FOR REFERENCE

Do Not Take From This Room

Ward's Business Directory™
of U.S. Private and Public Companies

ISSN 1048-8707

ard's Business Directory™

of U.S. Private and Public Companies

- A Comprehensive Guide to over 113,000 Companies in Alphabetic, Geographic, and Industry Arrangements
- Ranks Companies by Sales Within 4-Digit SIC and 6-Digit NAICS
- Provides Rankings and Analyses of the Industry Activity of Leading Companies

55th Edition

Volume 5: Ranked by Sales within 4-Digit SIC

Virgil L. Burton III, Project Editor

GALE
CENGAGE Learning

Detroit • New York • San Francisco • New Haven, Conn • Waterville, Maine • London

Ward's Business Directory of U.S. Private and Public Companies, 55th Edition

Project Editor: Virgil L. Burton III

Editorial: Kimberly N. Hunt-Lowrance

Editorial Support Services: Scott Flaugher

Product Management: Jenai Drouillard

Product Design: Pam Galbreath

Composition Department: Gary Leach, Evi Seoud

Manufacturing: Rita Wimberley

This publication is a creative work fully protected by all applicable copyright laws, as well as by misappropriation, trade secret, unfair competition, and other applicable laws. The authors and editors of this work have added value to the underlying factual material herein through one or more of the following: unique and original selection, coordination, expression, arrangement, and classification of the information.

For product information and technology assistance, contact us at **Gale Customer Support, 1-800-877-4253.**
For permission to use material from this text or product, submit all requests online at **www.cengage.com/permissions.**
Further permissions questions can be emailed to **permissionrequest@cengage.com**

While every effort has been made to ensure the reliability of the information presented in this publication, Gale, Cengage Learning, does not guarantee the accuracy of the data contained herein. Gale accepts no payment for listing; and inclusion in the publication of any organization, agency, institution, publication, service, or individual does not imply endorsement of the editors or publisher. Errors brought to the attention of the publisher and verified to the satisfaction of the publisher will be corrected in future editions.

EDITORIAL DATA PRIVACY POLICY. Does this publication contain information about you as an individual? If so, for more information about our editorial data privacy policies, please see our Privacy Statement at www.gale.com.

Gale
27500 Drake Rd.
Farmington Hills, MI, 48331-3535

ISBN-13: 978-1-4144-6018-5 (8 Volume set)
ISBN-10: 1-4144-6018-X (8 Volume set)
ISBN-13: 978-1-4144-6017-8 (5 Volume set)
ISBN-10: 1-4144-6017-1 (5 Volume set)
ISBN-13: 978-1-4144-6016-1 (4 Volume set)
ISBN-10: 1-4144-6016-3 (4 Volume set)
ISBN-13: 978-1-4144-6026-0 (2 Volume set)
ISBN-10: 1-4144-6026-0 (2 Volume set)
ISBN-13: 978-1-4144-6020-8 (Volume 1)
ISBN-10: 1-4144-6020-1 (Volume 1)
ISBN-13: 978-1-4144-6021-5 (Volume 2)
ISBN-10: 1-4144-6021-X (Volume 2)
ISBN-13: 978-1-4144-6022-2 (Volume 3)
ISBN-10: 1-4144-6022-8 (Volume 3)
ISBN-13: 978-1-4144-6023-9 (Volume 4)
ISBN-10: 1-4144-6023-6 (Volume 4)
ISBN-13: 978-1-4144-6024-6 (Volume 5)
ISBN-10: 1-4144-6024-4 (Volume 5)
ISBN-13: 978-1-4144-6025-3 (Volume 6)
ISBN-10: 1-4144-6025-2 (Volume 6)
ISBN-13: 978-1-4144-6027-7 (Volume 7)
ISBN-10: 1-4144-6027-9 (Volume 7)
ISBN-13: 978-1-4144-6028-4 (Volume 8)
ISBN-10: 1-4144-6028-7 (Volume 8)

ISSN 1048-8707

Printed in the United States of America
1 2 3 4 5 6 7 16 15 14 13 12

Contents

Ward's Business Directory of U.S. Private and Public Companies is a premiere business resource profiling more than 113,000 U.S. companies—90 percent of which are private. Whether it be for contacting a company or calculating its market share, the *Ward's* series is an invaluable tool for librarians, executives, students, analysts, marketers, and all other professionals who require current company and industry profiles.

Complete Company Listings

Volumes 1, 2, and 3 provide current company information in a single A-Z arrangement and offer hard-to-find data on small and mid-sized companies as well as complete profiles of large corporations. In addition to full contact information, listings include:

- Financial figures
- Number of employees
- Up to four 4-digit SICs and one 5- or 6- digit NAICS code with descriptions of products and services offered
- Up to five executive officers' names and titles
- Year founded
- Ticker symbol and stock exchange of publicly traded companies
- Immediate parent name for corporate tree linkage

Geographic Arrangement

Volume 4 contains a geographic listing of the companies in Volumes 1, 2, and 3 arranged by zip code within state.

Total number of companies, employees, and sales is provided at the end of each state section.

Rankings and Tables for Industry Analysis

Special Features in Volume 4 offer at-a-glance evaluations of industry activity through a series of ranked lists, including:

- 1,000 Largest Privately Held Companies
- 1,000 Largest Publicly Held Companies
- 1,000 Largest Employers
- Analysis of Private and Public Companies by State
- Analysis by Revenue per Employee of the Top 1,000 Companies by SIC and NAICS
- Analysis of Private and Public Companies by SIC and NAICS

Volume 5 offers national rankings by sales within SIC codes at the 4-digit level, while *Volume 8* provides national rankings by sales within NAICS codes at the 5- and 6-digit level. Both volumes provide the total number of companies, sales, and employees for each SIC and NAICS industry— the data needed to estimate marketshare more precisely than in other business directories.

Volumes 6 and 7 offer state rankings by sales within 4-digit SIC and provide the total number of companies, sales, and employees for each SIC covered in each state. Each state section also features rankings and analysis of

- 100 Largest Privately Held Companies
- 100 Largest Publicly Held Companies
- 100 Largest Employers

Since 1960, *Ward's Business Directory of U.S. Private and Public Companies* has been the leading source for hard-to-find information on private companies. Librarians, business executives, students, professional planners, job hunters, and others have come to rely on *Ward's* for reliable and accessible information on private and public companies. For example, *Ward's* assists market researchers in identifying market participants and analyzing market share. It also helps sales managers identify potential clients, create targeted mailings, and determine parent/subsidiary relationships. In addition, merger and acquisition specialists find *Ward's* a valuable tool in analyzing market position and locating specific data on targeted companies.

Scope

Ward's Business Directory covers domestic private and public companies. The directory is published in eight volumes. Up to twenty items of information are provided for each company listed. In addition to names, addresses, telephone numbers, e-mails, and URLs, hard-to-find data such as sales (which is generally considered more valuable information than net worth), employee figures, and up to five names and titles of executive officers may be provided.

Four-digit Standard Industrial Classification (SIC) codes are given in all volumes except Volume 8, in which five- and six-digit North American Industry Classification System (NA-ICS) codes are given. Both SIC and NAICS codes are provided in Volumes 1-4. The divisions of Private Households (SIC 8811; NAICS 81411), Public Administration (SIC 9111-9721; NAICS 92111-92812), and Nonclassifiable Establishments (SIC 9999; NAICS 99999) are not covered in *Ward's* as public and private companies are not found in these classifications.

Following the introductory matter in each volume of *Ward's* are two guides to the four-digit SIC system. In addition, Volumes 1-4 and Volume 8 include two guides to using the SIC with the newer NAICS codes. Below is a list of all the tables provided in *Ward's*:

- Numeric listing of SIC codes
- Alphabetic listing of SIC codes
- Numeric listing of NAICS codes
- Alphabetic listing of NAICS codes
- SIC codes with NAICS equivalents
- NAICS codes with SIC equivalents

Arrangement

Ward's volumes are arranged as follows:

Alphabetic Listing—Volumes 1, 2, and 3 contain profiles of private and public companies arranged alphabetically by company name. The alphabetic arrangement allows easy access to complete information and company details for all entries in *Ward's*.

Geographic Listing—Volume 4 includes all of the companies in the *Alphabetic Listing* organized by state in ascending zip code order. This arrangement facilitates the identification of market share within specific regions. Volume 4 also contains a *Special Features* section that provides rankings and analyses of companies that have actual or estimated sales figures available. See the User's Guide for details.

Ranked by Sales within 4-Digit SIC—Volume 5 includes all of the companies profiled in the *Alphabetic Listing*. Companies are organized by the 4-digit SIC code that most closely resembles their principal industry and ranks them according to revenues.

State Rankings by Sales within 4-Digit SIC—Volumes 6 and 7 include all of the companies that are profiled in the *Alphabetic Listing*. Both volumes organize companies by state (including listings for the District of Columbia, Puerto Rico, and the Virgin Islands), then by the 4-digit SIC code that most closely resembles their principal industry and ranks them according to revenues.

Volumes 6 and 7 also contain rankings of the top private and public companies, as well as the top employers at the state level. Only those companies with sales figures are included in the rankings. See *User's Guide* for details.

Ranked by Sales within 6-Digit NAICS—Volume 8 organizes all companies profiled in the *Alphabetic Listing* by the 5- or 6-digit NAICS code that most closely resembles their principal industry and ranks them according to revenues.

Indexes

A *Company Name Index* listing all companies alphabetically appears in Volumes 5, 7, and 8. In addition to the com name, these indexes include each company's primary SIC or NAICS codes, rankings based on sales, and state code.

Method of Compilation

Ward's Business Directory is compiled and maintained through the efforts of the *Ward's* research staff of The Gale Group. Information is gathered from annual reports, trade associations, government documents, company web sites, and telephone interviews.

Every effort has been made to edit for data comparability, but some differences in figures may be found due to availability of data, fiscal year configurations, and accounting practices. Financial data on the public companies is compiled from fiscal year 2008 through 2011. Recent reorganizations or mergers may not be reflected in parent company data. Primary and secondary SIC codes are either provided by the company or are assigned by Gale's staff. Primary NAICS codes are provided by The Gale Group's staff based on government tables of NAICS equivalents of SIC codes. The primary SIC and NAICS code represents the industry from which a company derives the most revenue.

Available in Electronic Formats

Licensing. Ward's Directory of U.S. Private and Public Companies is available for licensing as a component of Gale's "Company Profile" database. The database is provided in a fielded format and is deliverable via FTP (File Transfer Protocol) and in other media. Licenses generally include daily updates of the database. For more information, contact Gale's Business Development Group at 1-800-877-GALE, or visit us on our web site at www.gale.cengage.com/bizdev.

Online. Ward's is available as part of the Business and Company Resource Center, which is available on a subscrip-

tion basis through InfoTrac, Gale's online information resource that features an easy-to-use end-user interface, powerful search capabilities, and ease of access through the World-Wide Web. For more information, call 1-800-877-GALE.

The Directory is also available online as part of the Gale Directory Library. For more information, call 1-800-877-GALE.

Acknowledgments

The editors are grateful to those who generously responded to our requests for updated information, provided additional data by telephone, fax, email or website and helped in the shaping of this edition with their comments and suggestions throughout the year.

Comments and Suggestions Welcome

Although every effort is made to maintain accuracy, errors may occasionally occur; we will be grateful if these are called to our attention. In addition, if a user of this edition of *Ward's* knows of a company that is not currently listed, please send the company name, address, and phone number to the address below. Also, suggestions regarding the format and coverage of *Ward's* are always welcome. Please contact:

Ward's Business Directory
Gale
27500 Drake Rd.
Farmington Hills, Michigan 48331-3535
Phone: (248) 699-4253
Toll-free: (800) 347-4253
Fax: (248) 699-8069
URL: www.gale.cengage.com

Volumes 1-3: Alphabetic Listing

Volumes 1-3 provide one complete alphabetic sequence. Companies beginning with numerics and letters A through F are listed in Volume 1; companies beginning with letters G through O are listed in Volume 2; and companies beginning with letters P through Z are listed in Volume 3. Listings are generally organized by the first element in the company name. When the company name is a personal name, the company name is alphabetized by the surname unless the first name or initial is part of a trade name. The user is advised to try to locate a company first by surname, and if unsuccessful, to try the first element in the name.

The tabular format of Volumes 4-8 does not permit all elements of each entry to be printed. Users should refer to the listings in Volumes 1-3 for complete information on a company.

A fabricated sample entry illustrating the information provided in a typical alphabetic listing is shown below. The number preceding each portion of the entry designates an item of information that is described in the following paragraph of the same number.

▌1▐ **R.L.A. Entertainment Group**
▌2▐ 11362 Savannah
▌3▐ Santa Fe Springs, NM 87559
▌4▐ **Phone:** (605)827-9000
▌5▐ **Fax:** (605) 827-9011
▌6▐ **Free:** (800) 961-1313
▌7▐ **E-mail:** info@rla.com
▌8▐ **URL:** http://www.rla.com
▌9▐ **Import/Export** ▌10▐ **Type:** Division ▌11▐ **FY End:** 3-94
  ▌12▐ **Sales:** $45.3* million ▌13▐ **Exchange:** NYSE ▌14▐ **Ticker Symbol:** RLAE ▌15▐ **Employees:** 787 ▌16▐ **Founded:** 1953 ▌17▐ **Immediate Parent:** R.L.A. Inc. ▌18▐ **SIC(s):** 7833 Drive-In Motion Picture Theaters; 7941 Video Tape Rental; 7933 Bowling Centers; 6719 Offices of Holding Companies. ▌19▐ **NAICS:** 512132 Drive-In Motion Picture Theaters. ▌20▐ **Description:** Manages and services drive-in theaters. ▌21▐ **Officer(s):** J.L. Johnson, CEO; Kenneth Scott, Senior VP; P.C. O 'Brien, VP of Sales.

Description of Numbered Elements

▌1▐ **Company Name.** Abbreviations are sometimes used to allow the full name to appear in subsequent volumes. See *Abbreviations, Codes, and Symbols.*

▌2▐ **Street Address.**

▌3▐ **City, State, Zip.**

▌4▐ **Phone Number.**

▌5▐ **Fax Number.**

▌6▐ **Toll-Free Number.**

▌7▐ **E-mail Address.**

▌8▐ **URL.**

▌9▐ **Import/Export Designation.** Companies may have the designation "Import, "Export," or "Import/Export" if the company engages in such activities.

▌10▐ **Type.** The company type will be designated as one of the following:

- Private
- Public
- Public Subsidiary
- Private Subsidiary
- Division
- Joint Venture
- Investment Fund

▌11▐ **FY End.** Fiscal year end is provided, if available.

▌12▐ **Financial Information.** The most recent financial information available is provided, preceded by one of the following rubrics:

- Sales
- Total Assets
- Gross Billings
- Operating Revenues

An asterisk (*) indicates that the *Ward's* staff has estimated the information.

▌13▐ **Exchange.** The stock exchange on which the company is traded will be one of the following:

- AMEX — American Stock Exchange
- Balt/Phil/DC – Baltimore, MD/Philadelphia, PA/Washington, DC Stock Exchange
- Boston – Boston Stock Exchange
- Midwest – Midwest Stock Exchange
- NASDAQ – National Association of Securities Dealers' Automated Quotations
- National – National Stock Exchange

TABLE 1

Sample Entry: Geographic Listing by ZIP Code Within State

GEOGRAPHIC LISTING BY ZIP CODE WITHIN NEW MEXICO

1	2	3	4	5	6	7	8	9
R.L.A. Entertainment Group	11362 Savannah, Santa Fe Springs	87559	505-827-9000	7833	512132	D	46	8
Southwest Express	PO Box 2389, Santa Fe Springs	87559	505-813-8267	2099	311423	R	234	.6
New Mexico Biotech Company	2138 W. Church St., Santa Fe Springs	87560	505-971-2104	3999	337127	S	21	<.1
Precision Electronics Inc	456 4th St., Sante Fe Springs	87560	505-254-3400	3651	33431	P	496	1.3

- NYSE – New York Stock Exchange
- OTC – Over-the-Counter
- Pacific – Pacific Stock Exchange
- Pittsburgh – Pittsburgh Stock Exchange

❙14❙ Ticker Symbol. For a publicly traded company, the ticker symbol used to identify it on a stock exchange (see Exchange above) is provided. When the stock exchange is provided, but not the ticker symbol, the rubric is followed by the notation "Not Avail."

❙15❙ Employees. The number of individuals employed by the company is provided when available.

❙16❙ Founded. The year of the company's founding is given if provided by the company.

❙17❙ Immediate Parent. Not all immediate parents will be found as separate entries in the directory. Non-U.S. parents do not meet the selection criteria for *Ward's*; other companies may not have responded to our requests for updated information.

❙18❙ Standard Industrial Classification (SIC) Codes. Up to four 4-digit SIC codes and their descriptions are provided (See *About Industrial Classification* for information on SIC codes and *Standard Industrial Classification Numeric and Alphabetic Listings* for a complete reference to SIC codes.)

❙19❙ North American Industry Classification System (NAICS) Codes. One 5- or 6-digit NAICS code and its description is provided (see *About Industry Classification* for information on NAICS codes and North American Industry Classification System Numeric and Alphabetic Listings for a complete reference to NAICS codes).

❙20❙ Description. An additional description of the type of business or products manufactured may be provided.

❙21❙ Officer(s). Up to five of the company's executive officers and their titles may be provided. When officer information is not available, a staff contact name may be provided.

Volume 4: Geographic Listing and Special Features

Volume 4 contains a *Geographic Listing* of all the companies contained in the *Alphabetic Listing*. Entries are arranged alphabetically by state and within state by zip code in ascending order. Within zip code, companies are arranged alphabetically by company name. Total number of compa- nies, total financial data (including estimates when avail- able), and total number of employees are provided at the end of each state section. Space considerations make it necessary to provide rounded financial figures for individual companies. However, "Totals" figures are actual, not rounded numbers.

A fabricated sample entry illustrating the information typically contained in each geographic listing is shown in Table 1. The boldface number preceding each portion of the entry designates the column heading of each item of informa- tion described in the corresponding paragraph following the same number below. State name and zip code are given in the running head at the top of each page.

Volume 4 also contains *Special Features* to assist the user in interpreting the information provided in *Ward's*. The follow- ing rankings and analysis are included:

1,000 Largest Privately Held Companies—ranked by sales; companies at the same sales level are ranked by number of employees.

1,000 Largest Publicly Held Companies—ranked by sales; companies at the same sales level are ranked by number of employees.

1,000 Largest Employers— ranked by number of employees; companies with the same number of employees are ranked by sales.

Analysis of Private and Public Companies by State—lists the number of private and public companies within each state, with the total amount of sales and the number of employees.

Analysis by Revenue per Employee of Top 1,000 Companies by SIC—lists the top 1,000 companies based on the 1,000 Largest Privately Held Companies and the 1,000 Largest Publicly Held Companies tables and ranking them by revenue per employee ratio within SIC codes.

Analysis by Revenue per Employee of Top 1,000 Companies by NAICS—lists the top 1,000 companies based on the 1,000 Largest Privately Held Companies and the 1,000 Largest Publicly Held Companies tables and ranking them by revenue per employee ratio within NAICS codes.

TABLE 2

Sample Entry: Company Rankings by Sales Within 4-Digit SIC

1	2	3	4	5	6	7	8	9
0211	Beef Cattle Feedlots	1	Cactus Feeders Inc—*Paul F Engler*	PO Box 3050, Armarillo TX 79116	806-373-2333	R	750	.5
		2	Walter Lasley and Sons Inc—*Walter Lasley*	PO Box 168, Stratford TX 79084	806-753-4411	R	16*	<.1
		3	Kerany County Feeders Inc—*Bradner A Tate*	9000 N Hwy 25, Lakin KS 67860	620-355-6630	R	12*	<.1
		4	El Toro Land and Cattle Co—*Robert Odell*	PO Box G, Heber CA 92249	760-352-6312	R	6*	<.1

Analysis of Private and Public Companies by 4-Digit SIC—provides sales and employee information for both private and public companies within each industry.

Analysis of Private and Public Companies by 6-Digit NAICS—provides sales and employee information for both private and public companies within each industry.

Description of Numbered Elements

▌1▐ **Company Name.**

▌2▐ **Address, City.**

▌3▐ **Zip Code.**

▌4▐ **Phone.**

▌5▐ **SIC.** Primary SIC code is listed.

▌6▐ **NAICS.** Primary NAICS code is listed

▌7▐ **Type.** One of the following codes will designate company type:

R   Private
P   Public
S   Private Subsidiary
B   Public Subsidiary
D   Division
J   Joint Venture
I   Investment Fund
U   Not Available

▌8▐ **Fin.** Sales, total assets, gross billings, or operating revenues in millions is given. If sales are less than one million, <1 is given; other sales figures are rounded to the nearest million. If financial data is unknown, the notation N/A is given.

▌9▐ **Empls.** Number of employees in thousands is provided. If the number of employees is less than 100, <.1 is given; other employee figures are rounded to the nearest hundred. If the number of employees is unknown, the notation N/A is given.

Volume 5: Ranked by Sales within 4-Digit SIC

Volume 5 ranks all companies profiled in the *Alphabetic Listing* by sales within 4-digit SIC. If sales information is not provided, companies are listed alphabetically within their respective SICs following those companies with financial information. Total number of companies, total financial data (including estimates when available), and total number of employees are provided at the end of each 4-digit SIC listing. The total financial and employee figures reflect the totals for only those companies listing financial and employee information. Company totals include all companies within a 4-digit SIC, including those without financial and employee figures. Approximate market share can be calculated for the companies listed by comparing individual companies to the totals provided at the end of each SIC group.

Where the immediate parent of a group shares a primary SIC with the company listed, the immediate parent will be indented directly below. Space limitations make it necessary to provide rounded financial figures for individual companies. However, "Totals" figures are actual, not rounded numbers.

A fabricated sample entry is shown in Table 2. The boldface number preceding each portion of the entry designates the column heading of each corresponding item of information described below. The SIC code and alphabetic description are provided at the top of each page.

Description of Numbered Elements

▌1▐ **SIC.**

▌2▐ **SIC Description.**

▌3▐ **Rank.** The ranking of the company within its primary 5- or 6-digit NAICS code, based on sales.

▌4▐ **Company Name—Executive Officer's Name.** The name of the chief executive officer is provided when available. For additional officers and their titles, see Volumes 1, 2, and 3.

▌5▐ **Address, City, State, and Zip Code.** The street address, city, state code, and zip code are provided. See *Abbreviations, Codes, and Symbols* for more information.

▌6▐ **Phone.**

▌7▐ **Type.** The type of company is designated by one of the following codes:

R   Private

TABLE 3

Sample Entry: State Rankings by Sales Within 4-Digit SIC

1	2	3	4	5	6	7	8	9
5511	New & Used Car Dealers	1	Edwards Chevrolet Company Inc.— *Leon W Edwards*	1400 3rd Ave N, Birmingham AL 35203	205-716-3300	R	51*	.1
		2	Carl Cannon Chevrolet-Olds Inc.— *James Cannon*	PO Box 1211, Jasper AL 35501	205-252-1954	R	33*	.1
		3	Capitol Motor Co.—*G Harris McGough*	405 Eastern Bypass, Montgomery AL 36117	334-271-1730	R	33*	.1
		4	Jim Burke Medical Center Inc.—*Earl Holley*	2415 7th Ave S, Birmingham AL 35233	205-252-8154	R	28*	.1

P	Public
S	Private Subsidiary
B	Public Subsidiary
D	Division
J	Joint Venture
I	Investment Fund
U	Not Available

∎8∎ Fin. Sales, total assets, gross billings, or operating revenues are provided in millions. If total amount is less than one million, <1 is given; other sales figures are rounded to the nearest million. Financial data of parent companies will generally reflect the financial data of the subsidiary companies. Companies without financial information will be listed alphabetically below those companies with a financial figure.

∎9∎ Empls. Number of employees in thousands is given. If the total number of employees is less than 100, <.1 is given; other employee figures are rounded to the nearest hundred. If number of employees is unknown or not applicable, the notation N/A is given.

∎10∎ Immediate Parent. The name of the immediate parent company, when available, will be indented below the company name.

Volumes 6 and 7: State Rankings by Sales within 4-Digit SIC

Volumes 6 and 7 rank all companies described in the *Alphabetic Listing* by sales within 4-digit SIC for each state (including listings for District of Columbia, Puerto Rico, and the Virgin Islands). If sales information is not provided, companies are listed alphabetically within their respective SICs following those companies with financial information. Total number of companies, total financial figures (including estimates when available), and total number of employees are provided at the end of each 4-digit SIC listing. The total financial and employee figures reflect the totals for only those companies listing financial and employee information. Company totals include all companies within a 4-digit SIC for that state, including those without financial and employee figures.

Where the immediate parent of a group shares a primary SIC with the company listed and is located in the same state, the immediate parent will be indented directly below. Space limitations make it necessary to provide rounded financial figures for individual companies. However, "Totals" figures are actual, not rounded numbers. Approximate market share can be calculated for the companies listed by comparing individual companies to the totals provided at the end of each SIC group.

Each state listing also includes a map and special rankings and analysis to assist the user in interpreting the information provided in *Ward's*. The following tables are included:

100 Largest Privately Held Companies— ranked by sales for each state; companies at the same sales level are ranked by number of employees

100 Largest Publicly Held Companies— ranked by sales for each state; companies at the same sales level are ranked by number of employees

100 Largest Employers— ranked by number of employees for each state; companies with the same number of employees are ranked by sales

A fabricated sample entry is shown in Table 3. The number preceding each portion of the entry designates the column heading of each corresponding item of information described below. The state name, SIC code, and alphabetic description are provided at the top of each page.

Description of Numbered Elements

∎1∎ SIC.

∎2∎ SIC Description.

∎3∎ State Rank. The ranking of the company within 4-digit SIC code for that state, based on sales.

∎4∎ Company Name–Executive Officer's Name. The name of the chief executive officer is provided. For additional officers and their titles, see Volumes 1, 2, and 3.

∎5∎ Address, City, State, and Zip Code. The street address, city, state code, and zip code are provided. See *Abbreviations, Codes, and Symbols* for more information.

TABLE 4

Company Rankings by Sales within 6-Digit NAICS

1	2	3	4	5	6	7	8	9
112112	Cattle Feedlots	1	Cactus Feeders Inc.—*Paul F Engler*	PO Box 3050, Amarillo TX 79116	806-373-2333	R	750	.5
		2	Walter Lasley and Sons Inc.—*Walter Lasley*	PO Box 168, Stratford TX 79084-0168	806-753-4411	R	16*	<.1
		3	Kearny Country Feeders Inc.—*Bradner A Tate*	9000 N Hwy 25, Lakin KS 67860	620-355-6630	R	12*	<.1
		4	El Toro Land and Cattle Co.—*Robert Odell*	PO Box G, Heber CA 92249	760-352-6312	R	6*	<.1

❚6❚ Phone.

❚7❚ Type. The type of company is designated by one of the following codes:

R	Private
P	Public
S	Private Subsidiary
B	Public Subsidiary
D	Division
J	Joint Venture
I	Investment Fund
U	Not Available

❚8❚ Fin. Sales, total assets, gross billings, or operating revenues are provided in millions. If total amount is less than one million, <1 is given; other sales figures are rounded to the nearest million. Financial data of parent companies will generally reflect the financial data of the subsidiary companies.

❚9❚ Empls. Number of employees in thousands is given. If the total number of employees is less than 100, <.1 is given; other employee figures are rounded to the nearest hundred. If number of employees is unknown or not applicable, the notation N/A is given.

❚10❚ Immediate Parent. The name of the immediate parent company, when available, will be indented below the company name

Volume 8: Ranked by Sales within 5- or 6-Digit NAICS

Volume 8 provides a ranking of all companies profiled in the *Alphabetic Listing* by sales within 5- or 6-digit NAICS code. If sales information is not provided, companies are listed alphabetically within their respective NAICS codes after those companies with financial information. Total number of companies, total financial figures (including estimates when available), and total number of employees are provided at the end of each NAICS listing. The total financial and employee figures reflect the totals for only those companies listing financial and employee information. Company totals include all companies within a 5- or 6-digit NAICS code, including those without financial and employee figures.

Where the immediate parent of a group shares a primary NAICS code with the company listed, the immediate parent will be indented directly below. Space limitations make it necessary to provide rounded financial figures for individual companies. However, "Totals" figures are actual, not rounded numbers. Approximate market share can be calculated for the companies listed by comparing individual companies to the totals provided at the end of each NAICS group.

A fabricated sample entry is shown in Table 4. The number preceding each portion of the entry designates the column heading of each corresponding item of information described below. The NAICS code and alphabetic description are provided at the top of each page.

Description of Numbered Elements

❚1❚ NAICS.

❚2❚ NAICS Description.

❚3❚ Rank. The ranking of the company within its primary 5- or 6-digit NAICS code, based on sales. name of the chief executive officer is provided. For additional officers and their titles, see Volumes 1, 2, and 3.

❚4❚ Company Name—Executive Officer's Name. The name of the chief executive officer is provided when available. For additional officers and their titles, see Volumes 1, 2, and 3.

❚5❚ Address, City, State, and Zip Code. The street address, city, state code, and zip code are provided. See *Abbreviations, Codes, and Symbols* for more information.

❚6❚ Phone.

❚7❚ Type. The type of company is designated by one of the following codes:

R	Private
P	Public
S	Private Subsidiary
B	Public Subsidiary
D	Division
J	Joint Venture

TABLE 5

Sample Entry: Company Name Index			
1	**2**	**3**	**4**
Abbot Corp.	CA	6361	113
Andrew Abbott Corp	MI	5912	39
A. R. L. Entertainment, Inc	NY	7833	32

I	Investment Fund
U	Not Available

█8█ Fin. Sales, total assets, gross billings, or operating revenues are provided in millions. If total amount is less than one million, <1 is given; other sales figures are rounded to the nearest million. Financial data of parent companies will generally reflect the financial data of the subsidiary companies. Companies without financial information will be listed alphabetically below those companies with a financial figure.

█9█ Empls. Number of employees in thousands is given. If the total number of employees is less than 100, <.1 is given; other employee figures are rounded to the nearest hundred. If number of employees is unknown or not applicable, the notation N/A is given.

█10█ Immediate Parent. The name of the immediate parent company, when available, will be indented below the company name

Company Name Index

Volumes 5, 7, and 8 contain an alphabetic listing of all the companies in each volume. In addition to company name, these indexes include ranking by sales (Volume 5), state code (Volume 7), ranking by state within primary SIC (Volume 7) or NAICS (Volume 8), and the primary SIC (Volumes 5 and 7) or NAICS (Volume 8).

A fabricated sample entry is shown in Table 5. The number preceding each portion of the entry designates the column heading of each corresponding item of information described below.

Description of Numbered Elements
█1█ Company Name.

█2█ State Code. State in which company is located is provided in Volume 7.

█3█ SIC or NAICS. Primary SIC code is listed in Volumes 5 and 7, and primary NAICS is listed in Volume 8.

█4█ Rank. The company's ranking within SIC is provided in Volume 5, the state ranking by sales within primary 4-digit SIC is provided in Volume 7, and the ranking within primary 5- or 6-digit NAICS code is provided in Volume 8.

Financial Figures Used in *Ward's*

When the financial data from private companies is unavailable, *Ward's* usually offers an estimate based on several considerations. These include number of employees, comparisons to like companies within an industry, and previously verified data. Estimates are so noted with an asterisk (*). Sales estimates are rounded to the nearest million. Companies without financial information are included if their address information was confirmed.

The basis for financial figures for most companies is sales. Some companies, however, list total assets, operating revenues, or gross billings. Advertising agencies, for example, list gross billings. These distinctions are not given in the entries in Volumes 4, 5, and 8. Therefore, to assist in analysis of the financial figures, both the SIC and NAICS codes for companies listing total assets, gross billings, and operating revenues are listed in Table 6 at their four-digit classification for SICs, and their three-to six-digit classification for NAICS.

About Industry Classification

Ward's offers tools to analyze companies in two industry classification systems. The primary system, the Standard Industrial Classification (SIC) system, was established by the U.S. government to provide a uniform means for collecting, presenting, and analyzing data. SIC codes are widely used by federal, state, and local government agencies, trade associations, private research organizations, and business professionals to promote comparability in the presentation of statistical data. The system to replace the SIC, the North American Industry Classification System (NAICS), was jointly

TABLE 6

Industries Reporting by Assets, Billings, and Revenue							
Total Assets		**Gross Billings**		**Operating Revenues**			
SIC	NAICS	SIC	NAICS	SIC		NAICS	
4911-4971	221	7311	54181	1521-1799	4512-4522	233-235	531
6011-6163	521-525	7313	54184	4011	4724-4731	481	541618
6311-6399	551			4111-4151	6211-6231	482111	561
6710-6799	813			4212-4215	6531	483-487	62191
				4311-4489		48851	81222
						49111	81399
						523	

TABLE 7

SIC Structure	
Codes	Title
Division E	Transportation, Communications, Electric, Gas, and Sanitary Services
48	Communications
481	Telephone Communications
4812	Radiotelephone Communications

TABLE 8

NAICS Structure	
Codes	Title
51	Information
513	Broadcasting and Telecommunications
5133	Telecommunications
51332	Wireless Telecommunications
513321	Paging

developed beginning in 1994 by the governments of Canada, Mexico, and the United States, and implemented in 1997 by the U.S. government as its new standard for processing data. The six-digit NAICS code allows for the classification of newer industries not previously covered by the SIC. It also classifies industries based upon a production/process-oriented basis instead of the mix of production- and market-based categories used by the SIC system.

1987 Standard Industrial Classification (SIC)

Each SIC code classifies an Establishment by the types of activity in which it is engaged. An Establishment is an economic unit where a service is performed or a product is manufactured or sold, generally at a single physical location. Each Establishment is classified according to its primary activity, which is determined by the main product or group of products that it produces or distributes, or by the services it renders. To be recognized as a separate industry within the SIC system, a set of Establishments must be statistically significant according to criteria such as the number of persons employed and the volume of business conducted. See Table 7. The SIC system comprises four levels of classification:

Divisions. The broadest SIC categories are divisions that define an activity in very general terms and are labeled with a letter. These divisions are: Agriculture, Forestry, and Fishing; Mining; Construction; Manufacturing; Transportation, Communications, Electric, Gas, and Sanitary Services; Wholesale Trade; Retail Trade; Finance, Insurance, and Real Estate; Services; and Public Administration.

Major Groups. Within these broad categories are major groups. Each major group has a two-digit code that makes up the first two numbers of the complete four-digit SIC code. In the case of Manufacturing, the major group codes range between 20 and 39. Examples of two-digit groups in Manufacturing are: Food and Kindred Products (20); Tobacco Products (21); Furniture and Fixtures (25); Printing, Publishing, and Allied Industries (27); and Industrial and Commercial Machinery and Computer Equipment (35).

Industry Groups. Major groups are further subdivided into three-digit industry groups. Each industry group is assigned a three-digit code based on the two-digit code for its major group. For example, Printing, Publishing and Allied

Industries is broken down into: 271 for Newspapers, 272 for Periodicals, and 273 for Books.

Industries. Industry groups are divided still further into specific Industry classifications which are assigned complete, four-digit codes based on the three-digit code assigned to its industry group. For example: 2731 for Book Publishing and 2732 for Book Printing.

1997 North American Industry Classification System (NAICS)

The NAICS system is similar in principle to the SIC system but differs in industry specificity and grouping. It includes broad classifications that are common among the three nations and unique national-level classifications. Whereas the SIC is classified by a letter and four digits, NAICS classifies industries by up to six digits. Industries common among all three nations are specified by five digits; national detail of the five-digit code is presented in the six-digit form. See Table 8. The NAICS comprises five levels of classification:

Industry Sector. The broadest NAICS categories, comparable to SIC divisions, consist of the first two numbers of the six-digit NAICS code. The industry sectors are: Agriculture, Forestry, Fishing and Hunting; Mining; Utilities; Construction; Manufacturing; Wholesale Trade; Retail Trade; Transportation and Warehousing; Information; Finance and Insurance; Real Estate and Rental Leasing; Professional, Scientific, and Technical Services; Management of Companies; and Enterprises; Administrative and Support, Waste and Remediation Services; Educational Services; Health Care and Social Assistance; Arts, Entertainment, and Recreation; Accommodation and Foodservices; Other Services (except Public Administration); and Public Administration.

Industry Subsector. Within the industry sector are industry subsectors, denoted by a three-digit number. For example, in the Information (51) sector, there is the Broadcasting Telecommunications (513) subsector.

Industry Group. Each industry subsector is further divided into four-digit industry groups. Within Broadcast and Telecommunications (513), for example, there are Radio and Television Broadcasting (5131); Cable Networks and Program Distribution (5132); and Telecommunications (5133).

TABLE 9

NAICS/SIC Structure Comparison

NAICS	Level	SIC
Two-Digit	Industry Sector	Division
Three-Digit	Industry Subsector	Two-Digit
Four-Digit	Industry Group	Three-Digit
Five-Digit	NAICS Industry	Four-Digit
Six-Digit	U.S. National Industry	Four-Digit

NAICS Industry. The industries that are common to all three nations have the five-digit classification, and are somewhat comparable to the four-digit classification in the SIC system. Within Telecommunications (5133) is Wireless Telecommunications Carriers (51332), which is similar to the four-digit SIC classification 4812: Radiotelephone Communications.

U.S. National Industry. The NAICS codes given on the six-digit level are specific to one nation. The United States further breaks down the code of Wireless Telecommunications Carriers (51332) into Paging (513321) and Cellular and Other Wireless Telecommunications 513322). Canada, Mexico, and the United States have agreed to use the same six-digit codes whenever possible. The sixth digit is optional,

however, and in many cases the five-digit code represents the most specific NAICS category. See Table 9.

SIC and NAICS Tables in *Ward's*

Following the introductory matter in each volume are two arrangements of SIC codes. The first is a numeric listing that provides a text description of each 4-digit SIC number. The second is an alphabetic listing of each SIC, which allows users to find the code that corresponds to an industry description. In addition to the two SIC tables, Volumes 1-4 and 8 include a numeric listing that provides a text description of each NAICS number and an alphabetic listing that allows users to find the NAICS code that corresponds to an industry description. These volumes also include a SIC table showing corresponding NAICS codes and a NAICS table with respective SIC codes.

The data conversion tables provided in this book reflect the U.S. version of the NAICS. The NAICS codes presented in *Ward's* were assigned by the Gale Group staff based on official U.S. government mapping between the SIC system and NAICS. The information is not official government classification, and some NAICS assignments may change for specific companies as NAICS becomes more widely implemented.

Miscellaneous Abbreviations

A

Acad	Academy
Admin	Administration
Amer	American
AMEX	American Stock Exchange
Apt	Apartment
Assn	Association
Assoc	Associate, Associated
Asst	Assistant
Auto	Automobile, Automotive
Avail	Available
Ave	Avenue

B

Balt/Phil/ DC	Baltimore, MD/Philadelphia, PA/Washington, DC Stock Exchange
Bd	Board
Bldg	Building
Blvd	Boulevard
Br	Branch
Bros	Brothers
Bur	Bureau
Bus	Business

C

CEO	Chief Executive Officer
CFO	Chief Financial Officer
Chem(s)	Chemical(s)
Chm	Chairman
Cnty	County
c/o	Care Of
Co	Company
Coll	College
Comm	Committee
Commn	Commission
Conf	Conference
Confed	Confederation
Cong	Congress
Cons	Consolidated
Constr	Construction
Conv	Convention
COO	Chief Operating Officer
Co-op	Co-operative

Corp	Corporation
Cos	Companies
Coun	Council
Ct	Court
Ctr	Center, Centre

D

D	Division
Dept	Department
Devel	Development
Dir	Director
Dist	Distribution
Div	Division
Dr	Drive

E

E	East
Empls	Employees
Equip	Equipment
Est	Establishment
Exc	Except
Exec	Executive
Expy	Expressway

F

Fed	Federal
Fin	Finance, Financial
Fl(s)	Floor(s)
Ft	Fort
Fwy	Freeway
FY	Fiscal Year

G

Gen	General
Govt	Government

H

HQ	Headquarters
Hwy	Highway

I

I	Investment Fund
Inc	Incorporated

Incl	Including
Indus	Industrial, Industries
Inst	Institute, Institution
Intl	International

J

J	Joint Venture

L

Labs	Laboratories
LLC	Limited Liability Company
LLP	Limited Liability Partnership
LP	Limited Partnership
Ln	Lane
Ltd	Limited

M

Metro	Metropolitan
Mfg	Manufacturing
Mfr(s)	Manufacturers
Mgr	Manager
Mgt	Management
Misc	Miscellaneous
Mktg	Marketing
Mt	Mount
Mtn	Mountain

N

N	North
NA	National Association
NAICS	North American Industry Classification System
NASDAQ	National Association of Securities Dealers' Automated Quotations
Natl	National
NE	Northeast
NEC	Not Elsewhere Classified
No	Number
NW	Northwest
NYSE	New York Stock Exchange

O

Oper(s)	Operation(s)
Org	Organization

OTC	Over-the-Counter

P

P	Public
Pkwy	Parkway
Pl	Place
PLC	Public Limited Company
Plz	Plaza
PO	Post Office
Pres	President
Pty	Proprietary

R

R	Private
Rd	Road
RD	Rural Delivery
Rep	Republic
RFD	Rural Free Delivery
Rm	Room
RR	Rural Route
Rte	Route

S

S	South, Subsidiary
SE	Southeast
Sec	Secretary
Sect	Section
SIC	Standard Industrial Classification
Soc	Society
Sq	Square
St	Saint, Street
Sta	Station
Std	Standard
Ste	Sainte, Suite
Sub	Subsidiary
Svc(s)	Service(s)
SW	Southwest
Sys	Systems

T

Tech	Technical
Ter	Terrace
Tpke	Turnpike
Treas	Treasurer
TV	Television

U

UN	United Nations
Univ	University
US	United States
USA	United States of America

V

VP	Vice President

W

W	West
Whsle	Wholesale

Standard Industrial Classification (SIC) Codes Numeric Listings

01—Agricultural Production—Crops

0111	Wheat
0112	Rice
0115	Corn
0116	Soybeans
0119	Cash Grains NEC
0131	Cotton
0132	Tobacco
0133	Sugarcane & Sugar Beets
0134	Irish Potatoes
0139	Field Crops Except Cash Grains NEC
0161	Vegetables & Melons
0171	Berry Crops
0172	Grapes
0173	Tree Nuts
0174	Citrus Fruits
0175	Deciduous Tree Fruits
0179	Fruits & Tree Nuts NEC
0181	Ornamental Nursery Products
0182	Food Crops Grown Under Cover
0191	General Farms—Primarily Crop

02—Agricultural Production—Livestock

0211	Beef Cattle Feedlots
0212	Beef Cattle Except Feedlots
0213	Hogs
0214	Sheep & Goats
0219	General Livestock NEC
0241	Dairy Farms
0251	Broiler, Fryer & Roaster Chickens
0252	Chicken Eggs
0253	Turkeys & Turkey Eggs
0254	Poultry Hatcheries
0259	Poultry & Eggs NEC
0271	Fur-Bearing Animals & Rabbits
0272	Horses & Other Equines
0273	Animal Aquaculture
0279	Animal Specialties NEC
0291	General Farms—Primarily Animal

07—Agricultural Services

0711	Soil Preparation Services
0721	Crop Planting, Cultivating & Protecting
0722	Crop Harvesting
0723	Crop Preparation Services for Market
0724	Cotton Ginning
0741	Veterinary Services—Livestock
0742	Veterinary Services—Specialties
0751	Livestock Services
0752	Animal Specialty Services
0761	Farm Labor Contractors
0762	Farm Management Services
0781	Landscape Counseling & Planning
0782	Lawn & Garden Services
0783	Ornamental Shrub & Tree Services

08—Forestry

0811	Timber Tracts
0831	Forest Products
0851	Forestry Services

09—Fishing, Hunting & Trapping

0912	Finfish
0913	Shellfish
0919	Miscellaneous Marine Products
0921	Fish Hatcheries & Preserves
0971	Hunting, Trapping & Game Propagation

10—Metal Mining

1011	Iron Ores
1021	Copper Ores
1031	Lead & Zinc Ores
1041	Gold Ores
1044	Silver Ores
1061	Ferroalloy Ores Except Vanadium
1081	Metal Mining Services
1094	Uranium, Radium & Vanadium Ores
1099	Metal Ores NEC

12—Coal Mining

1221	Bituminous Coal & Lignite-Surface
1222	Bituminous Coal-Underground
1231	Anthracite Mining
1241	Coal Mining Services

13—Oil & Gas Extraction

1311	Crude Petroleum & Natural Gas
1321	Natural Gas Liquids
1381	Drilling Oil & Gas Wells
1382	Oil & Gas Exploration Services
1389	Oil & Gas Field Services NEC

14—Nonmetallic Minerals Except Fuels

1411	Dimension Stone
1422	Crushed & Broken Limestone
1423	Crushed & Broken Granite
1429	Crushed & Broken Stone NEC
1442	Construction Sand & Gravel
1446	Industrial Sand
1455	Kaolin & Ball Clay
1459	Clay & Related Minerals NEC
1474	Potash, Soda & Borate Minerals
1475	Phosphate Rock
1479	Chemical & Fertilizer Mining NEC
1481	Nonmetallic Minerals Services
1499	Miscellaneous Nonmetallic Minerals

15—General Building Contractors

1521	Single-Family Housing Construction
1522	Residential Construction NEC

1531	Operative Builders
1541	Industrial Buildings & Warehouses
1542	Nonresidential Construction NEC

16—Heavy Construction Except Building Construction

1611	Highway & Street Construction
1622	Bridge, Tunnel & Elevated Highway
1623	Water, Sewer & Utility Lines
1629	Heavy Construction NEC

17—Special Trade Contractors

1711	Plumbing, Heating & Air-Conditioning
1721	Painting & Paper Hanging
1731	Electrical Work
1741	Masonry & Other Stonework
1742	Plastering, Drywall& Insulation
1743	Terrazzo, Tile, Marble & Mosaic Work
1751	Carpentry Work
1752	Floor Laying & Floor Work NEC
1761	Roofing, Siding & Sheet Metal Work
1771	Concrete Work
1781	Water Well Drilling
1791	Structural Steel Erection
1793	Glass & Glazing Work
1794	Excavation Work
1795	Wrecking & Demolition Work
1796	Installing Building Equipment NEC
1799	Special Trade Contractors NEC

20—Food & Kindred Products

2011	Meat Packing Plants
2013	Sausages & Other Prepared Meats
2015	Poultry Slaughtering & Processing
2021	Creamery Butter
2022	Cheese—Natural & Processed
2023	Dry, Condensed & Evaporated Dairy Products
2024	Ice Cream & Frozen Desserts
2026	Fluid Milk
2032	Canned Specialties
2033	Canned Fruits & Vegetables
2034	Dehydrated Fruits, Vegetables & Soups
2035	Pickles, Sauces & Salad Dressings
2037	Frozen Fruits & Vegetables
2038	Frozen Specialties NEC
2041	Flour & Other Grain Mill Products
2043	Cereal Breakfast Foods
2044	Rice Milling
2045	Prepared Flour Mixes & Doughs
2046	Wet Corn Milling
2047	Dog & Cat Food
2048	Prepared Feeds NEC
2051	Bread, Cake & Related Products

2052	Cookies & Crackers
2053	Frozen Bakery Products Except Bread
2061	Raw Cane Sugar
2062	Cane Sugar Refining
2063	Beet Sugar
2064	Candy & Other Confectionery Products
2066	Chocolate & Cocoa Products
2067	Chewing Gum
2068	Salted & Roasted Nuts & Seeds
2074	Cottonseed Oil Mills
2075	Soybean Oil Mills
2076	Vegetable Oil Mills NEC
2077	Animal & Marine Fats & Oils
2079	Edible Fats & Oils NEC
2082	Malt Beverages
2083	Malt
2084	Wines, Brandy & Brandy Spirits
2085	Distilled & Blended Liquors
2086	Bottled & Canned Soft Drinks
2087	Flavoring Extracts & Syrups NEC
2091	Canned & Cured Fish & Seafoods
2092	Fresh or Frozen Prepared Fish
2095	Roasted Coffee
2096	Potato Chips & Similar Snacks
2097	Manufactured Ice
2098	Macaroni & Spaghetti
2099	Food Preparations NEC

21—Tobacco Products

2111	Cigarettes
2121	Cigars
2131	Chewing & Smoking Tobacco
2141	Tobacco Stemming & Redrying

22—Textile Mill Products

2211	Broadwoven Fabric Mills—Cotton
2221	Broadwoven Fabric Mills—Manmade
2231	Broadwoven Fabric Mills—Wool
2241	Narrow Fabric Mills
2251	Women's Hosiery Except Socks
2252	Hosiery NEC
2253	Knit Outerwear Mills
2254	Knit Underwear Mills
2257	Weft Knit Fabric Mills
2258	Lace & Warp Knit Fabric Mills
2259	Knitting Mills NEC
2261	Finishing Plants—Cotton
2262	Finishing Plants—Manmade
2269	Finishing Plants NEC
2273	Carpets & Rugs
2281	Yarn Spinning Mills
2282	Throwing & Winding Mills
2284	Thread Mills
2295	Coated Fabrics—Not Rubberized
2296	Tire Cord & Fabrics
2297	Nonwoven Fabrics
2298	Cordage & Twine
2299	Textile Goods NEC

23—Apparel & Other Textile Products

2311	Men's/Boys' Suits & Coats
2321	Men's/Boys' Shirts
2322	Men's/Boys' Underwear & Nightwear
2323	Men's/Boys' Neckwear
2325	Men's/Boys' Trousers & Slacks
2326	Men's/Boys' Work Clothing
2329	Men's/Boys' Clothing NEC
2331	Women's/Misses' Blouses & Shirts
2335	Women's/Misses' Dresses
2337	Women's/Misses' Suits & Coats
2339	Women's/Misses' Outerwear NEC
2341	Women's/Children's Underwear
2342	Bras, Girdles & Allied Garments
2353	Hats, Caps & Millinery
2361	Girls'/Children's Dresses & Blouses
2369	Girls'/Children's Outerwear NEC
2371	Fur Goods
2381	Fabric Dress & Work Gloves
2384	Robes & Dressing Gowns
2385	Waterproof Outerwear
2386	Leather & Sheep-Lined Clothing
2387	Apparel Belts
2389	Apparel & Accessories NEC
2391	Curtains & Draperies
2392	Housefurnishings NEC
2393	Textile Bags
2394	Canvas & Related Products
2395	Pleating & Stitching
2396	Automotive & Apparel Trimmings
2397	Schiffli Machine Embroideries
2399	Fabricated Textile Products NEC

24—Lumber & Wood Products

2411	Logging
2421	Sawmills & Planing Mills—General
2426	Hardwood Dimension & Flooring Mills
2429	Special Product Sawmills NEC
2431	Millwork
2434	Wood Kitchen Cabinets
2435	Hardwood Veneer & Plywood
2436	Softwood Veneer & Plywood
2439	Structural Wood Members NEC
2441	Nailed Wood Boxes & Shook
2448	Wood Pallets & Skids
2449	Wood Containers NEC
2451	Mobile Homes
2452	Prefabricated Wood Buildings
2491	Wood Preserving
2493	Reconstituted Wood Products
2499	Wood Products NEC

25—Furniture & Fixtures

| 2511 | Wood Household Furniture |

2512	Upholstered Household Furniture	2824	Organic Fibers—Noncellulosic	3161	Luggage
2514	Metal Household Furniture	2833	Medicinals & Botanicals	3171	Women's Handbags & Purses
2515	Mattresses & Bedsprings	2834	Pharmaceutical Preparations	3172	Personal Leather Goods NEC
2517	Wood T.V. and Radio Cabinets	2835	Diagnostic Substances	3199	Leather Goods NEC
2519	Household Furniture NEC	2836	Biological Products Except Diagnostic		
2521	Wood Office Furniture	2841	Soap & Other Detergents		**32—Stone, Clay & Glass Products**
2522	Office Furniture Except Wood	2842	Polishes & Sanitation Goods	3211	Flat Glass
2531	Public Building & Related Furniture	2843	Surface Active Agents	3221	Glass Containers
2541	Wood Partitions & Fixtures	2844	Toilet Preparations	3229	Pressed & Blown Glass NEC
2542	Partitions & Fixtures Except Wood	2851	Paints & Allied Products	3231	Products of Purchased Glass
2591	Drapery Hardware, Blinds & Shades	2861	Gum & Wood Chemicals	3241	Cement—Hydraulic
2599	Furniture & Fixtures NEC	2865	Cyclic Crudes & Intermediates	3251	Brick & Structural Clay Tile
		2869	Industrial Organic Chemicals NEC	3253	Ceramic Wall & Floor Tile
	26—Paper & Allied Products	2873	Nitrogenous Fertilizers	3255	Clay Refractories
2611	Pulp Mills	2874	Phosphatic Fertilizers	3259	Structural Clay Products NEC
2621	Paper Mills	2875	Fertilizers—Mixing Only	3261	Vitreous Plumbing Fixtures
2631	Paperboard Mills	2879	Agricultural Chemicals NEC	3262	Vitreous China Table & Kitchenware
2652	Setup Paperboard Boxes	2891	Adhesives & Sealants	3263	Semivitreous Table & Kitchenware
2653	Corrugated & Solid Fiber Boxes	2892	Explosives	3264	Porcelain Electrical Supplies
2655	Fiber Cans, Drums & Similar Products	2893	Printing Ink	3269	Pottery Products NEC
2656	Sanitary Food Containers	2895	Carbon Black	3271	Concrete Block & Brick
2657	Folding Paperboard Boxes	2899	Chemical Preparations NEC	3272	Concrete Products NEC
2671	Paper Coated & Laminated-Packaging			3273	Ready-Mixed Concrete
			29—Petroleum & Coal Products	3274	Lime
2672	Coated & Laminated Paper NEC	2911	Petroleum Refining	3275	Gypsum Products
2673	Bags—Plastics, Laminated & Coated	2951	Asphalt Paving Mixtures & Blocks	3281	Cut Stone & Stone Products
2674	Bags—Uncoated Paper & Multiwall	2952	Asphalt Felts & Coatings	3291	Abrasive Products
2675	Die-Cut Paper & Board	2992	Lubricating Oils & Greases	3292	Asbestos Products
2676	Sanitary Paper Products	2999	Petroleum & Coal Products NEC	3295	Minerals—Ground or Treated
2677	Envelopes			3296	Mineral Wool
2678	Stationery Products		**30—Rubber & Miscellaneous Plastics Products**	3297	Nonclay Refractories
2679	Converted Paper Products NEC	3011	Tires & Inner Tubes	3299	Nonmetallic Mineral Products NEC
		3021	Rubber & Plastics Footwear		
	27—Printing & Publishing	3052	Rubber & Plastics Hose & Belting		**33—Primary Metal Industries**
2711	Newspapers	3053	Gaskets, Packing & Sealing Devices	3312	Blast Furnaces & Steel Mills
2721	Periodicals	3061	Mechanical Rubber Goods	3313	Electrometallurgical Products
2731	Book Publishing	3069	Fabricated Rubber Products NEC	3315	Steel Wire & Related Products
2732	Book Printing	3081	Unsupported Plastics Film & Sheet	3316	Cold-Finishing of Steel Shapes
2741	Miscellaneous Publishing	3082	Unsupported Plastics Profile Shapes	3317	Steel Pipe & Tubes
2752	Commercial Printing—Lithographic	3083	Laminated Plastics Plate & Sheet	3321	Gray & Ductile Iron Foundries
2754	Commercial Printing—Gravure	3084	Plastics Pipe	3322	Malleable Iron Foundries
2759	Commercial Printing NEC	3085	Plastics Bottles	3324	Steel Investment Foundries
2761	Manifold Business Forms	3086	Plastics Foam Products	3325	Steel Foundries NEC
2771	Greeting Cards	3087	Custom Compound of Purchased Resins	3331	Primary Copper
2782	Blankbooks & Looseleaf Binders	3088	Plastics Plumbing Fixtures	3334	Primary Aluminum
2789	Bookbinding & Related Work	3089	Plastics Products NEC	3339	Primary Nonferrous Metals NEC
2791	Typesetting			3341	Secondary Nonferrous Metals
2796	Platemaking Services		**31—Leather & Leather Products**	3351	Copper Rolling & Drawing
		3111	Leather Tanning & Finishing	3353	Aluminum Sheet, Plate & Foil
	28—Chemicals & Allied Products	3131	Footwear Cut Stock	3354	Aluminum Extruded Products
2812	Alkalies & Chlorine	3142	House Slippers	3355	Aluminum Rolling & Drawing NEC
2813	Industrial Gases	3143	Men's Footwear Except Athletic	3356	Nonferrous Rolling & Drawing NEC
2816	Inorganic Pigments	3144	Women's Footwear Except Athletic	3357	Nonferrous Wiredrawing & Insulating
2819	Industrial Inorganic Chemicals NEC	3149	Footwear Except Rubber NEC	3363	Aluminum Die-Castings
2821	Plastics Materials & Resins	3151	Leather Gloves & Mittens	3364	Nonferrous Die-Castings Except Aluminum
2822	Synthetic Rubber			3365	Aluminum Foundries
2823	Cellulosic Manmade Fibers			3366	Copper Foundries
				3369	Nonferrous Foundries NEC

3398	Metal Heat Treating
3399	Primary Metal Products NEC

34—Fabricated Metal Products

3411	Metal Cans
3412	Metal Barrels, Drums & Pails
3421	Cutlery
3423	Hand & Edge Tools NEC
3425	Saw Blades & Handsaws
3429	Hardware NEC
3431	Metal Sanitary Ware
3432	Plumbing Fixtures Fittings & Trim
3433	Heating Equipment Except Electric
3441	Fabricated Structural Metal
3442	Metal Doors, Sash & Trim
3443	Fabricated Plate Work—Boiler Shops
3444	Sheet Metal Work
3446	Architectural Metal Work
3448	Prefabricated Metal Buildings
3449	Miscellaneous Metal Work
3451	Screw Machine Products
3452	Bolts, Nuts, Rivets & Washers
3462	Iron & Steel Forgings
3463	Nonferrous Forgings
3465	Automotive Stampings
3466	Crowns & Closures
3469	Metal Stampings NEC
3471	Plating & Polishing
3479	Metal Coating & Allied Services
3482	Small Arms Ammunition
3483	Ammunition Except for Small Arms
3484	Small Arms
3489	Ordnance & Accessories NEC
3491	Industrial Valves
3492	Fluid Power Valves & Hose Fittings
3493	Steel Springs Except Wire
3494	Valves & Pipe Fittings NEC
3495	Wire Springs
3496	Miscellaneous Fabricated Wire Products
3497	Metal Foil & Leaf
3498	Fabricated Pipe & Fittings
3499	Fabricated Metal Products NEC

35—Industrial Machinery & Equipment

3511	Turbines & Turbine Generator Sets
3519	Internal Combustion Engines NEC
3523	Farm Machinery & Equipment
3524	Lawn & Garden Equipment
3531	Construction Machinery
3532	Mining Machinery
3533	Oil & Gas Field Machinery
3534	Elevators & Moving Stairways
3535	Conveyors & Conveying Equipment
3536	Hoists, Cranes & Monorails
3537	Industrial Trucks & Tractors
3541	Machine Tools—Metal Cutting Types

3542	Machine Tools—Metal Forming Types
3543	Industrial Patterns
3544	Special Dies, Tools, Jigs & Fixtures
3545	Machine Tool Accessories
3546	Power-Driven Handtools
3547	Rolling Mill Machinery
3548	Welding Apparatus
3549	Metalworking Machinery NEC
3552	Textile Machinery
3553	Woodworking Machinery
3554	Paper Industries Machinery
3555	Printing Trades Machinery
3556	Food Products Machinery
3559	Special Industry Machinery NEC
3561	Pumps & Pumping Equipment
3562	Ball & Roller Bearings
3563	Air & Gas Compressors
3564	Blowers & Fans
3565	Packaging Machinery
3566	Speed Changers, Drives & Gears
3567	Industrial Furnaces & Ovens
3568	Power Transmission Equipment NEC
3569	General Industrial Machinery NEC
3571	Electronic Computers
3572	Computer Storage Devices
3575	Computer Terminals
3577	Computer Peripheral Equipment NEC
3578	Calculating & Accounting Equipment
3579	Office Machines NEC
3581	Automatic Vending Machines
3582	Commercial Laundry Equipment
3585	Refrigeration & Heating Equipment
3586	Measuring & Dispensing Pumps
3589	Service Industry Machinery NEC
3592	Carburetors, Pistons, Rings & Valves
3593	Fluid Power Cylinders & Actuators
3594	Fluid Power Pumps & Motors
3596	Scales & Balances Except Laboratory
3599	Industrial Machinery NEC

36—Electronic & Other Electrical Equipment

3612	Transformers Except Electronic
3613	Switchgear & Switchboard Apparatus
3621	Motors & Generators
3624	Carbon & Graphite Products
3625	Relays & Industrial Controls
3629	Electrical Industrial Apparatus NEC
3631	Household Cooking Equipment
3632	Household Refrigerators & Freezers
3633	Household Laundry Equipment

3634	Electric Housewares & Fans
3635	Household Vacuum Cleaners
3639	Household Appliances NEC
3641	Electric Lamps
3643	Current-Carrying Wiring Devices
3644	Noncurrent-Carrying Wiring Devices
3645	Residential Lighting Fixtures
3646	Commercial Lighting Fixtures
3647	Vehicular Lighting Equipment
3648	Lighting Equipment NEC
3651	Household Audio & Video Equipment
3652	Prerecorded Records & Tapes
3661	Telephone & Telegraph Apparatus
3663	Radio & T.V. Communications Equipment
3669	Communications Equipment NEC
3671	Electron Tubes
3672	Printed Circuit Boards
3674	Semiconductors & Related Devices
3675	Electronic Capacitors
3676	Electronic Resistors
3677	Electronic Coils & Transformers
3678	Electronic Connectors
3679	Electronic Components NEC
3691	Storage Batteries
3692	Primary Batteries—Dry & Wet
3694	Engine Electrical Equipment
3695	Magnetic & Optical Recording Media
3699	Electrical Equipment & Supplies NEC

37—Transportation Equipment

3711	Motor Vehicles & Car Bodies
3713	Truck & Bus Bodies
3714	Motor Vehicle Parts & Accessories
3715	Truck Trailers
3716	Motor Homes
3721	Aircraft
3724	Aircraft Engines & Engine Parts
3728	Aircraft Parts & Equipment NEC
3731	Ship Building & Repairing
3732	Boat Building & Repairing
3743	Railroad Equipment
3751	Motorcycles, Bicycles & Parts
3761	Guided Missiles & Space Vehicles
3764	Space Propulsion Units & Parts
3769	Space Vehicle Equipment NEC
3792	Travel Trailers & Campers
3795	Tanks & Tank Components
3799	Transportation Equipment NEC

38—Instruments & Related Products

3812	Search & Navigation Equipment
3821	Laboratory Apparatus & Furniture

3822	Environmental Controls
3823	Process Control Instruments
3824	Fluid Meters & Counting Devices
3825	Instruments to Measure Electricity
3826	Analytical Instruments
3827	Optical Instruments & Lenses
3829	Measuring & Controlling Devices NEC
3841	Surgical & Medical Instruments
3842	Surgical Appliances & Supplies
3843	Dental Equipment & Supplies
3844	X-Ray Apparatus & Tubes
3845	Electromedical Equipment
3851	Ophthalmic Goods
3861	Photographic Equipment & Supplies
3873	Watches, Clocks, Watchcases & Parts

39—Miscellaneous Manufacturing Industries

3911	Jewelry & Precious Metal
3914	Silverware & Plated Ware
3915	Jewelers' Materials & Lapidary Work
3931	Musical Instruments
3942	Dolls & Stuffed Toys
3944	Games, Toys & Children's Vehicles
3949	Sporting & Athletic Goods NEC
3951	Pens & Mechanical Pencils
3952	Lead Pencils & Art Goods
3953	Marking Devices
3955	Carbon Paper & Inked Ribbons
3961	Costume Jewelry
3965	Fasteners, Buttons, Needles & Pins
3991	Brooms & Brushes
3993	Signs & Advertising Displays
3995	Burial Caskets
3996	Hard Surface Floor Coverings NEC
3999	Manufacturing Industries NEC

40—Railroad Transportation

4011	Railroads—Line-Haul Operating
4013	Switching & Terminal Services

41—Local & Interurban Passenger Transit

4111	Local & Suburban Transit
4119	Local Passenger Transportation NEC
4121	Taxicabs
4131	Intercity & Rural Bus Transportation
4141	Local Bus Charter Service
4142	Bus Charter Service Except Local
4151	School Buses
4173	Bus Terminal & Service Facilities

42—Trucking & Warehousing

4212	Local Trucking Without Storage
4213	Trucking Except Local
4214	Local Trucking With Storage
4215	Courier Services Except by Air
4221	Farm Product Warehousing & Storage
4222	Refrigerated Warehousing & Storage
4225	General Warehousing & Storage
4226	Special Warehousing & Storage NEC
4231	Trucking Terminal Facilities

43—U.S. Postal Service

4311	U.S. Postal Service

44—Water Transportation

4412	Deep Sea Foreign Transportation of Freight
4424	Deep Sea Domestic Transportation of Freight
4432	Freight Transportation on the Great Lakes
4449	Water Transportation of Freight NEC
4481	Deep Sea Passenger Transportation Except Ferry
4482	Ferries
4489	Water Passenger Transportation NEC
4491	Marine Cargo Handling
4492	Towing & Tugboat Services
4493	Marinas
4499	Water Transportation Services NEC

45—Transportation by Air

4512	Air Transportation-Scheduled
4513	Air Courier Services
4522	Air Transportation-Nonscheduled
4581	Airports, Flying Fields & Services

46—Pipelines Except Natural Gas

4612	Crude Petroleum Pipelines
4613	Refined Petroleum Pipelines
4619	Pipelines NEC

47—Transportation Services

4724	Travel Agencies
4725	Tour Operators
4729	Passenger Transportation Arrangement NEC
4731	Freight Transportation Arrangement
4741	Rental of Railroad Cars
4783	Packing & Crating
4785	Inspection & Fixed Facilities
4789	Transportation Services NEC

48—Communications

4812	Radiotelephone Communications
4813	Telephone Communications Except Radiotelephone
4822	Telegraph & Other Communications
4832	Radio Broadcasting Stations
4833	Television Broadcasting Stations
4841	Cable & Other Pay Television Services
4899	Communications Services NEC

49—Electric, Gas & Sanitary Services

4911	Electric Services
4922	Natural Gas Transmission
4923	Gas Transmission & Distribution
4924	Natural Gas Distribution
4925	Gas Production & Distribution NEC
4931	Electric & Other Services Combined
4932	Gas & Other Services Combined
4939	Combination Utility NEC
4941	Water Supply
4952	Sewerage Systems
4953	Refuse Systems
4959	Sanitary Services NEC
4961	Steam & Air-Conditioning Supply
4971	Irrigation Systems

50—Wholesale Trade—Durable Goods

5012	Automobiles & Other Motor Vehicles
5013	Motor Vehicle Supplies & New Parts
5014	Tires & Tubes
5015	Motor Vehicle Parts-Used
5021	Furniture
5023	Homefurnishings
5031	Lumber, Plywood & Millwork
5032	Brick, Stone & Related Materials
5033	Roofing, Siding & Insulation
5039	Construction Materials NEC
5043	Photographic Equipment & Supplies
5044	Office Equipment
5045	Computers, Peripherals & Software
5046	Commercial Equipment NEC
5047	Medical & Hospital Equipment
5048	Ophthalmic Goods
5049	Professional Equipment NEC
5051	Metals Service Centers & Offices
5052	Coal, Other Minerals & Ores
5063	Electrical Apparatus & Equipment
5064	Electrical Appliances-Television & Radio
5065	Electronic Parts & Equipment NEC
5072	Hardware
5074	Plumbing & Hydronic Heating Supplies
5075	Warm Air Heating & Air-Conditioning
5078	Refrigeration Equipment & Supplies

5082	Construction & Mining Machinery
5083	Farm & Garden Machinery
5084	Industrial Machinery & Equipment
5085	Industrial Supplies
5087	Service Establishment Equipment
5088	Transportation Equipment & Supplies
5091	Sporting & Recreational Goods
5092	Toys & Hobby Goods & Supplies
5093	Scrap & Waste Materials
5094	Jewelry & Precious Stones
5099	Durable Goods NEC

51—Wholesale Trade—Nondurable Goods

5111	Printing & Writing Paper
5112	Stationery & Office Supplies
5113	Industrial & Personal Service Paper
5122	Drugs, Proprietaries & Sundries
5131	Piece Goods & Notions
5136	Men's/Boys' Clothing
5137	Women's/Children's Clothing
5139	Footwear
5141	Groceries—General Line
5142	Packaged Frozen Foods
5143	Dairy Products Except Dried or Canned
5144	Poultry & Poultry Products
5145	Confectionery
5146	Fish & Seafoods
5147	Meats & Meat Products
5148	Fresh Fruits & Vegetables
5149	Groceries & Related Products NEC
5153	Grain & Field Beans
5154	Livestock
5159	Farm—Product Raw Materials NEC
5162	Plastics Materials & Basic Shapes
5169	Chemicals & Allied Products NEC
5171	Petroleum Bulk Stations & Terminals
5172	Petroleum Products NEC
5181	Beer & Ale
5182	Wines & Distilled Beverages
5191	Farm Supplies
5192	Books, Periodicals & Newspapers
5193	Flowers & Florists' Supplies
5194	Tobacco & Tobacco Products
5198	Paints, Varnishes & Supplies
5199	Nondurable Goods NEC

52—Building Materials & Garden Supplies

5211	Lumber & Other Building Materials
5231	Paint, Glass & Wallpaper Stores
5251	Hardware Stores
5261	Retail Nurseries & Garden Stores
5271	Mobile Home Dealers

53—General Merchandise Stores

5311	Department Stores
5331	Variety Stores
5399	Miscellaneous General Merchandise Store

54—Food Stores

5411	Grocery Stores
5421	Meat & Fish Markets
5431	Fruit & Vegetable Markets
5441	Candy, Nut & Confectionery Stores
5451	Dairy Products Stores
5461	Retail Bakeries
5499	Miscellaneous Food Stores

55—Automotive Dealers & Service Stations

5511	New & Used Car Dealers
5521	Used Car Dealers
5531	Automobile & Home Supply Stores
5541	Gasoline Service Stations
5551	Boat Dealers
5561	Recreational Vehicle Dealers
5571	Motorcycle Dealers
5599	Automotive Dealers NEC

56—Apparel & Accessory Stores

5611	Men's & Boys' Clothing Stores
5621	Women's Clothing Stores
5632	Women's Accessory & Specialty Stores
5641	Children's & Infants' Wear Stores
5651	Family Clothing Stores
5661	Shoe Stores
5699	Miscellaneous Apparel & Accessory Stores

57—Furniture & Homefurnishings Stores

5712	Furniture Stores
5713	Floor Covering Stores
5714	Drapery & Upholstery Stores
5719	Miscellaneous Home Furnishings Stores
5722	Household Appliance Stores
5731	Radio, Television & Electronics Stores
5734	Computer & Software Stores
5735	Record & Prerecorded Tape Stores
5736	Musical Instruments Stores

58—Eating & Drinking Places

5812	Eating Places
5813	Drinking Places

59—Miscellaneous Retail

5912	Drug Stores & Proprietary Stores
5921	Liquor Stores
5932	Used Merchandise Stores
5941	Sporting Goods & Bicycle Shops
5942	Book Stores
5943	Stationery Stores
5944	Jewelry Stores
5945	Hobby, Toy & Game Shops

5946	Camera & Photographic Supply Stores
5947	Gift, Novelty & Souvenir Shops
5948	Luggage & Leather Goods Stores
5949	Sewing, Needlework & Piece Goods
5961	Catalog & Mail-Order Houses
5962	Merchandising Machine Operators
5963	Direct Selling Establishments
5983	Fuel Oil Dealers
5984	Liquefied Petroleum Gas Dealers
5989	Fuel Dealers NEC
5992	Florists
5993	Tobacco Stores & Stands
5994	News Dealers & Newsstands
5995	Optical Goods Stores
5999	Miscellaneous Retail Stores NEC

60—Depository Institutions

6011	Federal Reserve Banks
6019	Central Reserve Depository NEC
6021	National Commercial Banks
6022	State Commercial Banks
6029	Commercial Banks NEC
6035	Federal Savings Institutions
6036	Savings Institutions Except Federal
6061	Federal Credit Unions
6062	State Credit Unions
6081	Foreign Banks-Branches & Agencies
6082	Foreign Trade & International Banks
6091	Nondeposit Trust Facilities
6099	Functions Related to Deposit Banking

61—Nondepository Institutions

6111	Federal & Federally-Sponsored Credit
6141	Personal Credit Institutions
6153	Short-Term Business Credit
6159	Miscellaneous Business Credit Institutions
6162	Mortgage Bankers & Correspondents
6163	Loan Brokers

62—Security & Commodity Brokers

6211	Security Brokers & Dealers
6221	Commodity Contracts Brokers & Dealers
6231	Security & Commodity Exchanges
6282	Investment Advice
6289	Security & Commodity Services NEC

63—Insurance Carriers

6311	Life Insurance
6321	Accident & Health Insurance
6324	Hospital & Medical Service Plans
6331	Fire, Marine & Casualty Insurance
6351	Surety Insurance

6361	Title Insurance
6371	Pension, Health & Welfare Funds
6399	Insurance Carriers NEC

64—Insurance Agents, Brokers & Service

6411	Insurance Agents, Brokers & Service

65—Real Estate

6512	Nonresidential Building Operators
6513	Apartment Building Operators
6514	Dwelling Operators Except Apartments
6515	Mobile Home Site Operators
6517	Railroad Property Lessors
6519	Real Property Lessors NEC
6531	Real Estate Agents & Managers
6541	Title Abstract Offices
6552	Subdividers & Developers NEC
6553	Cemetery Subdividers & Developers

67—Holding & Other Investment Offices

6712	Bank Holding Companies
6719	Holding Companies NEC
6722	Management Investment—Open-End
6726	Investment Offices NEC
6732	Educational & Religious Trusts
6733	Trusts NEC
6792	Oil Royalty Traders
6794	Patent Owners & Lessors
6798	Real Estate Investment Trusts
6799	Investors NEC

70—Hotels & Other Lodging Places

7011	Hotels & Motels
7021	Rooming & Boarding Houses
7032	Sporting & Recreational Camps
7033	Trailer Parks & Campsites
7041	Membership-Basis Organization Hotels

72—Personal Services

7211	Power Laundries—Family & Commercial
7212	Garment Pressing & Cleaners' Agents
7213	Linen Supply
7215	Coin-Operated Laundries & Cleaning
7216	Dry Cleaning Plants Except Rug
7217	Carpet & Upholstery Cleaning
7218	Industrial Launderers
7219	Laundry & Garment Services NEC
7221	Photographic Studios—Portrait
7231	Beauty Shops
7241	Barber Shops
7251	Shoe Repair & Shoeshine Parlors

7261	Funeral Services & Crematories
7291	Tax Return Preparation Services
7299	Miscellaneous Personal Services NEC

73—Business Services

7311	Advertising Agencies
7312	Outdoor Advertising Services
7313	Radio, T.V. & Publisher Representatives
7319	Advertising NEC
7322	Adjustment & Collection Services
7323	Credit Reporting Services
7331	Direct Mail Advertising Services
7334	Photocopying & Duplicating Services
7335	Commercial Photography
7336	Commercial Art & Graphic Design
7338	Secretarial & Court Reporting
7342	Disinfecting & Pest Control Services
7349	Building Maintenance Services NEC
7352	Medical Equipment Rental
7353	Heavy Construction Equipment Rental
7359	Equipment Rental & Leasing NEC
7361	Employment Agencies
7363	Help Supply Services
7371	Computer Programming Services
7372	Prepackaged Software
7373	Computer Integrated Systems Design
7374	Data Processing & Preparation
7375	Information Retrieval Services
7376	Computer Facilities Management
7377	Computer Rental & Leasing
7378	Computer Maintenance & Repair
7379	Computer Related Services NEC
7381	Detective & Armored Car Services
7382	Security Systems Services
7383	News Syndicates
7384	Photofinishing Laboratories
7389	Business Services NEC

75—Automobile Repair, Services & Parking

7513	Truck Rental & Leasing Without Drivers
7514	Passenger Car Rental
7515	Passenger Car Leasing
7519	Utility Trailer Rental
7521	Automobile Parking
7532	Top & Body Repair & Paint Shops
7533	Automobile Exhaust System Repair Shops
7534	Tire Retreading & Repair Shops
7536	Automotive Glass Replacement Shops

7537	Automotive Transmission Repair Shops
7538	General Automotive Repair Shops
7539	Automotive Repair Shops NEC
7542	Car Washes
7549	Automotive Services NEC

76—Miscellaneous Repair Services

7622	Radio & T.V. Repair
7623	Refrigeration Services Repair
7629	Electrical Repair Shops NEC
7631	Watch, Clock & Jewelry Repair
7641	Reupholstery & Furniture Repair
7692	Welding Repair
7694	Armature Rewinding Shops
7699	Repair Services NEC

78—Motion Pictures

7812	Motion Picture & Video Production
7819	Services Allied to Motion Pictures
7822	Motion Picture & Tape Distribution
7829	Motion Picture Distribution Services
7832	Motion Picture Theaters Except Drive-In
7833	Drive-In Motion Picture Theaters
7841	Video Tape Rental

79—Amusement & Recreation Services

7911	Dance Studios, Schools & Halls
7922	Theatrical Producers & Services
7929	Entertainers & Entertainment Groups
7933	Bowling Centers
7941	Sports Clubs, Managers & Promoters
7948	Racing Including Track Operations
7991	Physical Fitness Facilities
7992	Public Golf Courses
7993	Coin-Operated Amusement Devices
7996	Amusement Parks
7997	Membership Sports & Recreation Clubs
7999	Amusement & Recreation NEC

80—Health Services

8011	Offices & Clinics of Medical Doctors
8021	Offices & Clinics of Dentists
8031	Offices of Osteopathic Physicians
8041	Offices & Clinics of Chiropractors
8042	Offices & Clinics of Optometrists
8043	Offices & Clinics of Podiatrists
8049	Offices of Health Practitioners NEC
8051	Skilled Nursing Care Facilities

8052	Intermediate Care Facilities
8059	Nursing & Personal Care NEC
8062	General Medical & Surgical Hospitals
8063	Psychiatric Hospitals
8069	Specialty Hospitals Except Psychiatric
8071	Medical Laboratories
8072	Dental Laboratories
8082	Home Health Care Services
8092	Kidney Dialysis Centers
8093	Specialty Outpatient Facilities NEC
8099	Health & Allied Services NEC

81—Legal Services

8111	Legal Services

82—Educational Services

8211	Elementary & Secondary Schools
8221	Colleges & Universities
8222	Junior Colleges
8231	Libraries
8243	Data Processing Schools
8244	Business & Secretarial Schools
8249	Vocational Schools NEC
8299	Schools & Educational Services NEC

83—Social Services

8322	Individual & Family Services
8331	Job Training & Related Services
8351	Child Day Care Services
8361	Residential Care
8399	Social Services NEC

84—Museums, Botanical & Zoological Gardens

8412	Museums & Art Galleries
8422	Botanical & Zoological Gardens

86—Membership Organizations

8611	Business Associations
8621	Professional Organizations
8631	Labor Organizations
8641	Civic & Social Associations
8651	Political Organizations
8661	Religious Organizations
8699	Membership Organizations NEC

87—Engineering & Management Services

8711	Engineering Services
8712	Architectural Services
8713	Surveying Services
8721	Accounting, Auditing & Book-keeping
8731	Commercial Physical Research
8732	Commercial Nonphysical Research
8733	Noncommercial Research Organizations
8734	Testing Laboratories
8741	Management Services

8742	Management Consulting Services
8743	Public Relations Services
8744	Facilities Support Services
8748	Business Consulting Services NEC

88—Private Households

8811	Private Households

89—Services Not Elsewhere Classified

8999	Services NEC

91—Executive, Legislative & General

9111	Executive Offices
9121	Legislative Bodies
9131	Executive and Legislative Combined
9199	General Government NEC

92—Justice, Public Order & Safety

9211	Courts
9221	Police Protection
9222	Legal Counsel & Prosecution
9223	Correctional Institutions
9224	Fire Protection
9229	Public Order & Safety NEC

93—Finance, Taxation & Monetary Policy

9311	Finance, Taxation & Monetary Policy

94—Administration of Human Resources

9411	Administration of Educational Programs
9431	Administration of Public Health Programs
9441	Administration of Social and Manpower Programs
9451	Administration of Veterans' Affairs

95—Environmental Quality & Housing

9511	Air, Water & Solid Waste Management
9512	Land, Mineral and Wildlife Conservation
9531	Housing Programs
9532	Urban & Community Development

96—Administration of Economic Programs

9611	Administration of General Economic Programs
9621	Regulation & Administration of Transportation
9631	Regulation & Administration of Utilities
9641	Regulation of Agricultural Marketing
9651	Regulation of Miscellaneous Commercial Sectors
9661	Space Research & Technology

97—National Security & International Affairs

9711	National Security
9721	International Affairs

99—Nonclassifiable Establishments

9999	Nonclassifiable Establishments

Standard Industrial Classification (SIC) Codes Alphabetic Listings

Company Rankings by Sales within 4-Digit SIC

This section features rankings by sales within 4-digit SIC and the total number of companies, sales, and employees for each SIC. Financial figures are in millions. If sales are less than one million, <1 is given. Employees are in thousands. If the number of employees is less than 100, <.1 is given. The total financial and employee figures provided at the end of each SIC reflect the totals for only those companies listing financial and employee information. An indented line indicates immediate parent of the preceding company when they share a 4-digit SIC. Abbreviations, codes and symbols are defined in the introductory section. See Volumes 1, 2, and 3 for complete company information.

Rank	Company Name—*Executive Officer*	Address, City, State, Zip	Phone	Type	Fin	Empls
0111 Wheat						
1	Central Washington Grain Growers Inc—*Kevin Whitehall*	PO Box 649, Waterville WA 98858	509-745-8551	R	9*	.1
0112 Rice						
1	Mcfadden Farm—*Eugene Mcfadden*	16000 Powerhouse Rd, Potter Valley CA 95469	707-743-1122	R	2*	.1
0115 Corn						
1	Pioneer Hi-Bred International Inc—*Dean Oestreich*	PO Box 1000, Johnston IA 50131	515-270-3200	S	1,899*	5.2
2	Moews Seed Co—*Bettina Moews*	PO Box 214, Granville IL 61326	815-339-2201	R	3*	.1
3	Hillhouse Naturals Farm Ltd—*Shelly Batts*	7070 Wickliffe Rd, Wickliffe KY 42087	270-335-3585	R	1*	<.1
TOTALS: SIC 0115 Corn						
	Companies: 3				1,903	5.3
0119 Cash Grains Nec						
1	JD Heiskell and Co—*Duane Fischer*	PO Box 1379, Tulare CA 93275	559-685-6100	R	840*	.3
2	John I Haas Inc	5185 MacArthur Blvd NW, Washington DC 20016	202-777-4800	S	160*	2.0
3	Jewett-Cameron Seed Co—*Donald M Boone*	PO Box 816, North Plains OR 97133	503-647-2293	S	12*	<.1
4	Caswell Booe—*Booe Caswell*	3732 Hartman Rd, Yadkinville NC 27055	336-463-5938	R	1*	<.1
TOTALS: SIC 0119 Cash Grains Nec						
	Companies: 4				1,013	2.3
0131 Cotton						
1	Gerli and Co—*John M Sullivan*	41 Madison Ave, New York NY 10010	212-213-1919	R	3*	<.1
0132 Tobacco						
1	National Cigar Corp—*James Pogue*	PO Box 97, Frankfort IN 46041	765-659-3326	R	3*	<.1
0134 Irish Potatoes						
1	Agri-Empire—*Jim Minor*	PO Box 490, San Jacinto CA 92581	909-654-7311	R	46*	.2
2	Anthony Farms Inc—*Victor Anthony Jr*	PO Box 4, Scandinavia WI 54977	715-467-2212	R	16*	.1
TOTALS: SIC 0134 Irish Potatoes						
	Companies: 2				62	.3
0139 Field Crops Except Cash Grains Nec						
1	Pike Creek Turf Farms Inc—*Jaimie Allen*	427 Pike Creek Turf Ci, Adel GA 31620	229-896-7581	R	31*	.1
2	Laurel Valley Farms Inc—*Clint Blackwell*	PO Box 640, Avondale PA 19311	610-268-2075	R	20*	<.1
3	ML Macadamia Orchards LP—*Dennis J Simonis*	26-238 Hawaii Belt, Hilo HI 96720	808-969-8057	P	15	.3
4	Bruce Seed Farm—*Arden Bruce*	91 Lower Deep Creek Rd, Townsend MT 59644	406-266-3103	S	5*	<.1
5	Barenbrug USA Inc—*John Thyssen*	PO Box 239, Tangent OR 97389	541-926-5801	S	4*	.1
6	Back Acre Hop Farms Inc—*Paul Serres*	11283 Serres Ln Ne, Woodburn OR 97071	503-981-6098	R	3*	<.1
TOTALS: SIC 0139 Field Crops Except Cash Grains Nec						
	Companies: 6				78	.5
0161 Vegetables & Melons						
1	Fresh Del Monte Produce Inc—*Mohammad Abu-Ghazaleh*	PO Box 149222, Coral Gables FL 33114	305-520-8400	P	3,590	42.0
2	Tanimura and Antle Inc—*Rick Antle*	PO Box 4070, Salinas CA 93912	831-455-2950	R	589*	2.5
3	A Duda and Sons Inc—*Joseph Duda*	PO Box 620257, Oviedo FL 32762	407-365-2111	R	425*	1.0
4	Taylor and Fulton Inc—*Brian Turner*	PO Box 99, Palmetto FL 34220	941-729-3883	R	220*	1.0
5	William Bolthouse Farms Inc—*Andre Radandt*	7200 E Brundage Ln, Bakersfield CA 93307	661-366-7205	R	167*	2.0
6	Merrill Farms Inc—*Russ Merrill*	PO Box 659, Salinas CA 93902	831-424-7365	R	90*	.4
7	Wilson Farms Inc—*Paul Nanula*	1780 Wehrle Dr, Williamsville NY 14221	716-204-4300	R	88*	.4
8	Growers Express LLC—*Jamie Strachan*	PO Box 948, Salinas CA 93902	831-757-9700	R	73*	.4
9	Deardorff-Jackson Co—*Tom Deardorff*	PO Box 1188, Oxnard CA 93032	805-487-7801	R	56*	.3
10	Earthbound Farm Inc—*Drew Goodman*	1721 San Juan Hwy, San Juan Bautista CA 95045		R	35*	.2
11	Royal Packing Co—*Eric Schwartz*	639 Sanborn Pl, Salinas CA 93901	831-424-0975	S	21*	.2
12	Russo Farms Inc—*Thomas Russo*	1962 S East Ave, Vineland NJ 08360	856-692-5942	R	21*	.1
13	Harry Singh and Sons—*Harry Singh*	PO Box 1850, Oceanside CA 92051	760-758-9299	R	17*	.1
14	Bianchi and Sons Packing Co—*John Bianchi*	PO Box 190, Merced CA 95341	209-722-8134	R	12*	.1
15	Grimmway Farms Enterprises—*Robert Grimm*	PO Box 81498, Bakersfield CA 93380	661-845-5200	R	8*	.1
16	Harris Farms Inc—*John Harris*	27366 W Oakland Ave, Coalinga CA 93210	559-884-2859	R	8*	<.1
17	Nunes Company Inc—*Tom Nunes Jr*	PO Box 673, Salinas CA 93902	831-751-7500	R	7*	<.1

Note: An asterisk (*) indicates an estimated financial figure. The company type code used is as follows: R = Private, P = Public, S = Private Subsidiary, B = Public Subsidiary, D = Division, J = Joint Venture, I = Investment Fund.

COMPANY RANKINGS BY SALES WITHIN 4-DIGIT SIC

Rank	Company Name—Executive Officer	Address, City, State, Zip	Phone	Type	Fin	Empls
18	Sundia Corp—Jim Watkins	70 Washington St Ste 4, Oakland CA 94607	415-762-0600	R	5*	<.1
19	Foster Family Farm—Chris Foster	11006 W Ct St, Pasco WA 99301	509-266-4609	R	2*	.1
20	Asia Green Agriculture Corp—Zhan Youdai	174 FM 1830, Argyle TX 76226	972-233-0300	P	1	.3
21	Leach Farms Inc—Thomas Leach	W1102 Buttercup Ct, Berlin WI 54923	920-361-1880	R	1*	<.1

TOTALS: SIC 0161 Vegetables & Melons
Companies: 21 — 5,435 / 51.1

0171 Berry Crops

Rank	Company Name—Executive Officer	Address, City, State, Zip	Phone	Type	Fin	Empls
1	Naturipe Farms—Rich Amirsehhi	999 Vanderbilt Beach R, Naples FL 34108	239-591-1664	R	17*	.1
2	Robert Rothschild Farms LLC—Mary O'donnell	3143 E Us Hwy 36, Urbana OH 43078	937-653-7397	R	2*	<.1
3	Adkin and Son Associated Food Products Inc—Roy Adkin	6645 107th Ave, South Haven MI 49090	269-637-7450	R	2*	<.1

TOTALS: SIC 0171 Berry Crops
Companies: 3 — 21 / .1

0172 Grapes

Rank	Company Name—Executive Officer	Address, City, State, Zip	Phone	Type	Fin	Empls
1	Symms Fruit Ranch Inc—RA Symms	14068 Sunny Slope Rd, Caldwell ID 83607	208-459-4821	R	125*	.2
2	Delicato Vineyards—Chris Indelicato	12001 S Hwy 99, Manteca CA 95336	209-824-3501	R	110*	.2
3	Giumarra Vineyards Corp—Sal Giumarra	PO Box 1969, Bakersfield CA 93303	661-395-7000	R	100*	3.5
4	National Raisin Co—Ernie Bedrosian	PO Box 219, Fowler CA 93625	559-834-5981	R	63*	.3
5	John Kautz Farms—John Kautz	5920 E Live Oak Rd, Lodi CA 95240	209-334-4786	R	35*	.2
6	Scheid Vineyards Inc—Scott D Scheid	305 Hilltown Rd, Salinas CA 93908	831-455-9990	P	30	.1
7	Domaine Carneros—Eileen Crane	PO Box 5420, Napa CA 94581	707-257-0101	R	19*	.1
8	Jordan Vineyard and Winery—John Jordan	PO Box 878, Healdsburg CA 95448	707-431-5250	R	19*	.1
9	Luna Vineyards—Mary Ann Tsai	2921 Silverado Trail, Napa CA 94558		R	14*	<.1
10	Gainey Vineyard—Daniel Gainey	PO Box 910, Santa Ynez CA 93460	805-688-0558	R	6*	<.1
11	Diamond Creek Vineyards—Phil Steinschriber	1500 Diamond Mountain, Calistoga CA 94515	707-942-6926	R	6*	<.1
12	New Vavin Inc—Kristen Holzman	154 Winery Ln, Leon VA 22725	540-547-3707	R	4*	<.1
13	Byron Vineyard and Winery—Ken Brown	5475 Chardonnay Ln, Santa Maria CA 93454	805-934-4770	S	3*	<.1
14	Swanson Vineyards and Winery—W Clarke Swanson Jr	PO Box 459, Rutherford CA 94573	707-754-4018	R	3*	<.1
15	Raymond Vineyard and Cellar Inc—Jean Boisset	849 Zinfandel Ln, Saint Helena CA 94574	707-963-3141	R	2*	<.1
16	Fisher Vineyard—Fred Fisher	6200 St Helena Rd, Santa Rosa CA 95404	707-539-7511	R	2*	<.1
17	H Edwin Hauler—Edwin Auler	1402 San Antonio St St, Austin TX 78701	512-476-4477	R	2*	<.1
18	Chateau Operations Ltd—Robert Begin	15900 Rue De Vin, Traverse City MI 49686	231-223-4110	R	2*	<.1
19	Palmer Vineyards Inc—Robert Palmer	PO Box 2125, Aquebogue NY 11931	631-722-9463	R	1*	<.1
20	Sakonnet Vineyards LP—Earl Samson	PO Box 197, Little Compton RI 02837	401-635-4356	R	1*	<.1
21	Mcdowell Valley Vineyards Inc	PO Box 449, Hopland CA 95449	707-744-1053	R	1*	<.1
22	Dalla Valle Vineyards—Naoko Dalla Valle	PO Box 329, Oakville CA 94562	707-944-2676	R	1*	<.1
23	Boordy Vineyards—Robert Deford	12820 Long Green Pke, Hydes MD 21082	410-592-5015	R	1*	<.1
24	RH Keenan Co—Robert Keenan	3660 Spring Mountain R, Saint Helena CA 94574	707-963-9177	R	<1*	<.1

TOTALS: SIC 0172 Grapes
Companies: 24 — 550 / 5.0

0173 Tree Nuts

Rank	Company Name—Executive Officer	Address, City, State, Zip	Phone	Type	Fin	Empls
1	C Brewer and Company Ltd—James Andrasick	26-238 Hawaii Belt Rd, Hilo HI 96720	808-969-1826	R	1,654*	.8
2	Wailuku Water Company LLC—Avery B Chumbley	255 E Waiko Rd, Wailuku HI 96793	808-244-9590	R	10*	.1
3	MacFarms of Hawaii—Jeff Gilbrech	89-406 Mamalahoa Hwy, Captain Cook HI 96704	808-328-2435	R	9*	.1
4	Pape's Pecan House—Kenneth Pape	101 S 123rd Byp, Seguin TX 78155	830-379-7442	R	5*	<.1
5	Columbia Empire Farms Inc—Floyd Aylor	PO Box 1, Dundee OR 97115	503-538-2156	R	4*	.1

TOTALS: SIC 0173 Tree Nuts
Companies: 5 — 1,683 / 1.1

0174 Citrus Fruits

Rank	Company Name—Executive Officer	Address, City, State, Zip	Phone	Type	Fin	Empls
1	Lykes Agriculture—John Gose	7 Lykes Rd, Lake Placid FL 33852	863-465-4127	S	358*	.4
2	Ben Hill Griffin Inc—Ben Hill Griffin IV	PO Box 127, Frostproof FL 33843	863-635-2251	R	344*	.3
3	Jack M Berry Inc—Jack M Berry Jr	PO Box 459, LaBelle FL 33935	863-675-2769	R	234*	.9
4	Limoneira Co—Harold S Edwards	1141 Cummings Rd, Santa Paula CA 93060	805-525-5541	R	169*	.3
5	Alico Inc—JD Alexander	10070 Daniels Intersta, Fort Myers FL 33913	239-226-2000	P	99	.1
6	Bob Paul Inc—John R Paul Jr	PO Box 898, Winter Haven FL 33882	863-293-6317	R	13*	<.1
7	Peace River Citrus Products Inc—R Becker	PO Box 730, Arcadia FL 34265	772-492-4050	R	8*	.1

TOTALS: SIC 0174 Citrus Fruits
Companies: 7 — 1,224 / 2.1

0175 Deciduous Tree Fruits

Rank	Company Name—Executive Officer	Address, City, State, Zip	Phone	Type	Fin	Empls
1	Ontelaunee Orchards Inc—Walter Pohl	PO Box 182, Leesport PA 19533	610-926-2187	R	1,800*	<.1
2	CM Holtzinger Fruit Company LLC—C Mark Holtzinger	PO Box 989, Yakima WA 98907	509-457-5115	R	40*	.4
3	Auvil Fruit Company Inc—Mike Claphan	21902 State Rte 97, Oroville WA 98844	509-784-1033	R	32	.1
4	P-R Farms Inc—Pat V Ricchiuti	2917 E Shepherd, Clovis CA 93619	559-299-0201	R	20*	.2
5	Rice Fruit Co—John Rice	PO Box 66, Gardners PA 17324	717-677-8131	R	15*	.1
6	Mike Jensen Farms—Mike Jensen	13138 S Bethel Ave, Kingsburg CA 93631	559-897-4192	R	10*	.2
7	Lyman Farm Inc—Donald Richards	PO Box 453, Middlefield CT 06455	860-349-1793	R	3*	.1
8	Meadowbrook Orchards Inc—David Chandler	209 Chace Hill Rd, Sterling MA 01564	978-365-7617	R	1*	<.1
9	Oakwood Fruit Farm Inc—John Louis	31128 Apple Ridge Rd, Richland Center WI 53581	608-585-2701	R	1*	<.1
10	Apple Farm—Steven Meyerhans	104 Back Rd, Fairfield ME 04937	207-453-7656	R	1*	<.1
11	Country Mill Farms LLC	4648 Otto Rd, Charlotte MI 48813	517-543-1019	R	1*	<.1

TOTALS: SIC 0175 Deciduous Tree Fruits
Companies: 11 — 1,924 / 1.1

0179 Fruits & Tree Nuts Nec

Rank	Company Name—Executive Officer	Address, City, State, Zip	Phone	Type	Fin	Empls
1	Chiquita Brands International Inc—Fernando Aguirre	250 E 5th St, Cincinnati OH 45202	513-784-8000	P	3,139	21.0
2	Calavo Growers Inc—Lecil E Cole	1141A Cummings Rd, Santa Paula CA 93060	805-525-1245	P	523	1.5
3	Crest Fruit Inc—Val Gersting	PO Box 3090, Mission TX 78573	956-205-7300	D	17*	.2
4	D DeFranco and Sons Inc—Jerald DeFranco	1000 Lawrence St, Los Angeles CA 90021	213-627-8575	R	7*	.1
5	CC Graber Co—Clifford Graber	PO Box 511, Ontario CA 91762	909-983-1761	R	2*	<.1

TOTALS: SIC 0179 Fruits & Tree Nuts Nec
Companies: 5 — 3,687 / 22.8

0181 Ornamental Nursery Products

Rank	Company Name—Executive Officer	Address, City, State, Zip	Phone	Type	Fin	Empls
1	Ruppert Nurseries Inc—Craig Ruppert	7950 Hawkins Creamery, Laytonsville MD 20882		R	1,087*	2.0

Rank	Company Name—*Executive Officer*	Address, City, State, Zip	Phone	Type	Fin	Empls
2	Seminis Inc—*Glenn Stith*	2700 Camino del Sol, Oxnard CA 93030	805-647-1572	S	503*	3.0
3	Stark Brothers Nurseries—*Clay Stark Logan*	PO Box 1800, Louisiana MO 63353		R	439*	.4
4	LG Seeds Inc	22827 Shissler Rd, Elmwood IL 61529		R	247*	.2
5	Bell Nursery USA LLC—*Tony Moa*	3838 Bell Rd, Burtonsville MD 20866	301-421-1500	R	146*	<.1
6	W Atlee Burpee Co—*Christos Romas*	300 Park Ave, Warminster PA 18974	215-674-4900	R	117*	.4
7	Gurney Seed and Nursery Corp—*Niles Kinerk*	PO Box 4178, Greendale IN 47025	513-354-1492	R	88*	.7
8	Zelenka Nursery Inc—*Bob Berry*	16127 Winans St, Grand Haven MI 49417		R	88*	.7
9	Aris Horticulture Inc—*William Rasbach*	PO Box 230, Barberton OH 44203	330-745-2143	R	74*	.7
10	Mycogen Seeds—*Jerome Peribere*	9330 Zionsville Rd, Indianapolis IN 46268	317-337-3000	S	65*	1.1
11	Miller Plant Farms Inc—*James Estill*	PO Box 755, Winona TX 75792	903-877-2099	S	47	.3
12	Conard-Pyle Co—*Steve Hutton*	25 Lewis Rd, West Grove PA 19390	610-869-2426	R	38*	.3
13	Green Circle Growers Inc—*John Vanwingerden*	51051 US Hwy 20, Oberlin OH 44074	440-775-1411	R	25*	.2
14	Thomsen Greenhouses and Garden Center Inc—*Arno Shermock*	29754 156th Ave, St Joseph MN 56374	320-363-7375	R	24*	<.1
15	Van Wingerden International Inc	4112 Haywood Rd, Mills River NC 28759	828-891-4116	R	20*	.3
16	Alf Christianson Seed Co—*Hideo Takahashi*	11857 Bay Ridge Dr, Burlington WA 98233	360-336-9727	D	15*	.1
17	Speedling Inc—*Greg Davis*	PO Box 7220, Sun City FL 33586	813-645-3261	R	15*	.3
18	Margo Caribe Inc—*Michael J Spector*	Call Box 1370, Dorado PR 00646	787-883-2570	P	10	.1
19	Veldheer Tulip Garden Inc—*Vernon Veldheer*	12755 Quincy St, Holland MI 49424	616-399-1900	R	4*	.1
20	Charles C Hart Seed Co—*Charles H Hart*	PO Box 9169, Wethersfield CT 06129	860-529-2537	R	3*	<.1

TOTALS: SIC 0181 Ornamental Nursery Products
Companies: 20   3,054   10.6

0182 Food Crops Grown Under Cover

Rank	Company Name—*Executive Officer*	Address, City, State, Zip	Phone	Type	Fin	Empls
1	Monterey Mushrooms Inc—*Shah Kazmi*	260 Westgate Dr, Watsonville CA 95076	831-763-5300	R	744*	3.0
2	Village Farms LP—*Albert Vanzeyst*	7 Christopher Way, Eatontown NJ 07724	732-676-3000	S	53	.8
3	Sylvan Inc—*Mark Snyder*	90 Glade Dr, Kittanning PA 16201	724-543-3900	R	43*	.4
4	Modern Mushroom Farms Inc—*Charles Ciarrocchi*	PO Box 340, Avondale PA 19311	610-268-3535	R	15*	.5
5	Phillips Mushroom Farms LP—*Bill Stellar*	PO Box 190, Kennett Square PA 19348	610-444-4492	R	13*	.3
6	J-M Farms Inc—*Curtis Jurgensmeyer*	7001 S 580 Rd, Miami OK 74354	918-540-1567	R	8*	.3
7	Gourmet Mushrooms—*Malcom Clark*	PO Box 515, Graton CA 95444	707-829-7301	R	7*	<.1
8	Sylvan America Inc / Sylvan Inc	90 Glade Dr, Kittanning PA 16201	724-352-7520	S	3*	<.1
9	Calco Sprouts Inc—*Jino Yen*	2751 Minnehaha Ave, Minneapolis MN 55406	612-724-0276	R	2*	<.1
10	Shanghai Company Inc—*Chester Louie*	2800 Se Division St, Portland OR 97202	503-235-2525	R	2*	<.1

TOTALS: SIC 0182 Food Crops Grown Under Cover
Companies: 10   889   5.4

0191 General Farms—Primarily Crop

Rank	Company Name—*Executive Officer*	Address, City, State, Zip	Phone	Type	Fin	Empls
1	Agrinorthwest—*Don Sleight*	PO Box 2308, Pasco WA 99302	509-734-1190	R	134*	.5
2	DM Camp and Sons—*Don Camp Sr*	PO Box 80007, Bakersfield CA 93380	661-399-5511	R	65*	.3
3	JC Watson Company Inc—*Jon C Watson*	PO Box 300, Parma ID 83660	208-722-5141	R	10*	.1
4	US Farms Inc—*Jim Farooquer*	5404 Alton Pky Ste 5A3, Irvine CA 92604		P	10	<.1
5	Earthrise Nutritionals LLC—*Taro Ichimoto*	2151 Michelson Dr Ste, Irvine CA 92612	949-623-0980	R	3*	.1
6	Wolfsen Land and Cattle Co—*Donald C Skinner*	1269 W I St, Los Banos CA 93635	209-827-7700	R	<1	.1

TOTALS: SIC 0191 General Farms—Primarily Crop
Companies: 6   222   1.0

0211 Beef Cattle Feedlots

Rank	Company Name—*Executive Officer*	Address, City, State, Zip	Phone	Type	Fin	Empls
1	Cactus Feeders Inc—*Michael Engler*	PO Box 3050, Amarillo TX 79116	806-373-2333	R	750*	.5
2	Hitch Enterprises Inc—*Chris Hitch*	PO Box 1308, Guymon OK 73942	580-338-8575	R	635*	.3
3	Cargill Cattle Feeders—*Gregory Page*	151 N Main, Wichita KS 67202	316-291-2500	S	584*	.9
4	Agri Beef Co—*Robert Rebholtz Jr*	PO Box 6640, Boise ID 83707	208-338-2500	R	281*	.4
5	AzTx Cattle Co—*John Josserand*	PO Box 390, Hereford TX 79045	806-364-8871	R	169*	.2
6	Great Bend Feeding Inc—*Bill Bunker*	355 NW 30th Ave, Great Bend KS 67530	620-792-2508	R	63*	<.1
7	Barrett-Crofoot Inc—*Edward C Barrett*	PO Box 670, Hereford TX 79045	806-364-6081	R	37*	<.1
8	Ingalls Feed Yard—*Eddie Nichols*	10505 US Hwy 50, Ingalls KS 67853		D	17*	<.1
9	Oshkosh FeedYard Corp—*Terry Jessen*	PO Box 440, Oshkosh NE 69154	308-772-3237	R	17*	<.1
10	Walter Lasley and Sons Inc—*Walter E Lasley*	PO Box 168, Stratford TX 79084	806-753-4411	R	15*	<.1
11	Kearny County Feeders Inc—*Pat Koons*	PO Box 109, Lakin KS 67860	620-355-6630	R	12*	<.1
12	Reeve Cattle Co—*MP Reeve*	30 Old Chamiso Rd, Santa Fe NM 78501	620-275-0234	R	9*	<.1
13	Fall River Feedyard LLC—*Lonnie Dunn*	PO Box 892, Hot Springs SD 57747	605-745-4109	R	8*	<.1
14	Amistad Cattle Co—*Olijandro Elizando*	PO Box 7218, Eagle Pass TX 78853	830-757-1111	R	4*	<.1
15	Schaake Corp—*John Kincaid*	3901 Fairbanks Ave, Yakima WA 98902	509-249-8955	R	3*	<.1
16	Haskell Livestock Auction Company Inc—*Carter Fore*	Hwy 277 S, Haskell TX 79521	940-864-2624	R	2*	<.1
17	Aqua Pellet—*Odessa Jardim*	222 Quarry Ridge Ct, Elizabethtown KY 42701		R	1	<.1

TOTALS: SIC 0211 Beef Cattle Feedlots
Companies: 17   2,607   2.6

0212 Beef Cattle Except Feedlots

Rank	Company Name—*Executive Officer*	Address, City, State, Zip	Phone	Type	Fin	Empls
1	King Ranch Inc—*Jack Hunt*	Three Riverway Ste 160, Houston TX 77056	832-681-5700	R	214*	.5
2	Ford County Feed Yard Inc—*George Herrmann*	12466 US Hwy 400, Ford KS 67842	620-369-2252	R	23*	.1

TOTALS: SIC 0212 Beef Cattle Except Feedlots
Companies: 2   237   .6

0213 Hogs

Rank	Company Name—*Executive Officer*	Address, City, State, Zip	Phone	Type	Fin	Empls
1	Murphy-Brown LLC—*Jerry Godwin*	2822 Hwy 24 W, Warsaw NC 28398	910-293-3434	S	14,278*	6.0
2	Maschhoffs—*Ken Maschhoff*	7475 State Rte 127, Carlyle IL 62231	618-594-2125	R	3,006*	.5
3	Nebraska Pork Partners LLC—*Gary Preister*	PO Box 1920, Columbus NE 68602	402-564-9464	R	2,270*	.5
4	Progressive Swine Technologies—*James D Pillen*	3214 25th St, Columbus NE 68601	402-564-0407	R	1,057*	.5
5	Swine Graphics Enterprises LP—*Gene Barrick*	PO Box 668, Webster City IA 50595	515-832-5481	R	1,011*	.2
6	Schwartz Farms Inc—*John Schwartz*	32296 190th St, Sleepy Eye MN 56085	507-794-5774	R	574*	.2
7	New Fashion Pork Inc—*Brad Freking*	PO Box 244, Jackson MN 56143	507-847-4610	R	503*	.2
8	Prestage Farms Inc—*William H Prestage*	PO Box 438, Clinton NC 28329	910-592-5771	R	502*	1.0
9	Christensen Family Farms—*Bob Christensen*	PO Box 3000, Sleepy Eye MN 56085	507-794-5310	R	244*	.5
10	Circle 4 Farms—*John Morrell*	PO Box 100, Milford UT 84751	435-387-2107	S	231*	.5
11	Iowa Select Farms LP—*Jeff Hansen*	PO Box 400, Iowa Falls IA 50126	641-648-4479	R	219*	.9
12	AMVC Management Services—*Daryl Olsen*	508 Market St, Audubon IA 50025	712-563-2080	R	216*	<.1

Note: An asterisk (*) indicates an estimated financial figure. The company type code used is as follows: R = Private, P = Public, S = Private Subsidiary, B = Public Subsidiary, D = Division, J = Joint Venture, I = Investment Fund.

COMPANY RANKINGS BY SALES WITHIN 4-DIGIT SIC

Rank	Company Name—*Executive Officer*	Address, City, State, Zip	Phone	Type	Fin	Empls
13	Cargill Pork—*Waren Staley*	PO Box 699, Russellville AR 72811	479-968-4560	D	191*	<.1
14	Texas Farm LLC—*Yoshikiyo Fujii*	4200 S Main St, Perryton TX 79070	806-435-5935	S	142*	.3
15	Wakefield Pork Inc—*Chuck Peters*	PO Box 327, Gaylord MN 55334	507-237-5581	R	99*	<.1
16	Coastal Plains Pork LLC—*Henry Moore III*	791 Wallace Hwy, Harrells NC 28444	910-532-6006	R	44*	<.1
17	Coharie Farms Inc—*Nelson Waters Jr*	300 Westover Rd, Clinton NC 28328	910-592-1122	R	37*	.2
18	Robert Winner Sons Inc—*Brian Winner*	PO Box 39, Osgood OH 45351	419-582-4321	R	23*	.1
19	Furnas County Farms—*Ivan Backes*	4774 33rd Ave, Columbus NE 68601	402-824-3674	R	13*	<.1
20	Nutrition Services Inc—*Ken Lorenzen*	PO Box 386, York NE 68467	402-362-1633	R	9*	<.1
21	Pffj Inc—*Lori Connellech*	PO Box 398, Taylor AZ 85939	928-536-9106	R	4*	.1
22	Boe Farms Inc—*Ronald Boe*	803 Moselle Seminary R, Moselle MS 39459	601-752-5971	R	2*	<.1

TOTALS: SIC 0213 Hogs
Companies: 22 — 24,674 | 11.7

0241 Dairy Farms

Rank	Company Name—*Executive Officer*	Address, City, State, Zip	Phone	Type	Fin	Empls
1	Anderson-Erickson Dairy Co—*Miriam Erickson-Brown*	2420 E University Ave, Des Moines IA 50317	515-263-6349	R	147*	.5
2	Coach Farm Inc—*Miles Cahn*	105 Mill Hill Rd, Pine Plains NY 12567	518-398-5325	R	8*	<.1
3	High View Inc—*William Itle*	517 Vale Wood Rd, Loretto PA 15940	814-886-7171	R	5*	<.1
4	Monument Farms Inc—*Robert James*	2107 James Rd, Middlebury VT 05753	802-545-2119	R	4*	<.1
5	Faith Dairy Inc—*Jelle Mensonides*	3509 72nd St E, Tacoma WA 98443	253-531-3398	R	4*	<.1
6	Perry Dell Farms—*Diane Gibble*	90 Indian Rock Dam Rd, York PA 17403	717-741-3485	R	3*	<.1
7	Jackson Farms Dairy—*William Jackson*	6718 National Pke, New Salem PA 15468	724-246-7010	R	2*	<.1
8	Wright's Dairy Farm Inc—*Edward Wright*	200 Woonsocket Hill Rd, North Smithfield RI 02896	401-767-3014	R	2*	<.1

TOTALS: SIC 0241 Dairy Farms
Companies: 8 — 175 | .8

0251 Broiler, Fryer & Roaster Chickens

Rank	Company Name—*Executive Officer*	Address, City, State, Zip	Phone	Type	Fin	Empls
1	Koch Meat Company Inc—*Joseph C Grendys*	1300 Higgins Rd Ste 10, Park Ridge IL 60068	847-384-5940	R	1,251	7.1
2	Aviagen Group—*Randall Ennis*	5015 Bradford Dr, Huntsville AL 35805	256-890-3800	R	960*	1.0
3	Sylvest Farms Inc—*Dean Falk*	3500 Western Blvd, Montgomery AL 36108	334-281-0400	R	94*	1.3
4	Clark's Feed Mills Inc—*Robert Clark*	PO Box W, Shamokin PA 17872	570-648-4351	R	2*	<.1

TOTALS: SIC 0251 Broiler, Fryer & Roaster Chickens
Companies: 4 — 2,307 | 9.4

0252 Chicken Eggs

Rank	Company Name—*Executive Officer*	Address, City, State, Zip	Phone	Type	Fin	Empls
1	Cal-Maine Foods Inc—*Adolphus B Baker*	3320 Woodrow Wilson Dr, Jackson MS 39209	601-948-6813	P	942	2.1
2	Michael Foods Group Inc—*James Dwyer*	301 Carlson Pkwy Ste 4, Minnetonka MN 55305	952-258-4000	R	178*	3.8
3	Michael Foods Investors LLC	301 Carlson Pkwy Ste 4, Minnetonka MN 55305	952-258-4000	S	160*	3.8
4	Cal-Maine Partnership Ltd—*Fred R Adams Jr*	3320 Woodrow Wilson Dr, Jackson MS 39209	601-948-6813	S	30*	.1
5	Weaver Brothers Inc—*Timothy Weaver*	PO Box 333, Versailles OH 45380	937-526-3331	R	27*	.2
6	Lake Weiss Egg Company Inc—*Jeffrey Bradley*	PO Box 190, Centre AL 35960	256-927-5546	R	13*	<.1
7	Daylay Egg Farm Inc—*Kurt Lausecker*	11177 Township Rd 133, West Mansfield OH 43358	937-355-6531	R	9*	.1
8	CWT Farms International Inc—*Cees Boudewrjn*	PO Box 1396, Gainesville GA 30501	770-532-3181	R	8*	<.1
9	Hillandale-Gettysburg LP—*Syed Fyedrizvi*	370 Spicer Rd, Gettysburg PA 17325	717-334-9117	R	5*	.1
10	Eggland's Best Inc—*Charles Lanktree*	1400 S Trooper Rd Rm 2, King of Prussia PA 19406	610-265-6500	R	3*	<.1
11	Elkin Co—*Lee Fisher*	W 222 N 833 Cheaney Dr, Waukesha WI 53186	262-548-0864	R	3*	<.1

TOTALS: SIC 0252 Chicken Eggs
Companies: 11 — 1,377 | 10.2

0253 Turkeys & Turkey Eggs

Rank	Company Name—*Executive Officer*	Address, City, State, Zip	Phone	Type	Fin	Empls
1	Nicholas Turkey Breeding Farms—*Jihad Douglas*	31186 Midland Trail E, Lewisburg WV 24901	304-793-2680	S	19*	.2
2	Jaindl's Farms LLC—*Pat Seng*	3150 Ceffeetown Rd, Orefield PA 18069	610-395-3333	R	18*	.1

TOTALS: SIC 0253 Turkeys & Turkey Eggs
Companies: 2 — 37 | .3

0254 Poultry Hatcheries

Rank	Company Name—*Executive Officer*	Address, City, State, Zip	Phone	Type	Fin	Empls
1	Nash Johnson and Sons' Farms Inc—*Don Taber*	415 John Rich Rd, Warsaw NC 28398	910-289-6842	R	82*	.7
2	Draper Valley Holdings LLC—*Mark Anderson*	PO Box 838, Mount Vernon WA 98273	360-424-7947	R	80*	.5
3	Harrison Poultry Inc—*Michael Welch*	PO Box 550, Bethlehem GA 30620	770-867-7511	R	68*	.8
4	Hubbard Isa LLC—*Ann Davenport*	PO Box 415, Walpole NH 03608	603-756-3311	R	29*	.7
5	Wadeken Industries Inc—*Wally Cloud*	PO Box 1149, Canton GA 30169	770-479-5551	R	3*	<.1

TOTALS: SIC 0254 Poultry Hatcheries
Companies: 5 — 263 | 2.7

0259 Poultry & Eggs Nec

Rank	Company Name—*Executive Officer*	Address, City, State, Zip	Phone	Type	Fin	Empls
1	Maple Leaf Inc—*John Tucker*	PO Box 308, Milford IN 46542	574-658-4121	R	114*	1.1
2	Palmetto Pigeon Plant—*Anthony Barwick*	PO Box 3060, Sumter SC 29151	803-775-1204	R	4*	.1

TOTALS: SIC 0259 Poultry & Eggs Nec
Companies: 2 — 118 | 1.2

0272 Horses & Other Equines

Rank	Company Name—*Executive Officer*	Address, City, State, Zip	Phone	Type	Fin	Empls
1	Darley at Jonabell Farm—*James Bell Jr*	3333 Bowmans Mill Rd, Lexington KY 40513	859-255-8537	R	19*	.1
2	News Tribune Co—*Betty Weldon*	PO Box 420, Jefferson City MO 65102	573-636-3131	R	16*	.2
3	Calumet Farm Inc—*Bill Wittman*	3301 Versailles Rd, Lexington KY 40510	859-231-8272	R	8*	.1

TOTALS: SIC 0272 Horses & Other Equines
Companies: 3 — 43 | .3

0273 Animal Aquaculture

Rank	Company Name—*Executive Officer*	Address, City, State, Zip	Phone	Type	Fin	Empls
1	Motivatit Seafoods LLC—*Wayne Dehart*	PO Box 3916, Houma LA 70361	985-868-7191	R	31*	.2

0279 Animal Specialties Nec

Rank	Company Name—*Executive Officer*	Address, City, State, Zip	Phone	Type	Fin	Empls
1	Fluker Farms Inc—*David Fluker*	1333 Plantation Rd, Port Allen LA 70767	225-343-7035	R	39*	.1

0291 General Farms—Primarily Animal

Rank	Company Name—*Executive Officer*	Address, City, State, Zip	Phone	Type	Fin	Empls
1	Larson Products Inc—*Larry Larson*	PO Box 5, Sargeant MN 55973	507-584-2269	R	17*	<.1
2	Nevada Nile Ranch Inc—*Richard McDougal*	1375 E Reservation Rd, Lovelock NV 89419	775-273-2646	R	8*	<.1

TOTALS: SIC 0291 General Farms—Primarily Animal
Companies: 2 — 25 | <.1

Rank	Company Name—*Executive Officer*	Address, City, State, Zip	Phone	Type	Fin	Empls
0711 Soil Preparation Services						
1	Agricultural Supply Inc—*Richard Arias*	1435 Simpson Way, Escondido CA 92029	760-737-2442	S	10*	<.1
2	Golden Furrow Fertilizer Inc—*Thomas Fullenkamp*	PO Box 99, Eldon IA 52554	641-652-3535	R	6*	.1
3	Coggin and Fairchild Environmental Consultants Inc—*Jim Fairchild*	1144 Siesta Key Ln, Elgin IL 60120	630-497-9700	R	3*	<.1
4	Muller Erosion Control Inc—*David Muller*	PO Box 2723, Merrifield VA 22116	703-560-4040	R	3*	<.1
5	Waste Stream Technology Inc—*Joseph Giacomazza*	302 Grote St, Buffalo NY 14207	716-876-5290	S	2*	<.1
TOTALS: SIC 0711 Soil Preparation Services						
	Companies: 5				24	.2
0721 Crop Planting, Cultivating & Protecting						
1	San Miguel Produce Inc—*John Nishimori*	4444 Navalair Rd, Oxnard CA 93033	805-488-0981	R	30*	.1
2	Farming Technology Inc—*Pat Goolsby*	PO Box 14532, Houston TX 77221	713-923-5807	R	26*	.2
3	Paumanok Vineyards Ltd—*Charles Massoud*	PO Box 741, Aquebogue NY 11931	631-722-8800	R	1*	<.1
TOTALS: SIC 0721 Crop Planting, Cultivating & Protecting						
	Companies: 3				57	.3
0722 Crop Harvesting						
1	Hay Morrill Company Inc—*George Morrill*	1175 Morris Ave, Larned KS 67550	620-285-6941	R	1*	<.1
0723 Crop Preparation Services for Market						
1	Wyckoff Farms Inc—*David Wyckoff*	PO Box 249, Grandview WA 98930	509-882-3934	R	3,179*	4.8
2	Universal Blanchers LLC—*Michael Fisher*	2077 Convention Ctr, College Park GA 30337	404-209-2600	R	549*	.2
3	Stadelman Fruit LLC—*Rob Stuart*	111 Meade St, Zillah WA 98953	509-829-5145	R	155*	.7
4	Paramount Farms Inc—*Stewart Resnick*	11444 W Olympic Blvd, Los Angeles CA 90064	310-966-4650	R	150*	.6
5	Ramco Enterprises LP—*Vice Pomo*	PO Box 6729, Salinas CA 93912	831-758-5272	R	147*	2.3
6	Inland Fruit Co—*Susan Putman*	300 N Frontage Rd, Wapato WA 98951	509-877-2126	R	111*	.5
7	Ocean Mist Farms—*Edward Boutonnet*	10855 Ocaen Mist Parkw, Castroville CA 95012	831-633-2144	R	64*	.1
8	Milne Fruit Products Inc—*Michael Sorenson* Wyckoff Farms Inc	804 Bennett Ave, Prosser WA 99350	509-786-2611	S	36*	.1
9	Bluebird Inc—*Ron Gonsalves*	PO Box 378, Peshastin WA 98847	509-548-1700	R	35*	.5
10	LA Hearne Co—*Francis Giudici*	512 Metz Rd, King City CA 93930	831-385-5441	R	28*	.1
11	Mooney Farms—*Richard Monkes*	1220 Fortress St, Chico CA 95973	530-899-2661	R	28*	.1
12	American Copak Corp—*Steven A Brooker*	9175 Eton Ave, Chatsworth CA 91311	818-576-1000	R	23*	.1
13	Oxnard Lemon Co—*Sam Mayhew*	2001 Sunkist Cir, Oxnard CA 93033	805-483-1173	R	21*	.2
14	Auburn Bean and Grain—*Clifford Vennix*	PO Box 67, Auburn MI 48611	989-662-4423	R	20*	<.1
15	Wilkins-Rogers Inc—*Samuel Rogers*	PO Box 308, Ellicott City MD 21041	410-465-5800	R	13*	.2
16	Blue Star Growers Inc—*Terry Twitchell*	100 Blue Star Rd, Cashmere WA 98815	509-782-2922	R	12*	.3
17	American Custom Drying Co—*Michael Geiger*	109 Elbow Ln, Burlington NJ 08016	609-387-3933	R	10*	<.1
18	Sessions Company Inc—*William Ventress*	PO Box 311310, Enterprise AL 36331	334-393-0200	R	9*	.1
19	Baird-Neece Packing Corp—*Dick Neece Sr*	PO Box 791, Porterville CA 93258	559-784-3393	R	8*	.2
20	R D Bowman and Sons Inc—*Dale Bowman*	PO Box 658, Westminster MD 21158	410-848-3733	R	6*	.1
21	Rice Belt Warehouse Inc—*Richard Odis*	PO Box 1545, El Campo TX 77437	979-543-6221	R	6*	.1
22	Murakami Farms Inc—*Grant Kitamura*	PO Box 9, Ontario OR 97914	541-889-3131	R	3*	<.1
23	Golden River Fruit Company Inc—*George Lambeth*	PO Box 2090, Vero Beach FL 32961	772-562-8610	R	2*	<.1
24	Triple S Produce and Orchards—*Joseph Hassle*	Berry Brk Enterprises2, Dowagiac MI 49047	269-427-8205	R	2*	<.1
25	De Bruyn Produce Company Inc—*Margret De Bruyn*	PO Box 76, Zeeland MI 49464	616-772-2102	R	2*	<.1
26	Great Lakes Packing Co—*Jon Beliqutte*	6556 Quarterline Rd, Kewadin MI 49648	231-264-5561	R	2*	<.1
27	Ada Feed and Seed Inc—*Tim Wagner*	12 W Thorpe Ave, Ada MN 56510	218-784-7158	R	2*	<.1
28	Pabst Farms—*August Pabst*	35303 Pabst Rd, Oconomowoc WI 53066	262-567-4474	R	1*	<.1
29	Price Milling Company Inc—*Jack Price*	PO Box 398, Russellville AR 72811	479-968-1662	R	1*	<.1
30	Bio Plus Inc—*Rete R Odom*	1135 S Main St, Madison GA 30650	706-342-2599	R	1*	<.1
TOTALS: SIC 0723 Crop Preparation Services for Market						
	Companies: 30				4,626	11.2
0724 Cotton Ginning						
1	Roche Manufacturing Company Inc—*Edgar Roche*	PO Box 4156, Dublin GA 31040	478-272-3340	R	22*	.1
2	Anderson Clayton Corp—*Richard Haire*	PO Box 12506, Fresno CA 93778	559-447-1390	S	20*	.1
3	Lyford Gin Association—*Russell Klostermann*	PO Box 70, Lyford TX 78569	956-347-3541	R	8*	<.1
TOTALS: SIC 0724 Cotton Ginning						
	Companies: 3				50	.1
0741 Veterinary Services—Livestock						
1	Pipestone Veterinary Clinic—*Gerald Kennedy*	PO Box 188, Pipestone MN 56164	507-825-4211	R	12*	<.1
0742 Veterinary Services—Specialties						
1	VCA Antech Inc—*Robert L Antin*	12401 W Olympic Blvd, Los Angeles CA 90064	310-571-6500	P	1,485	9.9
2	Pet DRx Corp—*Gene E Burleson*	215 Centerview Dr Ste, Brentwood TN 37027	615-369-1914	R	64	.6
3	Smartpak Equine LLC—*Paal Gisholt*	40 Grissom Rd Ste 500, Plymouth MA 02360	774-773-1100	R	24*	.1
4	Webster Veterinary Supply Inc—*Scott P Anderson*	137 Barnum Rd, Devens MA 01434	978-353-6000	S	23*	.1
TOTALS: SIC 0742 Veterinary Services—Specialties						
	Companies: 4				1,596	10.7
0751 Livestock Services						
1	Cooperative Resources International—*R Doug Wilson*	PO Box 469, Shawano WI 54166	715-526-2141	R	205*	1.3
2	Pig Improvement Company USA—*Phillip David*	PO Box 348, Franklin KY 42135		S	179*	.7
3	Cooperative Resources International Inc—*Rd Wilson*	PO Box 469, Shawano WI 54166	715-526-2141	R	142*	1.3
4	ABS Global Inc—*Ian Biggs*	PO Box 459, De Forest WI 53532	608-846-3721	S	91*	.3
5	American Beef Co—*Vincent Paletta*	PO Box 30, Rockville MO 64780	660-598-2045	R	30*	.1
6	Genex Cooperative Inc—*Paul Greene* Cooperative Resources International	100 MBC Dr, Shawano WI 54166	715-526-2141	S	17*	.1
7	Select Sires Inc—*John Schouten*	11740 US 42 N, Plain City OH 43064	614-873-4683	R	17*	.1
8	New Market Poultry Products Inc—*Whitt Carr*	PO Box 220, New Market VA 22844	540-740-4260	R	5*	.2
9	AJ Peachey and Sons Inc—*Joseph Peachey*	72 Barrville Rd, Belleville PA 17004	717-667-2185	R	5*	.1
10	Abf Packing Inc—*D Funderburgh*	8758 S Us Hwy 377, Dublin TX 76446	254-968-4919	R	5*	.1
11	Avco Meat Company Inc—*Dennis Contris*	2820 E Meighan Blvd, Gadsden AL 35903	256-492-3682	R	3*	<.1
12	Universal Pig Genes Inc—*Steve Kerns*	30355 260th S, Eldora IA 50627	641-336-2952	R	2*	<.1

Note: An asterisk (*) indicates an estimated financial figure. The company type code used is as follows: R = Private, P = Public, S = Private Subsidiary, B = Public Subsidiary, D = Division, J = Joint Venture, I = Investment Fund.

COMPANY RANKINGS BY SALES WITHIN 4-DIGIT SIC

Rank	Company Name—Executive Officer	Address, City, State, Zip	Phone	Type	Fin	Empls
13	Edgewood Locker Inc—Terry Kerns	PO Box 245, Edgewood IA 52042	563-928-6814	R	1*	<.1

TOTALS: SIC 0751 Livestock Services
Companies: 13 — 701 — 4.3

0752 Animal Specialty Services

Rank	Company Name—Executive Officer	Address, City, State, Zip	Phone	Type	Fin	Empls
1	FURminator Inc—David Porter	1638 Headland Dr, Fenton MO 63026	636-680-9387	R	34*	<.1
2	Marine Animals Productions Inc—Moby Solangi	PO Box 207, Gulfport MS 39502	228-896-9182	R	11*	<.1
3	Dog Lovers Central—Rosemary Williams	5702 S Crenshaw Blvd, Los Angeles CA 90043	323-298-8811	R	4*	<.1
4	PetRays—Melissa Fields Tugwell	200 Valley Wood Rd Ste, The Woodlands TX 77380		R	4	<.1

TOTALS: SIC 0752 Animal Specialty Services
Companies: 4 — 53 — .1

0762 Farm Management Services

Rank	Company Name—Executive Officer	Address, City, State, Zip	Phone	Type	Fin	Empls
1	Hines Horticulture Inc—James R Tennant	12621 Jeffrey Rd, Irvine CA 92620	949-559-4444	R	233	2.7

0781 Landscape Counseling & Planning

Rank	Company Name—Executive Officer	Address, City, State, Zip	Phone	Type	Fin	Empls
1	The Brickman Group—Scott Brickman	18227D Flower Hill Way, Gaithersburg MD 20879	301-987-9200	R	900	3.0
2	ValleyCrest Cos—Burton S Sperber	24151 Ventura Blvd, Calabasas CA 91302	818-223-8500	R	344*	5.2
3	Valleycrest Landscape Maintenance/Tree Care Services—Roger Zino ValleyCrest Cos	2375 Pleasantdale Rd, Doraville GA 30340	770-662-8775	S	94*	.3
4	Aquascape Inc—Ed Beaulieu	901 Aqualand Way, Saint Charles IL 60174	630-659-2000	R	45*	.1
5	Gibbs Landscape Co—Jim Gibbs	4055 Atlanta Rd SE, Smyrna GA 30080	770-432-7761	R	30*	.1
6	SWA Group—Joe Runco	PO Box 5904, Sausalito CA 94966	415-332-5100	R	19*	.1
7	Dye Designs International Inc—Perry O Dye	88 Inverness Cir E Ste, Englewood CO 80112		R	18*	.1
8	Unique Environmental Concepts Inc—Todd Guilmette	7021 Mableton Pkwy SE, Mableton GA 30126	404-691-9310	R	15*	.1
9	Greenleaf Landscapes Inc—Al Lang	414 Muskingum Dr, Marietta OH 45750	740-373-1639	R	14*	<.1
10	Simpson Norton Corp—Tom Knecht	4144 S Bullard Ave, Goodyear AZ 85338	623-932-5116	R	12*	<.1
11	Complete Landscaping Systems Inc—Peter Salmeron	1727 E 2nd N, Wichita KS 67214	316-832-0061	R	12	.2
12	Frank's Commercial and Home Services Inc—Frank DiMaria	90 Pearce Ave, Tonawanda NY 14150	716-877-3008	R	11*	.1
13	TBG Partners Inc—Earl P Broussard	901 S MoPac Bldg 2 Ste, Austin TX 78746	512-327-1011	R	10*	.1
14	Aquatic and Wetland Consultants Inc—Jay Windell	9999 Weld County Rd 25, Fort Lupton CO 80621	303-442-4766	R	9*	.1
15	Amerine Systems Inc—Gary Amerine	10866 Cleveland Ave, Oakdale CA 95361	209-847-5968	R	4*	.1
16	ELITE Landscaping Inc—David B Katz	4 Commerce St Ext, Poughkeepsie NY 12603		R	4*	<.1
17	TurfstoreCom Inc—John Tidwell	237 Boling IndustrialW, Calhoun GA 30701	706-629-1675	R	3*	.1
18	Clark Condon Associates Inc—Sheila Condon	10401 Stella Link Rd, Houston TX 77025	713-871-1414	R	3*	<.1
19	Landscape Masterpiece—Casey Gilley	PO Box 2266, Carlsbad CA 92018	760-591-3800	R	2	<.1
20	Sweitzer and Associates Landscape Architects Inc—William Sweitzer	13300 Katy Fwy, Houston TX 77079	281-496-3111	R	2*	<.1
21	Tilson Landscape Co—Robert B Tilson	386 Maple Ave E Ste 21, Vienna VA 22180	703-242-6077	R	2*	<.1
22	Rademann Stone and Landscape Company Inc—Keith Hademann	W5551 County Rd B, Fond Du Lac WI 54937	920-922-7612	R	2*	<.1
23	McCaren Designs Inc—McRae Anderson	760 Vandalia St Ste 10, Saint Paul MN 55114	651-646-4764	R	1*	<.1
24	McKinnon Associates—Mark McKinnon	1137 W 26th St, Houston TX 77008	713-869-2797	R	1*	<.1
25	Colourscape Inc—Greg Wilson	16318 Pecan Dr, Richmond TX 77469	281-277-6122	R	1*	<.1
26	Land and Water Resources Inc—John Ryan	9575 W Higgins Rd Ste, Rosemont IL 60018	847-692-7170	R	1*	<.1

TOTALS: SIC 0781 Landscape Counseling & Planning
Companies: 26 — 1,559 — 9.7

0782 Lawn & Garden Services

Rank	Company Name—Executive Officer	Address, City, State, Zip	Phone	Type	Fin	Empls
1	TruGreen LandCare LLC—Richard Ascolese	860 Ridge Lake Blvd, Memphis TN 38120	901-681-1800	S	655*	13.1
2	O'Connell Landscape Maintenance Inc—George O'Connell	23091 Arroyo Vista, Rancho Santa Margarita CA 92688	949-589-2007	R	325*	1.0
3	Sungrow Horticulture Canada Inc—Mitch Weaver	15831 Ne 8th St Ste 10, Bellevue WA 98008	425-641-7577	R	175*	<.1
4	Valley Crest Landscape Maintenance—Burton Sperber	24151 Ventura Blvd, Calabasas CA 91302	818-223-8500	S	86*	2.0
5	Rma Land Construction Inc—Roy Mohammad	3061 E La Palma Ave, Anaheim CA 92806	714-985-2888	R	35*	.2
6	Superior Maintenance Co—Kevin Shurn	618 Westport Rd Ste D, Elizabethtown KY 42701	270-769-2553	R	25*	.6
7	Nature Scapes Inc—Rick Upchurch	1270-A Turner Rd, Lilburn GA 30047	770-923-7023	R	13*	.1
8	TruGreen Inc—Rick Ascolese	860 Ridge Lake Blvd, Memphis TN 38120		S	9*	.1
9	Mccall Service Inc—J Cooksey	2861 College St, Jacksonville FL 32205	904-389-5561	R	9*	.1
10	Spring-Green Lawn Care Corp—Ted Hofer	11909 S Spaulding Scho, Plainfield IL 60585	815-436-8777	R	8*	.1
11	Greenscape Environmental Services—Terry Walton	11100 Jones Bridge Rd, Alpharetta GA 30022	770-475-1226	R	6*	<.1
12	White Oak Landscape Company Inc—James Davis	3220 Moon Station Rd, Kennesaw GA 30144	770-427-0524	R	3*	.1
13	P and K Condo Management Inc—Jack Kroeker	PO Box 463100, Escondido CA 92046	760-746-9127	R	2*	<.1
14	NaturaLawn of America Inc—Phillip Catron	1 E Church St, Frederick MD 21701	301-694-5440	R	<1*	<.1
15	Knox Fertilizer Company Inc—Robert Shaw	PO Box 248, Knox IN 46534	574-772-6275	R	<1*	<.1

TOTALS: SIC 0782 Lawn & Garden Services
Companies: 15 — 1,351 — 17.4

0783 Ornamental Shrub & Tree Services

Rank	Company Name—Executive Officer	Address, City, State, Zip	Phone	Type	Fin	Empls
1	Asplundh Tree Expert Co—Scott M Asplundh	708 Blair Mill Rd, Willow Grove PA 19090	215-784-4200	R	2,486*	28.0
2	Davey Tree Expert Co—Karl Warnke	PO Box 5193, Kent OH 44240	330-673-9511	R	592	6.8
3	Wright Tree Service Inc—Scott Packard	PO Box 1718, Des Moines IA 50306	515-277-6291	R	430*	1.4
4	Terry Tree Service LLC—Thomas Terry III	225 Ballantyne Rd, Rochester NY 14623	585-436-2900	R	3*	<.1

TOTALS: SIC 0783 Ornamental Shrub & Tree Services
Companies: 4 — 3,511 — 36.2

0811 Timber Tracts

Rank	Company Name—Executive Officer	Address, City, State, Zip	Phone	Type	Fin	Empls
1	Treeland Nursery Co—John Boething	23475 Long Valley Rd, Woodland Hills CA 91367	818-883-1222	R	112*	.8
2	Powell Group—Nannette Noland	PO Box 788, Baton Rouge LA 70809	225-922-4540	R	63*	.2
3	Pope Resources LP—David L Nunes	19245 10th Ave NE, Poulsbo WA 98370	360-697-6626	P	31	<.1
4	Sterling Forest LLC—Louis Heimbach	16 Sterling Lake Rd, Tuxedo NY 10987	845-351-2151	R	14*	<.1
5	Merrill and Ring Inc—Richard Stroble	813 E 8th St, Port Angeles WA 98362	360-452-2367	R	10*	<.1
6	Pankratz Lumber Co—Kevin Capelle	PO Box 58388, Tukwila WA 98138	206-575-2525	R	3*	.1
7	Northwoods Evergreen—John Schultz	W3125 Ctr Rd, Merrill WI 54452	715-536-6060	R	1*	.1
8	Arrow Resources Development Inc—Peter Frugone	152 W 57th St 27th Fl, New York NY 10019	212-262-2300	P	<1	N/A

TOTALS: SIC 0811 Timber Tracts
Companies: 8 — 234 — 1.2

Rank	Company Name—*Executive Officer*	Address, City, State, Zip	Phone	Type	Fin	Empls
0831 Forest Products						
1	Westervelt Co—*Michael Case*	PO Box 48999, Tuscaloosa AL 35404	205-562-5000	R	152*	.7
2	International Paper Co Land and Timber Div—*John V Faraci*	22620 Hwy 8 W, Trout LA 71371	318-992-2181	D	14*	.1
TOTALS: SIC 0831 Forest Products						
	Companies: 2				166	.7
0851 Forestry Services						
1	Plum Creek Southern Timber LLC—*Rick R Holley*	999 3rd Ave Ste 4300, Seattle WA 98104	206-467-3600	S	528*	1.2
2	Plum Creek South Central Timberlands LLC	999 3rd Ave Ste 4300, Seattle WA 98104	206-467-3600	S	114*	.2
3	US Timberlands Company LP—*John M Rudey*	625 Madison Ave, New York NY 10022	212-755-1100	R	49*	<.1
4	Cascade Timber Consulting Inc—*Dave Furtwangler*	PO Box 446, Sweet Home OR 97386	541-367-2111	R	14*	<.1
5	Georgia Timberlands Inc—*Ed Hutcheson*	PO Box 1403, Macon GA 31202	478-788-4660	R	14*	<.1
6	Poyry Management Consulting	52 Vanderbuilt AveSte, New York NY 10017	646-651-1547	S	9*	<.1
TOTALS: SIC 0851 Forestry Services						
	Companies: 6				728	1.5
0912 Finfish						
1	O'hara Corp—*Francis O'hara*	120 Tillson Ave Ste 1, Rockland ME 04841	207-594-4444	R	6*	.1
0913 Shellfish						
1	John Keeler and Company Inc—*John Keeler*	3000 NW 109th Ave, Doral FL 33172	305-836-6858	R	28	<.1
2	JH Miles Company Inc—*John Miles*	PO Box 178, Norfolk VA 23501	757-622-9264	R	16*	.1
3	Little Bay Lobster Co—*Johnathan Shafmaster*	158 Shattack Way, Newington NH 03801	603-431-3170	R	4*	<.1
4	Bluffton and Oyster Co—*Larry Toomer*	PO Box 1124, Bluffton SC 29910	843-757-4010	R	1*	<.1
TOTALS: SIC 0913 Shellfish						
	Companies: 4				49	.1
1011 Iron Ores						
1	Cliffs Natural Resources Inc—*Joseph A Carrabba*	200 Public Sq Ste 3300, Cleveland OH 44114	216-694-5700	P	4,682	6.6
2	Cliffs Mining Co Cliffs Natural Resources Inc	200 Public Square Ste, Cleveland OH 44114	216-694-5700	S	1,207	3.8
3	Cliffs Mining Services Co Cliffs Natural Resources Inc	200 Public Square Ste, Cleveland OH 44114	216-694-5700	S	1,207	3.8
4	Coeur Bullion Corp—*Dennis E Wheeler*	505 Front Ave, Coeur D Alene ID 83814	208-667-3511	S	217*	.8
5	Hibbing Taconite Co—*Jack Tomey*	PO Box 589, Hibbing MN 55746	218-262-5950	R	139*	.7
6	Petron Pacific Inc—*Niraj Balasaria*	3931 Avion Park Ste C1, Chantilly VA 20151	703-330-7882	R	122*	.2
7	Northshore Mining Co—*Donald Gallagher* Cliffs Natural Resources Inc	10 Outer Dr, Silver Bay MN 55614	218-226-4125	S	120*	.5
8	Tilden Mining Company LC—*Bob Berglund* Cliffs Natural Resources Inc	PO Box 2000, Ishpeming MI 49849	906-475-3400	D	40*	.8
9	Quantum Materials Corp—*Stephen Squires*	7700 S River Pkwy, Tempe AZ 85284	214-701-8779	P	<1	<.1
TOTALS: SIC 1011 Iron Ores						
	Companies: 9				7,734	17.1
1021 Copper Ores						
1	Freeport-McMoRan Copper and Gold Inc—*Richard C Adkerson*	333 N Central Ave, Phoenix AZ 85004	602-366-8100	P	18,982	29.7
2	Southern Copper Corporation USA—*Oscar Gonzalez Rocha*	1440 E Missouri Ave St, Phoenix AZ 85014	602-264-1375	B	6,819	12.1
3	Asarco Inc—*Joseph Lapinsky*	5285 E Williams Circle, Tucson AZ 85711	520-798-7500	S	2,233	11.1
4	PT Freeport Indonesia Co—*James Moffett* Freeport-McMoRan Copper and Gold Inc	PO Box 51777, New Orleans LA 70151	504-582-4000	S	1,968*	10.0
5	Kennecott Utah Copper Corp—*Kelly Sanders*	PO Box 6001, Magna UT 84044	801-204-2000	S	1,206*	3.0
6	Alacer Gold Corp—*Edward C Dowling*	10333 E Dry Creek Rd S, Englewood CO 80112	303-292-1299	P	282	.1
7	Rio Tinto Procurement—*Paul Skinner*	P O Box 926, Valencia CA 91355	661-287-5450	S	281*	.1
TOTALS: SIC 1021 Copper Ores						
	Companies: 7				31,771	66.2
1031 Lead & Zinc Ores						
1	Doe Run Resources Corp—*A Bruce Neil*	1801 Park 270 Dr Ste 3, Saint Louis MO 63146	314-453-7100	R	131*	1.5
2	US Zinc Corp	PO Box 611, Houston TX 77001	713-926-1705	R	81*	.1
3	St Cloud Mining Co—*Patrick S Freeman*	PO Box 196, Winston NM 87943	575-743-5215	R	4*	.1
4	Kennecott Greens Creek Mining A JV—*Caroline Cave*	PO Box 32199, Juneau AK 99803	907-789-8100	R	<1*	<.1
TOTALS: SIC 1031 Lead & Zinc Ores						
	Companies: 4				216	1.7
1041 Gold Ores						
1	Newmont Mining Corp—*Richard T O'Brien*	6363 S Fiddler's Green, Greenwood Village CO 80111	303-863-7414	P	9,540	15.5
2	Coeur d'Alene Mines Corp—*Mitchell Krebs*	505 E Front Ave, Coeur D Alene ID 83814		P	1,021	1.9
3	Newmont Gold Co—*Richard T O'Brien* Newmont Mining Corp	6363 S Fiddlers Green, Greenwood Village CO 80111	303-863-7414	S	730	4.0
4	Hecla Mining Co—*Phillips S Baker Jr*	6500 N Mineral Dr Ste, Coeur d Alene ID 83815	208-769-4100	P	478	.7
5	Golden Star Resources Ltd—*Thomas G Mair*	10901 W Toller Dr Ste, Littleton CO 80127	303-830-9000	P	471	2.4
6	Cripple Creek and Victor Gold Mining Co—*Ray Dubois*	PO Box 191, Victor CO 80860	719-689-4220	J	337*	.3
7	SPDR Gold Trust—*Jason Toussaint*	424 Madison Avenue 3rd, New York NY 10017	212-317-3800	P	231	N/A
8	Jaguar Mining Inc—*Daniel R Titcomb*	125 N State St, Concord NH 03301	603-224-4800	P	171	1.8
9	Marigold Mining Company—*Charles Jeannes*	PO Box 160, Valmy NV 89438	775-623-9571	R	144*	.3
10	NA Degerstrom Inc—*Chris Myers*	3303 N Sullivan Rd, Spokane WA 99216	509-928-3333	R	132*	.2
11	International Minerals Corp—*Stephen J Kay*	7950 E Acoma Dr Ste 21, Scottsdale AZ 85260	480-483-9932	P	54	.2
12	Solitario Exploration and Royalty Corp—*Christopher E Herald*	4251 Kipling St Ste 39, Wheat Ridge CO 80033	303-534-1030	R	26*	<.1
13	Golden Star Holdings Ltd Golden Star Resources Ltd	10901 W Toller Dr, Littleton CO 80127	303-830-9000	S	20*	<.1
14	Addwest Minerals International Ltd—*Charles S Williams*	5460 Ward Rd Ste 202, Arvada CO 80002	303-424-5134	R	20*	<.1
15	Golden Sunlight Mines Inc—*Greg Lang*	453 Mt Hwy 2 E, Whitehall MT 59759	406-287-3257	R	12*	<.1
16	Golden Minerals Co—*Jeffrey G Clevenger*	350 Indiana St Suite 8, Golden CO 80401	303-839-5060	P	11	.2
17	Taranis Resources Inc—*John J Gardiner*	14247 W Iliff Ave, Lakewood CO 80228	303-716-5922	P	5	N/A
18	Western States Minerals Corp—*Stephen Alfers*	1658 Cole Blvd Ste 210, Lakewood CO 80401	303-425-7042	R	3*	<.1
19	Capital Gold Corp—*Colin P Sutherland*	76 Beaver St 14th Fl, New York NY 10005	212-344-2785	P	<1	.2
20	Gold Reserve Inc—*Rockne J Timm*	926 W Sprague Ave Ste, Spokane WA 99201		P	<1	.1

Note: An asterisk (*) indicates an estimated financial figure. The company type code used is as follows: R = Private, P = Public, S = Private Subsidiary, B = Public Subsidiary, D = Division, J = Joint Venture, I = Investment Fund.

COMPANY RANKINGS BY SALES WITHIN 4-DIGIT SIC

Rank	Company Name—*Executive Officer*	Address, City, State, Zip	Phone	Type	Fin	Empls
21	Vista Gold Corp—*Michael B Richings*	7961 Shaffer Pky Ste 5, Littleton CO 80127	720-981-1185	P	<1	<.1
22	Applied Minerals Inc—*Andre Zeitoun*	110 Greene St Ste 1101, New York NY 10012	212-226-4256	P	<1	<.1
23	Original Sixteen to One Mine Inc—*Michael M Miller*	PO Box 909, Alleghany CA 95910	530-287-3223	P	<1	<.1
24	Tara Minerals Corp—*Francis Biscan Jr*	2162 Acorn St, Wheaton IL 60189	630-752-4447	P	<1	<.1
25	Wits Basin Precious Minerals Inc—*Stephen D King*	900 IDS Ctr 80 S 8th S, Minneapolis MN 55402	612-349-5277	P	<1	<.1
26	Global Gold Corp—*Van Z Krikorian*	555 Theodore Fremd Ave, Rye NY 10580	914-925-0020	P	<1	<.1
27	GreenChek Technology Inc—*Lincoln Parke*	101 California St Ste, San Francisco CA 94111	315-710-1277	P	<1	<.1
28	American International Ventures Inc—*Steven Davis*	4058 Histead Way, Evergreen CO 80439	303-670-7378	P	<1	N/A
29	Fischer-Watt Gold Company Inc—*Peter Bojtos*	2582 Taft Ct, Lakewood CO 80215	303-232-0292	P	<1	N/A
30	Piedmont Mining Company Inc—*Robert M Shields Jr*	18124 Wedge Pky Ste 21, Reno NV 89511	704-523-6866	P	<1	N/A

TOTALS: SIC 1041 Gold Ores
Companies: 30   13,406   27.9

1061 Ferroalloy Ores Except Vanadium

1	Molycorp Inc—*Mark Smith*	5619 DTC Pkwy Ste 1000, Englewood CO 80111	303-843-8040	B	397	.9
2	Montana Resources LLP—*Tad Dale*	600 Shields Ave, Butte MT 59701	406-723-4081	R	16*	.3

TOTALS: SIC 1061 Ferroalloy Ores Except Vanadium
Companies: 2   413   1.3

1081 Metal Mining Services

1	Decisionpoint Systems Inc—*Nicholas Toms*	19655 Descartes, Foothill Ranch CA 92610	949-465-0065	P	67	.1
2	UNICO Inc—*Mark A Lopez*	8880 Rio San Diego Dr, San Diego CA 92108	619-209-6124	P	42*	<.1
3	Nana Dynatec Mining LLC—*Steve Borell*	1001 E Benson Blvd, Anchorage AK 99508	907-265-4110	R	16*	.2
4	Kennecott Exploration Co—*John V Main*	224 N 2200 W, Salt Lake City UT 84116	801-238-2400	D	9*	.1
5	Mines Management Inc—*Glenn Dobbs*	905 W Riverside Ave St, Spokane WA 99201	509-838-6050	P	<1	<.1
6	General Moly Inc—*Bruce D Hansen*	1726 Cole Blvd Ste 115, Lakewood CO 80401	303-928-8599	P	<1	<.1
7	Tara Gold Resources Corp—*Francis R Biscan Jr*	2162 Acorn Ct, Wheaton IL 60189	630-462-2079	P	<1	<.1

TOTALS: SIC 1081 Metal Mining Services
Companies: 7   134   .4

1094 Uranium, Radium & Vanadium Ores

1	Rio Algom Mining LLC—*Tim Kamphaus*	PO Box 208, Grants NM 87020	505-287-8851	R	6*	.1

1099 Metal Ores Nec

1	Stillwater Mining Co—*Francis R McAllister*	1321 Discovery Dr, Billings MT 59102	406-373-8700	B	906	1.6
2	Halco (Mining) Inc—*Pat Fyore*	12 Federal St Ste 320, Pittsburgh PA 15212	412-235-0265	R	163*	2.4
3	C-E Minerals Inc—*Steven Fortier*	100 Mansell Ct E Ste 6, Roswell GA 30076	770-225-7900	R	150*	.3
4	Materion Natural Resources Inc—*Alex Boulton*	PO Box 815, Delta UT 84624	435-864-2701	R	145*	1.9
5	Altair Nanomaterials Inc—*Alan Gotcher*	204 Edison Way, Reno NV 89502	775-858-3742	S	53*	<.1
6	Tulsa Metal Processing Co—*Sarah Smithey*	PO Box 36795, Phoenix AZ 85067	602-222-3560	R	16*	<.1
7	MPM Technologies Inc—*Michael J Luciano*	199 Pomeroy Rd, Parsippany NJ 07054	973-428-5009	P	1	<.1

TOTALS: SIC 1099 Metal Ores Nec
Companies: 7   1,433   6.2

1221 Bituminous Coal & Lignite—Surface

1	Alpha Natural Resources Inc—*Kevin S Crutchfield*	PO Box 2345, Abingdon VA 24212	276-619-4410	P	7,109	14.5
2	Peabody Energy Corp—*Gregory H Boyce*	701 Market St, Saint Louis MO 63101	314-342-3400	P	6,860	7.2
3	CONSOL Energy Inc—*J Brett Harvey*	1000 Consol Energy Dr, Canonsburg PA 15317	724-485-4000	P	5,236	8.6
4	Arch Coal Inc—*Steven F Leer*	1 CityPlace Dr Ste 300, St Louis MO 63141	314-994-2700	P	4,286	7.4
5	Massey Energy Co—*Baxter F Phillips Jr*	PO Box 26765, Richmond VA 23261	804-788-1800	P	3,039	7.4
6	Westmoreland Coal Sales Co—*Christopher K Seglem* Westmoreland Coal Co	2 N Cascade Ave Ste 14, Colorado Springs CO 80903	719-442-2600	S	2,188*	.9
7	Patriot Coal Company LP—*Richard M Whiting*	12312 Olive Blvd, St Louis MO 63141	314-275-3600	P	2,035	3.7
8	Alliance Holdings GP LP—*Joseph W Craft III*	1717 S Boulder Ave Ste, Tulsa OK 74119	918-295-1415	P	1,843	2.6
9	Drummond Company Inc—*Garry N Drummond*	PO Box 10246, Birmingham AL 35202	205-945-6300	R	1,798*	5.1
10	Alliance Resource Partners LP—*Joseph W Craft III*	PO Box 22027, Tulsa OK 74121	918-295-7600	P	1,610	3.6
11	Cloud Peak Energy Inc—*Colin Marshall*	PO Box 3009, Gillette WY 82717	307-687-6000	B	1,554	1.6
12	North American Coal Corp—*Robert Benson*	5340 Legacy Drive Buil, Plano TX 75024	972-448-5400	S	545*	1.1
13	Westmoreland Coal Co—*Keith E Alessi*	9540 S Maroon Cir Ste, Englewood CO 80112	303-922-6463	P	506	1.1
14	Oxford Resource Partners LP—*Charles C Ungurean*	41 S High St Ste 3450, Columbus OH 43215	614-643-0337	P	357	.8
15	Rhino Resource Partners LP—*David G Zatezalo*	424 Lewis Hargett Cir, Lexington KY 40503	859-389-6500	P	306	.9
16	Natural Resource Partners LP—*Corbin J Robertson Jr*	601 Jefferson St Ste 3, Houston TX 77002	713-751-7507	P	301	N/A
17	Western Energy Co—*Kent Saltros* Westmoreland Coal Co	PO Box 99, Colstrip MT 59323	406-748-5100	S	242*	.4
18	Baukol-Noonan Inc—*Mike Hummel*	PO Box 897, Bismarck ND 58502	701-222-8828	S	234*	.1
19	Caballo Coal Co—*Gregory Boyce*	2298 Bishop Rd, Gillette WY 82718	307-686-1991	S	166*	.3
20	Buckskin Mining Co—*Mike Nimmo*	PO Box 3027, Gillette WY 82717	307-682-9144	S	158*	.3
21	Hobet Mining Inc Arch Coal Inc	PO Box 305, Madison WV 25130	304-369-6780	S	144*	.4
22	Bridger Coal Co	PO Box 68, Point of Rocks WY 82942	307-922-7600	S	132	.4
23	Webster County Coal LLC—*Eric Blanford*	1586 Balls Hill Rd, Nebo KY 42441	270-249-2205	R	108*	1.4
24	Apogee Coal Co—*Steven Leer* Arch Coal Inc	PO Box 156, Yolyn WV 25654	304-792-8200	S	90*	.3
25	Amerikohl Mining Inc—*John Stilley*	202 Sunset Dr, Butler PA 16001	724-282-2339	R	58*	.1
26	Coal-Mac Inc—*Gary Bennett* Arch Coal Inc	PO Box 1050, Holden WV 25625	304-792-8400	S	47*	.1
27	Usibelli Coal Mine Inc—*Joseph E Usibelli Jr*	PO Box 1000, Healy AK 99743	907-683-2226	R	27*	.1
28	Oxford Mining Company Inc—*Charles Ungurean*	PO Box 427, Coshocton OH 43812	740-622-6302	R	24*	.5
29	Solar Sources Inc—*Felson Bowman*	PO Box 47068, Indianapolis IN 46247	317-788-0084	R	24*	.2
30	Nally and Hamilton Enterprises Inc—*Thomas Hamilton*	PO Box 157, Bardstown KY 40004	502-348-0084	R	23*	.2
31	Cordero Rojo Mining Co—*Joe Vaccari*	PO Box 1449, Gillette WY 82717	307-682-8005	R	22*	.6
32	Lambert Coal Company Inc—*AJ Lambert*	PO Box 490, Nora VA 24272	276-835-8666	R	21*	.1
33	Sun Coal and Coke Co—*Lynn L Elsenhans*	1111 Northshore Dr Ste, Knoxville TN 37919	865-558-0300	S	17*	<.1
34	A and G Coal Corp—*Jerry Wharton*	PO Box 1010, Wise VA 24293	276-328-3421	R	15*	.2
35	Pine Branch Coal Sales Inc—*David Duff*	PO Box 246, Chavies KY 41727	606-436-3712	R	15*	.2
36	Vigo Coal Operating Company Inc—*John Harman*	528 Main St Ste 202, Evansville IN 47708	812-759-8446	R	13*	.1
37	Valley Mining Inc—*Kreg Shuman*	PO Box 152, Uhrichsville OH 44683	740-922-3942	R	11*	.1
38	Knott Floyd Land Company Inc—*Jeff Joyce*	436 Daniels Creek, Banner KY 41603	606-946-2290	R	8*	.1
39	River Hill Coal Company Inc—*Harry Hanchar*	PO Box 141, Kylertown PA 16847	814-345-5642	R	7*	.1

Rank	Company Name—*Executive Officer*	Address, City, State, Zip	Phone	Type	Fin	Empls
40	Blue Blaze Coal Company and Capital Resource—*Ron Starnes*	PO Box 40, Canton IL 61520	309-647-2000	R	6*	.1
41	Pittston Coal Co—*Michael Dan*	PO Box 18100, Richmond VA 23226	804-289-9600	S	3*	<.1
42	Holmes Limestone Co—*Merle Mullet*	PO Box 295, Berlin OH 44610	330-893-2721	R	1*	<.1
43	Evergreen Energy Inc—*Ilyas Khan*	1225 17th St Ste 1300, Denver CO 80202	303-293-2992	P	<1	<.1

TOTALS: SIC 1221 Bituminous Coal & Lignite—Surface
Companies: 43   41,189   72.6

1222 Bituminous Coal—Underground

Rank	Company Name—*Executive Officer*	Address, City, State, Zip	Phone	Type	Fin	Empls
1	Utahamerican Energy Inc—*David Hibbs*	PO Box 910, East Carbon UT 84520	435-888-4000	S	70,080*	.4
2	Jim Walter Resources Inc—*Joseph B Leonard*	PO Box 133, Brookwood AL 35444	205-554-6150	D	1,361*	1.5
3	Arch Coal Sales Company Inc—*John W Eaves*	1 City Pl Dr Ste 300, Saint Louis MO 63141	314-994-2700	S	714*	<.1
4	American Coal Co—*Bob Murray*	9085 State Rte 34 N, Galatia IL 62935	618-268-6317	R	298*	.6
5	Mettiki Coal LLC (Oakland Maryland)—*Joseph W Craft III*	293 Table Rock Rd, Oakland MD 21550	301-334-3952	S	248*	.2
6	Twentymile Coal Co—*Gregory Boyce*	29515 Routt County Rd, Oak Creek CO 80467	970-879-3800	S	192*	.6
7	Rhino Energy LLC—*Paris Charles*	424 Lewis Hargett Cir, Lexington KY 40503	859-389-6500	R	137*	.6
8	Cumberland Resources Corp—*Richard Gilliam*	PO Box 2560, Wise VA 24293	276-679-0804	S	133*	.2
9	Ohio County Coal Co—*Gregory Boyce*	12312 Olive Blvd, Saint Louis MO 63141	314-275-3600	S	132*	.1
10	ENERGY WEST Mining Co—*Kevin J Degenstein*	PO Box 310, Huntington UT 84528	435-687-9821	S	77*	.4
11	Beech Fork Processing Inc—*James Booth*	PO Box 190, Lovely KY 41231	606-395-6841	R	33*	.3
12	Genwal Resources Inc—*David Hibbs* Utahamerican Energy Inc	PO Box 910, East Carbon UT 84520	435-888-4000	S	16*	.3
13	Roxcoal Inc—*Robert Scott*	PO Box 149, Friedens PA 15541	814-445-3876	R	10*	.1
14	Humphrey's Enterprises Inc—*Ron McCall*	P o Box 668, Norton VA 24273	276-679-1400	R	8*	.1
15	Knife River Corp—*William E Schneider*	1150 W Century Ave, Bismarck ND 58503	701-530-1400	S	N/A	5.0

TOTALS: SIC 1222 Bituminous Coal—Underground
Companies: 15   73,438   10.3

1231 Anthracite Mining

Rank	Company Name—*Executive Officer*	Address, City, State, Zip	Phone	Type	Fin	Empls
1	Reading Anthracite Coal Co—*Brian Rich*	PO Box 1200, Pottsville PA 17901	570-622-5150	R	9*	.1
2	Carbon Sales Inc—*Frederick Dewees*	PO Box 1600, Wilkes Barre PA 18705	570-823-7664	R	3*	<.1
3	Boyer's Sand and Rock Inc—*Bill Boyer*	4162 Birch Ave, Hawarden IA 51023	712-552-2308	R	2*	<.1

TOTALS: SIC 1231 Anthracite Mining
Companies: 3   14   .2

1241 Coal Mining Services

Rank	Company Name—*Executive Officer*	Address, City, State, Zip	Phone	Type	Fin	Empls
1	Penn Virginia Resource Partners LP—*William H Shea Jr*	5 Radnor Corporate Cen, Radnor PA 19087	610-975-8204	P	1,160	N/A
2	Penn Virginia GP Holdings LP—*William H Shea Jr*	4 Radnor Corporate Ctr, Radnor PA 19087	610-687-8900	R	864	N/A
3	Teco Coal Corp—*Jim J Shackleford*	200 Allison Blvd, Corbin KY 40701	606-523-4444	S	413*	.6
4	Alpha Natural Resources Virginia LLC—*Hermann Buerger*	PO Box 2345, Abingdon VA 24212	276-619-4410	R	147*	2.0
5	Calandra Frank Inc—*John Calandra*	PO Box 111253, Pittsburgh PA 15238	412-963-9071	R	47*	.7
6	Evergreen Mining Co—*Mike Duvall*	U S Rt 82, Cowen WV 26206	304-226-2120	R	25*	.2
7	Ohio Valley Coal Co—*Robert Murray*	56854 Pleasant Ridge R, Alledonia OH 43902	740-926-1351	R	20*	.4
8	Kmmc LLC—*Denis Bryant*	15 New Steamport Rd, Sebree KY 42455	270-835-7643	R	15*	.2
9	CQ Inc—*Clark D Harrison*	414 Innovation Dr, Blairsville PA 15717	724-459-8500	R	5*	.1

TOTALS: SIC 1241 Coal Mining Services
Companies: 9   2,696   4.1

1311 Crude Petroleum & Natural Gas

Rank	Company Name—*Executive Officer*	Address, City, State, Zip	Phone	Type	Fin	Empls
1	Exxon Mobil Corp—*Rex W Tillerson*	5959 Las Colinas Blvd, Irving TX 75039	972-444-1000	P	370,125	83.6
2	Marathon Oil Corp—*Clarence P Cazalot Jr*	5555 San Felipe Rd, Houston TX 77056	713-629-6600	P	72,321	29.7
3	BP Amoco Chemical Co—*Reyad Fezzani*	150 W Warrenville Rd, Naperville IL 60563	630-420-5111	S	36,745*	44.0
4	Occidental Oil and Gas Corp—*Ray R Irani* Occidental Petroleum Corp	10889 Wilshire Blvd, Los Angeles CA 90024	310-208-8800	S	33,155*	8.5
5	Spectra Energy Corp—*Gregory L Ebel*	PO Box 1642, Houston TX 77251	713-627-5400	P	26,686	5.4
6	Occidental Petroleum Corp—*Ray R Irani*	10889 Wilshire Blvd, Los Angeles CA 90024	310-208-8800	P	19,045	11.0
7	CMS Energy Corp—*John G Russell*	1 Energy Plz, Jackson MI 49201	517-788-0550	P	15,616	7.8
8	Dominion Exploration and Production Inc—*Mark McGettrick*	1415 Louisiana St Ste, Houston TX 77002	504-593-7000	S	12,729*	16.5
9	Apache Corp—*G Steven Farris*	PO Box 27709, Houston TX 77227	713-296-6000	P	12,092	4.4
10	Anadarko Petroleum Corp—*James T Hackett*	PO Box 1330, Houston TX 77251	832-636-1000	P	10,842	4.4
11	Devon Energy Corp—*John Richels*	20 N Broadway, Oklahoma City OK 73102	405-235-3611	P	9,940	5.0
12	Chesapeake Energy Corp—*Jeffrey A Fisher*	PO Box 18496, Oklahoma City OK 73154	405-848-8000	P	9,366	10.0
13	XTO Energy Inc—*Keith A Hutton* Exxon Mobil Corp	810 Houston St, Fort Worth TX 76102	817-870-2800	S	9,064	3.3
14	EOG Resources Inc—*Mark G Papa*	PO Box 4362, Houston TX 77210	713-651-7000	P	6,100	2.3
15	Southwestern Energy Production Co—*Steven L Mueller*	2350 N Sam Houston Pkw, Houston TX 77032	281-618-4700	S	5,581*	1.5
16	DCP Midstream LLC—*Thomas O'Connor*	370 17th St Ste 2500, Denver CO 80202	303-595-3331	J	4,555*	2.5
17	Coffeyville Resources Inc—*Jack Lipinski*	10 E Cambridge Cir Ste, Kansas City KS 66103	913-982-0500	S	3,100*	.4
18	Noble Energy Inc—*Charles D Davidson*	100 Glenborough Dr Ste, Houston TX 77067	281-872-3100	P	3,022	1.8
19	Pioneer Natural Resources Co—*Scott D Sheffield*	5205 N O' Connor Blvd, Irving TX 75039	972-444-9001	P	2,472	2.2
20	Nicor Gas—*John W Somerhalder*	PO Box 632, Aurora IL 60568	630-305-9500	S	2,406*	3.0
21	Arctic Slope Regional Corp—*Rex A Rock Sr*	PO Box 129, Barrow AK 99723	907-339-6000	R	2,193*	10.0
22	Denbury Resources Inc—*Wieland Wettstein*	PO Box 251289, Plano TX 75025	972-673-2000	P	1,922	1.2
23	Newfield Exploration Co—*Lee K Boothby*	363 N Sam Houston Pkwy, Houston TX 77060	281-847-6000	P	1,883	1.4
24	American Trading and Production Corp—*Daniel B Hirschhorn*	10 E Baltimore St Ste, Baltimore MD 21202	410-347-7150	R	1,644*	3.0
25	Cimarex Energy Co—*FH Merelli*	1700 Lincoln St Ste 18, Denver CO 80203	303-295-3995	P	1,614	.8
26	SM Energy Co—*Anthony Best*	1775 Sherman St Ste 12, Denver CO 80203	303-861-8140	P	1,603	.6
27	Plains Exploration and Production Co—*James C Flores*	700 Milam St Ste 3100, Houston TX 77002	713-579-6000	P	1,545	.8
28	Whiting Petroleum Corp—*James J Volker*	1700 Broadway Ste 2300, Denver CO 80290	303-837-1661	P	1,516	.6
29	JM Huber Corp—*Mike Marberry*	499 Thornall St 8th Fl, Edison NJ 08837	732-549-8600	R	1,507*	4.0
30	MarkWest Energy Partners LP—*Frank M Semple*	1515 Arapahoe St Twr 1, Denver CO 80202	303-925-9200	P	1,505	.7
31	Regency Energy Partners LP—*Michael J Bradley*	2001 Bryan St Ste 3700, Dallas TX 75201	214-750-1771	P	1,434	.7
32	SandRidge Energy Inc—*Tom L Ward*	123 Robert S Kerr Ave, Oklahoma City OK 73102	405-429-5500	P	1,415	2.4
33	Range Resources Corp—*Jeffrey L Ventura*	100 Throckmorton St St, Fort Worth TX 76102	817-870-2601	P	1,219	.8
34	Unit Corp—*Larry D Pinkston*	PO Box 702500, Tulsa OK 74170	918-493-7700	P	1,208	2.2
35	Questar Corp—*Ronald W Jibson*	PO Box 45433, Salt Lake City UT 84145	801-324-5000	P	1,194	1.7
36	Linn Energy LLC—*Mark E Ellis*	600 Travis Ste 5100, Houston TX 77002	281-840-4000	P	1,162	.8
37	Genesis Pipeline Texas LP—*John R Millar*	919 Milam St Ste 2100, Houston TX 77002	713-860-2577	S	1,122*	.6
38	Eagle Rock Energy Partners LP—*Joseph A Mills*	PO Box 9268, Houston TX 77261	281-408-1200	P	1,027	.5

Note: An asterisk (*) indicates an estimated financial figure. The company type code used is as follows: R = Private, P = Public, S = Private Subsidiary, B = Public Subsidiary, D = Division, J = Joint Venture, I = Investment Fund.

COMPANY RANKINGS BY SALES WITHIN 4-DIGIT SIC

Rank	Company Name—*Executive Officer*	Address, City, State, Zip	Phone	Type	Fin	Empls
39	Cabot Oil and Gas Corp—*Dan O Dinges*	840 Gessner, Houston TX 77024	281-589-4600	P	980	.5
40	Ultra Petroleum Corp—*Michael D Watford*	400 N Sam Houston Pky, Houston TX 77060	281-876-0120	P	979	.1
41	Concho Resources Inc—*Timothy A Leach*	550 W Texas Ave Ste 10, Midland TX 79701	432-683-7443	P	973	.4
42	Quicksilver Resources Inc—*Glenn M Darden*	801 Cherry St Ste 3700, Fort Worth TX 76102	817-665-5000	P	928	.5
43	Berry Petroleum Co—*Robert F Heinemann*	1999 Broadway Ste 3700, Denver CO 80202	303-999-4400	P	920	.3
44	Continental Resources—*Harold G Hamm*	PO Box 1032, Enid OK 73702	580-233-8955	P	839	.5
45	Atlas Energy Resources LLC—*Edward E Cohen*	1550 Coraopolis Height, Moon Township PA 15108	412-262-2830	S	787	N/A
46	Murphy Exploration and Production Co—*Kevin Fitzgerald*	16290 Katy Fwy Ste 600, Houston TX 77094	281-675-9000	S	742*	.3
47	Maxus Energy Corp—*Mario Rosso*	1330 Lake Robbins Dr S, The Woodlands TX 77380	281-681-7200	S	716*	2.1
48	Forest Oil Corp—*H Craig Clark*	707 17th St Ste 3600, Denver CO 80202	303-812-1400	P	705	.7
49	CNX Gas Corp—*J Brett Harvey*	1000 CONSOL Energy Dr, Canonsburg PA 15317	724-485-4000	S	683	.2
50	Swift Energy Co—*Terry E Swift*	16825 Northchase Dr St, Houston TX 77060	281-874-2700	P	599	.3
51	Geokinetics Inc—*Richard F Miles*	1500 CityWest Blvd Ste, Houston TX 77042	713-850-7600	P	558	5.2
52	Enbridge Energy East Texas LLC—*Steve Letwin*	1100 Louisiana St Ste, Houston TX 77002	713-650-8900	S	518*	.3
53	EXCO Resources Inc—*Douglas H Miller*	12377 Merit Dr Ste 170, Dallas TX 75251	214-368-2084	P	515	.9
54	Pioneer Natural Resources USA Inc—*Scott Sheffield* Pioneer Natural Resources Co	5205 N O'Connor Blvd S, Irving TX 75039		S	503*	.5
55	Pure Resources Inc—*Anthony J Best*	500 W Illinois St, Midland TX 79701	482-498-8600	S	490*	.3
56	Breitburn Energy Partners LP—*Halbert S Washburn*	515 S Flower St Ste 48, Los Angeles CA 90071	213-225-5900	P	480	.4
57	South Jersey Energy—*Michael J Renna*	1 S Jersey Plz, Folsom NJ 08037		S	467*	.1
58	Swift Energy International Inc—*Terry E Swift* Swift Energy Co	16825 Northchase Dr, Houston TX 77060	281-874-2700	S	443*	.2
59	ATP Oil and Gas Corp—*T Paul Bulmahn*	4600 Post Oak Pl Ste 1, Houston TX 77027	713-622-3311	P	438	.1
60	McMoran Exploration Co—*James R Moffett*	1615 Poydras St, New Orleans LA 70112	504-582-4000	P	434	.1
61	Thums Long Beach Co—*Frank Komin* Occidental Petroleum Corp	PO Box 2900, Long Beach CA 90801	562-624-3400	S	388*	.2
62	Hiland Partners LP—*Joseph L Griffin*	205 W Maple Ste 1100, Enid OK 73701	580-242-6040	S	388	N/A
63	Eastern American Energy Corp—*John Mork*	501 56th St, Charleston WV 25304	304-925-6100	S	353*	.3
64	Genesis Crude Oil LP	919 Milam Ste 2100, Houston TX 77002	713-860-2500	S	348*	.2
65	PAA Natural Gas Storage LLC—*Greg L Armstrong*	333 Clay St Ste 1100, Houston TX 77002	713-646-4100	P	343	.1
66	Legacy Reserves LP—*Cary D Brown*	303 W Wall St Ste 1400, Midland TX 79701	432-689-5200	P	337	.2
67	Comstock Resources Inc—*M Jay Allison*	5300 Town and Country, Frisco TX 75034	972-668-8800	P	332	.1
68	Oasis Petroleum Inc—*Thomas B Nusz*	1001 Fannin St Ste 150, Houston TX 77002	281-404-9500	P	330	.1
69	Venoco Inc—*Timothy Marquez*	370 17th St Ste 3900, Denver CO 80202	303-626-8300	P	329	.4
70	EV Energy Partners LP—*John B Walker*	1001 Fannin St Ste 800, Houston TX 77002	713-651-1144	P	262	.8
71	Penn Virginia Corp—*H Baird Whitehead*	100 Matsonford Rd Ste, Radnor PA 19087	610-687-8900	P	254	.2
72	Yates Petroleum Inc—*Frank Yates*	1004 W Richey Ave, Artesia NM 88210	575-748-4489	R	248*	.5
73	Aramco Services Co—*Ali I Al-Naimi*	9009 W Loop S, Houston TX 77096	713-432-4000	J	243*	.5
74	Energy Partners Ltd—*Gary Hanna*	201 St Charles Ave Ste, New Orleans LA 70170	504-569-1875	P	240	.1
75	Frontier El Dorado Refining Co—*Josh Goodmanson*	PO Box 1121, El Dorado KS 67042	316-321-2200	S	232*	.4
76	Gulfport Energy Corp—*James Palm*	14313 N May Ave Ste 10, Oklahoma City OK 73134	405-848-8807	P	229	.1
77	Pioneer Southwest Energy Partners LP—*Scott D Sheffield*	5205 N O'Connor Blvd S, Irving TX 75039	972-969-3586	P	213	3.3
78	Contango Oil and Gas Co—*Kenneth R Peak*	3700 Buffalo Speedway, Houston TX 77098	713-960-1901	P	204	<.1
79	Goodrich Petroleum Corp—*Walter G Goodrich*	801 Louisiana Ste 700, Houston TX 77002	713-780-9494	P	201	.1
80	SEECO Inc—*Steven L Mueller*	PO Box 13408, Fayetteville AR 72703	479-521-1141	S	200*	.2
81	Jay Management LLC—*Yossi Levy* Isramco Inc	2425 W Loop S Ste 810, Houston TX 77027	713-621-3882	S	200*	.2
82	Jay Petroleum LLC—*Yossi Levy* Isramco Inc	2425 W Loop S Ste810, Houston TX 77027	713-621-3882	S	200*	.2
83	Wexpro Co—*Bruce Williamson*	PO Box 45601, Salt Lake City UT 84139	801-324-2600	S	191*	.1
84	Nexen Petroleum USA Inc	5601 Granite Pky Ste 1, Plano TX 75024	972-450-4600	D	184*	.2
85	Encore Energy Partners LP—*Scott Smith*	5847 San Felipe Ste 30, Houston TX 77057	832-327-2255	P	184	N/A
86	Parallel Petroleum LLC—*Larry C Oldham*	PO Box 10587, Midland TX 79702	432-684-3727	R	183	<.1
87	PGS Data Processing Inc—*Jon Erik Reinhardsen*	15150 Memorial Dr, Houston TX 77079	281-509-8525	S	180*	.3
88	Petroquest Energy Inc—*Charles T Goodson*	400 E Kaliste Saloom R, Lafayette LA 70508	337-232-7028	P	179	.1
89	Lewis Energy Group LP—*Rod Lewis*	10101 Reunion Pl Ste 1, San Antonio TX 78216	210-384-3200	R	175*	.4
90	Resolute Energy Corp—*Nicholas Sutton*	1675 Broadway Ste 1950, Denver CO 80202	303-534-4600	R	173*	.2
91	Brigham Exploration Co—*Ben M Brigham*	6300 Bridge Point Pky, Austin TX 78730	512-427-3300	P	170	.1
92	Five States Energy Company LLC—*Arthur Budge*	1220 One Energy Sq 492, Dallas TX 75206	214-363-3008	P	157*	<.1
93	Seneca Resources Corp—*Matthew D Cabell*	1201 Louisiana Ste, Houston TX 77002	713-654-2600	S	154*	.1
94	Ward Petroleum Corp—*William Ward*	Box 1187, Enid OK 73702	580-234-3229	R	149*	.1
95	Delta Petroleum Corp—*Carl E Lakey*	370 17th St Ste 4300, Denver CO 80202	303-293-9133	P	147	<.1
96	St Mary Minerals Inc—*Tony Best* SM Energy Co	1775 Sherman St Ste 12, Denver CO 80203	303-861-8140	S	146*	.1
97	Brigham Oil and Gas LP—*Ben M Brigham* Brigham Exploration Co	6300 Bridge Point Pkwy, Austin TX 78730	512-427-3300	S	146*	.1
98	TXCO Resources Inc—*James E Sigmon*	777 E Sonterra Blvd St, San Antonio TX 78258	210-496-5300	P	144	.1
99	Callon Petroleum Operating Co—*Fred Callon*	PO Box 1287, Natchez MS 39121	601-442-1601	R	141*	.1
100	Carrizo Oil and Gas Inc—*SP Chip Johnson IV*	1000 Louisiana St Ste, Houston TX 77002	713-328-1000	P	140	.1
101	VAALCO Energy Inc—*Robert L Gerry III*	4600 Post Oak Pl Ste 3, Houston TX 77027	713-623-0801	P	135	.1
102	VAALCO Gabon Etame Inc—*Robert L Geary III* VAALCO Energy Inc	4600 Post Oak Pl Ste 3, Houston TX 77027	713-623-0801	S	134	<.1
103	Magnum Hunter Resources Corp—*Gary C Evans*	777 Post Oak Blvd Ste, Houston TX 77056	832-369-6986	P	129	.3
104	Cockrell Oil Corp—*Ernest H Cockrell*	1000 Main St Ste 3250, Houston TX 77002	713-209-7300	R	125*	.1
105	PrimeEnergy Corp—*Charles E Drimal Jr*	1 Landmark Sq Ste 1100, Stamford CT 06901	203-358-5700	P	118	.2
106	RAM Energy Resources Inc—*Larry E Lee*	5100 E Skelly Dr Ste 6, Tulsa OK 74135	918-663-2800	P	112	.2
107	Panhandle Oil and Gas Inc—*Michael C Coffman*	5400 N Grand Blvd Ste, Oklahoma City OK 73112	405-948-1560	P	111	<.1
108	BPZ Resources Inc—*Manuel Pablo Zuniga Pflucker*	580 Westlake Park Blvd, Houston TX 77079	281-556-6200	P	111	.3
109	GeoResources Inc—*Frank A Lodzinski*	110 Cypress Station Dr, Houston TX 77090	281-537-9920	P	107	.1
110	Constellation Energy Partners LLC—*Stephen R Brunner*	1801 Main St Ste 1300, Houston TX 77002		B	105	.1
111	Apco Oil and Gas International Inc—*Ralph A Hill*	1 Williams Ctr 35th Fl, Tulsa OK 74172	918-573-2164	B	105	<.1
112	Taylor Energy Co—*Patrick Taylor*	1 Lee Cir, New Orleans LA 70130	504-581-5491	R	100*	.2
113	GMX Resources Inc—*Ken L Kenworthy Jr*	9400 N Broadway Ste 60, Oklahoma City OK 73114	405-600-0711	P	97	.1
114	Crimson Exploration Inc—*Allen D Keel*	717 Texas Ave Ste 2900, Houston TX 77002	713-236-7400	P	97	.1
115	Goodrich Petroleum Corporation Incorporated of Louisiana Goodrich Petroleum Corp	333 Texas Ste 1375, Shreveport LA 71101	318-429-1375	S	94*	.1
116	Vanguard Natural Resources LLC—*Scott W Smith*	5847 San Felipe Ste 30, Houston TX 77057	832-327-2255	P	93	.1
117	JP Oil Company Inc—*Chris M Van Way*	PO Box 52584, Lafayette LA 70505	337-234-1170	R	91*	.1
118	Compass Energy Services Inc—*Ted Fritz*	1313 E Main St Ste 240, Richmond VA 23219	804-320-6900	S	91*	<.1
119	Callon Petroleum Inc—*Fred L Callon*	200 N Canal St, Natchez MS 39120	601-442-1601	P	90	.1

Rank	Company Name—*Executive Officer*	Address, City, State, Zip	Phone	Type	Fin	Empls
120	Signal Hill Petroleum Inc—*Craig Barto*	2633 Cherry Ave, Signal Hill CA 90755	562-595-6440	R	76*	.1
121	Great Western Drilling Company Inc—*Bruce M Brady*	PO Box 1659, Midland TX 79702	432-682-5241	R	75*	<.1
122	Endeavour International Corp—*William L Transier*	1001 Fannin St Ste 160, Houston TX 77002	713-307-8700	P	72	<.1
123	Wagner and Brown Ltd—*Cyril Wagner Jr*	1331 Lamar Ste 1370, Houston TX 77010	713-951-9200	R	71*	.1
124	Dorchester Minerals LP—*William Casey McManemin*	3838 Oak Lawn Ave Ste, Dallas TX 75219	214-559-0300	P	70	<.1
125	Headington Oil Co—*Timothy Headington*	2711 N Haskell Ste 280, Dallas TX 75204	214-696-0606	R	69*	.1
126	BMB Munai Inc—*Gamal Kulumbetov*	324 S 400 W Ste 225, Salt Lake City UT 84101	801-355-2227	P	64	.4
127	VAALCO Energy USA Inc—*Robert L Geary III* VAALCO Energy Inc	4600 Post Oak Pl Ste 3, Houston TX 77027	713-623-0801	S	63*	<.1
128	Abraxas Petroleum Corp—*Robert L G Watson*	18803 Meisner Dr, San Antonio TX 78258	210-490-4788	P	59	.1
129	Petrobras America Inc	10777 Westheimer Rd St, Houston TX 77042	713-781-9798	S	58*	.1
130	Benton Offshore China Co Harvest Natural Resources Inc	1177 Enclave Pky Ste 3, Houston TX 77077	281-899-5700	S	58*	<.1
131	Approach Resources Inc—*J Ross Craft*	1 Ridgmar Ctr 6500 Wes, Fort Worth TX 76116	817-989-9000	P	58	.1
132	Equitable Energy LLC—*David L Porges*	625 Liberty Ave Ste 17, Pittsburgh PA 15222	412-553-5700	S	57*	.3
133	Dominion Appalachian Development Inc—*Thomas Capps*	PO Box 1248, Jane Lew WV 26378	304-884-2000	S	56*	.1
134	Toreador Exploration and Production Inc—*Nigel JB Lovett*	13760 Noel Rd Ste 1100, Dallas TX 75240	214-559-3933	S	56*	<.1
135	Double Eagle Petroleum Co—*Richard Dole*	1675 Broadway Ste 2200, Denver CO 80202	303-794-8445	P	55	.1
136	Howard Energy Company Inc—*David Howard*	125 Park St Ste 250, Traverse City MI 49684	231-995-7850	R	54*	.1
137	Charles Holston Inc—*Brian J Recatto*	PO Box 728, Jennings LA 70546	337-824-8348	R	53*	.1
138	Lario Oil and Gas Co—*Michael O'Shaughnessy*	301 S Market St, Wichita KS 67202	316-265-5611	R	50*	.1
139	Mosbacher Energy Co—*Robert Mosbacher Jr*	712 Main St Ste 2200, Houston TX 77002	713-546-2565	R	48	.1
140	BTA Oil Producers—*Barry Beal*	16825 Northchase Dr St, Houston TX 77060	281-872-5022	R	47*	.1
141	North Coast Energy Inc—*Wendy L Straatmann* EXCO Resources Inc	One GOJO Plaza Ste 325, Akron OH 44311	330-572-8500	S	46*	.2
142	Keener Oil and Gas Co—*Dewey F Bartlett Jr*	1648 S Boston Ave Ste, Tulsa OK 74119	918-587-4154	R	45*	<.1
143	Citation Oil and Gas Corp—*Curtis Harrell*	14077 Cutten Rd, Houston TX 77069	281-891-1000	R	44*	.4
144	Gastar Exploration Ltd—*J Russell Porter*	1331 Lamar St Ste 650, Houston TX 77010	713-739-1800	P	43	<.1
145	Isramco Inc—*Haim Tsuff*	2425 W Loop S Ste 810, Houston TX 77027	713-621-3882	P	42	<.1
146	Unit Texas Drilling LLC—*Larry Pinkston*	PO Box 5320, Borger TX 79008	806-273-7573	S	40	.2
147	Barnwell Industries Inc—*Morton H Kinzler*	1100 Alakea St Ste 290, Honolulu HI 96813	808-531-8400	P	39	<.1
148	Wagner Oil Co—*Bryan Wagner*	500 Commerce St Ste 60, Fort Worth TX 76102	817-335-2222	R	37*	<.1
149	EnergynetCom Inc—*William W Britain*	7201 I-40 W Ste 319, Amarillo TX 79106	806-351-2953	S	35*	<.1
150	Output Exploration LLC—*James E Sigmon* TXCO Resources Inc	777 E Sonterra Blvd St, San Antonio TX 78258	210-496-5300	S	35*	<.1
151	GeoMet Inc—*J Darby Sere*	909 Fannin Ste 1850, Houston TX 77010	713-659-3855	P	33	.1
152	Hanson Production Co—*Neal Hanson*	6363 Woodway Dr Ste 60, Houston TX 77057	713-789-6202	R	29*	<.1
153	Caerus Oil and Gas LLC—*David H Keyte*	600 17th St Ste 1600 N, Denver CO 80202	303-565-4600	R	29	<.1
154	Dugan Production Corp—*Thomas A Dugan*	PO Box 420, Farmington NM 87499	505-325-1821	R	28*	.2
155	Manziel Interests—*DN Manziel*	PO Box 6005, Tyler TX 75711	903-592-4315	R	28*	<.1
156	US Energy Corp—*Keith G Larsen*	877 N 8th St W, Riverton WY 82501	307-856-9271	P	27	<.1
157	Lenape Resources Inc—*John C Holko*	9489 Alexander Rd, Alexander NY 14005	585-344-1200	R	27*	<.1
158	Cano Petroleum Inc—*Jim Latimer*	6500 N Belt Line Rd St, Irving TX 75063	214-687-0030	P	26	<.1
159	Grynberg Production Corp—*Jack J Grynberg*	5000 South Quebec St S, Denver CO 80237	303-850-7490	S	26	<.1
160	FX Energy Inc—*David N Pierce*	3006 Highland Dr Ste 2, Salt Lake City UT 84106	801-486-5555	P	25	<.1
161	Breck Operating Corp—*Fred F Dueser*	PO Box 911, Breckenridge TX 76424	254-559-3355	R	24*	<.1
162	BWAB Inc—*Steven Roitman*	475 17th St Ste 1390, Denver CO 80202	303-295-7444	R	24*	<.1
163	Tidelands Oil Production Co—*Scott Hara*	301 E Ocean Blvd, Long Beach CA 90802	562-436-9918	R	23*	.2
164	Miller Energy Resources Inc—*Scott M Boruff*	PO Box 130, Huntsville TN 37756	865-223-6575	P	23	.1
165	RBC Exploration Co—*Roger B Collins*	2627 E 21st, Tulsa OK 74114	918-744-5607	R	22*	<.1
166	Tri-C Resources Inc—*Michael S Cone*	909 Wirt Rd, Houston TX 77024	713-685-3600	R	21*	<.1
167	Enpro Inc	3617 Lexington Rd, Winchester KY 40391	859-744-6171	S	21*	<.1
168	Gasco Energy Inc—*W King Grant*	8 Inverness Dr E Ste 1, Englewood CO 80112	303-483-0044	P	20	<.1
169	Bridwell Oil Co—*GH Shores*	PO Box 1830, Wichita Falls TX 76307	940-723-4351	R	20*	.1
170	Graham-Michaelis Corp—*Walter A Michaelis Jr*	PO Box 247, Wichita KS 67201	316-264-8394	R	20*	<.1
171	Venus Exploration Inc—*Eugene L Ames Jr*	19240 Redland Rd Ste 2, San Antonio TX 78259	210-824-8882	R	20*	<.1
172	Houston American Energy Corp—*John F Terwilliger*	801 Travis St Ste 1425, Houston TX 77002	713-222-6966	P	20	<.1
173	Maguire Oil Co—*Cary Maguire*	5950 Berkshire Ln Ste, Dallas TX 75225	214-741-5137	R	19*	<.1
174	Enservco Corp—*Michael D Herman*	501 S Cherry St Ste 32, Denver CO 80246	303-333-3678	P	19	<.1
175	Burk Royalty Co—*David A Kimbell*	PO Box 94903, Wichita Falls TX 76308	940-397-8600	R	18*	.1
176	Davis Cos—*Lee Davis*	110 W 7th Ste 1000, Tulsa OK 74119	918-584-3581	R	18*	<.1
177	Avenue Energy Inc—*Levi Mochkin* Avenue Group Inc	17547 Ventura Blvd, Sherman Oaks CA 91401	818-465-1200	S	18*	<.1
178	Storm Cat Energy Corp—*Keith Knapstad*	1125 17th St Ste 2310, Denver CO 80202	303-991-5070	P	17	<.1
179	Hallador Energy Co—*Victor P Stabio*	1660 Lincoln St Ste 27, Denver CO 80264	303-839-5504	P	17	.3
180	CREDO Petroleum Corp—*Marlis E Smith Jr*	1801 Broadway Ste 900, Denver CO 80202	303-297-2200	P	17	<.1
181	Duncan Oil Inc—*Ray T Duncan*	1777 S Harrison St Pen, Denver CO 80210	303-759-3303	R	16*	<.1
182	Read and Stevens Inc—*Charles B Read*	PO Box 1518, Roswell NM 88202	575-622-3770	R	16*	<.1
183	GHK Co—*Robert A Hefner III*	6305 Waterford Blvd St, Oklahoma City OK 73118	405-858-9800	R	15*	<.1
184	Seven J Stock Farm Inc—*John R Parten*	16945 Northchase Dr St, Houston TX 77060	281-874-2101	R	15*	<.1
185	Samson Resources Co—*C Tholen*	PO Box 21022, Tulsa OK 74121	918-583-1791	R	14*	.1
186	Tengasco Inc—*Jeffrey R Bailey*	11121 Kingston Pk Ste, Knoxville TN 37934	865-675-1554	P	13	<.1
187	Transcom Communications Inc—*Scott Birdwell*	1925 W John Carpenter, Irving TX 75063	972-792-3700	R	13*	<.1
188	Benson Mineral Group Inc—*Bruce D Benson*	1560 Broadway Ste 1900, Denver CO 80202	303-863-3500	R	13*	<.1
189	HKN Inc—*Mikel D Faulkner*	180 State St Ste 200, Southlake TX 76092	817-424-2424	P	13	<.1
190	Seagull Operating Company Inc—*Scott S Lowe*	416 Travis St Ste 1215, Shreveport LA 71101	318-226-9170	R	12*	<.1
191	Davis Brothers Oil Producers Inc	110 West 7th Ste 10, Tulsa OK 74119	918-584-7272	S	12*	<.1
192	Sierra Resources LLC—*John Eads*	333 Clay St Ste 3660, Houston TX 77002	713-464-8183	R	12*	<.1
193	Royale Energy Inc—*Donald H Hosmer*	7676 Hazard Center Dr, San Diego CA 92108	619-881-2800	P	12	<.1
194	Gallagher Drilling Inc—*Victor R Gallagher Jr*	PO Box 3046, Evansville IN 47730	812-425-8256	R	11*	<.1
195	CA Properties Inc Daleco Resources Corp	17 Wilmont Mews 5th Fl, West Chester PA 19382	610-429-0181	S	11*	<.1
196	Deven Resources Inc—*Gary Novinskie*	17 Wilmont Mews 5th Fl, West Chester PA 19382	610-429-0181	R	11*	<.1
197	DRI Operating Company Inc—*Gary Novinskie* Daleco Resources Corp	17 Wilmont Mews 5th Fl, West Chester PA 19382	610-429-0181	S	11*	<.1
198	Harvest Natural Resources Inc—*James A Edmiston*	1177 Enclave Pkwy Ste, Houston TX 77077	281-899-5700	P	11	<.1
199	Hudson Oil Company of Texas—*William Hudson*	616 Texas St, Fort Worth TX 76102	817-336-7109	R	10*	<.1
200	Anglo-Dutch Petroleum International Inc—*Scott V Van Dyke*	8 Greenway Plz Ste 900, Houston TX 77046	713-993-9303	R	10*	<.1
201	JR Resources—*Randy Doverspike*	PO Box 188, Ringgold PA 15770	814-365-5821	R	10	<.1
202	Pioneer Oil and Gas—*Don J Colton*	1206 W South Jordan Pk, South Jordan UT 84095	801-566-3000	R	10	<.1

Note: An asterisk (*) indicates an estimated financial figure. The company type code used is as follows: R = Private, P = Public, S = Private Subsidiary, B = Public Subsidiary, D = Division, J = Joint Venture, I = Investment Fund.

COMPANY RANKINGS BY SALES WITHIN 4-DIGIT SIC

Rank	Company Name—Executive Officer	Address, City, State, Zip	Phone	Type	Fin	Empls
203	Syntroleum Corp—Edward G Roth	5416 S Yale Ave Ste 40, Tulsa OK 74135	918-592-7900	P	8	<.1
204	Earthstone Energy Inc—Ray Singleton	633 17th St Ste 1900, Denver CO 80202	303-296-3076	P	8	<.1
205	Bayou State Oil Corp—Ellis Brown	PO Box 7886, Shreveport LA 71137	318-222-0737	R	8*	<.1
206	Wheeler Oil Co—Randy McCall	6320 Southwest Blvd St, Fort Worth TX 76109	817-332-6145	R	8*	<.1
207	Clear Fork Inc—Robert W Eagle	PO Box 3095, Abilene TX 79604	325-677-1309	R	8*	<.1
208	Baird Oil Company Inc—Jim R Baird	PO Box 428, Logan KS 67646	785-689-7456	R	8*	<.1
209	Spindletop Oil and Gas Co—Chris G Mazzini	One Spindletop Centre, Dallas TX 75230	972-644-2581	P	8	.1
210	Evolution Petroleum Corp—Robert S Herlin	2500 CityWest Blvd Ste, Houston TX 77042	713-935-0122	P	8	<.1
211	Doyle Hartman Oil Producer—Doyle Hartman	500 N Main St, Midland TX 79701	432-684-4011	R	7*	<.1
212	Wisenbaker Production Co—Royce E Wisenbaker Jr	218 N Broadway Ave, Tyler TX 75702	903-593-2588	R	7*	<.1
213	Tri-Valley Oil and Gas Co—Maston Cunningham Tri-Valley Corp	4550 California Ave St, Bakersfield CA 93309	661-864-0500	S	7*	<.1
214	NCEY Holding LLC—Edward R DeStefano	1770 St James Pl Ste 3, Houston TX 77056	713-266-4344	R	7*	<.1
215	Lighting Oil Co—Walter Light	PO Box 6598, San Antonio TX 78209	210-828-6203	R	7*	<.1
216	Post Oak Oil Co—Carri A Bell	13300 N MacArthur, Oklahoma City OK 73142	405-621-1300	R	7	<.1
217	TM Hopkins Operating Inc—Tom Hopkins	PO Box 2859, Kilgore TX 75663	903-984-7721	R	7*	<.1
218	Fieldpoint Petroleum Corp—Ray D Reaves	1703 Edelweiss Dr, Cedar Park TX 78613	512-250-8692	P	7	<.1
219	Texas Vanguard Oil Co—William G Watson	PO Box 202650, Austin TX 78720	512-331-6781	P	6	<.1
220	Trans Energy Inc—John G Corp	PO Box 393, Saint Marys WV 26170	304-684-7053	P	6	<.1
221	Raymond Oil Company Inc—William S Raymond	155 N Market Ste 800, Wichita KS 67202	316-267-4214	R	6*	<.1
222	Redman Energy Corp—Jeff Voncannon	10375 Richmond Ave Ste, Houston TX 77042	713-782-1377	R	6*	<.1
223	Continental Resources of Illinois Inc—Richard Straeter	PO Box 749, Mount Vernon IL 62864	618-242-1717	R	5*	.1
224	Samson Oil and Gas LLC—Terrance Maxwell Barr	1726 Cole Blvd Ste 210, Lakewood CO 80401	303-295-0344	S	5	<.1
225	Waco Oil and Gas Company Inc—Ira Morris	PO Box 397, Glenville WV 26351	304-462-5741	R	5*	<.1
226	Mull Drilling Company Inc—Lewis M Mull	1700 N Waterfront Pkwy, Wichita KS 67206	316-264-6366	R	5*	<.1
227	Fair Oil Ltd—John R Garrett	PO Box 689, Tyler TX 75710	903-592-3811	R	5*	<.1
228	Ben M Patterson Jr—Ben Patterson Jr	613 NW Loop 410 Ste 68, San Antonio TX 78216	210-377-3703	R	5*	<.1
229	Tri-Valley Corp—Maston Cunningham	4550 California Ave St, Bakersfield CA 93309	661-864-0500	P	5	<.1
230	Pyramid Oil Co—John H Alexander	PO Box 832, Bakersfield CA 93302	661-325-1000	P	5	<.1
231	Pennaco Energy Inc Marathon Oil Corp	PO Box 3128, Houston TX 77253	713-629-6600	S	5	.1
232	New Concept Energy Inc—Gene S Bertcher	1603 Lyndon B Johnson, Dallas TX 75234	972-407-8400	P	4	.1
233	Muskegon Development Co—William Myler Jr	1425 S Mission Rd Ste, Mount Pleasant MI 48858	989-772-4900	R	4*	<.1
234	Stelbar Oil Corp—John C Shawver	155 N Market Ste 500, Wichita KS 67202	316-264-8378	R	4*	<.1
235	Nortex Corp—Al W Dugan	1415 Louisiana St, Houston TX 77002	713-658-1142	R	4*	<.1
236	Three Star Drilling and Producing Corp—Ira M Patton	PO Box 350, Lawrenceville IL 62439	618-936-2301	R	4*	<.1
237	Cree Oil Ltd—Ira J Cree	3250 Cherry Ave, Long Beach CA 90807	562-424-8647	R	4*	<.1
238	CRM Energy Inc—John Stranger	6301 N Western Ave, Oklahoma City OK 73118	405-848-5420	R	4*	<.1
239	Sefton Resources Inc—Karl Arleth	2050 S Oneida St Ste 1, Denver CO 80224	303-759-2700	P	4	N/A
240	Capital City Energy Group Inc—Timothy S Shear	PO Box 156, Burbank OH 44214	614-485-3110	P	3	<.1
241	Mexco Energy Corp—Nicholas C Taylor	PO Box 10502, Midland TX 79702	432-682-1119	P	3	<.1
242	Aladdin Petroleum Corp—George Bruce	123 S Market St, Wichita KS 67202	316-265-9602	R	3*	<.1
243	Canyon Energy Inc—David A Kemmer	7701 E Kellogg Dr Ste, Wichita KS 67207	316-263-3103	R	3*	<.1
244	EnMark Gas Corp—RG Miller	17430 Campbell Rd, Dallas TX 75252	214-368-5050	R	3*	<.1
245	Blue Dolphin Energy Co—Ivar Siem	801 Travis St Ste 2100, Houston TX 77002	713-568-4725	P	3	<.1
246	American Natural Energy Corp—Michael Paulk	6100 S Yale Ave Ste 30, Tulsa OK 74136	918-481-1440	P	3	<.1
247	Jerry Scott Drilling Company Inc—JG Scott	P O Box 271, Seminole OK 74818	405-382-2202	R	2*	<.1
248	Corda Corp—Paul De Cleva Jr	350 N St Paul St Ste 1, Dallas TX 75201	214-922-8023	R	2*	<.1
249	Banks Oil Co—Lee Banks	7701 E Kellog Ave Ste, Wichita KS 67207	316-612-1186	R	2*	<.1
250	Northland Royalty Co—Peter Sheehan	3030 4th Ave N, Billings MT 59101	406-259-5400	R	2*	<.1
251	Petroleum Inc—John K Garvey	300 W Douglas Ste 1050, Wichita KS 67202	316-291-8200	R	2*	<.1
252	Bayou City Exploration Inc—Charles T Bukowski	632 Adams St Ste 710, Bowling Green KY 42101		B	2	<.1
253	Glen Rose Petroleum Corp—Andrew Taylor-Kimmins	22762 Westheimer Pky, Katy TX 77450	832-437-0329	P	1	<.1
254	Oakridge Energy Inc—Arbie M Ray	4613 Jacksboro Hwy, Wichita Falls TX 76302	940-322-4772	P	1	<.1
255	Galaxy Energy Corp—Mark E Bruner	1331 17th St Ste 730, Denver CO 80202	303-293-2300	R	1*	<.1
256	Oceanic Exploration Co—James Blue	7800 E Dorado Pl Ste 2, Englewood CO 80111	303-220-8330	P	1	<.1
257	Voyager Oil and Gas Inc—James Russell Reger	2718 Montana Ave Ste 2, Billings MT 59101	406-245-4901	P	1	<.1
258	GSV Inc—Gilad Gat	191 Post Rd W, Westport CT 06880	203-221-2690	P	1	<.1
259	Ness Energy International Inc—David M Boyce	PO Box 162687, Fort Worth TX 76161	405-513-7733	R	1	<.1
260	Daleco Resources Corp—Gary Novinskie	17 Wilmont Mews 5th Fl, West Chester PA 19382	610-429-0181	P	1	<.1
261	EnDevCo Inc—Chris A Dittmar	2425 Fountainview Dr S, Houston TX 77057	713-977-4662	P	1	<.1
262	New Frontier Energy Inc—Samyak Veera	1801 Broadway Ste 920, Denver CO 80202	303-730-9994	R	1	<.1
263	Alternative Technologies—Len Maniscalco	PO Box 831, Bensenville IL 60106	630-766-7755	R	<1*	<.1
264	Merlon International—John Barnwell	3 Riverway Ste 750, Houston TX 77056	713-365-9936	R	<1	<.1
265	Altex Industries Inc—Steven H Cardin	PO Box 1057, Breckenridge CO 80424	303-265-9312	P	<1	<.1
266	Arete Industries Inc—Donald W Prosser	PO Box 141, Westminster CO 80036	303-427-8688	P	<1	N/A
267	Cobalt International Energy LP—Joseph H Bryant	1980 Post Oak Blvd Ste, Houston TX 77056	713-579-9100	P	<1	.1
268	Hyperdynamics Corp—Ray Leonard	12012 Wickchester Ln S, Houston TX 77079	713-353-9400	P	<1	<.1
269	Far East Energy Corp—Michael R McElwrath	363 N Sam Houston Pkwy, Houston TX 77060	832-598-0470	P	<1	<.1
270	Empire Energy Corp—Malcolm Bendall	4500 College Blvd, Leawood KS 66211	913-663-2310	P	<1	<.1
271	ERHC Energy Inc—Peter C Ntephe	5444 Westheimer Rd Ste, Houston TX 77056	713-626-4700	P	<1	<.1
272	Avenue Group Inc—Levi Mochkin	405 Lexington Ave 26th, New York NY 10174		P	<1	<.1
273	Evolution Fuels Inc—Dennis G McLaughlin III	3001 Knox St Ste 403, Dallas TX 75205	214-389-9800	P	<1	<.1
274	Surge Global Energy Inc—E Jamie Schloss	990 Highland Dr Ste 20, Solana Beach CA 92075	858-720-9900	P	<1	<.1
275	TX Holdings Inc—William Shrewsbury	12080 Virginia Blvd, Ashland KY 41102	606-928-1131	P	<1	<.1
276	American Energy Group Ltd—R Pierce Onthank	1 Gorham Island Ste 30, Westport CT 06880	203-222-7315	P	<1	<.1
277	Empire Petroleum Corp—Albert E Whitehead	4444 E 66th St, Tulsa OK 74136	918-488-8068	P	<1	<.1
278	PetroHunter Energy Corp—Martin B Oring	1600 Stout St Ste 450, Denver CO 80202	303-572-8900	P	<1	<.1
279	Holloman Energy Corp—Mark Stevenson	333 N Sam Houston Pkwy, Houston TX 77060	281-260-0193	P	<1	N/A
280	Parafin Corp—Sidney B Fowlds	5190 Neil Rd Ste 430, Reno NV 89502	213-985-3136	P	<1	N/A
281	Continental Energy Corp—Richard L McAdoo	1413 S Howard Ave Suit, Tampa FL 33606	813-387-3309	P	N/A	<.1
282	Aviva Petroleum Inc—Ronald Suttill	8235 Douglas Ave Ste 4, Dallas TX 75225	214-691-3464	R	N/A	<.1

TOTALS: SIC 1311 Crude Petroleum & Natural Gas
Companies: 282

					720,319	312.3

1321 Natural Gas Liquids

Rank	Company Name—Executive Officer	Address, City, State, Zip	Phone	Type	Fin	Empls
1	Enterprise Products Partners LP—Michael Creel	PO Box 4324, Houston TX 77210	713-381-6500	P	44,313	6.6
2	Williams Partners LP—Alan S Armstrong	1 Williams Ctr, Tulsa OK 74172	918-573-2000	P	14,380	N/A
3	Dynegy Inc—Thomas W Elward	1000 Louisiana St Ste, Houston TX 77002	713-507-6400	P	10,013	1.7
4	Dynegy Energy Partners LP—Bruce A Williamson	1000 Louisiana, Houston TX 77002	713-507-6400	S	3,067*	.3

Rank	Company Name—*Executive Officer*	Address, City, State, Zip	Phone	Type	Fin	Empls
	Dynegy Inc					
5	Energy Corporation of America—*John Mork*	4643 S Ulster St Ste 1, Denver CO 80237	303-694-2667	R	276*	.7
6	Ceramic Industries Inc—*John Denman*	4208 Versailles Ave, Dallas TX 75205	214-635-2727	R	6*	.1

TOTALS: SIC 1321 Natural Gas Liquids
Companies: 6   72,055   9.3

1381 Drilling Oil & Gas Wells

Rank	Company Name—*Executive Officer*	Address, City, State, Zip	Phone	Type	Fin	Empls
1	Pioneer Drilling Services Ltd—*Wm Stacy Locke* Pioneer Drilling Co	1250 NE Loop 410 Ste 1, San Antonio TX 78209	210-828-7689	S	7,798*	1.5
2	Anadrill Schlumberger	300 Schlumberger Dr, Sugar Land TX 77478	281-285-8000	S	6,002*	3.5
3	Chesapeake Operating Inc—*Aubrey McClendon*	PO Box 18496, Oklahoma City OK 73154	405-848-8000	S	4,589*	1.0
4	Boggs Natural Gas Co—*Harry Boggs*	1248 Charleston Rd, Spencer WV 25276	304-927-1286	R	3,807*	<.1
5	Diamond Offshore Drilling Inc—*Lawrence R Dickerson*	15415 Katy Fwy Ste 100, Houston TX 77094	281-492-5300	B	3,322	5.3
6	Patterson-UTI Energy Inc—*Douglas J Wall*	450 Gears Rd Ste 500, Houston TX 77067	281-765-7100	P	2,566	8.2
7	Key Energy Services Inc—*Dick Alario*	1301 McKinney Ste 1800, Houston TX 77010	713-651-4300	P	1,847	8.0
8	Helmerich and Payne Inc—*Hans Helmerich*	1437 S Boulder Ave, Tulsa OK 74119	918-742-5531	P	1,502	7.7
9	SOLOCO LLC—*Paul L Howes*	207 Town Center Pkwy 1, Lafayette LA 70506	337-988-4516	S	1,305*	.3
10	Noble Drilling Services Inc—*David W Williams*	13135 S Dairy Ashford, Sugar Land TX 77478	281-276-6100	S	997*	.2
11	Unit Drilling Co—*John Cromling*	PO Box 702500, Tulsa OK 74170	918-493-7700	S	942*	1.7
12	Rowan Companies Inc—*W Matt Ralls*	2800 Post Oak Blvd Ste, Houston TX 77056	713-621-7800	P	939	2.7
13	Pioneer Drilling Co—*Stacy Locke*	1250 NE Loop 410 Ste 1, San Antonio TX 78209	210-828-7689	P	716	3.3
14	Parker Drilling Co—*David C Mannon*	5 Greenway Plz Ste 100, Houston TX 77046	281-406-2000	P	659	2.0
15	Hercules Offshore Inc—*John Rynd*	9 Greenway Plz Ste 220, Houston TX 77046	713-350-5100	P	658	2.2
16	Atwood Oceanics Inc—*Robert J Saltiel*	PO Box 218350, Houston TX 77218	281-749-7800	P	645	1.3
17	Nabors Drilling USA Inc	515 W Greens Rd Ste 10, Houston TX 77067	281-874-0035	S	441*	5.6
18	Parker Drilling Company North America Inc—*David C Mannon* Parker North America Operations Inc	5 Greenway Plz Ste 100, Houston TX 77046	281-406-2000	S	429*	.1
19	Parker North America Operations Inc—*David C Mannon* Parker Drilling Co	5 Greenway Plz Ste 100, Houston TX 77046	281-406-2000	S	429*	.1
20	Bigard and Huggard Drilling Inc—*Steven Bigard*	5880 Ventura Way, Mount Pleasant MI 48858	989-775-6608	R	410*	.1
21	Atwood Hunter Co—*Robert J Saltiel* Atwood Oceanics Inc	PO Box 218350, Houston TX 77218	281-749-7800	R	407*	.1
22	Petroleum Development Corp—*James M Trimble*	PO Box 43078, Providence RI 02940	303-860-5800	P	348	.3
23	Cyclone Drilling Inc—*James J Hladky*	PO Box 908, Gillette WY 82717	307-682-4161	R	267*	.8
24	Fairman Corp—*Ron Fairman*	PO Box 288, Du Bois PA 15801	814-371-8410	R	263*	.1
25	Supreme Contractors LLC—*Paul L Howes*	110 Emerald Dr, Lafayette LA 70506	337-233-7357	S	257*	.1
26	QR Energy LP—*Alan L Smith*	5 Houston Ctr 1401 McK, Houston TX 77010	713-452-2200	P	253	N/A
27	Intermarine LLC—*Andre Grikitis*	16801 Greenspoint Pk D, Houston TX 77060	281-885-3500	R	217*	.1
28	WO Operating Co—*Miles O'Loughlin*	PO Box 960, Pampa TX 79066	806-665-8298	R	217*	<.1
29	Applied Drilling Technology Inc—*Rob Long*	15375 Memorial Dr Ste, Houston TX 77079	281-925-7100	S	207*	.1
30	Union Drilling Inc—*Christopher D Strong*	4055 International Plz, Fort Worth TX 76109	817-735-8793	P	193	1.2
31	Challenger Minerals Inc—*Charles B Hauf*	1311 Broadfield Blvd S, Houston TX 77084	832-587-5400	S	192*	<.1
32	Nabors Offshore Corp—*Jerry Shanklin*	515 W Greens Rd Ste 50, Houston TX 77067	281-874-0406	R	160*	.7
33	Nabors International Inc—*Sigfried Meissner*	515 W Greens Rd Ste 60, Houston TX 77067	281-874-0035	R	152*	1.7
34	BP Exploration Inc (Anchorage Alaska)—*Steve Marshall*	PO Box 196612, Anchorage AK 99519	907-564-5111	S	108*	1.3
35	Justiss Oil Company Inc—*JF Justiss Jr*	PO Box 2990, Jena LA 71342	318-992-4111	R	100*	.5
36	David New Drilling Company Inc—*DA New Jr*	PO Box 1487, Natchez MS 39120	601-442-1607	R	75*	<.1
37	Barnwell Kona Corp—*Morton H Kinzler*	1100 Alakea St Ste 290, Honolulu HI 96813	808-531-8400	S	72*	<.1
38	Nabors Drilling International Ltd	515 W Greens Rd Ste 12, Houston TX 77067	281-874-0035	R	49*	.5
39	Ardmore Production and Exploration Co—*CE Teacle*	PO Box 1988, Ardmore OK 73402	580-223-2292	R	46*	<.1
40	Helmerich and Payne International Drilling Co—*Hans Helmerich* Helmerich and Payne Inc	1437 S Boulder Ave, Tulsa OK 74119	918-742-5531	S	40*	.3
41	American Shoreline Inc—*Paul Strunk*	802 N Carancahua 1250, Corpus Christi TX 78401	361-888-4496	R	37*	<.1
42	Torch Energy Services—*James P Bryan*	1331 Lamar St, Houston TX 77010	713-650-1246	S	36*	.1
43	Dynamic Inc—*John Harvison*	2801 Glenda St, Haltom City TX 76117	817-838-1800	R	32*	<.1
44	Leonard Hudson Drilling Company Inc—*Leonard Hudson*	PO Box 1876, Pampa TX 79066	806-665-1816	S	30*	.2
45	Noble Properties Inc—*Vivian DuBois*	3475 Lenox Rd NE, Atlanta GA 30326	404-233-3011	R	28*	<.1
46	McVay Drilling Co—*Mike McVay*	PO Box 924, Hobbs NM 88241	505-397-3311	R	27*	.1
47	BT Operating Co—*Cambell Evans*	2425 Fountain View Dr, Houston TX 77057	713-977-9200	R	24*	<.1
48	Leede Operating Company LLC—*Ed H Leede*	6400 S Fiddler's Green, Greenwood Village CO 80111	303-721-8000	R	19*	<.1
49	Gardes Energy Services Inc—*Robert Gardes*	PO Box 92593, Lafayette LA 70509	337-234-6544	R	18*	<.1
50	RL Bolin—*Beverly Bolin*	4245 Kemp Blvd Ste 316, Wichita Falls TX 76308	940-691-7676	R	14*	<.1
51	Ramos Oil Company Inc—*Kent Ramos*	PO Box 401, West Sacramento CA 95691	916-371-2570	R	13*	.2
52	Imperial Petroleum Inc—*Jeffrey T Wilson*	PO Box 1006, Evansville IN 47706	812-867-1433	P	11	<.1
53	Brammer Engineering Inc—*Randy Beauclair*	400 Texas St Rm 600, Shreveport LA 71101	318-429-2345	R	9*	.1
54	Jacobs Financial Group Inc—*John M Jacobs*	300 Summers St Ste 970, Charleston WV 25301	304-343-8171	P	9	<.1
55	ONEOK Energy Resources Co	PO Box 871, Tulsa OK 74102	918-588-7000	S	6*	.1
56	Wisco-Moran Drilling Company Inc—*Joel Bouldin*	PO Box 939, Fresno TX 77545	281-431-2600	R	6*	.1
57	Black Dragon Resource Companies Inc—*Thomas Neely*	PO Box 458, Oil City LA 71061	318-995-0404	P	5	<.1
58	Les Wilson Inc—*Robert Wilson*	PO Box 331, Carmi IL 62821	618-382-4667	R	5*	.1
59	Zenith Drilling Corp—*C Robert Buford*	1223 N Rock Rd Bldg A, Wichita KS 67206	316-684-9777	R	5*	.1
60	Nabors Alaska Drilling Inc—*Dennis Smith*	2525 C St Ste 200, Anchorage AK 99503	907-263-6000	S	4	.3
61	Denali Drilling Inc—*Hal Ingalls*	8240 Petersburg St, Anchorage AK 99507	907-562-2312	R	4*	<.1
62	Berenergy Corp—*Miriam Beren*	PO Box 5850, Denver CO 80203	303-295-2323	R	2*	<.1
63	Great Northern Gas Co—*Thomas L DiGrappa*	621 17th St Ste 2150, Denver CO 80293	303-295-0938	R	2*	<.1
64	T-C Oil Co—*Robert Hewitt*	427 FM 774, Refugio TX 78377	361-526-4693	R	1*	<.1

TOTALS: SIC 1381 Drilling Oil & Gas Wells
Companies: 64   43,973   63.9

1382 Oil & Gas Exploration Services

Rank	Company Name—*Executive Officer*	Address, City, State, Zip	Phone	Type	Fin	Empls
1	GM Offshore Inc GulfMark Offshore Inc	10111 Richmond Ave Ste, Houston TX 77042	713-963-9522	S	17,305*	.5
2	Geokinetics USA Inc—*Jim White*	1500 Citywest Blvd Ste, Houston TX 77042	713-850-7600	S	4,575*	.1
3	ChevronTexaco Overseas Petroleum Inc—*David O'Reilly*	PO Box 5046, San Ramon CA 94583		S	3,180*	5.7
4	Bright and Company Production Co—*Clay Bright*	4228 N Central Expy St, Dallas TX 75206	214-559-9200	R	3,169*	.1
5	QEP Resources Inc—*Charles B Stanley*	1050 17th St Ste 500, Denver CO 80265	303-672-6900	P	3,159	.9
6	Hunt Consolidated Inc—*Ray L Hunt*	1445 Ross Ave Ste 1500, Dallas TX 75202	214-978-8000	R	2,120*	3.0
7	Gary-Williams Co—*Ronald Williams*	370 17th St Ste 5300, Denver CO 80202	303-628-3800	R	1,727*	.3

Note: An asterisk (*) indicates an estimated financial figure. The company type code used is as follows: R = Private, P = Public, S = Private Subsidiary, B = Public Subsidiary, D = Division, J = Joint Venture, I = Investment Fund.

COMPANY RANKINGS BY SALES WITHIN 4-DIGIT SIC

Rank	Company Name—*Executive Officer*	Address, City, State, Zip	Phone	Type	Fin	Empls
8	Harvey E Yates Co—*George M Yates*	PO Box 1933, Roswell NM 88202	575-623-6601	R	1,145*	.1
9	Davis Petroleum Corp—*Greg Davis*	1360 Post Oak Blvd Ste, Houston TX 77056	713-626-7766	R	1,078*	<.1
10	W and T Offshore Inc—*Tracy W Krohn*	9 Greenway Plz Ste 300, Houston TX 77046	713-626-8525	P	971	.3
11	Grynberg Petroleum Co—*Jack J Grynberg*	5299 DTC Blvd Ste 500, Greenwood Village CO 80111	303-850-7490	R	844*	<.1
12	Sharp Water Inc—*D J Shannahan*	1033 Fowler Ct, Dover DE 19901	302-677-0300	S	765*	<.1
13	Blue Ridge Group Inc—*Robert D Burr*	632 Adams St Ste 700, Bowling Green KY 42101	270-842-2421	R	754*	<.1
14	Tensas Delta Exploration Company LLC—*Scott Sinclair*	333 Texas St Ste 2121, Shreveport LA 71101	318-222-0026	R	550*	<.1
15	Pruet Oil Co—*William R James*	217 W Capitol St Ste 2, Jackson MS 39201	601-948-5279	R	508*	<.1
16	Modern Exploration Inc—*Gary Yost*	213 N Travis St 3rd Fl, Sherman TX 75090	903-893-1129	R	473*	<.1
17	Opicoil America Inc—*CH Chang*	3040 Post Oak Blvd, Houston TX 77056	713-297-8100	R	460*	<.1
18	ION Geophysical Corp—*Robert P Peebler*	2105 Citywest Blvd Bld, Houston TX 77042	281-933-3339	P	455	.9
19	Global Geophysical Services Inc—*Richard Degner*	13927 S Gessner Rd, Missouri City TX 77489	713-972-9200	P	385	1.3
20	GulfMark Offshore Inc—*Bruce A Streeter*	10111 Richmond Ave Ste, Houston TX 77042	713-963-9522	P	382	1.7
21	Black Hills Exploration And Production Inc—*Tim Hopkins*	350 Indiana St Ste 400, Golden CO 80401	720-210-1300	S	370*	.1
22	Dawson Geophysical Co—*Stephen C Jumper*	508 W Wall Ste 800, Midland TX 79701	432-684-3000	P	333	1.5
23	Clayton Williams Energy Inc—*Clayton W Williams*	6 Desta Dr Ste 3000, Midland TX 79705	432-682-6324	P	332	.4
24	Cleary Petroleum Corp—*Douglas B Cleary*	PO Box 7678, Edmond OK 73034	405-848-5019	R	308*	<.1
25	Madden Systems Inc—*Raymond Madden*	1801 E Pearl St, Odessa TX 79761	432-332-0255	R	249*	<.1
26	Unit Petroleum Co—*Larry D Pinkston*	PO Box 702500, Tulsa OK 74136	918-493-7700	D	222*	.3
27	New Jersey Natural Gas Co—*Laurence M Downes*	1415 Wyckoff Rd, Farmingdale NJ 07727	732-938-7977	S	217*	.5
28	Raydon Exploration Inc—*Steve Raybourn*	1601 Express Way Ste 1, Oklahoma City OK 73118	405-478-8585	R	200*	<.1
29	Mitenergy Upstream LLC—*Norman F Haisler*	9 Greenway Plz Ste 125, Houston TX 77046	713-960-0598	R	168*	<.1
30	Geo Frontiers Corp—*Gary K Rice*	5130 Boyd Blvd Ste A, Rowlett TX 75088	972-412-7939	R	167*	<.1
31	Xeron Inc—*David E Snyder*	2500 Citywest Blvd Ste, Houston TX 77042	713-988-0051	S	153*	<.1
32	Seahawk Drilling—*Louis Raspino*	1198 Barrow St, Houma LA 70360	985-872-4700	S	144*	1.7
33	Ellora Energy Inc—*T Scott Martin*	5665 Flatiron Pkwy, Boulder CO 80301	303-444-8881	S	142	.1
34	Petro-Hunt Corp—*Bruce W Hunt*	1601 Elm St Ste 3400, Dallas TX 75201	214-880-8400	R	122*	.2
35	Kodiak Oil and Gas Corp—*Lynn A Peterson*	1625 Broadway Ste 250, Denver CO 80202	303-592-8075	P	120	.1
36	Seitel Inc—*Robert D Monson*	10811 S Westview Cir D, Houston TX 77043	832-295-8300	R	114*	.1
37	Amerind Oil Company Ltd—*Robert M Leibrock*	415 W Wall St, Midland TX 79701	432-682-8217	R	92*	<.1
38	Warren Resources Inc—*Norman F Swanton*	1114 Ave of the Americ, New York NY 10036	212-697-9660	P	88	.1
39	Lively Exploration Co—*Bruce Lively*	2450 Fondren Rd Ste 26, Houston TX 77063	713-840-1905	R	86*	<.1
40	Anschutz Corp—*Sy Harvey*	555 17th St Ste 2400, Denver CO 80202	303-298-1000	R	84*	.2
41	Phibro Energy Production Inc—*Brian A Lavers*	500 Nyala Farms Rd, Westport CT 06880	203-221-5800	S	79	.3
42	Maple Companies of Texas—*Rex W Canon*	2626 Cole Ave Ste 610, Dallas TX 75204	214-880-0400	R	75*	.1
43	Pearson Technologies Inc—*William C Pearson*	1801 Broadway St Ste 5, Denver CO 80202	303-989-2014	R	49*	<.1
44	Walter Oil and Gas Corp—*JC Walter III*	1100 Louisiana St Ste, Houston TX 77002	713-659-1221	R	41*	.1
45	Arena Offshore LP	4200 Res Forest Dr 230, The Woodlands TX 77381	281-681-9500	R	38*	<.1
46	Texas Crude Energy Inc—*Peter Fluor*	PO Box 56586, Houston TX 77256	713-599-9900	R	33*	.1
47	Kriti Holdings Inc—*Allen M Crawford*	1010 Lamar St Ste 750, Houston TX 77002	713-655-7070	R	32*	<.1
48	Manti Resources Inc—*Lee Barberito*	800 N Shoreline Blvd, Corpus Christi TX 78401	361-888-7708	R	29*	<.1
49	Texland Petroleum Inc—*Jim Wilkes*	777 Main St Ste 3200, Fort Worth TX 76102	817-336-2751	R	28*	.1
50	Trek Resources Inc—*Michael E Montgomery*	4925 Greenville Ave St, Dallas TX 75206	214-373-0318	R	24*	<.1
51	Magellan Petroleum Corp—*J Thomas Wilson*	7 Custom House St 3rd, Portland ME 04101	207-619-8500	P	18	<.1
52	Alcorn Exploration Inc—*George Alcorn*	2000 Post Oak Blvd Ste, Houston TX 77056	713-622-3800	R	18	<.1
53	Infinity Energy Resources Inc—*Stanton Ross*	11900 College Blvd Ste, Overland Park KS 66210	913-948-9512	R	16*	<.1
54	Dan A Hughes Co—*Dan A Hughes*	PO Box 669, Beeville TX 78104	361-358-3752	R	15*	<.1
55	Wavetech Geophysical Inc—*Monica Kosi*	1401 17th St Ste 510, Denver CO 80202	303-534-3383	R	15*	<.1
56	Reserve Petroleum Co—*Cameron R McLain*	6801 Broadway Ext Ste, Oklahoma City OK 73116	405-848-7551	P	14	<.1
57	Jack Lawton Inc—*Jack E Lawton Jr*	101 N Huntington St, Sulphur LA 70663	337-497-0137	R	12*	<.1
58	South Texas Oil Co—*Michael J Pawelek*	300 E Sonterra Blvd St, San Antonio TX 78258	210-545-5994	P	9	<.1
59	D and J Oil Co—*John E Donaldson*	PO Box 10129, Enid OK 73706	580-242-3636	R	9*	<.1
60	Gunn Oil Co—*Vince Gunn*	PO Box 97508, Wichita Falls TX 76307	940-723-5585	R	8*	<.1
61	Century Geophysical Corp—*John Mccormick*	1223 S 71st E Ave, Tulsa OK 74112	918-838-9811	R	7*	.1
62	Central Resources Inc—*Paul J Zecchi*	1775 Sherman St Ste 26, Denver CO 80203	303-830-0100	R	6*	<.1
63	Corlena Oil Co—*Jeff Chestnut*	619 S Tyler St Ste 210, Amarillo TX 79101	806-372-5044	R	3*	<.1
64	Martin-Marks Minerals LLC—*Everard Marks*	2424 Edenborn Ave Ste, Metairie LA 70001	504-828-2564	R	3*	<.1
65	Ramsey Property Management Inc—*Steve Nichols*	2932 NW 122nd St Ste 4, Oklahoma City OK 73120	405-302-6200	R	3*	<.1
66	Rangeland Exploration Co—*Terry Michael*	201 W Wall St, Midland TX 79701	432-686-8983	R	3*	<.1
67	Byrd Operating Co—*Jack Byrd*	24 Smith Rd, Midland TX 79705	432-682-6523	R	2*	<.1
68	Grigsby Petroleum Inc	333 Texas St Ste 2285, Shreveport LA 71101	318-425-5306	R	2*	<.1
69	Austin Resources Corp—*Anthony Constantino*	4265 San Felipe Ste 14, Houston TX 77027	713-533-9052	R	2*	<.1
70	Cornell Oil Co—*Brian Modie*	1911 N Lamar Ste 300, Dallas TX 75202	972-386-5729	R	2*	<.1
71	Ferguson Resources Inc—*Richard R Setser*	PO Box 2508, Bakersfield CA 93303	661-327-4811	R	2*	<.1
72	Weber Energy Corp—*Ben R Weber Jr*	200 Crescent Ct Ste 18, Dallas TX 75201	214-855-8990	R	1*	<.1
73	Akm Enterprise Inc—*Amit Mehta*	5177 Richmond Ave Ste, Houston TX 77056	713-622-1082	R	1*	<.1
74	Energas Resources Inc—*George G Shaw*	800 NE 63rd St 3rd Fl, Oklahoma City OK 73105	405-879-1752	P	<1	<.1
75	Triton Distribution Systems Inc—*Gregory Lykiardopoulos*	105 Barbary Wy, Tiburon CA 94920	415-381-3271	P	<1	<.1
76	Zion Oil and Gas Inc—*Richard Rindberg*	6510 Abrams Rd Ste 300, Dallas TX 75231	214-221-4610	P	<1	<.1
77	EGPI Firecreek Inc—*Dennis Alexander*	6564 Smoke Tree Ln, Scottsdale AZ 85253	480-948-6581	P	<1	N/A

TOTALS: SIC 1382 Oil & Gas Exploration Services
Companies: 77

					48,315	21.3

1389 Oil & Gas Field Services Nec

Rank	Company Name—*Executive Officer*	Address, City, State, Zip	Phone	Type	Fin	Empls
1	Schlumberger Ltd—*Paal Kibsgaard*	5599 San Felipe FL 17, Houston TX 77056	713-513-2000	P	27,447	108.0
2	Halliburton Co—*David J Lesar*	3000 N Sam Houston Pkw, Houston TX 77032	281-575-3000	P	17,973	58.0
3	Energy Maintenance Services Group I LLC—*Tim H Nesler*	2000 Bering Dr Ste 600, Houston TX 77057	713-595-7600	R	7,000*	2.0
4	BJ Services Co—*Andy O'Donnell*	PO Box 4442, Houston TX 77210	713-462-4239	S	4,122	14.4
5	Oceaneering International Inc—*M Kevin McEvoy*	PO Box 40494, Houston TX 77240	713-329-4500	P	2,193	9.6
6	Superior Energy Services Inc—*David Dunlop*	601 Poydras St Ste 240, New Orleans LA 70130	504-587-7374	P	2,070	6.5
7	Helix Energy Solutions Group Inc—*Owen Kratz*	400 N Sam Houston Pky, Houston TX 77060	281-618-0400	P	1,399	1.7
8	Basic Energy Services Inc—*Kenneth V Huseman*	PO Box 10460, Midland TX 79702	432-620-5500	P	1,243	5.6
9	Willbros Group Inc—*Randy Harl*	4400 Post Oak Pkwy Ste, Houston TX 77027	713-403-8000	P	1,192	7.3
10	RPC Inc—*Richard A Hubbell*	2801 Buford Hwy Ste 52, Atlanta GA 30329	404-321-2140	P	1,096	2.5
11	Complete Production Services Inc—*Joseph C Winkler*	11700 Katy Fwy Ste 300, Houston TX 77079	281-372-2300	P	1,085	6.6
12	BJ Services Company USA LP—*John O'donnell* BJ Services Co	PO Box 4442, Houston TX 77210	713-462-4239	S	774*	.3
13	Allis-Chalmers Energy Inc—*Jorgen P Rasmussen*	11125 Equity Dr Ste 20, Houston TX 77041	713-856-4222	P	660	3.8
14	Global Industries Ltd—*John B Reed Jr*	PO Box 442, Sulphur LA 70664	337-583-5000	S	568	2.3
15	Superior Well Services Inc—*David Wallace*	121 Airport Profession, Indiana PA 15701	724-465-8904	S	399	1.4

Rank	Company Name—Executive Officer	Address, City, State, Zip	Phone	Type	Fin	Empls
16	Toledo Oil and Gas Services Inc—Andrew B Schmitt	1900 Shawnee Mission P, Mission Woods KS 66205	913-677-6800	S	344	2.6
17	Nabors Offshore Corp Inland Div—Rick Atwell	PO Box 466, Houma LA 70361	985-868-1874	D	207*	.1
18	Ensign United States Drilling Inc—Bob Geddes	PO Box 17805, Denver CO 80217	303-292-1206	S	189*	.1
19	Nabors Well Services Ltd—Eugene Isenberg	515 W Greens Rd Ste 12, Houston TX 77067	281-874-0035	S	178*	2.9
20	Protein Inc—Dana Montgomery	2833 Leonis Blvd Ste 2, Vernon CA 90058	323-583-1645	R	151*	.1
21	TETRA Production Testing GP LLC—Stuart Brightman	24955 I-45 N, The Woodlands TX 77380	281-367-1983	S	148*	<.1
22	WWL Industries—Billy D White	PO Box 4574, Odessa TX 79760	432-362-0326	R	140*	.1
23	Rfps Management Company Ii LP—Randall Rollins	2170 Piedmont Rd Ne, Atlanta GA 30324	404-888-2000	R	140*	2.5
24	ProTechnics International Inc—John Thomas (Tom) Hampton III	6316 Windfern, Houston TX 77040	713-328-2673	D	129*	.1
25	Danos and Curole Marine Contractors Inc—Garret Danos	PO Box 1460, Larose LA 70373	985-693-3313	R	90*	.9
26	Stallion Oilfield Services Inc—Craig M Johnson	PO Box 1486, Houston TX 77251	713-528-5544	R	82*	.9
27	Nana Regional Corporation Inc—Helvi Sandvik	PO Box 49, Kotzebue AK 99752	907-442-3301	R	73*	.5
28	Rex Energy Corp—Thomas Stabley	476 Rolling Ridge Dr S, State College PA 16801	814-278-7267	P	69	.2
29	Peak Oilfield Services Co—Michael R O'Connor	2525 C St Ste 201, Anchorage AK 99503	907-263-7000	R	65	.4
30	Dune Energy Inc—James A Watt	777 Walker St Ste 2300, Houston TX 77002	713-229-6300	B	64	<.1
31	Reliable Production Service Inc—James L Moore	PO Box 176, Livonia LA 70755	225-637-4835	R	63*	.1
32	Lufkin Industries Inc Automation Div	811 Willow Oak Dr, Missouri City TX 77489	281-495-1100	D	55*	<.1
33	Petrochem Field Services Inc—Sergio Sanchez	PO Box 60047, Houston TX 77205	281-441-2550	R	37*	.1
34	Greystar Corp—John Patton	10375 Richmond Ave Ste, Houston TX 77042	713-953-7007	R	37*	.7
35	MV Oil Trust—Michael J Ulrich	919 Congress St 5th Fl, Austin TX 78701		P	36	N/A
36	Associated Mechanical Erectors Company Inc—Ronnie Campbell	PO Box 909, Fort Mill SC 29716	803-548-7766	R	35*	.2
37	Offshore Energy Services Inc—Charles Garber	PO Box 53508, Lafayette LA 70505	337-233-3442	R	32*	.5
38	Natural Gas Services Group Inc—Stephen C Taylor	508 W Wall Ste 550, Midland TX 79701	432-262-2700	P	23	.2
39	Oil Well Service Co—James Sipprelle	1241 E Burnett St, Signal Hill CA 90755	562-595-4501	R	18*	.2
40	Tubular Services LLC—Sharon Biancardi	1010 Mccarty St, Houston TX 77029	713-675-6212	R	18*	.4
41	Diamond Construction Company Of Shattuck Inc—Kerry Martin	PO Box 1025, Woodward OK 73802	580-256-3385	R	18*	.1
42	Berry Brothers General Contractors	PO Box 253, Berwick LA 70342	985-384-8770	R	16*	.1
43	Schlumberger/EMR—Andrew Gould	300 Schlumberger Dr, Sugar Land TX 77478	281-285-8500	R	15*	.1
44	Pinnacle Gas Resources Inc—Peter G Schoonmaker	1 E Alger St, Sheridan WY 82801	307-673-9710	P	15	<.1
45	Mudlogging Company USA LP—Kenny Baucum	6741 Satsuma Dr, Houston TX 77041	713-466-7400	R	12*	.1
46	Western Steel Inc—Gene Calhoun	PO Box 3610, Hueytown AL 35023	205-744-2230	R	10*	.1
47	Max Welders Inc—Mcarthur Giroir	PO Box 500, Gibson LA 70356	985-631-3113	R	9*	.1
48	Prater Enterprises Inc—Wyman Prater	95 W Birch St, Canadian TX 79014	806-323-5383	R	8*	<.1
49	Central Industries Inc (Lafayette Louisiana)—William F Stevenson Jr	329 Westgate Rd, Lafayette LA 70506	337-233-3171	R	7*	.1
50	Charco Inc—Charles Kilgore	PO Box 609, Flomaton AL 36441	251-296-5460	R	7*	.1
51	Particle Drilling Technologies Inc—Jim B Terry	11050 W Little York Fa, Houston TX 77041	713-223-3031	P	5	<.1
52	Hunting Tubular Threading Inc—Philip Kemp	PO Box 520, Marrero LA 70073	504-348-3011	R	5*	.1
53	Leo and Sons Inc—Wyn King	PO Box 802, Iraan TX 79744	432-639-2729	R	5*	<.1
54	Hollingsworth Construction Co—Gary Hollingsworth	886 Hwy 531, Minden LA 71058	318-377-0610	R	4*	.1
55	KG Construction Co—Jerry Means	PO Box 1024, Gillette WY 82717	307-682-4311	R	4*	<.1
56	Baker Marine Corp—Larry Baker Jr	PO Box 190, Ingleside TX 78362	361-776-7585	H	3*	<.1
57	Gulf Coast Machine Services LLC—Bradley Stutes	PO Box 526, Broussard LA 70518	337-837-3175	R	3*	<.1
58	A F Industries Inc—Clint Fontenot	PO Box 91731, Lafayette LA 70509	337-232-3238	R	2*	<.1
59	Tejas Machines Inc—Debra Jackson	2115 Riley Fuzzell Rd, Spring TX 77386	281-350-8890	R	2*	<.1
60	Lease Management Inc—John Harkins	PO Box 290, Mount Pleasant MI 48804	989-773-5948	R	2*	<.1
61	Triton Engineering Services Co—James C Day	13135 S Dairy Ashford, Sugar Land TX 77478	281-276-6100	S	2*	<.1
62	ResTech Inc—James J Lorenzen	4201 FM 1960 W Ste 500, Houston TX 77068	281-537-8300	R	2*	<.1
63	Hallador Petroleum LLP	1660 Lincoln StSte 270, Denver CO 80264	303-839-5504	S	2*	<.1
64	CF and S Tank And Equipment Co—Ricky Frederick	PO Box 10070, New Iberia LA 70562	337-367-1217	R	2*	.1
65	Liberty Energy Corp—Ian Spowart	2 Allen Ctr Ste 1600 1, Houston TX 77002	713-353-4700	P	<1	<.1

TOTALS: SIC 1389 Oil & Gas Field Services Nec
Companies: 65   71,804   244.7

1411 Dimension Stone

Rank	Company Name—Executive Officer	Address, City, State, Zip	Phone	Type	Fin	Empls
1	Martin Marietta Materials Inc—C Howard Nye	2710 Wycliff Rd, Raleigh NC 27607	919-781-4550	P	1,714	5.0
2	Coburg Road Quarry LLC—Val Stilwell	90436 Coburg Rd, Eugene OR 97408	541-484-2000	R	20*	<.1
3	Eden Stone Company Inc—Dave Wirtz	W4520 Lime Rd, Eden WI 53019	920-477-2521	R	18*	.2
4	Fletcher Granite Company LLC—Matt Peterson	534 Groton Rd, Westford MA 01886	978-251-4031	R	13*	.2
5	Fox River Stone Inc—Nathan Creech	7N394 McLean Blvd, South Elgin IL 60177	847-742-6060	R	11*	<.1
6	Indiana Limestone Company Inc—Michael Lundin	PO Box 1560, Bedford IN 47421	812-275-3341	R	10*	.1
7	Carolina Quarries Inc—Doug Smith	805 Harris Granite Rd, Salisbury NC 28146	704-636-6780	R	7*	.1
8	Joliet Sand And Gravel Company Inc—George Comerford	2509 Mound Rd, Rockdale IL 60436	815-741-2090	R	7*	.1
9	Biesanz Stone Co—Charles Biesanz	4600 Goodview Rd, Winona MN 55987	507-454-4336	R	5*	<.1
10	Bjoin Limestone Inc—Howard Bjoin	PO Box 3220, Janesville WI 53547	608-876-6959	R	5*	<.1
11	Coolspring Stone Supply Inc—William Snoddy	PO Box 1328, Uniontown PA 15401	724-437-8663	R	4*	<.1
12	Wade Sand and Gravel Company Inc—R Wade	PO Box 39048, Birmingham AL 35208	205-324-6691	R	4*	<.1
13	Weber Stone Co—Mike Deutmeyer	12791 Stone City Rd X2, Anamosa IA 52205	319-462-3581	R	4*	<.1
14	BG Hoadley Quarries Inc—Patsy Fell	PO Box 1224, Bloomington IN 47402	812-332-1447	R	4*	<.1
15	Stonewall Materials Inc—Bart Barnett	1405 Hess Rd, Mineral Wells TX 76067	940-327-8722	R	4*	.1
16	Vinci Stone Products Inc—A Vinci	798 Marriottsville Rd, Marriottsville MD 21104	410-442-1460	R	3*	<.1
17	Anna Quarries Inc—Edward Simonds	PO Box 180, Anna IL 62906	618-833-5121	R	3*	<.1
18	Galassi Gary Stone and Steel Inc—Gary Galassi	44 Devonwood Ave, Romeoville IL 60446	815-886-3906	R	3*	<.1
19	Hilltop Slate Inc—David Thomas	PO Box 201, Middle Granville NY 12849	518-642-1453	R	3*	<.1
20	Harley Gray Stone Co—Carl Gray	PO Box 323, Paulden AZ 86334	928-636-2436	R	3*	.1
21	Media Quarry Company Inc—John Scala	PO Box 667, Media PA 19063	610-566-6667	R	2*	<.1
22	Indiana Stone Works—Donovan Short	PO Box 1406, Bedford IN 47421	812-279-0448	R	2*	<.1
23	Tile Collection Granite LLC	10901 Office Park Dr, Charlotte NC 28273	704-583-3080	R	2*	<.1
24	Architectural Stone Sales Inc—Gary Evans	1728 30th St, Bedford IN 47421	812-279-2421	R	2*	<.1
25	Jacobs Creek Stone Company Inc—Rj Mckinney	PO Box 608, Denton NC 27239	336-857-2602	R	2*	<.1

TOTALS: SIC 1411 Dimension Stone
Companies: 25   1,856   6.3

1422 Crushed & Broken Limestone

Rank	Company Name—Executive Officer	Address, City, State, Zip	Phone	Type	Fin	Empls
1	US Enrichment Corp—John K Welch	6903 Rockledge Dr, Bethesda MD 20817	301-564-3200	P	2,035	2.9
2	United States Lime and Minerals Inc—Timothy W Byrne	5429 LBJ Fwy Ste 230, Dallas TX 75240	972-991-8400	P	133	<.1
3	E Dillon and Co—Otey C Dudley	PO Box 160, Swords Creek VA 24649	276-873-6816	R	92*	.1

Note: An asterisk (*) indicates an estimated financial figure. The company type code used is as follows: R = Private, P = Public, S = Private Subsidiary, B = Public Subsidiary, D = Division, J = Joint Venture, I = Investment Fund.

COMPANY RANKINGS BY SALES WITHIN 4-DIGIT SIC

Rank	Company Name—Executive Officer	Address, City, State, Zip	Phone	Type	Fin	Empls
4	Laurel Sand and Gravel Inc—Ronald Matovick	14504 Greenview Dr Ste, Laurel MD 20708	301-953-7650	R	44*	.2
5	Mississippi Limestone Corp—Clifford Davis	1500 Port Rd, Friars Point MS 38631	662-383-2207	R	40*	.1
6	Wendling Quarries Inc—Anthony Manatt	PO Box 230, De Witt IA 52742	563-659-9181	R	36*	.2
7	NR Hamm Quarry Inc—N Rodney Hamm	609 Perry Pl, Perry KS 66073	785-597-5111	R	31*	.2
8	Cobleskill Stone Products Inc—Emil Galasso	112 Rock Rd, Cobleskill NY 12043	518-234-0221	R	30*	.2
9	Glenn O Hawbaker Inc—Daniel Hawbaker	1952 Waddle Rd Ste 203, State College PA 16803		R	30*	.3
10	Mulzer Crushed Stone Inc—James Mulzer	PO Box 249, Tell City IN 47586	812-547-7921	R	24*	.5
11	Stuart M Perry Inc—DW Perry	117 Limestone Ln, Winchester VA 22602	540-662-3431	R	22*	.2
12	White Rock Quarry LP—Ray Advnia	PO Box 119, Clay Center OH 43408	419-855-8388	R	21*	.6
13	Bussen Quarries Inc—Mark Bussen	5000 Bussen Rd, Saint Louis MO 63129	314-487-2300	R	20*	.1
14	Waterloo Coal Company Inc—T Darlington	PO Box 626, Jackson OH 45640	740-286-5633	R	17*	.1
15	Meshberger Brothers Stone Corp—Carolyn Fryback	PO Box 345, Berne IN 46711	260-334-5311	R	15*	.1
16	Greenville Quarries Inc—John Stovall	PO Box 388, Greenville KY 42345	270-338-2300	R	14*	.1
17	Elmhurst-Chicago Stone Co—Charles P Hammerschmidt Jr	400 W 1st St, Elmhurst IL 60126	630-832-4000	R	13*	.2
18	Columbia River Carbonates—Joerg A Bleeck	PO Box 2350, Woodland WA 98674	360-225-6505	R	12*	.1
19	Omni Materials Inc—Ed Pherson	PO Box 458, Mount Carmel IL 62863	618-262-5118	R	11*	<.1
20	Texas Crushed Stone Company Inc—W Snead	PO Box 1000, Georgetown TX 78627	512-863-5511	R	10*	.1
21	Meckley's Limestone Products Inc—Matt Markunas	1543 State Route 225, Herndon PA 17830	570-758-3011	R	10*	.1
22	Pounding Mill Quarry Corp—William Hunter	171 Saint Clair Xing, Bluefield VA 24605	276-326-1145	R	10*	.1
23	National Limestone Quarry Inc—Eric Stahl	PO Box 397, Middleburg PA 17842	570-837-1635	R	8*	<.1
24	Dolomite Inc—David Sloan	PO Box 1568, Marianna FL 32447	850-482-5570	S	8*	.1
25	L R Falk Construction Co—David Falk	PO Box 189, Saint Ansgar IA 50472	641-713-4569	R	7*	<.1
26	Pryor Stone Inc—James Kemp	PO Box 968, Pryor OK 74362	918-825-3370	R	7*	<.1
27	Colorado Lime Co—Tracy Gunn United States Lime and Minerals Inc	1468 Hwy 50, Delta CO 81416		S	7*	<.1
28	Everett Quarries Company Inc—Stephan Clarkson	499 Se Everett Ln Ste, Plattsburg MO 64477	816-539-2151	R	7*	.1
29	Magruder Limestone Company Inc—Warren Magruder	255 Watson Rd, Troy MO 63379	636-528-4180	R	6*	.1
30	Frazier Quarry Inc—Robert Frazier	PO Box 588, Harrisonburg VA 22803	540-434-6192	R	6*	.1
31	Ash Grove Aggregates Inc—Mike Lutz	PO Box 70, Butler MO 64730	660-679-4128	R	6*	.1
32	Charleston Stone Co—Jerald Tarble	PO Box 260, Charleston IL 61920	217-345-6292	R	6*	<.1
33	Liter's Inc—Robert Liter	5918 Haunz Ln, Louisville KY 40241	502-241-7637	R	5*	.1
34	Stewart Stone Inc—Larry Stewart	PO Box 1797, Cushing OK 74023	918-285-5600	R	5*	.1
35	Callender Construction Company Inc—Bruce Callender	928 W Washington St, Pittsfield IL 62363	217-285-2161	R	5*	.1
36	Quality Lime Co—Jerald Tarble	PO Box 439, Marshall IL 62441	217-826-2343	R	5*	<.1
37	Bailey Quarries Inc—David Bailey	PO Box 430, Republic MO 65738	417-732-8286	R	4*	<.1
38	Castle Concrete Co—Jerry Schnabe	PO Box 2379, Colorado Springs CO 80901	719-598-0214	S	4*	<.1
39	Miami River Stone Co—Thomas Milligan	PO Box 419, Sidney OH 45365	937-492-5412	R	4*	<.1
40	Conag Inc—Robert Hirschfeld	16672 County Rd 66a, Saint Marys OH 45885	419-394-8870	R	3*	<.1
41	Valley View Industries Inc—Richard Hatzer	7551e 2500 N Rd, Cornell IL 61319	815-358-2236	R	3*	<.1
42	Bryan Rock Products Inc—William Bryan	13040 Dem Con Dr, Shakopee MN 55379	952-445-3900	R	3*	<.1
43	CA Langford Company Inc—Charles Langford	2120 Warrenton Rd, Guntersville AL 35976	256-582-5723	R	3*	<.1
44	Wade Agricultural Products Inc—Ron Wade	PO Box 38, Lacygne KS 66040	913-757-2255	R	3*	<.1
45	Hoover Inc—Thomas Hoover	PO Box 400, La Vergne TN 37086	615-793-2600	R	3*	<.1
46	Schaefer Enterprises Of Deposit Inc—Larry Schaefer	315 Old Rte 10, Deposit NY 13754	607-467-4990	R	3*	<.1
47	Yahara Materials Inc—Larry Burcalow	PO Box 277, Waunakee WI 53597	608-849-4162	R	3*	<.1
48	Halquist Stone Company Inc—Thomas Halquist	N51w23563 Lisbon Rd N, Sussex WI 53089	262-246-9000	R	3*	.1
49	New Hope Crushed Stone And Lime Co—John Mehok	6970 Phillips Mill Rd, New Hope PA 18938	215-862-5295	R	3*	<.1
50	S S S Lumber Company Inc—Gerald Smith	PO Box 474, Louisiana MO 63353	573-754-5361	R	2*	<.1
51	Parker and Sons Stone LLC	PO Box 146, Whitefield OK 74472	918-967-8825	R	2*	<.1
52	MA Walker Company LLC—Lyle Walker	12146 Hwy 421 N, Mc Kee KY 40447	606-965-3151	R	2*	<.1
53	Jml Quarries Inc—Rodney Cornelius	420 Bernas Rd, Cochecton NY 12726	845-932-8206	R	2*	<.1
54	Ivey Construction Inc—Richard Ivey	1020 Bollerud St, Mineral Point WI 53565	608-987-2967	R	2*	<.1
55	King Limestone Inc—Duane King	53681 Spencer Rd, Cumberland OH 43732	740-638-3942	R	2*	<.1
56	L And W Quarries Inc—Jay Johnson	PO Box 335, Centerville IA 52544	641-437-4830	R	2*	<.1
57	Limerock Industries Inc—Nancy Bennett	2811 N Young Blvd, Chiefland FL 32626	352-493-1447	R	2*	<.1
58	Coots Materials Company Inc—David Coots	1700 W D St, Vinton IA 52349	319-472-4480	R	2*	<.1
59	Duff Quarry Inc—James Duff	PO Box 305, Huntsville OH 43324	937-686-2488	R	2*	<.1
60	MMD Stone LLC	600 Ne Quarry Dr, Jackson MO 63755	573-339-5800	R	2*	<.1
61	Bourbon Limestone Co—Arthur Walker	PO Box 218, Paris KY 40362	859-987-4425	R	2*	<.1
62	Clever Stone Company Inc—David Donnelson	1075 Wise Hill Rd, Clever MO 65631	417-743-2694	R	2*	<.1
63	Tiger Rock—Charles Turner	11469 W 9 Hwy, Stigler OK 74462	918-799-5859	R	1*	<.1

TOTALS: SIC 1422 Crushed & Broken Limestone
Companies: 63

					2,825	7.7

1423 Crushed & Broken Granite

Rank	Company Name—Executive Officer	Address, City, State, Zip	Phone	Type	Fin	Empls
1	Wake Stone Corp—Theodore Bratton	PO Box 190, Knightdale NC 27545	919-266-1100	R	48*	.1
2	Lafarge Aggregates Southeast Inc—Frederick Kemph	12735 Morris Rd Ext St, Alpharetta GA 30004	678-746-2000	R	22*	.4
3	Buffalo Crushed Stone Inc—Richard Garman	2544 Clinton St, Buffalo NY 14224	716-631-7500	S	20*	.2
4	Fletcher Granite Corp—Jonathan Maurer	534 Groton Rd, Westford MA 01886	401-232-2040	R	19*	.2
5	Mccullough Crushing Inc—Frederick Mccullough	548 Mccullough Hill Rd, Middlesex VT 05602	802-223-5693	R	4*	<.1
6	Charlotte Instyle Inc—Lennart Wiktorin	801 Pressley Rd Ste 10, Charlotte NC 28217	704-665-8880	R	3*	<.1
7	Ararat Rock Products Co—James Crossingham	PO Box 988, Mount Airy NC 27030	336-786-4693	R	3*	<.1
8	Granite Canyon Quarry A JV—Darrell Moran	636 I-80 Service Rd, Granite Canyon WY 82059	307-638-3582	R	1*	<.1

TOTALS: SIC 1423 Crushed & Broken Granite
Companies: 8

					120	1.0

1429 Crushed & Broken Stone Nec

Rank	Company Name—Executive Officer	Address, City, State, Zip	Phone	Type	Fin	Empls
1	Vulcan Materials Co—Donald M James	PO Box 385014, Birmingham AL 35242	205-298-3000	P	2,407	7.1
2	Luck Stone Corp—Charles Luck IV	PO Box 29682, Richmond VA 23242	804-784-6300	R	129*	.7
3	Tilcon New York Inc—John Cooney	162 Old Mill Rd, West Nyack NY 10994	845-358-4500	R	34*	.3
4	Dyer Quarry Inc—James Anderson	PO Box 188, Birdsboro PA 19508	610-582-6010	R	18*	<.1
5	Carolina Sunrock LLC—Bill Jones	PO Box 25, Butner NC 27509	919-575-4502	R	14*	.2
6	Naselle Rock and Asphalt Co—Arnie Wirkkala	PO Box 5, Naselle WA 98638	360-484-3443	R	11*	<.1
7	Lesueur-Richmond Slate Corp—Sam Berger	PO Box 8, Arvonia VA 23004	434-581-3214	R	11*	.1
8	Graymont Materials Inc (Plattsburgh New York)—Todd Kempainen	111 Quarry Rd, Plattsburgh NY 12901	518-561-5321	R	9*	.1
9	Ferrell Excavating Co—Vernon Ferrell	PO Box 367, Pecks Mill WV 25547	304-752-7950	R	7*	.1
10	Sterling Breen Crushing Inc—Sterling Breen	PO Box 1347, Chehalis WA 98532	360-736-4240	R	5*	<.1
11	Amis Materials Co—WD Amis Jr	PO Box 1871, Oklahoma City OK 73101	405-235-3555	R	4*	<.1
12	Sisson and Ryan Inc—Clyde Sisson	PO Box 128, Shawsville VA 24162	540-268-2413	R	3*	.1

Rank	Company Name—*Executive Officer*	Address, City, State, Zip	Phone	Type	Fin	Empls
13	Kemp Stone Inc—*William Kemp*	PO Box 968, Pryor OK 74362	918-825-3370	R	3*	<.1
14	Cedar Mountain Stone Corp—*Edward Dalrymple*	PO Box 12, Mitchells VA 22729	540-825-3370	R	3*	<.1
15	Johnson County Aggregates—*Shirley Annis*	23555 W 151st St, Olathe KS 66061	913-764-2127	R	2*	<.1
16	Lakeview Dirt Company Inc—*Greg Wilson*	497 S Holmes Blvd, Saint Augustine FL 32084	904-824-2586	R	2*	<.1
17	York Hill Trap Rock Quarry Co—*Leonardo Suzio*	PO Box 748, Meriden CT 06450	203-237-8421	R	2*	<.1
18	Coos Bay Timber Operators Inc—*David Gould*	PO Box D, North Bend OR 97459	541-756-6254	R	2*	<.1
19	Cayuga Crushed Stone Inc—*Tom Besemer*	PO Box 41, Lansing NY 14882	607-533-4273	R	2*	<.1
20	Superior Silica Sands LLC—*James Ferrell*	3014 Lime Stone C, Kosse TX 76653	254-746-7977	R	2*	<.1

TOTALS: SIC 1429 Crushed & Broken Stone Nec
Companies: 20

					2,669	8.9

1442 Construction Sand & Gravel

Rank	Company Name—*Executive Officer*	Address, City, State, Zip	Phone	Type	Fin	Empls
1	Hanson Building Materials America Inc—*Alan J Murray*	1350 Campus Pky Ste 30, Neptune NJ 07753	732-919-9777	S	9,628*	7.5
2	Martin Marietta Aggregates—*Stephen P Zelnak Jr*	2710 Wycliff Rd, Raleigh NC 27607	919-781-4550	S	290*	.2
3	Big River Industries Inc—*Joel Hammond*	3600 Mansell Rd Ste 57, Alpharetta GA 30022	678-461-2830	S	212*	.2
4	Stabler Companies Inc—*Cyril C Dunmire Jr*	635 Lucknow Rd, Harrisburg PA 17110	717-234-3106	R	200*	1.2
5	LG Everist Inc—*Rick Everist*	PO Box 5829, Sioux Falls SD 57117	605-334-5000	R	108*	.3
6	JC Compton Contractor—*Mike Flanagan Sr*	PO Box 768, McMinnville OR 97128	503-472-4155	R	98*	.1
7	Material Service Corp—*Michael Stanczak*	181 W Madison St Ste 1, Chicago IL 60602	312-372-3600	S	52*	.3
8	Titan America Inc—*Aris Papadoopoulos*	11000 NW 121st Way, Medley FL 33178	305-364-2230	R	45*	.3
9	Thelen Sand and Gravel Inc—*Steve Thelen*	28955 W Il Rte 173 Ste, Antioch IL 60002	847-838-8800	R	37*	.2
10	Cleveland Quarries Inc—*Russell Ciphers Sr*	850 W River Rd, Vermilion OH 44089	440-963-4008	R	32*	<.1
11	Wyoming Sand and Stone Co—*William Eyar-Price Jr*	6 Wyoming Sand Rd, Tunkhannock PA 18657	570-746-7250	R	26	.2
12	Hanson Building Materials West	PO Box 368, Green Cove Springs FL 32043	904-284-3213	S	24*	.1
13	Hastie Mining and Trucking—*Donald Hastie*	RR 1 Box 55, Cave In Rock IL 62919	618-289-4536	R	19*	<.1
14	Hilltop Basic Resources Inc—*John Steele*	1 W 4th St Ste 1100, Cincinnati OH 45202	513-651-5000	R	19*	.2
15	BV Hedrick Gravel and Sand Co—*Jeffrey Goodman*	PO Box 1040, Salisbury NC 28145	704-633-5982	R	17*	.4
16	Gravel Products Inc—*Joel Schriock*	2920 Railway Ave, Minot ND 58703	701-852-4751	R	17*	.1
17	D and J Construction Company Inc—*Richard Richardson*	PO Box 1889, West Monroe LA 71294	318-388-2764	R	16*	.2
18	River Bend Sand and Gravel Co—*Jeff Schaffer*	PO Box 12095, Salem OR 97309	503-363-9281	S	15*	.1
19	Dalrymple Gravel And Contracting Company Inc—*Robert Dalrymple*	2105 S Broadway, Pine City NY 14871	607-737-6200	R	13*	.1
20	Nugent Sand Co—*Vick Donlon*	PO Box 6072, Louisville KY 40206	502-584-0158	R	12*	.1
21	S M Lorusso and Sons Inc—*Antonio Lorusso*	PO Box 230, Walpole MA 02081	508-668-2600	R	12*	.1
22	Brett Aggregates Inc—*William Brett*	4794 Finlay St, Richmond VA 23231	804-222-5788	R	11*	<.1
23	Randles Sand and Gravel Inc—*David Randles*	19209 Canyon Rd E, Puyallup WA 98375	253-531-6800	R	10*	.1
24	Tiller Corp—*Gary Sauer*	PO Box 1480, Maple Grove MN 55311	763-425-4191	R	10*	.1
25	Sky Ute Sand and Gravel LLC—*David Piotrowski*	PO Box 350, Ignacio CO 81137	970-382-0609	R	9*	.1
26	Albrecht Sand and Gravel Co—*Robert Albrecht*	3790 W Sanilac Rd, Snover MI 48472	810-672-9272	R	7*	<.1
27	Beaver Gravel Corp—*Allyn Beaver*	16101 River Ave, Noblesville IN 46062	317-773-0679	R	6*	.1
28	Watson Gravel Inc—*Ronald Watson*	2728 Hamilton Cleves R, Hamilton OH 45013	513-863-0070	R	6*	.1
29	Delta Sand and Gravel Co—*Avon Babb*	999 Division Ave, Eugene OR 97404	541-688-2233	R	6*	.1
30	Northwest Rock—*Scott Rollin*	642 Nowekah Rd, Aberdeen WA 98520	360-533-3050	R	6*	.1
31	Capital Sand Company Inc—*Michael Farmer*	PO Box 104990, Jefferson City MO 65110	573-635-2255	R	5*	.1
32	Stansley Mineral Resources Inc—*Jeff Stansley*	5648 Main St Ste 3, Sylvania OH 43560	419-843-2813	R	5*	.1
33	Irving Gravel Co—*James Irving*	13415 Coldwater Rd, Fort Wayne IN 46845	260-637-3101	R	5*	<.1
34	A Lindberg and Sons Inc—*Roger Crimmins*	PO Box 308, Ishpeming MI 49849	906-486-4459	R	5*	.1
35	Hammett Gravel Company Inc—*Harold Hammett*	PO Box 209, Lexington MS 39095	662-834-1867	R	5*	.1
36	Palumbo Sand and Gravel Company Inc—*Fortunato Palumbo*	PO Box 810, Dover Plains NY 12522	845-832-6791	R	5*	<.1
37	Mega Sand Enterprises Inc—*Brenda Moore*	PO Box 656, Highlands TX 77562	281-843-3000	R	4*	<.1
38	Bonita Grande Mining LLC—*Rob Schneider*	25501 Bonita Grande Dr, Bonita Springs FL 34135	239-947-6411	R	4*	.1
39	Elam Sand and Gravel Corp—*Joseph Spezio*	PO Box 65, West Bloomfield NY 14585	585-657-8001	R	4*	.1
40	Shumaker Enterprises Inc—*Wade Shumaker*	2900 N Fm 973, Austin TX 78725	512-928-0008	R	4*	<.1
41	Dennis Fehn Gravel and Excavating Inc—*Dennis Fehn*	PO Box 256, Albertville MN 55301	763-497-2428	R	4*	<.1
42	Kraemer Company LLC—*Lary Schraepfer*	PO Box 235, Plain WI 53577	608-546-2255	R	4*	.1
43	Pinnacle Materials Inc—*Christine Yakman*	1200 Tices Ln Ste 202, East Brunswick NJ 08816	732-254-7676	R	4*	<.1
44	Con-Wear Products Inc—*Robert Alvarado*	449 W Navarro Ave, Mesa AZ 85210	480-892-4176	R	4*	<.1
45	Stewart Mining Industries Inc—*Nick Stewart*	13575 Indrio Rd, Fort Pierce FL 34945	772-464-4499	R	4*	<.1
46	Brookfield Sand and Gravel Inc—*Charles Curdy*	8587 N 850 W, Fairland IN 46126	317-835-2235	R	4*	<.1
47	Madison Sand and Gravel Company Inc—*Karen Ziegler*	5349 Norway Grove Scho, De Forest WI 53532	608-244-6726	R	4*	<.1
48	Brown and Watson Company Inc—*Lewis Watson*	PO Box 1890, Butler GA 31006	478-862-5426	R	4*	<.1
49	Ricci Brothers Sand Company—*Anthony Ricci*	PO Box 664, Port Norris NJ 08349	856-785-0166	R	4*	<.1
50	Roundtree Materials Inc—*Danny Roundtree*	PO Box 5327, Valdosta GA 31603	229-242-5158	R	4*	<.1
51	Tuckahoe Sand and Gravel Company Inc—*James Johnston*	PO Box 991, Pleasantville NJ 08232	609-981-2082	R	4*	<.1
52	Golden Gravel Co—*Jim Adam*	21 S Sunset St, Longmont CO 80501	303-776-1003	R	4*	.1
53	Fischer Sand and Aggregate LLP—*Peter Fischer*	14698 Galaxie Ave, Saint Paul MN 55124	952-432-7132	R	4*	<.1
54	Fred Radandt Sons Inc—*Josh Radandt*	1800 Johnston Dr, Manitowoc WI 54220	920-682-7758	R	4*	<.1
55	Small Sand and Gravel Inc—*Michael Small*	PO Box 617, Gambier OH 43022	740-427-3677	R	3*	<.1
56	Peck Road Gravel Pit—*Steve Bubalo*	PO Box 1286, Monrovia CA 91017	626-574-1855	R	3*	<.1
57	Harmony Sand and Gravel Inc—*Richard Hummer*	PO Box 277, Belvidere NJ 07823	908-475-4690	R	3*	<.1
58	Poudre Tech Aggregates Inc—*Martin Lind*	1625 Pelican Lakes Poi, Windsor CO 80550	970-686-5828	R	3*	<.1
59	Watkins Sand Co—*Frank Watkins*	PO Box 687, Bixby OK 74008	918-369-5238	R	3*	<.1
60	Susag Sand and Gravel Inc—*Mack Susag*	PO Box 23, Harvey ND 58341	701-324-4609	R	3*	<.1
61	Cosby-Carmichael Inc—*P Carmichael*	PO Box 100, Selma AL 36702	334-874-7411	R	3*	<.1
62	Lakeland Sand and Gravel Inc—*James Adzima*	7013 Atlantic Lake Rd, Hartstown PA 16131	814-382-8178	R	3*	<.1
63	Welch Holdings Inc—*James Welch*	8953 E Miami River Rd, Cincinnati OH 45247	513-353-3220	R	3*	<.1
64	Colorado County Sand and Gravel Company LLC	PO Box 866, El Campo TX 77437	979-543-3791	R	3*	<.1
65	Southeast Gravel Company Inc—*Larry Smith*	10529 State Hwy 54 E, Star City AR 71667	870-628-3451	R	3*	<.1
66	P K Guido Inc—*Kelly Guido*	640 Shady Dr, Roseburg OR 97471	541-673-1088	R	3*	<.1
67	Mottes Materials Inc—*Eugene Mottes*	PO Box 112, Iron River MI 49935	906-265-9955	R	3*	<.1
68	Varra Companies Inc—*Christopher Varra*	PO Box 2049, Broomfield CO 80038	303-666-6657	R	3*	<.1
69	Brown Brothers Sand Co—*Carl Brown*	PO Box 82, Howard GA 31039	706-269-3257	R	3*	<.1
70	Saxton Falls Sand and Gravel Co—*Richard Schindelar*	PO Box 576, Stanhope NJ 07874	908-852-0121	R	3*	<.1
71	Broadfoots Sand and Gravel Inc—*Terry Broadfoot*	716 2nd Ave S, Kearney NE 68847	308-236-5301	R	2*	<.1
72	Stocker Sand and Gravel Co—*Bill Stocker*	PO Box 176, Gnadenhutten OH 44629	740-254-4635	R	2*	<.1
73	Lucky Sand and Gravel Company Inc—*Bernard Udelson*	PO Box 823, Mantua OH 44255	330-562-6196	R	2*	<.1
74	Natural Aggregates Corp—*Daniel Pevos*	3362 Muir Rd, Milford MI 48380	248-685-1502	R	2*	<.1
75	Irvco Asphalt and Gravel Inc—*Wayne Irvin*	PO Box 931, Fruitland ID 83619	208-452-5835	R	2*	<.1
76	Seville Sand and Gravel Inc—*George Cross*	PO Box 360, Lodi OH 44254	330-948-1812	R	2*	<.1

Note: An asterisk (*) indicates an estimated financial figure. The company type code used is as follows: R = Private, P = Public, S = Private Subsidiary, B = Public Subsidiary, D = Division, J = Joint Venture, I = Investment Fund.

COMPANY RANKINGS BY SALES WITHIN 4-DIGIT SIC

Rank	Company Name—*Executive Officer*	Address, City, State, Zip	Phone	Type	Fin	Empls
77	Miller Excavating Inc—*Peter Miller*	3636 Stagecoach Trl N, Stillwater MN 55082	651-439-1637	R	2*	<.1
78	Lakeview Rock Products Inc—*Glenn Hughes*	PO Box 540700, North Salt Lake UT 84054	801-292-7161	R	2*	<.1
79	Charlotte County Mining and Material Inc—*Richard Neslund*	16070 Tamiami Trl, Punta Gorda FL 33955	239-567-1800	R	2*	<.1
80	Oster Sand And Gravel Inc—*Marlene Oster*	5947 Whipple Ave Nw, Canton OH 44720	330-494-5472	R	2*	<.1
81	Stancills Inc—*Terry Stancills*	499 Mountain Hill Rd, Perryville MD 21903	410-939-2224	R	2*	<.1
82	Ernest C Anderson Gravel and Ready Mixed Inc—*Ernest Anderson*	28741 County Hwy 26, Detroit Lakes MN 56501	218-847-4614	R	2*	<.1
83	Construction Aggregates Corporation Of Michigan—*David Sensibar*	PO Box 121, Grand Haven MI 49417	616-842-7900	R	2*	<.1
84	Prairie Sand and Gravel—*Blair Dillman*	PO Box 210, Prairie Du Chien WI 53821	608-326-6471	R	2*	<.1
85	Prior Lake Aggregates Inc—*William Pearson*	PO Box 309, Prior Lake MN 55372	952-447-5593	R	2*	<.1
86	Lingo Sand Company Inc—*Billy Lingo*	3634 Lingo Rd, Dothan AL 36303	334-983-4015	R	2*	<.1
87	C and J Gravel Products Inc—*John Gilleland*	27661 Hwy 160, Durango CO 81301	970-385-4112	R	1*	<.1
88	Dale E Percy Inc—*Dana Percy*	269 Weeks Hill Rd, Stowe VT 05672	802-253-8503	R	1*	<.1
89	Rupp Construction Inc—*Gary Radabaugh*	18228 Fulton Rd, Marshallville OH 44645	330-855-2781	R	1*	<.1
90	Tomahawk Sand and Gravel Company Inc—*Duane Winger*	PO Box 350, Tomahawk WI 54487	715-453-3616	R	1*	<.1
91	Washington Sand Company Inc—*Mitch Parish*	PO Box 2029, Washington MO 63090	636-239-0061	R	<1*	<.1

TOTALS: SIC 1442 Construction Sand & Gravel
Companies: 91

					11,144	14.1

1446 Industrial Sand

1	US Silica Co—*Bryan Shinn*	PO Box 187, Berkeley Springs WV 25411		S	519*	.7
2	ER Jahna Industries Inc—*Allen Keesler*	PO Drawer 840, Lake Wales FL 33859	863-676-9431	R	74*	.3
3	Short Mountain Silica Co—*RL Wallen*	170 Silica Rd, Mooresburg TN 37811	423-272-5700	R	45*	.1
4	Reserve Silica Corp—*William Melfi* Reserve Industries Corp	20 First Plaza Ctr NW, Albuquerque NM 87102	505-247-2384	S	42*	<.1
5	Zeochem LLC—*Martin Iseli*	1600 W Hill St, Louisville KY 40210	502-634-7600	R	20*	.2
6	Standard Sand and Silica Co—*L Carnes*	PO Box 1059, Davenport FL 33836	863-422-7100	R	14*	.1
7	Nugent Sand Company Inc—*Robert Chandonnet*	2925 Lincoln St, Norton Shores MI 49441	231-755-1686	R	4*	<.1
8	Holliston Sand Company Inc—*Robert Kimball*	PO Box 1168, Slatersville RI 02876	401-766-5010	R	3*	<.1
9	Northern Filter Media Inc—*David Reusswig*	2509 Pettibone Ave, Muscatine IA 52761	563-263-2711	R	3*	<.1
10	Ash Meadows Zeolite LLC—*Timothy Wuest*	PO Box 328, Berlin WI 54923	920-361-2388	R	3*	.1
11	Reserve Industries Corp—*Frank Melfi*	20 1st Plz Ctr NW Ste, Albuquerque NM 87102	505-247-2384	R	2*	<.1
12	Wexford Sand Co—*Charles Fowler*	8770 W 28 Rd, Harrietta MI 49638	231-389-2819	R	2*	<.1
13	Atwater-General Corp—*John Klug*	N57w13636 Carmen Ave S, Menomonee Falls WI 53051	262-781-3767	R	1*	<.1

TOTALS: SIC 1446 Industrial Sand
Companies: 13

					731	1.5

1455 Kaolin & Ball Clay

1	Imerys USA Inc—*Gerard Buffiere*	100 Mansell Ct E Ste 3, Roswell GA 30076	770-594-0660	R	474*	4.0
2	Thiele Kaolin Co—*Sam Smith*	PO Box 1056, Sandersville GA 31082	478-552-3951	R	30*	.6
3	Nord Resources Corp—*Wayne M Morrison*	PO Box 384, Dragoon AZ 85609	520-292-0266	P	29	.1
4	Kentucky-Tennessee Clay Co Imerys USA Inc	PO Box 232, Gleason TN 38229	731-648-2503	S	10*	.1
5	Spinks H C Clay Company Inc—*Harry Carothers*	PO Box 820, Paris TN 38242	731-642-5414	S	9*	.1
6	Arcilla Mining And Land Company LLC—*Joni Martin*	9474 Ga Hwy 57, Mc Intyre GA 31054	478-946-3664	R	4*	.1
7	WKA LLC—*Christina Marshon*	121 Milledgeville Hwy, Gordon GA 31031	478-628-5293	R	4*	.1

TOTALS: SIC 1455 Kaolin & Ball Clay
Companies: 7

					559	4.9

1459 Clay & Related Minerals Nec

1	AMCOL International Corp—*Ryan F McKendrick*	1500 W Shure Dr Ste 50, Arlington Heights IL 60004	847-394-8730	P	942	2.6
2	Black Hills Bentonite LLC—*Tom Thorson*	PO Box 9, Mills WY 82644	307-265-3740	R	63*	.1
3	Wyo-Ben Inc—*David Brown*	PO Box 1979, Billings MT 59103	406-652-6351	R	42*	.1
4	MFM Industries Inc—*Michael Wilkinson*	PO Box 68, Reddick FL 32686	352-732-7227	R	11*	.1
5	G K Construction Inc—*Richard Grandalen*	1169 Ln 11 1/2, Lovell WY 82431	307-548-6324	R	10*	.1
6	Milwhite Inc—*Mike Hughes*	5487 S Padre Isld Hwy, Brownsville TX 78521	956-547-1970	R	9*	<.1
7	E J Bognar Inc—*Nadine Bognar*	733 Washington Rd Ste, Pittsburgh PA 15228	412-344-9900	R	8*	<.1

TOTALS: SIC 1459 Clay & Related Minerals Nec
Companies: 7

					1,085	3.0

1474 Potash, Soda & Borate Minerals

1	Oci Chemical Corp—*Kevin Boyle*	5 Concourse Pkwy Ne, Atlanta GA 30328	770-261-0368	R	1,155*	.5
2	Searles Valley Minerals—*Stephen Cole*	9401 Indian Creek Pky, Overland Park KS 66210	913-344-9500	R	840*	3.2
3	General Chemical (Soda Ash) Inc—*Chris Douville*	PO Box 551, Green River WY 82935	307-875-3350	R	36*	.6

TOTALS: SIC 1474 Potash, Soda & Borate Minerals
Companies: 3

					2,031	4.3

1475 Phosphate Rock

1	Apac Mid-South Inc—*Sean O'sullivan*	500 Riverhills Busines, Birmingham AL 35242	205-995-5900	R	300*	.5
2	Natural Materials LLC—*Margaret Schenck*	1408 Hwy 44 Ste 800, Harlan IA 51537	712-755-2563	R	4*	.1

TOTALS: SIC 1475 Phosphate Rock
Companies: 2

					304	.6

1479 Chemical & Fertilizer Mining Nec

1	Compass Minerals International Inc—*Angelo Brisimitzakis*	9900 W 109th St Ste 10, Overland Park KS 66210	913-344-9200	P	1,106	1.8
2	Freeport-McMoRan Sulphur Co—*James R Moffett*	1615 Poydras St, New Orleans LA 70112	504-582-4000	R	159*	.3
3	Cooperstone Products Inc	PO Box 214, Subiaco AR 72865	479-858-2792	R	31*	<.1
4	United Salt Corp—*Jim O'donnell*	4800 San Felipe St, Houston TX 77056	713-877-2600	R	27*	.2
5	Potash Corporation Of Saskatchewan Sales—*William Doyle*	1101 Skokie Blvd Ste 4, Northbrook IL 60062		R	18*	.2
6	Agrifos Fertilizer LP—*Linda Alexander*	2001 Jackson Rd, Pasadena TX 77506	713-920-5300	R	16*	.2
7	New Riverside Ochre Company Inc—*Tom Deems*	PO Box 460, Cartersville GA 30120	770-382-4568	R	3*	<.1

TOTALS: SIC 1479 Chemical & Fertilizer Mining Nec
Companies: 7

					1,360	2.7

1481 Nonmetallic Minerals Services

1	Intrepid Potash Inc—*Robert P Jornayvaz III*	707 17th St Ste 4200, Denver CO 80202	303-296-3006	P	443	.9
2	Boart Longyear Co—*Richard Swayne*	PO Box 27314, Salt Lake City UT 84127	801-972-6430	S	78*	.7

Rank	Company Name—*Executive Officer*	Address, City, State, Zip	Phone	Type	Fin	Empls
3	Zemex Corp—*Ignacio Bustamant*	1040 Crown Pointe Pky, Atlanta GA 30338	770-392-8680	R	74*	.4
4	Lightbridge Corp—*Seth Grae*	1600 Tyson's Blvd Ste, McLean VA 22102	571-730-1200	P	6	<.1
5	Crystal Ceres Industries Inc—*Robin Cellino*	2250 Liberty Dr, Niagara Falls NY 14304	716-283-0445	R	3*	.1
6	Chief Mining Inc—*Ken Calloway*	PO Box 446, Glen Daniel WV 25844	304-294-8718	R	3*	<.1
7	Dixie Drilling Corp—*Russell Boren*	1940 Pinson Valley Pkw, Birmingham AL 35217	205-849-1727	R	3*	<.1

TOTALS: SIC 1481 Nonmetallic Minerals Services
Companies: 7   611   2.1

1499 Miscellaneous Nonmetallic Minerals

Rank	Company Name—*Executive Officer*	Address, City, State, Zip	Phone	Type	Fin	Empls
1	World Minerals Inc—*John Oskan*	130 Castilian Dr, Santa Barbara CA 93117	805-737-2454	S	173*	1.5
2	American Rock Salt Company LLC—*Joseph G Bucci*	PO Box 230, Union Dale PA 18470	585-991-6827	R	88*	.2
3	Martin Marietta Composites LLC	PO Box 30013, Raleigh NC 27622	919-882-2303	S	18*	<.1
4	Nano-C LLC—*Viktor Vejins*	33 Southwest Park, Westwood MA 02090	781-407-9417	R	14*	<.1
5	Natural Resources USA Corp—*Brad Bunnett*	3200 County Rd 31, Rifle CO 81650	720-876-2373	R	9	<.1
6	Millburn Peat Company Inc—*Robert Render*	PO Box 1160, Milan IL 61264	219-362-7025	R	8*	<.1
7	Yellow Hair Trading and Mining Limited Inc—*Monte Nichols*	200 W Ash St, Globe AZ 85501	928-425-7625	R	4*	<.1
8	Professional Gem Sciences Inc—*Myriam Tashtey*	5 S Wabash Ave Ste 315, Chicago IL 60603	312-920-1541	R	1*	<.1
9	Hall's Arkansas Oilstones Inc—*Richard Hall*	3800 Amity Rd, Pearcy AR 71964	501-525-8595	R	<1*	<.1
10	Chancery Resources Inc—*Rafael A Pinedo*	4400 Westgrove Dr Ste, Addison TX 75001	972-655-9870	P	<1	<.1
11	Tiger International Resources Inc—*Patric Barry*	26981 Highwood Cir, Laguna Hills CA 92653	949-362-1600	P	<1	N/A

TOTALS: SIC 1499 Miscellaneous Nonmetallic Minerals
Companies: 11   314   1.9

1521 Single-Family Housing Construction

Rank	Company Name—*Executive Officer*	Address, City, State, Zip	Phone	Type	Fin	Empls
1	Choice Homes Inc—*Bob Ladd*	PO Box 155929, Fort Worth TX 76155	817-684-2400	R	2,507*	2.2
2	US Home Corp—*Robert J Strudler*	PO Box 2863, Houston TX 77252	713-877-2311	S	1,813*	2.4
3	KB Home Nevada Inc—*Leah Bryant*	750 Pilot Rd Ste F, Las Vegas NV 89119	702-266-8500	S	1,499*	.4
4	WL Homes LLC—*H Lawrence Webb*	895 Dove St Ste 200, Newport Beach CA 92660	949-265-2400	R	1,480*	1.1
5	Drees Co—*David G Drees*	211 Grandview Dr Ste 3, Fort Mitchell KY 41017	859-578-4200	R	822*	.9
6	Richmond American Homes Inc—*Larry A Mizel*	4350 S Monaco St, Denver CO 80237	303-773-1100	S	785	N/A
7	Continental Homes Inc	16430 N Scottsdale Rd, Scottsdale AZ 85254	480-483-0006	D	754*	.2
8	GL Homes of Florida Corp—*Itchko Ezratti*	1600 Sawgrass Corporat, Sunrise FL 33323	954-753-1730	R	681*	.3
9	Holiday Builders Inc—*Bruce Assam*	2293 W Eau Gallie Blvd, Melbourne FL 32935		R	672*	.5
10	Warmington Group—*Timothy P Hogan*	3090 Pullman St, Costa Mesa CA 92626	714-557-5511	R	653*	.7
11	McMillin Homes	2750 Womble Rd, San Diego CA 92106	619-477-4117	S	534*	.3
12	Perry Homes - A Joint Venture Inc—*William O Perry*	PO Box 34306, Houston TX 77234		R	518	N/A
13	HITT Contracting Inc—*Brett R Hitt*	2900 Fairview Park Dr, Falls Church VA 22042	703-846-9000	R	499*	.7
14	Elliott Homes Inc—*Harry C Elliott III*	340 Palladio Pky Ste 5, Folsom CA 95630	916-984-1300	R	483*	.1
15	American West Homes Inc—*Lawrence D Canarelli*	250 Pilot Rd Ste 140, Las Vegas NV 89119	702-736-6434	R	481*	.5
16	Fralin and Waldron Inc—*Karen Waldron*	90 Town Center Street, Daleville VA 24083	540-774-4415	R	442*	.4
17	Arthur Rutenberg Homes Inc—*Alan Weiner*	13922 58th St N, Clearwater FL 33760	727-536-5900	R	440*	.1
18	KB Home Colorado Ino—*Joffroy Mezger*	7807 E Peakview Ave St, Centennial CO 80111	303-323-1100	S	436	.1
19	Pasquinelli Construction Co—*Bruno A Pasquinelli Sr*	6880 N Frontage Rd Ste, Burr Ridge IL 60527	630-455-5400	H	429*	.2
20	John Wieland Homes and Neighborhoods Inc—*Terry Russel*	4125 Atlanta Rd SE, Smyrna GA 30080	770-907-3400	R	404*	.6
21	HJ Stabile and Son Inc—*John P Stabile II*	20 Cotton Rd, Nashua NH 03063	603-889-0318	R	403*	.1
22	Simonini Builders Inc—*Ray A Killian*	1910 S Boulevard Ste 2, Charlotte NC 28203	704-358-9940	R	378*	.1
23	CI Mitchell and Best Inc—*Bob Mitchell Corgan*	1686 E Gude Dr, Rockville MD 20850	301-762-9511	R	375*	.1
24	KB Home South Bay Inc—*Drew Kusnick*	6700 Koll Center Pkwy, Pleasanton CA 94566	925-750-1700	S	375*	.1
25	Town and Country Homes Inc	1806 S Highland Ave, Lombard IL 60148	630-953-2222	S	359*	.3
26	John Mourier Construction Inc—*John Mourier III*	1430 Blue Oaks Blvd St, Roseville CA 95747	916-782-8879	R	351*	.3
27	William Lyon Homes—*William Lyon Sr*	4490 Von Karmen Ave, Newport Beach CA 92660	949-833-3600	R	350*	.4
28	Intervest Construction Inc—*Mori Hosseini*	2379 Beville Rd, Daytona Beach FL 32119	386-788-0820	R	325	N/A
29	Albert D Seeno Construction Co—*Thomas Albert Seeno*	PO Box 4113, Concord CA 94524	925-671-7711	R	316*	.5
30	Paul Davis Restoration Inc—*Scott Baker*	1 Independent Dr Ste 2, Jacksonville FL 32202	904-737-2779	R	289*	.1
31	Tom Johnson Construction—*Tom R Johnson*	100 Midland Park Dr, O Fallon MO 63366	636-887-4120	R	267*	.2
32	Pacific Bay Homes LLC—*John Markely*	4041 MacArthur Blvd St, Newport Beach CA 92660	949-440-7200	R	266	.2
33	Polygon Northwest Company Inc—*Jeff Gow*	11624 SE 5th St Ste 20, Bellevue WA 98005	425-586-7700	R	251	N/A
34	Eastwood Construction Company Inc—*Joe Stewart*	2857 Westport Rd, Charlotte NC 28208	704-399-4663	R	235*	.2
35	Midwest Drywall Company Inc—*Steve Nienke*	PO Box 771170, Wichita KS 67277	316-722-9559	R	233*	.9
36	Paper Valley Corp—*Thomas Boldt*	PO Box 419, Appleton WI 54912	920-739-6321	S	229*	.2
37	Ryan Homes	11700 Plaza America Dr, Reston VA 20190	703-956-4000	S	222*	1.0
38	Century Homebuilders LLC—*Sergio Pino*	7270 NW 12th St Ste 41, Miami FL 33126	305-599-8100	R	209*	.1
39	Key Construction Inc (Gilbert Arizona)—*Reed Porter*	890 W Elliot Rd Ste 10, Gilbert AZ 85233	480-556-1216	R	207	N/A
40	Sun Lakes Construction Company Inc—*Edward J Robson*	9532 E Riggs Rd, Sun Lakes AZ 85248	480-895-9200	S	203*	.1
41	Fischer Homes Inc—*Henry K Fischer*	2670 Chancellor Dr Ste, Crestview Hills KY 41017	859-341-4709	R	199*	.4
42	Parker and Lancaster Corp—*Jeffrey P Orleans*	711 Moorefield Park Dr, Richmond VA 23236	804-323-3100	S	195*	.3
43	Kullman Industries Inc—*Avi Telyas*	1 Kullman Corporate Ca, Lebanon NJ 08833	908-236-0220	R	191*	.2
44	Peachtree Residential Properties—*Mike Ruland*	7380 McGinnis Ferry Rd, Suwanee GA 30024	770-622-2522	R	178	.1
45	T and R Properties Inc—*Ron Sabatino*	3895 Stoneridge Ln, Dublin OH 43017	614-923-4000	R	176*	.2
46	Champion Home Builders Inc—*Phyllis Knight*	755 W Big Beaver Rd St, Troy MI 48084	248-614-8200	R	173*	2.5
47	DR Horton (Scottsdale Arizona)—*Karl Spangler*	16430 N Scottsdale Rd, Scottsdale AZ 85254	480-483-0006	S	148*	.2
48	TH Properties—*Tim Hendricks*	345 Main St, Harleysville PA 19438	215-513-4270	R	143*	.2
49	Kean Development Co—*John Kean*	5 Main St 3rd Fl, Cold Spring Harbor NY 11724	631-367-9696	R	142*	<.1
50	Venture Homes Inc—*Robert C White Sr*	1580 Terrell Mill Rd S, Marietta GA 30067	770-955-8300	R	140*	.1
51	Sears Home Improvement Products Inc—*Allwyn Lewis*	PO Box 522290, Longwood FL 32752	407-767-0990	R	139*	2.9
52	Miller and Smith Inc—*Douglas Smith*	8401 Greensboro Dr Ste, McLean VA 22102	703-821-2500	R	138*	.2
53	Croom Construction Co—*David Croom*	1201 19th Pl Ste A400, Vero Beach FL 32960	772-562-7474	R	119*	.1
54	Wesseln Construction Company Inc—*Henry B Wesseln*	292 N Wilshire Ave Ste, Anaheim CA 92801	714-772-0808	R	116*	.3
55	Bielinski Brothers Builders Inc—*Harry Bielinski*	PO Box 1615, Waukesha WI 53187	262-542-9494	R	110*	.2
56	Pedcor Cos—*Bruce A Cordingley*	770 3rd Ave SW, Carmel IN 46032	317-587-0320	R	107*	.2
57	Achen-Gardner Inc—*Douglas Gardner*	550 S 79th St, Chandler AZ 85226	480-940-1300	R	106*	.1
58	Rector Phillips Morse Inc—*Ronald L Goss*	PO Box 7300, Little Rock AR 72217	501-664-7807	R	105	.1
59	Cooper Communities Inc—*John Cooper III*	903 N 47th St, Rogers AR 72756	479-246-6500	R	104*	.4
60	William E Buchan Inc—*William E Buchan*	2630 116th Ave NE Ste, Bellevue WA 98004	425-828-6424	R	101*	.1
61	CR Meyer and Sons Co—*Phillip J Martini*	895 W 20th Ave, Oshkosh WI 54902	920-235-3350	R	98	.5
62	Burnstead Construction Co—*Fred H Burnstead*	11980 NE 24th St Ste 2, Bellevue WA 98005	425-454-1900	R	95*	.1
63	Wildish Land Co—*James A Wildish*	PO Box 40310, Eugene OR 97401	541-485-1700	R	94*	.1
64	Chapman Homes Inc—*Michael Chapman*	404 Brunn School Rd Bl, Santa Fe NM 87505	505-983-8100	R	94*	<.1
65	Miller Construction Co—*Thomas J Miller*	614 S Federal Hwy, Fort Lauderdale FL 33301	954-764-6550	R	89*	.1

Note: An asterisk (*) indicates an estimated financial figure. The company type code used is as follows: R = Private, P = Public, S = Private Subsidiary, B = Public Subsidiary, D = Division, J = Joint Venture, I = Investment Fund.

COMPANY RANKINGS BY SALES WITHIN 4-DIGIT SIC

Rank	Company Name—Executive Officer	Address, City, State, Zip	Phone	Type	Fin	Empls
66	Segal and Morel Inc—Ken Segal	991 US Hwy 22 W Ste 10, Bridgewater NJ 08807	908-722-0505	R	88*	.1
67	Comstock Homes Inc—Chris Clemente	11465 Sunset Hills Rd, Reston VA 20190	703-883-1700	R	84*	.1
68	Amedore Homes Inc—George A Amedore Sr	1900 Western Ave, Albany NY 12203	518-456-1010	R	76*	<.1
69	Hayden Homes Inc—Dennis Hayden	7 The Pines Ct Ste A, Saint Louis MO 63141	314-434-5820	R	75*	<.1
70	DRH Cambridge Homes Inc—George Seagraves	800 S Milwaukee Ave, Libertyville IL 60048	847-362-9100	S	73*	.2
71	Providence Homes Inc—Willliam J Cellar	4901 Belfort Rd Ste 14, Jacksonville FL 32256	904-262-9898	R	71*	<.1
72	Andrew Roby General Contractor Inc—Trent Haston	PO Box 221416, Charlotte NC 28222	704-334-5477	R	67*	.1
73	Bozzuto Group—Thomas S Bozzuto	7850 Walker Dr Ste 400, Greenbelt MD 20770	301-220-0100	R	62*	.5
74	Stonebridge Builders Inc—Robert Bowman	1190 Dillerville Rd, Lancaster PA 17601	717-560-1400	R	61*	.1
75	Grand Homes Inc—Stephen H Brooks	15455 Dallas Pkwy Ste, Addison TX 75001	214-750-6528	R	61*	.1
76	Landstar Development Corp Central Florida Div	550 Biltmore Way, Coral Gables FL 33134	305-461-2440	D	60*	.1
77	JI Garcia Construction Inc—Joseph V Garcia	5591 N Golden State Bl, Fresno CA 93722	559-276-7726	R	59*	.1
78	Fischer and Frichtel Inc—John W Fischer	695 Trade Ctr Blvd Ste, Chesterfield MO 63005	314-576-0500	R	55*	<.1
79	Mayer Homes Inc—Randy Mayer	755 S New Ballas Rd St, Saint Louis MO 63141	314-997-2300	R	54*	<.1
80	Steve Klein Custom Builders—Steve Klein	103 Deer Chase, Victoria TX 77901	361-572-4663	R	51*	<.1
81	Beazer Homes Holdings Inc	5775 Peachtree Dunwood, Atlanta GA 30342	770-829-3700	S	47*	<.1
82	Saussy Burbank Inc—George Casey	3730 Glen Lake Dr Ste, Charlotte NC 28208	704-945-1515	R	47	<.1
83	Nordaas American Homes—Mike Redig	PO Box 116, Minnesota Lake MN 56068	507-462-3331	R	44*	<.1
84	Maracay Homes Arizona I LLC—Andy Warren	15279 N Scottsdale Rd, Scottsdale AZ 85254	480-970-6000	S	43*	.1
85	Foster Management Inc—Art Foster	3975 University Dr Ste, Fairfax VA 22030	703-385-8900	R	43*	<.1
86	Southern Homes and Remodelling Inc—Robert Newton	108 Ole Towne Sq Ste B, Central SC 29630	864-654-9360	R	41*	<.1
87	Paul Risk Associates Inc—Steven Risk	11 W State St, Quarryville PA 17566	717-786-7308	R	38*	.1
88	Christopher Homes Development Co—Christopher Gibbs	19 Corporate Plz, Newport Beach CA 92660	949-721-9777	R	38*	.1
89	Coastal Contractors Inc (Beaufort South Carolina)—Tim Rentz	39 Burton Hill Rd, Beaufort SC 29906	843-524-3191	R	38*	.1
90	All Pool and Spa Inc—John King	905 Kalanianaole Hwy, Kailua HI 96734	808-261-8991	R	38*	<.1
91	Mitchell-Carroll Homes Inc—Ronny Carroll	PO Box 218449, Houston TX 77218	281-578-6777	R	38*	<.1
92	Blue Tangerine Solutions Inc—Greg Bray	PO Box 651307, Vero Beach FL 32965	321-309-6900	R	36*	.1
93	Hedgewood Properties Inc—Pam Sessions	5860 Clarion St Ste 10, Cumming GA 30040	678-807-8144	R	36	.1
94	R and J Homes LLC—Steven Gabbard	927 Red Oak Cir, Benton AR 72019	501-316-1183	R	36*	<.1
95	Longford Group—John Murtagh	3077 E Warm Springs, Las Vegas NV 89120	702-454-5300	R	35*	.1
96	Denney Construction Co—Carl Denney	164 W Oak St, Lawrenceville GA 30046	770-995-5733	R	35*	<.1
97	Palace Construction Company Inc—Rick Carter	7 S Galapago St, Denver CO 80223	303-777-7999	R	34*	.1
98	William Trotter Co—Paul H Trotter	1515 Mockingbird Ln St, Charlotte NC 28209	704-525-1783	R	32*	<.1
99	Arlinghaus Builders Inc—Bob Schroder	142 Barnwood Dr, Edgewood KY 41017	859-392-8900	R	31*	.1
100	Martel Construction Inc—Tony Martel	1203 S Church Ave, Bozeman MT 59715	406-586-8585	R	30*	.2
101	Gateway Homes Inc—Tom Walker	PO Box 27943, Houston TX 77227	713-622-3737	R	30*	<.1
102	McKelvey Homes LLC—Jim Brennan	218 Chesterfield Towne, Chesterfield MO 63005	636-530-6900	R	30*	<.1
103	Richmond American Homes of Maryland Inc—Larry A Mizel	5171 California Ave St, Irvine CA 92617	949-467-2600	S	27*	.1
104	Pernix Group Inc—Nidal Z Zayed	151 E 22nd St, Lombard IL 60148	630-620-4787	P	26	.2
105	Bauer Construction Inc—Mark Bauer	PO Box 1406, Solana Beach CA 92075	858-481-0909	R	26*	<.1
106	Comstock Homebuilding Companies Inc—Christopher Clemente	11465 Sunset Hills Rd, Reston VA 20190	703-883-1700	P	24	<.1
107	BOWA Builders Inc—Larry Weinberg	7900 Westpark Dr Ste A, McLean VA 22102	703-734-9050	R	23*	.1
108	Sheffield Homes—James E Sheffield	6777 Wadsworth Blvd, Arvada CO 80003	303-420-0056	R	22*	<.1
109	Simplex Industries Inc—Patrick Fricchione	1 Simplex Dr, Scranton PA 18504	570-346-5113	R	21*	.2
110	Hampton Homes—Seth Lincoln	12206 1/2 Walraven Dr, Huffman TX 77336	713-366-3510	R	21	<.1
111	Storm Smart Building Systems—Brian Rist	6182 Idlewild St, Fort Myers FL 33966	239-278-9092	R	20*	.2
112	Amir Amirfar and Associates Inc—Amir Amirfar	26 Executive Park Ste, Irvine CA 92614	949-681-1900	R	19*	.1
113	Rockford Homes Inc—Robert Yoakam Sr	999 Polaris Pkwy Ste 2, Columbus OH 43240	614-785-0015	R	18*	<.1
114	Snyder Cos—Bob Snyder	15 Brickyard Rd, Essex Junction VT 05452	802-985-5722	R	15*	<.1
115	Neumann Enterprises Inc—Mark W Neumann	W330 Hasslinger Dr, Nashotah WI 53058	262-966-1001	R	15*	<.1
116	Joe Chronister Construction Co—Joe Chronister	PO Box 35, Lavaca AR 72941	479-674-5201	R	15*	<.1
117	Maryl Group Inc—Mark Richards	55 Merchant St Ste 290, Honolulu HI 96813	808-545-6464	R	14*	<.1
118	Connor and Company Inc—William S Connor	1101 Central Ave, Indianapolis IN 46202	317-637-0046	R	14*	<.1
119	FaxonGillis Homes Inc—Jerry Gillis	825 Timber Creek Dr, Cordova TN 38018	901-759-7000	R	14*	<.1
120	Dynamic Homes Inc—Paul Okeson	PO Box 1137, Detroit Lakes MN 56502	218-847-2611	R	13*	.1
121	Knestrick Contractor Inc—William Knestrick	2617 Grandview Ave, Nashville TN 37211	615-259-3755	R	13*	<.1
122	Bigelow Group Inc—Jamie Bigelow	860 Serendipity Dr, Aurora IL 60504	630-631-0700	R	13*	<.1
123	Fogarty Homes Inc—Brad Haubert	4550 Westbranch Hwy, Lewisburg PA 17837	570-523-3203	R	12	<.1
124	Ryan Olsen Development—Ryan Olsen	7911 NE 33rd Dr, Portland OR 97211	503-880-1776	R	12*	<.1
125	Klutts Property Management—J Vaughn Klutts Jr	1433 Emerywood Dr, Charlotte NC 28210	704-554-8861	R	12*	<.1
126	Sunrooms Plus Inc—Larry Chavez	7401 Indian School Rd, Albuquerque NM 87110	505-881-6004	R	12*	<.1
127	Meridian Homes Inc (Houston Texas)—Gary Cleary	9186 Old Katy Road Ste, Houston TX 77079	713-973-0003	R	11*	<.1
128	Grady Environmental Services Inc—Michael F Grady	6100 Westchester Park, College Park MD 20740	301-440-8697	R	11*	<.1
129	International Housing Div—Randy Saxton	999 S Main St, Smithfield UT 84335	435-563-3232	R	11*	<.1
130	JR Roberts Enterprises Inc—Robert C Hall Jr	7745 Greenback Ln Ste, Citrus Heights CA 95610	916-729-5600	R	11*	<.1
131	Deluxe Building Systems Inc—Donald Shiner	499 W 3rd St, Berwick PA 18603	570-752-5914	R	10*	<.1
132	Domes International Inc—Dicky Sparks	5 Murphy St, Tishomingo MS 38873	662-438-7186	R	10*	<.1
133	Avtec Homes—Larry Sietsma	1663 Georgia St NE, Palm Bay FL 32907	321-676-4668	R	10*	<.1
134	MB Visnic Custom Homes—Theodore Visnic	1684 E Gude Dr Ste 102, Rockville MD 20850	301-309-6470	R	10*	<.1
135	Schaefer Homes—Ron Brazell	6031 Flower Mdw, San Antonio TX 78222	210-648-9944	R	10*	<.1
136	Woodhaven Homes Inc—Jack Wilson	8721 Warden Rd, Sherwood AR 72120	501-835-6258	R	9*	<.1
137	Thompson Brooks Inc—Judith Thompson	375 Rhode Island St, San Francisco CA 94103	415-581-2600	R	8*	.1
138	Carolina Home Exteriors LLC—David Thereault	3224 Us Hwy 70 E, New Bern NC 28560	252-637-6599	R	8*	<.1
139	A and B Construction Development Inc—Jeremy Bonner	PO Box 15370, Asheville NC 28813	828-258-2000	R	8*	<.1
140	Manufactured Housing Enterprises Inc—James Newman	9302 Us Hwy 6, Bryan OH 43506	419-636-4511	S	7*	.1
141	Hamptons Luxury Homes Inc—Roy Dalene	PO Box 871, Bridgehampton NY 11932	631-537-1600	P	7	<.1
142	Eid-Co Buildings Inc—Gerald D Eid	1701 32nd Ave S, Fargo ND 58103	701-237-0510	R	7*	<.1
143	Southern Flair Builders Inc—B Jan Griffin	PO Box 481923, Charlotte NC 28269	704-948-6100	R	7*	<.1
144	Bosley Construction Inc—Bill Bosley	9107 N Rodney Parham R, Little Rock AR 72205	501-225-2729	R	7*	<.1
145	Leigh Custom Homes Inc—William Leigh	PO Box 7002, The Woodlands TX 77387	281-363-9152	R	7*	<.1
146	Bob Schmitt Homes Inc—Michael P Schmitt	9095 Gatestone Rd, North Ridgeville OH 44039	440-327-9495	R	6*	<.1
147	Sattler Homes Inc—Tom Sattler	PO Box 876, Littleton CO 80160	303-771-5995	R	6*	<.1
148	Yellowstone Log Homes LLC—Scott Norman	280 N Yellowstone Hwy, Rigby ID 83442	208-745-8108	R	5*	.1
149	Lindstrom Cleaning and Construction Inc—Charles Lindstrom	9621 10th Ave N, Minneapolis MN 55441	763-544-8761	R	5*	<.1
150	Bureau Veritas North America Inc—Dennis Ryan	1000 Jupiter Rd Ste 80, Plano TX 75074	469-241-1834	R	5*	<.1
151	Menendez-Donnell and Associates—Maria L Menendez	11767 Katy Frwy Ste 34, Houston TX 77079		R	5*	<.1
152	Donoso Inc—Roy Donoso	3701 N Ravenswood Ave, Chicago IL 60613	773-857-7904	R	5	<.1
153	R A Designs Inc—Susan Kennedy	1007 Buckingham Rd, Grosse Pointe MI 48230	313-885-0616	R	5*	<.1
154	K Carrender Construction Company Inc—Melvin Carrender	200 Ringgold Rd, Somerset KY 42503	606-679-2328	R	4*	<.1

Rank	Company Name—Executive Officer	Address, City, State, Zip	Phone	Type	Fin	Empls
155	Richardson Enterprises—Joel Richardson	360 Adams Ave, Valparaiso FL 32580	850-678-2584	R	4*	<.1
156	Ponds and Sons Construction Company Inc—Willis Ponds	24 Gabriel Dr, Lodge SC 29082	843-846-2500	S	4*	<.1
157	HA Cumber Inc—Aftab A Cumber	10100 W Sample Rd Ste, Coral Springs FL 33065	954-753-4242	R	4*	<.1
158	Winn Design LLC—Michael S Winn	100 W Jefferson St, Falls Church VA 22046	703-876-9697	R	4*	<.1
159	R/S Development Co—Randall Schaefer	12 A Sunset Way Ste 11, Henderson NV 89014	702-458-6820	R	4*	<.1
160	Medallion Homes Inc—Will Worth	6391 DeZavala Rd Ste 1, San Antonio TX 78249	210-494-2555	R	4*	<.1
161	Carolina Model Home Corp—William Dudley	PO Box 53278, Fayetteville NC 28305	910-323-5000	R	3*	.1
162	Suntide Homes Development Inc—David Nothum	2025 Lemay Ferry Rd, Saint Louis MO 63125	314-892-5106	R	3*	<.1
163	AFS and Associates Inc—Al Fazelpoor	81 Rt 130, Trenton NJ 08620	609-324-8380	R	3*	<.1
164	Cascade Contracting Inc—John Pate	582 Lynnhven Pkwy Ste, Virginia Beach VA 23452	757-368-0299	R	3*	<.1
165	Boston Lightning Rod Co—Parker Willard	PO Box 890, Dedham MA 02027	781-326-2807	R	2*	<.1
166	Stanley T Naudus Corp—Nick Flevarakis	109 Park Ave Ste B, Falls Church VA 22046	703-820-3660	R	2*	<.1
167	Valente Builders Inc—Daniel A Valente	1075 Dix Ave, Hudson Falls NY 12839	518-746-9040	R	2	<.1
168	John L Ulmer and Son Builders—John L Ulmer	12417 Cantrell Rd, Little Rock AR 72212	501-224-8481	R	2*	<.1
169	Kit Contractors Inc—Eugene Carson Sr	4619 Auburn Blvd Ste B, Sacramento CA 95841	916-481-9128	R	2*	<.1
170	Lone Star Siding and Windows—Brain Sonnier	17814 Windtree, Spring TX 77379	281-773-1255	R	1*	<.1
171	Summit Habitats Inc—Sandford M Treat	PO Box 1829, Edwards CO 81632	970-926-1743	R	1*	<.1
172	Joedy Sharpe Construction Company Inc—Joedy Sharpe	385 Spears Ln, Danville KY 40422	859-236-1479	R	1*	<.1
173	The Gear Group Inc—MC Ruedinger	1500 W Hampden Ave Ste, Englewood CO 80110	303-221-1511	R	<1	<.1
174	Pulte Diversified Companies Inc—Richard J Dugas Jr	100 Bloomfield Hills P, Bloomfield Hills MI 48304	248-647-2750	S	<1	N/A
175	Platinum Builders LLC—Steve Mellinger	PO Box 1091, New Carlisle IN 46552	574-654-7516	R	N/A	<.1
176	Hersh Levitt Investments Corp—Hersh Levitt	4914 Bissonnet St Ste, Bellaire TX 77401	713-661-0211	R	N/A	<.1

TOTALS: SIC 1521 Single Family Housing Construction
Companies: 176   27,979   30.5

1522 Residential Construction Nec

Rank	Company Name—Executive Officer	Address, City, State, Zip	Phone	Type	Fin	Empls
1	Benjamin Development Company Inc—Alvin Benjamin	377 Oak St Ste 401, Garden City NY 11530	516-745-0150	R	8,536*	2.3
2	Branch Group Inc—J William Karbach	PO Box 40004, Roanoke VA 24022	540-982-1678	R	1,625*	.7
3	Rooney Holdings Inc—L Francis Rooney III	3520 Kraft Rd, Naples FL 34105	239-403-0375	R	1,443*	2.6
4	KB Home—Jeffrey T Mezger	10990 Wilshire Blvd, Los Angeles CA 90024	310-231-4000	P	1,316	1.2
5	Hovnanian Enterprises Inc—Ara K Hovnanian	PO Box 500, Red Bank NJ 07701	732-747-7800	P	1,135	1.5
6	Modern Continental Companies Inc—Kenneth Anderson	600 Memorial Dr, Cambridge MA 02139	617-864-6300	R	1,098*	4.2
7	Boyd and Co—Darnall W Boyd	PO Box 23589, Columbia SC 29224	803-788-3800	R	840*	.2
8	David Weekley Homes—David Weekley	1111 N Post Oak Rd, Houston TX 77055	713-963-0500	D	624*	1.3
9	Pardee Construction Co—Michael V McGee	10880 Wilshire Blvd St, Los Angeles CA 90024	310-475-3525	S	538*	.7
10	Edward Rose Building Enterprises—Sheldon Rose	30057 Orchard Lake Rd, Farmington Hills MI 48333	248-539-2255	R	340*	1.5
11	Hunt Building Company Ltd—Woody Hunt	PO Box 12220, El Paso TX 79913	915-533-1122	R	273*	.3
12	Streeter Associates Inc—Jeffery B Streeter Jr	PO Box 118, Elmira NY 14902	607-734-4151	R	248*	.1
13	Kraft Construction Company Inc—F Fred Pezeshkan	3520 Kraft Rd, Naples FL 34105	239-643-6000	R	247*	.2
14	PN Hoffman Inc—Monty Hoffman	4725 Wisconsin Ave NW, Washington DC 20016	202-686-0010	R	216*	.1
15	JPI Investments Inc—Mark Bryant	600 E Las Colinas Blvd, Irving TX 75039	972-556-1700	R	200*	1.0
16	Gemcraft Homes Group Inc—Vickie Luther	2205 Commerce Rd Ste A, Forest Hill MD 21050	410-893-8458	R	180*	.1
17	Kopf Builders Inc—HR 'Bucky' Kopf	420 Avon Belden Rd, Avon Lake OH 44012	440-933-6908	R	178*	.2
18	Gillis Gilkerson Inc—Palmer Gillis	212 W Main St Ste 305, Salisbury MD 21801	410-749-4821	R	171*	.1
19	Colson and Colson Construction Co—William E Colson	2260 McGilchrist, Salem OR 97302	503-586-7401	R	125*	.1
20	Harkins Builders Inc—Richard M Lombardo	2201 Warwick Way, Marriottsville MD 21104	410-750-2600	R	120*	.2
21	Avatar Retirement Communities Inc—Jonathan Fels	201 Alhambra Cir, Coral Gables FL 33134	305-442-7000	S	111*	.1
22	Hardaway Construction Corp—Stan H Hardaway	615 Main St, Nashville TN 37206	615-254-5461	R	110*	.3
23	Shaw Construction LLC—Steve Meyer	300 Kalamath St, Denver CO 80223	303-825-4740	R	108*	.1
24	Heartland Inc—Terry Lee	PO Box 4320, Harrogate TN 37752	606-248-7323	P	99	.2
25	Apartment Housebuilders Inc—John A Kincannon	PO Box 959, North Little Rock AR 72115	501-758-2842	R	91*	.1
26	Weintraub Construction—Avi Weintraub	7760 W 20th Ave Ste 1, Miami FL 33016	305-557-9398	R	73*	<.1
27	Component Assembly Systems Inc—John Rapaport	620 Fifth Ave, Pelham NY 10803	914-738-5400	R	71*	.1
28	Motel Development Inc	4735 S Durango Dr Ste, Las Vegas NV 89147	702-227-9800	S	60*	<.1
29	Traton Corp—Bill Poston	720 Kennesaw Av, Marietta GA 30060	770-427-9064	R	59*	.1
30	Moretrench American Corp—Arthur B Corwin	100 Stickle Ave, Rockaway NJ 07866	973-627-2100	R	57*	.2
31	Green Valley Corp—Barry Swenson	777 N 1st St 5th Fl, San Jose CA 95112	408-287-0246	R	55*	.1
32	Thor Construction Inc—Ravi Norman	5400 Main St NE Ste 20, Minneapolis MN 55421	763-571-2580	R	54*	.1
33	GWL Construction LLC—Roger K Landry	275 Glen Lake Dr NW, Atlanta GA 30327	404-760-0064	R	45	<.1
34	McStain Neighborhoods—Tom Hoyt	7100 N Broadway Rm 5-H, Denver CO 80221	303-494-5900	R	45*	.1
35	Nationwide Housing Systems LP—Chuck Kearney Jr	2450 S Shore Blvd, League City TX 77573	281-334-9700	S	37*	.3
36	Birtcher Group—Brandon Birtcher	31910 Del Obispo Ste 1, San Juan Capistrano CA 92675	949-502-0500	R	37*	.1
37	Kettler Forlines Homes Inc—Clifford Forlines	9426 Stewartown Rd Ste, Montgomery Village MD 20886	301-258-0980	R	37*	.1
38	Winter Park Construction Co—Tracy Forrest	221 Circle Dr, Maitland FL 32751	407-644-8923	R	36*	.1
39	Bush Construction Corp—Marc B Sharp	4029 Ironbound Rd Ste, Williamsburg VA 23188	757-220-2874	R	35*	<.1
40	Majestic Construction Co—Harvey A Coleman	PO Box 369, Ramsey NJ 07446	201-327-1919	R	30*	.1
41	Trillacorpe Construction—Frank Campanaro	30100 Telegraph Rd Ste, Bingham Farms MI 48025	248-433-0585	R	29	.1
42	Nordic Construction Ltd—Wayne Melnyk	1099 Alakea St Ste 156, Honolulu HI 96813	808-541-9101	R	25*	.1
43	Kiska Construction Corp—Oliver Gursel	1034 44th Dr, Long Island City NY 11101	718-943-0400	R	25*	.1
44	Granor Price Homes—Bernard Granor	721 Dresher Rd Ste 100, Horsham PA 19044	215-830-1100	R	24*	.1
45	Beaver Builders Ltd	3130 47th Ave, Rock Island IL 61201	309-786-1491	R	20*	<.1
46	CL Carson Inc—Stuart Thomajan	826 Wagon Trail, Austin TX 78758	512-339-1140	R	17*	.1
47	GSG Builders Inc—Gilbert Godbold	PO Box 42142, Houston TX 77242	713-988-4847	R	17*	<.1
48	Thomas Electric Inc—David Thomas	7601 N 74th Ave, Glendale AZ 85303	623-842-3842	R	12*	.2
49	Park West Development Co—Stewart Jean	7077 E Bell Rd Ste 210, Scottsdale AZ 85254	602-264-1300	R	10*	<.1
50	Meade And Shepherd Coal Company Inc—Talmage Meade	12816 Hwy 160, Whitesburg KY 41858	606-633-7084	R	9*	.1
51	Greater Missouri Builders Inc—Dan Barnard	1551 Wall St Ste 220, Saint Charles MO 63303	636-946-1341	R	9*	<.1
52	Fairfield Homes Inc—David Williamson	5775 S Camino del Sol, Green Valley AZ 85622	520-625-1642	R	9*	<.1
53	ProTec Building Services Inc—J David Rauch	5555 Kearny Villa Rd, San Diego CA 92123	858-569-1080	R	6*	.1
54	Merchant Solutions USA Inc—Chesna Klaes	1420 Cypress Creek Rd, Cedar Park TX 78613	512-627-7182	R	5*	.1
55	Hernandez Companies Inc—Chris Hernandez	3734 E Anne St, Phoenix AZ 85040	602-438-7825	R	4*	.1
56	Futura Builders Group Inc—Sheikh Soni	30-02 72nd St, East Elmhurst NY 11370	718-424-4760	R	4*	.1
57	Ralph Hodge—Ralph Hodge	3335 Beulahtown Rd, Kenly NC 27542	919-284-2580	R	4*	.1
58	Exovations Of Atlanta LLC	1550 Oak Industrial Ln, Cumming GA 30041	770-205-2995	R	3*	<.1
59	Miceli Homes—Bud Miceli	536 Trade Center Blvd, Chesterfield MO 63005	636-537-1771	R	3*	<.1
60	Supreme Builders—Robert Baierl	1491 S 98th St, West Allis WI 53214	414-774-1491	R	2*	<.1

TOTALS: SIC 1522 Residential Construction Nec
Companies: 60   20,941   21.3

Note: An asterisk (*) indicates an estimated financial figure. The company type code used is as follows: R = Private, P = Public, S = Private Subsidiary, B = Public Subsidiary, D = Division, J = Joint Venture, I = Investment Fund.

COMPANY RANKINGS BY SALES WITHIN 4-DIGIT SIC

Rank	Company Name—*Executive Officer*	Address, City, State, Zip	Phone	Type	Fin	Empls

1531 Operative Builders

Rank	Company Name—*Executive Officer*	Address, City, State, Zip	Phone	Type	Fin	Empls
1	Centex Homes—*Timothy Eller* PulteGroup Inc	2728 N Harwood, Dallas TX 75201	214-981-5000	S	8,326*	6.9
2	PulteGroup Inc—*Richard J Dugas Jr*	100 Bloomfield Hills P, Bloomfield Hills MI 48304	248-647-2750	P	4,034	3.6
3	Centex Corp—*Richard J Dugas* PulteGroup Inc	PO Box 199000, Dallas TX 75219	214-981-5000	S	3,827	2.5
4	DR Horton Inc—*Donald J Tomnitz*	301 Commerce St Ste 50, Fort Worth TX 76102	817-390-8200	P	3,550	3.0
5	Lennar Corp—*Stuart A Miller*	700 NW 107th Ave Ste 4, Miami FL 33172	305-559-4000	P	3,095	4.1
6	NVR Inc—*Paul C Saville*	Plaza America Tower I, Reston VA 20190	703-956-4000	P	2,611	2.8
7	Shea Homes—*Bert Selva*	655 Brea Canyon Rd, Walnut CA 91789	909-594-9500	D	2,334*	.6
8	Artistic Homes Inc—*Jerry Wade*	4420 Tower Rd SW Ste A, Albuquerque NM 87121	505-247-8400	R	1,875*	<.1
9	Weyerhaeuser Real Estate Co—*Peter Orser*	PO Box 9777, Federal Way WA 98063	253-924-2345	S	1,767*	1.8
10	DR Horton Schuler Div—*James K Schuler* DR Horton Inc	828 Fort St Mall 4th F, Honolulu HI 96813	808-521-5661	S	1,603*	1.1
11	AG Spanos Cos—*Alexander G Spanos*	10100 Trinity Pkwy 5th, Stockton CA 95219	209-478-7954	R	1,562*	.6
12	Toll Brothers Inc—*Douglas C Yearley Jr*	250 Gibraltar Rd, Horsham PA 19044	215-938-8000	P	1,476	2.2
13	St Joe Towns and Resorts LP—*W Britton Greene*	245 Riverside Ave Ste, Jacksonville FL 32202		S	1,414*	1.2
14	Weekley Homes LP—*David M Weekley*	1111 N Post Oak Rd, Houston TX 77055	713-963-0500	R	1,336*	1.5
15	Kimball Hill Inc—*Ken Love*	5999 New Wilke Rd Ste, Rolling Meadows IL 60008	847-364-7300	R	1,164	.9
16	Taylor Woodrow Inc—*David Joyce*	8430 Enterprise Cir St, Bradenton FL 34202	941-554-2000	S	1,133*	.1
17	Robson Communities Inc—*Edward J Robson*	9532 E Riggs Rd, Sun Lakes AZ 85248		R	1,119*	1.0
18	Ryland Group Inc—*Larry T Nicholson*	24025 Park Sorrento St, Calabasas CA 91302	818-223-7500	P	1,064	1.0
19	Woodside Group Inc (Las Vegas Nevada)—*Ezra K Nilson*	39 E Eagle Ridge Dr St, North Salt Lake UT 84054	801-299-6700	R	1,033*	<.1
20	Standard Pacific Corp—*Scott D Stowell*	15360 Barranca Pky, Irvine CA 92618	949-789-1600	P	894	.8
21	Mercedes Homes Inc—*Keith Beuscher*	6767 N Wickham Blvd St, Melbourne FL 32940	321-259-6972	R	868*	1.3
22	Meritage Homes Corp—*Steven J Hilton*	17851 N 85th St Ste 30, Scottsdale AZ 85255	480-515-8100	P	861	.7
23	MDC Holdings Inc—*Larry A Mizel*	4350 S Monaco St, Denver CO 80237	303-773-1100	P	844	.9
24	Villages of Lake Sumter Inc—*H Gary Morse*	1000 Lake Sumter Landi, The Villages FL 32162	352-753-2270	R	802*	2.0
25	Ashton Residential LLC—*Thomas C Krobot*	1080 Holcombe Bridge R, Roswell GA 30076	770-642-6123	S	747	N/A
26	Beazer Homes USA Inc—*Allan P Merrill*	1000 Abernathy Rd Ste, Atlanta GA 30328	770-829-3700	P	742	.8
27	McBride and Son Homes Inc—*John Eillerman* McBride and Son Enterprises Inc	16091 Swingley Ridge R, Chesterfield MO 63017	636-537-2000	S	660*	.5
28	Orleans Homebuilders Inc—*George E Casey Jr*	3333 Street Rd Ste 101, Bensalem PA 19020	215-245-7500	P	583	.5
29	M/I Homes Inc—*Robert H Schottenstein*	3 Easton Oval Ste 500, Columbus OH 43219	614-418-8000	P	566	.6
30	McGuyer Homebuilders Inc—*Frank McGuyer*	7676 Woodway Ste 104, Houston TX 77063	713-952-6767	R	553*	.3
31	K Hovnanian at Washington LLC—*Ara K Hovnanian*	1802 Brightseat Rd 6th, Landover MD 20785	301-772-8900	S	506*	.5
32	K Hovnanian Forecast LLC—*James P Previti*	3536 Concours St Ste 1, Ontario CA 91764	909-483-7320	S	482*	.3
33	JTS Communities Inc—*Jack T Sweigart*	401 Watt Ave, Sacramento CA 95864	916-487-3434	R	456*	.4
34	Bowen Family Homes—*David J Bowen*	6650 Sugarloaf Pkwy St, Duluth GA 30097	678-325-4500	R	425*	.4
35	WCI Communities Inc—*David L Fry*	24301 Walden Ctr Dr, Bonita Springs FL 34134	239-498-8200	R	422*	1.1
36	Matthews Homes—*Pat Matthews*	3202 W March Ln Ste A, Stockton CA 95219	209-951-5444	R	401*	.2
37	Shapell Industries Inc—*Nathan Shapell*	8383 Wilshire Blvd Ste, Beverly Hills CA 90211	323-655-7330	R	378*	.3
38	Highland Homes Inc—*Rodger Sanders*	5601 Democracy Dr Ste, Plano TX 75024	972-789-3500	R	353*	.3
39	Fieldstone Communities Inc—*Frank S Foster*	2 Ada, Irvine CA 92618	949-790-5400	R	345*	.2
40	McBride and Son Enterprises Inc—*Richard Sullivan*	1 McBride and Son Corp, Chesterfield MO 63005	636-537-2000	R	340*	1.0
41	Jones Co—*Richard J Dugas* Centex Homes	16640 Chesterfield Gro, Chesterfield MO 63005	636-537-7000	S	338*	.6
42	Ivory Homes A Utah LP—*Clark D Ivory*	978 Woodoak Ln, Salt Lake City UT 84117	801-747-7000	R	330*	.1
43	Reynen and Bardis Development LLC—*John D Reynen*	9848 Business Park Dr, Sacramento CA 95827	916-366-3665	R	326	N/A
44	Olson Co—*Stephen E Olson*	3010 Old Ranch Pwky St, Seal Beach CA 90740	562-596-4770	R	306*	.3
45	Crosswinds Communities Inc—*Bernie Glieberman*	41050 Vincenti Ct, Novi MI 48375	248-615-1313	R	295*	.2
46	Sunrise Co—*William Bone*	300 Eagle Dance Cir, Palm Desert CA 92211	760-772-7227	R	255*	.3
47	Brighton Builders Inc	PO Box 500, Red Bank NJ 07701	732-383-2200	S	246*	.1
48	Homewood Corp—*John H Bain*	2700 E Dublin-Granvill, Columbus OH 43231	614-898-7200	R	241*	.4
49	Horst Group Inc—*Randall L Horst*	PO Box 3330, Lancaster PA 17604	717-581-9800	R	241*	.2
50	MJC Cos—*Michael A Chirco*	46600 Romeo Plank Rd S, Macomb MI 48044	586-263-1203	R	238	N/A
51	Ryan Building Group Inc—*William J Ryan*	945 N Plum Grove Rd St, Schaumburg IL 60173	847-995-8700	R	229*	.2
52	First Texas Homes—*Randall Van Wolfswinkel*	500 Crescent Ct Ste 35, Dallas TX 75201	214-613-3400	R	218*	.2
53	Century Vintage Homes—*John Pavelak*	1505 South D St Ste 20, San Bernardino CA 92408	909-381-6007	R	218*	.2
54	Landstar Development Corp—*Rudolfo Stern*	120 Fairway Woods Blvd, Orlando FL 32824	407-240-0044	R	204*	.2
55	Kalian Cos—*Patrick Kalian*	225 Hwy 35 Navesink N, Red Bank NJ 07701	732-741-0054	R	201*	.2
56	Hills Communities Inc—*Steven Guttman*	4901 Hunt Rd, Cincinnati OH 45242	513-984-0300	R	196*	.3
57	Mitchell Company Inc—*John B Saint*	PO Box 160306, Mobile AL 36616	251-380-2929	R	158	N/A
58	Pulte Homes of New Mexico Inc—*Richard Dugas* PulteGroup Inc	100 Bloomfield Hills P, Bloomfield Hills MI 48304	248-647-2750	S	152	N/A
59	Dominion Homes Inc—*Douglas G Borror*	PO Box 5000, Dublin OH 43016	614-356-5000	R	148	.2
60	Legend Home Corp—*Scott Bauer*	10410 Windermere Lakes, Houston TX 77065		R	148*	.1
61	First Home Builders of Florida Inc—*Ara Hovnanian*	1870 Colonial Blvd, Fort Myers FL 33907	239-458-8000	S	148	N/A
62	Aho Construction I Inc—*Melvin Aho*	5512 Ne 109th Ct Ste 1, Vancouver WA 98662	360-254-0493	R	145*	.1
63	Dan Ryan Builders—*Dan Ryan*	60 Thomas Johnson Dr, Frederick MD 21702	301-696-0200	R	143*	.2
64	Rottlund Company Inc—*David Rotter*	3065 Centre Pointe Dr, Roseville MN 55113	651-638-0500	R	137*	.1
65	Brayson Homes Inc—*Sonny Deavours*	780 Buford Hwy Bldg C, Suwanee GA 30024	770-831-2460	R	123*	.1
66	Westfield Homes USA Inc—*David Pelletz* Standard Pacific Corp	5100 W Lemon St Ste 30, Tampa FL 33609	813-282-1616	S	117*	.1
67	IDI Group Cos—*Giuseppe Cecchi*	1700 N Moore St Ste 20, Arlington VA 22209	703-558-7300	R	113*	.1
68	Corey Barton Homes—*Corey Barton*	PO Box 369, Meridian ID 83680	208-955-9900	R	110*	.1
69	Capital Pacific Holdings Inc—*Hadi Makarechian*	4100 MacArthur Blvd St, Newport Beach CA 92660	949-622-8400	R	109*	.1
70	Graham Cos—*Stuart Wyllie*	6843 Main St, Hialeah FL 33014	305-821-1130	R	109*	.7
71	Brown Family Communities LLC—*David M Brown*	2164 E Broadway Rd Ste, Tempe AZ 85282	480-921-1400	R	106*	.2
72	K Hovnanian Windward Homes LLC—*Ara K Hovnanian*	110 W Front St, Red Bank NJ 07701	813-885-7744	S	88*	.1
73	Plaster Development Company Inc—*Richard Plaster*	801 S Rancho Dr Ste E4, Las Vegas NV 89106	702-385-5031	R	83*	.1
74	Gehan Homes Ltd—*John Winneford*	14901 Quorum Dr, Dallas TX 75254	972-383-4300	R	83*	.1
75	Fulton Homes Inc—*Doug Fulton*	9140 S Kyrene Ste 202, Tempe AZ 85284	480-753-6789	R	82*	.1
76	Lake Erie Construction Co—*David Bleile*	PO Box 777, Norwalk OH 44857	419-668-3302	R	77*	.2
77	Hubble Homes—*Don Hubble*	701 S Allen St Ste 104, Meridian ID 83642	208-433-8800	R	65*	.1
78	Avatar Holdings Inc—*Jon M Donnell*	395 Village Dr, Poinciana FL 34759	863-427-7180	P	59	.2
79	Lakewood Homes Inc—*Buz Hoffman*	2700 W Higgins Rd Ste, Hoffman Estates IL 60169	847-884-8800	R	55*	.1
80	California Coastal Communities Inc—*Raymond J Pacini*	6 Executive Cir Ste 25, Irvine CA 92614	949-250-7700	R	47	<.1
81	Fox Ridge Homes of Tennessee Inc—*Paul Saville* NVR Inc	93 Seaboard Ln Ste 201, Brentwood TN 37027	615-377-6840	S	47*	.1

Rank	Company Name—*Executive Officer*	Address, City, State, Zip	Phone	Type	Fin	Empls
82	Ole South Properties Inc—*John D Floyd*	275 Robert Rose Dr, Murfreesboro TN 37129	615-896-0019	R	46*	<.1
83	Mulvaney Homes Inc—*Peter E Gilgan*	PO Box 7444, Charlotte NC 28241	704-375-9373	S	31*	<.1
84	Woodbridge Holdings Corp (Fort Lauderdale Florida)—*Alan B Levan*	PO Box 5403, Fort Lauderdale FL 33310	954-940-4950	S	26	.1
85	The Penna Group LLC—*Michael Evangelista-Ysasaga*	111 N Houston St Ste 2, Fort Worth TX 76102		R	16*	.3
86	Consolidated-Tomoka Land Co—*John Albright*	PO Box 10809, Daytona Beach FL 32120	386-274-2202	P	13	<.1
87	Jensen's Inc (Southington Connecticut)—*Kristian Jensen III*	PO Box 608, Southington CT 06489	860-793-0281	R	13*	.1
88	John Crosland Co—*Todd Mansfield*	227 W Trade St Ste 800, Charlotte NC 28202	704-529-1166	R	10	<.1
89	Ranon Construction—*Jason Dynan*	658 S Military Trail, Deerfield Beach FL 33442	954-427-1113	R	6*	<.1
90	Trine Construction Corp—*Michael Rendina*	27w364 N Ave, West Chicago IL 60185	630-668-4626	R	3*	<.1
91	Still Waters Design/Build Group—*Dinah Martinec*	7105 Golf Club Dr Ste, Fort Worth TX 76179	817-236-2090	R	2*	<.1

TOTALS: SIC 1531 Operative Builders
Companies: 91

					63,451	54.3

1541 Industrial Buildings & Warehouses

Rank	Company Name—*Executive Officer*	Address, City, State, Zip	Phone	Type	Fin	Empls
1	Bechtel Group Inc—*Riley P Bechtel*	PO Box 193965, San Francisco CA 94119	415-768-1234	R	15,559*	40.0
2	Turner Construction Co—*Peter Davoren*	375 Hudson St, New York NY 10014	212-229-6000	S	3,597*	5.0
3	McCarthy Building Companies Inc—*Michael D Bolen*	1341 N Rock Hill Rd, St Louis MO 63124	314-968-3300	R	3,500	4.8
4	Walbridge Aldinger Co—*John Rakolta Jr*	777 Woodward Ave Ste 3, Detroit MI 48226	313-963-8000	R	3,287*	2.0
5	Skanska USA Building Inc—*William Flemming*	1633 Littleton Rd, Parsippany NJ 07054	973-753-3500	S	2,969*	3.0
6	Parsons Corp—*Charles L Harrington*	100 W Walnut St, Pasadena CA 91124	626-440-2000	R	2,957*	10.0
7	Tishman Realty and Construction Company Inc—*Daniel R Tishman*	666 5th Ave, New York NY 10103	212-399-3600	R	2,868*	1.0
8	HBE Corp—*Fred S Kummer*	PO Box 419039, Saint Louis MO 63141	314-567-9000	R	2,841*	4.5
9	Day and Zimmermann Group Inc—*Harold L Yoh III*	1500 Spring Garden St, Philadelphia PA 19130	215-299-8000	R	2,400*	24.0
10	JE Dunn Construction Group Inc—*Terrence P Dunn*	1001 Locust St, Kansas City MO 64106	816-474-8600	R	2,300*	4.0
11	JE Dunn Construction—*Terrence P Dunn*	1001 Locust St, Kansas City MO 64106	816-474-8600	R	2,278*	2.7
12	Turner Industries Ltd—*Roland M Toups*	PO Box 2750, Baton Rouge LA 70821	225-922-5050	R	1,590*	15.0
13	TIC Holdings Inc—*Ronald W McKenzie*	PO Box 774848, Steamboat Springs CO 80477	970-879-2561	S	1,570*	9.0
14	Brasfield and Gorrie LLC—*Miller Gorrie*	PO Box 10383, Birmingham AL 35202	205-328-4000	R	1,508*	3.0
15	Barton Malow Co—*Ben C Maibach III*	26500 American Dr, Southfield MI 48034	248-436-5000	R	1,380*	1.3
16	Gilbane Inc—*Thomas Gilbane Jr*	7 Jackson Walkway, Providence RI 02903	401-456-5800	R	1,331*	1.9
17	Caddell Construction Company Inc—*John A Caddell*	PO Box 210099, Montgomery AL 36121	334-272-7723	R	1,189*	1.8
18	TIC - The Industrial Co—*Ron W McKenzie* TIC Holdings Inc	PO Box 774848, Steamboat Springs CO 80477	970-879-2561	S	1,134*	5.1
19	Yates Companies Inc—*William G Yates Jr*	PO Box 456, Philadelphia MS 39350	601-656-5411	R	1,123*	4.5
20	Opus Corp—*Mark Rauenhorst*	10350 Bren Rd W, Minnetonka MN 55343	952-656-4444	R	1,091*	.3
21	Weitz Group LLC—*Glenn H De Stigter*	5901 Thornton Ave, Des Moines IA 50321	515-698-4260	R	1,027*	1.4
22	Pepper Construction Companies LLC—*David Pepper*	643 N Orleans St, Chicago IL 60610	312-266-4700	R	913*	1.3
23	Kokosing Construction Company Inc—*William B Burgett*	PO Box 226, Fredericktown OH 43019	740-694-6315	R	911*	2.2
24	WG Yates and Sons Construction Co—*William G Yates Jr* Yates Companies Inc	One Gully Ave, Philadelphia MS 39350	601-656-5411	S	742*	3.0
25	Haskell Co—*Steve Halverson*	PO Box 44100, Jacksonville FL 32231	904-791-4500	R	718	1.0
26	Rudolph and Sletten Inc—*Martin B Sisemore*	1600 Seaport Blvd Ste, Redwood City CA 94063	650-216-3600	S	700*	.8
27	Austin Commercial Inc—*Ronald J Gafford*	1301 S Mopac Expy Ste, Austin TX 78746	512-306-9880	S	638*	1.0
28	Okland Construction Company Inc—*JRandy Okland*	1978 S W Temple, Salt Lake City UT 84115	801-486-0144	R	488*	.5
29	Flintco LLC—*David Kollmann*	1624 W 21st St, Tulsa OK 74107	918-587-8451	R	453*	.7
30	Manhattan Construction Co—*Leonard Rejchek*	6300 N Central Expy, Dallas TX 75206	214-357-7400	S	425*	.9
31	Kraus-Anderson Inc—*Bruce Engelsma*	523 S 8th St, Minneapolis MN 55404	612-305-2934	R	425*	.6
32	Walsh Construction—*George Anderson*	929 W Adams St, Chicago IL 60607	312-563-5400	S	424*	1.0
33	Berry Holdings LP—*Edward Martin*	PO Box 9908, Corpus Christi TX 78469	361-693-2100	R	421*	3.0
34	Stellar Group Inc—*Ronald H Foster Jr*	2900 Hartley Rd, Jacksonville FL 32257	904-260-2900	R	413*	1.0
35	Oscar J Boldt Construction Div—*Thomas J Boldt*	PO Box 419, Appleton WI 54912	920-739-6321	D	403*	2.0
36	O'Neil Industries Inc—*Richard Erickson*	2751 N Clybourn Ave, Chicago IL 60614	773-755-1611	R	367*	.5
37	McMillin Commercial	2750 Womble Rd, San Diego CA 92106	619-477-4117	S	342*	.5
38	Perini Building Company Inc—*Craig W Shaw*	2955 N Green Valley Pk, Henderson NV 89014	702-792-9209	S	337*	.7
39	Frank Messer and Sons Construction Co—*Peter Strange*	5158 Fishwick Dr, Cincinnati OH 45216	513-242-1541	R	314*	.5
40	SJ Amoroso Construction Company Inc—*Dana McManus*	390 Bridge Pkwy, Redwood City CA 94065	650-654-1900	R	300*	.4
41	Kimmins Contracting Corp—*Joseph M Williams*	1501 E 2nd Ave, Tampa FL 33605	813-248-3878	S	291*	.4
42	Sletten Inc—*Erik Sletten*	PO Box 2467, Great Falls MT 59403	406-761-7920	R	289*	.5
43	Seaboard Construction Group—*Vincent Fiore*	1518 Hwy 138, Wall NJ 07719	732-556-0080	R	270*	.1
44	Industrial Design and Construction—*Donald R Barden*	14061 Hwy 73, Prairieville LA 70769	225-343-1145	R	264*	.4
45	WA Klinger Inc—*Doug Ohlfest*	PO Box 8800, Sioux City IA 51102	712-277-3900	R	260*	.6
46	MB Kahn Construction Company Inc—*William H Neely*	PO Box 1179, Columbia SC 29202	803-736-2950	R	252*	.6
47	Powell Construction Company Inc—*James Powell*	3622 Bristol Hwy, Johnson City TN 37601	423-282-0111	R	246*	.5
48	Condon-Johnson and Associates Inc—*Gerard Condon*	PO Box 12368, Oakland CA 94604	510-636-2100	R	246*	.4
49	BMW Constructors Inc—*Brian Acton*	PO Box 22210, Indianapolis IN 46222	317-267-0400	R	245*	.6
50	Lauren Engineers and Constructors Inc—*C Cleve Whitener*	PO Box 1761, Abilene TX 79604	325-670-9660	R	235*	1.5
51	Doster Construction Company Inc—*T Duane Watson*	2100 International Par, Birmingham AL 35243	205-443-3800	R	207*	.5
52	BBL Construction Services LLC—*Kevin Gleason*	302 Washington Ave, Albany NY 12203	518-452-8200	S	206*	.5
53	Holder Construction Co—*Thomas Holder*	3333 Riverwood Pky SE, Atlanta GA 30339	770-988-3000	R	205*	.5
54	Horst Construction Company Inc—*Harry Scheid*	PO Box 3310, Lancaster PA 17604	717-581-9800	S	185*	.5
55	Reiman Corp—*TR (Tom) Reiman*	PO Box 1007, Cheyenne WY 82003	307-632-8971	R	183*	.3
56	Ruscilli Construction Company Inc—*L Jack Ruscilli*	2201 Arthur Ave, Columbus OH 43228	614-876-9484	R	180*	.2
57	Pacific Coast Steel—*David Perkins*	4805 Murphy Canyon Rd, San Diego CA 92123	858-737-7700	S	175*	1.0
58	Bast Hatfield Inc—*Kit Bast*	1399 Vischers Ferry Rd, Halfmoon NY 12065	518-373-2000	R	173*	.4
59	Tellepsen Builders LP—*Howard Tellepsen Jr*	777 Benmar Ste 400, Houston TX 77060	281-447-8100	R	166*	.4
60	Bette and Cring LLC	22 Century Hill Dr Ste, Latham NY 12110	518-213-1010	R	165*	.4
61	Tonn and Blank Construction—*Jon Glimore*	1623 Greenwood Ave, Michigan City IN 46360	219-879-7321	R	160*	.3
62	Berg Inc—*Robert B Hamm*	531 W 61 St, Shreveport LA 71106		R	152*	.4
63	FORTIS Construction Inc—*Jim Kilpatrick*	1705 SW Taylor St Ste, Portland OR 97205	503-459-4477	R	151*	.1
64	New South Construction Company Inc—*Douglas Davidson*	1132 W Peachtree St Nw, Atlanta GA 30309	404-443-4000	R	150*	.2
65	Geometrica Inc—*Francisco Castano*	12300 Dundee Ct Ste 20, Cypress TX 77429	832-220-1200	R	149*	.2
66	Dimeo Construction Co—*Bradford Dimeo*	75 Chapman St, Providence RI 02905	401-781-9800	R	149*	.2
67	Cox and Schepp Inc—*Robert Cox*	PO Box 36884, Charlotte NC 28236	704-716-2100	R	145*	.2
68	Winter Group of Cos—*Brent Reid*	191 Peachtree St NE St, Atlanta GA 30303	404-588-3300	R	144*	.4
69	CG Schmidt Inc—*Richard L Schmidt Jr*	PO Box 11609, Milwaukee WI 53211	414-577-1177	R	142*	.3
70	Bucon Inc—*Jan Lewis*	PO Box 419917, Kansas City MO 64141	816-245-6000	S	137*	.2
71	Conlon Construction Co—*Steve D Conlon*	PO Box 3400, Dubuque IA 52004	563-583-1724	R	134*	.2

Note: An asterisk (*) indicates an estimated financial figure. The company type code used is as follows: R = Private, P = Public, S = Private Subsidiary, B = Public Subsidiary, D = Division, J = Joint Venture, I = Investment Fund.

COMPANY RANKINGS BY SALES WITHIN 4-DIGIT SIC

Rank	Company Name—Executive Officer	Address, City, State, Zip	Phone	Type	Fin	Empls
72	BlueScope Construction Inc—Dan Kumm	PO Box 419917, Kansas City MO 64141	816-245-6000	S	133*	.2
73	Browning Construction Inc—Michael G Browning	6100 W 96th St Ste 250, Indianapolis IN 46278	317-344-7300	R	129*	<.1
74	Bethlehem Construction Inc—Michael Addleman	PO Box 505, Cashmere WA 98815	509-782-1001	R	126*	.2
75	Mcabee Construction Inc—Leroy Mcabee	PO Box 1460, Tuscaloosa AL 35403	205-349-2212	R	123*	.8
76	Architectural Utilities Inc—Doug Alumbaugh	PO Box 11586, Fort Worth TX 76110	817-926-4377	R	123*	.3
77	Opus US Corp—Tim Murnane	PO Box 59110, Minneapolis MN 55459	952-656-4444	R	120*	.3
78	Elkins Constructors Inc—Barry L Allred	701 W Adams St, Jacksonville FL 32204	904-353-6500	R	120*	.2
79	Performance Mechanical Inc—Don Silva	PO Box 1516, Pittsburg CA 94565	925-432-4080	S	117*	.7
80	MECS Global—PJ Desai	14522 S Outer Forty Rd, Chesterfield MO 63017	314-275-5700	R	117*	.4
81	WE O'Neil Construction Co—Richard Erickson O'Neil Industries Inc	2751 N Clybourn Ave, Chicago IL 60614	773-755-1611	S	115*	.1
82	H and M Construction Company Inc—Chris Carroll	PO Box 200, Jackson TN 38302	731-664-6300	R	109*	.3
83	Bond Brothers Inc—Edward A Bond Jr	145 Spring St, Everett MA 02149	617-387-3400	R	108*	.3
84	Sletten Construction of Nevada—Ron McCullough	5825 S Polaris Ave, Las Vegas NV 89118	702-739-8770	D	108*	.3
85	DeMaria Building Co—Richard DeMaria	3031 W Grand Blvd Ste, Detroit MI 48202	248-348-9720	R	107*	.2
86	Alvarado Construction Inc—Linda G Alvarado	1266 Santa Fe Dr, Denver CO 80204	303-629-0783	R	106*	.2
87	Nab Construction Corp—Gary Simpson	11220 14th Ave, College Point NY 11356	718-762-0001	R	104*	.4
88	GE Johnson Construction Company Inc—James M Johnson	25 N Cascade Ave Ste 4, Colorado Springs CO 80904	719-473-5321	R	104*	.3
89	Martin-Harris Construction Enterprises Inc—Frank Martin	3030 S Highland Dr, Las Vegas NV 89109	702-385-5257	R	102*	.3
90	Klinger Constructors LLC—Tom Novak	PO Box 90850, Albuquerque NM 87199	505-822-9990	S	101*	.1
91	RM Shoemaker Co—John K Ball	PO Box 888, West Conshohocken PA 19428	610-941-5500	R	100*	.1
92	BGI Contractors Inc—AB Bernard	PO Box 22077, Beaumont TX 77720	409-833-0303	R	96*	.2
93	ASW Services Inc—Andre Thornton	3375 Gilchrist Rd, Mogadore OH 44260	330-733-6291	R	95*	.2
94	R and H Construction Co—John Bradley	1530 SW Taylor St, Portland OR 97205	503-228-7177	R	90*	.3
95	TE Ibberson Co—Steve Kimes	828 5th St S, Hopkins MN 55343	952-938-7007	R	89*	.3
96	Morganti Group—Gerry Kelly	1450 Centrepark Blvd S, West Palm Beach FL 33401	561-689-0200	S	85*	.2
97	Congleton Hacker Co—Larry Cowgill	PO Box 22640, Lexington KY 40577	859-254-6481	R	83*	.2
98	Toledo Engineering Company Inc—Fred Paulson	PO Box 2927, Toledo OH 43606	419-537-9711	S	83*	.2
99	Greenfield Builders Inc	6831 E 32nd St Ste 300, Indianapolis IN 46226	317-860-2940	R	83	<.1
100	Saxon Group Inc—Jeni Bogdan	790 Brogdon Rd, Suwanee GA 30024	770-271-2174	R	82	.3
101	Wolverine Building Group—Michael Kelly	4045 Barden SE, Grand Rapids MI 49512	616-949-3360	R	81*	.1
102	Inman Construction Corp—Page Inman	88 Union Ave Ste 400, Memphis TN 38103	901-682-4100	S	80*	.2
103	Epoch Management Inc—James H Pugh	359 Carolina Ave, Winter Park FL 32789	407-629-5004	R	80*	.1
104	Kraemer Brothers LLC—Norm Kraemer	925 Park Ave, Plain WI 53577	608-546-2411	R	76*	.3
105	Albert M Higley Co—Bruce G Higley	2926 Chester Ave, Cleveland OH 44114	216-861-2050	R	75*	.2
106	Shelco Inc—D Edwin Rose	5016 Parkway Plz Blvd, Charlotte NC 28217	704-367-5613	R	75*	.2
107	MW Builders Inc—Peter Kelley	10955 Lowell Ave Ste 3, Overland Park KS 66210	913-345-0007	S	73*	.2
108	RL Turner Corp—Greg Turner	PO Box 40, Zionsville IN 46077	317-873-2712	R	73*	.2
109	Ragnar Benson Inc—Marty Guimon	250 S Norhtwest Hwy, Park Ridge IL 60068	847-698-4900	S	72*	.2
110	Cleary Building Corp—Sean Cleary	PO Box 930220, Verona WI 53593	608-845-9700	R	71*	.9
111	LYDIG Construction Inc—Larry Swartz	11001 E Montgomery, Spokane Valley WA 99206	509-534-0451	R	71*	.3
112	Law Company Inc—Richard Kerschen	PO Box 1139, Wichita KS 67201	316-268-0200	R	70*	.2
113	Alder Construction Co—Bruce Alder	3939 S 500 W, Salt Lake City UT 84123	801-266-8856	R	70*	.2
114	Williams Development and Construction Inc—Craig Williams	8990 Hempstead Hwy Ste, Houston TX 77008	713-683-8444	R	70*	.1
115	McCrory Construction Company LLC—Allen Amsler	PO Box 145, Columbia SC 29202	803-799-8100	R	68*	.2
116	BSI Constructors Inc—Paul Shaughnessy	6767 Southwest Ave, Saint Louis MO 63143	314-781-7820	R	66*	.1
117	EF Wall and Associates Inc—Joseph Bordas	PO Box 259, Barre VT 05641	802-479-1013	R	66*	.1
118	Benchmark Group Inc—Isha Francis	4053 Maple Rd Ste 200, Amherst NY 14226	716-833-4986	R	65*	.3
119	Embrey Partners Ltd—Walter M Embrey	1020 NE Loop 410 Ste 7, San Antonio TX 78209	210-824-6044	R	65*	.1
120	Armada/Hoffler Construction Co—Louis S Haddad	222 Central Park Ave S, Virginia Beach VA 23462	757-366-4000	R	63*	.2
121	Gamma Construction Co—Keith Williams	PO Box 22047, Houston TX 77227	713-963-0086	R	63*	.1
122	JE Abercrombie Inc—JE Abercrombie	9111 Galveston Ave, Jacksonville FL 32211	904-724-4471	R	63*	.1
123	VRH Construction Corp—Victor D Wortmann Jr	320 Grand Ave, Englewood NJ 07631	201-871-4422	R	63*	.1
124	Ozanne Construction Company Inc—Dominic Ozanne	1635 E 25th St, Cleveland OH 44114	216-696-2876	R	63*	<.1
125	C Overaa and Co—Jerry Overaa	200 Parr Blvd, Richmond CA 94801	510-234-0926	R	62*	.2
126	GL Morris General Building Co—GL Morris	PO Box 3632, Chatsworth CA 91313	818-341-5135	R	62*	.2
127	Rogers-O'Brien Construction Co—Preston L McAfee	1901 Regal Row, Dallas TX 75235	214-962-3000	R	62*	.2
128	Scrufari Construction Company Inc—Gary Sankes	3925 Hyde Park Blvd, Niagara Falls NY 14305	716-282-1225	R	62*	.2
129	Weaver-Bailey Contractors Inc—Charles T Weaver	PO Box 60, El Paso AR 72045	501-796-2301	R	62*	.2
130	Whitesell Construction Company Inc—Robert A Richards	PO Box 1605, Delran NJ 08075	856-764-2600	R	62	.1
131	Herm Hughes and Sons Inc—GE Hughes	PO Box 540700, North Salt Lake UT 84054	801-292-1411	R	61*	.3
132	Ruhlin Co—Jim Ruhlin	PO Box 190, Sharon Center OH 44274	330-239-2800	R	60*	.4
133	Henry Carlson Co—Henry Carlson III	1205 W Russell St, Sioux Falls SD 57104	605-336-2410	R	60*	.1
134	Levernier Construction Inc—Paul Levernier	7620 E Spear Ave, Spokane Valley WA 99212	509-927-3000	R	60*	.1
135	Dawson Building Contractors Inc—Judd Dawson	106 Rainbow Industrial, Rainbow City AL 35906	256-442-7280	R	59	.1
136	Williams Co (Orlando Florida)—Bruce Williams	2301 Silver Star Rd, Orlando FL 32804	407-295-2530	R	58*	.1
137	Pinkard Construction Co—Jim W Pinkard Jr	9195 W 6th Ave, Lakewood CO 80215	303-986-4555	R	57*	.2
138	RS Mowery and Sons Inc—Donald H Mowery	1000 Bent Creek Blvd, Mechanicsburg PA 17050	717-506-1000	R	56*	.1
139	Abrams Power Inc—Alan R Abrams	1945 The Exchange Ste, Atlanta GA 30339	770-953-0304	S	56*	.1
140	Smoot Construction—Lewis Smoot Sr	1907 Leonard Ave, Columbus OH 43219	614-253-9000	R	52*	.1
141	Sun Builders Co—Gilda Aiello Thompson	5870 Hwy 6 N Ste 206, Houston TX 77084	281-815-1020	R	51*	.1
142	Brookstone Corp—Steve J Dishman	3715 Dacoma St, Houston TX 77092	713-683-8800	R	51*	.1
143	Commerce Construction Company Inc—Edward Roski	13191 Crossroads Pky N, City of Industry CA 91746	562-692-9581	R	50*	.1
144	Dan Vos Construction Co—Gordon DeYoung	PO Box 189, Ada MI 49301	616-676-9169	R	50*	.1
145	Miller-Davis Co (Kalamazoo Michigan)—Rex Bell	1029 Portage St, Kalamazoo MI 49001	269-345-3561	R	48*	<.1
146	Commodore Builders—Joe Albanese	80 Bridge St, Newton MA 02458	617-614-3500	R	47*	.1
147	Blach Construction Co—Mike Blach	469 El Camino Real Ste, Santa Clara CA 95050	408-244-7100	R	47*	.1
148	Tuttle Construction Inc—Clyde R Rauch	PO Box 1153, Lima OH 45802	419-228-6262	R	46*	.2
149	Stevens Painton Corp—Tom Snyder	7850 Freeway Cir Ste 1, Cleveland OH 44130	440-234-7888	R	45*	.3
150	SSI Inc—Leo Anhalt	2817 S Yuma St, Fort Smith AR 72901	479-646-2901	R	45*	.2
151	Bartlett Brainard Eacott Inc—James H Eacott III	70 Griffin Rd S, Bloomfield CT 06002	860-242-5565	R	45*	.1
152	Wright Construction Group—Fred Edman	5811 Youngquist Rd, Fort Myers FL 33912	239-481-5000	R	45*	<.1
153	Structural Associates Inc—Dennis Weller	5903 Fisher Rd, East Syracuse NY 13057	315-463-0001	R	44*	.1
154	Cincinnati United Contractors Inc—Charles Kubicki	7175 E Kemper Rd, Cincinnati OH 45249	513-677-0060	R	43*	.1
155	BRB Contractors Inc—Michael C Welch	PO Box 750940, Topeka KS 66675	785-232-1245	R	42*	.3
156	Alex E Paris Contracting Company Inc—Alex Paris III	1595 Smith Twp State R, Atlasburg PA 15004	724-947-2235	R	42*	.1
157	Emerick Construction Co—Larry Sitz	PO Box 66100, Portland OR 97290	503-777-5531	R	42*	.1
158	Site Development Inc—Leonard Theisen	30850 Stephenson Hwy, Madison Heights MI 48071	248-583-1200	R	42*	.1
159	Summit Builders Construction Co—Jeffery C Stone	3333 E Camelback Rd St, Phoenix AZ 85018	602-840-7700	R	42*	.1

Rank	Company Name—*Executive Officer*	Address, City, State, Zip	Phone	Type	Fin	Empls
160	Wickersham Construction and Engineering Inc—*Bradford B Smith*	PO Box 4397, Lancaster PA 17604	717-397-8282	R	42*	.1
161	BH Craig Construction Company Inc—*Dave Marbury*	835 Wall St, Florence AL 35630	256-766-3350	R	41*	.1
162	Frank Mercede and Sons Inc—*Frank J Mercede*	1200 High Ridge Rd, Stamford CT 06905	203-322-8000	R	41*	.1
163	Lippert Brothers Inc—*Rick Lippert*	PO Box 17450, Oklahoma City OK 73136	405-478-3580	R	41*	.1
164	SDB Inc—*Dominic Spagnuolo*	810 W 1st St, Tempe AZ 85281	480-967-5810	R	41*	.1
165	Hyder Construction Inc—*Thomas N McLagan*	543 Santa Fe Dr, Denver CO 80204	303-825-1313	R	41*	<.1
166	DAW TECH—*James C Collings*	1600 W 2200 S Ste 201, Salt Lake City UT 84119	801-977-3100	R	41	.2
167	AKM LLC—*LaVerne King*	17474 Old Jefferson Hw, Prairieville LA 70769	225-753-5713	R	40*	.6
168	Hunzinger Construction Co—*John Hunzinger*	21100 Enterprise Ave, Brookfield WI 53045	262-797-0797	R	40*	.1
169	AJ Martini Inc—*Peter Martini*	5 Lowell Ave, Winchester MA 01890	781-569-6900	R	40*	.1
170	Glenn and Wright Inc—*Francis Glenn*	PO Box 100339, Birmingham AL 35210	205-836-0188	R	39*	.3
171	Jokake Construction Co—*Rozlyn Lipsey*	5013 E Washington Ste, Phoenix AZ 85034	602-224-4500	R	39*	.1
172	RW Setterlin Building Co—*Rob Setterlin*	560 Harmon Ave, Columbus OH 43223	614-459-7077	R	38*	.1
173	Spaw-Glass Construction Corp—*Joel Stone*	13800 West Rd, Houston TX 77041	281-970-5300	S	37*	.1
174	Rand Construction Co—*Kenneth M Hageman*	1428 W 9th St, Kansas City MO 64101	816-421-4143	R	37*	.1
175	FCL Builders Inc—*Michael J Boro*	1150 Spring Lake Dr, Itasca IL 60143	630-773-0050	R	37*	.1
176	Bonnette Page and Stone Corp—*Randy Remick*	91 Bisson Ave, Laconia NH 03246	603-524-3411	R	37*	.1
177	Riverstar Inc—*Stephen Craney*	1705 Wilkie Dr, Winona MN 55987	507-452-5109	R	36*	<.1
178	Hickory Construction Co—*Mark Baucom*	PO Box 1769, Hickory NC 28603	828-322-9234	R	36*	.1
179	RT Dooley Construction Co—*David Dooley*	4024 Barringer Dr, Charlotte NC 28217	704-527-6111	S	36*	.1
180	Kirco Manix—*Douglas Manix*	101 W Big Beaver Rd St, Troy MI 48084	248-354-5100	R	36*	.1
181	DeMattia Group—*Gary D Roberts*	45501 Helm St, Plymouth MI 48170	734-453-2000	R	35*	.1
182	Clark and Sullivan Constructors Inc—*BJ Sullivan*	4180 W Dewey Dr, Las Vegas NV 89118	702-798-5400	R	35*	<.1
183	Polu Kai Services LLC—*Sean Jensen*	137 N Washington St St, Falls Church VA 22046	703-533-0039	R	33	.1
184	Delta Fabrication And Machine Inc—*Gerald Williams*	PO Box 980, Daingerfield TX 75638	903-645-3458	R	31*	.2
185	Charles A Gaetano Construction Corp—*Charles A Gaetano*	258 Genesee St Mezanin, Utica NY 13502	315-733-4611	R	31*	.1
186	Culp Construction Co—*Charles H Culp*	2320 S Main St, Salt Lake City UT 84115	801-486-2064	R	31*	.1
187	SEDALCO Inc—*Tom Kader*	2554 E Long Ave, Fort Worth TX 76137		R	31*	.1
188	ARCO Construction Company Inc—*Richard Schultze*	380 Interstate N Pkwy, Atlanta GA 30339	770-541-1700	R	31*	.1
189	Dunlap and Company Inc—*Dennis E King*	PO Box 328, Columbus IN 47202	812-376-3021	R	30*	.2
190	Ben M Radcliff Contractor Inc—*Ben M Radcliff Jr*	PO Box 8368, Mobile AL 36689	251-666-7252	R	30*	.1
191	Graycor Industrial Constructors Inc	2 Mid America Plz Ste, Oakbrook Terrace IL 60181	630-684-7110	S	29*	.1
192	O'Harrow Construction—*Marv Swanson*	4575 Ann Arbor Rd, Jackson MI 49202	517-764-4770	R	29*	.1
193	Commercial Building Specialists Inc—*Mike Frasinetti*	401 Derek Pl, Roseville CA 95678	916-780-9680	R	29*	.1
194	Tesoro Corp—*Dennis Gilbert*	520 S Independence Blv, Virginia Beach VA 23452	757-518-8491	S	28*	.1
195	RACO General Contractors Inc—*Kevin Cleveland*	1401 Dalon Rd NE, Atlanta GA 30306	404-873-3567	R	28*	.1
196	Stanker and Galetto Inc—*Peter Galetto Jr*	317 W Elmer Rd, Vineland NJ 08360	856-692-8098	R	28*	<.1
197	Denver Commercial Builders Inc—*John R Barna Jr*	909 E 62nd Ave, Denver CO 80216	303-287-5525	R	28*	<.1
198	Global Performance—*Dennis Braasch*	30 Patewood Dr Ste 200, Greenville SC 29615	864-288-3009	R	27*	.1
199	Burlington Construction Company Inc—*Roderic M Oneglia*	67 Prospect St, Torrington CT 06790	860-482-5017	R	27*	<.1
200	Ellis Stone Construction Company Inc—*Jim Anderson*	PO Box 366, Stevens Point WI 54481	715-345-5000	R	26*	.1
201	Arizona Building Systems Inc—*Deborah M Dubree*	3636 E Anne St Ste A, Phoenix AZ 85040	602-437-0371	R	26*	.1
202	San Antonio Constructors Inc—*Roy Heath*	PO Box 682008, San Antonio TX 78268	210-681-0211	R	26*	.1
203	Borton LC—*Wayne Stewart*	PO Box 2108, Hutchinson KS 67504	620-669-8211	R	25*	.3
204	Clark DCC Builders LLC	PO Box 521108, Longwood FL 32752	407-834-3300	S	25*	.1
205	Eric F Anderson Inc—*Don K Anderson*	PO Box 2076, San Leandro CA 94577	510-430-8404	R	25*	.1
206	Fogel-Anderson Construction Co—*Ted A Anderson*	1212 E 8th St, Kansas City MO 64106	816-842-6914	R	25*	.1
207	Matt Construction Services Inc	6600 Grant Ave, Cleveland OH 44105	216-641-0030	S	25*	.1
208	Jack Jennings and Sons Inc—*Toni Jennings*	1030 Wilfred Dr, Orlando FL 32803	407-896-8181	R	25*	<.1
209	Bse Industrial Contractors Inc—*Randy Whisonant*	PO Box 5563, Birmingham AL 35207	205-254-8027	R	25*	.2
210	Ayuda Management Corp—*Maria Vogt*	11800 Ridge Pky Ste 55, Broomfield CO 80021	303-999-2020	R	24	<.1
211	DeLuca Enterprises Inc—*Alfonso DeLuca*	370 East Maple Ave Ste, Langhorne PA 19047	215-860-6500	R	24*	.1
212	Interwest Construction Company Inc—*Mark L Brown*	35 N Redwood Rd, North Salt Lake UT 84054	801-936-6200	R	24*	.1
213	Concorp Inc—*Randall McDavid*	PO Box 429, Nitro WV 25143	304-755-8178	R	23*	<.1
214	Alvin E Benike Inc—*John Benike*	PO Box 6547, Rochester MN 55903	507-288-6575	R	22*	.1
215	Dyad Constructors Inc—*Joe Pigford*	8505 Holt St, Houston TX 77054	713-799-9380	R	22*	.1
216	Ellis-Walker Builders Inc—*J W Walker*	PO Box 41109, Fayetteville NC 28309	910-485-8111	R	22*	<.1
217	Liberty Building Systems Inc—*Anthony Idle*	1540 Genessee St, Kansas City MO 64102		S	22*	<.1
218	S and M Sakamoto Inc—*Gerard Sakamoto*	500 Alakawa St Ste 220, Honolulu HI 96817	808-456-4717	R	22*	<.1
219	Muskegon Construction Co—*Kevin Donovan*	111 W Western Ave, Muskegon MI 49442	231-726-3177	S	21*	.2
220	Dixie Southern Industrial Inc—*Grover Curry*	1060 N Commonwealth Av, Polk City FL 33868	863-984-1900	R	21*	.1
221	Benchmark Development Corp—*Marty DelleBovi* Benchmark Group Inc	4053 Maple Rd Ste 200, Amherst NY 14226	716-832-4986	S	21*	.1
222	Hale-Mills Construction Inc—*Kendall Phinney*	3700 Buffalo Speedway, Houston TX 77098	713-665-1100	R	21*	.1
223	Peris Companies Inc—*Jeffrey R Pellegrino*	282 N Washington St, Falls Church VA 22046	703-533-4700	R	21*	.1
224	RT Milord Co—*Mike Thomas*	9801 S Industrial Dr, Bridgeview IL 60455	708-598-7900	R	21*	<.1
225	Sheridan Corp—*Bradley Nelson*	PO Box 359, Fairfield ME 04937	207-453-9311	R	20*	<.1
226	Beam Construction Company Inc—*Susan Lewis*	PO Box 129, Cherryville NC 28021	704-435-3206	R	20*	.2
227	Jarvis Downing and Emch Inc—*Kim Carfagna*	PO Box 6253, Wheeling WV 26003	304-232-5000	R	20*	.1
228	Linde-Griffith Construction Co—*Raymond A Finley*	152 Passaic St, Newark NJ 07104	973-481-1106	R	20*	.1
229	Wade Construction—*Michael W Lackey*	2950 Country Pkwy Ste, San Antonio TX 78216	210-490-9000	R	20*	.1
230	James Steele Construction Co—*Richard Naughton*	1410 Sylvan St, Saint Paul MN 55117	651-488-6755	R	20*	<.1
231	Hauptly Construction and Equipment Company Inc—*Carroll Hauptly*	2906 Violet Dr, Waterloo IA 50701	319-240-7253	R	20*	<.1
232	Milestone Construction Services Inc—*Keith Whitener*	21495 Ridgetop Cir Ste, Sterling VA 20166	703-406-0960	R	20*	<.1
233	Zandri Construction Corp—*Richard Zandri*	PO Box 140, Cohoes NY 12047	518-237-1411	R	20*	<.1
234	Zellner Construction Company Inc	3252 Linda Dr, Memphis TN 38118	901-794-1100	R	20*	<.1
235	Kjellstrom and Lee Inc—*Don Garber* Gilbane Inc	1607 Ownby Ln, Richmond VA 23220	804-288-0082	S	19*	<.1
236	Duffey Construction Company Inc—*Robert B Talley*	1395 NW 21st St, Miami FL 33142	305-325-0001	R	19*	<.1
237	Brae Burn Construction Co—*Timothy Pixley*	PO Box 742288, Houston TX 77274	713-777-0063	R	19*	.1
238	HG Reynolds Company Inc—*Jeffrey G Reynolds*	PO Box 2728, Aiken SC 29802	803-641-1401	R	18*	.1
239	Speegle Construction Inc—*Troy D Speegle*	210 Government Ave, Niceville FL 32578	850-729-2484	R	18*	.1
240	Erhardt Construction Co—*Joseph P Erhardt*	PO Box 208, Ada MI 49301	616-676-1222	R	18	.1
241	CMI Construction Inc—*Mike Mason*	11279 Perry Hwy Ste 50, Wexford PA 15090	724-934-8000	S	18*	.1
242	Edison Foard Inc—*Edison Cassels*	PO Box 19888, Charlotte NC 28219	704-329-8000	R	18*	<.1
243	Jackson Builders Inc—*Tim Robbins*	PO Box 148, Goldsboro NC 27533	919-734-5428	R	18*	<.1
244	Swindell-Dressler International Co—*James Hopkins*	5100 Casteel Dr, Coraopolis PA 15108	412-788-7100	R	18*	.1

Note: An asterisk (*) indicates an estimated financial figure. The company type code used is as follows: R = Private, P = Public, S = Private Subsidiary, B = Public Subsidiary, D = Division, J = Joint Venture, I = Investment Fund.

COMPANY RANKINGS BY SALES WITHIN 4-DIGIT SIC

Rank	Company Name—*Executive Officer*	Address, City, State, Zip	Phone	Type	Fin	Empls
245	Pickus Construction and Equipment Company Inc—*James L Pickus*	3330 Skokie Valley Rd, Highland Park IL 60035	847-681-8811	R	17*	.1
246	Borghesi Building and Engineering Co—*Allan R Borghesi*	2155 E Main St, Torrington CT 06790	860-482-7613	R	17*	<.1
247	Geis Construction Co—*Erwin Geis*	10020 Aurora Hudson Rd, Streetsboro OH 44241	330-528-3500	R	16*	<.1
248	Bouten Construction Co—*Bill Bouten*	PO Box 3507, Spokane WA 99220	509-535-3531	R	16*	<.1
249	George C Hopkins Construction Company Inc—*Gary Hopkins*	919 W Glenoaks Blvd, Glendale CA 91202	818-956-0533	R	16*	<.1
250	Renfrow Brothers Inc—*William Renfrow*	PO Box 4786, Spartanburg SC 29305	864-579-0558	R	15*	.1
251	ACC Construction Company Inc—*Mason McKnight III*	PO Box 211900, Augusta GA 30917	706-868-1037	R	15*	.1
252	ARB Inc (Paramount California)	26000 Commercentre Dr, Lake Forest CA 92630	949-598-9242	S	15*	.1
253	SubZero Constructors Inc—*Dean Soll*	30055 Comercio, Rancho Santa Margarita CA 92688	949-216-9500	R	15*	.1
254	TU Parks Construction Co—*Larry S Parks*	PO Box 3308, Chattanooga TN 37404	423-648-3800	R	15*	.1
255	Bascon Inc—*Frank Tamanko*	607 Redna Ter Ste 500, Cincinnati OH 45215	513-772-1674	R	15*	<.1
256	Magill Construction Company Inc—*Steve Knudson*	977 Koopman Ln, Elkhorn WI 53121	262-723-2283	R	15*	<.1
257	Industrial Construction Co (Cleveland Ohio)—*Walter Kerr*	10060 Brecksville Rd, Cleveland OH 44141	440-746-9200	R	14*	.1
258	Joseph Schmitt and Sons Construction Company Inc—*Steven J Schmitt*	2104 Union Ave, Sheboygan WI 53082	920-457-4426	R	14*	.1
259	Dill Construction Company Inc—*Stella S Ridilla*	PO Box 472, Latrobe PA 15650	724-537-3386	R	14*	<.1
260	Roepnack Corp—*Robert A Roepnack*	3195 N Powerline Rd St, Pompano Beach FL 33069	954-691-2400	R	14*	<.1
261	Willard Dunham Construction Co—*Clifford Dunham Jr*	85 Tyler Pl, South Plainfield NJ 07080	908-226-5533	R	13*	.1
262	Concorde Construction Co—*David Privitera*	2015 Ayrsley Town Blvd, Charlotte NC 28273	407-583-2116	R	13*	<.1
263	deb Construction Inc—*Adam A Vali*	2230 E Winston Rd, Anaheim CA 92806	714-632-6680	R	13*	<.1
264	Morgen and Oswood Construction Company Inc—*Gregory A Oswood*	PO Box 3009, Great Falls MT 59403	406-761-1420	R	13*	<.1
265	Curtis-Layer Construction Co—*Michael J Curtis*	PO Box 404, Aurora OH 44202	330-562-5269	R	13*	<.1
266	Retrotech Inc—*David Reh*	PO Box 586, Fishers NY 14453	585-924-6333	R	12*	.1
267	O'Connor Constructors Inc—*Thomas H O'Connor Jr*	45 Industrial Dr, Canton MA 02021	617-364-9000	R	12*	.1
268	Sun Construction and Design Services Inc—*Stephen B Strong*	1232 Boston Ave, Longmont CO 80501	303-444-4780	R	12*	.1
269	Smith and Green Construction Company Inc—*Dick Lowrey*	PO Box 727, Dalton GA 30722	706-278-4959	R	12*	<.1
270	Elder Construction Company Inc—*David Elder*	10197 Bunsen Way, Louisville KY 40299	502-491-8005	R	12*	<.1
271	Harold Macquinn Inc—*Ronald Macquinn*	PO Box 789, Ellsworth ME 04605	207-667-4653	R	11*	.1
272	Triad Corp—*J Wood*	1007 E Main St, Chattanooga TN 37408	423-267-2288	R	11*	.1
273	John T Jones Construction Co—*Jeffrey Jones*	PO Box 2424, Fargo ND 58108	701-232-3358	R	10*	.1
274	Vanman Companies Architects and Builders Inc—*Jack Holmes*	669 Winnetka Ave N, Minneapolis MN 55427	763-541-9552	R	10*	<.1
275	CF Haglin Sons—*Gary Gunderson*	3939 W 69th St, Edina MN 55435	952-920-6123	R	9*	.1
276	Brencal Contractors Inc—*Charles J Brickel*	6686 E McNichols Rd, Detroit MI 48212	313-365-4300	R	9*	.1
277	CPM Construction Planning and Management Inc—*Jerry Williams*	10053 N Hague Rd, Indianapolis IN 46256	317-842-8040	R	9*	<.1
278	Hillhouse Construction—*Kenneth B Huesby*	140 Charcot Ave, San Jose CA 95131	408-467-1000	R	9*	<.1
279	JD Taylor Construction—*James D Taylor III*	PO Box 155, Syracuse NY 13206	315-463-5204	R	9*	<.1
280	P and C Construction Co—*Steve Malany*	2133 NW York St, Portland OR 97210	503-665-0165	R	9*	<.1
281	Laughlin-Sutton Construction Co—*Steve Ambrose*	PO Box 13226, Greensboro NC 27415	336-375-0095	H	8*	.1
282	Dynamic Construction Inc—*Mark Gray*	172 Coors Blvd, Pataskala OH 43062	740-927-8898	R	8*	<.1
283	Construction Supervisors Inc—*Ron Mostyn*	4545 Bissonnet Ste 110, Bellaire TX 77401	713-667-0123	R	8*	<.1
284	EW Thorpe Inc—*EW Thorpe*	6600 Koll Center Pky S, Pleasanton CA 94566	925-846-3500	R	8*	<.1
285	Construction Ltd—*Timothy Dixon*	1825 Upland Dr, Houston TX 77043	713-984-9444	R	8*	<.1
286	Costanza Contracting Co—*John Costanza*	PO Box 2370, Cherry Hill NJ 08034	856-489-1850	R	7*	<.1
287	Canyon Construction Corp—*James Ferrell*	5712 Industry Ln Ste F, Frederick MD 21704	301-694-6686	R	7*	<.1
288	Jos L Muscarelle Inc—*Joseph L Muscarelle Jr*	Essex St Rte 17, Maywood NJ 07607	201-845-8100	R	7*	<.1
289	Smith's Machine and Welding Company Inc—*Shelby Smith*	PO Box 470, Brookhaven MS 39602	601-833-8787	R	6*	<.1
290	D and W Industries Inc—*Dale Kelling*	1401 N Ellis Rd, Sioux Falls SD 57107	605-336-0435	R	6*	<.1
291	Duggins Construction Inc—*Jim Duggins*	341 W Crown Ct, Imperial CA 92251	760-352-5600	R	6*	<.1
292	JW Bailey Construction Co—*W R Bailey*	PO Box 506, Santa Barbara CA 93102	805-963-1855	R	6*	<.1
293	Murphy Consolidated Industries Inc—*Alan McLaughlin*	PO Box 687, Follansbee WV 26037	304-527-0426	R	6*	<.1
294	Construction and Service Solutions Corp—*Suzanne Witnauer*	700 Howard St, Buffalo NY 14206	716-852-1219	R	6	<.1
295	Rock Hill Industrial Piping and Fabrication Inc—*Dean Archie*	450 Hall Spencer Rd, Catawba SC 29704	803-329-4781	R	6*	.1
296	Andrew General Contractors Inc—*Todd Andrew*	2301 Mercator Dr, Orlando FL 32807	407-681-7070	R	5*	<.1
297	Bonitz Contracting Co—*Tom Banks*	PO Box 82, Columbia SC 29202	803-799-0181	R	5*	<.1
298	James Luterbach Construction Company Inc—*Bill Luterbach*	2880 S 171st St, New Berlin WI 53151	262-782-1990	R	4*	<.1
299	Dunn Investment Co—*James S Overstreet Jr*	3900 Airport Hwy, Birmingham AL 35222	205-592-8908	R	4*	<.1
300	Pyramid Building Systems Inc—*Jay Hedges*	4775 N Fwy, Fort Worth TX 76106	817-926-4377	R	4*	<.1
301	A and R Construction Inc—*Alvin Connerly*	PO Box 881, Lewiston ID 83501	208-746-3394	R	3*	<.1
302	Carmel Contractors Inc—*Scott Tuttle*	8030 England St, Charlotte NC 28273	704-552-2338	R	3*	<.1
303	Atkinson Construction Company Inc—*Larry Atkinson*	PO Box 1104, Marion SC 29571	843-423-4931	R	2*	<.1
304	Gilbert H Moen Co—*Donald G Moen*	516 S 5th Ave, Yakima WA 98902	509-248-8740	R	2*	<.1
305	Ultimate Solutions LLC—*Margaret Jenkins*	1183 E Laketon Ave, Muskegon MI 49442	231-722-1560	R	2*	<.1
306	T Gene Edwards Inc—*Gene Edwards*	1309 Appling St, Chattanooga TN 37406	423-629-5828	R	2*	<.1
307	Bosell Foods Inc—*Bernie Polen*	17212 Miles Ave, Cleveland OH 44128	216-991-7600	R	1*	<.1
308	Howell Metal Corp—*Ralph Blowe*	PO Box 220, Murfreesboro NC 27855	252-398-4048	R	1*	<.1
309	Myers and Crow Company Ltd—*J Marc Myers*	3811 Turtle Creek Blvd, Dallas TX 75219	214-520-7800	R	1*	<.1
310	Quadrants Inc—*William G Clark*	30475 S Wixom Rd, Wixom MI 48393	248-960-3900	R	1*	<.1
311	Dogwood Industries LLC	PO Box 1491, Woodinville WA 98072	425-482-4422	R	1*	<.1
312	Iron Eagle Group Inc—*Michael J Bovalino*	448 W 37th St Ste 9G, New York NY 10018		P	<1	.1
313	McGraw/Kokosing Inc—*Chris Bergs* Kokosing Construction Company Inc	101 Clark Blvd, Middletown OH 45044	513-422-4521	S	N/A	.3

TOTALS: SIC 1541 Industrial Buildings & Warehouses
Companies: 313 | | | | | 82,810 | 204.7

1542 Nonresidential Construction Nec

Rank	Company Name—*Executive Officer*	Address, City, State, Zip	Phone	Type	Fin	Empls
1	Tutor Perini Corp—*Ronald N Tutor*	15901 Olden St, Sylmar CA 91342	818-362-8391	P	3,716	5.8
2	Turner Corp	901 Main St Ste 4900, Dallas TX 75202	214-915-9600	S	3,676*	3.0
3	Hensel Phelps Construction Co—*Jerry L Morgensen*	420 6th Ave, Greeley CO 80631	970-352-6565	R	2,950	2.3
4	Structure Tone Organization—*Robert Mullen*	770 Broadway, New York NY 10003	212-481-6100	R	2,592*	1.5
5	MA Mortenson Co—*Tom Gunkel*	700 Meadow Ln N, Minneapolis MN 55422	763-522-2100	R	2,512*	2.3
6	Clark Construction Group LLC—*Peter Forster*	7500 Old Georgetown Rd, Bethesda MD 20814	301-272-8100	R	2,425*	3.5
7	Whiting-Turner Contracting Co—*Willard Hackerman*	300 E Joppa Rd, Baltimore MD 21286	410-821-1100	R	2,359*	1.7
8	Neosho Construction Company Inc	5 Penn Plaza, New York NY 10001	212-502-7900	S	2,358*	1.3
9	JE Dunn Construction Co—*Terrence B Dunn*	2000 S Colorado Blvd S, Denver CO 80222	303-753-8988	S	1,936*	4.0
10	Walsh Group Ltd—*Matthew M Walsh*	929 W Adams St, Chicago IL 60607	312-563-5400	R	1,714*	5.0
11	Austin Industries Inc—*Ronald J Gafford*	PO Box 1590, Dallas TX 75221	214-443-5500	R	1,700	5.6
12	Swinerton Inc—*Mike Re*	260 Townsend St, San Francisco CA 94107	415-421-2980	R	1,700*	1.4

Rank	Company Name—*Executive Officer*	Address, City, State, Zip	Phone	Type	Fin	Empls
13	Lincoln Property Co—*Tim Byrne*	2000 McKinney Ave Ste, Dallas TX 75201	214-740-3300	R	1,530*	5.0
14	AG Spanos Cos—*Alex G Spanos*	10100 Trinity Pkwy 5th, Stockton CA 95219	209-478-7954	R	1,411*	.6
15	Suffolk Construction Company Inc—*John F Fish*	65 Allerton St, Boston MA 02119	617-445-3500	R	1,360*	.8
16	Morette Company Inc—*Michael Morette*	1201 N Tarragona, Pensacola FL 32501	850-432-4084	R	1,267*	1.0
17	DPR Construction Inc—*Doug Woods*	1450 Veterans Blvd, Redwood City CA 94063	650-474-1450	R	1,238*	2.0
18	Webcor Builders Inc—*Andrew Ball*	207 King St Ste 300, San Francisco CA 94107	415-978-1000	S	1,196*	.8
19	Rudolph/Libbe Inc—*Tim Alter* Rudolph/Libbe Companies Inc	6494 Latcha Rd, Walbridge OH 43465 •	419-241-5000	S	1,141*	.5
20	Brand Energy Inc—*Paul T Wood*	1325 Cobb Internationa, Kennesaw GA 30152	678-285-1400	S	1,090*	12.3
21	Suitt Construction Company Inc—*Luther Cochrane* KBR Inc (Birmingham Alabama)	201 E McBee Ave Ste 40, Greenville SC 29601	864-250-5000	S	1,011*	.7
22	Mosser Construction Inc—*Robert Moyer* WMOG Inc	122 S Wilson Ave, Fremont OH 43420	419-334-3801	S	1,005*	.7
23	Plaza Construction Corp—*Steve Fisher*	260 Madison Ave, New York NY 10016	212-849-4800	R	984*	.5
24	KBR Inc (Birmingham Alabama)—*T Michael Goodrich*	2000 International Par, Birmingham AL 35243	205-972-6000	R	983*	7.4
25	US Engineering Co—*Tyler Nottberg*	3433 Roanoke Rd, Kansas City MO 64111	816-753-6969	R	877*	.6
26	Alberici Corp—*Gregory Kozicz*	8800 Page Ave, Saint Louis MO 63114	314-733-2000	R	839*	.4
27	Buford-Thompson Co—*Richard Thompson*	PO Box 150449, Arlington TX 76015	817-467-4981	R	698*	.3
28	New South Construction Co—*Douglas C Davidson*	1132 W Peachtree St NW, Atlanta GA 30309	404-443-4000	R	696*	.5
29	Bartlett Cocke Inc—*Randal J Pawelek*	8706 Lockway, San Antonio TX 78217	210-655-1031	R	687*	.3
30	Sundt Corp—*David Crawford*	2015 W River Rd Ste 10, Tucson AZ 85704	520-750-4600	R	657*	1.5
31	Danis Building Construction Co—*John Danis*	3233 Newmark Drive, Miamisburg OH 45342	937-228-1225	R	640*	1.5
32	Hagerman Construction Corp—*Mark Hagerman*	510 W Washington Blvd, Fort Wayne IN 46853	260-424-1470	S	637*	.4
33	Dick Corp—*David E Dick*	PO Box 10896, Pittsburgh PA 15236	412-384-1000	R	629*	2.0
34	Shawmut Design and Construction—*Thomas E Goemaat*	560 Harrison Ave, Boston MA 02118	617-622-7000	R	576*	.7
35	Sampson Construction Company Inc—*John Sampson*	3730 S 14th St, Lincoln NE 68502	402-434-5450	R	575*	.3
36	Kitchell Corp—*William C Schubert*	1707 E Highland Ave St, Phoenix AZ 85016	602-264-4411	R	500	.8
37	Layton Construction Co—*David Layton*	9090 S Sandy Pkwy, Sandy UT 84070	801-568-9090	R	492*	.8
38	Barnhart Inc—*Eric Stenman*	10760 Thornmint Rd, San Diego CA 92127	858-385-8200	R	485*	.3
39	Beck Group—*Peter Beck*	1807 Ross Ave Ste 500, Dallas TX 75201	214-303-6200	R	484*	.5
40	Haskell Corp—*Fred M Haskell*	PO Box 917, Bellingham WA 98227	360-734-1200	R	478*	.3
41	Hargrove and Associates—*Ralph A Hardgrove*	P O Box 2687, Mobile AL 36652	251-476-0605	R	469*	.3
42	Engelberth Construction Inc—*Pierre LaBlanc*	463 Mountain View Dr S, Colchester VT 05446	802-655-0100	R	463*	.2
43	Hoar Construction LLC—*Robert O Burton*	2 Metroplex Dr Ste 400, Birmingham AL 35209	205-803-2121	R	450*	.5
44	Hathaway Dinwiddie Construction Co—*Greg Cosko*	275 Battery St Ste 300, San Francisco CA 94111	415-986-2718	R	444*	.4
45	Wohlsen Construction Co—*Gary Langmuir*	PO Box 7000, Lancaster PA 17604	717-299-2500	R	441*	.2
46	Jaynes Corp—*Donald A Power*	2906 Broadway NE, Albuquerque NM 87101	505-345-8591	R	416*	.2
47	Henegan Construction Company Inc—*Maureen A Henegan*	250 W 30th St, New York NY 10001	212-947-6441	R	403*	.2
48	Clancy and Theys Construction Co—*Tim Clancy*	PO Box 27608, Raleigh NC 27611	919-834-3601	R	401*	.5
49	Vratsinas Construction Co—*Sam Alley*	PO Box 2558, Little Rock AR 72203	501-376-0017	R	400*	.2
50	Faulkner USA Inc—*Greg Eden*	PO Box 722, Austin TX 78767	512-652-4000	R	382*	.3
51	Eichelberger Construction Inc—*William P Eichelberger*	PO Box 459, Dillsburg PA 17019	717-638-3000	R	347*	.2
52	Weaver Cooke Construction LLC—*Dan Estes*	8401 Key Blvd, Greensboro NC 27409	336-378-7900	R	344*	.2
53	Camosy Inc—*John Camosy*	PO Box 1070, Waukegan IL 60079	847-395-0800	R	333*	.2
54	Hardin Construction Company LLC—*William A Pinto*	3301 Windy Ridge Pkwy, Atlanta GA 30339	404-264-0404	R	331*	.5
55	Nabholz Construction Corp—*Bill Hannah*	PO Box 2090, Conway AR 72032		R	321*	.9
56	Big D Construction Corp—*Robert S Moore*	404 W 400 South, Salt Lake City UT 84101	801-415-6000	R	320	N/A
57	Wehr Constructors Inc—*Dale Berry*	PO Box 32185, Louisville KY 40232	502-491-9250	R	314*	.2
58	United Interior Resources Inc—*Neal Holden*	8200 Lovett Ave, Dallas TX 75227	214-381-0101	R	313*	.2
59	Devcon Construction Inc—*Gary Filizetti*	690 Gibraltar Dr, Milpitas CA 95035	408-942-8200	R	298*	.4
60	Matzen Construction Services LLC—*Peter T Matzen*	200 Ford Rd, Melrose NY 12121	518-663-5500	R	296*	.1
61	Graycor Inc—*Melvin Gray*	1 Graycor Dr, Homewood IL 60430	708-206-0500	R	284*	1.5
62	Andersen Construction Company Inc—*David Andersen*	6712 N Cutter Cir, Portland OR 97217	503-283-6712	R	280*	.4
63	Higgerson-Buchanan Inc—*Larry Hickerson*	PO Box 1128, Chesapeake VA 23327	757-545-4665	R	270*	.1
64	Titan Construction Organization—*Tom Saul*	11865 S Conley St, Olathe KS 66061	913-782-6700	R	255*	.2
65	RE Purcell Construction Co—*Raymond E Purcell*	1550 Starkey Rd, Largo FL 33771	727-584-3329	R	253*	.2
66	Lease Crutcher Lewis Builds—*Bill Lewis*	107 Spring St, Seattle WA 98104	206-622-0500	R	250	.5
67	Haselden Construction Inc—*Ed Haselden*	6950 S Potomac St, Centennial CO 80112	303-751-1478	R	244*	.4
68	McGough Construction Co—*Thomas J McGough*	2737 Fairview Ave N, Saint Paul MN 55113	651-633-5050	R	241*	.6
69	DL Withers Construction Inc—*Daniel L Withers*	3220 E Harbour Dr, Phoenix AZ 85034	602-438-9500	R	240*	.1
70	Kinsley Construction Inc (York Pennsylvania)—*Robert Kinsley*	PO Box 2886, York PA 17405	717-741-3841	R	239*	1.0
71	Fisher Development Inc—*Robert S Fisher*	201 Spear St, San Francisco CA 94105	415-228-3060	R	237*	.2
72	WMOG Inc—*Royce Kohman*	122 S Wilson Ave, Fremont OH 43420	419-334-3801	R	234*	.6
73	Grunley Construction Co—*Kenneth M Grunley*	15020 Shady Grove Rd S, Rockville MD 20850	240-399-2000	R	234*	.3
74	Tompkins Builders Inc—*Edward Small*	1110 Vermont Ave NW St, Washington DC 20005	202-789-0770	S	233*	.2
75	Pizzagalli Construction Co—*Peter Bernhardt*	193 Tilley Dr, South Burlington VT 05403	802-658-4100	R	230*	1.0
76	Joseph J Henderson and Son Inc—*David A Henderson*	PO Box 9, Gurnee IL 60031	847-244-3222	R	230*	.2
77	Forest City Erectors Inc—*Bette Mirgliotta*	8200 Boyle Pky, Twinsburg OH 44087	330-425-7185	R	230*	.1
78	Boldt Group Inc—*Tom Boldt*	PO Box 419, Appleton WI 54912	920-739-6321	R	228*	1.5
79	Osborne Construction Co—*George Osborne Jr*	PO Box 97010, Kirkland WA 98083	425-827-4221	R	228*	.5
80	Linbeck Construction Corp—*Charles L Greco*	3900 Essex Ln Ste 1200, Houston TX 77027	713-621-2350	R	220*	.3
81	Hawaiian Dredging Construction Co—*William J Wilson*	PO Box 4088, Honolulu HI 96812	808-735-3211	S	219*	1.5
82	Leopardo Companies Inc—*James A Leopardo*	5200 Prairie Stone Pky, Hoffman Estates IL 60192	847-783-3000	R	217*	.5
83	Jacobsen Construction Company Inc—*Lonnie M Bullard*	3131 W 2210 St, Salt Lake City UT 84119	801-973-0500	R	214*	.7
84	ROEL Construction Inc—*Wayne Hickey*	PO Box 80216, San Diego CA 92138	619-297-4156	R	209*	.5
85	Key Construction Inc	741 W 2nd St, Wichita KS 67203	316-263-9515	R	207*	.2
86	FA Wilhelm Construction Company Inc—*Philip G Kenney*	PO Box 516, Indianapolis IN 46206	317-359-5411	S	200*	.6
87	McBride Construction Resources Inc—*Ken McBride*	224 Nickerson St, Seattle WA 98109	206-283-7121	R	197*	.1
88	Bread Loaf Corp—*Maynard F McLaughlin*	1293 Rte 7 S, Middlebury VT 05753	802-388-9871	R	195*	.1
89	Guardian Companies Inc—*Joseph Cunane*	101 Rogers Rd Ste101, Wilmington DE 19801		R	194*	.1
90	GLY Construction Company Inc—*Lee Kilcup*	PO Box 6728, Bellevue WA 98008	425-451-8877	R	193*	.5
91	Owen-Ames-Kimball Co—*Bill Schoonveld*	300 Ionia NW, Grand Rapids MI 49503	616-456-1521	R	191*	.2
92	Conner Development Co—*Charles Conner*	846 108th Ave NE, Bellevue WA 98004	425-455-9280	R	184*	.1
93	John S Clark Company Inc—*Barry Hennings*	PO Box 1468, Mount Airy NC 27030	336-789-1000	S	181*	.4
94	Rudolph/Libbe Companies Inc—*Tim Alter*	6494 Latcha Rd, Walbridge OH 43465	419-241-5000	R	179*	.7
95	Trumbull-Nelson Construction Company Inc—*Lawrence J Ufford*	PO Box 1000, Hanover NH 03755	603-643-3658	R	176*	.1
96	LeChase Construction Services LLC—*William H Goodrich*	300 Trolley Blvd, Rochester NY 14606	585-254-3510	R	175*	.4
97	Milton J Wood Co—*Mark S Wood*	PO Box 26829, Jacksonville FL 32226	904-353-5527	R	175*	.4
98	WM Jordan Company Inc—*John R Lawson II*	11010 Jefferson Ave, Newport News VA 23601	757-596-6341	R	175*	.4

Note: An asterisk (*) indicates an estimated financial figure. The company type code used is as follows: R = Private, P = Public, S = Private Subsidiary, B = Public Subsidiary, D = Division, J = Joint Venture, I = Investment Fund.

COMPANY RANKINGS BY SALES WITHIN 4-DIGIT SIC

Rank	Company Name—*Executive Officer*	Address, City, State, Zip	Phone	Type	Fin	Empls
99	XI Construction Corp—*Eric Raff*	851 Buckeye Ct, Milpitas CA 95035	408-240-6000	R	175*	.2
100	Lathrop Company Inc—*Steven J Klepper*	460 W Dussel Dr, Maumee OH 43537	419-893-7000	S	174*	.4
101	Pcl Construction Inc—*Luise Wentoza*	1711 W Greentree Dr St, Tempe AZ 85284	480-829-6333	S	174*	.3
102	Kvaerner North American Construction Inc—*Steve Harker*	701 Technology Dr, Canonsburg PA 15317	724-416-6900	R	172*	1.5
103	Adolfson and Peterson Inc—*Douglas W Jaeger*	PO Box 9377, Minneapolis MN 55440	952-544-1561	R	171*	.4
104	JA Tiberti Construction Inc—*John T Tiberti*	PO Box 15250, Las Vegas NV 89114	702-248-4000	R	171*	.1
105	SD Deacon Corp—*Steven Deacon*	7745 Greenback Ln Ste, Citrus Heights CA 95610	916-969-0900	R	168*	.2
106	GH Phipps Construction Companies—*Charlie Graft*	5995 Greenwood Plaza B, Greenwood Village CO 80111	303-571-5377	R	168*	.3
107	Alexander Constructors Inc—*Greg Butz*	315 Vaughn St, Harrisburg PA 17110	717-234-7041	R	166*	.1
108	CR Pittman Construction Company Inc—*Charles R Pittman*	3021 Franklin Ave, New Orleans LA 70122	504-947-4771	R	165*	.1
109	Pepper-Lawson Construction LP—*Paul Lawson*	PO Box 219227, Houston TX 77218	281-371-3100	S	165*	.1
110	Hill and Wilkinson Ltd—*Greg Wilkinson*	800 Klein Rd Ste 100, Plano TX 75074	214-299-4300	R	163*	.3
111	RD Olson Construction LP—*Robert D Olson*	2955 Main St 3rd Fl, Irvine CA 92614	949-474-2001	R	162*	.1
112	Chugach Industries Inc—*Timothy Hopper*	3800 Centerpoint Dr St, Anchorage AK 99503	907-563-8866	R	162*	.8
113	Berglund Construction Co—*Fred Berglund*	8410 S S Chicago Ave, Chicago IL 60617	773-374-1000	R	160*	.4
114	Itasca Construction Associates Inc (Itasca Illinois)—*Steve Hicks*	300 Park Blvd Ste 305W, Itasca IL 60143	630-773-6700	R	160*	.1
115	Ray Fogg Building Methods Inc—*Micheal Merle*	981 Keynote Cir Ste 15, Cleveland OH 44131	216-351-7976	R	158*	.1
116	Stone and Webster Construction Inc—*Robert Belk*	100 Technology Ctr Dr, Stoughton MA 02072	617-589-5111	R	158*	2.4
117	Drymalla Construction Company Inc—*Earl Pitchford*	PO Box 698, Columbus TX 78934	979-732-5731	R	158*	.2
118	Power Construction Co—*Jeff Carp*	2360 Palmer Dr, Schaumburg IL 60173	847-925-1300	R	157*	.2
119	Miles-McClellan Construction Company Inc—*Lonnie Miles*	2100 Builders Pl, Columbus OH 43204	614-487-7744	R	157*	.1
120	Conlan Co—*Gary Condron*	1800 Pky Pl Se Ste 100, Marietta GA 30067	770-423-8000	R	157*	.1
121	Pavarini Construction Company Inc—*Jim Hurley* Structure Tone Organization	1111 Summer St, Stamford CT 06905	203-327-0100	S	156*	.1
122	EMJ Corp—*James F Sattler*	6148 Lee Hwy 1 Park Pl, Chattanooga TN 37421	615-855-1550	R	155	.2
123	Charles Pankow Builders Ltd—*Rik Kunnath*	199 SLos Robles AveSte, Pasadena CA 91101	626-304-1190	R	154*	.2
124	Batson-Cook Co—*Raymond L Moody Jr*	PO Box 151, West Point GA 31833	706-643-2500	R	150*	.4
125	Lemoine Company LLC	PO Box 92027, Lafayette LA 70509	337-896-7720	R	150*	.3
126	Sigal Construction Corp—*Gerald R Sigal*	2231 Crystal Dr Ste 20, Arlington VA 22202	703-302-1500	R	150*	.1
127	Aireko Construction Corp—*Lorenzo Dragoni*	PO Box 2128, San Juan PR 00922	787-653-6300	R	149*	.8
128	Gamma Construction Company Inc—*Keith Williams*	PO Box 22047, Houston TX 77227	713-963-0086	R	148*	.2
129	Sletten Construction Co—*Erik Sletten*	1000 25th St N, Great Falls MT 59401	406-761-7920	S	147*	.5
130	WELBRO Building Corp—*Steve Davis*	2301 Maitland Center P, Maitland FL 32751	407-475-0800	R	147*	.4
131	Oltmans Construction Co—*Joe Oltmans II*	PO Box 985, Whittier CA 90608	562-948-4242	R	147*	.3
132	Paric Corp—*P Joseph Mc Kee*	1001 Brdwlk Spgs Pl St, O Fallon MO 63368	636-561-9500	R	147*	.2
133	Wilhelm Construction Inc—*Philip Kenney*	PO Box 516, Indianapolis IN 46206	317-359-5411	R	145*	1.2
134	Mapp Construction LLC—*Mary Jones*	344 3rd St, Baton Rouge LA 70801	225-757-0111	R	145*	.2
135	Renaissance Woodworking Company Inc—*Scott Schoel*	13 Walnut St Ne, Decatur AL 35601	256-308-1231	R	144*	<.1
136	H and M Constructors Co	PO Box 16589, Asheville NC 28816	828-254-6141	S	142*	.1
137	John C Grimberg Company Inc—*John Grimberg*	3200 Tower Oaks Blvd S, Rockville MD 20852	301-881-5120	R	142*	.2
138	Imperial Construction Group Inc—*Frank Dominguez*	PO Box 720, Pine Brook NJ 07058	908-354-7400	R	141*	.1
139	Shiel Sexton Company Inc—*Andy Shiel*	902 N Capital Ave, Indianapolis IN 46204	317-423-6000	R	140*	.3
140	Choate Construction Co—*William M Choate*	8200 Roberts Dr Ste 60, Atlanta GA 30350	678-892-1200	R	134*	.3
141	Roy Anderson Corp—*Roy Anderson III*	PO Box 2, Gulfport MS 39502	228-896-4000	R	132*	.3
142	SM Wilson and Co—*Scott Wilson*	2185 Hampton Ave, Saint Louis MO 63139	314-645-9595	R	132*	.3
143	Sellen Construction Company Inc—*Robert P McCleskey*	227 Westlake Ave N, Seattle WA 98109	206-682-7770	R	131*	.3
144	Brice Building Company Inc—*Felix Drennen III*	PO Box 1028, Birmingham AL 35201	205-930-9911	R	126*	.3
145	DE Harvey Builders Inc—*David E Harvey Jr*	PO Box 42008, Houston TX 77242	713-783-8710	R	126*	.3
146	Mosites Construction Co—*Steve Mosites*	4839 Campbells Run Rd, Pittsburgh PA 15205	412-923-2255	R	126	.3
147	Anderson-Moore Construction Corp—*Michael J Anderson*	1568 Watertower Rd, Lake Park FL 33403	561-753-7400	R	126*	.1
148	J Calnan and Associates Inc—*Jay Calnan*	3 Batterymarch park 5, Quincy MA 02169	617-801-0200	R	126*	.1
149	Korte Co—*Todd Korte*	5700 Oakland Ave Ste 2, Saint Louis MO 63110	314-231-3700	R	120*	.3
150	Swerdlow Group—*Brett M Dill*	3390 Mary St Ste 200, Coconut Grove FL 33133	305-476-0100	R	119*	.1
151	Shaw-Lundquist Associates Inc—*Fred Shaw*	2757 W Service Rd, Saint Paul MN 55121	651-454-0670	R	116*	.1
152	T and G Constructors Inc—*David Grabosky*	8623 Commodity Cir, Orlando FL 32819	407-352-4443	R	116*	.1
153	Joseph J Duffy Co—*Michael Mozal*	4994 N Elston Ave, Chicago IL 60630	773-777-6700	R	115*	.1
154	Anson Industries Inc	1959 Anson Dr, Melrose Park IL 60160	708-681-1300	R	114*	1.2
155	Drake Construction Co (Cleveland Ohio)—*Steve Ciuni*	1545 E 18th St, Cleveland OH 44114	216-664-6500	R	114*	.1
156	Catamount Constructors Inc—*Jeff Cochran*	1250 Bergen Pkwy Ste B, Evergreen CO 80439	303-679-0087	R	111*	.1
157	EW Howell Company Inc—*Howard Rowland*	245 Newtown Rd Ste 600, Plainview NY 11803	516-921-7100	S	111*	.1
158	WS Bellows Construction Corp—*Tom Bellows*	PO Box 2132, Houston TX 77252	713-680-2132	R	108*	.2
159	Azteca Enterprises Inc—*Luis Spinola*	2518 Chalk Hill Rd, Dallas TX 75212	214-689-3815	R	108*	.1
160	Schweiger Construction Company Inc—*Carol Meharry*	8300 Troost Ave, Kansas City MO 64131	816-523-5875	R	108*	.1
161	Donley's Inc—*Mac Donley*	5430 Warner Rd, Cleveland OH 44125	216-524-6800	R	107*	.3
162	William Blanchard Co—*RF Blanchard*	PO Box 298, Springfield NJ 07081	973-376-9100	R	103*	.1
163	John F Otto Inc—*Mike Feuz*	PO Box 2858, Sacramento CA 95812	916-441-6870	R	101*	.2
164	Thos S Byrne Ltd—*John Avila*	3100 W 7th St Ste 200, Fort Worth TX 76107		R	100*	.3
165	JH Findorff and Son Inc—*Rich Lynch*	300 S Bedford St, Madison WI 53703	608-257-5321	R	98*	.4
166	Meinecke-Johnson Company Inc—*Randall E Johnson*	PO Box 2643, Fargo ND 58108	701-293-1040	R	97*	.1
167	James A Cummings Inc—*William R Derrer* Tutor Perini Corp	3575 NW 53rd St, Fort Lauderdale FL 33309	954-733-4211	S	96*	.1
168	Bernards Builders Management Services—*Doug Bernards*	555 1st St, San Fernando CA 91340	818-898-1521	R	95*	.2
169	Kapp Construction Co—*Randy Kapp*	PO Box 629, Springfield OH 45501	937-324-0134	R	95*	.1
170	Constructors and Associates Inc—*Daniel Busch* Structure Tone Organization	3333 Welborn St Ste200, Dallas TX 75219	214-520-3353	S	94*	.1
171	Renier Construction Corp—*William R Heifner*	2164 CityGate Dr, Columbus OH 43219	614-866-4580	R	94*	.1
172	Fortney and Weygandt Inc—*Robert L Fortney*	31269 Bradley Rd, North Olmsted OH 44070	440-716-4000	R	88*	.2
173	Quandel LLC—*Noble C Quandel*	4755 Linglestown Rd St, Harrisburg PA 17112	717-657-0909	R	87*	.2
174	George Sollitt Construction Co—*Howard Strong*	790 N Central Ave, Wood Dale IL 60191	630-860-7333	R	86*	<.1
175	Ferguson Construction Co (Sidney Ohio)—*Martin L Given*	PO Box 726, Sidney OH 45365	937-498-2381	R	85*	.2
176	John Deklewa and Sons Inc—*David J Deklewa*	1273 Washington Pke, Bridgeville PA 15017	412-257-9000	R	85*	.2
177	Murnane Building Contractors Inc—*Patrick Murnane*	PO Box 3048, Plattsburgh NY 12901	518-561-4010	R	85*	.2
178	SD Deacon Corp of California—*Steve Deacon*	7745 Greenback Ln Ste, Citrus Heights CA 95610	916-969-0900	R	85*	.2
179	Kettelhut Construction Inc—*Mark Meyer*	PO Box 5000, Lafayette IN 47903	765-447-2181	R	84*	.2
180	O and G Industries Inc—*Gregory S Oneglia*	112 Wall St, Torrington CT 06790	860-489-9261	R	84*	.2
181	Swinerton Builders Inc—*Tony Seashore* Swinerton Inc	4310 SW Macadam Ave St, Portland OR 97239	503-222-2000	S	83*	.2
182	Panzica Construction Co—*Anthony Panzica*	739 Beta Dr, Mayfield Village OH 44143	440-442-4300	R	82*	.1
183	LeCesse Construction Co—*Andrew Hislop*	75 Thruway Park Dr, West Henrietta NY 14586	585-334-4490	R	82*	.1
184	March-Westin Company Inc—*Phillip Weser*	360 Frontier Ave, Morgantown WV 26505	304-599-4880	R	81*	.3

Rank	Company Name—*Executive Officer*	Address, City, State, Zip	Phone	Type	Fin	Empls
185	Walker and Co (Winter Park Florida)—*Lance Walker Sr*	PO Box 754, Winter Park FL 32790	407-645-0500	R	81*	.1
186	Whaley Construction Company Inc—*Alex Whaley*	225 W Madison St, Troy AL 36081	334-566-4630	R	81*	.1
187	BOR-SON Cos—*Gary Heppelmann*	2001 Killebrew Dr Ste, Minneapolis MN 55425	952-854-8444	R	80*	.2
188	John Gallin and Son Inc—*Mark Varian*	102 Madison Ave 9th Fl, New York NY 10016	212-252-8900	R	80*	.1
189	Johnson Carlier Inc—*Carol Warner*	738 S 52nd St, Tempe AZ 85281	602-275-2222	R	80*	.1
190	Condotte America Inc—*Enrique I Espino*	10790 NW 127th St, Medley FL 33178	305-670-7585	R	78*	.2
191	Lincoln Builders Inc—*Danny Graham*	1910 Farmerville Hwy, Ruston LA 71270	318-255-3822	R	78*	.2
192	Perera Construction and Design Inc—*Henry Perera Jr*	2890 Inland Empire Blv, Ontario CA 91764	909-484-6350	R	78*	.1
193	Keene Construction Company of Central Florida Inc—*David Whitehill*	1400 Hope Rd, Maitland FL 32751	407-740-6116	R	77*	.1
194	Colville Tribal Services Corp—*John MacClain*	PO Box 184, Coulee Dam WA 99116	509-634-2537	R	74*	.2
195	Howell Construction	550 Lipan St, Denver CO 80204	303-825-6257	R	71*	<.1
196	Grinder Taber and Grinder Inc—*Edward I Grinder*	1919 Lynnfield Rd, Memphis TN 38119	901-767-2400	R	71*	<.1
197	Hoffman Construction Co—*Wayne Drinkward*	805 SW Broadway Ste 21, Portland OR 97205	503-221-8811	R	69*	.2
198	Tusca Construction—*Larry LaMette*	PO Box 4136, Grand Junction CO 81502	970-245-4071	R	69*	<.1
199	Linkous Construction Company Inc—*RE Linkous*	1661 Aaron Brenner Dr, Memphis TN 38120	901-754-0700	R	68*	.2
200	Tocci Building Corp—*John L Tocci*	660 Main St, Woburn MA 01801	781-935-5500	R	65	.1
201	Septagon Industries Inc—*Stace Anderson*	113 E 3rd St, Sedalia MO 65301	660-827-5955	R	64*	.3
202	Hogg Construction Inc—*James W Hogg*	2351 Freedom Way, York PA 17402	717-741-0839	R	64*	<.1
203	Dublin Construction Company Inc—*Ben Hall Jr*	PO Box 870, Dublin GA 31040	478-272-0721	R	63*	.2
204	Lewis Contractors—*Warren Miller*	55 Gwynns Mill Ct, Owings Mills MD 21117	410-356-4200	R	63*	.1
205	Joeris Inc—*Gary Joeris*	PO Box 790086, San Antonio TX 78279	210-494-1638	R	63*	.1
206	Deerfield Construction Company Inc—*Joe Bitzer*	8960 Glendale Milford, Loveland OH 45140	513-984-4096	R	63*	<.1
207	RE Lee and Son Inc—*Stan Binsted*	PO Box 7226, Charlottesville VA 22906	434-973-1321	R	62*	.2
208	JP Cullen and Sons Inc—*David Cullen*	PO Box 1957, Janesville WI 53547	608-754-6601	R	60*	.5
209	Peterson Construction Co—*Donald Bergfeld*	PO Box 2058, Wapakoneta OH 45895	419-941-2233	R	60*	.2
210	Kaplan Cos—*Michael Kaplan*	433 River Rd, Highland Park NJ 08904	732-846-5900	R	59*	.2
211	Rentenbach Constructors Inc—*Donald W Freeman*	2400 Sutherland Ave, Knoxville TN 37919	865-546-2440	R	59*	.2
212	UW Marx Inc—*Peter Marx*	20 Gurley Ave, Troy NY 12182	518-272-2541	R	59*	.1
213	Weitz Company Inc Denver Div—*Leonard Martling*	4725 S Monaco St Ste 1, Denver CO 80237	303-860-6600	D	59*	<.1
214	Sun Eagle Corp—*Martin Alvarez*	461 N Dean Ave, Chandler AZ 85226	481-961-0004	R	59*	<.1
215	Powers and Sons Construction Company Inc—*Mamon Powers Jr*	2636 W 15th Ave, Gary IN 46404	219-949-3100	R	58*	.1
216	Baldwin and Shell Construction Co—*Bob Shell*	PO Box 1750, Little Rock AR 72203	501-374-8677	R	57*	.2
217	Bridges pbt—*Paul Bridges*	1300 Brighton Rd, Pittsburgh PA 15233	412-321-5400	R	56*	.1
218	Calcon Constructors Inc—*James P Bosshart*	2270 W Dates Ave, Englewood CO 80110	303-762-1554	R	56*	.1
219	Hamann Construction Co—*Stephan M Hamann*	PO Box 245, Manitowoc WI 54221	920-682-8282	R	56*	<.1
220	Oak Contracting Corp—*Douglas Eder*	1000 Cromwell Bridge R, Towson MD 21286	410-828-1000	R	56*	<.1
221	Ford Development Corp—*Robert J Henderson*	11148 Woodward Ln, Sharonville OH 45241	513-772-1521	R	55*	.1
222	HBD Construction Inc—*Michael J Perry*	5517 Manchester Ave, Saint Louis MO 63110	314-781-8000	R	55*	.1
223	RN Rouse and Company Inc—*Dwight Best*	PO Box 10249, Goldsboro NC 27532	919-778-8800	R	54*	.3
224	Charles C Brandt Construction Co—*Steven E Lankton*	1505 N Sherman Dr, Indianapolis IN 46201	317-375-1111	R	54*	.1
225	Badgett Constructors LLC—*Bobby Oberhausen*	217 E Burnett Ave, Louisville KY 40208	502-636-3746	R	54*	.1
226	Tribble and Stephens Co—*Van Mart*	8588 Katy Fwy Ste 100, Houston TX 77024	713-465-8550	R	53*	.6
227	Building Service Inc—*Peter Kordus*	11925 W Carmen Ave, Milwaukee WI 53225	414-353-3600	R	53	.2
228	Perlo McCormack Pacific—*Jeff Perala*	7190 SW Sandberg St, Portland OR 97223	503-624-2090	R	53*	.1
229	Lakehead Constructors Inc—*Don Odermann*	2916 Hill Ave, Superior WI 54880	715-392-5181	R	52*	1.4
230	Granger Construction Co—*Glenn D Granger*	PO Box 22187, Lansing MI 48909	517-393-1670	R	52*	.1
231	Allen L Bender Inc—*Blake Bender*	2798 Industrial Blvd, West Sacramento CA 95691	916-372-2190	R	51*	.1
232	Turelk Inc—*Michael G Turi*	3700 Santa Fe Ave Ste, Long Beach CA 90810	310-835-3736	R	51*	.1
233	Beauchamp Construction Co—*Jim Beauchamp*	2100 Ponce De Leon Blv, Coral Gables FL 33134	305-445-0819	R	51*	<.1
234	Johnson and Galyon Contractors—*Doug Kennedy*	PO Box 3070, Knoxville TN 37917	865-688-1111	R	50*	.2
235	Ken Bratney Co—*Paul Bratney*	3400 109th St, Des Moines IA 50322	515-270-2417	R	50*	.2
236	Aui Contractors LLC—*Doug Alumbaugh*	4775 N Fwy, Fort Worth TX 76106	817-926-4377	R	49*	.3
237	Powell Building Group—*John D Finch*	1000 Northchase Dr Ste, Goodlettsville TN 37072	615-256-2200	R	48*	.1
238	TBI Construction and Construction Management Inc—*Tony P Mirenda*	1960 The Alameda Ste 2, San Jose CA 95126	408-246-3691	R	48*	<.1
239	Leapley Construction Group of Atlanta LLC—*Meredith Leapley*	294 Interstate N Cir S, Atlanta GA 30339	770-850-8711	R	48*	<.1
240	Max J Kuney Co—*Max J Kuney III*	PO Box 4008, Spokane WA 99220	509-535-0651	R	47*	.2
241	Continental Building Systems—*Todd Alexander*	150 E Broad St, Columbus OH 43215	614-221-1800	R	47*	.1
242	Warrior Group Inc—*V Gail Warrior-Lawrence*	1624 Falcon Dr Ste 100, DeSoto TX 75115	972-228-9955	R	47*	<.1
243	Pepper Lawson Construction Inc—*Paul Lawson*	PO Box 219227, Houston TX 77218	281-371-3100	S	46*	.1
244	HJ High Construction Co—*Robert John High*	1015 W Amelia St, Orlando FL 32805	407-422-8171	R	46*	<.1
245	Rollins-PCI Construction—*Barry Lake*	1302 Rising Ridge Rd S, Mount Airy MD 21771	301-831-5031	R	45*	<.1
246	McInnis Brothers Construction Inc—*Harry McInnis Jr*	PO Box 610, Minden LA 71058	318-377-6134	R	44*	.1
247	Gerace Construction Co—*Tom Valent*	4055 S Saginaw Rd, Midland MI 48640	989-496-2440	R	44*	.1
248	Hannig Construction Inc—*Troy Biddle*	PO Box 569, Terre Haute IN 47808	812-235-6218	R	44*	.1
249	Joe N Guy Company Inc—*Joe Guy*	2028 Powers Ferry Rd S, Atlanta GA 30339	770-955-4224	R	44*	.1
250	Martin K Eby Construction Company Inc—*Richard Bean*	PO Box 1679, Wichita KS 67201	316-268-3500	R	43*	.2
251	Story Construction Co—*Mike Espeset*	PO Box 1668, Ames IA 50010	515-232-4358	R	43*	.2
252	Dargan Construction Company Inc—*Shaw Dargan*	PO Box 1468, Myrtle Beach SC 29577	843-626-7602	R	43*	.2
253	Dugan and Meyers Construction Co—*Jay Meyers*	11110 Kenwood Rd, Cincinnati OH 45242	513-891-4300	R	43*	.1
254	LP Cox Co—*John F Myles III*	PO Box 10, Sanford NC 27331	919-774-4800	R	43*	.1
255	Mistick Construction—*L Makosky*	1300 Brighton Rd, Pittsburgh PA 15233	412-322-1121	R	43*	.1
256	Paul Hemmer Cos—*Paul Hemmer Jr*	250 Grandview Dr, Fort Mitchell KY 41017	859-341-8300	R	43*	.1
257	Pepper Construction Company of Indiana—*Bill McCarthy*	1850 W 15th St, Indianapolis IN 46202	317-681-1000	S	43*	.1
258	Selzer-Ornst Company Inc—*Robert Ornst Jr*	PO Box 13097, Milwaukee WI 53213	414-258-9900	R	43*	.1
259	Colarelli Construction Inc—*Vince Colarelli*	111 S Tejon Ste 112, Colorado Springs CO 80903	719-475-7997	R	43*	<.1
260	Atherton Construction Inc—*Matt Muretto*	50 N Gibson Rd Rm 115, Henderson NV 89014	702-889-3600	R	43*	<.1
261	Exxcel Contract Management Inc—*F Douglas Reardon*	2 Miranova Pl Ste 250, Columbus OH 43215	614-621-4500	R	42*	.1
262	Harbison-Mahony-Higgins Builders Inc—*Dave Higgins Jr*	15 Business Park Way S, Sacramento CA 95828	916-383-4825	R	42	.1
263	JR Abbott Construction Inc—*John Abbott*	PO Box 84048, Seattle WA 98124	206-467-8500	R	42*	.1
264	GL Barron Construction Inc—*Greg Barron*	6221 Southwest Blvd St, Fort Worth TX 76132	817-231-8100	R	42*	<.1
265	Trepte Construction Co	8195 Ronson Rd Ste E, San Diego CA 92111	858-279-8100	R	42*	<.1
266	RUST Constructors Inc—*Chris L Philips*	2 Perimeter Park S Ste, Birmingham AL 35243	205-995-7171	S	40*	.5
267	Alberici Constructors—*Greg Kozicz*, Alberici Corp	2150 Keinlen Ave, St Louis MO 63121		S	40*	.1
268	Strand Hunt Construction Inc—*Rollie Hunt*	18915 142nd Ave NE Ste, Woodinville WA 98072	425-488-1954	R	40*	.1
269	George A Grant Inc—*Richard Richter*	PO Box 789, Richland WA 99352	509-946-6188	R	40*	<.1
270	DS Simmons Inc—*Cleve Paul*	PO Box 287, Goldsboro NC 27533	919-734-4700	R	39*	.1

Note: An asterisk (*) indicates an estimated financial figure. The company type code used is as follows: R = Private, P = Public, S = Private Subsidiary, B = Public Subsidiary, D = Division, J = Joint Venture, I = Investment Fund.

COMPANY RANKINGS BY SALES WITHIN 4-DIGIT SIC

Rank	Company Name—*Executive Officer*	Address, City, State, Zip	Phone	Type	Fin	Empls
271	MLB Industries Inc—*Thomas Eckert*	1 Stone Break Rd, Malta NY 12020	518-289-1371	R	39*	.1
272	Quasius Construction Inc—*David Quasius*	1716 N 16th St, Sheboygan WI 53081	920-457-5585	R	39*	.1
273	Universal Construction Company Inc	11200 W 79th St, Lenexa KS 66214	913-342-1150	R	38*	.1
274	DG Beyer Inc—*George M Beyer*	3080 S Calhoun Rd, New Berlin WI 53151	262-789-6040	R	38*	.1
275	TEDCO Construction Corp—*James T Frantz*	Tedco Pl, Carnegie PA 15106	412-276-8080	R	38*	.1
276	Cornell and Company Inc—*Delor Cornell*	PO Box 807, Woodbury NJ 08096	856-742-1900	R	36*	.4
277	J Coleman Alvin and Son Inc—*Calvin Coleman*	9 Nh Rte 113, Albany NH 03818	603-447-5936	R	36*	.1
278	Valley View Building Services Inc—*Jaime Votaw*	106 W 2950 S, Salt Lake City UT 84115	801-576-0067	R	36*	.1
279	Beverly-Grant Inc—*Jerry Grant*	64 Peachtree Rd Ste 20, Asheville NC 28803	828-274-7084	R	35*	.1
280	Midstate Construction Corp—*Roger Nelson*	1180 Holm Rd, Petaluma CA 94954	707-762-3200	R	35*	.1
281	Downey Contracting LLC—*Eileen Hearn*	3217 Ne 63rd St, Oklahoma City OK 73121	405-478-5277	R	34*	.1
282	Codina Group Inc—*Armando Codina*	135 San Lorenzo Ave St, Coral Gables FL 33146	305-529-1300	S	34*	<.1
283	Nemanco Inc—*Don Fulton*	PO Box 268, Philadelphia MS 39350	601-656-7361	R	34*	.1
284	Speed-Fab-Crete Corporation International—*David Bloxom*	PO Box 15580, Fort Worth TX 76119	817-478-1137	R	32*	.1
285	Ross Brothers and Company Inc—*Steven M Ross*	3501 Brooklake Rd N, Salem OR 97303	503-393-5885	R	32*	.1
286	Ferguson Construction—*Gene Colin*	PO Box 80867, Seattle WA 98108	206-767-3810	R	32*	.1
287	Sain Construction Co—*Jimmy Sain*	PO Box 1078, Manchester TN 37349	931-728-7644	R	32*	.1
288	Stiles Construction Co—*Terry Stiles*	301 SE 2nd St, Fort Lauderdale FL 33301	954-627-9150	D	32*	.1
289	IBC Southwest Inc—*Dan Thomas*	23027 N 15th Lane Ste, Phoenix AZ 85027	623-581-5300	R	32*	<.1
290	Stobs Brothers Construction—*J Robert Stobs II*	580 NE 92nd S, Miami FL 33138	305-751-1692	R	32*	<.1
291	Tri-State Design Construction Inc—*Ronald U Davis*	7401 Old York Rd, Elkins Park PA 19027	215-782-8200	R	32*	<.1
292	Acme Construction Company Inc (Modesto California)—*Philip Mastagni*	PO Box 4710, Modesto CA 95352	209-523-2674	R	31*	.1
293	Irmscher Inc—*Tom Irmscher*	1030 Osage St, Fort Wayne IN 46808	260-422-5572	R	31*	.1
294	KOO Construction Inc—*Keith O Odister*	PO Box 348540, Sacramento CA 95834	916-371-3388	R	31*	<.1
295	Mardrian Group Inc—*Teresa L Bridgewaters*	PO Box 16069, Louisville KY 40256	502-776-2749	R	31*	<.1
296	Broadbent Co—*George P Broadbent*	117 E Washington St St, Indianapolis IN 46204	317-237-2900	R	30*	.1
297	CD Moody Construction Company Inc—*C David Moody Jr*	6017 Redan Rd, Lithonia GA 30058	770-482-7778	R	30*	<.1
298	Latco Inc—*James Latta*	PO Box 9, Lincoln AR 72744	479-824-3282	R	29*	.3
299	Mici Inc—*Brad Schmidt*	1206 Tappan Cir, Carrollton TX 75006	972-245-1022	R	29*	.2
300	Pioneer Contract Services Inc—*Ed Fritcher*	8090 Kempwood Dr, Houston TX 77055	713-464-8200	R	29*	.3
301	Johnston Applegate Inc—*Jim Applegate*	1016 12th St, Modesto CA 95354	209-538-4449	R	29*	.2
302	Advanced Office Interiors Inc—*Mick Jensen*	8801 S 137th Cir, Omaha NE 68138	402-896-5520	R	29*	.1
303	Shook Inc—*Frank Klein*	PO Box 138806, Dayton OH 45413	937-276-6666	S	29*	.1
304	Snyder-Langston Real Estate and Construction Services Inc—*Stephen Jones*	17962 Cowan, Irvine CA 92614	949-863-9200	R	29*	.1
305	Rochon Corp—*Jerry Braton*	3650 Annapolis Ln N St, Plymouth MN 55447	763-559-9393	R	29*	<.1
306	Rafn Co—*Tom Ambrey*	1721 132nd Ave NE, Bellevue WA 98005	425-702-6600	R	28*	.1
307	Pangea Inc—*Michael A Zambrana*	2604 S Jefferson Ave, Saint Louis MO 63118	314-333-0600	R	28*	.1
308	MSI General Corp—*Dirk J Debbink*	PO Box 7, Oconomowoc WI 53066	262-367-3661	R	28*	.1
309	Ramtech Building Systems Inc—*Michael Slataper*	1400 Hwy 287 S, Mansfield TX 76063	817-473-9376	R	28*	<.1
310	Monahan Co—*Michael J Monahan*	21321 Kelly Rd, Eastpointe MI 48021	586-774-3800	R	28*	<.1
311	William H Lane Inc—*William H Lane*	111 - 115 Court St, Binghamton NY 13901	607-775-0600	R	28*	<.1
312	Agri-Systems Inc—*Robert Hamlin*	1300 Minnesota Ave, Billings MT 59101	406-245-6231	R	28*	.3
313	Warfel Construction Co—*Ralph E Simpson Jr*	1110 Enterprise Rd, East Petersburg PA 17520	717-299-4500	R	26*	.1
314	Turner Steiner International Inc—*Peter Davoren* Turner Corp	375 Hudson St 6th Fl, New York NY 10014	212-229-6000	S	26*	.1
315	Ajax Building Corp—*Bill Byrne*	1080 Commerce Blvd, Midway FL 32343	850-224-9571	R	25*	.2
316	Engel Holdings Inc—*Matthew Engel*	3065 Rosecrans Pl Ste, San Diego CA 92110	310-834-3430	R	25*	.1
317	Landau Building Co—*Thomas Landau*	9855 Rinaman Rd, Wexford PA 15090	724-935-8800	R	25*	.1
318	LBM Construction Company Inc—*Gary D Lloyd*	11421 Blankenbaker Acc, Louisville KY 40299	502-452-1151	R	25*	.1
319	Bowen and Watson Inc—*Kevin C Watson*	PO Box 877, Toccoa GA 30577	706-886-3197	R	25*	.1
320	Voorhees International Inc—*Stephen Voorhees*	1656 Headland Dr, Fenton MO 63026	636-349-1555	R	25*	<.1
321	Mitchell Enterprises Inc—*Steve Mitchell*	PO Box 3109, Sherman TX 75091	903-893-6593	R	24*	.1
322	HC Merchandisers Inc—*Myron Harpole*	19844 Quiroz Ct, Walnut CA 91789	909-598-0509	R	24*	<.1
323	Pdc Facilities Inc—*William Maslowski*	700 Walnut Ridge Dr St, Hartland WI 53029	262-367-7700	R	24*	<.1
324	Designed Mobile Systems Industries Inc—*David Smith*	PO Box 367, Patterson CA 95363	209-892-6298	R	24*	.1
325	Maloney and Bell General Contractors Incorporated of California—*Michael C Blixt*	2620 Mercantile Dr, Rancho Cordova CA 95742	916-635-7600	R	23*	.1
326	Oliver Construction Co—*Robb Wierdsma*	PO Box 65, Oconomowoc WI 53066	262-567-6677	R	23*	.1
327	Wilcon Corp	3176 Kettering Blvd, Dayton OH 45439	937-299-9920	R	23*	.1
328	Pinkerton and Laws of Georgia Inc—*Jeffery S Jernigan*	1165 Northchase Pkwy S, Marietta GA 30067	770-956-9000	R	22*	.1
329	Sullivan Corp (Noblesville Indiana)—*Terrence Sullivan*	15299 Stony Creek Way, Noblesville IN 46060	317-776-2770	R	22*	.1
330	J-A-G Construction Co—*James Coffin*	PO Box 1493, Dodge City KS 67801	620-225-0061	R	22*	.1
331	Browning Construction Co—*James C Browning*	903 Basse Dr, San Antonio TX 78212	210-736-1701	R	21*	.1
332	Haverstick-Borthwick Co—*William A Cobb Jr*	PO Box 766, Plymouth Meeting PA 19462	610-825-9300	R	21*	.1
333	C Construction Company Inc—*Bryan P Rossman*	PO Box 8270, Tyler TX 75711	903-597-1500	R	21*	.1
334	CT Wilson Construction Company Inc—*Charles T Wilson Jr*	PO Box 2011, Durham NC 27702	919-383-2535	R	21*	.1
335	EC Kenyon Construction Company Inc—*Douglas Herring*	10028 San Jose Blvd, Jacksonville FL 32257	904-389-2353	R	21*	.1
336	Giordano Construction Company Inc—*Michael F Giordano*	PO Box 802, Branford CT 06405	203-488-7264	R	21*	.1
337	Lincoln Construction Inc—*Kurt N Schmitt*	4790 Shuster Rd, Columbus OH 43214	614-457-6015	R	21*	.1
338	Millie and Severson Inc—*Jonathan E Severson*	PO Box 3601, Los Alamitos CA 90720	562-493-3611	R	21*	.1
339	Peter R Brown Construction Inc—*Kevin Bowen*	PO Box 4100, Clearwater FL 33758	727-535-6407	R	21*	.1
340	Steele and Freeman Inc—*Mike Freeman*	1301 Lawson Rd, Fort Worth TX 76131	817-232-4742	R	21*	.1
341	Carothers Construction Inc—*Ben Logan*	PO Box 189, Taylor MS 38673	662-513-8820	R	21*	<.1
342	AL Huber and Son Inc—*August L Huber III*	10770 El Monte St, Overland Park KS 66211	913-341-4880	R	21*	<.1
343	Cox Construction Co—*Nigel Cary*	3170 Scott St, Vista CA 92083	760-727-9020	R	21*	<.1
344	Deig Brothers Lumber and Construction Company Inc—*Charles Martin*	PO Box 6429, Evansville IN 47719	812-423-4201	R	20*	.2
345	Peyronnin Construction Company Inc—*Edward Peyronnin*	PO Box 3317, Evansville IN 47711	812-423-6241	R	20*	.1
346	Eckman Construction Inc—*Mark Walsh*	84 Palomino Ln, Bedford NH 03110	603-623-1713	R	20*	.1
347	Jendoco Construction Corp—*Dom Dozzi*	2000 Lincoln Rd, Pittsburgh PA 15235	412-361-4500	R	20*	.1
348	KL House Construction Company Inc—*Michael O Brogdon*	6409 SE Acoma Rd, Albuquerque NM 87108	505-268-4361	R	20*	<.1
349	Rycon Construction Inc—*Todd A Dominick*	2525 Liberty Ave, Pittsburgh PA 15222	412-392-2525	R	20*	<.1
350	Summit Construction Company Inc—*Mike Martin*	PO Box 88126, Indianapolis IN 46208	317-634-6112	R	20*	<.1
351	WM Schlosser Company Inc—*Wil Schlosser*	2400 51st Pl, Hyattsville MD 20781	301-773-1300	R	19*	.3
352	Bruns-Gutzwiller Inc—*Tom Bruns*	305 S John St, Batesville IN 47006	812-934-2105	R	19*	.1
353	Teal Construction Co—*John Murray Jr*	1335 Brittmoore Rd, Houston TX 77043	713-465-8306	R	19*	<.1
354	Oberle and Associates Inc—*Ronald Oberle*	PO Box 398, Richmond IN 47375	765-966-7715	R	18*	.1
355	Roy Kirby and Sons Inc—*Leroy E Kirby Jr*	1421 Clarkview Rd Ste, Baltimore MD 21209	410-583-0808	R	18*	.1

Rank	Company Name—*Executive Officer*	Address, City, State, Zip	Phone	Type	Fin	Empls
356	New Era Builders Inc—*Joe Lopez*	36445 Biltmore Pl Ste, Willoughby OH 44094	440-942-4900	R	18*	<.1
357	HP Cummings Construction Co—*Dallas N Folk*	PO Box 29, Ware MA 01082	413-967-6251	R	17*	.1
358	Dublin Building Systems Inc—*Victor D Irelan*	PO Box 370, Dublin OH 43017	614-889-1445	R	17*	<.1
359	Gioffre Construction Inc—*John Gioffre*	6262 Eiterman Rd, Dublin OH 43016	614-764-0032	R	17*	<.1
360	Austin General Contracting Inc—*Michael Austin*	6440 Polaris Ave, Las Vegas NV 89118	702-730-0078	R	16*	.1
361	Biltmore Construction Company Inc—*Edward Parker Jr*	1055 Ponce DeLeon Blvd, Belleair FL 33756	727-585-2084	R	16*	.1
362	Tomlinson-Hawley-Patterson Inc—*Richard F Jagoe*	2225 Reservoir Ave, Trumbull CT 06611	203-372-3583	R	16*	<.1
363	JBM Builders Inc—*Steve Luebbenuse*	PO Box 50129, Fort Worth TX 76105	817-531-3913	R	16*	<.1
364	Shaver Construction Inc—*Ed Birch*	1430 Greg St Ste 501, Sparks NV 89431	775-359-4555	R	16*	<.1
365	Sicoli and Massaro Inc—*Dominick Massaro*	8525 Porter Rd, Niagara Falls NY 14304	716-297-0484	R	16*	<.1
366	Skaf Construction Co—*Antoine Ghosn*	5757 Blue Lagoon Dr St, Miami FL 33126	305-640-3010	R	16*	<.1
367	Baybutt Construction Corp—*Frederick L Baybutt*	PO Box 463, Keene NH 03431	603-352-6846	R	15*	.1
368	Bryan Construction Co—*Larry Ridgway*	1007 Earl Rudder Frwy, Bryan TX 77802	979-776-6000	R	15*	.1
369	Hench Brothers Inc—*Baron Hench*	508 E Pleasant Valley, Altoona PA 16602	814-944-0851	R	15*	.1
370	Creative Contractors Inc—*Alan C Bomstein*	620 Drew St, Clearwater FL 33755	727-461-5522	R	15*	<.1
371	Computer Sites Inc—*Linda Springs*	1225 S Huron St, Denver CO 80223	303-871-0550	R	15*	<.1
372	Mader Construction Corp—*Kevin Biddle*	PO Box 420, Elma NY 14059	716-655-3400	R	14*	.1
373	Henkel Construction Co—*Alan Kittleson*	P O Box 920, Mason City IA 50402	641-423-5674	R	14*	.1
374	Buquet and LeBlanc Inc—*William T Firesheets II*	PO Box 549, Baton Rouge LA 70821	225-753-4150	R	14*	.1
375	Gethmann Construction Company Inc—*JB Gethmann*	PO Box 160, Marshalltown IA 50158	641-753-3555	R	13*	.1
376	Randolph and Son Builders Inc—*Ray Randolph*	PO Box 410283, Charlotte NC 28241	704-588-7116	R	13*	.1
377	Langer Construction Co—*Thomas M Langer*	54 E Moreland Ave E, Saint Paul MN 55118	651-457-5993	R	13*	.1
378	Lebanon Building Systems Inc—*Carol Young*	601 E Main Ave, Myerstown PA 17067	717-866-4312	R	13*	.1
379	HSU Development Company Inc—*Walter Hsu*	1335 Rockville Pke Ste, Rockville MD 20852	301-881-3500	R	13*	<.1
380	Abco Builders Inc—*Charles Richards*	2680 Abco Ct, Lithonia GA 30058	770-981-0350	R	13*	<.1
381	Frymire Co—*Larry Frymire*	3000 Shotts St, Fort Worth TX 76107	817-336-4514	R	13*	<.1
382	United Construction Corp—*Craig Willcut*	5500 Equity Ave, Reno NV 89502	775-858-8090	R	13*	<.1
383	Specialty Piping Corp—*L Romine*	1230 S Meadville Rd, Davisville WV 26142	304-424-5347	R	12*	.1
384	Omega Qse Inc—*James Jordan*	6505 Collamer Rd, East Syracuse NY 13057	315-438-4426	R	12*	.1
385	Evans Construction Co—*Donald Evans*	1900 E Washington St, Springfield IL 62703	217-525-1456	R	12*	.1
386	Ambassador Construction Company Inc—*Cory Koven*	317 Madison Ave 12th F, New York NY 10017	212-922-1020	R	12*	<.1
387	Engineering Automation and Design Inc—*Stephen M Lichter*	4610 S 133rd St Ste 10, Omaha NE 68137	402-884-8650	R	12*	<.1
388	Rgm Constructors Of Texas LLC—*Joann Sharp*	15603 Interstate 35, Pflugerville TX 78660	512-990-8313	R	12*	<.1
389	Ivey's Construction Inc—*Kevin W Ivey*	4060 Courtenay Pkwy, Merritt Island FL 32953	321-453-3812	R	12*	<.1
390	Multicon Construction Inc—*Randy Bosscawen*	1320 McKinley Ave Ste, Columbus OH 43222	614-351-2683	S	12*	<.1
391	Obayashi Construction Inc	577 Airport Blvd Ste 6, Burlingame CA 94010	650-952-4910	S	12*	<.1
392	Bruce Kreofsky and Sons Inc—*Dennis Kreofsky*	865 Enterprise Dr Sw, Plainview MN 55964	507-534-3855	R	12*	.1
393	Whitley Manufacturing Company Inc—*Simon Dragan*	PO Box 496, South Whitley IN 46787	260-723-5131	R	11*	.2
394	Lloyd's Refrigeration Inc—*Walt P Lloyd*	5701 W Sunset Rd, Las Vegas NV 89118	702-798-1010	R	11*	.2
395	Sordoni Construction Services Inc—*William E Sordoni*	45 Owen St, Forty Fort PA 18704	570-287-3161	R	11*	<.1
396	Component Construction Co—*Randall Haefli*	6333 Airport Fwy, Fort Worth TX 76117	817-834-6274	R	11*	<.1
397	Sierra View Company Inc—*Mark Davis*	4202 Douglas Blvd Ste, Granite Bay CA 95746	916-774-7000	R	11*	<.1
398	H and A Construction Co—*Scott Olsen*	PO Box 23755, Tigard OR 97281	503-639-6148	R	11*	<.1
399	Webb and Sons Construction Company Inc—*Michael Webb*	PO Box 388, Athens TN 37371	423-745-1774	R	10*	.1
400	Tilden-Coil Constructors Inc—*Brian Jaramillo*	3612 Mission Inn Ave, Riverside CA 92507	951-684-5901	R	10*	<.1
401	Lund Martin Construction—*Willard Haro*	3023 Randolph St NE, Minneapolis MN 55418	612-782-2250	R	10*	<.1
402	Gierczyk Inc—*James P Gierczyk*	16200 Clinton St, Harvey IL 60426	708-596-9696	R	10*	<.1
403	Henley Group—*Henley Jones Jr*	2876 Hwy 9, Cheraw SC 29520	843-537-5924	R	10*	<.1
404	Christiansen Construction Company LLC	210 Main St, Pender NE 68047	402-385-3027	R	10*	<.1
405	Topline Building Inc—*Gene Waldron*	PO Box 2046, Alma GA 31510	912-632-4440	R	9*	.1
406	Ellerbe Becket Construction Services Inc—*Rick Lincicome*	800 LaSalle Ave, Minneapolis MN 55402	612-376-2000	S	9*	.4
407	Cbm Inc—*Larry Levy*	PO Box 8327, Cherry Hill NJ 08002	856-793-2200	R	9*	<.1
408	Erect-A-Tube Inc—*Susan Wagner*	PO Box 100, Harvard IL 60033	815-943-4091	R	8*	<.1
409	Heidenberger Construction Inc—*Steven Heidenberger*	10524 Detrick Ave 2nd, Kensington MD 20895	301-942-6444	R	8*	<.1
410	Illig Construction Co—*Rita Illig-Liebelt*	3577 N Figueroa St, Los Angeles CA 90065	323-227-1411	R	8*	<.1
411	D/B Constructors—*Alan Jackson*	2400 Great Southwest P, Fort Worth TX 76106	817-626-7300	R	8*	<.1
412	Clean Air Technology Inc—*Jeffrey Waller*	41105 Capital Dr, Canton MI 48187	734-459-6320	R	8*	<.1
413	Hoffman-Cortes Contracting Co—*Rita M Cortes*	1600 Baltimore Ste 102, Kansas City MO 64108	816-842-6170	R	7*	<.1
414	Quest Construction Engineering and Management Inc—*Leslie Schotz*	5995 Del Mar Mesa Rd, San Diego CA 92130	858-847-9307	R	7*	<.1
415	Triangle Construction Inc—*Thomas Baer*	PO Box 3304, Greenwood SC 29648	864-288-5500	R	7*	<.1
416	Centerre Construction Inc—*Steve Hritz*	4100 E Mississippi Ave, Denver CO 80246	303-220-9400	R	7*	<.1
417	Sessoms Construction Company Inc—*Fletcher Sessoms*	7485 Davie Rd Ext, Hollywood FL 33024	954-431-7900	R	7*	<.1
418	James H Cone Inc—*James Cone Jr*	PO Box 22297, Little Rock AR 72203	501-224-1058	R	6*	<.1
419	Miller and Norford Inc—*Ryan J Silvagio*	700 Ayers Ave, Lemoyne PA 17043	717-763-7014	R	6*	<.1
420	DJ Rose and Son Inc—*Dillon W Rose*	PO Drawer 2426, Rocky Mount NC 27802	252-442-6105	R	6*	<.1
421	Charles and Vinzant Construction Company LLC—*Charles Ferlisi*	500 Southland Dr Ste 1, Birmingham AL 35226	205-823-6761	R	6*	<.1
422	Roslovic and Partners Inc—*John Roslovic*	600 Morrison Rd, Gahanna OH 43230	614-328-0600	R	6*	<.1
423	TCWeiser Construction Co—*Todd Weiser*	360 W Waterloo St, Canal Winchester OH 43110	614-837-2166	R	6*	<.1
424	Pacific Construction Services Inc—*Ike Hong*	4700b N Ravenswood Ave, Chicago IL 60640	773-290-1600	R	6*	<.1
425	American Tennis Courts Inc—*Perry Rossi*	4051 N Point Rd, Baltimore MD 21222	410-477-4400	R	5*	<.1
426	RaDec Construction Company Inc—*Edwin J Bottolfsen*	PO Box 667, Hartington NE 68739	402-254-3345	R	5*	<.1
427	Dave's Construction Service Inc—*David Sexton*	PO Box 2215, Eden NC 27289	336-623-9906	R	5*	<.1
428	Colorado Tower Work—*Jack Johanson*	14824 E Greenwood Pl, Aurora CO 80014	303-690-0129	R	5*	.1
429	Leighton Consulting Inc—*Terrence Brennan*	17781 Cowan Ste 200, Irvine CA 92614	949-253-9836	R	4*	<.1
430	Lee Reger Builds Inc—*Lee Reger*	PO Box 1872, Shinnston WV 26431	304-592-2083	R	4*	<.1
431	Baltimore Contractors LLC—*John Rouse*	6609 Moravia Park Dr, Baltimore MD 21237	410-276-2800	R	4*	<.1
432	Ed Parker Inc—*Anthony Vera*	2108 West Fwy, Fort Worth TX 76102	817-332-8481	R	4*	<.1
433	Constructech Inc—*Bill Frantz*	31805 8 Mile Rd, Livonia MI 48152	248-476-1310	R	4*	<.1
434	Salon Interiors Inc—*Walter Siegordner*	62 Leuning St, South Hackensack NJ 07606	201-488-7888	R	3*	<.1
435	Chief Electric Co—*Mark Quinton*	1435 National St, Memphis TN 38122	901-323-1408	R	3*	<.1
436	AG Gaston Construction Inc—*Walter Howlett*	PO Box 697, Birmingham AL 35201	205-328-0376	S	3*	<.1
437	Dugan Construction Company Inc—*Thomas Dugan*	400 N Church St Ste 13, Moorestown NJ 08057	856-778-9455	R	3*	<.1
438	Cable Plus Inc—*Leo Ricca*	12316 John Lambert Rd, Gonzales LA 70737	225-647-6750	R	3*	<.1
439	Daniels Real Estate—*Stanley Daniels*	PO Box 6216, Gulfport MS 39506	228-896-5307	R	3*	<.1
440	Senez Roofing LLC—*Ericka Senez*	1060 E Industrial Dr K, Orange City FL 32763	386-774-4950	R	3*	<.1
441	Newbern Fabricating Inc—*Bud Cude*	980 E Hwy 77, Newbern TN 38059	731-627-3234	R	3*	<.1
442	Burnham Lumber Company Inc—*Ronald Austin*	839 County Rd G, Rewey WI 53580	608-943-6323	R	2*	<.1
443	Moody Construction Company Inc—*Wayne Moody*	816 S Church Ave, Louisville MS 39339	662-773-3778	R	2*	<.1

Note: An asterisk (*) indicates an estimated financial figure. The company type code used is as follows: R = Private, P = Public, S = Private Subsidiary, B = Public Subsidiary, D = Division, J = Joint Venture, I = Investment Fund.

COMPANY RANKINGS BY SALES WITHIN 4-DIGIT SIC

Rank	Company Name—*Executive Officer*	Address, City, State, Zip	Phone	Type	Fin	Empls
444	Pacific Domes Inc—*Asha Deliverance*	PO Box 1047, Ashland OR 97520	541-488-7737	R	2*	<.1
445	Head Inc—*Jim Head*	4477 E 5th Ave, Columbus OH 43219	614-338-8501	R	2*	<.1
446	Arris Builders Inc—*Terry Lysek*	25910 Acero Ste 330, Mission Viejo CA 92691	949-261-3113	S	2*	<.1
447	Pew Corp—*Thomas R Pew*	PO Box 2100, Missoula MT 59806	406-721-2001	R	2*	<.1
448	Laschober Construction Inc—*Gerry Laschober*	6840 Harp Ave, Port Saint John FL 32927	321-639-1153	R	2*	<.1
449	AR Merante Corp—*Rick Merante*	24353 Walnut St, Santa Clarita CA 91321	661-645-1218	R	1*	<.1
450	Lowder Construction Co—*James K Lowder*	2000 Interstate Park D, Montgomery AL 36109	334-270-6789	S	1*	<.1
451	RH Hoover Inc—*Ronald H Hoover*	9209 E Mission Ste F, Spokane WA 99206	509-924-9520	R	1	<.1
452	TA Loving Co—*Samuel Hunter*	400 Patetown, Goldsboro NC 27530	919-734-8400	R	N/A	.3
453	WL Butler Construction Inc—*William L Butler*	204 Franklin St, Redwood City CA 94063	650-361-1270	R	N/A	.1
454	J Caldarera and Company Inc—*Joe Caldarera*	201 Woodland Dr, LaPlace LA 70068	985-652-7676	R	N/A	<.1

TOTALS: SIC 1542 Nonresidential Construction Nec
Companies: 454   88,610   148.5

1611 Highway & Street Construction

Rank	Company Name—*Executive Officer*	Address, City, State, Zip	Phone	Type	Fin	Empls
1	Lane Industries Inc—*Robert E Alger*	90 Fieldstone Court, Cheshire CT 06410	203-235-3351	R	16,417*	4.5
2	Peter Kiewit Sons' Inc—*Bruce E Grewcock*	3555 Farnam St, Omaha NE 68131	402-342-2052	R	6,240	19.1
3	Vecellio and Grogan Inc—*Leo Vecellio Jr*	PO Box 2438, Beckley WV 25802	304-252-6575	R	4,404*	1.2
4	Barnhill Contracting Co—*Robert E Barnhill II*	PO Box 1529, Tarboro NC 27886	252-823-1021	R	3,290*	1.0
5	JD Abrams LP—*Jon Abrams*	111 Congress Ave Ste 2, Austin TX 78701	512-322-4000	R	2,945*	.9
6	Kiewit Construction Group Inc—*Bruce Grewcock* Peter Kiewit Sons' Inc	3555 Farnam St Ste 100, Omaha NE 68131	402-342-2052	S	2,250*	10.0
7	Granite Construction Inc—*James H Roberts*	585 W Beach St, Watsonville CA 95076	831-724-1011	P	2,010	3.0
8	Bacco Construction Co—*John A Fortier*	PO Box 458, Iron Mountain MI 49801	906-774-2616	R	1,835*	.5
9	Granite Halmar Construction Company Inc—*David H Ward* Granite Construction Inc	585 W Beach St, Watsonville CA 95076	831-724-1011	S	1,726*	4.5
10	CC Mangum Inc—*Chris Mangum*	PO Box 98895, Raleigh NC 27624	919-422-8606	R	1,331*	.5
11	Transfield Services North America—*Richard Herlich*	203 E Cary St Ste 200, Richmond VA 23219	804-261-8000	S	1,135*	.4
12	FNF Construction Inc—*Jed S Billings*	115 S 48th St, Tempe AZ 85281	480-784-2910	S	1,082*	.4
13	Hardrives of Delray Inc—*George T Elmore*	2101 S Congress Ave, Delray Beach FL 33445	561-278-0456	R	990*	.3
14	Kiewit Western Co—*Kenneth E Stinson* Peter Kiewit Sons' Inc	7926 S Platte Canyon R, Littleton CO 80128	303-979-9330	S	880*	2.5
15	American Civil Constructors—*Randy Maher*	1601 W Belleview Ave, Littleton CO 80120	303-795-2582	R	851*	.3
16	Nielsons Inc—*Curtis Broughton*	22419 County Rd G, Cortez CO 81321	970-565-8000	S	811*	.3
17	Grace Pacific Corp—*Robert Wilkinson*	PO Box 78, Honolulu HI 96810	808-245-9680	R	786*	.5
18	McHugh Enterprises Inc—*Bruce Lake*	PO Box 77939, Charlotte NC 28271	312-986-8000	R	746	.5
19	Rifenburg Construction Inc—*George Rifenburg*	159 Brick Church Rd, Troy NY 12180	518-279-3265	R	681*	.3
20	IA Construction Corp—*Robert Doucet* Barrett Paving Materials Inc	3 Becker Farm Rd Ste 3, Roseland NJ 07068	973-533-1004	S	593*	.3
21	Cleveland Cement Contractors Inc—*Michael H Simonetti*	4823 Van Epps Rd, Cleveland OH 44131	216-741-3954	R	557*	.3
22	Rogers Group Inc—*Gerard Geraghty*	PO Box 25250, Nashville TN 37202	615-242-0585	R	541*	1.6
23	LC Whitford Company Inc—*Brad Whitford*	164 N Main St, Wellsville NY 14895	585-593-3601	H	460*	.2
24	D'Addario Industries Inc—*David D'Addario*	PO Box 7056, Bridgeport CT 06601	203-333-9788	R	427*	.2
25	Road Constructors Inc—*William Quick*	6415 Bandel Rd NW, Rochester MN 55901	507-285-1211	R	425*	.2
26	Vecellio Contracting Corp—*Leo Vecillio Jr* Vecellio and Grogan Inc	PO Box 15065, West Palm Beach FL 33416	561-793-2102	S	422*	1.2
27	Lehman-Roberts Co—*Richard Moore*	PO Box 1603, Memphis TN 38101	901-774-4000	R	419*	.4
28	Brannan Paving Company Inc—*Waylon Brannan Jr*	PO Box 3403, Victoria TX 77903	361-573-3130	R	331*	.1
29	Community Asphalt Corp—*Jose Fernandez*	9725 Nw 117th Ave Ste, Medley FL 33178	305-884-9444	R	331*	.6
30	Cold Spring Construction Co—*Stephen Forrestel*	PO Box 358, Akron NY 14001	716-542-2011	R	330*	.1
31	Interstate Highway Construction Inc—*J Kenyon Schaeffer*	7135 S Tucson Way, Englewood CO 80112	303-790-9100	R	329*	.1
32	Barrett Paving Materials Inc—*Robert Doucet*	3 Becker Farm Rd Ste 3, Roseland NJ 07068	973-533-1001	R	305*	.3
33	Staker Paving and Construction Company Inc—*Scott Parson*	PO Box 27598, Salt Lake City UT 84127	801-258-3900	R	293*	2.2
34	Milestone Contractors LP—*Mark Blade*	PO Box 421459, Indianapolis IN 46242	317-788-1040	R	290*	.3
35	Skanska USA Civil West California District Inc—*Salvatore Mancini*	1995 Agua Mansa Rd, Riverside CA 92509	951-684-5360	R	284*	.9
36	Driggs Corp—*John Driggs*	8700 Ashwood Dr, Capitol Heights MD 20743	301-336-6700	R	273*	2.0
37	Striping Technology LP—*Linda Rudd*	PO Box 4279, Tyler TX 75712	903-595-6800	S	240*	.1
38	Garey Construction Company Inc—*Jack Garey*	11607 N Lamar Blvd, Austin TX 78753	512-837-5916	R	214*	.1
39	Ranger Construction Industries Inc—*Michael Slade*	PO Box 15065, West Palm Beach FL 33416	561-793-9400	R	213*	.8
40	Hubbard Construction Co—*Jean-Noel Velly*	PO Box 547217, Orlando FL 32854	407-645-5500	R	200*	1.3
41	Grady Brothers Inc	PO Box 421520, Indianapolis IN 46242	317-244-3343	R	183*	.1
42	Infrastructure Holdings Company LLC	115 S 48th St, Tempe AZ 85281	480-784-2910	R	180*	.9
43	L L Pelling Company Inc—*Chuck Finnegan*	PO Box 230, North Liberty IA 52317	319-626-4600	R	171*	.2
44	Orange County Transportation Authority—*Arthur Leahy*	PO Box 14184, Orange CA 92863	714-560-6282	R	167*	2.0
45	Aurora Blacktop Inc—*Jerry Leifheit*	1065 Sard Ave, Montgomery IL 60538	630-892-9389	R	166*	.1
46	Zachry Construction and Materials Inc—*David Zachry*	PO Box 33240, San Antonio TX 78265	210-871-2700	R	158*	2.7
47	Washington Group International Inc—*Stephen Hanks*	PO Box 73, Boise ID 83729	208-386-5000	R	150*	1.5
48	Poole and Kent Company Of Florida—*Steven Jordan*	PO Box 420556, Miami FL 33242	305-325-1930	R	150*	.3
49	Posillico Civil Inc—*Joseph Posillico*	1750 New Hwy, Farmingdale NY 11735	631-390-5738	R	149*	.4
50	Pciroads LLC—*Thomas Sloan*	14123 42nd St Ne, Saint Michael MN 55376	763-497-6100	R	149*	.1
51	Gohmann Asphalt And Construction Inc—*Jame Gohman*	1630 Broadway St, Clarksville IN 47129	812-282-1349	R	148*	.2
52	New Enterprise Stone and Lime Company Inc—*Donald Detwiler*	PO Box 77, New Enterprise PA 16664	814-766-2211	R	147*	1.5
53	T L Wallace Construction Inc—*Thomas Wallace*	PO Box 523, Columbia MS 39429	601-736-4525	R	141*	.4
54	Standard Construction Company Inc—*Clifton Hunt*	PO Box 38289, Germantown TN 38183	901-754-5181	R	140*	.2
55	Ceco Concrete Construction Inc—*Michael Moorehouse*	9135 Barton, Overland KS 66214	913-362-1855	S	138*	2.3
56	CC Myers Inc—*Clinton Myers*	3286 Fitzgerald Rd, Rancho Cordova CA 95742	916-635-9370	R	133*	.4
57	James McHugh Construction Co—*Michael Meagher* McHugh Enterprises Inc	1737 S Michigan Ave, Chicago IL 60616	312-986-8000	S	131*	.4
58	Herzog Contracting Corp—*Stanley Herzog*	PO Box 1089, Saint Joseph MO 64502	816-233-9001	R	130*	.9
59	APAC-Georgia Inc—*R Kirk Randolph*	900 Ashwood Pky Ste 70, Atlanta GA 30338	770-392-5300	S	130*	.4
60	Chester Bross Construction Service—*Chester Bross*	PO Box 430, Hannibal MO 63401	573-221-5958	R	126*	.3
61	Hunter Contracting Co—*Steve Padilla*	PO Box 900, Gilbert AZ 85299	480-892-0521	R	120*	.5
62	Redgwick Construction Co—*Bob Rahebi*	8150 Enterprise Dr, Newark CA 94560	510-782-0400	R	114*	<.1
63	Western Mobile Denver Paving Div—*Patrick Walker*	PO Box 21588, Denver CO 80221	303-657-4200	R	105*	.3
64	Hardrives Inc—*Steven Hall*	14475 Quiram Dr Ste 1, Rogers MN 55374	763-428-8886	R	104*	.3
65	RS Audley Inc—*Samuel Audley*	609 Rte 3-A, Bow NH 03304	603-224-7724	R	92*	.2
66	Royal Contracting Company Ltd—*Dave Hulihee*	677 Ahua St, Honolulu HI 96819	808-839-9006	R	89*	.2
67	Anderson Columbia Company Inc—*Joe Anderson*	PO Box 1829, Lake City FL 32056	386-752-7585	R	89*	1.0

Rank	Company Name—*Executive Officer*	Address, City, State, Zip	Phone	Type	Fin	Empls
68	JH Lynch and Sons Inc—*Stephen Lynch*	50 Lynch Pl, Cumberland RI 02864	401-333-4300	R	85*	.3
69	Peterson Contractors Inc—*Cordell Peterson*	PO Box A, Reinbeck IA 50669	319-345-2713	R	83*	.3
70	Kenmore Construction Company Inc—*William Scala*	700 Home Ave, Akron OH 44310	330-762-9373	R	83*	.3
71	McMurry Ready Mix Co—*W N McMurry*	PO Box 2488, Casper WY 82602	307-473-9581	R	82*	.3
72	Koss Construction Company Inc—*David Howard*	5830 SW Drury Ln, Topeka KS 66604	785-228-2928	R	81*	.3
73	Lakeside Industries Inc—*Timothy Lee*	PO Box 7016, Issaquah WA 98027	425-313-2600	R	78*	.8
74	Highway Construction Company Ltd—*Randy Ching*	720 Umi St, Honolulu HI 96819	808-841-5511	R	78*	<.1
75	CA Rasmussen Inc—*C A Rasmussen*	28548 Livingston Ave, Valencia CA 91355	661-367-9400	R	75*	.6
76	P Flanigan And Sons Inc—*Pierce Flanigan*	2444 Loch Raven Rd, Baltimore MD 21218	410-467-5900	R	74*	.3
77	Ecological Restoration and Management Inc	9475 Deereco Rd Ste 40, Timonium MD 21093	410-337-4899	S	70*	<.1
78	Cedar Valley Corp—*Steve R Jackson*	2637 Wagner Rd, Waterloo IA 50703	319-235-9537	R	64*	.1
79	Dmg Equipment Company Ltd—*James Armstrong*	PO Box 691, Conroe TX 77305	936-756-6960	R	64*	.2
80	Blythe Construction Inc—*Bill Carphardt*	PO Box 31635, Charlotte NC 28231	704-375-8432	S	64*	.6
81	Summers-Taylor Inc—*Rab Summers*	PO Box 1628, Elizabethton TN 37644	423-543-3181	R	63*	.4
82	Palmer Paving Corp—*David Callahan*	PO Box 47, Palmer MA 01069	413-283-8354	R	60*	<.1
83	PCI Roads Inc—*Thomas Sloan*	14123 42nd St NE, Saint Michael MN 55376	763-497-6100	R	60*	.5
84	Shelly And Sands Inc—*Richard Mcclelland*	PO Box 1585, Zanesville OH 43702	740-453-0721	R	58*	.6
85	Omg Midwest Inc—*Jim Gauger*	PO Box 3365, Des Moines IA 50316	515-266-9928	S	56*	.4
86	Reliable Contracting Company Inc—*Joseph Baldwin*	1 Churchview Rd, Millersville MD 21108	410-987-0313	R	55*	.5
87	White Construction Company Inc—*Luther White*	PO Box 790, Chiefland FL 32644	352-493-1444	R	54*	.7
88	Kamminga and Roodvoets Inc—*Dan Ringnalda*	3435 Broadmoor Ave SE, Grand Rapids MI 49512	616-949-0800	R	52*	.3
89	Bizzack Inc—*Lester Wimpy*	PO Box 12530, Lexington KY 40583	859-299-8001	R	51*	.3
90	LH Lacy Company Inc—*Mike Lacy*	1880 Crown Rd, Dallas TX 75234	214-357-0146	R	51*	.3
91	Simon Contractors Co—*Tim Gossman*	PO Box 209, Cheyenne WY 82003	307-632-7900	R	51*	.3
92	E and B Paving Inc—*Gary Stebbins*	286 W 300 N, Anderson IN 46012	765-643-5358	S	51*	.6
93	Mt Carmel Stabilization Group Inc—*Ed Pherson*	PO Box 458, Mount Carmel IL 62863	618-262-5118	R	50*	.1
94	CJ Mahan Construction Company Inc—*C Jeffery Mahan*	PO Box 670, Grove City OH 43123	614-875-8200	R	50*	.2
95	Ballenger Div—*Lee Powell*	PO Box 127, Greenville SC 29602	864-292-9550	D	49*	.2
96	Johnson Brothers Corp—*Walter D Johnson*	7500 Municipal Dr, Orlando FL 32819	407-948-6275	R	48*	.4
97	Leo Journagan Construction Co—*Allen Journagan*	3003 E Chestnut Expy S, Springfield MO 65802	417-869-7222	R	48*	.3
98	Paulsen Inc—*Larry Paulsen*	PO Box 17, Cozad NE 69130	308-784-3333	R	46*	.1
99	Laredo Paving Inc—*Bob Price*	PO Box 1029, Big Spring TX 79721	432-267-1691	R	46*	.1
100	PA Landers Inc—*Richard Mansfield*	PO Box 217, Hanover MA 02339	781-826-8818	R	46*	.3
101	Weekley Asphalt Paving Inc—*Daniel Weekley*	20701 Stirling Rd, Southwest Ranches FL 33332	954-680-8005	R	45*	.2
102	JD Posillico Inc—*Joseph Posillico*	1750 New Hwy, Farmingdale NY 11735	631-249-1872	R	43*	.4
103	Pulice Construction Inc—*WR Pulice*	2033 W Mountain View R, Phoenix AZ 85021	602-944-2241	R	43*	.3
104	Tucci and Sons Inc—*Michael F Tucci*	4224 Waller Rd, Tacoma WA 98443	253-922-6676	R	43*	.3
105	Hempt Brothers Inc—*George Hempt*	PO Box 278, Camp Hill PA 17001	717-737-3411	R	43*	.3
106	Reilly Construction Company Inc—*Chris Reilly*	110 E Main St, Ossian IA 52161	563-532-9211	R	42*	.3
107	McCarthy Improvement Co—*Joseph D Bush*	5401 Victoria Ave Ste, Davenport IA 52807	563-359-0321	R	41*	.3
108	Walter Toebe Construction—*Tom Stover*	29001 Wall St, Wixom MI 48393	248-349-7500	R	41*	.1
109	Petricca Industries Inc—*Basil Petricca*	PO Box 1145, Pittsfield MA 01202	413-442-6926	R	41*	.5
110	Nesbitt Contracting Company Inc—*James L Nesbitt*	100 S Price Rd, Tempe AZ 85281	480-423-7600	R	40*	.1
111	Shelly Daniels Asphalt—*Shelly Daniels*	16801 Delft Pl, Spring Hill FL 34610	727-056-4307	R	40*	<.1
112	Century Companies Inc—*Tim Robertson*	PO Box 579, Lewistown MT 59457	406-535-1200	R	39*	.1
113	Charles Blalock and Sons Inc—*Sidney Blalock*	PO Box 4750, Sevierville TN 37864	865-453-2808	R	39*	.3
114	Ferrell Paving Inc—*Dwight Ferrell*	2174 E Person Ave, Memphis TN 38114	901-324-3894	R	38*	.3
115	Oldcastle Sw Group Inc—*Craig Lambargy*	PO Box 3609, Grand Junction CO 81502	970-243-4900	R	36*	.4
116	ME Companies Inc—*Timothy R Foley*	635 Brooksedge Blvd, Westerville OH 43081	614-818-4900	R	36*	.1
117	Capitol Paving of DC Inc—*Francisco Neto*	2211 Channing St NE, Washington DC 20018	202-529-7225	R	36*	.1
118	W - L Construction and Paving Inc—*Kenneth Taylor*	PO Box 927, Chilhowie VA 24319	276-646-3804	R	36*	.2
119	Duininck Cos—*W Duininck*	PO Box 208, Prinsburg MN 56281	320-978-6011	R	35*	.3
120	Scott Construction Inc—*John D Scott*	PO Box 340, Lake Delton WI 53940	608-254-2555	R	35*	.2
121	WE Blain and Sons Inc—*Bill Blain*	PO Box 1208, Mount Olive MS 39119	601-797-4551	R	35*	.2
122	Hills Materials Co—*Lynn Kading*	PO Box 2320, Rapid City SD 57709	605-394-3300	R	35*	.3
123	Dement Construction Co—*William D Dement*	PO Box 1812, Jackson TN 38302	731-424-6306	R	34*	.3
124	Gary Merlino Construction Co—*Gary M Merlino*	9125 10th Ave S, Seattle WA 98108	206-762-9125	R	34*	.3
125	Dickerson Group Inc—*John Joyner*	PO Box 5011, Monroe NC 28111	704-289-3111	R	34*	.2
126	Everett Dykes Grassing Company Inc—*Van Dykes*	1339 GA Hwy 112, Cochran GA 31014	478-934-2707	S	34*	.1
127	Greggo and Ferrara Inc—*Nicholas Ferrara Jr*	4048 New Castle Ave, New Castle DE 19720	302-658-5241	R	34*	.1
128	Gilvin-Terrill Ltd—*Martha Chow*	PO Box 9027, Amarillo TX 79105	806-944-5200	R	33*	.1
129	Perez Interboro Asphalt Company Inc—*Robert Perez*	99 Paidge Ave, Brooklyn NY 11222	718-383-4100	R	33*	.2
130	Holland Corporation Inc—*James Holland*	PO Box 14130, Shawnee Mission KS 66285	913-888-5277	R	32*	<.1
131	Ser Construction Inc—*Rosbel Ramos*	PO Box 891145, Houston TX 77289	713-473-7900	R	31*	.2
132	Western Paving Contractors Inc—*Dorna Seanez*	15533 E Arrow Hwy, Irwindale CA 91706	626-338-7889	R	31*	.1
133	Richard F Kline Inc—*Thomas Kline*	7700 Grove Rd, Frederick MD 21704	301-662-8211	R	31*	.3
134	Eddins Electric Company Inc—*William Dunton*	PO Box 3455, West Columbia SC 29171	803-796-9078	R	31*	.1
135	Robert T Winzinger Inc—*JoAnn Winzinger*	1704 Marne Hwy, Hainesport NJ 08036	609-267-8600	R	30*	.2
136	Barber Brothers Contracting Company Inc—*Lionel H Barber*	PO Box 66296, Baton Rouge LA 70896	225-355-5611	R	30*	.2
137	Halifax Paving Inc—*James Davis*	PO Box 730549, Ormond Beach FL 32173	386-676-0200	R	27*	.2
138	Grg Construction Company Inc—*Glen Greer*	3740 E 43rd Pl, Tucson AZ 85713	520-544-8933	R	27*	.1
139	Matich Corp—*Martin Matich*	PO Box 50000, San Bernardino CA 92412	909-382-7400	R	26*	.2
140	Berns Construction Company Inc—*Dan C Keys*	PO Box 19815, Indianapolis IN 46219	317-545-8714	R	26*	.2
141	BR Amon and Sons Inc—*Tom Amon*	W-2950 Hwy 11, Elkhorn WI 53101	262-723-2547	R	26*	.2
142	Buckley and Co—*Joseph Martosella*	3401 Moore St, Philadelphia PA 19145	215-334-7500	R	26*	.2
143	General Construction Co—*Ron Morford* Peter Kiewit Sons' Inc	19472 Powder Hill Pl N, Poulsbo WA 98370	360-779-3200	S	26*	.2
144	Valley Construction Co—*William Hass*	PO Box 2020, Rock Island IL 61204	309-787-0292	R	26*	.2
145	Evans and Associates Enterprises Inc—*Linda Brown*	PO Box 30, Ponca City OK 74602	580-765-6693	R	25*	.3
146	DH Blattner and Sons Inc—*Scott Blattner*	392 County Rd 50, Avon MN 56310	320-356-7351	R	25*	.3
147	Ford Construction Co—*John H Ford*	PO Box 527, Dyersburg TN 38025	731-285-5185	R	25*	.2
148	Harper Co—*Michael Shayeson*	PO Box 420, Hebron KY 41048	859-586-8890	R	25*	.2
149	Amarillo Road Co—*Charles Schmidt*	PO Box 32075, Amarillo TX 79102	806-335-2922	R	25*	.1
150	Arrow Road Construction Co—*John Healy*	PO Box 334, Mount Prospect IL 60056	847-437-0700	R	25*	.2
151	Elmo Greer and Sons LLC—*Rex Greer*	PO Box 730, London KY 40743	606-843-6136	R	25*	.3
152	Kankakee Valley Construction Co—*Leonard Tobey*	PO Box 767, Kankakee IL 60901	815-937-8700	R	24*	.2
153	Cutler Repaving Inc—*Bob Veskerna*	921 E 27th St, Lawrence KS 66046	785-843-1524	R	24*	.1
154	Louisville Paving Company Inc—*William Dougherty*	1801 Payne St, Louisville KY 40206	502-583-1726	R	23*	.2
155	Flasher Ltd—*Curt Nichols*	PO Box 12637, San Antonio TX 78212	210-736-4251	R	23*	.1
156	Francis O Day Company Inc—*Francis Day*	850 E Gude Dr Ste A, Rockville MD 20850	301-762-6643	R	22*	.2

Note: An asterisk (*) indicates an estimated financial figure. The company type code used is as follows: R = Private, P = Public, S = Private Subsidiary, B = Public Subsidiary, D = Division, J = Joint Venture, I = Investment Fund.

COMPANY RANKINGS BY SALES WITHIN 4-DIGIT SIC

Rank	Company Name—*Executive Officer*	Address, City, State, Zip	Phone	Type	Fin	Empls
157	Jim Smith Contracting Company LLC—*Karen Lichgenberg*	1108 Dover Rd, Grand Rivers KY 42045	270-362-8661	R	22*	.2
158	Williamson Company Incorporated SL—*Blair Williamson*	PO Box 648, Charlottesville VA 22902	434-295-6137	R	22*	.1
159	Baker Rock Resources—*Todd Baker*	21880 Sw Farmington Rd, Beaverton OR 97007	503-642-2531	R	20*	.2
160	D and J Enterprises Inc—*Richard Starr*	3495 Lee Rd 10, Auburn AL 36832	334-821-8205	R	20*	.1
161	Ace Paving Company Inc—*Richard Christopherson*	PO Box 4520, Bremerton WA 98312	360-479-4200	R	20*	.1
162	Pittman Construction Co—*Arnie Pittman*	PO Box 155, Conyers GA 30012	770-922-8660	R	20*	.1
163	Ralph L Wadsworth Construction Company Inc—*Kip Wadsworth*	166 E 14000 South Rm 2, Draper UT 84020	801-553-1661	R	20*	.1
164	Russell Standard Corp—*James Johnson*	285 Kappa Dr Ste 300, Pittsburgh PA 15238	412-449-0700	R	20*	<.1
165	Midland Asphalt Materials Inc—*Timothy Sanders* Barrett Paving Materials Inc	PO Box 388, Tonawanda NY 14151	716-692-0730	S	19*	.1
166	Graves and Associates Inc—*Don C Graves*	PO Box 1549, Pine Bluff AR 71613	870-535-4123	R	19*	.1
167	Asphalt Contractors Inc—*Charles Brassell*	PO Box 241447, Montgomery AL 36124	334-279-5228	R	19*	.1
168	Ashmore Brothers Inc—*Richard Ashmore*	PO Box 529, Greer SC 29652	864-879-7311	R	18*	.1
169	Phillips Contracting Co—*Stuart Phillips*	PO Box 2069, Columbus MS 39704	662-328-6250	R	18*	.1
170	Oakgrove Construction Inc—*Douglas May*	PO Box 103, Elma NY 14059	716-652-2200	R	18*	.1
171	Crisdel Construction Group Inc—*Frank Criscola Sr*	240 Ryan St, South Plainfield NJ 07080	908-561-7550	R	17*	.1
172	F Miller and Sons Inc—*Joe T Miller*	PO Box 16863, Lake Charles LA 70616	337-439-4552	R	17*	.1
173	Hoover Construction Company Inc—*Peter G Johnson*	PO Box 1007, Virginia MN 55792	218-741-3280	R	17*	.1
174	JA Johnson Paving Co—*Dale Johnson*	1025 E Addison Ct, Arlington Heights IL 60005	847-439-2025	R	17*	.1
175	RL Rider and Co—*Charles W Rider*	PO Box 73, Warrenton VA 20188	540-347-1611	R	17*	.1
176	Allen Company Inc—*Hugh Gabbard*	3009 Atkinson Ave Ste, Lexington KY 40509	859-543-3361	R	17*	.1
177	Asphalt Paving Co—*Jeffrey Keller*	14802 W 44th Ave, Golden CO 80403	303-279-6611	R	16*	.1
178	Koski Construction Co—*Donald R Koski*	PO Box 1038, Ashtabula OH 44005	440-997-5337	R	16*	.1
179	Kaikor Construction Company Inc—*Garrett Sullivan*	PO Box 30162, Honolulu HI 96820	808-841-3110	R	16*	.1
180	Rockford Blacktop Construction Co—*Ben Holmstrom*	PO Box 2071, Loves Park IL 61130	815-654-4700	R	16*	.1
181	H-K Contractors Inc—*Wade Foster*	PO Box 51450, Idaho Falls ID 83405	208-523-6600	R	15*	.1
182	Peavy and Son Construction Company Inc—*Magnus Peavy*	PO Box 2369, Havana FL 32333	850-539-5019	R	15*	.1
183	JH Strain and Sons Inc—*Steve Strain*	PO Box 277, Tye TX 79563	325-692-0067	R	14*	.1
184	Edward Kraemer and Sons Inc—*Scott Peterson*	PO Box 220, Plain WI 53577	608-546-2311	R	14*	.1
185	Bowes Construction Inc—*Lyle Bowes*	2915 22nd Ave S, Brookings SD 57006	605-693-3557	R	14*	.1
186	Interstate Concrete And Asphalt Co—*Jeff Schaffer*	849 W Kathleen Ave, Coeur D Alene ID 83815	208-765-1144	R	14*	.1
187	Brystar Contracting Inc—*Bryan Phelps*	8385 Chemical Rd, Beaumont TX 77705	409-842-6768	R	13*	.1
188	Frederick Derr and Company Inc—*Fredrick M Derr*	3801 N Orange Ave, Sarasota FL 34234	941-355-8575	R	13*	.1
189	Rogers Construction Inc—*AJ Urbanek*	1220 SE 190th Ave, Portland OR 97233	503-254-5517	R	13*	.1
190	Millstone Bangert Inc—*Thom Kuhn*	601 Fountain Lakes Blv, Saint Charles MO 63301	636-949-0038	R	13*	.1
191	East Alabama Paving Company Inc—*Charles Lawler*	PO Box 2630, Opelika AL 36803	334-749-8865	R	13*	.1
192	Gallagher and Burk Inc—*Edwin Gallagher*	PO Box 7227, Oakland CA 94601	510-261-0466	R	13*	.1
193	Hudson River Construction Company Inc—*Eugene D Hallock Jr*	101 Dunham Dr Port of, Albany NY 12202	518-434-6677	R	12*	.1
194	Short and Son Paving Company Incorporated B P—*Burton Short*	PO Box 2007, Petersburg VA 23804	804-732-8412	R	12*	.1
195	Midwest Asphalt Corp—*Blair Bury*	PO Box 5477, Hopkins MN 55343	952-937-8033	R	12*	.1
196	Duffek Sand and Gravel Inc—*Calvin Krueger*	PO Box 190, Antigo WI 54409	715-623-7616	R	12*	<.1
197	Tampa Steel Erecting Co—*Robert Clark*	5127 Bloomingdale Ave, Tampa FL 33619	813-677-7184	R	11*	.1
198	Curran Group Inc—*Michael Curran*	286 Memorial Ct, Crystal Lake IL 60014	815-455-5100	R	11*	.1
199	James H Drew Corp—*Kennith L Sipe*	PO Box 68935, Indianapolis IN 46268	317-876-3739	R	11*	.1
200	AJ Walker Construction Co—*Charles Armstrong*	PO Box 118, Mattoon IL 61938	217-235-5647	R	11*	<.1
201	Rogers Construction Company Ltd—*W Rogers*	4915 S Interstate 35, Georgetown TX 78626	512-930-1155	R	11*	.1
202	U S Asphalt Co—*Nancy Cagle*	PO Box 45209, Omaha NE 68145	402-895-6666	R	10*	.1
203	Copeland Paving Inc—*Robert Copeland*	PO Box 608, Grants Pass OR 97528	541-476-4441	R	10*	.1
204	Teal Construction Inc—*Robert Edgell*	PO Box 779, Dover DE 19903	302-678-9500	R	10*	.1
205	Dalton Enterprises Inc—*Peter Dalton*	131 Willow St, Cheshire CT 06410	203-272-3221	R	10*	.1
206	Rupp Construction Company Inc—*Douglas Rupp*	PO Box 1, Slayton MN 56172	507-836-8555	R	10*	.1
207	D'ambra Construction Company Inc—*Michael D'ambra*	800 Jefferson Blvd Ste, Warwick RI 02886	401-737-1300	R	9*	.1
208	Nevada Barricade and Sign Company Inc—*Tamara Dethmers*	PO Box 20459, Reno NV 89515	775-331-5100	R	9*	.1
209	Baxter's Asphalt And Concrete Inc—*David Sloan*	PO Box 938, Marianna FL 32447	850-482-4621	R	9*	.1
210	Brown Brothers Construction Co—*Dewitt Brown*	10801 Us Hwy 421 N, Zionville NC 28698	828-297-2131	R	9*	.1
211	Folsom Construction Co—*Rann Folsom*	PO Box 817, Cordele GA 31010	229-273-6626	R	9*	.1
212	Colwell Construction Company Inc—*Carlton Colwell*	PO Box 850, Blairsville GA 30514	706-745-6239	R	8*	.1
213	Tony Angelo Cement Construction Co—*Carl Evangelista*	46850 Grand River, Novi MI 48374	248-344-4000	R	8*	.1
214	Burgreen Contracting Company Inc—*Richard Burgreen*	PO Box 49, Athens AL 35612	256-232-5666	R	8*	.1
215	SE Cline Construction Inc—*Sam Cline*	PO Box 354425, Palm Coast FL 32135	386-446-6444	R	8*	.1
216	Loch Sand And Construction Co—*Robert Loch*	PO Box 647, Maryville MO 64468	660-562-3100	R	8*	.1
217	Joseph Mccormick Construction Company Inc—*Owen Cormick*	PO Box 176, Erie PA 16512	814-899-3111	R	8*	<.1
218	Kibler Construction Company Inc—*Warren Kibler*	PO Box 408, Finksburg MD 21048	410-833-5345	R	7*	.1
219	Babler Brothers Inc—*Lloyd Babler Jr*	PO Box 11269, Portland OR 97211	503-285-7133	R	7*	<.1
220	RSE Grading Company Inc—*Roddy Sturdivant*	PO Box 210, Stephens GA 30667	770-921-3207	R	7*	.1
221	Templeton Paving LLC—*Marvin Templeton*	PO Box 4339, Lynchburg VA 24502	434-239-0383	R	6*	.1
222	Gallagher Asphalt Corp—*Charles Gallagher*	18100 Indiana Ave, Thornton IL 60476	708-877-7160	R	6*	<.1
223	Chapman Grading and Concrete Company Inc—*Robert Chapman*	2180 Chesnee Hwy, Spartanburg SC 29303	864-585-8133	R	6*	<.1
224	Weststar Construction Inc—*C Morgan*	9345 Pettit Rd, Baker LA 70714	225-775-6343	R	6*	<.1
225	Salt Lake Sand And Gravel Inc—*David Balls*	PO Box 2348, Sandy UT 84091	801-571-2721	R	6*	<.1
226	Jet Asphalt and Rock Co—*Jim Bennett*	PO Box 1567, El Dorado AR 71731	870-863-7801	R	6*	<.1
227	E D Baker Company Ltd—*Donnie Cornell*	PO Box 3190, Borger TX 79008	806-273-7501	R	5*	<.1
228	Heaton Brothers Construction Company Inc—*Charles Heaton*	5805 Saufley Field Rd, Pensacola FL 32526	850-453-1253	R	5*	<.1
229	Inland Asphalt Co—*Randy Wild*	PO Box 3366, Spokane WA 99220	509-534-6221	R	5*	<.1
230	Accurate Patterns Inc—*John Guidice*	246 W 38th St Fl 3, New York NY 10018	212-391-8626	R	5*	<.1
231	Superior Asphalt Of Central Florida Inc—*Howard Hewitt*	PO Box 490697, Leesburg FL 34749	352-383-2889	R	4*	<.1
232	Metroclean Express Corp—*Michael Strasser*	5301 Vernon Blvd, Long Island City NY 11101	718-482-0080	R	4*	<.1
233	Advanced Asphalt Co—*Richard Nelson*	PO Box 234, Princeton IL 61356	815-872-9911	R	4*	<.1
234	Allendale Gravel Company Inc—*James Litherland*	18306 Wabash 18 Ave, Allendale IL 62410	618-263-3521	R	4*	<.1
235	Spartan Asphalt Paving Co—*Scott Huber*	16777 Wood Rd, Lansing MI 48906	517-482-9611	R	4*	<.1
236	Hunt Paving Corp—*Bill Palmer*	2450 S Tibbs Ave, Indianapolis IN 46241	317-227-7800	S	4*	<.1
237	Mft Construction Inc—*Kathy Lienemann*	1426 9th Ave, Council Bluffs IA 51501	712-323-7926	R	4*	<.1
238	Hutch-N-Son Construction—*Harold Hutchinson*	PO Box 1874, Seneca SC 29679	864-885-1688	R	4*	<.1
239	Troop Construction and Electric Inc—*Frank Dominguez*	PO Box 754, Pine Brook NJ 07058	908-354-5585	R	4*	<.1
240	King Construction Inc—*John King*	16 Northwood Dr, Bloomfield CT 06002	860-242-2263	R	4*	<.1
241	Freeman Contracting Inc—*David Freeman*	PO Box 5690, Brookings OR 97415	541-469-4435	R	3*	<.1

Rank	Company Name—*Executive Officer*	Address, City, State, Zip	Phone	Type	Fin	Empls
242	Arawak Paving Company Inc—*John Barrett*	7503 Weymouth Rd, Hammonton NJ 08037	609-561-4100	R	3*	<.1
243	Bdk Group Of Northern Michigan Inc—*Thomas Irwin*	6795 Us Hwy 31 N, Charlevoix MI 49720	574-875-5183	R	3*	<.1
244	Western Construction Inc—*Steve Heaton*	PO Box 15569, Boise ID 83715	208-345-1440	R	3*	<.1
245	Commonwealth Stone—*Donald Fetterolf*	PO Box 66, Boswell PA 15531	814-629-6999	R	3*	<.1
246	Keystone Lime Co—*Melinda Walker*	PO Box 278, Springs PA 15562	814-662-2711	R	3*	.1
247	EZ Sweep Corp—*Teresa Nichols*	PO Box 1231, Tarpon Springs FL 34688	727-939-8600	R	3*	<.1
248	Geneva Construction Co—*John Bryan*	PO Box 998, Aurora IL 60507	630-892-4357	R	2*	<.1
249	JF Barton Contracting Co—*James F Barton Jr*	PO Box 73525, Houston TX 77273	281-443-3800	R	2*	<.1
250	Wallace Construction Inc—*Richard Wallace*	PO Box 1432, Martinsville IN 46151	317-422-5356	R	2*	<.1
251	Prosser Construction Co—*David Cruitt*	Rr 3 Box 75, Shelbyville IL 62565	217-774-5032	R	1*	<.1
252	Asphalt Patching Inc—*R Brillhart*	2810 Columbia Ave, Indianapolis IN 46205	317-925-6391	R	1*	<.1
253	Madden Contracting Company Inc—*James Madden*	PO Box 856, Minden LA 71058	318-377-0928	R	1*	.2
254	Angelo Iafrate Cos—*Angelo E Lafrate*	26300 Sherwood Ave, Warren MI 48091	586-756-1070	R	N/A	2.0
255	Leon E Wintermyer Inc—*Leon E Wintermyer*	220 Yocumtown Rd, Etters PA 17319	717-938-1468	R	N/A	.1

TOTALS: SIC 1611 Highway & Street Construction
Companies: 255   66,419   110.4

1622 Bridge, Tunnel & Elevated Highway

Rank	Company Name—*Executive Officer*	Address, City, State, Zip	Phone	Type	Fin	Empls
1	J Ray McDermott Holdings Inc—*Bob Deason* J Ray McDermott SA	757 N Eldridge Pky, Houston TX 77079	281-870-5000	S	2,529*	3.0
2	J Ray McDermott SA—*Stephen Johnson*	757 N Eldridge Pkwy, Houston TX 77079	281-870-5000	S	816*	7.1
3	Crowder Construction Co—*Otis A Crowder*	PO Box 30007, Charlotte NC 28230	704-372-3541	R	557*	.7
4	Guy F Atkinson Construction LLC—*Scott Lynn*	385 Interlocken Cresce, Broomfield CO 80021	303-410-2542	S	469	1.1
5	Allan A Myers Inc—*Allen Myers*	PO Box 1340, Worcester PA 19490	610-222-8800	R	435*	2.0
6	Jensen Construction Co—*Kurt Rasmussen*	PO Box 3345, Des Moines IA 50316	515-266-5173	R	238*	.8
7	CONTECH Bridge Solutions Inc—*Ronald C Keating*	PO box 20266, Dayton OH 45420	937-254-2233	S	184*	.2
8	Traylor Brothers Inc—*Thomas W Traylor*	PO Box 5165, Evansville IN 47716	812-477-1542	R	175*	.9
9	Vcc LLC—*Raouf Kassissieh*	600 Colinas Blvd E Ste, Irving TX 75039	214-574-4500	R	161*	.2
10	DA Collins Construction Co—*Thomas F Longe*	269 Ballard Road, Wilton NY 12831	518-664-9855	R	160*	.4
11	DeFoe Corp—*John Amicucci*	800 S Columbus Ave, Mount Vernon NY 10550	914-699-7440	R	160*	.2
12	Sehgal Sons Inc—*Nikhil Sehgal*	1234 Park Ave, New York NY 10128	987-184-0812	R	150*	5.9
13	Lunda Construction Co—*Larry Lunda*	PO Box 669, Black River Falls WI 54615	715-284-9491	R	148*	.7
14	Bradbury and Stamm Construction Company Inc—*Monique Blackman*	PO Box 10850, Albuquerque NM 87184	505-765-1200	R	145*	.3
15	George Harms Construction Co—*Ed Nyland*	PO Box 817, Farmingdale NJ 07727	732-938-4004	R	141*	.2
16	MCM Construction Inc—*Jim Carter*	PO Box 620, North Highlands CA 95660	916-334-1221	R	131*	.4
17	CW Matthews Contracting Company Inc—*Q Hammack*	PO Box 970, Marietta GA 30061	770-422-7520	R	105*	1.4
18	Word Constructors LLC—*Andy Cotten*	PO Box 310330, New Braunfels TX 78131	830-625-2365	R	62*	.4
19	Steve P Rados Inc—*Wally Rados* Rados Co	2002 E McFadden Ave St, Santa Ana CA 92705	714-835-4612	S	60*	.2
20	James D Morrissey Inc—*James D Morrissey Jr*	9119 Frankford Ave, Philadelphia PA 19114	215-333-8000	R	58*	.3
21	JF White Contracting Co—*Peter T White*	10 Burr St, Framingham MA 01701	508-879-4700	R	52*	.4
22	Rasmussen Group Inc—*Kurt Rasmussen*	PO Box 3333, Des Moines IA 50316	515-266-5173	R	42*	.1
23	George and Lynch Inc—*Dennis J Dinger*	150 Lafferty Ln, Dover DE 19901	302-736-3031	R	40*	.2
24	Rados Co—*Steve P Rados*	PO Box 15128, Santa Ana CA 92735	714-835-4612	R	38*	.3
25	Brutoco Engineering and Construction Inc—*Michael J Murphy*	PO Box 310189, Fontana CA 92331	909-350-3535	R	38*	.2
26	Skanska Koch Inc—*Robert Koch*	400 Roosevelt Ave, Carteret NJ 07008	732-969-1700	S	36*	.5
27	GAL Construction Company Inc—*Luis Ruscitto*	PO Box 127, Belle Vernon PA 15012	724-929-3000	R	36*	.2
28	CA Hull Company Inc—*Joseph R Malloure*	8177 Goldie Rd, Walled Lake MI 48390	248-363-3813	R	32*	.2
29	Adams and Smith Inc—*James Smith*	1380 W Center St, Lindon UT 84042	801-576-1200	R	29*	.1
30	R Zoppo Corp—*David Zoppo*	160 Old Maple St, Stoughton MA 02072	781-344-8822	R	26*	.2
31	AS Horner Construction Company Inc—*Dave Krueger*	5801 Bobby Foster Rd S, Albuquerque NM 87106	505-873-1577	R	19*	.2
32	Kiewit Southern Co (Atlanta Georgia)	450 Dividend Dr, Peachtree City GA 30269	770-487-2300	S	19*	<.1
33	J J Ferguson Sand and Gravel Co—*Jerry Steen*	PO Box 660, Greenwood MS 38935	662-453-5451	R	19*	.2
34	Pressure Concrete Inc—*Tony McDougle*	4158 Musgrove Dr, Florence AL 35630	256-764-5941	R	17*	.1
35	Beaty Construction Inc—*Dan Beaty*	5292 W 100N, Boggstown IN 46110	317-835-2254	R	14*	.1
36	Cowin and Company Inc—*John Cowin*	PO Box 19009, Birmingham AL 35219	205-945-1300	R	13*	.1
37	Meccor Industries Ltd—*Jonathan Eng*	3933 Oakton St, Skokie IL 60076	847 676 0202	R	12*	.1
38	Kubricky Construction Corp—*William Donnelly* DA Collins Construction Co	PO Box 3202, Glens Falls NY 12801	518-792-5864	S	12*	<.1
39	Ideker Inc—*Roger Ideker*	PO Box 7140, Saint Joseph MO 64507	816-364-3970	R	11*	.1
40	Merco Inc—*M Mergentime*	1117 Rte 31 S, Lebanon NJ 08833	908-730-8622	R	10*	.1
41	K Herron Construction Co—*Betty Herron*	4288 SW 12th St, Fort Lauderdale FL 33317	954-306-6170	R	10*	.1
42	Marra Corp—*Anthony Marra*	700 E 73rd St, Cleveland OH 44103	440-543-1412	R	9*	<.1
43	Mid Eastern Builders—*George B Clark*	PO Box 6748, Chesapeake VA 23323	757-487-5858	R	6*	.2
44	Capitol Tunneling Inc—*Kyle Lucas*	2216 Refugee Rd, Columbus OH 43207	614-444-0255	R	4*	<.1
45	Mac Const Inc—*Mark Mcclanahan*	PO Box 927, Chilhowie VA 24319	276-498-4300	R	3*	<.1
46	Tidwell And Associates Construction Company Inc—*Cheryl Tidwell*	PO Box 483, Booneville MS 38829	662-728-9709	R	3*	<.1

TOTALS: SIC 1622 Bridge, Tunnel & Elevated Highway
Companies: 46   7,431   29.6

1623 Water, Sewer & Utility Lines

Rank	Company Name—*Executive Officer*	Address, City, State, Zip	Phone	Type	Fin	Empls
1	Emcor Group Inc—*Anthony J Guzzi*	301 Merritt Seven 5th, Norwalk CT 06851	203-849-7800	P	5,614	25.0
2	MasTec Inc—*Jose R Mas*	800 S Douglas Rd 12th, Coral Gables FL 33134	305-599-1800	P	3,009	10.0
3	Zachry Construction Corp—*John B Zachry*	PO Box 33240, San Antonio TX 78265	210-871-2700	R	1,594*	11.5
4	Dycom Industries Inc—*Steven E Nielsen*	11770 US Hwy 1 Ste 101, Palm Beach Gardens FL 33408	561-627-7171	P	1,036	8.3
5	InfraSource Services Inc—*Paul Daily*	100 W 6th St Ste 300, Media PA 19063	610-480-8073	S	992	4.0
6	Insituform Technologies Inc—*Joseph Burgess*	17988 Edison Ave, Chesterfield MO 63005	636-530-8000	R	915	3.2
7	Rockdale Pipeline Inc—*Kenneth Richardson*	PO Box 1157, Conyers GA 30012	770-922-4123	R	620*	.1
8	Henkels and McCoy Inc—*Roderick Henkels*	985 Jolly Rd, Blue Bell PA 19422	215-283-7600	R	617*	5.1
9	MYR Group Inc—*William A Koertner*	1701 W Golf Rd Ste 101, Rolling Meadows IL 60008	847-290-1891	B	597	2.8
10	UniTek Global Services Inc—*C Scott Hisey*	1777 Sentry Pky Ste 30, Blue Bell PA 19422	267-464-1700	P	402	5.0
11	Ansco and Associates Inc Dycom Industries Inc	PO Box 18445, Greensboro NC 27410	336 852 3433	S	348*	.6
12	CableCom Inc Dycom Industries Inc	8602 Maltby Rd, Woodinville WA 98072	360-668-1300	S	290*	.5
13	STS LLC—*Dennis Tarosky* Dycom Industries Inc	2575 Westsdie Pkwy, Alpharetta GA 30004	678-461-3900	S	255*	.7

Note: An asterisk (*) indicates an estimated financial figure. The company type code used is as follows: R = Private, P = Public, S = Private Subsidiary, B = Public Subsidiary, D = Division, J = Joint Venture, I = Investment Fund.

COMPANY RANKINGS BY SALES WITHIN 4-DIGIT SIC

Rank	Company Name—*Executive Officer*	Address, City, State, Zip	Phone	Type	Fin	Empls
14	Meadow Valley Corp—*Bradley Larson*	PO Box 60726, Phoenix AZ 85082	602-437-5400	R	206*	.5
15	Yantis Co—*Blake Yantis*	3611 Paesanos Pky, San Antonio TX 78231	210-655-3780	R	203*	.5
16	CW Wright Construction Company Inc—*Jay E Sprull*	PO Box 3810, Chester VA 23831	804-768-1054	R	183*	.5
17	Reynolds Inc (Orleans Indiana)—*Jeff Reynolds*	4520 N State Rd 37, Orleans IN 47452	812-865-3232	R	180*	.5
18	New River Electrical Corp—*Thomas M Wolden*	PO Box 70, Cloverdale VA 24077	540-966-1650	R	175*	.5
19	Star Construction LLC Dycom Industries Inc	PO Box 6297, Knoxville TN 37914	865-521-6795	S	174*	.3
20	North Houston Pole Line Corp—*Earl Austin*	1608 Margaret St, Houston TX 77093	713-691-3616	R	173*	2.0
21	Power Line Services Inc—*Mark Crowson*	10077 Grogans Mill Rd, Spring TX 77380	281-651-2991	R	170*	1.0
22	Garney Construction Co—*Michael Heitman*	1333 NW Vivion Rd, Kansas City MO 64118	816-741-4600	R	169*	.7
23	Northeast Utilities Service Company Inc—*Charles Shivery*	PO Box 270, Hartford CT 06141	860-665-5000	R	155*	1.6
24	W M Lyles Co—*Richard Nemmer*	PO Box 4377, Fresno CA 93744	559-441-1900	R	145*	.2
25	Henkels and McCoy East Region Headquarters—*T Roderick Hinkels* Henkels and McCoy Inc	PO Box 19422, Blue Bell PA 19422	215-283-7600	D	144*	.2
26	Flippo Construction Company Inc—*Brian Flippo*	3820 Penn-Belt Pl, Forestville MD 20747	301-967-6800	R	141*	.4
27	Underground Construction Company Inc—*Chris Ronco*	5145 Industrial Way, Benicia CA 94510	707-746-8800	S	137*	.4
28	Oscar Renda Contracting Inc—*Oscar Renda*	608 Henrietta Creek Rd, Roanoke TX 76262	817-491-2703	R	136*	.4
29	EEI Holding Corp—*Robert Egizii*	700 N MacArthur Blvd, Springfield IL 62702	217-528-4001	R	121*	.3
30	Strike Construction LLC—*Steve Pate*	831 Crossbridge Dr, Spring TX 77373		R	118*	.6
31	Locating Inc—*Steven E Nielsen* Dycom Industries Inc	2575 Westside Pkwy Ste, Alpharetta GA 30004	678-461-3900	S	118*	.3
32	Atrex Inc—*David W Bradford*	175 Industrial Loop S, Orange Park FL 32073	904-264-9086	R	117*	.3
33	Apex Digital LLC (Sturgis Kentucky)—*David Ji* Dycom Industries Inc	PO Box 10, Sturgis KY 42459	270-333-3360	S	116*	.2
34	Irby Construction Co—*Bill Korlath*	PO Box 1819, Jackson MS 39215	601-969-1811	S	114*	.7
35	Berwick Electric Co—*Jim Peterson*	PO Box 7286, Colorado Springs CO 80933	719-632-7683	R	106*	.3
36	UTILX Corp—*John Connolly*	PO Box 97009, Kent WA 98064	253-395-0200	S	105	.9
37	Niels Fugal Sons Co—*Guy Fugal* Dycom Industries Inc	1005 S Main, Pleasant Grove UT 84062	801-785-3152	S	104*	.3
38	B Frank Joy Company Inc—*T Kenneth Joy*	5355 Kilmer Pl, Hyattsville MD 20781	301-779-9400	R	97*	.3
39	Lambert's Cable Splicing Company LLC—*Steven Nielson* Dycom Industries Inc	PO Box 563, Sharpsburg NC 27878	252-442-9777	S	93*	.2
40	Solo Construction Corp—*Randy Pierson*	3855 Commerce Pky, Miramar FL 33025	305-944-3922	R	90*	.2
41	Mountain Cascade Inc—*Michael Fuller*	PO Box 5050, Livermore CA 94551	925-373-8370	R	89*	.3
42	Colich and Sons	547 W 140th St, Gardena CA 90248	323-770-2920	R	83*	.2
43	Asplundh Construction Corp—*Christopher Asplundh Sr*	93 County Rd 101, Yaphank NY 11980	631-205-9340	S	80*	.6
44	Argonaut Constructors Inc—*Michael D Smith*	PO Box 639, Santa Rosa CA 95402	707-542-4862	R	80*	.2
45	GSE Construction Company Inc—*Orlando Gutierrez*	6950 Preston Ave, Livermore CA 94551	925-447-0292	R	70*	.2
46	Intren Inc—*Loretta Rosenmayer*	18202 W Union Rd, Union IL 60180	815-923-2300	R	68*	.3
47	Ranger Pipelines Inc—*Thomas Hunt*	PO Box 24109, San Francisco CA 94124	415-382-3700	R	66*	.1
48	L D'agostini and Sons Inc—*Antonio D'agostini*	15801 23 Mile Rd, Macomb MI 48042	586-781-3193	R	61*	.1
49	Wilson Construction Co—*Don Wilson*	PO Box 1190, Canby OR 97013	503-263-6882	R	61*	.2
50	Western Water Constructors Inc—*John Mcgarva*	707 Aviation Blvd, Santa Rosa CA 95403	707-540-9640	R	59*	<.1
51	Penn Line Service Inc—*Paul Mongell*	300 Scottdale Ave, Scottdale PA 15683	724-887-9110	R	58*	.8
52	Williams Brothers Construction—*Barry Curtis*	PO Box 1459, Billings MT 59103	406-259-9395	R	54*	.1
53	Sheehan Pipe Line Construction Co—*David Sheehan*	2431 E 61st St Ste 700, Tulsa OK 74136	918-747-3471	R	50*	.1
54	Irish Construction—*Gregory C Warde*	2641 River Ave, Rosemead CA 91770	626-288-8530	R	49*	.3
55	C-2 Utility Contractors LLC—*Curt Saunders* Dycom Industries Inc	33005 Roberts Ct, Coburg OR 97408	541-741-2211	S	49*	.1
56	Associated Pipe Line Contractors Inc—*Paul Somerville*	3535 Briarpark Ste 135, Houston TX 77042	713-789-4311	R	48*	.5
57	Woodruff and Sons Inc—*Roy Woodruff*	PO Box 10127, Bradenton FL 34282	941-756-1871	R	48*	.3
58	Troy Construction LLP—*David Dacus*	PO Box 450862, Houston TX 77245	281-437-8214	R	47*	.6
59	Affholder Inc—*J Joseph Burgess* Insituform Technologies Inc	17988 Edison Ave, Chesterfield MO 63005	636-530-8000	S	47*	.1
60	Linkus Enterprises Inc—*Horacio Guzman*	18631 Lloyd Ln, Anderson CA 96007	530-229-9197	R	45*	.7
61	Ellendale Electric Co—*John Anderson*	7722 Hwy 70, Bartlett TN 38133	901-382-0045	R	45*	.2
62	Kimmins Corp—*Francis M Williams*	1501 2nd Ave E, Tampa FL 33605	813-248-3878	R	42	.3
63	WL Hailey—*Don Ackerman*	PO Box 40646, Nashville TN 37204	615-255-3161	R	41*	.3
64	Diversified Utility Services Inc—*Leigh Anderson*	PO Box 80417, Bakersfield CA 93380	661-325-3212	R	41*	.3
65	Hassell Construction Company Inc—*James Hassell*	12211 Duncan Rd, Houston TX 77066	281-893-2570	R	40*	.2
66	Tucker Technology Inc (Oakland California)—*Frank Tucker*	300 Frank H Ogawa Plz, Oakland CA 94612	510-836-0422	R	40*	.1
67	P Gioioso and Sons Inc—*Francesco Gioioso*	50 Sprague St, Hyde Park MA 02136	617-364-5800	R	38*	.2
68	Max Foote Construction Company Inc—*Max E Foote*	PO Box 1208, Mandeville LA 70470	985-624-8569	R	37*	.2
69	Grady Crawford Construction Company Incorporated Of Baton Rouge—*Hugh Johnson*	PO Box 967, Baton Rouge LA 70821	225-275-7334	R	37*	.2
70	MA Bongiovanni Inc—*Michael Bongiovanni*	PO Box 147, Syracuse NY 13205	315-475-9937	R	36*	.1
71	Conatser Construction I Inc—*Jerry Conatser*	PO Box 15804, Fort Worth TX 76119	817-534-1743	R	35*	.2
72	Telcom Construction Inc—*Mark Muller*	PO Box 189, Clearwater MN 55320	320-558-9485	R	34*	.5
73	WorleyParsons—*John Grill*	125 W Huntington Dr, Arcadia CA 91007	626-294-3300	R	34*	.3
74	Brent Scarbrough and Company Inc—*Brent Scarbrough*	155 Robinson Dr, Fayetteville GA 30214	770-461-8603	R	34*	.2
75	Bayer Construction Company Inc—*Neil Horton*	PO Box 889, Manhattan KS 66505	785-776-8839	R	34*	.1
76	CJ Hughes Construction Co—*Dwight Randolph*	PO Box 7305, Huntington WV 25776		R	33*	.2
77	Nts Inc—*Robert Newberry*	8200 Stockdale Hwy, Bakersfield CA 93311	661-588-8514	R	33*	.4
78	M M C Inc—*Greg Paulk*	408 E Gowan Rd, North Las Vegas NV 89032	702-642-3332	R	31*	.2
79	E Sambol Corp—*Eric Sambol*	PO Box 5110, Toms River NJ 08754	732-349-2900	R	31*	.2
80	Dynamic Cable Construction LP—*Sue Mccoy*	591 Vz County Rd 4823, Ben Wheeler TX 75754	903-849-2747	R	30*	<.1
81	Westra Construction Corp—*Kenneth Beukema*	PO Box 1149, Palmetto FL 34220	941-723-1611	R	29*	.2
82	Probst Electric Inc—*Redgie Probst*	PO Box 126, Heber City UT 84032	435-657-1955	R	29*	.1
83	KH Smith Communications Inc Lambert's Cable Splicing Company LLC	2521 S Wesleyan Blvd, Rocky Mount NC 27803	252-442-1331	S	29*	.1
84	Raco Inc—*Dallas Riddle*	PO Box 265, Gretna VA 24557	434-656-6676	R	27*	.3
85	Smith Contractors Inc—*Kerry Smith*	PO Box 480, Lawrenceburg KY 40342	502-839-4196	R	27*	.1
86	Cash Construction Company Inc—*Bruce Cash*	PO Box 1279, Pflugerville TX 78691	512-251-7872	R	27*	.2
87	Watkins Construction Company Ltd—*Jerry Watkins*	PO Box 570, Corsicana TX 75151	903-874-6587	R	27*	.2
88	Shiya-Strephans Contracting Co—*Mark Shiya*	2735 E Rose Garden Ln, Phoenix AZ 85050	602-997-6308	R	26*	.4
89	Piping and Equipment Company Inc—*Arthur Farnham*	PO Box 1065, Wichita KS 67201	316-838-7511	R	26*	.1
90	Yates Construction Company Inc—*Robert Yates*	9220 Nc Hwy 65, Stokesdale NC 27357	336-548-9621	R	26*	.2
91	Hydaker-Wheatlake Co—*Charles Holmquist*	420 S Roth St Ste B, Reed City MI 49677	231-832-2258	R	25*	.2
92	Napp-Grecco Co—*Joseph M Napp*	1500 McCarter Hwy, Newark NJ 07104	973-482-3500	R	25*	.2

Rank	Company Name—*Executive Officer*	Address, City, State, Zip	Phone	Type	Fin	Empls
93	Montana Construction Corporation Inc—*Lisa Santaite*	80 Contant Ave, Lodi NJ 07644	973-478-5200	R	25*	<.1
94	Jf2 LLC—*Rita Bilodeau*	617 Water St, Gardiner ME 04345	207-588-4514	R	24*	.2
95	Kay and Kay Contracting Inc—*William Robinson*	1355 Keavy Rd, London KY 40744	606-864-7384	R	24*	.2
96	Suburban Pipeline Company Inc—*Stephen Barge*	5947 E Molloy Rd, Syracuse NY 13211	315-454-4441	R	23*	.2
97	Delta Construction Corp—*Kenneth Kobatake*	91-255 Oihana St, Kapolei HI 96707	808-682-1315	R	23*	.1
98	Jrcruz Corp—*Evaristo Cruz*	675 Line Rd, Matawan NJ 07747	732-290-0700	R	23*	.1
99	William J Schultz Inc—*William Schultz*	PO Box 40328, Fort Worth TX 76140	817-293-1864	R	23*	.3
100	Johnson - Davis Inc—*Scott Johnson*	604 Hillbrath Dr, Lantana FL 33462	561-588-1170	R	23*	.2
101	Blois Construction Inc—*Jim Blois*	PO Box 672, Oxnard CA 93032	805-656-1432	R	22*	.2
102	Crescent Construction Co—*Cornelius White*	PO Box 545, Metairie LA 70004	504-834-9286	R	22*	.4
103	Utility Contractors Inc—*Charles Grier*	PO Box 2079, Wichita KS 67201	316-265-9506	R	22*	.2
104	Hollico Inc—*C Holloway*	PO Box 96322, Houston TX 77213	713-453-0146	R	22*	.3
105	Mid-Ohio Pipeline Company Inc—*Chuck Austin*	PO Box 3049, Mansfield OH 44904	419-884-3772	R	21*	<.1
106	Floyd King and Sons Inc—*Terry King*	PO Box 3128, Matthews NC 28106	704-821-9273	R	20*	.2
107	Johnny Cat Inc—*John Holmes*	PO Box 89, Jacksonville OR 97530	541-899-4494	R	20*	.1
108	Wilson Brothers Construction Company Inc—*Bransen Harris*	PO Box 580, Alma AR 72921	479-632-2338	R	20*	.1
109	Straight Line Construction Inc—*Joe Garza*	PO Box 342, Freer TX 78357	361-394-7656	R	20*	.2
110	Latour Construction Inc—*Theodore Latour*	2134 County Rd Ste 8nw, Maple Lake MN 55358	320-963-5993	R	20*	.1
111	Robert J Devereaux Corp—*Michael Devereaux*	10 Emerson Pl Ste 2e, Boston MA 02114	617-742-3830	R	19*	.1
112	A-1 Excavating Inc—*Terry Pecha*	PO Box 90, Bloomer WI 54724	715-568-4141	R	19*	.1
113	William B Hopke Company Inc—*Michael Hopke*	PO Box 10400, Alexandria VA 22310	703-971-0404	R	19*	.1
114	WR Hodgson Company LP—*Steve Nickman*	10165 County Rd 106, Celina TX 75009	972-382-4800	R	18*	.1
115	Long Utility Corp—*Lee Long*	PO Box 727, Simpsonville SC 29681	864-967-2813	R	18*	.1
116	Southern Diversified Technologies Inc—*Charlie Smith*	130 N 2nd St, Brookhaven MS 39601	601-823-9440	R	18*	<.1
117	W W Payton Corp—*Wesley Payton*	PO Box 1056, Katy TX 77492	281-371-7068	R	18*	<.1
118	Reesman's Excavating and Grading Inc—*Greg Reesman*	28815 Bushnell Rd, Burlington WI 53105	262-539-2124	R	18*	<.1
119	Nutter Corp—*Jerry Nutter*	7211 Ne 43rd Ave Ste A, Vancouver WA 98661	360-573-2000	R	18*	.1
120	Mercer Construction Co—*David Gregory*	PO Box 888, Edna TX 77957	361-782-7163	R	18*	.1
121	Lafayette Utility System—*Lj Durel*	PO Box 4024, Lafayette LA 70502	337-291-8280	R	18*	.2
122	Future Telecom Inc—*Donald Riggs*	PO Box 852728, Mesquite TX 75185	972-329-6400	R	17*	.1
123	Hood Corp—*Bruce Svatos*	PO Box 5716, Norco CA 92860	951-520-4282	R	17*	.1
124	Precision Valley Communications—*J Roger Cawvey* Dycom Industries Inc	333 River St, Springfield VT 05156	802-885-9317	S	17*	<.1
125	Jk Communications and Construction Inc—*Jerry Kleven*	PO Box 62013, Phoenix AZ 85082	480-736-8400	R	17*	.2
126	Jmb Construction Inc—*Margaret Burke*	132 S Maple Ave, South San Francisco CA 94080	650-267-5300	R	17*	.1
127	Kana Pipeline Inc—*Dan Locke*	1639 E Miraloma Ave, Placentia CA 92870	714-986-1400	R	17*	.1
128	Barlovento LLC—*Jane Solomen*	431 Technology Dr, Dothan AL 36303	334-983-9979	R	16*	.1
129	Interwest Construction Inc—*Eben Twaddle*	609 N Hill Blvd, Burlington WA 98233	360-757-7574	R	16*	.1
130	Suburban Grading and Utilities Inc (Norfolk Virginia)—*Jerry Womack*	1190 Harmony Rd, Norfolk VA 23502	757-461-1800	R	16*	.1
131	American Utility Corporation Inc—*Robert Stannard*	PO Box 6658, Bloomington IN 47407	812-372-3259	R	16*	.1
132	King Pipeline And Utility Company Inc—*Forrest King*	1512 8th Ave S, Nashville TN 37203	615-256-6363	R	16*	.1
133	Kandey Company Inc—*Marie Kandefer*	19 Ransier Dr Ste 10, West Seneca NY 14224	716-675-7245	R	16*	<.1
134	Lewis Contractors Inc—*Ronald Lewis*	PO Box 1623, Bertram TX 78605	512-355-9094	R	16*	.1
135	Sellenriek Construction Inc—*Robert Sellenriek*	PO Box 237, Jonesburg MO 63351	636-488-3151	R	16*	.1
136	Fleming Construction Company LLC—*Jack Fleming*	23 E Airline Hwy, Kenner LA 70062	504-464-4000	R	15*	.1
137	Florida Design Contractors Inc—*Thomas Clarke*	1326 S Killian Dr, West Palm Beach FL 33403	561-845-1233	R	15*	<.1
138	Super Excavators Inc—*Jeff Weakle*	N59 W14601 Boblink Ave, Menomonee Falls WI 53051	262-252-3200	R	15*	.1
139	HN Donahoo Contracting Company Inc—*Lann Moore*	520 1st Ave N, Birmingham AL 35204	205-252-9246	R	15*	.1
140	Maverick Construction Corp—*Michael McNally*	1 Westinghouse Plz, Hyde Park MA 02136	617-361-6700	R	15*	.1
141	EA Services Inc—*Kevin Stern*	13850 Gulf Fwy, Houston TX 77034	281-922-4412	R	15	.1
142	Burtech Pipeline Inc—*Dominic Burtech*	102 2nd St, Encinitas CA 92024	760-634-2822	R	15*	.1
143	Allgood Construction Company Inc—*Sterling Moore*	PO Box 766, Fulshear TX 77441	281-499-9621	R	15*	.1
144	John Burns Construction Company Of Texas Inc—*John O'malley*	PO Box 1117, Lewisville TX 75067	972-434-6789	R	14*	.1
145	Eagle Mountain Construction Company Inc—*Marco Spagnuolo*	3885 E Industrial Dr, Flagstaff AZ 86004	928-526-2587	R	14*	.1
146	Mike Bubalo Construction Company Inc—*Mike Bubalo*	5102 Gayhurst Ave, Baldwin Park CA 91706	626-960-7787	R	14*	<.1
147	Sunset Excavating Inc—*Peter Konen*	PO Box 510720, Livonia MI 48151	734-427-3615	R	14*	.1
148	Cruz Construction Corp—*Licinio Cruz*	952 Holmdel Rd, Holmdel NJ 07733	732-946-8400	R	14*	.1
149	Reddico Construction Company Inc—*Stephen Redd*	10083 Fm 1484 Rd, Conroe TX 77303	936-539-6500	R	14*	.1
150	Energy Group Inc—*Keith Stallworth*	PO Box 36934, Grosse Pointe MI 48236	313-491-8411	R	14*	.1
151	Nelson Pipeline Constructors Inc—*Phil Scott*	PO Box 979, Fort Lupton CO 80621	303-857-1580	R	14*	.1
152	R D Crumley and Sons Inc—*R Crumley*	12705 Market St Rd, Houston TX 77015	713-451-1605	R	13*	.1
153	Kukurin Contracting Inc—*William Kukurin*	1169 Rte 286, Export PA 15632	724-325-2136	R	13*	.1
154	Spurlock Inc—*Jewel Spurlock*	PO Box 9171, Searcy AR 72145	501-268-6389	R	13*	.1
155	Beacon Piping Co—*Thomas Connor*	45 Industrial Dr, Canton MA 02021	617-364-9008	R	13*	.1
156	Cpf Underground Utilities Inc—*Charles Frederick*	PO Box 409, Prince Frederick MD 20678	410-535-5210	R	13*	.1
157	Komtech Cable Services—*Theron Blossom*	1887 Otoole Ave, San Jose CA 95131	408-416-0600	R	13*	.2
158	Pennsylvania Drilling Co—*Thomas Sturges*	500 Thompson Ave, Mc Kees Rocks PA 15136	412-771-2110	R	13*	<.1
159	Standard Construction Corp—*Emil Lienau*	PO Box 111, Rhinebeck NY 12572	845-876-8040	R	13*	<.1
160	Ward-Henshaw Construction Company Inc—*Ronald Ward*	PO Box 950, Canby OR 97013	503-266-1986	R	13*	<.1
161	CBC Services Inc—*Greg Caskey*	1059 Hwy 501, Goldonna LA 71031	318-727-8920	R	13*	.1
162	Ceroni Piping Co—*Steve Ceroni*	1372 Ipsen Rd, Belvidere IL 61008	815-332-7777	R	13*	<.1
163	Larrett Inc—*Andra Lands*	6712 Fm 1836, Kaufman TX 75142	972-962-3400	R	12*	.1
164	Cable Ventures Inc—*Cynthia Vivoli*	PO Box 47744, San Antonio TX 78265	210-653-1672	R	12*	.1
165	R Roese Contracting Company Inc—*Richard Roese*	PO Box 158, Kawkawlin MI 48631	989-684-5121	R	12*	.2
166	Loftis Construction Corp—*Linda Loftis*	PO Box 30504, Charlotte NC 28230	704-597-5811	R	12*	.1
167	Energy Economics Inc—*Ruth Donaldson*	PO Box 220, Dodge Center MN 55927	507-374-2557	R	12*	.1
168	United Electric Company Inc—*Dan Walsh*	4333 Robards Ln, Louisville KY 40218	502-459-5242	R	12*	<.1
169	Bodine Services Of Evansville LLC	5350 E Firehouse Rd, Decatur IL 62521	217-428-4381	R	12*	.1
170	WE Curling Welding Service Inc—*William Curling*	4125 S Military Hwy, Chesapeake VA 23321	757-485-8703	R	12*	.1
171	Digioia/Suburban Excavating LLC—*Carrie Thorndyke*	11293 Royalton Rd, North Royalton OH 44133	440-237-1978	R	12*	.1
172	Sommer Construction Inc—*Steve Sommer*	PO Box 1248, Nampa ID 83653	208-465-4778	R	12*	.1
173	South Carolina Tel-Con Inc—*Lee Powell*	PO Box 27131, Greenville SC 29616	864-322-5743	R	12*	<.1
174	Robinson Brothers Construction Inc—*Patrick Tate*	6150 Ne 137th Ave, Vancouver WA 98682	360-576-5359	R	12*	.1
175	Glenn Johnston Inc—*Cara Halloran*	663 Fork Run Rd, Clearfield PA 16830	412-751-4642	R	12*	.1
176	Colorado River Materials Inc—*Susan Montgomery*	8359 W Tangerine Rd, Marana AZ 85658	520-682-2855	R	12*	.1
177	Edwards Telecommunications Inc—*James Edwards*	777 Old Clemson Rd, Columbia SC 29229	803-750-2472	R	11*	.1
178	Merritt Contracting Inc—*William Merritt*	PO Box 7790, Gainesville GA 30504	770-532-6828	R	11*	.1
179	Professional Pipeline Contractors Inc—*Mark Norris*	PO Box 2035, Lancaster CA 93539	661-949-9799	R	11*	.1

Note: An asterisk (*) indicates an estimated financial figure. The company type code used is as follows: R = Private, P = Public, S = Private Subsidiary, B = Public Subsidiary, D = Division, J = Joint Venture, I = Investment Fund.

COMPANY RANKINGS BY SALES WITHIN 4-DIGIT SIC

Rank	Company Name—*Executive Officer*	Address, City, State, Zip	Phone	Type	Fin	Empls
180	Rast Construction Inc—*Thomas Rast*	PO Box 2072, Birmingham AL 35201	205-942-6888	R	11*	.1
181	Midwestern Contractors—*Tim Bell* Electric Conduit Construction Co	245 W Roosevelt Rd Ste, West Chicago IL 60185	630-668-3420	D	11*	.2
182	Culy Construction and Excavating Inc—*Ronald Culy*	PO Box 29, Winchester IN 47394	765-584-8509	R	11*	.1
183	S Diamond Co—*Enoch Smith*	1443 Beck St, Salt Lake City UT 84116	801-364-4445	R	11*	<.1
184	Ram Construction General Contractors Inc—*Michael Hammes*	4290 Pacific Hwy, Bellingham WA 98226	360-715-8643	R	11*	<.1
185	WH C Inc—*Randolph Warner*	PO Box 2340, Lafayette LA 70502	337-837-8765	R	11*	.1
186	Akerman Construction Company Inc—*Steven Akerman*	PO Box 1626, Purcell OK 73080	405-527-1232	R	11*	.1
187	Two Rivers Pipeline and Construction Company Inc—*Tommy Cronk*	PO Box 11189, Odessa TX 79760	432-333-9587	R	11*	.1
188	De Micco Brothers Inc—*Frank Micco*	1580 Stillwell Ave Fl, Bronx NY 10461	718-892-2505	R	11*	.1
189	C and S Companies Inc—*Lee Steinman*	12760 Ridge Dr, New London MO 63459	573-221-8789	R	11*	<.1
190	Felix LLC	90 Lincoln Ave 3, Bronx NY 10454	718-401-1235	R	11*	.1
191	Grand Bluff Construction Services LLC—*Deborah Peavy*	4464 Us Hwy 59 N, Beckville TX 75631	903-693-7886	R	11*	.1
192	Hobby Construction Company Inc—*Raymond Hobby*	PO Box 457, Newberry SC 29108	803-276-8828	R	11*	.1
193	Jimmy Closner and Sons Construction Company Inc—*David Closner*	PO Box 170, Mercedes TX 78570	956-565-2688	R	11*	.1
194	Balkema Excavating Inc—*Daniel Balkema*	1500 River St, Kalamazoo MI 49048	269-345-5289	R	11*	.1
195	Linco Construcion Company Inc—*Stephen Brown*	15490 Voss Rd, Sugar Land TX 77498	281-498-6882	R	11*	.1
196	CA Murren and Sons Company Inc—*Charles Murren*	2275 Ga Hwy 20, Grayson GA 30017	770-682-2940	R	10*	.1
197	J and L Utility Service Co—*Pierce Boyd*	PO Box 501, Edgewood TX 75117	903-896-4653	R	10*	.1
198	D and M Contracting Inc—*Dennis Castelli*	1868 Lions Club Rd, New Alexandria PA 15670	724-668-8775	R	10*	.1
199	Mabus Brothers Construction Company Inc—*Tommy Mabus*	920 Molly Pond Rd, Augusta GA 30901	706-722-8941	R	10*	.1
200	Williams Welding Inc—*Wayne Williams*	PO Box 553, Canadian TX 79014	806-323-6654	R	10*	.1
201	Team Construction LLC—*Ray Peoples*	434 Atlas Dr, Nashville TN 37211	615-781-2096	R	10*	.1
202	Trust Pipe Inc—*Terry Rosell*	1838 119th St, College Point NY 11356	718-539-6575	R	10*	.1
203	Trico Contracting Inc—*Brian Wolfe*	PO Box 409, Burlington WA 98233	360-757-2373	R	10*	.1
204	Van Peenen Contractors Inc—*Raymond Peenen*	213 Hamburg Tpke, Wayne NJ 07470	973-904-3100	R	10*	<.1
205	HBC Company Inc—*Jerry Hoogendoon*	131 Washington St, Lodi NJ 07644	973-777-4472	R	10*	<.1
206	N and T Digmore Inc—*Thomas Taylor*	1525 Tahoe Ct, Redding CA 96003	530-241-2992	R	10*	<.1
207	Continental Electric—*Robert King*	3012 Academy Way, Sacramento CA 95815	916-387-1105	R	10*	<.1
208	Pipelayers Inc—*Johnny Becker*	7580 Grissom Rd, San Antonio TX 78251	210-684-7400	R	10*	.1
209	Intermountain West Civil Constructors Inc—*Reese Randall*	PO Box 2790, Payson AZ 85547	928-474-4988	R	10*	<.1
210	Franchelli Enterprises Inc—*Patricia Frankelli*	PO Box 1668, Wilkes Barre PA 18705	570-829-5385	R	10*	.1
211	RA Scott Construction Co—*Mark Scott*	PO Box 9667, Daytona Beach FL 32120	386-238-1234	R	10*	.1
212	Swanberg Construction Inc—*Mark Swanberg*	PO Box 728, Valley City ND 58072	701-845-6946	R	10*	<.1
213	Patterson and Wilder Construction Company Inc—*Frank Patterson*	PO Box 86, Pelham AL 35124	205-663-7531	R	9*	.1
214	Kck Utility Construction Inc—*Mackie Klingbell*	103 N Allen Dr, Allen TX 75013	214-547-9152	R	9*	.1
215	CVA Inc—*Anthony Campellone*	110 Central Ave, Fairless Hills PA 19030	215-946-4500	R	9*	.1
216	A and W Contractors Inc—*James Archbell*	530 Woodlake Cir Ste 2, Chesapeake VA 23320	757-523-8668	R	9*	.1
217	R L Jones Company Inc—*David Jones*	18946 Redland Rd, San Antonio TX 78259	210-496-6223	R	9*	.1
218	Spiess Construction Company Inc—*Scott Coleman*	PO Box 2849, Santa Maria CA 93457	805-937-5859	R	9*	.1
219	Crain Brothers Inc (Grand Chenier Louisiana)—*Albert Crain*	300 Rita Dr, Bell City LA 70630	337-538-2411	R	9*	.1
220	Persistent Construction Inc—*Anthony Grano*	58 Industrial Ave, Fairview NJ 07022	201-941-9888	R	9*	<.1
221	Mid-South Builders Inc—*Ronald Grice*	PO Box 878, Lithonia GA 30058	770-484-9600	R	9*	<.1
222	Utility Constructors Inc—*Terry Lovelace*	PO Box 13627, Jackson MS 39236	601-922-9355	R	9*	.1
223	Nash Brothers Construction Company Inc—*Patrick Nash*	1840 S Kilbourn Ave, Chicago IL 60623	773-762-1800	R	9*	.1
224	Rossi Contractors Inc—*Gloria Rossi*	201 W Lake St, Northlake IL 60164	773-287-7545	R	9*	.1
225	Jwwtew LLC—*Carrie Ellis*	PO Box 6, Semmes AL 36575	251-649-9914	R	9*	.1
226	Town and Country Underground Utility Construction Inc—*William Muche*	W2899 Dunn Rd, Mayville WI 53050	920-387-2394	R	9*	.1
227	Kline's Construction Company Inc—*Wayne Kline*	20455 Centerville Cons, Centreville MI 49032	269-467-7870	R	9*	.1
228	Cossentino Contracting Company Inc—*John Cossentino*	8505 Contractors Rd, Baltimore MD 21237	410-574-5800	R	9*	.1
229	Stevens and Layton Inc—*V Dean*	11260 Palm Beach Blvd, Fort Myers FL 33905	239-693-1400	R	9*	.1
230	Dcci LLC—*Robert Gonzales*	PO Box 670, Wilbur OR 97494	541-957-2331	R	9*	.1
231	Tel-Power Inc—*Teddy Lykens*	809 Tel Power Rd, Hollidaysburg PA 16648	814-695-5331	R	9*	.1
232	Owens and Dove Inc—*William Owens*	9109 Owens Dr, Manassas Park VA 20111	703-330-0012	R	9*	.1
233	Amchel Communications Inc—*Ronald Robinson*	2800 Capital St, Wylie TX 75098	972-442-1030	R	9*	<.1
234	Kelco Contracting LLC	936 E Javelina Ave Ste, Mesa AZ 85204	480-926-6000	R	8*	.1
235	Midwest Mole Inc—*Daniel Liotti*	2460 N Graham Ave, Indianapolis IN 46218	317-545-1335	R	8*	.1
236	Vms Construction Co—*Victor Serrambana*	162 Lake St, Vernon CT 06066	860-871-0278	R	8*	<.1
237	Tommy Beasley Construction Company Inc—*Tommy Beasley*	PO Box 70515, Tuscaloosa AL 35407	205-330-9944	R	8*	.2
238	Chaz Equipment Company Inc—*Gary Czajkowski*	3180 Frlane Frms Rd St, Wellington FL 33414	561-333-2109	R	8*	.1
239	Edwards/Wilmington Inc—*Derrill Edwards*	3530 Us Hwy 421 N, Wilmington NC 28401	910-772-9777	R	8*	<.1
240	Cr Cable Construction Inc—*Matthew Buresh*	400 Blue Sky Pkwy, Lexington KY 40509	859-543-8289	R	8*	.1
241	C D Brown Const Inc—*Don Brown*	PO Box 675, Sulphur OK 73086	580-622-6363	R	8*	.1
242	B and C Construction Company Inc—*W Koeneman*	PO Box 488, Ellendale TN 38029	901-386-7040	R	8*	.1
243	Bay Country Enterprises Inc—*Eugene Clair*	26825 Point Lookout Rd, Leonardtown MD 20650	301-475-3902	R	8*	.1
244	Gulbranson Excavating-West Inc—*Tamara Mckenzie*	PO Box 2547, Helendale CA 92342	928-757-4379	R	8*	.1
245	Bdz Developers Inc—*Jim Henricks*	3207 Pacific Ave, Everett WA 98201	425-259-2290	R	8*	<.1
246	Gulf Coast Boring and Pipeline Inc—*William Fisher*	1065 George Jenkins Bl, Lakeland FL 33815	863-686-2263	R	8*	<.1
247	Tenetix Inc—*Mary A Stolecki*	PO Box 4470, El Dorado Hills CA 95762	916-638-1221	R	8*	<.1
248	Certified Environmental Services Inc—*Thomas Mclaughlin*	8892 Normandy Blvd, Jacksonville FL 32221	904-695-1911	R	8*	.1
249	Daleo Inc—*David Levisay*	7190 Forest St, Gilroy CA 95020	408-846-9621	R	8*	.1
250	Basile Construction Inc—*Allen Basile*	7952 Armour St, San Diego CA 92111	858-586-7800	R	8*	.1
251	C and M Construction Inc—*Conrad Sproul*	PO Box 1624, Sherwood OR 97140	503-625-5289	R	8*	.1
252	Highlander Energy Products Inc—*Brett Cleer*	98 S Fraley St Ste 1, Kane PA 16735	814-837-7743	R	8*	<.1
253	Camo Construction Company Inc—*Mike Grantham*	PO Box 178, Vidalia LA 71373	318-336-9121	R	8*	.1
254	Nodland Construction Co—*Rich Nodland*	PO Box 338, Alexandria MN 56308	320-763-5159	R	8*	.1
255	Township Builders Inc—*H Churchill*	PO Box 7252, Little Rock AR 72217	501-664-2036	R	8*	.1
256	K and W Underground Inc—*Rex Schick*	15608 S Keeler Ter, Olathe KS 66062	913-782-7387	R	8*	.1
257	Three Sons LLC—*Ben Austin*	PO Box 600, Hanna WY 82327	307-325-6532	R	8*	<.1
258	G and W Construction Company Inc—*Gabriel Alderman*	6730 Flemingsburg Rd, Morehead KY 40351	606-784-2396	R	8*	<.1
259	JWJ Inc—*J Yarbrough*	2300 Sw 3rd Ave, Ocala FL 34471	352-732-0550	R	7*	.1
260	Chandler Construction Services Inc—*Hubert Chandler*	1511 Ninety Six Hwy, Ninety Six SC 29666	864-227-3221	R	7*	.1
261	D and H Construction Company Inc—*Henry Graham*	1915 James Jackson Pkw, Atlanta GA 30318	404-792-1941	R	7*	.1
262	Larry Smith Contractor's Inc—*Larry Smith*	5737 Dry Fork Rd, Cleves OH 45002	513-367-0218	R	7*	.1
263	Lfg and E International Inc—*Ronald Brookshire*	663 Greenfield Dr, El Cajon CA 92021	619-593-3690	R	7*	.1
264	Zednem Pipeline Construction Inc—*Maryann Mendez*	13024 Euclid Ave, Chino CA 91710	909-986-0800	R	7*	.1

Rank	Company Name—*Executive Officer*	Address, City, State, Zip	Phone	Type	Fin	Empls
265	Jossart Brothers Inc—*Konrad Jossart*	1682 Swan Rd, De Pere WI 54115	920-339-8500	R	7*	<.1
266	Rickabaugh Pentecost Development LLC—*Krysten Pelland*	PO Box 310, Spanaway WA 98387	253-875-0212	R	7*	.1
267	Callaway Contracting Inc—*Patrick Callaway*	PO Box 11435, Jacksonville FL 32239	904-751-8944	R	7*	.1
268	Powercomm Construction Inc—*David Kwasnik*	21 Belmont Pl, Springfield MA 01108	571-259-8773	R	7*	.1
269	Dahme Construction Company Inc—*Gary Dahme*	PO Box 407, Aberdeen SD 57402	605-225-3917	R	7*	<.1
270	Direct Utility Contractors LLC—*Becky Woods*	PO Box 6760, Chandler AZ 85246	480-730-1537	R	7*	.1
271	Pride Utility Construction Co—*Tom Pridemore*	PO Box 7005, Chestnut Mountain GA 30502	770-844-8140	R	7*	.1
272	Vazzana Underground Construction Inc—*Bruce Vazzana*	1414 Industrial Rd, Las Vegas NV 89102	702-656-2333	R	7*	.1
273	Merryman Company Excavation—*Patrick Merryman*	PO Box 905, Woodstock IL 60098	815-337-1700	R	7*	.1
274	Rodarte Construction Inc—*Frank Rodarte*	PO Box 1875, Auburn WA 98071	253-939-0532	R	7*	<.1
275	Tiede's Line Construction Inc—*Eugene Tiede*	PO Box 342, Haysville KS 67060	316-529-2937	R	7*	<.1
276	C and L Construction Inc—*Nathan Currey*	PO Box 154, Collinsville OK 74021	918-376-2324	R	7*	<.1
277	Daley Tower Service Inc—*Dennis Leblanc*	1223 W Gloria Switch R, Carencro LA 70520	337-896-6719	R	7*	.1
278	T G Mercer Consulting Services Inc—*George Mercer*	2300 Tin Top Rd, Weatherford TX 76087	817-613-1058	R	7*	.1
279	Utah Pacific Construction Co—*Craig Young*	40940 Eleanora Way, Murrieta CA 92562	951-677-9876	R	7*	.1
280	Brett Construction Co—*Shaye Johnson*	PO Box 598, Hico TX 76457	254-796-4817	R	7*	.1
281	Ronny Turner Construction Company Inc—*Ronald Turner*	3571 S Nc 127 Hwy, Hickory NC 28602	828-294-1844	R	7*	.1
282	Brock G And L Construction Company Inc—*Lynne Brock*	4145 Calloway Ct, Stockton CA 95215	209-931-3626	R	7*	.1
283	Moore and Son Site Contractors Inc—*Ricky Moore*	103 Mcdowell Rd, Mills River NC 28759	828-891-8900	R	7*	.1
284	Brysan Utility Contractors Inc—*Chris Barber*	PO Box 3375, Loganville GA 30052	770-985-4606	R	7*	.1
285	Versatile Construction Inc—*F Smith*	PO Box 336, Logan NM 88426	575-487-2259	R	7*	.1
286	Milwaukee Waterworks—*Gary Gibson*	3850 N 35th St Rm 155, Milwaukee WI 53216	414-286-2870	R	7*	.1
287	DBI Services Inc—*Derek Crombie*	743 Cochran St Ste B, Simi Valley CA 93065	805-732-8029	R	7*	.1
288	New Mexico Underground Contractors Inc—*Willie Montano*	6201 Industry Way Se, Albuquerque NM 87105	505-877-2300	R	7*	.1
289	Ralph Hodge Construction Co—*Ralph Hodge*	PO Box 1179, Wilson NC 27894	252-237-3663	R	7*	.1
290	J-2 Contracting Co—*Chris Leone*	PO Box 129, Greeley CO 80632	970-392-0694	R	7*	<.1
291	Sun Coast Underground Utility Construction Corp—*Robert Laforce*	17259 Jean St, Fort Myers FL 33967	239-454-2600	R	7*	<.1
292	Great Lakes Cable Communications Inc—*Paul Braam*	5473 Wild Cherry Cir, Greendale WI 53129	414-427-8460	R	7*	.1
293	GEM Contractors Inc—*Wayne Marcinko*	1499 Old 41 Hwy Nw, Marietta GA 30060	770-421-1499	R	7*	.1
294	Joseph Canova and Son Inc—*Charles Canova*	13313 Virginia Manor R, Laurel MD 20707	301-419-2020	R	7*	<.1
295	Mainline Contracting Inc—*Floyd Schaffer*	PO Box 3448, Rapid City SD 57709	605-348-7068	R	7*	<.1
296	Kuechle Underground Inc—*Jerome Kuechle*	PO Box 509, Kimball MN 55353	320-398-8888	R	7*	.1
297	Lewis Lee Inc—*Michael Lewis*	PO Box 2586, Georgetown TX 78627	512-863-5151	R	7*	<.1
298	Line Construction Inc—*Luke Gunter*	PO Box 3937, Sanford NC 27331	919-775-5454	R	6*	.1
299	B Robert Our Company Inc—*Robert Our*	PO Box 1539, Harwich MA 02645	508 432 0530	R	6*	<.1
300	Mar-Con Services LLC	PO Box 837, Deer Park TX 77536	713-473-1800	R	6*	.1
301	Gulf Coast Underground Inc—*Steven Goble*	3093 Hunter St, Fort Myers FL 33916	239-274-9504	R	6*	.1
302	John Plott Company Inc—*John Plott*	PO Box 20183, Tuscaloosa AL 35402	205-345-5678	R	6*	.1
303	Mge Underground Inc—*Michael Goldstein*	PO Box 4189, Paso Robles CA 93447	805-238-3510	R	6*	<.1
304	W Walsh Company Inc—*William Walsh*	32 Walton St, Attleboro MA 02703	508-226-4300	R	6*	.1
305	Prillaman and Pace Inc—*F Carter*	PO Box 4667, Martinsville VA 24115	276-632-6308	R	6*	.1
306	Compton Construction Company Inc—*Milton Compton*	PO Box 1010, Princeton WV 24740	304-487-3467	R	6*	.1
307	CRJ Contracting Inc—*James Ciacciarelli*	1340 3 Ave, Plainfield NJ 07002	900-000-7900	R	6*	.1
308	S and S Communication Services Inc—*Merle Shields*	Keyser Rd, Acme PA 15610	724-423-6735	R	6*	.1
309	Telecommunications Contracting Company Inc—*Richard Taschek*	2242 Marlton Pke, Marlton NJ 08053	856-810-1658	R	6*	.1
310	W D Wright Contracting Inc—*Bryan Wright*	134 Glendale Rd, Beaver Falls PA 15010	724-847-0234	R	6*	.1
311	Tri-State Utilities Co—*Steven Mcsweeny*	2111 Smith Ave, Chesapeake VA 23320	757-366-9505	R	6*	<.1
312	Joseph T Hardy and Son Inc—*John Hardy*	425 Old Airport Rd, New Castle DE 19720	302-328-9457	R	6*	<.1
313	Schoon Construction Inc—*Le Roy Schoon*	PO Box 800, Cherokee IA 51012	712-225-5736	R	6*	.1
314	Nti LLC—*Robin Jeeter*	6586 Meadowridge Rd, Elkridge MD 21075	410-796-7770	R	6*	.1
315	Qc Communications Inc—*Mark Holland*	7925 W 100 S, Wabash IN 46992	260-563-4453	R	6*	.1
316	Kris Mechanical Inc—*Robert Medlin*	PO Box 1773, Easley SC 29641	864-859-5831	R	6*	<.1
317	RL Coolsaet Construction Co—*Jeffrey A Coolsaet*	28800 Goddard Rd, Romulus MI 48174	734-946-9300	R	6*	.1
318	Forest Construction Company Inc—*Paul Mongell*	PO Box 462, Scottdale PA 15683	724-887-9110	R	6*	.1
319	Coastline Utility Contractors Inc—*Thomas Luke*	PO Box 26068, Jacksonville FL 32226	904-425-4085	R	6*	.1
320	Warrco Inc—*Joyce Warren*	PO Box 4185, Danville VA 24540	434-836-7750	R	6*	.1
321	Nelson Lewis Inc—*Janet Lewis*	PO Box 235, Marble Falls TX 78654	830-693-8874	R	6*	.1
322	Swenke Company Inc—*Richard Swenke*	PO Box 5, Kasson MN 55944	507-634-7778	R	6*	.1
323	Frank Semeraro Construction Company Inc—*Charles Semeraro*	333 Ratzer Rd, Wayne NJ 07470	973-694-3038	R	6*	<.1
324	Deneau Construction Inc—*Glen Fritz*	7861 Beechcraft Ave, Gaithersburg MD 20879	301-840-1007	R	6*	<.1
325	Fydaq Company Inc—*Mike Craft*	301 1/2 S Richman Ave, Fullerton CA 92832	714-447-9760	R	6*	<.1
326	Smith Pipeline Inc—*Ricky Smith*	400 Bohannon Rd, Fairburn GA 30213	770-964-0503	R	6*	<.1
327	Orion Construction Company Inc—*Thomas Mehegan*	PO Box 1290, New Smyrna Beach FL 32170	386-423-1191	R	6*	<.1
328	Coal Creek Construction Inc—*Denny Portra*	PO Box 1068, Underwood ND 58576	701-442-3188	R	6*	<.1
329	Hopkins Construction Inc—*R Hopkins*	18904 Maranatha Way St, Bridgeville DE 19933	302-337-3366	R	6*	<.1
330	North Slope Telecom Inc—*Bill Laxson*	2020 E Dowling Rd Ste, Anchorage AK 99507	907-562-4693	R	6*	<.1
331	C Spirito Inc—*A Spirito*	1382 Pleasant St, East Weymouth MA 02189	781-331-8866	R	6*	<.1
332	Frank Horne Construction Inc—*Frank Horne*	PO Box 338, Fair Bluff NC 28439	910-649-7803	R	6*	<.1
333	Rwl Construction Inc—*Richard Lewis*	PO Box 1209, Sealy TX 77474	979-627-7866	R	6*	<.1
334	JF Wilkerson Contracting Company Inc—*Joseph Wilkerson*	PO Box 183, Morrisville NC 27560	919-467-1829	R	6*	.1
335	Intercounty Engineering Inc—*Maurice Hynes*	PO Box 50553, Lighthouse Point FL 33074	954-972-9800	R	6*	<.1
336	Walker Utilities Inc—*Gary Walker*	PO Box 54122, Hurst TX 76054	817-268-2318	R	6*	<.1
337	Jeremy Hiltz Excavating Inc—*Jeremy Hiltz*	PO Box 1142, Ashland NH 03217	603-968-9694	R	6*	<.1
338	Golden State Boring and Pipe Jacking Inc—*Jeffrey Johnson*	2028 E Cedar St, Ontario CA 91761	909-930-5811	R	6*	<.1
339	Cooperative Development LLC—*Bonnie Wichern*	1831 Anne St Nw Ste 10, Bemidji MN 56601	218-444-1143	R	6*	<.1
340	J Letterman and Associates Inc—*Jency Mills*	PO Box 23259, Columbia SC 29224	803-736-1141	R	6*	<.1
341	Nerone and Sons Inc—*Rick Nerone*	19501 S Miles Rd Ste 1, Cleveland OH 44128	216-662-2235	R	6*	<.1
342	Hudson Paving Inc—*Norman Pelletier*	19 Barretts Hill Rd, Hudson NH 03051	603-882-6854	R	6*	<.1
343	Pole Line Contractors Inc—*Spencer Porter*	169 Rockin Chair Rd, Spring Creek NV 89815	775-777-7001	R	6*	<.1
344	Appling Boring Company Inc—*Carey Appling*	426 Baxter Cemetary Rd, Forest City NC 28043	828-657-6397	R	6*	<.1
345	Urban Contractors Inc—*James Parrish*	7113 N Bryant Ave, Oklahoma City OK 73121	405-478-5370	R	6*	<.1
346	Widman Construction Inc—*Terry Widman*	27199 State Hwy 3, Godfrey IL 62035	618-466-1036	R	6*	<.1
347	Gilmore And Son Construction Corp—*James Gilmore*	PO Box 1411, Hammond LA 70404	225-567-3795	R	6*	<.1
348	Fountain Engineering Inc—*Freddie Fountain*	PO Box 700457, Miami FL 33170	305-256-2700	R	5*	<.1
349	Danrik Construction Inc—*Danny White*	PO Box 92868, Lafayette LA 70509	337-232-2488	R	5*	<.1
350	Southwest Contracting Inc—*Matthew Fulford*	PO Box 788, Odessa FL 33556	813-792-0180	R	5*	<.1
351	BUT Inc—*Ted Burton*	240 Maple Ave, Beaumont CA 92223	951-769-0647	R	5*	<.1

Note: An asterisk (*) indicates an estimated financial figure. The company type code used is as follows: R = Private, P = Public, S = Private Subsidiary, B = Public Subsidiary, D = Division, J = Joint Venture, I = Investment Fund.

COMPANY RANKINGS BY SALES WITHIN 4-DIGIT SIC

Rank	Company Name—Executive Officer	Address, City, State, Zip	Phone	Type	Fin	Empls
352	Prince Ventures LLC—William Prince	1444 Municipal Pkwy, Douglasville GA 30134	404-622-3468	R	5*	<.1
353	Trax Company Inc—Billy Gann	PO Box 857, Iuka MS 38852	662-423-6044	R	5*	<.1
354	Herschap Backhoe and Ditching Inc—Bill Herschap	PO Box 489, Bastrop TX 78602	512-303-3834	R	5*	<.1
355	Construction Specialty Service Inc—Daniel George	8801 Crippen St Unit A, Bakersfield CA 93311	661-663-7000	R	5*	.1
356	Anderson Piping Contractors Inc—Richard Schmicker	PO Box 20517, El Cajon CA 92021	619-579-1628	R	5*	<.1
357	Herion Co—Randall Herion	PO Box 206, Rogersville MO 65742	417-767-1005	R	5*	<.1
358	Larson Plumbing And Utility Co—Nicolas Llanes	PO Box 10709, Corpus Christi TX 78460	361-887-6234	R	5*	<.1
359	Rain For Rent—Darren Flood	100 Oil Ct, Rifle CO 81650	970-625-4600	R	5*	.1
360	Johnson Brothers Construction Company Inc—Bartt Johnson	PO Box 205, Bigelow AR 72016	501-759-9999	R	5*	<.1
361	Anthony Construction Company Inc—Al Anthony	8110 7th Ave S, Seattle WA 98108	206-762-3780	R	5*	<.1
362	Metro Equipment Service Inc—Jorge Godoy	7171 Sw 62nd Ave Ste 5, South Miami FL 33143	305-740-3303	R	5*	<.1
363	Trinet Construction Inc—Nora Hickey	2560 Marin St, San Francisco CA 94124	415-695-7814	R	5*	<.1
364	Tri State Tower Inc—Ricky Ellison	625 51st St, Marion IA 52302	319-373-5040	R	5*	.2
365	Whiting Construction Company Inc—Frank Whiting	PO Box 485, Troutman NC 28166	704-528-9395	R	5*	<.1
366	Lowe-North Construction Inc—Lawrence North	800 S A Line Dr, Spring Hill KS 66083	913-686-3080	R	5*	<.1
367	Ramos and Associates Inc—Hector Ramos	PO Box 837, Lytle TX 78052	210-628-4277	R	5*	<.1
368	United Pipeline Systems USA Inc—Dale Kneller Insituform Technologies Inc	135 Turner Dr, Durango CO 81303	970-259-0354	D	5*	<.1
369	Gordon-Palmgren Inc—Gordon Palmgren	PO Box 545, Pell City AL 35125	205-338-2017	R	5*	<.1
370	Cone Construction Corporation Inc—Daniel East	515 Wheeler Ave Se, Albuquerque NM 87102	505-342-2898	R	5*	<.1
371	J Tropeano Inc—Louisa Tanner	1780 Osgood St, North Andover MA 01845	978-689-2745	R	5*	<.1
372	Texoma Underground Utilities—Buddy Holder	PO Box 519, Durant OK 74702	972-329-2570	R	5*	<.1
373	Deichman Excavating Company Inc—Stanley Deichman	PO Box 12, Logansport IN 46947	574-722-7677	R	5*	<.1
374	F and D Oilfield Maintenance Inc—Fred Varner	PO Box 88, Baker MT 59313	406-778-3542	R	5*	<.1
375	Sharpe and Preszler Construction Company Inc—Neal Lumper	605 E Kennewick Ave, Kennewick WA 99336	509-586-1138	R	5*	<.1
376	Fiber Optic Concepts And Lighting LLC	106 Arabian Dr, Lafayette LA 70507	337-886-0403	R	5*	<.1
377	Bradley Sutton—Brad Sutton	1310 County Rd 46, Mount Hope AL 35651	256-974-6627	R	5*	<.1
378	Schneider's Trucking Inc—Fred Schneider	PO Box 216, Lake Villa IL 60046	847-395-2810	R	5*	<.1
379	Rk Cable Contractors Partnership Ltd—Richard Kinsey	PO Box 1141, Tomball TX 77377	281-351-4100	R	5*	<.1
380	Clark Power Corp—Michael Hocutt	PO Box 45188, Little Rock AR 72214	501-558-4901	R	5*	<.1
381	Finway Inc—Eric Vogel	PO Box 682, Conroe TX 77305	936-756-9205	R	5*	<.1
382	Northwinds Of Wyoming Inc—Russell Underwood	PO Box 599, Douglas WY 82633	307-358-6550	R	5*	<.1
383	Wolf Landscape Co—Lynn Wolf	1965 Mount View Rd, Marriottsville MD 21104	301-607-4346	R	5*	<.1
384	Maintenance Division City Shops—Rich Barstad	830 Mcclaine St, Silverton OR 97381	503-873-6359	R	5*	.1
385	Insituform Of New England Inc—Anthony Hooper	253b Worcester Rd, Charlton MA 01507	508-248-1700	R	5*	<.1
386	Holladay Construction Company Inc—Benjamin Holladay	5419 Hickory Ridge Rd, Spotsylvania VA 22551	540-582-2700	R	5*	<.1
387	Urban Telecommunications Inc—Donna Torres	3318 Delavall Ave, Bronx NY 10475	718-862-0500	R	5*	<.1
388	M-Co Construction Inc—Ricky Main	PO Box 489, Springtown TX 76082	817-589-7601	R	5*	<.1
389	J and R Construction Co—Richard Marbury	337 Fore Ln, Mason TN 38049	901-294-3211	R	5*	<.1
390	SL Cable Construction Inc—Steve Livesay	PO Box 304, Colbert GA 30628	706-540-1418	R	5*	<.1
391	Urban Electrical Services Inc—Don Urban	PO Box 219, Carrizo Springs TX 78834	830-876-2685	R	5*	<.1
392	Kenneth West Inc—Joel West	2821 Jones Franklin Rd, Raleigh NC 27606	919-233-2282	R	5*	<.1
393	Phil Reome Inc—Phillip Reome	13263 Bill Francis Dr, Auburn CA 95603	530-823-7501	R	5*	<.1
394	Sajasa Construction Inc—Branston Weyer	PO Box 1488, Woodinville WA 98072	425-487-0808	R	5*	<.1
395	B and Z Co—Bruce Binger	1171 Milton St, Benton Harbor MI 49022	269-925-6999	R	5*	<.1
396	SC Valley Engineering Inc—Sam Wathen	656 Front St, El Cajon CA 92020	619-444-2366	R	5*	<.1
397	Vishnu Inc—Jay Shah	504 Ross Dr, Sunnyvale CA 94089	408-223-8600	R	5*	<.1
398	Bill Enyart and Sons Contracting Inc—William Enyart	412 Solida Rd, South Point OH 45680	740-377-4208	R	5*	<.1
399	Ogden City Utilities—John Patterson	PO Box 410480, Salt Lake City UT 84141	801-629-8321	R	5*	.1
400	Hartco Cable Inc—Jerry Hart	PO Box 32, Geneseo IL 61254	309-944-2026	R	5*	<.1
401	R D Braswell Construction Co—Richard Braswell	3241 Us Hwy 70 E Ste 1, Smithfield NC 27577	919-965-3131	R	5*	<.1
402	Bates Utility Company Inc—Tom Bates	841 Westwood Industria, Weldon Spring MO 63304	636-939-5628	R	5*	<.1
403	S E Macmillan Company Inc—Stanley Macmillan	PO Box 1539, Bangor ME 04402	207-942-2169	R	5*	<.1
404	Terra Firm Inc—E Shelton	400 S Aston Dr, Mesquite TX 75182	972-226-1306	R	5*	<.1
405	WLW Construction Inc—Wendy Wagner	PO Box 377, Mount Dora FL 32756	352-383-7305	R	5*	<.1
406	Unity Construction Company Inc—Joel Holcomb	PO Box 651, Mableton GA 30126	770-943-9886	R	5*	<.1
407	Northwest Cable Construction Inc—Kenneth Kannard	PO Box 339, Big Bend WI 53103	262-662-4918	R	5*	<.1
408	Stately Contractors Inc—Glenn Bower	6028 33rd St E, Bradenton FL 34203	941-756-4700	R	5*	<.1
409	Stapleton Services and Manufacturing Inc—Howard Stapleton	PO Box 840, Donna TX 78537	956-781-2922	R	5*	<.1
410	Lupe Rubio Construction Company Inc—Lupe Rubio	PO Box 1838, Kingsland TX 78639	325-388-8500	R	4*	<.1
411	Hoot Johnson Construction Inc—Hoot Johnson	700 H Cr 1313, Hillsboro TX 76645	254-582-7473	R	4*	<.1
412	Air Weld Inc—Adolfo Carrasco	PO Box 3095, Laredo TX 78044	956-722-1960	R	4*	<.1
413	DJ Pinciotti Construction Company Inc—Daniel Pinciotti	6 Commerce Dr, Warminster PA 18974	215-443-8655	R	4*	<.1
414	Eleccomm Corp—Stephen Martin	785 Woburn St, Wilmington MA 01887	978-657-0091	R	4*	<.1
415	James F Pedersen Company Inc—James Pedersen	PO Box 310, Hollywood SC 29449	843-889-8210	R	4*	<.1
416	Rocky Kohl Excavating Inc—Delores Kohl	3330 E Valley Rd, Renton WA 98057	425-251-8820	R	4*	<.1
417	Forest Hill Communications Inc—John Healy	2024 Eden Mill Rd, Pylesville MD 21132	410-452-0478	R	4*	<.1
418	Ed Braswell and Sons Inc—David Braswell	632 Quarry Ln, Rocky Mount NC 27803	252-937-3877	R	4*	<.1
419	Marcellus Construction Company Inc—Don Carsto	PO Box 201, Mannsville NY 13661	315-872-4024	R	4*	<.1
420	Ronkin Construction Inc—James Barron	1201 Pauls Ln, Joppa MD 21085	410-679-4750	R	4*	<.1
421	Lantier Construction Company Inc—Douglas Lantier	145 Dey Grove Rd, Monroe NJ 08831	732-446-1437	R	4*	<.1
422	Raymow Construction Company Inc—E Bradley	101 Dunbar Ave Ste F, Oldsmar FL 34677	813-855-8484	R	4*	<.1
423	Flowline Alaska Inc—Richard Schok	1881 Livengood Ave, Fairbanks AK 99701	907-456-4911	R	4*	<.1
424	Sterling Excavation Inc—Patrick Ryan	511 Gateway Dr, Jefferson City MO 65109	573-893-4455	R	4*	<.1
425	D and D Utility Contractors Inc—David Gizzi	272 W Ave, Long Branch NJ 07740	732-222-6810	R	4*	<.1
426	Scheck Mechanical Corp—Richard Scheck	500 E Plainfield Rd, Countryside IL 60525	708-482-8100	R	4*	<.1
427	S Holland Company Inc—Stephyn Holland	19425 Haude Rd, Spring TX 77388	281-651-7272	R	4*	<.1
428	Freiday Construction Inc—William Freiday	PO Box 4267, Kingman AZ 86402	928-757-2176	R	4*	<.1
429	Darnell and Dickson Construction Inc—David Darnell	5039 N Chadbourne St, San Angelo TX 76903	325-653-1920	R	4*	<.1
430	Buck's Communication Co—Buck Buchanan	PO Box 1874, High Point NC 27261	336-869-8538	R	4*	.1
431	Antill Pipeline Construction Company Inc—Marvin Antill	PO Box 3897, Houma LA 70361	985-879-2626	R	4*	<.1
432	Enterprise Communications Utility Contractors Of Florida Inc—Dalas Mccalf	160 W Evergreen Ave St, Longwood FL 32750	407-834-5505	R	4*	<.1
433	St Clair Jack Inc—Terry Stclair	PO Box 12961, Roanoke VA 24030	540-344-1657	R	4*	<.1
434	Bouchard Communications Inc—Mona Bouchard	11231 Burbank Blvd, North Hollywood CA 91601	818-761-2154	R	4*	<.1
435	A/K/A Services Inc—Josephine Basile	15551 Okeechobee Blvd, Loxahatchee FL 33470	561-791-7561	R	4*	<.1
436	Jaeger Construction Inc—William Jaeger	PO Box 1300, Yuba City CA 95992	530-673-3885	R	4*	<.1
437	Con Cast Co—Ross Kallenberger	4808 Stine Rd Ste D, Bakersfield CA 93313	661-832-4546	R	4*	<.1
438	G and S Electric—Gary Krezman	1604 Basler St, Sacramento CA 95811	916-442-7714	R	4*	<.1
439	Turnure Telecom LLC—Loara Davis	2679 151st Pl Ne, Redmond WA 98052	425-822-6588	R	4*	<.1

Rank	Company Name—Executive Officer	Address, City, State, Zip	Phone	Type	Fin	Empls
440	Pride Environmental Construction Inc—Jo Gambrazzio	PO Box 547, East Taunton MA 02718	508-880-6009	R	4*	<.1
441	BD Evans Construction Inc—Brian Evans	6380 Preston Ave, Livermore CA 94551	925-447-7642	R	4*	<.1
442	Nick Jorae Excavating Inc—Nicholas Jorae	7172 Shepardsville Rd, Laingsburg MI 48848	517-333-0668	R	4*	<.1
443	Leifer Construction Inc—Stephen Leifer	12717 State Ave, Marysville WA 98271	360-659-3322	R	4*	<.1
444	Williams Construction—Charles Williams	2164 Dyches Rd, Statesboro GA 30461	912-842-2027	R	4*	<.1
445	Baird Contracting Company Inc—Mitch Kell	276 Snow Dr, Birmingham AL 35209	205-942-1095	R	4*	<.1
446	Joel A Trimm Construction Company Inc—Joel Trimm	PO Box 1599, Brookshire TX 77423	281-375-5886	R	4*	<.1
447	Lone Star Utilities LLC—Richard Lesnar	10553 Fm 1390, Scurry TX 75158	972-486-3373	R	4*	<.1
448	Floyd's Construction Inc—Bruce Floyd	1201 S Hwy 160 Ste 100, Pahrump NV 89048	775-727-5606	R	4*	<.1
449	Globe Contractors Inc—Ramon Olson	PO Box 450, Pewaukee WI 53072	262-246-0600	R	4*	<.1
450	J De Sigio Construction Inc—Julian Desigio	5055 Bleecker St, Baldwin Park CA 91706	626-480-8900	R	4*	<.1
451	Corzo Contracting Company Inc—Gloria Lema	78 Richfield St, Plainview NY 11803	516-349-0061	R	4*	<.1
452	Hawley Construction Inc—Tony Hawley	8156 Nc Hwy 42 W, Kenly NC 27542	919-284-4020	R	4*	<.1
453	Saenz Utility Contractors Ltd—Fernando Saenz	22290 Fm 88, Edcouch TX 78538	956-262-8506	R	4*	<.1
454	Dean Dallas Inc—Cindy Tyler	PO Box 296, Harrodsburg KY 40330	859-734-7071	R	4*	<.1
455	JD Dye—J Dye	1308 Descanso Ave, San Marcos CA 92069	760-471-9531	R	4*	<.1
456	Melvin Bush Construction Inc—Melvin Bush	2748 Sw Casella St, Port Saint Lucie FL 34953	772-336-0623	R	4*	<.1
457	Plumbing Planning Corp—Eddie Hill	11860 Dorsett Rd, Maryland Heights MO 63043	314-739-0057	R	4*	<.1
458	Ross And Son Utility Contractor Inc—Robert Ross	913 Ventures Way, Chesapeake VA 23320	757-436-2018	R	4*	<.1
459	Wiegand and Storrer Inc—Leslie Savant	PO Box 2068, East Peoria IL 61611	309-699-6457	R	4*	<.1
460	International Towers Inc—Douglas Gratzer	911 W Grant Rd, Tucson AZ 85705	520-742-0457	R	4*	<.1
461	Kiowa Line Builders Inc—David Ray	PO Box 721, Tipton MO 65081	660-433-2677	R	4*	<.1
462	Rent A Tech Inc—Rick Fleming	6838 Ellicott Dr Ste 2, East Syracuse NY 13057	315-463-7656	R	4*	<.1
463	Five JAB Oilfield Construct—Jennifer Bohannon	PO Box 1063, Tomball TX 77377	281-356-7767	R	4*	<.1
464	Clay Pipeline Inc—Kay Garrison	70 Fox Hollow Rd, Manchester KY 40962	606-598-6239	R	4*	<.1
465	WRBS Inc—William Harrison	PO Box 11357, Houston TX 77293	713-692-7103	R	4*	<.1
466	Pipemasters Inc—Hoy Fellure	PO Box 1088, Hurricane WV 25526	304-562-2382	R	4*	<.1
467	Darlington County Water And Sewer Authority—Larry Mcdowell	1701 Harry Byrd Hwy, Darlington SC 29532	843-393-8131	R	4*	<.1
468	Butterworth and Scheck Inc—Donald Butterworth	10 Thompson St, Stratford CT 06615	203-377-5723	R	4*	<.1
469	Eaker Construction LLC—Jon Eaker	PO Box 398, Pineville NC 28134	704-643-1011	R	4*	<.1
470	MJ Halgard Construction—Michael Halgard	2785 Mathia Rd, Hardin KY 42048	270-474-8424	R	4*	.1
471	A and C Communications Corp—Heyward Adams	1118 Garrett Creek Rd, Burkesville KY 42717	270-433-7676	R	4*	.1
472	Summit Pipeline Inc—James Collins	886 Bradford St Sw, Gainesville GA 30501	770-531-1661	R	4*	<.1
473	Westtower Communications—Cal Payne	2017 Opportunity Dr St, Roseville CA 95678	916-783-6400	R	4*	<.1
474	Tri County Tower Service—Bill Klingensmith	8900 Mahoning Ave, North Jackson OH 44451	330-538-9878	R	4*	<.1
475	Tugaloo Pipeline Inc—Edward Hare	975 Cleveland Pke Rd, Westminster SC 29693	864-647-7441	R	4*	<.1
476	Alsterda Cartage and Construction Company Inc—Jack Summers	11832 S Harding Ave, Chicago IL 60803	708-385-1834	R	4*	<.1
477	Doherty Giannini Reitz Construction Co—Patrick Doherty	304 N York Rd, Bensenville IL 60106	630-766-3230	R	4*	<.1
478	Allen D Ormond—Allen Ormond	702 Summit Ave, Kinston NC 28501	252-523-9250	R	4*	<.1
479	Crilly Communication Co—Aaron Crilly	165 Ron St, Duncansville PA 16635	814-696-7323	R	4*	<.1
480	Fuller Contracting Company LLC	980 Salisbury Rd, Mocksville NC 27028	336-751-3712	R	4*	<.1
481	Mago Construction Co—Rinaldo Quadrini	1284 Parks Rd, Oakland MI 48363	586-752-7018	R	4*	<.1
482	Modern Cable Technology Inc—Robert Walker	7015 Euc Dr Ste 101, Ooltewah TN 37063	423-094-9300	R	3*	<.1
483	OCI Construction Company Inc—Robert Wantz	8560 Pekin Rd, Novelty OH 44072	440-338-3166	R	3*	<.1
484	Rp Schroeder Construction Inc—Patti Schroeder	26657 146th St Nw, Zimmerman MN 55398	763-856-2230	R	3*	<.1
485	Mikab Corp—Wesley Weis	PO Box 36, Dumont NJ 07628	201-387-7700	R	3*	<.1
486	Blackmon Contracting Company Inc—Jerry Blackmon	PO Box 991, Smithfield NC 27577	919-989-9998	R	3*	<.1
487	Don Moorhead Construction Inc—Donald Moorhead	1513 Anderson St, Belton SC 29627	864-338-0888	R	3*	<.1
488	Giannetti Contracting Corp—Rick Giannetti	6340 Sims Dr, Sterling Heights MI 48313	586-268-2090	R	3*	<.1
489	Pacific Utility Construction—Joseph Souza	1350 E Beamer St, Woodland CA 95776	530-669-7812	R	3*	<.1
490	Allied Contracting Company Inc—John Burke	6039 Statesboro Hwy, Sylvania GA 30467	912-863-4584	R	3*	<.1
491	Central Virginia Maintenance Inc—Danny Elder	PO Box 300, Buckingham VA 23921	434-969-1779	R	3*	<.1
492	Gluth Brothers Construction Inc—Frank Gluth	1151 Lake Ave, Woodstock IL 60098	815-338-1662	R	3*	<.1
493	Powers Construction	1775 Alpine Dr, Clarksville TN 37040	931-503-9070	R	3*	<.1
494	Global Mechanical Inc—Robert Powell	225 Scarlet Rd, Kennett Square PA 19348	610-444-2100	R	3*	<.1
495	Kincaid Construction Inc—Scott Kincaid	PO Box 28323, Kansas City MO 64188	816-436-4000	R	3*	<.1
496	Redding City Electric Utility—Jim Feider	17120 Clear Creek Rd, Redding CA 96001	530-245-7050	R	3*	<.1
497	GB and G Construction—J Gray	2937 Fm 1569, Greenville TX 75401	903-455-9412	R	3*	<.1
498	J and D Construction—Curtis Hall	Rr 2 Box 338, Bronson TX 75930	936-275-2464	R	3*	<.1
499	Mccizer Pipeline Inc—Lana Mccabe	PO Box 1190, Bald Knob AR 72010	501-724-9947	R	3*	<.1
500	Roese Pipeline Company Inc—Robert Roese	PO Box 489, Linwood MI 48634	989-684-5121	R	3*	<.1
501	Ten Brink Underground—Bruce Ten-Brink	40509 Chancey Rd, Zephyrhills FL 33542	813-788-0184	R	3*	<.1
502	Fayette Tree And Trench Inc—Eugene Nottenkamper	PO Box 471, Fayetteville AR 72702	479-521-5559	R	3*	<.1
503	Liberty Underground Inc—James Burkhardt	PO Box 20892, Rochester NY 14602	585-346-0971	R	3*	<.1
504	Owyhee Construction Inc—Monte Clure	6434 W Gowen Rd, Boise ID 83709	208-376-2240	R	3*	<.1
505	Stone Mountain Contracting Inc—Larry Fawcett	2021 Bentley Dr, Stone Mountain GA 30087	770-413-4210	R	3*	<.1
506	C and N Electric Power and Line Construction Inc—Steve King	PO Box 1154, Ozark AR 72949	479-667-5220	R	3*	<.1
507	Kdm Construction LLC—Mike Blackwell	1531 Cooters Point Rd, Gilbert LA 71336	318-724-7394	R	3*	<.1
508	Locklear Contracting Inc—Rencil Locklear	469 Lonnie Farm Rd, Pembroke NC 28372	910-521-4767	R	3*	<.1
509	Schmidt Construction Company Inc—Richard Schmidt	PO Box 90337, Austin TX 78709	512-288-1511	R	3*	<.1
510	H and W Contractors Inc—Michael Watkins	PO Box 876, Massillon OH 44648	330-833-0982	R	3*	<.1
511	A E Shull and Co—Alfred Shull	5750 Reed Rd, Tyler TX 75707	903-561-5061	R	3*	<.1
512	Aponte Construction Company Inc—Francis Aponte	PO Box 925, Flemington NJ 08822	908-788-4046	R	3*	<.1
513	Building and Utility Contractors Inc—Kourosh Malek	PO Box 68, Redfield AR 72132	501-397-2594	R	3*	<.1
514	Patnick Inc—Pat Divito	205 W Grand Ave Ste 10, Bensenville IL 60106	630-350-8422	R	3*	<.1
515	Schroeder Construction Company Ltd—Kathy Comer	13625 Pond Springs Rd, Austin TX 78729	512-219-6001	R	3*	<.1
516	Fibertech Inc—Burt Preisinger	PO Box 5510, Granbury TX 76049	817-326-5227	R	3*	<.1
517	Juan Mendoza—Juan Mendoza	3701 Jade St, Mercedes TX 78570	956-565-5222	R	3*	<.1
518	Cleburne Utility Construction Inc—Billy Shaw	1429 County Rd 426, Cleburne TX 76031	817-558-1590	R	3*	<.1
519	E and R Construction Inc—Russell Conroy	5141 Calmview Ave, Baldwin Park CA 91706	626-338-8405	R	3*	<.1
520	Environmental Consultants LLC	PO Box 3148, Poughkeepsie NY 12603	845-486-1030	R	3*	<.1
521	Abe Utilities Inc—Justus Everett	PO Box 33413, Raleigh NC 27636	919-834-3421	R	3*	<.1
522	Bc Underground LLC—Dana Watson	3260 Cargo St, Fort Myers FL 33916	239-482-4826	R	3*	<.1
523	Prunty Construction Company Inc—Ernest Knoll	3120 Us Hwy 14 Byp, Brookings SD 57006	605-693-3511	R	3*	<.1
524	Summit Underground Companies Inc—James Collins	886 Bradford St Sw, Gainesville GA 30501	770-531-1661	R	3*	<.1
525	Besco Utilities Inc—Christine Higgins	6900 Ne 4th Ct, Miami FL 33138	305-759-1668	R	3*	<.1
526	C J Calamia Construction Company Inc—Carl Calamia	PO Box 668, Metairie LA 70004	504-467-8782	R	3*	<.1
527	Hughey Construction Company Inc—Larry Hughey	PO Box 478, Waverly TN 37185	931-296-4320	R	3*	<.1
528	Jms Construction LLC	208 Massengill Rd, Benson NC 27504	919-894-4850	R	3*	<.1

Note: An asterisk (*) indicates an estimated financial figure. The company type code used is as follows: R = Private, P = Public, S = Private Subsidiary, B = Public Subsidiary, D = Division, J = Joint Venture, I = Investment Fund.

COMPANY RANKINGS BY SALES WITHIN 4-DIGIT SIC

Rank	Company Name—Executive Officer	Address, City, State, Zip	Phone	Type	Fin	Empls
529	Krueger Excavating Inc—Jane Krueger	2400 N 4th Ave, Sioux Falls SD 57104	605-336-7617	R	3*	<.1
530	Line Contracting Company Inc—Earl Hobbs	PO Box D, Brownstown IN 47220	812-358-2956	R	3*	<.1
531	Whitesides Construction Inc—Hugh Whitesides	PO Box 1070, Duncan SC 29334	864-439-6820	R	3*	<.1
532	B and B Land Clearing Company Inc—Mark Hyde	6815 Hwy Blvd, Katy TX 77494	281-391-7089	R	3*	<.1
533	Happel Excavating Inc—Dennis Happel	PO Box 336, Waverly IA 50677	319-352-2193	R	3*	<.1
534	Hughes Plumbing and Utility Contractors Inc—Preston Hughes	2473 Eslava Creek Pkwy, Mobile AL 36606	251-476-5002	R	3*	<.1
535	Over And Under General Contractors Inc—Jerry Blackwell	PO Box 53, Suwanee GA 30024	770-682-9160	R	3*	<.1
536	Coastal Contractors Inc—Edward Penuel	116 N Creek Dr, Jacksonville NC 28546	910-347-5126	R	3*	<.1
537	Savala Construction Co—Leonard Savala	16402 Construction Cir, Irvine CA 92606	949-651-0221	R	3*	<.1
538	Turpin Inc—Judy Turpin	PO Box 1172, Forest Park GA 30298	404-366-8569	R	3*	<.1
539	Barnette Construction Inc—William Barnette	PO Box 859, Wise VA 24293	276-328-2000	R	3*	<.1
540	Tamerrel Excavation Inc—John Miner	PO Box 128, Parachute CO 81635	970-876-0845	R	3*	<.1
541	Dorfman Construction Company Inc—Gerald E Dorfman	5525 Oakdale Ave Ste 1, Woodland Hills CA 91364	818-702-9731	R	3*	<.1
542	Gulf Coast Remediation LLC	3414 Persimmon St, Houston TX 77093	713-699-9313	R	3*	<.1
543	L and H Construction Inc—Ansel Mcclam	1302 Fork Retch Ct, Mullins SC 29574	843-464-0803	R	3*	<.1
544	Zubeck Inc—Bill Zubeck	8047 Kenai Spur Hwy, Kenai AK 99611	907-283-3991	R	3*	<.1
545	Utility Systems Construction and Engineering LLC—Max Nia-kini	255 N Washington St St, Rockville MD 20850	301-610-9194	R	3*	<.1
546	Gahr Line and Cable LLC	PO Box 63, Saint James MO 65559	573-265-7000	R	3*	<.1
547	Sanders Pipeline Construction Co—Bill Sanders	PO Box 598, Cuero TX 77954	361-275-5622	R	3*	<.1
548	Site Solution Contractors LLC	6895 Pickerington Rd, Carroll OH 43112	614-920-0142	R	3*	<.1
549	Mercer and Ussery Inc—Arthur Mercer	7940 Arthur Cemetery R, Troy TX 76579	254-984-2225	R	3*	<.1
550	Don E Kelly Contractor Inc—Don Kelly	299 NW Outer Rd, Norwood MO 65717	417-746-4545	R	3*	<.1
551	Karsten Equipment Co—Kenneth Karsten	3955 Industrial Dr, Saint Ann MO 63074	314-429-2221	R	3*	<.1
552	RD Blue Construction Inc—Robert Blue	20474 Monument Rd, Crescent IA 51526	712-328-0068	R	3*	<.1
553	Transamerican Underground Ltd—Cara Bailey	1904 Peninsula Dr, Flower Mound TX 75022	972-691-8600	R	3*	<.1
554	Wal-Con Construction Co—John Artukovich	PO Box 462, Surfside CA 90743	562-592-3344	R	3*	<.1
555	Citi Lites Inc—Dennis Peterson	PO Box 440, Pequot Lakes MN 56472	218-568-4744	R	3*	<.1
556	Com-Tech Construction Inc—Randall Candler	PO Box 609, Westfield IN 46074	317-867-4486	R	3*	<.1
557	Robert Mcclure Trenching Inc—William Mcclure	7722 Pleasant Grove Rd, Charlotte NC 28216	704-399-3763	R	3*	<.1
558	Vdi Communications Inc—Jazmine Galeaz	9189 Winkler Dr Ste E, Houston TX 77017	713-776-3237	R	3*	<.1
559	Mainline Supply of Jonesboro Inc—Ken Smith	1045 Post Industrial W, Jonesboro GA 30238	770-471-1303	R	3*	<.1
560	Man-Con Inc—Guy Mancini	3460 Sw 11th St, Deerfield Beach FL 33442	954-427-0230	R	3*	<.1
561	Don Hubbard Contracting Co—Donald Hubbard	1015 Linda Vista Dr, San Marcos CA 92078	760-736-3241	R	3*	<.1
562	Green River Construction Company Inc—Jerry Knudson	6402 S 144th St Ste 1, Tukwila WA 98168	206-246-9456	R	3*	<.1
563	S and W Utility Contractors Inc—Gary Jones	9416 Front St S Ste A, Lakewood WA 98499	253-584-0660	R	3*	<.1
564	Gwaltney Drilling Inc—Michael Crouch	PO Box 520, Washington IN 47501	812-254-5085	R	3*	<.1
565	Sloan Utility Contracting Inc—David Sloan	6949 Turner Mountain R, Gadsden AL 35903	256-492-6177	R	3*	<.1
566	Waterworks District No 3—Jimmie French	1306 Third St, Pineville LA 71360	318-640-4707	R	3*	<.1
567	Lazzati Construction Company Inc—John Lazzati	PO Box 65206, Baltimore MD 21209	410-296-0433	R	3*	<.1
568	Lakeside Contracting Inc—Carl Featche	PO Box 232, Huffman TX 77336	281-812-7078	R	3*	<.1
569	Amerine Utilities Construction Inc—Glen Amerine	PO Box 1546, Great Bend KS 67530	620-792-1223	R	3*	<.1
570	James River Mechanical Inc—Charles Fitchett	PO Box 946, Smithfield VA 23431	757-357-3613	R	3*	<.1
571	Blurton Banks and Associates—Joe Blurton	PO Box 12448, Jackson MS 39236	601-957-2055	R	3*	<.1
572	Marocco Construction Company Inc—Raymond Marocco	PO Box 19021, Baltimore MD 21284	410-828-9033	R	3*	<.1
573	Arete Construction Corp—Ed Sessions	PO Box 35018, Juneau AK 99803	907-780-6866	R	3*	<.1
574	Basnight Construction Company Inc—Marc Basnight	PO Box 1025, Manteo NC 27954	252-473-3474	R	3*	<.1
575	Guerrero Construction Corp—Joe Guerrero	PO Box 1100, Ontario CA 91762	909-590-0031	R	3*	<.1
576	Harvey Construction Company Inc—Lucian Harvey	523 W Mayes St, Jackson MS 39213	601-366-5246	R	3*	<.1
577	Joao And Bradley Construction Company Inc—Fernando Joao	PO Box 20345, Lehigh Valley PA 18002	610-867-1500	R	3*	<.1
578	PKD Inc—David Kiyohara	7829 S 206th St, Kent WA 98032	253-872-7916	R	3*	<.1
579	Silva's Pipeline Inc—Teresa Silva	PO Box 751, Hayward CA 94543	510-786-2722	R	3*	<.1
580	Mountain Valley Contracting Inc—Richard Davis	605 28 1/4 Rd Unit B, Grand Junction CO 81506	970-245-1990	R	3*	<.1
581	Morris Construction Inc—Andy Morris	901 S Tamm Ln, Harlingen TX 78552	956-535-2264	R	3*	.1
582	Allcom Electric Inc—Charles Neil	80 Whitney Pl, Fremont CA 94539	510-656-7099	R	3*	<.1
583	Florida Tel-Con Inc—Edwin Rock	1513 County Rd 315, Green Cove Springs FL 32043	904-529-5200	R	3*	<.1
584	Cline Construction Inc—Greg Cline	PO Box 832, Big Spring TX 79721	432-267-6006	R	3*	<.1
585	Huff Grading and Pipeline Company Inc—Jerry Huff	117b Commerce Dr, Dallas GA 30132	770-445-4028	R	3*	<.1
586	Blazek Corp—Don Blazek	2005 Union Ave, Lawler IA 52154	563-238-7150	R	3*	<.1
587	Ramey Contractor Engineers Inc—Steven Ramey	112 Marston St, Lawrence MA 01841	978-683-6791	R	3*	<.1
588	Brown Construction Inc—Richard Brown	PO Box 495, Nampa ID 83653	208-465-0274	R	3*	<.1
589	Earth-Tech Services Corp—Ronald Waldron	6730 Industrial Ave, Port Richey FL 34668	727-846-9525	R	3*	<.1
590	F Rizzo Construction Inc—Joseph Rizzo	162 York St, Auburn NY 13021	315-252-1872	R	3*	<.1
591	Innovative Cabling Systems Inc—Randall Rossetti	50 Northwestern Dr, Salem NH 03079	603-898-0764	R	3*	<.1
592	James A Hahn Inc—James Hahn	1102 Sunset Pl, Ojai CA 93023	805-646-3635	R	3*	<.1
593	Mikels Construction Co—Jeanine Little	PO Box 5499, Kingwood TX 77325	713-691-5192	R	3*	<.1
594	Hcm and J Inc—Diana Hydrick	PO Box 1324, Gatesville TX 76528	254-865-2400	R	3*	<.1
595	Rossi and Company Incorporated SC—Stephen Rossi	1410 16th St Se, Roanoke VA 24014	540-342-6600	R	3*	<.1
596	Diamond Danco Construction—William Wright	1300 E 13th St, North Little Rock AR 72114	501-374-2241	R	3*	<.1
597	Tele-Communication Installation and Technology—Tommy Tharp	PO Box 1074, Elephant Butte NM 87935	575-744-5951	R	3*	<.1
598	BK Utility Contractors Inc—Alan Krohn	1775 Bryson Ln, Midlothian TX 76065	972-723-2919	R	3*	<.1
599	Seger Communications Inc—Edward W Seger	3786 Broadway St, Buffalo NY 14227	716-681-4646	R	3	<.1
600	Specialty Tower Lighting Ltd—George Jackson	1630 Elmview Dr, Houston TX 77080	713-722-8123	R	3*	<.1
601	Weimer Construction Co—Fred Weimer	PO Box 1228, Pearland TX 77588	281-485-2222	R	3*	<.1
602	Bankston Construction Inc—Versie Bankston	8901 Schaefer Hwy, Detroit MI 48228	313-931-8640	R	3*	<.1
603	Capital Contracting Co—Ernesto Rotondo	6336 Millett Ave, Sterling Heights MI 48312	586-276-0222	R	3*	<.1
604	Cornell Harbison Excavating—Roger Harbison	2014 Edwardsville Gale, Georgetown IN 47122	812-923-5811	R	3*	<.1
605	Francis Brothers Sewer and Drainage—Ernie Francis	PO Box 40, Brookhaven NY 11719	631-345-3537	R	3*	<.1
606	Joseph L Balkan Inc—Joseph Balkan	13001 Jamaica Ave, Richmond Hill NY 11418	718-641-1222	R	3*	<.1
607	Kozik Brothers Inc—Ronald Kozik	213 Executive Dr Ste 3, Cranberry Township PA 16066	724-443-2230	R	3*	<.1
608	M Marlon Ivy and Associates Inc—Mark Ivy	PO Box 9, Spring TX 77383	281-651-1618	R	3*	<.1
609	Montgomery County Of Public Service Authority P S A—Jeff Mersch	755 Roanoke St Ste 1d, Christiansburg VA 24073	540-382-6930	R	3*	<.1
610	Underground Systems Construction Inc—Dane Beckworth	PO Box 386, Fairbury NE 68352	402-729-5502	R	3*	<.1
611	Cla Construction Diversified LLC—Jennifer Vonperbandt	8414 Farm Rd Ste 180-5, Las Vegas NV 89131	702-387-2688	R	3*	<.1
612	Electrical Line Services Inc—Frank Kovar	14200 S Tulsa Dr, Oklahoma City OK 73170	405-691-4910	R	3*	<.1
613	RM Hiner Construction Company Inc—Rex Hiner	11 Austin Rd, Lamar CO 81052	719-336-3467	R	3*	<.1
614	Bill Siler Contracting Inc—William Siler	PO Box 460, South Range MI 49963	906-482-8518	R	3*	<.1
615	Design Point Inc—Doug Lautenbach	2 84th St Sw Unit C, Byron Center MI 49315	616-988-5300	R	3*	<.1

Rank	Company Name—*Executive Officer*	Address, City, State, Zip	Phone	Type	Fin	Empls
616	ER Zeiler Excavating Inc—*Edmund Zeiler*	125 W Sub Station Rd, Temperance MI 48182	734-847-5745	R	3*	<.1
617	L Harper Everett And Son Inc—*Don Harper*	345 College Pkwy Ste 1, Parkersburg WV 26104	304-428-2083	R	3*	<.1
618	Mlaskoch Utility Construction Inc—*Ron Mlaskoch*	PO Box 65, Willow River MN 55795	218-372-3977	R	3*	<.1
619	Annandale Contracting Inc—*Marvin Smith*	6646 County Rd 5 Nw, Annandale MN 55302	320-274-8296	R	3*	<.1
620	Amarillo Utility Contractors Inc—*Monte Taylor*	PO Box 19745, Amarillo TX 79114	806-342-0255	R	3*	<.1
621	Integrity Tower Inc—*Marc Gates*	402 Airport Rd Ste 3, Endicott NY 13760	607-754-3542	R	3*	<.1
622	Precision Management and Construction Inc—*Gary Beene*	PO Box 1467, Forney TX 75126	972-564-3133	R	3*	<.1
623	American Sewer Services Inc—*Dennis Biondish*	N2768 County Rd P, Rubicon WI 53078	262-966-3393	R	3*	<.1
624	CCI Spectrum Inc—*Robert Klopfenstein*	PO Box 24354, Jacksonville FL 32241	904-268-4951	R	3*	<.1
625	John R Walker Inc—*John Walker*	4038 475 Industrial Bl, Macon GA 31210	478-474-8841	R	3*	<.1
626	Pacitto and Forest Construction Co—*Steve Pacitto*	52500 Pontiac Trl, Wixom MI 48393	248-685-7050	R	3*	<.1
627	Silas White Construction Inc—*Silas White*	PO Box 551025, Dallas TX 75355	972-272-1004	R	3*	<.1
628	Tackle Construction Inc—*Daniel Smith*	32255 Morton Rd, Brookshire TX 77423	281-391-3232	R	3*	<.1
629	Brent Woodward Inc—*Brent Woodward*	3743 N Hwy 97, Redmond OR 97756	541-504-5538	R	3*	<.1
630	Double R Utilities Inc—*Ronnie Welch*	466 Poetry Rd, Royse City TX 75189	972-772-9060	R	3*	<.1
631	Pestana Pacific Ltd—*Ernest Pestana*	1431 Atteberry Ln, San Jose CA 95131	408-954-1000	R	3*	<.1
632	Usi Cable Corp—*Carol Gaston*	PO Box 820, Piqua OH 45356	937-778-8318	R	2*	<.1
633	Nexgen Constructors Inc—*George Woodland*	PO Box 1080, Eagle CO 81631	970-328-4946	R	2*	<.1
634	Brook Hill Communications Inc—*Edward Barnette*	6384 Power Rd, Mechanicsville VA 23111	804-730-8400	R	2*	<.1
635	J and C Meador Inc—*Jerry Meador*	358 Southwind Cir, Abilene TX 79602	325-793-1082	R	2*	<.1
636	Dix and Associates Pipeline Contractors Inc—*Robert Dix*	210 Industry Pkwy, Nicholasville KY 40356	859-887-2661	R	2*	<.1
637	Behr Drilling Systems Inc—*Robert Behrens*	20229 N 67th Ave Pmb 1, Glendale AZ 85308	623-266-2673	R	2*	<.1
638	Falcon Contracting Company Of Bartow—*Gilbert Olinger*	840 E Lemon St, Bartow FL 33830	863-533-5479	R	2*	<.1
639	Grant Street Construction Inc—*David Compagni*	48 Grant St, Cortland NY 13045	607-753-1690	R	2*	<.1
640	Middlecreek Corp—*David Oursler*	PO Box 136, Peabody KS 66866	620-983-2532	R	2*	<.1
641	Rothenberger Construction Inc—*Daniel Rothenberger*	PO Box 457, Concord MI 49237	517-524-8944	R	2*	<.1
642	Sterling Construction Company A Colorado Corp—*S Simpson*	PO Box 792, Rifle CO 81650	970-625-8606	R	2*	<.1
643	Amazing Man Inc—*Richard Beshears*	78 Forest Ave, Nesconset NY 11767	516-852-9004	R	2*	<.1
644	Silva Construction Company Inc—*Joseph Silva*	1325 Old Fall River Rd, North Dartmouth MA 02747	508-644-2724	R	2*	<.1
645	Flecha Construction Inc—*Roberto Ferreira*	PO Box 5128, Newark NJ 07105	973-344-7618	R	2*	<.1
646	Navasota Odessa Energy Partners LP—*Frank Giacalone*	PO Box 3189, Odessa TX 79760	432-332-3197	R	2*	<.1
647	Talon Industries Inc—*Valarie Meyer*	1104 Enterprise Pl, Arlington TX 76001	817-265-5511	R	2*	<.1
648	Arox Land Development Corp—*John Tunstall*	700 Bell Rd, Sarasota FL 34240	941-377-2520	R	2*	<.1
649	Barnhart And Son Inc—*James Barnhart*	6355 Holt Rd, Holt MI 48842	517-646-6926	R	2*	<.1
650	Billy D Johnson Contractors Inc—*Billy Johnson*	402 Pine Dr, Four Oaks NC 27524	919-963-6096	R	2*	<.1
651	Blood Hound Inc—*Mark Mason*	750 Patrick Pl Ste B, Brownsburg IN 46112	317-858-9830	R	2*	<.1
652	Cmc Trenching Inc—*Lawrence Stumph*	620 Hardwicke Ave, Birmingham MO 64161	816-455-2570	R	2*	<.1
653	Cruz Tec Inc—*Andres Cruz*	12210 Ann Ln, Houston TX 77064	281-469-2888	R	2*	<.1
654	Forsyth Water And Sewer Construction Inc—*Randy Leonard*	10414 N Nc Hwy 150, Clemmons NC 27012	336-764-1665	R	2*	<.1
655	Gar-Con Inc—*R Breazeale*	PO Box 413, Pickens SC 29671	864-878-6346	R	2*	<.1
656	John Neri Construction Company Inc—*Nicholas Neri*	770 W Factory Rd Ste B, Addison IL 60101	630-629-8384	R	2*	<.1
657	Web Construction Inc—*Betty Crawford*	13004 N Navarro St, Victoria TX 77904	361-574-9589	R	2*	<.1
658	Citation Construction Co—*Pat Lackey*	8515 Ingrid Dr, Elgin TX 78621	512-272-9702	R	2*	<.1
659	Delta Pipeline Inc—*Richard Vance*	1407 Foothill Blvd Ste, La Verne CA 91750	909-596-2632	R	2*	<.1
660	Cecil Construction Corp—*Paul Stringer*	680 Cherry Grove Rd, Earleville MD 21919	410-275-1047	R	2*	<.1
661	G Helmer Construction Company Inc—*George Helmer*	1061 W Malaga Rd, Williamstown NJ 08094	856-629-3347	R	2*	<.1
662	Vls Construction Inc—*Sharon Gillis*	PO Box 630, Ravensdale WA 98051	425-432-3306	R	2*	<.1
663	Manhole Builders Inc—*Edward Jaureguy*	5021 Stone Ave, Riverside CA 92509	951-681-0601	R	2*	<.1
664	Mc Cleary Jp Offshore Construction Inc—*James Mccleary*	PO Box 3562, Morgan City LA 70381	985-631-2121	R	2*	<.1
665	North Central Excavating Trucking and Masonry Inc—*Richard Townsend*	1135 Gornick Ave, Gaylord MI 49735	989-732-2125	R	2*	<.1
666	Bob Hull Inc—*Richard Hull*	PO Box 202, Frankfort KS 66427	785-292-4790	R	2*	<.1
667	DC and R Construction Inc—*Billy Brackins*	251 Cedarwood Dr, Sevierville TN 37876	865-453-4496	R	2*	<.1
668	Didicom Towers Inc—*Jimmy Didier*	PO Box 180727, Fort Smith AR 72918	479-424-1100	R	2*	<.1
669	Llll Construction Company Inc—*Billie Loftin*	4545 Kent Rd, Shreveport LA 71107	318-929-3506	R	2*	<.1
670	Harrison and Harrison Inc—*James Harrison*	PO Box 5635, Athens GA 30604	706-549-2555	R	2*	<.1
671	P and E Construction Inc—*John Elliott*	169 Old Worcester Rd, Charlton MA 01507	508-248-9060	R	2*	<.1
672	All Purpose Contracting Inc—*Ann Kaverman*	24533 Rd U20, Delphos OH 45833	419-695-4165	R	2*	<.1
673	Baker Underground and Construction LLC	3403 Stmboat Island Rd, Olympia WA 98502	360-493-1680	R	2*	<.1
674	Custom Cable Services Inc—*Glenn Dyer*	646 Anchors St Nw Ste, Fort Walton Beach FL 32548	850-301-9322	R	2*	<.1
675	Stone-Circle Underground Inc—*Becky Laman-Hynes*	3830 Sw 30th Ave, Fort Lauderdale FL 33312	954-797-9455	R	2*	<.1
676	Tng Utility Corp—*Chip Callegari*	PO Box 2749, Spring TX 77383	281-350-0895	R	2*	<.1
677	Burr Plumbing And Pumping Inc—*Eric Burr*	1645 Almaden Rd, San Jose CA 95125	408-287-2877	R	2*	<.1
678	Leatherwood Construction Inc—*Michael Leatherwood*	17050 Bushard St Ste 2, Fountain Valley CA 92708	714-593-6575	R	2*	<.1
679	R L Coward Construction Inc—*R Coward*	PO Box 1089, Roebuck SC 29376	864-576-4134	R	2*	<.1
680	Gonzales Boring and Tunneling Company Inc—*James Gonzales*	PO Box 187, North Plains OR 97133	503-647-2218	R	2*	<.1
681	N Pandelena Construction Company Inc—*Abigail Pandelena*	6 Starwood Dr, Hampstead NH 03841	603-329-1111	R	2*	<.1
682	My-Con Inc—*Kevin Hager*	3801 Perry St, Hudsonville MI 49426	616-896-9049	R	2*	<.1
683	Totman Enterprises Inc—*Martha Totman*	PO Box 355, Scituate MA 02066	781-545-6604	R	2*	<.1
684	Heller Company Inc—*Lynn Heller*	PO Box 1438, Hot Springs AR 71902	501-623-7241	R	2*	<.1
685	Brenda W Paul—*Brenda Paul*	482 Nc State Hwy 121, Greenville NC 27834	252-830-0989	R	2*	<.1
686	Arizona Road Specialties Inc—*Terry Daniel*	PO Box 51957, Mesa AZ 85208	480-558-0331	R	2*	<.1
687	Castrejon Inc—*Bert Castrejon*	9201 Ifanti St, Minneapolis MN 55449	763-450-2055	R	2*	<.1
688	Coutts Brothers Inc—*Dennis Coutts*	PO Box 58, Gardiner ME 04345	207-582-6146	R	2*	<.1
689	Neie Construction Services LLC—*Tom Williams*	3175 Rte 10 E Ste 700, Denville NJ 07834	973-537-3600	R	2*	<.1
690	HR Bookstrom Construction Inc—*Eric Bookstrom*	PO Box 4492, Lincoln NE 68504	402-464-4342	R	2*	<.1
691	Metro Construction Inc—*Giles Long*	2526 Caney Branch Rd, Leesville SC 29070	803-532-2795	R	2*	<.1
692	Granbury Contracting and Utilities Inc—*Wayne Wienecky*	PO Box 1176, Granbury TX 76048	817-573-5006	R	2*	<.1
693	Longhorn Construction Inc—*Don Harmon*	PO Box 249, Lander WY 82520	307-349-1281	R	2*	<.1
694	Reddy Construction Company Inc—*Eugene Richard*	4 Turner Dr, Spencerport NY 14559	585-352-3777	R	2*	<.1
695	Arc Underground Inc—*Christine Savoia*	2114 W Thomas St, Chicago IL 60622	773-235-4648	R	2*	<.1
696	Wg Stang LLC	2403 Jacksonburg Rd, Hamilton OH 45011	513-863-6924	R	2*	<.1
697	Emh Environmental Inc—*Edward Halley*	3060 Rte 97 Ste 190, Glenwood MD 21738	410-489-9630	R	2*	<.1
698	Flanigan Plumbing Company Inc—*Gary Flanigan*	2707 Palmyra Rd, Albany GA 31707	229-436-2501	R	2*	<.1
699	L and L Utilities Inc—*Lorri Lewis*	746 Robert Webb Rd, Dublin GA 31027	478-274-0876	R	2*	<.1
700	D L Kellerman Company Inc—*Don Kellerman*	1275 Us 50, Milford OH 45150	513-831-6298	R	2*	<.1
701	B and A Construction Inc—*Allen Bowen*	15842 Boyle Ave, Fontana CA 92337	909-355-4380	R	2*	<.1
702	GH Smith Construction Inc—*Gerald Smith*	430 Shuler Ct, Columbia SC 29212	803-781-5460	R	2*	<.1
703	Illinois Underground Inc—*Terry Havens*	PO Box 236, Wenona IL 61377	815-853-0801	R	2*	<.1

Note: An asterisk (*) indicates an estimated financial figure. The company type code used is as follows: R = Private, P = Public, S = Private Subsidiary, B = Public Subsidiary, D = Division, J = Joint Venture, I = Investment Fund.

COMPANY RANKINGS BY SALES WITHIN 4-DIGIT SIC

Rank	Company Name—*Executive Officer*	Address, City, State, Zip	Phone	Type	Fin	Empls
704	Mcconnell Grading And Utilities and Co—*Harold Mcconnell*	238 John Mcconnell Rd, Easley SC 29640	864-836-5263	R	2*	<.1
705	Northland Technology Inc—*Peter Downey*	348 Park St Ste 205, North Reading MA 01864	978-664-9904	R	2*	<.1
706	Quality Underground Inc—*Jeffery Richardson*	PO Box 7281, Colorado Springs CO 80933	719-522-0300	R	2*	<.1
707	RW Scott Construction Inc—*Steve Scott*	PO Box 2160, Orcutt CA 93457	805-925-5540	R	2*	<.1
708	Bohler Well Service LLC	PO Box 685, Sterling CO 80751	970-522-3078	R	2*	<.1
709	Lmk Pipe Renewal LLC	1131 Nw 55th St, Fort Lauderdale FL 33309	954-772-0075	R	2*	<.1
710	Rilo Electric and Communication Construction LLC	1822 Skyway Dr Unit O, Longmont CO 80504	303-774-2029	R	2*	<.1
711	Double Diamond Construction Company Inc—*Paul Smelly*	3200 38th St, Northport AL 35473	205-361-3473	R	2*	<.1
712	Robinson Tower Inc—*Stanley Robinson*	PO Box 143, Greenville NC 27835	252-758-1453	R	2*	<.1
713	Aldridge Jordan Inc—*J Jordan*	PO Box 1158, Albany GA 31702	229-432-7737	R	2*	<.1
714	Cherokee Grading and Utility Contractors Inc—*Kem Cook*	4390 Earney Rd Ste 130, Woodstock GA 30188	770-664-0362	R	2*	<.1
715	East Carolina Builders Inc—*William Boyd*	PO Box 1300, Newport NC 28570	252-223-5277	R	2*	<.1
716	Larry Baker Contracting—*Larry Baker*	1203 State Rte 170, East Palestine OH 44413	330-426-1037	R	2*	<.1
717	Milco Utilities Inc—*Richard Copa*	911 Ravendale Dr, Shreveport LA 71107	318-464-2299	R	2*	<.1
718	Southeastern Utilities Contractors Inc—*Ray Long*	PO Box 821, Farmington GA 30638	770-725-2076	R	2*	<.1
719	OFT Construction Inc—*Roland Silva*	PO Box 403, Kirtland NM 87417	505-320-6158	R	2*	<.1
720	Pickarski Inc—*Benjamin Pickarski*	PO Box 1200, Gouldsboro PA 18424	570-676-9320	R	2*	<.1
721	Colt Contracting Co—*David Byrd*	PO Box 899, Clinton NC 28329	910-592-2789	R	2*	<.1
722	Site Rite Construction Company Inc—*Kathryn Anderson*	PO Box 30240, Kansas City MO 64112	816-561-4890	R	2*	<.1
723	Civil Engineering Construction Inc—*Michael Hogan*	PO Box 1669, Loomis CA 95650	916-652-9884	R	2*	<.1
724	Ddh Apple Valley Construction Inc—*Douglas Hamilton*	9312 Deep Creek Rd, Apple Valley CA 92308	760-247-4810	R	2*	<.1
725	Merrick Utility Associates Inc—*Frank Diorio*	91 Marine St, Farmingdale NY 11735	631-249-2560	R	2*	<.1
726	Michael A Long Construction Inc—*Michael Long*	7930 Cook Riolo Rd, Antelope CA 95843	916-722-5215	R	2*	<.1
727	Spiva Construction Inc—*Lowell Spiva*	PO Box 1909, Camarillo CA 93011	805-987-1772	R	2*	<.1
728	JB Construction Inc—*Harvey Jahner*	PO Box 397, Linton ND 58552	701-254-4533	R	2*	<.1
729	EW Harmon Inc—*Ernest Harmon*	3344 Hamner Ave, Norco CA 92860	951-371-0272	R	2*	<.1
730	Haydon Construction Inc—*E Haydon*	PO Box 185, Clovis CA 93613	559-251-5522	R	2*	<.1
731	Texacable Inc—*Alton Sheppard*	PO Box 3157, Temple TX 76505	254-773-1163	R	2*	<.1
732	May Gruhn Inc—*Ronald May*	6897 Phillips Pkwy Dr, Jacksonville FL 32256	904-262-9544	R	2*	<.1
733	Roadhole Utility Systems Inc—*Russell Britt*	8020 Hankins Industria, Toano VA 23168	757-566-2572	R	2*	<.1
734	Rocky Mountain Fiber Plus Inc—*Jesse Hill*	PO Box 452, Kiowa CO 80117	303-621-2820	R	2*	<.1
735	Bryson and Bryson Builders Inc—*Christopher Bryson*	3714 Nc Hwy 111 S, Seven Springs NC 28578	252-569-1200	R	2*	<.1
736	Buckeye Excavating and Construction Inc—*David Nickoli*	191 State Rte 61, Norwalk OH 44857	419-663-3113	R	2*	<.1
737	DT Utility Contractors Inc—*Dennis Tollett*	2614 Causbie Rd, Weatherford TX 76087	817-596-0169	R	2*	<.1
738	Prince and Sons Contractors LLC—*Larry Prince*	1233 S Jackson St, Tullahoma TN 37388	931-455-0041	R	2*	<.1
739	Anderson Contracting Inc—*Kenneth Anderson*	PO Box 652, Williamsburg KY 40769	606-549-9961	R	2*	<.1
740	Excel Construction Inc—*Joseph Watson*	PO Box 87, Conway SC 29528	843-347-6662	R	2*	<.1
741	Kinnan Engineering Inc—*Keith Kinnan*	320 Baldwin Rd, Camas Valley OR 97416	541-445-2271	R	2*	<.1
742	Pipe Inc—*Lance Thueson*	455 S Kings Rd Ste B2, Nampa ID 83687	208-466-2503	R	2*	<.1
743	Superior Pipelines Inc—*Walter Alexander*	PO Box 81387, Bakersfield CA 93380	661-588-8081	R	2*	<.1
744	Kiva Inc—*Gary Griffin*	1501 Hillside Ter, Buda TX 78610	512-295-8900	R	2*	<.1
745	Val-Com Field Services Inc—*Daniel Valdemar*	333 N Sam Houston Pkwy, Houston TX 77060	281-405-5520	R	2*	<.1
746	Digco Utilities—*Derrel Isenberg*	481 Fortson St Stb, Shreveport LA 71107	318-221-9693	R	2*	<.1
747	Stringer Construction Company LLC	PO Box 1188, Stringer MS 39481	601-670-0652	R	2*	<.1
748	Town Shop—*Jade Robinson*	PO Box 26, Jena LA 71342	318-992-5160	R	2*	<.1
749	William Pattison Moblie Welding—*William Pattison*	11619 Graywood Dr, Houston TX 77089	281-481-9590	R	2*	<.1
750	ZZ Liner Inc—*Chris Scarratt*	539 W 140th St, Gardena CA 90248	310-329-8717	R	2*	<.1
751	Sandhills Contractors Inc—*Ronnie Turner*	PO Box 1, Sanford NC 27331	919-775-3828	R	2*	<.1
752	Pinnacle Cable South Inc—*Erik Carlson*	PO Box 51505, Summerville SC 29485	843-873-1012	R	2*	<.1
753	HIE Contractors Inc—*James Houston*	324 Markus Ct, Newark DE 19713	302-224-3032	R	2*	<.1
754	Casey Construction Inc—*Mel Casey*	620 Handley Trl, Emerald Hills CA 94062	650-369-1876	R	2*	<.1
755	Coakley Company Inc—*Kevin Coakley*	6822 Albert Pke Rd, Royal AR 71968	501-767-5800	R	2*	<.1
756	Eubank Construction Company Inc—*Kevin Eubank*	2011 N 2nd St, Booneville MS 38829	662-728-2046	R	2*	<.1
757	Holiday Sewer And Construction Inc—*John Digidio*	1000 N Rand Rd Ste 116, Wauconda IL 60084	847-526-1646	R	2*	<.1
758	J T V Inc—*Joyce Velitschkowski*	PO Box 28397, Saint Petersburg FL 33709	727-528-1998	R	2*	<.1
759	Northeast Services Inc—*John Laughlin*	2921 S Clinton Ave, South Plainfield NJ 07080	908-756-0560	R	2*	<.1
760	Secord Contracting Corp—*Thomas Secord*	PO Box 26372, Tampa FL 33623	813-870-0630	R	2*	<.1
761	B and M Telecom Inc—*James Ballard*	PO Box 654, Mansfield TX 76063	817-473-8080	R	2*	<.1
762	Pipevision Products Inc—*Richard Fast*	PO Box 1546, La Salle IL 61301	815-220-1919	R	2*	<.1
763	L W Fritts Construction Company Inc—*Luther Fritts*	PO Box 518, Florence AL 35631	256-764-5693	R	2*	<.1
764	Gasline Service Co—*Jeffrey Lambert*	4391 Gibsonia Rd, Gibsonia PA 15044	724-444-7788	R	2*	<.1
765	Lasiter Utility Backhoe Inc—*Terry Lasiter*	504 Cir View Dr, Pipe Creek TX 78063	830-510-6113	R	2*	<.1
766	Cable Tv Construction And Installations Inc—*Dana Martin*	7710 Harms Rd, Houston TX 77041	713-896-4252	R	2*	<.1
767	Hoffman and Hoffman Trenching Inc—*Duane Hoffman*	PO Box 866, Cedar Falls IA 50613	319-232-4807	R	2*	<.1
768	John Boyd Inc—*Paul Boyd*	5299 Asbury Ave, Tinton Falls NJ 07753	732-922-1770	R	2*	<.1
769	Ritchie Construction Company Inc—*Jacille Herrin*	PO Box 523, Mount Pleasant NC 28124	704-436-6313	R	2*	<.1
770	RL Utilities Inc—*Russ Lundemo*	PO Box 1154, La Porte TX 77572	281-479-6567	R	2*	<.1
771	HR Candee Construction Inc—*Scott Candee*	3255 Fairfield Ave Ste, Bridgeport CT 06605	203-368-0002	R	2*	<.1
772	Pathcomm LLC—*Claudia Metzler*	18340 Valley Blvd, Bloomington CA 92316	909-874-7698	R	2*	<.1
773	Dakota Line Contractors LLC—*Lorraine Richard*	6731 Sterling Dr, Bismarck ND 58504	701-224-8654	R	2*	<.1
774	American Tank Inc—*Alisa Leyden*	PO Box 30054, Chicago IL 60630	312-808-1444	R	2*	<.1
775	B and E Aqatics Inc—*Jim Barnes*	826 Weston Ct, Elburn IL 60119	630-365-5488	R	2*	<.1
776	Dave Perkins Contracting Inc—*David Perkins*	7060 143rd Ave Nw Ste, Anoka MN 55303	763-427-0109	R	2*	<.1
777	Fsh Utility Services Inc—*Ron Kaloust*	3166 Hrsless Carraige, Norco CA 92860	951-520-4399	R	2*	<.1
778	Utilityworks Inc—*Richard Jolly*	4714 Renee Ford Rd, Stanfield NC 28163	704-888-4964	R	2*	<.1
779	3f Utility Construction Inc—*Mike Flores*	5114 N Inspiration Rd, Mission TX 78573	956-585-3477	R	2*	<.1
780	DW Tower Inc—*Dale Wilson*	5601c San Francisco Rd, Albuquerque NM 87109	505-872-8400	R	2*	<.1
781	Action Pipeline Contractors Inc—*Carlos Amado*	121 S Olsen Ave, Tucson AZ 85719	520-792-4302	R	2*	<.1
782	Davis Excavation Inc—*Drew Davis*	PO Box 1169, Van Alstyne TX 75495	214-733-8042	R	2*	<.1
783	Municipal Utilities Inc—*Judy Jones*	PO Box 25094, Fort Worth TX 76124	817-429-7100	R	2*	<.1
784	Richard D Schafer Company Inc—*Richard Schafer*	PO Box 451, Churchville MD 21028	410-399-4013	R	2*	<.1
785	Midwest Utility Trenching Service—*Jim Stoll*	3804 Hwy 67, Camanche IA 52730	563-259-1346	R	2*	<.1
786	Bramble Construction Company Inc—*Sammuel Bramble*	812 E Market St, Georgetown DE 19947	302-856-6723	R	2*	<.1
787	Poleset Inc—*Bruce Livingood*	5355 Prosperity Pke, Prosperity PA 15329	724-222-9414	R	2*	<.1
788	Silver Creek Communications Inc—*Peggy Marty*	PO Box 1, Park City UT 84060	801-450-0405	R	2*	<.1
789	Mofield Brothers Construction Co—*John Mofield*	644 Lebanon Hwy, Carthage TN 37030	615-735-1313	R	2*	<.1
790	Ronnie Mullins and Sons Inc—*Bonnie Mullins*	PO Box 427, Elkhorn City KY 41522	606-754-8969	R	2*	<.1
791	Modern Sewer Service—*Ron Foco*	512 Mcgraw St, Bay City MI 48708	989-892-6375	R	1*	<.1
792	BH Holmes Construction Company Inc—*Randy Holmes*	PO Box 726, La Vergne TN 37086	615-793-3133	R	1*	<.1
793	Cofer Pipe Construction LLC	1865 Sharp Springs Rd, Winchester TN 37398	931-962-0927	R	1*	<.1

Rank	Company Name—*Executive Officer*	Address, City, State, Zip	Phone	Type	Fin	Empls
794	Romtec Utilities Inc—*Tim Bogan*	18240 N Bank Rd, Roseburg OR 97470	541-496-4752	R	1*	<.1
795	Service Construction LLC	28475 Greenfield Rd, Southfield MI 48076	248-569-4200	R	1*	<.1
796	Delfelice Corp—*George Defelice*	28 Silva Ln, Dracut MA 01826	978-319-9849	R	1*	<.1
797	Smart Pipe Company Inc—*Steve Catha*	1426 Vanderwilt Ln Bld, Katy TX 77449	281-945-5700	R	1*	<.1
798	Global Controls LLC	PO Box 780548, Orlando FL 32878	407-381-9060	R	1*	<.1
799	Brandt Construction Co—*Michael Fricke*	PO Box 1138, Moorpark CA 93020	805-523-7818	R	1*	<.1
800	Cherry Brothers Inc—*Michael Cherry*	PO Box 117, Pinson AL 35126	205-681-7991	R	1*	<.1
801	Chris-Lin Construction Inc—*Paul Dragone*	PO Box 17891, West Palm Beach FL 33416	561-790-0192	R	1*	<.1
802	Dennis Myers Contracting Corp—*Dennis Myers*	PO Box 665, Fenton MI 48430	772-473-7114	R	1*	<.1
803	Lewis Construction Of Virginia Inc—*Kevin Lewis*	7716 Quaker Dr, Suffolk VA 23437	757-986-2273	R	1*	<.1
804	Cnr Contractors Inc—*Carrie Johnson*	3632 Bedow Rd, Fort Ripley MN 56449	218-829-4618	R	1*	<.1
805	Lazarus Group Inc—*Al Hoffer*	PO Box 2447, Palm City FL 34991	772-288-2326	R	1*	<.1
806	Nicassio Enterprises Inc—*Gloria Nicassio*	1002 Attilio Ct, Harrison City PA 15636	724-744-0756	R	1*	<.1
807	Sanders General Construction LLC	16541 Redmond Way, Redmond WA 98052	425-401-0090	R	1*	<.1
808	Freedom Underground LLC	6555 W Gary Ave Ste 1, Las Vegas NV 89139	702-263-4992	R	1*	<.1
809	Network Services Group Inc—*Gary Flynn*	5105 Mcclanahan Dr Ste, North Little Rock AR 72116	501-758-6058	R	1*	<.1
810	Precision Boring Technology Inc—*Daniel Smith*	PO Box 3570, Olathe KS 66063	913-206-4734	R	1*	<.1
811	Collins Construction Of Saint George Island Inc—*John Collins*	PO Box 1007, Eastpoint FL 32328	850-670-5790	R	1*	<.1
812	Consolidated Productions Groups Inc—*Delroy Saunders*	1403 Se Ohio Ave, Arcadia FL 34266	863-993-3665	R	1*	<.1
813	Henley Construction Inc—*Larry Henley*	PO Box 1636, Harrison AR 72602	870-743-1500	R	1*	<.1
814	Pacifica Contracting Inc—*Sandra Sperber*	PO Box 90668, San Diego CA 92169	858-483-9988	R	1*	<.1
815	Colan Contracting Inc—*George Colan*	183 Orlando Dr, Sicklerville NJ 08081	856-262-8510	R	1*	<.1
816	De-Bar Contracting Company Inc—*Louis Baratta*	PO Box 140337, Staten Island NY 10314	718-447-1115	R	1*	<.1
817	E Aiudi And Sons Inc—*Ettro Aiudi*	24 Depot Rd, Kensington CT 06037	860-828-4464	R	1*	<.1
818	Lawler and Stanz Inc—*Clyde Lawler*	3725 Serrano St, Martinez CA 94553	925-370-7698	R	1*	<.1
819	Lykins Contracting Inc—*David Lykins*	12783 N State Rd 101, Sunman IN 47041	812-623-2244	R	1*	<.1
820	Major Sewer and Water Contractors Inc—*Robert Vigorito*	285 Metropolitan Ave, Brooklyn NY 11211	718-388-0300	R	1*	<.1
821	Tnt Underground Contracting Inc—*Todd Taughinbaugh*	3930 York Rd, New Oxford PA 17350	717-624-1954	R	1*	<.1
822	Caron Pipe Jacking Inc—*Jackie Mals*	77 Willow Brook Dr, Berlin CT 06037	860-828-0050	R	1*	<.1
823	Seedorf Construction—*Tom Seedorf*	3425 N Wheatridge Rd, Enid OK 73703	580-242-0309	R	1*	<.1
824	Sergi Construction Inc—*Frank Sergi*	775 Jewett Holmwood Rd, East Aurora NY 14052	716-652-8014	R	1*	<.1
825	Sutton Wj Company Inc—*William Sutton*	28100 Jones Loop Rd, Punta Gorda FL 33982	941-639-7470	R	1*	<.1
826	A and E Leasing and Construction—*Alice Sosa-Wolfford*	PO Box 687, Aransas Pass TX 78335	361-758-6588	R	1*	<.1
827	Alpine Development Inc—*Mark Vanderwel*	20415 150th Ave Se, Monroe WA 98272	425-402-1014	R	1*	<.1
828	Asbuilt Construction Inc—*Dan Higgins*	535 Commercial Ave, Reedsburg WI 53959	608-524-4663	R	1*	<.1
829	DA Parrish and Sons Inc—*Darryl Parrish*	PO Box 8580, Stockton CA 95208	209-466-3831	R	1*	<.1
830	D-Kal Engineering Inc—*David Loughran*	PO Box 1919, San Luis Obispo CA 93406	805-543-7758	R	1*	<.1
831	Schuler Engineering Corp—*Bruce Schuler*	564 Bateman Cir, Corona CA 92880	951-738-9215	R	1*	<.1
832	Star Equipment Corp—*Charlene Foran*	30 Heath Rd, South Easton MA 02375	508-238-2808	R	1*	<.1
833	Tvd Inc—*Tom D'angelo*	47 Marchwood Rd Ste 2a, Exton PA 19341	610-594-7520	R	1*	<.1
834	Glen Mauldon Construction—*Glen Mauldon*	1345 Lamb Rd, Mason MI 48854	517-676-4363	R	1*	<.1
835	O'donnell Line Construction Company Inc—*Anita O'donnell*	PO Box 613, Pepperell MA 01463	978-433-6224	R	1*	<.1
836	Dominion Inc—*Mike Olmstead*	PO Box 48, Scottsbluff NE 69363	308-635-3372	R	1*	<.1
837	Longo Sewer Construction Co—*Mike Longo*	4107 Groonvalo Rd, Clovoland OH 44121	216-201-6680	R	1*	<.1
838	Deevan Inc—*Van Williams*	1450 Kinetic Rd Ste A, West Palm Beach FL 33403	561-844-5518	R	1*	<.1
839	Construction By Camco Inc—*Mark Marchiniak*	2125 Oak Leaf St, Joliet IL 60436	815-741-4455	R	1*	<.1
840	Kg Solutions Inc—*Keith Grim*	79 Daily Dr Ste 510, Camarillo CA 93010	805-312-4114	R	1*	<.1
841	Shore Connection Inc—*James Lally*	304 Forge Rd Unit 10, West Creek NJ 08092	609-294-4990	R	1*	<.1
842	GCPS Inc—*Chris Heule*	PO Box 590002, Houston TX 77259	281-291-7955	R	1*	<.1
843	C B Developers Inc—*Sherry Breland*	938 Old Rifle Range Rd, Petal MS 39465	601-582-1600	R	1*	<.1
844	Cr Contracting Ltd—*Melanie Danklefs*	20770 N Hwy 281 108-29, San Antonio TX 78258	210-274-5286	R	1*	<.1
845	Orf Construction Inc—*William Orf*	15181 Pke 313, Bowling Green MO 63334	573-324-3552	R	1*	<.1
846	Underground Industries Inc—*Bernard Vito*	179 N Jog Rd, West Palm Beach FL 33413	561-689-1566	R	1*	<.1
847	Grattan Line Construction Corp—*Charles Rubeski*	35 Sullivan Rd, North Billerica MA 01862	978-663-7723	R	1*	<.1
848	Bishop Construction Inc—*Theodore Bishop*	1637 Billy Casper Dr, El Paso TX 79936	915-592-4477	R	1*	<.1
849	Pilgrim Communications Inc—*Michael Whitecotton*	3402 C St Ne Ste 101, Auburn WA 98002	253-887-8464	R	1*	<.1
850	Smith's Construction Inc—*Alvin Smith*	11238 Dobson Rd, Gulfport MS 39503	228-832-5446	R	1*	<.1
851	CPI Contracting Inc—*Charles Smith*	1805 Saint Clair River, Algonac MI 48001	810-794-7256	R	1*	<.1
852	Didier Communications Tower Inc—*Jimmy Didier*	PO Box 180727, Fort Smith AR 72918	479-424-1100	R	1*	<.1
853	HL Bennett Jr Inc—*Jay Bennett*	60 F Bennett Sq Ste 60, Southbury CT 06488	203-264-5645	R	1*	<.1
854	Pacific Tank and Pipeline—*Landan Cheney*	PO Box 990, Sidney MT 59270	406-652-1769	R	1*	<.1
855	Hsa Construction Inc—*Margaret Hamann*	6546 N 15000e Rd, Grant Park IL 60940	815-465-6956	R	1*	<.1
856	Tec Enterprises Inc—*Wesley Jinks*	395 Tom Dean Rd, Farmerville LA 71241	318-368-3616	R	1*	<.1
857	Broadcast Tower Technologies Inc—*Diana Boone*	4551 San Siro Dr, Sarasota FL 34235	941-359-8833	R	1*	<.1
858	Inland Valley Engineering Inc—*Stephanie Aanestad*	27475 Ynez Rd 627, Temecula CA 92591	951-303-8309	R	1*	<.1
859	Sedaghat and Associates Engineers—*Mansour Sedaghat*	512 S San Vicente Blvd, Los Angeles CA 90048	323-653-4906	R	1*	<.1
860	Sitetech LLC	PO Box 261, Charlotte TN 37036	615-789-3940	R	1*	<.1
861	Consortium Communications Inc—*William Dolbow*	6475 E Main St Ste 106, Reynoldsburg OH 43068	614-759-4949	R	1*	<.1
862	May Construction Inc—*Troy Hahn*	PO Box 402, Madison SD 57042	605-997-2895	R	1*	<.1
863	Larry Clark Construction Inc—*Larry Clark*	5427 Bardstown Rd Ste, Louisville KY 40291	502-239-8400	R	1*	<.1
864	Angle Tower Corp—*Calvin Waller*	PO Box 475, Gainesville FL 32602	352-375-7734	R	1*	<.1
865	Da Neal Construction Inc—*David Erickson*	36296 Ne Wilsonville R, Newberg OR 97132	503-682-0585	R	1*	<.1
866	Wondra Construction Inc—*Robert Mayer*	W2874 Graylog Rd, Iron Ridge WI 53035	920-387-5840	R	1*	<.1
867	Intag Inc—*Victor Intag*	10805 Sunset Ste 300, Saint Louis MO 63127	314-822-1102	R	1*	<.1
868	Larson Crane Service Inc—*Don Larson*	2119 E Clary St, Worthington MN 56187	507-376-3420	R	<1*	<.1
869	Bill Mcgowan Inc—*Bill Mcgowan*	77170 Hwy 1082, Covington LA 70435	985-893-1468	R	<1*	<.1
870	Tri Dal Ltd—*Cris Csho*	540 Commerce St, Southlake TX 76092	817-481-2886	R	<1*	.3

TOTALS: SIC 1623 Water, Sewer & Utility Lines
Companies: 870 — 26,454 — 132.5

1629 Heavy Construction Nec

Rank	Company Name—*Executive Officer*	Address, City, State, Zip	Phone	Type	Fin	Empls
1	Jacobs Engineering Group Inc—*Craig L Martin*	PO Box 7084, Pasadena CA 91109	626-578-3500	P	10,382	45.7
2	TIC-Industrial Company Southeast Inc	PO Box 774848, Steamboat Springs CO 80487	970-871-7209	D	6,480*	9.0
3	Skanska USA Civil Inc—*Salvatore Mancini*	1616 Whitestone Expy S, Whitestone NY 11357	718-767-2600	S	1,994*	5.0
4	Siemens Water Technologies	250 N Barrington Rd, Hoffman Estates IL 60192	724-772-1402	D	1,200*	5.8
5	Weeks Marine Inc—*Richard S Weeks*	4 Commerce Dr 2nd Fl, Cranford NJ 07016	908-272-4010	R	859*	1.0
6	Siemens Energy Inc—*Randy Zwirn*	4400 N Alafaya Trl, Orlando FL 32826	407-736-2000	R	748*	6.1
7	Phillips and Jordan Inc—*Ben Turner*	PO Box 52050, Knoxville TN 37912	865-688-8342	R	661*	.8
8	Sterling Construction Company Inc—*Patrick Manning*	20810 Fernbush Ln, Houston TX 77073	281-821-9091	P	460	1.3

Note: An asterisk (*) indicates an estimated financial figure. The company type code used is as follows: R = Private, P = Public, S = Private Subsidiary, B = Public Subsidiary, D = Division, J = Joint Venture, I = Investment Fund.

COMPANY RANKINGS BY SALES WITHIN 4-DIGIT SIC

Rank	Company Name—*Executive Officer*	Address, City, State, Zip	Phone	Type	Fin	Empls
9	Burns and Roe Enterprises Inc—*K Keith Roe*	800 Kinderkamack Rd, Oradell NJ 07649	201-265-2000	R	408*	1.6
10	Cherry Hill Construction Inc—*James Laing*	8211 Washington Blvd, Jessup MD 20794	410-799-3577	R	399*	.5
11	David A Bramble Inc—*David Bramble*	705 Morgnec Rd, Chestertown MD 21620	410-778-3023	R	375*	.3
12	Orion Marine Group—*Mike Pearson*	12000 Aerospace Ave St, Houston TX 77034	713-852-6500	P	353	1.5
13	Sargent Corp—*Herb Sargent*	PO Box 435, Stillwater ME 04489	207-827-4435	R	352*	.4
14	King Fisher Marine Service Inc—*Mike Pearson* Orion Marine Group	PO Box 108, Port Lavaca TX 77979	361-552-6751	S	331*	.4
15	Tutor-Saliba Corp—*Ronald N Tutor*	15901 Olden St, Sylmar CA 91342	818-362-8391	S	321*	1.2
16	Ashton Company Inc—*Bill Vail*	PO Box 26927, Tucson AZ 85726	520-624-5500	R	271*	.3
17	Great Lakes Dredge and Dock Co (Oak Brook Illinois)—*Jonathan W Berger*	2122 York Rd, Oak Brook IL 60523	630-574-3000	R	270*	.8
18	Slattery Skanska Inc—*Richard Cavallaro* Skanska USA Civil Inc	1616 Whitestone Expy, Whitestone NY 11357	718-767-2600	S	262*	.3
19	Irwin Industries Inc—*John Dewey*	1580 W Carson St, Long Beach CA 90810	310-233-3000	R	250*	1.0
20	SNC-Lavalin Constructors Inc—*Mike Ranz*	PO Box 3037, Bothell WA 98041	425-489-8000	S	240*	.3
21	Keppel Amfels Inc—*T Tan*	PO Box 3107, Brownsville TX 78523	956-831-8220	R	190*	1.5
22	Shook National Corp—*Frank Klein*	PO Box 138806, Dayton OH 45413	937-276-6666	R	185*	.3
23	Dutra Group—*Bill T Dutra*	2350 Kerner Blvd Ste 2, San Rafael CA 94901	415-258-6876	R	184*	.2
24	Snelson Companies Inc—*Ed Shannon*	601 W State St, Sedro Woolley WA 98284	360-856-6511	R	173*	.2
25	Sherwood Construction Company Inc—*John Curtis*	PO Box 9163, Wichita KS 67277	316-943-0211	R	172*	.2
26	Landscapes Unlimited LLC—*William Kubly*	1201 Aries Dr, Lincoln NE 68512	402-423-6653	R	169*	1.0
27	Knife River Construction—*Bill Schneider*	1764 Skyway, Chico CA 95928	530-891-6555	S	167*	.3
28	Foster Wheeler Pyropower—*Raymond J Milchovich*	Perryville Corporate P, Clinton NJ 08809	908-730-4000	R	166*	.2
29	Ellard Contracting Company Inc—*DW Ellard*	PO Box 101477, Birmingham AL 35210	205-956-2846	R	162*	.3
30	Bmwc Group Inc—*Thomas Obrien*	1740 W Michigan St, Indianapolis IN 46222	317-267-0400	R	157*	.7
31	Hughes Group Inc—*James P Hughes*	6200 E Hwy 62 Ste100, Jeffersonville IN 47130	812-282-4393	R	150*	.3
32	Ventech Engineers International Corp—*Bill Stanley*	1149 Ellsworth Dr Ofc, Pasadena TX 77506	713-477-0201	S	147*	.3
33	US Contractors Ltd—*Lynn Monical*	PO Box 447, Clute TX 77531	979-265-7451	R	144*	2.0
34	Entact LLC—*Lawrence Day*	3129 Bass Pro Dr, Grapevine TX 76051	972-580-1323	R	140*	.5
35	Monterey Mechanical Co—*Milt Burleson*	8275 San Leandro St, Oakland CA 94621	510-632-3173	R	136*	.4
36	International Generating Co—*Neil H Smith*	15 Wayside Rd, Burlington MA 01803	781-993-3000	S	123*	.2
37	JR Filanc Construction Company Inc—*Mark E Filanc*	740 N Andreasen Dr, Escondido CA 92029	760-941-7130	R	120*	.2
38	Aurora Contractors Inc—*Frank Vero Sr*	100 Raynor Ave, Ronkonkoma NY 11779	631-981-3785	R	120*	.2
39	Ref-Chem LP (Odessa Texas)—*Harvey J Page*	PO Box 2588, Odessa TX 79760	432-332-8531	R	114*	.8
40	Northern Improvement Co—*Tom McKormick*	PO Box 2846, Fargo ND 58108	701-277-1225	R	112*	.9
41	Leonard B Hebert Jr and Company Inc—*Leonard B Hebert Jr*	PO Box 26245, New Orleans LA 70186	504-241-6363	R	111*	.3
42	Skanska USA Civil Southeast Inc—*Peter Kenna*	295 Bendix Rd Ste 400, Virginia Beach VA 23452	757-420-4140	R	111*	.8
43	Grupe Co—*Fritz Grupe*	3255 W March Ln Ste 40, Stockton CA 95219	209-473-6000	R	100*	.4
44	ValleyCrest Landscape Inc—*Richard Sperber*	24151 Ventura Blvd, Calabasas CA 91302	818-223-8500	S	88*	1.1
45	Tarco Inc (Arvada Colorado)—*Todd E Thomas*	4781 W 58th Ave, Arvada CO 80002	303-429-2221	R	88*	.4
46	Gemma Power Systems LLC—*William F Griffin*	2461 Main St, Glastonbury CT 06033	860-659-0509	R	86*	.1
47	Swanson Contracting Co—*Ted Swanson*	11701 S Mayfield Ave, Alsip IL 60803	708-388-0623	R	83*	.1
48	PF Moon And Company Inc—*Phillip Moon*	PO Box 346, West Point GA 31833	706-643-1524	R	78*	.1
49	Azco Inc—*Mark Loper*	PO Box 567, Appleton WI 54912	920-734-5791	R	73*	.7
50	ASI Constructors Inc	1850 E Platteville Blv, Pueblo West CO 81007	719-647-2821	R	68*	.1
51	Dashiell Corp—*Steve Hicks*	12301 Kurland Dr Ste 4, Houston TX 77034	713-558-6600	S	65*	.3
52	Lyles Diversified Inc—*William M Lyles III*	PO Box 4376, Fresno CA 93744	559-441-1900	R	62*	.3
53	Massman Construction Co—*Henry J Massman IV*	PO Box 8458, Kansas City MO 64114	816-523-1000	R	62*	.3
54	Isemoto Contracting Company Ltd—*Leslie Isemoto*	648 Piilani St, Hilo HI 96720	808-935-7194	R	58*	.2
55	WM Lyles Co—*Michael A Burson* Lyles Diversified Inc	PO Box 4377, Fresno CA 93744	559-441-1900	S	55*	.2
56	Nicholson Construction Co—*Andrew D Walker*	12 McClane St, Cuddy PA 15031	412-221-4500	S	54*	.2
57	Megen Construction Company Inc—*Evans Nwankwo*	11130 Ashburn Rd, Cincinnati OH 45240	513-742-9191	R	52*	.1
58	Bowen Engineering Corp—*Doug Bowen*	8802 North Meridian St, Indianapolis IN 46260	317-842-2616	R	50*	.3
59	McLean Contracting Co—*Richard F Hoffman*	6700 McLean Way, Glen Burnie MD 21060	410-553-6700	R	50*	.2
60	Tarlton Corp—*Tracy Elsperman Hart*	5500 W Park Ave, Saint Louis MO 63110	314-633-3300	R	48*	.3
61	Manson Construction Co—*Eric Haug*	PO Box 24067, Seattle WA 98124	206-762-0850	R	48*	.2
62	Mathiowetz Construction Co—*Brian Mathiowetz*	30676 County Rd 24, Sleepy Eye MN 56085	507-794-6953	R	46*	.2
63	Crom Corp—*James Copley*	250 Sw 36th Ter, Gainesville FL 32607	352-372-3436	R	46*	.6
64	Foster Wheeler Constructors Inc—*Umberto Della Sala*	Perryville Corporate P, Clinton NJ 08809	908-730-4000	D	42*	.4
65	O Weaver Hosea And Sons Inc—*Paul Weaver*	PO Box 8039, Mobile AL 36689	251-342-3025	R	42*	.1
66	Norfolk Dredging Co—*G Dudley Ware*	PO Box 1706, Chesapeake VA 23327	757-547-9391	R	39*	.2
67	Carl Bolander and Sons Co—*Mark Ryan*	PO Box 7216, Saint Paul MN 55107	651-224-6299	R	38*	.2
68	Luedtke Engineering Co—*Kurt Luedtke*	PO Box 111, Frankfort MI 49635	231-352-9631	R	34*	.1
69	Harrison Western Construction Corp—*Chris Hassel*	1208 Quail St, Lakewood CO 80215	303-234-0273	R	30*	.1
70	Dutra Materials—*William Dutra* Dutra Group	2350 Kerner Blvd Ste 2, San Rafael CA 94901	415-258-6876	S	29*	.3
71	Healey Railroad Corp—*Glenn V Healey*	P0 Box 190, Midlothian VA 23113	804-379-3904	R	29*	.1
72	Foundation Constructors Inc—*Peter Brandl*	PO Box 97, Oakley CA 94561	925-754-6633	R	28*	.2
73	Railroad Construction Company Inc—*Alfonso Daloisio Jr*	75-77 Grove St, Paterson NJ 07503	973-684-0362	R	25*	.5
74	Luhr Brothers Inc—*Alois Luhr*	PO Box 50, Columbia IL 62236	618-281-4106	R	24*	.2
75	Johnston Construction Co—*George Johnston*	PO Box 98, Dover PA 17315	717-292-3606	R	24*	.1
76	Aubrey Silvey Enterprises Inc—*Tommy Muse*	371 Hamp Jones Rd, Carrollton GA 30117	770-834-0738	R	23*	.3
77	Knik Construction Co—*Steve Jansen*	18000 International Bl, Seattle WA 98188	206-439-5525	S	21*	<.1
78	Matous Construction Ii Ltd—*Maria Kaesberg*	8602 State Hwy 317, Belton TX 76513	254-780-1400	R	21*	.1
79	R and L Development Company Inc—*Dale Latimer*	PO Box 529, New Alexandria PA 15670	724-668-2223	R	20*	.2
80	Spearin Preston Burrows Inc—*John Eckerd*	3365 Richmond Ter, Staten Island NY 10303	718-720-8039	R	20*	.2
81	Atlantic-Meeco Inc—*Paul Durlacher*	PO Box 3939, Mcalester OK 74502	918-423-6833	R	20*	.1
82	AJ Johns Inc—*Archie Johns*	3225 Anniston Rd, Jacksonville FL 32246	904-641-2055	R	19*	.2
83	Atlas Railroad Construction Co—*William M Stout*	PO Box 8, Eighty Four PA 15330	724-228-4500	R	18*	.2
84	Stone Hill Contracting Company Inc—*Samuel Mott*	PO Box 1370, Doylestown PA 18901	215-340-1840	R	18*	<.1
85	Industrial Resources Inc—*Charles Miller*	PO Box 2648, Fairmont WV 26555	304-363-4100	R	17*	.1
86	AES Warrior Run LLC—*Paul Hanrahan*	11600 Mexico Farms Rd, Cumberland MD 21502	301-777-0055	S	17*	.1
87	First Golf Corp	3605 E Hialea Ct Ste 4, Phoenix AZ 85044	480-345-7857	R	17*	<.1
88	Scotty's Contracting And Stone LLC—*George Walenga*	PO Box 4500, Bowling Green KY 42102	270-781-3998	R	15*	.4
89	Intensus Engineering Incorporated LLC—*J Carlos Salcedo*	PO Box 123, Cold Spring NY 10516	845-265-6000	R	13*	<.1
90	Enviro-Tech Services Inc—*Sammy Wyatt*	PO Box 51653, Bowling Green KY 42102	270-781-5126	R	12*	<.1
91	Durham Pump Inc—*Thomas Martin*	PO Box 60, Durham CA 95938	530-891-4821	R	10*	<.1
92	Yanke Energy Inc—*Sheldon Schultz*	PO Box 5405, Boise ID 83705	208-338-2205	R	10*	<.1
93	Lafayette Utility Construction Company Inc—*David Powell*	PO Box 944, Pleasantville NJ 08232	609-645-2600	R	9*	<.1

Rank	Company Name—*Executive Officer*	Address, City, State, Zip	Phone	Type	Fin	Empls
94	WR Townsend Contracting Inc—*William Townsend*	1465 County Rd 210 W, Jacksonville FL 32259	904-354-9202	R	8*	.1
95	Stanmar Inc—*Jim Wakely*	321 Common Wealth Rd S, Wayland MA 01778	978-443-9922	R	7*	<.1
96	Orion Associates Inc—*Allan Gibbs*	1317 Cavalier Blvd, Chesapeake VA 23323	757-558-6400	R	6*	.1
97	Pae and Associates Inc—*John Elder*	PO Box 429, Brookville OH 45309	937-833-0013	R	6*	.1
98	Mgk Industries Inc—*Michael Kachmar*	PO Box 276, Pottstown PA 19464	610-705-5700	R	6*	<.1
99	Jackson-Cook LC—*Geraldine Cook*	PO Box 2763, Tallahassee FL 32316	850-576-4187	R	5*	.1
100	Bartek Construction Co—*Larry Bartek*	PO Box 200203, San Antonio TX 78220	210-648-4780	R	5*	<.1
101	Famco Inc—*Richard Smailes*	PO Box 157, Huntington WV 25716	304-529-3328	R	5*	<.1
102	Blue Ridge Construction Inc—*Gary D Haglund*	PO Box 76000, Colorado Springs CO 80970	719-578-5225	R	5*	<.1
103	P and M Communications Contractors Inc—*Paul Mangan*	1242 Olive St, Lakeland FL 33815	863-683-5599	R	4*	<.1
104	Showalter Incorporated F L—*Louis Kiger*	PO Box 11525, Lynchburg VA 24506	434-845-2388	R	4*	.1
105	Clark Brothers Inc	19772 S Elgin Rd, Dos Palos CA 93620	209-392-6144	R	4*	<.1
106	Crofton Construction Services Inc—*Kenneth Crofton*	PO Box 7756, Portsmouth VA 23707	757-397-1131	R	4*	<.1
107	Virginia West Pipeline Inc—*David Bolton*	PO Box 970, Princeton WV 24740	304-425-4053	R	3*	<.1
108	Nunn Constructors Ltd—*David Nunn*	23602 Botkins Rd, Hockley TX 77447	281-351-8383	R	3*	<.1
109	Chemical Design Service Company Inc—*Walter Schmid*	PO Box 513, Lockport NY 14095	716-433-6744	R	2*	<.1
110	Farnham and Pfile Company Inc—*Douglas Farnham*	1200 Maronda Way Ste 4, Monessen PA 15062	724-653-1010	R	2*	<.1
111	Ida-West Energy Co—*Mark Stokes*	PO Box 7867, Boise ID 83707	208-395-8930	S	2*	<.1
112	Zimmerman and Co—*Michael Zimmerman*	PO Box 467, Delaware OH 43015	740-369-7594	R	2*	<.1
113	QSS International Inc—*Pramond Banavar*	3917 Old Lee Hwy Ste 1, Fairfax VA 22030	703-766-0211	R	2*	<.1
114	Total Containment Systems LP—*John K Hagopian II*	28 1/2 Alice St, Binghamton NY 13904	607-723-3066	R	2*	<.1
115	Dolphin Marine Equipment Inc—*Larry Fisk*	13056 Faxton St, Clearwater FL 33760	727-391-1479	R	1*	<.1
116	Linde Enterprises Inc—*Scott Linde*	PO Box A, Honesdale PA 18431	570-253-2643	R	1*	.1
117	Complete Water Services LLC—*Jim Lewis*	340 Cherokee St Ne, Marietta GA 30060	678-355-9270	R	1*	<.1
118	Frontier-Kemper Constructors Inc—*Galyn Rippentrop*	PO Box 6690, Evansville IN 47719	812-426-2741	R	N/A	.3

TOTALS: SIC 1629 Heavy Construction Nec
Companies: 118

					32,001	106.0

1711 Plumbing, Heating & Air-Conditioning

Rank	Company Name—*Executive Officer*	Address, City, State, Zip	Phone	Type	Fin	Empls
1	Cohesant Inc—*Morris H Wheeler*	23400 Commerce Park, Beachwood OH 44122	216-910-1700	P	12,685	N/A
2	American Residential Services LLC—*Donald K Karnes*	965 Ridge Lake Blvd St, Memphis TN 38120	901-271-9700	S	3,312	N/A
3	Van's Comfortemp—*Jason Tota*	135 S Congress Ave, Delray Beach FL 33445	561-278-5232	R	3,007*	.1
4	Service Experts Inc—*Robert Schjerven*	1207 Ave L, Plano TX 75074	972-730-3535	S	967*	8.0
5	Sterling Boiler And Mechanical Inc—*Daniel Felker*	PO Box 8004, Evansville IN 47716	812-479-5447	R	360*	.8
6	Egan Mechanical Contractors Inc—*Craig Sulentic* Egan Co	7625 Boone Ave N, Brooklyn Park MN 55428	763-544-4131	S	357*	.7
7	Monumental Investment Corp—*Adam E Snavely*	4530 Hollins Ferry Rd, Baltimore MD 21227	410-247-2200	R	320*	1.0
8	Kirk and Blum Manufacturing Company Inc—*Richard J Blum*	3120 Forrer St, Cincinnati OH 45209	513-458-2600	S	265*	.4
9	Nagelbush Mechanical Inc—*Stephen H Kornfeld*	1800 NW 49th St Ste 11, Fort Lauderdale FL 33309	954-736-3000	R	237*	.4
10	August Winter and Sons Inc—*Jerry Hietpas*	2323 N Roemer Rd, Appleton WI 54911	920-739-8881	R	236*	.1
11	Wiginton Corp—*Debbie Bien*	699 Aero Ln, Sanford FL 32771	407-936-1922	R	208*	.4
12	Cox Engineering Co—*Jeff Chase*	35 Industrial Dr, Canton MA 02021		R	196*	.3
13	TDIndustries Inc—*Bob Ferguson*	13850 Diplomat Dr, Dallas TX 75234	972-888-9500	R	191*	1.4
14	Corval Group—*Paul Jordan*	1633 Eustis St, Saint Paul MN 55108	651-645-0451	R	191*	.6
15	Shumate Air Conditioning and Heating Company Inc—*Sandy Shumate*	2805 Premiere Pky NW, Duluth GA 30097	678-584-0880	R	180*	.4
16	Stromberg Sheet Metal Works Inc—*Robert B Gawne*	6701 Distribution Dr, Beltsville MD 20705	301-931-1000	R	169*	.3
17	Way Holding Co—*Peter Way*	5308 Ashbrook, Houston TX 77081	713-666-3541	R	165*	.3
18	Brainer And Brown Plumbing Inc—*Ken Brainer*	217 Steedly Dr, Louisville KY 40214	502-361-3747	R	162*	<.1
19	Waldinger Corp—*Thomas Koehn*	PO Box 1612, Des Moines IA 50306	515-323-5107	R	156*	.9
20	Western States Fire Protection Company Inc—*Gene Postma*	7026 S Tucson Way, Centennial CO 80112	303-792-0022	R	151*	1.4
21	Trinity Mechanical Systems Inc—*Terry Logan*	14036 S Lakes Dr, Charlotte NC 28273	704-391-1412	R	150*	<.1
22	Fluidics Inc—*Edward A Quinn*	9815 Roosevelt Blvd St, Philadelphia PA 19114	215-671-7930	S	146*	.3
23	P1 Group Inc—*Smitty Belcher*	16210 W 108th St, Lenexa KS 66219	913-529-5000	R	136*	.8
24	Egan Co—*Jim Malecha*	7625 Boone Ave N, Brooklyn Park MN 55428	763-544-4131	R	136*	.7
25	Batchelor's Mechanical Contractors Inc—*Don F Rhodes*	PO Box 7504, Mobile AL 36670	251-470-6800	R	130*	.2
26	John E Green Co—*Peter J Green*	220 Victor St, Highland Park MI 48203	313-868-2400	R	124*	.3
27	Reedy Industries Inc—*William Reedy*	2440 Ravine Way Ste 20, Glenview IL 60025	847-729-9450	R	122	.8
28	Warwick Plumbing and Heating Corp—*GRoyden Goodson III*	11048 Warwick Blvd, Newport News VA 23601	757-599-6111	R	121*	.4
29	ColonialWebb Contractors—*Mitch Haddon*	2820 Ackley Ave, Richmond VA 23228	804-916-1400	R	120*	1.4
30	Therma Corp—*Joseph Parisi*	1601 Las Plumas Ave, San Jose CA 95133	408-347-3400	R	120*	1.2
31	McClure Co—*Thomas Brown*	PO Box 1579, Harrisburg PA 17110	717-232-9743	D	111*	.1
32	Alaka'i Mechanical Corp—*Clark Morgan*	2655 Waiwai Loop, Honolulu HI 96819	808-834-1085	R	110*	.3
33	Industrial Contractors Inc (Bismarck North Dakota)—*Lloyd Bushong*	PO Box 5519, Bismarck ND 58506	701-258-9908	S	108*	.3
34	Total Mechanical—*Dennis Braun*	W234 N2830 Paul Rd, Pewaukee WI 53072	262-523-2500	R	106*	.3
35	RS Andrews Enterprises Inc—*Jack Dowling*	3510 Dekalb Technology, Atlanta GA 30340	770-454-1820	R	103*	.2
36	Riggs Distler and Company Inc—*Stephen M Zemaitatis*	4 Esterbrook Ln, Cherry Hill NJ 08003	856-433-6000	R	99*	.5
37	Cropp-Metcalfe Inc—*Mitchell Cropp*	8421 Hilltop Rd, Fairfax VA 22031	703-698-8855	R	99*	.2
38	Dee Cramer Inc—*Matt Cramer*	4221 E Baldwin, Holly MI 48442	248-674-7589	R	99*	.2
39	B and W Mechanical Contractors Inc—*W Chandler White Jr*	PO Box 2223, Norcross GA 30091	770-449-6000	R	93*	.1
40	Elliott-Lewis Corp—*William Sautter*	2900 Black Lake Pl, Philadelphia PA 19154	215-698-4400	S	91*	.6
41	MCC Group LLC—*Joseph A Jaeger Jr*	3001 17th St, Metairie LA 70002	504-833-8291	R	90*	.6
42	Roth Brothers Inc	PO Box 4209, Youngstown OH 44515	330-793-5571	S	90*	.6
43	Grunau Company Inc—*Larry Loomis*	PO Box 479, Milwaukee WI 53201	414-216-6900	R	86*	.4
44	CCI Mechanical Inc—*Davis Mullholand*	PO Box 25788, Salt Lake City UT 84125	801-973-9000	R	81*	.2
45	JWP Gowan Inc—*Anthony Guzzi*	5550 Airline Dr, Houston TX 77076	713-696-5400	S	80*	.8
46	Letsos Co—*James N Letsos III*	P0 Box 36927, Houston TX 77236	713-783-3200	R	80*	.4
47	Stegall Metal Industries Inc—*Greg Smith*	PO Box 2207, Birmingham AL 35201	205-251-0330	R	80*	.1
48	WW Gay Mechanical Contractor Inc—*William W Gay*	524 Stockton St, Jacksonville FL 32204	904-388-2696	R	76*	.9
49	Illingworth Corp—*Dan Pfeifer*	PO Box 314, Milwaukee WI 53201	414-476-5790	S	74*	.2
50	Mckinstry Company LLC—*Dean Baker*	PO Box 24567, Seattle WA 98124	206-762-3311	R	74*	.7
51	Corrigan Brothers Inc—*Dennis Corrigan*	3545 Gratiot St, Saint Louis MO 63103	314-771-6200	R	72*	.7
52	Cobb Mechanical Contractors Inc—*Tom F Cobb*	2906 W Morrison St, Colorado Springs CO 80904	719-471-8958	R	69*	.2
53	Environmental Air Systems Inc—*James Bullock*	PO Box 13006, Greensboro NC 27415	336-273-1975	R	68*	.2
54	Southern Air Inc—*Ronald Kidd Jr*	PO Box 4205, Lynchburg VA 24502	434-385-6200	R	66*	.8
55	Wenzel Plumbing and Heating Inc—*Fred Hanson*	1959 Shawnee Rd, Saint Paul MN 55122	651-452-7565	R	66*	.1
56	Quality Mechanical Inc—*Doug Lea*	3175 Westwood Dr, Las Vegas NV 89109	702-732-2545	R	65*	.3
57	Great Lakes Plumbing and Heating Co—*George Treutelaar*	4521 W Diversey Ave, Chicago IL 60639	773-489-0400	R	60*	.4

Note: An asterisk (*) indicates an estimated financial figure. The company type code used is as follows: R = Private, P = Public, S = Private Subsidiary, B = Public Subsidiary, D = Division, J = Joint Venture, I = Investment Fund.

COMPANY RANKINGS BY SALES WITHIN 4-DIGIT SIC

Rank	Company Name—*Executive Officer*	Address, City, State, Zip	Phone	Type	Fin	Empls
58	Tweet-Garot Mechanical Inc—*Tim Howald*	PO Box 11767, Green Bay WI 54307	920-498-0400	R	60*	.4
59	Western Air Limbach—*Leonard Hayward* Limbach Facility Services LLC	12442 Knott St, Garden Grove CA 92841	714-653-7000	D	60*	.3
60	McCrea Equipment Company Inc—*Wayne E Lanhardt*	4463 Beech Rd, Temple Hills MD 20748	301-423-6623	R	58*	.4
61	Aldag/Honold Mechanical Inc—*David Aldag*	PO Box 1265, Sheboygan WI 53082	920-458-5558	R	57*	.1
62	Heating and Plumbing Engineers—*Bill Eustace*	407 W Filmore Pl, Colorado Springs CO 80907	719-633-5414	R	56*	.3
63	Comfort Systems USA—*Jody Vowell*	9745 Bent Oak Dr, Houston TX 77040	832-590-5700	S	55*	.2
64	Shoffnerkalthoff Mechanical Electrical Service Inc—*David Dugger*	PO Box 10048, Knoxville TN 37939	865-523-1129	R	55*	.5
65	Fagan Co—*Bill Adams*	PO Box 15238, Kansas City KS 66115	913-621-4444	S	54*	.2
66	Plyler Construction—*Mike Plyler*	PO Box 912406, Sherman TX 75091	903-893-6393	R	54*	.2
67	Harder Mechanical Contractors Inc—*Steve Harder*	PO Box 5118, Portland OR 97208	503-281-1112	R	50*	.5
68	Meccon Industries Inc—*John D Curran*	PO Box 206, Lansing IL 60438	708-474-8300	R	50	.3
69	Yearout Mechanical and Engineering Inc—*Kevin Yearout*	PO Box 3508, Albuquerque NM 87190	505-884-0994	R	50*	.3
70	Holaday-Parks-Fabricators Inc—*Gerald Parks*	PO Box 69208, Seattle WA 98168	206-248-9700	R	49*	.3
71	Owens Companies Inc—*John J Owens*	930 E 80th St, Bloomington MN 55420	952-854-3800	R	49*	.1
72	Wayne Automatic Fire Sprinklers Inc—*Wayne Gey*	222 Capitol Ct, Ocoee FL 34761	407-656-3030	R	48*	.3
73	Morrison Construction Co—*Daniel Sharpe*	PO Box 747, Hammond IN 46325	219-932-5036	R	47*	.3
74	Western Allied Mechanical Inc—*James Muscarella*	1180 Obrien Dr, Menlo Park CA 94025	650-326-0750	R	46*	.2
75	SunDurance Energy LLC—*Al Bucknam*	2045 Lincoln Hwy Ediso, Edison NJ 08817	732-520-5000	R	45	<.1
76	Cosco Fire Protection Inc—*Daniel Pool*	321 E Gardena Blvd, Gardena CA 90248	323-321-5155	S	45	.4
77	Bassett Mechanical Contractors and Engineers Inc—*Kim Bassett Heitzman*	PO Box 7000, Kaukauna WI 54130	920-759-2500	R	45*	.3
78	Precision Piping And Mechanical Inc—*Scott Jones*	5201 Middle Mt Vernon, Evansville IN 47712	812-425-5052	R	43*	.2
79	Donnelly Mechanical Corp—*Cathy Donnelly*	96-59 222nd St, Queens Village NY 11429	718-886-1500	R	43*	.1
80	Joseph Davis Inc—*Jeffrey Davis*	120 W Tupper St, Buffalo NY 14201	716-842-1500	R	42*	.4
81	Temp-Control Mechanical Corp—*James Culbertson*	PO Box 11065, Portland OR 97211	503-285-9851	R	42*	.3
82	Bonland Industries Inc—*William Boniface*	PO Box 200, Wayne NJ 07474	973-694-3211	R	41*	.3
83	Airco Mechanical Inc—*Steve Humason*	8210 Demetre Ave, Sacramento CA 95828	916-381-4523	R	41*	.3
84	Herre Brothers Inc—*Richard Mcbride*	4417 Valley St, Enola PA 17025	717-732-4454	R	40*	.3
85	John W Danforth Co—*Kevin G Reilly*	300 Colvin Woods Pky, Tonawanda NY 14150	716-832-1940	R	40*	.3
86	Central Air Conditioning Company Inc—*Joe Samia*	3435 W Harry St, Wichita KS 67213	316-945-0797	R	40*	.1
87	CommAir Mechanical Services—*Jack Lofy*	1266 14th St Fl 2, Oakland CA 94607	510-839-1050	D	38*	.3
88	William G Tomko and Son Inc—*Martha J Tomko*	859 Missionary Dr, Pittsburgh PA 15236		R	38*	.2
89	Lewis and Lambert LLLP—*Richard Brandon*	PO Box 14439, Fort Worth TX 76117	817-834-7146	R	37*	.2
90	Edwards Engineering Inc—*Edward Lieske*	1000 Touhy Ave, Elk Grove Village IL 60007	847-364-8100	R	37*	.3
91	Goyette Mechanical Company Inc—*Dominic Goyette*	PO Box 33, Flint MI 48501	810-743-6883	R	37*	.1
92	Lutz Frey Corp—*Richard Donnelly*	1195 Ivy Dr, Lancaster PA 17601	717-898-6808	R	36*	.2
93	Luckinbill Inc—*Dennis Luckinbill*	304 E Broadway, Enid OK 73701	580-233-2026	R	35*	.2
94	Ray L Hellwig Plumbing and Heating Inc—*Glen Bollenbacher*	1301 Laurelwood Rd, Santa Clara CA 95054	408-727-5612	R	35*	.1
95	eSolar Inc—*John Van Scoter*	3355 W Empire Ave Ste, Burbank CA 91504	626-685-1810	R	35*	.1
96	Fountain Construction Company Inc—*Brad Fountain*	PO Box 10506, Jackson MS 39289	601-373-4162	R	34*	.3
97	Wayne Crouse Inc—*William P Lugaila*	PO Box 4349, Pittsburgh PA 15204	412-771-5176	R	34*	.2
98	Charles E Jarrell Contracting Company Inc—*Michael Jarrell*	4208 Rider Trl N, Earth City MO 63045	314-291-0100	R	34*	.3
99	Mollenberg-Betz Inc—*H Van Mollenberg*	300 Scott St, Buffalo NY 14204	716-614-7473	R	33*	.2
100	Rock Hill Mechanical Corp—*Robert Schnitzer*	524 Clark Ave, Saint Louis MO 63122	314-966-0600	R	33*	.2
101	SI Goldman Co—*John C Martin*	PO Box 526100, Longwood FL 32752	407-830-5000	S	33*	.2
102	Automatic Fire Sprinklers Inc—*Gary Peterson*	7272 Mars Dr, Huntington Beach CA 92647	714-841-2066	R	32*	.2
103	C and R Mechanical Co—*George Edinger*	12825 Pennridge Dr, Bridgeton MO 63044	314-739-1800	R	31*	.2
104	Viking Automatic Sprinkler Company Inc—*Ryan Johnston*	301 York Ave, Saint Paul MN 55130	651-558-3300	R	31*	.2
105	Bassett Inc—*William Bassett*	PO Box 7000, Kaukauna WI 54130	920-759-2500	R	30*	.3
106	Climatemp Inc—*John Comforte*	315 N May St, Chicago IL 60607	312-829-3131	R	30*	.2
107	Hutchinson Contracting Co—*Fredrick J Hutchinson*	621 Chapel Ave, Cherry Hill NJ 08034	856-429-6677	R	30*	.2
108	Himec Inc—*Greg Donley*	1400 7th St Nw, Rochester MN 55901	507-281-4000	R	30*	.2
109	United Group Services Inc—*Daniel Freese*	9740 Near Dr, Cincinnati OH 45246	513-874-2004	R	30*	.2
110	Baker Group Iowa—*Gary Bridgewater*	4224 Hubbell Ave, Des Moines IA 50317	515-262-4000	R	29*	.2
111	Victoria Air Conditioning Inc—*Gay Heilker*	PO Box 3882, Victoria TX 77903	361-578-5241	R	29*	.2
112	Harry Grodsky and Company Inc—*Ronald D Grodsky*	PO Box 880, Springfield MA 01101	413-785-1947	R	29*	.2
113	Edward Joy Co—*LP Markert*	PO Box 338, Syracuse NY 13210	315-474-3360	R	28*	<.1
114	WW Gay Fire Protection Inc—*Nandu Paryani*	522 Stockton St, Jacksonville FL 32204	904-387-7973	R	28*	.2
115	Dauenhauer Plumbing Inc—*Gary Thieneman*	3416 Robards Ct, Louisville KY 40218	502-451-2233	R	27*	.2
116	Jackson and Blanc Inc—*Kirk Jackson*	7929 Arjons Dr, San Diego CA 92126	858-831-7900	R	27*	.2
117	AirTemp Inc—*William Murdy*	11 Wallace Ave, South Portland ME 04106	207-774-2300	S	27*	.1
118	Hermanson Co—*Rick Hermanson*	1221 2nd Ave N, Kent WA 98032	206-575-9700	R	26*	.2
119	Mckamish Inc—*David Mckamish*	50 55th St, Pittsburgh PA 15201	412-781-6262	R	25*	.3
120	Charles P Blouin Inc—*Joe Cullen*	203 New Zealand Rd, Seabrook NH 03874	603-474-3400	R	25*	.1
121	Neas Inc—*Stephen Bartlett*	PO Box 525, Williston VT 05495	802-864-3800	R	25*	.2
122	Brewer-Garrett Co—*Lou Joseph*	6800 Eastland Rd, Cleveland OH 44130	440-243-3535	R	24*	.2
123	Comfort Engineers Inc—*Alan Williams*	PO Box 2955, Durham NC 27715	919-383-2502	R	24*	.2
124	Halo Sheet Metal Company Inc—*Patricia Pellegrino*	140 Lehigh Ave, Lakewood NJ 08701	732-901-0080	R	23*	.2
125	MJ Daly and Sons Inc—*Richard Peters*	PO Box 2797, Waterbury CT 06723	203-753-5131	R	23*	.2
126	Starcon International Inc—*Mike Uremovich*	260 Market Pl, Manhattan IL 60442	815-478-4615	S	23*	.2
127	Vermont Heating and Ventilating Company Inc—*David Brown*	16 Tigan St Ste A, Winooski VT 05404	802-655-8805	R	22*	.1
128	Columbus Heating and Ventilating Co—*Charles Gulley*	182 N Yale Ave, Columbus OH 43222	614-274-1177	R	22*	.1
129	Bolton Corp—*Michael Bolton*	PO Box 10186, Raleigh NC 27605	919-828-9021	R	22*	.2
130	Mallory and Evans Inc—*Tim Sidwell*	PO Box 447, Decatur GA 30031	404-297-1000	R	22*	.1
131	Universal Enterprises Inc—*Ralph Ridenour*	545 Beer Rd, Ontario OH 44906	419-529-3500	R	22*	.2
132	Albers Sheetmetal And Ventilating Inc—*George Albers*	200 Plato Blvd W Ste A, Saint Paul MN 55107	651-224-3100	R	21*	.2
133	New England Sheet Metal Works—*James Boone*	PO Box 11158, Fresno CA 93771	559-268-7375	R	21*	.1
134	Dunbar Mechanical Inc—*Stephen Dunbar*	PO Box 352350, Toledo OH 43635	419-537-1900	R	21*	.2
135	Brewer and Company of West Virginia Inc—*J Meeks*	PO Box 3108, Charleston WV 25331	304-744-5314	R	21*	.1
136	Jacobs Mechanical Co—*John Mc Donald*	1366 Hopple St, Cincinnati OH 45225	513-681-6800	R	19*	.1
137	Valley Mechanical Inc—*David Stutz*	608 Salem Rd, Rossville GA 30741	706-866-8812	R	19*	.2
138	Modern Piping Inc—*Dave Brown*	PO Box 128, Cedar Rapids IA 52406	319-364-0131	R	19*	.1
139	Robert Lloyd Sheet Metal Inc—*Robert Lloyd*	PO Box 307, Independence OR 97351	503-838-3863	R	19*	.1
140	Hoyt Brumm and Link Inc—*Todd Hoyt*	1400 E 9 Mile Rd, Ferndale MI 48220	248-548-3355	R	19*	.1
141	Heide and Cook Ltd—*Earle Matsuda*	1714 Kanakanui St, Honolulu HI 96819	808-841-6161	R	18	.1
142	Estes Heating and Air Conditioning Inc—*Thomas Estes*	PO Box 16548, Atlanta GA 30321	404-361-6560	R	18*	.1
143	William E Walter Inc—*Doug Wyrwicki*	PO Box 391, Flint MI 48501	810-232-7459	R	18*	.1
144	Hurckman Mechanical Industries Inc—*John Hurckman*	PO Box 10977, Green Bay WI 54307	920-499-8771	R	18*	.1

Rank	Company Name—*Executive Officer*	Address, City, State, Zip	Phone	Type	Fin	Empls
145	FLS Energy—*Michael Shore*	239 Amboy Rd, Asheville NC 28806	828-350-3993	R	18	.1
146	General Sheet Metal Corp—*Jim Wiggem*	2330 Louisiana Ave N, Minneapolis MN 55427	763-544-8747	R	17*	.2
147	JE Shekell Inc—*John E Shekell*	424 W Tennessee St, Evansville IN 47710	812-425-9131	R	17*	.2
148	OC McDonald Company Inc—*Jim McDonald*	1150 W San Carlos St, San Jose CA 95126	408-295-2182	R	17*	.1
149	Scobell Company Inc—*Charles Haise*	1356 E 12th St, Erie PA 16503	814-453-4361	R	17*	.1
150	Specific Systems Ltd—*Mike Bolick*	7655 E 41st St, Tulsa OK 74145	918-663-9321	R	17*	.1
151	Admiral Heating and Ventilating Inc—*Daniel Krueger*	4150 Litt Dr, Hillside IL 60162	708-544-3100	R	17*	.1
152	Fhc Holding Co—*Robert Holt*	PO Box 9100, Grand Rapids MI 49509	616-538-1811	R	16*	.1
153	EM Duggan Inc—*Vincent F Petroni*	PO Box 306, Canton MA 02021	781-828-2292	R	16*	.1
154	Moncrief Heating and Air Conditioning Inc—*Frank Mutz*	935 Chattahoochee Ave, Atlanta GA 30318	404-350-2300	R	16*	.1
155	KSW Mechanical Inc—*Floyd Warkol*	37-16 23rd St, Long Island City NY 11101	718-340-1409	S	16*	<.1
156	ACE Duraflo Systems LLC—*Larry Gillanders*	3122 W Alpine St, Santa Ana CA 92704	714-564-7600	R	16*	<.1
157	Allied Fire Protection—*Ted Vinther*	555 High St, Oakland CA 94601	510-533-5516	R	16*	.1
158	Piedmont Mechanical Inc—*Albert Smith*	PO Box 4925, Spartanburg SC 29305	864-578-9114	R	16*	.1
159	H Lamm Industries Inc—*Helmut Lamm*	4425 Ne 6th Ter, Oakland Park FL 33334	954-491-8929	R	15*	.1
160	Power Cooling Inc—*Lloyd Larsen*	4343 Vernon Blvd, Long Island City NY 11101	718-784-1300	R	15*	.1
161	Airvac Inc—*Mark Jones*	PO Box 528, Rochester IN 46975	574-223-3980	S	15*	.1
162	CFM/VR-Tesco Inc—*Siegfried Schulz*	1875 Fox Ln, Elgin IL 60123		R	15	.1
163	Rabe Environmental Systems Inc—*Mark Patrizia*	2300 W 23rd St, Erie PA 16506	814-456-5374	R	15*	.1
164	Champion Industrial Contractors Inc—*Darrell Champion*	PO Box 4399, Modesto CA 95352	209-524-6601	R	15*	.1
165	Air-Rite Service—*Lawrence M Van Someren*	100 Overland Dr, North Aurora IL 60542	630-264-1150	R	14*	.1
166	Daigle Oil Co—*Richard Daigle*	PO Box 328, Fort Kent ME 04743	207-834-5027	R	14*	.1
167	Quality Sprinkler Company Inc—*Robert Kluttz*	10301 Old Concord Rd, Charlotte NC 28213	704-549-8220	R	14*	.1
168	Miller Engineering Co—*Henry E Fortney*	1616 S Main St, Rockford IL 61102	815-963-4878	R	14*	.1
169	Boone and Darr Inc—*Michael Darr*	PO Box 1718, Ann Arbor MI 48106	734-665-0648	R	14*	.1
170	Air Conditioning by Luquire Inc—*Conrad Missildine*	PO Box 211328, Montgomery AL 36121	334-264-9666	R	14*	<.1
171	Shelley's Septic Tank Inc—*David Shelly*	PO Box 249, Zellwood FL 32798	407-889-8042	R	14*	.1
172	Palmetto Automatic Sprinkler Company Inc—*William Mill*	PO Box 2927, West Columbia SC 29171	803-794-1602	R	14*	.1
173	Welsch Furnace Co—*George Welsch*	PO Box 28545, Saint Louis MO 63146	314-872-8070	R	14*	.1
174	Owens Services Corp—*John Owens* Owens Companies Inc	930 E 80th St, Bloomington MN 55420	952-854-3800	S	13*	.2
175	James McCullagh Company Inc—*William H Doremus*	PO Box 6011, Plainview NY 11803	516-293-8800	R	13*	.1
176	Kirk Williams Company Inc—*James Williams*	PO Box 189, Grove City OH 43123	614-875-9023	R	13*	.1
177	Kaelber Co—*Don E Kaelber*	PO Box 488, Kenosha WI 53141	262-654-3589	R	13*	.1
178	Crawford Heating and Cooling Co—*Robert Frink*	1306 Mill St, Rock Island IL 61201	309-788-4573	R	13*	.1
179	Superior Automatic Sprinkler Inc—*Robert Lawson*	308 Sango Ct, Milpitas CA 95035	408-946-7272	R	13*	.1
180	Giese Sheet Metal Company Inc—*Charles Giese*	2125 Kerper Blvd, Dubuque IA 52001	563-588-2023	R	12*	.1
181	Mid-State Contracting LLC—*Ron Earnhardt*	PO Box 1425, Wausau WI 54402	715-675-2388	R	12*	.1
182	Palmer And Sicard Inc—*Mark Hodsdon*	140 Epping Rd Ste 102, Exeter NH 03833	603-778-1841	R	12*	.1
183	C and B Services—*Troy Crochet*	346 Twin City Hwy, Port Neches TX 77651	409-722-9697	R	12*	.1
184	Harold G Butzer Inc—*Jason Thomson*	730 Wicker Ln, Jefferson City MO 65109	573-636-4115	R	12*	.1
185	Limbach Facility Services LLC—*Charlie Bacon*	31- 35th St, Pittsburgh PA 15201	412-359-2100	R	12*	.1
186	Air Comfort Corp—*Tim Smerz*	2550 Braga Dr, Broadview IL 60155	708-345-1900	R	11*	.1
187	Straus Systems Inc—*Rick Beeler*	7 Straus Crt, Stafford TX 77477	281-498-1689	R	11*	.1
188	Fred McGilvray Inc—*Fred McGilvray*	PO Box 522204, Miami FL 33152	305-592-5910	R	11*	.1
189	McAllister—*Charles McAllister*	30 Mays Landing Rd, Somers Point NJ 08244	856-665-4545	R	11*	<.1
190	Bjc Management Inc—*Cheryl Allison*	7700 Hwy 287, Arlington TX 76001	817-561-1149	R	11*	.1
191	Springfield Engineering Company Inc—*Jerry Fielder*	1528 E Trafficway St, Springfield MO 65802	417-869-1539	R	11*	.1
192	Big Tex Air Conditioning LP—*Jack Hicks*	PO Box 23296, Houston TX 77228	713-631-7738	R	10*	.1
193	re2g—*Jude Webster*	122 Turnpike Rd, Westborough MA 01581	508-939-7324	R	10	<.1
194	Jones Automatic Sprinkler Inc—*Steven Ledbetter*	PO Box 588, Americus GA 31709	229-928-0111	R	10*	.1
195	Infinity Contractors Inc—*Jim Salter*	2563 E Loop 820 N, Fort Worth TX 76118	817-838-8700	R	10*	<.1
196	Brigade Fire Protection Inc—*Douglas Irvine*	5701 Safety Dr Ne, Belmont MI 49306	616-784-1644	R	10*	.1
197	OnForce Solar Inc—*Charles Feit*	1 Bridge Plz 2nd Fl, Fort Lee NJ 07024		R	9	<.1
198	All Arctic Sheet Metal Inc—*Douglas McQuown*	2310 NE Columbia Blvd, Portland OR 97211	503-288-5844	R	9*	.1
199	Sullivan Mechanical Contractors Inc—*Malcolm Sullivan*	PO Box 304, Shenandoah VA 22849	540-652-8188	R	9*	.1
200	Pi Mechanical Inc—*John Bishop*	PO Box 22054, Greensboro NC 27420	336-274-1533	R	9*	.1
201	Bfp Fire Protection Inc—*Chris Amos*	17 Janis Way, Scotts Valley CA 95066	831-461-1100	R	9*	.1
202	Petrie Heating and Cooling—*Randal Petrie*	649 Horace Lewis Rd, Cookeville TN 38506	931-528-8888	R	9*	<.1
203	Lyons Company Inc—*Thomas Lyons*	PO Box 393, Glasgow KY 42142	270-651-2733	R	9*	.1
204	Johns Brothers Inc—*Dwight Schaubach*	1384 Ingleside Rd, Norfolk VA 23502	757-852-3300	R	8*	.1
205	Real Mechanical Inc—*Robert Fritsche*	475 Gradle Dr, Carmel IN 46032	317-846-9299	R	8*	.1
206	Sierra Pacific Home and Comfort Inc—*Jason Hanson*	2550 Mercantile Dr Ste, Rancho Cordova CA 95742	916-638-0543	R	8*	.1
207	Soehnlen Piping Company Inc—*Eric Siefert*	1400 W Main St, Louisville OH 44641	330-875-5513	R	8*	.1
208	Coleman Spohn Corp—*Lonnie Coleman*	1775 E 45th St, Cleveland OH 44103	216-431-8070	R	8*	<.1
209	Weather Makers Inc—*John Roland*	1741 W Rd, Chesapeake VA 23323	757-421-2665	R	7*	.1
210	B and L Mechanical Inc—*James Sink*	PO Box 6682, Greenville SC 29606	864-277-5487	R	7*	<.1
211	Gillespie and Powers Refractory and Engineering Inc—*John Gillespie*	9550 True Dr, Saint Louis MO 63132	314-423-9460	R	7*	.1
212	Continental Mechanical of the Pacific—*Robert K Fujikawa*	2146 Puuhale Pl, Honolulu HI 96819	808-845-5936	R	7*	.1
213	Griffin Tommy L Plumbing and Heating Co—*Tommy Griffin*	PO Box 2346, Macon GA 31203	478-477-5171	R	7*	.1
214	GreenLogic LLC—*Marc Clejan*	425 County Rd 39A Ste, Southampton NY 11968	631-771-5152	R	7*	<.1
215	L and H Mechanical—*Kevin Kolesar*	4038 E Superior Ave St, Phoenix AZ 85040	602-437-4822	R	7*	<.1
216	EL Payne Co—*Gordon Payne Jr*	1529 S Robertson Blvd, Los Angeles CA 90035	310-275-5331	R	7*	<.1
217	Tri-State Fire Protection Inc—*Walter Howard*	PO Box 70, Newburgh IN 47629	812-853-9229	R	7*	.1
218	FJ Murphy and Son Inc—*John Pasko*	1800 Factory St, Springfield IL 62702	217-528-4081	R	6*	.1
219	Smith Filter Corp—*Roger Smith*	5000 41st St Ct, Moline IL 61265	309-764-8324	R	6*	<.1
220	Helfrich Brothers Boiler Works Inc—*Vincent Helfrich*	39 Merrimack St, Lawrence MA 01843	978-683-7244	R	6*	.1
221	Teachey Mechanical Inc—*Ben Teachey*	PO Box 339, Simpsonville SC 29681	864-967-2917	R	6*	.1
222	Energy Management Specialists Inc—*Marc Mapel*	15800 Industrial Pky, Cleveland OH 44135	216-676-9045	R	6*	<.1
223	McMullen Air Conditioning and Refrigeration Service—*Joe Conti*	4877 28th St N, Saint Petersburg FL 33714	727-527-0000	R	6*	<.1
224	Central Fire Protection Inc—*Dan Dotson*	PO Box 19309, Birmingham AL 35219	205-942-0200	R	6*	<.1
225	AA Samuels Sheet Metal Company Inc—*Andrew Samuels*	PO Box 2407, Youngstown OH 44509	330-793-9326	R	6*	.1
226	National Automatic Sprinkler Co—*Gerald Lind*	10351 Jamestown St Ne, Minneapolis MN 55449	763-784-8902	R	6*	.1
227	Allied Ventilation Inc—*Mary Seraphinoff*	21714 Schmeman Ave, Warren MI 48089	586-779-4300	R	6*	<.1
228	Fire Protection Testing Inc—*Edwin Nichols*	1701 Highland Ave Ste, Cheshire CT 06410	203-250-1115	R	5*	<.1
229	Benedict Refrigeration Service Inc—*Timothy Benedict*	PO Box 3008, Eau Claire WI 54702	715-834-3191	R	5*	<.1
230	Ce Acquisition LLC—*Judy Evans*	7469 E Monte Cristo Av, Scottsdale AZ 85260	480-513-1600	R	5*	<.1
231	Certified Fire Protection Inc—*Karl Walker*	3140 S 460 W, Salt Lake City UT 84115	801-281-0746	R	5*	<.1

Note: An asterisk (*) indicates an estimated financial figure. The company type code used is as follows: R = Private, P = Public, S = Private Subsidiary, B = Public Subsidiary, D = Division, J = Joint Venture, I = Investment Fund.

COMPANY RANKINGS BY SALES WITHIN 4-DIGIT SIC

Rank	Company Name—Executive Officer	Address, City, State, Zip	Phone	Type	Fin	Empls
232	Garland Heating and Air Conditioning Co—Raymond Estrello	2113 S Garland Ave, Garland TX 75041	972-278-3506	R	5*	<.1
233	Stamar Inc—Bryan Stansell	2331 Adams Dr NW, Atlanta GA 30318	404-352-3478	R	5*	<.1
234	Wilson of Wallingford Inc—David O'Connell	221 Rogers Ln, Wallingford PA 19086	610-566-7600	R	5*	<.1
235	321 Plumbing Inc—Dawn Bittar	2510 Kirby Cir Ste 105, Palm Bay FL 32905	321-728-2888	R	5*	<.1
236	Lowry Mechanical Inc—Samuel Lowry	PO Box 162, Laurens SC 29360	864-984-2589	R	5*	<.1
237	Magic City Sprinkler Inc—Melanie Obenchain	1601 Granby St Ne, Roanoke VA 24012	540-345-9818	R	5*	.1
238	Clark Harry Plumbing and Heating—Brad Marshall	3026 Broadway, Oakland CA 94611	510-652-5787	R	4*	<.1
239	Eagle Fire Protection Inc—Myron Heath	1205 Crown Park Cir, Winter Garden FL 34787	407-656-8387	R	4*	<.1
240	On Time Electric and Air—John Karbowski	2312 Western Trails Bl, Austin TX 78745	512-346-6800	R	4*	<.1
241	Aztec Mechanical Inc—Nancy Martin	2509 Comanche Rd NE, Albuquerque NM 87107	505-884-2770	R	4*	<.1
242	Southern Mechanical Systems Co—Michael Glasner	8709 Meta St, Houston TX 77022	713-691-6400	R	4*	<.1
243	Hazel Heating and Air Conditioning Inc—Ashley Rowe	PO Box 522, Newberry SC 29108	803-276-0501	R	4*	<.1
244	Komodo Enterprises Inc—Matthew Mccullough	8915 Research Dr Ste 1, Irvine CA 92618	949-748-5996	R	4*	<.1
245	Wissco Irrigation Inc—Bryan Wynen	1820 S Bend Ave, South Bend IN 46637	574-277-9851	R	4*	<.1
246	Central Mechanical Systems Inc—Darrell Cordes	PO Box 126, Marshfield WI 54449	715-387-4568	R	4*	<.1
247	Refractory Maintenance Corp—William Cook	PO Box 98, Williamson NY 14589	315-589-4441	R	4*	<.1
248	TS C Inc—Larry Sinn	3385 Brushy Creek Rd, Greer SC 29650	864-770-8000	R	3*	<.1
249	CRFireline Inc—Clarence Robichaud	108 Ctr Ave, Pacheco CA 94553	925-685-9008	R	3*	<.1
250	Korral Kool Inc—Larry Gordon	3355 N Reseda Ste 1, Mesa AZ 85215	480-807-0290	R	3*	<.1
251	CA Wilson Electric Service Inc—Dennis Wilson	PO Box 745, Highlands NC 28741	828-526-2568	R	3*	<.1
252	Tropic-Kool Engineering Inc—Ken Bray	1232 Donegan Rd, Largo FL 33771	727-581-2824	R	3*	<.1
253	Empire Heating and Cooling Co—Greg Beers	PO Box 31514, Billings MT 59107	406-259-5538	R	3*	<.1
254	Cary Services Inc—Mark Cary	PO Box 5101, Abilene TX 79608	325-695-7283	R	3*	<.1
255	Absolute Fire Protection Inc—Dan Mathias	836 Ritchie Hwy Ste 1, Severna Park MD 21146	410-544-7771	R	3*	<.1
256	Superior Heating and Cooling Corp—Jack Artz	115 Triple Diamond Blv, Venice FL 34292	941-484-0627	R	3*	<.1
257	Pioneer Plumbing Inc—Michael Motzkin	1312 E Wieding Rd, Tucson AZ 85706	520-623-4444	R	3*	<.1
258	Airtrol Inc—Stephen W Pol	3960 North St, Baton Rouge LA 70806	225-383-2617	R	3*	<.1
259	Hydro-Tech Fire Protection Inc—Barrett Baker	PO Box 40, Brush Prairie WA 98606	360-256-2816	R	3*	<.1
260	Service Experts LLC—Jamey Iebema	1225 E Sioux Ave, Pierre SD 57501	605-224-1991	R	3*	<.1
261	Snelling Co—Philip Krinkie	1404 Concordia Ave, Saint Paul MN 55104	651-646-7381	R	3*	<.1
262	GJ Hopkins Inc—James Harrison	PO Box 12467, Roanoke VA 24025	540-982-1873	S	3*	<.1
263	Chris Agee—Chris Agee	516 Plantation Park Dr, Loganville GA 30052	770-466-6678	R	3*	<.1
264	Tri-State Automatic Sprinkler Corp—Gary Penniston	5570 Carey Ave, Davenport IA 52807	563-386-8707	R	3*	<.1
265	Alward Electric Inc—Milton Alward	PO Box 434, Gladwin MI 48624	989-426-9228	R	2*	<.1
266	National Turf Inc—James Haines	11843 Tug Boat Ln, Newport News VA 23606	757-873-2424	R	2*	<.1
267	High Point Sprinkler Inc—Joe Harrison	PO Box 2478, High Point NC 27261	336-475-6181	R	2*	.1
268	Air Masters Inc—Kyle Haufman	62b Rector St, Staten Island NY 10310	718-727-4547	R	2*	<.1
269	Air Conditioning Store Inc—Gary Mckinzie	1581 Crosswind Dr Ste, Bryan TX 77808	979-779-6700	R	2*	<.1
270	Pecos Valley Pump Inc—David Bratcher	PO Box 94, Artesia NM 88211	575-746-3713	R	2*	<.1
271	Fire Protection Systems Inc—David Goodridge	PO Box 100, Pelham NH 03076	603-635-7512	R	2*	<.1
272	TEC Mechanical Service Co—Doug Francis	PO Box 3550, Redmond WA 98073	425-881-3247	R	2*	<.1
273	Joe Lombardo Plumbing and Heating of Rockland Inc—Ron Lombardo	321 Spook Rock Rd, Suffern NY 10901	845-357-6537	R	2*	<.1
274	Houston Air Inc—Kevin Linear	PO Box 1321, Tavernier FL 33070	305-852-2960	R	2*	<.1
275	Serveco Inc—Will Mayo	4129 N Davis Hwy, Pensacola FL 32503	850-438-8541	R	2*	<.1
276	Haugk Companies Inc—Christopher Kortenber	PO Box 730, Decatur IN 46733	260-724-9184	R	2*	<.1
277	Ram Freezers And Coolers—Raul Montes	783 W 18th St, Hialeah FL 33010	305-887-1000	R	2*	<.1
278	Omaha Sprinkler Co—Greg Higginbotham	PO Box 3745, Omaha NE 68103	712-322-0724	R	2*	<.1
279	Math Mechanical Inc—Craig Mathias	902 Dunedin Rd, Portsmouth VA 23701	757-465-0500	R	2*	<.1
280	Stokley's Services Inc—Richard Shortt	2500 Almeda Ave Ste 20, Norfolk VA 23513	757-857-7247	R	2*	<.1
281	Lewis Fire Protection Inc—Walter Lewis	PO Box 176, Villa Rica GA 30180	770-459-3636	R	1*	<.1
282	RH Tinney Inc—Robert Tinney	296 Wright Brothers Av, Livermore CA 94551	925-373-6101	R	1*	<.1
283	Garawco Inc—Steve Hall	PO Box 508, Rock Hill SC 29731	803-324-4381	R	1*	<.1
284	Hawkins Company Inc—Robert Hawkins	222 Towson Ave, Fort Smith AR 72901	479-785-2891	R	1*	<.1
285	BCH Mechanical Inc—Daryl Blume	6354 118th Ave N, Largo FL 33773	727-546-3561	S	1*	.5
286	Metropolitan Mechanical Contractors Inc—Mark Anderson	7450 Flying Cloud Dr, Eden Prairie MN 55344	952-941-7010	S	N/A	.5

TOTALS: SIC 1711 Plumbing, Heating & Air-Conditioning
Companies: 286

					31,212	58.4

1721 Painting & Paper Hanging

	Company	Address	Phone	Type	Fin	Empls
1	Brock Enterprises Inc—Jeff Davis	PO Box 306, Beaumont TX 77704	409-833-6226	R	1,218*	15.0
2	ML McDonald Sales Company Inc—Kevin O'Donnell	PO Box 315, Watertown MA 02471	617-923-0900	R	177*	.2
3	M Ecker and Company Inc—Frank Marrese	9525 W Bryn Mawr Ave S, Rosemont IL 60018	847-994-6000	D	71*	.3
4	Swanson and Youngdale Inc—Robert E Swanson	PO Box 26070, Saint Louis Park MN 55426	612-545-2541	R	52*	.2
5	Long Painting Co—Mike Cassidy	21414 68th Ave S, Kent WA 98032	253-234-8050	R	25*	.2
6	Arrow Striping and Manufacturing Inc—Kymmberly Stark	PO Box 1622, Billings MT 59103	406-248-2463	R	11*	<.1
7	C and Z Enterprises LLC—Luke Robinson	20109 B Mashburn St, Pflugerville TX 78660	512-989-8377	R	11*	.1
8	Land-Ron Inc—Ronald Karpiuk	6753 Kingspointe Pkwy, Orlando FL 32819	407-816-7035	R	9*	<.1
9	N Chasen and Son Inc—Jeff Chasen	2924 W Marshall St, Richmond VA 23230	804-353-4563	R	6*	<.1
10	Vivax Pro Painting—Jeremiah Owen	1100 W Littleton Blvd, Littleton CO 80120	720-331-9735	R	5	<.1
11	Hartman-Walsh Painting Co—Edward C Smith	7144 N Market St, Saint Louis MO 63133	314-863-1800	R	4*	.1
12	Wilson Office Interiors LLC—Cathy Gallacher	1444 Oak Lawn Ave Ste, Dallas TX 75207	972-488-4100	R	4*	.1

TOTALS: SIC 1721 Painting & Paper Hanging
Companies: 12

					1,593	16.2

1731 Electrical Work

	Company	Address	Phone	Type	Fin	Empls
1	Quanta Services Inc—James F O'Neal	2800 Post Oak Blvd Ste, Houston TX 77056	713-629-7600	P	4,624	17.5
2	Harris Technical Services Corp—Sheldon Fox	1000 Charles J Herbert, Palm Bay FL 32905	703-739-1713	S	2,518	N/A
3	Hatzel and Buehler Inc—William A Goeller	PO Box 7499, Wilmington DE 19803	302-478-4200	R	1,806*	.7
4	Sasco Electric SASCO	2750 Moore Ave, Fullerton CA 92833	714-870-0217	D	1,399*	.6
5	Comfort Systems USA Inc—Brian E Lane	675 Bering Ste 400, Houston TX 77057	713-830-9600	P	1,240	7.1
6	Contra Costa Electric Inc—Michael Dias	825 Howe Rd, Martinez CA 94553	925-229-4250	S	1,032	.4
7	Zwicker Electric Company Inc—David P Pinter	360 Park Ave S 4th Fl, New York NY 10010	212-477-8400	R	922*	.4
8	Fisk Corp—Kenneth J Orlowski	PO Box 4417, Houston TX 77210	713-868-6111	R	896*	3.1
9	Fox Electric Ltd—Wes Shahan	PO Box 13338, Arlington TX 76094	817-461-2571	R	884*	.4
10	Pike Electric Corp—J Eric Pike	PO Box 868, Mount Airy NC 27030	336-789-2171	R	594	4.6
11	SASCO—Larry Smead	2750 Moore Ave, Fullerton CA 92833	714-870-0217	R	490*	1.8
12	Integrated Electrical Services Inc—James Lindstrom	4801 Woodway Dr Ste 20, Houston TX 77056	713-860-1500	P	482	2.7
13	Faith Technologies Inc—Rollie Stephenson	225 Main St, Menasha WI 54952	920-225-6500	R	413*	1.4

Rank	Company Name—*Executive Officer*	Address, City, State, Zip	Phone	Type	Fin	Empls
14	Power City Electric Inc—*Dan Aga*	3327 E Olive Ave, Spokane WA 99202	509-535-8500	R	399*	.2
15	White Mountain Cable—*John Dowd*	PO Box 459, Epsom NH 03234	603-736-4766	S	387*	1.5
16	Klingler Electric Corp—*Anton Klinger*	222 Marketridge Dr, Ridgeland MS 39157	601-956-7774		386	.2
17	Ceitronics Inc—*Scott Mitchell*	2460 Zanker Rd, San Jose CA 95131		S	384*	.2
	Cupertino Electric Inc					
18	Rosendin Electric Inc—*Tom Sorley*	PO Box 49070, San Jose CA 95161	408-286-2800	R	358*	3.3
19	Emcor Construction Services—*Anthony J Guzzi*	1420 Spring Hill Rd St, Mc Lean VA 22102	703-556-8000	S	350*	2.7
20	No Time Inc—*Donna Stewart*	11237 E Riggs Rd, Chandler AZ 85249	480-895-7500	R	350*	<.1
21	Electro Management Inc—*Britt Baker*	111 SW Jackson Ave, Des Moines IA 50315	515-288-6774	R	333*	.4
22	Mass Electric Construction Co—*Rick Lanoha*	180 Guest St, Boston MA 02135	617-254-1015	R	326*	1.4
23	Jess Howard Electric Co—*Jesse Howard*	PO Box 95, Blacklick OH 43004	614-861-1300	R	314*	.1
24	Volt Telecommunications Group Inc—*Sam Edmondson*	6400 Regency Pkwy Ste, Norcross GA 30071	770-806-4616	S	273*	1.8
25	Gaylor Electric—*John Gaylor*	11711 N College Ave St, Carmel IN 46032	317-843-0577	R	273*	1.0
26	Sachs Electric Co—*Clayton M Scharff*	1572 Larkin Williams R, Fenton MO 63026	636-532-2000	R	270*	1.0
27	Shelby Electric Company Inc—*Al Quarin*	112 E E H Crump Blvd, Memphis TN 38106	901-948-1545	R	251*	.1
28	Cupertino Electric Inc—*John Boncher*	1132 N Seventh St, San Jose CA 95112	408-808-8000	R	238*	1.4
29	Hunt Electric Corp—*Michael Hanson*	2300 Territorial Rd St, Saint Paul MN 55114	651-646-2911	R	232*	.6
30	Helix Electric Inc—*Gary Shekhter*	8260 Camino Santa Fe S, San Diego CA 92121	858-535-0505	R	226*	1.5
31	Morrow-Meadows Corp—*Karen Price*	231 Benton Ct, City of Industry CA 91789	909-598-7700	R	222*	.8
32	Harris Electric Inc—*Dick Sundholm*	4020 23rd Ave W, Seattle WA 98199	206-282-8080	R	194*	.1
33	Argan Inc—*Rainer H Bosselmann*	1 Church St Ste 401, Rockville MD 20850	301-315-0027	P	183	.2
34	Johnson Electric Company Inc—*Padgett Johnson*	PO Box 8511, Greenville SC 29604	864-220-6164	R	162*	.1
35	Construction Management Services Inc—*John Adams*	PO Box 7499, Wilmington DE 19803	302-478-4200	R	162*	1.3
36	Wachter Inc—*Brad Botteron*	16001 W 99th St, Lenexa KS 66219	913-541-2500	R	160*	1.0
37	Cannon and Wendt Electric Company Inc—*Albert G Wendt*	4020 N 16th St, Phoenix AZ 85016	602-279-1681	R	160*	.3
38	A/Z Corp—*Perry Lorenz*	PO Box 370, North Stonington CT 06359		R	157*	.3
39	Dynalectric Co—*Brian Burns*	22930 Shaw Rd Ste 100, Dulles VA 20166	703-742-3500	S	146*	.9
40	Vallejo Electric Inc—*Maria Fennell*	2629 Foothill Blvd 273, La Crescenta CA 91214	818-248-8438	R	145*	<.1
41	Gaylor Inc—*John Gaylor*	5750 Castle Creek Pkwy, Indianapolis IN 46250	317-843-0577	R	144*	.8
42	Electrical Construction Co—*George Adams*	PO Box 10286, Portland OR 97296	503-224-3511	R	136*	.5
43	JF Electric Inc—*Greg Fowler*	PO Box 570, Edwardsville IL 62025	618-797-5353	R	136*	.6
44	Harlan Electric Co—*Willaim A Koertner*	2695 Crooks Rd, Rochester Hills MI 48309	248-853-4601	S	125	.5
45	Cleveland Electric Inc—*James R Cleveland Jr*	1281 Fulton Industrial, Atlanta GA 30336	404-696-4550	R	121*	.5
46	KDC Systems/Dynalectric—*Chris Pesavento*	4462 Corporate Center, Los Alamitos CA 90720	714-828-7000	S	114*	.5
47	Barth Electric Company Inc—*Michael Barth Jr*	1934 N Illinois St, Indianapolis IN 46202	317-924-6226	R	108*	.4
48	Hiram Electrical Contractors Inc—*Christine Cilio*	1351 W Foster Ave, Chicago IL 60640	773-878-0703	R	108*	<.1
49	Miller Electric Co (Jacksonville Florida)—*Henry E Autrey*	PO Box 1799, Jacksonville FL 32201	904-388-8000	R	107*	1.0
50	Rex Moore Electrical Contractors and Engineers—*David Rex Moore*	6001 Outfall Cir, Sacramento CA 95828	916-372-1300	R	107*	.8
51	Town and Country Electric Inc—*Roland G Stephenson*	2662 American Dr, Appleton WI 54914	920-225-6500	D	107*	.1
	Faith Technologies Inc					
52	Crime Alert Alarm Co—*Julie Buller*	690 Lenfest Rd, San Jose CA 95133		R	104*	<.1
53	Egizii Electric Inc—*Robert Egizii*	700 N MacArthur Blvd, Springfield IL 62702	217-528-4001	D	103*	.4
54	Wasa Electrical Service Inc	2908 Kaihikapu St, Honolulu HI 90819	808-839-2741	R	101*	.4
55	L and S Electric Inc—*Allan Lewitzke*	PO Box 740, Schofield WI 54476	715-359-3155	R	87*	.3
56	City Lights Electrical Company Inc—*Maryanne Cataldo*	290 Pine St, Canton MA 02021	617-822-3300	R	86*	.3
57	American Inc—*Butch Oldfield*	1345 N American St, Visalia CA 93291	559-651-1776	R	84*	.3
58	Polk Mechanical—*Ken Polk*	2425 Dillard St, Grand Prairie TX 75051	972-339-1200	R	84*	.3
59	Cochran Inc—*Leeann Cochran*	PO Box 33524, Seattle WA 98133	206-367-1900	R	83*	.6
60	Ludvik Electric Co—*James Ludvik*	3900 S Teller St, Lakewood CO 80235	303-781-9601	R	83*	.3
61	Gardner Zemke Co—*Rivka Zemke*	6100 Indian School Rd, Albuquerque NM 87110	505-881-0555	R	81*	.3
62	Electric Machinery Enterprises Inc—*Theresa Jurado*	2515 E Hanna Ave, Tampa FL 33610	813-238-5070	S	80*	.5
63	Mona Electric Group Inc—*Vincent Mona*	7915 Malcolm Rd Ste 40, Clinton MD 20735	301-868-8400	R	80*	.4
64	Meade Electric Company Inc—*Frank J Lizzadro*	9550 W 55th St, McCook IL 60525	708-588-2500	R	80*	.3
65	Vaughn Industries LLC—*Mark Greer*	1201 E Findlay St, Carey OH 43316	419-396-3900	R	79*	.4
66	Willmar Electric Service Inc—*David Chapin*	2405 Trott Ave SW, Willmar MN 56201	320-235-4386	R	77*	.3
67	Guarantee Electrical Co—*Rick Oertli*	3405 Bent Ave, Saint Louis MO 63116	314-772-5400	R	76*	.7
68	Bay Electric Company Inc—*John Biagas*	627 36th St, Newport News VA 23607	757-595-2300	R	75*	.2
69	Cleveland Electric Co—*James R Cleveland Jr*	1281 Fulton Industrial, Atlanta GA 30336	404-696-4550	S	74*	.6
	Cleveland Electric Inc					
70	Eii Inc—*Richard Guempel*	PO Box 128, Cranford NJ 07016	908-276-1000	R	71*	.3
71	Truland Systems Corp—*Robert Truland*	1900 Oracle Way Ste 70, Reston VA 20190	703-464-3000	R	70*	.3
72	Interstates Construction Services Inc—*Larry Den Herder*	PO Box 260, Sioux Center IA 51250	712-722-1662	R	66*	.3
73	Colorado Industrial Construction Services Company Inc—*James Prall*	651 Corporate Cir Ste, Golden CO 80401	303-754-2501	R	66*	<.1
74	Mwmpc Corp—*Mitchell Cappadonna*	3828 Pinemont Dr, Houston TX 77018	713-681-0627	R	62*	.2
75	Starr Electric Company Inc—*John D Starr*	6 Battleground Ct, Greensboro NC 27408	336-275-0241	R	61*	.4
76	Newkirk Electric Associates Inc—*Chris Anton*	1875 Roberts St, Muskegon MI 49442	231-722-1691	R	60*	.2
77	O'Connell Electric Company Inc—*Victor Salerno*	830 Phillips Rd, Victor NY 14564	585-924-2176	R	58*	.5
78	Arrow Electric Company Inc—*Barry Saylor*	PO Box 36215, Louisville KY 40233	502-367-0141	R	55*	.2
79	API Electric Co—*Brad Bows*	4330 W 1st St, Duluth MN 55807	218-628-3323	S	54*	.2
80	Broadway Electrical Company Inc—*Lawrence Hurwitz*	295 Freeport St, Boston MA 02122	617-288-7900	R	54*	.2
81	General Sound Co (Richardson Texas)—*Joe A Durham*	PO Box 832367, Richardson TX 75083	972-231-2541	R	53*	<.1
82	Miller-Eads Company Inc—*Tom Chastain*	PO Box 55234, Indianapolis IN 46205	317-545-7101	R	51*	.2
83	LE Myers Co—*William S Koertner*	PO Box 3100, Decatur IL 62524	217-877-0430	S	51*	.2
84	Broadway Electric Service Corp—*Wayne Wojciechowski*	1800 N Central St, Knoxville TN 37917	865-524-1851	R	50*	.6
85	Sargent Electric Co—*Stephan Dake*	PO Box 30, Pittsburgh PA 15230	412-391-0588	R	50*	.4
86	CrossCom National Inc—*Greg Miller*	9 Pky N Ste 250, Deerfield IL 60015	847-520-9200	R	50*	.2
87	Comm-Works Holdings LLC—*Alan Lampe*	3550 Annapolis Ln Ste, Minneapolis MN 55447	763-475-1300	R	50*	.2
88	Gilbert Mechanical Contractors Inc—*Dan Gilbert*	4451 W 76th St, Minneapolis MN 55435	952-835-3810	R	50*	.2
89	City Electric Inc—*Gabriel Marian*	819 Orca St, Anchorage AK 99501	907-272-4531	R	48*	.1
90	Daidone Electric Inc—*John Daidone*	200 Raymond Blvd, Newark NJ 07105	973-690-5216	R	48*	.2
91	Steiny and Company Inc—*Susan Steiny*	221 N Ardmore Ave, Los Angeles CA 90004	770-552-6900	R	47*	.3
92	Mcs Of Tampa Inc—*Gilbert Gonzales*	3926 W S Ave, Tampa FL 33614	813-872-0217	R	47*	.3
93	Huen New York Inc—*Michael Hughes*	6695 Old Collamer Rd, East Syracuse NY 13057	315-432-5060	R	46*	.8
94	Kearney Electric Inc—*Mike Kearney*	3609 E Superior Ave, Phoenix AZ 85040	602-437-0235	R	46*	.3
95	Pritchard Electric Company Inc—*Harvey Morrison*	2425 8th Ave, Huntington WV 25703	304-529-2566	R	46*	.3
96	Staff Electric Company Inc—*James Sullivan*	W133N5030 Campbell Dr, Menomonee Falls WI 53051	262-781-8230	R	46*	.3
97	G and M Electrical Contractors Inc—*Thomas Rivi*	1746 N Richmond St, Chicago IL 60647	773-278-8200	R	46*	.2
98	NetPlanner Systems Inc—*J Clinton Bridges*	3100 Northwoods Pl Ste, Norcross GA 30071	770-662-5482	R	46*	.2

Note: An asterisk (*) indicates an estimated financial figure. The company type code used is as follows: R = Private, P = Public, S = Private Subsidiary, B = Public Subsidiary, D = Division, J = Joint Venture, I = Investment Fund.

COMPANY RANKINGS BY SALES WITHIN 4-DIGIT SIC

Rank	Company Name—Executive Officer	Address, City, State, Zip	Phone	Type	Fin	Empls
99	Northern Electric Inc—Orville Fleming	1275 W 124th Ave, Denver CO 80234	303-428-6969	R	45*	.3
100	Meisner Electric Incorporated Of Florida—Tim Onnen	220 Ne 1st St, Delray Beach FL 33444	561-278-8362	R	45*	.3
101	Eas Contracting LP—John Wall	2941 Trade Ctr Ste 200, Carrollton TX 75007	972-590-5576	R	44*	.1
102	Aerial Contractors Inc—Kevin Ellenson	3030 24th Ave S, Moorhead MN 56560	701-277-1737	S	44*	<.1
103	HB Frazer Co—Franklin P Holleran	514 Shoemaker Rd, King of Prussia PA 19406	610-768-0400	R	43*	.3
104	Energy Systems Group LLC—Jim Adams	4655 Rosebud Ln, Newburgh IN 47630	812-471-5000	S	43*	.2
105	Electrico Inc—Buddie Boyer	1300 Racquet Rd Ste 1, Baltimore MD 21209	410-828-0040	R	43*	.2
106	Davis H Elliot Co—David Haskins AEW Inc	PO Box 12707, Roanoke VA 24027	540-344-1294	S	42*	.5
107	H and H Group Inc—Michael Christensen	PO Box 44267, Madison WI 53744	608-273-3434	R	42*	.4
108	Mcmillan Brothers Electric Inc—Patrick Mcmillan	1515 S Van Ness Ave, San Francisco CA 94110	415-826-5100	R	42*	.2
109	Industrial Power and Lighting Corp—George R Schlemmer	701 Seneca St Ste 500, Buffalo NY 14210	716-854-1811	R	42*	.2
110	Shaw Electric Company Inc—Dick Shaw	3600 Fuller Ave, Kansas City MO 64129	816-921-0033	R	42*	.2
111	Sprig Electric Co—Medford Snyder	1860 S 10th St, San Jose CA 95112	408-298-3134	R	42*	.3
112	D and N Electric Co—Robert Nix	3015 R N Martin St, Atlanta GA 30344	404-254-4200	R	41*	.2
113	Schmidt Electric Company LP—Terri Needham	9701 Fm 1625, Austin TX 78747	512-243-1450	R	39*	.5
114	Van Ert Electric Company Inc—Jason Smith	7019 W Stewart Ave, Wausau WI 54401	715-845-4308	R	39*	.4
115	Hilscher Clarke Electric Co—Ronald D Becker	519 4th St NW, Canton OH 44703	330-452-9806	R	39*	.3
116	All City Electric	6201 Enterprise Dr, Diamond Springs CA 95619	530-626-5802	R	39*	.1
117	Matrix Communications Group Corp—James Annese	126 Dwight Park Cir St, Syracuse NY 13209	315-451-4777	R	39*	.1
118	Commonwealth Electric Company of the Midwest—David Firestone	PO Box 80638, Lincoln NE 68501	402-474-1341	R	38*	.3
119	Albino Construction Inc—Albino Martinez	12568 W Wash Blvd Ste, Los Angeles CA 90066	310-454-9908	R	38*	<.1
120	Merit Electrical Inc—Thom Bonner	PO Box 86710, Baton Rouge LA 70879	225-673-8850	R	38*	.3
121	Armour and Sons Electric Inc—Raymond Armour	23 Cabot Blvd E, Langhorne PA 19047	215-943-4400	R	38*	.1
122	Gel Inc—John Gardner	2101 N Main St, East Peoria IL 61611	309-694-1468	R	37*	.1
123	Lake Erie Electric Inc—Peter J Corogin	25730 1st St, Westlake OH 44145	440-835-5565	R	36*	.1
124	Huston Electric Inc—Jeff Cardwell	1915 E N St, Kokomo IN 46901	765-457-9137	R	36*	.3
125	Tru-Val Electric Corp—Christopher Totaro	205 S Newman St, Hackensack NJ 07601	201-498-9200	R	36*	.3
126	Miller Electric Co (Omaha Nebraska)—Ray A Bruegman	2501 St Marys Ave, Omaha NE 68105	402-341-6479	R	35*	.2
127	Motive Energy Telecommunication Group Inc—Bob Istwan	125 E Commercial St Un, Anaheim CA 92801	714-888-2525	S	35*	.1
128	Pomeroy Electric Inc—Steve Pomeroy	3131 SW 13th Dr, Deerfield Beach FL 33442	954-427-0705	R	35*	.1
129	Del Monte Electric Company Inc—John Hunter	6998 Sierra Ct Ste A, Dublin CA 94568	925-829-6000	R	35*	.1
130	Open Systems Technologies Inc—Daniel Behm	605 Seward Ave Nw Ste, Grand Rapids MI 49504	616-574-3619	R	34*	.1
131	Valley Communications Inc—Kenneth R Hurst	4616 Roseville Rd Ste, North Highlands CA 95660	916-349-7300	R	34*	.4
132	Midwest Electric—RJ Nicolosi	4601 Homer Ohio Ln, Groveport OH 43125	614-482-8022	R	34*	.2
133	Aschinger Electric Co—Emily Martin	PO Box 26322, Fenton MO 63026	636-343-1211	R	34*	.2
134	Alliant Systems LLC—John Rozell	1600 NW 167th Pl, Beaverton OR 97006	503-230-8991	R	34*	.1
135	Adman Electric Inc—Todd Moreland	2311 E 28th St, Chattanooga TN 37407	423-622-5103	R	34*	.3
136	Marathon Electrical Contractors Inc—Larry Argo	PO Box 320067, Birmingham AL 35232	205-323-8500	R	34*	.2
137	Goldfield Corp—John H Sottile	1684 W Hibiscus Blvd, Melbourne FL 32901	321-724-1700	P	33	.1
138	Dale C Rossman Inc—Kenneth Brown	PO Box 1021, Mulberry FL 33860	863-904-1077	R	33*	.3
139	Edna West Associates Ltd—Dennis Nelson	3755 W Hacienda Ave, Las Vegas NV 89118	702-798-2970	R	33*	.3
140	Shawver and Son Inc—John Shawver III	144 NE 44th St, Oklahoma City OK 73105	405-525-9451	R	33*	.1
141	Collins Electric Company Inc—Joseph A Collins	53 2nd Ave, Chicopee MA 01020	413-592-9221	R	33*	.1
142	Calaveras Power Partners LP—Jim Hengel	PO Box 240130, San Antonio TX 78224	210-475-8000	R	33*	.5
143	Kst Electric Ltd—Kristen Fiebig	14215 Fm 973 N, Manor TX 78653	512-272-8841	R	32*	.5
144	TexCom Inc—Eric D Wesley	600 Washington St, Portsmouth VA 23704	757-397-0035	R	32*	.3
145	EnergyConnect Group Inc—Kevin R Evans	901 Campisi Way Ste 26, Campbell CA 95008	408-370-3311	P	32	<.1
146	Environmental Management Systems Consultants Inc—Glen Smith	2134 Espey Ct Ste 9, Crofton MD 21114	301-858-0220	R	32*	.2
147	Thompson Electric Inc—Larry Thompson	49 Northmoreland Ave, Munroe Falls OH 44262	330-686-2300	R	31*	.2
148	Valley Electrical Consolidated Inc—Rex Ferry	977 Tibbetts Wick Rd, Girard OH 44420	330-539-4044	R	30*	.2
149	Kelso-Burnett Co—Brad Weir	5200 Newport Dr, Rolling Meadows IL 60008	847-259-0720	R	30*	.4
150	Electrical and Instrumentation Unlimited Inc—Dennis Howe	204 S Bernard Rd, Broussard LA 70518	337-837-9172	R	30*	.3
151	Kleinknecht Electric Company Inc—Lisa Canty	252 W 37th St Fl 9, New York NY 10018	212-728-1800	R	30*	.2
152	Intermountain Electric Inc—Ed Will Quanta Services Inc	14100 E 35th Pl Ste 10, Aurora CO 80011	303-733-7248	S	30*	.2
153	Continuant—Doug Graham	2001 48th Ave, Fife WA 98424		R	30*	.2
154	World Fiber Technologies Inc—Mark Battle	4070 Nine Mcfarland Dr, Alpharetta GA 30004	770-619-0118	R	30*	.2
155	Deem LLC—Robert Leffler	6831 E 32nd St Ste 200, Indianapolis IN 46226	317-860-2990	R	29*	.2
156	Wolfe and Travis Electric Company Inc—Donald Wolfe	2001 Gladstone Ave, Nashville TN 37211	615-244-6800	R	29*	.1
157	Allison-Smith Co—Lanny S Thomas	2284 Marietta Blvd, Atlanta GA 30318	404-351-6430	R	29*	.3
158	Gephart Electric Company Inc—Carol Heinsch	3550 Labore Rd Ste 11, Saint Paul MN 55110	651-484-4900	R	29*	.2
159	Chain Electric Co—Bobby Chain	PO Box 2058, Hattiesburg MS 39403	601-545-3800	R	28*	.2
160	Fox Valley Fire and Safety Company Inc—Kenneth Volkening	2730 Pinnacle Dr, Elgin IL 60124	847-695-5990	R	28*	.2
161	Spenser Communications Inc—John N Poole	800 E Arrow Hwy, Covina CA 91722	626-593-3131	R	28*	.1
162	Laney's Inc—Keven Wolf	55 27th St S, Fargo ND 58103	701-237-0543	R	28*	.1
163	N J D Wiring and Electric Inc—Peter Karageorgiou	21308 99th Ave, Queens Village NY 11429	718-479-5400	R	28*	.1
164	Brennan Electric Inc—Robert Brennan	460 S Stoddard Ave Ste, San Bernardino CA 92401	909-884-0233	R	27*	.2
165	United Electric Enterprise Ltd—Rj Nicolosy	4601 Homer Ohio Ln, Groveport OH 43125	614-482-8008	R	27*	.1
166	ACI Mechanical Inc—Michael G McCoy Comfort Systems USA Inc	PO Box 192, Ames IA 50010	515-232-1236	S	27*	.1
167	Clear Connection Corp—Kurk Moody	801 Striker Ave, Sacramento CA 95834	916-567-0144	R	27*	.2
168	Frischhertz Electric Company Inc—James Frischhertz	PO Box 19266, New Orleans LA 70179	504-482-1146	R	27*	.2
169	Spencer Technologies Inc—David Strickler	102 Otis St, Northborough MA 01532	508-595-9496	R	27*	.2
170	Roland's Electric Inc—Roland Cadieux	307 Suburban Ave Ste A, Deer Park NY 11729	631-242-8080	R	26*	.1
171	Neal Electric Corp—Clark Thompson	13250 Kirkham Way, Poway CA 92064	858-513-2525	R	26*	.3
172	Bruce and Merrilees Electric Co—Jay H Bruce	930 Cass St, New Castle PA 16101	724-652-5566	R	26*	.4
173	Long Electric Company Inc—Jerry Chlystun	1310 S Franklin Rd, Indianapolis IN 46239	317-356-2455	R	26*	.3
174	Tri-City Electrical Contractors Inc	430 W Dr, Altamonte Springs FL 32714	407-788-3500	R	26*	.1
175	Sunwest Electric Inc—Brien Pariseau	3064 E Miraloma Ave, Anaheim CA 92806	714-630-8700	R	26*	.2
176	EPE Corp—James Bell	645 Harvey Rd Ste 1, Manchester NH 03103	603-669-9181	R	26*	.2
177	Mayers Electric Company Inc—Howard Mayers	4004 Erie Ct Ste B, Cincinnati OH 45227	513-272-2900	R	26*	.2
178	Atlas Electric Company Inc—William Sherrod	PO Box 6233, Knoxville TN 37914	865-524-8615	R	26*	.2
179	Knight Electrical Services Corp—Bartholomew Carmody	111 8th Ave Fl 9, New York NY 10011	212-989-2333	R	26*	.2
180	Veca Electric Company Inc—Tom Fairbanks	PO Box 80467, Seattle WA 98108	206-436-5200	R	26*	.2
181	Trans-Tel Central Inc—Jack Morgan	2805 Broce Dr, Norman OK 73072	405-447-5025	R	25*	.1
182	Ermco Inc—Darrell Gossett	PO Box 1507, Indianapolis IN 46206	317-780-2923	R	25*	.3
183	A M Ortega Construction Inc—Archie Ortega	10125 Channel Rd, Lakeside CA 92040	619-390-1988	R	25*	.2

Rank	Company Name—*Executive Officer*	Address, City, State, Zip	Phone	Type	Fin	Empls
184	Peoples Electrical Contractors Inc—*Bill Lindberg*	277 E Fillmore Ave, Saint Paul MN 55107	651-227-7711	R	25*	.2
185	Paul E Smith Company Inc—*Eric Salder*	5150 Elmwood Ste 200, Indianapolis IN 46203	317-489-0682	R	25*	.1
186	Kimbrell Electric Inc—*Paul Kimbrell*	7593 N 73rd Dr, Glendale AZ 85303	602-265-2111	R	25*	.1
187	Franke Con J Electric Inc—*Lewis Frain*	317 N Grant St, Stockton CA 95202	209-462-0717	R	25*	.1
188	Southland Electric Inc—*Mark Peterson*	4950 Greencraig Ln, San Diego CA 92123	858-634-5050	R	25*	.1
189	John E Kelly and Sons Electrical Construction Inc—*Stephen Kelly*	8431 Old Marlboro Pke, Upper Marlboro MD 20772	301-736-2250	R	25*	.1
190	Rathje Enterprises Inc—*David Rathje*	PO Box 976, Decatur IL 62525	217-423-2593	R	25*	.3
191	RK Electric Inc—*Lonnie Robinson*	42021 Osgood Rd, Fremont CA 94539	510-770-5660	R	25*	.1
192	Miller Bonded Inc—*Keith Wilson*	4538 Mcleod Rd Ne, Albuquerque NM 87109	505-881-0220	R	24*	.2
193	Big State Electric Ltd—*William Johsnon*	PO Box 8237, San Antonio TX 78208	210-735-1051	R	24*	.2
194	Romanoff Electric Inc—*Matthew Romanoff*	1288 Research Rd, Gahanna OH 43230	614-755-4500	R	24*	.3
195	Erb Electric Co—*Tom Knight*	500 Hall St Ste 1, Bridgeport OH 43912	740-633-5055	R	24*	.2
196	Bill's Electric Inc—*Roy Wilson*	PO Box 707, Webb City MO 64870	417-624-6660	R	23*	.2
197	Pyro-Communication Systems Inc—*Michael Donahue*	15531 Container Ln, Huntington Beach CA 92649	714-902-8000	R	23*	.2
198	Electric Resource Contractors Inc—*Dana Daniels*	4024 Washington Ave N, Minneapolis MN 55412	612-522-6511	R	23*	.2
199	Alabama Electric Company Incorporated Of Dothan—*John Sloop*	PO Box 8277, Dothan AL 36304	334-792-5164	R	23*	.2
200	Anderson Electric Inc—*Wes Anderson*	PO Box 758, Springfield IL 62705	217-529-5471	R	23*	.2
201	Egan-McKay Electrical Contractors Inc—*Duane Hendricks*	7625 Boone Ave N, Brooklyn Park MN 55428	763-544-4131	S	23*	.2
202	Schoonover Electric Co—*Robert Reick*	1063 US Hwy 22, Mountainside NJ 07092	908-233-2400	R	23*	.2
203	1st Electric Inc—*Richard China*	2340 Monumental Ave St, Baltimore MD 21227	410-242-0303	R	23*	.1
204	Mared Mechanical Contractors Corp—*Hank Brancaccio*	4230 W Douglas Ave, Milwaukee WI 53209	414-536-0411	R	23*	.1
205	Apollo Electric—*Leroy Holt*	330 N Basse Ln, Brea CA 92821	714-256-8414	R	23*	.1
206	Kaiser Electric Inc—*Steve Giacin*	1552 Fencorp Dr, Fenton MO 63026	636-305-1515	R	23*	.2
207	Pratt Communications Inc—*Kevin Pratt*	2913 Tech Ctr, Santa Ana CA 92705	714-540-6840	R	23*	.2
208	Five Star Electric Corp—*Gary Segal*	10132 101st St, Ozone Park NY 11416	718-641-5000	R	23*	.2
209	Spieler and Ricca Electrical Company Inc—*Ronald Spieler*	5209 Van Dam St, Long Island City NY 11101	718-392-4100	R	23*	.2
210	Excel Security Corp—*Neal Garelik*	505 8th Ave Rm 1700, New York NY 10018	212-239-8086	R	22*	.2
211	Borrell Inc—*Anthony Borrell*	PO Box 172119, Tampa FL 33672		R	22*	.2
212	Lacorte Companies Inc—*Eileen Lacorte*	630 7th Ave, Troy NY 12182	518-286-6000	R	22*	.3
213	Nathan Alterman Electric Company Inc—*Jerry Kolinek*	PO Box 700490, San Antonio TX 78270	210-496-6888	R	22*	.3
214	Custom Computer Cable Inc—*Courtney Matthews*	43766 Trade Ctr Pl, Dulles VA 20166	703-662-2401	R	22*	.2
215	Vexillum Inc—*Clifford Zachman*	1250 Birchwood Dr, Sunnyvale CA 94089	408-734-4282	R	22*	.2
216	Truland Service Corp—*Nazeeh Kidoawi*	5701j General Wash Dr, Alexandria VA 22312	703-642-5222	R	22*	.2
217	Dooley Electric Company Inc—*Robert A Hemsing*	4014 3rd Ave, Brooklyn NY 11232	718-840-2200	H	22*	.1
218	Electricians Inc—*Melvyn Iwaki*	2875 Paa St Ste B, Honolulu HI 96819	808-839-2242	R	22*	.1
219	Mel-Kay Electric Company Inc—*Linda Garrett*	1511 N Garvin St, Evansville IN 47711	812-423-1128	R	22*	.1
220	Northgate Electric Corp—*Karen Bass*	63 Depot Rd, Huntington Station NY 11746	631-271-2242	R	22*	.1
221	Barnes and Powell Electrical Company Inc—*William Powell*	PO Box 849, Elm City NC 27822	252-236-3111	R	22*	.1
222	Bay Area Systems And Solutions Inc—*Jeffrey Yee*	856 Folsom St, San Francisco CA 94107	415-295-1600	R	22*	<.1
223	Budget Electrical Contractors Inc—*William Diesel*	25051 5th St, San Bernardino CA 92410	909-381-2646	R	22*	.2
224	Nikkel and Associates Inc—*Dennis Tiernan*	728 E Lincoln Way, Ames IA 50010	515-232-8606	R	21*	.1
225	Perlectric Inc—*Micheal Perle*	2711 Prosperity Ave St, Fairfax VA 22031	703-352-5151	R	21*	.2
226	Gettle Inc—*Jonathan Kinsley*	2745 Black Bridge Rd, York PA 17406	717-843-1231	R	21*	.1
227	Hallmark Air Conditioning Inc—*Bill Fortner*	3300 Bingle Rd, Houston TX 77055	713-690-8800	R	21*	.3
228	Vector Electric And Controls Inc—*Reynolds Moran*	39423 Babin Rd, Gonzales LA 70737	225-450-2020	R	21*	.2
229	Varney Inc—*Paul Bratton*	PO Box 3187, Roanoke VA 24015	540-343-0155	R	21*	.2
230	Albarell Electric Inc—*Michael Albarell*	PO Box 799, Bethlehem PA 18016	610-691-8606	R	21*	.2
231	D P Electric Inc—*Daniel Puente*	6002 S Ash Ave, Tempe AZ 85283	480-858-9070	R	20*	.2
232	Contemporary Electrical Services Inc—*Christopher Broadbent*	112 Glyndon St Ne Ste, Vienna VA 22180	703-255-9226	R	20*	.1
233	CW Henderson Electric Inc—*Clifford Henderson*	PO Box 91051, Houston TX 77291	281-447-3426	R	20*	.1
234	Wade Electric Inc—*Ira Harris*	3091 12th St, Long Island City NY 11102	718-932-9233	R	20*	.1
235	Maxwell Electrical Services Inc—*Richard Hood*	2601 N Arlington Ave, Indianapolis IN 46218	317-546-9600	R	20*	.1
236	Rydalch Electric Inc—*Robert Rydalch*	250 Plymouth Ave, Salt Lake City UT 84115	801-265-1813	R	20*	.1
237	Scalfo Electric Inc—*Richard Grouser*	3539 N Mill Rd, Vineland NJ 08360	856-692-5196	R	20*	.1
238	Yale Mechanical Inc—*John Dedlon*	220 W 81st St, Minneapolis MN 55420	952-884-1661	R	20*	.1
239	Namaste Solar Electric Inc—*Blake Jones*	4571 Broadway St, Boulder CO 80304	303-447-0300	R	20*	.1
240	Kleinberg Electric Inc—*Carol Kleinberg*	437 W 16th St Fl 4, New York NY 10011	212-206-1140	R	20*	.2
241	Claypool Electric Inc—*Charles Claypool*	1275 Lancaster Kirkers, Lancaster OH 43130	740-653-5683	R	20*	.2
242	Southeast Electric Of Central Florida Inc—*Alan Deese*	PO Box 530103, Orlando FL 32853	407-895-7075	R	20*	.2
243	Barrier Electric Company Inc—*John Barrier*	181 Ave A Ste A, Bayonne NJ 07002	201-823-2542	R	19*	<.1
244	Delta Diversified Enterprises Inc—*LR Donelson*	425 W Gemini Dr, Tempe AZ 85283	480-831-0532	R	19*	.4
245	Smith and Keene Electric Service Inc—*Tim Smith*	833 Live Oak Dr, Chesapeake VA 23320	757-420-1231	R	19*	.4
246	SM Lawrence Co—*Vincent Matlock* Comfort Systems USA Inc	245 Preston St, Jackson TN 38301	731-423-0112	D	19*	.1
247	Kelly Electric LLC—*Ed Lomas*	2100 Consulate Dr Ste, Orlando FL 32837	407-859-8801	R	19*	.2
248	Spg Solar Inc—*Thomas Rooney*	20 Leveroni Ct, Novato CA 94949	415-883-7657	R	19*	.1
249	Auburn Electrical Construction Company Inc—*Greg Lanier*	PO Box 2310, Auburn AL 36831	334-821-7360	R	19*	.1
250	Security Equipment Inc—*Sidney Meridith*	13505 C St, Omaha NE 68144	402-333-3233	R	18*	.1
251	Baroco Electric Construction Co—*J Gill*	75 Brent Ln, Pensacola FL 32503	850-438-5636	R	18*	.1
252	Larry Causey Inc—*Larry Causey*	3521 Gilbert Rd, Grand Prairie TX 75050	972-790-0703	R	18*	.2
253	Moore Electrical Contracting Inc—*Roscoe Moore*	PO Box 730, Rialto CA 92377	951-371-4202	R	18*	.1
254	Superior Group—*Greg Stewart*	740 Waterman Ave, Columbus OH 43215	614-488-8025	R	18*	.2
255	Sme Incorporated Of Seattle—*Steve Marvich*	828 Poplar Pl S, Seattle WA 98144	206-329-2040	R	18*	.1
256	ESI Inc—*Tom Schroth*	4696 Devitt Dr, Cincinnati OH 45246	513-454-3741	R	18*	.1
257	William J Shaeffer's Sons Inc—*Gerald Shaeffer*	169 Boro Line Rd, King Of Prussia PA 19406	610-962-5500	R	18*	.1
258	Joseph Weinstein Electric Corp—*Martin Weinstein*	9424 88th St, Ozone Park NY 11416	718-843-5555	R	18*	.2
259	Tricomm Services Corp—*Joseph Walsh*	1247 N Church St Ste 8, Moorestown NJ 08057	856-914-9001	R	18*	.1
260	F and W Electrical Contractors Inc—*James Freasier*	PO Box 98, Floresville TX 78114	830-393-0083	R	18*	<.1
261	Cherry Lane Electrical Service Inc—*Robert Muir*	8750 3 Cherry Ln, Laurel MD 20707	301-575-2433	R	17*	.2
262	Robert A Denton Inc—*Chris Oconner*	47460 Galleon Dr, Plymouth MI 48170	734-451-7878	R	17*	.2
263	Main Electric Ltd—*Charles Trent*	PO Box 563, Pueblo CO 81002	719-542-4114	R	17*	.1
264	Ready Electric Company Inc—*Andy Windhorst*	2030 Frankfort Ave, Louisville KY 40206	502-893-2511	R	17*	.2
265	Adams Electric Co—*Steve Rasmussen*	1338 Biglerville Rd, Gardners PA 17324	717-334-9211	R	17*	.2
266	DC Group Inc—*Jon Frank*	1977 W River Rd N, Minneapolis MN 55411		R	17*	.1
267	Aether Dbs LLC—*Rob Adams*	PO Box 4738, Naperville IL 60567	630-637-9470	R	17*	.1
268	Bana Electric Corp—*Michael Bender*	50 Gazza Blvd, Farmingdale NY 11735	631-249-6110	R	17*	.1
269	Brothers Air and Heat Inc—*Roger Costner*	1320 E Main St, Rock Hill SC 29730	803-327-4040	S	17*	.1
270	Nuline Technologies Inc—*Kimberly Martin*	520 Quail Hollow Dr St, Wheeling IL 60090	847-520-9300	R	17*	.2

Note: An asterisk (*) indicates an estimated financial figure. The company type code used is as follows: R = Private, P = Public, S = Private Subsidiary, B = Public Subsidiary, D = Division, J = Joint Venture, I = Investment Fund.

COMPANY RANKINGS BY SALES WITHIN 4-DIGIT SIC

Rank	Company Name—*Executive Officer*	Address, City, State, Zip	Phone	Type	Fin	Empls
271	Masters Electrical Services Ltd—*Abel Hawkins*	4239 W Ih 10, Seguin TX 78155	830-303-6330	R	17*	.1
272	Tap Electrical Contracting Service Inc—*Anthony Cardillo*	926 Lincoln Ave Ste C, Holbrook NY 11741	631-567-7600	R	17*	.1
273	Johnson Electric Inc—*Richard Gaumond*	2919 Meade Ave Ste A, Las Vegas NV 89102	702-433-1777	R	17*	.2
274	American Fire Equipment Sales and Service Corp—*Ann Papuga*	3107 W Virginia Ave, Phoenix AZ 85009	602-433-2484	R	17*	.1
275	Beckstrom Electric Co—*Kenneth Beckstrom*	37277 E Richardson Ln, Purcellville VA 20132	540-338-2344	R	17*	.1
276	Tom Hagan Enterprises Inc—*Tom Hagan*	PO Box 2290, Corrales NM 87048	505-897-7140	R	17*	.1
277	S and L Electric Inc—*Leo Villeneuve*	5313 State Hwy 56, Colton NY 13625	315-262-2631	R	16*	.1
278	Hall Electrical Contractor Incorporated John E—*John Hall*	3303 Airline Blvd Ste, Portsmouth VA 23701	757-465-1658	R	16*	.1
279	Defender Security Company Inc—*David Lindsey*	6100 N Keystone Ave St, Indianapolis IN 46220		R	16*	.3
280	Gulf Electric Company Incorporated Of Mobile—*Charles Freeman*	PO Box 2385, Mobile AL 36652	251-666-0654	R	16*	.2
281	Corky Wells Electric Inc—*Shannon Wells*	PO Box 203, Rush KY 41168	606-928-2074	R	16*	.1
282	Teknon Corp—*Gordon Spencer*	15443 Ne 95th St, Redmond WA 98052	425-895-8535	R	16*	.1
283	Moody's Electric Inc—*Linda Moody*	40150 State Hwy 59, Bay Minette AL 36507	251-937-0678	R	16*	.1
284	Bell Electrical Contractors Inc—*Charlie Pavelec*	128 Millwell Dr, Maryland Heights MO 63043	314-878-0878	S	16*	.1
285	Kelly Km Inc—*Kevin Menard*	106 Huntoon Memorial H, Rochdale MA 01542	508-892-8117	R	16*	.1
286	Ace Electrical Contractors Inc—*Larry Palm*	5465 Hwy 169 N, Minneapolis MN 55442	763-694-8800	R	16*	.1
287	Fullford Electric Inc—*James Fullford*	303 E Van Horn Rd, Fairbanks AK 99701	907-456-7356	R	16*	.1
288	Van's Comfortemp Air Conditioning Inc—*David Owens*	135 S Congress St, Delray Beach FL 33445	561-859-0303	R	16*	.1
289	MCA Communications Inc—*Richard Cortez*	PO Box 38391, Houston TX 77238	281-591-2434	R	16*	.1
290	JW Electric Inc—*Rebecca Mccolley*	2900 E Randol Mill Rd, Arlington TX 76011	817-795-0858	R	16*	.1
291	Hellman Electric Corp—*Steve Lazzaro*	855 Brush Ave Frnt 2, Bronx NY 10465	718-931-9900	R	16*	.1
292	Bopat Electric Company Inc—*Robert Driggers*	9130 Red Branch Rd Ste, Columbia MD 21045	410-995-1715	R	15*	.1
293	Amf Electrical Contractors Inc—*John Frisella*	PO Box 16140, Saint Louis MO 63105	314-647-4066	R	15*	.1
294	Metro Electric Company Inc—*Randolph Harley*	PO Box 71228, North Charleston SC 29415	843-554-0621	R	15*	.1
295	Ennis Electric Company Inc—*John Ennis*	7851 Wellingford Dr, Manassas VA 20109	703-631-9431	R	15*	.1
296	Evelyn Baird Gentry Corp—*Wade Ingram*	4303 Glebe Rd, Houston TX 77018	713-681-7339	R	15*	.2
297	Globe Communications Inc—*Victor R Lundy III*	PO Box 2445, Durham NC 27715	919-383-5544	S	15*	.2
298	Divane Brothers Electric Co—*Danial J Divane*	2424 N 25th Ave, Franklin Park IL 60131	847-455-7143	R	15*	.1
299	Abbett Electric Corp—*Jeffrey Abbett*	1850 Bryant St, San Francisco CA 94110	415-864-7500	R	15*	.1
300	Acme Electric Co—*Donald Barrigar*	PO Box 247, Cedar Rapids IA 52406	319-365-8677	R	15*	.1
301	Bullet Electric Inc—*Don Stern*	290 Lodi St, Hackensack NJ 07601	201-441-9450	R	15*	.1
302	Decker Electric Company Inc—*Paul Fischer*	1282 Folsom St, San Francisco CA 94103	415-552-1622	R	15*	.1
303	EC Ernst Inc—*Jim Hegarty*	132 Log Canoe Cir, Stevensville MD 21666	301-350-7770	S	15*	.1
304	Shaw Electric Co—*Robert Minielly*	33200 Schoolcraft Rd, Livonia MI 48150	734-425-6800	R	15*	.1
305	GMA Electrical Corp—*Gina Addeo*	201 Edward Curry Ave, Staten Island NY 10314	718-477-9600	R	15*	.1
306	Rjp Electric LLC—*Pamela Ames*	3608 S Big Bend Blvd, Saint Louis MO 63143	314-781-2400	R	15*	.1
307	Sumter Utilities Inc—*Tim Moore*	PO Box 579, Sumter SC 29151	803-469-8585	R	15*	.1
308	US Voice and Data—*Jim Hogan*	11500 Blankenbaker Acc, Louisville KY 40299	502-479-8030	S	15*	.1
309	Ray S Pantel Inc—*Ray Pantel*	71 Wisner Ave, Middletown NY 10940	845-343-7250	R	15*	<.1
310	Seravalli Inc—*Charles Seravalli*	10059 Sandmeyer Ln, Philadelphia PA 19116	215-969-6500	R	15*	.1
311	Glow Electric Co—*Barbara Donnelly*	13437 Kolmar Ave, Midlothian IL 60445	708-389-7447	R	15*	.1
312	Suburban Electrical Engineers/Contractors Inc—*Guy Smith*	709 N Hickory Farm Ln, Appleton WI 54914	920-739-5156	R	15*	.1
313	Neshaminy Electrical Contractors Inc—*John Lyons*	PO Box 329, Bensalem PA 19020	215-638-2900	R	15*	.1
314	Jaroth Inc—*Thomas Keane*	2001 Crow Canyon Rd, San Ramon CA 94583	925-553-3650	R	14*	.1
315	Kirkwood Electric Inc—*Wayne Kirkwood*	PO Box 152000, Cape Coral FL 33915	239-574-3449	R	14*	.1
316	Birckhead Electric Inc—*Michael Birckhead*	2408 Crofton Blvd, Crofton MD 21114	301-858-0373	R	14*	.1
317	Picatti Brothers Inc—*Donald Picatti*	PO Box 9576, Yakima WA 98909	509-248-2540	R	14*	.1
318	Wilson Electric Co—*Lewis Maffioli*	113 S Madison St, Rockford IL 61104	815-963-0434	R	14*	.1
319	Westgate Inc—*John Thigpen*	PO Box 1948, Baton Rouge LA 70821	225-749-2635	R	14*	.3
320	High Power Technical Services Inc—*Scott Weis*	2230 Ampere Dr, Louisville KY 40299	502-254-0768	R	14*	.3
321	Datawatch Systems Inc—*William Peel*	4401 E W Hwy Ste 500, Bethesda MD 20814	301-654-3282	R	14*	.1
322	Benson Security Systems Inc—*Shawn Benson*	2065 W Obispo Ave Ste, Gilbert AZ 85233	480-892-8688	R	14*	.1
323	Sabah International Inc—*Michele Sabah*	5925 Stoneridge Dr, Pleasanton CA 94588	925-463-0431	R	14*	.1
324	Bridgefield Electrical Services Inc—*Chad Havens*	PO Box 130, Bridge City TX 77611	409-886-3200	R	14*	.1
325	Bob Biter Electrical Enterprises Inc—*Robert Biter*	PO Box 227, Cresson PA 16630	814-886-7111	R	14*	.1
326	Indianapolis Electric Company Inc—*Linville Coner*	241 S State Ave, Indianapolis IN 46201	317-636-3391	R	14*	.1
327	Wesley Crow Electric Inc—*Wesley Crow*	PO Box 70, Lampasas TX 76550	512-556-6532	R	14*	.1
328	Levangie Electric Company Inc—*Stephen Vangie*	978 Washington St, Weymouth MA 02189	781-331-4900	R	14*	<.1
329	TRC Electrical Construction Services Inc—*Walt Ratterman*	PO Box 289, New Park PA 17352	717-993-0403	R	14*	.1
330	Totem Electric Of Tacoma Inc—*Scott Stephens*	PO Box 1093, Tacoma WA 98401	253-383-5022	R	14*	.1
331	Front Range Wireless Inc—*Aaron Kingstrom*	7476 S Eagle St Ste A, Centennial CO 80112	303-703-4667	R	14*	<.1
332	Ferry Electric Co—*James Ferry*	250 Curry Hollow Rd, Pittsburgh PA 15236	412-892-2100	R	13*	.1
333	Aa/Acme Locksmiths Inc—*Steven Harris*	1922 Republic Ave, San Leandro CA 94577	510-483-6584	R	13*	.1
334	Pieper Electric Inc—*Richard Pieper*	5070 N 35th St Ste 1, Milwaukee WI 53209	414-462-7700	R	13*	.1
335	Superior Light and Sign Maintenance Company Inc—*John Kenney*	2121 S 24th St, Omaha NE 68108	402-345-0800	R	13*	.1
336	Lea Electric LLC—*Julie Gardner*	PO Box 190130, Boise ID 83719	208-888-2523	R	13*	.1
337	Elliott Contracting Inc—*Harold Breahm*	PO Box 3038, Pikeville KY 41502	606-437-7368	R	13*	.1
338	C and R Systems Inc—*Robert Cross*	1835 Capital St, Corona CA 92880	951-270-0255	R	13*	.1
339	S and W Contracting Company Inc—*Richie Bolin*	952 New Salem Rd, Murfreesboro TN 37129	615-893-2511	R	13*	.1
340	Hurst Electric LP—*Gerald Jordan*	136 S Norwood Dr, Hurst TX 76053	817-268-3000	R	13*	<.1
341	Security Instrument Corporation Of Delaware—*Arthur Mattei*	309 W Newport Pke, Wilmington DE 19804	302-998-2261	R	13*	.1
342	IK Electric Co—*Scott Korenblat*	PO Box 2140, Little Rock AR 72203	501-376-2081	R	13*	.1
343	McDaniel Fire Systems Inc—*Richard Bledsoe*	1055 W Joliet Rd, Valparaiso IN 46385	219-462-0571	R	13*	.1
344	Hjd Capital Electric Inc—*Henry Davila*	5424 Hwy 90 W, San Antonio TX 78227	210-681-0954	R	13*	.1
345	WW Enterprises Inc—*Larry Willis*	4144 S Mingo Rd, Tulsa OK 74146	918-234-7110	R	13*	.1
346	Ward's Marine Electric Inc—*Ward Eshleman*	617 Sw 3rd Ave, Fort Lauderdale FL 33315	954-523-2815	R	13*	.1
347	Faith Enterprises Inc—*Steve Trutna*	129 S Corona St, Colorado Springs CO 80903	719-578-8281	R	13*	.1
348	Marcum Electric Inc—*Ralph Marcum*	200 Commerce Dr, Pelham AL 35124	205-664-1415	R	13*	.2
349	Wigdahl Electric Co—*David Wigdahl*	625 Pratt Blvd Ste 2, Elk Grove Village IL 60007	847-439-8200	R	13*	.1
350	Volunteer Electric Inc—*John Pruitt*	195 River Hills Dr, Nashville TN 37210	615-391-5555	R	13*	.1
351	PS Development Corp—*Adam Saitman*	7760 Deering Ave, Canoga Park CA 91304	818-340-0965	R	13*	.1
352	Total Electric Service Inc—*Bradford Haessly*	PO Box 217, Marshfield WI 54449	715-384-3311	R	13*	.1
353	Netversant - Northern California Inc—*Russell Hayslip*	1411 S Milpitas Blvd, Milpitas CA 95035	510-771-1200	R	13*	.1
354	W K Jennings Electric Company Inc—*Glen Herring*	1707 Dungan Lnne, Austin TX 78754	512-834-8677	R	13*	.1
355	Bigman Brothers Inc—*Stephen Bigman*	4340 34th St, Long Island City NY 11101	718-786-1421	R	13*	.1
356	Gillis Electric Inc—*John Gillis*	34133 Schoolcraft Rd, Livonia MI 48150	734-425-1011	R	13*	.1
357	Partners Electrical Services LLC	7303 Windfern Rd Ste 2, Houston TX 77040	832-399-4000	R	12*	.1

Rank	Company Name—Executive Officer	Address, City, State, Zip	Phone	Type	Fin	Empls
358	Afc Electric Inc—Michael Quinn	10550 Abernathy St, Bonita Springs FL 34135	239-498-3131	R	12*	.1
359	Diverse Electrical Company Inc—George Bryan	8801b Creedmoor Rd, Raleigh NC 27615	919-848-4652	R	12*	.1
360	West-Fair Electric Contractors Inc—James Farina	PO Box 298, Hawthorne NY 10532	914-769-8050	R	12*	.1
361	Dpi LLC—Angela Holnagel	5005 N State Line Ave, Texarkana TX 75503	281-476-0900	R	12*	<.1
362	Bay Harbour Electric Inc—Carolyn Dolak	2007 W 32nd St Ste 2, Erie PA 16508	814-864-7383	R	12*	.1
363	Schmidt Kaplan Electric Inc—Laurance Kaplan	PO Box 23625, Rochester NY 14692	585-328-0130	R	12*	.1
364	Y-Delta Inc—Jimmy Rogers	5657 Lakeview Rd, Statesboro GA 30461	912-587-5839	R	12*	.1
365	Fran Corp—James Johannemann	100 Snake Hill Rd, West Nyack NY 10994	845-358-1200	R	12*	.1
366	Crosby Electric Company Inc—Kenneth Crosby	PO Box 240368, Montgomery AL 36124	334-272-2085	R	12*	.1
367	Jordano Electric Company Inc—Vincent Piccolo	200 Hudson St, Hackensack NJ 07601	201-489-4800	R	12*	.1
368	JP Rainey and Company Inc—Thomas Moore	3548 K St, Philadelphia PA 19134	215-743-1376	R	12*	.1
369	Bestco Electric Inc—Dimitri Guzman	1322 7th St, Modesto CA 95354	209-569-0120	R	12*	.1
370	Ideacom Mid-America Inc—Laurence Anderson	30 Water St W, Saint Paul MN 55107	651-292-0102	R	12*	.1
371	Howe Electric Construction Inc—Ty Howe	4682 E Olive Ave, Fresno CA 93702	559-255-8992	R	12*	.1
372	Clawson Communications Inc—Glenn Clawson	474 Park 800 Dr, Greenwood IN 46143	317-887-9250	R	12*	.1
373	High Voltage Maintenance Corp—Tom Nation	PO Box 13059, Dayton OH 45413	937-278-0811	S	12*	.1
374	Andersen Services Inc—Don Andersen	PO Box 561897, Charlotte NC 28256	704-596-2525	R	12*	.1
375	Kogap Electrical Division Inc—Jerry Lausman	PO Box 1608, Medford OR 97501	541-776-6547	R	12*	.1
376	Suppressions Systems Inc—Jeff Lambert	PO Box 610, Blue Springs MO 64013	215-679-6291	R	12*	.1
377	Transtar Electric Inc—Daniel Bollin	767 Warehouse Rd Ste B, Toledo OH 43615	419-385-7573	R	12*	.1
378	Evans Services Inc—Eric Saltzer	2406 Valleydale Rd, Birmingham AL 35244	205-588-4385	R	12*	<.1
379	Morrow-Meadows Corporation Northern California—James Goetz Morrow-Meadows Corp	385 Oyster Point Blvd, South San Francisco CA 94080	650-634-0682	S	12*	<.1
380	Kent Electric Co—Elmer Kent	11631 Industry Ave, Fontana CA 92337	951-681-2910	R	12*	.1
381	Briner Electric Co—John Fogarty	PO Box 1329, Maryland Heights MO 63043	314-298-0800	R	12*	.1
382	Kinder Electric Company Inc—David Kinder	9087 Technology Ln, Fishers IN 46038	317-842-0809	R	12*	.1
383	L And O Electric Inc—John Lambert	11302 Pollyanna Ave, Austin TX 78753	512-339-9340	R	12*	.1
384	Interface Cable Assemblies And Services Corp—Matthew Bonfitto	4219 23rd Ave, Long Island City NY 11105	718-278-1100	R	12*	<.1
385	Walsh Electric Company Inc—Patrick Walsh	101 Sentry Cir, Yorktown VA 23692	757-890-0636	R	12*	.1
386	Dakota Security Systems Inc—James Yunag	2201 E 54th St N, Sioux Falls SD 57104	605-271-7000	R	12*	.1
387	Sunpro Inc—M Kozak	7640 Whipple Ave Nw, Canton OH 44720	330-966-0910	R	12*	.1
388	Audio Command Systems Inc—Robert Kaufman	694 Main St, Westbury NY 11590	516-997-5800	R	12*	.1
389	Operational Security Systems Inc—James Coleman	1231 Collier Rd Nw Ste, Atlanta GA 30318	404-352-0025	R	12*	.1
390	Pjs Electric Inc—Eileen Scariano	10 43rd St L15, Brooklyn NY 11232	718-832-9609	R	12*	<.1
391	Ellendale Electric Company Inc—John Anderson	7722 Us Hwy 70, Memphis TN 38133	901-382-0045	R	12*	.1
392	S and H Lone Star Electric Inc—Mark Huston	2008 W 5th St, Fort Worth TX 76107	817-335-8044	R	12*	.1
393	Kidwell Inc—Chris Kidwell	3333 Folkways Cir, Lincoln NE 68504	402-475-9151	R	11*	.1
394	Lei Companies Inc—Brandon Berumen	2017 Curtis St, Denver CO 80205	303-934-5631	R	11*	.1
395	Network Cabling Infrastructures Inc—William Valentine	PO Box 1325, Buford GA 30515	770-495-0798	R	11*	.1
396	Dixon Electric Inc—Doug Dixon	516 W 4th St, Lexington KY 40508	859-276-2575	R	11*	.1
397	Carter Electric Company Inc—Walter Carter	3940 Washington Rd Ste, Augusta GA 30907	706-863-1385	R	11*	.1
398	Perram Electric Inc—Zoltan Kovacs	6882 Ridge Rd, Wadsworth OH 44281	330-239-2661	P	11*	<.1
399	JL Maupin Enterprises Inc—James Maupin	8508 Rannie Rd, Houston TX 77080	713-460-2115	R	11*	.1
400	Apex Electric—Mel Hawkins	3280 W Hacienda Ave St, Las Vegas NV 89118	702-791-2739	R	11*	.1
401	P SC Industrial Outsourcing Inc—Bryan Landry	2104 Engineers Rd, Belle Chasse LA 70037	504-394-7490	R	11*	.1
402	Tomco Electric Inc—Dennis Thompson	PO Box 6388, Bend OR 97708	541-389-5424	R	11*	.1
403	Allbrite Electrical Contractors Inc—Lloyd Gerber	4450 Nw 126th Ave Ste, Coral Springs FL 33065	954-583-6788	R	11*	.1
404	CNS Communications LLC—Wade Herter	16631 N 91st St Ste 10, Scottsdale AZ 85260	480-473-2440	R	11*	<.1
405	Jim Smith Electric Service Inc—James Smith	12931 Metro Pkwy Ste 2, Fort Myers FL 33966	239-277-1301	R	11*	.1
406	Mts Services Inc—Thomas Banks	13 Delta Dr Unit 7, Londonderry NH 03053	603-845-1100	R	11*	.1
407	Jack T Hill Electric Co—Dana Hill	10100 N Lamar Blvd, Austin TX 78753	512-836-3950	R	11*	.1
408	Lytle Electric Co—Jeff Reinoehl	PO Box 32, Robinson IL 62454	618-546-1113	R	11*	<.1
409	Arc Electric Company Inc—Lawrence Cooper	PO Box 1187, Millington TN 38083	901-872-1911	R	11*	.1
410	Pyramid Electric Inc—Anita Haines	7555 Appling Ctr Dr, Memphis TN 38133	901-382-2000	R	11*	.1
411	Colvin Electric Inc—Charles Colvin	3901 Kelly Ln, Pflugerville TX 78660	512-388-2271	R	11*	.1
412	Control Specialist Inc—George Brown	PO Box 1479, Decatur TX 76234	817-638-2629	R	11*	.1
413	Schetter Electric Inc—Frank Schetter	PO Box 1377, Sacramento CA 95812	916-446-2521	R	11*	.1
414	Trans-Alarm Inc—Terrance Mullett	500 E Travelers Trl St, Burnsville MN 55337	952-894-1700	R	11*	.1
415	Gregg Electric Inc—Randall Fehlman	608 W Emporia St, Ontario CA 91762	909-983-1794	R	11*	.1
416	Brown Electric Company Inc—Robert Sylvester	1100 Charles Ave, Dunbar WV 25064	304-768-0407	R	11*	.1
417	Jerry Pybus Electric Inc—Jerry Pybus	PO Box 6500, Panama City FL 32404	850-784-2766	R	11*	.1
418	A and F Electric Company Inc—Terry Atwood	2300 Kline Ave, Nashville TN 37211	615-244-4443	R	11*	.1
419	Malko Electric Company Inc—Steve Diamond	6200 Lincoln Ave, Morton Grove IL 60053	847-967-9500	R	11*	.1
420	Sentry Electric Incorporated of Central Florida—John Muchard	1313 28th St, Orlando FL 32805	407-843-0207	R	11*	.1
421	Icomm Corp—Frederick Shuart	PO Box 930299, Wixom MI 48393	248-960-3700	R	11*	.1
422	Lan-Tel Communications Services Inc—Kristi Mcbee	520 N M7 Hwy, Independence MO 64056	816-650-5038	R	10*	.1
423	Electrical Controls And Maintenance Inc—Michael Wynne	PO Box 128, Mechanicsville VA 23111	804-741-2280	R	10*	.1
424	Fpi Electrical Inc—Terry Ambrosino	11 Green Mountain Dr, Cohoes NY 12047	518-782-7400	R	10*	.1
425	Allied Electrical Contractors Inc—Hugh Kelley	1425 Lindbergh Dr, Beaumont TX 77707	409-842-5100	R	10*	.1
426	Gerstner Electric Inc—John Gerstner	2400 Cassens Dr, Fenton MO 63026	636-349-5999	R	10*	.1
427	Zeig Electric Inc—James Zeig	8224 White Settlement, Fort Worth TX 76108	817-732-7895	R	10*	.1
428	Tiger Electric Inc—Stanley Longenecker	650 N Berry St, Brea CA 92821	714-529-8061	R	10*	.1
429	G L Frederick—Gene Frederick	9835 Kitty Ln, Oakland CA 94603	510-430-0399	R	10*	.1
430	Securecom Inc—Kevin Mcelwee	1940 Don St Ste 100, Springfield OR 97477	541-343-5565	R	10*	.1
431	Ava Electric Company Inc—Alvin Biagas	1410 Marblewood Ave, Capitol Heights MD 20743	301-636-9555	R	10*	.1
432	Beachem Brothers Electric Inc—William Beauchamp	921 N Lime Ave, Sarasota FL 34237	941-365-1919	R	10*	.1
433	Connors - Haas Inc—Brian Haas	6337 Dean Pkwy, Ontario NY 14519	585-265-1810	R	10*	.1
434	Union Electric Contracting Co—Beverly Bortz	350 Commerce Dr, Fort Washington PA 19034	215-643-2990	R	10*	.1
435	Goldsmith Associates Inc—Gary Goldsmith	3 Larwin Rd Ste A, Cherry Hill NJ 08034	856-751-4747	R	10*	.1
436	Capitol Electric Company Inc—Darrell Mcneel	11401 Ne Marx St, Portland OR 97220	503-255-9488	R	10*	.1
437	Associated Companies Inc—Herbert Varner	4985 Spirit Lake Rd, Winter Haven FL 33880	863-294-9292	R	10*	.1
438	Southwestern Electrical Company Inc—H Boyles	PO Box 1602, Wichita KS 67201	316-263-1264	R	10*	.1
439	Laibe Electric Co—Gerald Deaton	404 N Byrne Rd, Toledo OH 43607	419-531-4251	R	10*	.1
440	Jim Luca Electrical Contractor Inc—Jim Luca	4575 Brownsville Rd St, Powder Springs GA 30127	770-439-0000	R	10*	.1
441	Dennis Electric Incorporated—Charles Dennis	7560 Bartlett Corp Dr, Bartlett TN 38133	901-382-8150	R	10*	.1
442	Parsons Electric Inc—Tim Parsons	PO Box 13038, Lexington KY 40583	859-233-9823	R	10*	.1
443	C O Christian and Sons Company Inc—C Christian	2139 Canady Ave, Nashville TN 37211	615-254-3491	R	10*	.1
444	CDL Electric Company Inc—Larry Seward	201 N Joplin St, Pittsburg KS 66762	620-231-6420	R	10*	.1

Note: An asterisk (*) indicates an estimated financial figure. The company type code used is as follows: R = Private, P = Public, S = Private Subsidiary, B = Public Subsidiary, D = Division, J = Joint Venture, I = Investment Fund.

COMPANY RANKINGS BY SALES WITHIN 4-DIGIT SIC

Rank	Company Name—*Executive Officer*	Address, City, State, Zip	Phone	Type	Fin	Empls
445	Recore Electrical Contractors Inc—*Michael Recore*	PO Box 1972, Gastonia NC 28053	704-867-1647	R	10*	.1
446	Richard A Heaps Electrical Contractor Inc—*Diane K Meehan*	8909 Florin Rd, Sacramento CA 95829	916-386-8857	R	10*	.1
447	Evets Electric Inc—*Rex Ferry*	977 Tibbetts Wick Rd, Girard OH 44420	330-539-4044	R	10*	.1
448	Daniel's Electrical Construction Company Inc—*Thomas Ispas*	10881 Business Dr, Fontana CA 92337	909-427-9000	R	10*	<.1
449	A-1 Mechanical Lansing Inc—*Tim White*	3610 Old Lansing Rd, Lansing MI 48917	517-322-2300	R	10*	<.1
450	Axxis Network and Telecommunications Inc—*Mostafa Moghadassi*	22817 Ventura Blvd Ste, Woodland Hills CA 91364	818-713-8262	R	10*	<.1
451	Inglett and Stubbs LLC—*Don Davidson*	5200 Riverview Rd, Mableton GA 30126	404-881-1199	R	10*	<.1
452	Dvl Automation Inc—*Michael Murphy*	115 Sinclair Rd, Bristol PA 19007	215-785-6750	R	10*	<.1
453	Shew Electric Inc—*James Shew*	2628 River Rd Liberty, North Wilkesboro NC 28659	336-838-6920	R	10*	<.1
454	F K Everest Inc—*Mike Martin*	140 Business Park Dr, Fairmont WV 26554	304-363-8830	R	10*	.1
455	Harrington Electric Co—*Thomas Morgan*	3800 Perkins Ave, Cleveland OH 44114	216-361-5101	R	10*	.1
456	Ives Corporation E H—*Robert Hurst*	2115 Springfield Ave, Norfolk VA 23523	757-543-1444	R	10*	.1
457	Lakey Electric Company Inc—*Craig Carr*	PO Box 40279, Houston TX 77240	713-460-5882	R	10*	.1
458	Mcf Services Inc—*Sharon Ponticello*	621 W Washington St, Norristown PA 19401	610-239-9400	R	10*	.1
459	Rml Electric Inc—*Robert Lafferty*	3749 E Atlanta Ave, Phoenix AZ 85040	602-244-2080	R	10*	.1
460	Independent Investors Inc—*Daniel Smith*	PO Box 3686, Omaha NE 68103	402-346-1881	R	10*	.1
461	Evers and Whatley Electric Inc—*Randall Evers*	311 Campbell Rd, El Dorado AR 71730	870-863-4494	R	10*	.1
462	Greg A Vietri Inc—*Greg Vietri*	105 Independence Way, Coatesville PA 19320	610-857-1110	R	10*	<.1
463	Pacific Design and Construction Corp—*Jim Peys*	3225 Pine Ave, Long Beach CA 90807	562-427-5050	R	10*	.1
464	Northwest Electric Inc—*Steve Porter*	PO Box 37, Reisterstown MD 21136	410-526-4555	R	10*	.1
465	Cove Electric Inc—*Garlan Hulslander*	77824 Wildcat Dr, Palm Desert CA 92211	760-360-0036	R	10*	.1
466	Sonitrol Security Systems Of Hartford Inc—*Douglas Curtiss*	PO Box 4006, Rocky Hill CT 06067	860-247-4500	R	10*	.1
467	Network Cabling Systems Inc—*Louis Romero*	2430 Whitehall Park Dr, Charlotte NC 28273	704-523-8606	R	10*	.1
468	Boz Electrical Contractors Inc—*John Bosma*	6 Warren Dr, Vernon NJ 07462	973-764-2800	R	10*	<.1
469	Rt Electric Inc—*Kevin Tegmeyer*	480 N 17th St, Las Cruces NM 88005	575-523-9252	R	10*	.1
470	Electric Controls And Systems Inc—*Gregory Bray*	PO Box 100816, Birmingham AL 35210	205-833-9900	R	10*	.1
471	Doyle's Electric Inc—*Robert Leitner*	15035 Jefferson Hwy, Baton Rouge LA 70817	225-752-5112	R	10*	.1
472	Wireless Advanced Communications Inc—*Andrew Bellendir*	3901 W Service Rd, Evans CO 80620	970-330-9415	R	10*	.1
473	Pinnacle Electronic Systems Inc—*Robert Betty* Construction Management Services Inc	3600 Silverside Rd, Wilmington DE 19810	302-478-4200	S	10*	<.1
474	Krug Associates Inc—*Jeffrey Krug*	26269 Research Pl, Hayward CA 94545	510-887-1117	R	10*	<.1
475	Hallmark Energy Economics Inc—*Leonard Piazza*	22923 Quicksilver Dr S, Sterling VA 20166	703-574-5001	R	10*	<.1
476	Moon Security Services Inc—*Ruth Pound*	PO Box B, Pasco WA 99302	509-543-3814	R	9*	.2
477	Grant Contracting Inc—*Earl Grant*	303 Koon St, West Columbia SC 29169	803-794-1251	R	9*	<.1
478	Walsh Electrical Contracting Inc—*Kevin Walsh*	76 Midland Ave, Staten Island NY 10306	718-351-3399	R	9*	<.1
479	Sulphur Electric Company Inc—*James Stark*	PO Box 30, Sulphur LA 70664	337-882-0454	R	9*	.1
480	JH Electric Of New York Inc—*Raina Herrick*	1 Detroit Rd, Huntington Station NY 11746	631-423-6969	R	9*	.1
481	Cable Communications Inc—*Susan Hurley*	6200 S Oakley Ave, Chicago IL 60636	773-925-1344	R	9*	<.1
482	Consolidated Electrical Contractors And Engineers Inc—*Terry Wallace*	PO Box 1528, Dothan AL 36302	334-793-4974	R	9*	.1
483	Us Communications And Electric Inc *Patricia Kendig*	4933 Neo Pkwy, Cleveland OH 44128	216-478-0810	R	9*	.1
484	Circle A Electric Inc—*David Allen*	1051 Kennedy Ln, Saginaw TX 76131	817-625-0880	R	9*	.1
485	Oilfield Electric Co—*Allen Fletcher*	1801 N Ventura Ave, Ventura CA 93001	805-648-3131	R	9*	.1
486	A Randy's Electric Inc—*Charles Spitzer*	PO Box 42577, Saint Petersburg FL 33742	727-573-1400	R	9*	.1
487	Davenport Electric Contract Co—*Frederick Fuessel*	PO Box 4229, Davenport IA 52808	563-326-6475	R	9*	.1
488	East Coast Electrical Contractors Inc—*Robert Walker*	2 Lan Dr, Westford MA 01886	978-692-3232	R	9*	.1
489	Southwest Telecom Services Inc—*C Boyd*	PO Box 1239, Rockwall TX 75087	214-381-3333	R	9*	.1
490	Super Electric Construction Co—*William A Schult*	4300 W Chicago Ave, Chicago IL 60651	773-489-4400	R	9*	.1
491	Southeast Power Corp—*Robert Jones* Goldfield Corp	1805 Hammock Rd, Titusville FL 32796	321-268-0540	S	9*	.1
492	Ans Advanced Network Services LLC—*Robert Hebert*	12 Elmwood Rd Ste 1, Albany NY 12204	518-292-6555	R	9*	.1
493	Design Electric Inc—*Douglas Bischoff*	PO Box 1252, Saint Cloud MN 56302	320-252-1658	R	9*	.1
494	Elk Electric Inc—*Mike Kanetzky*	4707 Weidemar Ln, Austin TX 78745	512-442-8085	R	9*	.1
495	A Murphy Inc—*Arthur Murphy*	35 Hanover St, Hanover MA 02339	781-826-0222	R	9*	<.1
496	Telecommunications Management Solutions Inc—*Bruce Jaftok*	570 Division St, Campbell CA 95008	408-866-5495	R	9*	<.1
497	Marine Electric Company Inc—*Charles Wirth*	PO Box 3319, Louisville KY 40201	502-587-6514	R	9*	<.1
498	Genovese and Massaro Inc—*Michael Massaro*	2466 State St, Hamden CT 06517	203-230-9055	R	9*	<.1
499	Lakeland Electric Inc—*Terry Kendall*	PO Box 809, Cookeville TN 38503	931-526-7216	R	9*	.1
500	Hall Brothers Electrical Contractors Inc—*James Hall*	2611 Whitehouse Rd, South Chesterfield VA 23834	804-526-0911	R	9*	.1
501	College Station Electric Inc—*Jack Matthews*	PO Box 3906, Bryan TX 77805	979-774-8948	R	9*	.1
502	Applied Technical Systems Inc—*Robert Kumpula*	6024 Jean Rd Ste E200, Lake Oswego OR 97035	503-684-9611	R	9*	.1
503	Commercial Electric Inc—*Nicholas Teves*	1010 Paapu St, Honolulu HI 96819	808-841-4595	R	9*	.1
504	Diamond Electric Inc—*Tom Hartley*	PO Box 996, Dover DE 19903	302-697-3296	R	9*	.1
505	Pfeiffer Electric Company Inc—*William Pfeiffer*	448 Queens Ln, San Jose CA 95112	408-436-8523	R	9*	<.1
506	A and B Electric Company Inc—*Gregory Akers*	2530 Jmt Industrial Dr, Apopka FL 32703	407-293-5984	R	9*	.1
507	Quality Communications of Florida Inc—*John Hood*	3700 SW 30th Ave, Fort Lauderdale FL 33312	954-584-4111	R	9*	.1
508	Alliance Telecommunications Contractors Inc—*Richard Knapp*	323 New Rd Ste 2, Parsippany NJ 07054	973-276-0909	R	9*	<.1
509	Hargrove Electric Co—*Steve Hargrove*	PO Box 566077, Dallas TX 75356	214-742-8665	R	9*	.1
510	Technical Management Associates Inc—*Terri Russillo*	245 Pittsburgh Rd Ste, Butler PA 16001	724-282-4800	R	9*	.1
511	Mascal Electric Inc—*John Corsiglia*	PO Box 398, Dekalb IL 60115	815-758-8164	R	9*	.1
512	C and G Electric Inc—*Brad Carrell*	4801 W University Dr S, Denton TX 76207	940-387-4331	R	9*	.1
513	Industrial Electric Co—*Gary Novak*	660 Taft St Ne, Minneapolis MN 55413	612-331-1268	R	9*	.1
514	Hitt Electric Corp—*Robert Hitt*	2972 Holland Rd, Virginia Beach VA 23453	757-422-2740	R	9*	<.1
515	Enertech Electrical Inc—*Gregory Haren*	101 Yngstown Lwllville, Lowellville OH 44436	330-536-2131	R	9*	<.1
516	Adco Electric Inc—*Whit Adams*	PO Box 7395, Jackson MS 39282	601-922-3575	R	9*	.1
517	Electric Maintenance And Construction Inc—*Edward Roseman*	9513 N Trask St, Tampa FL 33624	813-886-3733	R	8*	.1
518	Lighting Maintenance Inc—*Hilary Yoder*	5193 Raynor Ave, Linthicum MD 21090		R	8*	.1
519	Miller Communications Inc—*Paul Curry*	4088 Alpha Dr Ste 101, Allison Park PA 15101	412-781-5000	R	8*	.1
520	Pagoda Electric Inc—*Vincent Mills*	6516 W Archer Ave, Chicago IL 60638	773-229-8800	R	8*	<.1
521	Delta California Contractors Inc—*Deborah Patchett*	1940 W Cheryl Dr, Phoenix AZ 85021	602-997-7111	R	8*	.1
522	Action Services Group Inc—*Jon Frandisco*	1400 N 6th Ave, Knoxville TN 37917	865-595-3333	R	8*	.1
523	Fiber-Tel Contractors Inc—*Mike Mansfield*	PO Box 264, Midway AR 72651	870-481-1000	R	8*	.1
524	Fowler Electric Co—*Jeffrey Boring*	7777 First Pl, Bedford OH 44146	440-786-9777	R	8*	.1
525	Triple R Electric Inc—*Randal Amescua*	19892 Fm 2252 Unit 1, San Antonio TX 78266	210-946-7770	R	8*	.1
526	Glesco Electric Inc—*Kevin Mitchell*	3103 E Tatman Ct Ste 1, Urbana IL 61802	217-328-7700	R	8*	.1
527	Electrex Company Inc—*Lawrence Page*	41775 Production Dr, Harrison Township MI 48045	586-468-7571	R	8*	<.1
528	Levinson and Santoro Electric Corp—*Fred Levinson*	1820 130th St, College Point NY 11356	718-961-9600	R	8*	.1
529	Blake Electric Contracting Company Inc—*Peter Blake*	311 E 150th St, Bronx NY 10451	718-292-8080	R	8*	<.1
530	JN Electric Of Tampa Bay Inc—*John Narcisi*	2441 Old Cypress Creek, Land O Lakes FL 34639	813-948-1608	R	8*	.1

Rank	Company Name—*Executive Officer*	Address, City, State, Zip	Phone	Type	Fin	Empls
531	Universal Atlantic Systems Inc—*Ronald Schwartz*	700 Abbott Dr, Broomall PA 19008	610-328-1000	R	8*	.1
532	Artistic Lighting And Electric—*Duane Johnson*	PO Box 151106, San Rafael CA 94915	415-456-1656	R	8*	<.1
533	Border Electric Inc—*John Smith*	59 River Rd, Calais ME 04619	207-454-8619	R	8*	<.1
534	Cavanaugh Electrical Contracting Inc—*Joseph Cavanaugh*	PO Box 1511, Wilkes Barre PA 18703	570-826-0389	R	8*	.1
535	Mister Sparky Inc—*Patrick Kennedy*	2064 Canton Rd, Marietta GA 30066	770-422-3400	S	8*	.1
536	Rowan Inc—*Paul Rowan*	2782 Loker Ave W, Carlsbad CA 92010	760-692-0700	R	8*	.1
537	Brush Contractors Inc—*Stephen Brush*	5000 Transamerica Dr, Columbus OH 43228	614-850-8500	R	8*	.1
538	Carter and Crawley Inc	PO Box 5069, Greenville SC 29606	864-288-6250	R	8*	.1
539	Baker Electric Inc—*Britt W Baker* Electro Management Inc	111 Jackson Ave, Des Moines IA 50315	515-288-6774	S	8*	.1
540	Elrod Electrical Service Inc—*Terry Elrod*	3800 Waldenbrook Rd, Greensboro NC 27407	336-852-7776	R	8*	.1
541	Newtron Group Inc—*NB Thomas*	PO Box 46059, Baton Rouge LA 70895	225-927-8921	R	8*	.1
542	Nucero Electrical Construction Company Inc—*Sally Nucero*	7210 Wissinoming St, Philadelphia PA 19135	215-338-9500	R	8*	<.1
543	Fisource Inc—*Charles Womack*	471 E 124th Ave, Thornton CO 80241	303-922-4900	R	8*	.1
544	Polo Electric Corp—*Sam Stathis*	497 Canal St, New York NY 10013	212-627-8220	R	8*	.1
545	Johnny B Electric Inc—*Johnny Davis*	1100 W 1st Ave, Amarillo TX 79106	806-371-7361	R	8*	.1
546	Biven's Electric Inc—*Stephnie Biven*	94-1388 Moaniani St St, Waipahu HI 96797	808-676-5550	R	8*	.1
547	Adirondack Cabling Inc—*John Womer*	10 Petra Ln, Albany NY 12205	518-452-0124	R	8*	<.1
548	American Alarm Company Inc—*Jared Kilgore*	5365 N 99th Ave Ste 12, Glendale AZ 85305	623-536-2522	R	8*	.1
549	Southwest Surveillance Systems Inc—*Scott Bartlett*	6265 S Valley View Blv, Las Vegas NV 89118	702-876-0807	R	8*	.1
550	Forest Dixieland Corp—*William Brown*	PO Box 502, Abita Springs LA 70420	985-892-3210	R	8*	.1
551	Brown Electric Construction Company Inc—*Lonnie Nuttelman*	1309 Watts Ln, Quincy IL 62305	217-222-3483	R	8*	<.1
552	R E W Group Inc—*Ronnie Wright*	9105 Old Marlboro Pke, Upper Marlboro MD 20772	301-599-5500	R	8*	<.1
553	Atlas/Pellizzari Electric Inc—*Steven Pellizzari*	450 Howland St, Redwood City CA 94063	650-364-1204	R	8*	<.1
554	Giles Electric Co—*Bradley Giles*	PO Box 214176, Daytona Beach FL 32121	386-767-5895	R	8*	<.1
555	Electri-Tec Electrical Construction Inc—*John Forseth*	100 David Cir, Arena WI 53503	608-753-2442	R	8*	.1
556	Advanced Electrical Solutions Inc—*Terry Kerchie*	4051 Sw 47th Ave Ste 1, Davie FL 33314	954-327-9212	R	8*	.1
557	Carpenter Electric Inc—*Vance Carpenter*	1333 53rd St, West Palm Beach FL 33407	561-848-7881	R	8*	.1
558	Altel Systems Inc—*Andrew Musci*	601 N Main St, Brewster NY 10509	845-278-4400	R	8*	<.1
559	Gregory Electric Inc—*Rodney Bryant*	3317 N Lincoln Ave, Loveland CO 80538	970-669-7609	R	8*	.1
560	Comtel Systems Technology Inc—*Richard Nielsen*	1294 Hammerwood Ave, Sunnyvale CA 94089	408-543-5600	R	8*	.1
561	Telstar Instruments—*Robert Marston*	1717 Solano Way Ste 34, Concord CA 94520	925-671-2888	R	8*	.1
562	Copper Mountain Electric LLC	2530 W 14200 S, Riverton UT 84065	801-302-8354	R	8*	<.1
563	Hitt Electric Company Inc—*James Hitt*	216 Two Mile Pke, Goodlettsville TN 37072	615-859-3451	R	8*	.1
564	J D Parrella Electric Inc—*Stephen Parrella*	299 Washington St Ste, Newburgh NY 12550	845-562-4112	R	7*	.1
565	Nesko Electric Co—*Thomas Luby*	3111 S 26th Ave, Broadview IL 60155	708 681 6116	R	7*	.1
566	Pomalee Electric Company Inc—*Frank Depaola*	450 7th Ave Ste 1501, New York NY 10123	212-564-6810	R	7*	.1
567	Secur-Com Inc—*Jody Williamson*	3714 Bluestein Dr Ste, Austin TX 78721	512-458-2288	R	7*	.1
568	Star Installations Inc—*Humberto Garced*	3420 State Rte 66, Neptune NJ 07753	732-643-5788	R	7*	.1
569	Mafco Electrical Contractors Inc—*George Brescia*	69 Fishfry St, Hartford CT 06120	860-728-0209	R	7*	<.1
570	Wm H Clinger Corp—*Michael Clinger*	PO Box 158, Concordville PA 19331	610-459-1234	R	7*	.1
571	Agc Electric Inc—*Tomas Curbelo*	2660 W 79th St, Hialeah FL 33016	305-823-2280	R	7*	.1
572	Carl I Schaeffer Electric Co—*Daniel Schaeffer*	4667 Green Park Rd, Saint Louis MO 63123	314-892-7800	R	7*	.1
573	Gessin Electrical Contractor Inc—*David Wasserman*	791 E 139th St, Bronx NY 10454	710-292-0100	R	7*	.1
574	Falcon Communications Inc—*Donald Cook*	1708 N Douglass St, Malden MO 63863	573-276-5169	R	7*	.1
575	Dimensional Communications Inc—*Paul Hagman*	1220 Anderson Rd, Mount Vernon WA 98274	360-424-6164	R	7*	.1
576	Elliott Electric Service Inc—*Thomas Elliott*	PO Box 233, South Boston VA 24592	434-572-2349	R	7*	<.1
577	Corporate Electric Services—*Michael Neswold*	6855 Hanging Moss Rd, Orlando FL 32807	407-677-4080	R	7	.1
578	Cable East Inc—*Robert Wall*	PO Box 1367, Statham GA 30666	678-753-1410	R	7*	.1
579	May-Han Electric Inc—*David Hanson*	1600 Auburn Blvd, Sacramento CA 95815	916-929-0150	R	7*	.1
580	Universal Electrical Service Inc—*Ronald Bilger*	255 Schoolhouse Rd Ste, Souderton PA 18964	215-721-7400	R	7*	.1
581	Brittashan Enterprises Corp—*Ed Rembish*	7 Park Dr, Franklin NJ 07416	973-827-8001	R	7*	.1
582	Lynco Electric Company Inc—*Raylyn Wilcox*	1520 W Amador Ave, Las Cruces NM 88005	575-523-9066	R	7*	<.1
583	Gm Cable Contractors Inc—*Gil Matherne*	9232 Joor Rd, Baton Rouge LA 70818	225-261-9800	R	7*	.1
584	Rapier Electric Inc—*N Rapier*	4845 Augspurger Rd, Hamilton OH 45011	513-868-9087	R	7*	.1
585	WL Sturm Electric Inc—*William Sturm*	6830 Power Line Dr, Florence KY 41042	859-342-6620	R	7*	.1
586	Mohegan It Group LLC—*Susan Griffin*	620 Nrwich New London, Uncasville CT 06382	860-848-0787	R	7*	<.1
587	DJ Electrical Contractors Inc—*Dennis Kennelly*	217 Fordham St, Bronx NY 10464	718-885-2680	R	7*	.1
588	Wallace Electrical Incorporated Tommy—*R Merryman*	3410 Shannon Park Dr, Fredericksburg VA 22408	540-899-2334	R	7*	.1
589	Bagby Electric Of Virginia Inc—*Dave Tribble*	10491 Lakeridge Pkwy, Ashland VA 23005	804-550-5203	R	7*	.1
590	Ostroff Electrical Contractors Inc—*Kevin Ostroff*	10215 159th Rd, Howard Beach NY 11414	718-323-5200	R	7*	.1
591	Page Electrical Corp—*Kenneth Page*	60 Elm Hill Ave, Leominster MA 01453	978-537-8437	R	7*	.1
592	United Electric Of Wheeling Inc—*Robert Kubovicz*	PO Box 6897, Wheeling WV 26003	304-232-1330	R	7*	.1
593	N J Shaum and Son Incorporated Electrical Contractors— *Frank Patton*	PO Box 819, Flagstaff AZ 86002	928-774-4564	R	7*	<.1
594	Electro-Communications Co—*David Moore*	6815 216th St Sw, Lynnwood WA 98036	425-774-6600	R	7*	<.1
595	RE Yates Electric Inc—*William Yates*	1623 E Poland Rd, New Castle PA 16102	724-667-1100	R	7*	<.1
596	Tel-Communication Inc—*Frank Barrett*	1215 Howard St, Elk Grove Village IL 60007	847-593-8480	R	7*	<.1
597	Jelec USA Inc—*Jean Jacques Paufiques*	103 Row Three, Lafayette LA 70508	337-266-6060	R	7*	<.1
598	Westfield Electric Inc—*Sheri Busdeker*	PO Box 93, Gibsonburg OH 43431	419-862-0078	R	7*	<.1
599	Cummins Electric Inc—*M Cummins*	PO Box 638, Richmond IN 47375	765-962-6332	R	7*	.1
600	Monacacy Valley Electric Inc—*Jay Wantz*	1925 Frederick Pke, Littlestown PA 17340	717-359-9500	R	7*	<.1
601	Crisp Fire Sprinklers Inc—*AW Crisp*	5201 Saunders Rd, Fort Worth TX 76119	817-572-3663	R	7*	<.1
602	Total Security Solutions—*John Richards*	170 National Park Dr, Fowlerville MI 48836	517-223-7807	R	7	<.1
603	Lake Charles Electric Company LLC—*Connie Hoffpauir*	617 Gray St, Westlake LA 70669	337-436-0634	R	7*	.1
604	Midwest Interstate Electrical Construction Co—*Peter Chaput*	1355 W N Ave, Chicago IL 60642	773-342-2600	R	7*	.1
605	Faith Electric Service Inc—*H Blackman*	611 Grassdale Rd Ste A, Cartersville GA 30121	770-386-5418	R	7*	.1
606	Copeland Electric Company Inc—*Lonnie Copeland*	PO Box 4051, Monroe LA 71211	318-322-9865	R	7*	.1
607	A B C Electric Company Inc—*John Whitmer*	PO Box 82466, Lincoln NE 68501	402-435-3514	R	7*	.1
608	Commercial Fire And Communications Inc—*Gregory Wooten*	PO Box 1350, Largo FL 33779	727-530-4521	R	7*	.1
609	Harold R Clune Inc—*Judith Clune*	30 Prospect St, Ballston Spa NY 12020	518-885-6199	R	7*	<.1
610	Olympic Electrical Wiring Corp—*Mikhail Koltunov*	133 50th St, Brooklyn NY 11232	718-768-2262	R	7*	.1
611	Traylor Electric Company Inc—*Laurie Traylor*	4240 W Hillsboro Blvd, Coconut Creek FL 33073	954-421-3300	R	7*	.1
612	T and T G and S Electrical Contractors—*Thomas Tuton*	531 2nd St, Everett MA 02149	617-381-0765	R	7*	.1
613	Allegheny City Electric Inc—*Michael Septak*	1139 Woodland Ave, Pittsburgh PA 15212	412-734-0818	R	7*	.1
614	D W Evans Electric Inc—*Michael Evans*	4200 Old Nc 10, Durham NC 27705	919-383-6020	R	7*	.1
615	Sidney Electric Co—*John Frantz*	840 S Vandemark Rd, Sidney OH 45365	937-498-2357	R	7*	.1
616	Milton Electric Company Inc—*John Borz*	3618 E Lombard St, Baltimore MD 21224	410-276-3420	R	7*	.1
617	Dec Electrical Contractors Inc—*Dorothy Turner*	PO Box 326, Berlin NJ 08009	856-767-6000	R	7*	.1
618	Garner Electric Inc—*Charles Garner*	2920 Se Brookwood Ave, Hillsboro OR 97123	503-226-6445	R	7*	.1

Note: An asterisk (*) indicates an estimated financial figure. The company type code used is as follows: R = Private, P = Public, S = Private Subsidiary, B = Public Subsidiary, D = Division, J = Joint Venture, I = Investment Fund.

COMPANY RANKINGS BY SALES WITHIN 4-DIGIT SIC

Rank	Company Name—Executive Officer	Address, City, State, Zip	Phone	Type	Fin	Empls
619	King Brothers Electric Company Inc—Donald King	1701 Camden Ave, Durham NC 27704	919-682-3489	R	7*	<.1
620	Darr Construction Inc—Wayne Darr	2863 Brotherton Rd, Berlin PA 15530	814-267-3615	R	7*	<.1
621	Bates Electric Inc—William Goldthorp	7901 Hopi Pl, Tampa FL 33634	813-888-7050	R	7*	.1
622	Hoskins Electric Co—Fred Hoskins	414 Thompson Ln, Austin TX 78742	512-385-8831	R	7*	.1
623	Dexter Fortson Associates Inc—Andrew Fortson	910 Ploof Dr, Bessemer AL 35023	205-432-2700	R	7*	.1
624	C and H Electric Inc—Robert Cordeau	1999 S Main St, Waterbury CT 06706	203-754-3231	R	7*	.1
625	Hawkins Electric Service Inc—Eric Shatzer	12126 Conway Rd, Beltsville MD 20705	301-210-0900	R	7*	.1
626	Phone Masters Ltd—Barb Davis	523 N Old Saint Louis, Wood River IL 62095	618-254-7330	R	7*	<.1
627	Electrical Dynamics Inc—Gregory Schick	11900 Livingston Rd St, Manassas VA 20109	703-455-3561	R	7*	<.1
628	Whitney Electric Co—Craig Whitney	PO Box 1596, Colorado Springs CO 80901	719-260-0266	R	7*	<.1
629	B and B Designed Systems Inc—Brian Miller	21334 Croghan Pke Ste, Orbisonia PA 17243	814-259-3991	R	7*	.1
630	South Side Electric Inc—David Wintheiser	9201 E Bloomington Fwy, Bloomington MN 55420	952-888-5500	R	7*	.1
631	Cantu Electric Company Inc—Amparo Cantu	PO Box 3166, Laredo TX 78044	956-723-3062	R	7*	.1
632	H and H Utility Contractors Inc—Gordon Heath	225 W Franklin Rd, Meridian ID 83642	208-888-6876	R	7*	.1
633	Imperial Electric Inc—Jeffrey Hatch	5005 S Peachtree Rd, Mesquite TX 75180	972-288-7191	R	7*	.1
634	Monroe And Meadows Systems Inc—William Monroe	PO Box 550939, Dallas TX 75355	214-553-6103	R	7*	.1
635	Solar Electric Systems Inc—Peter Borducci	2 Tibbits Ave, White Plains NY 10606	914-793-0805	R	7*	.1
636	SOS Electric Inc—Sandra Scherer	PO Box 1800, Chillicothe OH 45601	740-773-2828	R	7*	.1
637	Treadwell Electric Contractors Inc—Donald Treadwell	5301 Polk St Bldg 9, Houston TX 77023	713-921-9450	R	7*	.1
638	Chrome Electric LLC—William Butcher	PO Box 2804, Titusville FL 32781	321-267-0990	R	7*	.1
639	Accunex Inc—Farid Jadali	20700 Lassen St, Chatsworth CA 91311	818-882-5858	R	7*	.1
640	Tennyson Electric Inc—Michael Tennyson	7275 National Dr Ste A, Livermore CA 94550	925-606-1038	R	7*	.1
641	Power Service Concepts Inc—John Deangelo	599 Albany Ave, Amityville NY 11701	631-841-2300	R	7*	<.1
642	Burner Fire Control Inc—Sam Cruse	PO Box 53482, Lafayette LA 70505	337-237-4547	R	7*	.1
643	Wagner Electric Company Inc—Michael Wagner	PO Box 24373, Louisville KY 40224	502-267-8384	R	7*	.1
644	Cities Electric Inc—Steve Sowieja	3100 225th St W, Farmington MN 55024	651-463-3810	R	7*	.1
645	B and D Electrical Contractors Inc—William Slack	PO Box 150482, Longview TX 75615	903-297-3001	R	7*	.1
646	Acree-Daily Corp—Dan Blend	4501 Hilton Corporate, Columbus OH 43232	614-416-6600	R	7*	.1
647	Bradford Electric Company Inc—Richard Bradford	912 Winchester Rd Ne, Huntsville AL 35811	256-859-3413	R	7*	.1
648	Gregg Electric Co—Frank Dush	3521 N 22nd St, Lincoln NE 68521	402-476-6463	R	7*	.1
649	All Systems Designed Solutions Inc—Gary Venable	3241 N 7th St Trfy, Kansas City KS 66115	913-281-5100	R	7*	<.1
650	Robert Bailey Electric Inc—Robert Bailey	620 Merriman St, Conway AR 72032	501-327-3955	R	7*	<.1
651	Stilian Electric Inc—James Stilian	108 Tenney St, Georgetown MA 01833	978-352-9994	R	7*	<.1
652	R and L Electric Inc—Ron Canion	1826 Barnett Dr, Weatherford TX 76087	817-613-0819	R	7*	.2
653	Stellos Electric Supply Inc—James Stellos	PO Box 409, Nashua NH 03061	603-882-3126	R	6*	.1
654	Courtesy Electric Co—Kevin Curtis	1356 S Jason St, Denver CO 80223	303-778-8180	R	6*	.1
655	RIS Electrical Contractors Inc—Bob Hayes	7330 Sycamr Cayn Blvd, Riverside CA 92508	951-653-2611	R	6*	.1
656	Skeels Electric Co—Clyde Wetsch	PO Box 5009, Bismarck ND 58502	701-223-5440	R	6*	.1
657	Robertson Electric Company Inc—William Robertson	2131 Berkmar Dr, Charlottesville VA 22901	434-973-4348	R	6*	<.1
658	Valley Electrical Contracting Inc—Frank Nurse	2820 Latimer St Ste A, Missoula MT 59808	406-541-4444	R	6*	<.1
659	All-Mode Communications Inc—David Yeater	1725 Dryden Rd, Freeville NY 13068	607-347-4164	R	6*	<.1
660	Sunstrand Electric Company Inc—Eugene Aguirre	1616 Berkley St, Elgin IL 60123	847-742-0266	R	6*	<.1
661	Shelly Electric Company Inc—Bruce Shelly	1126 Callowhill St, Philadelphia PA 19123	215-627-0400	R	6*	.1
662	Oneida Communications Inc—Charles Higgins	5400 Dower House Rd, Upper Marlboro MD 20772	301-772-4000	R	6*	.1
663	Pcs-Phone Inc—Jeffery Hartman	1121 Boyce Rd Ste 1600, Pittsburgh PA 15241	724-942-4844	R	6*	.1
664	Double "r" Electrical Contractors LP—Jennifer Campbell	521 W Walnut St, Garland TX 75040	972-272-5595	R	6*	.1
665	T and M Electric Of Clay County Inc—James Linton	200 College Dr, Orange Park FL 32065	904-272-0272	R	6*	.1
666	Enerlume Energy Management Corp—John Ekregen	2 Broadway, Hamden CT 06518	203-248-4100	P	6	.1
667	Brand Electric Inc—Jeff Brand	6274 E 375 S, Lafayette IN 47905	765-296-3437	R	6*	.1
668	Electric Contractors Inc—William Lawson	442 Browns Cove Rd, Ridgeland SC 29936	843-384-9899	R	6*	.1
669	Midland Electric Co—Timothy Freedman	8003 Vine Crest Ave St, Louisville KY 40222	502-339-7835	R	6*	.1
670	Pinnacle Services Inc—Lori Olander	1337 Industrial Dr, Itasca IL 60143	630-773-8660	R	6*	.1
671	Ault Electric Company Inc—Bernedette Kay	2348 Holgate St, Tacoma WA 98402	253-383-5109	R	6*	<.1
672	E F Belk and Son Inc—Donald Belk	933 Oak Ridge Farm Hwy, Mooresville NC 28115	704-664-5959	R	6*	.1
673	New United Inc—Joseph Incandela	1544 Burgundy Pkwy, Streamwood IL 60107	630-289-1187	R	6*	.1
674	Re-Con Co—Gary Bowker	12 Ne 52nd St, Oklahoma City OK 73105	405-525-8084	R	6*	.1
675	Electric Service Of Clinton Inc—Steven Heysinger	PO Box 1116, Clinton IA 52733	563-242-8231	R	6*	.1
676	Forster Electrical Services Inc—Thomas Forster	PO Box 1021, Columbus IN 47202	812-376-0715	R	6*	.1
677	Hinson Electric Inc—Ronald Hinson	2200 Stafford St Ext, Monroe NC 28110	704-283-1051	R	6*	.1
678	Rume Corp—Matthew Sack	100 Carolyn Blvd, Farmingdale NY 11735	631-694-3709	R	6*	.1
679	Bi-Jamar Inc—James Bryan	PO Box 5501, Stockton CA 95205	209-948-2104	R	6*	<.1
680	Cenpro Services Inc—Andrew Kohler	PO Box 259, Madison IL 62060	618-876-1000	R	6*	<.1
681	STE Electrical Systems Inc—Clarence Tibbs	PO Box 2011, Apopka FL 32704	407-884-7383	R	6*	.1
682	Preston Casteel Electric Company Inc—Darrel Casteel	PO Box 421, Monroe GA 30655	770-921-0499	R	6*	.1
683	Thunderhorse Investments—Christina Antee	1565 W Main St 208-152, Lewisville TX 75067	214-222-3949	R	6*	.1
684	Fuellgraf Electric Co—CHarles L Fuellgraf III	600 S Washington St, Butler PA 16001	724-282-4800	R	6*	.1
685	Instrument Technical Services Inc—David Lannie	8235 Padgett Switch Rd, Irvington AL 36544	251-957-1095	R	6*	.1
686	Corrigan Electric Company Inc—Thomas Corrigan	2621 Holloway Rd, Louisville KY 40299	502-267-4600	R	6*	.1
687	Ideal Electric Inc—Michael Wales	3777 Quentin St Unit 1, Denver CO 80239	303-307-4949	R	6*	.1
688	Louisiana Nesco Ltd—Pam Harrell-Odom	PO Box 146, Baytown TX 77522	281-422-4730	R	6*	.1
689	Universal Security Systems Inc—Theodore Meshover	310 Oser Ave, Hauppauge NY 11788	631-951-0604	R	6*	.1
690	Global Netoptex Inc—Alan Etterman	75 E Santa Clara Ste 8, San Jose CA 95113	408-289-9395	R	6*	.1
691	Nec Service Co—Donald Williamson	PO Box 50362, Midwest City OK 73140	405-237-1311	R	6*	.1
692	Premier Electric Inc—David White	120 E Louisiana St, Evansville IN 47711	812-429-1122	R	6*	.1
693	Vaughan Electric Company Inc—Sam Vaughan	3007 Wake Forest Rd, Durham NC 27703	919-596-1327	R	6*	.1
694	G-C Electric Company Inc—Michael Gross	705 E Rock Rd, Allentown PA 18103	610-797-3500	R	6*	<.1
695	CCC Technologies Inc—Vincent Willas	700 Nicholas Blvd Ste, Elk Grove Village IL 60007	847-427-2330	R	6*	<.1
696	Network Electric Inc—Ben Hansen	2995 S 460 W, Salt Lake City UT 84115	801-972-5600	R	6*	<.1
697	West Star Electrical Contractors Inc—Joan Howard	963 N Burnt Hickory Rd, Douglasville GA 30134	770-949-7800	R	6*	<.1
698	Rodda Electric Inc—Raymond Rodda	2155 Elkins Way Ste D, Brentwood CA 94513	925-240-6024	R	6*	<.1
699	Lenni Electric Corp—Ray Meehan	1020 Andrew Dr, West Chester PA 19380	610-436-9922	R	6*	<.1
700	Miller Electric and Technology Inc—Beth Miller	9010 Brentwood Blvd St, Brentwood CA 94513	925-516-5922	R	6*	<.1
701	Neco LLC	724 Ave F, Bogalusa LA 70427	985-732-4624	R	6*	<.1
702	Bent Electrical Contractors Inc—Thomas Bent	59a Innerbelt Rd, Somerville MA 02143	617-628-0831	R	6*	<.1
703	Fanshawe Inc—John Fanshawe	143 Main St, Nanuet NY 10954	845-627-3232	R	6*	<.1
704	PACE Electrical Construction Inc—Obie Peterson	PO Box 85340, Tucson AZ 85754	520-884-5972	R	6*	<.1
705	Campbell Electric Inc—Judy Campbell	2310 Schramm Rd, Indian River MI 49749	231-238-8014	R	6*	<.1
706	Mid-State Mechanical Inc—Charles Harper	PO Box 607, Bridgeport WV 26330	304-623-3171	R	6*	<.1
707	Orion Integration Group—Greg Chavez	8880 W Barnes St, Boise ID 83709	208-321-8000	R	6*	<.1
708	Maurer Electric Inc—Lawrence Maurer	28 Westland Dr, Bad Axe MI 48413	989-269-8171	R	6*	<.1

Rank	Company Name—*Executive Officer*	Address, City, State, Zip	Phone	Type	Fin	Empls
709	Electro Illumination and Design Inc—*Stanley Durst*	34777 Via Josefina, Rancho Mirage CA 92270	760-770-0061	R	6*	<.1
710	Kenco Enterprises Inc—*Mark Chaput*	3416 1st Ave N, Billings MT 59101	406-245-4946	R	6*	.1
711	King Electric LLC—*Tammy Dye*	PO Box 1367, El Reno OK 73036	405-262-3446	R	6*	.1
712	Secom Group Inc—*David Gagnon*	49 Macomb Pl Ste 1, Mount Clemens MI 48043	586-493-5828	R	6*	.1
713	Izzo Electric and Sons Inc—*Joseph Izzo*	22 Minnesota Ave, Warwick RI 02888	401-921-2403	R	6*	.1
714	Millennium Enterprises Unlimited Inc—*Gary Trotter*	4340 Edgewater Dr, Orlando FL 32804	407-420-2001	R	6*	.1
715	MJ Losito Electrical Contractors Inc—*Michael Losito*	98 Wooster St, Bethel CT 06801	203-790-9225	R	6*	.1
716	Rewald Electric Company Inc—*Robert Ebbers*	1607 S Teut Rd, Burlington WI 53105	262-763-3573	R	6*	.1
717	Cable Utilties Inc—*George Corriveau*	PO Box 396, Sparta NJ 07871	973-726-7301	R	6*	.1
718	C and F Contracting And Rental LLC	PO Box 395, Choudrant LA 71227	318-768-4478	R	6*	.1
719	Progressive Electric Inc—*Ted Brady*	PO Box 3695, Charleston WV 25336	304-345-1253	R	6*	.1
720	Edlen Electrical Exhibition Services Inc—*Leonard Swimmer*	3010 Builders Ave, Las Vegas NV 89101	702-385-6911	R	6*	.1
721	Big John's Electric Company Inc—*Tim Baysden*	1305 Halltown Rd, Jacksonville NC 28546	910-455-2480	R	6*	.1
722	Heard Brothers Electrical Contractors Inc—*Anthony Heard*	PO Box 490205, Lawrenceville GA 30049	770-962-1881	R	6*	.1
723	Kohlhase Electric Inc—*David Kohlhase*	121 Lafayette Rd Unit, North Hampton NH 03862	603-964-7700	R	6*	.1
724	Reed and Thomas Electrical Contractors Inc—*Stephen Reed*	621 Hanover Pke, Hampstead MD 21074	410-239-9680	R	6*	.1
725	Summit Electrical Contractors Inc—*Harold Hurst*	13790 Ranch Rd, Jacksonville FL 32218	904-741-4898	R	6*	<.1
726	G and G Electric Service Company Inc—*Danny Garrett*	3805 Weatherford Hwy, Granbury TX 76049	817-279-7777	R	6*	<.1
727	Cranney Companies Inc—*Brian Cranney*	10 Rainbow Ter, Danvers MA 01923	978-750-6900	R	6*	<.1
728	Sea-Tac Electric Inc—*Thomas Hargreaves*	7056 S 220th St, Kent WA 98032	253-872-5553	R	6*	<.1
729	Myers Electric Of Eastern New Mexico Inc—*Kevin Myers*	3700 N Prince St Ste A, Clovis NM 88101	575-763-5323	R	6*	<.1
730	High-Tech-Tronics Inc—*Marc Bradley*	PO Box 271493, Oklahoma City OK 73137	405-495-0215	R	6*	<.1
731	K and T Electrical Contractors Inc—*Avinash Kagade*	403 County Rd Ste 1, Cliffwood NJ 07721	732-583-1133	R	6*	<.1
732	Empire Electric M and S Inc—*Antonio Hernandez*	1041 Sw 67th Ave, Miami FL 33144	305-264-9982	R	6*	.1
733	Current Electric Co—*Denis Nowak*	440 N Elmwood Rd, Marlton NJ 08053	856-783-6620	R	6*	.1
734	Commcorp Inc—*Harold Boston*	86 Rte 526, Allentown NJ 08501	609-259-5480	R	6*	.1
735	K - W Electric Inc—*Gerry Krebsbach*	N5875 County Rd M, Plymouth WI 53073	920-467-2000	R	6*	.1
736	Sorensen Electric Inc—*Robert Sorensen*	1770 Millard Dr Ste D, Plano TX 75074	972-578-9395	R	6*	.1
737	Superior Electric Service Co—*Jane Fitzsimmons*	36 Germay Dr, Wilmington DE 19804	302-658-5949	R	6*	.1
738	Total Video Products—*Larry Gallner*	414 Southgate Ct, Mickleton NJ 08056	856-423-7400	R	6*	<.1
739	TT and E Enterprises Inc—*Shirley Thomas*	PO Box 188, Lizella GA 31052	478-935-8622	R	6*	<.1
740	Linkmont Technologies Inc—*Sergio Gutierrez*	4b Inverness Ct E Ste, Englewood CO 80112	303-433-2333	R	6*	.1
741	Burriss Electrical Inc—*Christine Burris*	1251 N Lake Dr, Lexington SC 29072	803-957-3350	R	6*	.1
742	Estes Electric Inc—*Gary Estes*	PO Box 5, Waxahachie TX 75168	972-938-8290	R	6*	.1
743	Hegge Electrical Contractors Inc—*James Hegge*	83852 Ave 45, Indio CA 92201	760-776-5560	R	6*	.1
744	Inner City Electrical Contractors Inc—*Sal Anelli*	160 21st St, Brooklyn NY 11232	718-768-7003	R	6*	.1
745	Allstate Energy Inc—*Thomas Willis*	1717 W 3rd St, Tempe AZ 85281	480-967-0220	R	6*	.1
746	Delta Electrical Contractors Of Lansing Inc—*Melissa Austin*	PO Box 80980, Lansing MI 48908	517-322-2177	R	6*	.1
747	Mc Crary Electric Inc—*Roy Mc Crary*	8409 4th St Nw, Los Ranchos NM 87114	505-898-6983	R	6*	.1
748	Shrader Electric Company Inc—*Stephen Shrader*	2824 Loch Raven Rd, Baltimore MD 21218	410-235-5255	R	6*	.1
749	Ace Electric Company Inc—*A Pickles*	PO Box 6721, Richmond VA 23230	804-266-2429	R	6*	<.1
750	Aldon Electric Inc—*Donald Mullaney*	38 Greenwood Ave, Weymouth MA 02189	781-337-0222	R	6*	<.1
751	Grove Gill Electric Co—*Brad Gill*	2410 Webster St, Oakland CA 94612	510-451-2929	R	6*	<.1
752	Jack Moorman Electrical Contractors Inc—*John Bates*	PO Box 1631, Shreveport LA 71165	318-221-8348	R	6*	<.1
753	Prairie Technologies Incorporated Of Minnesota—*Michael Day*	5600 Queens Ave Ne Ste, Elk River MN 55330	763-255-3200	R	6*	<.1
754	Guard Tronic Inc—*David Gilbert*	PO Box 567, Fort Smith AR 72902	479-785-2323	R	6*	.1
755	Meyer Global Security Inc—*Timothy Meyer*	PO Box 1800, Joshua TX 76058	817-426-1199	R	6*	.1
756	Acra Electric Inc—*Robert Greco*	842 SE 46th Ln, Cape Coral FL 33904	239-542-1624	R	6*	.1
757	Consolidated Electrical and Mechanical Inc—*Bruce Hundelt*	1432 Kingsland Ave, Saint Louis MO 63133	314-721-2530	R	6*	.1
758	Demco New York Corp—*Peter Donohoe*	6701 Manlius Ctr Rd St, East Syracuse NY 13057	315-437-7100	R	6*	.1
759	Izzo And Sons—*Joseph Izzo*	PO Box 20498, Cranston RI 02920	401-921-2403	R	6*	.1
760	Pasquariello Electric Corp—*Ken Horton*	PO Box 65, New Haven CT 06513	203-787-1061	R	6*	.1
761	Humphrey Electric Company Inc—*Cleveland Humphrey*	724 Grove Rd, Midlothian VA 23114	804-794-4877	R	6*	<.1
762	Am-Tex Electric Inc—*Jay Langen*	300 S Travis St, Amarillo TX 79106	806-373-8461	R	6*	<.1
763	Indicom Electric Co—*Roy Cracraft*	3402 E Wier Ave, Phoenix AZ 85040	602-276-6343	R	6*	<.1
764	Sound and Signal Systems Of New Mexico Inc—*Albert Jorgensen*	3233 Stanford Dr Ne, Albuquerque NM 87107	505-884-1217	R	6*	<.1
765	Huneke Enterprises LLC	307 S Elm St, Waxahachie TX 75165	972-935-0310	R	6*	<.1
766	Jmg Security Systems Inc—*Kenneth Jacobs*	17150 Newhope St Ste 1, Fountain Valley CA 92708	714-545-8882	R	6*	<.1
767	Moore Electric Company Inc—*Johnny Moore*	700 Sprott Dr, Montgomery AL 36117	334-215-7200	R	6*	<.1
768	JM Corporation and Son Inc—*James Corp*	7612 113th St E, Puyallup WA 98373	253-845-6745	R	6*	<.1
769	Amtrak/Lirr JV—*National Corporation*	400 W 31st St, New York NY 10001	212-630-7745	R	5*	.1
770	Armstrong Electric Company Inc—*Wayne Proffitt*	PO Box 10444, Lynchburg VA 24506	434-528-4066	R	5*	.1
771	Hensel Electric Co—*Alan Hensel*	PO Box 8438, Waco TX 76714	254-776-3411	R	5*	.1
772	M and M Electric Inc—*Steven Wadsworth*	3655 W Dewey Dr, Las Vegas NV 89118	702-798-1077	R	5*	.1
773	Progressive Services Inc—*Michael Hirst*	300 Commercial Dr, Wilmington DE 19805	302-658-7260	R	5*	.1
774	Kidron Electric Inc—*Arthur Neuenschwander*	PO Box 248, Kidron OH 44636	330-857-2871	R	5*	<.1
775	Sabino Electric Inc—*Douglas Jones*	945 W 29th St, Tucson AZ 85713	520-623-6061	R	5*	<.1
776	California Retrofit Inc—*Richard Mitten*	1375 N Brasher St, Anaheim CA 92807	714-779-1156	R	5*	<.1
777	Columbia Electric Inc—*Joann Scruggs*	1980 Davis St, San Leandro CA 94577	510-430-9505	R	5*	<.1
778	ME C Inc—*Clinton Staggers*	221 Mcrand Ct Ste 100, Hagerstown MD 21740	301-293-1000	R	5*	<.1
779	WA Chester LLC	3400 Benning Rd Ne, Washington DC 20019	202-398-1630	R	5*	.1
780	Imagen USA Inc—*Jaime Zabala*	2409 J And C Blvd, Naples FL 34109	239-594-7722	R	5*	.1
781	Capitol Valley Electric Inc—*David Reis*	8550 Thys Ct, Sacramento CA 95828	916-686-3244	R	5*	<.1
782	Aatronics Inc—*Paul Orlovich*	10 N Liberty St Ste 12, Boise ID 83704	208-343-0900	R	5*	<.1
783	Low Voltage Wiring Ltd—*John Borchert*	1540 Quail Lake Loop, Colorado Springs CO 80906	719-540-8900	R	5*	<.1
784	Applied Communications Group Inc—*Mike Meilahn*	345 W Irving Park Rd, Roselle IL 60172	630-529-1020	R	5*	<.1
785	Ahlstrom-Schaeffer Electric Corp—*John Dale*	46 Hopkins Ave, Jamestown NY 14701	716-665-6510	R	5*	<.1
786	Detention Electronic Consultants Inc—*Edward Weiss*	1981 Whitesville Rd, Toms River NJ 08755	732-244-7327	R	5*	<.1
787	Win-Sam Inc—*James Samis*	1300 S University Dr S, Fort Worth TX 76107	817-370-0009	R	5*	.1
788	Md Electric Co—*Jim Dobson*	PO Box 9, Shelbyville KY 40066	502-633-9034	R	5*	.1
789	Ops Plus Inc—*Bridgette Pregliasco*	4530 Bishop Ln Ste 109, Louisville KY 40218	502-454-9767	R	5*	.1
790	Tc Electric Company Inc—*Thomas Curley*	6701 Governor Printz B, Wilmington DE 19809	302-791-9100	R	5*	<.1
791	Deberry Electric Company Inc—*David Deberry*	PO Box 26037, Jacksonville FL 32226	904-757-8424	R	5*	<.1
792	Mid-South Electric Contractors Inc—*Wesley Wells*	3951 Homewood Rd, Memphis TN 38118	901-365-1818	R	5*	<.1
793	Stilsing Electric Inc—*Kathleen Stilsing*	PO Box 27, Rensselaer NY 12144	518-463-4451	R	5*	<.1
794	Gbm Managment Group LP—*Gary Menzies*	PO Box 1554, Azle TX 76098	817-444-5371	R	5*	<.1
795	Harper Electric Construction Company Inc—*Johnny Harper*	PO Box 698, Andalusia AL 36420	334-222-7022	R	5*	<.1
796	Hei Inc—*Will Humbard*	PO Box 31310, Albuquerque NM 87190	505-880-1819	R	5*	<.1
797	Dks Enterprises Inc—*Trever Crick*	250 N Main St, Brighton CO 80601	720-685-0041	R	5*	<.1

Note: An asterisk (*) indicates an estimated financial figure. The company type code used is as follows: R = Private, P = Public, S = Private Subsidiary, B = Public Subsidiary, D = Division, J = Joint Venture, I = Investment Fund.

COMPANY RANKINGS BY SALES WITHIN 4-DIGIT SIC

Rank	Company Name—Executive Officer	Address, City, State, Zip	Phone	Type	Fin	Empls
798	Truckee Meadows Electric Inc—Scott Peterson	4607 Aircenter Cir Ste, Reno NV 89502	775-825-2414	R	5*	<.1
799	Integrity Electric Inc—Darren Bogan	3498 Hwy 20 Ste 1, Decatur AL 35601	256-560-0775	R	5*	.1
800	Jade Communications Inc—Serge Leblanc	6610 E Rogers Cir, Boca Raton FL 33487	561-997-8552	R	5*	.1
801	Long Electric Co—Fred Armbruster	PO Box 5391, Abilene TX 79608	325-672-2112	R	5*	.1
802	Electricity and Lighting Inc—Philip Mash	PO Box 530991, Birmingham AL 35253	205-879-2997	R	5*	<.1
803	Infinite Energy Construction Inc—Nilson Goes	13625 Oak St, Kansas City MO 64145	816-763-7471	R	5*	<.1
804	Data Electric Corp—Lawrence Simon	205 W Blueridge Ave, Orange CA 92865	714-282-1717	R	5*	<.1
805	Oliveira-Lucas Enterprises Inc—Frank Lucas	PO Box 766, Turlock CA 95381	209-667-2851	R	5*	<.1
806	Weydman Electric Inc—Lisa Hobba	747 Young St, Tonawanda NY 14150	716-692-7667	R	5*	<.1
807	Esc Automation Inc—John Tiesi	22121 17th Ave Se Ste, Bothell WA 98021	425-487-8613	R	5*	<.1
808	Pirkle Electric Company Inc—Willis Pirkle	PO Box 310685, Atlanta GA 31131	404-346-7733	R	5*	<.1
809	Ellsworth Electric Of PA Inc—John Barr	131 Sunset Blvd W, Chambersburg PA 17202	717-264-2888	R	5*	<.1
810	Piedmont Telecommunications Inc—Robert Newell	976 E Governor Rd, Hershey PA 17033	717-534-8560	R	5*	.2
811	Fowler Electrical Contractors Inc—H Mc Leod Fowler	PO Box 901, Southern Pines NC 28388	910-692-7288	R	5*	.1
812	J Frank Blakely Co—Danny Phillips	371 E Kennedy St, Spartanburg SC 29302	864-583-7215	R	5*	.1
813	Cablecom LLC—Teri Severinsen	3701 W Burnham St Ste, Milwaukee WI 53215	414-226-2205	R	5*	.1
814	Anmar Electrical Contractor—Mark Rusden	2570 W Maple Ave, Feasterville Trevose PA 19053	215-702-8393	R	5*	.1
815	D'andrea Enterprises—Robert D'andrea	8100 Ulmerton Rd Ste 1, Largo FL 33771	727-536-3535	R	5*	.1
816	Aulds and Garner Tele-Com Services Inc—Ralph Aulds	PO Box 750668, Houston TX 77275	281-484-2900	R	5*	<.1
817	Arens Electric Inc—Steve Arens	4735 S Santa Fe Cir, Englewood CO 80110	303-761-1289	R	5*	<.1
818	Teledynamics Communications Service Corp—Robert Pullman	330 7th Ave Fl 21, New York NY 10001	212-594-7333	R	5*	<.1
819	Trans Electric Inc—Oscar Baker	2700 Diode Ln, Louisville KY 40299	502-266-6669	R	5*	<.1
820	Arose Inc—Kemp Cook	PO Box 27, Westville NJ 08093	856-931-2045	R	5*	<.1
821	Crescent Engineering Company Inc—Clarence Broze	PO Box 36, La Marque TX 77568	409-935-2416	R	5*	<.1
822	Electronic Security Corporation Of America—Gregory Torre	254 Fairview Rd, Woodlyn PA 19094	610-544-9555	R	5*	<.1
823	Hawkins Service Co—Troy Hawkins	9260 Bay Plz Blvd Ste, Tampa FL 33619	813-849-2411	R	5*	<.1
824	Holt Electrical Contractors Inc—J Holt	7620 Rickenbacker Dr G, Gaithersburg MD 20879	301-294-8899	R	5*	<.1
825	Telecom Networking Systems Inc—Michael Kokoletsos	26250 Industrial Blvd, Hayward CA 94545	510-723-0062	R	5*	<.1
826	Precision Electric Contractors LLC—Jack Schmidt	PO Box 816, Medford OR 97501	541-773-6279	R	5*	<.1
827	Core Communication Inc—Nicholas Rozzi	PO Box 7269, Redwood City CA 94063	650-968-9300	R	5*	<.1
828	Farnham Electric Co—Waldo Farnham	1050 Ne Lafayette Ave, Mcminnville OR 97128	503-472-2186	R	5*	<.1
829	Putnam Electrical Contractors LLC—Jasmine Putnam	423 Carolina Rd, Aberdeen NC 28315	910-944-1625	R	5*	<.1
830	Taunt Electric Company Inc—Craig Taunt	PO Box 153, Gladwin MI 48624	989-426-9306	R	5*	<.1
831	ARC Electric Construction Company Inc—Wiliam Callahan	739 2nd Ave, New York NY 10016	212-573-9600	R	5*	<.1
832	Atlantic Power and Light Company Inc—Mark Donovan	17 Dickens St, Dorchester MA 02122	617-436-2758	R	5*	<.1
833	Santa Maria Electric Inc—Steve Mussell	408 N Broadway, Santa Maria CA 93454	805-922-7777	R	5*	<.1
834	Snowden Electric Company Inc—Fred Snowden	6820 Orangethorpe Ave, Buena Park CA 90620	714-522-1690	R	5*	<.1
835	Garrett Electric Company Inc—Nick Naccarato	284 Wellsian Way, Richland WA 99352	509-946-5656	R	5*	<.1
836	L and L Electrical Inc—Thomas Manders	2688 Brickton N Dr, Buford GA 30518	678-482-9014	R	5*	<.1
837	El Paso ARC Electric Inc—Cano Ortiz	PO Box 370087, El Paso TX 79937	915-593-3700	R	5*	<.1
838	Palace Electrical Contractors Inc—Gerard Palazzo	3558 Park Ave, Wantagh NY 11793	516-781-3500	R	5*	<.1
839	Robert Colburn Electric Inc—Robert Colburn	PO Box 3667, Eureka CA 95502	707-445-8474	R	5*	<.1
840	Carrol Electric Co—Daniel Stamper	1111 Nw T St, Richmond IN 47374	765-962-6553	R	5*	<.1
841	Intercities Electric Company Inc—Don Buchanan	417 Jetxe St Ste A, Grand Prairie TX 75051	972-647-0109	R	5*	<.1
842	Industrial Electrical Systems Inc—Steven Taylor	PO Box 6296, Lafayette IN 47903	765-449-9418	R	5*	<.1
843	Emblaze Vcon Inc—Ran Sharon	2 University Plz Ste 2, Hackensack NJ 07601	201-883-1220	R	5*	<.1
844	Deployment Solutions LLC—Martin Keith	332 Bandini Pl, Vista CA 92083	317-281-9682	R	5*	.1
845	Hubbell Electric Products Inc—Kevin Brenson	16750 Vincennes Ave St, South Holland IL 60473	708-339-1713	R	5*	.1
846	Commercial Energy Systems Inc—William Staffieri	PO Box 697, Frederick MD 21705	301-371-7000	R	5*	<.1
847	Chatfield Electric Inc—Martin Tomic	3217 Doolittle Dr, Northbrook IL 60062	847-509-1660	R	5*	<.1
848	Rosset Electric Co—Sherwin Rosset	1754 N Paulina St, Chicago IL 60622	773-486-6210	R	5*	<.1
849	Pick Electric Inc—Patrick Priddy	PO Box 6770, Spokane WA 99217	509-532-1975	R	5*	<.1
850	Stutts Corporation Inc—James Stutts	PO Box 7188, Huntsville AL 35807	256-536-8726	R	5*	<.1
851	Marcanti Electric Inc—John Marcanti	PO Box 3130, Globe AZ 85502	928-425-0269	R	5*	<.1
852	Begley Enterprises Inc—Dennis Dragotta	19904 Pollyanna Dr, Livonia MI 48152	248-474-6059	R	5*	.1
853	Center Line Technologies Inc—Clyde Jones	26560 Liberal, Center Line MI 48015	586-754-0309	R	5*	.1
854	Abc Electric Service Inc—Joseph Abraham	210 5th St, Fort Myers FL 33907	239-936-3355	R	5*	.1
855	Horizon Services Corp—Frank Davis	PO Box 380972, Birmingham AL 35238	205-988-9553	R	5*	.1
856	Alexander Electric Inc—Gary Alexander	1602 E Denman Ave, Lufkin TX 75901	936-637-3762	R	5*	<.1
857	Marshall's Electric Inc—Stanley Marshall	3621 E 66th Ave, Anchorage AK 99507	907-349-3516	R	5*	<.1
858	Maverick Communications Inc—Ben Blackmon	PO Box 2233, Beaumont TX 77704	409-840-5223	R	5*	<.1
859	Performance Imaging LLC—Ken Bluma	550 W Ave Ste 2, Stamford CT 06902	203-504-5200	R	5*	<.1
860	Quantum Controls Inc—Richard Lebrun	802 Interchange Blvd, Newark DE 19711	302-737-7042	R	5*	<.1
861	Trojan Electric Inc—Manuel Gonzales	2515 Miller Ln, Pantego TX 76013	817-467-1137	R	5*	<.1
862	Whf Electrical Contractors Inc—James Hilborn	2903 Capital St, Wylie TX 75098	972-442-5738	R	5*	<.1
863	Craftsman Electric Inc—Kathleen Fischer	3855 Alta Ave Ste 1, Cincinnati OH 45236	513-891-4426	R	5*	<.1
864	Hawk Electric Inc—Russell Mellor	PO Box 540150, North Salt Lake UT 84054	801-397-1020	R	5*	<.1
865	Compasstools Inc—Steve Chiles	12353 E Ester Ave Ste, Centennial CO 80112	303-627-1810	R	5*	<.1
866	Masters Electrical Contractors Association—Joe Ryan	8242 N Dixie Dr, Dayton OH 45414	937-264-0418	R	5*	.1
867	Southland Electrical Company Inc—Michael Mccain	5640 Clifford Cir Ste, Birmingham AL 35210	205-833-5400	R	5*	.1
868	Tekmate LLC—Bill Mclean	3003 Minnesota Dr Ste, Anchorage AK 99503	907-561-6283	R	5*	.1
869	Coastal Electric Inc—Dennis Palmer	3660 S Scotts Blvd, Columbia MO 65203	573-875-2200	R	5*	.1
870	Enterprise Electrical Contracting Inc—Jame Bill	9401 NW 106th St Ste 1, Miami FL 33178	305-884-6540	R	5*	.1
871	Essential Energy Services Inc—Nat Harrison	113 State Ave Ste 103, Clayton NC 27520	919-550-7675	R	5*	.1
872	General Electrical Services Of Texas Inc—Jerry Huckabay	PO Box 31029, Amarillo TX 79120	806-622-8430	R	5*	.1
873	Shoals Electric Company Inc—Adrian Yarbrough	PO Box 2448, Muscle Shoals AL 35662	256-381-4146	R	5*	<.1
874	Master Technology Group Inc—Ryan Blundell	8555 W 123rd St, Savage MN 55378	952-960-1212	R	5*	<.1
875	Fleenor Security Systems Inc—Norman Fleenor	PO Box 3903, Johnson City TN 37602	423-282-3755	R	5*	<.1
876	Advanced Electrical Services Inc—Johnathan Mason	9527 51st Ave, College Park MD 20740	301-220-3400	R	5*	<.1
877	Bonded Electric Construction Inc—Ronald Jay	4284 Sawtelle Blvd, Los Angeles CA 90066	310-636-1060	R	5*	<.1
878	Johnson Group Inc—Aubrey Johnson	3600 Chamberlain Ln St, Louisville KY 40241	502-412-6343	R	5*	<.1
879	Allstate Electric Inc—David Longstreet	1961 Pine Ridge Dr Sw, Jenison MI 49428	616-669-2520	R	5*	<.1
880	Collett Electric Inc—Steve Collett	4790 Quality Ct, Las Vegas NV 89103	702-871-1963	R	5*	<.1
881	Four C Construction Inc—Daniel Curling	1745 W Rd, Chesapeake VA 23323	757-421-2057	R	5*	<.1
882	Homeland Solutions Inc—Frank Gomez	15942 Los Serranos, Chino Hills CA 91709	760-431-5255	R	5*	<.1
883	Mcclendon Electrical Services—Mike Mcclendon	1506 Ferguson Ln, Austin TX 78754	512-833-7330	R	5*	<.1
884	Morris Heating and Cooling Inc—Lewis Morris	1467 Production Dr, Burlington KY 41005	859-282-8300	R	5*	<.1
885	Fall River Electrical Associates Inc—Dana Johnston	PO Box 1248, Fall River MA 02722	508-675-0523	R	5*	<.1
886	Lea Albert Electric Co—Mitchell Delgar	1410 Olsen Dr, Albert Lea MN 56007	507-373-6650	R	5*	<.1
887	Portland Electrical Construction Inc—Mike Donohue	PO Box 460, Oregon City OR 97045	503-655-2281	R	5*	<.1

Rank	Company Name—*Executive Officer*	Address, City, State, Zip	Phone	Type	Fin	Empls
888	Mcdaniel Electric Corp—*Bryan Mcdaniel*	63 Via Pico Plz Ste 14, San Clemente CA 92672	949-369-8678	R	5*	<.1
889	Electric Supply Company Inc—*Wilfred Gooding*	3225 Pacific St, North Charleston SC 29418	843-740-1710	R	5*	.1
890	Access Data Network Solutions Inc—*John Castellaw*	4077 Viscount Ave, Memphis TN 38118	901-365-1571	R	5*	<.1
891	Colony Electric Company Inc—*Joseph Provato*	178 Industrial Loop St, Staten Island NY 10309	718-948-1313	R	5*	<.1
892	Walker Electric Company Inc—*Michael Walker*	4511 Kentucky Ave, Nashville TN 37209	615-292-4336	R	5*	<.1
893	Graves Inc—*Gary Graves*	312 W 17th Ave, Hutchinson KS 67501	316-669-1282	R	5*	<.1
894	A and J Electric Company Inc—*Joseph Fellner*	9623 Philadelphia Rd F, Baltimore MD 21237	410-687-5151	R	5*	<.1
895	Aurora Electric Inc—*Veronica Rose*	JFK International Airp, Jamaica NY 11430	718-371-0385	R	5	<.1
896	Bayshore Electric Inc—*Mike Whaley*	804 Root St, Daytona Beach FL 32114	386-252-2287	R	5*	<.1
897	Beach Electric Co—*Thomas Canty*	10411 Baur Blvd, Saint Louis MO 63132	314-863-0344	R	5*	<.1
898	James W Knight Electric Inc—*James Knight*	PO Box 5992, Tampa FL 33675	813-248-3877	R	5*	<.1
899	R J Skelding Company Inc—*Robert Skelding*	PO Box 503, Allentown PA 18105	610-437-4036	R	5*	<.1
900	Trio Electrical Contracting Company Inc—*Charles Collum*	PO Box 1475, Pelham AL 35124	205-664-7902	R	5*	<.1
901	Tri-Tech Electric Inc—*Elizabeth Zupancic*	1320 Enterprise Dr Ste, Romeoville IL 60446	630-378-0600	R	5*	<.1
902	Cowart Electric and Industrial Contractors Inc—*Ronald Cowart*	PO Box 2345, Valdosta GA 31604	229-241-1685	R	5*	<.1
903	Electro Acoustics and Video Inc—*Chris Jordan*	2905 Suffolk Dr Ste 20, Fort Worth TX 76133	817-924-2756	R	5*	<.1
904	WEC Electric Inc—*William Coleman*	21516 Palm Ave, Grand Terrace CA 92313	909-825-8535	R	5*	<.1
905	Arizona Traffic Signal Inc—*Mark Mahl*	7150 W Roosevelt St, Phoenix AZ 85043	602-943-3040	R	5*	<.1
906	Hlk Construction Inc—*Donna Kath*	PO Box 1169, Loomis CA 95650	916-652-9632	R	5*	.1
907	Kulak Electric Inc—*Gerald Kulak*	4202 E Elwood St Ste 3, Phoenix AZ 85040	602-438-8808	R	5*	.1
908	Proton Electric LLC—*Tammy O'connor*	510 Whitney Ave Ste A8, Lantana FL 33462	561-547-0027	R	5*	.1
909	Smith Brothers Electric Inc—*Mitchael Slagle*	18445 Weaver St, Detroit MI 48228	313-837-1234	R	5*	.1
910	Total Electric Contracting Inc—*Joe Wright*	12830 Metro Pkwy Ste 9, Fort Myers FL 33966	239-278-0002	R	5*	.1
911	JRD Electric Company Inc—*Joseph Duggan*	1051 Van Buren Ave, Franklin Square NY 11010	516-352-1140	R	5*	.1
912	Wilco Electrical LLC—*Kimberly Nemic*	3651 NW 79th Ave, Miami FL 33166	305-248-9911	R	5*	.1
913	LJ Construction Inc—*Lloyd Jones*	PO Box 6129, Kinston NC 28501	252-520-7592	R	5*	<.1
914	Cook Industrial Electric Company Inc—*Joseph Cook*	PO Box 839, Cordele GA 31010	229-273-1516	R	5*	<.1
915	Firecraft Of New York Inc—*Donald Oellerich*	51 N Prospect Ave, Lynbrook NY 11563	516-256-2700	R	5*	<.1
916	Smc Electrical Corp—*Fred March*	185 Lively Blvd, Elk Grove Village IL 60007	847-290-8500	R	5*	<.1
917	Delta Electric Company Inc—*Robert Baggaley*	3261 Fitzgerald Rd, Rancho Cordova CA 95742	916-638-1772	R	5*	<.1
918	Barry Communications Inc—*Barry Gerhardt*	146 W Boylston Dr, Worcester MA 01606	508-853-7110	R	5*	<.1
919	Kale Companies Inc—*Thomas Kale*	122 River Dr, Moline IL 61265	309-797-9290	R	5*	<.1
920	Wyoming Electric Inc—*Dave Nelson*	125 N Sheridan Ave, Sheridan WY 82801	307-674-6846	R	5*	<.1
921	Andy Klein Electrical Contracting Inc—*Andrew Klein*	1501 Truman St Ste C, San Fernando CA 91340	818-365-1478	R	5*	<.1
922	Oliver Electric Construction Inc—*Robert Oliver*	PO Box 3529, Lawrence KS 66046	785-748-0777	R	5*	<.1
923	Amt Systems Inc—*Glen Glancy*	26810 Oak Ave Ste A, Santa Clarita CA 91351	661-251-4206	R	5*	<.1
924	Nordick Electric and Sheet Metal Inc—*Rod Nordick*	1310 4th Ave S, Wahpeton ND 58075	701-642-5550	R	5*	<.1
925	Mulrooney and Sporer Inc—*Joseph Mulrooney*	103 Birch Dr, Roaring Brook Township PA 18444	570-342-9254	R	5*	<.1
926	Vetter Electric Inc—*Ray Vetter*	PO Box 41645, Nashville TN 37204	615-391-0354	R	5*	<.1
927	Wang Electric Inc—*Nils Wang*	4107 E Winslow Ave Ste, Phoenix AZ 85040	602-324-5350	R	4*	.1
928	Heights Electric Services Inc—*Joseph Hebert*	PO Box 70021, Houston TX 77270	281-850-5100	R	4*	.1
929	RMT Electric Corp—*Richard Spenelli*	23819 Braddock Ave, Bellerose NY 11426	718-347-4517	R	4*	.1
930	West Side Electric Company Inc—*Karl Jensen*	1834 Se 8th Ave, Portland OR 97214	503-231-1548	R	4*	<.1
931	B D B Inc—*Blake Barregar*	11743 Cardinal Cir, Garden Grove CA 92843	714-530-8150	R	4*	<.1
932	Aladdin Electric Inc—*Barry Duff*	PO Box 600, Manitou KY 42436	270-821-1463	R	4*	<.1
933	AM La Salle Electric Inc—*Gary Salle*	PO Box 2859, Cathedral City CA 92235	760-328-1088	R	4*	<.1
934	Arcom Systems Inc—*David Watson*	5200 Northshore Ln, North Little Rock AR 72118	501-753-3667	R	4*	<.1
935	Burtner Electric Inc—*David Burtner*	787 N 10th St, Noblesville IN 46060	317-848-5765	R	4*	<.1
936	Energy Electric Company Inc—*Bruce Dubeau*	740 Quaker Hwy, Uxbridge MA 01569	508-883-6445	R	4*	<.1
937	HP Electrical Designs Inc—*Louis Perri*	321 W 44th St Ste 405, New York NY 10036	212-581-3400	R	4*	<.1
938	KL Bradley Electric Inc—*Keith Bradley*	PO Box 238, Piedmont OK 73078	405-943-2442	R	4*	<.1
939	State Electrical and Motor Service Inc—*Michael Rosenberg*	411 Macopin Rd, West Milford NJ 07480	973-838-4800	R	4*	<.1
940	Lock-Wood Electric Inc—*Jeffrey Lock*	PO Box 2661, Conway AR 72033	501-327-0303	R	4*	<.1
941	Moore J B Electrical Contractor Inc—*Gene Moore*	PO Box 4306, Lynchburg VA 24502	434-239-2686	R	4*	<.1
942	Townsquare Electric Inc—*Emil Szot*	101 State Rte 94, Blairstown NJ 07825	908-362-5100	R	4*	<.1
943	Serban's Background Music Inc—*Brian Richards*	PO Box 9602, Bakersfield CA 93389	661-324-9044	R	4*	<.1
944	A/Coe Electric Corp—*Scott Le Febvre*	695 Littleton Rd, Parsippany NJ 07054	973-334-0045	R	4*	<.1
945	Jorge Vasquez Labor Contractor—*Jorge Vasquez*	8036 Meridian Rd Ne, Silverton OR 97381	503-874-0127	R	4*	.1
946	Ksmeg Cable Marketing And Installation Company Inc—*Mary Gretler*	11444 Rojas Dr Ste C14, El Paso TX 79936	915-591-9877	R	4*	<.1
947	Morlandt Electric Company LLC—*James Morlandt*	9425 Old Crpus Christi, San Antonio TX 78223	210-633-0181	R	4*	<.1
948	Paige Electric Company LLC	18308c Commission Rd, Long Beach MS 39560	228-863-6072	R	4*	<.1
949	Acorn Electrical Specialists Inc—*Nancy Murphy*	PO Box 550, Piney Flats TN 37686	423-928-6969	R	4*	<.1
950	Finesse Electric Inc—*Curt Wagner*	PO Box 6837, Freehold NJ 07728	732-577-9671	R	4*	<.1
951	Wanko Electric Inc—*John Wanko*	7965 Kensington Ct Ste, Brighton MI 48116	248-437-5500	R	4*	<.1
952	Stewart's Electrical Contractors Inc—*Glen Stewart*	40680 State Hwy 59, Bay Minette AL 36507	251-937-6393	R	4*	<.1
953	Automated Controls Inc—*Raymond Douglas*	111 Ne 14th St, Lamesa TX 79331	806-872-8341	R	4*	<.1
954	Signal Service Industries Inc—*Patricia Robbins*	12200 Sw 129th Ct, Miami FL 33186	305-254-7702	R	4*	<.1
955	Welburn Electric Inc—*Gary Welburn*	PO Box 329, Phoenix OR 97535	541-535-3727	R	4*	<.1
956	Donco and Sons Inc—*Donavon Fink*	1410 N Daly St, Anaheim CA 92806	714-254-0099	R	4*	<.1
957	Kyle Electric Inc—*Thomas Kyle*	PO Box 410, North Bend OR 97459	541-756-2723	R	4*	<.1
958	Hicks Electrical Company Inc—*Elmer Hicks*	PO Box 19448, Shreveport LA 71149	318-688-3360	R	4*	<.1
959	I W Macfarlane Corp—*William Anderson*	2115 N Main St, Santa Ana CA 92706	714-543-9265	R	4*	<.1
960	Acpi Systems Inc—*Laura Meyer*	3445 Hamilton New Lond, Hamilton OH 45013	513-738-3840	R	4*	<.1
961	Colorado Custom Electric Inc—*Michael Chapman*	14405 W Colfax Ave 101, Lakewood CO 80401	303-552-0474	R	4*	.1
962	Central Electric LLC	2618 Copper Ridge Cir, Steamboat Springs CO 80487	970-871-9611	R	4*	.1
963	Ralph White Electric Company Inc—*Ralph White*	5776 Reeds Bridge Rd, Ringgold GA 30736	706-861-1083	R	4*	.1
964	Stetson Electric LLC—*Donna Marshall*	21001 N Tatum Blvd Ste, Phoenix AZ 85050	623-434-7751	R	4*	<.1
965	Fiske Inc—*Clifford Fiske*	1023 S Lincoln Ave, Loveland CO 80537	970-667-9569	R	4*	<.1
966	CA D Electric Inc—*Carol Doyle*	2 Thornpath Ln, Rose Valley PA 19063	610-565-8544	R	4*	<.1
967	Ldh Electrical Contractor Inc—*Dennis Heleine*	PO Box 496, Falling Waters WV 25419	304-274-2754	R	4*	<.1
968	Abc Communications Corp—*Andrew Burns*	1776 N Pine Island Rd, Plantation FL 33322	954-321-9000	R	4*	<.1
969	Accord Electric Corp—*Daniel Bala*	17852 Jamestown Ln, Huntington Beach CA 92647	714-841-5180	R	4*	<.1
970	All Industrial Electric Inc—*Michael Pokorny*	432 E State Pkwy Ste 1, Schaumburg IL 60173	847-885-9600	R	4*	<.1
971	Florida Fire And Sound Inc—*Richard O'rourke*	637 Triumph Ct, Orlando FL 32805	407-298-8812	R	4*	<.1
972	Stiegler Company Inc—*Ron Klossner*	PO Box 3644, Green Bay WI 54303	920-494-0224	R	4*	<.1
973	Dean Brothers Inc—*Eddie Dean*	PO Box 625, Harrisonburg VA 22803	540-433-8873	R	4*	<.1
974	Angelica Brothers Electrical Contracting Inc—*John Angelica*	724 Main St, Holyoke MA 01040	413-533-2062	R	4*	<.1
975	Ken Nix and Associates Inc—*Ken Nix*	700 Dividend Dr Ste 10, Peachtree City GA 30269	770-460-0671	R	4*	<.1
976	Superior Electrical Contractors Inc—*Reynaldo Madiedo*	2151 Nw 93rd Ave, Doral FL 33172	305-477-6328	R	4*	.1

Note: An asterisk (*) indicates an estimated financial figure. The company type code used is as follows: R = Private, P = Public, S = Private Subsidiary, B = Public Subsidiary, D = Division, J = Joint Venture, I = Investment Fund.

COMPANY RANKINGS BY SALES WITHIN 4-DIGIT SIC

Rank	Company Name—*Executive Officer*	Address, City, State, Zip	Phone	Type	Fin	Empls
977	Tri-Star Electric Inc—*Robert Kerns*	PO Box 7038, Chesapeake VA 23323	757-485-9511	R	4*	.1
978	Act Electric Co—*Allan Tate*	PO Box 202069, Arlington TX 76006	817-267-0026	R	4*	.1
979	Nrk Inc—*Randy Keyes*	1126 S 13th St, Terre Haute IN 47802	812-232-1800	R	4*	<.1
980	Peachtree Electric Lighting Inc—*David Prevatt*	105 Industrial Way Ste, Fayetteville GA 30215	770-461-5015	R	4*	<.1
981	Alvarez Electric Inc—*Juan Alvarez*	104 S 25th St, Mcallen TX 78501	956-682-0440	R	4*	<.1
982	Mckenzie and Associates Electrical LLC—*Cheryl Moulder*	PO Box 1919, West Monroe LA 71294	318-323-6357	R	4*	<.1
983	Mgh Enterprises Inc—*Ginger Hook*	2540 Cactus Ave, Chico CA 95973	530-894-2537	R	4*	<.1
984	Alpine Electric Corp—*John Findley*	PO Box 1065, Traverse City MI 49685	231-947-3600	R	4*	<.1
985	Fast Electrical Contractors Inc—*George Scalf*	335 Wilhagan Rd, Nashville TN 37217	615-360-2300	R	4*	<.1
986	Krieger Electric Inc—*Robert Krieger*	1115 6th St Sw, Winter Haven FL 33880	863-294-1650	R	4*	<.1
987	Summit Electrical Construction Inc—*Mark Bratton*	3710 Messer Airport Hw, Birmingham AL 35222	205-591-0155	R	4*	<.1
988	Twin City Electric Company Inc—*Robert Ross*	PO Box 4513, Lafayette IN 47903	765-474-1463	R	4*	<.1
989	Tom Watson Inc—*Tom Watson*	1199 Industry Way, El Centro CA 92243	760-352-7776	R	4*	<.1
990	New Way Electric Inc—*Rick Paslay*	PO Box 21503, Eugene OR 97402	541-686-2365	R	4*	<.1
991	Hebbard Electric Inc—*John Hebbard*	2002 Westside Dr, Augusta GA 30907	706-447-4337	R	4*	<.1
992	Native Tele-Data Solutions Inc—*Marilyn Steeber*	4443 N Flowing Wells R, Tucson AZ 85705	520-888-5860	R	4*	<.1
993	Banks Electric Inc—*John Banks*	399 Distribution Pkwy, Collierville TN 38017	901-853-4920	R	4*	.1
994	Driscoll Electric Co—*Joan Driscoll*	980 N Michigan Ave Ste, Chicago IL 60611	312-214-4994	R	4*	.1
995	Fiber Logic Inc—*Doug Leigh*	3601 Canyon Lake Dr, Rapid City SD 57702	605-343-2061	R	4*	.1
996	Global Optics San Antonio LP—*Denise Sanchez*	1235 Safari St, San Antonio TX 78216	210-545-3477	R	4*	.1
997	Heco Inc—*Don Harris*	7151 Gateway Ct, Manassas VA 20109	703-369-1660	R	4*	.1
998	Pylman Power Inc—*Edward Pylman*	1132 Electric Ave, Wayland MI 49348	616-877-0949	R	4*	.1
999	Service Electric Corporation Of Va—*Jean Alexander*	PO Box 14004, Chesapeake VA 23325	757-543-1340	R	4*	.1
1000	Dan Gilbson Electric Company Inc—*Harry Gibson*	PO Box 20, Chula GA 31733	229-386-8583	R	4*	<.1
1001	Wade Electric Company Inc—*Jerry Barrix*	503 Airways Blvd, Jackson TN 38301	731-423-2800	R	4*	<.1
1002	Raven Electric Inc—*Donald Lederhos*	8015 Schoon St, Anchorage AK 99518	907-349-9668	R	4*	<.1
1003	Sadler Electric Inc—*Robert Sadler*	5855 S 77th St, Omaha NE 68127	402-331-3217	R	4*	<.1
1004	Sievers Security Systems Inc—*Michael Sievers*	18210 Saint Clair Ave, Cleveland OH 44110	216-383-1234	R	4*	<.1
1005	Slbs LLC—*Charlie Williams*	1024 Executive Park Av, Baton Rouge LA 70806	225-927-7725	R	4*	<.1
1006	TS Electric Inc—*Scott Shepard*	6220 S 300 W, Salt Lake City UT 84107	801-263-0188	R	4*	<.1
1007	Contrologic Environmental Inc—*Anthony Battista*	PO Box 2809, Atlantic Beach NC 28512	252-726-3204	R	4*	<.1
1008	J Corliss Electric Inc—*John Corliss*	374 Congress St Rear 2, Boston MA 02210	617-423-3939	R	4*	<.1
1009	Aero Electrical Contractors Inc—*George Wolfenbarker*	8020 Dove Pkwy, Canal Winchester OH 43110	614-834-8181	R	4*	<.1
1010	DL Williams Electric Company Inc—*David Williams*	11630 Columbia Park Dr, Jacksonville FL 32258	904-262-8005	R	4*	<.1
1011	KCE Electric Inc—*Kevin Gaston*	8460 Maple Pl Ste 104, Rancho Cucamonga CA 91730	909-483-0769	R	4*	<.1
1012	C and R Electric Inc—*Robert Burns*	899 Airport Park Rd St, Glen Burnie MD 21061	410-760-4224	R	4*	<.1
1013	Cox's Electrical Contracting And Engineering Inc—*Danny Cox*	5918 Hwy 27 S, Dequincy LA 70633	337-786-5764	R	4*	<.1
1014	Greer Electric Company Inc—*Floyd Greer*	2424 Quaker Ave, Lubbock TX 79410	806-797-9977	R	4*	<.1
1015	Hy-Power Electric Co—*Edward Kosteck*	14531 Edison Dr, New Lenox IL 60451	815-462-6680	R	4*	<.1
1016	Joyner Electric Inc—*Cecile Joyner*	PO Box 20029, Tallahassee FL 32316	850-576-1125	R	4*	<.1
1017	Mariano Construction Inc—*Martin Mariano*	PO Box 127, Bloomsburg PA 17815	570-387-0713	R	4*	<.1
1018	Quailiy Electric Of Valdosta Inc—*Frank Wotherington*	PO Box 2705, Valdosta GA 31604	229-244-3560	R	4*	<.1
1019	Skyler Electric Company Inc—*David Ferguson*	12911 Loma Rica Dr, Grass Valley CA 95945	530-273-5100	R	4*	<.1
1020	Alkat Electrical Contractors Inc—*Katherine Mickens*	PO Box 6903, Richmond VA 23230	804-354-0944	R	4*	<.1
1021	Feris Electric Co—*Mitchell Feris*	3909 Broadway Ave, Fort Worth TX 76117	817-831-1288	R	4*	<.1
1022	Beta Electric Inc—*Douglas Tarnopoll*	228 Lackawanna Ave Ste, West Paterson NJ 07424	973-837-1222	R	4*	<.1
1023	Electric Service Group Inc—*Rhodney Honeycutt*	212 2nd St Nw, Hickory NC 28601	828-322-8120	R	4*	<.1
1024	Jordan High Voltage Inc—*Thomas Jordan*	4901 Sw 51st St, Davie FL 33314	954-587-7754	R	4*	<.1
1025	Killen Contractors Inc—*Charles Killen*	PO Box 786, Brandon MS 39043	601-854-6522	R	4*	<.1
1026	Rosher Electric Company Inc—*James Mcarthur*	4670 Halls Mill Rd, Mobile AL 36693	251-666-3510	R	4*	<.1
1027	Streff Electric Inc—*Nicholas Streff*	751 Ctr Point Rd Ne, Cedar Rapids IA 52402	319-363-7033	R	4*	<.1
1028	Becker Electric Company Inc—*William Becker*	820 Gibbon St Ste 300, Alexandria VA 22314	703-683-5888	R	4*	<.1
1029	Inland Electric Inc—*Laurie Benjamin*	360 Se Baseline St, Hillsboro OR 97123	503-681-4700	R	4*	<.1
1030	Hour Electric Company Inc—*Simeon A Hunsdon*	PO Box 325, Fort Edward NY 12828	518-747-4144	R	4*	<.1
1031	SCO Inc—*Randy Opperman*	6789 Fish Lake Rd, North Branch MI 48461	810-245-1676	R	4*	<.1
1032	Tri State Electric Inc—*Wolfgang Poth*	PO Box 22770, Bakersfield CA 93390	661-635-0261	R	4*	<.1
1033	ME Pfahler Construction Inc—*Michael Pfahler*	PO Box 81141, Cleveland OH 44181	440-234-5600	R	4*	<.1
1034	Foley Electric Inc—*John Philpott*	919 Arguello St, Redwood City CA 94063	650-369-2878	R	4*	<.1
1035	Central Electrical Service Corp—*Sean Westervelt*	PO Box 249, Brookfield CT 06804	203-740-8994	R	4*	<.1
1036	Stephenson Electric Co—*Dennis Smith*	PO Box 610841, Port Huron MI 48061	810-987-5777	R	4*	<.1
1037	Sage Telecommunications Corp (Denver Colorado)—*Robert Gudka*	6700 Race St, Denver CO 80229	303-227-0986	R	4*	<.1
1038	Productions Unlimited Inc—*Brian Phillips*	870 Anderson Ridge Rd, Greer SC 29651	864-675-6146	R	4*	<.1
1039	Emergency Power Controls Inc—*Patrick Carolan*	3940 Prospect Ave Ste, Yorba Linda CA 92886	714-777-5993	R	4*	<.1
1040	J and S Electric Inc—*James Wong*	44 Woodland Ave, San Rafael CA 94901	415-454-3620	R	4*	<.1
1041	J Mac Electric Inc—*Gerald Call*	1805 E Haskell Pl, Tulsa OK 74110	918-583-4949	R	4*	<.1
1042	Jador International Corp—*Dorothy Brown-Alfaro*	PO Box 171268, Hialeah FL 33017	786-486-2377	R	4*	<.1
1043	Jrd Electric Corp—*Joseph Duggan*	6711 79th St, Middle Village NY 11379	718-326-1666	R	4*	.1
1044	Costello Electric Company Inc—*Karol Costello*	PO Box 1138, Acworth GA 30101	770-966-1946	R	4*	<.1
1045	Lakewood Electric Company Inc—*John Cord*	4535 S Santa Fe Dr Ste, Englewood CO 80110	303-783-0600	R	4*	<.1
1046	Pennsylvania Networks Inc—*Randy Brooks*	21334 Croghan Pke Ste, Orbisonia PA 17243	814-259-3999	R	4*	<.1
1047	Clyde Electrical and Mechanical Construction Inc—*Claude Guillemette*	PO Box 5931, Kingwood TX 77325	281-359-4625	R	4*	<.1
1048	Lynn Electric Inc—*George Grieb*	PO Box 248, Lawrence KS 66044	785-843-5079	R	4*	<.1
1049	Vallee Electrical Services Inc—*Steve Vallee*	3716 Park Pl, Montrose CA 91020	818-248-9671	R	4*	<.1
1050	Prim Industrial Contractors Inc—*David Prim*	PO Box 507, Bolingbroke GA 31004	478-742-0420	R	4*	<.1
1051	Royal Electric Company Of Central Florida Inc—*Blake Ferguson*	645 Newburyport Ave, Altamonte Springs FL 32701	407-834-2345	R	4*	<.1
1052	Custom Electric Inc—*David Laraia*	52 Main St, Manchester CT 06042	860-643-7110	R	4*	<.1
1053	MPK Enterprises—*Kenneth Powell*	5625 W Washington Blvd, Los Angeles CA 90016	310-836-8076	R	4*	<.1
1054	Parker and Cowing Electric Inc—*Peter Gillis*	19607 Prairie St, Northridge CA 91324	818-772-5030	R	4*	<.1
1055	RCG Technology Systems Of North Carolina Inc—*John Vereen*	PO Box 340, Oak Island NC 28465	910-278-9254	R	4*	<.1
1056	Environmental Controls Corp—*Richard Schweiger*	15860 Upper Bnes Ferry, Lake Oswego OR 97035	503-620-4228	R	4*	<.1
1057	Ibew Local 441—*Chuck Downing*	309 N Rampart St Ste M, Orange CA 92868	714-939-3131	R	4*	<.1
1058	Jin Electric Co—*John Jin*	4468 N Elston Ave, Chicago IL 60630	773-777-9992	R	4*	<.1
1059	Dixie Electric Company Inc—*John Yelverton*	580 Trade Ctr St, Montgomery AL 36108	334-262-2946	R	4*	<.1
1060	Brandenburg Electric Inc—*Richard Pastor*	PO Box 519, Frederick MD 21705	301-662-0144	R	4*	<.1
1061	Extel Communications Corp—*Scot Keifer*	8301 Crest Industrial, Saint Louis MO 63123	314-352-2266	R	4*	<.1
1062	Nelson B Cooney And Sons Inc—*Nelson Cooney*	PO Box 53, Medford NJ 08055	609-654-2292	R	4*	<.1
1063	Nrg Power Inc—*Than Nguyen*	3011 S Shennen St, Santa Ana CA 92704	714-424-6484	R	4*	<.1

Rank	Company Name—*Executive Officer*	Address, City, State, Zip	Phone	Type	Fin	Empls
1064	Van Maanen Electric Inc—*Nathan Maanen*	PO Box 1131, Newton IA 50208	641-791-9473	R	4*	<.1
1065	Crystal Electric Inc—*Garry Kamas*	1270 Rock Creek Cir, Lafayette CO 80026	303-666-0667	R	4*	<.1
1066	Hi-Tech Electric Inc—*Richard Rosenthal*	7006 S Alton Way E-200, Centennial CO 80112	303-796-8800	R	4*	<.1
1067	Open Options Systems Inc—*Janet Dixon*	6480 Chupp Rd Ste C8, Lithonia GA 30058	770-482-7040	R	4*	<.1
1068	S and H Electric Company Inc—*James Heffernan*	1235 E Davis St, Arlington Heights IL 60005	847-255-7300	R	4*	<.1
1069	Blatt and Myers Inc—*Eldon Dieffenbach*	PO Box 345, Myerstown PA 17067	717-866-6468	R	4*	<.1
1070	Dba Electric Inc—*Dennis Laplante*	766 Vertin Ave Ste C, Salinas CA 93901	831-422-8308	R	4*	<.1
1071	Central Electric Company Of Tulsa Inc—*Dan Brown*	PO Box 690236, Tulsa OK 74169	918-437-8423	R	4*	<.1
1072	Duff Electric Corp—*Antonio Cipolla*	1525 Old Louisquisset, Lincoln RI 02865	401-722-2300	R	4*	<.1
1073	James Babcock Inc—*David Babcock*	2925 N Mitthoeffer Pl, Indianapolis IN 46229	317-898-1172	R	4*	<.1
1074	Joe Claud Electric Inc—*Joe Claud*	1428 Ashland City Rd, Clarksville TN 37040	931-648-4391	R	4*	<.1
1075	Leer Electric Inc—*Stephen Leer*	3 Barlo Cir Ste A, Dillsburg PA 17019	717-432-9756	R	4*	<.1
1076	Vintage Electric Inc—*Mike Mcgraw*	2421 Nw 71st Pl, Gainesville FL 32653	352-371-8021	R	4*	<.1
1077	Stokes Electric Of Central Florida Inc—*Charles Stokes*	3711 Nw 27th Ave, Ocala FL 34475	352-351-4605	R	4*	<.1
1078	Robert P Lepley Electrical Contractor—*Robert Lepley*	232 Valley St, Lewistown PA 17044	717-248-1182	R	4*	<.1
1079	C W Fischer Electric Inc—*Charles Fischer*	4057 Ne 5th Ter, Oakland Park FL 33334	954-566-5689	R	4*	<.1
1080	Alpine Electric Inc—*Tom Maestas*	PO Box 1012, Alamosa CO 81101	719-589-9144	R	4*	<.1
1081	Itz Electric Inc—*Charles Itz*	804 E Main St, Fredericksburg TX 78624	830-997-4535	R	4*	<.1
1082	Henry's Electric Inc—*G Scott*	PO Box 384, Lee MA 01238	413-243-0690	R	4*	<.1
1083	National Electrical Co—*Dhanraj Inderdeo*	11775 Airport Park Dr, Orlando FL 32824	407-859-0578	R	4*	<.1
1084	Hovey Electric Inc—*Rita Hovey*	2936 E Venture Dr Ste, Midland MI 48640	989-631-2023	R	4*	.1
1085	Jesses Enterprise Electric—*Jesse Ruiz*	34734 California Rd, Los Fresnos TX 78566	956-350-9919	R	4*	<.1
1086	US First Energy—*Micheal Jarmana*	2203 Commerce St, Dallas TX 75201	214-231-2120	R	4*	.1
1087	Otto Electric Inc—*Jack Otto*	4469 S Mendenhall Rd S, Memphis TN 38141	901-795-8876	R	4*	<.1
1088	United Security Associates Ltd—*Michael Backer*	28 Willett Ave, Port Chester NY 10573	914-937-2600	R	4*	<.1
1089	US Energy Corp—*James Bernard*	1455 Alderman Dr Bldg, Alpharetta GA 30005	770-752-7325	R	4*	<.1
1090	S Randall Electric Inc—*Randy Pomikahl*	PO Box 340059, Austin TX 78734	512-263-7990	R	4*	<.1
1091	Vollmer Electric Company Inc—*F Vollmer*	4702 Dodge St Ste A, San Antonio TX 78217	210-824-6313	R	4*	<.1
1092	Dovetail Construction Company Inc—*Alan Frasz*	16675 Cnaanville Hills, Athens OH 45701	740-592-1800	R	4*	<.1
1093	Erickson Electrical Contractors Inc—*Mary Erickson*	2804 St Johns Blf Ste, Jacksonville FL 32246	904-641-9090	R	4*	<.1
1094	Excel Electric Inc—*Shane Heil*	PO Box 160, Niwot CO 80544	303-530-3333	R	4*	<.1
1095	Intellitec Security Services LLC—*Marty Millan*	2000 Shames Dr, Westbury NY 11590	516-876-2000	R	4*	<.1
1096	Southern Electricom Co—*Dawn Huckeba*	PO Box 1490, Lizella GA 31052	478-935-9432	R	4*	<.1
1097	Stoiber Electric Company Inc—*William Stoiber*	12425 Knoll Rd Stop 9, Elm Grove WI 53122	262-782-2226	R	4*	<.1
1098	Bradley Electric Inc—*Bradley Floyd*	2605 E Adams St, Phoenix AZ 85034	602-273-3838	R	4*	<.1
1099	D and J Quality Electric Inc—*Dennis Hathcock*	PO Box 88283, Colorado Springs CO 80908	719-495-4321	R	4*	<.1
1100	Opperman Electric Company Inc—*Scott Opperman*	1025 W Enon Ave, Fort Worth TX 76140	817-293-3828	R	4*	<.1
1101	Mountain City Electric Inc—*Robert Mc Dade*	PO Box 5319, Chattanooga TN 37406	423-756-6777	R	4*	<.1
1102	Crocker Electrical Company Inc—*Edward Crocker*	115 Sagamore St, Quincy MA 02171	617-773-1030	R	4*	<.1
1103	Elec-Tech Electrical Services Inc—*Larry Page*	PO Box 78129, Nashville TN 37207	615-860-3007	R	4*	<.1
1104	Gamble Electric Inc—*Ronald Gamble*	2934 N Stone Ave Ste 1, Tucson AZ 85705	520-622-3780	R	4*	<.1
1105	Honeycutt Electric Inc—*Brad Honeycutt*	2750 Armstrong Dr, Winston Salem NC 27103	336-768-5887	R	4*	<.1
1106	Jasper Lightning Protection Inc—*Jasper Thompson*	PO Box 422941, Kissimmee FL 34742	407-932-4219	R	4*	<.1
1107	Mathieu Electric Company Inc—*Gerald Mathieu*	1222 Laredo St, Corpus Christi TX 78401	361-884-7702	R	4*	<.1
1108	Specialty Communications And Electronics Inc—*Roderick Roy*	5920 Serena St, Simi Valley CA 93063	805-577-7551	R	4*	<.1
1109	Westmaas Electric Co—*Harvey Westmaas*	2400 Clyde Park Ave Sw, Grand Rapids MI 49509	616-247-1185	R	4*	<.1
1110	Wil-Cal Lighting Management Company Inc—*Kinya Pollard*	1688 Pomona Ave, San Jose CA 95110	408-297-6118	R	4*	<.1
1111	Interconnect Computer Cabling Services Inc—*Philip Tilton*	406 Libbey IndustrialP, East Weymouth MA 02189	781-331-9811	R	4*	<.1
1112	Colvico Inc—*Cory Colvin*	PO Box 2682, Spokane WA 99220	509-536-1875	R	4*	<.1
1113	Ray Electric Co—*Lyle Ray*	PO Box 2511, Amarillo TX 79105	806-374-0041	R	4*	<.1
1114	Belec Electrical Inc—*Roy Belluomini*	7720 Gross Point Rd, Skokie IL 60077	847-967-6111	R	4*	<.1
1115	Union Electric Inc—*James Lawrence*	PO Box 1453, Battle Creek MI 49016	269-962-7583	R	4*	<.1
1116	Terry Spell Mechanical Services Inc—*Terry Spell*	PO Box 310, Autryville NC 28318	910-525-4030	R	4*	<.1
1117	Powerhouse Electrical Services Inc—*Bryan Neil*	13119 Lookout Way, San Antonio TX 78233	210-495-3800	R	4*	.1
1118	Charlie Mann Electric Inc—*Charlie Mann*	811 Charlie Mann Ct, Gambrills MD 21054	301-262-0105	R	4*	<.1
1119	D and M Electrical Services Inc—*Dennis Williams*	307 Mcgowan Dr, Fredericksburg VA 22408	540-898-7507	R	4*	<.1
1120	Telephone Man Inc—*Sam Schetrompf*	302 Industrial Dr, Avondale PA 19311	610-268-0277	R	4*	<.1
1121	Thiel Electric Inc—*David Thiel*	7920 Mccarty Rd, Saginaw MI 48603	989-702-1100	R	4*	<.1
1122	Central State Elootric Inc—*Robert Morrow*	19030 1st St Ne, Lutz FL 33549	813-948-1341	R	4*	<.1
1123	H and L Electric Inc—*Harold Newman*	11130 Legion Dr, Saint George KS 66535	785-494-8989	R	4*	<.1
1124	Easton Enterprises Inc—*Nicholas Luparelli*	3151 Sw 14th Pl Ste 1, Boynton Beach FL 33426	561-375-9404	R	4*	<.1
1125	A and M Electrical Contractors Inc—*Marty Kocurek*	5214 Hillsborough St, Raleigh NC 27606	919-852-3772	R	4*	<.1
1126	Alliance Service and Control Specialists Inc—*Ben Hodder*	4846 S 40th St, Phoenix AZ 85040	602-431-8434	R	4*	<.1
1127	Cochise Electric Inc—*William Hendrix*	21424 N 20th Ave, Phoenix AZ 85027	602-272-6161	R	4*	<.1
1128	Driscoll Light and Power Inc—*Kevin Driscoll*	218 Atlantic Ave, Wells ME 04090	207-646-3538	R	4*	<.1
1129	Great Western Electrical Inc—*Scott Burson*	3310 Girard Blvd Ne, Albuquerque NM 87107	505-881-6525	R	4*	<.1
1130	M and M Harrison Electric Company Inc—*Mark Harrison*	911 N Sumner St, Colfax WA 99111	509-397-2333	R	4*	<.1
1131	Miller Electric Company Of Indiana Inc—*Richard Bellich*	PO Box 10808, Merrillville IN 46411	219-738-1770	R	4*	<.1
1132	National Electric Company Inc—*John Milota*	4115 S 57th St, Omaha NE 68117	402-341-4008	R	4*	<.1
1133	RE Lee Electric Company Inc—*Roy Lee*	PO Box 280, Newington VA 22122	703-550-7500	R	4*	<.1
1134	Turri Inc—*Raymond Turri*	766 Riverside Ave, Torrington CT 06790	860-482-2972	R	4*	<.1
1135	Wilkins Electric Company Inc—*David Wilkins*	2735 Huff Dr, Lawrenceville GA 30044	770-279-8594	R	4*	<.1
1136	Associated Electrical Services LLC—*Russell Breton*	255 S Hickory Blvd, Pleasant Hill IA 50327	515-262-5703	R	4*	<.1
1137	Intelectric Inc—*Mitchell Weiner*	3718 Overland Ave, Los Angeles CA 90034	310-838-5486	R	4*	<.1
1138	Moye Electric Company Inc—*Doyle Moye*	PO Box 4097, Dublin GA 31040	478-275-9054	R	4*	<.1
1139	Caldwell Electrical Contractors Inc—*Joe Caldwell*	2035 Atlas Cir, Gainesville GA 30501	770-531-7890	R	4*	<.1
1140	Steiner Electric Inc—*Richard Steiner*	2323 Sylvan Way, West Bend WI 53095	262-334-5517	R	4*	<.1
1141	Leed Electric Inc—*Joann Sedita*	11907 Front St, Norwalk CA 90650	562-868-5771	R	4*	<.1
1142	Patrick Electric Service Inc—*Bobby Patrick*	1602 S Monroe St, Amarillo TX 79102	806-374-0407	R	4*	.1
1143	JM Walters and Son Inc—*James Walters*	401 Ferry St Ste 101, Metropolis IL 62960	618-524-4934	R	4*	<.1
1144	Alert Security Services By Kiser Group Inc—*Chris Becker*	2179 Lawrenceville Hwy, Lawrenceville GA 30044	770-682-7877	R	4*	<.1
1145	Allstate Electric Company Inc—*Kenneth Harrison*	4322 3rd Ave S, Birmingham AL 35222	205-591-4150	R	4*	<.1
1146	Bill Black Electric Inc—*Rose Black*	PO Box 126, Myra TX 76253	940-736-2227	R	4*	<.1
1147	Morocco Electric Inc—*Paul Morocco*	201 S Pleasant Ave, Somerset PA 15501	814-445-4267	R	4*	<.1
1148	RKS Electric Corp—*Steve Weinstein*	9424 90th St, Ozone Park NY 11416	718-843-5555	R	4*	<.1
1149	Boggs Electric Company Inc—*Michael Boggs*	5303 Buford Jett Ln, Mesquite TX 75180	972-557-5906	R	4*	<.1
1150	Carr Technologies Group Inc—*Pam Atkins*	497 Muller Ln, Newport News VA 23606	757-269-0080	R	4*	<.1
1151	Delcon Inc—*Dean Lewis*	PO Box 1748, Jackson WY 83001	307-733-2240	R	4*	<.1
1152	Electrical Services Ltd—*Randy Howard*	PO Box 2941, Washington NC 27889	252-946-5766	R	4*	<.1
1153	Crist Electrical Contractor Inc—*Philip Crist*	2432 Matthew Talbot Rd, Forest VA 24551	434-525-6249	R	4*	<.1

Note: An asterisk (*) indicates an estimated financial figure. The company type code used is as follows: R = Private, P = Public, S = Private Subsidiary, B = Public Subsidiary, D = Division, J = Joint Venture, I = Investment Fund.

COMPANY RANKINGS BY SALES WITHIN 4-DIGIT SIC

Rank	Company Name—Executive Officer	Address, City, State, Zip	Phone	Type	Fin	Empls
1154	A and H Electrical Services Inc—Charles Himes	PO Box 82981, Tampa FL 33682	813-972-3880	R	4*	<.1
1155	A D Electric Inc—Andrew Deditch	PO Box 1209, Sabattus ME 04280	207-375-6616	R	4*	<.1
1156	Arnett Electric Inc—Michael Arnett	611 Schoolhouse Rd, Lakeland FL 33813	863-644-9702	R	4*	<.1
1157	Baish Electric Company Ltd—Vann Riley	10808 Hillpoint, San Antonio TX 78217	210-599-2259	R	4*	<.1
1158	Bollinger Electric Inc—William Dietrich	514 N Madison St, Allentown PA 18102	610-437-4763	R	4*	<.1
1159	Broken Arrow Electric Company Inc—Steve Kelley	4330 Broadway Blvd Se, Albuquerque NM 87105	505-873-3380	R	4*	<.1
1160	CW Pond Contractors Inc—Patricia Pond	PO Box 1170, Norwalk CT 06856	203-866-1530	R	4*	<.1
1161	Hyde Electric Inc—Kenneth Hyde	1717 E Van Buren St St, Phoenix AZ 85006	602-257-0057	R	4*	<.1
1162	Lewis Electric LLC	98-487 Koauka Loop Apt, Aiea HI 96701	808-927-2482	R	4*	<.1
1163	PR Faulk Electrical Corp—Phillip Faulk	3103 Hal Siler Dr, Sanford NC 27332	919-775-1990	R	4*	<.1
1164	Robert Lloyd Electric Co—Robert Lloyd	PO Box 9055, Wichita Falls TX 76308	940-766-3213	R	4*	<.1
1165	Stalco Inc—Steven Landry	850 Lawrence St, Lowell MA 01852	978-459-9139	R	4*	<.1
1166	Pcs Power and Communications Solutions Inc—Edward Castillo	279 E Helen Rd, Palatine IL 60067	847-358-8900	R	4*	<.1
1167	Contract Electric Co—Shirley Preston	723 6 Mile Rd Nw, Comstock Park MI 49321	616-784-2393	R	4*	<.1
1168	Driscoll Electric Company Inc—Brendan Driscoll	83 Newbern Ave, Medford MA 02155	781-393-9299	R	4*	<.1
1169	Fox Electrical Co—Terry Fox	PO Box 187, Austin MN 55912	507-433-7184	R	4*	<.1
1170	Model Electric Inc—Rodney Kanter	PO Box 98, Norfolk NE 68702	402-371-7111	R	4*	<.1
1171	Bunting Electric Inc—Danny Bunting	PO Box 358, Dardanelle AR 72834	479-229-2479	R	4*	<.1
1172	Balanced Rock Electric Inc—Anna Knutz	268 Victory Ave, Twin Falls ID 83301	208-735-9578	R	4*	<.1
1173	Lauderdale Electric Inc—Roxanna Lauderdale	205 Prairie Lake Rd St, East Dundee IL 60118	847-426-9900	R	4*	<.1
1174	Ervin Electric Inc—Jacqueline Wilson	1846 N 106th E Ave, Tulsa OK 74116	918-832-0808	R	4*	<.1
1175	Media Design Inc—Bill Maxey	2510 Van Buren St, Houston TX 77006	713-520-0023	R	4*	<.1
1176	Accurate Electric NW Inc—Clint Keely	PO Box 30003, Spokane WA 99223	509-921-9473	R	4*	<.1
1177	Elijah Electric—Luis Martinez	PO Box 323, Kelseyville CA 95451	209-577-4636	R	4*	<.1
1178	West Virginia Signal and Light Inc—Charles Mcbrayer	PO Box 134, Kenna WV 25248	304-372-9648	R	4*	<.1
1179	Sentry Watch Inc—Carl Loye	PO Box 10362, Greensboro NC 27404	336-292-6470	R	3*	.1
1180	West Bay Electric Inc—David Wilks	95 Chestnut Rd, North Kingstown RI 02852	401-295-2452	R	3*	.1
1181	Mcgaha Electric Company Inc—Matthew Mcgaha	PO Box 3621, Knoxville TN 37927	865-523-8373	R	3*	<.1
1182	Choice Electric Corp—Bob Grassia	2080 W 60th Ave, Denver CO 80221	303-430-7200	R	3*	<.1
1183	Falcon Electrical Contractors Inc—Jeffrey Shaute	PO Box 282, South Amboy NJ 08879	732-727-0660	R	3*	<.1
1184	RS Electrical Contractors Inc—John Lillie	PO Box 607, Buena NJ 08310	856-697-3310	R	3*	<.1
1185	Sass J and J Electric Inc—James Sass	PO Box 1910, Kingston NY 12402	845-331-8666	R	3*	<.1
1186	Ave Electric Inc—David Bellehumeur	1499 Pomona Rd Ste H, Corona CA 92882	951-279-7407	R	3*	<.1
1187	Rayburn Electric Company Inc—Greg Rayburn	2 Dude St Nw, Rome GA 30165	706-235-8272	R	3*	<.1
1188	Beebe Electric Inc—Steve Beebe	106 Hillside Dr, Lewisville TX 75057	972-436-5652	R	3*	<.1
1189	Kween Industries Inc—Kingsley Wientge	PO Box 382, Lebanon OH 45036	513-932-2293	R	3*	<.1
1190	Adobe Electric Inc—Dennis Newberry	4360 W Tompkins Ave St, Las Vegas NV 89103	702-362-5557	R	3*	<.1
1191	All-Electric Construction and Communication LLC	97 Crestwood Rd, Milford CT 06460	203-882-8160	R	3*	<.1
1192	American Electric Company Inc—Bruce Cordray	7067 Galen Dr W, Avon IN 46123	317-272-9000	R	3*	<.1
1193	Eagle Electric Inc—Kurt Brooks	7000 Commerce Park Dr, Midvale UT 84047	801-255-8089	R	3*	<.1
1194	Harbor Construction Company Inc—Thomas Gibson	PO Box 9145, Hampton VA 23670	757-722-9823	R	3*	<.1
1195	Meridian Electrical Associates Inc—Gary Tuerk	2501 Bristol Rd, Warrington PA 18976	215-918-0277	R	3*	<.1
1196	Mid States Electric Co—Brian Henschen	PO Box 215, Lawton IA 51030	712-202-0977	R	3*	<.1
1197	Tjc Holdings Inc—Terry Chapman	6600 Royal St Ste B, Pleasant Valley MO 64068	816-415-2252	R	3*	<.1
1198	Tom Branighan Inc—Thomas Branighan	PO Box 791188, New Orleans LA 70179	504-486-1233	R	3*	<.1
1199	Ca-Par Electric Inc—William Cain	63396 Old Military Rd, Pearl River LA 70452	504-465-3750	R	3*	<.1
1200	Kilowatt Electric Co—Edward Flack	1700 Nw 22nd Ave, Pompano Beach FL 33069	954-975-8200	R	3*	<.1
1201	Sare Electric Inc—Rick Sare	PO Box 12870, Olympia WA 98508	360-352-2628	R	3*	<.1
1202	Ambient Sound Inc—Tom Barrett	75 New England Way, Warwick RI 02886	401-941-8500	R	3*	<.1
1203	Treehouse Productions Management Inc—David La Porte	812 Charles St, Providence RI 02904	401-751-3121	R	3*	<.1
1204	AJ Kirkwood and Associates Inc—Arch Kirkwood	2115 Mannix Dr, San Antonio TX 78217	210-824-0590	R	3*	<.1
1205	All Coast Communications Inc—Edward Haber	2612 Calliandra Ter, Coconut Creek FL 33063	954-973-3637	R	3*	<.1
1206	H and M Electric Co—Donald Grimes	909 S Highland Ave, Covington VA 24426	540-962-3953	R	3*	<.1
1207	Quality Electric Company Inc—Lewis Fletcher	3033 Holloway St, Durham NC 27703	919-596-8113	R	3*	<.1
1208	Contel Inc—Mike Diamond	2101 Stonington Ave, Hoffman Estates IL 60169	847-839-9700	R	3*	<.1
1209	EWM Electric Inc—Greg Entsminger	718 Fairgate Rd Sw, Marietta GA 30064	770-426-5448	R	3*	<.1
1210	Honda Electric Inc—Jeff Plzak	PO Box 236, Loretto MN 55357	763-498-8433	R	3*	<.1
1211	McGrath Electric Inc—Michael Grath	PO Box 1739, Janesville WI 53547	608-752-0508	R	3*	<.1
1212	Ruder Electric Inc—David Ruder	1075 Lesco Rd, Kankakee IL 60901	815-932-8660	R	3*	<.1
1213	Wft Communications Inc—William Thompson	3699 Industry Ave, Lakewood CA 90712	562-490-2900	R	3*	<.1
1214	Electrical Production Services Inc—Carla Struble	2431 Galpin Ct Ste 140, Chanhassen MN 55317	952-401-1888	R	3*	<.1
1215	Jupiter Electric Inc—Wayne Marshall	126 Main St Ste 5, North Reading MA 01864	978-664-2800	R	3*	<.1
1216	Next Level Data and Telephone Systems Inc—Tomas Garcia	7074 Commerce Cir Ste, Pleasanton CA 94588	925-730-0140	R	3*	<.1
1217	World Security and Electric Inc—Santiago Serrano	7963 Nw 14th St, Doral FL 33126	305-477-9640	R	3*	<.1
1218	Riverside Electric Inc—Paul Gangloff	680 Redna Ter, Cincinnati OH 45215	513-936-0100	R	3*	<.1
1219	Sonak Electrical Contractors—Akin Sonuga	5341 N Sawyer Ave, Chicago IL 60625	773-866-1065	R	3*	<.1
1220	Enerpro Inc—Frank Bourbeau	5780 Thornwood Dr, Goleta CA 93117	805-683-2114	R	3*	<.1
1221	California Associated Power Inc—Michael Cullen	3724 Park Pl, Glendale CA 91201	818-957-8961	R	3*	<.1
1222	Fulton Communications Inc—Benny Treadway	3146 Reps Miller Rd, Norcross GA 30071	770-446-3100	R	3*	<.1
1223	Huntington Security Systems Inc—Scott Mullins	1070 N Batavia St Ste, Orange CA 92867	714-288-0855	R	3*	<.1
1224	Crosstown Electrical and Data Inc—Dave Heermance	5463 Diaz St, Irwindale CA 91706	626-813-6693	R	3*	<.1
1225	Mccarley Electric Inc—Loretta Mccarley	276 Wilbur Ave, Yuba City CA 95991	530-671-0565	R	3*	<.1
1226	Mcdiarmid Controls Inc—Ardell Diarmid	85579 Hwy 99 S, Eugene OR 97405	541-726-1677	R	3*	<.1
1227	Pendleton Creek Farms Construction Inc—Jeff Page	PO Box 1125, Vidalia GA 30475	912-537-6210	R	3*	<.1
1228	Pet Safety Systems Inc—Dick Pattison	PO Box 798, Mercer Island WA 98040	206-232-3068	R	3*	<.1
1229	Rdm Electric Company Inc—Robert Mcdonnell	13867 Redwood Ave, Chino CA 91710	909-591-0990	R	3*	<.1
1230	Telecable Systems Inc—Sidney Mizukami	73-4165 Hulikoa Dr Uni, Kailua Kona HI 96740	808-329-2480	R	3*	<.1
1231	Enterprise Technologies Inc—John Mitchum	4465 Tile Dr, North Charleston SC 29405	843-744-0150	R	3*	<.1
1232	Tri County Electric Co—Henery Trost	960 Eureka Dr, Turlock CA 95380	209-667-8476	R	3*	<.1
1233	Hawkins Electric Company Inc—A Phelps	5400 Berwyn Rd Ste 205, Berwyn Heights MD 20740	301-474-4470	R	3*	<.1
1234	Gulf Atlantic Electrical Constructors Inc—Michael Reny	416 S County Hwy 393 3, Santa Rosa Beach FL 32459	850-622-2225	R	3*	<.1
1235	Unisys Electric Inc—Frances Rubel	19 Irving Pl, Staten Island NY 10304	718-815-0625	R	3*	<.1
1236	Northstar Electric Co—Jon Boone	PO Box 772886, Eagle River AK 99577	907-688-5551	R	3*	<.1
1237	Telecom Enterprises Inc—Sandra Burdette	PO Box 1326, Lagrange GA 30241	706-882-1777	R	3*	<.1
1238	Rush Electric Company Inc—Alan Rush	PO Box 10376, Alexandria VA 22310	703-971-3900	R	3*	<.1
1239	AEC Electrical Contractors Inc—Wayne Alderman	7005 Lloyd Rd W, Jacksonville FL 32220	904-766-6848	R	3*	<.1
1240	B and B Electric Inc—Albert Blaha	1303 Western Ave, Eau Claire WI 54703	715-832-1676	R	3*	<.1
1241	Beltran Electrical Contractor—Alfredo Beltran	860 Kastrin St, El Paso TX 79907	915-599-8777	R	3*	<.1
1242	Cattaneo Electric Co—Sharon Cattaneo	8171 S Lemont Rd, Darien IL 60561	630-910-9400	R	3*	<.1

Rank	Company Name—*Executive Officer*	Address, City, State, Zip	Phone	Type	Fin	Empls
1243	Donovan Electric Inc—*Tim Bilek*	1706 N 102nd Ave, Omaha NE 68114	402-339-8833	R	3*	<.1
1244	Elect General Contractors Inc—*Timothy Covell*	27634 Jackson Rd, Circleville OH 43113	740-420-9248	R	3*	<.1
1245	Gordon and Zoerb Electrical Contractors Inc—*Tony Girone*	420 S Harris Hill Rd, Williamsville NY 14221	716-633-1166	R	3*	<.1
1246	Homeguard Inc—*Arthur Davis*	2325 Black Rock Tpke, Fairfield CT 06825	203-371-0311	R	3*	<.1
1247	Mer-Cal Electric Inc—*Wes Myers*	104 E 13th St, Merced CA 95341	209-383-3442	R	3*	<.1
1248	Nelco Electric Inc—*Bruce Nelson*	PO Box 157, Germantown WI 53022	262-502-9950	R	3*	<.1
1249	Optec Communications Inc—*Thomas Leong*	1134 49th Ave, Long Island City NY 11101	212-727-2313	R	3*	<.1
1250	Tes Electrical Construction Inc—*Wallace Nelson*	5306 Aldrin Ct, Bakersfield CA 93313	661-834-0900	R	3*	<.1
1251	Kenco Electric Inc—*Kenneth Edwards*	PO Box 300, Tobaccoville NC 27050	336-924-0216	R	3*	<.1
1252	Royal Electrical Services Inc—*Royal Trivett*	820 W 2nd St, Pueblo CO 81003	719-546-0442	R	3*	<.1
1253	Parker Electric Co—*Charles Parker*	3916 Sw 29th St, Oklahoma City OK 73119	405-682-1461	R	3*	<.1
1254	American Alarms Inc—*Gerald Gaciobbi*	569 Park Ave 575, Cranston RI 02910	401-781-1000	R	3*	<.1
1255	Brad's Electric Inc—*Brad Phillips*	604 Greenwood Rd, West Columbia SC 29169	803-791-7344	R	3*	<.1
1256	Ec Electric Inc—*Chris Kelleher*	PO Box 464787, Lawrenceville GA 30042	770-822-2006	R	3*	<.1
1257	Harbinger Communications Inc—*Edward Rodrigues*	27 Dunstan St, Newton MA 02465	617-965-1466	R	3*	<.1
1258	All Service Electric Inc—*Donna Gathard*	57 Aberdeen Rd, Smithtown NY 11787	631-265-6800	R	3*	<.1
1259	USA Electrical Construction Contractors Inc—*Rudy Cicco*	630 S Broadway, Pitman NJ 08071	856-582-5251	R	3*	<.1
1260	Electro Design Inc—*Mark Morrison*	1033 Montana St, Orlando FL 32803	407-228-4211	R	3*	<.1
1261	Gab Construction Inc—*George Brilla*	670 Coleman Ave, San Jose CA 95110	408-280-0900	R	3*	<.1
1262	Integrated Communications Services Inc—*Michael Smith*	6216 Angus Dr Ste B, Raleigh NC 27617	919-781-9916	R	3*	.1
1263	Powertec Inc—*Frank Patterson*	1708 Mactavish Ave, Richmond VA 23230	804-359-3600	R	3*	.1
1264	Delta Electric Services Inc—*Neal De Marcus*	136 Hickory St, Madison TN 37115	615-865-2198	R	3*	<.1
1265	Southern Installations Inc—*Ernest Frost*	PO Box 865, Lexington SC 29071	803-359-5151	R	3*	<.1
1266	Cameron Electric Inc—*Richard Beckom*	4771 N Franklin Rd Ste, Indianapolis IN 46226	317-547-5474	R	3*	<.1
1267	Haas Electric Inc—*Frederick Haas*	82 Main St, South Hadley MA 01075	413-536-1474	R	3*	<.1
1268	Morgan and Burt Electric Company Inc—*Wilbur Morgan*	12503 Creekside Dr, Largo FL 33773	727-507-0997	R	3*	<.1
1269	RE Newcomb Electric Inc—*Roy Newcomb*	9247 Whiskey Bottom Rd, Laurel MD 20723	301-953-1935	R	3*	<.1
1270	Bloomfield Electric Company Inc—*Kevin Calhoun*	3 Alcap Rdg, Cromwell CT 06416	860-632-8448	R	3*	<.1
1271	Intergrated Networking Technologies LLC—*Angela Columber*	6111 Hrltg Pk Dr Ste A, Chattanooga TN 37416	423-265-5454	R	3*	<.1
1272	Area Utilities Inc—*Paul Granger*	101 Peninsula Dr Ste 1, North East MD 21901	410-287-0077	R	3*	<.1
1273	Dony Electric Inc—*Doug Barbeau*	200 Nw 12th St Ste 1, Florida City FL 33034	305-245-3533	R	3*	<.1
1274	Great Lakes Power and Lighting Inc—*Charles Schwab*	9646 Marine City Hwy, Casco MI 48064	586-716-4000	R	3*	<.1
1275	JE Reedy Inc—*Greg Reedy*	PO Box 1265, Seymour IN 47274	812-497-3380	R	3*	<.1
1276	Residential Electric Inc—*Ronald Tripp*	3240 S Standard Ave, Santa Ana CA 92705	714-556-3813	R	3*	<.1
1277	Roshell Electric Inc—*Jeff Roshell*	14896 County Hwy S, Chippewa Falls WI 54729	715-723-2881	R	3*	<.1
1278	Waypoint Systems Inc—*Roger Bennett*	1455 Old Alabama Rd St, Roswell GA 30076	770-649-6100	R	3*	<.1
1279	Computer Cabling and Telephone Service—*Daniel Beam*	961 Acorn Dr, Harrisonburg VA 22802	540-437-4201	R	3*	<.1
1280	Pro-Arc Electrical Construction Company Inc—*Dominic Rossi*	1229 E Algonquin Rd St, Arlington Heights IL 60005	847-427-1111	R	3*	<.1
1281	Amer Electric Inc—*Dennis Amer*	PO Box 1090, Keene NH 03431	603-357-8553	R	3*	<.1
1282	Okc Electrical Contractors Inc—*Jesse Degeare*	1644 Nw 3rd St, Oklahoma City OK 73106	405-232-7153	R	3*	<.1
1283	Suncoast Electric Inc—*Donald Penner*	7199 30th Ave N, Saint Petersburg FL 33710	727-347-2176	R	3*	<.1
1284	Hurt Electric Inc—*Henry Hurt*	N57w14502 Shawn Cir, Menomonee Falls WI 53051	262-252-0500	R	3*	<.1
1285	Lippolis Electric Inc—*Carmine Lippolis*	25 7th St 2, Pelham NY 10803	914-738-3550	R	3*	<.1
1286	Tosone Electric Inc—*James Flaherty*	PO Box 3057, Upper Montclair NJ 07043	973-746-8888	R	3*	<.1
1287	White Electric Inc—*Dennis White*	1106 Se Stallings Dr, Nacogdoches TX 75964	936-564-5180	R	3*	<.1
1288	Applied Electric Inc—*James Slotnick*	4549 Tabor St Ste A, Wheat Ridge CO 80033	303-420-1518	R	3*	<.1
1289	Capodanno Electric Inc—*William Capodanno*	455 Ludlow Ave, Cranford NJ 07016	908-272-8850	R	3*	<.1
1290	DFG Electric Inc—*Mark Lungo*	218 Foxon Rd, East Haven CT 06513	203-467-1081	R	3*	<.1
1291	Gropp Electric Inc—*Tad Gropp*	PO Box 3246, Spokane WA 99220	509-534-4000	R	3*	<.1
1292	Hire Electric Inc—*Ronald Mchale*	2700 W 2nd St, The Dalles OR 97058	541-296-5574	R	3*	<.1
1293	Richmar Controls and Service Company Inc—*Thomas Gorman*	851 Mclean Ave Ste 1, Yonkers NY 10704	914-776-6060	R	3*	<.1
1294	Roy Spittle Associates Inc—*Thomas Spittle*	5 Heritage Way, Gloucester MA 01930	978-283-2299	R	3*	<.1
1295	Summit Electric Inc—*Robert Roberts*	2544 Acacia Dr, Troy MI 48083	248-689-0300	R	3*	<.1
1296	Triangle Electric Inc—*Don Hoffelt*	PO Box 789, Williston ND 58802	701-572-6783	R	3*	<.1
1297	Wright 1 Electric—*Robert Lane*	5618 Se 135th Ave, Portland OR 97236	503-760-8522	R	3*	<.1
1298	Electrical Design and Motor Control Inc—*Kevin Robertson*	500 Giuseppe Ct Ste 4, Roseville CA 95678	916-773-2869	R	3*	<.1
1299	Magnum Electric Service Inc—*Greg Galpin*	1537 Fowler St, Richland WA 99352	509-783-7411	R	3*	<.1
1300	Timmons Electric Company Inc—*Samuel Timmons*	130 N Ct St, Morganfield KY 42437	270-389-2420	R	3*	<.1
1301	Schmidt Electric Inc—*Ron Roberts*	5330 Distribution Dr, Fort Wayne IN 46825	260-484-0313	R	3*	<.1
1302	APS Corp—*Daniel Jacquish*	465 Union Ave Ste 3, Bridgewater NJ 08807	908-725-2222	R	3*	<.1
1303	Electro Maintenance Inc—*Joseph Sole*	5133 W Hurley Pond Rd, Wall Township NJ 07727	732-751-9639	R	3*	<.1
1304	Mountain Vista Development Inc—*Chuck King*	2675 E Patrick Ln Ste, Las Vegas NV 89120	702-458-9700	R	3*	<.1
1305	Mike's Electric Inc—*Michael Pappalardo*	494 Morse Rd, Jay VT 05859	802-988-9678	R	3*	.1
1306	Lucas Underground Utilities—*Patricia Lucas*	PO Box 90, Melfa VA 23410	757-787-3510	R	3*	<.1
1307	Gonzales Communications Inc—*Alfred Gonzales*	10821 Lakeview Ave, Lenexa KS 66219	913-829-7601	R	3*	<.1
1308	Iowa One Call—*Nancy Jensen*	320 Leclaire St Ste 1, Davenport IA 52801	563-322-2400	R	3*	<.1
1309	Daniel Electric Company Inc—*William Woodhull*	3000 Auburn Rd, Auburn Hills MI 48326	248-299-0900	R	3*	<.1
1310	Diversified Electrical Systems Inc—*Donald Heard*	4283 Sw High Meadows A, Palm City FL 34990	772-219-9942	R	3*	<.1
1311	B Lipman and Associates Inc—*Peter Elmo*	326 E 25th St, Baltimore MD 21218	410-366-3373	R	3*	<.1
1312	Energy Electric Inc—*Charles Sanford*	PO Box 8125, Tampa FL 33674	813-932-7146	R	3*	<.1
1313	MCD International Inc—*Darrell Masters*	PO Box 91675, Albuquerque NM 87199	505-822-6306	R	3*	<.1
1314	Advent Security Inc—*Richard Owens*	101 Roesch Ave, Oreland PA 19075	215-576-7111	R	3*	<.1
1315	Comet Electric And Equipment LLC—*Mark Lurtz*	197 65th Ter N, West Palm Beach FL 33413	561-689-4401	R	3*	<.1
1316	A and W Electric Of Hollywood Inc—*Jimmy Artigas*	3100 Se 4th Ave, Fort Lauderdale FL 33316	954-527-5599	R	3*	<.1
1317	Adam Shelton Electric Inc—*Adam Shelton*	PO Box 2292, Advance NC 27006	336-998-5198	R	3*	<.1
1318	Advanced Electrical Systems Inc—*Jeff Poe*	PO Box 126, Calhoun GA 30703	706-629-8383	R	3*	<.1
1319	Albritton Electrical Service Inc—*Keith Albritton*	4821 Six Oaks Dr, Tallahassee FL 32303	850-562-1193	R	3*	<.1
1320	Artel Electrical Contractors Inc—*Eugene Jordan*	76 Union Ave Ste B, Ronkonkoma NY 11779	631-738-7600	R	3*	<.1
1321	Bemci Electric Inc—*Christian Masarik*	PO Box 522, Saint Augustine FL 32085	904-829-2700	R	3*	<.1
1322	Blankenship Electric Inc—*Charles Blankenship*	PO Box 2427, Greenville SC 29602	864-246-7200	R	3*	<.1
1323	N Gil Electric Company Inc—*Felicano Gil*	10134 Olga Ln, Houston TX 77041	713-462-1896	R	3*	<.1
1324	Automated Entry Systems Inc—*Alan King*	130 Iowa Ln Ste 202, Cary NC 27511	919-678-6380	R	3*	<.1
1325	D and W Electric Company Inc—*Daniel Carter*	2601 Pickettville Rd, Jacksonville FL 32220	904-786-3420	R	3*	<.1
1326	Haitz Electric Company Inc—*Fred Haitz*	108 Greenwood Ave, Midland Park NJ 07432	201-689-9600	R	3*	<.1
1327	M Sakuma Electric Inc—*Melvin Sakuma*	720 Moowaa St Ste A, Honolulu HI 96817	808-847-7173	R	3*	<.1
1328	Phillips Electric Inc—*Edward Phillips*	PO Box 105, Thornton IL 60476	708-877-1100	R	3*	<.1
1329	Ramsey Ward Electric Co—*Jeff Ward*	621 Moore St Sw, Ardmore OK 73401	580-223-2221	R	3*	<.1
1330	Decker and Bruce Electric Inc—*Charlie Bruce*	22 Corporate Cir Ste 3, East Syracuse NY 13057	315-432-1835	R	3*	<.1
1331	ACS Security Systems Inc—*Herbert Morris*	PO Box 16596, Jacksonville FL 32245	904-725-2240	R	3*	<.1
1332	Enterprise Electric Inc—*Jean Keith*	PO Box 5431, Boise ID 83705	208-344-0441	R	3*	<.1

Note: An asterisk (*) indicates an estimated financial figure. The company type code used is as follows: R = Private, P = Public, S = Private Subsidiary, B = Public Subsidiary, D = Division, J = Joint Venture, I = Investment Fund.

COMPANY RANKINGS BY SALES WITHIN 4-DIGIT SIC

Rank	Company Name—*Executive Officer*	Address, City, State, Zip	Phone	Type	Fin	Empls
1333	Marvin Bill Electric Inc—*Don Roberts*	2705 N Larkin Ave, Fresno CA 93727	559-291-2575	R	3*	<.1
1334	Advanced Security Systems Of New Jersey—*Robert Penna*	11 Chestnut St, Tenafly NJ 07670	201-567-8363	R	3*	<.1
1335	Alva Electric Inc—*Lori Ricketts*	118 W Franklin St, Evansville IN 47710	812-401-2582	R	3*	<.1
1336	BN Systems Inc—*Cindy Reid*	PO Box 347, Orchard Park NY 14127	716-662-9199	R	3*	<.1
1337	CH Attick Electric Inc—*Harry Attick*	10485 Theodore Green B, White Plains MD 20695	301-870-3700	R	3*	<.1
1338	Diamond Electrical Contractors Inc—*Ken Mckuhen*	6999 02 Merill Rd, Jacksonville FL 32277	904-565-4424	R	3*	<.1
1339	Dms-Electric Inc—*Sergey Mishchuk*	8504 Se Stark St, Portland OR 97216	503-252-6611	R	3*	<.1
1340	Fouts Electric Corp—*Scott Fouts*	5238 Kazuko Ct, Moorpark CA 93021	805-529-0385	R	3*	<.1
1341	Gulf States Electric Inc—*Martin Rogers*	4585 Progress Ave, Naples FL 34104	239-263-7137	R	3*	<.1
1342	Hangtown Electric Inc—*Terri Smith*	PO Box 630, Shingle Springs CA 95682	916-859-0500	R	3*	<.1
1343	Ingram J D "buck" Electric Company Inc—*Robert Ingram*	PO Box 414, Pensacola FL 32591	850-433-8266	R	3*	<.1
1344	Jaymor Electric Inc—*Maureen Jung*	500 Park Ave Ste 204, Lake Villa IL 60046	847-245-4700	R	3*	<.1
1345	Keithly Electric Co—*Daniel Keithly*	827 S Director St, Seattle WA 98108	206-763-6875	R	3*	<.1
1346	Moody and Phillips Electric Company Inc—*Ernest Phillips*	1205 S Bennett St, Tyler TX 75701	903-597-5001	R	3*	<.1
1347	Nicotri Electric Inc—*Judy Nicotri*	9195 Mammoth Ave, Baton Rouge LA 70814	225-929-9867	R	3*	<.1
1348	Noblitt Electric Inc—*Henry Noblitt*	PO Box 1271, Pascagoula MS 39568	228-769-8327	R	3*	<.1
1349	Ohio Valley Communications Inc—*Lester Hammer*	20 E Sycamore St, Evansville IN 47713	812-425-4416	R	3*	<.1
1350	Snake River Electrical—*Chris Jensen*	PO Box 1006, Blackfoot ID 83221	208-785-0140	R	3*	<.1
1351	Teldata Communications Inc—*Vipul Kapila*	19211 Chennault Way St, Gaithersburg MD 20879	301-670-0122	R	3*	<.1
1352	Tracy Electric Inc—*Robert Tracy*	1308 Jefferson St, Lawrenceville IL 62439	618-943-2243	R	3*	<.1
1353	Troy's Contracting Inc—*Troy Reese*	3026 San Bruno Ave Ste, San Francisco CA 94134	415-468-9066	R	3*	<.1
1354	GE Jones Electric Company Inc—*George Stratton*	212 N Polk St, Amarillo TX 79107	806-372-5505	R	3*	<.1
1355	Golden State Electrical Contractors Inc—*Sean Salveson*	5830 Sunset Dr Ste 60, Foresthill CA 95631	530-367-4802	R	3*	<.1
1356	Stephens Electric Company Inc—*Carl Stephens*	34008 18th Pl S Ste B, Federal Way WA 98003	253-838-1296	R	3*	<.1
1357	Aafp Systems Inc—*Ken Hoffman*	PO Box 520279, Longwood FL 32752	407-830-6302	R	3*	<.1
1358	Anbro Electric Company Inc—*Greg Anderson*	PO Box 1622, Bloomington IN 47402	812-336-4992	R	3*	<.1
1359	BEC Electric Inc—*Brian Vardiman*	419 Main St Ste 217, Huntington Beach CA 92648	714-890-1602	R	3*	<.1
1360	Bell Electrical Contractors LLC	PO Box 575, Torrington CT 06790	860-482-2222	R	3*	<.1
1361	Decision Systems Plus Inc—*Randy Wear*	1011 E Touhy Ste 170, Des Plaines IL 60018	847-699-9960	R	3*	<.1
1362	Esi Contracting—*Chris Altomare*	5431 Production Dr, Huntington Beach CA 92649	714-893-3768	R	3*	<.1
1363	Schwan Electric Inc—*Thomas Schwan*	PO Box 1733, Aberdeen SD 57402	605-225-9211	R	3*	<.1
1364	PC Pricer Inc—*Patrick Pricer*	PO Box 130, Weslaco TX 78599	956-969-0232	R	3*	<.1
1365	Signal Service Co—*Joseph Freck*	4341 Cranwood Pkwy, Cleveland OH 44128	216-662-4820	R	3*	<.1
1366	Cabling Services Corp—*Clayton Schaefer*	6901 E Fish Lake Rd St, Maple Grove MN 55369	763-463-6370	R	3*	<.1
1367	Cei Electric Co—*William Peters*	3140 Ruler Dr Ste D, Commerce Township MI 48390	248-960-3534	R	3*	<.1
1368	Polarity Electric Inc—*Jeff Smith*	4922 146th Ave, Holland MI 49423	269-751-8928	R	3*	<.1
1369	Ecm Enterprises Inc—*Thomas Roberts*	5a Lafayette St, Plattsburgh NY 12901	518-561-7923	R	3*	<.1
1370	Lawrence Cable Service Inc—*Glenn Lawrence*	20705 S Western Ave St, Torrance CA 90501	310-328-4689	R	3*	<.1
1371	Master Service Mid-Atlantic Inc—*Patrick Smith*	PO Box 2417, Elkins WV 26241	304-636-8170	R	3*	<.1
1372	Premier Control Systems LLC—*Tino Dalmau*	13918 Airline Hwy, Baton Rouge LA 70817	225-408-1004	R	3*	<.1
1373	A Boesch Corporation Electric—*Edward Boesch*	PO Box 2756, Slidell LA 70459	985-641-1361	R	3*	<.1
1374	Clarity Audio/Video Systems Inc—*Tom Brandabur*	15831 Hwy 55 Ste C, Minneapolis MN 55447	763-551-2300	R	3*	<.1
1375	Current Electric Of Battle Creek Inc—*Stan Schultz*	322 Mcintyre Ln, Springfield MI 49037	269-660-0100	R	3*	<.1
1376	Standard Electric Company Inc—*Doug Hulse*	2006 E Prairie Cir, Olathe KS 66062	913-782-5409	R	3*	<.1
1377	Florida Towers Service Inc—*Sid Richards*	17930 Cook Ln, Spring Hill FL 34610	813-679-5750	R	3*	<.1
1378	Industrial Electric Inc—*Mark Moody*	PO Box 41218, Phoenix AZ 85080	623-582-5204	R	3*	<.1
1379	Channel Electric Inc—*Chris Herby*	625 Stedman St, Ketchikan AK 99901	907-225-9725	R	3*	<.1
1380	Radford Tech Services Inc—*John Gilley*	14869 Holden Cir, Horizon City TX 79928	915-852-9511	R	3*	<.1
1381	Guardian Radon Mitigation and Electrical Services LLC—*Andrew Leihsing*	451 Burr Oak Dr, Oswego IL 60543	630-768-9836	R	3*	<.1
1382	Communication Power Solutions Inc—*Dan Washburn*	6100 S Maple St Ste 11, Tempe AZ 85283	480-345-9801	R	3*	<.1
1383	Expert Comfort Solutions	35 Barber Pond Rd, Bloomfield CT 06002	860-242-2050	S	3*	<.1
1384	Puffin Electric Inc—*Bruce Hess*	PO Box 1724, Homer AK 99603	907-235-8160	R	3*	<.1
1385	Safe T Lighting LLC—*Melba Harrison*	2301 E Goliad Ave Ste, Crockett TX 75835	936-544-3833	R	3*	<.1
1386	Square V Electric Co—*Vahig Dan*	277 Chestnut Hill Rd, Colchester CT 06415	860-537-0342	R	3*	<.1
1387	T and T Equipment Inc—*Thomas Reilly*	PO Box 2652, Cinnaminson NJ 08077	856-786-7752	R	3*	<.1
1388	Teksolutions Inc—*Keith Bowman*	2820 Roe Ln Ste R, Kansas City KS 66103	913-432-9335	R	3*	<.1
1389	Hoyt Communications Inc—*Martin Hoyt*	10054 Vista Ct, Myersville MD 21773	301-293-1013	R	3*	<.1
1390	G and B Electrical Co—*Jaren Braun*	726 Tennyson Downs Ct, Bloomfield Hills MI 48304	248-647-2647	R	3*	<.1
1391	Scott Boatner Construction Inc—*Scott Boatner*	602 W Main St Ste A, Louisville MS 39339	662-773-8025	R	3*	<.1
1392	Bdr Management Inc—*Richard Barbato*	245 Ronkonkoma Ave, Ronkonkoma NY 11779	631-738-7374	R	3*	<.1
1393	Mesa Brothers Inc—*Raul Mesa*	5215 Sw 103rd Ave, Miami FL 33165	305-630-2549	R	3*	.1
1394	Design Consultants and Constructors—*Frederick Graefe*	2148 Richardson Rd, Westminster MD 21158	410-477-5011	R	3*	<.1
1395	Action Electrical Contracting Company Inc—*Anthony Spina*	1955 37th St, Astoria NY 11105	718-728-7770	R	3*	<.1
1396	Michael J Manfredi—*Michael Manfredi*	6 Shady Ln Dr, Burlington MA 01803	781-648-7594	R	3*	<.1
1397	All Phase Electrical Contractors—*Barbara Tornes*	5250 Waterford Rd, Marietta OH 45750	740-373-5151	R	3*	<.1
1398	All-Tech Electric Inc—*Clarence Allred*	PO Box 608, Tooele UT 84074	435-843-0185	R	3*	<.1
1399	Electrical Contracting Services LLC—*Billy Hudson*	PO Box 244, Waverly TN 37185	931-296-5585	R	3*	<.1
1400	Jesco Electric Inc—*John Smith*	PO Box 416, Hopkinsville KY 42241	270-886-9410	R	3*	<.1
1401	Hoefler Communications Inc—*Daniel Hoefler*	5894 E Seneca Tpke, Jamesville NY 13078	315-492-7930	R	3*	<.1
1402	Sunrise Electric Of Central Florida Inc—*Howard Dougherty*	1708 Old River Trl, Chuluota FL 32766	407-365-4493	R	3*	<.1
1403	Integrated Media Systems Inc—*Mohammad Ahmadi*	655 Hawaii St, El Segundo CA 90245	310-725-8500	R	3*	<.1
1404	Line - Load Electrical Contractor's Inc—*Stephen Pfeiffer*	27 Henry Ford Cir Ste, Waldorf MD 20602	301-932-4033	R	3*	<.1
1405	1 Quality Electric Inc—*Joe Sanchez*	22784 San Miguel St, Harlingen TX 78552	956-421-2078	R	3*	<.1
1406	A-1 Electrical Contractors Inc—*Carl Orgeron*	2783 Lapalco Blvd, Harvey LA 70058	504-368-1575	R	3*	<.1
1407	Bartoli Electric Co—*Richard Bartoli*	22 Knight St, Norwalk CT 06851	203-838-4895	R	3*	<.1
1408	Busy Bee Electric Inc—*James Oehlschlaeger*	PO Box 10, Hooven OH 45033	513-353-3553	R	3*	<.1
1409	Communications Technology Inc—*Matthew Duray*	1306 Central Ave, Billings MT 59102	406-248-8900	R	3*	<.1
1410	Davison Electric Company Inc—*David Defelice*	305 N 1st St, Martins Ferry OH 43935	740-633-2972	R	3*	<.1
1411	Diane Electric Inc—*Steven Kopec*	1371 Seabury Ave, Bronx NY 10461	718-931-1300	R	3*	<.1
1412	Edison Electric Inc—*Charles Hayden*	2417 104th St Ct S, Lakewood WA 98499	253-583-0700	R	3*	<.1
1413	Four D Electric Inc—*John Noone*	4 Raymond Dr Ste D, Havertown PA 19083	610-789-8900	R	3*	<.1
1414	Godfrey Electric Inc—*Albert Godfrey*	1222 Omar Rd, West Palm Beach FL 33405	561-833-3753	R	3*	<.1
1415	Group Electric Company LLC	330 Woodycrest Ave, Nashville TN 37210	615-259-3284	R	3*	<.1
1416	Hamilton Brothers Electric Inc—*Stuart Hamilton*	PO Box 715, Springville UT 84663	801-489-9449	R	3*	<.1
1417	Shaum Electric Company Inc—*Gary Shaum*	1125 N Nappanee St, Elkhart IN 46514	574-264-4189	R	3*	<.1
1418	Telelink Communications Inc—*Cheryl Corser*	397 Herndon Pkwy Ste 1, Herndon VA 20170	703-810-8400	R	3*	<.1
1419	Timm Electric Inc—*Theodora Mcgann*	17832 Mills Rd, Joliet IL 60433	815-723-4501	R	3*	<.1
1420	Yates Electric Service Inc—*William Yates*	88a Dover Rd, Durham NH 03824	603-868-8295	R	3*	<.1
1421	Its Telecommunications Systems Inc—*Robert Post*	PO Box 277, Indiantown FL 34956	772-597-2111	R	3*	<.1

Rank	Company Name—*Executive Officer*	Address, City, State, Zip	Phone	Type	Fin	Empls
1422	On Line Inc—*Ward Hostetler*	1732 Mayfair Pl, Crofton MD 21114	410-451-9881	R	3*	<.1
1423	Mccraken Electric Inc—*Daniel Mccracken*	PO Box 3800, Amarillo TX 79116	806-372-8339	R	3*	<.1
1424	Defiance Electric Inc—*Jay Boucher*	86 Chosen Vale Ln Ste, Enfield NH 03748	603-632-4982	R	3*	<.1
1425	Power Electric Co—*Joe Gormally*	218 W 3620 S, Salt Lake City UT 84115	801-288-1064	R	3*	<.1
1426	Austin Telecommunications and Electrical Inc—*James Austin*	290 Pratt St, Meriden CT 06450	203-630-1822	R	3*	.1
1427	Buckhorn Land Development Corp—*Jay Howell*	221 E Albert St, Portage WI 53901	608-742-2222	R	3*	<.1
1428	Robinson Electric Inc—*Bob Robinson*	2314 N 12th Ave, Paragould AR 72450	870-215-5360	R	3*	<.1
1429	Duranet Inc—*R Thornton*	663 Eharlee Five Forks, Kingston GA 30145	770-424-5442	R	3*	<.1
1430	Worksafe Iowa—*Craig Zwerling*	100 Oakdale Campus, Iowa City IA 52242	319-335-4428	R	3*	<.1
1431	Horace Sullivan Inc—*Horace Sullivan*	PO Box 100843, Nashville TN 37224	615-254-7791	R	3*	<.1
1432	Kreg Electric Inc—*Patrick Kriegel*	3799 Ne 12th Ave, Pompano Beach FL 33064	954-786-1642	R	3*	<.1
1433	Stonecipher Corp—*Steven Stonecipher*	479 W Bedford Ave Ste, Fresno CA 93711	559-431-5839	R	3*	<.1
1434	Sun Electric Inc—*Harold Chyle*	411 39th St Nw, Fargo ND 58102	701-281-9140	R	3*	<.1
1435	Two-L Electric Co—*Larry Gingery*	1363 Heistan Pl, Memphis TN 38104	901-274-2232	R	3*	<.1
1436	Rick's Gate Works Inc—*Richard Hendrix*	8724 Remmet Ave, Canoga Park CA 91304	818-993-1989	R	3*	<.1
1437	Quality Electrical Service Inc—*Ramiro Onate*	2758 Ernest St, Jacksonville FL 32205	904-388-9198	R	3*	<.1
1438	Alert Alarm System Inc—*Steve Nolte*	1118 S Greenwood Ave, Fort Smith AR 72901	479-782-4954	R	3*	<.1
1439	Cain Security Systems Inc—*Ronald Cain*	PO Box 6575, Alexandria VA 22306	703-360-1900	R	3*	<.1
1440	Central Electrical Systems Inc—*Kim Holtzendorf*	77 Three Rivers Dr Ne, Rome GA 30161	706-235-3858	R	3*	<.1
1441	Cochran Electric Inc—*Donna Cochran*	90 Grace Dr, Powell OH 43065	614-847-0035	R	3*	<.1
1442	Energy Conservation Techniques Ltd—*Kathryn Fisher*	1501 S Preston St Ste, Louisville KY 40217	502-636-2402	R	3*	<.1
1443	Grow Electric Inc—*Kimberly Grow*	160 Whiteford Way, Lexington SC 29072	803-951-2099	R	3*	<.1
1444	Hara Electrical Contractors Inc—*Albert Bednarik*	9311 Old Marlboro Pke, Upper Marlboro MD 20772	301-856-0292	R	3*	<.1
1445	Locust Valley Electric Inc—*Philip Straus*	93 Glen Cove Ave Unit, Glen Cove NY 11542	516-759-2500	R	3*	<.1
1446	Panko Electrical and Maintenance Inc—*Barbara Panko*	1080 Chenango St Ste B, Binghamton NY 13901	607-722-6455	R	3*	<.1
1447	S-Con Services Inc—*Richard Creed*	PO Box 953, Bryan TX 77806	979-822-4445	R	3*	<.1
1448	Static Electric Co—*Anthony Maturo*	1456 Skees Rd Ste A, West Palm Beach FL 33411	561-684-6100	R	3*	<.1
1449	Stokes Electrical Service Inc—*Robert Stokes*	4306 Austin Ave, Richmond VA 23222	804-329-9380	R	3*	<.1
1450	Straddick Electric and Systems Inc—*Ryan Stradling*	3 Chester Ave, Medford NJ 08055	609-654-7790	R	3*	<.1
1451	T and F Inc—*Lakesha Freeman*	PO Box 320036, Birmingham AL 35232	205-591-5231	R	3*	<.1
1452	Tanasa Inc—*Garland Horn*	617 N Retta St, Fort Worth TX 76111	817-834-3238	R	3*	<.1
1453	Wj Electric Company Inc—*Ramona Johnson*	PO Box 619, Orland Park IL 60462	708-599-3343	R	3*	<.1
1454	Conveyor Services Inc—*Brian Buckingham*	10252 Decoursey Pke, Ryland Hght KY 41015	859-356-5145	R	3*	<.1
1455	Bagnall Electric Inc—*Glen Bagnall*	PO Box 577, Sherburne NY 13460	607-674-9460	R	3*	<.1
1456	Coburn Electric Inc—*Daniel Peterson*	PO Box 118, Hood River OR 97031	541-354-1163	R	3*	<.1
1457	Kingston Contracting Inc—*Martin Gillman*	512 S Airport Blvd, South San Francisco CA 94080	650-635-7410	R	3*	<.1
1458	New Canaan Alarm Company Inc—*Paul Chludzinski*	PO Box 597, New Canaan CT 06840	203-966-8713	R	3*	<.1
1459	MBE Electric Inc—*Erwin Mendoza*	PO Box 7339, Riverside CA 92513	951-352-2490	R	3*	<.1
1460	Pro-Tech International Security Systems Inc—*Rudi Yzer*	7485 Davie Rd Ext, Hollywood FL 33024	954-433-4333	R	3*	<.1
1461	Standard Communications Group LLC	155 Webster St Ste O, Hanover MA 02339	781-982-8982	R	3*	<.1
1462	Quality Standby Services LLC—*Karl Gretzinger*	PO Box 674408, Marietta GA 30006	770-916-1747	R	3*	<.1
1463	Central Sierra Electric Company Inc—*Susan Franklin*	PO Box 698, Jackson CA 95642	209-223-3363	R	3*	<.1
1464	Kasc Inc—*Karen Cody*	9910 W 190th St Ste J, Mokena IL 60448	708-478-7400	R	3*	<.1
1465	Pgi Group Inc—*Eric Uhrenholt*	3860 Industrial Way, Benicia CA 94510	707-751-5900	R	3*	.1
1466	Claywell Electric Company Inc—*Pamela Hill*	297 Woodfield Xing, Glastonbury CT 06033	860-652-0094	R	3*	<.1
1467	Contact Electric LLC	PO Box 10445, Raleigh NC 27605	919-572-6969	R	3*	<.1
1468	Emms Electric Inc—*Mary Mccormick*	2230 Farmington Ave, Boyertown PA 19512	610-369-7174	R	3*	<.1
1469	Grey Electric Company Inc—*Chris Carroll*	205 Arden Rd, Emerald Isle NC 28594	252-354-4040	R	3*	<.1
1470	Indrolect Co—*Joseph Schlager*	PO Box 15492, Cincinnati OH 45215	513-821-4788	R	3*	<.1
1471	Powerhouse Electric Of Nc Inc—*Michael Carrieri*	1030 Classic Rd Ste 10, Apex NC 27539	919-362-1608	R	3*	<.1
1472	Pro Electric Inc—*Gary Hillis*	2012 Poole Dr Nw, Huntsville AL 35810	256-851-2041	R	3*	<.1
1473	R Palmieri Electrical Contractor Inc—*Raymond Palmieri*	PO Box 490, Buena NJ 08310	856-697-3218	R	3*	<.1
1474	Sajiun Electric Inc—*Manny Sajiun*	105 W 27th St, New York NY 10001	212-675-2800	R	3*	<.1
1475	Sentry Electric and Controls Inc—*Donnie Daniels*	PO Box 385, Harrisburg NC 28075	704-455-5538	R	3*	<.1
1476	Sonco Electric Company Inc—*Nat Rodriquez*	PO Box 7435, Odessa TX 79760	432-337-6380	R	3*	<.1
1477	Holicong Locksmith's and Central Security Inc—*William Croce*	PO Box 126, Holicong PA 18928	215-794-7542	R	3*	<.1
1478	Advanced Electric Company Inc—*James Stevens*	PO Box 1087, Pelham AL 35124	205-664-4500	R	3*	<.1
1479	Apple Electric Inc—*Lisa Prestipino*	18854 John J Williams, Rehoboth Beach DE 19971	302-645-5105	R	3*	<.1
1480	C T Electrical Corp—*Robert Cox*	2500 Coxshire Ln, Davidsonville MD 21035	301-261-3341	R	3*	<.1
1481	CH Electric Co—*Charles Hansborough*	PO Box 690092, San Antonio TX 78269	210-690-7600	R	3*	<.1
1482	East Alabama Electric Company Inc—*Jeff Franklin*	PO Box 1030, Auburn AL 36831	334-821-9158	R	3*	<.1
1483	Gehl Electric Inc—*Timothy Hepburn*	PO Box 1085, Whittier CA 90609	714-257-1081	R	3*	<.1
1484	J and M Electrical Service—*James Mills*	280 Rum Gully Rd, Murrells Inlet SC 29576	843-651-8226	R	3*	<.1
1485	Smink Electric Inc—*John Smink*	PO Box 1103, Elyria OH 44036	440-322-5518	R	3*	<.1
1486	United Automation LLC—*Connie Smith*	315 Wallace Dean Rd, West Monroe LA 71291	318-397-0208	R	3*	<.1
1487	United Electrical Services Inc—*Robert Faiss*	2231 Meridian Blvd Ste, Minden NV 89423	775-782-4303	R	3*	<.1
1488	Willamette Electric Inc—*Dan Fife*	PO Box 230547, Portland OR 97281	503-624-3631	R	3*	<.1
1489	Safeguard Alarm Systems Inc—*Richard Morales*	PO Box 506, Houma LA 70361	985-879-1212	R	3*	<.1
1490	Cuadra Construction Inc—*Henry Rosales*	3200 Osgood Cmn, Fremont CA 94539	510-353-1260	R	3*	<.1
1491	Qn Electric Inc—*Kenneth Quirin*	PO Box 129, Kailua HI 96734	808-263-9813	R	3*	<.1
1492	Bay Electric Inc—*Mark Rosenlund*	PO Box 297, Dollar Bay MI 49922	906-482-8784	R	3*	<.1
1493	Advanced Alarm Service Inc—*Edward Zimmerman*	1253 Okeechobee Rd Ste, West Palm Beach FL 33401	561-833-7099	R	3*	<.1
1494	Touch Stone Solutions Inc—*Teresa Gawrys*	830 Park Ave, Meadville PA 16335	814-336-6201	R	3*	<.1
1495	Lackey's Electrical Inc—*Judy Clement*	2204 Lackey Rd, Corinth MS 38834	662-286-6989	R	3*	<.1
1496	J Grothe Electric Inc—*John Grothe*	15632 El Prado Rd, Chino CA 91710	909-993-9400	R	3*	<.1
1497	Brannan and Son Electric—*Dennis Brannan*	11122 Woodbury Rd, Garden Grove CA 92843	714-537-3235	R	3*	<.1
1498	Ace Electric Service Company LLC	10304 Washington Pke, Corryton TN 37721	865-688-3003	R	3*	<.1
1499	Gil-Men Electric Company Inc—*Charles Gilcrease*	PO Box 4584, Santa Fe NM 87502	505-982-2456	R	3*	<.1
1500	O'fallon Electric Co—*Carol Eichholz*	PO Box 488, O Fallon IL 62269	618-632-3577	R	3*	<.1
1501	Alpha Acme Electric Inc—*Brent Cox*	PO Box 20406, Montgomery AL 36120	334-281-4074	R	3*	<.1
1502	Altec Electrical Inc—*Earl Hooper*	902 Main St, La Marque TX 77568	409-935-6313	R	3*	<.1
1503	Crawford Electric and Welding Inc—*Gene Mccoy*	PO Box 1788, Milledgeville GA 31059	478-452-8661	R	3*	<.1
1504	Crowe and Sons Electrical Corp—*James Crowe*	576 Middlesex St, Lowell MA 01851	978-453-6696	R	3*	<.1
1505	Electronic Systems Consultants Inc—*Anson Fogeo*	109 Abc, Aspen CO 81611	970-925-1700	R	3*	<.1
1506	Iwired Inc—*Maggie George*	16573 N 92nd St Ste 10, Scottsdale AZ 85260	480-922-2500	R	3*	<.1
1507	Mc Leod Electric Company Inc—*Alonzo Mc Leod*	PO Box 4190, Blue Mountain AL 36204	256-236-1331	R	3*	<.1
1508	Quality Electric Of Douglas County Inc—*Mike Hutton*	1011 E 31st St, Lawrence KS 66046	785-843-9211	R	3*	<.1
1509	Rapides Station LLC	4003 Lee St, Alexandria LA 71302	318-445-3711	R	3*	<.1
1510	Ray's Electric Inc—*Richard Kretchmar*	PO Box 4001, Wichita KS 67204	316-838-8231	R	3*	<.1
1511	Snell-Northcutt Electric Inc—*Bob Snell*	PO Box 24601, Little Rock AR 72221	501-224-2832	R	3*	<.1

Note: An asterisk (*) indicates an estimated financial figure. The company type code used is as follows: R = Private, P = Public, S = Private Subsidiary, B = Public Subsidiary, D = Division, J = Joint Venture, I = Investment Fund.

COMPANY RANKINGS BY SALES WITHIN 4-DIGIT SIC

Rank	Company Name—*Executive Officer*	Address, City, State, Zip	Phone	Type	Fin	Empls
1512	Wirtz Electric Inc—*James Wirtz*	1675 S Sheridan Dr, Muskegon MI 49442	231-773-0018	R	3*	<.1
1513	David Crowell Electric Inc—*David Crowell*	3100 Airway Ave Ste 12, Costa Mesa CA 92626	714-444-3592	R	3*	<.1
1514	Gulfcoast Telephone Company Inc—*Russ Arpasi*	12590 Metro Pkwy, Fort Myers FL 33966	239-275-0011	R	3*	<.1
1515	J and J Electric Inc—*Jeff Baltazar*	3410 S 1500 W, Ogden UT 84401	801-622-0270	R	3*	<.1
1516	JSS Electric Inc—*John Stankiewicz*	17515 S Miles Rd, Cleveland OH 44128	216-581-7434	R	3*	<.1
1517	Bryant Electric Repair and Construction Inc—*Robert Davis*	PO Box 1658, Gastonia NC 28053	704-864-5703	R	3*	<.1
1518	Faulk Electric Corp—*Dennis Helinski*	PO Box 26645, Tucson AZ 85726	520-294-1683	R	3*	<.1
1519	Jim's Electric Inc—*Ken Nair*	PO Box 580541, Tulsa OK 74158	918-258-5101	R	3*	<.1
1520	Electri-Tech Inc—*Michael Wallis*	82 Tuckahoe Rd, Dorothy NJ 08317	609-476-0822	R	3*	<.1
1521	San Antonio Telephone Co—*Peggy Hines*	1425 Universal City Bl, Universal City TX 78148	210-657-5757	R	3*	<.1
1522	Service Electric Inc—*Laura Crowell*	726 Walsh Rd, Madison WI 53714	608-241-3377	R	3*	<.1
1523	Weisman Electric Co—*Thomas Weisman*	42 Hudson St Ste 102, Annapolis MD 21401	410-266-3522	R	3*	<.1
1524	Mark Olson Electric Inc—*Mark Olson*	1385 Donner Ave, San Francisco CA 94124	415-822-3508	R	3*	<.1
1525	Thomas Hughes—*Thomas Hughes*	160 Mccormick Ave, Costa Mesa CA 92626	714-641-1809	R	3*	<.1
1526	Fla Electric and Design—*Alan Howse*	1964 Carroll St, Clearwater FL 33765	727-446-2100	R	3*	<.1
1527	Pyramid Sound and Light Inc—*Randy Hansen*	5133 State Rd 54, New Port Richey FL 34652	727-372-0809	R	3*	<.1
1528	Jack Peirce Electric—*Jack Peirce*	1504 13th St, Wichita Falls TX 76301	940-322-1812	R	3*	<.1
1529	B and K Electrical and Mechanical Contractors Inc—*Gary Hunter*	PO Box 490, Alexander AR 72002	501-847-0200	R	3*	<.1
1530	Tico Electric Inc—*Richard Maley*	PO Box 414, Mckeesport PA 15134	412-678-6105	R	3*	.1
1531	Cde Electrical Contracting Inc—*Kevin Coffey*	305 Southdowne Dr, Maryville TN 37801	865-379-2949	R	3*	<.1
1532	Fox Electric Limited Co	PO Box 2069, Los Lunas NM 87031	505-866-7957	R	3*	<.1
1533	Ingalls and Son Electrical Contr—*Linda Spazian*	36 Holland Dr, Hartford CT 06111	860-667-1948	R	3*	<.1
1534	Marzuco Electric Inc—*Charles Marzuco*	425 Market St, Sainte Genevieve MO 63670	573-883-5347	R	3*	<.1
1535	Oak Electric Company Inc—*Michael Coscia*	PO Box 575, Oakland NJ 07436	201-337-6613	R	3*	<.1
1536	Omni Electrical and Constructors Inc—*Bill Fowler*	PO Box 4335, Lynchburg VA 24502	804-768-8641	R	3*	<.1
1537	Sam's Electrical Contractors Inc—*Hassan Shehayeb*	PO Box 1448, Palm Harbor FL 34682	727-934-7252	R	3*	<.1
1538	Jerry Zabel Electric Company Inc—*Jerrold Zabel*	3065 Brewster, West Bloomfield MI 48322	248-851-7624	R	3*	<.1
1539	Sonitrol Of Southern Oregon Inc—*Robert Duncan*	546 Business Park Dr, Medford OR 97504	541-779-5611	R	3*	<.1
1540	Curren Environmental Inc—*Richard Foley*	10 Penn Ave, Cherry Hill NJ 08002	856-662-7005	R	3*	<.1
1541	Lachappelle Electric Co—*Gary Lachappelle*	1423 Brady Blvd, San Antonio TX 78237	210-432-1881	R	3*	<.1
1542	Control and Equipment Company Of El Paso Inc—*John Holland*	2001 E Yandell Dr, El Paso TX 79903	915-545-2256	R	3*	<.1
1543	Gueldner Electric Co—*John Gueldner*	247 W Olmos Dr, San Antonio TX 78212	210-828-1378	R	3*	<.1
1544	J T Yates Electric Service Inc—*John Yates*	PO Box 2206, Rockingham NC 28380	910-895-5520	R	3*	<.1
1545	Sierra Industries Inc—*David Robards*	1918 Frazer Ave, Sparks NV 89431	775-359-5130	R	3*	<.1
1546	Bieker Electric Inc—*Richard Bieker*	3001 N Albert Pke Ave, Fort Smith AR 72904	479-783-3086	R	3*	<.1
1547	Bob Ward Electric—*Bob Ward*	6924 Canby Ave Ste 120, Reseda CA 91335	818-881-8499	R	3*	<.1
1548	Brown Electric Inc—*Dianne Brown*	17450 Indian Head Hwy, Accokeek MD 20607	301-283-3602	R	3*	<.1
1549	Gilliam Electric Inc—*Steve Gilliam*	PO Box 714, Anderson MO 64831	417-845-3956	R	3*	<.1
1550	Goodin Electric Inc—*John Goodin*	605 Garfield Ave Ste A, Newark OH 43055	740-522-3113	R	3*	<.1
1551	Greater Phoenix Electric Inc—*Paul Robinson*	2432 W Peoria Ave Ste, Phoenix AZ 85029	602-674-3072	R	3*	<.1
1552	Howard Systems Voice Data And Video Wiring LLC—*Everett Howard*	10 Commerce Way, Barrington NH 03825	603-335-9900	R	3*	<.1
1553	Jensen Electric Co—*Gary Jensen*	1460 Huntington Cir, Reno NV 89509	775-322-3100	R	3*	<.1
1554	Medley Electric Company Inc—*Orien Medley*	PO Box 368, Rockwell NC 28138	704-279-2186	R	3*	<.1
1555	Murphy Electric Company Inc—*Bruce Murphy*	22863 Bryant Ct Ste 10, Sterling VA 20166	703-435-1920	R	3*	<.1
1556	Presco Telecommunications Inc—*Michael Preston*	32420 148th Ave Se, Auburn WA 98092	253-833-8088	R	3*	<.1
1557	Roman Electric Inc—*Roman Bettencort*	1750 Augusta Ct, Visalia CA 93277	559-651-1007	R	3*	<.1
1558	Tci Electric Inc—*Siobhan Tully*	PO Box 1080, Windham NH 03087	603-898-8058	R	3*	<.1
1559	Commercial Electric Company Of Alexandria LLC	PO Box 12446, Alexandria LA 71315	318-442-8608	R	3*	<.1
1560	Wiley Davis Electrical Inc—*Wiley Davis*	4236 S 76th E Ave, Tulsa OK 74145	918-627-5406	R	3*	<.1
1561	CW Campbell Electric Inc—*Randy Eulenfel*	802 Cantwell Ln, Corpus Christi TX 78408	361-887-0766	R	3*	<.1
1562	Matzinger Electric—*Tim Matzinger*	907 Bridger Dr, Bozeman MT 59715	406-587-7290	R	3*	<.1
1563	Wil's Electrical Service Contractors Inc—*Wilford Sonnier*	PO Box 927, Carencro LA 70520	337-233-4620	R	3*	<.1
1564	Adams Electric Inc—*Ben Adams*	504a Nathan Ln, Elkhorn WI 53121	262-248-6995	R	3*	<.1
1565	Custom Controls Corp—*Tom Gibelyou*	4630 16th St E Ste B24, Fife WA 98424	253-922-5874	R	3*	<.1
1566	Kobo Utility Construction Corp—*Kevin O'neil*	PO Box 483, West Hyannisport MA 02672	508-771-9363	R	3*	<.1
1567	Palman Electric Inc—*Jeffrey Palman*	1957 Pioneer Rd Ste E4, Huntingdon Valley PA 19006	215-443-5500	R	3*	<.1
1568	Roger Electric Inc—*Daniel Blanc*	73 Lake Ave Ext Ste 1, Danbury CT 06810	203-744-2265	R	3*	<.1
1569	P J Ellis Electric Company Inc—*Elsie Ellis*	1219 Brookpark Rd, Cleveland OH 44109	216-749-3450	R	3*	<.1
1570	Williams Electronics LLC—*Donna Kriete*	702 W 155 S, Angola IN 46703	260-665-7499	R	3*	<.1
1571	Astro Company Inc—*Philip Catania*	PO Box 847, Azusa CA 91702	626-969-7615	R	3*	<.1
1572	Azar Electric Inc—*Judy Najour*	4580 Thicket Trl, Snellville GA 30039	770-979-8226	R	3*	<.1
1573	Dietz-Nauman Inc—*Scott Nauman*	33 N 4th St 797, Mount Wolf PA 17347	717-266-1551	R	3*	<.1
1574	E and P Electrical Contracting Company Inc—*Parviz Nekoumand*	3418 Azalea Garden Rd, Norfolk VA 23513	757-858-8100	R	3*	<.1
1575	Frank B Lesher Company Inc—*Edmund Lesher*	1680 Edgar Ave, Chambersburg PA 17201	717-263-9248	R	3*	<.1
1576	Hein Lighting And Electric Inc—*Jim Hein*	5030 Blum Rd, Martinez CA 94553	925-939-1528	R	3*	<.1
1577	Lantelligence Inc—*Peter Buswell*	6072 Corte Del Cedro, Carlsbad CA 92011	760-918-0150	R	3*	<.1
1578	Moeller Electric Inc—*Joseph Moeller*	308 E Pennsylvania Blv, Feasterville Trevose PA 19053	215-396-2830	R	3*	<.1
1579	Petrusha Enterprises Inc—*Chuck Petrusha*	3302 T St, Eureka CA 95503	707-443-6366	R	3*	<.1
1580	Rakoz Electric Inc—*Mary Rakoz*	1583 Bishop Rd, Chehalis WA 98532	360-748-7700	R	3*	<.1
1581	Rotor Electric Co—*Benjamin Rosenberg*	9522 Grinnell St, Detroit MI 48213	313-891-0511	R	3*	<.1
1582	Smallcomb Wiring Inc—*Thomas Smallcomb*	136 E Garry Ave, Santa Ana CA 92707	714-556-8591	R	3*	<.1
1583	Zata Corp—*Lester Zatko*	PO Box 980, Warren OH 44482	330-399-8921	R	3*	<.1
1584	A-1 Electric Of Lake City Inc—*David Cheatham*	188 Ne Osburn Way, Lake City FL 32055	386-752-5488	R	3*	<.1
1585	Premiere Music And Film Systems Inc—*Kenneth Johnson*	1400 N Kingsbury St, Chicago IL 60642	312-274-0220	R	3*	<.1
1586	Comelco Inc—*Jesse Gonzalez*	410 N St Unit 130, Longwood FL 32750	407-830-5884	R	3*	<.1
1587	Fleming Electric Inc—*Tom Gray*	325 Meadow Ave Ste C, East Peoria IL 61611	309-694-6277	R	3*	<.1
1588	E and R Electric—*Rick Blickenstaff*	5172 W Patrick Ln Ste, Las Vegas NV 89118	702-877-0105	R	3*	<.1
1589	Electrical Sales Corp—*Allan Bissinger*	PO Box 1095, Metairie LA 70004	504-833-3646	R	3*	<.1
1590	Four Directions Inc—*Jeffrey Ford*	11 Railroad Ave, Farmingdale NJ 07727	732-256-4864	R	3*	<.1
1591	Fredricks Electric Inc—*Jason Fredricks*	2211 Newcastle Ave, Cardiff By The Sea CA 92007	760-436-9172	R	3*	<.1
1592	Sunstream Inc—*James Talmadge*	808 Keyser Ave, Natchitoches LA 71457	318-352-1400	R	3*	<.1
1593	Southern Sun Electric Corp—*Mark Nelson*	2303 W Division St, Springfield MO 65802	417-865-6377	R	3*	<.1
1594	Northern Industrial Electric—*Dori Cramer*	2435 Radio Ln, Redding CA 96001	530-246-2366	R	3*	<.1
1595	Ron Pfaff Electric Inc—*Ron Pfaff*	6440 Norwalk Rd Ste A, Medina OH 44256	330-723-9901	R	3*	<.1
1596	William R Sharpe Inc—*Timothy Sharpe*	PO Box 789, Clarksburg WV 26302	304-622-4681	R	3*	<.1
1597	Bartley Bob Electric Inc—*Donna Bartley-Clark*	PO Box 621, Lindsay OK 73052	405-756-2091	R	3*	<.1

Rank	Company Name—*Executive Officer*	Address, City, State, Zip	Phone	Type	Fin	Empls
1598	Baswell Electrical Construction—*Bruce Baswell*	93 Leighann Pl, Windsor CA 95492	707-837-7345	R	3*	<.1
1599	Diverse Communications Solutions—*Barbara Canfield*	1800 Ne 25th Ave Ste 4, Hillsboro OR 97124	503-690-9107	R	3*	<.1
1600	Northstar Electrical Service LLC	8926 County Rd 156, Kaufman TX 75142	214-708-6629	R	3*	<.1
1601	Apex Manufacturing Services Ltd—*David Lewis*	PO Box 80410, Billings MT 59108	406-248-7728	R	3*	<.1
1602	H and M Ventures LLC—*Hazen Schulz*	408 S Queen Anne Dr, Fairless Hills PA 19030	215-547-0192	R	3*	<.1
1603	Christenson Communication—*Rene Biggs*	PO Box 61627, Sunnyvale CA 94088	408-744-9400	R	3*	<.1
1604	Agfa Construction Inc—*Julia Tarlo*	11325 Queens Blvd Ste, Forest Hills NY 11375	718-332-5466	R	2*	.1
1605	B Electric Inc—*John Baldwin*	PO Box 94270, Albuquerque NM 87199	505-828-0241	R	2*	<.1
1606	Gaudette Electric Inc—*Gerard Gaudette*	PO Box 2820, Homosassa Springs FL 34447	352-628-3064	R	2*	<.1
1607	Co-Been Electric Company LLC—*Kathy Shive*	5796 Ferguson Rd, Memphis TN 38134	901-388-8601	R	2*	<.1
1608	Stec Enterprizes Inc—*Chuck Stec*	483 Collingswood Blvd, Port Charlotte FL 33954	941-627-4039	R	2*	<.1
1609	Talco Electrical Construction Inc—*Fred Talarico*	6250 Kestrel Ct Ste 4, Missoula MT 59808	406-721-5242	R	2*	<.1
1610	Tekota Electric Inc—*Douglas Worley*	17005 Proffits Pt, Peyton CO 80831	719-570-6100	R	2*	<.1
1611	Midwest Detection Systems Inc—*Michelle Brickle*	144 Ashman Cir, Midland MI 48640	989-631-2451	R	2*	<.1
1612	Gulf Coast Electric Co—*David Tate*	2700 Market St, Baytown TX 77520	281-422-8336	R	2*	<.1
1613	Williamson Electrical Company Inc—*Charles Williamson*	PO Box 728, Milton FL 32572	850-623-0282	R	2*	<.1
1614	Worcester Electrical Associates Inc—*Robert Blanchette*	PO Box 924, Worcester MA 01613	508-754-4175	R	2*	<.1
1615	Meer Electrical Contractors Inc—*Richard Meer*	PO Box 1902, Roswell GA 30077	770-993-8028	R	2*	<.1
1616	Combine Systems Inc—*Shannon Fitzgerald*	PO Box 1085, Waldorf MD 20604	301-870-4300	R	2*	<.1
1617	Ecco Engineering And Construction Company Inc—*Terry Hay*	4882 E 2nd St, Benicia CA 94510	707-745-9660	R	2*	<.1
1618	Gold Coast Security Inc—*Jan Purvis*	1710 SW Blvd, Coos Bay OR 97420	541-267-5000	R	2*	<.1
1619	Hobbs Electric Inc—*William Lewis*	822 Silver Palm Ave, Melbourne FL 32901	321-723-5434	R	2*	<.1
1620	Landmark Electric Inc—*John Guarre*	PO Box 93280, Rochester NY 14692	585-359-0800	R	2*	<.1
1621	M and L Electric Inc—*Don Myers*	9331 Pleasant Plain Rd, Brookville OH 45309	937-833-5154	R	2*	<.1
1622	Munro Electric Company Inc—*John Munro*	PO Box 930178, Wixom MI 48393	248-344-9990	R	2*	<.1
1623	PC Electric Inc—*William Nuttall*	6892 Doolittle Ave Ste, Riverside CA 92503	951-689-1430	R	2*	<.1
1624	Ramcomm Inc—*Jesus Ramirez*	359 Lake Park Rd Ste 1, Lewisville TX 75057	972-221-3577	R	2*	<.1
1625	Rizzo and Sons Industrial Service Company Inc—*John Rizzo*	PO Box 96, Mentcle PA 15761	814-948-5381	R	2*	<.1
1626	Walker Electric Inc—*Dee Schoenfield*	3725 S Saginaw St Ste, Flint MI 48507	810-233-5111	R	2*	<.1
1627	Weber Electric Inc—*John Weber*	200 E Lafayette St, Bloomington IL 61701	309-827-7337	R	2*	<.1
1628	Smartworks Inc—*Rachael Richards*	7913 S Castlebay St, Tucson AZ 85747	520-574-7477	R	2*	<.1
1629	Stevens Electric Of Quincy Inc—*C Stevens*	PO Box 771, Quincy IL 62306	217-222-5220	R	2*	<.1
1630	Boston Electric And Telephone Corp—*Gerard Gardillo*	1854 Dorchester Ave, Dorchester Center MA 02124	617-288-0700	R	2*	<.1
1631	Coffey Electric Inc—*Doug Coffey*	3575 Darien Hwy, Brunswick GA 31525	912-267-9648	R	2*	<.1
1632	IES Texoma Inc—*Ronald Stogner*	PO Box 271, Sadler TX 76264	903-564-3231	R	2*	<.1
1633	ESS Inc—*Joe Arnold*	PO Box 240211, Montgomery AL 36124	334-279-9141	R	2*	<.1
1634	Mauro Electric Inc—*Kevin Mauro*	PO Box 2099, Snohomish WA 98291	360-653-5300	R	2*	<.1
1635	Transel Elevator and Electric Inc—*Mark Gregiorio*	509 W 34th St Fl 4, New York NY 10001	212-727-3200	R	2*	<.1
1636	C and R Electrical Service Inc—*Charles Emmons*	PO Box 98, Stapleton AL 36578	251-937-6386	R	2*	<.1
1637	Aa Electric Ltd—*Qonnie Laughlin*	500 Alakawa St Rm 100, Honolulu HI 96817	808-841-4131	R	2*	<.1
1638	Alert Electric Inc—*Gale Hatleberg*	1970 N 28th St, Springfield OR 97477	541-747-2213	R	2*	<.1
1639	Candor Electric Inc—*Vincent Di Fiore*	7825 S Claremont Ave, Chicago IL 60620	773-778-2626	R	2*	<.1
1640	Central States Electric Inc—*J Schneider*	3220 S Hoover Rd, Wichita KS 67215	316-942-6333	R	2*	<.1
1641	Coats Electric Company Inc—*Carl Coats*	845 Wall St, Florence AL 35630	256-766-9104	R	2*	<.1
1642	Coli Electric Contractors Inc—*Dante Colaianni*	1 Sears Dr Ste 403, Paramus NJ 07652	201-265-4822	R	2*	<.1
1643	Electrical Construction Management Inc—*Douglas Ford*	10801 Electron Dr Ste, Louisville KY 40299	502-267-6867	R	2*	<.1
1644	Engler Electric Inc—*James Engler*	PO Box 1745, Utica NY 13503	315-724-0135	R	2*	<.1
1645	E-Tel Systems Corp—*Victor Watts*	43766 Trade Ctr Pl Ste, Sterling VA 20166	703-904-1700	R	2*	<.1
1646	Island Electric Maui Inc—*Rick Haylor*	PO Box 844, Wailuku HI 96793	808-879-3145	R	2*	<.1
1647	L and M Electric Inc—*William Mccartney*	2567 Oscar Johnson Dr, Charleston SC 29405	843-529-6329	R	2*	<.1
1648	Mars Electrical LLC—*Dan Reginelli*	190 White St, Danbury CT 06810	203-790-6425	R	2*	<.1
1649	Sanford Electric Company Inc—*Lorri Willick*	PO Box 2025, Sanford FL 32772	407-322-1562	R	2*	<.1
1650	Westway Electric Systems Inc—*Christopher Lang*	PO Box 8645, Glendale CA 91224	323-663-3756	R	2*	<.1
1651	B and E Communications Inc—*H Ellis*	PO Box 7656, Jackson MS 39284	601-922-6031	R	2*	<.1
1652	Demand Electric Inc—*Richard Dion*	711 Valley St, Manchester NH 03103	603-625-2309	R	2*	<.1
1653	Vision Communications Inc—*Keli Kleidosty*	PO Box 1027, Kekaha HI 96752	316-744-7527	R	2*	<.1
1654	Bob Maisano—*Bob Maisano*	38 Cypress Ter Ste Rd3, Springfield NJ 07081	973-912-8224	R	2*	<.1
1655	ID Corp—*Randy Hand*	PO Box 21031, Billings MT 59104	406-259-1180	R	2*	<.1
1656	Goold Electric Inc—*Ruben Santana*	1040 Serpentine Ln Ste, Pleasanton CA 94566	925-484-1551	R	2*	<.1
1657	Juniper Group Inc—*Vlado Hreljanovic*	20283 State Rd Ste 400, Boca Raton FL 33498	516-829-4670	P	2	<.1
1658	H and L Electrical of Raleigh Nc Inc—*Jack Harper*	PO Box 878, Garner NC 27529	919-779-0337	R	2*	<.1
1659	Chubb Electric Service Inc—*Timothy Chubb*	1005 Trident St, Hanahan SC 29410	843-744-8400	R	2*	<.1
1660	Fishel Co—*Jeff Keeler*	1372 McGaw Ave, Irvine CA 92614	949-221-9350	R	2*	<.1
1661	Hodge Electrical Contractors Inc—*William Hodge*	264 Allison Rd, Piney Flats TN 37686	423-538-8410	R	2*	<.1
1662	Northeast Security Systems Inc—*Ronald Spinney*	PO Box 1566, Wiscasset ME 04578	207-882-9531	R	2*	<.1
1663	OD Miller Electric Company Inc—*Dale Miller*	1115 W Main St, Louisville OH 44641	330-875-1651	R	2*	<.1
1664	Cheyenne Electric Inc—*Randy Mcdowell*	702 Mccann Rd, Longview TX 75601	903-757-7797	R	2*	<.1
1665	Electrical and Mechanical Systems Inc—*Stephen Herbstritt*	316 Cherry St, Erie PA 16507	814-453-2518	R	2*	<.1
1666	Airways Electric Inc—*James Dickey*	PO Box 140008, Memphis TN 38114	901-744-1221	R	2*	<.1
1667	Bayou Electrical Services Inc—*Gregory Rachal*	1205 W Bessemer Ave St, Greensboro NC 27408	336-389-9600	R	2*	<.1
1668	Casa Technology Systems LLC	1745 W Deer Valley Rd, Phoenix AZ 85027	623-537-0110	R	2*	<.1
1669	Coker Electric Company LLC—*Jimmy Coker*	6712 Dollarway Rd, Pine Bluff AR 71602	870-247-4800	R	2*	<.1
1670	Cougar Communication Services LLC—*Jack Arneson*	11907 W 48th Ave Unit, Wheat Ridge CO 80033	303-421-9854	R	2*	<.1
1671	Doss Electric Inc—*Phillip Doss*	PO Box 652, Maben MS 39750	662-324-2524	R	2*	<.1
1672	Eastec Inc—*Frederick Pierce*	PO Box 1748, Belmar NJ 07719	732-751-2600	R	2*	<.1
1673	Edwards George D Electric Company Inc—*James Edwards*	706 3rd Ave S, Nashville TN 37210	615-256-6196	R	2*	<.1
1674	Lightmore Electric Associates Inc—*Andrew Popik*	1 Blue Hill Plz Ste 15, Pearl River NY 10965	845-735-0274	R	2*	<.1
1675	Majestic Electric Company Inc—*Hank Byram*	PO Box 358, North Vernon IN 47265	812-346-2110	R	2*	<.1
1676	Mid Florida Electrical and Controls Inc—*Michael Music*	56 W Central Ave, Lake Wales FL 33853	863-679-5303	R	2*	<.1
1677	Ne Inc—*Wendy Bertini*	PO Box 31380, Las Vegas NV 89173	702-364-8877	R	2*	<.1
1678	Pacifica Electrical Contractors—*Thomas Puga*	14120 Paramount Blvd, Paramount CA 90723	562-634-3561	R	2*	<.1
1679	Pine Valley Electric Inc—*David Diederich*	PO Box 4895, Parker CO 80134	303-841-1032	R	2*	<.1
1680	Walters Electric Inc—*James Rabun*	225 E Wilbur Ave, Lake Mary FL 32746	407-321-8444	R	2*	<.1
1681	Aladdin's Electrical—*Michael Hoefer*	PO Box 7351, Cotati CA 94931	707-795-7207	R	2*	<.1
1682	Zapata Enterprises Inc—*William Zapata*	7675 Carley Dr, Port Tobacco MD 20677	301-843-9117	R	2*	<.1
1683	A-1 Electric Service Inc—*Gaylen Jones*	2525b E Livingston St, Springfield MO 65803	417-831-7770	R	2*	<.1
1684	Island Lighting and Power Systems—*Jim O'neil*	6 Hill St, Norfolk MA 02056	508-384-3882	R	2*	<.1
1685	K Bar Texas Electric Inc—*Donny Barry*	PO Box 1287, Levelland TX 79336	806-894-6189	R	2*	<.1
1686	Quantum Electric Inc—*Bill Tidmore*	3711 E Admiral Pl, Tulsa OK 74115	918-835-0546	R	2*	<.1
1687	Central/Long-Mcgehee Inc—*Robert Slaton*	PO Box 70218, Montgomery AL 36107	334-834-6600	R	2*	<.1

Note: An asterisk (*) indicates an estimated financial figure. The company type code used is as follows: R = Private, P = Public, S = Private Subsidiary, B = Public Subsidiary, D = Division, J = Joint Venture, I = Investment Fund.

COMPANY RANKINGS BY SALES WITHIN 4-DIGIT SIC

Rank	Company Name—Executive Officer	Address, City, State, Zip	Phone	Type	Fin	Empls
1688	Engineered Services Inc—Kevin Madden	7983 Sw Jack James Dr, Stuart FL 34997	772-283-2320	R	2*	<.1
1689	Inhouse Systems Inc—Kody Shed	PO Box 3989, Temple TX 76505	254-774-8271	R	2*	<.1
1690	Romac Electric Inc—Steve Worbington	10025 Camelot Ln, Rogers AR 72758	479-621-9909	R	2*	<.1
1691	Tele-Solutions Inc—Michael Finaldi	1767 Us Hwy 22 W Ste 1, Union NJ 07083	908-851-0444	R	2*	<.1
1692	Central Business Communications Inc—Mark Lynn	560 Eagle Manor Ln, Chesterfield MO 63017	314-576-1301	R	2*	<.1
1693	Cg Electrical Services Inc—Steven Gulick	12895 Temple Blvd, West Palm Beach FL 33412	561-333-8200	R	2*	<.1
1694	Chick-A-Chop Electrical Contractor Inc—Joe Chickachop	103 Lakeside Ave, Cherry Hill NJ 08003	856-428-4800	R	2*	<.1
1695	Expert Electric Inc—Larry Wright	1119 Grand Ave, Phoenix AZ 85007	602-254-6741	R	2*	<.1
1696	Fibernext LLC—Shawn Parker	41 Locke Rd, Concord NH 03301	603-226-2400	R	2*	<.1
1697	Grady R Jolley Electrical Contractors Inc—Grady Jolley	1014 Industry Dr Ste 1, Shelby NC 28152	704-481-1144	R	2*	<.1
1698	Gregg Electric Corp—Gregg Brown	PO Box 380370, Murdock FL 33938	941-764-6565	R	2*	<.1
1699	Henry Electric Inc—Charles Henry	3709 Transportation Dr, Fort Wayne IN 46818	260-490-7777	R	2*	<.1
1700	Huffman Engineering Inc—Howard Huffman	5301 N 57th St Ste 101, Lincoln NE 68507	402-464-6823	R	2*	<.1
1701	Keypoint Services International Inc—Wade Norman	3882 Crater Lake Ave, Medford OR 97504	541-857-8070	R	2*	<.1
1702	Reece Electric Inc—Krystal Reece	PO Box 204, Stockbridge GA 30281	770-474-2379	R	2*	<.1
1703	Richardson Logic Control Inc—Charles Hicks	8115 Hicks Holw, Mckinney TX 75071	972-542-7375	R	2*	<.1
1704	Sal Electric Company Inc—Philip Chianetta	83 Fleet St, Jersey City NJ 07306	201-798-4406	R	2*	<.1
1705	Stone Electric Company Inc—Paula Woodall	4624 5th Ave S, Birmingham AL 35222	205-592-6313	R	2*	<.1
1706	T and J Electric Corp—Anne Newton	PO Box 1051, Westford MA 01886	978-692-1591	R	2*	<.1
1707	Totalcom Management Inc—Moses Oroian	PO Box 460230, San Antonio TX 78246	210-366-1116	R	2*	<.1
1708	Venture Electric Co—Donald Hatchett	10136 Hull St Rd C, Midlothian VA 23112	804-276-6422	R	2*	<.1
1709	Windsor Electric Contracting Inc—Pramanand Rambharose	9501 Brisbin St, Jamaica NY 11435	718-850-6523	R	2*	<.1
1710	Bodiford Electric Inc—Wallace Bodiford	3976 N Monroe St Ste 9, Tallahassee FL 32303	850-562-8118	R	2*	<.1
1711	Star 3 Corp—Robert Urban	6395 E Platte Ave, Colorado Springs CO 80915	719-591-8658	R	2*	<.1
1712	Annette LLC—Stephanie Stoll	926 Diablo Ave Ste 332, Novato CA 94947	415-893-1677	R	2*	<.1
1713	Ablecomm Inc—Michael Marcus	230 Woodmont Rd Ste 15, Milford CT 06460	203-878-8383	R	2*	<.1
1714	Phoenix Commercial Electric Inc—Vincent Gagliardi	8901 N 79th Ave Ste 10, Peoria AZ 85345	623-879-0112	R	2*	<.1
1715	Bernard Eckert—Bernard Eckert	15712 Willets Point Bl, Whitestone NY 11357	718-746-8438	R	2*	<.1
1716	JC Electric—Jose Cardenas	11144 Devan Dr, Mission TX 78573	956-519-2701	R	2*	<.1
1717	Moore Electrical Contractors Inc—Johnny Moore	PO Box 350579, Jacksonville FL 32235	904-645-6807	R	2*	<.1
1718	Los Angles Hwc—Dave Cathcraft	14402 Carmenita Rd, Norwalk CA 90650	562-623-9787	R	2*	<.1
1719	Cr Electric Company LLC	153 Hilbert Cir, Jonesborough TN 37659	423-913-3888	R	2*	<.1
1720	B and D Electric Inc—Stephen Hannahs	7606 Northport Dr, Lansing MI 48917	517-322-0252	R	2*	<.1
1721	Direct Communications Inc—Steve Vandervort	13701 S Hwy 75, Glenpool OK 74033	918-291-0092	R	2*	<.1
1722	Durham and Sons Inc—Ralph Durham	1947 N Harbor City Blv, Melbourne FL 32935	321-259-2665	R	2*	<.1
1723	Electrical Systems and Solutions Inc—Don Laut	7879 Cessna Ave, Gaithersburg MD 20879	301-948-0101	R	2*	<.1
1724	Hall Electric Co—Rodney Dobb	PO Box 785, Muskegon MI 49443	231-726-5001	R	2*	<.1
1725	Multi Services Inc—Connie Thompson	PO Box 9, Harkers Island NC 28531	252-504-2180	R	2*	<.1
1726	Nycom Networks Corp—Michael Fusco	PO Box 585, Washingtonville NY 10992	212-462-2000	R	2*	<.1
1727	Price Electric Company Inc—Boyce Swink	1422 Okeechobee Rd, West Palm Beach FL 33401	561-832-5657	R	2*	<.1
1728	R and R Electric Of Southwest Florida Inc—Richard Armbrust	568 Commercial Blvd, Naples FL 34104	239-643-5221	R	2*	<.1
1729	Richard J Curley Inc—Richard Curley	25 School Ln, Norristown PA 19403	610-539-5245	R	2*	<.1
1730	Salzman Electric Company Inc—John Blerkon	12307 20th Ave, College Point NY 11356	718-229-5520	R	2*	<.1
1731	T and S Fire And Security Inc—James Testerman	3025 Randleman Rd, Greensboro NC 27406	336-273-0859	R	2*	<.1
1732	Bowne Electric Inc—Bob Bowne	2210 Denton Dr Ste 109, Austin TX 78758	512-454-5325	R	2*	<.1
1733	CS Hurd Electrical Contracting Inc—Carter Hurd	PO Box 1626, Richmond Hill GA 31324	912-756-5881	R	2*	<.1
1734	Wacor Electronic Systems Inc—Henry Hall	1830 State St, East Petersburg PA 17520	717-581-1008	R	2*	<.1
1735	Bettis Electric Company Inc—Bill Bettis	Macy Dr Ste 1304, Roswell GA 30076	770-518-7820	R	2*	<.1
1736	C Williams Electrical Construction Inc—Chrisopher Williams	464 S 10th Ave, Mount Vernon NY 10550	914-667-5754	R	2*	<.1
1737	J Adams Electrical Contractor Inc—Mark Adams	1240 Old Bells Ferry R, Marietta GA 30066	770-428-3797	R	2*	<.1
1738	Joyner Cable Telecommunications Inc—Johnny Joyner	105 Channel Dr, Lake Mary FL 32746	407-324-9434	R	2*	<.1
1739	Mc Com Inc—Rod Mcleod	PO Box 536329, Grand Prairie TX 75053	972-445-8668	R	2*	<.1
1740	Samm Enterprises Inc—Melanie Adams	PO Box 410, Defuniak Springs FL 32435	850-892-4377	R	2*	<.1
1741	T and S Electric Inc—Archie Tyson	PO Box 1339, Knightdale NC 27545	919-217-2821	R	2*	<.1
1742	Wea Electrical Contractor Inc—William Escorcia	7701 W 26th Ave Unit 2, Hialeah FL 33016	305-820-3208	R	2*	<.1
1743	A-C-Y Communications Contractors Inc—Fred Ludwig	342 Hower St Ne, North Canton OH 44720	330-494-6933	R	2*	<.1
1744	Advanced Detection Systems Inc—William Walden	4450 W Eau Gallie Blvd, Melbourne FL 32934	321-777-6655	R	2*	<.1
1745	Geniac Electric Inc—Robert Geniac	3503 Greenleaf Blvd St, Kalamazoo MI 49008	269-321-1700	R	2*	<.1
1746	Veltri Electric Inc—John Veltri	1045 Jefferson Ave Ste, Washington PA 15301	724-222-3811	R	2*	<.1
1747	Apl Electric Inc—Beverly Applebee	2131 Aetna Rd, Ashtabula OH 44004	440-998-2688	R	2*	<.1
1748	Baldridge Electric Inc—Judy Baldridge	1825 S Eisenhower St, Wichita KS 67209	316-267-0058	R	2*	<.1
1749	Benjamin Hr Inc—Richard Hoffman	3525 Amber St Ste 1, Philadelphia PA 19134	215-535-5200	R	2*	<.1
1750	Clayco Electric Co—Gabe Brull	319 E 11th Ave, Kansas City MO 64116	816-221-0593	R	2*	<.1
1751	E and M O'hara Inc—Edward O'hara	144 Main St, West Orange NJ 07052	973-325-3626	R	2*	<.1
1752	Elco Electric—Paul Philbrick	311 Perry Rd, Bangor ME 04401	207-942-4659	R	2*	<.1
1753	Frost Electric Company Inc—Craig Martin	749 Morton Ave, Aurora IL 60506	630-897-3900	R	2*	<.1
1754	Harvey Preston Electric Co—Russell Thomas	12110 Old Hwy 71, Fort Smith AR 72916	479-646-0433	R	2*	<.1
1755	M Gitlin Company Inc—Michael Gitlin	133 Andrien Rd, Glen Mills PA 19342	610-558-0680	R	2*	<.1
1756	Mas Electrical Services Inc—Michael Struble	32940 Capitol St, Livonia MI 48150	734-425-0950	R	2*	<.1
1757	Metroplex Inc—Thomas Gage	1115 S Waldron Rd Ste, Fort Smith AR 72903	479-646-6624	R	2*	<.1
1758	MP Baker Electric Inc—Michael Baker	PO Box 5836, Lafayette IN 47903	765-447-4658	R	2*	<.1
1759	Reliance Electric Inc—Kelly Johnson	25945 Main St, Zimmerman MN 55398	763-856-4371	R	2*	<.1
1760	S and S Electric Inc—Teresa Legrys	608 N Loudoun St, Winchester VA 22601	540-665-2033	R	2*	<.1
1761	Smoky Mountain Systems Inc—Charles D'ascoli	19 Smoky Mountain Dr, Franklin NC 28734	828-369-6067	R	2*	<.1
1762	Twin City Electric Inc—Cheryl Mulcahey	1701 Easy St Ste 5, Bloomington IL 61701	309-827-0636	R	2*	<.1
1763	Ulinski Electric Inc—Jon Ulinski	12379 31 Mile Rd, Washington MI 48095	586-752-5226	R	2*	<.1
1764	Vitel Communications Inc—Andrew Corcoran	8111 Nw 33rd St, Doral FL 33122	305-382-1000	R	2*	<.1
1765	Holm Electric Inc—Kevin Holm	PO Box 6856, Incline Village NV 89450	775-831-3781	R	2*	<.1
1766	Tim Brown Electric Inc—Timothy Brown	3088 Winkle Ave Ste B, Santa Cruz CA 95065	831-465-9870	R	2*	<.1
1767	Quality Electric And Controls Inc—Mark Richards	604 32 1/2 Rd, Clifton CO 81520	970-434-7600	R	2*	<.1
1768	Field Communications Inc—Robert Minarick	957 Alps Rd, Wayne NJ 07470	973-305-8500	R	2*	<.1
1769	Kap Contracting Company Inc—Sherry Kolbush	705 S Camden Ave, Fruitland MD 21826	410-742-9244	R	2*	<.1
1770	Ace Electrical Service of North Florida Inc—David Woody	4659 Hwy Ave Unit 3, Jacksonville FL 32254	904-322-7138	R	2*	<.1
1771	Cable Systems Installations Inc—John Hutchinson	PO Box 261, Sparta WI 54656	608-269-3159	R	2*	<.1
1772	East Pasco Electric—Tony Leger	4841 Allen Rd, Zephyrhills FL 33541	813-782-8622	R	2*	<.1
1773	Fusion Electric LLC	PO Box 936, Prosper TX 75078	972-347-2387	R	2*	<.1
1774	Bobby Davis Electric Company Inc—Robert Davis	2979 Sandbrook St, Memphis TN 38116	901-345-1636	R	2*	<.1
1775	Harley Electric Company Inc—Harry Katz	1817 Unionport Rd, Bronx NY 10462	718-823-8885	R	2*	<.1
1776	Tri-City Electric Service Inc—Kathleen Hill	9638 W 143rd St Ste 1, Orland Park IL 60462	708-349-9505	R	2*	<.1
1777	East Texas Alarm Inc—Gary Hodge	315 S Vine Ave, Tyler TX 75702	903-593-3225	R	2*	<.1

Rank	Company Name—Executive Officer	Address, City, State, Zip	Phone	Type	Fin	Empls
1778	Eyemax Security LLC	5665 Atlanta Hwy, Alpharetta GA 30004	678-523-5780	R	2*	<.1
1779	Lightech Inc—Librado Anglero	549 E Brambleton Ave S, Norfolk VA 23510	703-725-3340	R	2*	<.1
1780	Genessee Electric Inc—Bryan Fleming	14309 N Fenton Rd, Fenton MI 48430	810-750-8899	R	2*	<.1
1781	Hbi Electric Inc—Jeff Demoss	10164 County Rd 10, East Liberty OH 43319	937-666-5088	R	2*	<.1
1782	Schmidtlein Electric Inc—Debbie Schmidtlein	305 Ne Croco Rd, Topeka KS 66616	785-357-4572	R	2*	<.1
1783	Tim Reinhold Enterprises LLC—Reinhold Eiliena	751 N Service Rd E, Sullivan MO 63080	573-860-2514	R	2*	<.1
1784	Mueske Electric Inc—Duane Mueske	PO Box 286, Spirit Lake IA 51360	712-336-1986	R	2*	<.1
1785	Ainsworth Electric Inc—Richard Ainsworth	3763 Lapeer Rd Ste E, Port Huron MI 48060	810-984-5768	R	2*	<.1
1786	Davila Electric Company Inc—Albert Davila	1842 Bandera Rd, San Antonio TX 78228	210-436-1551	R	2*	<.1
1787	Electrical Contractors Inc—Thomas Moreland	PO Box 1191, Cape Girardeau MO 63702	573-335-4556	R	2*	<.1
1788	Electrix Company Inc—Dave Goldsworthy	4452 Ocean View Blvd S, Montrose CA 91020	818-790-9200	R	2*	<.1
1789	Htis Inc—Earl Jones	6001 Stonington St Ste, Houston TX 77040	713-462-0977	R	2*	<.1
1790	Kyne and Son Electric Co—John Kyne	201 Janney Rd, Dayton OH 45404	937-237-7150	R	2*	<.1
1791	Middlebury Electric Inc—Philip Wogoman	65725 Us Hwy 33, Goshen IN 46526	574-825-5741	R	2*	<.1
1792	Rice and Brouillard Electric Inc—Phillip Rice	PO Box 1626, Haverhill MA 01831	978-372-8734	R	2*	<.1
1793	Sub Station Specialists—Veronica Marsh	42044 Winchester Rd 3c, Temecula CA 92590	951-296-9526	R	2*	<.1
1794	Tel-Net Group Inc—Michael Ballis	9351 Philadelphia Rd E, Baltimore MD 21237	410-661-9510	R	2*	<.1
1795	Chuck's Electrical Service Inc—Charles Lansinger	105 Brown St, Centreville MD 21617	410-758-0808	R	2*	<.1
1796	BK Signs Inc—Brian Kanner	1028 W Kirkwall Rd, Azusa CA 91702	626-334-5600	R	2*	<.1
1797	C and C Electrical Contractors—Fred Cialdea	19 Crossman Rd, Woburn MA 01801	781-932-8778	R	2*	<.1
1798	Jefferson Current Electric Inc—Judy Davis	N3085 County Rd K, Jefferson WI 53549	920-674-6444	R	2*	<.1
1799	Completecomm Telecommunications Inc—Shaun Alger	PO Box 1126, Carlsbad CA 92018	760-477-7700	R	2*	<.1
1800	Dever Electric Inc—Matthew Dever	95 Rte 50, Ocean View NJ 08230	609-390-3434	R	2*	<.1
1801	American Electrical Contracting Inc—Earl Frick	5065 Saint Augustine R, Jacksonville FL 32207	904-737-7770	R	2*	.1
1802	Harbor Electric Inc—James Vonplinsky	1745 Aurora Rd, Melbourne FL 32935	321-254-7959	R	2*	.1
1803	Electrical Solutions LLC	6011 Leewood Dr, Alexandria VA 22310	703-765-3136	R	2*	<.1
1804	Stanley Alarm Systems Inc—Clude Roy	PO Box 628, Kawkawlin MI 48631	989-686-3194	R	2*	<.1
1805	Baumgartner's Electric Inc—Gary Baumgartner	1601 W 1st St, Sioux Falls SD 57104	605-336-2889	R	2*	<.1
1806	Bill Anderson and Associates Inc—William Anderson	7600 Appling Ctr Dr St, Memphis TN 38133	901-377-8030	R	2*	<.1
1807	Hou-Tex Power Inc—Jim Cochran	720 W 20th St, Houston TX 77008	713-869-9113	R	2*	<.1
1808	Cochran Electric Co—Ron Cochran	2103 S Jackson St, Jackson MI 49203	517-784-7106	R	2*	<.1
1809	James D Gilliam Electric Inc—James Gilliam	119 Buena Vista Rd, Hot Springs AR 71913	501-525-1381	R	2*	<.1
1810	N and D Technical Services Inc—Norman Barnett	8717 Stagecoach Rd, Little Rock AR 72210	501-455-5222	R	2*	<.1
1811	Pace Electric Inc—Mark Prusinski	12015 W Janesville Rd, Hales Corners WI 53130	414-425-3305	R	2*	<.1
1812	RAR Electric Inc—Micheal Dufrene	209 W S St, Ithaca MI 48847	989-875-3988	R	2*	<.1
1813	Twa Industries Inc—Terry Atkins	207 E Holly Ave Ste 10, Sterling VA 20164	703-450-9253	R	2*	<.1
1814	Comer Electric Company Inc—R Comer	2302 W Andrew Johnson, Morristown TN 37814	423-587-2360	R	2*	<.1
1815	Ross Electric Inc—Robert Ross	4200 Blanco Rd, San Antonio TX 78212	210-733-5452	R	2*	<.1
1816	Boasso Construction LLC—Raymond Boasso	4600 E Saint Bernard H, Meraux LA 70075	504-628-4233	R	2*	<.1
1817	Cobalt Electric Inc—Mark Watkins	75 Maddox Rd Ste 100, Buford GA 30518	770-564-1826	R	2*	<.1
1818	Genesis Electrical Systems Inc—Russel Davis	9675 Wendell Rd, Dallas TX 75243	214-343-3565	R	2*	<.1
1819	Harrison Electrical Construction Inc—Kevin Harrison	304 Pine Bark Ln, North Augusta SC 29860	803-663-4006	R	2*	<.1
1820	Huss Electric Company Inc—James Huss	7768 Service Ctr Dr, West Chester OH 45069	513-759-9470	R	2*	<.1
1821	Maximum Communication Inc—Michael Lockette	PO Box 140095, Saint Louis MO 63114	314-423-0007	R	2*	<.1
1822	O H Burg Corp—Barry Kesselman	181 Tosca Dr, Stoughton MA 02072	781-344-0522	R	2*	<.1
1823	Robert Anderson Electrical Contracting Inc—Robert Anderson	466 N Nassau St, Charleston SC 29403	843-577-5775	R	2*	<.1
1824	Virginia Electrical Services Inc—Robert Simmons	PO Box 400, Daleville VA 24083	540-777-0393	R	2*	<.1
1825	Brent Electric Inc—Gene Brent	1245 Se 2nd St, Pryor OK 74361	918-824-1134	R	2*	<.1
1826	Innovation Industries Inc—Keith Hughes	PO Box 1906, Eustis FL 32727	352-357-4459	R	2*	<.1
1827	West Star Electric Inc—James Houg	603 Lake St E Ste 201, Wayzata MN 55391	763-537-0807	R	2*	<.1
1828	Bca Electric—Jennifer Harrol	5081 Leonard Rd, Bryan TX 77807	979-823-4000	R	2*	<.1
1829	CW Harrelson Electric Co—Clarence Harrelson	PO Box 4136, Wilmington NC 28406	910-762-1001	R	2*	<.1
1830	Edmondson Allen H Electrical Contractor—Allen Edmondson	7313 Central Ave Pke, Powell TN 37849	865-938-5299	R	2*	<.1
1831	Hts LLC	2020 Land O Lkes Blvd, Lutz FL 33549	813-751-1030	R	2*	<.1
1832	Angeloni Electric Inc—David Angeloni	670 E Parkridge Ave St, Corona CA 92879	951-354-9544	R	2*	<.1
1833	Comroe Advance Power Inc—Donald Pusey	3061 Pheasant Dr, Northampton PA 18067	610-837-6664	R	2*	<.1
1834	Engles and Fahs Inc—Michael Fahs	3564 Gillespie Dr, York PA 17404	717-792-0100	R	2*	<.1
1835	Mr Wire—Herbert Gaines	1427 Mission Rd Ste D, South San Francisco CA 94080	650-992-9473	R	2*	<.1
1836	Stirling And Associates Of Flager Inc—Kipp Gardner	PO Box 1350, Bunnell FL 32110	386-437-3369	R	2*	<.1
1837	Lee Davis Electric Inc—Lee Davis	1104 Birch St, Park Rapids MN 56470	218-732-8304	R	2*	<.1
1838	Piece of Work Corporation of Boynton Beach—Phil Barone	1021 S Rogers Cir Ste, Boca Raton FL 33487	561-989-0930	R	2*	<.1
1839	Blackfoot Electric Corp—Jennifer Scott	3921 76th Ave N, Pinellas Park FL 33781	727-546-0002	R	2*	<.1
1840	Blumenthal-Kahn Electric LP Truland Systems Corp	PO Box 369, Owings Mills MD 21117	410-363-1200	S	2*	<.1
1841	Chicagoland Cabling Solutions Inc—Lawrence Mathieu	784 Oak Creek Dr, Lombard IL 60148	708-233-3700	R	2*	<.1
1842	Cotner Electric Co—Ronald Cotner	2049 Southern Expy, Cape Girardeau MO 63703	573-335-8110	R	2*	<.1
1843	Division 16 Electrical Inc—Jennifer Harvey	6025 Technology Dr, West Melbourne FL 32904	321-727-1006	R	2*	<.1
1844	Five State Electric LLC	PO Box 8455, Greenville SC 29604	864-232-3411	R	2*	<.1
1845	Full Range Security Protection Inc—Louis Buzzeo	3000 47th Ave, Long Island City NY 11101	718-392-6666	R	2*	<.1
1846	FV Casno Electrical Contractor Inc—Francis Casano	1161 Old Dixie Hwy, Vero Beach FL 32960	772-567-8134	R	2*	<.1
1847	G and T Electric Inc—George White	551 Easton Rd Ste B, Warrington PA 18976	215-918-2565	R	2*	<.1
1848	Jewell Electric Inc—Don Jewell	PO Box 1102, Du Bois PA 15801	814-371-8174	R	2*	<.1
1849	Johnson Electric Co—Audie Bradshaw	PO Box 845, Addison TX 75001	972-387-4770	R	2*	<.1
1850	K and H Corp—Gerald Peterson	1927 W 2nd St, Webster City IA 50595	515-832-1762	R	2*	<.1
1851	Madruga Electric Inc—Melvin Madruga	3216 State Rd, Bakersfield CA 93308	661-399-3750	R	2*	<.1
1852	Mazza Electric Corp—John Mazza	494 8th Ave Fl 6, New York NY 10001	212-564-0322	R	2*	<.1
1853	Prism Technology Group Inc—Doreen Mcerlean	820 Riverside Ave, Lyndhurst NJ 07071	201-804-7700	R	2*	<.1
1854	Reliable Voice and Data Systems Inc—Robert Lovejoy	366 E Meadow Ave, East Meadow NY 11554	516-542-1130	R	2*	<.1
1855	Schwann Electric Company Inc—Dorothy Schwan	5292 N NW Hwy, Chicago IL 60630	773-467-2900	R	2*	<.1
1856	Shamrock Companies Inc—Jim Wyckoff	PO Box 5806, Katy TX 77491	281-492-0206	R	2*	<.1
1857	Smartwatch Security and Sound LLC—Dean Farrel	PO Box 1215, Mount Dora FL 32756	352-383-2479	R	2*	<.1
1858	Techtele Communications LLC—Mary Chealina	120 Willow Brook Dr, Berlin CT 06037	860-829-3000	R	2*	<.1
1859	Ukasik Electric—Carl Ukasik	5509 W Lake Rd, Erie PA 16505	814-833-6020	R	2*	<.1
1860	US Electric and Telecom—Patrick Naughton	13 Wild Rd, Hopkinton MA 01748	508-435-0111	R	2*	<.1
1861	Wagner Electric And Construction LLC—Scottie Cameron	326 Cycle Dr, Portersville PA 16051	724-368-3482	R	2*	<.1
1862	City Electric Of Plainview Inc—Ricky Mason	4428 Olton Rd, Plainview TX 79072	806-296-5111	R	2*	<.1
1863	Roberts Electric Company Inc—Alan Butler	2210 Foreman St, Cayce SC 29033	803-796-3710	R	2*	<.1
1864	Three Phase Electric Inc—Ronald Riopelle	493 Ne 3rd Ave Ste B20, Canby OR 97013	503-263-2558	R	2*	<.1
1865	Digitech Custom Audio and Video Inc—Mark Vyain	612 Station Dr, Carmel IN 46032	317-580-1922	R	2*	<.1
1866	Gallegos Electric Inc—Juan Gallegos	1350 El Jardin Heights, Brownsville TX 78526	956-542-0058	R	2*	<.1

Note: An asterisk (*) indicates an estimated financial figure. The company type code used is as follows: R = Private, P = Public, S = Private Subsidiary, B = Public Subsidiary, D = Division, J = Joint Venture, I = Investment Fund.

COMPANY RANKINGS BY SALES WITHIN 4-DIGIT SIC

Rank	Company Name—*Executive Officer*	Address, City, State, Zip	Phone	Type	Fin	Empls
1867	Kaiser Electrical Contractors Inc—*Edward Kaiser*	PO Box 427, Morton IL 61550	309-263-8355	R	2*	<.1
1868	Response Electric Inc—*Michael Weiss*	680 Lorimer St, Brooklyn NY 11211	718-599-9753	R	2*	<.1
1869	Tibbetts Electric Inc—*Robert Bettencourt*	PO Box 285, Canton MA 02021	781-821-2124	R	2*	<.1
1870	Duffy's Electric Inc—*Monique Duff*	PO Box 291, Bradley ME 04411	207-843-7375	R	2*	<.1
1871	Tyrrell Electrical Contractors Inc—*Jeremiah Tyrrell*	56808 Grand River Ave, New Hudson MI 48165	248-437-3233	R	2*	<.1
1872	Advanced Communications Group Inc—*Lynn Cockrum*	355 Old Oxford Rd, Covington GA 30014	770-385-1422	R	2*	<.1
1873	Mid-Counties Electric Inc—*Michael Flores*	12901 N Tully Rd, Lodi CA 95240	209-931-7110	R	2*	<.1
1874	Acme Electric Inc—*Chuck Orr*	96 N Precision Dr Ste, Pueblo West CO 81007	719-547-3335	R	2*	<.1
1875	Chris Electric Company Inc—*Chris Syrpes*	1501 W Cedar Ave, Denver CO 80223	303-778-8281	R	2*	<.1
1876	D and E Electric Inc—*Douglas Fritz*	7055 Okeana Drewsburg, Okeana OH 45053	513-738-1172	R	2*	<.1
1877	G Bishop and Co—*Gary Bishop*	756 E Edna Pl, Covina CA 91723	626-966-5000	R	2*	<.1
1878	Hartline Supply Inc—*Curtis Hartline*	PO Box 6836, Lakeland FL 33807	863-425-6000	R	2*	<.1
1879	Jarrett Electric Inc—*Carl Jarrett*	3321 Sillect Ave, Bakersfield CA 93308	661-327-8046	R	2*	<.1
1880	S and G Waldrop Electric Inc—*D Waldrop*	1506 2nd Ave N, Bessemer AL 35020	205-426-4168	R	2*	<.1
1881	T and J Electric Company Inc—*Mike Taylor*	2627 Allentown Rd, Pekin IL 61554	309-347-2196	R	2*	<.1
1882	Weaver Electric Inc—*Dennis Burnett*	626 Ave E, Bayonne NJ 07002	201-339-1909	R	2*	<.1
1883	Automated Cable Services Inc—*Nathan Flowers*	PO Box 607, Waldorf MD 20604	301-888-9223	R	2*	<.1
1884	Cliff Delsart Electric Inc—*Steve Delsart*	2065 S Oneida St, Green Bay WI 54304	920-494-7070	R	2*	<.1
1885	Macnichol Electric Inc—*Stephen Macnichol*	2 Wildewood Dr, Lynnfield MA 01940	781-334-4849	R	2*	<.1
1886	Quinn Electric Corp—*Greg Quinn*	26185 190th Ave, Eldridge IA 52748	563-285-4530	R	2*	<.1
1887	K Rieger Company Inc—*Kent Rieger*	PO Box 326, Elmhurst IL 60126	630-530-7515	R	2*	<.1
1888	Carl Hall—*Carl Hall*	PO Box 1847, Yuba City CA 95992	530-673-4682	R	2*	<.1
1889	Crafts Electric Inc—*Jeff Diederichs*	1602 N 30th St, Manitowoc WI 54220	920-682-4684	R	2*	<.1
1890	Eldridge Electric and Son Inc—*Chris Eldridge*	380 S Main St, Bishop CA 93514	760-873-9140	R	2*	<.1
1891	Entec Systems Inc—*Brent Laws*	450 Satellit Blvd Ne P, Suwanee GA 30024	770-931-0800	R	2*	<.1
1892	John Coyne Electrical Contracting Inc—*John Coyne*	43 Langenbach Rd, East Greenbush NY 12061	518-479-3255	R	2*	<.1
1893	Leddy Electric Inc—*Thomas Leddy*	22 Lark Industrial Pkw, Greenville RI 02828	401-949-0910	R	2*	<.1
1894	Northeast Temperature Controls Inc—*John Mulkerin*	32 Swanton St, Winchester MA 01890	781-729-0087	R	2*	<.1
1895	Quality Cctv Systems Inc—*Dianne Rust*	3513 Gregory Pond Rd, Richmond VA 23236	804-276-7300	R	2*	<.1
1896	Sure-Lock-Homes Security and Communications Inc—*Donald Hains*	14450 Ewing Ave S Ste, Burnsville MN 55306	952-224-5450	R	2*	<.1
1897	Sweetwater Electronic Construction and Maintenance Inc—*W Whisenant*	PO Box 1292, Sweetwater TX 79556	325-235-3456	R	2*	<.1
1898	Data Cabling Solutions Inc—*Andrew Dever*	636 Coventry Pl, Amherst OH 44001	440-985-1402	R	2*	<.1
1899	Paul Wiley Electrical Contractors Inc—*Paul Wiley*	PO Box 491210, Atlanta GA 30349	404-763-5681	R	2*	<.1
1900	Stealth Ltd—*J Mondy*	PO Box 7617, Charleston WV 25356	304-776-0047	R	2*	<.1
1901	Brevard Electric Co—*James Newman*	5133 Boylston Hwy, Mills River NC 28759	828-890-0064	R	2*	<.1
1902	Commworld Of Kern County Inc—*Tamra Sturges*	5401 Woodmere Dr, Bakersfield CA 93313	661-833-6361	R	2*	<.1
1903	Electro Systems Electric Inc—*Mitch Cottrell*	16932 Gothard St Ste I, Huntington Beach CA 92647	714-848-5646	R	2*	<.1
1904	Freedom Electrical Company Inc—*Michael Lamkin*	117 Ashburnham St, Fitchburg MA 01420	978-343-0500	R	2*	<.1
1905	G and S Electrical Company LLC	79 2nd St, Medford MA 02155	617-293-6777	R	2*	<.1
1906	Paradigm Energy Inc—*Raymond Gerton*	20692 Corsair Blvd, Hayward CA 94545	510-785-9441	R	2*	<.1
1907	Spectrum Systems Integration Inc—*Frances Coumes*	9905 Painter Ave Ste A, Whittier CA 90605	562-944-5747	R	2*	<.1
1908	Watkins Construction Company Inc—*Debra Watkins*	PO Box 968, Stevenson WA 98648	509-427-5525	R	2*	<.1
1909	Richardson Electrical Company Inc—*Linda Richardson*	PO Box 1330, Seabrook NH 03874	603-474-3900	R	2*	<.1
1910	A 1 Quality Electric Inc—*Jim Richardson*	6268 W 10th St Ste 1, Greeley CO 80634	970-352-9040	R	2*	<.1
1911	Albright Electric Inc—*Steve Shuck*	2245 E Mckinley Ave, Fresno CA 93703	559-227-6450	R	2*	<.1
1912	Americom Telecommunications Inc (Houston Texas)—*George R Adelson*	3544 East TC Jester, Houston TX 77018	713-688-8299	R	2*	<.1
1913	Chicopee Electronics—*Sandra F Averill*	277 Grattan St, Chicopee MA 01020	413-533-6743	R	2*	<.1
1914	Future Home Co—*Murray Kunis*	2034 Cotner Ave 1st Fl, West Los Angeles CA 90025	310-966-9442	R	2*	<.1
1915	Muleshoe Valley Inc—*Steven Stancell*	PO Box 631, Muleshoe TX 79347	806-272-4266	R	2*	<.1
1916	Performance Electric Inc—*Timothy Lindsay*	22625 Mojave St, Apple Valley CA 92308	760-961-2132	R	2*	<.1
1917	Alight Electric—*Bill Wong*	263 Crown Cir, South San Francisco CA 94080	650-991-3282	R	2*	<.1
1918	Beekman Co—*Thomas Beekman*	1410 Fm 2855 Rd, Katy TX 77493	281-371-0552	R	2*	<.1
1919	Carm's Electric Company Inc—*Paul Gurriero*	16130 Cleophus Ave, Allen Park MI 48101	313-382-7631	R	2*	<.1
1920	Hooper Electric—*Rick Hooper*	319 Freeman Rd, Livingston TX 77351	936-327-4250	R	2*	<.1
1921	Medical Communications Systems Inc—*William Wilson*	17595 Paxton Ave, Lansing IL 60438	708-895-4500	R	2*	<.1
1922	Network Connections USA Inc—*Graham Barker*	221 Soldiers Creek Pl, Longwood FL 32750	407-321-7394	R	2*	<.1
1923	Total Systems Integration Inc—*Jorge Tinajero*	PO Box 227249, Los Angeles CA 90022	323-346-0161	R	2*	<.1
1924	Cumberland Services Group Inc—*Lygetta Morgan*	PO Box 564, Rockwood TN 37854	865-354-3652	R	2*	<.1
1925	Giberson Electric Inc—*E Giberson*	310 S Rte 121, Warrensburg IL 62573	217-672-3579	R	2*	<.1
1926	Bennett Electric And Industrial Contractors Inc—*Rickey Bennett*	PO Box 2273, Valdosta GA 31604	229-253-1971	R	2*	<.1
1927	Mac General Inc—*Mike Carignan*	111 Carpenter Dr Ste G, Sterling VA 20164	703-707-0606	R	2*	<.1
1928	National Design Group Inc—*Michael Hall*	10281 Frosty Ct Ste 15, Manassas VA 20109	703-530-1400	R	2*	<.1
1929	Pat's Electric Inc—*Pat Smith*	104 Cedar Ave, Orange City FL 32763	386-775-7776	R	2*	<.1
1930	Chiv Electrical—*John Chivington*	530 Williams Ditch Rd, Cantonment FL 32533	850-937-1094	R	2*	<.1
1931	Don Johnson Electric Service—*Don Johnson*	3506 Westwood Cir, Rowlett TX 75088	972-412-6314	R	2*	<.1
1932	H and L Electrical Inc—*Howard Locklear*	PO Box 626, Laurinburg NC 28353	910-276-9655	R	2*	<.1
1933	Mastertech Security Services Inc—*Buck Millican*	PO Box 299, Mesquite NV 89024	702-346-2576	R	2*	<.1
1934	Multi Two Electric Inc—*Glenn Wideman*	70 Pitney Rd, Lancaster PA 17602	717-735-7706	R	2*	<.1
1935	Biship Electric Of Ocala Inc—*Robin Bishop*	11027 Se 24th St Rd, Silver Springs FL 34488	352-625-9022	R	2*	<.1
1936	Blackwelder and Associates Electric Company Inc—*Al Tondreault*	6965 38th St N, Pinellas Park FL 33781	727-526-1873	R	2*	<.1
1937	Brian Electric Inc—*Brian Sullivan*	82 Deep Spring Ln, Stamford CT 06907	203-348-2454	R	2*	<.1
1938	Cablecom Corp—*Thomas Looney*	3825 N Elston Ave, Chicago IL 60618	773-539-6000	R	2*	<.1
1939	Col-Bran Electric Inc—*Rob Cheshier*	109 Pky, Boerne TX 78006	210-479-5553	R	2*	<.1
1940	Englewood Electric Inc—*William Yager*	7341 Sawyer Cir, Port Charlotte FL 33981	941-698-9799	R	2*	<.1
1941	Gray Audograph Agency Inc—*John Collins*	PO Box 726, New Castle DE 19720	302-658-1700	R	2*	<.1
1942	JDK Electrical Inc—*Ken Wischmeyer*	5282 Research Dr, Huntington Beach CA 92649	714-893-1993	R	2*	<.1
1943	Sammarco Electric Company Inc—*Tim Sammarco*	1183 N Mclean Blvd, Memphis TN 38108	901-728-4173	R	2*	<.1
1944	Sayre Electric—*Betty Smith*	PO Box 1001, East Liverpool OH 43920	330-385-2520	R	2*	<.1
1945	Scotty's Construction Company LLC	4838 N Dietz Rd, Webberville MI 48892	517-468-3200	R	2*	<.1
1946	Swing Electrical Company Inc—*Lynn Gantt*	PO Box 6187, Newport News VA 23606	757-873-0245	R	2*	<.1
1947	Titan Electrical Construction and Design Inc—*Curtis Johnson*	735 Cross Pointe Rd, Columbus OH 43230	614-501-6744	R	2*	<.1
1948	Vanguard Security System Inc—*Stan Sikorski*	995 John A Papalas Dr, Lincoln Park MI 48146	313-383-5115	R	2*	<.1
1949	WF Anderson Electric Inc—*William Anderson*	1850 Williams St, San Leandro CA 94577	510-351-4612	R	2*	<.1
1950	Central Florida Alarm Services Inc—*Troy Deal*	1235 W Fairbanks Ave, Orlando FL 32804	407-622-7760	R	2*	<.1
1951	Four Star Electric Inc—*Gerald Hale*	PO Box 976, Nampa ID 83653	208-941-5700	R	2*	<.1
1952	Kinter Electric Inc—*Greg Kinter*	2761 E Edison Rd, Sunnyside WA 98944	509-882-1000	R	2*	<.1

Rank*	Company Name—*Executive Officer*	Address, City, State, Zip	Phone	Type	Fin	Empls
1953	Climate Masters and Electrical Company Inc—*Jack Morrison*	PO Box 7109, Spanish Fort AL 36577	251-626-9231	R	2*	<.1
1954	Elliott's Air Conditioning And Electrical Inc—*Delbert Elliott*	PO Box 578, Granbury TX 76048	817-573-9698	R	2*	<.1
1955	Home Protection Center Inc—*Peter Leftin*	16519 Addison Rd, Addison TX 75001	972-733-7200	R	2*	<.1
1956	Conserv Inc—*Jerry Kirklin*	9855 Crppint Blvd Ste, Indianapolis IN 46256	317-578-9860	R	2*	<.1
1957	Jemco Electrical Contractors Inc—*James Magriples*	9213 180th St, Jamaica NY 11433	718-658-9500	R	2*	<.1
1958	Merit Electric Company Inc—*Larry Neuman*	751 Payne Ave, Saint Paul MN 55130	651-774-9671	R	2*	<.1
1959	Allied Security Alarms—*Rudy Alva*	269 Wattis Way, South San Francisco CA 94080	650-871-8959	R	2*	<.1
1960	Alarms Unlimited Inc—*Benjamin Bland*	339 Egidi Dr, Wheeling IL 60090	847-410-0000	R	2*	<.1
1961	Chet's Electric Inc—*Michael Hodges*	PO Box 262, Redmond OR 97756	541-548-1825	R	2*	<.1
1962	Ssi Systems Inc—*Randy Walker*	PO Box 393, Westminster CA 92684	714-899-8725	R	2*	<.1
1963	Taurus Industries Inc—*Bruce Towhey*	PO Box 15088, Tumwater WA 98511	360-754-8491	R	2*	<.1
1964	Ebersole Electric Inc—*Daniel Ebersole*	6790 Penn Ave, Wernersville PA 19565	610-693-5938	R	2*	<.1
1965	Kruts Electric Inc—*Brian Krutsinger*	PO Box 6511, Champaign IL 61826	217-688-3100	R	2*	<.1
1966	Nationwide Electrical Testing Inc—*Shashikant Bagle*	6050 Southard Trce, Cumming GA 30040	770-667-1875	R	2*	<.1
1967	Cannon Electric Co—*Bonny Yorkston*	2801 Roeder Ave, Bellingham WA 98225	360-733-4070	R	2*	<.1
1968	Tucknott Electrical Co—*Robert Tucknott*	6850 Regional St Ste 1, Dublin CA 94568	925-931-0800	R	2*	<.1
1969	LEB Electric Ltd—*William Parker*	85 Ralph Ave, Copiague NY 11726	631-842-0500	R	2*	.1
1970	Automated Energy Controls Inc—*Candice Hunte*	PO Box 702, Hartland MI 48353	248-887-0297	R	2*	<.1
1971	Ayala Electric Company Inc—*Francisco Ayala*	1904 Tameria Dr, Irving TX 75060	214-298-4382	R	2*	<.1
1972	Story Electrical Service Inc—*Glenda Story*	6335 Hill Chappel Rd, Paducah KY 42001	270-534-1655	R	2*	<.1
1973	A and A Electric Inc—*Runette Ansley*	3699 Bc Grant Rd, Cornelia GA 30531	706-778-7306	R	2*	<.1
1974	BVJ Company Inc—*John Jones*	PO Box 1189, Clinton NC 28329	910-592-1858	R	2*	<.1
1975	Ibex Tech Corp—*Eduardo Perez*	12355 Sw 129th Ct Ste, Miami FL 33186	786-242-4930	R	2*	<.1
1976	Jk Electric Inc—*Jason Knapp*	PO Box 5723, Lincoln NE 68505	402-327-8436	R	2*	<.1
1977	Union Lightning Protection Installers Inc—*Chris Wessels*	470 Keller Dr, Waukegan IL 60085	847-775-1520	R	2*	<.1
1978	M and M Power LLC	645 Long Corner Rd, Mount Airy MD 21771	301-317-9050	R	2*	<.1
1979	Bodie Electrical Contractors Of Fla Inc—*William Bodie*	2973 Edgewood Ave W, Jacksonville FL 32209	904-766-8611	R	2*	<.1
1980	C and W Electric Company Inc—*Derrill Chapman*	PO Box 1842, Anderson SC 29622	864-226-2762	R	2*	<.1
1981	Dillie And Kuhn Inc—*Larry Dillie*	2875 Akers Dr, Colorado Springs CO 80922	719-591-9900	R	2*	<.1
1982	Global Electric Inc—*Michael Biehl*	701 Farnsworth Ave, Oconto WI 54153	920-834-2234	R	2*	<.1
1983	Grivet Electric Inc—*Dan Grivet*	3008 S Fairway Dr, Tempe AZ 85282	480-820-0114	R	2*	<.1
1984	High Plains Electric—*Wayne Brown*	409 E 4th St, Dalhart TX 79022	806-244-2232	R	2*	<.1
1985	Turbo Electrical Contractors Inc—*Jack Deboer*	12502 Taylor Rd, Houston TX 77041	713-937-8098	R	2*	<.1
1986	American Electric Of Virginia Inc—*Paul Stanley*	899 Norfolk Sq, Norfolk VA 23502	757-455-5171	R	2*	<.1
1987	Budwine Service Electric Company Inc—*Dewain Healey*	PO Box 1599, Carlsbad NM 88221	575-885-3195	R	2*	<.1
1988	Engineered Systems Inc—*Charles Higgins*	14775 Grover St, Omaha NE 68144	402-333-0100	R	2*	<.1
1989	Fresch Electric Inc—*Albert Fresch*	1414 Milan Rd, Sandusky OH 44870	419-626-2535	R	2*	<.1
1990	Howard Electric Inc—*Richard Howard*	PO Box 749, Stinnett TX 79083	806-878-2060	R	2*	<.1
1991	Ib Electric Inc—*John Blagoi*	7008 Cherty Dr, Pls Vrds Pnsl CA 90275	310-544-9996	R	2*	<.1
1992	Lavandera Electric Co—*Ralph Lavandera*	PO Box 15715, Tampa FL 33684	813-870-3486	R	2*	<.1
1993	Mcneill Sound and Security Systems—*Richard Mcneil*	PO Box 961, West Covina CA 91793	626-968-3291	R	2*	<.1
1994	Nor Tec Electric Inc—*Barry Norton*	683 Sw Whitmore Dr, Port Saint Lucie FL 34984	772-785-6001	R	2*	<.1
1995	North Town Electric Company Inc *Steve Hope*	2429 Fabens Rd Ste 100, Dallas TX 75229	972-620-1995	R	2*	<.1
1996	Nu-Court Electrical Construction Inc—*James Courtney*	75 Hancock St Ste 101, Braintree MA 02184	781-843-1406	R	2*	<.1
1997	Quality Electric Service Company LLC	PO Box 613, Ocean View NJ 08230	609-861-1409	R	2*	<.1
1998	Vern's Electric Inc—*Marlene Gillenberger*	1917 Brownsville Rd St, Pittsburgh PA 15210	412-881-7899	R	2*	<.1
1999	Wmr Contracting Inc—*Bill Raper*	PO Box 10988, Glendale AZ 85318	602-315-0331	R	2*	<.1
2000	Burglar Alarm And Security Company Inc—*Danny Northcutt*	PO Box 90532, Lafayette LA 70509	337-234-0396	R	2*	<.1
2001	AJ Giannattasio Electrical Contractors Inc—*A Giannattasio*	203 Main St, Matawan NJ 07747	732-290-8940	R	2*	<.1
2002	Detech Inc—*Richard Holley*	37 Industrial Park Dr, Hendersonville TN 37075	615-822-7425	R	2*	<.1
2003	Frankl Electric Inc—*William Frankl*	PO Box 453, Mc Kees Rocks PA 15136	412-331-1611	R	2*	<.1
2004	G and G Electric Inc—*Randy Cruickshank*	3126 Reynolds Rd Units, Lakeland FL 33803	863-665-5400	R	2*	<.1
2005	Mcdonald Electric Service Inc—*Barry Mcdonald*	6915 W Beaver St, Jacksonville FL 32254	904-356-9473	R	2*	<.1
2006	Hubbard Electric Inc—*Jerry Hubbard*	1806 Ralph Ave, Louisville KY 40216	502-449-0588	R	2*	<.1
2007	Wamco Electric Inc—*William Moser*	150 School St Ste D, Westbury NY 11590	516-333-4444	R	2*	<.1
2008	Port Jervis Electric Inc—*Albert Sardina*	50 Barcelow St, Port Jervis NY 12771	845-856-1744	R	2*	<.1
2009	Dalton Electric Co—*Joe Spezialy*	3511 132nd St Sw Ste 4, Lynnwood WA 98087	425-787-1826	R	2*	<.1
2010	Farmers Electric Inc—*Frank Booth*	30 E Hemlock St, Othello WA 99344	509-488-2822	R	2*	<.1
2011	Priority Electric Inc—*Paul Prior*	381 Allen St, New Britain CT 06053	860-827-8504	R	2*	<.1
2012	Pyrotection Specialists Inc—*Kelly Palmer*	25570 Rye Canyon Rd St, Santa Clarita CA 91355	661-294-9187	R	2*	<.1
2013	Bagley Electric LLC	PO Box 228, Manchester TN 37349	931-728-5848	R	2*	<.1
2014	Kee Electrical Contractors Inc—*Chris Demeter*	PO Box 400, Brookville OH 45309	937-833-4848	R	2*	<.1
2015	Petrelli Electric Inc—*Salvatore Petrelli*	PO Box 801148, Santa Clarita CA 91380	661-268-7312	R	2*	<.1
2016	Berks Electric Inc—*Joseph Frymoyer*	PO Box 127, Geigertown PA 19523	610-372-8900	R	2*	<.1
2017	Concord Electrical Contractors Inc—*Mark Topley*	219 Ne 35th St, Miami FL 33137	305-576-1717	R	2*	<.1
2018	Mannino Electric Inc—*Robert Mannino*	4 Buckingham Ave, Poughkeepsie NY 12601	845-452-3520	R	2*	<.1
2019	Phil Hall Electric Inc—*Phil Hall*	PO Box 1845, Dickson TN 37056	615-446-0348	R	2*	<.1
2020	Automatic Door Systems LLC	86 Porete Ave, North Arlington NJ 07031	201-955-5311	R	2*	<.1
2021	Bock Electric Inc—*Bill Bock*	3510 Rhodes Rd, Rhodes MI 48652	989-879-4256	R	2*	<.1
2022	Canzan Electric Inc—*Colin Jaques*	184a Morris Ln Ste A, Campbell CA 95008	408-559-4673	R	2*	<.1
2023	Dhc Inc—*David Hansen*	7960 Silverton Ave Ste, San Diego CA 92126	858-547-3815	R	2*	<.1
2024	Alfredo Malatesta Inc—*Alfredo Malatesta*	26650 Isabella Pkwy, Canyon Country CA 91351	661-424-1150	R	2*	<.1
2025	Northland Corrosion Services Ltd—*Rob Engh*	1405 Willow Dr, Laurel MT 59044	406-628-2213	R	2*	<.1
2026	Gala Homes Ltd—*Jason Delarnau*	105 Sunset Oaks Dr, Holly Springs NC 27540	919-629-2058	R	2*	<.1
2027	Austin Electric Co—*Robert Mann*	PO Box 2106, Chesapeake VA 23327	757-420-2143	R	2*	<.1
2028	Custom Security—*Andrew Conci*	4694 Cemetery Rd Ste 2, Hilliard OH 43026	614-861-2300	R	2*	<.1
2029	Aristotle Electric—*Tom Lernet*	2961 Industrial Rd, Las Vegas NV 89109	702-731-5024	R	2*	<.1
2030	Allen Electric Co—*Richard Allen*	111 W 20th St, Joplin MO 64804	417-624-3121	R	2*	<.1
2031	Best Electric Contractors Inc—*J Harrison*	15018 Marine Rd, Humble TX 77396	281-441-4454	R	2*	<.1
2032	Castillo Electric LLC	142 Alcazar St, Royal Palm Beach FL 33411	561-753-2301	R	2*	<.1
2033	Viking Energy Of Lincoln Inc—*Rick Hoeksema*	509 W Traverse Bay Rd, Lincoln MI 48742	989-736-6618	R	2*	<.1
2034	Bingemann G Electric LLC	PO Box 2388, Vincentown NJ 08088	609-859-4266	R	2*	<.1
2035	Dukes Electric Company Inc—*Charles Dukes*	PO Box 1284, Lagrange GA 30241	706-883-6750	R	2*	<.1
2036	Kd Electric Inc—*Jerry Kleffer*	989 Pedigo Way Ste A, Bowling Green KY 42103	270-782-9992	R	2*	<.1
2037	Northern Electric Of Durham Inc—*Robin King*	1611 Camden Ave, Durham NC 27704	919-682-8919	R	2*	<.1
2038	P2 Electric Inc—*Pat Ton*	416 Graham Ave, Brooklyn NY 11211	718-349-3737	R	2*	<.1
2039	Prime Cabling Services Inc—*Myron Veil*	528 Palisades Dr 170, Pacific Palisades CA 90272	310-835-3824	R	2*	<.1
2040	Scarponi Electric LLC—*Thomas Ferland*	45 Allen St Ste 5, Rochester NH 03867	603-332-5011	R	2*	<.1
2041	Southeastern Electrical Contractors Inc—*Derek Weigle*	1550 Johnson Rd, Macon GA 31220	478-994-6247	R	2*	<.1
2042	Buffalo Electric Inc—*Steve Demun*	106 Ash St Ste A, Bellevue ID 83313	208-788-9659	R	2*	<.1

Note: An asterisk (*) indicates an estimated financial figure. The company type code used is as follows: R = Private, P = Public, S = Private Subsidiary, B = Public Subsidiary, D = Division, J = Joint Venture, I = Investment Fund.

COMPANY RANKINGS BY SALES WITHIN 4-DIGIT SIC

Rank	Company Name—*Executive Officer*	Address, City, State, Zip	Phone	Type	Fin	Empls
2043	Carter Electric—*John Carter*	PO Box 711, Galion OH 44833	419-468-9019	R	2*	<.1
2044	Chandler Electric Inc—*Sherry Chandler*	905 Spyglass Cir, Vine Grove KY 40175	270-877-2185	R	2*	<.1
2045	Labella Electric Inc—*Jerry Labella*	145 S Main St, Port Chester NY 10573	914-937-7050	R	2*	<.1
2046	Payne Electric Co—*Mike Simon*	PO Box 81008, Austin TX 78708	512-339-2232	R	2*	<.1
2047	Rebel Electric Heating and Air Conditioning Inc—*Cliff Richardson*	12025 Sullivan Rd, Baton Rouge LA 70818	225-261-6400	R	2*	<.1
2048	Smb Electrical Contractors Inc—*Sussan Rhoades*	616 Old Edmondson Ave, Catonsville MD 21228	410-747-2400	R	2*	<.1
2049	Strouse Electric Company Inc—*David Strouse*	411 Oak St, South Amboy NJ 08879	732-727-6161	R	2*	<.1
2050	Circle City Security Systems Inc—*Jack Jordan*	5355 E 38th St Ste 110, Indianapolis IN 46218	317-542-7087	R	2*	<.1
2051	Nasin Electric LLC	PO Box 797, Baltic CT 06330	860-822-9250	R	2*	<.1
2052	Nsi-Systems Inc—*Rosa Murtha*	2357 De La Cruz Blvd, Santa Clara CA 95050	408-844-8161	R	2*	<.1
2053	M and M Electric Of N W Florida Inc—*Mark Nelson*	8247 E Bay Blvd, Gulf Breeze FL 32566	850-939-0404	R	2*	<.1
2054	Moody Electric Inc—*John Moody*	669 Nw 90th St, El Portal FL 33150	305-758-2000	R	2*	<.1
2055	Power Solutions Electrical Contractors Inc—*Keith Steele*	444 Lincoln Blvd, Middlesex NJ 08846	732-356-7668	R	2*	<.1
2056	Sheridan Electric Inc—*Raymond Sheridan*	133 Hallene Rd, Warwick RI 02886	401-732-4515	R	2*	<.1
2057	Advanced Lighting and Sound Inc—*Robert Sullivan*	2722 Elliott Dr, Troy MI 48083	248-298-2995	R	2*	<.1
2058	Cadri Company Inc—*Norman Cadaret*	540 3rd St, Lake Elsinore CA 92530	951-674-1435	R	2*	<.1
2059	Circuit-Tron Corp—*Larry Studley*	1635 S Alvernon Way, Tucson AZ 85711	520-790-4960	R	2*	<.1
2060	Haveco Electric Inc—*Paul Haveruk*	PO Box 698, San Clemente CA 92674	949-492-4924	R	2*	<.1
2061	Hirst Electric Company—*Michael Hirst*	2326 Brooklyn Rd, Jackson MI 49203	517-782-5091	R	2*	<.1
2062	Mclain Electric Company Inc—*Jeffrey Lain*	263 Stamm Rd, Newington CT 06111	860-667-9280	R	2*	<.1
2063	Robeson Electric Company Inc—*Jack Floyd*	PO Box 1526, Lumberton NC 28359	910-739-6076	R	2*	<.1
2064	Southport Electrical Service Inc—*Patricia Evans*	5559 Anchor Village Ln, Southport NC 28461	910-457-6193	R	2*	<.1
2065	Texas Technical Services Inc—*Diego Ramirez*	10405 Rockley Rd, Houston TX 77099	281-568-8874	R	2*	<.1
2066	VM Leasing Inc—*Nancy Van Duyne*	2433 Reeves Rd, Joliet IL 60436	815-725-7883	R	2*	<.1
2067	Heaton Electric Inc—*Russell Heaton*	15 Meridian Ct, Kalispell MT 59901	406-755-2669	R	2*	<.1
2068	Randel Electric Inc—*Tobey Sheridan*	2307 W N Ave, Chicago IL 60647	773-342-0383	R	2*	<.1
2069	Sound Security Inc—*Thomas Trentman*	2500 Viking Ct, Cincinnati OH 45244	513-474-0380	R	2*	<.1
2070	PGS Enterprises—*George Saldana*	7823 Marina Dr Ste 2, San Antonio TX 78250	210-680-3615	R	2*	<.1
2071	Valure Electrical And Air Conditioning Inc—*Louis Valure*	PO Box 148, Bourg LA 70343	985-594-2566	R	2*	<.1
2072	Russell Electric Incorporated Of Rocky Mount—*John Christian*	PO Box 7874, Rocky Mount NC 27804	252-446-5005	R	2*	<.1
2073	All Star Electrical Services Inc—*Jorda Armas*	11871 Sw 207th St, Miami FL 33177	305-971-5292	R	2*	<.1
2074	E and K Electric Inc—*Myrna Kunkel*	306 E 25th St, Jasper IN 47546	812-482-3161	R	2*	<.1
2075	Ryan Electric Inc—*Dennis Ryan*	1305 W Enos Ave, Springfield IL 62702	217-698-4877	R	2*	<.1
2076	A and O Electric Inc—*Clyde Allen*	PO Box 67, Grosse Tete LA 70740	225-648-2528	R	2*	<.1
2077	Canoe Country Electric—*William Ronn*	765 Kawishiwi Trl, Ely MN 55731	218-365-3633	R	2*	<.1
2078	Jf Electrical Contractors Inc—*Jane Fiore*	249 E Prospect Ave, Mount Prospect IL 60056	847-818-0134	R	2*	<.1
2079	Mid-Atlantic Control Systems LLC—*Brendan Mannix*	11706 Parklawn Dr, Rockville MD 20852	301-587-6551	R	2*	<.1
2080	Phase Masters Inc—*James Hightower*	12054 Miramar Pkwy, Miramar FL 33025	305-655-0927	R	2*	<.1
2081	S J Electric Inc—*Joe Davidovich*	4459 Renaissance Pkwy, Cleveland OH 44128	216-765-1855	R	2*	<.1
2082	Electric Systems Of Duluth Inc—*John Michalski*	4731 Grand Ave Ste 1, Duluth MN 55007	218-722-0764	R	2*	<.1
2083	Fibertech Communications Inc—*Jason Knight*	6424 Derry St, Harrisburg PA 17111	717-657-3427	R	2*	<.1
2084	Boscar Electric Inc—*Peter Borello*	745 Lafayette St, Utica NY 13502	315-724-8874	R	2*	<.1
2085	Horizon Electric Inc—*Ken Bacon*	PO Box 2828, Lagrange GA 30241	706-845-9007	R	2*	<.1
2086	Shelby Electric Inc—*James Shelby*	588 Burton Cemetery Rd, Mitchell IN 47446	812-849-5636	R	2*	<.1
2087	Logic Systems Sound And Lighting Inc—*Howard Self*	255 Marshall Rd Ste 16, Valley Park MO 63088	314-968-4050	R	2*	<.1
2088	Economy Wiring Company Inc—*Jay Smith*	633 Sw 148th St, Burien WA 98166	206-424-7542	R	2*	<.1
2089	High Country Electric Construction Inc—*Paul Easley*	PO Box 347, Sedalia CO 80135	303-933-6467	R	2*	<.1
2090	Homestead Electric Co—*Michael Ahern*	27839 W Concrete Dr St, Ingleside IL 60041	815-363-1222	R	2*	<.1
2091	New England Communications Corp—*William Tokarz*	1275a Cromwell Ave Ste, Rocky Hill CT 06067	860-529-3200	R	2*	<.1
2092	Pavlik Electric Company Inc—*Emanuel Pavlik*	PO Box 17107, Missoula MT 59808	406-543-8783	R	2*	<.1
2093	Ward Electric Inc—*Michael Ward*	6080 Fulton St E Ste C, Ada MI 49301	616-676-9675	R	2*	<.1
2094	Pathcom Inc—*Robert Gannon*	40 Lloyd Ave Ste 106, Malvern PA 19355	610-640-3724	R	2*	<.1
2095	John C Myres Jr Inc—*John Myres*	8211 Valencia Ave, Lubbock TX 79424	806-795-7929	R	2*	<.1
2096	Sound and Communication Inc—*Algie Broome*	5830 N State St, Jackson MS 39206	601-957-5830	R	2*	<.1
2097	Sousa Electric Corp—*Jeffrey Sousa*	PO Box 352, Livermore CA 94551	925-456-3838	R	2*	<.1
2098	Entertainment Arts Inc—*Timothy Huff*	4637 Parkbreeze Ct, Orlando FL 32808	407-299-9678	R	2*	<.1
2099	Cbs Electric Inc—*Martin Stacks*	296 County Rd 2446, Guntown MS 38849	662-348-3152	R	2*	<.1
2100	Cleveland Enterprises LLC—*Keitha Depanion*	356493 E 1030 Rd, Prague OK 74864	405-567-0066	R	2*	<.1
2101	Mccullough Electric Company LLC	801 19th Ave N, Nashville TN 37208	615-320-1550	R	2*	.1
2102	Murdock Electric Inc—*Maryjane Fiedler*	1444 Market Cir Unit H, Port Charlotte FL 33953	941-629-4280	R	2*	<.1
2103	Seven-O-Electric Inc—*William Byrd*	2005 Thorn Rd, Lake Charles LA 70605	337-474-8181	R	2*	<.1
2104	M-R Electric and Security Alarms Inc—*Michael Locklear*	9525 Rennert Rd, Shannon NC 28386	910-843-2989	R	2*	<.1
2105	R and T Electric Inc—*Jonathan Ruggles*	315 S Main St, Concord NH 03301	603-224-4782	R	2*	<.1
2106	Dave Pybus Electric—*David Pybus*	6600 E Hwy 22, Panama City FL 32404	850-871-5613	R	2*	<.1
2107	Etheridge Electric Company Inc—*Gary Ethridge*	6711 Shiloh Rd, Hahira GA 31632	229-794-2148	R	2*	<.1
2108	Fischer and Hoehn Electric Inc—*Karen Fischer*	1653 Stadium Rd, Mankato MN 56001	507-345-6368	R	2*	<.1
2109	MGI Inc—*Tommy Moore*	2714 W Mercury Blvd, Hampton VA 23666	757-838-9525	R	2*	<.1
2110	Ozarks Electric Inc—*Jeffrey Fuzzell*	2925 E Chestnut Expy J, Springfield MO 65802	417-865-3938	R	2*	<.1
2111	Rkknb Inc—*Rod Barenberg*	4305 Harlan St, Wheat Ridge CO 80033	303-424-7200	R	2*	<.1
2112	Automatic Electric Inc—*John Radford*	PO Box 248, Ashland City TN 37015	615-792-5141	R	2*	<.1
2113	Centerpointe Electric LLC	PO Box 1440, Novi MI 48376	248-465-8800	R	2*	<.1
2114	Clear Communications Inc—*Noah Fissehazion*	8311 Fenton St, Silver Spring MD 20910	301-495-8989	R	2*	<.1
2115	Current Electrical Contractors Inc—*James Eberle*	1946 Lehigh Ave Ste D, Glenview IL 60026	847-832-0700	R	2*	<.1
2116	Pacific Energy Construction Corp—*John Wilkins*	19631 Prairie St, Northridge CA 91324	818-700-5300	R	2*	<.1
2117	Hamker Enterprises Corp—*Joseph Hamker*	520 Nw 9th Ave, Homestead FL 33030	305-247-8281	R	2*	<.1
2118	Kallies Electric Inc—*Randall Kallies*	1280 Engel Dr, Shawano WI 54166	715-524-3201	R	2*	<.1
2119	Mc Gervey Electric Inc—*Charles Gervey*	3571 Valley Dr Ste 1, Pittsburgh PA 15234	412-854-4436	R	2*	<.1
2120	Sailfish Communications Inc—*Albert Sasso*	3135 39th Ave N Ste 3, Saint Petersburg FL 33714	727-302-0901	R	2*	<.1
2121	Sparks Electrical Inc—*Art Caudle*	1924 Frazer Ave, Sparks NV 89431	775-359-2177	R	2*	<.1
2122	Techteriors LLC—*Holly Day*	12308 Corp Pkwy 12w 12, Mequon WI 53092	262-243-9800	R	2*	<.1
2123	911 VehicleCom Inc—*Mark Attaway*	2130 E Winston Rd, Anaheim CA 92806	714-808-0911	R	2*	<.1
2124	Accord Electric Co—*R Daniel Mc Cord*	PO Box 248, Arnold MO 63010	636-942-9101	R	2*	<.1
2125	Advantage Security Integration Ltd—*Gary Roberson*	5611 Hoover St, Houston TX 77092	713-490-2020	R	2*	<.1
2126	Allen Electric Company Inc—*William Allen*	12545 Perrywood Ln, Dunkirk MD 20754	301-812-1190	R	2*	<.1
2127	Asset Protection Partnership Ltd—*Brian Dickinson*	PO Box 349, Forest Grove OR 97116	503-359-4344	R	2*	<.1
2128	Bernardoni Electric Inc—*Thomas Bernardoni*	830 Tollgate Rd, Elgin IL 60123	847-697-2600	R	2*	<.1
2129	Bowen Electric Service Inc—*James Rowe*	7856 Beechcraft Ave, Gaithersburg MD 20879	301-258-9200	R	2*	<.1
2130	Circuit Shop Electronic Systems Inc—*Chris Reindollar*	PO Box 8437, Lancaster PA 17604	717-625-7199	R	2*	<.1
2131	Communications Cable And Wireless Inc—*Jeff O'bryan*	PO Box 261, Blowing Rock NC 28605	704-588-0508	R	2*	<.1

Rank	Company Name—*Executive Officer*	Address, City, State, Zip	Phone	Type	Fin	Empls
2132	Day Electrical Inc—*Tina Day*	PO Box 102, Montgomery PA 17752	570-547-7983	R	2*	<.1
2133	Granite Ledge Electrical Contractors Inc—*Rhonda Brown*	15436 130th St, Foreston MN 56330	320-294-5557	R	2*	<.1
2134	Guardian Systems Inc—*Richard Helstrom*	102 S 54th St, Chandler AZ 85226	480-940-8900	R	2*	<.1
2135	International Tela-Com Inc—*Edmund Horgan*	45 Park Ridge Dr, Fletcher NC 28732	828-651-9801	R	2*	<.1
2136	Jordan Valley Electric Inc—*Brent Wiens*	4225 W 8270 S Ste A, West Jordan UT 84088	801-282-2310	R	2*	<.1
2137	Mc Elwee Electric Inc—*Susan Elwee*	560 Oakland Ave Sw, Grand Rapids MI 49503	616-454-7788	R	2*	<.1
2138	Modern System Concepts Inc—*Mark Popkowski*	PO Box 5028, Katy TX 77491	281-599-7388	R	2*	<.1
2139	Naperville Electrical Contractors Inc—*Robert Fornecker*	PO Box 424, Oswego IL 60543	630-554-0077	R	2*	<.1
2140	Sisam Electric Inc—*Richard Sisam*	2970 S W Temple, Salt Lake City UT 84115	801-466-8906	R	2*	<.1
2141	T Volt Inc—*Wesley Tole*	3808 Davie Blvd, Fort Lauderdale FL 33312	954-792-4535	R	2*	<.1
2142	Tcp Business System Inc—*Terry Walzman*	PO Box 1219, New York NY 10113	973-984-1100	R	2*	<.1
2143	Tom Shuster Electrical Inc—*Tom Shuster*	PO Box 50306, Kalamazoo MI 49005	269-343-3880	R	2*	<.1
2144	Digital Security And Electronics Inc—*John Becker*	610 Calle Plano, Camarillo CA 93012	805-987-4246	R	2*	<.1
2145	Doug's Electrical Service Inc—*Doug Hottinger*	60 Shiloh Rd, Russellville AR 72802	479-968-6842	R	2*	<.1
2146	Nordby Electric Inc—*Keith Nordby*	PO Box 12026, Santa Rosa CA 95406	707-579-1240	R	2*	<.1
2147	Torrisi Electric Inc—*Michael Torrisi*	3305 Ridge Pke, Eagleville PA 19403	610-539-5054	R	2*	<.1
2148	FEC Electric Inc—*Johnny Moore*	PO Box 77, Redlands CA 92373	909-793-0965	R	2*	<.1
2149	Howard County Electric Company Inc—*Eric Santmyer*	9693 Gerwig Ln Ste T, Columbia MD 21046	410-290-9888	R	2*	<.1
2150	James Lynah Electric Company Inc—*Savage Lynah*	34 Echols Ave, Savannah GA 31406	912-355-0261	R	2*	<.1
2151	Rite Way Electric Inc—*Emerson Smoker*	2904 Three Lakes Rd Se, Albany OR 97322	541-926-0504	R	2*	<.1
2152	Total Electric Construction Co—*Jim Leonard*	PO Box 13247, Edwardsville KS 66113	913-441-0192	R	2*	<.1
2153	Associated Electrical Contractors Inc—*John Quinn*	PO Box 8353, Saint Joseph MO 64508	816-233-6888	R	2*	<.1
2154	DBS Communications Inc—*David Schrembeck*	5061 W 161st St, Cleveland OH 44142	216-265-3200	R	2*	<.1
2155	Leibold Communications Inc—*Nick Leibold*	1448 Elliott Ave W, Seattle WA 98119	206-286-8981	R	2*	<.1
2156	Pcd—*Henry Beaumont*	1032 Maxwell Dr, Santa Rosa CA 95401	707-546-3633	R	2*	<.1
2157	Spike Electric Inc—*Scott Brown*	2990 E La Palma Ave St, Anaheim CA 92806	714-238-1400	R	2*	<.1
2158	Voice And Data Cable Specialists Inc—*Rick Colaw*	16441 N 91st St Ste 10, Scottsdale AZ 85260	480-483-0606	R	2*	<.1
2159	Morrissey Electric Company Inc—*Jim Morrissey*	14225 Dayton Cir Ste 1, Omaha NE 68137	402-331-4173	R	2*	<.1
2160	Ron's Electric Inc—*Randy Nishimura*	PO Box 311, Lihue HI 96766	808-245-4611	R	2*	<.1
2161	Airport Mechanical Services Inc—*Mary Nelson*	PO Box 305, Enumclaw WA 98022	360-802-9904	R	2*	<.1
2162	Ben's Electric Co—*Ben Jochim*	1390 Randall Dr, Cambria CA 93428	805-927-4374	R	2*	<.1
2163	Castle Rock Electric Inc—*Ben Mosco*	24915 Chicory Ct, Newhall CA 91381	661-253-0020	R	2*	<.1
2164	Communications Unlimited—*Don Allen*	PO Box 551501, Dallas TX 75355	214-340-6001	R	2*	<.1
2165	Kirtland Inc—*Patricia Kirtland*	3274 Hwy 61 N, Saint Paul MN 55110	651-704-9338	R	2*	<.1
2166	Scout Electric Inc—*Robert Fathers*	18 Fox Run, Denville NJ 07834	973-627-2556	R	2*	<.1
2167	C-Tec Electric Corp—*Cal Classi*	10170 99th St, Ozone Park NY 11416	718-323-4400	H	2*	<.1
2168	Doyle Electric Company Inc—*Gene Doyle*	10078 Hatch Pkwy N, Baxley GA 31513	912-367-4433	R	2*	<.1
2169	Facility Improvement Corp—*John Phillips*	800 7th Ave N, Great Falls MT 59401	406-452-0009	R	2*	<.1
2170	Fda Enterprises Inc—*Les Freeman*	1521 Central Park Dr, Hurst TX 76053	817-589-1200	R	2*	<.1
2171	I-C Electrical Systems Inc—*Anthony Pelino*	50 Park Ln, Highland NY 12528	845-883-5161	R	2*	<.1
2172	Ken Curran Electric Inc—*Steven Curran*	234 N 1st Ave, Barstow CA 92311	760-256-9441	R	2*	<.1
2173	Arrow Communications Inc—*Jeff Leslie*	PO Box 560, Indiantown FL 34956	772-692-3000	R	2*	<.1
2174	Savant Software Sciences Inc—*Joshua Cintron*	PO Box 7454, Princeton NJ 08543	609-799-9664	R	2*	<.1
2175	Fjm Electric Inc—*Forrest Kinley*	1186 Ctr St Ste A, Riverside CA 92507	951-779-2900	H	2*	<.1
2176	Tel-Tech Systems—*Yuenyee Kwong*	2946 W Valley Blvd, Alhambra CA 91803	626-282-8228	R	2*	<.1
2177	Whiskey Hill Electric Inc—*Curt Cribbins*	PO Box 391, Hubbard OR 97032	503-981-4640	R	2*	<.1
2178	O'connor Technologies LLC	PO Box 9897, Panama City FL 32417	301-602-2808	R	2*	<.1
2179	Stemco LLC—*Todd Hirsch*	111 John St Rm 1020, New York NY 10038	212-608-7802	R	1*	.1
2180	Multi-Con Inc—*Joe Collins*	PO Box 9325, Jackson MS 39286	601-922-7777	R	1*	<.1
2181	Webber's World—*Marshall Myers*	33155 Camino Capistran, Mission Viejo CA 92675	949-496-7738	R	1*	<.1
2182	International Electric—*Ric Harshman*	8369 Southpark Ln, Littleton CO 80120	303-778-0884	R	1*	<.1
2183	Pmm Electric Inc—*Mike Avery*	47914 Amite River Rd, Saint Amant LA 70774	225-675-6973	R	1*	<.1
2184	Neff Electric Company Inc—*William Neff*	PO Box 392, Altoona PA 16603	814-943-5257	R	1*	<.1
2185	Sign-Tech Electric LLC	5113 Pacific Hwy E Ste, Fife WA 98424	253-922-2146	R	1*	<.1
2186	Corkill Electric Service Co—*Gary Corkill*	1645 Carboy Rd, Arlington Heights IL 60005	847-228-7015	R	1*	<.1
2187	JR Linn Electric Inc—*Jeff Linn*	PO Box 1785, Destin FL 32540	850-837-8474	R	1*	<.1
2188	Nightlight Electric Company Inc—*Roger Sheak*	PO Box 1241, Farmington NM 87499	505-327-6565	R	1*	<.1
2189	RS Communication—*Max Ray*	3091 Directors Row, Memphis TN 38131	901-398-9324	R	1*	<.1
2190	Triangle Electric Corp—*Nancy Bradshaw*	560 Bouldin Rd, Ridgeway VA 24148	276-957-2281	R	1*	<.1
2191	Dor-San Electric Washington Inc—*Fred Edwards*	PO Box 5712, Hacienda Heights CA 91745	909-869-6024	R	1*	<.1
2192	Larry De George—*Larry George*	PO Box 2669, Ashtabula OH 44005	440-964-2817	R	1*	<.1
2193	Michael O'connor—*Michael O'connor*	1 Fawn Meadow Rd, Weston CT 06883	203-454-9995	R	1*	<.1
2194	Parks Electric and Quality Controls Inc—*Larry Parks*	2285 Rubart Dr, Marietta GA 30066	770-509-9257	R	1*	<.1
2195	Precision Tech Electric Inc—*Mario Lima*	4 Ikes Ln, Manalapan NJ 07726	732-780-3131	R	1*	<.1
2196	Quarry Electric Inc—*Clay Goins*	2400 Sw 57th Way, West Park FL 33023	954-981-4802	R	1*	<.1
2197	Ric Electrical Services LLC—*Dianne Sax*	7480 State Blvd Ext, Meridian MS 39305	601-482-9161	R	1*	<.1
2198	Southwest Alarm Systems—*Tommy Henson*	10701 Plano Rd Ste 100, Dallas TX 75238	214-503-6188	R	1*	<.1
2199	Accurate Cabling Inc—*Tony Kinsman*	PO Box 2221, Mount Vernon WA 98273	425-259-2342	R	1*	<.1
2200	Data Phone Wiring and Cable—*Gary Gunter*	208 Davie Blvd, Fort Lauderdale FL 33315	954-761-7171	R	1*	<.1
2201	Guadalupe Electric Inc—*John Flowers*	PO Box 291606, Kerrville TX 78029	830-895-2148	R	1*	<.1
2202	Heart Of Texas Controls LLC	17898 Fm 16 W, Lindale TX 75771	903-882-8945	R	1*	<.1
2203	Italk Telecontracting Inc—*Ken Harbison*	7642 N Oak Trfy, Kansas City MO 64118	816-436-8080	R	1*	<.1
2204	Kep Electric Inc—*Kevin Padgett*	4026 Bach Buxton Rd, Batavia OH 45103	513-752-3043	R	1*	<.1
2205	M Trudeau Electric Inc—*Michael Trudeau*	5066 W Ave M2, Lancaster CA 93536	661-722-8818	R	1*	<.1
2206	Ridgeway Electric—*Michael Jalilie*	PO Box 1009, Burlingame CA 94011	650-344-8716	R	1*	<.1
2207	Allen and Whalen Company Incorporated Of Md—*Bruce Steele*	647 Lofstrand Ln Ste N, Rockville MD 20850	301-762-5333	R	1*	<.1
2208	Johnson Electric Motors Inc—*Douglas Kammeyer*	2925 Commerce Way, Ogden UT 84401	801-621-3853	R	1*	<.1
2209	Liberty Electric Company Corp—*Joseph Hall*	16 Prospect St, Columbiana OH 44408	330-757-8472	R	1*	<.1
2210	Mark's Electric Inc—*Mark Vierkant*	114 Grant St W, Detroit Lakes MN 56501	218-847-2149	R	1*	<.1
2211	A and B Electric Inc—*Ron Atkins*	5906 W Victory Rd, Boise ID 83709	208-362-9061	R	1*	<.1
2212	Alief Electro Mechanical Inc—*Joe Leal*	811 Park Two Dr, Sugar Land TX 77478	281-565-3900	R	1*	<.1
2213	Banner Security Systems Inc—*Tony Spann*	620 Sigman Rd Ne Ste 4, Conyers GA 30013	770-922-6720	R	1*	<.1
2214	Bpl Global Ltd—*Pete Londa*	500 Cranberry Woods Dr, Cranberry Township PA 16066	724-933-7700	R	1*	<.1
2215	Casa Vieja Contractors—*Mario Alaspriste*	6102 Melvin Ave, Tarzana CA 91356	818-774-1423	R	1*	<.1
2216	Central Communications Installers Inc—*Roger Culver*	805 Ne 7th Ter, Cape Coral FL 33909	239-772-7717	R	1*	<.1
2217	Coyote Cabling LLC—*Melissa Parra*	1771 W Hadley Ave, Las Cruces NM 88005	575-525-1422	R	1*	<.1
2218	Fire Management Associates Inc—*Steven Ervin*	6587 Denver Industrial, Denver NC 28037	704-483-8588	R	1*	<.1
2219	Gunnar Electric Inc—*Lois Walters*	7960 Eden Prairie Rd, Eden Prairie MN 55347	952-937-9262	R	1*	<.1
2220	Hydes Business Services Inc—*Frank Hyde*	PO Box 362067, Birmingham AL 35236	205-278-7900	R	1*	<.1
2221	Juneau Electric Co—*Carla Meek*	2770 Sherwood Ln Ste J, Juneau AK 99801	907-789-0811	R	1*	<.1

Note: An asterisk (*) indicates an estimated financial figure. The company type code used is as follows: R = Private, P = Public, S = Private Subsidiary, B = Public Subsidiary, D = Division, J = Joint Venture, I = Investment Fund.

COMPANY RANKINGS BY SALES WITHIN 4-DIGIT SIC

Rank	Company Name—*Executive Officer*	Address, City, State, Zip	Phone	Type	Fin	Empls
2222	Mathias Electric and Plumbing Inc—*Glen Mathias*	PO Box 375, Altamont IL 62411	618-483-6975	R	1*	<.1
2223	MicrocomNet Inc—*Les Asrouch*	1200 E Ctr St, Marion OH 43302	740-387-1826	R	1*	<.1
2224	MN Badeaux Construction Services Inc—*Maurice Badeaux*	215 Persimmon Ln, Lake Jackson TX 77566	979-299-0117	R	1*	<.1
2225	Modern Electric Of F M Inc—*David Olson*	PO Box 225, Fargo ND 58107	701-232-2986	R	1*	<.1
2226	National Wiretec Communications Inc—*John Clemmer*	26370 Ruether Ave, Santa Clarita CA 91350	661-298-5606	R	1*	<.1
2227	Professional Electrical Services Inc—*Richard Tanner*	PO Box 8605, Mobile AL 36689	251-473-7888	R	1*	<.1
2228	Progressive Telephone Systems and Communications Inc—*Greg Patterson*	PO Box 190, Gresham OR 97030	503-665-4900	R	1*	<.1
2229	R and T Electric LLC—*Doug Jeningas*	PO Box 612, Ohatchee AL 36271	256-892-1997	R	1*	<.1
2230	Raborne Electric Corp—*Kenneth Rameau*	633 Parker St, Gardner MA 01440	978-632-2740	R	1*	<.1
2231	Rose Electric Inc—*Malcolm Wortham*	PO Box 849, Hutto TX 78634	512-759-3700	R	1*	<.1
2232	So Cal Air and Electric Inc—*Don Daltan*	1590 S Milliken Ave St, Ontario CA 91761	909-464-2300	R	1*	<.1
2233	Summit City Electric Company Inc—*William Brown*	512 Hayden St, Fort Wayne IN 46802	260-422-3232	R	1*	<.1
2234	United Electric Contractors Inc—*Lianne Anderson*	5301 S 2nd Ave, Everett WA 98203	425-252-7811	R	1*	<.1
2235	Westbrook Electric Construction LLC—*Chris Stoll*	9550 W Sergo Dr Ste 11, La Grange Highlands IL 60525	708-485-0001	R	1*	<.1
2236	Yates Electric Inc—*Thomas Yates*	PO Box 335, Blue Grass IA 52726	563-386-5930	R	1*	<.1
2237	Z-Non Electric Inc—*Zenon Verver*	PO Box 17425, Austin TX 78760	512-442-2002	R	1*	<.1
2238	Bettwy Electric Inc—*Tim Bettwy*	PO Box 388, Newry PA 16665	814-695-7644	R	1*	<.1
2239	Bunkley Electric Company Inc—*Garry Bunkley*	1173 Woodlawn Dr, Abilene TX 79603	325-677-4460	R	1*	<.1
2240	Charlotte Sound and Visual Systems Inc—*John Roach*	2923 Griffith St, Charlotte NC 28203	704-527-2004	R	1*	<.1
2241	Eagle Electric Of Grand Forks Inc—*Darryl Beauchamp*	PO Box 637, East Grand Forks MN 56721	701-746-0449	R	1*	<.1
2242	Mike Gibson Electric Inc—*Mike Gibson*	3675 Hewatt Ct Ste A2, Snellville GA 30039	770-985-2404	R	1*	<.1
2243	R and B Electric Inc—*Robert Deyoung*	4545 W Dickman Rd, Springfield MI 49037	269-963-2665	R	1*	<.1
2244	Talbott Electric Inc—*Kirk Talbott*	1887 E Washington Blvd, Pasadena CA 91104	626-798-1105	R	1*	<.1
2245	Trico Electric Corp—*Peter Trilivas*	495 Graham Ave, Brooklyn NY 11222	718-853-7070	R	1*	<.1
2246	White William D Company Inc—*Aria White*	3505 Magnolia St, Oakland CA 94608	510-658-8167	R	1*	<.1
2247	Wire's Electrical Shop Inc—*Dale Durling*	107 W Valley View Ave, Hackettstown NJ 07840	908-852-4450	R	1*	<.1
2248	Altimate Electric Inc—*Harry Holmes*	1008 Rising Ridge Rd, Mount Airy MD 21771	301-607-8003	R	1*	<.1
2249	Electrical Technologies Inc—*H Hutmacher*	PO Box 308, Chickasha OK 73023	405-224-9100	R	1*	<.1
2250	J L Davis Electrical Contractor Inc—*Jack Davis*	PO Box 1028, Barbourville KY 40906	606-546-8491	R	1*	<.1
2251	Richmond Communications Group Inc—*Richard Osborn*	2750 Northaven Rd Ste, Dallas TX 75229	972-241-1982	R	1*	<.1
2252	Bauer Electric Inc—*Frederick Bauer*	517 41st Ave, Winona MN 55987	507-454-5564	R	1*	<.1
2253	Better-Way Electric and Data Communication Inc—*Greg Hall*	1813 Sunset Pl Ste B, Longmont CO 80501	303-772-8003	R	1*	<.1
2254	Elyon Inc—*Robert Beaudoin*	PO Box 7093, Plainville CT 06062	860-747-5903	R	1*	<.1
2255	Icn Integrated Communication Networks Inc—*C Barnes*	3800 Camp Creek Pkwy S, Atlanta GA 30331	678-904-0727	R	1*	<.1
2256	Jax Asphalt Company Inc—*Robert Metcalf*	1800 Waterworks Rd, Mount Vernon IL 62864	618-244-0500	R	1*	<.1
2257	Pacific Northwest Telco Inc—*John Bogaty*	10200 Sw Greenburg Rd, Portland OR 97223	503-802-4000	R	1*	<.1
2258	Team Electric Inc—*Robert Gilliland*	PO Box 81, Harbor City CA 90710	310-325-0315	R	1*	<.1
2259	V and H Electric Company Inc—*Vernon Green*	801 S Lincoln St, Stockton CA 95206	209-463-6975	R	1*	<.1
2260	Valley Flood Lite Service Inc—*Dave Young*	7023 Valjean Ave, Van Nuys CA 91406	818-785-8850	R	1*	<.1
2261	Queen Capital Group LLC	5031 B U Bowman Dr Ste, Buford GA 30518	770-532-0046	R	1*	<.1
2262	Reliable Business Concerns Inc—*William Miller*	PO Box 1298, Everett WA 98206	425-353-5512	R	1*	<.1
2263	Henzel Electric Company Inc—*Donald Henzel*	18 Gingerbread Ln, Albany NY 12208	518-489-6007	R	1*	<.1
2264	Victoria Electric Company Inc—*Gary Charpula*	PO Box 2116, Victoria TX 77902	361-572-8266	R	1*	<.1
2265	Claxton Electric Inc—*Ray Claxton*	15125 Water Oak Pl, Huntertown IN 46748	260-637-0040	R	1*	<.1
2266	Scholl Electric Inc—*Lavere Scholl*	908 S Westgate St, Addison IL 60101	630-458-9000	R	1*	<.1
2267	Brunswick Electric Inc—*Richard Livsey*	290 Hoosick St, Troy NY 12180	518-270-3695	R	1*	<.1
2268	Sansing Electric—*Robert Sansing*	PO Box 60141, San Angelo TX 76906	325-655-3165	R	1*	<.1
2269	Utterback Electrical Inc—*L Utterback*	13500 Orlando Rd, Nokesville VA 20181	703-791-6400	R	1*	<.1
2270	Isd Audio Video Inc—*John Maxson*	PO Box 4876, El Dorado Hills CA 95762	916-939-8118	R	1*	<.1
2271	Bcs Communications Systems Inc—*Linda Geier*	PO Box 2455, Vacaville CA 95696	707-448-6217	R	1*	<.1
2272	Viking Electrical Contracting Incorporated LLC—*Scott Lidle*	2434 Hamilton Ave, Cleveland OH 44114	216-771-6988	R	1*	<.1
2273	M Rivenburg Inc—*Marshal Rivenburg*	PO Box 881, Oswego IL 60543	630-327-7400	R	1*	<.1
2274	DG and G Electric Inc—*Donnie Grounds*	PO Box 120, Midlothian TX 76065	972-775-3788	R	1*	<.1
2275	DM Stone Electrical Construction Inc—*Donnie Stone*	515 International Cir, Summerville SC 29483	843-873-7515	R	1*	<.1
2276	Hicks Electric Inc—*James Hicks*	1075 Orienta Ave Ste B, Altamonte Springs FL 32701	407-831-4881	R	1*	<.1
2277	Cache Valley Electric—*Jim Laub*	4301 Iverson Blvd, Trinity AL 35673	256-308-9900	R	1*	<.1
2278	Conley Electric Inc—*David Conley*	PO Box 561, Cleveland TN 37364	423-472-7712	R	1*	<.1
2279	Dr J Electric Inc—*Ali Olli*	12 Adair St, Stanhope NJ 07874	973-347-5926	R	1*	<.1
2280	KC Mini Storage—*Kevin Classen*	4300 S Van Buren St, Enid OK 73703	580-242-2297	R	1*	<.1
2281	Kern Maintenance and Construction Corp—*Joe Johnston*	3520 College Blvd Ste, Oceanside CA 92056	661-833-1446	R	1*	<.1
2282	Universal Electric LLC	95 Mcclendon Ave, West Monroe LA 71291	318-366-0991	R	1*	<.1
2283	Access and Video Integration Corp—*John Koci*	5226 E 50 N, Lafayette IN 47905	765-446-2696	R	1*	<.1
2284	CK Electric Inc—*Karen Gwin*	78 Masters Dr, Saint Augustine FL 32084	904-825-1571	R	1*	<.1
2285	Greylock Electrical Company Inc—*Bernard Schneider*	9 Elm St, Adams MA 01220	413-743-8458	R	1*	<.1
2286	Volz Electric Inc—*Corrine Volz*	4534 S Grand Blvd, Saint Louis MO 63111	314-832-3070	R	1*	<.1
2287	Mountain States Electric—*Jay Maddox*	5435 W 59th Ave Unit P, Arvada CO 80003	303-432-0175	R	1*	<.1
2288	Reynolds Electric Inc—*Cary Reynolds*	16931 Belle Isle Dr, Cornelius NC 28031	704-892-8003	R	1*	<.1
2289	Asbill Electric Service Inc—*W Asbill*	3818 Columbia Hwy, Leesville SC 29070	803-532-0369	R	1*	<.1
2290	Derouen Electrical Service Incorporated—*Donnie Derouen*	105 Lloyd Rd, Lafayette LA 70506	337-981-0440	R	1*	<.1
2291	Hodges Triad Electric LLC	1484 Hampton Plz Dr, Kernersville NC 27284	336-788-8731	R	1*	<.1
2292	King Electric Of Ocaloosa Inc—*Larry King*	PO Box 1798, Crestview FL 32536	850-682-4511	R	1*	<.1
2293	T Di Russo Electric Contractor Inc—*Anthony Russo*	63 23 Metropolitan Ave, Middle Village NY 11379	718-821-1646	R	1*	<.1
2294	Wiring Unlimited Inc—*Mark Hebebrand*	13911 Lorain Ave, Cleveland OH 44111	216-671-1800	R	1*	<.1
2295	Ashley Electric Inc—*William Ashley*	PO Box 308, Whiteville NC 28472	910-642-3057	R	1*	<.1
2296	BCL Electric Inc—*Brent Loney*	PO Box 9221, Moscow ID 83843	208-882-0136	R	1*	<.1
2297	Ekstrom Electric Inc—*Ronald Ekstrom*	106 N Raddant Rd, Batavia IL 60510	630-761-0300	R	1*	<.1
2298	George Benson Electric Inc—*Richard Hage*	112 Greenwood Ave, Midland Park NJ 07432	201-445-0200	R	1*	<.1
2299	Ibid Power Inc—*Mark Lallemand*	143 NW Ave B201, Tallmadge OH 44278	330-633-4880	R	1*	<.1
2300	Kebalo Electric Company Inc—*Walter Kebalo*	175 Wheeler Rd, South Windsor CT 06074	860-644-5124	R	1*	<.1
2301	Photo-Scan Of Los Angeles Inc—*Richard Balcom*	743 Cochran St Ste C, Simi Valley CA 93065	805-581-4448	R	1*	<.1
2302	Ronsco Electric Inc—*Rhonda Grunther*	PO Box 388, Long Beach NY 11561	516-897-8703	R	1*	<.1
2303	Westland Electric Inc—*Kyle Jackson*	PO Box 63, Nephi UT 84648	435-623-0906	R	1*	<.1
2304	Block Electrical Contracting Inc—*Steven Block*	PO Box 444, Springfield NE 68059	402-253-3030	R	1*	<.1
2305	Castellino Electric—*Steve Castellino*	448 Elm Ave, San Bruno CA 94066	650-873-7445	R	1*	<.1
2306	Colburn Communications Inc—*Mike Colburn*	1830 Telegraph Rd, Manning SC 29102	803-473-5152	R	1*	<.1
2307	D and S Electric Inc—*Denny Taylor*	16427 88th St E, Sumner WA 98390	253-863-0989	R	1*	<.1
2308	Loftus Electric Inc—*Michael Loftus*	4451 Enterprise Ct Ste, Melbourne FL 32934	321-253-4333	R	1*	<.1
2309	Puget Sound Alarm Company Inc—*Michael Corrigan*	17555 15th Ave Ne, Shoreline WA 98155	206-365-3155	R	1*	<.1
2310	Alvin Wynn Electric Company Inc—*James Wynn*	PO Box 1002, Fitzgerald GA 31750	229-423-5495	R	1*	<.1

Rank	Company Name—Executive Officer	Address, City, State, Zip	Phone	Type	Fin	Empls
2311	Communications Solutions Inc—Scott Perkins	6195 Lake Gray Blvd St, Jacksonville FL 32244	904-777-6656	R	1*	<.1
2312	E Haberli Electric LLC—Bonnie Majka	17 River Rd, Meriden CT 06451	203-235-5653	R	1*	<.1
2313	Electrical Systems Inc—David Dauffenbach	1815 S Pattie St, Wichita KS 67211	316-263-2415	R	1*	<.1
2314	George A Green Inc—Kenneth Green	PO Box 594, Woodbury CT 06798	203-263-2640	R	1*	<.1
2315	J and M Electric Inc—Michael Mielke	2222 Minnesota St, Oshkosh WI 54902	920-303-2073	R	1*	<.1
2316	Miljavac Electric Corp—John Miljavac	PO Box 7201, Saint Joseph MO 64507	816-233-0108	R	1*	<.1
2317	Network Communications Installation Inc—Merle Mcentee	2478 Fender Ave Ste H, Fullerton CA 92831	714-278-1019	R	1*	<.1
2318	Signal Engineering Corp—Kenneth Gatley	503 Industry Dr, Hampton VA 23661	757-826-1518	R	1*	<.1
2319	All Pro Electrical Contractors Inc—William Sylvia	1101 S Rogers Cir, Boca Raton FL 33487	561-988-0460	R	1*	<.1
2320	Atlantic Ordinance International Inc—John Byrd	PO Box 3924, Portsmouth VA 23701	757-673-0790	R	1*	<.1
2321	Dolinger Electric Inc—Jesse Dolinger	224 Old Baltimore Pke, Nottingham PA 19362	610-932-8200	R	1*	<.1
2322	F and N Enterprises Inc—Frank Renfro	PO Box 3340, Amarillo TX 79116	806-372-5665	R	1*	<.1
2323	House Electric Company Inc—Dennis House	PO Box 373, Wentzville MO 63385	636-327-4763	R	1*	<.1
2324	Inman Electric Company Inc—Thomas Inman	15 S 6th St, Estherville IA 51334	712-362-2203	R	1*	<.1
2325	Internal Telecommunication Systems Inc—Gene Kershner	2700 Lodi St, Syracuse NY 13208	315-472-6611	R	.1*	<.1
2326	JB Miller Electric Company Inc—J Miller	PO Box 1579, Keystone Heights FL 32656	352-473-0022	R	1*	<.1
2327	Lifeline Amplification Systems Inc—Scott Wright	41 Means Dr Ste A, Platteville WI 53818	608-348-3057	R	1*	<.1
2328	Positive Power LLC—George Langlois	4658 W 1150 S, Ogden UT 84404	801-732-0680	R	1*	<.1
2329	Southern Electrical Services Inc—John Karbowski	2602 Charles Ln Ste 5, Sugar Land TX 77498	281-242-0048	R	1*	<.1
2330	Tow Electric Company Inc—David Tow	1099 E Champlain Dr A1, Fresno CA 93720	559-434-7432	R	1*	<.1
2331	Vs-Communication Inc—Wulf Bieschke	23785 Cabot Blvd Ste 3, Hayward CA 94545	510-723-3320	R	1*	<.1
2332	William M Wetmore Inc—William Wetmore	232 Rolling Rd, Gaithersburg MD 20877	301-948-0072	R	1*	<.1
2333	Arthur Diefenbach Inc—Arthur Diefenbach	PO Box 263, Montgomery NY 12549	845-457-5744	R	1*	<.1
2334	George S Drummey Company Inc—Stephen Drummey	PO Box 179, North Easton MA 02356	781-963-0782	R	1*	<.1
2335	Home Menders Inc—Jeffrey Widness	2112 Ponderosa Cir, Duluth MN 55811	218-722-6181	R	1*	<.1
2336	Rel Inc—Randy Langton	PO Box 1683, Muskogee OK 74402	918-682-4961	R	1*	<.1
2337	Westin Industries Inc—Ted Donnelly	3020 Callie Still Rd, Lawrenceville GA 30045	770-458-3437	R	1*	<.1
2338	Aerobee Electric Inc—Timothy Craddock	2026 Massoit Rd, Royal Oak MI 48073	248-549-2044	R	1*	<.1
2339	Dollard Enterprises LLC	2714 Veritas Dr, Oviedo FL 32765	407-366-7498	R	1*	<.1
2340	Kucera Electric Inc—Robert Kucera	PO Box 1828, Winner SD 57580	605-842-1510	R	1*	<.1
2341	Safety Net Corp—Anthony Rinaldi	164 Kingsland Rd, Boonton NJ 07005	973-263-2500	R	1*	<.1
2342	Clc Cabling Service—Cynthia Carey	154 New Beaver Creek R, Markleysburg PA 15459	724-329-0828	R	1*	<.1
2343	Massaro Electric Corp—John Massaro	879 Nassau Rd, Uniondale NY 11553	516-481-3759	R	1*	<.1
2344	C and R Security Inc—Terrill Rigsby	1102 Forest Hill Dr, Atmore AL 36502	251-368-4786	R	1*	<.1
2345	Systems Electrical Services Inc—Nicholas Dangelo	387 Prospect Pl, Revere MA 02151	781-289-7864	R	1*	<.1
2346	Primary Electrical Contracting And Design Inc—Glen Gersten-slager	3605 S Clvland Mssllon, Barberton OH 44203	330-825-5800	R	1*	<.1
2347	Schmidt Electric LLC	66 Naugatuck Dr, Naugatuck CT 06770	203-723-1082	R	1*	<.1
2348	Pico Wholesale Electric and Lighting Supplies Inc—Farhad Pourshalimi	4365 W Pico Blvd, Los Angeles CA 90019	323-934-9400	R	1*	<.1
2349	Professional Video and Sound—Curtis Wright	PO Box 576687, Modesto CA 95357	209-521-2141	R	1*	<.1
2350	Gonzales Electric Service Inc—Arthur Scanlan	2023 S Philippe Ave, Gonzales LA 70737	225-644-7008	R	1*	<.1
2351	AC Electrical Contractor Inc—Dayira Hernandez	3451 Nw 48th St, Miami FL 33142	305-805-9580	R	1*	<.1
2352	Rfb Electric Inc—Raywood Baudoin	400 Breaux Rd, Lafayette LA 70506	337-216-0506	R	1*	<.1
2353	3 G Electric Inc—Sandra Crone	PO Box 40, Garden City KS 67846	620-276-2421	R	1*	<.1
2354	A H Electrical Service Inc—Moses Sanchez	PO Box 1338, Denton TX 76202	940-320-2041	R	1*	<.1
2355	American Business Information Systems—Jackie Miller	PO Box 165978, Irving TX 75016	972-513-2247	R	1*	<.1
2356	Audio West—Glenn Hatch	PO Box 978, Yorba Linda CA 92885	714-528-2285	R	1*	<.1
2357	Communications Plus Inc—David Staples	8910 Research Blvd Ste, Austin TX 78758	512-834-9696	R	1*	<.1
2358	Grns Electrical Contractors Corp—Gregory Spina	7 Carro Ct, Dover NJ 07801	973-537-7755	R	1*	<.1
2359	O'neal Electirc Co—John O'neal	1705 E Summit St, Red Oak IA 51566	712-623-3764	R	1*	<.1
2360	Redden Electrical Contractors Inc—B Redden	PO Box 270699, Dallas TX 75227	214-388-8543	R	1*	<.1
2361	Elco Electric Service Corp—Kenneth Reuter	948 Pontiac Ave, Cranston RI 02920	401-946-2000	R	1*	<.1
2362	Gholson Electric Inc—John Gholson	PO Box 470322, Fort Worth TX 76147	817-332-1010	R	1*	<.1
2363	Osborne Brothers LLC	PO Box 43, Saint Marys KS 66536	785-437-6287	R	1*	<.1
2364	Sam Nichols Electrical Inc—Samuel Nichols	785 Kiowa Ave Ste 102, Lake Havasu City AZ 86403	928-855-4121	R	1*	<.1
2365	Ag Electrical Contractors Inc—Aldo Gallelli	222 Harvard Ave, Metuchen NJ 08840	732-548-3995	R	1*	<.1
2366	Anton Electric Inc—Joseph Anton	31 Lynn Ave, Oreland PA 19075	215-886-4360	R	1*	<.1
2367	I Phase Electric Inc—Charles Ginns	253 E Market St, West Chester PA 19382	610-436-9252	R	1*	<.1
2368	Owen Electric Inc—Lois Owen	8889 Archibald Ave, Rancho Cucamonga CA 91730	909-987-7782	R	1*	<.1
2369	Reed Electric Company Inc—James Reed	221 Oak St, San Francisco CA 94102	415-861-6522	R	1*	<.1
2370	Sacon Inc—Kenneth Matheny	PO Box 581, Elgin SC 29045	803-779-8200	R	1*	<.1
2371	Seifert Electric Inc—George Seifert	PO Box 281, Bismarck ND 58502	701-223-5367	R	1*	<.1
2372	Altec Systems Inc—Tim Feury	1395 S Marietta Pkwy S, Marietta GA 30067	770-420-0055	R	1*	<.1
2373	Rhode Island Telephone Inc—George Shaheen	81 Western Industrial, Cranston RI 02921	401-944-8388	R	1*	<.1
2374	Tpc Technologies Inc—Kenneth Kuespert	185 Bell Rd, Niles MI 49120	269-687-9798	R	1*	<.1
2375	Alpha Audio Systems Inc—John Virden	24846 Ave Rockefeller, Valencia CA 91355	661-257-3593	R	1*	<.1
2376	Cemco Electric Inc—Cliff Morgan	PO Box 38100, Charlotte NC 28278	704-529-0394	R	1*	<.1
2377	Tech-Time Communication Inc—Jim Selfridge	5801 Norris Rd, Bakersfield CA 93308	661-397-0792	R	1*	<.1
2378	Therrell Alarm Protection Service Inc—John Restivo	1618 Exchange Pkwy, Waco TX 76712	254-776-8887	R	1*	<.1
2379	Mcmillan Study Guides Inc—Gayle Smith	PO Box 1153, San Luis Obispo CA 93406	805-545-0112	R	1*	<.1
2380	Myron Zucker Inc—Donna Zobel	36825 Metro Ct, Sterling Heights MI 48312	586-979-9955	R	1*	<.1
2381	Waatti and Sons Electric Co—Marvin Waatti	58914 Romeo Plank Rd, Ray MI 48096	586-781-2760	R	1*	<.1
2382	Binford Electric LLC	5949 S Valdai Way, Aurora CO 80015	303-699-5848	R	1*	<.1
2383	County Electric Inc—John Lajoie	PO Box 954, Caribou ME 04736	207-498-8231	R	1*	<.1
2384	Daniel John Electric Inc—Sigrid Broderick	PO Box 192, Columbia City IN 46725	260-356-2981	R	1*	<.1
2385	Touchton Electric Inc—David Touchton	111 N Broadway St, Pittsburg KS 66762	620-232-9294	R	1*	<.1
2386	Computer Enterprise Inc—Vera Preto	1530 Saint Charles Ave, Lakewood OH 44107	216-228-7156	R	1*	<.1
2387	Joe Pizik Electric Inc—Joseph Pizik	375 Oliver Dr, Troy MI 48084	248-362-3608	R	1*	<.1
2388	Lords Electric Inc—Robert Gratton	587 N County Line Rd, Jackson NJ 08527	732-928-9681	R	1*	<.1
2389	Energy Consulting Service Inc—Jack Davidoff	351 Kent Ave, Brooklyn NY 11211	718-963-2556	R	1*	<.1
2390	Kansas City Telecom—Lyddon Lee	111 W 31st St, Kansas City MO 64108	816-756-5934	R	1*	<.1
2391	P 2 P Technologies Inc—Merrill Hall	233 E Davis St, Culpeper VA 22701	540-727-8100	R	1*	<.1
2392	Tom Smith Electrical Service Inc—David Smith	2016 Natchez Dr, Mccomb MS 39648	601-684-5781	R	1*	<.1
2393	Brothers Electric Co—Dennis Letson	3447 Cedar Ave S, Minneapolis MN 55407	612-721-1606	R	1*	<.1
2394	Don Grubb—Don Grubb	PO Box 181715, Dallas TX 75218	214-321-1511	R	1*	<.1
2395	Michigan Electric LLC—Robert Mazzocco	3855 Kiefer Ave, Warren MI 48091	586-754-1580	R	1*	<.1
2396	Advance Electric Inc—Kent Anderson	PO Box 5932, Grand Forks ND 58206	701-746-5222	R	1*	<.1
2397	Advanced Video Surveillance Inc—Joseph Riotto	66 Clinton Rd, Fairfield NJ 07004	973-882-1920	R	1*	<.1
2398	Classic Electric Inc—Roger Honey	8531 Ablette Rd, Santee CA 92071	619-449-8580	R	1*	<.1

Note: An asterisk (*) indicates an estimated financial figure. The company type code used is as follows: R = Private, P = Public, S = Private Subsidiary, B = Public Subsidiary, D = Division, J = Joint Venture, I = Investment Fund.

COMPANY RANKINGS BY SALES WITHIN 4-DIGIT SIC

Rank	Company Name—*Executive Officer*	Address, City, State, Zip	Phone	Type	Fin	Empls
2399	Pacific Coast Electric—*Tom Shell*	180 Huffaker Rd, Rio Oso CA 95674	530-633-2200	R	1*	<.1
2400	Schneider Electrical Inc—*Pamela Schneider*	PO Box 433, Mount Vernon IN 47620	812-838-0125	R	1*	<.1
2401	Star Tel Systems Inc—*Donald Wyatt*	PO Box 515, Glasgow KY 42142	270-651-5597	R	1*	<.1
2402	Vectordyne Inc—*Francis Di Paolo*	14 York Rd, Willow Grove PA 19090	215-657-3386	R	1*	<.1
2403	Intranet Communications Group Inc—*Craig Blease*	3500 Nw 2nd Ave Ste 72, Boca Raton FL 33431	561-367-7276	R	1*	<.1
2404	Realtime Enterprise Networks Communications LLC	5450 Katella Ave Ste 1, Los Alamitos CA 90720	562-431-1300	R	1*	<.1
2405	Westphal Electric Inc—*Denise Hersch*	6409 Hamilton Dr E, Holland OH 43528	419-865-8888	R	1*	<.1
2406	Argus Electric Inc—*Chuck Collings*	PO Box 1024, Twin Falls ID 83303	208-733-4422	R	1*	<.1
2407	Chadwick Electric Inc—*Blye Chadwick*	1281 E Magnolia St Ste, Fort Collins CO 80524	970-484-0544	R	1*	<.1
2408	Code Electric Inc—*Jack Haggard*	2717 22nd St Se, Salem OR 97302	503-581-8684	R	1*	<.1
2409	Electrical Technology Inc—*Irv Weinstein*	35 Doyle Ct, East Northport NY 11731	631-499-0300	R	1*	<.1
2410	Florida Sound Engineering Company Inc—*Robert Cole*	5570 Flrda Mining Bldg, Jacksonville FL 32257	904-396-0444	R	1*	<.1
2411	Gulf Coast Downhole Technologies LLC—*Paul Hobbs*	6407 Eppes St, Houston TX 77087	713-667-4238	R	1*	<.1
2412	Neemar Inc—*Robert Dimarco*	2 Anco Dr, Deptford NJ 08096	856-227-2323	R	1*	<.1
2413	Quality Wiring Inc—*Sophia Dandrinos*	10145 Nw 19th St, Doral FL 33172	305-593-8306	R	1*	<.1
2414	Benson Sound Inc—*Larry Benson*	3900 E Innerstate 240, Oklahoma City OK 73135	405-670-4461	R	1*	<.1
2415	Deltacom Corp—*Paul Dalbero*	11 Old Bradley St Ste, East Haven CT 06512	203-469-4566	R	1*	<.1
2416	C Tech Corp—*Chris Villarreall*	5865 W 9600 N, Highland UT 84003	801-492-0669	R	1*	<.1
2417	Frazee Electric Inc—*Michael Kern*	PO Box 278, Frazee MN 56544	218-334-2382	R	1*	<.1
2418	Advanced Wireworks Inc—*Kevin Bogenreif*	631 W 96th St, Chanhassen MN 55317	952-403-9519	R	1*	<.1
2419	Productive Electric Inc—*Robert Bruns*	PO Box 810, Lewisburg OH 45338	937-962-3021	R	1*	<.1
2420	Advanced Telemetry Systems International Inc—*Paul Johnson*	PO Box 461659, Escondido CA 92046	760-738-6804	R	1*	<.1
2421	US Media Corp—*William Brookins*	218 High St, Dedham MA 02026	781-329-0447	R	1*	<.1
2422	C and C Equipment Sales and Repairs Inc—*Butch Goff*	PO Box 26100, Jacksonville FL 32226	904-751-6020	R	1*	.2
2423	Marsh Creek—*Mick Mckay*	41522 N Bay Hill Way, Anthem AZ 85086	623-322-8460	R	1*	.1
2424	Permaloc Security Devices Inc—*James Wolfe*	PO Box 4699, Silver Spring MD 20914	301-681-3200	R	1*	<.1
2425	Hightower Electric Company Inc—*William Hightower*	6115 Theall Rd, Houston TX 77066	281-440-4405	R	1*	<.1
2426	Swanson Enterprises Inc—*Willie Swanson*	303 Swansons Rd, Louisburg NC 27549	919-853-3533	R	1*	<.1
2427	Ashpaugh Electric Inc—*David Ashpaugh*	17902 Us Hwy 31 N D, Westfield IN 46074	317-896-2605	R	1*	<.1
2428	Ldt Ltd—*Lauren Templeton*	2920 W Woodstock Rd St, Woodstock VT 05091	802-457-3340	R	1*	<.1
2429	Turnage Corp—*James Turnage*	PO Box 1677, Morehead City NC 28557	252-727-0740	R	1*	<.1
2430	Tim Inc—*Sammuel Timmons*	130 N Ct St, Morganfield KY 42437	270-389-2420	R	1*	<.1
2431	Basson Sound Equipment—*Victor Basson*	1954 Kellogg Ave, Carlsbad CA 92008	760-929-0457	R	1*	<.1
2432	Cmacm Technologies Inc—*James Wilson*	38 Mill Gulch Rd, Sheridan MT 59749	406-842-5339	R	1*	<.1
2433	HES Electric Co—*Virgil Versteeg*	1881 S Dayton St, Denver CO 80247	303-368-1100	R	1*	<.1
2434	Storm Communications—*Kacee Walls*	PO Box 424, Knightdale NC 27545	919-261-8968	R	1*	<.1
2435	Advanced Technology LLC—*David Ansehl*	804 Horan Dr, Fenton MO 63026	314-991-5050	R	1*	<.1
2436	Bunnell Electric Inc—*Joseph Bunnell*	9966 Cincinnati Dayton, West Chester OH 45069	513-779-8778	R	1*	<.1
2437	Laughlin Electric Co—*Gloria Laughlin*	400 Selby Ave Ste E, Saint Paul MN 55102	651-224-2585	R	1*	<.1
2438	Advance Data Communications Inc—*Arnold Damian*	167 Darcy Pkwy, Lathrop CA 95330	209-858-4442	R	1*	<.1
2439	Gerdes Electric Inc—*Jeffrey Gerdes*	14781 Jenny St, Hesperia CA 92345	760-949-8617	R	1*	<.1
2440	Jvb Enterprises Inc—*James Brown*	5433 Charrin Dr, Houston TX 77032	281-449-4565	R	1*	<.1
2441	OR Communications Contractor LLC	PO Box 309, Santa Cruz NM 87567	505-753-9866	R	1*	<.1
2442	PKD Professional Systems Inc—*Kurt Davidsen*	2100 E Norse Ave, Cudahy WI 53110	414-747-1100	R	1*	<.1
2443	Shawnee Lighting Systems Inc—*Ronald Odell*	36609 45th St, Shawnee OK 74804	405-275-7275	R	1*	<.1
2444	Varco Inc—*Don Varni*	PO Box 790007, Paia HI 96779	808-579-9479	R	1*	<.1
2445	Greater Texas Electric Inc—*John Swanson*	PO Box 96274, Houston TX 77213	281-458-0634	R	1*	<.1
2446	Leslie Electric Services Inc—*Michele Remrey*	1801 Camanche Ave, Clinton IA 52732	563-242-2868	R	1*	<.1
2447	Schmitt Telecom Partners Inc—*Steve Schmitt*	PO Box 2213, Waterloo IA 50704	319-232-3701	R	1*	<.1
2448	Sierra Electric Inc—*Mitchell Murphy*	4120 N Swallow Ave, Pasco WA 99301	509-542-8682	R	1*	<.1
2449	Bennett Electric Inc—*Rosa Bennett*	6956 E 13th St, Tulsa OK 74112	918-622-9331	R	1*	<.1
2450	Ckb Inc—*Ernest Hart*	90 Lowell Rd, Salem NH 03079	603-894-5820	R	1*	<.1
2451	Dyer Electric Co—*W Dyer*	2135 E Indian School R, Phoenix AZ 85016	602-955-3770	R	1*	<.1
2452	Electric Masters Service Inc—*Nancy Sebastian*	9375 Gerwig Ln Ste A, Columbia MD 21046	410-381-8940	R	1*	<.1
2453	Elliott Controls Inc—*Glen Elliott*	10 Northern Blvd Ste 4, Amherst NH 03031	603-883-7975	R	1*	<.1
2454	Loramar Technologies Inc—*Mark C Johnson*	13 Woodland Ave, Fox Lake IL 60020	847-587-0670	R	1*	<.1
2455	Lundquist Associates Ltd—*Donald Lundquist*	610 Naval Base Rd Ste, Norfolk VA 23505	757-480-1046	R	1*	<.1
2456	Pursell Construction Inc—*Mark Pursell*	804 Estates Dr Ste 202, Aptos CA 95003	831-688-9400	R	1*	<.1
2457	SK Electric Inc—*Harold Sunada*	3523 Ala Haukulu Pl, Honolulu HI 96818	808-841-8852	R	1*	<.1
2458	Tropical Communications Inc—*William Devierno*	6937 Nw 82nd Ave, Miami FL 33166	305-599-2114	R	1*	<.1
2459	West End Electric Inc—*Greg Otto*	896 E Mountain Rd, Hegins PA 17938	570-682-9292	R	1*	<.1
2460	Electrical Work Inc—*Jon Reuter*	20481 Via Palo Pinto, Murrieta CA 92562	951-698-7758	R	1*	<.1
2461	Magnus Inc—*Paul Magnuson*	PO Box 39, Milaca MN 56353	320-982-8060	R	1*	<.1
2462	Micron Electrical Contracting Inc—*Dwayne Coleman*	13640 Elmira St, Detroit MI 48227	313-934-5945	R	1*	<.1
2463	Montoya Electric Service Inc—*Thomas Montoya*	PO Box 948, Auburndale FL 33823	863-967-9432	R	1*	<.1
2464	Ripon Electric Inc—*Michael Walgenbach*	510 Aspen St, Ripon WI 54971	920-748-6606	R	1*	<.1
2465	Stahl Electric Inc—*Ira Stahl*	2860 Mount Carmel Ave, Glenside PA 19038	215-572-6242	R	1*	<.1
2466	American Detection Systems Inc—*Kevin Gallagher*	6763 Market St Ste A, Wilmington NC 28405	910-799-7172	R	1*	<.1
2467	National Security Alliance Consultants LLC—*Bob Kishk*	2507 E Yandell Dr, El Paso TX 79903	915-533-8524	R	1*	<.1
2468	Accurate Electric Inc—*Ron Stratman*	510 N Santa Fe Ave, Salina KS 67401	785-825-4010	R	1*	<.1
2469	Life Line Communications Of Long Island Inc—*Lisa Cohn*	235 Glen Cove Ave, Sea Cliff NY 11579	516-759-0550	R	1*	<.1
2470	Cable Guyz Communications Inc—*Mary Johnson*	PO Box 22804, Lincoln NE 68542	402-742-4899	R	1*	<.1
2471	Electrical And Communications Services Inc—*Gary Jarrell*	2847 43rd Ave Sw, Lanett AL 36863	334-576-1200	R	1*	<.1
2472	Scherping Electric Inc—*Kurt Scherping*	38489 Tristan Rd, Freeport MN 56331	320-836-2865	R	1*	<.1
2473	Tri-R Telecommunications Inc	110 E 9th St Ste B286, Los Angeles CA 90079	213-239-8491	R	1*	<.1
2474	Access Computer Systems Corp—*Michael Herbert*	2174 Mar Vista Ave, Altadena CA 91001	626-692-6233	R	1*	<.1
2475	Dial One Telecommunications—*Paul Kalmakoff*	PO Box 873, Stanwood WA 98292	360-629-2085	R	1*	<.1
2476	Gas Control Technologies—*Mark Beckner*	PO Box 86, Newbury Park CA 91319	805-382-6035	R	1*	<.1
2477	Globus Inc—*Michael Napal*	4005 N Verdugo Rd, Los Angeles CA 90065	323-257-8300	R	1*	<.1
2478	Gregory Electric Company Inc—*Robert E Livingston Jr*	PO Drawer 1419, Columbia SC 29202	803-748-1122	R	1*	<.1
2479	Normandeau Communications Inc—*Brett Normandeau*	2097 Riverdale St, West Springfield MA 01089	413-584-3131	R	1*	<.1
2480	StealthCom Solutions Inc—*Jason Aguilar*	6190 Lake Shore Ct Ste, Colorado Springs CO 80915	719-359-5410	R	1*	<.1
2481	Steven K Smith—*Steven Smith*	547 W 20th St, Idaho Falls ID 83402	208-528-5499	R	1*	<.1
2482	Antennas Unlimited Inc—*Ray Willhoite*	1003 Highland Park Dr, Lexington KY 40505	859-255-8190	R	1*	<.1
2483	Connect Technology Inc—*Tom Glensgard*	2743 N Wolcott Ave Ste, Chicago IL 60614	847-981-9745	R	1*	<.1
2484	Joseph H Smith—*Joseph Smith*	5 Saint James St, Lowell MA 01852	978-453-6472	R	1*	<.1
2485	MMR Group Inc—*James B Rutland*	PO Box 84210, Baton Rouge LA 70884	225-756-5090	R	1*	<.1
2486	Oasis Telecommunications Data and Records Inc—*Tom Hinrichs*	PO Box 1985, Bozeman MT 59771	406-586-4667	R	1*	<.1
2487	All Island Electrical Contracting Inc—*John Murphy*	PO Box 1008, Amityville NY 11701	631-598-0010	R	1*	<.1

Rank	Company Name—*Executive Officer*	Address, City, State, Zip	Phone	Type	Fin	Empls
2488	Direct Electric Co—*John Large*	40399 Clybourne Cir, Murrieta CA 92562	951-965-1014	R	1*	<.1
2489	Minuteman Electric LLC	PO Box 1017, Branford CT 06405	203-457-6908	R	1*	<.1
2490	e2e Communications Inc—*Frank Lemons*	PO Box 1148, Jacksonville NC 28541	910-375-5100	R	1*	<.1
2491	Southern Media Systems Inc—*David Major*	1523 N Pinebark Ln, Charleston SC 29407	843-556-3112	R	1*	<.1
2492	Telcom Corp—*Bobra Bush*	1499 W Palmetto Park R, Boca Raton FL 33486	561-394-5448	R	1*	<.1
2493	Data Tel US—*Toby Morris*	20404 71st St E, Bonney Lake WA 98391	253-891-7775	R	1*	<.1
2494	Jerry Barnes Electric Inc—*Jerry Barnes*	PO Box 347, Red Oak NC 27868	252-977-8845	R	1*	<.1
2495	Electrical and Lighting Incorporated of Virginia A/K/A ELI Inc—*Rita Kazarian*	7661d Fullerton Rd, Springfield VA 22153	703-440-5745	R	1*	<.1
2496	West Electric Inc—*Timothy West*	PO Box 54, Bremen OH 43107	740-689-8800	R	1*	<.1
2497	Telephone Technical Services Inc—*Terry Evans*	703 E Main St, Humble TX 77338	281-446-6988	R	1*	<.1
2498	Art O Lite Electric Company Inc—*Brad Williams*	230 52nd St, Moline IL 61265	309-797-2548	R	1*	<.1
2499	Deere Electric Inc—*Thomas Deere*	10684 Carson Hwy, Tecumseh MI 49286	517-431-2220	R	1*	<.1
2500	DSL Sound Inc—*William Hetzer*	PO Box 2527, Hagerstown MD 21741	301-797-1070	R	1*	<.1
2501	Enviromation Inc—*Dennis Mcnamee*	11135 Leadbetter Rd, Ashland VA 23005	804-798-7717	R	1*	<.1
2502	Jeffco Electric Inc—*Jeff Myers*	3716 Clifton Pl, Montrose CA 91020	818-249-9900	R	1*	<.1
2503	Pyrometric Company Inc—*Bill Kennedy*	1312 S 96th St, Seattle WA 98108	206-762-8307	R	1*	<.1
2504	Riley CA Electric Construction Corp—*Charlotte Birck*	911 Lee St, Elk Grove Village IL 60007	847-437-3851	R	1*	<.1
2505	Sierra Electric LLC—*Kevin Wayman*	5565 Leo Park Rd, West Jordan UT 84081	801-280-6106	R	1*	<.1
2506	Involve Test And Control Inc—*Louis Perry*	50508 Central Industri, Shelby Township MI 48315	586-254-3165	R	1*	<.1
2507	Photo Specialty Shop Inc—*Mark Pedley*	303 5th St, Eureka CA 95501	707-442-4462	R	1*	<.1
2508	Rocky Mountain Technologies LLC—*Anthony Baca*	PO Box 4026, Durango CO 81302	970-259-5200	R	1*	<.1
2509	Selectric LLC—*Sharron Crownley*	2124 Priest Bridge Dr, Crofton MD 21114	410-451-7260	R	1*	<.1
2510	Wright Brothers Electric Company Inc—*Phillip Stroud*	711 N Person St Ste A, Raleigh NC 27604	919-839-5660	R	1*	<.1
2511	A and B Construction Corp—*Terryl Adams*	2530 Marion Dr, Las Vegas NV 89115	702-644-7757	R	1*	<.1
2512	Central Coast Electronics Inc—*John Weiss*	510 Quintana Rd, Morro Bay CA 93442	805-772-5303	R	1*	<.1
2513	Air Tek Inc—*M Dwinnell*	PO Box 1187, Soldotna AK 99669	907-262-9391	R	1*	<.1
2514	Beckett Electrical Services LLC	PO Box 81381, Austin TX 78708	512-346-7462	R	1*	<.1
2515	Florida Electric Inc—*James Ratliff*	PO Box 20191, Tallahassee FL 32316	850-574-3355	R	1*	<.1
2516	Shir-Omar Inc—*Arthur Walker*	PO Box 1722, Shreveport LA 71166	318-424-0400	R	1*	<.1
2517	Computerized Meter Corp—*Jerry Fund*	450 7th Ave Ste 403, New York NY 10123	212-279-7215	R	1*	<.1
2518	Hawkeye Alarm and Signal Co—*Kenneth Samek*	PO Box 2431, Waterloo IA 50704	319-232-0490	R	1*	<.1
2519	HWS Energy Partners LLC	2805 Research Rd Ste 1, Champaign IL 61822	217-356-3749	R	1*	<.1
2520	Sun Elect—*James Parker*	901 Van Ness Ave, Torrance CA 90501	310-376-7319	R	1*	<.1
2521	Carr Electric Company Inc—*Robert David*	PO Box 210218, Montgomery AL 36121	334-279-5623	R	1*	<.1
2522	Excel Communications Worldwide Inc—*George Nolte*	1527 Gehman Rd, Harleysville PA 19438	215-256-6776	R	1*	<.1
2523	Rocco J Russo Ltd—*Mark Russo*	PO Box 589, Port Chester NY 10573	914-937-0001	R	1*	<.1
2524	Seneca Energy Ii LLC—*Peter Zeliff*	2999 Judge Rd, Oakfield NY 14125	585-948-8580	R	1*	<.1
2525	Sound Masters Inc—*Jerry Reske*	PO Box 31728, Seattle WA 98103	206-632-4313	R	1*	<.1
2526	Freeze Frame Video Surveillance—*Lawrence Footlick*	1509 Aviation Blvd, Redondo Beach CA 90278	310-379-4223	R	1*	<.1
2527	Micro Generation Technologies Inc—*Diane Swartwood*	315 Ken Mar Industrial, Broadview Heights OH 44147	440-838-5035	R	1*	<.1
2528	Padd Electrical Inc—*Scherrie Addyman*	22635 State St, Steger IL 60475	708-756-2132	R	1*	<.1
2529	Aqoom Inc—*John Jurik*	201 Stuyvesant Ave, Lyndhurst NJ 07071	201-438-2244	R	1*	<.1
2530	Energy Management Strategies—*Ann Rodenberg*	PO Box 16, Thurmont MD 21788	301-241-5020	R	1*	<.1
2531	Intellicom Technologies—*Jesse Hindemith*	PO Box 27056, San Diego CA 92198	858-486-1115	R	1*	<.1
2532	Kabel-X USA LLC—*Darin Clause*	1400 Nw 107th Ave Fl 4, Doral FL 33172	305-392-4123	R	1*	<.1
2533	Tele Data Contractors Inc—*Roger Bradford*	13008 2nd St, Grandview MO 64030	816-943-1957	R	1*	<.1
2534	Commworld Of Cumberland LLC	PO Box 664, Cameron WI 54822	715-234-1344	R	1*	<.1
2535	SS Electric and Service Company LLC—*Maria Shrebe*	114 Slocum Rd, Calhoun LA 71225	318-397-1172	R	1*	<.1
2536	Amp Check Electric—*George Twiggs*	444 Garfield Ave Ne, Lake Placid FL 33852	863-465-4162	R	1*	<.1
2537	Coastal Power Solutions LLC—*Dale Rice*	6135 Rangeline Rd, Theodore AL 36582	251-443-8600	R	1*	<.1
2538	Mercier Electric and Communications Inc—*Joseph Mercier*	567 Mammoth Rd, Dracut MA 01826	978-957-4954	R	1*	<.1
2539	Darella Maintenance And Electric Corporation Inc—*Edward Darella*	21 E 16th St, Paterson NJ 07524	973-684-6016	R	1*	<.1
2540	Diversified Concepts Inc—*David May*	2533 Cherry Valley Tpk, Marcellus NY 13108	315-673-2088	R	1*	<.1
2541	Guys Electric Service Of Westchester Inc—*Guy Fuschetto*	216 Eastchester Rd, New Rochelle NY 10801	914-235-4069	R	1*	<.1
2542	Control Engineering Group Inc—*Wayne Deming*	175 Smran Commercee Pl, Apopka FL 32703	407-889-2432	R	1*	<.1
2543	Smooth Technologies LLC	4747 Res Frest Dr Ste, Spring TX 77381	281-362-1012	R	1*	<.1
2544	Paul Patrick Electric Inc—*Paul Patrick*	5755 Windover St, Milton FL 32583	850-623-8047	R	1*	<.1
2545	Blacks Electric—*R Black*	1117 Chitwood Ave Se, Fort Payne AL 35967	256-845-1133	R	1*	<.1
2546	Brico Electric Inc—*Karen Flaherty*	107 N M Luther King Jr, Clearwater FL 33755	727-787-0091	R	1*	<.1
2547	Custom Electric and Design Inc—*Matt Degennaro*	9853 Tamiami Trl N Ste, Naples FL 34108	239-514-2296	R	1*	<.1
2548	Mackay Telephone Systems Inc—*Scott Mackay*	1219 E Ctr St, Marion OH 43302	740-387-4403	R	1*	<.1
2549	Fs Alarms Inc—*Michael Jennings*	555 Summit Ave, Jersey City NJ 07306	201-963-4030	R	1*	<.1
2550	Advanced Technical Systems Inc—*Gretchen Fawcett*	PO Box 265, Canton IL 61520	309-647-4463	R	1*	<.1
2551	Hoagland Electric Inc—*Daniel Hoagland*	3622 Goshen Rd, Fort Wayne IN 46818	260-489-5990	R	1*	<.1
2552	Power Technical Services Inc—*Ronald Scott*	PO Box 77310, Baton Rouge LA 70879	225-272-2113	R	1*	<.1
2553	Becovic Management Group Inc—*Muhamed Becovic*	4520 N Clarendon Ave S, Chicago IL 60640	773-271-6143	R	1*	<.1
2554	Drl Services Inc—*Sharon Yasemsky*	PO Box 3368, Virginia Beach VA 23454	757-481-3003	R	1*	<.1
2555	Leitner Electric Co—*Perry Leitner*	10939 Reed Hartman Hwy, Blue Ash OH 45242	513-351-9024	R	1*	<.1
2556	Cable Systems Inc—*David Lanni*	PO Box 26, Macedon NY 14502	315-986-4823	R	1*	<.1
2557	Huntsville Electrical Services—*Randall Rierson*	4811 Commercial Dr Nw, Huntsville AL 35816	256-533-5555	R	1*	<.1
2558	American Access Controls Inc—*Cheryl Keeley*	14237 N Florida Ave, Tampa FL 33613	813-265-8820	R	1*	<.1
2559	Great River Contractors LLC	220 S Warsaw St, Nauvoo IL 62354	319-208-0171	R	1*	<.1
2560	Advance Cable Company LLC—*Randy Larson*	PO Box 620033, Middleton WI 53562	608-831-1688	R	1*	<.1
2561	ITM Electronics Inc—*Brad Holton*	PO Box 309, Greenleaf ID 83626	208-459-1882	R	1*	<.1
2562	Hatley's Electrical Service—*Larry Hatley*	PO Box 975, Norwood NC 28128	704-474-5777	R	1*	<.1
2563	Pacific Power Testing Inc—*Steve Emmert*	14280 Doolittle Dr, San Leandro CA 94577	510-351-8811	R	1*	<.1
2564	CMH Sound And Video Inc—*Carlton Hearne*	134 Hillcrest Ave Nw, Canton OH 44720	330-497-8100	R	1*	<.1
2565	Vital Energy Inc—*Steve Steinberg*	905 Greenwich Dr, Thousand Oaks CA 91360	805-230-1130	R	1*	<.1
2566	Goodson Electric Inc—*Mark Goodson*	620 17th St W, Palmetto FL 34221	941-729-5633	R	<1*	<.1
2567	Maguire Electrical Construction LLC—*Deborah Maguire*	2547 Fire Rd A, Egg Harbor Township NJ 08234	609-645-8600	R	<1*	<.1
2568	3M Pacific Security Systems Inc—*Seymour Hoff*	214 Cristich Ln Ste 20, Campbell CA 95008	408-295-0500	R	<1*	<.1
2569	Connections USA Inc—*Sidney Hull*	2200 Marietta Hwy Ste, Canton GA 30114	770-479-7508	R	<1*	<.1
2570	EAS Industries Inc—*Steven Clark*	PO Box 7696, Sebring FL 33872	954-525-8700	R	<1*	<.1
2571	Acupower Inc—*Thomas Rabolli*	7154 N University Dr, Tamarac FL 33321	954-726-4756	R	<1*	<.1
2572	Possidento Electric LLC—*Stephen Possidento*	18 Sunset Ln, Wolcott CT 06716	203-879-1046	R	<1*	<.1
2573	Rmf Inc—*Gary Retter*	1661 N Amber St, Boise ID 83706	208-322-5789	R	<1*	<.1
2574	Landes Audio and Video LLC	35 Perry St Ste 2, Chester NJ 07930	908-879-6999	R	<1*	<.1
2575	Howard Borress Enterprises Inc—*Howard Borress*	494 Greenwich St, New York NY 10013	212-334-0220	R	<1*	<.1

Note: An asterisk (*) indicates an estimated financial figure. The company type code used is as follows: R = Private, P = Public, S = Private Subsidiary, B = Public Subsidiary, D = Division, J = Joint Venture, I = Investment Fund.

COMPANY RANKINGS BY SALES WITHIN 4-DIGIT SIC

Rank	Company Name—Executive Officer	Address, City, State, Zip	Phone	Type	Fin	Empls
2576	Tidal Communication LLC—Chris Faddis	2 Elm Sq Frnt 3, Andover MA 01810	978-475-4168	R	<1*	<.1
2577	Audiss-Thorsen Inc—John Wayson	PO Box 225, Sonoma CA 95476	707-938-8005	R	<1*	<.1
2578	Westshore Data Inc—Christopher Bartel	1331 Linda St, Rocky River OH 44116	440-356-6363	R	<1*	<.1
2579	Built-In-Systems Inc—Jeffrey Simon	4987 Cleveland St Ste, Virginia Beach VA 23462	757-499-1111	R	<1*	<.1
2580	Faceshot LLC	3457 Ringsby Ct Unit 2, Denver CO 80216	303-698-1132	R	<1*	<.1
2581	Synchronized Networking Solutions LLC—Chad Biddinger	265 Samuels Rd, Coxs Creek KY 40013	719-371-2315	R	<1*	<.1
2582	Acx Inc—Ismael Guadalupe	PO Box 191124, Dallas TX 75219	214-522-0836	R	<1*	<.1
2583	Lighting Control Systems Inc—Albert Suarez	4735 Sw 74th Ave, Miami FL 33155	305-267-1013	R	<1*	<.1
2584	Arrel Enterprises Inc—Richard Lattanzi	2800 Bob Wallace Ave S, Huntsville AL 35805	256-534-5853	R	<1*	<.1
2585	Control Line Electric Inc—Anthony Voroshuck	1425 Koll Cir Ste 106, San Jose CA 95112	408-451-9361	R	<1*	<.1
2586	Custom Audio And Lighting Inc—Andy Sykora	3087 Old Hodges Rd, Abbeville SC 29620	864-446-3492	R	<1*	<.1
2587	Lawn Fire Co—Carl Etler	PO Box 12, Lawn PA 17041	717-964-2369	R	<1*	<.1
2588	Oxford Alarm And Communications—William Vick	179 Hwy 6 E, Oxford MS 38655	662-236-5520	R	<1*	<.1
2589	American Defense Services Inc—Ken Lanvalaco	PO Box 6378, Metairie LA 70009	504-832-0026	R	<1*	<.1
2590	Fpc Services Inc—Joyce Papich	1771 Sublette Rd, Sublette IL 61367	815-849-5135	R	<1*	<.1
2591	PBC Sound Technologies—Neal Wetmore	71 3 Freedom Pkwy, Hermon ME 04401	207-947-0712	R	<1*	<.1
2592	Aec Electric Inc—Michel Castonguay	1105 N Allen Ave, Pasadena CA 91104	626-398-3664	R	<1*	<.1
2593	Boundless Security Systems Inc—Steve Morton	3 Simm Ln Ste 1f, Newtown CT 06470	203-445-0562	R	<1*	<.1
2594	Coolidge Electric LLC	1347 Heller Dr, Yardley PA 19067	215-369-3595	R	<1*	<.1
2595	Donaldson Electric Company Inc—Gordon Donaldson	9625 S Main St Ste C, Jonesboro GA 30236	770-471-9500	R	<1*	<.1
2596	Robb's Electric Inc—Ronald Robb	7414 Frances Dr, Morris AL 35116	205-681-0494	R	<1*	<.1
2597	Mac Brothers Electric—Dennis Cuen	5310 Hereford St, Detroit MI 48224	313-881-9799	R	<1*	<.1

TOTALS: SIC 1731 Electrical Work
Companies: 2,597   42,462   188.1

1741 Masonry & Other Stonework

Rank	Company Name—Executive Officer	Address, City, State, Zip	Phone	Type	Fin	Empls
1	Dee Brown Inc—Robert V Barnes Jr	PO Box 570335, Dallas TX 75357	214-321-6443	R	240*	.5
2	Navillus Tile Inc—Donald Sullivan	460 Park Ave Rm 801, New York NY 10022	212-750-1808	R	172*	.4
3	Otto Baum Company Inc—Kenneth D Baum	PO Box 161, Morton IL 61550	309-266-7114	R	143*	.4
4	Seedorff Masonry Inc—Mark H Guetzko	408 W Mission St, Strawberry Point IA 52076	563-933-2296	R	109*	.3
5	Sun Valley Masonry Inc—Robert L Baum	10828 N Cave Creek Rd, Phoenix AZ 85020	602-943-6106	R	71*	.6
6	Hamon-Custodis—William P Dillon	58 E Main St, Somerville NJ 08876	908-685-4000	S	51*	.1
7	International Chimney Corp—Richard Lohr	PO Box 260, Buffalo NY 14231	716-634-3967	R	31*	.3
8	Wasco Inc—Brad Procter	1138 2nd Ave N, Nashville TN 37208	615-244-9090	R	28*	.4
9	Thermal Specialties Inc—Robert Caffey	PO Box 3623, Tulsa OK 74101	918-836-4800	R	18*	.1
10	Satco Inc—Gerald Satawa	PO Box 83377, Baton Rouge LA 70884	225-291-0352	R	14*	<.1
11	Blue Rock Industries—Dick Wilson	737 Spring St, Westbrook ME 04092	207-772-6770	R	12*	.1
12	V J Mattson Co—Thomas Morack	9200 W 191st St Ste 1, Mokena IL 60448	708-479-1990	R	11*	.1
13	Thatcher Engineering Corp—R Parkison	7100 Industrial Hwy, Gary IN 46406	219-949-2084	R	10*	.1
14	Intrepid Enterprises Inc—Harold Prestenburg	1848 Industrial Blvd, Harvey LA 70058	504-348-2861	R	6*	.1
15	Pacific Pavingstone—Terry Morrill	2729 Foothill Blvd, La Crescenta CA 91214	818-244-4000	R	6*	.1
16	Pagliaro Brothers Stone Company Inc—Joseph Pagliaro	6301 Foxley Rd Ste 201, Upper Marlboro MD 20772	301-599-6066	R	5*	.1
17	Glass Design Inc—Roger Weilacher	PO Box 568, Sapulpa OK 74067	918-224-4371	R	5*	<.1
18	Paddock Masonry Inc—Jamie Paddock	PO Box 2447, Eugene OR 97402	541-345-4629	R	3*	<.1
19	Ben Porto and Sons Ltd—Robert Deg	PO Box 34300, Bethesda MD 20827	301-365-1915	R	2*	<.1
20	Pyro Industrial Services Inc—John Carlson	PO Box 237, Portage IN 46368	219-787-5700	R	2*	<.1
21	O'brien Cut Stone Co—John O'brien	19100 Miles Rd, Cleveland OH 44128	216-663-7800	R	2*	<.1

TOTALS: SIC 1741 Masonry & Other Stonework
Companies: 21   941   3.6

1742 Plastering, Drywall & Insulation

Rank	Company Name—Executive Officer	Address, City, State, Zip	Phone	Type	Fin	Empls
1	API Group Inc—Russell Becker	1100 Old Hwy 8 NW, Saint Paul MN 55112		R	1,440*	9.0
2	Performance Contracting Group Inc—Craig Davis	16400 College Blvd, Lenexa KS 66219	913-888-8600	R	716*	6.8
3	Acousti Engineering Company of Florida—James R Verner	4656 34th St SW, Orlando FL 32811	407-425-3467	R	120*	1.5
4	King and Company Inc (New Orleans Louisiana)—Cyril P Geary Jr	PO Box 50263, New Orleans LA 70150	504-486-9195	R	82*	.6
5	Anning-Johnson Co—John Andrzejewski	1959 Anson Dr, Melrose Park IL 60160	708-681-1300	D	74*	.1
6	Manganaro MidatlanticLLC—Tom Vagrin	6405-D Ammendale Rd, Beltsville MD 20705	301-937-0580	R	28*	.2
7	Jacobson and Company Inc—Thomas G Jacobson	PO Box 511, Elizabeth NJ 07207	908-355-5200	R	22*	.2
8	Grayhawk LLC—Jim Robinson	PO Box 12111, Lexington KY 40580	859-255-2754	R	21*	.2
9	Sullivan Brothers Inc—Patrick Sullivan	2515 S Stoughton Rd, Madison WI 53716	608-222-1277	R	18*	.2
10	Entrx Corp—Peter L Hauser	800 Nicollet Mall Ste, Minneapolis MN 55402	612-333-0614	P	17	<.1
11	Anchor Insulation Company Inc—Gregory Fiske	435 Narragansett Park, Pawtucket RI 02861	401-438-6720	R	16*	.1
12	BJ McGlone and Company Inc—Brian McGlone	PO Box 594, Edison NJ 08818	732-287-8600	R	13*	.2
13	Cardinal Industrial Insulation Company Inc—Mark Mueller	PO Box 2258, Louisville KY 40201	502-589-5794	R	11*	.1
14	Valcom Enterprises Inc—Harry Lafkas	120 Ctr St, Newport KY 41071	859-655-4400	R	8*	<.1
15	Baker Drywall Fort Worth Ltd—Brian Baker	2213 W Broadway St, Fort Worth TX 76102	817-810-0180	R	7*	.1
16	Central Coating Company Inc—Luke Nolan	670 S Pine St, Madera CA 93637	559-673-0074	R	6*	<.1
17	Allied Construction Services Inc—Robert L Maddox III	PO Box 937, Des Moines IA 50304	515-288-4855	R	4*	<.1
18	Airtite Contractors Inc—Ron Fletcher	343 Carol Ln, Elmhurst IL 60126	630-530-9001	R	3*	.1
19	Drywall Distributors Inc—Scott Mcdonald	PO Box 14, Woodinville WA 98072	425-488-4888	R	3*	<.1
20	Zander Insulation—William Zander	3316 Meadow Rd, Verona WI 53593	608-833-6620	R	2*	<.1
21	Ceiling Solutions—Todd Abrams	171 N Ethel Ave, Hawthorne NJ 07506	973-423-1655	R	1*	<.1

TOTALS: SIC 1742 Plastering, Drywall & Insulation
Companies: 21   2,609   19.4

1743 Terrazzo, Tile, Marble & Mosaic Work

Rank	Company Name—Executive Officer	Address, City, State, Zip	Phone	Type	Fin	Empls
1	Twin City Tile and Marble Co—Jim Hidding	900 Montreal Circle, Saint Paul MN 55102		R	78*	.1
2	Imperial Marble and Tile Company Inc—Lloyd Colgate	651 3rd Ave N, Birmingham AL 35203	205-252-8982	R	1*	<.1

TOTALS: SIC 1743 Terrazzo, Tile, Marble & Mosaic Work
Companies: 2   79   .1

1751 Carpentry Work

Rank	Company Name—Executive Officer	Address, City, State, Zip	Phone	Type	Fin	Empls
1	Closet World Inc—Frank Melkonian	3860 Capitol Ave, City Of Industry CA 90601	562-699-9945	R	621*	.7
2	Carpenter Contractors Of America Inc—Donald Reiter	3900 Ave G Nw, Winter Haven FL 33880	863-294-6449	R	442*	1.0
3	Center Brothers Inc—Henry Tuten III	PO Box 22278, Savannah GA 31403	912-232-6491	R	198*	.2
4	BT Mancini Company Inc—Skip Weaver	PO Box 361930, Milpitas CA 95036	408-942-7900	R	42*	.2
5	Sloan and Company Inc—Scott Casabona	PO Box 2845, Caldwell NJ 07007	973-227-3555	R	26*	.3
6	Maxons Restorations Inc—Damon Gersh	280 Madison Ave, New York NY 10016	212-447-6767	R	19*	.1

Rank	Company Name—Executive Officer	Address, City, State, Zip	Phone	Type	Fin	Empls
7	Century Stair Company Inc—Donald Costello	15175 Washington St, Haymarket VA 20169	703-754-4163	R	15*	.2
8	Eklips Enterprises Inc—Joseph Klips	3674 Dayton Park Dr, Dayton OH 45414	937-235-0157	R	9*	<.1
9	Concraft Restoration Services—Tony Crimando	1171 Centre Rd, Auburn Hills MI 48326	248-276-9400	R	5	.1
10	Blackrock Construction LLC	3433 1st Ave, Fernandina Beach FL 32034	904-591-9810	R	5*	<.1
11	Solidsurface Designs Inc—Matthew Baiada	1651 Sherman Ave, Pennsauken NJ 08110	856-910-7720	R	4*	<.1
12	Midwest Stainless Technologies LLC—Jen Ford	5408 3m Dr Ste B, Menomonie WI 54751	715-235-5472	R	4*	<.1
13	United Construction Co—Barry Clarambeau	4431 Shanewood Ct, Orlando FL 32837	407-908-8883	R	2*	.1
14	Apex Group LLC—Jim Mette	8213 Old Jumpers Hole, Millersville MD 21108	410-315-7776	R	2*	<.1
15	Jasco Window Corp—Joseph Carbone	11 Denton Ave S, New Hyde Park NY 11040	516-354-5772	R	1*	<.1
16	F and R Installers Corp—Barbara Foster	63 Flushing Ave Unit 2, Brooklyn NY 11205	718-855-1600	R	1*	<.1
17	Wallside Inc—Stanford Blanck	27000 Trlley Industral, Taylor MI 48180	313-292-4400	R	1*	<.1

TOTALS: SIC 1751 Carpentry Work
Companies: 17   1,396   2.8

1752 Floor Laying & Floor Work Nec

Rank	Company Name—Executive Officer	Address, City, State, Zip	Phone	Type	Fin	Empls
1	Shaw Contract Flooring—Kyle Harding	410 Old Mill Rd, Cartersville GA 30120		S	200*	.4
2	Peninsula Group Inc—Kelli Finale	PO Box 71, Livermore CA 94551	925-449-6000	R	182*	.5
3	Irvine Access Floors Inc—Larry Worthington	9425 Washington Blvd N, Laurel MD 20723	301-617-9333	R	54*	.1
4	Kalman Floor Company Inc—Carl N Ytterberg	1202 Bergen Pky Ste 11, Evergreen CO 80439	303-674-2290	R	16*	<.1
5	Ari Products Inc—Ross Gilfillan	102 Gaither Dr Ste 3, Mount Laurel NJ 08054	856-234-0757	R	16*	<.1
6	Hoover and Wells Inc—Margaret Hoover	PO Box 8398, Toledo OH 43605	419-691-9220	R	12*	.1
7	Hagopian Fire and Flood Services Inc—Edmond Hagopian	14050 W 8 Mile Rd, Oak Park MI 48237	248-541-6500	D	10*	<.1
8	Covington Flooring Co—Joe Covington Jr	PO Box 19968, Birmingham AL 35219	205-328-2330	R	10*	<.1
9	Continental Flooring Co (Scottsdale Arizona)—Chris Coleman	9319 N 94th Way Ste 10, Scottsdale AZ 85258	480-949-8509	R	7*	<.1
10	Superior Floor Covering Inc—Karen O'connor	PO Box 314, Posen IL 60469	708-371-0515	R	5*	<.1
11	Ruggieri Brothers Inc—William Ruggieri	1191 Pontiac Ave, Cranston RI 02920	401-463-9100	R	5*	<.1
12	Tera-Lite Inc—David Palomino	1631 S 10th St, San Jose CA 95112	408-288-8655	R	4*	<.1
13	Staticworx Inc—David H Long	PO Box 590069, Newton Centre MA 02459	617-923-2000	R	3*	<.1
14	Associated Acc International Ltd—Richard Goodman	306 Main St Ste 1, Millburn NJ 07041	908-686-6011	R	2*	<.1
15	Morlang Flooring—Mike Morlang	3823 NW Arlington, Lawton OK 73505	580-695-1170	R	2*	<.1

TOTALS: SIC 1752 Floor Laying & Floor Work Nec
Companies: 15   528   1.3

1761 Roofing, Siding & Sheet Metal Work

Rank	Company Name—Executive Officer	Address, City, State, Zip	Phone	Type	Fin	Empls
1	Centimark Corp—Brian Altvater	12 Grandview Cir, Canonsburg PA 15317	724-743-7777	R	1,002*	2.5
2	Tecta America Corp—Mark F Santacrose	5215 Old Orchard Rd St, Skokie IL 60077	847-581-3888	R	979*	2.6
3	Mountain Co—Harry H Esbenshade	PO Box 5310, Vienna WV 26105	304-295-3311	R	219*	.6
4	North American Roofing Services Inc—Brian Verble	41 Dogwood Rd, Asheville NC 28806	828-687-7767	R	55*	.3
5	Aduddell Industries—Tim Aduddell	PO Box 89550, Oklahoma City OK 73189	405-703-4316	P	47	.4
6	Field Investments Inc—Stephen Field	PO Box 1425, Springfield OH 45501	937-323-5518	R	41*	.1
7	Distinctive Roofing LLC—Daniel W Grifford Jr	2606 W Townley Ave Ste, Phoenix AZ 85021	602-943-2047	R	40*	<.1
8	Tri-State Roofing and Sheet Metal Company Of West Virginia—Harry Esbenshade	PO Box 188, Davisville WV 26142	304-485-6593	R	38*	.1
9	Pangere Corp—Steve Pangere	4050 W 4th Ave, Gary IN 46406	219-949-1368	R	37*	.2
10	Crown Corr Inc—Richard Pellar	7100 W 21st Ave, Gary IN 46406	219-949-8080	R	37*	.2
11	United Sheet Metal Inc—Jimmie Roberts	51 Ritchie Rd, Capitol Heights MD 20743	301-350-4200	R	35*	.3
12	Streimer Sheet Metal Works Inc—Frederick Streimer	740 N Knott St, Portland OR 97227	503-288-9393	R	35*	.2
13	CMR Construction and Roofing—Steve Soule	10734 Trenton Ave, St Louis MO 63132		R	31*	.1
14	Preferred Inc—Jerry D Brown	6021 Highview Dr, Fort Wayne IN 46818	260-483-8383	R	30*	.1
15	Midland Engineering Company Inc—Charles W Frazier	52369 SR 933 N, South Bend IN 46637	574-272-0200	R	24*	.3
16	Knox Industries Inc—Jack Knox	PO Box 1337, Smyrna GA 30081	770-434-7401	R	24*	.2
17	Kalkreuth Roofing and Sheet Metal Inc—John Kalkreuth	PO Box 6399, Wheeling WV 26003	304-232-8540	R	24*	.3
18	PI Roof Maintenance Inc—Joel Johnson	6109 Remount Rd, North Little Rock AR 72118	501-687-6246	R	23*	.1
19	Academy Roofing and Sheet Metal Co—John L McDermott	1501 NW 12th Ave, Pompano Beach FL 33069	954-935-9996	R	21*	.1
20	Winona Heating and Ventilating Company Inc—Michael Gostomski	PO Box 77, Winona MN 55987	507-452-2064	R	20*	.1
21	Sessa Sheet Metal Contractors Inc—Tom Sessa	529 N Haven St, Baltimore MD 21205	410-327-7000	R	20*	.2
22	Charles F Evans Company Inc—William Norton	PO Box 228, Elmira NY 14902	607-734-8151	S	19*	.1
23	Gooding Simpson and Mackes Inc—Reed Gooding	PO Box 476, Ephrata PA 17522	717-733-1241	R	19*	.1
24	B-H-W Sheet Metal Co—Keith Harris	PO Box 995, Jonesboro GA 30237	770-471-9303	R	17*	.1
25	Mccusker-Gill Inc—Dale Hatfield	75 Industrial Park Rd, Hingham MA 02043	781-740-5800	R	17*	.2
26	Stainless Specialists Inc—Roger Prochnow	PO Box 687, Wausau WI 54402	715-675-4155	R	16*	.1
27	Prate Installations Inc—Michael Prate	1120 N Rand Rd Frnt 1, Wauconda IL 60084	847-526-6402	R	16*	.2
28	Ferber Sheet Metal Works Inc—Frances Ferber	PO Box 26069, Jacksonville FL 32226	904-356-3042	R	16*	.2
29	Gastonia Sheet Metal Works Inc—Ronald Long	PO Box 12216, Gastonia NC 28052	704-864-0344	R	16*	.1
30	Snyder Roofing and Sheet Metal Inc—James F King	12650 SW Hall Blvd, Tigard OR 97223	503-620-5252	R	15*	.1
31	Turner Roofing And Sheet Metal Inc—Chirs Myer	1200 E Memphis St, Broken Arrow OK 74012	918-258-2585	R	15*	.1
32	Fred Christen and Sons Co—Fredrick Christen	PO Box 547, Toledo OH 43697	419-243-4161	R	14*	.1
33	Johnson Contracting Company Inc—C Johnson	2750 Morton Dr, East Moline IL 61244	309-755-0601	R	13*	.2
34	N E Tech-Air Inc—Robert Lilly	16 Manson Libby Rd, Scarborough ME 04074	207-347-7577	R	13*	.1
35	CEI West Roofing Co—Frederick Holland	1881 W 13th Ave, Denver CO 80204	303-573-5953	R	11*	.1
36	East Muskegon Roofing and Sheet Metal Company Inc—Gregory Kanaar	1665 Holton Rd, Muskegon MI 49445	231-744-2461	R	10*	.1
37	Standard-Taylor Industries Inc—George L Taylor	P O Box 1309, Montgomery AL 36102	334-265-1262	R	10*	.1
38	Robert Mitchell Company Inc—Arthur Bois	PO Box 2008, Portland ME 04104	207-797-6771	R	10*	.1
39	E and M Dissolution Corp—Eric Grohler	PO Box 3007, Decatur IL 62524	217-875-0831	R	9*	.2
40	M and J Materials Inc—Frank Hopson	PO Box 428, Trussville AL 35173	205-655-7451	R	8*	.1
41	Airway Sheet Metal Company Inc—Timothy Saunders	110 Oakgrove Rd Ste 10, Sterling VA 20166	703-471-4300	R	7*	.1
42	Professional Roofing and Exteriors—Daniel Cupit	5790 Lamar St, Arvada CO 80002	303-420-0986	R	7*	<.1
43	Custom Product Development Corp—Gerald Ammirato	4603 Las Positas Rd St, Livermore CA 94551	925-960-0577	R	7*	.1
44	Ducts Inc—Patricia Sickle Mc Elroy	883 Addison Rd, Cleveland OH 44103	216-391-2400	R	6*	.1
45	Hanset Stainless Inc—James Hanset	PO Box 11350, Portland OR 97211	503-283-8822	R	5*	.1
46	J and H Aluminum—Michael Hill	187 Enterprise Dr, Somerset KY 42501	606-679-8660	R	5*	.1
47	National Metal Fabricators LLC—William Tom Bonine	2395 Greenleaf Ave, Elk Grove Village IL 60007	847-439-5321	R	5*	<.1
48	Premier Roofing and Construction—Brian Eaton	695 S Jason St, Denver CO 80223	303-697-5000	R	5*	.1
49	RS Roofing and Sheet Metal Company Inc—Richard Shand	39 W Prospect St, Nanuet NY 10954	845-623-8404	R	4*	<.1
50	All Pro Roofing—Richard Grogan	1616 Cloister Way, Plano TX 75075	972-596-7777	R	4*	<.1
51	Keas Stainless Steel Fabricators Inc—Jack Keas	PO Box 15747, Oklahoma City OK 73155	405-232-0869	R	4*	<.1
52	Northeastern Sheet Metal Company Inc—Thomas Messenger	32 Lawnacre Rd, Windsor Locks CT 06096	860-292-6883	R	4*	<.1

Note: An asterisk (*) indicates an estimated financial figure. The company type code used is as follows: R = Private, P = Public, S = Private Subsidiary, B = Public Subsidiary, D = Division, J = Joint Venture, I = Investment Fund.

COMPANY RANKINGS BY SALES WITHIN 4-DIGIT SIC

Rank	Company Name—*Executive Officer*	Address, City, State, Zip	Phone	Type	Fin	Empls
53	Sylvester Sheet Metal Corp—*Michael Sylvester*	451 Pepsi Rd Ste B, Manchester NH 03109	603-624-4586	R	3*	<.1
54	WnR Inc—*Kimberly May*	5740 Big River Dr, The Colony TX 75056	972-741-9770	R	3*	<.1
55	Pcy Enterprises Inc—*Roger Young*	2118 Winchell Ave, Cincinnati OH 45214	513-241-5566	R	3*	<.1
56	Dill and Norris Company Inc—*Edwin Norris*	PO Box 2099, Columbus MS 39704	662-328-4532	R	3*	<.1
57	Bri-Car Roofing and Sheet Metal Inc—*Leonard Briston*	4597 Garfield Rd, Auburn MI 48611	989-631-8078	R	2*	<.1
58	Metal Fabrications—*Steve Wright*	399 E Harrison St Ste, Corona CA 92879	951-272-4272	R	2*	<.1
59	Engineering and Manufacturing Services Inc—*Merrill Walker*	PO Box 1111, Huntsville AL 35807	256-536-2810	R	2*	<.1
60	Dc and B Hot Shot And Trucking—*Carol Sorenson*	14129 Hwy 2 Ste 303, Williston ND 58801	701-572-5075	R	2*	<.1
61	Superior Commercial Roofing Inc—*Robert Heins*	16486 Grove Rd, Lansing MI 48906	517-321-2044	R	1*	<.1

TOTALS: SIC 1761 Roofing, Siding & Sheet Metal Work
Companies: 61 .... 3,127 ... 11.6

1771 Concrete Work

Rank	Company Name—*Executive Officer*	Address, City, State, Zip	Phone	Type	Fin	Empls
1	DRYCO Construction Inc—*Daren Young*	42745 Boscell Rd, Fremont CA 94538	510-438-6500	R	700*	.1
2	Penhall Co	320 N Crescent Way, Anaheim CA 92801	714-772-6450	R	601*	.8
3	Baker Concrete Construction Inc—*Daniel L Baker*	900 N Garver Rd, Monroe OH 45050	513-539-4000	R	480*	4.0
4	Stewart Builders Ltd—*Donald Stewart*	PO Box 41450, Houston TX 77241	713-983-8002	R	144*	1.4
5	Plant Improvement Co—*W Clyde Shepherd III*	PO Box 8088 Station F, Atlanta GA 31106	404-633-3600	R	101*	.3
6	Mike Hage Distinctive Concrete and Masonry—*Michael Hage*	6820 Washington Ave, Minneapolis MN 55344	612-328-0807	R	96*	<.1
7	Superior Gunite—*Anthony L Federico*	12306 Van Nuys Blvd, Lake View Terrace CA 91342	818-896-9199	R	83*	.2
8	Cavico Corp—*Ha Quang Bui*	17011 Beach Blvd Ste 1, Huntington Beach CA 92647	714-843-5456	P	61	3.4
9	Zenith Tech Inc—*Ned W Bechthold*	PO Box 1028, Waukesha WI 53187	262-524-1800	R	60	.5
10	Case Foundation Co—*John OMalley*	1325 W Lake St, Roselle IL 60172	630-529-2911	S	58*	.5
11	Miller and Long Company Inc—*Dannie Burke*	4824 Rugby Ave, Bethesda MD 20814	301-657-8000	R	52*	.5
12	Jersey Precast Corp—*Amir Ulis*	853 Nottingham Way, Trenton NJ 08638	609-689-3700	R	48*	.1
13	B and B Concrete Company Inc—*Henry C Brevard Jr*	PO Box 407, Tupelo MS 38802	662-842-6312	R	42*	.1
14	Border States Paving Inc—*Dan L Thompson*	PO Box 2586, Fargo ND 58108	701-237-4860	R	37*	.2
15	Conco Cement Co—*Steve Gonsalves*	5141 Commercial Cir, Concord CA 94520	925-685-6799	R	32*	.2
16	Daniel G Schuster Inc—*Daniel Schuster*	PO Box 604, Owings Mills MD 21117	410-363-9620	R	31*	.5
17	Anderson Brothers Construction Company Of Brainerd Inc—*James Anderson*	PO Box 668, Brainerd MN 56401	218-829-1768	R	26*	.2
18	Wille Brothers Co—*Curt Wille*	12600 S Hamlin Ct, Alsip IL 60803	708-388-9000	R	25*	.1
19	S D Ireland Concrete Construction Corp—*Scott Ireland*	PO Box 2286, South Burlington VT 05407	802-863-6222	R	24*	.2
20	Infrastructure Services Inc—*Tim Herbert*	5215 Fidelity St, Houston TX 77029	281-233-8000	R	21*	.2
21	American Pan and Engineering Company Inc—*Nader Jarun*	53 Johnston Cir, Palmetto GA 30268	770-463-1448	R	20*	.1
22	Newcastle Construction Inc—*Glen Siddle*	3978 Parkwood Rd, Bessemer AL 35022	205-426-2307	R	20*	<.1
23	Precision Concrete Construction Company Inc—*William Kline*	PO Box 217, White Marsh MD 21162	410-256-2800	R	20*	.2
24	Colorado Asphalt Services Inc—*H Leiser*	PO Box 329, Commerce City CO 80037	303-292-3434	R	18*	.2
25	Dance Brothers Inc—*Anderson Dance*	825 C Hammonds Ferry, Linthicum Heights MD 21090	410-789-8200	R	17*	.1
26	Elmer's Crane And Dozer Inc—*Russell Broad*	PO Box 6150, Traverse City MI 49696	231-943-5541	R	16*	.2
27	Richard O'brien Companies Inc—*Richard O'brien*	640 W Tnnecoee Ave Uni, Denver CO 80223	303-778-8771	R	15*	.2
28	C and C Concrete Pumping Inc—*Pepi Cancio Jr*	12599 NW 107th Ave, Medley FL 33178	305-885-1522	R	15*	.2
29	Carson Concrete and Decking Inc	3475 N Dodge Blvd, Tucson AZ 85716	520-325-0557	R	12*	.2
30	Shotcrete Systems Inc—*Rob Vonarb*	12965 San Fernando Rd, Sylmar CA 91342	818-833-1293	R	10*	<.1
31	Gateway Concrete Forming Services Inc—*Robert Bilz*	5938 Hamilton Cleves R, Miamitown OH 45041	513-353-2000	R	9*	.1
32	Modern Concrete Inc—*Scott Reutner*	PO Box 5711, Elko NV 89802	775-753-5100	R	7*	.1
33	Gaddie Shamrock Inc—*Roy Beard*	PO Box 280, Columbia KY 42728	270-384-2665	R	7*	.1
34	Cornerstone Construction Services Inc—*Amadita Stone*	4205 Edgewater Dr, Orlando FL 32804	407-299-3299	R	5*	<.1
35	Northern Plains Construction—*Doug Osborn*	390 Hillside Dr, Winner SD 57580	605-842-2471	R	4*	.1
36	Walker B-C Inc—*Kevin Walker*	7311 Kelley Ln, Harrah OK 73045	405-454-1487	R	3*	<.1
37	Alloy Industrial Contractors Inc—*Daniel Mac Millan*	PO Box 15058, Savannah GA 31416	912-355-6315	R	3*	<.1
38	Armor Deck Inc—*Tim Maas*	6315 S Kyrene Rd Ste 1, Tempe AZ 85283	480-456-0555	R	2*	<.1

TOTALS: SIC 1771 Concrete Work
Companies: 38 .... 2,924 ... 15.4

1781 Water Well Drilling

Rank	Company Name—*Executive Officer*	Address, City, State, Zip	Phone	Type	Fin	Empls
1	Beylik Drilling Inc—*Robert S Beylik*	3000 W MacArthur Blvd, Santa Ana CA 92704	714-434-4747	R	61*	.2
2	Stamm-Scheele Inc—*Andrew B Schmitt*	202 W Louisiana Ave, Rayne LA 70578	337-334-3126	S	13*	<.1
3	Water Resources International Inc—*Blaise Clay*	PO Box 44520, Kamuela HI 96743	808-882-7207	S	4*	<.1
4	Case Boring Corp—*Mark Case*	8585 Bunkerhill Rd, Gasport NY 14067	716-433-5923	R	2*	<.1

TOTALS: SIC 1781 Water Well Drilling
Companies: 4 .... 80 3

1791 Structural Steel Erection

Rank	Company Name—*Executive Officer*	Address, City, State, Zip	Phone	Type	Fin	Empls
1	Joseph T Ryerson and Son Inc—*Steve Makarewicz*	2621 W 15th Pl, Chicago IL 60608	773-762-2121	S	568*	1.5
2	Schuff Steel Co—*Scott Schuff* Schuff International Inc	420 S 19th Ave, Phoenix AZ 85009	602-252-7787	S	338*	.9
3	Schuff International Inc—*Scott A Schuff*	420 S 19th Ave, Phoenix AZ 85009	602-252-7787	P	288	1.6
4	Derr and Gruenewald Construction Co—*Robert Derr*	PO Box 218, Henderson CO 80640	303-287-3456	R	284*	.3
5	Sme Industries Inc—*Craig Moyes*	5801 Wells Park Rd, West Jordan UT 84081	801-280-0711	R	170*	.9
6	High Concrete Group LLC—*Jeffrey Smith*	PO Box 10008, Lancaster PA 17605	717-336-9300	R	105*	.9
7	Fought and Company Inc—*Rex Smith*	PO Box 23759, Tigard OR 97281	503-639-3141	R	37*	.2
8	Rebar Engineering Inc—*Charles Krebs*	PO Box 3986, Santa Fe Springs CA 90670	562-946-2461	R	28*	.2
9	Southern Erectors Inc—*N Jernigan*	6540 W Nine Mile Rd, Pensacola FL 32526	850-944-0013	R	20*	.1
10	Brunton Enterprises Inc—*John Brunton*	8815 Sorensen Ave, Santa Fe Springs CA 90670	562-945-0013	R	18*	.1
11	Douglas Steel Fabricating Corp—*James Buzzie*	PO Box 27277, Lansing MI 48909	517-322-2050	R	18*	.1
12	Artimex Iron Company Inc—*Jose Padilla*	315 Cypress Ln, El Cajon CA 92020	619-444-3155	R	16*	.1
13	Snodgrass and Sons Construction Inc—*David L Snodgrass*	2700 S George Washingt, Wichita KS 67210	316-687-3110	R	16*	.1
14	Universal Steel Buildings Inc—*Robert Kennington*	2472 Sunset Dr, Grenada MS 38901	662-226-4512	R	16*	.1
15	Allens Steel Products Inc—*T Allen*	PO Box 463, Arlington TN 38002	901-867-0171	R	12*	.1
16	Alliance Riggers and Constructors Ltd—*Paul Cordova*	1200 Kastrin St, El Paso TX 79907	915-591-4513	R	11*	.1
17	Derrick Loadmaster and Equipment Inc—*Tommy Welsh*	1084 Cruse Ave, Broussard LA 70518	337-837-5429	R	11*	.1
18	Caldwell Tanks Alliance LLC	PO Box 608, Newnan GA 30264	770-253-3232	S	10*	.1
19	Steel Supply and Engineering Co—*R Dean*	2020 Newark Ave Se, Grand Rapids MI 49507	616-452-3281	R	9*	.1
20	Bellis Steel Company Inc—*Theron Ghrist*	8740 Vanalden Ave, Northridge CA 91324	818-886-5601	R	8*	.1
21	Heartland Tank LLC—*Nancy Wehunt*	6750 E Coleman Rd, Ponca City OK 74604	580-762-0368	R	7*	.1
22	Pro Industrial Welding Inc—*Keith Crabtree*	732 Ridge Rd, Saltville VA 24370	276-624-3888	R	7*	.1
23	Waffle-Crete International Inc—*Jerry Kramer*	2500 E 9th St, Hays KS 67601	785-625-3486	R	5*	<.1
24	Lucey Boiler Co—*A Troxler*	PO Box 3239, Chattanooga TN 37404	423-267-5541	R	3*	<.1

Rank	Company Name—*Executive Officer*	Address, City, State, Zip	Phone	Type	Fin	Empls
25	Southland Erectors And Riggers Inc—*Wray Powell*	117 Chickamauga Ave, Knoxville TN 37917	865-525-2183	R	3*	<.1
26	SEF Stainless Steel Inc—*Monica De Luca*	7950 E Baltimore St, Baltimore MD 21224	410-284-8032	R	2*	<.1
27	RW Sowers and Associates Inc—*Robert Sowers*	1004 Talton Ave, Deland FL 32720	386-822-4588	R	1*	<.1
28	Masterform Tool Co—*Richard Perales*	9510 Fullerton Ave, Franklin Park IL 60131	847-455-5674	R	1*	<.1

TOTALS: SIC 1791 Structural Steel Erection
Companies: 28   2,011   7.7

1793 Glass & Glazing Work

Rank	Company Name—*Executive Officer*	Address, City, State, Zip	Phone	Type	Fin	Empls
1	Permasteelisa North America Corp—*Alberto Gobbi*	123 Day Hill Rd, Windsor CT 06095	860-298-2000	R	300*	1.0
2	Harmon Contract Inc—*Russell Huffer*	6325 Sandburg Rd Ste 1, Golden Valley MN 55427	763-525-2300	S	85*	.3
3	Harmon Contract Asia Ltd—*Chuck Mowrey* Harmon Contract Inc	6325 Sandburg Ste 100, Golden Valley MN 55427	763-525-2300	S	47*	.1
4	Fairfax Glass Co—*Robert Caplan*	7728 Lee Hwy, Falls Church VA 22042	703-560-1140	R	22*	<.1
5	Lynbrook Glass and Architectural Metals Corp—*Joseph Torsiello*	941 Motor Pkwy, Hauppauge NY 11788	631-582-3060	R	20*	.1
6	Ch Holdings USA Inc—*Greg Sage*	10733 Sunset Office Dr, Saint Louis MO 63127	314-984-8484	R	17*	.3
7	Calibre Door Closers Inc—*John Linder*	1481 N Main St, Orange CA 92867	714-633-5100	R	7*	<.1
8	Willet Hauser Architectural Glass Inc—*Michael Hauser*	1685 Wilkie Dr, Winona MN 55987	507-457-3500	R	6*	.1
9	Arrow Glass and Mirror Inc—*Danny Davis*	9201 Brown Ln Ste 280, Austin TX 78754	512-336-0400	R	6*	<.1
10	Shoreline Glass Company Inc—*Jerry Schor*	1 Mth Plz, Hillside IL 60162	312-829-9500	R	5*	.1
11	Kennedy Glass Inc—*Gary Kennedy*	PO Box 681, Lawrence KS 66044	785-843-4416	R	3*	<.1
12	All Action Architectural Metal and Glass—*John Quinones*	146-G Sylvania Pl, South Plainfield NJ 07080	732-738-6655	R	3*	<.1
13	Dunn-Rite Glass Inc—*Sharon Dunn*	4131 Carnation Ave, Haltom City TX 76111	817-831-4282	R	3*	<.1
14	North Star Glass Industries Inc—*Timothy Casey*	4135 Coon Rapids Blvd, Minneapolis MN 55433	763-421-7072	R	1*	<.1

TOTALS: SIC 1793 Glass & Glazing Work
Companies: 14   525   2.1

1794 Excavation Work

Rank	Company Name—*Executive Officer*	Address, City, State, Zip	Phone	Type	Fin	Empls
1	Mckinney Drilling Co—*George Cloud*	PO Box 5005, Odenton MD 21113	410-874-1235	R	22,167*	.5
2	Ryan Incorporated Central—*Patrick Ryan*	2700 E Racine St, Janesville WI 53545	608-754-2291	R	472*	.6
3	DBM Contractors Inc—*Tom Armour*	PO Box 6139, Federal Way WA 98063	253-838-1402	R	276*	.4
4	Pleasant Excavating Co—*WD Pleasants Jr*	24024 Frederick Rd Ste, Clarksburg MD 20871	301-428-0800	R	245*	.2
5	Schnabel Foundation Co—*Hubert Deaton III*	45240 Business Ct Ste, Sterling VA 20166	703-742-0020	R	180*	1.5
6	Mario Sinacola and Sons Excavating Inc—*James Sinacola*	10950 Research Rd, Frisco TX 75033	214-387-3900	R	150*	.4
7	Bay Cities Paving and Grading Inc—*Benjamin Rodriguez*	5029 Forni Dr, Concord CA 94520	925-687-6666	R	96*	.3
8	United Contractors Midwest Inc—*James Buhlig*	PO Box 13420, Springfield IL 62791	217-546-6192	R	75*	.1
9	Harper Contracting Inc—*Rulon Harper*	8201 W 5400 S, Salt Lake City UT 84118	801-250-0132	R	68*	.3
10	Independence Excavating Inc—*Victor DiGeronimo Sr*	5720 Schaaf Rd, Independence OH 44131	216-524-1700	R	64*	.4
11	Kanawha Stone Co—*Arthur L King*	PO Box 503, Nitro WV 25143	304-755-8271	R	60*	.4
12	Fox Contractors Corp—*Dallas Day*	8902 Airport Dr Ste B, Fort Wayne IN 46809	260-747-7461	R	50*	.4
13	George J Igel and Company Inc—*John B Igel*	2040 Alum Creek Dr, Columbus OH 43207	614-445-8421	R	50*	.3
14	Beaver Excavating Co—*Mark Sterling*	PO Box 6059, Canton OH 44706	330-478-2151	R	46*	.4
15	PT Ferro Construction Co—*Phil Hess*	PO Box 156, Joliet IL 60434	815-726-6284	R	45*	.1
16	RA Bright Construction Inc—*Robert Bright*	23808 W Andrew Rd, Plainfield IL 60585	815-439-5760	R	40*	.3
17	Dykema Excavators Inc—*James Dykema*	1730 3 Mile Rd NE, Grand Rapids MI 49505	616-363-6895	R	40*	.1
18	American Construction Supply Inc—*Stephen Kilper*	1 American Way, Warren OH 44484	330-856-8800	S	39*	<.1
19	Brubacher Excavating Inc—*Keith A Brubacher*	PO Box 528 Rte 625, Bowmansville PA 17507	717-445-4571	R	38*	.3
20	Plote Inc—*Raymond Plote*	1100 Brandt Dr, Hoffman Estates IL 60192	847-695-9300	R	38*	.1
21	Tschiggfrie Excavating—*Ed Tschiggfrie*	425 Julien Dubuque Dr, Dubuque IA 52003	563-557-7450	R	32*	.2
22	A Williams Trucking and Trenching Inc—*Dolly Williams*	225 3rd Ave, Brooklyn NY 11217	718-923-9600	R	32*	<.1
23	Shoosmith Brothers Inc—*Tony Lucas*	PO Box 2770, Chesterfield VA 23832	804-748-5823	R	32*	.2
24	Geo-Con Inc—*Brian Jasperse*	4075 Monroeville Blvd, Monroeville PA 15146	412-856-7700	R	28*	.1
25	Haines And Kibblehouse Inc—*John Haines*	PO Box 196, Skippack PA 19474	610-584-8500	R	23*	.2
26	Charles J Miller—*Charles Miller*	3514 Basler Rd, Hampstead MD 21074	410-239-8006	R	22*	.4
27	West Valley Construction Company Inc—*Mike Kelly*	580 McGlincy Ln, Campbell CA 95008		R	21*	.3
28	Perry Engineering Company Inc—*Rupert Werner*	1945 Millwood Pike, Winchester VA 22602	540-667-4310	R	20*	.3
29	Sukut Construction Inc—*Michael Crawford*	4010 W Chandler Ave, Santa Ana CA 92704	714-540-5351	R	18*	.2
30	Jay Dee Contractors Inc—*Thomas S Di Ponio*	38881 Schoolcraft Rd, Livonia MI 48150	734-591-3400	R	16*	.1
31	Kass Brothers Inc—*Jean Connick*	PO Box 487, Westwego LA 70096	504-348-9018	R	14*	.1
32	Young and Son Inc—*Laverne Young*	315 Kelly Rd, Niceville FL 32578	850-729-1321	R	10*	.1
33	John Eramo and Sons Inc—*Anthony Eramo*	3670 Lacon Rd, Hilliard OH 43026	614-777-0020	R	10*	<.1
34	Swinney Brothers Excavating Inc—*Gregg Huey*	11140 N State Rd 67, Mooresville IN 46158	317-831-2081	R	10*	.1
35	Wadsworth-Phillips Contractors Inc—*Malcolm Wadsworth*	5036 Coosada Ferry Rd, Montgomery AL 36110	334-263-2563	R	9*	.1
36	Millgard Corp—*D Millgard*	PO Box 510027, Livonia MI 48151	734-425-8550	R	8*	.1
37	Bean Inc—*David Schomp*	1800 Wood Ave, Easton PA 18042	610-253-4265	R	8*	<.1
38	CJ Mabardy Inc—*Charles Mabardy*	PO Box 329, Winchendon MA 01475		R	7*	<.1
39	Schlichting and Sons Excavating Inc—*Bruce Schlichting*	1178 Barberry Ln, Belvidere IL 61008	815-332-3333	R	6*	.1
40	Bradley Excavating Inc—*Bradley Grubaugh*	2220 Busch Ave, Colorado Springs CO 80904	719-685-9755	R	5*	<.1
41	Beer And Slabaugh Inc—*Rodney Beer*	23965 Us Hwy 6, Nappanee IN 46550	574-773-3413	R	4*	<.1
42	Gurney Brothers Construction Inc—*Daniel Gurney*	N Springfield Gurney R, North Springfield VT 05150	802-886-2210	R	4*	<.1
43	Lester Brothers Excavation Inc—*James Lester*	5405 E Michigan Ave, Jackson MI 49201	517-764-7888	R	4*	<.1
44	Desiato Sand and Gravel Corp—*Phillip Desiato*	999 Stafford Rd, Storrs Mansfield CT 06268	860-429-6479	R	3*	<.1
45	J and K Pipeline Inc—*Joseph Goetz*	4951 S Rio Grande St, Littleton CO 80120	720-889-1940	R	3*	<.1
46	Cato Drilling Co—*Jack Morrison*	PO Box 200736, San Antonio TX 78220	210-337-6165	R	3*	<.1
47	Griffin Contracting—*Gerald Griffin*	25742 State Hwy 25, Bloomfield MO 63825	573-568-3196	R	2*	<.1
48	Morrow and Sons Inc—*Robert Morrow*	PO Box 37, Fraser CO 80442	970-726-5624	R	2*	<.1

TOTALS: SIC 1794 Excavation Work
Companies: 48   24,596   9.4

1795 Wrecking & Demolition Work

Rank	Company Name—*Executive Officer*	Address, City, State, Zip	Phone	Type	Fin	Empls
1	Ghilotti Brothers Inc—*Mike Ghilotti*	525 Jacoby St, San Rafael CA 94901	415-454-7011	R	141*	.3
2	National Wrecking Co—*Sheldon J Mandell*	2441 N Leavitt St, Chicago IL 60647	773-384-2800	R	81*	.2
3	Brandenburg Industrial Service Co—*Thomas Little*	2625 S Loomis St, Chicago IL 60608	312-326-5800	R	75*	.4
4	Cleveland Wrecking Co—*Jim Sheridan*	628 E Edna Pl, Covina CA 91723	626-967-9799	R	64*	.6
5	Veit Cos—*Vaugh Veit*	14000 Veit Pl, Rogers MN 55374	763-428-2242	R	60*	.5
6	US Dismantlement LLC—*T Harry Gieschen*	2600 S Throop St, Chicago IL 60608	312-328-1400	R	10*	.1
7	Plant Reclamation—*Fred Glueck*	912 Harbour Way S, Richmond CA 94804	510-233-6552	R	8*	<.1
8	American Traders Inc—*Joseph E Yovanovitch*	3934 New Vision Dr, Fort Wayne IN 46845	260-338-2640	R	6*	<.1

Note: An asterisk (*) indicates an estimated financial figure. The company type code used is as follows: R = Private, P = Public, S = Private Subsidiary, B = Public Subsidiary, D = Division, J = Joint Venture, I = Investment Fund.

COMPANY RANKINGS BY SALES WITHIN 4-DIGIT SIC

Rank	Company Name—*Executive Officer*	Address, City, State, Zip	Phone	Type	Fin	Empls
9	Tristar Of America Inc—*Joseph Barillari*	2731 Simpson Cir, Norcross GA 30071	770-368-8700	R	1*	<.1

TOTALS: SIC 1795 Wrecking & Demolition Work
Companies: 9

					446	2.1

1796 Installing Building Equipment Nec

Rank	Company Name—*Executive Officer*	Address, City, State, Zip	Phone	Type	Fin	Empls
1	Bragg Companies Inc—*Marilynn Bragg*	PO Box 727, Long Beach CA 90801	562-984-2400	R	127*	.5
2	Belding Walridge LLC—*John Rakolta Jr*	1275 Aurora Ln, Aurora IL 60505	630-906-6860	S	87*	.1
3	Atlas Industrial Holdings LLC—*George Ghanem*	5275 Sinclair Rd, Columbus OH 43229	614-841-4500	R	75*	.5
4	Mercury Solar Systems Inc—*Frank J Alfano*	36 Midland Ave, Port Chester NY 10573	914-637-9700	R	55	.3
5	TriMark Raygal Inc—*Jack Mervis*	2719 White Rd, Irvine CA 92614	949-474-1000	R	37*	.1
6	DW Nicholson Corp—*John L Nicholson*	PO Box 4197, Hayward CA 94540	510-887-0900	R	33*	.2
7	Integrated Power Corp—*Eric Pollock*	504 Redwood Blvd Ste 2, Novato CA 94947	415-884-5555	R	33*	<.1
8	Mid-American Elevator Company Inc—*Robert Bailey*	820 N Wolcott Ave, Chicago IL 60622	773-486-6900	R	30*	.2
9	Professional Meters Inc—*Robert Dullard*	3605 N SR 47 Ste E, Morris IL 60450	815-942-7000	R	16	.1
10	Hopkins Illinois Elevator Company Inc—*Carol Siemion*	832 N Wolcott Ave, Chicago IL 60622	773-486-3350	R	14*	<.1
11	Lovegreen Industrial Services Inc—*Vernon Lovegreen*	2280 Sibley Ct, Saint Paul MN 55122	651-890-1166	R	13*	.1
12	Newell Machinery Company Inc—*Timothy Grissel*	1405 Mitchell Dr, Hiawatha IA 52233	319-393-1610	R	12*	.1
13	Regis Belt Maintenance Inc—*Jim Angus*	900 S Campbell Ave, Chicago IL 60612	312-733-4100	R	12*	.1
14	Marshall Elevator Co—*Robert Jamison*	2015 Mary St, Pittsburgh PA 15203	412-431-1340	R	11*	.1
15	Egenolf Machine Inc—*James Egenolf*	2916 Bluff Rd Ste A, Indianapolis IN 46225	317-787-5301	R	10*	.1
16	Process Mechanical Piping And Erection Inc—*Lynn Godwin*	PO Box 209, Peachland NC 28133	704-272-7646	R	10*	.1
17	Coast Machinery Movers—*Larry Beard*	2431 Chico Ave, S El Monte CA 91733	626-579-4510	R	9*	.1
18	Koger/Air Corp—*Donna Koger*	PO Box 2098, Martinsville VA 24113	276-638-8821	R	9*	.1
19	Rees Companies Inc—*Roderick Rees*	PO Box 26835, Collegeville PA 19426	610-489-9007	R	8*	.1
20	Taylor Elevator Corp—*John Taylor*	3573 Plover Ave, Naples FL 34117	239-643-0490	R	8*	.1
21	Collins and Jewell Company Inc—*Christopher Jewell*	43 Wisconsin Ave, Norwich CT 06360	860-887-8813	R	8*	<.1
22	Detroit Elevator Co—*Donald Purdie*	2121 Burdette St, Ferndale MI 48220	248-591-7484	R	7*	.1
23	Mid-States Millwright and Builders Inc—*Kevin Vier*	PO Box 404, Nevada IA 50201	515-382-6280	R	6*	<.1
24	Morris Kreitz and Sons Inc—*Don Jacobs*	220 N Park Rd, Wyomissing PA 19610	610-376-7187	R	5*	<.1
25	Fabricating/Distributor Inc—*Donald Peacock*	6410 S Sossaman Rd, Mesa AZ 85212	480-988-2477	R	5*	<.1
26	Southern Converting Machinery Erectors Inc—*James Zager*	PO Box 1287, Valdosta GA 31603	229-242-9872	R	4*	<.1
27	Colt Temperature Control and Tube Inc—*Rual Coray*	2332 Rockview Dr, Sandy UT 84092	801-943-4195	R	4*	<.1
28	Atlanta Bin and Shelving Corp—*David Wentz*	4295 International Blv, Norcross GA 30093	678-380-8493	R	4*	<.1
29	Mcdal Corp—*Frank Mullan*	475 E Church Rd, King Of Prussia PA 19406	610-277-5484	R	3*	<.1
30	Grisham Industries Inc—*Bill Grisham*	13609 110th Ave Ste 2, Davenport IA 52804	563-381-3525	R	3*	<.1
31	Northwest Installations Inc—*Tracy Lopez*	PO Box 1563, Findlay OH 45839	419-423-5738	R	3*	.1
32	Barclay Mechanical Services Inc—*Rick Hall*	PO Box 360, Paul ID 83347	208-438-8108	R	2*	.1
33	Jeffrey Elevator Company Inc—*Nick Budmats*	570 Estes Ave, Schaumburg IL 60193	847-524-2400	R	2*	<.1
34	Industrial Automation Specialists Corp—*Kathy Burton*	17 Research Dr, Hampton VA 23666	757-766-7520	R	1*	<.1
35	Simco Erectors Inc—*Paul Smith*	2447 Meredith Dr, Loganville GA 30052	770-466-0686	R	1*	<.1
36	Bob Mitchell Associates Inc—*Charles Mitchell*	11717 Unicorn Rd, Temple Terrace FL 33637	813-985-2642	R	1*	<.1
37	Hegwood Electric Service Inc—*Kirk Hegwood*	2528 Pleasantdale Rd A, Atlanta GA 30340	770-447-8853	R	1*	<.1
38	Alfa Tec Manufacturing Company Inc—*Alfred Hoff*	220 5th St, Bridgeport CT 06607	203-367-8498	R	<1*	<.1

TOTALS: SIC 1796 Installing Building Equipment Nec
Companies: 38

					668	3.2

1799 Special Trade Contractors Nec

Rank	Company Name—*Executive Officer*	Address, City, State, Zip	Phone	Type	Fin	Empls
1	Lend Lease—*Murray Coleman*	200 Park Ave, New York NY 10166		R	4,850*	7.5
2	Layne Christensen Co—*Andrew B Schmitt*	1900 Shawnee Mission P, Mission Woods KS 66205	913-677-6800	P	1,026	4.4
3	LVI Services Inc—*Scott E State*	80 Broad St 3rd Fl, New York NY 10004	212-951-3660	R	977*	1.5
4	Matrix Service Co—*John R Hewitt*	5100 E Skelly Dr Ste 7, Tulsa OK 74135	918-838-8822	P	627	2.6
5	Brisk Waterproofing Co—*Michael Radigan* Western Construction Group	720 Grand Ave, Ridgefield NJ 07657	201-945-0210	S	609*	1.1
6	Hayward Baker Inc—*George R Grisham*	1130 Annapolis Rd Ste, Odenton MD 21113	410-551-8200	S	504*	.7
7	Sauer Inc (Pittsburgh Pennsylvania)—*William N Steitz Jr*	30 51st St, Pittsburgh PA 15201	412-687-4100	S	461*	.6
8	Shasta Industries Inc—*Skip Ast*	3750 W Indian School R, Phoenix AZ 85019		R	406*	.6
9	Furmanite Corp—*Charles R Cox*	2435 N Central Expy, Richardson TX 75080	972-699-4000	P	286	1.5
10	Kinetic Systems Inc—*Michael D Appolonia*	48400 Fremont Blvd, Fremont CA 94538	510-683-6000	S	214*	.4
11	Keller Foundations Inc—*Robert Rubright*	1130 Annapolis Rd Ste, Odenton MD 21113	410-551-8200	R	162*	3.0
12	Anthony and Sylvan Pools Corp—*Stuart D Neidus*	6690 Beta Dr Ste 300, Mayfield Village OH 44143	440-720-3301	R	137*	.4
13	CST Environmental Inc—*Subhas Khara*	404 N Berry St, Brea CA 92821	714-672-3500	R	132*	.6
14	A and B Process Systems Corp—*Anthony J Hilgemann*	PO Box 86, Stratford WI 54484	715-687-4332	R	128*	.2
15	Western Construction Group—*Benjamin M Bishop Jr*	1637 N Warson Rd, Saint Louis MO 63132	314-427-1637	R	123*	1.2
16	Bragg Crane and Rigging Co—*Marilynn Bragg*	PO Box 727, Long Beach CA 90801	562-984-2400	S	114*	.2
17	Primus Builders Inc—*Richard O'Connell*	8294 Hwy 92 Ste 210, Woodstock GA 30189	770-928-7120	R	100*	<.1
18	CRC-Evans Automatic Welding	PO Box 3227, Houston TX 77253	281-999-8920	D	97*	.2
19	Bankhead Enterprises Inc—*Glenda Cole*	1080 Donald L Hollowel, Atlanta GA 30318	404-894-7950	R	80*	.5
20	Abington Group Inc—*Michael J Carr*	195 West Rd, Portsmouth NH 03801	603-436-5800	R	77*	.1
21	Rmd Holdings Ltd—*Robert Demil*	53861 Gratiot Ave, Chesterfield MI 48051	586-749-6900	R	74*	.1
22	BRH-Garver Construction LP—*Edward Boswell*	7600 S Santa Fe Bldg A, Houston TX 77061	713-921-2929	R	71*	.1
23	Minnotte Contracting Corp—*David W Minnotte*	1 Minnotte Sq, Pittsburgh PA 15220	412-922-1633	R	70*	.1
24	NEO Corp—*Todd Escaravage*	289 Silkwood Dr, Canton NC 28716	828-456-4332	R	51*	.1
25	Regent Aerospace Corp—*Fariba Bolourchi*	28110 W Harrison Pkwy, Valencia CA 91355	661-257-3000	R	47*	.7
26	King Kitchens Inc	6075 E Shelby Dr E Ste, Memphis TN 38141	901-362-9651	R	45*	<.1
27	PetroChem Insulation Inc—*Arthur Lewis*	110 Corporate Pl, Vallejo CA 94590	707-644-7455	R	40*	<.1
28	Troon Construction—*Ray Garcia*	1515 N Greenfield Rd S, Mesa AZ 85205	480-443-7744	R	27*	<.1
29	Earth Exploration Inc—*Scott Ludlow*	7770 W New York St, Indianapolis IN 46214	317-273-1690	R	26*	<.1
30	Secoa Inc—*Jeff Jones*	8650 109th Ave N, Champlin MN 55316	763-506-8800	R	25*	.1
31	Environmental Design and Construction LLC—*Dennis J Garbis*	1104 Good Hope Rd SE, Washington DC 20020	202-373-5200	R	25*	.1
32	Transaction Technology Corp—*Ed Harrison*	75 Beattie Pl Ste 410, Greenville SC 29601	864-271-6522	R	23*	.1
33	Iris Window Coverings—*Dick Benton*	505 S 4th St, Renton WA 98057	425-793-9398	R	23*	<.1
34	Cable Services Company Inc—*Ken Michaels*	2113 Marydale Ave, Williamsport PA 17701	570-323-8518	R	22*	.1
35	Gary Pools Inc—*Leif Zars*	438 Sandau Rd, San Antonio TX 78216	210-341-5153	R	21*	.1
36	Joseph M Zimmer Inc—*Joseph Zimmer III*	8860 Citation Rd, Baltimore MD 21221	410-780-0600	R	21*	.1
37	Prospect Waterproofing Co—*James Stamer*	118 Acacia Ln, Sterling VA 20166	703-450-2355	R	20*	.4
38	Classy Closets Etc Inc—*Duane Standage*	1251 S Nelson Dr, Chandler AZ 85226	480-478-0924	R	19*	.2
39	Orlando Rock and Sealing Corp—*Scott Altman*	9530 Sidney Hayes Rd, Orlando FL 32824	407-859-5990	R	19*	.1
40	Larson Themed Construction Company Inc—*Andrew Messing*	107 Mt Zion, Florence KY 41042	513-917-9301	R	18*	.1
41	Production Fenceworks Inc—*Chris Palicastro*	5155 Watson Fain Rd, Loganville GA 30052	678-873-3628	R	18*	<.1
42	Crown Fence Co—*Cecil Gates*	12118 Bloomfield Ave, Santa Fe Springs CA 90670	562-864-5177	R	18*	.1
43	Empire City Iron Works—*Harvey Heffner*	1037 46th Rd, Long Island City NY 11101	718-361-0100	R	18*	.2

Rank	Company Name—*Executive Officer*	Address, City, State, Zip	Phone	Type	Fin	Empls
44	Pci Energy Services Inc—*Jimmy Morgan*	1 Energy Dr, Lake Bluff IL 60044	847-680-8100	R	17*	.3
45	Industrial Coatings Contractors Inc—*Norman Bercegeay*	PO Box 1320, Prairieville LA 70769	225-673-4490	R	17*	.2
46	Alcorn Fence Co—*Greg Erikson*	PO Box 1249, Sun Valley CA 91353	818-983-0650	R	16*	.2
47	Griffin Dewatering Corp—*Kazem Khonsari*	5306 Clinton Dr, Houston TX 77020	713-676-8000	R	16*	.1
48	Facilitech Inc—*Kathy White*	1111 Valley View Ln, Irving TX 75061	817-858-2000	R	16*	.1
49	Tower Systems Inc—*William Carlson*	PO Box 1474, Watertown SD 57201	605-886-0930	R	16*	.1
50	E L Wagner Company Inc—*John Gedney*	PO Box 3679, Bridgeport CT 06605	203-335-3960	R	15*	.1
51	Universal Builders Supply Inc—*Kevin O'callaghan*	27 Horton Ave Ste 5, New Rochelle NY 10801	914-699-2400	R	15*	.1
52	Custom Biologicals Inc—*Clarence L Baugh*	1239 E Newport Center, Deerfield Beach FL 33442	561-998-1699	R	15*	<.1
53	Offshore Cleaning Systems LLC—*Baer Anderson*	9525 Us Hwy 167, Abbeville LA 70510	337-898-2104	R	15*	.2
54	Genie Electronics Company Inc—*B Snyder*	PO Box 395, Red Lion PA 17356	717-244-1099	R	15*	.1
55	Premier Electrical Corp—*Fred Jahnke*	4401 85th Ave N, Brooklyn Park MN 55443	763-424-6551	R	14*	.1
56	Modernfold/Styles Inc—*Robert Styles*	PO Box 3180, South Hackensack NJ 07606	201-329-6226	R	14*	.1
57	C E Toland and Son—*Blake Toland*	5300 Industrial Way, Benicia CA 94510	707-747-1000	R	14*	.1
58	Tsf Investments Inc—*Kenneth Smith*	5725 N 55th Ave, Glendale AZ 85301	623-934-5380	R	13*	.2
59	Cannon Sline Inc	2 Lukens Dr Ste 600, New Castle DE 19720	302-658-1420	S	13*	.2
60	Gulf Crane Services Inc—*Charles Bollinger*	PO Box 1843, Covington LA 70434	985-892-0056	R	13*	.1
61	Marek Brothers Co—*R Stan Marek*	2115 Judiway St, Houston TX 77018	713-681-9213	R	12*	.2
62	Harlan Laws Corp—*Steven Laws*	PO Box 15070, Durham NC 27704	919-596-2124	R	11*	.1
63	Janson Industries—*Eric Janson*	PO Box 6090, Canton OH 44706	330-455-7029	R	11*	.1
64	PW Stephens Inc—*Scott Johnson*	15201 Pipeline Ln Unit, Huntington Beach CA 92649	714-892-2028	R	11*	.1
65	Industrial Video LLC—*Tim Czyzak*	14885 W Sprague Rd, Cleveland OH 44136	440-325-2309	R	10*	<.1
66	Servpro (Bear Deleware)—*Richard Massey*	301 Carson Dr, Bear DE 19701	302-392-6000	R	10*	<.1
67	Colorado Lining International Inc—*John Heap*	1062 Singing Hills Rd, Parker CO 80138	303-841-2022	R	10*	<.1
68	J Marion Bryan and Sons Inc—*Allen Bryan*	PO Box 1519, Easton MD 21601	410-819-3001	R	10*	<.1
69	Southeastern Products Inc—*Tyler Burgess*	PO Box 4178, Greenville SC 29608	864-233-9023	R	9*	.1
70	Welcome Industrial Corp—*Tony Lin*	95 Marcus Blvd, Deer Park NY 11729	631-392-1731	R	9*	.1
71	Entera Inc—*Larry Presley*	1200 Bell Ave, Panama City FL 32401	850-763-7982	R	9*	.1
72	Designer Surfaces Unlimited Inc—*Gregory Fisher*	5103 Pegasus Ct Ste D, Frederick MD 21704	301-831-4443	R	9*	.1
73	S Kivett Inc—*Robert Kivett*	PO Box 590, Clinton NC 28329	910-592-0161	R	7*	.1
74	Metalclad Insulation Corp—*David Trueblood*	1818 E Rosslyn Ave, Fullerton CA 92831	714-634-9050	S	7*	.1
75	Joan Smith Enterprises Inc—*Jeremy Smith*	1660 S Alma School Rd, Mesa AZ 85210	480-345-0005	R	7*	.1
76	Support Construction Inc—*Bruce Jones*	PO Box 5397, Titusville FL 32783	321-267-4495	R	7*	<.1
77	Berlin Food and Lab Equipment Co—*Michael Urlich*	43 S Linden Ave, South San Francisco CA 94080	650-589-4231	R	7*	<.1
78	Capital Fire Protection Co—*William Jolley*	3360 Valleyview Dr, Columbus OH 43204	614-279-9448	R	6*	.1
79	Carlisle Road Associates Inc—*Joe Wiehbercht*	2320 Tower Dr, Dover PA 17315	717-308-0001	R	6*	.1
80	Controlled Air Inc—*Michael Broyles*	1509 Riverport Rd, Kingsport TN 37660	423-245-6761	R	6*	<.1
81	DPC General Contractors Inc—*David Sever*	1860 NW 21 Terrace, Miami FL 33142	305-325-0447	R	6*	<.1
82	LVR Inc (Hannacroix New York)—*Gary Peterson*	139 US Rte 9 W, Hannacroix NY 12087	518-756-9188	R	6*	<.1
83	Construction Partnership Inc—*Terry Meyer*	1700 Broadway Ave N, Rochester MN 55906	507-288-6466	R	6*	<.1
84	Rubber Applications Inc—*Stanley Hobby*	PO Box 826, Mulberry FL 33860	863-425-5626	R	6*	<.1
85	J R Clancy Inc—*Michel Murthy*	7041 Interstate Island, Syracuse NY 13209	315-451-3440	R	6*	.1
86	Nassau Pools Construction Inc—*Thomas Threlkeld*	3420 Westview Dr, Naples FL 34104	239-643-0990	R	6*	.1
87	Sanitary Process Systems Inc—*Tom Fischer*	945 Fruitville Pke, Lititz PA 17543	717-627-6630	R	6*	<.1
88	L R Borelli Inc—*Sandra Borelli*	1220 S Pasadena, Mesa AZ 85210	480-969-6606	R	5*	.1
89	National Maintenance Inc—*Jonathan Bragoli*	185 Sweet Hollow Rd, Old Bethpage NY 11804	516-249-8960	R	5*	<.1
90	Veolia Es Alaron LLC—*Kimberly Tindall*	2138 State Rte 18, Wampum PA 16157	724-535-5777	R	5*	<.1
91	West Tower Communications—*Calvin Payne*	112 E State St, Ridgeland MS 39157	601-898-4450	R	5*	<.1
92	Delta Disaster Services Inc—*Michael Mastous*	5535 W 56th Ave Ste 10, Arvada CO 80002	303-933-4888	R	5*	<.1
93	APEXteriors—*Jim Stringham*	PO Box 132, South Beloit IL 61080	815-624-2161	R	5*	<.1
94	Stealth Concealment Solutions Inc—*Sean Mclernon*	6549 Fain St, North Charleston SC 29406	843-207-8000	R	5*	<.1
95	Texoma Contracting Inc—*Randel Scott*	PO Box 979, Muskogee OK 74402	918-682-1435	R	5*	<.1
96	Eagle Scaffolding Services Inc—*Michael Paladino*	67 Mill St, Amityville NY 11701	631-842-1700	R	5*	.1
97	Sim-Co Fabricators Inc—*Dave Simmons*	15174 Vista Del Rio Av, Chino CA 91710	909-597-7804	R	4*	<.1
98	Jacob Licht Inc—*Gary Licht*	765 Westminster St, Providence RI 02903	401-331-4000	R	4*	<.1
99	Integrated Housekeeping Management Inc—*John Borders*	PO Box 50708, Indianapolis IN 46250	317-841-7777	R	4*	.1
100	LCS Site Services LLC—*Kevin Birrell*	PO Box 5983, Springfield VA 22150	703-372-2461	R	4	<.1
101	Capitol City Fence Company Inc—*John Roop*	920 E Ohio St, Indianapolis IN 46202	317-638-3381	R	4*	<.1
102	Blasters Inc—*Scott Boos*	7813 Professional Pl S, Tampa FL 33637	813-985-4500	R	4*	<.1
103	Pacific Coast Installations Inc—*Darris Egger*	16130 Gundry Ave, Paramount CA 90723	562-630-1733	R	4*	<.1
104	Browning's Welding Service Inc—*Tommy Browning*	PO Box 190, Wooster AR 72181	501-679-2184	R	4*	<.1
105	Devcon Group Inc—*Dan Sardi*	2379 Haystack Rd, Castle Rock CO 80104	720-733-3667	R	4*	<.1
106	Permanent Concrete Solutions Inc—*Pete Christensen*	3702 W Valley Hwy N St, Auburn WA 98001	206-878-4612	R	4*	<.1
107	Miller Machine and Welding LLC	PO Box 991, Hillsboro TX 76645	254-582-2185	R	4*	<.1
108	Montana Lines Inc—*Jan Livesay*	2800 Upper River Rd, Great Falls MT 59405	406-727-1316	R	4*	<.1
109	Oasis Supply and Trade Inc—*Jide Famuagun*	5350 S Western Ave Ste, Oklahoma City OK 73109	405-605-1930	R	4	<.1
110	New Jersey Mirror And Bath Accessories Inc—*Leonard Yan-char*	Hainesport Industrial, Hainesport NJ 08036	609-261-2100	R	3*	<.1
111	LG Hetager Drilling Inc—*Roland Gearhart*	1857 Woodland Ave Ext, Punxsutawney PA 15767	814-938-7370	R	3*	<.1
112	First Restoration Inc—*James Farley*	PO Box 173307, Arlington TX 76003	817-557-6810	R	3*	<.1
113	Stokes Dock Co—*Shane Stokes*	3797 Hwy 54 Ste E-11, Osage Beach MO 65065	573-348-2334	R	3	<.1
114	Custom Fiberglass Molding Inc—*Richard Discher*	E5880 Little River Rd, Weyauwega WI 54983	920-867-2606	R	3*	<.1
115	St Louis Conveyor Co—*Steve Mason*	12981 Maurer Industria, Saint Louis MO 63127	314-842-5400	R	3*	<.1
116	Marine Steel Painting Corp—*Leon Hatzitetros*	2064 Zoeller Rd, Alden NY 14004	716-937-3765	R	3*	<.1
117	NW Metal Fabricators Inc—*Kerry Karlson*	PO Box 1666, Hermiston OR 97838	541-567-7171	R	3*	<.1
118	Rak Corrosion Control Inc—*Guy Reph*	7455 S Dewey Rd, Amherst OH 44001	440-985-2171	R	3*	<.1
119	Carson And Roberts Site Construction And Engineering Inc—*Daniel Carson*	171 Rte 94, Lafayette NJ 07848	973-579-4100	R	3*	<.1
120	Rollie's Sales and Service Inc—*Dale Walsh*	PO Box E, Osakis MN 56360	320-859-4811	R	3*	<.1
121	Aufderworld Corp—*James Aufderheide*	2750 Niagara Ln N, Plymouth MN 55447	952-941-8000	R	3*	<.1
122	AAA Pool Services Inc—*Brad Hughes*	4856 Haygood Rd Ste 10, Virginia Beach VA 23455	757-499-5852	R	3*	.3
123	HE Installations—*W Poillucci*	14804 Hwy 176, Woodstock IL 60098	815-337-1071	R	3*	<.1
124	Badeco Inc—*Carolyn Bade*	402 Callaghan Rd, San Antonio TX 78228	210-299-4714	R	2*	.1
125	Schmelzer Industries Inc—*Jean Schmelzer*	PO Box 249, Somerset OH 43783	740-743-2866	R	2*	<.1
126	House Of Closets—*Igal Hever*	9649 Owensmouth Ave St, Chatsworth CA 91311	818-341-0755	R	2*	<.1
127	Custom Pipe Coating Inc—*O Rabon*	PO Box 445, Galena Park TX 77547	713-675-2324	R	2*	<.1
128	Demand Communications Inc—*Susan Holgate*	28 Rockwell Rd, Newfield NY 14867	607-687-1861	R	2*	<.1
129	Glasslock Inc—*R Haddock*	22 W Dover St, Easton MD 21601		R	2*	<.1
130	W E Neal Slate Co—*Eugene Ziemer*	2840 Hwy 25, Watertown MN 55388	952-955-3340	R	2*	<.1
131	Custom Tree Care Inc—*Greg Gathers*	3722 SW Spring Creek L, Topeka KS 66610	785-478-9805	R	2	<.1

Note: An asterisk (*) indicates an estimated financial figure. The company type code used is as follows: R = Private, P = Public, S = Private Subsidiary, B = Public Subsidiary, D = Division, J = Joint Venture, I = Investment Fund.

COMPANY RANKINGS BY SALES WITHIN 4-DIGIT SIC

Rank	Company Name—Executive Officer	Address, City, State, Zip	Phone	Type	Fin	Empls
132	US Aluminum Services Corp—Thiago Davila	5528 Force Four Pky, Orlando FL 32839	407-237-3128	R	2	<.1
133	Burden's Machine and Welding Inc—Donald Burden	PO Box 177, Newark OH 43058	740-345-9246	R	2*	<.1
134	Knight's Fabrication and Welding Inc—Gary Knight	PO Box 23908, Eugene OR 97402	541-607-0392	R	2*	<.1
135	R and H Systems Inc—Randy Hammel	2030 W Washington St, Petersburg VA 23803	804-796-9405	R	2*	<.1
136	Delaware Valley Custom Marble Inc—Stephen Embler	4 Briar Dr, West Grove PA 19390	610-345-0800	R	2*	<.1
137	Carmel Engineering Inc—Paul Weaver	PO Box 67, Kirklin IN 46050	765-279-8955	R	2*	<.1
138	Bohn Fiberglass Industries Inc—Gale Bohn	PO Box 58490, Louisville KY 40268	502-933-3515	R	2*	<.1
139	Penn-Tech International Inc—Thomas Hedberg	3 S Bacton Hill Rd Uni, Malvern PA 19355	484-395-0145	R	2*	<.1
140	American Technology and Research Industries Inc—Robert Link	790 W Andrew Johnson H, Greeneville TN 37745	423-638-5847	R	2*	<.1
141	CA International Inc—Daniel Shen	9730 Industrial Blvd, Lenexa KS 66215	913-338-4488	R	2*	<.1
142	Shaw's Fiberglass And Plastics Inc—Alan Shaw	19402 Se Foster Rd, Damascus OR 97089	503-658-7429	R	2*	<.1
143	Sunwest Engineering Constructors Inc—Pamela Lawrence	2766 Pomona Blvd, Pomona CA 91768	909-594-9850	R	1*	<.1
144	Orman's Welding and Fab Inc—David Orman	3322 Curtis Orman Rd, West Point MS 39773	662-494-9471	R	1*	<.1
145	Baril Coatings—David Harman	401 Growth Pkwy, Angola IN 46703	260-665-8431	R	1*	<.1
146	One Way Service Corp—Ken Morrow	234 S Hibbert, Mesa AZ 85210	480-731-9700	R	1*	<.1
147	Fiberglass Pool Resurfacing—Dan Tucker	5031 Blum Rd Ste 1, Martinez CA 94553	925-723-0400	R	1*	<.1
148	Mdm Scaffolding Services Inc—Eugene Morgan	1084 Texan Trl, Grapevine TX 76051	817-329-4994	R	1*	<.1
149	Weather Seal Products Inc—Lisa Nigro	PO Box 248, Carteret NJ 07008	732-969-0700	R	1*	<.1
150	Lightspeed Networks LLC—Robert Carter	331 S River Dr Ste 12, Tempe AZ 85281	480-377-0178	R	1*	<.1
151	Dsp Network Inc—Judy Bell	5352 Plata Rosa Ct, Camarillo CA 93012	805-482-0898	R	1*	<.1
152	Nott Ltd—Judy Nott	3801 La Plata Hwy, Farmington NM 87401	505-327-5646	R	1*	<.1
153	Commercial Care Services Inc—Gary Carville	6100 Westline Dr, Houston TX 77036	713-774-9922	R	1*	<.1
154	Industrial Machine and Hydraulics Inc—Jack Kenney	785 N 9th Ave, Brighton CO 80603	303-659-0620	R	1*	<.1
155	R and S Welding and Fabricating—Robert Rosenbaum	961 W 25 S, Winamac IN 46996	574-946-6816	R	1*	<.1

TOTALS: SIC 1799 Special Trade Contractors Nec
Companies: 155   12,504   36.3

2011 Meat Packing Plants

Rank	Company Name—Executive Officer	Address, City, State, Zip	Phone	Type	Fin	Empls
1	Tyson Fresh Meats Inc	800 Stevens Port Dr, Dakota Dunes SD 57049	605-235-2061	S	13,899*	41.0
2	Smithfield Foods Inc—C Larry Pope	200 Commerce St, Smithfield VA 23430	757-365-3000	P	12,203	46.4
3	Hormel Foods Corp—Jeffrey M Ettinger	1 Hormel Pl, Austin MN 55912	507-437-5611	P	7,221	19.3
4	Seaboard Corp—Steven J Bresky	9000 W 67th St, Merriam KS 66202	913-676-8800	P	5,747	10.6
5	American Foods Group LLC—Tom Rosen	4430 S 110th St, Omaha NE 68137	920-436-6523	R	1,778*	4.0
6	ContiGroup Companies Inc—Paul J Fribourg	277 Park Ave, New York NY 10172	212-207-5930	R	1,537*	13.5
7	Nebraska Beef Ltd—Robert Reams	4501 S 36th St, Omaha NE 68107	402-734-6823	R	900*	.9
8	Gwaltney of Smithfield Ltd—Larry Pope Smithfield Foods Inc	PO Box 489, Smithfield VA 23431	757-365-3000	S	552	1.4
9	Clougherty Packing LLC Hormel Foods Corp	3049 E Vernon Ave, Los Angeles CA 90058	323-583-4621	S	414*	1.3
10	JBS USA Holdings Inc—Wesley Mendonca Batista	1770 Promontory Cir, Greeley CO 80634	970-506-8000	S	409*	.5
11	Sam Kane Beef Processors Inc—Jerry Kane	PO Box 9254, Corpus Christi TX 78469	361-241-5000	R	402*	.9
12	Pine Ridge Farms LLC—Lori Spearman	1800 Maury St, Des Moines IA 50317	515-266-4100	R	303*	.4
13	Richwood Meat Co—Mike Wood	2751 N Santa Fe Dr, Merced CA 95348	209-722-8171	R	278*	.1
14	Carolina Pride Foods Inc—Bill Barnette	PO Box 188, Greenwood SC 29648	864-229-5611	R	262*	.9
15	GFI America Inc—Mitchell Goldberger	2815 Blaisdell Ave, Minneapolis MN 55408	612-872-6262	R	220*	.8
16	Gusto Packing Company Inc—Rafael Caballero	2125 Rochester Rd, Montgomery IL 60538	630-896-8608	R	195*	.4
17	Field Packing Company LLC—Tony Clair	PO Box 20003, Owensboro KY 42304	270-926-2324	S	191*	.5
18	Smithfields Lykes Div Smithfield Foods Inc	PO Box 518, Plant City FL 33564	813-752-1102	D	178	2.0
19	Cimpl's LLC—Thomas Rosen	PO Box 80, Yankton SD 57078	605-665-1665	R	153*	2.0
20	Jbs Packerland Inc—Richard Vesta	PO Box 23000, Green Bay WI 54305	920-468-4000	R	147*	1.5
21	Kayem Foods Inc—Romuald Monkiewicz	75 Arlington St, Chelsea MA 02150	617-889-1600	R	135*	.5
22	Oberto Sausage Co—Tom Campanile	PO Box 429, Kent WA 98032	253-437-6100	R	134*	1.0
23	Grote and Weigel Inc—Michael Greiner	76 Granby St, Bloomfield CT 06002	860-242-8528	R	124*	<.1
24	Indiana Packers Corp—Masao Watanabe	PO Box 318, Delphi IN 46923	765-564-3680	R	121*	1.4
25	Green Bay Dressed Beef LLC—Lou Bannon	PO Box 8547, Green Bay WI 54308	920-437-6330	R	119*	1.4
26	Sioux-Preme Packing Co—Gary Malenke	PO Box 255, Sioux Center IA 51250	712-722-2555	R	113*	.3
27	J and B Meats Corp—Jeff Jobe	2302 1st St, Coal Valley IL 61240	309-799-7341	R	107*	.1
28	Dietz and Watson Inc—Louis Eni	5701 Tacony St, Philadelphia PA 19135	215-831-9000	R	96*	.9
29	Bruce Packing Company Inc—Larry Bruce	PO Box 540, Silverton OR 97381	503-873-8334	R	96*	.4
30	Leidy's Inc—Jim V Stone	PO Box 2, Harleysville PA 19438	215-723-4606	R	96*	.3
31	Ellison Meat Co—Brian Karels	1401 Sioux Dr, Pipestone MN 56164	507-825-5486	R	82*	.2
32	Eddy Packing Company Inc—Ronald Beeman	PO Box 392, Yoakum TX 77995	361-293-2361	R	82*	.2
33	Rabe's Quality Meat Inc—Ronald Rabe	PO Box 45602, Omaha NE 68145	402-895-5399	R	80*	.1
34	Harris Ranch Beef Co—John Harris	PO Box 220, Selma CA 93662	559-896-3081	R	67*	.7
35	Raber Packing Co—Carol Wetterauer	1413 N Raber Rd, Peoria IL 61604	309-673-0721	R	62*	<.1
36	Wolverine Packing Co—A Bonahoom	2535 Rivard St, Detroit MI 48207	313-259-7500	R	58*	.3
37	United Food Group LLC—Dale Nakashima	PO Box 58506, Los Angeles CA 90058	323-826-3236	S	55*	.5
38	John R Morreale Inc—John Lucaccioni	216 N Peoria St, Chicago IL 60607	312-421-3664	R	51*	.1
39	Transhumance Colorado Inc—Jan Hines	4900 Clarkson St, Denver CO 80216	303-296-1466	R	50*	.1
40	Kunzler and Company Inc—Christian Kunzler	PO Box 4747, Lancaster PA 17604	717-299-6301	R	50*	.5
41	Beef Packers Inc—Dennis Roth	3115 S Fig Ave, Fresno CA 93706	559-268-5586	R	48*	.5
42	Chicago Meat Authority Inc—Jordan Dorfman	1120 W 47th Pl, Chicago IL 60609	773-254-3811	R	47*	.3
43	Brown Packing Company Inc—Brian Oedzes	PO Box 703, South Holland IL 60473	708-849-7990	R	47*	.1
44	Reichel Foods Inc—Craig Reichel	3706 Enterprise Dr Sw, Rochester MN 55902	507-289-7264	R	43*	.3
45	Independent Food Corp—Patrick Florence	PO Box Ee, Twin Falls ID 83303	208-733-0980	R	43*	.2
46	Washington Agricultural Development Inc—Gayland Pedhirney	PO Box 832, Toppenish WA 98948	509-865-2121	R	41*	.6
47	John Morrell and Co Smithfield Foods Inc	PO Box 405020, Cincinnati OH 45240		S	40*	.2
48	Quality Pork International Inc—Larry Lubeck	10404 F Plz, Omaha NE 68127	402-339-1911	R	39*	.4
49	Carlton Farms Inc—John Duyn	PO Box 580, Carlton OR 97111	503-852-7166	R	37*	.1
50	Fairbank Reconstruction Corp—Rick Fahle	PO Box 170, Ashville NY 14710	716-782-2000	R	35*	.1
51	Central Valley Meat Company Inc—Lawrence Coelho	10431 8 3/4 Ave, Hanford CA 93230	559-583-9624	R	34*	.2
52	Family Brands International LLC—John Wampler	PO Box 429, Lenoir City TN 37771	865-986-8005	R	33*	.2
53	Red Castle Bakeries—Marco Minuto	30 Inez Dr, Bayshore NY 11706	631-231-1330	R	33*	<.1
54	Ohio Packing Co—Walter Wilke	1306 Harmon Ave, Columbus OH 43223	614-239-1600	R	32*	.2
55	Pork King Packing Inc—Tom Miles	8808 S State Rte 23, Marengo IL 60152	815-568-8024	R	31*	.2
56	Martin S Abattoir And Wholesale Meats Inc—Carlton Martin	1600 Martin Rd, Godwin NC 28344	910-567-6102	R	29*	.2
57	Provimi Foods Inc—Brian Friesen	W2103 County Rd W V, Seymour WI 54165	920-833-6861	R	29*	.1

Rank	Company Name—*Executive Officer*	Address, City, State, Zip	Phone	Type	Fin	Empls
58	Lone Star Beef Processors LP—*John Cross*	2150 E 37th St, San Angelo TX 76903	325-658-5555	R	29*	.2
59	Creekstone Farms Premium Beef—*Dennis Buhlke*	604 Goff Industrial Rd, Arkansas City KS 67005	620-741-3366	R	28*	<.1
60	Kent Quality Foods Inc—*Charles Soet*	703 Leonard St Nw, Grand Rapids MI 49504	616-459-4595	R	26*	.1
61	Chef's Requested Foods Inc—*John Williams*	PO Box 82096, Oklahoma City OK 73148	405-239-2610	R	26*	.2
62	Hill Meat Co—*James Cheney*	PO Box 1066, Pendleton OR 97801	541-276-7621	R	24*	.1
63	Meats Plus Inc—*Bob Nadarski*	PO Box 155, Loda IL 60948	217-386-2381	R	23*	<.1
64	Masami Foods Inc—*Masami Ishida*	5222 Tingley Ln, Klamath Falls OR 97603	541-884-1735	R	23*	.2
65	Bubba Foods LLC	PO Box 2823, Jacksonville FL 32203	904-482-1900	R	21*	.2
66	Henry's Hickory House Inc—*William Morris*	PO Box 2823, Jacksonville FL 32203	904-354-6839	R	19*	.1
67	Swan Packing Inc—*Gerald Rowles*	700 Corning Ave, Des Moines IA 50313	515-262-1111	R	19*	.1
68	Beltex Corp—*Eric Nauwalaers*	3801 N Grove St, Fort Worth TX 76106		R	19*	.1
69	Curtis Packing Co—*Douglas Curtis*	PO Box 1470, Greensboro NC 27402	336-275-7684	R	19*	.1
70	Gem Meat Packing Co—*Brent Compton*	515 E 45th St, Boise ID 83714	208-375-9424	R	18*	<.1
71	First Class Foods Inc—*Salomon Benzimra*	PO Box 2397, Hawthorne CA 90251	310-676-2500	R	18*	.1
72	Central Beef Industry LLC—*Paul Beautler*	PO Box 399, Center Hill FL 33514	352-793-3671	R	18*	.1
73	Southern Quality Meats Inc—*B Haynie*	PO Box 617, Pontotoc MS 38863	662-489-1524	R	17*	.1
74	Fremont Beef Co—*Les Leech*	PO Box 908, Fremont NE 68026	402-727-7200	R	17*	.1
75	Calco International Inc—*Seiko Armstrong*	10065 E Harvard Ave St, Denver CO 80231	303-671-4550	R	16*	<.1
76	Burnett and Son Meat Company Inc—*Donald Burnett*	1420 S Myrtle Ave, Monrovia CA 91016	626-357-2165	R	16*	.1
77	Fuji Foods US Inc—*Ken Omura*	4340 Glencoe St, Denver CO 80216	303-377-3738	R	15*	<.1
78	Harper's Country Hams Inc—*Gary Harper*	PO Box 122, Clinton KY 42031	270-653-2081	R	15*	.1
79	Chisesi Brothers Meat Packing Company Inc—*Philip Chisesi*	PO Box 23827, New Orleans LA 70183	504-822-3550	R	15*	.1
80	Freirich Foods Inc—*Paul Bardinas*	PO Box 1529, Salisbury NC 28145	704-636-2621	R	15*	.1
81	Bush Brothers Provision Co—*Harry Bush*	1931 N Dixie Hwy, West Palm Beach FL 33407	561-832-6666	R	14*	<.1
82	Rupari Food Services Inc—*Robert Mintz*	1208 W Newport Ctr Dr, Deerfield Beach FL 33442	954-480-6320	R	14*	<.1
83	Polk's Meat Products Inc—*John Polk*	PO Box 1190, Magee MS 39111	601-849-9997	R	13*	.1
84	City Foods Inc—*Kenneth Kohn*	PO Box 09190, Chicago IL 60609	773-523-1566	R	13*	.1
85	Iowa Lamb Corp—*William Brennan*	PO Box 352, Hawarden IA 51023	712-551-1126	R	13*	.1
86	Manning's Beef LLC—*Olivia Tamayo*	PO Box 1156, Pico Rivera CA 90660	562-908-1089	R	12*	.1
87	H and B Packing Company Inc—*Jake Bauer*	PO Box 2344, Waco TX 76703	254-752-2506	R	12*	.1
88	Ena Meat Packing Inc—*Ali Kucukkarca*	240 E 5th St, Paterson NJ 07524	973-742-4790	R	11*	<.1
89	Colorado Meat Packers Inc—*Roy Moore*	PO Box 16552, Denver CO 80216	303-295-0207	R	11*	.1
90	RBR Meat Company Inc—*Irwin Miller*	PO Box 58225, Los Angeles CA 90058	323-826-2155	R	11*	.1
91	Cartwright's Valley Meat Co—*Jamie Cartwright*	825 Union Ave, Grants Pass OR 97527	541-479-0321	R	11*	<.1
92	Grogan's Farm Inc—*Roger Williams*	PO Box 39, Arlington KY 42021	270-655-6421	S	11*	<.1
93	Custom Meats Corp—*James E Melady*	1802 Levee St, Dallas TX 75207	214-747-9606	R	11*	<.1
94	Iowa Pacific Processors Inc—*Michael Everett*	2606 Sunset Rd, Des Moines IA 50321	515-288-5435	R	11*	.1
95	Dakota Pack Inc—*Douglas Skinner*	PO Box 77, Estherville IA 51334	712-362-2225	R	11*	.1
96	Peoria Packing Ltd—*Harry Katsiavelos*	1307 W Lake St, Chicago IL 60607	312-226-2600	R	11*	.1
97	Beef International Inc—*Biagio Mento*	7010 Central Hwy, Pennsauken NJ 08109	856-663-6763	R	11*	.1
98	West Lake Food Corp—*Chimin Yenson*	2430 Cape Cod Way, Santa Ana CA 92703	714-973-2286	R	10*	.1
99	Karn Meats Inc—*Richard Karn*	922 Taylor Ave, Columbus OH 43219	614-252-3712	R	10*	.1
100	Swaggerty Sausage Company Inc—*Kyle Swaggerty*	2827 Swaggerty Rd, Kodak TN 37764	865-933-2625	R	10*	.1
101	Manchester Packing Company Inc—*Robert Dogner*	349 Wetherell St, Manchester CT 06040	860-646-5000	R	10*	.1
102	Ham Stevison Co—*Michael Stevison*	PO Box 219, Portland TN 37148	615-325-4161	R	10*	.1
103	Empire Packing—*Debra Robinson*	7430 32nd Ave Ne, Olympia WA 98516	360-459-3745	R	10*	.1
104	Atlantic Veal and Lamb Inc—*Phillip Peerless*	275 Morgan Ave, Brooklyn NY 11211		R	9*	<.1
105	Verschoor Meats Inc—*Dan Kiser*	PO Box 2410, Sioux City IA 51106	712-252-1847	R	9*	.1
106	S and S Quality Meats LLC—*Steve Younger*	PO Box 629, Emporia KS 66801	620-342-6354	R	8*	.1
107	Nations Best Delicatessen Company Inc—*Ira Rosner*	D7 Hunts Point Co Op M, Bronx NY 10474	718-328-5270	R	8*	.1
108	Dayton Meat Co—*Bob Dickson*	13245 SE Fletcher Rd, Dayton OR 97114	503-864-2237	S	8*	<.1
109	Lowell Packing Co—*Lowell Downing*	PO Box 220, Fitzgerald GA 31750	229-423-2051	R	8*	.1
110	Gulf Packing Company LP—*Charlie Booth*	PO Box 357, San Benito TX 78586	956-399-2631	R	8*	.1
111	Nordic Foods Inc—*Jason Hall*	4747 Speaker Rd, Kansas City KS 66106	913-281-1167	R	7*	.1
112	Spectrum Preferred Meats Inc—*Kevin Rude*	6194 W Pines Rd, Mount Morris IL 61054	815-946-3816	R	7*	.1
113	Morrilton Packing Company Inc—*David Ruff*	51 Blue Diamond Dr, Morrilton AR 72110	501-354-2474	R	7*	.1
114	Elkhorn Valley Packing Co—*Lynn Grant*	101 Central St, Harper KS 67058	620-896-2300	R	6*	.1
115	Noah's Ark Processors Corp—*Steven Krausnan*	1821 311th Ave, Dawson MN 56232	320-769-2020	R	6*	.1
116	Bartlow Brothers Inc—*Dan Reynolds*	PO Box 207, Rushville IL 62681		R	6*	.1
117	Schaefers Market—*Mark Schaefer*	411 Sinclair Lewis Ave, Sauk Centre MN 56378	320-352-6490	R	6*	<.1
118	OHSN Inc—*Lavern Gisinger*	PO Box 2037, Lawton OK 73502	580-248-1299	R	6*	<.1
119	Needham Inc—*William Needham*	1204 Jones St, Omaha NE 68102	402-344-3820	R	5*	<.1
120	Bass Farms Inc—*John Bass*	PO Box 126, Spring Hope NC 27882	252-478-4147	R	5*	.1
121	Hazle Park Packing Co—*Gary Kreisl*	260 Washington Ave, Hazle Township PA 18202	570-455-7571	R	5*	<.1
122	Caughman's Meat Plant Inc—*Ronald Caughman*	PO Box 457, Lexington SC 29071	803-356-3216	R	5*	<.1
123	Wampler's Farm Sausage Company Inc—*Ted Wampler*	781 Hwy 70 W, Lenoir City TN 37771	865-986-2056	R	5*	.1
124	Roe's Of San Antonio LLC	PO Box 7265, San Antonio TX 78207	210-224-5441	R	5*	.1
125	Nagle's Veal Inc—*Michael Lemler*	PO Box 30960, San Bernardino CA 92413	909-383-7075	R	5*	<.1
126	VJ Provision Inc—*Sam Jacobellis*	410 S Varney St, Burbank CA 91502	818-843-3945	R	5*	<.1
127	Troyer's Trail Bologna Inc—*Dale Troyer*	6552 State Rte 515, Dundee OH 44624	330-893-2414	R	5*	<.1
128	Silver Springs Farm Inc—*Daniel Fillippo*	PO Box 268, Harleysville PA 19438	215-256-4321	R	4*	<.1
129	Southern Packing Corp—*Hyman Brooke*	4004 Battlefield Blvd, Chesapeake VA 23322	757-421-2131	R	4*	<.1
130	Curtis Packing Company Inc—*W Branch*	115 Sycamore St, Tifton GA 31794	229-382-4014	R	4*	<.1
131	Central Nebraska Packing Inc—*Matt Litt*	PO Box 550, North Platte NE 69103	308-532-1250	R	4*	<.1
132	Carl Rittberger Sr Inc—*Andrew Rittberger*	1900 Lutz Ln, Zanesville OH 43701	740-452-2767	R	4*	<.1
133	Tri-State Beef Company Inc—*Robert Runtz*	2124 Baymiller St, Cincinnati OH 45214	513-579-1722	R	4*	<.1
134	Ralph's Packing Co—*Gary Crane*	PO Box 249, Perkins OK 74059	405-547-2464	R	4*	<.1
135	Fieldstone Meats Of Alabama Inc—*Donald Wilson*	PO Box 1014, Oneonta AL 35121	205-625-3686	R	4*	<.1
136	Hampton Meat Processing Company Inc—*E Hampton*	PO Box 545, Hopkinsville KY 42241	270-885-8474	R	4*	<.1
137	Great Lakes Packing Company International Inc—*Robert Oates*	1535 W 43rd St, Chicago IL 60609	773-927-6660	R	4*	<.1
138	Iowa Lamb Buyers	402 10th St, Hawarden IA 51023	712-551-2627	R	3*	.1
139	Mahan Packing Company Inc—*K Mahan*	6540 State Rte 45, Bristolville OH 44402	330-889-2454	R	3*	<.1
140	Eickman's Processing Company Inc—*Michael Eickman*	PO Box 118, Seward IL 61077	815-247-8451	R	3*	<.1
141	Balley Foods LLC	PO Box 908, Bailey NC 27807	252-235-3558	R	3*	<.1
142	Heinkel's Packing Company Inc—*Miles Wright*	PO Box 2134, Decatur IL 62524	217-428-4401	R	3*	<.1
143	A To Z Kosher Meat Products Company Inc—*Edward Weinberg*	123 Grand St Ext, Brooklyn NY 11211	718-384-7400	R	3*	<.1
144	Union County Livestock Inc—*James Baird*	350 T Frank Wathen Rd, Uniontown KY 42461	270-822-4866	R	3*	<.1
145	Lakeview Packing Company Inc—*Jacob Turnage*	604 Lakeview Rd, La Grange NC 28551	252-747-8166	R	3*	<.1

Note: An asterisk (*) indicates an estimated financial figure. The company type code used is as follows: R = Private, P = Public, S = Private Subsidiary, B = Public Subsidiary, D = Division, J = Joint Venture, I = Investment Fund.

COMPANY RANKINGS BY SALES WITHIN 4-DIGIT SIC

Rank	Company Name—*Executive Officer*	Address, City, State, Zip	Phone	Type	Fin	Empls
146	Robertson's Hams Inc—*Clay Robertson*	110 Wanda St, Marietta OK 73448	580-276-3395	R	2*	<.1
147	NS Troutman and Sons Inc—*Lynn Troutman*	PO Box 65, Freeburg PA 17827	570-374-4949	R	2*	<.1
148	C Roy Inc—*Richard Roy*	444 Roy Dr, Yale MI 48097	810-387-3957	R	2*	<.1
149	Hot Springs Packing Company Inc—*John Stubblefield*	PO Box 2312, Hot Springs AR 71914	501-767-2363	R	2*	<.1
150	G and C Packing Co—*Frank Grindinger*	PO Box 6639, Colorado Springs CO 80934	719-634-1587	R	2*	<.1
151	M Robzen Inc—*Mark Robzen*	1285 Main St, Swoyersville PA 18704	570-331-4507	R	2*	<.1
152	Salem Packing Co—*Josephine Bonaccurso*	PO Box 131, Salem NJ 08079	856-935-1206	R	2*	<.1
153	Triangle Packing Inc—*John Hoyt*	PO Box 551, Choteau MT 59422	406-466-2342	R	2*	<.1
154	Merrick's Of Nebraska LLC—*Rich Carpenter*	PO Box 727, Oxford NE 68967	308-824-3261	R	2*	<.1
155	Heffelfinger's Meats Inc—*Rick Heffelfinger*	469 County Rd 30a, Jeromesville OH 44840	419-368-7131	R	2*	<.1
156	Eunice Superette Inc—*Jerome Moore*	1044 Hwy 91, Eunice LA 70535	337-546-6041	R	2*	<.1
157	Clay Center Locker—*Brad Dieckmann*	212 6th St, Clay Center KS 67432	785-632-5550	R	1*	<.1
158	Premium Meats Inc—*Michael Kassos*	241 Logan Ave Ne, Warren OH 44483	330-394-8651	R	1*	<.1
159	Gold Medal Packing Inc—*Joseph Rocco*	PO Box 652, Oriskany NY 13424	315-337-1911	R	1*	.1
160	Venus Foods Inc—*Robert Tsai*	770 S Stimson Ave, City Of Industry CA 91745	626-369-5188	R	1*	<.1
161	Greer's Inc—*David Greer*	PO Box 98, Pryor OK 74362	918-825-1710	R	1*	<.1

TOTALS: SIC 2011 Meat Packing Plants

Companies: 161					50,361	166.9

2013 Sausages & Other Prepared Meats

Rank	Company Name—*Executive Officer*	Address, City, State, Zip	Phone	Type	Fin	Empls
1	BEF Holding Company Inc—*Steven A Davis*	3776 S High St, Columbus OH 43207	614-491-2225	S	45,145*	42.0
2	JBS USA LLC—*Wesley Batista*	PO Box 337570, Greeley CO 80633	970-506-8000	S	11,479*	24.8
3	Sara Lee Corp—*Marcel H M Smits*	3500 Lacey Rd, Downers Grove IL 60515	630-598-6000	P	10,793	33.4
4	Farmland Foods Inc—*Mike Brown*	PO Box 20121, Kansas City MO 64195	816-801-4300	S	6,570	.3
5	Keystone Foods LLC—*Larry S McWilliams*	300 Barr Harbor Dr Ste, West Conshohocken PA 19428	610-667-6700	D	5,379*	13.0
6	Sara Lee Foods—*Brenda C Barnes* Sara Lee Corp	10151 Carver Rd, Cincinnati OH 45242		D	3,704	N/A
7	Smithfield Packing Company Inc—*Timothy O Schellpeper*	200 Commerce St, Smithfield VA 23430	757-365-3000	S	1,554*	5.8
8	Oscar Mayer Foods Corp—*Nick Meriggioli*	910 Mayer Ave, Madison WI 53704	608-241-3311	D	1,300*	3.0
9	Willow Brook Foods Inc	PO Box 9300, Minneapolis MN 55440	952-742-7575	S	955*	1.2
10	Hatfield Quality Meats—*Douglas C Clemens* Clemens Family Corp	PO Box 902, Hatfield PA 19440	215-368-2500	S	857*	1.6
11	Fresh Mark Inc—*David Cochenour*	PO Box 571, Massillon OH 44648	330-455-5253	R	796*	1.6
12	Clemens Family Corp—*Philip A Clemens*	PO Box 902, Hatfield PA 19440	215-368-2500	R	781*	1.7
13	Zartic Inc—*James E Mauer*	438 Lavender Dr NW, Rome GA 30165	706-234-3000	R	582*	1.3
14	Lopez Foods Inc—*Ed Sanchez*	6016 Nw 120th Ct, Oklahoma City OK 73162	405-603-7500	R	466*	1.6
15	Patrick Cudahy Inc—*William G Otis*	1 Sweet Apple-Wood Ln, Cudahy WI 53110	414-744-2000	S	454*	1.0
16	Jimmy Dean Foods Sara Lee Corp	3500 Lacey Rd, Downers Grove IL 60515	630-598-6000	S	400	<.1
17	Manda Packing Company LLC	PO Box 3374, Baton Rouge LA 70821	225-344-7636	R	323*	.2
18	Bridgford Food Processing Corp *William L Bridgford* Bridgford Foods Corp	1308 N Patt StBox 3773, Anaheim CA 92801	714-526-5533	R	318*	.7
19	Bridgford Marketing Co—*William L Bridgford* Bridgford Foods Corp	1308 N Patt St Box 377, Anaheim CA 92801	714-526-5533	S	318*	.7
20	Afa Foods Inc—*Barry Renninger*	860 1st Ave Ste 866, King Of Prussia PA 19406	610-277-5010	R	305*	.8
21	Ball Park Brand Sara Lee Corp	10151 Carver Rd, Cincinnati OH 45242		D	264*	.5
22	Bar-S Foods Co—*Timothy Day*	PO Box 29049, Phoenix AZ 85038	602-264-7272	R	192*	1.6
23	Home Market Foods Inc—*Wesley Atamian*	140 Morgan Dr, Norwood MA 02062	781-948-1500	R	191*	1.7
24	Gallo Salame	2411 Baumann Ave, San Lorenzo CA 94580	510-276-1300	S	158*	.3
25	S and S Foods LLC—*Robert Horowitz*	1120 W Foothill Blvd, Azusa CA 91702	626-633-1609	R	158*	.2
26	Mountain City Meat Co—*Ron Divin*	5905 E 42nd Ave, Denver CO 80216	303-320-1116	R	142*	.3
27	Johnsonville Sausage LLC—*Ralph Stayer*	PO Box 906, Sheboygan Falls WI 53085	920-453-6900	R	140*	1.4
28	Dold Foods Inc	PO Box 4339, Wichita KS 67204	316-838-9101	S	137*	.3
29	Abbyland Foods Inc—*Harland Schraufnagel*	PO Box 69, Abbotsford WI 54405	715-223-6386	R	127*	.5
30	Bridgford Foods Corp—*John V Simmons*	PO Box 3773, Anaheim CA 92803	714-526-5533	P	118	.5
31	Park 100 Foods Inc—*Gary Meade*	326 E Adams St, Tipton IN 46072	765-675-3480	R	114*	.3
32	Sugar Creek Packing Co—*John Richardson*	2101 Kenskill Ave, Wshngtn Ct Hs OH 43160	740-335-3586	R	107*	1.2
33	Oregon Freeze Dry Inc—*James Merryman*	PO Box 1048, Albany OR 97321	541-967-6531	R	106*	<.1
34	Westin Inc—*Scott Carlson*	11808 W Ctr Rd Ste 1, Omaha NE 68144	402-691-8800	R	100*	.3
35	Maid-Rite Steak Company Inc—*Don Bernstein*	PO Box 509, Dunmore PA 18512	570-343-4748	R	98*	.2
36	Lloyd's Barbecue Co—*Jeffrey M Ettinger*	1455 Mendota Heights R, St Paul MN 55120	651-688-6000	S	97*	.3
37	Thumann Inc—*Henry Thumann*	670 Dell Rd Ste 1, Carlstadt NJ 07072	201-935-3636	R	92*	.3
38	SYSCO Food Services of Hampton Roads—*John Hall*	7000 Harbour View Blvd, Suffolk VA 23435	757-673-4000	R	87	.2
39	Stampede Meat Inc—*Joseph Ligas*	7351 S 78th Ave, Bridgeview IL 60455	773-376-4300	R	84*	.5
40	JC Potter Sausage Co—*Steve Englander*	1914 Hwy 70 E, Durant OK 74701	580-924-2414	R	82*	.3
41	J and B Sausage Company Inc—*Danny V Janecka*	PO Box 7, Waelder TX 78959	830-788-7511	R	82*	.3
42	Quaker Maid Meats Inc—*Stanley Szortyka*	PO Box 350, Reading PA 19607	610-376-1500	R	79*	.2
43	Sadler's Smokehouse Ltd—*Ernie Younger*	PO Box 1088, Henderson TX 75653	903-657-5581	R	78*	.3
44	Appert's Food Inc—*Joe Omann*	900 Hwy 10 S, Saint Cloud MN 56304	320-251-3200	R	78*	.1
45	Devro Inc—*Dogulas Stewart*	PO Box 11925, Columbia SC 29211	803-796-9730	S	70*	.4
46	Cloverdale Foods Co—*T Russell*	PO Box 667, Mandan ND 58554	701-663-9511	R	70*	.3
47	D L Lee and Sons Inc—*W Lee*	PO Box 206, Alma GA 31510	912-632-4406	R	67*	.3
48	Fair Oaks Farms LLC—*Mike Thompson*	7600 95th St, Pleasant Prairie WI 53158	262-947-0320	R	56*	.2
49	Best Kosher Foods Corp Sara Lee Corp	3500 Lacey Rd, Downers Grove IL 60515	630-598-6000	S	55*	.4
50	Williams Sausage Company Inc—*Roger Williams*	5132 Old Troy Hickman, Union City TN 38261	731-885-5841	R	55*	.3
51	Carl Buddig And Co—*Robert Buddig*	950 175th St, Homewood IL 60430	708-798-0900	R	53*	.5
52	Carlton Foods Corp—*Randy Rust*	880 S State Hwy 46, New Braunfels TX 78130	830-625-7583	S	50*	.1
53	Daniele International Inc—*Stefano Dukcevich*	105 Davis Dr, Pascoag RI 02859	401-568-6228	R	50*	.2
54	Jtm Provisions Company Inc—*Anthony Maas*	PO Box 711134, Cincinnati OH 45271	513-367-4900	R	48*	.3
55	Quality Sausage Company Inc—*Gene Eisen*	1925 Lone Star Dr, Dallas TX 75212	214-634-3400	R	48*	.3
56	Kronos Foods Corp—*Michael Austin*	1 Kronos, Glendale Heights IL 60139	224-353-5353	R	47*	.3
57	Richards Cajun Foods Corp—*Ronnie Doucet*	PO Box 414, Church Point LA 70525	337-684-6309	S	47*	.1
58	Cti-Ssi Food Services LLC—*Todd Carson*	PO Box 700, Caldwell ID 83606	208-482-7844	R	45*	.5
59	Pocino Foods Co—*Frank Pocino*	PO Box 2219, La Puente CA 91746	626-968-8000	R	45*	.1
60	Liguria Foods Inc—*Jehan Saulnier*	1515 15th St N, Humboldt IA 50548	515-332-4121	R	45*	.1
61	Skylark Meats LLC—*Belinda Mawhiney*	4430 S 110th St, Omaha NE 68137	402-592-0300	R	44*	.3
62	Surlean Meat Co—*Darryl Scott*	PO Box 831449, San Antonio TX 78283	210-227-4370	R	43*	.3
63	Bridgford Food Processing of Texas LP—*William L Bridgford*	1707 S Good Latimer Ex, Dallas TX 75226	214-428-1535	S	42*	.1

Rank	Company Name—*Executive Officer*	Address, City, State, Zip	Phone	Type	Fin	Empls
	Bridgford Foods Corp					
64	Roger Wood Foods Inc—*David Solana*	PO Box 2926, Savannah GA 31402	912-964-6335	R	41*	.3
65	Taylor Provision Company Inc—*John T Cumbler*	P O Box 5108, Trenton NJ 08638	609-392-1113	R	41*	.1
66	Bruss Co—*John Tyson*	3548 N Kostner Ave, Chicago IL 60641	773-282-2900	S	40*	.2
67	Al and John Inc—*Alexander Oldja*	444 Marshall St, Paterson NJ 07503	973-742-4990	R	38*	.2
68	Daily Foods Inc—*Warren Wilcox*	3535 S 500 W, Salt Lake City UT 84115	801-269-1998	R	38*	.2
69	Quincy Street Inc—*Douglas Hekman*	13350 Quincy St, Holland MI 49424	616-399-3330	R	37*	.1
70	John Soules Foods Inc—*John Soules*	PO Box 4579, Tyler TX 75712	903-592-9800	R	35*	.4
71	Holten Meat Inc—*Michael Holten*	1682 Sauget Business B, East Saint Louis IL 62206	618-337-8400	R	34*	.2
72	Allied Foods Inc (Scranton Pennsylvania)—*Michael Peloucci*	PO Box 142, Scranton PA 18504	570-961-5801	R	34*	.1
73	Nitta Casings Inc—*Frank Caroselli*	141 Southside Ave, Bridgewater NJ 08807	908-218-4400	R	33*	.2
74	Dean Sausage Company Inc—*George Grabner*	PO Box 750, Attalla AL 35954	256-538-6082	R	33*	.1
75	Casa Di Bertacchi Corp—*Robert Rich*	PO Box 245, Buffalo NY 14240	856-696-5600	R	33*	.2
76	Jones Dairy Farm—*Philip Jones*	PO Box 808, Fort Atkinson WI 53538	920-563-2431	R	32*	.4
77	Rosina Food Products Inc—*James Corigliano*	170 French Rd, Buffalo NY 14227		R	32*	.2
78	SIL Inc—*Troy Link*	PO Box 549, New Glarus WI 53574	608-527-2131	R	31*	.2
79	Koegel Meats Inc—*John Koegel*	3400 W Bristol Rd, Flint MI 48507	810-238-3685	R	31*	.1
80	Sunnyvalley Smoked Meats Inc—*William Andreetta*	PO Box 2158, Manteca CA 95336	209-825-0288	R	30*	.1
81	John Hofmeister and Son Inc—*Ed Hofmeister*	2386 S Blue Island Ave, Chicago IL 60608	773-847-0700	R	29*	.1
82	Allen Brothers Inc—*Todd Allen Hatoff*	3737 S Halsted St, Chicago IL 60609	773-890-5100	R	28*	.1
83	Premio Foods Inc—*Marc Cinque*	50 Utter Ave, Hawthorne NJ 07506	973-427-1106	R	27*	.2
84	Louie's Finer Meats Inc—*Louie Muench*	PO Box 774, Cumberland WI 54829	715-822-4728	R	27*	.1
85	Burger's Ozark Country Cured Hams Inc—*Steven Burger*	32819 Hwy 87, California MO 65018	573-796-3134	R	27*	.2
86	Kowalski Companies Inc—*Michael Kowalski*	2270 Holbrook St, Detroit MI 48212	313-873-8200	R	27*	.2
87	Adams Ralph and Paul Inc—*Milo Jones* Jones Dairy Farm	PO Box 219, Bridgeville DE 19933	302-337-8208	S	26*	.4
88	Global Foods Processing Inc—*David Guest*	1826 Chicago Ave, Sioux City IA 51106	712-255-6000	R	26*	.2
89	Square H Brands Inc—*Henry Haskell*	2731 S Soto St, Vernon CA 90058	323-267-4600	R	26*	.2
90	Fred Usinger Inc—*Frederick Usinger*	1030 N Old World 3rd S, Milwaukee WI 53203	414-276-9100	R	25*	.1
91	Farmington Foods Inc—*Frank Dijohn*	7419 Franklin St, Forest Park IL 60130	708-771-3600	R	25*	.2
92	Sparrer Sausage Company Inc—*Brian Graves*	4325 W Ogden Ave, Chicago IL 60623	773-762-3334	R	25*	.1
93	Frick's Meat Products Inc—*David Frick*	360 M E Frick Dr, Washington MO 63090	636-239-2200	R	25*	.2
94	Hansel 'n Gretel Brand Inc—*Milton Rattner*	7936 Cooper Ave, Glendale NY 11385	718-326-0041	R	24*	.2
95	Kiolbassa Provision Co—*Robert Kiolbassa*	1325 S Brazos St, San Antonio TX 78207	210-226-8127	R	24*	.1
96	C and F Packing Company Inc—*Joseph Freda*	PO Box 209, Lake Villa IL 60046	847-245-2000	R	22*	.1
97	Kings Command Foods Inc—*Ronald Baer*	7622 S 188th St, Kent WA 98032	425-251-6788	R	22*	.1
98	International Casings Group Inc—*Paul Lankveld*	4420 S Wolcott Ave, Chicago IL 60609	773-376-9200	R	21*	.1
99	Webster City Custom Meats Inc—*Dean Bowden*	1611 E 2nd St, Webster City IA 50595	515-832-1130	R	21*	.2
100	Alderfer Inc—*Earl Manhold*	PO Box 2, Harleysville PA 19438	215-256-8818	R	20*	.1
101	Aidells Sausage Co—*Bob McHenry*	1625 Alvarado St, San Leandro CA 94577	510-614-5450	R	20*	.1
102	Copaz Packing Corp—*Charles Finkel*	PO Box 40268, Cincinnati OH 45240	513-671-1676	R	19*	.3
103	Seaport Meat Co—*Nancy Camarda*	PO Box 91979, Spring Valley CA 91979	619-713-2278	R	19*	<.1
104	Cher-Make Sausage Co—*Arthur Chermak*	PO Box 1267, Manitowoc WI 54221	920-683-5980	R	19*	.1
105	John Volpi and Company Inc—*Loronza Pasetti*	5203 Northrup Ave, Saint Louis MO 63110	314-772-8550	R	18*	.1
106	Flanders Provision Co—*Chris Huff*	PO Box 720, Waycross GA 31502	912-283-5191	R	17*	.1
107	Vincent Giordano Corp—*Guy Giordano*	2600 Washington Ave, Philadelphia PA 19146	215-467-6629	R	17*	.1
108	Prime-Pak Foods Inc—*Todd Robson*	2076 Memorial Park Dr, Gainesville GA 30504	770-536-8708	R	17*	.2
109	Bert Hazekamp and Son Inc—*David Hazekamp*	3933 S Brooks Rd, Muskegon MI 49444	231-773-6425	R	17*	.1
110	Best Provision Company Inc—*Floyd Jayson*	144 Avon Ave, Newark NJ 07108	973-242-5000	R	17*	.1
111	Randolph Packing Co—*Angelo Carmignani*	275 Roma Jean Pkwy, Streamwood IL 60107	630-830-3100	R	16*	.1
112	Premium Protein Products LLC—*Michael Cooper*	4611 W Adams St, Lincoln NE 68524	402-470-4300	R	16*	.2
113	Diluigi's Inc—*Louis Diluigi*	41 Popes Ln, Danvers MA 01923	978-750-9900	R	16*	.1
114	Derek And Constance Lee Corp—*Derek Lee*	19355 San Jose Ave, City Of Industry CA 91748	909-595-8831	R	15*	.1
115	Msn Corp—*Leo Sprecher*	431 Somerville St, Manchester NH 03103	603-623-3528	R	15*	.1
116	Engelhart Gourmet Foods Inc—*Robert Englehart*	2475 Courage Dr, Fairfield CA 94533	707-422-6300	R	15*	.1
117	Carolina Packers Inc—*John Jones*	PO Box 1109, Smithfield NC 27577	919-934-2181	R	14*	.1
118	Allied Specialty Foods Inc—*Mark Broccoli*	313 Hickory Pl, Vineland NJ 08360	856-507-1100	R	14*	.1
119	Harrington's In Vermont Inc—*Peter Klinkenberg*	PO Box 288, Richmond VT 05477	802-434-7500	R	14*	.1
120	Hi-Grade Meats Inc—*Kenneth Lippmann*	2160 S W Temple, Salt Lake City UT 84115	801-487-5818	R	14*	.1
121	Standard Meat Company LP—*Jonathan Savell*	5105 Investment Dr, Dallas TX 75236	214-561-0561	R	13*	.1
122	Silver Star Meats Inc—*Robert Germony*	PO Box 393, Mc Kees Rocks PA 15136	412-771-5539	R	13*	.1
123	Prime Food Processing Corp—*Yee Chan*	300 Vandervoort Ave, Brooklyn NY 11211	718-963-2323	R	13*	.1
124	Tower Isles Frozen Foods Ltd—*Beryl Levi*	PO Box 330625, Brooklyn NY 11233	718-495-2626	R	13*	.1
125	Premium Iowa Pork LLC—*Bart Bickley*	PO Box 188, Hospers IA 51238	712-752-8666	R	13*	.1
126	Schaller Manufacturing Corp—*Ralph Schaller*	2235 46th St, Astoria NY 11105	718-721-5480	R	12*	.1
127	Appetito Provisions Company Inc—*Michael Tota*	PO Box 8098, Union City NJ 07087	201-864-3410	R	12*	.1
128	High Top Products Corp—*Mariano Vazquez*	1034 Nw 23rd St, Miami FL 33127	305-633-1646	R	12*	.1
129	Dewied International Inc—*Howard Dewied*	PO Box 200165, San Antonio TX 78220	210-661-6161	R	11*	.1
130	Stevens Sausage Company Inc—*N Stevens*	PO Box 2304, Smithfield NC 27577	919-934-3159	R	11*	.1
131	B and H Foods Inc—*Stanley Bracey*	PO Box 668568, Charlotte NC 28266	704-332-4106	R	11*	.1
132	Smith Provision Company Inc—*Michael Weber*	1300 Cranberry St, Erie PA 16501	814-459-4974	R	10*	<.1
133	O'brien and Company Inc—*Dave Hascall*	3302 Harlan Lewis Rd, Bellevue NE 68005	402-291-3600	R	10*	.1
134	Savoie's Sausage And Food Products Inc—*Eula Savoie*	1742 Hwy 742, Opelousas LA 70570	337-942-7241	R	10*	.1
135	Suncrest Farms Country Hams Inc—*Randall Gambill*	PO Box 634, Wilkesboro NC 28697	336-667-4441	R	10*	.1
136	Uncle Charlie's Meats Inc—*A Parsons*	406 N Estill Ave, Richmond KY 40475	859-623-1967	R	10*	.1
137	Uncle Charley's Sausage Co—*Charles Armitage*	1135 Industrial Park R, Vandergrift PA 15690	724-845-3302	R	10*	<.1
138	Kansas City Sausage Company LLC—*Bruce Ginn*	8001 Nw 106th St, Kansas City MO 64153	816-891-9600	R	10*	<.1
139	Pinellas Provision Corp—*Todd Reese*	PO Box 20124, Saint Petersburg FL 33742	727-822-2701	R	10*	<.1
140	McKenzie of Vermont—*Ralph Smith*	PO Box 4059, Burlington VT 05406	802-864-4585	R	10*	<.1
141	Papa Cantella's Inc—*Thomas Cantella*	3341 E 50th St, Vernon CA 90058	323-584-7272	R	10*	.1
142	Zweigle's Inc—*Roberta Camardo*	651 Plymouth Ave N, Rochester NY 14608	585-546-1740	R	10*	.1
143	Yonekyu USA Inc—*Osamu Saito*	3615 E Vernon Ave, Vernon CA 90058	323-581-4194	R	10*	.1
144	Werner Gourmet Meat Snacks Inc—*Ken Werner*	PO Box 579, Tillamook OR 97141	503-842-7577	R	10*	.1
145	Kesslers Inc—*Robert E Kessler Jr*	PO Box 126, Lemoyne PA 17043	717-763-7162	R	9*	.1
146	Isc Inc—*Frank Isernio*	5600 7th Ave S, Seattle WA 98108	206-762-6207	R	9*	<.1
147	Palmyra Bologna Co—*Craig Seltzer*	PO Box 111, Palmyra PA 17078	717-838-6336	R	9*	.1
148	Busseto Foods Inc—*G Grazier*	PO Box 12403, Fresno CA 93777	559-485-9882	R	9*	.1
149	Serv-Rite Meat Company Inc—*Gary Marks*	PO Box 65026, Los Angeles CA 90065	323-227-1911	R	8*	.1
150	Hummel Brothers Inc—*William Hummel*	180 Sargent Dr, New Haven CT 06511	203-787-4113	R	8*	.1
151	Cibao Meat Products Inc—*Lutzi Isidor*	630 Saint Anns Ave, Bronx NY 10455	718-993-5072	R	8*	.1

Note: An asterisk (*) indicates an estimated financial figure. The company type code used is as follows: R = Private, P = Public, S = Private Subsidiary, B = Public Subsidiary, D = Division, J = Joint Venture, I = Investment Fund.

COMPANY RANKINGS BY SALES WITHIN 4-DIGIT SIC

Rank	Company Name—*Executive Officer*	Address, City, State, Zip	Phone	Type	Fin	Empls
152	Cherry Meat Packers Inc—*Keith Pozulp*	4750 S California Ave, Chicago IL 60632	773-927-1200	R	8*	<.1
153	Crofton and Sons Inc—*Noble Crofton*	PO Box 698, Brandon FL 33509	813-685-7745	R	8*	<.1
154	Bear Creek Smokehouse LLC—*Shelly Jones*	10857 State Hwy 154, Marshall TX 75670	903-935-5217	R	8*	.1
155	Corky's Food Manufacturing LP—*Barry Pelts*	5255 Poplar Ave, Memphis TN 38119	901-396-9888	R	8*	.1
156	Chandler Foods Inc—*Jeff Chandler*	2727 Immanuel Rd, Greensboro NC 27407	336-299-1934	R	8*	<.1
157	Omaha Meat Processors Inc—*David Kousgaard*	6016 Grover St, Omaha NE 68106	402-554-1965	R	8*	<.1
158	Meadow-Farms Sausage Co—*Joe Toia*	6215 S Western Ave, Los Angeles CA 90047		R	8*	<.1
159	Miller Packing Co—*Michael De Benedetti*	PO Box 1390, Lodi CA 95241	209-339-2310	R	8*	.1
160	Plumrose USA Inc—*Carsten Jakobsen*	14 Jonergin Dr, Swanton VT 05488	802-868-7314	R	8*	.1
161	Karl Ehmer Inc—*Mark Hanssler*	PO Box 716, Locust Valley NY 11560	718-456-8100	R	8*	.1
162	Hobes Country Hams Inc—*Hobert Gambill*	PO Box 350, Wilkesboro NC 28697	336-670-3401	R	8*	.1
163	Larry S Sausage Co—*Larry Godwin*	PO Box 4, Fayetteville NC 28302	910-483-5148	R	8*	<.1
164	Caribbean Products Ltd—*Brian Hartman*	3624 Falls Rd Ste 2, Baltimore MD 21211	410-235-7700	R	7*	.1
165	Gunnoe Sausage Co—*Charles Gunnoe*	3989 Cifax Rd, Goode VA 24556	540-586-1091	R	7*	.1
166	Kirby and Holloway Provisions Company Inc—*Russell Kirby*	PO Box 222, Harrington DE 19952	302-398-3705	R	7*	.1
167	New Best Packers Inc—*Michael Drew*	1122 Bronson St, Palatka FL 32177	386-328-5127	R	7*	<.1
168	Mese Hsin Tung Yang Foods Company Inc—*Su Mai*	405 S Airport Blvd, South San Francisco CA 94080	650-589-7689	R	7*	<.1
169	Gold Star Sausage Co—*Phil Pisciotta*	2800 Walnut St, Denver CO 80205	303-295-6400	R	7*	<.1
170	Redondo's LLC—*Hoa Heather Tom Ngu*	94-140 Leokane St, Waipahu HI 96797	808-671-5444	R	7*	<.1
171	Queen City Sausage and Provision Inc—*Elmer Hensler*	PO Box 25213, Cincinnati OH 45225	513-541-5581	R	7*	<.1
172	Clair D Thompson and Sons Inc—*Ronald Thompson*	PO Box 506, Jersey Shore PA 17740	570-398-1880	R	7*	<.1
173	Frank Wardynski and Sons Inc—*Raymond Wardynski*	PO Box 336, Buffalo NY 14240	716-854-6083	R	7*	<.1
174	January Co—*Jim Ding*	9844 40th Ave S, Seattle WA 98118	206-725-9919	R	7*	<.1
175	Wohrle's Foods Inc—*Walter Pickwell*	PO Box 224, Pittsfield MA 01202	413-442-1518	R	7*	<.1
176	Atk Foods Inc—*Richard Kurzawski*	1143 W Lake St, Chicago IL 60607	312-829-2250	R	7*	<.1
177	Fabbri Sausage Manufacturing—*Ray Fabbri*	166 N Aberdeen St, Chicago IL 60607	312-829-6363	R	6*	<.1
178	Niagara Tying Service Inc—*Albert Barrato*	176 Dingens St, Buffalo NY 14206	716-825-0066	R	6*	<.1
179	814 Americas Inc—*Bill Otis*	814 2nd Ave, Elizabeth NJ 07202	908-354-2674	R	6*	.1
180	Jenkins Foods Inc—*Harry Mauney*	2119 New House Rd, Shelby NC 28150	704-434-2347	R	6*	<.1
181	Denmark Sausage Company Inc—*Dennis Vandenberg*	7713 W Golden Ln, Peoria AZ 85345	623-979-4234	R	6*	<.1
182	Dombrovski Meats Co—*Patrick Dombrovski*	PO Box 308, Foley MN 56329	320-968-6275	R	6*	<.1
183	Atlantic Pork and Provisions Inc—*Jack Antinori*	14707 94th Ave, Jamaica NY 11435	718-272-9550	R	6*	<.1
184	Makowski's Real Sausage Co—*Nicole Makowski*	2710 S Poplar Ave, Chicago IL 60608	312-842-5330	R	6*	<.1
185	Wendel Aquisition Inc—*Donald Wendl*	1638 Saint Louis Ave, Kansas City MO 64101	816-221-6283	R	6*	<.1
186	Hi Country Snack Foods Inc—*James Johnson*	PO Box 159, Lincoln MT 59639	406-362-4203	R	6*	.1
187	Conecuh Sausage Company Inc—*Shelia Sessions*	PO Box 327, Evergreen AL 36401	251-578-3380	R	6*	<.1
188	Drexel Foods Inc—*Gary Kanellopoulos*	7035 N American St, Philadelphia PA 19122	215-425-9900	R	6*	<.1
189	Oversea Casing Company LLC—*Tina Moore*	601 S Nevada St, Seattle WA 98108	206-682-6845	R	6*	<.1
190	Parker House Sausage Co—*Michael Parker*	4605 S State St, Chicago IL 60609	773-538-1112	R	6*	<.1
191	Schonwetter Enterprises Inc—*Steven Schonwetter*	41 Lark St, Cohoes NY 12047	518-237-0171	R	6*	<.1
192	Pender Packing Company Inc—*Danny Baker*	4520 Nc Hwy 133, Rocky Point NC 28457	910-675-3311	R	5*	<.1
193	Neese Country Sausage Inc—*Thomas Neese*	1452 Alamance Church R, Greensboro NC 27406	336-275-9548	R	5*	<.1
194	Case Pork Roll Company Inc—*Thomas Greib*	PO Box 33019, Trenton NJ 08629	609-396-8171	R	5*	<.1
195	Daniel Weaver Company Inc—*Robert Trider*	PO Box 525, Lebanon PA 17042	717-274-6100	R	5*	<.1
196	Wisconsin Sausage Co—*Stephen Sorrer*	2560 Cir Dr, Stoughton WI 53589	608-873-5867	R	5*	<.1
197	De An's Pork Products Inc—*Frank Angelis*	899 4th Ave, Brooklyn NY 11232	718-788-2464	R	5*	<.1
198	Alexander and Hornung Inc—*Bernard Polen*	20643 Stephens Rd, St Clair Shores MI 48080	586-771-9880	R	5*	<.1
199	Lord's Sausage and Country Ham Inc—*Wayne Lord*	PO Box 1000, Dexter GA 31019	478-875-3101	R	5*	<.1
200	Chicopee Provision Company Inc—*Tina Vezina*	PO Box 7, Chicopee MA 01014	413-594-4765	R	5*	<.1
201	Camellia General Provision Company Inc—*Edmund Cichocki*	1333 Genesee St, Buffalo NY 14211	716-893-5352	R	5*	<.1
202	Pet Food Services Inc—*Tim Chism*	1201 Sw 76th Ave, Amarillo TX 79118	806-371-8775	R	5*	<.1
203	Dankworth Packing Company Inc—*Michael Dankworth*	PO Box 584, Ballinger TX 76821	325-365-3553	R	5*	<.1
204	Pulaski Meat Products Co—*Ronald Preiss*	123 N Wood Ave, Linden NJ 07036	908-925-5380	R	5*	<.1
205	Dora Dee's Products Inc—*Jay Bernath*	973 Confederate Ave Se, Atlanta GA 30312	404-627-3547	R	5*	<.1
206	Lincoln Packing Co—*Giovanni Colagiovanni*	7 Industrial Rd, Cranston RI 02920	401-943-0876	R	4*	<.1
207	P G Molinari and Sons Inc—*Frank Giorgi*	1401 Yosemite Ave, San Francisco CA 94124	415-822-5555	R	4*	<.1
208	Papa Charlie's Inc—*Joe Hall*	1800 S Kostner Ave, Chicago IL 60623	773-522-7900	R	4*	<.1
209	Enslin And Son Packing Co—*August Enslin*	2500 Glendale Ave, Hattiesburg MS 39401	601-582-9300	R	4*	<.1
210	Longhorn Barbecue Production Center—*Walter Fette*	10420 E Montgomery Dr, Spokane Valley WA 99206	509-922-0702	R	4*	<.1
211	Hofmann Sausage Company Inc—*Rusty Flook*	6196 Eastern Ave, Syracuse NY 13211	315-437-7257	R	4*	<.1
212	Crawford Sausage Company Inc—*John Zicha*	2310 S Pulaski Rd, Chicago IL 60623	773-277-3095	R	4*	<.1
213	Carmelita Provision Company Inc—*Mario Lopez*	2901 W Floral Dr, Monterey Park CA 91754	323-262-6751	R	4*	<.1
214	Old Trapper Smoked Products Inc—*Dennis Evenson*	PO Box 730, Forest Grove OR 97116	503-359-5425	R	4*	<.1
215	Arnold's Meat Food Products Inc—*Sheldon Dosik*	274 Heyward St, Brooklyn NY 11206	718-963-1400	R	4*	<.1
216	Lipari's Sausage Inc—*Joe Manganella*	220 6th Ave, Hawthorne NJ 07506	973-304-0137	R	4*	<.1
217	Vandco Inc—*Robert Vollwerth*	PO Box 239, Hancock MI 49930	906-482-1550	R	4*	<.1
218	Kruse And Son Inc—*David Kruse*	PO Box 945, Monrovia CA 91017	626-358-4536	R	4*	<.1
219	Fratelli Beretta USA Inc—*Lorenzo Beretta*	210 Green St, South Hackensack NJ 07606	201-343-5161	R	3*	<.1
220	Country Snacks Manufacturing Inc—*Dwight Frazier*	513 Commerce Dr, Henderson NC 27537	252-433-4644	R	3*	<.1
221	Original Greek Specialties Inc—*Andre Papantoniou*	5757 W 59th St, Chicago IL 60638	773-735-2250	R	3*	<.1
222	Mosby Packing Company Inc—*Joseph Mosby*	PO Box 4253, Meridian MS 39304	601-485-5615	R	3*	<.1
223	Demes Gourmet Corp—*Randy Martin*	327 N State College Bl, Fullerton CA 92831	714-870-6040	R	3*	<.1
224	Miller's Country Hams Inc—*Jan Frick*	7110 Hwy 190, Dresden TN 38225	731-364-3940	R	3*	<.1
225	Counts Sausage Company Inc—*Jimmy Counts*	PO Box 390, Prosperity SC 29127	803-364-2392	R	3*	<.1
226	Lewis Sausage Company Inc—*Edgar Hardy*	PO Box 1296, Burgaw NC 28425	910-259-2642	R	3*	<.1
227	Ham Wayco Co—*George Worrell*	506 N William St, Goldsboro NC 27530	919-735-3962	R	3*	<.1
228	Silver Creek Specialty Meats Inc—*William Kramlich*	PO Box 3307, Oshkosh WI 54903	920-232-3581	R	3*	<.1
229	Wycen Foods Inc—*Arthur Leong*	560 Estabrook St, San Leandro CA 94577	510-351-1988	R	3*	<.1
230	Butcher Boy Meats LLC—*Dennis Lapensee*	20643 Stephens St, St Clair Shores MI 48080	586-771-9880	R	3*	<.1
231	Sheinman Provision Company Inc—*Stan Rultenberg*	4192 Viola St 96, Philadelphia PA 19104	215-473-7065	R	3*	<.1
232	Niester Sausage Co—*Randy Ray*	4426 E Hwy 377, Granbury TX 76049	817-573-0211	R	3*	<.1
233	Williams Incorporated T O—*Huyn Chay*	PO Box C, Portsmouth VA 23705	757-397-0771	R	3*	<.1
234	Baudin's Sausage Kitchen Inc—*Leona Baudin*	4636 Bridge St Hwy, Saint Martinville LA 70582	337-845-4920	R	3*	<.1
235	Bavaria Sausage Kitchen Inc—*Fred Voll*	PO Box 930275, Verona WI 53593	608-845-6691	R	3*	<.1
236	Jennings Premium Meats Inc—*Jason Jennings*	PO Box 116, New Franklin MO 65274	660-848-2229	R	3*	<.1
237	Rabideaux's Sausage Kitchen Inc—*Joseph Daigle*	105 Hwy 165, Iowa LA 70647	337-582-3184	R	3*	<.1
238	Martin Rosol's Inc—*Robert Rosol*	45 Grove St, New Britain CT 06053	860-223-2707	R	2*	<.1
239	Lisbon Sausage Company Inc—*Antonio Rodrigues*	PO Box 2028, New Bedford MA 02741	508-993-7645	R	2*	<.1
240	Domestic Casing Co—*Harold Klagsbald*	410 3rd Ave, Brooklyn NY 11215	718-522-1902	R	2*	<.1
241	Honey Bear Ham—*Julie Connell*	1160 W Grand Ave Ste 1, Chicago IL 60642	312-942-1160	R	2*	<.1

Rank	Company Name—*Executive Officer*	Address, City, State, Zip	Phone	Type	Fin	Empls
242	Lou's Sausage Ltd	14723 Miles Ave, Cleveland OH 44128	216-752-5060	R	2*	<.1
243	First Quality Sausage—*Donald Gehrig*	5110 E Washington Ave, Las Vegas NV 89110	702-399-7675	R	2*	<.1
244	Jesse's Fine Meats Inc—*Greg Allen*	PO Box 832, Cherokee IA 51012	712-225-3637	R	2*	<.1
245	Meat-O-Mat Corp—*Ron Fatato*	320 2nd St, Brooklyn NY 11215	718-965-7250	R	2*	<.1
246	Meyer's Sausage Co—*Betty Meyer*	PO Box 940, Elgin TX 78621	512-285-3331	R	1*	<.1
247	Cattaneo Brothers Inc—*Mike Kaney*	769 Caudill St, San Luis Obispo CA 93401	805-543-7188	R	1*	<.1
248	Mack's Liver Mush Inc—*B Mckee*	PO Box 227, Polkville NC 28136	704-434-6188	R	1*	<.1
249	Trailsteaks LLC	4295 Cromwell Rd Ste 2, Chattanooga TN 37421	423-648-7888	R	1*	.1
250	Real Kosher Sausage Company Inc—*Jacob Hill*	9 Euclid Ave, Newark NJ 07105	973-690-5394	R	1*	<.1
251	Blue and Gold Sausage Inc—*Donald Ramsey*	PO Box 657, Jones OK 73049	405-399-2954	R	1*	<.1

TOTALS: SIC 2013 Sausages & Other Prepared Meats
Companies: 251   98,575   164.2

2015 Poultry Slaughtering & Processing

Rank	Company Name—*Executive Officer*	Address, City, State, Zip	Phone	Type	Fin	Empls
1	Tyson Foods Inc—*Kathleen M Bader*	PO Box 2020, Springdale AR 72764		P	32,266	115.0
2	Pilgrim's Corp—*Bill Lovette*	1770 Promontory Cir, Greeley CO 80634		P	7,536	34.5
3	West Central Turkeys Inc—*Bob Tegt*	704 N Broadway, Pelican Rapids MN 56572	218-863-6816	S	6,515*	7.0
4	Perdue Inc—*James A Perdue*	PO Box 1656, Horsham PA 19044	410-543-3000	R	4,381*	20.0
5	Sanderson Farms Inc—*Joe F Sanderson Jr*	PO Box 988, Laurel MS 39441	601-649-4030	P	1,978	11.3
6	Michael Foods Inc—*James E Dwyer Jr*	301 Carlson Pkwy Ste 4, Minnetonka MN 55305	952-258-4000	R	1,543	3.8
7	Moroni Feed Co—*Kent Braton*	PO Box 368, Moroni UT 84646	435-436-8221	R	1,449*	.7
8	ConAgra Frozen Foods—*Gary Rodkin*	PO Box 3768, Omaha NE 68103	402-595-6000	D	1,400*	7.5
9	Foster Poultry Farms Inc—*Ron Foster*	PO Box 306, Livingston CA 95334	209-357-1121	R	1,382*	10.0
10	Cal-Maine Farms Inc—*Adolphus Baker*	PO Box 2960, Jackson MS 39207	601-948-6813	S	598	1.6
11	Fort Recovery Equity Inc—*William Glass*	PO Box 307, Fort Recovery OH 45846	419-375-4119	R	525*	.2
12	Jennie-O Turkey Store Inc—*Glenn Leitch*	PO Box 778, Willmar MN 56201	320-235-2622	S	467*	7.0
13	Fieldale Farms Corp—*Thomas Hensley*	PO Box 558, Baldwin GA 30511	706-778-5100	R	460*	4.8
14	Cagle's Inc—*J Douglas Cagle*	1385 Collier Rd NW, Atlanta GA 30318	404-355-2820	P	310	1.9
15	Marjac Holdings LLC—*Byron Phillips*	PO Box 1017, Gainesville GA 30503	770-531-5000	R	260*	1.2
16	George's Inc—*Gary C George*	PO Drawer G, Springdale AR 72765	479-927-7000	R	250*	2.0
17	Case Farms Of Ohio Inc—*Thomas Shelton*	PO Box 185, Winesburg OH 44690	330-359-7141	R	246*	.3
18	Gentrys Poultry Co—*Wes Gentry III*	PO Box 38, Ward SC 29166	864-445-2161	R	232*	.2
19	Triumph Foods LLC—*Steven Moore*	5302 Stockyards Expy, Saint Joseph MO 64504	816-396-2700	R	179*	2.0
20	West Liberty Foods LLC—*Rick Porter*	PO Box 318, West Liberty IA 52776	319-627-2126	R	156*	1.7
21	Sara Lee Refrigerated Foods Foodservice—*Brenda Barnes*	PO Box 25111, Cincinnati OH 45225		R	148*	.9
22	Primera Foods Corp—*Ron Ashton*	PO Box 373, Cameron WI 54822	715-458-4075	R	100*	.1
23	Farmers Pride Inc—*J Good*	PO Box 39, Fredericksburg PA 17026	717-865-6626	R	97*	1.1
24	Albertville Quality Foods Inc—*Don Haynie*	PO Box 756, Albertville AL 35950	256-840-9923	R	92*	.1
25	Farbest Foods Inc—*Ted J Seger*	PO Box 480, Huntingburg IN 47542	812-683-4200	R	85*	.5
26	Barber Foods—*David Barber*	PO Box 4821, Portland ME 04112	207-482-5500	R	67*	.7
27	Southern Hens Inc—*John Comino*	329 Moselle Seminary R, Moselle MS 39459	601-582-2262	R	58*	.6
28	Henningsen Foods Inc—*Gary Lorimor*	14334 Industrial Rd, Omaha NE 68144	402-330-2500	R	52*	.2
29	Suzanna's Kitchen Inc—*Bradley Howard*	4025 Buford Hwy, Duluth GA 30096	770-476-9900	R	50*	.2
30	RW Sauder Inc—*Paul Sauder*	570 Furnace Hills Pke, Lititz PA 17543	717-626-2074	R	50	.3
31	Sunrise Foods LLC	5000 Us Hwy 431, Albertville AL 35950	256-894-3339	R	44*	.5
32	Petaluma Acquistion LLC—*Susy Silva*	PO Box 7368, Petaluma CA 94955	707-763-1904	R	43*	.2
33	American Dehydrated Foods Inc—*Kurt Hellweg*	PO Box 4087, Springfield MO 65808	417-881-7755	R	38*	.2
34	Brakebush Brothers Inc—*William Brakebush*	N4993 6th Dr, Westfield WI 53964	608-296-2121	R	33*	.4
35	Tony Downs Foods Co—*Richard Downs*	54934 210th Ln, Mankato MN 56001	507-387-3663	R	32*	.4
36	Tur-Pak Foods Inc—*Stanley Sherman*	PO Box 116, Sioux City IA 51102	712-277-8484	R	31*	.2
37	Northern Pride Inc—*Glen Jaenicke*	PO Box 598, Thief River Falls MN 56701	218-681-1201	R	31*	.2
38	Holmes Foods Inc—*Phillip Morris*	101 S Liberty Ave, Nixon TX 78140	830-582-1551	R	30*	.3
39	Pvf Acquisitions LLC—*Elisa Allan*	1767 Denver W Marriott, Golden CO 80401	303-468-2500	R	28*	.2
40	Forest Packing Co—*Willis Haralson*	PO Box D, Forest MS 39074	601-469-3321	R	26*	.2
41	B and B Poultry Company Inc—*Benjamin Fisher*	PO Box 307, Norma NJ 08347	856-692-8893	R	25*	.2
42	Classic Egg Products Inc—*Paul Osborne*	409 N Wood St, Neosho MO 64850	417-451-2050	R	21*	.3
43	Michigan Turkey Producers Cooperative Inc—*Dan Lennon*	2140 Chicago Dr Sw, Wyoming MI 49519	616-245-2221	R	20*	.6
44	Culver Duck Farms Inc—*Herbert Culver*	PO Box 910, Middlebury IN 46540	574-825-9537	R	20*	.1
45	Eastern Shore Poultry Company Inc—*Harry Dukes*	21724 Broad Creek Ave, Georgetown DE 19947	302-855-1350	R	20*	.4
46	Estherville Foods Inc—*Phillip Sonstegard*	PO Box 158, Estherville IA 51334	712-362-3527	R	19*	.2
47	Fulton Processors Inc—*Valentino Petrusich*	PO Box 2, Fulton CA 95439	707-546-8482	R	19*	.1
48	Tip Top Poultry Inc—*Robin Burruss*	PO Box 6338, Marietta GA 30065	770-973-8070	R	15*	1.3
49	BE Products Inc—*Criag Ballas*	PO Box 2217, Zanesville OH 43702	740-453-0386	R	15*	.1
50	Whitewater Processing Co—*Kelly Kopp*	10964 Campbell Rd, Harrison OH 45030	513-367-4133	R	12*	.1
51	Butterfield Foods Co—*Richard Downs*	PO Box 229, Butterfield MN 56120	507-956-5103	R	12*	.1
52	ISE America Inc—*NH Ise*	PO Box 267, Galena MD 21635	410-755-6300	R	11	.1
53	H and L Poultry Processing LLC—*Paul Gant*	PO Box 905, Warren AR 71671	870-226-3339	R	10*	.3
54	Shelton's Poultry Inc—*Gary Flannigan*	204 N Loranne Ave, Pomona CA 91767	909-623-4361	R	10*	<.1
55	Oskaloosa Food Products Corp—*Blair Van Zetten*	PO Box 7, Oskaloosa IA 52577	641-673-3486	R	9*	.1
56	St Partners LLC—*David Cathey*	2118 Centennial Dr, Gainesville GA 30504	770-536-4520	R	9*	.1
57	Wapsie Produce Inc—*Marc Nichols*	PO Box 378, Decorah IA 52101	563-382-4271	R	9*	.1
58	Butcher Block Inc—*Joseph Frazzica*	14 Food Mart Rd, Boston MA 02118		R	8*	.1
59	Siouxpreme Egg Products Inc—*Phillip Songstegard*	PO Box 297, Sioux Center IA 51250	712-722-4787	R	7*	.1
60	Phoenix Foods Inc—*Paul Nicholson*	PO Box 23886, Nashville TN 37202	615-742-4989	R	7*	.1
61	Chick N Portions Inc—*Tom Higgobotham*	12725 NW 38th Ave, Opa Locka FL 33054	305-687-0000	R	7*	.1
62	Deb-El Foods Corp—*Elliot Gibber*	PO Box 876, Elizabeth NJ 07207	908-351-0330	R	7*	.1
63	Golden Platter Foods Inc—*Scott Bennett*	37 Tompkins Point Rd, Newark NJ 07114	973-242-0290	R	6*	.1
64	Schiltz Foods Inc—*Richard Schiltz*	PO Box 267, Sisseton SD 57262	605-698-7651	R	6*	<.1
65	Crescent Duck Farm Inc—*Douglas Corwin*	PO Box 500, Aquebogue NY 11931	631-722-8700	R	5*	.1
66	Bally United Produce Ltd—*Sergio Wong*	429 Forest Gate Dr, Garland TX 75042	972-487-7788	R	5*	<.1
67	Mr B's Of Abbotsford Inc—*Jim Brodhagen*	PO Box 91, Abbotsford WI 54405	715-223-3742	R	4*	<.1
68	Starkel Poultry Inc—*Elsie Starkel*	34303 27th Ave E, Roy WA 98580	253-845-2876	R	3*	<.1
69	Premium Poultry Co—*Chad Verdi*	PO Box 8828, Warwick RI 02888	401-467-3200	R	3*	<.1
70	Npc Processing Inc—*Daniel Desautels*	15 Holmes Rd, South Burlington VT 05403	802-660-0496	R	3*	<.1
71	Elwell Farms Inc—*Richard Elwell*	PO Box 11443, Santa Ana CA 92711	714-546-9280	R	3*	<.1
72	Greenberg Smoked Turkeys Inc—*Sam Greenberg*	PO Box 4818, Tyler TX 75712	903-595-0725	R	2*	<.1
73	Golden Duck Inc—*Binh Vo*	2619 Texas St, Houston TX 77003	713-222-9262	R	2*	<.1
74	Marshall Egg Products Inc—*Lois Rust*	123 N Miami Ave, Marshall MO 65340	660-886-3381	S	1*	<.1

Note: An asterisk (*) indicates an estimated financial figure. The company type code used is as follows: R = Private, P = Public, S = Private Subsidiary, B = Public Subsidiary, D = Division, J = Joint Venture, I = Investment Fund.

COMPANY RANKINGS BY SALES WITHIN 4-DIGIT SIC

Rank	Company Name—*Executive Officer*	Address, City, State, Zip	Phone	Type	Fin	Empls
75	Townsends Inc—*Tom Weisser*	22855 DuPont Blvd, Georgetown DE 19947	302-855-7100	R	<1	4.0

TOTALS: SIC 2015 Poultry Slaughtering & Processing
Companies: 75   63,603   248.8

2021 Creamery Butter

Rank	Company Name—*Executive Officer*	Address, City, State, Zip	Phone	Type	Fin	Empls
1	Land O'Lakes Inc—*Chris Policinski*	PO Box 64101, Saint Paul MN 55164	651-481-2222	R	11,100	9.0
2	Dairy Farmers of America Inc—*Rick Smith*	10220 N Ambassador Dr, Kansas City MO 64153	816-801-6455	R	2,521*	3.5
3	Belgium Co—*Nino Mazzaro*	1100 Grape Ave, Saint Cloud FL 34769	407-957-1886	R	145*	<.1
4	Grassland Dairy Products Inc—*Dallas Wuethrich*	PO Box 160, Greenwood WI 54437	715-267-6182	R	39*	.2
5	Graf Creamery Inc—*Jim Bleick*	PO Box 49, Zachow WI 54182		R	29*	.1
6	Wuethrich Brothers-Nebraska LLC—*Tayt Wuethrich*	N8790 Fairground Ave, Greenwood WI 54437	715-267-5181	R	8*	.1

TOTALS: SIC 2021 Creamery Butter
Companies: 6   13,842   12.9

2022 Cheese—Natural & Processed

Rank	Company Name—*Executive Officer*	Address, City, State, Zip	Phone	Type	Fin	Empls
1	Kraft Foods Inc—*Irene Rosenfeld*	3 Lakes Dr, Northfield IL 60093	847-646-2000	P	49,207	127.0
2	Kraft Foods North America Inc—*W Anthony Vernon* Kraft Foods Inc	3 Lakes Dr, Northfield IL 60093	847-646-2000	S	21,907	N/A
3	Schreiber Foods Inc—*Mike Haddad*	PO Box 19010, Green Bay WI 54307	920-437-7601	R	3,000*	5.0
4	Leprino Foods Co—*James Leprino*	1830 W 38th Ave, Denver CO 80211	303-480-2600	R	2,239*	3.0
5	Great Lakes Cheese Company Inc—*Gary Vanic*	PO Box 1806, Hiram OH 44234	440-834-2500	R	2,150	1.7
6	Hilmar Cheese Company Inc—*John Jeter*	PO Box 910, Hilmar CA 95324	209-667-6076	R	1,042*	1.0
7	Swiss Colony Inc—*John Baumann*	PO Box 2816, Monroe WI 53566	608-328-8400	R	600*	1.2
8	Zausner Foods Corp—*James M Williams*	400 S Custer Ave, New Holland PA 17557	717-355-8505	S	504*	.4
9	Lactalis American Group Inc—*Frederick Bouisset*	2376 S Park Ave, Buffalo NY 14220	716-823-6262	R	168*	1.5
10	Conagra Dairy Foods Company Inc—*Richard Scalise*	215 W Diehl Rd, Naperville IL 60563	630-857-1000	R	154*	1.6
11	Gehl Foods Inc—*John Gehl*	PO Box 1004, Germantown WI 53022	262-251-8570	R	150*	.2
12	Le Sueur Cheese Co—*Marc Davis*	11000 W 78th St Ste 21, Eden Prairie MN 55344	952-914-0400	S	119*	.1
13	Minerva Cheese Factory Inc—*Phil Mueller*	PO Box 60, Minerva OH 44657	330-868-4196	R	109*	.1
14	Miceli Dairy Products Co—*Joseph Miceli*	2721 E 90th St, Cleveland OH 44104	216-791-6222	R	105*	.2
15	Ellsworth Cooperative Creamery—*Paul Bauer*	PO Box 610, Ellsworth WI 54011	715-273-4311	R	96*	.1
16	Weyauwega Star Dairy Inc—*James Knaus*	PO Box 658, Weyauwega WI 54983	920-867-2870	R	85*	.1
17	Burnett Dairy Co-Operative Association—*Dan Strabel*	11631 State Rd 70, Grantsburg WI 54840	715-689-2468	R	85*	.2
18	Berner Food and Beverage Inc—*Stephen Kneubuehl*	2034 E Factory Rd, Dakota IL 61018	815-563-4222	R	78*	.2
19	Emmi Roth USA Inc—*Fermo Jaeckle*	657 2nd St, Monroe WI 53566	608-329-7666	R	69*	.1
20	McCadam Cheese Company Inc—*Brian Lee*	1 Home Farm Way, Montpelier VT 05602		R	66*	.2
21	Nelson-Ricks Creamery Co—*Calvin L Nelson*	1755 Freemont Dr, Salt Lake City UT 84104	801-364-3607	R	66*	<.1
22	Ariza Cheese Co—*Ausencio Ariza*	7602 Jackson St, Paramount CA 90723	562-630-4144	R	64*	<.1
23	Comstock Dairy Enterprises Inc—*Tony Curella*	PO Box 36, Comstock WI 54826	715-822-2437	R	58*	.1
24	Klondike Cheese Co—*Ronald Buholzer*	PO Box 234, Monroe WI 53566	608-325-3021	R	51*	.1
25	Tillamook County Creamery Association—*James Mcmullen*	4185 Hwy 101 N, Tillamook OR 97141	503-842-4481	R	51*	.6
26	Sierra Cheese Manufacturing Co—*Charlene Franco*	916 S Santa Fe Ave, Compton CA 90221	310-635-1216	R	51*	<.1
27	Biery Cheese Co—*Dennis Biery*	6544 Paris Ave, Louisville OH 44641	330-875-3381	R	47*	.3
28	Sartori Food Corp—*Jeffrey Schwager*	PO Box 258, Plymouth WI 53073	920-893-6061	R	42*	.3
29	Alpine Cheese Co—*Robert Ramseyer*	PO Box 181, Winesburg OH 44690	330-359-6291	R	35*	<.1
30	Gossner Foods Inc—*Dolores Wheeler*	PO Box 3247, Logan UT 84323	435-752-9365	R	32*	.4
31	Belgioioso Cheese Inc—*Errico Auricchio*	4200 Main St, Green Bay WI 54311	920-863-3003	R	32*	.2
32	Trega Foods Ltd—*Douglas Simon*	PO Box 223, Little Chute WI 54140	920-788-2115	R	29*	.3
33	Turner Dairy Farms Inc—*Charles Turner*	1049 Jefferson Rd, Pittsburgh PA 15235	412-372-2211	R	29*	.2
34	Saputo Cheese And Protein LLC—*Mike Goad*	800 E Paige Ave, Tulare CA 93274	559-687-8411	S	26*	.3
35	Galaxy Nutritional Foods Inc—*Michael E Broll*	66 Whitecap Dr, North Kingstown RI 02852	401-667-5000	R	25*	<.1
36	Valley Queen Cheese Factory Inc—*Mark Leddy*	PO Box 351, Milbank SD 57252	605-432-4563	R	23*	.1
37	Franklin Foods Inc—*Jon Gutknecht*	PO Box 486, Enosburg Falls VT 05450	802-933-4338	R	22*	.1
38	Excelpro Inc—*Peter Ernster*	3760 E 26th St, Vernon CA 90058	323-415-8544	R	22*	<.1
39	Terranova Of California Inc—*Frank Terranova*	PO Box 578, Newman CA 95360	209-862-1732	S	20*	.1
40	Baker Cheese Factory Inc—*Richard Baker*	N5279 County Rd G, Saint Cloud WI 53079	920-477-7871	R	19*	.1
41	Cedar Grove Cheese Inc—*Robert Wills*	PO Box 185, Plain WI 53577	608-546-5284	R	12*	<.1
42	Sun-Re Cheese Corp—*Thomas Aiello Jr*	178 Lenker Ave, Sunbury PA 17801	570-286-1511	R	9*	.1
43	Old Fashioned Foods Inc—*Bernard Youso*	PO Box 111, Mayville WI 53050	920-387-4444	R	9*	.1
44	Aunt Lizzie's Cheese Straws Inc—*Ginna Kelly*	1531 Overton Park Ave, Memphis TN 38112	901-266-3372	R	8*	<.1
45	Rizo-Lopez Foods Inc—*Ivan Rizo*	PO Box 797, Riverbank CA 95367	209-869-5232	R	8*	.1
46	Masson Cheese Corp—*Morris Farinella*	6180 Alcoa Ave, Vernon CA 90058	323-583-1251	R	8*	<.1
47	Wohlt Cheese Corp—*Marilyn Taylor*	PO Box 203, New London WI 54961	920-982-9000	R	8*	.1
48	A and M Cheese Co—*Antonio Sofo*	253 Waggoner Blvd, Toledo OH 43612	419-476-8369	R	7*	.1
49	Lewis County Dairy Corp—*Moshe Banayan*	110 Beard St, Brooklyn NY 11231	718-243-0400	R	7*	.1
50	Twin County Dairy Inc—*John Roetlin*	2206 540th St Sw, Kalona IA 52247	319-656-2776	R	7*	.1
51	Biazzo Dairy Products Inc—*John Iapichino*	1145 Edgewater Ave, Ridgefield NJ 07657	201-941-6800	R	7*	.1
52	Simons Speicalty Cheese—*Doug Simon*	2735 Freedom Rd, Appleton WI 54913	920-788-6311	R	6*	.1
53	Original Herkimer County Cheese Company Inc—*Sheldon Basloe*	PO Box 310, Herkimer NY 13350	315-895-7428	R	6*	.1
54	Deutsch Kase Haus Inc—*Richard Guggisber* Guggisberg Cheese Inc	11275 W 250 N, Middlebury IN 46540	574-825-9511	S	6*	.1
55	Cady Cheese Factory Inc—*Dale Marcott*	126 State Rd 128, Wilson WI 54027	715-772-4218	R	6*	<.1
56	Hans Rothenbuhler and Son Inc—*John Rothenbuhler*	15815 Nauvoo Rd, Middlefield OH 44062	440-632-5228	R	6*	<.1
57	Thiel Cheese Inc—*Stephen Thiel*	N7630 County Rd Bb, Hilbert WI 54129	920-989-1440	R	6*	.1
58	Maytag Dairy Farms Inc—*James Stevens*	PO Box 806, Newton IA 50208	641-792-1133	R	5*	.1
59	Bunker Hill Cheese Company Inc—*Peter Dauwalder*	6005 County Rd 77, Millersburg OH 44654	330-893-2131	R	5*	.1
60	Antonio Mozzarella Factory Inc—*Thomas Pugliese*	631 Frelinghuysen Ave, Newark NJ 07114	973-353-9411	R	5*	<.1
61	Guggisberg Cheese Inc—*Richard Guggisberg*	5060 State Rte 557, Millersburg OH 44654	330-893-2500	R	5*	.1
62	Cedar Valley Cheese Inc—*Jeff Hiller*	W3111 Jay Rd, Belgium WI 53004	920-994-4415	R	5*	<.1
63	Westby Co-Operative Creamery—*Mark Levendoski*	401 S Main St, Westby WI 54667	608-634-3181	R	5*	<.1
64	Avanti Foods Co—*Anthony Zueger*	PO Box 457, Walnut IL 61376	815-379-2155	R	5*	<.1
65	F Cappiello Dairy Products Inc—*Peter Cappiello*	115 Van Guysling Ave, Schenectady NY 12305	518-374-5064	R	5*	<.1
66	Edelweis Cheese Company Inc—*Gordon Moen*	M447 County Trak C, Marshfield WI 54449	715-687-4148	R	4*	<.1
67	Springside Cheese Corp—*Wayne Hintz*	7989 Arndt Rd, Oconto Falls WI 54154	920-829-6395	R	4*	<.1
68	Capital Foods Inc—*Joseph Falcone*	1701 E Elizabeth Ave, Linden NJ 07036	908-587-9050	R	3*	<.1
69	Holmes Cheese Co—*Robert Ramseyer*	9444 State Rte 39, Millersburg OH 44654	330-674-6451	R	3*	<.1
70	Warren Cheese Plant Inc—*John Bussman*	PO Box 686, Warren IL 61087	815-745-2627	R	3*	<.1
71	Castle Cheese Inc—*George Myrter*	PO Box 378, Portersville PA 16051	724-368-3850	R	3*	<.1
72	Montena/Taranto Foods Inc—*Wade Montena*	400 Victoria Ter, Ridgefield NJ 07657	201-943-8484	R	3*	<.1
73	Zimmerman Cheese Inc—*Mark Witke*	6853 State Rd 78, South Wayne WI 53587	608-968-3414	R	3*	<.1

Rank	Company Name—Executive Officer	Address, City, State, Zip	Phone	Type	Fin	Empls
74	Mancuso Cheese Co—Michael Berta	612 Mills Rd, Joliet IL 60433	815-722-2475	R	3*	<.1
75	Cacique USA Inc—Jose Cuiriz	5631 N Golden State Bl, Fresno CA 93722	559-276-5147	R	3*	<.1
76	Chalet Cheese Coop—Myron Olson	N4858 County Rd N, Monroe WI 53566	608-325-4343	R	2*	<.1
77	Laura Chenel's Chevre Inc—Hugues Triballat	22085 Carneros Vinyrd, Sonoma CA 95476	707-996-1252	R	2*	<.1
78	Widmer's Cheese Cellars Inc—Joseph Widmer	PO Box 127, Theresa WI 53091	920-488-2503	R	2*	<.1
79	Pearl Valley Cheese Inc—John Stalder	54760 Township Rd 90, Fresno OH 43824	740-545-6002	R	2*	<.1
80	Via Cheese LLC	12 Jonergin Dr, Swanton VT 05488	802-868-7301	R	2*	<.1
81	Middlefield Original Cheese Coop—Eli Miller	PO Box 237, Middlefield OH 44062	440-632-5567	R	2*	<.1
82	Taylor Cheese Corp—James Taylor	PO Box 639, Weyauwega WI 54983	920-867-2337	R	2*	<.1
83	Valley Cheese Inc—Steve Majors	PO Box 9, Spring Valley MN 55975	507-346-2591	R	2*	<.1
84	Edelweiss Townhall Cheese—Bruce Workman	890 N Twin Grove Rd, Monroe WI 53566	608-938-4094	R	2*	<.1
85	Graham Cheese Corp—Ura Miller	Hwy 57 N, Elnora IN 47529	812-692-5237	R	2*	<.1
86	Mozzarella Co—Paula Lambert	2944 Elm St, Dallas TX 75226	214-741-4072	R	2*	<.1
87	Marin French Cheese Company Inc—James Boyce	7500 Red Hill Rd, Petaluma CA 94952	707-762-6001	R	1*	<.1
88	Lifeline Food Company Inc—Jone Chappell	426 Orange Ave, Seaside CA 93955	831-899-5040	R	1*	<.1
89	Gilman Cheese Corp—Thomas Hand	PO Box 187, Gilman WI 54433	715-447-8241	R	1*	.1
90	Loleta Cheese Factory—Lowell Bright	252 Loleta Dr, Loleta CA 95551	707-733-5470	R	1*	<.1
91	Pace Dairy Foods Co—Jim Lehman	2700 Valleyhigh Dr NW, Rochester MN 55901	507-288-6315	S	N/A	.4

TOTALS: SIC 2022 Cheese— Natural & Processed
Companies: 91   82,897   149.1

2023 Dry, Condensed & Evaporated Dairy Products

Rank	Company Name—Executive Officer	Address, City, State, Zip	Phone	Type	Fin	Empls
1	Rich Products Corp—Bill Gisel	1 Robert Rich Way, Buffalo NY 14213	716-878-8000	R	2,900	8.0
2	First District Association—Clinton Fall	101 S Swift Ave, Litchfield MN 55355	320-693-3236	R	391*	.2
3	Guida's Milk and Ice Cream Co—Michael Guida	433 Park St, New Britain CT 06051	860-224-2404	R	314*	.4
4	Kohler Mix Specialties LLC—JD Clarkson	4041 Hwy 61, White Bear Lake MN 55110	651-426-1633	S	300*	.2
5	Synutra International Inc—Liang Zhang	2275 Research Blvd Ste, Rockville MD 20850	301-840-3888	P	249	5.2
6	O-At-Ka Milk Products Cooperative Inc—Robert Hall	PO Box 718, Batavia NY 14021	585-343-0536	R	237*	.3
7	Commercial Creamery Co—Michael Gilmartin	PO Box 93, Spokane WA 99210	509-747-4131	R	160*	.1
8	CFI Of Wisconsin Inc—Tom Miskowski	400 Century Ct, Sparta WI 54656	608-269-1900	S	150*	.3
9	Davisco Foods International Inc—Mark Davis	11000 W 78th St Ste 21, Eden Prairie MN 55344	952-914-0400	R	88*	<.1
10	Dietrich's Milk Products LLC	100 Mckinley Ave, Reading PA 19605	610-929-5736	R	73*	.2
11	Crest Foods Company Inc—Jeffery Meiners	PO Box 371, Ashton IL 61006	815-453-7411	R	64*	.5
12	Foster Dairy Farms—Jeff Foster	572 Hwy 1, Fortuna CA 95540	707-725-6182	R	48*	.3
13	Bongards' Creameries—Brent Ziegler	13200 County Rd 51, Norwood MN 55368	952-466-5521	R	47*	.3
14	Milk Products LLC—David Kuehnel	PO Box 150, Chilton WI 53014	920-849-2348	R	44*	.1
15	Standard Candy Company Inc—James Spradley	PO Box 101025, Nashville TN 37224	615-889-6360	R	41*	.4
16	Valentine Enterprises Inc—Donald Mcdaniel	940 Collins Hill Rd, Lawrenceville GA 30043	770-995-0661	R	33*	.2
17	Food Sciences Corp—Robert Schwartz	821 E Gate Dr, Mount Laurel NJ 08054	856-778-9200	R	24*	.2
18	Dakota Country Cheese Company Inc—Virgil Johnson	PO Box 488, Mandan ND 58554	701-663-0246	R	15*	<.1
19	Glasgow Spray-Dry Inc—Billy Williams	1117 Cleveland Ave, Glasgow KY 42141	270-651-2146	R	14*	.1
20	Maple Island Inc—Daniel O'brien	2497 7th Ave E Ste 105, Saint Paul MN 55109	651-773-1000	R	14*	.1
21	Elgin Dairy Foods Inc—Ed Gignac	3707 W Harrison St, Chicago IL 60624	630-408-9222	R	12*	.1
22	Tova Industrics LLC—Theresa Overberz	PO Box 24410, Louisville KY 40224	502-267-7333	R	9*	.1
23	Farbest-Tallman Foods Corp—Daniel Meloro	160 Summit Ave, Montvale NJ 07645	201-573-4900	R	9*	.1
24	Vern Dale Products Inc—Laverne Johnson	8445 Lyndon St, Detroit MI 48238	313-834-4190	R	6*	<.1
25	Farmers Cooperative Creamery Of Mcminnville Oregon—Michael Anderson	700 Ne Hwy 99w, Mcminnville OR 97128	503-472-2157	R	5*	<.1
26	Jackson-Mitchell Inc—Robert Jackson	PO Box 934, Turlock CA 95381	209-667-2019	R	5*	<.1
27	Command Nutritionals LLC—Scott Biedron	10 Washington Ave Ste, Fairfield NJ 07004	973-227-8210	R	5*	<.1
28	Tropical Oasis LLC—Chris Maher	3602 N Hwy 121, Melissa TX 75454		R	4*	<.1
29	Lynn Protein Inc—William Schwantes	W1933 Us Hwy 10, Granton WI 54436	715-238-7129	R	4*	<.1
30	Caps and Tabs Inc—Jeffery Grossman	3111 Camino Del Rio N, San Diego CA 92108	619-285-5400	R	3*	<.1
31	Midor- Ltd—Debra Parrish	PO Box 168, Elroy WI 53929	608-462-8275	R	3*	<.1
32	Grow Company Inc—Andrew Szalay	55 Railroad Ave, Ridgefield NJ 07657	201-941-8777	R	3*	<.1
33	Mbp Company LLC—Mike Thomas	PO Box 15, Harrison NY 10528	914-967-2442	R	3*	<.1
34	Meadowvale Inc—Steve Steinwart	109 Beaver St, Yorkville IL 60560	630-553-0202	R	2*	<.1
35	Vitamin Power Incororated—David Friedlander	75 Commerce Dr, Hauppauge NY 11788	631-676-5790	R	1*	<.1

TOTALS: SIC 2023 Dry, Condensed & Evaporated Dairy Products
Companies: 35   5,277   17.4

2024 Ice Cream & Frozen Desserts

Rank	Company Name—Executive Officer	Address, City, State, Zip	Phone	Type	Fin	Empls
1	Dreyer's Grand Ice Cream Holdings Inc—Mike Mitchell	5929 College Ave, Oakland CA 94618	510-652-8187	S	1,594*	6.0
2	J and J Snack Foods Corp/Mia—Gerald B Shreiber	PO Box 3777, Scranton PA 18505	570-457-7431	S	1,241*	2.3
3	Haagen-Dazs Company Inc—Mike Paxton	5929 College Ave, Oakland CA 94618	763-293-2691	S	883*	1.6
4	Wells' Dairy Inc—Mike Wells	PO Box 1310, Le Mars IA 51031	712-546-4000	R	729*	2.5
5	Roberts Dairy Co—Tim Nelson	PO Box 3825, Omaha NE 68103	402-344-4321	R	260*	.9
6	Bruster's Real Ice Cream Inc—Jim Sahene	1005 S Bee St, Pittsburgh PA 15220	412-919-2100	R	240*	.3
7	TCBY Enterprises Inc—Herren Hickingbotham	2855 E Cottonwood Pky, Salt Lake City UT 84121	801-736-5600	R	109*	<.1
8	Fieldbrook Foods Corp—Kenneth Johnson	1 Ice Cream Dr, Dunkirk NY 14048	716-366-5400	R	104*	.4
9	Baldwin Richardson Foods Co—Eric G Johnson	20201 S LaGrange Rd St, Frankfort IL 60423	815-464-9994	R	103*	.2
10	Hershey Creamery Co—George Holder	301 S Cameron St, Harrisburg PA 17101	717-238-8134	R	94*	.5
11	Perry's Ice Cream Company Inc—Robert Denning	1 Ice Cream Plz, Akron NY 14001	716-542-5492	R	86*	.3
12	Ben and Jerry's Homemade Inc—Jostein Solheim	30 Community Dr, South Burlington VT 05403	802-846-1500	S	85*	.3
13	Turner Holdings LLC—Ed Fleming	653 Turner Ln, Covington TN 38019	901-476-2643	R	77*	.9
14	House Of Flavors Inc—Whit Gallagher	110 N William St, Ludington MI 49431	231-845-7369	R	66*	.2
15	Asael Farr and Sons Co—Michael Farr	2575 S 300 W, Salt Lake City UT 84115	801-484-8724	R	62*	.1
16	Fike's Dairy Inc—Joseph Carson	PO Box 1247, Uniontown PA 15401	724-438-8581	S	59*	.2
17	Big Apple Dairy Desserts—Terry Tucci	4175 Veterans Hwy, Ronkonkoma NY 11779	631-585-0900	S	53*	.1
18	Jel Sert Co—Gary Ricco	PO Box 261, West Chicago IL 60186	630-231-7590	R	51*	.2
19	Yocream International Inc—John N Hanna	5858 NE 87th Ave, Portland OR 97220	503-256-3754	R	51	.1
20	Cold Stone Creamery—Dan Beem	9311 E Via de Ventura, Scottsdale AZ 85258	480-362-4800	S	49*	.2
21	Yarnell Ice Cream Company Inc—Albert Yarnell	PO Box 78, Searcy AR 72145	501-268-2414	R	37*	.2
22	Royal Ice Cream Co—Rochelle Roth	6200 Euclid Ave, Cleveland OH 44103	216-432-1144	R	37*	.1
23	Mini Melts—Tom Mosey	245 Asylum St, Norwich CT 06360	860-889-7300	R	36*	.1
24	Graeter's Manufacturing Co—Katherine Graeter	2145 Reading Rd, Cincinnati OH 45202	513-721-3323	R	33*	.4
25	Dippin' Dots Inc—Curt Jones	PO Box 890743, Charlotte NC 28289	270-443-8994	R	30*	.2
26	Luvel Dairy Products Inc—James H Briscoe	PO Box 1229, Kosciusko MS 39090	662-289-3344	R	25*	.1
27	Rich Ice Cream Co—John Rich	2915 S Dixie Hwy, West Palm Beach FL 33405	561-833-7585	R	22*	.1

Note: An asterisk (*) indicates an estimated financial figure. The company type code used is as follows: R = Private, P = Public, S = Private Subsidiary, B = Public Subsidiary, D = Division, J = Joint Venture, I = Investment Fund.

COMPANY RANKINGS BY SALES WITHIN 4-DIGIT SIC

Rank	Company Name—*Executive Officer*	Address, City, State, Zip	Phone	Type	Fin	Empls
28	Calip Dairies Operating Co Big Apple Dairy Desserts	4175 Veterans Memorial, Ronkonkoma NY 11779	631-585-0900	S	21*	<.1
29	Philly's Famous Water Ice Inc—*Jan Grywczynski*	1102 N 28th St, Tampa FL 33605	813-353-8645	R	19*	.1
30	Newport Creamery LLC—*Nicholas Janikies*	35 Sockanosset Cross R, Cranston RI 02920	401-946-4000	R	18*	.4
31	Tofutti Brands Inc—*David Mintz*	PO Box 786, Cranford NJ 07016	908-272-2400	P	18	<.1
32	Deep Foods Inc—*Arvind Amin*	1090 Springfield Rd St, Union NJ 07083	908-810-7500	R	16*	.2
33	Klinke Brothers Ice Cream Co—*John Klinke*	2450 Scaper St, Memphis TN 38114	901-743-8250	R	16*	.1
34	Baskin Robbins—*Jon Luther*	130 Royall St, Canton MA 02021	781-737-3000	S	15*	.1
35	Natural Fruit Corp—*Simon Bravo*	770 W 20th St, Hialeah FL 33010	305-887-7525	R	14*	<.1
36	Lappert's Ice Cream and Coffee—*Michael Lappert*	223 Ohio Ave, Richmond CA 94804	510-231-2340	R	13*	.1
37	Belfonte Ice Cream Co—*Roger Capps*	1511 Brooklyn Ave, Kansas City MO 64127	816-483-9070	S	13*	.1
38	Heisler's Cloverleaf Dairy Inc—*Leonard Ostergard*	743 Catawissa Rd, Tamaqua PA 18252	570-668-3399	R	11*	.1
39	Reinhold Ice Cream Co—*Robert Mandell*	800 Fulton St, Pittsburgh PA 15233	412-321-7600	R	11*	.1
40	Olympic Ice Cream Company Inc—*Mike Barone*	12910 91st Ave, Richmond Hill NY 11418	718-849-6200	R	10*	.1
41	Good Old Days Foods Inc—*Phillip Steele*	PO Box 191470, Little Rock AR 72219	501-565-1257	R	9*	.1
42	Rhino Foods Inc—*Ted Castle*	79 Industrial Pky, Burlington VT 05401	802-862-0252	R	9*	.1
43	Ziegenfelder Co—*Lisa Railing*	PO Box 6645, Wheeling WV 26003	304-232-6360	R	9*	.1
44	Caspers Ice Cream Inc—*Paul Merrill*	11805 N 200 E, Richmond UT 84333	435-258-2477	R	8*	.1
45	Kopp's Frozen Custard	18880 W Bluemound Rd, Brookfield WI 53045	262-789-9490	R	8*	<.1
46	Guernsey Dairy Stores Inc—*Martin Mcguire*	21300 Novi Rd, Northville MI 48167	248-349-1466	R	8*	.1
47	Nadolife Inc—*David Spatafore*	PO Box 182225, Coronado CA 92178	619-522-6890	R	7*	.1
48	Royalston Foods LLC—*John Kenney*	2327 Wycliff St Ste 1, Saint Paul MN 55114	651-312-0912	R	7*	.1
49	Driggs Farms of Indiana Inc—*Howard Driggs*	PO Box 820, Decatur IN 46733	260-724-2136	R	7*	.1
50	Superior Dairy Products Co—*Tim Jones*	325 N Douty St, Hanford CA 93230	559-582-0481	R	7*	<.1
51	Independent Dairy Inc—*Michael Cheney*	126 N Telegraph Rd, Monroe MI 48162	734-241-6016	R	7*	.1
52	Washburn's Dairy Inc—*Richard Washburn*	PO Box 551, Gloversville NY 12078	518-725-0629	R	5*	.1
53	Rainbow Glacier Inc—*Jim Jackson*	PO Box 2289, Lake Oswego OR 97035	360-693-1605	R	5*	.1
54	Triple Sondae Enterprises—*Clark Goehring*	29337 Fresno Ave, Shafter CA 93263	661-746-3692	R	5*	.1
55	Jms Ices Inc—*Michael Scolaro*	501 Port Richmond Ave, Staten Island NY 10302	718-448-0853	R	5*	<.1
56	Titusville Dairy Products Co—*Charles Turner*	PO Box 186, Titusville PA 16354	814-827-1833	R	4*	<.1
57	Ciao Bella Gelato Company Inc—*Charlie Apt*	25A Vreeland Rd Ste 10, Florham Park NJ 07932	973-373-1200	S	4*	.1
58	Sugar Creek Foods International Inc—*Scott Horn*	PO Box 747, Russellville AR 72811	479-968-1005	R	4*	<.1
59	Jamal's Enterprises Inc—*Charles Shamieh*	868 Burlway Rd, Burlingame CA 94010	650-347-2122	R	4*	<.1
60	La Brisa Ice Cream Company LLC—*Jose Flores*	7842 Canal St, Houston TX 77012	713-926-3460	R	4*	<.1
61	Greenwood Ice Cream Company Limited Inc—*Mitchell Williams*	4829 Peachtree Rd, Atlanta GA 30341	770-455-6166	R	4*	<.1
62	Angelo's Italian Ices—*Angelo Rana*	1548 E Cocopah St, Phoenix AZ 85034	602-254-2125	R	3*	<.1
63	Balian Ice Cream CoInc—*Alexander Balian*	2916 E Olympic Blvd 30, Los Angeles CA 90023	323-261-6111	R	3*	<.1
64	Fono Unlimited Inc—*Paulette Fono*	99 Stanford Shopping C, Palo Alto CA 94304	650-322-4664	R	3*	<.1
65	Schwan's Sales Inc—*David Belcher*	5 Dean Dr Ne, Cartersville GA 30121	770-382-2432	R	3*	<.1
66	Leon's Frozen Custard—*Ronald Schneider*	3131 S 27th St, Milwaukee WI 53215	414-383-1784	R	3*	<.1
67	Garber Ice Cream Co—*David Garber*	PO Box 3265, Winchester VA 22604	540-662-5422	R	3*	<.1
68	Pierre's French Ice Cream Inc—*Sol Roth*	6519 Carnegie Ave, Cleveland OH 44103	216-431-2555	Π	3*	<.1
69	Express Corde Enterprises LLC	931 S Cypress St, La Habra CA 90631	714-680-6558	R	3*	<.1
70	Warwick Ice Cream Co—*Gerard Bucci*	743 Bald Hill Rd, Warwick RI 02886	401-821-8403	R	2*	<.1
71	Lezza Spumoni And Desserts Inc—*Edward Lezza*	4009 Saint Charles Rd, Bellwood IL 60104	708-547-5969	R	2*	<.1
72	Culvers Frozen Custard—*Liza Metz*	219 Central Bridge St, Wausau WI 54401	715-845-6994	R	2*	<.1
73	Ray's Ice Cream Company Inc—*Dale Stevens*	4233 Coolidge Hwy, Royal Oak MI 48073	248-549-5256	R	2*	<.1
74	Homer's Ice Cream Inc—*Stephen Poulos*	1237 Green Bay Rd, Wilmette IL 60091	847-251-0477	R	2*	<.1
75	Sunset Ice Cream—*John Fritz*	1849 Lycoming Creek Rd, Williamsport PA 17701	570-326-7475	R	2*	<.1
76	Gifford's Dairy Inc—*Roger Gifford*	25 Hathaway St, Skowhegan ME 04976	207-474-2604	R	2*	<.1
77	Big Dipper—*Sharon Roberge*	222 Rte 108, Somersworth NH 03878	603-742-7075	R	2*	<.1
78	Moomers Homemade Ice Cream LLC—*Nancy Plummer*	7263 N Long Lake Rd, Traverse City MI 49685	231-941-4122	R	2*	<.1
79	Kellerhaus Inc—*Bettina Potter*	PO Box 5337, Laconia NH 03247	603-366-4466	R	1*	<.1
80	Purity Ice Cream Company Inc—*Bruce Lane*	700 Cascadilla St, Ithaca NY 14850	607-272-1545	R	1*	<.1
81	Uncle Harry's Fine Food Products—*Mike Artery*	100 S Jefferson St, Waterford WI 53185	262-534-4757	R	1*	<.1
82	Milk Products LLC—*Tom Neitzel*	5327 S Lamar St, Dallas TX 75215	214-565-0332	S	1*	<.1
83	Dr Mike's Ice Cream Inc—*Robert Allison*	158 Greenwood Ave, Bethel CT 06801	203-792-4388	R	<1*	<.1

TOTALS: SIC 2024 Ice Cream & Frozen Desserts
Companies: 83   6,583   21.0

2026 Fluid Milk

Rank	Company Name—*Executive Officer*	Address, City, State, Zip	Phone	Type	Fin	Empls
1	Dean Foods Co—*Gregg L Engles*	2711 N Haskell Ave Ste, Dallas TX 75204	214-303-3400	P	12,123	25.8
2	Southern Foods Group LP Dean Foods Co	PO Box 279000, Dallas TX 75227	214-824-8163	S	6,883*	5.0
3	Prairie Farms Dairy Inc—*Ed Mullins*	1100 N Broadway St, Carlinville IL 62626	217-854-2547	R	6,467*	5.0
4	Crystal Cream and Butter Co—*Michael Newell*	8340 Belvedere Ave, Sacramento CA 95826	916-444-7200	R	4,907*	.6
5	HP Hood LLC—*John A Kaneb*	6 Kimball Ln Ste 400, Lynnfield MA 01940	617-887-3000	R	2,200*	4.5
6	Foremost Farms USA Coop—*David Fuhrmann*	PO Box 111, Baraboo WI 53913	608-355-8700	R	1,480*	1.4
7	Dairy Fresh Corp Cowarts Div	509 MLK Dr, Prichard AL 36610		D	1,053*	.7
8	Barber Milk Inc—*Johnny Collins* Dean Foods Co	36 Barber Ct, Birmingham AL 35209	205-942-2351	S	906*	.8
9	United Dairymen Of Arizona—*Keith Murfield*	PO Box 26877, Tempe AZ 85285	480-966-7211	R	613*	.2
10	Instantwhip Foods Inc—*Douglas A Smith*	PO Box 333, Columbus OH 43216	614-488-2536	R	604*	.6
11	Hiland Dairy Foods Company LLC—*Gary Aggus*	PO Box 2270, Springfield MO 65801	417-862-9311	R	589*	1.3
12	Dannon Company Inc—*Gustavo Valle*	PO Box 90296, Allentown PA 18109		S	521*	.9
13	United Dairy Inc—*Joseph Carson*	PO Box 280, Martins Ferry OH 43935	740-633-1451	R	473*	.7
14	Horizon Organic Farms Maryland Inc—*Charles Marcy* Horizon Organic Holding Corp	11471 Augustine Herman, Kennedyville MD 21645	410-348-5472	S	442*	.3
15	Stremicks Heritage Foods LLC—*Lori Arias*	4002 Westminster Ave, Santa Ana CA 92703	714-775-5000	R	358*	.4
16	Wayne Dairy Products Inc—*Dale Gray*	PO Box 250, Richmond IN 47375	765-935-7521	R	191*	.5
17	Mayfield Dairy Farms LLC—*Scottie Mayfield* Dean Foods Co	PO Box 310, Athens TN 37371	423-745-2151	S	180*	1.2
18	Yoplait USA—*Robert Waldron*	1055 E Sandhill Ave, Carson CA 90746	310-605-6100	S	178*	.6
19	Byrne Dairy Inc—*Carl Byrne*	240 Oneida St, Syracuse NY 13202	315-475-2111	R	170*	.5
20	Horizon Organic Holding Corp—*Charles F Marcy* Dean Foods Co	PO Box 17577, Boulder CO 80308		S	167*	.3
21	Berkeley Farms Inc Dean Foods Co	PO Box 4616, Hayward CA 94540	510-265-8600	S	163*	.6
22	Northwest Dairy Association—*Jim Wegner*	PO Box 34377, Seattle WA 98124	206-284-7220	R	140*	1.3
23	Reiter Dairy LLC—*Bill Riley*	1961 Commerce Cir, Springfield OH 45504	937-323-5777	S	132*	.4

Rank	Company Name—*Executive Officer*	Address, City, State, Zip	Phone	Type	Fin	Empls
	Dean Foods Co					
24	Milkco Inc—*Keith Collins*	PO Box 16160, Asheville NC 28816	828-254-9560	S	103*	.3
25	Maola Milk And Ice Cream Company LLC—*Wayne Russell*	PO Box S, New Bern NC 28563	252-638-1131	S	100*	.4
26	Bareman Dairy Inc—*Stanley Bareman*	PO Box 8157, Holland MI 49422	616-396-0306	R	97*	.3
27	TG Lee Foods Inc	315 N Bumby Ave, Orlando FL 32803		S	95*	.6
	Dean Foods Co					
28	Agri-Mark Inc—*Paul Johnston*	PO Box 5800, Lawrence MA 01842	978-689-4442	R	91*	.9
29	Country Fresh LLC—*Gregg L Engles*	355 Mart St SW, Grand Rapids MI 49548	616-243-0173	S	90*	.5
	Dean Foods Co					
30	Producers Dairy Food Inc—*Larry Shehadey*	250 E Belmont Ave, Fresno CA 93701	559-264-6583	R	85*	.4
31	H Meyer Dairy Co—*Gregg Engles*	415 John St, Cincinnati OH 45215	513-948-8811	R	80*	.2
32	California Dairies Inc—*Richard Cotta*	2000 N Plz Dr, Visalia CA 93291	559-625-2200	R	80*	.8
33	Anderson Dairy Inc—*Harold Bellinger*	801 Searles Ave, Las Vegas NV 89101	702-642-7507	R	76*	.2
34	Dean Dairy Products Co—*Frank Chrastina*	1690 Oneida Ln, Sharpsville PA 16150	724-962-7801	S	75*	.2
	Dean Foods Co					
35	Schenkel's All-Star Dairy LLC—*Larry Brown*	PO Box 642, Huntington IN 46750	260-356-3425	S	73*	.1
	Dean Foods Co					
36	Liberty Dairy Co—*Gregg Engles*	PO Box 575, Evart MI 49631	231-734-5592	S	71*	.2
	Dean Foods Co					
37	Gore's Inc—*Kenneth Harvick*	PO Box 1000, Comanche TX 76442	325-356-3045	R	67*	.2
38	Umpqua Dairy Products Co—*Douglas Feldkamp*	PO Box 1306, Roseburg OR 97470	541-672-2638	R	65*	.2
39	Yofarm Co—*Charles Marcy*	162 Spring St, Naugatuck CT 06770	203-720-0000	R	64*	.1
40	Robinson Dairy LLC—*Charlie Walling*	646 Bryant St, Denver CO 80204	303-825-2990	S	64*	.2
	Dean Foods Co					
41	Swiss Premium Dairy Inc	2401 Walnut St, Lebanon PA 17042	717-273-2658	S	59*	.2
	Dean Foods Co					
42	Dairy Fresh LLC—*B Meredith*	PO Box 4009, Winston Salem NC 27115	336-723-0311	S	56*	.2
	Dean Foods Co					
43	Meadow Brook Dairy Co—*Jed Davis*	2365 Buffalo Rd, Erie PA 16510	814-899-3191	D	56*	.2
	Dean Foods Co					
44	Broughton Foods LLC—*David Broughton*	PO Box 656, Marietta OH 45750	740-373-4121	D	51*	.3
	Dean Foods Co					
45	Hastings Cooperative Creamery Co—*Robert Winter*	PO Box 217, Hastings MN 55033	651-437-9414	R	50*	<.1
46	Clover Farms Dairy Company Inc—*Richard Hartman*	PO Box 14627, Reading PA 19612	610-921-9111	R	49*	.3
47	Lakeview Farms Inc—*Ernest Graves*	PO Box 98, Delphos OH 45833	419-695-9925	R	41*	.2
48	Elmhurst Dairy Inc—*Henry Schwartz*	15525 Styler Rd, Jamaica NY 11433	718-526-3442	R	39*	.2
49	Sinton Dairy Foods Company LLC—*Matt Conner*	PO Box 578, Colorado Springs CO 80901	719-633-3821	R	38*	.2
50	Kleinpeter Farms Dairy LLC—*Stephen Kleinpeter*	14444 Airline Hwy, Baton Rouge LA 70817	225-753-2121	R	37*	.2
51	Winder Farms—*Gordon Liddle*	4400 W 4100 S, Salt Lake City UT 84120	801-969-3401	R	36*	.2
52	Clover-Stornetta Farms Inc—*Kevin Imm*	PO Box 750369, Petaluma CA 94975	707-778-8448	R	34*	.2
53	Galliker Dairy Co—*Charles Price*	PO Box 159, Johnstown PA 15907	814-266-8702	R	33*	.4
54	Kan-Pak LLC—*Dennis Cohlman*	1016 S Summit St, Kansas City KS 66103	620-442-6820	R	28*	.1
55	Smith Brothers Farms Inc—*Scott Highland*	PO Box 778, Kent WA 98035	253-852-1000	R	21*	.1
56	Springfield Creamery Inc *Joe Kesey*	29440 Airport Rd, Eugene OR 97402	541-689-2911	R	20*	.1
57	Toft Dairy Inc—*Eugene Meisler*	PO Box 2558, Sandusky OH 44871	419-625-4376	R	18*	.1
58	Cumberland Dairy Inc—*Carmine Catalana*	PO Box 308, Rosenhayn NJ 08352	856-451-1300	R	18*	.1
59	Harrisburg Dairies Inc—*Frederick Dewey*	PO Box 2001, Harrisburg PA 17105	717-233-8701	R	17*	.1
60	Andersen Dairy Inc—*Jack Dunn*	PO Box 310, Battle Ground WA 98604	360-687-7171	R	16*	.1
61	Central Dairy Co—*Chris Hackman*	610 Madison St, Jefferson City MO 65101	573-635-6148	R	16*	.1
62	Inland Northwest Dairies LLC—*Sterling Bess*	PO Box 7310, Spokane WA 99207	509-489-8600	R	16*	.1
63	Creamland Dairies Inc—*Bill Andes*	PO Box 25067, Albuquerque NM 87125	505-247-0721	S	15*	<.1
	Dean Foods Co					
64	Western Quality Food Products LC—*Kim Ritz*	997 N Airport Rd, Cedar City UT 84721	435-586-6577	S	15*	.1
	Stremicks Heritage Foods LLC					
65	Dairy Maid Dairy Inc—*Mike Dorsette*	259 E 7th St, Frederick MD 21701	301-663-5114	R	14*	.1
66	Southeast Dairy Processors Inc—*William Tiller*	PO Box 5088, Tampa FL 33675	813-621-3233	R	11*	.1
67	Old Europe Cheese Inc—*Francisco Garcia*	1330 E Empire Ave, Benton Harbor MI 49022	269-925-5003	R	11*	.1
68	Farmdale Creamery Inc—*Scott Hofferber*	1049 W Base Line St, San Bernardino CA 92411	909-889-3002	R	10*	.1
69	Hy-Point Dairy Farms Inc—*John Meany*	425 Beaver Valley Rd, Wilmington DE 19803	302-478-1414	R	10*	.1
70	Mason Dixon Farms Inc—*Richard Waybright*	1800 Mason Dixon Rd, Gettysburg PA 17325	717-334-4056	R	9*	.1
71	High Desert Milk Inc—*Randall Robinson*	1033 Idaho St, Burley ID 83318	208-878-6455	R	7*	.1
72	AB Munroe Dairy Inc—*Robert Armstrong*	151 N Brow St, East Providence RI 02914	401-438-4450	R	7*	.1
73	BL Cream Co—*Lee Hurwitz*	1505 Metropolitan St, Pittsburgh PA 15233	412-321-7700	R	7*	.1
74	Maple Hill Farms Inc—*William A Miller*	PO Box 767, Bloomfield CT 06002	207-622-2708	R	6*	<.1
75	Eberhard Creamery Inc—*John Eberhard*	PO Box 845, Redmond OR 97756	541-548-5181	R	6*	<.1
76	Regis Milk Company Inc—*Thad Mitchum*	578 Meeting St, Charleston SC 29403	843-723-3418	R	5*	.1
77	Arps Dairy Inc—*Stephen Boomer*	PO Box 803, Defiance OH 43512	419-782-9116	R	5*	<.1
78	Country Classic Dairies Inc—*Mike Monforton*	PO Box 968, Bozeman MT 59771	406-586-5425	R	5*	<.1
79	Willard J Stearns and Sons Inc—*Willard Stearns*	50 Stearns Rd, Storrs Mansfield CT 06268	860-423-9289	R	4*	<.1
80	Lochmead Dairy Inc—*Jock Gibson*	1120 Ivy St, Junction City OR 97448	541-998-8544	R	4*	<.1
81	Reed's Dairy Inc—*Alan Reed*	2660 W Broadway St, Idaho Falls ID 83402	208-522-0123	R	4*	<.1
82	Brown Cow West Corp—*Steve Ford*	3810 Delta Fair Blvd, Antioch CA 94509	925-757-9209	R	3*	<.1
83	Verifine Dairy Products Corporation of Sheboygan Inc—*Harrald F Kroeker*	PO Box 879, Sheboygan WI 53082	920-457-7733	S	3*	.1
	Dean Foods Co					
84	Livingston Chocolate Company Inc—*Julia Bishop*	PO Box 189, Livingston TN 38570	931-823-6451	R	3*	<.1
85	Hanan Products Company Inc—*Stuart Hanan*	196 Miller Pl, Hicksville NY 11801	516-938-1000	R	2*	<.1
86	Instantwhip-Dayton Inc—*Donald Tiller*	5820 Executive Blvd, Dayton OH 45424	937-235-5930	R	2*	<.1
87	Longacre's Modern Dairy Inc—*Daniel Longacre*	PO Box 69, Barto PA 19504	610-845-7551	R	2*	<.1

TOTALS: SIC 2026 Fluid Milk
Companies: 87 | | | | | 43,233 | 63.7

2032 Canned Specialties

1	Campbell Soup Co—*Denise Morrison*	1 Campbell Pl, Camden NJ 08103	856-342-4800	P	7,719	17.5
2	Gerber Products Co—*Dr Kathleen Reidy*	445 State St, Fremont MI 49413	231-928-2000	S	2,960*	9.0
3	TreeHouse Foods Inc—*Sam K Reed*	2021 Spring Rd Ste 600, Oak Brook IL 60523	708-483-1300	P	2,050	3.9
4	Steuben Foods Inc—*Kenneth Schlossberg*	15504 Liberty Ave, Jamaica NY 11433	718-291-3333	R	837*	.3
5	Bruce Foods Corp—*Joseph Brown*	PO Box 1030, New Iberia LA 70562	337-365-8101	R	396*	1.6
6	Beech-Nut Nutrition Corp—*Christopher Rudolf*	13 British American Bl, Latham NY 12110	518-595-6600	S	345*	.4

Note: An asterisk (*) indicates an estimated financial figure. The company type code used is as follows: R = Private, P = Public, S = Private Subsidiary, B = Public Subsidiary, D = Division, J = Joint Venture, I = Investment Fund.

COMPANY RANKINGS BY SALES WITHIN 4-DIGIT SIC

Rank	Company Name—*Executive Officer*	Address, City, State, Zip	Phone	Type	Fin	Empls
7	Goya Foods Inc—*Robert I Unanue*	100 Seaview Dr, Secaucus NJ 07094	201-348-4900	R	288*	.7
8	Truesoups LLC—*Mark Rogers*	26401 79th Ave S, Kent WA 98032	253-872-0403	S	143*	.2
9	Spring Glen Fresh Foods Inc—*John Warehime*	PO Box 518, Ephrata PA 17522		D	58*	.2
10	Morgan Foods Inc—*John Morgan*	90 W Morgan St, Austin IN 47102	812-794-1170	R	49*	.6
11	Vanee Foods Co—*Aloysius Eekeren*	5418 Mcdermott Dr, Berkeley IL 60163	708-449-7300	R	47*	.3
12	Nest Collective—*Neil Grimmer*	1485 Park Ave Ste 200, Emeryville CA 94608	510-225-4018	R	44	.8
13	Juanita's Foods—*Mark De La Torre*	PO Box 847, Wilmington CA 90748	310-834-5339	R	35*	.1
14	Slim-Fast Foods Co—*John Rice*	PO Box 3625, West Palm Beach FL 33402	561-833-9920	S	28*	.1
15	Kettle Cuisine Inc—*Jeremiah Shafir*	270 2nd St, Chelsea MA 02150	617-884-1219	R	21*	.1
16	Ebro Foods Inc—*Zenaida Abreu*	1330 W 43rd St, Chicago IL 60609	773-696-0150	R	14*	.1
17	Advanced Fresh Concepts Corp—*Ryuji Ishii*	19205 S Laurel Park Rd, Compton CA 90220	310-604-3200	R	14*	.1
18	Nurture Inc—*Shazi Visram*	139 Fulton St Ste 907, New York NY 10038	212-374-2779	R	13	.1
19	Beckman and Gast Company Inc—*William Gast*	282 W Kremer Hoying Rd, Saint Henry OH 45883	419-678-4195	R	13*	<.1
20	New Mexico Food Distributors Inc—*Larry Gutierrez*	3041 University Blvd S, Albuquerque NM 87106	505-888-0199	R	13*	.1
21	Riba Foods Inc—*Miguel Barrios*	PO Box 630461, Houston TX 77263	713-975-7001	R	12*	.1
22	Page's Produce Co—*Gene Page*	4601 Pacific Blvd, Vernon CA 90058	323-277-3660	R	12*	.1
23	Corn Maiden Foods Inc—*Pascal Dropsy*	24201 Frampton Ave, Harbor City CA 90710	310-784-0400	R	12*	.1
24	Foodswing Inc—*Roger Hoffman*	904 Woods Rd, Cambridge MD 21613	410-228-1644	R	11*	.1
25	Mancini Packing Co—*Richard Mancini*	PO Box 157, Zolfo Springs FL 33890	863-735-2000	R	11*	.1
26	Superior Quality Foods Inc—*Linda Owen*	2355 E Francis St, Ontario CA 91761	909-923-4733	S	10*	.1
27	Pastorelli Food Products Inc—*Richard Pastorelli*	162 N Sangamon St, Chicago IL 60607	312-666-2041	R	7*	<.1
28	Stir Foods LLC	1581 N Main St, Orange CA 92867	714-637-6050	R	7*	.1
29	Wonton Food Corp—*Roger Young*	2902 Caroline St, Houston TX 77004	832-366-1280	R	5*	<.1
30	Catalina Finer Food Corp—*Alejandro Cepero*	PO Box 15815, Tampa FL 33684	813-876-3910	R	5*	<.1
31	Taif Inc—*Joseph Talluto*	600 Kaiser Dr Ste A, Folcroft PA 19032	610-522-0122	R	5*	<.1
32	Deli Food Manufacturing Inc—*George Tsai*	10875 Indian Head Indu, Saint Louis MO 63132	314-426-7273	R	4*	<.1
33	Rocky Mountain Food Factory Inc—*Mercedes Huang*	2825 S Raritan St, Englewood CO 80110	303-761-3330	R	4*	<.1
34	La Indiana Tamales Inc—*Raul Ramos*	PO Box 23600, Los Angeles CA 90023	626-333-6098	R	4*	<.1
35	Golden Specialty Foods LLC—*Javed Atcha*	14605 Best Ave, Norwalk CA 90650	562-802-2537	R	4*	<.1
36	Michael B's LLC	22625 S Western Ave, Torrance CA 90501	310-320-0141	R	3*	<.1
37	Oliverio's Italian Style Peppers Inc—*Deanna Mason*	280 N Ohio Ave, Clarksburg WV 26301	304-622-4959	R	3*	<.1
38	Bien Padre Foods Inc—*Benito Lim*	PO Box 3748, Eureka CA 95502	707-442-4585	R	3*	<.1
39	Hume Specialties Inc—*Christine Hume*	PO Box 4329, Winston Salem NC 27115	802-875-3117	R	3*	<.1
40	Uncle Dave's Kitchens Inc—*Tim Goodwin*	PO Box 961, White River Junction VT 05001	802-333-4141	R	3*	<.1
41	El Alteno Foods Inc—*Rene Reynoso*	PO Box 91088, City Of Industry CA 91715	213-623-7815	R	3*	<.1
42	Expro Manufacturing Corp—*Peter Ernster*	2800 Ayers Ave, Vernon CA 90058	323-415-8544	R	3*	<.1
43	Homestead Ravioli Company Inc—*Terry Hall*	315 S Maple Ave Bldg 1, South San Francisco CA 94080	650-615-0750	R	2*	<.1
44	Los Potros Distribution Center LLC Dist Of Mexican and American Products—*Griselda Lopez*	3925 W Adams St Ste 2, Phoenix AZ 85009	602-272-8952	R	2*	<.1
45	Mi Ranchito Food Inc—*Joe Ramirez*	PO Box 159, Bayard NM 88023	575-537-3868	R	2*	<.1
46	Spanish Gardens Food Manufacturing Company Inc—*Norma Miller*	2301 Metropolitan Ave, Kansas City KS 66106	913-831-4242	R	1*	<.1
47	National Coney Island Chili Co—*James Giftos*	6700 E Davison St, Detroit MI 48212	313-365-5611	R	1*	<.1
48	Arizona Cactus Ranch—*Natalie McGee*	PO Box 8, Green Valley AZ 85622	520-625-4419	R	1*	<.1
49	Ray's Brand Products Inc	PO Box 793, Decatur IL 62525	217-422-6153	R	1*	<.1
50	Bloemer Food Sales Co—*Lawrence Bloemer*	925 S 7th St, Louisville KY 40203	502-584-8338	R	1*	<.1
51	Suzanne Chalet Foods Inc—*Vita Hinshaw*	3800 Chalet Suzanne Dr, Lake Wales FL 33859	863-676-6011	R	1*	<.1

TOTALS: SIC 2032 Canned Specialties
Companies: 51

					15,234	37.1

2033 Canned Fruits & Vegetables

Rank	Company Name—*Executive Officer*	Address, City, State, Zip	Phone	Type	Fin	Empls
1	HJ Heinz Co—*William R Johnson*	PO Box 57, Pittsburgh PA 15230	412-456-5700	P	10,707	34.8
2	Dole Food Company Inc—*David A DeLorenzo*	PO Box 5132, Westlake Village CA 91359	818-879-6600	P	6,893	74.3
3	JM Smucker Co—*Timothy P Smucker*	PO Box 197, Orrville OH 44667	330-682-3000	P	4,826	4.5
4	Del Monte Foods Co—*Neil Harrison*	PO Box 193575, San Francisco CA 94119	415-247-3000	S	3,700	5.2
5	Dole Fresh Vegetables Inc—*Richard Dahl* Dole Food Company Inc	PO Box 1759, Salinas CA 93902	831-422-8871	S	2,267*	3.0
6	JM Smucker Pennsylvania Inc—*Timothy P Smucker* JM Smucker Co	300 Keck Ave, New Bethlehem PA 16242	814-275-1323	S	2,155*	3.5
7	Seneca Foods Corp—*Kraig H Kayser*	3736 S Main St, Marion NY 14505	315-926-8100	P	1,195	3.4
8	Ocean Spray Cranberries Inc—*Randy Papadellis*	1 Ocean Spray Dr, Middleboro MA 02349	508-946-1000	R	1,133*	2.0
9	Red Gold Inc—*Brian Reichart*	PO Box 83, Elwood IN 46036	765-754-7527	R	818*	1.3
10	Morinda Inc—*Kerry Asay*	PO Box 4000, Orem UT 84059	801-234-1000	R	421*	1.2
11	Tree Top Inc—*Thomas Stokes*	PO Box 248, Selah WA 98942	509-697-7251	R	365*	1.3
12	Morning Star Packing Co—*Chris Rufer*	13448 Volta Rd, Los Banos CA 93635	209-826-8000	R	350*	3.0
13	Hanover Foods Corp—*John A Warehime*	PO Box 334, Hanover PA 17331	717-632-6000	R	288*	2.0
14	Honee Bear Canning—*Steve Packer*	72100 M 40, Lawton MI 49065		R	225*	.3
15	Cliffstar Corp—*Sean McGir*	1 Cliffstar Ave, Dunkirk NY 14048	716-366-6100	R	224*	1.1
16	Allens Inc—*Roderick Allen*	PO Box 250, Siloam Springs AR 72761	479-524-6431	R	216*	2.0
17	Kagome Inc—*Wataru Kise*	333 Johnson Rd, Los Banos CA 93635	209-826-8850	R	187*	1.9
18	Nation Pizza Products LP—*Marshall Bauer*	601 E Algonquin Rd, Schaumburg IL 60173	847-397-3320	R	150*	.6
19	Ultimate Juice Co—*Kenneth G Romanzi*	180 Mount Airy Rd, Basking Ridge NJ 07920	908-367-6200	S	130	.8
20	Knouse Foods Cooperative Inc—*Kenneth Guise*	800 Pach Glen Idaville, Peach Glen PA 17375	717-677-8181	R	129*	1.2
21	Langers Juice Company Inc—*David Langer*	16195 Stephens St, City of Industry CA 91745	626-336-1666	R	120*	.2
22	Freshco Ltd—*Cliff Burg*	7929 SW Jack James Dr, Stuart FL 34997	772-287-2111	R	112*	.1
23	Mullins Food Products Inc—*Jeanne Gannon*	2200 S 25th Ave, Broadview IL 60155	708-344-3224	R	105*	.4
24	Oregon Cherry Growers Inc—*Ed Johnson*	PO Box 7357, Salem OR 97303	503-364-8421	R	96*	.4
25	JM Smucker LLC—*Timothy P Smucker* JM Smucker Co	1050 Stanton St, Ripon WI 54971	920-745-6100	S	90*	.2
26	S Martinelli and Co—*John Martinelli*	PO Box 1868, Watsonville CA 95077		R	90*	.2
27	Lidestri Foods Inc—*John Lidestri*	815 Whitney Rd W, Fairport NY 14450	585-377-7700	R	85*	.8
28	SK Foods LP—*Glen McClaran*	PO Box 160, Lemoore CA 93245	831-655-5400	R	81*	.4
29	Deep South Products Inc—*Peter A Lynch*	PO Box 1448, Fitzgerald GA 31750	229-423-1121	S	74*	.3
30	Bush Brothers and Co—*James Ethier*	PO Box 52330, Knoxville TN 37950	865-588-7685	R	72*	.7
31	Nantucket Allserve Inc—*Tom First*	4 Easy St, Nantucket MA 02554	508-228-8170	R	66*	.1
32	Clement Pappas and Company Inc—*Dean Pappas*	1 Collins Dr, Carneys Point NJ 08069		R	63*	.4
33	Smucker Specialty Foods Co—*Richard Smucker* JM Smucker Co	PO Box 345, Ripon WI 54971	920-745-6100	D	60*	.1
34	Del Mar Food Products Corp—*P Mecozzi*	PO Box 891, Watsonville CA 95077	831-722-3516	R	57*	.1
35	Johanna Foods Inc—*Robert Facchina*	PO Box 272, Flemington NJ 08822	908-788-2200	R	53*	.5

Rank	Company Name—*Executive Officer*	Address, City, State, Zip	Phone	Type	Fin	Empls
36	Fremont Co—*Richard Smith*	802 N Front St, Fremont OH 43420	419-334-8995	R	52*	.2
37	Spectrum Organic Products LLC—*Neil G Blomquist*	5341 Old Redwood Hwy S, Petaluma CA 94954	707-778-8900	S	50*	.1
38	Ingomar Packing Company LLC—*Matt Bianchi*	PO Box 1448, Los Banos CA 93635	209-826-9494	R	48*	.3
39	Bell-Carter Foods Inc—*Ken Wienholz*	3742 Mt Diablo Blvd, Lafayette CA 94549	925-284-5933	R	47*	.5
40	Country Pure Foods Inc—*Raymond Lee*	681 W Waterloo Rd, Akron OH 44314	330-753-2293	R	43*	.5
41	Indian Summer Coop—*Roy D Hackert*	3958 W Chauvez Rd, Ludington MI 49431	231-845-6248	R	43*	.3
42	Furman Foods Inc—*David Geise*	PO Box 500, Northumberland PA 17857	570-473-3516	R	43*	.3
43	Lawrence Foods Inc—*Lester Lawrence*	2200 Lunt Ave, Elk Grove Village IL 60007	847-437-2400	R	42*	.3
44	American Beverage Corp Daily Juice Products Div	1 Daily Way, Verona PA 15147	412-828-9020	D	38*	.5
45	New Era Canning Co—*Rick Ray*	4856 1st St, New Era MI 49446	231-861-2151	R	37*	.3
46	Texas Citrus Exchange—*Judy Rodriguez*	702 E Expwy 83, Mission TX 78572	956-585-8321	R	36*	.1
47	Moody Dunbar Inc—*Stanley K Dunbar*	PO Box 6048, Johnson City TN 37602	423-952-0100	R	35*	.2
48	Smuckers Quality Beverages of Havre de Grace—*Dan Hastings* JM Smucker Co	340 Old Bay Ln, Havre de Grace MD 21078	410-939-1403	S	35*	.1
49	Stonewall Kitchen LLC—*Jonathan King*	2 Stonewall Ln, York ME 03909	207-351-2713	R	34*	.4
50	Vie-Del Co—*Dianne Nury*	PO Box 2908, Fresno CA 93745	559-834-2525	R	34*	.1
51	Valley Processing Inc—*Mary Bliesner*	PO Box 246, Sunnyside WA 98944	509-837-8084	R	33*	.1
52	SEW Friel LLP—*Joseph Green*	PO Box 10, Queenstown MD 21658	410-827-8811	R	32*	.2
53	Juice Tyme Inc—*Philip Scott*	4401 S Oakley Ave, Chicago IL 60609	773-579-1291	R	30*	.1
54	Olive Musco Products Inc—*Nicholas Musco*	17950 Via Nicolo, Tracy CA 95377	209-836-4600	R	29*	.3
55	Smucker Natural Foods Inc—*Julia Sabin* JM Smucker Co	PO Box 369, Chico CA 95927	530-899-5000	S	29*	.1
56	Sun Orchard Inc—*Marc Isaacs*	1198 W Fairmont Dr, Tempe AZ 85282	480-966-1770	R	26*	.1
57	MA Gedney Co—*Jeff Tuttle*	PO Box 8, Chaska MN 55318	952-448-2612	R	26*	.1
58	Vita-Pakt Citrus Products Co—*James Boyles*	PO Box 309, Covina CA 91723	626-332-1101	R	26*	.2
59	Stanislaus Food Products Co—*Thomas Cortopassi*	PO Box 3951, Modesto CA 95352	209-522-7201	R	26*	.1
60	Henry and Henry Inc—*William Day*	3765 Walden Ave, Lancaster NY 14086	716-685-4000	R	25*	.1
61	Dairy Fresh Of Louisiana Inc—*Steve Mccormic*	PO Box 600, Baker LA 70704	225-774-0690	S	25*	.1
62	Beaumont Juice Inc—*Tom Carmody*	550 B St, Beaumont CA 92223	951-769-7171	R	25*	.1
63	Orange Bang Inc—*David Fox*	13115 Telfair Ave, Sylmar CA 91342	818-833-1000	R	24*	<.1
64	Tip Top Canning Co—*George Timmer*	PO Box 126, Tipp City OH 45371	937-667-3713	R	22*	.2
65	Fruit Dynamics LLC—*Rich Cahoon*	4176 Mercantile Ave, Naples FL 34104	239-643-7373	R	22*	.1
66	Wizard's Cauldron Ltd—*Cecilia Redding*	878 Firetower Rd, Yanceyville NC 27379	336-694-5665	R	22*	<.1
67	Mccall Farms Inc—*Marion Swink*	6615 S Irby St, Effingham SC 29541	843-662-2223	R	22*	.1
68	TW Garner Food Co—*Ralph E Garner*	PO Box 4329, Winston Salem NC 27115	336-661-1550	R	20*	.1
69	Hirzel Canning Co—*Karl Hirzel*	411 Lemoyne Rd, Northwood OH 43619	419-693-0531	R	18*	.1
70	Paradise Tomato Kitchens Inc—*Ronald Peters*	1500 S Brook St, Louisville KY 40208	502-637-1700	R	18*	.1
71	Escalon Premier Brands Inc HJ Heinz Co	1905 McHenry Ave, Escalon CA 95320	209-838-7341	S	17	.1
72	Brady Farms Inc—*Robert Brady*	14786 Winans St, West Olive MI 49460	616-842-3916	R	16*	.1
73	The Mushroom Co—*Dennis Newhard*	902 Woods Rd, Cambridge MD 21613	410-221-8972	R	16*	.1
74	Apple and Eve LLC—*Jonathan Alpert*	2 Seaview Blvd Fl 3, Port Washington NY 11050	516-621-1122	R	15*	.1
75	M and D Products Inc—*Dale Clellan*	0001 Harney Rd Ste 4, Tampa FL 33637	813-988-2211	R	15*	.1
76	Maui Land and Pineapple Company Inc—*Warren H Haruki*	870 Hali'imaile Rd, Makawao HI 96768	808-877-3351	P	15	<.1
77	Bear-Stewart Corp—*Melvin Bressler*	1025 N Damen Ave, Chicago IL 60622	773-276-0400	R	13*	<.1
78	Creamery Corp—*Joseph Vantreeck*	550 W 7th Ave Ste 1410, Anchorage AK 99501	907-561-5223	R	12*	.1
79	Jasper Wyman and Son—*Edward Flanagan*	PO Box 100, Milbridge ME 04658	207-546-3800	R	11*	.1
80	Delgrosso Foods Inc—*James Grosso*	PO Box 337, Tipton PA 16684	814-684-5880	R	11*	.1
81	R and Z Ventures Inc—*Len Roseberg*	1300 Sw 1st Ct, Pompano Beach FL 33069	954-782-9800	R	10*	.1
82	Cherryfield Foods Inc—*Raginr Kamp*	4 Park St, Cherryfield ME 04622	207-546-7573	R	10*	.1
83	St Julian Wine Company Inc—*David Braganini*	PO Box 127, Paw Paw MI 49079	269-657-5568	R	10*	.1
84	Simply Smucker's Inc—*Timothy P Smucker* JM Smucker Co	333 Wadsworth Rd, Orrville OH 44667	330-684-1500	S	9*	<.1
85	Triple H Food Processors Inc—*Thomas Harris*	5821 Wilderness Ave, Riverside CA 92504	951-352-5700	R	9*	.1
86	Odwalla Inc	120 Stone Pine Rd, Half Moon Bay CA 94019		S	8*	.1
87	Newman's Own Inc—*Mike Havard*	246 Post Rd E, Westport CT 06880	203-222-0136	R	8*	<.1
88	Santa Barbara Olive Co—*Craig Makela*	12477 Calle Real, Santa Barbara CA 93117	805-562-1456	R	8*	<.1
89	Northwest Naturals Corp—*Tom Hursen*	11805 North Creek Pkwy, Bothell WA 98011	425-881-2200	R	7*	<.1
90	Sam S Acccursio and Sons Packing and Produce Inc—*Sam Accursio*	PO Box 901767, Homestead FL 33090	305-246-3455	R	7*	.1
91	Blue Runner Foods Inc—*Richard Thomas*	726 S Burnside Ave, Gonzales LA 70737	225-647-3016	R	7*	<.1
92	Citrus Systems Inc—*Tom Boehland*	125 Jackson Ave N, Hopkins MN 55343	952-935-0410	R	6*	.1
93	Oasis Foods Inc—*Eric Bocks*	PO Box 217, Planada CA 95365	209-382-0263	R	6*	.1
94	Manzana Products Company Inc—*Suzanne Kaido*	PO Box 209, Sebastopol CA 95473	707-823-5313	R	6*	<.1
95	Svz USA Washington Inc—*Jenny Billups*	PO Box 715, Othello WA 99344	509-488-6563	R	6*	.1
96	Florida Food Products Inc—*Jerry Brown*	PO Box 1300, Eustis FL 32727	352-357-4141	R	6*	<.1
97	Jardine Foods Inc—*Robert Mcgee*	PO Box 1530, Buda TX 78610	512-295-4600	R	6*	<.1
98	Biad Chili Co—*Chris Biad*	8927 N Valley Dr, Las Cruces NM 88007	575-525-1101	R	5*	.1
99	American Spoon Foods Inc—*Justin Rashid*	PO Box 566, Petoskey MI 49770	231-347-9030	R	5*	<.1
100	JG Boswell Tomato Company - Kern LLC—*Larisa Arambula*	PO Box 515, Buttonwillow CA 93206	661-764-9000	R	5*	<.1
101	Pfeiffer's California Custom Packing Inc—*Jeff Pfeiffer*	400 3rd St, Exeter CA 93221	559-592-5327	R	5*	.1
102	Cahoon Farms Inc—*Donald Cahoon*	PO Box 190, Wolcott NY 14590	315-594-8081	R	5*	<.1
103	Ray Brothers and Noble Canning Company Inc—*Mark Noble*	PO Box 314, Hobbs IN 46047	765-675-7451	R	5*	.1
104	Private Label Foods Of Rochester Inc—*Frank Lavorato*	PO Box 60805, Rochester NY 14606	585-254-9205	R	5*	<.1
105	HK Canning Inc—*Henry Knaust*	130 N Garden St, Ventura CA 93001	805-652-1392	R	4*	<.1
106	Leonard Mountain Inc—*Deborah Berckefeldt*	PO Box 67, Leonard OK 74043	918-366-2800	R	4*	<.1
107	Florida Fruit Juices Inc—*Donald Franko*	7001 W 62nd St, Chicago IL 60638	773-586-6200	R	4*	<.1
108	Tropical Preserving Company Inc—*Ronald Randall*	1711 E 15th St, Los Angeles CA 90021	213-748-5108	R	4*	<.1
109	Lodi Canning Company Inc—*Robert Goeres*	PO Box 315, Lodi WI 53555	608-592-4236	R	3*	<.1
110	Alaska Wild Berry Products Inc—*Peter G Eden*	5225 Juneau St, Anchorage AK 99518	907-562-8858	R	3*	<.1
111	Elliott's Amazing Juices—*Elliott Hirsh*	1921 Wharton Rd, Jenkintown PA 19046	215-886-9356	R	3*	<.1
112	Fong Huy Foods Inc—*David Tran*	5001 Earle Ave, Rosemead CA 91770	626-286-8328	R	2*	<.1
113	Louis Maull Co—*Louis Maull*	219 N Market St, Saint Louis MO 63102	314-241-8410	R	2*	<.1
114	HA Rider and Sons—*George Rider*	2482 Freedom Blvd, Watsonville CA 95076	831-722-3882	R	2*	<.1
115	Wicker's Food Products Inc—*Glen Hemmingway*	PO Box 129, Hornersville MO 63855	573-737-2416	R	2*	<.1
116	Judah Manufacturing Corp—*Lynn Trimble*	10440 E NW Hwy, Dallas TX 75238	214-340-6200	R	2*	<.1
117	Rc Industries Inc—*Steve Cress*	PO Box 5, Navarre OH 44662	330-879-5486	R	2*	<.1
118	Cincinnati Preserving Co—*Andrew Liscow*	3015 E Kemper Rd, Cincinnati OH 45241	513-771-2000	R	1*	<.1
119	Carolina Treet Inc—*Joe King*	PO Box 1017, Wilmington NC 28402	910-762-1950	R	1*	<.1

Note: An asterisk (*) indicates an estimated financial figure. The company type code used is as follows: R = Private, P = Public, S = Private Subsidiary, B = Public Subsidiary, D = Division, J = Joint Venture, I = Investment Fund.

COMPANY RANKINGS BY SALES WITHIN 4-DIGIT SIC

Rank	Company Name—*Executive Officer*	Address, City, State, Zip	Phone	Type	Fin	Empls
120	Palmetto Canning Co—*Jonathan Greenlaw*	PO Box 155, Palmetto FL 34220	941-722-1100	R	1*	<.1
121	Pepper Patch—*Dorothy Smith*	1250 Old Hillsboro Rd, Franklin TN 37069	615-790-1012	R	1*	<.1
122	Cherith Valley Gardens Inc—*V Alan Werner*	PO Box 12040, Fort Worth TX 76110	817-922-8822	R	1*	<.1
123	Arcadia Dairy Farms Inc—*James Arthur*	PO Box 631, Arden NC 28704	828-684-3556	R	1*	<.1
124	Muirhead Canning Co—*James Barrett*	5267 Mill Creek Rd, The Dalles OR 97058	541-298-1660	R	1*	<.1
125	Crown Processing Company Inc—*John Bowen*	PO Box 1, Bellflower CA 90707	562-865-0293	R	1*	<.1
126	Hawaiian Fruit Specialties LLC—*Karen Howard*	2-2741 Kaumualii Hwy, Kalaheo HI 96741	808-332-9333	R	1*	<.1
127	Gib's Classics Inc—*Paul Inclan*	2123 Watterson Tr, Louisville KY 40219		R	<1	<.1
128	NuVim Inc—*Richard P Kundrat*	18327 Port Cir, Lewes DE 19958	302-827-4054	P	<1	<.1

TOTALS: SIC 2033 Canned Fruits & Vegetables
Companies: 128

					39,065	160.3

2034 Dehydrated Fruits, Vegetables & Soups

Rank	Company Name—*Executive Officer*	Address, City, State, Zip	Phone	Type	Fin	Empls
1	Basic American Foods Inc—*Jack Parks*	2185 North California, Walnut Creek CA 94596	925-472-4000	R	392*	2.0
2	Sunsweet Growers Inc—*Arthur Driscoll*	901 N Walton Ave, Yuba City CA 95993	530-674-5010	R	262*	.6
3	Sun-Maid Growers Of California—*Barry F Kriebel*	13525 S Bethel Ave, Kingsburg CA 93631	559-896-8000	R	221*	.6
4	Zoria Farms Inc—*John Zoria*	3487 McKee Rd Ste 54, San Jose CA 95127	559-673-6368	R	198*	.5
5	Sensient Dehydrated Flavors LLC—*Patrick Laubacher*	PO Box 1524, Turlock CA 95381	209-667-2777	S	110*	.6
6	Valley View Packing Company Inc—*Salvadore Rubino*	PO Box 5699, San Jose CA 95150	408-289-8300	R	75*	.1
7	Murakami Produce Co—*Sig Murakami*	1431 SE 1st St, Ontario OR 97914	541-889-3181	R	71*	.1
8	Nonpareil Corp—*Chris Abend*	40 N 400 W, Blackfoot ID 83221	208-785-5880	R	46*	.5
9	Lion Raisins Inc—*Alfred Lion*	PO Box 1350, Selma CA 93662	559-834-6677	R	39*	.4
10	Oregon Potato Co—*Frank Tiegs*	PO Box 169, Boardman OR 97818	541-481-2715	R	38*	.4
11	Idaho Supreme Potatoes Inc—*Wilford Chapman*	PO Box 246, Firth ID 83236	208-346-6841	R	38*	.4
12	Setton's International Foods Inc—*Joshua Setton*	85 Austin Blvd, Commack NY 11725	631-543-8090	R	32*	.4
13	Precision Foods Inc—*W Trent*	11457 Olde Cabin Rd St, Saint Louis MO 63141	314-567-7400	S	30*	.2
14	Joyce Food LLC—*Yakov Ostreicher*	80 Ave K, Newark NJ 07105	973-491-9696	R	27*	.2
15	Idaho Fresh-Pak Inc—*Ryan Clement*	PO Box 130, Lewisville ID 83431	208-754-4686	R	25*	.4
16	Winnemucca Farms Inc—*John Brien*	1 Potato Pl Unit 3, Winnemucca NV 89445	775-623-2900	R	24*	.2
17	Jade Food Products Inc—*Hollis Ho*	94-476 Koaki St, Waipahu HI 96797	808-678-8886	R	20*	<.1
18	Cascade Specialties Inc—*Jack Sollazzo*	PO Box 603, Boardman OR 97818	541-481-2522	R	15*	.1
19	Graceland Fruit Inc—*Alan Devore*	1123 Main St, Frankfort MI 49635	231-352-7181	R	12*	.2
20	Eatem Corp—*Robert Buono*	1829 Gallagher Dr, Vineland NJ 08360	856-692-1663	R	12*	.1
21	Chooljian Brothers Packing Company Inc—*Michael Chooljian*	PO Box 395, Sanger CA 93657	559-875-5501	R	11*	.1
22	Minnesota Dehydrated Vegetables Inc—*James Stewart*	PO Box 245, Fosston MN 56542	218-435-1997	R	10*	.1
23	Major Products Company Inc—*Daniel Rose*	PO Box 675, Little Ferry NJ 07643	201-641-5555	R	8*	.1
24	Rio Valley Chili Inc—*Nick Carson*	PO Box 131, Rincon NM 87940	575-267-4636	R	7*	.1
25	Victor Packing Inc—*Victor Sahatdjian*	11687 Rd 27 1/2, Madera CA 93637	559-673-5908	R	7*	.1
26	Breedlove Dehydrated Food Inc—*Angela Warner*	1818 N Martin Luther K, Lubbock TX 79403	806-741-0404	R	6*	.1
27	Pacific Pure-Aid Co—*Timothy Root*	PO Box 157, Silverton OR 97381	503-873-3600	R	6*	<.1
28	MA and Sons—*Mary Garay*	PO Box 302, Derry NM 87933	575-267-1122	R	6*	.1
29	Swiss Food Products LP—*Paul Schwankee*	4333 W Division St, Chicago IL 60651	312-829-0100	R	6*	<.1
30	Tec Foods Inc—*Anastasios Costianis*	4300 W Ohio St, Chicago IL 60624	773-638-5310	R	5*	<.1
31	New Season Foods Inc—*Mark Frandsen*	PO Box 157, Forest Grove OR 97116	503-357-7124	S	5*	<.1
32	JUST TOMATOES Co—*Karen Cox*	PO Box 807, Westley CA 95387	209-894-5371	R	5*	<.1
33	Kamish Food Products—*Ted Kamish*	5846 N Kolmar Ave, Chicago IL 60646	773-725-6959	R	5*	<.1
34	Cherry Chukar Co—*Pamela Auld*	PO Box 510, Prosser WA 99350	509-786-2055	R	5*	<.1
35	New Mexico Chili Products Inc—*David Ramos*	3225 Hwy 418, Deming NM 88030	575-546-3636	R	4*	.1
36	Rabbit Creek Products Inc—*Donna Cook*	PO Box 1059, Louisburg KS 66053	913-837-2757	R	2*	<.1
37	L'esprit De Campagne—*Carey Lokey*	PO Box 3130, Winchester VA 22604	540-955-1014	R	1*	<.1
38	W and G Flavors Inc—*J Wheeler*	PO Box 1434, Cockeysville MD 21030	410-771-6606	R	1*	<.1

TOTALS: SIC 2034 Dehydrated Fruits, Vegetables & Soups
Companies: 38

					1,784	8.2

2035 Pickles, Sauces & Salad Dressings

Rank	Company Name—*Executive Officer*	Address, City, State, Zip	Phone	Type	Fin	Empls
1	Carriage House Companies Inc—*Richard R Koulouris*	196 Newton St, Fredonia NY 14063	716-673-1000	S	1,462	1.0
2	T Marzetti Co—*Bruce Rosa*	PO Box 29163, Columbus OH 43229	614-846-2232	D	613*	1.5
3	B and G Foods Inc—*David L Wenner*	4 Gatehall Dr Ste 110, Parsippany NJ 07054	973-401-6500	P	544	.7
4	Kikkoman Foods Inc—*Kazuo Shimizu*	PO Box 69, Walworth WI 53184	262-275-6181	R	447*	.2
5	Claussen Pickle Co—*Irene Rosenfeld*	1500 E Walnut St, Fullerton CA 92831	714-870-8235	D	130*	.4
6	Clements Foods Co—*Edward Clements*	PO Box 14538, Oklahoma City OK 73113	405-842-3308	R	74*	.3
7	Naturally Fresh Inc—*Jerry Greene*	1000 Naturally Fresh B, Atlanta GA 30349	404-765-9000	R	62*	.3
8	Piggie Park Enterprises Inc—*Lee Scott*	PO Box 6847, West Columbia SC 29171		R	61*	.3
9	Chelten House Products Inc—*Steven Dabrow*	PO Box 434, Bridgeport NJ 08014	856-467-1600	R	52*	.1
10	Bowman Apple Products Company Inc—*Gordon D Bowman II*	PO Box 817, Mount Jackson VA 22842	540-477-3111	R	51*	.2
11	Pfeiffer Foods Inc—*John Gerlach* T Marzetti Co	PO Box 29163, Columbus OH 43229		D	49*	.2
12	E McIlhenny and Sons Corp—*Paul CP McIlhenny*	1 Main Rd, Avery Island LA 70513	337-365-8773	R	41*	.1
13	Meduri Farms Inc—*Joe Meduri*	PO Box 636, Dallas OR 97338	503-623-0308	R	41*	.5
14	Gielow Pickles Inc—*Douglas Gielow*	5260 Main St, Lexington MI 48450	810-359-7680	R	26*	.2
15	Spring Silver Foods Inc—*Ed Schaefer*	PO Box 360, Eau Claire WI 54702	715-832-9739	R	24*	.2
16	Mrs Stratton's Salads Inc—*George Bradford*	PO Box 190187, Birmingham AL 35219	205-940-9640	R	22*	.1
17	Beaverton Foods Inc—*William Small*	7100 Nw Century Blvd, Hillsboro OR 97124	503-646-8138	R	22*	.1
18	Kruger Foods Inc—*Kara Kruger*	PO Box 220, Farmington CA 95230	209-941-8518	R	21*	.1
19	Smithfield Companies Ham and Products Company Inc—*Jim Groves*	PO Box 487, Smithfield VA 23431	757-357-2121	S	19	.1
20	Lee Brothers Inc—*Gene Lee*	420 Clyde Ave, Mountain View CA 94043	650-964-9650	R	14*	.1
21	G L Mezzetta Inc—*Ronald Mezzetta*	105 Mezzetta Ct, American Canyon CA 94503	707-648-1050	R	13*	.1
22	Gold Pure Food Products Company Inc—*Steven Gold*	1 Brooklyn Rd, Hempstead NY 11550	516-483-5600	R	12*	.1
23	Marjon Specialty Foods Inc—*John Miller*	3508 Sydney Rd, Plant City FL 33566	813-752-3482	R	11*	.1
24	Cascade Ag Services Inc—*Craig Stafferson*	13459 Dodge Valley Rd, Mount Vernon WA 98273	360-466-0491	R	11*	.1
25	JG Van Holten And Son Inc—*James Byrnes*	PO Box 66, Waterloo WI 53594	920-478-2144	R	11*	.1
26	Heritage Family Specialty Foods Inc—*Daniel Brackeen*	901 Santerre St, Grand Prairie TX 75050	972-660-6511	R	10*	.1
27	World Harbors Inc—*Steven Arthurs*	176 First Flight Dr, Auburn ME 04210	207-786-3200	R	10*	<.1
28	Kajun Kettle Foods Inc—*Pierre Hilzim*	PO Box 23722, New Orleans LA 70183	504-733-8800	R	10*	<.1
29	Cajun Chef Products Inc—*James Bulliard*	PO Box 248, Saint Martinville LA 70582	337-394-7112	R	9*	.1
30	Aloha Shoyu Company Ltd—*Brian Tanigawa*	96 1205 Waihona St, Pearl City HI 96782	808-456-5929	R	9*	<.1
31	Batampte Pickle Products Inc—*Barry Silberstein*	77 Brooklyn Terminal M, Brooklyn NY 11236	718-251-2100	R	8*	.1
32	United Pickle Products Corp—*Marvin Weishaus*	4366 Park Ave, Bronx NY 10457	718-933-6060	R	8*	.1
33	Jurado Inc—*Arturo Jurado*	300 S Motel Blvd, Las Cruces NM 88007	575-526-4971	R	8*	<.1

Rank	Company Name—*Executive Officer*	Address, City, State, Zip	Phone	Type	Fin	Empls
34	Green Garden Food Products Inc—*Mark Hockman*	5851 S 194th St, Kent WA 98032	253-395-4460	R	8*	.1
35	Plochman Inc—*Carl Plochman*	1333 N Boudreau Rd, Manteno IL 60950	815-468-3434	R	7*	.1
36	Kaplan and Zubrin—*Ronald Kaplan*	PO Box 1006, Camden NJ 08101	856-964-1083	R	7*	<.1
37	Morehouse Foods Inc—*David Latter*	760 Epperson Dr, City Of Industry CA 91748	626-854-1655	R	7*	.1
38	Bartush-Schnitzius Foods Co—*John Rubi*	PO Box 396, Lewisville TX 75067	972-219-1270	R	7*	.1
39	Del Sol Food Company Inc—*Jerry Brown*	PO Box 2243, Brenham TX 77834	979-836-5978	R	6*	.1
40	Yamasa Corporation USA—*Masura Ogura*	3500 Fairview Industri, Salem OR 97302	503-363-8550	R	6*	<.1
41	Griffin Holdings Inc—*John W Griffin*	PO Box 1928, Muskogee OK 74402	918-687-6311	R	6*	<.1
42	Schlotterbeck and Foss Company Inc—*Paul Dioli*	117 Preble St, Portland ME 04101	207-772-4666	R	6*	<.1
43	Swanson Pickle Company Inc—*John Swanson*	PO Box 211, Ravenna MI 49451	231-853-2289	R	5*	<.1
44	Lancaster Fine Foods Inc—*Michael Thompson*	2320 Norman Rd, Lancaster PA 17601	717-397-9578	R	5*	<.1
45	Arcobasso Foods Inc—*Pat Newsham*	8014 N Broadway, Saint Louis MO 63147	314-381-8083	R	4*	<.1
46	San-J International Inc—*Takayoshi Sato* Yamasa Corporation USA	2880 Sprouse Dr, Richmond VA 23231	804-226-8333	S	4*	<.1
47	Sechlers Pickles Inc—*Max Troyer*	PO Box 152, Saint Joe IN 46785	260-337-5461	R	4*	<.1
48	Rob Salamida Company Inc—*Robert Salamida*	71 Pratt Ave Ste 1, Johnson City NY 13790	607-729-4868	R	4*	<.1
49	A-1 Eastern-Home-Made Pickle Company Inc—*Martin Morhar*	1832 Johnston St, Los Angeles CA 90031	323-223-1141	R	4*	<.1
50	Renfro Foods Inc—*Bill Renfro*	PO Box 321, Fort Worth TX 76101	817-336-3849	R	3*	<.1
51	Ginger Golden Products Inc—*Koichi Takeuchi*	5860 Bandini Blvd, Commerce CA 90040	323-838-1070	R	3*	<.1
52	Cosmo's Food Products Inc—*Cosmo Laudano*	200 Callegari Dr, West Haven CT 06516	203-933-9323	R	3*	<.1
53	Walden Farms Inc—*Mitchell Berko*	1209 W Saint Georges A, Linden NJ 07036	908-925-9494	R	3*	<.1
54	Mandarin Soy Sauce Inc—*Michael Wu*	4 Sands Station Rd, Middletown NY 10940	845-343-1505	R	3*	<.1
55	Flamm Pickle And Packaging Company Inc—*Gina Flamm*	PO Box 500, Eau Claire MI 49111	269-461-6916	R	3*	<.1
56	Custom Foods Inc—*John Hausbeck*	634 Kendrick St, Saginaw MI 48602	989-249-8061	R	2*	<.1
57	Tapatio Foods LLC	4685 District Blvd, Vernon CA 90058	323-587-8933	R	2*	<.1
58	Howard Foods Inc—*Charles Waite*	PO Box 2072, Danvers MA 01923	978-774-6207	R	2*	<.1
59	Hudson Valley Homestead—*John King*	102 Sheldon Ln, Craryville NY 12521	518-851-7336	R	2*	<.1
60	Ashman Distributing Co—*Tim Ashman*	PO Box 1068, Virginia Beach VA 23451	757-428-6734	R	1*	<.1
61	Seasons Harvest Inc—*Charley Moore*	PO Box 91, Union Pier MI 49129	269-469-7899	R	1*	<.1

TOTALS: SIC 2035 Pickles, Sauces & Salad Dressings
Companies: 61 — 4,025 / 8.1

2037 Frozen Fruits & Vegetables

Rank	Company Name—*Executive Officer*	Address, City, State, Zip	Phone	Type	Fin	Empls
1	JR Simplot Company Inc—*Bill Whitacre*	PO Box 27, Boise ID 83707	208-336-2110	R	4,500*	10.0
2	Mott's Inc—*Gil Cassagne*	6 High Ridge Park, Stamford CT 06905	203-329-0911	S	488	1.3
3	Norpac Foods Inc—*George Smith*	930 W Washington St, Stayton OR 97383	503-769-2101	R	476*	4.0
4	Tropicana Products Inc—*Greg Shearson*	PO Box 338, Bradenton FL 34206	941-747-4461	S	321*	2.5
5	Seneca Foods International Ltd	3736 S Main St, Marion NY 14505	315-926-8100	S	190*	.6
6	National Frozen Foods Corp—*Richard Grader*	PO Box 9366, Seattle WA 98109	206-322-8900	R	189*	1.0
7	Sabroso Co—*Jim Root*	Po Box 4310, Medford OR 97501	541-772-5653	S	161*	.3
8	Langer Juice Company Inc—*Nathan Langer*	16195 Stephens St, City Of Industry CA 91745	626-336-3100	R	160*	.2
9	Tampico Beverages Inc—*Scott Miller*	3106 N Campbell Ave, Chicago IL 60618		R	137*	.2
10	Twin City Foods Inc—*Roger Lervick*	PO Box 699, Stanwood WA 98292	360-629-2111	R	135*	.8
11	Vitality Beverages Inc—*Jorge Sadurni*	400 N Tampa St Ste 150, Tampa FL 33602	801-301-4600	R	131*	.4
12	Pictsweet Co—*James Tankersley*	PO Box 119, Bells TN 38006	731-663-7600	R	114*	1.2
13	Seabrook Brothers and Sons Inc—*James Seabrook*	PO Box 5103, Bridgeton NJ 08302	856-455-8080	R	94*	.2
14	Citrus World Inc—*Stephen Caruso*	PO Box 1111, Lake Wales FL 33859	863-676-1411	R	82*	.8
15	Hansen Fruit and Cold Storage Inc—*Harley Hansen*	PO Box 9755, Yakima WA 98909	509-457-4153	R	77*	.1
16	Dole Packaged Foods LLC—*Florisel Samudio*	PO Box 545, Atwater CA 95301	209-358-5643	R	73*	.8
17	Coloma Frozen Foods Inc—*Bradley Wendzel*	4145 Coloma Rd, Coloma MI 49038	269-849-0500	R	64*	.2
18	Rainsweet—*George Crispin*	PO Box 6109, Salem OR 97304	503-363-4293	R	59*	.2
19	Louis Dreyfus Citrus Inc—*Peter Hahn*	355 9th St, Winter Garden FL 34787	407-656-1000	R	36*	.4
20	Silver Springs Citrus Inc—*John Rees*	PO Box 155, Howey In The Hills FL 34737	352-324-2101	R	36*	.2
21	Value Frozen Foods Inc—*Ray Walker*	PO Box 487, Patterson CA 95363	956-262-4723	R	30*	.6
22	Smith Frozen Foods Inc—*Sharon Smith*	101 Depot St, Weston OR 97886	541-566-3515	R	26*	.3
23	Penobscot Mccrum LLC—*Dawn Macleod*	28 Pierce St, Belfast ME 04915	207-338-4360	R	24*	.2
24	Wawona Frozen Foods Inc—*William Smittcamp*	100 W Alluvial Ave, Clovis CA 93611	559-299-2901	R	23*	.1
25	Parrot-Ice Drink Products of America Inc—*Greg Johnson*	7121 Perimeter Park Dr, Houston TX 77041	713-937-9496	R	23*	.1
26	Scenic Fruit Co—*Hugh Eisele*	7510 Se Altman Rd, Gresham OR 97080	503-663-3434	R	20*	.2
27	Holly Hill Fruit Products Inc—*Louis McKnight*	PO Box 708, Davenport FL 33836	863-422-1131	R	17*	.1
28	Smeltzer Companies Inc—*Tim Brian*	6032 Joyfield Rd, Frankfort MI 49635	231-882-4421	R	15*	.2
29	Garrett Packing Co—*Roy Rachor* Smith Frozen Foods Inc	11 NW 4th Ave, Milton Freewater OR 97862	541-938-3325	S	15*	.1
30	Interstate Food Processing Corp—*Douglas Oppenheimer*	877 W Main St Ste 700, Boise ID 83702	208-343-2602	R	14*	.1
31	Ventura Coastal LLC—*Maxine Gould*	PO Box 69, Ventura CA 93002	805-653-7000	R	13*	.1
32	Mr Dell Foods Inc—*Kurt Johnsen*	PO Box 494, Kearney MO 64060	816-628-4644	R	10*	<.1
33	J Hellman Frozen Foods Inc—*Bryce Hellman*	1601 E Olympic Blvd, Los Angeles CA 90021	213-627-1093	R	10*	.1
34	Paris Foods Corp	PO Box 121, Trappe MD 21673	410-476-3185	R	9*	.1
35	Oregon Fruit Products Co—*Joe Peterson*	PO Box 5283, Salem OR 97304	503-581-6211	R	8*	.1
36	Sno Pac Foods Inc—*Peter Gengler*	521 Enterprise Dr, Caledonia MN 55921	507-725-5281	R	8*	.1
37	Florida Bottling Inc—*Tom Fuhrman*	1035 Nw 21st Ter, Miami FL 33127	305-324-5932	R	8*	.1
38	National Fruit Vegetable Technology Corp—*Daniel Cashman*	PO Box 67, Baltimore OH 43105	740-862-6300	R	8*	.1
39	Brownwood Acres Foods Inc—*Bob Underwood*	PO Box 486, Eastport MI 49627	231-599-3101	R	6*	<.1
40	California Citrus Producers Inc—*Tommy Elliot*	PO Box 310, Cutler CA 93615	559-562-5169	R	6*	<.1
41	JG Townsend Jr and Company Inc—*Roger Townsend*	PO Box 430, Georgetown DE 19947	302-856-2525	R	5*	<.1
42	Naumes Concentrates Inc—*Michael Naumes*	PO Box 69, Wapato WA 98951	509-877-8882	R	5*	<.1
43	Allen's Blueberry Freezer Inc—*Roy Allen*	PO Box 536, Ellsworth ME 04605	207-667-5561	R	4*	<.1
44	Bel Aire Foods Inc—*Kenneth Kalb*	530 Camp Horne Rd, Pittsburgh PA 15237	412-364-7277	R	4*	<.1
45	Sunsation Inc—*Perry Eichor*	100 S Cambridge Ave, Claremont CA 91711	909-542-0280	R	3*	<.1
46	Big Gus Onion Rings Inc—*Peter George*	4500 Turney Rd, Cleveland OH 44105	216-883-9045	R	3*	<.1
47	Johnson Concentrates Inc—*George Johnson*	PO Box 955, Sunnyside WA 98944	509-837-4600	R	3*	<.1
48	Patterson Frozen Foods Inc—*John Ielmini*	PO Box 487, Patterson CA 95363	209-892-5060	R	1*	<.1
49	California Concentrate Co—*Dennis Alexander*	18678 N Hwy 99, Acampo CA 95220	209-334-9112	R	1*	<.1
50	GM Allen and Son Inc—*Wayne Allen*	PO Box 454, Blue Hill ME 04614	207-469-7060	R	1	.4

TOTALS: SIC 2037 Frozen Fruits & Vegetables
Companies: 50 — 7,845 / 28.3

2038 Frozen Specialties Nec

Rank	Company Name—*Executive Officer*	Address, City, State, Zip	Phone	Type	Fin	Empls
1	Kellogg Co—*John A Bryant*	PO Box 3599, Battle Creek MI 49016		P	12,397	30.6

Note: An asterisk (*) indicates an estimated financial figure. The company type code used is as follows: R = Private, P = Public, S = Private Subsidiary, B = Public Subsidiary, D = Division, J = Joint Venture, I = Investment Fund.

COMPANY RANKINGS BY SALES WITHIN 4-DIGIT SIC

Rank	Company Name—*Executive Officer*	Address, City, State, Zip	Phone	Type	Fin	Empls
2	Schwan Food Co—*Gregory Flack*	115 W College Dr, Marshall MN 56258	507-532-3274	R	2,775*	18.0
3	Heinz Frozen Food Co—*Dave Moran*	1062 Progress St, Pittsburgh PA 15212	412-237-5757	S	1,948*	.4
4	Nestle USA - Prepared Foods Division Inc—*Angelo Iantosca*	30003 Bainbridge Rd, Solon OH 44139	440-349-5757	S	1,800*	5.0
5	Chef America Inc—*Paul Merage*	20 Inverness Pl E, Englewood CO 80112	303-790-0303	S	565*	1.6
6	Bellisio Foods Inc—*Joel Conner*	PO Box 16630, Duluth MN 55816	218-723-5555	R	312*	1.4
7	Lady Little Foods Inc—*John Geocaris*	2200 Pratt Blvd, Elk Grove Village IL 60007	847-806-1440	R	250*	.4
8	Overhill Farms Inc—*James Rudis*	PO Box 58806, Vernon CA 90058	323-582-9977	P	169	.7
9	Kraft Pizza Company Inc—*David Johnson*	1 Kraft Ct, Glenview IL 60025	847-998-2000	R	161*	1.5
10	Kerry Ingedients and Flavors—*Jerry Behan*	100 E Grand Ave, Beloit WI 53511	608-363-1200	S	130*	.6
11	Edible Arrangements LLC—*Tariq Farid*	95 Barnes Rd, Wallingford CT 06492	203-774-8000	R	100*	.1
12	Amy's Kitchen Inc—*Andy Berliner*	PO Box 4759, Petaluma CA 94955	707-578-7188	R	92*	.9
13	GA Food Services Of Pinellas County Inc—*James Lobianco*	12200 32nd Ct N, Saint Petersburg FL 33716	727-573-2211	R	88*	.4
14	State Fair Foods Inc—*Robert Taggart*	3900 Meacham Blvd, Haltom City TX 76117	817-427-7700	D	87*	.5
15	Simeus Foods International Inc	812 S 5th Ave, Mansfield TX 76063		S	78*	.3
16	Processed Foods Corp—*Graham Hunter*	3600 Pleasant Ridge Rd, Knoxville TN 37921	865-525-0401	R	75*	.3
17	Sanderson Farms Inc (Jackson Mississippi)—*Joe Sanderson*	PO Box 988, Laurel MS 39441		S	73	.4
18	Joseph Seviroli Inc—*Joseph Seviroli*	601 Brook St, Garden City NY 11530	516-222-6220	R	70*	.2
19	Wei-Chuan USA Inc Chicago Div—*Steve Lin* Wei-Chuan USA Inc	6845 Santa Fe Dr, Hodgkins IL 60525	708-352-8886	S	70*	<.1
20	Chef Francisco Inc	250 Hansen Access Rd, King of Prussia PA 19406	610-265-7400	S	67*	.3
21	Brooks Food Group Inc—*Robin C Brooks*	940 Orange St, Bedford VA 24523	540-586-8284	R	63*	.3
22	Goodman Food Products—*Donald Goodman*	200 E Beach Ave, Inglewood CA 90302	310-674-3180	R	51*	.3
23	Ajinomoto Frozen Foods USA Inc—*Haruo Kurata*	7124 N Marine Dr, Portland OR 97203	503-286-6548	R	50*	.3
24	De Wafelbakkers LLC—*Ed Hansberry*	PO Box 13570, Maumelle AR 72113	501-791-3320	R	50*	.2
25	Wei-Chuan USA Inc—*Steve Lin*	6655 S Garfield Ave, Bell Gardens CA 90201	562-372-2020	R	47*	.2
26	Gardenburger Inc—*Scott C Wallace*	15615 Alton Pky Ste 35, Irvine CA 92618	949-255-2000	R	46	.2
27	Valley Fine Foods Company Inc—*Chia-Chi Tu*	3909 Park Rd Ste H, Benicia CA 94510	707-746-6888	R	45*	.3
28	Portionables Inc—*Patrick Calliari*	2825 Roeder Ave Ste 4, Bellingham WA 98225	360-676-9140	R	41*	.3
29	Camino Real Foods Inc—*Rob Cross*	PO Box 30729, Los Angeles CA 90030	323-585-6599	R	39*	.4
30	ASK Foods Inc—*Wendy Di Matteo Holsi*	PO Box 388, Palmyra PA 17078	717-838-6356	R	39*	.2
31	Bernatello's Pizza Inc—*William Ramsay*	200 Congress St W, Maple Lake MN 55358	320-963-6191	R	38*	.2
32	El Encanto Inc—*Jacqueline Baca*	2001 4th St Sw, Albuquerque NM 87102	505-243-2722	R	36*	.4
33	Request Foods Inc—*Jack Dewitt*	PO Box 2577, Holland MI 49422	616-786-0900	R	36*	.4
34	Milmar Food Group Ii LLC—*Roy Makinen*	1 6 1/2 Station Rd, Goshen NY 10924	845-294-5400	R	30*	.3
35	Buddy's Kitchen Inc—*Dave Smith*	12105 Nicollet Ave, Burnsville MN 55337	952-894-2540	R	25*	.2
36	Kahiki Foods Inc—*Alan L Hoover*	1100 Morrison Rd, Gahanna OH 43230	614-322-3180	R	23	.2
37	Ateeco Inc—*Thomas F Twardzik*	PO Box 606, Shenandoah PA 17976	570-462-2745	R	23*	.2
38	Armanino Foods of Distinction Inc—*Edmond J Pera*	30588 San Antonio St, Hayward CA 94544	510-441-9300	P	23	<.1
39	Chung's Products LP—*Danny Beal*	3907 Dennis St, Houston TX 77004	713-741-2118	R	21*	.1
40	Dufour Pastry Kitchens—*Judi Arnold*	251 Locust Ave, Bronx NY 10454	718-402-8800	R	21*	<.1
41	Ragozzino Foods Inc—*Gloria Ragozzino*	PO Box 116, Meriden CT 06450	203-238-2553	R	21*	.1
42	M C I Foods Inc—*Daniel Southard*	12835 S Atlantic Ave, Compton CA 90221	310-635-5664	R	20*	.1
43	Sierra Madre Foods Inc—*Mauro Robles*	608 Monterey Pass Rd, Monterey Park CA 91754	626-289-5054	R	19*	.1
44	Old Fashioned Kitchen Inc—*Jay Conzen*	1045 Towbin Ave, Lakewood NJ 08701	732-364-4100	R	19*	.1
45	International Dehydrated Foods Inc—*Kirk Hellweg*	PO Box 10347, Springfield MO 65808	417-881-7820	R	16*	.1
46	Choice Products USA Inc—*Richard Mchugh*	PO Box 307, Eau Claire WI 54703	715-833-8761	R	15	.3
47	Louisa Food Products Inc—*Thomas Baldetti*	1918 Switzer Ave, Saint Louis MO 63136	314-868-3000	R	15*	.1
48	Golden Krust Caribbean Bakery Inc—*Lowell Hawthorne*	3958 Park Ave, Bronx NY 10457	718-655-7878	R	15	.1
49	Pasco Corporation Of America—*Tsunehisa Kikkawa*	6500 N Marine Dr, Portland OR 97203	503-289-6500	R	14*	.1
50	Riverside Foods Inc—*Mark Kornely*	2520 Wilson St, Two Rivers WI 54241	920-793-4511	R	14*	.1
51	SA Piazza And Associates LLC—*Gary Gunderson*	PO Box 1603, Clackamas OR 97015	503-657-3123	R	13*	<.1
52	O'tasty Foods Inc—*Ming Huang*	160 S Hacienda Blvd, City Of Industry CA 91745	626-330-1229	R	13*	.1
53	On-Cor Frozen Foods LLC—*John Statis*	627 Landwehr Rd, Northbrook IL 60062	847-205-1040	R	11*	.1
54	Five Star Frozen Foods Inc—*Rick Pfrang*	PO Box 740, Kaukauna WI 54130	920-766-9930	R	10*	.1
55	Elena's Food Specialties Inc—*Peter Sartorio*	405 Allerton Ave, South San Francisco CA 94080	650-871-8700	R	9*	.1
56	Leonetti Frozen Foods Inc—*Beth DiPietro*	5935 Woodland Ave, Philadelphia PA 19143	215-729-4200	R	9*	<.1
57	Codino's Foods Inc—*Scott Devantier*	704 Corporation Park S, Scotia NY 12302	518-372-3308	R	9*	<.1
58	Fry Foods Inc—*Norman Fry*	PO Box 837, Tiffin OH 44883	419-448-0831	R	8*	.1
59	Amy Food Inc—*Phyllis Hsu*	3324 S Richey St, Houston TX 77017	713-910-5860	R	8*	.1
60	Harvest Food Products Company Inc—*Danny Kha*	710 Sandoval Way, Hayward CA 94544	510-675-0383	R	7*	<.1
61	La Mousse—*Nadine Korman*	11150 La Grange Ave, Los Angeles CA 90025	310-478-6051	R	7*	.1
62	Savignano Food Corp—*Michael Savignano*	107 S Jefferson St, Orange NJ 07050	973-673-3355	R	7*	.1
63	Pedro's Tamales—*Mark Hale*	PO Box 3571, Lubbock TX 79452	806-745-9531	R	6*	<.1
64	Finger Food Products Inc—*Robert Cordova*	PO Box 560, Niagara Falls NY 14304	716-297-4555	R	6*	.1
65	Pizza Corner Inc—*David Zubrod*	1031 4th St Sw, Valley City ND 58072	701-845-0104	R	5*	.1
66	Garland Ventures Ltd—*Leon Hsu*	115 S International Rd, Garland TX 75042	972-485-8878	R	5*	<.1
67	Pierino Frozen Foods Inc—*Pierino Guglielmetti*	1695 Southfield Rd, Lincoln Park MI 48146	313-928-0950	R	4*	<.1
68	Mh Inc—*Eric Lecaptain*	706 Daniel St Ste 2, Billings MT 59101	406-259-2930	R	4*	<.1
69	Emil's Pizza Inc—*Rick Roedl*	PO Box 168, Watertown WI 53094	920-262-9756	R	4*	<.1
70	Mama Rosie's Company Inc—*Anthony Sardo*	10 Dorrance St, Boston MA 02129	617-242-4300	R	4*	<.1
71	Bee Bee Que Inc—*David Barnes*	7033 E 49th Ave, Commerce City CO 80022	303-287-2856	R	4*	<.1
72	Lucias Pizza Co—*Darrell Long*	10989 Gravois Industri, Saint Louis MO 63128	314-843-2553	R	4*	<.1
73	Les Chateaux De France Inc—*Gerald Shapiro*	1 Craft Ave, Inwood NY 11096	516-239-6795	R	4*	<.1
74	Italia Foods Inc—*Filippo Carabetta*	2365 Hammond Dr, Schaumburg IL 60173	847-397-4479	R	4*	<.1
75	Appetizers Made Easy Inc—*Matt Brown*	25 Branca Rd, East Rutherford NJ 07073	201-531-1212	R	4*	<.1
76	Crave Foods Inc—*Shaheda Sayed*	2043 Imperial St, Los Angeles CA 90021	213-627-8887	R	3*	<.1
77	Putney Pasta Company Inc—*Carol Berry*	28 Vernon St Ste 434, Brattleboro VT 05301	802-257-4800	R	3*	<.1
78	O Chilli Frozen Foods Inc—*Jeffrey Rothschild*	1251 Shermer Rd, Northbrook IL 60062	847-562-1991	R	3*	<.1
79	Tien Tien Food Company Inc—*Fred Tang*	1415 Van Dyke Ave, San Francisco CA 94124	415-671-2089	R	3*	<.1
80	Peppy's Foods Inc—*Frieda Gozza*	PO Box 293, Westtown NY 10998	845-457-5868	R	2*	.1
81	TJ Pizza's Inc—*Tom Jones*	150 Shepley Dr, Saint Louis MO 63137	314-869-9404	R	2*	<.1
82	Chef-Co Wholesale Distributors Inc—*Eric Hammons*	PO Box 1848, West Monroe LA 71294	318-396-8625	R	2*	<.1
83	Namias Of Arizona Inc—*Raymond Flores*	4644 E Fort Lowell Rd, Tucson AZ 85712	520-884-1333	R	2*	<.1
84	King Kold Inc—*Douglas Smith*	331 N Main St, Englewood OH 45322	937-836-2731	R	2*	<.1
85	Portesi's Italian Foods Inc—*Joseph Mitch*	3201 Business Park Dr, Stevens Point WI 54482	715-344-7974	R	2*	<.1
86	Teresa Foods Inc—*Robert Nagel*	PO Box 1028, Peotone IL 60468	708-258-6200	R	2*	<.1
87	Luige's Pizza Factory Ltd—*Larry Drake*	W3830 Hwy K, Belgium WI 53004	920-994-4884	R	2*	<.1
88	Dudek Foods Inc—*Mark Dudek*	PO Box 12378, Detroit MI 48212	313-891-5226	R	2*	<.1
89	Tapas International Inc—*Herbert Prokscha*	6929 Nrcooflee Rd Ste, Orlando FL 32822	407-857-6699	R	1*	<.1
90	Lucky Foods LLC—*Tammy Jo*	7774 Sw Nimbus Ave Ste, Beaverton OR 97008	503-641-6602	R	1*	<.1

Rank	Company Name—*Executive Officer*	Address, City, State, Zip	Phone	Type	Fin	Empls
91	Campobello Foods—*Vincent Totta*	1008 SE Blue Pky, Lees Summit MO 64063	816-554-1161	R	1*	<.1
92	Upscale Foods Inc—*Edith Katz*	4630 Quebec Ave N Lwer, Minneapolis MN 55428	763-533-0521	R	1*	<.1
93	Dinewise Inc—*Paul Roman*	500 Bi-County Blvd Ste, Farmingdale NY 11735	631-694-1111	P	1	<.1
94	Ruiz Food Products Inc—*Fred Ruiz*	PO Box 37, Dinuba CA 93618	559-591-5510	R	1*	2.5

TOTALS: SIC 2038 Frozen Specialties Nec
Companies: 94 — 22,423 — 73.1

2041 Flour & Other Grain Mill Products

Rank	Company Name—*Executive Officer*	Address, City, State, Zip	Phone	Type	Fin	Empls
1	Cargill Inc—*Gregory R Page*	PO Box 9300, Minneapolis MN 55440	952-742-7575	R	119,469	138.0
2	CHS Inc—*Chris Casale*	5500 Cenex Dr, Inver Grove Heights MN 55077	651-355-6000	P	36,916	9.6
3	General Mills Inc—*Samir Behl*	PO Box 9452, Minneapolis MN 55440	763-764-7600	P	14,797	33.0
4	Corn Products International Inc—*Ilene S Gordon*	PO Box 7100, Westchester IL 60154	708-551-2600	P	6,544	11.1
5	Alabama Farmers Coop—*Tommy Paulk*	PO Box 2227, Decatur AL 35609	256-353-6843	R	2,201*	2.3
6	Bartlett and Co (Kansas City Missouri)—*James B Heberstreit*	4900 Main St Ste 1200, Kansas City MO 64112	816-753-6300	R	1,894*	.7
7	Knoxville Milling Co—*Scott Petty* C H Guenther and Son Inc	1605 Prosser Rd, Knoxville TN 37914	865-546-5511	S	472*	.8
8	Star Of The West Milling Co—*Arthur Loeffler*	PO Box 146, Frankenmuth MI 48734	989-652-9971	R	294*	.2
9	Cargill Corn Milling North America—*Greg Page* Cargill Inc	PO Box 9300, Minneapolis MN 55440	612-742-4144	D	211*	2.3
10	C H Guenther and Son Inc—*Dale Tremblay*	PO Box 118, San Antonio TX 78291	210-227-1401	R	79*	.8
11	King Arthur Flour Inc—*Steve Voigt*	PO Box 1010, Norwich VT 05055	802-649-3361	R	76	.2
12	Azteca Milling Co—*Don Schleppegrell*	1159 Cottonwood Ln Ste, Irving TX 75038	972-232-5300	D	58*	.2
13	Thymly Products Inc—*Harry Muller-Thym*	PO Box 65, Colora MD 21917	410-658-4820	R	52*	.1
14	Birkett's International Inc—*Wayne Wagner*	PO Box 440, Penn Yan NY 14527	315-536-3311	R	52*	<.1
15	Spartan Foods Of America Inc—*Robert Utecht*	PO Box 1003, Fairforest SC 29336	864-595-6262	R	51*	.2
16	Keynes Brothers Inc—*William Keynes*	PO Box 628, Logan OH 43138	740-385-6824	R	47*	.1
17	Guttenplan's Frozen Dough Inc—*Abe Littenberg*	100 Hwy 36 E, North Middletown NJ 07748	732-495-9480	R	46*	.1
18	Stafford County Flour Mills Company Inc—*Alvin Brensing*	PO Box 7, Hudson KS 67545	620-458-4121	R	46*	<.1
19	King Milling Co—*Brian Doyle*	PO Box 99, Lowell MI 49331	616-897-9264	R	38*	<.1
20	Bay State Milling Co—*Brian Rothwell*	100 Congress St Ste 2, Quincy MA 02169	617-328-4400	R	38*	.3
21	Food Should Taste Good Inc—*Peter Lescoe*	PO Box 776, Needham Heights MA 02494	781-455-8500	R	34	<.1
22	NutraCea Inc—*W John Short*	6720 N Scottsdale Rd S, Scottsdale AZ 85253	602-522-3000	P	32	.3
23	Chelsea Milling Co—*Howdy Holmes*	PO Box 460, Chelsea MI 48118	734-475-1361	R	31*	.3
24	Sun Rich LLC—*John Myer*	PO Box 128, Hope MN 56046	507-451-4724	R	29*	.2
25	Valley Grain Products—*Roberto G Barrera*	5301 Industrial Park D, Henderson KY 42420	270-826-2533	D	28	.1
26	Hodgson Mill Inc—*Robert Goldstein*	PO Box 1048, Effingham IL 62401	217-347-0105	R	26*	.1
27	Morrison Milling Co—*Scott Petty* C H Guenther and Son Inc	319 E Prairie St, Denton TX 76201	940-387-6111	S	26*	.2
28	Canadian Harvest-USA LP—*David Belaney*	1001 Cleveland St S, Cambridge MN 55008	763-689-5800	R	25*	<.1
29	Agricor Inc—*Steve Wickes*	PO Box 807, Marion IN 46952	765-662-0606	R	25*	<.1
30	Midstate Mills Inc—*Steven Arndt*	PO Box 350, Newton NC 28658	828-464-1611	R	20*	.1
31	Mcshares Inc—*Monte White*	PO Box 1460, Salina KS 67402	785-825-2181	R	20*	.1
32	Pendleton Flour Mills LLC—*Alan Kessler*	PO Box 400, Pendleton OR 97801	541-276-6511	R	19*	.1
33	Cargill Dry Corn Ingredients Inc—*Rex Winter*	616 S Jefferson St, Paris IL 61944	217-465-5331	R	16*	.1
34	Blendex Company LLC—*John Beadle*	11208 Electron Dr, Louisville KY 40299	502-267-1003	R	16*	.1
35	Sftc LLC—*Aleta Palva*	18 Bisbee Ct, Santa Fe NM 87508	505-473-7000	R	16*	.1
36	Central Milling LLC—*Keith Giusto*	PO Box 7, Richmond UT 84333	435-258-2425	R	14*	.1
37	Yh Products Corp—*Jason Nova*	400 Lombard St, Oxnard CA 93030	805-983-1130	R	13*	<.1
38	House-Autry Mills Inc—*Roger Mortenson*	PO Box 460, Four Oaks NC 27524	919-963-6200	R	12*	.1
39	R Ibarra's Inc—*Hilda Ibarra*	201 Ne 35th St, Fort Worth TX 76106	817-625-8300	R	11*	.1
40	H Nagel and Son Co—*Bill Nagel*	2428 Central Pkwy, Cincinnati OH 45214	513-665-4550	R	11*	<.1
41	Atkinson Milling Co—*Glen Wheeler*	95 Atkinson Mill Rd, Selma NC 27576	919-965-3547	R	10*	<.1
42	Knappen Milling Co—*Charles Knappen III*	PO Box 245, Augusta MI 49012	269-731-4141	R	9*	<.1
43	Quinoa Corp—*David F Schnorr*	PO Box 279, Gardena CA 90248	310-217-8125	R	8*	<.1
44	Hopkinsville Milling Co—*Robert Harper*	PO Box 669, Hopkinsville KY 42241	270-886-1231	R	8*	<.1
45	ADM Milling Co—*Craig Fisher*	8000 W 110th St Ste 30, Overland Park KS 66210	913-491-9400	D	7*	.1
46	Cornell Brothers Inc—*D Cornell*	PO Box 101, Middlebury Center PA 16935	570-376-2471	R	7*	<.1
47	Giusto's Speciality Foods LLC	344 Littlefield Ave, South San Francisco CA 94080	650-873-6566	R	7*	<.1
48	Bay Foods Inc—*James Bay*	PO Box 1455, Chicago IL 60690	312-346-5757	R	6*	<.1
49	Lakeside Mills Inc—*Bryan King*	PO Box 230, Rutherfordton NC 28139	828-286-4866	R	6*	<.1
50	Big Spring Mill Inc—*David Long*	PO Box 305, Elliston VA 24087	540-268-2267	R	5*	<.1
51	Mayab Happy Tacos Inc—*Jorge Alamilla*	450 Florida Grove Rd, Perth Amboy NJ 08861	732-293-0400	R	5*	<.1
52	Quality Ingredients Corp—*Thomas Schmidt Sr*	PO Box 306, Chester NJ 07930	908-879-2227	R	5*	<.1
53	Corn Flour Producers LLC—*Leo Olabarrieta*	PO Box 2, Worthington IN 47471	812-875-3113	R	4*	<.1
54	Pappy's Enterprises Inc—*Robert Geller*	2605 N Rolling Rd Ste, Baltimore MD 21244	410-265-1600	R	4*	<.1
55	Allen Brothers Milling Company Inc—*Ewart Edgerton*	PO Box 1437, Columbia SC 29202	803-779-2460	R	4*	<.1
56	McIntosh Farm Service Co—*Robert Kringlen*	350 State St SW, McIntosh MN 56556	218-563-3735	R	4*	<.1
57	Ashland Roller Mills Inc—*Linwood Attkisson*	PO Box 1775, Ashland VA 23005	804-798-8329	R	4*	<.1
58	Pete-Za-Ria Pizza Inc—*Harry Peters*	PO Box 608, Portville NY 14770	716-933-7100	R	4*	<.1
59	Big J Milling and Elevator Company Inc—*John Reese*	PO Box 717, Brigham City UT 84302	435-723-3459	R	4*	<.1
60	El Merendero Posas Inc—*Antonio Posa*	PO Box 5797, Santa Fe NM 87502	505-471-4766	R	4*	<.1
61	Wilson's Corn Products Inc—*Thomas Wilson*	PO Box 97, Rochester IN 46975	574-223-3177	R	3*	<.1
62	Ohio Baking Company Inc—*Joseph Spano*	PO Box 4010, Utica NY 13504	315-724-2033	R	3*	<.1
63	Wpp Dough Company Inc—*Michael Omahne*	1280 Saint Clair Rd, Johnstown PA 15905	814-539-7799	R	2*	<.1
64	Nilson Farms Inc—*Bradley Nilson*	14105 74th St Ne, Hoople ND 58243	701-894-6413	R	2*	<.1
65	Uhlmann Co—*Paul Uhlmann*	1009 Central St, Kansas City MO 64105	816-221-8200	R	1*	<.1
66	War Eagle Mill Inc—*Martin Roenigk*	12017 Sellers Pl Rd, Hindsville AR 72738	479-789-5343	R	1*	<.1
67	Kiwa Bio-Tech Products Group Corp—*Wei Li*	310 N Indian Hill Blvd, Claremont CA 91711	626-715-5855	P	<1	<.1

TOTALS: SIC 2041 Flour & Other Grain Mill Products
Companies: 67 — 183,929 — 202.7

2043 Cereal Breakfast Foods

Rank	Company Name—*Executive Officer*	Address, City, State, Zip	Phone	Type	Fin	Empls
1	Quaker Oats Co—*Robert S Morrison*	PO Box 04003, Chicago IL 60604	312-821-1000	S	5,040	11.9
2	Malt-O-Meal Co—*Chris Neugent*	80 S 8th St Ste 2700, Minneapolis MN 55402	612-338-8551	R	168*	1.4
3	Small Planet Foods Inc—*Michele Meyer*	719 Metcalf St, Sedro Woolley WA 98284	360-855-0100	S	78*	.1
4	Weetabix Company Inc—*Richard George*	20 Cameron St, Clinton MA 01510	978-368-0991	R	49*	.3
5	Echo Lake Foods Inc—*Scott Meinerz*	PO Box 279, Burlington WI 53105	262-763-9551	R	35*	.2
6	Kashi Co—*Philip Tauber*	PO Box 8557, La Jolla CA 92038	858-274-8870	R	32*	.1
7	Dakota Specialty Milling Inc—*William Matthaei*	PO Box 46, Fargo ND 58107	701-282-9656	R	13*	.1

Note: An asterisk (*) indicates an estimated financial figure. The company type code used is as follows: R = Private, P = Public, S = Private Subsidiary, B = Public Subsidiary, D = Division, J = Joint Venture, I = Investment Fund.

COMPANY RANKINGS BY SALES WITHIN 4-DIGIT SIC

Rank	Company Name—*Executive Officer*	Address, City, State, Zip	Phone	Type	Fin	Empls
8	Little Crow Foods—*Denny Fuller*	PO Box 1038, Warsaw IN 46581	574-267-7141	R	6*	<.1

TOTALS: SIC 2043 Cereal Breakfast Foods
Companies: 8

					5,421	14.0

2044 Rice Milling

Rank	Company Name—*Executive Officer*	Address, City, State, Zip	Phone	Type	Fin	Empls
1	MasterFoods USA Inc—*John Franklyn Mars*	295 Brown St, Elizabethtown PA 17022	717-367-1500	S	12,192*	27.0
2	Riceland Foods Inc—*Daniel Kennedy*	PO Box 927, Stuttgart AR 72160	870-673-5500	R	1,132*	1.6
3	Producers Rice Mill Inc—*Keith Glover*	PO Box 1248, Stuttgart AR 72160	870-673-4444	R	483*	.7
4	Pacific International Rice Mills Inc—*Soren W Schroder*	PO Box 652, Woodland CA 95776	530-666-1691	S	75*	.1
5	Farmers Rice Milling Company Inc—*Jamie Warshaw*	PO Box 3704, Lake Charles LA 70602	337-433-5205	R	62*	.1
6	Rice Planters Mill LLC—*Edward Gaspard*	403 S Washington St, Abbeville LA 70510	337-898-3056	R	60*	<.1
7	Pacific Grain Products Intl—*Zachary S Wochok*	PO Box 2060, Woodland CA 95776	530-662-5056	D	45*	.2
8	Ricetec Inc—*John Nelson*	PO Box 1305, Alvin TX 77512	281-756-3180	R	36*	.2
9	Farmers Rice Coop—*Robert Sandrock*	PO Box 15223, Sacramento CA 95851	916-568-4300	R	33*	.3
10	Indian Harvest Specialtifoods Inc	PO Box 428, Bemidji MN 56619	218-751-8500	R	15*	<.1
11	Far West Rice Inc—*C Johnson*	PO Box 370, Durham CA 95938	530-891-1339	R	13*	<.1
12	Sage V Foods LLC—*V Pete Vegas*	12100 Wilshire Blvd St, Los Angeles CA 90025	310-820-4496	R	12*	<.1
13	Doguet's Rice Milling Co—*Mike Doguet*	795 S Major Dr, Beaumont TX 77707	409-866-2297	R	10*	<.1
14	Cormier Rice Milling Company Inc—*J Ferguson*	PO Box 152, De Witt AR 72042	870-946-3561	R	8*	<.1
15	Seaberg Rice and Co-op—*Roy Seaberg*	PO Box 100, Dayton TX 77535	936-258-2627	R	3*	<.1

TOTALS: SIC 2044 Rice Milling
Companies: 15

					14,178	30.5

2045 Prepared Flour Mixes & Doughs

Rank	Company Name—*Executive Officer*	Address, City, State, Zip	Phone	Type	Fin	Empls
1	Continental Mills Inc—*John Heily*	PO Box 88176, Seattle WA 98138	253-872-8400	R	183*	.6
2	Bruegger's Enterprises—*James J Greco*	PO Box 374, Burlington VT 05402	802-660-4020	R	178*	.3
3	Value Creation Partners Inc—*G Humphrey*	445 Hutchinson Ave Ste, Columbus OH 43235	614-785-6401	R	148*	1.5
4	TNT Crust Inc—*Roger LeBreck*	PO Box 8929, Green Bay WI 54308	920-431-7240	S	98*	.3
5	Lavoi Corp—*Bob Gansel*	1749 Tullie Cir Ne, Atlanta GA 30329	404-325-1016	R	54*	.3
6	Watson Foods Company Inc—*James Watson*	301 Heffernan Dr, West Haven CT 06516	203-932-3000	R	36*	.2
7	Drayton Foods LLC—*Tim Roach*	PO Box 9018, Fargo ND 58106	701-277-9947	R	29*	.2
8	Hydroblend Inc—*Mike Guthrie*	1801 N Elder St, Nampa ID 83687	208-467-7441	R	22*	.1
9	Langlois Co—*Richard Langlois*	10810 San Sevaine Way, Mira Loma CA 91752	951-360-3900	R	11*	.1
10	Cohen's Bakery Inc—*Mark Didomenico*	1132 Broadway St, Buffalo NY 14212	716-892-8149	R	10*	<.1
11	T R Rizzuto Pizza Crust Inc—*Tony Rizzuto*	3420 E Riverside Ave, Spokane WA 99202	509-536-9268	R	8*	<.1
12	Modern Products Inc—*Anthony A Palermo*	6425 W Executive Dr, Mequon WI 53092	262-242-2400	R	8*	<.1
13	Dover Foods Inc—*Kathy Milner*	353 Banner Farm Rd, Mills River NC 28759	828-890-8344	R	7*	<.1
14	PACA Foods LLC—*Michael Shepardson*	5212 Cone Rd, Tampa FL 33610	813-628-8228	R	6*	<.1
15	Daylight Corp—*John Bond*	PO Box 691150, Tulsa OK 74169	918-438-0800	R	6*	<.1
16	Shenandoah Mills Inc—*Dale Nunnery*	PO Box 369, Lebanon TN 37088	615-444-0841	R	5*	<.1
17	Wind and Willow Inc—*Rozena Shackelford*	PO Box 191, Mount Vernon MO 65712	417-466-4646	R	4*	<.1
18	Flour Power Inc—*James Mattson*	6867 Martindale Rd, Shawnee Mission KS 66218	913-441-4787	R	3*	<.1

TOTALS: SIC 2045 Prepared Flour Mixes & Doughs
Companies: 18

					815	3.7

2046 Wet Corn Milling

Rank	Company Name—*Executive Officer*	Address, City, State, Zip	Phone	Type	Fin	Empls
1	AE Staley Manufacturing Co—*D Lynn Grider*	2200 E El Dorado St, Decatur IL 62521	217-423-4411	S	2,828*	2.8
2	Grain Processing Corp—*Gage Kent*	1600 Oregon St, Muscatine IA 52761	563-264-4829	R	448*	.8
3	Penford Corp—*Thomas D Malkoski*	7094 S Revere Pkwy, Centennial CO 80112	303-649-1900	P	315	.3
4	Penford Products Co—*Thomas D Malkoski* Penford Corp	7094 S Revere Pkwy, Centennial CO 80112	303-649-1900	S	272*	.3
5	Manildra Group USA—*Gerry Degnan*	4210 Shawnee Mission P, Shawnee Mission KS 66205	913-362-0777	R	84*	.1
6	Corn Products Development Inc—*Ilene Gordon*	PO Box 6129, Stockton CA 95206	209-982-1920	S	32*	.1
7	Cargill Specialy Canola Oils—*Gregory Page*	2300 N Yellowstone Hwy, Idaho Falls ID 83401	208-522-4113	S	16*	<.1
8	Western Polymer Corp—*Linda Jagger*	32 Rd R Se, Moses Lake WA 98837	509-765-1803	R	14*	.1

TOTALS: SIC 2046 Wet Corn Milling
Companies: 8

					4,010	4.5

2047 Dog & Cat Food

Rank	Company Name—*Executive Officer*	Address, City, State, Zip	Phone	Type	Fin	Empls
1	Nestle Purina PetCare Co—*W Patrick McGinnis*	Checkerboard Sq, Saint Louis MO 63164	314-982-1000	S	2,763	19.2
2	Hill's Pet Nutrition Inc—*Neil Thompson*	PO Box 148, Topeka KS 66601		S	1,179	2.7
3	ReConserve of Illinois—*Bob McMullen* Scope Products Inc	6160 S River Rd, Hodgkins IL 60525	708-354-5882	S	1,035*	.4
4	Recycle to Conserve Inc—*Bob McMullen* Scope Products Inc	704 Zephyr St, Stockton CA 95206	209-982-5085	S	1,035*	.4
5	Recycle to Conserve TX Inc—*Bob McMullen* Scope Products Inc	3610 Duncanville Rd, Dallas TX 75236	214-339-4755	S	1,035*	.4
6	International Transportation Service Inc—*Bob McMullen* Scope Products Inc	2811 Wilshire Blvd, Santa Monica CA 90403	310-458-1574	S	847*	.4
7	Reconserve of Colorado—*Bob McMullen* Scope Products Inc	5801 Franklin St, Denver CO 80216	303-295-0750	S	847*	.4
8	Reconserve of Maryland—*Bob McMullen* Scope Products Inc	3220 Sun St, Baltimore MD 21226	410-354-1417	S	847*	.4
9	Reconserve of Texas—*Bob McMullen* Scope Products Inc	3610 Duncanville Rd, Dallas TX 75236	214-339-4755	S	847*	.4
10	Scope Energy Resources Inc—*Bob McMullen* Scope Industries Inc	2811 Wilshire Blvd Ste, Santa Monica CA 90403	310-458-1574	S	847*	.4
11	Scope Products Inc—*Bob McMullen* Scope Industries Inc	2811 Wilshire Blvd Ste, Santa Monica CA 90403	310-458-1574	S	847*	.4
12	Scope Properties Inc—*Bob McMullen* Scope Industries Inc	2811 Wilshire Blvd Ste, Santa Monica CA 90403	310-458-1574	S	847*	.4
13	Topnotch Foods Inc—*Bob McMullen* Scope Products Inc	1988 E 57th St, Vernon CA 90058	323-586-2007	S	847*	.4
14	Kal Kan Foods Inc—*John Franklyn Mars*	PO Box 58853, Los Angeles CA 90058	323-587-2727	S	220*	1.2
15	Scope Industries Inc—*Meyer Luskin*	2811 Wilshire Blvd Ste, Santa Monica CA 90403	310-458-1574	P	81	.4
16	Northwest Pet Products Inc—*Bill Behnken*	PO Box 810, Woodland WA 98674	360-225-8855	R	60*	.1
17	Bil-Jac Foods Inc—*Robert Kelly*	3337 Medina Rd, Medina OH 44256	330-722-7888	R	56*	.1
18	Meow Mix Co—*Richard Thompson*	PO Box 1594, Secaucus NJ 07096	201-520-4000	S	47*	.1
19	Kass Products Inc—*Brent Weinmann*	PO Box 33, Bowling Green OH 43402	419-832-1641	R	47*	.1

Rank	Company Name—*Executive Officer*	Address, City, State, Zip	Phone	Type	Fin	Empls
20	Karem Inc—*Gregg Sheil*	549 Karem Dr, Marshall WI 53559	608-655-3439	R	40*	<.1
21	Royal Canin USA Inc—*Stan Howton*	500 Fountain Lakes Blv, Saint Charles MO 63301	636-926-0003	S	40*	.2
22	Safeway Pet Food Plant—*Steven Burd*	PO Box 29093, Phoenix AZ 85038		D	38*	<.1
23	Hi-Tek Rations Inc—*Leonard Powell*	PO Box 1223, Dublin GA 31040	478-272-8826	R	35*	.1
24	Spf North America Inc—*David Berry*	5300 Hwy 25 N, Hodges SC 29653	864-374-3239	R	27*	.2
25	Schell and Kampeter Inc—*Gary Schell*	PO Box 156, Meta MO 65058	573-229-4203	R	26*	.3
26	Wellpet LLC—*Steve Harris*	200 Ames Pond Dr Ste 1, Tewksbury MA 01876	978-289-5500	R	26*	.1
27	Triple - T Foods Inc—*Chris Terlip*	PO Box 943, Frontenac KS 66763	620-231-7779	R	17*	.1
28	Pet Factory Inc—*Tom Miller*	845 E High St, Mundelein IL 60060	847-837-8900	R	16*	.1
29	Yukon Nutritional—*Mark Heyward*	13506 Summerport Ste 4, Windermere FL 34786	407-877-8779	R	16*	<.1
30	Dogswell LLC—*Marco Gianni*	1964 Westwood Blvd Ste, Los Angeles CA 90025	310-651-5200	R	16*	<.1
31	Three Dog Bakery Inc—*Scott Ragan*	1843 N Topping Ave, Kansas City MO 64120	816-474-3647	R	15*	.1
32	Treatco Inc—*Margie Thomas*	PO Box 4047, Wichita KS 67204	316-265-7900	R	15*	.1
33	Chenango Valley Pet Foods Inc—*Donald Fingerman*	PO Box 720, Sherburne NY 13460	607-674-2121	R	14*	.1
34	Hyland Co—*Barbara Hinton*	PO Box 5129, Ashland KY 41105	606-928-4011	R	14*	<.1
35	Specialty Feeds Inc—*Joseph Coscia*	PO Box 9600, Memphis TN 38190	901-774-9080	R	14*	<.1
36	Nature's Recipe Pet Foods—*Robert M Leibowitz*	1 Maritime Plaza, San Francisco CA 94111	415-247-3000	S	13*	.1
37	Pro-Pet LLC—*W Wright*	PO Box 369, Saint Marys OH 45885	419-394-3374	R	12*	.1
38	Wow-Bow Distributors Ltd—*Mikelle Salimbene*	70-D Corbin Ave, Bay Shore NY 11706	631-254-6064	R	10*	<.1
39	Redbarn Pet Products Inc—*Jeff Baikie*	2148 W 16th St, Long Beach CA 90813	562-495-7315	R	9*	.1
40	Selective Petfood Services Inc—*John Morrell*	101 Virginia St, Sioux City IA 51101	712-255-2545	S	9*	<.1
41	C J Foods Inc—*John Kuenzi*	PO Box 348, Pawnee City NE 68420	402-852-2341	R	6*	<.1
42	Bench and Fields Pet Foods LLC—*Mark Bennett*	PO Box 6, Mishawaka IN 46546	574-534-7843	R	4*	<.1
43	Hy Win Foods Inc—*R Bingham*	8620 S Regency Dr, Tulsa OK 74131	918-227-0004	R	3*	<.1
44	Willard Milling Inc—*Sally Sexton*	PO Box 129, Willard KY 41181	606-474-5754	R	3*	<.1
45	C and R International Sales Inc—*Charles Toledo*	2403 Navy Dr, Stockton CA 95206	209-943-1777	R	3*	<.1
46	Evanger Dog and Cat Food Company Inc—*Holly Sher*	221 Wheeling Rd, Wheeling IL 60090	847-537-0102	R	1*	<.1

TOTALS: SIC 2047 Dog & Cat Food

	Companies: 46				14,776	30.2

2048 Prepared Feeds Nec

Rank	Company Name—*Executive Officer*	Address, City, State, Zip	Phone	Type	Fin	Empls
1	Mountaire Corp—*Ronald Cameron*	1901 Napa Valley Dr, Little Rock AR 72212	501-372-6524	R	145,200*	6.0
2	ConAgra Foods Inc—*Gary M Rodkin*	1 ConAgra Dr, Omaha NE 68102	402-240-4000	P	12,303	23.2
3	Goldsboro Milling Company Inc—*H Gordon Maxwell*	PO Box 10009, Goldsboro NC 27532	919-778-3120	R	1,584*	1.2
4	Purina Mills LLC—*Chris Policinski*	PO Box 66812, Saint Louis MO 63166	636-742-6100	R	1,112*	2.5
5	Provimi North America Inc—*Charles Shininger*	10 Collective Way, Brookville OH 45309	937-770-2400	R	712*	.5
6	American Proteins Inc—*Thomas Bagwell*	4705 Leland Dr, Cumming GA 30041	770-886-2250	R	450*	.7
7	OK Industries Inc—*Randall Goins*	PO Box 1119, Fort Smith AR 72902	479-783-4186	R	402*	4.0
8	Valley Proteins Inc—*Gerald Smith*	PO Box 3588, Winchester VA 22604	540-877-2590	R	300*	1.4
9	Global Harvest Foods Ltd—*Eric Mills*	16000 Christensen Rd S, Seattle WA 98188	206-957-1350	R	206*	.1
10	Furst-Mcness Co—*Martha Furst*	120 E Clark St, Freeport IL 61032	815-235-6151	R	176*	.2
11	Effingham Equity—*Dennis Montavon*	PO Box 488, Effingham IL 62401	217-342-4101	R	162*	.4
12	Farmers Union Industries LLC—*Dennis Rosen*	PO Box 319, Redwood Falls MN 56283	507-637-2938	R	148*	.3
13	JD Heiskell and Holdings LLC—*Duane Fischer*	PO Box 1379, Tulare CA 93275	559-685-6100	R	147*	.3
14	Kalmbach Feeds Inc—*Paul Kalmbach*	PO Box 38, Upper Sandusky OH 43351	419-294-3838	R	138*	.3
15	Milk Specialties Co—*Trevor Tomkins*	260 S Washington St, Carpentersville IL 60110	847-426-3411	R	137*	.5
16	Endres Processing Ltd—*Leon J Endres*	13420 Courthouse Blvd, Rosemount MN 55068	651-438-3113	R	109*	.1
17	TriOak Foods Inc—*Randy Pflum*	PO Box 68, Oakville IA 52646	319-766-4411	R	89*	.1
18	Mid-Kansas Cooperative Association—*Dave Christiansen*	PO Box D, Moundridge KS 67107	620-345-6328	R	84*	.2
19	Stillwater Milling Co—*Alice Fowler*	PO Box 2407, Stillwater OK 74076	405-372-3445	R	80*	.2
20	Golden Sun Feeds Inc—*Fernando Palacios* Purina Mills LLC	PO Box 517, Estherville IA 51334	712-362-3551	S	79*	.3
21	Ag Partners Coop—*Gary Yotter*	PO Box 467, Lake City MN 55041	651-345-3328	R	60*	.1
22	Penny Newman Milling LLC—*Micheal Nicoletci*	PO Box 12147, Fresno CA 93776	559-448-8800	R	57*	.1
23	Gorman Milling Company Inc—*Harold Fritts*	PO Box 276, Gorman TX 76454	254-734-2252	R	51*	.1
24	Fishbelt Feeds Inc—*Joe Oglesby*	PO Box 609, Moorhead MS 38761	662-246-5065	R	49*	<.1
25	Farmers Cooperative Elevator Co (Echo Minnesota)—*Scott Dubbelde*	PO Box 59, Hanley Falls MN 56245	507-768-3448	R	46*	<.1
26	HJ Baker and Bro Inc—*Christopher Smith*	228 Saugatuck Ave Ste, Westport CT 06880	203-682-9200	R	46*	.2
27	Kreamer Feed Inc—*William Robinson*	PO Box 38, Kreamer PA 17833	570-374-8148	R	38*	<.1
28	Willowbrook Feeds Inc—*Susie Silva*	PO Box 7368, Petaluma CA 94955	707-795-7190	S	38*	.2
29	D and D Commodities Ltd—*Dick Hebert*	PO Box 359, Stephen MN 56757	218-478-3308	R	37*	.1
30	Merrick's Inc	PO Box 620307, Middleton WI 53562	608-831-3440	R	35*	.1
31	White Oak Mills Inc—*Mark Wagner*	419 W High St, Elizabethtown PA 17022	717-367-1525	R	35*	.1
32	Hatch Milling Co—*Amanda Machado*	9400 W Main St, Turlock CA 95380	209-669-9089	S	35*	<.1
33	Texas Farm Products Co—*Bud Wright*	915 South Fredonia St, Nacogdoches TX 75964	936-564-3711	R	32*	.2
34	Dekalb Feeds Inc—*Kelly Keaschall*	PO Box 111, Rock Falls IL 61071	815-625-4546	R	31*	.1
35	Pine Manor Inc—*Galen Miller*	2704 S Main St, Goshen IN 46526	574-533-4186	R	30*	.2
36	Lackawanna Products Corp—*David Olshan*	PO Box 660, Clarence NY 14031	716-633-1940	R	28*	.1
37	EJ Houle Inc—*Jeff Houle*	55 SW 2nd St, Forest Lake MN 55025	651-464-3326	R	28*	<.1
38	Akron Hg Inc—*Thomas Hall*	101 W Railroad Ave, Akron CO 80720	970-345-2206	R	26*	<.1
39	Gramco Inc—*Robert Mattison*	299 Waverly St, Springville NY 14141	716-592-2845	R	26*	<.1
40	Alaska Garden And Pet Supply Inc—*Kenneth Sherwood*	PO Box 101246, Anchorage AK 99510	907-279-4519	R	26*	.1
41	Zinpro Corp—*Michael Anderson*	10400 Viking Dr Ste 24, Eden Prairie MN 55344	952-944-2736	R	25*	.1
42	Integrated Grain and Milling Inc—*Richard Zacky*	PO Box 11127, Fresno CA 93771	559-443-6500	R	25*	<.1
43	Farmer's Cooperative Elevator (Hudsonville Michigan)—*Jim Roskam*	PO Box 219, Hudsonville MI 49426	616-669-9596	R	23*	<.1
44	Premier Feeds LLC—*John Heinz*	292 N Howard St, Sabina OH 45169	937-584-2411	R	22*	.1
45	Farmers Cooperative Co (New Hartford Iowa)	PO Box 307, New Hartford IA 50660	319-983-2259	S	22*	<.1
46	Garland Farm Supply Inc—*Ernest Smith*	PO Box 741, Garland NC 28441	910-529-9731	R	21*	<.1
47	Fromm Family Foods LLC	PO Box 365, Thiensville WI 53092	262-242-2200	R	20*	<.1
48	Big "v" Feeds Inc—*William Verner*	PO Box 943, Mcalester OK 74502	918-423-1565	R	20*	.1
49	Elenbaas Company Inc—*Dennis Elenbaas*	PO Box 39, Sumas WA 98295	360-988-5811	R	20*	.1
50	Form-A-Feed Inc *Steve Nelson*	PO Box 9, Stewart MN 55385	320-562-2413	R	19*	.1
51	Big Gain Inc—*Elton Klaustemeier*	PO Box 308, Mankato MN 56002	507-387-7971	R	18*	.1
52	Star Milling Co—*William Cramer*	PO Box 1987, Perris CA 92572	951-657-3143	R	18*	.1
53	Biozyme Inc—*Robert Norton*	PO Box 4428, Saint Joseph MO 64504	816-238-3326	R	17*	.1
54	Hergert Milling Inc—*Clarence Hergert*	1424 Ave B, Scottsbluff NE 69361	308-632-2315	R	16*	.1
55	Ralco Nutrition Inc—*Jon Knochenmus*	PO Box 1083, Marshall MN 56258	507-532-5748	R	15*	.1

Note: An asterisk (*) indicates an estimated financial figure. The company type code used is as follows: R = Private, P = Public, S = Private Subsidiary, B = Public Subsidiary, D = Division, J = Joint Venture, I = Investment Fund.

COMPANY RANKINGS BY SALES WITHIN 4-DIGIT SIC

Rank	Company Name—Executive Officer	Address, City, State, Zip	Phone	Type	Fin	Empls
56	Ranch-Way Inc—Phyllis Bixler	PO Box 2026, Fort Collins CO 80522	970-482-1662	R	15*	.1
57	Kay-Dee Feed Co—Tom Lohry	1919 Grand Ave, Sioux City IA 51106	712-277-2011	R	15*	.1
58	Minn-Dak Growers Ltd—Harris Peterson	PO Box 13276, Grand Forks ND 58208	701-746-7453	R	15*	.1
59	Flint River Mills Inc—Henry Metcalf	PO Box 280, Bainbridge GA 39818	229-246-2232	R	14*	.1
60	Caldwell Milling Company Inc—Henry Caldwell	PO Box 179, Rose Bud AR 72137	501-556-5226	R	14*	.1
61	Strauss Veal Feeds Inc—David Grant	PO Box 149, North Manchester IN 46962	260-982-8611	R	14*	.1
62	Indi-Bel Inc—Lester Myers	PO Box 878, Indianola MS 38751	662-887-1226	R	14*	.1
63	Jupe Feeds Inc—Dennis Jupe	PO Box 40, Temple TX 76503	254-773-5211	R	13*	<.1
64	Dfs Inc—David Kier	PO Box 3, Newell IA 50568	712-272-3396	R	13*	.1
65	Waterloo Mills Co—Donald Michels	PO Box 1227, Waterloo IA 50704	319-234-7756	R	13*	<.1
66	Albion International Inc—Duane Ashmead	PO Box 750, Clearfield UT 84089	801-773-4631	R	13*	.1
67	John A Van Den Bosch Co—David Vanden Bosch	PO Box 1786, Holland MI 49422	616-848-2000	R	12*	<.1
68	Cooperative Sampo Corp—Dave Blomfeth	Box 220, Menahga MN 56464	218-564-4534	R	11*	.1
69	F Triple Inc—Leroy Hanson	6165 Nw 86th St Ste A, Johnston IA 50131	515-727-1715	R	11*	.1
70	Ragland Mills Inc—Eloise Ragland	14079 Hammer Rd, Neosho MO 64850	417-451-2510	R	11*	<.1
71	Mid-South Milling Company Inc—John Petty	710 Oakleaf Office Ln, Memphis TN 38117	901-767-0071	R	11*	<.1
72	Kassik Milling Company Inc—Michael Kassik	PO Box 128, Milligan NE 68406	402-629-4241	R	11*	<.1
73	Domain Inc—William Buell	156 High St Ste 1, New Richmond WI 54017	715-246-6525	R	10*	.1
74	Lyssy and Eckel LP—Gerald Eckel	PO Box 128, Poth TX 78147	830-484-3314	R	10*	.1
75	Braswell Milling Co—Ronald Braswell	PO Box 669, Nashville NC 27856	252-459-2143	R	10*	.1
76	Burkmann Feeds Of Glasgow LLC—Bonnie Vernon	100 Georgetown Ln, Glasgow KY 42141	270-651-8000	R	10*	.1
77	Kerber Milling Co—John Kerber	PO Box 96, Emmetsburg IA 50536	712-852-2712	R	10*	.1
78	Bomac Vets Plus Inc—John Gale	102 3rd Ave E, Knapp WI 54749	715-665-2118	R	9*	<.1
79	Jupe Mills Inc—Ervin Jupe	PO Box 474, West TX 76691	254-826-5301	R	9*	<.1
80	Vitalix Inc—Greg Olson	2692 County Rd 57, Alliance NE 69301	308-762-8358	R	9*	.1
81	Fur Breeders Agricultural Coop—Chris Falco	8700 S 700 W, Sandy UT 84070	801-255-4228	R	9*	<.1
82	Vit-E-Men Company Inc—Scott Watson	PO Box 1252, Norfolk NE 68701	402-379-0311	R	9*	<.1
83	Holmes By Products Co—Abe Miller	3175 Township Rd 411, Millersburg OH 44654	330-893-2322	R	9*	.1
84	Jerico Products Inc—Mike Lind	100 E D St, Petaluma CA 94952	707-762-7251	R	9*	<.1
85	San Francisco Bay Brand Inc—Andreas Schmidt	8239 Enterprise Dr, Newark CA 94560	510-792-7200	R	9*	<.1
86	Southern States Hopkinsville Coop—Bruce Sanders	501 E 13th St, Hopkinsville KY 42240	270-885-8461	R	8*	<.1
87	Hi Plains Feed LLC—John Mcclelland	1650 N Sherlock Rd, Garden City KS 67846	620-277-2886	R	8*	<.1
88	Seed Resources LLC—Frank Hoogland	1650 Broadway Ave Nw, Grand Rapids MI 49504	616-365-0009	R	8*	<.1
89	Alfa-Pet Inc—Ben Schulein	4914 Daggett Ave, Saint Louis MO 63110	314-865-0400	R	8*	<.1
90	H Rockwell and Son Inc—James Rockwell	PO Box 197, Canton PA 17724	570-673-5148	R	8*	<.1
91	Animal Science Products Inc—Bailey Reynolds	PO Box 631408, Nacogdoches TX 75963	936-560-0003	R	8*	<.1
92	Cumberland Valley Cooperative Association—Vernon Horst	PO Box 350, Shippensburg PA 17257	717-532-2197	R	8*	<.1
93	Valley Feed Mill Incorporated Of Paris—David Edzards	315 W Ctr St, Paris TX 75460	903-785-3501	R	8*	.1
94	Ohio Pet Foods Inc—Jim Golladay	38251 Industrial Park, Lisbon OH 44432	330-424-1431	R	8*	<.1
95	Hbh Enterprises—Frank Ballard	PO Box 967, Springville UT 84663	801-489-3815	R	7*	.1
96	Lucta USA Inc—Jim Bouc	1829 Stanley St, Northbrook IL 60062	847-272-6650	S	7*	<.1
97	Robt Morgan Inc—Robert Morgan	PO Box 877, Paris IL 61944	217-466-4777	R	7*	<.1
98	Deal-Rite Feeds Inc—Ronald Deal	109 Anna Dr, Statesville NC 28625	704-873-8646	R	7*	<.1
99	Martins Elevators Inc—Alvin Martin	13219 Maugansville Rd, Hagerstown MD 21740	301-733-2553	R	7*	<.1
100	Bagdad Roller Mills Inc—Eugene Weakley	PO Box 7, Bagdad KY 40003	502-747-8968	R	6*	<.1
101	Freeport Roller Mills Inc—Al Beste	PO Box 7, Freeport MN 56331	320-836-2145	R	6*	<.1
102	Channel Fish Company Inc—Rosario Silvestro	370 E Eagle St, Boston MA 02128	617-569-3200	R	6*	<.1
103	Scott's Feed Inc—Scott Collins	245 Elm St, Malone NY 12953	518-483-3110	R	6*	<.1
104	Gateway Products Inc—Arthur Simon	PO Box 529, Holly CO 81047	719-537-6351	R	6*	<.1
105	Pied Piper Mills Inc—Robert Moore	PO Box 309, Hamlin TX 79520	325-576-3684	R	6*	<.1
106	Syfrett Feed Company Inc—Charles Syfrett	PO Box 1287, Okeechobee FL 34973	863-763-5586	R	6*	<.1
107	Strauss Feeds LLC—David Grant Strauss Veal Feeds Inc	W7507 Provimi Rd, Watertown WI 53098	920-261-7882	S	6*	<.1
108	Postive Feed Inc—Gary Inglish	PO Box 1049, Sealy TX 77474	979-885-2903	R	6*	<.1
109	Kropf/Chs LLC	815 S 2nd St, Harrisburg OR 97446	541-995-6384	R	6*	<.1
110	English River Pellets Inc—Edwin Hershberger	PO Box 1203, Kalona IA 52247	319-656-2285	R	6*	<.1
111	JS West Milling Company Inc—D West	PO Box 1041, Modesto CA 95353	209-529-4232	R	6*	<.1
112	Elk Grove Milling Inc—Robert Lent	8320 Eschinger Rd, Elk Grove CA 95757	916-684-2056	R	6*	<.1
113	Nrv Inc—Sabiem Fontaine	N8155 American St, Ixonia WI 53036	262-567-8989	R	5*	<.1
114	RGR Inc—Jerry Lollis	1 4 Mile S Intersectio, Kingston OK 73439	580-564-2324	R	5*	<.1
115	Union Grove Feed LLC—Michael Keller	PO Box 8, Union Grove NC 28689	704-539-5109	R	5*	<.1
116	Ahrberg Milling Of Cushing Inc—Fredrick Ahrberg	PO Box 968, Cushing OK 74023	918-225-0267	R	5*	<.1
117	Triple Crown Nutrition Inc—Robert Daugherty	319 Barry Ave S Ste 30, Wayzata MN 55391	952-473-6330	R	5*	<.1
118	Seed Factory Northwest Inc—Randall Steele	PO Box 245, Ceres CA 95307	209-634-8522	R	5*	<.1
119	Biokyowa Inc—Toshi Hirai	PO Box 1550, Cape Girardeau MO 63702	573-335-4849	R	5*	<.1
120	Mccauley Brothers Inc—Dennis Longmire	PO Box 604, Versailles KY 40383	859-873-3333	R	5*	<.1
121	Ezell-Key Grain Company Inc—Weldon Key	PO Box 1062, Snyder TX 79550	325-573-9373	R	5*	<.1
122	Blair Milling and Elevator Company Inc—Thomas Bishop	PO Box 437, Atchison KS 66002	913-367-2310	R	5*	<.1
123	WB Fleming Company Inc—William Scott	PO Box 1409, Tifton GA 31793	229-382-7821	R	4*	<.1
124	Cammack Ranch Supply Inc—Gary Cammack	PO Box 100, Union Center SD 57787	605-985-5591	R	4*	<.1
125	Leach Grain and Milling Company Inc—Willis Leach	8131 Pivot St, Downey CA 90241	562-869-4451	R	4*	<.1
126	Behrends Feed and Fertilizer LP—Kim Behrends	3599 Ranch Rd 1376, Fredericksburg TX 78624	830-997-3410	R	4*	<.1
127	Canine Caviar Pet Foods Inc—Jeff Baker	4131 Tigris Way, Riverside CA 92503	714-223-1800	R	4*	<.1
128	Cochecton Mills Inc—Dennis Nearing	30 Depot Rd, Cochecton NY 12726	845-932-8282	R	4*	<.1
129	Western Yeast Company Inc—Keith Turner	305 W Ash St, Chillicothe IL 61523	309-274-3160	R	4*	<.1
130	Ashley-Martin Manufacturing Inc—Diane Keegan	90160 Us Hwy 93, Arlee MT 59821	406-726-3700	R	4*	<.1
131	Bird Pretty International Inc—Michael Massie	31008 Foxhill Ave, Stacy MN 55079	651-462-1799	R	3*	<.1
132	West End Milling Company Inc—Doyle Weltzbarker	702 W Screven St, Quitman GA 31643	229-263-4157	R	3*	<.1
133	Laurinburg Milling Co—Ronnie Reese	108 James St, Laurinburg NC 28352	910-276-1621	R	3*	<.1
134	Island Dehy Inc—David Burkholder	PO Box 88, Cozad NE 69130	308-784-2115	R	2*	<.1
135	Robinson Farms Feed Co—Michael Robinson	7000 S Inland Dr, Stockton CA 95206	209-466-7915	R	2*	<.1
136	Brookhurst Mill—Bradley Pope	3315 Van Buren Blvd, Riverside CA 92503	951-688-3511	R	2*	<.1
137	Heath and Son Feed and Supply Inc—Dwight Heath	PO Box 578, Ava MO 65608	417-683-4161	R	2*	<.1
138	Lakin Milling Company Inc—Charles Lakin	4456 S Dysart Rd, Avondale AZ 85323	623-932-3970	R	2*	<.1
139	Nutriad Inc—Keith Klanderman	420 Airport Rd Ste C, Elgin IL 60123	847-214-4860	R	2*	<.1
140	Republic Mills Inc—William Koon	PO Box 50146, Okolona OH 43550	419-758-3511	R	2*	<.1
141	John Roth and Son Inc—Robert Buscher Sr	5425 S 43rd St, Omaha NE 68107	402-731-7500	R	2*	<.1
142	Smith Southside Feed and Grain Inc—L Eugene Smith	PO Box 446, Bowling Green KY 42102	270-529-5651	R	2*	<.1
143	Aquatrol Inc—Bill Miller	237 N Euclid Way Ste H, Anaheim CA 92801	714-533-3381	R	2*	<.1
144	Richdel Inc—Richard Merriner	PO Box 1968, Carson City NV 89702	775-246-3022	R	2*	<.1

Rank	Company Name—*Executive Officer*	Address, City, State, Zip	Phone	Type	Fin	Empls
145	Menezes Brothers Inc—*Richard Menezes*	2532 E Pacheco Blvd, Los Banos CA 93635	209-826-5561	R	2*	<.1
146	Blue Lily Farms LLC—*Karen Schmidt*	PO Box 10, Le Center MN 56057	507-357-2339	R	2*	<.1
147	Oxford Alfalfa Inc—*R Sawyer*	PO Box 368, Oxford KS 67119	620-455-2411	R	1*	<.1
148	Woody's Feed And Grain—*Allan Woodberry*	PO Box 1934, Dickinson ND 58602	701-225-5161	R	1*	<.1
149	Alba International Inc—*RK Arundale II*	PO Box 111, North Aurora IL 60542		R	1	<.1
150	Savory Creations International—*Amy Hollon*	2121 S El Camino Real, San Mateo CA 94403	650-638-1024	R	1*	<.1
151	Pet Ecology Brands Inc—*Ralph Steckel*	14822 Venture Dr, Dallas TX 75234	972-759-8080	R	<1	<.1

TOTALS: SIC 2048 Prepared Feeds Nec
Companies: 151

					165,314	48.3

2051 Bread, Cake & Related Products

Rank	Company Name—*Executive Officer*	Address, City, State, Zip	Phone	Type	Fin	Empls
1	Flowers Foods Inc—*George E Deese*	1919 Flowers Cir, Thomasville GA 31757	229-226-9110	P	2,773	9.4
2	Hostess Brands Inc—*Brian J Driscoll*	6031 Connection Dr, Irving TX 75039	972-532-4500	R	2,500	20.0
3	Pepperidge Farm Inc—*Patrick J Callaghan*	595 Westport Ave, Norwalk CT 06851	203-846-7000	S	1,494*	5.1
4	McKee Foods Corp—*Mike McKee*	PO Box 750, Collegedale TN 37315	423-238-7111	R	978*	6.0
5	Dawn Food Products Inc—*Carrie Jones-Barber*	3333 Sargent Rd, Jackson MI 49201	517-789-4400	R	845*	3.2
6	East Balt Inc—*Frank Kuchuris*	1801 W 31st Pl, Chicago IL 60608	773-376-4444	R	640*	1.6
7	Loaf 'N Jug Inc—*Art Stawski*	442 Keeler Pkwy, Pueblo CO 81001	719-948-3071	S	557*	1.7
8	Fresh Start Bakeries Inc—*Russ Doll*	145 S State Cckg Blvd, Brea CA 92821	714-256-8900	R	420*	.6
9	Mrs Baird's Bakeries Inc	7301 S Fwy, Fort Worth TX 76134	817-615-3000	S	300*	3.4
10	Tasty Baking Co—*Charles P Pizzi* Flowers Foods Inc	3 Crescent Dr Ste 200, Philadelphia PA 19112	215-221-8500	S	289	.7
11	Alfred Nickles Bakery Inc—*David Gardner*	26 Main St N, Navarre OH 44662	330-879-5635	R	196*	1.7
12	Perfection Bakeries Inc—*John Popp*	350 Pearl St, Fort Wayne IN 46802	260-424-8245	R	175*	1.6
13	Roskam Baking Co—*Robert Roskam*	PO Box 202, Grand Rapids MI 49501	616-574-5757	R	115*	1.0
14	Orograin Bakeries Manufacturing Inc—*Peter Rollins*	255 Bsnepa Ctr Dr Ste, Horsham PA 19044	518-463-2221	R	109*	1.3
15	Maplehurst Bakeries LLC—*Dave Winiger*	50 Maplehurst Dr, Brownsburg IN 46112	317-858-9000	R	106*	1.0
16	Way Bakery—*John Popp* Perfection Bakeries Inc	2100 Enterprise St, Jackson MI 49203	517-787-6720	S	101*	1.6
17	Hostess Cake Div—*Craig D Jung* Hostess Brands Inc	6007 S St Andrews Pl, Los Angeles CA 90047	323-753-3521	D	91*	.9
18	Steven Roberts Original Deserts LLC—*Charles Kosmont*	4990 Oakland St, Denver CO 80239	303-375-9925	R	81*	.3
19	George Weston Bakeries Inc—*Gary J Prince*	PO Box 535, Totowa NJ 07511	631-273-6100	D	80*	.6
20	Benson's Inc—*Larry Benson*	PO Box 429, Bogart GA 30622	770-725-5711	R	80*	.4
21	Schulze And Burch Biscuit Co—*Kevin Boyle*	1133 W 35th St, Chicago IL 60609	773-927-6622	R	75*	.4
22	Schmidt Baking Company Inc—*John Paterakis*	PO Box 418770, Boston MA 02241	410-668-8200	R	66*	.7
23	Maple Leaf Foods USA Inc—*Douglas Macfarlane*	1011 E Touhy Ave Ste 5, Des Plaines IL 60018	847-655-8100	R	63*	.6
24	Klosterman Baking Co—*Kenneth Klosterman*	4760 Paddock Rd, Cincinnati OH 45229	513-242-1004	R	63*	.6
25	Fullbloom Baking Company Inc—*Karen Trilevsky*	6500 Overlake Pl, Newark CA 94560	510-494-1700	R	56*	.3
26	King Soopers Inc Bakery Div—*Russ Dispence*	PO Box 5567, Denver CO 80217	303-778-3100	S	56*	.4
27	Rotella's Italian Bakery Inc—*Louis Rotella*	6949 S 108th St, La Vista NE 68128	402-592-6600	R	52*	.3
28	Indianapolis Bakery—*David Dillon*	6801 English Ave, Indianapolis IN 46219	317-322-5000	S	52*	.4
29	Tasty Baking Oxford Inc—*Charles Pizzi* Tasty Baking Co	700 Lincoln St, Oxford PA 19363	610-932-2300	S	50*	.2
30	Table Talk Pies Inc—*Christos Cocaine*	120 Washington St Ste, Worcester MA 01610	508-798-8811	R	50*	.1
31	Lepage Bakeries Inc—*Andrew Barowski*	PO Box 1900, Auburn ME 04211	207-783-9161	R	48*	.5
32	Italian Peoples Bakery Inc—*Patrick Gachetti*	63 Butler St, Trenton NJ 08611	609-394-7161	R	48*	.2
33	Maple Donuts Inc—*Charles Burnside*	3455 E Market St, York PA 17402	717-757-7826	R	47*	.3
34	Turano Baking Co—*Renato Turano*	6501 W Roosevelt Rd, Berwyn IL 60402	708-788-9220	R	46*	.5
35	Cajoleben Inc—*Jeannette Galasso*	10820 San Sevaine Way, Mira Loma CA 91752	951-360-1211	R	46*	.4
36	Sterling Foods LLC—*Mike Brehm*	PO Box 790370, San Antonio TX 78279	210-490-1669	R	46*	.3
37	Gold Medal Bakery Inc—*Roland Lecomte*	PO Box I, Fall River MA 02724	508-674-5766	R	45*	.5
38	Lawler Foods Inc—*William Lawler*	PO Box 2558, Humble TX 77347	281-446-0059	R	44*	.3
39	Piantedosi Baking Company Inc—*Thomas Piantedosi*	240 Commercial St, Malden MA 02148	781-321-3400	R	43*	.2
40	Caravan Bakery and Trading Co—*Joseph Maroun*	33300 Western Ave, Union City CA 94587	510-487-2600	R	42*	.3
41	A Angonoa Inc—*Peter Zampieri*	PO Box 560089, College Point NY 11356	718-762-4466	R	42*	.1
42	Wenner Bread Products Inc—*Richard Wenner*	33 Rajon Rd, Bayport NY 11705	631-563-6262	R	41*	.4
43	Pechter's Baking Group LLC—*George Thomas*	840 Jersey St, Harrison NJ 07029	973-483-3374	R	39*	.3
44	Rockland Bakery Inc—*Ignazio Battaglia*	94 Demarest Mill Rd W, Nanuet NY 10954	845-623-5800	R	39*	.5
45	Franklin Baking Company Inc—*Tom Buffkin* Flowers Foods Inc	PO Box 228, Goldsboro NC 27533	919-735-0344	S	39*	.3
46	Balboa Dessert Co—*Rudy Pollak*	1760 E Wilshire Ave, Santa Ana CA 92705		R	38*	.1
47	Puritan Bakery Inc—*Matthew Grimes*	1624 E Carson St, Carson CA 90745	310-830-5451	R	38*	.2
48	Freund Baking Co—*James Freund*	PO Box 3791, Glendale CA 91221	818-502-1400	R	36*	.2
49	Orlando Baking Co—*Chester Orlando*	7777 Grand Ave, Cleveland OH 44104	216-361-1872	R	36*	.4
50	Flowers Baking Company of Texarkana LLC—*Debbie Broussard* Flowers Foods Inc	7 Jim Walter Dr, Texarkana AR 71854	870-773-7523	S	34*	.1
51	Multigrains Inc—*Joseph Faro*	117 Water St, Lawrence MA 01841	978-373-0055	R	34*	.2
52	Gonnella Baking Co—*Nick Marcucci*	2002-14 W Erie St, Chicago IL 60612	312-733-2020	R	33*	.4
53	Two Chefs On A Roll Inc—*Jeff Goh*	18201 Central Ave, Carson CA 90746	310-436-1600	R	33*	.2
54	Calise and Sons Bakery Inc—*Michael Calise*	2 Quality Dr, Lincoln RI 02865	401-334-3444	R	32*	.2
55	Delight Grecian Foods Inc—*Peter Parthenis*	1201 Tonne Rd, Elk Grove Village IL 60007	847-364-1010	R	31*	.2
56	New Bakery Company Of Ohio Inc—*Sam McLaughlin*	3005 Eastpointe Dr, Zanesville OH 43701		S	31	.2
57	Bailey Street Bakery LLC—*Wayne Chandler*	165 Bailey St Sw, Atlanta GA 30314	404-584-9540	R	31*	.2
58	Carolina Foods Inc—*Paul Scarborough*	PO Box 36816, Charlotte NC 28236	704-333-9812	R	31*	.3
59	Le Pafe Inc—*Jonathan Lau*	7547 Telegraph Rd, Montebello CA 90640	323-888-2929	R	30*	.2
60	Tbb Inc—*Manuel Teixeira*	113 Kossuth St Ste 129, Newark NJ 07105	973-589-8875	R	29*	.2
61	Bunny Bread Inc—*George Deese* Flowers Foods Inc	PO Box 26368, New Orleans LA 70186	504-241-1206	D	29*	.2
62	Love's Bakery Inc—*Michael Walters*	PO Box 294, Honolulu HI 96809	808-841-2088	R	29*	.3
63	Modern Italian Bakery Of West Babylon Inc—*James Turco*	301 Locust Ave, Oakdale NY 11769	631-589-7300	R	29*	.2
64	Holsum Of Fort Wayne Inc—*Wayne Davidson*	PO Box 11468, Fort Wayne IN 46858	260-456-2130	S	28*	2.5
65	Lucks Co—*Rick Ellison*	3003 S Pine St, Tacoma WA 98409	206-674-7200	R	28	.1
66	Zaro Bake Shop Inc—*Stewart Zaro*	138 Bruckner Blvd, Bronx NY 10454	718-993-5600	R	27*	.3
67	New Horizons Baking Company Inc—*Tilmon F Brown*	211-A Woodlawn Ave, Norwalk OH 44857		R	27*	.2
68	Twin City Bagel Inc—*Shimon Harosh*	130 Hardman Ave S, South Saint Paul MN 55075	651-554-0200	R	26*	.2
69	Oak State Products Inc—*Stephen Goulding*	PO Box 549, Wenona IL 61377	815-853-4348	R	26*	.4
70	Flowers Baking Company Inc—*George E Deese*	PO Box 12579, Jacksonville FL 32209	904-354-3771	S	26*	.2

Note: An asterisk (*) indicates an estimated financial figure. The company type code used is as follows: R = Private, P = Public, S = Private Subsidiary, B = Public Subsidiary, D = Division, J = Joint Venture, I = Investment Fund.

COMPANY RANKINGS BY SALES WITHIN 4-DIGIT SIC

Rank	Company Name—*Executive Officer*	Address, City, State, Zip	Phone	Type	Fin	Empls
	Flowers Foods Inc					
71	Toufayan Bakery Inc—*Harry Toufayan*	175 Railroad Ave, Ridgefield NJ 07657	201-941-2000	R	26*	.1
72	Amoroso's Baking Co—*Daniel Amoroso*	PO Box 1226, Lansdowne PA 19050	215-471-4740	R	26*	.3
73	Baldinger Baking Company LP—*Bob Baldinger*	215 Eva St, Saint Paul MN 55107	651-224-5761	R	26*	.1
74	Wolferman's Inc	PO Box 9100, Medford OR 97501		S	25	.2
75	Solana Beach Baking Co—*David Wells*	5927 Farnsworth Ct, Carlsbad CA 92008	760-931-0148	R	24*	.2
76	Mrs Smith's Bakeries of Spartanburg LLC—*David Stanaland*	PO Box 4367, Spartanburg SC 29305	864-503-9101	S	24*	.1
77	Beckmann's Old World Bakery Ltd—*Beth Holland*	104 Bronson St Ste 6, Santa Cruz CA 95062	831-423-9242	R	23*	.2
78	Grebes' Bakeries Inc—*James Grebe*	5132 W Lincoln Ave, Milwaukee WI 53219	414-543-7001	R	23*	.2
79	Michel's Bakery Inc—*Jon Liss*	5698 Rising Sun Ave, Philadelphia PA 19120	215-742-3900	R	22*	.1
80	Ne-Mo's Bakery Inc—*Michael Morales*	416 N Hale Ave, Escondido CA 92029	760-741-5725	R	22	.2
81	Flowers Baking Company of Houston—*Andy Brown*	PO Box 7568, Houston TX 77270	713-869-5701	D	22*	.2
	Flowers Foods Inc					
82	Roman Meal Co—*Bill Mattheai*	PO Box 11126, Tacoma WA 98411	253-475-0964	R	22*	.1
83	Ozark Empire Distributors Inc—*Bill Suggs*	PO Box 129, Rogers AR 72757	479-636-3313	R	21*	.2
84	Herman Seekamp Inc—*Kent Bickford*	1120 W Fullerton Ave, Addison IL 60101	630-628-6555	R	21*	.1
85	Morabito Baking Company Inc—*Michael Morabito*	757 Kohn St, Norristown PA 19401	610-275-5419	R	21*	.1
86	Koffee Kup Bakery Inc—*Ronald Roberge*	436 Riverside Ave, Burlington VT 05401	802-863-2696	R	21*	.1
87	Bakery Express-Mid Atlantic Inc—*Charles Burman*	4711 Hollins Ferry Rd, Halethorpe MD 21227	410-281-2000	R	21*	.1
88	Oven Fresh Baking Company Inc—*George Spanos*	250 N Washtenaw Ave, Chicago IL 60612	773-638-1234	R	20*	.1
89	Fb Sale LLC—*Richard Kestenblatt*	1688 N Wayneport Rd, Macedon NY 14502	315-986-9999	R	20*	.1
90	Kangaroo Brands Inc—*John Kashou*	7620 N 81st St, Milwaukee WI 53223	414-355-9696	R	20*	.1
91	Athens Baking Company LLC—*Dave Smart*	4589 W Jacquelyn Ave, Fresno CA 93722	559-485-3024	R	20*	<.1
92	Nickles Bakery Inc—*David Gardner*	1000 Broadway St, Martins Ferry OH 43935	740-633-1711	S	20*	.2
	Alfred Nickles Bakery Inc					
93	Flowers Baking Company of Birmingham LLC—*Carter Wood*	900 16th St N, Birmingham AL 35203	205-252-1161	S	19	.2
	Flowers Foods Inc					
94	Aladdin Bakers Inc—*Joseph Ayoub*	240 25th St, Brooklyn NY 11232	718-499-1818	R	19*	.1
95	Texas French Bread Inc—*Judy Wilcott*	2900 Rio Grande St, Austin TX 78705	512-499-0035	R	19*	.1
96	Bon Appetit Danish Inc—*Rick Mashoon*	4525 District Blvd, Vernon CA 90058	323-584-9500	R	19*	.1
97	South Florida Bakery Inc—*Lourdes Bernardo*	14159 Sw 144th St, Miami FL 33186	305-256-1777	R	18*	.1
98	Best Express Foods Inc—*Jim Burt*	1730 Sabre St, Hayward CA 94545	510-782-5338	R	18*	.1
99	Sunrise Baking Company LLC—*Nat Printz*	4564 2nd Ave, Brooklyn NY 11232	718-499-0800	R	17*	.1
100	Bread Garden Ltd	1001 S 344th St Ste C, Federal Way WA 98003	604-639-9229	R	17*	.1
101	Ace Baking Co—*Kevan Johnson*	1803 E 58th Ave Ste A, Denver CO 80216	303-296-7482	S	17*	<.1
102	Harting's Bakery Inc—*Jere Heft*	PO Box 220, Bowmansville PA 17507	717-445-5644	R	17*	<.1
103	Greyston Bakery Inc—*Julius Walls*	104 Alexander St, Yonkers NY 10701	914-375-1510	R	17*	.1
104	Salem Baking Co—*Dewey Wilkerson*	224 S Cherry St, Winston Salem NC 27101	336-748-0230	R	16*	.1
105	Suncoast Bakeries Inc—*Bernard Vroom*	2811 59th Ave Dr E, Bradenton FL 34203	941-753-7494	R	16*	.1
106	ACME Bread Co—*Steve Sullivan*	2730 9th St, Berkeley CA 94710	510-843-2978	R	16*	.1
107	Palagonia Bakery Company Inc—*Christopher Palagonia*	508 Junius St, Brooklyn NY 11212	718-272-5400	R	16*	.1
108	Frisco Baking Company Inc—*James Pricco*	621 W Ave 26, Los Angeles CA 90065	323-225-6111	R	16*	.1
109	Gb Foods Inc—*Emmanuel Megrelis*	12824 Hempstead Rd Ste, Houston TX 77092	713-460-9503	R	16*	.1
110	Pacific Northwest Baking Co—*Micheal Stevens*	1307 Puyallup St, Sumner WA 98390	253-863-0373	R	15*	.1
111	Neomonde Baking Co—*Sam Saleh*	10235 Chpil Hl Rd Ste, Morrisville NC 27560	919-469-8009	R	15*	.1
112	Giuliano-Pagano Corp—*Gregory Ritmire*	1117 E Walnut St, Carson CA 90746	310-537-7700	R	15*	.1
113	Corbin-Hill Inc—*A Moreno*	PO Box 28139, Santa Ana CA 92799	714-966-6695	R	14*	.1
114	Oteri's Italian Pastries Co—*Lisa Oteri*	4919 N 5th St, Philadelphia PA 19120	215-457-4958	R	14*	.1
115	Tennessee Bun Co—*Cordia Harrington*	197 Printwood Dr, Dickson TN 37055	615-441-4600	R	13*	.1
116	Metropolitan Baking Co—*James Kordas*	8579 Lumpkin St, Detroit MI 48212	313-875-7246	R	13*	.1
117	First Toro Family LP—*Helmer Toro*	2239 Broadway, New York NY 10024	212-595-8000	R	12*	.1
118	Creme Curls Bakery Inc—*Gary Bierling*	PO Box 276, Hudsonville MI 49426	616-669-6230	R	12*	.1
119	Montana Mills Bread Company Inc—*Eugene O'Donovan*	2171 Monroe Ave Ste 20, Rochester NY 14618	585-242-7544	S	11*	.4
120	Valley Lahvosh Baking Co—*Janet Saghatelian*	502 M St, Fresno CA 93721	559-485-2700	R	11*	<.1
121	Anne and Molly's Inc—*Molly Bolanos*	22330 68th Ave S, Kent WA 98032	253-872-8390	R	11*	.1
122	Countryside Baking Inc—*Carrie Barber*	1711 Kettering, Irvine CA 92614	949-851-9654	R	10*	.1
123	Mrs Cubbison's Foods Inc	7240 E Gage Ave, Commerce CA 90040	562-231-1680	S	10	.1
	Hostess Brands Inc					
124	M and M Bakery Products Inc—*Dennis Maggiora*	1900 Garden Tract Rd, Richmond CA 94801	510-235-0274	R	10*	.1
125	San Luis Sourdough—*Dave West*	3877 Long St, San Luis Obispo CA 93401	805-782-8933	S	10*	.1
126	Orange Bakery Inc—*Torahito Hyashi*	17751 Cowan Ave, Irvine CA 92614	949-863-1377	S	9*	.1
127	Melrose Baking Co—*George Goetz*	7356 Melrose Ave, Los Angeles CA 90046	323-651-3165	R	9*	<.1
128	Dutch Country Apple Dumplings Inc—*Andrew Hamsher*	PO Box 603, Orrville OH 44667	330-683-0646	R	9*	.1
129	Rocky Mountain Baking Co—*Chet Anderson*	8835 W 116th Cir Ste A, Broomfield CO 80021	303-991-2331	R	8*	.1
130	Haas Baking Company Inc—*Joseph Haas*	9769 Reavis Park Dr, Saint Louis MO 63123	314-631-6100	R	8*	.1
131	Jtm Foods Inc—*Jeff Mcmillin*	2126 E 33rd St, Erie PA 16510	814-899-0886	R	8*	.1
132	Quinzani's Bakery Inc—*Steven Quinzani*	380 Harrison Ave, Boston MA 02118	617-426-2114	R	8*	.1
133	Theodoro Baking Company Inc—*Michael Daniels*	6038 N Lindbergh Blvd, Hazelwood MO 63042	314-731-3777	R	8*	.2
134	Bagelry Inc—*John Hamstra*	320 Cedar St Ste A, Santa Cruz CA 95060	831-429-8049	R	8*	<.1
135	Eilenberger Baking Co—*Kenneth D Smith*	PO Box 710, Palestine TX 75802	903-729-2175	R	8*	<.1
136	Gold Standard Baking Inc—*Yianny Caparos*	3700 S Kedzie Ave Ste, Chicago IL 60632	773-523-2333	R	8*	<.1
137	Otterbein's Bakery—*Mark Otterbein*	2603 N Rolling Rd Ste, Baltimore MD 21244	410-265-8700	R	8*	.1
138	Homestead Baking Co—*Peter Vican*	145 N Broadway, Rumford RI 02916	401-434-0551	R	8*	.1
139	Cellone Bakery Inc—*Jay Cellone*	PO Box 16288, Pittsburgh PA 15242	412-922-5335	R	7*	.1
140	Hometown Bagel Inc—*Troy Schwartzberg*	11800 Nw 102nd Rd Ste, Medley FL 33178	305-887-5200	R	7*	.1
141	Middle East Bakery Inc—*John Boghos*	30 International Way, Lawrence MA 01843	978-688-2221	R	7*	.1
142	Bagel Boy Inc—*Chaouki Bouchrouche*	485 S Union St, Lawrence MA 01843	978-682-8646	R	7*	.1
143	Roma Bakery Inc—*Robert Pera*	PO Box 348, San Jose CA 95103	408-294-0123	R	7*	.1
144	Bakery De France Inc—*John Salameh*	603 Dover Rd Ste 6, Rockville MD 20850	301-762-8770	R	7*	.1
145	Napoleon Bakery Inc—*Kevin Chapchin*	7356 Melrose Ave, Los Angeles CA 90046	323-651-3165	R	7*	.1
146	Grimaldi's Home Of Bread Inc—*Vito Grimaldi*	2101 Menahan St, Ridgewood NY 11385	718-497-1425	R	7*	.1
147	Cold Spring Bakery Inc—*Dale Schurman*	308 Main St, Cold Spring MN 56320	320-685-8681	R	7*	.1
148	Rolf's Patisserie Inc—*Lloyd Culbertson*	4343 W Touhy Ave, Lincolnwood IL 60712	847-675-6565	R	7*	.1
149	Glen Wayne Wholesale Bakery Inc—*Wayne Stelz*	1800 Artic Ave, Bohemia NY 11716	631-289-9200	R	7*	.1
150	Freed's Bakery LLC—*John Brennan*	299 Pepsi Rd, Manchester NH 03109	603-627-7746	R	7*	.1
151	Dipaolo Baking Company Inc—*Dominick Massa*	598 Plymouth Ave N, Rochester NY 14608	585-232-3510	R	6*	.1
152	Teeny Foods—*Rick Teeny*	3434 Ne 170th Pl, Portland OR 97230	503-252-3006	R	6*	.1
153	Cannoli Factory—*Ezequiel Montemayor*	75 Wyandanch Ave, Wyandanch NY 11798	631-643-2700	R	6*	.1
154	Paielli's Bakery Inc—*Dino Paielli*	6020 39th Ave, Kenosha WI 53142	262-654-0785	R	6*	.1
155	Super Bakery Inc—*Franco Harris*	5700 Corporate Dr Ste, Pittsburgh PA 15237	412-367-2518	R	6*	<.1

Rank	Company Name—*Executive Officer*	Address, City, State, Zip	Phone	Type	Fin	Empls
156	Paramount Bakeries Inc—*Shraga Zabludousky*	61 Davenport Ave, Newark NJ 07107	973-482-6638	R	5*	.1
157	Bakery Express Of Central Texas LP—*Charles Burman*	PO Box 293328, Lewisville TX 75029	972-221-8394	R	5*	.1
158	Goldilocks Corporation Of California—*Mendrei Leelin*	10329 Painter Ave, Santa Fe Springs CA 90670	562-946-9995	R	5*	.1
159	Zingerman's Bakehouse Inc—*Frank Carollo*	3711 Plz Dr Ste 5, Ann Arbor MI 48108	734-761-7255	R	5*	.1
160	Bordenav's Marin Baking LLC—*Fred Radwan*	1512 4th St, San Rafael CA 94901	415-453-2957	R	5*	<.1
161	Neuman Bakery Specialties Inc—*George Neuman*	PO Box 216, Addison IL 60101	630-916-8909	R	5*	<.1
162	Reginas Bay Bakery	423 E Silver Spring Dr, Whitefish Bay WI 53217	414-332-5340	R	5*	<.1
163	Sacramento Baking Company Inc—*Samir Elajou*	9221 Beatty Dr, Sacramento CA 95826	916-361-2000	R	5*	<.1
164	Acme Bread Co—*Drew Wescott*	846 Independence Ave, Mountain View CA 94043	650-938-2978	R	5*	.1
165	G H Leidenheimer Baking Company Ltd—*Robert Whann*	1501 Simon Bolivar Ave, New Orleans LA 70113	504-525-1575	R	5*	.1
166	Bernardino's Bakery Inc—*Victor Augusto*	PO Box 180, Chicopee MA 01014	413-592-1944	R	5*	.1
167	Prestige Bread Company Of Jersey City Inc—*Mariusz Kolodziej*	5601-5711 Tonnelle Ave, North Bergen NJ 07047	201-422-7900	R	5*	.1
168	S and S Bakery Inc—*Jesse Fadick*	2545 Britannia Blvd, San Diego CA 92154	619-489-2000	R	5*	.1
169	Flowers Baking Company Of Denton LLC—*Keith Wheeler*	4210 Edwards Rd, Denton TX 76208	940-383-5280	R	5*	.1
170	Felix Roma and Sons Inc—*Eugene Roma*	PO Box 5547, Endicott NY 13763	607-748-3336	R	5*	.1
171	Termini Brothers Inc—*Vincent Termini*	1523 S 8th St 25, Philadelphia PA 19147	215-334-1816	R	5*	.1
172	Capistrano's Bakery Inc—*Jim White*	807 W Geneva Dr, Tempe AZ 85282	480-968-0468	R	4*	.1
173	Baker Brownie Inc—*Dennis Perkins*	4870 W Jacquelyn Ave, Fresno CA 93722	559-277-7070	R	4*	.1
174	Miller Bakery Inc—*Brian Miller*	1415 N 5th St, Milwaukee WI 53212	414-347-2300	R	4*	.1
175	Bay's Southern Bread Inc—*Charles Bay*	211 Hartman Dr, Lebanon TN 37087	615-449-6444	R	4*	.1
176	Joe Fazio Bakery Inc—*Charles Fazio*	1717 Sublette Ave, Saint Louis MO 63110	314-645-6239	R	4*	.1
177	Pratzel Bakery Company Inc—*Ron Pratzel*	PO Box 21510, Saint Louis MO 63132	314-993-5511	R	4*	<.1
178	Mikawaya—*Frances Hashimoto*	5563 Alcoa Ave, Vernon CA 90058	323-587-5504	R	4*	.1
179	Ener-G Foods Inc—*Sam Wylde*	PO Box 84487, Seattle WA 98124	206-767-6660	R	4*	<.1
180	ATV Bakery Inc—*Joseph Alber*	36 S 3rd St, Reading PA 19602	610-374-5577	R	4*	<.1
181	Creative Cakes Inc—*Spencer Biles*	8814 Brookville Rd, Silver Spring MD 20910	301-587-1599	R	4*	<.1
182	Superior Baking Company Inc—*Michael Debenedictis*	176 N Warren Ave, Brockton MA 02301	508-586-6601	R	4*	.1
183	Brothers Baking Co—*Donald Wegner*	PO Box 680, Edwardsburg MI 49112	269-663-8591	R	4*	<.1
184	Great American Dessert Company LLC	PO Box 780208, Flushing NY 11378	718-894-3494	R	4*	.1
185	Best Harvest LLC—*Brandon Beavers*	530 S 65th St, Kansas City KS 66111	913-287-6300	R	4*	.1
186	Egypt Star Inc—*Esther Erdessy*	608 N Front St, Allentown PA 18102	610-434-8516	R	4*	.1
187	Brown's Bun Baking Co—*George Dinu*	4817 W Vernor Hwy, Detroit MI 48209	734-348-6034	R	4*	.1
188	Claddah Corp—*Shannon Talty*	207 Reece Way Ste 1625, Casselberry FL 32707	407-388-0400	R	4*	.1
189	Schaller's Bakery Inc—*Weddell Schaller*	826 Highland Ave, Greensburg PA 15601	724-837-3660	R	4*	<.1
190	Avb Inc—*Glenn Dahl*	5209 Se International, Portland OR 97222	503-335-8077	R	4*	<.1
191	Commitment 2000 Inc—*William Sam*	105 Monsignor Valente, Buffalo NY 14206	716-853-1071	R	4*	<.1
192	Bread Alone and Bakery Cafe—*Daniel Leader*	PO Box 358, Boiceville NY 12412	845-657-3328	R	4*	.1
193	Oakhouse Farm Inc—*William Stanger*	2221 Mustang Way, Madison WI 53718	608-223-9808	R	4*	<.1
194	Alrajs Inc—*Mike Solomon*	146 Albany Ave, Lindenhurst NY 11757	631-225-0300	R	3*	<.1
195	Turnbull Bakeries Incorporated Of La—*Wayne Turnbull*	523 1st St, New Orleans LA 70130	504-581-5383	R	3*	.1
196	Capitol Cake Co—*John Kunkel*	PO Box 3797, Baltimore MD 21217	410-669-8600	R	3*	<.1
197	Angel's Bakeries Inc—*Joseph Angel*	29 Norman Ave, Brooklyn NY 11222	718-389-1400	R	3*	<.1
198	Fiesta Mexican Foods Inc—*Raymond Armenta*	979 G St, Brawley CA 92227	760-344-3580	R	3*	<.1
199	Langlinais Baking Company Inc—*Bobby Langlinais*	815 S Saint Antoine St, Lafayette LA 70501	337-235-2644	R	3*	<.1
200	Stagno's Bakery Inc—*Frank Stagno*	PO Box 5254, Pittsburgh PA 15206	412-441-3485	R	3*	<.1
201	Venice Baking Co—*James Sisto*	134 Main St, El Segundo CA 90245	310-322-7357	R	3*	<.1
202	Pain D'avignon 11 Inc—*Toma Stamenkovic*	15 Hinckley Rd Unit C, Hyannis MA 02601	508-778-8588	R	3*	<.1
203	Marin Baking LLC	PO Box 150505, San Rafael CA 94915	415-453-2957	R	3*	.1
204	Hansen's Cakes Inc—*Patrick Hansen*	1072 S Fairfax Ave, Los Angeles CA 90019	323-936-4332	R	3*	.1
205	Liliha Bakery Ltd	515 N Kuakini St, Honolulu HI 96817	808-531-1651	R	3*	.1
206	Tripoli Bakery Inc—*Rosario Zappella*	104 Common St Ste 6, Lawrence MA 01840	978-682-7754	R	3*	.1
207	Franco-American Mezzaluna—*Frank Bastoni*	202 W 7th St, Santa Rosa CA 95401	707-545-7528	R	3*	<.1
208	North's Bakery California Inc—*Graham North*	5430 Satsuma Ave, North Hollywood CA 91601	818-761-2892	R	3*	<.1
209	Pastries By Edie Inc—*Edie Gour*	21608 Sherman Way, Canoga Park CA 91303	818-340-0203	R	3*	<.1
210	Jaarsma Bakery—*Kristi Jaarsma*	727 Franklin St, Pella IA 50219	641-628-2940	R	3*	<.1
211	Seasons' Enterprises Ltd—*Michael Season*	PO Box 965, Addison IL 60101	630-628-0211	R	3*	<.1
212	Superior Cake Products Inc—*Kevin Mccafferty*	105 Ashland Ave, Southbridge MA 01550	508-764-3276	R	3*	<.1
213	BAB Inc—*Michael W Evans*	500 Lake Cook Rd Ste 4, Deerfield IL 60015	847-948-7520	P	3	<.1
214	New Mount Pleasant Bakery—*Joe Riitano*	941 Crane St, Schenectady NY 12303	518-374-7577	R	3*	.1
215	Dakota Brands International Inc—*Rex King*	2121 13th St Ne, Jamestown ND 58401	701-252-5073	R	3*	<.1
216	Quality Croutons Inc—*David Moore*	4031 S Racine Ave, Chicago IL 60609	773-927-8200	R	3*	<.1
217	Coeur D'alene French Baking Co—*Teresa Boukal*	6701 S 216th St, Kent WA 98032	253-395-9695	R	3*	<.1
218	Hron Management LLC	5613 Salmen St, Harahan LA 70123	504-734-9188	R	3*	<.1
219	Ander-Beacon Corp—*Barbara Nuetzel*	101 Convention Center, Las Vegas NV 89109	702-365-6348	R	3*	<.1
220	Heidelberg Group Inc—*Boyd Bissell*	PO Box 787, Herkimer NY 13350	315-866-0999	R	3*	<.1
221	RBJ Inc—*Jonathan Robins*	1135 W Geneva Dr, Tempe AZ 85282	480-921-4161	R	3*	<.1
222	Costanzo's Bakery Inc—*Angelo Costanzo*	30 Innsbruck Dr, Cheektowaga NY 14227	716-656-9093	R	3*	<.1
223	Jaciva's Inc—*Jacob Elmer*	4733 Se Hawthorne Blvd, Portland OR 97215	503-234-8115	R	3*	<.1
224	La Esperanza Baking—*Herbert Santos*	148 W Forest Ave, Englewood NJ 07631	201-871-1933	R	3*	<.1
225	Chef Jays Food Products—*Monica Littmann*	2510 E Sunset Rd Ste 5, Las Vegas NV 89120	702-873-7777	R	3*	<.1
226	Sciambra-Passini French Bakery Inc—*Micheal Sciambra*	685 S Fwy Dr, Napa CA 94558	707-252-3072	R	3*	<.1
227	Royale Cheesecake Inc—*Dino Roidopoulous*	9016 Garland Rd, Dallas TX 75218	214-328-9102	R	3*	<.1
228	Breadworks—*Karl Bock*	2110 Brighton Rd, Pittsburgh PA 15212	412-231-7555	R	2*	<.1
229	Simon Hubig Company Inc—*Thomas Bowman*	2417 Dauphine St, New Orleans LA 70117	504-945-2181	R	2*	<.1
230	Ani's Inc—*Abe Tanaka*	99-840 Iwaiwa St Unit, Aiea HI 96701	808-488-2193	R	2*	<.1
231	Edner Corp—*Ehud Kirshner*	1200 Zephyr Ave, Hayward CA 94544	510-441-8504	R	2*	<.1
232	Quebrada Bakery Co—*Kay Kretchmar*	208 Mass Ave, Arlington MA 02474	781-648-0700	R	2*	.1
233	International Food Bakeries Inc—*John Panas*	7949 Wellingford Dr, Manassas VA 20109	703-369-2890	R	2*	<.1
234	United Bakery Inc—*Daniel Sanchez*	727 S Flower St, Burbank CA 91502	818-843-1892	R	2*	<.1
235	Fresno French Bread Bakery Inc—*Al Lewis*	2625 Inyo St, Fresno CA 93721	559-268-7088	R	2*	<.1
236	Alois J Binder Bakery Inc—*Alois Binder*	940 Frenchmen St, New Orleans LA 70116	504-947-1111	R	2*	<.1
237	Harrison Bakery West—*James Rothfeld*	1306 W Genesee St, Syracuse NY 13204	315-422-1468	R	2*	<.1
238	Hearthbread LLC—*Ronda Stacy*	PO Box 1282, Coeur D Alene ID 83816	509-487-7687	R	2*	<.1
239	Gourmet Bakery Inc—*Teresio Musso*	PO Box 1858, Union City CA 94587	510-441-0311	R	2*	<.1
240	Alice Corp—*Yoshi Yuyama*	529 Church St, Ridgefield NJ 07657	201-943-5877	R	2*	<.1
241	Jr Bakery—*Janet Rosing*	2841 W Howard St, Chicago IL 60645	773-465-6733	R	2*	<.1
242	Chow Time Foods Inc—*Cris Gunter*	PO Box 610, Statham GA 30666	678-753-1761	R	2*	<.1
243	Pierre Country Bakery Inc—*Marsha Smith*	3239 E 3300 S, Salt Lake City UT 84109	801-486-0900	R	2*	<.1
244	Hawaii Star Bakery Inc—*Liane Smalls*	944 Akepo Ln, Honolulu HI 96817	808-841-3602	R	2*	<.1

Note: An asterisk (*) indicates an estimated financial figure. The company type code used is as follows: R = Private, P = Public, S = Private Subsidiary, B = Public Subsidiary, D = Division, J = Joint Venture, I = Investment Fund.

COMPANY RANKINGS BY SALES WITHIN 4-DIGIT SIC

Rank	Company Name—*Executive Officer*	Address, City, State, Zip	Phone	Type	Fin	Empls
245	Caravan Bakery Inc—*Joseph Maroun*	33300 Western Ave, Union City CA 94587	510-487-2600	R	2*	<.1
246	Neighborhood Baking Co—*Carolyn Mistell*	4200 Ne Wygant St, Portland OR 97218	503-221-1829	R	2*	.1
247	Swiss Oven Bakery—*Gary Wise*	PO Box 1322, Mesa AZ 85211	480-483-2774	R	2*	.1
248	Continental Baking Co—*Jeff Babka*	3818 Woodville Rd, Northwood OH 43619	419-697-0100	R	2*	<.1
249	Yost Dutch Maid Bakery Inc—*Tim Yost*	809 Scalp Ave, Johnstown PA 15904	814-266-3191	R	2*	<.1
250	Golden Boy Pies Inc—*Terry Hunt*	4945 Hadley St, Overland Park KS 66203	913-384-6460	R	2*	<.1
251	Pettit's Pastry Inc—*Brett Pettit*	502 N 16th St, Omaha NE 68102	402-345-1111	R	2*	<.1
252	Tasty Bake Inc—*Peter Johnson*	1945 8th St, Baker City OR 97814	541-523-5323	R	2*	<.1
253	Gregory's Wheat Shop Inc—*Jim Coltrin*	930 S 500 W, Woods Cross UT 84010	801-295-3405	R	2*	<.1
254	Pyrenees French Bakery Inc—*Marianne Laxague*	PO Box 3626, Bakersfield CA 93385	661-322-7159	R	2*	<.1
255	Palermo Bakery Inc—*Rosario Zito*	1620 Fremont Blvd, Seaside CA 93955	831-394-8212	R	2*	<.1
256	Frank Korinek and Company Inc—*George Korinek*	4828 W 25th St, Cicero IL 60804	708-652-2870	R	2*	<.1
257	Del Buono Bakery Inc—*Constantino Buono*	319 Black Horse Pke, Haddon Heights NJ 08035	856-546-9585	R	2*	<.1
258	Buono Brothers Bakery Inc—*David Buono*	301 W 2nd St, Chester PA 19013	610-876-9224	R	2*	<.1
259	New England Country Pies Inc—*Joseph Lannan*	736 Milford Rd, Merrimack NH 03054	603-883-7111	R	2*	<.1
260	Adam Matthews Inc—*Adam Burckle*	2104 Plantside Dr, Louisville KY 40299	502-499-2253	R	2*	<.1
261	Amiram Dror Inc—*Amiram Dror*	226 India St, Brooklyn NY 11222	718-349-0650	R	2*	<.1
262	Schmell And Azman Bakery—*Scott Zangwill*	7006 Reisterstown Rd E, Baltimore MD 21215	410-484-7343	R	2*	<.1
263	Stella's Kitchen And Bakery—*James Ziegler*	2525 1st Ave N, Billings MT 59101	406-248-3060	R	2*	<.1
264	Geddes Bakery Company Inc—*Vasilios Pappas*	421 S Main St, North Syracuse NY 13212	315-437-8084	R	2*	<.1
265	Bakery Management Corp—*Luis Lacal*	15625 Nw 15th Ave, Miami FL 33169	305-623-3838	R	2*	<.1
266	Knickerbocker Baking Inc—*Steven Corinatis*	26040 Pinehurst Dr, Madison Heights MI 48071	248-541-2112	R	2*	<.1
267	Weiman's Bakery Inc—*Morton Weiman*	125 N 17th St, Richmond VA 23219	804-644-7412	R	2*	<.1
268	Bread Factory LLC—*Jean Lebris*	30 Grove Ave, New Rochelle NY 10801	914-637-9514	R	2*	<.1
269	Laura's French Baking Company Inc—*Laura Kim*	6721 S Alameda St, Los Angeles CA 90001	323-585-5144	R	2*	<.1
270	Johnson's Bakery Inc—*Dennis Johnson*	820 W 5th St, Waterloo IA 50702	319-232-8154	R	2*	<.1
271	Dalo's Bakery Inc—*Donato Dalo*	1201 Freas Ave, Berwick PA 18603	570-752-4519	R	2*	<.1
272	Queen's Bakery Inc—*Jack Yen*	2311 Pasadena Ave, Los Angeles CA 90031	323-222-6447	R	2*	<.1
273	New French Bakery—*Pascale Rigo*	4231 Transport St, Ventura CA 93003	805-339-9495	R	2*	<.1
274	Jeannine's Baking Company Of Santa Barbara—*Eleanor Hardey*	15 E Figueroa St, Santa Barbara CA 93101	805-966-1717	R	2*	<.1
275	Bagels Forever Inc—*Barry Berman*	PO Box 5547, Madison WI 53705	608-231-2427	R	2*	<.1
276	Vaccaro's Inc—*Nicholas Vaccaro*	8949 Brookville Rd, Silver Spring MD 20910	301-587-8700	R	2*	<.1
277	Rosemark Bakery Inc—*Carol Rosemark*	258 Snelling Ave S, Saint Paul MN 55105	651-698-3838	R	1*	<.1
278	Four Daughters Inc—*Allen Harris*	14391 Penasquitos Dr, San Diego CA 92129	858-578-8995	R	1*	<.1
279	Norcia Bakery—*Donald Horne*	624 Belden Ave Ne, Canton OH 44704	330-454-1077	R	1*	<.1
280	Blackey's Bakery Inc—*Robert Reding*	PO Box 18667, Minneapolis MN 55418	612-789-5326	R	1*	<.1
281	Patisserie Poupon Inc—*Joseph Poupon*	820 E Baltimore St, Baltimore MD 21202	410-332-0390	R	1*	<.1
282	Vallos Bakery LLC—*Scott Hanuschak*	1800 Broadway, Bethlehem PA 18015	610-866-1012	R	1*	<.1
283	Demello and Sorli Enterprises Inc—*Christian Sorli*	PO Box 2171, Honolulu HI 96805	808-262-5307	R	1*	<.1
284	More Bakery Inc—*Raymond More*	2512 N 15th St, Tampa FL 33605	813-248-1531	R	1*	<.1
285	Pesce Baking Company Ltd—*Gary Cellone*	45 N Hine St, Youngstown OH 44506	330-746-6537	R	1*	<.1
286	Munster Donut—*Elaine Butynaski*	8314 Calumet Ave, Munster IN 46321	219-836-1709	R	1*	<.1
287	Middle East Baking Co—*Isaac Cohen*	1380 Marsten Rd, Burlingame CA 94010	650-348-7200	R	1*	<.1
288	Clear Lake Specialty Products Inc—*Rocco Violi*	2205 6th Ave S, Clear Lake IA 50428	641-357-5916	R	1*	<.1
289	Missouri Baking Co—*Chris Gambaro*	2027 Edwards St, Saint Louis MO 63110	314-773-6566	R	1*	<.1
290	Scholars Inn Bakehouse—*Albert Trevino*	125 N College Ave, Bloomington IN 47404	812-331-6029	R	1*	.1
291	Maxwell Bakery Inc—*George Jograj*	2700 Atlantic Ave, Brooklyn NY 11207	718-498-2200	R	1*	<.1
292	Bountiful Bread—*Mark Burgasser*	1475 Western Ave Ste 2, Albany NY 12203	518-438-3540	R	1*	<.1
293	Yorkville Bagels Inc—*Helmer Toro*	1551 2nd Ave, New York NY 10028	212-734-7441	R	1*	<.1
294	Blackhawk Bakery Ltd—*Don Dixon*	PO Box 7805, Paducah KY 42002	270-442-3631	R	1*	<.1
295	Oceanside Knish Factory Inc—*Leonard Model*	PO Box 154, Oceanside NY 11572	516-766-4445	R	1*	<.1
296	Graber's Kountry Korner—*Stephen Graber*	8902 N 900 E, Odon IN 47562	812-636-8035	R	1*	<.1
297	Jasmine Bakery Inc—*Robert Miller*	1001 S 344th St Ste 2, Federal Way WA 98003	253-838-6683	R	1*	<.1
298	Triboro Bagel Company Inc—*Abe Moskowitz*	18312 Horace Harding E, Flushing NY 11365	718-539-8484	R	1*	<.1
299	Mary Of Puddin Hill Inc—*Ken Bain*	PO Box 241, Greenville TX 75403	903-455-2651	R	1*	<.1
300	Hahn's Old Fashioned Cake Company Inc—*Regina Hahn*	75 Allen Blvd, Farmingdale NY 11735	631-249-3456	R	1*	<.1
301	Hostess Cake—*Ed Ro*	6325 San Fernando Rd, Glendale CA 91201	818-246-1803	R	1*	<.1
302	Mom's Apple Pie Co—*Avis Renshaw*	220 Loudoun St Se, Leesburg VA 20175	703-771-8590	R	1*	<.1
303	Acadian Bakery Inc—*Duane Broussard*	112 W Brentwood Blvd, Lafayette LA 70506	337-984-7698	R	1*	<.1
304	Bagel Grove Inc—*Matthew Grove*	5 Burrstone Rd, Utica NY 13502	315-724-8015	R	1*	<.1
305	Nantucket Bake Shop Inc—*Margarette Detmer*	PO Box 539, Nantucket MA 02554	508-228-2797	R	1*	<.1
306	Sunrise Bakery Inc—*Virginia Forti*	1813 3rd Ave E, Hibbing MN 55746	218-263-4985	R	<1*	<.1
307	Ofb Industries LLC—*Tashyanna Enriquez*	4941 W Magnolia St, Phoenix AZ 85043	602-269-7563	R	<1*	<.1
308	Rubschlager Baking Corp—*Paul Rubschlager*	3220 W Grand Ave Ste 1, Chicago IL 60651	773-826-1245	R	<1*	<.1

TOTALS: SIC 2051 Bread, Cake & Related Products
Companies: 308

					15,533	92.4

2052 Cookies & Crackers

1	Ralcorp Holdings Inc—*J Patrick Mulcahy*	PO Box 618, Saint Louis MO 63188	314-877-7000	P	4,741	11.0
2	Nabisco Biscuit Co	PO Box 1911, East Hanover NJ 07936	973-503-2000	S	3,695	6.0
3	Keebler Foods Co—*David MacKay*	721 N Larch Ave, Elmhurst IL 60126	630-833-2900	S	2,757	12.5
4	J and J Snack Foods Corporation of California—*Gerald B Shreiber* J and J Snack Foods Corp	5353 S Downey Rd, Vernon CA 90058	323-581-0171	S	2,320*	2.3
5	Snyder's-Lance Inc—*David V Singer*	PO Box 32368, Charlotte NC 28232	704-554-1421	P	1,635	6.1
6	J and J Snack Foods Corp—*Gerald B Shreiber*	6000 Central Hwy, Pennsauken NJ 08109	856-665-9534	P	744	3.1
7	Beth's Fine Desserts Inc	591 Mercantile Dr, Cotati CA 94931	707-792-0375	R	286*	<.1
8	Snyder's Of Hanover Inc—*Carl Lee*	PO Box 6917, Hanover PA 17331	717-632-4477	R	273*	2.4
9	Mrs Field's Original Cookies Inc—*Michael Ward*	1141 W 2400 S, Salt Lake City UT 84104	801-736-5600	R	233*	.8
10	Bremner Inc—*Rich Koulouris* Ralcorp Holdings Inc	1475 US Hwy 62 W, Princeton KY 42445	270-365-5505	S	176*	.6
11	Ralston Foods Inc—*Dave Skarie* Ralcorp Holdings Inc	800 Market St 27th Fl, Saint Louis MO 63101	314-877-7000	S	139*	.5
12	Lance Private Brands—*Jim Hartschuh* Snyder's-Lance Inc	PO Box 888, Burlington IA 52601	319-754-6551	S	138*	.7
13	J and J Snack Foods Corp Bakery Div—*Gerald Schreiber* J and J Snack Foods Corp	6000 Central Hwy, Pennsauken NJ 08109		D	100*	.3
14	Joy Cone Co—*David George*	3435 Lamor Rd, Hermitage PA 16148	724-962-5747	R	90*	.5
15	DF Stauffer Biscuit Company Inc—*Taka Kataoka*	PO Box 1426, York PA 17405	717-843-9016	S	84*	.5

Rank	Company Name—*Executive Officer*	Address, City, State, Zip	Phone	Type	Fin	Empls
16	Stella D' Oro Biscuit Company Inc—*David V Singer*	8600 South Blvd, Charlotte NC 28273		S	75	.4
17	Snyder's-Lance Inc Th Foods Inc—*Sam Mori*	2134 Harlem Rd, Loves Park IL 61111	815-636-9500	R	52*	.3
18	Biscomerica Corp—*Ayad Fargo*	PO Box 1070, Rialto CA 92377	909-877-5997	R	50*	.3
19	Manischewitz Co—*Paul Bensabat*	1 Harmon Plz Ste 1002, Secaucus NJ 07094	201-553-1100	R	47*	.2
20	Pretzels Inc—*William Mann*	PO Box 503, Bluffton IN 46714	260-824-4838	R	45*	.2
21	Silver Lake Cookie Company Inc—*Joseph Vitarelli*	141 Freeman Ave, Islip NY 11751	631-581-4000	R	44*	.3
22	Westminster Cracker Company Inc—*Dennis Keaveny*	1 Scale Ave Ste 81, Rutland VT 05701	802-773-8888	R	43*	<.1
23	Petri Baking Products Inc—*Amelia Habib*	18 Main St, Silver Creek NY 14136	716-934-2661	R	36*	.2
24	Todd's Snax Inc—*David Humbert*	680 W Chestnut St, Hanover PA 17331	717-637-5931	R	34*	.2
25	Fehr Foods Inc—*Steve Fehr*	5425 N 1st St, Abilene TX 79603	325-691-5425	R	33*	.2
26	Bachman Co—*Joseph Welch*	PO Box 15053, Reading PA 19612	610-320-7800	R	32*	.4
27	Daddy Ray's—*Dave Morris*	PO Box 186, Moscow Mills MO 63362	636-366-9900	S	31*	.1
28	J and J Snack Foods Corp Smith Cookie Co—*Murray Albers*	1388 Ne Hwy 99w, Mcminnville OR 97128	503-472-5145	R	30*	.2
29	Steven-Robert Originals LLC—*Roslyn Berry*	4990 Oakland St, Denver CO 80239	303-375-9925	R	28*	.2
30	Richmond Baking Co—*James Quigg*	PO Box 698, Richmond IN 47375	765-962-8535	R	24*	.1
31	DBC Corp—*Peter Beukelaer*	PO Box 456, Madison MS 39130	601-856-7454	R	22*	.3
32	Cookietree Inc—*Greg Schenk*	PO Box 57888, Salt Lake City UT 84157	801-268-2253	R	22*	.1
33	Keebler USA Inc—*John Bryant*	PO Box CAMB, Battle Creek MI 49016	269-961-2000	S	21*	.1
34	Willmar Cookie and Nut Co—*Michael Mickelson*	PO Box 88, Willmar MN 56201	320-235-0600	R	17*	.1
35	Condor Corp—*George Phillips*	124 W Airport Rd, Lititz PA 17543	717-560-1882	R	17*	.1
36	Bud's Best Cookies Inc—*Bud Cason*	2070 Pkwy Office Cir, Hoover AL 35244	205-987-4840	R	15*	.1
37	Cookie Kingdom Inc—*Cliff Sheppard*	1201 E Walnut St, Oglesby IL 61348	815-883-3331	R	15*	.1
38	Basic Grain Products Inc—*Michael Chu*	300 E Vine St, Coldwater OH 45828	419-678-2304	R	14*	.1
39	Chattanooga Bakery Inc—*Samuel Campbell*	PO Box 111, Chattanooga TN 37401	423-267-3351	R	14*	.2
40	Shirley's Cookie Company Inc—*William Feathers*	PO Box 312, Claysburg PA 16625	814-239-2208	R	14*	.1
41	Fairfield Gourmet Food Corp—*Ari Margulies*	12 Commerce Rd, Fairfield NJ 07004	973-227-2800	R	14*	.1
42	Country Fresh Batter Inc—*Hope Spivak*	221 King Manor Dr Ste, King Of Prussia PA 19406	610-272-4673	R	14*	.1
43	Gilda Industries Inc—*Juan Blazquez*	2525 W 4th Ave, Hialeah FL 33010	305-887-8286	R	11*	.1
44	Traditional Baking Inc—*Kathleen Cunningham*	2575 S Willow Ave, Bloomington CA 92316	909-877-8471	R	11*	.1
45	Enjoy Life Natural Brands—*Scott Mandell*	3810 N River Rd, Schiller Park IL 60176	847-260-0300	R	10*	.1
46	Makkos Of Brooklyn Ltd—*Thomas Makkos*	200 Moore St, Brooklyn NY 11206	718-366-9800	R	9*	.1
47	Charlies Specialties Inc—*Jay Thier*	2500 Freedland Rd, Hermitage PA 16148	724-346-2350	R	9*	.1
48	Amay's Bakery and Noodle Company Inc—*Kee Hom*	837 E Commercial St, Los Angeles CA 90012	213-626-2713	R	8*	.1
49	Adrienne's Gourmet Foods—*John O'donnell*	849 Ward Dr, Santa Barbara CA 93111	805-964-6848	R	8*	.1
50	Davis Cookie Co—*Dana Davis*	PO Box 430, Rimersburg PA 16248	814-473-3125	R	7*	.1
51	President Global Corp—*Ping Wu*	6965 Aragon Cir, Buena Park CA 90620	714-994-2990	R	7*	.2
52	Aron Streit Inc—*Malka Kubersky*	148-154 Rivington St, New York NY 10002	212-475-7000	R	6*	.1
53	Cavanagh Co—*Brian Cavanagh*	610 Putnam Pke, Greenville RI 02828	401-949-4000	R	6*	.1
54	Pure's Food Specialties Inc—*Elliott Pure*	2929 S 25th Ave, Broadview IL 60155	708-344-8884	R	6*	.1
55	Elizabeth's Food Company Inc—*Elizabeth Bastasch*	19301 S Santa Fe Ave S, Compton CA 90221	310-638-2168	R	6*	<.1
56	Linden Cookies Inc—*Paul Sturz*	25 Brenner Dr, Congers NY 10920	845-268-5050	R	6*	.1
57	Diamond Bakery Company Ltd—*Brent Kunimoto*	756 Moowaa St, Honolulu HI 96817	808-847-3551	R	6*	.1
58	Christie Cookie Co—*Toby Wilt*	1205 3rd Ave N, Nashville TN 37208	615-242-3817	R	5*	<.1
59	Bakers Choice Co—*Wayne Sonkin*	21400 Telegraph Rd, Southfield MI 48033	248-827-7500	R	5*	<.1
60	Falcone's Cookie Land Ltd—*Angelo Falcone*	1648 61st St, Brooklyn NY 11204	718-236-4200	R	5*	<.1
61	Tom Sturgis Pretzels Inc—*Thomas Sturgis*	2267 Lancaster Pike, Reading PA 19607	610-775-0335	R	5*	<.1
62	Local Baking Products Inc—*Aaron Aihini*	135 Manchester Pl, Newark NJ 07104	973-482-1400	R	5*	<.1
63	Uncle Ralph's Cookie Co—*Margaret Wight*	PO Box 1673, Frederick MD 21702	301-695-6224	R	4*	<.1
64	Oktex Baking LP—*Steve Fehr*	600 N Hwy 77, Marietta OK 73448	580-276-4100	R	4*	.1
65	Byrd Cookie Co—*Benny Curl*	PO Box 13086, Savannah GA 31416	912-355-1716	R	4*	<.1
66	Eleni's Nyc Inc—*Eleni Gianopulos*	4725 34th St Ste 305, Long Island City NY 11101		R	4*	<.1
67	First Grade Food Corp—*Jimmy Luong*	5134 W Hanna Ave, Tampa FL 33634	813-886-6118	R	4*	<.1
68	Umeya Inc—*Tak Hamano*	414 Crocker St, Los Angeles CA 90013	213-626-8341	R	3*	<.1
69	Spaans Cookie Company Inc—*Jim Spaans*	456 C St, Galt CA 95632	209-745-1974	R	3*	<.1
70	Direct Sales and Service Inc—*Marilyn Caine*	141 Lanza Ave Bldg 8, Garfield NJ 07026	973-340-4480	R	3*	<.1
71	Martin's Pretzel Bakery—*Clarence Martin*	1229 Diamond St, Akron PA 17501	717-859-1272	R	3*	<.1
72	Uncle Henry's Pretzel Bakery—*A Martin*	PO Box 219, Bowmansville PA 17507	717-445-4690	R	3*	<.1
73	Novelty Cone Company Inc—*Steven Marinucci*	807 Sherman Ave, Pennsauken NJ 08110	856-665-9525	R	3*	<.1
74	Venus Wafers Inc—*Luke Barmakian*	100 Research Rd Ste 3, Hingham MA 02043	781-740-1002	R	3*	<.1
75	Pati Petite Butter Cookies Inc—*Keith Graham*	1785 Mayview Rd, Bridgeville PA 15017	412-221-4033	R	3*	<.1
76	Barney's Bakery Inc—*George Barney*	PO Box 2782, Weirton WV 26062	304-748-4370	R	2*	<.1
77	YZ Enterprises Inc—*Yuval Zaliouk*	1930 Indian Wood Cir S, Maumee OH 43537	419-893-8777	R	2*	<.1
78	Roma Bakery and Imported Foods—*Philomania Castriciano*	428 N Cedar St, Lansing MI 48912	517-485-9466	R	2*	<.1
79	De Baufre Bakeries Inc—*Charles Debaufre*	2900 Waterview Ave, Baltimore MD 21230	410-752-5175	R	2*	<.1
80	E and C Olson Inc—*Edmund Olson*	3731 Clack Rd, Madison GA 30650	706-342-1861	R	1*	<.1
81	Hammond Pretzel Bakery Inc—*Thomas Nicklaus*	716 S W End Ave, Lancaster PA 17603	717-392-7532	R	1*	<.1
82	Granny B's Cookies LLC—*Paul Homolik*	1357 W 400 S, Orem UT 84058	801-226-1555	R	1*	<.1
83	Fortunately Yours—*Dawn Maynard*	5405 Lancaster Circlev, Lancaster OH 43130		R	1	<.1
84	Cookie Specialties Inc—*Quentin Pierce*	482 N Milwaukee Ave Re, Wheeling IL 60090	847-537-3888	R	1*	<.1
85	GH Bent Co—*Eugene Pierotti*	7 Pleasant St, Milton MA 02186	617-698-5945	R	1*	<.1
86	JMS Enterprises Inc—*Matt Scheeren*	1300 Hopeman Pkwy, Waynesboro VA 22980	540-943-6350	R	1*	<.1
87	Aunt Beth's Products Inc—*Beth Modlin*	1828 Clover Rd, Mishawaka IN 46545	574-259-6244	R	1*	<.1

TOTALS: SIC 2052 Cookies & Crackers
Companies: 87   18,413   53.7

2053 Frozen Bakery Products Except Bread

Rank	Company Name—*Executive Officer*	Address, City, State, Zip	Phone	Type	Fin	Empls
1	Bama Companies Inc—*Paula Marshall*	PO Box 4829, Tulsa OK 74159	918-732-2000	R	250*	1.2
2	Pillsbury Co	PO Box 9452, Minneapolis MN 55440		S	130*	.5
3	Sweet Street Desserts Inc—*Sandy Solmon*	PO Box 15127, Reading PA 19612	610-921-8113	R	66*	.7
4	Granny's Kitchens LLC—*Kevin Mcdonough*	178 Industrial Park Dr, Frankfort NY 13340	315-735-5000	R	47*	.3
5	Love and Quiches Ltd—*Irwin Axelrod*	178 Hanse Ave, Freeport NY 11520	516-623-8800	R	42*	.3
6	Lone Star Bakery Inc—*Mac Morris*	PO Box 201960, San Antonio TX 78220	210-648-6400	R	42*	4
7	Eli's Cheesecake Co—*Marc Schulman*	6701 W Forest Preserve, Chicago IL 60634	773-736-3417	R	38*	.2
8	Labree's—*Bernard Labree*	PO Box 555, Old Town ME 04468	207-827-6121	R	25*	.3
9	Galaxy Desserts—*Paul Levitan*	1100 Marina Way S Ste, Richmond CA 94804	510-439-3160	R	20*	.2
10	Main Street Gourmet LLC—*Nate Searles*	170 Muffin Ln, Cuyahoga Falls OH 44223	330-929-0000	R	19*	.1
11	Panarama Inc—*Margret Sapp*	1300 Shiloh Rd Nw Ste, Kennesaw GA 30144	770-427-4896	R	17*	.1

Note: An asterisk (*) indicates an estimated financial figure. The company type code used is as follows: R = Private, P = Public, S = Private Subsidiary, B = Public Subsidiary, D = Division, J = Joint Venture, I = Investment Fund.

COMPANY RANKINGS BY SALES WITHIN 4-DIGIT SIC

Rank	Company Name—*Executive Officer*	Address, City, State, Zip	Phone	Type	Fin	Empls
12	Plush Pippin Corp—*Henry Lambert*	21331 88th Pl S F, Kent WA 98031	253-872-7300	S	12*	.1
13	James Skinner Co—*James Skinner*	4657 G St, Omaha NE 68117	402-734-1672	R	11*	.1
14	Van's International Foods Inc—*Eric Kufel*	2525 E Arizona Ste D, Phoenix AZ 85016	480-751-6777	R	9*	.1
15	Horizon Snack Foods Inc—*Robert Sharp*	7066 Las Positas Rd St, Livermore CA 94551	925-373-7700	R	9*	.1
16	Hadley Farms Inc—*Frank Haan*	47 S Main St, Smithsburg MD 21783	301-824-2558	R	8*	.1
17	Cloverhill Pastry Vending Corp—*William Gee*	2035 N Narragansett Av, Chicago IL 60639	773-745-9800	R	8*	.1
18	Tast-I-Twist Bakers Inc—*Benjamin De Lorio*	2200 Bleecker St, Utica NY 13501	315-732-7612	R	6*	<.1
19	Wicks Pies Inc—*Michael Wickersham*	PO Box 268, Winchester IN 47394	765-584-8401	R	6*	.1
20	Les Boulangers Associes Inc—*Michel Robert*	18842 13th Pl S, Seatac WA 98148	206-241-9343	R	6*	<.1
21	Field's Inc—*Chris Field*	PO Box 7, Pauls Valley OK 73075	405-238-7381	R	5*	<.1
22	Croissant Etc Corp—*Mark Carollo*	6940 Industrial Loop, Greendale WI 53129	414-421-5226	R	3*	<.1
23	Albies Foods Inc—*Albert Quaal*	1534 Orourke Blvd, Gaylord MI 49735	989-732-2800	R	3*	<.1

TOTALS: SIC 2053 Frozen Bakery Products Except Bread
Companies: 23

					778	4.8

2061 Raw Cane Sugar

1	Okeelanta Corp	PO Box 85, South Bay FL 33493	561-993-1600	S	1,270*	2.0
2	United States Sugar Corp—*Robert H Buker Jr*	111 Ponce de Leon Ave, Clewiston FL 33440	863-983-8121	R	398*	2.5
3	Rio Grande Valley Sugar Growers Inc—*Ralph Barrera*	PO Box 459, Santa Rosa TX 78593	956-636-1411	R	62*	.5
4	St Mary Sugar Shipping Company Inc—*Wilson Terry*	PO Box 269, Jeanerette LA 70544	337-276-6761	R	56*	<.1
5	Alma Plantation Ltd—*David B Stewart*	Rte 1 Box 210, Lakeland LA 70752	225-627-6746	R	52*	.2
6	Sugar Cane Growers Cooperative Of Florida—*George Wedgworth*	PO Box 666, Belle Glade FL 33430	561-996-5556	R	48*	.5
7	Sterling Sugars Inc—*Craig P Callier*	611 Irish Bend Rd, Franklin LA 70538	337-828-0620	R	37*	.2
8	MA Patout and Son Ltd—*Craig P Caillier*	3512 J Patout Burns Rd, Jeanerette LA 70544	337-276-4592	R	32*	.2
9	Lula Westfield LLC—*Mike Daigle*	PO Box 10, Paincourtville LA 70391	985-369-6450	R	13*	.1
10	Harry L Laws and Co—*Glenn R Timmons*	5133 S Florence Ave, Port Allen LA 70767	225-749-2861	R	11*	<.1
11	Lafourche Sugars LLC—*Greg Noland*	141 Leighton Quarters, Thibodaux LA 70301	985-447-3210	R	10*	.1
12	Cajun Sugar Co-Operative Inc—*Frank Minville*	2711 Northside Rd, New Iberia LA 70563	337-365-3401	R	7*	.1
13	Louisiana Sugar Cane Cooperative Inc—*Michael Melancon*	6092 Resweber Hwy, Saint Martinville LA 70582	337-394-3255	R	5*	.1
14	Sugar Jeanerette Company Inc—*Robert Roane*	2304 Main St, Jeanerette LA 70544	337-276-4238	R	4*	.1
15	Gay and Robinson Inc—*Charlie Okamoto*	PO Box 156, Kaumakani HI 96747	808-335-3133	R	2*	<.1

TOTALS: SIC 2061 Raw Cane Sugar
Companies: 15

					2,008	6.5

2062 Cane Sugar Refining

1	Tate and Lyle Inc—*Iain Ferguson*	1403 Foulk Rd Ste 102, Wilmington DE 19803	302-478-4773	S	1,280*	8.0
2	Imperial Sugar Co—*John C Sheptor*	PO Box 9, Sugar Land TX 77487	281-491-9181	P	848	.5
3	Savannah Foods and Industries Inc—*William Sprague* Imperial Sugar Co	PO Box 4225, Savannah GA 31407	912-234-1261	D	283*	.5
4	Diamond Crystal Brands Inc—*Walt Lehneis*	PO Box 9177, Savannah GA 31412	912-651-5112	S	147*	.2
5	Hawaiian Commercial and Sugar Co—*Rick W Volner*	PO Box 266, Puunene HI 96784	808-877-0081	D	75*	.8
6	Cargill Kitchen Solutions—*David Maclennan*	Po Box 9300, Minneapolis MN 55440	763-271-5600	D	49*	.3

TOTALS: SIC 2062 Cane Sugar Refining
Companies: 6

					2,682	10.3

2063 Beet Sugar

1	American Crystal Sugar Co—*David Berg*	101 3rd St N, Moorhead MN 56560	218-236-4400	R	1,204*	1.4
2	Southern Minnesota Beet Sugar Coop—*John Richmond*	PO Box 500, Renville MN 56284	320-329-8305	R	440*	.6
3	Western Sugar Coop—*Indur Mathur*	7555 E Hampden Ave Ste, Denver CO 80231	303-830-3939	R	157*	.7

TOTALS: SIC 2063 Beet Sugar
Companies: 3

					1,800	2.6

2064 Candy & Other Confectionery Products

1	Mars Inc—*Paul S Michaels*	6885 Elm St, McLean VA 22101	703-821-4900	R	27,857*	65.0
2	See's Candy Shops Inc—*Brad Kinstler*	210 El Camino Real, South San Francisco CA 94080		R	2,243*	2.0
3	UIS Inc—*Andrew E Pietrini*	15 Exchange Pl Ste 112, Jersey City NJ 07302	201-946-2600	R	1,105*	9.2
4	Farley's and Sathers Candy Company Inc—*Liam C Lively*	1 Sather Plz, Round Lake MN 56167	507-945-8181	R	630*	1.2
5	Russell Stover Candies Inc—*Thomas Ward*	4900 Oak St, Kansas City MO 64112	816-842-9240	R	610*	6.0
6	Tootsie Roll Industries Inc—*Melvin Gordon*	7401 S Cicero Ave, Chicago IL 60629	773-838-3400	P	517	2.2
7	Dahlgren and Company Inc	PO Box 609, Crookston MN 56716	218-281-2985	S	158*	.1
8	Sweet Candy Co—*R Anthony Sweet*	PO Box 22450, Salt Lake City UT 84112	801-886-1444	R	147*	.1
9	Mantrose-Hauser Company Inc—*Susan Coleman*	1175 Post Rd E, Westport CT 06880	203-454-1800	S	138*	.6
10	Warrell Corp—*Patrick Huffman*	1250 Slate Hill Rd, Camp Hill PA 17011	717-761-5440	R	126*	.3
11	Cambridge Brands Inc—*Melvin Gordon* Tootsie Roll Industries Inc	810 Main St, Cambridge MA 02139	617-491-2500	S	107*	.2
12	Cherrydale Farms Inc—*Ross Cherry*	1900 AM Dr, Quakertown PA 18951		R	100	1.0
13	Bestsweet Inc—*Richard Zulman*	PO Box 329, Mooresville NC 28115	704-664-4300	R	95*	.3
14	Gertrude Hawks Chocolate Inc—*Bill Aubrey*	9 Keystone Park, Dunmore PA 18512	570-342-7556	R	60*	1.0
15	Ferrara Pan Candy Company Inc—*Salvatore Ferrara*	7301 Harrison St, Forest Park IL 60130	708-366-0500	R	58*	.5
16	Just Born Inc—*David Shaffer*	1300 Stefko Blvd, Bethlehem PA 18017	610-867-7568	R	57*	.6
17	Ce De Candy Inc—*Jonathan Dee*	1091 Lousons Rd, Union NJ 07083	908-964-0660	R	43*	.2
18	Andes Manufacturing LLC—*Melvin J Gordon* Tootsie Roll Industries Inc	1400 E Wisconsin St, Delavan WI 53115	262-728-9121	S	42*	.2
19	New England Confectionery Co—*Richard Krause*	135 American Legion Hw, Revere MA 02151	781-485-4500	R	41*	.5
20	Zachary Confections Inc—*John Zachary*	PO Box 219, Frankfort IN 46041	765-659-4751	R	40*	.3
21	American Licorice Co—*John Kretchmer*	2796 Nw Clearwater Dr, Bend OR 97701	541-617-0800	R	39*	.4
22	Kenny's Candy Company Inc—*Kenneth Nelson*	PO Box 269, Perham MN 56573	218-346-2340	R	38*	.2
23	Waymouth Farms Inc—*Gerard Knight*	5300 Boone Ave N, Minneapolis MN 55428	763-533-5300	R	38*	.2
24	Sconza Candy Co—*James Sconza*	1 Sconza Candy Ln, Oakdale CA 95361	209-845-3700	R	37*	.1
25	Glade's Taffy Town Inc—*David Glade*	PO Box 1949, Salt Lake City UT 84110	801-355-4637	R	36*	<.1
26	Anthony Thomas Candy Co—*Tom Zanetos*	PO Box 21865, Columbus OH 43221	614-274-8405	R	34*	.2
27	Doumak Inc—*Barry Blum*	2201 Touhy Ave, Elk Grove Village IL 60007	847-437-2100	R	33*	.2
28	Sherwood Brands Inc—*Uziel Frydman*	9601 Blackwell Rd Ste, Rockville MD 20850	301-309-6161	P	32	.2
29	Kencraft Inc—*R Murray*	119 E 200 N, Alpine UT 84004	801-756-6916	R	32*	.2
30	Morley Candy Makers Inc—*Ronald Rapson*	23770 Hall Rd, Clinton Township MI 48036	586-468-4300	R	31*	.2
31	Primrose Candy Co—*Mark Puch*	4111 W Parker Ave, Chicago IL 60639	773-276-9522	R	31*	.2
32	Hospitality Mints LLC—*Richard Townsend*	PO Box 3140, Boone NC 28607	828-264-3045	R	29*	.1
33	Pearson Candy Co—*Larry Hassler*	PO Box 64459, Saint Paul MN 55164	651-698-0356	R	28*	.2

Rank	Company Name—*Executive Officer*	Address, City, State, Zip	Phone	Type	Fin	Empls
34	Powerbar Inc—*Brian Maxwell*	800 N Brand Blvd Fl 19, Glendale CA 91203	818-549-6000	R	25*	.3
35	Atkinson Candy Co—*B Atkinson*	PO Box 150220, Lufkin TX 75915	936-639-2333	R	25*	.2
36	Goldenrod—*Lea Melchior*	PO Box 1140, York Beach ME 03910	207-363-2621	R	24	.1
37	Maxfield Candy Co—*R Murray*	PO Box 554, Salt Lake City UT 84110	801-355-5321	R	24*	.1
38	Clasen Quality Coatings Inc—*Jay Jensen*	5126 W Ter Dr Ste 100, Madison WI 53718	608-467-1130	R	24*	.1
39	Palmer and Co—*Martin Palmer*	PO Box 326, Sioux City IA 51102	712-258-5543	R	22*	.1
40	Moonstruck Chocolate Co—*Dan Hossley*	6600 N Baltimore Ave, Portland OR 97203	503-247-3448	R	22*	.2
41	Judson-Atkinson Candies Inc—*Basil E Atkinson*	PO Box 200669, San Antonio TX 78220	210-359-8380	R	21*	.1
42	Ed and Don's Of Hawaii Inc—*Vladimir Grave*	4462 Malaai St, Honolulu HI 96818	808-423-8200	R	21*	.1
43	Arway Confections Inc—*Craig Leva*	3425 N Kimball Ave, Chicago IL 60618	773-267-5770	R	20*	.1
44	Wasserstein Partners LP—*Ellis B Jones*	1301 Ave of the Americ, New York NY 10019	212-702-5600	R	18*	<.1
45	Albanese Confectionery Group Inc—*Scott Albanese*	5441 E Lincoln Hwy, Merrillville IN 46410	219-769-6887	R	18*	.1
46	Pez Manufacturing Corp—*Alliette Laughran*	35 Prindle Hill Rd, Orange CT 06477	203-795-0531	R	15*	.1
47	Purdyco Ltd—*Michael Purdy*	2846 Ualena St, Honolulu HI 96819	808-839-5222	R	15*	.1
48	Boyer Candy Company Inc—*Robert Faith*	821 17th St, Altoona PA 16601	814-944-9401	R	15*	.1
49	Goetze's Candy Company Inc—*Spaulding Goetze*	3900 E Monument St, Baltimore MD 21205	410-342-2010	R	13*	.1
50	Fran's Chocolates Ltd—*Fran Bigelow*	1300 E Pike St, Seattle WA 98122	206-322-0233	R	12*	.1
51	Thompson Candy Co—*Jeffrey White*	80 S Vine St, Meriden CT 06451	203-235-2541	R	12*	.1
52	Lammes Candies Since 1885 Inc—*Pam Teich*	PO Box 1885, Austin TX 78767	512-310-1885	R	12*	.1
53	LA Burdick Chocolates—*Paula Burdick*	PO Box 593, Walpole NH 03608	603-756-3701	R	11*	.1
54	Dogleg Properties Inc—*Robert Rivard*	2870 Yellow Goose Rd, Lancaster PA 17601	717-898-7131	R	11*	.1
55	Fenton Enterprises Inc—*Rob Peterson*	PO Box 1962, Orem UT 84059	801-224-9500	R	11*	.1
56	Thompson Brands LLC—*Julie Bender*	80 S Vine St, Meriden CT 06451	203-235-2541	R	10*	.1
57	Sweet Shop Candies Inc—*James Webb*	1316 Industrial Rd, Mount Pleasant TX 75455	903-575-0033	R	10*	.1
58	Harbor Sweets Inc—*Phyllis Leblanc*	85 Leavitt St, Salem MA 01970	978-745-7648	R	10*	.1
59	Ames International Inc—*George Paulose*	4401 Industry Dr E Ste, Fife WA 98424	253-946-4779	R	10*	.1
60	Annabelle Candy Company Inc—*Susan Karl*	PO Box 3665, Hayward CA 94540	510-783-2900	R	10*	.1
61	Liberty Orchards Company Inc—*Gregory Taylor*	PO Box C, Cashmere WA 98815	509-782-2191	R	9*	.1
62	Joyva Corp—*Milton Radutzky*	53 Varick Ave, Brooklyn NY 11237	718-497-0170	R	9*	.1
63	Innovative Candy Concepts LLC—*Eric Loadman*	3765 Atlanta Industria, Atlanta GA 30331	404-505-7332	R	9*	.1
64	Decko Products Inc—*F Niggemyer*	2105 Superior St, Sandusky OH 44870	419-626-5757	R	8*	.1
65	Crown Candy Corp—*James Weatherford*	PO Box 6273, Macon GA 31208	478-781-4911	R	7*	.1
66	Piedmont Candy Co—*Chris Reid*	PO Box 1722, Lexington NC 27293	336-248-2477	R	7*	.1
67	Chris Candies Inc—*Tim Rogers*	1557 Spring Garden Ave, Pittsburgh PA 15212	412-322-9400	R	7	.1
68	HB Hunter Co—*Bill Barrett*	PO Box 1599, Norfolk VA 23501	757-664-5200	R	7*	<.1
69	Lehman Sugarfree Confections Inc—*Brian Berry*	PO Box 48099, Philadelphia PA 19144		R	7*	<.1
70	Squirrel Brand Co—*Brent Meyer*	113 Industrial Blvd St, McKinney TX 75069	214-585-0100	R	7*	<.1
71	La Tempesta Bakery Confections Inc—*Robert Sharp*	7066 Las Positas Rd St, Livermore CA 94551	650-873-8944	R	7*	.1
72	Kopper's Chocolate Specialty Company Inc—*Lorie Alexander*	39 Clarkson St, New York NY 10014	212-243-0220	R	7*	.1
73	WA Dehart Inc—*Christian Trate*	1130 Rte 15, New Columbia PA 17856	570-568-1551	R	7*	.1
74	Affy Tapple LLC—*Bill Henry*	6300 W Gross Point Rd, Niles IL 60714	847-588-2900	R	7*	.1
75	Marich Confectionery Company Inc—*Bradley Van Dam*	PO Box 1477, Hollister CA 95024	831-634-4700	R	7*	.1
76	Hawaiian Host Candies Of LA Inc *Keith Sakamoto*	15601 S Avalon Blvd, Gardena CA 90248	310-532-0543	R	7*	.1
77	Hilliard's House Of Candy—*Charles Carthy*	316 Main St, North Easton MA 02356	508-238-6231	R	7*	.1
78	Munson's Candy Kitchen Inc—*Robert B Munson*	PO BOX 9217, Bolton CT 06043	860-649-4332	R	6*	.2
79	Rajbhog Foods Inc—*Ajit Mody*	4123 Murray St, Flushing NY 11355	718-358-5105	R	6*	<.1
80	Jo's Candies—*Tom King*	2530 W 237th St, Torrance CA 90505	310-257-0260	R	6*	<.1
81	Forbes Candies Inc—*William Lawton*	1300 Taylor Farm Rd, Virginia Beach VA 23453	757-468-6602	R	6*	<.1
82	Candy Basket Inc—*Dale Fuhr*	1924 Ne 181st Ave, Portland OR 97230	503-666-2000	R	6*	<.1
83	World Candies Intl Ltd—*Samuel Cohen*	185 30th St, Brooklyn NY 11232	718-768-8100	R	6*	.1
84	FB Washburn Candy Corp—*James Gilson*	PO Box 3277, Brockton MA 02304	508-588-0820	R	5*	.1
85	Huckleberry People—*Lois Richardson*	1021 Waverly St, Missoula MT 59802	406-721-6024	R	5*	.1
86	Cerreta Candy Company Inc—*James Cerreta*	5345 W Glendale Ave, Glendale AZ 85301	623-930-9000	R	5*	<.1
87	Gimbal Brothers Inc—*Lance Gimbal*	PO Box 876, South San Francisco CA 94083	650-588-4844	R	4*	<.1
88	Food Technology And Design LLC—*John Cleveland*	PO Box 3677, Whittier CA 90605	562-944-7821	R	4*	<.1
89	Dietrich's Specialty Processing LLC	61 Vanguard Dr, Reading PA 19606	610-582-2170	R	4*	<.1
90	Ozark Delight Candy Co—*Don Churchwell*	1 Lollipop Ln, Prairie Grove AR 72753	479-846-5300	R	4*	<.1
91	Stutz Candy Co—*John Glaser*	400 S Warminster Rd, Hatboro PA 19040	215-675-2630	R	4*	<.1
92	Lucky Country Inc—*Lenka Dransfield*	3333 Finger Mill Rd, Lincolnton NC 28092	828-428-8313	R	4*	<.1
93	Mave Enterprises Inc—*Amy Grawitzky*	PO Box 480620, Los Angeles CA 90048	818-767-4533	R	4*	<.1
94	Tyler Candy Company LLC—*Vivian Walker*	PO Box 6556, Tyler TX 75711	903-561-3046	R	4*	<.1
95	Boston Fruit Slice and Confectionery Corp—*John Morrissey*	250 Canal St Ste 3, Lawrence MA 01840	978-686-2699	R	3*	<.1
96	Imaginings 3 Inc—*Sidney Diamond*	6401 W Gross Point Rd, Niles IL 60714	847-647-1370	R	3*	<.1
97	Euphoria Chocolate Company Inc—*Robert Bury*	4090 Stewart Rd, Eugene OR 97402	541-344-4914	R	3*	<.1
98	Hake Head LLC—*Alex Freytag*	1855 E 17th Ave, Columbus OH 43219	614-291-2244	R	3*	<.1
99	Toad-Ally Snax Inc—*Darlette Jenkins*	1410 Farragut Ave, Bristol PA 19007	215-788-7500	R	3*	<.1
100	Wagers Inc—*David Wagers*	PO Box 1217, Boise ID 83701	208-342-5505	R	3*	<.1
101	926 Partners Inc—*Joseph Hilbert*	2530 Parade St, Erie PA 16503	814-452-4026	R	3*	<.1
102	Yost Candy Co—*Sofie Yost*	51 N Cochran St, Dalton OH 44618	330-828-2777	R	3*	<.1
103	Glazers Distributers Of Iowa—*Thomas Rowen*	4377 112th St, Urbandale IA 50322	515-252-7173	R	3*	<.1
104	Pearl River Pastries LLC—*Joanne Lacroix*	4 Dexter Plz, Pearl River NY 10965	845-735-5100	R	3*	<.1
105	Chase Candy Co—*Barry M Yantis*	PO Box 698, Saint Joseph MO 64502	816-279-1625	R	3	<.1
106	Vande Walle's Candies Inc—*Steven Vandewalle*	400 N Mall Dr, Appleton WI 54913	920-738-7799	R	3*	<.1
107	Florida Candy Factory Inc—*Gerald Rehm*	721 Lakeview Rd, Clearwater FL 33756	727-446-0024	R	3*	<.1
108	Dilco Enterprises Inc—*Oscar Cook*	19927 Hwy 84 E, Boston GA 31626	229-498-2051	R	3*	<.1
109	Hawaii Candy Inc—*Keith Ohta*	2928 Ualena St Ste 4, Honolulu HI 96819	808-836-8955	R	3*	<.1
110	Mr Bs Fun Foods Inc—*Craig Pittman*	PO Box 218, Valdese NC 28690	828-879-1901	R	3*	<.1
111	Nancy's Homemade Fudge Inc—*Nancy Galli*	PO Box 860, Meadows Of Dan VA 24120	276-952-2112	R	3*	<.1
112	Louis J Rheb Candy Company Inc—*Edwin Harger*	3352 Wilkens Ave, Baltimore MD 21229	410-644-4321	R	3*	<.1
113	Mcjak Candy Company LLC	1087 Branch Rd, Medina OH 44256	330-722-3531	R	3*	<.1
114	Rainbow Cotton Candy LLC—*Marvin Eisenteraut*	503 S Rockford Dr, Tempe AZ 85281	480-829-8918	R	2*	<.1
115	Trappistine Nuns Inc—*Mthr Fitzpatrick*	8400 Abbey Hill Ln, Dubuque IA 52003	563-556-6330	R	2*	<.1
116	Dye Candy Corp—*Barry Yantis*	PO Box 698, Saint Joseph MO 64502	816-279-1625	R	2*	<.1
117	Clyde Cummings Candy Inc—*Marlon Cummings*	679 E 900 S, Salt Lake City UT 84105	801-328-4858	R	2*	<.1
118	Betty Jane Home Made Candies Inc—*John Heinz*	3049 Asbury Rd, Dubuque IA 52001	563-582-4668	R	2*	<.1
119	Jay R King—*Jay King*	PO Box 766, West Liberty OH 43357	937-465-3061	R	2*	<.1
120	Anderson's Candies Inc—*Goldie Anderson*	1010 W State St, Baden PA 15005	724-869-3018	R	2*	<.1
121	CranBerry Sweets Co—*Clayton B Shaw*	1005 Newmark Ave, Coos Bay OR 97420		R	2*	<.1
122	Andrews Caramel Apples Inc—*Daniel Demarco*	5001 W Belmont Ave, Chicago IL 60641	773-286-2224	R	2*	<.1
123	Fenton and Lee Confections	PO Box 3244, Eugene OR 97403	541-343-7629	R	2*	<.1

Note: An asterisk (*) indicates an estimated financial figure. The company type code used is as follows: R = Private, P = Public, S = Private Subsidiary, B = Public Subsidiary, D = Division, J = Joint Venture, I = Investment Fund.

COMPANY RANKINGS BY SALES WITHIN 4-DIGIT SIC

Rank	Company Name—*Executive Officer*	Address, City, State, Zip	Phone	Type	Fin	Empls
124	Andrews Candy Company Inc—*Gary Andrews*	2606 Pine St, Arkadelphia AR 71923	870-246-2796	R	2*	<.1
125	Harbor Candy Shop Inc—*Eugenie Sotiropoulos-Fo*	PO Box 2064, Ogunquit ME 03907	207-646-8078	R	2*	<.1
126	Len Libby's Inc—*Maureen Hemond*	419 Us Rte 1, Scarborough ME 04074	207-883-4897	R	2*	<.1
127	Dumas Candy Company Inc—*Dave Johnson*	153 Superior Dr, Delhi LA 71232	318-878-2294	R	2*	<.1
128	Kendon Candies Inc—*Kathleen Glass*	460 Perrymont Ave, San Jose CA 95125	408-297-6133	R	2*	<.1
129	3300 South Associates LLC—*Marilyn Oakey*	2057 E 3300 S, Salt Lake City UT 84109	801-485-1031	R	1*	<.1
130	Winfrey's Olde English Fudge Inc—*Christine Winfrey*	40 Newburyport Tpke St, Rowley MA 01969	978-948-7448	R	1*	<.1
131	Brigittine Monks Gourmet Confections—*James Adamson*	23300 Walker Ln, Amity OR 97101	503-835-8080	R	1*	<.1
132	Art Coco Chocolate Co—*Mark Callahan* Silvestri Sweets Inc	2248 Gary Ln, Geneva IL 60134	630-232-2500	S	1*	<.1
133	Morkes Inc—*Rhonda Morkes*	1890 N Rand Rd, Palatine IL 60074	847-359-3454	R	1*	<.1
134	Abbott's Candy And Gifts Inc—*Suanna Goodnight*	48 E Walnut St, Hagerstown IN 47346	765-489-4442	R	1*	<.1
135	Victoria's Candies Inc—*Paul Esposito*	51 N Laurel St, Hazleton PA 18201	570-455-6341	R	1*	<.1
136	MrchocolateCom LLC—*Louise Geller*	66 Water St Ste 2, Brooklyn NY 11201	718-875-9772	R	1*	<.1
137	Silvestri Sweets Inc—*Mary Silvestri*	2248 Gary Ln, Geneva IL 60134	630-232-2500	R	1*	<.1
138	Sherm Edwards Candies Inc—*David Golembeski*	509 Cavitt Ave, Trafford PA 15085	412-372-4331	R	1*	<.1
139	Rosalind Candy Castle Inc—*James Crudden*	PO Box 93, New Brighton PA 15066	724-843-1144	R	1*	<.1
140	Eden Processing Inc—*Louis Tenore*	100 E St, Poplar Grove IL 61065	815-765-2000	R	1*	<.1
141	Truan's Candies Inc—*Mark Truan*	13716 Tireman St, Detroit MI 48228	313-584-3400	R	1*	<.1
142	Dorothy Cox Candies Inc—*Francis Cox*	115 Huttleston Ave, Fairhaven MA 02719	508-996-2465	R	1*	<.1
143	Dorothy's Candies—*Robert Gastel*	1228 Long Run Rd, White Oak PA 15131	412-678-2723	R	1*	<.1
144	Russos' Inc—*Vincent Vannah*	329 Main St, Saugus MA 01906	781-233-1737	R	1*	<.1
145	Mona Lisa Chocolates and Confection Company LLC/Mona Lisa Chocolatier	PO Box 1632, Arlington VA 22210	703-524-8888	R	1*	<.1
146	R and S Roberts Enterprises Inc—*Mellissa Armstrong*	116 A St Se, Auburn WA 98002	253-333-7567	R	<1*	<.1
147	Light Vision	1776 Mentor Ave, Cincinnati OH 45212	513-351-9444	R	<1*	<.1
148	Jelly Belly Candy Co—*Robert Simpson*	1 Jelly Belly Ln, Fairfield CA 94533	707-428-2800	R	<1*	.7

TOTALS: SIC 2064 Candy & Other Confectionery Products
Companies: 148   35,353   100.2

2066 Chocolate & Cocoa Products

Rank	Company Name—*Executive Officer*	Address, City, State, Zip	Phone	Type	Fin	Empls
1	Nestle USA Inc—*Brad Alford*	800 N Brand Blvd, Glendale CA 91209	818-549-6000	S	8,250	14.0
2	Hershey Co—*James Nevels*	100 Crystal A Dr, Hershey PA 17033	717-534-4200	P	5,671	13.5
3	Godiva Chocolatier Inc—*Jim Goldman*	355 Lexington Ave, New York NY 10017	212-984-5900	R	770*	2.2
4	Lyons-Magnus Inc—*Robert Smittcamp*	3158 E Hamilton Ave, Fresno CA 93702	559-268-5966	R	171*	.3
5	TR Toppers Inc—*Tim Rode*	PO Box 6308, Boise ID 83707	719-948-4902	R	74*	<.1
6	Ghirardelli Chocolate Co—*Fabrizio Parini* Lindt and Sprungli (USA) Inc	1111 139th Ave, San Leandro CA 94578	510-483-6970	S	71*	.7
7	Blommer Chocolate Co—*Joseph Blommer*	600 W Kinzie St, Chicago IL 60654	312-226-7700	R	71*	.4
8	Lindt and Sprungli (USA) Inc—*Thomas Linemayr*	1 Fine Chocolate Pl, Stratham NH 03885	603-778-8100	R	63*	.7
9	Madelaine Chocolate Novelties Inc—*Jorge Farber*	9603 Beach Channel Dr, Rockaway Beach NY 11693	718-945-1500	R	50*	.5
10	ADM Cocoa—*Patricia A Woertz*	12500 W Carmen Ave, Milwaukee WI 53225	414-358-5700	D	48*	.3
11	Buddy Squirrel LLC—*Margaret Gile*	PO Box 07581, Milwaukee WI 53207	414-483-4500	R	48*	.2
12	Guittard Chocolate Co—*Gary Guittard*	PO Box 4308, Burlingame CA 94011	650-697-4427	R	47*	.2
13	World's Finest Chocolate Inc—*Howard Zodikoff*	4801 S Lawndale Ave, Chicago IL 60632	773-847-4600	R	41*	.4
14	Mars Retail Group Inc—*Lynn Moran*	1 Sunset Way, Henderson NV 89014	702-458-8864	S	38*	.5
15	Linette James P Inc	PO Box 212, Womelsdorf PA 19567	610-589-4526	D	35*	.1
16	Elmer Candy Corp—*Robert Nelson*	PO Box 788, Ponchatoula LA 70454	985-386-6166	R	26*	.3
17	Dws Inc—*Ric Lashway*	102 Kimball Ave Ste 2, South Burlington VT 05403	802-862-6004	R	26*	<.1
18	Very Special Chocolats Inc—*Gerald Morris*	760 N Mckeever Ave, Azusa CA 91702	626-334-7838	R	15*	.3
19	Champlain Chocolate Company Inc—*James Lampman*	750 Pine St, Burlington VT 05401	802-864-1808	R	14*	.1
20	Lake Country Foods Inc—*Phillip Kemppianen*	132 S Concord Rd, Oconomowoc WI 53066	262-567-5521	D	13*	.1
21	Calico Cottage Inc—*Mark Wurzel*	210 New Hwy, Amityville NY 11701	631-841-2100	R	11*	.1
22	Seattle Chocolate Company LLC—*Joe Slye*	1180 Andover Park W, Tukwila WA 98188	425-264-2800	R	10*	.1
23	Storck of the Americas Inc—*Liam Killeen*	325 N LaSalle St Rm 40, Chicago IL 60654	312-467-5700	S	10*	.1
24	Frankford Candy and Chocolate Company Inc—*Stuart Selarnick*	9300 Ashton Rd, Philadelphia PA 19114	215-735-5200	R	8*	.2
25	Vosges Chocolates Inc—*Katrina Markoff*	2211 N Elston Ave Ste, Chicago IL 60614	773-388-5560	R	8*	.1
26	Totally Chocolate Inc—*Jeffrey Robinson*	2025 Sweet Rd, Blaine WA 98230	360-332-3900	R	6*	.1
27	Bloomer Candy Co—*William S Barry*	PO Box 3450, Zanesville OH 43702	740-452-7501	R	6*	<.1
28	Judy's Candy Co—*Jerry Shelton*	1225 8th St, Berkeley CA 94710		R	6*	<.1
29	Omanhene Cocoa Bean Co—*Steven C Wallace*	PO Box 22, Milwaukee WI 53201	414-744-8780	R	6*	<.1
30	Giannios Candy Company Inc—*John Giannios*	430 Youngstown Poland, Struthers OH 44471	330-755-5727	R	6*	.1
31	Fralingers Inc—*Frank Glaser*	1325 Boardwalk Ste 1, Atlantic City NJ 08401	609-345-2177	R	5*	.1
32	Holiday Candy Corp—*Roger Mceldowney*	PO Box 40, Buffalo NY 14217	716-877-0879	R	4*	<.1
33	Chocolate In Topographic Co—*Kenneth Wolf*	2660 Walnut St, Denver CO 80205	303-292-6364	R	3*	<.1
34	Dietsch Brothers Inc—*Jeffery Dietsch*	400 W Main Cross St, Findlay OH 45840	419-422-4474	R	3*	.1
35	Alethea's Chocolates Inc—*Gust Tassy*	8301 Main St, Williamsville NY 14221	716-633-8620	R	3*	<.1
36	Ernex Corporation Inc—*Ernest Grunhut*	5518 Ave N, Brooklyn NY 11234	718-951-2251	R	3*	<.1
37	Green Mountain Chocolate Company Inc—*William Campbell*	1 Rosenfeld Dr, Hopedale MA 01747	508-473-9060	R	3*	<.1
38	Parkside Candy Company Inc—*Phillip Buffamonte*	3208 Main St, Buffalo NY 14214	716-833-7540	R	2*	<.1
39	Premise Maid Candies Inc—*Joseph Damiano*	10860 Hamilton Blvd, Breinigsville PA 18031	610-395-3221	R	2*	<.1
40	Philadelphia Candies Inc—*Spyros Macris*	1546 E State St, Hermitage PA 16148	724-981-6341	R	2*	<.1
41	Mary Ann's Chocolate Factory Inc—*Joan Abraham*	4695 44th St Se Ste 14, Grand Rapids MI 49512	616-241-6411	R	2*	<.1
42	Baraboo Candy Co—*Dennis Roney*	PO Box 63, Baraboo WI 53913	608-356-7425	R	1*	<.1
43	Schenone Specialty Foods Inc—*Ernie Schenone Jr*	PO Box 730, Clements CA 95227	209-759-3340	R	1*	<.1
44	Anderson's Candy Shop Inc—*Lars Anderson*	10301 N Main St, Richmond IL 60071	815-678-6000	R	1*	<.1

TOTALS: SIC 2066 Chocolate & Cocoa Products
Companies: 44   15,654   35.7

2067 Chewing Gum

Rank	Company Name—*Executive Officer*	Address, City, State, Zip	Phone	Type	Fin	Empls
1	Wm Wrigley Jr Co—*Dushan Petrovich*	PO Box 3900, Peoria IL 61612	312-644-2121	S	5,389*	16.4
2	Ford Gum and Machine Company Inc—*George Stege*	18 Newton Ave, Akron NY 14001	716-542-4561	R	23*	.1
3	Lotte USA Inc—*Tetsuo Kaneko*	5243 Wayne Rd, Battle Creek MI 49037	269-963-6664	R	7*	<.1

TOTALS: SIC 2067 Chewing Gum
Companies: 3   5,419   16.5

2068 Salted & Roasted Nuts & Seeds

Rank	Company Name—*Executive Officer*	Address, City, State, Zip	Phone	Type	Fin	Empls
1	Nabisco Inc—*Roger Deromedi*	7 Campus Dr, Parsippany NJ 07054	973-682-5000	D	1,100*	6.0

Rank	Company Name—*Executive Officer*	Address, City, State, Zip	Phone	Type	Fin	Empls
2	Diamond Foods Inc—*Michael Mendes*	1050 S Diamond St, Stockton CA 95205	209-467-6000	P	966	1.8
3	John B Sanfilippo and Son Inc—*Jeffrey T Sanfilippo*	1703 N Randall Rd, Elgin IL 60123	847-289-1800	P	674	1.4
4	Berberian Nut Co—*Rex Lewis*	6100 Wilson Landing Rd, Chico CA 95973	530-891-4900	R	65*	.2
5	Suntree LLC—*Jim Bear*	40897 Rd 120, Orosi CA 93647	559-528-5454	R	42*	.1
6	AL Bazzini Company Inc—*Rocco Damato*	200 Food Center Dr, Bronx NY 10474	718-842-8644	R	41*	.1
7	Soft Pretzel Franchise Systems Inc—*Dan DiZio*	7368 Frankford Ave, Philadelphia PA 19136	215-338-4606	R	40*	.1
8	Mountain Man Nut and Fruit Co—*David Conner*	10338 S Progress Way, Parker CO 80134	303-841-4041	R	39*	.1
9	Kelley Manufacturing Co (Tifton Georgia)—*Bennie Branch*	PO Box 1467, Tifton GA 31793	229-382-9393	R	38*	.2
10	King Nut Co—*Martin Kanan*	31900 Solon Rd, Solon OH 44139	440-248-8484	R	35*	.2
11	Durham Ellis Pecan Co—*HL Dollins*	308 S Houston St, Comanche TX 76442		R	32*	.1
12	Hazelnut Growers Of Oregon Inc—*Compton Lansdale*	PO Box 626, Cornelius OR 97113	503-648-4176	R	32*	.1
13	Priester Pecan Company Inc—*Thomas Ellis*	208 Old Fort Rd E, Fort Deposit AL 36032	334-227-4301	R	28*	.1
14	Stahmann Farms Inc—*Sally Rovirosa*	PO Box 70, San Miguel NM 88058	575-526-2453	R	28*	.2
15	Trophy Nut Co—*Gerald Allen*	PO Box 199, Tipp City OH 45371	937-667-8478	R	24*	.1
16	Continental Dining and Refreshment Services—*Jim Bardy*	44800 N I-94 Service D, Belleville MI 48111	734-699-4100	R	24*	.3
17	Terri Lynn Inc—*Terri Graziano*	PO Box 5118, Elgin IL 60121	847-741-1900	R	17*	.1
18	Barcelona Nut Company Inc—*Tony Psonis*	502 S Mount St, Baltimore MD 21223	410-233-5252	R	15*	.1
19	Nutcracker Brands Inc—*Kevin J Hunt*	26 Cook St, Billerica MA 01821	978-663-5400	S	12*	.1
20	A L Schutzman Company Inc—*Gordon Liebl*	N21 W-23560 Rdgview Pk, Waukesha WI 53188	262-832-8200	R	11*	.1
21	Hammons Products Co—*Brian Hammons*	105 Hammons Dr, Stockton MO 65785	417-276-5181	R	10*	.1
22	Beer Nuts Inc—*James Shirk*	PO Box 1327, Bloomington IL 61702	309-827-8580	R	10*	.1
23	Pardoe's Perky Peanuts Inc—*Carl Pardoe*	PO Box 90, Montandon PA 17850	570-524-9595	R	8*	<.1
24	Indianola Pecan House Inc—*Wheeler Timbs*	PO Box 367, Indianola MS 38751	662-887-5420	R	7*	.1
25	Superior Nut Company Inc—*Harry Hintlian*	PO Box 410086, Cambridge MA 02141	617-876-3808	R	5*	<.1
26	Regal Health Foods International Inc—*Gregory Piatigorsky*	3705 W Grand Ave, Chicago IL 60651	773-252-1044	R	5*	.1
27	Klein Brothers Holdings Ltd—*Thomas Klein*	1515 S Fresno Ave, Stockton CA 95206	209-942-1020	R	4*	<.1
28	Quality Packaging Inc—*Ronald Mozingo*	1820 Industrial Dr, Stockton CA 95206	209-944-7200	R	3*	<.1
29	California Nuggets Inc—*Steve Gikas*	23073 S Frederick Rd, Ripon CA 95366	209-599-7131	R	3*	<.1
30	Nut Factory Inc—*Gene Cohen*	PO Box 815, Greenacres WA 99016	509-926-6666	R	3*	<.1
31	Eagle Ranch Pistachio Groves—*George Schweers*	7288 Hwy 54-70, Alamogordo NM 88310	575-434-0035	R	2*	<.1
32	Sundial Orchards Hulling and Drying—*Brad Barrow*	1500 Kirk Rd, Gridley CA 95948	530-846-6155	R	1*	<.1

TOTALS: SIC 2068 Salted & Roasted Nuts & Seeds
Companies: 32 — 3,324 — 11.7

2074 Cottonseed Oil Mills

1	Yazoo Valley Oil Mill Inc—*W Clark*	PO Box 1320, Greenwood MS 38935	662-453-4312	R	116*	.2
2	Delta Oil Mill—*Scott Middleton*	PO Box 29, Jonestown MS 38639	662-358-4481	R	33*	.1
3	Pyco Industries—*Gail Kring*	PO Box 841, Lubbock TX 79408	806-747-3434	R	21*	.1
4	Planters Cotton Oil Mill Inc—*Bob Norsworthy*	2901 Planters Dr, Pine Bluff AR 71601	870-534-3631	R	11*	.1

TOTALS: SIC 2074 Cottonseed Oil Mills
Companies: 4 — 180 — .4

2075 Soybean Oil Mills

1	Bunge North America Inc—*Soren Schroder*	11720 Borman Dr, Saint Louis MO 63146	314-292-2000	S	9,536*	3.4
2	DuPont Protein Technologies International Inc—*Tony Armold*	PO Box 88940, Saint Louis MO 63188	314-659-3000	J	4,734*	3.5
3	Solae Co—*Torkel Rhenman*	4300 Duncan Ave, Saint Louis MO 63110	314-982-1010	R	3,053*	2.4
4	AG Processing Inc—*Marty P Reagan*	PO Box 2047, Omaha NE 68103	402-496-7809	R	1,743*	3.8
5	Owensboro Grain Co—*Robert Hicks*	PO Box 1787, Owensboro KY 42302	270-926-2032	R	400*	.1
6	South Dakota Soybean Processors LLC—*Thomas Kersting*	PO Box 500, Volga SD 57071	605-647-9240	R	288*	.1
7	Solae LLC—*Tony Arnold*	4300 Duncan Ave, Saint Louis MO 63110	314-659-3000	R	178*	1.6
8	Riceland Foods Inc Lecithin Div—*Danny Kennedy*	PO Box 927, Stuttgart AR 72160	501-225-0936	D	170*	.5
9	House Foods America Corp—*Shigeru Shirasaka*	7351 Orangewood Ave, Garden Grove CA 92841	714-901-4350	R	11*	.1
10	WA Cleary Corp—*Margaret Cleary*	PO Box 10, Somerset NJ 08875	732-329-8399	R	8*	<.1
11	American Soy Products Inc—*Hiroyasu Iwatsuki*	1474 Woodland Dr, Saline MI 48176	734-429-2310	R	5*	<.1

TOTALS: SIC 2075 Soybean Oil Mills
Companies: 11 — 20,126 — 15.6

2076 Vegetable Oil Mills Nec

1	Archer Daniels Midland Co—*Patricia A Woertz*	PO Box 1470, Decatur IL 62525	217-424-5200	P	80,676	30.7
2	Fuji Vegetable Oil Inc—*Tomoyuki Yoshida*	120 Brampton Rd, Savannah GA 31408	912-966-5900	R	92*	.1
3	Agri-Fine Inc—*Mike Hoelzeman*	2701 E 100th St, Chicago IL 60617	773-978-5130	R	6*	<.1

TOTALS: SIC 2076 Vegetable Oil Mills Nec
Companies: 3 — 80,774 — 30.8

2077 Animal & Marine Fats & Oils

1	Daybrook Holdings Inc—*Gregory Holt*	PO Box 1931, Morristown NJ 07960	973-538-6766	R	356*	.3
2	Omega Protein Corp—*Joseph L von Rosenberg III*	2105 City West Blvd St, Houston TX 77042	713-623-0060	P	168	.5
3	Captek Softgel International Inc—*James Hao*	16218 Arthur St, Cerritos CA 90703	562-921-9511	R	35*	.1
4	Kane-Miller Corp—*Stanley Kane*	1991 Main St Ste 260, Sarasota FL 34236	941-906-7700	R	23*	.3
5	Kodiak Fishmeal Co—*Dan James*	915 Gibson Cove Rd, Kodiak AK 99615	907-486-3171	R	10*	<.1
6	Riegel By-Products Company Inc—*Allen Riegel*	PO Box 7064, Shreveport LA 71137	318-222-3309	R	6*	<.1
7	Geo Pfau's Sons Company Inc—*Norman Pfau*	PO Box 7, Jeffersonville IN 47131	812-283-6697	R	5*	.1
8	Inland Products Inc—*Gary Baas*	PO Box 2228, Columbus OH 43216	614-444-1127	R	5*	.1
9	Src Milling Company LLC—*Bill Eckstien*	11350 Kiefer Blvd, Sacramento CA 95830	916-363-4821	R	5*	.1
10	Harbinger Group Inc—*Philip A Falcone*	450 Park Ave 27th Fl, New York NY 10022	212-906-8555	P	4	<.1
11	Mendota Agri-Products Inc—*Joseph Baka*	448 N 3973rd Rd, Mendota IL 61342	815-539-5633	R	3*	<.1
12	WB Riggins Tallow Company Inc—*Wallace Riggins*	4474 Camp Coleman Rd, Trussville AL 35173	205-655-3612	R	3*	<.1
13	Western Mass Rendering Company Inc—*David Plakias*	94 Foster Rd, Southwick MA 01077	413-569-6265	R	3*	<.1
14	Nevada Byproducts Inc—*Michael Koewler*	1705 N Wells Ave, Reno NV 89512	775-323-0791	R	2*	<.1
15	Tucson Tallow Company Inc—*Glorie Haugh*	3928 N Fairview Ave, Tucson AZ 85705	520-887-0440	R	2*	<.1
16	Kostelac Grease Service Inc—*John Kostelac*	3330 Kostelac Ln, Belleville IL 62223	618-538-5421	R	2*	<.1
17	Bio-Oregon Inc—*Walter Kost*	PO Box 429, Warrenton OR 97146	503-861-2256	R	1*	<.1

TOTALS: SIC 2077 Animal & Marine Fats & Oils
Companies: 17 — 632 — 1.5

2079 Edible Fats & Oils Nec

| 1 | Darling International Inc—*Randall Stuew* | 251 O'Connor Ridge Blv, Irving TX 75038 | 972-717-0300 | P | 1,797 | 3.3 |
| 2 | ACH Food Co's Inc—*Richard Rankin* | 7171 Goodlett Farms Pk, Cordova TN 38016 | 901-381-3000 | R | 1,346* | .2 |

Note: An asterisk (*) indicates an estimated financial figure. The company type code used is as follows: R = Private, P = Public, S = Private Subsidiary, B = Public Subsidiary, D = Division, J = Joint Venture, I = Investment Fund.

COMPANY RANKINGS BY SALES WITHIN 4-DIGIT SIC

Rank	Company Name—*Executive Officer*	Address, City, State, Zip	Phone	Type	Fin	Empls
3	Ventura Foods LLC—*Christopher Furman*	40 Pointe Dr, Brea CA 92821	714-257-3700	S	1,008*	3.0
4	CF Sauer Company Inc—*Conrad Sauer IV*	PO Box 27366, Richmond VA 23261	804-342-8572	R	264*	.8
5	Oasis Trading Company Inc—*Anthony Alves*	635 Ramsey Ave Ste 201, Hillside NJ 07205	908-964-0477	R	26*	.2
6	Mahoney Environmental—*John Mahoney*	1819 Moen Ave, Rockdale IL 60436	815-730-2080	R	17*	.1
7	Aarhus Karlshamn USA Inc—*Jean Rotsaert*	499 Thornall St Ste 5, Edison NJ 08837	973-344-1300	R	14*	.1
8	Barlean's Organic Oils LLC—*Karen Martin*	4936 Lake Terrell Rd, Ferndale WA 98248	360-384-0485	R	7*	.1
9	Catania-Spagna Corp—*Anthony Basile*	PO Box 847315, Boston MA 02284	978-772-7900	R	7*	<.1
10	Liberty Vegetable Oil Co—*Irwin Field*	PO Box 4207, Cerritos CA 90703	562-921-3567	R	5*	<.1
11	California Olive Ranch Inc—*Gregory Kelly*	2675 Lone Tree Rd, Oroville CA 95965	530-846-8000	R	4*	<.1
12	Nick Sciabica and Sons A Corp—*Joseph Sciabica*	2150 Yosemite Blvd, Modesto CA 95354	209-577-5067	R	2*	<.1

TOTALS: SIC 2079 Edible Fats & Oils Nec
Companies: 12   **4,497**   **7.9**

2082 Malt Beverages

Rank	Company Name—*Executive Officer*	Address, City, State, Zip	Phone	Type	Fin	Empls
1	Anheuser-Busch Companies Inc—*David A Peacock*	1 Busch Pl, Saint Louis MO 63118		S	18,989	30.8
2	Molson Coors Brewing Co—*Peter Swinburn*	1225 17th St Ste 3200, Denver CO 80202	303-927-2337	P	3,254	14.7
3	Boston Beer Company Inc—*Martin F Roper*	1 Design Center Ste 85, Boston MA 02210	617-368-5000	P	661	.8
4	MillerCoors LLC—*Tom Long*	4000 W State St, Milwaukee WI 53208		R	605*	.8
5	Boston Brewing Company Inc—*Martin F Roper* Boston Beer Company Inc	One Design Center Ste, Boston MA 02116	617-368-5000	S	475*	.8
6	Independent Brewers United Inc—*Martin Kelly*	431 Pine St Ste G-14, Burlington VT 05401	802-658-2739	R	434*	.6
7	High Falls Brewing Company Inc—*Norman Snyder*	445 St Paul St, Rochester NY 14605		R	250*	.5
8	BBC Mass Inc—*Jim Koch* Boston Beer Company Inc	One Design Center Ste, Boston MA 02110	617-368-5000	S	245*	.4
9	Craft Brewer's Alliance Inc—*Terry E Michaelson*	929 North Russell St, Portland OR 97227	503-331-7270	P	141	.6
10	Anheuser-Busch Inc—*David A Peacock* Anheuser-Busch Companies Inc	1 Busch Pl, Saint Louis MO 63118	314-577-2000	S	122	N/A
11	San Diego Brewery Co—*Scott Stamp*	10450 Friars Rd Ste L, San Diego CA 92120	619-284-2739	R	92*	.2
12	Four Peaks Brewing Co—*Jim Scussel*	1340 E 8th St Ste 104, Tempe AZ 85281	480-303-9967	R	82*	.2
13	Pearl Brewing Co—*Paul Beard*	PO Box 792627, San Antonio TX 78279	210-226-0231	R	80*	.2
14	D G Yuengling And Son Inc—*Richard Yuengling*	501 Mahantongo St, Pottsville PA 17901	570-622-4141	R	80*	.2
15	Lion Brewery Inc—*Cliford Riseos*	700 N Pennsylvania Ave, Wilkes Barre PA 18705	570-823-8801	R	72*	.1
16	Carolina Beer and Beverage LLC—*Michael Brown*	PO Box 1183, Mooresville NC 28115	704-799-2337	R	64*	.2
17	Mike's Hard Lemonade Co—*Philip O'Neil*	159 S Jackson St 4th F, Seattle WA 98104	206-267-4400	S	62*	.1
18	Pyramid Breweries Inc—*Robert M Kelly* Independent Brewers United Inc	91 S Royal Brougham Wa, Seattle WA 98134	206-682-8322	S	51*	.5
19	Carver Brewing Co—*William Carver*	1022 Main Ave, Durango CO 81301	970-259-2545	R	47*	.1
20	Boundary Bay Brewing Co—*Ed Bennett*	1107 Railroad Ave, Bellingham WA 98225	360-647-5593	R	46*	.1
21	Deschutes Brewery Inc—*Gary Fish*	901 Sw Simpson Ave, Bend OR 97702	541-385-8606	R	44*	.3
22	Pittsburgh Brewing Co—*Thomas Gephart*	3340 Liberty Ave, Pittsburgh PA 15201	412-682-7400	R	41*	.3
23	Steamworks Brewing Co—*Kris Oyler*	801 E 2nd Ave, Durango CO 81301	970-259-9200	R	41*	.1
24	Brooklyn Brewery Ltd—*Steve Hindy Potter*	79 N 11th St, Brooklyn NY 11211	718-486-7422	R	41*	.1
25	New Belgium Brewing Company Inc—*Kimberly Jordan*	500 Linden St, Fort Collins CO 80524	970-221-0524	R	38*	.2
26	Roosters 25th St Brewing Co—*Peter Buttschardt*	253 Historic 25th St, Ogden UT 84401	801-627-6171	R	36*	.1
27	Mendocino Brewing Company Inc—*Yashpal Singh*	1601 Airport Rd, Ukiah CA 95482	707-463-6610	P	36	.1
28	Los Gatos Brewing Co—*Andy Pavicich*	130 N Santa Cruz Ave S, Los Gatos CA 95030	408-395-9929	R	35*	.2
29	Breckenridge Brewery and Pub—*Ed Cerkovink*	471 Kalamath St, Denver CO 80204	303-623-2739	R	34*	.1
30	Leinenkugel Jacob Brewing Co—*Thomas J Leinenkugel*	PO Box 337, Chippewa Falls WI 54729		R	33*	.1
31	KMT Management Inc—*Leo Townsell*	6861 Main St, Williamsville NY 14221	716-632-0552	R	27*	<.1
32	Anchor Brewing Co—*Frederick Maytag*	1705 Mariposa St, San Francisco CA 94107	415-863-8350	R	27*	.1
33	Skagit River Brewing Co—*Charles Sullivan*	404 S 3rd St, Mount Vernon WA 98273	360-336-2884	R	26*	<.1
34	Fountain Rock Management Corp—*Philip Bowers*	124 N Market St, Frederick MD 21701	301-631-0089	R	26*	.2
35	Snowshoe Brewing Co—*Jeff Yarnell*	PO Box 2224, Arnold CA 95223	209-795-2272	R	21*	<.1
36	Boulevard Brewing Associates LP—*John McDonald*	2501 Southwest Blvd, Kansas City MO 64108	816-474-7095	R	20*	.1
37	Southern Eagle Distributing LLC	243 Ocilla Hwy, Fitzgerald GA 31750	229-423-4679	R	17*	.2
38	Backdraft Brewing Co—*Michael Reddy*	35122 W Michigan Ave, Wayne MI 48184	734-722-7639	R	17*	.1
39	Louis Saint Brewery Inc—*Thomas Schlafly*	2100 Locust St, Saint Louis MO 63103	314-241-2337	R	17*	.1
40	Mount St Helena Brewing Co—*Nancy Simon*	PO Box 1430, Middletown CA 95461	707-987-3361	R	17*	<.1
41	Snake River Brewing Co—*Joni Upsher*	PO Box 3317, Jackson WY 83001	307-739-2337	R	16*	<.1
42	Morgan Street Brewery and Tavern Inc—*Dennis Harper*	721 N 2nd St, Saint Louis MO 63102	314-231-9970	R	15*	<.1
43	Stevens Point Brewery—*John Zappa*	2617 Water St, Stevens Point WI 54481	715-344-9310	R	14*	<.1
44	Stone Brewing Co—*Greg Koch*	1999 Citracado Pky, Escondido CA 92029	760-471-4999	R	12*	.1
45	Santa Barbara Brewing Company LLC—*Wayne Drella*	501 State St, Santa Barbara CA 93101	805-730-1040	R	10*	<.1
46	Steinbeck Brewing Co—*Geoffrey Harries*	1082 B St, Hayward CA 94541	510-886-9823	R	9*	.1
47	Summit Brewing Co—*Mark Stutrud*	910 Montreal Cir, Saint Paul MN 55102	651-265-7800	R	9*	<.1
48	Saint Arnold Brewing Co—*Brock L Wagner*	2000 Lyons Ave, Houston TX 77020	713-686-9494	R	9*	<.1
49	Tracks Brewing Co—*James Bride*	1641 N Main St, Tooele UT 84074	435-882-4040	R	9*	.1
50	Mass Bay Brewing Company Inc—*Richard Doyle*	306 Northern Ave Ste 2, Boston MA 02210	617-574-9551	R	9*	.1
51	Creekside Kitchen—*Jean Wilson*	11 S Beaver St Ste 1, Flagstaff AZ 86001	928-779-0079	R	8*	.1
52	Silver Creek Brewing Corp—*Todd Schnaberger*	N 57 W6172 Portland Rd, Cedarburg WI 53012	262-375-4444	R	8*	<.1
53	BC Marketing Concepts Inc—*Irene Firmat*	506 Columbia St, Hood River OR 97031	541-386-2281	R	8*	.1
54	North Coast Brewing Company Inc—*Mark Ruedrich*	455 N Main St, Fort Bragg CA 95437	707-964-2739	R	8*	.1
55	Magic Hat Brewing Company and Performing Arts Center Inc— *Martin Kelly*	5 Bartlett Bay Rd, South Burlington VT 05403	802-658-2739	R	7*	.1
56	1316 Commonwealth Ave Corp—*Martin Murphy*	1316 Commonwealth Ave, Allston MA 02134	617-566-6699	R	7*	.1
57	Labatt USA LLC—*Shari Keisow*	50 Fountain Plz Ste 90, Buffalo NY 14202	716-604-1050	R	7*	.1
58	Anderson Valley Brewing Inc—*Kenneth Allen*	PO Box 505, Boonville CA 95415	707-895-2337	R	7*	<.1
59	Appalachian Brewing Company Inc—*Shawn Gallagher*	50 N Cameron St, Harrisburg PA 17101	717-221-1080	R	6*	.1
60	Willoughby Brewing Co—*Jeff Halkertston*	4057 Erie St, Willoughby OH 44094	440-975-0202	R	6*	.1
61	Long Trail Brewing Co—*Brian Walsh*	Us Rte 4, Bridgewater Corners VT 05035	802-672-5011	R	6*	.1
62	Alaskan Brewing LLC—*Dave Wilson*	5429 Shaune Dr, Juneau AK 99801	907-780-5866	R	6*	.1
63	Sundayriver Brewing Company Inc—*Grant Wilson*	PO Box 847, Bethel ME 04217	207-824-4253	R	6*	.1
64	Boulder Beer Inc—*Jeff Brown*	2880 Wilderness Pl, Boulder CO 80301	303-444-8448	R	5*	.1
65	5 Seasons Brewing LLC	3655 Old Milton Pkwy, Alpharetta GA 30005	770-521-5551	R	5*	.1
66	Stoudt Brewing Co—*Carol Stoudt*	PO Box 880, Adamstown PA 19501	717-484-4387	R	5*	.1
67	Texas Ingredient Corp—*Fred Brown*	2701 Pipeline Rd, Cleburne TX 76033	817-645-1328	R	5*	.1
68	Sundance Food Service Inc—*Steve Islam*	19461 Main St Ste 101, Huntington Beach CA 92648	714-969-8000	R	5*	<.1
69	Victory Brewing Co—*Ron Barchet*	420 Acorn Ln, Downingtown PA 19335	610-873-0881	R	5*	<.1
70	August Schell Brewing Co—*Ted Marti*	PO Box 128, New Ulm MN 56073	507-354-5528	R	4*	<.1
71	Cambridge Brewing Company Inc—*Phillip Bannatyne*	1 Kendall Sq Ste B1102, Cambridge MA 02139	617-494-1994	R	4*	<.1

Rank	Company Name—*Executive Officer*	Address, City, State, Zip	Phone	Type	Fin	Empls
72	Table Bluff Brewing Inc—*Barbara Groom*	617 4th St, Eureka CA 95501	707-445-4480	R	4*	<.1
73	Rocky River Brewing Co—*Gary Cintron*	21290 Ctr Ridge Rd, Rocky River OH 44116	440-895-2739	R	4*	.1
74	Sprecher Brewing Company Inc—*Randal Sprecher*	701 W Glendale Ave, Milwaukee WI 53209	414-964-7837	R	4*	<.1
75	Mc Kenzie Brewing Co—*Cordy Jensen*	PO Box 11006, Eugene OR 97440	541-686-2739	R	3*	<.1
76	Elysian Brewing Co—*Joe Bisacca*	1221 E Pke St, Seattle WA 98122	206-860-1920	R	3*	<.1
77	Jones Brewing Company Inc—*Gabriel Podlucky*	PO Box 746, Smithton PA 15479	724-872-2337	R	3*	<.1
78	Legend Brewing Co—*Thomas Martin*	321 W 7th St, Richmond VA 23224	804-232-8871	R	3*	.1
79	Big Sky Brewing Co—*Neal Leathers*	PO Box 17170, Missoula MT 59808	406-549-2777	R	3*	<.1
80	Left Hand and Tabernash Brewing—*Eric Wallace*	1265 Boston Ave, Longmont CO 80501	303-772-0258	R	3*	<.1
81	Atlanta Brewing Co—*Robert Budd*	2323 Defoor Hills Rd N, Atlanta GA 30318	404-355-5558	R	3*	<.1
82	United Distributing Company LLC	1158 Jordon Ave, Dothan AL 36303	334-793-2688	R	3*	<.1
83	Otter Creek Brewing Inc—*Morgan Wolaver*	793 Exchange St, Middlebury VT 05753	802-388-0727	R	3*	<.1
84	Weiss Ltd—*Marc Weiss*	800 New Loudon Rd Ste, Latham NY 12110	518-786-6258	R	3*	<.1
85	Lagunitas Brewing Co—*Tony Magee*	1280 N Mcdowell Blvd, Petaluma CA 94954	707-769-4495	R	3*	<.1
86	West Mountain Brewing Co—*John Schmuecker*	21 W Mountain St, Fayetteville AR 72701	479-442-9090	R	2*	<.1
87	Silver City Brewing Company Inc—*Roger Houmes*	PO Box 3606, Silverdale WA 98383	360-698-5879	R	2*	.1
88	Free State Brewing Co—*Chuck Magerl*	636 Massachusetts St, Lawrence KS 66044	785-843-4555	R	2*	.1
89	D L Geary Brewing Company Inc—*David Geary*	38 Evergreen Dr, Portland ME 04103	207-878-2337	R	2*	<.1
90	Maritime Pacific Brewing Company Inc—*George Hancock*	PO Box 17812, Seattle WA 98127	206-782-6181	R	2*	<.1
91	San Juan Brewing Company Inc—*Ronald Tekatch*	1 Front St, Friday Harbor WA 98250	360-378-2337	R	2*	<.1
92	Big Time Brewery Company Inc—*Reid Martin*	4133 University Way Ne, Seattle WA 98105	206-545-4509	R	2*	<.1
93	New Glarus Brewing Co—*Deborah Carey*	PO Box 759, New Glarus WI 53574	608-527-5850	R	2*	<.1
94	Estes Park Brewery Inc—*Eric Bratrud*	PO Box 2136, Estes Park CO 80517	970-586-5421	R	1*	<.1
95	Sarasota Brewing Co—*Tony Francano*	6607 Gateway Ave, Sarasota FL 34231	941-925-2337	R	1*	<.1
96	Shipyard Brewing Company LLC—*Fred Forsley*	86 Newbury St, Portland ME 04101	207-761-0807	R	1*	<.1
97	Lakefront Brewery Inc—*Russell Klisch*	1872 N Commerce St, Milwaukee WI 53212	414-372-8800	R	1*	<.1
98	Bayhawk Ales Inc—*Karl Zappa*	2000 Main St Ste A, Irvine CA 92614	949-442-7565	R	1*	<.1
99	Fish Brewing Co—*Lyle Morse*	515 Jefferson St SE, Olympia WA 98501	360-943-6480	R	1	<.1
100	New England Brewing Co—*Robert Leonard*	7 Selben St, Woodbridge CT 06525	203-387-2222	R	<1*	<.1
101	Kona Brewing Co—*Jeremiah Neal*	75-5629 Kuakini Hwy, Kailua Kona HI 96740	808-334-2739	R	N/A	<.1

TOTALS: SIC 2082 Malt Beverages
Companies: 101 — 26,750 — 56.6

2083 Malt

Rank	Company Name—*Executive Officer*	Address, City, State, Zip	Phone	Type	Fin	Empls
1	Great Western Malting Co—*Greg Friberg*	PO Box 1529, Vancouver WA 98668	360-693-3661	S	584*	.3
2	Cargill Malt Co—*Greg Page*	704 S 15th St, Sheboygan WI 53081	920-459-4148	R	152*	.3
3	Malt Products Corporation Of Nj—*Amy Targen*	PO Box 898, Saddle Brook NJ 07663	201-845-4420	R	52*	.7

TOTALS: SIC 2083 Malt
Companies: 3 — 787 — 1.2

2084 Wines, Brandy & Brandy Spirits

Rank	Company Name—*Executive Officer*	Address, City, State, Zip	Phone	Type	Fin	Empls
1	LVMH Moet Hennessy Louis Vuitton—*Bernard Arnault*	85 10th ave, New York NY 10011	212-251-8200	R	15,677*	56.0
2	Constellation Brands Inc—*Robert Sands*	207 High Point Dr Bldg, Victor NY 14564		P	4,097	4.3
3	E and J Gallo Winery—*Joseph E Gallo*	PO Box 1130, Modesto CA 95353	209-341-3111	R	1,957*	5.0
4	Wente Brothers—*Eric Wente*	5565 Tesla Rd, Livermore CA 94550	925-456-2300	R	493*	.8
5	Trinchero Family Estates—*Bob Trinchero*	277 St Helena Hwy S, St Helena CA 94574		R	375*	.6
6	Beringer Wine Estates Co—*Walter T Klenz*	PO Box 111, Saint Helena CA 94574	707-967-4412	R	356*	.7
7	Sutter Home Winery Inc—*Louis B Trinchero*	PO Box 248, Saint Helena CA 94574	707-963-3104	R	323*	.6
8	Biltmore Estate Wine Company Inc—*Poslusny Beth*	1 Antler Hill Rd, Asheville NC 28803	828-255-1776	R	295*	.1
9	Banfi Products Corp—*Harry Mariani*	1111 Cedar Swamp Rd, Old Brookville NY 11545	516-626-9200	R	250	.1
10	Mondavi Marc and Peter Jr Enterprises—*Peter Mondavi Sr*	PO Box 191, Saint Helena CA 94574	707-967-2200	R	120*	.1
11	Rodney Strong Vineyards—*Carmen Castaldi* Klein Foods Inc	PO Box 6010, Healdsburg CA 95448	707-431-1533	D	112*	.2
12	Fetzer Vineyards—*Paul Dolan*	13601 Old River Rd, San Rafael CA 94903	707-744-7600	R	100	.3
13	Hogue Cellars Ltd—*Gary Hogue*	PO Box 31, Prosser WA 99350	509-786-4557	R	62*	.1
14	J Wine Co—*Judy Jordan*	PO Box 6009, Healdsburg CA 95448	707-431-5400	R	57*	<.1
15	Weibel Inc—*Fred E Weibel Jr*	PO Box 87, Woodbridge CA 95258		R	49*	<.1
16	Chateau St Jean—*Jim Watkins*	PO Box 293, Kenwood CA 95452	707-833-4134	S	46*	.1
17	Caymus Vineyards—*Churck Wagner*	PO Box 268, Rutherford CA 94573	707-963-4204	R	42*	<.1
18	Domaine Chandon Inc—*Fredric Cumenal*	1 California Dr, Yountville CA 94599	707-944-8844	R	41*	.2
19	Charles Jacquin Et Cie Inc—*Norton Cooper*	2633 Trenton Ave, Philadelphia PA 19125	215-425-9300	R	41*	.1
20	Elan Chateau Resorts LLC—*Tony Mastandrea*	100 Rue Charlemagne Dr, Braselton GA 30517	678-425-0900	R	40*	.5
21	Fess Parker Winery and Vineyard—*Eli Parker* Parker Station Inc	PO Box 908, Los Olivos CA 93441	805-688-1545	S	40*	<.1
22	Chateau Montelena Winery—*James L Barrett*	1429 Tubbs Ln, Calistoga CA 94515	707-942-5105	R	35*	<.1
23	Viansa Winery and Tuscan Club—*Sam Sebastiani*	25200 Arnold Dr, Sonoma CA 95476	707-935-4700	R	31*	.3
24	Sequoia Grove Winery Partnership—*Michael Trujillo*	8338 St Helena Hwy, Napa CA 94558	707-944-2945	R	28*	.1
25	Ravenswood Winery Inc—*Joel Peterson* Franciscan Vineyards Inc	18701 Gehricke Rd, Sonoma CA 95476	707-933-2332	S	28*	<.1
26	San Antonio Winery Inc—*Steve Riboli*	737 Lamar St, Los Angeles CA 90031	323-223-1401	R	26*	.2
27	Newton Vineyard LLC—*Rudolpho Hrosz*	2555 Madrona Ave, Saint Helena CA 94574	707-963-9000	R	25*	.2
28	Ferrari-Carano Vineyards/Wine LLC—*Hoss Milone*	PO Box 1549, Healdsburg CA 95448	707-433-6700	R	20*	.1
29	Klein Foods Inc—*Thomas B Klein*	PO Box 6010, Healdsburg CA 95448	707-433-6511	R	20*	.1
30	Hess Collection Winery—*Tom Selfridge*	PO Box 4140, Napa CA 94558	707-255-1144	R	18*	.1
31	Tedeschi Vineyards Ltd—*Paula Hegele*	PO Box 953, Kula HI 96790	808-878-6058	R	18*	<.1
32	Old Mill Winery—*A Paul Cantwell*	33 Tegam Way, Geneva OH 44041	440-466-5560	R	18*	<.1
33	Willamette Valley Vineyards—*James W Bernau*	8800 Enchanted Way SE, Turner OR 97392	503-588-9463	P	17	.1
34	Franciscan Vineyards Inc—*Augustin Huneeus* Constellation Brands Inc	1178 Galleron Rd, Saint Helena CA 94574	707-963-7111	D	17	.1
35	King Estate Winery Inc—*Edward King*	80854 Territorial Hwy, Eugene OR 97405	541-942-9874	R	15*	.1
36	Far Niente Winery Inc—*Larry Maguire*	PO Box 327, Oakville CA 94562	707-944-2861	R	15*	.1
37	Stag's Leap Wine Cellars—*Jeff Mcbride*	5766 Silverado Trl, Napa CA 94558	707-944-2020	R	15*	.1
38	Clos LaChance Wines Inc—*Bill Murphy*	1 Hummingbird, San Martin CA 95046	408-686-1050	R	13*	<.1
39	Sine Qua Non	1750 N Ventura Ave No, Ventura CA 93001	805-640-8910	R	13*	<.1
40	Stone Hill Wine Company Inc—*L Held*	1110 Stone Hill Hwy, Hermann MO 65041	573-486-2221	R	12*	.1
41	Markham Vineyards—*Bryan Bondio*	PO Box 636, Saint Helena CA 94574	707-963-5292	R	12*	<.1
42	Peter Michael Winery Inc—*Scott Rodde*	12400 Ida Clayton Rd, Calistoga CA 94515	707-942-4459	R	12*	<.1
43	Skalli Corp—*Michaela Rodeno*	PO Box 38, Rutherford CA 94573	707-963-4507	R	11*	.1
44	Edna Valley Vineyard—*Harry Hansen*	2585 Biddle Ranch Rd, San Luis Obispo CA 93401	805-544-5855	S	11*	<.1

Note: An asterisk (*) indicates an estimated financial figure. The company type code used is as follows: R = Private, P = Public, S = Private Subsidiary, B = Public Subsidiary, D = Division, J = Joint Venture, I = Investment Fund.

COMPANY RANKINGS BY SALES WITHIN 4-DIGIT SIC

Rank	Company Name—*Executive Officer*	Address, City, State, Zip	Phone	Type	Fin	Empls
45	Grgich Hills Cellar—*Miljenko Grgich*	PO Box 450, Rutherford CA 94573	707-963-2784	R	10*	.1
46	Gundlach-Bundschu Winery—*Jeff Bundschu*	PO Box 1, Vineburg CA 95487	707-938-5277	R	9*	<.1
47	Sebastiani Vineyards Inc—*Mary Ann Cuneo*	389 4th St E, Sonoma CA 95476	707-933-3200	R	8	.1
48	Falkner Winery Inc—*Ray Falkner*	40620 Calle Contento, Temecula CA 92591	951-676-8231	R	7*	.1
49	Clos Pegase Winery Inc—*Jan Shrem*	PO Box 305, Calistoga CA 94515	707-942-4981	R	7*	<.1
50	Tualatin Vineyards—*Jim Bernau* Willamette Valley Vineyards Inc	10850 NW Seavey Rd, Forest Grove OR 97116	503-357-5005	S	7*	<.1
51	Navarro Winery—*Edward Bennett*	PO Box 47, Philo CA 95466	707-895-3686	R	7*	.1
52	Laetitia Vineyards and Winery Inc—*Selim Zilkha*	453 Laetitia Vineyard, Arroyo Grande CA 93420	805-481-1772	R	6*	.1
53	Cakebread Cellars—*Bruce Cakebread*	PO Box 216, Rutherford CA 94573	707-963-5221	R	6*	.1
54	Thornton Winery—*John Thornton*	PO Box 9008, Temecula CA 92589	951-699-0099	R	6*	.1
55	Frasinetti Winery—*Howard Frasinetti*	7395 Frasinetti Rd, Sacramento CA 95829	916-383-2444	R	6*	<.1
56	Old Medina Winery—*Roy Crowder*	2894 Old Medina Rd, Jackson TN 38305	731-256-1400	R	6*	<.1
57	Fenestra Winery—*Lanny Replogle*	PO Box 582, Sunol CA 94586	925-447-5246	R	6*	<.1
58	Oak Knoll Winery Inc—*Greg Lint*	29700 SW Burkhalter Rd, Hillsboro OR 97123	503-648-8198	R	6*	<.1
59	Provenance Vineyard—*Tom Rinaldi*	PO Box 668, Rutherford CA 94573	707-968-3633	S	6*	<.1
60	Clos Du Val Wine Company Ltd—*Bernard Portet*	PO Box 4350, Napa CA 94558	707-259-2200	R	5*	.1
61	Messina Hof Wine Cellars Inc—*Paul Bonarrigo*	4545 Old Reliance Rd, Bryan TX 77808	979-778-9463	R	5*	<.1
62	Sven And Ole's Fishing Company Inc—*Kent Rosenblum*	2900 Main St Ste 1100, Alameda CA 94501	510-865-7007	S	5*	.1
63	Overlook Vineyards LLC—*Margaret Benelli*	PO Box 340, Kenwood CA 95452	707-833-0053	R	5*	<.1
64	Williamsburg Winery Ltd—*Patrick Duffeler*	5800 Wessex Hundred, Williamsburg VA 23185	757-229-0999	R	5*	.1
65	Freixenet Sonoma Caves Inc—*Diego Jimenez*	PO Box 1949, Sonoma CA 95476	707-996-7256	R	5*	<.1
66	St James Winery Inc—*Patricia Hofherr*	540 Sidney St, Saint James MO 65559	573-265-7912	R	4*	.1
67	Hazlitt 1852 Vineyards Inc—*Elaine Hazlitt*	PO Box 53, Hector NY 14841	607-546-9463	R	4*	<.1
68	Round Hill Cellars—*Marco Zaninovich*	1680 Silverado Trl S, Saint Helena CA 94574	707-963-5251	R	4*	<.1
69	Seavin Inc—*C Cox*	19239 Us Hwy 27, Clermont FL 34715	352-394-8627	R	4*	.1
70	Pina John Jr and Sons—*David Pina*	PO Box 373, Oakville CA 94562	707-944-2229	R	4*	.1
71	Merryvale Vineyards LLC—*Sean Foster*	1451 Stanley Ln, Napa CA 94559	707-963-2225	R	4*	<.1
72	Mount Palomar Winery Inc—*Carol Darwish*	33820 Rancho Californi, Temecula CA 92591	951-676-5047	R	4*	<.1
73	Stags' Leap Winery Inc—*Christophe Pauber*	6150 Silverado Trl, Napa CA 94558	707-944-1303	R	4*	<.1
74	Brotherhood America's Oldest Winery Ltd—*Hernan Donoso*	PO Box 190, Washingtonville NY 10992	845-496-3661	R	4*	<.1
75	Dry Creek Vineyard No 1 LLC—*Don Wallace*	PO Box T, Healdsburg CA 95448	707-433-1000	R	4*	<.1
76	Lynfred Winery Inc—*Fred Koehler*	15 S Roselle Rd, Roselle IL 60172	630-529-9463	R	4*	<.1
77	Napa Wine Company LLC—*Sheldon Parker*	PO Box 434, Oakville CA 94562	707-944-8669	R	3*	<.1
78	Vale Coventry Winery Inc—*David Conrad*	PO Box 249, Grandview WA 98930	509-882-4100	R	3*	<.1
79	Matanzas Creek Winery—*Jeff Jackson*	6097 Bennett Valley Rd, Santa Rosa CA 95404	707-528-6464	R	3*	<.1
80	Imagery State Wine Art Gallery—*Joe Benziger*	1883 London Ranch Rd, Glen Ellen CA 95442	707-935-4500	R	3*	.1
81	Central Coast Wine Warehouse—*Lynn Brogren*	2717 Aviation Way Ste, Santa Maria CA 93455	805-928-9210	R	3*	<.1
82	Kunde Enterprises Inc—*Dawn Chase*	PO Box 639, Kenwood CA 95452	707-833-5501	R	3*	.1
83	Goldstone Land Company LLC—*Donna Rowe*	11900 Furry Rd, Lodi CA 95240	209-368-3113	R	3*	<.1
84	Montinore Vineyard Limited Inc *Rudy Marchesi*	PO Box 490, Forest Grove OR 97116	503-359-5012	R	3*	<.1
85	Brutocao Cellars—*Steve Bruticao*	PO Box 780, Hopland CA 95449	707-744-1066	S	3*	<.1
86	Cain Cellars Inc—*James Meadlock*	3800 Langtry Rd, Saint Helena CA 94574	707-963-1616	R	3*	<.1
87	Chateau Grand Travers Ltd—*Edward O'keefe*	12239 Ctr Rd, Traverse City MI 49686	231-223-7355	R	3*	<.1
88	Glenora Wine Cellars Inc—*Eugene Pierce*	5435 State Rte 14, Dundee NY 14837	607-243-5511	R	3*	<.1
89	Swedish Hill Vineyard Inc—*Richard Peterson*	4565 State Rte 414, Romulus NY 14541	315-549-8326	R	3*	<.1
90	Gibson Wine Co—*Leland Herman*	1720 Academy Ave, Sanger CA 93657	559-875-2505	R	3*	<.1
91	Seghesio Wineries Inc—*Eugene Seghesio*	700 Grove St, Healdsburg CA 95448	707-433-3579	R	3*	<.1
92	Quady Winery Inc—*Andrew Quady*	PO Box 728, Madera CA 93639	559-673-8068	R	3*	<.1
93	Chaumette Inc—*Hank Johnson*	24345 State Rte Ww, Sainte Genevieve MO 63670	573-747-1000	R	3*	<.1
94	Ozeki Sake U S A Inc—*Bunjiro Osabe*	249 Hillcrest Rd, Hollister CA 95023	831-637-9217	R	3*	<.1
95	Tomasello Winery Inc—*Charles Tomasello*	225 N White Horse Pke, Hammonton NJ 08037	609-561-0567	R	3*	<.1
96	Cosentino Signature Wineries—*Mitch Cosentino*	PO Box 2818, Yountville CA 94599	707-944-1220	R	3*	<.1
97	Wagner Vineyards and Brewing Co—*Stanley Wagner*	9322 State Rte 414, Lodi NY 14860	607-582-6450	R	2*	<.1
98	Silverado Vineyards—*Diane Miller*	6121 Silverado Trl, Napa CA 94558	707-257-1770	R	2*	<.1
99	Lemon Creek Winery Ltd—*Tim Lemon*	533 E Lemon Creek Rd, Berrien Springs MI 49103	269-471-1321	R	2*	<.1
100	Twin Peaks Winery Inc—*Cliff Lede*	1473 Yountville Cross, Yountville CA 94599	707-945-0855	R	2*	<.1
101	L Foppiano Wine Co—*Louis Foppiano*	PO Box 606, Healdsburg CA 95448	707-433-7272	R	2*	<.1
102	Orfila Vineyards—*Alejandro Orfila*	13455 San Pasqual Rd, Escondido CA 92025	760-738-6500	R	2*	<.1
103	Chateau Morrisette Inc—*David Morrisette*	PO Box 766, Meadows Of Dan VA 24120	540-593-2865	R	2*	<.1
104	Justin Vineyards and Winery—*Justin Baldwin*	11680 Chimney Rock Rd, Paso Robles CA 93446	805-238-6932	R	2*	<.1
105	Codorniu Napa Inc—*Michael Kenton*	1345 Henry Rd, Napa CA 94559	707-224-1668	R	2*	<.1
106	Washington Wine and Beverage Company Inc—*Salvatore Leone*	15029 Woodinvle Redmnd, Woodinville WA 98072	425-485-2437	R	2*	<.1
107	Dreyer Wine LLC—*Jonathan Dreyer*	PO Box 484, Graton CA 95444	650-851-9448	R	2*	<.1
108	El Molino Winery—*Lilly Oliver*	PO Box 306, Saint Helena CA 94574	707-963-3632	R	2*	<.1
109	Executive Wine and Spirits Inc—*Ed Parker*	34 First St, Bedford NH 03110	603-647-8048	R	2*	<.1
110	Jarvis—*William Jarvis*	2970 Monticello Rd, Napa CA 94558	707-255-5280	R	2*	<.1
111	Jug Shop Inc—*Dan Ravetti*	1590 Pacific Ave, San Francisco CA 94109	415-885-2922	R	2*	<.1
112	Newt Red Cellars Inc—*David Whiting*	3675 Tichenor Rd, Hector NY 14841	607-546-4100	R	2*	<.1
113	Flora Springs Wine Co—*John Komes*	1978 Zinfandel Ln, Saint Helena CA 94574	707-963-5711	R	2*	<.1
114	Freemark Abbey Winery LP—*Tim Bell*	PO Box 410, Saint Helena CA 94574	707-963-9694	R	2*	<.1
115	Kuleto Villa LLC—*Xandaria Neal*	2470 Sage Canyon Rd, Saint Helena CA 94574	707-963-9750	R	2*	<.1
116	Chateau Potelle Inc—*Jean Fourmeaux*	528 Coombs St, Napa CA 94558	707-255-9440	R	2*	<.1
117	Duck Walk Vinyards—*Herodotus Damianos*	PO Box 962, Water Mill NY 11976	631-726-7555	R	2*	<.1
118	Tesla Vineyards LP—*Margie Crowell*	4590 Tesla Rd, Livermore CA 94550	925-456-2500	R	2*	<.1
119	David Bruce Winery Inc—*David Bruce*	21439 Bear Creek Rd, Los Gatos CA 95033	408-354-4214	R	2*	<.1
120	Eric Trump Wine Manufacturing LLC—*Gregory Brun*	100 Grand Cru Dr, Charlottesville VA 22902	434-220-5908	R	1*	<.1
121	Windgate Vineyards Inc—*Daniel Enerson*	1998 Hemlock Acres Rd, Smicksburg PA 16256	814-257-8797	R	1*	<.1
122	Edmeades LLC—*Robert Love*	18700 Geyserville Ave, Geyserville CA 95441	707-895-3232	R	1*	<.1
123	Augusta Wine Inc—*Connie Ezeshim*	PO Box 147, Augusta MO 63332	636-228-4464	R	1*	<.1
124	Parker Station Inc—*Fess G Parker III*	6200 Foxen Canyon Rd, Los Olivos CA 93441	805-688-1545	R	1*	<.1
125	Foley Estates Vineyard and Winery—*William Foley II*	6121 E Hwy 246, Lompoc CA 93436	805-737-6222	R	1*	<.1
126	Alambic Inc—*Ansley J Coale Jr*	PO Box 1059, Ukiah CA 95482	707-462-3221	R	1*	<.1
127	Warner Vineyards Inc—*Patrick Warner*	706 S Kalamazoo St, Paw Paw MI 49079	269-657-3165	R	1*	<.1
128	Thomas Leonardini—*Thomas Leonardini*	1563 Saint Helena Hwy, Saint Helena CA 94574	707-963-9454	R	1*	<.1
129	Mayacamas Vineyards—*Robert Travers*	1155 Lokoya Rd, Napa CA 94558	707-224-4030	R	1*	<.1
130	Turnbull Wine Cellars—*Patrick O'dell*	PO Box 29, Oakville CA 94562	707-963-5839	R	1*	<.1
131	Galleano Winery Inc—*Donald Galleano*	4231 Wineville Ave, Mira Loma CA 91752	951-685-5376	R	1*	<.1
132	Alderbrook Vineyards and Winery LLC—*Mike Braga*	2306 Magnolia Dr, Healdsburg CA 95448	707-433-9154	R	1*	<.1

Rank	Company Name—*Executive Officer*	Address, City, State, Zip	Phone	Type	Fin	Empls
133	Prejean Winery Inc—*Elizabeth Prejean*	2634 State Rte 14, Penn Yan NY 14527	315-536-7524	R	1*	<.1
134	Stryker Winery—*Craig Macdonald*	5110 Hwy 128, Geyserville CA 95441	707-433-1944	R	1*	<.1
135	Clear Creek Distillery Ltd—*Stephen Mccarthy*	2389 Nw Wilson St, Portland OR 97210	503-248-9470	R	1*	<.1
136	Mission Mountain Winery—*Thomas Campbell*	PO Box 100, Dayton MT 59914	406-849-5524	R	1*	<.1
137	Spring Oak Winery Inc—*Silvia Scharff*	Hc 220, Altoona PA 16601	814-946-3799	R	1*	<.1
138	Duplin Wine Cellars Inc—*David Fussell*	PO Box 756, Rose Hill NC 28458	910-289-3888	R	1*	.1
139	Von Stiehl Winery—*William Schmiling*	115 Navarino St, Algoma WI 54201	920-487-5208	R	1*	<.1
140	Hermann J Wiemer Vineyard Inc—*Hermann Wiemer*	PO Box 38, Dundee NY 14837	607-243-7971	R	<1*	<.1
141	Cap Rock Winery—*Don Roark*	408 E Woodrow Rd, Lubbock TX 79423	806-863-2704	R	<1	<.1
142	Benmarl Wine Company Ltd—*Mark Miller*	156 Highland Ave, Marlboro NY 12542	845-236-4265	R	<1*	<.1

TOTALS: SIC 2084 Wines, Brandy & Brandy Spirits
Companies: 142 — — — — 25,302 74.7

2085 Distilled & Blended Liquors

Rank	Company Name—*Executive Officer*	Address, City, State, Zip	Phone	Type	Fin	Empls
1	Beam Inc—*Matt Shattock*	510 Lake Cook Rd, Deerfield IL 60015	847-948-8888	P	7,142	24.6
2	Brown-Forman Corp—*Paul C Varga*	850 Dixie Hwy, Louisville KY 40210	502-585-1100	P	3,404	3.9
3	Jim Beam Brands Co—*Matt Shattock* Beam Inc	510 Lake Cook Rd, Deerfield IL 60015	847-948-8888	S	1,093*	1.2
4	Robert Mondavi Corp—*Gregory Evans*	PO Box 2129, Yountville CA 94599	707-226-1395	S	978	.9
5	Heaven Hill Distilleries Inc—*Max Shapira*	PO Box 729, Bardstown KY 40004	502-348-3921	R	300*	.4
6	Jack Daniel Distillery Brown-Forman Corp	PO Box 199, Lynchburg TN 37352	931-759-4221	S	246*	.3
7	Bowman Distillery Incorporated A Smith—*John Adams*	1 Bowman Dr Ste 100, Fredericksburg VA 22408	540-373-4555	R	207*	.4
8	Bacardi Corp—*Joaquin Bacardi*	PO Box 363549, San Juan PR 00936	787-788-1500	R	204*	.4
9	Barton Inc—*Robert Sands*	1 S Dearborn St Ste 17, Chicago IL 60603	312-873-9600	D	73*	.5
10	Bacardi Bottling Corp—*Ausker Suarez*	PO Box 26368, Jacksonville FL 32226	904-757-1290	R	52*	.3
11	Skyy Spirits LLC—*Gerry Ruvo*	1 Beach St Fl 300, San Francisco CA 94133	415-315-8000	S	46	.1
12	Majestic Distilling Company Inc—*Lee Schuman*	PO Box 7372, Baltimore MD 21227	410-242-0200	R	36*	<.1
13	Tri-Tech Laboratories Inc—*Steven Fullerton*	PO Box 10341, Lynchburg VA 24506	434-845-7073	R	32*	.2
14	Castle Brands Inc—*Richard J Lampen*	122 E 42nd St Ste 4700, New York NY 10168	646-356-0200	P	32	<.1
15	Luxco Inc—*Donn Lux*	5050 Kemper Ave, Saint Louis MO 63139	314-772-2626	R	27*	.2
16	Mccormick Distilling Company Inc—*Jim Zargo*	1 Mc Cormick Ln, Weston MO 64098	816-640-2276	R	25*	.2
17	United States Distilled Products Co—*Bradley Johnson*	1607 12th St S, Princeton MN 55371	763-389-4903	R	23*	.2
18	Maker's Mark Distillery Inc—*Bill Samuels Jr*	3350 Burks Spring Rd, Loretto KY 40037	502-459-7884	R	19*	.1
19	American Distilling Inc—*Edward Jackowitz*	31 E High St, East Hampton CT 06424	860-267-4444	R	7*	.1
20	Hood River Distillers Inc—*Ronald Dodge*	PO Box 240, Hood River OR 97031	541-386-1588	R	5*	<.1
21	Montebello Brands Inc—*Leo Conte*	1919 Willow Spring Rd, Baltimore MD 21222	410-282-8800	R	4*	.1
22	Takara Sake USA Inc—*Kazuyoshi Ito*	708 Addison St, Berkeley CA 94710	510-540-8250	R	3*	<.1
23	Gekkeikan Sake USAInc—*Tetsuyoshi Suizu*	1136 Sibley St, Folsom CA 95630	916-985-3111	R	3*	<.1
24	Bartow Ethanol Of Florida LC—*Anthony Senagore*	1705 E Mann Rd, Bartow FL 33830	863-533-2498	R	3*	<.1
25	Prince Black Distillery Inc—*Robert Guttag*	PO Box 1999, Clifton NJ 07015	973-365-2050	R	3*	<.1
26	Sakeone Corp—*Steve Boone*	820 Elm St, Forest Grove OR 97116	503-357-7056	R	2*	<.1
27	Chambord Et Cie SARL—*Claude Kistner*	2633 Trenton Ave, Philadelphia PA 19125	215-425-9300	R	2*	<.1
28	Kentucky Bourbon Distillers Ltd—*Even Kulsveen*	PO Box 785, Bardstown KY 40004	502-348-0081	R	1*	<.1
29	Drinks Americas Holdings Ltd—*J Patrick Kenny*	372 Danbury Road Ste 1, Wilton CT 06897	203-762-7000	P	1	<.1

TOTALS: SIC 2085 Distilled & Blended Liquors
Companies: 29 — — — — 13,973 33.9

2086 Bottled & Canned Soft Drinks

Rank	Company Name—*Executive Officer*	Address, City, State, Zip	Phone	Type	Fin	Empls
1	PepsiCo Inc—*Indra K Nooyi*	700 Anderson Hill Rd, Purchase NY 10577	914-253-2000	P	57,838	294.0
2	Dr Pepper Snapple Group Inc—*Larry D Young*	PO Box 869077, Plano TX 75086	972-673-7000	P	5,903	19.0
3	Hansen Natural Corp—*Rodney C Sacks*	550 Monica Cir Ste 201, Corona CA 92880	909-739-6200	P	1,951	1.5
4	Coca-Cola Bottling Company Consolidated—*J Frank Harrison III*	PO Box 31487, Charlotte NC 28231	704-551-4000	P	1,515	5.2
5	Gatorade Co—*Rich Beck* PepsiCo Inc	PO Box 049003, Chicago IL 60604	312-821-1000	S	1,224*	2.6
6	Honickman Affiliates—*Jeffrey Honickman*	8275 Rte 130, Pennsauken NJ 08110	856-665-6200	R	1,215*	5.0
7	Snapple Beverage Group Inc Dr Pepper Snapple Group Inc	900 King St, Port Chester NY 10573	—	S	1,000*	.5
8	Coca-Cola Bottling Company of Chicago—*John Brock* Coca-Cola Enterprises Inc	7400 N Oak Park Ave, Niles IL 60714	847-647-0200	D	913*	4.0
9	Coca-Cola Bottling Company of Northern New England Inc—*Lawrence Lordi*	1 Executive Park Dr, Bedford NH 03110	603-627-7871	S	853*	1.0
10	Coca-Cola Enterprises Inc—*John F Brock*	2500 Windy Ridge Pkwy, Atlanta GA 30339	678-260-3000	P	624	13.5
11	Wis - Pak Inc—*Barbara Parish*	PO Box 496, Watertown WI 53094	920-262-6300	R	605*	.6
12	National Beverage Corp—*Nick A Caporella*	8100 SW 10th St Ste 40, Ft Lauderdale FL 33324	954-581-0922	P	600	1.2
13	Philadelphia Coca-Cola Bottling Co—*James Bruce Llewellyn*	725 E Erie Ave, Philadelphia PA 19134	215-427-4500	R	483*	2.0
14	Coca-Cola Bottling Company of St Louis—*John Brock* Coca-Cola Enterprises Inc	3800 Mueller Rd, Saint Charles MO 63301	636-443-0800	S	470*	.5
15	Swire Coca-Cola USA—*Jack Pelo* Coca-Cola Swire Pacific Holdings Inc	12634 S 265 W, Draper UT 84020	801-816-5300	D	460*	1.7
16	Arrowhead Mountain Spring Water Co—*Kim Jeffery*	2767 E Imperial Hwy St, Brea CA 92821	714-792-2100	S	382*	1.6
17	Coca-Cola Swire Pacific Holdings Inc—*Jack Pelo*	12634 S 265 W, Draper UT 84020	801-816-5300	S	352*	1.7
18	Coca-Cola Bottling Company of Ohio Coca-Cola Enterprises Inc	1560 Triplett Blvd, Akron OH 44306	330-784-2653	S	320*	.8
19	Hansen Beverage Co—*Rodney Sacks* Hansen Natural Corp	550 Monica Cir Ste 201, Corona CA 92880	—	S	308*	.5
20	Coca-Cola Bottling Company of New York—*Brian Wynne* Coca-Cola Enterprises Inc	555 Taxter Rd, Elmsford NY 10523	914-789-1100	D	304*	.2
21	Abarta Inc—*John F Bitzer III*	1000 Gamma Dr Ste 500, Pittsburgh PA 15238	412-963-6226	R	280*	1.2
22	Coca-Cola Bottling Company of West Virginia—*J Frank Harrison* Coca-Cola Bottling Company Consolidated	640 Winfield Rd, Saint Albans WV 25177	304-759-0300	S	278*	.3
23	Coca-Cola Bottling Company of Little Rock—*Gary James* Coca-Cola Enterprises Inc	7000 Interstate 30, Little Rock AR 72209	501-569-2700	S	269*	.3
24	Beverage Capital Corp—*Harold Honickman*	3051 Washington Blvd C, Baltimore MD 21230	410-242-1998	R	247*	.4
25	Florida Coca-Cola Bottling Co—*John Terry* Coca-Cola Enterprises Inc	3350 Pembroke Rd, Hollywood FL 33021	954-985-5000	D	234*	.7
26	Louisiana Coca-Cola Bottling Company Ltd—*Lowry Kline*	5601 Citrus Blvd, New Orleans LA 70123	504-818-7000	R	166*	1.7

Note: An asterisk (*) indicates an estimated financial figure. The company type code used is as follows: R = Private, P = Public, S = Private Subsidiary, B = Public Subsidiary, D = Division, J = Joint Venture, I = Investment Fund.

COMPANY RANKINGS BY SALES WITHIN 4-DIGIT SIC

Rank	Company Name—*Executive Officer*	Address, City, State, Zip	Phone	Type	Fin	Empls
27	Midwest Coca-Cola Bottling Co Coca-Cola Enterprises Inc	2750 Eagandale Blvd, Saint Paul MN 55121	651-454-5460	S	160*	1.0
28	Central Investment LLC—*John F Coons Jr*	4600 McAuley Place Sui, Cincinnati OH 45242	513-563-9700	R	151*	1.0
29	G and J Pepsi-Cola Bottlers Inc—*Stanley Kaplan*	9435 Waterstone Blvd S, Cincinnati OH 45249	513-785-6060	R	151*	1.6
30	Hinckley and Schmitt Inc—*David Krishcok*	6055 S Harlem Ave, Chicago IL 60638	773-586-8600	R	148*	2.2
31	CC Clark Inc—*Albert Clark*	PO Box 966, Starkville MS 39760	662-323-4317	R	148*	.8
32	Pepsi Midamerica Co—*Harry Crisp*	PO Box 1070, Marion IL 62959	618-997-1377	R	125*	.7
33	Royal Crown Bottling Corp—*Nancy Hodge*	PO Box 2870, Evansville IN 47728	812-424-7978	R	118*	.3
34	Ouachita Coca-Cola Bottling Co—*John F Brock* Coca-Cola Enterprises Inc	1300 Martin Luther Kin, Monroe LA 71202	318-388-4900	S	117*	.3
35	Ozarka Spring Water Co—*Peter Brabeck-Letmathe*	PO Box 2313, Greenwich CT 06830	203-531-4100	S	115*	.4
36	Pepsi-Cola Bottling Company of Yakima—*Rodger Noel* Noel Corp	PO Box 111, Yakima WA 98907	509-248-1313	S	112*	.4
37	Pepsi-Cola Bottling Co (Nashville Tennessee)—*Zein Abdalla*	715 Thompson Ln, Nashville TN 37204	615-383-7000	R	108*	.3
38	Tuscaloosa Coca-Cola Inc—*John F Brock*	6501 McFarlind Blvd E, Tuscaloosa AL 35405	205-345-7717	R	108*	.1
39	Northeast Mississippi Coca-Cola Bottling Co—*Robert H Clark* CC Clark Inc	PO Box 966, Starkville MS 39760	662-338-3400	S	102*	.2
40	Coca-Cola Bottling Company of Mississippi—*Kenneth Williams* Coca-Cola Enterprises Inc	PO Box 239, Corinth MS 38835	662-287-1433	D	97*	.1
41	Gulf States Canners Inc—*Albert Clark*	1006 Industrial Park D, Clinton MS 39056	601-924-0511	R	95*	.1
42	Chesterman Co—*Cy Chesterman*	PO Box 3657, Sioux City IA 51102	712-255-8814	R	93*	.9
43	Blue Rock Products Co—*John L Olson*	PO Box 1708, Sidney MT 59270	406-433-3403	R	91*	.1
44	Kalil Bottling Co—*George Kalil*	PO Box 26888, Tucson AZ 85726	520-624-1788	R	88*	.8
45	Magnolia Coca-Cola Bottling Co—*Clark McKean* Coca-Cola Enterprises Inc	11001 Gateway Blvd W, El Paso TX 79935	915-593-2653	S	83*	.4
46	Coca-Cola Bottling Company Texarkana—*Ricky Anderson* Coca-Cola Enterprises Inc	1930 New Boston Rd, Texarkana TX 75501	903-794-5135	S	82*	.1
47	Bernick Cos	PO Box 7008, Saint Cloud MN 56302	320-252-6441	R	81	.6
48	Culligan of Greater Kansas City—*Connie Rishworph*	19625 W Old 56 Hwy, Olathe KS 66061	913-782-4141	R	73*	.1
49	Adirondack Beverages Inc—*Doug Martin*	701 Corporations Park, Scotia NY 12302	518-370-3621	R	73	.2
50	Coca-Cola Bottling Company of Colorado—*Matt Wilson* Coca-Cola Enterprises Inc	PO Box 17100, Denver CO 80217	303-292-2653	S	60*	.3
51	Pepsi Bottling Ventures Of Idaho Inc—*Keith Reimer*	8925 Birch Ln, Nampa ID 83687	208-475-1250	R	60*	.2
52	Columbus Coca-Cola Bottling Co—*J Frank Harrison* Coca-Cola Bottling Company Consolidated	1334 Washington St, Columbus IN 47201	812-376-3381	S	48*	.1
53	Fiji Water LLC—*John Cochran*	11444 W Olympic Blvd S, Los Angeles CA 90064	310-312-2850	S	44*	<.1
54	Varni Brothers Corp—*John Varni*	400 Hosmer Ave, Modesto CA 95351	209-521-1777	R	44*	.3
55	Noel Corp—*Roger Noel*	PO Box 111, Yakima WA 98907	509-248-4545	R	43*	.3
56	Coca-Cola Bottling Company of West Point-LaGrange Coca-Cola Enterprises Inc	1700 E 10th St, West Point GA 31833	706-645-1397	S	42*	.1
57	Niagara Bottling LLC—*Ria Dasuki*	2560 E Philadelphia St, Ontario CA 91761	909-230-5000	R	37*	.3
58	Cleveland Coca-Cola Bottling Company Inc—*Charles Bitzer*	25000 Miles Rd, Cleveland OH 44146	216-690-2653	R	36*	.2
59	Abita Springs Water Company Inc—*Stewart E Allen*	5660 New Northside Dr, Atlanta GA 30328	504-828-2222	R	36*	.1
60	Lehrkind's Inc—*Carl Lehrkind*	PO Box 10580, Bozeman MT 59719	406-586-2029	R	36*	.1
61	Springfield Coca-Cola Bottling Co—*Corey Jones* Coca-Cola Enterprises Inc	3495 Sangamon Ave, Springfield IL 62707	217-544-4891	D	36*	.1
62	Coca-Cola Bottling Company Rutland—*Franklin Bower* Coca-Cola Enterprises Inc	182 Quality Rd, Rutland VT 05701	802-773-2768	S	32*	<.1
63	Big Springs Inc—*Paul Fowler*	PO Box 2709, Huntsville AL 35804	256-533-9450	R	30*	.2
64	Talking Rain Beverage Co—*Doug MacLean*	PO Box 549, Preston WA 98050	425-222-4900	R	30*	.1
65	Dr Pepper/7-Up Bottling Company Of The West—*Edward Frazer*	PO Box 7200, Reno NV 89510	775-322-3456	R	30*	.1
66	Louisiana Coca-Cola Bottling Co—*Bob Rosa* Coca-Cola Enterprises Inc	5601 Citrus Blvd, Harahan LA 70123	504-818-7000	D	29*	.1
67	Ito En (USA) Inc—*Yosuke Honjo*	125 Puuhale Rd, Honolulu HI 96819	808-847-4477	R	29*	.1
68	Middlesboro Coca-Cola Bottling Works Inc—*Neil Barry*	PO Box 1485, Middlesboro KY 40965	606-248-2660	R	29*	.1
69	Coca-Cola Bottling Works Of Tullahoma Inc—*Russell Whitis*	1502 E Carroll St, Tullahoma TN 37388	931-455-3466	R	28*	.1
70	Carolina Canners Inc—*Brantley Burnett*	PO Box 1628, Cheraw SC 29520	843-537-5281	R	27*	.3
71	Southwest Canners Inc—*Dave Jones*	PO Box 809, Portales NM 88130	575-356-6623	R	26*	.2
72	Harrington Co—*Donald Harrington*	PO Box 3178, Butte MT 59702	406-494-3200	R	26*	.2
73	Corinth Coca-Cola Bottling Works Inc—*HL Williams*	PO Box 239, Corinth MS 38834	662-287-1433	R	25*	.1
74	Maplewood Beverage Packers LLC—*Nick Dimaria*	45 Camptown Rd, Maplewood NJ 07040	973-416-4582	R	24*	.2
75	Gulf Distributing Company Of Mobile LLC	3378 Moffett Rd, Mobile AL 36607	251-476-9600	R	21*	.3
76	Amcan Beverages Inc—*Don Soetaert*	1201 Commerce Blvd, American Canyon CA 94503	707-557-0500	R	21*	.1
77	Reed's Inc—*Christopher Reed*	13000 S Spring St, Los Angeles CA 90061	310-217-9400	P	20	<.1
78	Coca-Cola Bottling Group Southwest—*Christy Wallace* Coca-Cola Enterprises Inc	PO Box 15050, Amarillo TX 79105	806-324-5300	D	20*	.1
79	Maui Soda and Ice Works Ltd—*Michael Nobriga*	PO Box 1170, Wailuku HI 96793	808-244-7951	R	19*	.1
80	Natchez Coca-Cola Bottling Co—*Moe Leblanc* Coca-Cola Enterprises Inc	191 Devereaux Dr, Natchez MS 39120	601-442-1641	D	19*	<.1
81	Canada Dry Bottling Company of Meriden Inc—*Anthony D Tomassetti*	PO Box 910, Meriden CT 06450	203-235-5751	R	19*	<.1
82	Love Bottling Co—*William Love*	PO Box 625, Muskogee OK 74402	918-682-3434	R	19*	.1
83	Jones Soda Co—*Bill Meissner*	234 9th Ave N, Seattle WA 98109	206-624-3357	P	18	<.1
84	Ahf Industries Inc—*Alan Friedman*	PO Box 391, French Lick IN 47432	812-936-9988	R	17*	.2
85	Castle Co-Packers LLC—*Greg Ewing*	204 B Schreiber Indust, New Kensington PA 15068	724-339-4040	R	17*	.1
86	Southeastern Bottling Company Of Arizona Inc—*Karl Schade*	PO Box 1076, Safford AZ 85548	928-428-2192	R	16*	.1
87	Beverage South Inc—*Brantlet T Burnett Sr*	PO Box 3567, Greenville SC 29608	864-242-6041	R	16*	.1
88	Pepsi-Cola Bottling Company Incorporated Of Norton Va—*George Hunnicutt*	PO Box 158, Norton VA 24273	276-679-1122	R	15*	.2
89	Ada Coca-Cola and Dr Pepper Bottling Co—*Thomas Crabtree*	PO Box 1607, Ada OK 74821	580-332-0257	R	13*	.1
90	Sanford Coca-Cola Bottling Co—*Charles Ingram*	PO Box 1207, Sanford NC 27331	919-774-4111	R	13*	.1
91	Snappy Snack Vending—*Bob Brown*	4705 S Perkins Rd, Stillwater OK 74074	405-372-8332	R	12*	.1
92	Coca-Cola Enterprises—*Don Harkness* Coca-Cola Enterprises Inc	216 Peekstock Rd, Kalamazoo MI 49001	269-343-1277	S	12*	.1
93	Portland Bottling Co—*Tom Kennan*	1321 Ne Couch St, Portland OR 97232	503-231-5035	R	12*	<.1
94	Independent Beverage Corp—*Marc Robinson*	3936 Corporation Cir, Charlotte NC 28216	704-399-2504	R	12*	.1
95	Capitol Beverage Packers—*Millard Tonkin*	2670 Land Ave, Sacramento CA 95815	916-929-7777	R	11*	.1
96	Drinkmore Delivery Inc—*Bob Perini*	7595 Rickenbacker Dr S, Gaithersburg MD 20879		R	10*	.1
97	Temple Bottling Company Ltd—*T Floca*	PO Box 308, Temple TX 76503	254-773-3376	R	10*	.1

Rank	Company Name—*Executive Officer*	Address, City, State, Zip	Phone	Type	Fin	Empls
98	Northern Bottling Co—*William Gokey*	PO Box 639, Minot ND 58702	701-852-0544	R	10*	.1
99	Cpf Inc—*John Webster*	25 Copeland Dr, Ayer MA 01432	978-772-9287	R	10*	.1
100	Birrell Bottling Co—*Kelly Clay*	940 Spring Creek Pl, Springville UT 84663	801-491-3366	R	9*	.1
101	Coca-Cola Bottling Co—*Richard Pelo*	PO Box 794, Walla Walla WA 99362	509-529-0753	R	9*	.1
102	Green Spot Packaging Inc—*John Tsu*	100 S Cambridge Ave, Claremont CA 91711	909-625-8771	R	9*	<.1
103	Celsius Holdings Inc—*Stephen C Haley*	2424 N Federal Hwy Ste, Boca Raton FL 33431	561-276-2239	P	8	N/A
104	Mahaska Bottling Co—*Brad G Muhl*	PO Box 50, Oskaloosa IA 52577	641-673-3481	R	8*	.1
105	Ale-8-One Bottling Co—*Frank Rogers Lll*	PO Box 645, Winchester KY 40392	859-744-3484	R	8*	.1
106	Burks Beverage—*WE Burks*	2555 Burks Pl, Dyersburg TN 38024	731-285-3671	R	7	.1
107	Clear Mountain Spring Water—*Breck Speed*	3201 S Elm St, Little Rock AR 72204	501-664-6700	R	7*	.1
108	Coca-Cola Bottling Company Of Cape Cod Inc—*John Kayajan*	PO Box 779, Sandwich MA 02563	508-888-0001	R	7*	.1
109	Pepsi-Cola Champaign Urbana Bottler Company Inc—*John Trebellas*	1306 W Anthony Dr, Champaign IL 61821	217-352-4126	R	6*	.1
110	Coca-Cola Bottling Company Of Hot Springs—*Van Lyell*	321 Market St, Hot Springs AR 71901	501-623-7707	R	6*	.1
111	Supreme Manufacturing Company Inc—*Clifford Krause*	5 Connerty Ct, East Brunswick NJ 08816	732-254-0087	R	6*	<.1
112	American Purpac Technologies LLC	2924 Wyetta Dr, Beloit WI 53511	608-362-5012	R	6*	.1
113	Michigan Bottling and Custom Pack Co—*Sal Landa*	13940 Tireman St, Detroit MI 48228	313-846-1717	R	6*	.1
114	Shonan USA Inc—*Akira Nozaka*	PO Box 128, Grandview WA 98930	509-882-5583	R	5*	.1
115	Dr Pepper/7-Up Bottling Co—*Mike Pomweoy*	4419 Robert C Byrd Dr, Beckley WV 25801	304-253-3532	R	5*	.1
116	Pepsi-Cola Ogdensburg Inc—*Scott Wright* PepsiCo Inc	PO Box 708, Ogdensburg NY 13669	315-393-1720	S	5*	<.1
117	Pepsi-Cola Bottling Of Aroostook—*J Freeman*	52 Industrial St Ste 1, Presque Isle ME 04769	207-760-3000	R	5*	<.1
118	Dry Soda Co—*Sharelle Klaus*	410 1st Ave S, Seattle WA 98104	206-652-2345	R	5*	<.1
119	Chesapeake Treatment Company LLC—*Ray Fuentes* Coca-Cola Bottling Company Consolidated	4847 Chesapeake Dr, Charlotte NC 28216	704-398-0369	S	5*	<.1
120	Jefferson City Coca-Cola Bottling Company Inc—*Carl Vogel*	604 Jefferson St, Jefferson City MO 65101	573-636-6165	R	5*	<.1
121	New Leaf Brands Inc—*Eric Skae*	1 DeWolf Rd Ste 208, Old Tappan NJ 07675	201-784-2400	P	4	<.1
122	Sun-Drop Bottling Company Of Rocky Mount NC Inc—*John Berry*	2550 Raleigh Rd, Rocky Mount NC 27803	252-977-4586	R	4*	<.1
123	Cawy Bottling Company Inc—*Vincent Cossio*	2440 Nw 21st Ter, Miami FL 33142	305-634-8669	R	4*	.1
124	Deep Rock Water Co—*Colleen Porterfield*	2640 California St, Denver CO 80205	303-292-2020	S	4*	.1
125	Union City Coca-Cola Bottling Company LLC—*Rhonda Kincade*	PO Box 748, Union City TN 38281	731-885-5140	R	4*	<.1
126	Mile High Beverages Inc—*Ronald Godbout*	520 Cobban St, Butte MT 59701	406-723-3984	R	3*	<.1
127	Coca-Cola Bottling Company Of Hopkinsville Ky—*John Jige*	5401 Commerce Dr, Paducah KY 42001	270-538-4600	R	3*	.1
128	North Star Beverage Company Inc—*Richard Doucette*	PO Box 188, Hurley WI 54534	715-561-5270	R	3*	<.1
129	Ozarks Coca-Cola/Dr Pepper Bottling Co—*John Schaefer*	PO Box 11250, Springfield MO 65808	417-865-9900	R	3*	.3
130	A and W Bottling Company Inc—*R Christiansen*	7620 Hardeson Rd, Everett WA 98203	425-355-0100	R	3*	<.1
131	Atl Coca-Cola Btl Company Att Acct—*Rudd Cummings*	75 Andrews Way, Villa Rica GA 30180	770-459-9023	R	3*	<.1
132	Dr Pepper Bottling Company Of Dublin—*Mark Kloster*	221 S Patrick St, Dublin TX 76446	254-445-3466	R	3*	<.1
133	Stueber Beverages Inc—*Mary Luethmers*	PO Box 506, Park Falls WI 54552	715-762-3773	R	3*	<.1
134	Lipsey Mountain Spring Water—*Joe Lipsey III*	PO Box 1246, Norcross GA 30093	770-449-0001	R	3*	<.1
135	Coca-Cola Bottling Company Of Minot—*Jeff Miller*	405 9th St Se, Minot ND 58701	701-852-4431	R	3*	<.1
136	High Bridge Spring Water Company Inc—*Linda Slagel*	3830 High Bridge Rd, Wilmore KY 40390	859-858-4407	R	3*	<.1
137	Southern Beverage Packers Inc—*David Byrd*	PO Box 560, Appling GA 30802	706-541-9222	R	3*	<.1
138	Douglas County Bottling Co—*Bruce Hanna*	612 Nw Cecil Ave, Roseburg OR 97470	541-672-6596	R	3*	<.1
139	Saratoga Spring Water Co—*Adam Madkour*	11 Geyser Rd, Saratoga Springs NY 12866	518-584-6363	R	2*	<.1
140	Pepsi-Cola Memphis Bottling Co—*John Johnson*	PO Box 277, Memphis MO 63555	660-465-8553	R	2*	<.1
141	Cole Water Company LLC—*John Spencer*	PO Box 1244, Peru IN 46970	765-472-4254	R	2*	<.1
142	Truetoniqs LLC	7440 N 49th St, Longmont CO 80503	303-530-4533	R	2*	<.1
143	Sunny Maid Corp	632 Monterey Pass Rd, Monterey Park CA 91754	626-289-5671	R	2*	<.1
144	Amazing Beverages Inc—*Elliott Hirsh*	1921 Wharton Rd, Jenkintown PA 19046	215-886-9356	R	2*	<.1
145	Cadbury Schweppes Inc—*Gilbert Cassagne*	2809 Ajax Ave Ste 106, Rogers AR 72758	479-631-4800	R	2*	<.1
146	Clovis Bottlers Inc—*Terry Lusk*	5700 Mabry Dr, Clovis NM 88101	575-763-0230	R	2*	<.1
147	Northern Neck Coca-Cola Bottling Company Inc—*Gregory Purcell*	PO Box 395, Montross VA 22520	804-493-8051	R	2*	<.1
148	Palomar Mountain Premium Spring Water LLC—*Jim Mahoney*	1270 W Mission Ave, Escondido CA 92029	760-743-0140	R	2*	<.1
149	Three Rivers Bottling LLC—*Robert Yates*	204b Schreiber Inductr, New Kensington PA 15068	724-339-4040	R	2*	<.1
150	Ohio Beverage Systems Inc—*James Rickon*	9200 Midwest Ave, Cleveland OH 44125	216-267-2871	R	2*	<.1
151	Apani Southwest Inc—*Arden Hawkins*	PO Box 12031, Lubbock TX 79452	806-744-1606	R	2*	<.1
152	Johnnie Ryan Company Inc—*Paul Janik*	3084 Niagara St, Niagara Falls NY 14303	716-282-1606	R	2*	<.1
153	Aqua Blox LLC—*Christina Hurn*	12000 E Slauson Ave St, Santa Fe Springs CA 90670	562-693-9599	R	1*	<.1
154	DC Brands International Inc—*Richard Pearce*	9500 W 49th Ave Ste D-, Wheat Ridge CO 80033	303-279-3800	P	1	<.1
155	Innermountain Distributing Co—*William Bois*	PO Box 650, New Castle CO 81647	970-240-0720	R	<1*	<.1
156	Hall of Fame Beverages Inc—*Jessica A Gutierrez*	500 N Estrella Pkwy St, Goodyear AZ 85338	623-387-2997	P	<1	<.1
157	Seawright Holdings Inc—*Joel Sens*	600 Cameron St, Alexandria VA 22314	703-340-1629	P	<1	<.1
158	Prime Star Group Inc—*Edward Braniff*	4560 S Decatur, Las Vegas NV 89117	702-497-0736	P	<1	N/A

TOTALS: SIC 2086 Bottled & Canned Soft Drinks

	Companies: 158				82,806	382.6

2087 Flavoring Extracts & Syrups Nec

Rank	Company Name—*Executive Officer*	Address, City, State, Zip	Phone	Type	Fin	Empls
1	Coca-Cola Co (Atlanta Georgia)—*Muhtar Kent*	PO Box 1734, Atlanta GA 30301		P	35,119	139.6
2	MacAndrews and Forbes Holdings Inc—*Ronald O Perelman*	35 E 62nd St, New York NY 10021	212-572-8600	R	5,700*	19.8
3	Pointing Color Inc—*Kenneth P Manning*	2515 N Jefferson, Saint Louis MO 63106	314-889-7600	S	2,756*	3.6
4	Sensient Flavors International Inc—*Kenneth P Manning*	5600 W Raymond St, Indianapolis IN 46241	317-243-3521	S	2,756*	3.6
5	Sensient Food Colors LP—*Kenneth P Manning*	777 E Wisconsin Ave St, Milwaukee WI 53202	414-271-6755	S	2,756*	3.6
6	Sensient Health Care Management Co—*Kenneth P Manning*	330 S Mill St, Juneau WI 53039	920-386-2691	S	2,756*	3.6
7	Sensient Holding Inc—*Kenneth P Manning*	777 E Wisconsin Ave St, Milwaukee WI 53202	414-271-6755	S	2,756*	3.6
8	Sensient Imaging Technologies Inc—*Kenneth P Manning*	777 E Wisconsin Ave St, Milwaukee WI 53202	414-272-6755	S	2,756*	3.6
9	Flavor Burst Inc	499 Commerce Dr, Danville IN 46122	317-745-2952	R	2,693*	3.5
10	M and F Worldwide Corp—*Barry F Schwartz*	35 E 62nd St, New York NY 10065	212-572-8600	P	1,783	8.2
11	Sensient Flavors Inc—*James P McCarthy*	777 E Wisconsin Ave, Milwaukee WI 53202		S	809*	.3
12	Sensient Flavors LLC—*Fonda Baumgartner*	5600 W Raymond St, Indianapolis IN 46241	317-243-3521	R	165*	1.5
13	Sensient Colors Inc—*Kenneth Manning*	PO Box 14538, Saint Louis MO 63178	314-889-7600	S	154*	.3
14	Red Arrow Products Company LLC—*Cathy Suckey*	PO Box 1537, Manitowoc WI 54221	920-769-1100	R	76*	.2
15	Mafco Holdings Inc—*Ronald Perelman* MacAndrews and Forbes Holdings Inc	35 E 62nd St, New York NY 10021	212-572-8600	S	52*	.3
16	Autocrat LLC—*Joan Lefrancois*	10 Blackstone Valley P, Lincoln RI 02865	401-333-3300	R	50*	.1
17	Murphy S Mother Laboratories Inc—*David Murphy*	PO Box 16846, Greensboro NC 27416	336-273-1737	R	45*	.1

Note: An asterisk (*) indicates an estimated financial figure. The company type code used is as follows: R = Private, P = Public, S = Private Subsidiary, B = Public Subsidiary, D = Division, J = Joint Venture, I = Investment Fund.

COMPANY RANKINGS BY SALES WITHIN 4-DIGIT SIC

Rank	Company Name—*Executive Officer*	Address, City, State, Zip	Phone	Type	Fin	Empls
18	A M Todd Co—*Henry Todd*	1717 Douglas Ave, Kalamazoo MI 49007	269-343-2603	R	42*	.3
19	Monin Inc—*William Lombardo*	2100 Range Rd, Clearwater FL 33765	727-461-3033	R	41*	.1
20	Frutarom Inc—*Ori Yehudai*	9500 Railroad Ave, North Bergen NJ 07047	201-861-9500	S	40	.1
21	Lemon-X Corp—*James Grassi*	PO Box 20800, Huntington Station NY 11746	631-424-2850	R	39*	.2
22	Baldwin Richardson Foods Co—*Eric Johnson*	3268 Blue Heron Dr, Macedon NY 14502	315-986-2727	R	38*	.2
23	Saratoga Food Specialties	771 W Crossroads Pkwy, Bolingbrook IL 60490	630-833-3810	S	33*	.1
24	Masterson Company Inc—*Joe Masterson*	PO Box 691, Milwaukee WI 53201	414-647-1132	R	33*	.2
25	Virginia Dare Extract Company Inc—*Howard Smith*	882 3rd Ave Ste 2, Brooklyn NY 11232	718-788-1776	R	32*	.2
26	Fona International Inc—*Joseph Slawek*	1900 Averill Rd, Geneva IL 60134	630-578-8600	R	31*	.2
27	Synergy Flavors Inc—*Roderick Sowders*	1230 Karl Ct, Wauconda IL 60084	847-487-1011	R	29*	.1
28	California Custom Fruits And Flavors Inc—*Mike Mulhausen*	15800 Tapia St, Irwindale CA 91706	626-736-4130	R	24*	.1
29	Flavorchem Corp—*Salvatore Sprovieri*	1525 Brook Dr, Downers Grove IL 60515	630-932-8100	R	22*	.1
30	Henry H Ottens Manufacturing Company Inc—*George Robinson*	7800 Holstein Ave, Philadelphia PA 19153	215-365-7800	R	21*	.1
31	Flavor Systems International Inc—*William Wasz*	10139 Commerce Park Dr, Cincinnati OH 45246	513-870-4900	R	20*	.1
32	R Torre and Company Inc—*Melanie Dulbecco*	233 E Harris Ave, South San Francisco CA 94080	650-875-1200	R	20*	.1
33	Whitfield Foods Inc—*Les Massey*	PO Box 791, Montgomery AL 36101	334-263-2541	R	20*	.1
34	Federal Flavors Inc—*Robert Manchick*	3116 Berea Rd, Cleveland OH 44111	216-671-6300	R	19*	.1
35	Da Vinci Gourmet Ltd—*William R Cotter*	7224 First Ave S, Seattle WA 98108	206-768-7401	R	17*	.1
36	Agilex Flavor Div—*Tom Lamb*	30322 Esperanza Ste 40, Rancho Santa Margarita CA 92688	949-635-1000	S	17*	.1
37	Felbro Food Products Inc—*Michael Feldmar*	5700 W Adams Blvd, Los Angeles CA 90016	323-936-5266	R	16*	<.1
38	Edlong Corp—*Laurie Johnson*	225 Scott St, Elk Grove Village IL 60007	847-439-9230	R	16*	.1
39	Fruitcrown Products Corp—*Robert Jagenburg*	250 Adams Blvd, Farmingdale NY 11735	631-694-5800	R	16*	.1
40	Bi Nutraceuticals Inc—*George Pontiakos*	2550 E El Presidio St, Long Beach CA 90810	310-669-2100	R	16*	.1
41	American Fruits And Flavors—*Fred Farago*	PO Box 331060, Pacoima CA 91333	818-899-9574	R	16*	.1
42	Brand Aromatics—*Karl E Brand*	PO Box 3033, Lakewood NJ 08701	732-363-8080	R	12*	<.1
43	Sethness Products Co—*Charles Sethness*	PO Box 597963, Chicago IL 60659	847-329-2080	R	11*	.1
44	Carolina Beverage Corp—*Cliff Ritchie*	PO Box 697, Salisbury NC 28145	704-637-5881	R	10*	.1
45	Robertet Inc—*Peter N Lombardo*	125 Bauer Dr, Oakland NJ 07436	201-405-1000	R	9*	<.1
46	D D Williamson and Company Inc—*Theodore Nixon*	1901 Payne St, Louisville KY 40206	502-895-2438	R	9*	.1
47	Belton Foods Inc—*David Sipos*	PO Box 13605, Dayton OH 45413	937-890-7768	R	9*	<.1
48	Kerr Concentrates Inc—*Andy Stormant*	2340 Hyacinth St Ne, Salem OR 97301	503-378-0493	R	9*	.1
49	American Almond Products Company Inc—*Victor Frumolt*	103 Walworth St, Brooklyn NY 11205	718-875-8310	R	8*	.1
50	Monarch Beverage Co—*Phil Terry*	1123 Zonolite Rd NE St, Atlanta GA 30306	404-262-4040	R	8*	<.1
51	Star Kay White Inc—*Walter Katzenstein*	85 Brenner Dr, Congers NY 10920	845-268-2600	R	8*	.1
52	Sunopta Fruit Group Inc—*Michael Jacobs*	PO Box 2218, South Gate CA 90280	323-774-6000	R	8*	.1
53	Elan Chemical Co—*David Weisman*	268 Doremus Ave, Newark NJ 07105	973-344-8014	R	8*	.1
54	Illes Food Ingredients Ltd—*George Illes*	2200 Luna Rd Ste 120, Carrollton TX 75006	214-631-8499	R	7*	.1
55	Sqwincher Corp—*Tommy Howard*	PO Box 8250, Columbus MS 39705	662-328-0400	R	6*	<.1
56	Sea Breeze Fruit Flavors Inc—*Steven Sanders*	441 Rte 202, Towaco NJ 07082	973-334-7777	R	6*	.1
57	John Hogan Interests Inc—*Brooke Hogan*	PO Box 560029, Dallas TX 75356	214-637-0214	R	5*	.1
58	THasegawa USAInc—*Mark Scott*	14017 183rd St, Cerritos CA 90703	714-522-1900	R	5*	.1
59	International Fruit Inc—*Gene Hays*	1201 S Orlando Ave Ste, Winter Park FL 32789	407-628-1121	S	5*	<.1
60	H and H Products Co—*Morris Hartley*	6600 Magnolia Homes Rd, Orlando FL 32810	407-299-5410	R	5*	<.1
61	Malolo Beverages and Supplies Ltd—*Sanford Young*	120 Sand Island Access, Honolulu HI 96819	808-845-4830	R	4*	<.1
62	Centrome Inc—*Robert Simone*	85 5th Ave Ste 5, Paterson NJ 07524	973-357-0577	R	4*	<.1
63	Three Vee Food and Syrup Products Inc—*Samuel Gombo*	110 Bridge St, Brooklyn NY 11201	718-858-7333	R	4*	<.1
64	Flavor House Inc—*Richard Staley*	PO Box 997, Adelanto CA 92301	760-246-9131	R	4*	<.1
65	Florida Natural Flavors Inc—*Dave Erdman*	PO Box 181125, Casselberry FL 32718	407-834-5979	R	4*	<.1
66	H Fox and Company Inc—*David Fox*	416 Thatford Ave, Brooklyn NY 11212	718-385-4600	R	4*	<.1
67	Vineland Syrup Inc—*Meilech Kornbluh*	PO Box 1326, Vineland NJ 08362	856-691-5772	R	3*	<.1
68	Delano Growers Grape Products—*Ray Cox*	32351 Bassett Ave, Delano CA 93215	661-725-3255	R	3*	<.1
69	Sethness-Greenleaf Inc—*J Mcraith*	1826 N Lorel Ave, Chicago IL 60639	773-889-1400	R	3*	.1
70	H B Taylor Co—*Leon Juskaitis*	4830 S Christiana Ave, Chicago IL 60632	773-254-4805	R	3*	<.1
71	KJ International Inc—*Alnoor Dhanani*	537 Market St Ste 100, Chattanooga TN 37402	423-267-5691	R	2*	<.1
72	Blossom Valley Foods—*Robert Wagner*	20 Casey St, Gilroy CA 95020	408-848-5520	R	2*	<.1
73	Edgar A Weber and Co—*Andrew Plennert*	PO Box 546, Wheeling IL 60090	847-215-1980	R	2*	<.1
74	Flavor Dynamics Inc—*Dolf Rovira*	640 Montrose Ave, South Plainfield NJ 07080	908-822-8855	R	2*	<.1
75	International Bakers Services Inc—*William Busse*	3839 Progress Dr, South Bend IN 46628	574-287-7111	R	2*	<.1
76	Mane-California—*Kent Hunter*	411 Pendleton Way, Oakland CA 94621	510-562-2371	S	2*	<.1
77	Dr Smoothie Enterprises—*Bill Haugh*	1730 Raymer Ave, Fullerton CA 92833	714-449-9787	R	2*	<.1
78	C S Steen Syrup Mill Inc—*Albert Steen*	PO Box 339, Abbeville LA 70511	337-893-1654	R	2*	<.1
79	Southern Flavoring Company Inc—*John Messier*	PO Box 341, Bedford VA 24523	540-586-8565	R	2*	<.1
80	Distributors Processing Inc—*Randy Walker*	17656 Ave 168, Porterville CA 93257	559-781-0297	R	2*	<.1
81	Calevas Laboratories Inc—*Mark Simon*	1222 1st St Ne, Washington DC 20002	202-842-2324	R	2*	<.1
82	National Flavors Inc—*John Hinkle*	PO Box 2153, Kalamazoo MI 49003	269-344-3640	R	2*	<.1
83	Kosto Food Products Co—*Donald Colby*	1325 N Old Rand Rd, Wauconda IL 60084	847-487-2600	R	2*	<.1
84	RH Bauman and Company Inc—*Russell H Bauman*	21021 Devonshire St #2, Chatsworth CA 91311	818-709-1093	R	1*	<.1
85	Nedlog Co—*Glenn Golden*	92 Messner Dr, Wheeling IL 60090	847-541-0924	R	1*	<.1

TOTALS: SIC 2087 Flavoring Extracts & Syrups Nec
Companies: 85 — 64,007 — 200.0

2091 Canned & Cured Fish & Seafoods

Rank	Company Name—*Executive Officer*	Address, City, State, Zip	Phone	Type	Fin	Empls
1	Bumble Bee Seafoods LLC—*Christopher D Lischewski*	PO Box 85362, San Diego CA 92186	858-715-4000	R	1,191*	4.0
2	StarKist Foods Inc—*In Soo Cho*	225 N Shore Dr Ste 400, Pittsburgh PA 15212	412-323-7400	S	630	.6
3	Tri-Union Seafood LLC—*Thiraphong Chansiri*	9330 Scranton Rd Ste 5, San Diego CA 92121	858-558-9662	S	400*	2.9
4	Texas Pack Inc—*Ray McLaughlin*	PO Box 1643, Port Isabel TX 78578	956-943-5461	R	321*	.4
5	Singleton Seafood Co—*Gary Rodkin*	1804 Turkey Creek Rd, Plant City FL 33566	813-750-1850	S	58*	.4
6	Minterbrook Oyster Co—*Erica Wicksten*	PO Box 432, Gig Harbor WA 98335	253-857-5251	R	55*	.1
7	Boyajian Inc—*John Boyajian*	144 Will Dr, Canton MA 02021	781-828-9966	R	42*	.1
8	Coast Seafoods Co—*Tim Morris*	14711 NE 29th Pl Ste 1, Bellevue WA 98007	425-702-8800	R	38*	<.1
9	Cape May Foods LLC—*Lance Harrison*	PO Box 309, Millville NJ 08332	856-825-8111	R	28*	.2
10	Alabama Catfish Inc—*Jerry Whittington*	PO Box 769, Uniontown AL 36786	334-628-3474	R	21*	.3
11	Pacific Smoking Co—*Eugene Meyer*	1175 Edgewater St NW, Salem OR 97304	503-905-4946	R	21*	<.1
12	Oregon Lox Co—*Mik Bryant*	4828 W 11th Ave, Eugene OR 97402	541-726-7824	R	18*	<.1
13	Acme Smoked Fish Corp—*Eric Caslow*	30 Gem St, Brooklyn NY 11222	718-383-8585	R	16*	.1
14	Salmolux Inc—*George Kuetgens*	34100 9th Ave S Ste A, Federal Way WA 98003	253-874-2026	R	14*	.1
15	Copper River Seafoods Inc—*Scott Blake*	PO Box 158, Cordova AK 99574	907-424-3721	R	14*	.1
16	Galilean Seafood Inc—*Mark Montopoli*	PO Box 1140, Bristol RI 02809	401-253-3030	R	9*	.1
17	Bevans Oyster Co—*Ronald Bevans*	1090 Skipjack Rd, Kinsale VA 22488	804-472-2331	R	7*	.1

Rank	Company Name—*Executive Officer*	Address, City, State, Zip	Phone	Type	Fin	Empls
18	Quality Foods From The Sea Inc—*William Barclift*	PO Box 1837, Elizabeth City NC 27906	252-338-5455	R	6*	.1
19	Ameripure Processing Company Inc—*John Tesvich*	803 Willow St, Franklin LA 70538	337-413-8000	R	5*	.1
20	Carolyn Collins Caviar Co—*Carolyn M Collins*	113 York St, Michigan City IN 46360	219-809-8100	R	5*	<.1
21	Aquamar Inc—*Hugo Yamakawa*	10888 7th St, Rancho Cucamonga CA 91730	909-481-4700	R	4*	<.1
22	Spence and Company Ltd—*Charles Spence*	76 Campanelli Industri, Brockton MA 02301	508-427-5577	R	4*	<.1
23	Quinault Pride Seafoods—*Rudy Tsucada*	100 W Quinault St, Taholah WA 98587	360-276-4431	R	4*	<.1
24	Weigardt Brothers Inc—*Fritz Weigardt*	PO Box 309, Ocean Park WA 98640	360-665-4111	R	3*	<.1
25	Alaska Sausage Company Inc—*Herbert Eckmann*	PO Box 92157, Anchorage AK 99509	907-562-3636	R	3*	<.1
26	Bay City Crab Inc—*Chris Fulcher*	PO Box 608, Aurora NC 27806	252-322-5291	R	3*	<.1
27	Yamasa Enterprises—*Frank Kawana*	515 Stanford Ave, Los Angeles CA 90013	213-626-2211	R	3*	<.1
28	Kool Ice And Seafood Company Inc—*Dave Nickerson*	110 Washington St, Cambridge MD 21613	410-228-2300	R	3*	<.1
29	American-Canadian Fisheries Inc—*Andy Vitaljic*	PO Box 728, Bellingham WA 98227	360-398-1117	R	3*	<.1
30	Trader Bay Ltd—*Lindsey Babich*	PO Box 429, Lakebay WA 98349	253-884-5249	R	2*	<.1
31	C-Pak Sea Foods Inc—*Edmund Gonzales*	742 E 61st St, Los Angeles CA 90001	323-231-7077	R	2*	<.1
32	Ducktrap River Fish Farm LLC—*Rafaeo Puga*	57 Little River Dr, Belfast ME 04915	207-338-6280	R	1*	<.1
33	Hillard Bloom Packing Company Inc—*Hillard Bloom*	2601 Ogden Ave, Port Norris NJ 08349	856-785-0120	R	1*	<.1

TOTALS: SIC 2091 Canned & Cured Fish & Seafoods
Companies: 33 ... 2,935 ... 10.0

2092 Fresh or Frozen Prepared Fish

Rank	Company Name—*Executive Officer*	Address, City, State, Zip	Phone	Type	Fin	Empls
1	California Shellfish Company Inc—*Eugene Bugatto*	PO Box 2028, San Francisco CA 94126	415-923-7400	R	3,543*	.7
2	Sea Watch International Ltd—*Robert Brennan*	8978 Glebe Park Dr, Easton MD 21601	410-822-7500	R	586*	.5
3	Gortons—*Judson Reis*	128 Rogers St, Gloucester MA 01930	978-283-3000	S	462*	1.0
4	Consolidated Catfish Companies LLC—*Dick Stevens*	PO Box 271, Isola MS 38754	662-962-3101	R	454*	.6
5	American Seafoods Group LLC—*Bernt O Bodal*	2025 1st Ave Ste 900, Seattle WA 98121	206-374-1515	R	411*	1.1
6	Icicle Seafoods Inc—*Dennis Guhlke*	PO Box 79003, Seattle WA 98119	206-282-0988	R	403*	.5
7	Ocean Beauty Seafoods LLC—*Mark Palmer*	PO Box 70739, Seattle WA 98127	206-285-6800	R	387*	2.5
8	Trident Seafoods Corp—*Charles Bundrant*	5303 Shilshole Ave Nw, Seattle WA 98107	206-783-3818	R	309*	2.5
9	Chugach Alaska Corp—*Ed Herndon*	3800 Centerpoint Dr Rm, Anchorage AK 99503	907-563-8866	R	273*	5.1
10	High Liner Foods USA Inc—*Henry E Demone*	PO Box 839, Portsmouth NH 03802	603-431-6865	S	231*	.3
11	Orca Bay Seafoods Inc—*Ryan Mackey*	PO Box 9010, Renton WA 98057	425-204-9100	R	144*	.2
12	Pacific Coast Seafoods Co—*Frank Dulcich*	PO Box 70, Warrenton OR 97146	503-861-2201	R	109*	.2
13	Seatrade International Company Inc—*Stephen Barndollar*	105 Bartlett St, Portsmouth NH 03801	603-431-5184	R	94*	<.1
14	Bering Select Seafoods Co—*Paul Gilliland*	641 W Ewing St, Seattle WA 98119	206-284-3474	R	75*	.1
15	First Republic Corporation of America—*Jonathan P Rosen*	302 5th Ave, New York NY 10001	212-279-6100	R	51	.4
16	Unisea Inc—*Terry Shaff*	PO Box 97019, Redmond WA 98073	425-881-8181	R	48*	.3
17	Lafitte Frozen Foods Corp—*Kam Poon*	5165 Caroline St, Lafitte LA 70067	504-689-2041	R	47*	<.1
18	Viking Seafoods LLC—*Joe Novello*	50 Crystal St, Malden MA 02148	781-322-2000	R	45*	.1
19	Tampa Bay Fisheries Inc—*Robert Patterson*	3060 Gallagher Rd, Dover FL 33527	813-752-8883	R	44*	.5
20	American Seafood Co—*Tom Cassidy*	3657 Old Getwell Rd, Memphis TN 38118	901-542-5100	R	43*	.1
21	Blount Seafood Corp—*F Blount*	630 Currant Rd, Fall River MA 02720	774-888-1300	R	41*	.2
22	North Coast Sea-Foods Corp—*Norman Stavis*	5 Drydock Ave, Boston MA 02210	617-345-4400	R	37*	.2
23	Peter Pan Seafoods Inc—*Barry Collier*	2200 6th Ave Ste 1000, Seattle WA 98121	200-728-0000	R	37*	.4
24	Fish House Foods Inc—*Ron Butler*	1263 Linda Vista Dr, San Marcos CA 92078	760-597-1270	R	36*	.4
25	Chesapeake Bay Packing LLC—*Rick Robins*	800 Terminal Ave, Newport News VA 23607	757-244-8440	R	34*	.1
26	Netuno USA Inc—*Luciano R Bonaido*	18501 Pines Blvd Rm 20, Pembroke Pines FL 33029	305-513-0904	R	34*	<.1
27	Westward Seafoods Inc—*Rick Dutton*	2101 4th Ave Ste 1700, Seattle WA 98121	206-682-5949	R	33*	.4
28	Bell Buoy Crab Co—*Dwight Eager*	PO Box 316, Chinook WA 98614	360-777-8272	R	30*	<.1
29	Simmons Farm Raised Catfish Inc—*Harry Simmons*	2628 Erickson Rd, Yazoo City MS 39194	662-746-5687	R	27*	.2
30	Eastern Shore Seafood Products LLC—*Arthur Myers*	PO Box 48, Mappsville VA 23407	757-854-4422	R	26*	.2
31	Chesapeake Fish Company Inc—*Mark Bailey*	535 Harbor Ln, San Diego CA 92101	619-238-0526	R	25*	.1
32	Ocean Gold Seafoods Inc—*Dennis Rydman*	PO Box 1104, Westport WA 98595	360-268-2510	R	25*	.2
33	Shining Ocean Inc—*Robert Bleu*	1515 Puyallup St, Sumner WA 98390	253-826-3700	R	22*	.1
34	Leavins Seafood Inc—*Grady Leavins*	PO Box 520, Apalachicola FL 32329	850-653-8823	R	22*	.1
35	Hillman Shrimp and Oyster Co—*Clifford Hillman*	10700 Hillman Dr, Dickinson TX 77539	281-339-1506	R	21*	.3
36	Chef John Folse and Company Inc—*John Folse*	2517 S Philippe Ave, Gonzales LA 70737	225-644-6000	R	20*	.3
37	Gasllc LLC—*Lou Fleming*	2200 Alaskan Way Ste 4, Seattle WA 98121	206-441-1990	R	20*	.1
38	Sun Coast Calamari Inc—*John Borman*	PO Box 151, Oxnard CA 93032	805-385-0056	R	19*	.2
39	Magnolia Processing Inc—*William Gidden*	PO Box 609, Tunica MS 38676	662-363-3600	R	18*	.2
40	Carolina Classics Catfish Inc—*Robert Mayo*	PO Box 10, Ayden NC 28513	252-746-2818	R	18*	.1
41	Seafreeze LP—*Michel Harris*	PO Box 24978, Seattle WA 98124	206-767-7350	R	16*	.1
42	Washington Crab Producers Inc—*Frank Dulcich*	PO Box 1488, Westport WA 98595	360-268-9161	R	16*	.1
43	Maryland Seafood Inc—*Joseph Scrivener*	PO Box 191, Valley Lee MD 20692	301-994-1525	R	15*	.2
44	Handy International Inc—*Terry Conway*	700 E Main St, Salisbury MD 21804	410-912-2000	R	15*	.1
45	Norquest Seafoods Inc—*Terry Gardiner* Trident Seafoods Corp	5245 Shilshole Ave Nw, Seattle WA 98107	206-281-7022	S	15*	.1
46	Carrington Foods Inc—*David Carrington*	PO Box 509, Mobile AL 36601	251-675-9700	R	15*	.1
47	Sugiyo USA Inc—*Mitsuo Takahashi*	PO Box 468, Anacortes WA 98221	360-293-0180	R	15*	.1
48	Belle Southern Frozen Foods Inc—*Howard Shaw*	PO Box 28620, Jacksonville FL 32226	904-768-1591	R	15*	.1
49	Capt Neill's Seafood Inc—*Phillip Carawan*	PO Box 164, Columbia NC 27925	252-796-0795	R	14*	.1
50	Noxubee County Producers Inc—*Norman Koehn*	PO Box 700, Macon MS 39341	662-726-2502	R	14*	.1
51	Caito Fisheries Inc—*Joseph Caito*	PO Box 1370, Fort Bragg CA 95437	707-964-6368	R	14*	.1
52	Pamlico Packing Company Inc—*W Cross*	PO Box 336, Grantsboro NC 28529	252-745-3688	R	12*	.1
53	Bon Secour Fisheries Inc—*John Nelson*	PO Box 60, Bon Secour AL 36511	251-949-5050	R	12*	.2
54	MS Intertrade Inc—*Matthew Mariani*	PO Box 6083, Santa Rosa CA 95406	707-579-2123	R	9*	.1
55	C F Gollott And Son Seafood Inc—*Brian Gollott*	PO Box 1191, Biloxi MS 39533	228-392-2747	R	8*	.1
56	Independent Packers Corp—*Jeffery Buske*	2001 W Grfeld St Ste C, Seattle WA 98119	206-285-6000	R	7*	.1
57	Good Harbor Fillet Company LLC—*Marc Tillis*	PO Box 1595, Gloucester MA 01931	978-675-9100	R	7*	.1
58	Gulf Crown Seafood Company Inc—*Jon Floyd*	PO Box 198, Delcambre LA 70528	337-685-4721	R	7*	.1
59	Home Port Seafood—*Glen Binschus*	2875 Roeder Ave Ste 11, Bellingham WA 98225	360-676-4707	R	6*	.1
60	Sea Snack Foods Inc—*Fred Ockrim*	PO Box 21467, Los Angeles CA 90021	213-622-2204	R	6*	.1
61	Maruhide Marine Products Inc—*Hideo Kawamura*	2145 W 17th St, Long Beach CA 90813	562-435-6509	R	6*	.1
62	Sea Harvest Packing Co—*Charles Wells*	PO Box 818, Brunswick GA 31521	912-264-3212	R	5*	.1
63	Okuhara Foods Inc—*James Okuhara*	881 N King St, Honolulu HI 96817	808-848-0581	R	5*	<.1
64	Q Sea Specialty Services Qss LLC—*Melody Juarez*	6069 Hannegan Rd, Bellingham WA 98226	360-398-9708	R	5*	.1
65	Seabrook Seafood Inc—*Thomas Hults*	PO Box 776, Kemah TX 77565	281-334-2546	R	4*	.1
66	Fish Processors Inc—*Leo Ray*	PO Box 479, Hagerman ID 83332	208-837-6114	R	4*	<.1
67	Atchafalaya Crawfish Processing LLC—*Linda Constantine*	PO Box 528, Breaux Bridge LA 70517	337-228-7515	R	4*	.1
68	Top Catch Inc—*Arthur Gentile*	60 Commerce St Ste 64, Brooklyn NY 11231		R	4*	.1

Note: An asterisk (*) indicates an estimated financial figure. The company type code used is as follows: R = Private, P = Public, S = Private Subsidiary, B = Public Subsidiary, D = Division, J = Joint Venture, I = Investment Fund.

COMPANY RANKINGS BY SALES WITHIN 4-DIGIT SIC

Rank	Company Name—*Executive Officer*	Address, City, State, Zip	Phone	Type	Fin	Empls
69	Coal Point Trading Co—*Nancy Hillstrand*	4306 Homer Spit Rd, Homer AK 99603	907-235-3877	R	4*	<.1
70	R A Lesso Seafood Inc—*Rudy Lesso*	PO Box 1428, Biloxi MS 39533	228-374-7200	R	4*	.1
71	Water Street Seafood Inc—*Steven Rash*	PO Box 121, Apalachicola FL 32329	850-653-8902	R	4*	.1
72	Cozy Harbor Seafood Inc—*John Norton*	PO Box 389, Portland ME 04112	207-879-2665	R	4*	.1
73	Fulcher S Point Pride Seafood Inc—*Chris Fulcher*	PO Box 250, Oriental NC 28571	252-249-0123	R	4*	<.1
74	Bay Ocean Seafood LLC	PO Box 3136, Bay City OR 97107	503-322-3316	R	3*	<.1
75	EJ Conrad and Sons Seafood Inc—*James Conrad*	1947 Rocky Neck Rd, Lancaster VA 22503	804-462-7400	R	3*	.1
76	Prince Of The Sea Ltd—*Roy Tuccillo*	PO Box 887, Westbury NY 11590	516-333-6344	R	3*	<.1
77	High Tide Seafoods—*Ernest J Vail*	PO Box 2141, Port Angeles WA 98362	360-452-8488	R	3*	<.1
78	Silver Creek Farms Inc—*David Mccollum*	450 Locust St S, Twin Falls ID 83301	208-736-0829	R	3*	<.1
79	CB Caroon Crab Company Inc—*Keith Caroon*	PO Box 10340, Southport NC 28461	910-457-6384	R	3*	<.1
80	Seafood International Distributor Inc—*Roy Roberts*	PO Box 432, Breaux Bridge LA 70517	337-228-2912	R	3*	<.1
81	Seafreeze Ltd—*Richard Goodwin*	100 Davisville Pier Rd, North Kingstown RI 02852	401-295-2585	R	3*	<.1
82	Long Beach Enterprise Inc—*Tai Tran*	PO Box 3048, Santa Fe Springs CA 90670	562-944-8945	R	3*	<.1
83	North Atlantic Fish Company Inc—*Frank Cefalo*	88 Commercial St Ste 1, Gloucester MA 01930	978-283-4121	R	3*	<.1
84	North Star Cold Storage—*John Boggs*	PO Box 1359, Stanwood WA 98292	425-778-8189	R	2*	<.1
85	Van Dyke's Chesapeake Seafood Inc—*Eleanor Dyke*	300 Lecompte St, Cambridge MD 21613	410-228-9000	R	2*	<.1
86	Nelson Crab Inc—*Kristi Nelson*	PO Box 520, Tokeland WA 98590	360-267-2911	R	2*	<.1
87	Sea Star Seafood Corp—*James Faro*	128 Bartlett St, Marlborough MA 01752	508-429-6860	R	2*	<.1
88	Nichirei Foods Inc	2201 6th Ave Ste 1350, Seattle WA 98121	206-448-7800	S	2*	<.1
89	Sahlman Seafoods Inc—*Marty Williams*	PO Box 5009, Tampa FL 33675	813-248-5726	R	2*	<.1
90	Cape Seafoods Inc—*Martin Howley*	3 State Pier Unit A, Gloucester MA 01930	978-283-8522	R	2*	<.1
91	Jensen Tuna Inc—*Ken Trinh*	5885 Hwy 311, Houma LA 70360	985-868-8809	R	2*	<.1
92	Boja's Foods Inc—*Kay Kramer*	PO Box 602, Bayou La Batre AL 36509	251-824-4186	R	2*	<.1
93	Southeastern Sea Products Inc—*Mark Maynard*	1500 Maple Ave, Melbourne FL 32935	321-259-1914	R	2*	<.1
94	Chiefland Crab Company Inc—*Howard Hart*	PO Box 174, Steinhatchee FL 32359	352-493-4887	R	2*	<.1
95	WT Ruark and Company Inc—*William Ruark*	PO Box 99, Fishing Creek MD 21634	410-397-3133	R	2*	<.1
96	Cajun Gold Catfish Processors Inc—*Wayne Branton*	PO Box 271, Wilmot AR 71676	870-473-2360	R	1*	<.1
97	Jubilee Foods Inc—*C Kraver*	PO Box 39, Bayou La Batre AL 36509	251-824-2110	R	1*	<.1
98	Harvest Time Seafood Inc—*Kevin Dartez*	208 W Elina St, Abbeville LA 70510	337-893-9029	R	1*	<.1
99	Southern Pride Catfish LLC—*John Cummings*	PO Box 436, Greensboro AL 36744	334-624-4021	R	1*	<.1
100	Charles H Parks and Company Inc—*Virgil Ruark*	PO Box 100, Fishing Creek MD 21634	410-397-3400	R	1*	<.1
101	Alaska Seafood Company Inc—*J Hand*	5731 Concrete Way, Juneau AK 99801	907-780-5111	R	1*	<.1
102	Sea Safari Ltd—*W Bateman*	PO Box 369, Belhaven NC 27810	252-943-3091	R	<1*	<.1
103	Herb's Seafood LLC—*Lee Gutkin*	1920 Swarthmore Ave St, Lakewood NJ 08701	732-730-9310	R	<1*	<.1
104	Pacific Star Seafoods Inc—*Randy Patrick*	PO Box 190, Kenai AK 99611	907-283-7787	R	<1*	<.1
105	Seafood Producers Coop—*Thomas Mclaughlin*	2875 Roeder Ave Ste 2, Bellingham WA 98225	360-733-0120	R	N/A	<.1

TOTALS: SIC 2092 Fresh or Frozen Prepared Fish
Companies: 105

					8,654	23.7

2095 Roasted Coffee

Rank	Company Name—*Executive Officer*	Address, City, State, Zip	Phone	Type	Fin	Empls
1	Java City—*Ross McMahon*	1300 Del Paso Rd, Sacramento CA 95834	916-565-5500	R	3,414*	.4
2	Montana Coffee Traders Inc—*Robby Beall*	5810 US Hwy 93 S, Whitefish MT 59937	406-862-7633	R	3,072*	.1
3	Green Mountain Coffee Roasters Inc—*Larry Blanford*	33 Coffee Ln, Waterbury VT 05676	802-244-5621	P	2,651	5.6
4	Nestle USA - Beverages Division Inc—*Joe Weller*	800 N Brand Blvd, Glendale CA 91203	818-549-6000	D	754*	1.2
5	Community Coffee Company LLC—*Annette Vaccaro*	PO Box 791, Baton Rouge LA 70821	225-368-3900	R	623*	1.0
6	S and D Coffee Inc—*Ron Hinson*	PO Box 1628, Concord NC 28026	704-782-3121	R	551*	.6
7	Farmer Brothers Co—*Jeffrey A Wahba*	20333 S Normandie Ave, Torrance CA 90502	310-787-5200	P	464	1.8
8	Peet's Coffee and Tea Inc—*Patrick J O'Dea*	PO Box 12509, Berkeley CA 94712	510-594-2100	P	334	3.5
9	Torrefazione Italia LLC	2401 Utah Ave S, Seattle WA 98134		S	187*	.3
10	Coffee Holding Company Inc—*Andrew Gordon*	3475 Victory Blvd, Staten Island NY 10314	718-832-0800	P	147	.1
11	Boyd Coffee Co—*Jeffrey Newman*	19730 Ne Sandy Blvd, Portland OR 97230	503-666-4545	R	99*	.4
12	Rogers Family Co—*Jon B Rogers*	1933 Davis St, San Leandro CA 94577	916-258-8000	R	92*	.2
13	Peerless Coffee Co—*George Vukasin Sr*	260 Oak St, Oakland CA 94607		R	79*	.1
14	Mountanos Brothers Coffee Co—*Michael Stratis Mountanos*	380 Swift Ave Ste 13, South San Francisco CA 94080		R	74*	.1
15	Royal Cup Inc—*Hatton Smith*	PO Box 170971, Birmingham AL 35217	205-849-5836	R	69*	.6
16	Hawaii Coffee Co—*Jim Wayman*	1555 Kalani St, Honolulu HI 96817		R	62*	.1
17	F Gavina and Sons Inc—*Pedro Gavina*	2700 Fruitland Ave, Vernon CA 90058	323-582-0671	R	56*	.3
18	New England Tea and Coffee Inc—*James Kaloyanides*	100 Charles St, Malden MA 02148	781-324-8094	R	46*	.2
19	Leroy Hill Coffee Company Inc—*Debra Hill*	PO Box 6219, Mobile AL 36660	251-476-1234	R	39*	.1
20	Espresso Disposition Corporation 1—*Jose Souto*	5605 Nw 82nd Ave, Doral FL 33166	305-594-9062	R	37*	.2
21	Javo Beverage Company Inc—*Stanley L Greanias*	1311 Specialty Dr, Vista CA 92081	760-560-5286	R	23	.1
22	White Coffee Corp—*Carol White*	1835 38th St, Astoria NY 11105	718-204-7900	R	20*	.1
23	Melitta North America Inc—*Martin Miller*	13925 58th St N, Clearwater FL 33760	727-535-2111	R	19*	.2
24	Excellent Coffee Company Inc—*William Kapos*	259 E Ave, Pawtucket RI 02860	401-724-6393	R	18*	.1
25	Rogers Gourmet Coffee and Tea Market—*Jon B Rogers* Rogers Family Co	1731 Aviation Blvd, Lincoln CA 95648		S	18	<.1
26	Caffe' D'amore Inc—*Chris Julias*	PO Box 1047, Monrovia CA 91017	626-792-9146	R	18*	.1
27	Paul De Lima Company Inc—*Paul De Lima*	7546 Morgan Rd, Liverpool NY 13090	315-457-3725	R	16*	.1
28	Barrie House Coffee Company Inc—*Paul Goldstein*	945 Nepperhan Ave, Yonkers NY 10703	914-423-8400	R	16*	.1
29	BRJ Inc—*Jon Rogers*	1731 Aviation Blvd, Lincoln CA 95648	916-258-8000	R	15*	.1
30	Executive Coffee Service Co—*Fred Neighbors*	3105 E Reno Ave, Oklahoma City OK 73117	405-236-3932	R	14*	.1
31	H and C Coffee Co—*David L Booth*	PO Box 11686, Roanoke VA 24022	540-982-0941	S	14	<.1
32	First Colony Coffee And Tea Inc—*Nicholas Giraldo*	PO Box 11005, Norfolk VA 23517	757-622-2224	R	13*	.1
33	Jeremiah Pick Coffee Co—*Jeremiah Pick*	1495 Evans Ave, San Francisco CA 94124	415-206-9900	R	12*	<.1
34	John A Vassilaros and Son Inc—*John Vassilaros*	2905 120th St, Flushing NY 11354	718-886-4140	R	11*	<.1
35	Peerless Coffee And Tea—*George Vukasin*	260 Oak St, Oakland CA 94607	510-763-1763	R	10*	.1
36	European Roasterie Inc—*Timothy Tulloch*	250 W Bradshaw St, Le Center MN 56057	507-357-2272	R	8*	.1
37	Cascade Coffee Inc—*Tim Kirstein*	1525 75th St Sw Ste 10, Everett WA 98203	425-347-3995	R	8*	.1
38	Schapira's Coffee and Tea Company Inc—*Joel Schapira*	PO Box 327, Pine Plains NY 12567	518-398-7100	R	7*	<.1
39	S J Mccullagh Inc—*Warren Emblidge*	245 Swan St, Buffalo NY 14204	716-856-3473	R	6*	.1
40	Colonial Coffee Roasters Inc—*Rafael Acevedo*	3250 Nw 60th St, Miami FL 33142	305-634-1843	R	6*	<.1
41	Omar Coffee Co—*Diane Bokron*	41 Commerce Ct, Newington CT 06111	860-667-8889	R	5*	.1
42	Clean Foods Inc—*Chris Shephard*	760 E Santa Maria St, Santa Paula CA 93060	805-933-3027	R	5*	<.1
43	Stewarts Private Blend Foods Inc—*Donald Stwewart*	4110 W Wrightwood Ave, Chicago IL 60639	773-489-2500	R	5*	<.1
44	Counter Culture Coffee Inc—*Brett Smith*	4911 S Alston Ave, Durham NC 27713	919-361-5282	R	4*	<.1
45	Campbell Coffee Roasting Co—*Fred Nagger*	1875 S Bascom Ave Ste, Campbell CA 95008	408-559-8040	R	4*	<.1
46	Arbuckle Coffee Co—*Denay Willis*	3550 E Corporate Dr, Tucson AZ 85706	520-790-5282	R	4*	<.1
47	Caffe Calabria Coffee Roasters LLC	3933 30th St, San Diego CA 92104	619-683-7787	R	4*	<.1
48	Empire Coffee Company Inc—*Steven Dunefsky*	106 Purdy Ave, Port Chester NY 10573	914-934-1100	R	4*	.1

Rank	Company Name—*Executive Officer*	Address, City, State, Zip	Phone	Type	Fin	Empls
49	Gillies Coffee Co—*Donald Schoenholt*	PO Box 320206, Brooklyn NY 11232	718-499-7766	R	3*	<.1
50	Araban Coffee Company Inc—*Joseph Leary*	2 Keith Way, Hingham MA 02043	781-740-4441	R	3*	<.1
51	Piacere International Inc—*Richard Forquer*	11680 Goldring Rd Unit, Arcadia CA 91006	626-357-9380	R	3*	<.1
52	Brisk Rcr Coffee Company Inc—*Richard Perez*	402 N 22nd St, Tampa FL 33605	813-248-6264	R	3*	<.1
53	Lingle Brothers Coffee Inc—*James Lingle*	6500 Garfield Ave, Bell Gardens CA 90201	562-927-3317	R	3*	<.1
54	BK Associates International Inc—*Paul Karabinis*	PO Box 1238, Oneonta NY 13820	607-432-1499	R	2*	<.1
55	Door County Coffee and Tea Co—*Victoria Wilson*	PO Box 319, Sturgeon Bay WI 54235	920-743-8870	R	2*	<.1
56	Torke Coffee Company Inc—*Ward Torke*	PO Box 694, Sheboygan WI 53082	920-458-4114	R	2*	<.1
57	Rae' Launo Corp—*Benjamin Rayfield*	2717 E Adamo Dr, Tampa FL 33605	813-242-4281	R	2*	<.1
58	Bargreen Coffee Company Inc—*Howie Bargreen*	2821 Rucker Ave, Everett WA 98201	425-252-3161	R	2*	<.1
59	Nicholas Coffee and Tea Co—*Nicholas G Nicholas*	23 Market Pl, Pittsburgh PA 15222	412-261-4225	R	2*	<.1
60	Sunfresh Citrus and Flavors Inc—*Karyl Golden*	92 E Messner Dr, Wheeling IL 60090	847-541-0890	R	2*	<.1
61	European Coffee Classics Inc—*Helmut Radtke* Melitta North America Inc	1401 Berlin Rd Ste A, Cherry Hill NJ 08034	856-428-7202	S	2*	<.1
62	Oasis Coffee Corp—*Ralph Sandolo*	327 Main Ave, Norwalk CT 06851	203-847-0554	R	1*	<.1
63	Ryan Coffee Co—*Gregory B Ryan*	2993 Teagarden St, San Leandro CA 94577	510-357-1425	R	1*	<.1
64	Wheeling Coffee and Spice Company Inc—*Mary Lokmer*	13 14th St, Wheeling WV 26003	304-232-0141	R	1*	<.1

TOTALS: SIC 2095 Roasted Coffee
Companies: 64   13,190   18.8

2096 Potato Chips & Similar Snacks

Rank	Company Name—*Executive Officer*	Address, City, State, Zip	Phone	Type	Fin	Empls
1	Frito-Lay Inc—*Albert P Carey*	PO Box 660634, Dallas TX 75266	972-334-7000	S	16,620*	45.0
2	Gruma Corp—*Jairo Senise*	PO Box 167847, Irving TX 75016	972-232-5000	S	600*	2.0
3	Shearer's Foods Inc—*Scott Smith*	692 Wabash Ave N, Brewster OH 44613	330-767-3426	R	173*	1.6
4	Barrel O' Fun Snack Foods Co—*Kenneth Nelson*	PO Box 230, Perham MN 56573	218-346-7000	R	160*	.4
5	Bickel's Snack Foods—*John A Warehime*	PO Box 2427, York PA 17405	717-843-0738	S	158*	.6
6	Herr Foods Inc—*Edwin Herr*	PO Box 300, Nottingham PA 19362	610-932-9330	R	152*	1.5
7	Golden Enterprises Inc—*Mark W McCutcheon*	1 Golden Flake Dr, Birmingham AL 35205	205-458-7316	P	131	.8
8	Golden Flake Snack Foods Inc—*Mark McCutcheon* Golden Enterprises Inc	PO Box 2447, Birmingham AL 35201	205-323-6161	S	116	1.2
9	Uncle Rays LLC—*Raymond Jenkins*	14245 Birwood St, Detroit MI 48238	313-834-0800	S	50*	.2
10	Azteca Foods Inc—*Arthur Velasquez*	5005 S Nagle Ave, Berwyn IL 60402	708-563-6600	R	50*	.1
11	Cape Cod Potato Chip Co—*Jeff Newell*	100 Breeds Hill Rd, Hyannis MA 02601	508-775-3358	S	48*	.2
12	Mike-Sell's Potato Chip Co—*Leslie Mapp*	PO Box 115, Dayton OH 45404	937-228-9400	R	41*	.3
13	Better Made Snack Foods Inc—*Robert Marracino*	10148 Gratiot Ave, Detroit MI 48213	313-925-4774	R	40*	.2
14	South Georgia Pecan Company Inc—*Jim Worn*	PO Box 5366, Valdosta GA 31603	229-244-1321	R	39*	.2
15	Jacob Group Ltd—*Jim Speak*	4118 S Halsted St, Chicago IL 60609	773-254-7400	R	38*	.2
16	Rudolph Foods Company Inc—*James Rudolph*	PO Box 509, Lima OH 45802	419-648-3611	R	36*	.4
17	Auntie Anne's Inc—*William P Dunn Jr*	48-50 W Chestnut St St, Lancaster PA 17603	717-435-1435	R	36*	.1
18	Martin's Potato Chips Inc—*Kenneth Potter*	PO Box 28, Thomasville PA 17364	717-792-3565	R	34*	.2
19	Ideal Snacks Corp—*Zeke Alenick*	89 Mill St, Liberty NY 12754	845-292-7000	R	32*	.2
20	Wyandot Inc—*Nick Chilton*	135 Wyandot Ave, Marion OH 43302	740-383-4031	R	31*	.4
21	Barbara's Bakery Inc—*Ken Wood*	3900 Cypress Dr, Petaluma CA 94954	707-765-2273	R	29*	.2
22	Mccleary Inc—*Pat Mccleary*	PO Box 187, South Beloit IL 61080	815-389-3053	R	25*	.1
23	Keystone Food Products Inc—*William Corriere*	PO Box 326, Easton PA 18044	610-258-0888	R	24*	.2
24	Fresca Mexican Foods LLC—*Karen Wynia*	11193 W Emerald St, Boise ID 83713	208-376-6922	R	22*	.1
25	Anita's Mexican Foods Corp—*Mauro Robles*	1390 W 4th St, San Bernardino CA 92411	909-884-8706	R	20*	.1
26	Tim's Cascade Style Potato Chips—*Neil Harrison*	1150 Industry Dr N, Algona WA 98001	253-833-0255	D	18*	.1
27	Variety Foods Inc—*James Champane*	7001 Chicago Rd, Warren MI 48092	586-268-4900	R	17*	.1
28	Condor Snack Co—*George Phillips*	4300 Oneida St, Denver CO 80216	303-333-6075	R	15*	.1
29	Terra Chips	4600 Sleepytime Dr, Boulder CO 80301		D	14	.1
30	Brimhall Food Company Inc—*Terry Brimhall*	PO Box 34185, Memphis TN 38184	901-377-9016	R	13*	.1
31	Severance Foods Inc—*Richard Stevens*	3476 Main St, Hartford CT 06120	860-724-7063	R	12*	<.1
32	Warnock Food Products Inc—*Donald Warnock*	20237 Masa St, Madera CA 93638	559-661-4845	R	11*	.1
33	Backer's Potato Chip Co—*Vicki Mcdaniel*	PO Box 128, Fulton MO 65251	573-642-2833	R	8*	.1
34	Ara Food Corp—*Alberto Abrante*	PO Box 520631, Miami FL 33152	305-592-5558	R	8*	.1
35	Grippo Potato Chip Company Inc—*Ralph Pagel*	6750 Colerain Ave, Cincinnati OH 45239	513-923-1900	R	7*	.1
36	Terrell's Potato Chip Company Inc—*Jack Terrell*	218 Midler Park Dr, Syracuse NY 13206	315-437-2786	R	7*	.1
37	Ira Middleswarth and Son Inc—*Bob Middleswarth*	PO Box 354, Middleburg PA 17842	570-837-1431	R	7*	.1
38	Ralph Good Inc—*Ralph Good*	PO Box 924, Adamstown PA 19501	717-484-4884	R	7*	.1
39	Great Western Tortilla Co—*William Ralston*	1761 E 58th Ave, Denver CO 80216	303-298-0705	R	6*	.1
40	Hacienda Mexican Foods LLC—*Lydia Guttierrez*	PO Box 10678, Detroit MI 48210	313-895-8823	R	5*	.1
41	Jones Potato Chip Co—*Robert Jones*	823 Bowman St, Mansfield OH 44903	419-529-9424	R	5*	.1
42	Mister Bee Potato Chip Co—*Douglas Klein*	PO Box 1645, Parkersburg WV 26102	304-428-6133	R	5*	<.1
43	Ballreich Brothers Inc—*Brian Reis*	PO Box 186, Tiffin OH 44883	419-447-1814	R	4*	<.1
44	Burkey Acquisition Inc—*Tony Tsonis*	1 Popcorn Ln, Dover PA 17315	717-292-5611	R	4*	.1
45	Unique Pretzel Bakery Inc—*William P Spannuth*	215 E Bellevue Ave, Reading PA 19605	610-929-3172	R	4*	<.1
46	El-Ranchero Food Products—*Salvador Hernandez*	2547 S Kedzie Ave, Chicago IL 60623	773-847-9167	R	4*	.1
47	Kitchen Cooked Inc—*Richard Blackhurst*	PO Box 200, Farmington IL 61531	309-245-2191	R	4*	.1
48	Mitchum Inc—*John Wilson*	PO Box 36639, Charlotte NC 28236	704-372-6744	R	3*	<.1
49	Prime Choice Foods West—*Jose Gomez*	1761 E 58th Ave, Denver CO 80216	303-298-0705	R	3*	<.1
50	Ixpalia Inc—*Jaime Picos*	PO Box 17563, Austin TX 78760	512-389-0389	R	3*	<.1
51	Festida Foods Ltd—*Kyle Kurtiss*	PO Box 326, Cedar Springs MI 49319	616-696-0400	R	3*	<.1
52	Turkey Creek Pork Skins Inc—*Laddie Fulcher*	PO Box 69, Thomaston GA 30286	706-647-8841	R	2*	<.1
53	American Skin LLC—*Brenda Phelps*	PO Box 1445, Burgaw NC 28425	910-259-2232	R	2*	<.1
54	Porkie Company Of Wisconsin Inc—*Gerald Rydeski*	PO Box 100346, Cudahy WI 53110	414-483-6562	R	2*	<.1
55	Mutt and Jeff Enterprises Inc—*Timothy Scaff*	PO Box 82226, Atlanta GA 30354	404-767-2411	R	2*	<.1
56	Igh Enterprises Inc—*John Wilson*	PO Box 36639, Charlotte NC 28236	704-372-6744	R	2*	<.1
57	Sterzing Food Co—*Thomas Blackwood*	1819 Charles St, Burlington IA 52601	319-754-8467	R	1*	<.1
58	Dakota Style Inc—*Kevin Dandurand*	PO Box 220, Clark SD 57225	605-532-5271	R	1*	<.1
59	Kitch N Cook D Potato Chip Company Inc—*George Curry*	1703 W Beverley St, Staunton VA 24401	540-886-4473	R	1*	<.1
60	Roberts American Gourmet Food Inc	PO Box 326, Sea Cliff NY 11579	516-656-4545	R	1*	<.1

TOTALS: SIC 2096 Potato Chips & Similar Snacks
Companies: 60   18,918   58.2

2097 Manufactured Ice

Rank	Company Name—*Executive Officer*	Address, City, State, Zip	Phone	Type	Fin	Empls
1	Home City Ice Co—*Thomas Sedler*	PO Box 111116, Cincinnati OH 45211	513-574-1800	R	3,200*	1.2
2	Reddy Ice Holdings Inc—*Gilbert M Cassagne*	8750 N Central Expy St, Dallas TX 75231	214-526-6740	P	316	2.7
3	Reddy Ice Corp—*Gilbert M Cassagne*	8750 N Central Expy St, Dallas TX 75231	214-526-6740	S	206*	1.7

Note: An asterisk (*) indicates an estimated financial figure. The company type code used is as follows: R = Private, P = Public, S = Private Subsidiary, B = Public Subsidiary, D = Division, J = Joint Venture, I = Investment Fund.

COMPANY RANKINGS BY SALES WITHIN 4-DIGIT SIC

Rank	Company Name—*Executive Officer*	Address, City, State, Zip	Phone	Type	Fin	Empls
	Reddy Ice Holdings Inc					
4	Airgas Dry Ice—*Phil Filer*	6340 Sugarloaf Pky Ste, Duluth GA 30097	770-717-2200	S	15*	.1
5	Knowlton Enterprises Inc—*Norman Knowlton*	1755 Yeager St, Port Huron MI 48060	810-987-7100	R	14*	.1
6	AT Reynolds and Sons Inc—*Harold Reynolds*	PO Box 168, Kiamesha Lake NY 12751	845-794-7040	R	10*	.1
7	Growers Ice Co—*Dennis Stevens*	PO Box 298, Salinas CA 93902	831-424-5781	R	7*	<.1
8	Ice Products Inc—*George Moll*	650 E Division St, Evansville IN 47711	812-425-8191	R	7*	.1
9	Triangle Ice Company Of Beaufort Inc—*Larry Naylor*	431 Harmon St, Savannah GA 31401	912-234-8866	R	5*	.1
10	Arizona Ice Man Inc—*Eugene Oliver*	447 W Watkins Rd Ste 3, Phoenix AZ 85003	602-470-1010	R	5*	<.1
11	York Ice Company Inc—*Edward Neuman*	281 Kings Mill Rd, York PA 17401	717-848-2639	R	4*	<.1
12	Saxony Ice Co	500 Fenimore Rd, Mamaroneck NY 10543	914-698-8808	S	4*	.1
13	Blue American Ice Co—*David Peters*	PO Box 1497, Whitney TX 76692	254-694-3613	R	3*	<.1
14	Maplewood Ice Company Inc—*David Wood*	PO Box 62, Whitehall NY 12887	518-499-2345	R	2*	<.1
15	Arctic Glacier Oregon Inc—*James Porcelli*	909 N Columbia Blvd Ct, Portland OR 97217	503-285-2800	R	2*	<.1
16	Pelican Ice and Cold Storage Inc—*Todd Roberts*	PO Box 2131, Kenner LA 70063	504-525-4193	R	2*	<.1
17	Baker's Ice Company Inc—*Tim Baker*	2120 Ice St, Pacific MO 63069	636-271-4603	R	2*	<.1
18	Gainsville Ice—*Rick Bunch*	508 Se 11th Ave, Gainesville FL 32601	352-376-6653	R	2*	<.1
19	Aquatech Of Birmingham Inc—*Thomas Seale*	PO Box 68, Pelham AL 35124	205-663-6250	R	2*	<.1
20	U S Ice Corp—*Saad Abbo*	10625 W 8 Mile Rd, Detroit MI 48221	313-862-3344	R	2*	<.1
21	Rose Ice and Coal Company Inc—*Archie Harris*	1202 Market St, Wilmington NC 28401	910-762-2464	R	2*	<.1
22	Millersburg Ice Co—*Lewis Ritchey*	25 S Grant St, Millersburg OH 44654	330-674-3016	R	2*	<.1
23	Little Woodrows—*Little Woodrows*	5611 Morningside Dr, Houston TX 77005	713-521-2337	R	1*	<.1
24	City Ice Co—*Mark Resnick*	13600 Permilla Springs, Chester VA 23836	804-796-9423	R	1*	<.1
25	Jefferson Ice Co—*Robert Rustman*	PO Box 2248, Chicago IL 60690	773-622-9400	R	1*	<.1
26	Kar Ice Service Inc—*Tom Lewis*	PO Box 1197, Barstow CA 92312	760-256-2648	R	1*	<.1
27	NC Frozen Foods Inc—*Michael Thomas*	PO Box 2601, Kill Devil Hills NC 27948	252-441-2136	R	1*	<.1
28	Sea Gardens Seafoods Inc—*Andy Amason*	PO Box 181, Valona GA 31319	912-832-4437	R	1*	<.1
29	Northwest Gel Inc—*Norman Campbell*	PO Box 671530, Chugiak AK 99567	907-688-2044	R	1*	<.1

TOTALS: SIC 2097 Manufactured Ice
Companies: 29   3,821   6.5

2098 Macaroni & Spaghetti

Rank	Company Name—*Executive Officer*	Address, City, State, Zip	Phone	Type	Fin	Empls
1	New World Pasta Co—*Peter Smith*	PO Box 126457, Harrisburg PA 17112	717-526-2200	R	463*	1.3
2	Nissin Foods Company Inc (Gardena California)—*Shawn Masaki*	2001 W Rosecrans Ave, Gardena CA 90249		S	150*	.4
3	Monterey Gourmet Foods Inc—*Eric C Eddings*	1528 Moffett St, Salinas CA 93905	831-753-6262	R	109*	.4
4	Maruchan Inc—*Kiyoshi Fukagawa*	15800 Laguna Canyon Rd, Irvine CA 92618	949-789-2300	R	63*	.6
5	A Zerega's Sons Inc—*John Vermylen*	PO Box 241, Fair Lawn NJ 07410	201-797-1400	R	47*	.2
6	Dakota Growers Pasta Company Inc—*Timothy Dodd*	1 Pasta Ave, Carrington ND 58421	701-652-2855	S	30*	.4
7	Wing Hing Noodles Co—*Kenny Yee*	1659 E 23rd St, Los Angeles CA 90011	323-232-8899	R	27*	.1
8	Baily International Inc—*George Tsai*	1751 Burns Ave, Saint Louis MO 63132	314-487-4616	R	26*	.3
9	Venda Ravioli Inc—*Alan Costantino*	265 Atwells Ave Ste 1, Providence RI 02903	401-421-9105	R	17*	.1
10	Noodles By Leonardo Inc—*Leonard Gasparre*	PO Box 860, Devils Lake ND 58301	701-662-8300	R	15*	.1
11	Pasta Montana LLC—*Randy Gilbertson*	1 Pasta Pl, Great Falls MT 59401	406-761-1516	R	11*	.1
12	Twin Marquis Inc—*Joseph Tang*	328 Johnson Ave, Brooklyn NY 11206	718-386-6868	R	8*	.1
13	D'orazio Foods Inc—*Anthony Orazio*	PO Box 243, Bellmawr NJ 08099	856-931-1900	R	8*	.1
14	New Hong Kong Noodle Company Inc—*Steven Lum*	360 Swift Ave Ste 22, South San Francisco CA 94080	650-952-9404	R	4*	<.1
15	Rossi Pasta Factory Inc—*John Hammat*	PO Box 930, Marietta OH 45750	740-376-2065	R	4*	<.1
16	Food City USA Inc—*Monika Piz-Wilson*	4752 W 60th Ave Ste A, Arvada CO 80003	303-321-4447	R	4*	<.1
17	Florence Macaroni Manufacturing Company Inc—*Roy Dominici*	4334 W Chicago Ave, Chicago IL 60651	773-252-6113	R	3*	<.1
18	Dimares Italian Specialty Food—*Charles Fazio*	2363 59th St, Saint Louis MO 63110	314-781-1125	R	3*	<.1
19	Quon Yick Noodle Company Inc—*Margaret Leong*	9668 Telstar Ave, El Monte CA 91731	626-350-1882	R	3*	<.1
20	H and U Inc—*Hidehito Uki*	1933 Colburn St, Honolulu HI 96819	808-841-5808	R	3*	<.1
21	Tsue Chong Company Inc—*Kenneth Louie*	800 S Weller St, Seattle WA 98104	206-623-0801	R	2*	<.1
22	Hong Kong Noodle Company Inc—*Glenn Der*	2350 S Wentworth Ave, Chicago IL 60616	312-842-0480	R	2*	<.1
23	Nanka Seimen Co—*Shoichi Sayano*	3030 Leonis Blvd, Vernon CA 90058	323-585-9967	R	2*	<.1
24	US Durum Products Ltd—*Michael Florescu*	PO Box 10126, Lancaster PA 17601	717-293-8698	R	2	<.1
25	Hong Hop Company Inc—*Dai Hee*	10 Bowery, New York NY 10013	212-732-0735	R	2*	<.1
26	Carso's Pasta Company Inc—*Dave Brown*	PO Box 77003, Seattle WA 98177	425-670-1302	R	2*	<.1
27	O B Macaroni Co—*Jenni Ratliff*	PO Box 53, Fort Worth TX 76101	817-335-4629	R	2*	<.1
28	Gabriele Macaroni Company Inc—*Ann Fusano*	PO Box 90564, City Of Industry CA 91715	626-964-2324	R	1*	<.1
29	Riviera Ravioli Inc—*Joseph Giordano*	643 Morris Park Ave, Bronx NY 10460	718-823-0260	R	1*	<.1
30	Star Ravioli Manufacturing Company Inc—*Lawrence Piretra*	2 Anderson Ave Ste 2, Moonachie NJ 07074	201-933-6427	R	1*	<.1

TOTALS: SIC 2098 Macaroni & Spaghetti
Companies: 30   1,016   4.5

2099 Food Preparations Nec

Rank	Company Name—*Executive Officer*	Address, City, State, Zip	Phone	Type	Fin	Empls
1	Bunge Ltd—*Alberto Weisser*	50 Main St 6th Fl, White Plains NY 10606	914-684-2800	P	45,707	33.0
2	WhiteWave Foods Co—*Gregg Engles*	12002 Airport Way, Broomfield CO 80021	303-635-4000	S	4,800*	1.2
3	Lamb-Weston Inc—*Richard Porter*	PO Box 1900, Tri Cities WA 99302	509-735-4651	S	3,495*	6.0
4	McCormick and Company Inc—*Alan D Wilson*	18 Loveton Cir, Sparks MD 21152	410-771-7301	P	3,337	7.5
5	Unilever Bestfoods North America—*Paul Polman*	800 Sylvan Ave, Englewood Cliffs NJ 07632	201-894-7760	D	3,000	7.4
6	Pinnacle Foods Group LLC—*Robert Gamgort*	PO Box 3900, Peoria IL 61612	856-969-7100	S	2,440	4.5
7	Hain Celestial Group Inc—*Irwin D Simon*	58 South Service Rd, Melville NY 11747	631-730-2200	P	1,130	2.0
8	Lancaster Colony Corp—*John B Gerlach Jr*	37 W Broad St, Columbus OH 43215	614-224-7141	P	1,090	3.1
9	Ready Pac Produce Inc—*Dennis Gertmenian*	4401 Foxdale Ave, Irwindale CA 91706	626-856-8686	R	915*	1.0
10	Tia Rosa Bakery—*Juan Muldoon*	14401 Statler Blvd, Fort Worth TX 76155	817-864-2500	S	705*	3.9
11	Griffith Laboratories Inc—*Dean Griffith*	1 Griffith Ctr, Alsip IL 60803	708-371-0900	R	700*	2.5
12	Chef Solutions Inc—*Steve Silk*	120 W Palatine Rd, Wheeling IL 60090	847-325-7500	R	645*	6.8
13	American Italian Pasta Co—*John P Kelly*	4100 N Mulberry Dr Ste, Kansas City MO 64116	816-584-5000	R	628	.7
14	Fresh International Corp—*Fernando Aguierre*	PO Box 80002, Salinas CA 93912	831-422-5334	R	625*	3.0
15	Gilster-Mary Lee Corp—*Donald Welge*	PO Box 227, Chester IL 62233	618-826-2361	R	615*	4.0
16	Old Sturbridge Inc—*Jim Donahue*	1 Old Sturbridge Villa, Sturbridge MA 01566	508-347-3362	R	528*	.3
17	Fresh Express Inc / Fresh International Corp	PO Box 80599, Salinas CA 93912	831-424-2921	S	400*	2.5
18	Riviana Foods Inc—*Bastiaan G de Zeeuw*	PO Box 2636, Houston TX 77252	713-529-3251	S	396*	2.8
19	NutraSweet Co—*Nick E Rosa*	10 S Wacker Dr, Chicago IL 60606	312-873-5013	S	280*	.3
20	Golden Peanut Company LLC—*James Dorsett*	100 N Point Ctr E Ste, Alpharetta GA 30022	770-752-8160	J	269*	1.0
21	Medifast Inc—*Michael S McDevitt*	11445 Cronhill Dr, Owings Mills MD 21117	410-581-8042	P	258	.5
22	Ameriqual Group LLC—*Mark Bradley*	18200 Hwy 41 N, Evansville IN 47725	812-867-1444	R	249*	.7
23	Reser's Fine Foods Inc—*Mark Reser*	PO Box 8, Beaverton OR 97075	503-643-6431	R	239*	2.1

Rank	Company Name—*Executive Officer*	Address, City, State, Zip	Phone	Type	Fin	Empls
24	Minn-Dak Farmers Cooperative Inc—*David Roche*	7525 Red River Rd, Wahpeton ND 58075	701-642-8411	R	214*	.3
25	Celestial Seasonings Inc—*Steven List* Hain Celestial Group Inc	4600 Sleepytime Dr, Boulder CO 80301	303-530-5300	S	185*	.2
26	Natural Nutrition Group Inc Hain Celestial Group Inc	58 S Service Rd, Melville NY 11747	516-237-6200	S	168*	.3
27	ConAgra Snack Foods Group—*Gary Rodkin*	7700 France Ave S Ste, Minneapolis MN 55435	952-835-6900	D	160*	.9
28	Penzeys Spices Inc—*William Penzey*	12001 W Capitol Dr, Wauwatosa WI 53222	262-785-7676	R	160*	.3
29	Lesaffre Yeast Corp—*John Riesch*	7475 W Main St, Milwaukee WI 53214		R	149*	.7
30	Tone Brothers Inc—*Doug Alridge*	2301 SE Tones Dr, Ankeny IA 50021	515-965-2711	S	146*	.4
31	Unico Inc (Lake Worth Florida)—*Mark Lopez*	2201 4th Ave N, Lake Worth FL 33461	561-582-3030	R	143*	.2
32	ConAgra Grocery Products Co	3353 Michelson Dr, Irvine CA 92612	949-437-1000	S	142*	.6
33	Twinlab Corp—*Bill Nicholson*	600 E Quality Dr, American Fork UT 84003	801-763-0700	R	138*	.2
34	Inventure Foods Inc—*Terry McDaniel*	5415 E High St Ste 350, Phoenix AZ 85054	623-932-6200	P	134	.4
35	LSG Sky Chefs Inc	6191 N State Hwy 161, Irving TX 75038	972-793-9000	S	131*	.6
36	Mission Foods Corp	PO Box 167847, Irving TX 75038	972-232-5000	D	113*	.2
37	Romero Foods Inc—*Leon Romero*	15155 Valley View Ave, Santa Fe Springs CA 90670	562-802-1858	R	104*	.1
38	Orval Kent Food—*Steven B Kent* Chef Solutions Inc	120 W Palatine Rd, Wheeling IL 60090	973-779-2090	D	100*	.3
39	Jacmar Food Service Distribution	12761 Schabarum Ave, Irwindale CA 91706		R	99*	.9
40	Dutch Gold Honey Inc—*Nancy Gamber*	2220 Dutch Gold Dr, Lancaster PA 17601	717-393-1716	R	99*	.1
41	Balance Bar Co—*Hendrick J Hartong*	115 E Stevens Ave Ste, Valhalla NY 10595		S	95*	.1
42	Vaughan Foods Inc—*Herbert B Grimes*	216 NE 12th St, Moore OK 73160	405-794-2530	R	94	.5
43	Link Snacks Inc—*Dr John Link*	PO Box 397, Minong WI 54859	715-466-2234	R	91*	.3
44	Cedarlane Natural Foods Co—*Robert Atallah*	1135 E Artesia Blvd, Carson CA 90746	310-886-7720	R	90*	.3
45	International Food Solutions—*Michael Wetterauer*	1930 California Ave, Corona CA 92881	909-737-4800	R	89*	.4
46	Cuisine Solutions Inc—*Stanislas Vilgrain*	2800 Eisenhower Ave St, Alexandria VA 22312	703-270-2900	R	88*	.3
47	La Reina Inc—*Richard Robles*	316 N Ford Blvd, Los Angeles CA 90022	323-268-2791	R	88*	.2
48	EA Sween Deli Express—*Robert Linner*	16101 W 78th St, Eden Prairie MN 55344	952-937-9440	R	87*	.9
49	Gel Spice Company Inc—*Andre Engel*	PO Box 285, Bayonne NJ 07002	201-339-0700	R	76*	.2
50	Old Dutch Mustard Company Inc—*Paul Santich*	98 Cuttermill Rd Ste 2, Great Neck NY 11021	516-466-0522	R	72*	.1
51	Northern Star Co	3171 5th St SE, Minneapolis MN 55414	612-339-8981	S	71*	.3
52	Greencore USA Inc—*Liam Mcclennon*	2 Opportunity Way, Newburyport MA 01950	978-462-3663	R	70*	.5
53	CC Pollen Co—*Bruce Brown*	3627 E Indian School R, Phoenix AZ 85018	602-957-0096	R	69*	.1
54	Prolab Nutrition Inc—*Frank Cameron*	21411 Prairie St, Chatsworth CA 91311	818-739-6000	S	66*	.3
55	Fuchs North America Inc—*Jack Irvin*	9740 Reisterstown Rd, Owings Mills MD 21117	410-363-1700	R	66*	.2
56	Lifeway Foods Inc—*Julie Smolyansky*	6431 W Oakton St, Morton Grove IL 60053		P	64	.3
57	ME Thompson Inc—*Jerry Thompson*	2178 W 21st St, Jacksonville FL 32209	904-356-6258	R	61*	.1
58	American Pie LLC—*Alan Mitzner*	130 Crossways Park Dr, Woodbury NY 11797	516-921-6800	R	61*	<.1
59	Crider Inc—*W Crider*	PO Box 398, Stillmore GA 30464	912-562-4435	R	61*	.7
60	Clif Bar and Co—*Gary Erickson*	1451 66th St, Emeryville CA 94608	510-558-7855	R	57*	.2
61	RJ Van Drunen and Sons Inc—*Edward Van Drunen*	PO Box 9, Momence IL 60954	815-472-3100	R	54*	.3
62	Vita Food Products Inc—*Clifford K Bolen*	2222 W Lake St, Chicago IL 60612	312-738-4500	R	54	.2
63	Ole' Mexican Foods Inc—*Eduardo Moreno*	6585 Crescent Dr, Norcross GA 30071	770-582-9200	R	52*	.5
64	Victoria Packing Corp *Gorald Aquilina*	443 E 100th St, Brooklyn NY 11236	718-927-3000	S	50*	.3
65	Puratos Corp—*Ed Belle*	1941 Old Cuthbert Rd, Cherry Hill NJ 08034	856-428-4300	R	50*	.3
66	Service Foods Inc—*Stanley Sax*	4355 International Blv, Norcross GA 30093	770-662-5562	R	48*	.2
67	Good Earth Teas—*Barbara Roth*	890 Mountain Ave Ste 1, New Providence NJ 07974		S	47*	.1
68	Asiana Cuisine Enterprises Inc—*Harlan Chin*	1447 W 178th St Ste 30, Gardena CA 90248	310-327-2233	R	46*	.6
69	Harris Soup Co—*Rod Harris*	17711 Ne Riverside Pkw, Portland OR 97230	503-257-7687	R	46*	.3
70	Kalsec Inc—*Paul Todd*	PO Box 50511, Kalamazoo MI 49005	269-349-9711	R	44*	.3
71	Maramont Corp—*Harry Reichman*	5600 1st Ave Bldg C, Brooklyn NY 11220	718-439-8900	R	44*	.5
72	Elite Spice Inc—*Linda Allen*	7151 Montevideo Rd, Jessup MD 20794	410-796-1900	R	44*	.3
73	El-Milagro Inc—*Raphael Lopez*	3050 W 26th St, Chicago IL 60623	773-523-5627	R	43*	.5
74	Sandridge Food Corp—*Mark Sandridge*	PO Box 278, Medina OH 44258	330-725-2348	R	43*	.2
75	California Natural Products—*Pat Mitchell*	PO Box 1219, Lathrop CA 95330	209-858-2525	R	42*	.2
76	Brady Enterprises Inc—*Kevin Maguire*	PO Box 890099, East Weymouth MA 02189	781-337-5000	R	42*	.1
77	Joe Corbi's Wholesale Pizza Inc—*Rocco Violi*	1430 Desoto Rd, Baltimore MD 21230	410-525-3810	R	40*	.2
78	Baumer Foods Inc—*Alvin Baumer*	2424 Edenborn Ave Ste, Metairie LA 70001	504-482-5761	R	40*	.2
79	Tortilleria El Maizal Inc—*Marcelo Reyes*	1920 Shiloh Rd Nw 4-10, Kennesaw GA 30144	770-427-1570	R	39*	.2
80	Landshire Inc—*Dale Musick*	727 N 1st St, Saint Louis MO 63102		R	39*	.4
81	El Lago Tortillas Inc—*Luis Centeno*	1700 E 4th St, Austin TX 78702	512-476-0945	R	39*	.1
82	Williams Foods Inc—*Dale Tremblay*	13301 W 99th St, Lenexa KS 66215	913-888-4343	S	39*	.2
83	Diversified Foods And Seasonings Inc—*Richard Chapman*	1115 N Causeway Blvd S, Mandeville LA 70471	985-809-3600	R	38*	.5
84	Winter Gardens Quality Foods Inc—*Jason Bross*	PO Box 339, New Oxford PA 17350	717-624-4911	R	38*	.3
85	Concord Foods Inc—*Peter Neville*	10 Minuteman Way, Brockton MA 02301	508-580-1700	R	38*	.2
86	Proliant Inc—*Roger Jacobsen*	2425 Se Oak Tree Ct, Ankeny IA 50021	515-289-5100	R	38*	.2
87	Southeastern Mills Inc—*Robert Grizzard*	PO Box 908, Rome GA 30162	706-291-6528	R	38*	.2
88	Better Baked Foods Inc—*David Christopher*	56 Smedley St, North East PA 16428	814-725-8778	R	38*	.4
89	Del Rey Tortilleria Inc—*Jeanette Toledo*	5201 W Grand Ave, Chicago IL 60639	773-637-8900	R	37*	.2
90	Watkins Inc—*Mark Jacobs*	PO Box 5570, Winona MN 55987	507-457-3300	R	35*	.3
91	Signature Foods Inc—*Charles McAtee*	73 Enterprise Dr Ste D, Pendergrass GA 30567		R	35*	.1
92	Gourmet Boutique LLC—*Denise Baxter*	14402 158th St, Jamaica NY 11434	718-977-1200	R	35*	.3
93	Ramona's Mexican Food Products Inc—*Romana Banuelos*	PO Box 1275, Gardena CA 90249	310-323-1950	R	34*	.2
94	Wonton Food Inc—*Ching Wong*	220 Moore St 222, Brooklyn NY 11206	718-628-6868	R	33*	.2
95	Ruiz Mexican Foods Inc—*Edward Ruiz*	2151 E Francis St, Ontario CA 91761	909-947-7811	R	33*	.2
96	RC Bigelow Inc—*Cynthia Bigelow*	201 Black Rock Tpke, Fairfield CT 06825	203-334-1212	R	33*	.4
97	Southern Tea LLC—*Maria Roberts*	1267 Cobb Industrial D, Marietta GA 30066	770-428-5555	R	32*	.2
98	Mane Inc—*Michell Mane*	999 Tech Dr, Milford OH 45150	513-248-9876	S	32*	.2
99	Hpc Foods Ltd—*Eric Enomoto*	288 Libby St, Honolulu HI 96819	808-848-2431	R	31*	.2
100	Rocky Mountain Chocolate Factory Inc—*Franklin E Crail*	265 Turner Dr, Durango CO 81303	970-259-0554	P	31	.3
101	Gold Star Chili Inc—*John Sullivan*	650 Lunken Park Dr, Cincinnati OH 45226	513-231-4541	R	31*	.2
102	La Canasta Mexican Food Products Inc—*Josie Ippelito*	PO Box 6939, Phoenix AZ 85005	602-269-7721	R	30*	.2
103	Redco Foods Inc—*Debo Mukherjee*	1 Hansen Island, Little Falls NY 13365	315-823-1300	S	30*	.1
104	Flora Inc—*Thomas Greither*	PO Box 73, Lynden WA 98264	360-354-2110	R	30*	.1
105	Italian Rose Garlic Products Inc—*Ken Berger*	1380 W 15th St Ste A, Riviera Beach FL 33404	561-863-5556	R	30*	.1
106	American Pop Corn Co—*Garrett Smith*	PO Box 178, Sioux City IA 51102	712-239-1232	R	30*	.2
107	La Tapatia Tortilleria Inc—*Helen Chavez-Hansen*	104 E Belmont Ave, Fresno CA 93701	559-441-1030	R	30*	.2
108	La Espiga De Oro Inc—*Alfredo Lira*	1202 W 15th St, Houston TX 77008	713-861-4200	R	29*	.2
109	Miller's American Honey Inc—*George Murdock*	PO Box 500, Colton CA 92324	909-825-1722	R	29*	<.1
110	Hulman and Co—*Anton George*	PO Box 150, Terre Haute IN 47808	812-478-7216	R	29*	.2

Note: An asterisk (*) indicates an estimated financial figure. The company type code used is as follows: R = Private, P = Public, S = Private Subsidiary, B = Public Subsidiary, D = Division, J = Joint Venture, I = Investment Fund.

COMPANY RANKINGS BY SALES WITHIN 4-DIGIT SIC

Rank	Company Name—Executive Officer	Address, City, State, Zip	Phone	Type	Fin	Empls
111	Vigo Importing Co—Anthony Alessi	PO Box 15584, Tampa FL 33684	813-884-3491	R	28*	.1
112	Sunland Inc—Jimmy Schearer	PO Box 1059, Portales NM 88130	575-356-6638	R	28*	.1
113	National Vinegar Company Inc—Alex Wolff	PO Box 2761, Houston TX 77252	713-223-4214	R	28*	.1
114	Jpc Pasta Company LLC	262 Primrose St, Haverhill MA 01830	978-521-1718	R	27*	.2
115	Exquisita Tortillas Inc—J Rodriguez	PO Box 1078, Edinburg TX 78540	956-383-6712	R	27*	.2
116	Diana's Mexican Food Products Inc—Samuel Magana	PO Box 369, Norwalk CA 90651	562-926-5802	R	27*	.3
117	Austin Packaging Co—James Heimark	1118 N Main St, Austin MN 55912	507-433-6623	R	25*	.3
118	Opta Food Ingredients Inc—Doug Schreves	100 Apollo Dr, Chelmsford MA 01824	781-276-5100	S	25	.1
119	SunOpta Sunflower—Steven Bromley	5850 Opus Pkwy Ste 150, Minnetonka MN 55343	218-643-8467	S	25*	.1
120	Quality Formulations Inc	110 Pennsylvania Ave, Paterson NJ 07503	973-977-8800	R	25	<.1
121	Schiff Food Products Company Inc—David Deutscher	7401 W Side Ave, North Bergen NJ 07047	201-868-6800	R	25*	<.1
122	Hans Kissle Company Inc—Steven Zenlea	9 Creek Brook Dr, Haverhill MA 01832	978-556-4500	R	25*	.1
123	Paradise Inc—Randy S Gordon	PO Box 4230, Plant City FL 33563		P	24	.2
124	Uno Foods Inc—Frank W Guidara	100 Charles Park Rd, Boston MA 02132	617-323-9200	S	24*	.1
125	Peking Noodle Company Inc—Frank Tong	1514 San Fernando Rd, Los Angeles CA 90065	323-223-2023	R	24*	.1
126	National Vinegar Co (St Louis Missouri)—John Placio	1750 S Brentwood Blvd, Saint Louis MO 63144	314-962-4111	R	24*	<.1
127	Border Foods Inc—Randy Clark	4065 J St Se, Deming NM 88030	575-546-8863	R	24*	.2
128	Mojave Foods Corp—Margarita Taylor McCormick and Company Inc	6200 E Slauson Ave, Los Angeles CA 90040	323-890-8900	S	24	.1
129	Kf Foods Inc—Timothy Neerdaels	1375 Gruber Rd, Green Bay WI 54313	920-434-8874	R	23*	.2
130	Latino Enterprises Inc—Marcelino Solis	3451 Atlnta Industrial, Atlanta GA 30331	404-351-9822	R	23*	.1
131	Proven Partners Group LLC	1111 Bowes Rd, Elgin IL 60123	847-888-1230	R	23*	.2
132	Leavitt Corp—James Hintlian	100 Santilli Hwy, Everett MA 02149	617-389-2600	R	23*	.1
133	Albuquerque Tortilla Company Inc—Luther Martinez	4300 Alexander Blvd Ne, Albuquerque NM 87107	505-344-4011	R	23*	.1
134	Nasoya Foods Inc—Robert Jones	1 New England Way, Ayer MA 01432	978-772-6880	R	22*	.2
135	Made Rite Sandwich Company Of Chattanooga Inc—B Sullivan	PO Box 27, Ooltewah TN 37363	423-238-5492	R	22*	.2
136	Simplexity Health Inc—Jerry Anderson	PO Box 609, Klamath Falls OR 97601	541-882-5406	R	22	.1
137	Woeber Mustard Manufacturing Co—Raymond Woeber	PO Box 388, Springfield OH 45501	937-323-6281	R	22*	.1
138	Foran Spice Company Inc—Patrica Goto	PO Box 109, Oak Creek WI 53154	414-764-1220	R	21*	.1
139	St Clair Foods Inc—Oscar Edmonds	3100 Bellbrook Dr, Memphis TN 38116	901-396-8680	R	21*	.1
140	Wisconsin Spice Inc—Phillip Sass	PO Box 190, Berlin WI 54923	920-361-3555	R	21*	<.1
141	Leon's Fine Foods Inc—Bob Clements	PO Box 1850, Mckinney TX 75070	972-529-5050	R	21*	.2
142	King Tortilla Inc—Juan Guardiola	PO Box 763, Moundridge KS 67107	620-345-2674	R	21*	.1
143	World Flavors Inc—Robert Holmquist	76 Louise Dr, Warminster PA 18974	215-672-4400	R	20*	.1
144	Lee Kum Kee Foods Inc (City of Industry California)—David Lee	14455 Don Julian Rd, City Of Industry CA 91746	626-336-3886	R	20*	.1
145	AC Legg Inc—Jim Purvis	PO Box 709, Calera AL 35040	205-324-3451	R	19*	.1
146	Turtle Mountain LLC—Ken Demangelaere	PO Box 21938, Eugene OR 97402	541-338-9400	R	19*	<.1
147	Sokol And Co—John Novak	5315 Dansher Rd, Countryside IL 60525	708-482-8250	R	19*	.1
148	FS S Inc—Stephen Lineer	5202 Moundview Dr, Red Wing MN 55066	651-388-5568	R	18*	<.1
149	ZonePerfect Nutrition Co—J Scott White	625 Cleveland Ave, Columbus OH 43215		D	18*	<.1
150	Romero's Food Products Inc—Richard Scandalito	15155 Valley View Ave, Santa Fe Springs CA 90670	562-802-1858	H	18*	.1
151	RL Schreiber Inc—Tom Schreiber	1741 Nw 33rd St, Pompano Beach FL 33064	954-972-7102	R	18*	.1
152	Bakers Best/Trotter Soft Prtzl—Gary Powell	1880 N Penn Rd, Hatfield PA 19440	215-822-3511	S	17*	.1
153	Custom Culinary Inc—Scott Gilbert	2021 Swift Dr, Oak Brook IL 60523	630-928-4898	R	17*	.1
154	Don Pancho Authentic Mexican Foods Inc—George Puentes Reser's Fine Foods Inc	3060 Industrial Way Ne, Salem OR 97301	503-370-9710	S	17*	.1
155	Abco Laboratories Inc—Allen Baron	PO Box 2519, Fairfield CA 94533	707-432-2200	R	16*	.1
156	El Popocatapetl Industries Inc—Ernesto Avina	1854 W 21st St, Chicago IL 60608	312-421-6143	R	16*	.1
157	Maple Grove Farms Of Vermont Inc—Dave Wenner	1052 Portland St, Saint Johnsbury VT 05819	802-748-5141	R	16*	.1
158	Sunrise Foods Inc—Dave Thorud	3120 Valleyview Dr, Columbus OH 43204	614-276-2880	R	16*	.1
159	My Own Meals Inc—Mary Jackson	400 Lake Cook Rd Ste 1, Deerfield IL 60015	847-948-1118	R	15*	<.1
160	Aranda's Tortilla Factory—Victor Aranda	1318 E Scotts Ave, Stockton CA 95205	209-464-8675	R	15*	<.1
161	Heather Creek Foods LLC	12485 Commissioner Dr, North Jackson OH 44451	330-538-9722	R	15*	<.1
162	ST Specialty Foods Inc—Dale Schulz	8700 Xylon Ave N, Minneapolis MN 55445	763-493-9600	R	15*	.1
163	Isabelle's Kitchen Inc—Vincent Pupillo	417 Main St, Harleysville PA 19438	215-256-1012	S	13*	.1
164	Honest Tea Inc—Seth Goldman	4827 Bethesda Ave, Bethesda MD 20814	301-652-3556	S	13*	<.1
165	Durkee-Mower Inc—Donald D Durkee	PO Box 470, Lynn MA 01903	781-593-8007	R	13*	.1
166	Aldon Food Corp—Victor Skloff	4461 Township Line Rd, Schwenksville PA 19473	484-991-1000	R	12*	.1
167	Fishers Bakery And Sandwich Company Inc—Winfield Fisher	1519 Brookside Dr, Raleigh NC 27604	919-901-0739	R	11*	.1
168	El Tapatio Market—Larry Flores	310 E Florence Ave Ste, Los Angeles CA 90003	323-751-1330	R	11*	.1
169	La Fortaleza Inc—Tony Cassillia	501 N Ford Blvd, Los Angeles CA 90022	323-261-1211	R	11*	.1
170	Cornfields Inc—Phyllis Cretors	3898 Sunset Ave, Waukegan IL 60087	847-263-7000	R	11*	.1
171	PR Nutrition Inc—Bill Louge	5900 Sea Lion Pl Ste 1, Carlsbad CA 92010		R	11*	<.1
172	Mrs Gerry's Kitchen Inc—Alan Oliver	PO Box 1127, Albert Lea MN 56007	507-373-6384	R	11*	.1
173	Chef Merito Inc—Jose Corugedo	7915 Sepulveda Blvd, Van Nuys CA 91405	818-787-0100	R	11*	.1
174	ForeverGreen IP LLC—Ronald M Williams	972 N 1430 W, Orem UT 84057	801-655-5500	P	11	<.1
175	Magic Seasoning Blends Inc—Shawn Mcbribe	PO Box 23342, New Orleans LA 70183	504-731-3590	R	10*	.1
176	Tortillas Mexico Mexico Inc—Jose Rangel	840 W 11th Ave, Denver CO 80204	303-623-7875	R	10*	.1
177	Bearden Sandwich Company Inc—Lloyd Bearden	PO Box 45130, Baton Rouge LA 70895	225-927-4670	R	10*	.1
178	RC Fine Foods Inc—Susan Goldman	PO Box 236, Belle Mead NJ 08502	908-359-5500	R	10*	.1
179	Fresh Meal Solutions Inc—James Baird	410 T Frank Wathen Rd, Uniontown KY 42461	270-822-2743	R	10*	.1
180	Prime Deli Corp—Harry Nakamura	1301 A Ridgeview Dr St, Lewisville TX 75057	972-219-7110	R	10*	.1
181	Los Angeles Salad Company Inc—Robert Hana	600 S 6th Ave, City Of Industry CA 91746	626-322-9000	R	9*	.1
182	Sensory Effects Powder Systems Inc—Charles Nicolais	136 Fox Run Dr, Defiance OH 43512	419-782-5010	R	9*	.1
183	Jones Popcorn Inc—James Jones	PO Box 48, New Albany IN 47151	812-941-8810	R	9*	.1
184	Midas Foods International—Richard Elias	10750 Capital St, Oak Park MI 48237	248-544-4574	R	9*	<.1
185	CC Foods Inc—Ralph Casillas	3348 E Wier Ave, Phoenix AZ 85040	602-276-7974	R	9*	.1
186	La Mexicana Inc—Keith Bloxham	10020 14th Ave Sw, Seattle WA 98146	206-763-1488	R	9*	.1
187	Super Lopez Food Products And Tortilla Factory Inc—Ramiro Lopez	7314 Harrisburg Blvd, Houston TX 77011	713-921-1237	R	8*	.1
188	Walker Foods Inc—Robert Walker	237 N Mission Rd, Los Angeles CA 90033	323-268-5191	R	8*	.1
189	House Of Thaller Inc—John Thaller	1600 Harris Rd, Knoxville TN 37924	865-689-5893	R	8*	.1
190	El Tortillero LLC—Priscilla Cazares	5330 S 12th Ave, Tucson AZ 85706	520-889-2279	R	8*	.1
191	El Mirasol Inc—Guillermo Gama	4008 Airport Rd, Plant City FL 33563	813-754-5857	R	8*	.1
192	Los Amigos Tortilla Manufacturing Inc—Ruben Rodriguez	251 Armour Dr Ne, Atlanta GA 30324	404-876-8153	R	8*	.1
193	Jacobs Management Corp—Irwin Jacobs	80 S 8th St Ste 2900, Minneapolis MN 55402	612-339-9500	R	8*	<.1
194	Michigan Dessert Corp—Richard Elias	10750 Capital St, Oak Park MI 48237	248-544-4574	R	8*	<.1
195	Popcorn Factory Inc—Nancy Hensel	13970 W Laurel Dr, Lake Forest IL 60045		S	8*	<.1
196	Honey Silverbow Company Inc—Gary Grigg	1120 E Wheeler Rd, Moses Lake WA 98837	509-765-6616	R	8*	<.1

Rank	Company Name—*Executive Officer*	Address, City, State, Zip	Phone	Type	Fin	Empls
197	LesserEvil Brand Snack Co—*Bunker West*	PO Box 4098, Greenwich CT 06831	914-779-3000	R	8*	<.1
198	SmartPrice Sales and Marketing Inc—*Andrew Topus*	651 Landwehr, Northbrook IL 60062	847-637-8390	R	8*	<.1
199	Taste It Presents Inc—*John Alair*	200 Sumner Ave, Kenilworth NJ 07033	908-241-9191	R	8*	.1
200	Produce World Inc—*Joseph Fereira*	30611 San Antonio St, Hayward CA 94544	510-441-1449	R	8*	.1
201	Cantare Foods Inc—*Olivier Fischer*	7651 Saint Andrews Ave, San Diego CA 92154	619-690-7550	R	8*	.1
202	Sincere Orient Commercial Corp—*Andy Khun*	15222 Valley Blvd, City Of Industry CA 91746	626-333-8882	R	8*	.1
203	Hannah International Foods Inc—*George Hannah*	PO Box 458, Seabrook NH 03874	603-474-5805	R	7*	.1
204	Mrs Grissom's Salads Inc—*Grace Grissom*	PO Box 40231, Nashville TN 37204	615-255-4137	R	7*	.1
205	Redstar Yeast and Products	7475 W Main St, Milwaukee WI 53214		R	7	<.1
206	FBC Industries Inc—*Robert Bloom*	1933 N Meacham Rd 550, Schaumburg IL 60173	847-839-0880	R	7*	<.1
207	Barnard Nut Company Inc—*Jose Menendez*	PO Box 453636, Miami FL 33245	305-836-9999	R	7*	.1
208	Louisburg Cider Mill—*Tom Schierman*	14730 Hwy 68, Louisburg KS 66053	913-837-5202	R	7*	.1
209	Future Foods—*Stan Solomonson*	3829 Sacramento Ave, Santa Rosa CA 95405	707-542-5599	R	7	N/A
210	Mi Mama's Tortillas Inc—*Art Velasquez*	828 S 17th St, Omaha NE 68108	402-345-2099	R	7*	.1
211	Griffin Food Co—*John Griffin*	PO Box 1928, Muskogee OK 74402	918-687-6311	R	7*	.1
212	R and S Mexican Food Products Inc—*Danny Franks*	PO Box 2262, Glendale AZ 85311	602-272-2727	R	7*	.1
213	Mi Rancho Tortilla Incorporated—*Dorthy Cruz*	801 Purvis Ave, Clovis CA 93612	559-299-3183	R	7*	.1
214	Red Eagle Enterprises Inc—*Serapio Terrones*	12946 W Santa Fe Dr, Surprise AZ 85378	623-583-0291	R	7*	.1
215	La Barca Tortilleria Inc—*Jose Arevalo*	PO Box 23548, Los Angeles CA 90023	323-268-1744	R	7*	.1
216	Hunter Spice Inc—*Conrad Sauer*	184 Suburban Rd, San Luis Obispo CA 93401	805-544-4466	R	6*	.1
217	Pugsley's Sandwiches Inc—*Gary Senger*	PO Box 116, Devils Lake ND 58301	701-662-2309	R	6*	.1
218	Foulds Inc—*Christopher Bradley*	520 E Church St, Libertyville IL 60048	847-362-3062	R	6*	<.1
219	Sidaris Italian Foods—*Joseph Sidari*	3820 Lakeside Ave E, Cleveland OH 44114	216-431-3344	R	6*	.1
220	Sugar Vermont Maple Company Inc—*David Marvin*	37 Industrial Park Dr, Morrisville VT 05661	802-888-8349	R	6*	.1
221	MRS Foods Inc—*Laura Perez*	4408 W 5th St, Santa Ana CA 92703	714-554-2791	R	6*	.1
222	Kerry Co—*Wendy Pairazaman*	21612 88th Ave S, Kent WA 98031	253-395-9400	R	6*	.1
223	Old Dominion Peanut Corp—*William Chiaro*	PO Box 11165, Norfolk VA 23517	757-622-1633	R	6*	.1
224	Spice King Corp—*Anne Stern*	438 El Camino Dr, Beverly Hills CA 90212	310-277-7487	R	6*	<.1
225	A-1 Wholesale Sandwich Co—*John Musser*	429 Cabot Rd, South San Francisco CA 94080	650-869-7090	R	6*	.1
226	Kiko Foods Inc—*Max Burnell*	2628 Lexington Ave, Kenner LA 70062	504-466-2090	R	6*	.1
227	La Fama Foods Inc—*Raul Roel*	303 S Ave A, Longview TX 75604	903-759-7704	R	6*	.1
228	Linden Nut Company Inc—*John Martini*	8452 Demartini Ln, Linden CA 95236	209-887-3731	R	6*	.1
229	Sweet Harvest Foods Management Inc—*Curt Riess*	515 Cannon IndustrialB, Cannon Falls MN 55009	507-263-8599	R	6*	.1
230	Andy's Seasoning Inc—*Katherine Anderson*	2829 Chouteau Ave, Saint Louis MO 63103	314-664-3004	R	6*	<.1
231	Zateca Foods LLC	PO Box 1420, Greeley CO 80632	970-351-6000	R	5*	.1
232	Van Bennett Food Company Inc—*Patrick Emmett*	101 N Carroll St, Reading PA 19611	610-374-8348	R	5*	<.1
233	La Mexicana Tortilleria Inc—*Rudolph Guerrero*	2703 S Kedzie Ave, Chicago IL 60623	773-247-5443	R	5*	.1
234	Risvold's Inc—*Tim Brandon*	1234 W El Segundo Blvd, Gardena CA 90247	323-770-2674	R	5*	<.1
235	Famous Natchitoches Louisiana Meat Pie Co—*Harold Mccain*	PO Box 540, Coushatta LA 71019	318-932-3472	R	5*	<.1
236	Manuels Mexican American Fine Foods Inc—*Orlando Torres*	PO Box 789, Bountiful UT 84011	801-484-1431	R	5*	<.1
237	Ilyssa Manufacturing Corp—*Jeffrey Levi*	57 Commerce St 59, Brooklyn NY 11231	718-625-4180	R	5*	.1
238	Hood River Juice Company Inc—*David Ryan*	1590 Country Club Rd, Hood River OR 97031	541-386-3003	R	5*	.1
239	Revolution Tea LLC *Chris Ramzio*	5080 N 40th St Ste 375, Phoenix AZ 85018	602-393-3737	R	5*	<.1
240	Nina's Mexican Foods Inc—*Ruben Vasquez*	20631 Valley Blvd Ste, Walnut CA 91789	909-468-5888	R	5*	<.1
241	DRM Management Inc—*Ronald Digiore*	3430 Transit Rd, Depew NY 14043	716-668-0333	R	5*	<.1
242	Woolery Enterprises Inc—*Daniel Woolery*	2099 Burroughs Ave, San Leandro CA 94577	510-357-5700	R	5*	<.1
243	All American Seasonings Inc—*Carlos Rodriguez*	10600 E 54th Ave Unit, Denver CO 80239	303-623-2320	R	5*	<.1
244	S and K Industries Inc—*Eugene Suarez*	9209 Enterprise Ct, Manassas Park VA 20111	703-369-0232	R	5*	<.1
245	Johnny's Fine Foods Inc—*John Crabill*	319 E 25th St, Tacoma WA 98421	253-383-4597	R	5*	<.1
246	Rama Food Manufacture Corp—*Karen Bing*	2131 S Parco Ave, Ontario CA 91761	909-923-5305	R	5*	<.1
247	El Burrito Mexican Food Products Inc—*Mark Roth*	PO Box 90125, City of Industry CA 91715	626-369-7828	R	5*	<.1
248	Morton Bassett LLC—*Morton Gothelf*	84 Galli Dr, Novato CA 94949	415-883-8530	R	5*	<.1
249	Triland Foods Inc—*Joe Rieger*	PO Box 744, Sergeant Bluff IA 51054	712-943-7675	R	5	<.1
250	New Mexico Mexican Foods—*Robert Estrada*	916 E Amador Ave, Las Cruces NM 88001	575-526-8351	R	5*	.1
251	Tom Harris Inc—*Tom Harris*	5821 Wilderness Ave, Riverside CA 92504	951-352-5700	R	5*	.1
252	Oasis Mediterranean Cuisine—*Francois Hashem*	PO Box 8881, Toledo OH 43623	419-269-1459	R	5*	<.1
253	Annandale Foods LLC—*Jamie Deakins*	435 Annandale Blvd, Annandale MN 55302	320-274-1081	R	5*	.1
254	Golding Farms Foods Inc—*Ernest Golding*	6061 Gun Club Rd, Winston Salem NC 27103	336-766-6161	R	5*	<.1
255	J and K Ingredients Inc—*James Sausville*	160 E 5th St Fl 2, Paterson NJ 07524	973-340-8700	R	5*	<.1
256	Ingallina's Box Lunch Inc—*Chris Ingallina*	135 S Lucile St, Seattle WA 98108	206-756-9400	R	5*	<.1
257	Del Castillo Foods Inc—*Marciano Castillo*	2346 Maggio Cir, Lodi CA 95240	209-368-6650	R	5*	<.1
258	Lasco Foods Inc—*Thomas Ellinwood*	4553 Gustine Ave, Saint Louis MO 63116	314-832-1906	R	5*	<.1
259	Essen Nutrition Corp—*Madhavan Anirudhan*	1414 Sherman Rd, Romeoville IL 60446	630-739-6700	R	5*	<.1
260	Everson Spice Company Inc—*Kim Everson*	2667 Gundry Ave, Long Beach CA 90755	562-988-1223	R	4*	<.1
261	Fiore Di Pasta Inc—*Bernadetta Primavera*	4776 E Jensen Ave, Fresno CA 93725	559-457-0431	R	4*	<.1
262	Armando G Martinez—*Armando Martinez*	215 W Ave N, San Angelo TX 76903	325-653-5640	R	4*	<.1
263	Carmel Food Group Inc—*John Personeni*	31128 San Clemente St, Hayward CA 94544	510-429-0356	R	4*	<.1
264	Robles Brothers Inc—*George Robles*	1700 Rogers Ave, San Jose CA 95112	408-436-5551	R	4*	<.1
265	Delori Products Inc—*Jaime Brown*	PO Box 92668, City Of Industry CA 91715	626-965-3006	R	4*	<.1
266	Datrex Inc—*John Simonsen*	PO Box 1537, Kinder LA 70648	337-738-4511	R	4*	<.1
267	Dawn's Foods Inc—*Gregory Drewsen*	1530 La Dawn Dr, Portage WI 53901	608-742-2494	R	4*	<.1
268	Famarco Inc—*Bruce Martin*	1381 Air Rail Ave, Virginia Beach VA 23455	757-460-3573	R	4*	<.1
269	Old Mansion Inc—*J Patton*	PO Box 1838, Petersburg VA 23805	804-862-9889	R	4*	<.1
270	Panola Pepper Corp—*Grady Brown*	1414 Holland Delta Rd, Lake Providence LA 71254	318-559-1774	R	4*	<.1
271	Survivor Industries Inc—*Howard Wallace*	1621 Emerson Ave, Oxnard CA 93033	805-385-5560	R	4*	<.1
272	Fire and Flavor Grilling Co—*Davis Knox*	375 Commerce Blvd Ste, Bogart GA 30622		R	4*	<.1
273	MAS Sales Ltd—*Michael Sica*	11225 W Grand Ave, Melrose Park IL 60164	847-451-0005	R	4*	<.1
274	Mexamerica Foods Inc—*Gerald Riddle*	1037 Trout Run Rd, Saint Marys PA 15857	814-781-1447	R	4*	<.1
275	La Princesita Tortilleria Inc—*Francisco Ramirez*	3432 E Cesar Chavez Av, Los Angeles CA 90063	323-267-0673	R	4*	<.1
276	Finest Food Company Inc—*Derek Shiraki*	743 Waiakamilo Rd Ste, Honolulu HI 96817	808-848-0365	R	4*	<.1
277	Uncle Lee's Tea Inc—*Kuo-Lin Lee*	11020 Rush St, El Monte CA 91733	626-350-3309	R	4*	<.1
278	Culinarte Marketing Group LLC—*Jim Vann*	808 Packerland Dr, Green Bay WI 54303	920-498-3004	R	4*	<.1
279	Dallas Tortillas Inc—*Ruben Leal*	309 N Marsalis Ave, Dallas TX 75203	214-943-7681	R	4*	<.1
280	Saranac Brand Foods Inc—*Dennis Nowak*	PO Box 264, Saranac MI 48881	616-642-9463	R	4*	<.1
281	Beverage House Inc—*Jim Gollhofer*	400 High Point Rd Se S, Cartersville GA 30120	770-387-0451	R	4*	<.1
282	Dawson Dorothy Food Products Inc—*Phillip Dawson*	PO Box 312, Jackson MI 49204	517-788-9830	R	4*	<.1
283	La Superior Food Products Inc—*George Young*	PO Box 3866, Shawnee KS 66203	913-432-4933	R	4*	<.1
284	Plantain Products Co—*Margaret Argudo*	5821 Causeway Blvd, Tampa FL 33619	813-626-9486	R	3*	<.1
285	La Bonita Inc—*Albert Ornelas*	1813 E California Ave, Bakersfield CA 93307	661-324-1632	R	3*	<.1
286	Dominguez Family Enterprises Inc—*Luis Dominguez*	2885 Van Horn Dr, Hood River OR 97031	541-386-6311	R	3*	<.1

Note: An asterisk (*) indicates an estimated financial figure. The company type code used is as follows: R = Private, P = Public, S = Private Subsidiary, B = Public Subsidiary, D = Division, J = Joint Venture, I = Investment Fund.

COMPANY RANKINGS BY SALES WITHIN 4-DIGIT SIC

Rank	Company Name—*Executive Officer*	Address, City, State, Zip	Phone	Type	Fin	Empls
287	Blendco Inc—*Charles Mccaffrey*	8 J M Tatum Industrial, Hattiesburg MS 39401	601-544-9800	R	3*	<.1
288	Usm Manufacturing LLC	2206 114th St, Lubbock TX 79423	806-745-2727	R	3*	<.1
289	Walker's Food Products Co—*Shawn Boyce*	PO Box 34762, Kansas City MO 64116	816-472-8121	R	3*	<.1
290	Taste Maker Foods LLC—*Jack Beasley*	1415 E Mclemore Ave, Memphis TN 38106	901-274-4407	R	3*	<.1
291	Specialty Rice Inc—*Ojus Ajmera*	1000 W 1st St, Brinkley AR 72021	870-734-1233	R	3*'	<.1
292	Tata Tea Inc—*Ravi Sankararaman*	1001 W Dr Mlk Jr Blvd, Plant City FL 33563	813-754-2602	R	3*	<.1
293	Lehman Foods Inc—*Charles Lehman*	1145 Arroyo St Ste B, San Fernando CA 91340	818-837-7600	R	3*	<.1
294	Rodriguez Company Inc—*Henry Rodriguez*	7060 N Rodriquez Rd, Mc Neal AZ 85617	520-364-3926	R	3*	<.1
295	St Laurent Brothers Inc—*Keith Whitney*	PO Box 117, Bay City MI 48707	989-893-7522	R	3*	<.1
296	Wm E Martin And Sons Company Inc—*William Martin*	9339 170th St, Jamaica NY 11433	718-291-1300	R	3*	<.1
297	Cosmos Food Company Inc—*David Kim*	2405 Forney St, Los Angeles CA 90031	323-221-9142	R	3*	<.1
298	Hi Mountain Jerky Inc—*John Hummel*	1000 College View Dr, Riverton WY 82501	307-856-6626	R	3*	<.1
299	Colorado Tortilla Company Inc—*Margaret Buerkle*	5672 E 58th Ave Ste A, Commerce City CO 80022	303-288-5417	R	3*	<.1
300	Papy's Foods Inc—*Matthew Gallimore*	4131 W Albany St, Mchenry IL 60050	815-385-3313	R	3*	<.1
301	Sinaloa Hawaiian Tortillas Inc—*Ysidro Macias*	PO Box 31013, Honolulu HI 96820	808-833-3695	R	3*	<.1
302	East Shore Specialty Foods Inc—*Jeri Mesching*	PO Box 379, Hartland WI 53029	262-367-8988	R	3*	<.1
303	Scandinavian Formulas Inc—*Catherine P Peklak*	140 E Church St, Sellersville PA 18960	215-453-2507	R	3*	<.1
304	Snack Factory Inc—*Warren Wilson*	PO Box 3562, Princeton NJ 08543	609-683-5400	R	3*	<.1
305	La Tolteca Foods Inc—*Philip Hilvitz*	PO Box 1437, Pueblo CO 81002	719-543-5733	R	3*	<.1
306	Vivolac Cultures Corp—*Wesley Sing*	3862 E Washington St, Indianapolis IN 46201	317-359-9528	R	3*	<.1
307	Dakota Tom's Sandwiches Inc—*Richard Bordewyk*	PO Box 271, Corsica SD 57328	605-946-5123	R	3*	<.1
308	Cain Food Industries Inc—*Gary Cain*	PO Box 35066, Dallas TX 75235	214-630-4511	R	3*	<.1
309	Cathay Food Corp—*Victor Wong*	960 Msschusetts Ave St, Boston MA 02118	617-427-1507	R	3*	.1
310	Sanitary Tortilla Manufacturing Company Inc—*Jesse Villarreal*	623 Urban Loop, San Antonio TX 78204	210-226-9209	R	3*	<.1
311	Marx Brothers Inc—*Edgar Marx*	3100 2nd Ave S, Birmingham AL 35233	205-251-3139	R	3*	<.1
312	Country Home Creations Inc—*Shirley Ann Kautman Jon*	PO Box 126, Goodrich MI 48438	810-244-7348	R	3*	<.1
313	Herold Salads Inc—*Cathy Herold*	17512 Miles Ave, Cleveland OH 44128	216-991-7500	R	3*	<.1
314	Desert Pepper Trading Co—*W Kerr*	PO Box 1761, El Paso TX 79949	915-544-3434	R	3*	<.1
315	Everfresh Food Corp—*Oren Steinfeldt*	501 Huron Blvd Se, Minneapolis MN 55414	612-331-6393	R	3*	<.1
316	Gmp Manufacturing Inc—*Gregory Pickett*	4795 Industrial Way, Benicia CA 94510	707-751-3942	R	3*	<.1
317	Aloha Tofu Factory Inc—*Paul Uyehara*	961 Akepo Ln, Honolulu HI 96817	808-845-2669	R	3*	<.1
318	J O Spice And Cure Company Inc—*M Mcphaul*	3721 Old Georgetown Rd, Baltimore MD 21227	410-247-5205	R	3*	<.1
319	Zina's Salads Inc—*Zina Shaknovich*	11 Great Meadow Ln, East Hanover NJ 07936	973-428-0660	R	3*	<.1
320	Renaissance Restaurant Group LLC	120 Thistle Top Trl, Apex NC 27502	919-624-7101	R	2*	.1
321	Delrio Tortilla Factory—*Esta Perez*	1402 Gillette Blvd, San Antonio TX 78224	210-922-4810	R	2*	<.1
322	Pop's Bakery Inc—*Antonio Garcia*	208 E Ave J, San Angelo TX 76903	325-655-1170	R	2*	<.1
323	Pappy's Meat Company Inc—*Edward Papulias*	PO Box 5257, Fresno CA 93755	559-291-0218	R	2*'	<.1
324	US Mills Inc—*Charles Verde*	200 Reservoir St Ste 3, Needham Heights MA 02494	415-486-2101	R	2*	<.1
325	Alamo Tamale Company LP—*Jose Herendez*	3713 Jensen Dr, Houston TX 77026	713-228-6445	R	2*	.1
326	Mccutcheon Apple Products Inc—*Robert Mc Cutcheon*	PO Box 243, Frederick MD 21705	301-662-3261	R	2*	<.1
327	Tortilleria La California Inc—*Sergio Sanchez*	2241 Cypress Ave, Los Angeles CA 90065	323-221-8940	R	2*	<.1
328	Chef's Catering Inc—*Chuck Hammerle*	3770 W Whitton Ave, Phoenix AZ 85019	602-233-9420	R	2*	<.1
329	Dixie Dew Products Inc—*Robert Carl*	PO Box 18310, Erlanger KY 41018	859-283-1050	R	2*	<.1
330	Houlihan's Culinary Traditions Ltd—*Elaine Houlihan*	2650 Paldan Dr, Auburn Hills MI 48326	248-373-1100	R	2*	<.1
331	Tee Lee Popcorn Inc—*James Weaver*	PO Box 108, Shannon IL 61078	815-864-2363	R	2*	.1
332	Casa Valdez Inc—*Jose Valdez*	502 E Chicago St, Caldwell ID 83605	208-459-6461	R	2*	.1
333	Azar's Natural Foods Inc—*Tony Saady*	108 Prescott Ave, Virginia Beach VA 23452	757-486-7778	R	2*	.1
334	Matador Processors Inc—*Betty Wood*	PO Box 2200, Blanchard OK 73010	405-485-3567	R	2*	<.1
335	Mexi-Snax Corp—*Armando Viescas*	6860 El Paso Dr, El Paso TX 79905	915-779-5709	R	2*	<.1
336	Tomanetti Food Products Inc—*George Michel*	631 Allegheny Ave, Oakmont PA 15139	412-828-3040	R	2	<.1
337	China Mist Tea Co—*Rommie Flammer*	7435 E Tierra Buena Ln, Scottsdale AZ 85260	480-998-8807	R	2*	<.1
338	Galca Mexican Food Inc—*Hector Galvan*	3805 Aldine Mail Rd, Houston TX 77039	281-442-9800	R	2*	<.1
339	T W Burleson and Son Inc—*Thomas Burleson*	PO Box 578, Waxahachie TX 75168	972-937-4810	R	2*	<.1
340	Minn-Dak Yeast Company Inc—*Steve Caspers* Minn-Dak Farmers Cooperative Inc	18175 Red River Rd W, Wahpeton ND 58075	701-642-3300	S	2*	<.1
341	Ellis Popcorn Company Inc—*Ann Ellis*	101 Poplar St, Murray KY 42071	270-753-5451	R	2*	<.1
342	Hoople Country Kitchens Inc—*David Caskey*	714 N 5th St, Rockport IN 47635	812-649-2351	R	2*	<.1
343	Producers Peanut Company Inc—*James R Pond Jr*	PO Box 250, Suffolk VA 23439	757-539-7496	R	2*	<.1
344	Popcorn County USA Inc—*William Brush*	PO Box 40, North Loup NE 68859	308-496-4781	R	2*	<.1
345	Old World Specialties Inc—*Scott Webb*	12431 Boxwood Farms Dr, Catharpin VA 20143		R	2*	<.1
346	Esperanzas Tortilleria Inc—*Victor Martinez*	750 Rock Springs Rd, Escondido CA 92025	760-743-5908	R	2*	<.1
347	Reidco Inc—*John Reid*	1351 W Us Hwy 50, Brownstown IN 47220	812-358-3000	R	2*	<.1
348	Snak-Time Foods Inc—*Vance Clark*	PO Box F, Fraziers Bottom WV 25082	704-434-5400	R	2*	<.1
349	Adelita Tortilla Factory—*Roberto Borrego*	1130 Fresno, San Antonio TX 78201	210-733-5352	R	2*	<.1
350	Five Star Foods Inc—*Donald Richards*	PO Box 550, Spooner WI 54801	715-635-6401	R	2*	<.1
351	La Tapatia Inc—*Esther Rosencrans*	8941 Old County Dr, El Paso TX 79907	915-859-9616	R	2*	<.1
352	SOS Food Lab Inc—*Stella Koniecpolski*	9399 Nw 13th St, Doral FL 33172	305-594-9933	R	2*	<.1
353	Lau Lau Plant—*Michael Irish*	966 Robello Ln, Honolulu HI 96817	808-832-9500	R	2*	<.1
354	Circle U Foods Inc—*Lynn Ulmer*	751 Eight Twenty Blvd, Fort Worth TX 76106	817-626-6918	R	2*	<.1
355	Pure Foods Inc—*Michael Ingalls*	PO Box 989, Sultan WA 98294	360-793-2241	R	2*	<.1
356	Rmr Inc—*Richard Kaneda*	515 Ward Ave Ste B, Honolulu HI 96814	808-591-8205	R	1*	<.1
357	Family Loompya Corp—*Alen Enriquez*	2626 Southport Way Ste, National City CA 91950	619-477-2125	R	1*	<.1
358	Art's Mexican Products Inc—*Robert Gutierrez*	615 Kansas Ave, Kansas City KS 66105	913-371-2163	R	1*	<.1
359	Al Dente Inc—*Monique Deschaine*	9815 Main St, Whitmore Lake MI 48189	734-449-8522	R	1*	<.1
360	Test Laboratories Inc—*Gregory Brewster*	7121 Canby Ave, Reseda CA 91335	818-881-4268	R	1*	<.1
361	Tropical Blossom Honey Co—*John Douglas Mc Ginn*	PO Box 8, Edgewater FL 32132	386-428-9027	R	1*	<.1
362	Venture Foods Inc—*Dale Entringer*	177 Sibley St, Fond Du Lac WI 54935	920-922-9033	R	1*	<.1
363	La Jalisciense Inc—*Sergio Abundis*	2650 Bagley St, Detroit MI 48216	313-237-0008	R	1*	<.1
364	Harbar LLC—*Heidi Hartung*	320 Turnpike St, Canton MA 02021	781-828-0848	R	1*	<.1
365	Toby's Family Foods—*Jonah Alves*	1160 Shelley St, Springfield OR 97477	541-689-8506	R	1*	<.1
366	Tague Technologies Inc—*Wesley Tague*	PO Box 29137, Denver CO 80229	303-287-3852	R	1*	<.1
367	Moon Shine Trading Co—*Ishai Zeldner*	1250-A Harter Ave, Woodland CA 95776	530-668-0660	R	1*	<.1
368	PB Leiner USA—*Gerard Marchand*	366 N Broadway Ste 307, Jericho NY 11753	516-822-4040	S	1*	<.1
369	Grandma LaMure's Spice'n Slice Inc	436 N Washington Ave, Prescott AZ 86301	928-778-7260	R	1*	<.1
370	LMZ Soluble Coffee Inc—*Jonathan Feuer*	111 Great Neck Rd Ste, Great Neck NY 11021	516-773-8500	R	1*	<.1
371	Das Brot Inc—*Steven Holtsclaw*	3324 Towerwood Dr, Dallas TX 75234	972-243-8443	R	1*	<.1
372	Bolner's Fiesta Products Inc—*Timothy Bolner*	426 Menchaca St, San Antonio TX 78207	210-734-6404	R	1*	<.1
373	Stout's Cider Mill—*Ron Stout*	PO Box 1100, Willcox AZ 85644	520-384-3696	R	1*	<.1
374	Chugwater Chili Corp—*Karl Wilkerson*	PO Box 92, Chugwater WY 82210	307-422-3345	R	<1*	<.1
375	Mi Rancho Tortilla Factory—*Robert Berber*	425 Hester St, San Leandro CA 94577	510-553-0444	R	<1*	<.1

Rank	Company Name—*Executive Officer*	Address, City, State, Zip	Phone	Type	Fin	Empls
376	Santa Fe Ole Inc—*Jim Wrench*	1212 Pky Dr Ste A, Santa Fe NM 87507	505-660-2449	R	<1*	<.1

TOTALS: SIC 2099 Food Preparations Nec
Companies: 376   80,366   135.0

2111 Cigarettes

Rank	Company Name—*Executive Officer*	Address, City, State, Zip	Phone	Type	Fin	Empls
1	Philip Morris International Inc—*Louis C Camilleri*	120 Park Ave, New York NY 10017	917-663-2000	P	67,713	78.3
2	Altria Group Inc—*Martin J Barrington*	6601 W Broad St, Richmond VA 23230	804-274-2200	P	24,363	10.0
3	Philip Morris USA Inc—*William F Gifford Jr* Altria Group Inc	6601 W Broad St, Richmond VA 23230		S	21,229*	13.0
4	Reynolds American Inc—*Daniel Delen*	PO Box 2990, Winston-Salem NC 27102	336-741-2000	P	8,551	5.8
5	RJ Reynolds Tobacco Co—*Daniel Delen* Reynolds American Inc	PO Box 2959, Winston Salem NC 27102	336-741-5000	S	7,350	4.0
6	Lorillard Inc—*Murray S Kessler*	PO Box 21688, Greensboro NC 27408	336-335-7000	P	5,932	2.7
7	Lorillard Tobacco Co—*Martin L Orlowsky* Lorillard Inc	PO Box 10529, Greensboro NC 27404	336-335-7000	S	1,888	3.7
8	Vector Group Ltd—*Howard M Lorber*	100 SE 2nd St 32nd Fl, Miami FL 33131	305-579-8000	P	1,133	.6
9	S and M Brands Inc—*Malcolm Bailey*	3662 Ontario Rd Ste B, Keysville VA 23947	434-736-2130	R	100*	.2
10	Jose Carlos Cigars—*Bill Davies*	17506 Brighton Ave Uni, Port Charlotte FL 33954	941-429-6621	R	2*	<.1
11	Star Scientific Inc—*Jonnie R Williams*	4470 Cox Rd Ste 110, Glen Allen VA 23060	804-527-1970	P	1	<.1

TOTALS: SIC 2111 Cigarettes
Companies: 11   138,262   118.2

2121 Cigars

Rank	Company Name—*Executive Officer*	Address, City, State, Zip	Phone	Type	Fin	Empls
1	Swisher International Inc (Jacksonville Florida)	PO Box 2230, Jacksonville FL 32203	904-353-4311	S	267*	1.3
2	Altadis USA Inc—*Theo W Folz*	PO Box 407166, Fort Lauderdale FL 33340	954-772-9000	S	233*	.1
3	J C Newman Cigar Co—*Eric Newman*	PO Box 2030, Tampa FL 33601	813-248-2124	R	24*	.2
4	Finck Cigar Co—*William Finck Jr*	PO Box 831007, San Antonio TX 78283	210-226-4191	R	12*	.1

TOTALS: SIC 2121 Cigars
Companies: 4   536   1.7

2131 Chewing & Smoking Tobacco

Rank	Company Name—*Executive Officer*	Address, City, State, Zip	Phone	Type	Fin	Empls
1	UST LLC—*Murray S Kessler*	6 High Ridge Park Bldg, Stamford CT 06905	203-817-3000	S	1,500	4.6
2	United States Smokeless Tobacco Co—*Peter P Paoli*	2325 Bells Rd, Richmond VA 23234	804-274-2200	S	1,056*	4.0
3	North Atlantic Operating Co—*Lawrence S Wexler*	PO Box 32980, Louisville KY 40232	203-202-9547	R	130*	.3
4	Swedish Match North America—*Lars Dahlgren*	PO Box 13297, Richmond VA 23225	804-787-5100	D	80*	.8
5	TOP Tobacco LP—*Claus Platt*	PO Box 205, Lake Waccamaw NC 28450	910-646-3014	S	17*	.1
6	Oregon Mint Co—*Bill WA Geiger*	PO Box 1530, Manzanita OR 97130		R	15	.2
7	Smokey Mountain Chew Inc—*Dave Savoca*	PO Box 1028, Grand Rapids MN 55745		R	15*	<.1

TOTALS: SIC 2131 Chewing & Smoking Tobacco
Companies: 7   2,813   9.9

2141 Tobacco Stemming & Redrying

Rank	Company Name—*Executive Officer*	Address, City, State, Zip	Phone	Type	Fin	Empls
1	Flue-Cured Tobacco Cooperative Stabilization Corp—*Tommy Bunn*	PO Box 12300, Raleigh NC 27605	919-821-4560	R	80*	<.1

2211 Broadwoven Fabric Mills—Cotton

Rank	Company Name—*Executive Officer*	Address, City, State, Zip	Phone	Type	Fin	Empls
1	Milliken and Co—*Joe Salley*	PO Box 1926, Spartanburg SC 29304	864-503-2020	R	2,043*	9.0
2	Intier Automotive Inc (Novi Michigan)—*Donald J Walker*	39600 Lewis Dr, Novi MI 48377	248-567-4000	S	975*	1.0
3	Joan Fabrics Corp—*Elkin B McCallum*	100 Vesper Executive P, Tyngsboro MA 01879	978-649-5626	R	624	4.2
4	Hamrick Mills—*W Hamrick*	PO Box 48, Gaffney SC 29342	864-489-4731	R	582*	.4
5	Culp Inc—*Franklin Saxon*	PO Box 2686, High Point NC 27261	336-889-5161	P	217	1.1
6	Copen Associates Inc—*Carin Trundle*	1 W 37th St 10th Fl, New York NY 10018	212-819-0008	R	211*	.2
7	DesignTex Inc—*Tom Hamilton*	200 Varick St 8th Fl, New York NY 10014	212-886-8100	S	164*	.2
8	Thomaston Manufacturing LLC—*Jerome M Zaslow*	135 Greenwood Ave, Wyncote PA 19095	215-576-6352	S	159*	1.6
9	Associated Textile Converters Inc—*Jeff Thomas*	15 E 26th St 7th Fl, New York NY 10010	212-532-8670	R	104*	.1
10	Crown Crafts Inc—*E Randall Chestnut*	PO Box 1028, Gonzales LA 70707	225-647-9100	P	90	.2
11	Burlington Fabrics Inc—*John Bakane*	804 Green Valley Rd St, Greensboro NC 27408	336-379-4675	D	75*	1.0
12	Greenwood Mills Inc—*James C Self III*	300 Morgan Ave, Greenwood SC 29646	864-229-2571	R	61*	.7
13	Holliston LLC—*Keith A Polak*	PO Box 478, Kingsport TN 37662	423-357-6141	R	57*	.3
14	Bloomsburg Mills Inc (Bloomsburg Pennsylvania)—*James P Marion III*	PO Box 420, Bloomsburg PA 17815	570-784-4262	R	54*	.3
15	American Fiber and Finishing Inc—*Paul Robichaud*	PO Box 2488, Albemarle NC 28002	704-983-6102	R	50*	.9
16	Polartec LLC—*Greg Segall*	46 Stafford St, Lawrence MA 01841	987-685-6341	R	49*	.8
17	Bonded Fiberloft Inc—*Mark Bidner*	2748 Tanager Ave, Commerce CA 90040	323-726-7820	R	48*	.4
18	Alice Manufacturing Company Inc—*Ellison Kissick*	PO Box 369, Easley SC 29641	864-859-6323	R	37*	.6
19	Allison Corp—*David Dennison*	15-33 Okner Pkwy, Livingston NJ 07039	973-992-3800	R	29*	.1
20	Rubin Manufacturing Inc—*David Rubin*	2241 S Halsted St, Chicago IL 60608	312-738-0222	R	29*	.3
21	Shavel Home Products—*Matty Shavel*	13 Roszel Rd, Princeton NJ 08540	609-452-1800	R	24*	<.1
22	S I Jacobson Manufacturing Co—*Larry Futterman*	1414 Jacobson Dr, Waukegan IL 60085	847-623-1414	R	23*	.2
23	Engineered Specialty Textiles LLC	25 E Ct St Ste 302, Greenville SC 29601	864-335-4004	R	16*	.2
24	A Lakhany International Inc—*Hashim Lakhany*	12011 Westbrae Pkwy, Houston TX 77031	713-266-8799	R	14*	.2
25	Homtex Inc—*Jerry Wootten*	15295 Al Hwy 157, Vinemont AL 35179	256-734-3937	R	14*	.1
26	Absecon Mills Inc—*Randolph Taylor*	PO Box 672, Cologne NJ 08213	609-965-5373	R	12*	.1
27	Vectorply Corp—*Donald Massey*	3500 Lakewood Dr, Phenix City AL 36867	334-291-7704	R	8*	.1
28	Sherman Textile Co—*Frank Ewing*	PO Box 596, Dallas NC 28034	704-922-5254	R	6*	.1
29	Northwest Co—*Ross Auerbach*	49 Bryant Ave, Roslyn NY 11576	516-484-6996	R	6*	<.1
30	Ferncrest Fashions Inc—*Steve Seaborn*	4813 Starcrest Dr, Monroe NC 28110	704-283-6422	R	6*	.1
31	Wolf Manufacturing Company Inc—*Jeffrey Wolf*	PO Box 3100, Waco TX 76707	254-753-7301	R	5*	.1
32	Dazian LLC—*Jon Weingarten*	18 Central Blvd, South Hackensack NJ 07606	201-549-1000	R	5*	<.1
33	DesignCraft Fabric Corp—*Jeffrey Weiner*	2230 Ridge Dr, Glenview IL 60025	847-904-7000	R	5*	<.1
34	Rivers West Apparel Inc—*Michael McGinley*	2900 4th Ave S, Seattle WA 98134	206-682-8574	R	5*	<.1
35	Brecon Knitting Mills Inc—*Allen Mcmillan*	PO Box 478, Talladega AL 35161	256-362-6141	R	4*	<.1
36	Advanced Textile Composites Inc—*Paul J Bocchino*	700 E Parker St, Scranton PA 18509	570-207-7000	R	4*	<.1
37	Wilcom America Inc—*Ed Harof*	PO Box 920008, Norcross GA 30010	770-409-9503	R	2*	<.1
38	KBC of America Inc	1350 Broadway Ste 1612, New York NY 10018	212-244-2955	R	1*	<.1
39	Akron Cotton Products Inc—*Michael Zwick*	437 W Cedar St, Akron OH 44307	330-434-7171	R	1*	<.1

TOTALS: SIC 2211 Broadwoven Fabric Mills—Cotton
Companies: 39   5,818   24.6

Note: An asterisk (*) indicates an estimated financial figure. The company type code used is as follows: R = Private, P = Public, S = Private Subsidiary, B = Public Subsidiary, D = Division, J = Joint Venture, I = Investment Fund.

COMPANY RANKINGS BY SALES WITHIN 4-DIGIT SIC

Rank	Company Name—Executive Officer	Address, City, State, Zip	Phone	Type	Fin	Empls
2221 Broadwoven Fabric Mills—Manmade						
1	Polymer Group Inc—Veronica Hagen	9335 Harris Corners Pk, Charlotte NC 28269	704-697-5100	S	883	3.1
2	Albany International Corp—Jospeh Morone	PO Box 1907, Albany NY 12201	518-445-2200	P	815	4.3
3	Unifi Inc—Williams Jasper	PO Box 19109, Greensboro NC 27419	336-294-4410	P	713	2.7
4	RB Pamplin Corp—Robert B Pamplin Jr	805 SW Broadway Ste 24, Portland OR 97205	503-248-1133	R	538*	4.5
5	Twitchell Corp—John Nash	PO Box 8156, Dothan AL 36304	334-792-0002	S	277*	.4
6	Keyston Brothers—Dee Duncan	2801 Academy Way Rm A, Sacramento CA 95815	916-927-5851	R	258*	.2
7	Springfield LLC—James C Tennyson	PO Box 250, Gaffney SC 29342	864-489-2513	R	192*	.3
8	Hallwood Group Inc—Anthony J Gumbiner	3710 Rawlins St Ste 15, Dallas TX 75219	214-528-5588	P	168	.5
9	Propex Inc—Joseph F Dana	6025 Lee Highway Ste 4, Chattanooga TN 37421	423-855-1466	R	116*	.2
10	Poly-Pak Industries Inc—Peter Levy	125 Spagnoli Rd, Melville NY 11747	631-293-6767	R	103*	.4
11	Microfibres Inc—James Mcculloch	PO Box 1208, Pawtucket RI 02862	401-725-4883	R	76*	1.1
12	Owens Corning Solutions Group—Michael H Thaman	303 Hurstbourne Pkwy, Louisville KY 40222	502-394-5800	D	53*	<.1
13	Texollini Inc—Danial Kadisha	2575 El Presidio St, Carson CA 90810	310-537-3400	R	48*	.3
14	Guilford Fibers—Shannon White	1001 Militwary Cutoff, Wilmington NC 28405	910-794-5800	S	46*	.4
15	Belding Hausman Inc—BillD Morton	2130 E Main St, Lincolnton NC 28092	704-735-2581	R	44*	.6
16	Highland Industries Inc—David Jackson	629 Green Valley Rd St, Greensboro NC 27408	336-547-1600	S	39*	.6
17	Southern Mills Inc—Donald Olsen	PO Box 289, Union City GA 30291	770-969-1000	S	38*	.5
18	Seaman Corp—Richard Seaman	1000 Venture Blvd, Wooster OH 44691	330-262-1111	R	37*	.3
19	Charles D Owen Manufacturing Co—Charles Owen	PO Box 457, Swannanoa NC 28778	828-298-6802	R	37*	.7
20	Biederlack Of America Corp—Richard Alford	11501 Bedford Rd Ne, Cumberland MD 21502	301-759-3633	R	37*	.4
21	Carole Fabrics Corp—W 'bill' Geiger	PO Box 1436, Augusta GA 30903	706-863-4742	R	29*	.5
22	Carthage Fabrics Corp—Phil Landau	PO Box 1573, Port Chester NY 10573	910-947-2211	R	24*	.2
23	Dewitt Company Inc—Larry Dewitt	905 S Kingshighway St, Sikeston MO 63801	573-472-0048	R	21*	.1
24	Rose America Corp—Regina Hanna	3100 S Meridian Ave, Wichita KS 67217	316-941-1100	R	20*	.4
25	Julius Koch USA Inc—Lewis M Coco	387 Church St, New Bedford MA 02745		R	18*	.2
26	Kings Plush Inc—John Kay	PO Box 398, Kings Mountain NC 28086	704-739-4503	R	17*	.2
27	Albany International Corp (Menasha Wisconsin) Albany International Corp	435 6th St, Menasha WI 54952	920-725-2600	D	17*	.2
28	Dsm Dyneema LLC—Edward Sheu	PO Box 1887, Greenville NC 27835	252-758-3436	R	16*	.2
29	Bloomsburg Mills Inc—James Marion	1065 Av Of The Amrcs F, New York NY 10018	212-221-6114	R	16*	.3
30	Superior Glass Fibers Inc—David Miller	PO Box 89, Bremen OH 43107	740-569-4175	R	15*	.2
31	Stern and Stern Industries Inc—Peter Thornton	188 Thacher St, Hornell NY 14843	212-972-4040	R	14*	.1
32	Juniata Fabrics Inc—Terry Wray	PO Box 1806, Altoona PA 16603	814-944-9381	R	12*	.1
33	Thibaut Inc—Bob Senior	480 Frelinghuysen Ave, Newark NJ 07114	973-643-1118	S	10*	.1
34	Nordic Fiberglass Inc—Susan Haugen	PO Box 27, Warren MN 56762	218-745-5095	R	10*	.1
35	American Technical Solutions Inc—Robert Sandee	PO Box 10, Walkertown NC 27051	336-595-2763	R	9*	.1
36	Shuford Mills LLC—Stephen Shuford	PO Box 2228, Hickory NC 28603	828-328-2131	S	9*	.1
37	Lamar International Inc—Frederick Burnett	2903 Governors Dr Sw, Huntsville AL 35805	256-533-5375	R	8*	.1
38	Wayne Mills Company Inc—Martin Heilman	130 W Berkley St, Philadelphia PA 19144	215-842-2134	R	8*	.1
39	Thrace-Linq Inc—Scott Womack	2550 W 5lh N St, Summerville SC 29483	843-873-5000	R	7*	.1
40	Valdese Textiles Inc—Yasmine Safadi	PO Box 490, Valdese NC 28690	828-874-4216	R	7*	.1
41	Premier Quilting Corp—Robert Katen	720 W Industry Dr, Oxford NC 27565	919-693-1151	R	5*	.1
42	Cramer Fabrics Inc—Hans Cramer	20 Venture Dr, Dover NH 03820	603-742-3838	R	5*	<.1
43	D and T Fiberglass Inc—Donald Stommel	PO Box 293330, Sacramento CA 95829	916-383-9012	R	5*	<.1
44	Steele Plastics Inc—Robert Steele	PO Box 1076, Conway AR 72033	501-327-5122	R	4*	<.1
45	Burlington House Upholstery—Ken Kunverger	PO Box 21207, Greensboro NC 27420	336-379-6220	D	3	<.1
46	J Robert Scott Textiles Inc—Sally Sirkin Lewis	500 N Oak St, Inglewood CA 90302	310-659-4300	D	2*	<.1
47	Glassline Inc—Guy Kenny	199 W Ann Arbor Trl, Plymouth MI 48170	734-453-2728	R	1*	<.1
48	Florida SpA Covers and Vinyl Specialties Inc—Cathy Jones	PO Box 34, Hayesville NC 28904	727-535-8282	R	1*	<.1
49	Alex Silk Company Inc—John Hryncewich	53 Braen Ave, Hawthorne NJ 07506	973-427-0499	R	1*	<.1

TOTALS: SIC 2221 Broadwoven Fabric Mills—Manmade
Companies: 49   4,830 24.7

Rank	Company Name—Executive Officer	Address, City, State, Zip	Phone	Type	Fin	Empls
2231 Broadwoven Fabric Mills—Wool						
1	Haartz Corp—John Fox	87 Hayward Rd, Acton MA 01720	978-264-2600	R	209*	.4
2	American Woolen Company Inc—Richard Marcus	PO Box 521399, Miami FL 33152	305-635-4000	R	100*	1.5
3	Cannon County Knitting Mills Inc—Stanley Kaskel	237 Castlewood Dr Ste, Murfreesboro TN 37129	615-890-2938	R	35*	1.5
4	Swan Finishing Company Inc—Pat Guerriero	372 Stevens St, Fall River MA 02721	508-674-4611	R	23*	.2
5	National Nonwovens Inc—Anthony Centofanti	PO Box 150, Easthampton MA 01027	413-527-3445	R	22*	.2
6	Town House Home Furnishings LLC—Sendy Maiers	PO Box 360, Smithville MS 38870	662-651-5441	R	18*	.1
7	Lantal Textiles Inc—Scott Walker	PO Box 965, Rural Hall NC 27045	336-969-9551	R	15*	.2
8	Voith Fabrics Waycross Sales Inc—Kevin Frank	2500 Scapa Rd, Waycross GA 31503	912-490-4000	R	12*	.2
9	Voith Fabrics Florence Inc—David Barefield	220 Price St, Florence MS 39073	601-845-2202	R	9*	.1
10	Orr Felt Co—Dimitri Nicholas	PO Box 908, Piqua OH 45356	937-773-0551	R	6*	.1
11	Premier Yarn Dyers Inc—Edward Jones	128 George St, Adairsville GA 30103	770-773-3695	R	4*	<.1
12	Radon Inc—Ramona Whipps	1111 4th Ave Nw, New Prague MN 56071	952-758-5155	R	1*	<.1

TOTALS: SIC 2231 Broadwoven Fabric Mills—Wool
Companies: 12   455 4.4

Rank	Company Name—Executive Officer	Address, City, State, Zip	Phone	Type	Fin	Empls
2241 Narrow Fabric Mills						
1	Worldtex—Stewart Little	PO Box 2189, Hickory NC 28603	828-322-2242	R	487*	1.4
2	Narrow Fabrics of America Corp—Ronald Casty	850 Boylston St Ste 42, Chestnut Hill MA 02467	617-232-6060	R	113*	1.0
3	Tape-Craft Corp—Scott Najasaki	200 Tape Craft Dr, Oxford AL 36203	256-236-2535	S	39*	.4
4	S-Line—Jerry Squyres	PO Box 59509, Dallas TX 75229	972-402-9000	R	39*	.1
5	Bacova Guild Ltd—Charlie Bowers	1000 Commerce Ctr Dr, Covington VA 24426	540-863-2600	S	36*	.4
6	Bally Ribbon Mills—Raymond Harries	PO Box D, Bally PA 19503	610-845-2211	R	34*	.3
7	United Elastic Corp Stuart Div	201 S Main St, Stuart VA 24171	276-694-7171	S	30*	.3
8	Labeltex Mills Inc—Torag Pourshamtobi	6100 Wilmington Ave, Los Angeles CA 90001	323-582-0228	R	23*	.2
9	Murdock Webbing Company Inc—Craig Pilgrim	27 Foundry St, Central Falls RI 02863	401-724-3000	R	20*	.2
10	Narrow Fabric Industries Corp—Charles Miller	701 Reading Ave, Reading PA 19611	610-376-2891	R	19*	.2
11	Hofmann and Leavy Inc—Roger Leavy	3251 Sw 13th Dr Ste 3, Deerfield Beach FL 33442	954-698-0000	R	17*	.2
12	Southern Weaving Co—Rodney Grandy	PO Box 487, Greenville SC 29602	864-233-1635	R	17*	.3
13	Ribbon Webbing Corp—Jae Chang	4711 W Division St, Chicago IL 60651	773-287-1221	R	15*	.1
14	Carolina Narrow Fabric Co—Horace Freeman	PO Box 1485, Winston Salem NC 27102	336-631-3000	R	13*	.1
15	Mitchellace Inc—Steven Keating	PO Box 89, Portsmouth OH 45662	740-354-2813	R	13*	.1
16	Conrad-Jarvis Corp—William Jarvis	PO Box 878, Pawtucket RI 02862	401-722-8700	R	11*	.1
17	North East Knitting Inc—Rosalie Darosa	PO Box 7247, Cumberland RI 02864	401-727-0500	R	11*	.1
18	Newtex Industries Inc—Jerome Joliet	8050 Victor Mendon Rd, Victor NY 14564	585-924-9135	R	10*	.1

Rank	Company Name—*Executive Officer*	Address, City, State, Zip	Phone	Type	Fin	Empls
19	Pittsfield Weaving Co—*Gilbert Bleckmann*	PO Box 8, Pittsfield NH 03263	603-435-8301	R	9*	.1
20	RVL Packaging Inc—*Kim MacAulay*	31330 Oak Crest Dr, Westlake Village CA 91361	818-735-5000	S	8*	.1
21	Universal Strap Inc—*Thomas Johnson*	W209n17500 Industrial, Jackson WI 53037	262-677-3641	R	8*	.1
22	Mcmichael Mills Inc—*Daltnel Mcmichael*	PO Box 126, Elon College NC 27244	336-584-0134	R	7*	.1
23	Sturges Manufacturing Company Inc—*Richard Griffith*	PO Box 59, Utica NY 13503	315-732-6159	R	7*	.1
24	Hickory Brands Inc—*Nisson Joseph*	PO Box 429, Hickory NC 28603	828-322-2600	R	7*	.1
25	Bechik Products Inc—*Bill Simon*	1020 Discovery Rd Ste, Eagan MN 55121	651-698-0364	R	6*	<.1
26	Jrm Industries Inc—*Lou Simon*	1 Mattimore St, Passaic NJ 07055	973-779-9340	R	6*	.1
27	Bell Manufacturing Co—*Tom Seder*	777 Main St, Lewiston ME 04240	207-784-2961	R	5*	.1
28	Snapco Manufacturing Corp—*Jeffrey Spitz*	140 Central Ave Ste 1, Hillside NJ 07205	973-282-0300	R	3*	<.1
29	Massasoit/Tackband Inc—*Samuel Rickless*	118 Dulong Cir, Chicopee MA 01022	413-593-6731	R	2*	<.1
30	Darlington Fabrics Corp—*Leonard Rautenberg*	1407 Broadway Ste 1220, New York NY 10018	212-938-1054	S	2*	<.1
31	Ramsay Fabrics Inc—*John Shulman*	570 7th Ave Ste 1200, New York NY 10018	212-944-4826	R	2*	<.1
32	Trims—*Perrin Weschler*	720 Sheridan Dr Ste C, Easton PA 18045	610-559-7700	R	1*	<.1

TOTALS: SIC 2241 Narrow Fabric Mills
Companies: 32   1,020   6.4

2251 Women's Hosiery Except Socks

Rank	Company Name—*Executive Officer*	Address, City, State, Zip	Phone	Type	Fin	Empls
1	Hampshire Group Ltd—*Heath Golden*	114 W 41st St, New York NY 10036	212-840-5666	P	135	.2
2	GoldToeMoretz LLC	7110 E Washington St S, Mebane NC 27302	919-563-0233	R	116*	.6
3	Bossong Hosiery Mills Inc—*F Bossong*	PO Box 789, Asheboro NC 27204	336-625-2175	R	28*	.3
4	Slane Hosiery Mills Inc—*Jim Cobb*	PO Box 2486, High Point NC 27261	336-883-4136	R	26*	.2
5	Star America Inc—*Harry Hemphill*	PO Box 1501, Concord NC 28026	704-788-4700	R	20*	.2
6	Hci Direct Inc—*Jean Vernor*	1150 Northbrook Dr Ste, Trevose PA 19053	215-494-2900	R	16*	.3
7	Lemco Mills Inc—*Chester Mayer*	PO Box 2098, Burlington NC 27216	336-226-5548	R	15*	.2
8	USA Knit Inc—*Patrick Smith*	PO Box 680196, Fort Payne AL 35968	256-845-6456	R	11*	.1
9	Central Carolina Hosiery Inc—*Serge Babayan*	211 Shady Oak Dr, Biscoe NC 27209	910-428-9688	R	6*	.1
10	Highland Mills Inc—*Samuel Kaplan*	PO Box 33775, Charlotte NC 28233	704-375-3333	R	6*	.1
11	Sue-Lynn Textiles Inc—*Thurman Oakley*	PO Box 939, Haw River NC 27258	336-578-0871	R	3*	.1
12	American Essentials Inc—*Jordon Lipson*	358 5th Ave 2nd Fl, New York NY 10001	212-695-7025	R	1*	<.1

TOTALS: SIC 2251 Women's Hosiery Except Socks
Companies: 12   382   2.3

2252 Hosiery Nec

Rank	Company Name—*Executive Officer*	Address, City, State, Zip	Phone	Type	Fin	Empls
1	Royce Hosiery Mills Inc—*Steven J Lowenthal*	350 5th Ave Ste 300, New York NY 10118	212-695-5113	R	355*	.3
2	Kayser-Roth Corp—*Kevin Toomey*	PO Box 26530, Greensboro NC 27415		R	160*	2.2
3	Carolina Hosiery Mills Inc—*Maurice Koury*	PO Box 850, Burlington NC 27216	336-226-5581	R	128*	.3
4	Cooper Hosiery Mills Inc—*Mack Cooper*	PO Box 680909, Fort Payne AL 35968	256-845-1491	R	81*	1.0
5	Twin City Knitting Company Inc—*Francis Davis*	PO Box 1179, Conover NC 28613	828-464-4830	R	36*	.2
6	ThorLo Inc—*James Throneburg*	PO Box 5399, Statesville NC 28687	704-872-6522	R	32*	.3
7	Crescent Inc—*Sandra Boyd*	PO Box 669, Niota TN 37826	423-568-2101	R	26*	.3
8	Harriss and Covington International Inc—*Edward Covington*	PO Box 1909, High Point NC 27261	336-882-6811	R	26*	.2
9	Lea-Wayne Knitting Mills Inc—*Butch Ratcliff*	5937 Commerce Blvd, Morristown TN 37814	423 586 7513	R	20*	.2
10	Cricket Hosiery Inc—*Vic Mulaire*	1341 Railroad Ave, Bridgeport CT 06605	203-336-4901	R	17*	<.1
11	Robin Lynn Mills Inc—*R Chisenhall*	PO Box 680647, Fort Payne AL 35968	256-845-4910	R	17*	.2
12	Johnson Hosiery Mills Inc—*Charles Johnson*	3395 Young Ave Ne, Fort Payne AL 35967	256-845-1560	R	16*	.4
13	Fox River Mills Inc—*John Lessard*	PO Box 298, Osage IA 50461	641-732-3798	R	14*	.3
14	Valley Mills Inc—*Robert Cooper*	PO Box 282, Valley Head AL 35989	256-635-6211	R	14*	.1
15	Parker Hosiery Company Inc—*Edgar Parker*	PO Box 699, Old Fort NC 28762	828-668-7628	R	13*	.2
16	Cherokee Hosiery Mills Inc—*Bobby Cold*	PO Box 680708, Fort Payne AL 35968	256-845-0004	R	13*	.2
17	Catawba Sox LLC—*Ron Bowman*	PO Box 517, Conover NC 28613	828-464-1690	R	13*	.1
18	For Bare Feet Inc—*Sharon Rivenbark*	PO Box 159, Helmsburg IN 47435	812-988-6674	R	13*	.1
19	W Y Shugart and Sons Inc—*Jonathan Shugart*	PO Box 680289, Fort Payne AL 35968	256-845-1251	R	12*	.1
20	Pickett Hosiery Mills Inc—*J Harris*	PO Box 877, Burlington NC 27216	336-227-2716	R	12*	.1
21	Huffman Finishing Company Inc—*A Huffman*	PO Box 170, Granite Falls NC 28630	828-396-1741	R	12*	.3
22	Mayo Knitting Mill Inc—*Ben Mayo*	PO Box 160, Tarboro NC 27886	252-823-3101	R	9*	.1
23	Ben Mar Inc—*Eddy Everett*	4313 Williams Ave Ne, Fort Payne AL 35967	256-845-6218	R	9*	.2
24	Crawford Knitting Company Inc—*John Mccuiston*	PO Box 1360, Ramseur NC 27316	336-824-1065	R	8*	.1
25	Baker Hosiery Inc—*James Baker*	PO Box 680649, Fort Payne AL 35968	256-845-3019	R	7*	.1
26	Trimfit Inc—*Arnold Kramer Jr*	1900 Frost Rd Ste 111, Bristol PA 19007	215-781-0600	R	5*	.1
27	C and M Mills Inc—*Howard Cohn*	2315 Homewood Ave, Baltimore MD 21218	410-366-8800	R	5*	.1
28	Elder Hosiery Mills Inc—*Delos Elder*	PO Box 2377, Burlington NC 27216	336-226-2229	R	4*	.1
29	Burke Hosiery Mills Inc—*David Dale*	PO Box 368, Hildebran NC 28637	828-328-1725	R	4*	.1
30	Robinson Hosiery Mill Inc—*Kenneth Robinson*	PO Box 730, Valdese NC 28690	828-874-2228	R	3*	.1

TOTALS: SIC 2252 Hosiery Nec
Companies: 30   1,080   7.8

2253 Knit Outerwear Mills

Rank	Company Name—*Executive Officer*	Address, City, State, Zip	Phone	Type	Fin	Empls
1	Russell Corp—*John F Ward*	3330 Cumberland Blvd S, Atlanta GA 30339	678-742-8000	S	1,435	15.5
2	Russell Financial Services Inc—*John F Ward* Russell Corp	3300 Cumberland Blvd S, Atlanta GA 30339	678-742-8000	S	1,110*	1.4
3	Anvil Holdings Inc—*Anthony Corsano*	228 E 45th St, New York NY 10017	212-476-0300	R	180*	3.7
4	Vf Imagewear Inc (Martinsville Virginia)—*George Derhofer*	3375 Joseph Martin Hwy, Martinsville VA 24112	276-956-7200	R	179*	4.2
5	Passport Brands Inc—*Robert Stephen Stec*	252 W 37th St, New York NY 10018	646-459-2600	P	37	.1
6	Knitcraft Corp—*Bernhard Brenner*	4020 W 6th St, Winona MN 55987	507-454-1163	R	31*	.3
7	Skip's Cutting Inc—*Daniel Miller*	55 New St Ste 15, Ephrata PA 17522	717-354-4370	R	30*	.4
8	Paris Accessories Inc—*Peter Markson*	1385 Broadway Fl 21, New York NY 10018	212-868-0500	R	27*	.4
9	Contempora Fabrics Inc—*Brent Bass*	351 Contempora Dr, Lumberton NC 28358	910-738-7131	R	16*	.2
10	Textile Piece Dyeing Company Inc—*Dan Doherr*	PO Box 370, Lincolnton NC 28093	704-732-4200	R	15*	.1
11	Reliable Of Milwaukee—*Mark Blutstein*	PO Box 563, Milwaukee WI 53201	414-272-5084	R	14*	.1
12	Volunteer Knit Apparel Inc—*Gary West*	403 Old Knoxville Hwy, New Tazewell TN 37825	423-626-8000	R	12*	.2
13	Quake City Casuals Inc—*John Glucksman*	1800 S Flower St, Los Angeles CA 90015	213-746-0540	R	12*	.1
14	High Sierra Sport Co—*Harry Bernbaum*	880 Corporate Woods Pk, Vernon Hills IL 60061		R	9*	<.1
15	Delta Pacific Activewear Inc—*Imran Parekh*	1301 E Wilshire Ave St, Santa Ana CA 92705	714-541-6747	R	8*	.1
16	Artex Knitting Mills Inc—*Arthur Pottash*	PO Box 183, Westville NJ 08093	856-456-2800	R	7*	.1
17	Jacques Moret Inc	1411 Broadway 8th Fl, New York NY 10018	212-354-2400	R	7*	.1
18	Charlotte Trimming Company Inc—*Antonio Ibanez*	900 Pressley Rd, Charlotte NC 28217	704-527-3435	R	6*	.1
19	Park Shirt Co—*Rajan Shamdasani*	422 Industrial Dr, Jamestown TN 38556	931-879-5894	R	6*	.1
20	Project E—*Mike Hecht*	743 Lambert Dr NE, Atlanta GA 30324	404-347-9393	R	4*	<.1

Note: An asterisk (*) indicates an estimated financial figure. The company type code used is as follows: R = Private, P = Public, S = Private Subsidiary, B = Public Subsidiary, D = Division, J = Joint Venture, I = Investment Fund.

COMPANY RANKINGS BY SALES WITHIN 4-DIGIT SIC

Rank	Company Name—Executive Officer	Address, City, State, Zip	Phone	Type	Fin	Empls
21	Michael Simon Inc—Michael Simon	250 W 39th St Ste 202, New York NY 10018	212-382-1910	R	2*	<.1
22	Columbiaknit Inc—Jakob Kryszek	5200 Se Harney Dr, Portland OR 97206	503-774-2008	R	1*	<.1
23	Marble Knits Inc—Kalman Sinay	544 Park Ave Ste 3, Brooklyn NY 11205	718-237-7990	R	1*	<.1
24	Russell Servicing Company Inc—John F Ward Russell Corp	755 Lee St, Alexander City AL 35010	256-500-4000	S	N/A	14.4

TOTALS: SIC 2253 Knit Outerwear Mills
Companies: 24 — 3,150 — 41.6

2254 Knit Underwear Mills

Rank	Company Name—Executive Officer	Address, City, State, Zip	Phone	Type	Fin	Empls
1	Fruit of the Loom Inc—John B Holland	1 Fruit of the Loom Dr, Bowling Green KY 42103	270-781-6406	S	1,841	9.4
2	Jockey International Inc—Debra Waller	PO Box 1417, Kenosha WI 53141	262-658-8111	R	550*	5.0
3	Alpha Mills Corp—Richard Biever	122 S Margaretta St, Schuylkill Haven PA 17972	570-385-0511	R	18*	.2
4	Cressona Knit Products Inc—Bernard Wise	PO Box 68, Bernville PA 19506	570-385-3301	R	17*	.2
5	Rubens and Marble Inc—Richard Rubens	2340 N Racine Ave, Chicago IL 60614	847-256-1149	R	7*	.1

TOTALS: SIC 2254 Knit Underwear Mills
Companies: 5 — 2,433 — 14.9

2257 Weft Knit Fabric Mills

Rank	Company Name—Executive Officer	Address, City, State, Zip	Phone	Type	Fin	Empls
1	Engine Textiles—James Kim	12537 Cerise Ave, Hawthorne CA 90250	310-644-4001	R	59*	.4
2	McMurray Fabrics Inc—Brian L McMurray	PO Box 67, Aberdeen NC 28315	910-944-2128	R	45*	.3
3	Alamac American Knits LLC—Mark Cabral	PO Box 1347, Lumberton NC 28359	910-618-2200	R	26*	.2
4	Mohican Mills Inc—Steve Myers	PO Box 190, Lincolnton NC 28093	704-735-3343	S	21*	.2
5	United Knitting Limited Partnership I—Jean Headrick	310 Industrial Dr Sw, Cleveland TN 37311	423-476-9163	R	21*	.1
6	Siny Corp—Daniel Sinykin	PO Box 271, Janesville WI 53547	608-754-2866	R	17*	.1
7	Tenenblatt Corp—William Tenenblatt	3750 Broadway Pl, Los Angeles CA 90007	323-232-2061	R	16*	.3
8	Adele Knits Inc—Bruce Brown	3304 Old Lexington Rd, Winston Salem NC 27107	336-784-2111	R	14*	.2
9	Mocaro Dyeing and Finishing Inc—T Spell	PO Box 6689, Statesville NC 28687	704-878-6645	R	10*	.1
10	Mocaro Industries Inc—T Spell	PO Box 6689, Statesville NC 28687	704-878-6645	R	6*	.1
11	South Fork Industries Inc—Fred Poovey	PO Box 1220, Lincolnton NC 28093	704-732-6946	R	4*	.1
12	Accent Fabrics Inc—Charles Hall	PO Box 1506, Lumberton NC 28359	910-739-8115	R	3*	<.1

TOTALS: SIC 2257 Weft Knit Fabric Mills
Companies: 12 — 242 — 2.0

2258 Lace & Warp Knit Fabric Mills

Rank	Company Name—Executive Officer	Address, City, State, Zip	Phone	Type	Fin	Empls
1	Guilford Mills Inc—Cy Alexander	6001 W Market St, Greensboro NC 27409	336-316-4000	S	446	2.6
2	GFD Services Inc—David Thursfield Guilford Mills Inc	4925 W Market St, Greensboro NC 27407	336-316-4000	S	436*	2.0
3	Elastic Fabrics of America Inc—James F Robbins	PO Box 21986, Greensboro NC 27420	336-378-2677	D	153*	.2
4	Milco Industries Inc—Norman Belmonte	149 Madison Ave 10th F, New York NY 10016	212-683-0826	R	67*	.6
5	FAB Industries Corp—Steve Myers	98 Cutter Mill Rd Ste, Great Neck NY 11021	516-498-3200	R	50*	.5
6	Guilford Mills Michigan Inc—Shannon White Guilford Mills Inc	1001 Military Cut Off, Wilmington NC 28405	910-794-5800	S	44*	.2
7	Hornwood Inc—Charles Horne	766 Haileys Ferry Rd, Lilesville NC 28091	704-848-4121	R	41*	.4
8	Gold Mills Inc—Shannon White Guilford Mills Inc	141 N Wideawake St, Pine Grove PA 17963	570-345-2611	S	37*	.3
9	Klauber Brothers Inc—Roger Klauber	980 Ave of the America, New York NY 10018	212-686-2531	R	10*	.1
10	Lace Lastics Company Inc—Bruce Heerema	PO Box 508, Oxford NC 27565	919-693-2100	R	9*	.1
11	Carolina Cotton Works Inc—Page Ashby	14 Commerce Dr, Gaffney SC 29340	864-488-2824	R	8*	.1
12	Gehring Textiles Inc—G Gehring	1225 Franklin Ave Ste, Garden City NY 11530	516-747-4555	R	2*	<.1

TOTALS: SIC 2258 Lace & Warp Knit Fabric Mills
Companies: 12 — 1,304 — 7.0

2259 Knitting Mills Nec

Rank	Company Name—Executive Officer	Address, City, State, Zip	Phone	Type	Fin	Empls
1	Inventec Manufacturing (North America) Corp—Richard Lee	6215 W By NW Blvd B, Houston TX 77040	713-996-5200	R	22*	.3
2	Shelby Elastics Of North Carolina LLC—Nathan Bowden	PO Box 2405, Shelby NC 28151	704-487-4301	R	4*	.1

TOTALS: SIC 2259 Knitting Mills Nec
Companies: 2 — 26 — .3

2261 Finishing Plants—Cotton

Rank	Company Name—Executive Officer	Address, City, State, Zip	Phone	Type	Fin	Empls
1	Burlington House Div—Joseph L Gorga	804 Green Valley Rd St, Greensboro NC 27408	336-379-6220	D	120	.6
2	Namifiers Lanyards and Name Tags—Bryan Welton	280 W 900 N, Springville UT 84663	801-491-8068	R	100*	.1
3	Cranston Print Works Co—George Shuster	1381 Cranston St, Cranston RI 02920	401-943-4800	R	86*	.4
4	Santee Print Works—Martin Barocas	PO Box 340, Sumter SC 29151	803-773-1461	R	68*	1.1
5	American Textile Co—Jack Ouellette	10 N Linden St, Duquesne PA 15110	412-948-1020	R	33*	.2
6	Yates Bleachery Co—P Yates	PO Box 800, Flintstone GA 30725	706-820-1531	R	32*	.3
7	Pisgah Yarn And Dyeing Company Inc—Juanita Lonon	PO Box 606, Old Fort NC 28762	828-668-7667	R	30*	.1
8	Duro Textiles LLC—Patriarch Partners	110 Chace St, Fall River MA 02724	508-675-0101	R	30*	.2
9	Caitac Garment Processing Inc—Muneyuki Ishii	14725 S Broadway, Gardena CA 90248	310-217-9888	R	29*	.5
10	Fabricut Inc—David Finer	9303 E 46th St, Tulsa OK 74145	918-622-7700	R	28*	.4
11	Rockland Industries Inc—Mark Berman	PO Box 17293, Baltimore MD 21297	410-522-2505	R	27*	.5
12	Central Textiles Inc—James Kinnon	PO Box 68, Central SC 29630	864-639-2491	R	27*	.2
13	Crystal Springs Print Works Inc—Thomas Tarvin	PO Box 750, Chickamauga GA 30707	706-375-2125	R	24*	.2
14	Timeline Inc—Verne Holoubek	W238n1800 Rockwood Dr, Waukesha WI 53188	262-547-0500	R	17*	.2
15	Sherry Manufacturing Company Inc—Quentin Sandler	PO Box 470550, Miami FL 33247	305-693-7000	R	15*	.2
16	Denim Processing Inc—James West	PO Box 4450, Oneida TN 37841	423-569-9100	R	12*	.4
17	Screenworks USA Inc—Sharad Mehta	2234 Taft Vineland Rd, Orlando FL 32837	407-245-3600	R	12*	.1
18	A Usdf California Corp—Robert Lee	12641 Industry St, Garden Grove CA 92841	714-891-8234	R	11*	.1
19	Liquid Blue Inc—Paul Roidoulis	1 Crownmark Dr, Lincoln RI 02865	401-333-6200	R	10*	.1
20	Back Alley Printers Inc—Jeff Swartzendruber	PO Box 657, Waterloo IA 50704	319-234-3109	R	8*	<.1
21	Cutting Edge Texstyles LLC—Bob Cosgrove	PO Box 249, Bedford MA 01730	781-271-0000	R	7*	.1
22	Specialty Shearing and Dyeing Inc—James Gaino	PO Box 2087, Greenville SC 29602	864-233-1255	R	6*	<.1
23	JC Viramontes Inc—J Viramontes	PO Box 9777, El Paso TX 79995	915-857-4545	R	5*	<.1
24	Nuance Industries Inc—Sammy Namroody	212 W 35th St Ste 64, New York NY 10001	212-695-8060	R	4*	<.1
25	Textile Graphics Inc—Jeff Chapman	3138 NE Rivergate St S, McMinnville OR 97128	503-472-1493	R	2*	<.1
26	Silver Screen Design Inc—Cheryl Termo	324 Wells St, Greenfield MA 01301	413-773-1692	R	2*	<.1
27	Amalgamated Culture Work Inc—Wayne Turiansky	420 Pine St, Burlington VT 05401	802-864-7630	R	1*	<.1

TOTALS: SIC 2261 Finishing Plants—Cotton
Companies: 27 — 745 — 6.1

Rank	Company Name—*Executive Officer*	Address, City, State, Zip	Phone	Type	Fin	Empls
2262 Finishing Plants—Manmade						
1	Raxon Fabrics Corp—*Ruud Averson*	261 5th Ave Rm 501, New York NY 10016	212-532-6816	R	62*	.1
2	Pageland Screen Printers Inc—*Robert Neal*	PO Box 339, Pageland SC 29728	843-672-6123	R	18*	.1
3	Peace Textile America Inc—*Chang Bae*	PO Box 1148, Sumter SC 29151	803-773-2177	R	13*	.1
4	Tex Flock Inc—*Edward Abramek*	200 Founders Dr, Woonsocket RI 02895	401-765-2340	R	10*	<.1
5	Customs Screens Inc—*John Mcmichael*	2216 Us Hwy 311, Madison NC 27025	336-427-0265	R	7*	.1
6	Reid and Clark Screen Arts Co—*Alejandro Melero*	722 33rd St, San Diego CA 92102	619-233-7541	R	1*	<.1
TOTALS: SIC 2262 Finishing Plants—Manmade						
	Companies: 6				**111**	**.4**
2269 Finishing Plants Nec						
1	Franco Manufacturing Company Inc—*Louis Franco*	555 Prospect St, Metuchen NJ 08840	732-494-0500	R	230*	.8
2	Chris Stone and Associates—*Mark Aizawa*	PO Box 58606, Vernon CA 90058	323-583-9857	R	214*	.3
3	Ronile Inc—*Phillip Essig*	PO Box 1059, Rocky Mount VA 24151	540-483-0261	R	199*	1.4
4	Meridian Industries Inc—*Robert Matz*	735 North water Street, Milwaukee WI 53202	414-224-0610	R	161*	1.1
5	Matchmaster Dyeing and Finishing Inc—*William Tenenblatt*	3700 S Broadway, Los Angeles CA 90007	323-233-4281	R	23*	.4
6	Brittany Dyeing And Printing Corp—*Kenneth Joblon*	PO Box 3106, New Bedford MA 02741	508-999-3281	R	18*	.2
7	Color Spectrum Inc—*James Crane*	PO Box 1207, La Fayette GA 30728	706-638-4878	R	14*	.2
8	Berkshire Corp—*Whitmore Kelley*	21 River St, Gt Barrington MA 01230	413-528-2602	R	9*	.1
9	India Ink—*Richard Benaron*	2457 E 27th St, Los Angeles CA 90058	323-589-6471	R	7*	.1
10	Wolfe Dye And Bleach Works Inc—*Andrew Wolfe*	25 Ridge Rd, Shoemakersville PA 19555	610-562-7639	R	5*	<.1
11	Austin Horn Collection—*Arthur Rosenstein*	2331 Tubeway Ave, Los Angeles CA 90040	323-838-7808	R	5*	<.1
12	Almore Dye House Inc—*Jeffery Teichner*	6850 Tujunga Ave, North Hollywood CA 91605	818-506-5444	R	4*	<.1
13	Rezex Corp—*Shahrzad Rezai*	1901 Sacramento St, Los Angeles CA 90021	213-622-2015	R	4*	<.1
14	ArcticShield Inc—*JT Griffin*	1700 W Albany St Ste A, Broken Arrow OK 74012	918-258-8788	R	2*	<.1
15	Consolidated Jet Printers Inc—*Mark Ladley*	2115 Radcliffe Ave, Charlotte NC 28207	704-375-1920	R	2*	<.1
TOTALS: SIC 2269 Finishing Plants Nec						
	Companies: 15				**897**	**4.5**
2273 Carpets & Rugs						
1	Mohawk Industries Inc—*Jeffrey S Lorberbaum*	PO Box 12069, Calhoun GA 30703	706-629-7721	P	5,642	26.2
2	Shaw Industries Group Inc—*Vance Bell*	PO Drawer 2128, Dalton GA 30722	706-278-3812	S	4,000*	25.0
3	Bentley Prince Street Inc—*Anthony Minite* Interface Inc	14641 Don Julian Rd, City of Industry CA 91746	626-333-4585	S	2,046*	.7
4	Beaulieu of America LLC—*Carl M Bouckaert*	PO Box 1248, Dalton GA 30722	706-876-2900	R	1,179*	7.5
5	Interface Inc—*Daniel T Hendrix*	2859 Paces Ferry Rd St, Atlanta GA 30339	770-437-6800	P	1,057	3.6
6	Dixie Group Inc—*Daniel K Frierson*	104 Nowlin Ln Ste 101, Chattanooga TN 37421	423-510-7000	P	231	1.2
7	Mountville Mills Inc—*David Hart*	1729 S Davis Rd, Lagrange GA 30241	706-882-2961	R	169*	.5
8	The New Patcraft and Designweave—*Robert Chandler* Shaw Industries Group Inc	PO Box 2128, Dalton GA 30722	706-517-7700	S	117*	.2
9	Atlas Carpet Mills Inc—*James Horwich*	2200 Saybrook Ave, Los Angeles CA 90040	323-724-9000	R	116*	.3
10	Magee Rieter Automotive Systems—*Harry M Katerman*	480 W 6th St, Bloomsburg PA 17815	570-784-4100	J	100*	.7
11	Tandus Flooring Inc—*Glen Hussmann*	311 Smith Industrial B, Dalton GA 30721	706-259-9711	R	99*	1.6
12	Maples Industries Inc—*John Maples*	PO Box 40, Scottsboro AL 35768	256-259-1327	R	92*	1.5
13	Masland Carpets Inc—*Kenneth L Dempsey* Dixie Group Inc	PO Box 11467, Mobile AL 36671	251-675-9080	S	86	.6
14	Newmark Rug Co—*Hill Eaton* Mohawk Industries Inc	PO Box 3637, Dalton GA 30719	706-278-8661	S	55*	.3
15	Royalty Carpet Mills Inc—*Mike Derderian*	17111 Red Hill Ave, Irvine CA 92614	949-474-4000	R	54*	.8
16	InterfaceFLOR LLC Interface Inc	PO Box 1503, LaGrange GA 30241	706-882-1891	S	50*	.8
17	Abbyson Corp	20701 Nordhoff St, Chatsworth CA 91311	818-534-3400	R	42*	.1
18	Brumlow Mills Inc—*Mitchell Brumlow*	PO Box 1779, Calhoun GA 30703	706-625-4428	R	40*	.4
19	Blue Ridge Acquisition Company LLC—*Chris Dillon*	PO Box 507, Ellijay GA 30540	706-276-2001	R	40*	.2
20	Lexmark Carpet Mills Inc—*Todd White*	285 Kraft Dr, Dalton GA 30721	706-277-3000	R	39*	.2
21	Apache Mills Inc—*Steven Wildstein*	PO Box 907, Calhoun GA 30703	706-629-7791	R	34*	.3
22	Georgia Carpet Finishers Inc—*Larry Oxford*	PO Box 1285, Chatsworth GA 30705	706-695-3600	R	25*	.1
23	Bloomsburg Carpet Industries Inc—*Thomas Habib*	4999 Columbia Blvd, Bloomsburg PA 17815	570-784-9188	R	22*	.2
24	Feizy Import and Export Co—*John Feizy*	1949 N Stemmons Fwy, Dallas TX 75207	214-747-6000	R	21*	.2
25	Global Textile Services LLC—*C Lee*	PO Box 188, Dalton GA 30722	706-226-5647	R	21*	.2
26	Orian Rugs Inc—*Lucien Vanwynsberghe*	PO Box 2276, Anderson SC 29622	864-224-0271	R	18*	.2
27	Flemish Master Weavers Inc—*Joan Moulin*	155 Brookside Ave, West Warwick RI 02893	401-828-0300	R	17*	.1
28	Millennium Carpet Mills Inc—*Jimmy Davis*	PO Box 1079, Chatsworth GA 30705	706-695-6763	R	16*	<.1
29	Monterey Carpets Inc—*Larry Jones* Tandus Flooring Inc	1231 E Dyer Rd Ste 155, Santa Ana CA 92705	714-557-8615	S	16*	.2
30	Chem-Tech Finishers Inc—*Shelby Peeples*	PO Box 2083, Dalton GA 30722	706-278-8312	R	14*	.2
31	Edward Fields Inc—*Eleanor Fields*	150 E 58th St Ste 1101, New York NY 10155	212-310-0400	R	11*	.2
32	Viam Manufacturing Inc—*Takashi Hayakawa*	9440 Norwalk Blvd, Santa Fe Springs CA 90670	562-695-0651	R	11*	.1
33	Flortek Corp—*Warren Harris*	39 W 55th St, Bayonne NJ 07002	201-436-7700	R	9*	.1
34	Dorsett Industries LP—*Tammy Basler*	PO Box 805, Dalton GA 30722	706-278-1961	R	9*	.1
35	Barrett Carpet Mills Inc—*Frank Guthier*	PO Box 2045, Dalton GA 30722	706-277-2114	R	8*	.1
36	Al Knoch Interiors Inc—*Al Knoch*	PO Box 484, Canutillo TX 79835	915-886-5800	R	7*	.1
37	Payne and Cambron Inc—*Bill Payne*	70 Commerce Dr, Chatsworth GA 30705	706-695-9888	R	6*	.1
38	Mat Cactus Manufacturing Co—*Debra Hartranft-Derin*	930 W 10th St, Azusa CA 91702	626-443-9369	R	5*	<.1
39	Noreen Seabrook Marketing Inc—*Michael Nichols Marcy*	7545 N Broadway, Red Hook NY 12571	845-758-0084	R	3*	<.1
40	J And H Carpets Inc—*Jimmy Davis*	PO Box 1079, Chatsworth GA 30705	706-695-6761	R	3*	<.1
41	Custom Loom's Rug Mills Inc—*Terry Oster*	225 Roslyn Rd Ste C, Roslyn Heights NY 11577	516-484-0522	R	2*	.1
42	Lacey-Champion Inc—*Aimee Lacey*	PO Box 99, Fairmount GA 30139	706-337-5355	R	1*	<.1
TOTALS: SIC 2273 Carpets & Rugs						
	Companies: 42				**15,531**	**74.6**
2281 Yarn Spinning Mills						
1	Pharr Yarns LLC—*Mike Radford*	PO Box 1939, Mc Adenville NC 28101	704-824-3551	R	21,300*	1.8
2	Parkdale Mills Inc—*Anderson D Warlick*	PO Box 1787, Gastonia NC 28053	704-874-5000	R	686*	2.5
3	Fiberweb Inc—*Dean Gaskins*	70 Old Hickory Blvd, Old Hickory TN 37138	615-847-7000	R	253*	.6
4	Unifi Manufacturing Inc—*Bill Jasper*	PO Box 19109, Greensboro NC 27419	336-316-5545	R	161*	2.4
5	Parkdale America LLC—*Kim Bamonte*	PO Box 1787, Gastonia NC 28053	704-864-8761	R	147*	2.1
6	National Spinning Company Inc—*Jim Chesnutt*	1481 W 2nd St, Washington NC 27889	252-975-7111	R	110*	1.0

Note: An asterisk (*) indicates an estimated financial figure. The company type code used is as follows: R = Private, P = Public, S = Private Subsidiary, B = Public Subsidiary, D = Division, J = Joint Venture, I = Investment Fund.

COMPANY RANKINGS BY SALES WITHIN 4-DIGIT SIC

Rank	Company Name—*Executive Officer*	Address, City, State, Zip	Phone	Type	Fin	Empls
7	Carolina Mills Inc—*Stephen G Dobbins Jr*	PO Box 157, Maiden NC 28650	828-428-9911	R	103*	.6
8	Inman Mills—*Robert Chapman*	PO Box 207, Inman SC 29349	864-472-2121	R	62*	.5
9	Swift Spinning Inc—*Owen Hodges*	PO Box 8767, Columbus GA 31908	706-568-9929	R	49*	.4
10	Tuscarora Yarns Inc—*Martin Foil*	PO Box 218, Mount Pleasant NC 28124	704-436-6527	R	35*	.3
11	Ultrafab Inc—*Joseph Bridgeford*	1050 Hook Rd, Farmington NY 14425	585-924-2186	R	30*	.2
12	Kentwool Co—*Mark Kent*	PO Box 67, Pickens SC 29671	864-878-6367	R	24*	.1
13	American House Spinning Inc—*Adel Agha*	PO Box 668, Central SC 29630	864-639-2461	R	20*	.3
14	Richmond Yarns Inc—*R Goodman*	Hwy 220, Ellerbe NC 28338	910-652-5554	R	19*	.3
15	Wyndmoor Industries Inc—*William Kaplan*	PO Box 818, Lincolnton NC 28093	704-732-1171	R	19*	.2
16	Jones Companies Limited LP—*Richard Ayers*	PO Box 367, Humboldt TN 38343	731-784-2832	R	16*	.3
17	Sylvania Yarn Systems Inc—*Harry Batty*	405 Mims Rd, Sylvania GA 30467	912-564-7183	R	12*	.2
18	Kraemer Textiles Inc—*David Schmidt*	PO Box 72, Nazareth PA 18064	610-759-4030	R	12*	.1
19	Palmetto Synthetics LC—*Nik Casstevens*	PO Box 889, Kingstree SC 29556	843-382-4000	R	9*	.1
20	Hanora Spinning Inc—*Gerald Beyer*	PO Box 104, Woonsocket RI 02895	401-767-3360	S	9	.1
21	Chesterfield Yarn Mills Inc—*Miller Neisler*	PO Box 427, Pageland SC 29728	843-672-7211	R	9*	.1
22	Extruded Fibers Inc—*Robert Mcentire*	112 Westcott Way, Dalton GA 30720	706-226-2275	R	9*	.1
23	American Knitting Corp—*Ernest Capizzi*	655 S 10th St, Allentown PA 18103	610-435-7988	R	8*	.1
24	Southern Yarn Dyers Inc—*John Whittenburg*	101 Conyers Industrial, Cartersville GA 30120	770-382-3800	R	8*	.1
25	Waverly Mills Inc—*Robert Kunik*	PO Box 240416, Charlotte NC 28224	910-276-1441	R	4*	<.1
26	Chima Inc—*Douglas Heydt*	PO Box 6236, Reading PA 19610	610-372-6508	R	3*	<.1
27	Oakdale Cotton Mills—*William Ragsdale*	710 Oakdale Rd, Jamestown NC 27282	336-454-1144	R	2*	<.1

TOTALS: SIC 2281 Yarn Spinning Mills
Companies: 27

					23,120	14.3

2282 Throwing & Winding Mills

1	Sapona Manufacturing Company Inc—*Steele Redding*	PO Box 1287, Asheboro NC 27204	336-625-2727	R	65*	.2
2	Mini Fibers Inc—*Charles Keith*	2923 Boones Creek Rd, Johnson City TN 37615	423-282-4242	R	11*	<.1
3	Texturing Services Inc—*Linton Tillman*	PO Box 3631, Martinsville VA 24115	276-632-3130	R	11*	.1
4	Plymkraft Inc—*Doug Southard*	479 Export Cir, Newport News VA 23601	757-595-0364	R	8*	.1
5	Hickory Dyeing And Winding Company Inc—*Robert Miller*	PO Box 1975, Hickory NC 28603	828-322-1550	R	6*	.1
6	Atwater Inc—*Elmo Begliomini*	627 W Main St, Plymouth PA 18651	570-779-9568	R	4*	.1

TOTALS: SIC 2282 Throwing & Winding Mills
Companies: 6

					106	.6

2284 Thread Mills

1	American and Efird Inc—*Fred Jackson*	PO Box 507, Mount Holly NC 28120	704-827-4311	S	297*	2.9
2	UKI Supreme Corp—*Bill Buchanan*	PO Box 848, Hickory NC 28603	828-322-6975	R	14	.1
3	Eddington Thread Manufacturing Company Inc—*Massoud Mat-infar*	PO Box 446, Bensalem PA 19020	215-639-8900	R	12*	.1
4	Fiber Innovation Technology Inc—*Michael Holt*	398 Innovation Dr, Johnson City TN 37604	423-232-0072	R	10*	.1
5	Aerobics Inc—*Gordon Boggis*	34 Fairfield Pl, West Caldwell NJ 07006	973-276-9700	R	8*	.1
6	Liberty Threads NA Inc—*Robert S Hegen Jr*	41 Meadow St, Winsted CT 06098	860-379-2920	R	4*	<.1
7	Miami Thread—*Ron Daugherty*	PO Box 3166, Drexel NC 28619	828-438-2791	R	3*	<.1

TOTALS: SIC 2284 Thread Mills
Companies: 7

					348	3.3

2295 Coated Fabrics—Not Rubberized

1	Duro-Last Inc—*Thomas Hollingsworth*	525 W Morley Dr, Saginaw MI 48601	989-753-6486	R	129*	.5
2	Cooley Inc—*Jeffrey Flath*	50 Esten Ave, Pawtucket RI 02860	401-724-9000	R	90*	.2
3	Intex Corp—*T Zee*	PO Box 1440, Long Beach CA 90801	310-549-5400	R	46*	.1
4	Tonoga Inc—*Andrew Russell*	PO Box 69, Petersburg NY 12138	518-658-3202	R	29*	.5
5	J D Lincoln Inc—*Jim Davis*	851 W 18th St, Costa Mesa CA 92627	949-650-8106	S	27*	.1
6	Shawmut Corp—*James Wyner*	208 Manley St, West Bridgewater MA 02379	508-588-3300	R	26*	.4
7	Perma Glas-Mesh Inc—*Dominique Objois*	PO Box 220, Dover OH 44622	330-343-4441	S	24*	<.1
8	Schneller LLC—*Richard Organ*	6019 Powdermill Rd, Kent OH 44240	330-673-1400	R	24*	.2
9	Adell Plastics Inc—*Arthur Dellheim*	4530 Annapolis Rd, Baltimore MD 21227	410-789-7780	R	23*	.1
10	Alpha Associates Inc—*Christopher Avallone*	PO Box 128, Woodbridge NJ 07095	732-634-5700	R	22*	.2
11	Bradford Industries Inc—*Richard Satin*	1857 Middlesex St Ste, Lowell MA 01851	978-459-4100	R	17*	.1
12	Bondcote Corp—*Theodore Anderson*	PO Box 729, Pulaski VA 24301	540-980-2640	R	13*	.1
13	Laminating Services Inc—*Phillip Tarullo*	PO Box 32159, Louisville KY 40232	502-458-2614	R	12*	.1
14	Bruin Plastics Company Inc—*Dennis Angelone*	PO Box 700, Glendale RI 02826	401-568-3081	R	11*	.1
15	Deitsch Plastic Company Inc—*Mordecoi Deitsch*	PO Box 26005, West Haven CT 06516	203-934-6603	R	11*	.1
16	Majilite Corp—*Michael Willwerth*	1530 Broadway Rd, Dracut MA 01826	978-441-6800	R	11*	.1
17	Polyguard Products Inc—*Shawn Eastham*	PO Box 755, Ennis TX 75120	972-875-8421	R	5*	<.1
18	Beaver Manufacturing Company Inc—*Edward Needham*	PO Box 279, Mansfield GA 30055	770-786-1622	R	5*	<.1
19	Bio Plastics Co—*Frank Boron*	34655 Mills Rd, North Ridgeville OH 44039	440-327-0485	R	5*	<.1
20	Industrial Polymers and Chemicals Inc—*Susan Dacey*	508 Boston Tpke, Shrewsbury MA 01545	508-845-6112	R	3*	<.1
21	Architectural Fiberglass Corp—*Charles Wittman*	1395 Marconi Blvd, Copiague NY 11726	631-842-4772	R	2*	<.1
22	Swift Textile Metalizing LLC—*Robert Hartley*	PO Box 66, Bloomfield CT 06002	860-243-1122	R	2*	<.1
23	Ava Industries Inc—*Eva Stark*	1975 Midland Rd, Rock Hill SC 29730	803-366-3151	R	1*	<.1

TOTALS: SIC 2295 Coated Fabrics—Not Rubberized
Companies: 23

					539	3.1

2296 Tire Cord & Fabrics

1	Firestone Fibers and Textiles Co	PO Box 1369, Kings Mountain NC 28086	704-734-2100	D	64*	.5
2	Southeastern Converting Inc—*Lowell Bivens*	227 Harvest St, Winfield AL 35594	205-487-8700	R	6*	.1

TOTALS: SIC 2296 Tire Cord & Fabrics
Companies: 2

					70	.6

2297 Nonwoven Fabrics

1	Lydall Thermal/Acoustical Inc—*Joe Abbruzzi*	PO Box 109, Hamptonville NC 27020	336-468-8522	S	179	N/A
2	Foss Manufacturing Company Inc—*Pam Fenstermaker*	PO Box 5000, Hampton NH 03843	603-929-6000	R	37*	.6
3	Hobbs Bonded Fibers Inc—*C Hobbs*	PO Box 2521, Waco TX 76702	254-741-0040	R	25*	.2
4	Sellars Absorbent Materials Inc—*John Sellars*	6565 N 60th St, Milwaukee WI 53223	414-353-5650	R	21*	.1
5	Fiber Bond Corporation Illinois—*John Marienau*	110 Menke Rd, Trail Creek IN 46360	219-879-4541	R	14*	.1
6	Cerex Advanced Fabrics Inc—*James Walker*	610 Chemstrand Rd, Cantonment FL 32533	850-968-0100	R	14*	.1
7	Hyosung Inc (New York New York)—*SR Cho*	1 Penn Plz Ste 2020, New York NY 10119	212-736-7100	S	8*	<.1

Rank	Company Name—*Executive Officer*	Address, City, State, Zip	Phone	Type	Fin	Empls
8	Sellars Nonwovens—*Thomas Fellars* Sellars Absorbent Materials Inc	PO Box 270, Atglen PA 19310	610-593-5145	S	3*	<.1

TOTALS: SIC 2297 Nonwoven Fabrics
Companies: 8   301   1.2

2298 Cordage & Twine

Rank	Company Name—*Executive Officer*	Address, City, State, Zip	Phone	Type	Fin	Empls
1	American Manufacturing Company Inc—*Robert Strouse*	555 Croton Rd Ste 305, King Of Prussia PA 19406	610-962-3770	R	139*	1.0
2	Connection Concepts Inc—*John Lavitola*	1419 Centre Cir, Downers Grove IL 60515	630-599-0330	R	24*	.3
3	Bridon Cordage LLC—*James Dean*	909 E 16th St, Albert Lea MN 56007	507-377-1601	R	18*	.2
4	Samson Rope Technologies Inc—*Tony Bon* American Manufacturing Company Inc	2090 Thornton St, Ferndale WA 98248	360-384-4669	S	16*	.3
5	Yale Cordage Inc—*Tom Yale*	77 Industrial Park Rd, Saco ME 04072	207-282-3396	R	16*	.1
6	Western Filament Inc—*Wayne Wright*	630 Hollingsworth St, Grand Junction CO 81505	970-241-8780	R	12*	.1
7	Rocky Mount Cord Co—*Joseph Bunn*	PO Box 4304, Rocky Mount NC 27803	252-977-9130	R	10*	.1
8	Cortland Line Company Inc—*Brian Ward*	PO Box 5588, Cortland NY 13045	607-756-2851	R	10*	.1
9	Gladding Braided Products LLC—*D Christakos*	PO Box 164, South Otselic NY 13155	315-653-7211	R	6*	<.1
10	Wall Rope/Yale Technology—*Tom Yale* Yale Cordage Inc	PO Box 25, Spencer NC 28159	207-282-3396	S	4*	.1
11	Novus Technologies Inc—*Michael Springer*	PO Box 2506, Opelika AL 36803	334-749-6300	R	3*	<.1
12	Alan Baird Industries Inc—*Robert Mitchell*	1 Hollywood Ave Ste 9, Ho Ho Kus NJ 07423	201-652-6335	R	3*	<.1
13	Manufacture Resource Products Inc—*Mark Lu*	19907 E Walnut Dr S St, Walnut CA 91789	909-839-2988	R	2*	<.1
14	Dynamex Corp—*Ben Bravin*	155 E Albertoni St, Carson CA 90746	310-329-0399	R	2*	<.1
15	Fitec International Inc	3525 Ridge Meadow Pky, Memphis TN 38115	901-366-9144	R	2*	<.1
16	Proflex Manufacturing Inc—*Ben Whitaker*	5301 Rivoli Dr, Macon GA 31210	478-781-4335	R	2*	<.1
17	Nca Inc—*Richard Whipple*	PO Box 345, Pomfret Center CT 06259	860-974-2310	R	1*	<.1

TOTALS: SIC 2298 Cordage & Twine
Companies: 17   268   2.2

2299 Textile Goods Nec

Rank	Company Name—*Executive Officer*	Address, City, State, Zip	Phone	Type	Fin	Empls
1	Wm T Burnett Holding LLC—*Jeff Nassner*	1500 Bush St, Baltimore MD 21230	410-837-3000	R	2,061*	.5
2	Dan River Inc—*Barry F Shea*	PO Box 261, Danville VA 24543	434-799-7000	R	327*	3.5
3	Royal Ten Cate USA Inc—*David Clarke*	365 S Holland Dr, Pendergrass GA 30567	706-693-2226	R	151*	1.5
4	James Thompson and Company Inc—*Robert Judell*	381 Park Ave S Rm 718, New York NY 10016	212-686-4242	R	65*	.1
5	Atkins and Pearce Inc—*Jeb Head*	1 Braid Way, Covington KY 41017	859-356-2001	R	40*	.3
6	Nexcel Synthetics—*Rom Reddy*	799 Industrial Blvd, Chatsworth GA 30705		R	20*	.3
7	Union Wadding Co—*Kenneth Washburn*	123 Dyer St Ste 2, Providence RI 02903	401-725-3500	R	22*	.2
8	Leigh Fibers Inc—*Keith Taylor*	1101 Syphrit Rd, Wellford SC 29385	864-439-4111	R	20*	.3
9	First Performance Fabrics Inc—*Amber M Brookman*	25 W 45th St 11th Fl, New York NY 10036	212-551-0100	D	19*	<.1
10	Noble BioMaterials—*Jeff B Keane*	300 Palm St, Scranton PA 18505	570-955-1800	R	18*	<.1
11	Newark Fibers Inc—*Bruce Burgermaster*	28 Piermont Rd, Rockleigh NJ 07647	201-768-6800	R	17*	.1
12	Columbia Recycling Corp—*Albert Goldberg*	PO Box 2101, Dalton GA 30722	706-278-4701	R	15*	.3
13	Belton Industries Inc—*Carroll Hart*	PO Box 127, Belton SC 29627	864-338-5711	R	14*	.1
14	Hendrix Batting Co—*Kenneth Hendrix*	PO Box 7400, High Point NC 27264	336-431-1101	R	13*	.2
15	Kasbar National Industries Inc—*Steven Derman*	370 Reed Rd Ste 200, Broomall PA 19008	610-544-7117	R	13*	.1
16	Prodesco Inc—*Stephen Chadwick*	PO Box 237, Perkasie PA 18944	215-257-6566	S	11*	.1
17	Spectro Coating Corp—*Hemendra Shah*	101 Scott Dr, Leominster MA 01453	978-534-1800	R	9*	.1
18	Felters Of South Carolina LLC—*Roger Fehrman*	PO Box 228, Roebuck SC 29376	864-576-7900	R	9*	.1
19	Johnston-Morehouse-Dickey Company Inc—*Herbert Forse*	PO Box 173, Bethel Park PA 15102	412-833-7100	R	8*	<.1
20	Deccofelt Corp—*Gerald Heinrich*	PO Box 156, Glendora CA 91740	626-963-8511	R	8*	.1
21	Optimum Technologies Inc—*Lewis Mcdermott*	PO Box 1537, Cartersville GA 30120	770-386-3470	R	6*	.1
22	Buffalo Industries Inc—*Mark Benezra*	99 S Spokane St, Seattle WA 98134	206-682-9900	R	5*	.1
23	Domestic Fabrics And Blankets Corp—*David Wilfong*	2002 W Vernon Ave, Kinston NC 28504	252-523-7948	R	4*	<.1
24	Fp Woll and Co—*Frederick Woll*	10060 Sandmeyer Ln, Philadelphia PA 19116	215-934-5966	R	4*	<.1
25	Swatchworks Inc—*Mike Vold*	7995 Main St Ne, Minneapolis MN 55432	763-781-2560	R	3*	<.1
26	Frankel Associates Inc—*Salvatore Palina*	69 Cleveland Ave, Bay Shore NY 11706	631-242-7337	R	2*	<.1
27	Mighty Mat Inc—*Matthew Smith*	1400 Cntrepark Blvd 31, West Palm Beach FL 33401	561-683-5090	R	2*	<.1

TOTALS: SIC 2299 Textile Goods Nec
Companies: 27   2,896   7.9

2311 Men's/Boys' Suits & Coats

Rank	Company Name—*Executive Officer*	Address, City, State, Zip	Phone	Type	Fin	Empls
1	Tommy Hilfiger USA Inc—*Fred Gehring*	601 W 26th St, New York NY 10001	212-549-6388	S	1,877	N/A
2	Oxford Industries Inc—*J Hicks Lanier*	222 Piedmont Ave NE, Atlanta GA 30308	404-659-2424	P	604	4.0
3	John H Daniel Company Inc—*Richard Bryan*	120 W Jackson Ave, Knoxville TN 37902	865-637-6441	R	359*	.3
4	Woolrich Inc—*James Griggs*	2 Mill St, Woolrich PA 17779	570-769-6464	R	95*	.8
5	Barco Uniforms Inc—*Danny Robertson*	350 W Rosecrans Ave, Gardena CA 90248	310-323-7315	R	56*	.2
6	Hugo Boss USA Inc—*Anthony Lucia*	601 W 26th St Rm 845, New York NY 10001	212-940-0600	R	36*	.9
7	Alpha Industries Inc (Knoxville Tennessee)—*Alan Cirker*	14200 Park Meadow Dr S, Chantilly VA 20151	703-378-1420	R	31*	.4
8	Valley Apparel LLC	PO Box 20157, Knoxville TN 37940	865-577-2923	R	18*	.3
9	Hardwick Clothes Inc—*Thomas Hopper*	PO Box 2310, Cleveland TN 37320	423-476-6534	R	18*	.3
10	Union Apparel Inc—*Leo Borg*	PO Box 709, Masontown PA 15461	724-423-4900	R	16*	.6
11	George Weintraub and Sons Inc—*Jeff Weintraub*	641 Lexington Ave, New York NY 10022	212-581-8708	R	15*	<.1
12	Lanier Clothes Co—*Dennis MacCullough* Oxford Industries Inc	11 W 42nd St 15th Fl, New York NY 10036	212-247-7712	D	15	.2
13	Joseph Abboud Manufacturing Corp—*Anthony Sapienza*	689 Belleville Ave, New Bedford MA 02745	508-999-1301	R	14*	.5
14	Bremen-Bowdon Investment Company Inc—*E Plunkett-Buttim*	141 Commerce St, Bowdon GA 30108	770-258-3315	R	14*	.4
15	Tennessee Apparel Corp—*Ricky Francis*	PO Box 670, Tullahoma TN 37388	931-455-3491	R	14*	.3
16	Stanbury Uniforms Inc—*Gary Roberts*	PO Box 100, Brookfield MO 64628	660-258-2246	R	14*	.3
17	Sterlingwear Of Boston Inc—*Frank Fredella*	175 William F Mcclella, Boston MA 02128	617-567-6465	R	13*	.2
18	Fruhauf Uniforms Inc—*Fred Fruhauf*	PO Box 16159, Wichita KS 67216	316-263-7500	R	13*	.2
19	Blauer Manufacturing Company Inc—*T Attalah*	20 Aberdeen St, Boston MA 02215	617-536-6606	R	13*	.3
20	Golden Manufacturing Company Inc—*James Fennell*	PO Box 390, Golden MS 38847	662-454-3428	R	12*	.4
21	Southwick Clothing LLC—*Estelle Berry*	20 Computer Dr, Haverhill MA 01832	978-686-3833	R	12*	.2
22	Nu-Look Fashions Inc—*Larry Fannin*	5080 Sinclair Rd, Columbus OH 43229	614-885-4936	R	12*	.1
23	Correctional Industries Georgia Administration—*Jerry Watson*	2984 Clifton Springs R, Decatur GA 30034	404-244-5100	R	11*	.2
24	De Rossi and Son Company Inc—*Donald Rossi*	PO Box 1324, Vineland NJ 08362	856-691-0061	R	9*	.2
25	Mv Corporation Inc—*Josh Peyser*	PO Box 9171, Bay Shore NY 11706	631-273-8020	R	8*	.2
26	Crown Clothing Co—*Howard Levin*	609 Paul St, Vineland NJ 08360	856-691-0343	R	7*	.2
27	Martin Greenfield Clothiers Ltd—*Martin Greenfield*	239 Varet St, Brooklyn NY 11206	718-497-5480	R	7*	.1
28	New Maryland Clothing Manufacturing Inc—*August Piccinini*	3023 E Madison St, Baltimore MD 21205	410-675-8800	R	7*	.1
29	Check Group LLC—*Charlie Kass*	1385 Broadway Fl 16, New York NY 10018	212-221-4700	R	6*	.1
30	Romart Inc—*Edwin Brandes*	101 Pittston Ave Ste 3, Scranton PA 18505	570-342-9257	R	2*	<.1

Note: An asterisk (*) indicates an estimated financial figure. The company type code used is as follows: R = Private, P = Public, S = Private Subsidiary, B = Public Subsidiary, D = Division, J = Joint Venture, I = Investment Fund.

COMPANY RANKINGS BY SALES WITHIN 4-DIGIT SIC

Rank	Company Name—*Executive Officer*	Address, City, State, Zip	Phone	Type	Fin	Empls
31	W Seitchik and Sons Inc—*Richard Seitchik*	PO Box 6812, Philadelphia PA 19132	215-743-0319	R	2*	<.1
32	Universal Merchandise Inc—*Itender Singh*	PO Box 572152, Tarzana CA 91357	818-344-2044	R	1*	<.1

TOTALS: SIC 2311 Men's Boys' Suits & Coats
Companies: 32   3,330   11.8

2321 Men's/Boys' Shirts

Rank	Company Name—*Executive Officer*	Address, City, State, Zip	Phone	Type	Fin	Empls
1	PVH Corp—*Emanuel Chirico*	200 Madison Ave, New York NY 10016	212-381-3500	P	4,637	22.7
2	Quiksilver Inc—*Robert B McKnight Jr*	15202 Graham St, Huntington Beach CA 92649	714-889-2200	P	1,953	6.6
3	Perry Ellis International Inc—*George Feldenkreis*	3000 NW 107th Ave, Miami FL 33172	305-592-2830	P	764	2.4
4	Marc Ecko Enterprises Inc—*Seth Gerszberg*	40 W 23rd St, New York NY 10010	917-262-1002	R	731*	1.3
5	American Apparel Inc—*Dov Charney*	747 Warehouse St, Los Angeles CA 90021	213-488-0226	P	533	11.3
6	Seattle Pacific Industries Inc—*Steven Richey*	1633 Westlake Ave N, Seattle WA 98109	206-282-8889	R	340*	.3
7	Cross Creek Apparel LLC—*Hank Spires*	755 Lee St, Alexander City AL 35010		R	100*	2.0
8	CGS Industries Inc—*Ashok Sani*	3409 Queens Blvd, Long Island City NY 11101	718-482-0700	R	82*	.2
9	Ike Behar Inc—*Alan Behar*	13955 NW 60th Ave, Miami Lakes FL 33014	305-557-5212	R	53*	.3
10	Mossimo Inc	1450 Broadway 4th Fl, New York NY 10018	212-730-0030	D	31	<.1
11	Cherokee Inc—*Henry Stupp*	6835 Valjean Ave, Van Nuys CA 91406	818-908-9868	P	31	<.1
12	Elder Manufacturing Company Inc—*Ron Sher*	PO Box 273, Saint Louis MO 63166	314-469-1120	R	24*	.6
13	Regina Behar Enterprises—*Ike Behar*	13955 Nw 60th Ave, Hialeah FL 33014	305-557-5212	R	23*	.1
14	M Hidary and Company Inc—*Morris Hidary*	10 W 33rd St 9th Fl, New York NY 10001	212-736-6540	R	21*	.1
15	Ashland Shirt Inc—*Robert Opie*	2309 Chestnut St, Ashland PA 17921	570-875-3100	D	21*	.3
16	Buck Wear Inc—*David Trapp*	2900 Cowan Ave, Baltimore MD 21223	410-646-6400	R	20*	<.1
17	M Rubin and Sons Inc—*Eric Rubin*	3401 38th Ave, Long Island City NY 11101	718-361-2800	R	15*	.1
18	Pentland USA	3333 New Hyde Park Rd, New Hyde Park NY 11042	516-365-1333	D	15*	<.1
19	Sport-Haley Inc—*Catherine Blair*	4600 E 48th Ave, Denver CO 80216		P	12	<.1
20	TSF Sportswear LLC—*Barry Shulman*	1501 W Copans Rd Ste 3, Pompano Beach FL 33064	954-563-4433	R	9*	.1
21	Karman Inc—*Gary Mandelbaum*	14707 E 2nd Ave Ste 30, Aurora CO 80011	303-893-2320	R	7*	.1
22	Ruddock Manufacturing Company Inc—*Leon Ruddock*	PO Box 10205, El Paso TX 79995	915-544-3530	R	5*	.1
23	Haddad Brothers Inc—*Alan Haddad*	112 W 34th St Rm 1555, New York NY 10120	212-563-2117	R	5*	.1
24	In Private Inc—*Michael Castle*	1350 Broadway Ste 800, New York NY 10108	212-279-0786	R	4*	<.1
25	Westmoor Manufacturing Co—*Jeffrey Hochster*	PO Box 162749, Fort Worth TX 76161	817-625-2841	R	3*	.1
26	Granite Knitwear Inc—*Michael Jones*	PO Box 498, Granite Quarry NC 28072	704-279-5526	R	3*	.1
27	Spell LLC Cherokee Inc	6835 Valjean Ave, Van Nuys CA 91406	818-908-9868	S	3*	<.1
28	Generra Co—*Dan Shamdasani*	823 Washington St, New York NY 10018	212-594-5801	R	2*	<.1
29	LS Men's Clothing Co—*Rachel Sheinbaum*	49 W 45th St 3rd Fl, New York NY 10036	212-575-0933	R	2*	<.1
30	BRENTS Inc—*Julie Brents*	217 N Locust Ave, Fayetteville AR 72701	318-347-7500	R	1*	<.1
31	Ramstar Mills Inc—*Richard Feiertag*	1107 Commercial St, Athens TX 75751	903-292-1174	R	1	<.1
32	Pine Island Sportswear Ltd—*James Winter*	1609b N Rocky River Rd, Monroe NC 28110	704-289-5600	R	<1*	<.1
33	FITT Highway Products Inc—*Michael R Dunn*	5840 El Camino Real St, Carlsbad CA 92008	949-582-5933	R	<1	<.1

TOTALS: SIC 2321 Men's/Boys' Shirts
Companies: 33   9,451   48.8

2322 Men's/Boys' Underwear & Nightwear

Rank	Company Name—*Executive Officer*	Address, City, State, Zip	Phone	Type	Fin	Empls
1	Robinson Manufacturing Co—*T Robinson*	PO Box 338, Dayton TN 37321	423-775-2212	R	138*	.5
2	JE Morgan Knitting Mill Inc—*Tom Scheitrum*	PO Box 390, Tamaqua PA 18252	570-668-3330	S	27*	.3
3	Royal Textile Mills Inc—*Mark Atwater*	PO Box 250, Yanceyville NC 27379	336-694-4121	R	10*	.1

TOTALS: SIC 2322 Men's Boys' Underwear & Nightwear
Companies: 3   175   .8

2323 Men's/Boys' Neckwear

Rank	Company Name—*Executive Officer*	Address, City, State, Zip	Phone	Type	Fin	Empls
1	Robert Talbott Carmel—*Robb Talbott*	PO Box 996, Carmel Valley CA 93924	831-649-6000	R	41*	.3
2	MMG Corp (St Louis Missouri)—*Don Eisenberg*	PO Box 14346, Saint Louis MO 63178	314-421-2182	R	20*	.2
3	MJB Manufacturing Company Inc—*Harry Kraly*	PO Box 2538, Wilmington NC 28402	910-762-5663	R	6*	.1

TOTALS: SIC 2323 Men's Boys' Neckwear
Companies: 3   67   .5

2325 Men's/Boys' Trousers & Slacks

Rank	Company Name—*Executive Officer*	Address, City, State, Zip	Phone	Type	Fin	Empls
1	VF Corp—*Eric C Wiseman*	PO Box 21488, Greensboro NC 27420	336-424-6000	P	7,703	47.0
2	Levi Strauss and Co—*John Anderson*	1155 Battery St, San Francisco CA 94111	415-501-6000	R	4,674	17.0
3	Lee Apparel Company Inc—*Mackey McDonald* VF Corp	PO Box 2940, Shawnee Mission KS 66201	913-384-4000	S	510	10.4
4	Haggar Clothing Co—*Paul Buxbaum*	11511 Luna Rd, Dallas TX 75234	214-352-8481	R	473*	3.2
5	True Religion Apparel Inc—*Jeffrey Lubell*	2263 E Vernon Ave, Vernon CA 90058	323-266-3072	P	420	1.7
6	Savane International Corp	3000 NW 107th Ave, Miami FL 33172	305-592-2830	S	277*	4.0
7	VF Jeanswear LP—*Eric C Wiseman* VF Corp	PO Box 21488, Greensboro NC 27420	336-424-6000	S	100*	.3
8	Fox Apparel Inc—*Wallace Thompson*	100 Industrial Park Av, Asheboro NC 27205	336-629-7641	R	32*	.2
9	Ardmore Manufacturing Inc—*Tammy Engram*	824 Moore St Sw, Ardmore OK 73401	580-226-3626	R	18*	.1
10	Oxxford Clothes Xx Inc—*Mike Cohen*	1220 W Van Buren St Fl, Chicago IL 60607	312-829-3600	S	14*	.3
11	Calhoun Apparel Inc—*Bobby Steele*	PO Box 1204, Calhoun City MS 38916	662-628-6636	R	11*	.4
12	Ameri-Tech Dist Inc—*Alfred Fernandez*	5201 El Paso Dr, El Paso TX 79905	915-772-9861	R	8*	.1
13	Astro Apparel Inc—*James Alperin*	PO Box 3627, Scranton PA 18505	570-346-1700	R	4*	.1
14	W Thomas Company Inc—*Bill Thomas*	531 Canal St Ste 201, Reading PA 19602	610-372-9765	R	4*	.1
15	Y and W Sportswear Inc—*Julian Yarbrough*	242 Frank Rd, Fitzgerald GA 31750	229-423-9349	R	4*	.1
16	Stone County Garment Inc—*Thomas Heydt*	309 N Jefferson Ave St, Springfield MO 65806	417-723-5229	R	3*	.1
17	After Six Inc—*Kathy Peskens*	240 Collins Industrial, Athens GA 30601	706-543-5286	S	3*	<.1
18	Berle Manufacturing Company Inc—*Robert Stine*	PO Box 7393, Columbia SC 29202	843-762-7150	R	3*	<.1

TOTALS: SIC 2325 Men's Boys' Trousers & Slacks
Companies: 18   14,261   85.0

2326 Men's/Boys' Work Clothing

Rank	Company Name—*Executive Officer*	Address, City, State, Zip	Phone	Type	Fin	Empls
1	Cintas Corp—*Scott D Farmer*	PO Box 625737, Cincinnati OH 45262	513-459-1200	P	3,810	30.0
2	Appel Uniforms—*Michael Benstock*	10055 Seminole Blvd, Seminole FL 33772	727-397-9611	D	598*	.9
3	Carhartt Inc—*Bryan Adams*	PO Box 600, Dearborn MI 48121	313-271-8460	R	551*	3.3
4	Williamson-Dickie Manufacturing Co—*Philip Williamson*	PO Box 1779, Fort Worth TX 76101		R	460*	4.0
5	Elbeco Inc—*David L Lurio*	PO Box 13099, Reading PA 19612	610-921-0651	R	162*	.7
6	Fechheimer Brothers Company Inc—*Brad Kinstler*	4545 Malsbary Rd, Cincinnati OH 45242	513-793-5400	S	90*	1.0
7	Superior Uniform Group Worldwide Distribution Center	304 Superior Dr, Eudora AR 71640	870-355-8381	D	41*	.2

Rank	Company Name—Executive Officer	Address, City, State, Zip	Phone	Type	Fin	Empls
8	Landau Uniforms Inc—Nathaniel Landau	PO Box 516, Olive Branch MS 38654	662-895-7200	R	35*	1.0
9	American Uniform Co—Gary Smith	4363 Ocoee St N Ste 3, Cleveland TN 37312	423-476-6561	R	34*	.4
10	United Pioneer Corp—Bernard Braverman	2777 Summer St Ste 206, Stamford CT 06905	203-504-6260	R	32*	.6
11	Strategic Partners Inc—Michael Singer	9800 De Soto Ave, Chatsworth CA 91311	818-671-2100	R	19*	.5
12	Border Apparel Laundry Ltd—Enrique Cervantes	6969b Industrial Ave, El Paso TX 79915	915-772-7170	R	18*	1.5
13	Workrite Uniform Company Inc—Keith Suddaby	1701 Lombard St Ste 20, Oxnard CA 93030	805-483-0175	S	16*	.4
14	Eagle Work Clothes Inc—Charles Fruchter	PO Box 388, Union NJ 07083	908-964-8888	R	15*	<.1
15	Knk Apparel Inc—John Kang	223 W Rosecrans Ave, Gardena CA 90248	310-768-3333	R	14*	.3
16	Berne Apparel Co—Ronald Nussbaum	PO Box 530, Ossian IN 46777	260-622-1500	R	12*	.4
17	CC Filson Co—Bill Kulczycki	PO Box 34020, Seattle WA 98124	206-624-4437	R	11*	.2
18	Rubin Brothers Inc—David Rubin	2241 S Halsted St, Chicago IL 60608	312-942-1111	R	10*	.1
19	AME's Uniforms Inc—Mark Forst	700 NW 57th Pl, Fort Lauderdale FL 33309	945-739-7507	R	8*	<.1
20	Acme Laundry Products Inc—Doubbie Byers	21600 Lassen St, Chatsworth CA 91311	818-341-0700	R	7*	.1
21	Raven Rock Workwear Inc—Steve Thomas	7610 McEwen Rd, Dayton OH 45459	937-222-7700	R	7*	.1
22	Choi Brothers Inc—Tony Choi	3401 W Division St, Chicago IL 60651	773-489-2800	R	6*	.1
23	Euclid Garment Manufacturing Co—Charles Rosenblatt	PO Box 550, Kent OH 44240	330-673-7413	R	5*	.1
24	Southeastern Shirt Corp—Edward Straight	PO Box 308, Mount Pleasant TN 38474	931-379-3231	R	5*	.1
25	Team Safety Apparel Inc—Heyward Hodges	PO Box 113, Crystal Springs MS 39059	601-892-3571	R	4*	.1
26	Helga Designs Inc—Helga S James	1966 Spring House Rd, Kirkwood MO 63122	314-614-4362	R	4*	<.1
27	Universal Overall Co—Sanford Eckerling	1060 W Van Buren St, Chicago IL 60607	312-226-3336	R	3*	.1
28	Pgi Inc—James Sonntag	PO Box 307, Green Lake WI 54941	920-294-4300	R	3*	.1
29	Five-M Apparel Inc—Jim Milligan	PO Box 210, Trenton TN 38382	731-855-0026	R	1*	.1

TOTALS: SIC 2326 Men's Boys' Work Clothing
Companies: 29 — 5,983 / 46.3

2329 Men's/Boys' Clothing Nec

Rank	Company Name—Executive Officer	Address, City, State, Zip	Phone	Type	Fin	Empls
1	Calvin Klein Inc—Paul T Murry III	205 W 39th St, New York NY 10018		S	6,700	.9
2	Columbia Sportswear Co—Timothy P Boyle	14375 NW Science Park, Portland OR 97229	503-985-4000	P	1,694	4.2
3	Fishman and Tobin Inc—Mark Fishman	4000 Chemical Rd Ste 5, Plymouth Meeting PA 19462	610-828-8400	R	1,437*	2.5
4	Warnaco Inc—Joseph R Gromek	501 7th Ave, New York NY 10018	212-287-8000	S	584*	12.0
5	Fox Head Inc	18400 Sutter Blvd, Morgan Hill CA 95037	408-776-8800	R	216*	.5
6	Holloway Sportswear Inc—Mark S Vondenhuevel	PO Box 4489, Sidney OH 45365	937-497-7575	R	174*	.3
7	Vf Sportswear Inc—Karen Murray	40 W 57th St Fl 3, New York NY 10019	212-541-5757	R	152*	3.3
8	Delong Sportswear Inc—G Lannom	PO Box 189, Grinnell IA 50112	641-236-3106	R	113*	.3
9	Dunbrooke Sportswear Co—Matt Gray	PO Box 1900, Independence MO 64055	816-795-7722	R	57*	.1
10	No Fear Inc—Mark Simo	2251 Faraday Ave, Carlsbad CA 92008	760-931-9550	R	52*	.3
11	PremiumWear Inc—Jayme Weber	5500 Feltl Rd, Minnetonka MN 55343		S	46*	.1
12	Indiana Knitwear Corp—Eugene Bate	PO Box 309, Greenfield IN 46140	317-462-4413	R	43*	<.1
13	Pomare Ltd—Donald Kang	700 N Nimitz Hwy, Honolulu HI 96817	808-973-3266	R	41*	.5
14	Antigua Group Inc—Ron McPherson	16651 N 84th Ave, Peoria AZ 85382	623-523-6000	R	38*	.2
15	Hong Yuan Industrial Company Ltd—Robert Huang	11911 Clark St, Arcadia CA 91006	626-303-4658	R	23*	<.1
16	Pro Look Sports Inc—Dustin Rhodes	37 E Ctr St, Provo UT 84606	801-374-8530	R	21*	<.1
17	Refriglwear Inc—Ronald Breakstone	PO Box 30, Dahlonega GA 30533	706-867-9770	R	21*	.1
18	Nsg Corp—Jeff Webb	PO Box 660359, Dallas TX 75266	972-840-1233	R	18*	.6
19	Melmarc Products Inc—Brian Hirth	4040 W Carriage Dr, Santa Ana CA 92704	714-549-2170	R	15*	.2
20	RB Iii Associates Inc—Matthew Lehrer	166 Newport Dr, San Marcos CA 92069	760-471-5370	R	12*	.2
21	Speedline Athletic Wear Inc—Steven Malzone	PO Box 2498, Tampa FL 33601	813-876-1375	R	10*	.2
22	Craig Industries Inc—Larry Crolley	PO Box 845, Lamar SC 29069	843-326-5561	R	10*	.2
23	Ripon Award Jackets Inc—Henry Derleth	PO Box 25, Berlin WI 54923	920-361-1500	R	10*	.2
24	Antaeus Fashions LLC—Peter Lin	2411 Loma Ave, South El Monte CA 91733	626-452-0797	R	10*	<.1
25	Roytex Inc—Dennis Mourry	16 E 34th St 17th Fl, New York NY 10016	212-686-3500	R	9*	.2
26	Wilson Sporting Goods Co Clothing and Pad Div	4600 Roberts Matthews, Sparta TN 38583	931-738-7500	D	8*	.2
27	Alleson Of Rochester Inc—Elena Olive	2921 Brighton Henriett, Rochester NY 14623	585-272-0606	R	8*	.1
28	Brooklyn Industries Corp—Lexy Funk	43 Hall St Fl 6 Ste A1, Brooklyn NY 11205		R	7*	.1
29	Bristol Products Corp—Richard Horner	PO Box 158, Bristol TN 37621	423-968-4140	R	7*	.1
30	Andari Fashion Inc—Lillian Wang	9626 Telstar Ave, El Monte CA 91731	626-575-2759	R	7*	.1
31	Streamline Design and Silkscreen Inc—Thom Hill	1299 S Wells Rd, Ventura CA 93004	805-884-1025	R	6*	.1
32	Liggett Corp—Patricia Liggett	1200 Industrial Park R, South Fulton TN 38257	731-479-1631	R	5*	.1
33	Rigo International—Peter Ma	1527 Newton St, Los Angeles CA 90021	213-746-1737	R	5*	<.1
34	Bogner of America Inc—Peter Born	172 Bogner Dr, Newport VT 05855	802-334-6507	R	4*	<.1
35	Augusta Sportswear Inc—Brian Marks	PO Box 14939, Augusta GA 30919	706-860-4633	R	3*	.4
36	Racoe Inc—Ray Coe	327 College St, Red Boiling Springs TN 37150	615-699-6580	R	3*	.1
37	Weatherproof Garment Co—Frederick Stollmack	1071 Ave of the Americ, New York NY 10018	212-695-7716	R	3*	<.1
38	Imago Ltd—Laura Hlavac	1190 James Ave, Saint Paul MN 55105	651-690-9724	R	1*	.1
39	Pro Dive—John Hudson	429 Seabreeze Blvd, Fort Lauderdale FL 33316	954-776-3483	R	1*	<.1

TOTALS: SIC 2329 Men's Boys' Clothing Nec
Companies: 39 — 11,573 / 28.3

2331 Women's/Misses' Blouses & Shirts

Rank	Company Name—Executive Officer	Address, City, State, Zip	Phone	Type	Fin	Empls
1	Beall's Inc—Stephen M Knopik	1806 38th Ave E, Bradenton FL 34208	941-747-2355	R	1,227*	10.7
2	Donna Karan International Inc—Mark Weber	550 7th Ave, New York NY 10018	212-789-1500	S	660*	2.1
3	Land N Sea Inc (New York New York)—Robert Sobel	1375 Broadway 2nd Fl, New York NY 10018	212-444-6000	R	469*	1.0
4	St John Knits International Inc—Glenn McMahon	17622 Armstrong Ave, Irvine CA 92614	949-863-1171	B	396	4.9
5	Notations Inc—Kurt Erman	539 Jacksonville Rd, Warminster PA 18974	215-259-2000	R	194*	.1
6	Elie Tahari Ltd—Elie Tahari	16 Bleeker St, Millburn NJ 07041	973-671-6300	R	51*	.7
7	Peoples Liberation Inc—Colin Dyne	1212 S Flower St 5th F, Los Angeles CA 90015		P	31	<.1
8	eFashion Solutions LLC—Ed Foy Jr	80 Enterprise Ave S, Secaucus NJ 07094	201-601-4200	R	23*	.1
9	Adrianna Papell Ltd—Gary Briskman	512 7th Ave, New York NY 10018	212-695-5244	R	11*	<.1
10	Fashion Life Inc—Tony Kim	18455 S Figueroa St, Gardena CA 90248	310-808-9922	R	10*	.2
11	Cynthia Rowley—Cynthia Rowley	376 Bleecker St, New York NY 10014	212-242-0847	R	8*	<.1
12	Marie Anna Designs Inc—Donald Farley	PO Box 777, Ashland WI 54806	715-682-9569	R	4*	.1
13	Rhoda Lee Inc—Michael Laufer	525 Fashion Ave Rm 312, New York NY 10018	212-840-5700	R	4*	.1
14	Basham Industries—Glenn Basham	10325 Sr 56, Coalmont TN 37313	931-692-3218	R	4*	.1
15	Double B Textiles Inc—Thomas Box	939 Washington St, Franklinton LA 70438	985-839-3063	R	<1*	<.1

TOTALS: SIC 2331 Women's Misses' Blouses & Shirts
Companies: 15 — 3,091 / 20.1

2335 Women's/Misses' Dresses

Rank	Company Name—Executive Officer	Address, City, State, Zip	Phone	Type	Fin	Empls
1	Kellwood Co—Michael M Saunders	PO Box 14374, St Louis MO 63178	314-576-3100	R	2,102*	30.0

Note: An asterisk (*) indicates an estimated financial figure. The company type code used is as follows: R = Private, P = Public, S = Private Subsidiary, B = Public Subsidiary, D = Division, J = Joint Venture, I = Investment Fund.

COMPANY RANKINGS BY SALES WITHIN 4-DIGIT SIC

Rank	Company Name—*Executive Officer*	Address, City, State, Zip	Phone	Type	Fin	Empls
2	Maggy London International Ltd—*Milton Kahn*	530 7th Ave 16th Fl, New York NY 10018	212-944-7199	R	30*	.1
3	JLM Couture Inc—*Joseph L Murphy*	525 7th Ave Ste 1703, New York NY 10018	212-921-7058	P	25	.1
4	Jodi Kristopher Inc—*Ira Rosenberg*	6015 Bandini Blvd, Los Angeles CA 90040	323-890-8000	R	14*	.2
5	Milady Bridals Inc—*Eve Muscio*	1375 Broadway, New York NY 10018	212-302-0050	R	12*	<.1
6	Oscar De La Renta LLC—*Alexander Bolen*	550 7th Ave Fl 8, New York NY 10018	212-282-0500	R	9*	.1
7	Necessary Objects Ltd—*Ady Frankel*	3000 47th Ave Ste F601, Long Island City NY 11101	718-392-0226	R	5*	.1
8	Demetrios Designs Ltd—*Demetrios Elias*	222 W 37th St Frnt, New York NY 10018	212-967-5222	R	5*	.1
9	Quality Pattern Corp—*Mario Lipari*	246 W 38th St Fl 9, New York NY 10018	212-704-0355	R	5*	.1
10	William Rondina Inc—*William Rondina*	16 E 52nd St Fl 10, New York NY 10022	212-838-1944	R	4*	<.1
11	Eileen West—*Eileen West*	525 Brannan St Ste 410, San Francisco CA 94107	415-957-9378	R	3*	<.1
12	Volumecocomo Apparel Inc—*Andrew Ahn*	4160 Bandini Blvd, Vernon CA 90058	323-881-1830	R	2*	<.1
13	Ursula Of Switzerland Inc—*Ursula Rickenbacher*	31 Mohawk Ave, Waterford NY 12188	518-237-2580	R	2*	<.1
14	Private Brand Merchandising Corp—*William Berman*	214 W Olympic Blvd, Los Angeles CA 90015	213-749-0191	R	1*	<.1

TOTALS: SIC 2335 Women's Misses' Dresses
Companies: 14   2,216   30.8

2337 Women's/Misses' Suits & Coats

Rank	Company Name—*Executive Officer*	Address, City, State, Zip	Phone	Type	Fin	Empls
1	The Jones Group Inc—*Wesley R Card*	1411 Broadway, New York NY 10018	212-642-3860	P	3,734	12.1
2	Sag Harbor—*Michael W Kramer*	600 Kellwood Pkwy, Chesterfield MO 63017	314-576-3100	D	162*	.2
3	Levy Group Inc—*Donald Levy*	512 7th Ave, New York NY 10018	212-398-0707	R	150*	.2
4	Leon Max Inc—*Leon Max*	3100 New York Dr, Pasadena CA 91107		R	68*	.1
5	Pendleton Woolen Mills Inc—*Bill Lawrence*	PO Box 3030, Portland OR 97208	503-226-4801	R	42*	1.0
6	Graff California Wear Inc—*Franco Morielli*	1515 E 15th St, Los Angeles CA 90021	213-749-0171	R	16*	.1
7	Searle Blatt Ltd—*Alice Blatt*	119 W 40th St, New York NY 10018	212-730-7717	R	7*	<.1
8	Bromley Coats Inc—*Barry Kay*	463 Fashion Ave, New York NY 10018	212-239-2025	R	5*	.1
9	Executive Apparel Inc—*Donald Singer*	7912 Dungan Rd, Philadelphia PA 19111	215-464-5400	R	5*	.1
10	Item House Inc—*Greg Davis*	2920 S Steele St, Tacoma WA 98409	253-627-7168	R	4*	<.1
11	RCM Design Inc—*Michael Kaufman*	500 7th Ave 6th Fl, New York NY 10018	212-827-0370	S	2*	<.1
12	Byer California—*Allan Byer*	66 Potrero Ave, San Francisco CA 94103	415-626-7844	R	N/A	.9

TOTALS: SIC 2337 Women's Misses' Suits & Coats
Companies: 12   4,194   14.7

2339 Women's/Misses' Outerwear Nec

Rank	Company Name—*Executive Officer*	Address, City, State, Zip	Phone	Type	Fin	Empls
1	Guess Retail Inc Guess Inc	1444 S Alameda St, Los Angeles CA 90021	213-765-5578	S	3,270*	6.8
2	Guesscom Inc Guess Inc	1444 S Alameda St, Los Angeles CA 90021	213-765-5578	S	3,270*	6.8
3	Guess Inc—*Paul Marciano*	1444 S Alameda St, Los Angeles CA 90021	213-765-3100	P	2,487	15.0
4	Liz Claiborne Inc—*William L McComb*	1441 Broadway, New York NY 10018	212-354-4900	P	1,519	6.1
5	Bebe Stores Inc—*Manny Mashouf*	400 Valley Dr, Brisbane CA 94005	415-715-3900	P	493	3.4
6	MJ Soffe Company Inc—*Kenneth Spires*	1 Soffe Dr, Fayetteville NC 28312	910-483-2500	S	433*	.9
7	Koret Of California Inc—*Steve Power*	13077 E Temple Ave, City of Industry CA 91746		S	300*	1.4
8	Hamrick's Inc—*Barry Hamrick*	742 Peachoid Rd, Gaffney SC 29341	864-489-6095	R	220*	2.5
9	Body Glove International LLC—*Bob Meistrell*	201 Herondo St, Redondo Beach CA 90277	310-374-3441	R	200*	.1
10	Tarrant Apparel Group—*Gerard Guez*	3151 E Washington Blvd, Los Angeles CA 90023	323-780-8250	R	156	.1
11	AH Schreiber Company Inc—*Joel Schreiber*	460 W 34th St, New York NY 10001	212-564-2700	R	147*	.3
12	Jones Apparel Group Holdings Inc—*Peter Boneparth*	250 Rittenhouse Cir, Bristol PA 19007	215-785-4000	R	147*	4.4
13	Jaya Apparel Group LLC—*John Francia*	5175 S Soto St, Vernon CA 90058	323-584-3500	R	140*	.2
14	Liz Claiborne Incorporated Special Markets Liz Claiborne Inc	1441 Broadway Fl 22, New York NY 10018		S	130*	.1
15	Triumph Apparel Corp—*Carol J Hochman*	1411 Broadway Fl 8, New York NY 10018		P	100	.5
16	Josephine Chaus—*Josephine Chaus*	530 7th Ave, New York NY 10018	212-354-1280	P	85	.1
17	Creative Apparel Associates LLC—*Sharon Rybarczyk*	PO Box 208, Belfast ME 04915	207-342-5830	R	43*	.4
18	Everlast Worldwide Inc—*Dave Forsey*	1350 Broadway Ste 2300, New York NY 10018	212-239-0990	R	40	.1
19	skinnyCorp LLC—*Tom Ryan*	1260 W Madison St, Chicago IL 60607	773-878-3557	R	37*	.1
20	Apparel Ventures Inc—*Marvin Goodmen*	13809 S Figueroa St, Los Angeles CA 90061	310-538-4980	R	26*	.2
21	Kentucky Textiles Inc—*Cliff Shumate*	1800 Main St, Paris KY 40361	859-987-5228	R	25*	.6
22	A and H Sportswear Company Inc—*Mark Waldman*	500 William St, Pen Argyl PA 18072	610-759-9550	R	25*	.7
23	Robby Len Fashions—*Brian Ebstein* AH Schreiber Company Inc	1411 Broadway 25th Fl, New York NY 10018	212-391-2525	D	24*	.4
24	Scotty's Fashions Company Inc—*Joe Palma*	636 Pen Argyl St, Pen Argyl PA 18072	610-863-6454	R	24*	<.1
25	Sugartown Worldwide Inc—*Scott Beaumont*	800 3rd Ave, King of Prussia PA 19406	610-878-5550	R	23*	.1
26	Elite Sportswear LP—*Al Berryman*	PO Box 16400, Reading PA 19612	610-921-1469	R	15*	.3
27	Karen Kane Inc—*Lonnie Kane*	2275 E 37th St, Vernon CA 90058	323-588-0000	R	15*	.3
28	Stony Apparel Corp—*Tony Litman*	1500 S Evergreen Ave, Los Angeles CA 90023	323-981-9080	R	14*	.2
29	National Spirit Group Ltd—*Joel Hallford*	PO Box 660359, Dallas TX 75266	972-840-1233	S	14*	.1
30	Unger Fabrik LLC—*Celso Ong*	1515 E 15th St, Los Angeles CA 90021	213-222-1010	R	14*	.2
31	Citizens Of Humanity LLC—*Miller Tomy*	5715 Bickett St, Huntington Park CA 90255	323-923-1240	R	13*	.2
32	Swimwear Anywhere Inc—*Rosemarie Dilorenzo*	85 Sherwood Ave, Farmingdale NY 11735	631-420-1400	R	11*	.2
33	5 B's Inc—*Leland Biles*	PO Box 520, Zanesville OH 43702	740-454-8453	R	10*	.4
34	Just For Wraps Inc—*Vrajesh Lal*	5815 Smithway St, Commerce CA 90040	213-239-0503	R	10*	.1
35	American Rag CIE—*Mark Werts*	150 S LaBrea Ave, Los Angeles CA 90036	323-935-3154	R	10*	<.1
36	Aaron Corp—*Paul Shechet*	1820 E 41st St, Vernon CA 90058	323-235-5959	R	8*	.2
37	Laundry By Shelli Segal—*Paula Schneider*	5835 S Eastern Ave Ste, Commerce CA 90040	323-767-1810	R	8*	.1
38	Counter-Fit Inc—*Michael Macaluso*	1 Ironside Ct, Willingboro NJ 08046	609-871-8888	R	8*	.1
39	K-L Manufacturing Company Inc—*Joseph Doohan*	2726 N Monroe St, Spokane WA 99205	509-326-2350	R	8*	.1
40	Tripp Nyc Inc—*Natharorn Goodman*	5200 W Side Ave, North Bergen NJ 07047	201-333-5873	R	8*	<.1
41	Paris Blues LLC—*Alma Gonzalez*	3040 E Ana St, Compton CA 90221	310-605-2000	R	7*	.1
42	Golf Apparel Brands Inc—*Edward Kahn*	13301 S Main St, Los Angeles CA 90061	310-327-5188	R	7*	.1
43	Maingate Inc—*David Morokek*	7900 Rockville Rd, Indianapolis IN 46214	317-243-2000	R	7*	.1
44	Lebanon Apparel Corp—*Jeoffrey Bodenhorst*	70 Thornhill Dr, Lebanon VA 24266	276-889-3656	R	7*	.1
45	IguanaMed—*Gregory Lilien*	2444 W 16th St 5th Fl, Chicago IL 60608		R	6	<.1
46	Bill Sills Sportswear Inc—*Bill Sills*	PO Box 855, Huntingdon TN 38344	731-986-2217	R	6*	.1
47	Da-Rue Of California Inc—*Richard Elrath*	PO Box 59918, Los Angeles CA 90059	310-323-1350	R	5*	.1
48	Japanese Weekend Inc—*Barbara White*	222 Dore St, San Francisco CA 94103	415-621-0555	R	5*	.1
49	Clover Garments Inc—*Florence Lo*	2565 3rd St Ste 232, San Francisco CA 94107	415-826-6909	R	5*	.1
50	Great Circle Ventures Holdings LLC—*Mike Rusinko*	PO Box 98, Columbus GA 31902	305-638-2650	R	5*	.1
51	Winkie Manufacturing Company Inc—*Edward Harris*	1900 N Narragansett Av, Chicago IL 60639	773-889-7700	R	3*	.1
52	Jowett Garments Factory Inc—*Charly Chiang*	10359 Rush St, South El Monte CA 91733	626-350-0515	R	3*	<.1
53	Team Apparel Inc—*Lowell Potter*	320 Huntsville Industr, Huntsville TN 37756	423-663-4164	R	3*	.1

Rank	Company Name—*Executive Officer*	Address, City, State, Zip	Phone	Type	Fin	Empls
54	HC Contracting Inc—*Carolyn Ferrara*	318 W 39th St Fl 4, New York NY 10018	212-643-9292	R	3*	.1
55	Mustang Sportswear Inc—*Marvin Poster*	10214 37th Ave, Corona NY 11368	718-898-2500	R	3*	<.1
56	Henry-Lee and Company LLC—*Gregg Pavalon*	549 W Randolph St Ste, Chicago IL 60661	312-648-1575	R	2*	<.1
57	Perazzi Apparel Co—*Daniel Jason*	4679 Hugh Howell Rd St, Tucker GA 30084	678-387-6660	R	2*	<.1
58	Cee Sportswear—*Paul Bogner*	5808 Wilmington Ave, Vernon CA 90058	323-585-8500	R	2*	<.1
59	Saw Textiles Inc—*Sue Lankford*	3025 Appling Rd, Memphis TN 38133	901-377-2968	R	1*	<.1
60	Raj Manufacturing Inc—*Aziz Jlelati*	2692 Dow Ave, Tustin CA 92780	714-838-3110	R	1*	<.1
61	Hgl Inc—*Humberto Gonzales*	2001 Hawkins Cir, Los Angeles CA 90001	323-581-5997	R	1*	<.1
62	Jantzen LLC—*George Feldenkreis*	PO Box 3001, Portland OR 97208	503-238-5000	D	N/A	.2

TOTALS: SIC 2339 Women's Misses' Outerwear Nec
Companies: 62 — 13,612 — 54.8

2341 Women's/Children's Underwear

Rank	Company Name—*Executive Officer*	Address, City, State, Zip	Phone	Type	Fin	Empls
1	Warnaco Group Inc—*Joseph R Gromek*	501 7th Ave, New York NY 10018	212-287-8000	P	2,513	7.1
2	Sid Greenberg Inc—*Steve Klein*	6 E 32nd St Fl 10, New York NY 10016	212-689-3131	R	218*	1.2
3	Charles Komar and Sons Inc—*Charles E Komar*	16 E 34th St 10th Fl, New York NY 10016	212-725-1500	R	69*	.4
4	Management Industries Inc—*Jeff Mirvis*	13889 S Figueroa St, Los Angeles CA 90061	310-516-5900	R	56*	.1
5	Mayer Berkshire Corp—*Michael Mayer*	PO Box 244, Wayne NJ 07470	973-696-6200	R	17*	.2
6	Carolina Apparel Group Inc—*Pamela Ball*	425 Hwy 52 S, Wadesboro NC 28170	704-694-6544	R	16*	.1
7	Russell-Newman Inc—*Eric Hamburg*	PO Box 2306, Denton TX 76202	940-898-8888	R	15*	.2
8	Burlen Corp—*Steve Klein*	PO Box 168, Tifton GA 31793	229-382-4100	R	10*	.4
9	Hemingway Apparel Manufacturing Inc—*Jack Marsh*	PO Box 459, Hemingway SC 29554	843-558-2525	R	9*	.2
10	Irwin Manufacturing Corp—*Jeff Heller*	PO Box 507, Ocilla GA 31774	229-468-9481	R	8*	.2
11	Obbi LLC—*Michael O'bryan*	16 E 34th St Fl 10, New York NY 10016	212-725-1500	R	7*	.1
12	Miss Elaine Inc—*James Seldin*	8430 Valcour Ave, Saint Louis MO 63123	314-631-1900	R	5*	.1
13	Waterbury Garment LLC—*Daniel Livingston*	16 E 34th St Fl 10, New York NY 10016	212-725-1500	R	4*	<.1
14	Afr Apparel International Inc—*Amir Moghadam*	19401 Business Ctr Dr, Northridge CA 91324	818-773-5000	R	3*	.1

TOTALS: SIC 2341 Women's Children's Underwear
Companies: 14 — 2,950 — 10.3

2342 Bras, Girdles & Allied Garments

Rank	Company Name—*Executive Officer*	Address, City, State, Zip	Phone	Type	Fin	Empls
1	Gelmart Industries Inc—*Ezra Nasser*	136 Madison Ave 4th Fl, New York NY 10016	212-743-6900	R	26*	.2
2	Vanity Fair Intimates LP	PO Box 90015, Bowling Green KY 42102	270-781-6400	S	16*	.1
3	Metric Products Inc—*Shirley Magidson*	4671 Leahy St, Culver City CA 90232	310-815-9000	R	1*	<.1

TOTALS: SIC 2342 Bras, Girdles & Allied Garments
Companies: 3 — 43 — .3

2353 Hats, Caps & Millinery

Rank	Company Name—*Executive Officer*	Address, City, State, Zip	Phone	Type	Fin	Empls
1	Rhe Hatco Inc—*Paul Lavoie*	601 Marion Dr, Garland TX 75042	972-494-0511	R	79*	.5
2	New Era Cap Company Inc—*Christopher Koch*	160 Delaware Ave, Buffalo NY 14202	716-549-0445	R	61*	1.4
3	Imperial Headwear Inc—*Rick White*	17101 E Ohio Dr, Aurora CO 80017	303-597-0206	S	44*	.3
4	Bollman Hat Co—*Donald Rongione*	PO Box 517, Adamstown PA 19501	717-484-4361	R	39*	1.0
5	Paramount Apparel International Inc—*Bruce Levinson*	PO Box 98, Bourbon MO 65441	573-732-4411	R	27*	.8
6	Ahead Headgear Inc—*Kenneth A Shwartz*	270 Samuel Barnet Blvd, New Bedford MA 02745	508-985-9898	R	24*	.3
7	Cookies Inc—*Charles Dweck*	1 E 33rd St Fl 6, New York NY 10016	646-452-5552	R	14*	.6
8	Bernard Cap Company Inc—*Lawrence Weinstein*	9800 NW 79th Ave, Hialeah FL 33016	305-822-4800	R	11*	.2
9	Cali-Fame Of Los Angeles Inc—*Michael Kennedy*	20934 S Santa Fe Ave, Carson CA 90810	323-268-3187	R	8*	.1
10	Coolibar—*John Barrow*	2401 Edgewood Ave S, Minneapolis MN 55426	952-922-1445	R	8*	<.1
11	Legendary Holdings Inc—*Thomas Smith*	8653 Avenida Costa Nor, San Diego CA 92154	619-872-6100	R	8*	<.1
12	Cap America Inc—*Phillip Page*	PO Box 229, Fredericktown MO 63645	573-783-3394	R	8*	.2
13	Arlington Hat Company Inc—*Lewis Strongin*	4725 34th St Ste 301, Long Island City NY 11101	718-361-3000	R	8*	.2
14	M and B Headwear Company Inc—*Sheldon Bigler*	PO Box 8180, Richmond VA 23223	804-648-1603	R	6*	.1
15	R and H Solutions Inc—*Robert Tomaseski*	26 Town Ctr Way 719, Hampton VA 23666	757-838-8380	R	5*	.1
16	Pro Line Headwear Inc—*Scott Kirk*	1332 N Main St, Fort Worth TX 76164	817-246-1978	R	5*	.1
17	New Jersey Headwear Corp—*Mitch Cahn*	PO Box 7009, Newark NJ 07107	973-497-0102	R	5*	.1
18	Town Talk Manufacturing Company Inc—*Wayne Joplin*	PO Box 58157, Louisville KY 40268	502-933-7575	R	4*	.1
19	Higgins Acquisition Inc—*Alicia Webb*	1511 Main St, Oran MO 63771	573-262-3567	R	3*	.1
20	Northern Cap And Glove Manufacturing LLC—*Sam Rafowitz*	2633 Minnehaha Ave, Minneapolis MN 55406	612-729-3000	R	3*	.1
21	Sew Cal Logo Inc—*Richard Songer*	207 W 138th St, Los Angeles CA 90061		P	2	.1
22	DVE Manufacturing Inc—*Donald Loiselle*	PO Box 2005, Lewiston ME 04241	207-783-9895	R	2*	<.1
23	Baam Inc—*Jon Bernstein*	20847 Betron St, Woodland Hills CA 91364	818-716-1818	R	2*	<.1

TOTALS: SIC 2353 Hats, Caps & Millinery
Companies: 23 — 373 — 6.1

2361 Girls'/Children's Dresses & Blouses

Rank	Company Name—*Executive Officer*	Address, City, State, Zip	Phone	Type	Fin	Empls
1	Forever 21 Inc—*Don Chang*	2001 S Alameda St, Los Angeles CA 90058	213-741-5100	R	1,300*	12.5
2	VF Playwear Inc—*Gary Simmons*	PO Box 21488, Greensboro NC 27420	336-424-1000	S	937*	1.6
3	Garan Inc—*Seymour Lichtenstein*	350 Fifth Ave, New York NY 10118	212-563-2000	S	227*	4.5
4	Baby Togs Inc—*Sharon Wax*	100 W 33rd St Ste 1100, New York NY 10001	212-868-2100	R	183*	.3
5	Cl Castro and Co—*Cl Castro*	1107 W Laurel, San Antonio TX 78201	210-733-3961	R	125*	.2
6	Jalate Ltd—*V Bacon*	1675 South Alameda St, Los Angeles CA 90021	213-765-5000	R	54*	.1
7	Gerson and Gerson Inc—*Matthew Gerson*	112 W 34th St Ste 1710, New York NY 10120	212-279-1130	R	53*	.1
8	Star Children's Dress Company Inc—*Edward Rosen*	100 W 33rd St Ste 1005, New York NY 10001	212-279-1524	R	32*	.1
9	Diane Von Furstenberg Studio—*Diane Von Furstenberg*	389 W 12th St, New York NY 10014	212-741-6607	R	18*	<.1
10	Dive N' Surf Inc—*Robert Meistrell*	504 N Broadway, Redondo Beach CA 90277	310-372-8423	R	9*	<.1
11	JM Originals Inc—*Martha Arginsky*	PO Box 628, Ellenville NY 12428	845-647-3003	R	7*	.1

TOTALS: SIC 2361 Girls' Children's Dresses & Blouses
Companies: 11 — 2,945 — 19.7

2369 Girls'/Children's Outerwear Nec

Rank	Company Name—*Executive Officer*	Address, City, State, Zip	Phone	Type	Fin	Empls
1	Carter's Inc—*Michael D Casey*	1170 Peachtree St Ste, Atlanta GA 30309	404-745-2700	P	2,110	2.6
2	OshKosh B'Gosh Inc—*David A Brown* Carter's Inc	PO Box 300, Oshkosh WI 54903	920-231-8800	S	399	5.1
3	Spencers Inc—*James Crossingham*	238 Willow St, Mount Airy NC 27030	336-789-9111	R	334*	1.7
4	General Sportwear Company Inc—*Herbert Rosenstock*	PO Box 588, Ellenville NY 12428	845-647-4411	R	96*	.2
5	Third Street Sportswear Manufacturing Inc—*W Thomas*	PO Box 145, Ozark MO 65721	417-485-3881	R	7*	.1
6	Easyfine Asia Ltd—*Peter Sheintoch*	431 E Tioga St, Philadelphia PA 19134	215-739-0200	R	7*	.1

Note: An asterisk (*) indicates an estimated financial figure. The company type code used is as follows: R = Private, P = Public, S = Private Subsidiary, B = Public Subsidiary, D = Division, J = Joint Venture, I = Investment Fund.

COMPANY RANKINGS BY SALES WITHIN 4-DIGIT SIC

Rank	Company Name—*Executive Officer*	Address, City, State, Zip	Phone	Type	Fin	Empls
7	Valtex LLC—*Paul Kunitz*	PO Box 159, Scottsboro AL 35768	256-259-2599	R	1*	<.1
TOTALS: SIC 2369 Girls' Children's Outerwear Nec						
Companies: 7					2,953	9.8
2371 Fur Goods						
1	Flemington Fur Co—*Robert Benjamin*	8 Spring St, Flemington NJ 08822	908-782-2212	R	10*	<.1
2	Albert and Marc Kaufman Inc—*Marc Kaufman*	232 West 30th St, New York City NY 10001	212-564-0050	R	2*	<.1
TOTALS: SIC 2371 Fur Goods						
Companies: 2					12	<.1
2381 Fabric Dress & Work Gloves						
1	Boss Holdings Inc—*G Louis Graziadio III*	1221 Page St, Kewanee IL 61443	309-852-2131	R	48*	.2
2	Choctaw-Kaul Distribution—*Kenny Tubby*	3540 Vinewood St, Detroit MI 48208	313-894-9494	R	32*	.2
3	Southern Glove Manufacturing Company Inc—*Brent Fidler*	749 Ac Little Dr, Newton NC 28658	828-464-4884	R	11*	.3
4	North Star Glove Co—*Rob Wekell*	PO Box 1214, Tacoma WA 98401	253-627-7107	R	6*	<.1
5	Fairfield Line Inc—*Fred Hunt*	PO Box 500, Fairfield IA 52556	641-472-3191	R	5*	.1
6	Hercules Glove Manfacturing Company Inc—*Arvind Joshi*	740 Driving Park Ave, Rochester NY 14613	585-663-1949	R	1*	<.1
7	Illinois Glove Co—*David Shmikler*	3701 Commercial Ave, Northbrook IL 60062	847-291-1700	R	1*	<.1
8	Tempo Glove Manufacturing Inc—*Michael Mandlman*	3820 W Wisconsin Ave, Milwaukee WI 53208	414-344-1100	R	1*	<.1
9	Brooks Tactical Systems—*Brooks Speier*	296 N Shore Blvd Fi, Fox Island WA 98333	253-549-2866	R	1*	<.1
TOTALS: SIC 2381 Fabric Dress & Work Gloves						
Companies: 9					105	.8
2384 Robes & Dressing Gowns						
1	Natori Company Inc—*Josie Natori*	180 Madison Ave Fl 19, New York NY 10016	212-532-7796	R	12*	.2
2385 Waterproof Outerwear						
1	Neese Industries Inc—*Timothy Sands*	PO Box 1059, Gonzales LA 70707	225-647-6553	R	16*	.1
2	Harris Manufacturing Company Inc—*S Harris*	550 W Ingham Ave, Ewing NJ 08638	609-393-3717	R	15*	.1
3	Whaling Distributors Inc—*Thomas Savage*	451 Quarry St, Fall River MA 02723	508-678-9061	R	6*	<.1
TOTALS: SIC 2385 Waterproof Outerwear						
Companies: 3					36	.2
2386 Leather & Sheep-Lined Clothing						
1	Lb Fragrance LLC—*Lisa Lehrein*	5233 Alcoa Ave, Vernon CA 90058	323-282-4100	R	9*	.2
2	Distinctive Industries Of Texas Inc—*Dwight Forrester*	PO Box 140949, Austin TX 78714	512-491-3500	R	6*	.1
3	Vanson Leathers Inc—*Mike Vanson*	951 Broadway Ste 1, Fall River MA 02724	508-678-2000	R	4*	.1
TOTALS: SIC 2386 Leather & Sheep-Lined Clothing						
Companies: 3					19	.4
2387 Apparel Belts						
1	Tandy Brands Accessories Inc—*N Roderick McGeachy*	690 E Lamar Blvd Ste 2, Arlington TX 76011	817-548-0090	P	142	.6
2	Trafalgar Ltd—*Marley Hodgson*	1 Selleck St Ste 3I, Norwalk CT 06855	203-853-2107	R	30*	.4
3	Amiee Lynn Accessories—*Steven Spolansky*	366 5th Ave, New York NY 10001	212-268-4747	R	10*	.1
4	American Belt Co—*Allan Ford*	1355 Adams Rd, Bensalem PA 19020	215-639-8000	R	10*	.2
5	Madison Company Inc—*Fred Burke*	PO Box 657, Madison NC 27025	336-548-9624	R	6*	<.1
TOTALS: SIC 2387 Apparel Belts						
Companies: 5					197	1.2
2389 Apparel & Accessories Nec						
1	Rennoc Corp—*Mike Bruzzese*	3501 S East Blvd, Vineland NJ 08360	856-327-5400	R	19,648*	.1
2	Gymboree Corp—*Matthew McCauley*	500 Howard St, San Francisco CA 94105	415-278-7000	P	1,100	12.4
3	Liz Claiborne Accessories—*William McComb*	1441 Broadway, New York NY 10018	212-354-4900	D	765*	1.0
4	Volcom Inc—*Richard R Woolcott*	1740 Monrovia Ave, Costa Mesa CA 92627	949-646-2175	S	323	.5
5	Gerber Childrenswear LLC—*Gary F Simmons*	1333 Broadway, New York NY 10018	212-863-2400	S	210*	2.4
6	Nautica Jeans Co—*Eric C Wiseman*	105 Corporate Center B, Greensboro NC 27408	212-541-5757	S	193*	.3
7	Standard Textile Company Inc—*Gary Heiman*	PO Box 371805, Cincinnati OH 45222	513-761-9255	R	168*	3.5
8	Varsity Spirit Fashions and Supplies Inc—*Jeffrey G Webb* Varsity Spirit Corp	6745 Lenox Center Ct S, Memphis TN 38115		S	155*	.3
9	C Brewer Co—*Charles Brewer III*	3630 Miraloma Ave, Anaheim CA 92806	714-630-6810	R	113*	.2
10	CafepressCom Inc—*Fred Durham*	1850 Gateway Dr Ste 30, San Mateo CA 94404	650-655-6610	R	100*	.4
11	Skip Hop Inc—*Michael Diamant*	50 W 23rd St 10th Fl, New York NY 10010	212-868-9850	R	95*	.3
12	Varsity Spirit Corp	PO Box 751210, Memphis TN 38175	901-387-4370	S	64*	.5
13	Nixon Uniform Service Inc—*Murray Berstein*	500 Cemterpoint Blvd, New Castle DE 19720	302-764-7550	R	54*	.3
14	EarthCom Inc—*Phillip Meynard*	135 2nd Ave, Waltham MA 02451	781-893-7474	R	42*	.1
15	ER Moore Co—*Karen Hartmann*	840 Union St, Salem VA 24153	540-387-0000	R	39*	.4
16	Ogio International Inc—*Tony Palma*	14926 Pony Express Rd, Bluffdale UT 84065	801-619-4100	R	32*	.1
17	Chasing Fireflies LLC—*Lori Liddle*	350 Midland Dr, Seattle WA 98188	206-574-4500	R	32	.1
18	Safe Reflections Inc—*Robert Koppes*	3220 N Granada Ave Ste, Saint Paul MN 55128	651-773-8199	R	27*	<.1
19	JanSport Inc	2011 Farallon Dr, San Leandro CA 94577	510-614-4000	S	22*	.4
20	180s LLC—*Susan Schafton*	701 E Pratt St Ste 180, Baltimore MD 21202	410-534-6320	R	21*	.1
21	I Shalom and Company Inc—*Isaac Shalom*	411 5th Ave, New York NY 10016	212-532-7911	R	17	.1
22	Pacon Manufacturing Corp—*A Shannon*	400 Pierce St, Somerset NJ 08873	732-764-9070	R	14*	.2
23	Foot Petals LLC—*Tina Aldatz*	6615 E Pacific Coast H, Long Beach CA 90803	562-795-1700	R	13*	<.1
24	Demoulin Brothers and Co—*William Marsden*	1025 S 4th St, Greenville IL 62246	618-664-2000	R	11*	.2
25	Mar-Mac Manufacturing Company Inc—*John Mc Leod*	PO Box 447, Mc Bee SC 29101	843-335-5814	R	10*	.3
26	Royal Park Uniforms Inc—*William Royal*	PO Box 24, Prospect Hill NC 27314	336-562-3345	R	7*	.1
27	Regency Cap and Gown Co—*David Crisp*	PO Box 8988, Jacksonville FL 32239	904-724-3500	R	6*	.1
28	Weissman's Theatrical Supplies Inc—*Howard Weissman*	6750 Manchester Ave, Saint Louis MO 63139	314-773-9000	R	6*	.1
29	Prep Sportswear—*Chad Hartvigson*	4660 Ohio Ave S Ste A, Seattle WA 98134	206-876-2800	R	6*	.1
30	Jannette Hughes—*Jannette Hughes*	5920 Martn Luthr Kng J, Seattle WA 98118	206-722-1412	R	5*	.1
31	Wedding Brand Investors LLC—*Steven Kahn*	2510 Commonwealth Ave, North Chicago IL 60064	847-775-4800	R	5*	.1
32	Army and Air Force Exchange Service—*Bruce A Casella*	PO Box 660202, Dallas TX 75266	214-312-2011	R	4*	43.6
33	Macoy Publishing and Masonic Supply Company Inc—*John Emory*	PO Box 9759, Richmond VA 23228	804-262-6551	R	3*	<.1
34	Southern Soldier Mercantile Inc—*Charlie Wilton*	1002 N 20th St, Morehead City NC 28557	252-393-8426	R	3*	.1
35	Johnny Cupcakes—*Johnny Earle*	106 Finnell Dr Ste 24, Weymouth MA 02188		R	3*	<.1
36	MensRedTagcom—*Lee Ferry*	1031 Stewart Ct, Joliet IL 60431		R	3*	<.1
37	Costume Specialists Inc—*Wendy Goldstein*	211 N 5th St, Columbus OH 43215	614-464-2115	R	3*	<.1

Rank	Company Name—*Executive Officer*	Address, City, State, Zip	Phone	Type	Fin	Empls
38	Gavson Inc—*Kevin Gavson*	PO Box 551030, Dallas TX 75355	972-840-2273	R	2*	<.1
39	Rose Solomon Co—*Mendel Reichman*	63 Flushing Ave Unit 3, Brooklyn NY 11205	718-855-1788	R	1*	<.1
40	Endless Road Products Inc—*Gary Watson*	1413 Airway, Waterford MI 48327	248-666-9496	R	1*	<.1
41	Simon Worldwide Inc—*Greg Mays*	5200 W Century Blvd St, Los Angeles CA 90045	310-417-4660	P	<1	<.1
42	Respect Your Universe Inc—*Christopher Martens*	6533 Octave Ave, Las Vegas NV 89139	702-664-1246	P	<1	N/A

TOTALS: SIC 2389 Apparel & Accessories Nec
Companies: 42   23,326   68.4

2391 Curtains & Draperies

1	Chf Industries Inc—*Frank Foley*	PO Box 410727, Charlotte NC 28241	704-522-5000	R	468*	.5
2	Miller Curtain Company Inc—*Gerd Miller*	211 New Laredo Hwy, San Antonio TX 78211	210-483-1000	R	80*	1.1
3	Housatonic Curtain Company Inc—*John Fitzpatrick*	PO Box 659, Housatonic MA 01236	413-274-6173	R	65*	.1
4	Malnove Incorporated Of Utah—*Paul Malnove*	Freeport Ctr Bldg A 16, Clearfield UT 84016	801-773-7400	R	22*	.6
5	Croscill Inc—*Marc Navarre*	261 5th Ave Fl 25, New York NY 10016	212-689-7222	R	21*	.6
6	Haleyville Drapery Manufacturing Company Inc	PO Box 695, Haleyville AL 35565	205-486-9257	D	8*	.1
7	Wesco Fabrics Inc—*Richard Gentry*	PO Box 16604, Denver CO 80216	303-388-4101	R	8*	.1
8	Seamless Sensations Inc—*Juergen Hanebrink*	PO Box 668, Chester SC 29706	803-581-0909	R	6*	.1
9	Aero Drapery Corp—*William Bathke*	75 W Viking Dr, Little Canada MN 55117	952-890-6393	R	6	<.1
10	Richloom Fabrics Corp—*Fred Richman*	261 5th Ave Fl 12, New York NY 10016	212-685-5400	R	6*	<.1
11	Virginia Quilting Inc—*John Wesley McAden*	PO Box 99, La Crosse VA 23950	434-757-1809	R	5*	.1
12	Beacon Looms Inc—*Seymour Sadinoff*	411 Alfred Ave, Teaneck NJ 07666	201-833-1600	R	5*	<.1
13	Fred Wilkinson Associates Inc—*Fred Wilkinson*	PO Box 1264, Valdosta GA 31603	229-242-4072	R	5*	.1
14	Merrill Y Landis Ltd—*Steven Landis*	PO Box 249, Telford PA 18969	215-723-8177	R	3*	.1
15	Decorative Novelty Company Inc—*Leonard Feldman*	74 20th St, Brooklyn NY 11232	718-965-8600	R	1*	<.1
16	Vocational Services Inc—*Robert Comben*	2239 E 55th St, Cleveland OH 44103	216-431-8085	R	1*	.2

TOTALS: SIC 2391 Curtains & Draperies
Companies: 16   709   3.7

2392 Housefurnishings Nec

1	WestPoint Home Inc—*Joseph Pennacchio*	28 E 28th St 8th Fl, New York NY 10016	212-930-2000	R	1,646	13.9
2	Springs Global US Inc—*Tom O'connor*	PO Box 70, Fort Mill SC 29716	803-547-1500	R	1,081*	8.0
3	UNICOR—*Harley Lappin*	320 1st St NW, Washington DC 20534	202-305-3500	R	625*	23.2
4	Arden Cos—*Robert S Sachs*	30400 Telegraph Rd Rm, Bingham Farms MI 48025	248-415-8500	R	424*	1.2
5	MIT International Inc—*Norman Plotkin*	PO Box 23847, Houston TX 77228	713-675-0075	R	334*	.3
6	Jay Franco and Sons Inc—*Joseph A Franco*	295 5th Ave 3rd Fl, New York NY 10016	212-679-3022	R	240*	.1
7	SK Textiles Inc—*Robert Paul Schwartz*	2938 E 54th St, Vernon CA 90058	323-581-8986	R	143*	.4
8	Barclay Home Products Corp—*Richard Whiting*	PO Box 306, Cherokee NC 28719	828-497-7902	R	71*	.2
9	Brentwood Originals Inc—*Loren Sweet*	20639 S Fordyce Ave, Carson CA 90810	310-637-6804	R	59*	.4
10	Pacific Coast Feather Co—*Eric Moen*	PO Box 80385, Seattle WA 98108	206-624-1057	R	54*	1.2
11	Louisville Bedding Company Inc—*Steve Elias*	10400 Bunsen Way, Louisville KY 40299	502-491-3370	R	33*	.8
12	CDS Ensembles Inc—*Joe Nettles*	PO Box 930, Greer SC 29652	864-848-3499	R	31	.3
13	John R Lyman Co—*William Wright*	2255 Westover Rd, Chicopee MA 01022	413-598-8344	R	26*	.1
14	Bardwil Inductrioc Inc—*George Bardwil*	1071 Avenue of the Ame, New York NY 10018	212-944-1870	R	25*	.2
15	Madison Industries Inc—*Michael Schwartz*	279 5th Ave Fl 2, New York NY 10016	212-679-5110	R	20*	.6
16	Easy Way Leisure Corp—*Jon Randman*	412 S Cooper Ave, Cincinnati OH 45215	513-731-5640	R	19*	.3
17	Quickie Manufacturing Corp—*Michael Magerman*	PO Box 156, Cinnaminson NJ 08077	856-829-7900	R	19*	.5
18	Park B Smith Inc—*Linda Smith*	230 5th Ave, New York NY 10016	212-889-1818	R	16*	.1
19	Down-Lite International Inc—*Larry Werthaiser*	8153 Duke Blvd, Mason OH 45040	513-229-3696	R	16*	.2
20	Klear-Vu Corp—*Jack Mintz*	PO Box 4128, Fall River MA 02723	508-674-5723	R	15*	.3
21	Phoenix Down Corp—*John Facateselis*	85 Rte 46 W, Totowa NJ 07512	973-812-8100	R	15*	.1
22	Bucky Products Inc—*Thomas Shoaf*	1200 W Nickerson St, Seattle WA 98119	206-545-8790	R	15*	<.1
23	Latex Foam International LLC—*Steven Watson*	510 River Rd, Shelton CT 06484	203-924-0700	R	14*	.2
24	Freudenberg Household Products LP—*Tim Molek*	2188 Diehl Rd, Aurora IL 60502	630-270-1400	R	13*	.4
25	Kleen Maid Inc—*Shaham Solouki*	6015 Randolph St, Commerce CA 90040	323-581-3000	R	12*	<.1
26	Sports Coverage Inc—*Ricardo Schulz*	5555 Military Pkwy, Dallas TX 75227	214-381-3096	R	11*	.1
27	Kimlor Mills Inc—*Wade Svicarovich*	2630 Saint Matthews Rd, Orangeburg SC 29118	803-531-2037	R	10*	.1
28	Josie Accessories Inc—*Mark Siegel*	261 5th Ave Fl 10, New York NY 10016	212-889-6376	R	10*	.2
29	Reliance Upholstery Supply Company—*Stanley Grietzer*	PO Box 58584, Los Angeles CA 90058	323-321-2300	R	10*	.1
30	Sweet Dreams Inc—*F Sansing*	1300 E Upas Ave, Mcallen TX 78501	956-687-2737	R	9*	.1
31	Anderson Fabrics Inc—*Ron Anderson*	PO Box 311, Blackduck MN 56630	218-835-6677	R	8*	.3
32	Hospi-Tel Manufacturing Co—*David Freedland*	545 N Arlington Ave St, East Orange NJ 07017	973-678-7100	R	8*	.1
33	Hedaya Home Fashions Inc—*Nathan Hedaya*	1111 Jefferson Ave, Elizabeth NJ 07201	908-352-0808	R	8*	.1
34	Berkshire Blanket Holdings Inc—*Thomas Bowles*	PO Box 420, Ware MA 01082	413-967-5964	R	8*	.1
35	Crane Interiors Inc—*Larry Bucklin*	PO Box 459, Woodbury TN 37190	615-563-4800	R	8*	.2
36	Royale Comfort Seating Inc—*Clyde Goble*	PO Box 235, Taylorsville NC 28681	828-632-2865	R	8*	.1
37	Initials Interiors Inc—*Mario Morales*	PO Box 3860, Cookeville TN 38502	931-520-1523	R	7*	.1
38	Dallco Industries Inc—*Douglas Dallmeyer*	PO Box 2727, York PA 17405	717-854-7875	R	7*	.2
39	Bramson House Inc—*Jules Abramson*	151 Albany Ave, Freeport NY 11520	516-764-5006	R	6*	.1
40	SIS Enterprises Inc—*Shari Hammer*	6707 Shingle Creek Pkw, Minneapolis MN 55430	763-789-0956	R	6*	.1
41	Saturday Knight Ltd—*Franklin Kling*	2100 Section Rd, Cincinnati OH 45237	513-641-1400	R	6*	.1
42	Stevens Linen Associates Inc—*Gregory Kline*	PO Box 95, Dudley MA 01571	508-943-0813	R	6*	.1
43	Comfort Research LLC—*Chip George*	3860 Roger B Chaffee B, Grand Rapids MI 49548	616-475-5000	R	6*	<.1
44	Ltpc Inc—*Michael Mitch*	900 Conroy Pl, Easton PA 18040	610-438-2418	R	6*	.1
45	Pro-Mart Industries Inc—*Azad Sabounjian*	17421 Von Karman Ave, Irvine CA 92614	949-428-7700	R	4*	<.1
46	Gp Foam Fabricators Inc—*Bobby Pace*	PO Box 7483, High Point NC 27264	336-434-3600	R	4*	<.1
47	Chief Manufacturing Co—*Susan Hall*	PO Box 191, Thomaston GA 30286	706-647-1162	R	3*	<.1
48	Postcraft Co—*Bruce Beyer*	625 W Rillito St, Tucson AZ 85705	520-624-2531	R	2*	<.1
49	Dakotah Inc	530 Park Ln, Webster SD 57274	605-345-2268	S	2*	<.1
50	GI Roth Inc—*Judith Roth*	470 E Brown St, Blairsville PA 15717	724-459-6600	R	2*	<.1
51	Better Sleep Inc—*William Emery*	100 Readington Rd, Branchburg NJ 08876	908-464-2200	R	2*	<.1
52	Frederick Hart Company Inc—*Frederick Hart*	2617 Talley St Ste A, Decatur GA 30030	404-373-4030	R	1*	<.1
53	Heartland USA Inc—*Helen Higgins*	6435 Us 45 S, Carrier Mills IL 62917	618-994-4343	R	1*	<.1

TOTALS: SIC 2392 Housefurnishings Nec
Companies: 53   5,136   55.3

2393 Textile Bags

1	Adco Products Inc—*Alan Ein*	10920 Ventura Blvd, Studio City CA 91604	818-998-6655	R	35*	1.0
2	Outdoor Recreation Group Incorporated Outdoor Products—*Joel Altshule*	1919 Vine Burn Ave, Los Angeles CA 90032	323-226-0820	R	23*	.1

Note: An asterisk (*) indicates an estimated financial figure. The company type code used is as follows: R = Private, P = Public, S = Private Subsidiary, B = Public Subsidiary, D = Division, J = Joint Venture, I = Investment Fund.

COMPANY RANKINGS BY SALES WITHIN 4-DIGIT SIC

Rank	Company Name—Executive Officer	Address, City, State, Zip	Phone	Type	Fin	Empls
3	Gleason Corp—Howard Kay	10474 Santa Monica Blv, Los Angeles CA 90025	310-470-6001	R	15*	.5
4	Outdoor Research Inc—Dann Nordstrom	2203 1st Ave S Ste 700, Seattle WA 98134	206-467-8197	R	14*	.2
5	Fka Distributing Co—Roman Ferber	3000 N Pontiac Trl, Commerce Township MI 48390	248-863-3000	R	13*	.4
6	Starr Aircraft Products Inc—Shelby Barnette	PO Box 158, Sherman TX 75091	903-893-1106	R	12*	.3
7	J and M Industries Inc—Maurice Gaudet	300 Ponchatoula Pkwy, Ponchatoula LA 70454	985-386-6000	R	12*	.2
8	Outdoor Recreation Group Inc—Joel Altshule	1919 Vineburn Ave, Los Angeles CA 90032	323-226-0820	R	12*	.1
9	Polytex Fibers Corp—Isaac Bazbaz	9341 Baythorne Dr, Houston TX 77041	713-690-9055	R	10*	.1
10	A D M Corp—Mary Mota	100 Lincoln Blvd, Middlesex NJ 08846	732-469-0900	R	10*	.1
11	Clear Edge Crosible Inc—Mark Angus	PO Box 271, Moravia NY 13118	315-497-2960	R	9*	.2
12	Kenneth Fox Supply Co—Kenneth Fox	PO Box 2288, Mcallen TX 78502	956-682-6176	R	9*	.2
13	Action Bag and Cover Inc—Byung Lee	18401 Mount Langley St, Fountain Valley CA 92708	714-964-9144	R	8*	.1
14	Dow Cover Company Inc—Mark Steinhardt	373 Lexington Ave, New Haven CT 06513	203-469-5394	R	7*	.1
15	A Rifkin Co—Paul Lantz	PO Box 878, Wilkes Barre PA 18703	570-825-9551	R	6*	.1
16	OBC Northwest Inc—Tracy Boyce	PO Box 759, Canby OR 97013	503-266-2021	R	5*	.1
17	Acadia Industries Inc—Danny Rogers	PO Box 361, Crowley LA 70527	337-783-8182	R	5*	.1
18	American Bag and Burlap Co—Elliot Corman	PO Box 505649, Chelsea MA 02150	617-884-7600	R	3*	<.1
19	JAC Custom Pouches Inc—Kimberly Sirovica	PO Box 29, Dowagiac MI 49047	269-782-3190	R	2*	<.1

TOTALS: SIC 2393 Textile Bags
Companies: 19

					212	3.5

2394 Canvas & Related Products

1	Bestop Inc—Rick Sabourin	PO Box 307, Broomfield CO 80038	303-465-1755	S	2,380*	.4
2	CRDaniels Inc—Gary Abel	PO Box 17211, Baltimore MD 21297	410-461-2100	R	69*	.4
3	Estex Manufacturing Company Inc—Brent Wilkes	PO Box 368, Fairburn GA 30213	770-964-3322	R	59*	.1
4	Rainier Industries Ltd—Scott Campbell	18375 Olympic Ave S, Tukwila WA 98188	425-251-1800	R	21*	.1
5	Great Lakes Boat Top Co—Jim Wilson	15 Quality Cir, Vonore TN 37885	423-884-6761	R	20*	.1
6	Speck Products Inc—Irene Baran	227 Forest Ave, Palo Alto CA 94301	650-462-2040	R	16*	<.1
7	Outdoor Venture Corp—James Egnew	30 Venture Dr, Stearns KY 42647	606-376-5021	R	15*	.2
8	Reyes Industries Inc—Fernando Reyes	PO Box 241687, San Antonio TX 78224	210-924-3190	R	15*	.3
9	Service Manufacturing Corp (Aurora Illinois)	5414 W Roosevelt Rd, Chicago IL 60644	773-287-5600	R	14*	.1
10	Hendee Enterprises Inc—John Macfarlane	9350 S Point Dr, Houston TX 77054	713-796-2322	R	12*	.1
11	Covercraft Industries Inc—Martin Lichtmann	100 Enterprise, Pauls Valley OK 73075	405-238-9651	R	11*	.4
12	Holland Awning Co—Steven Schaftenaar	10875 Chicago Dr, Zeeland MI 49464	616-772-2052	R	10*	.1
13	John Johnson Co—Richard Dancy	274 S Waterman St, Detroit MI 48209	313-496-0600	R	10*	.1
14	Sunsetter Products LP—Heidi Coy	184 Charles St, Malden MA 02148	781-321-9600	R	9*	.1
15	Vapc Liquidating Inc—Kevin Shea	12 Forbes Rd, Newmarket NH 03857	603-659-6439	R	8*	.1
16	Integrated Textile Solutions Inc—Joanne Thornehill	865 Cleveland Ave, Salem VA 24153	540-389-8113	R	8*	.1
17	Eide Industries Inc—Don Araiza	16215 Piuma Ave, Cerritos CA 90703	562-402-8335	R	8*	.1
18	Mountain Tarp And Awning Inc—Jeff Bowling	PO Box 186, Middlesboro KY 40965		R	8*	.1
19	E-Z On Auto Tops Inc—Leo Davis	PO Box 130, Iva SC 29655	864-348-7772	R	6*	.1
20	Broton Industries Inc—G Lewis	1 Sam Stratton Rd, Amsterdam NY 12010	518 842 3030	R	6*	.1
21	Western Ag Enterprises Inc—Richard Carter	8121 W Harrison St, Tolleson AZ 85353	623-907-4034	R	6*	.1
22	Air Structures American Technologies Inc—Donato Fraioli	211 S Ridge St Ste 3, Port Chester NY 10573	914-937-4500	R	5*	.1
23	Transportation Equipment Inc—Lynn Chenowth	1404 N Marshall Ave, El Cajon CA 92020	619-449-8860	R	5*	<.1
24	RJ Hanlon Company Inc—Robert Hanlon	17408 Tiller Ct Ste 60, Westfield IN 46074	317-867-2900	R	5*	.1
25	MM Reif Ltd—Harry Miller	PO Box 191490, Boston MA 02119	617-442-9500	R	5*	.1
26	Marine Mooring Inc—Randall Pollen	3404 N 600 E, Warsaw IN 46582	574-594-5787	R	4*	<.1
27	Lomont Holdings Company Inc—Dan Lomont	PO Box 537, Angola IN 46703	260-665-7492	R	4*	<.1
28	Gosport Manufacturing Company Inc—Joseph King	PO Box 26, Gosport IN 47433	812-879-4224	R	3*	<.1
29	Dawson Tarpaulins Inc—Melvin Gilley	PO Box 666, Dawson GA 39842	229-995-3018	R	3*	<.1
30	Baraboo Tent and Awning Inc—Clyde Moon	PO Box 57, Baraboo WI 53913	608-356-8303	R	2*	<.1
31	California Industrial Fabrics—Robert White	2325 Marconi Ct, San Diego CA 92154	619-661-7166	R	2*	<.1
32	Clamshell Structures Inc—Gregory J Mangan	1101 Maulhardt Ave, Oxnard CA 93030	805-988-1340	R	2*	<.1
33	Zamzow Manufacturing Company Inc—Ellis Schmidt	3201 N Broadway, Saint Louis MO 63147	314-231-5034	R	2*	<.1
34	Albax Inc—William Picciotti	500 W Wrightwood Ave, Elmhurst IL 60126	630-758-1072	R	1*	<.1
35	Quadro Corp—Wayne Jenum	21796 Hwy 55 N, Glenwood MN 56334	320-634-5353	R	1*	<.1
36	Innovative Designs Inc (Pittsburg Pennsylvania)—Joseph Riccelli	223 N Main St Ste 1, Pittsburgh PA 15215	412-799-0350	P	1	<.1
37	Canamer Intl LLC—George Cipov	5701 Industrial Park R, Winona MN 55987	507-452-1700	R	1*	<.1
38	FOF Products Inc—Richard Roeder	PO Box 904, Delavan WI 53115	262-728-2686	R	1*	<.1
39	Contemporary Computerwear Corp—Joseph D'aura	PO Box 320117, San Francisco CA 94132	415-664-0164	R	1*	<.1

TOTALS: SIC 2394 Canvas & Related Products
Companies: 39

					2,755	3.7

2395 Pleating & Stitching

1	Airborne Systems Group—Elek Puskas	5800 Magnolia Ave, Pennsauken NJ 08109	856-663-8120	R	134*	.6
2	Fabri-Quilt Inc—Adlai Kunst	901 E 14th Ave, Kansas City MO 64116	816-421-2000	R	39*	.2
3	Avanti Linens Inc—Arthur Tauber	PO Box 415, Wood Ridge NJ 07075	201-641-7766	R	31*	.2
4	Sansegal Sportswear Inc—Macon Rudick	611 W 9560 S, Sandy UT 84070	801-566-3248	R	25*	.3
5	World Emblem International Inc—Randy Carr	1500 Ne 131st St, North Miami FL 33161	305-899-9006	R	21*	.3
6	National Emblem Inc—Milton Lubin	PO Box 5325, Carson CA 90749	310-537-4900	R	16*	.3
7	Liberty Embroidery Inc—Phillip Ray	PO Box 707, Madison NC 27025	336-548-1802	R	16*	.6
8	Lakeshirts Inc—Mark Fritz	PO Box 52, Detroit Lakes MN 56502	218-847-2171	R	15*	.5
9	Lg Inc—Susan Ganz	10246 Reisterstown Rd, Owings Mills MD 21117	410-363-1000	R	12*	.4
10	Ensign Emblem Ltd—Gayle Zreliak	1746 Keane Dr, Traverse City MI 49696	231-946-7703	R	9*	.2
11	New Buffalo Shirt Factory Inc—John Weiss	4055 Casillio Pkwy, Clarence NY 14031	716-759-6273	R	8*	.1
12	Penn Emblem Co—Stephen Grady	PO Box 16243, Philadelphia PA 19114	215-632-7800	R	7*	.1
13	Creative Embroidery Corp—Steven Diamond	305 3rd Ave W Ste 3, Newark NJ 07107	973-497-5700	R	6*	<.1
14	Janlynn Corp—John Kozub	2070 Westover Rd, Chicopee MA 01022	413-206-0002	R	6*	.1
15	Time Square Development Corp—Norton Handler	PO Box 39203, Denver CO 80239	303-375-1011	R	4*	.1
16	Regal Originals Inc—Rodger Cohen	247 W 37th St Frnt 3, New York NY 10018	212-921-0270	R	3*	.1
17	Gregory A Scott Inc—Greg Scott	PO Box 11058, Kansas City KS 66111	913-287-5390	R	2*	<.1
18	Pleating Plus Ltd—Ernest Vega	527 40th St, Union City NJ 07087	201-863-2991	R	1*	<.1
19	Yoonimex Inc—Edward Yoon	12941 Sunnyside Pl, Santa Fe Springs CA 90670	562-906-2100	R	1*	.1

TOTALS: SIC 2395 Pleating & Stitching
Companies: 19

					354	3.9

2396 Automotive & Apparel Trimmings

1	Findlay Industries Inc—Philip D Gardner	4000 Fostoria Ave, Findlay OH 45840	419-422-1302	R	1,141*	5.0

Rank	Company Name—*Executive Officer*	Address, City, State, Zip	Phone	Type	Fin	Empls
2	Travel Tags Inc—*Barb Cederberg*	5842 Carmen Ave, Inver Grove Heights MN 55076	651-450-1201	R	918*	.4
3	Berwick Offray LLC—*Scott Shea*	PO Box 428, Berwick PA 18603	570-752-5934	S	252*	2.1
4	Vomela Specialty Company Inc—*Thomas Auth*	274 Fillmore Ave E, Saint Paul MN 55107	651-228-2200	R	35*	.3
5	QST Industries Inc—*Thomas Danch*	525 W Monroe St Ste 14, Chicago IL 60661	312-930-9400	R	29*	.1
6	Dayton Bag and Burlap Co—*Samuel Lumby*	PO Box 8, Dayton OH 45401	937-258-8000	R	21*	.1
7	Hi-Tech Seating Products Inc—*Ronald Belk*	40 E Verdugo Ave 2, Burbank CA 91502	323-564-4481	R	14*	.2
8	Allied Printing Services Inc—*John Sommers*	PO Box 850, Manchester CT 06045	860-643-1101	R	13*	.4
9	Romatic Manufacturing Co—*Roger Hebert*	PO Box 470, Southbury CT 06488	203-264-8203	R	13*	.2
10	American Process Lettering Inc—*Gary Huddell*	PO Box 251, Clifton Heights PA 19018	610-623-9000	R	11*	.2
11	Sharpline Converting Inc—*Jack Snyder*	PO Box 9608, Wichita KS 67277	316-722-9080	R	10*	.3
12	SS Designs Inc—*Bob Carter*	PO Box 834, Winter Haven FL 33882	863-965-2576	R	9*	.1
13	Rennen International—*TK Lee*	120-19 Rockaway Blvd, South Ozone Park NY 11420	718-978-6722	R	9*	<.1
14	Diemasters Manufacturing Inc—*Virgil Dela*	2100 Touhy Ave, Elk Grove Village IL 60007	847-640-9900	R	8*	.1
15	Pointsmith Point-Of-Purchase Management Services LP—*Thomas Ashe*	21202 Park Row Dr, Katy TX 77449	281-599-5900	R	8*	.1
16	American Stitchco Inc—*Steve Luelf*	4662 Hwy 62 W, Mountain Home AR 72653	870-425-7777	R	8*	.2
17	Greenfield Research Inc—*Michael Penn*	PO Box 239, Greenfield OH 45123	937-981-2154	R	8*	.3
18	Starline USA Inc—*Joshua Lapsker*	3036 Alt Blvd, Grand Island NY 14072	716-773-0100	R	7*	.1
19	Petra Manufacturing Co—*Norman Hoffberg*	6600 W Armitage Ave, Chicago IL 60707	773-622-1475	R	7*	.1
20	ES Sports Corp—*Eric Suher*	47 Jackson St, Holyoke MA 01040	413-534-5634	R	7*	.1
21	Artisans Inc—*Gordon Dukerschein*	PO Box 278, Glen Flora WI 54526	715-322-5285	R	6*	.1
22	Lending Trimming Company Inc—*John Benis*	179 Christopher St, New York NY 10014	212-242-7502	R	6*	.1
23	International Foam Products Inc—*Steve Sklow*	PO Box 545, Stanhope NJ 07874	704-588-0080	R	6*	.1
24	Dallas Bias Fabrics Inc—*Stewart Kipness*	1401 N Carroll Ave, Dallas TX 75204	214-824-2036	R	6*	.1
25	Dash Designs Inc—*Brad Schiff*	6014 S Ash Ave, Tempe AZ 85283	480-967-1675	R	5*	.1
26	Kid-U-Not Inc—*Linda Rubel*	1201 Central Park Dr, Sanford FL 32771	407-324-2112	R	5*	.1
27	Sugar Creek Designs Inc—*Jayne Erwin*	202 S Joplin Ave, Joplin MO 64801	417-781-9696	R	5*	.1
28	Graphic Prints Inc—*Alan Greenberg*	16540 S Main St, Gardena CA 90248	310-768-0474	R	5*	<.1
29	Karibe Inc—*Karen Carroll*	PO Box 681, Pittston PA 18640	570-655-9173	R	5*	.1
30	Hot Action Sportswear Inc—*Melissa Penland*	307 Division Ave Ste 1, Ormond Beach FL 32174	386-677-5680	R	5*	<.1
31	Admark Graphic Systems Inc—*Larry Sloop*	PO Box 2789, Huntersville NC 28070	704-596-5180	R	5*	<.1
32	Adcolor Screenprinting Inc—*Kurt Hulliger*	620 Adcolor Dr, Lexington KY 40511	859-253-1046	R	4*	.1
33	Prinzing Enterprises Inc—*Robert Lasky*	PO Box 2131, Milwaukee WI 53201		S	4*	<.1
34	National Bias Fabric Co—*James Engelbert*	4516 Saint Clair Ave, Cleveland OH 44103	216-361-0530	R	4*	<.1
35	Western Textile Products Co—*Charles Van Dyke*	3400 Tree Ct Industry, Saint Louis MO 63122	636-225-9400	R	4*	<.1
36	Htm Concepts Inc—*John Hughes*	118 County Farm Rd, Windsor NC 27983	252-794-2122	R	2*	<.1
37	Goodbye Blue Monday Inc—*Robert Haney*	2865 Wilderness Pl Ste, Boulder CO 80301	303-786-7220	R	2*	<.1
38	Automatic Printing Company Inc—*George Prescott*	1713 Cuming St 15, Omaha NE 68102	402-341-2351	R	1*	<.1

TOTALS: SIC 2396 Automotive & Apparel Trimmings
Companies: 38   2,607   11.3

2397 Schiffli Machine Embroideries

1	United Embroidery Inc—*Lawrence Severrini*	17 Wondoll Pl, Fairview NJ 07022	201-863-0070	R	9*	.2

2399 Fabricated Textile Products Nec

1	G-III Apparel Group Ltd—*Morris Goldfarb*	512 7th Ave, New York NY 10018	212-403-0500	P	1,063	2.2
2	TRW Vehicle Safety Systems Inc	14761 East 32 Mile Rd, Romeo MI 48065	586-232-7200	S	500*	7.0
3	G-III License Company LLC G-III Apparel Group Ltd	512 7th Ave, New York NY 10018	212-403-0500	S	254*	.4
4	Annin and Co—*Carter Beard*	105 Eisenhower Pky Ste, Roseland NJ 07068	973-228-9400	R	216*	.5
5	Bridgewater Interiors LLC—*Ronald Hall*	4617 W Fort St, Detroit MI 48209	313-842-3300	J	147*	.3
6	Superior Uniform Group Inc—*Michael Benstock*	10055 Seminole Blvd, Seminole FL 33772	727-397-9611	P	112	.6
7	Joe's Jeans Inc—*Marc B Crossman*	2340 S Eastern Ave, Commerce CA 90040	323-837-3700	P	95	.3
8	G-III Brands Ltd G-III Apparel Group Ltd	512 7th Ave, New York NY 10018	212-403-0500	S	93*	.3
9	Asco Division of Win Craft Inc—*John Killen*	PO Box 888, Winona MN 55987	507-452-3386	D	75*	.4
10	Pioneer Aerospace Corp—*John Smith*	PO Box 207, South Windsor CT 06074	860-528-0092	S	25*	.6
11	Britten Banners Inc—*Paul Britten*	2322 Cass Rd, Traverse City MI 49684	231-941-8200	R	25*	.1
12	Artfx Inc—*Thomas Groce*	PO Box 128, Rich Square NC 27869	757-853-1703	R	19*	.2
13	Decorator Industries Inc—*William A Johnson*	12240 SW 53rd St Ste 5, Cooper City FL 33330	954-689-0370	R	19	.2
14	Mills Manufacturing Corp—*James Turner*	PO Box 8100, Asheville NC 28814	828-645-3061	R	17*	.2
15	Vesture Corp—*Byron Owens*	120 E Pritchard St, Asheboro NC 27203	336-629-3000	R	15*	.1
16	Nor'eastern Trawl Systems Inc—*Tomomi Ishii*	7910 Ne Day Rd, Bainbridge Island WA 98110	206-842-5623	R	15*	.1
17	VH Blackinton and Company Inc—*Peter Roque*	PO Box 1300, Attleboro Falls MA 02763	508-699-4436	R	13*	.2
18	National Banner Company Inc—*Marc Goldfarb*	PO Box 842372, Dallas TX 75284	972-241-2131	R	11*	.2
19	Action Embroidery Corp—*Ira Newman*	1315 Brooks St, Ontario CA 91762	909-983-1359	R	11*	.2
20	Fenner Inc—*Nick Hobson*	311 W Stiegel St, Manheim PA 17545	717-665-2421	R	10*	.3
21	Performance Designs Inc—*William Coe*	1300 E International S, Deland FL 32724	386-738-2224	R	10*	.2
22	USA Products Group Inc—*Stephen Jackson*	PO Box 1750, Lodi CA 95241	209-334-1460	R	7*	.1
23	Valeo—*Brian Anderson*	19275 W Capitol Dr, Brookfield WI 53045		R	7*	<.1
24	Carolina Visuals LLC—*Micheal Liberman*	PO Box 160, Smoaks SC 29481	843-562-2010	R	6*	.2
25	Prestige Flag and Banner Company Inc—*Mike Roberts*	591 Camino Dela Reina, San Diego CA 92108	619-497-2220	R	6*	.1
26	RJS Racing Equipment Inc—*Robert Farmer*	23506 John R Rd, Hazel Park MI 48030	248-548-5727	R	4*	.1
27	Blackburn Manufacturing Co—*James Blackburn*	PO Box 86, Neligh NE 68756	402-887-4161	R	4*	.1
28	Osp Sling Inc—*Todd Negus*	PO Box 1207, Sequim WA 98382	360-683-4109	R	4*	<.1
29	Aircraft Industries Inc—*Susan Klemm*	PO Box 549, Edwardsburg MI 49112	269-663-8544	R	4*	<.1
30	Mcleod Belting Company Inc—*John Andrew*	PO Box 2310, Greensboro NC 27402	336-299-7216	R	3*	<.1
31	Basic Concepts Inc—*Edward Romer*	1310 Harris Bridge Rd, Anderson SC 29621	864-224-7227	R	3*	<.1
32	Mount Everest Contract Sewing—*Myung Jun*	867 Isabella St, Oakland CA 94607	510-834-9478	R	3*	<.1
33	Photo Emblem Inc—*Sherman Richardson*	5010 S Main St, Winston Salem NC 27107	336-784-4000	R	2*	<.1
34	Starkor Manufacturing Inc—*Phyllis Atwood*	3454 Ne Hwy 101, Lincoln City OR 97367	541-994-3939	R	1*	<.1
35	Applied Visual Sciences—*Michael W Trudnak*	250 Exchange Pl Ste H, Herndon VA 20170	703-464-5495	P	1	<.1
36	Arlington Sample Book Company Inc—*James Nichol*	100 Fernwood Point Rd, Sunapee NH 03782	603-763-9082	R	1*	<.1
37	Flameret Inc—*Christopher Glover*	1810 E Sahara Ave Ste, Las Vegas NV 89104		P	<1	<.1

TOTALS: SIC 2399 Fabricated Textile Products Nec
Companies: 37   2,803   15.0

2411 Logging

1	Simpson Investment Co—*Colin Moseley*	917 E 11th St, Tacoma WA 98421	253-779-6400	R	780	4.3

Note: An asterisk (*) indicates an estimated financial figure. The company type code used is as follows: R = Private, P = Public, S = Private Subsidiary, B = Public Subsidiary, D = Division, J = Joint Venture, I = Investment Fund.

COMPANY RANKINGS BY SALES WITHIN 4-DIGIT SIC

Rank	Company Name—Executive Officer	Address, City, State, Zip	Phone	Type	Fin	Empls
2	Sealaska Corp—Chris E McNeil Jr	1 Sealaska Plz Ste 400, Juneau AK 99801	907-586-1512	R	495*	1.4
3	MAXXAM Property Inc—Charles E Hurwitz	1330 Post Oak Blvd Ste, Houston TX 77056	713-975-7600	S	370*	1.2
4	Klukwan Inc—Tom Crandall	PO Box 209, Haines AK 99827	907-766-2211	R	300*	.6
5	Canal Wood LLC—Jim Pridgen	4311- D Ludgate St, Lumberton NC 28358	910-739-2885	R	33*	.1
6	Pride Manufacturing Company LLC	10 N Main St, Burnham ME 04922	207-487-3322	R	29*	.5
7	Miller Shingle Company Inc—Bruce Miller	PO Box 29, Granite Falls WA 98252	360-691-7727	R	27*	.2
8	Peterson Pacific Inc—Larry Cumming	PO Box 40490, Eugene OR 97404	541-689-6520	R	22*	.2
9	Siller Brothers Inc—Tom Siller	1250 Smith Rd, Yuba City CA 95991	530-673-0734	R	11*	.1
10	Pine Timber Wood Production Inc—Dennis Carey	PO Box 579, Montezuma GA 31063	478-472-8213	R	7*	.1
11	Shaan Seet Inc—Leona Casey	PO Box 690, Craig AK 99921	907-826-3251	R	2*	<.1
12	Soterra LLC—Michael Gasser	PO Box 18, Jackson MS 39205	601-933-0088	S	1*	<.1

TOTALS: SIC 2411 Logging
Companies: 12 2,077 8.7

2421 Sawmills & Planing Mills—General

Rank	Company Name—Executive Officer	Address, City, State, Zip	Phone	Type	Fin	Empls
1	New South Companies Inc—James Singleton	PO Box 9089, Myrtle Beach SC 29578	843-236-9399	R	14,210*	.7
2	Stimson Lumber Co—Andrew Miller	520 SW Yamhill St Ste, Portland OR 97204	503-222-1676	R	8,435*	1.2
3	Georgia-Pacific LLC—James Hannan	PO Box 105605, Atlanta GA 30348	404-652-4000	S	1,933*	45.0
4	Universal Forest Products Inc—Matthew J Missad	2801 E Beltline Ave NE, Grand Rapids MI 49525	616-364-6161	P	1,891	5.1
5	Sierra Pacific Industries—Archie Aldis (Red) Emmerson	PO Box 496028, Redding CA 96049	530-378-8000	R	1,608*	4.4
6	J Paul Levesque and Sons Inc—Dan Levesque	PO Box 749, Ashland ME 04732	207-435-6401	R	1,429*	.3
7	Louisiana-Pacific Corp—Richard W Frost	414 Union St Ste 2000, Nashville TN 37219	615-986-5600	P	1,357	3.9
8	Hampton Affiliates Inc—Steve Zika	9600 SW Barnes Rd Ste, Portland OR 97225	503-297-7691	R	1,170*	1.8
9	Pope and Talbot Inc—Harold N Stanton	1500 SW 1st Ave Ste 20, Portland OR 97201	503-228-9161	P	841	2.4
10	Batson Mill LLC—Paul L Howes	PO Box 444, Batson TX 77519	936-262-8000	S	791*	1.7
11	Temple-Inland Forest Products Corp—DoyleR Simons	1300 S Mopac Expwy 3rd, Austin TX 78746	512-434-5800	S	787*	3.1
12	Cranberry Hardwoods Inc—J Jarrell	PO Box 7290, Beckley WV 25802	304-255-2240	R	662*	.1
13	Louisiana-Pacific Corporation Division Office—Rick Frost Louisiana-Pacific Corp	PO Box 4000, Hayden Lake ID 83835	208-772-6011	D	350*	2.8
14	Jemison Investment Company Inc—James Davis	2001 Park Pl Ste 320, Birmingham AL 35203	205-324-7681	R	300*	<.1
15	Rex Lumber Co—Benjamin Forester	840 Main St, Acton MA 01720	978-263-0055	R	272*	.3
16	Anthony Timberlands Inc—Steve Anthony	PO Box 137, Bearden AR 71720	870-687-3611	R	252*	.3
17	Taylor-Ramsey Corp—Pete Ramsey	PO Box 11888, Lynchburg VA 24506	434-929-7443	R	176*	.5
18	Swanson Group Inc—Steven Swanson	PO Box 250, Glendale OR 97442	541-832-1121	R	176*	.7
19	Deltic Timber Corp—Ray C Dillon	PO Box 7200, El Dorado AR 71731	870-881-9400	P	142	.5
20	Gilman Building Products LLC—Bobby Strickland	581705 White Oak Rd, Yulee FL 32097	904-548-1000	R	131*	.8
21	Piedmont Lumber and Mill Co—Bill Myer	395 Taylor Blvd Ste 22, Pleasant Hill CA 94523	925-674-8970	R	122*	.1
22	Kitchens Brothers Manufacturing Co—D Kitchens	PO Box 217, Utica MS 39175	601-885-6001	R	105*	.3
23	Potlatch Corp Wood Products Western Div—Michael Covey	PO Box 1016, Lewiston ID 83501	509-835-1500	D	71*	.4
24	Manke Lumber Company Inc—Charles Manke	1717 Marine View Dr, Tacoma WA 98422	253-572-6252	R	65*	.5
25	Guy Bennett Lumber Co—Janice Dimke	PO Box 875, Clarkston WA 99403	208-875-1121	R	64*	.3
26	Anderson-Tully Co—Chip Dickinson	775 Ridge Lake Blvd St, Memphis TN 38120	901-576-1400	R	63*	.3
27	Buchanan Hardwoods Inc—Doug Fikes	PO Box 424, Selma AL 36701	334-872-0491	R	53*	.4
28	Corbitt Manufacturing Inc—Hosea Corbitt	854 NW Guerdon St, Lake City FL 32055	386-755-2555	R	52*	.3
29	Rsg Forest Products Inc—Robert Sanders	985 Nw 2nd St, Kalama WA 98625	360-673-2825	R	51*	.8
30	Freeman Brothers Lumber Inc—Terry Freeman	PO Box 490, Russellville AR 72811	479-968-4986	R	47*	.2
31	Shuqualak Lumber Company Inc—Bill Thomas	69 College St, Shuqualak MS 39361	662-793-4528	R	46*	.2
32	Anderson and Middleton Co—Jim Middleton	815 8th St, Hoquiam WA 98550	360-533-2410	R	46*	.1
33	Cal-Tex Lumber Company Inc—George Schmidbauer	PO Box 631010, Nacogdoches TX 75963	936-564-6426	R	42*	.2
34	Mason County Forest Products LLC	PO Box 1626, Shelton WA 98584	360-427-3500	R	41*	.2
35	Cersosimo Lumber Company Inc—Dominic Cersosimo	1103 Vernon St, Brattleboro VT 05301	802-254-4508	R	38*	.2
36	Welco Lumber Co—Dick Stroble	813 E 8th St, Port Angeles WA 98362	360-651-1580	R	38	.2
37	Vaagen Brothers Lumber Inc Ione Div—Duane Vaagen Vaagen Brothers Lumber Inc	565 W 5th Ave, Colville WA 99114	509-684-5071	D	38*	.1
38	Warm Springs Forest Products Industries	PO Box 810, Warm Springs OR 97761		R	35*	.1
39	Frank Miller Lumber Company Incorporated Union City—Martha Miller Mathias	1690 Frank Miller Rd, Union City IN 47390	765-964-3196	R	33*	.2
40	Taylor Lumber Inc—Joe Churak	18253 State Rte 73, Mc Dermott OH 45652	740-259-6222	R	32*	.3
41	Southern Lumber Company Inc—Jeff Pohle	1402 Monterey Hwy, San Jose CA 95110	408-297-9663	R	31*	.1
42	Buse Timber and Sales Inc—Mark Hecker	3812 28th Pl Ne, Everett WA 98201	425-258-2577	R	30*	.1
43	Cascade Hardwoods LLC—Kelley Hekinson	PO Box 269, Chehalis WA 98532	360-748-0178	R	30*	.3
44	Gutchess Lumber Company Inc—Andrew Middleton	PO Box 5478, Cortland NY 13045	607-753-3393	R	29*	.3
45	Pacific Fibre Products Inc—Larry Lemmons	PO Box 278, Longview WA 98632	360-577-7112	R	29*	.2
46	Moose River Lumber Company Inc—C Lumbert	PO Box 454, Jackman ME 04945	207-668-4193	R	29*	.1
47	Collum's Lumber Products LLC—Craig Harper	PO Box 535, Allendale SC 29810	803-584-3451	R	29*	.3
48	Ralph Hamel Forest Products Inc—Ralph Hamel	5401 County Rd D, Vesper WI 54489	715-569-4186	R	28*	.1
49	Hardwoods Of Michigan Inc—Robert Vogel	PO Box 620, Clinton MI 49236	517-456-7431	R	28*	.1
50	Collins Pine Co—Eric Schooler	1618 Sw 1st Ave Ste 50, Portland OR 97201	503-227-1219	R	28*	.4
51	North American Forest Products Inc—John Wiley	PO Box 600, Edwardsburg MI 49112	269-663-8500	R	28*	.2
52	SDS Lumber Co—Jason Spadero	PO Box 266, Bingen WA 98605	509-493-2155	R	27*	.3
53	Begley Lumber Company Inc—George Begley	PO Box 2800, Hazard KY 40743	606-877-1228	R	27*	.3
54	Seneca Sawmill Co—Aaron Jones	PO Box 851, Eugene OR 97440	541-689-1011	R	27*	.2
55	Vaagen Brothers Lumber Inc—Duane Vaagen	565 W 5th Ave, Colville WA 99114	509-684-5071	R	26*	.2
56	Rebel Lumber Company Inc—Winfred Little	PO Box 340, Marshville NC 28103	704-272-7623	R	26*	.2
57	Swift Lumber Inc—George Swift	PO Box 1298, Atmore AL 36504	251-368-8800	R	25*	.1
58	Pacific Topsoils Inc—Dave Forman	805 80th St Sw, Everett WA 98203	425-337-2700	R	25*	.2
59	Pyramid Mountain Lumber Inc—Roger Johnson	PO Box 549, Seeley Lake MT 59868	406-677-2201	R	24*	.1
60	Forest Tmi Products Inc—Peter Fograscher	318 State Hwy 7, Morton WA 98356	360-496-6777	R	24*	.2
61	D R Johnson Lumber Co—Don Johnson	PO Box 66, Riddle OR 97469	541-874-2231	R	23*	.2
62	Neiman Enterprises Inc—James Neiman	PO Box 218, Hulett WY 82720	307-467-5252	R	23*	.3
63	Jordan Lumber and Supply Inc—Robert Jordan	PO Box 98, Mount Gilead NC 27306	910-439-6121	R	23*	.4
64	Canfor USA Corp—George Layton	4395 Curtis Rd, Bellingham WA 98226	360-647-2434	R	23*	.2
65	JD Lumber Inc—Jeff Weimer	PO Box 55, Priest River ID 83856	208-448-2671	R	22*	.2
66	Hassell and Hughes Lumber Company Inc—Ralph Hughes	PO Box 68, Collinwood TN 38450	931-724-9191	R	22*	.2
67	American Testing Laboratories Inc—N Horton	PO Box 4230, Eatonton GA 31024	706-485-7796	R	21*	.2
68	Memphis Hardwood Flooring Company Inc—Tom Cathey	PO Box 382093, Germantown TN 38183	901-526-7306	R	20*	.2
69	Yoder Lumber Company Inc—Eli Yoder	4515 Township Rd 367, Millersburg OH 44654	330-893-3121	R	20*	.2
70	Independence Lumber Inc—Randall Eller	407 Lumber Ln, Independence VA 24348	276-773-3744	R	20*	.2
71	Dunaway Timber Co—Robert Christ	PO Box 157, Fordsville KY 42343	270-276-3367	R	20*	.1
72	Wisconsin Veneer And Plywood Co—John Besse	PO Box 140, Mattoon WI 54450	715-489-3611	R	19*	.2

Rank	Company Name—*Executive Officer*	Address, City, State, Zip	Phone	Type	Fin	Empls
73	Sanders Wood Products Inc—*Robert Sanders*	PO Box 169, Molalla OR 97038	503-829-7200	R	19*	.3
74	Wilkins Kaiser and Olsen Inc—*William Wilkins*	PO Box 8, Carson WA 98610	509-427-8413	R	19*	.1
75	Parton Lumber Company Inc—*Carl Parton*	251 Parton Rd, Rutherfordton NC 28139	828-287-4257	R	19*	.1
76	Cortland Wood Products Inc—*Homer Gutchess*	PO Box 5508, Cortland NY 13045	607-753-1081	R	17*	.2
77	Kretz Lumber Company Inc—*Troy Brown*	PO Box 548, Antigo WI 54409	715-623-5410	R	17*	.2
78	Mid-Willamette Lumber Products Inc—*John Taylor*	38054 Jefferson Scio D, Scio OR 97374	503-394-2089	R	17*	.2
79	Forest Products Inc—*W Robinson*	PO Box 541, Corbin KY 40702	606-528-3553	R	17*	.2
80	Menominee Tribal Enterprises—*Adrian Miller*	PO Box 10, Neopit WI 54150	715-756-2311	R	17*	.2
81	South Everson Lumber Company Inc—*Hardarshan Johal*	PO Box 309, Everson WA 98247	360-966-2188	R	17*	.1
82	Thompson Hardwoods Inc—*Stephen Johnson*	PO Box 646, Hazlehurst GA 31539	912-375-7703	R	16*	.2
83	RY Timber Inc—*Don Richardson*	PO Box 220, Townsend MT 59644	406-266-3111	R	15*	.2
84	Fred Netterville Lumber Co—*Charles Netterville*	PO Box 857, Woodville MS 39669	601-888-4343	R	15*	.1
85	Replogle Enterprises—*Giles Replogle*	PO Box 130, Henry TN 38231	731-243-7268	R	14*	.2
86	Durgin And Crowell Lumber Company Inc—*Peter Crowell*	231 Fisher Corner Rd, New London NH 03257	603-763-2860	R	13*	.1
87	Norstam Veneers Inc—*George Bowlin*	PO Box 32, Mauckport IN 47142	812-732-4391	R	13*	.1
88	Robbins Lumber Inc—*Jenness Robbins*	PO Box 9, Searsmont ME 04973	207-342-5221	R	13*	.1
89	Southern Forest Products LLC—*Tony Damron*	PO Box 207, Bon Wier TX 75928	409-397-4221	S	13*	.1
90	Jasper Lumber Company Inc—*Freddy Thompson*	PO Box 1425, Jasper AL 35502	205-384-9088	R	13*	.1
91	Washington Alder LLC—*Richard Ammons*	13421 Farm To Market R, Mount Vernon WA 98273	360-428-8583	R	13*	.1
92	Sierra Forest Products Inc—*Kent Duysen*	PO Box 10060, Terra Bella CA 93270	559-535-4893	R	12*	.1
93	PH Chadbourne and Co—*Robert P Chadbourne*	PO Box 88 Rte 26, Bethel ME 04217	207-824-2166	R	12*	.1
94	Coxe-Lewis Corp—*Thomas C Coxe*	PO Box 5, Gatesville NC 27938	252-357-0050	R	12*	.1
95	Lewis Brothers Land and Timber Inc—*Jeff Lewis*	PO Box 334, Aliceville AL 35442	205-373-2496	R	12*	.1
96	AJD Forest Products LP—*Jerry Goodmore*	PO Box 629, Grayling MI 49738	989-348-5412	R	12*	.1
97	Balfour Lumber Company Inc—*Michael Warren*	PO Box 1337, Thomasville GA 31799	229-226-0611	R	12*	.1
98	Flc Timber Inc—*Dennis Frank*	PO Box 79, Mill City OR 97360	503-897-2371	R	11*	.1
99	Merritt Brothers Lumber Company Inc—*Wilbur Merritt*	PO Box 190, Athol ID 83801	208-683-3321	R	11*	.1
100	Hazlehurst Lumber Company Inc—*G Adams*	PO Box 900, Hazlehurst MS 39083	601-894-1064	R	10*	.1
101	North Florida Lumber Company Inc—*C Finley Mc Rae*	PO Box 610, Bristol FL 32321	850-643-2238	R	10*	.1
102	Ray White Lumber Company Inc—*Don White*	PO Box 7, Sparkman AR 71763	870-678-2277	R	10*	.1
103	Riley Creek Lumber Co—*Marc Brinkmeyer*	PO Box 220, Laclede ID 83841	208-255-3200	R	10*	<.1
104	Keadle Lumber Enterprises Inc—*Steve Keadle*	889 Railroad St, Thomaston GA 30286	706-647-8981	R	10*	.1
105	Snider Industries Inc—*Julianna Parr*	PO Box 668, Marshall TX 75671	903-938-9221	R	10*	.1
106	Jerry Williams and Son Inc—*John Williams*	PO Box 2430, Smithfield NC 27577	919-934-4115	R	10*	.1
107	Hedstrom Lumber Company Inc—*Howard Hedstrom*	1504 Gunflint Trl, Grand Marais MN 55604	218-387-2995	R	10*	.1
108	Middle Tennessee Lumber Company Inc—*William Joyce*	PO Box 427, Burns TN 37029	615-446-3461	R	9*	.1
109	Travis Lumber Company Inc—*Gilbert Travis*	PO Box 39, Mansfield AR 72944	479-928-4446	R	9*	.1
110	East Perry Lumber Co—*Marvin Petzoldt*	PO Box 105, Frohna MO 63748	573-824-5272	R	9*	.1
111	Corley M L and Sons Sawmill Inc—*Dwight Corley*	PO Box 2519, Lexington SC 29071	803-356-2133	R	0*	.1
112	Hough and Ready Lumber Co—*Lincoln Phillippi*	PO Box 519, Cave Junction OR 97523	541-592-3116	R	9*	.1
113	Forest Shaniko Products Inc—*Lloyd Ziebert*	PO Box 557, Scio OR 97374	503-859-3698	R	9*	.1
114	Leesville Lumber Company Inc—*Glenn Williams*	PO Box 320, Leesville LA 71496	337-238-1387	R	9*	.1
115	WM Sheppard Lumber Company Inc—*William Sheppard*	PO Box 38, Brooklet GA 30415	912-842-2197	R	8*	.1
116	Algoma Lumber Company Inc—*Reinhart Krause*	1400 Perry St, Algoma WI 54201	920-407-3511	R	8*	<.1
117	Almond Brothers Lumber Co—*Ardis Almond*	403 Ringgold Ave, Coushatta LA 71019	318-932-4041	R	8*	.1
118	Dickerson Lumber Co—*Mack Dickerson*	3939 Burkesville Rd, Glasgow KY 42141	270-428-3644	R	8*	.1
119	Griffin Lumber Co—*W Griffin*	PO Box 237, Cordele GA 31010	229-273-3113	R	8*	.1
120	Harrigan Lumber Company Inc—*Patrick Harrigan*	PO Box 926, Monroeville AL 36461	251-575-4821	R	7*	.1
121	Beckwith Lumber Company Inc—*Ralph Beckwith*	PO Box 39, Slatyfork WV 26291	304-572-1220	R	7*	.1
122	Tuscarora Hardwoods Inc—*Aquillas Peachey*	PO Box 64, Elliottsburg PA 17024	717-582-4122	R	7*	.1
123	Owens and Hurst Lumber Co—*James Hurst*	PO Box 1316, Eureka MT 59917	406-297-3114	R	6*	.1
124	P E Barnes and Sons Ltd—*P Barnes*	700 Mill Rd, Hamburg AR 71646	870-853-8288	R	6*	.1
125	Wayne Lumber Company Inc—*Walter Richardson*	PO Box 576, Monticello KY 42633	606-348-9889	R	6*	.1
126	Forest Products Sales Inc—*Thomas Butterfield*	PO Box 57367, Salt Lake City UT 84157	801-262-6428	R	6*	<.1
127	East Alabama Lumber Company Inc—*Wayne Welch*	PO Box 110, Lafayette AL 36862	334-864-7120	R	5*	.1
128	Precision Prefinishing Inc—*Melvin Hartmeier*	PO Box 25277, Portland OR 97298	541-995-1655	R	5*	<.1
129	Artesia Sawdust Products Inc—*Brigitte Laura-Espinoza*	13434 S Ontario Ave, Ontario CA 91761	909-947-5983	R	5*	<.1
130	Maine Woods Company LLC—*Ken Carl*	PO Box 111, Portage ME 04768	207-435-4393	R	5*	.1
131	Donver Inc—*Donald Vershay*	PO Box 181, Kill Buck NY 14748	716-945-1910	R	4*	<.1
132	Burroughs-Ross-Colville Company LLC—*Pete Blankenship*	PO Box 610, Mcminnville TN 37111	931-473-2111	R	4*	<.1
133	Peace Flooring Company Inc—*John Duke*	PO Box 87, Magnolia AR 71754	870-234-2310	R	3*	<.1
134	Long Beach Redwood Shavings Company Inc—*Jack Price*	PO Box 1020, Long Beach CA 90801	310-639-4524	R	2*	<.1
135	Reuser Inc—*Bruce Reuser*	370 Santana Dr, Cloverdale CA 95425	707-431-1111	R	2*	<.1
136	Tigerton Lumber Co—*Gerald Ort*	PO Box 70, Tigerton WI 54486	715-535-2181	R	2*	<.1
137	Tolleson Lumber Company Inc—*Whitney Wood*	PO Box 970, Perry GA 31069	478-987-2105	R	1*	.4
138	Granite State Forest Products Inc—*Richard French*	1104 Old Concord Rd, Henniker NH 03242	603-428-7890	R	1*	<.1

TOTALS: SIC 2421 Sawmills & Planing Mills—General
Companies: 138   39,450   93.3

2426 Hardwood Dimension & Flooring Mills

Rank	Company Name—*Executive Officer*	Address, City, State, Zip	Phone	Type	Fin	Empls
1	Collins Companies Inc—*Eric L Schooler*	1618 SW 1st Ave, Portland OR 97201	503-227-1219	R	312*	.8
2	Weaber Inc—*Galen G Weaber*	1231 Mt Wilson Rd, Lebanon PA 17042	717-867-2212	R	213*	.5
3	Glen Oak Lumber and Milling Inc—*Tom Talbot*	2885 N County Rd Ste F, Montello WI 53949	608-297-2161	R	50*	.4
4	Babcock Lumber Co—*Carl Borntraeger*	2220 Palmer St, Pittsburgh PA 15218	412-351-3515	R	46*	.6
5	Robbins Inc—*James Stoehr*	4777 Eastern Ave, Cincinnati OH 45226	513-871-8988	R	36*	.3
6	American Hardwood Industries LLC—*John O'dea*	567 N Charlotte Ave, Waynesboro VA 22980	540-946-9150	R	33*	.6
7	Century Flooring Company LLC—*Roger Branscum*	PO Box 480, Melbourne AR 72556	870-368-4000	R	32*	.3
8	St Croix Valley Hardwoods Inc—*Gordon Fick*	PO Box 120, Luck WI 54853	651-407-2800	R	30*	.3
9	Havco Wood Products LLC—*Alan Austin*	PO Box 1342, Cape Girardeau MO 63702	573-334-6024	R	28*	.5
10	Robbins Hardwood Flooring Inc—*James H Stoehr III* Robbins Inc	4777 Eastern Ave, Cincinnati OH 45226	513-871-8988	D	26	.3
11	Darlington Veneer Company Inc—*John Ramsey*	PO Box 1087, Darlington SC 29540	843-393-3861	R	24*	.2
12	Anderson Wood Products Co—*Sidney Anderson*	PO Box 11517, Louisville KY 40251	502-778-5591	R	23*	.2
13	Frank Miller Lumber Company Inc—*Dan Hackett*	1690 Frank Miller Rd, Union City IN 47390	765-964-3196	R	22*	.2
14	Matson Lumber Co—*Becky Matson*	PO Box L, Brookville PA 15825	814-849-5334	R	19*	.1
15	Carolina North Lumber Co—*Bruce Hughes*	PO Box 340, Randleman NC 27317	336-498-6600	R	19*	.2
16	Maxwell Hardwood Milling—*Thomas Maxwell*	190 Wilson Mill Rd, Monticello AR 71655	870-367-2436	R	19*	.2
17	Stuart Flooring Corp—*Buddy Williams*	PO Box 947, Stuart VA 24171	276-694-4547	R	18*	.2
18	Appalachian Wood Products Inc—*Dennis Mccahan*	PO Box 1408, Clearfield PA 16830	814-765-2003	R	17*	.3

Note: An asterisk (*) indicates an estimated financial figure. The company type code used is as follows: R = Private, P = Public, S = Private Subsidiary, B = Public Subsidiary, D = Division, J = Joint Venture, I = Investment Fund.

COMPANY RANKINGS BY SALES WITHIN 4-DIGIT SIC

Rank	Company Name—Executive Officer	Address, City, State, Zip	Phone	Type	Fin	Empls
19	Inter-State Hardwoods Company Inc—Edward Frazee	PO Box 7, Bartow WV 24920	304-456-4597	R	17*	.2
20	Northwest Hardwoods Div—Steven R Rogel	10220 SW Greenburg Rd, Portland OR 97223	503-246-5700	D	16*	<.1
21	Commercial Carving Co—Bill Murphy	PO Box 878, Thomasville NC 27361	336-475-2301	R	14*	.2
22	Young's Furniture Manufacturing Co—William Young	PO Box 217, Whitesburg TN 37891	423-235-6548	R	14*	.1
23	Monticello Flooring and Lumber Company Inc—Connie Young	PO Box 637, Monticello KY 42633	606-348-5941	R	12*	.1
24	Kitko Wood Products Inc—Robert Kitko	6098 Glen Hope Blvd, Glen Hope PA 16645	814-672-3606	R	12*	.1
25	Calion Lumber Company Inc—Edwin Thomas	PO Box 348, Calion AR 71724	870-748-2411	R	12*	.1
26	Smith Flooring Inc—Jon Smith	PO Box 99, Mountain View MO 65548	417-934-2291	R	11*	.1
27	Alabama Interforest Corp—Robert Newsom	PO Box 100, Eufaula AL 36072	334-687-8009	R	11*	.1
28	Fitzpatrick And Weller Inc—Gregory Fitzpatrick	PO Box 490, Ellicottville NY 14731	716-699-2393	R	10*	.1
29	Action Floor Systems LLC—Thomas Abendroth	4781 N Us Hwy 51, Mercer WI 54547	715-476-3512	R	10*	.1
30	Indiana Wood Products Inc—Mary Hetler	PO Box 1168, Middlebury IN 46540	574-825-2129	R	9*	.1
31	Mcminnville Manufacturing Co—David Wootten	PO Box 151, Mcminnville TN 37111	931-473-2131	R	8*	.1
32	Whitson Lumber Company Inc—Albert Whitson	PO Box 705, Clarksville TN 37041	931-645-4831	R	7*	.1
33	Woodcraft Inc—Tim Elliott	PO Box 1819, Morristown TN 37816	423-581-5413	R	7*	.1
34	Buchanan Lumber Birmingham Inc—William Buchanan	PO Box 424, Aliceville AL 35442	205-373-8717	R	7*	.1
35	Baxstra Inc—Allan Stratford	1224 W 132nd St, Gardena CA 90247	323-770-4171	R	7*	.1
36	Partee Flooring Mill LLP—Larry Burrow	PO Box 667, Magnolia AR 71754	870-234-4081	R	6*	.1
37	Scepter Hardwoods Inc—Garney Scott	1485 Scepter Ln, Waverly TN 37185	931-738-5264	R	6*	.1
38	Rutland Lumber Company Inc—Leslie Rutland	PO Box 2349, Collins MS 39428	601-765-8892	R	5*	.1
39	Davis Mining and Manufacturing Inc—W Jack Davis	613 Front St E, Coeburn VA 24230	276-395-3354	R	5*	<.1
40	Cherrybark Flooring Inc—Greg Kitchens	PO Box 151, Hazlehurst MS 39083	601-894-4441	R	4*	.1
41	Brookville Wood Products Inc—Joseph Mitchell	PO Box 1, Brookville PA 15825	814-849-7331	R	4*	<.1
42	Adams Wood Products Inc—Larry Swinson	PO Box 728, Morristown TN 37815	423-587-2942	R	3*	.1
43	Blackstone Wood Products Inc—Richard Keyes	PO Box 730, Lenoir NC 28645	828-433-4747	R	3*	<.1
44	Kentwood Manufacturing Co—James Fennema	4849 Barden Ct Se, Grand Rapids MI 49512	616-698-6370	R	2*	<.1
45	Hardwoods Of Morristown Inc—James Elliot	PO Box 1196, Morristown TN 37816	423-317-9417	R	2*	<.1

TOTALS: SIC 2426 Hardwood Dimension & Flooring Mills
Companies: 45

					1,189	8.3

2429 Special Product Sawmills Nec

Rank	Company Name—Executive Officer	Address, City, State, Zip	Phone	Type	Fin	Empls
1	Shakertown 1992 Inc—Scott Clark	PO Box 400, Winlock WA 98596	360-785-3501	R	5*	.1

2431 Millwork

Rank	Company Name—Executive Officer	Address, City, State, Zip	Phone	Type	Fin	Empls
1	JELD-WEN Inc—Roderick C Wendt	3250 Lakeport Blvd, Klamath Falls OR 97601	541-882-3451	R	2,632*	20.0
2	Andersen Corp—Jay Lund	100 4th Ave N, Bayport MN 55003	651-264-5150	R	2,550*	10.2
3	Nortek Inc—Richard L Bready	50 Kennedy Plz, Providence RI 02903	401-751-1600	S	2,064*	8.0
4	Sne Enterprises Inc—Edward Schield	888 S View Dr, Mosinee WI 54455	715-693-7000	R	1,842*	1.5
5	Pella Corp—Pat Meyer	102 Main St, Pella IA 50219	641-628-1000	R	1,299*	9.0
6	Ply Gem Holdings Inc—Gary Robinette	5020 Weston Pky, Cary NC 27513	919-677-3900	R	951	4.2
7	Croft LLC—Susan Bellipanni	PO Box 826, Mccomb MS 39649	601-684-6121	R	568*	.3
8	Woodgrain Millwork Inc—Reed Dame	PO Box 566, Fruitland ID 83619		R	412*	.8
9	Weather Shield Manufacturing Inc—Jim Brost	PO Box 309, Medford WI 54451	715-748-2100	R	280*	4.0
10	Patrick Industries Inc—Todd M Cleveland	PO Box 638, Elkhart IN 46515	574-294-7511	P	235	.7
11	Eggers Industries Inc—Jay Streu	PO Box 88, Two Rivers WI 54241	920-793-1351	R	217*	.5
12	Sierrapine A California LP—Al Oneto	3010 Lava Ridge Ct Ste, Roseville CA 95661	916-772-3422	R	150*	.4
13	Ampco Products LLC—Ricardo Garcia	11400 Nw 36th Ave, Miami FL 33167	305-821-5700	R	131*	.1
14	Kolbe and Kolbe Millwork Company Inc—Judy Gorski	1323 S 11th Ave, Wausau WI 54401	715-842-5666	R	105*	1.6
15	Lyman Lumber Co—Jim Hurd	18900 W 78th St, Chanhassen MN 55317	952-470-4800	S	103*	.7
16	Black Millwork Company Inc—Ted Councilor	PO Box 27, Allendale NJ 07401	201-934-0100	R	100*	.2
17	Truth Hardware Corp—Greg Wobschall	700 W Bridge St, Owatonna MN 55060	507-451-5620	R	95*	1.4
18	Funder America Inc—Peter Funder	PO Box 729, Mocksville NC 27028	336-751-3501	R	81*	.1
19	Cascade Wood Products Inc—Gary Moore	PO Box 2429, White City OR 97503	541-826-2911	R	72*	1.0
20	Sierra Lumber Manufacturers—Joe Eger	PO Box 6216, Stockton CA 95206	209-943-7777	R	71*	.2
21	Advanced Environmental Recycling Technologies Inc—Joe G Brooks	914 N Jefferson St, Springdale AR 72764	479-756-7400	P	70	.4
22	Southern Staircase Inc—Paul Miro	6025 Shiloh Rd Ste E, Alpharetta GA 30005	770-888-7333	R	65*	.4
23	Contact Lumber Co—Frank Pearson	9200 SE Sunnybrook Blv, Clackamas OR 97015	503-228-7361	R	59*	.5
24	Mcdonough Holdings Inc—Dale Knight	21050 N Pima Rd Ste 10, Scottsdale AZ 85255	602-544-5900	R	52*	1.0
25	Haley Brothers Inc—Scot Baker	6291 Orangethorpe Ave, Buena Park CA 90620	714-670-2112	R	52*	.4
26	Gossen Corp—Bob Simon	2030 W Bender Rd, Milwaukee WI 53209	414-228-9800	R	50*	.3
27	HB and G Building Products Inc—Lance Servais	PO Box 589, Troy AL 36081	334-566-5000	R	50*	.3
28	Bayer Built Woodworks—Joseph Bayer	24614 US Hwy 71 N, Belgrade MN 56312	320-254-3651	R	48*	.3
29	Cox Interior Inc—Barry Cox	1751 Old Columbia Rd, Campbellsville KY 42718	270-465-2624	R	42*	.8
30	Marshfield Doorsystems Inc—Donald Bergman	1401 E 4th St, Marshfield WI 54449	715-384-2141	R	42*	.7
31	Marvin Windows Of Tennessee Inc—John Marvin	101 Marvin Dr, Ripley TN 38063	731-635-5190	R	40*	.7
32	Cascade Ohio Inc—Nicholas Nierzejewski	1209 Maple Ave, Conneaut OH 44030	440-593-5800	R	39*	.3
33	Bilt Best Windows—Jay Hoffer	175 10th St, Sainte Genevieve MO 63670	573-883-3571	R	38*	.3
34	Automated Building Components Inc—Tom Lowe	PO Box 40, Excelsior MN 55331	952-474-4374	R	36*	.3
35	Automated Building Components Millwork Div Automated Building Components Inc	PO Box 950, Chanhassen MN 55317	952-937-9060	D	35*	.1
36	Coffman Stairs LLC—Chris Clear	1000 Industrial Rd, Marion VA 24354	276-783-7251	R	33*	.6
37	Barnett Millworks Inc—Paul Barnett	PO Box 389, Theodore AL 36590	251-443-7710	R	33*	.3
38	Mohawk Flush Doors Inc—Barry Shovlin	980 Point Township Dr, Northumberland PA 17857	570-473-3557	R	32*	.3
39	Manassa Stock Building Supply	8020 Arco Corporate Dr, Raleigh NC 27617	919-431-1000	D	32*	.1
40	Menzner Lumber And Supply Co—Philip Menzner	PO Box 217, Marathon WI 54448	715-443-2354	R	31*	.2
41	Timber Blind Manufacturing Ltd—Pete Boleneus	1400 Lavon, McKinney TX 75069	214-544-2051	R	31*	.3
42	Ideal Door Co—Gene Colleran	320 10th Ave, Baldwin WI 54002	715-684-3223	S	30*	.4
43	Legere Group Ltd	PO Box 1527, Avon CT 06001	860-674-0392	R	30*	.1
44	Hwd Acquisition Inc—Domnic Truniger	PO Box 319, Medford WI 54451	715-748-2011	R	29*	.5
45	Parenti and Raffaelli Ltd—Bob Parenti	215 E Prospect Ave, Mount Prospect IL 60056	847-253-5550	R	29*	.2
46	Odl Inc—Jeff Mulder	215 E Roosevelt Ave, Zeeland MI 49464	616-772-9111	R	29*	.4
47	Lincoln Wood Products Inc—Jane Bierman	PO Box 375, Merrill WI 54452	715-536-2461	R	29*	.5
48	Rich Millwork—Tom Rich	1070 Quesada Ave, San Francisco CA 94124	415-282-8336	R	25*	.2
49	Fetzers Inc—Wallace Fetzer	6223 W Double Eagle Ci, Salt Lake City UT 84118	801-484-6103	R	25*	.2
50	Mid-America Hardwoods Inc—Gary Shepard	PO Box 160, Sarcoxie MO 64862	417-548-2191	R	25*	.2
51	Grabill Cabinet Company Inc—Scott Sommer	PO Box 40, Grabill IN 46741	260-627-2131	R	25*	.2
52	Rogue Valley Door Inc—John Dunkin	PO Box 2710, Grants Pass OR 97528	541-479-5354	R	23*	.2
53	Morgan Brothers Millwork Inc—Steve Morgan	PO Box 4343, Laurel MS 39441	601-649-9188	R	22*	.2
54	Vision Products Inc—Kirk Wolff	PO Box 830107, San Antonio TX 78283	830-755-4719	R	21*	.2

Rank	Company Name—*Executive Officer*	Address, City, State, Zip	Phone	Type	Fin	Empls
55	Clear Pine Mouldings Inc—*Frank Pearson*	PO Box 309, Prineville OR 97754	541-447-4195	R	20*	.4
56	Middlebury Hardwood Products Inc—*Charles Lamb*	PO Box 1429, Middlebury IN 46540	574-825-9524	R	20*	.2
57	Koetter Woodworking Inc—*Randall Koetter*	533 Louis Smith Rd, Borden IN 47106	812-923-8875	R	20*	.3
58	Designed Stairs Inc—*Michelle Ducharme*	1251 E 6th St, Sandwich IL 60548	815-786-7600	R	20*	.2
59	Delta Enterprises—*Spencer Nash*	PO Box 588, Greenville MS 38702	662-335-5291	R	20*	.2
60	Mathews Brothers Co—*John Hawthorne*	PO Box 345, Belfast ME 04915	207-338-3360	R	19*	.2
61	Alexandria Moulding Inc—*Jacques Cholette*	PO Box 169, Moxee WA 98936	509-248-2120	R	19*	.3
62	Dorris Lumber And Moulding Co—*Joshua Tyler*	2601 Redding Ave, Sacramento CA 95820	916-452-7531	R	18*	.1
63	Nordic Interior Inc—*Helge Halvorsen*	5601 Maspeth Ave, Maspeth NY 11378	718-456-7000	R	18*	.2
64	Riverdale Window And Door Corp—*Kenneth Caito*	2 Esmond St, Smithfield RI 02917	401-231-6000	R	17*	.2
65	RSL Woodworking Products Co—*Ron Lewkowitz*	3092 English Creek Ave, Egg Harbor Township NJ 08234	609-484-1600	R	17*	.2
66	Annandale Millwork And Allied Systems Corp—*Gene Frogale*	PO Box 2600, Winchester VA 22604	540-665-9600	R	17*	.2
67	Nationwide Industries Inc—*Christopher Kliefoth*	10333 Windhorst Rd, Tampa FL 33619	813-988-2628	S	17*	<.1
68	Nickell Moulding Company Inc—*George Nickell*	PO Box 1502, Elkhart IN 46515	574-264-3129	R	17*	.2
69	Karona Inc—*Ronald Sisson*	PO Box 888410, Grand Rapids MI 49588	616-554-3551	R	17*	.2
70	Columbia Woodworking Inc—*David Seagraves*	935 Brentwood Rd Ne, Washington DC 20018	202-526-2387	R	16*	.1
71	Doellken- Woodtape Inc—*Marty Martin*	7104 Cessna Dr, Greensboro NC 27409	425-319-2605	R	16*	.2
72	Clifton Moulding Corp—*C Burton*	PO Box 77, Clifton TX 76634	254-675-8641	R	16*	.2
73	Basileia Investments Inc—*Brant O'Hair*	PO Box 2764, Lubbock TX 79408	806-765-5791	R	15*	.1
74	LE Smith Co—*Laura Smith-Nolte*	PO Box 766, Bryan OH 43506	419-636-4555	R	15*	.1
75	Toms Quality Millwork And Hardwoods Inc—*Thomas Fleischman*	N1308 Drumlin Dr, Campbellsport WI 53010	920-533-4860	R	14*	.1
76	Annona Manufacturing Co—*James Peek*	PO Box 287, Annona TX 75550	903-697-3591	R	14*	.2
77	Northwestern Inc—*C Wayne Noecker*	15054 Oxnard St, Van Nuys CA 91411	818-786-1581	R	14*	.1
78	L and L Custom Shutters Inc—*Larry Allen*	1907 Nancita Cir, Placentia CA 92870	714-996-2500	R	14*	.1
79	Reilly Worldwide Inc—*Michael Reilly*	901 Burman Blvd, Calverton NY 11933	631-208-0710	R	14*	.1
80	Schuco USA LP—*Patrice Oleary*	240 Pane Rd, Newington CT 06111	860-666-0505	R	13*	.1
81	SR Door Inc—*Scott Miller*	PO Box 1414, Pataskala OH 43062	740-927-3558	R	13*	.1
82	Loudoun Stairs Inc—*Brent Mercke*	341 N Maple Ave, Purcellville VA 20132	540-338-7400	R	13*	.2
83	Os Stephenson Millwork Company Inc—*Russell Stephenson*	PO Box 699, Wilson NC 27894	252-237-1141	R	13*	.1
84	Durawood Products Inc—*Craig Mcdonald*	18 Industrial Way, Denver PA 17517	717-336-0220	R	13*	.1
85	Cana Inc—*David Geiger*	29194 Phillips St, Elkhart IN 46514	574-262-4664	R	12*	.1
86	Oshkosh Architectural Door Co—*Todd Robinson*	PO Box 2468, Oshkosh WI 54903	920-233-6161	R	12*	.1
87	Memphis Sash and Door Co—*Ron Bonds*	PO Box 18449, Memphis TN 38181	901-363-6040	D	12*	.1
88	Pacific Mdf Products Inc—*Douglas Hanzlick*	4312 Anthony Ct Ste A, Rocklin CA 95677	916-660-1882	R	12*	.1
89	Hollywood Woodwork Inc—*Yves Desmarais*	2951 Pembroke Rd, Hollywood FL 33020	954-920-5009	R	12*	.1
90	City Aluminum Company Inc—*Mindy Twer*	1909 E Hagert St, Philadelphia PA 19125	215-425-7373	R	12*	.1
91	Herrick and White Ltd—*Kenneth Bertram*	3 Flat St, Cumberland RI 02864	401-658-0440	R	11*	.1
92	Grubb Lumber Company Inc—*David Arronson*	PO Box 627, Wilmington DE 19899	302-652-2800	R	11*	.1
93	Kaufman Stairs Inc—*Alan Kaufman*	150 E Inman Ave, Rahway NJ 07065	732-388-9870	R	11*	.1
94	Meyer and Lundahl Manufacturing Co—*William R Lundahl*	PO Box 6158, Phoenix AZ 85005	602-254-9286	R	11*	.1
95	Quantum Windows and Doors Inc—*Hugh Matheson*	2720 34th St, Everett WA 98201	425-259-6650	R	11*	.1
96	Ohline Corp—*William Conn*	1930 W 139th St, Gardena CA 90249	310-327-4630	R	10*	.1
97	Ornamental Products Inc—*Tom Highley*	PO Box 4068, Archdale NC 27263	336-431-1127	R	10*	.2
98	AKA Michaelangelo Stairbuilder LLC—*Joshua Jacobs*	31 Randall St, North Easton MA 02356	508-238-9054	R	10*	.2
99	Taney Corp—*Eric Glass*	PO Box 29, Taneytown MD 21787	410-756-6671	R	10*	.1
100	Clearspan Components Inc—*Daniel Holland*	PO Box 4195, Meridian MS 39304	601-483-3941	R	10*	.1
101	American Millwork Corp—*Vaughn Nickell*	4840 Beck Dr, Elkhart IN 46516	574-295-4158	R	9*	.1
102	Somerset Door And Column Co—*Dean Hottle*	PO Box 755, Somerset PA 15501	814-445-9608	R	9*	.1
103	Memphis Folding Stairs Inc—*Dwight Henry*	PO Box 820305, Memphis TN 38182	901-458-1161	R	8*	.1
104	General Stair Corp—*Saby Behar*	690 W 83rd St, Hialeah FL 33014	305-769-9900	R	8*	.1
105	Renaissance French Doors and Sash Inc—*Michael Jenkins*	2425 W Commonwealth Av, Fullerton CA 92833	714-578-0090	R	8*	.1
106	LWO Corp—*Phil Conti*	PO Box 17125, Portland OR 97217	503-286-5372	R	8*	.1
107	Southern Screen Products Ltd—*Ilona Plager*	5143 Oak Leaf Ter, Stone Mountain GA 30087	770-469-2800	R	8*	.1
108	Carolina Hardwoods Inc—*Robert Green*	105 Clover Dr Sw, Lenoir NC 28645	828-728-8402	R	7*	.1
109	Yuba River Moulding and Mill Work Inc—*Thomas Williams*	PO Box 1078, Yuba City CA 95992	530-742-2168	R	7*	<.1
110	Lynden Door Inc—*Ted Bargen*	PO Box 528, Lynden WA 98264	360-354-5676	R	7*	.1
111	Anderco Inc—*Peter Johnson*	540 Airpark Dr, Fullerton CA 92833	714-992-4162	R	7*	.1
112	Amron Stair Works Inc—*Ron Thorson*	152 Industrial Dr, Gilberts IL 60136	847-426-4800	R	7*	.1
113	Owen Manufacturing Inc—*Richard Asdel*	331 N Oak St, Owen WI 54460	715-229-2126	R	6*	.1
114	American Stairway Inc—*Brad Hudspeth*	3807 Lamar Ave, Memphis TN 38118	901-795-9200	R	6*	.1
115	Maiman Co—*David Paulo*	3839 E Mustard Way, Springfield MO 65803	417-862-0681	R	6*	<.1
116	Klise Manufacturing Co—*Phillip Veen*	601 Maryland Ave Ne, Grand Rapids MI 49505	616-459-4283	R	6*	<.1
117	Forest Siskiyou Products—*Fred Duchi*	PO Box 811, Anderson CA 96007	530-378-6980	R	6*	<.1
118	Frederick and May Lumber Co—*James Frederick*	PO Box 218, West Liberty KY 41472	606-743-3136	R	6*	.1
119	Alexander Moulding Mill Co—*John Alexander*	PO Box 312, Hamilton TX 76531	254-386-3187	R	5*	.1
120	Quality Cabinet And Fixture Co—*Tim Paradise*	885 Gateway Ctr Way A, San Diego CA 92102	619-266-1011	R	5*	<.1
121	Buffelen Woodworking Co—*Joseph Guizzetti*	1901 Taylor Way, Tacoma WA 98421	253-627-1191	R	4*	<.1
122	Ron's Cabinets Inc—*John Packert*	PO Box 515, Sauk Rapids MN 56379	320-252-7667	R	4*	<.1
123	US Window and Door	1355 Grand Ave, San Marcos CA 92078	760-471-7452	R	4*	<.1
124	Almega Enterprises Inc—*Richard Brosius*	1305 W 17th St, Vancouver WA 98660	360-573-1711	R	4*	<.1
125	Midwest Prefinishing Inc—*Georgia Larson*	2310 Pinehurst Dr, Middleton WI 53562	608-836-3667	R	4*	<.1
126	Artistic Stairs Inc—*Jeff Steiger*	PO Box 1222, Tinley Park IL 60477	815-464-9090	R	3*	<.1
127	Ash Millworks Inc—*A Herring*	65 Springfield Rd, Petal MS 39465	601-544-3962	R	3*	<.1
128	Swiss Woodcraft Inc—*Ken Maibach*	15 Industrial St, Rittman OH 44270	330-925-1807	R	3*	<.1
129	Alps Technologies Inc—*Robert Wagner*	500 Memorial Dr Ste 1, Somerset NJ 08873	732-764-0777	R	3*	<.1
130	Lindsay Sash Inc—*John Roise*	1995 Commerce Ln, North Mankato MN 56003	507-625-4278	R	3*	<.1
131	Somerset Wood Products Co—*Lester Bloch*	10 Johnson Dr, Raritan NJ 08869	908-526-0030	R	3*	<.1
132	Absolute Windows Inc—*Ronald Baker*	9630 S 76th Ave, Oak Lawn IL 60457	708-599-9191	R	2*	<.1
133	Beechcraft Products Inc—*Richard Misner*	1100 N Saginaw St, Durand MI 48429	989-288-2606	R	2*	<.1
134	Continental Display and Store Fixtures Inc—*Leta Nichols*	2324 Auburn Blvd, Sacramento CA 95821	916-482-3545	R	2*	<.1
135	Desert Millwork Inc—*Wm Heller*	1702 W Roosevelt St St, Phoenix AZ 85007	602-258-7517	R	2*	<.1
136	Lemica Corp—*Gary Brown*	11201 Manning St, Detroit MI 48234	313-839-0900	R	2*	<.1
137	Mr Foamy Southwest Fl LLC—*Karen Fiorillo*	3411 Hanson St, Fort Myers FL 33916	239-461-3110	R	2*	<.1
138	Ultimate Windows Inc—*Jack Perrino*	110 Chelsea St, Everett MA 02149	617-387-5566	R	1*	<.1
139	Universal Level Company Inc—*Christopher Janik*	440 Fredonia Ave, Fredonia WI 53021	262-692-9505	R	1*	<.1
140	California Millworks Corp—*Lay Cho*	27772 Ave Scott, Santa Clarita CA 91355	661-294-2345	R	<1*	<.1
141	ROW Window Co—*Glen Brooks*	13404 Wood Duck Dr, Plainfield IL 60585	815-725-5491	R	<1*	<.1

TOTALS: SIC 2431 Millwork
Companies: 141   16,065   85.4

Note: An asterisk (*) indicates an estimated financial figure. The company type code used is as follows: R = Private, P = Public, S = Private Subsidiary, B = Public Subsidiary, D = Division, J = Joint Venture, I = Investment Fund.

COMPANY RANKINGS BY SALES WITHIN 4-DIGIT SIC

Rank	Company Name—*Executive Officer*	Address, City, State, Zip	Phone	Type	Fin	Empls
	2434 Wood Kitchen Cabinets					
1	RSI Home Products Inc—*Alex Calabrese*	400 E Orange Thorpe Av, Anaheim CA 92801	714-449-2200	R	917*	5.0
2	Merillat Industries Inc—*Karen Strauss*	PO Box 1946, Adrian MI 49221	517-263-0771	D	681*	5.1
3	Kraftmaid Cabinetry Inc—*Mike Newton*	PO Box 1055, Middlefield OH 44062	440-632-5333	S	498*	3.0
4	Woodcraft Industries Inc—*John Fitzpatrick*	525 Lincoln Ave Se, Saint Cloud MN 56304	320-252-1503	R	249*	1.5
5	Norcraft Companies LP	3020 Denmark Ave Ste 1, Eagan MN 55121		S	247	1.6
6	Omega Cabinets Ltd—*Greg Stoner*	1205 Peters Dr, Waterloo IA 50703	319-235-5700	R	169*	2.4
7	Zenith Products Corp—*Joseph Mahon*	400 Lukens Dr, New Castle DE 19720	302-326-8200	R	146*	.5
8	US Remodelers Inc	1884 S Elmhurst Rd, Mount Prospect IL 60056	847-758-2310	S	128	.6
9	Canyon Creek Cabinet Co—*Bill Weaver*	16726 Tye St SE, Monroe WA 98272	206-674-0800	R	102*	.3
10	Kitchen Kompact Inc—*W Gahm*	PO Box 868, Jeffersonville IN 47131	812-282-6681	R	84*	.3
11	Wood-Mode Inc—*Robert Gronlund*	PO Box 250, Kreamer PA 17833	570-374-2711	R	82*	1.3
12	Wellborn Cabinet Inc—*Paul Wellborn*	PO Box 1210, Ashland AL 36251	256-354-7151	R	73*	1.2
13	Bertch Cabinet Manufacturing Inc—*Gary Bertch*	PO Box 2280, Waterloo IA 50704	319-296-2987	R	59*	.9
14	B J Tidwell Industries Inc—*Bryan Tidwell*	PO Box 200850, San Antonio TX 78220	210-225-0290	R	57*	.9
15	Dura Supreme Inc—*Keith P Stotts*	300 Dura Dr, Howard Lake MN 55349	320-543-3872	R	55*	.6
16	Republic Industries Inc—*Brian Roper*	1400 Warren Dr, Marshall TX 75672	903-935-3680	R	49*	.2
17	Primewood Inc—*John Fitzpatrick* Woodcraft Industries Inc	2217 9th St N, Wahpeton ND 58075	701-642-2727	S	48*	.5
18	Royal Cabinets Inc—*Clay Smith*	1260 E Grand Ave, Pomona CA 91766	909-629-8565	R	42*	.6
19	Tru-Wood Cabinets Inc—*David Rush*	PO Box 640, Ashland AL 36251	256-354-3378	R	41*	.3
20	Starmark—*John Swedeen*	PO Box 84810, Sioux Falls SD 57118	605-335-8600	R	37*	.6
21	American Woodmark Corp (Kingman Arizona)—*Kent B Guichard*	PO Box 1980, Winchester VA 22601	928-757-7106	S	36*	.4
22	Plain 'N Fancy Kitchens Inc—*George Achey*	208 Rte 501 N, Schaefferstown PA 17088	717-949-6571	R	34*	.2
23	Koch and Company Inc—*Jim Koch*	1809 N St, Seneca KS 66538	785-336-6022	R	34*	.3
24	Lanz Cabinet Shop Inc—*Brent Lanz*	3025 W 7th Pl, Eugene OR 97402	541-485-4050	R	33*	.3
25	Woodcase Fine Cabinetry Inc—*Angie Harkness*	3255 W Osborn Rd, Phoenix AZ 85017	602-269-9731	R	30*	.3
26	Haas Cabinet Company Inc—*Jeffrey Haas*	625 W Utica St, Sellersburg IN 47172	812-246-4431	R	30*	.3
27	Quality Custom Cabinetry Inc—*Glen Good*	PO Box 189, New Holland PA 17557	717-661-6900	R	29*	.3
28	Woodharbor Doors and Cabinetry Inc—*Curtis Lewerke*	3277 9th St SW, Mason City IA 50401	641-423-0444	R	28*	.5
29	Medallion Cabinetry Inc—*Tom Cook*	1 Medallion Way, Waconia MN 55387	952-442-5171	D	26*	.3
30	Walzcraft Industries Inc—*Richard Walz*	2600 Hemstock St, La Crosse WI 54603	608-781-6355	R	25*	.4
31	Candlelight Cabinetry Inc—*John Yakich*	24 Michigan St, Lockport NY 14094	716-434-6543	R	25*	.2
32	Regal Kitchens LLC—*Americo Castipellanas*	8600 Nw S River Dr Ste, Miami FL 33166	305-885-0111	R	24*	.2
33	Forest Wellborn Products Inc—*Tim Wellborn*	2212 Airport Blvd, Alexander City AL 35010	256-234-7900	R	23*	.2
34	Valley Cabinet Inc—*Dean Stoller*	845 Prosper St, De Pere WI 54115	920-336-3174	R	23*	.2
35	Cabinetry By Karman Inc—*Paul Wellborn* Wellborn Cabinet Inc	6000 Stratler St, Salt Lake City UT 84107	801-268-3581	S	23*	.2
36	Evans Cabinet Corp—*Mark Trexter*	1321 N Franklin St, Dublin GA 31021	478-272-2530	R	22*	.2
37	Mastercraft Industries Inc—*David West*	120 W Allen St, Rice Lake WI 54868	715-234-8111	R	22*	.2
38	Leedo Manufacturing Company Inc—*Ken Hirshman*	PO Box 520, East Bernard TX 77435	979-335-4885	R	22*	.4
39	California Kitchen Cabinet Door Corp—*Edward Rossi*	400 Cochrane Cir, Morgan Hill CA 95037	408-782-5700	R	22*	.3
40	Zee Manufacturing Ltd—*Judy Brown*	4600 W Us Hwy 90, San Antonio TX 78237	210-684-1611	R	21*	.2
41	Shamrock Cabinet and Fixture Corp—*William Price*	10201 E 65th St, Raytown MO 64133	816-737-2300	R	21*	.2
42	Crestwood Inc—*Mike Junk*	601 E Water Well Rd, Salina KS 67401	785-827-0317	R	19*	.2
43	Lsi Corporation Of America Inc—*Dave Eberhardt*	2100 Xenium Ln N, Minneapolis MN 55441	763-559-4664	R	18*	.2
44	United Cabinet Company LLC—*Marla Riggan*	PO Box 110774, Nashville TN 37222	615-833-1961	R	18*	.1
45	Custom Wood Products LLC—*Kim Malus*	PO Box 4500, Roanoke VA 24015	540-342-0363	R	17*	.2
46	Bass Cabinets And Related Products Inc—*J Hamlin*	503 W 3rd Ave, Mesa AZ 85210	480-962-5249	R	17*	.2
47	Kountry Wood Products LLC—*Perry Miller*	PO Box 530, Nappanee IN 46550	574-773-5673	R	17*	.1
48	Grandview Products Company Inc—*Emil Zetmeir*	PO Box 874, Parsons KS 67357	620-421-6970	R	16*	.1
49	Mid-America Cabinets Inc—*Bob Hosteter*	PO Box 219, Gentry AR 72734	479-736-2671	R	15*	.1
50	Dutch Made Inc—*Martin Graber*	PO Box 310, Grabill IN 46741	260-657-3311	R	15*	.1
51	Moralmar Kitchen Cabinets Inc—*Eduardo Moreno*	3130 W 15th Ave, Hialeah FL 33012	305-556-1520	R	14*	.1
52	Kountry Kraft Kitchens Inc—*Elvin Hurst*	PO Box 570, Newmanstown PA 17073	610-589-4575	R	13*	.1
53	Plato Woodwork Inc—*Tim Pinske*	PO Box 98, Plato MN 55370	320-238-2193	R	13*	.1
54	Cullman Cabinet and Supply Company Inc—*James Edge*	PO Box 1150, Cullman AL 35056	256-734-1540	R	12*	.1
55	Wm Ohs Inc—*William Ohs*	5095 Peoria St, Denver CO 80239	303-371-6550	R	12*	.1
56	Tacoma Fixture Company Inc—*Jim Ryan*	1815 E D St, Tacoma WA 98421	253-383-5541	R	12*	.1
57	Romar Cabinet and Top Company Inc—*Anthony Angelis*	23949 S Northern Ill D, Channahon IL 60410	815-467-9900	R	11*	.1
58	Strata Design Inc—*Charles Cady*	PO Box 6250, Traverse City MI 49696	231-929-2140	R	11*	<.1
59	Brandom Holdings LLC—*Leanette Alen*	404 Hawkins St, Hillsboro TX 76645	254-580-1200	R	11*	.1
60	Tri Star Cabinet And Top Company Inc—*James Thomas*	PO Box 338, New Lenox IL 60451	815-485-2564	R	9*	.1
61	Carolina Cabinet Company Inc—*Carolyn Daniel*	PO Box 219, Wilson NC 27894	252-291-5181	R	9*	.1
62	Nature's Blend Wood Products Inc—*Ted Wohlin*	717 1st Ave, Ford City PA 16226	724-763-7057	R	8*	.1
63	Woodpro Cabinetry Inc—*Leland Walls*	PO Box 70, Cabool MO 65689	417-962-5127	R	8*	.1
64	Reborn Cabinets—*Brenda Nardo*	2981 E La Palma Ave, Anaheim CA 92806	714-630-2220	R	8*	.1
65	Corona Millworks Co—*Jose Corona*	5572 Edison Ave, Chino CA 91710	909-628-4411	R	8*	.1
66	Meridian Products Inc—*Marty Ness*	124 Earland Dr Bldg 2, New Holland PA 17557	717-355-7700	R	8*	.1
67	Valley Casework Inc—*Susan Raymond*	585 Vernon Way, El Cajon CA 92020	619-579-6886	R	7*	.1
68	Pioneer Cabinetry Inc—*Jack Dixon*	PO Box 280, Davison MI 48423	810-658-2075	R	7*	.1
69	Donald Dean and Sons Inc—*Sue Dean*	PO Box 246, Montrose PA 18801	570-278-1179	R	7*	.1
70	Brown County Cabinets Inc—*Terence Vercauteren*	998 Glory Rd, Green Bay WI 54304	920-336-9691	R	7*	.1
71	Quality Wood Products Inc—*David Stry*	7400 E 12th St, Kansas City MO 64126	816-231-4601	R	7*	.1
72	W L Rubottom Co—*Gary Mccoy*	320 W Lewis St, Ventura CA 93001	805-648-6943	R	6*	.1
73	Florida Plywoods Inc—*John Maultsby*	PO Box 458, Greenville FL 32331	850-948-2211	R	6*	.1
74	Southcoast Cabinet Inc—*Cadante Senese*	755 Pinefalls Ave, Walnut CA 91789	909-594-3089	R	6*	.1
75	Great Northern Cabinetry Inc—*Phil Staat*	749 Kennedy St, Rib Lake WI 54470	715-427-5255	R	6*	.1
76	Ton Ken Fabricators Inc—*Robert Saj*	2505 Main St, Buffalo NY 14214	716-832-1200	R	5*	<.1
77	ShelfGenie—*Ben Rozenblat*	1642 Powers Ferry Rd S, Marietta GA 30067	770-955-4375	R	5	<.1
78	Siematic Corp—*Ulrich W Siekmann*	3 Interplex Dr Ste 101, Feasterville PA 19053	215-604-1350	R	5*	.1
79	Rosebud Manufacturing Company Inc—*Don Grayson*	PO Box 409, Madison SD 57042	605-256-4561	R	4*	.1
80	Schmidt Cabinet Company Inc—*John Schmidt*	PO Box 68, New Salisbury IN 47161	812-347-2434	R	4*	<.1
81	Supply One Corp—*Richard Flaute*	PO Box 636, Dayton OH 45401	937-297-1111	R	3*	<.1
82	Nixon Cabinet Company Inc—*Bobby Nixon*	17048 Blackburn Rd, Athens AL 35611	256-232-5722	R	3*	<.1
83	Pars Industries Inc—*Mehdi Govari*	1520 Corprt Ctr Dr Ste, San Diego CA 92154	619-671-9663	R	1*	<.1

TOTALS: SIC 2434 Wood Kitchen Cabinets
Companies: 83

					4,720	36.7

Rank	Company Name—Executive Officer	Address, City, State, Zip	Phone	Type	Fin	Empls
2435 Hardwood Veneer & Plywood						
1	RLC Industries Co—Allyn Ford	PO Box 1088, Roseburg OR 97470	541-679-3311	R	1,193*	3.0
2	Roseburg Forest Products Co—Allyn C Ford RLC Industries Co	PO Box 1088, Roseburg OR 97470	541-679-3311	S	1,100	3.9
3	Columbia Forest Products Inc—Brad Thompson	7900 Triad Ctr Dr Ste2, Greensboro NC 27409		R	656*	2.5
4	MacBeath Hardwood Company Inc—Rick McDaniel	930 Ashby Ave, Berkeley CA 94710	510-843-4390	R	134*	.1
5	International Veneer Company Inc—O Edwards	1551 Montgomery St, South Hill VA 23970	434-447-7100	R	50*	.2
6	Birchwood Best	PO Box 68 600 E Hwy 48, Birchwood WI 54817	715-354-3441	S	40	.2
7	David R Webb Company Inc—Greg Lottes	PO Box 8, Edinburgh IN 46124	812-526-2601	R	38*	.4
8	Murphy Co—John Murphy	2350 Prairie Rd, Eugene OR 97402	541-461-4545	R	34*	.5
9	Marion Plywood Corp—Peter Rogers	PO Box 497, Marion WI 54950	715-754-5231	R	28*	.5
10	Rutland Plywood Corp—Jack Barrett	PO Box 6180, Rutland VT 05702	802-747-4400	R	28*	.3
11	Freeman Corp—George Freeman	PO Box 96, Winchester KY 40392	859-744-4311	R	28*	.3
12	G-L Veneer Company Inc—Leslie Levin	2224 E Slauson Ave, Huntington Park CA 90255	323-582-5203	R	23*	.1
13	Ferche Millwork Inc—Gerald Grider	400 Division St N, Rice MN 56367	320-393-5700	R	22*	.2
14	Coldwater Veneer Inc—Dean Calhoun	548 Race St, Coldwater MI 49036	517-278-5676	R	22*	.1
15	Swanson Group Manufacturing LLC—Steven Swanson	PO Box 1168, Roseburg OR 97470	541-492-1121	S	20*	.3
16	Flexible Materials Inc—Ronald Humin	1202 Port Rd, Jeffersonville IN 47130	812-280-7000	R	18*	.1
17	Miller Veneers Inc—Thomas Miller	PO Box 11085, Indianapolis IN 46201	317-638-2326	R	18*	.1
18	Pavco Industries Inc—Robert Boland	PO Box 612, Pascagoula MS 39568	228-762-3172	R	17*	.1
19	Amos-Hill Associates Inc—Susanne Renner	PO Box 7, Edinburgh IN 46124	812-526-2671	R	16*	.2
20	Bessemer Plywood Corp—Richard Thomason	PO Box 76, Bessemer MI 49911	906-667-0277	R	13*	.1
21	Indiana Veneers Corp—Werner Lorenz	1121 E 24th St, Indianapolis IN 46205	317-926-2458	R	12*	.1
22	BL Curry and Sons Inc—Jon Curry	PO Box 439, New Albany IN 47151	812-945-6623	R	8*	.1
23	Quality Plywood Company Inc—Virgil Palmer	PO Box 187, Waynesboro MS 39367	601-735-3106	R	7*	.1
24	Keller Products Inc—John Hudson	PO Box 4105, Manchester NH 03108	603-627-7887	R	7*	<.1
25	Capital Veneer Works Inc—R Adams	PO Box 240785, Montgomery AL 36124	334-264-1401	R	6*	.1
26	West Point Veneer LLC—Brian Davis Coldwater Veneer Inc	320 Dupont St, West Point VA 23181	804-843-2900	S	4*	.1
27	Appalaphian—Andrew Kimball	PO Box 228, Lyons GA 30436	828-837-2914	S	3*	.1
28	Tailor Cut Wood Products Inc—Ricky Price	PO Box 99, Taylorsville NC 28681	828-632-2808	R	2*	<.1
29	Manthei Inc—Thomas Manthei	3996 Charlevoix Ave, Petoskey MI 49770	231-347-4672	R	2*	.2
30	Lokota Woods International—Don Steffy	9735 Tall Timber Dr, Cincinnati OH 45241	812-989-8516	R	1*	<.1
TOTALS: SIC 2435 Hardwood Veneer & Plywood Companies: 30					3,550	13.9
2436 Softwood Veneer & Plywood						
1	Georgia-Pacific Corp Building Products Div—John Terry	PO Box 105605, Atlanta GA 30348	404-652-4000	D	7,486	15.0
2	Baltek Inc—Georg Reif	PO Box 16148, High Point NC 27261	201-767-1400	S	1,691*	1.0
3	Timber Products Co—Joseph H Gonyea	PO Box 269, Springfield OR 97477	541-747-4577	R	600*	1.5
4	International Wood Industries Inc—Robert Rotticci	18101 SW Boones Ferry, Tualatin OR 97062	503-670-0365	R	91	<.1
5	Hardel Mutual Plywood Corp—Sang Teng	PO Box 540, Chehalis WA 98532	360-740-0232	R	89*	.2
6	Idaho Veneer Co—Pat Malloy	PO Box 339, Post Falls ID 83877	200-773-4511	R	82*	.1
7	Pacific Veneer Ltd	PO Box 9777, Federal Way WA 98063	253-924-2345	S	79*	.1
8	Pacific Wood Laminates Inc—Ronald Fallert	PO Box 820, Brookings OR 97415	541-469-4177	R	70*	.3
9	Scotch Plywood Company Inc—Thomas O'melia	PO Box 38, Fulton AL 36446	334-636-4424	R	62*	.4
10	South Coast Lumber Co—Ronald Fallert	PO Box 670, Brookings OR 97415	541-469-2136	R	33*	.2
11	Forest Hunt Products Inc—D Young	PO Box 1263, Ruston LA 71273	318-255-2245	R	31*	.6
12	Rosboro LLC—Rich Babcock	PO Box 20, Springfield OR 97477	541-746-8411	R	28*	.4
13	Freres Lumber Company Inc—Theodore Freres	PO Box 276, Lyons OR 97358	503-859-2121	R	28*	.4
14	Coastal Forest Resources Co—Kevin Luzak	PO Box 1128, Havana FL 32333	850-539-6432	R	24*	.4
15	Emerald Forest Products Inc—Gerald Vickers	PO Box 2746, Eugene OR 97402	541-683-1984	R	22*	.4
16	Atlantic Veneer International Corp—Christian Weygoldp	PO Box 660, Beaufort NC 28516	252-728-3169	R	18*	.4
17	Veneer Products Acquisitions LLC—Adams Tindel	PO Box 278, Fitzgerald GA 31750	229-424-0294	R	17*	.2
18	Giles and Kendall Inc—Beverly Head	PO Box 188, Huntsville AL 35804	256-776-2978	R	17*	.2
19	Hoquiam Plywood Company Inc—Mark Mcfeely	PO Box 737, Hoquiam WA 98550	360-533-3060	R	15*	.1
TOTALS: SIC 2436 Softwood Veneer & Plywood Companies: 19					10,483	21.8
2439 Structural Wood Members Nec						
1	iLevel by Weyerhaeuser—Thomas H Denig	200 E Mallard Dr, Boise ID 83706	208-364-1200	S	876*	4.0
2	American Hardwood Industries—Theodore Rossi	567 N Charlotte Ave, Waynesboro VA 22980	540-946-9150	R	473*	.7
3	American Woodmark Corp—Kent B Guichard	PO Box 1980, Winchester VA 22604	540-665-9100	P	453	3.7
4	Trussway Manufacturing Inc—Jim Thomas	PO Box 111577, Houston TX 77293	713-691-6900	R	264*	.7
5	Steel of West Virginia Inc—Tim Duke	PO Box 2547, Huntington WV 25726	304-696-8200	S	97*	.5
6	A C Houston Lumber Co—Ron Mason	PO Box 401000, Las Vegas NV 89140	702-633-5100	R	57*	.2
7	Laminate Technologies Inc—Frederick Zoeller	161 Maule Rd, Tiffin OH 44883	419-448-0812	R	36*	.1
8	Schuck Component Systems—Craig Steele	8205 N 67th Ave, Glendale AZ 85308	623-931-3661	R	35*	.2
9	Redbuilt LLC—Dallas Anderson	PO Box 60, Boise ID 83707		R	32*	.2
10	James Truss Co A Nevada Corp—James Harrington	2080 Mondo Ct, Las Vegas NV 89123	702-642-7548	R	31*	.3
11	Brooks Manufacturing Co—Dwayne Carter	PO Box 7, Bellingham WA 98227	360-733-1700	R	30*	.1
12	California Truss Co—Ken Cloyd	23665 Cajalco Rd, Perris CA 92570	951-657-7491	R	28*	.3
13	Shelter Systems Corp—Dwight Hikel	PO Box 450, Hainesport NJ 08036	609-261-2000	R	27*	.2
14	Spates Family Consulting Inc—Tom Spates	85435 Middleton, Thermal CA 92274	760-397-4122	R	25*	.2
15	W Kost Manufacturing Company Inc—Bradley Kost	75 Koppie Dr, Gilberts IL 60136	847-428-0600	R	25*	.2
16	Lumber Specialties Ltd—Carl Schoenhard	PO Box 38, Dyersville IA 52040	563-875-2858	R	23*	.2
17	JC Snavely and Sons Inc—Charles Fessler	150 Main St, Landisville PA 17538	717-898-2241	R	22*	.2
18	Okaw Truss Inc—Fred Helmuth	368 E State Rte 133, Arthur IL 61911	217-543-3371	R	22*	.4
19	Aviston Lumber Co—Maurice E Netemeyer	101 S Clement Dr, Aviston IL 62216	618-228-7247	R	21*	.1
20	Structural Component Systems Inc—E Christoffersen	1255 Front St, Fremont NE 68025	402-721-5622	R	20*	.3
21	Desert Truss Inc—Don Buttrum	5404 W Montebello Ave, Glendale AZ 85301	623-516-0586	R	20*	.2
22	Ken Luneack Construction Inc—Paul Luneack	PO Box 239, Saint Louis MI 48880	989-681-5774	R	20*	.2
23	Timber Truss Housing Systems Inc—Gary Saunders	PO Box 996, Salem VA 24153	540-387-0273	R	19*	.2
24	DMC West Corp—Peter C Alexander	PO Box 70006, Boise ID 83707	208-331-4300	S	19*	.1
25	Younger Brothers Components Inc—James III	8525 N 75th Ave, Peoria AZ 85345	623-412-7979	R	18*	.2
26	Shelter Systems Ltd—Dwight Hikel	1025 Meadow Branch Rd, Westminster MD 21158	410-876-3900	R	17*	.2
27	Hanson Truss Inc—Donald Hanson	13950 Yorba Ave, Chino CA 91710	909-591-9256	R	15*	.1

Note: An asterisk (*) indicates an estimated financial figure. The company type code used is as follows: R = Private, P = Public, S = Private Subsidiary, B = Public Subsidiary, D = Division, J = Joint Venture, I = Investment Fund.

COMPANY RANKINGS BY SALES WITHIN 4-DIGIT SIC

Rank	Company Name—*Executive Officer*	Address, City, State, Zip	Phone	Type	Fin	Empls
28	Dade Truss Company Inc—*Salvador Jurado*	6401 Nw 74th Ave, Miami FL 33166	305-592-8245	R	15*	.1
29	General Building Systems LLC—*Kenneth Black*	5795 Rogers St Ste A, Las Vegas NV 89118	702-642-1010	R	14*	.1
30	Southeastern Materials Inc—*Tony Dennis*	PO Box 279, Albemarle NC 28002	704-983-1144	R	14*	.1
31	True House Inc—*Barry Dixon*	10411 Alta Dr, Jacksonville FL 32226	904-757-7500	R	13*	.1
32	Truss Specialists Inc—*Dean Ashbacher*	PO Box 177, La Crescent MN 55947	507-895-8400	R	13*	.1
33	Truss-Tech Industries Inc—*Alec Asgari*	4883 Roy Carlson Blvd, Buford GA 30518	770-271-1347	R	12*	.2
34	Capital Structures Inc—*Steven Spradlin*	900 Atlanta St, Fort Smith AR 72901	479-783-8666	R	12*	.1
35	Automated Products Inc—*Gary Korpela*	1812 Karau Dr, Marshfield WI 54449	715-387-3426	R	12*	.1
36	Heart Truss and Engineering Corp—*Curtis Schaberg*	1830 N Grand River Ave, Lansing MI 48906	517-372-0850	R	11*	.1
37	Madera Component Systems Inc—*Frank Singh*	6323 W Van Buren St, Phoenix AZ 85043	623-245-1001	R	11*	.1
38	K and K Industries Inc—*Abe Knepp*	8518 E 550 N, Montgomery IN 47558	812-486-3281	R	11*	.1
39	Best Building Components LLC—*Phillip Martin*	17950 Maugens Ave, Maugansville MD 21767	301-739-4220	R	11*	<.1
40	Montgomery Truss and Panel Inc—*Charles Montgomery*	PO Box 866, Grove City PA 16127	724-458-7500	R	11*	.1
41	Piercefield Corporation Inc—*Roy Piercefield*	PO Box 18665, Erlanger KY 41018	859-341-7767	R	10*	.1
42	Woodbury Roof Truss Inc—*Richard Phalines*	PO Box 215, Woodbury Heights NJ 08097	856-845-3848	R	10*	.1
43	Stock Components Systems Inc—*Ron Alltop*	PO Box 1547, Kernersville NC 27285	336-993-4541	R	10*	.1
44	W Kost Inc—*Walter Kost*	4175 Sw Martin Hwy, Palm City FL 34990	772-286-3700	R	10*	.1
45	Ridgway Roof Truss Co—*Karl Losen*	PO Box 1309, Gainesville FL 32602	352-376-4436	R	9*	.1
46	Stark Truss Of Summerville Limited LLC—*Ron Groom*	351 International Cir, Summerville SC 29483	843-875-0550	R	9*	.1
47	Kerkhoff Associates Inc—*Timothy Kerkhoff*	PO Box 578, Otterbein IN 47970	765-583-4491	R	8*	.1
48	Anderson Truss Company Inc—*John Prospero*	PO Box 33, Alcoa TN 37701	865-983-9485	R	8*	.1
49	King Filler Co—*Wayne King*	PO Box 185, Homedale ID 83628	208-337-3134	R	8*	.1
50	Letherer Truss Inc—*Steven Letherer*	851 Industrial Dr, Clare MI 48617	989-386-4999	R	8*	.1
51	Harrison Industries Inc—*Carol Harrison*	PO Box 250, Greenville AL 36037	334-382-6534	R	7*	.1
52	Florida Quality Truss Industries Inc—*Rasmin Adak*	3635 Park Central Blvd, Pompano Beach FL 33064	954-975-3384	R	5*	<.1
53	Supress Products LLC—*Bruce Donaldson*	PO Box 3472, San Rafael CA 94912	415-233-4317	R	5*	<.1
54	Truss Partners LLC—*Julie Patterson*	PO Box 344, Tipton IN 46072	317-896-2571	R	5*	.1
55	Mainely Trusses Inc—*Michael Boulet*	PO Box 377, Fairfield ME 04937	207-453-4911	R	3*	<.1
56	Dawkins Inc—*Clinton Dawkins*	PO Box 40706, Jacksonville FL 32203	904-350-6600	R	3*	<.1
57	Kintec LLC	PO Box 587, Pewee Valley KY 40056	502-241-9456	R	3*	<.1
58	Wisconsin Truss Inc—*Daniel Schulner*	609 Industrial Park Rd, Cornell WI 54732	715-239-6465	R	2*	<.1
59	International Building Technologies Group—*Kenneth Yeung*	17800 Castleton St Ste, City of Industry CA 91748	626-581-8500	P	<1	<.1

TOTALS: SIC 2439 Structural Wood Members Nec
Companies: 59

					3,006	16.3

2441 Nailed Wood Boxes & Shook

Rank	Company Name—*Executive Officer*	Address, City, State, Zip	Phone	Type	Fin	Empls
1	WII Components Inc—*John Fitzpatrick*	525 Lincoln Ave SE, Saint Cloud MN 56304	320-252-1503	R	260*	1.7
2	North American Container Corp—*John Grigsby*	1811 W Oak Ave Ste D, Marietta GA 30062	770-431-4858	R	43*	.6
3	Ruszel Woodworks Inc—*Jack Ruszel*	2980 Bayshore Rd, Benicia CA 94510	707-745-6979	R	26*	.1
4	Complete Packaging Inc—*Robert Maul*	PO Box 735, Monroe MI 48161	734-241-2794	R	5*	.1

TOTALS: SIC 2441 Nailed Wood Boxes & Shook
Companies: 4

					334	2.4

2448 Wood Pallets & Skids

Rank	Company Name—*Executive Officer*	Address, City, State, Zip	Phone	Type	Fin	Empls
1	IFCO Systems North America—*David Russell*	6829 Flintlock Rd, Houston TX 77040	713-332-6200	S	387*	3.6
2	Millwood Inc—*Lionel W Trebilcock*	PO Box 960, Vienna OH 44473	330-393-4400	R	361*	1.0
3	Battle Lumber Company Inc—*J Battle*	PO Box 1147, Wadley GA 30477	478-252-5210	R	72*	.4
4	Palletone Inc—*Howe Wallace*	PO Box 819, Bartow FL 33831	863-533-1147	R	72*	1.1
5	Elberta Crate and Box Co—*Ramsey Simmons*	PO Box 760, Bainbridge GA 39818	229-246-2266	R	57*	.7
6	Tasler Inc—*Greg Tasler*	PO Box 726, Webster City IA 50595	515-832-5200	R	43*	.1
7	Berry Industrial Group Inc—*Debra Berry*	30 Main St, Nyack NY 10960	845-353-8338	R	39*	.1
8	Northwest Pallet Supply—*Walter Pollack*	3648 Morreim Dr, Belvidere IL 61008		R	35	.3
9	American Fibertech Corp—*Rob Meister*	PO Box 220, Remington IN 47977	219-261-3586	R	34*	.3
10	Pallet Factory Inc—*Michael Doyle*	3740 Arnold Rd, Memphis TN 38118	901-795-8300	R	33*	.2
11	Litco International Inc—*Lionel Trebilcock*	PO Box 150, Vienna OH 44473	330-539-5433	R	24*	<.1
12	Allied Pallet Co—*William Newman*	PO Box 367, Providence Forge VA 23140	804-966-5597	R	23*	.3
13	Edwards Wood Products Inc—*Jeff Edwards*	PO Box 219, Marshville NC 28103	704-624-5098	R	22*	.4
14	Timber Creek Resource LLC—*Stephanie Mustin*	5059 N 119th St, Milwaukee WI 53225	414-466-1645	R	20*	.2
15	Lumber And Things Industries Inc—*Jack Amoruso*	PO Box 386, Jacksonville WV 26726	304-788-5600	R	19*	.2
16	Bae Systems Container Solutions Inc—*Robert Carr*	19750 County Rd 7, Berthoud CO 80513	970-532-2268	R	19*	.2
17	Wooden Pallets Gp LLC—*Jacob Goeffston*	PO Box 555, Silsbee TX 77656	409-385-1234	R	18*	.2
18	United Pallet Services Inc—*Wayne Randall*	4043 Crows Landing Rd, Modesto CA 95358	209-538-5844	R	17*	.2
19	Ongweoweh Corp—*Frank C Bonamie*	PO Box 3300, Ithaca NY 14852	607-266-7070	R	16*	<.1
20	Arrington Lumber And Pallet Company Inc—*Ernest Arrington*	PO Box 1900, Jacksonville TX 75766	903-586-4070	R	16*	.2
21	Kamps Inc—*Bernard Kamps*	2900 Peach Ridge Ave N, Grand Rapids MI 49534	616-453-9676	R	15*	.5
22	B and B Lumber Company Inc—*Jeffrey Booher*	PO Box T, Jamesville NY 13078	315-492-1786	R	14*	.1
23	Libla Industries Inc—*David Libla*	1450 Rowe Pky, Poplar Bluff MO 63901	573-778-1211	R	14*	.2
24	Girard Wood Products Inc—*Steve Vipond*	PO Box 830, Puyallup WA 98371	253-845-0505	R	12*	.1
25	Nelson Co—*David Caltrider*	2116 Sparrows Point Rd, Baltimore MD 21219	410-477-3000	R	9*	.1
26	Fai Industries Inc—*Heather Davis*	1601 Holland St, Cumberland MD 21502	301-777-0461	R	8*	.1
27	Alan Gorzlancyk Enterprises Inc—*Alan Gorzlancyk*	PO Box 486, Plover WI 54467	715-344-5015	R	8*	.1
28	M and H Crates Inc—*Andy Mccown*	Rr Ste 7 Box 96, Jacksonville TX 75766	903-683-5351	R	8*	.1
29	Pallet Resource Of NC Inc—*Forrest Grimes*	4572 N Nc Hwy 150, Lexington NC 27295	336-731-8338	R	8*	.1
30	Associated Pallets Inc—*Mike Perry*	PO Box 400, Bremen KY 42325	270-754-4087	R	8*	.1
31	Hinchcliff Lumber Co—*Jay Phillips*	PO Box 386, Parsons WV 26287	304-478-2500	R	7*	.1
32	Southern Packaging Inc—*Kenneth Tuminello*	7271 Hwy 190 W, Port Allen LA 70767	225-343-9674	R	7*	.1
33	Williamsburg Millwork Corp—*M Piland*	PO Box 427, Bowling Green VA 22427	804-994-2151	R	7*	.1
34	Pallet Masters Inc—*Stephen Anderson*	655 E Florence Ave, Los Angeles CA 90001	323-758-6559	R	6*	.1
35	Nelson Company Inc (Baltimore Maryland)—*Jim Peregoy*	2116 Sparrows Point Rd, Baltimore MD 21219	410-477-3000	R	6*	.1
36	Anderson Forest Products Inc—*Billy Anderson*	PO Box 520, Tompkinsville KY 42167	270-487-6778	R	6*	.1
37	Packaging Technology Inc—*Richard Difilippo*	118 Pickering Way Ste, Exton PA 19341	610-363-8830	R	4*	<.1
38	Cooperative Workshops Inc—*Roger Garlich*	1500 Ewing Dr, Sedalia MO 65301	660-827-2100	R	4*	.3
39	Carolina Base - Pac Corp—*Weidner Abernathy*	PO Box 783, Hudson NC 28638	828-728-7304	R	3*	<.1
40	Lanport Chassis Pool—*Steven Miller*	124 Prosperity St, Garden City GA 31408	912-964-0547	R	2*	<.1
41	Acme Pallet Company Inc—*Tom Vassiliou*	45-10 Court Sq, Long Island City NY 11101	718-784-8020	R	2*	<.1

TOTALS: SIC 2448 Wood Pallets & Skids
Companies: 41

					1,484	11.7

2449 Wood Containers Nec

Rank	Company Name—*Executive Officer*	Address, City, State, Zip	Phone	Type	Fin	Empls
1	Independent Stave Company Inc—*John Boswell*	PO Box 104, Lebanon MO 65536	417-588-4151	R	144*	1.0

Rank	Company Name—*Executive Officer*	Address, City, State, Zip	Phone	Type	Fin	Empls
2	Corbett Package Co—*W Albert Corbett*	PO Box 210, Wilmington NC 28402	910-763-9991	R	140*	.1
3	Brown Forman Cooperage Co—*Bill Coleman*	914 Boonville Hwy, Lynchburg TN 37352	931-759-4334	R	89*	.2
4	Overseas Packing LLC—*Susan Murray*	19800 Alexander Rd, Bedford OH 44146	440-232-2917	S	21*	.1
5	Georgia Crate and Basket Company Inc—*Bolling Jones*	PO Box 46, Thomasville GA 31799	229-226-2541	R	19*	.1
6	Index Packaging Inc—*Bruce Lander*	1055 White Mountain Hw, Milton NH 03851	603-652-4406	R	16*	.1
7	Hinton Lumber Products Inc—*Larry Howell*	PO Box 1846, Tuscaloosa AL 35403	205-758-2761	R	15*	.1
8	Great American Wirebound Box Company Inc—*J Sharp*	PO Box 179, Fernwood MS 39635	601-684-7311	R	13*	.2
9	Tosca Ltd—*Jere Dhein*	PO Box 8127, Green Bay WI 54308	920-617-4013	R	13*	.1
10	T and R Lumber Co—*Cheryl Guardia*	PO Box 2484, Rancho Cucamonga CA 91729	909-899-3312	R	9*	.1
11	Ljm Packaging Company Inc—*John Pezza*	28 Mason St, North Kingstown RI 02852	401-295-2660	R	6*	.1
12	Johnston's Trading Post Inc—*James Johnston*	11 N Pioneer Ave, Woodland CA 95776	530-661-6152	R	6*	.1
13	French Packaging Services Inc—*Brian French*	249 Oceana Way, Norwood MA 02062	617-558-5225	R	4*	<.1
14	Industrial Wood Fab and Packaging Co—*Richard Ott*	18620 Fort St, Riverview MI 48193	734-284-4808	R	2*	<.1
15	Nelson Case Corp—*John Bovadilla*	650 S Jefferson St Ste, Placentia CA 92870	714-528-2215	R	2*	<.1
16	Smith Kramer Inc	1622 Westport Rd, Kansas City MO 64111	816-756-3777	R	1*	<.1
17	United Basket—*Phil Hanfling*	58-01 Grand Ave, Maspeth NY 11378	718-894-5454	R	N/A	<.1
18	Texas Crating Inc—*Eloy Martinez*	19051 Kenswick Dr Ste, Humble TX 77338	281-446-0553	R	N/A	<.1

TOTALS: SIC 2449 Wood Containers Nec
Companies: 18   **498**   **2.3**

2451 Mobile Homes

Rank	Company Name—*Executive Officer*	Address, City, State, Zip	Phone	Type	Fin	Empls
1	Clayton Homes Inc—*Kevin T Clayton*	PO Box 9790, Maryville TN 37802	865-380-3000	S	3,200*	14.0
2	Champion Enterprises Inc—*Timothy Bernlohr*	755 W Big Beaver Ste 1, Troy MI 48084	248-340-9090	R	1,033	4.1
3	Redman Industries Inc—*Robert Linton* Champion Enterprises Inc	2550 Walnut Hill Ln St, Dallas TX 75229	214-353-3600	S	614	3.7
4	HSTR Manufacturing Holdings Inc	2450 S Shore Blvd Ste, League City TX 77573	281-334-9700	S	463*	.7
5	Bellcrest Homes—*David A Roberson* Cavalier Homes Inc	PO Box 630, Millen GA 30442	478-982-4000	S	268*	.4
6	Southern Energy Homes Inc—*Keith O Holdbrooks* Clayton Homes Inc	PO Box 390, Addison AL 35540	256-747-8589	S	203	1.5
7	Cavco Industries Inc—*Joseph H Stegmayer*	1001 N Central Ave 8th, Phoenix AZ 85004	602-256-6263	P	172	1.3
8	Cavalier Homes Inc—*Bobby Tesney* Southern Energy Homes Inc	PO Box 300, Addison AL 35540	256-747-1575	S	164*	1.0
9	Skyline Corp—*Thomas G Deranek*	PO Box 743, Elkhart IN 46515	574-294-6521	P	162	1.3
10	Ritz-Craft Corporation of Penna Inc—*Paul D John*	PO Box 70, Mifflinburg PA 17844	570-966-1053	R	110*	1.1
11	Horton Homes Inc—*N Horton*	PO Box 4410, Eatonton GA 31024	706-485-8506	R	83*	1.5
12	Homes Of Merit Inc Champion Enterprises Inc	PO Box 2097, Lake City FL 32056	386-755-3073	S	82*	.7
13	Golden West Homes—*Kevin T Clayton* Clayton Homes Inc	3100 N Perris Blvd, Perris CA 92571	951-943-8055	S	75*	.7
14	Redman Homes Inc—*William C Griffiths* Redman Industries Inc	298 Harvey Faulk Rd, Sanford NC 27332	919-774-4439	S	58*	.2
15	Jacobsen Manufacturing Inc—*Bob Jacobsen*	600 Packard Ct, Safety Harbor FL 34695	727-726-1138	R	41*	.2
16	Indiana Building Systems LLC—*John Guequierre*	51700 Lovejoy Dr, Middlebury IN 46540	574-825-3700	R	37*	.3
17	Oak Creek Homes LP—*Finis F Teeter*	4805 E Loop 820 S, Fort Worth TX 76119	817-478-5551	S	33	.2
18	Giles Industries Inc—*Alan Neely*	405 S Broad St, New Tazewell TN 37825	423-626-7243	R	32*	.3
19	Fleetwood Homes of Florida Cavco Industries Inc	700 Main St, Auburndale FL 33823	863-967-7575	S	30*	.3
20	Legacy Housing Ltd—*Sharlotte Farley*	4801 Mark Iv Pkwy, Fort Worth TX 76106	817-624-7565	R	29*	.5
21	Deer Valley Corp—*Charles G Masters*	3111 W Dr MLK Blvd Ste, Tampa FL 33607	813-418-5250	P	29	.2
22	Fuqua Homes Inc—*Phillip Daniels*	7100 S Cooper St, Arlington TX 76001	817-465-3211	R	28*	.4
23	Valley Manufactured Housing Inc—*Arthur Berger*	1717 S 4th St, Sunnyside WA 98944	509-839-9409	R	24*	.2
24	River Birch Homes Inc—*Delmo Payne*	400 River Birch Dr, Hackleburg AL 35564	205-935-1997	R	19*	.2
25	Majestic Homes Inc—*Tom Trexler* Prestige Home Centers Inc	PO Box 1659, Ocala FL 34474	352-732-5157	S	17*	.1
26	F F and P Mobile Modular Technologies Inc—*John Fillingham*	PO Box 657, Gering NE 69341	308-436-3131	R	16*	.1
27	Nashua Homes Of Idaho Inc—*Kenneth Goodrich*	PO Box 170008, Boise ID 83717	208-345-0222	R	16*	.1
28	Nobility Homes Inc—*Terry E Trexler*	PO Box 1659, Ocala FL 34478	352-732-5157	P	15	.1
29	Cappaert Manufactured Housing Inc—*Michael Cappaert*	PO Box 820567, Vicksburg MS 39182	601-636-5401	R	14*	.1
30	Pine Grove Manufactured Homes Inc—*Wayne Fanelli*	PO Box 128, Pine Grove PA 17963	570-345-2011	R	14*	.1
31	Mark Line Industries Of Pennsylvania Inc—*L Arnold*	502 Alexander Dr, Ephrata PA 17522	717-733-1315	R	14*	.1
32	King's Custom Builders Inc—*Russell Taylor*	PO Box 584, Ellaville GA 31806	229-937-2538	R	13*	.2
33	Franklin Homes Inc—*Jerry James*	10655 Hwy 43, Russellville AL 35653	256-332-4510	R	12*	.1
34	Quality Housing Supply LLC Cavalier Homes Inc	PO Box 940, Hamilton AL 35570	205-921-2880	S	10*	<.1
35	Skyline Homes Inc—*Thomas Deranek* Skyline Corp	PO Box 743, Elkhart IN 46515	574-755-6521	S	9*	.1
36	Oliver Technologies Inc—*James Oliver*	PO Box 9, Hohenwald TN 38462	931-796-4555	R	9*	.1
37	Home Place Inc—*Jim Tidmore*	5305 Veterans Memorial, Adamsville AL 35005	205-674-0304	R	5*	<.1
38	Homark Company Inc—*James Violette*	100 3rd St Sw, Red Lake Falls MN 56750	218-253-2777	R	4*	.1
39	Prestige Home Centers Inc—*Tom Trexler* Nobility Homes Inc	PO Box 1659, Ocala FL 34478	352-622-2955	S	<1	.1

TOTALS: SIC 2451 Mobile Homes
Companies: 39   **7,159**   **36.1**

2452 Prefabricated Wood Buildings

Rank	Company Name—*Executive Officer*	Address, City, State, Zip	Phone	Type	Fin	Empls
1	Irish Homes Inc—*John Hussey* Liberty Homes Inc	721 N Nappanee St, Elkhart IN 46514	574-522-2233	S	365*	.8
2	Waverlee Homes Inc—*Edward J Hussey* Liberty Homes Inc	2039 Bexar Ave E, Hamilton AL 35570	205-921-1887	S	365*	.8
3	Excel Homes Inc—*Steve Scharnhorst*	RR 2 Box 683, Liverpool PA 17045	717-444-3395	R	293*	.7
4	Lester Building Systems LLC—*John Hall*	1111 2nd Ave S, Lester Prairie MN 55354	320-395-2531	R	187*	.4
5	All American Homes LLC—*Steven E Kerr*	PO Box 451, Decatur IN 46733	260-724-9171	S	159*	.5
6	American Homestar Corp—*Finis F Teeter*	2450 S Shore Blvd Ste, League City TX 77573	281-334-9700	P	145	.6
7	Karsten Co—*Rick Boyd*	1200 Wilco Rd, Stayton OR 97383		R	136*	.1
8	Muncy Homes Inc—*Thomas Saltsgiver*	1567 Rt 442 Hwy, Muncy PA 17756	570-546-2261	R	94*	.5
9	Modtech Holdings Inc—*Dennis L Shogren*	2830 Barrett Ave, Perris CA 92571	951-943-4014	P	87	.4
10	Liberty Homes Inc—*Edward J Hussey*	PO Box 35, Goshen IN 46527	574-533-0431	P	84	.8
11	Nationwide Custom Homes Inc—*Tony Watson*	PO Box 5511, Martinsville VA 24115	276-632-7100	S	62*	.5

Note: An asterisk (*) indicates an estimated financial figure. The company type code used is as follows: R = Private, P = Public, S = Private Subsidiary, B = Public Subsidiary, D = Division, J = Joint Venture, I = Investment Fund.

COMPANY RANKINGS BY SALES WITHIN 4-DIGIT SIC

Rank	Company Name—Executive Officer	Address, City, State, Zip	Phone	Type	Fin	Empls
12	Adrian Homes—Stan Daughtry	PO Box 266, Adrian GA 31002	478-668-4800	D	58*	.1
13	Walden Structures Inc—Charles Walden	3100 Jefferson St, Riverside CA 92504	951-351-3155	R	48*	.4
14	Philadelphia Sign Co—Bill Trucksess	707 W Spring Garden St, Palmyra NJ 08065	856-829-1460	R	42*	.3
15	Lindal Cedar Homes Inc—Robert W Lindal	PO Box 24426, Seattle WA 98124	206-725-0900	R	40*	.2
16	Vfp Inc—Jerry Arnold	PO Box 21269, Roanoke VA 24018	540-977-0500	R	35*	.2
17	Structural Systems Inc—Bruce Gordon	PO Box 322, Walkersville MD 21793	301-271-7734	R	34*	.6
18	Rjf - Keiser Industries LLC—Tim Farrar	PO Box 9000, Oxford ME 04270	207-539-8883	R	23*	.2
19	Apex Homes Inc—Chriss Nipple	7172 Rte 522, Middleburg PA 17842	570-837-2333	R	22*	.2
20	Enviroplex Inc—Glenn Owens	4777 E Carpenter Rd, Stockton CA 95215	209-466-8000	S	22*	.1
21	Lincoln Logs Ltd—John D Shepherd	PO Box 135, Chestertown NY 12817	518-494-5500	R	22	.1
22	Palm Harbor Manufacturing LP—Larry Keener	15305 Dallas Pkwy Ste, Addison TX 75001	512-385-5880	S	21*	<.1
23	Blazer Industries Inc—Marvin Shetler	PO Box 489, Aumsville OR 97325	503-749-1900	R	19*	.2
24	Karsten Homes LLC—Larry Nelson	2700 Karsten Ct Se, Albuquerque NM 87102	505-242-5580	R	19*	.2
25	Fleetwood Homes of Oregon	PO Box 628, Woodburn OR 97071	503-981-3136	S	19*	.2
26	Component Manufacturing Co—Tom Reaves	PO Box 84808, Sioux Falls SD 57118	605-339-3647	R	19*	.2
27	Barna Log Homes LLC—Gilbert Phillips	PO Box 5124, Oneida TN 37841		R	19*	.2
28	Future Home Technology Inc—John Longabucco	PO Box 4255, Port Jervis NY 12771	845-856-9033	R	16*	.1
29	Foremost Industries Inc—Ralph Michael	2375 Buchanan Trl W, Greencastle PA 17225	717-597-7166	R	15*	.2
30	Westchester Modular Homes Inc—Charles Hatcher	Reagans Mill Rd, Wingdale NY 12594	845-832-9400	R	15*	.1
31	Modern Building Systems Inc—James Rasmussen	PO Box 110, Aumsville OR 97325	503-749-4949	R	14*	.1
32	Modular Structures of PA Inc—Jay Swartz	1910 N Old Trl, Selinsgrove PA 17870	570-743-2012	R	14*	.1
33	Alliance Homes Inc—G Spann	PO Box 266, Adrian GA 31002	478-668-3232	R	14*	.2
34	Penn Lyon Homes Corp—Roger Lyons	PO Box 27, Selinsgrove PA 17870	570-374-4004	R	14	.1
35	Design Homes of Minnesota—Randy Weeks	600 N Marquette Rd, Prairie du Chien WI 53821		R	14*	<.1
36	Epoch Corp—Douglas Basnett	PO Box 235, Suncook NH 03275	603-225-3907	R	14*	.1
37	American Modular Systems Inc—Daniel Sarich	787 Spreckels Ave, Manteca CA 95336	209-825-1921	R	14*	.1
38	Mccall Of The Wild Inc—Dave Ochoa	9652 W State St, Star ID 83669	208-238-5858	R	12*	.2
39	Indicom Buildings Inc—Scott Mattson	PO Box 1567, Burleson TX 76097	817-447-1213	R	12*	.1
40	Heritage Homes Of Nebraska Inc—Rod Tompkins	PO Box 37, Wayne NE 68787	402-375-4770	R	12*	.1
41	New England Homes Inc—Daniel Donahue	270 Ocean Rd, Greenland NH 03840	603-436-8830	R	11*	.1
42	Wisconsin Homes Inc—Lamont Nienast	PO Box 250, Marshfield WI 54449	715-384-2161	R	10*	.1
43	Virginia Homes Manufacturing Corp—Roger Mitchell	PO Box 410, Boydton VA 23917	434-738-6107	R	10*	.1
44	Cardinal Homes Inc—Bret Berneche	PO Box 10, Wylliesburg VA 23976	434-735-8111	R	10*	.1
45	Manternach Development Co—Galen Manternach	1553 11th Dr, Friendship WI 53934	608-339-7888	R	10*	.1
46	Sunshine Manufactured Structures Inc—Dean Bodine	PO Box 1439, Rockwell NC 28138	704-279-6600	R	9*	.1
47	Superior Homes LLC—Julie Cluts	715 21st St Sw, Watertown SD 57201	605-886-3270	R	9*	.1
48	Hi-Tech Housing Inc—Charles Fanaro	1103 Maple St, Bristol IN 46507	574-848-5593	R	9*	.1
49	Stratford Homes LP—John William	PO Box 37, Stratford WI 54484	715-687-3133	R	9*	.1
50	Murray Building and Crane Industries Inc—Jerry Murray	PO Box 800334, Houston TX 77280	713-464-6506	R	9*	.1
51	Rmd Manufacturing Ltd—Harleene Hackler	1402 Hwy 287 S, Mansfield TX 76063	817-477-5321	R	9*	.1
52	Hoge Lumber Co—John Hoge	PO Box 159, New Knoxville OH 45871	419-753-2263	R	8*	.1
53	Beracah Homes Inc—R Collison	9590 Manticoke Dr, Greenwood DE 19950	302-349-4561	R	6*	.1
54	Timberland Homes Inc—Gilbert Wood	1201 37th St Nw, Auburn WA 98001	253-735-3435	R	4*	<.1
55	S S Steele and Company Inc—Robert Steele	4951 Government Blvd, Mobile AL 36693	251-661-9600	R	3*	<.1
56	Unibilt Industries Inc—Douglas Scholz	PO Box 373, Vandalia OH 45377	937-890-7570	R	<1*	.1

TOTALS: SIC 2452 Prefabricated Wood Buildings
Companies: 56

					2,744	12.1

2491 Wood Preserving

Rank	Company Name—Executive Officer	Address, City, State, Zip	Phone	Type	Fin	Empls
1	Koppers Inc—Walter W Turner	436 7th Ave, Pittsburgh PA 15219	412-227-2001	R	1,170*	2.0
2	McFarland Cascade—Charles Casanave	PO Box 1496, Tacoma WA 98401	253-572-3033	R	150*	.4
3	Cox Industries Inc—R Johnson	PO Box 1124, Orangeburg SC 29116	803-534-7467	R	117*	.4
4	JH Baxter and Co—Georgia Baxter Krause	PO Box 10797, Eugene OR 97440	541-689-3801	R	86*	.2
5	Hoover Treated Wood Products Inc—Barry Holden	154 Wire Rd, Thomson GA 30824	706-595-1264	R	86*	.2
6	Jefferson Homebuilders Inc—Joseph Daniel	PO Box 1148, Culpeper VA 22701	540-825-5898	R	84*	.2
7	Burke-Parsons-Bowlby Corp—Richard E Bowlby	PO Box 231, Ripley WV 25271	304-372-1202	R	63*	.4
8	Atlantic Wood Industries Inc—William Crossman	PO Box 1608, Savannah GA 31402	912-966-7008	R	44*	.3
9	Robbins Manufacturing Company Inc—Laurence Hall	PO Box 17939, Tampa FL 33682	813-971-3030	R	33*	.5
10	Texas Electric Cooperatives Inc—Mike Williams	1122 Colorado St Ste 2, Austin TX 78701	512-454-0311	R	29*	.2
11	Elder Wood Preserving Company Inc—Joe Elder	PO Box 522, Mansura LA 71350	318-964-2196	R	28*	.1
12	Boatright Railroad Products Inc—Rush Boatright	PO Box 43889, Birmingham AL 35243	205-991-0750	R	28*	.3
13	California Cascade Industries—Stu Heath	PO Box 130026, Sacramento CA 95853	916-736-3353	R	27*	.2
14	Osmose Inc—Paul Goydan	1016 Everee Inn Rd, Griffin GA 30224	770-233-4200	R	26*	.2
15	Potomac Supply Corp—William Carden	1398 Kinsale Rd, Kinsale VA 22488	804-472-2527	R	24*	.2
16	Burke-Parsons-Bowlby Corp Appalachian Div—Richard Bowlby Burke-Parsons-Bowlby Corp	PO Box 86, Goshen VA 24439	540-997-9251	D	20*	.1
17	Exterior Wood Inc—Stanley Bishoprick	PO Box 206, Washougal WA 98671	360-835-8561	R	17*	.1
18	General Wood Preserving Company Inc—Karl Boatright	PO Box 370, Leland NC 28451	910-371-3131	R	7*	.1
19	Appalachian Wood Floors Inc—Jim Graf	838 Campbell Ave, Portsmouth OH 45662	740-354-4572	R	4*	.1
20	Romco Inc—Ole Rommesmo	PO Box 2044, Fargo ND 58107	701-282-7025	R	3*	<.1
21	Land And Sea Forest Products Of Pennsylvania Corp—Wade Carden	400 Rock Run Rd, Fairless Hills PA 19030	215-295-5460	R	2*	<.1

TOTALS: SIC 2491 Wood Preserving
Companies: 21

					2,047	6.0

2493 Reconstituted Wood Products

Rank	Company Name—Executive Officer	Address, City, State, Zip	Phone	Type	Fin	Empls
1	Collins Products LLC—Dale Slate	PO Box 16, Klamath Falls OR 97601	541-884-2241	S	157*	.6
2	Homasote International Sales Company Inc—Craig Stiffler Homasote Co	PO Box 7240, West Trenton NJ 08628	609-883-3300	S	135*	.1
3	Martco LP—Jonathan Martin	PO Box 1110, Alexandria LA 71309	318-448-0405	R	56*	.9
4	Tectum Inc—Mike Massaro	PO Box 3002, Newark OH 43058	740-345-9691	R	43*	.1
5	Dominance Industries Inc—Ed McDonald	RR 4 Box 371, Broken Bow OK 74728	580-584-6247	R	24*	.2
6	Langboard Inc—John Langdale	PO Box 837, Quitman GA 31643	229-263-8943	R	19*	.3
7	Fiberesin Industries Inc—Larry Starkweather	PO Box 88, Oconomowoc WI 53066	262-567-4427	R	17*	.1
8	Norbord Minnesota Inc—Joanne Lewis	4409 Northwood Rd Nw, Solway MN 56678	218-751-2023	R	16*	.1
9	Homasote Co—Warren L Flicker	PO Box 7240, West Trenton NJ 08628	609-883-3300	P	16	.1
10	Kronospan LLC	1 Kronospan Way, Eastaboga AL 36260	256-741-8755	R	14*	.1
11	Norbord Alabama Inc—Bruce Brebe	4400 Barton Industrial, Lanett AL 36863	334-576-1500	R	14*	.1
12	Forest Hambro Products Inc—Dwayne Reichlin	PO Box 129, Crescent City CA 95531	707-464-6131	R	10*	.3
13	Alcan Baltek Corp—Ronald Tassello	PO Box 16148, High Point NC 27261	201-767-1400	R	9*	.1

Rank	Company Name—*Executive Officer*	Address, City, State, Zip	Phone	Type	Fin	Empls
14	Masonite US Holdings Inc—*Fred Bench*	1 N Dale Mabry Hwy Ste, Tampa FL 33609	813-877-2726	D	7*	.1
15	Conwed Designscape—*Russell A Leighton Jr*	800 Gustafson Rd, Ladysmith WI 54848	715-532-5548	D	6*	.1
16	LI Cultured Marble Inc—*Doris Holder*	1184 Maple Grove Ch Rd, Mount Airy NC 27030	336-789-5320	R	2*	<.1

TOTALS: SIC 2493 Reconstituted Wood Products
Companies: 16 — 544, 3.3

2499 Wood Products Nec

Rank	Company Name—*Executive Officer*	Address, City, State, Zip	Phone	Type	Fin	Empls
1	Leucadia National Corp—*Joseph S Steinberg*	315 Park Ave S, New York NY 10010	212-460-1900	P	9,350	2.4
2	Pro-Build Holdings Inc—*Fred Marino*	7595 Technology Way 5t, Denver CO 80237	303-262-8500	S	4,653*	17.0
3	Koppers Holdings Inc—*Walter W Turner*	436 7th Ave, Pittsburgh PA 15219	412-227-2001	P	1,539	1.7
4	Longaberger Co—*Tami Longaberger*	1500 E Main St, Newark OH 43055	740-322-5000	R	1,206*	8.7
5	Simpson Manufacturing Company Inc—*Thomas J Fitzmyers*	PO Box 10789, Pleasanton CA 94588	925-560-9032	P	603	2.0
6	Atrium Companies Inc—*Gregory T Faherty*	PO Box 226597, Dallas TX 75220	214-630-5757	R	598	4.5
7	Trex Company Inc—*Ronald W Kaplan*	160 Exeter Dr, Winchester VA 22603	540-542-6300	P	318	.6
8	Burnes of Boston/Connoisseur Group—*William D Marohn*	3103 Clairmont Rd Suit, Atlanta GA 30329		D	258*	1.0
9	Wood Resources LP	1 Sound Shore Dr Ste 3, Greenwich CT 06830	203-302-3343	S	200*	.7
10	Midwest Towers Inc—*Larry Brown*	PO Box 1465, Chickasha OK 73023	405-224-4622	R	86*	.2
11	Sanderson Plumbing Products Inc—*Sandra Sanderson*	PO Box 1367, Columbus MS 39703	662-328-4000	R	55*	.8
12	California Cedar Products Co—*Charles Berolzheimer*	400 S Fresno St, Stockton CA 95203	209-944-5800	R	31*	.6
13	Solon Manufacturing Company Inc	PO Box 441, North Haven CT 06473		R	30*	.4
14	Timberlane Woodcrafters Inc—*Rick Skidmore*	150 Domorah Dr, Montgomeryville PA 18936	215-616-0600	R	30*	.1
15	Armstrong Wood Products Inc—*Michael D Lockhart*	16803 Dallas Pkwy, Addison TX 75001	214-887-2000	S	28*	.1
16	Southern Finishing Company Inc—*Edgar Brown*	PO Box 888, Stoneville NC 27048	336-573-3537	R	27*	.3
17	Aakron Rule Corp—*Danielle Robillard*	PO Box 418, Akron NY 14001	716-542-5483	R	25*	.2
18	Walpole Woodworkers Inc—*Louis Maglio*	PO Box 151, Walpole MA 02081	508-668-2800	R	23*	.4
19	Matthews Four Seasons—*Paul Bolt*	6677 E Hardaway Rd, Stockton CA 95215	209-931-1695	S	23*	.1
20	Simpson Strong-Tie International Inc—*Thomas J Fitzmyers* Simpson Manufacturing Company Inc	PO Box 10789, Pleasanton CA 94588	925-560-9000	S	23*	.1
21	Structural Industries Inc—*Stanley Hirsch*	2950 Vtrans Memorial H, Bohemia NY 11716	516-822-5200	R	20*	.2
22	White River Hardwoods-Woodworks Inc—*Joan Johnson*	1197 S Happy Hollow Rd, Fayetteville AR 72701	479-442-6986	R	20*	.1
23	W R Vermillion Company Inc—*William Thomas*	1207 S Scenic Ave, Springfield MO 65802	417-862-3785	R	19*	.2
24	Madison Mill Inc—*Thomas Mckelvey*	PO Box 90886, Nashville TN 37209	615-269-8969	R	16*	.1
25	Ginsey Industries Inc—*Herbert Briggs*	281 Benigno Blvd, Bellmawr NJ 08031	856-933-1300	R	16*	.1
26	Automated Routing Inc—*Barry Schaefer*	16920 N State Rd 545, Saint Meinrad IN 47577	812-357-2429	R	13*	.1
27	Cranford Woodcarving Inc/Plant 1—*Jessie Cranford*	PO Box 9007, Hickory NC 28603		R	12*	.2
28	Gemline Frame Company Inc—*Neil Gold*	2623 Medford St Ste B, Los Angeles CA 90033	323-223-1178	R	12*	.1
29	Amorim Cork Composites Inc—*Gary Fell*	PO Box 25, Trevor WI 53179	262-862-2311	R	12*	.1
30	Matthews Redwood Inc—*Robert Matthews*	6677 E Hardaway Rd, Stockton CA 95215	209-931-1695	R	11*	.1
31	Cherry Creek Woodcraft Inc—*Martin Goldman*	PO Box 267, South Dayton NY 14138	716-988-3211	R	11*	.1
32	Rochester Shoe Tree Company Inc—*John Fox*	PO Box 746, Ashland NH 03217	603-968-3301	R	11*	.1
33	Lowe Products Company Inc—*John Lowe*	PO Box D, Shepherdstown WV 25443	304-876-2546	R	10*	.1
34	Mccrorie Group LLC	PO Box 9007, Hickory NC 28603	828-328-4538	R	10*	.1
35	Applegate Insulation Systems Inc—*Aaron Applegate*	1000 Highview Dr, Webberville MI 48892	517-521-3545	R	9*	.1
36	Ramrod Enterprises LLC—*William Mitchell*	12286 Hwy 105 E, Conroe TX 77306	936-756-4846	R	9*	.1
37	JK Adams Company Inc—*Malcolm E Cooper Jr*	PO Box 248, Dorset VT 05251	802-362-2303	R	9*	<.1
38	Mid America Frame Inc—*Fred Trayler*	PO Box 243, Plattsburg MO 64477	816-539-3701	R	9*	.1
39	West Wood Products Inc—*Golan Levy*	2943 E Las Hermanas St, Compton CA 90221	310-631-8978	R	9*	<.1
40	Robert's Wood Products Inc—*Rick Robert*	1070 County Rd 3770, Mountain View MO 65548	417-934-2092	R	8*	.1
41	Malden International Designs Inc—*John Aucello*	19 Cowan Dr, Middleboro MA 02346	508-291-1104	R	8*	.1
42	FJ Designs Inc—*Faline Jones*	2163 Great Trails Dr, Wooster OH 44691	330-264-1377	R	7*	.1
43	Mossberg Industries Inc—*William Moyer*	204 N 2nd St, Garrett IN 46738	260-357-5141	R	7*	.1
44	Church Hill Classics Ltd—*Lucie Voves*	594 Pepper St, Monroe CT 06468	203-268-1535	R	7*	.1
45	Heartfelt Inc—*Linwood Metts*	PO Box 21305, Roanoke VA 24018	540-387-2032	R	6*	.1
46	Gemini Mouldings Inc—*Frederick Campbell*	2755 Spectrum Dr, Elgin IL 60124	847-426-9243	R	6*	.1
47	Walter T Kelley Company LLC—*Kay Bohn*	PO Box 240, Clarkson KY 42726	270-242-2012	R	5*	.1
48	Sand Creek Post and Beam—*Len Dickinson*	116 W 1st St, Wayne NE 68787	402-833-5600	R	5	<.1
49	Happy Co—*Mark Juarez*	26203 Production Ave S, Hayward CA 94545	510-300-1260	S	5*	<.1
50	Opus Inc	PO Box 327, Lititz PA 17543		S	5	.1
51	Gallery Graphics Inc—*Richard Bright*	PO Box 502, Noel MO 64854	417-475-6191	R	5*,	.1
52	Ward's Cabinetry Inc—*Rob Jennings*	PO Box 531394, Birmingham AL 35253	205-646-3344	R	4*	<.1
53	Shelbyville Pencil Company Inc—*George Townes*	PO Box 727, Shelbyville TN 37162	931-684-7700	R	3*	<.1
54	P and R Specialty Inc—*Greg Blankenship*	PO Box 741, Piqua OH 45356	937-773-0263	R	3*	<.1
55	Wood Ventures—*John Hendriksen*	PO Box 563, Grass Valley CA 95945	530-272-4972	R	3*	<.1
56	Prodyne Enterprises Inc	9611 Santa Anita Ave, Rancho Cucamonga CA 91730	909-484-1212	R	3*	<.1
57	Mille Fabricators	52 Mill St, Arcade NY 14009	585-492-5690	R	3*	<.1
58	Hartford Fine Art and Framing Co—*William E Plage*	80 Pitkin St, East Hartford CT 06108	860-528-1409	R	3*	<.1
59	Fancy Fixtures OnlineCom—*Robert Milkowski*	132 Dupont St, Plainview NY 11803	516-349-3003	R	3*	<.1
60	Hygolet Inc—*Andre Stucki*	349 Se 2nd Ave, Deerfield Beach FL 33441	954-481-8601	R	3*	<.1
61	Channel Manufacturing Inc—*Jordan Klein*	55 Channel Dr, Port Washington NY 11050	516-944-6271	R	2*	<.1
62	Forest Cowee Products Inc—*William Stallkamp*	PO Box 248, Berlin NY 12022	518-658-2233	R	2*	<.1
63	Cumberland Wood Products Inc—*Mark Love*	PO Box 68, Helenwood TN 37755	423-569-6363	R	2*	<.1
64	S and S Acrylic Inc—*Chih-Kuei Hsu*	4690a S Old Peachtree, Norcross GA 30071	770-729-0650	R	1*	<.1
65	HA Stiles Co—*Ambrose Berry*	PO Box 779, Westbrook ME 04098	207-854-8458	R	1*	<.1
66	Fordyce Picture Frame Company Inc—*Joe Barnes*	PO Box 1026, Fordyce AR 71742	870-352-2115	R	1*	.1
67	Wolf Creek Products Inc—*Marcia Gunderson*	1425 Washington St, Eldora IA 50627	641-858-2332	R	<1*	<.1

TOTALS: SIC 2499 Wood Products Nec
Companies: 67 — 19,455, 44.9

2511 Wood Household Furniture

Rank	Company Name—*Executive Officer*	Address, City, State, Zip	Phone	Type	Fin	Empls
1	Ashley Furniture Industries Inc—*Todd Wanek*	1 Ashley Way, Arcadia WI 54612	608-323-3377	R	3,000*	14.0
2	Bernhardt Furniture Company Inc—*Anne Bernhardt*	PO Box 740, Lenoir NC 28645	828-758-9811	R	1,610*	2.1
3	Furniture Brands International Inc—*Ralph P Scozzafava*	1 N Brentwood Blvd 15t, Saint Louis MO 63105	314-863-1100	P	1,160	6.2
4	Ethan Allen Interiors Inc—*M Farooq Kathwari*	PO Box 1966, Danbury CT 06813	203-743-8000	P	679	4.7
5	Drexel Heritage Furnishings Inc HDM Furniture Industries	401 E Main St, Thomasville NC 27360		S	571*	1.3
6	Sauder Woodworking Co—*Kevin Sauder*	502 Middle St, Archbold OH 43502	419-446-2711	R	472*	2.7
7	L and JG Stickley Inc—*Aminy Audi*	PO Box 480, Manlius NY 13104	315-682-5500	R	379*	1.5
8	Whalen Furniture Manufacturing Inc—*Kenneth Whalen*	1578 Air Wing Rd, San Diego CA 92154	619-236-8455	R	263*	.2
9	Bassett Furniture Industries Inc—*Robert H Spilman Jr*	PO Box 626, Bassett VA 24055	276-629-6000	P	253	1.3

Note: An asterisk (*) indicates an estimated financial figure. The company type code used is as follows: R = Private, P = Public, S = Private Subsidiary, B = Public Subsidiary, D = Division, J = Joint Venture, I = Investment Fund.

COMPANY RANKINGS BY SALES WITHIN 4-DIGIT SIC

Rank	Company Name—*Executive Officer*	Address, City, State, Zip	Phone	Type	Fin	Empls
10	Pulaski Furniture Corp—*Lawerance E Webb*	3980 Premier Dr Suite, High Point NC 27265	540-980-7330	R	230*	2.5
11	Hooker Furniture Corp—*Paul B Toms Jr*	PO Box 4708, Martinsville VA 24115	276-632-0459	P	169	.7
12	Walter E Smithe Furniture Inc—*Walter E Smithe III*	1251 W Thorndale Ave, Itasca IL 60143		R	120*	.5
13	Stanley Furniture Company Inc—*R Glen Prillaman*	PO Box 30, Stanleytown VA 24168	276-627-2000	P	105	.5
14	Dolly Madison Industries Inc—*David Scheu*	9780 Ormsby Station Rd, Louisville KY 40223	502-426-4351	S	101*	.2
15	Bush Industries Inc—*Jim Sherbert*	PO Box 460, Jamestown NY 14702	716-665-2000	S	100*	.9
16	American Drew	4310 Regency Dr Ste 10, High Point NC 27265	336-294-5233	S	80*	.8
17	Ameriwood Industries—*Jim Kimminau*	410 E 1st St S, Wright City MO 63390	636-745-3351	S	71*	.6
18	Wexford Collection	16525 S Avalon Blvd, Carson CA 90746	310-538-4150	D	70*	.3
19	Manual Woodworkers and Weavers Inc—*Jay Zito*	272 Old Sunset Hill Rd, Hendersonville NC 28792	828-692-7333	R	68*	.3
20	Hekman Furniture Co—*Dan Masters*	860 E Main Ave, Zeeland MI 49464	616-748-2660	S	62*	.4
21	Zodax LP—*Philip Cohanim*	14040 Arminta St, Panorama City CA 91402	818-785-5626	R	61*	.1
22	Kincaid Furniture Company Inc—*Steve Kincaid*	240 Pleasant Hill Rd, Hudson NC 28638	828-728-3261	S	58*	.9
23	Chromcraft Revington Inc—*Ronald H Butler*	1330 Win Hentschel Blv, West Lafayette IN 47906	765-807-2640	P	56	.3
24	Sandberg Furniture Manufacturing—*John A Sandberg*	PO Box 58291, Los Angeles CA 90058	323-582-0711	R	56*	.5
25	Tmi Systems Design Corp—*Dean Rummel*	50 S 3rd Ave W, Dickinson ND 58601	701-456-6716	R	52*	.4
26	Riverside Furniture Corp—*Scott Ostrander*	PO Box 1427, Fort Smith AR 72902	479-785-8100	R	51*	.7
27	Standard Furniture Manufacturing Company Inc—*William Peters*	PO Box 1089, Bay Minette AL 36507	251-937-6741	R	49*	.7
28	La Barge Inc (Holland Michigan)—*Jeff Young*	2427 Penny Rd, High Point NC 27265	336-812-2400	R	47*	.1
29	Carolina Business Furniture Inc—*Hank Menke*	PO Box 4398, Archdale NC 27263	336-431-9400	S	41*	.1
30	Progressive Furniture Inc—*Kevin Sauder*	PO Box 308, Archbold OH 43502	419-446-4500	R	40*	.2
31	Harden Furniture Company Inc—*Gregory M Harden*	8550 Mill Pond Way, Mc Connellsville NY 13401	315-245-1000	R	35*	.5
32	Thomasville Furniture Industries Inc—*Nancy Webster* Furniture Brands International Inc	401 E Main St, Thomasville NC 27361	336-472-4000	S	34	.4
33	Crawford Furniture Manufacturing Corp—*Michael Cappa*	PO Box 668, Jamestown NY 14702	716-661-9100	R	33*	.3
34	Legacy Cabinets LLC—*Rodney Suggs*	PO Box 730, Eastaboga AL 36260	256-831-4888	R	32*	.4
35	Furniture Values International LLC—*Richard McMillan*	601 N 75th Ave, Phoenix AZ 85043	602-442-5600	R	30*	.3
36	Bausman And Company Inc—*Craig Johnson*	1425 S Campus Ave, Ontario CA 91761	909-947-0139	R	30*	.3
37	Kushwood Chair Inc—*Daniel Kusvhinikov*	1290 E Elm St, Ontario CA 91761	909-930-2100	R	29*	.3
38	Borkholder Corp—*Freeman D Borkholder*	PO Box 5, Nappanee IN 46550	574-773-3144	R	27*	.1
39	Whittier Wood Products Co—*Scott Whittier*	PO Box 2827, Eugene OR 97402	541-687-0213	R	27*	.1
40	Cresent Enterprises Inc—*Charles Tomkins*	PO Box 1438, Gallatin TN 37066	615-452-1671	R	27*	.3
41	Hickory Business Furniture—*Kevin Stark* Thomasville Furniture Industries Inc	PO Box 8, Hickory NC 28603	828-328-2064	D	26*	.3
42	Cramco Inc—*Paul Cramer*	2200 E Ann St, Philadelphia PA 19134	215-427-9500	R	23*	.2
43	A F Lorts Company Inc—*Michael Lorts*	PO Box 5550, Goodyear AZ 85338	623-936-1437	R	23*	.2
44	Frank Chervan Inc—*Gregory Terrill*	2005 Greeenbriar Ave, Roanoke VA 24013	540-586-5600	R	22*	.2
45	American Moulding and Millwork Co—*Lloyd Kent*	1620 S 3rd St, Sanford NC 27330	919-775-4111	R	22*	.3
46	Dubois Wood Products Inc—*Bryan Meyerholtz*	PO Box 386, Huntingburg IN 47542	812-683-3613	R	22*	.2
47	HDM Furniture Industries—*Jeff Young* Furniture Brands International Inc	1925 Eastchester Dr, High Point NC 27265	336-888-4800	S	21*	.1
48	Trendwood Inc—*Dan Ragland*	120 E Watkins St Ste 1, Phoenix AZ 85004	602-416-7800	R	20*	.2
49	Mobel Inc—*Paul Ruhe*	2130 Industrial Park R, Ferdinand IN 47532	812-367-1214	R	20*	.2
50	Big Tree Furniture and Industries Inc—*Young Lim*	2883 E Victoria St, Compton CA 90221	310-894-7500	R	20*	<.1
51	Orleans Furniture Inc—*Ed Marshall*	1481 N Main St, Columbia MS 39429	601-736-9002	R	19*	.4
52	Jimson Manufacturing Company Inc—*Jimmy Setliff*	676 Old Hamilton Rd, Haleyville AL 35565	205-486-9515	R	17*	.2
53	Lakewood Manufacturing Company Inc—*Doug Widlake*	1241 New Windsor Rd, Westminster MD 21158	410-876-7988	R	17*	.2
54	Wine Cellar Innovations—*James Deckebach*	4575 Eastern Ave, Cincinnati OH 45226	513-321-3733	R	17*	.2
55	Hitchcock Chair Company Ltd—*Ron Coleman*	13 Riverton Rd, Riverton CT 06065	860-738-9958	R	16*	.2
56	Grand Rapids Chair Co—*David Miller*	625 Chestnut St Sw, Grand Rapids MI 49503	616-774-0561	R	16*	.1
57	Henkel-Harris Company Inc—*William Henkel*	PO Box 2170, Winchester VA 22604	540-667-4900	R	16*	.3
58	Stow Co—*Eric Wolff*	3311 Windquest Dr, Holland MI 49424	616-399-3311	R	15*	.1
59	Dean Donald and Sons Inc—*Jeffrey Dean*	PO Box 246, Montrose PA 18801	570-278-1179	R	15*	.1
60	Brooks Furniture Manufacturingrs Inc—*Jeremiah Brooks*	PO Box 199, Tazewell TN 37879	423-626-1111	R	15*	.2
61	American Atelier Inc—*David Goodman*	2132 Downyflake Ln, Allentown PA 18103	610-439-4040	R	15*	.2
62	Felix Manufacturing Company Inc—*Arthur Felix*	PO Box 4758, Compton CA 90224	310-635-6095	R	15*	.1
63	Philip Reinisch Company LLC—*Stanford Reinisch*	PO Box 127, Saint Anthony IN 47575	812-326-2626	R	14*	.2
64	Woodcrest Manufacturing Inc—*Walter Woodhams*	PO Box 848, Peru IN 46970	765-472-4471	R	14*	.2
65	Habersham Plantation Corp—*Matthew Eddy*	PO Box 1209, Toccoa GA 30577	706-886-1476	R	13*	.1
66	Land And Sky Inc—*Ronald Larson*	1401 W Bond Cir, Lincoln NE 68521	402-470-2468	R	13*	.1
67	H and H Furniture Manufacturers Inc—*Ken Hill*	PO Box 10, Seagrove NC 27341	336-873-7520	R	12*	.1
68	Karges Furniture Company Inc—*Joan Rogier*	PO Box 6517, Evansville IN 47719	812-425-2291	R	11*	.1
69	Lounora Industries Inc—*Kelli Berry*	PO Box 2128, Columbus MS 39704	662-328-1685	R	11*	.3
70	Trinity Furniture Inc—*Lorraine Moore*	P O Box 7835, Waco TX 76714		D	11*	.1
71	Perdues Inc—*Richard Perdue*	2415 Creek Dr, Rapid City SD 57703	605-341-2101	R	11*	.1
72	Caperton Furnitureworks LLC—*Terry Frost*	5270 Valley Rd, Berkeley Springs WV 25411	304-258-2343	R	11*	.1
73	Whitaker Furniture Company Inc—*Robert Thompson*	PO Box 1468, Searcy AR 72145	501-268-5377	R	10*	.1
74	Bentwood Furniture Inc—*Gary White*	310 Nw Morgan Ln, Grants Pass OR 97526	541-474-0996	R	10*	.1
75	Higdon Furniture Co—*J Higdon*	PO Box 1739, Quincy FL 32353	850-627-7564	R	10*	.1
76	J H Craver And Son Inc—*Janice Holcomb*	1709 Us 601 Hwy, Yadkinville NC 27055	336-463-5538	R	8*	.1
77	Quality Craft Inc—*Robert Qua*	4645 Fargo Ave, San Diego CA 92117	858-273-4962	R	8*	.1
78	Craftique LLC—*John Erwin*	PO Box 428, Mebane NC 27302	919-563-1212	R	8*	.1
79	Colby Furniture Company Inc—*August Strandberg*	236 Laurel Ave, Hamilton AL 35570	205-921-3333	R	7*	.1
80	Hinkle Chair Company Inc—*William Hinkle*	PO Box 410, Springfield TN 37172	615-384-8477	R	6*	.1
81	Ideal Frame Company Inc—*Phil Lackey*	PO Box 935, Taylorsville NC 28681	828-632-3771	R	6*	.1
82	Brownwood Furniture Inc—*Rick Vartanian*	9805 6th St Ste 104, Rancho Cucamonga CA 91730	909-945-5613	R	5*	.2
83	Industrial Woodworking Corp—*Bradford Davis*	PO Box 286, Zeeland MI 49464	616-741-9663	R	5*	<.1
84	Statton Industries Inc—*Philip Statton*	PO Box 530, Hagerstown MD 21741	301-739-0360	R	5*	.1
85	Baby's Dream Furniture Inc—*David Fellfeli*	PO Box 579, Buena Vista GA 31803	229-649-4404	R	5*	.1
86	Dawson Heritage Furniture Company Inc—*James Dawson*	PO Box 1371, Pulaski VA 24301	417-673-9000	R	4*	.1
87	Trend Manor Furniture Manufacturing Company Inc—*Theodore Vecchione*	17047 Gale Ave, City Of Industry CA 91745	626-964-6493	R	4*	.1
88	Union City Mirror and Table Company Inc—*Gene Russo*	PO Box 825, Union City NJ 07087	201-867-1827	R	4*	<.1
89	Textured Design Furniture Inc—*J Gonzales*	1303 S Claudina St, Anaheim CA 92805	714-502-9121	R	4*	.1
90	Brown Street Furniture LLC—*Kevin Bernadino*	PO Box 278, Whitefield NH 03598	603-837-2547	R	4*	<.1
91	Gateway Manufacturing Inc—*Douglas Gessford*	PO Box 445, Mount Sterling KY 40353	859-497-0058	R	4*	<.1
92	Five Star Industries Inc—*Byford Reidelberger*	PO Box 60, Du Quoin IL 62832	618-542-5421	R	3*	.1
93	Klaussner Casegoods Div—*JB Davis*	Drawer 220, Asheboro NC 27204	336-625-6174	D	3*	<.1
94	Tidewater Workshop—*Peter Caporilli*	PO Box 456, Egg Harbor City NJ 08215	609-965-4000	R	3*	<.1

Rank	Company Name—Executive Officer	Address, City, State, Zip	Phone	Type	Fin	Empls
95	WC Redmon Company Inc—C Redmon	PO Box 7, Peru IN 46970	765-473-6683	R	2*	<.1
96	Terra Furniture Inc—Ken Burrows	14819 Salt Lake Ave, City of Industry CA 91746	626-912-8523	R	2*	<.1
97	Woodlines—Mark Van Oort	301 20th Ave N, Hopkins MN 55343	952-746-5003	R	2*	<.1
98	Environments Inc (Beaufort South Carolina)—Mary Hampton	PO Box 1348, Beaufort SC 29901		R	2*	<.1
99	Lea Industries Inc—Lamont Hope	4310 Regency Dr Ste 10, High Point NC 27265	336-294-5233	S	1*	<.1
100	Through The Barn Door Properties Inc—John Tate	1034 S William St, Henderson NC 27536	252-492-9501	R	1*	<.1

TOTALS: SIC 2511 Wood Household Furniture
Companies: 100 — 11,045 — 55.4

2512 Upholstered Household Furniture

Rank	Company Name—Executive Officer	Address, City, State, Zip	Phone	Type	Fin	Empls
1	La-Z-Boy Inc—Kurt L Darrow	PO Box 2390, Monroe MI 48161	734-242-1444	P	1,187	7.9
2	Rowe Diversified Inc (McLean Virginia)—David L Dutton	239 Rowan St, Salem VA 24153	703-847-8670	S	1,043*	2.6
3	Rowe Properties Inc	239 Rowan St, Salem VA 24153	703-847-8670	S	1,043*	2.6
4	Rowe Worldwide Inc—David Dutton	239 Rowan St, Salem VA 24153	703-847-8670	S	1,043*	2.6
5	Klaussner Furniture Industries Inc	405 Lewallen Rd, Asheboro NC 27205	336-625-6174	R	729*	1.5
6	Broyhill Furniture Industries Inc—Tom Foy	1 Broyhill Park, Lenoir NC 28645	828-758-3111	S	450	7.0
7	Lane Furniture Industries Inc—Gregory P Roy	PO Box 7374, Tupelo MS 38802	662-566-7211	S	256	4.0
8	Berkline/Benchcraft Holdings LLC—Dal Ackard	PO Box 6003, Morristown TN 37815	423-585-1500	R	240*	<.1
9	Lexington Furniture Industries Inc—Phil Haney	1300 National Hwy, Thomasville NC 27360	336-474-5300	R	204*	3.0
10	Rowe Furniture Inc—Stephanie Lucas	2121 Gardner St, Elliston VA 24087	540-444-7693	R	159*	1.7
11	Bauhaus USA Inc—James Wiygul La-Z-Boy Inc	1 Bauhaus Dr, Saltillo MS 38866	662-869-2664	D	153*	.3
12	Hickory White Co—Chuck Auten Sherrill Furniture Company Inc	PO Box 998, Hickory NC 28603	828-322-8624	S	115*	.3
13	Benchcraft LLC—Junior Dick Berkline/Benchcraft Holdings LLC	PO Box 6003, Morristown TN 37815	662-685-4711	S	112*	1.2
14	Corinthian Inc—Vick Etheridge	PO Box 1918, Corinth MS 38835	662-287-7835	R	100*	1.0
15	Sherrill Furniture Company Inc—Harold Sherrill	PO Box 189, Hickory NC 28603	828-322-2640	R	96*	1.4
16	Albany Industries Inc—Shelby Mcclarty	504 N Glenfield Rd, New Albany MS 38652	662-534-9800	R	91*	.4
17	England and Corsair Upholstery—Otis Sawyer La-Z-Boy Inc	402 Old Knoxville Hwy, New Tazewell TN 37825	423-626-5211	S	86	1.0
18	Parkhill Furniture Company Inc—David Belford	PO Box 308, Okolona MS 38860	662-257-1811	R	81*	.9
19	Franklin Corp—Hassell Franklin	PO Box 569, Houston MS 38851	662-456-4286	R	79*	1.2
20	HM Richards Inc—William Quirk	PO Box 373, Baldwyn MS 38824	662-365-9485	R	70*	.5
21	Craftmaster Furniture Inc—Roy Calcagne	PO Box 759, Taylorsville NC 28681	828-632-9786	R	55*	.5
22	Mccreary Modern Inc—Bob Creary	PO Box 130, Newton NC 28658	828-464-6465	R	54*	.6
23	Brueton Industries Inc—Ralph Somma	146 Hanse Ave, Freeport NY 11520	516-379-3400	R	51*	.1
24	Bradington-Young LLC—C Scott Young	PO Box 487, Cherryville NC 28021	704-435-5881	S	50	.4
25	Thomasville Furniture Industries Inc Thomasville Upholstery Div	PO Box 500, Hickory NC 28603	828-345-6225	D	44*	.1
26	Minson Corp—Kenneth Chen	1 Minson Way, Montebello CA 90640	323-513-1041	R	39*	.3
27	Fairfield Chair Co—J Beall	PO Box 1710, Lenoir NC 28645	828-758-5571	R	37*	.7
28	Sam Moore Furniture Industries Inc—Alan Cole	1556 Dawn Dr, Bedford VA 24523	540-586-8253	D	34*	.4
29	Mastercraft Inc—Clifton Reynolds	PO Box 97, Lagrange IN 46761	260-463-8702	R	30*	.3
30	Southern Motion Inc—Roger Bland	PO Box 1064, Pontotoc MS 38863	662-488-4007	R	29*	.5
31	Alrs Inc—Arthur Fink	18626 S Reyes Ave, Compton CA 90221	310-223-4200	R	28*	.2
32	Life Style Furniture Company Inc—Daniel Dempsey	PO Box 146, Okolona MS 38860	662-447-3878	R	27*	.3
33	American Leather Inc—Robert Duncan	4501 Mountain Creek Pk, Dallas TX 75236	972-296-9599	R	25*	.4
34	March Furniture Manufacturing Inc—Brian Boyers	PO Box 875, Ramseur NC 27316	336-824-4413	R	25*	.2
35	Schnadig Corp—Howard Pan	4200 Tudor Ln, Greensboro NC 27410	336-389-5200	R	24*	.4
36	Kroehler Furniture Manufacturing Company Inc—Jay Schottenstein	PO Box 1178, Conover NC 28613	828-459-9865	R	23*	.4
37	Classic Leather Inc—Thomas Shores	PO Box 2404, Hickory NC 28603	828-328-2046	R	23*	.4
38	Hughes Furniture Industries Inc—Roy Hughes	PO Box 486, Randleman NC 27317	336-498-8700	R	22*	.3
39	Max Home LLC	101 Max Pl, Fulton MS 38843	662-862-9966	R	22*	.4
40	New England Woodcraft Inc—Harmon Thurston	PO Box 165, Forest Dale VT 05745	802-247-8211	R	21*	.1
41	E J Victor Inc—John Jokinen	PO Box 309, Morganton NC 28680	828-437-1991	R	20*	.2
42	Klote International Corp—Lars Johannessan	992 Industrial Park Rd, Dandridge TN 37725	865-397-1173	R	20*	.1
43	Wesley Hall Inc—Jack West	141 Firgrove Church Rd, Hickory NC 28603	828-324-7466	R	20*	.2
44	Golden Brothers Inc—Richard Golden	401 Bridge St, Old Forge PA 18518	570-451-7477	R	19*	.2
45	Capris Furniture Industries Inc—Pedro Interian	1401 Nw 27th Ave, Ocala FL 34475	352-629-8889	R	19*	.1
46	King Hickory Furniture Co—Robert Palmer	PO Box 1179, Hickory NC 28603	828-322-6025	R	19*	.2
47	Southwood Furniture Corp—Rocky Holscher	PO Box 2245, Hickory NC 28603	828-465-1776	R	18*	.2
48	Cisco Brothers Corp—Francisco Pinedo	1933 W 60th St, Los Angeles CA 90047	323-778-8612	R	15*	.2
49	Panache Designs—Scott Hunt	1773 N Sichel St, Los Angeles CA 90031	323-441-9600	R	15*	<.1
50	Van Sark Inc—Kevin Sarkisian	888 Doolittle Dr, San Leandro CA 94577	510-635-1111	R	15*	.1
51	Royal Custom Designs Inc—Darius Panah	1449 W Industrial Park, Covina CA 91722	626-967-5261	R	14*	.1
52	Home-Style Industries Inc—Jason Lippert	1323 11th Ave N, Nampa ID 83687	208-466-8481	R	13*	.3
53	Mayo Manufacturing Corp—Michael Mayo	PO Box 5338, Texarkana TX 75505	903-838-0518	R	13*	.1
54	Carsons Inc—TC Stout	PO Box 14186, High Point NC 27263	336-431-1101	R	13*	.2
55	Lodging By Liberty—Jim Fennell	PO Box 1269, Liberty NC 27298	336-622-2201	S	13*	.1
56	Style-Line Furn Inc—Margie Anderson	PO Box 2450, Verona MS 38879	662-566-1113	R	13*	.1
57	Charles Inc—Charles Schneider	600 N 10th St, Council Bluffs IA 51503		R	12*	.1
58	Mitchell Gold Plus Bob Williams Co—Bob Williams	135 1 Comfortable Pl, Taylorsville NC 28681		R	12*	.1
59	Michael Thomas Furniture Inc—Thomas Jordan	PO Box 1275, Liberty NC 27298	336-622-3075	R	12*	.1
60	Taylor King Furniture Inc—Del Starnes	286 County Home Rd, Taylorsville NC 28681	828-632-7731	R	12*	.1
61	Pfc Inc—Hoyl Priest	PO Box 705, Athens TN 37371	423-745-9127	R	11*	.1
62	Klaussner Corporate Services Inc—J Davis	PO Box 148, Milford IA 51351	712-338-4727	R	11*	.1
63	Edward Ferrell Lewis Mittman—Jobst Blachy	685 Southwest Dr, High Point NC 27260	336-841-3028	R	11*	.1
64	Marge Carson Inc—Jim Barge	PO Box 889, Rosemead CA 91770	626-571-1111	R	11*	.1
65	Leathercraft Inc—Herschel Keener	PO Box 639, Conover NC 28613	828-322-3305	R	11*	.1
66	Unique Originals Inc—Gregory Milu	3550 Nw 58th St, Miami FL 33142	305-634-2274	R	10*	.1
67	Chicago Textile Corp—Jean Joseph	4500 S Kolin Ave Ste 2, Chicago IL 60632	773-890-5445	R	9*	.1
68	Modern Of Marshfield Inc—William Mork	137 W 9th St, Marshfield WI 54449	715-387-1181	R	9*	.1
69	Cooke Manufacturing Company Inc—James Cooke	PO Box 4230, Cleveland TN 37320	423-476-5536	R	8*	.1
70	D R Kincaid Chair Company Inc—Danny Kincaid	PO Box 925, Lenoir NC 28645	828-754-0255	R	8*	.1
71	Key City Furniture Company Inc—F Forester	PO Box 680, Wilkesboro NC 28697	336-838-4191	R	8*	.1
72	Meadowbrook Furniture Inc—Phillip Gough	PO Box 219, Hickory Flat MS 38633	662-333-7200	R	8*	.1
73	Lancer Inc—Randy Deese	PO Box 848, Star NC 27356	910-428-2181	R	7*	.1

Note: An asterisk (*) indicates an estimated financial figure. The company type code used is as follows: R = Private, P = Public, S = Private Subsidiary, B = Public Subsidiary, D = Division, J = Joint Venture, I = Investment Fund.

COMPANY RANKINGS BY SALES WITHIN 4-DIGIT SIC

Rank	Company Name—*Executive Officer*	Address, City, State, Zip	Phone	Type	Fin	Empls
74	Massoud Furniture Manufacturing Co—*Charles Massoud*	8351 Moberly Ln, Dallas TX 75227	214-388-8655	R	7*	.1
75	Hallagan Manufacturing Company Inc—*Stephen Hallagan*	PO Box 268, Newark NY 14513	315-331-4640	R	7*	.1
76	Stanford Furniture Corp—*Randy Short*	PO Box 69, Claremont NC 28610	828-459-1992	R	7*	.1
77	Miss Eaton Inc—*Bill Cotter*	263 Coffee St, Pontotoc MS 38863	662-489-4242	R	6*	.1
78	Collums Furniture Inc—*Ken Collums*	120 E St, Houlka MS 38850	662-568-2412	R	5*	.1
79	Robertson Furniture Company Inc—*Scott Hodges*	PO Box 847, Toccoa GA 30577	706-886-1494	R	5*	.1
80	Golden Chair Inc—*Greg Washington*	958 Washington Rd, Houlka MS 38850	662-568-7830	R	5*	<.1
81	Westwood Industries Inc—*Rheena Tolbert*	PO Box 2354, Tupelo MS 38803	662-844-2187	R	5*	.1
82	Flores Design Fine Furniture Inc—*Jose Guerra*	4618 Pacific Blvd, Vernon CA 90058	323-585-3200	R	4*	<.1
83	Pacer Furniture Manufacturing Inc—*Ricardo Durazo*	PO Box 58087, Los Angeles CA 90058	323-235-3900	R	3*	<.1
84	Furnari Furniture Corp—*Richard Furnari*	1810 S Reservoir St, Pomona CA 91766	909-622-3079	R	3*	<.1
85	Med-Lift and Mobility Inc—*Linda Blount*	PO Box 1249, Calhoun City MS 38916	662-628-8196	R	3*	<.1
86	Smith and Watson—*Robert Ryan*	200 Lexington Ave Rm 8, New York NY 10016	212-686-6444	R	2*	<.1
87	Avon Workshop Inc—*Gene Saenger*	6245 Creek Rd, Cincinnati OH 45242	513-985-0606	R	2*	<.1
88	Southern Furniture Company Of Conover Inc—*Jerome Bolick*	PO Box 307, Conover NC 28613	828-464-0311	R	1*	.3

TOTALS: SIC 2512 Upholstered Household Furniture
Companies: 88

8,493   53.3

2514 Metal Household Furniture

Rank	Company Name—*Executive Officer*	Address, City, State, Zip	Phone	Type	Fin	Empls
1	Graco Children's Products Inc	150 Oaklands Blvd, Exton PA 19341	610-884-8000	D	447*	1.4
2	Douglas Furniture Of California LLC—*Richard Parker*	809 Tyburn Rd, Palos Verdes Estates CA 90274	310-749-0003	R	166*	2.4
3	Brown Jordan Co—*Frank Taff*	9860 Gidley St, El Monte CA 91731	626-443-8971	R	138*	.5
4	Kln Steel Products Company LLC—*Kris Benson*	PO Box 34690, San Antonio TX 78265	210-227-4747	R	120*	.4
5	Tropitone Furniture Company Inc—*Michael Echolds*	5 Marconi, Irvine CA 92618	949-951-2010	R	47*	.6
6	Corsican Table Co	PO Box 58647, Los Angeles CA 90058	323-587-3101	R	32*	.2
7	All Luminum Products Inc—*Warren Cohen*	10981 Decatur Rd, Philadelphia PA 19154	215-632-2800	R	32*	.3
8	Smith Brothers Of Berne Inc—*Steven Lehman*	PO Box 270, Berne IN 46711	260-589-2131	R	29*	.3
9	Dehler Manufacturing Company Inc—*Edward Herman*	5801 W Dickens Ave, Chicago IL 60639	773-637-1666	R	23*	<.1
10	Swaim Inc—*Andy Swaim*	PO Box 4189, Archdale NC 27263	336-885-6131	R	22*	.2
11	PremierGarage Systems LLC—*Don Shultz*	1616 W Williams Dr, Phoenix AZ 85027	480-483-3030	R	16*	.1
12	Pavilion Furniture Inc—*Michael Buzzella*	16200 Nw 49th Ave, Hialeah FL 33014	305-823-3480	R	15*	.1
13	Nambe LLC—*Gloria Olivas*	PO Box 15070, Santa Fe NM 87592	505-471-2912	R	14*	.1
14	Victor Martin Inc—*Martin Perfit*	2417 E 24th St, Vernon CA 90058	323-587-3101	R	12*	.1
15	Johnston Casuals Furniture Inc—*Joseph Johnston*	PO Box 668, North Wilkesboro NC 28659	336-838-5178	R	10*	.1
16	Metal Classics Inc—*Louis Koch*	PO Box 3436, Evansville IN 47733	253-476-1448	R	9*	<.1
17	Hard Manufacturing Company Inc—*William Godin*	230 Grider St, Buffalo NY 14215	716-893-1800	R	8*	.1
18	American Massage Products Inc—*Mary Park*	341 Central Ave, Silver Creek NY 14136	716-934-2648	R	4*	<.1
19	Elliott's Designs Inc—*Elliott Jones*	2473 E Rancho Del AMO, Compton CA 90220	310-631-4931	R	4*	<.1
20	Dwyer Products Corp—*Clayton Jacobs*	1000 Davey Rd Ste 100, Woodridge IL 60517	630-741-7900	R	3*	<.1
21	South Jersey Metal Inc—*Joseph Wagner*	PO Box 5148, Deptford NJ 08096	856-228-0642	R	3*	<.1
22	Jack-Post Corp—*John Bycraft*	800 E 3rd St, Buchanan MI 49107	269-695-7000	R	2*	<.1

TOTALS: SIC 2514 Metal Household Furniture
Companies: 22

1,154   6.9

2515 Mattresses & Bedsprings

Rank	Company Name—*Executive Officer*	Address, City, State, Zip	Phone	Type	Fin	Empls
1	Leggett and Platt Inc—*David S Haffner*	PO Box 757, Carthage MO 64836	417-358-8131	P	3,636	18.3
2	Tempur-Pedic International Inc—*Mark A Sarvary*	1713 Jaggie Fox Way, Lexington KY 40511	859-259-0754	P	1,418	1.8
3	Sealy Corp—*Louis R Bachicha*	1 Office Pkwy Rd, Trinity NC 27370	336-861-3500	B	1,230	4.3
4	Simmons Co (Atlanta Georgia)—*Steve Fendrich*	1 Concourse Pkwy Ste 8, Atlanta GA 30328	770-512-7700	R	1,029	2.8
5	Select Comfort Corp—*William R McLaughlin*	9800 59th Ave N, Minneapolis MN 55442	763-551-7000	P	743	2.3
6	Serta Inc—*Edward Lilly*	2600 Forbs Ave, Hoffman Estates IL 60192	847-645-0200	R	261*	3.1
7	Boyd Floatation/Royal Waterbeds Inc—*Dennis Boyd*	2440 Adie Rd, Maryland Heights MO 63043	314-569-3669	R	49*	.2
8	Winston-Salem Industries For The Blind Inc—*Daniel Boucher*	7730 N Point Blvd, Winston Salem NC 27106	336-759-0551	R	42*	.8
9	Corsicana Bedding Inc—*Carroll Moran*	PO Box 1050, Corsicana TX 75151	903-872-2591	R	33*	.6
10	Kolcraft Enterprises Inc—*Thomas Koltun*	1100 W Monroe St, Chicago IL 60607	312-361-6315	R	32*	.2
11	Blue Bell Mattress CoInc—*Mark Kolovson*	24 Thompson Rd, East Windsor CT 06088	860-292-6372	R	29*	.2
12	Amf Support Surfaces Inc—*Charles Wyatt*	1691 N Delilah St, Corona CA 92879	951-549-6800	R	26*	.2
13	Jamison Bedding Inc—*Frank Gorrell*	5301 Virginia Way Ste, Brentwood TN 37027	615-794-1883	R	23*	.2
14	Kingsdown Inc—*J Flippin*	PO Box 388, Mebane NC 27302	919-563-3531	R	22*	.3
15	Paramount Industrial Companies Inc—*James Diamonstein*	1112 Kingwood Ave, Norfolk VA 23502	757-855-3321	R	21*	.1
16	Spring Spiller Co—*J Coleman*	2216 S 24th St, Sheboygan WI 53081	920-457-3649	R	19*	.2
17	Dynasty Consolidated Industries Inc—*Amir Sunderji*	4646 Harry Hines Blvd, Dallas TX 75235	214-630-3132	R	15*	.1
18	Spring Air Mattress Corp—*John Grove*	PO Box 20028, Greensboro NC 27420	336-272-1141	R	13*	.1
19	Sealy Mattress Company Of New Jersey Inc—*Walter Hertz*	697 River St, Paterson NJ 07524	973-345-8800	R	12*	.1
20	Serta Restokraft Mattress Company Inc—*Lawrence Kraft*	38025 Jay Kay Dr, Romulus MI 48174	734-727-9000	R	12*	.1
21	Dixie Bedding Corp—*Dan Kamis*	4800 Nw 37th Ave, Miami FL 33142	305-634-1505	R	12*	.1
22	Omaha Bedding Co—*Irving Veitzer*	PO Box 27396, Omaha NE 68127	402-733-8600	R	11*	.1
23	Standard Mattress Co—*Robert Naboicheck*	PO Box 89, Hartford CT 06141	860-549-2000	R	11*	.1
24	Mattress Firm Holding Corp—*Steve Stagner*	5815 Gulf Fwy, Houston TX 77023	713-923-1090	P	10*	1.0
25	Dreamline Manufacturing Inc—*Steve Tipton*	PO Box 1250, Cabot AR 72023	501-843-3585	R	10*	.1
26	Lacrosse Furniture Co—*Chris Podschun*	1215 Oak St, La Crosse KS 67548	785-222-2541	R	10*	.1
27	Norka Futon—*Kevin Royer*	143 W Market St, Akron OH 44303	330-253-9330	R	6*	<.1
28	Popular Mattress Factory Inc—*George Yapor*	1049 Eastside Rd, El Paso TX 79915	915-774-4212	R	5*	<.1
29	Savvy Rest Inc—*Michael Penny*	4414 Ivy Commons, Charlottesville VA 22903		R	4	<.1
30	Rapid Air Systems—*John F Riley*	PO Box 20810, Milwaukee WI 53220	262-787-2500	R	4*	<.1
31	Blue Ridge Products Company Inc—*Charles Ingle*	PO Box 2028, Hickory NC 28603	828-322-7990	R	3*	<.1
32	Lions Volunteer Blind Industries Inc—*Don Britton*	758 W Morris Blvd, Morristown TN 37813	423-586-3922	R	2*	.2

TOTALS: SIC 2515 Mattresses & Bedsprings
Companies: 32

8,751   37.8

2517 Wood T.V. and Radio Cabinets

Rank	Company Name—*Executive Officer*	Address, City, State, Zip	Phone	Type	Fin	Empls
1	Eagle Industries LLC—*Amado Rivas*	PO Box 9697, Bowling Green KY 42102	270-843-3363	R	40*	.7
2	Parker House Manufacturing Co—*Sam Perone*	505 W Foothill Blvd, Azusa CA 91702		R	18*	.1
3	Sound-Craft Systems Inc—*Bruce McCullough*	1584 Petit Jean Mtn Rd, Morrilton AR 72110	501-727-5476	R	9*	<.1
4	Custom Shoppe—*Mike Smith*	300 Air Park Dr, Watertown WI 53094	920-262-9700	R	3*	<.1
5	Greenway Home Services LLC—*Whit Greenway*	3910 Windolyn Cir S, Memphis TN 38133	901-381-9001	R	2*	<.1
6	Cabinets Plus—*Chris Foster*	5650 District Blvd Ste, Bakersfield CA 93313	661-398-1589	R	2*	<.1

TOTALS: SIC 2517 Wood T.V. and Radio Cabinets
Companies: 6

74   .9

Rank	Company Name—*Executive Officer*	Address, City, State, Zip	Phone	Type	Fin	Empls
2519 Household Furniture Nec						
1	Flexsteel Industries Inc—*Ronald Klosterman*	PO Box 877, Dubuque IA 52004	563-556-7730	P	339	1.3
2	Rowe Cos—*Gerald M Birnbach*	1650 Tysons Blvd Ste 7, McLean VA 22102	703-847-8760	R	301	2.4
3	Suncast Corp—*Thomas Tisbo*	701 N Kirk Rd, Batavia IL 60510	630-879-2050	R	93*	.8
4	Flanders Industries Inc—*Dudley Flanders*	PO Box 1788, Fort Smith AR 72902	479-785-2351	R	66*	.4
5	Sunterrace Casual Furniture Inc—*Thom Lombardo*	2369 Chrles Rper Jnas, Stanley NC 28164	704-263-1967	R	22*	.2
6	Mcguire Furniture Company Inc—*Sarah Garcia*	1201 Bryant St, San Francisco CA 94103	415-626-1414	R	5*	<.1
7	Fremarc Industries Inc—*Maurice Donenfeld*	18751 E Railrd, City of Industry CA 91748	626-965-0802	R	5*	.1
8	Contemporary Products Of Texas Inc—*Ken Lucas*	PO Box 510, Walburg TX 78673	512-868-0346	R	5*	<.1
9	Southeastern Fiberglass Products Inc—*Richard Mitchum*	51 Sweet Pea Rd, Bamberg SC 29003	803-245-4393	R	4*	<.1
10	California Furniture Collections Inc—*Eric Vogt*	150 Reed Ct Ste A, Chula Vista CA 91911	858-693-6000	R	3*	<.1
11	Muniz Plastics Inc—*Julio Muniz*	2276 Nw 21st Ter, Miami FL 33142	305-634-8848	R	2*	<.1
TOTALS: SIC 2519 Household Furniture Nec Companies: 11					844	5.3
2521 Wood Office Furniture						
1	HNI Corp—*Stanley A Askren*	PO Box 1109, Muscatine IA 52761		P	1,834	9.5
2	Haworth Inc—*Franco Bianchi*	1 Haworth Ctr, Holland MI 49423	616-393-3000	R	1,660	8.0
3	Herman Miller Inc—*Brian C Walker*	PO Box 302, Zeeland MI 49464	616-654-3000	P	1,649	5.8
4	Kimball International Inc—*James C Thyen*	1600 Royal St, Jasper IN 47546	812-482-1600	P	1,203	6.4
5	Knoll Inc—*Andrew B Cogan*	1235 Water St, East Greenville PA 18041	215-679-7991	P	1,056	3.1
6	Kimball Electronics Inc—*Don Charron* Kimball International Inc	1600 Royal St, Jasper IN 47549	812-482-1600	S	989*	3.0
7	Brown Jordan International Inc—*Gene Moriarty*	9860 Gidley St, El Monte CA 91731	626-443-8971	R	355	1.2
8	Ofs Brands Holdings Inc—*Robert Menke*	PO Box 100, Huntingburg IN 47542		R	201*	2.0
9	Shelby Williams Industries Inc—*Franklin Jacobs*	5303 E Morris Blvd, Morristown TN 37813	423-586-7000	S	166*	1.7
10	Ivan Allen Furniture Co—*Louise Allen*	1000 Marietta St NW St, Atlanta GA 30318	404-760-8700	R	144*	.8
11	Paoli Inc—*Tom Graham* HNI Corp	PO Box 30, Paoli IN 47454	812-865-1525	S	82*	.7
12	Marco Display Specialists Gp LC—*Darrell Cooper*	PO Box 123439, Fort Worth TX 76121	817-244-8300	R	65*	.5
13	Goebel Fixture Co—*Robert Croatt*	528 S Dale St, Hutchinson MN 55350	320-587-2112	R	64*	.1
14	Herman Miller Greenhouse—*Brian Walker* Herman Miller Inc	10201 Adams St, Holland MI 49424	616-654-3000	S	60*	.6
15	Tesco Industries Inc—*Norman Kiecke*	1035 E Hacienda, Bellville TX 77418		R	49*	.1
16	A C Furniture Company Inc—*Kennon Robertson*	PO Box 200, Axton VA 24054	276-650-3356	R	40*	.5
17	Maxon Furniture Inc—*Jean Reynolds* HNI Corp	660 SW 39th St Ste 150, Renton WA 98057		S	38*	.2
18	Jasper Desk Company Inc—*James Arvin*	PO Box 111, Jasper IN 47547	812-482-4132	R	35*	.1
19	Nucraft Furniture Co—*Bob Bockheim*	5151 W River Dr Ne, Comstock Park MI 49321	616-784-6016	R	33*	.2
20	Balt Inc—*Lorraine Moore*	2885 Lorraine Ave, Temple TX 76501	254-778-4727	R	33*	.1
21	Jasper Seating Company Inc—*Michael Elliott*	PO Box 231, Jasper IN 47547	812-482-3204	R	32*	.5
22	Vecta—*Robert Beck*	1800 S Great SW Pky, Grand Prairie TX 75051	972-641-2860	D	29*	.3
23	Jofco Inc—*Bill Rubino*	PO Box 71, Jasper IN 47547	812-482-5164	R	26	.3
24	Dar-Ran Furniture Industries Inc—*Randall Hollingsworth*	PO Box 7614, High Point NC 27264	336-861-2400	R	21*	.3
25	Case Systems Inc—*Richard Vanderweele*	PO Box 2044, Midland MI 48641	989-496-9510	R	21*	.2
26	Tuohy Furniture Corp—*Daniel Tuohy*	42 Saint Albans Pl, Chatfield MN 55923	507-867-4280	R	20*	.2
27	High Point Furniture Industries Inc—*Spencer O'meara*	PO Box 2063, High Point NC 27261	336-431-7101	R	20*	.2
28	Taylor Chair Co—*Jeffrey Baldassari*	1 Taylor Pkwy, Bedford OH 44146	440-232-0700	R	19*	.1
29	Alc-Collegedale LLC—*Richard Rogers*	PO Box 159, Round Rock TX 78680	423-693-2140	R	15*	.2
30	Commercial Wood Products Co—*Craig Roberts*	10019 Yucca Rd, Adelanto CA 92301	760-246-4530	R	15*	<.1
31	Jsj Seating Company Texas LP—*Janet Cox*	4121 Rushton St, Florence AL 35630	256-767-4100	S	14*	.1
32	Princeton Upholstery Company Inc—*Stan Gottlieb*	PO Box 269, Middletown NY 10940	845-343-2196	R	12*	.1
33	Creative Wood Products Inc—*Jose Mendes*	PO Box 14367, Oakland CA 94614	510-635-5399	R	12*	.1
34	Inwood Office Furniture Inc—*Glen Sturm*	PO Box 646, Jasper IN 47547	812-482-6121	R	11*	.2
35	Taylor Desk Co—*Alan Paull* Taylor Chair Co	11020 Santa Fe Ave, Lynwood CA 90262	310-631-6727	S	11*	.1
36	Jasper Chair Co—*Fred Barth*	534 E 8th St, Jasper IN 47546	812-482-5239	R	11*	.1
37	Ccn International Inc—*Richard Conoyer*	200 Lehigh St, Geneva NY 14456	315-789-4400	R	11*	.1
38	Whitehall Furniture LLC—*Edward Wathen*	PO Box 30, Paoli IN 47454	270-683-3585	R	10*	.1
39	Chairmasters Inc—*Jeff Jahier*	200 E 146th St, Bronx NY 10451	718-292-0600	R	10*	.1
40	Crest Cabinet Manufacturing Corp—*Ron Weissman*	12490 49th St N, Clearwater FL 33762	727-572-5590	R	8*	<.1
41	Viking Acoustical Corp—*Bret Starkweather*	21480 Heath Ave, Lakeville MN 55044	952-469-3405	R	7*	.1
42	Murray Cabinet and Fixtures Inc—*Murray Greengrass*	3325 India St, San Diego CA 92103	619-295-1550	R	7*	.1
43	Marc Woodworking Inc—*Joseph Hirsch*	1719 English Ave, Indianapolis IN 46201	317-635-9663	R	7*	.1
44	Schu Industries Inc—*Wayne Schueller*	453 5th St, Random Lake WI 53075	920-994-9528	R	6*	.1
45	Sehrer Holding Co—*Thomas Sehrer*	PO Box 1354, Lynnwood WA 98046	425-776-2181	R	6*	.1
46	Rieke Office Interiors Inc—*Todd Rieke*	2000 Fox Ln, Elgin IL 60123	847-622-9711	R	6*	.1
47	FE Hale Manufacturing Company Inc—*Jim Benson*	PO Box 186, Frankfort NY 13340	315-894-5490	R	6*	.1
48	Ken Boudreau Inc—*Carly Boudreau*	20485 144th Ave Ne, Woodinville WA 98072	425-402-8001	R	6*	.1
49	Quaker Furniture Inc—*Clyde Lail*	PO Box 1973, Hickory NC 28603	828-322-1794	R	6*	.1
50	Scholar Craft Commercial Furniture—*Ken Goode*	PO Box 170748, Birmingham AL 35217	205-951-9800	R	4*	<.1
51	Arnold Furniture Manufacturerss Inc—*Julius Arnold*	400 Coit St, Irvington NJ 07111	973-399-0505	R	3*	<.1
52	Maury Office Systems Inc—*E Bean*	1330 Sycamore View Rd, Memphis TN 38134	901-388-8080	R	3*	.1
53	National Business Services Inc—*Mike Chambers*	1601 Magoffin Ave, El Paso TX 79901	915-544-1271	R	3*	<.1
54	Executive Office Concepts—*Richard Sinclair*	1705 S Anderson Ave, Compton CA 90220	310-537-1657	R	3*	<.1
55	Bourne Industries Inc—*Jeffrey Walters*	491 S Comstock St, Corunna MI 48817	989-743-3461	R	2*	<.1
56	Koster Construction Company Inc—*Don Koster*	PO Box 282, Spirit Lake IA 51360	712-336-4426	R	2*	<.1
57	Coen Furniture Inc—*Greg Mesler*	10865 Seaboard Loop, Houston TX 77099	281-983-0100	R	1*	<.1
58	Agati Inc—*Joe Agati*	1219 W Lake St, Chicago IL 60607	312-829-1977	R	1*	<.1
TOTALS: SIC 2521 Wood Office Furniture Companies: 58					10,159	48.7
2522 Office Furniture Except Wood						
1	Steelcase Inc—*James P Hackett*	901 44th St SE, Grand Rapids MI 49508	616-247-2710	P	2,437	10.0
2	Krueger International Inc—*Richard J Resch*	1330 Bellview St, Green Bay WI 54302	920-468-8100	R	397*	1.8
3	Gunlocke Co	1 Gunlocke Dr, Wayland NY 14572		S	252*	.9
4	Allsteel Inc—*Jeff Lorenger*	2210 2nd Ave, Muscatine IA 52761	563-262-4800	S	149*	1.4
5	Fire King International LLC—*Carlos Queiroz*	PO Box 559, New Albany IN 47151	812-948-8400	R	122*	.5
6	TAB Products Co—*Thaddeus Jaroszewicz*	605 4th St, Mayville WI 53050	920-387-3131	R	72*	.5

Note: An asterisk (*) indicates an estimated financial figure. The company type code used is as follows: R = Private, P = Public, S = Private Subsidiary, B = Public Subsidiary, D = Division, J = Joint Venture, I = Investment Fund.

COMPANY RANKINGS BY SALES WITHIN 4-DIGIT SIC

Rank	Company Name—*Executive Officer*	Address, City, State, Zip	Phone	Type	Fin	Empls
7	Tennsco Corp—*Stuart Speyer*	PO Box 1888, Dickson TN 37056	615-446-8000	R	71*	.6
8	Mity Enterprises Inc—*Randall Hales*	1301 W 400 N, Orem UT 84057	801-224-0589	S	60	.4
9	Stanley Vidmar Storage Technologies—*Ed Roma*	11 Grammes Rd, Allentown PA 18103		D	49	.3
10	e-Systems Group LLC—*Lisa Mack*	1250 W 124th Ave, Westminster CO 80234	303-465-2800	R	48*	.2
11	Hirsh Industries Inc—*G Stewart*	11229 Aurora Ave, Urbandale IA 50322	515-299-3200	R	47*	.6
12	American Seating Co—*Edward Clark*	401 Amrcan Seating Ctr, Grand Rapids MI 49504	616-732-6600	R	39*	.5
13	Norstar Office Products Inc—*Willaim Huang*	5353 Jillson St, Commerce CA 90040	323-262-1919	R	39*	.1
14	ErgoGenesis LLC—*Mark McMillian*	1 BodyBilt Place, Navasota TX 77868	936-825-1700	R	34*	.1
15	Scott Rice Co—*George Basore*	7501 N Broadway Ext, Oklahoma City OK 73116	405-848-2224	R	34*	.1
16	Marvel Group Inc—*John Dellamore*	3843 W 43rd St, Chicago IL 60632	773-843-2900	R	33*	.5
17	Michigan Tube Swagers And Fabricators Inc—*Phillip Swy*	7100 Industrial Dr, Temperance MI 48182	734-847-3875	R	32*	.5
18	APW Mayville LLC—*Dan Eder*	PO Box 28, Mayville WI 53050	920-387-3000	R	29*	.2
19	Office Star Products—*Rick Blumenthal*	PO Box 3520, Ontario CA 91761	909-930-2000	R	28*	.1
20	Pedigo Products Inc—*Richard Pedigo*	4000 Se Columbia Way, Vancouver WA 98661	360-695-3500	R	27*	.1
21	Ergotron Inc—*Joel Hazzard*	1181 Trapp Rd, St Paul MN 55121	651-681-7600	S	26*	.2
22	McDowell and Craig Manufacturing Co—*JC McDowell*	13146 Firestone Blvd, Norwalk CA 90650	562-921-4441	R	25*	.2
23	Affordable Interior Systems Inc—*Bruce Platzman*	4 Bonazzoli Ave, Hudson MA 01749	978-562-7500	R	24*	.1
24	Watson Furniture Group—*William S Haggerty*	26246 12 Trees Ln NW, Poulsbo WA 98370	360-394-1300	R	24*	.1
25	Arte De Mexico Inc—*Gerald Stoffers*	1000 Chestnut St, Burbank CA 91506	818-753-4559	R	22*	.2
26	Trendway Corp—*Mark Groulx*	PO Box 9016, Holland MI 49422	616-399-3900	R	21*	.3
27	Russ Bassett Corp—*Mike Dressendorfer*	8189 Byron Rd, Whittier CA 90606	562-945-2445	R	20*	.1
28	Kwik-File LLC—*John Lafond*	490 Northco Dr, Minneapolis MN 55432	763-572-1980	R	20*	.1
29	Luxor (Waukegan Illinois)—*Dixon Brooke Jr*	PO Box 830, Waukegan IL 60079		S	19*	.1
30	Davis Furniture Industries Inc—*Danny Davis*	PO Box 2065, High Point NC 27261	336-889-2009	R	18*	.2
31	Stylex Inc—*John Golden*	PO Box 5038, Delanco NJ 08075	856-461-5600	R	18*	.1
32	Stinger Medical—*Gary Coonan*	1152 Park Ave, Murfreesboro TN 37129	615-896-1652	R	16*	.1
33	Artone LLC—*Mark Moll*	107 Institute St, Jamestown NY 14701	716-664-2232	R	16*	.1
34	Datum Filing Systems Inc—*Thomas Potter*	PO Box 355, Emigsville PA 17318	717-764-6350	R	16*	.1
35	Nova Solutions Inc—*John Lechman*	PO Box 725, Effingham IL 62401	217-342-7070	R	15*	.1
36	Neutral Posture Ergonomics Inc—*David Ebner*	3904 N Texas Ave, Bryan TX 77803	979-778-0502	R	15*	.1
37	Metal Components LLC—*Norm Czurak*	3281 Roger B Chaffee S, Grand Rapids MI 49548	616-252-1900	R	14*	.1
38	Reconditioned Systems Inc—*Dirk D Anderson*	2636 S Wilson St Ste 1, Tempe AZ 85282		P	13	.1
39	National Electro-Coatings Inc—*Gregory Schneider*	15655 Brookpark Rd, Cleveland OH 44142	216-898-0080	R	13*	.1
40	Esi Ergonomic Solutions LLC—*Tracie Nelson*	4030 E Quenton Dr Ste, Mesa AZ 85215	480-517-1871	R	12*	.1
41	Afco Systems Inc—*Michael Mallia*	200 Finn Ct Ste 1, Farmingdale NY 11735	631-249-9441	R	10*	.1
42	American Interiors Inc—*Steven Essig*	302 S Byrne Rd Bldg 10, Toledo OH 43615	419-535-1808	R	10*	.1
43	Paragon Furniture LP—*Pamela Wade*	2224 E Randol Mill Rd, Arlington TX 76011	817-633-3242	R	10*	.1
44	Mills Co—*David Newberry*	112 River St, Upper Sandusky OH 43351	419-294-2321	R	10*	.1
45	Neutral Posture Inc—*David Ebner*	3904 N Texas Ave, Bryan TX 77803	979-778-0502	R	9*	.1
46	Cramer Inc—*Nick Christenson*	1222 Quebec St, Kansas City MO 64116	816-471-4433	R	9*	.1
47	Argc LLC—*Johnny Williams*	PO Box 1612, Gadsden AL 35902	256-442-2600	R	7*	.1
48	Cayman Manufacturing Inc—*Donald Ferguson*	1301 Sw 34th Ave, Deerfield Beach FL 33442	954-421-1170	R	7*	.1
49	Workplace Systems Inc—*Patricia Zeamans*	562 Mammoth Rd, Londonderry NH 03053	603-622-3727	R	5*	<.1
50	MLP Seating Corp—*Ralph D Samuel*	2125 Lively Blvd, Elk Grove Village IL 60007	847-956-1700	R	5*	<.1
51	Emeco Industries Inc—*Jay Buckbinder*	PO Box 179, Hanover PA 17331	717-637-5951	R	3*	<.1
52	Fortress Inc—*Donald Wolper*	11969 Arrow Rt, Rancho Cucamonga CA 91739	909-483-6092	R	2*	<.1
53	Jami Inc—*Gregg Masenthin*	7300 W 110th St Commer, Overland Park KS 66210	913-663-3459	R	2*	<.1
54	Rhamdec Inc—*Ronald H Arima*	PO Box 4296, Santa Clara CA 95050	408-496-5590	R	2*	<.1
55	Office Environments of New England LLC—*Bob Kelly*	22 Boston Wharf Rd, Boston MA 02210	617-439-4900	R	1*	.1
56	JBM DataCom	1001 Cramton NE, Ada MI 49301	616-676-3168	R	1*	<.1

TOTALS: SIC 2522 Office Furniture Except Wood
Companies: 56

					4,458	22.7

2531 Public Building & Related Furniture

Rank	Company Name—*Executive Officer*	Address, City, State, Zip	Phone	Type	Fin	Empls
1	Johnson Controls Inc—*Stephen A Roell*	PO Box 591, Milwaukee WI 53201	414-524-1200	P	40,833	162.0
2	Lear Corp—*Robert E Rossiter*	PO Box 5008, Southfield MI 48086	248-447-1500	P	10,955	86.8
3	BE Aerospace Inc—*Amin J Khoury*	1400 Corporate Center, Wellington FL 33414	561-791-5000	P	2,500	7.7
4	Wise Company Inc—*James Freudenberg*	5535 Pleasant View Rd, Memphis TN 38134	901-388-0155	R	1,787*	.6
5	Graco Children's Products Inc Century Products Div—*Mark D Ketchum*	3 Glenlake Pky, Atlanta GA 30328	770-418-7000	D	196*	1.4
6	Virco Manufacturing Corp—*Robert A Virtue*	PO Box 44846, Los Angeles CA 90044	310-533-0474	P	181	1.1
7	Air Cruisers Company LLC—*Dan Kline*	1747 State Rte 34, Wall Township NJ 07727	732-681-3527	S	174*	2.8
8	Hoover Universal Inc—*Keith Wandell*	49200 Halyard Dr, Plymouth MI 48170	734-254-5000	S	154*	2.0
9	Setex Inc—*Shinichirou Shirahama* Tachi-S Engineering USA Inc	1111 Mckinley Rd, Saint Marys OH 45885	419-394-7800	S	109*	.5
10	Brodart Co—*Arthur Brody*	500 Arch St, Williamsport PA 17701		R	92*	1.0
11	Stevens Industries Inc—*Todd Wegman*	704 W Main St, Teutopolis IL 62467	217-540-3100	R	68*	.5
12	Tachi-S Engineering USA Inc—*Hiroyuki Miki*	23227 Commerce Dr, Farmington Hills MI 48335	248-478-5050	R	67*	.9
13	Irwin Seating Co—*Earle Irwin*	PO Box 2429, Grand Rapids MI 49501	616-574-7400	R	58*	.7
14	American of Martinsville—*Noel Chitwood*	PO Box 5071, Martinsville VA 24112	276-632-2061	D	50*	.2
15	Buckstaff Company Inc—*John Buckstaff*	PO Box 2506, Oshkosh WI 54903	920-235-5890	R	50*	.2
16	Advanced Component Technologies Inc—*Robert Kluver*	91 16th St S, Northwood IA 50459	641-324-2231	S	48*	.9
17	Milsco Manufacturing Co—*Shawn Cummings*	PO Box 245021, Milwaukee WI 53224	414-354-0500	S	40*	.4
18	Brice Manufacturing Co—*Rick Salanitri*	10262 Norris Ave, Pacoima CA 91331	818-896-2938	S	37	.2
19	Greenpoint Technologies Inc—*Jon Buccola*	4600 Carillon Pt, Kirkland WA 98033	425-828-2777	R	29*	.1
20	Spectrum Industries Inc—*David Hancock*	PO Box 400, Chippewa Falls WI 54729	715-723-6750	R	27*	.2
21	Toyo Seat USA Corp—*Seizo Yamaguchi*	2155 S Almont Ave, Imlay City MI 48444	810-724-0300	R	27*	.4
22	Hussey Seating Co—*Timothy Hussey*	38 Dyer St Ext, North Berwick ME 03906	207-676-2271	R	27*	.3
23	Sauder Manufacturing Co—*Virgil Miller*	PO Box 230, Archbold OH 43502	419-445-7670	R	26*	.4
24	Artco-Bell Corp—*Darryl Rosser*	1302 Industrial Blvd, Temple TX 76504	254-778-1811	R	25*	.2
25	Freedman Seating Co—*Gerald Freedman*	4545 W Augusta Blvd, Chicago IL 60651	773-524-2440	R	22*	.3
26	Faurecia Automotive Seating—*Jacques Lemorvan*	PO Box 214680, Auburn Hills MI 48321	859-485-1700	R	21*	.2
27	Church Chair Industries Inc—*Ruth Sammons*	7007 New Calhoun Hwy N, Rome GA 30161	706-235-0115	R	20*	.3
28	Worden Co—*William Hendrick*	199 E 17th St, Holland MI 49423	616-392-1848	R	20*	.2
29	Ghent Manufacturing Inc—*George Leasure*	2999 Henkle Dr, Lebanon OH 45036	513-932-3445	R	18*	.2
30	Collegedale Casework Inc—*James C Wardlaw*	PO Box 810, Collegedale TN 37315	423-693-2163	R	18*	.1
31	Columbia Manufacturing Inc—*Kenneth Howard*	PO Box 1230, Westfield MA 01086	413-562-3664	R	18	.1
32	Interkal LLC—*Linda Zuverink*	PO Box 2107, Kalamazoo MI 49003	269-349-1521	R	18*	.2
33	Gasser Chair Company Inc—*Gary Gasser*	4136 Logan Way, Youngstown OH 44505	330-759-2234	R	17*	.2
34	Llebroc Industries—*Wayne Corbell*	3601 Conway St, Fort Worth TX 76111	817-831-6261	R	17*	.1

Rank	Company Name—*Executive Officer*	Address, City, State, Zip	Phone	Type	Fin	Empls
35	Serious Energy Inc—*Kevin Surace*	1250 Elko Dr, Sunnyvale CA 94089	408-541-8000	R	13*	.1
36	Tri-Way Industries Inc—*Bradley Johnson*	506 44th St NW, Auburn WA 98001	253-859-4585	R	11*	.1
37	Smith System Inc (Plano Texas)—*Charles Risdall*	PO Box 860415, Plano TX 75086	972-398-4050	R	11*	.1
38	Charter Of Lynchburg Inc—*Waldemar Oelschlager*	PO Box 11988, Lynchburg VA 24506	434-239-9000	R	10*	.1
39	Admc Inc—*Steve Sykes*	PO Box 608, Temple TX 76503		R	7*	.1
40	Dakat Inc—*R Bennett*	2500 Ada Dr, Elkhart IN 46514	574-264-9504	R	6*	.1
41	Omni International Inc—*Karl Jahn*	PO Box 1409, Vernon AL 35592	205-695-9173	R	6*	.1
42	Bytec Inc—*Rick Larkin*	44801 Centre Ct E, Clinton Township MI 48038	586-228-9410	R	6*	<.1
43	Georgia Chair Co—*James Bagwell*	PO Box 935, Gainesville GA 30503	770-536-1366	R	5*	.1
44	Mc Court Manufacturing Inc—*Julia Court*	1001 N 3rd St, Fort Smith AR 72901	479-783-2593	R	5*	<.1
45	Torrington Distributors Inc—*James Mazzarelli*	43 Norfolk St, Torrington CT 06790	860-482-4464	R	3*	<.1
46	Lexington Corp—*Richard Strefling*	2503 Banks Ct, Elkhart IN 46514	574-295-8166	R	2*	<.1
47	Artisans' Guild Inc—*Bruce Thomas*	311 Amhurst Ave, High Point NC 27260	336-841-4140	R	2*	<.1
48	London Church Furniture Inc—*David Abbott*	PO Box 281, London KY 40743	606-864-2230	R	1*	<.1

TOTALS: SIC 2531 Public Building & Related Furniture
Companies: 48   57,834   274.0

2541 Wood Partitions & Fixtures

Rank	Company Name—*Executive Officer*	Address, City, State, Zip	Phone	Type	Fin	Empls
1	Borroughs Corp—*Tim J Tyler*	3002 N Burdick St, Kalamazoo MI 49004		R	813*	.3
2	Lozier Corp—*Allan Lozier*	PO Box 3448, Omaha NE 68103	402-457-8000	R	378*	1.7
3	Knape and Vogt Manufacturing Co—*Peter Martin*	2700 Oak Industrial Dr, Grand Rapids MI 49505		R	157	.6
4	RC Smith Co—*Peter J Smith*	14200 Southcross Dr W, Burnsville MN 55306	952-854-0711	R	108*	.1
5	Structural Concepts Corp—*David Geerts*	888 E Porter Rd, Norton Shores MI 49441	231-798-6218	R	55*	.3
6	Pacific Fixture Company Inc—*Keith Stark*	12860 San Fernando Rd, Sylmar CA 91342	818-362-2130	R	41*	<.1
7	Hamilton Fixture Co—*John Schlegel*	3550 Symmes Rd, Hamilton OH 45015	513-874-2016	R	37*	.5
8	Harbor Industries Inc—*Henry Parker*	14130 172nd Ave, Grand Haven MI 49417	616-842-5330	R	35*	.3
9	Westmark Products Inc—*Dennis Milsten*	PO Box 44040, Tacoma WA 98448	253-531-3470	R	34*	.2
10	Wenger Corp—*William Beer*	555 Park Dr, Owatonna MN 55060	507-455-4100	R	28*	.4
11	Boden Store Fixtures Inc—*Carl Boden*	PO Box 301009, Portland OR 97294	503-252-4728	R	26*	.3
12	Imperial Woodworking Co—*Frank Huschitt*	310 N Woodwork Ln, Palatine IL 60067	847-358-6920	R	25*	.2
13	Columbus Show Case Co—*Chris Aschinger*	4401 Equity Dr, Columbus OH 43228	614-850-1460	R	25*	.2
14	Jahabow Industries Inc—*Addison Thomas*	1004 Industrial Dr, Owensville MO 65066	573-437-4151	R	22*	.2
15	National Partitions Inc—*Anthony D'andrea*	10300 Goldenfern Ln, Knoxville TN 37931	865-670-2100	R	21*	.2
16	University Products Inc—*Scott E Magoon*	517 Main St, Holyoke MA 01040	413-532-3372	R	21*	.1
17	The Miller Group	1112 Westmark Dr, Saint Louis MO 63131	314-822-8090	R	20*	.2
18	Modern Woodcrafts LLC—*Lisa Pelletier*	72 NW Dr, Plainville CT 06062	860-677-7371	R	19*	.2
19	Bay View Industries Inc—*Eugene Plitt*	7821 S 10th St, Oak Creek WI 53154	414-764-2120	R	18*	.1
20	Synsor Corp—*Gary Bullock*	1920 Merrill Creek Pkw, Everett WA 98203	425-551-1300	R	17*	.1
21	Columbia Showcase and Cabinet Company Inc—*Samuel Patterson*	11034 Sherman Way, Sun Valley CA 91352	818-765-9710	R	15*	.1
22	Bishop Fixture And Millwork Inc—*Morgan Nelson*	101 Eagle Dr, Balsam Lake WI 54810	715-485-9312	R	15*	.2
23	Quality One Woodwork LLC—*Randy Hartl*	3005 Millard Ave, Hastings MN 55033	651-480-8351	R	15*	.1
24	Brakur Custom Cabinetry Inc—*Kenneth Kurtz*	18656 S State Rte 59, Joliet IL 60404	815-436-4970	R	15*	.1
25	Hale Tj Co—*John Hale*	PO Box 250, Menomonee Falls WI 53052	262-255-5555	R	14*	.1
26	Milford Enterprises Inc—*Gary Fetterman*	450 Commerce Dr, Quakertown PA 18951	215-538-2778	R	13*	.1
27	Capitoline Tops Of Florida Inc—*Glavon Smith*	100 Capitoline Dr Ne, Rome GA 30165	706-235-5000	R	12*	.1
28	International Thermocast Corp—*Mark Anderson*	308 Bell Park Dr, Woodstock GA 30188	678-445-2022	R	12*	.1
29	Amtrend Corp—*Hamid Malik*	1458 Manhattan Ave, Fullerton CA 92831	714-630-2070	R	11*	.1
30	Colorado Counter-Tops Inc—*Carlos Ramirez*	3795 E 38th Ave, Denver CO 80205	303-388-0044	R	11*	.1
31	Albertsons Mill—*Duane Lundell*	959 W Utah Ave, Payson UT 84651	801-465-4853	R	11	.1
32	Universal Presentation Concepts Inc—*Daniel Levine*	1501 S Stoughton Rd, Madison WI 53716	608-222-5658	R	11*	.1
33	Fuller Marketing Inc—*Hugh Fuller*	512 S Main St, Carrollton MO 64633	660-542-1097	R	11*	.1
34	Architectural Woodworking Co—*John Heydorff*	582 Monterey Pass Rd, Monterey Park CA 91754	626-570-4125	R	10*	.1
35	Hallmark Center-Fixture	PO Box 1775, Center TX 75935	936-598-5645	S	10*	.1
36	Food Concepts Inc (Middleton Wisconsin)—*Brad Duesler*	2551 Parmenter St, Middleton WI 53562	608-831-5006	R	10*	.1
37	Benchmark Fixture Corp—*Henry Kelman*	775 Brookside Dr, Richmond CA 94801	510-232-3842	R	9*	.1
38	Mcgrory Inc—*Timothy Grory*	576 Rosedale Rd 1, Kennett Square PA 19348	610-444-1512	R	8*	.1
39	Modar Inc—*Dennis Rousseau*	1394 E Empire Ave, Benton Harbor MI 49022	269-925-0671	R	8*	.1
40	Giffin Interior and Fixture Inc—*Gordon D Giffin*	500 Scotti Dr, Bridgeville PA 15017	412-221-1166	R	8*	.1
41	Kosakura and Associates Inc—*Chris Kiepfer*	2215 S Standard Ave, Santa Ana CA 92707	714-668-3000	R	8*	.1
42	JR Jones Fixture Co—*Douglas Jones*	3216 Winnetka Ave N, Minneapolis MN 55427	763-398-4309	R	8*	.1
43	Ferrante Manufacturing Co—*Sante Ferrante*	6626 Gratiot Ave, Detroit MI 48207	313-571-1111	R	7*	.1
44	Accent Industries Inc—*David Shaw*	9629 58th Pl, Kenosha WI 53144	262-857-9450	R	7*	.1
45	Wind Mill Woodworking Inc—*Jay Hogfeldt*	200 Balsam Rd, Sheboygan Falls WI 53085	920-467-2402	R	6*	.1
46	Michigan Maple Block Company Inc—*James Reichart*	PO Box 245, Petoskey MI 49770	231-347-4170	R	6*	.1
47	Newood Display Fixture Manufacturing Co—*Gerald Moshofsky*	PO Box 21808, Eugene OR 97402	541-688-0907	R	6*	.1
48	Stanly Fixtures Acquisition LLC—*Arold Thomson*	PO Box 616, Norwood NC 28128	704-474-3184	R	6*	.1
49	Bernhard Woodwork Ltd—*Herta Bernhard*	3670 Woodhead Dr, Northbrook IL 60062	847-291-1040	R	6*	.1
50	View Rite Manufacturing—*Brad Somberg*	455 Allan St, Daly City CA 94014	415-468-3850	R	6*	.1
51	MMI of Mississippi Inc—*John Freels*	1022 Advance Ln, Hazlehurst MS 39083	601-892-1105	S	6*	<.1
52	Assi Fabricators LLC—*Janet Brown*	11270 Old Baltimore Pk, Beltsville MD 20705	301-937-2800	R	6*	<.1
53	Nagele Manufacturing Company Inc—*Fred Nagele*	5201 W 164th St, Cleveland OH 44142	216-433-1100	R	5*	<.1
54	Suba Manufacturing Inc—*Jack Bell*	921 Bayshore Rd, Benicia CA 94510	707-745-0358	R	5*	<.1
55	Arcy Plastic Laminates Inc—*Robert Cecucci*	PO Box 307, Waterford NY 12188	518-235-0753	R	4*	<.1
56	Wilbedone Inc—*Thomas Beames*	1133 State Rte 222, Cortland NY 13045	607-756-8813	R	4*	<.1
57	Jensen Cabinet Inc—*Dennis Jensen*	PO Box 10599, Fort Wayne IN 46853	260-456-2131	R	4*	<.1
58	Mark Bric Display Corp—*Larry Ragland*	4740 Chudoba Pkwy, Prince George VA 23875	804-862-4655	R	3*	<.1
59	Shur Fit Distributors Inc—*Paul Gross*	221 N Main St, Franklin OH 45005	937-746-0567	R	3*	<.1
60	Hurco Design and Manufacturing—*Micah Larsen*	PO Box 9119, Ogden UT 84409	801-334-3322	R	3*	<.1
61	Fabricor Inc—*Barbara Summers*	1342 Woodswether Rd, Kansas City MO 64105	816-221-8611	R	3*	<.1
62	Woodworkers of Denver Inc—*Jan Harvey*	1475 S Acoma St, Denver CO 80223	303-777-7656	R	3*	<.1
63	Brewster Panel Corp—*Jim Riley*	PO Box 669, Vernon AL 35592	205-695-6841	R	2*	<.1
64	August Lotz Company Inc—*Mark Schlichter*	PO Box 127, Fall Creek WI 54742		R	2*	<.1
65	Sinicrope and Sons Inc—*Gary Sinicrope*	1124 Westminster Ave, Alhambra CA 91803	323-283-5131	R	2*	<.1
66	Gulf States Marble Inc—*Leighton Dunham*	PO Box 1944, Slidell LA 70459	985-641-0925	R	1*	<.1
67	Pacific Home Products Inc—*Wesley Moore*	PO Box 55188, Hayward CA 94545	510-293-6909	R	1*	<.1
68	Hmc Industries Inc—*Craig Lundberg*	PO Box 67, Lynnwood WA 98046	425-778-3144	R	1*	<.1

TOTALS: SIC 2541 Wood Partitions & Fixtures
Companies: 68   2,251   9.3

Note: An asterisk (*) indicates an estimated financial figure. The company type code used is as follows: R = Private, P = Public, S = Private Subsidiary, B = Public Subsidiary, D = Division, J = Joint Venture, I = Investment Fund.

COMPANY RANKINGS BY SALES WITHIN 4-DIGIT SIC

Rank	Company Name—*Executive Officer*	Address, City, State, Zip	Phone	Type	Fin	Empls
2542 Partitions & Fixtures Except Wood						
1	Crenlo LLC—*Lance Fleming*	1600 4th Ave NW, Rochester MN 55901	507-289-3371	S	118*	1.1
2	Vira Manufacturing Inc—*James Smith*	1 Buckingham Ave, Perth Amboy NJ 08861	732-442-8472	R	40*	.2
3	Marlite Inc—*John Popa*	PO Box 250, Dover OH 44622	330-343-6621	R	38*	.3
4	Lyon Workspace Products LLC—*R Washington*	PO Box 671, Aurora IL 60507	630-892-8941	R	35*	.5
5	Racks Inc—*R Wall*	PO Box 530840, San Diego CA 92153	619-661-0987	R	31*	.5
6	Claas Concepts Corp—*Stephen Claas*	1255 Zephyr Ave, Hayward CA 94544	510-429-8390	R	31*	<.1
7	Packaging Concepts Ltd—*Leonard Grossman*	15 Wellington Rd, Lincoln RI 02865	401-334-4646	R	28*	.2
8	Pan-Oston Co—*Terry Scariot*	6944 Louisville Rd, Bowling Green KY 42101	270-783-3900	R	28*	.4
9	List Industries Inc—*Herbert List*	PO Box 9601, Deerfield Beach FL 33442	954-429-9155	R	28*	.2
10	Rwi Manufacturing Inc—*Manfred Haiderer*	600 S Lake St, Aurora IL 60506	630-897-6951	R	27*	.2
11	American Locker Security Systems Inc—*Edward Ruttenberg*	815 S Main St, Grapevine TX 76051	817-329-1600	S	27*	.1
12	Samson Products Inc—*Richard Mcnamara*	6285 Randolph St, Commerce CA 90040	323-726-9070	R	26*	.5
13	Store Kraft Manufacturing Co—*Gary Cook*	PO Box 807, Beatrice NE 68310	402-223-2348	R	26*	.5
14	Ridg-U-Rak Inc—*John Pellegrino*	PO Box 150, North East PA 16428	814-725-8751	R	25*	.4
15	A George Diack Inc—*T Gonzalez*	1250 S Johnson Dr, City of Industry CA 91745	626-961-2491	R	24*	.1
16	King Load Manufacturing Co—*Charlie Chupp*	1357 W Beaver St, Jacksonville FL 32209	904-354-8882	R	24*	.2
17	Cannon Equipment Southeast Inc—*Chuck Gruber*	PO Box 1446, Chattanooga TN 37401	423-752-1000	R	24*	.2
18	Kent Corp—*M Oztekin*	PO Box 170399, Birmingham AL 35217	205-853-3420	R	24*	.2
19	Rapid Rack Inc Rapid Rack Industries Inc	14421 E Bonelli Ave, City of Industry CA 91746	626-333-7225	D	23*	.2
20	Stylmark Inc—*Ken Ritterstach*	PO Box 32008, Minneapolis MN 55432	763-574-7474	R	20*	.2
21	Vision Woodworking Inc—*Don Gamboni*	7890 Hickory St NE, Fridley MN 55432	763-571-5767	R	20*	<.1
22	Ready Metal Manufacturing Co—*Edward Radek*	140 S Dearborn St Ste, Chicago IL 60603	773-376-9700	R	20*	.3
23	Consolidated Storage Companies Inc—*Robert Logemann*	225 Main St, Tatamy PA 18085	610-253-2775	R	19*	.2
24	Western Pacific Storage Solutions Inc—*Tom Rogers*	300 E Arrow Hwy, San Dimas CA 91773	909-451-0303	R	18*	.1
25	Testrite Instrument Company Inc—*Laurence Rubin*	216 S Newman St, Hackensack NJ 07601	201-543-0240	R	18*	.1
26	Steve's Plating Corp—*Terry Knezevich*	3111 N San Fernando Bl, Burbank CA 91504	818-842-2184	R	17*	.1
27	Discount Office Items—*Tim Horton*	302 Industrial Dr, Columbus WI 53925	920-623-9528	R	17	<.1
28	Presence From Innovation LLC—*Jennifer Mcartor*	2290 Ball Dr, Saint Louis MO 63146	314-423-9777	S	16*	.1
29	Showbest Fixture Corp—*James Schubert*	4112 Sarellen Rd, Henrico VA 23231	804-222-5535	R	16*	.1
30	Inscape Inc (Falconer New York)—*Mo Bhayana*	221 Lister Ave 1, Falconer NY 14733	716-665-6210	S	15*	.1
31	Emjac Industries Inc—*David Dorta*	1075 Hialeah Dr, Hialeah FL 33010	305-883-2194	R	14*	.1
32	Reeve Store Equipment Co—*John Frackelton*	PO Box 276, Pico Rivera CA 90660	562-949-2535	R	13*	.1
33	Carr Metal Products Inc—*Bernie Berry*	3735 N Arlington Ave, Indianapolis IN 46218	317-542-0691	R	13*	.1
34	Northway Industries Inc—*C Battram*	PO Box 277, Middleburg PA 17842	570-837-1564	R	13*	.1
35	Boston Retail Products Inc—*Richard Rubin*	400 Riverside Ave, Medford MA 02155	781-395-7417	R	12*	.1
36	Uniweb Inc—*Karl Weber*	222 S Promenade Ave, Corona CA 92879	951-279-7999	R	12*	.1
37	Metal Fabricating Corp—*Judy Kalski*	10408 Berea Rd, Cleveland OH 44102	216-631-2480	R	12*	.1
38	Kardex Systems Inc—*Ronald Miller*	25 Industrial Blvd, Paoli PA 19301	610-296-9730	S	12*	.1
39	T And D Metal Products LLC—*Carola Good*	602 E Walnut St, Watseka IL 60970	815-432-4938	R	11*	.1
40	Midland Metal Products Co—*Bernard Donald*	1200 W 37th St, Chicago IL 60609	773-927-5700	R	11*	.1
41	Capitol Wood Works LLC	1010 E Edwards St, Springfield IL 62703	217-522-5553	R	11*	.1
42	Handy Store Fixtures Inc—*Paul Kurland*	337 Sherman Ave, Newark NJ 07114	973-242-1600	R	11*	.1
43	Rapid Rack Industries Inc—*Vaughn Sucevich*	14421 Bonelli St, City Of Industry CA 91746	626-333-7225	R	11*	.1
44	Vulcan Industries Inc (Moody Alabama)—*William Hutson*	PO Box 1943, Birmingham AL 35201	205-640-2400	S	10*	<.1
45	General Partitions Manufacturing Corp—*George Zehner*	PO Box 8370, Erie PA 16505	814-833-1154	R	9*	.1
46	Leo Prager Inc—*Peter Schoenfeld*	138 W 25th St Ste 1000, New York NY 10001	212-243-4113	R	9*	.1
47	Advanced Equipment Corp—*W Dickson*	2401 W Commonwealth Av, Fullerton CA 92833	714-635-5350	R	8*	.1
48	Transwall—*Shaun Mannix*	PO Box 1930, West Chester PA 19380	610-429-1400	S	8*	.1
49	Laminated Products Inc—*Kevi Jacob*	5718 52nd St, Kenosha WI 53144	262-658-4114	R	8*	.1
50	Gerali Custom Design Inc—*David Gerali*	1482 Sheldon Dr, Elgin IL 60120	847-760-0500	R	8*	.1
51	Shaw and Slavsky Inc—*Thomas Smith*	13821 Elmira St, Detroit MI 48227	313-834-3990	R	7*	.1
52	Maro Display Inc—*Steven Censo*	St 112 Dillabur Ave, North Kingstown RI 02852	401-294-5551	R	7*	.1
53	Lingo Manufacturing Company Inc—*Mark Lingo*	7400 Industrial Rd, Florence KY 41042	859-371-2662	R	7*	.1
54	Glaro Inc—*Neal Glass*	735 Calebs Path Ste 1, Hauppauge NY 11788	631-234-1717	R	7*	.1
55	Industrial Enclosure Corp—*John Palmer*	PO Box 2817, Aurora IL 60507	630-898-0400	R	6*	.1
56	Wiremasters Inc—*Paul Scriba*	1040 1050 W 40 St, Chicago IL 60609	773-254-3700	R	6*	.1
57	Davis Bacon Material Handling Inc—*Judy Davis*	5000 Valley Blvd, Los Angeles CA 90032	323-227-1921	R	6	<.1
58	Teichman Enterprises Inc—*Ruth Teichman*	6100 Bandini Blvd, Commerce CA 90040	323-278-9000	R	5*	.1
59	Displays by Rioux—*Robert Rioux*	PO Box 3008, Syracuse NY 13220	315-458-3639	R	5*	<.1
60	Bull Metal Products Inc—*Steven Bull*	PO Box 738, Middletown CT 06457	860-346-9691	R	5*	<.1
61	Select Marketing Solutions—*Pam Zastrow*	1175 Lakeside Dr, Gurnee IL 60031	847-249-4939	R	4*	<.1
62	Trind Co—*Jay Trinder*	1004 Obici IndustrialB, Suffolk VA 23434	757-539-0262	R	4*	<.1
63	Asentria Inc—*Tim Stoner*	1200 N 96th St, Seattle WA 98103	206-344-8800	R	3*	.1
64	Imperial Counters Lllp—*Elaine Gove*	725 Spiral Blvd, Hastings MN 55033	651-437-3903	R	3*	<.1
65	Buckley Co—*Steve Buckley*	241 Forest Ave, Cohasset MA 02025	781-383-9962	R	3*	<.1
66	Clark Specialty Company Inc—*James Presley*	8440 State Rte 54, Hammondsport NY 14840	607-569-2191	R	3*	<.1
67	Plastic Line Manufacturing Inc—*Marjorie Wallace*	9070 Louisiana St, Merrillville IN 46410	219-769-8022	R	3*	<.1
68	Adapto Storage Products—*Joe Caridnan*	625 E 10th Ave, Hialeah FL 33010	305-887-9563	R	2*	<.1
69	Fmmb LLC	14600 E 7 Mile Rd, Detroit MI 48205	313-372-7420	R	2*	<.1
70	Cal Partitions Inc—*Alan Anderson*	23814 President Ave, Harbor City CA 90710	310-539-1911	R	2*	<.1
71	M Lavine Design Workshop Inc—*Jackie Bach*	2330 County Rd 137, Waite Park MN 56387	320-230-6650	R	2*	<.1
72	TechRack Systems—*Frank Sommerfield*	11615 Forest Central D, Dallas TX 75243	214-340-7594	R	2*	<.1
73	Sterling Rack Inc—*Ron Dalrymple*	176 Tarheel Dr, Gastonia NC 28056	704-866-9131	R	2*	<.1
74	Independent Welding Co—*Nelson Guevara*	PO Box 404, Wharton NJ 07885	973-361-9731	R	2*	<.1
75	Able Steel Equipment Company Inc—*Bonnie Tarkenton*	5002 23rd St, Long Island City NY 11101	718-361-9240	R	2*	<.1
76	Illinois Rack Enterprises Inc—*Brian Mooney*	480 Scotland Rd Ste A, Lakemoor IL 60051	815-385-5750	R	1*	<.1

TOTALS: SIC 2542 Partitions & Fixtures Except Wood
Companies: 76   1,134   9.9

Rank	Company Name—*Executive Officer*	Address, City, State, Zip	Phone	Type	Fin	Empls
2591 Drapery Hardware, Blinds & Shades						
1	Newell Rubbermaid Inc—*Michael B Polk*	3 Glenlake Pky, Atlanta GA 30328	770-418-7000	P	5,759	19.4
2	Springs Window Fashions LLC—*Scott Fawcett*	7549 Graber Rd, Middleton WI 53562	608-836-1011	R	2,174*	4.6
3	Levolor/Kirsh—*Stephanie Chattilon* Newell Rubbermaid Inc	4110 Premier Dr, High Point NC 27265	336-812-8181	D	565*	3.0
4	Lafayette Venetian Blind Inc—*Joseph Morgan*	PO Box 2838, West Lafayette IN 47996	765-464-2500	R	70*	1.0
5	Kenney Manufacturing Co—*Leslie Kenney*	1000 Jefferson Blvd, Warwick RI 02886	401-739-2200	R	58*	.6
6	Comfortex Corp—*Thomas Marusak*	21 Elm St, Watervliet NY 12189	518-273-3333	R	51*	.8

Rank	Company Name—*Executive Officer*	Address, City, State, Zip	Phone	Type	Fin	Empls
7	Hunter Douglas Fabrication-Northern California	2390 Zanker Rd, San Jose CA 95131	408-435-8844	S	33*	.2
8	Skagfield Corp—*Hilmar Skagfield*	PO Box 6566, Tallahassee FL 32314	850-878-1144	R	29*	.5
9	Douglas Hunter Fabrication Co—*Marv Hopkins*	2315 Luna Rd Ste 136, Carrollton TX 75006	972-484-9771	R	23*	.4
10	American Drapery Blind and Carpet Inc—*Donald Richmond*	PO Box 896, Renton WA 98057	425-255-3893	R	20*	.2
11	Selective Enterprises Inc—*John Hawkins*	PO Box 410149, Charlotte NC 28241	704-588-3310	R	17*	.1
12	Designer Blinds Of Omaha Inc—*Lloyd Woodworth*	4500 S 76th Cir, Omaha NE 68127	402-331-2283	R	15*	.2
13	Beauti-Vue Products Corp—*Jim Grumbeck*	8555 194th Ave, Bristol WI 53104	262-857-2306	R	15*	.1
14	C-Mor Co—*Brian Dautch*	1 Passaic St Unit 30, Wood Ridge NJ 07075	973-478-3900	R	12*	.1
15	Tentina Window Fashions Inc—*Frank Miritello*	PO Box 615, Lindenhurst NY 11757	631-957-9585	R	10*	.1
16	Finial Company Inc—*Martha Beck*	4030 La Reunion Pkwy, Dallas TX 75212	214-678-0805	R	8*	.1
17	Techniku Inc—*Robert Collett*	325 Interlocken Pkwy B, Broomfield CO 80021	303-355-9347	R	1*	<.1
18	Bautech Inc—*John Karas*	1550 N Old Rand Rd Ste, Wauconda IL 60084	847-526-1515	R	1*	<.1

TOTALS: SIC 2591 Drapery Hardware, Blinds & Shades
Companies: 18   8,860   31.2

2599 Furniture & Fixtures Nec

Rank	Company Name—*Executive Officer*	Address, City, State, Zip	Phone	Type	Fin	Empls
1	Kinetic Concepts Inc—*John Bibb*	PO Box 659508, San Antonio TX 78265	210-524-9000	P	2,018	6.9
2	Steward Carney Hospital Inc—*Ralph Delatorre*	299 Park Ave, New York NY 10171	212-894-5317	R	154*	3.0
3	Commercial Furniture Group—*Seamus Bateson*	810 West Hwy 25/70, Newport TN 37821	423-623-0031	R	153*	.8
4	Edsal Manufacturing Company Inc—*Bruce Saltzberg*	4400 S Packers Ave, Chicago IL 60609	773-254-0600	R	114*	1.3
5	Stryker Medical—*Stephen MacMillan*	3800 E Centre Ave, Portage MI 49002	269-329-2100	D	96*	.7
6	Plymold Furnishing Solutions—*Chuck Mayhew*	615 Centennial Dr, Kenyon MN 55946	507-789-5111	R	46*	.2
7	Koala Corp	6982 S Quentin St, Centennial CO 80112	303-539-8300	S	37	.3
8	UMBRA LLC—*Les Mandelbaum*	1705 Broadway St, Buffalo NY 14212		R	36*	.3
9	Kojo Worldwide Corp—*Joe Robertson*	9654 Siempre Viva Rd, San Diego CA 92154	619-205-5722	R	35*	.5
10	JBI Inc (Long Beach California)—*Jay Rothman*	2650 El Presidio, Long Beach CA 90810	310-537-8200	R	29*	.2
11	Awh Corp—*Henry Hopeman*	435 Evaex Ave Ste 103, Waynesboro VA 22980	540-949-9200	R	29*	.6
12	BK Industries—*Ken Goodwin*	PO Box 80400, Simpsonville SC 29680	864-963-3471	D	28*	.2
13	Triad Manufacturing Inc—*Dave Caito*	4321 Semple Ave, Saint Louis MO 63120	314-381-5280	R	25*	.3
14	Leland Manufacturing LLC—*Glenn Lange*	PO Box 9, Ferdinand IN 47532	812-367-1761	R	23*	.1
15	Lista International Corp—*Donald Brown*	106 Lowland St, Holliston MA 01746	508-429-1350	R	22*	.2
16	Fcc Commercial Furniture Inc—*Gary Crowe*	8452 Old Hwy 99 N, Roseburg OR 97470	541-673-3351	R	21*	.2
17	Barbosa Cabinets Inc—*Edward Barbosa*	2020 E Grant Line Rd, Tracy CA 95304	209-836-2501	R	20*	.3
18	Forbes Industries Div—*Tim Sweetland*	1933 E Locust St, Ontario CA 91761	909-923-4559	R	20*	.2
19	Genesis Fixtures Inc—*Scott Stewart*	3842 Redman Dr, Fort Collins CO 80524	970-416-9315	D	15*	.2
20	Barton Medical Corp—*Glynn Bloomquist*	5725 Hwy 290 W Ste 103, Austin TX 78735	512-476-7199	R	14*	<.1
21	Parisi Inc—*Joseph Parisi*	305 Pheasant Run, Newtown PA 18940	215-968-6677	R	14*	.1
22	American Locker Group Inc—*Allen D Tilley*	815 S Main St, Grapevine TX 76051	817-329-1600	P	12	.1
23	Hausmann Industries Inc—*David Hausmann*	130 Union St, Northvale NJ 07647	201-767-0255	R	12*	.1
24	Hunt Country Furniture Inc—*Randy Williams*	19 Dog Tail Corners Rd, Wingdale NY 12594	845-832-6601	R	12*	.1
25	Shoto Corp—*Nicole Thor*	6450 County Rd B, Two Rivers WI 54241	920-682-0196	R	12*	.1
26	Shafer Commercial Seating Inc—*Randall Shafer*	4101 E 48th Ave, Denver CO 80216	303-322-7792	R	11*	.1
27	Falcon Companies International Inc—*John Sumner* Commercial Furniture Group	10650 Gateway Blvd, Saint Louis MO 63132		S	10*	.2
28	Hanco Inc—*Kim Regan*	PO Box 48, Peru IN 46970	765-473-6691	R	9*	.1
29	United Metal Fabricators Inc—*Eileen Melvin*	1316 Eisenhower Blvd, Johnstown PA 15904	814-266-8726	R	9*	.1
30	Vitro Seating Products—*Stephen Scott*	PO Box 470159, Saint Louis MO 63147	314-241-2265	R	7*	.1
31	Bally Block Co—*James Reichart*	PO Box 188, Bally PA 19503	610-845-7511	R	7*	.1
32	Marlo Manufacturing Company Inc—*Salvatore Pirruccio*	301 Division St, Boonton NJ 07005	973-423-0226	R	6*	<.1
33	Industrial Management Inc—*David Lemons*	PO Box 829, Albany OR 97321	541-926-1463	R	5*	<.1
34	Paladin Industry Inc—*Larry Bell*	4990 W Greenbrooke Dr, Grand Rapids MI 49512	616-698-7495	R	5*	<.1
35	Medical Technology Industries Inc—*Jeff Baker*	3655 Ninigret Dr, Salt Lake City UT 84104	801-887-5114	R	3*	<.1
36	M L Rongo Inc—*Michael Rongo*	1281 Humbracht Cir, Bartlett IL 60103	708-343-8820	R	3*	<.1
37	Carlin Manufacturing Inc—*Kevin Carlin*	466 W Fallbrook Ave St, Fresno CA 93711		R	3*	<.1
38	Infanti International	1153 W Elizabeth Ave, Linden NJ 07036	718-447-5632	R	3*	<.1
39	Aldajo Inc—*Daniel Caballero*	PO Box 540921, Opa Locka FL 33054	305-685-3040	R	3*	<.1
40	Hospital Bed Remanufacturing Company Inc—*Roger Meyer*	2211 Williamsburg Pke, Richmond IN 47374	765-966-1400	R	2*	<.1
41	Vivax Medical Corp—*Thomas D Ellen*	89 Putter Ln Ste 85, Torrington CT 06790	860-489-7890	R	2*	<.1
42	Brandt Equipment LLC—*Richard Brandt*	4461 Bronx Blvd, Bronx NY 10470	718-994-0800	R	2*	<.1
43	Carts Of Colorado Inc—*Stanley Gallery*	5420 S Quebec St Ste 2, Greenwood Village CO 80111	303-329-0101	R	1*	<.1
44	Medreco Inc—*Gerald Paul*	PO Box 100, Liberty IN 47353	765-458-7444	R	1*	<.1
45	Caseworks Industries Inc—*Lester Weinman*	827 E 17th St Ste 125, Tucson AZ 85719	520-574-1000	R	1*	<.1

TOTALS: SIC 2599 Furniture & Fixtures Nec
Companies: 45   3,088   17.8

2611 Pulp Mills

Rank	Company Name—*Executive Officer*	Address, City, State, Zip	Phone	Type	Fin	Empls
1	Weyerhaeuser Co—*Daniel S Fulton*	PO Box 9777, Federal Way WA 98063	253-924-2345	P	6,552	14.3
2	Boise Inc—*Alexander Toeldte*	PO Box 990050, Boise ID 83799	208-384-7000	P	2,404	5.4
3	Parsons and Whittemore Inc—*George Landegger*	4 International Dr, Rye Brook NY 10573	914-937-9809	R	1,075*	2.5
4	Buckeye Technologies Inc—*John B Crowe*	PO Box 80407, Memphis TN 38108	901-320-8100	P	905	1.4
5	Buckeye Lumberton Corp—*Douglas Dowell* Buckeye Technologies Inc	1001 Tillman, Memphis TN 38112	901-320-8100	S	673	.1
6	Pratt Industries Inc—*Brian Mcpheely*	1800C Sarasota Pkwy Ne, Conyers GA 30013	770-918-5678	R	471*	4.0
7	American Paper Recycling Corp—*Kenneth Golden*	87 Central St Ste 8, Mansfield MA 02048	508-339-5551	R	34*	.1
8	Rapid Processing LLC—*Frank Sculzo*	860 Humboldt St, Brooklyn NY 11222	718-349-0500	R	6*	.1
9	Midwest Fibre Sales Corp—*F Wilcox*	PO Box 825, Springfield MO 65801	417-862-1976	R	5*	<.1
10	Cheney Pulp And Paper Co—*Mark Snyder*	PO Box 215, Franklin OH 45005	937-746-9991	R	4*	<.1
11	SGD Holdings Ltd—*Harry Johansing*	1860 Eastman Ave Ste 1, Ventura CA 93003	805-644-4462	P	4	<.1

TOTALS: SIC 2611 Pulp Mills
Companies: 11   12,132   27.9

2621 Paper Mills

Rank	Company Name—*Executive Officer*	Address, City, State, Zip	Phone	Type	Fin	Empls
1	Kimberly-Clark Corp—*Thomas J Falk*	PO Box 619100, Dallas TX 75261	972-281-1200	P	19,746	57.0
2	MeadWestvaco Corp—*John A Luke Jr*	501 S 5th St, Richmond VA 23219	804-444-1000	P	5,693	18.0
3	Fasson Roll North America—*Donald A Nolan*	8080 Norton Pkwy, Mentor OH 44060	440-534-6000	S	3,640	.8
4	NewPage Holding Corp—*George F Martin*	8540 Gander Creek Dr, Miamisburg OH 45342		R	3,600	6.0
5	NewPage Corp—*George Martin* NewPage Holding Corp	8540 Gander Creek Dr, Miamisburg OH 45342	937-242-9345	S	3,596	7.3
6	Pentair Inc—*Randall J Hogan*	5500 Wayzata Blvd Ste, Minneapolis MN 55416	763-545-1730	P	3,457	15.3

Note: An asterisk (*) indicates an estimated financial figure. The company type code used is as follows: R = Private, P = Public, S = Private Subsidiary, B = Public Subsidiary, D = Division, J = Joint Venture, I = Investment Fund.

COMPANY RANKINGS BY SALES WITHIN 4-DIGIT SIC

Rank	Company Name—Executive Officer	Address, City, State, Zip	Phone	Type	Fin	Empls
7	FiberMark DSI—Anthony MacLaurin	26 Sears Wy, West Springfield MA 01089	413-732-0141	S	2,565*	1.7
8	Johns Manville Corp—Steve Hochhauser	PO Box 5108, Denver CO 80217	303-978-2000	S	1,750*	7.0
9	Verso Paper Corp—Michael A Jackson	6775 Lenox Center Ct S, Memphis TN 38115	901-369-4100	P	1,605	2.8
10	PH Glatfelter Co—Dante Parrini	96 S George St Ste 500, York PA 17401	717-225-4711	P	1,455	4.3
11	Sappi Fine Paper North America—Ronee Hagen	225 Franklin St 28th F, Boston MA 02110	617-423-7300	S	1,442*	2.9
12	AbitibiBowater Newsprint—David J Paterson	5020 Hwy 11 S, Calhoun TN 37309	423-336-2211	D	1,118*	.7
13	Wausau Paper Corp—Thomas J Howatt	100 Paper Pl, Mosinee WI 54455	715-693-4470	P	1,035	2.3
14	Fonda Group Inc (Oshkosh Wisconsin)—Bob Korzenski	PO Box 2038, Oshkosh WI 54903	920-235-9330	R	920*	2.0
15	Appleton Papers Inc—Mark R Richards	PO Box 359, Appleton WI 54912	920-734-9841	R	826*	2.3
16	Schweitzer-Mauduit International Inc—Frederic Villoutreix	100 North Point Ctr E, Alpharetta GA 30022	770-569-4271	P	816	2.8
17	Kapstone Paper and Packaging Corp—Roger W Stone	1101 Skokie Blvd Ste 3, Northbrook IL 60062	847-239-8800	P	783	1.6
18	Neenah Paper Inc—John O'Donnell	3460 Preston Ridge Rd, Alpharetta GA 30005	678-566-6500	P	658	1.7
19	Gilman Investment Co—Bernard Bergreen	111 W 50th St, New York NY 10020	212-246-3300	R	575*	2.6
20	SP Newsprint Co—Joseph Gorman	245 Peachtree Center A, Atlanta GA 30303	404-979-6600	R	507*	.4
21	Potlatch Corp Pulp and Paperboard Market Services Div—Michael Covey	601 W 1st Ave Ste 1600, Spokane WA 99201		D	350*	1.0
22	Blue Heron Paper Co—Michael Siebers	419 Main St, Oregon City OR 97045	503-650-4211	S	305*	.2
23	Hollingsworth and Vose Company Inc—Valentine Hollingsworth	112 Washington St, East Walpole MA 02032	508-850-2000	R	220*	1.7
24	Simpson Tacoma Kraft Company LLC—Allan Trinkwald	917 E 11th St, Tacoma WA 98421	253-779-6400	S	189*	.4
25	Crane and Company Inc—Charles Kittrgdge	30 S St, Dalton MA 01226	413-684-2600	R	157*	1.4
26	Abitibi-Consolidated Corp—Breen Blain	18511 Beaumont Hwy, Houston TX 77049	936-634-8811	R	154*	1.6
27	Ahlstrom Filtration Inc—Jan Lang	PO Box 1410, Madisonville KY 42431	270-821-0140	S	147*	.1
28	Blue Ridge Holding Corp—Richard Lozyniak	41 Main St, Canton NC 28716	828-454-0676	R	143*	2.1
29	Lincoln Paper And Tissue LLC—Keith Scotter	PO Box 490, Lincoln ME 04457	207-794-0600	R	141*	.4
30	Burrows Paper Corp—RW Burrows	PO Box 987, Little Falls NY 13365	315-823-2300	R	123*	.7
31	Nice-Pak Products Inc—Robert Julius	2 Nice Pak Park, Orangeburg NY 10962	845-365-1700	R	116*	1.0
32	Resolute Forest Products Augusta Newsprint Co—Rich Zgol	PO Box 1647, Augusta GA 30903	706-798-3440	S	106*	.4
33	Thilmany Nicolet Mill—Russ Wanke	200 Main Ave, De Pere WI 54115	920-337-1203	D	97*	.4
34	Blandin Paper Co—Brend Eikens	115 Sw 1st St, Grand Rapids MN 55744	218-327-6200	R	90*	.9
35	Sabin Robbins Paper Co—Thomas Roberts	497 Circle Freeway Dr, Cincinnati OH 45246	513-874-5270	R	86*	.2
36	Erving Industries Inc—Morris Housen	97 E Main St, Erving MA 01344	413-422-2700	R	82*	.5
37	BPM Inc—James S Koronkiewicz	PO Box 149, Peshtigo WI 54157	715-582-4551	R	60*	.2
38	Norkol Converting Corp—Lawrence Kolinski	11650 W Grand Ave, Melrose Park IL 60164	708-531-1000	R	60*	.3
39	Base-Line Inc—Howard E Harper	4 Corporate Dr Ste 186, Shelton CT 06484	253-852-6681	R	58*	<.1
40	White Birch Paper Co—Peter M Brant	80 Field Point Rd Ste, Greenwich CT 06830	203-661-3344	R	58*	<.1
41	Inland Empire Paper Company Inc—Kevin Rasler	PO Box 2160, Spokane WA 99210	509-924-1911	R	56*	.1
42	Nippon Paper Industries USA Company Ltd—Teruo Tamaki	PO Box 271, Port Angeles WA 98362	360-457-4474	R	55*	.3
43	Monadnock Paper Mills Inc—Richard Verney	117 Antrim Rd, Bennington NH 03442	603-588-3311	R	50*	.2
44	Linn West Paper Co—Ron Stern	PO Box 68, West Linn OR 97068	503-557-6500	R	48*	.3
45	Smart Papers LLC—Larry Englund	601 N B St, Hamilton OH 45013	513-869-5000	R	45*	.4
46	Ennis Tag and Label Co—Chuck Hester	PO Box D, Wolfe City TX 75496	903-496-2244	D	40*	.2
47	TST Impreso Inc—Marshall D Sorokwasz	PO Box 506, Coppell TX 75019	972-462-0100	S	36*	.1
48	Ahlstrom West Carrollton Inc—Charles Huber	PO Box 44098, West Carrollton OH 45449	937-859-3821	R	35*	.1
49	Maryland Paper Company LP—Michael Carr	16144 Elliott Pkwy, Williamsport MD 21795	301-223-6550	R	33*	.2
50	Manistique Papers Inc—Wendy J Tilford	453 S Mackinac Ave, Manistique MI 49854	906-341-2175	S	32*	.2
51	Specialty Paper Mills Inc—Ronald Gabriel	PO Box 3188, Santa Fe Springs CA 90670	562-692-8737	S	30*	.2
52	French Paper Co—Jerry French	PO Box 398, Niles MI 49120	269-683-1100	R	28*	.1
53	Alabama River Newsprint Co—John Weaver	PO Box 10, Perdue Hill AL 36470	251-575-2800	R	26*	.2
54	Kurtz Brothers—Monty Kunes	PO Box 392, Clearfield PA 16830	814-765-6561	R	26*	.1
55	Pac-Paper Inc—Robert Fike	6416 Nw Whitney Rd, Vancouver WA 98665	360-695-7771	R	25*	.1
56	Putney Paper Company Inc—Fred Concklin	PO Box 226, Putney VT 05346	802-387-5571	R	24*	.2
57	Bonita Packaging Products Inc—John Gordon	7333 Sw Bonita Rd, Portland OR 97224	503-684-6542	R	22*	.1
58	Erving Paper Mills Inc—Morris Housen	97 E Main St, Erving MA 01344	413-422-2700	R	21*	.1
59	Ahlstrom Mount Holly Springs LLC—Mark Cassel	122 W Butler St, Mount Holly Springs PA 17065	717-486-3438	R	17*	.1
60	International Cellulose Corp—Steven Kempe	12315 Robin Blvd, Houston TX 77045	713-433-6701	R	13*	<.1
61	Brookdale Plastics Inc—Joseph Meixell	9909 S Shore Dr Ste 3, Plymouth MN 55441	763-797-1000	R	13*	.1
62	Great Lakes Tissue Company Inc—Clarence Roznowski	437 S Main St, Cheboygan MI 49721	231-627-0200	R	12*	.1
63	Package Design and Manufacturing Inc—David Rosser	12424 Emerson Dr, Brighton MI 48116	248-486-4390	R	9*	.1
64	Crocker Technical Papers Inc—Lawrence Gelsomini	431 Westminster St, Fitchburg MA 01420	978-345-7771	R	8*	.1
65	Dingman Data Systems Ltd—Victoria Dingman	55 Plant Ave, Hauppauge NY 11788	631-273-1001	R	6*	.1
66	Cottrell Paper Company Inc—Jack Cottrell	PO Box 35, Rock City Falls NY 12863	518-885-1702	R	5*	<.1
67	Caba Co—Ed Rabkin	1310 Don Gaspar St, Santa Fe NM 87505	505-983-1942	R	4*	<.1
68	B and B Paper Converters Inc—John Jazwa	12500 Elmwood Ave, Cleveland OH 44111	216-941-8100	R	4*	<.1
69	Graphic Resources Inc—Jack Schall	1911 Vernon St, Kansas City MO 64116	816-221-3555	R	3*	<.1
70	Caseys' Page Mill Ltd—Mike Casey	6528 S Oneida Ct, Centennial CO 80111	303-220-1463	R	3*	<.1
71	Ken Ag Inc—Bruce Perry	PO Box 326, Ashland OH 44805	419-281-1204	R	2*	<.1

TOTALS: SIC 2621 Paper Mills
Companies: 71   **59,261**   **156.8**

2631 Paperboard Mills

Rank	Company Name—Executive Officer	Address, City, State, Zip	Phone	Type	Fin	Empls
1	International Paper Co—John V Faraci	6400 Poplar Ave, Memphis TN 38197	901-419-9000	P	25,179	59.5
2	Rock-Tenn Co—James A Rubright	PO Box 4098, Norcross GA 30091	770-448-2193	P	5,400	26.6
3	Sonoco Products Co—Harris E DeLoach Jr	1 N 2nd St, Hartsville SC 29550	843-383-7000	P	4,499	19.6
4	Temple-Inland Inc—Doyle R Simons	1300 S Mopac Expwy 3rd, Austin TX 78746	512-434-5800	P	3,799	10.5
5	Caraustar Mill Group Inc	PO Box 115, Austell GA 30168	770-948-3101	S	2,420*	2.5
6	Chesapeake Corp—Jerry Kerins	1021 E Cary St, Richmond VA 23219	804-697-1000	P	1,055*	5.4
7	Weyerhaeuser Paper Co Containerboard Packaging Div—Daniel Fulton	PO Box 9777, Federal Way WA 98063	253-924-2345	D	885*	1.0
8	Newark Group Inc—Robert H Mullen	20 Jackson Dr, Cranford NJ 07016	908-276-4000	R	532*	2.5
9	FiberMark Inc—Anthony MacLaurin	PO Box 498, Brattleboro VT 05302	802-257-0365	R	438	1.7
10	ITW Angleboard	3600 W Lake Ave, Glenview IL 60025		D	257*	.3
11	MeadWestvaco Containerboard	501 S 5th St, Richmond VA 23219	256-437-2161	D	150	.5
12	Caraustar Recovered Fiber Group Inc	5000 Austell Powder Sp, Austell GA 30106	770-948-3101	S	134*	.2
13	Republic Paperboard Co	8801 SW Lee Blvd, Lawton OK 73505	580-510-2200	S	105	.9
14	Interstate Resources Inc—Charles Feghali	1300 Wilson Blvd Ste 1, Arlington VA 22209	703-243-3355	R	73*	.9
15	Walter G Anderson Inc—Marc Anderson	4535 Willow Dr, Hamel MN 55340	763-478-2133	R	70*	.2
16	Demco Inc—Bill Stroner	PO Box 7488, Madison WI 53707	608-241-1201	R	50*	.1
17	Cincinnati Paperboard Corp	5500 Wooster Rd, Cincinnati OH 45226	513-871-7112	D	35	.1
18	Gaylord Brothers—Guy Marhewka Demco Inc	PO Box 4901, Syracuse NY 13221		S	30*	.1

Rank	Company Name—*Executive Officer*	Address, City, State, Zip	Phone	Type	Fin	Empls
19	Newman and Company Inc—*Fred Herman*	6101 Tacony St, Philadelphia PA 19135	215-333-8700	R	28*	.2
20	Sweetwater Paperboard Company Inc—*Mike Keough*	PO Box 115, Austell GA 30168	770-944-9350	S	25*	.1
21	RTS Packaging LLC	PO Box 4098, Norcross GA 30091		J	23*	.1
22	Winston Printing Co—*James Gordon*	PO Box 11026, Winston Salem NC 27116	336-759-0051	R	18*	.1
23	Jackson Paper Manufacturing Co—*Tim Campbell*	PO Box 667, Sylva NC 28779	828-586-5534	R	18*	.1
24	Chesapeake Recycling Co—*Steve Cotner*	PO Box 160, Winamac IN 46996		R	16*	<.1
25	Lowell Paper Box Company Inc—*Paul Connolly*	3 Elliott St, Nashua NH 03064	603-595-0700	R	14*	.1
26	National Carton and Coating Co—*James Yost*	1439 Lavelle Dr, Xenia OH 45385	937-372-8001	R	11*	.1
27	Finn Industries Inc—*William Finn*	1921 S Business Pkwy, Ontario CA 91761	909-930-1500	R	7*	.1
28	Shell Packaging Corp—*Stephen Beckerman*	200 Connell Dr Ste 120, Berkeley Heights NJ 07922	908-871-7000	R	7*	<.1
29	United States Box Corp—*Alan Kossoff*	1296 Mccarter Hwy, Newark NJ 07104	973-481-2000	R	5*	<.1
30	Lodner Printing Inc—*Paul Locascio*	1205 Whitlock Ave, Bronx NY 10459	718-589-3660	R	3*	<.1
31	Printing and Packaging Inc—*Boyce Hanna*	PO Box 1558, Shelby NC 28151	704-482-3866	R	3*	<.1
32	Parsons Steel Rule Dies Inc—*James Parsons*	617 S Smallwood St, Baltimore MD 21223	410-945-4800	R	3*	<.1
33	Midwest Cortland Inc—*Roy Urbanek*	9535 River St, Schiller Park IL 60176	847-671-0376	R	2*	<.1
34	Mat Nuwood LLC—*Desy Holoway*	PO Box 578, Lenoir NC 28645	828-758-4463	R	1*	<.1

TOTALS: SIC 2631 Paperboard Mills
Companies: 34   45,294   133.6

2652 Setup Paperboard Boxes

Rank	Company Name—*Executive Officer*	Address, City, State, Zip	Phone	Type	Fin	Empls
1	Greif Inc—*Michael J Gasser*	425 Winter Rd, Delaware OH 43015	740-549-6000	P	4,248	15.7
2	Packaging Corporation of America—*Mark W Kowlzan*	1955 W Field Ct, Lake Forest IL 60045		P	2,620	8.3
3	Caraustar Industries Inc—*Michael J Keough*	PO Box 115, Austell GA 30168	770-948-3101	R	820	3.2
4	Tim-Bar Corp—*Matthew Heleva*	148 Penn St, Hanover PA 17331	717-632-4727	R	121*	1.1
5	Simkins Industries Inc—*Leon Simkins*	PO Box 1870, New Haven CT 06508	203-787-7171	R	102*	1.0
6	Rusken Packaging Inc—*Greg Rusk*	PO Box 2100, Cullman AL 35056	256-734-0092	R	82*	.3
7	Boxit Corp—*David Helm*	5555 Walworth Ave, Cleveland OH 44102	216-631-6900	R	53*	.3
8	Mclean Packaging Corp—*Joseph Fenkel*	1504 Glen Ave, Moorestown NJ 08057	856-359-2600	R	38*	.3
9	Simkins Corp—*Morton Simkins*	2824 N 2nd St, Philadelphia PA 19133	215-739-4033	R	34*	.2
10	F M Howell and Co—*Katherine Roehlke*	PO Box 286, Elmira NY 14902	607-734-6291	R	30*	.2
11	Plaza Packaging Corp—*Sandy Connor*	PO Box 520530, Bronx NY 10452	718-293-5900	R	23*	.2
12	A Klein and Company Inc—*Jesse Salwen*	PO Box 670, Claremont NC 28610	828-459-9261	R	19*	.1
13	Mason Box Co—*Hugh Mason*	PO Box 129, North Attleboro MA 02761	508-695-9381	R	17*	.1
14	Imperial Paper Box Corp—*Ira Sukoff*	252 Newport St, Brooklyn NY 11212	718-346-6100	R	17*	.1
15	Brick and Ballerstein Inc—*Gary Levinson*	1085 Irving Ave, Ridgewood NY 11385	718-497-1400	H	11*	.1
16	Austell Box Board Corp—*Michael J Keough* Caraustar Industries Inc	3300 Joe Jerkins Blvd, Atlanta GA 30303	770-948-3100	D	10*	.2
17	House Of Packaging Inc—*Jack Franck*	PO Box 90305, City Of Industry CA 91715	626-369-3371	R	5*	.1

TOTALS: SIC 2652 Setup Paperboard Boxes
Companies: 17   8,250   31.4

2653 Corrugated & Solid Fiber Boxes

Rank	Company Name—*Executive Officer*	Address, City, State, Zip	Phone	Type	Fin	Empls
1	Liberty Diversified International Inc—*Michael Fiterman*	5600 Hwy 169 N, Minneapolis MN 55428	763-536-6600	R	4,429*	1.8
2	Pactiv Corp—*Joseph E Doyle*	1900 W Field Ct, Lake Forest IL 60045	847-482-2000	S	2,800*	10.0
3	Dopaco California Inc—*Edward Fitts*	4545 Qantas Ln, Stockton CA 95206	209-983-1930	S	2,498*	1.3
4	Longview Fibre Paper and Packaging Inc—*Randy Nebel*	PO Box 639, Longview WA 98632	360-425-1550	S	951*	3.0
5	Green Bay Packaging Inc—*William F Kress*	1700 N Webster Ct, Green Bay WI 54302	920-433-5111	R	858*	3.0
6	Southland Container Corp—*David Katt*	6 Nesbitt Dr, Inman SC 29349	864-578-0085	R	531*	4.5
7	Great Northern Corp—*John Davis*	PO Box 939, Appleton WI 54912	920-739-3671	R	258*	1.0
8	Orange County Container Group LLC—*Carlos Conce*	PO Box 847, Forney TX 75126	214-515-6400	R	165*	1.7
9	Us Corrugated Inc—*Dennis Mehiel*	550 Broad St Ste 605, Newark NJ 07102	973-353-8088	R	136*	1.1
10	Tharco—*Oscar B Fears*	2222 Grant Ave, San Lorenzo CA 94580		R	127*	.8
11	Sayco Container Inc—*Michael Feterik* Orange County Container Group LLC	13400 Nelson Ave, City Of Industry CA 91746	619-440-4411	S	113*	1.0
12	Fleetwood Fibre Packaging and Graphics	15250 Don Julian Rd, City of Industry CA 91745	626-968-8503	R	100*	.2
13	Highland Containers Inc—*Doug Johnston*	100 Ragsdale Rd, Jamestown NC 27282	336-887-5400	R	92*	.5
14	Carolina Container Co—*Ronald Sessions*	PO Box 2166, High Point NC 27261	336-883-7146	R	87*	.3
15	President Container Inc—*Marvin Grossbard*	PO Box 387, Wood Ridge NJ 07075	201-933-7500	R	75*	.4
16	Tri-Wall A Weyerhaeuser Co—*John Faraci*	2626 County Rd 71, Butler IN 46721	260-868-2151	R	70*	.2
17	Key Container Company Inc—*Bob Watts*	4224 Santa Ana St, South Gate CA 90280	323-564-4211	R	66*	.1
18	Color-Box LLC—*Terry Cinotte*	623 S G St, Richmond IN 47374	765-966-7588	S	61*	.3
19	Afco Inc—*Jeffrey Feibelman*	PO Box 19720, Johnston RI 02919	401-943-5040	R	59*	.7
20	Innerpac LLC—*Anthony Ditommaso*	1942 S Laramie Ave, Cicero IL 60804	708-863-8300	R	58*	.4
21	York Container Co—*Charles Wolf*	PO Box 3008, York PA 17402	717-757-7611	R	58*	.2
22	Bates Container LLC—*Leah Crum*	PO Box 822028, Fort Worth TX 76182	817-498-3200	R	53*	.3
23	Connecticut Container Corp—*Harry Perkins*	455 Sackett Point Rd, North Haven CT 06473	203-248-2161	R	50*	.2
24	Advance Paper Box Co—*Martin Gardner*	6100 S Gramercy Pl, Los Angeles CA 90047	323-750-2550	R	49*	.3
25	Green Bay Packaging Kalamazoo Container Div—*Tom Herlihy* Green Bay Packaging Inc	PO Box 3007, Kalamazoo MI 49003	269-552-1000	D	43*	.1
26	Lawrence Paper Co—*Justin Hill*	2801 Lakeview Rd, Lawrence KS 66049	785-843-8111	R	43*	.2
27	Lewisburg Container Co—*Anthony Pratt*	PO Box 39, Lewisburg OH 45338	937-962-2681	R	42*	.3
28	Columbia Corrugated Box Company Inc—*Marvin Lince*	12777 Sw Tltin Shrwood, Tualatin OR 97062	503-692-3344	R	42*	.2
29	Ideal Box Co—*Scott Eisen*	4800 S Austin Ave, Chicago IL 60638	708-594-3100	R	41*	.2
30	Marfred Industries—*Marvin Fenster*	PO Box 2048, Sun Valley CA 91353		R	40*	.3
31	Akers Packaging Service Inc—*James Akers*	PO Box 610, Middletown OH 45042	513-422-6312	R	40*	.2
32	Longview Fibre Co Central Container Div Longview Fibre Paper and Packaging Inc	PO Box 639, Longview WA 98632	360-425-1550	D	39*	.2
33	Rand-Whitney Container LLC—*Robert Kraft*	1 Agrand St, Worcester MA 01607	508-791-2301	R	38*	.4
34	Acorn Paper Products Company Inc—*Max Weissberg*	PO Box 23965, Los Angeles CA 90023	323-268-0507	R	38*	.3
35	Bradford Co—*Thomas Bradford*	PO Box 1199, Holland MI 49422	616-399-3000	R	37*	.2
36	Miller Container Corp—*Gerald Van Severen*	PO Box 1130, Milan IL 61264	309-787-6161	R	37*	.3
37	Bell Container Corp—*Irwin Brafman*	PO Box 5728, Newark NJ 07105	973-344-4400	R	37*	.2
38	Doxes Of St Louis Inc—*Michael Patton*	PO Box 790100, Saint Louis MO 63179	314-781-2600	R	36*	.2
39	American River-PackageOne Inc—*Tom Kandris*	4225 Pell Dr, Sacramento CA 95838	916-858-1300	R	36*	.1
40	Key Container Corp—*David Strauss*	PO Box 2370, Pawtucket RI 02861	401-723-2000	R	36*	.2
41	Supplyone Weyers Cave Inc—*William Leith*	PO Box 126, Weyers Cave VA 24486	540-234-9292	R	34*	.1
42	Gabriel Container Co—*Ronald Gabriel*	PO Box 3188, Santa Fe Springs CA 90670	714-541-2897	R	34*	.2
43	Harbor Packaging Inc—*Jim Sorenson*	13100 Danielson St, Poway CA 92064	858-513-1800	R	34*	.2
44	Bay Corrugated Container Inc—*Connie Reuther*	1655 W 7th St, Monroe MI 48161	734-243-5400	R	34*	.2

Note: An asterisk (*) indicates an estimated financial figure. The company type code used is as follows: R = Private, P = Public, S = Private Subsidiary, B = Public Subsidiary, D = Division, J = Joint Venture, I = Investment Fund.

COMPANY RANKINGS BY SALES WITHIN 4-DIGIT SIC

Rank	Company Name—Executive Officer	Address, City, State, Zip	Phone	Type	Fin	Empls
45	Delta Corrugated Paper Products Corp—Walter Lieb	199 W Ruby Ave, Palisades Park NJ 07650	201-941-1910	R	33*	.2
46	H P Neun Company Inc—Michael Hanna	75 N Main St, Fairport NY 14450	585-388-1360	R	32*	.2
47	Kell Holdings Corp—John Kell	PO Box 28, Chippewa Falls WI 54729	715-723-1801	R	32*	.2
48	Advance Packaging Corp—Carol Hoyt	PO Box 888311, Grand Rapids MI 49588	616-949-6610	R	32*	.3
49	Mid-Atlantic Packaging—Andrew Pierson	PO Box 445, Montgomeryville PA 18936	215-362-5100	R	31*	.2
50	Specialty Industries Inc—Carl Cheek	PO Box 330, Red Lion PA 17356	717-246-1661	R	31*	.2
51	Beacon Container Corp—Jerome Grossman	700 W 1st St, Birdsboro PA 19508	610-582-2222	R	30*	.1
52	Integrated Packaging Corporation Inc—Albert D Fuller	122 Quentin Ave, New Brunswick NJ 08901	732-247-5200	R	30*	.1
53	Atlas Container Corp—Paul Centenari	8140 Telegraph Rd, Severn MD 21144	410-551-6300	R	30*	.4
54	Sobel Corrugated Containers Inc—Terry Sobel	18612 Miles Rd, Cleveland OH 44128	216-475-2100	R	30*	.2
55	Pride Container Corp—Benjamin Thompson	4545 W Palmer St, Chicago IL 60639	773-227-6000	R	30*	.2
56	Cano Container Corp—Juventino Cano	3920 Enterprise Ct, Aurora IL 60504	630-585-7500	R	29*	.1
57	Specialized Packaging Radisson LLC—Robert Gariepy	8800 Sixty Rd, Baldwinsville NY 13027	315-638-4355	R	29*	.2
58	Custom Packaging Inc—Jacqueline Cowden	1315 W Baddour Pkwy, Lebanon TN 37087	615-444-6025	R	26*	.2
59	Peachtree Packaging Inc—Wayne Morrison	770 Marathon Pkwy, Lawrenceville GA 30046	770-822-1304	R	26*	.2
60	St Hart Container—Mark Beyma	1901 E Rosslynn Ave, Fullerton CA 92831	714-278-6000	S	25*	.1
61	Harris Packaging Corp—Jana Bickford	PO Box 14437, Haltom City TX 76117	817-429-6262	R	25*	.1
62	Squire Corrugated Container Corp—James Beneroff	PO Box 405, South Plainfield NJ 07080	908-862-9111	R	25*	.1
63	Jones Lumber Company Inc—Brett Jones	PO Box 69, Sandy Hook MS 39478	601-876-2427	R	25*	.2
64	David Weber Company Inc—James Doherty	3500 Richmond St, Philadelphia PA 19134	215-426-3500	R	25*	.1
65	Lone Star Corrugated Container Corp—John Mc Leod	PO Box 177357, Irving TX 75017	972-579-1551	R	24*	.1
66	Sumter Packaging Corp—Ben Desollar	2341 Corporate Way, Sumter SC 29154	803-481-2003	R	24*	.1
67	Ferguson Supply And Box Manufacturing Co—Paige Burgess	10820 Quality Dr, Charlotte NC 28278	704-597-0310	R	23*	.1
68	Corrugated Container Corp—David Higginbotham	PO Box 20369, Roanoke VA 24018	540-774-0500	R	23*	.2
69	Colorado Container Corp—Bruce Kelley	4221 Monaco St, Denver CO 80216	303-331-0400	R	23*	.1
70	Drake Alliance Corp—John Carrico	PO Box 7948, Houston TX 77270	713-869-9121	R	23*	.1
71	New-Tech Packaging Inc—J Heotis	2718 Pershing Ave, Memphis TN 38112	901-324-5553	R	23*	.1
72	High Country Container Inc—Howard Deline	3700 Lima St, Denver CO 80239	303-373-1430	R	23*	.1
73	Bennett Packaging Of Kansas City Inc—Kathy Bennett	220 Nw Space Ctr Cir, Lees Summit MO 64064	816-379-5001	R	23*	.1
74	Dee Paper Company Inc—Jay Dee	100 Broomall St, Chester PA 19013	610-876-9285	R	22*	.1
75	Allpak Container Inc—Wayne Millage	1100 Sw 27th St, Renton WA 98057	425-227-0400	S	22*	.1
76	Great Southern Industries Inc—Charles Ellis	PO Box 5325, Jackson MS 39296	601-948-5700	R	21*	.1
77	Design Packaging Inc—Mark Boyd	6479 Chupp Rd, Lithonia GA 30058	770-482-5012	R	21*	.1
78	American Corrugated Products Inc—Donald Youell	4700 Alkire Rd, Columbus OH 43228	614-870-2000	R	21*	.2
79	Great Lakes Packaging Corp—Glen Arnold	W190n11393 Carnegie Dr, Germantown WI 53022	262-255-2100	R	20*	.1
80	Packaging Services Of Maryland Inc—Vernon Litzinger	16461 Elliott Pkwy, Williamsport MD 21795	301-223-6200	R	20*	.1
81	Mystic Ltd—Todd Thompson	301 Sw 27th St, Renton WA 98057	425-251-5959	R	20*	.1
82	Abex Display Systems Inc—Robbie Blumenfeld	7101 Fair Ave, North Hollywood CA 91605	818-503-0999	R	20*	.1
83	Minnesota Corrugated Box Inc—Richard Krebsbach	PO Box 610, Albert Lea MN 56007	507-373-5006	R	19*	.1
84	Knickerbocker Partition Corp—David Markbreiter	PO Box 3035, Freeport NY 11520	516-546-0550	R	19*	.1
85	Progress Container Corp—Jimmie Johnson	635 Patrick Mill Rd Sw, Winder GA 30680	678-425-2000	R	19*	.1
86	Action Box Company Inc—Terry Malloy	6207 N Houston Rosslyn, Houston TX 77091	713-869-7701	R	18*	.1
87	Thompson Norampac Inc—Peter Brook	PO Box 246, Thompson CT 06277	860-923-9563	R	18*	.1
88	Liberty Container Co—Robert Watts	PO Box 71, South Gate CA 90280	323-564-4211	R	18*	.1
89	Willard Packaging Company Inc—Dana Salkeld	PO Box 27, Gaithersburg MD 20884	301-948-7700	R	18*	.1
90	Northwest Paper Box Manufacturerss Inc—Brad Allen	5617 N Basin Ave, Portland OR 97217	503-240-2800	R	17*	.1
91	Cumberland Container Corp—Eugene Jared	PO Box 250, Monterey TN 38574	931-839-2227	R	17*	.1
92	Shillington Box Company LLC—Dawn Anglin	3501 Tree Ct Industria, Saint Louis MO 63122	636-225-5353	R	16*	.1
93	Lakeway Container Inc—A Jolley	5715 Superior Dr, Morristown TN 37814	423-581-2164	R	16*	.1
94	Ace Packaging Systems Inc—John V Faraci	6400 Poplar Ave, Memphis TN 38197	901-419-9000	D	16*	.2
95	Great Lakes-Triad Plastic Packaging Corp—Brian Burns	3939 36th St Se, Grand Rapids MI 49512	616-241-6441	R	16*	.1
96	Nysco Products LLC—Leonard Applebaum	PO Box 725, Bronx NY 10473	718-792-9000	R	15*	.1
97	Servants Inc—Sharon Montgomery	PO Box 848, Jasper IN 47547	812-634-2201	R	15*	.1
98	Metro Containers Inc—William Akers	4927 Beech St, Cincinnati OH 45212	513-351-6800	R	15*	.1
99	Cooper Container Corp—A Cooper	PO Box 730, Maynardville TN 37807	865-992-5700	R	14*	.1
100	General Fibre Products Corp—James Miller	170 Nassau Terminal Rd, New Hyde Park NY 11040	516-358-7500	R	14*	.1
101	General Container—Tim Black	5450 Dodds Ave, Buena Park CA 90621	714-562-8700	R	13*	.1
102	Commercial Corrugated Corp—John Pauley	PO Box 12099, Baltimore MD 21281	410-522-0900	R	12*	.1
103	Creative Packaging Inc—James Hamilton	175 James St, Worcester MA 01603	508-756-7275	R	12*	.1
104	Tecumseh Packaging Solutions Inc—William Akers	PO Box 427, Tecumseh MI 49286	517-423-2126	R	12*	.1
105	Carton Craft Corp—Louis Reiss	2549 Charlestown Rd St, New Albany IN 47150	812-949-4393	R	11*	.1
106	Chickasaw Container Co—Bud Davis	PO Box 49, Okolona MS 38860	662-447-3759	R	11*	.1
107	Inter-Continental Corp—Mark Radke	PO Box 1119, Conover NC 28613	828-464-8250	R	10*	.1
108	Burlington Rigid Box—Johnny Coffee	PO Box 240, Burlington NC 27216	336-226-1616	D	10*	.1
109	Tavens Container Inc—Richard Ames	22475 Aurora Rd, Bedford OH 44146	216-883-3333	R	10*	<.1
110	Custom Pad And Partition Inc—James Jones	1100 Richard Ave, Santa Clara CA 95050	408-970-9711	R	10*	.1
111	General Die And Die Cutting Inc—Peter Vallone	151 Babylon Tpke, Roosevelt NY 11575	516-623-5071	R	10*	.1
112	RDA Container Corp—Alan Brant	70 Cherry Rd, Gates NY 14624	585-247-2323	R	9*	.1
113	Vail Industries Inc—Robert Vail Jr	49 Ohio St, Navarre OH 44662	330-879-5653	R	9*	.1
114	All-Pak Manufacturing Corp—Don Smith	1221 Jackson St Ste A-, Aurora IL 60505	630-851-5859	R	9*	.1
115	Badger Packaging Corp—Tom Kiekow	2035 Stonebridge Rd, West Bend WI 53095	262-338-4080	R	9*	<.1
116	Accurate Die Cutting Inc—William Alguire	413 Interchange St, Mckinney TX 75071	972-562-7921	R	8*	.1
117	Rudd Container Corp—Darrell Rudd	4600 S Kolin Ave, Chicago IL 60632	773-847-7600	R	8*	<.1
118	Capitol City Container Corp—Richard Purcell	8240 Zionsville Rd, Indianapolis IN 46268	317-875-0290	R	8*	<.1
119	Sample Barn—Jimmy Bowers	PO Box 2017, Calhoun GA 30703	706-629-9003	R	7*	.1
120	Pyramid Paper Products Inc—Tom Binkowski	725 S Mapleton St, Columbus IN 47201	812-372-0288	R	6*	<.1
121	Montgomery Products Ltd—Gary Berman	PO Box 784, Phoenixville PA 19460	610-933-2500	R	6*	<.1
122	Nelson Container Corp—Thomas Nelson	W180n11921 River Ln, Germantown WI 53022	262-250-5000	R	5*	<.1
123	Corrugated Specialties Inc—Paul Henson	PO Box 6385, Fort Smith AR 72906	479-648-3292	R	5*	<.1
124	Dakota Corrugated Box Co—Robert S Bittner	PO Box 1664, Sioux Falls SD 57101	605-332-3501	R	4*	<.1
125	William T Peters LLC—Penny Banaszak	1370 Pineview St, Gaylord MI 49735	989-732-0660	R	2*	<.1
126	Prestige Display And Packaging LLC—Bill Witters	420 Distribution Cir, Fairfield OH 45014	513-285-1040	R	2*	<.1
127	Hugh Edward Sandefur Training Center Inc—F Reed	1449 Corporate Ct, Henderson KY 42420	270-827-2401	R	1*	.1
128	Victory Box Corp—Alex Landy	PO Box 842, Cranford NJ 07016	908-245-5100	R	1*	<.1

TOTALS: SIC 2653 Corrugated & Solid Fiber Boxes

Companies: 128					15,989	45.9

2655 Fiber Cans, Drums & Similar Products

| 1 | Matrix Packaging of Florida Inc—Joseph Artiga | 1001 Brickell Bay Dr, Miami FL 33131 | 305-358-9696 | R | 1,249* | .3 |
| 2 | Newark Paperboard Products | 20 Jackson Dr, Cranford NJ 07016 | 908-276-4000 | D | 800* | 3.2 |

Rank	Company Name—*Executive Officer*	Address, City, State, Zip	Phone	Type	Fin	Empls
3	Precision Paper Tube Co—*Rick Hatton*	1033 S Noel Ave, Wheeling IL 60090	847-537-4250	R	111*	.2
4	New England Paper Tube Company Inc—*Kenneth Douglas*	PO Box 186, Pawtucket RI 02862	401-725-2610	R	33*	.2
5	Schutz Container Systems Inc—*Frederick Wenzel*	PO Box 5950, North Branch NJ 08876	908-526-6161	R	32*	.3
6	Caraustar—*Paul Curtis*	1045 Industrial Park D, Kernersville NC 27284	336-996-4165	S	28	.2
7	Diemolding Corp—*Donald Dew*	125 Rasbach St, Canastota NY 13032	315-697-2221	R	15*	.1
8	Tube-Tainer Inc—*Mike Mundia*	8174 Byron Rd, Whittier CA 90606	562-945-3711	R	12*	<.1
9	Drilltec Technologies Inc—*Bryan Baker*	10875 Kempwood Dr Ste, Houston TX 77043	713-895-9852	R	12*	.1
10	American Spool and Packaging—*Lawrence Ridgeway*	PO Box 2225, Hartsville SC 29551	843-332-3314	R	10*	.1
11	M9 Defense Inc—*Brace Barber*	13110 Ne 177th Pl, Woodinville WA 98072	719-282-8242	R	10*	<.1
12	Crescent Paper Tube Co—*P Seltman*	PO Box 517, Florence KY 41022	859-371-0250	R	8*	.1
13	Sonoco Products Co Industrial Products Div	166 Baldwin Park Blvd, City of Industry CA 91746	626-369-6611	D	7*	.1
14	TJ Assemblies Inc—*Dolores Jarosz*	10349 Franklin Ave, Franklin Park IL 60131	847-671-0060	R	5*	.1
15	CF Maier Composites Inc—*Walter Thurner*	16351 Table Mountain P, Golden CO 80403	303-278-8013	R	3*	.1
16	Louisiana Container Company Inc—*Robert Doolittle*	PO Box 5048, Alexandria LA 71307	318-473-2526	R	2*	<.1

TOTALS: SIC 2655 Fiber Cans, Drums & Similar Products
Companies: 16   2,337   5.0

2656 Sanitary Food Containers

1	Huhtamaki Inc—*Clay Dunn*	9201 Packaging Dr, De Soto KS 66018	913-583-3025	R	25,425*	3.0
2	International Paper Foodservice Business	6400 Poplar Ave, Memphis TN 38197		D	1,094*	2.5
3	Menasha Corp—*James M Kotek*	PO Box 367, Neenah WI 54957	920-751-1000	R	621*	3.2
4	Letica Corp—*Ilija Letica*	PO Box 5005, Rochester MI 48308	248-652-0557	R	243*	1.8
5	Plastirunn Corp—*Jack Elyahouzadeh*	70 Emjay Blvd Bldg A, Brentwood NY 11717	631-273-2626	R	5*	<.1
6	PromoMedia Concepts Inc—*Marc Friedman*	599 11th Ave Fl 3, New York NY 10036	212-265-5431	R	2*	<.1

TOTALS: SIC 2656 Sanitary Food Containers
Companies: 6   27,390   10.5

2657 Folding Paperboard Boxes

1	Graphic Packaging Holding Co—*David W Scheible*	814 Livingston Ct, Marietta GA 30067	770-644-3000	P	4,206	12.3
2	Malnove Inc—*Paul Malnove*	10500 Canada Dr, Jacksonville FL 32218	904-757-5030	R	226*	.6
3	Caraustar Ashland Carton Plant—*Mike Keough*	PO Box 115, Austell GA 30168	770-948-3101	S	155*	.3
4	Dopaco Inc—*Robert Cauffman*	100 Arrandale Blvd, Exton PA 19341	610-269-1776	R	143*	1.3
5	All American Packaging—*Rafael Chagin*	6548 N Glenwood Ave, Chicago IL 60626	773-758-6655	R	80*	<.1
6	Barger Packaging Corp—*M Welch*	2901 Oakland Ave, Elkhart IN 46517	574-389-1860	R	65*	.4
7	Gibraltar Packaging Group Inc—*Walter E Rose*	PO Box 2148, Hastings NE 68902	402-463-1300	R	59*	.3
8	Standard Group Inc—*Steven Levkoff*	75-20 Astoria Blvd Ste, East Elmhurst NY 11370	718-335-5500	R	59*	.3
9	MOD-PAC Corp—*Daniel G Keane*	1801 Elmwood Ave, Buffalo NY 14207	716-873-0640	B	56	.4
10	Flower City Printing Inc—*Wayne Scheible*	PO Box 60680, Rochester NY 14606	585-663-9000	R	55*	.3
11	Los Angeles Paper Box and Board Mills Inc—*William Kewell III*	6027 S Eastern Ave, Commerce CA 90040	323-685-8900	R	53*	.2
12	Colbert Packaging Corp—*James Hamilton*	28355 N Bradley Rd, Lake Forest IL 60045	847-367-5990	R	50*	.2
13	Arkay Packaging Corp—*Mitchell Kaneff*	100 Marcus Blvd Ste 2, Hauppauge NY 11788	631-273-2000	R	44*	.2
14	Burd and Fletcher Co—*John Young*	5151 E Geospace Dr, Independence MO 64056	816-257-0291	R	40*	.4
15	Utah Paper Box Co—*Paul Keyser*	340 W 200 S, Salt Lake City UT 84101	801-363-0093	R	40*	.2
16	Seaboard Folding Box Corp—*Allen Rabinow*	35 Daniels St, Fitchburg MA 01420	978-342-8921	R	39*	.2
17	Bell Inc—*Benjamin Graham*	1411 N D Ave, Sioux Falls SD 57104	605-332-6721	R	38*	.2
18	Royal Paper Box Company Of California—*James Hodges*	PO Box 458, Montebello CA 90640	323-728-7041	R	35*	.2
19	Hub Folding Box Company Inc—*Alfred Dirico*	774 Norfolk St, Mansfield MA 02048	508-339-0005	R	34*	.3
20	Curtis Packaging Corp—*Donald Droppo*	44 Berkshire Rd, Sandy Hook CT 06482	203-426-5861	R	31*	.2
21	Carton Service Inc—*Robert Lederer*	PO Box 702, Shelby OH 44875	419-342-5010	R	29*	.3
22	Midlands Packaging Corp—*Richard Warman*	4641 N 56th St, Lincoln NE 68504	402-464-9124	R	28*	.2
23	Harvard Folding Box Company Inc—*Leon Simkins*	PO Box 327, Lynn MA 01905	781-598-1600	R	27*	.2
24	El Paso Press/Box Inc—*Paul Malooly*	222 N Concepcion St, El Paso TX 79905	915-779-3999	R	26*	.2
25	Sfbc LLC—*Gerald Boudreau*	35 Daniels St, Fitchburg MA 01420	978-342-8921	R	26*	.2
26	Card Pak Inc—*Lisa Thomas*	29601 Solon Rd, Solon OH 44139	440-542-3100	R	25*	.1
27	J and J Packaging Inc—*Augustine Delestrez*	PO Box 127, Sunman IN 47041	812-623-1140	R	21*	.1
28	Boelter Industries Inc—*Dennis Boelter*	PO Box 916, Winona MN 55987	507-452-2315	R	21*	.1
29	Gooby Industries Corp—*Joanna Kagan*	45 Chase St Ste 45, Methuen MA 01844	978-689-0100	R	20*	.1
30	Thoro-Packaging Inc—*Janet Steiner*	1467 Davril Cir, Corona CA 92880	951-278-2100	R	20*	.1
31	Dixie Printing And Packaging LLC—*James Downey*	7354-58 Baltimore Anna, Glen Burnie MD 21061	410-766-1944	R	17*	.1
32	Indiana Carton Company Inc—*David Petty*	PO Box 68, Bremen IN 46506	574-546-3848	R	16*	.1
33	Rice Packaging Inc—*Clifford Rice*	356 Somers Rd, Ellington CT 06029	860-872-8341	R	16*	.1
34	Americraft Carton Inc—*Rick N Johnson*	403 Fillmore Ave E, Saint Paul MN 55107	651-227-6655	R	14*	.1
35	Cartoncraft Inc—*Felipe Reyes*	2900 Dukane Dr Ste 2, Saint Charles IL 60174	630-377-1230	R	12*	.1
36	Johnson Printing And Packaging Corp—*Stu Weitzman*	40 77th Ave Ne, Minneapolis MN 55432	763-571-2000	R	12*	.1
37	Mccowat-Mercer Packaging Inc—*Thomas Betler*	PO Box 818, Jackson TN 38302	731-427-3376	R	11*	.1
38	F and S Carton Co—*Douglas Scranton*	PO Box 8606, Grand Rapids MI 49518	616-538-9400	R	10*	.1
39	Sterling Paper Co—*Martin Stein*	2155 Castor Ave, Philadelphia PA 19134	215-744-5350	R	9*	.1
40	Warneke Paper Box Co—*Stephen Warneke*	4500 Joliet St, Denver CO 80239	303-371-3071	R	8*	.1
41	Ott Packagings Inc—*Bernie Sarsfield*	719 Hwy 522, Selinsgrove PA 17870	570-374-2811	R	7*	.1
42	Economy Folding Box Corp—*J Moos*	2601 S La Salle St, Chicago IL 60616	312-225-2000	R	6*	.1
43	Ohio Valley Cartons Inc—*Charles Guenther*	3670 Werk Rd, Cincinnati OH 45248	513-922-6688	R	4*	<.1
44	Upco Graphics Inc—*Mark Ussery*	2633 Mckinney Ave Ste, Dallas TX 75204	214-634-2882	R	3*	<.1
45	Midvale Paper Box Company Inc—*David Frank*	19 Bailey St, Wilkes Barre PA 18705	570-824-3577	R	2*	<.1

TOTALS: SIC 2657 Folding Paperboard Boxes
Companies: 45   5,895   20.9

2671 Paper Coated & Laminated—Packaging

1	Sealed Air Corp—*William V Hickey*	200 Riverfront Blvd, Elmwood Park NJ 07407	201-791-7600	P	5,641	26.3
2	Bemis Company Inc—*Henry J Theisen*	PO Box 669, Neenah WI 54957	920-727-4100	P	5,323	20.2
3	Bagcraftpapercon III LLC—*Gaby Ajram*	2700 Apple Valley Rd N, Atlanta GA 30319	404-261-7205	R	1,943*	.2
4	Griffon Corp—*Ronald J Kramer*	712 Fifth Ave 18th Fl, New York NY 10019	212-957-5000	P	1,831	5.9
5	Pliant Solutions Corp—*Ronald Artzer* Pliant Corp	10 Greenfield Rd, South Deerfield MA 01373	413-665-2145	S	1,811*	3.0
6	Printpack Inc—*Dennis M Love*	PO Box 43687, Atlanta GA 30336	404-460-7000	R	1,240*	4.4
7	Pliant Corp—*Harold C Bevis*	1475 Woodfield Rd Ste, Schaumburg IL 60173	847-969-3300	R	1,097*	2.9
8	Cello-Foil Products Inc—*Kenneth Lesiow*	155 Brook St, Battle Creek MI 49037	269-964-7137	S	415*	.3
9	Minnesota Mining and Manufacturing Co Electronics Markets Materials Div—*George W Buckley*	3M Center Bldg 223-6S-, Saint Paul MN 55144		D	197*	1.2
10	Pacific Southwest Container LLC—*Sharon Borkowski*	PO Box 3351, Modesto CA 95353	209-526-0444	R	140*	.5

Note: An asterisk (*) indicates an estimated financial figure. The company type code used is as follows: R = Private, P = Public, S = Private Subsidiary, B = Public Subsidiary, D = Division, J = Joint Venture, I = Investment Fund.

COMPANY RANKINGS BY SALES WITHIN 4-DIGIT SIC

Rank	Company Name—*Executive Officer*	Address, City, State, Zip	Phone	Type	Fin	Empls
11	Clear Lam Packaging Inc—*James Sanfilippo*	1950 Pratt Blvd, Elk Grove Village IL 60007	847-439-8570	R	117*	.6
12	Amcor Flexibles Inc—*Peter Brues*	1919 S Butterfield Rd, Mundelein IL 60060	847-362-9000	R	61*	.5
13	Packaging Personified Inc—*Dominic Imburgia*	246 Kehoe Blvd, Carol Stream IL 60188	630-653-1655	R	61*	.2
14	Southern Missouri Containers Inc—*Richard Bachus*	900 N Belcrest Ave, Springfield MO 65802	417-831-2685	R	55*	.3
15	Daubert Industries Inc—*M Lawrence Garman*	1333 Burr Ridge Pky St, Willowbrook IL 60527	630-203-6800	R	54*	.2
16	Bomarko Incorporated Delaware—*Geza Verik*	PO Box 1510, Plymouth IN 46563	574-936-9901	R	50*	.3
17	Worthen Industries Inc	3 E Spit Brook Rd, Nashua NH 03060	603-888-5443	R	50*	.2
18	3M Label Materials	1030 Lake Rd, Medina OH 44256	330-725-1444	D	47*	.1
19	Bedford Industries Inc—*Kim Milbrandt*	PO Box 39, Worthington MN 56187	507-376-4136	R	42*	.3
20	Amgraph Packaging Inc—*Kenneth Fontaine*	PO Box 178, Versailles CT 06383	860-822-8231	R	40*	.1
21	Nordenia USA Inc—*William Burke*	14591 State Hwy 177, Jackson MO 63755	573-335-4900	R	40*	.4
22	Zellwin Farms Co—*Glen Rogers*	PO Box 188, Zellwood FL 32798	407-886-1891	R	35*	.2
23	Bpx Films LP—*Thomas Bryce*	PO Box 18338, Memphis TN 38181	901-369-4414	R	33*	.1
24	Venchurs Inc—*Jeffery Wyatt*	800 Liberty St, Adrian MI 49221	517-263-8937	R	32*	.2
25	Superpac Inc—*Lee Marchetti*	PO Box 189, Southampton PA 18966	215-322-1010	R	32*	.2
26	SGI Integrated Graphic Systems—*Scott D Ready*	14902 Sommermeyer St S, Houston TX 77041	713-744-4100	D	30*	.2
27	Trojan Lithograph Corp—*Hans Koch*	800 Sw 27th St, Renton WA 98057	425-873-2200	R	29*	.2
28	Paperboard Packaging Corp—*Mark Williams*	PO Box 3057, Yuba City CA 95992	530-671-9000	R	28*	.1
29	Hamilton Plastics Inc—*Hershad Shah*	PO Box 16579, Chattanooga TN 37416	423-622-2200	R	26*	.1
30	Stewart Sutherland Inc—*John Stewart*	PO Box 162, Vicksburg MI 49097	269-649-0530	R	25*	.1
31	H S Crocker Company Inc—*Ronald Giordano*	12100 Smith Dr, Huntley IL 60142	847-669-3600	R	23*	.1
32	Adhesive Packaging Specialties Inc—*Stephen Buchanan*	PO Box 31, Peabody MA 01960	978-531-3300	R	22*	.1
33	Vinyl Technology Inc—*Daniel Mullora*	200 Railroad Ave, Monrovia CA 91016	626-443-5257	R	22*	.2
34	Hampden Papers Inc—*Robert Fowler*	PO Box 149, Holyoke MA 01041	413-536-1000	R	22*	.1
35	Fibre Converters Inc—*James Stuck*	PO Box 130, Constantine MI 49042	269-279-1700	R	21*	<.1
36	Nitto Denko America Inc—*Masamichi Takemoto*	48500 Fremont Blvd, Fremont CA 94538	510-445-5400	S	21*	<.1
37	Bollore Inc—*Steve Brunetti*	PO Box 530, Dayville CT 06241	860-774-2930	R	20*	.1
38	Orion Pacific Inc—*J Fowler*	PO Box 4148, Odessa TX 79760	432-332-0058	R	19*	.2
39	ITW Electronic Component Packaging Systems—*Henry Swan*	95 Commerce Dr, Somerset NJ 08873	732-873-5500	S	19*	<.1
40	Audio Video Color Corp—*Moshe Begim*	20550 Denker Ave, Torrance CA 90501	310-533-5811	R	18*	.3
41	CSS Distribution Group—*Mindy Withrow*	10709 Electron Dr, Louisville KY 40299	502-423-1011	R	17*	<.1
42	Miller Technologies International—*Drayton Miller*	3928 Mcgregor Ct, Mobile AL 36608	251-343-9101	R	16*	.2
43	Kennedy Group Inc—*Bertram Kennedy*	38601 Kennedy Pkwy, Willoughby OH 44094	440-951-7660	R	14*	.1
44	J-Pac LLC—*Peter Larocke*	25 Centre Rd, Somersworth NH 03878	603-692-9955	R	14*	.1
45	Tapecon Inc—*Alan Davis*	PO Box 4004, Buffalo NY 14240	716-854-1322	R	13*	.2
46	Stratix Corp—*Bonney Stamper Shuman*	4920 Avalon Ridge Pky, Norcross GA 30071	770-326-7580	R	13*	.1
47	Andex Industries Inc—*John Anthony*	PO Box 887, Escanaba MI 49829	906-786-6070	R	12*	.1
48	Oliver-Tolas Healthcare Packaging Inc—*Gerald Bennish*	905 Pennsylvania Blvd, Feasterville Trevose PA 19053	215-322-7900	S	11*	.2
49	Protect-All Inc—*Tony Trajkovich*	109 Badger Pkwy, Darien WI 53114	262-724-3292	R	10*	.1
50	T and T Graphics Inc—*Todd R Walker*	PO Box 690, Miamisburg OH 45342	937-847-6000	R	10*	.1
51	Tarason Labels Inc—*Kevin McKenna*	PO Box 1207, Conovor NC 28613	828-464-4743	R	10*	<.1
52	Command Plastic Corp—*Richard Ames*	124 W Ave, Tallmadge OH 44278	330-434-3497	R	9*	.1
53	Bryce Johnson Inc—*Ron Purifoy*	PO Box 18707, Memphis TN 38181	901-942-6500	R	9*	.1
54	LF and P Inc—*James Landers*	3560 Lafayette Rd Ste, Portsmouth NH 03801	603-436-6374	R	9*	.1
55	Conductive Containers Inc—*Brad Ahlm*	4500 Quebec Ave N, Minneapolis MN 55428	763-537-2090	R	9*	.1
56	JC Parry and Sons Company Inc—*Beatrice Parry*	1920 Halethorpe Farms, Baltimore MD 21227	410-536-0400	R	8*	.1
57	International Tray Pads and Packaging Inc—*Robert Knorr*	PO Box 307, Aberdeen NC 28315	910-944-1800	R	7*	<.1
58	Norpak Corp—*Anthony Coraci*	70 Blanchard St, Newark NJ 07105	973-589-4200	R	7*	.1
59	Poly Print Inc—*Patrick Genova*	2300 W Wetmore Rd, Tucson AZ 85705	520-792-1061	R	6*	<.1
60	Flextech Packaging Ltd—*Robert Bellafronto*	10095 International Bl, Cincinnati OH 45246	513-874-3600	R	6*	<.1
61	Longhorn Packaging Inc—*Mary Carinhas*	PO Box 8337, San Antonio TX 78208	210-222-9686	R	5*	<.1
62	Vista Graphic Communications LLC—*David Marr*	7915 E 30th St, Indianapolis IN 46219	317-898-2000	R	5*	<.1
63	Package Printing Company Inc—*James Barnhart*	PO Box 378, West Springfield MA 01090	413-736-2748	R	5*	<.1
64	Mason Transparent Package Company Inc—*Richard Cole*	1180 Commerce Ave, Bronx NY 10462	718-792-6000	R	4*	<.1
65	Thermech Corp—*Jim Shah*	1773 W Lincoln Ave Ste, Anaheim CA 92801	714-533-3183	R	3*	<.1
66	Foxon Co—*William Ewing*	PO Box 1178, Providence RI 02901	401-421-2386	R	3*	<.1
67	Truan Family Partnership—*John Wilshire*	900 Dutch Valley Dr, Knoxville TN 37918	865-688-5264	R	3*	<.1
68	TP Franklin Inc—*Gerald Parish*	PO Box 126, Franklin OH 45005	937-743-8818	R	2*	<.1
69	Norman Paper And Foam Company Inc—*Norman Levine*	4501 S Santa Fe Ave, Vernon CA 90058	323-582-6101	R	2*	<.1
70	C Squared Communications Inc—*David F Carver*	PO Box 36, Hood VA 22723	540-948-5245	R	2*	<.1
71	BWE Ltd—*Jannetta Moscovits*	PO Box 652, Republic PA 15475	724-246-0470	R	1*	<.1
72	Life Line Packaging Inc—*Miguel Lackenbacher*	1250 Pierre Way, El Cajon CA 92021	619-444-2737	R	1*	<.1

TOTALS: SIC 2671 Paper Coated & Laminated—Packaging

	Companies: 72				20,974	72.1

2672 Coated & Laminated Paper Nec

Rank	Company Name—*Executive Officer*	Address, City, State, Zip	Phone	Type	Fin	Empls
1	3M Co—*George W Buckley*	PO Box 33121, Saint Paul MN 55133	651-737-6501	P	26,662	80.1
2	GE Plastics—*Charlene Begley*	1 Plastics Ave, Pittsfield MA 01201	413-448-5800	S	6,695*	14.0
3	Intertape Polymer Group (Columbia South Carolina)	2000 S Beltline Blvd, Columbia SC 29201	803-799-8800	D	580*	2.2
4	Computype Inc—*WE Roach*	2285 W County Rd C, Saint Paul MN 55113	651-633-0633	R	230*	.3
5	Morgan Adhesives Co—*Henry J Theisen*	4560 Darrow Rd, Stow OH 44224	330-688-1111	S	227*	.5
6	Kanzaki Specialty Papers Inc—*Stephen Hefner*	1350 Main St, Springfield MA 01103		S	183*	.2
7	Ipg Holdings Inc (Bradenton Florida)—*Dale Sween*	3647 Cortez Rd W Ste 1, Bradenton FL 34210	941-727-5788	S	170*	2.0
8	Shurtape Technologies LLC—*Jim Shuford*	1506 Highland Ave NE, Hickory NC 28601	828-322-2700	R	164*	.9
9	General Formulations Inc	309 S Union Ave, Sparta MI 49345	616-887-7387	R	130*	.2
10	PLC Enterprises Inc—*Burton Koffman*	300 Plz Dr, Vestal NY 13850	607-729-9331	R	126*	.7
11	Discount Labels Inc—*Robert Burton*	PO Box 709, New Albany IN 47151	812-945-2617	S	91*	.1
12	Nashua Label Products	3838 S 108th St, Omaha NE 68144	402-397-3600	D	88*	.3
13	Mohawk Fine Papers Inc—*John Haren*	PO Box 497, Cohoes NY 12047	518-237-1740	R	83*	.7
14	Riverside Paper Corp—*Kevin W Buckley*	PO Box 179, Appleton WI 54912	920-991-2333	R	68*	.4
15	Label Art	1 Riverside Way, Wilton NH 03086		R	65*	.1
16	National Label Co—*James Shacklett*	2025 Joshua Rd, Lafayette Hill PA 19444	610-825-3250	R	58*	.3
17	LeMaitre Vascular Inc—*George W LeMaitre*	63 2nd Ave, Burlington MA 01803	781-221-2266	P	56	.3
18	United Ad Label	300 Lang Blvd, Grand Island NY 14072		D	54	.2
19	Scapa Tapes North America Inc—*Heejae Chae*	111 Great Pond Dr, Windsor CT 06095	860-688-8000	R	48*	.2
20	Oliver-Tolas Healthcare Packaging LLC—*Gerald Bennish*	445 6th St Nw, Grand Rapids MI 49504	616-456-7711	R	45*	.4
21	Atlas Tag and Label Inc—*Mark Bissell*	PO Box 638, Neenah WI 54957	920-722-1557	R	40*	.1
22	Fortifiber Corp—*Stuart Yount*	300 Industrial Dr, Fernley NV 89408	775-333-6400	R	39*	.2
23	Custom Tapes Inc—*Joseph Palmer*	7125 W Gunnison St, Chicago IL 60706	708-867-6060	R	38*	.1
24	Chiyoda America Inc—*John Sato*	378 Thousand Oaks Blvd, Morgantown PA 19543	610-286-3100	R	38*	.1

Rank	Company Name—*Executive Officer*	Address, City, State, Zip	Phone	Type	Fin	Empls
25	Ritrama Inc—*Daryl Hanzal*	800 Kasota Ave Se, Minneapolis MN 55414	612-378-2277	R	38*	.2
26	Light Fabrications Inc—*James Cucinelli*	40 Hytec Cir, Rochester NY 14606	585-426-5330	R	37*	.2
27	Hazen Paper Co—*John Hazen*	PO Box 189, Holyoke MA 01041	413-538-8204	R	36*	.2
28	Timemed Labeling Systems Inc—*Jerry Nerad*	144 Tower Dr, Burr Ridge IL 60527	630-986-1800	S	34*	.2
29	Tesa Tape Inc—*Daniel Germain*	5825 Carnegie Blvd, Charlotte NC 28209	704-554-0707	R	30*	.2
30	Argent International Inc—*Fred Perenic*	41016 Concept Dr, Plymouth MI 48170	734-582-9800	R	30*	.1
31	Adchem Corp—*Joseph Pufahl*	1852 Old Country Rd, Riverhead NY 11901	631-727-6000	R	28*	.1
32	Kdv Label Company Inc—*Richard Vaughn*	PO Box 1006, Waukesha WI 53187	262-544-5891	R	28*	.1
33	Holland Manufacturing Co—*Jack Holland*	PO Box 404, Succasunna NJ 07876	973-584-8141	R	27*	.2
34	Ideal Tape Company Inc	1400 Middlesex St, Lowell MA 01851		S	27	.1
35	Continental Datalabel Inc—*Timothy Flynn*	1855 Fox Ln, Elgin IL 60123	847-742-1600	R	26*	.2
36	Acucote Inc—*John Leath*	PO Box 538, Graham NC 27253	336-578-1800	R	23*	.1
37	Label Systems Inc—*Michael Zubretsky*	56 Cherry St, Bridgeport CT 06605	203-333-5503	R	23*	.2
38	Lamart Corp—*Steven Hirsh*	PO Box 1648, Clifton NJ 07015	973-772-6262	R	21*	.1
39	Dewal Industries Inc—*Eric Walsh*	PO Box 372, Saunderstown RI 02874	401-789-9736	R	20*	.1
40	Seal Methods Inc—*Eugene Welter*	PO Box 2604, Santa Fe Springs CA 90670	562-944-0291	R	18*	.1
41	Budnick Converting Inc—*Ann Wegmann*	PO Box 197, Columbia IL 62236	618-281-8090	R	18*	.1
42	Spinnaker Coating LLC—*Louis A Guzzeti Jr*	518 E Water St, Troy OH 45373	937-332-6500	R	18*	.3
43	Lancer Label Inc—*Rick Fisher*	301 S 74th St, Omaha NE 68114	402-390-9119	R	17*	.2
44	Paper Coating Co—*Todd Yanke*	3536 E Medford St, Los Angeles CA 90063	323-264-2232	R	17*	.1
45	Crowell Corp—*Herbert Adelman*	PO Box 3227, Wilmington DE 19804	302-998-0557	R	17*	.1
46	Westmark Industries Inc—*Michael Offer*	6701 Mcewan Rd, Lake Oswego OR 97035	503-620-0945	R	16*	.1
47	Lofton Label Inc—*Richard Gajewski*	6290 Claude Way, Inver Grove Heights MN 55076	651-457-8118	R	16*	.1
48	Rjm Manufacturing Inc—*Thomas Dodd*	250 Canal Rd, Fairless Hills PA 19030	215-736-3644	R	15*	.1
49	Z-International Inc—*Fritz Zschietzschmann*	PO Box 34767, Kansas City MO 64116	816-474-4455	R	15*	.2
50	Paris Art Label Company Inc—*Ronald Tarantino*	217 River Ave, Patchogue NY 11772	631-648-6200	R	14*	.1
51	Richmark Company Inc—*William Donner*	PO Box 22310, Seattle WA 98122	206-322-8884	R	14*	.1
52	Syracuse Label Company Inc—*Kathleen Alaimo*	110 Luther Ave, Liverpool NY 13088	315-422-1037	R	14*	.1
53	Felix Schoeller North America Inc—*Paul Williamsson-Jon*	PO Box 250, Pulaski NY 13142	315-298-5133	R	12*	.1
54	Breathing Color Inc—*Nick M Friend*	1221 E Dyer Rd Ste 150, Santa Ana CA 92705	714-744-4085	R	12*	<.1
55	Unifoil Corp—*Joseph Funicelli*	12 Daniel Rd, Fairfield NJ 07004	973-244-9900	R	11*	.1
56	Oaklee International Inc—*Leo Lee*	125 Raynor Ave, Ronkonkoma NY 11779	631-436-7900	R	10*	.1
57	Label Aid Systems Inc—*Charles Bashore*	PO Box 550, Madison AL 35758	256-772-9356	R	9*	.1
58	Pallflex Products Co—*Lawrence D Kingsley*	PO Box 929, Putnam CT 06260	860-928-7761	R	9*	<.1
59	Aladdin Label Inc—*John Brunes*	4501 N Sawyer Rd, Oconomowoc WI 53066	262-544-4455	R	9*	.1
60	Shawsheen Rubber Company Inc—*Denis Kelley*	PO Box 4296, Andover MA 01810	978-475-1710	R	9*	.1
61	Tek Pak Inc—*Anthony Beyer*	1336 Paramount Pkwy, Batavia IL 60510	630-406-0560	R	9*	.1
62	Enviro-Cote Inc—*Chris Moffitt*	3380 Gilchrist Rd, Mogadore OH 44260	330-633-4700	R	8*	<.1
63	Brand Label Inc—*F Matlock*	8295 Western Way Cir, Jacksonville FL 32256	904-737-6433	R	8*	<.1
64	Lginternational Inc—*Lon Martin*	6700 Sw Bradbury Ct, Portland OR 97224	503-620-0520	R	8*	<.1
65	Rainier Plywood Co—*Doug Baum*	624 E 15th St, Tacoma WA 98421	253-383-5533	R	7*	<.1
66	Acro Labels Inc—*Robert Regan*	PO Box 444, Abington PA 19001	215-657-5366	R	7*	.1
67	Ample Industrico Ino *David Menzies*	PO Box 394, Nixa MO 65714	417-725-2657	R	6*	<.1
68	Stretchtape Inc—*Alex Mc Donald*	18460 Syracuse Ave, Cleveland OH 44110	216-486-9400	R	6*	<.1
69	Markal Finishing Company Inc—*Craig Sander*	PO Box 3466, Bridgeport CT 06606	203-384-8219	R	6*	<.1
70	Luminer Converting Group Inc—*Thomas Spina*	1925 Swarthmore Ave St, Lakewood NJ 08701	732-886-6557	R	6*	<.1
71	Viking Label And Packaging Inc—*Thomas Wetrosky*	PO Box 10, Nisswa MN 56468	218-963-2575	R	6*	<.1
72	Badger Tag And Label Corp—*Robert Thiel*	PO Box 306, Random Lake WI 53075	920-994-4348	R	5*	<.1
73	Coyne Graphic Finishing Inc—*Kevin Coyne*	1301 Newark Rd, Mount Vernon OH 43050	740-397-6232	R	5*	<.1
74	American Adhesive Coatings LLC—*Edward Krug*	PO Box 1708, Lawrence MA 01842	978-688-7400	R	4*	<.1
75	Opc Packaging Corp—*Thomas Mccaffrey*	320a Perimeter Point B, Winston Salem NC 27105	336-661-3300	R	4*	<.1
76	Buckley Graphics Inc—*Randall Buckley*	4980 Monroe St, Denver CO 80216	303-321-6833	R	4*	<.1
77	Holly Label Company Inc—*John Carr*	72 Hollyhill Dr, Nicholson PA 18446	570-222-9000	R	3*	<.1
78	Laminall Inc—*Jack Klebanow*	19 40 Hazen St, East Elmhurst NY 11370	718-947-3400	R	3*	<.1
79	J C Manufacturing Inc—*Roy Johnston*	506 Townsend Ave, High Point NC 27263	336-861-1666	R	3*	<.1
80	Tape and Label Converters Inc—*Robert Varela*	PO Box 398, Pico Rivera CA 90660	562-945-3486	R	3*	<.1
81	Gaston Systems Inc—*Gary Harris*	200 S Main St, Stanley NC 28164	704-263-6000	R	1*	<.1

TOTALS: SIC 2672 Coated & Laminated Paper Nec

	Companies: 81				36,809	109.6

2673 Bags—Plastics, Laminated & Coated

1	Ampac Holdings LLC—*John Baumann*	12025 Tricon Rd, Cincinnati OH 45246	513-671-1777	R	300*	1.1
2	Bryce Corp—*Thomas J Bryce*	4505 Old Lamar Ave, Memphis TN 38118	901-369-4400	R	279*	.5
3	Omega Plastic Corp—*Alfred Teo*	901 Commerce Cir, Shelbyville KY 40065	502-633-0168	S	150*	1.8
4	Bagcraft Packaging LLC—*Gene Gentili*	3900 W 43rd St, Chicago IL 60632	773-254-8000	S	130*	1.0
5	TGC Industries Inc—*Wayne A Whitener*	101 E Park Blvd Ste 95, Plano TX 75074	972-881-1099	P	108	.8
6	Trinity Packaging Corp—*David Williams*	84 Business Park Dr St, Armonk NY 10504	914-273-4111	R	85*	.7
7	Pacific Pier Inc—*Bijan Pakzad*	1180 Nw Maple St Ste 1, Issaquah WA 98027	425-646-8801	R	60*	<.1
8	Poly Pak America Inc—*Richard Gerwitz*	2939 E Washington Blvd, Los Angeles CA 90023	323-264-2400	R	58*	.1
9	Omega Extruding Co—*Marwan Issac*	9614 Lucas Ranch Rd, Rancho Cucamonga CA 91730	909-941-2800	R	50*	.1
10	Super Sack Bag Inc—*Robert Williamson*	11510 Data Dr, Dallas TX 75218	214-340-7060	R	43*	.6
11	Api Industries Inc—*Reuven Rosenberg*	2 Glenshaw St, Orangeburg NY 10962	845-365-2200	R	42*	.2
12	Wisconsin Film and Bag Inc—*Jack Riopelle*	3100 E Richmond St, Shawano WI 54166	715-524-2565	R	42*	.2
13	Trans Western Polymers Inc—*Stephen Bai*	6909 Las Positas Rd St, Livermore CA 94551	925-449-7800	R	41*	.4
14	Excelsior Packaging Group Inc—*Ronnie Shemesh*	159 Alexander St, Yonkers NY 10701	914-968-1300	R	40*	.2
15	Uniflex Industries Inc—*Rob Cunningham*	1600 Calebs Path Ext, Hauppauge NY 11788	516-932-2000	S	36*	.4
16	Zenith Specialty Bag Company Inc—*Scott Anderson*	PO Box 8445, Rowland Heights CA 91748	626-912-2481	R	35*	.2
17	Mexico Plastic Co—*Carl Fuemmeler*	PO Box 760, Mexico MO 65265	573-581-4128	R	34*	.2
18	Star Packaging Corp—*Michael Wilson*	453 Cir 85 St, College Park GA 30349	404-763-2800	R	32*	.2
19	Crown Poly Inc—*Abraham Simhaee*	5700 Bickett St, Huntington Park CA 90255	323-585-5522	R	30*	.2
20	Sigma Extruding Corp—*Alfred Teo*	PO Box 808, Lyndhurst NJ 07071	201-933-6000	R	29*	.2
21	Aargus Plastics Inc—*Jerome Starr*	540 Allendale Dr Ste A, Wheeling IL 60090	847-325-4444	R	28*	.2
22	Buckeye Boxes Inc—*Craig Hoyt*	601 N Hague Ave, Columbus OH 43204	614-274-8484	R	28*	.1
23	Tara Plastics Corp—*Ollie Wilson*	175 Lake Mirror Rd, Forest Park GA 30297	404-360-4464	R	25*	.1
24	X-L Plastics Inc—*Melvin Fischman*	220 Clifton Blvd, Clifton NJ 07011	973-777-1888	R	24*	.1
25	Bag Makers Inc—*Maribeth Sandford*	6606 S Union Rd, Union IL 60180	815-923-2247	R	23*	.1
26	Plastic Packaging Technologies LLC—*Crystal Romero*	750 S 65th St, Kansas City KS 66111	913-287-3383	R	22*	.1
27	Colormasters LLC—*Ben Fryre*	PO Box 2289, Albertville AL 35950	256-878-8880	R	21*	.1
28	Roplast Industries Inc—*Robert Bateman*	3155 S 5th Ave, Oroville CA 95965	530-532-9500	R	21*	.1

Note: An asterisk (*) indicates an estimated financial figure. The company type code used is as follows: R = Private, P = Public, S = Private Subsidiary, B = Public Subsidiary, D = Division, J = Joint Venture, I = Investment Fund.

COMPANY RANKINGS BY SALES WITHIN 4-DIGIT SIC

Rank	Company Name—Executive Officer	Address, City, State, Zip	Phone	Type	Fin	Empls
29	American Louver Co—Geoffrey Glass	PO Box 206, Skokie IL 60076	847-470-3300	R	20*	.1
30	Colonial Bag Corp—Howard Anderson	205 E Fullerton Ave, Carol Stream IL 60188	630-690-3999	R	19*	.1
31	JM Murray Center Inc—Floyd Moon	823 State Rte 13 Ste 1, Cortland NY 13045	607-756-9913	R	18*	.2
32	Portco Packaging Corp—Macy Wall	3601 SE Columbia Way S, Vancouver WA 98661	360-696-1641	R	15*	.1
33	Webster Industries Inc (Peabody Massachusetts)—James Nichols	PO Box 3119, Peabody MA 01960	978-532-2000	S	15*	.1
34	Accutech Films Inc—William Barga	PO Box 115, Coldwater OH 45828	419-678-8700	R	14*	.1
35	Fisher Container Corp—Donald Fisher	1111 Busch Pkwy, Buffalo Grove IL 60089	847-541-0000	R	14*	.1
36	Kapak Company LLC—Chuck Naynon Ampac Holdings LLC	5305 Parkdale Dr, Minneapolis MN 55416	952-541-0730	S	13*	.1
37	Durabag Company Inc—F Huang	1432 Santa Fe Dr, Tustin CA 92780	714-259-8811	R	13*	.1
38	Plaspack USA Inc—Michael Hunter	PO Box 428, Antigo WI 54409	715-623-4449	R	12*	.1
39	Quality Transparent Bag Inc—Stephen Kessler	PO Box 486, Bay City MI 48707	989-893-3561	R	12*	.1
40	Seal-Tite Plastic Packaging Company Inc—James Black	PO Box 558748, Miami FL 33255	305-264-9015	R	11*	.1
41	All American Arkansas Poly Corp—Jack Klein	309 Phillips Rd, North Little Rock AR 72117	501-945-5763	R	11*	.1
42	Protective Lining Corp—Steven Howard	601 39th St, Brooklyn NY 11232	718-854-3838	R	10*	.1
43	New Wave Converting Inc—Walter Clemmons	14808 Whittram Ave, Fontana CA 92335	909-356-0171	R	10*	<.1
44	Poly Craft Industries Corp—Samuel Brach	12 Franklin St, Brooklyn NY 11222	718-392-3636	R	10*	<.1
45	Clark Container Inc—Larry Chilton	PO Box 160, Lyles TN 37098	931-670-4400	R	10*	.1
46	Houston Poly Bag I Ltd—Judy Adaway	11726 Holderrieth Rd, Tomball TX 77375	281-351-1726	R	9*	.1
47	Fabricon Products Inc—Bruce Dinda	PO Box 18358, River Rouge MI 48218	313-841-8200	R	9*	.1
48	Caltex Plastics Inc—Ruth Rosenfeld	2380 E 51st St, Vernon CA 90058	323-583-4140	R	9*	.1
49	Parish Manufacturing Inc—Gary Smith	7430 New Augusta Rd, Indianapolis IN 46268	317-872-0172	R	9*	<.1
50	Diamond Cellophane Products Inc—Howard Diamond	2855 Shermer Rd, Northbrook IL 60062	847-418-3000	R	9*	.1
51	T-N-T Plastics Inc—Terry Carroll	701 Industrial Dr, Perryville MO 63775	573-547-1051	R	8*	.1
52	Bag Connection Inc—Pete Nelson	459 Sw 9th St, Dundee OR 97115	503-538-8180	R	8*	<.1
53	Waverly Plastics Company Inc—Rose Nieuwenhuyzen	PO Box 801, Waverly IA 50677	319-352-3333	R	8*	<.1
54	M and M Printed Bag Inc—Jeff Taylor	5651 Kimball Ct, Chino CA 91710	909-393-5537	R	8*	<.1
55	Products Resources Inc—Jeff Lukas	8647 W Ogden, Lyons IL 60534		R	7*	<.1
56	Winzen Film Inc—Robert Williamson Super Sack Bag Inc	PO Box 677, Sulphur Springs TX 75483	214-340-7060	S	7*	.1
57	Mohawk Western Plastics Inc—John Mordoff	PO Box 463, La Verne CA 91750	909-593-7547	R	7*	<.1
58	Pexco Packaging Corp—William Buri	PO Box 6540, Toledo OH 43612	419-470-5935	R	7*	<.1
59	Flexwrap Corp—Mark Loeffelman	40 Meta Ln, Lodi NJ 07644	973-777-5877	R	6*	<.1
60	Gemini Plastic Films Corp—Andrew Presto	PO Box 360, Garfield NJ 07026	973-340-0700	R	6*	<.1
61	Bags Inc—Scott Currie	1900 N Sooner Rd, Oklahoma City OK 73141	405-427-5473	R	6*	<.1
62	Basic Plastics Co—Erol Bulur	318 Mclean Blvd Bldg 5, Paterson NJ 07504	973-977-8151	R	5*	<.1
63	Shadow Plastics Inc—Terry Schissel	2301 Pioneer Ave, Rice Lake WI 54868	715-234-9186	R	5*	<.1
64	Plastics R Unique Inc—Kenneth Boersma	352 Mill St, Wadsworth OH 44281	330-334-4820	R	5*	<.1
65	Allied Converters Inc—Richard Ellenbogen	PO Box 548, New Rochelle NY 10802	914-235-1585	R	5*	<.1
66	Ace-Lon Corp—Harry Gentile	PO Box 642, Malden MA 02148	781-322-7121	R	5*	<.1
67	Blue Chip Group Inc—Jacqueline Augason	432 W 3440 S, Salt Lake City UT 84115	801-263-6667	R	4*	<.1
68	Bearse USA—Thomas Auer	3815 W Cortland St, Chicago IL 60647	773-235-8710	R	4*	.1
69	Jumbobag Corp—Jacob Bazbaz	9200 Baythorne Dr, Houston TX 77041	713-460-8545	R	4*	<.1
70	Vac Pac Inc—Hessa Tary	PO Box 6339, Baltimore MD 21230	410-685-5220	R	4*	<.1
71	Laminet Cover Co—Frank Lieber	4900 W Bloomingdale Av, Chicago IL 60639	773-622-6700	R	3*	<.1
72	Bags Unlimited Inc—Michael Macaluso	7 Canal St, Rochester NY 14608	585-436-9006	R	3*	<.1
73	Tdi2 Custom Packaging Inc—Mike Deniger	3400 W Fordham Ave, Santa Ana CA 92704	714-751-6782	R	3*	<.1
74	Monument Industries Inc—Lawrence Amos	PO Box 617, Bennington VT 05201	802-442-8187	R	2*	<.1
75	Ru-Nell Inc—Roy Thompson	PO Box 137, Dallas GA 30132	770-445-2503	R	2*	<.1
76	Plastic Manufacturers Inc—William Seiler	3510 Scotts Ln, Philadelphia PA 19129	215-438-1082	R	1*	<.1
77	Kage Poly Products LLC	96 Elm St, Manchester CT 06040	860-646-8228	R	<1*	<.1

TOTALS: SIC 2673 Bags— Plastics, Laminated & Coated
Companies: 77

                                                2,215   12.6

2674 Bags—Uncoated Paper & Multiwall

Rank	Company Name—Executive Officer	Address, City, State, Zip	Phone	Type	Fin	Empls
1	Exopack LLC—Jack E Knott II	3070 Southport Rd, Spartanburg SC 29302	864-596-7140	R	1,215*	2.2
2	Hood Packaging Corp—Rick Markell	25 Woodgreen Pl, Madison MS 39110	601-853-7260	R	504*	1.0
3	Mid-America Packaging—James Livingston	1793 Enterprise Pkwy, Twinsburg OH 44087	330-425-2700	R	178*	.6
4	Aspen Products Inc—Bill Biggins	4231 Clary Blvd, Kansas City MO 64130	816-921-0234	R	69*	.6
5	Bancroft Bag Inc—Bonnie Woods	PO Box 35807, West Monroe LA 71294	318-387-2550	R	60*	.6
6	Werthan Packaging Inc—Don Belmont	1515 5th Ave N, Nashville TN 37208	615-259-9331	R	58*	.3
7	Home Care Industries Inc—Robert Logemann	1 Lisbon St, Clifton NJ 07013	973-365-1600	R	46*	.3
8	Langston Companies Inc—Robert Langston	PO Box 60, Memphis TN 38101	901-774-4440	R	44*	.4
9	Colonial Bag Company Inc—David Drumheller	1 Ocean Pond Ave, Lake Park GA 31636	229-559-8484	R	41*	.3
10	Gift Box Corporation Of America—Clyde Brownstone	7 W 34th St Ste 1035, New York NY 10001	212-684-5113	R	28*	.2
11	El Dorado Paper Bag Manufacturing Company Inc—Louis Hall	PO Box 1585, El Dorado AR 71731	870-862-4977	R	27*	.2
12	Gateway Packaging Company Of Missouri—Roger Miller	5910 Winner Rd, Kansas City MO 64125	816-214-9605	R	26*	.2
13	Wright Packaging Inc—Mark Mclaughlin	PO Box 1147, Bettendorf IA 52722	563-324-5727	R	21*	.2
14	Dominick Terzuoli—Dominick Terzuoli	163 13th St, Brooklyn NY 11215	718-499-9717	R	19*	.1
15	Brown Paper Goods Co—Allen Mons	3530 Birchwood Dr, Waukegan IL 60085	847-688-1450	R	18*	.1
16	Ross And Wallace Paper Products Inc—Ken Ross	PO Box 2069, Hammond LA 70404	985-345-1321	R	9*	.1
17	DURO Bag Manufacturing Co—Charles Shor	7600 Empire Dr, Florence KY 41042	859-371-2150	R	6*	.1
18	JIT Reshippables—Josh Jones	14970 Berkshire Indust, Middlefield OH 44062	440-834-0727	R	6*	<.1
19	Rtr Packaging Corp—Ron Raznick	27 W 20th St, New York NY 10011	212-620-0011	R	4*	<.1
20	Cempro Inc—Steve Morrely	298 Keystone Dr, Bethlehem PA 18020	610-837-9696	R	3*	<.1

TOTALS: SIC 2674 Bags— Uncoated Paper & Multiwall
Companies: 20

                                                2,382   7.2

2675 Die-Cut Paper & Board

Rank	Company Name—Executive Officer	Address, City, State, Zip	Phone	Type	Fin	Empls
1	Nielsen and Bainbridge—Jack Forbes	40 Eisenhower Dr, Paramus NJ 07653	201-368-9191	R	219*	.9
2	Celeritas Group LLC—Hal Harvey	1250 W 124th Ave, Westminster CO 80234		R	115*	.2
3	Norampac New York City Inc—Marc-Andre Depin	5515 Grand Ave, Maspeth NY 11378	718-386-3200	S	53*	.3
4	Mid Island Die Cutting Corp—Robert Geier	77 Schmitt Blvd, Farmingdale NY 11735	631-293-0180	R	32*	.2
5	MarcomNordic—Deedee Foster	5017 Boone Ave N, New Hope MN 55428	763-535-6440	R	24*	.1
6	Fuller Box Company Inc—Peter Fuller	PO Box 9, North Attleboro MA 02761	508-695-2525	R	24*	.3
7	Bluff Springs Paper Company Ltd—Steve Frank	PO Box 1139, Kosciusko MS 39090	662-289-1022	R	19*	.1
8	Butler Merchandising Solutions Inc—Ken Butler	2233 Delmar Blvd, Saint Louis MO 63103	314-421-3295	R	15*	.1
9	Universal Diecutters Corp—Darrell Paddock	8480 Hwy 66, Wadesville IN 47638	812-985-5942	R	15*	.1
10	Phillips Graphic Finishing Inc—Doug Shelly	150 Arrowhead Dr, Manheim PA 17545	717-653-4565	R	12*	.1

Rank	Company Name—*Executive Officer*	Address, City, State, Zip	Phone	Type	Fin	Empls
11	Elbe-Cesco Inc—*Elliot Comenitz*	PO Box 3160, Fall River MA 02722	508-676-8531	R	10*	.1
12	Apex Die Corp—*Kevin Cullen*	840 Cherry Ln, San Carlos CA 94070	650-592-6350	R	8*	.1
13	Carrollton Specialty Products Co—*Erin Boster*	PO Box 529, Lexington MO 64067	660-542-0021	R	8*	.3
14	Murnane Packaging Corp—*Frank Murnane*	607 NW Ave, Northlake IL 60164	708-449-1200	R	8*	<.1
15	Presentation Folder Inc—*Joseph Tardie*	1130 N Main St, Orange CA 92867	714-289-7000	R	7*	<.1
16	Gfa Decorative Trade Services Inc—*Steven Hannigon*	4209 Folsom Ave, Saint Louis MO 63110	636-349-7700	R	6*	<.1
17	Bindery 1 Inc—*Erazm Rokitnicki*	PO Box 3335, Des Moines IA 50316	515-265-4091	R	6*	<.1
18	Shamrock Die Cutting Company Inc—*Carole Lorenzini*	3020 Meyerloa Ln, Pasadena CA 91107	323-266-4556	R	5*	<.1
19	New England Finishing Inc—*John Coale*	709 Main St, Holyoke MA 01040	413-532-7777	R	5*	<.1
20	Precise Die and Coating Inc—*Frank Barbarino*	9450 Topanga Canyon Bl, Chatsworth CA 91311	818-700-2768	R	5*	<.1
21	Southern Folder and Index Company Incorporated Del—*Dan Byrd*	PO Box 1139, Kosciusko MS 39090	870-863-5184	R	4*	<.1
22	Jacobsen Industries Inc—*Lee Jacobsen*	12173 Market St, Livonia MI 48150	734-591-6111	R	4*	<.1
23	Ross-Gage Inc—*Thomas Ross*	PO Box 8, Indianapolis IN 46206	317-283-2323	R	4*	.1
24	Windsor House Investments Inc—*Carl Price*	3750 Noakes St, Los Angeles CA 90023	323-261-0231	R	4*	<.1
25	Pacific Paper Box Company Inc—*James Faville*	2478 Sw Sherwood Dr, Portland OR 97201	503-248-0256	R	4*	.1
26	W and W Specialities Inc—*Mike Wilburn*	794 Ozark Baptist Ch R, Marietta MS 38856	662-365-5648	R	4*	.1
27	Label Technologies Inc—*Dean Tapp*	1125 Satellit Blvd Nw, Suwanee GA 30024	770-418-9005	R	3*	<.1
28	Amex Die Cutting Service Inc—*Jeanne Martin*	2454 Chico Ave, South El Monte CA 91733	626-579-6800	R	3*	<.1
29	Schwartz Manufacturing Co—*Alessandra Schwartz*	PO Box 328, Two Rivers WI 54241	920-793-1375	R	3*	<.1
30	Hexon Corp—*Abdullah Zubi*	700 E Whitcomb Ave, Madison Heights MI 48071	248-585-7585	R	3*	<.1
31	Accu-Shape Die Cutting Inc—*Preston Means*	4050 Market Pl, Flint MI 48507	810-230-2445	R	2*	<.1

TOTALS: SIC 2675 Die Cut Paper & Board
    Companies: 31   630   3.3

2676 Sanitary Paper Products

1	Attends Healthcare Products—*Michael Fagan*	1029 Old Creek Rd, Greenville NC 27834	252-752-1100	R	644*	.4
2	Hoffmaster Group Inc—*Roderick Leyden*	PO Box 2038, Oshkosh WI 54903	920-235-9330	R	582*	1.3
3	Tambrands Sales Corp—*Wolfgang Berndt*	1 Procter And Gamble P, Cincinnati OH 45202	513-983-1100	R	166*	1.9
4	Whitestone Acquisition Corp—*James Better*	4265 W Vernal Pke, Bloomington IN 47404	812-332-3703	S	56*	.1
5	US Alliance Paper Inc—*John Sarraf*	101 Heartland Blvd, Edgewood NY 11717	631-254-3030	R	45*	.2
6	Rose's Southwest Papers Inc—*Robert Espat*	1701 2nd St Sw, Albuquerque NM 87102	505-842-0134	R	33*	.3
7	Principle Business Enterprises Inc—*Charles Stocking*	PO Box 129, Dunbridge OH 43414	419-352-1551	R	23*	.1
8	Amjems Inc—*Roberto Baspanzuri*	3725 E 10th Ct, Hialeah FL 33013	305-835-8846	R	21*	.2
9	Georgia-Pacific Corp Professional Div—*W Babin*	PO Box 105605, Atlanta GA 30348	404-652-4000	D	18*	.3
10	Keystone Adjustable Cap Company Inc—*Andrew Feinstein*	1591 Hylton Rd Ste B, Pennsauken NJ 08110	856-663-5740	R	14*	<.1
11	Scott Paper Co	351 Phelps Dr, Irving TX 75038	972-281-1200	S	N/A	30.0

TOTALS: SIC 2676 Sanitary Paper Products
    Companies: 11   1,602   34.9

2677 Envelopes

1	Convoo Inc—*Robert G Burton Sr*	1 Canterbury Green 201, Stamford CT 06901	203-595-3000	P	1,909	8.4
2	National Envelope Corp—*Ken Winterhalter*	3211 Internet Blvd Ste, Frisco TX 75034	972-731-1100	R	1,353*	3.0
3	Champion Envelope Corporation-West—*Chris Bowles*	4450 Edison Ave, Chino CA 91710	909-364-1373	R	291*	3.0
4	Quality Park Products—*Robert G Burton Sr* Cenveo Inc	1200 Washington Ave S, Minneapolis MN 55415		S	90	.4
5	Western States Envelope Co—*Mark Lemberger*	PO Box 2048, Milwaukee WI 53201	262-781-5540	R	82*	.8
6	Mackay Mitchell Envelope Company LLC—*Michael Becker*	2100 Elm St Se, Minneapolis MN 55414	612-331-9311	R	75*	.4
7	Oles Envelope Corp—*John Young*	532 E 25th St, Baltimore MD 21218	410-243-1520	R	42*	.2
8	Wisco Envelope Company Inc—*Paul V Reilly*	PO Box 880, Tullahoma TN 37388		R	38*	.3
9	Worcester Envelope Co—*Eldon Pond*	PO Box 406, Auburn MA 01501	508-832-5394	R	36*	.2
10	Envelope 1 Inc—*James Jakubovic*	41969 State Rte 344, Columbiana OH 44408	330-482-3900	R	33*	.2
11	Papercone Corp—*Brooks Bower*	3200 Fern Valley Rd, Louisville KY 40213	502-961-9493	R	30*	.2
12	Colortree Incorporated Of Virginia—*Dennis Whitcomb*	PO Box 28990, Richmond VA 23228	804-358-4245	R	27*	.2
13	Frank G Love Envelopes Inc—*Michael Love*	10733 E Ute St, Tulsa OK 74116	918-836-3535	R	26*	.1
14	Rochester 100 Inc—*Nicholas Sfikas*	PO Box 92801, Rochester NY 14692	585-475-0200	R	23*	.2
15	National Church Supply Company Incorporated Envelope Service—*Rick Cronin*	PO Box 269, Chester WV 26034	304-387-5200	R	19*	<.1
16	Husky Envelope Products Inc—*William Settle*	PO Box 868, Walled Lake MI 48390	248-624-7070	R	15*	.1
17	Envelope Printery Inc—*David Hamilton*	8979 Samuel Barton Dr, Belleville MI 48111	734-398-7700	S	14*	.1
18	Hampton Envelope Co—*Richard Hayes*	200 Hanley Industrial, Saint Louis MO 63144	314-644-1222	R	11*	.1
19	Liberty Envelope Corp—*William Marver*	7550 Corporate Way, Eden Prairie MN 55344	952-975-5050	R	11*	.1
20	United Envelope LLC—*Ravi Pichu*	4890 Spring Grove Ave, Cincinnati OH 45232	513-542-4700	R	10*	.1
21	Envelope Service Inc—*Gary Hilgeman*	7101 Lincoln Pkwy, Fort Wayne IN 46804	260-432-6277	R*	7*	.1
22	Roodhouse Envelope Co—*Gary Randall*	PO Box A, Roodhouse IL 62082	217-589-4321	R	7*	.1
23	Ray Envelope Company Inc—*Chris Hester*	PO Box 19187, Indianapolis IN 46219	317-353-6251	R	7*	<.1
24	Tension Envelope Corp—*William Berkley*	819 E 19th St, Kansas City MO 64108	816-471-3800	R	6*	1.3
25	K C Envelope Company Inc—*Bogdan Wos*	8638 Ne Underground Dr, Kansas City MO 64161	816-455-3980	S	5*	.1
26	Tri-State Envelope Corp—*Joel W Orgler*	20 Market St, Ashland PA 17921	570-875-0433	R	<1	.5

TOTALS: SIC 2677 Envelopes
    Companies: 26   4,164   19.7

2678 Stationery Products

1	JJ Collins Sons Inc—*Jim Collins*	7125 Janes Ave Ste 200, Woodridge IL 60517	630-960-2525	R	77*	.2
2	Top Flight Inc—*E Robinson*	PO Box 927, Chattanooga TN 37401	423-266-8171	R	51*	.3
3	Blumberg Excelsior Inc—*Robert Blumberg*	62 White St, New York NY 10013	212-431-5000	R	45*	.4
4	Roaring Spring Blank Book Co—*Daniel Hoover*	740 Spang St, Roaring Spring PA 16673	814-224-5141	R	41*	.4
5	William Arthur Inc—*Paul Wainman*	PO Box 460, West Kennebunk ME 04094	207-985-6581	R	24*	.3
6	Roselle Paper Company Inc—*Samuel Lefkovits*	PO Box 381, Roselle NJ 07203	908-245-6758	R	22*	.1
7	Cpp International LLC—*Bill Stacks*	PO Box 7525, Charlotte NC 28241	704-588-3190	R	18*	.1
8	All Book Covers Inc—*Ivan Fishman*	1445 S Mcclintock Dr, Tempe AZ 85281	480-966-6283	R	16*	.1
9	Kleer-Fax Inc—*Elias Cruz*	750 New Horizons Blvd, Amityville NY 11701	631-225-1100	S	16*	.1
10	Green Field Paper Co—*Rick Smith*	7196 Clairemont Mesa B, San Diego CA 92111	858-565-2585	R	15*	<.1
11	Mrs Grossman's Paper Co—*Andrea Grossman*	3810 Cypress Dr, Petaluma CA 94954	707-763-1700	R	15*	<.1
12	Quotable Cards Inc—*Gillian Simon*	611 Broadway Ste 615, New York NY 10012	212-420-7552	R	9*	<.1
13	A and W Products Company Inc—*Dennis Broessel*	PO Box B, Port Jervis NY 12771		R	7*	.1
14	National Indexing Systems Inc—*Sheryl Batchelder*	1809 S Division Ave, Orlando FL 32805	407-423-7575	R	7*	<.1
15	Eternal Star Corp—*Hung Choi*	240 W 134th St, Los Angeles CA 90061	310-768-1945	R	5*	<.1
16	Reproducta Company Inc—*Thomas Schulhof*	30 E 33rd St Fl 10, New York NY 10016	212-685-0751	R	4*	<.1

Note: An asterisk (*) indicates an estimated financial figure. The company type code used is as follows: R = Private, P = Public, S = Private Subsidiary, B = Public Subsidiary, D = Division, J = Joint Venture, I = Investment Fund.

COMPANY RANKINGS BY SALES WITHIN 4-DIGIT SIC

Rank	Company Name—*Executive Officer*	Address, City, State, Zip	Phone	Type	Fin	Empls
17	Mbm Industries Inc—*Matthew Studner*	4717 Stenton Ave, Philadelphia PA 19144	215-844-2490	R	4*	<.1
18	Steel City Corp—*Rod Mitchell*	190 N Meridian Rd, Youngstown OH 44509	330-792-7663	R	4*	<.1
19	Acme Graphics Inc—*Jeff Scherrman*	PO Box 1348, Cedar Rapids IA 52406	319-364-0233	R	4*	<.1
20	File-Ez Folder Inc—*Laura Lawton*	PO Box 284, Spokane WA 99210	509-534-1044	R	3*	<.1
21	Memex Books Inc—*Michael Held*	200 Pond Ave, Middlesex NJ 08846	732-752-7220	S	1*	<.1

TOTALS: SIC 2678 Stationery Products
Companies: 21   385   2.3

2679 Converted Paper Products Nec

Rank	Company Name—*Executive Officer*	Address, City, State, Zip	Phone	Type	Fin	Empls
1	Smead Manufacturing Co—*Sharon Hoffman Avent*	600 Smead Blvd, Hastings MN 55033	651-437-4111	R	550*	2.6
2	Amscan Holdings Inc—*Gerald C Rittenberg*	80 Grasslands Rd, Elmsford NY 10523	914-345-2020	R	425*	2.2
3	Glitterwrap Inc—*Alfred Scott*	701 Ford Rd Ste 1, Rockaway NJ 07866	973-625-4200	R	307*	.1
4	AMCOR Sunclipse—*Eric Bloom*	6600 Valley View St, Buena Park CA 90620	714-562-6000	R	297*	2.0
5	Nashua Corp—*Thomas Brooker*	3838 South 108th St, Omaha NE 68144		S	265	.7
6	W/S Packaging Group Inc—*Terrence Fulwiler*	PO Box 127, Algoma WI 54201	920-866-6300	R	211*	2.0
7	Cleo Inc—*Andrew Kelly*	4025 Viscount Ave, Memphis TN 38118	901-369-6300	S	160	1.0
8	Shore To Shore Inc—*Howard Kurdin*	8170 Washington Villag, Dayton OH 45458	937-866-1908	R	133*	1.7
9	Tufco Technologies Inc—*Jim Robinson*	PO Box 23500, Green Bay WI 54305	920-336-0054	P	110	.3
10	Southern States Packaging Co—*Michael Lyon*	PO Box 650, Spartanburg SC 29304	864-579-3911	R	74*	.1
11	Caraustar Saint Paris—*Norman Pfeifer*	5000 Austell-Powder Sp, Austell GA 30106	937-663-4142	S	62*	.2
12	Compac Corp—*Carl Allieri*	103 Bilby Rd, Hackettstown NJ 07840		R	62*	.1
13	OMNOVA Wallcovering Inc—*Kevin McMullen*	175 Ghent Rd, Fairlawn OH 44333	330-869-4200	S	57*	.1
14	Ecological Fibers Inc—*Stephen F Quill*	40 Pioneer Dr, Lunenburg MA 01462	978-537-0003	R	51*	.2
15	Eco-Products Inc—*Michael Hastings*	4755 Walnut St, Boulder CO 80301	303-449-1876	R	49*	.1
16	Pacon Corp—*James Schmitz*	PO Box 7170, Appleton WI 54912	920-830-5050	R	44*	.2
17	Progressive Converting Inc—*Dan Curtin*	2430 E Glendale Ave, Appleton WI 54911	920-832-8844	R	41*	.2
18	Sullivan Paper Company Inc—*Richard Sullivan*	PO Box 88, West Springfield MA 01090	413-734-3107	R	41*	.3
19	Paper Systems Inc—*Lawrence Curk*	PO Box 150, Springboro OH 45066	937-746-6841	R	41*	.2
20	Pmco LLC—*Mike Webster*	9220 Glades Dr, Hamilton OH 45011	513-825-7626	R	40*	.1
21	Gateway Packaging Co—*Roger Miller*	20 Central Industrial, Granite City IL 62040	618-451-0010	R	38*	.2
22	Crescent Cardboard Company LLC—*C Ozmun*	100 W Willow Rd, Wheeling IL 60090	847-537-3400	R	35*	.2
23	Gordon Paper Company Inc—*Tavia Gordon*	PO Box 1806, Norfolk VA 23501	757-464-3581	R	35*	.1
24	TAPEMARK Company Inc—*Robert C Klas Jr*	1685 Marthaler Ln, West Saint Paul MN 55118	651-455-1611	R	29*	.2
25	FDS Manufacturing Co—*Robert Stevenson*	PO Box 3120, Pomona CA 91769	909-591-1733	R	26*	.2
26	Arkwright Advanced Coating Inc—*Phillip Hursh*	PO Box 139, Fiskeville RI 02823	401-821-1000	R	25*	.1
27	Panelfold Inc—*Guy Dixon*	PO Box 680130, Miami FL 33168	305-688-3501	R	25*	.2
28	Hub Labels Inc—*Abbud Dahbura*	18223 Shawley Dr, Hagerstown MD 21740	301-790-1660	R	24*	.2
29	Extra Packing Corp—*Gerald S Kramer*	631 Golden Harbour Dr, Boca Raton FL 33432	561-416-2060	R	24*	<.1
30	Marking Services Inc—*Jeff Dickinson*	PO Box 240027, Milwaukee WI 53224	414-973-1331	R	22*	.1
31	Admore Inc—*Bill Tignanelly*	24707 Wood Ct, Macomb MI 48042		S	22*	.2
32	Jacobson Hat Company Inc—*Howard Jacobson*	PO Box 1429, Scranton PA 18501	570-342-7887	R	21*	.1
33	Kadant AES—*Jonathan W Painter*	35 Sword St, Auburn MA 01501	518-793-8801	D	21*	.1
34	Mbw Inc—*James Jones*	184 Gov Dukakis Dr, Orange MA 01364	978-544-6462	R	19*	.1
35	Gardei Industries LLC	1087 Erie Ave, North Tonawanda NY 14120	716-693-7100	R	19*	<.1
36	Brooklace Inc—*Charles Foster*	PO Box 2038, Oshkosh WI 54903	203-937-4555	R	18*	.1
37	Wise Tag and Label Company Inc—*W Wise*	7035 Central Hwy, Pennsauken NJ 08109	856-663-2400	R	17*	.1
38	Phenix Label Company Inc—*Hans Peter*	11610 S Alden St, Olathe KS 66062	913-327-7000	R	17*	.1
39	Canson Inc—*Kevin Kelley*	PO Box 220, South Hadley MA 01075	413-538-9250	R	16*	.1
40	Interstate Paper Supply Company Inc—*Bart Raitano*	PO Box 670, Roscoe PA 15477	724-938-2218	R	16*	.1
41	Tag Allen-Bailey and Label Inc—*Eugene Tonucci*	PO Box 123, Caledonia NY 14423	585-538-2324	R	16*	.1
42	Deltapaper Corp—*Bill Bregman*	8295 National Hwy, Pennsauken NJ 08110	215-547-6000	R	15*	<.1
43	Kent Adhesive Products Co—*Edward Small*	PO Box 626, Kent OH 44240	330-678-1626	R	15*	.1
44	Pap-R Products Co—*Scott Ware*	PO Box N, Martinsville IL 62442	217-382-4141	R	14*	.1
45	Fine Impressions Inc—*Mike Schmidt*	1680 Roe Crest Dr, North Mankato MN 56003	507-625-4355	R	14*	.1
46	Hooven - Dayton Corp—*Christopher Che*	8060 Technology Blvd, Dayton OH 45424	937-233-4473	R	14*	.1
47	Mid-York Press Inc—*Michael Janitz*	PO Box 733, Sherburne NY 13460	607-674-4491	R	13*	.1
48	PC I Paper Conversions Inc—*Lloyd Withers*	6761 Thompson Rd, Syracuse NY 13211	315-437-1641	R	13*	.1
49	Bro Tex Company Inc—*Roger Greenberg*	800 Hampden Ave, St Paul MN 55114	651-645-5721	R	13*	.1
50	Epsen Hillmer Graphics Co—*Thomas Hillmer*	13748 F St, Omaha NE 68137	402-342-7000	R	13*	.1
51	Setterstix Corp—*Frederick Rossetti*	261 S Main St, Cattaraugus NY 14719	716-257-3451	R	13*	.1
52	Quality Circle Products Inc—*Gary Flaum*	PO Box 36, Montrose NY 10548	914-736-6600	R	11*	.1
53	Daret Inc—*Stephanie Muth*	33 Daret Dr, Ringwood NJ 07456	973-962-6001	R	10*	.1
54	Newco Inc—*James Berezny*	PO Box 836, Butler NJ 07405	973-383-7777	R	9*	.1
55	R and D Sleeves LLC—*Randy Barden*	PO Box 460, Plymouth FL 32768	407-886-9010	R	8*	<.1
56	Cortec Group Inc—*R Scott Schafler*	200 Park Ave, New York NY 10166	212-370-5600	R	7*	<.1
57	Lewis Label Products Corp—*Gibson Lewis*	2300 Race St, Fort Worth TX 76111	817-834-7334	R	6*	<.1
58	C L Downey Co—*Barry Blue*	PO Box 857, Hannibal MO 63401	573-221-8250	R	6*	.1
59	Kardol Quality Products LLC—*Eric Kahn*	285 S W St, Lebanon OH 45036	513-933-8206	R	6*	.1
60	Drummond Printing Inc—*Amberlea Barnes*	2114 S Main St, Stuttgart AR 72160	870-673-2726	R	6*	.1
61	Laminated Industries Inc—*Chaim Schvimmer*	2000 Brunswick Ave, Linden NJ 07036	908-862-5995	R	5*	<.1
62	Columbia Sales Inc—*John Palmer*	2233 Warwood Ave, Wheeling WV 26003	304-277-2233	R	5*	<.1
63	Carpet Rentals Inc—*A Gardner*	PO Box 5386, Statesville NC 28687	704-872-4461	R	5*	<.1
64	Fidelity Paper Supply Inc—*Pierre Guariglia*	PO Box 376, East Hanover NJ 07936	973-599-0222	R	5*	<.1
65	Parti Line International—*Ronee Holmes*	706 Royal St, New Orleans LA 70116	504-522-0300	R	4*	<.1
66	Plastic Tubing Industries Inc—*Michael Maroschak*	PO Box 607356, Orlando FL 32860	407-298-5121	R	4*	<.1
67	East-West Label Company Inc—*Christopher Wilson*	PO Box 306, Conshohocken PA 19428	610-825-0410	R	4*	<.1
68	Bryant Label Company Inc—*James Bryant*	2240 Hwy 75, Blountville TN 37617	423-323-5440	R	3*	<.1
69	Label Printing Systems Inc—*Greg Ebert*	3937 Westpoint Blvd, Winston Salem NC 27103	336-760-3271	R	13*	<.1
70	Wet-N-Stick LLC—*Lee Goldman*	2816 Morris Ave, Union NJ 07083	908-687-8273	R	3	<.1
71	Hartman Plastics Inc—*Robert Hartman*	373 Poplar Rd, Honey Brook PA 19344	610-273-7113	R	2*	<.1
72	Col-Tab Inc—*Denise Dowless*	PO Box 14928, Portland OR 97293	503-233-2248	R	2*	<.1
73	Labelcraft USA Inc—*Charles Schoenbachler*	PO Box 37205, Louisville KY 40233	502-454-4617	R	2*	<.1
74	Fritz Ken Tooling and Design Inc—*Kenneth Fritz*	PO Box 70, Petersburg VA 23804	804-862-4155	R	2*	<.1
75	Andrews Steel Rule Die Company Inc—*Thomas Andrews*	707 E 47th St, La Grange IL 60525	708-352-2555	R	2*	<.1
76	Cellu Tissue Holdings Inc—*Russ Taylor*	249 N Lake St, Neenah WI 54956	920-727-3913	R	2*	<.1
77	Veco Printing Inc—*Clive Roe*	3202 W Expy 83, Weslaco TX 78596	956-968-1589	R	1*	<.1
78	Aigner Index Inc—*Mark Aigner*	218 Mac Arthur Ave, New Windsor NY 12553	845-562-4510	R	1*	<.1
79	Freedom Industries Inc (Tullahoma Tennessee)—*Dale Ward*	1400 S Washington St, Tullahoma TN 37388	931-461-5125	R	1*	<.1
80	Flutter Fetti Fun Factory—*Ronee Homes* Parti Line International	9219 133rd Ave Unit 1E, Largo FL 33773	504-522-0300	D	1*	<.1

Rank	Company Name—*Executive Officer*	Address, City, State, Zip	Phone	Type	Fin	Empls
81	Party Time Manufacturing Co—*James Rosentel*	PO Box 447, Pittston PA 18640	570-655-1689	R	1*	<.1
82	A Bar Code Business Inc—*Steven Belford*	702 Duck Lake Rd Ste 1, Lady Lake FL 32159	352-750-0077	R	1*	<.1

TOTALS: SIC 2679 Converted Paper Products Nec
Companies: 82 — — — — 3,768 18.5

2711 Newspapers

Rank	Company Name—*Executive Officer*	Address, City, State, Zip	Phone	Type	Fin	Empls
1	News Corp—*Rupert Murdoch*	1211 Ave of the Americ, New York NY 10036	212-852-7000	P	33,405	51.0
2	Cox Enterprises Inc—*Jimmy W Hayes*	PO Box 105357, Atlanta GA 30348	678-645-0000	R	11,234*	50.0
3	Tribune Company Holdings Inc—*Gil Thelen*	PO Box 191, Tampa FL 33601	813-259-8225	S	8,157*	7.2
4	Advance Publications Inc—*Steven Newhouse*	4 Times Sq, New York NY 10036	718-981-1234	R	6,841*	26.0
5	Montgomery Media—*Wesley Rowe* Journal Register Co	6220 Ridge Ave, Philadelphia PA 19128	215-483-7300	S	6,001*	4.7
6	Gannett Company Inc—*Craig A Dubow*	7950 Jones Branch Dr, McLean VA 22107	703-854-6000	P	5,439	32.6
7	Tribune Co—*Eddy Hartenstein*	435 N Michigan Ave, Chicago IL 60611	312-222-9100	R	5,063*	19.6
8	Hearst Corp—*Frank A Bennack Jr*	1345 Ave of the Americ, New York NY 10105	212-649-2000	R	4,875*	22.0
9	Washington Post Co—*Donald E Graham*	1150 15th St NW, Washington DC 20071	202-334-6000	P	4,215	18.0
10	Newsday Inc—*Terry Jimenez* Tribune Co	235 Pinelawn Rd, Melville NY 11747	631-843-2175	S	4,092*	3.2
11	Morris Multimedia Inc—*Charles Morris*	27 Abercorn St, Savannah GA 31401	912-233-1281	R	3,926*	1.0
12	New York Times Co—*Arthur O Sulzberger Jr*	620 8th Ave, New York NY 10018	212-556-1234	P	2,323	7.3
13	Baltimore Sun Co Tribune Co	PO Box 1377, Baltimore MD 21278	410-332-6000	S	2,027*	2.0
14	Newspapers Of New England Inc—*George Wilson*	PO Box 1177, Concord NH 03302	603-224-5301	R	1,958*	.4
15	St Louis Post-Dispatch LLC—*Kevin Mowbray* Lee Enterprises Inc	900 N Tucker Blvd, Saint Louis MO 63101	314-340-8000	S	1,790*	1.4
16	Dow Jones and Company Inc—*Les Hinton* News Corp	1211 Ave of the Americ, New York NY 10036	212-416-2000	S	1,784*	7.4
17	American City Business Journals Inc—*Whitney Shaw* Advance Publications Inc	120 W Morehead St Ste, Charlotte NC 28202	704-973-1000	S	1,538*	1.8
18	Asbury Park Press Inc—*Thomas Donovan* Gannett Company Inc	Box 1550, Neptune NJ 07754	732-922-6000	S	1,538*	1.5
19	Miami Herald Publishing Co—*David Landsberg* McClatchy Co	1 Herald Plz, Miami FL 33132	305-350-2111	S	1,148*	2.4
20	Times Publishing Co—*Paul C Tash*	PO Box 1121, Saint Petersburg FL 33731	727-893-8111	R	1,104*	1.0
21	MediaNews Group Inc—*John Paton*	101 W Colfax Ave Ste 1, Denver CO 80202	303-954-6360	R	1,051*	12.7
22	McClatchy Co—*Gary B Pruitt*	2100 Q St, Sacramento CA 95816	916-321-1855	P	1,050	8.5
23	Orlando Sentinel Communications Co—*Kathleen Waltz* Tribune Co	633 N Orange Ave, Orlando FL 32801	407-420-5000	D	990*	.9
24	Register Company Inc	790 Township Line Rd, Yardley PA 19067	215-504-4200	S	938	N/A
25	Worcester Telegram and Gazette—*Bruce Gaultney* New York Times Co	PO Box 15012, Worcester MA 01615	508-793-9100	S	821*	.8
26	Central Newspapers Inc—*Douglas H McCorkindale* Gannett Company Inc	PO Box 1950, Phoenix AZ 85001	602-444-8000	S	805	5.0
27	Schurz Communications Inc—*Todd F Schurz*	1301 E Douglas Rd, Mishawaka IN 46545	574-247-7237	R	793*	2.9
28	EW Scripps Co—*Richard A Boehne*	312 Walnut St 2800 Scr, Cincinnati OH 45202	513-977-3000	P	777	4.6
29	Lee Enterprises Inc—*Mary E Junck*	201 N Harrison St, Davenport IA 52801	563-383-2100	P	756	6.2
30	Landmark Media Enterprises—*Frank Batten Jr*	PO Box 449, Norfolk VA 23501	757-446-2010	R	733*	5.0
31	Media General Inc—*Marshall N Morton*	PO Box 85333, Richmond VA 23293	804-649-6000	P	678	4.7
32	Star Publishing Co—*Mary F Junck* Lee Enterprises Inc	926 P St, Lincoln NE 68508	402-475-4200	S	641*	.5
33	Freedom Communications Inc—*Mitchell Stern*	17666 Fitch, Irvine CA 92614	949-253-2300	R	597*	5.2
34	GateHouse Media Inc—*Michael E Reed*	350 Willowbrook Office, Fairport NY 14450	585-598-0030	B	559	5.2
35	Morris Communications Company LLC—*William S Morris*	725 Broad St, Augusta GA 30901	706-724-0851	R	534*	6.0
36	Copley Press Inc—*David C Copley*	7776 Ivanhoe Ave, La Jolla CA 92037	858-454-0411	R	530*	3.5
37	Galveston Newspapers Inc—*Martha Walls*	PO Box 628, Galveston TX 77553	409-683-5200	R	527*	.7
38	Suburban Journal Newspapers—*Robert Jelenio* Journal Register Co	1714 Deer Tracks Trl, Saint Louis MO 63131	314-821-1110	S	526*	6.0
39	Dispatch Printing Co—*Mike Curtin*	34 S 3rd St, Columbus OH 43215	614-461-5000	R	488*	2.1
40	AH Belo Corp—*Robert W Decherd*	PO Box 224866, Dallas TX 75222	214-977-8200	B	487	2.5
41	Saint Paul Pioneer Press—*Guy Gilmore* MediaNews Group Inc	345 Cedar St, Saint Paul MN 55101	651-222-1111	S	486*	.9
42	Sun-Sentinel Co—*Bob Gremillin* Tribune Co	200 E Las Olas Blvd, Fort Lauderdale FL 33301	954-356-4000	S	466*	1.5
43	Southern Connecticut Newspapers Inc—*Mark Aldamm* Hearst Corp	1455 E Putnam Ave, Old Greenwich CT 06870	203-625-4400	S	465*	.5
44	Journal Register Co—*John Paton*	790 Township Line Rd 3, Yardley PA 19067	215-504-4200	R	463*	4.5
45	Iowa Newspapers Inc—*Joe Craig* Omaha World-Herald Co	317 5th St, Ames IA 50010	515-232-2160	S	436*	.2
46	Des Moines Register and Tribune Co—*Laura Hollingsworth* Gannett Company Inc	PO Box 957, Des Moines IA 50304	515-284-8000	S	428*	1.0
47	Fort Wayne Newspapers—*Michael J Christman*	PO Box 100, Fort Wayne IN 46801	260-461-8324	R	425*	.4
48	Community Newspaper Holdings Inc—*Donna Barrett*	445 Dexter Ave Ste 700, Montgomery AL 36104	334-293-5800	R	383*	6.5
49	Journal Communications Inc—*Steven J Smith*	PO Box 661, Milwaukee WI 53201	414-224-2000	P	377	2.2
50	Denver Newspaper Agency LLP—*Jerry Grilly* EW Scripps Co	PO Box 719, Denver CO 80201	303-892-5000	S	368*	2.4
51	Delaware Gazette—*Gary Merrell*	18 E William St, Delaware OH 43015	740-363-1161	S	367	.2
52	Forum Communications Co—*Lloyd Case*	PO Box 2020, Fargo ND 58107	701-451-5629	R	360*	.4
53	Pantagraph Publishing Co—*Henry Bird* Lee Enterprises Inc	PO Box 2907, Bloomington IL 61702	309-829-9000	S	358*	.3
54	Phoenix Newspapers Inc—*Kara Ritter* Gannett Company Inc	200 E Van Buren St, Phoenix AZ 85004	602-444-8000	S	357*	3.3
55	Caller-Times Publishing Co—*Libby Averyt*	PO Box 9136, Corpus Christi TX 78469	361-884-2011	R	349*	.4
56	Sun-Times Media Holdings LLC—*Jeremy L Halbreich*	350 N Orleans, Chicago IL 60654	312-321-3230	R	324	2.3
57	Dallas Morning News Inc—*James Moroney III* AH Belo Corp	508 Young St, Dallas TX 75202	214-977-8222	S	314	.3
58	Dolan Co—*James P Dolan*	222 S 9th St Ste 2300, Minneapolis MN 55402	612-317-9420	P	311	2.0
59	Columbus Ledger Enquirer—*Valerie Canepa* McClatchy Co	PO Box 711, Columbus GA 31902	706-571-8565	S	310*	.3
60	Star Tribune Co—*Par Ridder*	425 Portland Ave S, Minneapolis MN 55415	612-673-4000	S	280*	2.9

Note: An asterisk (*) indicates an estimated financial figure. The company type code used is as follows: R = Private, P = Public, S = Private Subsidiary, B = Public Subsidiary, D = Division, J = Joint Venture, I = Investment Fund.

COMPANY RANKINGS BY SALES WITHIN 4-DIGIT SIC

Rank	Company Name—*Executive Officer*	Address, City, State, Zip	Phone	Type	Fin	Empls
	McClatchy Co					
61	Chicago Sun-Times—*John Barron*	350 N Orleans, Chicago IL 60654	312-321-3000	S	266*	1.2
	Sun-Times Media Holdings LLC					
62	Ogden Newspapers Inc—*Robert Nutting*	1500 Main St, Wheeling WV 26003	304-233-0100	R	258*	.3
63	Wooster Daily Record Inc—*R Victor Dix*	212 E Liberty St, Wooster OH 44691	330-264-1125	S	254*	.2
64	Greater Media Inc—*Peter H Smyth*	35 Braintree Hill Pk S, Braintree MA 02184	781-348-8600	R	250*	1.5
65	Star-Telegram Newspaper Inc—*Wes Turner*	PO Box 1870, Fort Worth TX 76101	817-390-7400	S	229*	1.6
	McClatchy Co					
66	Herald Media Inc—*Patrick J Purcell*	1 Harold Square, Boston MA 02118	617-426-3000	R	224*	1.8
67	Stockton Newspapers Inc—*Roger Coover*	PO Box 900, Stockton CA 95201	209-546-8240	R	219*	.4
68	Antelope Valley Newspapers Inc—*William C Markham*	PO Box 4050, Palmdale CA 93590	661-273-2700	R	206*	.2
69	North Jersey Media Group Inc—*Stephen Borg*	150 River St, Hackensack NJ 07601	201-646-4000	R	202*	1.9
70	Boston Globe—*Christopher Mayer*	PO Box 55819, Boston MA 02205	617-929-2000	S	201*	2.2
	New York Times Co					
71	Detroit Media Partnership LP—*Rich Harshbarger*	615 W Lafayette Blvd, Detroit MI 48226	313-222-6500	S	185*	2.0
	Gannett Company Inc					
72	Kansas City Star Co—*Mac Tully*	1729 Grand Blvd, Kansas City MO 64108	816-234-4636	S	185	2.0
73	Philadelphia Newspapers Inc—*Kevin Donahue*	PO Box 8263, Philadelphia PA 19101		R	185	2.0
74	Moline Dispatch Publishing Co—*Kurt Allemeier*	1720 5th Ave, Moline IL 61265	309-764-4344	R	181*	1.0
75	Philadelphia Media Holdings LLC—*Gregory Osberg*	PO Box 13942, Philadelphia PA 19101	215-854-2000	R	180*	3.1
76	Diocese Of Camden New Jersey—*Curtis Johnson*	631 Market St, Camden NJ 08102	856-756-7900	R	178*	3.0
77	Chronicle Publishing Co (San Francisco California)—*Frank Vega*	901 Mission St, San Francisco CA 94103	415-777-1111	S	176	2.7
78	Lawrence Journal-World Co—*Dolph C Simons Jr*	PO Box 888, Lawrence KS 66044	785-843-1000	R	166*	.6
79	Lozano Enterprises Inc—*James Schumacher*	700 S Flower St 30th F, Los Angeles CA 90017	213-622-8332	R	165*	.6
80	Santa Cruz Sentinel Publishers—*Michael Turpin*	1800 Green Hills Rd St, Scotts Valley CA 95066	831-423-4242	D	155*	.2
	Dow Jones and Company Inc					
81	Auburn Journal Inc	PO Box 5910, Auburn CA 95604	530-885-5656	S	153*	.2
82	California Newspapers Partnership—*Don Borut*	PO Box 1259, Covina CA 91722	626-962-8811	R	145*	2.9
83	Globe Newspaper Company Inc—*Steven Ainsley*	PO Box 55819, Boston MA 02205	617-929-2000	R	144*	2.3
84	Macon Telegraph—*George McCanless*	PO Box 4167, Macon GA 31208	478-744-4200	S	144*	.3
	McClatchy Co					
85	Star Tribune Media Company LLC—*Kristie Alberty*	425 Portland Ave, Minneapolis MN 55488	612-673-4000	R	142*	2.7
86	Daily Racing Form LLC—*Brent Diamond*	100 Broadway 7th Fl, New York NY 10005	212-366-7600	S	139*	.1
87	WEHCO Media Inc—*Walter E Hussman Jr*	PO Box 2221, Little Rock AR 72203	501-378-3400	R	128*	.1
88	Detroit Free Press—*David Hunke*	600 W Fort St, Detroit MI 48226	313-222-6400	D	127*	.3
	Gannett Company Inc					
89	Pawtucket Times—*Dan Trafford*	PO Box 307, Pawtucket RI 02862	401-722-4000	S	117*	.1
	Journal Register Co					
90	Omaha World-Herald Co—*Terry Kroeger*	1314 Douglas St, Omaha NE 68102	402-444-1000	R	117*	2.3
91	Virginia Gazette Companies LLC—*WC O'Donovan*	216 Ironbound Rd, Williamsburg VA 23188	757-220-1736	S	116*	.1
	Daily Press Inc					
92	Saratogian LLC—*Michael F O'Sullivan*	20 Lake Ave, Saratoga Springs NY 12866	518-584-4242	S	115*	.1
	Journal Register Co					
93	St Louis Post-Dispatch	900 N Tucker Blvd, Saint Louis MO 63101	314-340-8000	S	111*	1.0
	Lee Enterprises Inc					
94	Durango Herald Inc—*Richard Ballantine*	PO Drawer A-0950, Durango CO 81301	970-247-3504	R	111*	.1
95	Contra Costa Newspapers Inc	2640 Shadelands Dr, Walnut Creek CA 94598	925-935-2525	S	110*	1.5
	MediaNews Group Inc					
96	Post Gazette Publishing Co—*John R Block*	34 Blvd of the Allies, Pittsburgh PA 15222	412-263-1100	S	110*	1.2
97	Delphos Herald Inc—*Murray Cohen*	405 N Main St, Delphos OH 45833	419-695-0015	R	110*	.1
98	St Lawrence County Newspapers—*Randall Stair*	PO Box 409, Ogdensburg NY 13669	315-393-1000	R	109*	.1
99	Guard Publishing Company Inc—*Tony Baker*	PO Box 10188, Eugene OR 97440	541-485-1234	R	108*	.4
100	Record Searchlight Co—*Shanna Cannon*	PO Box 492397, Redding CA 96049	530-243-2424	S	108*	.2
	EW Scripps Co					
101	News and Observer Publishing Co—*Orage Quarles III*	PO Box 191, Raleigh NC 27602	919-829-4500	S	105*	1.2
	McClatchy Co					
102	Advertiser Co—*Scott Brown*	PO Box 1000, Montgomery AL 36101	334-262-1611	S	105*	.4
	Gannett Company Inc					
103	Daily News LP—*Santhosh Benjamin*	450 W 33rd St Fl 3, New York NY 10001	212-210-2100	R	103*	1.6
104	Hanford Sentinel Inc—*Manuel Collazo*	PO Box 9, Hanford CA 93232	559-582-0471	S	103*	.1
	St Louis Post-Dispatch					
105	Hartford Courant Co	285 Broad St, Hartford CT 06115	860-241-6200	S	102*	1.1
	Tribune Co					
106	Freedom Newspapers Of NM—*Michael Stern*	17666 Fitch, Irvine CA 92614	949-253-2300	S	102*	.2
	Freedom Communications Inc					
107	Plain Dealer Publishing Co—*Terrance Egger*	PO Box 630504, Cincinnati OH 45263	216-999-5000	R	96*	1.5
108	Tower Media Inc—*Ike Massey*	PO Box 4200, Woodland Hills CA 91367	818-713-8300	R	95*	1.0
109	Messenger Post Newspapers—*Rick Jensen*	73 Buffalo St, Canandaigua NY 14424	585-394-0770	S	94*	.2
	GateHouse Media Inc					
110	Courier-Journal—*Arnold Garson*	PO Box 740031, Louisville KY 40201	502-582-4011	S	92*	1.0
	Gannett Company Inc					
111	San Jose Mercury News Inc—*Mark Zieman*	750 Ridder Park Dr, San Jose CA 95131	408-920-5000	S	92*	1.0
	MediaNews Group Inc					
112	Oklahoma Publishing Co—*David Thompson*	PO Box 25125, Oklahoma City OK 73125	405-475-3311	R	91*	1.0
113	Klamath Publishing Co—*David Lord*	PO Box 788, Klamath Falls OR 97601	541-885-4410	R	86*	.8
114	Evening Post Publishing Co—*Ivan Anderson*	134 Columbus St, Charleston SC 29403	843-577-7111	R	86*	1.5
115	Jonesboro Sun—*David Mosesso*	PO Box 1249, Jonesboro AR 72403	870-935-5525	D	84*	.2
116	The Ledger—*Jerome Ferson*	PO Box 408, Lakeland FL 33802	863-802-7323	S	78*	.5
	New York Times Co					
117	Findlay Publishing Co—*Karl Heminger*	PO Box 609, Findlay OH 45839	419-422-5151	R	78*	.2
118	Memphis Publishing Co—*Joseph Pepe*	495 Union Ave, Memphis TN 38103	901-529-2345	S	77*	.8
	EW Scripps Co					
119	New York Post—*Lloyd Williams*	1211 Ave of the Americ, New York NY 10036	212-930-8000	D	74*	.8
120	California Community News Corp—*Thomas Johnson*	5091 4th St, Irwindale CA 91706	626-472-5222	S	74*	.4
	Tribune Co					
121	Small Newspaper Group—*Len Small*	PO Box 632, Kankakee IL 60901	815-937-3300	R	72*	.3
122	Courier Div (Findlay Ohio)—*Edwin L Heminger*	PO Box 609, Findlay OH 45839	419-422-5151	S	72*	.1
	Findlay Publishing Company					
123	Oldham Associates Inc (Springville Utah)—*Don A Oldham*	1180 N Mountain Spring, Springville UT 84663	801-853-5353	R	71*	.1

Rank	Company Name—*Executive Officer*	Address, City, State, Zip	Phone	Type	Fin	Empls
124	Newark Morning Ledger Co—*Donald Newhouse*	1 Star Ledger Plz, Newark NJ 07102	973-877-4141	R	71*	1.2
125	Paddock Publications Inc/Daily Herald—*Daniel Baumann*	PO Box 280, Arlington Heights IL 60006	847-427-4300	R	70*	.8
126	Brehm Communications Inc—*Bill Brehm Jr*	PO Box 28429, San Diego CA 92198	858-451-6200	R	70*	.7
127	Gazette Co—*Chuck Peters*	PO Box 511, Cedar Rapids IA 52406	319-398-8211	R	70*	.6
128	Times-Citizen Communications Inc—*Jo Martin*	PO Box 640, Iowa Falls IA 50126	641-648-2521	R	69*	.1
129	Persis Corp—*Easton Manson*	900 Fort St Mall Ste 1, Honolulu HI 96813	808-599-8000	R	65*	.7
130	Sun-Gazette Co—*Bernard A Oravic* Ogden Newspapers Inc	PO Box 728, Williamsport PA 17701	570-326-1551	S	65*	.1
131	Times Herald Publishing Co—*Stan B Huskey* Journal Register Co	PO Box 409, Norristown PA 19401	610-272-2500	D	62*	.1
132	Lake County Record Bee—*Gary Dickson*	PO Box 849, Lakeport CA 95453	707-263-5636	R	61*	.1
133	Cape Publications Inc—*Mark Mikolajczyk*	PO Box 419000, Melbourne FL 32941	321-242-3600	R	60*	.7
134	Bakersfield Californian—*Richard Beene*	PO Box 440, Bakersfield CA 93302	661-395-7500	R	60*	.3
135	Wave Community Newspapers—*Pluria Marshall Jr*	1730 Olympic Blvd Se 5, Los Angeles CA 90015	323-556-5720	R	60*	.1
136	Detroit Legal News Publishing LLC—*Brad Thompson*	1409 Allen Dr Ste B, Troy MI 48083	248-577-6100	R	59*	.1
137	Shaw Newspapers—*Thomas Shaw*	PO Box 487, Dixon IL 61021	815-284-4000	R	58*	.6
138	Southern RI Newspapers—*David Dear Jr* Journal Register Co	187 Main St, Wakefield RI 02879	401-789-9744	D	58*	.1
139	TheStreet Inc—*Daryl Otte*	14 Wall St 15th Fl, New York NY 10005	212-321-5000	P	57	.3
140	Laramie Newspaper Inc—*Don Black*	320 E Grand Ave, Laramie WY 82070	307-742-2176	R	57*	.1
141	Territorial Newspapers—*Thomas Lee* Wick Communications Co	PO Box 27087, Tucson AZ 85726	520-294-1200	S	56*	.1
142	Meridian Star Inc—*Crystal Dupre*	PO Box 1591, Meridian MS 39302	601-693-1551	R	56*	.1
143	Prairie Mountain Publishing Company LLC—*Patrick Birmingham*	1048 Pearl St, Boulder CO 80302	303-442-1202	R	55*	1.1
144	Verde Valley Newspapers Inc—*Donald Soldwedel*	PO Box 429, Cottonwood AZ 86326	928-634-2241	R	55*	.5
145	Eagleherald Publishing LLC—*Rob Becker*	PO Box 77, Marinette WI 54143	715-735-6611	R	55*	.5
146	Beacon Journal Publishing Co—*Andrea Mathewson*	PO Box 640, Akron OH 44309	330-996-3000	S	54*	.6
147	Kroner Publications Inc—*John J Kroner Sr*	PO Box 150, Niles OH 44446	330-544-5500	R	54*	.1
148	Daily Southtown Inc Sun-Times Media Holdings LLC	6901 W 159th St, Tinley Park IL 60477	708-633-6700	S	53*	.6
149	Patuxent Publishing Co—*Jim Quimby*	10750 Little Patuxent, Columbia MD 21044	410-730-3990	R	53*	.3
150	Union Democrat Corp—*Robert Peres* Western Communications Inc	84 S Washington St, Sonora CA 95370	209-532-7151	D	53*	.1
151	Tni Partners—*Michael Jameson*	PO Box 26887, Tucson AZ 85726	520-573-4400	R	51*	.9
152	Courier Times Inc—*Mike Scobey*	8400 N Bristol Pike, Levittown PA 19057	215-949-4000	R	50*	1.0
153	Delaware County Daily Times Central States Publishing—*David Carr*	500 Mildred Ave, Primos PA 19018	610-622-8800	R	50	.2
154	Stephens Media Group—*Sherman R Frederick*	PO Box 70, Las Vegas NV 89125	702-383-0211	S	48*	.7
155	Daily Press Inc—*Digby A Solomon* Tribune Co	7505 Warwick Blvd, Newport News VA 23607	757-247-4600	S	47*	.5
156	Sierra Vista Herald—*Philip Vega* Wick Communications Co	102 Fab Ave, Sierra Vista AZ 85635	520-458-9440	D	47*	.1
157	News-Journal Corp—*Herbert Davidson*	PO Box 2831, Daytona Beach FL 32120	386-252-1511	R	46*	.9
158	The Providence Journal Co—*Howard G Sutton*	75 Fountain St, Providence RI 02902	401-277-7000	S	46*	.5
159	Lincoln Journal Star—*John Maher* Lee Enterprises Inc	PO Box 81609, Lincoln NE 68501	402-475-4200	D	45	.4
160	Chico Community Publishing Inc—*Jeff Kaenel*	353 E 2nd St, Chico CA 95928	530-894-2300	R	43*	.2
161	La Porte Publishing LLC—*Len Small*	701 State St, La Porte IN 46350	219-362-2161	R	43*	1.0
162	Alliance Publishing Company Inc—*Chuck Dix*	PO Box 2180, Alliance OH 44601	330-821-1200	R	41*	.9
163	Roanoke Times—*Debbie Meade* Landmark Media Enterprises	PO Box 2491, Roanoke VA 24010	540-981-3340	S	40*	.5
164	Appeal-Democrat Inc—*Dave Schmall* Freedom Communications Inc	1530 Ellis Lake Dr, Marysville CA 95901	530-741-2345	S	40*	.2
165	Pacific Publishing Co (Seattle Washington)—*Peter Bernhard*	PO Box 80156, Seattle WA 98108	206-461-1300	R	39*	<.1
166	Press and News in Osseo—*Jeff Coolman*	PO Box 280, Osseo MN 55369	763-425-3323	R	39*	<.1
167	Nevada County Publishing Co—*Lee Brant*	464 Sutton Way, Grass Valley CA 95945	530-273-9561	R	38*	1.0
168	Desert Sun Publishing Co—*Rich Ramhoff* Gannett Company Inc	PO Box 2734, Palm Springs CA 92263	760-322-8889	S	37*	.4
169	Evansville Courier and Press—*Jack Pate* EW Scripps Co	PO Box 268, Evansville IN 47702	812-464-7500	S	37*	.4
170	Oakland Tribune Inc—*John Armstrong*	7677 Oakport St Ste 95, Oakland CA 94621	510-208-6300	R	37*	.8
171	Republican Co—*David Starr* Newark Morning Ledger Co	1860 Main St, Springfield MA 01103	413-788-1000	S	36*	.7
172	Albuquerque Publishing Company Inc—*Nancy Wood*	7777 Jefferson St Ne, Albuquerque NM 87109	505-823-7777	R	36*	.6
173	Scranton Times LP—*Kevin Fitzgerald*	149 Penn Ave Ste 1, Scranton PA 18503	570-348-9100	R	35*	.7
174	Greensboro News and Record Inc—*Robin Saul*	200 E Market St, Greensboro NC 27401	336-373-7000	S	35*	.7
175	Harris Enterprises Inc (Hutchinson Kansas)—*Bruce Buchanan*	PO Box 190, Hutchinson KS 67504	620-694-5700	R	35*	.6
176	Detroit News Inc—*Jonathan Wolman* MediaNews Group Inc	615 W Lafayette Blvd, Detroit MI 48226	313-222-2300	S	35*	.3
177	Press Sentinel Newspapers Inc—*Eric Denty*	252 W Walnut St, Jesup GA 31545		R	35*	<.1
178	Daily Journal Corp—*Gerald L Salzman*	915 E 1st St, Los Angeles CA 90012	213-229-5300	P	35	.2
179	Eastern Colorado Publishing Co—*David Mcclain*	PO Box 1272, Sterling CO 80751	970-522-1990	R	33*	.1
180	Swift Communications—*Bill Toler*	580 Mallory Way, Carson City NV 89701	775-283-5500	R	32*	1.2
181	Hills Newspaper Inc—*David Rounds* MediaNews Group Inc	1516 Oak St, Alameda CA 94501	510-339-3939	S	32*	<.1
182	Cincinnati Enquirer Gannett Company Inc Newspaper Div	312 Elm St, Cincinnati OH 45202	513-721-2700	S	32*	<.1
183	Gazette Newspapers Inc—*Harry Saltzgaver* Washington Post Co	5225 E 2nd St, Long Beach CA 90803	562-433-2000	S	31*	<.1
184	Salina Journal Inc—*Tom Bell*	PO Box 740, Salina KS 67402	785-823-6363	R	31*	.7
185	News World Communications Inc—*Thomas Mcdevitt*	3600 New York Ave Ne, Washington DC 20002	202-636-3000	R	30*	1.0
186	Eagle Tribune Publishing Company Inc—*John Clymer*	PO Box 100, Lawrence MA 01842	978-685-1000	R	30*	.5
187	Wichita Eagle—*Kim Nussbaum* McClatchy Co	825 E Douglas, Wichita KS 67201		S	30*	.3
188	Sustain Technologies Inc Daily Journal Corp	915 E 1st St, Los Angeles CA 90012	213-229-5300	S	30*	<.1
189	Patriot-News Co—*John Kirkpatrick* Advance Publications Inc	PO Box 2265, Harrisburg PA 17105	717-255-8100	S	29*	.5
190	Ottumwa Courier—*Tom Hawley*	213 E 2nd St, Ottumwa IA 52501	641-684-4611	S	29*	.1

Note: An asterisk (*) indicates an estimated financial figure. The company type code used is as follows: R = Private, P = Public, S = Private Subsidiary, B = Public Subsidiary, D = Division, J = Joint Venture, I = Investment Fund.

COMPANY RANKINGS BY SALES WITHIN 4-DIGIT SIC

Rank	Company Name—*Executive Officer*	Address, City, State, Zip	Phone	Type	Fin	Empls
	Community Newspaper Holdings Inc					
191	Employment News LLC—*Gord Carley*	6753 E 47th Ave Ste A, Denver CO 80216	303-329-6300	R	29*	<.1
192	News-Press and Gazette Company Inc	PO Box 29, Saint Joseph MO 64502	816-271-8500	R	28*	.3
193	Cache Valley Publishing LLC—*Bruce Smith*	PO Box 487, Logan UT 84323	435-752-2121	R	28*	.1
194	Ojai Valley Newspapers LLC—*Lenny Roberts*	PO Box 277, Ojai CA 93024	805-646-1476	R	28*	<.1
195	Woodward Communications Inc—*Thomas Yunt*	PO Box 688, Dubuque IA 52004	563-588-5687	R	28*	.6
196	Denver Publishing Co—*John Temple*	PO Box 719, Denver CO 80201	303-892-5000	R	27*	.3
197	Clipper Publishing Co—*R Gail Stahle*	PO Box 267, Woods Cross UT 84010	801-295-2251	R	27*	.1
198	Olympic View Publishing LLC—*Brown Maloney*	PO Box 1750, Sequim WA 98382	360-683-3311	R	27*	<.1
199	Ecm Publishers Inc—*Jeff Athmann*	4095 Coon Rapids Blvd, Minneapolis MN 55433	763-712-2400	R	26*	.6
200	Mobile Press Register Inc—*Howard Bronson*	PO Box 2488, Mobile AL 36652	251-219-5400	R	26*	.5
201	C M Media Inc—*Max Brown*	PO Box 29913, Columbus OH 43229	614-888-4567	R	26*	.3
202	The Daily Herald Co—*Mike Benbow*	PO Box 930, Everett WA 98206	425-339-3000	S	26*	.3
	Washington Post Co					
203	Western Communications Inc—*Gordon Black*	PO Box 6020, Bend OR 97708	541-382-1811	R	26*	.2
204	HR Industries Inc—*Richard Beckman*	5055 Wilshire Blvd, Los Angeles CA 90036	323-525-2000	S	26*	.1
205	Baltimore Publishing Group—*Joy Bramble*	2513 N Charles St, Baltimore MD 21218	410-366-3900	R	26*	<.1
206	Sound Publishing Inc—*Manfred Tempelmayr*	19351 8th Ave Ne Ste 1, Poulsbo WA 98370	360-394-5800	R	26*	.6
207	American-Republican Inc—*W Pape*	PO Box 2090, Waterbury CT 06722	203-574-3636	R	26*	.3
208	Eagle Newspapers Inc—*Thomas Lanctot*	PO Box 12008, Salem OR 97309	503-393-1774	R	25*	.4
209	Hansan Group Inc—*Roy Battaglia*	1255 22nd St Nw Ste 70, Washington DC 20037	703-289-4670	R	25*	.1
210	Tallahassee Democrat—*Patrick Dorsey*	PO Box 990, Tallahassee FL 32302	850-599-2100	R	25*	.3
211	Seattle Times Co—*Frank A Blethen*	PO Box 70, Seattle WA 98111		R	25*	.2
212	East Oregonian Publishing Co—*Steve Forrester*	PO Box 1089, Pendleton OR 97801	541-276-2211	R	25*	<.1
213	Michigan Chronicle Publishing—*Sam Logan*	479 Ledyard St, Detroit MI 48201	313-963-5522	R	25*	<.1
214	Times Publishing Co—*Marilyn Mead*	205 W 12th St, Erie PA 16534	814-870-1600	R	25*	.3
215	Eau Claire Press Co—*Pieter Graaskamp*	PO Box 570, Eau Claire WI 54702	715-833-9200	R	24*	.3
216	Chesapeake Publishing Corp—*Thomas Bradlee*	PO Box 600, Easton MD 21601	410-822-1500	R	24*	.6
217	Jefferson County Publications Inc—*Bob Williams*	14522 S Outer Forty Rd, Town and Country MO 63017	314-821-1110	S	24*	<.1
	Suburban Journal Newspapers					
218	Prescott Newspapers Inc—*Joseph Soldwedel*	PO Box 312, Prescott AZ 86302	928-445-3333	R	24*	.5
219	Press-Enterprise Inc—*Paul Eyerly*	3185 Lackawanna Ave, Bloomsburg PA 17815	570-387-1234	R	23*	.3
220	Sun News (Myrtle Beach South Carolina)—*PJ Browning*	PO Box 406, Myrtle Beach SC 29578	843-626-8555	S	23	.3
	McClatchy Co					
221	Fayetteville Publishing Company Inc—*Charles Broadwell*	PO Box 849, Fayetteville NC 28302	910-323-4848	R	23*	.4
222	Abilene News Co—*Kim Nussbaum*	PO Box 30, Abilene TX 79604	325-673-4271	D	23*	.3
	EW Scripps Co					
223	Bradenton Herald—*Bob Turner*	PO Box 921, Bradenton FL 34206	941-748-0411	S	23*	.3
	McClatchy Co					
224	Times Herald Co—*Tim Dowd*	911 Military St, Port Huron MI 48060	810-985-7171	S	23*	.3
	Gannett Company Inc					
225	Paxton Media Group LLC—*Rick Bean*	PO Box 2092, Durham NC 27702	919-419-6500	R	23*	.2
226	Greater Jersey Press Inc—*Ben Cannizzaro*	PO Box 5001, Freehold NJ 07728	732-358-5200	S	23*	.1
	Greater Media Inc					
227	Sincell Publishing Company Inc—*Don Sincell*	PO Box 326, Oakland MD 21550	301-334-3963	R	23*	<.1
228	Shore Line Newspapers—*Erik Hesselberg*	PO Box 349, Guilford CT 06437	203-453-2714	D	23*	<.1
	Journal Register Co					
229	Reading Eagle Co—*William Flippin*	345 Penn St, Reading PA 19601	610-371-5000	R	23*	.4
230	Hour Publishing Co—*Jack Whitton*	PO Box 790, Norwalk CT 06852	203-846-3281	R	22*	.2
231	Uniontown Newspapers Inc—*Gary Shorts*	PO Box 848, Uniontown PA 15401	724-439-7500	R	22*	.3
232	Journal Graphics—*Phillip Bridge*	2840 NW 35th Ave, Portland OR 97210	503-790-9100	R	22*	.2
233	Nebraska Printing Cener—*Scott Stewart*	PO Box 5325, Lincoln NE 68501	402-466-8521	R	22*	<.1
234	ECM Publishers Forest Lake—*Julian Anderson*	4095 Coon Rapids Blvd, Coon Rapids MN 55433	763-712-2400	D	22*	<.1
	Ecm Publishers Inc					
235	Greeneway Enterprises Inc—*Sarah Greene*	PO Box 250, Gilmer TX 75644	903-843-2503	R	22*	<.1
236	Herald-Mail Co—*John League*	PO Box 439, Hagerstown MD 21741	301-733-5131	R	21*	.2
237	Telegraph Publishing Co—*Andrew Bickford*	17 Executive Dr, Hudson NH 03051	603-882-2741	R	21*	.2
238	Gaston Gazette LLP—*Sherry Collins*	PO Box 1538, Gastonia NC 28053	704-869-1700	R	21*	.2
239	Springfield Business Journal—*Dianne E Osis*	PO Box 1365, Springfield MO 65801	417-831-3238	R	21*	<.1
240	B and L Financial Service—*Steva Vialle*	205 S 13th St, Lexington MO 64067	660-259-2247	S	21*	<.1
241	News Printing Co—*Thomas Shaw*	200 1st Ave E, Newton IA 50208	641-792-3121	R	20*	.5
242	Turley Publications Inc—*Patrick Turley*	24 Water St, Palmer MA 01069	413-283-8393	R	20*	.2
243	White Mountain Publishing Co—*Greg Tock*	PO Box 1570, Show Low AZ 85902	928-537-5721	R	20*	<.1
244	Gazette Publishing Inc—*William N Kremer*	1114 Broadway, Wheaton MN 56296	320-563-8146	R	20*	<.1
245	Times Picayune Publishing Corp—*Ashton Phelps*	3800 Howard Ave, New Orleans LA 70125	504-826-3279	R	20*	.4
246	Grand Forks Herald—*Mary Jo Hotzler*	PO Box 6008, Grand Forks ND 58206	701-780-1100	S	20	.2
	Forum Communications Co					
247	News Media Corp—*John Tompkins*	PO Box 46, Rochelle IL 61068	815-562-2061	R	19*	.6
248	European and Pacific Stars And Stripes—*Thomas Kelsch*	529 14th St Nw Ste 350, Washington DC 20045	202-761-0900	R	19*	.5
249	Reminder Media Inc—*Kenneth Hovland*	PO Box 27, Vernon Rockville CT 06066	860-875-3366	R	19*	.2
250	San Ramon Valley Times	PO Box 5088, Walnut Creek CA 94596	925-935-2525	S	19*	.2
	Contra Costa Newspapers Inc					
251	Telegraph Herald Inc—*Jim Normandin*	PO Box 688, Dubuque IA 52004	563-588-5611	D	19	.2
	Woodward Communications Inc					
252	Sioux City Newspapers Inc—*Ron Peterson*	515 Pavonia St, Sioux City IA 51101	712-293-4250	S	19*	.2
	Lee Enterprises Inc					
253	Visalia Newspapers Inc—*Amy Pack*	PO Box 31, Visalia CA 93279	559-735-3200	S	19*	.1
	Gannett Company Inc					
254	Diversified Suburban Newspapers Inc—*Nan Chalat-Noaker*	PO Box 3688, Park City UT 84060	435-649-9014	R	19*	<.1
255	Joongang USA—*Tae Kang*	13749 Midvale Ave N, Seattle WA 98133	206-365-4000	R	19*	.4
256	Shearman Corp—*Thomas Shearman*	PO Box 2893, Lake Charles LA 70602	337-433-3000	R	19*	.3
257	Texas Community Newspapers Inc—*Roy Brown*	3509 Hulen St Ste 201, Fort Worth TX 76107	817-336-8300	R	19*	.5
258	Ironton Publications Inc—*James Boone*	2903 S 5th St, Ironton OH 45638	740-532-1441	R	18*	.5
259	Ogden Publishing Corp—*David Rau*	PO Box 12790, Ogden UT 84412	801-625-4200	S	18*	.4
260	Federated Publications Inc—*Idris Bond*	1175 N A St, Richmond IN 47374	765-962-1575	S	18	.2
	Gannett Company Inc					
261	Danbury Publishing Co—*Shawn Palmer*	333 Main St, Danbury CT 06810	203-744-5100	D	18*	.2
262	Joplin Globe Publishing Company Inc—*Christina Jones*	PO Box 64802, Joplin MO 64802	417-623-3480	D	18*	.2
	Community Newspaper Holdings Inc					
263	Central Wisconsin Publications—*Carol O'Leary*	PO Box 180, Medford WI 54451	715-748-2626	R	18*	<.1

Rank	Company Name—*Executive Officer*	Address, City, State, Zip	Phone	Type	Fin	Empls
264	Uintah Basin Standard Inc—*Craig Ashby* Brehm Communications Inc	268 S 200 E, Roosevelt UT 84066	435-722-5131	S	18*	<.1
265	Rust Communications Inc—*Rex Rust*	PO Box 699, Cape Girardeau MO 63702	573-335-6611	R	18*	.3
266	Consolidated Publishing Company Inc—*Phillip Sanguinetti*	PO Box 189, Anniston AL 36202	256-236-1551	R	18*	.2
267	Princeton Packet Inc—*James Kilgore*	PO Box 350, Princeton NJ 08542	609-924-3244	R	18*	.2
268	News-Gazette Inc—*John Foreman*	PO Box 677, Champaign IL 61824	217-351-5252	R	18*	.4
269	Day Publishing Co—*Gary Farrugia*	PO Box 1231, New London CT 06320	860-442-2200	R	18*	.4
270	High Point Enterprise Inc—*Fred Paxton*	PO Box 1009, High Point NC 27261	336-888-3500	R	18*	.2
271	Truth Publishing Company Inc—*John Dille III*	PO Box 487, Elkhart IN 46515	574-294-1661	R	18*	.2
272	Red Wing Publishing Co—*Arlin Albrecht*	1602 Hwy 71, International Falls MN 56649	218-285-7411	R	17*	.3
273	Post-Bulletin Company LLC—*Bill Lisser*	PO Box 6118, Rochester MN 55903	507-285-7600	R	17*	.4
274	New England Newspapers Inc—*Andrew Mick*	PO Box 1171, Pittsfield MA 01202	413-447-7311	R	17*	.4
275	Free Lance-Star Publishing Company Of Fredericksburg Va—*Josiah Rowe*	616 Amelia St, Fredericksburg VA 22401	540-374-5000	R	17*	.4
276	Sun Coast Media Group Inc—*Derek Dunn-Rankin*	23170 Harborview Rd, Port Charlotte FL 33980	941-206-1000	R	17*	.4
277	Kingsport Publishing Corp—*David Rau*	PO Box 479, Kingsport TN 37662	423-246-8121	S	17*	.2
278	Owensboro Messenger-Inquirer Inc—*Matt Francis*	PO Box 1480, Owensboro KY 42302	270-926-0123	R	17*	.2
279	Mail Tribune Co—*Grady Singletary*	PO Box 1108, Medford OR 97501	541-776-4411	S	17*	.2
280	Kearns-Tribune Corp—*Dominic Welch* MediaNews Group Inc	143 S Main St Ste 400, Salt Lake City UT 84111	801-237-2031	S	17*	.2
281	Baseball America Inc—*Catherine Silver*	4319 S Alston Ave, Durham NC 27713	919-682-9635	S	17*	<.1
282	North Lake Tahoe Bonanza—*Arne Hoel* Swift Communications	PO Drawer 7820, Incline Village NV 89452	775-831-4666	S	17*	<.1
283	News India Times—*Shomik Chaudhuri*	37 W 20th St Ste 1009, New York NY 10011	212-675-7515	R	17*	<.1
284	California Examiner—*Oscar Jornacion*	4515 Eagle Rock Blvd, Los Angeles CA 90041	323-344-3500	R	17*	<.1
285	Tuscola County Advertiser Inc—*Bob Edwards*	344 N State St, Caro MI 48723	989-673-3181	R	17*	.5
286	Northwest Media Washington LP—*Peter Horvitz*	PO Box 130, Kent WA 98035	425-274-4782	R	17*	.2
287	New Mexican Inc—*Stephen Watkins*	PO Box 2048, Santa Fe NM 87504	505-983-3303	R	17*	.2
288	Record-Journal Real Estate Co—*Eliot White*	PO Box 915, Meriden CT 06450	203-235-1661	R	17*	.3
289	Union Leader Corp—*Joseph Mcquaid*	PO Box 9555, Manchester NH 03108	603-668-4321	R	17*	.3
290	Douthit Communications Inc—*H Kenneth*	PO Box 760, Sandusky OH 44871	419-625-5825	R	17*	.2
291	Hi-Desert Publishing Co—*Cindy Melland*	56445 29 Palms Hwy, Yucca Valley CA 92284	760-365-3315	R	17*	.2
292	West County Journals—*Michelle Prusz*	14522 S Outer 40 Rd St, Town And Country MO 63017	314-821-2462	R	16*	.2
293	Mohave County Miner Inc—*Donald Soldwedel*	3015 Stockton Hill Rd, Kingman AZ 86401	928-753-6397	R	16*	.5
294	Breeze Corp—*George Nutting*	PO Box 151306, Cape Coral FL 33915	239-574-1110	R	16*	.4
295	Journal Times—*Rick Parrish* Lee Enterprises Inc	212 4th St, Racine WI 53403	262-634-3322	S	16*	.2
296	P and N Holdings Inc—*Paul Walser*	21 N Wyoming St, Hazleton PA 18201	570-455-3636	R	16*	.2
297	Helen Gordon Interests Ltd—*Kathy Douglass*	PO Box 2025, Houston TX 77252	713-371-3500	R	16*	.3
298	Commonwealth Publishing Inc—*Wyatt Emmerich*	PO Box 8050, Greenwood MS 38935	662-453-5312	R	16*	.2
299	Albany Herald Publishing Co—*Michael Gebhart*	PO Box 48, Albany GA 31702	229-888-9300	D	16	.2
300	Burlington Times Inc—*Grover Friend*	4284 Rte 130, Willingboro NJ 08046	609-871-8000	R	16*	.4
301	Citrus Publishing Inc—*Mike Abernathy*	PO Box 1899, Inverness FL 34451	352-563-6363	R	16*	.2
302	Bangor Publishing Co—*Richard Warren*	PO Box 1329, Bangor ME 04402	207-990-8000	R	15*	.3
303	Daily Lewiston Sun—*James Costello*	PO Box 4400, Lewiston ME 04243	207-784-5411	R	15*	.3
304	Observer Publishing Co—*Thomas Northrop*	122 S Main St, Washington PA 15301	724-222-2200	R	15*	.3
305	Daily Newstribune Inc—*Peter Miller*	426 2nd St, La Salle IL 61301	815-223-3200	R	15*	.2
306	Jewish Press Inc—*Sidney Klass*	338 3rd Ave, Brooklyn NY 11215	718-330-1100	R	15*	.1
307	Westfield News Publishing Inc—*Lawrence Hebert*	PO Box 930, Westfield MA 01086	413-562-4181	R	14*	.3
308	Homestead Publishing Co—*John D Worthington* Baltimore Sun Co	PO Box 189, Bel Air MD 21014	410-838-4400	S	14*	.2
309	Recorder Publishing Co—*Stephen Parker*	17 19 Morristown Rd, Bernardsville NJ 07924	908-766-3900	R	14*	.2
310	Santa Maria Times Inc—*Cynthia Schur* St Louis Post-Dispatch	PO Box 400, Santa Maria CA 93456	805-925-2691	S	14*	.2
311	Fairfield Publishing Co—*Foy McNaughton*	PO Box 47, Fairfield CA 94533	707-425-4646	R	14*	.1
312	Hellenic Times	823 11th Ave 5th Fl, New York NY 10019	212-333-7456	S	14*	<.1
313	Daily Chinese News Inc—*James Guon*	PO Box 2032, Monterey Park CA 91754	323-268-4982	R	14*	.2
314	Frank Mayborn Enterprises Inc—*Anyse Mayborn*	PO Box 6114, Temple TX 76503	254-778-4444	R	13*	.3
315	World Journal LLC—*Howard Lee*	14107 20th Ave Fl 2, Whitestone NY 11357	718-746-8889	R	13*	.3
316	Times-Shamrock Commuciations—*Ron Zacchi*	75 N Washington St, Wilkes Barre PA 18701	570-821-2000	R	13*	.3
317	Mankato Free Press Co—*Jim Santori* Community Newspaper Holdings Inc	418 S 2nd St, Mankato MN 56001	507-625-4451	S	13	.1
318	Kpc Media Group Inc—*Terry Housholder*	102 N Main St, Kendallville IN 46755	260-347-0400	R	13*	.2
319	Pottsville Republican Inc—*Duane Koch*	PO Box 209, Pottsville PA 17901	570-622-3456	R	13*	.1
320	News Communications Inc—*James A Finkelstein*	2 Park Ave, New York NY 10016	212-689-2500	R	12	.1
321	Southwest Newspapers—*Stan Rolfsrud*	PO Box 8, Shakopee MN 55379	952-445-3333	R	12*	.2
322	944 Media LLC—*Marc Lotenbergf*	4445 N Buckboard Tr, Scottsdale AZ 85251	480-423-1944	R	12	.1
323	Herald Publishing Co—*John Paton* Journal Register Co	50 Sargent Dr, New Haven CT 06511	203-789-5200	S	12*	.2
324	Victoria Advocate Publishing Co—*John Roberts*	PO Box 1518, Victoria TX 77902	361-575-1451	R	12*	.2
325	Richner Communications Inc—*Stuart Richner*	2 Endo Blvd, Garden City NY 11530	516-569-4000	R	12*	.1
326	Corvallis Gazette-Times—*Mike McInally* Lee Enterprises Inc	PO Box 368, Corvallis OR 97333	541-753-2641	S	12*	.1
327	Bristol Press Publishing Co—*Nancy Frede* Journal Register Co	PO Box 2158, Bristol CT 06011	860-584-0501	S	12*	.1
328	Herald Association Inc—*R John Mitchell*	PO Box 668, Rutland VT 05702	802-747-6121	R	12*	.1
329	Doings Newspapers Inc—*Paul A Carroll* Sun-Times Media Holdings LLC	920 N York Rd Ste 200, Hinsdale IL 60521	630-320-5400	S	12*	<.1
330	Minnesota Spokesman-Recorder—*Tracey Williams-Dillard*	3744 4th Ave S, Minneapolis MN 55409	612-827-4021	R	12*	<.1
331	Community Newspapers Inc—*WH NeSmith Jr*	PO Box 792, Athens GA 30603	706-548-0010	R	12*	<.1
332	Times Republic—*Larry Perrotto*	1492 E Walnut St, Watseka IL 60970	815-432-5227	R	12*	.2
333	Derrick Publishing Co—*Patrick Boyle*	PO Box 928, Oil City PA 16301	814-676-7444	R	12*	.1
334	West Virginia Newspaper Publishing Co—*David Raese*	1251 Earl L Core Rd, Morgantown WV 26505	304-292-6301	R	11*	.1
335	Tribune Publishing Company Inc—*Albert Alford*	505 C St, Lewiston ID 83501	208-743-9411	R	11*	.1
336	Retherford Holdings Inc—*Bill Retherford*	524 S Main St, Broken Arrow OK 74012	918-663-1414	R	11*	.1
337	Osteen Publishing Co—*H Osteen*	PO Box 1677, Sumter SC 29151	803-774-1200	R	11*	.1
338	Greater Media Newspapers Inc—*Ben Cannizzaro* Greater Media Inc	PO Box 5001, Freehold NJ 07728	732-358-5200	S	11*	.1
339	Computerworld Inc C W Database Div—*Matt Sweeney*	PO Box 9171, Framingham MA 01701	508-879-0700	D	11*	.1
340	Editor and Publisher Company Inc	17782 Cowan St Ste C, Irvine CA 92614	949-660-6150	S	11*	.1

Note: An asterisk (*) indicates an estimated financial figure. The company type code used is as follows: R = Private, P = Public, S = Private Subsidiary, B = Public Subsidiary, D = Division, J = Joint Venture, I = Investment Fund.

COMPANY RANKINGS BY SALES WITHIN 4-DIGIT SIC

Rank	Company Name—*Executive Officer*	Address, City, State, Zip	Phone	Type	Fin	Empls
341	Sentinel Standard Inc—*Cindy Conrad*	114 N Depot St, Ionia MI 48846	616-527-2100	R	11*	<.1
342	Lillie Suburban Newspapers Inc—*Beatrice Enright*	2515 7th Ave E, Saint Paul MN 55109	651-777-8800	R	11*	.1
343	Lafromboise Newspapers—*J Lafromboise*	PO Box 580, Centralia WA 98531	360-736-3311	R	11*	.1
344	Editorial Projects In Education Inc—*Virgina Edwards*	6935 Arlington Rd Ste, Bethesda MD 20814	301-280-3100	R	11*	.1
345	Ming Pao Inc (Long Island City New York)—*Paul Hui Hau Tung*	4331 33rd St, Long Island City NY 11101	718-786-2888	R	11*	.1
346	Keene Publishing Corp—*James Rousmaniere*	PO Box 546, Keene NH 03431	603-352-1234	R	11*	.1
347	Minnesota Suburban Publications LLC—*Dick Hendrickson*	10917 Valley View Rd, Eden Prairie MN 55344	952-829-0797	R	11*	.1
348	Times And News Publishing Co—*Philip Jones*	1570 Fairfield Rd, Gettysburg PA 17325	717-334-1131	R	11*	.1
349	Press Holding Corp—*Art Powers*	PO Box 1717, Johnson City TN 37605	423-929-3111	R	10*	.1
350	Eunice News Inc—*Tom Coleman*	PO Box 989, Eunice LA 70535	337-457-3061	R	10*	.1
351	Lawton Publishing Company Inc—*Donald Bentley*	PO Box 2069, Lawton OK 73502	580-353-0620	R	10*	.2
352	Buckner News Alliance Inc—*Philip Buckner*	2101 4th Ave Ste 2300, Seattle WA 98121	206-727-2727	R	10*	.1
353	Rapid City Journal—*Brad Slater* Lee Enterprises Inc	PO Box 450, Rapid City SD 57709	605-394-8300	S	10*	.1
354	Record Herald—*Pat Patterson* GateHouse Media Inc	30 Walnut St, Waynesboro PA 17268	717-762-2151	S	10*	<.1
355	Sun-Reporter Publishing Co—*Amelia Ashley-Ward*	1791 Bancroft Ave, San Francisco CA 94124	415-671-1000	R	10*	<.1
356	Ad-Mast Publishing Co—*James Washington*	PO Box 151789, Dallas TX 75315	214-428-8958	R	10*	<.1
357	River City Newspapers LLC—*Michael E Quinn*	2225 W Acoma Blvd W, Lake Havasu City AZ 86403	928-453-4237	R	10*	<.1
358	Tap Publishing Co—*Greg Walker*	PO Box 509, Crossville TN 38557	931-484-5137	R	10*	.1
359	Daily Woburn Times Inc—*Peter Haggerty*	1 Arrow Dr, Woburn MA 01801	781-933-3700	R	10*	.1
360	American Publishing Co—*Horacio Aguirre*	2900 Nw 39th St, Miami FL 33142	305-633-3341	R	10*	.1
361	Rockingham Publishing Company Inc—*Thomas Byrd*	PO Box 193, Harrisonburg VA 22803	540-574-6200	R	9*	.2
362	Dover Post Company Inc—*James Flood*	PO Box 664, Dover DE 19903	302-678-3616	R	9*	.1
363	Ashland Publishing Co—*Rick Rakes* Dow Jones and Company Inc	224 17th St, Ashland KY 41101	606-326-2600	D	9*	.1
364	Journal of Commerce Group—*Chris Brooks*	2 Penn Pl E, Newark NJ 07105	973-776-8660	D	9*	.1
365	The American News The Farm Form—*Jerome Ferson*	PO Box 4430, Aberdeen SD 57402	605-225-4100	R	9*	.1
366	Times Daily Inc New York Times Co	219 W Tennessee St, Florence AL 35630	256-766-3434	S	9*	.1
367	Tri-Lakes Newspapers Inc—*Ted Dulaney*	PO Box 1900, Branson MO 65615	417-334-3161	R	9*	.1
368	Missourian Publishing Co—*William Miller*	PO Box 336, Washington MO 63090	636-239-7701	R	9*	.1
369	Hagedorn Communications Inc—*Christopher Hagedorn*	PO Box 680, New Rochelle NY 10802	914-636-7400	R	9*	.1
370	Progressive Publishing Co—*Margaret Krebs*	PO Box 291, Clearfield PA 16830	814-765-5581	R	9*	.2
371	Suffolk Life Newspapers—*David Willmott*	PO Box 167, Riverhead NY 11901	631-369-0800	R	9*	.1
372	Hastings and Sons Publishing Co—*Peter Gamage*	PO Box 951, Lynn MA 01903	781-593-7700	R	8*	.1
373	Lee Publications Inc—*Fred Lee*	PO Box 121, Palatine Bridge NY 13428	518-673-3237	R	8*	.1
374	Edward A Sherman Publishing Co—*Albert Sherman*	PO Box 420, Newport RI 02840	401-849-3300	R	8*	.1
375	William Boyd Printing Company Inc—*Jane Carey*	4 Weed Rd Ste 1, Latham NY 12110	518-436-9686	R	8*	.1
376	Daily Beloit News—*Bill Barth*	149 State St, Beloit WI 53511	608-365-8811	R	8*	.1
377	Ottawa Publishing Company Inc—*Len Small*	110 W Jefferson St, Ottawa IL 61350	815-433-2000	R	8*	.1
378	Signal Newspapers Inc—*Morris Thomas* Morris Multimedia Inc	PO Box 801870, Santa Clarita CA 91380	661-259-1234	S	8*	.1
379	Cookson Hills Publishers Inc—*Jim Mayo*	111 N Oak St, Sallisaw OK 74955	918-775-4433	R	8*	<.1
380	Steffen Publishing Inc—*Sally Steffen*	PO Box 403, Holland Patent NY 13354	315-865-4100	R	8*	.1
381	Salem Times-Commoner Publishing Company Inc—*John Perrine*	120 S Broadway Ave, Salem IL 62881	618-548-3330	R	8*	.2
382	Carteret Publishing Company Inc—*Walter Phillips*	PO Box 1679, Morehead City NC 28557	252-726-7081	R	8*	.1
383	Reporter—*Jody Lodevick*	916 Cotting Ln, Vacaville CA 95688	707-448-6401	R	8*	.1
384	Courier Publishing Co—*John Voorhies*	PO Box 1468, Grants Pass OR 97528	541-474-3700	R	7*	.1
385	Scripps Treasure Coast Publishing—*Rebecca Hicks*	600 Edwards Rd, Fort Pierce FL 34982	772-461-2050	R	7*	.1
386	Corning Publishing Co—*J Rockwell*	PO Box 85, Corning AR 72422	870-857-6397	R	7*	.2
387	The Gadsden Times—*Roger Quinn* New York Times Co	PO Box 188, Gadsden AL 35901	256-549-2000	D	7*	.1
388	Worcester Publishing Ltd—*Allen Fletcher*	172 Shrewsbury St Ste, Worcester MA 01604	508-755-8004	R	7*	.1
389	Crawford Perspectives—*Arch Crawford*	6890 E Sunrise Dr Ste, Tucson AZ 85750	520-577-1158	R	7*	<.1
390	Kankakee Valley Publishing Co—*Larry Perrotto*	117 N Van Rensselaer S, Rensselaer IN 47978	219-866-5111	R	7*	.2
391	Winchester Evening Star Inc—*Thomas Byrd*	2 N Kent St, Winchester VA 22601	540-667-3200	R	7*	.1
392	Wayne Printing Company Inc—*Hal Tanner*	PO Box 10629, Goldsboro NC 27532	919-778-2211	R	7*	.1
393	Butler County Publishing Company Inc—*Don Schrieber*	PO Box 7, Poplar Bluff MO 63902	573-785-1414	R	7*	.1
394	Times-Argus Association Inc—*R Mitchell*	PO Box 707, Barre VT 05641	802-479-0191	R	7*	.1
395	Mayhill Publications Inc—*R Mayhill*	PO Box 90, Knightstown IN 46148	765-345-5133	R	7*	.1
396	Middletown Press Publishing Co—*Tom Wiley* Journal Register Co	386 Main St 4th Fl, Middletown CT 06457	860-347-3331	S	6	.1
397	Hub Kearney Publishing Company Inc—*Steven Chatelain*	PO Box 1988, Kearney NE 68848	308-237-2152	R	6*	.1
398	Las Vegas Sun Inc—*Brian Greenspun*	2290 Corp Cir Dr Ste 2, Henderson NV 89014	702-990-2494	R	6*	.1
399	Marshalltown Newspaper Inc—*George Nutting*	PO Box 1300, Marshalltown IA 50158	641-753-6611	R	6*	.1
400	Ithacan Publishing Company Inc—*Anna Funck*	269 Park Hall, Ithaca NY 14850	607-274-3207	R	6*	.1
401	Index Publishing—*Tim Keck*	1535 11th Ave Ste 300, Seattle WA 98122	206-323-7101	R	6*	.1
402	Chronicle Printing Co—*Lucy Crosbie*	One Chronicle Rd, Willimantic CT 06226	860-423-8466	R	6*	.1
403	Clarksburg Publishing Co	PO Box 2000, Clarksburg WV 26302	304-626-1400	R	6*	.1
404	Afro-American Newspaper—*John Oliver*	2519 N Charles St, Baltimore MD 21218	410-554-8200	R	6*	.1
405	Sun Publishing Corp—*Skip Whitson*	PO Box 5588, Santa Fe NM 87502	505-471-5177	R	6*	.1
406	Flagstaff Publishing Co—*Don Rowley* St Louis Post-Dispatch	PO Box 1849, Flagstaff AZ 86002	928-774-4545	S	6*	.1
407	Wilmington Star-News Inc—*Robert J Gruber* New York Times Co	PO Box 840, Wilmington NC 28402	910-343-2000	S	6*	.1
408	Jewish Exponent Inc—*Joseph Kemp*	2100 Arch St Fl 4, Philadelphia PA 19103	215-832-0700	R	6*	<.1
409	Forward Association Inc—*Jane Eisner*	125 Maiden Ln, New York NY 10038	212-889-8200	R	6*	<.1
410	Chartwell Inc—*Phillip I Dunklin*	2970 Peachtree Rd NW S, Atlanta GA 30305	404-237-9099	R	6*	<.1
411	Elwood Publishing Company Inc—*Jack Barnes*	PO Box 85, Elwood IN 46036	765-552-3355	R	6*	.1
412	Eagle Media Partners LP—*H Barclay*	2501 James St, Syracuse NY 13206	315-434-8889	R	6*	.1
413	Mcnaughton Newspapers—*Foy Mcnaughton*	PO Box 1470, Davis CA 95617	530-756-0800	R	6*	.1
414	American Marketing Services Inc—*M Griswold*	129000 Cloverleaf Ctr, Germantown MD 20874	301-258-1166	R	6*	.1
415	Daily Ludington News Inc—*David Jackson*	PO Box 340, Ludington MI 49431	231-845-5181	R	6*	.1
416	Hpc Of Pennsylvania Inc—*David Radler*	1120 N Carbon St Ste 1, Marion IL 62959	618-993-1711	R	6*	.1
417	Martinsville Bulletin Inc—*Antonette Haskell*	PO Box 3711, Martinsville VA 24115	276-638-8801	R	6*	.1
418	Seattle Business Journal Inc—*Emory Thomas*	801 2nd Ave Ste 210, Seattle WA 98104	206-583-0701	R	6*	.1
419	Helmer Printing Inc—*Mark Helmer*	PO Box 40, Beldenville WI 54003	715-273-4601	R	6*	.1
420	Philadelphia Tribune Co—*Robert Bogle*	520 S 16th St, Philadelphia PA 19146	215-893-4050	R	6*	.1

Rank	Company Name—*Executive Officer*	Address, City, State, Zip	Phone	Type	Fin	Empls
421	Log Cabin Democrat LLC—*Janiece Driscoll*	PO Box 969, Conway AR 72033	501-327-6621	R	6*	.1
422	World Newspaper Inc—*Peter Rogers*	PO Box 370, North Platte NE 69103	308-532-6000	R	5*	.1
423	William J Kline and Son Inc—*Sidney Lefavour*	1 Venner Rd, Amsterdam NY 12010	518-843-1100	R	5*	.1
424	Bay Guardian Co—*Bruce Brugman*	135 Micaicaippi St, San Francisco CA 94107	415-255-3100	R	5*	.1
425	Index-Journal Co—*Judith Burns*	PO Box 1018, Greenwood SC 29648	864-223-1411	R	5*	.1
426	Webb Communications Inc—*Mark Lundberg*	1 Maynard St, Williamsport PA 17701	570-326-7634	R	5*	.1
427	Augusta Focus Inc—*Charles Walker*	1143 Laney Walker Blvd, Augusta GA 30901	706-724-7855	R	5*	.1
428	Community Media Corp—*Kathy Verdugo*	9559 Valley View St, Cypress CA 90630	714-220-0292	R	5*	.1
429	Hunterdon County Democrat Inc—*Catherine Langley*	8 Minneakoning Rd, Flemington NJ 08822	908-782-4747	R	5*	.1
430	Finger Lakes Printing Company Inc—*William Mclean*	218 Genesee St, Geneva NY 14456	315-789-3333	R	5*	.1
431	Southern Lakes Newspapers LLC—*Marcy Mendicino*	700 N Pine St, Burlington WI 53105	262-763-3511	R	5*	.1
432	Greeneville Publishing Company Inc—*John Jones*	PO Box 1630, Greeneville TN 37744	423-638-4181	R	5*	.2
433	Idaho Press-Tribune Inc—*Stephanie Presley*	PO Box 9399, Nampa ID 83652	208-467-9251	R	5*	.2
434	Oconee Publishing Inc—*Jerry Edwards*	PO Box 547, Seneca SC 29679	864-882-2375	R	5*	.1
435	Seaton Publishing Company Inc—*Edward Seaton*	PO Box 787, Manhattan KS 66505	785-776-2200	R	5*	.1
436	Inter-County Co-Op Publishing Association Inc—*Vivian Byl*	PO Box 490, Frederic WI 54837	715-327-4236	R	5*	.1
437	The Smithfield Herald—*Scott Bolejack*	PO Box 1417, Smithfield NC 27577	919-934-2176	R	5*	.1
438	KK Stevens Publishing Co—*Thomas Stevens*	PO Box 590, Astoria IL 61501	309-329-2151	R	5*	<.1
439	Eagle Publications Inc—*Martin Norton*	2 Eastport Plz Dr Ste, Collinsville IL 62234	618-345-5400	R	5*	<.1
440	Louisiana Publishing—*Tony Taylor*	PO Box 1199, Boutte LA 70039	985-758-2795	R	5*	<.1
441	Denison Bulletin and Review—*Greg Wehle*	PO Box 550, Denison IA 51442	712-263-2122	R	5*	<.1
442	Northfield News Publishing Co—*Renee Huckle*	PO Box 58, Northfield MN 55057	507-645-5615	R	5*	<.1
443	Burlington Hawk Eye Co—*Steve Delaney*	PO Box 10, Burlington IA 52601	319-754-8461	R	5*	.1
444	Daily Wilson Times Inc—*Morgan Dickerman*	PO Box 2447, Wilson NC 27894	252-243-5151	R	5*	.1
445	Wednesday Journal Inc—*Dan Haley*	141 S Oak Park Ave Ste, Oak Park IL 60302	708-524-8300	R	5*	.1
446	Porterville Recorder Co—*Mark Mceachen*	PO Box 151, Porterville CA 93258	559-784-5000	R	5*	.1
447	Huse Publishing Co—*Eugene Huse*	PO Box 977, Norfolk NE 68702	402-371-1020	R	5*	.1
448	A Zimmer Ltd—*Arthur Zimmer*	4111 Sentinel Heights, Jamesville NY 13078	315-422-7011	R	5*	.1
449	Herburger Publications Inc—*Roy Herburger*	604 N Lincoln Way, Galt CA 95632	209-745-1551	R	5*	.1
450	Call Newspapers Inc—*Fred Knecht*	PO Box 178, Schuylkill Haven PA 17972	570-385-3120	R	5*	<.1
451	Cowl Inc—*Michael Massey*	PO Box 2981, Providence RI 02912	401-865-2214	R	5*	.1
452	Des Plaines Journal Inc—*Richard Wessell*	622 Graceland Ave, Des Plaines IL 60016	847-299-5511	R	5*	.1
453	Grace Communications Inc—*Joann Grace*	PO Box 60859, Los Angeles CA 90060	213-346-0033	R	5*	.1
454	Tracy Press Inc—*Robert Matthews*	PO Box 419, Tracy CA 95378	209-835-3030	R	5*	.1
455	Bee Publishing Co—*R Smith*	PO Box 5503, Newtown CT 06470	203-426-3141	R	5*	.1
456	Suburban Journals—*Tom Rees* St Louis Post-Dispatch	14522 S Outer Fourty R, Town and Country MO 63017	314-821-1110	S	5	.1
457	Sentinel Integrity Solutions - USA LP—*Ginger Corey*	6606 Miller Rd 2, Houston TX 77049	281-457-2225	R	5*	.1
458	Progressive Communications—*Kay Culbertson*	PO Box 791, Mount Vernon OH 43050	740-397-5333	R	5*	.1
459	China Times Printing Inc—*Franklin Yu*	PO Box 970, San Gabriel CA 91778	626-576-7006	R	5*	.1
460	Reed Print Inc—*Frank Reed*	5409 Aldrin Ct, Bakersfield CA 93313	661-834-0496	R	5*	.1
461	Tabloid Graphic Services Inc—*Steve Brosious*	7101 Westfield Ave, Pennsauken NJ 08110	856-486-0410	R	5*	.1
462	Gallup Independent Co—*Robert Zollinger*	PO Box 1210, Gallup NM 87305	505-863-6811	R	5*	.1
463	Vicksburg Printing And Publishing Co—*Louis Cashman*	PO Box 821668, Vicksburg MS 39182	601-636-4545	H	4*	.1
464	Maquoketa Newspapers Inc—*Robert Melvold*	108 W Quarry St, Maquoketa IA 52060	563-652-2441	R	4*	.1
465	Paso Del Norte Publishing Inc—*Adrian Rodriguez*	1801 Texas Ave, El Paso TX 79901	915-838-1601	R	4*	.1
466	USA Distributors Inc—*Antonio Ibarria*	3510 Bergenline Ave St, Union City NJ 07087	201-348-1959	R	4*	.1
467	Mother Lode Printing and Publishing Company Inc—*Joe Boydston*	PO Box 1088, Placerville CA 95667	530-622-1255	R	4*	.1
468	Managementf Paper Company LLC	650 Smithfield St Ste, Pittsburgh PA 15222	412-316-3342	R	4*	<.1
469	Argus Hillsboro Inc—*Clark Gallagher*	PO Box 588, Hillsboro OR 97123	503-648-1131	R	4*	<.1
470	Star Publishing Company Inc—*Rubert Phillips*	522 W 3rd St, Hope AR 71801	870-777-8841	R	4*	.1
471	Brunswick News Publishing Co—*Buff Leavy*	PO Box 1557, Brunswick GA 31521	912-265-8320	R	4*	.1
472	Commercial Dispatch Publishing Company Inc—*V Birney*	PO Box 511, Columbus MS 39703	662-328-2424	R	4*	.1
473	Ibj Corp—*Michael Maurer*	41 E Washington St Ste, Indianapolis IN 46204	317-634-6200	R	4*	.1
474	Leader Publications LLC—*David Compton*	217 N 4th St, Niles MI 49120	269-683-2100	R	4*	.1
475	State Hornet—*Layla Bohm*	6000 J St, Sacramento CA 95819	916-278-6583	R	4*	.1
476	India Abroad Publications Inc—*Ajit Balakrishnan*	42 Broadway Ste 1836, New York NY 10004	212-929-1727	R	4*	.1
477	Roswell Daily Record Inc—*Robert Beck*	PO Box 1897, Roswell NM 88202	575-622-7710	R	4*	.1
478	Star Printing Co—*John Sullivan*	PO Box 2000, Livingston MT 59047	406-222-2000	R	4*	.2
479	Feather Publishing Company Inc—*Michael Taborski*	PO Box B, Quincy CA 95971	530-283-0800	R	4*	.1
480	Bryan Publishing Co—*Christopher Cullis*	PO Box 471, Bryan OH 43506	419-636-1111	R	4*	.1
481	Rock Valley Publishing LLC—*Pete Cruger*	11512 N 2nd St, Machesney Park IL 61115	815-877-4044	R	4*	.1
482	Sherman Publications Inc—*James Sherman*	PO Box 108, Oxford MI 48371	248-628-4801	R	4*	.1
483	Ag Press Inc—*Verlla Coughenour*	PO Box 1009, Manhattan KS 66505	785-539-7558	R	4*	.1
484	Herald Reflector Inc—*David Rau*	PO Box 71, Norwalk OH 44857	419-668-3771	R	4*	.1
485	Tooele Transcript-Bulletin Publishing Company Inc—*Scott Dunn*	PO Box 390, Tooele UT 84074	435-882-0050	R	4*	.1
486	Hawaii Hochi Ltd—*Paul Yempuku*	PO Box 17430, Honolulu HI 96817	808-845-2255	R	4*	.1
487	Hometown News—*William Knox*	28 Milwaukee Ave W, Fort Atkinson WI 53538	920-563-5553	R	4*	.1
488	Village News Inc—*David Tennyson*	PO Box 1108, Blytheville AR 72316	870-763-4461	R	4*	<.1
489	Chillicothe Gazette—*Mike Throne* Gannett Company Inc	50 W Main St, Chillicothe OH 45601	740-773-2111	S	4*	<.1
490	Chippewa Herald—*Mark Baker* Lee Enterprises Inc	PO Box 69, Chippewa Falls WI 54729	715-723-5515	S	4*	<.1
491	Glastonbury Citizen Inc—*James Hallas*	PO Box 373, Glastonbury CT 06033	860-633-4691	R	4*	<.1
492	Business Publications Corp—*Connie Wimer*	100 4th St, Des Moines IA 50309	515-288-3336	R	4*	<.1
493	National Catholic Reporter Publishing Co—*Wally Reiter*	PO Box 411009, Kansas City MO 64141	816-531-0538	R	4*	<.1
494	Cannon Falls Beacon Inc—*Dick Dalton*	PO Box 366, Cannon Falls MN 55009	507-263-3991	R	4*	<.1
495	East Coast Publications Inc—*Thomas Murray*	PO Box 55, Accord MA 02018	781-878-4540	R	4*	.1
496	Almeda Times Star—*Dean Singleton*	1516 Oak St, Alameda CA 94501	510-748-1666	S	4*	<.1
497	Leader Publishing Inc—*Garrick Feldman*	PO Box 766, Jacksonville AR 72078	501-982-9421	R	4*	.1
498	Pilot LLC—*Hunter Chase*	145 W Pennsylvania Ave, Southern Pines NC 28387	910-692-7271	R	4*	.1
499	Polk County Publishing Co—*Alvin Holley*	PO Box 1276, Livingston TX 77351	936-327-4357	R	4*	.1
500	Shelbyville Newspapers Inc—*Paul Mahoney*	PO Box 750, Shelbyville IN 46176	317-398-6631	R	4*	.1
501	Burrell's Information Services—*Robert Wagner*	297 Care St Fl 1, Harrisburg PA 17109	717-671-3872	R	4*	.1
502	Riverfront Times—*Ray Hartmann*	6358 Delmar Blvd Ste 2, Saint Louis MO 63130	314-615-6666	R	4*	.1
503	Stonebridge Press Inc—*Frank Chilinski*	PO Box 90, Southbridge MA 01550	508-764-4325	R	4*	.1
504	Los Angeles Sentinel Inc—*Brik Booker*	3800 Crenshaw Blvd, Los Angeles CA 90008	323-299-3800	R	4*	.1
505	Los Angeles Jewish Publications Inc—*Kember Sax*	3580 Wilshire Blvd Ste, Los Angeles CA 90010	213-368-1661	R	4*	<.1
506	Norton Press Inc—*Michael Tate*	PO Box 380, Norton VA 24273	276-679-1101	R	4*	.1

Note: An asterisk (*) indicates an estimated financial figure. The company type code used is as follows: R = Private, P = Public, S = Private Subsidiary, B = Public Subsidiary, D = Division, J = Joint Venture, I = Investment Fund.

COMPANY RANKINGS BY SALES WITHIN 4-DIGIT SIC

Rank	Company Name—*Executive Officer*	Address, City, State, Zip	Phone	Type	Fin	Empls
507	Austin Chronicle Corp—*Nick Barbaro*	4000 N Interstate 35, Austin TX 78751	512-454-5766	R	4*	.1
508	Arkansas Valley Publishing Company Inc—*Merle Baranczyk*	125 E 2nd St, Salida CO 81201	719-539-6691	R	4*	.1
509	Allegheny Bar Association Inc—*David Blaener*	436 7th Ave Ste 4, Pittsburgh PA 15219	412-261-6255	R	4*	.1
510	Connection Publishing Inc—*Peter Labovitz*	PO Box 221374, Chantilly VA 20153	703-821-5050	R	4*	.1
511	Iowa Information Inc—*Peter Wagner*	PO Box 160, Sheldon IA 51201	712-324-5347	R	4*	<.1
512	Beacon Communications Inc—*John Howell*	1944 Warwick Ave Ste 4, Warwick RI 02889	401-732-3100	R	4*	<.1
513	RW Publications Division Of Waterhouse Publication Inc—*Robert Rozeski*	3770 Transit Rd, Orchard Park NY 14127	716-662-4200	R	4*	.2
514	News Reporter Company Inc—*James High*	PO Box 707, Whiteville NC 28472	910-642-4104	R	4*	.1
515	Bedford Gazette LLC—*George Sample*	424 W Penn St, Bedford PA 15522	814-623-1151	R	4*	.1
516	Waupaca County Publishing Company Inc—*Scott Turner*	PO Box 152, Waupaca WI 54981	715-258-5546	R	4*	.1
517	Alter Communications Inc—*Ronnie Buerger*	1040 Park Ave Ste 200, Baltimore MD 21201	410-752-3504	R	4*	.1
518	Observer Group Inc—*Matthew Walsh*	PO Box 8100, Longboat Key FL 34228	941-383-5509	R	4*	.1
519	Chicago Citizen Newspaper Group—*William Garth*	806 E 78th St, Chicago IL 60619	773-783-1251	R	4*	.1
520	Record Publishing Company Inc—*Bart Adams*	PO Box 1448, Dunn NC 28335	910-891-1234	R	3*	.1
521	Daily News Publishing Co—*Chris Miles*	PO Box 128, Mckeesport PA 15134	412-664-9161	R	3*	.1
522	Suburban Publishing Corp—*Richard Ayer*	10 1st Ave, Peabody MA 01960	978-532-5880	R	3*	<.1
523	Imes Communications Of El Paso—*V Imes*	516 Main St, Columbus MS 39701	662-328-2424	R	3*	.1
524	Weatherford News Inc—*Phillip Reid*	118 S Broadway St, Weatherford OK 73096	580-772-3301	R	3*	.1
525	Horizon Ohio Publications Inc—*Todd Boit*	102 E Spring St, Saint Marys OH 45885	419-394-7414	R	3*	.1
526	Cortland Standard Printing Company Inc—*Kevin Howe*	PO Box 5548, Cortland NY 13045	607-756-5665	R	3*	.1
527	Da Publishing Inc—*Deanna Nelson*	205 S New Madrid St, Sikeston MO 63801	573-471-1137	R	3*	.1
528	New York Press Inc—*Russ Smith*	79 Madison Ave Fl 16, New York NY 10016	212-268-8600	R	3*	.1
529	Roberson Advertising Service LLC—*Michael Roberson*	3010 Lausat St, Metairie LA 70001	504-832-1481	R	3*	.1
530	Tide Water Pulication LLC—*Terry Cassidy*	PO Box 497, Franklin VA 23851	757-562-3187	R	3*	.1
531	Argus Press Co—*Tom Campbell*	201 E Exchange St, Owosso MI 48867	989-725-5136	R	3*	.1
532	Journal-News Publishing Company Inc—*Jeffrey Fletcher*	PO Box 998, Ephrata WA 98823	509-754-4636	R	3*	.1
533	Columbia Basin Publishing Company Inc—*Duane Hagadone*	PO Box 910, Moses Lake WA 98837	509-765-4561	R	3*	.1
534	Gazette Media Inc—*William Bleakley*	PO Box 54649, Oklahoma City OK 73154	405-528-6000	R	3*	.1
535	International Daily News—*Jessica Elnitiarta*	870 Monterey Pass Rd, Monterey Park CA 91754	323-265-1317	R	3*	.1
536	Sun News Inc—*Robert Marshall*	PO Box 145, Marysville WA 98270	360-659-1300	R	3*	.1
537	Bee Publications Inc—*Trey Measer*	5564 Main St, Williamsville NY 14221	716-632-4700	R	3*	.1
538	Inter Mountain Company Inc—*George Nutting*	PO Box 1339, Elkins WV 26241	304-636-2121	R	3*	.1
539	Batesville Guard Record—*O Jones*	PO Box 2036, Batesville AR 72503	870-793-2383	R	3*	.1
540	Athol Press Inc—*Richard Chase*	PO Box 1000, Athol MA 01331	978-249-3535	R	3*	<.1
541	Gardena Valley News Inc—*George Algie*	PO Box 219, Gardena CA 90248	310-329-6351	R	3*	<.1
542	Ranger Riverton Inc—*Steven Peck*	PO Box 993, Riverton WY 82501	307-856-2244	R	3*	.1
543	Oelwein Publishing Company Inc—*John Perotto*	PO Box 511, Oelwein IA 50662	319-283-2144	R	3*	.1
544	Seaton Publishing Co—*Donald Seaton*	PO Box 788, Hastings NE 68902	402-462-2131	R	3*	.1
545	Forward Newspaper LLC—*Samuel Norich* Forward Association Inc	125 Maiden Ln, New York NY 10038	212-889-8200	S	3*	.1
546	Texoma Web Offset Printing Ltd—*Dwayne Crow*	PO Box 410, Gainesville TX 76241	940-665-6262	R	3*	.1
547	Polish Daily News—*Edward Moskal*	5711 N Milwaukee Ave, Chicago IL 60646	773-763-3343	R	3*	.1
548	Bicentennial Publishing Corp—*Ted Kondratowicz*	333 W 38th St, New York NY 10018	212-594-2266	R	3*	<.1
549	Brasilians Press And Publications Inc—*Joao Matos*	PO Box 985, New York NY 10185	212-764-6161	R	3*	<.1
550	JO Emmerich and Associates Inc—*John Emmerich*	PO Box 2009, Mccomb MS 39649	601-684-2421	R	3*	<.1
551	El Crepusculo Inc—*Robin Mc Kinney Marti*	PO Box 3737, Taos NM 87571	575-758-2241	R	3*	<.1
552	San Jose Business Journal—*James MacGregor* American City Business Journals Inc	125 S Market St 11th F, San Jose CA 95113	408-295-3800	S	3*	<.1
553	San Antonio Current Co—*George Lynett*	915 Dallas St, San Antonio TX 78215	210-227-0044	R	3*	<.1
554	San Antonio Informer Publishing—*Tom Moore*	333 S Hackberry St, San Antonio TX 78203	210-227-8300	R	3*	<.1
555	Tioga Publishing Co—*Larry Paerrotto*	PO Box 118, Wellsboro PA 16901	570-724-2287	R	3*	.1
556	Reub Williams and Sons Inc—*Michael Williams*	PO Box 1448, Warsaw IN 46581	574-267-3111	R	3*	.1
557	Standard Publishing Company Inc—*Kathleen Russell* Morris Multimedia Inc	PO Box 150, Mcminnville TN 37111	931-473-2191	S	3*	.1
558	Creston Publishing Co—*Thomas Shaw*	PO Box 126, Creston IA 50801	641-782-2141	R	3*	.1
559	Excel Promotions Corp—*Richard Freedman*	565 Broadhollow Rd Ste, Farmingdale NY 11735	631-454-1600	R	3*	.1
560	Houston Business Journals Inc—*Ray Shaw*	1233 W Loop S Ste 1300, Houston TX 77027	713-688-8811	R	3*	.1
561	Arkansas Times Inc—*Alan Leveritt*	PO Box 34010, Little Rock AR 72203	501-375-2985	R	3*	<.1
562	Hometown Publications Ii Inc—*Ken Ubert*	PO Box 335, Germantown WI 53022	262-238-6397	R	3*	<.1
563	King Media Enterprises Inc—*Don King*	PO Box 6297, Cleveland OH 44101	216-791-7600	R	3*	<.1
564	Hudson Reporter Associates LP—*Nancy Kist*	PO Box 3069, Hoboken NJ 07030	201-798-7800	R	3*	<.1
565	Union City Daily Messenger Inc—*David Critchlow*	PO Box 430, Union City TN 38281	731-885-0744	R	3*	<.1
566	Wyoming Newspapers—*John Tompkins*	PO Box 1058, Torrington WY 82240	307-532-2184	R	3*	.1
567	South County Newspaper Inc—*Albert Sherman*	PO Box 5679, Wakefield RI 02880	401-789-6000	R	3*	.1
568	Courier Herald Publishing Company Inc—*Griffin Lovett*	115 S Jefferson St, Dublin GA 31021	478-272-5522	R	3*	.1
569	Current Publishing LLC—*Ann Duddy*	PO Box 840, Westbrook ME 04098	207-854-2577	R	3*	.1
570	Green Banner Publications Inc—*Joseph Green*	PO Box 38, Pekin IN 47165	812-967-3176	R	3*	.1
571	Mark I Publications Inc—*Mark Wilder*	PO Box 747769, Rego Park NY 11374	718-205-8000	R	3*	.1
572	Iran Times Inc—*Javad Khabaz*	PO Box 9848, Washington DC 20016	202-659-9868	R	3*	<.1
573	Jewish Week Inc—*Gary Rosenblatt*	1501 Broadway Ste 505, New York NY 10036	212-921-7822	R	3*	<.1
574	Denver Business Journal—*Scott Bemis*	1700 Broadway Ste 515, Denver CO 80290	303-837-3500	R	3*	<.1
575	East Hampton Star Inc—*Helen Rattray*	PO Box 5002, East Hampton NY 11937	631-324-0002	R	3*	<.1
576	Bailey Publishing and Communications Inc—*James Bailey*	10 N Newnan St, Jacksonville FL 32202	904-356-2466	R	3*	<.1
577	Cycle News Inc—*Sharon Clayton*	PO Box 930, North Bend OR 97459	949-863-7082	R	3*	<.1
578	Livewire Printing Company Inc—*James Keul*	PO Box 208, Jackson MN 56143	507-847-3771	R	3*	.1
579	Town Cryer—*Roger Miller*	62 Black Mountain Rd, Brattleboro VT 05301	802-257-7771	R	3*	.1
580	Anteebo Publishers Inc—*Robert Edgar*	96 Kercheval Ave, Grosse Pointe MI 48236	313-882-6900	R	3*	.1
581	Morris Newspaper Corporation Of Kansas—*Charles Morris* Morris Multimedia Inc	PO Box 228, Great Bend KS 67530	620-792-1211	S	3*	<.1
582	Carter Publishing Company Inc—*John Owensby*	PO Box 337, Kernersville NC 27285	336-993-2161	R	3*	<.1
583	Winchester Sun Co—*George Tatman*	20 Wall St, Winchester KY 40391	859-744-3123	R	3*	<.1
584	City Of Roses Newspaper Co—*Richard Meeker*	2220 Nw Quimby St, Portland OR 97210	503-243-2122	R	3*	<.1
585	Hubbard Publishing Co—*Janet Hubbard*	PO Box 40, Bellefontaine OH 43311	937-592-3060	R	3*	<.1
586	Patchogue Advance Inc—*John Tuthill*	20 Medford Ave Ste 1, Patchogue NY 11772	631-475-1000	R	3*	<.1
587	Post Citizen Media—*Alice Queen*	PO Box 136, Conyers GA 30012	770-483-7108	S	3	<.1
588	Pipestone Publishing Company Inc—*James Kuel*	PO Box 277, Pipestone MN 56164	507-825-3333	R	3*	.4
589	Illini Media Co—*Tim Ditman*	512 E Green St, Champaign IL 61820	217-337-8300	R	3*	.4
590	Graphic Publications Inc—*Michael Mast*	123 W 3rd St, Dover OH 44622	330-343-4377	R	3*	.1
591	Specht Newspapers Inc—*David Specht*	PO Box 1339, Minden LA 71058	318-377-1866	R	3*	<.1

Rank	Company Name—*Executive Officer*	Address, City, State, Zip	Phone	Type	Fin	Empls
592	Consolidated Race Promoters Of Automobile Competition Inc—*Kathy Root*	PO Box 921, Vinton IA 52349	319-472-4763	R	3*	<.1
593	National Herald Inc—*Anthony Diamataris*	3710 30th St, Long Island City NY 11101	718-784-5255	R	3*	<.1
594	Enterprise Publishing Co—*Mark Rhoades*	PO Box 328, Blair NE 68008	402-426-2121	R	3*	.1
595	Suburban Newspapers Inc—*Shon Barenklau*	604 Fort Crook Rd N, Bellevue NE 68005	402-733-7300	R	3*	.1
596	Wappingers Falls Shopper Inc—*Albert Osten*	84 E Main St, Wappingers Falls NY 12590	845-297-3723	R	3*	.1
597	Hunter Publishing Inc—*Jon Hunter*	PO Box 348, Madison SD 57042	605-256-4444	R	3*	<.1
598	Larson Publishing Inc—*Robert Larson*	PO Box 619, Sedona AZ 86339	928-282-7795	R	3*	<.1
599	Windsor-Press Inc—*George Mitten*	PO Box 465, Hamburg PA 19526	610-562-2267	R	3*	<.1
600	Morris Publications—*Larry Mendonca*	122 S 3rd Ave, Oakdale CA 95361	209-847-3021	R	3*	<.1
601	Press And Journal Inc—*Joseph Sukle*	20 S Union St, Middletown PA 17057	717-944-4628	R	3*	<.1
602	Vermont Publishing Corp—*Emerson Lynn*	281 N Main St, Saint Albans VT 05478	802-524-9771	R	3*	<.1
603	Want Ads Of Omaha Inc—*Otis Seals*	PO Box 6569, Omaha NE 68106	402-342-4426	R	3*	<.1
604	Breeze Printing Co—*Mary Lasswell*	PO Box 440, Taylorville IL 62568	217-824-2233	R	2*	<.1
605	Hersam Publishing Co—*Martin Hersam*	38 Vitti St, New Canaan CT 06840	203-966-9541	R	2*	<.1
606	Bradford County Telegraph Inc—*John Miller*	135 W Call St, Starke FL 32091	904-964-6305	R	2*	<.1
607	Columbus Messenger Co—*Phillip Daubel*	3500 Sullivant Ave, Columbus OH 43204	614-272-5422	R	2*	<.1
608	Times Review Newspaper Corp—*Troy Gustavson*	PO Box 1500, Mattituck NY 11952	631-298-3200	R	2*	<.1
609	Lakeland Shopping Guide Green—*Bill Marcel*	225 7th Ave E, Alexandria MN 56308	320-763-3133	R	2*	.1
610	Boone Newspapers—*Todd Carpenter*	PO Box 1447, Natchez MS 39121	601-442-9101	R	2*	.1
611	Classified Display—*George Lynette*	812 Park Ave, Baltimore MD 21201	410-523-0300	R	2*	.1
612	Hardin County Publishing Company Inc—*Jeff Barnes*	PO Box 230, Kenton OH 43326	419-674-4066	R	2*	.1
613	Rutherford The Tennessean—*Mary Reeves*	224 N Walnut St, Murfreesboro TN 37130	615-225-4000	R	2*	.1
614	Waycross Journal Herald Inc—*Roger Williams*	400 Isabella St, Waycross GA 31501	912-283-2244	R	2*	<.1
615	Daily Ellensburg Record Inc—*Dave Lord*	401 N Main St, Ellensburg WA 98926	509-925-1414	R	2*	<.1
616	Hillsboro Journal Inc—*Joyce Connor*	431 S Main St, Hillsboro IL 62049	217-532-3933	R	2*	<.1
617	Oneida Publications Inc—*Maryann Hawthorne*	PO Box 120, Oneida NY 13421	315-363-5100	R	2*	<.1
618	O'bannon Publishing Company Inc—*Dennis Huber*	301 N Capitol Ave, Corydon IN 47112	812-738-2211	R	2*	<.1
619	Wakefield Item Co—*Robert Dolbeare*	26 Albion St, Wakefield MA 01880	781-245-0080	R	2*	<.1
620	James Digeorgia and Associates Inc—*James Digeorgia*	925 S Federal Hwy Ste, Boca Raton FL 33432	561-750-8483	R	2*	<.1
621	Times-Herald Publishing Company Inc—*Trent Bonner Mc Collu*	PO Box 1699, Forrest City AR 72336	870-633-3130	R	2*	.1
622	Gardner News Inc—*Alberta Bell*	PO Box 340, Gardner MA 01440	978-632-8000	R	2*	.1
623	Review—*Sandy Iverson*	325 Academy St Rm 201, Newark DE 19716	302-831-2771	R	2*	.1
624	Ball Publishing Company Inc—*Carol Ball*	5312 Sebring Warner Rd, Greenville OH 45331	937-548-3330	R	2*	<.1
625	Cabinet Press Inc—*Shana Hoch*	54 School St, Milford NH 03055	603-673-3100	R	2*	<.1
626	Tallapoosa Publishers Inc—*Tim Reeves*	PO Box 999, Alexander City AL 35011	256-234-4281	R	2*	<.1
627	Woodward Publishing Company Inc—*Sheila Gay*	PO Box 928, Woodward OK 73802	580-256-2200	R	2*	<.1
628	Daily Quill—*Frank Martin*	PO Box 110, West Plains MO 65775	417-256-9191	R	2*	<.1
629	Murray Newspapers Inc—*Alice Rouse*	PO Box 1040, Murray KY 42071	270-753-1916	R	2*	<.1
630	Hippopress LLC—*Dan Szczesny*	49 Hollis St, Manchester NH 03101	603-625-1855	R	2*	<.1
631	Marysville Newspaper Inc—*Daniel Behrens*	PO Box 226, Marysville OH 43040	937-644-9111	R	2*	<.1
632	Beeville Publishing Co—*Fred Latcham*	PO Box 10, Beeville TX 78104	361-358-2550	R	2*	<.1
633	Austin Newspapers Inc—*Dave Chruchill*	310 2nd St Ne, Austin MN 55912	507-433-8851	R	2*	<.1
634	Three Rivers Commercial News—*Richard Milliman*	PO Box 130, Three Rivers MI 49093	269-279-7488	R	2*	<.1
635	Washington Jewish Week Inc—*Preston Lequita*	11426 Rckvlle Pke Ste, Rockville MD 20852	301-230-2222	R	2*	<.1
636	News Daily Paper—*Herman Cawthon*	138 Church St, Jonesboro GA 30236	770-478-5753	R	2*	.1
637	Canon City Shopper Newspaper—*Gary Minor*	212 S 5th St, Canon City CO 81212	719-275-9131	R	2*	<.1
638	Bay St Louis Newspapers Inc—*Chark Lancaster*	PO Box 2009, Bay Saint Louis MS 39521	228-467-5473	R	2*	<.1
639	Carter-Hubbard Publishing Company Inc—*Julius Hubbard*	711 Main St, North Wilkesboro NC 28659	336-838-4117	R	2*	<.1
640	Daily Newspaper—*Daniel Baulmson*	385 Airport Rd Ste A, Elgin IL 60123	847-608-2700	R	2*	<.1
641	Delphos Herald Of Indiana Inc—*Murray Cohen*	PO Box 4128, Lawrenceburg IN 47025	812-537-0063	R	2*	.3
642	Students Publications Inc—*Bill Casey*	111 Communications Ctr, Iowa City IA 52242	319-335-5787	R	2*	.1
643	Washington News Publishing Company Inc—*Ashley Futrell*	PO Box 1788, Washington NC 27889	252-946-2144	R	2*	.1
644	Morrison County Record—*Carolyn Hoheisel*	216 1st St Se, Little Falls MN 56345	320-632-2345	R	2*	.1
645	American Classified Inc—*Robert Christensen*	1468 Roswell Rd, Marietta GA 30062	770-971-8333	R	2*	.1
646	Reflector Publishing/Printing—*Marvin Case*	PO Box 2020, Battle Ground WA 98604	360-687-5151	R	2*	.1
647	USA Printing Corp—*Wea Lee*	11122 Bellaire Blvd, Houston TX 77072	281-498-4310	R	2*	.1
648	Messenger Publication Inc—*Dick Norlander*	280 West Main St, Isle MN 56342	320-676-3123	R	2*	<.1
649	Star Journal Publishing Co—*Avis Tucker*	PO Box 68, Warrensburg MO 64093	660-747-8123	R	2*	<.1
650	Daily Sentinel Classified Advertising—*Jennifer Ricks*	PO Box 630068, Nacogdoches TX 75963	936-564-8361	R	2*	<.1
651	Jeffco Publishing Company Inc—*Scott Perrimann*	PO Box 17270, Golden CO 80402	303-279-5541	R	2*	<.1
652	Postal Systems Examiner—*Charles Cresswell*	102 E Columbia St, Farmington MO 63640	573-756-0280	R	2*	<.1
653	News Banner Publications Inc—*Mark F Miller*	PO Box 436, Bluffton IN 46714	260-824-0224	R	2*	<.1
654	Valley Newspaper Inc—*Nell Walls-Cowart*	PO Box 850, Lanett AL 36863	334-644-1101	R	2*	<.1
655	Biocentury Publications Inc—*David Flores*	PO Box 1246, San Carlos CA 94070	650-595-5333	R	2*	<.1
656	Vondrak Publishing Company Inc—*James Drak*	6225 S Kedzie Ave, Chicago IL 60629	773-476-4800	R	2*	<.1
657	Winnemucca Publishing Company Inc—*Peter Bernhard*	1022 Grass Valley Rd, Winnemucca NV 89445	775-623-5011	R	2*	<.1
658	Williamson County Sun Inc—*Linda Scarbrough*	PO Box 39, Georgetown TX 78627	512-930-4824	R	2*	<.1
659	Great Northern Wheels Deals Inc—*Bill Collins*	2321 Lincoln St, Oroville CA 95966	530-533-2134	R	2*	<.1
660	Fort Worth Weekly LP—*Lee Newquist*	3311 Hamilton Ave, Fort Worth TX 76107	817-877-3018	R	2*	<.1
661	Gannett Company Inc Newspaper Div—*Garacia Martone* Gannett Company Inc	7950 Jones Branch Dr, McLean VA 22102	703-854-6000	D	2*	<.1
662	Page One Inc—*Dolores Heim*	PO Box 278, Imlay City MI 48444	810-724-2615	R	2*	<.1
663	Thief River Falls Times Inc—*John P Mattson*	PO Box 100, Thief River Falls MN 56701	218-681-4450	R	2	<.1
664	Unger Enterprises Inc—*C Unger*	PO Box 8, Nitro WV 25143	304-755-0270	R	2*	<.1
665	Valley Courier Newspaper—*Keith R Cerny*	PO Box 1099, Alamosa CO 81101	719-589-2553	S	2*	<.1
666	Keynoter Publishing Co—*Wayne Markham*	PO Box 500158, Marathon FL 33050	305-743-5551	R	2*	<.1
667	Leader Publishing Co (Pontiac Illinois)—*Tom Hutson*	PO Box 170, Pontiac IL 61764	815-842-1153	R	2*	<.1
668	Lee Publishing Co—*Larry Lee*	2330 Alhambra Blvd, Sacramento CA 95817	916-452-4781	R	2*	<.1
669	Publishing Forest LLC—*Greg Allen*	PO Box 1919, Wake Forest NC 27588	919-556-3182	R	2*	<.1
670	Sonoma Index Tribune Corp—*Bill Lynch*	PO Box C, Sonoma CA 95476	707-938-2111	R	C	<.1
671	Extra Bilingual Publications Group	3906 W North Ave, Chicago IL 60647	773-252-3534	R	2*	<.1
672	India-West Publications Inc—*Ramesh Murarka*	933 Macarthur Blvd, San Leandro CA 94577	510-383-1140	R	2*	<.1
673	Milwaukee Catholic Press Apostolate Inc—*Brian Olszewski*	PO Box 070913, Milwaukee WI 53207	414-769-3500	R	2*	<.1
674	Pesch Publishing Company Inc—*Charles Gardon*	PO Box 187, Peshtigo WI 54157	715-582-4541	R	2*	<.1
675	Barnum Printing and Publishing Co—*Joe Rosenberg*	6899 Grove St, Denver CO 80221	303-936-2345	R	2*	<.1
676	Midwest Byline—*George Williams*	309 3rd St NW, Bemidji MN 56601	218-759-1139	R	2*	<.1
677	Delta Publications Inc—*Michael Mathes*	PO Box 237, Kiel WI 53042	920-894-2828	R	2*	<.1
678	Miami County Publishing Company Inc—*Greg Branson*	PO Box 389, Paola KS 66071	913-294-2311	R	2*	<.1
679	Suel Printing Company Inc—*Lois Wann*	PO Box 25, New Prague MN 56071	952-758-4435	R	2*	<.1

Note: An asterisk (*) indicates an estimated financial figure. The company type code used is as follows: R = Private, P = Public, S = Private Subsidiary, B = Public Subsidiary, D = Division, J = Joint Venture, I = Investment Fund.

COMPANY RANKINGS BY SALES WITHIN 4-DIGIT SIC

Rank	Company Name—Executive Officer	Address, City, State, Zip	Phone	Type	Fin	Empls
680	Coast Star—James Manser	13 Broad St, Manasquan NJ 08736	732-223-0076	R	2*	<.1
681	Hopewell Publishing Company Inc—James Lancaster	PO Box 481, Hopewell VA 23860	804-458-8511	R	2*	<.1
682	Bolton Newspapers Inc—Kermit Bolton	PO Box 826, Monroeville AL 36461	251-575-3282	R	2*	<.1
683	Realtimetraderscom—Andrew Marthiasan	1325 N Forest Rd Ste 3, Buffalo NY 14221	716-632-6600	R	2*	<.1
684	Bluffton News Publishing and Printing Company Inc—Thomas Edwards	PO Box 49, Bluffton OH 45817	419-358-8010	R	2*	<.1
685	Nuvo Inc—Kevin Mckinney	3951 N Meridian St Ste, Indianapolis IN 46208	317-254-2400	R	2*	<.1
686	AM News Corp—Wilbert Tatum	2340 Frdrick Douglas B, New York NY 10027	212-932-7400	R	2*	<.1
687	Herald Farmville Inc—William Wall	PO Box 307, Farmville VA 23901	434-392-4151	R	2*	<.1
688	Napoleon Inc—Christopher Cullis	595 E Riverview Ave, Napoleon OH 43545	419-592-5055	R	2*	<.1
689	Shelbyville Publishing Company Inc—Hugh Jones	PO Box 380, Shelbyville TN 37162	931-684-1200	R	2*	<.1
690	Vernon Publishing Inc—Dane Vernon	PO Box 315, Eldon MO 65026	573-392-5658	R	2*	<.1
691	Mineral Daily News Tribune—Kirk Davis	PO Box 879, Keyser WV 26726	304-788-3333	R	2*	<.1
692	La Tribuna Publication Inc—Ruth Molenaar	300 36th St Apt 1, Union City NJ 07087	201-617-1360	R	2*	<.1
693	Mexico Independent Inc—Mark Backus	PO Box 129, Mexico NY 13114	315-963-7813	R	2*	<.1
694	Purdue Student Publishing Foundation—Niagara Falls	PO Box 2506, West Lafayette IN 47996	765-743-1111	R	2*	<.1
695	Winfield Publishing Company Inc—Frederick Seaton	PO Box 543, Winfield KS 67156	620-221-1050	R	2*	<.1
696	Gold Nugget Publications Inc—Martin Jones	PO Box 440, Virden IL 62690	217-965-3355	R	2*	<.1
697	Pioneer Printing Company Inc—Tena Williams	PO Box 7900, Ketchikan AK 99901	907-225-3157	R	2*	<.1
698	Bear River Publishing Co—Dave Lord	PO Box 152, Preston ID 83263	208-852-1666	R	2*	<.1
699	Greenville Record Argus Inc—Robert Bracey	PO Box 711, Greenville PA 16125	724-588-5000	R	2*	<.1
700	Media Palmer Inc—Robert Palmer	PO Box 1177, Mount Pleasant TX 75456	903-572-1705	R	2*	<.1
701	Panhandle Buyers Guide—Thomas Aird	415 Wilson St, Martinsburg WV 25401	304-267-9983	R	2*	<.1
702	Mid America Publishers	PO Box 18095, Kansas City MO 64133	816-356-8790	R	2*	<.1
703	New Times Media Group—Fred Bohnhoff	1010 Marsh St, San Luis Obispo CA 93401	805-546-8208	R	2*	<.1
704	Paris Publishing Co—William Williams	PO Box 310, Paris TN 38242	731-642-1162	R	2*	<.1
705	Reporter Publishing Company Inc—Herbert Meyer	PO Box 869, Independence KS 67301	620-331-3550	R	2*	<.1
706	Rochester Business Journal—Susan Holliday	45 E Ave Ste 500, Rochester NY 14604	585-546-8303	R	2*	<.1
707	Voice Communications Corp—Debbie Loggins	51180 Bedford St, New Baltimore MI 48047	586-716-8100	R	2*	<.1
708	Rhinoceros Times—John Hammer	PO Box 9421, Greensboro NC 27429	336-273-0880	R	2*	<.1
709	Tidewater Newspapers Inc—Elsa Verbyla	PO Box 2060, Gloucester VA 23061	804-693-3101	R	2*	<.1
710	Okaloosa Publishing Company Inc—James Knudsen	295 W James Lee Blvd, Crestview FL 32536	850-682-6524	R	2*	<.1
711	James Newspapers Inc—Howard James	1 Pikes Hl, Norway ME 04268	207-743-7011	R	2*	<.1
712	Natchitoches Times Inc—Lonnie Thomas	PO Box 448, Natchitoches LA 71458	318-352-3618	R	2*	<.1
713	Vineyard Gazette Inc—Richard Reston	PO Box 66, Edgartown MA 02539	508-627-4311	R	2*	<.1
714	Fredericksburg Publishing Co—Terrill Collier	PO Box 1639, Fredericksburg TX 78624	830-997-2155	R	2*	<.1
715	Madison Courier—Jane Jacobs	310 Courier Sq, Madison IN 47250	812-265-3641	R	2*	<.1
716	Blade Empire Publishing Company Inc—J Lowell	PO Box 309, Concordia KS 66901	785-243-2424	R	2*	<.1
717	Chester County Independent Inc—Robin Belew	PO Box 306, Henderson TN 38340	731-989-4624	R	2*	<.1
718	Port Townsend Publishing Company Inc—Scott Wilson	226 Adams St, Port Townsend WA 98368	360-385-2900	R	2*	<.1
719	Welch Publishing Co—Robert Welch	PO Box 267, Perrysburg OH 43552	419-874-4491	R	2*	<.1
720	Bay City Tribune—Michael Reddell	PO Box 2450, Bay City TX 77404	979-245-5555	R	2*	<.1
721	Middle Tyger Times—Don Wilder	438 N Main St, Woodruff SC 29388	864-439-0068	R	2*	<.1
722	Martin Broadcasting Corp—Lynn Martin	620 Choctaw St, Alva OK 73717	580-327-2200	R	2*	<.1
723	North Wind Student Newspaper—Stefane Nichols	2310 University Ctr, Marquette MI 49855	906-227-2545	R	2*	<.1
724	L and M Publications Inc—Linda Toscano	1840 Merrick Ave, Merrick NY 11566	516-378-5320	R	2*	<.1
725	Easy Reader Inc—Kevin Cody	PO Box 427, Hermosa Beach CA 90254	310-372-4611	R	2*	<.1
726	Howe Printing Company Inc—Gary Howel	PO Box 149, Prairie Du Chien WI 53821	608-326-2441	R	2*	<.1
727	Schneps Publications Inc—Victoria Schneps	3815 Bell Blvd Ste 38, Bayside NY 11361	718-224-5863	R	2*	<.1
728	Bewick Publications Inc—Scott Beick	PO Box 706, Dearborn MI 48121	313-584-4000	R	2*	<.1
729	Enterprise Newspaper Group Inc—George Gregersen	PO Box 11778, Salt Lake City UT 84147	801-533-0556	R	2*	<.1
730	Homestead Newspapers Inc—Gary Shorts	PO Box 900340, Homestead FL 33090	305-245-2311	R	2*	<.1
731	Mortgage Press Ltd—Russell Sickmen	1220 Wantagh Ave, Wantagh NY 11793	516-409-1400	R	2*	<.1
732	New England Business Media LLC—Debra Amorelli	172 Shrewsbury St Ste, Worcester MA 01604	508-755-8004	R	2*	<.1
733	Campus Communications Inc—Patricia Carey	PO Box 14257, Gainesville FL 32604	352-376-4446	R	2*	<.1
734	Red And Black Publishing Company Inc—Harry Montevideo	540 Baxter St, Athens GA 30605	706-433-3000	R	2*	.1
735	Boston Sb Publishing Inc—Dawn Curtis	320 Congress St, Boston MA 02210	617-210-7905	R	2*	<.1
736	Seawave Corp—Arthur Hall	1508 Rte 47, Rio Grande NJ 08242	609-886-8600	R	2*	<.1
737	Denham Springs Publishing Company Inc—Jeff David	PO Box 1529, Denham Springs LA 70727	225-665-5176	R	2*	<.1
738	Martin Publishing Company Inc—Robert Martin	PO Box 380, Havana IL 62644	309-543-3311	R	2*	<.1
739	Appen Newspapers Inc—Raymond Appen	319 N Main St, Alpharetta GA 30009	770-442-3278	R	2*	<.1
740	Gaffney Ledger Inc—Cody Sossamon	1604 W Floyd Baker Blv, Gaffney SC 29341	864-489-1131	R	2*	<.1
741	Register Publishing Co—Ken Serota	PO Box 248, Harrisburg IL 62946	618-253-7146	R	2*	<.1
742	Southwest Publisher LLC—Vanessa Repass	PO Box 391, Pulaski VA 24301	540-980-5220	R	2*	<.1
743	Metro North Newspapers Inc—Scott Perriman	PO Box 350070, Westminster CO 80035	303-426-6000	R	2*	<.1
744	Dth Publishing Inc—Kevin Scawarz	PO Box 3257, Chapel Hill NC 27515	919-962-1163	R	1*	.1
745	Nucity Publications Inc—Christopher Johnson	2118 Central Ave Se 15, Albuquerque NM 87106	505-346-0660	R	1*	.1
746	Western Carolina Publishing Company Inc—Jerry Leedy	PO Box 40, Lincolnton NC 28093	704-735-3031	R	1*	<.1
747	Periodico El Vida—Manuel Munoz	130 Palm Dr, Oxnard CA 93030	805-483-1008	R	1*	<.1
748	Beach Beacon—Dan Autry	9911 Seminole Blvd, Seminole FL 33772	727-397-5563	R	1*	<.1
749	Cabot Star Harold—Dennis Byrd	PO Box 1058, Cabot AR 72023	501-843-3534	R	1*	<.1
750	News Chronicle Company Inc—Kenneth Wolfrom	PO Box 100, Shippensburg PA 17257	717-532-4101	R	1*	<.1
751	Berner Brothers Publishing Company Inc—Marie Berner	612 Superior St, Antigo WI 54409	715-623-4191	R	1*	<.1
752	Central Record Publications—Kandy Gates	PO Box 1027, Medford NJ 08055	609-654-5000	R	1*	<.1
753	Chronicle—Mike Ferris	PO Box 553, Omak WA 98841	509-826-1110	R	1*	<.1
754	Newport Publishing Company Inc—John Jones	PO Box 279, Newport TN 37822	423-623-6171	R	1*	<.1
755	News Eagle—Dun Doyle	303 Main Ave Ste C, Hawley PA 18428	570-226-4547	R	1*	<.1
756	Ogemaw County Herald Inc—Robert Perlberg	PO Box 247, West Branch MI 48661	989-345-0044	R	1*	<.1
757	People Sentinel—Billy Morris	PO Box 1255, Barnwell SC 29812	803-259-3501	R	1*	<.1
758	Providence Business News Inc—Roger Bergenheim	220 W Exchange St Ste, Providence RI 02903	401-273-2201	R	1*	<.1
759	South End—Davis Markeysha	5425 Woodward Ave Ste, Detroit MI 48202	313-577-3498	R	1*	<.1
760	Ckmt Associates Inc—Philip Cartwright	6405 Olcott St, Hammond IN 46320	219-924-2820	R	1*	<.1
761	Wisconsin Free Press—Andrew Johnson	PO Box 271, Mayville WI 53050	920-387-2211	R	1*	<.1
762	Paris Beacon News—Ned Jenison	218 N Main St, Paris IL 61944	217-465-6424	R	1*	<.1
763	City Press Publishing Co—Chris Farrell	210 12th Ave S Ste 100, Nashville TN 37203	615-244-7989	R	1*	<.1
764	Doncar Inc—Carol Margraf	100 Domino Dr 1, Concord MA 01742	978-371-2442	R	1*	<.1
765	Georgetown Newspapers Inc—Mike Scogin	1481 Cherry Blossom Wa, Georgetown KY 40324	502-863-1111	R	1*	<.1
766	Hesperia Resorter—Ray Pryke	PO Box 400937, Hesperia CA 92340	760-244-0021	R	1*	<.1
767	Kaechele Publications Inc—Cheryl Kaechele	PO Box 189, Allegan MI 49010	269-673-5534	R	1*	<.1
768	Louisa Publishing Company Ltd—Michael Hodges	PO Box 306, Wapello IA 52653	319-523-4631	R	1*	<.1

Rank	Company Name—Executive Officer	Address, City, State, Zip	Phone	Type	Fin	Empls
769	Tenn Tom Publishing Inc—William McKinzey	PO Box J, Aliceville AL 35442	205-373-2916	R	1*	<.1
770	Tribune Corp—Ray Dyer	PO Box 9, El Reno OK 73036	405-262-5180	R	1*	<.1
771	Village Publishing Company Inc—Robert Sweeney	8933 E Union Ave Ste 2, Greenwood Village CO 80111	303-773-8313	R	1*	<.1
772	Empire State Weeklies Inc—David Young	2010 Empire Blvd, Webster NY 14580	585-671-1533	R	1*	<.1
773	Cricket Press Inc—Harry Slade	PO Box 357, Manchester MA 01944	978-526-7131	R	1*	<.1
774	Mullen Publications Inc—Mason Smith	9629 Old Nations Ford, Charlotte NC 28273	704-527-5111	R	1*	<.1
775	Delta Press Publishing Company Inc—Wyatt Emmerich	123 E 2nd St, Clarksdale MS 38614	662-627-2201	R	1*	<.1
776	Sentinel Corp—Jack Overmyer	PO Box 260, Rochester IN 46975	574-223-2111	R	1*	<.1
777	Marlboro Publishing Co—William Kinney	PO Box 656, Bennettsville SC 29512	843-479-3815	R	1*	<.1
778	Van Zandt Newspapers LLC—Kelli Baxter	PO Box 60, Wills Point TX 75169	903-873-2525	R	1*	<.1
779	Banner News Publishing Company Inc—Walter Hussman	PO Box 100, Magnolia AR 71754	870-234-5130	R	1*	<.1
780	Chicago Maroon—Judy Marciniak	1212 E 59th St Rm 26, Chicago IL 60637	773-702-9555	R	1*	<.1
781	Liberty Group Publishing—Tim Evans	108 W 1st St, Geneseo IL 61254	309-944-2119	R	1*	<.1
782	Marshall Publishing Company LLC—Sandra Walters Rust Communications Inc	PO Box 100, Marshall MO 65340	660-886-2233	S	1*	<.1
783	Midvalley Publishing Inc—Pete Penner	740 N St, Sanger CA 93657	559-875-2511	R	1*	<.1
784	New Mexico Business Weekly Inc—Ray Shaw	116 Central Ave Sw Ste, Albuquerque NM 87102	505-348-8301	R	1*	<.1
785	Oxford Eagle Inc—Jesse Phillips	PO Box 866, Oxford MS 38655	662-234-4331	R	1*	<.1
786	Today Enterprises Inc—Michael Lewis	710 Brickell Ave, Miami FL 33131	305-358-2663	R	1*	<.1
787	Wayne County Publications Inc—Thomas George	10294 Rte 152, Wayne WV 25570	304-272-3433	R	1*	<.1
788	Webster Kirkwood Times Inc—Dwight Bitikofer	122 W Lockwood Ave Fl, Saint Louis MO 63119	314-968-2699	R	1*	<.1
789	Service Publication Inc—Richard Paulsin	7147 Kennedy Ave, Hammond IN 46323	219-845-4445	R	1*	<.1
790	Central Florida Publishing Inc—Robert Mason	700 W Fulton St, Sanford FL 32771	407-365-6604	R	1*	<.1
791	Pluim Publishing Inc—Robert Hulstein	113 Central Ave Se, Orange City IA 51041	712-737-4266	R	1*	<.1
792	Eagle Newspapers LLC—Dean Eckenorth	1116 10th St, Coronado CA 92118	619-437-8800	R	1*	<.1
793	Inde Enterprises Inc—Cheryl Wormley	671 E Calhoun St, Woodstock IL 60098	815-338-8040	R	1*	<.1
794	Rafu Shimpo—Michael Komai	138 Onizuka St, Los Angeles CA 90012	213-629-2231	R	1*	<.1
795	Republic Newspapers Inc—Douglas Horne	11863 Kingston Pke, Knoxville TN 37934	865-675-6397	R	1*	<.1
796	Russell Publications Inc—Gilbert Russell	PO Box 429, Peotone IL 60468	708-258-3474	R	1*	<.1
797	West Seattle Herald Inc—Gerald Robinson	14006 1st Ave S B, Burien WA 98168	206-932-0300	R	1*	<.1
798	Daily Greenbrier Newspapers Inc—John Moffitt	PO Box 471, Lewisburg WV 24901	304-645-1206	R	1*	<.1
799	Preston Citizen—Robert Marshall	77 S State St, Preston ID 83263	208-852-0155	R	1*	<.1
800	Express Publishing Inc—Evelyn Phillips	PO Box 1013, Ketchum ID 83340	208-726-8060	R	1*	<.1
801	San Patricio Publishing Company Inc—John Tracy	PO Box B, Sinton TX 78387	361-364-1270	R	1*	<.1
802	News-Telegraph Publishing Corp—Larry Perroto	PO Box 230, Atlantic IA 50022	712-243-2624	R	1*	<.1
803	Atlanta Latino Newspaper—Farid Sadri	3000 Northwoods Pkwy, Norcross GA 30071	770-416-7570	R	1*	<.1
804	Cape Gazette Ltd—Dennis Forney	PO Box 213, Lewes DE 19958	302-645-7700	R	1*	<.1
805	Herald Sanford Inc—J Paxton	PO Box 100, Sanford NC 27331	919-708-9000	R	1*	<.1
806	Southern Historical News Inc—James Rogers	PO Box 1068, Hiram GA 30141	770-943-1650	R	1*	<.1
807	Rust Publication Company Inc—Tom Stangl	PO Box 930, Le Mars IA 51031	712-546-7031	R	1*	<.1
808	Arens Corp—Gary Godfrey	PO Box 69, Covington OH 45318	937-473-2028	R	1*	<.1
809	Courier-Herald—John Natt	PO Box 157, Enumclaw WA 98022	360-825-2555	R	1*	<.1
810	FS View and Florida Flambeau Newspaper—Robert Parker	PO Box 20208, Tallahassee FL 32316	850-561-6653	R	1*	<.1
811	Litmor Publishing Corp—Edward Norris	81 E Barclay St, Hicksville NY 11801	516-931-0012	R	1*	<.1
812	Daily Atlanta World Inc—Alexis Scott	145 Auburn Ave Ne, Atlanta GA 30303	404-659-1110	R	1*	<.1
813	Franklin Web Printing Company Inc—Mary Anderson	115 Beasley Dr, Franklin TN 37064	615-794-7181	R	1*	<.1
814	North Country Publishing Co—John Coots	79 Main St, Lancaster NH 03584	603-788-4939	R	1*	<.1
815	Pueblo Publishers Inc—William Toops	7122 N 59th Ave, Glendale AZ 85301	623-842-6000	R	1*	<.1
816	Sylva Herald Publishing Company Inc—Steve Gray	PO Box 307, Sylva NC 28779	828-586-2611	R	1*	<.1
817	Daily Tryon Bulletin Inc—Jeffrey Byrd	16 N Trade St, Tryon NC 28782	828-859-9151	R	1*	<.1
818	Summerville Communications Inc—Janet Meyer	104 E Doty Ave, Summerville SC 29483	843-873-9424	R	1*	<.1
819	Kimbel Publication Inc—Mary Oelke	PO Box 8936, Baltimore MD 21222	410-288-6060	R	1*	<.1
820	Adair Progress Inc—Donna Crowe	PO Box 595, Columbia KY 42728	270-384-6471	R	1*	<.1
821	Addison Press Inc—Angelo Lynn	58 Maple St, Middlebury VT 05753	802-388-4944	R	1*	<.1
822	Champion Publications Of Chino Inc—Allen Mccombs	PO Box 607, Chino CA 91708	909-628-5501	R	1*	<.1
823	Collegian Inc—Gerry Hamilton	123 S Burrowes St, State College PA 16801	814-865-2531	R	1*	<.1
824	Chestnut Hill Local—Suzanne Biemiller	8434 Germantown Ave St, Philadelphia PA 19118	215-248-8800	R	1*	<.1
825	Downtown Denver News—Samantha Martel	1550 Larimer St Ste 22, Denver CO 80202	303-292-6397	R	1*	<.1
826	Forward Times Publishing Co—Lenora Carter	PO Box 8346, Houston TX 77288	713-526-4727	R	1*	<.1
827	Halifax Gazette Publishing Company Inc—Keith Shelton	PO Box 524, South Boston VA 24592	434-572-3945	R	1*	<.1
828	Parsons Publishing Company Inc—Ann Charles	PO Box 836, Parsons KS 67357	620-421-2000	R	1*	<.1
829	Santa Fe Reporter Inc—Richard Meeker	PO Box 2306, Santa Fe NM 87504	505-988-5541	R	1*	<.1
830	Kingsville Publishing Company Inc—Bob Odom	PO Box B, Kingsville TX 78364	361-592-4304	R	1*	<.1
831	Os Hood County News Inc—Jerry Tidwell	PO Box 879, Granbury TX 76048	817-573-7066	R	1*	.1
832	Booster Inc—Mark Hauser	31 W Sumner St, Hartford WI 53027	262-673-2900	R	1*	<.1
833	Bridge City Publishing Inc—Larry Atkinson	1413 E Grand Crossing, Mobridge SD 57601	605-845-3646	R	1*	<.1
834	Bulletin Net Inc—Bruce Herbert	PO Box 1788, Nokomis FL 34274	941-468-2569	R	1*	<.1
835	Curry Coastal Pilot—Charles Kocher Western Communications Inc	PO Box 700, Brookings OR 97415	541-469-3123	S	1*	<.1
836	Herald Harrodsburg Inc—Chris Freeman	PO Box 68, Harrodsburg KY 40330	859-734-2726	R	1*	<.1
837	Mcduffie County Newspapers Inc—James Lancaster	PO Box 1090, Thomson GA 30824	706-595-1601	R	1*	<.1
838	River Publishers Inc—Chris Barbee	115 W Burleson St, Wharton TX 77488	979-532-8840	R	1*	<.1
839	Walton Tribune—Patrick Graham	124 N Broad St, Monroe GA 30655	770-267-8371	R	1*	<.1
840	Covington Virginian Inc—Horton Beirne	PO Box 271, Covington VA 24426	540-962-2121	R	1*	<.1
841	Inyo Register—Shron Dare	450 E Line St, Bishop CA 93514	760-873-3535	R	1*	<.1
842	Lake Shore Weekly News—Mark Beckstrom	1001 Twelve Oaks Ctr D, Wayzata MN 55391	952-473-0890	R	1*	<.1
843	Catskill Delaware Publications Inc—Frederick Stabbert	PO Box 308, Callicoon NY 12723	845-887-5200	R	1*	<.1
844	Massapequa Post—Alfred Sams	1045b Park Blvd, Massapequa Park NY 11762	516-798-5100	R	1*	<.1
845	Albia Newspapers Inc—Charles Lancaster	PO Box 338, Albia IA 52531	641-932-7121	R	1*	<.1
846	Boone News Republican—Claudia Lovin	PO Box 100, Boone IA 50036	515-432-1234	S	1*	<.1
847	Calumet Publishing Inc—James Moran	PO Box 227, Chilton WI 53014	920-849-4551	R	1*	<.1
848	Chatham News Publishing Co—Alan Resch	PO Box 290, Siler City NC 27344	919-663-3232	R	1*	<.1
849	Houghton Lake Resorter Inc—Thoams Hamp	PO Box 248, Houghton Lake MI 48629	989-366-5341	R	1*	<.1
850	Richard's Publishing Company Inc—Richard Richards	Main St, Gonvick MN 56644	218-487-5225	R	1*	<.1
851	Romeo Observer Inc—Melvin Bliech	PO Box 96, Romeo MI 48065	586-752-3524	R	1*	<.1
852	Voice Publishing Company Inc—Robert Moore	4145 Travis St Ste 300, Dallas TX 75204	214-754-8710	R	1*	<.1
853	Colbert Courier Journal Inc—Robert Love	1828 Darby Dr, Florence AL 35630	256-764-4268	R	1*	<.1
854	Citrus Valley Publishing Co—Don Johnson	PO Box 431, Santa Paula CA 93061	805-525-1890	R	1*	<.1
855	Lewis Publishing Company Inc—Michael Lewis	PO Box 153, Lynden WA 98264	360-354-4444	R	1*	<.1
856	Daily Midway Driller Inc—John Watkins	PO Box 958, Taft CA 93268	661-763-3171	S	1*	<.1

Note: An asterisk (*) indicates an estimated financial figure. The company type code used is as follows: R = Private, P = Public, S = Private Subsidiary, B = Public Subsidiary, D = Division, J = Joint Venture, I = Investment Fund.

COMPANY RANKINGS BY SALES WITHIN 4-DIGIT SIC

Rank	Company Name—*Executive Officer*	Address, City, State, Zip	Phone	Type	Fin	Empls
857	LitWatch Inc—*John Toothman*	PO Box 8, Great Falls VA 22066	703-683-1224	R	1*	<.1
858	Metro Times Inc—*Lisa Rudy* Scranton Times LP	733 Saint Antoine St 2, Detroit MI 48226	313-961-4060	S	1*	<.1
859	Jackson Hole Magazine—*Michael Sellett*	PO Box 7445, Jackson WY 83002	307-733-2047	R	1*	<.1
860	Chronicle Inc—*Christopher Braithwaite*	PO Box 660, Barton VT 05822	802-525-3531	R	1*	<.1
861	Clarke County Publishing Inc—*Tom Shaw*	111 E Washington St, Osceola IA 50213	641-342-6006	R	1*	<.1
862	Hill Country Publishing Company Inc—*Fred Lowe*	PO Box 631, Lampasas TX 76550	512-556-6262	R	1*	<.1
863	Southern Siskiyou Newspapers Inc—*Jenny Axtman*	924b N Mount Shasta Bl, Mount Shasta CA 96067	530-926-5214	R	1*	<.1
864	Calitoday Newspaper—*Nam Nguyen*	540 S 10th St, San Jose CA 95112	408-297-8271	R	1*	<.1
865	Fulton Sun Gazette—*Karen Atkins*	PO Box 550, Fulton MO 65251	573-642-7272	R	1*	<.1
866	Hereford Brand Inc—*Mauri Montgomery*	PO Box 673, Hereford TX 79045	806-364-2030	R	1*	<.1
867	New York Daily Challenge Inc—*Thomas Watkins*	1195 Atlantic Ave Fl 2, Brooklyn NY 11216	718-636-9500	R	1*	<.1
868	Revere Independent—*Robert Lehmann*	385 Broadway Ste 105, Revere MA 02151	781-485-0588	R	1*	<.1
869	Shakour Publishers Inc—*Mitchell Shakour*	PO Box 487, Keene NH 03431	603-352-5250	R	1*	<.1
870	Ute City Tea Party Ltd—*David Danforth*	517 E Hopkins Ave Ste, Aspen CO 81611	970-925-2220	R	1*	<.1
871	Observer News Enterprise Inc—*Steve Garland*	PO Box 48, Newton NC 28658	828-464-0221	R	1*	<.1
872	Beaver Newspapers Inc—*Lisa Reest*	835 Lawrence Ave, Ellwood City PA 16117	724-758-5573	R	1*	<.1
873	Evening Bulletin Inc—*Thomas Rice*	1500 Walnut St Ste 300, Philadelphia PA 19102	215-735-9150	R	1*	<.1
874	Fayette County Union Inc—*Gerald Blue*	PO Box 153, West Union IA 52175	563-422-3888	R	1*	<.1
875	Winter Garden Times Inc—*Andrew Bailey*	720 S Dillard St, Winter Garden FL 34787	407-656-2121	R	1*	<.1
876	North Country This Week—*William Shumway*	PO Box 975, Potsdam NY 13676	315-265-1000	R	1*	<.1
877	Montgomery Communications Inc—*John Montgomery*	PO Box 129, Junction City KS 66441	785-762-5000	R	1*	.1
878	San Antonio Observer—*Jacquelyn Aly*	PO Box 200226, San Antonio TX 78220	210-212-6397	R	1*	<.1
879	Brooklyn Journal Publications Inc—*John Hasty*	30 Henry St, Brooklyn NY 11201	718-858-2300	R	1*	<.1
880	Commentator—*Zev Nagel*	500 W 185th St, New York NY 10033	212-795-4308	R	1*	<.1
881	Dickson Press Inc—*Ken Macdonald*	PO Box 550, Raeford NC 28376	910-875-2121	R	1*	<.1
882	Gazette—*Paul Newton*	PO Box 319, Galena IL 61036	815-777-0019	R	1*	<.1
883	South Carolina Black Media Group—*Isaac Washington*	PO Box 11128, Columbia SC 29211	803-799-5252	R	1*	<.1
884	Hasco Newspaper Inc—*Robert Haskell* Martinsville Bulletin Inc	PO Box 406, Mount Sterling KY 40353	859-498-2222	S	1*	<.1
885	Kanabec Publications Inc—*Eugene Johnson*	107 Park St S, Mora MN 55051	320-679-2661	R	1*	<.1
886	Rappahannock Record—*Fred Gaskins*	PO Box 400, Kilmarnock VA 22482	804-435-1701	R	1*	<.1
887	Oceana's Herald-Journal Inc—*James Young*	PO Box 190, Hart MI 49420	231-873-5602	R	1*	<.1
888	Clarke County Democrat Inc—*James Cox*	PO Box 39, Grove Hill AL 36451	251-275-3375	R	1*	<.1
889	W B Rogers Printing Co—*Wendell Lenhart*	PO Box 548, Trenton MO 64683	660-359-2212	R	1*	<.1
890	Citizens Publishing Company Inc—*Kim Anderson*	PO Box 309, Windom MN 56101	507-831-3455	R	1*	<.1
891	Customnews Inc—*Ross Heller*	PO Box 15009, Chevy Chase MD 20825	301-951-1881	R	1*	<.1
892	Al Dia Newspaper Inc—*Hernan Guaracao*	1500 Jf Kennedy Blvd S, Philadelphia PA 19102	215-569-4666	R	1*	<.1
893	Five D Newspapers—*James Herring*	PO Box 317, Bridgeport IL 62417	618-945-9310	R	1*	<.1
894	St Louis Argus Newspaper—*Eddie Hasan*	4595 Dr Mrtn Luther Ki, Saint Louis MO 63113	314-531-1323	R	1*	<.1
895	Bossier Newspaper Publishing Company Inc *Nila Johnson* Specht Newspapers Inc	4250 Viking Dr, Bossier City LA 71111	318-747-7900	S	1*	<.1
896	Hutchinson Leader—*Arlin Albrecht*	36 Washington Ave W, Hutchinson MN 55350	320-587-5000	R	1*	<.1
897	Winona Post Inc—*John Edstrom*	PO Box 27, Winona MN 55987	507-452-1262	R	1*	<.1
898	Foliage Enterprises Inc—*John Ricketson*	439 W Orange Blossom T, Apopka FL 32712	407-886-2777	R	1*	<.1
899	Black Chronicle Inc—*Russell Perry*	PO Box 17498, Oklahoma City OK 73136	405-424-4695	R	1*	<.1
900	Milton Newspapers Inc—*Carla Brnes*	6629 Elva St, Milton FL 32570	850-623-3616	R	1*	<.1
901	Boone Newspapers Inc—*Todd Carpenter*	PO Box 2370, Tuscaloosa AL 35403	205-330-4100	R	1*	<.1
902	Kaneland Publications Inc—*Stephen Cooper*	123 N Main St, Elburn IL 60119	630-365-6446	R	1*	<.1
903	Badger Herald Inc—*Sam Strobel*	326 W Gorham St, Madison WI 53703	608-257-4712	R	1*	.1
904	Hispanic Print Media LLC—*B Galloway*	PO Box 11398, Denver CO 80211	303-936-8556	R	1*	<.1
905	Kansas City Call—*Donna Stewart*	PO Box 410477, Kansas City MO 64141	816-842-3804	R	1*	<.1
906	Grove Sun Newspaper Company Inc—*Peter Crow*	27 W 3rd St Ste A, Grove OK 74344	918-786-2228	R	1*	<.1
907	Herald Of Randolph—*M Drysdale*	PO Box 309, Randolph VT 05060	802-728-3232	R	1*	<.1
908	Camas Washougal Post Record—*Brent Erickson*	PO Box 1013, Camas WA 98607	360-834-2141	R	1*	<.1
909	New Horizon Publishers—*Danno Wise*	PO Box 308, Port Isabel TX 78578	956-943-5545	R	1*	<.1
910	South Boston News Inc—*Sylvia Laughlin*	PO Box 100, South Boston VA 24592	434-572-2928	R	1*	<.1
911	Telescope Inc—*Mark Miller*	1314 19th St, Belleville KS 66935	785-527-2244	R	1*	<.1
912	Tomahawk Leader Inc—*Larry Tobin*	PO Box 345, Tomahawk WI 54487	715-453-2151	R	1*	<.1
913	Oregonian Publishing Company LLC—*John Mannex*	1320 Sw Broadway, Portland OR 97201	503-221-8327	R	<1*	1.2
914	Daily Orange Corp—*Becca Mcgovern*	744 Ostrom Ave, Syracuse NY 13210	315-443-2314	R	<1*	.1
915	Taylorsville Times—*Walter Sharpe*	PO Box 279, Taylorsville NC 28681	828-632-2532	R	<1*	<.1
916	Fayette County Record Inc—*Kyle Barton*	PO Box 400, La Grange TX 78945	979-968-3155	R	<1*	<.1
917	Fishermen's News Inc—*Peter Philipf*	2201 W Commodore Way, Seattle WA 98199	206-282-7545	R	<1*	<.1
918	Sheridan Newspapers Inc—*Edward Seaton*	PO Box 2006, Sheridan WY 82801	307-672-2431	R	<1*	<.1
919	Dartmouth Inc—*Rdex Tejera*	6175 Robinson Hall, Hanover NH 03755	603-646-2600	R	<1*	<.1
920	Northeast Nebraska Media Inc—*Kevin Peterson*	PO Box 70, Wayne NE 68787	402-375-2600	R	<1*	<.1
921	LDJ Inc—*Edward Danner*	PO Box 7, Lanse MI 49946	906-524-6194	R	<1*	<.1
922	Falls Church News Press—*Nicholas Benton*	450 W Broad St Ste 321, Falls Church VA 22046	703-532-3267	R	<1*	<.1
923	Tri County Publishing Inc—*Myron Schober*	PO Box 429, Rushford MN 55971	507-864-7700	R	<1*	<.1
924	Cartersville Newspaper Inc—*Carmage Walls*	PO Box 70, Cartersville GA 30120	770-382-4545	R	<1*	<.1
925	Young DC Inc—*Aimee Phelps*	1904 18th St NW Unit B, Washington DC 20009	202-232-5300	R	<1	.1
926	Truax Printing Inc—*Thomas Truax*	425 E Haskell St, Loudonville OH 44842	419-994-4166	R	<1*	<.1
927	Wick Communications Co—*John Mathew*	333 W Wilcox Dr Ste 30, Sierra Vista AZ 85635	520-458-0200	R	N/A	.7
928	Wooster Republican Printing Co—*Paul Williams*	PO Box 918, Wooster OH 44691	330-264-3511	R	N/A	.5
929	Central Michigan Newspapers—*Al Frattura*	PO Box 447, Mount Pleasant MI 48804	989-779-6000	R	N/A	.5
930	Evening Times—*Beth Brewer* GateHouse Media Inc	111 Green St, Herkimer NY 13350	315-823-3680	S	N/A	<.1
931	Closing the Gap Inc—*Connie Kneip*	PO Box 68, Henderson MN 56044	507-248-3294	R	N/A	<.1

TOTALS: SIC 2711 Newspapers
Companies: 931   146,605   528.2

2721 Periodicals

Rank	Company Name—*Executive Officer*	Address, City, State, Zip	Phone	Type	Fin	Empls
1	Bio-It World Inc—*Alan Bergstein*	250 First Ave Ste 300, Needham MA 02494	508-628-4700	S	19,881*	12.8
2	Thomson Reuters Corp—*David Thomson*	3 Times Sq, New York NY 10036	646-223-4000	P	13,100	55.0
3	Time Inc—*Laura Lang*	1271 Ave of the Americ, New York NY 10020	212-522-1212	S	3,675	1.4
4	Reed Elsevier Inc—*Andrew Prozes*	125 Park Ave 23rd Fl, New York NY 10017	212-309-5498	S	3,200*	11.0
5	Emmis Publishing Corp—*Jeffrey Smulyan*	1 Emmis Plz 40 Monumen, Indianapolis IN 46204	317-266-0100	S	2,217*	.4
6	Conde Nast Publications—*Charles Townsend*	4 Times Sq, New York NY 10036	212-286-2860	R	1,720*	2.2
7	EBSCO Industries Inc—*Dixon Brooke Jr*	PO Box 1943, Birmingham AL 35201	205-991-6600	R	1,542*	5.5

Rank	Company Name—*Executive Officer*	Address, City, State, Zip	Phone	Type	Fin	Empls
8	Reader's Digest Association Inc—*Robert E Guth*	Readers Digest Rd, Pleasantville NY 10570	914-238-1000	S	1,456	4.3
9	Meredith Corp—*Stephen M Lacy*	1716 Locust St, Des Moines IA 50309	515-284-3000	P	1,400	3.3
10	Advanstar Communications Inc—*Joseph Loggia* Advanstar Inc	6200 Canoga Ave 2nd Fl, Woodland Hills CA 91367	818-593-5000	S	1,353*	1.0
11	Dominion Enterprises—*Jack Ross*	150 Granby St, Norfolk VA 23510	757-351-7000	R	1,261*	.9
12	Nielsen Co	770 Broadway, New York NY 10003	646-654-4500	D	882*	.6
13	Reed Business Information—*Mark Kelsey* Reed Elsevier Inc	360 Park Ave S 18th Fl, New York NY 10010	646-746-6400	D	875*	5.7
14	United Business Media LLC—*David Levin*	600 Community Dr, Manhasset NY 11030	516-562-5000	S	797	3.4
15	Johnson Publishing Company LLC—*Desiree Rogers*	820 S Michigan Ave, Chicago IL 60605	312-322-9200	R	757*	2.6
16	TV Guide Magazine Group Inc—*Matt Webb Mitovich*	4 Radnor Corporate Ctr, Radnor PA 19087	610-293-8500	S	753*	3.3
17	Rovi Corp—*Alfred J Amoroso*	2830 De La Cruz Blvd, Santa Clara CA 95050	408-562-8400	P	691	2.0
18	Ziff Davis Media Inc—*Ce Vivek*	28 E 28th St, New York NY 10016	212-503-3500	S	592*	.4
19	American Media Inc—*David J Pecker*	1 Park Ave, New York NY 10016	212-545-4800	R	500*	2.1
20	Nielsen Business Media Inc—*Greg Farrar*	770 Broadway, New York NY 10003		S	490*	1.3
21	National Geographic Society Inc—*John M Fahey Jr*	1145 17th St NW, Washington DC 20036	202-857-7000	R	467*	2.0
22	Dennis Publishing	55 W 39th St 5th Fl, New York NY 10018	212-207-8787	S	466*	.3
23	Limra International Inc—*Robert Kerzner*	300 Day Hill Rd, Windsor CT 06095	860-688-3358	R	392*	.3
24	SNL Financial LC—*Mike Chinn*	212 7th Street NE, Charlottesville VA 22902	434-977-1600	R	373*	.3
25	American Girl LLC—*Ellen L Brothers*	8400 Fairway Pl, Middleton WI 53562	608-836-4848	S	350*	1.4
26	Bonnier Corp—*Terry Snow*	460 N Orlando Ave Ste, Winter Park FL 32789	407-628-4802	S	350*	1.0
27	Southern Progress Corp—*Laura Lang* Time Inc	PO Box 2581, Birmingham AL 35202	205-445-6000	S	344*	.5
28	Forbes Inc—*Steve Forbes*	60 5th Ave, New York NY 10011	212-620-2200	R	331*	.7
29	Advanstar Inc—*Joseph Loggia*	2501 Colorado Ave Ste, Santa Monica CA 90404	310-857-7500	R	324*	1.0
30	Belvoir Publications Inc—*Robert Englander*	800 Connecticut Ave 4w, Norwalk CT 06854	203-857-3100	R	270*	.3
31	Crain Communications Inc—*Rance E Crain*	1155 Gratiot Ave, Detroit MI 48207	313-446-6000	R	267*	1.0
32	Creatas Footage—*David Moffly*	6000 N Forest Park Dr, Peoria IL 61614	309-688-8080	D	265*	.2
33	Wenner Media LLC—*Jann S Wenner*	1290 Ave of the Americ, New York NY 10104	212-767-8209	R	247*	.3
34	Playboy Enterprises Inc—*Scott Flanders*	680 N Lake Shore Dr, Chicago IL 60611	312-751-8000	P	240	.5
35	PRIMEDIA Inc—*Charles Stubbs*	3585 Engineering Dr St, Norcross GA 30092	678-421-3000	S	232	.8
36	Martha Stewart Living Omnimedia Inc—*Lisa Gersh*	601 W 26th St, New York NY 10001	212-827-8000	P	231	.6
37	North American Membership Group Inc—*Steven F Burke*	12301 Whitewater Dr St, Minnetonka MN 55343	952-936-9333	R	230*	.4
38	Advertising Specialty Institute Inc (Trevose Pennsylvania)— *Norman Unger Cohn*	4800 E Street Rd, Trevose PA 19053	215-953-4000	R	229*	1.0
39	RISI Inc—*John Day*	4 Alfred Cir, Bedford MA 01730	781-734-8900	J	219*	.2
40	Rodale Inc—*Maria Rodale*	33 E Minor St, Emmaus PA 18098	610-967-5171	R	212*	1.2
41	Newsweek Inc—*Richard Smith*	395 Hudson St, New York NY 10014	212-445-4000	S	207*	1.0
42	Penton Media Inc—*Sharon Rowlands*	249 W 17th St, New York NY 10011	212-204-4200	R	204*	.7
43	American Lawyer Media LLC—*William L Pollak*	345 Park Ave S, New York NY 10010	212-779-8994	S	194*	1.0
44	Texas Monthly Inc—*Evan Smith*	PO Box 1569, Austin TX 78767	512-320-6900	S	192*	.1
45	Hoffman Media LLC—*Phyllis Hoffman DePiano*	1900 International Par, Birmingham AL 35243	205-995-8860	R	175*	.1
46	Jobson Medical Information LLC—*Michael Tansey*	100 Ave, New York NY 10013	212-274-7000	R	152*	.4
47	Highlights For Children Inc—*Kent Johnson*	PO Box 269, Columbus OH 43216	614-486-0631	R	147*	.1
48	Harvard Business School Publishing Corp—*Mark Bloomfield*	300 N Beacon St, Watertown MA 02472	617-783-7400	R	141*	.3
49	Essence Communications Partners—*Edward Lewis*	1500 Broadway 6th Fl, New York NY 10036	212-642-0600	J	138*	.1
50	Sandhills Publishing Co—*Tom Peed*	PO Box 82545, Lincoln NE 68501	402-479-2181	R	127*	.4
51	Xplain Corp—*John Alexander*	PO Box 5200, Westlake Village CA 91359	805-494-9797	R	126*	.1
52	Nature America Inc—*Steven Inchcoombe*	75 Varick St Fl 9, New York NY 10013	212-726-9200	R	125*	.4
53	Reed Construction Data—*Iain Melville*	30 Technology Pky S St, Norcross GA 30092	770-417-4000	S	125*	.4
54	Hachette Filipacchi Holdings Inc—*Gerald Roquemaurel*	1633 Broadway Ste 4001, New York NY 10019	212-767-6000	R	121*	2.1
55	Earl G Graves Publishing Company Inc—*Earl G Graves Jr* Earl G Graves Ltd	130 5th Ave Fl 10, New York NY 10011	212-242-8000	S	115*	.1
56	Watt Publishing Co—*Greg Watt*	303 N Main St, Rockford IL 61101	815-966-5400	R	114*	.1
57	Canon Communications Inc—*Rich Nass*	11444 W Olympic Blvd S, Los Angeles CA 90064	310-445-4200	S	102*	.1
58	Curtis Publishing Co—*Hank Zachry*	1000 Waterway Blvd, Indianapolis IN 46202	317-633-2070	R	92*	.6
59	Worth Media—*Bill Curtis*	29160 Heathercliff Rd, Malibu CA 90265	310-589-7700	R	88*	.1
60	Testa Communications—*Robin Hazan*	25 Willowdale Ave, Port Washington NY 11050	516-767-2500	R	84*	.1
61	iVillage International Holding Corp—*Jodi Kahn*	79 5th Ave, New York NY 10011	212-664-4444	S	83*	.3
62	Cygnus Business Media Inc—*John French*	12735 Morris Rd Bldg 2, Alpharetta GA 30004		R	82*	.7
63	Lebhar-Friedman Inc—*Roger Friedman*	425 Park Ave Ste 501, New York NY 10022	212-756-5000	R	76*	.3
64	Technical Analysis Inc—*Mary K Hutson*	4757 California Ave SW, Seattle WA 98116	206-938-0570	R	76*	<.1
65	IPC Print Services Inc—*Ken Kozminski*	2179 Maiden Ln, Saint Joseph MI 49085		S	73*	.1
66	Stagnito Publishing Co—*Cameron Bishop*	155 Pfingsten Rd Ste 2, Deerfield IL 60015	847-205-5660	R	73*	.1
67	Conway Data Inc—*Laura Lyne*	6625 The Corners Parkw, Norcross GA 30092	770-446-6996	R	73*	.1
68	California Offset Printers Inc—*William Rittwage*	620 W Elk Ave, Glendale CA 91204	818-291-1100	R	72*	.1
69	FUSE3—*Clifford Franklin*	802 N 1st St, St Louis MO 63102	314-421-4040	R	71*	<.1
70	Clipper Magazine Inc—*Steve Zuckerman*	3708 Hempland Rd, Mountville PA 17554	717-569-5100	S	69*	.3
71	Fastline Publications LLC—*Mary Hutchinson*	PO Box 248, Buckner KY 40010	502-222-0146	R	67*	.2
72	ComputerWire Inc—*Mark Meek*	245 5th Ave 4th Fl, New York NY 10016	212-652-5380	R	66*	.1
73	Latina Media Ventures LLC—*Fabio Freyre*	625 Madison Ave 3rd Fl, New York NY 10022	212-642-0200	R	65*	<.1
74	Ziff-Davis Inc—*Jason Young*	28 E 28th St, New York NY 10016	212-503-3500	S	62	.3
75	hcPro Inc—*Brian Bussey*	75 Sylvan St Ste A 101, Danvers MA 01923	781-639-1872	S	60*	.3
76	Operation Bass Inc—*Charlie Evans*	30 Gamble Ln, Benton KY 42025	270-252-1000	R	57*	.2
77	Bauer Publishing Company LP—*Hubert Boehle*	270 Sylvan Ave Ste 210, Englewood Cliffs NJ 07632	201-569-6699	R	55*	.5
78	Sunset Publishing Corp—*Kevin Lynch* Southern Progress Corp	80 Willow Rd, Menlo Park CA 94025	650-321-3600	S	54*	.2
79	Hearst Business Communications Inc—*Frank A Bennack*	50 Charles Lindbergh B, Uniondale NY 11553		R	54*	<.1
80	American Express Publishing—*Ed Kelly*	1120 Ave Of The Americ, New York NY 10036	212-382-5600	S	52*	.3
81	ARTnews LLC—*Milton Esterow*	48 W 38th St, New York NY 10018	212-398-1690	R	51*	<.1
82	Pennysaver Publications Inc—*Dean Deluca*	460 Rodi Rd, Penn Hills PA 15235	412-243-4215	S	50*	.2
83	Executive Business Media Inc—*Murray Greenwald*	PO Box 1500, Westbury NY 11590	516-334-3030	R	49*	.1
84	Vance Publishing Corp—*Donald Ransdell*	PO Box 1400, Lincolnshire IL 60069	847-634-2600	R	48*	.2
85	Lapidary Journal—*Jean Daniels*	300 Chesterfield Pky, Malvern PA 19355	610-232-5700	S	48*	.1
86	American Opinion Publishing Inc—*John McManus*	PO Box 8040, Appleton WI 54912	920-749-3784	R	48*	.1
87	Corporate Reports Inc—*Brooke Graydon*	3927 Peachtree Rd NE, Atlanta GA 30319	404-233-2230	R	47*	<.1
88	Dailycandy Inc—*Danielle Levy*	584 Broadway Ste 510, New York NY 10012	646-435-9199	R	46*	<.1
89	Horizon Publishing Co—*Charles Carlson*	7412 Calumet Ave Ste 1, Hammond IN 46324	219-852-3200	R	46*	<.1
90	Multi AG Media Company LLC—*Scott Smith*	6437 Collamer Rd, East Syracuse NY 13057		R	46*	<.1
91	Wiesner Publications LLC—*Dan Wiesner*	6160 S Syracuse, Greenwood Village CO 80111		R	45*	.2

Note: An asterisk (*) indicates an estimated financial figure. The company type code used is as follows: R = Private, P = Public, S = Private Subsidiary, B = Public Subsidiary, D = Division, J = Joint Venture, I = Investment Fund.

COMPANY RANKINGS BY SALES WITHIN 4-DIGIT SIC

Rank	Company Name—*Executive Officer*	Address, City, State, Zip	Phone	Type	Fin	Empls
92	CG Editorial—*Sam Kennedy* Ziff Davis Media Inc	101 2nd St, San Francisco CA 94105	415-547-8000	S	45*	<.1
93	Christie's Great Estates Inc—*Neil Palmer*	125 Lincoln Ste 300, Santa Fe NM 87501	505-983-8733	S	42*	<.1
94	Imagination Publishing—*James Meyers*	600 W Fulton Ave Ste 6, Chicago IL 60661	312-887-1000	R	41*	.1
95	American Psychiatric Publishing Inc—*Ron McMillen*	1000 Wilson Blvd Ste 1, Arlington VA 22209	703-907-7322	R	41*	.1
96	1105 Media Inc—*Neal Vitale*	9200 Oakdale Ave Rm 10, Chatsworth CA 91311	818-734-1520	R	40*	.4
97	Allen Press Inc—*Gerald Lillian*	PO Box 368, Lawrence KS 66044	785-843-1234	R	37*	.4
98	House Of White Birches Inc	306 E Parr Rd, Berne IN 46711	260-589-4000	S	37*	.1
99	Hunter Publishing LP—*Michael Hunter*	PO Box 746, Walpole MA 02081	561-835-2022	R	33*	.2
100	Earl G Graves Ltd—*Earl Graves Jr*	130 5th Ave 10th Fl, New York NY 10011	212-242-8000	R	32*	.1
101	Angstrom Graphics Inc—*Wayne Angstrom*	2025 Mckinley St, Hollywood FL 33020	954-920-7300	R	32*	.5
102	Upper Room—*Karen Greenwaldt*	PO Box 340004, Nashville TN 37203	615-340-7200	R	31*	.1
103	BookPage—*Michael A Zibart*	2143 Belcourt Ave, Nashville TN 37212	615-292-8926	R	31*	<.1
104	Sumner Communications Inc—*Scott Sumner*	24 Stony Hill Rd, Bethel CT 06801	203-748-2050	R	31*	<.1
105	Future Us Inc—*Jonathan Bint*	4000 Shoreline Ct Ste, South San Francisco CA 94080	650-872-1642	S	30*	.3
106	Homes and Land Publishing Ltd—*Blair Schmidt-Fellner*	1830 E Park Ave, Tallahassee FL 32301	850-574-2111	R	29*	.2
107	Kelley Blue Book Company Inc—*Paul Johnson*	PO Box 19691, Irvine CA 92623	949-770-7704	R	27*	.5
108	First Marketing Co—*Ronald Drenning*	3300 Gateway Dr, Pompano Beach FL 33069	954-979-0700	R	26*	.3
109	Gulf Publishing Co—*John T Royall*	PO Box 2608, Houston TX 77252	713-529-4301	S	26	.1
110	DC Comics—*Diane Nelson*	1700 Broadway 7th Fl, New York NY 10019	212-636-5400	S	25*	.2
111	New Hope Natural Media—*Fred Linder* Penton Media Inc	1401 Pearl St, Boulder CO 80302	303-939-8440	D	25*	.1
112	Midwest Publishing Inc—*Tina Gerke*	10844 N 23rd Ave, Phoenix AZ 85029	602-943-1244	R	23*	.3
113	BASS Inc—*Steven Yates*	PO Box 10000, Lake Buena Vista FL 32830	407-566-2277	S	23*	.1
114	NexGen Software Technologies Inc—*Richard L Halsten*	PO Box 9696, Naperville IL 60567	630-566-5192	R	23*	.1
115	SMR Research Corp—*Stuart A Feldstein*	300 Valentine St, Hackettstown NJ 07840	908-852-7677	R	23*	<.1
116	Alcohol and Drug Addiction Services—*Russell Kaye*	614 W Superior Ave Ste, Cleveland OH 44113	216-348-4830	R	22*	<.1
117	Tv Guide Distribution Inc—*Richard Julason*	100 Matsonford Rd, Wayne PA 19087	610-293-8500	R	21*	.5
118	Daily Variety Ltd—*Neil Stiles* Reed Business Information	5900 Wilshire Blvd Ste, Los Angeles CA 90036		S	21*	.1
119	Delicious Living—*Radha Marcum* Penton Media Inc	1401 Pearl St, Boulder CO 80302	303-939-8440	S	21*	.1
120	Kyra Communications—*Richard Doherty*	3864 Bayberry Ln, Seaford NY 11783	516-783-6244	R	21*	<.1
121	On-Board Media Inc—*Robert Eichner*	1691 Michigan Ave Ste, Miami Beach FL 33139	305-673-0400	S	21*	.1
122	Scientific American Inc—*Steven Yee*	75 Varick St 9th Fl, New York NY 10013	212-451-8200	S	20*	.1
123	Card Web—*Robert B McKinley*	PO Box 1700, Frederick MD 21702	301-631-9100	R	20*	<.1
124	Airline Tariff Publishing Co—*William Andres*	45005 Aviation Dr Ste, Dulles VA 20166	703-471-7510	R	20*	.4
125	Bowtie Inc—*Norman Ridker*	PO Box 57900, Los Angeles CA 90057	213-385-2222	R	20*	.4
126	Plenum Publishing Corp—*Peter Hendriks*	233 Spring St, New York NY 10013	212-620-8000	R	20*	.1
127	Primedia Enthusiast Publications Inc—*John Loughlin*	6375 Flank Dr Ste 100, Harrisburg PA 17112	717-657-9555	R	20*	.2
128	Babcox Publications Inc—*Bill Babcox*	3550 Embassy Pkwy, Akron OH 44333	330-670-1234	R	19*	.1
129	Publishing Group of America Inc—*Dick Porter*	341 Cool Springs Blvd, Franklin TN 37067	615-468-6000	R	19*	<.1
130	Mcmurry Publishing Inc—*Preston Mc*	1010 E Missouri Ave, Phoenix AZ 85014	602-395-5850	R	19*	.2
131	Farm Journal Inc—*Andrew Weber*	30 S 15th St Ste 900, Philadelphia PA 19102	215-557-8900	R	19*	.2
132	Merion Publications Inc—*Ann Kielinski*	2900 Horizon Dr, King Of Prussia PA 19406	610-278-1400	R	18*	.4
133	Active Interest Media Inc—*Efrem Zimbalist*	300 Continental Blvd S, El Segundo CA 90245	310-356-4100	R	17*	.1
134	New Stuff Company Inc—*Stephen Mindich*	126 Brookline Ave Ste, Boston MA 02215	617-859-3333	R	17*	.3
135	Primedia Enthusiast Publication Inc—*John Loughlin*	6405 Flank Dr, Harrisburg PA 17112	717-657-9555	R	17*	.1
136	Mariah Media Inc—*Lawrence Burke*	400 Market St, Santa Fe NM 87501	505-989-7100	R	17*	.1
137	Ideas Publishing Group—*Carlos Modia* Conde Nast Publications	1101 Brickell Ave Ste, Miami FL 33131	305-371-9393	D	17	.1
138	Jadent Inc—*Dennis O'Shea*	PO Box 881, Salem OR 97308	503-393-9500	R	16*	.1
139	Casiano Communications Inc—*Manuel A Casiano*	1700 Fernandez Juncos, San Juan PR 00909	787-728-3000	H	16*	.3
140	OAG Worldwide Ltd—*Stephen Bray*	3025 Highland Pkwy Ste, Downers Grove IL 60515	630-515-5307	S	16*	.1
141	Data Advantage Corp—*Hal Andrews*	1515 Story Ave, Louisville KY 40206	502-587-9500	R	16*	<.1
142	WestWorld Productions Inc—*Yuri Spiro*	420 N Camden Dr, Beverly Hills CA 90210	310-276-9600	R	16*	<.1
143	August Home Publishing Co—*Donald Peschke*	2200 Grand Ave, Des Moines IA 50312	515-282-7000	R	15*	.2
144	Schofield Media Ltd—*Andrew Schofield*	200 E Randolph St Ste, Chicago IL 60601	312-236-4090	R	15*	.2
145	GIE Media Inc—*Richard Foster*	PO Box 532, Richfield OH 44286	330-523-5400	R	15*	.1
146	Atlantic Monthly Group—*David G Bradley*	600 New Hampshire Ave, Washington DC 20037	202-266-6000	R	15*	.1
147	Carmel Trader Publishing Inc—*Ernie Blood*	4501 Hills and Dles Rd, Canton OH 44708	330-478-9200	R	15*	<.1
148	Grubb and Ellis Bissell Patrick—*Edward Curran*	200 Providence Rd Ste, Charlotte NC 28207	704-248-2180	R	15*	<.1
149	Beckett Publications LP—*Jeff Amano*	4635 Mcewen Rd, Dallas TX 75244	972-991-6657	R	15*	.1
150	Amos Press Inc—*Bruce Boyd*	PO Box 4129, Sidney OH 45365	937-498-2111	R	15*	.3
151	Trade Press Media Group Inc—*Robert Wisniewski*	2100 W Florist Ave, Milwaukee WI 53209	414-228-7701	R	15*	.1
152	Magazine Group Inc—*Jane Ottenberg*	1129 20th St NW Ste 70, Washington DC 20036	202-331-7700	R	14*	.1
153	Science Service Inc—*Dudley Herschbach*	1719 N St NW, Washington DC 20036	202-785-2255	R	14*	.1
154	Environmental Business International Inc—*Grant Ferrier*	4452 Park Blvd Ste 306, San Diego CA 92116	619-295-7685	R	14*	<.1
155	Maddux Publishing Inc—*Carlen Maddux*	PO Box 202, Saint Petersburg FL 33731	727-823-4394	R	14*	<.1
156	Entrepreneur Media Inc—*Neil Perlman*	PO Box 19787, Irvine CA 92623	949-261-2325	R	14*	.1
157	M Shanken Communications Inc—*Marvin Shanken*	387 Park Ave S Fl 8, New York NY 10016	212-684-4224	R	14*	.1
158	Harris Publications Inc—*Stanley Harris*	1115 Broadway Fl 8, New York NY 10010	212-807-7100	R	14*	.1
159	Penny Publications LLC—*Kathy Cappellieri*	6 Prowitt St, Norwalk CT 06855	203-866-6688	R	14*	.2
160	Municipal Code Corp—*A Langford*	PO Box 2235, Tallahassee FL 32316	850-576-3171	R	13*	.2
161	Skinder-Strauss Associates—*Andrew Strauss*	PO Box 50, Newark NJ 07101	973-642-1440	R	13*	.1
162	Uhlig LLC—*Janeen Borello*	8455 Lenexa Dr, Lenexa KS 66214	913-725-1000	R	13*	.1
163	New York Entertainment Corp—*Kevin Brown*	2446 E 65th St, Brooklyn NY 11234	718-763-7034	R	13*	.1
164	Miles Media Group Inc—*Roger Miles*	6751 Professional Pkwy, Sarasota FL 34240	941-342-2300	R	12*	.1
165	Fornax Corp—*Susan Lit*	90 Sherman St, Cambridge MA 02140	617-864-7360	R	12*	.1
166	Pace Communications Inc—*Bonnie Hunter*	1301 Carolina St Ste 2, Greensboro NC 27401	336-378-6065	R	12*	.1
167	Ogden Publications Inc—*Robert Nutting*	1503 Sw 42nd St, Topeka KS 66609	785-274-4300	R	12*	.1
168	LFP Inc—*Jim Kohls*	8484 Wilshire Blvd Ste, Beverly Hills CA 90211	323-651-5400	R	12*	.1
169	Pathway Press—*Joseph A Mirkovich*	PO Box 2250, Cleveland TN 37320	423-476-4512	R	12	.1
170	Nation Magazine Co—*Teresa Stack*	33 Irving Pl, New York NY 10003	212-209-5400	R	12*	<.1
171	Global Directions Inc—*Lisa Spivey*	3230 Scott St, San Francisco CA 94123	415-921-1316	R	12*	<.1
172	Playbill Inc—*Philip Birsh*	525 7th Ave Rm 1801, New York NY 10018	212-557-5757	R	12*	.1
173	Archie Comic Publications Inc—*Richard Goldwater*	325 Fayette Ave, Mamaroneck NY 10543	914-381-5155	R	12*	.1
174	Blood-Horse Inc—*Stacy Bearse*	3101 Beaumont Centre C, Lexington KY 40513	859-278-2361	R	12*	.1
175	Corporate Sports Marketing Group Inc—*Christopher King*	2120 Range Rd, Clearwater FL 33765	727-669-6972	R	12*	.1
176	Dupont Publishing Inc—*Steve Chapman*	3051 Tech Dr N, Saint Petersburg FL 33716	727-573-9339	R	11*	.1

Rank	Company Name—*Executive Officer*	Address, City, State, Zip	Phone	Type	Fin	Empls
177	Worcester Magazine Inc—*Paul Giorgio*	101 Water St Fl 3, Worcester MA 01604	508-749-3166	D	11*	.1
178	Georgia Electric Membership Corp—*A Paul Wood*	PO Box 1707, Tucker GA 30085	770-270-6950	R	11*	.1
179	Meister Media Worldwide Inc—*Gary Fitzgerald*	37733 Euclid Ave, Willoughby OH 44094	440-942-2000	R	11*	.1
180	Great Lakes Publishing Co—*Lute Harmon*	1422 Euclid Ave Ste 73, Cleveland OH 44115	216-771-2833	R	11*	.1
181	Daisy Publishing Company Inc—*Roland Hinz*	PO Box 957, Santa Clarita CA 91380	661-295-1910	R	11*	.1
182	Information Today Inc—*Thomas Hogan*	143 Old Marlton Pke, Medford NJ 08055	609-654-6266	R	11*	.1
183	Journal Of Bone And Joint Surgery Inc—*James Heckman*	20 Pickering St Ste 3, Needham MA 02492	781-449-9780	R	10*	<.1
184	Turnstile Publishing Company Inc—*Rance Crain*	1500 Park Ctr Dr, Orlando FL 32835	407-563-7000	R	10*	.1
185	Dark Horse Comics Inc—*Michael Richardson*	10956 Se Main St, Milwaukie OR 97222	503-652-8815	R	10*	.1
186	Diablo Country Magazine Inc—*Steven Rivera*	2520 Camino Diablo, Walnut Creek CA 94597	925-943-1111	R	10*	.1
187	Putman Media Inc—*John Cappelletti*	555 W Pierce Rd Ste 30, Itasca IL 60143	630-467-1300	R	10*	.1
188	Home And Away Inc—*Durand Achee*	PO Box 3535, Omaha NE 68103	402-592-5000	R	10*	<.1
189	Ideals Publications Inc	2636 Elm Hill Pike, Nashville TN 37241	615-333-0478	R	10*	<.1
190	San Diego Magazine Publishing Co—*James Fitzpatrick*	1450 Front St, San Diego CA 92101	619-230-9292	R	10*	<.1
191	Tobe Associates Inc	463 7th Ave Ste 202, New York NY 10018	212-867-8677	S	10*	<.1
192	Advanced Network Marketing Inc—*Robert Pittman*	5252 Orange Ave Ste 10, Cypress CA 90630	714-226-0585	R	10*	<.1
193	Metro Corp—*David Lipson*	1818 Market St Ste 360, Philadelphia PA 19103	215-564-7700	R	10*	.1
194	American Health Lawyers Association—*Peter Liebold*	1620 I St Nw Fl 6, Washington DC 20006	202-833-1100	R	10*	.1
195	Laurin Publishing Company Inc—*Teddi Laurin*	PO Box 4949, Pittsfield MA 01202	413-499-0514	R	10*	.1
196	Desert Publications Inc—*Milton Jones*	PO Box 2724, Palm Springs CA 92263	760-325-2333	R	10*	.1
197	Douglas Publications LLC—*Curtis Wharton*	2807 N Parham Rd Ste 2, Richmond VA 23294	804-762-9600	R	9*	.1
198	National Business Media Inc—*Robert Wieber*	PO Box 1416, Broomfield CO 80038	303-469-0424	R	9*	.1
199	Cutting Edge Media Inc—*Phillip Longnecker*	1595 S Mount Joy St Fr, Elizabethtown PA 17022	717-361-9007	R	9*	.1
200	St Media Group International Inc—*Tedd Swormstedt*	11262 Cornell Park Dr, Blue Ash OH 45242	513-421-2050	R	9*	.1
201	Harper's Magazine Foundation—*John Macarthur*	666 Broadway Fl 11, New York NY 10012	212-420-5720	R	9*	<.1
202	Journal Publications Inc—*Larry Kluger*	1500 Paxton St Fl 3, Harrisburg PA 17104	717-236-4300	R	9*	.1
203	Paper Publishing Company Inc—*David Hershkovits*	365 Broadway, New York NY 10013	212-226-4405	R	9*	.1
204	JV Rockwell Publishing Inc—*J Rockwell*	PO Box 85, Corning AR 72422	870-857-3531	R	9*	.1
205	Twelve Signs Inc—*Richard Housman*	3369 S Robertson Blvd, Los Angeles CA 90034	310-553-8000	R	9*	.1
206	Kappa Publishing Group Inc—*Despina Nulty*	PO Box 750, Fort Washington PA 19034	215-643-5800	R	9*	.1
207	Key Enterprises LLC—*Kevin Dunn*	220 S 6th St Ste 500, Minneapolis MN 55402	612-333-6700	R	9*	.1
208	Construction Journal Ltd—*Richard Goldman*	759 SW Federal Hwy Ste, Stuart FL 34994	772-781-2144	R	8*	.1
209	Education Center Inc—*Kate Brower*	PO Box 9753, Greensboro NC 27429	336-854-0309	R	8*	.1
210	Yankee Publishing Inc—*James Trowbridge*	PO Box 520, Dublin NH 03444	603-563-8111	R	8*	.1
211	Yoga Journal LLC—*Joy Aurelio* Active Interest Media Inc	475 Sansome St Ste 850, San Francisco CA 94111	415-591-0555	S	8*	<.1
212	Paisano Publications LLC—*John Lagana*	28210 Dorothy Dr, Agoura Hills CA 91301	818-889-8740	R	8*	.1
213	F-D-C Reports Inc—*Mike Squires*	5635 Fishers Ln Ste 60, Rockville MD 20852	240-221-4500	R	8*	.1
214	Village Shop Inc—*Robert Goff*	PO Box 968, Traverse City MI 49685	231-946-3712	R	8*	.1
215	Leisure Publishing Company Inc—*J Richard Wells*	PO Box 21535, Roanoke VA 24018	540-989-6138	R	8*	<.1
216	Coyne and Blanchard Inc—*Patrick Coyne*	110 Constitution Dr, Menlo Park CA 94025	650-326-6040	R	8*	<.1
217	Voicings Publications Inc—*James Colaianni*	PO Box 3102, Margate NJ 08402	609-822-9401	R	8*	<.1
218	Edgell Enterprises Inc—*Gabriele Edgell*	4 Middlebury Blvd Ste, Randolph NJ 07860	973-252-0100	R	8*	.1
219	DE Enterprise Inc—*Robert Fernald*	PO Box 679, Camden ME 04843	207-594-9544	R	8*	.1
220	Windhover Information Inc—*Alicia Mcniven*	383 Main Ave, Norwalk CT 06851	203-838-4401	R	8*	.1
221	Business Journals Inc—*Britton Jones*	PO Box 5550, Norwalk CT 06856	203-853-6015	R	8*	.1
222	Lyle Printing and Publishing Company Inc—*Scot Darling*	PO Box 38, Salem OH 44460	330-337-3419	R	7*	.1
223	Francis Emory Fitch Inc—*George Pavlides*	229 W 28th St Fl 9, New York NY 10001	212-619-3800	R	7*	.1
224	Urner-Barry Publications Inc—*Paul Brown*	PO Box 389, Toms River NJ 08754	732-240-5330	R	7*	.1
225	Panoff Publishing Inc—*Bill Panoff*	4517 Nw 31st Ave, Fort Lauderdale FL 33309	954-377-7777	R	7*	.1
226	Source Enterprises Inc—*Jeremy Miller*	11 Broadway Ste 315, New York NY 10004	212-253-3700	R	7*	.1
227	Gulfshore Media LLC—*Norma Machado*	330 S Pineapple Ave St, Sarasota FL 34236	941-487-1100	R	7*	<.1
228	Publications and Communications LP—*Gary Pittman*	13581 Pond Springs Rd, Austin TX 78729	512-250-9023	R	7*	<.1
229	New Republic Inc—*Mike Rancilio*	1331 H St NW Ste 700, Washington DC 20005	202-508-4444	R	7*	<.1
230	Equine Network—*Cathy Laws* Active Interest Media Inc	656 Quince Orchard Rd, Gaithersburg MD 20878	301-977-3900	S	7*	<.1
231	Haymarket Group Ltd—*Thomas Coffey*	45 W 34th St Ste 600, New york NY 10001	212-239-0855	R	7*	<.1
232	Montage Media Corp—*Steven Sweeney*	1000 Wyckoff Ave, Mahwah NJ 07430	201-891-3200	R	7*	<.1
233	Mac Fadden Holdings Inc—*Michael Boylan*	333 7th Ave Rm 1100, New York NY 10001	212-614-3980	R	7*	.1
234	Infoworld Media Group Inc—*Robert Ostrow*	501 2nd St Ste 500, San Francisco CA 94107	415-243-4344	R	7*	.1
235	Pollstar—*Gary Bongiovanni*	4697 W Jacquelyn Ave, Fresno CA 93722	559-271-7900	R	7*	.1
236	LIF Publishing Corp—*Richard Reina*	14 Ramsey Rd, Shirley NY 11967	631-345-5200	R	7*	.1
237	Hour Media LLC—*Ed Peabody*	117 W 3rd St, Royal Oak MI 48067	248-691-1800	R	6*	.1
238	Wiesnermedia LLC—*Dan Wiesner*	6160 S Syracuse Way St, Greenwood Village CO 80111	303-662-5200	R	6*	.1
239	Cities West Publishing Inc—*Bill Phalen*	PO Box 26810, Scottsdale AZ 85255	480-664-3960	R	6*	.1
240	Greenspring Media Group Inc—*Steve Fox*	600 U S Trust Bldg, Minneapolis MN 55402	612-371-5800	R	6*	.1
241	Hobby Publications Inc—*David Gherman*	207 Commercial Ct, Morganville NJ 07751	732-536-5160	R	6*	<.1
242	Clapper Publishing Company Inc—*Marie Clapper*	2400 E Devon Ave Ste 2, Des Plaines IL 60018	847-635-5800	R	6*	<.1
243	Exhibitor Magazine Group—*Lee Knight*	PO Box 368, Rochester MN 55903	507-289-6556	R	6*	.1
244	Latina Style Inc—*Robert Bard*	1701 Clarendon Blvd St, Arlington VA 22209	703-312-0904	R	6*	<.1
245	Children's Technology Review—*Warren Buckleitner*	120 Main St, Flemington NJ 08822	908-284-0404	R	6*	<.1
246	Fma Communicatons Inc—*Gerald Shankel*	833 Featherstone Rd, Rockford IL 61107	815-227-8284	R	6*	.1
247	Arthur L Davis Publishing Agency Inc—*Nancy Miller*	PO Box 216, Cedar Falls IA 50613	319-277-2414	R	6*	<.1
248	Pike and Fischer Inc—*Meg Hargraves*	8505 Fenton St Ste 208, Silver Spring MD 20910	301-562-1530	R	6*	.1
249	Ehlert Publishing Group Inc—*Stephen Hedlund*	6420 Sycamore Ln N Ste, Maple Grove MN 55369	763-383-4400	S	6*	<.1
250	Rodman Publishing Corp—*Rodman Zilenziger*	70 Hilltop Rd Ste 3000, Ramsey NJ 07446	201-825-2552	R	6*	<.1
251	Creative Age Publications Inc—*Deborah Carver*	7628 Densmore Ave, Van Nuys CA 91406	818-782-7328	R	6*	<.1
252	Nation Company LP—*Mary Valkenburg*	33 Irving Pl Fl 8, New York NY 10003	212-209-5400	R	6*	.1
253	Bz Media LLC—*H Bahr*	7 High St Ste 407, Huntington NY 11743	631-421-4158	R	6*	<.1
254	Herald Publishing House—*Greg Booth*	PO Box 390, Independence MO 64051	816-521-3015	R	5*	.1
255	National Review Inc—*Thomas Rhodes*	215 Lexington Ave Fl 1, New York NY 10016	212-679-7330	R	5*	.1
256	Moffly Publications Inc—*John Moffly*	205 Main St Ste 1, Westport CT 06880	203-869-0009	R	5*	<.1
257	Home Buyer Publications Inc—*John Kupferer*	4125 Lafayette Ctr Dr, Chantilly VA 20151	703-222-9411	R	5*	<.1
258	Icd Publications Inc—*Ian Gittlitz*	45 Research Way Ste 10, East Setauket NY 11733	631-246-9300	R	5*	<.1
259	Game and Fish Publication Inc—*Steven Vaughn*	2250 New Market Pkwy S, Marietta GA 30067	770-953-9222	R	5*	.1
260	Oak Tiger Publications Inc—*Craig Bednar*	900 S 3rd St, Minneapolis MN 55415	612-338-4125	R	5*	.1
261	Shoreline Creations Ltd—*Carl Wassink*	2465 112th Ave, Holland MI 49424	616-393-2077	R	5*	<.1
262	Miller Magazines Inc—*Jill Miller*	290 Maple Ct Ste 232, Ventura CA 93003	805-644-3824	R	5*	<.1
263	Columbus Bride—*Max Brown*	PO Box 29913, Columbus OH 43229	614-540-5900	R	5*	.1
264	Keller International Publishing LLC—*Brad Berger*	150 Great Neck Rd Ste, Great Neck NY 11021	516-829-9210	R	5*	.1

Note: An asterisk (*) indicates an estimated financial figure. The company type code used is as follows: R = Private, P = Public, S = Private Subsidiary, B = Public Subsidiary, D = Division, J = Joint Venture, I = Investment Fund.

COMPANY RANKINGS BY SALES WITHIN 4-DIGIT SIC

Rank	Company Name—*Executive Officer*	Address, City, State, Zip	Phone	Type	Fin	Empls
265	HIC Corp—*Doug Condra*	PO Box W, Newport Beach CA 92658	949-261-1636	R	5*	<.1
266	Physicians Postgraduate Press Inc—*John Shelton*	PO Box 752870, Memphis TN 38175	901-751-3800	R	5*	<.1
267	Board Member Inc—*T Kerstetter*	PO Box 3468, Brentwood TN 37024	615-309-3200	R	5*	.1
268	Cpw Inc—*Jennifer Starr*	201 N 17th St, Morehead City NC 28557	252-247-7442	S	5*	.1
269	Word Up Publications Inc—*Scott Figman*	210 E Hwy 4 Ste 211, Paramus NJ 07652	201-843-9018	R	5*	<.1
270	Gemini Corp—*John Zwarensteyn*	549 Ottawa Ave Nw Ste, Grand Rapids MI 49503	616-459-4545	R	5*	<.1
271	Davis Brothers Publishing Company Ltd—*Laura Cole*	4500 Speight Ave, Waco TX 76711	254-754-5636	R	5*	<.1
272	Duncan Mcintosh Company Inc—*Duncan Mcintosh*	17782 Cowan Ste A, Irvine CA 92614	949-660-6150	R	5*	<.1
273	Doyle Group—*Joseph Doyle*	5150 Palm Valley Rd St, Ponte Vedra Beach FL 32082	904-285-6020	R	5*	<.1
274	Triple D Publishing Inc—*Douglas Brown*	1300 S Dekalb St, Shelby NC 28152	704-482-9673	R	5*	<.1
275	Linguisystems Inc—*Linda Bowers*	3100 4th Ave, East Moline IL 61244	309-755-2300	R	5*	<.1
276	All American Crafts Inc—*Darren Cohen*	7 Waterloo Rd, Stanhope NJ 07874	973-347-6900	R	5*	<.1
277	Connell Communications Inc—*T Connell*	45 Main St Ste 102, Peterborough NH 03458	603-924-7271	R	4*	.1
278	Homes and Lifestyles Magazine Inc—*Fred Bradley*	11859 Lincolnway, Osceola IN 46561	574-674-5197	R	4*	.1
279	Solutions Magazine—*Wayne Gross*	15 Technology Pkwy S, Norcross GA 30092	770-209-7200	R	4*	.1
280	Associated Business Publications Company Ltd—*Joseph Pramberger*	1466 Broadway Ste 910, New York NY 10036	212-490-3999	R	4*	<.1
281	Bellerophon Publications Inc—*Horace Havemeyer*	61 W 23rd St Fl 4, New York NY 10010	212-627-9977	R	4*	<.1
282	Woodenboat Publications Inc—*James Miller*	PO Box 78, Brooklin ME 04616	207-359-4651	R	4*	<.1
283	Johnson Press Of America Inc—*Dale Flesburg*	PO Box 592, Pontiac IL 61764	815-844-5161	R	4*	<.1
284	Palm Beach Media Group Inc—*Ronald Woods*	PO Box 3344, Palm Beach FL 33480	561-659-0210	R	4*	<.1
285	Jes Publishing Corporation Management—*Margaret Shuff*	PO Box 820, Boca Raton FL 33429	561-997-8683	R	4*	<.1
286	Bedford Communications Inc—*Edward Brown*	1410 Brdwy Frnt 2 Fl 2, New York NY 10018	212-807-8220	R	4*	<.1
287	Silverchair Science Communications Inc—*Thane Kerner*	310 E Main St Ste 110, Charlottesville VA 22902	434-296-6333	R	4*	.1
288	Wall Street Reporter Magazine Inc—*Jack Marks*	419 Lafayette St Fl 2, New York NY 10003	212-363-2600	R	4*	.1
289	Business Word Inc—*Donald EL Johnson* hcPro Inc	11211 E Arapahoe Rd St, Centennial CO 80112		S	4*	.1
290	National Braille Press Inc—*Paul Parravano*	88 Saint Stephen St, Boston MA 02115	617-266-6160	R	4*	<.1
291	Athletic Business Publications Inc—*Gretchen Brown*	4130 Lien Rd, Madison WI 53704	608-249-0186	R	4*	<.1
292	Florida Magazine Administrators Inc—*Jeffrey Lichtenstein*	621 Nw 53rd St Ste 370, Boca Raton FL 33487	561-997-1660	R	4*	<.1
293	National Multiple Listing Inc—*Harris Small*	6601 N Andrews Ave, Fort Lauderdale FL 33309	954-772-8880	R	4*	<.1
294	Jones Publishing Inc—*Joseph Jones*	PO Box 5000, Iola WI 54945	715-445-5000	R	4*	<.1
295	Kenney Communications Inc—*Barbara Kenney*	1215 Spruce Ave, Orlando FL 32824	407-859-3113	R	4*	<.1
296	Insite Group LP—*Molly Barton*	123 E Wm J Bryan Pkwy, Bryan TX 77803	979-823-5567	R	4*	<.1
297	Decision Economics Inc—*Allen Sinai*	555 5th Ave 15th Fl, New York NY 10017	212-884-9440	R	4*	<.1
298	Beverage Media Group Inc—*Mike Roth*	116 John St Rm 2, New York NY 10038	212-571-3232	R	4*	<.1
299	ComputorEdge Magazine Inc—*Jack Dunning*	4740 Murphy Canyon Rd, San Diego CA 92123	858-573-0315	R	4*	<.1
300	Coprar Media Inc—*Justin Finocchiaro*	3551 SW 23rd Ter, Coral Gables FL 33145	305-529-0142	R	4*	<.1
301	PTO Today Inc—*Tim Sullivan*	100 Stonewall Blvd Ste, Wrentham MA 02093	508-384-0394	R	4*	<.1
302	Lundberg Survey Inc—*Trilby Lundberg*	911 Via Alondra, Camarillo CA 93012	805-383-2400	R	4*	<.1
303	Nyrev Inc—*Rae Hederman*	435 Hudson St Rm 300, New York NY 10014	212-757-8070	R	4*	<.1
304	Gambit Communications—*E Huffstutler*	3923 Bienville St, New Orleans LA 70119	504-486-5900	R	4*	<.1
305	Midwest Outdoors Ltd—*Eugene Laulunen*	111 Shore Dr, Burr Ridge IL 60527	630-887-7722	R	4*	<.1
306	Bell Press Inc—*Lawrence Bell*	2403 Champa St, Denver CO 80205	303-296-1600	R	4*	<.1
307	Mercury Publishing Services Inc—*Dan Drumheller*	1300 Piccard Dr Ste 10, Rockville MD 20850	240-631-1000	R	4*	<.1
308	Isthmus Publishing—*Vincent O'hern*	101 King St, Madison WI 53703	608-251-5627	R	4*	<.1
309	America Press Inc—*Thomas Reese*	106 W 56th St, New York NY 10019	212-581-4640	R	4*	<.1
310	Hunter Associates Inc—*Thomas Lemberger*	PO Box 13, Lynnfield MA 01940	781-233-9100	R	4*	<.1
311	Wall Street Transcript Corp—*Andrew Pickup*	48 W 37th St Rm 800, New York NY 10018	212-952-7400	R	4*	<.1
312	Hatton Brown Publishers Inc—*David Ramsey*	PO Box 2268, Montgomery AL 36102	334-834-1170	R	4*	<.1
313	Kci Communications Inc—*Phil Ash*	7600 Leesburg Pke Ste, Falls Church VA 22043	703-905-8000	R	3*	<.1
314	Csc Publishing Inc—*Richard Cress*	1155 Northland Dr, Saint Paul MN 55120	651-287-5600	R	3*	<.1
315	Media That Deelivers Inc—*Michael Dee*	8132 N 87th Pl, Scottsdale AZ 85258	480-460-5203	R	3*	<.1
316	Conquest Business Media Inc—*Glen White*	152 Conant St Ste 3, Beverly MA 01915	978-299-1200	R	3*	<.1
317	Idaho Law Review	PO Box 442321, Moscow ID 83844	208-885-7241	R	3*	<.1
318	Good News Publishing Company Inc—*Kirk Clinsclaes*	PO Box 96, Caney KS 67333	620-879-5460	R	3*	<.1
319	Alternative Publications Inc—*Louis Fortis*	207 E Buffalo St Ste 4, Milwaukee WI 53202	414-276-2222	R	3*	<.1
320	Weiss Communications Inc—*Mary Weiss*	6610 N Shadeland Ave S, Indianapolis IN 46220	317-585-5858	R	3*	<.1
321	Trade Publishing Inc—*Carl Hebenstreit*	287 Mokauea St Ste B, Honolulu HI 96819	808-848-0711	R	3*	<.1
322	Image Magazine Inc—*Dean Dingman*	5001 Birch St, Newport Beach CA 92660	714-689-3900	R	3*	<.1
323	Penny Marketing LP—*Cathrine Cappelliri*	6 Prowitt St, Norwalk CT 06855	203-866-6688	R	3*	<.1
324	Asa Publication Incorporated Mt—*Sally Buxkemper*	2 Simmental Way, Bozeman MT 59715	406-587-2778	R	3*	<.1
325	Wilks Publications Inc—*Gilbert Wilks*	PO Box 388, Portland TN 37148	615-325-4196	R	3*	<.1
326	Dana Chase Publications Inc—*Susan Korin*	6 Camelot Dr, Oak Brook IL 60523	630-990-3484	R	3*	<.1
327	Benjamin Media Inc—*Bernard Krzys*	PO Box 190, Peninsula OH 44264	330-467-7588	R	3*	<.1
328	brassMEDIA Inc—*Bryan Sims*	PO Box 1220, Corvallis OR 97339	541-753-8546	R	3*	<.1
329	Personal Selling Power Inc—*Gerhard Gschwandtner*	PO Box 5467, Fredericksburg VA 22403	540-752-7000	R	3*	<.1
330	Audio Amateur Inc—*Edward Dell*	PO Box 876, Peterborough NH 03458	603-924-9464	R	3*	<.1
331	Business Journal Of Portland Inc—*Lloyd Woods*	851 Sw 6th Ave Ste 500, Portland OR 97204	503-274-8733	R	3*	<.1
332	Digital Publishing Solutions—*Ira Penner*	46 3rd Ave, Somerville MA 02143	617-241-0163	R	3*	<.1
333	Career Communications Group Inc—*Tyrone Taborn*	729 E Pratt St Fl 5, Baltimore MD 21202	410-244-7101	R	3*	<.1
334	PA C Publishing Inc—*Paul Cianci*	PO Box 492, Palm Harbor FL 34682	813-814-1505	R	3*	<.1
335	Energy NewsData Corp—*Cyrus Noe*	PO Box 900928, Seattle WA 98109	206-285-4848	R	3*	<.1
336	Purcell Enterprises Inc—*John R Purcell*	PO Box 7628, Hilton Head Island SC 29938	843-842-6200	R	3*	<.1
337	Magazine I Spectrum E—*Willie Jones*	3 Park Ave Fl 17, New York NY 10016	212-419-7555	R	3*	<.1
338	Trend Publishing Inc—*William D'alexander*	625 N Michigan Ave Ste, Chicago IL 60611	312-932-1158	R	3*	<.1
339	Children and Families Inc—*Julie Antonio*	1651 Prince St, Alexandria VA 22314	703-739-7561	R	3*	<.1
340	United Publications Inc—*Brook Taliaferro*	PO Box 995, Yarmouth ME 04096	207-846-0600	R	3*	<.1
341	US Frontline News Inc—*Ryu Fujiwara*	330 Madison Ave Lbby 2, New York NY 10017	212-922-9090	R	3*	<.1
342	Lawrence Street Publications—*Lance Kamin*	24445 Nrthwstrn 218, Southfield MI 48075	248-945-4700	R	3*	<.1
343	Specpub Inc—*Caryn Goldberg*	6380 Wilshire Blvd Ste, Los Angeles CA 90048	323-960-5400	R	3*	<.1
344	Fantagraphics Books Inc—*Gary Groth*	7563 Lake City Way Ne, Seattle WA 98115	206-524-1967	R	3*	<.1
345	Summitt Publishing Co—*Lloyd Ferguson*	330 N Wabash Ave Ste 2, Chicago IL 60611	312-222-1010	R	3*	<.1
346	Clinical Chemistry Inc—*Mac Fancher*	1850 K St Nw Ste 625, Washington DC 20006	202-835-8737	R	3*	<.1
347	Cathedral Foundation Inc—*Daniel Medinger*	PO Box 777, Baltimore MD 21203	443-524-3150	R	3*	<.1
348	Reach Publishing Systems Inc—*Robert Slattery*	9933 Alliance Rd Ste 2, Blue Ash OH 45242	513-794-4100	R	3*	<.1
349	Chansen Publishing Inc—*Clint Pittman*	6 Horizon Ct, Rockwall TX 75032	972-882-1300	R	3*	<.1
350	Carmichael and Associates Inc—*Frank Carmichael*	1420 63rd St, Kenosha WI 53143	262-564-8800	R	3*	<.1
351	Newsgraphics Of Delmar Inc—*Richard Ahlstrom*	PO Box 100, Delmar NY 12054	518-439-5363	R	3*	<.1
352	CQ Communications Inc—*Richard Ross*	25 Newbridge Rd Ste 30, Hicksville NY 11801	516-681-2922	R	3*	<.1

Rank	Company Name—*Executive Officer*	Address, City, State, Zip	Phone	Type	Fin	Empls
353	Sussex Publishers Inc—*John Colman*	115 E 23rd St Fl 9, New York NY 10010	212-260-7210	R	3*	<.1
354	Ehlert Publishing Group—*Ralph Poole*	20700 Belshaw Ave, Carson CA 90746	310-537-6322	R	3*	<.1
355	Counsel For Secular Humanism—*Ronald Lindsay*	PO Box 664, Amherst NY 14226	716-636-7571	R	3*	<.1
356	Industrial Market Place—*Joel Wineberg*	7842 Lincoln Ave Ste 1, Skokie IL 60077	847-676-1900	R	3*	<.1
357	RA Rapaport Publishing—*Richard Rapaport*	150 W 22nd St Fl 8, New York NY 10011	212-989-0200	R	3*	<.1
358	Preparatory Magazine Group Inc—*Luciano Rammairone*	1200 S Ave Ste 202, Staten Island NY 10314	718-761-4800	R	3*	.1
359	Celebrity Service International Inc—*Vickey Bagley*	2301 Tracy Pl Nw, Washington DC 20008	202-745-9788	R	3*	<.1
360	Quarterly Review Of Wines—*Richard Elia*	24 Garfield Ave, Winchester MA 01890	781-729-7132	R	3*	<.1
361	Carstens Publications Inc—*Harold Carstens*	PO Box 700, Newton NJ 07860	973-383-3355	R	3*	<.1
362	Honolulu Publishing Company Ltd—*Nicholas Tinebra*	707 Richards St Ste 52, Honolulu HI 96813	808-524-7400	R	3*	<.1
363	Lockwood Trade Journal Company Inc—*George Lockwood*	26 Broadway Ste 9m2, New York NY 10004	212-391-2060	R	3*	<.1
364	Mckinnon Enterprises—*Gary Beneventi*	PO Box 719001, San Diego CA 92171	858-571-1818	R	3*	<.1
365	Five Star Publishing Inc—*Heidi Gorman*	PO Box 998, Fort Dodge IA 50501	515-955-6234	R	2*	<.1
366	Atlanta Metropolitan Publishing Inc—*Thomas Casey*	180 Allen Rd Ne Ste 20, Atlanta GA 30328	404-843-9800	R	2*	<.1
367	Leader Publishing Group Inc—*Gina Wright*	3379 Peachtree Rd Ne S, Atlanta GA 30326	404-760-1200	R	2*	<.1
368	Newsletters Ink Corp—*John Richey*	PO Box 4008, Lancaster PA 17604	717-393-1000	R	2*	<.1
369	Harvard Magazine Inc—*Kathrine Shute*	7 Ware St, Cambridge MA 02138	617-495-5746	R	2*	<.1
370	Michigan Contractor and Builder—*John Weatherhead* Reed Business Information	1200 Madison Ave Ste L, Indianapolis IN 46225	317-423-7080	D	2	<.1
371	Ann Arbor Observer Co—*Laura Mcreynolds*	201 Catherine St, Ann Arbor MI 48104	734-769-3175	R	2*	<.1
372	Bradley Communications Corp—*William Harrison*	PO Box 360, Broomall PA 19008	484-477-4220	R	2*	<.1
373	Forced Exposure Inc—*James Johnson*	PO Box 9102, Waltham MA 02454	781-321-0320	R	2*	<.1
374	Drug Delivery Technology LLC—*Mhsa Dekoven*	219 Changebridge Rd, Montville NJ 07045	973-299-1200	R	2*	<.1
375	Homebuyers Guide Real Estate Inc—*Harry Crowell*	17780 Fitch Ste 195, Irvine CA 92614	949-476-3055	R	2*	<.1
376	Mcmunn Associates—*Larry Mcmunn*	900 Haddon Ave Ste 302, Collingswood NJ 08108	856-858-3440	R	2*	<.1
377	Travel Trade Publications Inc—*Joel Abels*	PO Box 3781, New York NY 10163	212-343-3360	R	2*	<.1
378	Competitor Magazine—*Bob Babbitt*	10179 Hudiken St Ste 1, San Diego CA 92121	858-768-6800	R	2*	<.1
379	Editorial Experts Inc—*Claire Kincaid*	8945 Guilford Rd Ste 1, Columbia MD 21046	410-309-8200	R	2*	.2
380	Distinctive Properties Of Napa Valley—*Randy Principe*	1615 2nd St, Napa CA 94559	707-256-2251	R	2*	.1
381	Contemporary Media Inc—*Kenneth Neill*	460 Tennessee St, Memphis TN 38101	901-521-9000	R	2*	.1
382	Vogel Communications Inc—*Steve Vogel*	701 5th Ave Fl 42, Seattle WA 98104	206-262-8183	R	2*	<.1
383	Elevator World—*Ricia Sturgeon Hendrick*	PO Box 6507, Mobile AL 36606	251-479-4514	R	2*	<.1
384	Magna Publications Inc—*William Haight*	2718 Dryden Dr, Madison WI 53704	608-246-3590	R	2*	<.1
385	Chronicle Of The Horse Inc—*Robert Banner*	PO Box 46, Middleburg VA 20118	540-687-6341	R	2*	<.1
386	International Smart Tan Network Inc—*Dale Parrott*	PO Box 1630, Jackson MI 49204	517-784-1772	R	2*	<.1
387	Levas Inc—*Walter Lomax*	200 Highpoint Dr Ste 2, Chalfont PA 18914	215-822-7935	R	2*	<.1
388	Thaddeus Computing Inc—*Hal Goldstein*	110 N Ct St, Fairfield IA 52556	641-472-6330	R	2*	<.1
389	Business Publishers Inc—*Leonard Eiserer*	PO Box 17592, Baltimore MD 21297		R	2*	<.1
390	Inside Mortgage Finance Publications Inc—*Guy D Cecala*	7910 Woodmont Ave Ste, Bethesda MD 20814	301-951-1240	R	2*	<.1
391	Patricia Seybold Group—*Patricia Seybold*	PO Box 783, Needham Heights MA 02494	617-742-5200	R	2*	<.1
392	Grimes Publications of Georgia Inc—*Millard Grimes*	624 S Milledge Ave Ste, Athens GA 30605	706-354-0463	R	2*	<.1
393	Automundo Productions Inc—*Jorge Koechlin*	2960 SW 8th St 2nd Fl, Miami FL 33135	305-541-4198	R	2*	<.1
394	Truth Seeker Company Inc—*Bonnie Lange*	239 S Juniper St, Escondido CA 92025	760-489-5211	R	2*	<.1
395	Cholo Publishing Inc *Choh N Low*	125 Maiden Ln Ste 16A, New York NY 10030	212-947-4322	R	2*	<.1
396	Thinking Cap Solutions Inc—*Victor J Maliar*	PO Box 2925, Port Angeles WA 98362	360-452-6159	R	2*	<.1
397	Data Trace Chemistry Publishers Inc—*David Reicher*	110 W Rd Ste 227, Baltimore MD 21204	410-494-4994	R	2*	<.1
398	Varsity Communications Inc—*Ralph Boyle*	12510 33rd Ave Ne Ste, Seattle WA 98125	206-367-2420	R	2*	<.1
399	Luby Publishing Inc—*Keith Hamilton*	122 S Michigan Ave Ste, Chicago IL 60603	312-341-1110	R	2*	<.1
400	Northeast Scene Inc—*Richard Kabat*	1468 W 9th St Ste 805, Cleveland OH 44113	216-241-7550	R	2*	<.1
401	Country Standard Time—*Jeffrey Remz*	54 Ballard St, Newton MA 02459	617-969-0331	R	2*	<.1
402	Uptown Publications Inc—*Michael Portantino*	PO Box 34623, San Diego CA 92163	619-299-6397	R	2*	<.1
403	Maine Antique Digest Inc—*Samuel Pennington*	PO Box 1429, Waldoboro ME 04572	207-832-4888	R	2*	<.1
404	Challenge Publications Inc—*Edwin Schnepf*	9509 Vassar Ave Ste A, Chatsworth CA 91311	818-700-6868	R	2*	<.1
405	Idg International Sales Corp—*Patrick Mcgovern*	3 Post Office Sq Ste 4, Boston MA 02109	617-422-0930	R	2*	<.1
406	On The Go Magazines Inc—*George Kohn*	2945 Ne 3rd St Ste 203, Ocala FL 34470	352-732-2594	R	2*	<.1
407	Retail Reporting Corp—*Henry Burr*	302 5th Ave Fl 11, New York NY 10001	212-279-7000	R	2*	<.1
408	Rb Publishing Inc—*Ronald Brent*	PO Box 259098, Madison WI 53725	608-241-8777	R	2*	<.1
409	StarchefsCom Inc—*Antoinette Bruno*	9 E 19th St Fl 9, New York NY 10003	212-966-3775	R	2*	<.1
410	Joseph Co—*Carla Mignogna*	1406 Pittsburgh St, Cheswick PA 15024	412-781-1461	R	2*	<.1
411	Modern Drummer Publications Inc—*Isabel Spagnardi*	12 Old Bridge Rd, Cedar Grove NJ 07009	973-239-4140	R	2*	<.1
412	Liberty Media For Women LLC—*Marcia Gillespie*	433 S Beverly Dr, Beverly Hills CA 90212	310-556-2500	R	2*	<.1
413	Synthesis—*William Fishkin*	210 W 6th St, Chico CA 95928	530-899-7708	R	2*	<.1
414	Gulf Stream Media Group—*Mark Cormick*	800 E Broward Blvd Ste, Fort Lauderdale FL 33301	954-462-4488	R	2*	<.1
415	Instrumentalists Inc—*James Rohner*	200 Northfield Rd, Northfield IL 60093	847-446-5000	R	2*	<.1
416	Weiss and Hughes Publishing Inc—*Stuart Weiss*	189 Wind Chime Ct Ste, Raleigh NC 27615	919-870-1722	R	2*	<.1
417	Country Music Media Group—*Tony Seibert*	PO Box 420235, Palm Coast FL 32142	615-259-1111	R	2*	<.1
418	Avid Media Venture Inc—*Craig Rosengarden*	1825 W Walnut Hill Ln, Irving TX 75038	972-550-9000	R	2*	<.1
419	La Parent Magazine—*Madelyn Calabrese*	443 Irving Dr Ste A, Burbank CA 91504	818-846-0400	R	2*	<.1
420	Vacuum Dealers Trade Association—*Judy Patterson*	2724 2nd Ave, Des Moines IA 50313	515-282-9101	R	2*	<.1
421	Philadelphia Style Magazine LLC—*Haley Binn*	141 League St, Philadelphia PA 19147	215-468-6670	R	2*	<.1
422	Louisville Magazine Inc—*Dan Crutcher*	137 W Muhammad Ali Blv, Louisville KY 40202	502-625-0100	R	2*	<.1
423	Atlantic Publication Group LLC	PO Box 30007, Charleston SC 29417	843-747-0025	R	2*	<.1
424	Jazz Times Inc—*Glen Sabin*	10801 Margate Rd, Silver Spring MD 20901	301-588-4114	R	2*	<.1
425	Mag Inc—*Mark Goldberg*	31 Dutch Mill Rd, Ithaca NY 14850	607-257-6970	R	1*	<.1
426	Halcyon Business Publications Inc—*Dennis Shea*	400 Post Ave Ste 304, Westbury NY 11590	516-338-0900	R	1*	<.1
427	Alaska Quality Publishing Inc—*Robert Ulin*	8537 Corbin Dr, Anchorage AK 99507	907-562-9300	R	1*	<.1
428	Chesapeake Bay Communications Inc—*Richard Royer*	PO Box 4358, Annapolis MD 21403	410-263-2662	R	1*	<.1
429	Trades Publishing Inc—*Tim Wilson*	20 Our Way Dr, Crossville TN 38555	931-484-8819	R	1*	<.1
430	Renegade Publishing Inc—*Keith Skrzypczak*	PO Box 50499, Tulsa OK 74150	918-592-5550	R	1*	<.1
431	Turner Communications Inc—*Bruce White*	125 Strafford Ave Ste, Wayne PA 19087	610-975-4541	R	1*	<.1
432	UMI Publications Inc—*C Mothershead*	PO Box 30036, Charlotte NC 28230	704-374-0420	R	1*	<.1
433	Inside Council—*Charles Carman*	222 S Riverside Plz St, Chicago IL 60606	312-654-3500	R	1*	<.1
434	Oxendine Publishing Inc—*W Oxendine*	412 Nw 16th Ave, Gainesville FL 32601	352-373-6907	R	1*	<.1
435	Arizona Beverage Analyst—*Lawrence Bell*	2403 Champa St, Denver CO 80205	303-296-1600	R	1*	<.1
436	Bulletin Board Inc—*French Salter*	PO Box 2490, Montgomery AL 36102	334-272-1225	R	1*	<.1
437	Prime National Publishing Corp—*Eileen Devito*	470 Boston Post Rd, Weston MA 02493	781-899-2702	R	1*	<.1
438	Pam Printers And Publishers Inc—*Ronald Haubrich*	1012 Vermont St, Quincy IL 62301	217-222-4030	R	1*	<.1
439	Media Index Publishing Inc—*James Baker*	PO Box 24365, Seattle WA 98124	206-382-9220	R	1*	<.1
440	Madison Magazine Inc—*Jennifer Winiger*	PO Box 44965, Madison WI 53744	608-270-3600	R	1*	<.1
441	Family Publishing Group Inc—*Heather Hart*	141 Halstead Ave 3rd F, Mamaroneck NY 10543	914-381-7474	R	1*	<.1

Note: An asterisk (*) indicates an estimated financial figure. The company type code used is as follows: R = Private, P = Public, S = Private Subsidiary, B = Public Subsidiary, D = Division, J = Joint Venture, I = Investment Fund.

COMPANY RANKINGS BY SALES WITHIN 4-DIGIT SIC

Rank	Company Name—*Executive Officer*	Address, City, State, Zip	Phone	Type	Fin	Empls
442	FirehouseCom—*Dave Iannone*	11720 Bltsvlle Dr Ste, Beltsville MD 20705	301-486-7500	R	1*	<.1
443	New Car Test Drive Inc—*John Tipp*	1121 Kirts Blvd Unit D, Troy MI 48084	248-273-6020	R	1*	<.1
444	TKO/Real Estate Advisory Group—*Ted Kraus*	PO Box 2630, Trenton NJ 08690	609-587-6200	R	1*	<.1
445	Mio Publication Inc—*James Dygert*	1864 University Pkwy, Sarasota FL 34243	941-351-2411	R	1*	<.1
446	International Marketing Strategies Inc—*James Lawrence*	62 Southfield Ave Ste, Stamford CT 06902	203-406-0106	R	1*	<.1
447	High Society Magazine Inc—*Geoffrey Lurie*	801 2nd Ave Lbby, New York NY 10017	212-661-7878	R	1*	<.1
448	Plexus Publishing Inc—*Tom Hogan*	143 Old Marlton Pike, Medford NJ 08055	609-654-6500	R	1*	<.1
449	San Diego Metropolitan Business Magazine—*Robert Page*	3990 Old Town Ave Ste, San Diego CA 92110		R	1*	<.1
450	Omega 7 Inc—*Alonzo Washington*	PO Box 171046, Kansas City KS 66117	913-321-6764	R	1*	<.1
451	Zeitgeist Publishing Inc—*Mary Rudell*	PO Box 3000, Denville NJ 07834	301-729-6190	R	1*	<.1
452	Donley Technology—*Elizabeth M Donley*	PO Box 152, Colonial Beach VA 22443	804-224-9427	R	1*	<.1
453	Kart Marketing Group Inc—*Darrell E Sitarz*	PO Box 101, Wheaton IL 60189	630-653-7368	R	1*	<.1
454	WPL Associates Inc—*Paul Levin*	PO Box 1495, Bethesda MD 20827	301-765-9525	R	1*	<.1
455	Ace Publishing Inc—*William Orovan*	PO Box 16630, Phoenix AZ 85011	602-266-0550	R	1*	<.1
456	Vernon Publications LLC—*Gene Walters*	PO Box 970, Woodinville WA 98072	425-488-3211	R	1*	<.1
457	Herald And Banner Press—*Ray Crooks*	PO Box 4060, Shawnee Mission KS 66204	913-432-0331	R	1*	<.1
458	Magellan Publishing—*Tom Yunt*	PO Box 688, Dubuque IA 52004	563-588-5611	S	1*	<.1
459	Midsouth Media Group	6920 Oak Forest Dr, Olive Branch MS 38654	662-890-3359	R	1*	<.1
460	Lambda Publications Inc—*Tracy Baim*	5443 N Broadway St Ste, Chicago IL 60640	773-871-7610	R	1*	<.1
461	Jonesreport Inc—*Phil Stillerman*	PO Box 80209, Indianapolis IN 46280	317-844-9024	R	1	<.1
462	Real Estate Magazines Ltd—*Steve Bruhill*	16200 Dallas Pkwy Ste, Dallas TX 75248	972-248-8761	R	1*	<.1
463	Dees Communication Inc—*John Dees*	PO Box 931, Montgomery AL 36101	334-263-4436	R	1*	<.1
464	Black and White Inc—*Chuck Geis*	2210 2nd Ave N Fl 2, Birmingham AL 35203	205-933-0460	R	1*	<.1
465	Energy Publishing Inc—*Forest Hill*	PO Box 52210, Knoxville TN 37950	865-588-0645	R	1*	<.1
466	Quanturo Publishing Inc—*Esther Jackson*	4141 Ne 2nd Ave Ste 20, Miami FL 33137	305-373-3700	R	<1*	<.1
467	Ethikos Inc—*Andrew Singer*	PO Box 31, Mamaroneck NY 10543	914-381-7475	R	<1*	<.1
468	Suburban Publishing Inc—*Robert Martinelli*	3301 Lancaster Pke Ste, Wilmington DE 19805	302-656-1809	R	<1*	<.1
469	Bankruptcy Creditors' Service Inc—*Peter A Chapman*	301 N Harrison St Ste, Princeton NJ 08540	215-945-7000	R	<1	<.1
470	Rip Off Press Inc—*Gilbert Shelton*	11180 Edgewood Rd, Auburn CA 95603	530-885-8183	R	<1*	<.1
471	Offshore Press Inc—*Vernon Jacobs*	PO Box 8137, Shawnee Mission KS 66208	913-362-9667	R	<1*	<.1

TOTALS: SIC 2721 Periodicals
Companies: 471 — 70,706 — 167.9

2731 Book Publishing

Rank	Company Name—*Executive Officer*	Address, City, State, Zip	Phone	Type	Fin	Empls
1	McGraw-Hill Companies Inc—*Harold McGraw III*	1221 Ave of the Americ, New York NY 10020		P	6,246	22.7
2	Wiley Publishing Services Inc—*William J Pesce* John Wiley and Sons Inc	10475 Crosspoint Blvd, Indianapolis IN 46256	317-572-3000	S	4,007*	5.1
3	Random House Inc—*Peter Olson*	1745 Broadway, New York NY 10019	212-782-9000	D	2,039	N/A
4	Scholastic Inc—*Richard Robinson*	557 Broadway, New York NY 10012	212-343-6100	P	1,906	9.1
5	John Wiley and Sons Inc—*William J Pesce*	111 River St, Hoboken NJ 07030	201-748-6000	P	1,743	5.1
6	McGraw-Hill Education—*Harold McGraw* McGraw-Hill Companies Inc	860 Taylor Station Rd, Blacklick OH 43004	614-759-3644	D	1,540*	2.0
7	Houghton Mifflin Co—*Barry O'Callaghan*	222 Berkeley St, Boston MA 02116	617-351-5000	S	1,282*	3.1
8	Check Point Software Technologies Inc—*Gil Shwed*	800 Bridge Pky, Redwood City CA 94065	650-628-2000	S	1,247	2.2
9	RR Bowker LLC—*Andrew Meyer*	630 Central Ave, New Providence NJ 07974	908-286-1090	R	1,242*	.9
10	CAB International North American Office—*Hans Rutimann*	875 Massachusettes Ave, Cambridge MA 02139	617-395-4051	R	1,196*	.5
11	HarperCollins Publishers Inc—*Jane Friedman*	10 E 53rd St, New York NY 10022	212-207-7000	S	975*	3.0
12	Little Brown and Co—*David Young*	3 Center Plz, Boston MA 02108	617-227-0730	D	868*	.6
13	Bertelsmann Inc—*Hans Sorge*	1540 Broadway Fl 24, New York NY 10036	212-782-1000	R	840*	13.0
14	Simon and Schuster Inc—*Carolyn Reidy*	1230 Ave Of The Americ, New York NY 10020	212-698-7000	S	671*	1.5
15	Sage Publications USA—*Blaise Simqu*	2455 Teller Rd, Thousand Oaks CA 91320	805-499-0721	R	627*	.5
16	Commerce Clearing House Inc—*Robert Becker*	20101 Hamilton Ave Ste, Torrance CA 90502	310-800-9800	S	538	4.7
17	Matthew Bender and Company Inc	1275 Broadway, Albany NY 12204	518-487-3000	S	434*	.2
18	McGraw-Hill Higher Education McGraw-Hill Companies Inc	1333 Burr Ridge Pky, Burr Ridge IL 60527	630-789-4000	D	385*	1.0
19	Bureau Of National Affairs Inc—*Paul N Wojcik*	3 Bethesda Metro Ctr, Bethesda VA 20814		R	352*	1.7
20	Marvel Entertainment Group Inc—*Isaac Perlmutter*	417 5th Ave, New York NY 10016	212-576-4000	S	352*	.3
21	LifeWay Christian Resources—*Thom Rainer*	1 Lifeway Plz, Nashville TN 37234	615-251-2000	R	318*	1.3
22	McGraw-Hill Construction—*Robert D Stuono* McGraw-Hill Companies Inc	1221 Ave of the Americ, New York NY 10020	212-904-2000	D	266*	1.5
23	Thomas Nelson Inc—*Michael S Hyatt*	PO Box 141000, Nashville TN 37214	615-889-9000	R	238*	.6
24	Knopf Publishing Group—*Edward Volini* Random House Inc	1745 Broadway, New York NY 10019	212-782-9000	D	237*	.2
25	World Book Inc—*Paul Gazzolo*	233 North Michigan Ave, Chicago IL 60601	312-729-5800	R	232*	.2
26	Haights Cross Communications Inc—*Ronald Schlosser*	136 Madison Ave 8th Fl, New York NY 10016	212-209-0500	R	222*	.9
27	Southwestern/Great American Inc—*Henry Bedford*	PO Box 305140, Nashville TN 37230	615-391-2500	R	216*	1.0
28	Princeton Review Inc—*John Connolly*	111 Speen St Ste 550, Framingham MA 01701	508-663-5050	P	214	1.0
29	Zaner-Bloser Inc—*Robert Page*	PO Box 16764, Columbus OH 43216	614-486-0221	S	209*	.2
30	Carson-Dellosa Publishing LLC—*Judy L Harris*	PO Box 35665, Greensboro NC 27425	336-632-0084	S	208*	.2
31	LexisNexis Publishing—*Andrew Prozes*	PO Box 7587, Charlottesville VA 22906	434-972-7600	D	195*	.8
32	Penguin Group Inc (New York New York)—*David Shanks*	375 Hudson St, New York NY 10014	212-366-2372	S	194	.9
33	Key Curriculum Press Inc—*Steven Rasmussen*	1150 65th St, Emeryville CA 94608	510-595-7000	R	192*	.1
34	JJ Keller and Associates Inc—*Robert Keller*	PO Box 368, Neenah WI 54957	920-722-2848	R	186*	1.5
35	Baker and Taylor Acquisitions Corp—*Tom Morgan*	2550 W Tyvola Rd Ste 3, Charlotte NC 28217	704-998-3100	R	177*	3.6
36	Rand McNally and Co—*Michael K Hehir*	PO Box 7600, Chicago IL 60680	847-329-8100	R	173*	.9
37	William S Hein and Company Inc—*Kevin Marmion*	1285 Main St, Buffalo NY 14209	716-882-2600	R	165*	.1
38	Academic Press Inc—*Crispin Davis*	30 Corporate Dr Ste 40, Burlington MA 01803	781-313-4880	D	150	.3
39	Aspen Publishers Inc—*Mark Dorman*	76 9th Ave 7 Fl, New York NY 10011	212-771-0600	S	149*	.6
40	RSMeans—*David Walsh*	700 Longwater Dr, Norwell MA 02061	781-585-7880	D	144*	.1
41	University Of New Mexico Press—*Luther Wilson*	MSC04 2820 1 Universit, Albuquerque NM 87131	505-277-2346	R	143*	.1
42	Penguin Group (USA) Inc—*David Shanks*	375 Hudson St Bsmt 3, New York NY 10014	212-366-2000	R	140*	2.0
43	Zondervan Corp—*Moe Girkins* HarperCollins Publishers Inc	5300 Patterson Ave SE, Grand Rapids MI 49512	616-698-6900	S	133*	.4
44	Volt Directory Services—*Gerard DiPippo*	1 Sentry Pkwy E Ste 10, Blue Bell PA 19422	610-825-7720	D	125	.9
45	Jim Henson Company Inc—*Lisa Henson*	1416 N La Brea Ave, Hollywood CA 90028	323-802-1500	R	110*	.1
46	Time4 Media—*Thomas Beusse*	2 Park Ave Fl 9, New York NY 10016	212-779-5000	S	109*	.7
47	Mel Bay Publications Inc—*William Bay*	4 Industrial Dr, Pacific MO 63069	636-257-3970	R	98*	.1
48	Holt McDougal—*Anthony Lucki* Houghton Mifflin Co	1900 S Batavia, Geneva IL 60134		D	97*	.3
49	Lexis Nexis—*Garry Campbell*	245 Peachtree Center A, Atlanta GA 30303	404-577-1779	D	93*	.4

Rank	Company Name—*Executive Officer*	Address, City, State, Zip	Phone	Type	Fin	Empls
50	Taylor Publishing Co—*David Fiore*	1550 W Mockingbird Ln, Dallas TX 75235	214-637-2800	R	85*	1.4
51	Hoover's Inc—*David Mather*	5800 Airport Blvd, Austin TX 78752	512-374-4500	S	83*	.4
52	Klutz Press—*John Cassidy*	450 Lambert Ave, Palo Alto CA 94306	650-857-0888	S	83*	.1
	Scholastic Inc					
53	Oxford University Press Inc—*Tim Barton*	198 Madison Ave Fl 8, New York NY 10016	212-726-6000	R	82*	.6
54	Tyndale House Publishers Inc—*Mark Taylor*	PO Box 80, Wheaton IL 60187	630-668-8300	R	79*	.3
55	Wizards Of The Coast Inc—*Greg Leeds*	PO Box 707, Renton WA 98057	425-226-6500	S	76*	.3
56	William B Eerdmans Publishing Co—*William B Eerdmans Jr*	2140 Oak Industrial Dr, Grand Rapids MI 49505	616-459-4591	R	73*	.1
57	Jist Publishing—*Michael Farr*	875 Montreal Way, Saint Paul MN 55102	317-613-4200	R	70*	.1
58	Macmillan/McGraw-Hill	148 Princeton-Hightsto, Hightstown NJ 08520	609-426-5793	D	69*	.4
	McGraw-Hill Education					
59	W W Norton and Company Inc—*W Mcfeely*	500 5th Ave Fl 6, New York NY 10110	212-354-5500	R	67*	1.0
60	Deseret Book Co—*Sheri Dew*	40 E South Temple, Salt Lake City UT 84111	801-534-1515	S	67*	1.0
61	Lippincott Williams and Wilkins—*John Monahan*	530 Walnut St, Philadelphia PA 19106	215-521-8300	D	67*	.3
62	Salem Press Inc—*Jim Magill*	PO Box 50062, Pasadena CA 91115	626-584-0106	R	65*	<.1
63	McFarland and Company Incorporated Publishers—*Robert Franklin*	PO Box 611, Jefferson NC 28640	336-246-4460	R	62*	<.1
64	Agency for Instructional Technology—*Chuck Wilson*	1800 N Stonelake Dr Bo, Bloomington IN 47404	812-339-2203	R	60*	<.1
65	Graphic Services LLC	PO Box 418, Rockland MA 02370	781-871-7744	R	59*	.2
66	West LEGALworks—*Moneesh Arora*	195 Broadway 9th Fl, New York NY 10007	212-332-8444	S	59*	<.1
67	Glencoe/McGraw-Hill—*Harold McGraw III*	2 Penn Plaza, New York NY 10121	212-904-2000	S	58*	.6
	Macmillan/McGraw-Hill					
68	HighReach Learning Inc—*Steve Cooper*	5275 Parkway Plaza Blv, Charlotte NC 28217	704-357-0112	S	57*	<.1
69	Baker Book House Co—*Dwight Baker*	PO Box 6287, Grand Rapids MI 49516	616-676-9185	R	55*	.2
70	Thompson Publishing Group Inc—*Robert Mate*	805 15th St NW, Washington DC 20005	202-872-4000	R	53*	.1
71	Technical Training Inc—*Lori Blaker*	2750 Product Dr, Rochester Hills MI 48309	248-853-5550	R	52*	.8
72	FW Media Inc—*David Nussbaumm*	4700 E Galbraith Rd, Cincinnati OH 45236	513-531-2222	R	51*	.8
73	Synq Solutions Inc—*Michael Snyder*	655 Lambert Dr Ne, Atlanta GA 30324	404-874-8400	R	50*	.3
74	Thomson PDR—*Bill Schlegel*	5 Paragon Dr, Montvale NJ 07645	201-358-7200	R	50	N/A
75	Jane's Information Group USA—*Michael Dell*	110 N Royal St Ste 200, Alexandria VA 22314	703-683-3700	S	48*	.3
76	Steve Jackson Games Inc—*Steve Jackson*	PO Box 18957, Austin TX 78760	512-447-7866	R	48*	<.1
77	CRC Press LLC	6000 Broken Sound Pky, Boca Raton FL 33487		S	46	.3
78	O'Reilly and Associates Inc—*Tim O'Reilly*	1005 Gravenstein Hwy N, Sebastopol CA 95472	707-829-7000	R	45*	.3
79	Frank W Cawood and Associates Inc—*Frank Cawood*	PO Box 2528, Peachtree City GA 30269	770-487-6307	R	40*	.1
80	Informa USA Inc—*Kenneth Bohlin*	1 Research Dr Ste 400a, Westborough MA 01581	508-616-6600	R	40*	.8
81	Walt Disney Publications Inc	500 S Buena Vista St, Burbank CA 91521	818-560-1000	D	39	.1
82	Hay House Inc—*Louise L Hay*	PO Box 5100, Carlsbad CA 92018	760-431-7695	R	38*	.1
83	Craftsman Book Co—*Gary Moselle*	6058 Corte Del Cedro, Carlsbad CA 92011	760-438-7828	R	38*	<.1
84	Haworth Press Inc	270 Madison Ave, New York NY 10016		S	37*	.2
85	Jossey-Bass Inc—*Wiliam Pesce*	10475 Cross Point, Indianapolis IN 46256		S	37	.2
	John Wiley and Sons Inc					
86	Facts and Comparisons Inc—*Arvind Subramanian*	77 Westport Plz Ste 45, Saint Louis MO 63146	314-216-2100	S	36*	.1
87	TFH Publications Inc—*Glen Axelrod*	PO Box 427, Neptune NJ 07754	732-988-8400	S	35*	.3
88	Graphic Arts Ctr Publishing Co—*Charles M Hopkins*	3019 NW Yeon, Portland OR 97210	503-226-2702	R	35*	.2
89	Nevada Publishing Inc	4735 S Durango Dr Ste, Las Vegas NV 89147	702-227-9800	S	35*	<.1
90	Chronicle Books LLC—*Jack Jensen*	680 2nd St, San Francisco CA 94107	415-537-4200	S	34*	.2
91	Sasquatch Books Inc—*Gary Luke*	1904 3rd Ave Ste 710, Seattle WA 98101	206-467-4300	R	34*	<.1
92	Accent Publications—*Chris Doornbos*	4050 Lee Vance View, Colorado Springs CO 80918	719-536-0100	S	32*	.4
93	MBI Publishing Co—*Ken Fund*	400 1st Ave N Ste 300, Minneapolis MN 55401	612-344-8100	R	31*	.1
94	Bridge Publications Inc—*Lis Astrupgaard*	5600 E Olympic Blvd, Los Angeles CA 90022	323-953-3320	R	31*	.1
95	St Martin's Press LLC—*Mark Bargen*	175 5th Ave, New York NY 10010	646-307-5151	R	30*	.5
96	Sybex Inc—*William Pesce*	111 River St, Hoboken NJ 07030	201-748-6000	S	30	.1
	John Wiley and Sons Inc					
97	WestNet Inc—*Joe Scullion*	4070 Youngfield St, Wheat Ridge CO 80033		R	30*	<.1
98	Concordia Publishing House—*Bruce Kintz*	3558 S Jefferson Ave, Saint Louis MO 63118	314-268-1000	R	28*	.3
99	Sterling Publishing Company Inc—*Charles Numberg*	387 Park Ave S 11th Fl, New York NY 10016	212-532-7160	S	28*	.3
100	University Press of America Inc—*Judith Rothman*	4501 Forbes Blvd Ste 2, Lanham MD 20706	301-459-3366	R	28*	.2
101	Columbia Books Inc	8120 Woodmont Ave Ste, Bethesda DC 20814	202-464-1662	R	28*	<.1
102	James Ray International—*James Ray*	5927 Balfour Ct Ste 10, Carlsbad CA 92008		R	28*	<.1
103	Channing Bete Company Inc—*Michael Bete*	1 Community Pl, South Deerfield MA 01373	413-665-7611	R	28*	.3
104	Workman Publishing Company Inc—*Peter Workman*	225 Varick St Fl 9, New York NY 10014	212-254-5900	R	28*	.2
105	Storey Publishing LLC—*Maribeth Casey*	210 Mass Moca Way, North Adams MA 01247	413-346-2100	S	27*	.1
	Workman Publishing Company Inc					
106	William H Sadlier Inc—*William Sadlier-Dinger*	14 Wall St, New York NY 10005		R	26	.2
107	Newkirk Products Inc—*Raymond Newkirk*	15 Corporate Cir, Albany NY 12203	518-862-3200	R	26*	.3
108	Mike Murach and Associates Inc—*Mike Murach*	4340 N Knoll, Fresno CA 93722	559-440-9071	R	26*	<.1
109	Perfection Learning Corp—*Steven Keay*	PO Box 500, Logan IA 51546	515-278-0133	R	25*	.2
110	Elsevier Science Inc—*Ron Mobed*	360 Park Ave S, New York NY 10010	212-989-5800	D	25*	.2
111	Oxmoor House Inc	PO Box 11095, Des Moines IA 50336		S	25	.1
112	Sourcebooks Inc—*Dominique Raccah*	PO Box 4410, Naperville IL 60567	630-961-3900	R	25*	.1
113	A-R Editions Inc—*Patrick Wall*	8551 Research Way Ste, Middleton WI 53562	608-836-9000	R	25*	<.1
114	Merriam-Webster Inc—*John Morse*	PO Box 281, Springfield MA 01102	413-734-3134	R	25*	.1
115	Sheridan Group (Hunt Valley Maryland)—*John Saxton*	11311 McCormick Rd Ste, Hunt Valley MD 21031	410-785-7277	R	23*	<.1
116	American Institute Of Aeronautics And Astronautics Inc—*Robert Dickman*	1801 Alexander Bell Dr, Reston VA 20191	703-264-7500	R	22*	.1
117	Publications International Ltd—*Louis Weber*	7373 N Cicero Ave, Lincolnwood IL 60712	847-676-3470	R	21*	.4
118	National Journal Group Inc—*Charles Green*	The Watergate 600 New, Washington DC 20037	202-739-8400	R	21*	.2
119	Princeton University Press—*Peter Dougherty*	41 William St, Princeton NJ 08540	609-258-4900	R	20*	.1
120	Goodheart-Willcox Company Inc—*John F Flanagan*	18604 West Creek Dr, Tinley Park IL 60477	708-687-5000	R	20*	.1
121	Abacus Software Inc—*Jim Oldfield Jr*	5130 Patterson Ave SE, Grand Rapids MI 49512	616-698-0330	R	20*	.1
122	Warren Publishing Inc—*Cathy Brophy*	17039 Kenton Dr Ste101, Cornelius NC 28031	704-659-2183	R	20*	<.1
123	Nazarene Publishing House—*Hardy Weathers*	2923 Troost Ave, Kansas City MO 64109	816-931-1900	R	20*	.2
124	Avon Books	10 E 53rd St, New York NY 10022	212-207-7000	S	20	.1
	HarperCollins Publishers Inc					
125	Kendall/Hunt Publishing Co—*Chad Chandlee*	PO Box 1840, Dubuque IA 52004	563-589-1000	R	19*	.2
126	Tax Notes Magazine—*Chris Bergin*	400 N Washington St, Falls Church VA 22046	703-533-4400	R	18*	.2
127	Tax Analysts—*Christopher Bergin*	510 N Washington St, Falls Church VA 22046	703-533-4400	R	18*	.2
128	McGraw-Hill/Osborne Media—*Harold McGraw III*	2100 Powell St 10th Fl, Emeryville CA 94608		S	18*	.1
	McGraw-Hill Companies Inc					
129	New World Library—*Marc Allen*	14 Pamaron Way, Novato CA 94949	415-884-2100	R	18*	<.1

Note: An asterisk (*) indicates an estimated financial figure. The company type code used is as follows: R = Private, P = Public, S = Private Subsidiary, B = Public Subsidiary, D = Division, J = Joint Venture, I = Investment Fund.

COMPANY RANKINGS BY SALES WITHIN 4-DIGIT SIC

Rank	Company Name—*Executive Officer*	Address, City, State, Zip	Phone	Type	Fin	Empls
130	Children's Book Press	965 Mission St Ste 425, San Francisco CA 94103	415-543-2665	R	18*	<.1
131	Victor Graphics Inc—*Reese Hicks*	1211 Bernard Dr, Baltimore MD 21223	410-233-8300	R	18*	.2
132	Plus Communications Inc—*Stephen Strang*	600 Rinehart Rd, Lake Mary FL 32746	407-333-0600	R	17*	.2
133	Curriculum Associates LLC—*Anthony Giordano*	PO Box 2001, North Billerica MA 01862	978-667-8000	R	17*	.2
134	British American Publishing Ltd—*Bernard Conners*	4 British American Blv, Latham NY 12110	518-786-6000	R	17*	.1
135	Group Publishing Inc—*Thom Schultz*	PO Box 481, Loveland CO 80539	970-669-3836	R	16*	.3
136	Columbia University Press—*James D Jordan*	61 W 62nd St, New York NY 10023	212-459-0600	R	16*	.1
137	Hot Off the Press Inc—*Paulette Jarvey*	1250 NW 3rd Ave, Canby OR 97013	503-266-9102	R	16*	.1
138	Paragon Book Reprint Corp—*Gordon L Anderson*	1925 Oakcrest Ave Ste, Saint Paul MN 55113	651-644-3087	R	16*	<.1
139	National Underwriter Co—*Andy Goodenough*	5081 Olympic Blvd, Erlanger KY 41018	859-692-2100	R	16*	.2
140	Harry N Abrams Inc—*Michael Jacobs*	115 W 18th St Fl 6, New York NY 10011	212-206-7715	R	16*	.1
141	Ucg Information Services LLC	PO Box 9405, Gaithersburg MD 20898	301-287-2700	R	16*	.4
142	Gospel Light Publications—*Bill Greig*	PO Box 7047, Oxnard CA 93031	805-644-9721	R	15*	.1
143	Gibbs M Smith Inc—*Gibbs Smith*	PO Box 667, Layton UT 84041	801-544-9800	R	15*	.1
144	Classroom Connect—*Jim Bowler*	6277 Sea Harbor Dr 5th, Orlando FL 32887	650-351-5100	R	14*	.1
145	In-Fisherman Inc	PO Box 420235, Palm Coast FL 32142		R	14*	.1
146	Peter Lang Publishing Inc—*Peter Lang*	29 Broadway, New York NY 10006	212-647-7706	S	14*	<.1
147	The Scarecrow Press Inc—*Stephen Ryan*	4501 Forbes Blvd Ste 2, Lanham MD 20706	301-459-3366	S	14*	<.1
148	Kregel Inc—*James Kregel*	PO Box 2607, Grand Rapids MI 49501	616-451-4775	R	14*	.1
149	Rosen Publishing Group Inc—*Roger Rosen*	PO Box 29278, New York NY 10087	212-777-3017	R	13*	.2
150	J Weston Walch Publisher—*Al Noyes*	PO Box 658, Portland ME 04104	207-772-2846	R	13*	<.1
151	Good Will Publishers Inc—*John Briody*	PO Box 269, Gastonia NC 28053	704-865-1256	R	13*	.1
152	Interweave Press LLC—*Sandi Wiseheart*	201 E 4th St, Loveland CO 80537	970-669-7672	R	13*	.1
153	Pastoral Solutions Inc—*Chris Voisey*	160 Old State Rd, Ellisville MO 63021	636-394-7000	R	13*	.1
154	Harvest House Publishers Inc—*Robert Hawkins*	990 Owen Loop N, Eugene OR 97402	541-343-0123	R	13*	.1
155	Barron's Educational Series Inc—*Manuel Barron*	250 Wireless Blvd, Hauppauge NY 11788	631-434-3311	R	13*	.1
156	Library Publications Inc—*David Steinberg*	2300 Chestnut St Ste 2, Philadelphia PA 19103	215-567-5080	R	12*	.2
157	Annual Reviews—*Samuel Gubins*	PO Box 10139, Palo Alto CA 94303	650-493-4400	R	12*	.1
158	SIAM—*Douglas Arnold*	3600 Market St 6th Fl, Philadelphia PA 19104	215-382-9800	R	12*	.1
159	Krames Communications Inc	780 Township Line Rd, Yardley PA 19067	267-685-2500	D	12*	.1
160	McGraw-Hill Contemporary Learning Series McGraw-Hill Companies Inc	Sluice Dock, Guilford CT 06437		D	12*	.1
161	Lillenas Publishing Co—*Tim M Curtis* Nazarene Publishing House	PO Box 419527, Kansas City MO 64141	816-931-1900	S	12*	<.1
162	World-Wide Printing Co—*Gilbert Lindsay*	210 S Cedar Ridge Dr C, Duncanville TX 75116	972-780-2511	R	12*	<.1
163	Worth Publishers Inc—*Elizabeth Widdicombe*	41 Madison Ave Fl 35, New York NY 10010	212-475-6000	R	11*	.1
164	Amsco School Publications Inc—*Henry Brun*	315 Hudson St Fl 5, New York NY 10013	212-886-6500	R	11*	.1
165	Lerner Publishing Group—*Adam Lerner*	1251 Washington Ave N, Minneapolis MN 55401		R	11*	.1
166	Nolocom Inc—*Bob Dubow*	950 Parker St, Berkeley CA 94710	510-549-1976	R	11*	.1
167	Alpha Omega Publications Inc—*Robert Campbell*	300 N Mckemy Ave, Chandler AZ 85226	602-438-2717	R	11*	.1
168	Omnigraphics Inc—*Frederick G Ruffner Jr*	615 Griswold St, Detroit MI 48226	313-961-1340	R	11*	.1
169	Farrar Straus and Giroux LLC—*Kate Coombs*	18 W 18th St Fl 7, New York NY 10011	212-741-6900	R	11*	.1
170	Marshall Cavendish Corp—*Richard Fariley*	99 White Plains Rd, Tarrytown NY 10591	914-332-8888	R	11*	<.1
171	FA Davis Co—*Robert Craven*	1915 Arch St, Philadelphia PA 19103	215-568-2270	R	11*	.1
172	Doane Agricultural Services Co—*Lynn Henderson*	77 Westport Pl Ste 250, Saint Louis MO 63146	314-569-2700	S	10*	.1
173	Facts on File Inc—*Mark McDonald* InfoBase Holdings Inc	132 W 31st St Fl 17, New York NY 10001	212-967-8800	S	10*	<.1
174	Thorndike Press—*Jamie Knobloch*	10 Water St Ste 310, Waterville ME 04901		D	10*	<.1
175	Career Press Inc—*Ron Fry*	P O Box 687, Franklin Lakes NJ 07417	201-848-0310	R	10*	<.1
176	Florida Funding Publications Inc—*John Adams*	PO Box 561565, Miami FL 33256	305-251-2203	D	10*	<.1
177	Stry-Lenkoff Company LLC—*Herbie Larke*	PO Box 32120, Louisville KY 40232	502-587-6804	R	10*	.1
178	Lexi-Comp Inc—*Robert Kerscher*	1100 Terex Rd, Hudson OH 44236	330-650-6506	R	9*	.1
179	Walter Foster Publishing Inc—*Ross Sarracino*	3 Wrigley Ste A, Irvine CA 92618	949-380-7510	R	9*	<.1
180	Gleim Publications Inc—*Irvin Gleim*	PO Box 12848, Gainesville FL 32604	352-375-0772	R	9*	.1
181	Capstone Press Inc—*G Ahern*	PO Box 669, Mankato MN 56002	507-388-6650	R	9*	.1
182	Zweig White and Associates Inc—*Mark C Zweig*	320 Rollston Ave Ste 1, Fayetteville AR 72702	508-651-1559	R	9*	.1
183	Destiny Image Inc—*Donald Nori*	PO Box 310, Shippensburg PA 17257	717-532-3040	R	9*	<.1
184	InfoBase Holdings Inc—*Mark McDonnell*	132 W 31st 17 Fl, New York NY 10001	212-967-8800	R	9*	<.1
185	Stone Bridge Press—*Peter Goodman*	PO Box 8208, Berkeley CA 94707		R	9*	<.1
186	Weldon Owen Inc—*Terry Newell*	415 Jackson St Ste 200, San Francisco CA 94111	415-291-0100	R	9*	.1
187	American Printing House For The Blind—*Tuck Tinsley*	PO Box 6085, Louisville KY 40206	502-895-2405	R	9*	.3
188	Cookbook Publishers Inc—*Kevin Derry*	PO Box 15920, Shawnee Mission KS 66285	913-492-5900	R	8*	.1
189	Schroeder Publishing Company Inc—*William Schroeder*	PO Box 3009, Paducah KY 42002	270-898-6211	R	8*	.1
190	Continuum International Publishing Group Inc—*Kenneth Quig-ley*	4775 Linglestown Rd, Harrisburg PA 17112	717-541-8130	R	8*	.1
191	Knowles Publishing Inc—*Richard Knowles*	PO Box 911004, Fort Worth TX 76111	817-838-0202	R	8*	.1
192	Enslow Publishers Inc—*Mark Enslow*	PO Box 398, Berkeley Heights NJ 07922	908-771-9400	R	8*	.1
193	Penton Overseas Inc—*Hugh Penton*	1958 Kellogg Ave, Carlsbad CA 92008	760-431-0080	R	8*	<.1
194	Warner Press Inc—*C Eric King*	PO Box 2499, Anderson IN 46012	765-644-7721	R	8*	<.1
195	Beginning Press—*Paula Begoun*	1030 SW 34 th St Ste A, Renton WA 98057	206-444-1616	R	8*	<.1
196	Wheatmark Inc—*Sam G Henrie*	610 E Delano St Ste 10, Tucson AZ 85705	520-798-3306	R	8*	<.1
197	Dorling Kindersley Publishing Inc—*Chuck Lang*	375 Hudson St Bsmt 2, New York NY 10014	212-213-4800	R	8*	.1
198	Bon Venture Services Inc—*Tom Garde*	PO Box 850, Flanders NJ 07836	973-584-5699	R	7*	.1
199	Liguori Publications—*Mathew Kessler*	1 Liguori Dr, Liguori MO 63057	636-464-2500	R	7*	.1
200	Martin-Smith Publishing Inc—*Nathan Bisk*	PO Box 31043, Tampa FL 33631	813-621-6900	R	7*	.2
201	Samuel French Inc—*Charles Nostrand*	45 W 25th St Fl 2, New York NY 10010	212-206-8990	R	7*	.1
202	ABC-Clio Inc—*Ronald Boehm*	PO Box 1911, Santa Barbara CA 93116	805-968-1911	R	7*	.1
203	Presbyterian Publishing Corp—*Davis Perkins*	100 Witherspoon St, Louisville KY 40202	502-569-5000	R	7*	.1
204	STATS Inc—*Gary Walrath*	2775 Shermer Rd, Northbrook IL 60062	847-583-2100	R	7*	.1
205	Rockwell Publishing Co—*David L Rockwell*	13218 NE 20th St, Bellevue WA 98005		R	7*	<.1
206	Eakin Press Sunbelt Media Inc—*Virginia Messer*	PO Box 21235, Waco TX 76702	254-235-6161	R	7*	<.1
207	Octameon Associates—*Anna Leider*	PO Box 2748, Alexandria VA 22301	703-836-5480	R	7*	<.1
208	Online Training Solutions Inc—*Joan Lambert*	PO Box 951, Bellevue WA 98009		R	7*	<.1
209	Outer Edge Software—*John Paul Mendocha*	22421 Barton Rd, Grand Terrace CA 92313	909-783-2000	R	7	<.1
210	Forecast International Inc—*Edward Nebinger*	22 Commerce Rd, Newtown CT 06470	203-426-0800	R	7*	<.1
211	Hackett Publishing Company Inc—*James Hullett*	PO Box 44937, Indianapolis IN 46244	317-635-9250	R	7*	<.1
212	Phoenix Publishing Inc—*Douglas Brown*	PO Box 3829, Blaine WA 98231	360-366-2204	R	6*	.1
213	Urban Ministries Inc—*C Wright*	1551 Regency Ct, Calumet City IL 60409	708-868-7100	R	6*	.1
214	Bruccoli Clark Layman Inc—*Matthew Bruccoli*	2006 Sumter St, Columbia SC 29201	803-771-4642	R	6*	.1
215	Helen Dwight Reid Educational Foundation Inc—*James Denton*	1319 18th St Nw, Washington DC 20036	202-296-6267	R	6*	.1

Rank	Company Name—Executive Officer	Address, City, State, Zip	Phone	Type	Fin	Empls
216	Literary Classics Of The Us—Cheryl Hurley	14 E 60th St Fl 11, New York NY 10022	212-308-3360	R	6*	<.1
217	Inside Communications Inc—Rick Rundall	1830 55th St, Boulder CO 80301	303-440-0601	R	6*	.1
218	Euromonitor International Inc—Trevor Fenwick	224 S Michigan Ave Ste, Chicago IL 60604	312-922-1115	S	6*	<.1
219	Kregel Publications Inc—James Kregel	PO Box 2607, Grand Rapids MI 49501	616-451-4775	R	6*	<.1
220	Schiffer Publishing Ltd—Peter Schiffer	4880 Lower Valley Rd, Atglen PA 19310	610-593-1777	R	6*	<.1
221	Arte Publico Press—Nicolas Kanellos	4902 Gulf Fwy Bldg 19, Houston TX 77023	713-743-2998	R	6*	<.1
222	Beacon Press—Tom Hallock	25 Beacon St, Boston MA 02108	617-742-2110	R	6*	<.1
223	New Leaf Press Inc—Tim Dudley	PO Box 726, Green Forest AR 72638	870-438-5288	R	6*	<.1
224	QED Press—Cynthia Frank	155 Cypress St, Fort Bragg CA 95437	707-964-9520	R	6*	<.1
225	Greene Bark Press Inc—Thomas J Greene	PO Box 1108, Bridgeport CT 06601	601-434-2802	R	6*	<.1
226	Future Network USA—Jonathan Simpson-Dint	149 5th Ave Fl 9, New York NY 10010	212-768-2966	R	6*	.1
227	G and R Publishing Co—Gary Nelson	507 Industrial Rd, Waverly IA 50677	319-352-5391	R	6*	.1
228	Louisiana Binding Service Inc—Patrick Williams	300 Ampacet Dr, Deridder LA 70634	337-460-8323	R	6*	.1
229	Stf Services Inc—Michael Smith	PO Box 3251, Syracuse NY 13220	315-463-8506	R	6*	.1
230	National Academies Press—Barbara Pope	500 5th St Nw Ste 1, Washington DC 20001	202-334-3313	R	6*	.1
231	Mesorah Publications Ltd—Martin Zlotowitz	4401 2nd Ave, Brooklyn NY 11232	718-921-9000	R	6*	<.1
232	Brownlow Publishing Co—Paul Brownlow	6309 Airport Fwy, Fort Worth TX 76117	817-831-3831	R	6*	<.1
233	Monterey Learning Systems Inc—George Stern	PO Box 51590, Palo Alto CA 94303	650-969-5450	R	6*	.1
234	Precept Ministries Of Reach Out Inc—Jack Arthur	7324 Noah Reid Rd, Chattanooga TN 37421	423-892-6814	R	5*	.1
235	Spanish House Inc—David Ecklebarger	1360 Nw 88th Ave, Doral FL 33172	305-592-6136	R	5*	<.1
236	Island Press-Center For Resource Economics—Charles Savitt	1718 Connecticut Ave N, Washington DC 20009	202-232-7933	R	5*	<.1
237	University of North Carolina Press—Kate Douglas	PO Box 2288, Chapel Hill NC 27515	919-966-3561	R	5*	<.1
238	Great American Quilt Factory Inc—Lynda Milligan	8970 E Hampden Ave, Denver CO 80231	303-740-6206	R	5*	<.1
239	Martingale and Co—Daniel Martin	19021 120th Ave NE Ste, Bothell WA 98011	425-483-3313	R	5*	<.1
240	Babe Winkelman Productions Inc—Mike Weinkauf	PO Box 407, Brainerd MN 56401	218-822-4424	R	5*	<.1
241	Lorenz Publishing Co—Thomas Moore	3190 Rider Trail S, Earth City MO 63045	314-991-4220	R	5*	<.1
242	Public Utilities Reports Inc—Bruce Radford	8229 Boone Blvd Ste 40, Vienna VA 22182	703-847-7720	R	5*	<.1
243	Information USA Inc—Matthew Lesko	12138 Nebel St, Rockville MD 20852		R	5*	<.1
244	Beyond Words Publishing Inc—Cynthia M Black	20827 NW Cornell Road, Hillsboro OR 97124	503-531-8700	R	5*	<.1
245	American Legal Publishing Corp—Stephen Wolf	432 Walnut St Fl 12, Cincinnati OH 45202	513-421-4248	R	5*	<.1
246	Harber Industries Inc—Ann Dalager	PO Box 485, Anoka MN 55303	763-503-0340	R	5*	<.1
247	Willow Creek Press Inc—Thomas Petrie	PO Box 147, Minocqua WI 54548	715-358-7010	R	5*	<.1
248	Technology Publishing Co—Harold Hower	2100 Wharton St Ste 31, Pittsburgh PA 15203	412-431-8300	R	5*	<.1
249	Publication Services Inc—Barbara Meihoefer	1802 S Duncan Rd, Champaign IL 61822	217-398-2060	R	4*	.1
250	Free Spirit Publishing Inc—Judy Galbraith	217 5th Ave N Ste 200, Minneapolis MN 55401	612-338-2068	R	4*	<.1
251	Critical Thinking Co—Michael Baker	PO Box 1610, Seaside CA 93955	831-393-3288	R	4*	<.1
252	Hayden - Mcneil LLC—Patrick Olson	14903 Pilot Dr, Plymouth MI 48170	734-455-7900	R	4*	<.1
253	Chick Publications Inc—Jack Chick	PO Box 3500, Ontario CA 91761	909-987-0771	R	4*	<.1
254	Rebus Inc—Rodney Friedman	632 Broadway Fl 11, New York NY 10012	212-505-2255	R	4*	<.1
255	BB Kirkbride Bible Co—J Marshall Gage	PO Box 606, Indianapolis IN 46206	317-633-1900	R	4*	<.1
256	Academic Therapy Publications—Anna Arena	20 Commercial Blvd, Novato CA 94949		R	4*	<.1
257	SPI Publisher Services—Frank Stumpf	880 Technology Park Dr, Glen Allen VA 23059	804-262-4219	S	4*	<.1
258	Academic Communication Associates Inc—Larry Mattes	PO Box 4279, Oceanside CA 92052	760-722-9593	R	4*	<.1
259	Bristol Publishing Enterprises Inc—Aidan Wylde	2714 McCone Ave, Hayward CA 94545	510-783-5472	R	4*	<.1
260	Jester Company Inc—Barbara Saltzman	PO Box 817, Palos Verdes Peninsula CA 90274	310-544-4733	R	4*	<.1
261	DCI Technical Inc—Andrea Mannheim	475 Franklin Ave Fl 2, Franklin Square NY 11010	516-355-0464	R	4*	.1
262	Kansa Technology LLC—Dan Yust	3700 Oakes Dr, Emporia KS 66801	620-343-6700	R	4*	<.1
263	Fidelity Associates Inc—Chris Cherry	PO Box 550968, Gastonia NC 28055	704-864-3766	R	4*	<.1
264	Prometheus Books Inc—Paul Kurtz	59 John Glenn Dr, Amherst NY 14228	716-691-0133	R	4*	<.1
265	Timber Press Inc—Peter Workman	133 Sw 2nd Ave Ste 450, Portland OR 97204	503-227-2878	S	4*	<.1
	Workman Publishing Company Inc					
266	Evergreen Publications Inc—Steve Pfeiffer	701 Enterprise St N, Aberdeen SD 57401	605-229-1779	R	4*	.1
267	Turner Publishing Company LLC—Todd Bottorff	200 4th Ave N Ste 950, Nashville TN 37219	615-255-2665	R	4*	<.1
268	Good Enterprises Ltd—Merle Good	PO Box 419, Intercourse PA 17534	717-768-3008	R	4*	<.1
269	Snohomish Publishing Company Inc—Jeffrey Wise	605 2nd St, Snohomish WA 98290	360-568-1242	R	4*	<.1
270	Government Data Publication—Siegfried Lobel	1661 Mcdonald Ave, Brooklyn NY 11230	718-627-0819	R	3*	<.1
271	Pelican Publishing Company Inc—Milburn Calhoun	1000 Burmaster St, Gretna LA 70053	504-368-1175	R	3*	<.1
272	Sinauer Associates Inc—Andrew Sinauer	PO Box 407, Sunderland MA 01375	413-549-4300	R	3*	<.1
273	American Psychiatric Press Inc—Robert Hales	1000 Wilson Blvd Ste 1, Arlington VA 22209	703-907-7322	R	3*	.1
274	Elan Publishing Company Inc—Thomas Power	PO Box 683, Meredith NH 03253	603-253-7030	R	3*	<.1
275	Vantage Press Inc—Martin Kleinwald	419 Park Ave S Fl 18, New York NY 10016	212-736-1767	R	3*	<.1
276	Louis Neibauer Company Inc—Nathan Neibauer	20 Industrial Dr, Warminster PA 18974	215-322-6200	R	3*	<.1
277	Shambhala Publications Inc—Samuel Bercholz	PO Box 170358, Boston MA 02117	617-424-0030	R	3*	<.1
278	Saint Marys Press Of Minnesota—Brother Steger	702 Ter Hts, Winona MN 55987	507-457-7900	R	3*	.1
279	Beauty Handbook Corp—John McAuliffe	346 N Main St, Port Chester NY 10573	914-935-1000	R	3*	<.1
280	University Of Hawaii Press—William H Hamilton	2840 Kolowalu St, Honolulu HI 96822	808-956-8255	R	3*	<.1
281	Malhame and Company Publishers and Importers Inc—George Malhame	PO Box 608, Melville NY 11747	631-694-8600	R	3*	<.1
282	Insurance Publishing Plus Corp—Walter J Gdowski	11690 Technology Dr, Carmel IN 46032	317-843-2523	R	3*	<.1
283	Hayes School Publishing Co—Clair N Hayes III	321 Penwood Ave, Pittsburgh PA 15221	412-371-2373	R	3*	<.1
284	Shapolsky Publishers—Ian Shapolsky	99 Spring St 3rd Fl, New York NY 10012	212-431-5011	R	3*	<.1
285	Travelers' Tales—James O'Reilly	853 Alma St, Palo Alto CA 94301	650-462-2110	D	3*	<.1
	O'Reilly and Associates Inc					
286	Bennett and Curran Inc—Jeff Stephenson	1545 W Tufts Ave Ste M, Englewood CO 80110	303-783-2255	R	3*	<.1
287	Avery Publishing Group Inc—John C Makinson	375 Hudson St, New York NY 10014	212-366-2000	D	3*	<.1
	Penguin Group Inc (New York New York)					
288	Coldstream Press—Ellie Huggins	PO Box 2822, Arnold CA 95223	209-795-6339	R	3*	<.1
289	Teach America Corp—Frank Broen	121 N Love St, Quincy FL 32351	850-875-0491	R	3*	<.1
290	Scientific Therapeutics Information Inc—John Romankiewicz	505 Morris Ave Ste 3, Springfield NJ 07081	973-376-5655	R	3*	<.1
291	Orion Publishing Co—Roger Rohrs	14555 N Scottsdale Rd, Scottsdale AZ 85254	480-951-1114	R	3*	<.1
292	Concept Systems Inc—Eugene Mcneese	2619 Canton Ct, Fort Collins CO 80525	970-482-0883	R	3*	.1
293	Ave Maria Press Inc—Frank Cunningham	PO Box 428, Notre Dame IN 46556	574-287-2831	R	3*	.1
294	Fox Chapel Publishing Company Inc—J Giagnocavo	1970 Broad St, East Petersburg PA 17520	717-560-4703	R	3*	<.1
295	Quality Medical Publishing Inc—Karen Berger	2248 Welsch Industrial, Saint Louis MO 63146	314-878-7808	R	3*	<.1
296	Krieger Publishing Company Inc—Robert Krieger	1725 Krieger Ln, Malabar FL 32950	321-724-9542	R	2*	<.1
297	EP Global Communications—Joseph M Valenzano Jr	416 Main St, Johnstown PA 15901	814-361-3860	P	2	<.1
298	Chelsea Green Publishing Company Inc—Margaret Baldwin	PO Box 428, White River Junction VT 05001	802-295-6300	R	2*	<.1
299	Alliance Publishing and Marketing Inc—Greg Pappas	PO Box 3354, Cumberland MD 21504	301-777-1110	R	2*	<.1
300	Berrett-Koehler Publishers Inc—Steven Piersanti	235 Montgomery St Ste, San Francisco CA 94104	415-288-0260	R	2*	<.1
301	Beauty Fashion Inc—George Ledes	8 W 38th St Frnt 2, New York NY 10018	212-840-8800	R	2*	<.1

Note: An asterisk (*) indicates an estimated financial figure. The company type code used is as follows: R = Private, P = Public, S = Private Subsidiary, B = Public Subsidiary, D = Division, J = Joint Venture, I = Investment Fund.

COMPANY RANKINGS BY SALES WITHIN 4-DIGIT SIC

Rank	Company Name—*Executive Officer*	Address, City, State, Zip	Phone	Type	Fin	Empls
302	Orbis Books—*Michael Leach*	PO Box 30, Maryknoll NY 10545	914-941-7590	R	2*	<.1
303	Charles C Thomas Publisher—*Michael Thomas*	PO Box 19265, Springfield IL 62794	217-789-8980	R	2*	<.1
304	Historical Preservations of America—*JM Evans*	PO Box 31226, Raleigh NC 27622	919-781-8710	R	2*	<.1
305	Lanier Publishing International—*Pamela Lanier*	PO Box 2240, Petaluma CA 94953	707-763-0271	R	2*	<.1
306	Hawthorne Educational Services Inc—*Michele Jackson*	800 Gray Oak Dr, Columbia MO 65201	573-874-1710	R	2*	<.1
307	Military Marketing Services Inc—*Roy Crawford*	333 Maple Ave E Ste 31, Vienna VA 22180	703-237-0203	S	2*	<.1
308	AvCom International—*Ken Green*	101 1st St 2nd Fl, Utica NY 13501	315-797-4420	R	2*	<.1
309	H and H Publishing Company Inc—*Robert D Hackworth*	1231 Kapp Dr, Clearwater FL 33765	727-442-7760	R	2*	<.1
310	Academy Chicago Publishers—*Anita Miller*	363 W Erie St Ste 4W, Chicago IL 60654	312-751-7302	R	2*	<.1
311	River City Publishing—*Carolyn Newman*	1719 Mulberry St, Montgomery AL 36106	334-265-6753	R	2*	<.1
312	Just Us Books Inc—*Wade Hudson*	356 Glenwood Ave Ste 7, East Orange NJ 07017	973-672-7701	R	2*	<.1
313	Concepts Publishing Inc—*Jill Bobrow*	PO Box 1066, Waitsfield VT 05673	802-496-5580	R	2*	<.1
314	Anotek Inc—*Christopher Welty*	1121 Obispo Ave Ste 11, Long Beach CA 90804	310-450-5027	R	2*	<.1
315	Bull Publishing Co—*James Bull*	PO Box 1377, Boulder CO 80306	303-545-6350	R	2*	<.1
316	Police Shield Corp—*David Armitage*	323 Otter St, Bristol PA 19007	215-788-3489	R	2*	<.1
317	Rod And Staff Publishers Inc—*Melvin Horst*	PO Box 3, Crockett KY 41413	606-522-4348	R	2*	.1
318	Eleanor Ettinger Inc—*Eleanor Ettinger*	119 Spring St Fl 1, New York NY 10012	212-925-7474	R	2*	<.1
319	Foxhill Press Inc—*Deb Wood*	37 E 7th St Ste 2, New York NY 10003	212-995-9620	R	2*	<.1
320	Callaway Editions Inc—*Nicholas Callaway*	19 Fulton St Fl 5, New York NY 10038	212-929-5212	R	2*	<.1
321	Peachtree Publishers Ltd—*Margaret Quinlan*	1700 Chattahoochee Ave, Atlanta GA 30318	404-876-8761	R	2*	<.1
322	Carlevale John—*John Carlevale*	640 Weaver Hill Rd, West Greenwich RI 02817	401-397-9838	R	1*	<.1
323	Brethren In Christ Media Ministries Inc—*Mark Burford*	PO Box 189, Nappanee IN 46550	574-773-3164	R	1*	<.1
324	Bradford Publishing Co—*Candice Boyele*	1743 Wazee St Ste 100, Denver CO 80202	303-292-2500	R	1*	<.1
325	Pace Learning Systems Inc—*Susan Mckee*	3710 Resource Dr, Tuscaloosa AL 35401	205-758-2823	R	1*	<.1
326	Executive Excellence Publishing LLC—*Ken Shelton*	1806 N 1120 W, Provo UT 84604	801-375-4060	R	1*	<.1
327	WGI Corp—*Glenn Davis*	1875 Swarthmore Ave, Lakewood NJ 08701	732-370-2900	R	1*	<.1
328	Payler Corp—*Barry Havemann*	237 W Pky Fl 2, Pompton Plains NJ 07444	973-617-8700	R	1*	<.1
329	Summer Street Press LLC—*Miriam Aronin*	460 Summer St Ste 305, Stamford CT 06901	203-325-2217	R	1*	<.1
330	Industrial Press Inc—*Alex Luchars*	989 Ave Of The Amrcs 1, New York NY 10018	212-889-6330	R	1*	<.1
331	Frasernet Inc—*George Fraser*	2940 Noble Rd Ste 1, Cleveland OH 44121	216-691-6686	R	1*	<.1
332	Channel Publishing Ltd—*Martha Puckett*	4750 Longley Ln Ste 11, Reno NV 89502	775-825-0880	R	1*	<.1
333	Creative Technology Of Sarasota Inc—*Thomas Turner*	5959 Palmer Blvd, Sarasota FL 34232	941-371-2743	R	1*	<.1
334	Copper Canyon Press—*Kris Becker*	PO Box 271, Port Townsend WA 98368	360-385-4925	R	1*	<.1
335	Ggp Publishing Inc—*Generosa Protano*	138 Chatsworth Ave Ste, Larchmont NY 10538	914-834-8896	R	1*	<.1
336	Garrett Book Co—*Lionel H Garrett*	PO Box 1588, Ada OK 74821	580-332-6884	R	1*	<.1
337	Snow Lion Publications Inc—*Jeff Cox*	PO Box 6483, Ithaca NY 14851	607-273-8519	R	1*	<.1
338	Franklin Estimating Systems—*Hal Harrison*	PO Box 540202, N Salt Lake UT 84054	801-303-6083	R	1*	<.1
339	Heyday Books—*Michael McCone*	PO Box 9145, Berkeley CA 94709	510-549-3564	R	1*	<.1
340	Performance Resource Press Inc—*George Watkins*	PO Box 99515, Troy MI 48099	248-588-7733	R	1*	<.1
341	Pritchett and Hull Associates Inc—*Cecily Shull*	3440 Oakcliff Rd Ste 1, Atlanta GA 30340	770-451-0602	R	1*	<.1
342	Common Courage Press—*Greg Bates*	PO Box 702, Monroe ME 04951	207-525-0900	R	1*	<.1
343	Hunter House Inc—*Elizabeth Whelan*	PO Box 2914, Alameda CA 94501	510-865-5282	R	1*	<.1
344	TEACH Services Inc—*Timothy Hullquist*	8300 Hwy 41 Ste 107, Ringgold GA 30736	518-358-3494	R	1*	<.1
345	Computational Mechanics Inc—*David Anderson*	25 Bridge St, Billerica MA 01821	978-667-5841	R	1*	<.1
346	Parenting Press Inc—*Elizabeth Crary*	PO Box 75267, Seattle WA 98175	206-364-2900	R	1*	<.1
347	Coffee House Press—*Allan Kornblum*	79 13th Ave Ste 110, Minneapolis MN 55413	612-338-0125	R	1*	<.1
348	Princeton Book Company Publishers—*Charles Woodford*	PO Box 831, Hightstown NJ 08520	609-426-0602	R	1*	<.1
349	American Lawyer Media - Philadelphia	1617 John F Kennedy Bl, Philadelphia PA 19103	215-557-2300	R	1*	<.1
350	Americas Group—*Angela King*	654 N Sepulveda Blvd S, Los Angeles CA 90049	310-476-6374	S	1*	<.1
351	Bella Books—*Linda Hill*	PO Box 10543, Tallahassee FL 32302	850-576-2370	R	1*	<.1
352	Broadfoot Publishing Co—*Tom Broadfoot*	1907 Buena Vista Cir, Wilmington NC 28411	910-686-9591	R	1*	<.1
353	Federal Research Service Inc—*Sandy Harris*	PO Box 1708, Annandale VA 22003		R	1*	<.1
354	Lawyers and Judges Publishing Co—*Steve L Weintraub*	PO Box 30040, Tucson AZ 85751	520-323-1500	R	1*	<.1
355	Polebridge Press Inc—*Charlene Matejovsky*	900 State St, Salem OR 97301	503-375-5323	R	1*	<.1
356	Bay Press Inc—*Laura Moriarty*	115 W Denny Way, Seattle WA 98119		R	1*	<.1
357	Capra Press Inc—*Robert Bason*	155 Canon View Rd, Santa Barbara CA 93108	805-969-0203	R	1*	<.1
358	Computer Training Services—*Shelden NeedLe*	6108 Stonehenge Pl, Rockville MD 20852		R	1*	<.1
359	Good Advice Press—*Nancy Castleman*	PO Box 78, Elizaville NY 12523	845-532-1835	R	1*	<.1
360	Salk International Travel Premiums Inc—*Ronald Salk*	PO Box 1388, Sunset Beach CA 90742		R	1*	<.1
361	BiblioData—*Ruth Orenstein*	PO Box 61, Needham Heights MA 02494	781-444-1144	R	1*	<.1
362	New Era Publications—*Dave McCracken*	PO Box 47, Happy Camp CA 96039	530-493-2062	R	1*	<.1
363	Intrans Book Service—*Freek Lankhof*	PO Box 467, Kinderhook NY 12106	518-758-1755	R	1*	<.1
364	Kc Publications Inc—*Dennis Harper*	PO Box 3615, Wickenburg AZ 85358	702-433-3415	R	1*	<.1
365	Hippocrene Books Inc—*George Blagowidow*	171 Madison Ave Rm 160, New York NY 10016	212-685-4371	R	1*	<.1
366	John F Blair Publisher Inc—*Carolyn Sakowski*	1406 Plz Dr, Winston Salem NC 27103	336-768-1374	R	1*	<.1
367	Pacific Crest Software Inc—*Daniel Apple*	906 Lacey Ave Ste 206, Lisle IL 60532	630-737-1067	R	1*	<.1
368	New Directions Publishing Corp—*Peggy Fox*	80 8th Ave Fl 19, New York NY 10011	212-255-0230	R	1*	<.1
369	Westcliffe Publishers Inc—*John Fielder*	PO Box 1261, Englewood CO 80150	303-935-0900	R	1*	<.1
370	Maverick Publications Inc—*Gary Asher*	PO Box 5007, Bend OR 97708	541-382-6978	R	1*	<.1
371	Small Planet Communications Inc—*Joseph Buschini*	15 Union St Ste 5, Lawrence MA 01840	978-794-2201	R	1*	<.1
372	Inforom Inc—*Virginia Ramsey*	5 Hanover Sq Rm 1900, New York NY 10004	212-361-2400	R	1*	<.1
373	Blacklightning Publishing Inc—*Walter Jeffries*	252 Riddle Pond Rd, West Topsham VT 05086	802-439-6462	R	<1*	<.1
374	Soho Press Inc—*Juris Jurjevics*	853 Broadway Ste 601, New York NY 10003	212-260-1900	R	<1*	<.1
375	Picton Corp—*Lewis Rohrbach*	120 Union St, Rockport ME 04856	207-236-6565	R	<1*	<.1
376	Steerforth Press LLC—*Helga Schmidt*	25 Lebanon St Frnt, Hanover NH 03755	603-643-4787	R	<1*	<.1
377	Vocational Biographies Inc—*Toby Behnen*	PO Box 31, Sauk Centre MN 56378	320-352-6516	R	<1*	<.1
378	Barricade Books Inc—*Lyle Stuart*	185 Bridge Plz N Ste 3, Fort Lee NJ 07024	201-944-7600	R	<1*	<.1
379	State House Press—*Tom Munnerlyn*	PO Box 15247, Austin TX 78761		R	<1	<.1
380	Trudy Corp—*Christopher Glover*	1810 E Sahara Ave Ste, Las Vegas NV 89104	702-522-1914	P	<1*	<.1
381	Industrial Safety and Hygiene News—*Tagg Henderson*	2401 W Big Beaver Rd S, Troy MI 48084	248-244-6498	R	<1*	<.1
382	Infosources Publishing—*Arlene Eis*	140 Norma Rd, Teaneck NJ 07666	201-836-7072	R	<1*	<.1
383	Michael Edmond Gray—*Michael Gray*	242 Eagle Flight, Ozark MO 65721		R	<1*	<.1
384	Mustang Publishing Co—*Rollin A Riggs*	PO Box 770426, Memphis TN 38177	901-355-4885	R	<1	N/A
385	Tomato Enterprises Book Publishing—*Dorothy Leland*	PO Box 73892, Davis CA 95617	530-750-1832	R	<1	N/A
386	IDC Framingham—*Kirk Campbell*	5 Speen St, Framingham MA 01701	508-872-8200	S	N/A	5.0
387	SourceMedia Inc—*Douglas Manoni*	1 State St Plz 27th Fl, New York NY 10004	212-803-8200	S	N/A	1.0
388	Maximum Ventures Corp—*James W Hoskins*	605 Silverthorn Rd, Gulf Breeze FL 32561	850-934-0819	R	N/A	<.1
389	Compact Classics	1 N Sherri Ln, Spring Valley NY 10977	845-426-5710	R	N/A	<.1

TOTALS: SIC 2731 Book Publishing
Companies: 389   38,225   131.3

Rank	Company Name—*Executive Officer*	Address, City, State, Zip	Phone	Type	Fin	Empls
2732 Book Printing						
1	Offset Paperback Manufacturers Inc—*Michael J Gallagher*	PO Box N, Dallas PA 18612	570-675-5261	S	1,021*	.7
2	Sheridan Books Inc—*Robert Moore*	PO Box 370, Chelsea MI 48118	734-475-9145	R	495*	.4
3	Courier Kendallville Inc—*James F Conway III* Courier Corp	2500 Marion Dr, Kendallville IN 46755	978-251-6000	S	391*	1.9
4	Courier Corp—*James F Conway III*	15 Wellman Ave, North Chelmsford MA 01863	978-251-6000	P	259	1.6
5	Tweddle Group Inc—*Andrew Tweddle*	24700 Maplehurst Dr, Clinton Township MI 48036	586-307-3700	R	109*	.3
6	Bertlesmann Industry Services Inc—*Ron Leach*	29011 Commerce Center, Valencia CA 91355	661-702-2700	R	90*	.6
7	Press Of Ohio Inc—*Mike Duffield*	3765 Sunnybrook Rd, Kent OH 44240	330-678-5868	R	59*	.4
8	Edwards Brothers Inc—*Martin Edwards*	PO Box 1007, Ann Arbor MI 48106	734-769-1000	R	58*	.4
9	Webcrafters Inc—*Jac Garner*	PO Box 7608, Madison WI 53707	608-244-3561	R	50*	.5
10	Maple Press Co—*James Wisotzkey*	PO Box 2695, York PA 17405	717-764-5911	R	49*	.9
11	Vail-Ballou Press Inc—*James Wisotzkey* Maple Press Co	PO Box 2695, York PA 17405	607-723-7981	S	48*	.9
12	CJ Krehbiel Co—*Robert C Krehbiel III*	3962 Virginia Ave, Cincinnati OH 45227	513-271-6035	R	38*	.2
13	Congressional Quarterly Inc—*David Hawkings*	2300 North St NW Ste 8, Washington DC 20037	202-729-1900	D	34*	.3
14	Thomson-Shore Inc	7300 W Joy Rd, Dexter MI 48130	734-426-3939	R	28*	.3
15	Gateway Press Inc (Louisville Kentucky)—*Nick Burrice*	4500 Robards Ln, Louisville KY 40218	502-454-0431	R	25*	.2
16	Lightning Source Inc—*David Prichard*	1246 Heil Quaker Blvd, La Vergne TN 37086	615-213-5815	R	25*	.2
17	Mcnaughton and Gunn Inc—*Julie Farland*	PO Box 10, Saline MI 48176	734-429-5411	R	24*	.2
18	C-Point Inc—*Fred Forte*	3505 Independence Dr, Fort Wayne IN 46808	260-484-3186	R	24*	.2
19	Versa Press Inc—*Steven Kennell*	1465 Spring Bay Rd, East Peoria IL 61611	309-822-8272	R	19*	.2
20	Inland Press (Menomonee Falls Wisconsin)—*Craig Faust*	W141 N 9450 Fountain B, Menomonee Falls WI 53051	262-255-5800	S	18*	.1
21	Malloy Inc—*William Upton*	PO Box 1124, Ann Arbor MI 48106	734-665-6113	R	17*	.3
22	Lake Book Manufacturing Inc—*Ralph Genovese*	2085 Cornell Ave, Melrose Park IL 60160	708-345-7000	R	16*	.3
23	Rose Printing Company Inc—*Charles Rosenberg*	PO Box 5078, Tallahassee FL 32314	850-576-4151	R	15*	.2
24	Hamilton Printing Company Inc—*Brian Payne*	PO Box 232, Rensselaer NY 12144	518-732-4491	R	14*	.1
25	United Graphics Inc—*Ralph Scrimager*	PO Box 559, Mattoon IL 61938	217-235-7161	R	14*	.1
26	Data Reproductions Corp—*Dennis Kavanagh*	4545 Glenmeade Ln, Auburn Hills MI 48326	248-371-3700	R	13*	.1
27	Integrated Book Technology Inc—*John Paeglow*	18 Industrial Park Rd, Troy NY 12180	518-271-5117	R	13*	.1
28	Adair—*Dennis Adair*	7850 2nd St, Dexter MI 48130	734-426-2822	R	12*	.1
29	King Printing Company Inc—*Sid Chinai*	181 Industrial Ave E, Lowell MA 01852	978-458-2345	R	12*	.1
30	Dunn and Company Inc—*David Dunn*	PO Box 968, Clinton MA 01510	978-368-8505	R	11*	.1
31	PA Hutchison Co—*Chris Hutchison*	2225 Richmond St, Philadelphia PA 19125	570-876-4560	R	11*	.1
32	Roundtable Press Inc—*Susan Meyer*	102 bloome Corners Rd, Warwick NY 10990	212-691-0500	R	10*	<.1
33	Vaughan Printing Inc—*Charles Vaughan*	PO Box 70187, Nashville TN 37207	615-256-2244	R	9*	.1
34	Dicom Corp—*David Knight*	PO Box 7214, Madison WI 53707	608-246-2600	R	9*	.1
35	Fundcraft Publishing Inc—*David Bradley*	PO Box 340, Collierville TN 38027	901-853-7070	R	8*	.2
36	Mass Web Printing Company Inc—*Bradley Mindich*	314 Washington St, Auburn MA 01501	508-832-5317	R	7*	.1
37	Consolidated Printers Inc—*Larry Hawkins*	2630 8th St, Berkeley CA 94710	510-843-8524	R	7*	.1
38	C and M Press Corp—*Robert Malkin*	5200 Smith Rd, Denver CO 80216	303-375-9922	R	7*	.1
39	Cushing-Malloy Inc—*Thomas Weber*	1350 N Main St, Ann Arbor MI 48104	734-662-6238	R	7*	.1
40	Graphics East Inc—*Michael Easthope*	10005 Sturgeon St, Rooovillo MI 48066	586-598-1500	R	7*	<.1
41	Courier E P I C—*James Conway* Courier Corp	15 Wellman Ave, North Chelmsford MA 01863	978-251-6000	D	6*	.1
42	TPS Enterprises Inc—*Richard Lindemann*	PO Box 375, Newton IL 62448	618-783-2978	R	6*	<.1
43	Tobay Printing Company Inc—*Robert Rogers*	1361 Marconi Blvd, Copiague NY 11726	631-842-3300	R	4*	<.1
44	Kc Book Manufacturing LLC—*Darrell Smith*	110 W 12th Ave, Kansas City MO 64116	816-842-9770	R	4*	<.1
45	West Wind Litho Inc—*Joseph Mik*	2513 S 3270 W, Salt Lake City UT 84119	801-975-7105	R	4*	<.1
46	Copies Overnight Inc—*Stephen Johnson*	262 Commonwealth Dr, Carol Stream IL 60188	630-690-2000	R	4*	<.1
47	Phoenix Printing Companies Inc—*Jeffery Hadden*	601 11th St, Augusta GA 30901	706-722-5262	R	3*	<.1
48	Express Solutions LLC—*Christene Helpingstine*	PO Box 27611, Salt Lake City UT 84127	801-977-0699	R	3*	<.1
49	Sterling Press Inc—*Dale Parks*	420 W 1700 S, Salt Lake City UT 84115	801-486-4641	R	3*	<.1
50	Triangle Press Inc—*John Burkholder*	6720 Allentown Blvd, Harrisburg PA 17112	717-541-9315	R	3*	<.1
51	Sundance Graphic Enterprises Inc—*Alan Howard*	PO Box 26605, Tucson AZ 85726	520-622-5233	R	3*	<.1
52	Johnson Cox Company Inc—*Ken Creech*	726 Pacific Ave, Tacoma WA 98402	253-272-2238	R	3*	<.1
53	Wimmer Cookbooks (Memphis Tennessee)—*Chris Toomey*	4650 Shelby Air Dr, Memphis TN 38118	901-362-8900	D	2*	<.1
54	Dove Publications and Software Inc—*Lawrence Nylin*	PO Box 1080, Pecos NM 87552	505-757-6597	R	2*	<.1
55	Casto and Harris Inc—*John Denbigh*	PO Box 189, Spencer WV 25276	304-927-2222	R	2*	<.1
56	Opera House Printing Co—*Genevieve Trump*	140 E Main St, Westminster MD 21157	410-848-2844	R	1*	<.1
57	All Systems Colour Inc—*George Dick*	2032 S Alex Rd Ste A, Dayton OH 45449	937-859-9701	R	1*	<.1
58	Smith and Kraus Publishers Inc—*Marisa Smith*	PO Box 127, Lyme NH 03768	207-523-2585	R	<1*	<.1
TOTALS: SIC 2732 Book Printing Companies: 58					3,136	13.3
2741 Miscellaneous Publishing						
1	Harte-Hanks Shoppers Inc—*Larry Franklin* Harte-Hanks Inc	9601 McAllister Fwy St, San Antonio TX 78216	210-829-9000	S	3,493*	6.4
2	International Data Group Inc—*Bob Carrigan*	1 Exeter Plz 15th Fl, Boston MA 02116	617-534-1200	R	3,240	13.3
3	Standard and Poor's Financial Services LLC—*Douglas Peterson*	55 Water St, New York NY 10041	212-438-1000	S	2,720*	8.5
4	Dex Media Inc—*Brian Barnum*	198 Inverness Dr W, Englewood CO 80112	303-784-2900	S	1,658*	2.7
5	SuperMedia LLC—*Peter J McDonald*	PO Box 619810, Dallas TX 75261		P	1,642	3.4
6	Dex One Corp—*Alfred T Mockett*	1001 Winstead Dr, Cary NC 27513	919-297-1600	P	1,481	2.7
7	Moody's Investors Service Inc—*Raymond W McDaniel Jr*	250 Greenwich St, New York NY 10007	212-553-1658	S	1,372*	2.4
8	Zynga Inc—*Mark Pincus*	365 Vermont St, San Francisco CA 94103		P	1,140*	2.8
9	DK Publishing—*Christopher Davis*	375 Hudson St, New York NY 10014	646-674-4000	S	1,131*	2.0
10	Mitchell International—*Alex Sun*	6220 Greenwich Dr, San Diego CA 92122	858-368-7000	S	990*	1.7
11	Harte-Hanks Inc—*Larry Franklin*	PO Box 269, San Antonio TX 78291	210-829-9000	P	861	4.9
12	TransWestern Publishing Company LP—*Rick Puente* Yellow Book USA Inc	8344 Claremont Mesa Bl, San Diego CA 92111	858-467-2800	S	800*	1.9
13	ALM Properties Inc—*William L Pollak*	120 Broadway 5th Fl, New York NY 10271	212-457-9400	R	580*	1.0
14	Local Insight Regatta Holdings Inc—*Scott A Pomeroy*	188 Inverness Dr W Ste, Englewood CO 80112	303-867-1600	R	578	1.1
15	United Communications Group—*Todd Foreman*	9737 Washingtonian Blv, Gaithersburg MD 20878	301-287-2700	R	463*	.8
16	Hands-on Mobile Inc—*Judy Wade*	140 Geary St Ste 500, San Francisco CA 94108	415-848-0400	R	435*	.8
17	Thomson North American Legal—*Peter Warwick*	PO Box 64526, Saint Paul MN 55164	651-687-7000	S	418*	.8
18	Pearson Scott Foresman—*Paul L McFall*	1900 E Lake Ave, Glenview IL 60025	847-729-3000	S	416*	.5
19	Disney Interactive Studios—*Graham Hopper*	521 Cir Seven Dr, Glendale CA 91201	818-553-5000	R	410*	.7
20	Associated Desert Shoppers Inc—*Harold Paradis*	73400 Hwy 111, Palm Desert CA 92260	760-346-1729	R	355*	.2

Note: An asterisk (*) indicates an estimated financial figure. The company type code used is as follows: R = Private, P = Public, S = Private Subsidiary, B = Public Subsidiary, D = Division, J = Joint Venture, I = Investment Fund.

COMPANY RANKINGS BY SALES WITHIN 4-DIGIT SIC

Rank	Company Name—*Executive Officer*	Address, City, State, Zip	Phone	Type	Fin	Empls
21	Standard and Poor's Compustat—*Harold McGraw III*	7400 S Alton Ct, Centennial CO 80112	303-721-4857	D	333*	.4
22	RL Polk and Co—*Stephen R Polk*	26533 Evergreen Rd Ste, Southfield MI 48076	248-728-7000	R	332*	1.2
23	HW Wilson Co—*Harold Regan*	950 University Ave, Bronx NY 10452	718-588-8400	R	299*	.5
24	Wolters Kluwer Health—*Jeff McCaulley*	161 W Washington St, Conshohocken PA 19428	610-234-4345	D	291*	.4
25	Compuserve—*Audrey Weil*	5000 Arlington Ctr Blv, Columbus OH 43220		S	275*	.3
26	ProQuest LLC—*Kurt P Sanford*	PO Box 1346, Ann Arbor MI 48106	734-761-4700	S	270*	1.2
27	First American CoreLogic Inc—*George Livermore*	4 First American Way, Santa Ana CA 92707	714-250-6400	S	233*	1.2
28	Classified Ventures LLC—*Daniel A Jauernig*	175 W Jackson Blvd 8th, Chicago IL 60604	312-601-5000	R	210	.8
29	Hal Leonard Corp—*Keith Mardak*	PO Box 13819, Milwaukee WI 53213	414-774-3630	R	209*	.4
30	Society of Automotive Engineers—*David Schutt*	400 Commonwealth Dr, Warrendale PA 15086	724-776-4841	R	208*	.3
31	Oxford University Press Electronic Publishing Div—*Laura Brown*	198 Madison Ave, New York NY 10016		D	184*	.3
32	Yellow Book USA Inc—*Joseh Walsh*	398 RXR Plaza, Uniondale NY 11556	516-766-1900	S	149*	.2
33	CTB/McGraw Hill LLC—*Ellen Haley*	20 Ryan Ranch Rd, Monterey CA 93940	831-393-0700	D	146*	.8
34	Standard Rate and Data Service—*Tom Drouillard*	1700 Higgins Rd, Des Plaines IL 60018	847-375-5000	R	141*	.2
35	William M Mercer Inc—*M Michele Burns*	540 Lake Cook Rd Ste 6, Deerfield IL 60015	847-317-7400	R	140*	.3
36	38 Studios LLC—*Jennifer MacLean*	5 Clock Tower Pl Ste 1, Maynard MA 01754	978-461-9990	R	130*	.2
37	Trion World Network Inc—*Lars Buttler*	303 Twin Dolphin Dr St, Redwood City CA 94065	650-631-9800	R	124*	.2
38	American Dental Association—*John S Findley*	211 E Chicago Ave, Chicago IL 60611	312-440-2500	R	122	.5
39	Pioneer Electronics Inc—*Junichi Naito*	1925 E Dominguez St, Long Beach CA 90810	310-952-2000	S	113*	.2
40	Steck-Vaughn Publishing Corp—*Tim McEwen*	10801 N Mo Pac Expy, Austin TX 78759	512-343-8227	D	113*	.2
41	Stevens Graphics Inc—*William J Davidson*	713 RD Abernathy Blvd, Atlanta GA 30310	404-753-1121	R	111*	.6
42	101communications LLC—*Neil Vitale*	9121 Oakdale Ave, Chatsworth CA 91311	818-734-1520	S	104*	.2
43	DeLorme—*Jim Skillings*	PO Box 298, Yarmouth ME 04096	207-846-7000	R	91*	.2
44	PEACH DVD—*Jim Monroe*	15115 Califa St, Van Nuys CA 91411	818-908-9663	R	88*	.2
45	Viacom New Media (New York New York)—*Philippe Dauman*	1540 Broadway, New York NY 10036	212-258-6000	R	87*	.2
46	SRA/McGraw-Hill—*Joe Gavigan*	220 E Danieldale Rd, DeSoto TX 75115		D	84*	.2
47	Cision—*Joe Bernardo*	332 S Michigan Ave, Chicago IL 60604		R	77*	.4
48	Jeppesen Sanderson Inc—*Mark Van Tine*	55 Inverness Dr E, Englewood CO 80112	303-799-9090	S	76	1.0
49	Libredigital Inc—*Russell P Reeder*	1835B Kramer Ln Ste 15, Austin TX 78758	512-334-5102	R	71*	.1
50	Logos Research Systems Inc—*Bob Pritchen*	1313 Commercial St, Bellingham WA 98225	360-527-1700	R	69*	.2
51	SoBran Inc—*Amos L Otis*	2677 Prosperity Ave St, Fairfax VA 22031	703-352-9511	R	66*	.5
52	Economist Intelligence Unit—*Robin Bew*	111 W 57th St, New York NY 10019	212-554-0600	D	66*	.1
53	SYS-CON Media Inc—*Fuat A Kircaali*	135 Chestnut Ridge Rd, Montvale NJ 07645	201-802-3000	R	62*	<.1
54	Ads Group	2155 Niagra Ln N, Plymouth MN 55447	763-449-5500	S	60*	.1
55	Blair Packaging—*Ronn Unterreiner*	116 E Missouri Blvd, Scott City MO 63780	573-264-2146	R	57*	.1
56	Citation Technologies Inc—*David Boyle*	5111 N Scottsdale Rd S, Scottsdale AZ 85250		R	54*	.1
57	TV Data Technologies LP—*Kenneth H Carter*	435 N Michigan Ave Ste, Chicago IL 60611	312-222-4444	S	53*	.6
58	Montevideo Publishing Co—*Robert Bradford*	223 S 1st St, Montevideo MN 56265	320-269-2156	R	52*	.1
59	Professional Image Printing and Packaging—*Cynthia Calvert*	12437 E 60th St, Tulsa OK 74146	918-461-0609	R	47*	.1
60	Brentwood-Benson Music Publishing Inc—*Dale Mathews*	741 Cool Springs Blvd, Franklin TN 37067	615-261-3300	R	45*	.2
61	Agi Publishing Inc—*Siegfried Fischer*	1850 N Gateway Blvd St, Fresno CA 93727	559-251-8888	R	45*	.7
62	Ringside Creative LLC—*Doug Cheek*	13320 Northend Ave Ste, Oak Park MI 48237	248-548-2500	R	43*	.1
63	Adis International Inc	770 Township Line Rd S, Yardley PA 19067	267-757-3400	S	40	.3
64	Briefings Publishing Group—*Alan Douglas*	2807 N Parham Rd, Richmond VA 23294		R	39*	<.1
65	American Medical Association—*Michael Maves*	515 N State St, Chicago IL 60610	312-464-5000	R	39	N/A
66	MindLeaders—*Paul MacCartney*	5500 Glendon Court Ste, Dublin OH 43016	614-781-7300	R	38*	.3
67	Environmental Data Resources Inc—*Robert D Barber*	440 Wheelers Farms Rd, Milford CT 06460		R	38*	.2
68	Northstar Travel Media LLC—*Thomas Kemp*	100 Lighting Way, Secaucus NJ 07094	201-902-2000	S	38*	.2
69	Let's Go Inc—*Sarah Rotman*	67 Mount Auburn St, Cambridge MA 02138	617-495-9659	R	35*	1.0
70	Cell Division—*Jeff Bogursky*	625 Ave of the America, New York NY 10011	212-268-2100	R	35*	.1
71	UpToDate TM Inc—*Pete Randall*	95 Sawyer Rd, Waltham MA 02453	781-392-2000	R	35*	.1
72	Business and Legal Reports Inc—*Robert L Brady*	141 Mill Rock Rd E, Old Saybrook CT 06475		R	34*	.2
73	O'neil and Associates Inc—*Robert Heilman*	495 Byers Rd, Miamisburg OH 45342	937-865-0800	R	33*	.3
74	Spot Image Corp—*Antoine de Chassy*	14595 Avion Pkwy Ste 5, Chantilly VA 20151	703-715-3100	S	33*	<.1
75	Phone Directories Company Inc—*Marc Bingham*	PO Box 2277, Orem UT 84059	801-932-0316	R	32*	.6
76	Bethesda Softworks LLC—*Vlatko Andonov*	1370 Piccard Dr Ste 12, Rockville MD 20850	301-926-8300	S	32*	.1
77	Aviation Week Group—*Gregory Hamilton*	1200 G StNW Ste 922, Washington DC 20005	515-237-3682	S	31*	.1
78	Penn Energy—*Bob Bioochini*	1421 S Sheridan Rd, Tulsa OK 74112	918-831-9884	D	31*	<.1
79	Law Bulletin Publishing Company Inc—*Brewster Mcfarland*	415 N State St Ste 1, Chicago IL 60654	312-644-7800	R	30*	.3
80	Grandville Printing Company Inc—*Patrick Brewer*	PO Box 247, Grandville MI 49418	616-534-8647	R	30*	.3
81	Bizbash Media—*David Adler*	21 W 38th St 13th Fl, New York NY 10018	646-638-3600	R	29*	.1
82	Certpoint Systems Inc—*Ara Ohanian*	4 Expressway Plz Ste 2, Roslyn Heights NY 11577		R	29*	.1
83	JC Research	606 N 1st St, San Jose CA 95112		S	29*	.1
84	Strong Audiovisual Inc—*Thomas R Wilmers*	1235 Tradeport Dr, Orlando FL 32824	407-858-9866	R	29*	.1
85	Killer Tracks—*Gary Gross*	9255 W Sunset Blvd Ste, Los Angeles CA 90069		R	29*	<.1
86	Riverside Publishing—*Anthony Lucki*	3800 Golf Rd Ste 200, Rolling Meadows IL 60008	630-467-7000	S	28*	.1
87	Virgo Publishing LLC—*Amy Thorlin*	PO Box 40079, Phoenix AZ 85067	480-990-1101	R	28*	.1
88	SSB Inc	3702 Pender Dr Ste 402, Fairfax VA 22030	703-277-1070	R	28*	.1
89	Buckle Down Publishing—*Thomas Emrick*	2308 Heinz Rd, Iowa City IA 52240		S	28*	.1
90	Focus Features—*James Schamus*	65 Bleecker St 3rd Fl, New York NY 10012	212-539-4000	S	28*	.1
91	Playdom Inc—*John Pleasants*	295 Page Mill Rd 2nd F, Palo Alto CA 94306	650-963-8000	S	28*	.1
92	Vhayu Technologies Corp	425 Market St 6th Fl, San Francisco CA 94105	415-344-6000	S	28*	.1
93	Associated Content Inc—*Patrick Keane*	88 Steele St Ste 400, Denver CO 80206	720-214-1000	R	28*	.1
94	Dream Theater Inc—*Ali Dayoudian*	30699 Russell Ranch Rd, Westlake Village CA 91362	818-707-3660	R	26*	<.1
95	Technical Software Services Inc—*Thomas Pigoski*	31 W Garden St Ste 100, Pensacola FL 32502	850-469-0086	R	25*	<.1
96	Intelliquis—*Bernard Yaw*	PO Box 1138, Draper UT 84020		R	25*	<.1
97	Universal Map Enterprises Inc—*Greg Bond*	6198 Butler Pike, Blue Bell PA 19422	386-873-3010	D	24*	.2
98	Neil A Kjos Music Co—*Neil Kjos*	PO Box 178270, San Diego CA 92177	858-270-9800	R	24*	.1
99	Grey House Publishing Inc—*Richard Gottlieb*	PO Box B, Millerton NY 12546	518-789-8700	R	24*	.1
100	Thomas Publishing Company LLC—*Jose Andrade*	5 Penn Plz Fl 17, New York NY 10001	212-695-0500	R	23*	.4
101	Haines and Company Inc—*William Haines*	PO Box 2117, North Canton OH 44720	330-494-9111	R	23*	.2
102	Digital Juice Inc—*David Hebel*	600 Technology Pk Ste, Lake Mary FL 32746	407-531-5540	R	23*	.1
103	Consumer Source Inc—*Charles Stubbs*	3585 Engineering Dr St, Norcross GA 30092	678-421-3000	R	21*	.2
104	Hammond and Stephens Co—*Dave Vander Zanden*	PO Box 629, Fremont NE 68025	402-721-1800	S	21*	.1
105	Computer and Communications Information Group Inc—*Gene Hall*	600 Delran Pkwy, Delran NJ 08075	856-764-0100	D	20*	.1
106	Coteau Shopper Inc—*Tim Oviatt*	PO Box 1176, Watertown SD 57201	605-882-1358	R	20*	<.1
107	KW Brock Directories Inc—*Ken Brock*	PO Box 1479, Pittsburg KS 66762	620-231-4000	R	20*	.2
108	Access Intelligence LLC—*Yves Beguin*	PO Box 9187, Gaithersburg MD 20898	301-354-2000	R	19*	.2

Rank	Company Name—*Executive Officer*	Address, City, State, Zip	Phone	Type	Fin	Empls
109	Foundation Center Inc—*Bradford Smith*	79 5th Ave Ste 400, New York NY 10003	212-620-4230	R	19*	.1
110	Sundance/Newbridge Educational Publishing LLC—*Richard Naylor*	PO Box 740, Northborough MA 01532		R	18*	.2
111	Fodor's Travel Publications Inc—*David Naggar*	1745 Broadway, New York NY 10019	212-782-9586	D	18*	.1
112	Taproot Interactive Studio—*Brooke Nanberg*	400 N State St2nd Fl, Chicago IL 60610	312-494-9999	R	18*	<.1
113	Elastic Creative—*Drew Fiero*	550 Bryant St, San Francisco CA 94107	415-495-5595	R	18*	<.1
114	Weidt Group—*John Weidt*	5800 Baker Rd Ste 100, Minnetonka MN 55345	952-938-1588	R	18*	<.1
115	HBO Studio Productions—*Bill Nelson*	120 E 23rd St Ste A, New York NY 10010	212-512-7800	S	18*	<.1
116	LearnSomething Inc—*Steve Roden*	2457 Care Dr, Tallahassee FL 32308	850-385-7915	R	18*	<.1
117	School Annual Publishing Co	2568 Park Center Blvd, State College PA 16801	814-278-6600	R	17*	.1
118	Access Softek Inc—*Chris Doner*	727 Allston Way Ste C, Berkeley CA 94710	510-848-0606	R	17*	<.1
119	Altegris Investments Inc—*John Sundt*	1200 Prospect St Ste 4, La Jolla CA 92037	858-459-7040	S	17*	<.1
120	Fuse Design Inc—*Stefan Drust*	775 Laguna Canyon Rd, Laguna Beach CA 92651	949-376-0438	R	17*	<.1
121	World Library Publications Inc—*William Rafferty*	3708 River Rd Ste 400, Franklin Park IL 60131	847-678-9300	R	17*	.2
122	Center For Science In The Public Interest—*Michael Jacobson*	PO Box 96611, Washington DC 20090	202-332-9110	R	17*	.1
123	Mac Innes Enterprises Inc—*Robert Allen*	303 S Pioneer Dr, Abilene TX 79605	325-676-4032	R	17*	.1
124	National Insurance Law Service	130 Turner St 4th Fl, Waltham MA 02453		S	16*	.1
125	SOA Software Inc—*Paul R Gigg*	12100 Wilshire Blvd St, Los Angeles CA 90025	310-826-1317	R	16*	.1
126	Post Asylum—*Donald Stokes*	5642 Dyer St, Dallas TX 75206	214-363-0162	R	16*	<.1
127	Cpp Inc—*Jeffrey Hayes*	1055 Joaquin Rd Fl 2, Mountain View CA 94043	650-969-8901	R	16*	.2
128	Marcoa Publishing Inc—*Matt Benedict*	9955 Black Mountain Rd, San Diego CA 92126	858-695-9600	R	15*	.1
129	Scott and Daughters Publishing Inc—*Alexis Scott*	6762 Lexington Ave, Los Angeles CA 90038	323-856-0008	R	15*	.1
130	eInstruction Corp—*Steve Kaye*	308 N Carroll Blvd, Denton TX 76201	940-565-0004	R	15*	.1
131	Martin Graphics and Printing Services—*Charles Martin*	808 N Country Fair Dr, Champaign IL 61821	217-398-5000	R	15*	<.1
132	Pantone Inc—*Lawrence Herbert*	590 Commerce Blvd, Carlstadt NJ 07072	201-935-5500	S	14*	.1
133	FJH Music Co—*Frank J Hackinson*	2525 Davie Rd Ste 360, Fort Lauderdale FL 33317	954-382-6061	R	14*	.1
134	WRS Group Ltd—*Scott J Salmans*	PO Box 21207, Waco TX 76702	254-776-6461	R	14*	.1
135	ODS-Petrodata Inc—*Per Christian-Grytnes*	3200 Wilcrest Dr Ste 1, Houston TX 77042	832-463-3000	S	14*	.1
136	The Thomas Kinkade Co—*Craig Fleming*	900 Lightpost Way, Morgan Hill CA 95037	408-201-5000	R	14*	.1
137	Mann Consulting Multimedia—*Harold Mann*	282 2nd St 4th Fl, San Francisco CA 94105	415-546-6266	R	14*	<.1
138	Buckmaster Publishing—*Jack Speer*	6196 Jefferson Hwy, Mineral VA 23117	540-894-5777	R	14*	<.1
139	Pixfusion LLC—*Rich Collins*	5 W 19th 2nd Fl N, New York NY 10001	212-604-0064	R	14*	<.1
140	General Investments Corp—*Weldon Bankston*	PO Box 1353, Los Gatos CA 95031	408-356-7208	R	14*	<.1
141	Zagat Survey LLC—*Eugene Zagat*	4 Columbus Cir Fl 3, New York NY 10019	212-977-6000	R	13*	.1
142	MaoGrogor Publishing Co—*Bob Taylor* Yellow Book USA Inc	17869 State Rte 536, Mount Vernon WA 98273	360-336-6171	S	13*	.1
143	Publishing Concepts LP—*Andrew Clancy*	4835 Lbj Fwy Ste 1100, Dallas TX 75244		R	13*	.2
144	ComputerPREP Inc—*Barry Fingerhut*	1230 W Washington St S, Tempe AZ 85281	602-275-7700	R	13*	.1
145	Kapp Advertising Services Inc—*Robert Kapp*	PO Box 840, Lebanon PA 17042	717-273-8127	R	12*	.1
146	Simplicity Pattern Company Inc—*Frank Rizzo*	261 Madison Ave 4th Fl, New York NY 10016	212-372-0500	S	12*	.1
147	Hearst Interactive Media—*Kenneth A Bronfin*	300 W 57th St, New York NY 10019	212-649-2000	D	12*	.1
148	ID8 Media—*Bob Palioca*	44 Montgomery Ste 1000, San Francisco CA 94104	510-665-1111	R	12*	<.1
149	Hermitage Group Inc—*Robert Bronnor*	5151 N Ravenswood Ave, Chicago IL 60640	773-561-3773	R	12*	<.1
150	RKO Pictures—*Ted Hartley*	1875 Century Park E St, Los Angeles CA 90067	310-277-0707	R	12*	<.1
151	Visible Productions—*Paul Baker*	213 Linden St Ste 200, Fort Collins CO 80524	970-407-7240	R	12*	<.1
152	Xplana Inc—*Hakan Satiroglu*	137 Newbury St 3rd flo, Boston MA 02116	617-262-0202	R	12*	<.1
153	Carl Fischer LLC—*Hayden Connor*	65 Bleecker St Fl 8, New York NY 10012	212-777-0900	R	12*	<.1
154	Mass-Marketing Inc—*Donald Mueller*	PO Box 40427, Cincinnati OH 45240	513-870-9000	R	12*	<.1
155	InterCom—*Bob Yeager*	3 Grogan's Park Ste 20, The Woodlands TX 77380		R	11*	<.1
156	51 Entertainment Group LLC—*John Trickett*	2231 S Carmelina Ave, Los Angeles CA 90064	310-207-5181	R	11*	<.1
157	FOI Services Inc—*John Kerry*	704 Quince Orchard Rd, Gaithersburg MD 20878	301-975-9400	R	11*	<.1
158	Iconceptual—*Robert Edgar*	101 Navigator Dr, Scotts Valley CA 95066	408-481-3800	R	11*	<.1
159	OpenSystems Publishing LLC—*Mike Hopper*	30233 Jefferson Ave, Saint Clair Shores MI 48082	586-415-6500	R	11*	<.1
160	Verite Inc—*Kimberley A Jones*	608 W 9320 S, Sandy UT 84070	801-553-1101	R	11*	<.1
161	GlobalLearningSystems Inc—*Lawrence P Cates*	6030 Daybreak Circle, Clarksville MD 21029		R	11*	<.1
162	Community Shoppers Inc—*Stephen Karstaedt*	PO Box 367, Delavan WI 53115	262-728-3424	R	11*	.1
163	Micropatent LLC—*Tom DeTroy*	250 Dodge Ave, East Haven CT 06512	203-466-5055	S	11	.1
164	Garland Converting—*Robert Garland*	945 N Larch Ave, Elmhurst IL 60126	630-833-8881	R	11*	.1
165	Investorplace Media LLC—*Steve Lawrence*	9201 Corporate Blvd, Rockville MD 20850	301-250-2200	R	10*	.1
166	J-Ad Graphics Inc—*John Jacobs*	PO Box 188, Hastings MI 49058	269-945-9554	R	10*	.1
167	Aircraft Technical Publishers—*Caroline Daniels*	101 S Hill Dr, Brisbane CA 94005	415-330-9500	R	10*	.1
168	Manufacturers' News Inc—*Howard S Dubin*	1633 Central St, Evanston IL 60201	847-864-7000	R	10*	.1
169	Payne Publishers Inc—*John Barbour*	8707 Quarry Rd Ste B, Manassas VA 20110	703-369-5454	R	10*	.1
170	Diversified Printers Inc—*Kenneth Bittner*	16200 Trojan Way, La Mirada CA 90638	714-994-3400	R	10*	.1
171	Leadership Directories Inc—*Gretchen G Teichgraeber*	104 5th Ave, New York NY 10011	212-627-4140	R	10*	.1
172	Faulkner Information Services Inc—*Tom Hogan*	7905 Browning Rd, Pennsauken NJ 08109	856-662-2070	S	10*	.1
173	ADP Hayes-Ligon—*Arthur F Weinbach*	401 N Washington St St, Rockville MD 20850	301-296-7200	D	10*	.1
174	Apex Learning Inc—*Cheryl Vedoe*	315 Fifth Ave S Ste 60, Seattle WA 98104	206-381-5600	R	10*	.1
175	First Advantage Assessment Solutions—*Jon Haber*	113 Terrace Hall Ave, Burlington MA 01803	781-229-8388	R	10*	.1
176	MentorU—*Jesse L Wacht*	4025 Camino Del Rio S, San Diego CA 92108	858-268-0800	R	10*	<.1
177	Nickel Ads Newspaper Inc—*Mary E Junck*	PO Box 5667, Portland OR 97228	503-256-4210	D	10	.1
178	Primary Source Media—*Frank Menchaca*	12 Lunar Dr, Woodbridge CT 06525		D	10*	.1
179	Oakstone Publishing LLC—*Jonathon Cain*	100 Corporate Pkwy Ste, Birmingham AL 35242	205-991-5188	R	9*	.1
180	Nextag Inc—*Jeff Katz*	2955 Campus Dr Ste 300, San Mateo CA 94403	650-645-4700	R	9*	.1
181	Energy Intelligence Group Inc—*Thomas Wallin*	5 E 37th St Fl 5, New York NY 10016	212-532-1112	R	9*	.1
182	Master Teacher Inc—*Tracey Debruyn*	PO Box 1207, Manhattan KS 66505	785-539-0555	R	9*	.1
183	Anthem Media LLC	7101 College Blvd Ste, Overland Park KS 66210	913-894-6923	R	9*	.1
184	Flying Spot Entertainment—*Pat Sanford*	83 Columbia St, Seattle WA 98104	206-464-0744	R	9*	.1
185	GR Leonard and Co	49 E Huntington Dr, Arcadia CA 91006	626-574-1800	R	9*	.1
186	Traffiq—*Nick Pahade*	462 7th Ave 21st Fl, New York NY 10018	212-792-2294	R	9*	<.1
187	Chedd-Angier Production Co—*Graham Chedd*	119 Braintree St Ste 4, Boston MA 02134	617-393-3480	R	9*	<.1
188	Interactive Factory Inc—*Alen Yen*	33 Farnsworth, Boston MA 02210	617-426-0609	R	9*	<.1
189	Vision Wise Inc—*Tim Capper*	4329 Belmont Ave, Dallas TX 75204	214-823-2260	R	9*	<.1
190	Lawglc Publishing Co—*Judy Meadows*	35 Fairway Ln, Jacksonville Beach FL 32250	904-223-2223	R	9*	<.1
191	Digital Lagoon—*David Dunlap*	14685 W 105th St, Lenexa KS 66215	913-888-3468	R	9*	<.1
192	IFI Claims Patent Services—*Mike Baycroft*	PO Box 1148, Madison CT 06443	203-779-5301	R	9*	<.1
193	Library Systems and Services LLC—*Frank Pezzanite*	12850 Middlebrook Rd S, Germantown MD 20874	301-540-5100	R	9*	<.1
194	Manhattan Bridge Capital Inc—*Assaf Ran*	60 Cutter Mill Rd Ste, Great Neck NY 11021	516-444-3400	P	9	<.1
195	Publisher's Guild Inc—*W Bornmiller*	2309 Sawgrass Village, Ponte Vedra Beach FL 32082	904-273-5394	R	9*	<.1
196	Lakes Area Advertiser Inc—*Carol Anderson*	236 W State Rte 173, Antioch IL 60002	847-395-4444	R	8*	.1

Note: An asterisk (*) indicates an estimated financial figure. The company type code used is as follows: R = Private, P = Public, S = Private Subsidiary, B = Public Subsidiary, D = Division, J = Joint Venture, I = Investment Fund.

COMPANY RANKINGS BY SALES WITHIN 4-DIGIT SIC

Rank	Company Name—*Executive Officer*	Address, City, State, Zip	Phone	Type	Fin	Empls
197	Countryside Publishing Company Inc—*Yvonne Shawn*	PO Box 1735, Oldsmar FL 34677	813-925-0195	R	8*	.1
198	Polack Printing Inc—*Carl Galant*	PO Box 2461, Grand Rapids MI 49501	616-878-5200	R	8*	.1
199	Platts Global Energy—*Lawrence Neal*	2 Penn Plz 25th Fl, New York NY 10121	212-904-3070	D	8*	.9
200	HuffingtonPostcom Inc—*Eric Hippeau*	560 Broadway Ste 308, New York NY 10012	212-245-7844	S	8*	.1
201	United Marketing Solutions Inc—*Jerry Bernier*	7644 Dynatech Ct, Springfield VA 22153	703-644-0200	S	8*	.1
202	Lawrence Ragan Communications Inc—*Mark Ragan*	111 E Wacker Dr Ste 50, Chicago IL 60601	312-960-4100	R	8*	.1
203	Southeast Publications USa Inc—*Wally Warrick*	4360 Peters Rd, Plantation FL 33317	954-583-3900	R	8*	<.1
204	Aurora and Quanta Productions—*Jose Azel*	81 W Commercial St Ste, Portland ME 04101	207-828-8787	R	8*	<.1
205	Tec-Ed Inc—*Stephanie Rosenbaum*	4300 Varsity Dr Ste A, Ann Arbor MI 48108	734-995-1010	R	8*	<.1
206	AD2 Inc—*Brad Mooberry*	1990 E Grand Ave Ste 2, El Segundo CA 90245	310-356-7500	R	8*	<.1
207	Vicom Inc—*Salvatore Nolfo*	1866 Fernandez Juncos, San Juan PR 00909	787-728-5252	R	8*	<.1
208	Bullfrog Films—*John Hoskyns-Abrahall*	PO Box 149, Oley PA 19547	610-779-8226	R	8*	<.1
209	Thomas S Klise Co—*Thomas S Klise*	PO Box 720, Mystic CT 06355	860-536-4200	R	8*	<.1
210	Motion Over Time Inc—*Neilson Neuschotz*	18 W 21St St5th Fl, New York NY 10010	212-229-1148	R	8*	<.1
211	Hanlund Phillips Corporate Design and Communications—*Mike Hanlund*	121 S Wilke Rd Ste 615, Arlington Heights IL 60005	312-527-9692	R	8*	<.1
212	Farm And Home Publishers Limited Inc—*Cliff Sheakley*	PO Box 305, Belmond IA 50421	641-444-3508	R	8*	.1
213	Herald Durango Inc—*Morley Ballantine*	1275 Main Ave, Durango CO 81301	970-247-3504	R	8*	.1
214	Lorenz Corp—*Reiff Lorenz*	PO Box 802, Dayton OH 45401	937-228-6118	R	8*	.1
215	Legal Directories Publishing Company Inc—*Diane Chapman*	PO Box 189000, Dallas TX 75218	214-321-3238	R	7*	.1
216	Sheridan Printing Co—*James Sheridan*	1425 3rd Ave, Alpha NJ 08865	908-454-0700	R	7*	.1
217	Uniquest Inc—*Shawn Thomas*	PO Box 291509, Nashville TN 37229	615-259-4500	R	7*	.1
218	New Era Portfolio—*Joseph L Garcia*	2101 E St Elmo Rd Ste, Austin TX 78744		R	7*	.1
219	Financial Information Inc—*Steve Kappel*	1 Cragwood Rd 2nd Fl, South Plainfield NJ 07080	908-222-5300	R	7*	<.1
220	Datasis Corp—*Bob Thomas*	1687 Elmhurst Rd, Elk Grove Village IL 60007	847-427-0909	R	7*	<.1
221	EduSelf Multimedia Publishers Inc—*Mario Nissim Hallphone*	61 Grand Ave, Englewood NJ 07631	201-569-5667	R	7*	<.1
222	Dream Home Source Inc—*Jayne Fenton*	3275 W Ina Rd Ste 260, Tucson AZ 85741	503-452-8664	R	7*	<.1
223	Data Connection—*Ian Ferguson*	12007 Sunrise Valley D, Reston VA 20191	703-715-4914	S	7*	<.1
224	Digital Media Graphix—*Curtis Jenkins*	123 W Jackson Ave Ste, Knoxville TN 37902	865-584-9740	R	7*	<.1
225	Guilford Publications Inc—*Robert Matloff*	72 Spring St Fl 4, New York NY 10012	212-431-9800	R	7*	.1
226	iMedia International—*Henry Williamson*	117 E Colorado Blvd St, Pasadena CA 91105	626-441-5351	P	7	<.1
227	Commercial Newspaper Service—*Mke Crow*	PO Box 1788, Nampa ID 83653	208-888-2753	R	7*	.1
228	Vista-Graphics Inc—*Randy Thompson*	1264 Perimeter Pkwy, Virginia Beach VA 23454	757-422-8979	R	7*	.1
229	Intersphere Communications Ltd—*Michael Oryl*	8370 Wilshire Blvd Ste, Beverly Hills CA 90211	323-655-9550	R	7*	<.1
230	Computercraft Corp—*Gene Hill*	1360 Beverly Rd Ste 10, Mc Lean VA 22101	703-893-8308	R	7*	.1
231	Associated Music Publishers Inc—*Barry Edwards*	257 Park Ave S Fl 20, New York NY 10010	212-254-2100	R	6*	.1
232	Elliott Wave International Inc—*Robert Prechter*	PO Box 1618, Gainesville GA 30503	770-536-0309	R	6*	.1
233	Theodore Presser Co—*Hayden Connor*	588 N Gulph Rd Ste B, King Of Prussia PA 19406	610-592-1222	R	6*	.1
234	Ken Cook Co—*Kenneth Cook*	PO Box 250940, Milwaukee WI 53225	414-466-6060	R	6*	.1
235	Bulletin News LLC—*Melissa Gillis*	11190 Sunrise Valley D, Reston VA 20191	703-483-6100	R	6*	.1
236	Pnl Publications Inc—*Dan Beard*	3627 Sandhurst Dr, York PA 17406	717-854-7799	R	6*	.1
237	Independent Information Services Corp—*Brian Seguin*	3333 W Division St Ste, Saint Cloud MN 56301	320-253-8858	R	6*	<.1
238	Atlantic Information Services Inc—*Richard Biehl*	1100 17th St Nw Ste 30, Washington DC 20036	202-775-9008	R	6*	<.1
239	Big Nickel—*Chuck Elliott*	PO Box 1567, Joplin MO 64802	417-624-4100	D	6*	<.1
240	Carroll Publishing—*Thomas E Carroll*	4701 Sangamore Rd Ste, Bethesda MD 20816	301-263-9800	R	6*	<.1
241	V! Studios	8200 Greensboro Dr Ste, McLean VA 22102	703-760-0440	R	6*	<.1
242	Brookwood Media Arts—*Rob Seskin*	716 N Bethlehem Pke St, Lower Gwynedd PA 19002	215-643-8580	R	6*	<.1
243	Gingko Press Inc—*Mo Cohen*	1321 5th St, Berkeley CA 94710	510-898-1195	R	6*	<.1
244	Interactive Media Communications Inc—*James L Mason*	PO Box 401002, Cambridge MA 02140	617-868-8288	R	6*	<.1
245	Mapresources—*Barbara Fordyce*	PO Box 757, Lambertville NJ 08530	609-397-1611	R	6*	<.1
246	Octavo Corp—*Czeslaw Grycz*	PO Box 24421, Oakland CA 94623	510-315-8657	R	6*	<.1
247	OtterStream Multimedia Inc—*Jan Utterstrom*	5355 Muriel Dr, Bellingham WA 98226		R	6*	<.1
248	Per Annum Inc—*Alicia Settle*	555 8th Ave Ste 203, New York NY 10018	212-647-8700	R	6*	<.1
249	Richard Diercks Company Inc—*Richard Dierks*	3140 Harbor Ln N Ste 2, Minneapolis MN 55447	763-231-3303	R	6*	<.1
250	SmithLee Productions Inc—*David Smith*	7420 Manchester, Saint Louis MO 63143	314-647-3900	R	6*	<.1
251	Sbc Yellow Pages—*Ray Riedy*	205 Nw 63rd St Ste 200, Oklahoma City OK 73116	405-879-5000	R	6*	.1
252	Evergreen Country Shopper Inc—*Gary Lapean*	PO Box 408, Ashland WI 54806	715-682-8131	R	6*	.1
253	Hocking Printing Company Inc—*Julie Hocking*	PO Box 456, Ephrata PA 17522	717-738-1151	R	6*	.1
254	Surfside East Inc—*J Blue*	800 Seahawk Cir Ste 10, Virginia Beach VA 23452	757-468-0606	R	6*	<.1
255	Ideation Inc—*Thomas Ungrodt*	2910 Huron Pkwy Ste 10, Ann Arbor MI 48105	734-761-4360	R	6*	.1
256	John Patrick Publishing LLC—*George Gerlach*	1707 4th St, Ewing NJ 08638	609-883-2700	R	6*	.1
257	Bass-Mollett Publishers Inc—*Duane Flowers*	PO Box 189, Greenville IL 62246	618-664-3141	R	5*	.1
258	RR Donnelley and Sons Company Digital Media Center—*Thomas J Quinlan III*	111 South Wacker Dr, Chicago IL 60606	312-326-8000	D	5*	34.0
259	Hanson Directory Service Inc—*William Hanson*	PO Box 786, Newton IA 50208	641-792-2855	R	5*	.1
260	Portfolio Media Inc—*Magnus Hoglund*	860 Broadway Fl 6, New York NY 10003	212-537-6331	R	5*	.1
261	Sunpress Inc—*William Matthew*	PO Box 187, Dade City FL 33526	352-567-5639	R	5*	.1
262	Ar Media Inc—*Raul Martinez*	601 W 26th St Rm 810, New York NY 10001	212-352-0731	R	5*	.1
263	Birmingham Printing And Publishing Company Inc—*Arthur Henley*	PO Box 131298, Birmingham AL 35213	205-251-5113	R	5*	<.1
264	RCR Wireless News—*Keith Crane*	1746 Cole Blvd Ste 150, Golden CO 80401	303-733-2500	S	5*	<.1
265	Logic Factory—*Todd Templeman*	100 Dolores St Ste 251, Carmel CA 93923	831-625-1004	R	5*	<.1
266	Business Financial Publishing LLC—*Ian Wyatt*	1725 Desales Street NW, Washington DC 20036	802-651-4722	R	5*	<.1
267	Mixman Technologies Inc—*Richard A Appelbaum*	PO Box 330042, San Francisco CA 94133	415-403-1380	R	5*	<.1
268	Chemical Sources International Inc—*Dale Krone*	PO Box 1824, Clemson SC 29633	864-646-7840	R	5*	<.1
269	Computer Economics Inc—*Frank Scavo*	2082 Business Center D, Irvine CA 92612	949-831-8700	R	5*	<.1
270	All Star Funds Inc—*Ronald E Rowland*	11651 Jollyville Rd, Austin TX 78759	512-219-1183	R	5*	<.1
271	Centron Software Technologies Inc—*Ron Centner*	8 Lacosta Ln, Pinehurst NC 28374	910-215-5708	R	5*	<.1
272	Lynn Learning Labs—*Adele Lynn*	609 Broad Ave, Belle Vernon PA 15012	724-929-5352	R	5*	<.1
273	Sussex Printing Corp—*Layton Ayres*	PO Box 1210, Seaford DE 19973	302-629-5060	R	5*	.1
274	Allured Publishing Corp—*Janet Ludwig*	336 Gundersen Dr Ste A, Carol Stream IL 60188	630-653-2155	R	5*	.1
275	Business Press—*Pam Ayala*	3450 14th St, Riverside CA 92501	909-806-3100	R	5*	.1
276	Charlesbridge Publishing Inc—*Brent Farmer*	85 Main St Ste 5, Watertown MA 02472	617-926-0329	R	5*	.1
277	Impact Information Inc	PO Box 1570, Londonderry VT 05148	727-736-6228	R	5*	.1
278	Trogdon Publishing Inc—*Bruce Trogdon*	5164 Normandy Park Dr, Medina OH 44256	330-925-3040	R	5*	<.1
279	Blender—*Christoph Mainusch*	1040 Ave of the Americ, New York NY 10018	212-302-2626	R	5*	<.1
280	Boosey and Hawkes Inc—*Jennifer Bilfield*	35 E 21st St Fl 9, New York NY 10010	212-358-5300	R	5*	.1
281	Judy Diamond Associates Inc—*Judy Diamond*	1301 Connecticut Ave N, Washington DC 20036	202-728-0840	R	5*	.1
282	G I A Publications Inc—*Edward Harris*	7343 S Mason Ave, Chicago IL 60638	708-496-3800	R	4*	.1
283	Heritage Co—*Sharon Spadasore*	605 W Dewitt Henry Dr, Beebe AR 72012	501-882-2079	R	4*	.1

Rank	Company Name—*Executive Officer*	Address, City, State, Zip	Phone	Type	Fin	Empls
284	Bulletin News Network Inc—*Paul Roellig*	11190 Sunrise Va Ste 1, Reston VA 20191	703-749-0040	R	4*	<.1
285	Associates In Medical Marketing Company Inc—*Marvin Anzel*	6 Penns Trl Ste 215, Newtown PA 18940	215-860-9600	R	4*	<.1
286	Advanced Design Corp—*Stephen L Gageby*	9447B Lorton Market St, Lorton VA 22079	703-550-5510	R	4*	.1
287	Firstcom Music Inc—*Sharon Baer*	1325 Capital Pky Ste10, Carrollton TX 75006	972-446-8742	R	4*	<.1
288	Step Saver Inc—*Andrew Pape*	213 Spring St, Southington CT 06489	860-628-9645	R	4*	<.1
289	PhotoBooks Inc—*James Edwards*	200 Arizona Ave NE Ste, Atlanta GA 30307	404-589-1228	R	4*	<.1
290	SIMBA Information Inc—*Kathy Mickey*	60 Long Ridge Rd, Stamford CT 06902	203-325-8193	D	4*	<.1
291	Frames Data Inc—*Marc Ferrara*	100 Ave of the America, New York NY 10013	212-219-7831	D	4*	<.1
292	Techno - Graphics and Translations Inc—*David Bond*	1451 E 168th St, South Holland IL 60473	708-331-3333	R	4*	<.1
293	Medical Equipment Distributors Inc—*Bill Elliott*	3223 S Loop 289 Ste 60, Lubbock TX 79423	806-793-8421	R	4*	<.1
294	MarCole Enterprises Inc—*Ronald D Coleman*	2920 Camino Diablo Ste, Walnut Creek CA 94597	925-933-9792	R	4*	<.1
295	Compu-Teach Educational Software—*David Urban*	16541 Redmond Way Ste, Redmond WA 98052	425-885-0517	R	4*	<.1
296	Delaplaine Creative—*John D Delaplaine*	122 Calistoga Rd Ste 5, Santa Rosa CA 95409	415-927-4466	R	4*	<.1
297	Ian Ryan Interactive—*Laird R Crawford*	1400 E Touhy Ave Ste 2, Des Plaines IL 60018	847-803-2050	R	4*	<.1
298	Grafica Interactive—*Debra Taeschler*	525 E Main St, Chester NJ 07930	908-879-2169	R	4*	<.1
299	Britt Communications—*T Randall Britt*	PO Box 4123, Huntsville AL 35815	256-882-5514	R	4*	<.1
300	Crystal Canyon Interactive—*David Montague*	867 E 2260 S, Provo UT 84606	801-372-2728	R	4*	<.1
301	Easy Book Publishing Inc—*John Russum*	6 Executive Park Dr St, Albany NY 12203	518-459-6281	R	4*	<.1
302	Luminair Film Productions Inc—*George Elder*	1644 N Honore St Ste 2, Chicago IL 60622	773-227-3456	R	4*	<.1
303	Northtown Sounds—*Tom Northrop*	275 Wickerberry Hollow, Roswell GA 30075	770-587-9350	R	4*	<.1
304	Thesaurus Linguae Graecae—*Maria Pantelia*	220 University Tower U, Irvine CA 92697	949-824-7031	R	4*	<.1
305	Ferguson Publishing Inc—*Matt Ferguson*	132 W 31st St 17th Fl, New York NY 10001		S	4*	<.1
306	Interactive Knowledge Inc—*Tim Songer*	801-B Central Ave, Charlotte NC 28205	704-344-0055	R	4*	<.1
307	Omnimedia Group—*Ryan W Boros*	4721 Runway Blvd, Ann Arbor MI 48108	734-761-8872	R	4*	<.1
308	Resolutions Multimedia Group Inc—*Steven Haws*	3811 N 24th St, Phoenix AZ 85016	602-956-3330	R	4*	<.1
309	Standish Group International Inc—*James H Johnson*	60 State St Ste 700, Boston MA 02109	508-760-3600	R	4*	<.1
310	Yellow Books USA—*James Clarke*	800 S Barranca Ave Ste, Covina CA 91723	626-338-6612	R	4*	.1
311	Asay Publishing Co—*Roger Asay*	PO Box 670, Joplin MO 64802	417-781-9317	R	4*	<.1
312	In Publications Inc—*David Stern*	5657 Wilshire Blvd Fl, Los Angeles CA 90036	323-848-2200	R	4*	<.1
313	Senior Network Inc—*Frederick Adler*	1 Dock St Ste 608, Stamford CT 06902	203-969-2700	R	4*	<.1
314	Student Lifeline Inc—*Richard Signarino*	PO Box 570200, Whitestone NY 11357	516-327-0800	R	4*	<.1
315	New Era Publishing Inc—*Joseph Garcia*	2101 E Saint Elmo Rd S, Austin TX 78744	512-928-3200	R	4*	<.1
316	Priority Publications Inc—*Mary Larranaga*	6700 France Ave S Ste, Minneapolis MN 55435	952-920-9943	R	4*	<.1
317	US Games Systems Inc—*Stuart Kaplan*	179 Ludlow St, Stamford CT 06902	203-353-8400	R	4*	<.1
318	St Associates Inc—*Sheila Monastiero*	1 Teal Rd, Wakefield MA 01880	781-246-4700	R	4*	<.1
319	Knowledge Unlimited Inc—*Judith Laitman*	PO Box 52, Madison WI 53701	608-661-5666	R	4*	<.1
320	Smyth and Helwys Publishing Inc—*Cecil Staton*	6316 Peake Rd, Macon GA 31210	478-757-0564	R	4*	<.1
321	Kwik-Sew Pattern Company Inc—*Eric Mcmaster*	3000 Washington Ave N, Minneapolis MN 55411	612-521-7651	R	4*	<.1
322	Edwin F Kalmus Company Inc—*Leon Galison*	PO Box 5011, Boca Raton FL 33431	561-241-6340	R	4*	<.1
323	Regeneration Press Inc—*Virginia Hughes*	801 S Wells St Apt 103, Chicago IL 60607	312-554-0669	R	3*	<.1
324	Chronotype Publishing Co—*Warren Dorrance*	PO Box 30, Rice Lake WI 54868	715-234-2121	R	3*	<.1
325	Hagadone Directories Inc—*James Hail*	PO Box 1266, Coeur D Alene ID 83816	208-667-8744	R	3*	<.1
326	Human Synergistics Inc—*Thomas Cross*	39819 Plymouth Rd, Plymouth MI 48170	734-459-1030	R	3*	<.1
327	Megatech Corp—*Varant V Basmajian*	555 Woburn St, Tewksbury MA 01876	978-937-9600	P	3	<.1
328	Ad-Fax Media Marketing Inc—*Laurence Ross*	149 Madison Ave Rm 801, New York NY 10016	212-684-9665	R	3*	<.1
329	Canterbury Press LLC—*Allan Daniels*	120 Interstate N Park, Atlanta GA 30339	770-952-8309	R	3*	<.1
330	Merchants Coupon Exchange Inc—*Dick Davis*	824 Bennett Dr Ste 104, Longwood FL 32750	407-331-5811	R	3*	<.1
331	Christian Light Publications Inc—*Richard Shank*	PO Box 1212, Harrisonburg VA 22803	540-434-0768	R	3*	.1
332	Shopper's Press Of Memphis—*Fred Eason*	PO Box 34967, Memphis TN 38184	901-458-8030	R	3*	<.1
333	Totalworks Inc—*Gail Ludewig*	2240 N Elston Ave, Chicago IL 60614	773-489-4313	R	3*	<.1
334	Art Classics LLC	11 E Wisconsin St, Trenton IL 62293	618-224-9133	R	3*	<.1
335	Discovery House Publishers Inc—*Martin Dehaan*	PO Box 2222, Grand Rapids MI 49501	616-942-9218	R	3*	<.1
336	Sirius Information Inc—*James Sinkinson*	124 Linden St, Oakland CA 94607	510-596-9300	R	3*	<.1
337	World Tariff Ltd—*Scott Morse*	6075 Poplar Ave, Memphis TN 38119	716-879-1324	S	3*	<.1
338	Human Resource Development Press Inc—*Robert W Carkhuff*	22 Amherst Rd, Amherst MA 01002	413-253-3488	R	3*	<.1
339	Trade Dimensions USA—*David Calhoun*	55 Greens Farms Rd, Westport CT 06880	203-222-5750	S	3*	<.1
340	CF Peters Corp—*Martha Hinrichsen*	7030 80th St, Glendale NY 11385	718-416-7800	R	3*	<.1
341	Eastgate Systems Inc—*Mark Bernstein*	134 Main St, Watertown MA 02472	617-924-9044	R	3*	<.1
342	K-12 MicroMedia Publishing Inc—*Tony Schweiker*	16 McKee Dr, Mahwah NJ 07430	201-529-4500	D	3*	<.1
343	Interactive Training Inc—*Paul Earl*	500 Cummings Ctr Ste 4, Beverly MA 01915	978-921-1755	R	3*	<.1
344	Michael Diehl Design—*Michael Diehl*	1415 Norton Ave, Glendale CA 91202	818-552-4110	R	3*	<.1
345	Primal Media Corp—*Cheri Haley*	PO Box 924, Portsmouth NH 03802	603-436-1072	R	3*	<.1
346	RADCO Media Inc—*Richard Deircks* Richard Diercks Company Inc	3140 Harbor Ln N Ste 2, Minneapolis MN 55447	763-231-3303	S	3*	<.1
347	Woods and Poole Economics Inc—*Sally Poole*	1794 Columbia Rd NW St, Washington DC 20009	202-332-7111	R	3*	<.1
348	Harmonic Vision Inc—*Phil Rockenbach*	210 S 5th St Ste 12, St Charles IL 60174	630-584-8513	R	3*	<.1
349	Image Work Communications—*John Lawrence*	5166 Kelvin Ave Ste B, Woodland Hills CA 91364	818-712-9439	R	3*	<.1
350	IVID Communications—*Jack Spiegelberg*	5205 Kearny Villa Way, San Diego CA 92123	858-217-5460	R	3*	<.1
351	Jersey Cow Software Company Inc—*Robert Wickenden*	3031 State Rte 27 Ste, Franklin Park NJ 08823	732-422-0101	R	3*	<.1
352	Oilfield Publications Inc—*Julia Vanston*	1333 W Loop S Ste 1525, Houston TX 77027	713-334-8970	R	3*	<.1
353	Text-Trieve Inc—*Dwight Curtis*	400 E Pine St Ste 210, Seattle WA 98122	206-325-7780	S	3*	<.1
354	MGE Inc—*Arthur Mrozowski*	512 Gertrude Ave, Aptos CA 95003		R	3*	<.1
355	Walker Communications Inc—*Martin S Walker*	2 Park Ave 9th Fl, New York NY 10016	212-944-0011	S	3*	<.1
356	Design Wizards Inc—*Harlowe Jaden*	PO Box 1662, Bismarck ND 58502	701-224-1000	R	3*	<.1
357	Universal Directory Publishing Corp—*Stanley Pesner*	2995 E White Star Ave, Anaheim CA 92806	714-994-6025	R	3*	<.1
358	Guide Book Publishing—*Jim Masterson*	PO Box 240430, Ballwin MO 63024	636-391-2121	R	3*	<.1
359	Power Images—*John Floyd*	2333 Stirling Rd, Fort Lauderdale FL 33312	954-966-0260	R	3*	<.1
360	Trozzolo Creative Resources Inc—*Pasquale Trozzolo*	802 Broadway St Ste 30, Kansas City MO 64105	816-842-8111	R	3*	<.1
361	Kensington Group Inc—*Lawrence Crampsey*	PO Box 1080, Hampton NH 03843	603-926-6742	R	3*	<.1
362	Dow Theory Forecasts Inc—*Charles Carlson*	7412 Calumet Ave Ste 1, Hammond IN 46324	219-931-6480	R	3*	<.1
363	Want Ads Of Fort Worth Inc—*Victor Verstraeta*	2800 W Lancaster Ave, Fort Worth TX 76107	817-870-0055	R	3*	<.1
364	Equibase Company Inc—*Hank Zeitel*	821 Corporate Dr, Lexington KY 40503	859-224-2860	R	3*	<.1
365	Taylor and Ives Inc—*Murray Balley*	48 W 37th St Fl 7, New York NY 10018	212-921-9300	R	3*	<.1
366	Midweek Inc—*Rick Anderson*	PO Box 617, Fergus Falls MN 56538	218-739-3308	R	2*	<.1
367	Frey Media Inc—*Marc Frey*	PO Box 5926, Hilton Head Island SC 29938	843-842-7878	R	2*	<.1
368	Mulligan Printing Corp—*Charles Mulligan*	312 Mile Rd, Tunkhannock PA 18657	570-836-2066	R	2*	<.1
369	Sampson Resources—*Dan Sampson*	4887 Alpha Rd Ste 220, Dallas TX 75244		R	2*	<.1
370	Guest Communications Corp—*Richard Travers*	15009 W 101st Ter, Shawnee Mission KS 66215	913-888-1217	R	2*	<.1
371	Champions Printing and Publishing Inc—*Jim Callahan*	6608 Fm 1960 Rd W Ste, Houston TX 77069	281-583-7661	R	2*	<.1
372	Culver Company LLC—*Kristen Dine*	104 Bridge Rd, Salisbury MA 01952	978-463-1700	R	2*	<.1

Note: An asterisk (*) indicates an estimated financial figure. The company type code used is as follows: R = Private, P = Public, S = Private Subsidiary, B = Public Subsidiary, D = Division, J = Joint Venture, I = Investment Fund.

COMPANY RANKINGS BY SALES WITHIN 4-DIGIT SIC

Rank	Company Name—*Executive Officer*	Address, City, State, Zip	Phone	Type	Fin	Empls
373	Pioneer Telephone Directories Corp—*Walter Bracewell*	106 Parkwest Cir, Dothan AL 36303	334-794-4129	R	2*	<.1
374	Cathedral Press Inc—*Harris Hanson*	PO Box 419, Long Prairie MN 56347	320-732-6143	R	2*	<.1
375	Greater Rochester Advertiser Inc—*Peter Stahlbrodt*	201 Main St, East Rochester NY 14445	585-385-1974	R	2*	<.1
376	Ypne LLC—*Edwin Eisen*	95 Rte 6a, Sandwich MA 02563	508-833-7912	R	2*	<.1
377	American Classifieds—*Denny Merrifield*	PO Box 6688, Lawton OK 73506	580-357-5311	R	2*	<.1
378	Lpi Printing And Graphic Inc—*William Joseph*	18 Spencer St, Stoneham MA 02180	781-438-5400	R	2*	<.1
379	Media Ventures Inc—*David Persson*	200 Connecticut Ave 2d, Norwalk CT 06854	203-852-6570	R	2*	<.1
380	Advercolor Press Inc—*William Konchak*	460 W 83rd St, Hialeah FL 33014	305-821-6441	R	2*	<.1
381	Rgi Publications Inc—*Phillip Wacker*	PO Box 338, Olathe KS 66051	913-829-7577	R	2*	<.1
382	Champion Directories Inc—*P Meadows*	100 Old State Rd S, Norwalk OH 44857	419-668-1280	R	2*	<.1
383	Mcilvaine Co—*Robert Ilvaine*	191 Waukegan Rd Ste 20, Northfield IL 60093	847-784-0012	R	2*	<.1
384	American Map Inc	58 Norfolk Ave Unit 4, South Easton MA 02375	508-230-2112	R	2*	<.1
385	Multimedia Research Group Inc—*Gary Schultz*	1754 Technology Dr Ste, San Jose CA 95110		R	2*	<.1
386	Launch Media Inc—*Sue Decker*	2700 Pennsylvania Ave, Santa Monica CA 90404	310-526-4300	S	2*	<.1
387	Texas Publishing Co—*Dan Albey*	5733 S Padre Island Dr, Corpus Christi TX 78412	361-991-1306	R	2*	<.1
388	InteLex Corp—*Mark Rooks*	PO Box 859, Charlottesville VA 22902	434-970-2286	R	2*	<.1
389	Universal Music Publishing Group Nashville—*Pat Higdon*	1904 Adelicia St, Nashville TN 37212	615-340-5400	D	2*	<.1
390	Economic Insight Inc—*Samuel A Van Vactor*	3004 SW 1st Ave, Portland OR 97201	503-222-2425	R	2*	<.1
391	National Information Services Corp—*Fred Durr*	3100 Saint Paul St Ste, Baltimore MD 21218	410-243-0797	S	2*	<.1
392	Lane Guide—*Milo A Speriglio*	10399 Double R Blvd, Reno NV 89521		R	2*	<.1
393	Outside The Box Interactive LLC—*Frank DeMarco*	150 Bay St Ste 706, Jersey City NJ 07302	201-610-0625	R	2*	<.1
394	Heartwood Media Inc—*Chris Conroy*	83 Hanover St Ste 42, Manchester NH 03101	603-665-9191	R	2*	<.1
395	Image Plant—*Randy Tinfow*	420 US Hwy 46, Fairfield NJ 07004	973-244-9220	R	2*	<.1
396	Ribit Productions Inc—*Robin Moss*	4287 Beltline Rd Ste 1, Addison TX 75001	972-239-8866	R	2*	<.1
397	TourScan Inc—*Arthur W Mehmel*	PO Box 2367, Darien CT 06820	203-453-9992	R	2*	<.1
398	Wildside Press / Judson Rosebush Co—*Judson Rosebush*	630 Ninth Avenue #502, New York NY 10036	212-581-3000	R	2*	<.1
399	Astrolabe Pictures—*Sam Osman*	10765 Clocktower Dr St, Countryside IL 60525	630-495-3000	R	2*	<.1
400	Frame By Frame Productions—*Sean Frame*	1331 8th St Bldg D, Berkeley CA 94710	510-558-9100	R	2*	<.1
401	Interactive Multimedia Artists—*Henry Trettin*	1709 W Wildwood Dr, Phoenix AZ 85045	480-361-8935	R	2*	<.1
402	Khush Multimedia—*Hitesh Bhatt*	100 W Monroe Ste 501, Chicago IL 60603	312-346-2048	R	2*	<.1
403	Mozgomedia—*Myklos Philips*	667 Flower Ave Ste 3, Venice CA 90291	310-633-7639	R	2*	<.1
404	Parallax Design Group Inc—*Mary Helen Fein*	12840 Earhart Ave Ste, Auburn CA 95602	530-887-9400	R	2*	<.1
405	Seattle Support Group—*Lee Simpson*	21581 S Crestview, Oregon City OR 97045		R	2*	<.1
406	Summit Aviation—*John Woellhas*	PO Box 723, Mead CO 80542	801-446-5858	R	2*	<.1
407	Ziba Photographs—*Sasha Shamaszad*	64 Shattuck Sq, Berkeley CA 94704	510-849-0776	R	2*	<.1
408	Alan I Harris Group—*Robert Benfatto*	709 S Aiken Ave, Pittsburgh PA 15232	412-687-5700	R	2*	<.1
409	Angle Park—*Martin Baumgaertner*	367 W Chicago Ave, Hinsdale IL 60654	312-751-9494	R	2*	<.1
410	ARTSCI Inc—*Bill Smith*	PO Box 1428, Burbank CA 91507	818-843-4080	R	2*	<.1
411	Business Information Graphics Inc—*Bruce McKinzie*	242 W 36th St Ste 1010, New York NY 10018	212-477-4288	R	2*	<.1
412	Convivial Design Inc—*Patricia Roberts*	PO Box 935, Abiquiu NM 87510	505-685-4603	R	2*	<.1
413	Digital United Interactive Multimedia—*Mark Magel*	18 Briggs Ln, Croton on Hudson NY 10520	914-271-4959	R	2*	<.1
414	Harvest Moon Studio—*Heather Lindquist*	3516 Dover St, Los Angeles CA 90039	323-660-3444	R	2*	<.1
415	Keesing's Worldwide LLC—*Jonathan Hixson*	1010 Rockville Pike St, Rockville MD 20852	301-718-8770	R	2*	<.1
416	KSK Studios—*Manny Kivowitz*	598 Broadway Ste 10A, New York NY 10012	212-481-3111	R	2*	<.1
417	Penrose Press—*Ray Lauzzana*	PO Box 470925, San Francisco CA 94147	415-567-4157	R	2*	<.1
418	Phokus Inc—*Kurt Remmers*	56 Greenwood Ave, Madison NJ 07940	973-377-2341	R	2*	<.1
419	Rick Doyle Action Photography—*Rick Doyle*	91-110 Hanua St #207, Kapolei HI 96707	858-337-1000	R	2*	<.1
420	Transformyx Inc—*Claude W Bethea*	8510 Quarters Lake Rd, Baton Rouge LA 70809	225-761-0088	R	2*	<.1
421	Raymond Software Inc—*James Raymond*	347 Massol Ave Ste 105, Los Gatos CA 95030	408-395-6157	R	2*	<.1
422	MGA Investment Company Inc—*Greg Deline*	145 Prado Rd, San Luis Obispo CA 93401	805-543-9050	R	2*	<.1
423	Xchanger—*Carol Peters*	PO Box 210, Butler MO 64730	660-679-6126	R	2*	<.1
424	Alpha Publishing Inc—*Louise Setaro*	3336 Grand Blvd Ste 20, Holiday FL 34690	727-841-7793	R	2*	<.1
425	Bay Tact Corp—*O Grinde*	440 Rte 198, Woodstock Valley CT 06282	860-974-2223	R	2*	<.1
426	Homes Inc—*George Carney*	PO Box 172, Raynham MA 02767	508-824-4030	R	2*	<.1
427	Plymouth Publishing Inc—*Susan Burke*	PO Box 3494, Falls Church VA 22043	703-506-4400	R	2*	<.1
428	Southwest Daily Times—*Charles Lancaster*	PO Box 889, Liberal KS 67905	620-626-5083	R	2*	<.1
429	Ross Publications Inc—*June Wankier*	113 W Amerige Ave, Fullerton CA 92832	714-870-8800	R	2*	<.1
430	Dramatic Publishing Company Inc—*Christopher Sergel*	PO Box 129, Woodstock IL 60098	815-338-7170	R	2*	<.1
431	Erin Taylor Fine Art Inc—*William Mack*	5222 W 78th St, Minneapolis MN 55435	952-844-9999	R	2*	<.1
432	Jdc Enterprises Inc—*Deborah Newman*	PO Box 1701, Euless TX 76039	972-550-1880	R	2*	<.1
433	Physical Weekly—*Peter Sprague*	2127 2nd Ave N, Fort Dodge IA 50501	515-573-8691	R	2*	<.1
434	Green Line Media Inc—*Jeff Fobes*	PO Box 144, Asheville NC 28802	828-251-1333	R	2*	<.1
435	Harvard Health Publications—*Ed Coburn*	10 Shattuck St Ste 2, Boston MA 02115	617-432-4714	R	2*	<.1
436	Lightning Bolt Entertainment Inc—*Timothy Bedgood*	3342 S Sandhill Rd, Las Vegas NV 89121	702-699-9493	R	2*	<.1
437	Commonwealth Business Media—*Gary Blaine*	3400 Lakeside Dr Ste 5, Miramar FL 33027	954-628-0058	R	2*	<.1
438	Wave Publishing Inc—*Richard Buys*	165 S 100 W, Heber City UT 84032	435-654-1471	R	2*	<.1
439	New Millenium Directories Inc—*Terry Brininger*	324 1st Ave, Sterling IL 61081	815-626-5737	R	2*	<.1
440	Rake Publishing Inc—*Tom Bartell*	PO Box 3690, Minneapolis MN 55403	612-436-2880	R	2*	<.1
441	Worth Nickel's Publications Inc—*Martin Stacey*	PO Box 2048, Coeur D Alene ID 83816	208-667-0651	R	2*	<.1
442	Media Transcripts Inc—*Pat King*	41 W 83rd St Apt 1b, New York NY 10024	212-362-1481	R	2*	<.1
443	Arrow Shopper—*Robert Kraemer*	15811 Bridge St, Ettrick WI 54627	608-525-5771	R	2*	<.1
444	Executive Printing and Mailing Inc—*Scott Sutton*	2501 Nw 17th Ln Ste A, Pompano Beach FL 33064	954-935-2292	R	2*	<.1
445	Majesty Music Inc—*Frank Garlock*	PO Box 6524, Greenville SC 29606	864-242-6722	R	1*	<.1
446	Summit Catalog Co—*Brett Moore*	PO Box 370108, Denver CO 80237	303-694-4545	R	1*	<.1
447	Well-Tempered Music Library—*Erik Lindgren*	PO Box 465, Middleboro MA 02346	508-947-7387	R	1*	<.1
448	Kardmaster Graphics—*William Snyder*	3320 Trexler Blvd, Allentown PA 18104	610-434-5262	R	1*	<.1
449	News Data Corp—*Cyrus Noe*	PO Box 900928, Seattle WA 98109	206-285-4848	R	1*	<.1
450	Women S Enterprise—*Marie Muller*	11333 N Central Expy, Dallas TX 75243	214-369-9393	R	1*	<.1
451	Trader Carolina Bargain Inc—*Pam Parnell*	21 Howell St, Greenville NC 27834	252-756-1500	R	1*	<.1
452	Publishers Consulting Corp—*Robert Lake*	613 Franklin St, Michigan City IN 46360	219-874-4245	R	1*	<.1
453	Buy And Sell Press Inc—*Emilio Prunetti*	605 Broadway, Jackson CA 95642	209-223-3333	R	1*	<.1
454	Monticello Times Inc—*Donald Smith*	PO Box 420, Monticello MN 55362	763-295-3131	R	1*	<.1
455	New York Legal Publishing Corp—*Ernest Barvoets*	136 Railroad Ave, Albany NY 12205	518-459-1100	R	1*	<.1
456	LJ Lubin Inc—*Leslie Lubin*	13615 Pino Ridge Pl Ne, Albuquerque NM 87111	505-217-2772	R	1*	<.1
457	Rockford Map Publishers Inc—*Suzanne Young*	PO Box 6126, Rockford IL 61125	815-544-7440	R	1*	<.1
458	Whole Systems International—*Darrell Griffin*	255 Washington St Ste1, Newton MA 02458	617-795-5400	R	1*	<.1
459	Regency Typographic Services Inc—*David Kahn*	2867 E Allegheny Ave, Philadelphia PA 19134	215-425-8810	R	1*	<.1
460	Electronic Trend Publications Inc—*Randall Sherman*	337 Clay St Ste 101, Nevada City CA 95959	408-369-7000	S	1*	<.1
461	Picture Vision Inc—*Jon Small*	209 10th Ave Ste 425, Nashville TN 37203	615-244-2060	R	1*	<.1
462	Raven Maps and Images—*Stuart Allan*	PO Box 850, Medford OR 97501	541-773-1436	R	1*	<.1

Rank	Company Name—Executive Officer	Address, City, State, Zip	Phone	Type	Fin	Empls
463	Architectural Designs Inc—Joel Davis	57 Danbury Rd, Wilton CT 06897	262-521-4596	R	1*	<.1
464	Aridi Computer Graphics Inc—Marwan Aridi	PO Box 797702, Dallas TX 75379	972-381-1300	R	1*	<.1
465	Bauer Financial Newsletters Inc—Karen L Dorway	2655 LeJeune Rd, Coral Gables FL 33134	305-445-9500	S	1*	<.1
466	Business Research Services Inc—Thomas Johnson	7720 Wisconsin Ave Ste, Bethesda MD 20814		R	1*	<.1
467	Washington Information Source Co—Kenneth Reid	19-B Wirt St SW, Leesburg VA 20175	703-779-8777	R	1*	<.1
468	Zane Publishing Inc—Stewart Cross	PO Box 1697, Woodstock GA 30188	770-795-9195	R	1*	<.1
469	VMR International Inc	16 Blanchard Rd, Grafton MA 01519	508-839-6707	R	1*	<.1
470	Avatar NuMedia—David Wong	13580 N Meadow View Dr, Grass Valley CA 95945	650-619-8819	R	1*	<.1
471	MediaMorphosis—Timothy Gilchrist	20 Barn Hill Rd, Monroe CT 06468	203-268-2112	R	1*	<.1
472	Reeves Business Forms—Scott Reeves	PO Box 3569, Sunriver OR 97707	541-593-6290	R	1*	<.1
473	AniMEDIA—Kenneth Lasher	11736 N Williamsburg D, Knoxville TN 37922	865-951-1992	R	1*	<.1
474	Cambrix Consulting Group LLC—Bruce Edwards	22319 Delia Ct, Calabasas CA 91302	818-917-6821	R	1*	<.1
475	Dreamlight Inc—Michael Scaramozzino	323 Andover St Ste 6, Wilmington MA 01887	978-658-5110	R	1*	<.1
476	E-Tactics Inc—Sarah E Stambler	370 Central Park W Ste, New York NY 10025	212-222-1713	R	1*	<.1
477	Fontographics Inc—Hossein Farmani	844 S Robertson Blvd S, Los Angeles CA 90035	310-659-0122	R	1*	<.1
478	Glyph Media Group Inc—C B Cooke	315 Bleecker St Ste 19, New York NY 10014	212-929-2773	R	1*	<.1
479	Howl'n Dog Designs—Beth Garst	PO Box 514, Boones Mill VA 24065	540-334-3831	R	1*	<.1
480	International Science and Technology Associates Inc—Alen Engel	526 N Spring Mill Rd, Villanova PA 19085	610-527-4500	R	1*	<.1
481	McLean Media—Lois McLean	12489 Rough and Ready, Grass Valley CA 95945	530-271-5630	R	1*	<.1
482	Learning Design—Susan Donley	700 Tenth St, Oakmont PA 15139	412-828-8679	R	1*	<.1
483	Norman Horowitz Co—Norman Horowitz	9000 Clifton Way Ste 4, Beverly Hills CA 90211	310-288-0137	R	1*	<.1
484	Post Literate Productions—Paul Dougherty	410 E 6th St Ste 18F, New York NY 10009	212-505-7376	R	1*	<.1
485	Ross Publishing LLC—Norman Ross	392 Central Park West, New York NY 10025	212-765-8200	R	1*	<.1
486	SimGraphics Corp—Mike Fusco	1441 Huntington Dr Uni, South Pasadena CA 91030	323-255-0900	R	1*	<.1
487	Mary Elizabeth Bourne—Mary Bourne	5 W 37th St Fl 6, New York NY 10018	212-391-4300	R	1*	<.1
488	Aero Surveys Of Georgia Inc—Tom Roberts	PO Box 6036, Marietta GA 30065	770-422-1611	R	1*	<.1
489	Great Lakes Publishing Inc—Ken Kramer	212 Kent St Ste 6, Portland MI 48875	517-647-4444	R	1*	<.1
490	Mid-Florida Publications Inc—Donna Covert	4645 N Hwy 19a, Mount Dora FL 32757	352-589-8811	R	1*	<.1
491	Construction Monitor LLC—David Mineer	PO Box 2202, Cedar City UT 84721	435-586-1205	R	1*	<.1
492	Oxbridge Communications Inc—Louis Hagood	186 5th Ave Fl 6, New York NY 10010	212-741-0231	R	1*	<.1
493	Pegasus Communications Inc—Virginia Wiley	1 Moody St Ste 3, Waltham MA 02453	781-398-9700	R	1*	<.1
494	Russell's Guides Inc—Harold Halladay	PO Box 11276, Cedar Rapids IA 52410	319-364-6138	R	1*	<.1
495	City Directory Inc—Merle Been	PO Box 265, Belmond IA 50421	641-444-4468	R	1*	<.1
496	Port-To-Print Inc—James Devine	2017 S Stoughton Rd, Madison WI 53716	608-273-4887	R	1*	<.1
497	Investech Research—James Stack	2472 Birch Glen Dr, Whitefish MT 59937	406-862-7777	R	1*	<.1
498	Oasis Publishing Inc—David Abrahams	941 O St Ste 800, Lincoln NE 68508	402-476-0666	R	1*	<.1
499	Five Star Ltd—Rebecca Ramsey	1835 Paseo San Luis, Sierra Vista AZ 85635	520-458-3340	R	<1*	<.1
500	Texas State Directory Press Inc—Julie Sayers	PO Box 12186, Austin TX 78711	512-477-5698	R	<1*	<.1
501	Baby Bee Bright Corp—Fred Dahlman	364 Industrial Park Dr, Mount Juliet TN 37122	615-754-4051	P	<1	N/A
502	First Detroit Corp—Albert Scace	30033 Paul Ct, Warren MI 48092	586-573-0045	R	<1*	<.1
503	Interchange Inc—Sylvan Friedman	PO Box 47596, Minneapolis MN 55447	763-694-7596	R	<1*	<.1
504	JR O'dwyer Company Inc John Odwyer	271 Madison Ave Ste 60, New York NY 10016	212-679-2471	R	<1*	<.1
505	Pet-Friendly Publications Inc—Harvey Barish	7320 E 6th Ave, Scottsdale AZ 85251	480-483-6000	R	<1*	<.1
506	Kaplan Interactive—Andrew S Rosen	888 7th Ave, New York NY 10106	212-752-1840	R	<1	34.0
507	Legacy Publishing Co (Westbrook Maine)—Steve Anderson	10 Speirs St, Westbrook ME 04092	207-856-5600	R	<1	.1
508	Ubisoft Red Storm	2000 CentreGreen Way S, Cary NC 27513	919-460-1776	S	N/A	.1
509	iUniverse Inc—Kevin Weiss	1663 Liberty Dr Ste 30, Bloomington IN 47403	402-323-7800	R	N/A	.1
510	Side Eight Software—Wood Harter	PO Box 5004, Garden Grove CA 92846	949-464-1939	R	N/A	<.1

TOTALS: SIC 2741 Miscellaneous Publishing

Companies: 510					33,168	162.3

2752 Commercial Printing—Lithographic

Rank	Company Name—Executive Officer	Address, City, State, Zip	Phone	Type	Fin	Empls
1	Valassis Communications Inc—Alan F Schultz	19975 Victor Pkwy, Livonia MI 48152	734-591-3000	P	2,236	7.1
2	Transcontinental Direct USA Inc—Hans Nielsen	1044 Pulinski Rd, Warminster PA 18974	215-659-4000	S	1,858*	1.3
3	National Print Group Inc—Phil Harris	PO Box 5968, Chattanooga TN 37406	423-622-2254	R	1,194*	.4
4	Consolidated Graphics Inc—Joe R Davis	5858 Westheimer Ste 20, Houston TX 77057	713-787-0977	P	1,100	5.3
5	Merrill Corp—John Castro	1 Merrill Cir, Saint Paul MN 55108	651-646-4501	R	712*	5.2
6	Broadcaster Press Inc—William Morris	201 W Cherry St, Vermillion SD 57069	605-624-4429	R	648*	.1
7	Democrat Printing and Lithographing Company Inc—Haynes Whitney	PO Box 191, Little Rock AR 72203	501-374-0271	R	500*	.3
8	K/P Corp—Joseph Atturio	13951 Washington Ave, San Leandro CA 94578	510-351-5400	R	489*	.3
9	Schawk Inc—David A Schawk	1695 S River Rd, Des Plaines IL 60018	847-827-9494	P	461	3.2
10	Jordan Industries Inc—John W Jordan II	1751 Lake Cook Rd Arbo, Deerfield IL 60015	847-945-5591	R	433*	4.0
11	Brown Printing Company Inc—Volker Petersen	PO Box 1549, Waseca MN 56093	507-835-2410	S	312*	2.6
12	SFI-Delaware LLC—Dave Davis	PO Box 2418, Norfolk VA 23501	757-622-8001	S	274	.3
13	Segerdahl Corp—Richard Joutras	1351 Wheeling Rd, Wheeling IL 60090	847-465-3354	R	248*	.4
14	Madden Communications Inc—Sean Madden	901 Mittel Dr, Wood Dale IL 60191	630-787-2200	R	236*	.3
15	Arandell Corp—Donald Treis	PO Box 405, Menomonee Falls WI 53052	262-255-4400	R	230*	.8
16	Merrill/May Inc—Raymond J Goodwin Merrill Corp	4110 Clearwater Rd, Saint Cloud MN 56301	320-656-5000	S	208*	.9
17	Mickelberry Communications Inc—James C Marlas	405 Park Ave 10th Fl, New York NY 10022	212-832-0303	R	167*	.7
18	Publishers Printing Company LLC—Mark Beach	PO Box 37500, Louisville KY 40233	502-543-2251	R	148*	1.7
19	Workflow Holdings LLC—David Davis	220 E Monument Ave, Dayton OH 45402		R	143*	2.1
20	Berlin Industries Inc—Tina Tromiczak	175 Mercedes Dr, Carol Stream IL 60188	630-682-0600	R	133*	.8
21	Sharp Corp (Conshohocken Pennsylvania)—George Burke	7451 Keebler Way, Allentown PA 18106	610-279-3550	S	125*	.5
22	Wolters Kluwer Financial Services—Brian Longe	PO Box 1457, Saint Cloud MN 56302		S	100*	.9
23	Southwest Offset Printing Co—Greg McDonald	13650 Gramercy Pl, Gardena CA 90249	310-323-0112	R	100*	.5
24	Bowne Business Communications Inc—David Shea	215 County Ave, Secaucus NJ 07094	201-271-1000	S	98*	.4
25	Nationwide Graphics—Carl L Norton	2500 West Loop S Ste 5, Houston TX 77027	713-961-4700	R	95*	.5
26	Gannett Offset Marketing Services Group—David Worland	PO Box 34470, Louisville KY 40232	502-454-6660	D	81*	1.1
27	Measurement Inc—Henry Scherich	423 Morris St, Durham NC 27701	919-683-2413	R	80*	.4
28	National Posters Inc—Joel Stuart National Print Group Inc	PO Box 5968, Chattanooga TN 37406	423-622-1106	S	80*	.2
29	Henry Wurst Inc—Michael Wurst	PO Box 12598, Kansas City MO 64116	816-842-3113	R	80*	.5
30	Specialty Promotions Inc—Paul Lefebvre	6019 W Howard St, Niles IL 60714	847-588-2580	R	74*	.3
31	CGI North America—Peter Furlonge	100 Burma Rd, Jersey City NJ 07305	201-217-1990	S	74	.7
32	Colwell Industries Inc—Bill Byers	123 N 3rd St Ste 702, Minneapolis MN 55401	612-340-0365	R	72*	1.0
33	Clondalkin Pharma and Healthcare Inc—William Mitchell	PO Box 3, Evansville IN 47701	336-292-4555	R	71*	.9

Note: An asterisk (*) indicates an estimated financial figure. The company type code used is as follows: R = Private, P = Public, S = Private Subsidiary, B = Public Subsidiary, D = Division, J = Joint Venture, I = Investment Fund.

COMPANY RANKINGS BY SALES WITHIN 4-DIGIT SIC

Rank	Company Name—*Executive Officer*	Address, City, State, Zip	Phone	Type	Fin	Empls
34	Hbp Inc—*John Snyder*	952 Frederick St, Hagerstown MD 21740	301-733-2000	R	70*	.1
35	Japs-Olson Co—*Michael Beddor*	7500 Excelsior Blvd, Minneapolis MN 55426	952-932-9393	R	63*	.7
36	Bowne of Phoenix Inc—*David A Shea*	1500 N Central Ave, Phoenix AZ 85004	602-223-4455	S	61*	.3
37	Vox Medica Inc—*Lorna Weir*	601 Walnut St, Philadelphia PA 19106	215-238-8500	R	60*	.1
38	Schmidt Printing Inc—*Joe Ferguson*	1101 Frontage Rd Nw, Byron MN 55920	507-775-6400	R	58*	.5
39	Disc—*Donald Sinkin*	10 Gilpin Ave, Hauppauge NY 11788	631-234-1400	R	58*	.3
40	FOCUS Direct Inc—*Patrick Cronin*	PO Box 17568, San Antonio TX 78217	210-805-9185	R	53*	.2
41	Panel Prints Inc—*William M Abene*	1001 Moosic Rd, Old Forge PA 18518	570-457-8334	R	50*	.4
42	Continental Web Press Inc—*Diane Field*	1430 Industrial Dr, Itasca IL 60143	630-773-1903	R	50*	.3
43	Epi Printers Inc—*William Guzy*	PO Box 1025, Battle Creek MI 49016	269-964-4600	R	50*	.7
44	Kay Screen Printing Inc—*Joseph Kowalczyk*	PO Box 1000, Lake Orion MI 48361	248-377-4999	R	49*	.3
45	Angstrom Graphics Incorporated Midwest—*Mark Berkey*	4437 E 49th St, Cleveland OH 44125	216-271-5300	S	49*	.3
46	American Spirit Graphics Corp—*Darren Carlson*	801 SE 9th St, Minneapolis MN 55414	612-623-3333	R	49*	.2
47	Sheridan Press Inc—*John Saxton*	PO Box 465, Hanover PA 17331	717-632-3535	R	48*	.4
48	Npc Inc—*Mark Kelly*	PO Box 373, Claysburg PA 16625	814-239-8787	R	48*	.5
49	Wright Printing Co—*Mark Wright*	11616 I St, Omaha NE 68137	402-330-2356	R	48*	.2
50	Universal Printing Company Inc—*Robert Ebel*	1234 S Kingshighway Bl, Saint Louis MO 63110	314-771-6900	R	47*	.2
51	Regulus Integrated Solutions LLC	860 Latour Ct, Napa CA 94558	707-254-4000	R	47*	.6
52	Printing Inc (Wichita Kansas) Consolidated Graphics Inc	344 N Saint Francis St, Wichita KS 67202	316-265-1201	S	46*	.3
53	Progress Printing Company Inc (Lynchburg Virginia)—*Mike Thornton*	PO Box 4575, Lynchburg VA 24502	434-239-9213	R	44*	.3
54	Emerald City Graphics Inc—*Mark Steiner* Consolidated Graphics Inc	23328 66th Ave S, Kent WA 98032	253-520-2600	S	44*	.2
55	ABC Imaging LLC—*Medi Falsafi*	1155 21st St NW, Washington DC 20036	202-429-8870	R	43*	.6
56	Pictorial Offset Corp—*Donald Samuels*	PO Box 157, Carlstadt NJ 07072	201-935-7100	R	43*	.3
57	Commercial Communications Inc—*Chris Illman*	1225 Walnut Ridge Dr, Hartland WI 53029	262-369-6000	R	43*	.3
58	Print South Corp—*Samuel Peters*	880 Great SW Pkwy, Atlanta GA 30336	404-349-4514	R	43*	.1
59	Intelligencer Printing Co—*Michael Stief*	330 Eden Rd, Lancaster PA 17601	717-291-3100	R	42*	.2
60	Monarch Litho Inc—*Robert Lopez*	1501 Date St, Montebello CA 90640	323-727-0300	R	41*	.3
61	Hampton Transfer Prints Inc—*Tammy Ross*	2230 Eddie Williams Rd, Johnson City TN 37601	423-928-7247	R	41*	.2
62	Wynalda Litho Inc—*Robert Wynalda*	PO Box 370, Belmont MI 49306	616-866-1561	R	40*	.1
63	Marketing Alliance Group Inc—*Brian Hair*	PO Box 128, Dalton GA 30722	706-277-9707	R	40*	.6
64	Jet Lithocolor Inc—*George Bogdanovic*	1500 Centre Cir, Downers Grove IL 60515	630-932-9000	R	40*	.2
65	Standard Publishing—*Larry Carpenter*	8805 Governor's Hill D, Cincinnati OH 45249	513-931-4050	S	39*	.3
66	Fgs-Wi LLC—*Martin Liebert*	1101 S Janesville St, Milton WI 53563	608-373-6500	R	39*	.3
67	Classic Graphics Inc—*David Pitts*	PO Box 480127, Charlotte NC 28269	704-597-9015	R	39*	.2
68	Concord Litho Group—*Peter Cook*	92 Old Tpke Rd, Concord NH 03301	603-225-3328	R	39*	.2
69	Dethmers Manufacturing Co—*Robert Koerselman*	PO Box 189, Boyden IA 51234	712-725-2311	R	38*	.3
70	Goodway Graphics Inc—*Noel Doherty*	261 York Rd Ste 930, Jenkintown PA 19046	215-887-5700	R	38*	.4
71	Worth Higgins and Associates Inc—*E Worth Higgins*	8770 Park Central Dr, Richmond VA 23227	804-264-2304	R	38*	.2
72	Jarvis Press Inc—*Ned Steck* Consolidated Graphics Inc	9112 Viscount Row, Dallas TX 75247	214-637-2340	S	37*	.2
73	Douglas Press Inc—*Frank Fienberg*	2810 Madison St, Bellwood IL 60104	708-547-8400	R	37*	.3
74	Suttle-Straus Inc—*John Berthelsen*	PO Box 370, Waunakee WI 53597	608-849-1000	S	36*	.3
75	Owen G Dunn Company Inc—*Owen Andrews*	1719 Red Robin Ln, New Bern NC 28562	252-633-3197	R	35*	.1
76	F L Motheral Co—*James Motheral*	4251 Empire Rd, Fort Worth TX 76155	817-335-1481	R	35*	.2
77	Earth Color Barton Press Inc—*Robert Kashan*	249 Pomeroy Rd, Parsippany NJ 07054	973-884-1300	R	35*	.2
78	Perfect Plastic Printing Corp—*Christopher Smoczynski*	PO Box 568, Saint Charles IL 60174	630-584-1600	R	35*	.2
79	Kelly Press Inc—*Michael Kelly*	1701 Cabin Branch Dr, Cheverly MD 20785	301-386-2800	R	34*	.3
80	Challenge Printing Company Inc—*Theodore Sasso*	2 Bridewell Pl, Clifton NJ 07014	973-471-4700	R	34*	.4
81	Marketing Services By Vectra Inc—*Craig Taylor*	3950 Business Park Dr, Columbus OH 43204	614-351-6868	R	34*	.2
82	Windward Print Star Inc—*Ed Raine*	650 Century Plz Dr Ste, Houston TX 77073	281-821-5522	R	34*	.3
83	Meyers Co—*David Dillon*	7277 Boone Ave N, Minneapolis MN 55428	763-533-9730	R	34*	.3
84	Confort and Company Inc—*Thomas Quinlan III*	111 S Wacker Dr, Chicago IL 60606	312-326-8000	R	34*	.2
85	Pollard Games Inc—*Gordon Pollard*	504 34th Ave, Council Bluffs IA 51501	712-366-9553	R	34*	.3
86	Hm Graphics Inc—*James Sandstrom*	PO Box 14397, Milwaukee WI 53214	414-321-6600	R	34*	.2
87	Three-Z Printing Co—*Dan Zerrusen*	PO Box 550, Teutopolis IL 62467	217-857-3153	R	34*	.5
88	Upper Deck Company LLC—*Julie Rohrer*	5909 Sea Otter Pl Ste, Carlsbad CA 92010	760-929-6500	R	34*	.4
89	American Press Inc—*Marshall Pettygrove*	1 American Pl, Gordonsville VA 22942	540-832-2253	R	33*	.3
90	Schiele Group—*John Schiele*	1880 Busse Rd, Elk Grove Village IL 60007	847-434-5455	R	33*	.1
91	Mercury Print Productions Inc—*Valerie Mannix*	50 Holleder Pkwy, Rochester NY 14615	585-458-7900	R	33*	.2
92	Integracolor Ltd—*Bill Yost*	PO Box 180218, Dallas TX 75218	972-289-0705	R	33*	.5
93	Ross Network Inc—*Thomas White*	PO Box 350, Freeport NY 11520	516-223-7177	R	33*	.2
94	Aircap Industries Corp—*Ted Moll*	PO Box 2120, Tupelo MS 38803	662-566-2332	R	33*	.5
95	Dingley Press Inc—*Robert Moore*	119 Lisbon St, Lisbon ME 04250	207-353-4151	R	32*	.4
96	Bowne of Los Angeles Inc—*David J Shea*	10591 Humbolt St, Los Alamitos CA 90720	562-240-2600	S	32*	.2
97	Engle Printing and Publishing Company Inc—*Pauline Engle*	PO Box 500, Mount Joy PA 17552	717-653-1833	R	31*	.4
98	Strine Printing Company Inc—*Michael Strine*	PO Box 149, York PA 17405	717-767-6602	R	31*	.4
99	Bolger LLC—*Charles Bolger*	3301 Como Ave Se, Minneapolis MN 55414	651-645-6311	R	31*	.2
100	JKG Group Inc—*Robert Gittlin*	990 S Rogers Cir Ste 8, Boca Raton FL 33487	561-241-1999	R	31*	.2
101	Standard Offset Printing Company Inc—*Charlotte Cooper*	PO Box 1059, Reading PA 19603	610-375-6174	R	31*	.2
102	Southeastern Printing Company Inc—*Donald Mader*	3601 Se Dixie Hwy, Stuart FL 34997	772-287-2141	R	31*	.2
103	Cedar Graphics Inc (Ronkonkoma New York)—*Hassan Igram* Earth Color Barton Press Inc	1700 Ocean Ave, Ronkonkoma NY 11779	631-467-1444	S	30	.3
104	Phoenix Lithographing Corp—*Ralph Arnold*	11631 Caroline Rd Ste, Philadelphia PA 19154	215-698-9000	R	30*	.1
105	Ncl Graphic Specialties Inc—*Steven Klopp*	N29w22960 Marjean Ln, Waukesha WI 53186	262-542-0711	R	30*	.2
106	Customink LLC—*Marc Katz*	7900 Westpark Dr Ste T, McLean VA 22102	703-891-2273	R	30*	.1
107	Mac Naughton Lithograph Company Inc—*Andrew Merson*	100 Castle Rd, Secaucus NJ 07094	201-863-8100	R	30*	.2
108	Air Waves Inc—*Kevin Simpson*	PO Box 330, Lewis Center OH 43035	740-548-1200	R	30*	.3
109	BH G Inc—*Michael Gackle*	PO Box 309, Garrison ND 58540	701-463-2201	R	30*	.1
110	Papers Inc—*Ron Baumgartner*	PO Box 188, Milford IN 46542	574-658-4111	R	29*	.3
111	Kingery Printing Co—*John Kingery*	PO Box 727, Effingham IL 62401	217-347-5151	R	29*	.2
112	Uni-Graphic Inc—*Robert Quinlan*	110j Commerce Way, Woburn MA 01801	781-231-7200	R	29*	.2
113	Creel Printing and Publishing Company Inc—*Allan Creel*	6330 W Sunset Rd, Las Vegas NV 89118	702-735-8161	R	29*	.3
114	Jay Packaging Group Inc—*Richard Kelly*	100 Warwick Industrial, Warwick RI 02886	401-739-7200	R	29*	.2
115	Fong Brothers Printing Inc—*Tony Fong*	320 Valley Dr, Brisbane CA 94005	415-467-1050	R	29*	.2
116	Kelvyn Press Inc—*Richard Malacina*	2910 S 18th Ave, Broadview IL 60155	708-343-0448	R	29*	.2
117	Toppan Printing Company (America) Inc—*Seshi Tanoue*	650 5th Ave Fl 12, New York NY 10019	212-489-7740	R	29*	.2
118	D and J Printing Inc—*Chris Kurtzman*	PO Box 587, Brainerd MN 56401	218-829-2877	R	28*	.2

Rank	Company Name—*Executive Officer*	Address, City, State, Zip	Phone	Type	Fin	Empls
119	Sandy-Alexander Inc—*Michael Graff* Mickelberry Communications Inc	200 Entin Rd, Clifton NJ 07014	973-470-8100	S	28*	.2
120	Moore Wallace Andrews-Connecticut—*David La Broad*	151 RedStone Rd, Manchester CT 06040	860-649-5570	S	28	.3
121	Original Smith Printing Inc—*Rockie Zeigler*	2 Hardman Dr, Bloomington IL 61701	309-663-0325	R	28*	.2
122	Rock Communications Ltd—*Tim Rock*	PO Box 189, Newton IA 50208	641-792-8334	R	28*	.4
123	Coral Graphic Services Inc—*Frank Cappo*	840 S Broadway, Hicksville NY 11801	516-576-2100	R	27*	.2
124	Meriliz Inc—*Timothy Poole*	PO Box 2054, Sacramento CA 95812	916-923-3663	R	27*	.1
125	Lahlouh Inc—*John Lahlouh*	PO Box 4345, Burlingame CA 94011	650-692-6600	R	27*	.2
126	Synergy Graphics Inc—*Donald Dale*	14505 27th Ave N, Minneapolis MN 55447	763-586-3700	R	27*	.2
127	Lake County Press Inc—*Ralph Johnson*	PO Box 9209, Waukegan IL 60079	847-336-4333	R	27*	.2
128	Certified Ad Services—*Thomas Speck*	PO Box 12025, Fresno CA 93776	559-233-1891	R	27*	.2
129	Universal Millennium Inc—*Bill Fitzgerald*	26 Dartmouth St Ste 1, Westwood MA 02090	781-251-2700	R	26*	.3
130	Schumann Printers Inc—*Daniel Schumann*	PO Box 128, Fall River WI 53932	920-484-3348	R	26*	.2
131	Bowne Financial Print—*Thomas J Quinlan*	111 S Wacker Dr, Chicago IL 60606	312-326-8000	S	26*	.2
132	McAdams Graphics Inc—*Gerald McAdams*	7200 S 1st St, Oak Creek WI 53154	414-768-8080	R	26*	.1
133	Compucolor Associates—*Thomas Weitzmann*	47-50 30th St, Long Island City NY 11101	516-358-0000	R	26*	.1
134	Solo Printing Inc—*Manuel Hernandez*	7860 Nw 66th St, Miami FL 33166	305-594-8699	R	26*	.1
135	Ccl Insertco LLC—*William Obrien*	1831 Portal St Ste D, Baltimore MD 21224	410-633-6525	S	26*	.2
136	Abg Acquisition Corp—*Joel Luce*	3810 Wabash Dr, Mira Loma CA 91752	951-361-7100	R	26*	.2
137	AFL Quality Inc—*Dennis Forchic*	2 Executive Dr, Voorhees NJ 08043	856-566-1270	R	26*	.2
138	Integrated Print and Graphics Inc—*Gary Mozina*	645 Stevenson Rd, South Elgin IL 60177	847-695-6777	R	25*	.1
139	Ares Printing And Packaging Corp—*Mary Filippidis*	63 Flushing Ave Unit 2, Brooklyn NY 11205	718-858-8760	R	25*	.1
140	Frederic Printing Co—*Chris Green* Consolidated Graphics Inc	14701 E 38th Ave, Aurora CO 80011	303-371-7990	D	25*	.1
141	Segerdahl Graphics Inc—*Rick Joutras* Segerdahl Corp	385 Gilman Ave, Wheeling IL 60090	847-850-8800	S	25*	.1
142	Kolor View Press Div—*John Burkhart* Dexter Hospitality Inc	PO Box 261, Aurora MO 65605		D	25*	.1
143	Naylor Inc—*Steve Naylor*	350 Great SW Pkwy, Atlanta GA 30336	404-739-7299	R	25*	.1
144	Beyer Graphics Inc—*William Beyer*	30 Austin Blvd Ste A, Commack NY 11725	631-543-3900	R	25*	.1
145	Postal Instant Press—*Catherine Monson*	26722 Plaza Ste 200, Mission Viejo CA 92691	949-348-5000	S	25*	.1
146	Morris Printing Group Inc—*Scott Morris*	PO Box 2110, Kearney NE 68848	308-236-7888	R	24*	.3
147	Sigler Companies Inc—*Beth Cross*	PO Box 887, Ames IA 50010	515-232-6997	R	24*	.2
148	Allison Payment Systems LLC—*Joseph Thomas*	PO Box 102, Indianapolis IN 46206	317-808-2400	R	24*	.2
149	Corporate Press Inc—*Michael Marcian*	9700 Philadelphia Crt, Lanham MD 20706	301-499-9200	R	24*	.2
150	Sinclair Printing Co—*Robert J Sinclair*	4005 Whiteside St, Los Angeles CA 90063	323-264-4000	R	24*	.1
151	Vanguard Printing LLC—*Mark Ploucha*	PO Box 4560, Ithaca NY 14852	607-272-1212	R	24*	.1
152	Panini America Inc—*Ann Powell*	2300 E Randol Mill, Arlington TX 76011	817-983-0300	R	24*	.1
153	Fisher Printing Inc—*Thomas Fischer*	8640 S Oketo Ave, Bridgeview IL 60455	708-598-1500	R	24*	.3
154	Master Print Inc—*David Dickens*	PO Box 1467, Newington VA 22122	703-550-9555	R	24*	.2
155	Duplicator Sales And Service Inc—*Jerome Nash*	831 E Broadway, Louisville KY 40204	502-560-1440	R	24*	.2
156	DS Graphics Inc—*Jeffrey Pallis*	120 Stedman St, Lowell MA 01851	978-970-1359	R	24*	.2
157	United Litho Inc—*J Garner*	21800 Beaumeade Cir, Ashburn VA 20147	703-858-1000	R	24*	.2
158	Colour Concepts Inc—*Mark Sears*	6980 Sycamore Canyon B, Riverside CA 92507	951-787-9988	R	24*	.2
159	Fine Line Graphics Corp—*James Basch*	PO Box 163370, Columbus OH 43216	614-486-0276	R	23*	.1
160	Print-O-Stat Inc—*Silvia Dugan*	PO Box 15046, York PA 17405	717-854-7821	R	23*	.2
161	Nieman Printing—*Joan Nieman*	10615 Newkirk St Ste 1, Dallas TX 75220	972-506-7400	R	23*	.2
162	F C L Graphics Inc—*Thomas Speilburg*	4600 N Olcott Ave, Chicago IL 60706	708-867-5500	R	23*	.2
163	Darwill Press Inc—*Janice Dyke*	11900 Roosevelt Rd, Hillside IL 60162	708-449-7770	R	23*	.2
164	Consolidated Graphics Group Inc—*Kenneth Lanci*	1614 E 40th St, Cleveland OH 44103	216-881-9191	R	23*	.1
165	Print Communications Inc—*Lowell Morrison*	2457 E Washington St, Indianapolis IN 46201	317-266-8208	R	23*	.2
166	Alcom Printing Group Inc—*William Kuplen*	PO Box 570, Harleysville PA 19438	215-513-1600	R	23*	.2
167	Commercial Lithographing Company Inc—*William Pfeiffer*	1226 Chestnut Ave, Kansas City MO 64127	816-241-2218	R	22*	.2
168	Publication Printers Corp—*Gary Rosenberg*	2001 S Platte River Dr, Denver CO 80223	303-936-0303	R	22*	.2
169	Fontana Lithograph Inc—*Brendan Connors*	4801 Viewpoint Pl, Hyattsville MD 20781	301-927-3800	R	22*	.2
170	Cedar Graphics Inc—*Hassan Igram*	PO Box 185, Hiawatha IA 52233	319-393-3600	R	22*	.2
171	Bowne of Chicago Inc	111 South Wacker Drive, Chicago IL 60661	312-707-9790	S	22*	.2
172	IPD Printing	5800 Peachtree Rd, Chamblee GA 30341	770-458-6351	D	22*	.2
173	Custom Labels Inc (Bossier City Louisiana)—*Robert Waddell*	4924 Hazel Jones Rd, Bossier City LA 71111	318-747-7460	R	22*	.1
174	Data Source Inc—*David Holland*	1400 Universal Ave, Kansas City MO 64120	816-483-3282	R	22*	.1
175	Goodway Graphics Of Virginia Inc—*Donald Wolk*	6628 Electronic Dr, Springfield VA 22151	703-941-1160	R	22*	.2
176	American Web Inc—*Donald Hansen*	4040 Dahlia St, Denver CO 80216	303-321-2422	R	22*	.1
177	Stouse Inc—*Bary Marquardt*	PO Box 3, Gardner KS 66030	913-764-5757	R	22*	.3
178	Mines Press Inc—*Daniel Mines*	231 Croton Ave, Cortlandt Manor NY 10567	914-788-1800	R	22*	.1
179	Foxfire Printing And Packaging Inc—*John Ferretti*	750 Dawson Dr, Newark DE 19713	302-368-9466	R	21*	.1
180	Original Impressions LLC—*Franz Fernandez*	12900 Sw 89th Ct, Miami FL 33176	305-233-1322	R	21*	.2
181	Indiana Printing And Publishing Co—*Michael Donnelly*	PO Box 10, Indiana PA 15701	724-465-5555	R	21*	.3
182	Mossberg and Company Inc—*James Hillman*	301 E Sample St, South Bend IN 46601	574-289-9253	R	21*	.1
183	Westland Printers Inc—*Matthew Flippen* Consolidated Graphics Inc	14880 Sweitzer Ln, Laurel MD 20707	301-384-7700	S	21*	.2
184	Moran Printing	9125 Bachman Rd, Orlando FL 32824	407-859-2030	S	21*	.2
185	Midstates Printing Inc—*Roger Feickert*	PO Box 940, Aberdeen SD 57402	605-225-5287	R	21*	.1
186	Beechmont Press LLC—*Dennis Watkins*	9951 Bunsen Way, Louisville KY 40299	502-491-1396	R	21*	.1
187	National Mail Graphics Corp—*John Sikorski*	300 Old Mill Ln, Exton PA 19341	610-524-1600	R	21*	.1
188	Business Stationery Program—*James Marchessault*	3200 143rd Cir, Burnsville MN 55306	952-894-4904	R	21*	.2
189	Great Eastern Color Lithographic Corp—*Lawrence Perretta*	46 Violet Ave, Poughkeepsie NY 12601	845-454-7420	R	21*	.2
190	Whitmore Print And Imaging Inc—*George Shenk*	1982 Moreland Pkwy, Annapolis MD 21401	410-263-6660	R	20*	.1
191	Spg Graphics Inc—*David Harding*	4923 W 78th St, Indianapolis IN 46268	317-876-3355	R	20*	.1
192	Pro Document Solutions Inc—*George Phillips*	1760 Commerce Way, Paso Robles CA 93446	805-238-6680	R	20*	.2
193	Egt Printing Solutions LLC—*Jonathan Strager*	32031 Townley St, Madison Heights MI 48071	248-583-2500	R	20*	.1
194	Marek Group Inc—*Frank Marek*	W228n821 Westmound Dr, Waukesha WI 53186	262-549-8900	R	20*	.1
195	Handbill Printers LP—*David Lerveld*	14321 Corporate Dr, Garden Grove CA 92843	714-554-6220	R	20*	.1
196	Letter Systems Inc—*Richard Tardiff*	15 Darin Dr, Augusta ME 04330	207-622-6241	R	20*	.1
197	ABS Graphics Inc—*Kenneth Veen*	901 S Rohlwing Rd Ste, Addison IL 60101	630-495-2400	R	20*	.1
198	Pearl Pressman Liberty Communications Group—*Dave Van Dusen*	7625 Suffolk Ave, Philadelphia PA 19153	215-925-4900	R	20*	.1
199	Henderson Gleaner—*Steve Austin*	PO Box 4, Henderson KY 42419	270-827-2000	S	20*	.1
200	Shapco Printing Inc—*Robert Shapiro*	524 N 5th St, Minneapolis MN 55401	612-375-1150	R	20	.1
201	Valley Business Printers Inc—*Mike N Flannery*	16230 Filbert St, Sylmar CA 91342	818-362-7771	R	20*	.1
202	Monroe Litho—*Chris Pape*	39 Delevan St, Rochester NY 14605	585-454-3290	R	20*	.1

Note: An asterisk (*) indicates an estimated financial figure. The company type code used is as follows: R = Private, P = Public, S = Private Subsidiary, B = Public Subsidiary, D = Division, J = Joint Venture, I = Investment Fund.

COMPANY RANKINGS BY SALES WITHIN 4-DIGIT SIC

Rank	Company Name—*Executive Officer*	Address, City, State, Zip	Phone	Type	Fin	Empls
203	VQS Enterprises Inc—*Donald McCurdy*	1081 Poinsettia Ave, Vista CA 92081	760-597-1200	R	20*	.1
204	Process Displays Co—*Peter Strommen*	7108 31st Ave N, Minneapolis MN 55427	763-546-1133	R	20*	.1
205	Printer Inc—*William Benskin*	1220 Thomas Beck Rd, Des Moines IA 50315	515-288-7241	R	20*	.1
206	Rotary Offset Press Inc—*C Kelly*	6600 S 231st St, Kent WA 98032	253-813-9900	R	19*	.1
207	Hagadone Printing Company Inc—*Duane Hagadone*	274 Puuhale Rd, Honolulu HI 96819	808-847-5310	R	19*	.1
208	Sierra Office Systems And Products Inc—*Michael Kipp*	9950 Horn Rd Ste 5, Sacramento CA 95827	916-369-0491	R	19*	.1
209	ICS Corp—*Matt Bastian*	2225 Richmond St, Philadelphia PA 19125	215-427-3278	R	19*	.2
210	Johns-Byrne Co—*Corey S Gustafson*	6701 W Oakton St, Niles IL 60714	847-583-3100	R	19	.1
211	Lewisburg Printing Inc—*Thomas Hawkins*	PO Box 2608, Lewisburg TN 37091	931-359-1526	R	19*	.1
212	La Crosse Graphics Inc—*Tim Morgan*	3025 East Ave S, La Crosse WI 54601	608-788-2500	R	19*	.1
213	Strathmore Press Inc—*Michael R Kelly*	1600 Magnolia Dr, Cincinnati OH 45215		R	19*	.1
214	Rogers Printing Inc—*Tom Rogers*	PO Box 215, Ravenna MI 49451	231-853-2244	R	19*	.1
215	Fetter Printing Co—*Terrence Gill*	PO Box 33128, Louisville KY 40232	502-634-4771	R	19*	.1
216	Lew A Cummings Company Inc—*John Cummings*	PO Box 16495, Hooksett NH 03106	603-625-6901	R	19*	.1
217	EP Graphics Inc—*Tyler Kitt*	169 S Jefferson St, Berne IN 46711	260-589-2145	R	19*	.1
218	Flagship Press Inc—*Charles Poor*	150 Flagship Dr, North Andover MA 01845	978-975-3100	R	19*	.1
219	Philipp Lithographing Co—*Peter Buening*	PO Box 4, Grafton WI 53024	262-377-1100	R	19*	.1
220	Visual Controls/Champ Inc—*Paul Featherston*	75 Cascade Blvd, Milford CT 06460	203-882-8222	R	19*	.2
221	Prisma Graphic Corp—*Robert Anderson*	2909 E Broadway Rd, Phoenix AZ 85040	602-304-5283	R	19*	.1
222	Print Pad Ltd—*Brian O'keefe*	5 Latour Ave Ste 200, Plattsburgh NY 12901	518-561-4383	R	18*	.2
223	Chromasource Inc—*Alex Pursley*	PO Box 8300, Fort Wayne IN 46898	260-420-3000	R	18*	.1
224	Coyle Reproductions Inc—*Frank Cutrone*	14949 Firestone Blvd, La Mirada CA 90638	714-690-8200	R	18*	.1
225	F P Horak Co—*Timothy Dust*	PO Box 925, Bay City MI 48707	989-892-6505	R	18*	.1
226	Trabon Printing Company Inc—*Tim Trabon*	430 E Bannister Rd, Kansas City MO 64131	816-361-6279	R	18*	.1
227	Ginny's Printing Inc—*Micheal Martin*	8410 Tuscany Way Ste B, Austin TX 78754		R	18*	.2
228	Gist and Herlin Press Inc—*John Robinson*	475 Heffernan Dr, West Haven CT 06516	203-479-7500	R	18*	.2
229	VG Reed and Sons Inc—*Bobby Reed*	1002 S 12th St, Louisville KY 40210		R	18*	.1
230	J and A Printing Inc—*Scott Cadwallader*	PO Box 457, Hiawatha IA 52233	319-393-1781	R	18*	.1
231	Bfc Forms Service Inc—*Joseph Novak*	1051 N Kirk Rd, Batavia IL 60510	630-879-9240	R	18*	.1
232	Boyd Brothers Inc—*James Boyd*	PO Box 18, Panama City FL 32402	850-763-1741	R	18*	.1
233	Flashes Publishers Inc—*John Morgan*	595 Jenner Dr, Allegan MI 49010	269-673-2141	R	18*	.2
234	Jacob North Printing Company Inc—*Charles Calhoun*	PO Box 82406, Lincoln NE 68501	402-470-5335	R	18*	.1
235	National Ticket Co—*Earl Foura*	PO Box 547, Shamokin PA 17872	570-672-2900	R	18*	.1
236	OT Printing Co—*Mary Held*	100 Fornoff Rd, Columbus OH 43207	614-443-4852	R	18*	.1
237	Suncraft Technologies Inc—*Ronald Desanto*	1301 Frontenac Rd, Naperville IL 60563	630-369-7900	R	18*	.1
238	Franklin Communications LLC—*Richard Nettina*	5301 Nw 37th Ave, Miami FL 33142	305-633-9779	R	18*	.1
239	Huston-Patterson Corp—*Thomas Kowa*	PO Box 260, Decatur IL 62525	217-429-5161	R	17*	.1
240	M Lee Smith Publishers LLC—*M Smith*	PO Box 5094, Brentwood TN 37024	615-373-7517	R	17*	.2
241	Fisher Inc—*Martin Fisher*	PO Box 1366, Cedar Rapids IA 52406	319-393-5405	R	17*	.1
242	Southern California Graphics Inc—*Gregory Toomey*	8432 Steller Dr, Culver City CA 90232	310-559-3600	R	17*	.1
243	Robin Enterprises Co—*Bradley Hance*	PO Box 6180, Westerville OH 43086	614-891-0250	R	17*	.1
244	McKay Press Inc—*Kevin Strand* Consolidated Graphics Inc	7600 W Wackerly St, Midland MI 48640	989-631-2360	S	17	.2
245	Mail Handling Inc—*Brian Ostenso*	7550 Corporate Way, Eden Prairie MN 55344	952-975-5000	R	17*	.1
246	Nta Graphics Inc—*Gregory Tremonti*	5225 Telegraph Rd, Toledo OH 43612	419-476-8808	R	17*	.1
247	Bradford and Bigelow Inc—*John Galligan*	3 Perkins Way, Newburyport MA 01950	978-904-3100	R	17*	.1
248	Kayes Inc—*William Marcil*	PO Box 2065, Fargo ND 58107	701-476-2000	R	16*	.1
249	Boutwell Owens and Company Inc—*Ward Mc Laughlin*	251 Authority Dr, Fitchburg MA 01420	978-343-3067	R	16*	.2
250	Chocklett Press Inc—*Robert Chocklett*	2922 Nicholas Ave Ne, Roanoke VA 24012	540-345-1820	R	16*	.1
251	Dynagraf Inc—*William Roche*	5 Dan Rd, Canton MA 02021	781-575-1700	R	16*	.1
252	Great Lakes Integrated Inc—*James Schultz*	4005 Clark Ave, Cleveland OH 44109	216-651-1500	R	16*	.1
253	Dexter Hospitality Inc—*Chris Dale*	PO Box 261, Aurora MO 65605	417-678-2135	R	16*	.2
254	Gazette Printing Company Inc—*Jeffrey Lampson*	PO Box 166, Jefferson OH 44047	440-576-9115	R	16*	.1
255	McQuiddy Printing Co—*David McQuiddy* Nationwide Graphics	711 Spence Ln, Nashville TN 37217	615-366-6565	S	16*	.1
256	Plymouth Printing Company Inc—*Keith Dovel*	PO Box 68, Cranford NJ 07016	908-276-8100	R	16*	.1
257	Canfield and Tack Inc—*Daniel Mahany*	925 Exchange St, Rochester NY 14608	585-235-7710	R	16*	.1
258	Polytype America Corp—*Pieter S Van der Griendt*	10 Industrial Ave, Mahwah NJ 07430	201-995-1000	S	16*	.1
259	Chromatic Incorporated Lithographers—*Mary Sevigny*	127 Concord St, Glendale CA 91203	818-242-5785	R	16*	<.1
260	Valley Sales Corp—*Eric Hofmeister*	PO Box 263, Stevens Point WI 54481	715-344-5175	R	16*	.1
261	Southern Atlantic Label Company Inc—*John Mckernan*	1300 Cavalier Blvd, Chesapeake VA 23323	757-487-2525	S	16*	.1
262	Gls Co—*Gary Garner*	1280 Energy Park Dr, Saint Paul MN 55108	651-644-3000	R	16*	.1
263	Henderson's Printing Inc—*R Henderson*	PO Box 431, Altoona PA 16603	814-944-0855	R	16*	.1
264	AJ Bart Inc—*A Bart*	4130 Lindbergh Dr, Addison TX 75001	972-960-8300	R	16*	.1
265	Cohber Press Inc—*Eric Webber*	PO Box 93100, Rochester NY 14692	585-475-9100	R	16*	.1
266	Indexx Inc—*Jordan Finn*	303 Haywood Rd, Greenville SC 29607	864-234-1024	R	16*	.1
267	B and B Printing Company Inc—*Michael Bland*	521 Research Rd, Richmond VA 23236	804-794-8273	R	15*	.1
268	Southwest Precision Printers Inc—*Tim Tully*	1055 Conrad Sauer Dr, Houston TX 77043	713-777-3333	R	15*	.1
269	Print Direction Inc—*William Stanton*	1600 Indian Brook Way, Norcross GA 30093	770-446-6446	R	15*	.1
270	Burton and Mayer Inc—*Timothy Burton*	W140n9000 Lilly Rd, Menomonee Falls WI 53051	262-781-0770	R	15*	.1
271	Color Ink Inc—*James Meissner*	PO Box 191, Sussex WI 53089	262-246-5000	R	15*	.1
272	Child Evangelism Fellowship Inc—*Reese Kauffman*	PO Box 348, Warrenton MO 63383	636-456-4321	R	15*	.2
273	Delson Properties Ltd—*David Delana*	PO Box 1069, El Reno OK 73036	405-262-5005	R	15*	.1
274	Geo Graphics Inc—*Norvin Hagan*	3450 Browns Mill Rd Se, Atlanta GA 30354	404-768-5805	R	15*	.1
275	Omaha Printing Co—*Steven Hayes*	4700 F St, Omaha NE 68117	402-734-4400	R	15*	.1
276	Ambrose Printing Co—*John Ambrose*	PO Box 280387, Nashville TN 37228	615-256-1151	R	15*	.1
277	Chas P Young Co—*James Hill* Consolidated Graphics Inc	PO Box 2622, Houston TX 77252	713-652-2100	S	15	.1
278	FBProductions Inc—*David Wohl*	9450 Topanga Canyon Bl, Chatsworth CA 91311	818-773-9337	R	15*	.1
279	Daily Printing Inc—*R Jacobson*	2333 Niagara Ln N, Minneapolis MN 55447	763-475-2333	R	15*	.1
280	R L Bryan Co—*Chris Christiansen*	PO Box 368, Columbia SC 29202	803-779-3560	R	15*	.1
281	Superior Lithographics Inc—*Doug Rawson*	3055 Bandini Blvd, Los Angeles CA 90058	323-263-8400	R	15*	.1
282	San Dieguito Printers Inc—*Richard Lapham*	1880 Diamond St, San Marcos CA 92078		R	15*	.1
283	Signature Printing—*Anthony Andrade*	5 Almeida Ave, East Providence RI 02914	401-438-1200	R	15*	.1
284	Cosmos Communications Inc—*Arnold Weiss*	1105 44th Dr, Long Island City NY 11101	718-482-1800	R	15*	.1
285	Knepper Press Corp—*Edward Ford*	2251 Sweeney Dr, Clinton PA 15026	724-899-4200	R	15*	.1
286	Kirkwood Printing Company Inc—*Robert Coppinger*	904 Main St, Wilmington MA 01887	978-658-4200	R	15*	.1
287	Ed Garvey And Co—*Edward Garvey*	7400 N Lehigh Ave, Niles IL 60714	847-647-1900	R	15*	.1
288	Linemark Printing Inc—*Steven Bearden*	501 Prince Georges Blv, Upper Marlboro MD 20774	301-430-0254	R	15*	.1
289	Bibbero Systems Inc—*Michael Buckley*	1300 N Mcdowell Blvd, Petaluma CA 94954	707-778-3131	R	15*	.1

Rank	Company Name—*Executive Officer*	Address, City, State, Zip	Phone	Type	Fin	Empls
290	Butler Color Press Inc—*Vernon Wise*	PO Box 31, Butler PA 16003	724-283-9132	R	15*	.1
291	Ironwood Lithographers Inc—*Rob Nawsel* Consolidated Graphics Inc	455 S 52nd St, Tempe AZ 85281	480-829-7700	S	14	.1
292	Rapit Printing Inc—*Raymond Holloway*	1415 1st Ave Nw, Saint Paul MN 55112	651-633-4600	R	14*	.1
293	Branch-Smith Resources—*Michael Branch*	PO Box 1868, Fort Worth TX 76101	817-882-4110	R	14*	.1
294	Paragon Supply Co—*Jodi Griffiths*	2532 S 3270 W, Salt Lake City UT 84119	801-978-3500	R	14*	.1
295	C-Graphic LLC—*Ann Downey*	4601 S 5th St, Milwaukee WI 53207	414-481-3100	R	14*	.1
296	K and M Printing Company Inc—*Ken Stobart*	1410 N Meacham Rd, Schaumburg IL 60173	847-884-1100	R	14*	.1
297	Moore-Langen Printing Company Inc—*Ivan Brewer*	200 Hulman St, Terre Haute IN 47802	812-234-1585	R	14*	.1
298	Vivid Impact Corp—*Earl Shiring*	PO Box 99098, Louisville KY 40269	502-491-8201	R	14*	.1
299	Harty Press Inc—*George Platt*	PO Box 324, New Haven CT 06513	203-776-8196	R	14*	.1
300	Bowne of Dallas LP—*Thomas J Quinlan*	PO Box 565527, Dallas TX 75356	214-651-1001	S	14*	.1
301	Heeter Printing Company Inc—*Scott Heeter*	441 Technology Dr, Canonsburg PA 15317	724-746-8900	R	14*	.1
302	Visual Systems Inc—*John Burg*	8111 N 87th St, Milwaukee WI 53224	414-464-8333	R	14*	.1
303	American Financial Printing Inc—*William Dewitt*	404 Industrial Blvd Ne, Minneapolis MN 55413	612-643-3487	R	14*	.1
304	Nebraska Printing Inc—*Charles Cuervo*	PO Box 21232, Tampa FL 33622	813-873-7117	R	14*	.1
305	Grand River Printing Inc—*Ann Porster*	8455 Haggerty Rd, Belleville MI 48111	734-394-1400	R	14*	.1
306	Kay Toledo Tag Inc—*Thomas Kay*	PO Box 5038, Toledo OH 43611	419-729-5479	R	14*	.1
307	Ad-Sell Co—*Mark Schocker*	5001 S W Ave, Saint Louis MO 63110	314-773-0500	R	14*	.1
308	Acme Printing Company Inc—*Jerry Miller*	66 Washington Ave, Des Moines IA 50314	515-244-1723	R	14*	.1
309	Midwest Web Inc—*Dean Hart*	4900 Superior St Ste 1, Lincoln NE 68504	402-464-6900	R	14*	.1
310	Forest Corp—*Forest Bookman*	1665 Enterprise Pkwy, Twinsburg OH 44087	330-425-3805	R	14*	.1
311	Ries Graphics Ltd—*Donald Ries*	12727 W Custer Ave, Butler WI 53007	262-781-5720	R	14*	.1
312	Kopy Kween Inc—*Morris Friedman*	42 Broadway Ste 2, New York NY 10004	212-514-6500	R	14*	.2
313	Colornet Printing And Graphics Inc—*Bob Wepasnick*	18630 Woodfield Rd, Gaithersburg MD 20879	301-208-8200	R	14*	.1
314	Blanks Printing and Imaging Inc—*Leron Blanks*	2343 N Beckley Ave, Dallas TX 75208	214-741-3905	R	14*	.1
315	Merrick Printing Company Inc—*M Merrick*	PO Box 1626, Louisville KY 40201	502-584-6258	R	13*	.1
316	Drug Package Inc—*Michael Greco*	901 Drug Package Ln, O Fallon MO 63366	636-272-6261	R	13*	.1
317	Finlay Printing LLC—*Kevin Kalagher*	44 Tobey Rd, Bloomfield CT 06002	860-242-2800	R	13*	.1
318	Raff Printing Inc—*Fred Aheimer*	PO Box 42365, Pittsburgh PA 15203	412-431-4044	R	13*	.1
319	Mail Co—*Brian Dicker*	1700 Broadway St Fl 2, Kansas City MO 64108	816-756-2733	R	13*	.1
320	Lithotone Inc—*Robert Priebe*	1313 W Hively Ave, Elkhart IN 46517	574-294-5521	R	13*	.1
321	Nutis Press Inc—*Ira Nutis*	PO Box 27248, Columbus OH 43227	614-237-8626	R	13*	.2
322	Art Dreams Home Inc—*Donald Koszyk*	2433 Eastman Ave, Ventura CA 93003	805-642-6444	R	13*	.1
323	Warwick Publishing Co—*Robert Paschal*	2601 E Main St, Saint Charles IL 60174	630-584-3871	R	13*	.1
324	Aus-Tex Duplicators Inc—*John Eastty*	PO Box 141157, Austin TX 78714	512-476-7581	R	13*	.1
325	Greystone Graphics Inc—*Eugene Reynolds*	101 Greystone Ave, Kansas City KS 66103	913-342-1393	R	13*	.1
326	Dimension Graphics Inc—*Clifton Pummill*	13915 W 107th St, Shawnee Mission KS 66215	913-469-6800	R	13*	.1
327	Quebecor World Infiniti—*Jacques Mallette*	96 Phoenix Ave, Enfield CT 06082	860-741-0150	S	13*	.1
328	Tristar Web Graphics Inc—*Masaud Baaba*	4010 Airline Dr, Houston TX 77022	713-691-0001	R	13*	.1
329	Martin Printing Company Inc—*E Ragsdale*	PO Box 69, Easley SC 29641	864-859-4032	R	13*	.1
330	Spartan Graphics Inc—*Jim Clay*	PO Box 218, Sparta MI 49345	616-887-8243	R	13*	.1
331	Brodock Press Inc—*Craig Brodock*	502 Court St, Utica NY 13502	315-735-9577	R	13*	.1
332	Copy Craft Printers Inc—*Danny Stockton*	4413 82nd St, Lubbock TX 79424	806-794-7752	R	13*	.1
333	King Lithographers Inc—*Martin Rego*	245 S Fourth Ave, Mount Vernon NY 10550	914-667-4200	R	13*	.1
334	Thames Printing Company Inc—*Neil Blinderman*	1 Wisconsin Ave, Norwich CT 06360	860-887-3541	R	13*	.1
335	George H Dean Co—*Kenneth Michaud*	140 Campanelli Dr Ste, Braintree MA 02184	781-356-4100	R	13*	.1
336	Hammer Press Printers Inc—*Susan Hammer*	PO Box 1029, Millburn NJ 07041	973-334-4500	R	13*	.1
337	Mount Vernon Printing Co—*Russell Price* Consolidated Graphics Inc	3229 Hubbard Rd, Hyattsville MD 20785	301-341-5600	S	13	.1
338	Modern Litho-Print Co—*Jeanie Moore*	PO Box 2170, Jefferson City MO 65102	573-635-6119	R	13*	.1
339	Sun Inc—*Harvey Cook*	320 John C Calhoun Dr, Orangeburg SC 29115	803-536-1786	R	13*	.1
340	O'neil Printing Inc—*Ronald Lahey*	PO Box 685, Phoenix AZ 85001	602-258-7789	R	13*	.1
341	Artcraft Printers Inc—*Hiallary Graff*	241 E Main St, Bozeman MT 59715	406-587-0677	R	13*	<.1
342	Integrity Graphics Inc—*Joseph Valla*	1010 Day Hill Rd, Windsor CT 06095	860-688-5200	R	13*	.1
343	Gergel-Kellem Company Inc—*John Gergel*	4544 Hinckley Industri, Cleveland OH 44109	216-398-2000	R	13*	.1
344	Levon Graphics Corp—*Harry Dickran*	PO Box 9073, Farmingdale NY 11735	631-233-6686	R	13*	.1
345	Web Offset Printing Company Inc—*John Tevlin*	12198 44th St N, Clearwater FL 33762	727-572-7488	R	13*	.1
346	Inco Development Corp—*Richard Abood*	PO Box 237, Mason MI 48854	517-676-5188	R	13*	.1
347	V3 Printing Corp—*David Wilson*	200 N Elevar St, Oxnard CA 93030	805-981-2600	R	13*	.1
348	Chernay Printing Inc—*Edmond Ward*	7483 S Main St, Coopersburg PA 18036	610-282-3774	R	13*	.1
349	Color Craft Graphic Arts Inc—*Thomas Foster*	PO Box 1570, Manitowoc WI 54221	920-684-5571	R	13*	.1
350	Capital Printing Corp—*Nolan Russo*	420 S Ave, Middlesex NJ 08846	732-560-1515	R	13*	.1
351	Hogue Printing Inc—*John Hogue*	159 W 1st Ave, Mesa AZ 85210	480-964-2951	R	13*	.1
352	Colorcraft Of Virginia Inc—*James Mayes*	22645 Sally Ride Dr St, Sterling VA 20164	703-709-2270	R	12*	.1
353	Cockrell Printing Co—*John Cockrell*	PO Box 1568, Fort Worth TX 76101	817-336-0571	R	12*	.1
354	Print Shop—*Rick Garner*	1707 San Jacinto St, Dallas TX 75201	214-969-2436	R	12*	.2
355	Cps Gumpert Inc—*Thomas Ostenso*	1789 Mcguckian St, Annapolis MD 21401	410-280-6633	R	12*	.1
356	Western Lithograph Of Texas—*John Bobbitt* Consolidated Graphics Inc	4335 Directors Row, Houston TX 77092	713-681-2100	S	12	.1
357	Pantagraph Printing And Stationery Co—*Michael Dolan*	217 W Jefferson St, Bloomington IL 61701	309-829-1071	R	12*	.1
358	Foster Printing Service Inc—*Nicholas Griswold*	PO Box 2089, Michigan City IN 46361	219-879-8366	R	12*	.1
359	Molino Co—*Melchor Castano*	8033 Slauson Ave, Montebello CA 90640	323-726-1000	R	12*	.1
360	Casey Printing Inc—*Richard Casey*	PO Box 913, King City CA 93930	831-385-3221	R	12*	.1
361	Jones and Carpenter 2051 Inc—*Jeff Jones*	11601 Caroline Rd, Philadelphia PA 19154	215-969-4600	R	12*	.1
362	Colonial Press International Inc—*Jose Gomez*	3690 NW 50th St, Miami FL 33142	305-633-1581	R	12*	.2
363	Anro Inc—*Angelo Rossi*	931 S Matlack St, West Chester PA 19382	610-687-1200	R	12*	.2
364	Southern Graphic Systems Inc	626 W Main St Ste 500, Louisville KY 40202	502-637-5443	S	12*	.1
365	Delzer Lithograph Co—*Eric Delzer*	PO Box 679, Waukesha WI 53187	262-522-2600	R	12*	.1
366	Gray Printing Co—*Robert A Gray*	PO Box 840, Fostoria OH 44830	419-435-6638	R	12*	.1
367	KB Publishing Inc—*Daniell Kallemeyn*	924 E 162nd St, South Holland IL 60473	708-333-5901	R	12*	.1
368	Mercury Printing Company Inc—*Danny Bailey* Consolidated Graphics Inc	4650 Shelby Air Dr, Memphis TN 38118	901-345-8480	S	12*	.1
369	Southwestern Stationery And Bank Supply Inc—*Robert Allee*	PO Box 18697, Oklahoma City OK 73154	405-525-9411	R	12*	.1
370	Vista Color Corp—*Jesus Serrano*	3401 Nw 36th St, Miami FL 33142	305-635-2000	R	12*	.1
371	Mar Graphics—*Richard Roever*	523 S Meyer Ave, Valmeyer IL 62295	618-935-2111	R	12*	.1
372	Pride Printing LLC—*Bernie Treece*	7501 E Monte Cristo Av, Scottsdale AZ 85260	480-921-3806	R	12*	.1
373	Color West Inc—*Lynn Jensen*	PO Box 10879, Burbank CA 91510	818-840-8881	R	12*	.1
374	Park Printing Inc—*Ralph Koloski*	2801 California St NE, Minneapolis MN 55418	612-789-4333	R	12*	.1
375	AE Litho Offset Printers Inc—*Annette Yellin*	PO Box 9000, Beverly NJ 08010	609-239-0700	R	12*	.1

Note: An asterisk (*) indicates an estimated financial figure. The company type code used is as follows: R = Private, P = Public, S = Private Subsidiary, B = Public Subsidiary, D = Division, J = Joint Venture, I = Investment Fund.

COMPANY RANKINGS BY SALES WITHIN 4-DIGIT SIC

Rank	Company Name—*Executive Officer*	Address, City, State, Zip	Phone	Type	Fin	Empls
376	Tucker-Castleberry Printing Inc—*Wiley Tucker*	3500 Mccall Pl, Atlanta GA 30340	770-454-1580	R	12*	.1
377	Neyenesch Printers Inc—*Carol Bentley*	PO Box 81184, San Diego CA 92138	619-297-2281	R	12*	.1
378	Newman-Burrows Co—*Mike Digle*	1000 Andover Park E, Seattle WA 98144	206-324-5644	R	12*	.1
379	AAA Digital Imaging Inc—*Michael Norris*	PO Box 80710, Atlanta GA 30366	770-451-7861	R	12*	.1
380	House Of Doolittle Ltd—*Ronald Stavoe*	1751 Nicholas Blvd, Elk Grove Village IL 60007	847-228-9591	R	12*	<.1
381	Reinberger Printwerks—*Christopher J Reinberger*	20275 Paseo Del Prado, Walnut CA 91789	909-594-9377	R	12*	<.1
382	Abbey Conception—*Abbot Polan*	PO Box 501, Conception MO 64433	660-944-3100	R	12*	.1
383	Vox Printing Inc—*Laverna Reid*	4000 E Britton Rd, Oklahoma City OK 73131	405-478-7500	R	12*	<.1
384	Envelopes Only Inc—*Deborah Craig*	2000 S Park Ave, Streamwood IL 60107	630-213-2500	R	12*	.1
385	Reindl Printing Inc—*Richard Reindl*	PO Box 317, Merrill WI 54452	715-536-9537	R	12*	.1
386	Hartley Press Inc—*Michael Hartley*	4250 Saint Augustine R, Jacksonville FL 32207	904-398-5141	R	12*	.1
387	Observer Daily and Sunday Newspaper—*Janice Gee*	PO Box 391, Dunkirk NY 14048	716-366-3000	R	12*	.1
388	Patsons Press—*Patricia Dellamano*	970 Stewart Dr, Sunnyvale CA 94085	408-737-8191	R	12*	.1
389	5 Day Business Forms Manufacturing Inc—*Leslie Messick*	PO Box 6269, Anaheim CA 92816	714-632-8674	R	12*	.1
390	Global Soft Digital Solutions Inc—*Christopher Petro*	371 State Rt 17, Mahwah NJ 07430	201-684-0900	R	12*	.1
391	Herald Printing Co—*David Stump*	PO Box 367, New Washington OH 44854	419-492-2133	R	12*	.1
392	Tech Color Graphics Inc—*Richard Garavito*	PO Box 375, Chino CA 91708	909-590-4554	R	12*	.1
393	Prism Color Corp—*Edward Brown*	31 Twosome Dr Ste 1, Moorestown NJ 08057	856-234-7515	R	11*	.1
394	Capital Printing Co—*Danny Stockton*	PO Box 17548, Austin TX 78760	512-442-1415	R	11*	.1
395	Edwards Graphic Arts Inc—*James Edwards*	PO Box 655, Des Moines IA 50303	515-280-9765	R	11*	.1
396	HC Miller Co—*Craig Johnson*	PO Box 10447, Green Bay WI 54307	920-465-3030	R	11*	.1
397	Cardinal Color Group LLC	1270 Ardmore Ave, Itasca IL 60143	630-467-1000	R	11*	.1
398	LC Colormark—*Abgela Hall*	1840 Hutton Dr Ste 208, Carrollton TX 75006	972-243-1919	R	11*	.1
399	West-Camp Press Inc—*Chad Canterbury*	39 Collegeview Rd, Westerville OH 43081	614-882-2378	R	11*	.1
400	Repro-Graphics Inc—*John Schiele*	1900 Arthur Ave, Elk Grove Village IL 60007	847-439-1775	R	11*	.1
401	Huggins Printing Co—*Arthur Gustin*	PO Box 7607, Harrisburg PA 17113	717-561-8182	R	11*	.1
402	Kwik Kopy Printing	12715 Telge Rd, Cypress TX 77429	281-256-4100	R	11*	.1
403	Creative Printing Services Inc—*John Chesney*	1701 Birchwood Ave, Des Plaines IL 60018	847-803-2800	R	11*	.1
404	Meyercord Revenue Inc—*David B Speer*	475 Village Dr, Carol Stream IL 60188	630-682-6200	S	11*	.1
405	Paul S Amidon and Associates Inc—*Paul S Amidon*	1966 Benson Ave, Saint Paul MN 55116	651-690-2401	R	11*	.1
406	Pitney Bowes Management Services Inc—*Greg Porter*	2000 Hamilton St, Philadelphia PA 19130	215-751-9800	S	11*	.1
407	Printery—*Rich Beeson* Consolidated Graphics Inc	2405 S Moorland Rd, New Berlin WI 53151	262-785-4940	S	11*	.1
408	Hederman Brothers LLC—*Hap Hederman*	PO Box 6100, Ridgeland MS 39158	601-853-7300	R	11*	.1
409	Craftsman Printing Inc—*James Glenn*	120 Citation Ct, Birmingham AL 35209	205-942-3939	R	11*	.1
410	Bloomington Offset Process Inc—*Thomas Mercier*	PO Box 278, Bloomington IL 61702	309-662-3395	R	11*	.1
411	Interprint Inc—*James Morten*	12350 Us Hwy 19 N, Clearwater FL 33764	727-531-8957	R	11*	.1
412	Oklahoma Offset Inc—*Robert Lorton*	PO Box 2008, Tulsa OK 74101	918-732-8171	R	11*	.1
413	Dahlstrom Display Inc—*Ross Iazzetto*	2875 S 25th Ave, Broadview IL 60155	708-410-4500	R	11*	.1
414	Springdot Inc—*Josh Deutsch*	2611 Colerain Ave, Cincinnati OH 45214	513-542-4000	R	11*	.1
415	Westamerica Graphics Inc—*Doug Grant*	19682 Descartes, Foothill Ranch CA 92610	949-462-3600	R	11*	.1
416	Fineline Graphics Inc—*Richard Miller*	8081 Zionsville Rd, Indianapolis IN 46268	317-872-4490	R	11*	.1
417	Irwin-Hodson Co—*T J McDonald*	2838 SE 9th Ave, Portland OR 97202	503-231-9990	R	11*	.1
418	Ambassador Press—*Ed Engle*	1400 Washington Ave N, Minneapolis MN 55411	612-521-0123	R	11*	.1
419	Fidlar Printing Co—*Tim Kilfow*	PO Box 3370, Davenport IA 52808	563-386-2311	R	11*	.1
420	Omega Printing Inc—*Louis Finger*	201 William St, Bensenville IL 60106	630-595-6344	R	11*	.1
421	Universal Printing and Publishing—*Bob Moura*	2410 Hwy 54 E, Durham NC 27713	919-361-5809	R	11*	.1
422	Quest Graphics LLC—*Bruce Sparks*	2423 Northline Industr, Maryland Heights MO 63043	314-997-1400	R	11*	.1
423	Cps Printing—*Phillip Lurie*	2304 Faraday Ave, Carlsbad CA 92008	760-438-9411	R	11*	.1
424	Alexanders Print Stop Inc—*Jeff Alexander*	245 S 1060 W, Lindon UT 84042	801-224-8666	R	11*	.1
425	Prime Time Thermographics Inc—*Mike Matchinsky*	1130 W Geneva Dr, Tempe AZ 85282	480-829-8890	R	11*	.1
426	James Mulligan Printing Co—*Jerome Kiske*	1808 Washingtn Ave Ste, Saint Louis MO 63103	314-621-0875	R	11*	.1
427	Meridian Graphics Inc—*David Melin*	2652 Dow Ave, Tustin CA 92780	714-263-7060	R	11*	.1
428	Breese Publishing Company Inc—*Steven Mahlandt*	PO Box 405, Breese IL 62230	618-526-7211	R	11*	.1
429	Stephenson Printing Inc—*George Stephenson*	5731 General Wash Dr, Alexandria VA 22312	703-642-9000	R	11*	.1
430	Buhl Press Inc—*Charles Barkley*	5656 Mcdermott Dr, Berkeley IL 60163	708-449-8989	R	11*	.1
431	Drummond Press Inc—*Diane Falconetti*	PO Box 2421, Jacksonville FL 32203	904-354-2818	R	11*	.1
432	Western Graphics Inc—*Timothy Keran*	530 Wheeler St N, Saint Paul MN 55104	651-603-6400	R	11*	.1
433	McDonald and Eudy Printers Inc—*Michael McDonald*	4509 Beech Rd, Temple Hills MD 20748	301-423-8900	R	11*	.1
434	Morris County Duplicating Corp—*Ernest D'angelo*	1 Lafayette Ave, Morristown NJ 07960	973-993-8484	R	11*	.1
435	Mccormick-Armstrong Company Inc—*Jacob Shaffer*	PO Box 1377, Wichita KS 67201	316-264-1363	R	11*	.1
436	Rpi Color Service Inc—*Ken Rellar*	1950 Radcliff Dr, Cincinnati OH 45204	513-471-4040	R	11*	.1
437	Castle-Pierce Corp—*Michael Castle*	PO Box 2247, Oshkosh WI 54903	920-235-2020	R	11*	.1
438	Pacific West Litho Inc—*Chang Chou*	3291 E Miraloma Ave, Anaheim CA 92806	714-579-0868	R	10*	.1
439	Unique Printers And Lithographers Inc—*John Collins*	5500 W 31st St, Cicero IL 60804	708-656-8900	R	10*	.1
440	Rider Dickerson Inc—*William Barta*	815 25th Ave, Bellwood IL 60104	312-427-2926	R	10*	.1
441	Kng Inc—*Robert Mcdonagh*	2102 E Karcher Rd, Nampa ID 83687	208-318-0188	R	10*	.1
442	Digital Printing Systems Inc—*Donald Nores*	777 N Georgia Ave, Azusa CA 91702	626-334-1244	R	10*	.1
443	Eagle Xm LLC—*Howard Harris*	5105 E 41st Ave, Denver CO 80216	303-320-5411	R	10*	.1
444	Versa-Tags Inc—*Ronald Garden*	PO Box 730, Cuba MO 65453	573-885-2230	R	10*	.1
445	Electronic Data Magnetics Inc—*Richard Hallman*	PO Box 7208, High Point NC 27264	336-882-8115	R	10*	.1
446	One-Write Co—*Norman Boyd*	3750 State Rte 37 E, Lancaster OH 43130	740-654-2128	R	10*	.1
447	C and D Printing Co—*William Serata*	12150 28th St N, Saint Petersburg FL 33716	727-572-9999	R	10*	.1
448	Aldine Inc (New York New York)—*Frank Autuoro*	150 Varick St Fl 6, New York NY 10013	212-226-2870	R	10*	.1
449	K and D Graphics—*Don Chew*	1432 N Main St Ste C, Orange CA 92867	714-639-8900	R	10*	.1
450	Rainbow Graphics Inc—*Jeffrey Koszuta*	933 Tower Rd, Mundelein IL 60060	847-824-9600	R	10*	<.1
451	Wetzel Brothers Inc—*Corey Spencer* Consolidated Graphics Inc	2401 E Edgerton, Cudahy WI 53110	414-271-5444	S	10*	.1
452	Best Press Inc—*Wendy Kalisher*	4201 Airborn Dr, Addison TX 75001	972-930-1000	R	10*	.1
453	Triad Enterprises Inc—*James Kohn*	PO Box 5287, West Columbia SC 29171	803-796-4000	R	10*	.1
454	Di Graphics—*Scott McLean*	PO Box 208, Wheat Ridge CO 80034	303-425-0510	R	10*	.1
455	Global Group Inc—*James Wolf*	4901 N Beach St, Fort Worth TX 76137	817-831-2631	R	10*	.1
456	Mail Print Inc—*Gina Danner*	8300 Ne Underground Dr, Kansas City MO 64161	816-459-8404	R	10*	.1
457	Shelton-Turnbull Printers Inc—*Barry Miller*	PO Box 22008, Eugene OR 97402	541-687-1214	R	10*	.1
458	Colortech Graphics Inc—*Alleyne Kelly*	28700 Hayes Rd, Roseville MI 48066	586-779-7800	R	10*	.1
459	Landmark Print Inc—*Michael Dimitriou*	375 Fairfield Ave Bldg, Stamford CT 06902	203-978-5100	R	10*	.1
460	Offset Impressions Inc—*George Ruth*	122 Mountain View Rd, Reading PA 19607	610-378-1851	R	10*	.1
461	Paragon Forms Inc—*Warren Anderson*	6820 Shingle Creek Pkw, Minneapolis MN 55430	763-560-8044	R	10*	.1
462	Strathmore Co—*Chang Park*	PO Box 391, Geneva IL 60134	630-232-9677	R	10*	<.1
463	Sprint-Denver Inc—*Kent Zwingelberg*	4999 Kingston St, Denver CO 80239	303-371-0566	R	10*	.1

Rank	Company Name—*Executive Officer*	Address, City, State, Zip	Phone	Type	Fin	Empls
464	Bp Solutions Group Inc—*Robert Williams*	PO Box 6250, Asheville NC 28816	828-252-4476	R	10*	.1
465	Quick Tab Ii Inc—*Charles Daughenbaugh*	PO Box 723, Tiffin OH 44883	419-448-6622	R	10*	.1
466	Western Printing Co—*Steve Pfeiffer*	PO Box 1555, Aberdeen SD 57402	605-229-1480	R	10*	.1
467	Tursso Companies Inc—*Bruce Rankin*	223 Plato Blvd E, Saint Paul MN 55107	651-222-8445	R	10*	.1
468	Etheridge Printing Co—*Howard Etheridge*	4434 Mcewen Rd, Dallas TX 75244	214-827-8151	R	10*	.1
469	Phoenix Press Inc—*Anthony Jasaitis*	PO Box 347, New Haven CT 06513	203-865-5555	R	10*	.1
470	Man-Grove Industries Inc—*Bradley Thurman*	1201 N Miller St, Anaheim CA 92806	714-630-3020	R	10*	.1
471	Schiele Graphics Inc—*John Schiele*	1880 Busse Rd, Elk Grove Village IL 60007	847-434-5455	R	10*	.1
472	Blue Island Newspaper Printing Inc—*Gary Rice*	262 W 147th St, Harvey IL 60426	708-333-1006	R	10*	.1
473	Cp Direct Inc—*Matthew Trotta*	4600 Boston Way Ste A, Lanham MD 20706	301-577-3003	R	10*	.1
474	Batson Printing Inc—*William Batson*	195 Michigan St, Benton Harbor MI 49022	269-926-6011	R	10*	.1
475	Elanders Seiz Inc—*William Seiz*	4525 Acworth Industria, Acworth GA 30101	770-917-7000	R	10*	.1
476	Van Lanen Inc—*Larry Van Lanen*	1967 Allouez Ave, Green Bay WI 54311	920-468-5252	R	10*	<.1
477	Walls Printing Company Inc—*Andrew Walls*	915 Greenbag Rd, Morgantown WV 26508	304-292-3368	R	10*	.1
478	Sentinel Printing Company Inc—*Charles Manthey*	PO Box 666, Saint Cloud MN 56302	320-251-6434	R	10*	.1
479	Courier Graphics Corp—*Pam Carritt*	2621 S 37th St, Phoenix AZ 85034	602-437-9700	R	10*	.1
480	Pulaski Publishing Inc—*S Lake*	PO Box 905, Pulaski TN 38478	931-363-3544	R	10*	.1
481	DP Murphy Company Inc—*Timothy Schratwieser*	945 Grand Blvd, Deer Park NY 11729	631-673-9400	R	10*	.1
482	Tru Line Lithographing Inc—*Edward Garvey*	PO Box 565, Sturtevant WI 53177	262-554-7300	R	10*	.1
483	Marshall and Bruce Co—*Robert Smith*	689 Davidson St, Nashville TN 37213	615-256-3661	R	10*	.1
484	Park Printing House Ltd—*Gregory Bass*	550 E Verona Ave, Verona WI 53593	608-845-6505	R	10*	.1
485	Mainline Printing Inc—*John Parker*	3500 Sw Topeka Blvd, Topeka KS 66611	785-233-2338	R	9*	.1
486	Triune Color Inc—*Williams James*	2605 River Rd, Cinnaminson NJ 08077	856-829-5600	R	9*	.1
487	Arcade Printing Co—*Catie Schmidt*	8489 Delport Dr, Saint Louis MO 63114	314-427-4301	R	9*	.1
488	Rt Associates Inc—*Robert Radzis*	3727 N Ventura Dr, Arlington Heights IL 60004	847-577-0700	R	9*	.1
489	K and H Printers-Lithographers Inc—*Jay Ackley*	PO Box 388, Everett WA 98206		R	9*	.1
490	Donald Blyler Offset Inc—*Donald Blyler*	1621 Willow St, Lebanon PA 17042	717-272-5656	R	9*	.1
491	Redmond Bcms Inc—*Georgia Redmond*	495 State Rte 53, Denville NJ 07834	973-664-2000	R	9*	.1
492	Foster Printing Company Inc—*Dennis Blackburn*	700 E Alton Ave, Santa Ana CA 92705	714-731-2000	R	9*	.1
493	Arbor Press LLC—*Douglas Milroy*	4303 Normandy Ct, Royal Oak MI 48073	248-549-0150	R	9*	.1
494	Crossmark Graphics Inc—*Jim Dobrzynski*	16100 W Overland Dr, New Berlin WI 53151	262-821-1343	R	9*	.1
495	Meridian Printing Inc—*Robert Nangle*	1538 S County Trl, East Greenwich RI 02818	401-885-4882	R	9*	.1
496	Southgate Group Inc—*Donald Nab*	PO Box 388, Everett WA 98206	206-248-1700	R	9*	.1
497	Mccourt Label Cabinet Co—*David Ferguson*	20 Egbert Ln, Lewis Run PA 16738	814-362-3851	R	9*	.1
498	Klasek Letter Company Ino *Edward Coe*	2850 S Jefferson Ave, Saint Louis MO 63118	314-664-0023	R	9*	.1
499	Argus Avante Graphic Comunications—*Tim Koenig* Nationwide Graphics	6125 Howard Street, Niles IL 60714	847-647-2020	S	9*	.I
500	Courier Printing Company Inc—*Jeana Chicosky* Consolidated Graphics Inc	1 Courier Pl, Smyrna TN 37167	615-355-4000	S	9*	.1
501	Consolidated Printing Solutions—*Hef Matthews* Consolidated Graphics Inc	2757 S Memorial Dr, Tulsa OK 74129	918-664-6642	S	9*	.1
502	Ejrex Inc—*C Rexwinkle*	1818 Broadway Ave, Parsons KS 67357	620-421-6200	R	9*	.1
503	Keys Printing Co—*Joe Mabry* Consolidated Graphics Inc	1004 Keys Dr, Greenville SC 29615	864-288-6560	S	9*	.1
504	Tucker Printers Inc—*Dan Tucker* Consolidated Graphics Inc	270 Middle Rd, Henrietta NY 14467	585-359-3030	S	9*	.1
505	Rydin Sign and Decal Inc—*Mark Weiler*	700 Phoenix Lake Ave, Streamwood IL 60107	630-483-4321	R	9*	.1
506	Wendling Printing Co—*Hal M Wendling*	PO Box 400, Newport KY 41072	859-261-8300	R	9*	.1
507	John S Swift Company Inc—*Michael Ford*	PO Box 5529, Buffalo Grove IL 60089	847-465-3300	R	9*	.1
508	Precision Litho Service Inc—*John Blair*	4250 118th Ave N, Clearwater FL 33762	727-573-1763	R	9*	.1
509	Standard Press Inc—*Andy Shulman*	1210 Menlo Dr Nw, Atlanta GA 30318	404-351-6780	R	9*	.1
510	Calvert-McBride Printing Co—*William D Calvert*	PO Box 6337, Fort Smith AR 72906	479-646-8311	R	9*	.1
511	Mib Industries Inc—*Isaac Mutzen*	4805 Metro Ave Ste 1, Ridgewood NY 11385	718-497-2200	R	9*	.1
512	General Business Envelope—*Steven Grossman*	PO Box 750, Hartford CT 06142	860-727-9100	R	9*	<.1
513	Imperial Lithographing Corp—*Robert Stormowski*	2487 S Commerce Dr, New Berlin WI 53151	262-439-2800	R	9*	<.1
514	Fricke-Parks Press Inc—*David Brown*	33250 Transit Ave, Union City CA 94587	510-489-6543	R	9*	.1
515	Roark Group Inc—*Sharon Garman*	1600 N 35th St, Rogers AR 72756	479-636-1686	R	9*	.1
516	Interstate Printing Co—*Eugene Peter*	PO Box 3667, Omaha NE 68103	402-341-8028	R	9*	.1
517	Metro Web Corp—*Tristan Vogel*	5901 Tonnelle Ave, North Bergen NJ 07047	201-553-0700	R	9*	.1
518	Richmond Printing LLC	5825 Schumacher Ln, Houston TX 77057	713-952-0800	R	9*	.1
519	Artco Offset Inc—*Arthur Frank*	155 Will Dr, Canton MA 02021	781-830-7900	R	9*	.1
520	Donahue Printing Company Inc—*Thomas Donahue*	5716 W Jefferson Blvd, Los Angeles CA 90016	323-938-4545	R	9*	.1
521	Pocky Inc—*John Sabatino*	PO Box 9062, Freeport NY 11520	516-379-2122	R	9*	.1
522	Redfield and Company Inc—*Thomas Kearney*	1901 Howard St, Omaha NE 68102	402-341-0364	R	9*	.1
523	Emco/Fgs LLC—*Kevin Murphy*	99 E Elm St, Everett MA 02149	617-389-0076	R	9*	.1
524	Pierce Co—*Rick Graalum*	PO Box 2887, Fargo ND 58108	701-235-5586	R	9*	.1
525	Marathon Press Inc—*Rex Alewel*	PO Box 407, Norfolk NE 68702	402-371-5040	R	9*	.1
526	Sauers Group Inc—*Richard Sauers*	1585 Roadhaven Dr, Stone Mountain GA 30083	770-621-8888	R	9*	.1
527	Ussery Printing Company Inc—*Fran Ussery*	PO Box 165446, Irving TX 75016	972-438-8344	R	9*	.1
528	Lettercomm Type Inc—*William Harris*	310 Swann Ave, Alexandria VA 22301	703-683-3105	R	9*	.1
529	Rink Printing Co—*Michael Rink*	814 S Main St, South Bend IN 46601	574-232-7935	R	9*	.1
530	Vision International Inc—*Timothy Fullmer*	3030 Directors Row, Salt Lake City UT 84104	801-973-8929	R	9*	.1
531	Printmailers Inc—*Steve Johns*	707 W Rd, Houston TX 77038	832-201-2000	R	9*	.1
532	Lithotype Company Inc—*Penelope Rich*	333 Point San Bruno Bl, South San Francisco CA 94080	650-871-1750	R	9*	.1
533	De La Rue North America Inc—*Richard Smith*	100 Powers Ct, Dulles VA 20166	703-450-1300	S	9*	.1
534	Brenneman Printing Inc—*Jennifer Brenneman*	PO Box 11147, Lancaster PA 17605	717-299-2847	R	9*	.1
535	Captiva Group Inc—*Tony Fernandez*	3838 Bogan Ave Ne, Albuquerque NM 87109	505-872-2200	R	9*	.1
536	Microforms Inc—*James Safran*	5971 Product Dr, Sterling Heights MI 48312	586-939-7900	R	9*	.1
537	Watkins Lithographic Inc—*Eddy Watkins*	1515 Gentry St, Kansas City MO 64116	816-842-3667	R	9*	.1
538	Cooperative Printing Association—*Dennis Hanson*	1225 N 7th St, Minneapolis MN 55411	612-721-5731	R	9*	<.1
539	Sign Boys LLC	501 E Whitcomb Ave, Madison Heights MI 48071	248-616-9394	R	9*	<.1
540	Maracom Corp—*Gary Peterson*	PO Box 737, Willmar MN 56201	320-235-3300	R	8*	.1
541	Print Tech LLC—*Jackie Yagla*	1154 Rte 22, Mountainside NJ 07092	908-232-2287	R	8*	.1
542	Advertiser Printers Inc—*J Brauch*	320 Clay St, Dayton KY 41074	859-431-4901	R	8*	.1
543	Fox Company Inc—*Michael Fox*	11000 W Becher St, Milwaukee WI 53227	414-321-4700	R	8*	.1
544	Inland Mailing Services Inc—*Phillip Adishian*	160 W Fthill Pkwy Ste, Corona CA 92882	951-371-6245	R	8*	.1
545	Johnson Litho Graphics Of Eau Claire Ltd—*Everett Papke*	2219 Galloway St, Eau Claire WI 54703	715-832-3211	R	8*	.1
546	Kennickell Printing Co—*Alfred Kennickell*	PO Box 3813, Savannah GA 31414	912-233-4532	R	8*	.1
547	C and S Press Inc—*Daniel Ellis*	405 27th St, Orlando FL 32806	407-841-3000	R	8*	.1
548	Hutchison-Allgood Printing Co—*Allie Hutchison*	260 Business Park Dr, Winston Salem NC 27107	336-769-0000	R	8*	.1

Note: An asterisk (*) indicates an estimated financial figure. The company type code used is as follows: R = Private, P = Public, S = Private Subsidiary, B = Public Subsidiary, D = Division, J = Joint Venture, I = Investment Fund.

COMPANY RANKINGS BY SALES WITHIN 4-DIGIT SIC

Rank	Company Name—*Executive Officer*	Address, City, State, Zip	Phone	Type	Fin	Empls
549	Lyndee Press Inc—*Joe Trivelli*	649 Triumph Ct, Orlando FL 32805	407-297-8484	R	8*	.1
550	Printed Specialties Inc—*Karen Smith*	5200 Columbia Dr, Carrollton GA 30117	770-832-1341	R	8*	.1
551	Upper Valley Press Inc—*Charles Harris*	PO Box 459, North Haverhill NH 03774	603-787-7000	R	8*	.1
552	Chicago Envelope Inc—*Robert Ohr*	685 Kimberly Dr, Carol Stream IL 60188	630-668-0400	R	8*	.1
553	Alexander Clark Inc—*Robert Alexander*	10801 W Emerald St, Boise ID 83713	208-322-0611	R	8*	.1
554	Samorlana LLC—*Wayne Check*	3500 Marmenco Ct, Baltimore MD 21230	410-789-5300	R	8*	.1
555	Odyssey Digital Printing Inc—*John Roberds*	5301 S 125th E Ave, Tulsa OK 74146	918-660-0492	R	8*	.1
556	Candid Litho Printing Ltd—*Howard Weinstein*	2511 49th Ave, Long Island City NY 11101	212-431-3800	R	8*	.1
557	Multi-Craft Litho Inc—*Deborah Simpson*	PO Box 72960, Newport KY 41072	859-581-2754	R	8*	<.1
558	Pond-Ekberg Co—*Jonathan Kratovil*	PO Box 1021, Westfield MA 01086	413-594-7511	R	8*	.1
559	Rochelle Printing Company Inc—*Celeste Sax*	600 S 7th St, Rochelle IL 61068	815-562-2128	R	8*	.1
560	Abbott Printing Co—*Arthur Abbott*	110 Atlantic Dr Ste 11, Maitland FL 32751	407-831-2999	R	8*	.1
561	Bell Litho Inc—*Felix Ricci*	370 Crossen Ave, Elk Grove Village IL 60007	847-952-3300	R	8*	.1
562	Garner Printing Co—*Steve Jones* Consolidated Graphics Inc	1697 NE 53rd Ave, Des Moines IA 50313	515-266-2171	S	8*	.1
563	Burrow Family Corp—*Gary Burrow*	PO Box 2683, High Point NC 27261	336-887-3173	R	8*	.1
564	Barnhart Press—*Richard Caulk*	2600 Farnam St, Omaha NE 68131	402-341-1322	R	8*	.1
565	Foster Printing Co (Tustin California)—*Dennis Blackburn*	700 E Alton, Santa Ana CA 92705	714-731-2000	R	8*	.1
566	Daniels Business Services Inc—*James Daniels*	PO Box 40, Asheville NC 28802	828-277-8250	R	8*	.1
567	Sudden Printing Inc—*Cecil Bristol*	PO Box 81066, Seattle WA 98108	206-243-4444	R	8*	.1
568	Wolf Colorprint Inc—*Jack W Meier*	111 Holmes Rd, Newington CT 06111	860-666-1200	R	8*	.1
569	Benchemark Printing Inc—*Robert Kosineski*	PO Box 1031, Schenectady NY 12301	518-393-1361	R	8*	.1
570	Lynx Group Inc—*Richard Faith*	2746 Front St Ne, Salem OR 97301	503-588-9339	R	8*	.1
571	Merit Printing Inc—*Charles Klein*	117 N 2nd St, Minneapolis MN 55401	612-339-8193	R	8*	.1
572	Suniland Press Inc—*Peter Rood*	PO Box 561108, Miami FL 33256	305-235-8811	R	8*	.1
573	General Press Corp—*James V Wolff*	PO Box 316, Natrona Heights PA 15065	724-224-3500	R	8*	.1
574	Professional Image Inc—*Cynthia Calvert*	12437 E 60th St, Tulsa OK 74146	918-461-0609	R	8*	<.1
575	Shawmut Advertising Inc—*Dominick Peluso*	33 Cherry Hill Dr Ste, Danvers MA 01923	978-762-7500	R	8*	<.1
576	4 D Printing Inc—*Douglas N Silsbee*	1007 Irwin Bridge Rd N, Conyers GA 30012	770-929-8717	R	8*	<.1
577	Hudson Printing Incorporated Dba Hudson Digital Printing—*Angie Fairweather*	2780 Loker Ave W, Carlsbad CA 92010	760-602-1260	R	8*	<.1
578	Tewell-Warren Printing Co—*John Bruxoort* Consolidated Graphics Inc	4710 Lipan St, Denver CO 80211	303-458-8505	S	8*	<.1
579	Walnut Circle Press Inc—*Kevin Miller* Consolidated Graphics Inc	PO Box 18187, Greensboro NC 27419	336-855-8070	S	8*	<.1
580	Superior Colour Graphics Inc—*John Brussee* Consolidated Graphics Inc	381 S Pitcher St, Kalamazoo MI 49007	269-381-4830	S	8*	<.1
581	Graphic Forms and Labels Inc—*Paul Curry*	PO Box 468, Nevada IA 50201	515-382-6561	R	8*	.1
582	Vanguard Media LLC—*George Lagary*	PO Box 4560, Ithaca NY 14852	908-851-2222	R	8*	.1
583	Villanti and Sons Printers Inc—*Anthony Villanti*	15 Catamount Dr, Milton VT 05468	802-864-0723	R	8*	.1
584	Wells Printing Company Inc—*Gene Wells*	6030 Perimeter Pkwy, Montgomery AL 36116	334-281-3449	R	8*	.1
585	London Litho Services Inc—*Francis Kurek*	11110 Pepper Rd, Hunt Valley MD 21031	410-527-3701	R	8*	.1
586	Sun Lithographing And Printing Co—*Dave Cook*	2105 W 2300 S, Salt Lake City UT 84119	801-972-6120	R	8*	.1
587	Bassette Printers LLC—*Elizabeth Newman*	PO Box 999, Springfield MA 01101	413-781-7140	R	8*	.1
588	Campbell Printing Company Inc—*Betty Campbell*	2055 Cleveland Hwy, Dalton GA 30721	706-259-3344	R	8*	.1
589	Keyline Corp—*Charles Baker*	750 Canosa Ct, Denver CO 80204	303-893-5165	S	8*	.1
590	Puritan Press Inc—*Kurt Peterson*	95 Runnells Bridge Rd, Hollis NH 03049	603-889-4500	R	8*	.1
591	Today's Graphics Inc—*John Glacken*	4848 Island Ave, Philadelphia PA 19153	215-634-6200	R	8*	.1
592	Printing Images Inc—*Thomas Dolan*	12266 Wilkins Ave Ste, Rockville MD 20852	301-984-1140	R	8*	.1
593	J and M Reproductions Corp—*John Milanowski*	1200 Rochester Rd, Troy MI 48083	248-588-8100	R	8*	<.1
594	Quest Lithographers Ltd—*Dan Cribbin*	2423 Northline Industr, Maryland Heights MO 63043	314-997-1400	R	8*	.1
595	Teagle and Little Inc—*Gregory Jordan*	1048 W 27th St, Norfolk VA 23517	757-622-5793	R	8*	.1
596	Johnston Lithograph Inc—*Keith Johnston*	11334 Hunt St, Romulus MI 48174	734-941-3510	R	8*	.1
597	Roberts Quality Printing Inc—*Robert Davis*	2049 Calumet St, Clearwater FL 33765	727-442-4011	R	8*	.1
598	North Star Publishing LLC—*Sally Coates*	111 Nw 122nd St, Oklahoma City OK 73114	405-775-2400	R	8*	.1
599	Goes Lithographing Company Inc—*Charles Goes*	42 W 61st St, Chicago IL 60621		R	8*	.1
600	Graphic Partners Inc—*Arthur Larsen*	4300 Rte 173, Zion IL 60099	847-872-9445	R	8*	.1
601	Reed-Hann Litho Co—*Howard Morehart*	200 High Pines Rd, Williamsport PA 17701	570-326-6567	R	8*	.1
602	Precision Litho—*Stephen Gleason*	2305 S 1070 W, Salt Lake City UT 84119	801-908-3200	R	8*	.1
603	Journal-Chronicle Co—*Sabra Otteson*	PO Box 347, Owatonna MN 55060	507-446-5300	R	8*	.1
604	Cincinnati Color Press Inc—*Douglas Aleshire*	10601 Medallion Dr, Cincinnati OH 45241	513-769-5577	R	8*	.1
605	Southern Arizona Graphic Associates Inc—*John Davis*	383 N Commerce Park Lo, Tucson AZ 85745	520-622-7667	R	8*	.1
606	Superior Printers Inc—*C Sengel*	1884 W Fairbanks Ave, Winter Park FL 32789	407-644-3344	R	8*	.1
607	Midamerican Printing Systems Inc—*Gerald Freund*	400 S Jefferson St Ste, Chicago IL 60607	312-663-4720	R	8*	.1
608	Reidler Decal Corp—*Edward Reidler*	PO Box 8, Saint Clair PA 17970	570-429-1812	R	8*	.1
609	Sterling C Sommer Inc—*James Evans*	PO Box 217, Tonawanda NY 14151	716-694-3377	R	8*	.1
610	Woolverton Printing Co—*John Lynch*	PO Box 456, Cedar Falls IA 50613	319-277-2616	R	8*	<.1
611	Kansas Bank Note Company Inc—*William Falstad*	PO Box 360, Fredonia KS 66736	620-378-2146	R	7*	.1
612	James Printing Inc—*Evan James*	1340 Taney St, Kansas City MO 64116	816-561-6211	R	7*	.1
613	Badger Press Inc—*Frank Brown*	PO Box 610, Fort Atkinson WI 53538	920-563-5144	R	7*	.1
614	Martin Lithograph Inc—*Martin Saavedra*	PO Box 4240, Tampa FL 33677	813-254-1553	R	7*	.1
615	Atlantic Graphic Services Inc—*Ariel Schmidt*	PO Box 768, Clinton MA 01510	978-368-1262	R	7*	.1
616	Doyle Printing And Offset Company Inc—*Cecil Kuever*	5206 46th Ave, Hyattsville MD 20781	301-322-4800	R	7*	.1
617	Gohrs Printing Service Inc—*David Chrzanowski*	1107 Hess Ave, Erie PA 16503	814-455-0629	R	7*	.1
618	Toledo Ticket Co—*Roy Carter*	PO Box 6876, Toledo OH 43612	419-476-5424	R	7*	.1
619	Mercantile Printing—*Henry Michie*	70 Hartwell St, West Boylston MA 01583	508-835-1500	R	7*	.1
620	Cnp Solutions Inc—*Gary Sneed*	8948 Western Way Ste 1, Jacksonville FL 32256	904-363-0009	S	7*	.1
621	Gray Graphics Corp—*Saber Helal*	8607 Central Ave, Capitol Heights MD 20743	301-808-1000	R	7*	.1
622	Newsweb Corp—*Fred Eychaner*	1645 W Fullerton Ave, Chicago IL 60614	773-975-0400	R	7*	.1
623	Bruce Printing Inc—*Mike Robertson*	315 27th Ave Se, Minneapolis MN 55414	612-331-3373	R	7*	.1
624	Repco Printers and Lithographers Inc—*Fred Zaegel*	8405 St Charles Rock R, Saint Louis MO 63114	314-426-1800	R	7*	.1
625	Typecraft Press Inc—*Edward Major*	PO Box 4295, Pittsburgh PA 15203	412-488-1600	R	7*	<.1
626	In-Print Graphics Inc—*Joseph Racine*	4201 166th St, Oak Forest IL 60452	708-396-1010	R	7*	<.1
627	Ceprint Solutions Inc—*Tony Townsend*	PO Box 1229, Lexington NC 27293	336-956-6327	R	7*	.1
628	Harvey Press Inc—*Ken Allen*	246 Harbor Cir, New Orleans LA 70126	504-246-8974	R	7	.1
629	Tuttle Law Print Inc—*Joanne Cillo*	PO Box 110, Rutland VT 05702	802-773-9171	R	7*	.1
630	Harvard Printing Group—*Richard Bitetti*	175 Rte 46 W, Fairfield NJ 07004	973-672-0800	R	7*	.1
631	Graphic Research Unlimited Inc—*Richard Brach*	32 S Ave, Fanwood NJ 07023	908-322-2225	R	7*	.1
632	Graytor Printing Company Inc—*Stephen Toron*	PO Box 187, Lyndhurst NJ 07071	201-933-0100	R	7*	.1
633	Hc Holdings Inc—*Hugh Carter*	6215 Purdue Dr Sw, Atlanta GA 30336	404-344-2665	R	7*	.1

Rank	Company Name—Executive Officer	Address, City, State, Zip	Phone	Type	Fin	Empls
634	Mcclafferty Printing Co—Marybeth Mcclafferty	1600 N Scott St, Wilmington DE 19806	302-652-8112	R	7*	.1
635	Print Source Inc—Michael Stevenson	9040 Sw Burnham St, Tigard OR 97223	503-639-9835	R	7*	.1
636	Media Northstar Inc—Eugene Johnson	930 Cleveland St S, Cambridge MN 55008	763-689-1181	R	7*	.1
637	Good Printers Inc—Michal Fornadal	213 Dry River Rd, Bridgewater VA 22812	540-828-4663	R	7*	.1
638	Circle Press Inc—Richard Springer	121 Varick St Fl 8, New York NY 10013	212-924-4277	R	7*	.1
639	District Creative Printing Inc—Stephanie Daly	6350 Fallard Dr, Upper Marlboro MD 20772	301-868-8610	R	7*	.1
640	Skinner and Kennedy Co—Charles Pecher	9451 Natural Bridge Rd, Saint Louis MO 63134	314-426-2800	R	7*	.1
641	Liberty Lithographers Inc—Angela Hipelius	18625 W Creek Dr, Tinley Park IL 60477	708-633-7450	R	7*	<.1
642	R W Patterson Printing Co—Leroy Patterson	1550 Territorial Rd, Benton Harbor MI 49022	269-925-2177	R	7*	.1
643	Allegra Network—Carl Gerhardt	21680 Haggerty Rd, Northville MI 48167	248-596-8600	R	7*	.1
644	Zenger Group Inc—Stephen Zenger	525 Hertel Ave, Buffalo NY 14207	716-871-1058	R	7*	.1
645	Ennis Willie—Ennis Willie	6364 Warren Dr, Norcross GA 30093	770-449-7744	R	7*	.1
646	Michigan Web Press Inc—Rick Burrough	10450 Enterprise Dr, Davisburg MI 48350	248-620-2990	R	7*	.1
647	Swift Print Communication Services LLC—John Seibel	PO Box 28252, Saint Louis MO 63132	314-991-4300	R	7*	.1
648	Challenge Graphics Services Inc—Anthony Brancato	22 Connor Ln, Deer Park NY 11729	631-586-0171	R	7*	.1
649	Cyu Lithographics Inc—Wane Ru	13363 Molette St, Santa Fe Springs CA 90670	562-921-8111	R	7*	.1
650	Horizon Graphics—Mike Spann	2111 Grand Ave Pkwy, Austin TX 78728	512-989-0006	R	7*	.1
651	KB Offset Printing Inc—Raymond Caravan	3500 E College Ave Ste, State College PA 16801	814-238-8445	R	7*	.1
652	Oakland Printing Services Inc—Charles Rhmal	1754 Maplelawn Dr, Troy MI 48084	248-649-9000	R	7*	.1
653	Pacemaker Press Pp and S Inc—Matthew Whitney	6797 Bowmans Xing, Frederick MD 21703	301-696-9629	R	7*	.1
654	Bennett Brothers Printing Company Inc—David Bennett	125 Royal Woods Ct Ste, Tucker GA 30084	770-723-1192	R	7*	<.1
655	Paris Printing—John Rogers	1003 Canal Blvd, Richmond CA 94804	510-439-3100	R	7*	<.1
656	Toms Enterprises Inc—Tom Stanley	1200 Chase Ave, Elk Grove Village IL 60007	847-439-7834	R	7*	<.1
657	Con-Wald Corp—Michael George	PO Box 4592, Philadelphia PA 19131	215-879-1400	R	7*	<.1
658	Wallace Carlson Co—Ann Turbeville	10825 Greenbrier Rd, Minnetonka MN 55305	952-545-1645	R	7*	<.1
659	Nova Blue Inc (Chantilly Virginia)—Richard Bartlett	14119 Mariah Ct, Chantilly VA 20151	703-631-6700	R	7*	<.1
660	Press Media Corp—Darren Wooden	1601 W 820 N, Provo UT 84601	801-373-6996	R	7*	<.1
661	Garrison Printing Co—Jake Garrison	7155 Airport Hwy, Pennsauken NJ 08109	856-488-1900	R	7*	<.1
662	Merten Co	1515 Central Pkwy, Cincinnati OH 45214	513-721-5167	D	7*	<.1
663	Ryan Peters LLC	25448 Primehook Rd 400, Milton DE 19968	302-360-8072	R	7*	<.1
664	Shorett Printing Inc—Charles Shorett	PO Box 6560, San Bernardino CA 92412	909-888-7531	R	7*	.1
665	Graphic Communications Corp—Hoyt Tuggle	394 N Clayton St, Lawrenceville GA 30046	770-963-1871	R	7*	.1
666	Igi Printing Company Inc—David Wolk	PO Box 687, Foxcroft Square PA 19046	215-887-5700	R	7*	.1
667	Telepress Inc—Daren Loken	19241 62nd Ave S, Kent WA 98032	425-392-1660	R	7*	.1
668	Wayne Printing Co—Scott Hoerr	PO Box 125, Edwards IL 61528	309-691-2496	R	7*	.1
669	Zimmermann Printing Co—David Zimmermann	PO Box 931, Sheboygan WI 53082	920-457-5021	R	7*	.1
670	Lithographic Industries Inc—Louis Ebert	2445 Gardner Rd, Broadview IL 60155	708-865-1018	R	7*	<.1
671	Mac Donald and Evans Inc—Francesco Piazza	1 Rex Dr, Braintree MA 02184	781-848-9090	R	7*	.1
672	Tempo Graphics Inc—Peter Vouros	455 E N Ave, Carol Stream IL 60188	630-462-8200	R	7*	.1
673	Penmor Lithographers Inc—Paul Fillion	PO Box 2003, Lewiston ME 04241	207-784-1341	R	7*	.1
674	T K O Distributors Inc—Lillian Roberts	2921 Ctr Port Cir, Pompano Beach FL 33064	954-485-9880	R	7*	.1
675	Lake Lithograph Co—Howard Lake	10371 Central Park Dr, Manassas VA 20110	703-361-8030	R	7*	.1
676	O'dell Printing Company Inc—William O'dell	5460 State Farm Dr Ste, Rohnert Park CA 94928	707-585-2718	R	7*	<.1
677	Corley Printing Company LLC—Thomas Hanewinkel	3777 Rider Trl S, Earth City MO 63045	314-739-3777	R	7*	<.1
678	Waveline Direct LLC—Josh Massie	192 Hempt Rd, Mechanicsburg PA 17050	717-795-8830	R	7*	.1
679	American Brochure and Catalogue Company Inc—James Notte	880 Louis Dr, Warminster PA 18974	215-259-1600	R	7*	<.1
680	Goodwill Printing Co—Marvin Fishman	PO Box 21820, Detroit MI 48221	248-547-7500	R	7*	<.1
681	Simon Printing Co—Bernard Simon	10810 Craighead Dr, Houston TX 77025	713-666-1296	R	7*	<.1
682	Watkins Printing Co—Tammy Green	1401 E 17th Ave, Columbus OH 43211	614-297-8270	R	7*	<.1
683	Allen Stromberg And Co—G Kruchko	18504 W Creek Dr, Tinley Park IL 60477	773-847-7131	R	7*	<.1
684	Hpc Integrated Graphic Solutions LLC—Rick Deens	1034 Home Ave, Akron OH 44310	330-535-1566	R	7*	<.1
685	GraphTec Inc—Russ Hewitt　Consolidated Graphics Inc	8620 Old Dorsey Rd, Jessup MD 20794	301-317-0100	S	7	.1
686	Bpi Media Group Inc—Alan Davis	PO Box 600, Boaz AL 35957	256-593-2048	R	7*	.1
687	Shared Mail Aquisitions LLC—Keith Bartlett	72 Industrial Cir, Lancaster PA 17601	717-656-9865	R	7*	.1
688	Activities Press Inc—Ted Bullard	7181 Industrial Park B, Mentor OH 44060	440-953-1200	R	7*	.1
689	Press Printing Enterprises Inc—Larry Luettich	PO Box 220, Fort Myers FL 33902	239-334-1238	R	7*	.1
690	Ross Printing Inc—Erwin Ross	550 E 76th Ave, Denver CO 80229	303-287-3217	R	7*	.1
691	Genoa Business Forms Inc—David Paulson	PO Box 450, Sycamore IL 60178	815-895-2800	R	7*	<.1
692	Service Litho-Print Inc—Steven Elbing	PO Box 875, Oshkosh WI 54903	920-231-3060	R	7*	<.1
693	Universal Lithographers Inc—Donald Zastrow	PO Box 181, Sheboygan WI 53082	920-452-3401	R	7*	<.1
694	Valenti Brothers Graphics Ltd—Debi Halcro	PO Box 3026, Honolulu HI 96802	808-591-2166	R	7*	<.1
695	Chippewa Graphics Inc—Randy Blackorbay	8801 Bass Lake Rd, Minneapolis MN 55428	763-536-9889	R	7*	<.1
696	Custom Printers Inc—Dan Goris	2801 Oak Industrial Dr, Grand Rapids MI 49505	616-454-9224	R	7*	<.1
697	Data Management Inc—Daniel Hincks	PO Box 789, Farmington CT 06034	860-677-8586	R	7*	<.1
698	Pollard Group Inc—Robin Pollard	4824 S Tacoma Way, Tacoma WA 98409	253-473-7755	R	7*	<.1
699	Oliver Printing Company Inc—George Oliver	1760 Enterprise Pkwy, Twinsburg OH 44087	330-425-7890	R	7*	<.1
700	Kopco Inc—Kenneth George	PO Box 69, Caney KS 67333	620-879-2117	R	7*	.1
701	Thunder Projects Inc—Neil Rose	1 N Loder Ave, Endicott NY 13760	607-754-0020	R	7*	<.1
702	New Horizon Graphics Inc—Tony Guida	1200 Prime Pl, Hauppauge NY 11788	631-231-8055	R	7*	<.1
703	Mat-Co Business Forms Inc—Frank Matter	PO Box 100844, Nashville TN 37224	615-244-4404	R	7*	<.1
704	Janon Printing Corp—Alexander Jannone	4893 Mcgrath St, Ventura CA 93003	805-644-9212	R	7*	<.1
705	Kanet Pol Bridges Inc—Charley Lindemann	7107 Shona Dr, Cincinnati OH 45237	513-681-1450	R	7*	<.1
706	Multiscope Inc—Michael McCay	187 36th St, Pittsburgh PA 15201	412-456-1050	R	7*	<.1
707	Neoprint Inc—Thomas Bellomo	11 Alpha Rd, Chelmsford MA 01824	978-256-9939	R	7*	<.1
708	Graphic Arts Inc—Barbara Koontz	4100 Chestnut St, Philadelphia PA 19104	215-382-5500	R	7*	<.1
709	Nemi Publishing Inc—Gregory Nemi	PO Box 568, Farmington ME 04938	207-778-4801	R	6*	.1
710	Jones Printing Service Inc—Harry Jones	PO Box 1786, Chesapeake VA 23327	757-436-3331	R	6*	.1
711	Pacific Printing and Fulfillment Inc—Vince Lepera	11385 Sunrise Park Dr, Rancho Cordova CA 95742	916-638-2900	R	6*	.1
712	Color World Of Montana Inc—Jeff Burgard	PO Box 1088, Bozeman MT 59771	406-587-4508	R	6*	.1
713	P and P Press Inc—Bill Starks	6513 N Galena Rd, Peoria IL 61614	309-691-8511	R	6*	.1
714	Citizen Printing Co—David Shafer	1309 Webster Ave, Fort Collins CO 80524	970-482-2537	R	6*	<.1
715	Blue Ocean Press Inc—Tom Mounce	6299 Nw 27th Way, Fort Lauderdale FL 33309	954-973-1819	R	6*	<.1
716	City Press Inc—Richard Lau	W238n1650 Rockwood Dr, Waukesha WI 53188	262-523-3000	R	6*	<.1
717	Ram Printing Inc—Walter Zaremba	PO Box 900, East Hampstead NH 03826	603-382-7045	R	6*	<.1
718	Regal Printing Co—D Brown	10123 L St, Omaha NE 68127	402-339-9797	R	6*	<.1
719	Dellas Graphics Inc—Thomas Dellas	835 Canal St, Syracuse NY 13210	315-474-4641	R	6*	<.1
720	Envelopes and Forms Inc—Christopher Deedy	2505 Meadowbrook Pkwy, Duluth GA 30096	770-449-1755	R	6*	<.1
721	James W Smith Printing Co—Matthew Smith	1573 Saint Paul Ave, Gurnee IL 60031	847-244-6486	R	6*	<.1
722	Journeyman Press Inc—Steve Silverstein	PO Box 914, Newburyport MA 01950	978-465-8950	R	6*	<.1

Note: An asterisk (*) indicates an estimated financial figure. The company type code used is as follows: R = Private, P = Public, S = Private Subsidiary, B = Public Subsidiary, D = Division, J = Joint Venture, I = Investment Fund.

COMPANY RANKINGS BY SALES WITHIN 4-DIGIT SIC

Rank	Company Name—*Executive Officer*	Address, City, State, Zip	Phone	Type	Fin	Empls
723	Professional Duplicating Inc—*Thomas Gregory*	33 E State St, Media PA 19063	610-891-7979	R	6*	<.1
724	Haig Press Inc—*James Kalousdian*	690 Old Willets Path, Hauppauge NY 11788	631-582-5800	R	6*	<.1
725	Starline Printing Inc—*William Lang*	PO Box 1045, Albuquerque NM 87103	505-345-8900	R	6*	.1
726	Alliance Printing LP—*Jeff Birmingham*	5225 Hollister St, Houston TX 77040	713-688-2688	R	6*	.1
727	Central Printing Corp—*Michael Skelton*	PO Box 568, Delavan WI 53115	262-728-4231	R	6*	.1
728	Pm Graphics Inc—*Paul Mc Ghee*	10170 Philipp Pkwy, Streetsboro OH 44241	330-656-1230	R	6*	.1
729	Professional Printing Center Inc—*Norman Ward*	817 Yupo Ct, Chesapeake VA 23320	757-547-1990	R	6*	.1
730	Brian Paul Inc—*David Ebel*	3933 N Ventura Dr, Arlington Heights IL 60004	847-398-8677	R	6*	<.1
731	Baker Printing Company Inc—*John Bishop*	PO Box 450, Baker LA 70704	225-775-0137	R	6*	<.1
732	Triangle Printers Inc—*Harvey Saltzman*	3737 Chase Ave, Skokie IL 60076	847-675-3700	R	6*	<.1
733	Boomer's Inc—*Harold Klein*	PO Box 80697, Lincoln NE 68501	402-434-8500	R	6*	<.1
734	Metropolitan Graphic Arts Inc—*Joseph Szymanski*	930 Turret Ct, Mundelein IL 60060	847-566-9502	R	6*	<.1
735	Pollock Printing Inc—*Ronnie Pollock*	928 6th Ave S, Nashville TN 37203	615-255-0526	R	6*	<.1
736	Monahan Brothers Inc—*Thomas Monahan*	4100 Howard Ave, New Orleans LA 70125	504-524-8248	R	6*	.1
737	Northeast Printing and Distribution Company Inc—*Herb Carpenter*	12 Nepco Way, Plattsburgh NY 12903	518-563-8214	R	6*	.1
738	Thp Graphics Group Inc—*Jefferson Riley*	PO Box 81166, Conyers GA 30013	770-483-5973	R	6*	.1
739	Prestige Color Inc—*James Dommel*	19 Prestige Ln, Lancaster PA 17603	717-392-1711	R	6*	<.1
740	Brandt Enterprises Inc—*Marc Brandt*	PO Box 2673, Davenport IA 52809	563-386-9740	R	6*	<.1
741	Meeks Lithographing Co—*Jerry Crockett*	6749 E 12th St, Tulsa OK 74112	918-836-0900	R	6*	<.1
742	Marange Printing Company Inc—*Mario Autiero*	195 Cortlandt St, Belleville NJ 07109	973-751-3600	R	6*	<.1
743	Gordon Bernard Company LLC—*Jerry Kline*	22 Whitney Dr, Milford OH 45150	513-248-7600	R	6*	.1
744	Garrity Printing LLC—*Bernie Galligan*	109 Research Dr, Harahan LA 70123	504-733-9654	R	6*	<.1
745	Compucolor Associates Inc—*Thomas Weitzmann*	2200 Marcus Ave Ste C, New Hyde Park NY 11042	516-358-0000	R	6*	<.1
746	Graphic Design Inc—*James Kranz*	PO Box 307, Hastings MN 55033	651-437-6459	R	6*	<.1
747	Silver State Merchandisers—*William Wortman*	3721 Meade Ave, Las Vegas NV 89102	702-367-2544	R	6*	<.1
748	Brenholb Inc—*Eugene Brenner*	1234 Triplett St, San Antonio TX 78216	210-349-4024	R	6*	<.1
749	Piedmont Graphics Inc—*George Dyke*	1007 Industrial Park D, Marietta GA 30062	770-425-1222	R	6*	<.1
750	Pomco LLC—*Denise Benay*	4411 Whitaker Ave, Philadelphia PA 19120	215-455-9500	R	6*	<.1
751	Donihe Graphics Inc—*Sam Stiltner*	766 Brookside Dr, Kingsport TN 37660	423-246-2800	D	6*	.1
752	Bacchus Press Inc—*Monsoor Assadi*	1287 66th St, Emeryville CA 94608	510-420-5800	R	6*	.1
753	Bridgetown Printing Co—*Margo Yohner* Consolidated Graphics Inc	5300 N Channel Ave, Portland OR 97217	503-863-5300	S	6*	.1
754	Caskey Printing Inc—*Gregory Caskey*	850 Vogelsong Rd, York PA 17404	717-764-4500	R	6*	.1
755	century Marketing Solutions—*Dianne Acree*	PO Box 4032, Monroe LA 71201	318-387-4621	S	6*	.1
756	Golf Associates Advertising Company Inc—*Edward Pinkston*	PO Box 6917, Asheville NC 28816	828-252-9867	R	6*	.1
757	Lester Lithograph Inc—*Robert Miller*	1128 N Gilbert St, Anaheim CA 92801	714-491-3981	R	6*	.1
758	Tristar Graphics Group Inc—*Robert Devinney*	2830 Breard St, Monroe LA 71201	318-387-1725	R	6*	.1
759	Woodridge Press Inc—*Tom Sheffield* Consolidated Graphics Inc	3070 E Ceena Ct, Anaheim CA 92806	714-632-7690	S	6*	.1
760	Franzon Graphics-Ohio LLC—*Beverly Baker*	PO Box 715, Sheboygan WI 53082	216-361-4860	S	6*	<.1
761	Quality Assured Enterprises Inc—*Robert Westmeyer*	1600 5th St, Hopkins MN 55343		R	6*	<.1
762	Precision Printing Group Inc—*Joseph Cartafalsn*	117 Jackson Rd, Berlin NJ 08009	856-753-0900	R	6*	<.1
763	Champ Printing Company Inc—*Robert Champ*	730 4th Ave, Coraopolis PA 15108	412-269-0197	R	6*	<.1
764	Yorke Printe Shoppe Inc—*Philip Scull*	930 N Lombard Rd, Lombard IL 60148	630-627-4960	R	6*	<.1
765	Aspen Press Company LC	9423 S 670 W, Sandy UT 84070	801-748-2522	R	6*	<.1
766	Jms Graphics Inc—*James Stiles*	199 Park Rd Ext Ste B, Middlebury CT 06762	203-598-7555	R	6*	<.1
767	Palmer Printing Inc—*Edmund Rossini*	739 S Clark St Fl 1, Chicago IL 60605	312-427-7150	R	6*	<.1
768	Sunkist Graphics Inc—*Steven Black*	401 E Sunset Rd, Henderson NV 89011	702-566-9008	R	6*	<.1
769	American Infrastructure—*Robert Hellman*	950 Tower Ln Ste 800, Foster City CA 94404	650-854-6000	R	6*	<.1
770	Ross Printing Co—*Alan Ross*	PO Box 3267, Spokane WA 99220	509-534-0655	R	6*	<.1
771	Williams and Heintz Map Corp—*Holly Budd*	8119 Central Ave, Capitol Heights MD 20743	301-336-1144	R	6*	<.1
772	George Coriaty—*George Coriaty*	7240 Greenleaf Ave, Whittier CA 90602	562-698-7513	R	6*	<.1
773	Commerce Printing Co—*Steve Commerce*	8560 Cottonwood St NW, Coon Rapids MN 55433	612-332-2381	R	6*	<.1
774	Modern Printing Co—*Wayne Bress*	PO Box 1125, Laramie WY 82073	307-745-7344	R	6*	<.1
775	Summit Press Inc (Fort Worth Texas)—*Bill Guess*	2825 Bledsoe St, Fort Worth TX 76107	817-334-0521	R	6*	<.1
776	World Trade Printing Co	12082 Western Ave, Garden Grove CA 92841	714-903-2500	R	6*	<.1
777	Pittcraft Printing Inc—*Tim Collar*	PO Box 718, Pittsburg KS 66762	620-231-6200	R	6*	<.1
778	TBF Graphics—*Greg Turner*	803 S Washington Ave, Saginaw MI 48601	989-752-5540	R	6*	<.1
779	Ram Publications Inc—*Theresa Loisita*	2525 Michigan Ave Bldg, Santa Monica CA 90404	310-453-0043	R	6*	<.1
780	Audubon Media Corp—*Keith Glade*	PO Box 268, Audubon IA 50025	712-563-2661	R	6*	.1
781	C and J Forms and Label Inc—*J Calvert*	PO Box 2647, Fort Smith AR 72902	479-646-8716	R	6*	<.1
782	Industrial Printers Of California—*Darcy Hall*	PO Box 504, Santa Ana CA 92702	714-545-8484	R	6*	<.1
783	Print Tech Of Western Pennsylvania—*Robert Weingard*	250 Alpha Dr, Pittsburgh PA 15238	412-364-0114	R	6*	<.1
784	Jaco-Bryant Printers Inc—*Sam Lencke*	PO Box 751592, Memphis TN 38175	901-546-9600	R	6*	<.1
785	Cross Media Inc—*Michael Tobias*	PO Box 2509, Addison TX 75001	214-367-3600	R	6*	<.1
786	Sfc Graphics Cleveland Ltd—*Thomas Clark*	PO Box 877, Toledo OH 43697	419-255-1283	R	6*	<.1
787	Itek Graphics LLC—*John Rawlins*	2200 Intrstate N Dr St, Charlotte NC 28206	704-357-6002	R	6*	.1
788	Central Ohio Graphics Inc—*Suzanne Hilleary*	1020 W 5th Ave, Columbus OH 43212	614-294-3200	R	6*	<.1
789	Cereus Graphics Inc—*Tom Ginter*	2950 E Broadway Rd Ste, Phoenix AZ 85040	602-445-0680	R	6*	<.1
790	Capitol City Press Inc—*Michael Eisenmann*	2975 37th Ave Sw, Tumwater WA 98512	360-943-3556	R	6*	<.1
791	Chicago Press Corp—*Mitchell Harrison*	1112 N Homan Ave, Chicago IL 60651	773-276-1500	R	6*	<.1
792	Factors Etc Inc—*Harry Geissler*	1218 Pulaski Hwy Ste 4, Bear DE 19701	302-834-1625	R	6*	.1
793	Columbus Marble Works Inc—*Key Blair*	PO Box 791, Columbus MS 39703	662-328-1477	R	6*	.1
794	Goodwin Graphics Inc—*Timothy Goodwin*	PO Box 110917, Carrollton TX 75011	972-446-7313	R	6*	<.1
795	Millbrook Printing Co—*Larry Winkler*	3540 Jefferson Hwy, Grand Ledge MI 48837	517-627-4078	R	6*	<.1
796	Graphic Developments Inc—*George Davis*	PO Box 1415, Hanover MA 02339	781-878-2222	R	6*	<.1
797	Niknejad Inc—*Kamran Niknejad*	2216 Federal Ave, Los Angeles CA 90064	310-477-0407	R	6*	<.1
798	GSG LLC—*Paul Ferron*	177 Vallecitos De Oro, San Marcos CA 92069	760-752-9500	R	6*	<.1
799	Dynacolor Graphics Inc—*Donald Duncanson*	PO Box 699037, Miami FL 33269	305-625-5388	R	6*	<.1
800	Service Printers Of Duluth Inc—*Timothy Walsh*	127 E 2nd St, Duluth MN 55805	218-727-1513	R	6*	<.1
801	F J Remey Company Inc—*Richard Haas*	121 Willis Ave, Mineola NY 11501	516-741-5112	R	6*	<.1
802	Reed and Witting Co—*Edward Cyphers*	2900 Sassafras Way, Pittsburgh PA 15201	412-682-1000	R	6*	<.1
803	Printing Resource Inc—*Craig Brady*	125 S 1200 W, Lindon UT 84042	801-796-7200	R	6*	<.1
804	Fey Publishing Co—*Scott Gasch*	PO Box 8051, Wisconsin Rapids WI 54495	715-423-2400	R	6*	.1
805	Winona Printing Co—*Will Stoltman*	PO Box 31, Winona MN 55987	507-454-5743	R	6*	<.1
806	Castle Industries LLC—*Robert Chambers*	304 Arcadia Dr, Greenville SC 29609	864-233-0318	R	6*	<.1
807	Arkansas Graphics Inc—*Kenneth Wilcox*	PO Box 34080, Little Rock AR 72203	501-376-8436	R	6*	<.1
808	Webster Printing Company Inc—*Ernest Foster*	1069 W Washington St, Hanson MA 02341	781-447-5484	R	6*	<.1
809	Day and Night Printing Inc—*Peg Hillman*	8618 Westwood Ctr Dr L, Vienna VA 22182	703-734-4940	R	6*	<.1

Rank	Company Name—*Executive Officer*	Address, City, State, Zip	Phone	Type	Fin	Empls
810	J B Kreider Company Inc—*H Holsinger*	PO Box 4284, Pittsburgh PA 15203	412-246-0343	R	6*	<.1
811	Mark Lithography Inc—*Charles Tumminello*	PO Box 362, Cedar Knolls NJ 07927	973-538-5557	R	6*	<.1
812	Naples Graphics and Printing Inc—*David Wacker*	4408 Corporate Sq, Naples FL 34104	239-643-3430	R	6*	<.1
813	Orion Press Inc—*Cressa Nelson*	1224 W Melinda Ln, Phoenix AZ 85027	623-582-1010	R	6*	<.1
814	Typecraft Inc—*D Montgomery*	2040 E Walnut St, Pasadena CA 91107	626-795-8093	R	6*	<.1
815	Em Printing LLC	3081 Bartlett Corp Dr, Bartlett TN 38133	901-759-1220	R	6*	<.1
816	Springfield Printing Corp—*Mark Sanderson*	PO Box 19, North Springfield VT 05150	802-886-2201	R	6*	<.1
817	Faust Printing Inc—*Donald Faust*	PO Box 721713, Pinon Hills CA 92372	909-980-1577	R	6*	<.1
818	Lake Printing Company Inc—*Gary Lorenz*	6815 Hwy 54, Osage Beach MO 65065	573-346-0600	R	6*	<.1
819	R J Zappen Printers and Designers Inc—*Richard Zappen*	200 Wilson Ct, Bensenville IL 60106	630-694-1447	R	5*	.1
820	Dockins Graphics Inc—*Dennis Dockins*	PO Box 3933, Cleveland TN 37320	423-478-2540	R	5*	<.1
821	Superior Business Forms Inc—*Stan Ritter*	PO Box 400, Greeneville TN 37744	423-787-6000	R	5*	<.1
822	Imperial Printing Products Company Inc—*Stuart Cojac*	PO Box 240905, Charlotte NC 28224	704-554-1188	R	5*	<.1
823	JMH Printing Co—*James Highfill*	PO Box 530797, Grand Prairie TX 75053	972-263-1226	R	5*	<.1
824	Wright Larco Inc—*Michael Fullerton*	9051 Sunland Blvd, Sun Valley CA 91352	818-246-8877	R	5*	<.1
825	Automation Printing Co—*Herbert Tobman*	1230 Long Beach Ave, Los Angeles CA 90021	213-488-1230	R	5*	<.1
826	Craig Envelope Corp—*Lawrence Aaronson*	1201 44th Ave, Long Island City NY 11101	718-786-4277	R	5*	<.1
827	Roto Graphic Printing Inc—*William Hintz*	255 S 80th Ave, Wausau WI 54401	715-845-4443	R	5*	<.1
828	Stauffer Acquisition Corp—*Nicholas Schafer*	1160 Enterprise Ct, East Petersburg PA 17520	717-569-3200	R	5*	<.1
829	White Oak Group Inc—*David Wisehaupt*	PO Box 4945, Lancaster PA 17604	717-291-2222	R	5*	<.1
830	Fort Orange Press Inc—*Michael Witko*	PO Box 828, Albany NY 12201	518-489-3233	R	5*	<.1
831	Holiday Printing And Lithograph—*Robert Schluter*	PO Box 3177, Covina CA 91722	626-912-6008	R	5*	<.1
832	West Texas Printing Co—*James Blake*	2909 Stephen F Austin, Brownwood TX 76801	325-646-3598	R	5*	.1
833	Bison Printing Inc—*Franz Beisser*	1342 On Time Rd, Bedford VA 24523	540-586-3955	R	5*	<.1
834	Stuart Web Inc—*Thomas Hawken*	5675 Se Grouper Ave, Stuart FL 34997	772-287-8067	R	5*	<.1
835	Ellison Graphics Corp—*Nicholas Litwin*	1400 W Indiantown Rd, Jupiter FL 33458	561-746-9256	R	5*	<.1
836	Douglas Printing Company Inc—*David Douglas*	2601 Winford Ave, Nashville TN 37211	615-254-8429	R	5*	<.1
837	Elm Press Inc—*Victor Losure*	16 Tremco Dr, Terryville CT 06786	860-583-3600	R	5*	<.1
838	Finn Graphics Inc—*Robert Finn*	220 Stille Dr, Cincinnati OH 45233	513-941-6161	R	5*	<.1
839	Hertzberg Ernst and Sons—*Blair Clark*	1751 W Belmont Ave, Chicago IL 60657	773-525-4126	R	5*	<.1
840	Homewood Press Inc—*Eugene Dubuc*	400 E State Line Rd, Toledo OH 43612	419-478-0695	R	5*	<.1
841	Village Instant Printing Inc—*Austin Parks*	1515 10th St, Modesto CA 95354	209-576-2568	R	5*	<.1
842	Paramount Miller Graphics Inc—*Jon Cummins*	5299 Saint Augustine R, Jacksonville FL 32207	904-448-1700	R	5*	<.1
843	Prographics Inc—*Christina Stevens*	9200 Lower Azusa Rd, Rosemead CA 91770	626-287-0417	R	5*	<.1
844	Dual Printing Inc—*William Sabio*	340 Nagel Dr, Cheektowaga NY 14225	716-684-3825	R	5*	<.1
845	Spencer Evening World—*John Gillaspy*	PO Box 226, Spencer IN 47460	812-829-2255	R	5*	.1
846	Corporate Color—*Michael Marcian*	500 Monocacy Blvd, Frederick MD 21701	301-662-1195	R	5*	<.1
847	Mill Pond Press Inc—*Richard Mitchell*	250 Ctr Ct Unit A, Venice FL 34285	941-497-6020	R	5*	<.1
848	Letton Gooch Printers Inc—*Howard Unger*	PO Box 2842, Norfolk VA 23501	757-622-7567	R	5*	<.1
849	Fx Digital Media Inc—*Columbus Woodruff*	1600 E 23rd St, Cleveland OH 44114	216-241-4040	R	5*	<.1
850	Graphic Management Inc—*Scott Wright*	270 Sheffield St, Mountainside NJ 07092	908-654-8400	R	5*	<.1
851	Highlite Printers Inc—*John Putnick*	880 W Jefferson Ave, Trenton MI 48183	734-284-8944	R	5*	<.1
852	Paulsen Printing Co—*James Paulsen*	4753 S Mendenhall Rd, Memphis TN 38141	901-363-5988	R	5*	<.1
853	Printco Inc—*Kenneth Sperling*	PO Box 440, Omro WI 54963	920-685-5662	R	5*	<.1
854	Repro Acquisition Company LLC—*Joe Ferguson*	25001 Rockwell Dr, Cleveland OH 44117	216-738-3800	R	5*	<.1
855	Fencor Graphics Inc—*Robert Fennell*	1505 Ford Rd, Bensalem PA 19020	215-745-2266	R	5*	<.1
856	Glover Printing Inc—*Louis Goldberg*	2401 Atlantic Ave, Raleigh NC 27604	919-821-5535	R	5*	<.1
857	Coral Color Process Ltd—*Edward Aiello*	50 Mall Dr, Commack NY 11725	631-543-5200	R	5*	<.1
858	Fruitridge Printing and Lithograph Inc—*Susan Hausmann*	3258 Stockton Blvd, Sacramento CA 95820	916-452-9213	R	5*	<.1
859	Kellmark Corp—*George Kelly*	2501 Ada Dr, Elkhart IN 46514	574-264-9695	R	5*	.1
860	Kenyon Press Inc—*Ray Kenyon*	PO Box 710, Sherburne NY 13460	607-674-9066	R	5*	.1
861	Mccain Printing Company Inc—*Eugene Saunders*	PO Box 3443, Danville VA 24543	434-792-1331	R	5*	<.1
862	Edward Enterprises Inc—*Mark Ibara*	PO Box 30468, Honolulu HI 96820	808-841-4231	R	5*	<.1
863	Philip Holzer And Associates LLC—*Christina Bosco*	525 W 52nd St Fl 2, New York NY 10019	212-691-9500	R	5*	<.1
864	Quantum Color Inc—*Darry Finn*	8742 Buffalo Ave, Niagara Falls NY 14304	716-283-8700	R	5*	<.1
865	Dobb Printing Inc—*Jim Dobb*	2431 Harvey St, Muskegon MI 49442	231-722-1060	R	5*	<.1
866	Printing Center Inc—*Vincent Perrella*	1 White Lake Rd, Sparta NJ 07871	973-383-6362	R	5*	<.1
867	Richardson and Edwards Inc—*Edward Kolodziej*	1110 W National Ave, Addison IL 60101	630-543-1818	R	5*	<.1
868	T and C Graphics Inc—*Anthony Garbi*	PO Box 249, Addison IL 60101	630-932-8484	R	5*	<.1
869	New London Press Inc—*Howard Givens*	301 Curie Dr, Alpharetta GA 30005	770-442-1363	R	5*	<.1
870	Hatteras Inc—*Claudia Nesbitt*	12801 Prospect St, Dearborn MI 48126	313-624-3300	R	5*	<.1
871	Riegle Press Inc—*Gerald Carmody*	PO Box 207, Flint MI 48501	810-653-9631	R	5*	<.1
872	Shamrock Printing Inc—*Dennis Burke*	4211 Jvl Industrial Pk, Marietta GA 30066	770-924-7535	R	5*	<.1
873	Weber Printing Company Inc—*Richard Weber*	18700 S Ferris Pl, Compton CA 90220	310-639-5064	R	5*	<.1
874	Creative Imprints Inc—*Clifford Garnett*	15 Commerce Way Ste D, Norton MA 02766	508-285-7650	R	5*	<.1
875	Winnebago Color Press Inc—*Lawrence Busse*	PO Box 528, Menasha WI 54952	920-725-4365	R	5*	.1
876	Evolution Impressions Inc—*Thomas Gruber*	160 Commerce Dr, Rochester NY 14623	585-473-6600	R	5*	<.1
877	Ace Forms Of Kansas Inc—*Leon Bogner*	2900 N Rotary Ter, Pittsburg KS 66762	620-232-9290	R	5*	.1
878	Pavsner Press Inc—*Melvin Pavsner*	PO Box 18455, Baltimore MD 21237	410-687-7550	R	5*	.1
879	Clark Graphics Inc—*Charles Clark*	21914 Schmeman Ave, Warren MI 48089	586-772-4900	R	5*	.1
880	Daily Item Publishing Co—*Janet A Tippett*	PO Box 607, Sunbury PA 17801	570-286-5671	S	5*	.1
881	Sunray Printing Solutions Inc—*Thomas Wolke*	25123 22nd Ave, Saint Cloud MN 56301	320-253-8808	R	5*	.1
882	Unity Graphics and Engraving Company Inc—*Jerry Mandel*	PO Box 88, Englewood NJ 07631	201-569-6400	R	5*	<.1
883	Odyssey Press Inc—*Charles Parker*	PO Box 7307, Rochester NH 03839	603-749-4433	R	5*	<.1
884	Sekan Printing Company Inc—*Donald Banwart*	PO Box 631, Fort Scott KS 66701	620-223-5190	R	5*	<.1
885	Pioneer Printing and Stationery Inc—*Jerry Ziemann*	PO Box 466, Cheyenne WY 82003	307-635-4114	R	5*	<.1
886	Bayside Printing Inc—*Rosemary Bundscho*	PO Box 73687, Houston TX 77273	281-209-9500	R	5*	<.1
887	Eagle Graphics Inc—*John McIntosh*	5 Dan Rd, Canton MA 02021	781-830-1896	R	5*	<.1
888	Jersey Printing Associates Inc—*Gregory Heh*	PO Box 355, Atlantic Highlands NJ 07716	732-872-9654	R	5*	<.1
889	Queen City Printers Inc—*Alan Schillhammer*	701 Pine St, Burlington VT 05401	802-864-4566	R	5*	<.1
890	Harris Interactive Media Inc—*Harold Still*	1519 Stone Ridge Dr, Stone Mountain GA 30083	770-938-7650	R	5*	<.1
891	J D Graphic Company Inc—*James Blasio*	1101 Arthur Ave, Elk Grove Village IL 60007	847-364-4000	R	5*	<.1
892	John C Otto Company Inc—*Kevin Spall* Consolidated Graphics Inc	PO Box 367, East Longmeadow MA 01028	413-525-4131	D	5*	<.1
893	Lithocraft Inc—*Robert Brewer*	1502 Beeler St, New Albany IN 47150	812-948-1608	R	5*	<.1
894	United Printing Inc—*Ken Bischoff*	PO Box 936, Bismarck ND 58502	701-223-0505	R	5*	<.1
895	Grc Enterprises Inc—*Arvind Gupta*	4169 Bludau Dr, Warrenton VA 20187	540-428-7000	R	5*	<.1
896	Rapid Rater Co—*Lourdes Madsen*	PO Box 13055, Tallahassee FL 32317	850-893-7346	R	5*	<.1
897	Christmas City Printing Company Inc—*Paul Sicinski*	861 14th Ave, Bethlehem PA 18018	610-868-5844	R	5*	<.1
898	Citadel Communications—*Loretta Franzi*	3300 Business Dr, Sacramento CA 95820	916-456-6000	R	5*	<.1

Note: An asterisk (*) indicates an estimated financial figure. The company type code used is as follows: R = Private, P = Public, S = Private Subsidiary, B = Public Subsidiary, D = Division, J = Joint Venture, I = Investment Fund.

COMPANY RANKINGS BY SALES WITHIN 4-DIGIT SIC

Rank	Company Name—*Executive Officer*	Address, City, State, Zip	Phone	Type	Fin	Empls
899	Dancor Inc—*Dan Fronk*	2155 Dublin Rd, Columbus OH 43228	614-340-2155	R	5*	<.1
900	David A Smith Printing Inc—*David Smith*	742 S 22nd St, Harrisburg PA 17104	717-564-3719	R	5*	<.1
901	Tennant Printing Company Inc—*Murray Miller*	PO Box 432, Deland FL 32721	386-734-2233	R	5*	<.1
902	Tru Color Litho Inc—*Frank Daws*	511 Houston St, Nashville TN 37203	615-742-1281	R	5*	<.1
903	Mido Printing Company Inc—*Michael Dobrash*	6845 E 48th Ave, Denver CO 80216	303-287-2854	R	5*	<.1
904	Hammond Press Inc—*Michael Hammond*	PO Box 58167, Pittsburgh PA 15209	412-821-4100	R	5*	<.1
905	Harman Press Inc—*Jay M Goldner*	1227 N Highland Ave, Los Angeles CA 90038	323-463-7187	R	5*	<.1
906	General Printing Co—*Kenneth Slavik*	537 Kaaahi St, Honolulu HI 96817	808-597-2271	R	5*	<.1
907	Western Printing Company Inc—*Patrick Coughlin*	5129 S 95th E Ave, Tulsa OK 74145	918-665-2874	R	5*	<.1
908	JEM Sales Inc—*Chris Maer*	430 Lavender Dr NW, Rome GA 30165	706-232-1709	R	5*	<.1
909	Spectrum Printing Company LLC—*George Stewart*	4651 S Butterfield Dr, Tucson AZ 85714	520-571-1114	R	5*	<.1
910	Standwill Packaging Inc—*William Standwill*	220 Sherwood Ave, Farmingdale NY 11735	631-752-1236	R	5*	<.1
911	Tri M Graphics Co—*Jon Jensen*	625 E Main St, Owatonna MN 55060	507-451-3920	R	5*	<.1
912	Concept Press Inc—*Jimmy Lin*	4301 22nd St, Long Island City NY 11101	718-784-8899	R	5*	<.1
913	Honsa-Binder Printing Inc—*Kay Owens*	320 Spruce St, Saint Paul MN 55101	651-222-0251	R	5*	<.1
914	Joseph Berning Printing Co—*Michael Berning*	1850 Dalton Ave, Cincinnati OH 45214	513-721-0781	R	5*	<.1
915	Navrat's Office Products—*Richard Duncan*	PO Box N, Emporia KS 66801	620-342-2092	R	5*	<.1
916	Kelley Pagels Enterprises LLC—*Betty Benner*	500 Huron, Michigan City IN 46360	219-872-8552	R	5*	<.1
917	Ramsbottom Printing Inc—*P Ramsbottom*	135 Waldron Rd, Fall River MA 02720	508-730-2220	R	5*	.1
918	A and J Printing Inc—*Bill Dunton*	PO Box 518, Nixa MO 65714	417-725-2674	R	5*	<.1
919	First Impressions Lithographic Company Inc—*Sandra Triolo*	PO Box 9062, Freeport NY 11520	516-333-3343	R	5*	<.1
920	Southern Colortype Company Inc—*Kenneth Groomes*	2927 Sidco Dr, Nashville TN 37204	615-256-1631	R	5*	<.1
921	Arcade Lithographing Corp—*Clarence Urban*	2108 Whitfield Park Lo, Sarasota FL 34243	941-755-2655	R	5*	<.1
922	Jerry Berman Enterprises Inc—*Phyllis Berman*	5306 Beethoven St, Los Angeles CA 90066	310-577-6606	R	5*	<.1
923	Pargraphics Inc—*Joe Davis*	125 Mitchell Blvd Ste, San Rafael CA 94903	415-479-2171	R	5*	<.1
924	Earl D Arnold Printing Co—*Earl Arnold*	630 Lunken Park Dr, Cincinnati OH 45226	513-533-6900	R	5*	<.1
925	Harmony Press Inc—*Fred Grotenhuis*	717 W Berwick St, Easton PA 18042	610-559-9800	R	5*	<.1
926	Hoffman Brothers Inc—*Dean O'brien*	398 S Shell Rd, Debary FL 32713	386-668-1860	R	5*	<.1
927	Insua Graphics Inc—*Jose Insua*	9121 Glenoaks Blvd, Sun Valley CA 91352	818-767-7007	R	5*	<.1
928	Precision Offset Inc—*Larry Smith*	17422 Murphy Ave, Irvine CA 92614	949-752-1714	R	5*	<.1
929	Joe L Smith Jr Inc—*Nancy Smith*	PO Box 1309, Beckley WV 25802	304-253-7361	R	5*	<.1
930	Wendtco Web Printing Inc—*Edward Reichenbach*	1299 Stowe Ave, Medford OR 97501	541-772-7039	R	5*	<.1
931	Integraphx Inc—*Edward Nowokunski*	656 Michael Wylie Dr, Charlotte NC 28217	704-529-5044	R	5*	<.1
932	Foresight Group Inc—*William Christofferson*	2822 N Martin Luther, Lansing MI 48906	517-485-5700	R	5*	<.1
933	Kenwel Printers Inc—*David Starner*	4272 Indianola Ave, Columbus OH 43214	614-261-1011	R	5*	<.1
934	Heritage Instant Printing Company Inc—*Robert Wendt*	3575-N 124th St, Brookfield WI 53005	262-790-5000	R	5*	<.1
935	Hudson Printing Inc—*Gary Began*	9085 Fwy Dr, Macedonia OH 44056	330-467-9003	R	5*	<.1
936	Prime Printing Inc—*Gary Smith*	8929 Kingsridge Dr, Dayton OH 45458	937-438-3707	R	5*	<.1
937	Shipman Printing Industries Inc—*Gary Blum*	PO Box 357, Niagara Falls NY 14304	716-504-7700	R	5*	<.1
938	Capital Offset Company Inc—*Jay Stewart*	PO Box 2824, Concord NH 03302	603-225-3308	R	5*	<.1
939	Shanin Co—*Milton Shanin*	PO Box 597604, Chicago IL 60659	847-676-1200	R	5*	.1
940	Docu Mart Copy and Printing Inc—*Kevin Gravely*	5624 Citrus Blvd, Harahan LA 70123	504-733-4616	R	5*	<.1
941	Teg Corp—*William Beasley*	PO Box 4669, Roanoke VA 24015	540-772-7835	R	5*	<.1
942	J and M Printing Inc—*Harrison Mccleery*	PO Box 248, Gwinner ND 58040	701-678-2461	R	5*	<.1
943	Brookshire Publications Inc—*L Weaver*	PO Box 7145, Lancaster PA 17604	717-392-1321	R	5*	<.1
944	Empire Corporation Kit Of America Inc—*Ray Stormont*	2444 Nw 7th Pl, Miami FL 33127	305-634-3694	R	5*	<.1
945	King Business Forms Corp—*Jimmy King*	PO Box 1467, New Tazewell TN 37824	423-626-7700	R	5*	<.1
946	Clear Lake Press Inc—*Dan Nitz*	PO Box 29, Waseca MN 56093	507-835-4430	R	5*	<.1
947	Apple Press Ltd—*Gary Gehman*	307 Commerce Dr, Exton PA 19341	610-363-1776	R	5*	<.1
948	Color Inc—*Barry Hamm*	1600 Flower St, Glendale CA 91201	818-240-1350	R	5*	<.1
949	Howard Quinn Co—*Indar Prasad*	298 Alabama St, San Francisco CA 94103	415-621-3750	R	5*	<.1
950	Howe's Standard Publishing Company Inc—*Laurie Howe-Opromollo*	1980 S W Blvd, Vineland NJ 08360	856-691-2000	R	5*	<.1
951	Pr1mus Printing Inc—*Mark Kilchanman*	2540 24th Ave S, Minneapolis MN 55406	612-729-9000	R	5*	<.1
952	William Charles Printing Company Inc—*Joseph Pelligrini*	7 Fairchild Ct Ste 100, Plainview NY 11803	516-349-0900	R	5*	<.1
953	Register Lithographers Ltd—*Joseph Fishman*	1155 Bloomfield Ave, Clifton NJ 07012	973-916-2804	R	5*	<.1
954	Macomb Printing Inc—*Ronald Bracali*	44272 N Groesbeck Hwy, Clinton Township MI 48036	586-463-2301	R	5*	<.1
955	Office Supply Services Incorporated Of Charlotte—*Garry Vreugdenhil*	PO Box 5450, Concord NC 28027	704-786-4677	R	5*	<.1
956	Your Town Press Inc—*Charles Toll*	2773 Cherry Ave Ne, Salem OR 97301	503-364-2122	R	5*	<.1
957	Rogers Printing Company Inc—*Bruce Lynch*	136 Pond St, Leominster MA 01453	978-537-9791	R	5*	<.1
958	Sos Printing Inc—*Bradford Reimers*	8135 Ronson Rd, San Diego CA 92111	858-292-1800	R	5*	<.1
959	Brd Printing Inc—*Donald Hough*	912 W Saint Joseph St, Lansing MI 48915	517-372-0268	R	5*	<.1
960	Grand Blanc Printing Inc—*Morton Stebbins*	9449 Holly Rd, Grand Blanc MI 48439	810-694-1155	R	5*	<.1
961	Issgr Inc—*Debra Briggs*	6611 Portwest Dr Ste 1, Houston TX 77024	713-869-7700	R	5*	<.1
962	Boyertown Publishing Company Inc—*Dennis Lobaugh*	48-52 S Reading Ave, Boyertown PA 19512	610-367-2121	R	5*	<.1
963	Allied Lithographing Company Inc—*Tim Heier*	2199 E 9th St, Kansas City MO 64124	816-842-5770	R	5*	<.1
964	Expo Promotions Inc—*Andrew Alvarez*	137 N Gibson Rd 110, Henderson NV 89014	702-639-9777	R	5*	<.1
965	Miller O'connell Corp—*Dave Bosshard*	514 Wells St, Delafield WI 53018	262-782-1470	R	5*	<.1
966	Ameriprint Graphics Inc—*Elizabeth Nemecek*	2065 American Dr Ste C, Neenah WI 54956	920-733-0468	R	5*	<.1
967	F and S Holdings Inc—*Fred Brooks*	1800 Dolphin Dr Ste 10, Waukesha WI 53186	262-650-6300	R	5*	<.1
968	Humphrey Printing Company Inc—*Rudolph Miller*	PO Box 5025, Wichita Falls TX 76307	940-766-4255	R	5*	<.1
969	Modern Reproductions Inc—*Lawrence Winkowski*	127 Mckean St, Pittsburgh PA 15219	412-488-7700	R	5*	<.1
970	Mid-South Publishing Company Inc—*G May*	PO Box 1102, Shreveport LA 71163	318-222-1100	R	5*	<.1
971	Greenwell-Chisholm Printing Company Inc—*Carl Greenwell*	420 E Parrish Ave, Owensboro KY 42303	270-684-3267	R	5*	<.1
972	Tri-State Publishing Co—*Richard Pflug*	PO Box 1119, Steubenville OH 43952	740-283-3686	R	5*	<.1
973	Un Communications Inc—*William Corbin*	1429 Chase Ct, Carmel IN 46032	317-844-8622	R	5*	<.1
974	Midtown Printing Co—*Thomas Auffenberg*	2115 59th St, Saint Louis MO 63110	314-781-6505	R	5*	<.1
975	Johnson Company Of Rochester Minnesota—*Judith Brown*	1416 Valleyhigh Dr Nw, Rochester MN 55901	507-288-7788	R	5*	<.1
976	Paul Baker Printing Inc—*Paul Baker*	220 Riverside Ave, Roseville CA 95678	916-783-8317	R	5*	<.1
977	First Impression Group Inc—*Brian Shay*	2700 Blue Waters Rd St, Saint Paul MN 55121	651-683-1125	R	5*	<.1
978	Pentagraphix Offset Printing Inc—*Jonathan Chung*	629 Grove St Ste 701, Jersey City NJ 07310	201-526-9300	R	5*	<.1
979	Lawrence Printing Co—*George Ellis*	PO Box 886, Greenwood MS 38935	662-453-6301	R	4*	.1
980	Mayfield Printing Company Inc—*Kent Isbell*	PO Box 469, Mayfield KY 42066	270-247-5814	R	4*	<.1
981	Paradigm Printing Inc—*Todd Reigel*	429 Virgil Dr, Dalton GA 30721	706-226-7474	R	4*	<.1
982	A and E Printers And Mailers Inc—*Bradley Jodway*	3303 N E St, Lansing MI 48906	517-484-2535	R	4*	<.1
983	Kap Graphics Inc—*Kenneth Anderson*	PO Box 960, Mundelein IL 60060	312-454-1505	R	4*	<.1
984	Searles Graphics Inc—*Kenneth Searles*	56 Old Dock Rd, Yaphank NY 11980	631-345-2202	R	4*	<.1
985	Brodnax Printing Company I LLC—*Robert Singer*	2338 Reagan St, Dallas TX 75219	214-528-2622	R	4*	<.1
986	Lind-Remsen Printing Company Inc—*Robert Remsen*	3918 S Central Ave, Rockford IL 61102	815-969-0610	R	4*	<.1

Rank	Company Name—Executive Officer	Address, City, State, Zip	Phone	Type	Fin	Empls
987	Print Management Corp—Timothy O'leary	6700 S Glacier St, Tukwila WA 98188	425-251-5005	R	4*	<.1
988	Printmanagement LLC—Vickie Boughton	3950 Virginia Ave, Cincinnati OH 45227	513-272-7000	R	4*	<.1
989	Seaside Printing CoInc—Mark Cochrane	1220 E 4th St, Long Beach CA 90802	562-437-6437	R	4*	<.1
990	Talon Printing Inc—Loren Mansfield	1955 Pky Blvd, Salt Lake City UT 84119	801-977-9666	R	4*	<.1
991	Signature Printing And Graphics Company Inc—Mike Reda	889 Poplar Hall Dr, Norfolk VA 23502	757-461-5300	R	4*	<.1
992	B and B Printers Inc—Kevin Blankenkeckler	1706 W State St, Bristol TN 37620	423-764-5751	R	4*	<.1
993	Mcclung Printing Inc—Thomas Trevillian	550 N Commerce Ave, Waynesboro VA 22980	540-949-8139	R	4*	<.1
994	Carlisle Printing Of Walnut Creek Ltd—Marcus Wengerd	2673 Township Rd 421, Sugarcreek OH 44681	330-852-9922	R	4*	<.1
995	Commerce Financial Printers Corp—Thomas Montrone	305 Cox St, Roselle NJ 07203	908-241-9880	S	4*	<.1
996	Hudson Graphics Inc—Steven Cartwright	PO Box 7010, Longview TX 75607	903-758-1773	R	4*	<.1
997	Quick Tick International Inc—Don Andrews	12902 Haynes Rd Ste 4, Houston TX 77066	832-249-6400	R	4*	<.1
998	Steinhauser Inc—Tara Halpin	207 E 4th St, Newport KY 41071	859-491-7900	R	4*	<.1
999	Mitographers Inc—David Veldhuizen	PO Box 84910, Sioux Falls SD 57118	605-336-1818	R	4*	<.1
1000	Mountain Printing Company Inc—Rose Marie De Pasqua	PO Box 608, Berlin NJ 08009	856-767-7600	R	4*	<.1
1001	Admiral Products Company Inc—Vincent Hvizda	4101 W 150th St, Cleveland OH 44135	216-671-0600	R	4*	<.1
1002	St Louis Lithographing Co—Jack Rosen	6880 Heege Rd, Saint Louis MO 63123	314-352-1300	S	4*	<.1
1003	Dumont Printing Incorporated—Cheryl Pair	PO Box 12726, Fresno CA 93779	559-485-6311	R	4*	<.1
1004	Leo Lam Inc—Amy Chan	3589 Nevada St Ste A, Pleasanton CA 94566	925-484-3690	R	4*	<.1
1005	Spectra Measuring Systems Inc—Cory Mistric	11841 Coursey Blvd, Baton Rouge LA 70816	225-292-3953	R	4*	<.1
1006	Town Crier Ltd—Randy Rolffs	PO Box 103, Pella IA 50219	641-628-1130	R	4*	.1
1007	Modern Media Inc—James Griffin	8723 3rd Ave, Brooklyn NY 11209	718-238-6600	R	4*	.1
1008	Consolidated Printing and Stationery Company Inc—Donald Vandegrift	PO Box 1217, Salina KS 67402	785-825-5426	R	4*	<.1
1009	Catalogs By Design—Lorna Rudick	590 N Gulph Rd, King Of Prussia PA 19406	610-337-9133	R	4*	<.1
1010	1st Street Graphics Inc—Tim Burtner	PO Box 3237, Saint Joseph MO 64503	816-233-4567	R	4*	<.1
1011	Quick Print—Gary Gravely	6373 S Memorial Dr Ste, Tulsa OK 74133	918-250-5466	R	4*	<.1
1012	Englund Graphics Inc—Edward Englund	PO Box 41515, Minneapolis MN 55441	763-536-9100	R	4*	<.1
1013	Mi-Te Fast Printers Inc—Thomas Sackley	180 W Washington St St, Chicago IL 60602	312-236-3278	R	4*	<.1
1014	Transcript Press Inc—Ron Minnix	PO Box 6440, Norman OK 73070	405-360-7999	R	4*	<.1
1015	Duke Graphics Inc—Blake Leduc	33212 Lakeland Blvd, Willoughby OH 44095	440-946-0606	R	4*	<.1
1016	Stewart-Taylor Co—James Olson	114 W Superior St, Duluth MN 55802	218-722-4421	R	4*	<.1
1017	Central Blueprint Co—Margaret Smith	47 W 5th Ave, Eugene OR 97401	541-342-3624	R	4*	<.1
1018	Spartan Printing Inc—Jim Trebilcock	320 109th St, Arlington TX 76011	817-640-6341	R	4*	<.1
1019	Donlevy Lithograph Inc—Carolyn Black	PO Box 1298, Wichita KS 67201	316-262-7277	R	4*	<.1
1020	Erie Lake Graphics Inc—James Dietz	5372 W 130th St, Brookpark OH 44142	216-262-7575	R	4*	<.1
1021	Koke New Century Inc—Doug Koke	PO Box 1184, Eugene OR 97440	541-687-1184	R	4*	<.1
1022	Panoramic Press Inc—Jeffrey Erickson	2920 N 35th St, Phoenix AZ 85018	602-955-2001	R	4*	<.1
1023	Rush Graphics Inc—Zora Agheli	1122 Goffle Rd 32, Hawthorne NJ 07506	973-427-9393	R	4*	<.1
1024	Sioux Falls Shopping News Inc—K Lesnar	PO Box 5184, Sioux Falls SD 57117	605-339-3633	R	4*	.1
1025	All About Signs N Print Inc—Javed Rahmatullah	4261 Green Ridge Dr, Marietta GA 30062	770-321-6446	R	4*	.1
1026	Newman Printing Company Inc—Louis Newman	1300 E 29th St, Bryan TX 77802	979-779-7700	R	4*	<.1
1027	Utloy Brothers Inc—Duane Harrison	PO Box 1086, Troy MI 48099	248-585-1700	R	4*	<.1
1028	Northeast Offset Inc—Joseph Balboni	11 Alpha Rd, Chelmsford MA 01824	978-256-9939	R	4*	<.1
1029	Quadrangle Press Inc—James Fahrenthold	9111 Broadway St, San Antonio TX 78217	210-828-8191	R	4*	<.1
1030	Sheriar Press Inc—Sheila Krynski	3005 Hwy 17 Byp N, Myrtle Beach SC 29577	843-448-1102	R	4*	<.1
1031	Castle Communications Inc—John Gevelda	121 Industrial Dr, Dekalb IL 60115	815-758-5484	R	4*	<.1
1032	Roebuck Printing Inc—Charles Roebuck	4987 Mercantile Rd, Baltimore MD 21236	410-931-3300	R	4*	<.1
1033	Spectrum Printers Inc—Andy Staveren	400 E Russell Rd Ste 1, Tecumseh MI 49286	517-423-5735	R	4*	<.1
1034	Sim's Press Inc—Kenneth Simonetta	PO Box 207, Peterborough NH 03458	603-924-3804	R	4*	<.1
1035	D and K Printing Inc—Gary Bennett	2930 Pearl St, Boulder CO 80301	303-444-1123	R	4*	<.1
1036	Independent Graphics Inc—Louis Ciampi	PO Box 703, Pittston PA 18640	570-654-4040	R	4*	<.1
1037	Oakdale Printing Company Inc—Robert Ghegan	PO Box 2302, Riverton NJ 08077	856-829-7110	R	4*	<.1
1038	Press America Inc—Martin D'amico	661 Fargo Ave, Elk Grove Village IL 60007	847-228-0333	R	4*	<.1
1039	Spectrum Graphic Services Inc—Joseph Tripoli	601 N Edgewood Ave Ste, Wood Dale IL 60191	630-766-7673	R	4*	<.1
1040	Superior Print Inc—Dennis Amos	PO Box 401, Sellersburg IN 47172	812-246-6311	R	4*	<.1
1041	Goetz Printing Co—Stephen Smith	PO Box 2130, Springfield VA 22152	703-569-8232	R	4*	<.1
1042	Allen Printing Company Inc—Paul Heffington	PO Box 40583, Nashville TN 37204	615-642-0348	R	4*	<.1
1043	Arrowhead Press Inc—Dominic Sims	220 W Maple Ave Ste D, Monrovia CA 91016	626-358-1168	R	4*	<.1
1044	Printing Concepts Inc—Michael Martin	4982 Pacific Ave, Erie PA 16506	814-833-8080	R	4*	<.1
1045	Pyne-Davidson Co—Harry Davidson	237 Weston St, Hartford CT 06120	860-522-9106	R	4*	<.1
1046	QS I Inc—John Carrico	3024 Mishawaka Ave, South Bend IN 46615	574-282-1200	R	4*	<.1
1047	North Florida Web Press Inc—Richard Walsh	5164 Shawland Rd, Jacksonville FL 32254	904-783-3275	R	4*	.1
1048	Richardson Printing Corp—Dennis Ballantyne	PO Box 663, Marietta OH 45750	740-373-5362	R	4*	.1
1049	Bainbridge Post Searchlight Inc—Samuel Griffin	PO Box 277, Bainbridge GA 39818	229-246-2827	R	4*	<.1
1050	American Bank Systems Inc—James Bruce	PO Box 20668, Oklahoma City OK 73156	405-607-7000	R	4*	<.1
1051	Mitchell Graphics Inc—Gary Fedus	2363 Mitchell Park Dr, Petoskey MI 49770	231-347-4635	R	4*	<.1
1052	Fisher Printers Inc—Martin C Fisher	PO Box 1366, Cedar Rapids IA 52406	319-393-5405	R	4*	<.1
1053	Star Printing Corp—Mark Abrams	1200 W Chestnut St, Brockton MA 02301	508-583-9046	R	4*	<.1
1054	Clark's Printing Service Inc—Tom Clark	2 Westside Dr, Asheville NC 28806	828-254-1432	R	4*	<.1
1055	Fittje Brothers Printing—Matt Walenczak Consolidated Graphics Inc	2822 Delta Dr, Colorado Springs CO 80910	719-392-4286	S	4*	<.1
1056	Jost and Kiefer Printing Co—Kathy Ridder	PO Box 2, Quincy IL 62306	217-222-5145	R	4*	<.1
1057	Kolb Boyette and Assoc Inc—Al Thorn	PO Box 13345, Durham NC 27709	919-544-7839	R	4*	<.1
1058	Lockwood Company Inc—Buck Snowden	PO Box 128, Atchison KS 66002	913-367-0110	R	4*	<.1
1059	Colorlith Corp—Larry Pierce	818 Jefferson St, Fall River MA 02721	508-837-6100	R	4*	<.1
1060	L Brown And Sons Printing Inc—Lawrence Brown	14-20 Jefferson St, Barre VT 05641	802-476-3164	R	4*	<.1
1061	Southern Reprographics Inc—Phillip Mccoley	PO Box 1878, Little Rock AR 72203	501-372-4011	R	4*	<.1
1062	County Graphics Ltd—Gina Scarola	2 Stercho Rd, Linden NJ 07036	908-474-9797	R	4*	<.1
1063	Creative Printing and Graphic Design Inc—Rick Pearce	1009 Pine St, Orlando FL 32824	407-855-0202	R	4*	<.1
1064	Deschamps Printing Company Inc—Henry Deschamps	PO Box 127, Salem MA 01970	978-744-2152	R	4*	<.1
1065	Exacta Graphics Inc—Wolfhart Schubach	13050 W Custer Ave, Butler WI 53007	262-781-0000	R	4*	<.1
1066	Free Press Publishing Co—John Harrison	PO Box 1333, Tampa FL 33601	813-254-5888	R	4*	<.1
1067	Griffiths Services Inc—Ron Griffith	121 S Old Springs Rd, Anaheim CA 92808	714-685-7700	R	4*	<.1
1068	Latta Graphics Inc—Eileen Latta	PO Box 31, Little Ferry NJ 07643	201-440-4040	R	4*	<.1
1069	Lewis Advertising Company Inc—Marilyn Dickman	325 E Oliver St, Baltimore MD 21202	410-539-5100	R	4*	<.1
1070	Olympus Press Inc—Frank Vertrees	3400 S 150th St, Tukwila WA 98188	206-242-2700	R	4*	<.1
1071	Printing Corporation Of The Americas Inc—Jan Tuchman	620 Sw 12th Ave, Pompano Beach FL 33069	954-781-8100	R	4*	<.1
1072	Processors Mailing Inc—Anthony Perone	2396 Bateman Ave, Duarte CA 91010	626-358-5600	R	4*	<.1
1073	TL Krieg Offset Inc—Terry Krieg	10600 Chester Rd, Cincinnati OH 45215	513-542-1522	R	4*	<.1
1074	Voris Communication Company Inc—Scott Voris	PO Box 1090, Aurora IL 60507	630-898-0800	R	4*	<.1

Note: An asterisk (*) indicates an estimated financial figure. The company type code used is as follows: R = Private, P = Public, S = Private Subsidiary, B = Public Subsidiary, D = Division, J = Joint Venture, I = Investment Fund.

COMPANY RANKINGS BY SALES WITHIN 4-DIGIT SIC

Rank	Company Name—*Executive Officer*	Address, City, State, Zip	Phone	Type	Fin	Empls
1075	Schmidt Printing Company Inc—*Stephen Siegwald*	PO Box 3945, Louisville KY 40201	502-447-8724	R	4*	<.1
1076	Herdell Printing and Lithography Inc—*Ardis Herdell*	PO Box 72, Saint Helena CA 94574	707-963-3634	R	4*	<.1
1077	J-Peam LLC—*Britt Kauffman*	3300 S Fwy, Fort Worth TX 76110	817-927-1819	R	4*	<.1
1078	SP Mount Printing Company Inc—*Gerald L McGill Sr*	1306 E 55th St, Cleveland OH 44103	216-881-3316	R	4*	<.1
1079	Garrison Brewer Co—*Neal W Scaggs*	214 Stone Rd, Belpre OH 45714	740-423-1400	D	4*	<.1
1080	Hampden Press Inc—*Richard Blue*	9955 E Hampden Ave Uni, Denver CO 80231	303-750-2035	R	4*	<.1
1081	Menu Printers Inc—*Graham Clark*	2175 N Batavia St Ste, Orange CA 92865	714-921-1050	R	4*	<.1
1082	Tennessee Industrial Printing Services Inc—*Diane Jordan*	51 Miller Ave, Jackson TN 38305	731-668-3500	R	4*	<.1
1083	Wilson Printing—*Dale Wilson*	5777 Hollister Ave, Goleta CA 93117	805-964-8875	R	4*	<.1
1084	Thomas Printing—*Frank Thomas*	PO Box 9048, Kalispell MT 59904	406-755-5447	R	4*	<.1
1085	United Systems of Arkansas Inc	1201 Main St, Little Rock AR 72202		R	4*	<.1
1086	Ben Franklin Press Inc—*Ron Clark*	910 S Hohokam Dr Ste 1, Tempe AZ 85281	480-968-7959	R	4*	<.1
1087	Brooklyn Printing and Advertising Inc	7150 Boone Ave N, Brooklyn Park MN 55428	763-425-9575	R	4*	<.1
1088	Liberty Playing Cards LP—*Michael Ahmed*	2001 E Randal Mill Rd, Arlington TX 76011		S	4	<.1
1089	First Class Printing Inc—*Bruce Tanner*	PO Box 877, Fayetteville TN 37334	931-438-5165	R	4*	<.1
1090	Baton Rouge Printing Inc—*Kevin Bankston*	PO Box 97, Baton Rouge LA 70821	225-343-3423	R	4*	<.1
1091	Pete Keiger Printing Company Inc—*Louis Crockett*	3735 Kimwell Dr, Winston Salem NC 27103	336-760-0099	R	4*	<.1
1092	Avion Graphics Inc—*Craig Greiner*	27192 Burbank, Foothill Ranch CA 92610	949-472-0438	R	4*	<.1
1093	Agrecolor Inc—*Anthony Greco*	400 Sagamore Ave, Mineola NY 11501	516-741-8700	R	4*	<.1
1094	Georgia National Forms Inc—*Clem Havlik*	1199 Atlanta Industria, Marietta GA 30066	770-424-1000	S	4*	<.1
1095	Kehl-Kolor Inc—*Jon Kehl*	PO Box 770, Ashland OH 44805	419-281-3107	R	4*	<.1
1096	Southland Printing Inc—*Billy Davis*	1079 Majaun Rd, Lexington KY 40511	859-276-1965	R	4*	<.1
1097	Winchester Printers Inc—*Ronald Hottle*	212 Independence Rd, Winchester VA 22602	540-662-6911	R	4*	<.1
1098	Redding Printing Company Inc—*Ken Peterson*	1130 Continental St, Redding CA 96001	530-243-0525	R	4*	<.1
1099	Herrmann Printing and Litho Inc—*Eugene Herrmann*	1709 Douglas Dr, Pittsburgh PA 15221	412-243-4100	R	4*	<.1
1100	Poggi Press Inc—*Charles Poggi*	PO Box 668, Hoboken NJ 07030	201-659-0837	R	4*	<.1
1101	Spectrum Press Inc—*Stan Thomas*	1300 N Loesch Rd, Bloomington IN 47404	812-335-1945	R	4*	<.1
1102	Paulson Press Inc—*Ben Letto*	904 Cambridge Dr, Elk Grove Village IL 60007	847-290-0080	R	4*	<.1
1103	Artisan Press Inc—*Scott Kuehl*	3201 Northbrook Dr, Sioux City IA 51105	712-258-0684	R	4*	<.1
1104	KMS 2000 Inc—*Kevin Smith*	PO Box 21220, Canton OH 44701	330-454-9444	R	4*	<.1
1105	Inter-City Printing Company Inc—*Paul Murai*	614 Madison St, Oakland CA 94607	510-451-4775	R	4*	<.1
1106	Oscar T Smith Co—*John Porta*	901 E Fayette St, Baltimore MD 21202	410-727-4740	R	4*	<.1
1107	Marr Printing—*Howard Gropper*	49 Oakley St, Poughkeepsie NY 12601	845-452-2679	R	4*	<.1
1108	P and H Graphic Communications Inc—*Paul Hunt*	420 N 5th St Ste 475, Minneapolis MN 55401	612-338-7511	R	4*	<.1
1109	Kalil Printing Inc—*Walter Kalil*	21 S Limerick Rd, Royersford PA 19468	610-948-9330	R	4*	<.1
1110	Graphic Communications Inc—*Jerry Randall*	9603 Fallard Ter, Upper Marlboro MD 20772	301-599-2020	R	4*	<.1
1111	Brown Printing Inc—*Greg Meeker*	411 Madison St, Jefferson City MO 65101	573-636-8012	R	4*	<.1
1112	Compton and Sons Inc—*Bob Ruzicka*	10645 Baur Blvd, Saint Louis MO 63132	314-991-2201	R	4*	<.1
1113	Hadley Printing Company Inc—*Christopher Desrosiers*	58 Canal St, Holyoke MA 01040	413-536-8517	R	4*	<.1
1114	Lawson Printers Inc—*Betty Rankin*	685 W Columbia Ave, Battle Creek MI 49015	269-965-0525	R	4*	<.1
1115	New Image Press Inc—*David Brown*	4433 Howley St, Pittsburgh PA 15224	412-683-1300	R	4*	<.1
1116	Schutte Lithography Inc—*Gary Schutte*	2716 Kotter Ave, Evansville IN 47715	812-469-3500	R	4*	<.1
1117	Studley Press Inc—*Charles Gillett*	PO Box 214, Dalton MA 01227	413-684-0441	R	4*	<.1
1118	Lawton Printers Inc—*Kimberly Koon*	185 Anchor Rd, Casselberry FL 32707	407-260-0400	R	4*	<.1
1119	Print-Tech Inc—*James Ceely*	6800 Jackson Rd, Ann Arbor MI 48103	734-996-2345	R	4*	<.1
1120	Airo Graphics Inc—*John Rogers*	3055 S 44th St Ste 1, Phoenix AZ 85040	480-894-1630	R	4*	<.1
1121	Smith Print Inc—*Donald Smith*	90 Assinippi Ave, Norwell MA 02061	781-878-5555	R	4*	<.1
1122	Impact Printers and Lithographers Inc—*Robert Serna*	1401 Brummel Ave, Elk Grove Village IL 60007	847-981-9676	R	4*	<.1
1123	Julin Printing Company Inc—*John Williams*	PO Box 151, Monticello IA 52310	319-465-3558	R	4*	<.1
1124	Golden Banner Press Inc—*William Rand*	1248 S Padre Island Dr, Corpus Christi TX 78416	361-854-1933	R	4*	<.1
1125	Print Rite Inc—*Charles Wright*	PO Box 722130, Houston TX 77272	281-568-3333	R	4*	<.1
1126	Aa One Litho Inc—*Jay Kim*	PO Box 30055, Santa Ana CA 92735	714-641-8835	R	4*	<.1
1127	Advance Printing Inc—*Gerard Quinn*	6836 Harford Rd, Baltimore MD 21234	410-254-1111	R	4*	<.1
1128	Beauvais Printing Inc—*Charles Beauvais*	PO Box 422, Guilford CT 06437	203-453-6077	R	4*	<.1
1129	Calendar Press Inc—*Catherine Trainor*	PO Box 191, Peabody MA 01960	978-531-1860	R	4*	<.1
1130	Northern California Graphics Inc—*William Palma*	817 W Maude Ave, Sunnyvale CA 94085	408-738-3840	R	4*	<.1
1131	Sewell Printing Service Inc—*Hunter Tison*	2697 Apple Valley Rd N, Atlanta GA 30319	404-237-2553	R	4*	<.1
1132	Sun Press Inc—*Kevin Kieffer*	1800 Grand Ave, Wausau WI 54403	715-845-4911	R	4*	<.1
1133	W and C Printing Company Inc—*Dan Trainor*	PO Box 307, Winona MN 55987	507-452-2658	R	4*	<.1
1134	Courier Printing And Lithography Inc—*Robert Corirossi*	323 N 2nd St, Rockford IL 61107	815-968-6644	R	4*	<.1
1135	Carter Printing and Graphics Inc—*Gene Carter*	PO Box 385, Knightdale NC 27545	919-266-5280	R	4*	<.1
1136	Academy Graphic Communication Inc—*James Champion*	1000 Brookpark Rd, Cleveland OH 44109	216-661-2550	R	4*	<.1
1137	Leatherback Publishing Inc—*Ernie Rose*	681 7th Ave, Kirkland WA 98033	425-822-1202	R	4*	<.1
1138	Mclean Industries Inc—*Evan Mc Lean*	120 S Kenwood St, Glendale CA 91205	818-242-1146	R	4*	<.1
1139	Paladin Enterprises Inc—*Peder Lund*	PO Box 1307, Boulder CO 80306	303-443-7250	R	4*	<.1
1140	Plum Grove Printers Inc—*Peter Lineal*	2160 Stonington Ave, Hoffman Estates IL 60169	847-882-4020	R	4*	<.1
1141	Stoughton Printing Co—*Jack Stoughton*	130 N Sunset Ave, City Of Industry CA 91744	626-961-3678	R	4*	<.1
1142	Success Printing and Mailing Inc—*Robert Hurwitz*	10 Pearl St, Norwalk CT 06850	203-847-1112	R	4*	<.1
1143	Insta-Print Inc—*Gary Blancke*	7915 Penn Randall Pl, Upper Marlboro MD 20772	301-736-3390	R	4*	<.1
1144	Artcraft Inc—*Steve Chopard*	PO Box 35063, Des Moines IA 50315	515-285-3550	R	4*	<.1
1145	Sample Media Inc—*David Nahan*	112 E 8th St, Ocean City NJ 08226	609-399-5411	R	4*	<.1
1146	Direct Mail Lithographers Inc—*Kirk Swain*	231 Skipjack Rd, Prince Frederick MD 20678	301-855-1700	R	4*	<.1
1147	Fulton Press Inc—*Claude Fulton*	5610 W 65th St, Little Rock AR 72209	501-562-7007	R	4*	<.1
1148	Concord Printing Company Inc—*Ben Palmer*	420 Copperfield Blvd N, Concord NC 28025	704-786-3717	R	4*	<.1
1149	White Pines Corp—*Martha Edwards*	5204 Jackson Rd, Ann Arbor MI 48103	734-761-2670	R	4*	<.1
1150	Union-Hoermann Press Inc—*James Sigman*	PO Box 916, Dubuque IA 52004	563-582-3631	R	4*	<.1
1151	Crossfire Graphics Inc—*Richard Crosse*	3885 Forest St, Denver CO 80207	303-322-8772	R	4*	<.1
1152	Rg Acquisitions Inc—*Jeff Jump*	4236 W Ferguson Rd, Fort Wayne IN 46809	260-747-3195	R	4*	<.1
1153	Tempt Instore Productions—*Mike Draver*	N84w13480 Leon Rd Ste, Menomonee Falls WI 53051	262-293-0078	R	4*	<.1
1154	Globe Lithographing Company Inc—*Arthur Stanton*	1 Teaneck Rd Ste 1, Ridgefield Park NJ 07660	201-440-0800	R	4*	<.1
1155	Lebon Press Inc—*Andrew Lerner*	PO Box 320430, Hartford CT 06132	860-278-6355	R	4*	<.1
1156	Litho Press Inc—*Joseph Lacy*	1747 Massachusetts Ave, Indianapolis IN 46201	317-634-6468	R	4*	<.1
1157	Migu Press Inc—*Pam Mirabile*	260 Ivyland Rd, Warminster PA 18974	215-957-9763	R	4*	<.1
1158	Sherman Printing Company Inc—*Peter Sherman*	1020 Tpke St Ste 11, Canton MA 02021	781-828-8855	R	4*	<.1
1159	Qw Memphis Corp—*Frances Hayes*	PO Box 16037, Memphis TN 38186	901-348-6510	R	4*	<.1
1160	Team Printing Plus Inc—*Isaac Tristan*	2002 N 23rd Ave, Phoenix AZ 85009	602-252-5900	R	4*	<.1
1161	Pryntcomm Ltd—*Thomas Roberts*	PO Box 100, Pierre SD 57501	605-224-9999	R	4*	<.1
1162	Harris Press Inc—*Douglas Harris*	510 Mapleleaf Dr, Nashville TN 37210	615-889-8151	R	4*	<.1
1163	Computer Data Forms Inc—*Randy Unruh*	1901 E Levee St, Dallas TX 75207	214-741-3231	R	4*	<.1
1164	Mennonite Press Inc—*Steven Rudiger*	PO Box 867, Newton KS 67114	316-283-4680	R	4*	<.1

Rank	Company Name—*Executive Officer*	Address, City, State, Zip	Phone	Type	Fin	Empls
1165	Dave Shepard Enterprises Inc—*Dave Shepard*	5070 Nw 235th Ave Ste, Hillsboro OR 97124	503-693-6456	R	4*	<.1
1166	Reporter Company Inc—*Leonard Govern*	132 Delaware St Ste 2b, Walton NY 13856	607-865-4131	R	4*	<.1
1167	Conlan Corp—*Daniel Conlan*	PO Box 2763, South San Francisco CA 94083	650-871-8500	R	4*	<.1
1168	Wolverine Printing Company LLC—*Chris Peterson*	315 Grandville Ave Sw, Grand Rapids MI 49503	616-451-2075	R	4*	<.1
1169	Asheboro Piedmont Printing Inc—*Larry Presnell*	PO Box 430, Asheboro NC 27204	336-899-7910	R	4*	<.1
1170	Assistex Inc—*Doug O'dell*	9501 Console Dr Ste 10, San Antonio TX 78229	210-691-8900	R	4*	<.1
1171	Brennan's House Of Printing Inc—*Anne Brennan*	5612 Blessey St, Harahan LA 70123	504-734-7371	R	4*	<.1
1172	Eagle Printing and Thermographing—*Frank Rosienski*	2894 N Milwaukee Ave, Chicago IL 60618	773-252-0700	R	4*	<.1
1173	Imedia Inc—*Ron Williams*	4360 San Carlos Dr, Macon GA 31206	478-314-2285	R	4*	<.1
1174	Jupiter Communications LLC—*Ann Dosin*	860 Honeyspot Rd Ste 3, Stratford CT 06615	203-377-3555	R	4*	<.1
1175	Lake City Printing Inc—*Peter Romero*	1723 W Sale Rd, Lake Charles LA 70605	337-477-2595	R	4*	<.1
1176	Qwik Print and Bindery Of Florida Inc—*Candy Carnley*	1210 S Adams St, Tallahassee FL 32301	850-224-8717	R	4*	<.1
1177	Ram Offset Lithographers LLC—*Joe Milder*	2651 Ave G, White City OR 97503	541-826-3155	R	4*	<.1
1178	Dutton Press Inc—*Leonard Dutton*	280 W 79th Pl, Hialeah FL 33014	305-823-1101	R	4*	<.1
1179	Thompson Press Inc—*Frank Altino*	PO Box 4514, Hialeah FL 33014	305-625-8800	R	4*	<.1
1180	E V Yeuell Inc—*Andrew Hall*	8 Adele Rd, Woburn MA 01801	781-933-2984	R	4*	<.1
1181	Irving Press Inc—*Gerald Gaul*	2530 United Ln, Elk Grove Village IL 60007	847-595-6650	R	4*	<.1
1182	Kalnin Graphics Inc—*Dianne Kalnin*	PO Box 1011, Foxcroft Square PA 19046	215-887-6970	R	4*	<.1
1183	Mel Printing Company Inc—*Michael Filkovich*	19110 Allen Rd, Melvindale MI 48122	313-928-5440	R	4*	<.1
1184	Artistic Tape And Label Printers—*Wilford Bengtzen*	377 W 100 S, Salt Lake City UT 84101	801-532-5363	R	4*	<.1
1185	Berland Printing Inc—*Lawrence Berland*	3950 S Morgan St, Chicago IL 60609	773-327-7300	R	4*	<.1
1186	Kahny Printing Inc—*John Kahny*	4766 River Rd, Cincinnati OH 45233	513-251-2911	R	4*	<.1
1187	Tri-Star Offset Corp—*Brian Nawroth*	6020 59th Pl, Maspeth NY 11378	718-894-5555	R	4*	<.1
1188	Creative Print Group Inc—*Brian White*	1560 Caton Ctr Dr N, Baltimore MD 21227	410-242-8300	R	4*	<.1
1189	Huntford Printing—*George Loughborough*	275 Dempsey Rd, Milpitas CA 95035	408-957-5000	R	4*	<.1
1190	Official Offset Corp—*Ben Paulino*	8600 New Horizons Blvd, Amityville NY 11701	631-957-8500	R	4*	<.1
1191	Fort Wayne Printing Company Inc—*Gary Bastin*	909 Production Rd, Fort Wayne IN 46808	260-471-7744	R	4*	<.1
1192	Copy Cats—*Marino Gonzalez*	PO Box 4204, Santa Fe NM 87502	505-984-1336	R	3*	.1
1193	Cherry Lane Lithographing Corp—*William Citterbart*	15 E Bethpage Rd, Plainview NY 11803	516-293-9294	R	3*	<.1
1194	Golden Circle Printing Inc—*J Maners*	2252 Dr F E Wright Dr, Jackson TN 38305	731-423-2895	R	3*	<.1
1195	National Paper and Envelope Corp—*John Tachon*	99 Kero Rd, Carlstadt NJ 07072	201-935-9400	R	3*	<.1
1196	Newport Graphics Inc—*John Somma*	121 Varick St Rm 302, New York NY 10013	212-255-2727	R	3*	<.1
1197	King International Corp—*George Smith*	PO Box 1009, King NC 27021	336-983-5171	R	3*	<.1
1198	Semco Color Press Inc—*Bernard Semtner*	117 E Hill St, Oklahoma City OK 73105	405-528-1919	R	3*	<.1
1199	Town and Country Industries Inc—*Debera Hunchy*	1001 E Summit St, Crown Point IN 46307	219-924-0441	R	3*	<.1
1200	Dick Wildes Printing Company Inc—*Katie Stickel*	PO Box 1510, White Plains MD 20695	301-932-7171	R	3*	<.1
1201	Hooker Ballew Printing Co—*James Hooker*	133 Manufacturing St, Dallas TX 75207	214-748-5376	R	3*	<.1
1202	Berkshire Printing Inc—*Gregory Lacava*	PO Box 146, New Milford CT 06776	860-355-2675	R	3*	<.1
1203	Coprintco Business Forms Inc—*Ron Tienhaara*	PO Box 6, Longview WA 98632	360-425-1810	R	3*	<.1
1204	Deluxe Printing Company Inc—*Tom East*	PO Box 9467, Hickory NC 28603	828-322-1329	R	3*	<.1
1205	Four Star Reproductions Inc—*Charles Cioppa*	PO Box 10275, Fairfield NJ 07004	973-227-2001	R	3*	<.1
1206	Printers Trade Inc—*Saul Franks*	10081 Sandmeyer Ln, Philadelphia PA 19116	215-934-5666	R	3*	<.1
1207	Fowler Printing and Graphics Inc—*Stephen Brennan*	132 York Ave, Randolph MA 02368	781-986-8900	R	3*	<.1
1208	Nu-Way Printing and Envelope Co—*Vince Johnson*	306 Se 8th Ave, Portland OR 97214	503-232-7151	R	3*	<.1
1209	Gate City Printing Company Inc—*Chris Lassiter*	PO Box 1157, Burlington NC 27216	336-378-1163	R	3*	<.1
1210	Earle Press Inc—*Jerry Grevel*	PO Box 327, Muskegon MI 49443	231-773-2111	R	3*	<.1
1211	Gainesville Printing Co—*Roger Fleitman*	PO Box 1011, Gainesville TX 76241	940-665-5517	R	3*	<.1
1212	Riverrun Press—*Alfred Higdon*	600 Shoppers Ln, Kalamazoo MI 49004	269-349-7603	R	3*	<.1
1213	Wordsprint Inc—*Steve Lester*	PO Box 544, Wytheville VA 24382	276-228-6608	R	3*	<.1
1214	Alliance Press Inc—*Matthew Edwards*	5908 Weisbrook Ln, Knoxville TN 37909	865-584-3500	R	3*	<.1
1215	Eps Printing Inc—*Joe Salam*	490 Burnham St, South Windsor CT 06074	860-528-9426	R	3*	<.1
1216	Jewett Publications Inc—*Richard Jewett*	PO Box 390, Farmersburg IN 47850	812-696-2015	R	3*	<.1
1217	Mercantile Press Inc—*Coleman Bye*	3007 Bellevue Ave, Wilmington DE 19802	302-764-6884	R	3*	<.1
1218	Sprint Print Inc—*Craig Winstead*	PO Box 1250, Madisonville KY 42431	270-825-3376	R	3*	<.1
1219	Vanard Lithographers Inc—*Annette Fritzenkotter*	PO Box 87884, San Diego CA 92138	619-291-8350	R	3*	<.1
1220	D and D Printing Co—*Mike Bardwell*	342 Market Ave Sw Unit, Grand Rapids MI 49503	616-454-7710	R	3*	<.1
1221	Advertisers Duplicating Inc—*Doug Freeman*	PO Box 42307, Urbandale IA 50323	515-254-0080	R	3*	<.1
1222	American Printing and Envelope Inc—*Anthony Penny*	PO Box 347, Auburn MA 01501	508-832-6100	R	3*	<.1
1223	Breck Graphics Inc—*Ron Vetter*	3983 Linden Ave Se, Grand Rapids MI 49548	616-248-4000	R	3*	<.1
1224	Curry Printing Ltd—*Cody Curry*	1109 Pamela Dr, Euless TX 76040	817-545-7777	R	3*	<.1
1225	Farley Printing Co—*William Englehart*	96 Vandever Ave, Wilmington DE 19802	302-656-4466	R	3*	<.1
1226	Friendship Creative Printers Inc—*Gregg Palmer*	1120 Benfield Blvd Ste, Millersville MD 21108	410-987-2000	R	3*	<.1
1227	House Of Graphics—*Phillis Herbold*	370 Randy Rd, Carol Stream IL 60188	630-682-0810	R	3*	<.1
1228	Mandel Co—*Rick Mandel*	PO Box 12124, Milwaukee WI 53212	414-271-6970	R	3*	<.1
1229	Master Graphics—*Christopher Love*	1100a S Main St, Rochelle IL 61068	815-562-5800	R	3*	<.1
1230	Merrit Press Inc—*Merrit Lauderback*	700 Tidewater Dr, Norfolk VA 23504	757-460-2890	R	3*	<.1
1231	Sbpi Inc—*Bill Henry*	PO Box 8487, Saint Louis MO 63132	314-423-2424	R	3*	<.1
1232	Southern Company Enterprise Inc—*Mark Thompson*	54024 Cravey Rd, Callahan FL 32011	904-879-2101	R	3*	<.1
1233	Swift Print Inc—*Randy Leonard*	PO Box 49320, Wichita KS 67201	316-262-3789	R	3*	<.1
1234	Tom and Jerry Printcraft Forms Inc—*Thomas Guidice*	PO Box 743, Mamaroneck NY 10543	914-698-3453	R	3*	<.1
1235	White Eagle Printing Company Inc—*Eric Bielawski*	2550 Kuser Rd, Trenton NJ 08691	609-586-2032	R	3*	<.1
1236	Winner Press Inc—*Hermi Fu*	4331 33rd St 1, Long Island City NY 11101	718-937-7715	R	3*	<.1
1237	Busy Printing—*William Henry*	2464 S Tejon St, Englewood CO 80110	303-936-3441	R	3*	<.1
1238	Duley Press Inc—*Michael Lowenhar*	PO Box 484, Mishawaka IN 46546	574-259-5203	R	3*	<.1
1239	Suburban Press Inc—*William Mueller*	3818 Lorain Ave, Cleveland OH 44113	216-961-0766	R	3*	<.1
1240	Independent Printing Company Inc—*Margaret Bell*	8735 Bollman Pl Ste A, Savage MD 20763	410-792-8866	R	3*	<.1
1241	Phoenix Graphics Inc—*Sal Biase*	464 State St 470, Rochester NY 14608	585-232-4040	R	3*	<.1
1242	Just-Us Printers Inc—*Michael Justus*	PO Box 41, Springdale AR 72765	479-751-0385	R	3*	<.1
1243	Dowd - Witbeck Printing Corp—*Denise Padula*	599 Pawling Ave, Troy NY 12180	518-274-2421	R	3*	<.1
1244	424 Holdings LLC	217 5th Ave N Ste 200, Minneapolis MN 55401	612-338-2068	R	3*	<.1
1245	Presscraft Papers Inc—*Pamela Lorenz*	5140 River Rd, Benzonia MI 49616	231-882-5505	R	3*	<.1
1246	Image Group Inc—*James Plummer*	PO Box 248, Syracuse IN 46567	574-457-3111	R	3*	<.1
1247	Canaan Printing Inc—*Carolyn Misenheimer*	4820 Jefferson Davis H, Richmond VA 23234	804-271-4820	R	3*	<.1
1248	J and L Press Inc—*Mark Iwakiri*	600 Sonora Ave, Glendale CA 91201	818-549-8344	R	3*	<.1
1249	Molloy Corp—*John Molloy*	9000 Suthwest Fwy Ste, Houston TX 77074	713-771-9485	R	3*	<.1
1250	Professional Graphics Printing Co—*George Chesky*	9550 Lynn Buff Ct, Laurel MD 20723	301-470-7177	R	3*	<.1
1251	Lewis Color Lithographers Inc—*Thomas Lewis*	30 Joseph E Kennedy Bl, Statesboro GA 30458	912-681-6824	R	3*	<.1
1252	Tampa Bay Press Inc—*John Hedler*	4710 Eisenhower Blvd B, Tampa FL 33634	813-886-1415	R	3*	<.1
1253	American Printers Exchange Inc—*Daniel Brannon*	1606 Headway Cir Ste 1, Austin TX 78754	512-452-5058	R	3*	<.1
1254	Atkins Printing Service Inc—*James Mitchell*	155 Main St, Waterville ME 04901	207-872-5565	R	3*	<.1

Note: An asterisk (*) indicates an estimated financial figure. The company type code used is as follows: R = Private, P = Public, S = Private Subsidiary, B = Public Subsidiary, D = Division, J = Joint Venture, I = Investment Fund.

COMPANY RANKINGS BY SALES WITHIN 4-DIGIT SIC

Rank	Company Name—*Executive Officer*	Address, City, State, Zip	Phone	Type	Fin	Empls
1255	Bell Photographers Inc—*David Bell*	6600 Hwy 89, Ogden UT 84405	801-479-4624	R	3*	<.1
1256	Bri-Lee Marketing Inc—*Sandra Hedges*	404 W Powell Ln Ste 40, Austin TX 78753	512-836-6902	R	3*	<.1
1257	EFM Group Inc—*Del Crone*	PO Box 94958, Phoenix AZ 85070	602-256-2500	R	3*	<.1
1258	Goodwin Brothers Printing Co—*Patrick Goodwin*	2613 N Broadway, Saint Louis MO 63102	314-231-8732	R	3*	<.1
1259	Hall Letter Shop Inc—*Catherine Dounies*	5200 Rosedale Hwy, Bakersfield CA 93308	661-327-3228	R	3*	<.1
1260	Hanson Printing Company Inc—*Kim Taylor*	PO Box 1990, Brockton MA 02303	508-586-4737	R	3*	<.1
1261	Hudson Printing Company Inc—*Robert Bergman*	4809 34th St, Long Island City NY 11101	718-937-8600	R	3*	<.1
1262	Independent Resources Inc—*David Curbelo*	PO Box 23489, Tampa FL 33623	813-237-0945	R	3*	<.1
1263	Inkstone Inc—*Robert Donahoe*	129 Liberty St, Brockton MA 02301	508-587-5200	R	3*	<.1
1264	Irwin Enterprises Inc—*Larry Irwin*	3030 W Pasadena Ave, Flint MI 48504	810-732-0180	R	3*	<.1
1265	Northeast Wisconsin Printing Company Inc—*Mark Weinfurter*	1718 E Wisconsin Ave, Appleton WI 54911	920-735-6777	R	3*	<.1
1266	Trojan Press Inc—*Nancy Dreiling*	1635 Burlington St, North Kansas City MO 64116	816-221-6477	R	3*	<.1
1267	Crown Press Inc—*Scott Hauer*	2450 S 24th St, Phoenix AZ 85034	602-437-4444	R	3*	<.1
1268	Jaysell Inc—*Larry Lazarus*	317 N Orange Ave, Orlando FL 32801	407-423-2051	R	3*	<.1
1269	R G Management Inc—*Michael Rogers*	3640 Princeton Oaks St, Orlando FL 32808	407-889-3100	R	3*	<.1
1270	Image Systems Inc—*Mark Dexter*	37 W 28th St Fl 10, New York NY 10001	212-727-2600	R	3*	<.1
1271	Imperial Graphic Communications Inc—*David Emery*	600 Honeyspot Rd, Stratford CT 06615	203-377-2676	R	3*	<.1
1272	Lewis Printing Co—*Chris Lewis*	PO Box 27122, Richmond VA 23261	804-648-2000	R	3*	<.1
1273	Master Printing Co—*Donald Dobos*	3112 Broadview Rd, Cleveland OH 44109	216-351-2246	R	3*	<.1
1274	Mix Printing Company Inc—*Joanne Mix*	PO Box 112460, Carrollton TX 75011	972-248-9000	R	3*	<.1
1275	George H Buchanan—*Carl Zweigle*	PO Box 788, Swedesboro NJ 08085	856-241-3960	R	3*	<.1
1276	Dimension Photo Engraving Company Inc—*Douglas Drenberg*	1507 W Cass St, Tampa FL 33606	813-251-0244	R	3*	<.1
1277	Quality Quick Print Inc—*Roger Feickert*	PO Box 940, Aberdeen SD 57402	605-226-2541	R	3*	.1
1278	Lauderdale Graphics Corp—*Boon Tirasitipol*	10110 USA Today Way, Miramar FL 33025	954-450-0800	R	3*	<.1
1279	Warner Offset Inc—*Mark Warner*	640 Stevenson Rd, South Elgin IL 60177	847-695-9400	R	3*	<.1
1280	Decal Information Systems—*Nancy Matturi*	PO Box 2728, Huntersville NC 28070	704-688-0964	R	3*	<.1
1281	Stephenville Printing Company Inc—*Tommy Cochran*	1193 W S Loop, Stephenville TX 76401	254-965-5012	R	3*	<.1
1282	Central Texas Printing Inc—*A Price*	1522 Washington Ave, Waco TX 76701	254-754-4653	R	3*	<.1
1283	D S Wilson Enterprises Inc—*William Wilson*	815 Union St, Selma AL 36701	334-875-6214	R	3*	<.1
1284	Progressive Graphics Inc—*Norman Williams*	2860 Crusader Cir, Virginia Beach VA 23453	757-368-3321	R	3*	<.1
1285	Tops Printing Inc—*Steven Britton*	2023 S Texas Ave, Bryan TX 77802	979-779-1234	R	3*	<.1
1286	Ideal Printing Co—*Dan Goris*	2801 Oak Industrial Dr, Grand Rapids MI 49505	616-453-2433	R	3*	<.1
1287	Colorsource Inc—*Alfred Demarco*	5113 Central Hwy, Pennsauken NJ 08109	856-488-8100	R	3*	<.1
1288	Galvanic Printing and Plate Company Inc—*John Moss*	50 Commercial Ave, Moonachie NJ 07074	201-939-3600	R	3*	<.1
1289	Lafayette Printing Co—*David Sattler*	PO Box 206, Lafayette IN 47902	765-423-2578	R	3*	<.1
1290	A and A Printing Inc—*Atef Matni*	320 Queen Anne Ave N, Seattle WA 98109	206-285-3883	R	3*	<.1
1291	A-1 Printing Service Inc—*Frazer Windless*	810 E Brooks Rd, Memphis TN 38116	901-396-2023	R	3*	<.1
1292	Brujan Inc—*Jacqueline Bischoff*	855 Bloomfield Ave, Clifton NJ 07012	973-773-8950	R	3*	<.1
1293	City Printing Company Inc—*Joseph Valentini*	122 Oak Hill Ave, Youngstown OH 44502	330-747-5691	R	3*	<.1
1294	LC Dumac	2837 S 600 W, Salt Lake City UT 84115	801-328-8748	R	3*	<.1
1295	Popcorn Press Inc—*Al Glasby*	32400 Edward Ave Ste A, Madison Heights MI 48071	248-588-4444	R	3*	<.1
1296	Publications Printing Of Nebraska Inc—*Philip Crews*	PO Box 130, Waterloo NE 68069	402-779-4696	R	3*	<.1
1297	Real World Enterprises Inc—*Dave Haugland*	1754 University Ave W, Saint Paul MN 55104	651-644-5979	R	3*	<.1
1298	A and H Lithoprint Inc—*Patricia Ashley*	2540 S 27th Ave, Broadview IL 60155	708-345-1196	R	3*	<.1
1299	Johnston Printing Inc—*J Johnston*	PO Box 2525, Spokane WA 99220	509-624-4407	R	3*	<.1
1300	Physicians Record Company Inc—*John Voller*	3000 Ridgeland Ave, Berwyn IL 60402	708-749-3111	R	3*	.1
1301	Hansen Printing Company Inc—*Bruce Hansen*	9745 Industrial Dr Ste, Bridgeview IL 60455	708-599-1500	R	3*	<.1
1302	Art Communication Systems Inc—*Park Cook*	1340 N 17th St, Harrisburg PA 17103	717-232-0144	R	3*	<.1
1303	Marketing Team Alpha Inc—*Timothy Doan*	1871 Summit Rd, Cincinnati OH 45237	513-821-2275	R	3*	<.1
1304	A and L Litho Inc—*Lee Hayes*	PO Box 461149, Escondido CA 92046	760-752-9500	R	3*	<.1
1305	Armstrong Family Industries Inc—*Edward Armstrong*	1 Printers Dr, Hermon ME 04401	207-848-7300	R	3*	<.1
1306	Copy Express Inc—*Steve Daugherty*	1255 Eastland Dr, Lexington KY 40505	859-255-2679	R	3*	<.1
1307	Georges and Shapiro Lithograph Inc—*Jason Shapiro* Consolidated Graphics Inc	8386 Rovana Cir, Sacramento CA 95828	916-231-1410	S	3*	
1308	Howard Printing Company Inc—*Michael Smetana*	7419 S Sprinkle Rd, Portage MI 49002	269-329-0022	R	3*	<.1
1309	Johnson's Office Solutions Inc—*Derek Johnson*	PO Box 817, Hazlehurst GA 31539	912-375-4208	R	3*	<.1
1310	MFA Atelier Inc—*Al Marco*	201 Nevada St, El Segundo CA 90245	310-615-1818	R	3*	<.1
1311	Schulenburg Printing and Office Supplies Inc—*Randy Proske*	PO Box 429, Schulenburg TX 78956	979-743-4511	R	3*	<.1
1312	theprinterscom—*Raymond J Caravan*	3500 E College Ave Ste, State College PA 16801	814-237-7600	R	3*	<.1
1313	Unigraphic-Color Corp—*Donna Hansbury*	301 W Mn St, Plymouth PA 18651	570-779-9543	R	3*	<.1
1314	Angel Lithographing Co—*William Angel*	2700 90th St, Sturtevant WI 53177	262-637-7171	R	3*	<.1
1315	Bastian Brothers and Co—*John Waugh*	PO Box 260, Freeland MI 48623	989-695-5534	R	3*	<.1
1316	Print Shop Inc—*Phillip Rutledge*	PO Box 1868, Glasgow KY 42142	270-651-3751	R	3*	<.1
1317	Folks Creative Printers Inc—*James Saiter*	101 E George St, Marion OH 43302	740-383-6326	R	3*	<.1
1318	Beacon Printing Company Inc—*George Grimes*	2850 Old Washington Rd, Waldorf MD 20601	301-843-1995	R	3*	<.1
1319	Gallant Graphices Limited Inc—*Melvin Eiger*	242 Attlebury Hill Rd, Stanfordville NY 12581	845-868-1166	R	3*	<.1
1320	Aspen Graphics Inc—*Ted Reece*	4795 Oakland St, Denver CO 80239	303-371-2345	R	3*	<.1
1321	Brita Litho Inc—*Thomas Galante*	629 Grove St Ste 701, Jersey City NJ 07310	201-526-9314	R	3*	<.1
1322	Clearwater Packaging Inc—*John Hoover*	615 Grand Central St B, Clearwater FL 33756	727-442-2596	R	3*	<.1
1323	Crc Print Inc—*Brian Kowalski*	PO Box 95585, Palatine IL 60095	847-215-8611	R	3*	<.1
1324	Davis Printing And Business Forms—*Robert Davis*	PO Box 65249, Salt Lake City UT 84165	801-486-3851	R	3*	<.1
1325	Durra Print Inc—*Tim Durrance*	717 S Woodward Ave, Tallahassee FL 32304	850-222-4768	R	3*	<.1
1326	Galley Printing Company Inc—*Richard Stitch*	2892 Westway Dr, Brunswick OH 44212	330-220-5577	R	3*	<.1
1327	Gibbs General Printing Inc—*Kenneth Gibbs*	1910 N Providence Rd, Columbia MO 65202	573-443-8890	R	3*	<.1
1328	Keystone Press Inc—*Robert Trapani*	5683 New Peachtree Rd, Atlanta GA 30341	770-458-3174	R	3*	<.1
1329	Mccann-Southworth Printing Co—*Robert Mccann*	529 N Prince Ln, Springfield MO 65802	417-831-7207	R	3*	<.1
1330	Michael Graphics Inc—*Michael Caruso*	11 Terminal Rd, New Brunswick NJ 08901	732-846-8680	R	3*	<.1
1331	Shearer Printing Service Inc—*Brian Shearer*	PO Box 668, Kokomo IN 46903	765-457-3274	R	3*	<.1
1332	Trese Inc—*Michael Trese*	2040 Murrell Rd, Rockledge FL 32955	321-632-7272	R	3*	<.1
1333	Abc Printing Inc—*Robert Kagy*	PO Box 3309, Lacey WA 98509	360-456-4545	R	3*	<.1
1334	Lithoprint Company Inc—*Steven Smirl*	PO Box 498, Waukesha WI 53187	262-542-3520	R	3*	<.1
1335	Printing Port Inc—*Wayne Morris*	PO Box 2092, Myrtle Beach SC 29578	843-236-1225	R	3*	<.1
1336	Printing Services Of Greensboro Inc—*Eddie Brame*	PO Box 13242, Greensboro NC 27415	336-274-7663	R	3*	<.1
1337	Bacon Printing Inc—*Carlton Strout*	1070 Hammond St, Bangor ME 04401	207-942-5593	R	3*	<.1
1338	Columbine Trenton Co—*Robert Lesser*	10415 Trenton Ave, Saint Louis MO 63132	314-423-2580	R	3*	<.1
1339	Premier Color Graphics Inc—*Wayne Yada*	324 S Santa Fe St, Visalia CA 93292	559-625-8606	R	3*	<.1
1340	Tiger Business Forms Inc—*Mike Pina*	7765 W 20th Ave, Hialeah FL 33014	305-888-3528	R	3*	<.1
1341	Conkur Printing Inc—*Walter Pflumm*	629 W 54th St Fl 4, New York NY 10019	212-541-5980	R	3*	<.1
1342	Gateway Printing and Graphics Inc—*Jeffery Donner*	3970 Big Tree Rd, Hamburg NY 14075	716-823-3873	R	3*	<.1
1343	Gh Printing Company Inc—*Gail Herlin*	5207 Walnut Ave, Downers Grove IL 60515	630-960-4115	R	3*	<.1

Rank	Company Name—*Executive Officer*	Address, City, State, Zip	Phone	Type	Fin	Empls
1344	J and D Printing Inc—*John Vitzthum*	815 S 28th St Ste C, Tacoma WA 98409	253-272-3336	R	3*	<.1
1345	Mekong Printing Inc—*Hoan Truong*	2421 W 1st St, Santa Ana CA 92703	714-558-9595	R	3*	<.1
1346	Star Printing Company Inc—*Robert L'auck*	125 N Union St, Akron OH 44304	330-376-0514	R	3*	<.1
1347	Swifty Printing and Digital Imaging Inc—*Ben Nikfard*	2001 3rd Ave, Seattle WA 98121	206-441-0800	R	3*	<.1
1348	World Press Inc—*Adrian Peters*	1626 Manufacturers Dr, Fenton MO 63026	636-343-1167	R	3*	<.1
1349	Com Tec Printing and Graphics Inc—*Lorrie Culloton*	2219 E University Dr, Phoenix AZ 85034	602-273-9060	R	3*	<.1
1350	Harbor Duvall Graphics Inc—*Michael Duvall*	2604 Sisson St Ste 2, Baltimore MD 21211	410-243-9300	R	3*	<.1
1351	Holly's Custom Print Inc—*Steve Hollingshead*	PO Box 4454, Newark OH 43058	740-928-2697	R	3*	<.1
1352	Lombard Enterprises Inc—*Stephen Lombard*	3619 San Gbriel River, Pico Rivera CA 90660	562-692-7070	R	3*	<.1
1353	Pasa Services Inc—*Blanca Bichara*	2277 Nw 82nd Ave, Doral FL 33122	305-594-8662	R	3*	<.1
1354	APG Inc—*Rick Snodgrass*	5355 Oakbrook Pkwy, Norcross GA 30093	770-446-0256	R	3*	<.1
1355	Artisan Columbia Printing—*Alan Granat*	469 Union Ave, Westbury NY 11590	516-997-7990	R	3*	<.1
1356	Richards Graphic Communications Inc—*Mary Lawrence*	2700 Van Buren St, Bellwood IL 60104	708-547-6000	R	3*	<.1
1357	Terry Print Solutions—*Mark Terry*	PO Box 1839, Janesville WI 53547	608-752-1517	R	3*	<.1
1358	Action Printers LLC—*Del Orser*	PO Box 337, Coeur D Alene ID 83816	208-667-2488	R	3*	<.1
1359	Communication Graphics Inc (Glen Burnie Maryland)—*Diana O'Donnell*	6741 Baymeadow Dr, Glen Burnie MD 21060	410-768-1100	R	3*	<.1
1360	Johnson Graphics Inc—*Tom Peterson*	21 Fontana Ln Ste 101, Baltimore MD 21237	410-918-0600	R	3*	<.1
1361	VisionPs LLC	208 S Jefferson St Fl, Chicago IL 60661	312-263-6002	R	3*	<.1
1362	Bbc Corp—*Chris Mulligan*	4286 N Star Dr, Shingle Springs CA 95682	530-677-4009	R	3*	<.1
1363	Matthews Printing Company Inc—*Billy Lipscomb*	PO Box 1433, Gainesville GA 30503	770-536-3439	R	3*	<.1
1364	Youngstown Arc Engraving Co—*E Olsen*	380 Victoria Rd, Youngstown OH 44515	330-793-2471	R	3*	<.1
1365	Bromley Printing Inc—*Elizabeth Bromley*	514 Northdale Blvd Nw, Minneapolis MN 55448	763-767-0000	R	3*	<.1
1366	Crow River Press—*Christine Boesche*	PO Box 99, Hutchinson MN 55350	320-587-2062	R	3*	<.1
1367	Hauser Printing Company Inc—*J Alker*	1513 Sams Ave, New Orleans LA 70123	504-733-2022	R	3*	<.1
1368	Northern and Nye Printing Inc—*Randy Northern*	3115 Robinson Dr, Waco TX 76706	254-662-2292	R	3*	<.1
1369	Paradise Printing Inc—*Paul Pistone*	14657 Industry Cir, La Mirada CA 90638	714-228-9628	R	3*	<.1
1370	Printing Incorporated Of Louisville Kentucky—*Kelly Abney*	1600 Dutch Ln Ste A, Jeffersonville IN 47130	502-368-6555	R	3*	<.1
1371	Campbell Graphics Inc—*Laverne Lamar*	545 Westchester Dr, Campbell CA 95008	408-371-6411	R	3*	<.1
1372	Register Graphics Inc—*Robert Beach*	PO Box 98, Randolph NY 14772	716-358-2921	R	3*	<.1
1373	William N Cann Inc—*William Cann*	1 Meco Cir, Wilmington DE 19804	302-995-0820	R	3*	<.1
1374	All American Publishing Limited Co—*John Elliott*	5417 W Kendall St, Boise ID 83706	208-376-5080	R	3*	<.1
1375	Atlas Lithograph Co—*William Cary*	7807 Ostrow St, San Diego CA 92111	858-560-8273	R	3*	<.1
1376	Baldwin Press Inc—*Gary Baldwin*	110 Leslie St, Dallas TX 75207	214-631-0111	R	3*	<.1
1377	Carolina Graphic Arts Inc—*Ricky Owens*	10 Hendrix Dr, Greenville SC 29607	864-627-1881	R	3*	<.1
1378	Diego and Son Printing Inc—*Nicholas Aguilera*	PO Box 13100, San Diego CA 92170	619-233-5373	R	3*	<.1
1379	Nacci Printing Inc—*Frank Nacci*	1327 N 18th St, Allentown PA 18104	610-434-1224	R	3*	<.1
1380	Precision Graphics Of Oregon Inc—*Raymond Budd*	18500 Sw Teton Ave, Tualatin OR 97062	503-692-1000	R	3*	<.1
1381	Wells Print and Digital Services Inc—*Thomas Schorr*	3121 Watford Way, Madison WI 53713	608-274-7474	R	3*	<.1
1382	S Beckman Print and Graphic Solutions Inc—*Tracy Beckman*	376 Morrison Rd Ste D, Columbus OH 43213	614-864-2232	R	3*	<.1
1383	Unicom Grafix Inc—*Jerry Schuchardt*	PO Box 27226, Tucson AZ 85726	520-571-1740	R	3*	<.1
1384	West Shore Printing And Distribution Corp—*Robert Bruckner*	304 Mulberry Dr, Mechanicsburg PA 17050	717-691-8282	R	3*	<.1
1385	Hi-Lites Graphic Inc—*Jon Sovinski*	1212 Locust St, Fremont MI 49412	231-924-0630	R	3*	<.1
1386	Bps Printing and Graphics Inc—*Arvel Clark*	4474 White Plains Ln, White Plains MD 20695	301-753-4004	R	3*	<.1
1387	Starprint Publications Inc—*Eugene Stepp*	PO Box 216, Portage PA 15946	814-736-9666	R	3*	<.1
1388	Visual Art Graphic Services Inc—*George South*	5244 Goodell Rd, Mantua OH 44255	330-274-2775	R	3*	<.1
1389	Lebco Graphics Inc—*Lanne Brehmer*	31400 Interstate 10 W, Boerne TX 78006	830-755-8226	R	3*	<.1
1390	Hermitage Press Inc—*Michael Stoeckle*	1595 5th St, Ewing NJ 08638	609-882-3600	R	3*	<.1
1391	A To Z Offset Printing and Publishing Inc—*Joseph Zetouny*	9115 Terminal Ave, Skokie IL 60077	847-966-3016	R	3*	<.1
1392	Action Printing Of Norman Inc—*Steve Lindsay*	3400 Charleston Rd, Norman OK 73069	405-364-3615	R	3*	<.1
1393	Davis Printing Inc—*Joe Davis*	PO Box 51907, Bowling Green KY 42102	270-781-4770	R	3*	<.1
1394	Gateway Printing Company Inc—*Byrl Pointer*	PO Box 536, Bremen GA 30110	770-537-4329	R	3*	<.1
1395	Branner Printing Service Inc—*L Branner*	PO Box 307, Broadway VA 22815	540-896-8947	R	3*	<.1
1396	Top Graphics Inc—*Stephen Kodner*	658 Fee Fee Rd, Maryland Heights MO 63043	314-469-0505	R	3*	<.1
1397	Wholesale Envelope Inc—*Tommy Somers*	2410 Rice St, Lubbock TX 79415	806-762-2255	R	3*	<.1
1398	Cockle Printing Company Inc—*Andy Cockle*	2311 Douglas St, Omaha NE 68102	402-342-2831	R	3*	<.1
1399	Pencraft Corp—*John Pensinger*	4012 Kingston Ct Se St, Marietta GA 30067	770-612-0633	R	3*	<.1
1400	Golden Color Printing Inc—*Deng-Muh Yen*	9353 Rush St, South El Monte CA 91733	626-455-0850	R	3*	<.1
1401	James Conolly Printing Company Inc—*Robert Conolly*	72 Marway Cir, Rochester NY 14624	585-426-4150	R	3*	<.1
1402	Millennium Press Inc—*James Sullivan*	570 Silver St, Agawam MA 01001	413-821-0028	R	3*	<.1
1403	Tutt and Associates Inc—*Robert Tuttleman*	24154 Haggerty Rd, Farmington Hills MI 48335	248-476-3400	R	3*	<.1
1404	Ace Graphics Inc—*Rodney Kranz*	2052 Corporate Ln, Naperville IL 60563	630-357-2244	R	3*	<.1
1405	Advance Print and Graphics Inc—*Gary Hambell*	4553 Concourse Dr, Ann Arbor MI 48108	734-663-6816	R	3*	<.1
1406	Artcraft Engraving and Printing Inc—*Frederick Narup*	7921 W 26th Ave, Hialeah FL 33016	305-557-9449	R	3*	<.1
1407	Eveready Printing Inc—*Roger Wolfson*	20700 Miles Pkwy, Cleveland OH 44128	216-587-2389	R	3*	<.1
1408	J and K Resources Inc—*Jeff Seid*	PO Box 30717, Portland OR 97294	503-252-4009	R	3*	<.1
1409	Norcal Printing Inc—*Mei Lee*	1698 Evans Ave, San Francisco CA 94124	415-282-8856	R	3*	<.1
1410	Prime Investments Inc—*Alan Heywood*	856 E Main St, Mesa AZ 85203	480-833-8335	R	3*	<.1
1411	Wall Street Business Products Inc—*Steven Altman*	151 W 30th St Fl 8, New York NY 10001	212-563-4014	R	3*	<.1
1412	New City Communications—*Brian Hieggelke*	770 N Halsted St Ste 1, Chicago IL 60642	312-243-8786	R	3*	<.1
1413	Milford Printers—*Robert Heichel*	317 Main St, Milford OH 45150	513-831-6630	R	3*	<.1
1414	Quality Printing Service Inc—*George Keiser*	PO Box 1274, Bismarck ND 58502	701-255-3900	R	3*	<.1
1415	Decal Source Inc—*Anthony Johnson*	804 Knox Rd, Mc Leansville NC 27301	336-574-3141	R	3*	<.1
1416	Remlitho Inc—*Dominique Mattei*	PO Box 28, Terryville CT 06786	203-375-6990	R	3*	<.1
1417	Conti Publishing Inc—*Gerald Conti*	3030 Horseshoe Dr S St, Naples FL 34104	239-643-0047	R	3*	<.1
1418	Team Litho Inc—*Irwin Finkelstein*	629 W 54th St Fl 4, New York NY 10019	212-645-1380	R	3*	<.1
1419	Wholesale Printers Inc—*Ronald Ermshar*	10816 Ne 189th St, Battle Ground WA 98604	360-687-5500	R	3*	<.1
1420	Copy Center Of Topeka Inc—*Don Walters*	305 Se 17th St Ste C, Topeka KS 66607	785-234-6613	R	3*	<.1
1421	Morgan Printers Inc—*Jack Morgan*	PO Box 2126, Greenville NC 27836	252-355-5588	R	3*	<.1
1422	Rivkind Associates Inc—*Melvin Rivkind*	1735 Tpke St, Stoughton MA 02072	781-344-2650	R	3*	<.1
1423	Ben Franklin Press and Label Co—*Dennis Patterson*	480 Technology Way, Napa CA 94558	707-253-8250	R	3*	<.1
1424	Color Graphic Printing Inc—*Steve Johnson*	4150 W Division St, Springfield MO 65802	417-869-0848	R	3*	<.1
1425	Delta Pi Inc—*Chris Maloney*	2120 El Camino Ave, Sacramento CA 95821	916-446-3051	R	3*	<.1
1426	Garlic Inc—*Allen Gardner*	311 Ruthar Dr, Newark DE 19711	302-366-0848	R	3*	<.1
1427	Genie Repros Inc—*Barry Bishop*	2211 Hamilton Ave, Cleveland OH 44114	216-696-6677	R	3*	<.1
1428	Harris Lithographics Inc—*Harold Harris*	8516 Rainswood Dr, Landover MD 20785	301-322-1178	R	3*	<.1
1429	Illinois Office Supply Elect Printing Inc—*Robert Keeney*	1119 La Salle St, Ottawa IL 61350	815-434-0186	R	3*	<.1
1430	Qqc Printing LC	1152 W Riverdale Rd, Ogden UT 84405	801-621-7127	R	3*	<.1
1431	Skinner Printing Company Inc—*John Campbell*	PO Box 1787, Montgomery AL 36102	334-213-1116	R	3*	<.1
1432	Star Copy Printing and Promotion Center Inc—*Charles Kanney*	1911 Glazer Ave Ste 13, Naperville IL 60540	630-778-7827	R	3*	<.1

Note: An asterisk (*) indicates an estimated financial figure. The company type code used is as follows: R = Private, P = Public, S = Private Subsidiary, B = Public Subsidiary, D = Division, J = Joint Venture, I = Investment Fund.

COMPANY RANKINGS BY SALES WITHIN 4-DIGIT SIC

Rank	Company Name—Executive Officer	Address, City, State, Zip	Phone	Type	Fin	Empls
1433	Three Man Corp—John Barros	9190 Camino Santa Fe, San Diego CA 92121	858-684-5200	R	3*	<.1
1434	Travers Printing Inc—Ellen Courtemanche	PO Box 279, Gardner MA 01440	978-632-0530	R	3*	<.1
1435	Wooster Printing and Litho Inc—Andrew Kuntz	PO Box 71, Wooster OH 44691	330-264-5540	R	3*	<.1
1436	Dawson's Printing Inc—Gary Dawson	PO Box 455, Memphis TN 38101	901-525-3311	R	3*	<.1
1437	Claffey Printing Co—David Claffey	748 Greene St, Augusta GA 30901	706-724-3040	R	3*	<.1
1438	Courier Printing Corp—Hilton Evans	24 Laurel Bank Ave Ste, Deposit NY 13754	607-467-2191	R	3*	<.1
1439	First Impressions Printing Inc—Frank Spontelli	1847 Sw 27th Ave, Ocala FL 34471	352-237-6141	R	3*	<.1
1440	Su Printing Services—Michael Domachowske	1600 Jamesville Aave, Syracuse NY 13244	315-443-5145	R	3*	<.1
1441	Litho Graphics Print Communications Inc—Rod Lossner	1300 Sw Army Post Rd, Des Moines IA 50315	515-287-1795	R	3*	<.1
1442	Economy Printing Company Inc—Larry Smith	7837 Ocean Gateway, Easton MD 21601	410-822-3300	R	3*	<.1
1443	TR Wallis Graphics Inc—Tim Wallis	PO Box 1674, Rome GA 30162	706-234-7563	R	3*	<.1
1444	Pyramid Printing And Advertising Inc—Ronald Ciccolo	54-60 Mathewson Dr, Weymouth MA 02189	781-337-7609	R	3*	<.1
1445	12th Avenue Graphics Copy Service—Lazaro Valdes	PO Box 420010, Miami FL 33242	305-635-4441	R	3*	<.1
1446	Carlos Printing Concepts Inc—Greg Deusser	8803 S 218th St, Kent WA 98031	253-872-5454	R	3*	<.1
1447	Crescent Printing Company Inc—Roger Bjorge	1001 Commercial Ct, Onalaska WI 54650	608-781-1050	R	3*	<.1
1448	Custom Lithograph—Robert Hanel	7006 Stanford Ave, Los Angeles CA 90001	323-778-7751	R	3*	<.1
1449	Falcon Printing Inc—Juergen Lohrke	PO Box 280, Ada MI 49301	616-676-3737	R	3*	<.1
1450	Fine Line Litho Inc—Louis Lopardo	PO Box 6299, Cleveland OH 44101	216-426-5660	R	3*	<.1
1451	Future Reproductions Inc—Bryan Warras	21477 Bridge St Ste L, Southfield MI 48033	248-350-2060	R	3*	<.1
1452	Industrial Graphics Service Inc—James Chandler	5765 E N Ave, Kalamazoo MI 49048	269-381-1870	R	3*	<.1
1453	Kinaneco Inc—Greg Kinane	2925 Milton Ave, Syracuse NY 13209	315-468-6201	R	3*	<.1
1454	Largus Speedy Print Corp—Thomas Largus	732 W 45th St, Munster IN 46321	219-922-8414	R	3*	<.1
1455	Marquardt Printing Co—Barton Marquardt	7530 S Madison St Ste, Willowbrook IL 60527	630-887-8500	R	3*	<.1
1456	Minit Print It—Brad Warren	137 W Jefferson St, Louisville KY 40202	502-584-8386	R	3*	<.1
1457	Mundorff Graphics—Cynthia Mundorff	14400 Doolittle Dr, San Leandro CA 94577	510-895-1300	R	3*	<.1
1458	Navrat's Inc—Richard Duncan	PO Box N, Emporia KS 66801	620-342-2092	R	3*	<.1
1459	Premier Graphics Inc—Sal Madalone	500 Central Ave, Atlantic Highlands NJ 07716	732-872-9933	R	3*	<.1
1460	Folder Factory Inc—Mark Gentile	PO Box 308, Mount Jackson VA 22842	540-477-3852	R	3*	<.1
1461	Strickland Nick Quick Print Inc—Nick Strickland	109 E State St, Ridgeland MS 39157	601-898-1717	R	3*	.1
1462	Tj Printing Inc—Thomas Oswald	PO Box 510406, New Berlin WI 53151	262-784-1885	R	3*	<.1
1463	Schneidereith and Sons Inc—Wm Schneidereith Whitmore Print And Imaging Inc	2905 Whittington Ave, Baltimore MD 21230	410-525-0300	S	3*	<.1
1464	Saxon John Printing Inc—John Saxon	1440 Old Sq Rd, Jackson MS 39211	601-366-8246	R	3*	<.1
1465	Western Oregon Web Press Inc—Hubert Crowe	263 29th Ave Sw, Albany OR 97322	541-926-3000	R	3*	<.1
1466	Challenge Graphics Inc—Robert Ritter	16611 Roscoe Pl, North Hills CA 91343	818-892-0123	R	3*	<.1
1467	Latent Lettering Company Inc—Frances Stein	54 W 21st St Ste 10001, New York NY 10010	212-221-0055	R	3*	<.1
1468	Monroe Graphics Inc—Randolph Camp	1360 Us Hwy 78 E, Monroe GA 30655	770-267-0022	R	3*	<.1
1469	New Media Printing—Barbara Horlacher	PO Box 399, Bethpage NY 11714	516-681-0440	R	3*	<.1
1470	Page One Printers Inc—James Keul	1929 Engebretson Ave, Slayton MN 56172	507-836-6540	R	3*	<.1
1471	Tatman Inc—Marilyn Kinzler	PO Box 719, Connersville IN 47331	765-825-2164	R	3*	<.1
1472	Total Printing Company Inc—Gary Williams	4401 Sarellen Rd, Richmond VA 23231	804-222-3013	R	3*	<.1
1473	3-Day Envelopes Inc—Antoine Lahlouh	1649 Adrian Rd, Burlingame CA 94010	650-697-0505	R	3*	<.1
1474	Frye Printing Company Inc—John Frye	11801 Tecumseh Clinton, Clinton MI 49236	517-456-4466	R	3*	<.1
1475	Mr Quick Print Inc—Walter Turulis	PO Box 10814, Merrillville IN 46411	219-769-0049	R	3*	<.1
1476	Timbertech Inc—John Phillips	PO Box 546, Harbor Springs MI 49740	231-348-2750	R	3*	<.1
1477	Whitman Communications Inc—Stephen Whitman	PO Box 1156, Lebanon NH 03766	603-448-2600	R	3*	<.1
1478	William R Smith Co—Robert Smith	930 Winfield Rd, Petersburg VA 23803	804-732-0902	R	3*	<.1
1479	Oser Press Inc—Seth Oser	1239 University Ave, Rochester NY 14607	585-442-5621	R	3*	<.1
1480	Total Graphics Inc—James Crosslin	105 W High St, Manchester TN 37355	931-728-4487	R	3*	<.1
1481	G E M Litho-Print Inc—Steven Gregory	5800 Harvey Wilson Dr, Houston TX 77020	713-675-6171	R	3*	<.1
1482	Printing Island Corp—Philip Wang	11535 Martens River Ci, Fountain Valley CA 92708	714-668-1000	R	3*	<.1
1483	Streeter Printing and Graphics Inc—George Streeter	PO Box 1465, Augusta GA 30903	706-722-5781	R	3*	<.1
1484	Central Tape and Label Co—Albert Little	5525 Bingle Rd, Houston TX 77092	713-462-8585	R	3*	<.1
1485	Haas Printing Company Inc—Royce Haas	1000 Hummel Ave, Lemoyne PA 17043	717-761-0277	R	3*	<.1
1486	Trade Graphics Inc—Joseph Kish	8500 Baycenter Rd Ste, Jacksonville FL 32256	904-739-0505	R	3*	<.1
1487	VC P Inc—Herbert Vogt	901 W Algonquin Rd, Algonquin IL 60102	847-658-5090	R	3*	<.1
1488	Asia America Enterprise Inc—Macy Mak	1321 N Carolan Ave, Burlingame CA 94010	650-348-2333	R	3*	<.1
1489	Lopez Printing Inc—Leonard Lopez	427 Lombrano St, San Antonio TX 78207	210-732-3232	R	3*	<.1
1490	Mc Grath Press And Graphic Services Inc—Kevin Mcgrath	740 Duffy Dr, Crystal Lake IL 60014	815-356-5246	R	3*	<.1
1491	Michael's Printing Inc—Chris Babbitt	17300 Sw Upr Boone Rd, Portland OR 97224	503-598-0636	R	3*	<.1
1492	Rapid Printers Of Monterey—Mike Djubasak	201 Foam St, Monterey CA 93940	831-373-1822	R	3*	<.1
1493	Smithbates Printing and Design LLC—Jerry Henkel	537 Northern Heights B, Klamath Falls OR 97601	541-884-3714	R	3*	<.1
1494	Thorne Printing And Office Supplies Inc—Neil Thorne	623 12th Ave Rd, Nampa ID 83686	208-466-3682	R	3*	<.1
1495	Top Copi Reproductions Inc—Abraham Faerberg	111 John St Frnt 1, New York NY 10038	212-571-4141	R	3*	<.1
1496	Valley Press Inc—Aloysius Mc Carthy	5 E Montgomery Ave Ste, Bala Cynwyd PA 19004	610-664-7770	R	3*	<.1
1497	Zander Press Inc—Zane Zander	425 W Ryan St, Brillion WI 54110	920-756-2222	R	3*	<.1
1498	Zodiac Printing Corp—Thomas Zabroski	395 Oak Hill Rd Ste 10, Mountain Top PA 18707	570-474-9220	R	3*	<.1
1499	Crest Craft Co—Jack Johnson	3860 Virginia Ave, Cincinnati OH 45227	513-271-4858	R	3*	<.1
1500	Alliance Printing and Publishing Inc—Greg Brauch	PO Box 44925, Middletown OH 45044	513-423-7768	R	3*	<.1
1501	Tri-Town News Inc—Paul Hamilton	PO Box 570, Sidney NY 13838	607-561-3515	R	2*	<.1
1502	Capitol Litho Printing Corp—Ron Perryman	2301 N 16th St, Phoenix AZ 85006	602-252-6141	R	2*	<.1
1503	Color Impressions Inc—Jeff Johnson	3550 Comotara St, Wichita KS 67226	316-636-5505	R	2*	<.1
1504	Delta Forms Inc—Dominic Sabatino	31 Germay Dr, Wilmington DE 19804	302-652-3266	R	2*	<.1
1505	Park Press Quality Printing Inc—Dorothy Blommer	355 6th Ave N, Waite Park MN 56387	320-255-8937	R	2*	<.1
1506	Barton Industries Inc—Michael Barton	234 Redoubt Rd, Yorktown VA 23692	757-874-5958	R	2*	<.1
1507	Beechler's Printing Inc—Chris Beechler	350 Nw 39th Ave Ste A, Gainesville FL 32609	352-376-6565	R	2*	<.1
1508	Premier Prints Inc—Norman Hodges	PO Box 305, Sherman MS 38869	662-840-4060	R	2*	<.1
1509	Thermofast LLC	PO Box 671, Cockeysville MD 21030	410-602-2442	R	2*	<.1
1510	Cromwell Printing Company Inc—Corynn Bisi	4 Alcap Rdg, Cromwell CT 06416	860-635-3233	R	2*	<.1
1511	D Orser Inc—Del Orser	PO Box 337, Coeur D Alene ID 83816	208-667-2488	R	2*	<.1
1512	Japan Graphics Corp—Tai Makino	20817 S Western Ave, Torrance CA 90501	310-222-8639	R	2*	<.1
1513	Palm Springs Printing Inc—Virgil Thomas	PO Box 1686, Sanford FL 32772	407-682-1221	R	2*	<.1
1514	Baicy Communications Inc—John Baicy	2100 Glendale St, Winston Salem NC 27127	336-722-7768	R	2*	<.1
1515	Clobus Printing Inc—Garry Clobus	PO Box 5503, New Castle PA 16105	724-654-4361	R	2*	<.1
1516	Columbia Printing and Graphics Inc—Robert Wehrley	835 Se Hawthorne Blvd, Portland OR 97214	503-232-2212	R	2*	<.1
1517	Graessle-Mercer Co—George Graessle	100 N Pine St, Seymour IN 47274	812-522-5478	R	2*	<.1
1518	Millennium Marketing Solutions Inc—Janice Tippett	10900 Pump House Rd, Annapolis Junction MD 20701	301-725-8000	R	2*	<.1
1519	MPE Business Forms Inc—Twyla Edwards	1120 Oak St, Dekalb IL 60115	815-748-3676	R	2*	<.1
1520	Pride Printing Company Inc—Gerald Thorn	406 1st Ave W, Albany OR 97321	541-928-3322	R	2*	<.1
1521	RH Rosenfield and Company Inc—Robert Rosenfield	2066 Main St, Sanford ME 04073	207-324-5410	R	2*	<.1

Rank	Company Name—*Executive Officer*	Address, City, State, Zip	Phone	Type	Fin	Empls
1522	Flaire Print Communications Inc—*Mark Kuzma*	2110 Washington St Ne, Minneapolis MN 55418	612-789-2446	R	2*	<.1
1523	Seagull Printing Services Inc—*Linda Richards*	6969 High Tech Dr, Midvale UT 84047	801-565-1393	R	2*	<.1
1524	Everlasting Images Inc—*Rob Arra*	PO Box 830, Cape Neddick ME 03902	207-351-3277	R	2*	<.1
1525	La Dow and Spohn Inc—*Nancy Mahan*	PO Box 578, Fredonia KS 66736	620-378-2541	R	2*	<.1
1526	Tom White The Printer Inc—*H Graves*	PO Box 18485, Pensacola FL 32523	850-438-1602	R	2*	<.1
1527	Gesme Printing Inc—*Brian Pfeiffer*	PO Box 316, Marshall MN 56258	507-537-1577	R	2*	<.1
1528	Bigink LLC—*James Kaul*	1021 6th Ave S, Seattle WA 98134	206-340-1151	R	2*	<.1
1529	Bryan Enterprises Inc—*Kenneth Bryan*	1011 S Stimson Ave, City Of Industry CA 91745	626-961-9257	R	2*	<.1
1530	Car-Lin Offset Printing Company Inc—*John Geiger*	10 Colt Ct, Ronkonkoma NY 11779	631-737-1140	R	2*	<.1
1531	Fine Print Graphics Inc—*Nancy Baggett*	4712 N 125th St Ste A, Butler WI 53007	262-781-2255	R	2*	<.1
1532	Ipc Printing Inc—*David Doucet*	11632 Industriplex Blv, Baton Rouge LA 70809	225-751-4500	R	2*	<.1
1533	Kopico Inc—*Jess Chico*	1444 W 37th St, Chicago IL 60609	773-847-3213	R	2*	<.1
1534	Marfield Inc—*Lee Packard*	PO Box 814210, Dallas TX 75381	972-245-9122	R	2*	<.1
1535	Peacock Press Inc—*Brian Peacock*	PO Box 310, Rockland MA 02370	781-871-1645	R	2*	<.1
1536	Federal Letter Co—*Jill Intravartolo*	PO Box 411667, Kansas City MO 64141	816-421-5164	R	2*	<.1
1537	Joseph C Woodard Printing Company Inc—*Joyce Woodard*	2815 S Saunders St, Raleigh NC 27603	919-829-0634	R	2*	<.1
1538	Litho-Craft Company Inc—*Robert Mason*	W143 N 9358 Henry St W, Menomonee Falls WI 53051	262-255-4030	R	2*	<.1
1539	Beach Brothers Printing Inc—*Ronald Beach*	1010 Westmore Ave, Rockville MD 20850	301-424-9222	R	2*	<.1
1540	Gross Brothers Printing Company Inc—*Moses Gross*	3125 Summit Ave, Union City NJ 07087	201-865-4606	R	2*	<.1
1541	Hurt Companies LLC—*Steve Higdon*	518 W Main St, Louisville KY 40202	502-582-2679	R	2*	<.1
1542	Flare Multicopy Corp—*Steven Zeller*	1840 Flatbush Ave, Brooklyn NY 11210	718-258-8860	R	2*	<.1
1543	Adkins Printing Co—*Scott Pechout*	PO Box 2440, New Britain CT 06050	860-229-1673	R	2*	<.1
1544	Baucom Press Inc—*Alan Baucom*	5516 Susan Dr, Charlotte NC 28215	704-537-4323	R	2*	<.1
1545	Echo Communications Inc—*Katharyn Hoke*	PO Box 2300, New London NH 03257	603-526-6006	R	2*	<.1
1546	Horton and Horton Printing Co—*Roger Horton*	PO Box 447, Mabelvale AR 72103	501-455-3168	R	2*	<.1
1547	Piedmont Business Forms Inc—*Ken Ferguson*	PO Box 281, Newton NC 28658	828-464-0010	R	2*	<.1
1548	Schreiber Incorporated R G—*R Schreiber*	PO Box 998, Verona VA 24482	540-248-5300	R	2*	<.1
1549	Thomas Toscas—*Thomas Toscas*	3201 Halladay St, Santa Ana CA 92705	714-549-5002	R	2*	<.1
1550	WLINC Inc—*Annette Weber*	4402 11th St Ste 604, Long Island City NY 11101	718-361-8800	R	2*	<.1
1551	Southprint—*Tod Haman*	7525 Pingue Dr, Worthington OH 43085	614-888-7574	R	2*	<.1
1552	Louisiana Press Journal—*James Gierke*	3408 Georgia St, Louisiana MO 63353	573-754-5566	R	2*	<.1
1553	Custom Service Printers Inc—*Stephen Kamp*	916 E Keating Ave, Muskegon MI 49442	231-726-3297	R	2*	<.1
1554	Willey Printing Company Inc—*Jerry Sauls*	PO Box 886, Modesto CA 95353	209-524-4811	R	2*	<.1
1555	Instant Shade Trees Inc—*Thomas Cox*	23556 Coons Rd, Tomball TX 77375	281-376-8593	R	2*	<.1
1556	Tristate Blue Printing Inc—*George Marshall*	2401 Penn Ave, Pittsburgh PA 15222	412-281-3538	R	2*	<.1
1557	Curless Printing Co—*Donald Hadley*	202 E Main St Unit 1, Blanchester OH 45107	937-783-2403	R	2*	<.1
1558	Printcraft Press Inc—*Ray Johnson*	PO Box 39, Portsmouth VA 23705	757-397-0759	R	2*	<.1
1559	Craftsmen Photo Lithographers—*Samuel Newick*	38 Beach St, East Hanover NJ 07936	973-887-5761	R	2*	<.1
1560	Express Printing and Lithography Co—*Roger Raymond*	PO Box 3549, Hailey ID 83333	208-788-0022	R	2*	<.1
1561	Liberty Printing Inc—*Dorothy Baker*	PO Box 275, Clements CA 95227	209-467-8800	R	2*	<.1
1562	Mcclain Printing Co—*Kenneth Smith*	PO Box 403, Parsons WV 26287	304-478-2881	R	2*	<.1
1563	Metro Printers Guild Inc—*John Burley*	2009 Iris Dr Se, Conyers GA 30013	770-929-8198	R	2*	<.1
1564	Narragansett Business Forms Inc—*David Almeida*	PO Box 9448, Providence RI 02940	401-751-3440	R	2*	<.1
1565	Paragon Products Inc—*Richard Roy*	2300 Old Lake Mary Rd, Sanford FL 32771	407-322-1680	R	2*	<.1
1566	Sclm Enterprises Inc—*Scott Skinner*	11252 Leo Ln, Dallas TX 75229	972-243-1688	R	2*	<.1
1567	Stephen L Gangi Commercial Printing Inc—*Stephen Gangi*	PO Box 632, Somerville MA 02143	617-776-6071	R	2*	<.1
1568	Superior Printing Company Inc—*Carmen Morris*	1325 Logan Cir Nw, Atlanta GA 30318	404-522-9291	R	2*	<.1
1569	Western Robidoux Inc—*Connie Burri*	4006 S 40th St, Saint Joseph MO 64503	816-279-1617	R	2*	<.1
1570	Lesnau Printing Co—*Robert Lesnau*	6025 Wall St, Sterling Heights MI 48312	586-795-9200	R	2*	<.1
1571	Colorado Word Works Inc—*Wilbur Flachman*	PO Box 215, Westminster CO 80036	303-428-9529	R	2*	<.1
1572	Colortech Inc—*Rick Sullivan*	232 S 9th St, Lebanon PA 17042	717-273-8107	S	2*	<.1
1573	Minnesota Insty-Prints Inc—*Phillip Cheney*	618 2nd Ave S Ste B50, Minneapolis MN 55402	612-332-8669	R	2*	<.1
1574	Col-Pal Press Inc—*Ira Kirschenbaum*	3333 Lawson Blvd, Oceanside NY 11572	516-596-6500	R	2*	<.1
1575	Direct Impressions Inc—*Steve Delaney*	1335 Miramar St, Cape Coral FL 33904	239-549-4484	R	2*	<.1
1576	Stephen's-Nu-Ad Inc—*Mary Lane*	16576 Timberview Ct, Clinton Township MI 48036	248-737-4545	R	2*	<.1
1577	Dearborn Lithograph Inc—*Russell Masura*	12380 Globe St, Livonia MI 48150	734-464-4242	R	2*	<.1
1578	Corporate Visual Communications Inc—*Jaime Herrera*	9011 John W Carpenter, Dallas TX 75247	214-206-3763	R	2*	<.1
1579	Direct Digital Inc—*Jonathan Rich*	4012 S 24th St, Omaha NE 68107	402-733-5353	R	2*	<.1
1580	Exceptional Sale Promotion Inc—*Ernie Puopolo*	317 E 37th St Ste 5, Garden City ID 83714	208-345-4644	R	2*	<.1
1581	First California Press Inc—*James Donahue*	1075 Folsom St, San Francisco CA 94103	415-626-8965	R	2*	<.1
1582	Industry Color Printing Inc—*Rafael Osorio*	14307 Proctor Ave, La Puente CA 91746	626-961-2403	R	2*	<.1
1583	Micrgraphics Printing Inc—*Marcia Banninga*	2637 Emerson Blvd, Norton Shores MI 49441	231-733-3165	R	2*	<.1
1584	Presstime Graphics Inc—*Joseph Selliken*	1016 Poplar St, Terre Haute IN 47807	812-234-3815	R	2*	<.1
1585	Southern Printing Company Inc—*Leo Southern*	501 Industrial Park Rd, Blacksburg VA 24060	540-552-8352	R	2*	<.1
1586	Griffith's Printing Co—*Roy Bell*	404 E Baltimore Ave, Lansdowne PA 19050	610-623-3822	R	2*	<.1
1587	American Printing and Envelope Co—*Esther Amsterdam*	237 West 37th St Ste 3, New York NY 10018	212-730-0088	R	2*	<.1
1588	Barnhart Printing Corp—*John Waechter*	1107 Melchoir Pl Sw, Canton OH 44707	330-456-2279	R	2*	<.1
1589	Butts Ticket Company Inc—*Thomas Butts*	PO Box 70, Cochranville PA 19330	610-869-7450	R	2*	<.1
1590	Cmb Printing Inc—*Thomas Banis*	15w700 79th St Unit 4, Burr Ridge IL 60527	630-323-1110	R	2*	<.1
1591	Consolidated Reprographics—*Micheal Stockham*	345 Clinton St, Costa Mesa CA 92626	714-751-2680	S	2*	<.1
1592	Dallas Printing Company Inc—*Kirby J Taylor*	PO Box 64, Jackson MS 39205	601-355-4531	D	2*	<.1
1593	Henry N Sawyer Company Inc—*Johnathan Sawyer*	PO Box 290059, Charlestown MA 02129	617-242-4610	R	2*	<.1
1594	Lawrence Printing—*George Lawrence III*	3770-D Zip Industrial, Atlanta GA 30354	404-768-1936	R	2*	<.1
1595	Lilienthal Southeastern Inc—*Richard Lilienthal*	PO Box 580, Cambridge OH 43725	740-432-2448	R	2*	<.1
1596	Nugent Organization Inc—*Antonino Longo*	207 W 25th St Fl 9, New York NY 10001	212-645-6600	R	2*	<.1
1597	Quality Ultra Print Inc—*Aleese Kruse*	8811 Hwy 51 N, Southaven MS 38671	662-342-1512	R	2*	<.1
1598	Vermont Graphics Inc—*Albert Gehly*	18 Granger St, Bellows Falls VT 05101	802-463-9515	R	2*	<.1
1599	African American Corp—*Colleen Mackintosh*	222 Sw 4th Ave, Portland OR 97204	503-222-2942	R	2*	<.1
1600	AJT Enterprises Inc—*Dirk Hume*	2727 S Memorial Dr, Tulsa OK 74129	918-665-7083	R	2*	<.1
1601	James D Young Company Inc—*Steven Young*	1 Corporate Dr, North Haven CT 06473	203-234-1100	R	2*	<.1
1602	Arrow Printing Company Inc—*Robert Fellers*	PO Box 2898, Salina KS 67402	785-825-8124	R	2*	<.1
1603	Chroma-Tone Inc—*Matt Parulis*	PO Box 4, Saint Clair PA 17970	214-321-8601	R	2*	<.1
1604	Printing Palace Inc—*Eli Albek*	2300 Lincoln Blvd, Santa Monica CA 90405	310-451-5151	R	2*	<.1
1605	United Press Inc—*Robert Deer*	211 Northampton Ln, Lincolnshire IL 60069	847-427-1343	R	2*	<.1
1606	Collins Digital Imaging—*Hal Collins*	1218 Old Chtthchee Ave, Atlanta GA 30318	404-367-9840	R	2*	<.1
1607	Graphic Art Productions Inc—*James Gregoric*	2951 Sidco Dr, Nashville TN 37204	615-254-8122	R	2*	<.1
1608	St Vincent Press Inc—*Barbara Anzalone*	250 Cumberland St Ste, Rochester NY 14605	585-325-5320	R	2*	<.1
1609	Hotchkiss Inc—*Robert Heeter*	PO Box 390425, Denver CO 80239	303-371-3600	R	2*	<.1
1610	Hillis Printing Company Inc—*Charles Hillis*	525 Parrott St, San Jose CA 95112	408-294-2535	R	2*	<.1
1611	J and P Investments Inc—*Paul Erdman*	8100 Reading Rd, Cincinnati OH 45237	513-821-2299	R	2*	<.1

Note: An asterisk (*) indicates an estimated financial figure. The company type code used is as follows: R = Private, P = Public, S = Private Subsidiary, B = Public Subsidiary, D = Division, J = Joint Venture, I = Investment Fund.

COMPANY RANKINGS BY SALES WITHIN 4-DIGIT SIC

Rank	Company Name—*Executive Officer*	Address, City, State, Zip	Phone	Type	Fin	Empls
1612	Coloredge Visual LLC	127 W 30th St, New York NY 10011	212-594-4800	S	2	<.1
1613	Design Lithographers Inc—*Daniel Green*	519 8th Ave Ste 3, New York NY 10018	212-645-8900	R	2*	<.1
1614	Heliogramme America Inc—*Brenda Lupo*	3821 Homewood Rd, Memphis TN 38118	901-795-9006	R	2*	<.1
1615	Lee Corp—*Thomas Krieg*	12055 Mosteller Rd, Cincinnati OH 45241	513-771-3602	R	2*	<.1
1616	Cherokee Printing Inc—*Ray Boston*	1889 Southampton Rd, Jacksonville FL 32207	904-398-2852	R	2*	<.1
1617	LT Litho and Printing Co—*Mark Thomas*	16811 Noyes Ave, Irvine CA 92606	949-863-1340	R	2*	<.1
1618	Triangle Co—*Mike Cavert*	PO Box 3498, Tulsa OK 74101	918-592-5300	R	2*	<.1
1619	Britannia Press—*Mick Bond*	3652 Eastham Dr, Culver City CA 90232	310-839-3828	R	2*	<.1
1620	Office Dynamics Inc	5802 E Fowler Ave, Tampa FL 33617	813-980-3494	R	2*	<.1
1621	Progressive Partners Inc—*Kevin Cushing*	811 Lasalle Ave Ste 20, Minneapolis MN 55402	612-340-1111	R	2*	<.1
1622	Form Builders Inc—*David Riley*	715 S Country Club Dr, Mesa AZ 85210	480-835-0995	R	2*	<.1
1623	Ren-Cris Litho Inc—*Robert Guardia*	46 Ridgeview Dr, Ellington CT 06029	860-454-7074	R	2*	<.1
1624	West Coast Graphics Inc—*J Mayberry*	PO Box 6269, Anaheim CA 92816	562-941-4995	R	2*	<.1
1625	Castor Printing Company Inc—*Barry Spector*	6380 Castor Ave, Philadelphia PA 19149	215-535-1471	R	2*	<.1
1626	Highland Press Inc—*Rian Nodden*	304 Williams St, Fayetteville NC 28301	910-484-6007	R	2*	<.1
1627	High-Speed Process Printing Corp—*Ralph Wilbur*	130 Shepard St, Lawrence MA 01843	978-683-2766	R	2*	<.1
1628	Inline Digital Image LP—*Jane Holland*	608 112th St, Arlington TX 76011	817-640-1984	R	2*	<.1
1629	Pirolli Printing Company Inc—*Eugene Pirolli*	860 W Browning Rd, Bellmawr NJ 08031	856-933-1285	R	2*	<.1
1630	Quadco Printing Inc—*Richard Braak*	2535 Zanella Way, Chico CA 95928	530-894-4061	R	2*	<.1
1631	American Lithe and Publishing Inc—*George Tamms*	530 N 22nd St, Milwaukee WI 53233	414-342-5050	R	2*	<.1
1632	J W's Image Printing Inc—*Joann Garcia*	12246 Colony Ave, Chino CA 91710	909-393-6388	R	2*	<.1
1633	MS li Graphics Inc—*Michael Scordato*	327 W Jefferson St Ste, Rockford IL 61101	815-962-0655	R	2*	<.1
1634	A-B and C Enterprises Inc—*Bill Tatarka*	4111 S Natches Ct Ste, Englewood CO 80110	303-781-1788	R	2*	<.1
1635	Pelco Press Inc—*Paul Lear*	PO Box 147, Reeds Spring MO 65737	417-272-3507	R	2*	<.1
1636	Global Impressions Inc—*Dean Stevenson*	1299 Starkey Rd Ste 10, Largo FL 33771	727-535-4554	R	2*	<.1
1637	First Impressions Printing—*Gary Stang*	25030 Viking St, Hayward CA 94545	510-784-0811	R	2*	<.1
1638	Printing Mart Inc—*Virgina Collins*	301 Thomas French Dr, Scottsboro AL 35769	256-574-3755	R	2*	<.1
1639	Quality Press Inc—*C Walker*	222 S Orcas St, Seattle WA 98108	206-768-2655	R	2*	<.1
1640	Faith Printing Company Inc—*James Thompson*	4210 Locust Hill Rd, Taylors SC 29687	864-895-3822	R	2*	<.1
1641	Central Printing Co—*Rick Fazio*	205 Central Ave, Beckley WV 25801	304-252-5303	R	2*	<.1
1642	Cmyk Printing and Graphics Inc—*Bonnie Carter*	1947 Vanderhorn Dr, Memphis TN 38134	901-371-0391	R	2*	<.1
1643	Otto Printing And Entertainment Graphics—*David Otto*	PO Box 927, Cincinnati OH 45201	859-291-7700	R	2*	<.1
1644	Print Perfect Inc—*Frank Babich*	431 N Raddant Rd, Batavia IL 60510	630-406-1300	R	2*	<.1
1645	Ryder Election Services LLC—*Scott Ryder*	370 Sw Columbia St, Bend OR 97702	541-382-5934	R	2*	<.1
1646	Gandy Printers Inc—*Bernard Gandy*	1800 S Monroe St, Tallahassee FL 32301	850-222-5847	R	2*	<.1
1647	Gleason Printing Inc—*Jack Gleason*	3325 Republic Ave, Minneapolis MN 55426	952-925-1345	R	2*	<.1
1648	Printing Station Corp—*Mitch Eaton*	1420 Locust St, Des Moines IA 50309	515-243-8144	R	2*	<.1
1649	Rhs Enterprises Inc—*Roger Schlittler*	3303 Governors Dr Sw, Huntsville AL 35805	256-539-2279	R	2*	<.1
1650	Logan Brothers Printing Inc—*Ronald Maiers*	2619 E Michigan Ave, Lansing MI 48912	517-485-3771	R	2*	<.1
1651	Cascade Printing Co—*Mario Menconi*	3321 S Lawrence St, Tacoma WA 98409	253-472-5500	R	2*	<.1
1652	Dependable Lithographers Inc—*David Hananel*	3200 Skillman Ave, Long Island City NY 11101	718-472-4200	R	2*	<.1
1653	Heath Press Inc—*Donna Green*	4934 Fernlee Ave, Royal Oak MI 48073	248-288-5580	R	2*	<.1
1654	Hensley Printing and Graphics—*Doreen Staples*	PO Box 1068, Griffin GA 30224	770-227-4132	R	2*	<.1
1655	Joseph W Small Associates Inc—*Alice Small*	2003 Marsh Rd, Wilmington DE 19810	302-764-0820	R	2*	<.1
1656	Sheffield Press Printers And Lithographers—*Tom Rucinski*	PO Box 439, Schererville IN 46375	219-844-2520	R	2*	<.1
1657	Gordongraphics Inc—*Thomas Gordon*	21640 N 14th Ave Ste B, Phoenix AZ 85027	623-582-0099	R	2*	<.1
1658	North Shore Printers Inc—*Charlotte Wozniak*	PO Box 229, Waukegan IL 60079	847-623-0037	R	2*	<.1
1659	Gulf South Printing and Specialties Inc—*Marcel Babineaux*	1129 E Vermilion St, Lafayette LA 70501	337-235-5231	R	2*	<.1
1660	Mountain States Lithographing Co—*Paul Rhodes*	133 S Mckinley St, Casper WY 82601	307-234-9325	R	2*	<.1
1661	Brantley Printing Company and Office Supplies—*William Brantley*	PO Box 414, Waycross GA 31502	912-283-4831	R	2*	<.1
1662	Harris and Company Inc—*David Ritchie*	PO Box 527, Salem OH 44460	330-332-4127	R	2*	<.1
1663	Dover Litho Printing Co—*Michael Frebert*	1211 N Dupont Hwy, Dover DE 19901	302-678-1211	R	2*	<.1
1664	Matrix 20 Inc—*Kathy Romero*	1903 Nw 97th Ave, Doral FL 33172	305-591-7672	R	2*	<.1
1665	Paducah Printing Corp—*Bruce Shulman*	PO Box 193, Paducah KY 42002	270-443-5383	R	2*	<.1
1666	Anaconda Press Inc—*Catherine Cretu*	7908 Parston Dr, Forestville MD 20747	301-967-2300	R	2*	<.1
1667	Five Star Precision Printing Inc—*David Eilenberger*	PO Box 610, Shawnee On Delaware PA 18356	570-476-5400	R	2*	<.1
1668	Instant Print King Inc—*Rick Morgan*	81 Dutilh Rd, Cranberry Township PA 16066	724-776-5552	R	2*	<.1
1669	Peninsular Printing of Daytona Beach Inc—*William Maguire*	1814 Holsonback Dr, Daytona Beach FL 32117	386-274-4837	R	2*	<.1
1670	Print Wrap Corp—*Richard Neiman*	95 Sand Park Rd, Cedar Grove NJ 07009	973-239-1144	R	2*	<.1
1671	Union Printers Inc—*Wayne Burton*	1107 Phillips Ave, Knoxville TN 37920	865-573-6611	R	2	<.1
1672	Ace Printing Company Inc—*Lloyd Komoda*	1748 Mill St Ste A, Wailuku HI 96793	808-244-9033	R	2*	<.1
1673	Ready Industries Inc—*Eugene Reitz*	1212 S Olive St, Los Angeles CA 90015	213-749-2041	R	2*	<.1
1674	Behrmann Printing Company Inc—*Ivan Behrmann*	21063 Bridge St, Southfield MI 48033	248-799-7771	R	2*	<.1
1675	Raven Printing Inc—*Timothy Ballinger*	325 S Union Blvd, Lakewood CO 80228	303-989-9888	R	2*	<.1
1676	Maywood Printing Company Inc—*Colleen Munroe*	10211 E 18th St S, Independence MO 64052	816-252-8622	R	2*	<.1
1677	Newprint Offset Inc—*Anthony Soave*	108 Clematis Ave Ste 4, Waltham MA 02453	781-647-0331	R	2*	<.1
1678	Sherwood Printing Inc—*Laura Marsh*	4601 E 43rd St, North Little Rock AR 72117	501-945-0845	R	2*	<.1
1679	Cottonwood Printing Company Inc—*Victor Scherzinger*	2117 Osuna Rd Ne, Albuquerque NM 87113	505-345-5341	R	2*	<.1
1680	Dixie Printing Inc—*Harmon Jensen*	101 S Main St, Hurricane UT 84737	435-673-2274	R	2*	<.1
1681	A Forbes Company Inc—*Esley Forbes*	PO Box 2430, Lenoir NC 28645	828-758-0024	R	2*	<.1
1682	Associated Printing Professionals Inc—*Connie Brown*	2041 E Texas St, Bossier City LA 71111	318-747-5300	R	2*	<.1
1683	Lasting First Impressions Inc—*Douglas Rodenfels*	36 Carnegie Way, Cincinnati OH 45246	513-870-6900	R	2*	<.1
1684	Tom's Printing Inc—*Carol Chambers*	PO Box 70, Sardis TN 38371	504-733-0903	R	2*	<.1
1685	Alfred Envelope Co—*Owen Comer*	3536 N Mascher St, Philadelphia PA 19140	215-739-1500	R	2*	<.1
1686	Drafting Graphics Inc—*Jenantte Antink*	1250 Pratt Blvd, Elk Grove Village IL 60007	847-593-1223	R	2*	<.1
1687	Omaha Graphics Inc—*James Becher*	2956 Rainwood Rd, Omaha NE 68112	402-502-5526	R	2*	<.1
1688	Printing Ideas By Me Inc—*Mark Ellenburg*	997 W Kennedy Blvd A12, Orlando FL 32810	321-972-1820	R	2*	<.1
1689	Tracy Printing Inc—*Timothy Mezzenga*	3813 Chandler Dr Ne, Minneapolis MN 55421	612-788-2331	R	2*	<.1
1690	Andrepont Printing Inc—*Philip Andrepont*	5043 I 49 S Service Rd, Opelousas LA 70570	337-942-6385	R	2*	<.1
1691	Falconer Printing and Design Inc—*Stephen Roach*	PO Box 262, Falconer NY 14733	716-665-2504	R	2*	<.1
1692	Porath Business Services Inc—*Gerald Engelhart*	21000 Miles Pkwy, Cleveland OH 44128	216-626-0060	R	2*	<.1
1693	Printcraft Printing Inc—*Tom Turnbow*	1628 Main St, Lewiston ID 83501	208-743-2922	R	2*	<.1
1694	Dlux Printing Inc—*Gerald Mandel*	3814 W Fairfield Dr, Pensacola FL 32505	850-457-8494	R	2*	<.1
1695	Mcdonough Democrat Inc—*David Norton*	PO Box 269, Bushnell IL 61422	309-772-2129	R	2*	<.1
1696	Shreve Printing LLC	390 E Wood St, Shreve OH 44676	330-567-2341	R	2*	<.1
1697	Triad Business Products Inc—*Gene Cresswell*	PO Box 127, Rolla MO 65402	573-364-2485	R	2*	<.1
1698	Altman Printing Company Inc—*Tracie Altman*	201 Jones Rd, Spartanburg SC 29307	864-585-2474	R	2*	<.1
1699	Falcon Equity Inc—*Mark Avery*	2005 E Olive St, Decatur IL 62526	217-429-2125	R	2*	<.1
1700	Giant Horse Printing Inc—*Steve Ma*	1336 San Mateo Ave, South San Francisco CA 94080	650-875-7137	R	2*	<.1

Rank	Company Name—*Executive Officer*	Address, City, State, Zip	Phone	Type	Fin	Empls
1701	Keen Impressions Inc—*Jean Keen*	PO Box 6250, Asheville NC 28816	828-681-5881	R	2*	<.1
1702	Krieg - Taylor Lithograph Company Inc—*Richard Janelle*	5320 46th Ave, Hyattsville MD 20781	301-927-2412	R	2*	<.1
1703	Precision Press Inc—*Jake Anderson*	4525 41st St, Sioux City IA 51108	712-239-5555	R	2*	<.1
1704	Envelopes Of Nevada Inc—*Frank Rechtsteiner*	2287 Crestline Loop St, North Las Vegas NV 89030	702-644-8050	R	2*	<.1
1705	Steven James Media Inc—*Steven James*	12600 Belcher Rd S 106, Largo FL 33773	727-471-5020	R	2*	<.1
1706	Lowe's Printing Inc—*Robert Lowe*	PO Box 1116, Minot ND 58702	701-852-1211	R	2*	<.1
1707	Digital Press and Graphics LLC—*Nancy Breitenbach*	5015 Florida Blvd, Baton Rouge LA 70806	225-928-0524	R	2*	<.1
1708	South Central Printing Inc—*Ralph Waggener*	PO Box 339, Columbia KY 42728	270-384-4757	R	2*	<.1
1709	Angelus Pacific Company Inc—*Timothy Waddell*	PO Box 111, Fullerton CA 92836	714-871-1610	R	2*	<.1
1710	Masterprint Inc—*Jeffrey Berg*	1204 Declark St, Beaver Dam WI 53916	920-887-2260	R	2*	<.1
1711	Print Turnaround Inc—*Bruce Johnson*	3025 Malmo Dr, Arlington Heights IL 60005	847-228-1762	R	2*	<.1
1712	Franklin Graphics Inc—*David Franklin*	3103 S Cherokee Dr, Muskogee OK 74403	918-687-6149	R	2*	<.1
1713	Autographics Inc—*Chris Landy*	2025 Inverness Ave Ste, Baltimore MD 21230	410-539-4808	R	2*	<.1
1714	Cornerstone Press Inc—*James Ketchum*	705 N Ctr Point Rd, Hiawatha IA 52233	319-378-4451	R	2*	<.1
1715	Panther Graphics Inc—*Daryll Jackson*	465 Central Ave, Rochester NY 14605	585-546-7163	R	2*	<.1
1716	Print King Inc—*Dan Bowen*	7818 S Cicero Ave, Oak Lawn IL 60459	708-499-3777	R	2*	<.1
1717	Printers' Unlimited Inc—*Robert Mirabal*	112 Tarlton St, Corpus Christi TX 78415	361-883-1724	R	2*	<.1
1718	Rieck's Letter Service Inc—*Steven Post*	101 S 1st Ave, Reading PA 19611	610-375-8581	R	2*	<.1
1719	Sun Litho Print Inc—*Robert Mcmaster*	PO Box 444, East Stroudsburg PA 18301	570-421-3250	R	2*	<.1
1720	Brown Printers Of Troy Inc—*John Parry*	PO Box 388, Troy NY 12182	518-235-4080	R	2*	<.1
1721	Easy Graphics Inc—*Kenneth Seibel*	741 Alexander Rd Ste 3, Princeton NJ 08540	609-799-3279	R	2*	<.1
1722	Standard Printing and Mail Services Inc—*Kevin Walsh*	PO Box 11021, Fairfield NJ 07004	973-790-3333	R	2*	<.1
1723	Alpine Printing Inc—*Doug Groskopf*	5620 Kendall Ct Unit B, Arvada CO 80002	303-424-2089	R	2*	<.1
1724	Arkansas Printing Company Of Pine Bluff—*Donald Pearce*	PO Box 7232, Pine Bluff AR 71611	870-534-7202	R	2*	<.1
1725	Baise Enterprises Inc—*Craig Baise*	1103 N B St Ste F, Sacramento CA 95811	916-446-0167	R	2*	<.1
1726	Holm Graphic Services Inc—*Maryann Amundson*	1418 Walnut St, Des Moines IA 50309	515-288-8505	R	2*	<.1
1727	Wood River Printing and Publishing Co—*Bradney Racey*	PO Box 101, Wood River IL 62095	618-254-3134	R	2*	<.1
1728	Continental Printing Services Inc—*James Duduit*	4929 Toproyal Ln, Jacksonville FL 32277	904-743-6718	R	1*	<.1
1729	District Lithograph Company Inc—*William Voith*	12266 Wilkins Ave Ste, Rockville MD 20852	301-736-4444	R	1*	<.1
1730	Microscale Industries Inc—*David Williams*	18435 Bandilier Cir, Fountain Valley CA 92708	714-593-1422	R	1*	<.1
1731	Northwest Graphics Inc—*Donald Roberts*	940 Harmsted Ct, Saint Charles MO 63301	636-949-8136	R	1*	<.1
1732	B Harding Harry and Son Inc—*John Campbell*	PO Box 293, Whitman MA 02382	781-447-3941	R	1*	<.1
1733	American Printing Co—*Rick Whitledge*	249 N Main St, Madisonville KY 42431	270-821-5360	R	1*	<.1
1734	Fontana Enterprises Inc—*Kathy Fontana*	1534 Washington St, Waukegan IL 60085	847-244-2272	R	1*	<.1
1735	Luxon Printing Inc—*John Luxon*	375 Wegner Dr, West Chicago IL 60185	630-293-7710	R	1*	<.1
1736	RAD Printng LLC	PO Box 129, Syracuse NY 13211	315-437-4252	R	1*	<.1
1737	Graphic Image Corp—*John Markasovic*	2035 W Grand Ave, Chicago IL 60612	312-829-7800	R	1*	<.1
1738	Metro Printing and Publishing Inc—*Paul Adrignola*	109 W Washington St, Millstadt IL 62260	618-476-9587	R	1*	<.1
1739	Peerless Printing Co—*Kenneth Schrand*	2250 Gilbert Ave Ste 1, Cincinnati OH 45206	513-721-4657	R	1*	<.1
1740	Prestige Envelope and Lithographic Corp—*Gary Gingo*	81 Emjay Blvd Unit 1, Brentwood NY 11717	631-434-3399	R	1*	<.1
1741	Pride In Graphics Inc—*Mike Ekizian*	739 S Clark St Fl 2, Chicago IL 60605	312-427-2000	R	1*	<.1
1742	Quality Litho Inc—*James Muiller*	4627 Mission Rd, Kansas City KS 66103	913-262-5341	R	1*	<.1
1743	Grand Teton Lithography A Colorworld Printers Company Inc—*Jeff Burgard*	PO Box 4031, Jackcon WY 83001	307-733-8600	R	1*	<.1
1744	Monroe County Publishers Inc—*Zel Rice*	PO Box 252, Sparta WI 54656	608-269-3186	R	1*	<.1
1745	Elmira Quality Printers Inc—*David Curtis*	1580 Lake St, Elmira NY 14901	607-733-4695	R	1*	<.1
1746	Pro Printing and Graphics Inc—*Judy Peterson*	PO Box 608, North Platte NE 69103	308-532-1111	R	1*	<.1
1747	Quality Graphics and Forms Inc—*Doug Young*	1410 Gail Borden Pl B1, El Paso TX 79935	915-592-4500	R	1*	<.1
1748	Ddct Inc—*Dan Fogland*	365 N Broadwell Ave, Grand Island NE 68803	308-384-8520	R	1*	<.1
1749	Perfect Image Inc—*Ellen Carlisle*	8505 Crown Crescent Ct, Charlotte NC 28227	704-841-2466	R	1*	<.1
1750	Standard Forms Company of Tennessee—*Dixie Wooten*	PO Box 5040, Johnson City TN 37602	423-928-2125	R	1*	<.1
1751	Yelding Inc—*Christopher Yelding*	117 Great Hill Rd, Naugatuck CT 06770	203-723-1485	R	1*	<.1
1752	Color Concepts Printing and Design Co—*Robin Wahler*	2602 Tampa E Blvd, Tampa FL 33619	813-623-2921	R	1*	<.1
1753	Professional Graphics Inc—*Thomas Bumbolow*	25 Perry Ave, Norwalk CT 06850	203-846-4291	R	1*	<.1
1754	J-Con Reprographics Inc—*Connie Morris*	14324 W 96th Ter, Lenexa KS 66215	913-859-0800	R	1*	<.1
1755	Nova Graphics Inc—*Dianne Baldwin*	7805 E 89th St, Indianapolis IN 46256	317-577-6682	R	1*	<.1
1756	People's Graphics Inc—*Gaetano Senafe*	9745 Industrial Dr Ste, Bridgeview IL 60455	708-233-1250	R	1*	<.1
1757	Alabama Web Press Inc—*Hoyt Price*	1793 Eva Rd Ne, Cullman AL 35055	256-734-5104	R	1*	<.1
1758	Progress Printers Inc—*James Novak*	1445 Woodmere Ave, Traverse City MI 49686	231-947-5311	R	1*	<.1
1759	Mid-State Printing Inc—*Ed Belles*	PO Box 277, Ithaca MI 48847	989-875-4163	R	1*	<.1
1760	Rapid Circular Press Inc—*George Korecky*	526 N Western Ave, Chicago IL 60612	312-421-5611	R	1*	<.1
1761	Aladdin Graphics Inc—*Harold Vickers*	2016 N Tryon St, Charlotte NC 28206	704-377-2113	R	1*	<.1
1762	Best Copy and Printing Inc—*Rajendra Joshi*	7851 Beechcraft Ave St, Gaithersburg MD 20879	301-816-2820	R	1*	<.1
1763	Lone Star Printing And Office Supply LP—*Bonnie Bartels*	PO Box 1093, Seguin TX 78156	830-379-7771	R	1*	<.1
1764	Par Forms Corp—*Dan Nelson*	PO Box 372, Parsons KS 67357	620-421-0970	R	1*	<.1
1765	Qualified Printers Inc—*Jack Kenner*	2803 N Big Spring St, Midland TX 79705	432-683-4676	R	1*	<.1
1766	Briarwood Printing Company Inc—*David Drew*	301 Farmington Ave, Plainville CT 06062	860-747-6805	R	1*	<.1
1767	Utah Bank Note Company Inc—*Clyde Pannier*	4100 S W Temple Ste 10, Salt Lake City UT 84107	801-262-0074	R	1*	<.1
1768	Flp Group LLC—*Greg Kanane*	301 Clark St, Auburn NY 13021	315-252-7583	R	1*	<.1
1769	Cadore-Miller Printing Inc—*John Miller*	9901 S 78th Ave, Hickory Hills IL 60457	708-430-7091	R	1*	<.1
1770	Earl Litho Printing Company Inc—*Homer Earl*	1 Wagon Wheel Dr, Appleton WI 54913	920-734-0377	R	1*	<.1
1771	Miller Printing Company Inc—*Wayne Elliott*	4224 S Peoria Ave, Tulsa OK 74105	918-749-0981	R	1*	<.1
1772	Downeast Graphics and Printing Inc—*Charles Ferden*	PO Box 1103, Ellsworth ME 04605	207-667-5582	R	1*	<.1
1773	H2o Ltd—*M Hudson*	PO Box 55, Monticello IL 61856	217-762-8488	R	1*	<.1
1774	Brand Identity Inc—*Peter Stelmaszczyk*	1211 C St, Sacramento CA 95814	916-554-7554	R	1*	<.1
1775	Pools Press Inc—*Val Sampson*	3485 Commercial Ave, Northbrook IL 60062	847-498-9111	R	1*	<.1
1776	Carol Printing and Office Products Inc—*Martin Egeland*	147 W 35th St Frnt 2, New York NY 10001	212-594-5382	R	1*	<.1
1777	Systems Duplicating Company Inc—*Charles De Vito*	358 Robbins Dr, Troy MI 48083	248-585-7590	R	1*	<.1
1778	Craft Press Inc—*Robert Craft*	111 Quint St, San Francisco CA 94124	415-826-3000	R	1*	<.1
1779	T/O Printing Inc—*Michael Scher* Consolidated Graphics Inc	5334 Sterling Center D, Westlake Village CA 91361	818-706-8330	S	1*	.2
1780	Eagle Web Press Co—*Michael Gehring*	PO Box 12008, Salem OR 97309	503-393-7980	S	1*	.1
1781	Castle Press Inc—*Susan Kinney*	1222 N Fair Oaks Ave, Pasadena CA 91103		R	1*	.1
1782	JP Graphics Inc—*Rod Stoffel*	3001 E Venture Dr, Appleton WI 54911	920-733-4483	R	1*	.1
1783	Busin Valley Partners Inc—*Tom Ryan*	2381 Philmont Ave Ste, Huntingdon Valley PA 19006	215-947-9722	R	1*	<.1
1784	Charlie Chan Printing Inc	7402 W Sunset Blvd, Los Angeles CA 90046	323-850-5407	R	1*	<.1
1785	Heuss Printing Inc—*Donald Heuss*	903 N 2nd St, Ames IA 50010	515-232-6710	R	1*	<.1
1786	Frontline Printing and Design Inc—*John Louros*	204 S 20th St, Fairfield IA 52556	641-472-3574	R	1*	<.1
1787	Full Court Press Inc (Indianapolis Indiana)—*Dave Harding*	4923 W 78th St, Indianapolis IN 46268	317-876-1100	S	1*	<.1
1788	Florida Graphic Printing Inc—*Patricia Blythe*	503 Mason Ave, Daytona Beach FL 32117	386-253-4532	R	1*	<.1

Note: An asterisk (*) indicates an estimated financial figure. The company type code used is as follows: R = Private, P = Public, S = Private Subsidiary, B = Public Subsidiary, D = Division, J = Joint Venture, I = Investment Fund.

COMPANY RANKINGS BY SALES WITHIN 4-DIGIT SIC

Rank	Company Name—*Executive Officer*	Address, City, State, Zip	Phone	Type	Fin	Empls
1789	Communications Specialists Inc—*Spence Porter*	426 West Taft Ave, Orange CA 92865	714-998-3021	R	1*	<.1
1790	Furbush Roberts Printing Company Inc—*Thomas Roberts*	435 Odlin Rd, Bangor ME 04401	207-945-9409	R	1*	<.1
1791	Valliant Enterprises Inc—*Michael Canfield*	615 Gold Ave Sw, Albuquerque NM 87102	505-247-4175	R	1*	<.1
1792	Cardco Corp—*Stephen Schiefer*	1501 Cortland Ave, San Francisco CA 94110	415-285-4010	R	1*	<.1
1793	Beverly John Printers Inc—*Beverly Martin*	PO Box 3183, Sanford NC 27331	919-776-6022	R	1*	<.1
1794	Eichhorn Printing Inc—*David Eichhorn*	10534 York Rd Ste 103, Cockeysville MD 21030	410-584-7530	R	1*	<.1
1795	Potter and Associates Inc—*Joshua Potter*	4400 26th Ave W, Seattle WA 98199	206-623-8844	R	1*	<.1
1796	York Printing Co—*Katie North*	228 E 5th St, York NE 68467	402-362-3337	R	1*	<.1
1797	Adcraft Printers Inc—*Dallas Wheeler*	1355 W Jeffery St, Kankakee IL 60901	815-932-6432	R	1*	<.1
1798	Allcraft Printing Inc—*Don Williams*	1525 Edison St, Dallas TX 75207	214-742-6994	R	1*	<.1
1799	Chromatech Printing Inc—*Barbara Slambrouck*	16 Mary St, Des Plaines IL 60016	847-699-0333	R	1*	<.1
1800	Commercial Clear Print Inc—*Geoffrey Pick*	9025 Fullbright Ave, Chatsworth CA 91311	818-709-1220	R	1*	<.1
1801	Paperwork Co—*Jim Kirkpatrick*	11 E Dawes Ave, Bixby OK 74008	918-369-1014	R	1*	<.1
1802	Westar Graphics Inc—*John Terrell*	6442 Long Point Rd Ste, Houston TX 77055	713-957-4575	R	1*	<.1
1803	Middleton Printing Company Inc—*David Stewart*	1220 Corrugated Way, Columbus OH 43201	614-294-7277	R	1*	<.1
1804	Evans Printing Co—*John Holman*	PO Box 1870, Concord NH 03302	603-225-5529	R	1*	<.1
1805	Multicomp Inc—*Steve Cates*	PO Box 2761, Abilene TX 79604	325-676-0844	R	1*	<.1
1806	IPM Lithographics—*Dennis Berneberg*	9040 Carroll Way Ste 9, San Diego CA 92121	858-271-0771	R	1*	<.1
1807	Concorde Printing and Copying Inc—*Dominic Abbadi*	130E Randolph 2 Pruden, Chicago IL 60601	312-552-3006	R	1*	<.1
1808	Global Print and Design—*Linda Solt*	800 W Oak St, Old Forge PA 18518	570-347-3259	R	1*	<.1
1809	TRUMATCH Inc—*Steven Abramson*	71 Hill St, Southampton NY 11968	631-204-9100	R	1*	<.1
1810	Advantage Print Solutions LLC—*Debra Smith*	79 Acton Rd, Columbus OH 43214	614-519-2392	R	1*	<.1
1811	Quick Printing Plus—*Kevin Fitzgerald*	83 S Palm St, Ventura CA 93001	805-654-1707	R	1*	<.1
1812	Printing Arts Center Inc—*Allan Erickson*	211 W St James Pl, Longview WA 98632	360-636-1886	R	1*	<.1
1813	Star Printing Company LLC	2740 Locust St, Saint Louis MO 63103	314-652-2700	R	1*	<.1
1814	Barnaby Inc—*Paul Barnaby*	1620 Dekalb Ave, Sycamore IL 60178	815-895-6555	R	1*	<.1
1815	Hodgins Printing Company Inc—*Michael Hodgins*	56 Harvester Ave Ste 4, Batavia NY 14020	585-343-4429	R	1*	<.1
1816	Chantilly Printing and Graphics Inc—*James Swiatocha*	13808 Redskin Dr, Herndon VA 20171	703-471-2800	R	1*	<.1
1817	Printing Arts Inc—*Jon Otto*	8801 Wyoming Ave N, Minneapolis MN 55445	763-425-4251	R	1*	<.1
1818	Road America Inc—*Charles Mosier*	4580 Schaefer Ave, Chino CA 91710	909-591-6304	R	1*	<.1
1819	Edward Hine Co—*Bruce Simpson*	PO Box 1505, Peoria IL 61655	309-671-5500	R	1*	<.1
1820	Custom Telephone Printing Inc—*John Farella*	1002 Mchenry Ave, Woodstock IL 60098	815-338-0000	R	1*	<.1
1821	Havana Printing and Mailing—*Brenda Bryant*	PO Box 380, Havana IL 62644	309-543-2000	R	1*	<.1
1822	Metro Print Center Inc—*Rodney Silliman*	PO Box 65267, Washington DC 20035	202-833-2000	R	1*	<.1
1823	Thrasher Printing Inc—*Dale Thrasher*	814 Hanley Industrial, Saint Louis MO 63144	314-962-7979	R	1*	<.1
1824	Echo Appellate Press Inc—*Stuart Davis*	30 W Park Ave Ste 200, Long Beach NY 11561	516-432-3601	R	1*	<.1
1825	Best Printing And Duplicating Company Inc—*Gerald Gawrys*	11465 Schenk St, Maryland Heights MO 63043	314-298-7700	R	1*	<.1
1826	Alexander and Pamaro Inc—*Marc Tenzer*	4020 22nd St, Long Island City NY 11101	718-784-3201	R	1*	<.1
1827	Galaxy Design and Printing Inc—*Earnie Dieterich*	1888 N Market St, Frederick MD 21701	301-663-1345	R	1*	<.1
1828	Keener Printing Inc—*Duane Pecjak*	401 E 200th St, Cleveland OH 44119	216-531-7595	R	1*	<.1
1829	Lexington Press Inc—*Robert Sacco*	PO Box 51, Lexington MA 02420	781-862-8900	R	1*	<.1
1830	Breene Lithograph Inc—*Richard Breene*	9510 Vassar Ave, Chatsworth CA 91311	818-885-7900	R	1*	<.1
1831	Brooks Litho and Digital Group Inc—*David Brooks*	167 New Hwy, Amityville NY 11701	631-789-4500	R	1*	<.1
1832	SPC Graphics—*James Bastian*	201 N 3rd St Ste 300, Hannibal MO 63401	573-221-6300	R	1*	<.1
1833	Studio One Media Inc—*Larry Ryckman*	7650 E Evans Rd Ste C, Scottsdale AZ 85260	480-556-9303	P	1	<.1
1834	Optimun Print Solutions—*Dorothy Martin*	5051 Fwy Dr E, Columbus OH 43229	614-846-5959	R	1*	<.1
1835	Spaulding Press Inc—*Scott Putney*	PO Box 8, Bethel VT 05032	802-234-9550	R	1*	<.1
1836	Graphic Response Inc—*Ronald Mooney*	4460 Commerce Cir Sw, Atlanta GA 30336	404-696-9000	R	1*	<.1
1837	Printmail Inc—*James Folks*	1001 Dalworth Dr, Mesquite TX 75149	972-289-3344	R	1*	<.1
1838	Silicon Valley Industries Inc—*Steven Gossett*	525 Parrott St, San Jose CA 95112	408-277-0700	R	1*	<.1
1839	Loftin and Company Inc—*Walter Hobbs*	PO Box 669407, Charlotte NC 28266	704-393-9393	R	<1*	<.1
1840	Regal Art Press Inc—*Malcolm Baker*	PO Box 710, Saint Albans VT 05478	802-524-4855	R	<1*	<.1
1841	American Specialty Advertising And Printing Co—*Mark Isenstein*	899 Skokie Blvd Ste 11, Northbrook IL 60062	847-272-5255	R	<1*	<.1
1842	Cincinnati Printers Company Inc—*A Yockey*	9053 Le Saint Dr, Fairfield OH 45014	513-860-9053	R	<1*	<.1
1843	Aman Inc—*Rabah Raoof*	10710 Tucker St, Beltsville MD 20705	301-595-5999	R	<1*	<.1
1844	Rapid Print Inc—*Ronald Mcdonald*	6202 Ne Hwy 99 Ste 2, Vancouver WA 98665	360-695-6400	R	<1*	<.1
1845	Kona Printing And Graphics—*Mansfield Montizor*	PO Box 220, Kailua Kona HI 96745	808-329-8833	R	<1*	.1
1846	Marrs Printing Inc—*Walter Marrs*	860 Tucker Ln, Walnut CA 91789	626-965-7204	R	<1*	.1
1847	K and K Service—*K Jensen*	PO Box 1244, Independence KS 67301	620-331-7800	R	<1*	<.1
1848	Reprint! Inc—*Chris Checkles*	2035 Southwest Fwy, Houston TX 77098	713-522-9299	R	<1	<.1
1849	Burnett Engraving Company Inc—*Robert Poyar*	1351 N Hundley St, Anaheim CA 92806	714-632-0870	R	N/A	<.1

TOTALS: SIC 2752 Commercial Printing—Lithographic
Companies: 1,849   27,330   151.5

2754 Commercial Printing—Gravure

Rank	Company Name—*Executive Officer*	Address, City, State, Zip	Phone	Type	Fin	Empls
1	RR Donnelley and Sons Co—*Thomas J Quinlan III*	111 S Wacker Dr, Chicago IL 60606	312-326-8000	P	10,019	58.7
2	MPI Label Systems—*Randy Kocher*	450 Courtney Rd, Sebring OH 44672	330-938-2134	R	528*	.5
3	Gc Packaging LLC—*John Tinnon*	877 N Larch Ave, Elmhurst IL 60126	630-758-4100	R	334*	.2
4	McGaw Graphics—*Bruce McGaw*	450 Applejack Rd, Manchester Center VT 05255		R	140*	.1
5	Brown and Bigelow Inc—*William D Smith*	345 Plato Blvd E, Saint Paul MN 55107	651-293-7000	R	45*	.8
6	Transprint USA Inc—*William Boyd*	1000 Pleasant Valley R, Harrisonburg VA 22801	540-433-9101	R	17*	.2
7	O'neil Data Systems LLC—*Eugene Kumamoto*	12655 Beatrice St, Los Angeles CA 90066	310-448-6400	R	16*	.1
8	Vision Graphics Inc—*Mark Steputis*	5610 Boeing Dr, Loveland CO 80538	970-613-0608	R	16*	.1
9	Gemini Manufacturing LLC—*Damara Kotash*	30 Warren Pl Ste 2, Mount Vernon NY 10550	914-375-0855	R	15*	.2
10	General Packaging Products Inc—*William Kellogg*	1700 S Canal St, Chicago IL 60616	312-226-5611	R	13*	.1
11	Food Manufacturing—*Collin Ungaro*	PO Box 912, Rockaway NJ 07866	973-920-7000	R	12*	.2
12	Data Label Inc—*George Snyder*	1000 Spruce St, Terre Haute IN 47807	812-232-0408	R	12*	.2
13	Copac Inc—*Gerard Lux*	PO Box 2487, Spartanburg SC 29304	864-579-2554	R	11*	.1
14	Cooper Burdge—*Don Burdge*	PO Box 11306, Los Angeles CA 90011	213-747-7141	R	10*	.2
15	Label Tech Inc—*Peter Hall*	16 Interstate Dr, Somersworth NH 03878	603-692-2005	R	10*	.1
16	Clintrak Clinical Labeling Services LLC—*Darlene Lombardo*	2800 Veterans Hwy, Bohemia NY 11716	631-467-3900	R	9*	.1
17	Mutual Engraving Company Inc—*Salvatore Forelli*	PO Box 129, West Hempstead NY 11552	516-486-2996	R	8*	.1
18	Encore Studios Inc—*Robert Bloom*	PO Box 4000, Clifton NJ 07012	973-472-1800	R	8*	.1
19	Kim-Kraft Inc—*Timothy Mehl*	917 Bacon St, Erie PA 16511	814-870-9600	R	8*	.1
20	Raypress Corp—*Thomas Ray*	380 Riverchase Pkwy E, Birmingham AL 35244	205-989-3731	R	8*	.1
21	Continental-Anchor Ltd—*Jeffrey Zandt*	20 Jay St, Brooklyn NY 11201	718-784-7711	R	7*	.1
22	TFP Data Systems—*Rick Roddis*	PO Box 9012, Oxnard CA 93031	805-981-0992	S	7*	.1
23	Printing Associates Inc—*S White*	110 Windsor Pl, Central Islip NY 11722	631-231-7575	R	7*	.1
24	Western Shield Acquisitions LLC—*Edeliza Bundalien*	2146 E Gladwick St, Rancho Dominguez CA 90220	310-527-6212	R	6*	<.1

Rank	Company Name—*Executive Officer*	Address, City, State, Zip	Phone	Type	Fin	Empls
25	Constant Services Inc—*Vincent Pepe*	17 Commerce Rd Ste 2, Fairfield NJ 07004	973-227-2990	R	5*	<.1
26	Karr Graphics Corp—*Myron Karr*	2219 41st Ave Fl 2a, Long Island City NY 11101	212-645-6000	R	5*	<.1
27	Printswell Inc—*Ralph Dewberry*	135 Cahaba Valley Pkwy, Pelham AL 35124	205-985-9690	R	4*	<.1
28	Gooding Company Inc—*Gerald Hace*	5568 Davison Rd, Lockport NY 14094	716-434-5501	R	4*	<.1
29	Color Press Publishing Inc—*Larry Johnston*	1425 W Rose St, Walla Walla WA 99362	509-525-6030	R	4*	<.1
30	Stoyles Printing Co—*Bob Stoyles*	325 N Jackson Ave, Mason City IA 50401	641-424-4341	R	4*	<.1
31	Alna Envelope Company Inc—*Al Azus*	1567 E 25th St, Los Angeles CA 90011	323-235-3161	R	4*	<.1
32	Bcwest LLC—*Becky Venable*	PO Box 3938, Seattle WA 98124	206-323-8100	R	4*	<.1
33	Altwood Roll Label Company Inc—*Walter Kirchofer*	11 Wallace St, Elmwood Park NJ 07407	201-794-7855	R	4*	<.1
34	Midway Rotary Die Solutions—*Richard Seeley*	811 Progress Ct, Williamston MI 48895	517-655-5631	R	4*	<.1
35	Holmes Co—*John Lucas*	565 W Randolph St, Chicago IL 60661	312-930-0019	R	4*	<.1
36	International Gamco Inc—*Phillip Glassman*	9335 N 48th St, Omaha NE 68152	402-571-2449	R	3*	.2
37	Mc Allister Industries Inc—*Robert Allister*	731 S Hwy 101 Ste 2, Solana Beach CA 92075	858-755-0683	R	3*	<.1
38	Laplume and Sons Printing Inc—*Ronald Plume*	1 Farley St, Lawrence MA 01843	978-683-1009	R	3*	<.1
39	Pad And Publication Assembly Corp—*Joan Buehler*	PO Box 1536, Cherry Hill NJ 08034	856-424-0158	R	3*	<.1
40	Wells Legal Supply Inc—*Steven Houser*	PO Box 10554, Jacksonville FL 32247	904-399-1510	R	3*	<.1
41	Fongs Graphics and Printing Inc—*Chak Fong*	7743 Garvey Ave, Rosemead CA 91770	626-307-1898	R	3*	<.1
42	Pulaski Web Inc—*Richard Gaines*	908 9th St, Pulaski TN 38478	931-363-5005	R	2*	<.1
43	HF Anderson Engraving Co—*Kathleen Ellis*	4201 E 100th Ter, Kansas City MO 64137	816-761-9600	R	2*	<.1
44	Arzberger Engravers Inc—*Luther Dudley*	PO Box 36446, Charlotte NC 28236	704-333-7532	R	2*	<.1
45	Nussmeier Engraving Co—*David Nussmeier*	933 Main St, Evansville IN 47708	812-425-1339	R	2*	<.1
46	LR Lipps Impressive Printing Inc—*Sheila Morgan*	2708 Decatur St, Kenner LA 70062	504-466-5344	R	2*	<.1
47	Hodges and Irvine Inc—*Roger Powers*	PO Box 197, Saint Clair MI 48079	810-329-4787	R	2*	<.1
48	JM Gaske Inc—*Elizabeth Ginty*	PO Box 2088, Ellicott City MD 21041	410-750-7700	R	2*	<.1
49	Register Lakota Printing Inc—*Stephen Mayer*	PO Box 28, Chamberlain SD 57325	605-734-5548	R	1*	<.1
50	Bolind Inc—*Katherine Lukoskie*	PO Box 18714, Boulder CO 80308	303-443-3142	R	1*	<.1

TOTALS: SIC 2754 Commercial Printing—Gravure

Companies: 50					**11,340**	**63.1**

2759 Commercial Printing Nec

Rank	Company Name—*Executive Officer*	Address, City, State, Zip	Phone	Type	Fin	Empls
1	Quad/Graphics Inc—*David Blais*	N61 W23044 Harry's Way, Sussex WI 53089	414-566-6000	P	3,392	21.0
2	Deluxe Corp—*Pete J Godich*	3680 Victoria St N, Shoreview MN 55126	651-483-7111	P	1,418*	5.0
3	Corporate Graphics Commercial—*Dan Kvasnicka*	1750 Northway Dr, North Mankato MN 56003	507-388-3300	R	1,113	.2
4	Direct Checks Unlimited LLC—*Lee Schram* Deluxe Corp	PO Box 19000, Colorado Springs CO 80935	719-531-3900	S	1,101*	1.0
5	Harland Clarke Holdings Corp—*Chuck Dawson*	2939 Miller Rd, Decatur GA 30035	770-981-9460	S	1,056*	4.5
6	Direct Group—*Don McKenzie*	1595 Reed Rd, Pennington NJ 08534	856-241-9400	R	543*	.8
7	InnerWorkings Inc—*Eric Belcher*	600 W Chicago Ave Ste, Chicago IL 60654	312-642-3700	P	482	.7
8	Artcom Inc—*Geoffroy Martin*	2100 Powell St 10th Fl, Emeryville CA 94608	510-879-4700	R	462*	.7
9	Watson Label Products Corp—*Ilonka Rank*	10616 Trenton Ave, Saint Louis MO 63132	314-493-9300	R	458*	<.1
10	Multi-Color Corp—*Nigel Vinecombe*	4053 Clough Woods Dr, Batavia OH 45103	513-381-1480	P	338	1.4
11	SGS International Inc—*Hank Baughman*	626 West Main St Ste 5, Louisville KY 40202	502-637-5443	R	324	1.8
12	Topps Company Inc—*Ryan O'Hara*	1 Whitehall St, New York NY 10004	212-370-0300	R	294*	.5
13	York Tape and Label Inc—*John Mckernan*	PO Box 1309, York PA 17405	402-829-4594	S	224*	.8
14	RRD Direct—*Thomas Quinlan III*	111 S Wacker Dr, Chicago IL 60606	312-326-8000	D	217*	.3
15	Scientific Games International Inc—*A Lorne Weil*	1500 Bluegrass Lakes P, Alpharetta GA 30004	770-664-3700	S	213	1.4
16	Graphics Microsystems Inc—*Jerry Yochum*	480 Oakmead Pkwy, Sunnyvale CA 94085	408-731-2100	S	198*	.2
17	Chiswick Inc—*John Zecchino*	33 Union Ave, Sudbury MA 01776	978-443-9592	S	154*	.2
18	Imagine Print Solutions Inc—*Robert Lothenbach*	1000 Valley Park Dr, Shakopee MN 55379	952-903-4400	R	138*	.6
19	The Matlet Group LLC—*Gary Stiffler*	60 Delta Dr, Pawtucket RI 02860	401-834-3007	R	135*	.6
20	American Banknote Corp—*Steven Singer*	2200 Fletcher Ave, Fort Lee NJ 07024	201-592-3400	R	129*	2.0
21	Champion Industries Inc—*Marshall T Reynolds*	2450 1st Ave, Huntington WV 25728	304-528-2791	P	129	.7
22	Bowne International Inc—*David Shea*	55 Water St, New York NY 10041	212-924-5500	S	96*	.9
23	Packaging Specialties Of Georgia Inc—*Kaaren Biggs*	PO Box 360, Fayetteville AR 72702	479-521-2580	R	96*	.1
24	Hammer Packaging Corp—*James Hammer*	PO Box 22678, Rochester NY 14692	585-424-3880	R	94*	.4
25	Johnson Bryce Inc—*Ron Purifoy*	276 S Parkway W, Memphis TN 38109	901-942-6513	R	88*	.1
26	Outlook Group Corp—*Glen Yurjevich*	1180 American Dr, Neenah WI 54956	920-722-2333	R	76*	.4
27	Jacob North and Co—*Charles Calhoun*	3721 W Mathis, Lincoln NE 68524	402-470-5335	R	73*	.1
28	Bind-Rite/Union Graphics LLC—*Steve Cohen*	350 Michele Pl, Carlstadt NJ 07072	201-372-1000	R	72*	.2
29	Van Dam Machine—*Andy Stobbe*	81B Walsh Dr, Parsippany NJ 07054	973-257-7050	R	65*	.1
30	Barton Nelson Inc—*Dwight Nelson*	13700 Wyandotte St, Kansas City MO 64145	816-942-3100	R	63*	.5
31	MimeoCom Inc—*Adam Slutsky*	460 Park Ave S Fl 8, New York NY 10016	212-847-3000	R	60*	.4
32	Balmar Printing and Graphics Inc—*James A O'Hare*	2818 Fallfax Dr, Falls Church VA 22042	703-289-9000	R	58*	.6
33	Digital2Visual—*Gabe Lakatosh*	6159 Santa Monica Blvd, Los Angeles CA 90038	323-467-0700	R	49	.1
34	Pemcor Printing Company LLC—*Pamela Hershman*	30 Clipper Rd, West Conshohocken PA 19428	610-941-7290	R	49*	.1
35	Goodway Group Inc—*David Wolk*	261 Old York Road Ste, Jenkintown PA 19046	215-887-5700	R	48	.1
36	Ultra Flex Packaging Corp—*Eli Blatt*	975 Essex St, Brooklyn NY 11208	718-272-9100	R	46*	.3
37	Envelopes Unlimited Inc—*John Loudon*	649 N Horners Ln, Rockville MD 20850	301-424-3300	R	46*	.4
38	D B Hess Co—*Douglas Mann*	1530 Mcconnell Rd, Woodstock IL 60098	815-338-6900	R	45*	.4
39	Talon International Inc—*Lonnie D Schnell*	21900 Burbank Blvd Ste, Woodland Hills CA 91367	818-444-4100	P	42	.2
40	PrintPlacecom—*Shawn Petersen*	1130 Ave H E, Arlington TX 76011	817-701-3555	R	38	.2
41	Applied Printing Technologies LP—*Carl Grossman*	77 Moonachie Ave, Moonachie NJ 07074	201-896-6600	R	37*	.4
42	Creative Graphics Group LLC—*J Paul Dusseault*	PO Box 2626, Eugene OR 97402	541-484-2726	D	34*	.1
43	PAP Security Printing Inc—*Michael Robinson*	1813 Colonial Village, Lancaster PA 17601	717-399-3333	R	34*	.1
44	American Labelmark Company Incorporated Labelmaster—*Dwight Curtis*	5724 N Pulaski Rd, Chicago IL 60646	773-478-0900	R	33*	.3
45	George C Matteson Company Inc—*Kaye Summers*	PO Box 790, Blue Springs MO 64013	816-220-1300	R	31*	.2
46	Newspaper Agency Corp—*Brent Low*	PO Box 704005, Salt Lake City UT 84170	801-237-2800	R	30*	.5
47	Lisa Frank Inc—*Lisa Frank*	6760 S Lisa Frank Ave, Tucson AZ 85706	520-624-1903	R	30*	.3
48	Walle Corp—*Sean Keeney*	5900 Windward Pkwy Ste, Alpharetta GA 30005	770-667-3973	R	30*	.3
49	Nahan Printing Inc—*Michael Nahan*	PO Box 697, Saint Cloud MN 56302	320-251-7611	R	29*	.5
50	Robinette Inc—*Joseph Robinette*	PO Box 3567, Bristol TN 37625	423-968-7800	R	29*	.3
51	Abc Imaging Of Washington Inc—*Medi Salsafi*	1155 21st St Nw Lbby M, Washington DC 20036	202-429-8870	R	29*	.5
52	Intermountain Color Inc—*A Streit*	PO Box 4299, Boulder CO 80306	303-443-3800	R	28*	.3
53	Cincinnati Container Co—*Paul Johnson*	5060 Duff Dr, Cincinnati OH 45246	513-874-6874	R	27*	<.1
54	Garlock Printing And Converting Corp—*Peter Garlock*	164 Fredette St, Gardner MA 01440	978-630-1028	R	27*	.3
55	CI and D Graphics Inc—*Brian Dowling*	PO Box 644, Oconomowoc WI 53066	262-569-4060	R	27*	.3
56	Pioneer Packaging and Printing Inc—*Greg Polack*	1220 Lund Blvd, Anoka MN 55303	763-323-8308	R	26*	.2
57	Grafika Commercial Printing Inc—*Bernard Elzer*	PO Box 2153, Reading PA 19608	610-678-8630	R	26*	.3

Note: An asterisk (*) indicates an estimated financial figure. The company type code used is as follows: R = Private, P = Public, S = Private Subsidiary, B = Public Subsidiary, D = Division, J = Joint Venture, I = Investment Fund.

COMPANY RANKINGS BY SALES WITHIN 4-DIGIT SIC

Rank	Company Name—*Executive Officer*	Address, City, State, Zip	Phone	Type	Fin	Empls
58	Spear USA LLC—*Richard Spear*	5510 Courseview Dr, Mason OH 45040	513-459-1100	R	25*	.3
59	Britten Media Inc—*Paul Britten*	2322 Cass Rd, Traverse City MI 49684	231-941-8200	R	25*	.2
60	Dupli Graphics Corp—*J Matt*	PO Box 11500, Syracuse NY 13218	315-472-1316	R	25*	.1
61	ID Label Inc—*Neil Johnston*	461 Park Ave Ste 100, Lake Villa IL 60046		R	25*	<.1
62	Duratech Industries Inc—*Peter Johnson*	PO Box 2999, La Crosse WI 54602	608-781-2570	R	24*	.3
63	Universal Products Inc—*Al Bost*	PO Box 332, Goddard KS 67052	316-794-8601	R	23*	.3
64	Bartash Printing Inc—*Sidney Simon*	5400 Grays Ave, Philadelphia PA 19143	215-724-1700	R	23*	.2
65	Ronpak Inc—*Ronald Sedley*	PO Box 1005, South Plainfield NJ 07080	732-968-8000	R	23*	.2
66	AC Printing—*Artie Maydel*	3400-1 S Raider Dr, Euless TX 76040	817-267-8990	R	22*	<.1
67	Victor Envelope Manufacturing Corp—*Kent Gundlach*	301 Arthur Ct, Bensenville IL 60106	630-616-2750	R	22*	.2
68	Whitlam Label Company Inc—*Richard Shaieb*	24800 Sherwood, Center Line MI 48015	586-757-5100	R	21*	.1
69	National Printing Converters Inc—*Brian Buckley*	18 S Murphy Ave, Brazil IN 47834		R	21*	<.1
70	Belmark Inc—*Bruce Bell*	PO Box 5310, De Pere WI 54115	920-336-2848	R	21*	.4
71	Venture Encoding Service LLC—*Bryan Chilton*	4401 Cambridge Rd, Fort Worth TX 76155	817-283-9500	R	20*	.2
72	Bowne Of Houston Inc—*David J Shea*	PO Box 70087, Houston TX 77270	713-869-9181	D	20*	.2
73	Buffalo Newspress Inc—*Mark Korzelius*	PO Box 648, Buffalo NY 14240	716-852-1600	R	20*	.1
74	Data Associates Business Trust—*Lawrence Deangelis*	PO Box 267, Weston MA 02493	781-890-0110	R	20*	<.1
75	Milprint Inc—*Don Nimis*	3550 Moser St, Oshkosh WI 54901	920-527-2300	S	20*	<.1
76	Superior Printing Inc—*Robert Traut*	11930 Hamden Pl, Santa Fe Springs CA 90670	562-948-1866	R	20*	.1
77	C P Converters Inc—*Raymond King*	15 Grumbacher Rd, York PA 17406	717-764-1193	R	20*	.2
78	Briggs Medical Service Co—*Merwyn Dan*	PO Box 1698, Des Moines IA 50306	515-327-6400	R	19*	.4
79	Kappa Graphics LP—*Tom Brisbon*	50 Rock St, Hughestown PA 18640	570-655-9681	R	19*	.2
80	Communications Marketing And Distribution Services Inc—*Mark Nedza*	3060 Premiere Pkwy, Duluth GA 30097	678-466-7926	R	18*	.2
81	Sancoa International Company LP—*Michael Bachich*	92 Ark Rd, Lumberton NJ 08048	856-273-0700	R	18*	.3
82	Freeport Press Inc—*David Pilcher*	PO Box 198, Freeport OH 43973	740-658-4000	R	18*	.2
83	Empire Screen Printing Inc—*James Brush*	PO Box 218, Onalaska WI 54650	608-783-3301	R	18*	.4
84	Lane Press Inc—*Philip Drumheller*	PO Box 130, Burlington VT 05402	802-863-5555	R	18*	.3
85	Nelson Name Plate Co—*Thomas Cassutt*	2800 Casitas Ave, Los Angeles CA 90039	323-663-3971	S	18*	.3
86	Financial Graphic Services Inc—*Richard Malacina*	2910 S 18th Ave, Broadview IL 60155	708-343-0337	R	17*	.2
87	PrintingForLesscom Inc—*Andrew S Field*	100 PFL Way, Livingston MT 59047	406-222-2689	R	17*	.2
88	Trebnick Systems Inc—*Gregg Trebnick*	215 S Pioneer Blvd, Springboro OH 45066	937-743-1550	R	17*	<.1
89	Design Distributors Inc—*Adam Avrick*	300 Marcus Blvd, Deer Park NY 11729	631-242-2000	R	16*	.1
90	Kdm Signs Inc—*Robert Kissel*	10450 Medallion Dr, Cincinnati OH 45241	513-769-3500	R	16*	.3
91	Litho - Flexo Grafics Inc—*Freddy Versteeg*	2400 S 600 W, Salt Lake City UT 84115	801-484-8503	R	16*	.1
92	Bay State Envelope Inc—*Russell Frizzell*	440 Chauncy St, Mansfield MA 02048	508-337-8900	R	16*	<.1
93	Lowen Corp—*C Lowen*	PO Box 1528, Hutchinson KS 67504	620-663-2161	R	15*	.3
94	Modernistic Inc—*Scott Schulte*	1987 Industrial Blvd S, Stillwater MN 55082	651-291-7650	R	15*	.2
95	Alvin J Bart and Sons Inc—*Alvin Bart*	333 Johnson Ave, Brooklyn NY 11206	718-417-1300	R	15*	.2
96	Corporate Document Solutions—*Harold Percy*	11120 Ashburn Dr, Cincinnati OH 45240	513-595-8200	R	15*	.1
97	Print-O-Tape Inc—*Carl Walliser*	755 Tower Rd, Mundelein IL 60060	847-362-1476	R	15*	.1
98	J N White Associates Inc—*Randall White*	PO Box 219, Perry NY 14530	585-237-5191	R	15*	.1
99	Printworks South LP—*Tom Poruchny*	106 Western Dr, Portland TN 37148	615-325-5800	R	15*	.1
100	Fireball Industry Inc—*Roger Hansen*	700 Broadway Box B, Centerville SD 57014	605-563-2212	R	15*	<.1
101	SPI Communications Inc—*Lewis Saltzman*	2150 15th Ave, Melrose Park IL 60160		R	15*	<.1
102	Investment Enterprises Inc—*Michael Warner*	8230 8240 Haskell Ave, Van Nuys CA 91406	818-464-3800	R	15*	.2
103	Form Systems Inc—*Timothy Curtin*	PO Box 230759, Tigard OR 97281	503-256-5554	R	15*	<.1
104	Global Packaging Inc—*Tony Maginnis*	PO Box 187, Oaks PA 19456	610-666-1608	R	14*	.1
105	Butler Printing And Laminating Inc—*James Berezny*	PO Box 836, Butler NJ 07405	973-838-8550	R	14*	.1
106	R Buse Printing and Advertising—*Ray Buse*	1616 E Harvard, Phoenix AZ 85006	602-258-4757	R	14*	.1
107	Albert's Screen Print Inc—*Margaret Falkenstein*	PO Box 1041, Norton OH 44203	330-753-7559	R	14*	.1
108	Screenprint/Dow—*Walter Dowgiallo*	200 Research Dr, Wilmington MA 01887		R	14*	.1
109	Midland Press Corp—*Gene Blanc*	5440 Corporate Park Dr, Davenport IA 52807	563-359-3696	R	14*	.1
110	Mccallum Print Group Inc—*Terry Storms*	4700 9th Ave Nw, Seattle WA 98107	206-784-6892	R	14*	.1
111	Abigal Press Inc—*Salvatore Stratis*	PO Box 170704, Ozone Park NY 11417	718-641-5350	R	14*	.1
112	Whitley Printing Company LLC—*Dale Gaubatz*	4129 Commercial Ctr Dr, Austin TX 78744	512-476-7101	R	14*	.1
113	Dalb Inc—*Kevin Steeley*	73 Industrial Blvd, Kearneysville WV 25430	304-725-0300	R	13*	.2
114	Vaassen Inc—*Jean Philippe*	1200 Central Florida P, Orlando FL 32837	407-859-7780	R	13*	.1
115	Advanced Labelworx Inc—*Lana Sellers*	1006 Larson Dr, Oak Ridge TN 37830	865-966-8711	R	13*	.2
116	Priority Envelope Inc—*Ryan Wenning*	2920 Nw Blvd Ste 160, Minneapolis MN 55441	763-519-9190	R	13*	.1
117	Berman Printing Co—*William Pearson*	1441 Western Ave, Cincinnati OH 45214	513-421-1600	R	13*	.1
118	Infoimage Of California Inc—*Howard Lee*	141 Jefferson Dr, Menlo Park CA 94025	650-473-6388	R	13*	.1
119	Massachusetts Envelope Company Inc—*Steven Grossman*	PO Box 100, Somerville MA 02143	617-623-8000	R	13*	.1
120	Dard Products Inc—*Cary Shevin*	912 Custer Ave, Evanston IL 60202	847-328-5000	R	12*	.2
121	Harper Engraving and Printing Company Inc—*Donald Mueller*	PO Box 426, Columbus OH 43216	614-276-0700	R	12*	.1
122	Transfer Express Inc—*Ted Stahl*	7650 Tyler Blvd, Mentor OH 44060	440-918-1900	R	12*	.1
123	Mad Engine Inc—*Alby Amato*	13100 Gregg St Ste A, Poway CA 92064	858-558-5270	R	12*	.1
124	Crystal Print Inc—*Chris Hartwig*	PO Box 733, Appleton WI 54912	920-739-9135	R	12*	.1
125	Regal Press Inc—*William Duffey*	PO Box 126, Norwood MA 02062	781-769-3900	R	12*	.1
126	Highroad Press LLC—*Price Jackie*	233 Spring St Fl 9, New York NY 10013	212-675-6500	R	12*	<.1
127	Emmanuel County Newspapers Inc—*Wally Gallian*	PO Box 938, Swainsboro GA 30401	478-237-9971	R	12*	.2
128	Dupli-Systems Inc—*Bud Eldridge*	8260 Dow Cir, Strongsville OH 44136	440-234-9415	R	12*	.1
129	Post Printing Co—*Jane Thompson*	PO Box 101, Minster OH 45865	419-628-2321	R	12*	.1
130	Selecto-Flash Inc—*William Shondel*	PO Box 879, Orange NJ 07051	973-677-3500	R	11*	.1
131	Vincent Printing Company Inc—*Charles Casey*	PO Box 5967, Chattanooga TN 37406	423-697-0808	R	11*	.1
132	Cellotape Inc—*Peter Offermann*	47623 Fremont Blvd, Fremont CA 94538	510-651-5551	R	11*	.1
133	LP Macadams Company Inc—*D Macadams*	PO Box 5540, Bridgeport CT 06610	203-366-3647	R	11*	.1
134	Yunker Industries Inc—*Kari Yunker*	200 Sheridan Springs R, Lake Geneva WI 53147	262-249-5220	R	11*	.1
135	Documation LLC—*Roy Fuerstenberg*	1556 International Dr, Eau Claire WI 54701	715-839-8899	R	11*	.1
136	Mountain Products LP—*William Hartman*	PO Box 924647, Houston TX 77292	713-895-1350	R	11*	.1
137	Consolidated Graphic Communications—*Marshall Reynolds* Champion Industries Inc	PO Box A, Bridgeville PA 15017	412-221-2700	S	11*	.1
138	Mri Flexible Packaging Co—*James Moore*	122 Penns Trl, Newtown PA 18940	215-860-7676	R	11*	.1
139	Sierra Pacific Packaging Inc—*Allen Ennis*	525 Airport Pkwy, Oroville CA 95965	530-533-1058	R	11*	.1
140	Graphix Products Inc—*Diane Tews*	399 Wegner Dr, West Chicago IL 60185	630-231-2425	R	11*	.1
141	G-2 Graphic Service Inc—*Pamela Beard-Cotrupe*	5510 Cleon Ave, North Hollywood CA 91601	818-623-3100	R	11*	.1
142	Diversco Inc—*Russell Haraf*	1100 Venture Ct Ste 10, Carrollton TX 75006	972-478-6400	R	11*	.1
143	Paramount Games Inc—*Paul Swartz*	PO Box 428, Wheatland PA 16161	724-346-1671	R	11*	.1
144	Advanced Web Offset Inc—*Steve Shoemaker*	2260 Oak Ridge Way, Vista CA 92081	760-727-1700	R	11*	.1
145	Valley Screen Process Company Inc—*Jerome Bauer*	58740 Executive Dr, Mishawaka IN 46544	574-256-0901	R	10*	.1

Rank	Company Name—*Executive Officer*	Address, City, State, Zip	Phone	Type	Fin	Empls
146	Welch Printing Co—*S Welch*	350 Boxley Ave, Louisville KY 40209	502-636-3511	R	10*	.1
147	Giraffics—*Leonard Lee*	115 S State St, Lindon UT 84042	801-785-5000	R	10*	.1
148	Mcloone Metal Graphics Inc—*Nelson Jacobson*	PO Box 1117, La Crosse WI 54602	608-784-1260	S	10*	.1
149	Thelen Graphics Inc—*Andrew Thelen*	500 Simmon Dr, Osceola WI 54020	715-294-4990	R	10*	.1
150	Romo Inc—*Frederick Darling*	PO Box 800, De Pere WI 54115	920-336-5100	R	10*	.1
151	American Ad Bag Company Inc—*Virginia Semrow*	1510 Lamb Rd, Woodstock IL 60098	815-338-0300	R	10*	.1
152	Schawk USA Inc	45 Research Dr, Stamford CT 06906	203-348-6425	S	10*	.1
153	Wentworth Printing Corp—*Adam Geerts*	101 N 12th St, West Columbia SC 29169	803-796-9990	S	10*	.1
154	Hubbard Company Inc—*E Keith Hubbard*	PO Drawer 100, Defiance OH 43512	419-784-4455	R	10*	.1
155	AJ Parent Corp—*Arthur Parent*	6940 Aragon Cir Ste 6, Buena Park CA 90620	714-521-8784	R	10*	.1
156	Advanced Xerographics Imaging Systems Inc—*David Salazar*	6851 Tpc Dr Ste Ofc, Orlando FL 32822	407-351-0232	R	10*	.1
157	Printedd Products and Services Ltd—*Chris Herman*	PO Box 40, Arlington TX 76004	972-988-3133	R	10*	.1
158	Corporate Electronic Stationery Inc—*Bonnie Donald*	2708 American Dr, Troy MI 48083	248-583-7070	R	10*	.1
159	Fusion Imaging Inc—*Kathy Boydstun*	601 Boro St, Kaysville UT 84037	801-546-4567	R	9*	.1
160	Merrill Fine Arts Engraving Inc—*Joseph Fontana*	109 Shore Dr, Burr Ridge IL 60527	630-920-9300	R	9*	.1
161	Modagrafics Inc—*Lennard Carlson*	5300 Newport Dr, Rolling Meadows IL 60008	847-392-3980	R	9*	.1
162	Holland Litho Service Inc—*Jerry Baarman*	10972 Chicago Dr, Zeeland MI 49464	616-392-4644	R	9*	.1
163	Monarch Art Plastics LLC—*William Shanley*	3838 Church Rd, Mount Laurel NJ 08054	856-235-5151	R	9*	<.1
164	Drexel Technologies Inc—*Deron Taylor*	10840 W 86th St, Lenexa KS 66214	913-371-4430	R	9*	<.1
165	Seven Corners Printing—*Dan Winter*	1099 Snelling Ave N, Saint Paul MN 55108	651-222-8381	R	9*	<.1
166	Stellar Printing Inc—*Fred Newton*	3838 9th St, Long Island City NY 11101	718-361-1600	S	9*	.1
167	Designers' Press Inc—*David Simons*	6305 Chancellor Dr, Orlando FL 32809	407-843-3141	R	9*	.1
168	Communication Graphics Inc—*Richard Lawrance*	1765 N Juniper Ave, Broken Arrow OK 74012	918-258-6502	R	9*	.1
169	Pgi Fulfillment Inc—*Jeffory Brower*	11354 K Tel Dr, Minnetonka MN 55343	952-933-5745	R	9*	.1
170	Diocesan Publications Incorporated Of Ohio—*Robert Zielke*	6161 Wilcox Rd, Dublin OH 43016	614-718-9500	R	9*	.1
171	First American Printing And Direct Mail—*Joshua Breedlove*	6201 Hwy 57, Ocean Springs MS 39564	228-818-2300	R	9*	.1
172	Spectrum Label Corp—*Jerry Kwok*	30803 San Clemente St, Hayward CA 94544	510-477-0707	R	9*	.1
173	Creative Printing Company Inc—*Sheryl Leavey*	9014 W 51st Ter, Shawnee Mission KS 66203	913-262-5000	R	9*	<.1
174	Franzen Graphics Inc—*Craig Franzen*	PO Box 715, Sheboygan WI 53082	920-565-4656	R	8*	.1
175	Ac Label LLC—*Jack Rosen*	1305 S 630 E, American Fork UT 84003	801-642-3500	R	8*	.1
176	Art Wilson's Studio Inc—*William Goetsch*	501 S Acacia Ave, Fullerton CA 92831	714-870-7030	R	8*	.1
177	Independent's Service Co—*Susan Hibbard*	PO Box 231, Hannibal MO 63401	573-221-4615	R	8*	.1
178	Screen Tech Incorporated Of New Jersey Inc—*Dennis Berthiaume*	1800 W Blancke St, Linden NJ 07036	908-862-8000	R	8*	.1
179	Benchmark Graphics Inc—*John Miller*	165 Industrial Pkwy, Richmond IN 47374	705-935-0999	R	8*	<.1
180	Monroe Publishing Co—*Lonnie Moyer*	PO Box 1176, Monroe MI 48161	734-242-1100	R	8*	.2
181	International Color Posters Inc—*Eric Guerineau*	19651 Alter, Foothill Ranch CA 92610	949-380-2132	R	8*	.1
182	Shamrock Scientific Specialty Systems Inc—*Michael Greco*	PO Box 143, Bellwood IL 60104	708-547-9005	R	8*	.1
183	Wall Street Group Inc—*Philip Mc Gee*	1 Edward Hart Dr, Jersey City NJ 07305	201-333-4784	R	8*	.1
184	Sensical Inc—*John Haas*	31115 Aurora Rd, Solon OH 44139	216-641-1141	R	8*	.1
185	M and M Designs Inc—*Rob Myers*	PO Box 1049, Huntsville TX 77342	936-295-2682	R	8*	.1
186	American Cabin Supply—*Jim Claggett*	390 Enterprise Dr, Nicholasville KY 40356	859-887-1492	R	8*	.1
187	Cheringal Associates Inc—*William Cheringal*	500 Walnut St, Norwood NJ 07648	201-784-8721	R	8*	.1
188	Keith M Merrick Company Inc—*Michael Fleming*	PO Box 257, Sibley IA 51249	712-754-2503	R	8*	.1
189	Creel Printing Company Of California Inc—*Allan Creel*	151 Kalmus Dr Ste H11, Costa Mesa CA 92626	714-540-7005	S	7*	.1
190	Nordec Inc—*Christine Snyder*	900 Hampshire Rd, Stow OH 44224	330-940-3700	R	7*	.1
191	Argo Envelope Corp—*Lawrence Chait*	4310 21st St, Long Island City NY 11101	718-729-2700	R	7*	.1
192	Crowson-Stone Printing Co—*John De Loach*	PO Box 115, Columbia SC 29202	803-783-8770	R	7*	.1
193	Lasertec Inc—*Mark Schulte*	33472 Sterling Ponds B, Sterling Heights MI 48312	586-274-4500	R	7*	<.1
194	VictorystoreCom Inc—*Kelli Grubbs*	5200 30th St Sw, Davenport IA 52802	563-884-4464	R	7*	.1
195	Guynes Printing Company of Texas Inc—*Tim Gallegly*	927 Tony Lama St Ste C, El Paso TX 79915	915-772-2211	R	7*	.1
196	Graphics Group Inc—*Joe Davis*	2800 Taylor St, Dallas TX 75226	214-749-2222	S	7*	.1
197	Payne Printery Inc—*Thomas Gauntlett*	1101 Memorial Hwy, Dallas PA 18612	570-675-1147	R	7*	.1
198	Useful Products LLC—*Michael Warren*	429 W Jasper St, Goodland IN 47948	219-297-3154	R	7*	<.1
199	Bramkamp Printing Company Inc—*Larry Kuhlman*	9933 Alliance Rd Ste 2, Blue Ash OH 45242	513-241-1865	R	7*	<.1
200	Lambda Tech International—*Darwin Dahlgven*	3201 Stellhorn Rd, Fort Wayne IN 46835	260-407-1776	R	7*	<.1
201	Quality Assured Label Inc—*Robert Westmeyer*	1600 5th St S, Minnetonka MN 55343	952-933-7800	R	7*	.1
202	Dec-O-Art Inc—*Anthony Dosmann*	3914 Lexington Park Dr, Elkhart IN 46514	574-294-6451	R	7*	.1
203	Liberty Business Forms—*Willy Schumacher*	3230 E Main Ave, Spokane WA 99202	509-536-0515	R	7*	.1
204	Heinrich Ceramic Decal Inc—*Michael Mccall*	150 Goddard Memorial D, Worcester MA 01603	508-797-4800	R	7*	.1
205	Jda Lithographic Group LLC—*Kim Sarver*	2016 American Way, Kingsport TN 37660	423-230-6467	R	7*	.1
206	Scotti Graphics Inc—*Richard Scotti*	163 Varick St Fl 6, New York NY 10013	212-691-6644	R	7*	.1
207	Transpak Corp—*Thomas Wamser*	2 World Packaging Cir, Franklin WI 53132	414-855-9200	R	7*	.1
208	Team Concept Printing And Thermography Inc—*Anthony Rouse*	540 Tower Blvd, Carol Stream IL 60188	630-653-8326	R	7*	.1
209	Allen Screen Printing—*Joe Lepley*	25 Washington Ave, Scarborough ME 04074	207-510-6800	R	7*	<.1
210	Paragon Packaging Inc—*Rita Lewis*	1500 E Broad St, Mansfield TX 76063	817-477-5211	R	6*	<.1
211	Sunset Printing And Engraving Corp—*Mitchell Wainer*	10 Kice Ave, Wharton NJ 07885	973-537-9600	R	6*	.1
212	Select-A-Form Inc—*Dave Walters*	4717 Veterans Memorial, Holbrook NY 11741	631-981-3076	R	6*	.1
213	Richardson Printing Inc—*James Barker*	PO Box 4917, Kansas City MO 64120	816-421-2100	R	6*	<.1
214	Silver Communications Corp—*Sterling Schiffman*	102 Executive Dr Ste A, Sterling VA 20166	703-471-7339	R	6*	.1
215	Laser Image Inc—*Barbara Morris*	2451 N Stemmons Fwy, Dallas TX 75207	214-267-1313	R	6*	<.1
216	Russellville Newspapers Inc—*Chris Womack*	PO Box 887, Russellville AR 72811	479-968-5252	R	6*	.1
217	D-Lux Screen Printing Inc—*James Shuda*	PO Box 127, Holmen WI 54636	608-526-3308	R	6*	.1
218	Dickson's Inc—*Gary Dickson*	1484 Atlanta Industria, Atlanta GA 30331	404-696-9870	R	6*	.1
219	Round Two Inc—*Timothy Kilfoy*	1515 E Kimberly Rd, Davenport IA 52807	563-386-2311	R	6*	.1
220	Anderberg Innovative Print Solutions Inc—*Greg Anderberg*	6999 Oxford St, Minneapolis MN 55426	952-848-7300	R	6*	<.1
221	Baron Technology Inc—*David Baron*	62 Spring Hill Rd, Trumbull CT 06611	203-452-0515	R	6*	<.1
222	Threds Inc—*Keith Phillips*	10529 Lexington Dr, Knoxville TN 37932	865-525-2830	R	6*	<.1
223	Craftsman Printers Inc—*Ronald Peters*	PO Box 263, Lubbock TX 79408	806-744-4455	R	6*	<.1
224	Corporate Resource Systems Inc—*Todd Stanton*	525 Glenn Ave, Wheeling IL 60090	847-777-0230	R	6*	<.1
225	Motorsports Designs Inc—*John Kenzie*	300 Old Thomasville Rd, High Point NC 27260	336-454-1181	R	6*	<.1
226	Wallace Graphics Inc—*John Wallace*	PO Box 157, Decatur GA 30031	770-723-0202	R	6*	<.1
227	DMI USA Inc—*Mark Masters*	225 Ne Hillcrest Dr St, Grants Pass OR 97526	541-474-3535	R	6*	.1
228	Albert Basse Associates Inc—*Ellen Dietz*	175 Campanelli Pkwy, Stoughton MA 02072	781-344-3555	R	6*	<.1
229	Express Image Inc—*Roger Sarenpa*	2942 Rice St, Little Canada MN 55113	651-482-8602	R	6*	<.1
230	Twi Industries Inc—*Troy Wormell*	7498 E 46th Pl, Tulsa OK 74145	918-663-6655	R	6*	<.1
231	Docustar Inc—*Jay Brokamp*	1325 Glendale Milford, Cincinnati OH 45215	513-772-5400	R	6*	<.1
232	Tackett Volume Press Inc—*Larry Tackett*	PO Box 980503, West Sacramento CA 95798	916-374-8991	R	6*	<.1
233	Koza Inc—*Joseph Koza*	2910 S Main St, Pearland TX 77581	281-485-1462	R	6*	.1

Note: An asterisk (*) indicates an estimated financial figure. The company type code used is as follows: R = Private, P = Public, S = Private Subsidiary, B = Public Subsidiary, D = Division, J = Joint Venture, I = Investment Fund.

COMPANY RANKINGS BY SALES WITHIN 4-DIGIT SIC

Rank	Company Name—*Executive Officer*	Address, City, State, Zip	Phone	Type	Fin	Empls
234	Wbc Inc—*Waleed Ashoo*	PO Box 9862, Albuquerque NM 87119	505-243-8560	R	6*	<.1
235	Kjm Enterprises Inc—*Kevin Murray*	9590 Distribution Ave, San Diego CA 92121	858-537-2490	R	6*	<.1
236	Printing Enterprises Inc—*Dana Trainor*	1411 1st Ave Nw, Saint Paul MN 55112	651-636-9336	R	6*	<.1
237	Postpress Services Inc—*Aamir Anwar*	5693 New Peachtree Rd, Atlanta GA 30341	770-452-1982	R	5*	<.1
238	Ngs Printing Inc—*Gerhard Landrowski*	1400 Crispin Dr, Elgin IL 60123	847-741-4411	R	5*	<.1
239	Pagetek Printing and Design Inc—*Robert Richards*	PO Box 599, Hudson IA 50643	319-988-3306	R	5*	.1
240	Oak Printing Co—*James Helms*	19540 Progress Dr, Strongsville OH 44149	440-238-3316	R	5*	.1
241	Collectors Edition—*Michael Young*	9002 Eton Ave, Canoga Park CA 91304	818-885-0788	R	5*	.1
242	Tec Color Craft—*Gary Frenkiel*	1860 Wright Ave, La Verne CA 91750	909-392-9000	R	5*	<.1
243	American/Foothill Publishing Company Inc—*Doris Horwith*	10007 Commerce Ave, Tujunga CA 91042	818-352-7878	R	5*	<.1
244	P H I Group Inc—*Brian Bending*	555 E Business Ctr Dr, Mount Prospect IL 60056	847-824-5610	R	5*	<.1
245	Graphic Printing Corp—*Robert Stern*	751 Park Of Commerce D, Boca Raton FL 33487	561-994-3586	R	5*	<.1
246	Maverick Business Forms Inc—*James Chitwood*	PO Box 6195, Longview TX 75608	903-663-7503	R	5*	<.1
247	Schreiber Specialties Inc—*John Becker*	PO Box 273, Sussex WI 53089	262-246-9933	R	5*	<.1
248	Express Card And Label Company Inc—*John George*	PO Box 4247, Topeka KS 66604	785-233-0369	R	5*	<.1
249	Premier Southern Ticket Company Inc—*Kirk Schulz*	7911 School Rd, Cincinnati OH 45249	513-489-6700	R	5*	<.1
250	Quality Printing Inc—*Robert Mahaffey*	PO Box 23999, Jackson MS 39225	601-353-9663	R	5*	<.1
251	Priority Press Inc—*Jay Straka*	4026 W 10th St, Indianapolis IN 46222	317-241-4234	R	5*	<.1
252	Artcraft Company Inc—*John Dumochel*	PO Box E, Attleboro Falls MA 02763	508-695-4042	R	5*	.1
253	Ligature—*Christopher H Pennell*	4909 Alcoa Ave, Los Angeles CA 90058	323-585-6000	R	5*	.1
254	Winona Printing Company Inc (Winona Minnesota)—*William Stoltman*	1117 E Mark St, Winona MN 55987	507-454-5743	R	5*	<.1
255	Bizerba Label Solutions	PO Box 363, Forest Hill MD 21050	410-879-8220	S	5*	<.1
256	Twin City Printing and Litho Inc—*Walter Simpson*	PO Box 15368, Little Rock AR 72231	501-945-7165	R	5*	<.1
257	Vitachrome Graphics Group Inc—*Gary Durbin*	11517 Los Nietos Rd, Santa Fe Springs CA 90670	562-692-9200	R	5*	<.1
258	Gillespie Decals Inc—*Kerry Gillespie*	PO Box 1340, Wilsonville OR 97070	503-682-1122	R	5*	<.1
259	Flexo-Graphics LLC—*Mike Donough*	12820 W Glendale Ave, Butler WI 53007	262-790-2740	R	5*	<.1
260	Blue Ridge Printing Co—*Bruce Fowler* Champion Industries Inc	544 Haywood Rd, Asheville NC 28806	828-254-1000	S	5*	<.1
261	Centron Data Services Inc—*Darrel Stark*	1175 Devin Dr, Norton Shores MI 49441	231-798-1221	R	5*	<.1
262	President Enterprise Inc—*George Wu*	700 Columbia St, Brea CA 92821	714-671-9577	R	5*	<.1
263	Executive Printing—*Dena Wholey*	2219 E Thousand Oaks B, Thousand Oaks CA 91362	805-495-3630	R	5*	<.1
264	Echo Commercial Printing Inc—*Scott Keys*	PO Box 598, Sulphur Springs TX 75483	903-885-0861	R	5*	.1
265	Thoroughbred Times Company Inc—*Norman Ridker*	PO Box 8237, Lexington KY 40533	859-260-9800	S	5*	.1
266	Pro-Print Inc—*Creston Dorothy*	3920 Airpark Blvd, Duluth MN 55811	218-722-9805	R	5*	<.1
267	Nameplates For Industry Inc—*Donald Rudnick*	213 Theodore Rice Blvd, New Bedford MA 02745	508-998-9021	R	5*	<.1
268	Screen Graphics Of Florida Inc—*Nick Glaros*	2801 Nw 55th Ct Ste 7w, Fort Lauderdale FL 33309	954-485-4050	R	5*	.1
269	Images On Metal Inc—*Harlan Jacobson*	105 S Mantorville Ave, Kasson MN 55944	507-634-7776	R	5*	.1
270	Adcraft Inc—*James Kelly*	PO Box 130, South Sioux City NE 68776	402-494-5144	R	5*	<.1
271	Copperfield Publishing Inc—*John Saltas*	248 S Main St, Salt Lake City UT 84101	801-575-7003	R	5*	<.1
272	Harvest Productions Ltd—*Maryann Doe*	8050 E Crystal Dr, Anaheim CA 92807	714-279-2300	R	5*	<.1
273	Impact Label Corp—*Ronald Berry*	3434 S Burdick St, Kalamazoo MI 49001	269-381-4280	R	5*	.1
274	Ad-A-Day Company Inc—*Merrill Cross*	PO Box 950, Taunton MA 02780	508-824-8676	R	5*	<.1
275	Adams Lithographing Company Inc—*James Hogue*	PO Box 23865, Chattanooga TN 37422	423-899-9000	R	5*	<.1
276	Samuels Products Inc—*Millard Samuels*	9851 Redhill Dr, Blue Ash OH 45242	513-891-4456	R	5*	<.1
277	Lebanon Publishing Company Inc—*Dalton Wright*	100 E Commercial St, Lebanon MO 65536	417-532-9131	R	5*	<.1
278	Robert R Wix Inc—*Robert Wix*	2140 Pine St, Ceres CA 95307	209-537-4561	R	5*	<.1
279	Grafik Industries Ltd—*William Bentley*	640 E Diamond Ave Ste, Gaithersburg MD 20877	301-963-8600	R	5*	<.1
280	Lithographic Communications LLC—*Joyce Pietrzak*	9701 Indiana Pkwy, Munster IN 46321	219-924-9779	R	5*	.1
281	Arizona Embossing and Die Cutting Inc—*Lance Sennette*	2618 S 21st St, Phoenix AZ 85034	602-252-8123	R	5*	<.1
282	Western Screen Print Corp—*Charles Gullihur*	9401 Oso Ave, Chatsworth CA 91311	818-718-5757	R	5*	<.1
283	Excell Color Graphics Inc—*Jerry Blaising*	PO Box 80547, Fort Wayne IN 46898	260-482-2720	R	5*	<.1
284	Jackson Bates Engraving Company Inc—*Rozanne Flammer*	17-21 Elm St, Buffalo NY 14203	716-854-3000	R	5*	<.1
285	Mastro Graphic Arts Inc—*William Betteridge*	67 Deep Rock Rd, Rochester NY 14624	585-436-7570	R	5*	<.1
286	MW Periscope Inc—*Mary Wood*	2025 Royal Ln Ste 310, Dallas TX 75229	972-247-4202	R	4*	<.1
287	Parrot Press Inc—*R Parrot*	PO Box 8297, Fort Wayne IN 46898	260-422-6402	R	4*	<.1
288	American Graphic Systems Inc—*Tim Vernon*	7650 185th St Ste A, Tinley Park IL 60477	708-614-7007	R	4*	<.1
289	Champion Awards Inc—*Charles Bowen*	PO Box 751590, Memphis TN 38175	901-365-4830	R	4*	<.1
290	Laser Print Plus Inc—*Tim Delaney*	1261 1st St S Ext A, Columbia SC 29209	803-695-7090	R	4*	<.1
291	Logmatix Inc—*Philip Angevine*	1235 Kennestone Cir St, Marietta GA 30066	770-792-3777	R	4*	<.1
292	Merlin Printing Inc—*Steven Vid*	215 Dixon Ave, Amityville NY 11701	631-842-6666	R	4*	<.1
293	Matrix Label Systems Inc—*Gerald Perrill*	4692 S County Rd 600 E, Plainfield IN 46168	317-839-1973	R	4*	<.1
294	Libman Business Forms Inc—*Dennis Dickinson*	PO Box 11095, Green Bay WI 54307	920-496-0001	R	4*	<.1
295	Artisan Nameplate And Awards Corp—*Henry Weber*	2730 S Shannon St, Santa Ana CA 92704	714-556-6222	R	4*	<.1
296	M Rosenthal Co—*Edward Etter*	3125 Exon Ave, Cincinnati OH 45241	513-563-0081	R	4*	<.1
297	Carlton Industries LP—*Kay Carlton*	PO Box 280, La Grange TX 78945	979-242-5055	R	4*	<.1
298	Graphix Unlimited Inc—*Bernie Erickson*	3947 State Rd 106, Bremen IN 46506	574-546-3770	R	4*	<.1
299	Collinsville Printing Company Inc—*Jesse Bowles*	PO Box 505, Collinsville VA 24078	276-666-4400	R	4*	<.1
300	Central American Printing Inc—*Guardalupe Rodriguez*	2910 Nw 39th St, Miami FL 33142	305-633-9596	R	4*	<.1
301	Reliable Envelope and Graphics Inc—*Eugene Murphy*	85 Main Ave, Elmwood Park NJ 07407	201-794-7756	R	4*	<.1
302	Hawks and Associates Inc—*James Hawks*	PO Box 541207, Cincinnati OH 45254	513-752-4311	R	4*	<.1
303	Cb Graduation Announcements LLC—*Mary Lipnitz*	PO Box 781, Manhattan KS 66505	785-776-5018	R	4*	<.1
304	Butler Technologies Inc—*Bill Darney*	231 W Wayne St, Butler PA 16001	724-283-6656	R	4*	<.1
305	New Century Enterprises Inc—*Frank Vu*	601 Shepherd Dr, Garland TX 75042	972-926-6062	R	4*	<.1
306	Overt Press Inc—*Eileen Turcich*	4625 W 53rd St, Chicago IL 60632	773-284-0909	R	4*	<.1
307	K and M/Nordic Company Inc—*Bradford Kindberg*	5 Tripps Ln, Riverside RI 02915	401-431-9299	R	4*	<.1
308	Renze Display Co—*Douglas Buchanan*	2023 Harney St, Omaha NE 68102	402-342-1111	R	4*	<.1
309	Burns Publishing Company Inc—*Alan Redinger*	PO Box 995, Olathe KS 66051	913-782-0321	R	4*	<.1
310	ER Hitchcock Company Inc—*Edward R Young*	191 John Downey Dr, New Britain CT 06051	860-229-2024	R	4*	<.1
311	Troyk Screen Printing Corp—*Brian Troyk*	9980 S Oakwood Park Dr, Franklin WI 53132	414-423-2200	R	4*	<.1
312	Boosters Inc—*Jack Parks*	PO Box 70156, Montgomery AL 36107	334-263-4711	R	4*	<.1
313	Peacock Products Inc—*Eric Langslet*	PO Box 187, Bergenfield NJ 07621	201-385-5585	R	4*	<.1
314	OneSource Inc—*Mark Grosvenor*	305 Seaboard Ln Ste 30, Franklin TN 37067	615-591-7722	R	4*	<.1
315	Tiny Prints—*Ed Han*	884 Hermosa Ct Ste 100, Sunnyvale CA 94085	650-209-1341	S	4*	<.1
316	Brothers Printing and Lithography Inc	1227 N Highland, Los Angeles CA 90038	818-771-5252	R	4*	<.1
317	United Multi Media Inc—*Roy French*	9715 Carroll Centre Rd, San Diego CA 92126	858-695-1455	R	4*	<.1
318	S and S Promotions Inc—*Steve Saak*	1717 S Pennsylvania Av, Oklahoma City OK 73108	405-631-6516	R	4*	<.1
319	Ultrapak Printing and Packaging Inc—*Ted Steffen*	1600 S 92nd Pl Bldg I, Seattle WA 98108	206-763-0329	R	4*	<.1
320	Cole Screenprint Inc—*Ed Ogle*	4901 Ctr St, Tacoma WA 98409	253-564-4600	R	4*	<.1
321	Jeffrey and Foster Inc—*Thomas Matteini*	121 Varick St Fl 5, New York NY 10013	212-645-9818	R	4*	<.1

Rank	Company Name—*Executive Officer*	Address, City, State, Zip	Phone	Type	Fin	Empls
322	M and G Graphics Inc—*Josephine Meyer*	3500 W 38th St, Chicago IL 60632	773-247-1596	R	4*	<.1
323	Southern Finished Inc—*Heather Devries*	2171 Kingston Ct Se St, Marietta GA 30067	770-955-8850	R	4*	<.1
324	Bco Industries Of Western New York Inc—*Janet Soltzman*	PO Box 100, Tonawanda NY 14151	716-877-2800	R	4*	<.1
325	Sunrise Hitek Service Inc—*Libo Sun*	5915 N NW Hwy, Chicago IL 60631	773-792-8880	R	4*	<.1
326	Douglass Screen Printers Inc—*Lisa Hickey*	2710 New Tampa Hwy, Lakeland FL 33815	863-687-8545	R	4*	<.1
327	Fireball Industries Inc—*Roger Hansen*	PO Box B, Centerville SD 57014	605-563-2212	R	4*	<.1
328	DEW Graphics Inc—*Elaine Weisbrot*	44 W 28th St Fl 4, New York NY 10001	212-727-8820	R	4*	<.1
329	Wooten Graphics Inc—*James Wooten*	PO Box 819, Welcome NC 27374	336-731-4650	R	4*	<.1
330	Westland Enterprises Inc—*Jane Holden*	3621 Stewart Rd, Forestville MD 20747	301-736-0600	R	4*	<.1
331	Adcraft Decals Inc—*Robert Talion*	7708 Commerce Park Ova, Cleveland OH 44131	216-524-2934	R	4*	<.1
332	Color Q LLC—*Pam Lewin*	540 Richard St, Miamisburg OH 45342	937-866-4001	R	4*	<.1
333	Crisray Printing Corp—*Raymond Marro*	50 Executive Blvd Ste, Farmingdale NY 11735	631-293-3770	R	4*	<.1
334	Eastwood Litho Inc—*Justin Mohr*	PO Box 131, Syracuse NY 13206	315-437-2626	R	4*	<.1
335	Ideal Jacobs Corp—*Andrew Jacobs*	515 Valley St Bsmt 1, Maplewood NJ 07040	973-275-5100	R	4*	<.1
336	Frye-Williamson Press Inc—*Richard Serena*	PO Box 1057, Springfield IL 62705	217-522-7744	R	4*	<.1
337	Mountaineer Inc—*Jonathan Key*	PO Box 129, Waynesville NC 28786	828-452-0661	R	4*	<.1
338	Bay Area Business Cards Inc—*Steven Karp*	PO Box 488, Burlingame CA 94011	650-697-1988	R	4*	<.1
339	Service Printing Company Inc—*Melbourne Clarke*	PO Box 7994, Columbia SC 29202	803-799-6461	R	4*	<.1
340	Process Graphics Corp—*Timothy Farrell*	4801 Shepherd Trl, Rockford IL 61103	815-637-2500	R	4*	<.1
341	Trukmann's Inc—*Paul Korman*	4 Wing Dr, Cedar Knolls NJ 07927	973-538-7718	R	4*	<.1
342	Beltsville Service Center	6351 Ammendale Rd, Beltsville MD 20705	301-394-0400	R	4*	<.1
343	Daniel Label Printing Inc—*Irvin Daniel*	3125 E Washington Ave, North Little Rock AR 72114	501-945-1349	R	4*	<.1
344	Technical Screen Printing Inc—*Robert Golino*	1441 E Mcfadden Ave, Santa Ana CA 92705	714-541-8590	R	4*	<.1
345	Colortech Of Wisconsin Inc—*Conrad Reinhold*	1011 Ashwaubenon St, Green Bay WI 54304	920-337-0660	R	4*	<.1
346	Printech/Instant Ads Inc—*James Childs*	3670 Jefferson Ave Se, Grand Rapids MI 49548	616-245-0773	R	4*	<.1
347	Spinner Printing Co—*Raymond Spinner*	3335 Keller Springs Rd, Carrollton TX 75006	972-380-0789	R	4*	<.1
348	Fla Property Holdings Inc—*Jennifer Bly*	600 W 84th St, Hialeah FL 33014	305-821-1250	R	4*	<.1
349	Heyrman Printing LLC—*Cathy Miller*	2083 Holmgren Way, Green Bay WI 54304	920-499-4815	R	4*	<.1
350	Form Skillcraft Printers Inc—*Ken Eddelman*	3334 Nw Luzon St, Portland OR 97210	503-223-3489	R	4*	<.1
351	Walker Foil Stamping and Embossing Inc—*Robin Mizir*	664 Barry St Ste A, Orlando FL 32808	407-298-3645	R	4*	<.1
352	Ajc Printing Inc—*Anthony Compagnone*	207 W 25th St Frnt 4th, New York NY 10001	212-367-9801	R	4*	<.1
353	Delta Printing Company Inc—*Horace Hayden*	214 Columbia St, Bogalusa LA 70427	985-735-6544	R	3*	<.1
354	Unitech Deco Inc—*Merle Wurm*	19731 Bahama St, Northridge CA 91324	818-700-1373	R	3*	<.1
355	Waterhouse Publications Inc—*Robert Rozeski*	3770 Transit Rd, Orchard Park NY 14127	716-662-4182	R	3*	<.1
356	Beis Moshiach Inc—*Menachem Hendel*	744 Eactorn Pkwy, Brooklyn NY 11213	718-778-8000	R	3*	<.1
357	Specialized Screen Printing—*David Williams*	18435 Bandilier Cir, Fountain Valley CA 92708	714-964-1230	R	3*	<.1
358	Pepperite Thermographers Inc—*Mack Pepper*	PO Box 164, Memphis TN 38101	901-525-8257	R	3*	<.1
359	Aj Images Inc—*Janet Greebel*	259 E 1st Ave, Roselle NJ 07203	908-241-6900	R	3*	<.1
360	Label Art-Home Of Eas-E Stik Labels Inc—*David Masri*	290 27th St, Oakland CA 94612	510-465-1125	R	3*	<.1
361	Media Print Inc—*Attila Veres*	4002 N 36th Ave, Phoenix AZ 85019	602-256-6113	R	3*	<.1
362	Dister Inc—*Arthur Dister*	PO Box 10390, Norfolk VA 23513	757-857-1946	R	3*	<.1
363	Broken Arrow Productions Inc—*William Bodin*	PO Box 722095, Norman OK 73070	405-364-5034	R	3*	<.1
364	East Central Communications Co—*Dennis Kasler*	PO Box 5110, Rantoul IL 61866	217-892-9613	R	3*	<.1
365	Greenway Research Labs Inc—*Diane Altobelli*	14301 W Burnsville Pkw, Burnsville MN 55306	952-707-6904	R	3*	<.1
366	BC Graphics Inc—*Todd Grasle*	3155 Nw Yeon Ave Ste A, Portland OR 97210	503-239-7001	R	3*	<.1
367	Winsted Thermographers Inc—*Lester Jacobowitz*	917 Sw 10th St, Hallandale Beach FL 33009	954-454-9735	R	3*	<.1
368	Dasco Systems Inc—*Kenneth Schultz*	7787 Ranchers Rd Ne, Minneapolis MN 55432	763-574-2275	R	3*	<.1
369	Taylor Graphics Inc—*Dean Taylor*	1582 Browning, Irvine CA 92606	949-752-5200	R	3*	<.1
370	Cameo Crafts—*John Mckernan*	4995 Hillsdale Cir, El Dorado Hills CA 95762	916-933-4545	S	3*	<.1
371	Electronic Printing Solutions LLC	4898 Ronson Ct Ste B, San Diego CA 92111	858-576-3000	R	3*	<.1
372	Cityblue Technologies LLC—*Carolyn Mcwethy*	PO Box 1169, Peoria IL 61653	309-550-5000	R	3*	<.1
373	Chemtex Print USA Inc—*Carolyn Tan*	3061 E Maria St, Compton CA 90221	310-631-2454	R	3*	<.1
374	Walkerton Tool and Die Inc—*Scott Rizek*	PO Box 58, Walkerton IN 46574	574-586-3162	R	3*	<.1
375	Wandel Press—*Sandra Crosse*	1100 W 45th Ave, Denver CO 80211	303-561-1100	R	3*	<.1
376	Bovie Screen Process Printing Company Inc—*David Gintzler*	PO Box 720, Concord NH 03302	603-224-0651	R	3*	.1
377	ASAP Screen Printing—*Tom Sylvester*	8207 Cloverleaf Dr, Millersville MD 21108	410-969-4583	R	3*	<.1
378	Arch Crown Inc—*Craig Meadows*	460 Hillside Ave, Hillside NJ 07205		R	3*	<.1
379	Accumark Inc—*Theodore Bauer*	1540 Livingstone Rd, Hudson WI 54016	715-386-2525	R	3*	<.1
380	Bmc Productions Inc—*William Mcgough*	PO Box 652, Montgomery AL 36101	334-834-2013	R	3*	<.1
381	Marian Graphics Inc—*Werner Widmar*	11401 Pellicano Dr, El Paso TX 79936	915-542-0033	R	3*	<.1
382	Ponders Inc—*William Ponder*	117 N Madison St, Thomasville GA 31792	229-226-3341	R	3*	<.1
383	Stinehour Press—*Warren Bingham*	853 Lancaster Rd, Lunenburg VT 05906	802-328-2507	R	3*	<.1
384	Lesher Printers Inc—*Emiel Cool*	PO Box 565, Fremont OH 43420	419-332-8253	R	3*	<.1
385	A and B Label and Printing Inc—*Juan Barcena*	7245 Copperqueen Dr, El Paso TX 79915	915-774-0007	R	3*	<.1
386	Timsco Inc—*Walter Prichard*	5300 Beech Pl, Temple Hills MD 20748	301-423-1900	R	3*	<.1
387	Color Process Inc—*Mark Ingham*	13900 Prospect Rd, Strongsville OH 44149	440-268-7100	R	3*	<.1
388	Haywood Printing Company Inc—*Donald Benham*	PO Box 440, Lafayette IN 47902	765-742-4085	R	3*	<.1
389	Irwin Printing Company Inc—*R Irwin*	PO Box 9111, Springfield MO 65801	417-831-1878	R	3*	<.1
390	Label Maker Inc—*David Locker*	11445 Schenk Dr, Maryland Heights MO 63043	314-739-6773	R	3*	<.1
391	Printmasters Professional Printers Inc—*James Sheets*	7112 Augusta Rd, Piedmont SC 29673		S	3*	<.1
392	Rye Printing Inc—*Peter Nix*	2 Nursery Ln, Rye NY 10580	914-967-1400	R	3*	<.1
393	Anilox Roll Company Inc—*Michael Foran*	PO Box 60290, Charlotte NC 28260	704-588-1809	R	3*	<.1
394	Corporate Business Cards Ltd—*Richard Latarte*	9611 Franklin Ave, Franklin Park IL 60131	847-455-5760	R	3*	<.1
395	GC Lables Inc—*Justin Thompson*	PO Box 196, Stilwell KS 66085	913-897-6966	R	3*	<.1
396	Reed-Rite Inc—*Reed Callahan*	1427 Centre Circle Dr, Downers Grove IL 60515	630-620-8100	R	3*	<.1
397	Laser Light Technologies Inc—*Frank Hannan*	5 Danuser Dr, Hermann MO 65041	573-486-5500	R	3*	<.1
398	Aremco Products Inc—*Peter Schwartz*	PO Box 517, Valley Cottage NY 10989	845-268-0039	R	3*	<.1
399	Ace Label Systems Inc—*Darrell Wilk*	7101 Madison Ave W, Golden Valley MN 55427	763-277-7700	R	3*	<.1
400	LaserInkJetLablescom—*Mitch Holliday*	1075 Old Norcross RdSt, Norcross GA 30046	678-377-7575	R	3*	<.1
401	Searcy Newspapers Inc—*Scott Zeinemann*	PO Box 1379, Searcy AR 72145	501-268-8621	R	3*	<.1
402	Marco Fine Arts Galleries Inc—*Al Marco*	201 Nevada St, El Segundo CA 90245	310-615-1818	R	3*	<.1
403	Cooper and Clement Inc—*John Clement*	1840 Lemoyne Ave, Syracuse NY 13208	315-454-8135	R	3*	<.1
404	Copy Masters Inc—*Francisco Leitao*	106 Oak St Ste 2, Taunton MA 02780	508-824-1600	R	3*	<.1
405	Fair Publishing House Inc—*Kevin Doyle*	PO Box 350, Norwalk OH 44857	419-668-3746	R	3*	<.1
406	Keefer Printing Company Inc—*Richard Keefer*	3824 Transportation Dr, Fort Wayne IN 46818	260-424-4543	R	3*	<.1
407	Slide Works Inc—*Andrew Graham*	14 Industrial Way, Portland ME 04103	207-774-2689	R	3*	<.1
408	Yankee Printing Group Inc—*Harold Davis*	630 New Ludlow Rd, South Hadley MA 01075	413-532-9473	R	3*	<.1
409	Progress Printing Corp—*Martin Gapshis*	3324 S Halsted St Ste, Chicago IL 60608	773-927-0123	R	3*	<.1
410	Stevens Decal Company Inc—*Andrew Stevens*	3336 W Mcdowell Rd, Phoenix AZ 85009	602-269-7758	R	3*	<.1
411	R Graphics Inc—*Patricia Storlazzi*	1533 Glen Ave, Moorestown NJ 08057	856-231-8881	R	3*	<.1

Note: An asterisk (*) indicates an estimated financial figure. The company type code used is as follows: R = Private, P = Public, S = Private Subsidiary, B = Public Subsidiary, D = Division, J = Joint Venture, I = Investment Fund.

COMPANY RANKINGS BY SALES WITHIN 4-DIGIT SIC

Rank	Company Name—Executive Officer	Address, City, State, Zip	Phone	Type	Fin	Empls
412	Litehouse Custom Printing Inc—Mark Fuller	PO Box 216, Sandpoint ID 83864	208-263-9745	R	3*	<.1
413	Paul Wales Inc—Paul Wales	131 Se 10th Ave, Gainesville FL 32601	352-376-7646	R	3*	<.1
414	Screen America Inc—Matthew Dillon	44652 Guilford Dr Ste, Ashburn VA 20147	703-478-8974	R	3*	<.1
415	Graphics Type And Color Enterprises Inc—Manuel Perez	2300 Nw 7th Ave, Miami FL 33127	305-591-7600	R	3*	<.1
416	Lakeland Graphics Inc—Mark Johnson	6850 Shingle Creek Pkw, Minneapolis MN 55430	763-560-3606	R	3*	<.1
417	Ream Printing Company Inc—Jim Ream	PO Box 2891, York PA 17405	717-764-5663	R	3*	<.1
418	Crown Printing Inc—Mark Rust	1303 E Main St, Lakeland FL 33801	863-682-4881	R	3*	<.1
419	Artscroll Printing Corp—Elliot Schwartz	53 W 23rd St Fl 4, New York NY 10010	212-929-2413	R	3*	<.1
420	Marlow Printing Company Inc—Jack Freund	667 Kent Ave, Brooklyn NY 11249	718-625-4949	R	3*	<.1
421	Mdb Group Inc—Jim Fedders	9269 July Ln, Saint Augustine FL 32080	904-461-7784	R	3*	<.1
422	Cleveland Menu Printing Inc—Tom Ramella	1441 E 17th St, Cleveland OH 44114	216-241-5256	R	3*	<.1
423	Halifax Plastic Inc—Richard Schwarz	PO Box 9597, Daytona Beach FL 32120	386-252-2442	R	3*	<.1
424	Knight Media Inc—Charles Ehlers	412 W Mcneese St, Lake Charles LA 70605	337-478-8350	R	3*	<.1
425	Tripi Engraving Company Inc—Ed Lazarus	60 Meserole Ave, Brooklyn NY 11222	718-383-6500	R	3*	<.1
426	Label Source Inc—Chris Geeslin	3674 N Peachtree Rd, Atlanta GA 30341	770-936-8000	R	3*	<.1
427	Sayco Enterprises Inc—Sidney Young	2053 Premier Row, Orlando FL 32809	407-425-9490	R	3*	<.1
428	Rick's Quick Printing Inc—Richard Ozanick	2239 Banksville Rd, Pittsburgh PA 15216	412-571-0333	R	3*	<.1
429	All American Forms Manufacturing Inc—Paul Harris	1925 S Rosemary St Uni, Denver CO 80231	303-750-3005	R	3*	<.1
430	RITEC Corp—Carl Stella	940 Enchanted Way, Simi Valley CA 93065	805-577-9710	R	3*	<.1
431	Cooper Flexible Packaging Inc—Guy Cooper	789 Golf Ln, Bensenville IL 60106	630-595-6226	R	3*	<.1
432	Amigo Custom Screen Prints LLC	6351 Yarrow Dr Ste A a, Carlsbad CA 92011	760-452-7964	R	3*	<.1
433	Commercial Decal Of Ohio Inc—David Dunn	PO Box 2747, East Liverpool OH 43920	330-385-7178	R	3*	<.1
434	Designer Plastics Inc—Randy Mosley	PO Box 160, Arab AL 35016	256-586-2490	R	3*	<.1
435	Floor Productions LLC—Jeff Dahnert	324 Brickyard Rd, Dalton GA 30721	706-217-6462	R	3*	<.1
436	Burrell Printing Company Inc—Mark Bolles	901 Fm 685, Pflugerville TX 78660	512-990-1188	R	3*	<.1
437	First String Enterprises Inc—Ronald Strenge	18650 Graphic Ct, Tinley Park IL 60477	708-614-1200	R	3*	<.1
438	Universal Label Printers Inc—John Walsh	PO Box 3648, Santa Fe Springs CA 90670	562-944-0234	R	3*	<.1
439	Si-Cal Inc—Jaye Tyler	11 Walkup Dr, Westborough MA 01581	508-898-1800	R	3*	<.1
440	Pittsburgh City Paper Inc—Michael Fresling	650 Smithfield St Ste, Pittsburgh PA 15222	412-316-3342	R	3*	<.1
441	Dooley Co—Jim Knecht	PO Box 628, Olive Branch MS 38654	662-895-2778	R	3*	<.1
442	DSE Inc—Paul Saddler	PO Box 686, Columbus IN 47202	812-376-0310	R	3*	<.1
443	Screenwriters Inc—Kurt Tempelmeyer	4911 N 57th St, Lincoln NE 68507	402-437-8350	R	3*	<.1
444	Whithner Corp—Lee Whippo	6300 Blair Hill Ln, Baltimore MD 21209	410-769-9030	R	3*	<.1
445	Orffeo Printing Company Inc—Gregory Orffeo	PO Box 426, Lancaster NY 14086	716-681-5757	R	3*	<.1
446	Speedflo Business Forms Inc—Roger Parks	PO Box 1349, Glendale AZ 85311	623-934-3224	R	3*	<.1
447	Sms Communications Inc—Richard Santich	20116 Chagrin Blvd, Shaker Heights OH 44122	216-751-6686	R	3*	<.1
448	Universal Screen Graphics Inc—Tim Packrall	4422 N Church Ave Ste, Tampa FL 33614	813-623-5335	R	3*	<.1
449	Greenhaven Printing—Jeff Hyer	4575 Chatsworth St N, Saint Paul MN 55126	651-639-9822	R	3*	<.1
450	Arizona Commercial Printing Inc—Tim Moran	7466 E Monte Cristo Av, Scottsdale AZ 85260	480-607-9297	R	3*	<.1
451	Royer Group Inc—Amanda Schwartz	100 Independence Mall, Philadelphia PA 19106	215-592-3200	R	3*	<.1
452	Alabama Business Forms Inc—Donald Duffey	725 Memorial Pkwy Nw, Huntsville AL 35801	256-534-8038	R	3*	<.1
453	Cincinnati Convertors Inc—Donald Ellsworth	1730 Cleneay Ave, Cincinnati OH 45212	513-731-6600	R	3*	<.1
454	Content Management Corp—Zack Tsuji	37900 Central Ct, Newark CA 94560	510-505-1100	R	3*	<.1
455	Tennessee Valley Press Inc—James Johnson	PO Box 1514, Decatur AL 35602	256-353-8991	R	2*	.1
456	Datamark Graphics Inc—Don Byers	603 W Bailey St, Asheboro NC 27203	336-629-5282	R	2*	<.1
457	Subtle Impressions Inc—James Schaefer	1200 Industrial Ave, Gastonia NC 28054	704-583-1055	R	2*	<.1
458	Gazette Press Inc—Richard Martinelli	16 School St, Yonkers NY 10701	914-963-8300	R	2*	<.1
459	Sullivan Screen Print Company Inc—John Sullivan	3808 Fitzgerald Rd, Louisville KY 40216	502-776-5721	R	2*	<.1
460	Kap Tag and Label—Kenneth Anderson	PO Box 960, Mundelein IL 60060	312-454-1701	R	2*	<.1
461	US Laser—Rick Pope	344 Springhill Farm Rd, Fort Mill SC 29715	803-802-3946	R	2*	<.1
462	Igraphics—James Clay	165 Spring Hill Dr, Grass Valley CA 95945	530-273-2200	R	2*	<.1
463	MYS Designs Inc—Yvette Cohen	731 Ceres Ave, Los Angeles CA 90013	213-744-1183	R	2*	<.1
464	Apollo Printing and Graphics Center Inc—Gus Koucouthakis	731 S Michigan St, South Bend IN 46601	574-287-3707	R	2*	<.1
465	Custom Label and Decal LLC—Andries Wagenaar	3392 Investment Blvd, Hayward CA 94545	510-293-0889	R	2*	<.1
466	Griffin Publishing Inc—George Griffin	2210 N Dollar Rd, Spokane Valley WA 99212	509-534-3625	R	2*	<.1
467	Martin Glenn Scott Inc—Gerald Eastland	2051 W Geospace Dr, Independence MO 64056	816-257-0782	R	2*	<.1
468	Sapphire Envelope and Graphics Inc—Anthony Mellace	214 Davis Rd, Magnolia NJ 08049	856-782-2227	R	2*	<.1
469	Sourceone Graphics Inc—Jerry Cowan	7703 Central Ave Ne, Minneapolis MN 55432	763-786-5500	R	2*	<.1
470	Label Specialties Inc—James Medley	2501 Technology Dr, Louisville KY 40299	502-261-9000	R	2*	<.1
471	Symbology Inc—Theodore Schultze	7351 Kirkwood Ln N Ste, Maple Grove MN 55369	763-315-8080	R	2*	<.1
472	Lallie Inc—Nancy Lowell	210 Najoles Rd, Millersville MD 21108	443-679-1050	R	2*	<.1
473	Inter City Press Inc—Jack Aquila	143 Petticoat Ln, Lebanon NJ 08833	908-236-9911	R	2*	<.1
474	Fayette Publishing Inc—Calvin Beverly	PO Box 1325, Fayetteville GA 30214	770-719-1880	R	2*	<.1
475	Laser Ink Corp—Richard Smith	4018 Patriot Dr Ste 20, Durham NC 27703	919-361-5822	R	2*	<.1
476	Rheaume's House Of Lettering Inc—Janice Briggs	25113 21st Ave, Saint Cloud MN 56301	320-252-7680	R	2*	<.1
477	Ttc Trammell Company Inc—Bruce Trammell	PO Box 230493, Houston TX 77223	713-921-7121	R	2*	<.1
478	Venture Industries Inc—Norman Waters	PO Box 23923, Chattanooga TN 37422	423-894-9073	R	2*	<.1
479	Schofield Printing Inc—Robert Chito	211 Weeden St, Pawtucket RI 02860	401-728-6980	R	2*	<.1
480	Morrissey Brothers Printers Inc—Donisle Morrissey	929 E Slauson Ave, Los Angeles CA 90011	323-233-7197	R	2*	<.1
481	Seattle Chinese Post Inc—Assunta Ng	PO Box 3468, Seattle WA 98114	206-223-0623	R	2*	<.1
482	Colour Tech Marketing Inc—John Higgins	356 Sonwil Dr, Buffalo NY 14225	716-633-2520	R	2*	<.1
483	Fsi Label Co—Emily Kopko	PO Box 36480, Detroit MI 48236	586-776-4110	R	2*	<.1
484	Lincoln Press Company Inc—Paul Senra	PO Box 904, Fall River MA 02722	508-673-3241	R	2*	<.1
485	Palmer Envelope Co—Charles Stevenson	PO Box 428, Battle Creek MI 49016	269-965-1336	R	2*	<.1
486	Vistacraft Inc—J Feighner	PO Box 7275, Columbus GA 31908	706-561-9630	R	2*	<.1
487	ImageXpres Corp—John S Zankowski	333 Metro Park Ste N10, Rochester NY 14623		P	2	<.1
488	Mission Announcement Co—Gerald Cohen	PO Box 6133, Covina CA 91722	626-332-4084	R	2*	<.1
489	Tag Name Inc—Clyde Coller	175 W 2700 S Ste 101, Salt Lake City UT 84115	801-931-5000	R	2*	<.1
490	Whitney Printing Corp—Allen Nudelman	PO Box 1525, Buffalo NY 14205	716-852-3901	R	2*	<.1
491	Hi-Temperature Graphics Inc—John Rarey	PO Box 40, Columbia KY 42728	270-384-5587	R	2*	<.1
492	Jacksonville Specialty Advertising Inc	2727 Atlantic Blvd, Jacksonville FL 32207	904-398-7072	R	2*	<.1
493	Pony Corp—Lawrence Dehart	10794 Indian Hd Indust, Saint Louis MO 63132	314-423-3111	R	2*	<.1
494	Voss Signs LLC—Diane Voss	PO Box 553, Manlius NY 13104	315-682-6418	R	2*	<.1
495	Walter Haas Graphics Inc—Marianne Haas	123 W 23rd St, Hialeah FL 33010	305-883-2257	R	2*	<.1
496	Timberline Corp—Kenneth Katel	PO Box 9275, Rapid City SD 57709	605-342-6161	R	2*	<.1
497	Cummins Label Co—Phil Nagle	2230 Glendenning Rd, Kalamazoo MI 49001	269-345-3386	R	2*	<.1
498	Color Graphics Inc—Jim Petrole	7660 W Industrial Dr, Forest Park IL 60130	708-771-7660	R	2*	<.1
499	Franchise Times Corp—John Hamburger	2808 Anthony Ln S, Minneapolis MN 55418	612-767-3232	R	2*	<.1
500	Jim Buckley Offsetting Services Inc—Jim Buckley	3917 Penn Belt Pl, Forestville MD 20747	301-568-7600	R	2*	<.1
501	Oregon Blue Print Co	732 SE Hawthorne Blvd, Portland OR 97214	503-232-1161	R	2*	<.1

Rank	Company Name—*Executive Officer*	Address, City, State, Zip	Phone	Type	Fin	Empls
502	Desk Top Solutions Inc—*Brian Solov*	335 Bear Hill Rd, Waltham MA 02451	781-890-7500	R	2*	<.1
503	Lettergraphics - PFS Syracuse Letter Company Inc	141 Midland Ave, Syracuse NY 13202	315-476-8328	S	2*	<.1
504	On Demand Printing—*Jim Ronecker*	303 Mears Blvd, Oldsmar FL 34677	813-855-5559	R	2*	<.1
505	National Printing Co—*Megan Huston*	209 Bausman St, Pittsburgh PA 15210	412-431-5335	R	2*	<.1
506	Hal Mather and Sons Inc—*Douglas Mather*	11803 Hwy 120, Woodstock IL 60098	815-338-4000	R	2*	<.1
507	Business Images—*Linda Graham*	16297 W Nursery Rd, Hayward WI 54843	715-634-6228	R	2*	<.1
508	Monticel Inc—*Susan Weady*	588 Boston Post Rd, Guilford CT 06437	203-453-5887	R	2*	<.1
509	Larsen Graphics Inc—*Harold Larsen*	PO Box 1641, Vassar MI 48768	989-823-3000	R	2*	<.1
510	Feldman Printing Inc—*Terrian Feldman*	1732 N Sheridan Rd, Peoria IL 61604	309-682-7023	R	2*	<.1
511	Standard Pennant Company Inc—*James Casaday*	PO Box 415, Big Run PA 15715	814-427-2066	R	2*	<.1
512	Dement Printing Co—*John Dement*	2007 9th St, Meridian MS 39301	601-693-2721	R	2*	<.1
513	Bethel Park Printing Inc—*Anthony Zimmer*	5237 Brightwood Rd, Bethel Park PA 15102	412-835-4433	R	2*	<.1
514	LIC Screen Printing Inc—*Edward Rosenblum*	2949 Joyce Ln, Merrick NY 11566	516-546-7289	R	2*	<.1
515	Morgan Printing Co—*Shawn Goolsey*	1300 E Wise St, Bowie TX 76230	940-872-6285	R	2*	<.1
516	Briley's Designs and Signs—*Scott Briley*	14842 Robinson St, Shawnee Mission KS 66223	913-579-7533	R	2*	<.1
517	Polycraft Inc—*William Verstegen*	42075 Avenida Alvarado, Temecula CA 92590	951-296-0860	R	2*	<.1
518	Ama Precision Screening Inc—*George Pietropaolo*	456 Sanford Rd N, Churchville NY 14428	585-293-0820	R	2*	<.1
519	Digital Engraving Inc—*William Forman*	PO Box 1013, Woodacre CA 94973	415-252-9907	R	2*	<.1
520	Royal Label Company Inc—*Paul Clifford*	50 Park St, Dorchester MA 02122	617-825-6050	R	2*	<.1
521	Labeltape Inc—*Tom Carroll*	5100 Beltway Dr Se, Caledonia MI 49316	616-698-1830	R	2*	<.1
522	Graywood Inc—*Philip Gray*	12471 Dillingham Sq St, Woodbridge VA 22192	703-719-0050	R	2*	<.1
523	Frk/Jmk Investments Inc—*Fred Kelly*	PO Box 356, Columbus NE 68602	402-564-4443	R	2*	<.1
524	Mini Graphics Inc—*Jimmy Delise*	140 Commerce Dr, Hauppauge NY 11788	516-223-6464	R	2*	<.1
525	Wyoming Financial Publications—*Dale Bohren*	PO Box 80, Casper WY 82602	307-265-3870	R	2*	<.1
526	Tcc Printing And Imaging Inc—*Michael Crumpacker*	PO Box 14499, Seattle WA 98114	206-622-4050	R	2*	<.1
527	Eleven West Inc—*John Giesen*	6598 New River Rd, Fairlawn VA 24141	540-639-9319	R	2*	<.1
528	Rotary-Graphics Corp—*Randall Hake*	PO Box 789, Sheboygan WI 53082	920-458-5595	R	2*	<.1
529	Motson Graphics Inc—*Phillip Henderson*	PO Box 234, Flourtown PA 19031	215-233-0500	R	2*	<.1
530	Dot Thermography Inc—*Howard Davies*	4205 Lindbergh Dr, Addison TX 75001	972-701-8566	R	2*	<.1
531	North Star Nameplate Inc—*Steve Cooper*	5750 Ne Moore Ct, Hillsboro OR 97124	503-648-9208	R	2*	<.1
532	Catholic Printery Inc—*Kieth Sterling*	PO Box 81026, Seattle WA 98108	206-767-0660	R	2*	<.1
533	Newtech Imaging Inc—*Helen Godwin*	333 Queen St Ste B, Honolulu HI 96813	808-532-6566	R	2*	<.1
534	Ameriserv Inc—*Nancy Shearer*	630 W Carolina Ave, Hartsville SC 29550	843-383-5156	R	2*	<.1
535	Superior Advertising and Marketing Inc—*John Wharrie*	962 State Hwy Z, Cape Girardeau MO 63701	573-243-1446	R	2*	<.1
536	Aaa Printing and Graphics Inc—*John Madden*	1405 132nd Ave Ne Ste, Bellevue WA 98005	425-454-0156	R	2*	<.1
537	Hoppmann Printing Inc—*John Derpuy*	3000 N 117th St, Milwaukee WI 53222	414-476-2040	R	2*	<.1
538	Dimensional Graphics Industries—*Daniel Thomas*	2 Charles Brown Indust, Palmyra MO 63461	573-769-5570	R	2*	.1
539	Pioneer Announcements Inc—*Gregory Schenker*	PO Box 370904, Miami FL 33137	305-573-7000	R	2*	<.1
540	Screen Specialty Shop Inc—*Gary Prange*	8406 Nc Hwy 163, West Jefferson NC 28694	336-982-4135	R	2*	<.1
541	Business Printing Inc—*David Bonenberger*	3209 Commander Dr, Carrollton TX 75006	214-445-5000	R	2*	<.1
542	Howlan Inc—*Howard Moldofsky*	550 Northgate Pkwy, Wheeling IL 60090	847-279-1000	R	2*	<.1
543	Serigraphic Arts Inc—*David Johnson*	6806 Parke E Blvd, Tampa FL 33610	813-626-1070	R	2*	<.1
544	B and B Adcrafters Inc—*Jay Ostrander*	1712 Marshall St Ne, Minneapolis MN 55413	612-788-9461	R	2*	<.1
545	Erd Specialty Graphics Inc—*Larry Erd*	3250 Monroe St, Toledo OH 43606	419-242-9545	R	2*	<.1
546	Meridian Corp—*Mark Weibel*	1026 19th St S, La Crosse WI 54601	608-784-2110	R	2*	<.1
547	James Garner and Sons Screen Printing Inc—*James Garner*	5682 E Interstate 20, Abilene TX 79601	325-672-1402	R	2*	<.1
548	Kolorfusion International Inc—*Thomas Gerschman*	5401 Oswego St Unit C, Denver CO 80239	303-340-9994	P	2	<.1
549	Missouri Poster And Banner Company Inc—*Jerry Barham*	1331 Erie St, Kansas City MO 64116	816-474-6140	R	2*	<.1
550	Asn Inc—*Al Nawroth*	6020 59th Pl Ste 2, Maspeth NY 11378	718-894-0800	R	1*	<.1
551	JR Rowell Printing Company Inc—*James Rowell*	1929 Reynolds Ave, North Charleston SC 29405	843-747-0005	R	1*	<.1
552	Dana E Morrison Jr Co—*Dana Morrison*	800 Biermann Ct, Mount Prospect IL 60056		R	1*	<.1
553	Taylor Athletic Wear Inc—*William Taylor*	1533 Georgia Rd, Wetumpka AL 36092	334-567-4700	R	1*	<.1
554	Eaton Manufacturing Company Inc—*Joe Williams*	PO Box 1607, Houston TX 77251	713-223-2331	R	1*	<.1
555	Elkins-Swyers Printing Co—*Steven Nibert*	301 E Olive St, Springfield MO 65806	417-869-0506	R	1*	<.1
556	Sybar Press Inc—*Scott Beyer*	315 S 12th St Unit A, Montrose CO 81401	970-249-2611	R	1*	<.1
557	Meto-Grafics Inc—*Michael Emrich*	169 NW Hwy, Cary IL 60013	847-639-0044	R	1*	<.1
558	Perfection Printing—*Steve Myers*	9560 Le Saint Dr, Fairfield OH 45014	513-874-2173	R	1*	<.1
559	Golden Valley Products Inc—*Teresa Clark*	3607 Bryant Ave S, Minneapolis MN 55409	612-827-8216	R	1*	<.1
560	Sephardic Yellow Pages—*David Benhorren*	2150 E 4th St, Brooklyn NY 11223	718-998-0299	R	1*	<.1
561	Information Label Inc—*Mark Dufort*	12 Enterprise Ave, Clifton Park NY 12065	518-664-9411	R	1*	<.1
562	Syracuse Letter Company Inc—*Nancy Osborn*	PO Box 1295, Syracuse NY 13201	315-476-8328	R	1*	<.1
563	Van-Go Graphics—*Robert Vanasse*	5 S Main St, Millbury MA 01527	508-865-7300	R	1*	<.1
564	Walker Business Machines LLC—*Linda Harp*	4 W Ct Sq, Andalusia AL 36420	334-222-6255	R	1*	<.1
565	Hilsher Graphics—*John Hilsher*	1626 Riverside Dr, Williamsport PA 17702	570-326-9159	R	1*	<.1
566	Allied Decals-Fla Inc—*Bruce Landis*	5225 Nw 35th Ave, Fort Lauderdale FL 33309	954-776-0500	R	1*	<.1
567	National Las Vegas Inc—*Doug Newson*	4545 W Diablo Dr Ste A, Las Vegas NV 89118	702-257-2810	S	1*	<.1
568	Spring Hill Laser Services Corp—*Jeff Kulick*	PO Box 79, Sterling PA 18463	570-689-0970	R	1*	<.1
569	Keneal Industries Inc—*Wayne Cassells*	679 Parkwood Ave, Romeoville IL 60446	815-886-1300	R	1*	<.1
570	News Gazette Printing Co—*Dan Mills*	PO Box 1017, Lima OH 45802	419-227-2527	R	1*	<.1
571	Image Software Services Inc—*Jeffrey Schwarz*	2 Shaker Rd Ste D103, Shirley MA 01464	978-425-3600	R	1*	<.1
572	B and S Graphics Inc—*Ben Crum*	1000 Richfield Rd, Placentia CA 92870	714-572-0010	R	1*	<.1
573	Creative Screen Art Inc—*Alan Huegli*	17922 Lyons Cir, Huntington Beach CA 92647	714-842-4343	R	1*	<.1
574	B-W Graphics Inc—*Larry Boatright*	101 Westview Dr, Versailles MO 65084	573-378-6363	R	1*	<.1
575	Century Publishing—*Gerald Bean*	PO Box 727, Banning CA 92220	951-849-4586	R	1*	<.1
576	High Point Printing LLC—*Allen V Smith*	PO Box 142, Mantua OH 44255		R	1*	<.1
577	Pfaffco Inc—*Daniel Pfaff*	14329 Commerce Way, Hialeah FL 33016	305-635-0986	R	1*	<.1
578	Papercraft Inc	PO Box 04607, Milwaukee WI 53204	414-645-5760	S	1*	<.1
579	Crown Point Press—*Kathan Brown*	20 Hawthorne St, San Francisco CA 94105	415-974-6273	R	1*	<.1
580	Loren Company Industries Inc—*Jay Cugini*	25 Henry St, Bethel CT 06801	203-743-6962	R	1*	<.1
581	Print Box Inc (New York New York)—*Jeff Huvar*	PO Box 20687, New York NY 10118	631-421-8300	R	1*	<.1
582	CCL Label Inc—*Geoff T Martin*	161 Worcester Rd Ste 5, Framingham MA 01701	508-872-4511	D	1*	<.1
583	City Printing	7248 Clairemont Mesa B, San Diego CA 92111	858-278-5571	R	1*	<.1
504	Pro Mark Graphics—*Jan Greis*	751 Airport Rd, Metropolis IL 62960	618-524-2440	R	1*	<.1
585	Impression Point Inc—*Bob Labanca*	500 W Ave Ste 4, Stamford CT 06902	203-353-8800	R	1*	<.1
586	Better Living Concepts Inc—*Jeff Davies*	7233 Freedom Ave Nw, Canton OH 44720	330-494-2213	R	1*	<.1
587	Diversified Printing Services Inc—*Gilbert Salinas*	1927 W Commerce St, San Antonio TX 78207	210-226-2888	R	1*	<.1
588	Ashland Screening Corp—*Robert Starmann*	475 E Joe Orr Rd, Chicago Heights IL 60411	708-758-8800	R	1*	<.1
589	Sacramento Envelope Company Inc—*Dominic Tringali*	773 Northport Dr Ste C, West Sacramento CA 95691	916-371-4747	R	1*	<.1
590	Quality Printing Group Corp—*Roberto Gramatges*	2529 Nw 74th Ave, Miami FL 33122	305-639-2848	R	1*	<.1

Note: An asterisk (*) indicates an estimated financial figure. The company type code used is as follows: R = Private, P = Public, S = Private Subsidiary, B = Public Subsidiary, D = Division, J = Joint Venture, I = Investment Fund.

COMPANY RANKINGS BY SALES WITHIN 4-DIGIT SIC

Rank	Company Name—*Executive Officer*	Address, City, State, Zip	Phone	Type	Fin	Empls
591	Nicholas Bredice—*Nicholas Bredice*	10 Commerce St Ste 1, Norwalk CT 06850	203-866-6854	R	1*	<.1
592	Mark IV Graphics Inc—*Donn Singleton*	PO Box 55197, Stockton CA 95205	209-465-5441	R	1*	<.1
593	Grand Forms and Systems Inc—*Gregory Grana*	PO Box 1128, Arlington Heights IL 60006	847-259-4600	R	1*	<.1
594	Bailey Printing and Publishing Inc—*Sheridan Bailey*	PO Box 99, Coal City IL 60416	815-634-2102	R	1*	<.1
595	Light and Ink Corp—*Robert Fuchs*	2200 N Grand Ave, Evansville IN 47711	812-421-1400	R	1*	<.1
596	Checkerboard Ltd—*Micah Chase*	216 W Boylston St, West Boylston MA 01583	508-835-2475	R	1*	.2
597	Us1Com Inc—*Farid Elhami*	715 Southpoint Blvd St, Petaluma CA 94954	707-781-2560	R	1*	<.1
598	Enterprise Graphics Inc—*Steven Middleton*	200 32nd St Se Ste A, Grand Rapids MI 49548	616-247-8742	R	1*	<.1
599	Ep-Direct Inc—*Ron Langacker*	PO Box 1217, Fond Du Lac WI 54936	920-923-6310	R	1*	<.1
600	Riverhill Publications and Printing Inc—*James Tanzenhagen*	43954 N Groesbeck Hwy, Clinton Township MI 48036	586-468-6011	R	<1*	<.1
601	Breeze Reprographics Inc—*James Breeze*	9112 Hard Dr, Foley AL 36535	251-943-5532	R	<1*	<.1
602	Award/VisionPs Inc—*Steven Smits*	8301 183rd St, Tinley Park IL 60487	708-429-2000	R	<1*	<.1
603	John H Urban Inc—*Tracy Paugh*	80 Ridge Rd, Montague NJ 07825	973-948-4620	R	<1*	<.1
604	Glaser Corp—*Robert Glaser*	1512 Highland Ave, Duarte CA 91010	626-815-2716	R	<1*	<.1
605	Williams Stationery Company Inc—*Lance Williams*	PO Box 266, Camden NY 13316	315-245-0510	R	<1*	<.1
606	Patterson Office Supplies—*Jim Wiltz*	PO Box 9009, Champaign IL 61826	217-351-5400	S	N/A	.3
607	Alexander's Printing Company Inc—*Nannette Alexander*	PO Box 309, Dublin GA 31040	478-272-6495	R	N/A	<.1

TOTALS: SIC 2759 Commercial Printing Nec
Companies: 607

					17,323	82.2

2761 Manifold Business Forms

Rank	Company Name—*Executive Officer*	Address, City, State, Zip	Phone	Type	Fin	Empls
1	RR Donnelley	111 South Wacker Dr, Chicago IL 60606	847-607-6000	S	1,159*	19.0
2	Better Business Forms Inc—*Joseph Baker*	PO Box 250, Pinellas Park FL 33780	727-545-8703	R	724*	.4
3	Standard Register Co—*Joseph P Morgan Jr*	PO Box 1167, Dayton OH 45401	937-221-1000	P	668	2.6
4	Ennis Inc—*Keith S Walters*	PO Box 320, Midlothian TX 76065	972-775-9801	P	550	5.8
5	New England Business Service Inc—*Richard T Riley*	500 Main St, Groton MA 01471		S	493*	3.9
6	Flesh Co—*Roy Flesh*	2118 59th St, Saint Louis MO 63110	314-781-4400	R	267*	.3
7	Wilmer Service Line—*George Crump*	PO Box 109, Coldwater OH 45828		R	218*	.3
8	Northstar Computer Forms Inc—*Keith S Walters* Ennis Inc	7130 Northland Cir N, Brooklyn Park MN 55428	763-531-7340	S	148*	.5
9	DFS Group—*Michael Rudensky* New England Business Service Inc	500 Main St, Groton MA 01471		D	66*	.4
10	Impreso Inc—*Marshall D Sorokwasz*	PO Box 506, Coppell TX 75019	972-462-0100	P	64	.2
11	Calibrated Forms Company Inc—*Keith Walters* Ennis Inc	537 N East Ave, Columbus KS 66725	620-429-1120	S	58*	.3
12	Miami Systems Corp—*Richard Campbell*	10001 Alliance Rd Ste, Blue Ash OH 45242	513-793-0110	R	55*	.9
13	Paris Corp—*Jerry Toscani*	800 Highland Dr, Westampton NJ 08060		R	43*	.1
14	Highland Computer Forms Inc—*Robert Wilson*	PO Box 831, Hillsboro OH 45133	937-393-4215	R	30*	.1
15	Adams Investment Co—*Kenneth G Adams*	PO Drawer A, Bartlesville OK 74005	918-335-1010	R	29*	.3
16	Famous Hospitality Inc—*Allan Hare*	3493 Lamar Ave, Memphis TN 38118	901-365-4742	R	27*	.1
17	Apperson Print Resources Inc—*William Apperson*	13910 Cerritos Corp Dr, Cerritos CA 90703	562-356-3333	R	25*	.1
18	Kaye-Smith Enterprises Inc—*Alexander Smith*	PO Box 3010, Bellevue WA 98009	425-455-0923	R	25*	.2
19	Greatland Corp—*Bob R Nault*	PO Box 1157, Grand Rapids MI 49501	616-791-0100	R	24*	.2
20	Peachtree Business Products LLC—*Chris Ferrara*	PO Box 13290, Atlanta GA 30324	770-420-1978	R	22*	.2
21	Professional Office Services Inc—*H Williams*	PO Box 450, Waterloo IA 50704	319-235-6777	R	19*	.4
22	Ward-Kraft Inc—*Roger Kraft*	PO Box 938, Fort Scott KS 66701	620-223-5500	R	16*	.4
23	A-S Hospitality Div	3493 Lamar Ave, Memphis TN 38118	901-365-4742	R	16*	.1
24	Imperial Clinical Research Services Inc—*Matthew Bissell*	3100 Walkent Dr Nw, Grand Rapids MI 49544	616-784-0100	R	15*	.2
25	Advertisers Press Inc—*Linda Wild*	2222 Parview Rd, Middleton WI 53562	608-831-1222	R	15*	.2
26	Sterling Business Forms Inc—*Dave Goodnature*	PO Box 2486, White City OR 97503	541-779-3173	R	14*	.1
27	International Graphics Inc—*Bud Philbrook*	6 Ingersoll Rd, South Plainfield NJ 07080	908-753-5570	R	12*	.2
28	B and D Litho of Arizonia—*Kim Horner*	3820 N 38th Ave, Phoenix AZ 85018	602-269-2526	R	12*	.1
29	Royal Business Forms Inc—*Steve Ehlert* Ennis Inc	PO Box 5868, Arlington TX 76005	817-640-5248	S	12*	.1
30	Phoenix Data Inc—*Larry Lovell*	PO Box 200, Montgomery PA 17752	570-547-1665	R	12*	.1
31	PrintXcel	403 Westpark Ct Ste A, Peachtree City GA 30269		D	11*	.1
32	Arlington Printing And Stationers Inc—*Richard Ghelerter*	200 N Lee St, Jacksonville FL 32204	904-358-2928	R	10*	.1
33	Computer Forms Inc—*John Chapman*	PO Box 23456, Portland OR 97281	503-620-4433	R	10*	.1
34	Victor Printing Inc—*Terence Richards*	PO Box 707, Sharon PA 16146	724-342-2106	R	10*	.1
35	Formstore Inc—*Paul Edwards*	1614 Headland Dr, Fenton MO 63026	636-343-6910	R	10*	.1
36	Datatel Resources Corp—*Allen Simon*	1729 Penn Ave Ste 4, Monaca PA 15061	724-775-5300	R	9*	.1
37	Rmf Printing Technologies Inc—*Felipe Bautista*	PO Box 7500, Lancaster NY 14086	716-683-7500	R	9*	.1
38	Custom Business Forms Inc—*Don Gilles*	210 Edge Pl, Minneapolis MN 55418	612-789-0002	R	9*	.1
39	Eastern Business Forms Inc—*R Price*	PO Box 10, Mauldin SC 29662	864-288-2451	R	9*	.1
40	Maggio Data Forms Printing Ltd—*Robert Maggio*	1735 Expy Dr N, Hauppauge NY 11788	631-348-0343	R	9*	.1
41	Total Business Systems Inc—*Robert Finnerty*	30800 Montpelier Dr, Madison Heights MI 48071	248-588-9130	R	9*	.1
42	Hobby Press Inc—*David Gardner*	8001 NW 74th Ave, Miami FL 33166	305-887-4333	R	8*	<.1
43	Gulf Business Forms Inc—*Ross Doane*	PO Box 1073, San Marcos TX 78667	512-353-8313	R	8*	.1
44	Hygrade Business Group Inc—*Victor Albetta*	PO Box 1099, Clifton NJ 07014	973-249-6700	R	7*	.1
45	Bfi Print Communications Inc—*Arthur Graham*	PO Box 455, Whitman MA 02382	781-447-1199	R	7*	.1
46	Pummill Business Forms Inc—*Donald Pummill*	960 W River Center Rm, Comstock Park MI 49321	616-475-9000	R	7*	.1
47	American Business Printing Inc—*Eugene V Joynt*	560 Industrial Dr, Lewisberry PA 17339		R	7*	<.1
48	Quick Tech Graphics Inc—*Christopher Felker*	PO Box 607, Springboro OH 45066	937-743-5952	R	7*	<.1
49	Ames Computer Forms Inc—*Emmett Valline*	PO Box 1970, Ames IA 50010	515-232-3947	R	7*	.1
50	Bradley Graphic Solutions Inc—*Robert Bradley*	941 Mill Rd Ste 100, Bensalem PA 19020	215-638-8771	R	7*	<.1
51	Duffie Graphics Inc—*Gerald Duffie*	PO Box 1198, Danville VA 24543	434-797-4114	R	6*	.1
52	Bestforms Inc—*Ronald Eisele*	1135 Avenida Acaso, Camarillo CA 93012	805-388-0503	R	6*	<.1
53	Golden Business Forms Inc—*Joe Mccormick*	PO Box 306, Golden City MO 64748	417-537-4713	R	6*	.1
54	National Business Forms Inc—*Sharon Folk*	PO Box 1750, Greeneville TN 37744	423-638-7691	R	6*	.1
55	United Business Forms Inc—*William Davis*	8482 W Allens Bridge R, Greeneville TN 37743	423-639-5551	R	5*	.1
56	Shawnee Systems Inc—*Richard Rogers*	3616 Church St, Cincinnati OH 45244	513-561-4803	R	5*	.1
57	Puget Press Multiple Inc—*Janice Henning*	3431 Broadway, Everett WA 98201	425-259-9148	R	4*	<.1
58	Little Printing Co—*Tom Kinnison*	PO Box 1176, Troy OH 45356	937-773-4595	R	4*	<.1
59	Economy Printing Co—*Robert Strickland*	PO Box 2281, Jacksonville FL 32203	904-786-4070	R	4*	<.1
60	Speedflo Inc—*Harry Kruger*	PO Box 12268, Lexington KY 40582	859-233-3070	R	3*	<.1
61	Renfrow and Company Inc—*William Renfrow*	1123 Agnes St, Corpus Christi TX 78401	361-884-5541	R	3*	<.1
62	Cornelius Printed Products Inc—*John Cornelius*	PO Box 88888, Indianapolis IN 46208	317-923-1340	R	3*	<.1
63	Rotary Printing Company Inc—*Kevin F Doyle*	PO Box 260, Norwalk OH 44857	419-668-4821	R	3*	<.1
64	Rowan Business Forms Inc—*Richard Hardesty*	PO Box 1269, Salisbury NC 28145	704-638-3500	R	3*	<.1
65	Standard Printing Co—*Edmund Sobetski*	1008 N 16th St, Omaha NE 68102	402-342-3688	R	3*	<.1

Rank	Company Name—*Executive Officer*	Address, City, State, Zip	Phone	Type	Fin	Empls
66	Rough Notes Company Inc—*Walter J Gdowski*	PO Box 1990, Carmel IN 46082	317-582-1600	S	3*	<.1
67	Impressive Business Forms Inc—*Dale Eppler*	PO Box 131013, Tyler TX 75713	903-597-4599	R	3*	<.1
68	Datatech Business Forms Inc—*Jack Philips*	500 E Tioga St, Philadelphia PA 19134	215-739-2800	R	3*	<.1
69	Caprock Business Forms Inc—*Steve Hester*	1211 Ave F, Lubbock TX 79401	806-765-5541	R	3*	<.1
70	Stat Products Inc—*David Franco*	200 Butterfield Dr Ste, Ashland MA 01721	508-881-8022	R	3*	<.1
71	Grand Traverse Continuous Inc—*Walter Gallagher*	1661 Park Dr, Traverse City MI 49686	231-941-5400	R	2*	<.1
72	Journal Printing Co—*Pat Cashin*	4848 Industrial Park R, Stevens Point WI 54481	715-344-4084	R	2*	<.1
73	Pacific Multiforms Company Inc—*Brian Majeres*	6600 Ursula Pl S, Seattle WA 98108	206-762-5980	R	2*	<.1
74	Sef Inc—*James Doherty*	PO Box 40370, Mobile AL 36640	251-432-2936	R	2*	<.1
75	N And W Printing Associates Inc—*Joan Barbini*	14 Troy Hills Rd Ste 4, Whippany NJ 07981	973-428-0770	R	1*	<.1
76	Now Impressions Inc—*Kent Osborne*	17965 Ne 65th St, Redmond WA 98052	425-881-5911	R	1*	<.1
77	Williamson Law Book Co—*Greg Chwiecko*	790 Canning Pkwy, Victor NY 14564	585-924-3400	R	1*	<.1
78	Gem Acquisition Company Inc—*Katharine Owens*	5942 S Central Ave, Chicago IL 60638	773-735-3300	R	1*	<.1
79	Argontech Global—*Jason Feriante*	1185 Obrien Dr, Menlo Park CA 94025	650-557-2092	R	1*	<.1
80	White Graphics Inc—*Richard T White*	1411 Centre Circle Dr, Downers Grove IL 60515	630-629-9300	R	1*	<.1
81	Digimatics Inc—*Dennis Alumbaugh*	5 Crozerville Rd, Aston PA 19014	610-358-3900	R	1*	<.1
82	Rotary Forms Press Inc—*Jon Cassner*	835 S High St, Hillsboro OH 45133	937-393-3426	R	1*	.1

TOTALS: SIC 2761 Manifold Business Forms
	Companies: 82				5,102	39.9

2771 Greeting Cards

Rank	Company Name—*Executive Officer*	Address, City, State, Zip	Phone	Type	Fin	Empls
1	AG Interactive Inc—*Sally Babock-Schriner* American Greetings Corp	1 American Rd, Cleveland OH 44144	216-889-5000	S	4,423*	20.0
2	Hallmark Cards Inc—*Donald J Hall Jr*	PO Box 419034, Kansas City MO 64141	816-274-5111	R	4,039*	13.2
3	American Greetings Corp—*Zev Weiss*	1 American Rd, Cleveland OH 44144	216-252-7300	P	1,560	24.8
4	Taylor Corp—*Glen Taylor*	PO Box 3728, Mankato MN 56002	507-625-2828	R	1,137*	10.0
5	CSS Industries Inc—*Christopher J Munyan*	1845 Walnut St Ste 800, Philadelphia PA 19103	215-569-9900	P	451	1.8
6	Paper Magic Group Inc—*Robert Collins* CSS Industries Inc	PO Box 977, Scranton PA 18501	570-961-3863	D	44*	.2
7	Send Out Cards LLC—*Kody Bateman*	1825 W Research Way, Salt Lake City UT 84119	801-463-3800	R	33	.1
8	Marian Heath Greeting LLC—*Dan Stevers*	10 Renaissance Way, Sanford ME 04073	207-324-4153	R	30*	.1
9	Pep Direct Inc—*Sam Blackford*	19 Stoney Brook Dr, Wilton NH 03086	603-654-6141	R	28*	.1
10	Sunrise Greetings—*Susan Hare* Hallmark Cards Inc	1145 Sunrise Greetings, Bloomington IN 47404	812-336-9900	S	25*	.1
11	Leanin Tree Inc—*Thomas Trumble*	PO Box 9500, Boulder CO 80301	303-530-1442	R	24*	.2
12	New England Art Publishers Inc—*Richard Evans*	PO Box 67, Abington MA 02351	781-878-5151	R	23*	.3
13	P S Greetings Inc—*Mark Mccracken*	5730 N Tripp Ave, Chicago IL 60646	773-267-6150	R	18*	.2
14	Brick Mill Studios—*Dean Schulhof*	24 Mill Brook Rd, Wilton NH 03086	603-579-1600	R	11*	.1
15	Gallant Greetings Corp—*Catherine Moritz*	4300 United Pkwy, Schiller Park IL 60176	847-671-6500	R	10*	.1
16	Marian Heath Greeting Cards Inc—*Dan Steever*	PO Box 3130, Wareham MA 02571		R	9*	.1
17	Avanti Press Inc—*Frederic Ruffner*	155 W Congress St Ste, Detroit MI 48226	313-961-0022	R	5*	<.1
18	Paper House Productions Inc—*Donald Guidi*	PO Box 259, Saugerties NY 12477	845-246-7261	R	5*	<.1
19	Kalan LP—*Jeffrey Kalan*	PO Box 1029, Lansdowne PA 19050	610-623-1900	R	5*	<.1
20	Park Madison Group Inc—*Glen Biely*	1407 11th Ave, Seattle WA 98122	206-324-5711	R	5*	<.1
21	Gmr Enterprises Inc—*Gary Raskin*	2029 Verdugo Blvd, Montrose CA 91020	818-376-1226	R	4*	<.1
22	Perma-Greetings Inc—*James Vaughan*	2470 Schuetz Rd, Maryland Heights MO 63043	314-567-4606	R	4*	<.1
23	Meri Meri Inc—*Meridithe D'arcy*	PO Box 954, Belmont CA 94002	650-508-2300	R	3*	<.1
24	Claydon's Hallmark Shops—*Richard Claydon*	227 Bush St, Red Wing MN 55066	651-385-9080	R	2*	<.1
25	It Takes Two Inc—*Georgia Rettmer*	100 Minnesota Ave, Le Sueur MN 56058	507-665-6271	R	2*	<.1
26	Nobleworks Inc—*Ron Kanfi*	PO Box 1275, Hoboken NJ 07030	201-420-0095	R	2*	<.1
27	Blue Sky Publishing—*Bob Marqueen*	PO Box 19974, Boulder CO 80308	303-530-4654	R	1*	<.1
28	Elizabeth Lucas Designs—*Elizabeth Lucas*	518 Monrovia Ave, Long Beach CA 90814	562-714-7018	R	1*	<.1

TOTALS: SIC 2771 Greeting Cards
	Companies: 28				11,905	71.6

2782 Blankbooks & Looseleaf Binders

Rank	Company Name—*Executive Officer*	Address, City, State, Zip	Phone	Type	Fin	Empls
1	Esselte—*Gary J Brooks*	225 Broadhollow Rd Ste, Melville NY 11747	631-675-5700	S	926*	5.0
2	Harland dataPRINT Inc—*Timothy C Tuff*	PO Box 910, Milton WA 98354		S	853*	4.9
3	Safeguard Business Systems Inc—*Michael Magill*	8585 N Stemmons Fwy St, Dallas TX 75247	214-905-3935	S	155*	1.2
4	Designer Checks Inc—*Steve Berry*	PO Box 35620, Colorado Springs CO 80935	719-534-1164	S	85*	.5
5	Viatech Publishing Solutions Inc—*Michael Bertuch*	1440 5th Ave, Bay Shore NY 11706	631-968-8500	R	53*	.4
6	Day Runner Inc—*Mark Majeske*	PO Box 400, Sidney NY 13838		S	49*	.2
7	National Computer Print Inc—*Mike Graham*	5200 E Lake Blvd, Birmingham AL 35217	205-421-7000	R	36*	.6
8	Burnes of Boston—*Celia Clancy*	21 Cypress Blvd Ste 10, Round Rock TX 78665		D	36*	.2
9	Franklin Covey International Inc	2200 W Parkway Blvd, Salt Lake City UT 84119	801-975-1776	S	33*	.2
10	Samsill Corp—*James Bankes*	PO Box 15066, Fort Worth TX 76119	817-536-1906	R	32*	.4
11	Vulcan Information Packaging Inc—*Barry N Franklin*	PO Box 29, Vincent AL 35178		R	25*	.4
12	VIP Samples Inc—*Gary Dobson*	2800 112th St Ste 100, Grand Prairie TX 75050	972-647-8888	R	20*	.4
13	TROY Systems Inc (Santa Ana California)	940 S Coast Dr Ste 200, Costa Mesa CA 92626	714-241-4760	S	20*	.1
14	Dickard Widder Industries Inc—*Steven Slaven*	5602 Maspeth Ave, Maspeth NY 11378	718-326-3700	R	18*	.2
15	Trim Seal USA Inc—*Dan Semien*	17371 Ne 67th Ct Ste A, Redmond WA 98052	425-867-1522	R	16*	.3
16	Allied Group Inc—*Robert Clement*	25 Amflex Dr, Cranston RI 02921	401-946-6100	R	15*	.2
17	Napco Inc (Sparta North Carolina)—*Rocky Proffit*	120 Trojan Ave, Sparta NC 28675	336-372-5228	R	14*	.1
18	Ad Industries Inc—*Larry Wurzel*	PO Box 15997, North Hollywood CA 91615	818-765-4200	R	13*	.1
19	Pioneer Photo Albums Inc—*Shell Plutsky*	PO Box 2497, Chatsworth CA 91313	818-882-2161	R	12*	.2
20	Trendex Inc—*Jeffrey Polacek*	240 Maryland Ave E Ste, Saint Paul MN 55117	651-489-4655	R	12*	.1
21	Multi-Swatch Corp—*Keith Gordon*	2600 S 25th Ave Ste F, Broadview IL 60155	708-344-9440	R	11*	.1
22	Continental Binder And Specialty Corp—*Andrew Lisardi*	407 W Compton Blvd, Gardena CA 90248	310-324-8227	R	11*	.1
23	Leslie Company Inc—*Jerald Byrd*	PO Box 610, Olathe KS 66051	913-764-6660	R	10*	.1
24	Albumx Corp—*Terry Huang*	21 Grace Church St, Port Chester NY 10573	914-939-6878	R	10*	.1
25	Kambara USA Inc—*Sam Watanabe*	PO Box 747, Tualatin OR 97062	503-692-9818	R	9*	.1
26	Classic Album LLC	343 Lorimer St, Brooklyn NY 11206	718-388-2818	R	9*	.1
27	Napco Inc—*James Proffit*	PO Box 1029, Sparta NC 28675	336-372-5228	R	9*	.1
28	General Products—*Raymond Kalwajtys*	4045 N Rockwell St, Chicago IL 60618	773-463-2424	R	8*	.1
29	K and L Looseleaf Products Inc—*Ken Fairbanks*	425 Bonnie Ln, Elk Grove Village IL 60007	847-439-3300	R	8*	.1
30	Main Street Checks Inc—*Grady Burrow*	920 19th St N, Birmingham AL 35203	205-380-4000	R	8*	.1
31	Federal Sample Card Corp—*Michael Cronin*	4520 83rd St, Elmhurst NY 11373	718-458-1344	R	7*	.1
32	Silvanus Products Inc—*Sam Ewing*	PO Box 427, Sainte Genevieve MO 63670	573-883-3521	R	7*	.1
33	Eckhart and Company Inc—*Chris Eckhart*	4011 W 54th St, Indianapolis IN 46254	317-347-2665	R	7*	.1

Note: An asterisk (*) indicates an estimated financial figure. The company type code used is as follows: R = Private, P = Public, S = Private Subsidiary, B = Public Subsidiary, D = Division, J = Joint Venture, I = Investment Fund.

COMPANY RANKINGS BY SALES WITHIN 4-DIGIT SIC

Rank	Company Name—*Executive Officer*	Address, City, State, Zip	Phone	Type	Fin	Empls
34	Quickutz Inc—*Eric Ruff*	7 S 1550 W Ste 600, Lindon UT 84042	801-769-2480	R	7*	.1
35	Toron Inc—*Ronald Schilling*	1145 Wicomico St, Baltimore MD 21230	410-727-8520	R	6*	.1
36	Bear Graphics Inc—*Dan Youngblade*	PO Box 3290, Sioux City IA 51102	712-252-0169	R	6*	.1
37	First Healthcare Products Inc—*Paul Smith*	6125 Lendell Dr, Sanborn NY 14132	716-731-6608	R	6*	<.1
38	Docupak Inc—*William Lyons*	17515 Valley View Ave, Cerritos CA 90703	714-670-7944	R	6*	<.1
39	Reed Presentations Inc—*Barry Reed*	3480 S Clinton Ave, South Plainfield NJ 07080	908-753-8800	R	6*	.1
40	William Exline Inc—*William Exline*	12301 Bennington Ave, Cleveland OH 44135	216-941-0800	R	6*	<.1
41	Cadillac Looseleaf Products Inc—*Kurt Streng*	1195 Equity Dr, Troy MI 48084	248-288-9777	R	5*	<.1
42	Mueller Art Cover and Binding Co—*Edmond Mueller*	PO Box 360829, Strongsville OH 44136	440-238-0372	R	5*	<.1
43	Lennertson Sample Co—*Daniel Lennertson*	PO Box 110, Hermann MO 65041	573-486-8898	R	5*	<.1
44	General Loose Leaf Bindery Company Inc—*Glenn Nickow*	3811 Hawthorn Ct, Waukegan IL 60087	847-244-9700	R	5*	<.1
45	Design Concepts Inc—*Hal Kennerly*	341 S Rd, High Point NC 27262	336-887-1932	R	5*	<.1
46	Checkworks Inc—*Aloysious Uniack*	PO Box 60065, City Of Industry CA 91716	626-333-1444	R	4*	<.1
47	Vadis Quo Editions Inc—*Oliver Beltrami*	120 Elmview Ave, Hamburg NY 14075	716-648-2602	R	4*	<.1
48	Curb Records Inc—*Mike Curb*	48 Music Sq E, Nashville TN 37203	615-321-5080	R	4*	<.1
49	Advanced Looseleaf Technologies Inc—*Gary Cananzey*	PO Box 26, Dighton MA 02715	508-669-6354	R	4*	<.1
50	Space Age Laminating And Bindery Company Inc—*Shelly Nesloney*	3400 White Oak Dr, Houston TX 77007	713-868-1471	R	4*	<.1
51	Allied Binders And Packaging Inc—*Robert Pitt*	125 Wheeler St, La Vergne TN 37086	615-287-3166	R	4*	<.1
52	Data Print Ltd—*Charles Graham*	PO Box 2888, Amarillo TX 79105	806-324-4350	R	4*	<.1
53	Sperry Graphic Inc—*Harry Caruso*	PO Box 208, Folcroft PA 19032	610-534-8585	R	4*	<.1
54	United Loose Leaf Inc—*Isnar Brad Brados*	1941 E Watkins St, Phoenix AZ 85034	602-252-6056	R	4*	<.1
55	Johnthan Leasing Corp—*Eugene Kistler*	3480 S Clinton Ave, South Plainfield NJ 07080	908-226-3434	R	3*	<.1
56	Quality Sample Company Incorporated Of High Point NC—*James Bolden*	PO Box 7367, High Point NC 27264	336-434-0750	R	3*	<.1
57	Unipac Inc	2109 National Rd SW, Hebron OH 43025	740-929-2000	R	3*	<.1
58	Samples Inc—*David Tuttle*	623 SW St, High Point NC 27260	336-887-3646	R	3*	<.1
59	Promotion Associates Inc—*Seymour Bromberg*	540 Middlesex Ave, Metuchen NJ 08840	908-561-7710	R	3*	<.1
60	Abisco Products Co—*Angel Munoz*	10612 Pioneer Blvd, Santa Fe Springs CA 90670	562-906-9330	R	3*	<.1
61	A To Z Looseleaf Inc—*Mike Zanella*	2666 W Patapsco Ave, Baltimore MD 21230	410-525-0600	R	2*	<.1
62	Rogers Loose Leaf Company Inc—*James Stuercke*	1555 W Fulton St, Chicago IL 60607	312-226-1947	R	2*	<.1
63	Art Guild Binders Inc—*Timothy Hugenberg*	1068 Meta Dr, Cincinnati OH 45237	513-242-3000	R	2*	<.1
64	Performance Sample Inc—*Terrell Holtzclaw*	PO Box 309, Eton GA 30724	706-695-7676	R	2*	<.1
65	Creative Book Manufacturing Inc—*Patricia Foley*	1422 Callowhill St, Philadelphia PA 19130	215-567-2776	R	2*	<.1
66	Visual Products Inc—*Gail Wright*	1019 Porter St, High Point NC 27263	336-883-0156	R	2*	<.1
67	Walden Lang In-Pak Service—*Brian Billes*	468 Totowa Ave Ste 1, Paterson NJ 07522	973-595-5250	R	2*	<.1
68	Tamarack Packaging Ltd—*William De Arment*	PO Box 693, Meadville PA 16335	814-724-2860	R	2*	<.1
69	Continental Loose Leaf Inc—*Robert Andrews*	25 Cliff Rd W Ste 101, Burnsville MN 55337	612-378-4800	R	2*	<.1
70	High Tech Samples Inc—*Gerald Wilbanks*	PO Box 4227, Dalton GA 30719	706-275-6686	R	2*	<.1
71	Rainbow Samples Inc—*Tina Hudson*	PO Box 2031, Dalton GA 30722	706-226-1818	R	2*	<.1
72	Denver Bookbinding Company Inc—*Gail Lindley*	PO Box 11187, Denver CO 80211	303-455-5521	R	2*	<.1
73	Brewer-Cantelmo Company Inc—*Steve Kirschenbaum*	55 W 39th St Ste 205, New York NY 10018	212-244-4600	R	1*	<.1
74	Central Bindery and Looseleaf Co—*Todd Nickow*	PO Box 112, Evanston IL 60204	847-662-2418	R	1*	<.1
75	Dilley Manufacturing Company Inc—*Dave Dilley*	215 E 3rd St, Des Moines IA 50309	515-288-7289	R	1*	<.1
76	Tower Plastics Manufacturing Inc—*David Miller*	1430 E Davis St, Arlington Heights IL 60005	847-788-1700	R	1*	<.1
77	Roger Michael Press Inc—*Michael Held*	200 Pond Ave, Middlesex NJ 08846	732-752-0800	R	<1*	.1

TOTALS: SIC 2782 Blankbooks & Looseleaf Binders
Companies: 77   2,684   17.8

2789 Bookbinding & Related Work

1	Franklin Covey Mexico Inc Franklin Covey Co	2200 W Parkway Blvd, Salt Lake City UT 84119	801-817-1776	S	196*	1.5
2	Franklin Covey Co—*Robert A Whitman*	2200 W Parkway Blvd, Salt Lake City UT 84119	801-975-1776	P	161	.6
3	Bindagraphics Inc—*F Martin Anson*	2701 Wilmarco Ave, Baltimore MD 21223	410-362-7200	R	29*	.3
4	Roswell Bookbinding Co—*Mike Roswell*	2614 N 29th Ave, Phoenix AZ 85009	602-272-9338	R	28*	.2
5	Heckman Bindery Inc—*Stephen Heckman*	PO Box 89, North Manchester IN 46962	260-982-2107	R	25*	.4
6	Leed Selling Tools Corp—*Douglas Edwards*	PO Box 3088, Evansville IN 47730	812-867-4340	R	25*	.3
7	Spiral Binding Company Inc—*Robert Roth*	PO Box 286, Totowa NJ 07511	973-256-0666	R	22*	.2
8	Library Binding Service Inc—*Frederick James*	PO Box 1413, Des Moines IA 50306	515-262-3191	R	19*	.1
9	Booksource Inc—*Sanford Jaffe*	1230 Macklind Ave, Saint Louis MO 63110	314-647-0600	R	17*	.2
10	Bindtech Inc—*Dale Nichols*	1232 Antioch Pke, Nashville TN 37211	615-834-0404	R	15*	.2
11	R and R Bindery Service Inc—*Robert Mullins*	499 Rachel Rd, Girard IL 62640	217-627-2143	R	15*	.2
12	Bind Rite Service Inc—*Elliott Ward*	16 Horizon Blvd, South Hackensack NJ 07606	201-440-5585	R	14*	.2
13	Fox Bindery Inc—*Henry Fox*	2345 Milford Sq Pke, Quakertown PA 18951	215-538-5380	R	14*	.2
14	David Dobbs Enterprises Inc—*David Dobbs*	4600 Us Hwy 1 N, Saint Augustine FL 32095	904-824-6171	R	12*	.2
15	E and M Bindery Inc—*Gary Markovits*	11 Peekay Dr, Clifton NJ 07014	973-777-9300	R	12*	.1
16	Inserts USA Inc—*Frank Puisis*	4546 W 47th St, Chicago IL 60632	773-254-3366	R	11*	.1
17	John H Dekker and Sons Inc—*John Dekker*	2941 Clydon Ave Sw, Grand Rapids MI 49519	616-538-5160	R	11*	.1
18	Printwell Acquisition Company Inc—*Thomas Roach*	26975 Northline Rd, Taylor MI 48180	734-941-6300	R	11*	.1
19	Riverside Manufacturing Company Inc—*Peter Pape*	655 Driving Park Ave, Rochester NY 14613	585-458-2090	R	10*	.1
20	Seidl's Bindery Inc—*Bill Seidl*	PO Box 550229, Houston TX 77255	713-681-3815	R	10*	.1
21	Rosen Mandell and Immerman Inc—*Steve Visoky*	121 Varick St Rm 301, New York NY 10013	212-691-2277	R	10*	<.1
22	Graphic Solutions Group Inc—*Mark Pope*	8575 Cobb Internationa, Kennesaw GA 30152	770-424-2300	R	10*	.1
23	Acme Bookbinding Company Inc—*Paul Parisi*	PO Box 290699, Charlestown MA 02129	617-242-1100	R	9*	.1
24	Cavanaugh Press Inc—*Robert Atwell*	8960 Yellow Brick Rd, Baltimore MD 21237	410-391-1900	R	9*	.1
25	Impact Mailing of MN Inc—*Tim Johnson*	4600 Lyndale Ave N, Minneapolis MN 55412	612-521-6245	R	9*	.1
26	Bridgeport National Bindery Inc—*James Larsen*	PO Box 289, Agawam MA 01001	413-789-1981	R	9*	.1
27	Color House Graphics Inc—*Ken Postema*	3505 Eastern Ave Se, Grand Rapids MI 49508	616-241-1916	R	9*	<.1
28	Continental Bindery Corp—*Tim Hoffman*	700 Fargo Ave, Elk Grove Village IL 60007	847-439-6811	R	9*	.1
29	Centennial Bindery Inc—*Ron Haug*	1951 Landmeier Rd, Elk Grove Village IL 60007	847-437-9666	R	8*	.1
30	Olympic Bindery Inc—*Dan Mooney*	1829 Gardner Rd, Broadview IL 60155	708-344-7700	R	8*	.1
31	Southwest Plastic Binding Co—*Mark Mercer*	PO Box 150, Maryland Heights MO 63043	314-739-4400	R	8*	.1
32	Macke Brothers Inc—*Joseph Macke*	10355 Spartan Dr, Cincinnati OH 45215	513-771-7500	R	8*	.1
33	Superior Binding Inc—*John Brown*	6759 Baymeadow Dr, Glen Burnie MD 21060	410-582-9900	R	8*	.1
34	Advanced Graphic Products Inc—*Michael Standish*	PO Box 670992, Dallas TX 75367	972-471-5400	R	8*	.1
35	Rickard Circular Folding Co—*Jack Rickard*	325 N Ashland Ave, Chicago IL 60607	312-243-6300	R	7*	.1
36	BJ Bindery—*Naresh Arya*	833 S Grand Ave, Santa Ana CA 92705	714-835-7342	R	7*	.1
37	Summit Graphics Inc—*Herman Massa*	20 Andrews Dr, Woodland Park NJ 07424	201-342-2332	R	7*	.1
38	Franklin Press Inc—*Ernest Seals*	PO Box 1269, Baton Rouge LA 70821	225-387-0504	R	7*	.1
39	Cameo Samples LLC—*Tracy Paplett*	1420 N Park Dr, Fort Worth TX 76102	817-332-7088	R	7*	.1

Rank	Company Name—*Executive Officer*	Address, City, State, Zip	Phone	Type	Fin	Empls
40	D and D Display Group LLC	590 Bllvlle Tpke Bldg, Kearny NJ 07032	201-955-1145	R	7*	.1
41	Colorful Story Books Inc—*John Blewitt*	2 Hollywood Ct, South Plainfield NJ 07080	908-561-3333	R	7*	.1
42	Bindery and Specialties Pressworks Inc—*Dick Izzard*	PO Box 195, Plain City OH 43064	614-873-8129	R	6*	.1
43	Printer's Bindery Services Inc—*Ron Trotter*	925 Freeman Ave, Cincinnati OH 45203	513-821-8039	R	6*	.1
44	Houchen Bindery Ltd—*Don Osborne*	340 1st St, Utica NE 68456	402-534-2261	R	6*	.1
45	Paperfold/Graphic Finishers Inc—*Raymond M Friend*	951 Sampler Way, East Point GA 30344	404-767-4890	R	6*	<.1
46	JR Finishers Inc—*Frank Rocco*	616 Albion Ave, Schaumburg IL 60193	847-301-2556	R	6*	.1
47	Editors Press Inc—*Daniel Kelly*	1701 Cabin Branch Dr, Cheverly MD 20785	301-386-2800	S	5*	.1
48	Js Trade Bindery Services Inc—*Jai Kumar*	435 Harbor Blvd, Belmont CA 94002	650-637-9763	R	5*	.1
49	Central Bindery Co—*Andy Delph*	1329 N 29th Dr, Phoenix AZ 85009	602-269-3722	R	5*	.1
50	SB Liquidating Co—*Bruce Kappele*	1100 Touhy Ave, Elk Grove Village IL 60007	847-758-9500	R	5*	.1
51	GW Steffen Bookbinders Inc—*William Turoczy*	8212 Bavaria Dr E, Macedonia OH 44056	330-963-0300	R	5*	.1
52	FBC Enterprises Inc—*Clistia Williams*	5110 Rondo Dr, Fort Worth TX 76106	817-740-1951	R	5*	.1
53	Mascari and Mascari Services Inc—*John Mascari*	2601 Lively Blvd, Elk Grove Village IL 60007	630-860-9833	R	4*	.1
54	Wert Bookbinding Inc—*Gary Wert*	9975 Allentown Blvd, Grantville PA 17028	717-469-0626	R	4*	.1
55	ADR Bookprint Inc—*Patrick Tuttle*	2012 E Northern Ave, Wichita KS 67216	316-522-5599	R	4*	.1
56	Plastikoil Of Pennsylvania Inc—*Donald Barkley*	230 W Kensinger Dr, Cranberry Township PA 16066	724-935-9190	R	4*	<.1
57	Allied Bindery LLC—*Al Scott*	32451 N Avis Dr, Madison Heights MI 48071	248-588-5990	R	4*	<.1
58	Lander Bookbinding Corp—*Arthur Lander*	1439 Strassner Dr, Saint Louis MO 63144	314-963-1900	R	4*	<.1
59	Direct Mail Service Inc—*Raymond Fragale*	187 36th St, Pittsburgh PA 15201	412-471-6300	R	4*	.1
60	Wrap-Ups Inc—*Carl Niezing*	1700 Fenpark Dr, Fenton MO 63026	636-343-4010	R	4*	<.1
61	Mark Corp—*Mark Beard*	1900 Delaware Ave, Des Moines IA 50317	515-263-1800	R	4*	<.1
62	Big D Bindery Inc—*Diane Chapman*	PO Box 561408, Dallas TX 75356	214-634-8060	S	4*	<.1
63	United Bindery Service—*Bruce Kosaka*	1845 W Carroll Ave, Chicago IL 60612	312-243-0240	R	4*	<.1
64	Mc Cormick's Bindery Inc—*Dan Cormick*	5815 Magnolia Ave, Pennsauken NJ 08109	856-663-8035	R	4*	<.1
65	Wagner Printing Co—*Matt Wager*	PO Box 85, Freeport IL 61032	815-235-7656	R	4*	<.1
66	Southern Bindery Inc—*Wallace Jaco*	PO Box 161036, Memphis TN 38186	901-346-2749	R	4*	.1
67	Spi Binding Company Inc—*Linda Crispin*	PO Box 550, Darlington IN 47940	765-794-4992	R	4*	<.1
68	Meadowlands Bindery Inc—*Carmine Idone*	146 W Commercial Ave, Moonachie NJ 07074	201-935-6161	R	4*	<.1
69	Atlantic Coast Fulfillment Inc—*Wayne Suchy*	460 Sackett Point Rd, North Haven CT 06473	203-288-1220	R	4*	<.1
70	Bindery Associates Inc—*Robert Drummond*	2025 Horseshoe Rd, Lancaster PA 17602	717-295-7443	R	4*	<.1
71	Knopf and Sons Bindery Inc—*R Knopf*	1817 Florida Ave, Jacksonville FL 32206	904-353-5115	R	3*	<.1
72	Bindery Express Inc—*Thomas Silver*	7550 Corporate Way, Eden Prairie MN 55344	952-975-5075	R	3*	<.1
73	Kater-Crafts Inc—*Bruce Kavin*	4860 Gregg Rd, Pico Rivera CA 90660	562-692-0665	R	3*	<.1
74	National Library Bindery Company Of Georgia Inc—*Jack Tolbert*	PO Box 428, Roswell GA 30077	770-442-5490	R	3*	.1
75	Cal Bind—*Chris Stern*	4700 Littlejohn St, Baldwin Park CA 91706	626-338-3699	R	3*	.1
76	Rasch Graphic Services Corp—*Randy Rasch*	7211 Gessner Dr, Houston TX 77040	713-785-5750	R	3*	<.1
77	Rapid Bind Inc—*Sue Hein*	2728 Se 14th Ave, Portland OR 97202	503-231-8898	R	3*	<.1
78	Sample Concepts Inc—*Bryan Hair*	PO Box 128, Dalton GA 30722	706-278-0818	R	3*	<.1
79	Finishing and Mailing Center LLC—*Reagan Backer*	611 Fabrication St, Dallas TX 75212	214-747-6244	R	3*	<.1
80	Richard G Mirarchi—*Richard Mirarchi*	2538 Mission St, Pittsburgh PA 15203	412-481-8108	R	3*	<.1
81	Midwest Editions Inc—*Lance Johnson*	1060 33rd Ave Se, Minneapolis MN 55414	012-370-2020	R	0*	<.1
82	Quality Bindery Service Inc—*Kathleen Hartmans*	501 Amherst St, Buffalo NY 14207	716-883-5185	R	3*	<.1
83	Scott Lithographing Company Inc—*Phillip Scott*	1870 Tucker Industrial, Tucker GA 30084	770-938-0078	R	3*	<.1
84	Library Bindery Company Of PA Inc—*Stanley Ogdon*	63 E Broad St Ste 6, Hatfield PA 19440	215-855-2293	R	3*	<.1
85	Somerset Traveller Inc—*Allan Jaffe*	1221 Rollins Rd, Burlingame CA 94010	650-342-8545	R	3*	<.1
86	Erhard and Gilcher Inc—*Peter Coyne*	PO Box 84, Syracuse NY 13209	315-474-1072	R	3*	<.1
87	Prevaro Marketing Solutions LLC—*Kim Valerio*	PO Box 390014, Edina MN 55439	952-838-3500	R	3*	<.1
88	Fidelity Bindery Co—*Earl Williams*	2829 S 18th Ave, Broadview IL 60155	708-343-6833	R	3*	<.1
89	Graphic Finishing Services Inc—*Rick Olsby*	11490 Xeon St Nw Ste 1, Minneapolis MN 55448	763-767-3026	R	3*	<.1
90	Horizon Bindery—*Joseph Kiecana*	425 Meyer Rd, Bensenville IL 60106	630-860-1200	R	3*	<.1
91	J W Boarman Company Inc—*Edmund Eck*	1421 Ridgely St, Baltimore MD 21230	410-752-8800	R	3*	<.1
92	Lippo Binding Inc—*Sue-Yeh Lin*	1734 Tyler Ave, South El Monte CA 91733	626-575-8556	R	3*	<.1
93	Page Litho Inc—*Joy Pecherski*	6445 E Vernor Hwy, Detroit MI 48207	313-921-6880	R	3*	<.1
94	Stp Bindery Services Inc—*Steven Pensiero*	110 Prestige Park Rd, East Hartford CT 06108	860-528-1430	R	3*	<.1
95	Sterling Pierce Company Inc—*William Burke*	395 Atlantic Ave, East Rockaway NY 11518	516-593-1170	R	3*	<.1
96	Portland Bindery Inc—*John Wendland*	3342 Nw 26th Ave Ste 1, Portland OR 97210	503-223-1145	R	3*	<.1
97	Church Offset Printing Inc—*Michael Kruse*	PO Box 988, Albert Lea MN 56007	507-373-6485	R	2*	<.1
98	Marathon Bindery Services Inc—*Kerry Emmott*	7511 Langtry St Ste 10, Houston TX 77040	713-690-6040	R	2*	<.1
99	Oakwood Bindery—*Thomas Peterson*	1133 Manheim Pke, Lancaster PA 17601	717-396-9559	R	2*	<.1
100	C and C Bindery Company Inc—*Joe Spalone*	25 Central Ave Unit B, Farmingdale NY 11735	631-752-7078	R	2*	<.1
101	Seaboard Bindery Inc—*Frank Shear*	10 Linscott Rd, Woburn MA 01801	781-932-3908	R	2*	<.1
102	US Bindery Inc—*Celestino Carballo*	5330 NW 161st St, Hialeah FL 33014	305-622-7070	R	2*	<.1
103	Art Bindery Inc—*Carl Schaefer*	345 Industrial Ln, Birmingham AL 35211	205-945-8444	R	2*	<.1
104	Superior Sample Company Inc—*Nancy Hagen*	PO Box 550, Ligonier IN 46767	260-894-3136	R	2*	<.1
105	Red Book Credit Services—*Charlie Failes*	PO Box 2939, Shawnee Mission KS 66201	913-438-0606	R	2*	<.1
106	Binding Edge Inc—*Steve Penkala*	883 Blair Ave, Neenah WI 54956	920-725-5060	R	2*	<.1
107	Carolina Swatching Inc—*David Robinson*	PO Box 9255, Hickory NC 28603	828-327-9499	R	2*	<.1
108	Complete Hand Assembly And Finishing Inc—*Peter Sernoff*	500 E Luzerne St Ste 4, Philadelphia PA 19124	215-634-7490	R	2*	<.1
109	Quality Samples Inc—*Gary Gazaway*	PO Box 2451, Dalton GA 30722	706-226-2306	R	2*	<.1
110	Graphic Binding Inc—*Alan Greenbaum*	133 Maple St, Stoughton MA 02072	781-341-4445	R	2*	<.1
111	Puget Bindery Inc—*Richard Bayless*	7820 S 228th St, Kent WA 98032	253-872-5707	R	2*	<.1
112	Security Bindery Inc—*William Hinderer*	616 Industrial Blvd Ne, Minneapolis MN 55413	612-378-1553	R	2*	<.1
113	Service Bindery Enterprises Inc—*Richard Love*	3228 Morris St N, Saint Petersburg FL 33713	727-823-9866	R	2*	<.1
114	Freestate Bookbinders Inc—*Richard Wimbrough*	3110 Elm Ave Ste 1, Baltimore MD 21211	410-889-8098	R	2*	<.1
115	New Hampshire Bindery Inc—*Thomas Ives*	43 S Main St, Concord NH 03301	603-224-5055	R	2*	<.1
116	Jim Perry—*Jim Perry*	3178 Oakridge Dr, Chino CA 91709	909-947-0747	R	2*	<.1
117	Triad Container Inc—*Bobby Owens*	6543 Chupp Rd, Lithonia GA 30058	770-482-1478	R	2*	<.1
118	Mutual Library Bindery Inc—*Otto Rausch*	PO Box 6026, Syracuse NY 13217	315-455-6638	R	2*	<.1
119	Wesco Mounting and Finishing Inc—*Tim Black*	5465 Dodds Ave, Buena Park CA 90621	714-562-0122	R	2*	<.1
120	Modern Bindery Inc—*James Talley*	5555 S 104th E Ave, Tulsa OK 74146	918-250-9486	R	2*	<.1
121	Dillon Bindery Inc—*David Schroeckenthale*	424 W Walnut St, Milwaukee WI 53212	414-263-1411	R	2*	<.1
122	Joseph A Gilosa Bindery Inc—*Robert Gilosa*	555 20th Ave, Paterson NJ 07504	973-279-8006	R	2*	<.1
123	Efficiency Bindery Inc—*Robert Schlump*	95 Piper Rd, Hamden CT 06514	203-375-1011	R	2*	<.1
124	Sure Fold Company Inc—*Michael Duffy*	600 E Erie Ave Bldg 4, Philadelphia PA 19134	215-634-7480	R	2*	<.1
125	Garman Printing Company Inc—*Don Wiltfong*	1104 W Chicago Ave, East Chicago IN 46312	219-397-1985	R	2*	<.1
126	Wichita Bindery Inc—*John Marshall*	622 S Commerce St, Wichita KS 67202	316-262-3473	R	2*	<.1
127	Plastikoil Plus Inc—*Robert Kiley*	W136n5265 Campbell Ct, Menomonee Falls WI 53051	262-783-6500	R	2*	<.1
128	Dayton Bindery Service Inc—*Charles Bridges*	3757 Inpark Dr, Dayton OH 45414	937-235-3111	R	1*	<.1

Note: An asterisk (*) indicates an estimated financial figure. The company type code used is as follows: R = Private, P = Public, S = Private Subsidiary, B = Public Subsidiary, D = Division, J = Joint Venture, I = Investment Fund.

COMPANY RANKINGS BY SALES WITHIN 4-DIGIT SIC

Rank	Company Name—*Executive Officer*	Address, City, State, Zip	Phone	Type	Fin	Empls
129	H and H Bindery Inc—*Mitchell Haven*	3342 Bladensburg Rd St, Brentwood MD 20722	301-779-1011	R	1*	<.1
130	Young American Bindery—*Jack Hollick*	2157 E Del Amo Blvd, Compton CA 90220	310-898-1212	R	1*	<.1
131	Abby Bindery Company Inc—*Mark Burkowitz*	61 Blanchard St, Newark NJ 07105	973-690-5509	R	1*	<.1
132	Specialty Graphics Inc—*Angela Plowman*	1998 Republic Ave, San Leandro CA 94577	510-351-7705	R	1*	<.1
133	Kansas City Bindery and Mailing—*Philip Self*	12601 Kaw Dr Bonner Sp, Bonner Springs KS 66012	913-621-0500	R	1*	<.1
134	Printers Finishing Touch Inc—*Bruce Jones*	4604 Shepherdsville Rd, Louisville KY 40218	502-452-6104	R	1*	<.1
135	Bookcolor Bindery Services Inc—*Glenn Morrow*	1685 Woodland Ave, Columbus OH 43219	614-252-2941	R	1*	<.1
136	Performance Bindery Inc—*Sherwin Carter*	1120 N Franklintown Rd, Baltimore MD 21216	410-947-0707	R	1*	<.1
137	Printers Bindery Service Co—*Michael Wertz*	2121 S Harwood St, Dallas TX 75215	214-428-5111	R	1*	<.1
138	Russco Inc—*Ken Lont*	330 N 6th St, Prospect Park NJ 07508	973-942-2246	R	1*	<.1
139	Atlantic Bookbinders Inc—*David Bruso*	PO Box 1231, Sterling MA 01564	978-365-4524	R	1*	<.1
140	Darwin A Lewis Inc—*Darwin Lewis*	1837 W Woodstock Rd, Woodstock VT 05091	802-457-1205	R	1*	<.1
141	Custom Bindery—*Misty Hettinger*	1701 W 10th St Ste 9, Tempe AZ 85281	480-967-0500	R	<1*	<.1
142	Metro-Plex Bindery Inc—*Diane Williams*	1300 Lynn Ln, Allen TX 75002	972-727-1077	R	<1*	<.1
143	Praxis Bookbindery—*Peter Geraty*	1 Cottage St Unit 18, Easthampton MA 01027	413-527-7275	R	<1	<.1
144	Ridley's Book Bindery Inc—*Donald Ridley*	PO Box 4315, Ithaca NY 14852	607-257-0212	R	N/A	<.1

TOTALS: SIC 2789 Bookbinding & Related Work
Companies: 144

					1,103	10.5

2791 Typesetting

Rank	Company Name—*Executive Officer*	Address, City, State, Zip	Phone	Type	Fin	Empls
1	OEC Graphics Inc—*Jack Schloesser*	PO Box 2443, Oshkosh WI 54903	920-235-7770	R	28*	.2
2	Penn Industries Inc—*Jeff Alkazian*	PO Box 3117, Cerritos CA 90703	562-926-0455	S	21*	.2
3	Eagle Publishing Inc—*Jeffrey Carneal*	1 Massachusetts Ave Nw, Washington DC 20001	202-216-0600	R	21*	.2
4	Flm Graphics Corp—*Vincent Fiorello*	123 Lehigh Dr, Fairfield NJ 07004	973-575-9450	R	18*	.1
5	DATA2—*Jack Delo*	222 Turner Blvd, Saint Peters MO 63376	636-278-8888	R	14*	.1
6	Williams Typesetting Company Inc—*Earl Williams*	PO Box 21279, Chattanooga TN 37424	423-892-1328	R	12*	.1
7	Belk Printing Inc—*Lee Turnbull*	PO Box 471607, Charlotte NC 28247	704-588-4433	S	11*	.1
8	Carter Composition Corp—*Wayne Carter*	PO Box 6901, Richmond VA 23230	804-359-9206	R	11*	.1
9	Stafford Media Solutions Inc—*Chris Loiselle*	PO Box 340, Greenville MI 48838	616-754-9301	R	11*	.1
10	Muncie Novelty Company Inc—*David Broyles*	PO Box 823, Muncie IN 47308	765-288-8301	R	10*	.1
11	Mccarty Printing Corp—*Don Sieber*	PO Box 1136, Erie PA 16512	814-454-6337	R	10*	.1
12	CRW Graphics—*Harriet Weiss*	9100 Pennsauken Hwy, Pennsauken NJ 08110	856-662-9111	D	9*	.1
13	Printer Zink Inc—*Steve Harney*	1047 Broadway St, Anderson IN 46012	765-644-3959	R	8*	.1
14	Westchester Book/Rainsford Type Inc—*Dennis Pistone*	4 Old Newtown Rd, Danbury CT 06810	203-791-0080	R	8*	.1
15	Pal Graphics Inc—*Mary K McAllister*	10330 W Roosevelt Rd, Westchester IL 60154	708-344-8500	R	8*	.1
16	Joe Christensen Inc—*Brian Christensen*	PO Box 81269, Lincoln NE 68501	402-476-7535	R	8*	.1
17	Argosy Publishing Inc—*Andrew Bowditch*	109 Oak St Ste 102, Newton MA 02464	617-527-9999	R	8*	.1
18	TJ Metzgers Inc—*Thomas Metzger*	207 Arco Dr, Toledo OH 43607	419-861-8611	R	8*	.1
19	Folgergraphics Inc—*Richard Folger*	2339 Davis Ave, Hayward CA 94545	510-887-5656	R	8*	<.1
20	A-A Blueprint Company Inc—*John Scalia*	2757 Gilchrist Rd, Akron OH 44305	330-794-8803	R	7*	.1
21	Magnus Group Inc—*Richard Schiding*	PO Box 278, Emigsville PA 17318	717-764-5908	R	7*	.1
22	Albion-Holley Pennysaver Inc—*Karen Sawicz*	PO Box 231, Albion NY 14411	585-589-5641	R	6*	.1
23	Graphic Composition Inc—*Mark Jungen*	N1246 Technical Dr, Greenville WI 54942	920-757-6977	R	6*	<.1
24	Graphic World Inc—*Kevin Arrow*	11687 Adie Rd, Maryland Heights MO 63043	314-567-9854	R	6*	.1
25	New England Typographic Service Inc—*W Kern*	206 W Newberry Rd, Bloomfield CT 06002	860-242-2251	R	6*	.1
26	Ace Group Inc—*Anthony Gagliardi*	149 W 27th St Fl 3, New York NY 10001	212-255-7846	R	5*	<.1
27	Specialty Printing Inc—*Joseph Destefon*	PO Box 104, Charleroi PA 15022	724-489-9583	R	5*	<.1
28	Omegatype Typography Inc—*Yoram Mizrahi*	3101 W Clark Rd, Champaign IL 61822	217-352-1600	R	5*	<.1
29	Legal News Publishing Co—*Lucien Karlovec*	2935 Prospect Ave E, Cleveland OH 44115	216-696-3322	R	5*	<.1
30	Comercial Communications Inc—*Robert Hegwood*	525 W Alameda Dr Ste 1, Tempe AZ 85282	480-966-4003	S	5*	<.1
31	Jamik Associates Inc—*Michael O'Toole*	7852 Big Bend Blvd, Saint Louis MO 63119	314-962-5860	R	5*	<.1
32	Triangle Communications Group Inc—*Jeff Majewski*	191 Technology Dr, Garner NC 27529	919-878-6789	R	5*	<.1
33	Apollo Press Inc—*John Taylor*	270 Enterprise Dr, Newport News VA 23603		R	5*	<.1
34	Sun Newspapers Of Lincoln Inc—*Scott Stewart*	PO Box 5325, Lincoln NE 68505	402-466-8521	R	5*	<.1
35	Hot Graphics and Printing Inc—*Lynn Blurton*	5241 Elmore Rd, Memphis TN 38134	901-387-1717	R	4*	<.1
36	Business Card Express—*Kyle Grambrelle*	14000 63rd Way N, Clearwater FL 33760	727-535-7768	R	4*	.1
37	Serbin Printing Inc—*Mark J Serbin*	1500 N Washington Blvd, Sarasota FL 34236	941-366-0755	R	4*	<.1
38	R Miller Sales Company Inc—*Russell Miller*	9215 Cherokee Ln Ste 2, Shawnee Mission KS 66206	913-341-3727	R	4*	.1
39	Grunwald Printing Co—*John Grunwald*	PO Box 3219, Corpus Christi TX 78463	361-882-5654	R	4*	<.1
40	American Printing and Lithographing Company Inc—*Ronald Smith*	528 S 7th St, Hamilton OH 45011	513-867-0602	R	4*	<.1
41	Printcrafters Inc—*Howard Mintz*	4901 S 11th St, Philadelphia PA 19112	215-467-3660	R	4*	<.1
42	HOT Graphic Services Inc—*Gregory Shapiro*	PO Box 307, Toledo OH 43697	419-242-7000	R	3*	<.1
43	Word Tech Corp—*Daniel Picariello*	42 Pleasant St Ste D, Stoneham MA 02180	781-438-4111	R	3*	<.1
44	Graphic Composition Inc (Menasha Wisconsin)—*Mark Jungen*	N1246 Technical Dr, Greenville WI 54942	920-757-6977	R	3*	<.1
45	Starnet Digital Publishing Co—*Dave Mercers*	PO Box 1145, Bloomington IL 61702	309-664-6444	R	3*	<.1
46	Graphics III Advertising Inc—*Anita Schott*	832 Oregon Ave Ste L, Linthicum Heights MD 21090	410-789-7007	R	3*	<.1
47	Old Marietta Printers Inc—*Robert Irvin*	200 Cobb Pkwy N Ste 10, Marietta GA 30062	770-424-1107	R	3*	<.1
48	Harlan Graphic Arts Services Inc—*Larry Ehrman*	PO Box 643806, Cincinnati OH 45264	513-251-5700	R	3*	<.1
49	Laserwords Maine—*Vellayan Subbiah*	26 Forrestal St, Lewiston ME 04240	207-782-9595	R	2*	<.1
50	Commerce Color Inc—*Vincent Croghan*	1555 S 3rd St, Saint Louis MO 63104	314-781-7702	R	2*	<.1
51	Norco Printing Inc—*Ricky Damiani*	440 Hester St, San Leandro CA 94577	510-569-2200	R	2*	<.1
52	North American Graphics Inc—*John Mertz*	1629 W Lafayette Blvd, Detroit MI 48216	313-962-6969	R	2*	<.1
53	Oxford Hills Typesetting—*Howad James*	PO Box 269, Norway ME 04268	207-743-8958	R	2*	<.1
54	Artcraft Press Inc—*John Nicholas*	PO Box 7036, Mobile AL 36670	251-471-4383	R	2*	<.1
55	ET Lowe Publishing Company Inc—*Abert Ambrose*	2920 Sidco Dr, Nashville TN 37204	615-254-8866	R	2*	<.1
56	Lashore Press Inc—*Donald Cullough*	213 W Institute Pl Ste, Chicago IL 60610	312-427-7377	R	2*	<.1
57	Graphics Plus Inc—*Richard Hejna*	1808 Ogden Ave, Lisle IL 60532	630-968-9073	R	2*	<.1
58	Jtc Inc—*Jay Foust*	1820 W Ganson St, Jackson MI 49202	517-784-0576	R	2*	<.1
59	Newark Trade Typographers—*Robert Wislocky*	177 Oakwood Ave, Orange NJ 07050	973-674-3727	R	1*	<.1
60	Envisionink Co—*Mario Pisani*	1103 S Perkins St, Appleton WI 54914	920-730-0014	R	1*	<.1
61	Coghill Composition Company Inc—*John Coghill*	7640 Whitepine Rd, Richmond VA 23237	804-714-1100	R	1*	<.1
62	Montrose Publishing Company Inc—*David Spence*	498 S Main St, Montrose PA 18801	570-278-1141	R	1*	<.1
63	Computer Composition Corp—*Peter Fulton*	1401 W Girard Ave, Madison Heights MI 48071	248-545-4330	R	1*	<.1
64	Alpha Graphics Inc—*Christine Walsh*	3000 Chestnut Ave Ste, Baltimore MD 21211	410-727-1400	R	<1*	<.1
65	Adenine Press Inc—*Mukti Sarma*	PO Box 355, Guilderland NY 12084	518-456-0784	R	<1*	<.1
66	Technologies/Typography—*Kevin Krugh*	8 Church St, Merrimac MA 01860	978-346-4867	R	<1*	<.1
67	Spectracomp Inc—*Terry Fackler*	1609 Main St, Mechanicsburg PA 17055	717-697-9557	R	<1*	<.1
68	Rapid—*Dave Proze*	836 Harrison St, San Francisco CA 94107	415-957-5840	R	N/A	<.1

Rank	Company Name—*Executive Officer*	Address, City, State, Zip	Phone	Type	Fin	Empls
69	TR Desktop Publishing—*Kathy Tedsen*	46813 Fox Run Dr, Macomb MI 48044	586-228-8780	R	N/A	<.1

TOTALS: SIC 2791 Typesetting
Companies: 69　　　　　　　　　　　　　　　　　　　389　　3.4

2796 Platemaking Services

Rank	Company Name—*Executive Officer*	Address, City, State, Zip	Phone	Type	Fin	Empls
1	LaFrance Corp—*Joseph A Teti*	PO Box 5002, Concordville PA 19331	610-361-4300	R	263*	1.2
2	Southern Lithoplate Inc—*Clark Casson*	PO Box 9400, Wake Forest NC 27588	919-556-9400	R	60*	.2
3	Progress Printing Co—*Michael Thornton*	2677 Waterlick Rd, Lynchburg VA 24502	434-239-9213	R	45*	.2
4	Miller Dial Corp—*Jim Kaldem*	4400 Temple City Blvd, El Monte CA 91731	626-444-4555	R	36*	.1
5	Laser Graphic Systems Inc—*Francis D Gerace*	3520 Turfway Rd, Erlanger KY 41018	859-371-2244	S	34*	.2
6	Rex Three Inc—*Stephen Miller*	15431 Sw 14th St, Davie FL 33326	954-452-8301	R	20*	.2
7	Ggs Information Services Inc—*Paul Kilker*	3265 Farmtrail Rd, York PA 17406	717-764-2222	R	20*	.3
8	NAPP Systems Inc—*Trey Beckman*	5210 Phillip Lee Dr, Atlanta GA 30336	404-696-4565	S	19	.2
9	Csw Inc—*Laura Wright*	45 Tyburski Rd, Ludlow MA 01056	413-589-1311	R	17*	.2
10	Iridio Inc	5050 1st Ave S Ste 101, Seattle WA 98134		S	14*	.1
11	My Channellock Tools	PO Box 1853, Binghamton NY 13902	607-770-1005	S	14*	.1
12	Cnw Limited LLC—*Dave Pistole*	4710 Madison Rd, Cincinnati OH 45227	513-321-2775	R	13*	.1
13	Universal Engraving Inc—*Larry Hutchison*	PO Box 15090, Shawnee Mission KS 66285	913-599-0600	R	13*	.1
14	Classic Color Inc—*Raymond Bell*	2424 S 25th Ave, Broadview IL 60155	708-484-0000	R	13*	.1
15	Schawk Inc (Minneapolis Minnesota)	2626 2nd St NE, Minneapolis MN 55418	612-789-8514	D	12	.1
16	Desk Top Graphics Inc—*Eric Dyer*	65 Bay St, Dorchester MA 02125	617-350-8837	R	11*	.1
17	Stevenson Photo Color Company Inc—*Jeffrey Stevenson*	PO Box 26088, Cincinnati OH 45226	513-321-7500	R	10*	.1
18	Scan Group Inc—*David Patzer*	W222n625 Cheaney Rd, Waukesha WI 53186	262-521-1365	R	10*	.1
19	Ano-Coil Corp—*David Bujese*	PO Box 1318, Vernon Rockville CT 06066	860-871-1200	R	10*	.1
20	Great Atlantic Graphics Inc—*Fred Duffy*	280 Great Valley Pkwy, Malvern PA 19355	610-296-8711	R	10*	.1
21	Luminite Products Corp—*Richard Songer*	PO Box 27, Salamanca NY 14779	716-945-2270	R	10*	.1
22	Associates Engraving Co—*Stephen Wells*	PO Box 19452, Springfield IL 62794	217-523-4565	R	9*	.1
23	ONE Color Communications LLC—*Kimberly Croft*	1851 Harbor Bay Pkwy, Alameda CA 94502	510-263-1840	R	9*	.1
24	Creative Label Inc—*Jerry Koril*	2450 Estes Ave, Elk Grove Village IL 60007	847-956-6960	R	9*	.1
25	Digital Impressions Inc—*Peter Commandeur*	13338 Carrick Ave, Milpitas CA 95035	408-957-7444	R	7*	<.1
26	Effective Graphics Inc—*Roger Sanders*	19515 S Vermont Ave, Torrance CA 90502	310-323-2223	R	7*	.1
27	A-1 Digital Imaging—*Anthony Ferruza*	5670 Mcdermott Dr, Berkeley IL 60163	708-449-5858	R	7*	.1
28	Kramer Graphics Inc—*John Kramer*	2408 W Dorothy Ln, Moraine OH 45439	937-296-9600	R	6*	.1
29	Essex West Graphics Inc—*Donald Alldian*	305 Fairfield Ave, Fairfield NJ 07004	973-227-2400	R	6*	.1
30	Owosso Graphic Arts Inc—*Jerry Voight*	151 N Delaney Rd, Owosso MI 48867	989-725-7112	R	6*	<.1
31	Dixie Graphics Inc—*James Meadows*	636 Grassmere Park, Nashville TN 37211	615-832-7000	R	6*	.1
32	Color Service Inc—*Patrick Seeholzer*	595 Monterey Pass Rd, Monterey Park CA 91754	323-283-4793	R	5*	<.1
33	RS Graphic Services Inc—*Sharon Grant*	3300 S Jones St, Fort Worth TX 76110	817-921-6266	R	5*	<.1
34	Continental ColorCraft Inc—*Andy Scheidegger*	1166 W Garvey Ave, Monterey Park CA 91754	323-283-3000	R	5*	.1
35	Color Tek Inc—*Richard Reichert*	1280 Research Blvd, Saint Louis MO 63132	314-991-9003	R	5*	<.1
36	Adflex Corp—*Joseph Andolora*	300 Ormond St, Rochester NY 14605	585-454-2950	R	5*	<.1
37	Mcp Company Inc—*Jack Kellner*	2320 N 11th St, Milwaukee WI 53206	414-374-5660	R	5*	<.1
38	Saltzman Printers Inc—*Lewis Saltzman*	2150 N 15th Ave Ste C, Melrose Park IL 60160	708-344-4500	R	4*	<.1
39	Baltimore Color Plate Inc—*Eli Renn*	1030 Cromwell Bridge R, Baltimore MD 21286	410-823-9300	R	4*	<.1
40	Brophy Engraving Company Inc—*Howard Brophy*	626 Harper Ave, Detroit MI 48202	313-871-2333	R	4*	<.1
41	Adgravers Inc—*John Flanagan*	PO Box 7487, Detroit MI 48207	313-259-3780	R	4*	<.1
42	Precision Printing Inc—*David Miller*	2101 Hwy Dd, Moberly MO 65270	660-263-3620	R	4*	<.1
43	Acme Engraving Company Inc—*Roy Murat*	PO Box 1657, Passaic NJ 07055	973-778-0885	R	4*	.1
44	Park Lane Litho Plate—*Linda Salzhauer*	155 Ave Of The Amer, New York NY 10013	212-255-9100	R	3*	<.1
45	Zenith Engraving Company Inc—*Andy Graven*	PO Box 870, Chester SC 29706	803-377-1911	R	3*	<.1
46	Color House Company Ltd—*Joseph Cusick*	25 Council Rock Dr, Ivyland PA 18974	215-322-4310	R	3*	<.1
47	FCC LLC—*Andy Bost*	PO Box 35304, Greensboro NC 27425	336-883-7314	R	3*	<.1
48	Hollis Graphics Inc—*John Matey*	178 E Broadway Blvd, Tucson AZ 85701	520-623-7589	R	3*	<.1
49	North American Color Inc—*Lawrence Leto*	5960 S Sprinkle Rd, Portage MI 49002	269-323-0552	R	3*	<.1
50	Pressline Ink And Supply Company Inc—*Rafael Garcia*	12115 Slauson Ave, Santa Fe Springs CA 90670	562-907-1891	R	3*	<.1
51	Hughes Integrated Inc—*Robert Hughes*	PO Box 356, Plainwell MI 49080	269-685-5827	R	3*	<.1
52	GB Products International Corp—*Cynthia Gramling*	PO Box 6246, Concord CA 94524	925-825-3040	R	3*	<.1
53	Baltimore Office Supply Company Inc—*Ernest Atkinson*	641 Washington Blvd, Baltimore MD 21230	410-539-5184	R	3*	<.1
54	Moebius Design—*Peter Moebius*	9770 Carroll Centre Rd, San Diego CA 92126	858-450-4486	R	3*	<.1
55	Art-American Printing Plates Inc—*John Mc Sweeney*	1138 W 9th St Fl 4, Cleveland OH 44113	216-241-4420	R	3*	<.1
56	Lithographics Of Wisconsin Inc—*Henry Krauss*	16500 W Ryerson Rd, New Berlin WI 53151	262-782-7008	R	3*	<.1
57	Graphic Engravers Inc—*Charles Zidek*	691 Country Club Dr, Bensenville IL 60106	630-595-0400	R	2*	<.1
58	Ray Schumann and Associates Inc—*Dennis Schumann*	1347 January Ave, Saint Louis MO 63110	314-645-8700	R	2*	<.1
59	Your Images Inc—*John Tillman*	1300 Bailwood Rd Ste 2, Schaumburg IL 60173	847-437-6688	R	2*	<.1
60	Narup Engraving Company Inc—*Malcolm Vosbikian*	PO Box 1547, Palm City FL 34991	305-758-4435	R	2*	<.1
61	Computer Color Corp—*Walt Leroy*	228 Big Run Rd, Lexington KY 40503	859-277-2832	R	2*	<.1
62	Aft Corp—*William Andresen*	1815c Centinela Ave, Santa Monica CA 90404	310-576-1007	R	2*	<.1
63	R and S Digital Media—*Ronald Nelson*	2352 Eaken Ave Ne, Buffalo MN 55313	763-682-2628	R	2*	<.1
64	E C Schultz and Company Inc—*Michael Pautz*	333 Crossen Ave, Elk Grove Village IL 60007	847-640-1190	R	2*	<.1
65	Diamond Graphics Inc—*Clair Kirkpatrick*	2328 Lake St, Kalamazoo MI 49048	269-345-1164	R	2*	<.1
66	Midwest Imaging and Roller Services Inc—*Lawrence Shreve*	PO Box 390, Menasha WI 54952	920-722-6401	R	2*	<.1
67	James Banyon Photo Engraving Inc—*Nicholas Yanakas*	629 W 54th St Fl 4, New York NY 10019	212-239-1290	R	2*	<.1
68	Caporale Engraving Company Inc—*Louis Caporale*	30 Roberts Rd, Englewood Cliffs NJ 07632	201-569-8711	R	2*	<.1
69	RE May Inc—*Betty Pangrace*	1401 E 24th St, Cleveland OH 44114	216-771-6332	R	2*	<.1
70	Concord Photo Engraving Company Inc—*Peter Otto*	PO Box 1355, Concord NH 03302	603-225-3681	R	1*	<.1
71	Daniels Engraving Co—*William Daniels*	571 5th St Ste A, San Fernando CA 91340	818-837-3222	R	1*	<.1
72	Sterling Finishing Inc—*Robert Conover*	PO Box 595, Bristol PA 19007	215-788-4126	R	1*	<.1
73	Brenner Industries Inc—*Mark Brenner*	11121 W Rogers St, West Allis WI 53227	414-543-7290	R	<1	<.1
74	Johnson City Publishing Company Inc—*Donald Puglisi*	12 Hall St, Binghamton NY 13903	607-772-0687	R	<1*	<.1

TOTALS: SIC 2796 Platemaking Services
Companies: 74　　　　　　　　　　　　　　　　　844　　5.5

2812 Alkalies & Chlorine

Rank	Company Name—*Executive Officer*	Address, City, State, Zip	Phone	Type	Fin	Empls
1	Georgia Gulf Corp—*Paul D Carrico*	PO Box 105197, Atlanta GA 30348	770-395-4500	P	3,223	3.7
2	Olin Corp—*Joseph D Rupp*	190 Carondelet Plz Ste, Clayton MO 63105	314-480-1400	P	1,961	3.8
3	Celanese Chemicals - Americas—*David Weidman*	1601 W Lyndon B Johnso, Dallas TX 75234	972-443-4000	S	1,924*	5.2
4	Occidental Chemical Corp—*Ray Irani*	PO Box 809050, Dallas TX 75380	972-404-3800	S	525*	.6
5	FMC Wyoming Corp—*Pierre Brondeau*	PO Box 872, Green River WY 82935	307-875-2580	S	368*	.9
6	General Chemical Industrial Products Inc—*Ratan N Tata*	120 Eagle Rock Ave, East Hanover NJ 07936	973-599-5500	S	278	.7

Note: An asterisk (*) indicates an estimated financial figure. The company type code used is as follows: R = Private, P = Public, S = Private Subsidiary, B = Public Subsidiary, D = Division, J = Joint Venture, I = Investment Fund.

COMPANY RANKINGS BY SALES WITHIN 4-DIGIT SIC

Rank	Company Name—Executive Officer	Address, City, State, Zip	Phone	Type	Fin	Empls
7	JCI Jones Chemicals Inc—Jeffrey W Jones	1819 Main St Ste 100, Sarasota FL 34236	941-330-1537	R	266*	.8
8	Armand Products Co—W Patrick Fiedler	469 N Harrison St, Princeton NJ 08540	609-683-7090	S	174	N/A
9	Natural Soda Inc	3200 County Rd 31, Rifle CO 81650	970-878-3674	S	43*	<.1
10	Ashta Chemicals Inc—Reginald Baxter	PO Box 858, Ashtabula OH 44005	440-997-5221	R	20*	.1
11	Intrepid Potash - Moab LLC—Doug Garrett	PO Box 1208, Moab UT 84532	435-259-7171	R	10*	.1
12	Indian Springs Manufacturing Company Inc—Maurice Ferguson	PO Box 469, Baldwinsville NY 13027	315-635-6101	R	2*	<.1

TOTALS: SIC 2812 Alkalies & Chlorine
Companies: 12 — 8,793 — 16.0

2813 Industrial Gases

Rank	Company Name—Executive Officer	Address, City, State, Zip	Phone	Type	Fin	Empls
1	Air Liquide America LP—Michael J Graff	2700 Post Oak Blvd Ste, Houston TX 77056		R	14,000	35.0
2	Praxair Inc—Stephen F Angel	39 Old Ridgebury Rd, Danbury CT 06810	716-879-4077	P	10,166	26.3
3	Air Products and Chemicals Inc—John E McGlade	7201 Hamilton Blvd, Allentown PA 18195	610-481-4911	P	10,082	18.5
4	Matheson Tri-Gas Inc—William J Kroll	150 Allen Rd, Basking Ridge NJ 07920	973-257-1100	S	4,652*	2.8
5	Airgas Mid South Inc—Terry Lodge	31 N Peoria Ave, Tulsa OK 74120	918-582-0885	S	1,114*	.9
6	Airgas South—Jay Sullivan	125 Townpark Dr NW Ste, Kennesaw GA 30144	770-590-6200	S	1,113*	.5
7	American Air Liquide Holdings Inc—Michael Graff	2700 Post Oak Blvd Ste, Houston TX 77056		R	968*	5.0
8	Oxarc Inc—Greg Walmsley	PO Box 2605, Spokane WA 99220	509-535-7794	R	501*	.3
9	Airgas Carbonic Inc—Peter McCausland	6340 Sugarloaf Pkwy St, Duluth GA 30097	770-717-2200	S	331*	.2
10	Norco Inc—Jim Kissler	1125 W Amity Rd, Boise ID 83705	208-336-1643	R	211*	.7
11	Air Liquide Industrial US LP—Mark Lostak	2700 Post Oak Blvd Ste, Houston TX 77056	713-624-8000	R	153*	1.4
12	Airgas-Nor Pac Inc—Eddie Richards	11900 NE 95th St, Vancouver WA 98682	360-944-4000	S	69*	.4
13	Delta Airgas Inc	3503 W 7th St, Texarkana TX 75501	903-838-8516	D	62*	<.1
	Airgas Mid South Inc					
14	Pain Enterprises Inc—Jack Pain	101 Daniels Way, Bloomington IN 47404	812-330-1400	S	35*	.3
15	Trademark Nitrogen Corp—William Blevins	1216 Old Hopewell Rd, Tampa FL 33619	813-626-1181	R	35*	<.1
16	Industrial Enterprises of America Inc—Robert Renck Jr	711 3rd Ave Ste 1505, New York NY 10017	212-490-3100	P	31	.1
17	Cold Jet LLC—Judy Henline	455 Wards Corner Rd St, Loveland OH 45140	513-831-3211	R	29*	.1
18	Mountain States Airgas Inc—Peter McCausland	PO Box 1268, Charleston WV 25325	304-342-4124	S	25*	.2
19	Aeropres Corp—Kenneth Odom	PO Box 78588, Shreveport LA 71137	318-221-6282	R	18*	.1
20	Airgas North Central—Peter McCausland	601 C Avenue NE, Cedar Rapids IA 52401	319-366-1594	D	16*	<.1
21	Acetylene Gas Co—Peter McCausland	3500 Bernard St, Saint Louis MO 63103	314-533-3100	R	15*	.1
22	Chase Products Co—Robert Svendsen	PO Box 70, Maywood IL 60153	708-865-1000	R	14*	.1
23	Diversified Cpc International Inc—William Auriemma	24338 W Durkee Rd, Channahon IL 60410	815-423-5991	R	14*	.1
24	Dixon Investments Inc—J Dixon	PO Box 510, Orchard Hill GA 30266	770-227-8222	R	13*	<.1
25	Follmer Development Inc—Kit Follmer	840 Tourmaline Dr, Newbury Park CA 91320	805-498-4531	R	8*	<.1
26	Wellston Aerosol Manufacturing Company Inc—Norma Lockard	PO Box 326, Wellston OH 45692	740-384-2320	R	4*	<.1

TOTALS: SIC 2813 Industrial Gases
Companies: 26 — 43,677 — 93.1

2816 Inorganic Pigments

Rank	Company Name—Executive Officer	Address, City, State, Zip	Phone	Type	Fin	Empls
1	Valhi Inc—Steven L Watson	5430 LBJ Fwy Ste 1700, Dallas TX 75240	972-233-1700	P	1,593	.1
2	Ampacet Corp—Robert A DeFalco	660 White Plains Rd, Tarrytown NY 10591	914-631-6600	R	731*	1.5
3	Prince Minerals Inc—John Ropp	14 E 44th St Fl 5, New York NY 10017	646-747-4222	R	62*	.3
4	Silberline Manufacturing Company Inc—Lisa Scheller	PO Box B, Tamaqua PA 18252	570-668-6050	R	46*	.4
5	Solomon Colors Inc—Richard Solomon	PO Box 8288, Springfield IL 62791	217-522-3112	R	42*	.2
6	Kronos Inc (Cranbury New Jersey)—Lawrence A Wigdor	5 Cedar Brook Dr Ste 2, Cranbury NJ 08512	609-860-6200	D	28*	<.1
7	Colors For Plastics Inc—John Dalleska	2245 Pratt Blvd, Elk Grove Village IL 60007	847-437-0033	R	18*	.1
8	General Color and Chemical Company Inc—Carl Gartner	PO Box 7, Minerva OH 44657	330-868-4161	R	17*	.1
9	Magnetics Intl Inc—Walter Sieckmann	1111 N State Rd 149, Burns Harbor IN 46304	219-787-8055	R	14*	<.1
10	Rebus Inc (Aston Pennsylvania)—James Steever	205 W Bridgewater Rd, Aston PA 19014	610-497-4710	S	10*	<.1
11	Dynamic Color Solutions Inc—James Crawford	2024 S Lenox St, Milwaukee WI 53207	414-769-2580	R	6*	<.1
12	Kasha Industries Inc—E Kasha	PO Box 160, Grayville IL 62844	618-375-2511	R	4*	<.1
13	Ceramic Color And Chemical Manufacturing Co—William Wenning	PO Box 297, New Brighton PA 15066	724-846-4000	R	4*	<.1
14	Vwm-Republic Inc—Lynn Carlson	PO Box 605217, Cleveland OH 44105	216-641-2575	R	2*	<.1

TOTALS: SIC 2816 Inorganic Pigments
Companies: 14 — 2,577 — 2.9

2819 Industrial Inorganic Chemicals Nec

Rank	Company Name—Executive Officer	Address, City, State, Zip	Phone	Type	Fin	Empls
1	Dow Chemical Co—Andrew N Liveris	2030 Dow Ctr, Midland MI 48674	989-636-1000	P	53,674	49.5
2	El du Pont de Nemours and Co—Ellen J Kullman	1007 Market St, Wilmington DE 19801	302-774-1000	P	31,505	60.0
3	Champion Technologies Inc—Thomas Amonett	PO Box 27727, Houston TX 77227	713-627-3303	R	16,100*	2.3
4	Hanson North America Inc—Jim Kitzmiller	1333 Campus Pkwy, Neptune NJ 07753	732-919-2310	S	15,674	55.0
5	Honeywell International Specialty Materials—David Cote	101 Columbia Rd, Morristown NJ 07962	973-455-2000	R	8,309*	10.0
6	BWX Technologies Inc—Brandon C Bathards	PO Box 785, Lynchburg VA 24505	434-522-6800	S	4,752*	8.0
7	JBT FoodTech—Torbjorn Arvidsson	200 E Randolph St Fl 6, Chicago IL 60601	312-861-5900	S	3,775	14.8
8	Solvay Chemical Inc	PO Box 27328, Houston TX 77227	713-525-6800	D	3,298	8.7
9	WR Grace and Co—Fred E Festa	7500 Grace Dr, Columbia MD 21044	410-531-4000	P	3,212	6.3
10	EnergySolutions Inc—Val J Christensen	423 W 300 S Ste 200, Salt Lake City UT 84101	801-649-2000	P	1,752	5.0
11	ICC Industries Inc—John Oram	460 Park Ave, New York NY 10022	212-521-1700	R	1,629*	3.0
12	OM Group Inc—Joseph M Scaminace	127 Public Sq 1500 Key, Cleveland OH 44114		P	1,515	7.1
13	Catalytic Solutions Inc	4567 Telephone Rd Ste, Ventura CA 93003	805-473-4483	S	1,231*	.1
	Clean Diesel Technologies Inc					
14	Minerals Technologies Inc—Joseph Muscari	405 Lexington Ave, New York NY 10174	212-878-1800	P	1,045	2.1
15	Tetra Technologies Inc—Stuart M Brightman	24955 IH 45 N, The Woodlands TX 77380	281-367-1983	P	845	3.1
16	Adco Global Inc—John Knox	100 TriState Internati, Lincolnshire IL 60069	847-282-3485	R	844*	1.0
17	LSB Industries Inc—Jack E Golsen	16 S Pennsylvania Ave, Oklahoma City OK 73107	405-235-4546	P	805	1.8
18	Innophos Holdings Inc—Randy Gress	259 Prospect Plains Rd, Cranbury NJ 08512	609-495-2495	P	714	1.1
19	General Chemical Corp—William Redmond Jr	90 E Halsey Rd, Parsippany NJ 07054	973-515-0900	S	690*	4.5
20	Calgon Carbon Corp—John S Stanik	PO Box 717, Pittsburgh PA 15230	412-787-6700	P	541	1.1
21	Rockwood Specialties Group Inc—SEifi Ghasemi	100 Overlook Ctr, Princeton NJ 08540	609-514-0300	S	508*	10.0
22	Atotech USA Inc	1750 Overview Dr, Rock Hill SC 29730	803-817-3500	S	405*	.7
23	Dsm Chemicals North America Inc—J Boothe	PO Box 2451, Augusta GA 30903	706-849-6600	R	388*	.5
24	Manufacturers Chemicals LP—Chuck Stieg	PO Box 2788, Cleveland TN 37320	423-476-6518	S	362*	.4
25	Vertex Chemical Corp—Michael Moisio	11685 Manchester Rd, Saint Louis MO 63131	314-471-0500	R	293*	<.1
26	Haldor Topsoe Inc—Haldor Topsoe	17629 El Camino Real S, Houston TX 77058	281-228-5000	R	245*	.2
27	American Pacific Corp—Joseph Carleone	3883 Howard Hughes Pky, Las Vegas NV 89169	702-735-2200	P	210	.7
28	International Sulphur Inc—Jerry Jenett	PO Box 611, Mount Pleasant TX 75456	903-577-5500	R	191*	.3
29	Cormetech Inc—Steve Suttle	5000 International Dr, Durham NC 27712	919-620-3000	J	178*	.3

Rank	Company Name—*Executive Officer*	Address, City, State, Zip	Phone	Type	Fin	Empls
30	Ge-Hitachi Nuclear Energy Americas LLC—*Andrew White*	PO Box 5117, Schenectady NY 12301	910-675-5000	R	160*	1.6
31	ERCO Worldwide Inc—*Steve Hieger*	101 Hwy 73 S, Nekoosa WI 54457	715-887-4000	D	156*	.1
32	Solvay Interox Inc—*Gary Hall*	PO Box 27328, Houston TX 77227	713-525-6500	R	140*	.1
33	NL Industries Inc—*Harold Simmons*	5430 LBJ Fwy Ste 1700, Dallas TX 75240	972-233-1700	B	135	N/A
34	Twin Rivers Technologies Us Inc—*Lee Blank*	780 Washington St, Quincy MA 02169	617-472-9200	R	112*	.2
35	Phibro Animal Health Corp—*Gerald Carlson*	65 Challenger Rd, Ridgefield Park NJ 07660		R	111*	1.0
36	Indspec Chemical Corp—*Dave Dorka*	133 Main St, Petrolia PA 16050	724-756-2370	S	103*	.3
37	Technical Chemical Co—*Howard Dudley*	PO Box 139, Cleburne TX 76033	817-645-6088	R	100*	.2
38	Gulbrandsen Manufacturing Inc—*Donald Gulbrandsen*	2 Main St, Clinton NJ 08809	908-735-5458	R	83*	.1
39	Akzo Nobel Inc—*Hans Wijers*	525 W Van Buren St, Chicago IL 60607	312-544-7000	S	80*	.3
40	Mississippi Phosphates Corp	100 Webster Circle Ste, Madison MS 39110	601-898-9004	S	68*	.3
41	Gevo Inc—*Patrick R Gruber*	345 Inverness Dr S Bld, Englewood CO 80112	303-858-8358	P	65	.1
42	Dover Chemical Corp—*Dwain Colvin*	3676 Davis Rd Nw, Dover OH 44622	330-343-7711	R	60*	.3
43	Petro Hunt LLC—*Bruce Hunt*	1601 Elm St Ste 3400, Dallas TX 75201	214-880-8400	R	58*	.2
44	TETRA Process Services LC—*Geoffrey M Hertel*	25025 Interstate 45 N, The Woodlands TX 77380	281-367-1983	S	58*	.1
45	Altivia Corp—*J Jusbasche*	1100 La St Ste 3160, Houston TX 77002	713-658-9000	R	55*	.1
46	Imetal CE Minerals	1625 Snapps Ferry Rd, Greeneville TN 37745	423-639-9193	R	54*	.2
47	Cyanco LLC—*John Burrows*	9450 Double R Blvd Ste, Reno NV 89521	775-853-4300	S	53*	<.1
48	Hammond Group Inc—*W Wilke*	PO Box 6408, Hammond IN 46325	219-931-9360	R	51*	.3
49	United Chemical Technologies Inc	2731 Bartram Rd, Bristol PA 19007	215-781-9255	R	51*	.1
50	Amspec Chemical and Custom Compounding—*Kay Pali*	101 Carson Dr, Bear DE 19701	302-392-1702	R	50*	.1
51	Clean Diesel Technologies Inc—*Charles F Call*	4567 Telephone Road St, Ventura CA 93003	805-639-9458	P	48	.2
52	American Azide Corp (Cedar City Utah)—*Joseph Carleone* American Pacific Corp	3883 Howard Hughes Pkw, Las Vegas NV 89109	702-735-2200	S	48*	.1
53	Palm International Inc—*Bill Fields*	1717 JP Hennessy Dr, La Vergne TN 37086	615-641-1200	R	45*	<.1
54	Criterion Catalysts and Technologies LP—*Mike Albrecht*	16825 Northchase Dr St, Houston TX 77060	281-874-2600	R	43*	.4
55	Safetec of America Inc—*Scott Weinstein*	887 Kensington Ave, Buffalo NY 14215	716-895-1822	R	43*	.1
56	Erachem Comilog Inc—*Alain Pradoura*	610 Pittman Rd, Baltimore MD 21226	410-789-8800	R	40*	.2
57	Southern Ionics Inc—*Milton O Sundbeck Jr*	PO Box 1217, West Point MS 39773	662-494-3055	R	39*	.2
58	Sybron Chemicals Inc	PO Box 66, Birmingham NJ 08011	609-893-1105	S	37*	.1
59	Baerlocher Production USA LLC—*Ray Buehler*	5890 Highland Ridge Dr, Cincinnati OH 45232	513-482-6300	R	32*	.1
60	Peninsula Copper Industries Inc—*Kevin Codere*	PO Box 509, Hubbell MI 49934	906-296-9918	R	32*	.1
61	TOR Minerals International Inc—*Olaf Karasch*	722 Burleson St, Corpus Christi TX 78402	361-883-5591	P	31	.1
62	Heatbath Corp—*Ernest Walen*	PO Box 51048, Indian Orchard MA 01151	413-452-2000	R	30*	.1
63	Theochem Laboratories Inc—*John Theofilos*	7373 Rowlett Park Dr, Tampa FL 33610	813-237-6463	R	29*	.1
64	American Chemet Corp—*William Shropshire Jr*	PO Box 437, Deerfield IL 60015	847-948-0800	R	27*	.1
65	Odom Industries Inc—*Richard James*	PO Box 866, Waynesboro MS 39367	601-735-0088	R	26*	.2
66	Noah Technologies Corp—*Sonya Blumenthal*	1 Noah Park, San Antonio TX 78249	210-691-2000	R	25	.1
67	Jones-Hamilton Co—*J Kern Hamilton*	30354 Tracy Rd, Walbridge OH 43465	419-666-9838	R	24*	.1
68	AMPAC Farms Inc—*Joseph Carleone* American Pacific Corp	3883 Howard Hughes Pky, Las Vegas NV 89109	702-735-2200	S	24*	<.1
69	Valudor Products Inc—*Semyon Melamed*	7408 St Andrews Rd, Rancho Santa Fe CA 92067	858-759-0460	R	23	<.1
70	Afton Chemical Corp—*Warren Huang*	500 Spring St, Richmond VA 23219	804-788-5800	S	23*	<.1
71	Tessenderlo Kerley Inc—*Jordan Burns*	PO Box 15627, Phoenix AZ 85060	602-889-8300	S	22*	<.1
72	Fremont Industries Inc—*Mark Gruss*	PO Box 67, Shakopee MN 55379	952-445-4121	R	22*	.1
73	Intercat Inc—*Robert Talley*	PO Box 412, Sea Girt NJ 08750	732-223-4644	R	21*	.1
74	Iochem Corp—*Kenichi Onishi*	5801 Broadway Ext Ste, Oklahoma City OK 73118	405-848-8611	R	20*	<.1
75	Vandemark Chemical Inc—*Michael Kucharski*	1 N Transit Rd, Lockport NY 14094	716-433-6764	R	20*	.1
76	CHR Hansen Inc—*Peter Olesen*	9015 W Maple St, Milwaukee WI 53214	414-607-5700	S	17*	.1
77	Metals And Additives Corp—*Greg Stevens*	5929 Lakeside Blvd, Indianapolis IN 46278	317-290-5000	R	16*	.1
78	Protameen Chemicals Inc—*Emmanuel Balsamides*	PO Box 166, Totowa NJ 07511	973-256-4374	R	16*	.1
79	Mineral Research and Development—*Thorn Baccich* Rockwood Specialties Group Inc	5910 Pharr Mill, Harrisburg NC 28075	704-454-4811	D	16*	.1
80	Robb-Jack Corp—*David Baker*	3300 Nicolaus Rd Ste 1, Lincoln CA 95648	916-645-6045	R	15*	.1
81	Strem Chemicals Inc—*Michael Strem*	7 Mulliken Way, Newburyport MA 01950	978-499-1600	R	15*	.1
82	Birko Corp—*Florence Powers*	9152 Yosemite St, Henderson CO 80640	303-289-1090	R	14*	.1
83	Advance Research Chemicals Inc—*Dayal Meshri*	1110 Keystone Ave, Catoosa OK 74015	918-266-6789	R	14*	.1
84	Calvary Industries Inc—*John Morelock*	9233 Seward Rd, Fairfield OH 45014	513-874-1113	R	13*	.1
85	In-Cide Technologies Inc—*John Kenyon*	50 N 41st Ave Ste 2, Phoenix AZ 85009	602-233-0756	R	12*	<.1
86	Gac Chemical Corp—*David Colter*	PO Box 436, Searsport ME 04974	207-548-2525	R	12*	.1
87	Harperprints Inc—*Mike Harper*	One Industry Dr, Henderson NC 27537		D	10*	.1
88	Cowboy Charcoal LLC	PO Box 99, Albany KY 42602	606-387-8905	R	10*	.1
89	Park Chemical Co—*Ernest Walen* Heatbath Corp	8074 Military St, Detroit MI 48204	313-895-7215	S	10*	<.1
90	Asemblon Inc—*Michael D Ramage*	15340 NE 92nd St Ste B, Redmond WA 98052	425-558-5100	R	10*	.1
91	Reade Manufacturing Co—*James Gardella*	100 Ridgeway Blvd, Manchester NJ 08759	732-657-6451	S	9*	.1
92	Leech Carbide—*Daniel Leech*	PO Box 539, Meadville PA 16335	814-724-5454	R	8*	.1
93	Crystal Specialties Inc—*Janice Hendricks*	PO Box 17950, Colorado Springs CO 80935	719-540-0990	R	8*	<.1
94	Montana Sulphur and Chemical Co—*D Zink*	PO Box 31118, Billings MT 59107	406-252-9324	R	8*	<.1
95	Scotch Corp—*Lawrence Siegel*	PO Box 4466, Dallas TX 75208	214-943-4605	R	7*	<.1
96	Anachemia Chemicals Inc—*I Kudrnac*	3 Lincoln Blvd, Rouses Point NY 12979	518-297-4444	R	7*	<.1
97	Ucm Magnesia Inc—*Walter Johnson*	510 Mulberry Ln, Cherokee AL 35616	256-370-7102	R	7*	<.1
98	Frank Miller and Sons Inc—*James Miller*	13831 S Emerald Ave, Riverdale IL 60827	708-201-7200	R	7*	<.1
99	Giles Chemical Corp—*Richard Wrenn*	PO Box 370, Waynesville NC 28786	828-452-4784	R	7*	<.1
100	La-Mar-Ka Inc—*Yonette Lee*	10272 S Perdue Ave, Baton Rouge LA 70814	225-272-8125	R	7*	<.1
101	Pestco Inc—*Arnold Zlotnik*	290 Alpha Dr, Pittsburgh PA 15238	412-252-5200	R	7*	<.1
102	EmeraChem LLC—*Tom Girdlestone*	1729 Louisville Dr, Knoxville TN 37921	865-246-3000	R	7*	.1
103	Activated Metals and Chemicals Inc—*Daniel King*	1246 Airport Rd, Sevierville TN 37862	865-453-7177	S	7*	.1
104	Trigon Corp—*Bernard Tolotti*	PO Box 10207, Reno NV 89510	775-359-8494	R	6*	<.1
105	Syntech Chemicals Inc—*Christiaan Stevens*	14822 Hooper Rd, Houston TX 77047	713-433-5818	R	6*	<.1
106	Bethlehem Apparatus International Company Inc—*Bruce Lawrence*	PO Box Y, Hellertown PA 18055	610-838-7034	R	6*	<.1
107	Polyset Company Inc—*Bart Mcgonnigal*	PO Box 111, Mechanicville NY 12118	518-664-6000	R	6*	<.1
108	Southern Water Consultants Inc—*John Peters*	PO Box 1230, Decatur AL 35602	256-350-6133	R	6*	<.1
109	Masters Company Inc—*Garret Garcia*	890 Lively Blvd, Wood Dale IL 60191	630-238-9292	R	5*	<.1
110	EC Morris Corp—*Edward Morris*	201 Quadral Dr, Wadsworth OH 44281	330-335-2307	R	5*	<.1
111	Nyacol Nano Technologies Inc—*Robert Nehring*	PO Box 349, Ashland MA 01721	508-881-2220	R	5*	<.1
112	Freiborne Industries Inc—*Maureen Gill*	15 W Silverdome Indust, Pontiac MI 48342	248-333-2490	R	5*	<.1
113	Eagle Chemical Co—*Mark Celmer*	PO Box 107, Mobile AL 36601	251-452-9624	R	4*	<.1
114	Old Bridge Chemicals Inc—*Bruce Bzura*	PO Box 194, Old Bridge NJ 08857	732-727-2225	R	4*	<.1

Note: An asterisk (*) indicates an estimated financial figure. The company type code used is as follows: R = Private, P = Public, S = Private Subsidiary, B = Public Subsidiary, D = Division, J = Joint Venture, I = Investment Fund.

COMPANY RANKINGS BY SALES WITHIN 4-DIGIT SIC

Rank	Company Name—*Executive Officer*	Address, City, State, Zip	Phone	Type	Fin	Empls
115	Transene Company Inc—*Martin Hecht*	10 Electronics Ave, Danvers MA 01923	978-777-7860	R	4*	<.1
116	Astro American Chemical Company Inc—*Chris Moseley*	PO Box 878, Fountain Inn SC 29644	864-862-2731	R	4*	<.1
117	Fine Grinding Corp—*H Everett*	PO Box 71, Conshohocken PA 19428	610-828-7250	R	4*	<.1
118	Carbtrol Corp—*Kenneth Lanouette*	955 Connecticut Ave St, Bridgeport CT 06607	203-337-4347	R	4*	<.1
119	Deepwater Chemicals Inc—*Pamela Clem*	1210 Airpark Rd, Woodward OK 73801	580-256-0500	R	4*	<.1
120	Norit Americas Inc—*Maarten Knuttel*	PO Box 790, Marshall TX 75671	903-923-1000	R	3*	.3
121	Akron Dispersions Inc—*Michael Giustino*	PO Box 4195, Copley OH 44321	330-666-0045	R	3*	<.1
122	YS Inc—*Paul Young*	4531 County Rd 458, Collinsville AL 35961	256-845-5501	R	3*	<.1
123	California Carbon Company Inc—*Franklin Liu*	2825 E Grant St, Wilmington CA 90744	562-436-1962	R	2*	<.1
124	Cargille Laboratories Inc—*John Cargille*	55 Commerce Rd, Cedar Grove NJ 07009	973-239-6633	R	2*	<.1
125	Hummel Croton Inc—*Bernard Schoen*	10 Harmich Rd, South Plainfield NJ 07080	908-754-1800	R	2*	<.1
126	Chemical Corporation Of America Inc—*Frances Scher*	48 Leone Ln, Chester NY 10918	845-469-5800	R	2*	<.1
127	Esma Inc—*Tim Beezhold*	PO Box 734, South Holland IL 60473	708-331-1855	R	2*	<.1
128	Craft Laboratories Inc—*R Munsie*	1901 Lakeview Dr, Fort Wayne IN 46808	260-432-9467	R	2*	<.1
129	Wilkinson Chemical Corp—*Irene Wilkinson*	PO Box 407, Mayville MI 48744	989-843-6163	R	2*	<.1
130	Newchem Inc—*Robert Elefante*	Rr 2 Box 3000, New Cumberland WV 26047	304-387-3554	R	2*	<.1
131	Carbide Grinding Inc—*Philip Sanders*	9317 Gamebird Ln, Houston TX 77034	713-944-0015	S	2*	<.1
132	Pacific Sands Inc—*Michael L Michie*	1509 Rapids Dr, Racine WI 53404	262-619-3261	P	2	<.1
133	Chem-Met Co—*Arthur Fox*	PO Box 819, Clinton MD 20735	301-868-3355	R	2*	<.1
134	Popcorn Parlor Inc—*Alden J Glickman*	3857 Sheldon Dr, Ventura CA 93003	805-658-7369	R	1*	<.1
135	Benzsay and Harrison Inc—*Rudolph Benzsay*	PO Box 459, Delanson NY 12053	518-895-2311	R	1*	<.1
136	Beard Co—*Marc Messner*	301 NW 63rd St Ste 400, Oklahoma City OK 73116	405-842-2333	R	1	<.1
137	Cesco Chemicals Inc—*Joseph Noel*	106 Cesco Ln, Lafayette LA 70506	337-984-4227	R	1*	<.1
138	Servaas Manufacturing Corp—*David Servaas*	4897 Kessler Blvd E Dr, Indianapolis IN 46220	317-253-0454	R	<1*	<.1
139	GeNOsys Inc—*John W Miller*	86 N University Ave St, Provo UT 84601		P	<1	<.1

TOTALS: SIC 2819 Industrial Inorganic Chemicals Nec
Companies: 139

					157,673	268.3

2821 Plastics Materials & Resins

Rank	Company Name—*Executive Officer*	Address, City, State, Zip	Phone	Type	Fin	Empls
1	DuPont—*Ellen J Kullman*	1007 Market St, Wilmington DE 19898	302-774-1000	P	38,719	70.0
2	DuPont Delaware Inc—*Ellen J Kullman*	1007 Market St, Wilmington DE 19801	302-774-1000	S	30,529	60.0
3	Huntsman Polymers Corp	PO Box 2917, Wichita KS 67201	316-828-3477	S	7,000	14.0
4	Celanese Corp—*David N Weidman*	1601 W LBJ Fwy, Dallas TX 75234	972-443-4000	P	5,918	7.3
5	Eastman Chemical Co—*James P Rogers*	PO Box 431, Kingsport TN 37662	423-229-2000	P	5,842	10.0
6	InterTech Group Inc—*Anita Zucker*	PO Box 5205, North Charleston SC 29405	843-744-5174	R	3,830*	16.0
7	Chemtura Corp—*Craig A Rogerson*	199 Benson Rd, Middlebury CT 06749	203-573-2000	P	3,025	4.5
8	Albemarle International Corp—*Mark C Rohr* Albemarle Corp	330 S 4th St, Richmond VA 23219	804-788-6000	S	2,907*	3.7
9	Albemarle Corp—*Mark C Rohr*	Baton Rouge Twr 451 Fl, Baton Rouge LA 70801	225-388-7402	P	2,869	4.3
10	PolyOne Corp—*Stephen D Newlin*	33587 Walker Rd, Avon Lake OH 44012	440-930-1000	P	2,864	4.7
11	ThyssenKrupp Budd Co	3155 W Big Beaver Rd, Troy MI 48084	248-643-3500	S	2,500	13.0
12	WL Gore and Associates Inc—*Terri Kelly*	PO Box 9206, Newark DE 19714	410-506-7787	R	2,250*	9.0
13	Solvay North America LLC—*Alois Michielsen*	PO Box 27328, Houston TX 77227	713-525-6000	S	1,611*	4.0
14	Huntsman Chemicals Corp	500 Huntsman Way, Salt Lake City UT 84108	801-584-5700	S	1,300*	1.5
15	Kraton Polymers LLC—*Kevin M Fogarty* Polymer Holdings LLC	15710 John F Kennedy B, Houston TX 77032	281-504-4950	S	1,226	.9
16	Shell Chemical Co—*Lynn Elsenhans*	15536 River Rd, Norco LA 70079	504-465-7111	S	1,040*	4.2
17	Rogers L-K Corp—*Robert D Wachob* Rogers Corp	PO Box 188, Rogers CT 06263	860-774-9605	S	936*	1.2
18	Rogers Specialty Materials Corp—*Robert D Wachob* Rogers Corp	PO Box 188, Rogers CT 06263	860-774-9605	S	936*	1.2
19	TL Properties Inc—*Robert D Wachob* Rogers Corp	PO Box 188, Rogers CT 06263	860-774-9605	S	936*	1.2
20	Dyneon LLC—*Bill Myers*	6744 33rd St N, Oakdale MN 55128	651-733-1110	S	771*	.9
21	Rogers Corp—*Debra J Granger*	1 Technology Dr, Rogers CT 06263	860-774-9605	P	553	2.6
22	Dow Chemical—*Andrews Liveris*	1881 W Oak Pky, Marietta GA 30062	770-428-2684	D	463	N/A
23	Cytec Fiberite Inc—*David Lilley*	2085 E Technology Cr S, Tempe AZ 85284	480-730-2000	S	450	1.4
24	Dash Multi-Corp—*Marvin S Wool*	2500 Adie Rd, Maryland Heights MO 63043	314-432-3200	R	362*	.5
25	Aristech Acrylics LLC—*Rich Quinlan*	7350 Empire Dr, Florence KY 41042	859-283-1501	S	331*	.3
26	Toray Composites Inc—*Akira Takeo*	19002 50th Ave E, Tacoma WA 98446	253-846-1777	R	329*	.5
27	Formosa Plastics Corporation USA—*Chih-Tsuen Lee*	9 Peach Tree Hill Rd, Livingston NJ 07039	973-992-2090	R	314*	2.1
28	NOVA Chemicals Inc (Pittsburgh Pennslyvania)—*Randy G Woelfel*	400 Frankfort Rd, Monaca PA 15061		S	311*	.4
29	Landec Corp—*Gary T Steele*	3603 Haven Ave, Menlo Park CA 94025	650-306-1650	P	277	.3
30	Solvay Advanced Polymers LLC—*George Corbin* Solvay North America LLC	4500 McGinnis Ferry Rd, Alpharetta GA 30005	770-772-8760	S	267*	.4
31	Lewcott Corp—*Michael Buckstein*	86 Providence St, Millbury MA 01527	508-865-1791	R	250*	.1
32	Baker Petrolite Corp	12645 W Airport Blvd, Sugar Land TX 77478	281-276-5400	S	226*	.4
33	NB Coatings Inc—*Hidefumi Morita*	2701 E 170th St, Lansing IL 60438	708-474-7000	S	194*	.4
34	Myers Tire Supply International Inc	PO Box 1029, Akron OH 44309	330-253-5592	D	175	.5
35	Dsm Desotech Inc—*Steve Hartig*	1122 Saint Charles St, Elgin IL 60120	847-697-0400	S	161*	.2
36	Asahi Kasei Plastics North America Inc—*Nobuyuki Shunaga*	1 Thermofil Way, Fowlerville MI 48836	517-223-2000	R	140*	.2
37	Spartech Polycast—*Howard Kenney*	70 Carlisle Pl, Stamford CT 06902	203-327-6010	S	138*	.3
38	Specialty Polymers Inc—*Sheryl Southwell*	PO Box 299, Woodburn OR 97071		R	111*	.1
39	Trelleborg Sealing Solutions Great Lakes—*Ray Gillies*	3400 E Coliseum Blvd S, Fort Wayne IN 46805	260-482-4050	S	102*	1.0
40	Sterling Chemicals Inc—*John Genova* Eastman Chemical Co	333 Clay St Ste 3600, Houston TX 77002	713-650-3700	S	100	.2
41	MXL Industries Inc—*James A Eberle*	1764 Rohrerstown Rd, Lancaster PA 17601	717-569-8711	S	94*	.1
42	Cyclics Corp—*Ted Eveleth*	2135 Technology Dr, Schenectady NY 12308	518-881-1440	R	91*	.1
43	Brotech Corp—*Stefan Brodie*	150 Monument Rd Ste 20, Bala Cynwyd PA 19004	610-668-9090	R	90*	.8
44	Mg International Inc—*Junya Watanabe*	90 International Pkwy, Dallas GA 30157	770-505-0004	R	88*	.1
45	Mrc Polymers Inc—*Paul Binks*	3535 W 31st St, Chicago IL 60623	773-890-9000	R	73*	.1
46	Windsor Airmotive—*Patrick Dempsey*	7 Connecticut S Dr, East Granby CT 06026	860-653-5531	D	69*	.1
47	Tyco Fire Products CPVC Div—*Edward Breen*	245 Swancott Rd, Madison AL 35756	256-464-5633	S	69*	.1
48	Techmer Pm LLC—*Jeff Foster*	1 Quality Cir, Clinton TN 37716	865-457-6700	R	65*	.6
49	Polymeric Resources Corp—*Solomon Schlesinger*	PO Box 740, Wayne NJ 07474	973-694-4141	R	65*	.1
50	Plaskolite Inc—*James Dunn*	PO Box 1497, Columbus OH 43216	614-294-3281	R	61*	.5
51	Alloy Polymers Inc—*Charles Chiappone*	3310 Deepwater Termina, Richmond VA 23234	804-232-8000	R	55*	.3
52	Ensinger Inc—*Warren Phillips*	365 Meadowlands Blvd, Washington PA 15301	724-746-6050	R	53*	.5
53	Shintech Inc—*Chihiro Kanagawa*	3 Greenway Plz Ste 115, Houston TX 77046	713-965-0713	R	51*	.5

Rank	Company Name—*Executive Officer*	Address, City, State, Zip	Phone	Type	Fin	Empls
54	Poly Processing Company LLC—*Dixon Abell*	8055 Ash St, French Camp CA 95231	209-982-4904	R	48*	.3
55	Anderson Development Company Inc—*Joseph Greulich*	1415 E Michigan St, Adrian MI 49221	517-263-2121	S	47*	.1
56	Bulk Molding Compounds Inc—*Larry E Nunnery Jr*	1600 Powis Ct, West Chicago IL 60185	630-377-1065	R	45*	.1
57	ITW Philadelphia Resins	PO Box 309, Montgomeryville PA 18936	215-855-8450	R	43*	.1
58	MarChem Coated Fabrics Inc—*Marvin S Wool* Dash Multi-Corp	500 Orchard St, New Haven MO 63068	573-237-4444	S	43*	.1
59	Precision Coatings Inc—*Bob DeAngelis*	8120 Goldie St, Walled Lake MI 48390	248-363-8361	S	40*	.2
60	Teak Isle Inc—*Patrick Brown*	PO Box 417, Ocoee FL 34761	407-656-8885	R	37*	.2
61	Rust-Oleum Corp—*Michael Tellor*	11 Hawthorn Pkwy, Vernon Hills IL 60061	847-367-7700	S	37*	.3
62	Perstorp Compounds Inc—*Martin Lundin*	600 Matzinger Rd # 419, Toledo OH 43612	419-729-5448	S	33*	.1
63	Engineered Polymer Solutions—*Steve Linberg*	1400 N State St, Marengo IL 60152	815-568-3020	S	32*	.1
64	Plastics Engineering Company Inc—*Michael Brotz*	PO Box 758, Sheboygan WI 53082	920-458-2121	R	32*	.3
65	Springfield Products Inc—*Hidetsugi Kato*	PO Box 167, Springfield KY 40069	859-336-5116	R	31*	.4
66	Nina Plastic Bags Inc—*Satish Sharma*	1903 Cypress Lake Dr, Orlando FL 32837	407-851-6620	R	31*	.1
67	Hop Industries Corp—*Spencer Lin*	1251 Valley Brook Ave, Lyndhurst NJ 07071	201-438-6200	R	28*	.1
68	Styro Tek Inc—*Dale Arthur*	PO Box 1180, Delano CA 93216	661-725-4957	R	28*	.1
69	Capital Resin Corp—*Judithe Wensinger*	324 Dering Ave, Columbus OH 43207	614-445-7177	R	28*	.1
70	Epic Corp—*Donald Veenhuis*	600 Industrial Blvd, Palmyra WI 53156	262-495-3400	R	26*	<.1
71	River Recycling Industries Inc—*William Grodin*	4195 Bradley Rd, Cleveland OH 44109	216-459-2100	R	26*	<.1
72	Plastex Extruders Incorporated USA—*Jack White*	120 55th St Ne, Fort Payne AL 35967	256-845-8271	R	26*	<.1
73	Princeton Instruments Acton—*Don Templeman*	15 Discovery Way, Acton MA 01720	978-263-3584	D	25*	<.1
74	Crossfield Products Corp—*W Watt*	3000 E Harcourt St, Compton CA 90221	310-886-9100	R	24*	.1
75	Lakeside Plastics Inc—*Jeffery Seibold*	PO Box 2384, Oshkosh WI 54903	920-235-3620	R	24*	.1
76	Cass Polymers Inc—*Richard Bullock*	815 W Shepherd St Ste, Charlotte MI 48813	517-543-7510	R	22*	.1
77	HumiSeal—*Peter Chase*	PO Box 38355, Pittsburgh PA 15238	412-828-5470	D	22*	<.1
78	Hahl Inc—*Raymond M Trewhella*	PO Box 788, Lexington SC 29071	803-359-0706	S	20	.2
79	Reliant Worldwide Plastics LLC—*Craig Clark*	2800 N Dallas Pkwy, Plano TX 75093	940-668-7015	R	20*	.2
80	Rimtec Corp—*Atsuo Shinoda*	1702 Beverly Rd, Burlington NJ 08016	609-387-0011	R	19*	.1
81	Rapac Liquidating Company Inc—*Kenneth Adams*	65 Industrial Park, Oakland TN 38060	901-465-3607	R	18*	.1
82	New Hampshire Plastics Inc—*Gertrude Desmarais*	1 Bouchard St, Manchester NH 03103	603-669-8523	R	18*	.1
83	Elasco Inc—*Henry Larrucea*	11377 Markon Dr, Garden Grove CA 92841	714-891-1795	R	17*	.1
84	Esschem Inc—*Michael Norquist*	PO Box 1139, Linwood PA 19061	610-497-9000	R	16*	.1
85	KNF Corp—*Philip J Carcara*	734 W Penn Pke, Tamaqua PA 18252	570-386-3550	R	15	.1
86	DSM NeoSol Inc—*Warren Simmons*	199 Amaral St, Riverside RI 02915	401-435-8800	S	15*	<.1
87	Gallagher Corp—*Richard Gallagher*	3908 Morrison Dr, Gurnee IL 60031	847-249-3440	R	15*	.1
88	Ultimate Building Systems Ltd—*Chris Foit*	2725 Henkle Dr, Lebanon OH 45036	513-932-6923	R	15*	.1
89	Inchem Corp—*Stephen Crownshaw*	800 Celriver Rd, Rock Hill SC 29730	803-329-8000	R	14*	.1
90	Tembec Btlsr Inc—*Randy Fournier*	PO Box 2570, Toledo OH 43606	419-244-5856	R	13*	<.1
91	Jrlon Inc—*James Redmond*	PO Box 244, Palmyra NY 14522	315-597-4067	R	13*	.1
92	Interpolymer Corp—*Norwin Wolff*	200 Dan Rd, Canton MA 02021	781-828-7120	R	13*	.1
93	On Smooth Inc—*Sal Bianco*	2000 Saint John St, Easton PA 18042	610-252-5800	R	13*	.1
94	American Polymers Inc—*Harold Doherty*	PO Box 10, Andover MA 01810	508-756-1010	R	12*	.1
95	Nylon Corporation Of America Inc—*Greg Biederman*	333 Sundial Ave, Manchester NH 03103	603-627-5150	R	12*	.1
96	Dekalb Molded Plastics Co—*Jeff Rodgers*	PO Box 129, Butler IN 46721	260-868-2105	R	12*	.1
97	Reynolds Polymer Technology—*Roger Reynolds*	607 Hollingsworth St, Grand Junction CO 81505	970-241-4700	R	12*	.1
98	Atek Plastics Inc—*Christine Orris*	200 Holdsworth Dr, Kerrville TX 78028	830-896-6464	R	12*	.1
99	Austin Urethane Inc—*William Austin*	122 Crisp Dr, Americus GA 31719	229-924-0316	R	12*	.1
100	Arvron Inc—*Marvin Wynalda*	4720 Clay Ave Sw, Grand Rapids MI 49548	616-530-1888	R	12*	<.1
101	Rbc Industries Inc—*Kay Duckworth*	80 Cypress St, Warwick RI 02888	401-941-3000	R	12*	.1
102	Starrfoam Manufacturing Inc—*Gene Stanley*	1012 N Commerce St, Fort Worth TX 76164	817-654-4688	R	12*	.1
103	Georgia Foam Inc—*Joe Greene*	PO Box 303, Gainesville GA 30503	770-536-8888	R	11*	<.1
104	General Polymeric Corp—*Joseph Ferri*	PO Box 380, Reading PA 19607	610-374-5171	R	11*	.1
105	HK Research Corp—*Richard Higgins*	PO Box 1809, Hickory NC 28603	828-328-1721	R	11*	<.1
106	Roncelli Plastics Inc—*Gino Roncelli*	330 W Duarte Rd, Monrovia CA 91016	626-359-2551	R	11*	.1
107	Triangle Rubber Company LLC—*Keith Helfers*	PO Box 95, Goshen IN 46527	574-533-3118	R	10*	.1
108	Eastern Packaging Inc—*Erik Curtis*	283 Lowell St, Lawrence MA 01840	978-685-7723	R	10*	.1
109	BTLSR Toledo Inc	PO Box 2570, Toledo OH 43606	419-244-5856	R	10*	.1
110	Best Foam Fabricators Inc—*Keith A Hasty*	9633 S Cottage Grove A, Chicago IL 60628	773-721-1006	R	10*	<.1
111	Sunprene Co	350 N Buckeye St, Bellevue OH 44811	419-483-2931	S	10*	<.1
112	Total Systems Technology Inc—*Charles Piscatelli*	65 Terence Dr, Pittsburgh PA 15236	412-653-7690	R	10*	.1
113	Tsf Products Inc—*Kevin Farrell*	PO Box 2337, Martinsville VA 24113	276-638-3592	R	10*	.1
114	Crown Plastics Co—*Gary Ellerhorst*	116 May Dr, Harrison OH 45030	513-367-0238	R	10*	.1
115	Tiepet Inc—*Praveen Prabhu*	801 Pineview Rd, Asheboro NC 27203	336-672-0101	R	10*	.1
116	Everfab Inc—*Alan Everett*	12928 Big Tree Rd, East Aurora NY 14052	716-652-0772	R	9*	.1
117	Scandia Plastics Inc—*David Hallett*	PO Box 179, Plaistow NH 03865	603-382-6533	R	9*	.1
118	EV Roberts—*Ronald Cloud*	18027 Bishop Ave, Carson CA 90746	310-204-6159	R	9*	<.1
119	Sumter Coatings Inc—*Ross McKenzie*	2410 Hwy 15 S, Sumter SC 29154	803-481-3400	R	9*	.1
120	Terphane Inc—*Renan Bergmann*	2754 W Park Dr, Bloomfield NY 14469	585-657-5800	R	9*	.1
121	Dianal America Inc—*Hiroshi Sawa*	9675 Bayport Blvd, Pasadena TX 77507	713-758-2421	R	9*	<.1
122	Estron Chemicals Inc—*Alex Skora*	PO Box 127, Calvert City KY 42029	270-395-4195	R	9*	.1
123	Ultra-Poly Corp—*Alan Fiura*	PO Box 330, Portland PA 18351	570-897-7500	R	8*	.1
124	StrongGo LLC—*Riener Becker*	3296 E Hemisphere Loop, Tucson AZ 85706	520-547-3510	R	8*	<.1
125	Gmb Plastics Inc—*Marty Krauth*	PO Box 99, Cumming GA 30028	770-887-8008	R	8*	<.1
126	Sekisui Jushi America Inc—*Toshi Yamada*	110 Dent Dr Ne, Cartersville GA 30121	770-386-8837	R	8*	.1
127	Steinmetz Inc—*Michael Steinmetz*	PO Box 393, Moscow PA 18444	570-842-6161	R	7*	.1
128	Iowa E P S Products Inc—*Jerry Best*	5554 Ne 16th St, Des Moines IA 50313	515-262-0882	R	7*	.1
129	Dynachem Inc—*Keith Rife*	PO Box 19, Georgetown IL 61846	217-662-2136	R	7*	<.1
130	Nova Polymers Inc—*Roger Chapman*	PO Box 8460, Evansville IN 47716	812-476-0339	R	7*	<.1
131	Quadrant Chemical Corp—*Emmett Jamieson*	200 Industrial Blvd, Mckinney TX 75069	972-542-0072	R	7*	<.1
132	Agri Drain Corp—*Charles Schafer*	PO Box 458, Adair IA 50002	641-742-5211	R	7*	.1
133	Deck And Fence Services LLC—*Kathleen Doty*	106 S Elam Ave, Valley Park MO 63088	636-861-4525	R	7*	<.1
134	Cass Polymers Of Michigan Inc—*Diana Haynes*	31200 Stephenson Hwy, Madison Heights MI 48071	248-588-2270	R	7*	<.1
135	Petro Packaging Company Inc—*Rick Petrozziello*	PO Box 546, Cranford NJ 07016	908-272-4054	R	7*	<.1
136	Matrix Composites Inc—*David Nesbitt*	275 Barnes Blvd, Rockledge FL 32955	321 633 4480	R	7*	<.1
137	Adco International Plastics Corp—*John Adam*	1256 Sandtown Rd Sw, Marietta GA 30008	770-425-1234	R	6*	<.1
138	Buckeye Polymers Inc—*Jeffery Fisher*	104 Lee St, Lodi OH 44254	330-948-3007	R	6*	<.1
139	Cereplast Inc—*Frederic Scheer*	300 N Continental Blvd, El Segundo CA 90245	310-676-5000	P	6	<.1
140	Adc Acquisition Company Inc—*James Mondo*	407 Front St, Schenectady NY 12305	518-377-6471	R	6*	<.1
141	Polymer Concentrates Inc—*Phillips Christopherson*	PO Box 42, Clinton MA 01510	978-365-7335	R	6*	<.1
142	Ashley Resin Corp—*Philip Gottehrer*	1171 59th St, Brooklyn NY 11219	718-851-8111	R	6*	<.1

Note: An asterisk (*) indicates an estimated financial figure. The company type code used is as follows: R = Private, P = Public, S = Private Subsidiary, B = Public Subsidiary, D = Division, J = Joint Venture, I = Investment Fund.

COMPANY RANKINGS BY SALES WITHIN 4-DIGIT SIC

Rank	Company Name—*Executive Officer*	Address, City, State, Zip	Phone	Type	Fin	Empls
143	Pleiger Plastics Company LP—*Mary Kennedy*	PO Box 1271, Washington PA 15301	724-228-2244	R	6*	<.1
144	Ralco Industries Inc—*Robert Lebeaux*	1112 River St, Woonsocket RI 02895	401-767-2700	R	6*	<.1
145	Budd Chemical Company Inc—*Anthony Carsango*	431 Pennsville-Auburn, Penns Grove NJ 08069	856-299-1708	R	6*	<.1
146	Applied Polymer Systems Inc—*Steven Iwinski*	519 Industrial Dr, Woodstock GA 30189	678-494-5998	R	6*	<.1
147	Plastic Compounders Inc—*Phyllis Bowlin*	PO Box 664, Cambridge OH 43725	740-432-7371	R	6*	<.1
148	Plastic Design Inc—*Errol Flynn*	180 Middlesex St, North Chelmsford MA 01863	978-251-4830	R	6*	<.1
149	All Plastics And Fiberglass Inc—*Chris Bailey*	8201 Zeigler Blvd, Mobile AL 36608	251-633-2130	R	6*	<.1
150	Isotec International Inc—*Charles Knight*	PO Box 1249, Canton GA 30169	770-479-4775	R	6*	<.1
151	Plastic Specialties Inc—*George Manson*	10503 Metropolitan Dr, Austin TX 78758	512-835-5873	R	6*	<.1
152	Hro Inc—*Randol Owens*	PO Box 315, Wolcottville IN 46795	260-854-2772	R	5*	<.1
153	Hydroseal Polymers Inc—*Helena Lapper*	12151 Madera Way, Riverside CA 92503	951-272-2344	R	5*	<.1
154	Drs Industries Inc—*Dean Sparks*	1067 Hamilton Dr, Holland OH 43528	419-861-0334	R	5*	<.1
155	Zinn Polymers Inc—*Patricia Devita*	144 N Beverwyck Rd Ste, Lake Hiawatha NJ 07034	973-257-5500	R	5*	<.1
156	Forta Corp—*Rodger Lindh*	100 Forta Dr, Grove City PA 16127	724-458-5221	R	5*	<.1
157	QST Inc—*Bertram Lederer*	300 Industrial Park Rd, Saint Albans VT 05478	802-524-7704	S	5*	<.1
158	American Plastic Profiles Inc—*Larry Wallen*	PO Box 3540, Morristown TN 37815	423-586-3718	R	5*	<.1
159	Polyfil Corp—*Gerald Fabiano*	PO Box 130, Rockaway NJ 07866	973-627-4070	R	5*	<.1
160	Plastic Mart Inc—*James Nahigian*	43535 Gadsden Ave Ste, Lancaster CA 93534	310-268-1404	R	5*	<.1
161	Hapco Inc—*Steven Aronson*	353 Circuit St, Hanover MA 02339	781-826-8801	R	5*	<.1
162	K-Bin Inc—*Ervin Schroeder* Shintech Inc	5618 E Hwy 332, Freeport TX 77541	979-233-6610	S	5*	<.1
163	Axson North America Inc—*Lionel Pugel*	1611 Hults Dr, Eaton Rapids MI 48827	517-663-8191	R	4*	<.1
164	Crown Technology LLC	PO Box 789, Woodbury GA 30293	706-553-9500	R	4*	<.1
165	Oxford Industries Of Connecticut Inc—*Nicholas Defelice*	221 S St Ste 2, New Britain CT 06051	860-225-3700	R	4*	<.1
166	Replex Mirror Co—*Mark Schuetz*	PO Box 967, Mount Vernon OH 43050	740-397-5535	R	4*	<.1
167	Polychem Alloy Inc—*Chakra Gupta*	240 Polychem Ct, Lenoir NC 28645	828-754-7570	R	4*	<.1
168	Superior Products International II Inc—*Joseph E Pritchett*	10835 W 78th St, Shawnee KS 66214	913-962-4848	R	4*	<.1
169	Total Molding Solutions Inc—*Rajiv Naik*	416 E Cummins St, Tecumseh MI 49286	517-424-5900	R	4*	<.1
170	Polystyrene Products Company Inc—*Donald Gerard*	8875 Kelso Dr, Baltimore MD 21221	410-574-0680	R	4*	<.1
171	Dendritech Inc—*Emery Scheibert*	3110 Schuette Dr, Midland MI 48642	989-496-1152	R	4	<.1
172	Indusol Inc—*John Connor*	PO Box 723, Sutton MA 01590	508-865-9516	R	4*	<.1
173	Coastal Plastics Inc—*Robert Johnson*	PO Box 477, Hope Valley RI 02832	401-539-2446	R	3*	<.1
174	Steel Products Corp—*Charles Olson*	105 Huntoon Memorial H, Rochdale MA 01542	508-892-4770	R	3*	<.1
175	Replas Of Texas Inc—*Raymond Wright*	6754 Kirbyville St, Houston TX 77033	713-640-2040	R	3*	<.1
176	Magic Embedments Inc—*Mario Carosi*	PO Box 3260, Pawtucket RI 02861	401-729-1020	R	3*	<.1
177	Epolin Inc—*Greg Amato*	358-364 Adams St, Newark NJ 07105	973-465-9495	P	3	<.1
178	New Boston Rtm Inc—*Michael Angerer*	PO Box 188, New Boston MI 48164	734-753-9956	R	3*	<.1
179	Opco Inc—*Mike Payne*	PO Box 101, Latrobe PA 15650	724-537-9300	R	3*	<.1
180	American Polystyrene Corp—*Carolyn Tan*	1225 W 196th St, Torrance CA 90502	310-329-6379	R	3*	<.1
181	Reinforced Structures For Electronics Inc—*James Romeo*	50 Suffolk St, Worcester MA 01604	508-754-5316	R	3*	<.1
182	Aero Mold and Manufacturing Corp—*Vincent Bucaro*	1300 W National Ave St, Addison IL 60101	630-543-5465	R	3*	<.1
183	Plasti-Coat Corp—*Robert Mitchell*	137 Brookside Rd, Waterbury CT 06708	203-755-3741	R	3*	<.1
184	Corrosion Companies Inc—*Terry Glenn*	PO Box 1199, Washougal WA 98671	360-835-2171	R	3*	<.1
185	L-K Industry Inc—*Karen Stollings*	176 N W St, Versailles OH 45380	937-526-3000	R	3*	<.1
186	Eastern Molding International LLC—*Jessica Corsetti*	Elizabeth St, Batavia NY 14020	585-344-0220	R	3*	<.1
187	Unicore LLC	PO Box 324, Palmer MA 01069	413-284-9995	R	3*	<.1
188	C and D Enterprises Inc—*Charles Farley*	1929 N Opdyke Rd, Auburn Hills MI 48326	248-373-5553	R	2*	<.1
189	Pacific Plastics Design Inc—*Don Asenbauer*	15570 Roxford St, Sylmar CA 91342	818-364-6677	R	2*	<.1
190	Eezer Products Inc—*Leighton Sjostrand*	4734 E Home Ave, Fresno CA 93703	559-255-4140	R	2*	<.1
191	Majestic Mold and Tool Inc—*Timothy King*	177 Volney St, Phoenix NY 13135	315-695-2079	R	2*	<.1
192	Bromley Plastics Corp—*David Kattermann Jr*	PO Box 550, Fletcher NC 28732	828-651-8737	R	2*	<.1
193	Fiber Science Inc—*Steven D Fredricks*	2855 Kirby Ave NE Ste, Palm Bay FL 32905	321-726-6327	R	2*	<.1
194	Custom Films Inc—*Larry Bender*	PO Box 218, Marshall IL 62441	217-826-2326	R	2*	<.1
195	Abatron Inc—*Marsha Caporaso*	5501 95th Ave, Kenosha WI 53144	262-653-2000	R	2*	<.1
196	Photo Protective Technologies Inc—*James Gallas*	6610 Topper Ridge Rd, San Antonio TX 78233	210-493-6353	R	2*	<.1
197	Capital Plastics Company Inc—*Ed Sullivan*	10788 Tucker St, Beltsville MD 20705	301-595-1177	R	2*	<.1
198	Clarich Mold Corp—*John Buenger*	10119 W Roosevelt Rd, Westchester IL 60154	708-865-8120	R	2*	<.1
199	Elite Solutions Inc—*Jay Galvin*	15455 N Grnway Hyden L, Scottsdale AZ 85260	480-483-9242	R	2*	<.1
200	Jms Industries Inc—*Manjit Nagra*	PO Box 507, Springfield OH 45501	937-325-3502	R	2*	<.1
201	AP Pharma Inc—*John B Whelan*	123 Saginaw Dr, Redwood City CA 94063	650-366-2626	P	1	<.1
202	Axiom Industries Inc—*Cory Barge*	PO Box 1147, Tualatin OR 97062	503-620-2439	R	1*	<.1
203	Mrm Industries Inc—*Michael Mahan*	1655 Industrial Dr, Owosso MI 48867	989-723-7443	R	1*	<.1
204	Polymer Holdings LLC—*Kevin M Fogarty*	15710 John F Kennedy B, Houston TX 77032	281-504-4950	R	1*	.8
205	Sealing Systems Inc—*Steve Baker*	PO Box 920775, Houston TX 77292	985-542-8921	R	1*	<.1
206	Teflex Inc—*James Zigray*	PO Box 136, Factoryville PA 18419	570-945-9185	R	1*	<.1
207	Dip Seal Plastics Inc—*David Foran*	2311 23rd Ave, Rockford IL 61104	815-398-3533	R	1*	<.1
208	American Epoxy And Metal Inc—*Samer Daniel*	2470 Rowe St, Bronx NY 10461	718-828-7828	R	1*	<.1
209	Rohm and Haas Co—*Jerome A Peribere*	100 Independence Mall, Philadelphia PA 19106	215-592-3000	S	N/A	15.4
210	Shin-Etsu MicroSi Inc—*John J Sesody*	10028 S 51st St, Phoenix AZ 85044	480-893-8898	S	N/A	<.1

TOTALS: SIC 2821 Plastics Materials & Resins
Companies: 210   124,880   271.2

2822 Synthetic Rubber

Rank	Company Name—*Executive Officer*	Address, City, State, Zip	Phone	Type	Fin	Empls
1	Texas Petrochemicals LP—*Charles Shaver*	5151 San Felipe Ste 80, Houston TX 77056	713-627-7474	S	1,004*	.5
2	JMK International Inc—*Mike Micallef*	4800 Bryant Irvin Ct, Fort Worth TX 76107	817-737-3703	R	459*	.6
3	Dupont Performance Elastomers LLC—*Betty Ingram*	4417 Lancaster Pke, Wilmington DE 19805	302-774-1000	R	143*	1.4
4	Bridgestone APM Co—*Michael Filipek*	PO Box 1505, Findlay OH 45839	419-423-9552	S	118*	.2
5	Preferred Rubber Compounding Corp—*Kenneth Bloom*	1020 Lambert St, Barberton OH 44203	330-798-4790	R	106*	.2
6	Firestone Polymers LLC—*John Vincent*	381 W Wilbeth Rd, Akron OH 44301	330-379-7797	S	81*	.1
7	Arnco—*Larry Carapellotti*	5141 Firestone Pl, South Gate CA 90280	323-249-7500	R	70*	.1
8	Dicar Inc—*Daniel Freifeld*	PO Box 643, Pine Brook NJ 07058	973-575-1174	R	34*	.2
9	Liquid Molding Systems Inc—*Jim Manning*	2202 Ridgewood, Midland MI 48642	989-631-8030	S	30*	.1
10	US Poly Enterprises Inc—*Jerry Cooper*	PO Box 769, Dexter MO 63841	573-624-4266	R	21*	<.1
11	Ja-Bar Silicone Corp—*Gilbert Jacobs*	PO Box 1249, Andover NJ 07821	973-786-5000	R	14*	.1
12	Src Elastomerics Inc—*William Stockwell*	4749 Tolbut St, Philadelphia PA 19136	215-335-3005	R	13*	.1
13	Gaco Western LLC—*Peter Davis*	PO Box 9827, Seattle WA 98109	206-575-0450	R	13*	.1
14	Midwest Elastomers Inc—*George Wight*	PO Box 412, Wapakoneta OH 45895	419-738-9642	R	12*	.1
15	Shurclose Seal Rubber and Plastic—*Suzanne Blake*	PO Box 305, Lake Orion MI 48361	248-969-0500	R	12*	.1
16	Shincor Silicones Inc—*Jun Hamuro*	1150 Damar Dr, Akron OH 44305	330-630-9460	R	10*	.1
17	Crest Rubber Company Inc—*David Clark*	PO Box 312, Ravenna OH 44266	330-296-4015	R	8*	.1

Rank	Company Name—*Executive Officer*	Address, City, State, Zip	Phone	Type	Fin	Empls
18	Cri-Sil LLC—*Barbara Lavgine*	359 Hill St, Biddeford ME 04005	207-283-6422	R	6*	<.1
19	Medical Elastomer Development Inc—*Dennis Kaiser*	1700 Highland Rd, Twinsburg OH 44087	330-425-8352	R	6*	<.1
20	Contact Rubber Corp—*Louis Schroeder*	PO Box 97, Bristol WI 53104	262-857-2361	R	6*	<.1
21	Wayne County Rubber Inc—*Laurie Schang*	1205 E Bowman St, Wooster OH 44691	330-264-5553	R	6*	<.1
22	Polytek Development Corp—*David Salisbury*	55 Hilton St, Easton PA 18042	610-559-8620	R	5*	<.1
23	Immix Technologies LLC CRI-SIL—*Mark Stevens*	359 Hill St, Biddeford ME 04005	207-283-6422	R	5*	<.1
24	Peterson Systems International Inc—*Thomas Lubanski*	PO Box 1557, Duarte CA 91009	626-357-7051	R	5*	<.1
25	Michigan Composites Inc—*Jack Schoenthaler*	PO Box 1225, Niles MI 49120	269-684-0110	R	3*	<.1
26	Master Dynamics Of Vacaville—*Saied Sattari*	PO Box 6403, Vacaville CA 95696	707-451-0460	R	<1*	<.1

TOTALS: SIC 2822 Synthetic Rubber
Companies: 26 — 2,189 — 4.0

2823 Cellulosic Manmade Fibers

1	Rayonier Inc—*Lee Thomas*	50 N Laura St, Jacksonville FL 32202	904-357-9100	P	2,569	1.9
2	Rayonier Distribution Corp—*Lee M Thomas* Rayonier Inc	1301 Riverplace Blvd, Jacksonville FL 32207	904-357-9100	S	2,074*	1.8
3	BGF Industries Inc—*Robert Porcher*	3802 Robert Porcher Wa, Greensboro NC 27410	336-545-0011	S	363	2.0
4	Polymer Dynamics Inc—*William Peoples*	2200 S 12th St, Allentown PA 18103	610-798-2200	R	71*	.3
5	Newco Fibre Co—*Susan Weir*	PO Box 5585, Charlotte NC 28299	704-333-0751	R	11*	.1
6	Intermountain Design Inc—*Lloyd Barney*	2190 S 3270 W, Salt Lake City UT 84119	801-972-5252	R	4*	<.1

TOTALS: SIC 2823 Cellulosic Manmade Fibers
Companies: 6 — 5,092 — 6.1

2824 Organic Fibers—Noncellulosic

1	El du Pont de Nemours and Co Specialty Fibers Div	1007 N Market St, Wilmington DE 19898	302-774-1000	D	14,735*	45.0
2	Lydall Inc—*Dale G Barnhart*	1 Colonial Rd, Manchester CT 06042	860-646-1233	P	338	1.6
3	Wellman Inc—*Mark Ruday*	3303 Port and Harbor D, Bay Saint Louis MS 39520	228-533-4000	R	221*	.2
4	Quadrant Epp USA Inc—*Glenn Steady*	PO Box 14235, Reading PA 19612	610-320-6600	R	213*	1.0
5	Celanese Acetate—*David Weidman*	1601 W LBJ Fwy, Dallas TX 75234	972-443-4000	D	206*	.8
6	William Barnet and Son Inc Southern Div—*Bill McCrary*	PO Box 131, Arcadia SC 29320	864-576-7154	D	117*	.7
7	Universal Fibers Inc—*Marcus Ammen*	14401 Industrial Park, Bristol VA 24202	276-669-1161	R	82*	.5
8	Shakespeare Company LLC—*Jim Bennett*	6111 Shakespeare Rd, Columbia SC 29223		S	65*	.3
9	Formed Fiber Technologies LLC—*Kelly Mackinnon*	PO Box 1300, Auburn ME 04211	207-784-1118	R	60*	.5
10	Gudebrod Inc—*William Le Grande*	274 Shoemaker Rd, Pottstown PA 19464	610-327-4050	R	34*	.2
11	Fairfield Processing Corp—*Roy Young*	PO Box 1157, Danbury CT 06813	203-744-2090	R	32*	.2
12	Bontex Inc—*James Kostelni*	1 Bontex Dr, Buena Vista VA 24416	540-261-2181	P	25	.3
13	California Combining Corp—*Vincent Rosato*	5607 S Santa Fe Ave, Vernon CA 90058	323-589-5727	R	7*	<.1
14	Mirart Inc—*Stanley Oster*	2707 Gateway Dr, Pompano Beach FL 33069	954-974-5230	R	3*	<.1
15	Interplast Inc—*Allen Langman*	PO Box 1328, Burlington NJ 08016	609-386-4990	R	2*	<.1

TOTALS: SIC 2824 Organic Fibers—Noncellulosic
Companies: 15 — 16,140 — 51.3

2833 Medicinals & Botanicals

1	Johnson and Johnson—*William C Weldon*	1 Johnson and Johnson, New Brunswick NJ 08901	732-524-0400	P	61,587	114.0
2	Mead Johnson Nutrition Co—*Stephen W Golsby*	2701 Patriot Blvd 4th, Glenview IL 60026		B	3,142	6.5
3	Pfizer Animal Health Group—*Jeff Kindler*	235 E 42nd St, New York NY 10017	212-573-2323	D	1,220*	3.0
4	Takeda America Inc	767 3rd Ave, New York NY 10017	212-421-6950	S	1,086	N/A
5	Jason Pharmaceuticals Inc	19994 US Hwy 93 N, Arlee MT 59821		S	752*	.1
6	RT Vanderbilt Company Inc—*Hugh B Vanderbilt Jr*	30 Winfield St, Norwalk CT 06855	203-853-1400	R	611*	.6
7	USANA Health Sciences Inc—*David Wentz*	3838 W Parkway Blvd, Salt Lake City UT 84120	801-954-7100	P	582	1.2
8	Metagenics Inc—*Jeffrey Katke*	100 Avenida La Pata, San Clemente CA 92673	949-366-0818	R	578*	.6
9	Perrigo Company Of South Carolina	4615 Dairy Dr, Greenville SC 29607	864-288-5521	S	264*	.3
10	Natrol Inc—*Mo Patel*	21411 Prairie St, Chatsworth CA 91311	818-739-6000	S	247*	.3
11	Mitsubishi Chemicals America Inc—*Hiro Tanaka*	1 N Lexington Ave, White Plains NY 10601	914-286-3600	S	246*	1.5
12	Mannatech Inc—*Stephen D Fenstermacher*	600 S Royal Ln Ste 200, Coppell TX 75019	972-471-7400	P	228	.5
13	Nutraceutical International Corp—*Frank W Gay II*	1400 Kearns Blvd, Park City UT 84060	435-655-6000	P	188	.8
14	Pharmavite Corp—*Tatsuo Higuchi*	PO Box 9606, Mission Hills CA 91346	818-221-6200	S	131*	.8
15	Jeunique International Inc—*Mulford Nobbs*	19501 E Walnut Dr S, City of Industry CA 91748	909-598-8598	R	103*	.3
16	Novus International—*Thad Simons*	20 Research Park Dr, Saint Charles MO 63304	314-576-8886	J	97*	.2
17	Nova Biomedical Corp—*Francis Manganaro*	PO Box 9141, Waltham MA 02454	781-894-0800	R	79*	.7
18	Alfa Aesar—*Barry Singelais*	26 Parkridge Rd, Ward Hill MA 01835	978-521-6300	S	66*	.1
19	Optimum Nutrition Inc—*Anthony Costello*	700 N Commerce St, Aurora IL 60504	630-236-0097	R	64*	.3
20	GeoPharma Inc—*Mihir K Taneja*	6950 Bryan Dairy Rd, Largo FL 33777	727-258-4830	P	63	.3
21	Natural Alternatives International Inc—*Mark A LeDoux*	1185 Linda Vista Dr, San Marcos CA 92078	760-744-7700	P	56	.1
22	Neways Inc—*Scott Clair*	2089 Neways Dr, Springville UT 84663	801-418-2000	R	54*	.5
23	Pure World Inc—*Jacques Dikansky*	375 Huyler St, S Hackensack NJ 07606	201-440-5000	S	51*	.2
24	Naturex Corp—*Stephanie Ducroux*	375 Huyler St, South Hackensack NJ 07606	201-440-5000	S	50*	.2
25	Interchem Corp—*Ron Mannino*	120 Rte 17 N Ste 115, Paramus NJ 07652	201-261-7333	R	50*	.1
26	Bachem Bioscience Inc—*Damir Vidovic*	3700 Horizon Dr, King of Prussia PA 19406	610-382-2110	S	50*	.1
27	Suther Feeds Inc—*Jerry Suther*	105 S Kansas Ave, Frankfort KS 66427	785-292-4414	R	48*	<.1
28	All American Pharmaceutical—*Jeff Golini*	2376 Main St, Billings MT 59105	406-245-5793	R	45*	<.1
29	Archon Vitamin Corp—*Bill Lapensky*	209 40th St, Irvington NJ 07111	973-371-1700	R	42*	.1
30	Mylan Technologies Inc—*Robert J Coury*	110 Lake St, Saint Albans VT 05478	802-527-7792	S	41*	.3
31	Sciencebased Health—*Alain Magro*	500 Century Plaza Dr S, Houston TX 77073		R	41*	.1
32	Lane Labs - USA Inc—*Andrew J Lane*	3 North St, Waldwick NJ 07463	201-661-6000	R	40*	.1
33	Youngevity Inc—*Steve Wallach*	2400 Boswell Rd, Chula Vista CA 91914	619-934-3980	R	40*	<.1
34	One Lambda Inc—*George Ayoub*	21001 Kittridge St, Canoga Park CA 91303	818-702-0042	R	39*	.2
35	ProZyme—*Jo Wegstein*	3832 Bay Ctr Pl, Hayward CA 94545	510-638-6900	R	39	N/A
36	Gemini Pharmaceuticals Inc—*Michael Finamore*	87 Modular Ave, Commack NY 11725	631-543-3334	R	36*	.2
37	Monarch Nutritional Laboratories Inc—*Dave Johnson* Nutraceutical International Corp	PO Box 12217, Ogden UT 84412	801-334-3911	S	29*	.1
38	Nutricap Labs—*Jason Provenzano*	70 Carolyn Blvd, Farmingdale NY 11735		R	29*	<.1
39	Synovics Pharmaceuticals—*Ronald Lane*	5360 NW 35th Ave, Fort Lauderdale FL 33309	954-486-4590	P	26	.2
40	Haematologic Technologies Inc	57 River Rd Ste 1021, Essex Junction VT 05452	802-878-1777	R	23*	<.1
41	NSA International Inc—*A Jay Martin*	PO Box 18603, Memphis TN 38181	901-541-1223	R	23	<.1
42	Arnet Pharmaceutical Corp—*Jose Tabacinic*	2525 Davie Rd Ste 330, Plantation FL 33317	954-236-9053	R	22**	.2
43	Ryss Laboratory Inc—*Ming Lee*	29540 Kohoutek Way, Union City CA 94587	510-477-9570	R	18*	<.1
44	RITA Corp—*Brian Goode*	PO Box 457, Crystal Lake IL 60039	815-337-2500	R	18*	.1
45	Heel Inc—*Thierry Montsortr*	10421 Research Rd Se, Albuquerque NM 87123	505-293-3843	R	17*	.1

Note: An asterisk (*) indicates an estimated financial figure. The company type code used is as follows: R = Private, P = Public, S = Private Subsidiary, B = Public Subsidiary, D = Division, J = Joint Venture, I = Investment Fund.

COMPANY RANKINGS BY SALES WITHIN 4-DIGIT SIC

Rank	Company Name—Executive Officer	Address, City, State, Zip	Phone	Type	Fin	Empls
46	Cyanotech Corp—Brent Bailey	73-4460 Queen Kaahaman, Kailua Kona HI 96740	808-326-1353	P	17	.1
47	Medical Nutrition USA Inc—Robert Mathias	10 W Forest Ave, Englewood NJ 07631	201-569-1188	R	16	<.1
48	Nutritional Laboratories International—Michael Zeher	1001 S 3rd St W, Missoula MT 59801	406-273-5493	R	16*	.1
49	Boiron Inc—Ludovic Rassat	6 Campus Blvd, Newtown Square PA 19073	610-325-7464	S	14*	.1
50	Bio-Botanica Inc—Frank D'amelio	75 Commerce Dr, Hauppauge NY 11788	631-231-5522	R	13*	.1
51	Avanti Polar Lipids Inc—Walter Shaw	700 Industrial Park Dr, Alabaster AL 35007	205-663-2494	R	12*	.1
52	Unigene Laboratories Inc—Ashleigh Palmer	81 Fulton St, Boonton NJ 07005	973-265-1100	P	11	.1
53	Savient Pharmaceuticals Inc—John H Johnson	1 Tower Ctr 14th Fl, East Brunswick NJ 08816	732-418-9300	P	10	.2
54	Amt Labs Inc—Bing Fang	680 N 700 W, North Salt Lake UT 84054	801-299-1661	R	9*	.1
55	Dream Pharmaceuticals Inc	1911 Calle Dulce, Glendale CA 91208	818-291-0000	R	9*	<.1
56	Foster Corp—Lawrence Acquarulo	45 Ridge Rd, Putnam CT 06260	860-928-4102	R	8*	<.1
57	Promega Biosciences LLC—Jim Maurer	277 Granada Dr, San Luis Obispo CA 93401	805-544-8524	R	8*	.1
58	E Excel LLC	9957 Jordan Gateway, Sandy UT 84070	801-542-8900	R	7*	.1
59	Northridge Laboratories Inc—Jane Richman	20832 Dearborn St, Chatsworth CA 91311	818-882-5622	R	7*	.1
60	PacificHealth Laboratories Inc—Fred Duffner	100 Matawan Rd Ste 150, Matawan NJ 07747	732-739-2900	P	7	<.1
61	Konsyl Pharmaceuticals Inc—Anthony Cantaffa	8050 Industrial Park R, Easton MD 21601	410-822-5192	R	6*	.1
62	Highland Laboratories Inc—Kenneth Scott	PO Box 199, Mount Angel OR 97362	971-239-5283	R	6*	<.1
63	Pelron Corp—Floy Pelletier	PO Box 6, Lyons IL 60534	708-442-9100	R	5*	<.1
64	Toll Compaction Service Inc—Paul Pritchard	14 Memorial Dr, Neptune NJ 07753	732-776-8225	R	5*	<.1
65	Continental Manufacturing Chemist Inc—Stuart Miller	PO Box 68, Madrid IA 50156	515-795-2000	R	3*	<.1
66	Mega-Pro International Inc—Dave Smith	251 W Hilton Dr, Saint George UT 84770	435-673-1001	R	3*	<.1
67	Allermed Laboratories Inc—H Nielsen	7203 Convoy Ct, San Diego CA 92111	858-292-1060	R	3*	<.1
68	Peninsula Laboratories Inc—Damier Vidovich	305 Old County Rd, San Carlos CA 94070	650-592-5392	R	2*	<.1
69	Nutra Pharma Corp—Rik J Deitsch	2776 University Dr, Coral Springs FL 33065	954-509-0911	P	1	<.1
70	Advanced Nutritional Technology Inc—Lionel Borken	PO Box 2130, Dublin CA 94568	925-828-2128	R	1*	<.1
71	Vita Sea Products International Inc—Carrie Minucciani	550 Sylvan St, Daly City CA 94014	650-757-9851	R	1*	<.1
72	CTD Holdings Inc—CE Rick Strattan	14120 NW 126th Terr, Alachua FL 32615	386-418-8060	P	1	<.1
73	Nuvilex Inc—Robert Ryan	7702 E Doubletree Ranc, Scottsdale AZ 85258	480-348-8050	P	<1	<.1
74	Pangenex Corp—John Stanton	19337 US Hwy 19 N Ste, Clearwater FL 33764		P	<1	<.1

TOTALS: SIC 2833 Medicinals & Botanicals
Companies: 74

					72,460	135.9

2834 Pharmaceutical Preparations

Rank	Company Name—Executive Officer	Address, City, State, Zip	Phone	Type	Fin	Empls
1	Pfizer Inc—Ian Read	235 E 42nd St, New York NY 10017	212-733-2323	P	67,809	110.6
2	Merck and Company Inc—Kenneth C Frazier	PO Box 100, Whitehouse Station NJ 08889	908-423-1000	P	45,987	94.0
3	GlaxoSmithKline - USA—Jean-Pierre Garnier	PO Box 7929, Philadelphia PA 19101	919-483-2100	D	41,600*	24.0
4	Novartis Pharmaceuticals Corp—Daniel Vasella	1 Health Plz, East Hanover NJ 07936	862-778-8300	S	41,439	96.7
5	Abbott Laboratories—Miles D White	100 Abbott Park Rd, Abbott Park IL 60064	847-937-6100	P	35,167	90.0
6	Eli Lilly and Co—John C Lechleiter	Lilly Corporate Ctr, Indianapolis IN 46285	317-276-2000	P	23,076	38.4
7	Genentech Inc—Ian T Clark	1 DNA Way, South San Francisco CA 94080	650-225-1000	S	15,594*	13.0
8	Amgen Inc—Kevin W Sharer	1 Amgen Center Dr, Thousand Oaks CA 91320	805-447-1000	S	15,053	17.4
9	Schering Berlin Inc	PO Box 1000, Montville NJ 07045	973-487-2000	S	9,562*	25.5
10	Sicor Pharmaceuticals Sales Inc—William S Marth	19 Hughes, Irvine CA 92618	215-591-3000	S	8,938*	14.7
11	Teva Pharmaceuticals—William S Marth	19 Hughes, Irvine CA 92618	215-591-3000	S	8,938*	14.7
12	Mylan Inc (Canonsburg Pennsylvania)—Robert J Coury	1500 Corporate Dr, Canonsburg PA 15317	724-514-1800	P	5,451	13.0
13	Allergan Inc—David E I Pyott	PO Box 19534, Irvine CA 92623	714-246-4500	P	4,820	9.2
14	Watson Pharmaceuticals Inc—Paul M Bisaro	400 Interpace Pky, Parsippany NJ 07054	862-261-7000	P	4,584	6.7
15	Forest Laboratories Inc—Howard Solomon	909 3rd Ave, New York NY 10022	212-421-7850	P	4,420	5.6
16	Hospira Inc—John Staley	275 N Field Dr, Lake Forest IL 60045	224-212-2000	P	3,917	14.0
17	Nile Therapeutics Inc—Joshua Kazam	4 W 4th Ave Ste 400, San Mateo CA 94402	650-458-2670	P	3,666	<.1
18	Celgene Corp—Robert J Hugin	86 Morris Ave, Summit NJ 07901	908-673-9000	P	3,626	4.2
19	NBTY Inc—Jeffrey A Nagel	2100 Smithtown Ave, Ronkonkoma NY 11779	631-200-7327	S	2,959	14.4
20	Cephalon Inc—J Kevin Buchi	PO Box 4011, Frazer PA 19355	610-344-0200	P	2,761	3.7
21	Endo Pharmaceuticals Holdings Inc—David P Holveck	100 Endo Blvd, Chadds Ford PA 19317	610-558-9800	B	2,730	4.6
22	Barr Pharmaceuticals Inc	PO Box 1090, North Wales PA 19454	201-930-3300	S	2,501	8.9
23	Abbott Laboratories Ross Products Div—Miles White Abbott Laboratories	625 Cleveland Ave, Columbus OH 43215	614-624-7677	D	2,400*	5.0
24	GMP Companies Inc—Bart Chernow	1 E Broward Blvd Ste 1, Fort Lauderdale FL 33301	954-745-3510	R	2,352*	.1
25	Perrigo Co—Joseph C Papa	515 Eastern Ave, Allegan MI 49010	269-673-8451	P	2,269	7.7
26	AstraZeneca Pharmaceuticals LP	PO Box 15437, Wilmington DE 19850	302-886-3000	S	2,123*	12.0
27	Sanofi Pharmaceuticals Inc—Greg Irace	55 Corporate Dr, Bridgewater NJ 08807		S	2,029*	11.4
28	Merial Ltd—Gerald Belle	3239 Satellite Blvd Bl, Duluth GA 30096	678-638-3000	S	1,900*	5.0
29	Mylan Pharmaceuticals Inc—Robert Coury Mylan Inc (Canonsburg Pennsylvania)	PO Box 4310, Morgantown WV 26504	304-599-2595	S	1,844*	3.0
30	Colorcon Inc—Jean Deneuville	PO Box 24, West Point PA 19486	215-699-7733	R	1,842*	1.2
31	Teva Respiratory LLC—Neil Flanzraich	4400 Biscayne Blvd, Miami FL 33137	305-575-6100	S	1,837	10.1
32	King Pharmaceuticals Inc—Brian A Markison Pfizer Inc	501 5th St, Bristol TN 37620	423-989-8000	S	1,780	2.6
33	Berwind Corp—Michael McClelland	1500 Market St Ste 300, Philadelphia PA 19102	215-563-2800	R	1,710*	3.5
34	DSM Pharmaceuticals Products—Hans Engel	45 Waterview Blvd, Parsippany NJ 07054	252-758-3436	S	1,653*	2.6
35	Catalent Pharma Solutions Inc—John R Chiminski	14 Schoolhouse Rd, Somerset NJ 08873	732-537-6200	R	1,640	8.2
36	Vitaquest International LLC—Keith Frankel	8 Henderson Dr, West Caldwell NJ 07006	973-575-9200	R	1,563*	.6
37	Vertex Pharmaceuticals Inc—Matthew W Emmens	130 Waverly St, Cambridge MA 02139	617-444-6100	P	1,411	2.0
38	Sepracor Inc—Saburo Hamanaka	84 Waterford Dr, Marlborough MA 01752	508-481-6700	S	1,292	2.4
39	Eisai Inc—Haruo Naito	100 Tice Blvd, Woodcliff Lake NJ 07677	201-692-1100	S	1,143*	1.8
40	Sepracor Securities Corp—Saburo Hamanaka Sepracor Inc	84 Waterford Dr, Marlborough MA 01752	508-481-6700	S	1,092*	1.8
41	Sunovion Pharmaceuticals Inc—Saburo Hamanaka Sepracor Inc	84 Waterford Dr, Marlborough MA 01752	508-481-6700	S	1,092*	1.8
42	Elan Holdings Inc	1300 Gould Dr, Gainesville GA 30504	770-534-8239	S	1,081*	1.7
43	Par Pharmaceutical Companies Inc—Patrick G LePore	300 Tice Blvd, Woodcliff Lake NJ 07677	201-802-4000	P	926	.8
44	PurduePharma LP—John Stewart	201 Tresser Blvd, Stamford CT 06901	203-588-8000	R	892*	1.4
45	Forest Pharmaceuticals Inc Forest Laboratories Inc	13600 Shoreline Dr, Earth City MO 63045	314-493-7000	S	885*	5.0
46	Impax Laboratories Inc—Larry Hsu	30831 Huntwood Ave, Hayward CA 94544	510-476-2000	P	880	.9
47	Boehringer Ingelheim Corp—Werner Gerstenberg	PO Box 368, Ridgefield CT 06877	203-798-9988	R	867*	6.0
48	Alexion Pharmaceuticals Inc—Leonard Bell	352 Knotter Dr, Cheshire CT 06410	203-272-2596	P	783	1.0
49	Cubist Pharmaceuticals Inc—Michael W Bonney	65 Hayden Ave, Lexington MA 02421	781-860-8660	P	754	.7
50	United Therapeutics Corp—Martine A Rothblatt	1040 Spring St, Silver Spring MD 20910	301-608-9292	P	743	.5
51	Medicis Pharmaceutical Corp—Jonah Shacknai	7720 N Dobson Rd, Scottsdale AZ 85256	602-808-8800	P	721	.6

Rank	Company Name—*Executive Officer*	Address, City, State, Zip	Phone	Type	Fin	Empls
52	PolyMedica Corp—*Patrick T Ryan*	701 Edgewater Dr Ste 3, Wakefield MA 01880	781-486-8111	S	713*	2.3
53	Par Pharmaceutical Inc—*Patrick G LePore* Par Pharmaceutical Companies Inc	300 Tice Blvd, Woodcliff Lake NJ 07677	201-802-4000	S	690*	.7
54	TAP Pharmaceuticals Inc—*Alan MacKenzie* Abbott Laboratories	675 N Field Dr, Lake Forest IL 60045	847-582-2000	S	660*	3.3
55	Amylin Pharmaceuticals Inc—*Daniel M Bradbury*	9360 Towne Centre Dr, San Diego CA 92121	858-552-2200	P	651	.3
56	B Braun Inc (Irvine California)—*Carroll Neubauer*	PO Box 4027, Bethlehem PA 18018	610-691-5400	S	630*	1.6
57	F Hoffmann-La Roche Ltd—*David Austin*	3431 Hillview Ave, Palo Alto CA 94304	650-855-5050	S	625*	1.0
58	TEVA Pharmaceuticals USA—*William Marth*	1090 Horsham Rd, North Wales PA 19454	215-591-3000	S	606*	1.0
59	Vi-Jon Laboratories Inc—*Robert Kirby*	8515 Page Ave, Saint Louis MO 63114	314-427-1000	R	590*	1.5
60	Ben Venue Laboratories Inc—*Ben Murphy*	PO Box 46568, Bedford OH 44146	440-232-6264	S	585*	1.0
61	AstraZeneca LP—*Tony Zook*	PO Box 15437, Wilmington DE 19850	302-886-3000	S	533	1.2
62	Millennium Pharmaceuticals Inc—*Deborah Dunsire*	40 Landsdowne St, Cambridge MA 02139	617-679-7000	S	528	1.0
63	Alcon Laboratories Inc	6201 S Fwy, Fort Worth TX 76134	817-293-0450	S	526*	2.5
64	Melaleuca Inc—*Frank L VanderSloot*	3910 S Yellowstone Hwy, Idaho Falls ID 83402	208-522-0700	R	500*	2.5
65	Purdue Pharma LP—*John H Stewart*	1 Stamford Forum 201 T, Stamford CT 06901	203-588-8000	R	488*	1.4
66	Luitpold Pharmaceuticals Inc—*Mary Helenek*	PO Box 9001, Shirley NY 11967	631-924-4000	R	470*	.5
67	Sicor Inc—*Marvin Samson* TEVA Pharmaceuticals USA	19 Hughes, Irvine CA 92618		S	456	1.9
68	MonaVie LLC—*Dallin A Larson*	10855 S River Front Pk, South Jordan UT 84095	801-748-3100	R	455*	.5
69	Regeneron Pharmaceuticals Inc—*Leonard S Schleifer*	777 Old Saw Mill River, Tarrytown NY 10591	914-345-7400	P	446	1.7
70	BioMarin Pharmaceutical Inc—*Jean-Jacques Bienaime*	105 Digital Dr, Novato CA 94949	415-506-6700	P	441	1.0
71	Chattem Inc—*Chris Viehbacher*	1715 W 38th St, Chattanooga TN 37409	423-821-4571	S	438	.5
72	Medicines Co—*Clive A Meanwell*	8 Sylvan Way, Parsippany NJ 07054	973-290-6000	P	438	.4
73	Procter/Gamble Pharmaceutical—*Tom Finn*	PO Box 191, Norwich NY 13815	607-335-2111	D	420*	.7
74	Suncos Corp—*Paul Clark*	22021 20th Ave SE, Bothell WA 98021	425-485-1900	J	391*	.7
75	Dey Pharma LP Mylan Inc (Canonsburg Pennsylvania)	2751 Napa Valley Corpo, Napa CA 94558	707-224-3200	S	379*	1.0
76	Garden of Life Inc—*Jordan Rubin*	5500 Village Blvd Ste, West Palm Beach FL 33407	561-748-2477	R	364*	.1
77	Abraxis BioScience Inc—*Bruce Wendel* Celgene Corp	11755 Wilshire Blvd 20, Los Angeles CA 90025	310-883-1300	S	359	.9
78	Nature's Sunshine Products Inc—*Michael D Dean*	75 E 1700 S, Provo UT 84606	801-342-4300	P	350	1.1
79	Biovail Technologies Ltd—*David Tierney*	3701 Concorde Pkwy Ste, Chantilly VA 20151	703-480-6000	R	339*	.1
80	Reckitt Benckiser Pharmaceutical Inc—*Shaun Thaxter*	10710 Midlothian Tpke, Richmond VA 23235	804-379-1090	S	338*	.3
81	Prestige Brands Holdings Inc—*Matthew M Mannelly*	90 N Broadway, Irvington NY 10533	914-524-6810	B	337	.1
82	Endo Pharmaceuticals Inc—*David P Holveck* Endo Pharmaceuticals Holdings Inc	220 Lake Dr, Newark DE 19702	610-558-9800	S	328*	.5
83	Bausch and Lomb Pharmaceuticals Inc—*Gerald Ostrov*	1 Bausch and Lomb Phar, Rochester NY 14604	585-338-6000	S	322	.7
84	Prestige Brands Inc—*Matthew Mannelly* Prestige Brands Holdings Inc	90 N Broadway, Irvington NY 10533	914-524-6810	S	302	.1
85	Vintage Pharmaceutical Inc—*Marvin Samson*	120 Vintage Dr NE, Huntsville AL 35811	256-859-4011	S	293*	.5
86	Inwood Laboratories Inc—*Howard Solomon* Forest Laboratories Inc	909 3rd Ave, New York NY 10022	212-421-7850	S	287*	1.0
87	Emergent BioSolutions Inc—*Fuad El-Hibri*	2273 Research Blvd Ste, Rockville MD 20850	301-795-1800	P	286	.8
88	Ikaria Inc—*Daniel Tasse*	6 State Rte 173, Clinton NJ 08809	908-238-6600	R	275*	.5
89	Prometheus Laboratories Inc—*Joseph M Limber*	9410 Carroll Park Dr, San Diego CA 92121	858-824-0895	R	273*	.4
90	Jazz Pharmaceuticals Inc—*Bruce Cozadd*	3180 Porter Dr, Palo Alto CA 94304	650-496-3777	B	272	.4
91	Ribapharm Inc—*Kim David Lamon*	3300 Hyland Ave, Costa Mesa CA 92626	714-427-6236	S	270	.1
92	Cambrex Corp—*Steven Klosk*	1 Meadowlands Plz, East Rutherford NJ 07073	201-804-3000	P	255	.8
93	Beach Products Inc—*Richard Jenkins*	PO Box 13447, Tampa FL 33681	813-839-6565	R	254*	.3
94	Teva Animal Health Inc—*David S Cunningham* Teva Respiratory LLC	PO Box 8039, Saint Joseph MO 64508	816-364-3777	S	254*	.3
95	Caraco Pharmaceutical Laboratories Ltd—*GP Singh Sachera*	1150 Elijah McCoy Dr, Detroit MI 48202	313-871-8400	S	234	.5
96	Auxilium Pharmaceuticals Inc—*Adrian Adams*	40 Valley Stream Pkwy, Malvern PA 19355	484-321-5900	P	211	.6
97	Integrated Health Ideas Inc—*Robert L Erwin* iBio Inc	201 Rte 22, Hillside NJ 07205	973-926-0816	S	210*	.1
98	TCP Reliable Inc—*Maurice Barakat*	551 Raritan Ctr Pkwy, Edison NJ 08837	732-346-9200	R	203*	.2
99	Dpt Laboratories Ltd—*Joe Halbert*	PO Box 1659, San Antonio TX 78296	210-476-8100	R	196*	.6
100	Hi-Tech Pharmacal Company Inc—*David S Seltzer*	369 Bayview Ave, Amityville NY 11701	631-789-8228	P	191	.4
101	Alkermes Inc—*Richard F Pops*	852 Winter St, Waltham MA 02451	781-609-6000	P	187	.6
102	UCB Pharma—*Roch Doliveux*	1950 Lake Park Dr, Smyrna GA 30080	770-970-7500	S	184*	.5
103	OraPharma Inc—*Russell A Secter*	732 Louis Dr, Warminster PA 18974	215-956-2200	S	182*	.2
104	Acorda Therapeutics Inc—*Ron Cohen*	15 Skyline Dr, Hawthorne NY 10532	914-347-4300	P	182	.3
105	Organon Pharmaceuticals USA Inc—*Fred Hassan*	56 Livingston Ave, Roseland NJ 07068	973-325-4500	R	178*	1.7
106	Cordis International Corp—*Donald O'dwer*	PO Box 25700, Miami FL 33102	305-824-2000	R	176*	2.5
107	Unicity International Inc—*Stewart Hughes*	1201 North 800 E, Orem UT 84097	801-226-2600	R	176*	.3
108	Medivation Inc—*David T Hung MD*	201 Spear St 3rd Fl, San Francisco CA 94105	415-543-3470	P	175	.1
109	Neogen Corp—*James L Herbert*	620 Lesher Pl, Lansing MI 48912	517-372-9200	P	173	.7
110	Merck Holdings Inc—*Richard Henriques*	PO Box 100, Whitehouse Station NJ 08889	908-423-1000	S	171*	2.7
111	Gensia Sicor Inc—*Pierre Damien*	19 Hughes, Irvine CA 92618	949-455-4700	R	168*	1.9
112	Allergan USA Inc—*David Pyott*	PO Box 19534, Irvine CA 92623	714-246-4500	R	166*	2.0
113	Amneal Pharmaceuticals Of New York LLC—*Rashmi Agarwal*	85 Adams Ave, Hauppauge NY 11788	908-231-1911	R	163*	.2
114	Baylor Health Enterprises Inc—*Denward Freeman*	2625 Elm St Ste 216, Dallas TX 75226	214-820-2492	R	157*	.5
115	Experimental and Applied Sciences Inc—*Chris Scoggins* Abbott Laboratories	625 Cleveland Ave, Columbus OH 43215		S	155*	.2
116	Eurohealth (USA) Inc—*Micheal Raya*	401 Industrial Way W, Eatontown NJ 07724	732-542-1191	R	153*	.4
117	Bristol-Myers Squibb Holding Pharma LLC—*Luis Albors*	PO Box 30100, Manati PR 00674	787-815-1000	R	152*	.4
118	Galderma Laboratories Inc—*Albert Draaijer*	14501 N Fwy, Fort Worth TX 76177	817-961-5000	S	146*	.3
119	Anchen Pharmaceuticals Inc—*Bill Liu* Par Pharmaceutical Companies Inc	9601 Jeronimo Rd, Irvine CA 92618	949-837-6178	S	141*	.2
120	Boehringer Ingelheim Pharmaceuticals Inc—*Werner Gerstenberg* Boehringer Ingelheim Corp	PO Box 368, Ridgefield CT 06877	203-798-9988	S	140*	1.8
121	Roche Colorado Corp—*Don Fitzgerald* F Hoffmann-La Roche Ltd	2075 N 55th St, Boulder CO 80301	303-442-1926	D	136*	.4
122	Santarus Inc—*E David Ballard II*	3721 Valley Centre Dr, San Diego CA 92130	858-314-5700	P	125	.2
123	Rigel Pharmaceuticals Inc—*James M Gower*	1180 Veterans Blvd, South San Francisco CA 94080	650-624-1100	P	125	.1
124	Advanced Analytical Technologies Inc—*Steve Lasky*	2901 S Loop Dr Ste 415, Ames IA 50010	515-296-6600	R	118*	<.1
125	Universal Protein Supplements Corp—*Clyde Rockoff*	3 Terminal Rd, New Brunswick NJ 08901	732-545-3130	R	117*	.2
126	Questcor Pharmaceuticals Inc—*Don M Bailey*	1300 N Kellogg Dr SteD, Anaheim CA 92807	714-786-4200	P	115	.2

Note: An asterisk (*) indicates an estimated financial figure. The company type code used is as follows: R = Private, P = Public, S = Private Subsidiary, B = Public Subsidiary, D = Division, J = Joint Venture, I = Investment Fund.

COMPANY RANKINGS BY SALES WITHIN 4-DIGIT SIC

Rank	Company Name—Executive Officer	Address, City, State, Zip	Phone	Type	Fin	Empls
127	Noven Pharmaceuticals Inc—Jeffrey F Eisenberg	11960 SW 144th St, Miami FL 33186	305-253-5099	S	115*	.7
128	Lts Lohmann Therapy Systems Corp—Cornelia Bockhorn	21 Henderson Dr, West Caldwell NJ 07006	973-575-5170	R	114*	1.0
129	Obagi Medical Products Inc—Albert Hummel	3760 Kilroy Airport Wa, Long Beach CA 90806	562-628-1007	P	113	.2
130	Affymax Inc—John Orwin	4001-4015 Miranda Ave, Palo Alto CA 94304	650-812-8700	P	112	.1
131	Farnam Companies Inc—Rick Blomquist	PO Box 34820, Phoenix AZ 85067		S	108*	.3
132	Lannett Company Inc—Arthur P Bedrosian	13200 Townsend Rd, Philadelphia PA 19154	215-333-9000	P	107	.3
133	Scios Inc—James Mitchell	1900 Charleston Rd, Mountain View CA 94043	650-564-5050	S	105*	.5
134	Watson Pharma Inc—Paul M Bisaro Watson Pharmaceuticals Inc	PO Box 1953, Morristown NJ 07962	973-355-8300	S	102*	.6
135	Image Solutions Inc—Jinsoo Kim	100 S Jefferson Rd, Whippany NJ 07981	973-560-0404	S	100*	.5
136	Fisher Clinical Services Inc—Patrick Durbin	7554 Schantz Rd, Allentown PA 18106	610-391-0800	S	100*	.2
137	Isis Pharmaceuticals Inc—Stanley Crooke	2855 Gazelle Crt, Carlsbad CA 92010	760-931-9200	P	99	.3
138	Cody Laboratories—Richard Asherman Lannett Company Inc	601 Yellowstone Ave, Cody WY 82414	307-587-7099	S	96*	.1
139	Taro Pharmaceuticals USA Inc—Barry Levitt MD	3 Skyline Dr, Hawthorne NY 10532	914-345-9001	S	94*	.3
140	Alacer Corp—Ronald Fugate	80 Icon, Foothill Ranch CA 92610	949-454-3900	R	92*	.2
141	Armstrong Pharmaceuticals Inc—Ben Sheppard Amphastar Pharmaceuticals Inc	25 John Rd, Canton MA 02021	617-323-7404	S	89*	.2
142	Fortitech Inc—Walter Borisenok	2105 Technology Dr, Schenectady NY 12308	518-372-5155	R	89*	.2
143	Colgate Oral Pharmaceuticals Inc—Edward Filusch	300 Park Ave, New York NY 10022		S	88*	.4
144	Akorn Inc—Raj Rai	2500 Millbrook Dr, Buffalo Grove IL 60089	847-279-6100	P	86	.4
145	Targacept Inc—J Donald deBethizy	200 E 1st St Ste 300, Winston-Salem NC 27101	336-480-2100	P	86	.1
146	SciClone Pharmaceuticals Inc—Friedhelm Blobel	950 Tower Ln Ste 900, Foster City CA 94404	650-358-3456	P	85	.3
147	Xanodyne Pharmaceuticals Inc—Natasha Giordano	1 Riverfront Pl, Newport KY 41071	859-371-6383	R	84*	.3
148	Alnylam Pharmaceuticals Inc—John M Maraganore	300 3rd St 3rd Fl, Cambridge MA 02142	617-551-8200	P	83	.1
149	DepoMed Inc—James A Schoeneck	1360 O'Brien Dr, Menlo Park CA 94025	650-462-5900	P	81	.1
150	Bactolac Pharmaceutical Inc (Hauppauge New York)—Pailla Reddy Bactolac Pharmaceutical Inc	7 Oser Ave, Hauppauge NY 11788	631-951-4908	S	80*	.1
151	Endo Pharmaceuticals Solutions Inc—David P Holveck Endo Pharmaceuticals Holdings Inc	220 Lake Dr, Newark DE 19702	610-558-9800	S	78	.2
152	Apothecary Products Inc—Terrance Noble	11750 12th Ave S, Burnsville MN 55337	952-890-1940	R	78*	.2
153	Watson Laboratories Inc—Allen Chao Watson Pharmaceuticals Inc	620 N 51st Ave, Phoenix AZ 85043	602-278-1400	S	77*	.3
154	Spectrum Pharmaceuticals Inc—Rajesh C Shrotriya	11500 South Eastern Av, Henderson NV 89052	702-835-6300	P	74	.1
155	Array Biopharma Inc—Robert E Conway	3200 Walnut St, Boulder CO 80301	303-381-6600	P	72	.3
156	Nektar Therapeutics—Howard W Robin	455 Mission Bay Blvd S, San Francisco CA 94158	415-482-5300	P	72	.4
157	ICOS Corp—Mads Leustsen	22021 20th Ave SE, Bothell WA 98021	425-485-1900	R	71	.7
158	Infinity Pharmaceuticals Inc—Adelene Q Perkins	780 Memorial Dr, Cambridge MA 02139	617-453-1000	P	71	.2
159	Met-Rx USA Inc—Len Moskovitz	2100 Smithtown Ave, Ronkonkoma NY 11779		R	70*	.1
160	POZEN Inc—John R Plachetka	1414 Raleigh Rd, Chapel Hill NC 27517	919-913-1030	P	69	<.1
161	SurModics Inc—Gary R Maharaj	9924 W 74th St, Eden Prairie MN 55344	952-829-2700	P	68	.1
162	Matrixx Initiatives Inc—Dennis O'Donnell	PO Box 28486, Scottsdale AZ 85255	602-385-8888	R	67	<.1
163	Amphastar Pharmaceuticals Inc—Jack W Zhang	11570 6th St, Rancho Cucamonga CA 91730	909-980-9484	R	66*	1.0
164	Johnson and Johnson Merck Consumer Pharmaceutical Co	1 Merck Dr, Whitehouse Station NJ 08889	215-652-5000	S	66*	.2
165	Ironwood Pharmaceuticals Inc—Peter M Hecht	301 Binney Street 2nd, Cambridge MA 02142	617-621-7722	P	66	.3
166	SkinMedica Inc—Mary M Fisher	5909 Sea Lion Pl Ste H, Carlsbad CA 92008	760-448-3600	R	64*	.1
167	GTx Inc (Memphis Tennessee)—Mitchell S Steiner	175 Toyota Plz 7th Fl, Memphis TN 38103	901-523-9700	P	61	.1
168	Sucampo Pharmaceuticals Inc—Ryuji Ueno	4520 E West Hwy 3rd Fl, Bethesda MD 20814	301-961-3400	P	61	.1
169	G and W Laboratories Inc—Burton Greenblatt	111 Coolidge St, South Plainfield NJ 07080	908-753-2000	R	61*	.3
170	Nexgen Pharma Inc—Ian Gibson	46 Corporate Park #100, Irvine CA 92606	949-863-0340	R	60*	.2
171	ANI Pharmaceuticals Inc—Arthur S Przybal	210 Main St W, Baudette MN 56623	218-634-3500	S	59	.1
172	Vitamins Inc—James Carozza	200 E Randolph St Ste, Chicago IL 60601	312-861-0700	R	59*	.1
173	Applied Laboratories Inc—Anthony Moravec	PO Box 2127, Columbus IN 47202	812-372-2607	R	59*	.1
174	Heska Des Moines—Laurie Peterson	2538 SE 43rd St, Pleasant Hill IA 50327	515-263-8600	S	58*	.1
175	Nephron Pharmaceuticals Corp—Lou Kennedy	PO Box 547775, Orlando FL 32854	407-246-1389	R	57*	.6
176	Bactolac Pharmaceutical Inc—Pailla M Reddy	7 Oser Ave, Hauppauge NY 11788	631-951-4908	R	57	N/A
177	Ferndale Laboratories Inc—James Mcmillan	780 W 8 Mile Rd, Ferndale MI 48220	248-548-0900	R	57*	.3
178	Derma Sciences Inc—Edward J Quilty	214 Carnegie Ctr Ste 3, Princeton NJ 08540	609-514-4744	P	57	.2
179	Cima Labs Inc—Nick Valentine Cephalon Inc	7325 Aspen Ln, Brooklyn Park MN 55428	763-488-4700	S	56*	.2
180	DynPort Vaccine Company LLC—Robert V House	64 Thomas Johnson Dr, Frederick MD 21702	301-607-5000	S	55*	.1
181	Scientific Protein Laboratories Inc	PO Box 158, Waunakee WI 53597	608-849-5944	R	55*	.1
182	Jubilant Hollisterstier LLC—Charles Moore	PO Box 3145, Spokane WA 99220	509-489-5656	R	54*	.3
183	Astex Pharmaceuticals Inc—James S J Manuso	4140 Dublin Blvd Ste 2, Dublin CA 94568	925-560-0100	P	53	.1
184	EMD Pharmaceuticals Inc—Nancy J Wysenski	3211 Shannon Rd Ste 50, Durham NC 27707	919-401-7100	S	53*	.1
185	Nutrition Now Inc—Martin Rifkin	6350 Ne Campus Dr, Vancouver WA 98661	360-737-6800	R	53*	.1
186	Goodwin Biotechnology Inc—Bansi K Bhan	1850 NW 69th Ave, Plantation FL 33313	954-327-9639	R	51*	.1
187	QLT USA Inc—Robert Butchofsky	2579 Midpoint Dr, Fort Collins CO 80525	970-482-5868	S	50*	.2
188	Dendreon Corp—Mitchell H Gold	1301 2nd Ave Ste 3200, Seattle WA 98101	206-256-4545	P	48	1.5
189	ArQule Inc—Paolo Pucci	19 Presidential Way, Woburn MA 01801	781-994-0300	P	47	.1
190	Zalicus Inc—Mark HN Corrigan	245 1st St 3rd Fl, Cambridge MA 02142	617-301-7000	P	47	.1
191	Facet Biotech Corp—Faheem Hasnain Abbott Laboratories	1500 Seaport Blvd, Redwood City CA 94063	650-454-1000	S	46	.2
192	Cumberland Pharmaceuticals Inc—A J Kazimi	2525 W End Ave Ste 950, Nashville TN 37203	615-255-0068	P	46	.1
193	Columbia Laboratories Inc—Frank C Condella Jr	354 Eisenhower Pky Pla, Livingston NJ 07039	973-994-3999	P	46	<.1
194	AVEO Pharmaceuticals Inc—Tuan Ha-Ngoc	75 Sidney St, Cambridge MA 02139	617-299-5000	P	45	.1
195	New Chapter Inc—Larry Allgaier	90 Technology Dr, Brattleboro VT 05301	802-257-0018	R	44*	.2
196	ChemDesign Corp—David Mielke	20 Stanton St, Marinette WI 54143	715-735-9033	R	44*	.2
197	Adroit Medical Systems Inc—Gene Gammons	PO Box 277, Loudon TN 37774		R	44*	.1
198	Adolor Corp—Michael R Dougherty	700 Pennsylvania Dr, Exton PA 19341	484-595-1500	P	43	.1
199	Your Vitamins Inc—Andrew Lessman	430 Parkson Rd, Henderson NV 89011	702-564-9000	R	42*	.2
200	Mentholatum Co—Akiyoshi Yoshida	707 Sterling Dr, Orchard Park NY 14127	716-677-2500	R	42*	.2
201	Xcellerex Inc—Guy Broadbent	170 Locke Dr, Marlborough MA 01752	508-480-9235	SC	42*	.1
202	Aaron Industries Inc—James Medford	PO Box 305, Clinton SC 29325	864-833-0178	R	42*	.4
203	P F Laboratories Inc—Cheryl Bernardi	700 Union Blvd, Totowa NJ 07512	973-256-3100	R	41*	.2
204	Blistex Inc—Michael Donnantuono	1800 Swift Dr, Oak Brook IL 60523	630-571-2870	R	40*	.2
205	Vitatech International Inc—Thomas Tierney	2802 Dow Ave, Tustin CA 92780	714-832-9700	R	40*	.2
206	Carma Laboratories Inc—Donald Woelbing	5801 W Airways Ave, Franklin WI 53132	414-421-7707	R	40*	.2
207	Accentia BioPharmaceuticals Inc—Francis E O'Donnell Jr MD	324 S Hyde Park Ave St, Tampa FL 33606	813-864-2554	P	40	.1

Rank	Company Name—*Executive Officer*	Address, City, State, Zip	Phone	Type	Fin	Empls
208	Air Industries Group Inc—*Peter D Rettaliata*	1479 N Clinton Ave, Bay Shore NY 11706	631-968-5000	P	39 -	.2
209	Paddock Laboratories Inc—*Michael Graves*	3940 Quebec Ave N, Minneapolis MN 55427	763-546-4676	R	39*	.4
210	West-Ward Pharmaceutical Corp—*Michael Raya* Eurohealth (USA) Inc	401 Industrial Way W, Eatontown NJ 07724	732-542-1191	S	39*	.4
211	Lifevantage Corp—*Douglas C Robinson*	10813 S River Front Pk, South Jordan UT 84095	801-432-9300	P	39	<.1
212	Watson Laboratories Inc (Groveport Ohio)—*Paul Bisaro* Watson Pharmaceuticals Inc	311 Bonnie Cir, Corona CA 92880	951-493-5300	S	38*	.1
213	Country Life Inc—*Halbert Drexler*	180 Vanderbilt Motor P, Hauppauge NY 11788		R	38*	.1
214	DUSA Pharmaceuticals Inc—*Robert F Doman*	25 Upton Dr, Wilmington MA 01887	978-657-7500	P	37	.1
215	Delavau LLC—*Jaci Bodell*	10101 Roosevelt Blvd, Philadelphia PA 19154	215-671-1400	R	37*	.4
216	Pharmasol Corp—*Frederic Badia*	1 Norfolk Ave Ste 1, South Easton MA 02375	508-238-8501	R	37*	.2
217	Ritedose Corp—*Walter Zahn*	1 Technology Cir, Columbia SC 29203	803-806-3300	S	37*	.2
218	Manhattan Drug Company Inc—*Gerald Kay* iBio Inc	225 Long Ave, Hillside NJ 07205		S	36*	.1
219	Ferring Pharmaceuticals Inc—*Wayne Anderson*	4 Gatehall Dr 3rd Fl, Parsippany NJ 07054	973-796-1600	S	36*	.1
220	QuatRx Pharmaceuticals Co—*Robert L Zerbe*	777 E Eisenhower Pkwy, Ann Arbor MI 48108	734-913-9900	R	36*	.1
221	Vanda Pharmaceuticals Inc—*Mihael H Polymeropoulos*	9605 Medical Center Dr, Rockville MD 20850	240-599-4500	P	36	<.1
222	Magno-Humphries Labs Inc—*Thelma Magno*	8800 SW Commercial St, Tigard OR 97223	503-684-5464	R	35*	.1
223	MEDTOX Diagnostics Inc—*Richard Braun*	1238 Anthony Rd, Burlington NC 27215	336-226-6311	D	35*	.1
224	Noramco Inc	1440 Olympic Dr, Athens GA 30601	706-353-4400	S	34*	.2
225	XOMA Ltd—*John Varian*	2910 7th St, Berkeley CA 94710	510-204-7200	P	34	.2
226	Norac Inc—*Wallace Mccloskey*	405 S Motor Ave, Azusa CA 91702	626-334-2908	R	33*	.2
227	Tower Laboratories Ltd—*Norman Needleman*	PO Box 306, Centerbrook CT 06409	860-767-2127	R	32*	.1
228	National Vitamin Company Inc—*Earl Courtney*	1145 W Gila Bend Hwy, Casa Grande AZ 85122	520-423-1858	R	32*	.2
229	Pegasus Laboratories Inc—*Richard Martin*	8809 Ely St, Pensacola FL 32514	850-478-2770	S	32*	.2
230	Mikart Inc—*Cerie Mcdonald*	1750 Chattahoochee Ave, Atlanta GA 30318	404-351-4510	R	32*	.2
231	Veterinary Pharmaceuticals Inc—*Harold Des Jardins*	13159 13th Rd W, Hanford CA 93230	559-582-6800	R	32*	.1
232	Formatech Inc—*Benjamin S Isaacs*	200 Bulfinch Dr, Andover MA 01810	978-725-9077	R	32*	.1
233	Enzymatic Therapy Inc—*Randy Rose*	PO Box 22310, Green Bay WI 54305	920-469-1313	R	32*	.3
234	DURECT Corp—*James E Brown*	2 Results Way, Cupertino CA 95014	408-777-1417	P	32	.1
235	Best Medical International Inc—*Krishnan Suthanthiran*	PO Box 315, Springfield VA 22150	703-451-2378	R	30*	.2
236	Lloyd Inc—*W Eugene Lloyd*	PO Box 130, Shenandoah IA 51601	712-246-4000	R	30*	.1
237	BioVex Group Inc—*Philip Astley-Sparke*	34 Commerce Way, Woburn MA 01801	781-376-4900	R	30*	.1
238	Elona Bio Technologies Inc—*Ron Zimmerman* Teva Respiratory LLC	1040 Sierra Dr Ste 100, Greenwood IN 46143	317-865-4770	S	30*	.1
239	SSS Co—*Charles M Bentley*	PO Box 4447, Atlanta GA 30302	404-521-0857	R	30*	.1
240	Ligand Pharmaceuticals Inc—*John L Higgins*	11085 N Torrey Pines R, La Jolla CA 92037	858-550-7500	P	30	<.1
241	AVI BioPharma Inc—*Christopher Garabedian*	3450 Monte Villa Pkwy, Bothell WA 98021	425-354-5038	P	29	.1
242	Topifram Laboratories Inc—*Robert Neis*	PO Box 1613, Englewood Cliffs NJ 07632	201-894-9020	S	29*	.1
243	Unimed Pharmaceuticals Inc—*Laurence Downey MD*	901 Sawyer Rd, Marietta GA 30062	770-578-9000	S	29	N/A
244	Eurand Inc—*John Fraher*	845 Ctr Dr, Vandalia OH 45377	937-898-9669	R	28*	.1
245	Ardea Biosciences Inc—*Barry D Quart*	4939 Directors Pl, San Diego CA 92121	858-652-6500	P	27	.1
246	KV Pharmaceutical Co—*Gregory J Divis*	1 Corporate Woods Dr, Bridgeton MO 63044	314-645-6600	P	27	.2
247	Ther-Rx Corp KV Pharmaceutical Co	1 Corporate Woods Dr, Bridgeton MO 63044	314-646-3700	S	27	.2
248	Intarcia Therapeutics Inc—*K Alice Leung*	24650 Industrial Blvd, Hayward CA 94545	510-782-7800	R	27*	<.1
249	Perrigo Iowa Inc—*Dick Downing*	PO Box 1099, Ankeny IA 50021	515-243-3000	R	27*	.2
250	AIE Pharmaceuticals Inc—*Mike Youssef*	1845 S Vineyard Ave St, Ontario CA 91761	909-947-9898	R	26*	<.1
251	Intermune Inc—*Daniel G Welch*	3280 Bayshore Blvd, Brisbane CA 94005	415-466-2200	P	26	.2
252	iBio Inc—*Robert Kay*	9 Innovation Way Ste 1, Newark DE 19711	302-355-0650	P	25	.1
253	Botanical Laboratories Inc—*Jim Thornton*	PO Box 1596, Ferndale WA 98248	360-384-5656	R	25*	.1
254	Chester Packaging LLC—*John Deiters*	1900 Section Rd A, Cincinnati OH 45237	513-458-3840	R	24*	.1
255	PML Inc	100 Rodolphe St, Durham NC 27712	919-620-2000	S	24	.2
256	Dynavax Technologies Corp—*Dino Dina*	2929 7th St Ste 100, Berkeley CA 94710	510-848-5100	P	24	.1
257	Standard Homeopathic Co—*Mark Phillips*	PO Box 61067, Los Angeles CA 90061	310-768-0700	R	24*	.1
258	Zogenix Inc—*Roger L Hawley*	12671 High Bluff Dr St, San Diego CA 92130	858-259-1165	P	23	.1
259	Coating Place Inc—*Tim Breunig*	PO Box 930310, Verona WI 53593	608-845-9521	R	22*	.1
260	TolerRx Inc—*Douglas J Ringler*	300 Technology Sq 3rd, Cambridge MA 02139	617-354-8100	R	22*	<.1
261	Vetoquinol USA Inc—*Manny Martinez*	4250 N Sylvania Ave, Fort Worth TX 76137		S	22*	<.1
262	Vet Pharm Inc—*Chuck Ploeg*	PO Box 167, Sioux Center IA 51250	712-722-3836	R	22*	.1
263	Amicus Therapeutics Inc—*John Crowley*	6 Cedar Brook Dr, Cranbury NJ 08512	609-662-2000	P	21	<.1
264	Jost Chemical Co—*Jerry Jost*	8150 Lackland Rd, Saint Louis MO 63114	314-428-4300	R	21*	.1
265	Xttrium Laboratories Inc—*Kevin Creevy*	415 W Pershing Rd, Chicago IL 60609	773-268-5800	R	21*	.1
266	First Priority Inc—*Lawrence Schneider*	1590 Todd Farm Dr, Elgin IL 60123	847-289-1600	R	20*	.1
267	Soft Gel Technologies Inc—*Ronald Udell*	6982 Bandini Blvd, Commerce CA 90040	323-726-0700	R	20*	.1
268	Archimica Inc—*Steve Hancock*	PO Box 1246, Springfield MO 65801	417-866-7291	R	19*	.1
269	ImmunoGen Inc—*Daniel M Junius*	830 Winter St, Waltham MA 02451	781-895-0600	P	19	.2
270	SIGA Technologies Inc—*Eric A Rose*	35 E 62nd St, New York NY 10065	212-672-9100	P	19	.1
271	OHM Laboratories Inc—*Venkat Krishnan*	600 College Rd E, Princeton NJ 08540	609-720-9200	S	19*	.1
272	CPEX Pharmaceuticals Inc—*John A Sedor*	1105 N Market St Ste 1, Wilmington DE 19801	302-658-6100	R	19	<.1
273	Merz Inc—*Terry Conrad*	4215 Tudor Ln, Greensboro NC 27410	336-856-2003	R	18*	.1
274	Labrada Nutritional Systems Inc—*Lee Labrada*	14850 Woodham Dr, Houston TX 77073	281-209-2183	R	18	<.1
275	Gmp Laboratories Of America Inc—*Mohammad Ishaq*	2931 E La Jolla St, Anaheim CA 92806	714-630-2467	R	18*	.1
276	Voyager Pharmaceutical Corp—*Patrick S Smith*	8540 Colonnade Center, Raleigh NC 27615	919-846-4880	R	18*	<.1
277	Iso-Tex Diagnsotics Inc—*Tim Maloney*	PO Box 909, Friendswood TX 77549		R	18*	<.1
278	Cayman Chemical Company Inc—*Kirk Maxey*	1180 E Ellsworth Rd, Ann Arbor MI 48108	734-971-3335	R	17*	.1
279	Renew Life Formulas Inc—*Brenda Watson*	2076 Sunnydale Blvd, Clearwater FL 33765	727-450-1061	R	17*	.1
280	SkinCare Rx—*Mark B Taylor*	1055 S 700 W, Salt Lake City UT 84104	801-924-5818	R	17*	.1
281	CyDex Pharmaceuticals Inc—*Theron E Odlaug*	10513 W 84th Ter, Lenexa KS 66214	913-685-8850	R	17*	<.1
282	Interhealth Nutraceuticals Inc—*Paul Dijkstra*	5451 Industrial Way, Benicia CA 94510	707-751-2800	R	17*	<.1
283	Braintree Laboratories Inc—*HarryP Keegan*	PO Box 850929, Braintree MA 02185	781-843-2202	R	17*	<.1
284	Lake Consumer Products Inc—*John Wundrock*	PO Box 198, Jackson WI 53037	262-677-4121	R	17*	<.1
285	Arena Pharmaceuticals Inc—*Jack Lief*	6166 Nancy Ridge Dr, San Diego CA 92121	858-453-7200	P	17	.4
286	Mueller Sports Medicine Inc—*Curt Mueller*	PO Box 99, Prairie Du Sac WI 53578	608-643-8530	R	17	.1
287	GenVec Inc—*Paul H Fischer*	65 W Watkins Mill Rd, Gaithersburg MD 20878	240-632-0740	P	17	.1
288	Genesis Today Inc—*Lindsey Duncan*	14101 W Hwy 290 Bldg 1, Austin TX 78737	512-858-1977	R	16*	.1
289	Akorn (Somerset New Jersey)—*Arthur Przybyl* Akorn Inc	72-6 Veronica Ave, Somerset NJ 08873	732-846-8066	S	16*	.1
290	Nextpharma Technologies USA Inc—*William Wedlake*	5340 Eastgate Mall, San Diego CA 92121	858-450-3123	R	16*	<.1
291	Neos Therapeutics Inc—*Mark Tengler*	2940 N Hwy 360 Ste 400, Grand Prairie TX 75050	972-408-1300	R	15*	.1

Note: An asterisk (*) indicates an estimated financial figure. The company type code used is as follows: R = Private, P = Public, S = Private Subsidiary, B = Public Subsidiary, D = Division, J = Joint Venture, I = Investment Fund.

COMPANY RANKINGS BY SALES WITHIN 4-DIGIT SIC

Rank	Company Name—Executive Officer	Address, City, State, Zip	Phone	Type	Fin	Empls
292	NitroMed Inc—Kenneth Bate	6000 Fairview Rd Ste 6, Charlotte NC 28210	704-941-2020	R	15	<.1
293	Pacira Pharmaceuticals Inc—David Stack	5 Sylvan Way, Parsippany NJ 07054	973-254-3560	P	15	.1
294	ProPhase Labs Inc—Ted Karkus	PO Box 1349, Doylestown PA 18901	215-345-0919	P	15	<.1
295	United-Guardian Inc—Kenneth H Globus	PO Box 18050, Hauppauge NY 11788	631-273-0900	P	14	<.1
296	Ash Stevens Inc—Stephen Munk	5861 John C Lodge Fwy, Detroit MI 48202	313-872-6400	R	14*	.1
297	NYMOX Corp—Paul Averback	777 Terrace Ave, Hasbrouck Heights NJ 07604	514-332-3222	S	13*	<.1
298	Amerilab Technologies Inc—Fred Wehling	2765 Niagara Ln N, Minneapolis MN 55447	763-525-1262	R	13*	.1
299	Cangene bioPharma Inc—Vicki Wolff-Long	1111 S Paca St, Baltimore MD 21230	410-843-5000	S	12*	.1
300	Biotics Building Partnership—Daniel Deluca	6801 Biotics Research, Rosenberg TX 77471	281-344-0909	R	12*	.1
301	Health One Pharmaceutical Inc—Richard Yeh	9480 Telstar Ave Ste 5, El Monte CA 91731	626-279-9699	R	12*	<.1
302	InSite Vision Inc—Timothy Ruane	965 Atlantic Ave, Alameda CA 94501	510-865-8800	P	12	<.1
303	Sparhawk Laboratories Inc—Bert Hughes	12340 Santa Fe Trl Dr, Lenexa KS 66215	913-888-7500	R	12*	.1
304	Pain Therapeutics Inc—Remi Barbier	7801 N Capital of Texa, Austin TX 78731	512-501-2444	P	11	<.1
305	Dynatabs LLC—Harold Baum	1933 E 12th St, Brooklyn NY 11229	718-376-6084	R	11*	<.1
306	AVANIR Pharmaceuticals Inc—Keith A Katkin	20 Enterprise Ste 200, Aliso Viejo CA 92656	949-389-6700	P	11	.2
307	Icagen Inc—P Kay Wagoner	4222 Emperor Blvd Ste, Durham NC 27703	919-941-5206	P	11	<.1
308	Physicians' Pharmaceutical Corp—George E Riddle	10360 Deerborn Ln, Knoxville TN 37932	865-671-7800	R	11	<.1
309	American Bio Medica Corp—Stan Cipkowski	122 Smith Rd, Kinderhook NY 12106	518-758-8158	P	10	.1
310	Cortex Pharmaceuticals Inc—Mark A Varney PhD	15231 Barranca Pkwy, Irvine CA 92618	949-727-3157	P	10	<.1
311	Idenix Pharmaceuticals Inc—Ronald C Renaud Jr	60 Hampshire St, Cambridge MA 02139	617-995-9800	P	10	.1
312	Radix Laboratories Inc—Premchand Girdhari	1334 International Dr, Eau Claire WI 54701	715-833-0644	R	10*	<.1
313	Advanced Vision Research Inc—Jeffrey P Gilbard	660 Main St, Woburn MA 01801	781-932-8327	R	10*	.1
314	JV Northwest Inc—David Jones	390 S Redwood St, Canby OR 97013	503-263-2858	R	10*	.1
315	Halozyme Therapeutics Inc—Gregory Frost	11388 Sorrento Valley, San Diego CA 92121	858-794-8889	P	9	.1
316	ChemoCentryx Inc—Thomas J Schall	850 Maude Ave, Mountain View CA 94043	650-210-2900	R	9*	.1
317	Quality Bioresources Inc—Claudia Briell	1015 N Austin St, Seguin TX 78155	830-372-4797	R	9*	<.1
318	Napp Technologies Inc—Sheldon Wexler	401 Hackensack Ave 9th, Hackensack NJ 07601	201-843-4664	R	9*	<.1
319	Adamis Pharmaceuticals Corp—Dennis J Carlo	11455 El Camino Real, San Diego CA 92130	858-722-4242	R	9*	<.1
320	Rowell Laboratories Inc	5036 Dr Phillips Blvd, Orlando FL 32819		R	9*	<.1
321	Athersys Inc—Gil Van Bokkelen	3201 Carnegie Ave, Cleveland OH 44115	216-431-9900	P	9	.1
322	Pro Pac Labs Inc—Kim Wheelwright	PO Box 9691, Ogden UT 84409	801-621-0900	R	9*	<.1
323	Chattem Chemicals Inc—Jitendra Doshi	PO Box 9283, East Ridge TN 37412	423-822-5000	R	8*	.1
324	IVAX Diagnostics Inc—Kevin Clark Teva Respiratory LLC	2140 N Miami Ave, Miami FL 33127	305-324-2338	B	8	.1
325	Progenics Pharmaceuticals Inc—Mark R Baker	777 Old Saw Mill River, Tarrytown NY 10591	914-789-2800	P	8	.2
326	Trius Therapeutics Inc—Jeffrey Stein	6310 Nancy Ridge Dr St, San Diego CA 92121	858-452-0370	P	8	.1
327	H Reisman Corp—David Holmes	377 Crane St, Orange NJ 07050	973-677-9200	R	8*	<.1
328	Ion Laboratories Inc—William Oliver	5475 115th Ave N, Clearwater FL 33760	727-527-1072	R	8*	<.1
329	Apex Pharmaceuticals Inc—Alexander Saliman	28298 Constellation Rd, Valencia CA 91355	661-295-9772	R	8*	<.1
330	Advance Pharmaceutical Inc—Tasrin Hossain	2201 5th Ave Ste F, Ronkonkoma NY 11779	631-981-4600	R	8*	.1
331	Kelatron Corp—Robert Wilkins	1675 W 2750 S, Ogden UT 84401	801-394-4558	R	8*	.1
332	Synta Pharmaceuticals Corp—Safi R Bahcall	45 Hartwell Ave, Lexington MA 02421	781-274-8200	P	8	.1
333	Elge Inc—Larry Gremminger	1000 Cole Ave, Rosenberg TX 77471	281-342-8228	R	8*	.1
334	Mvp Laboratories Inc—Mary Chapek	4805 G St, Omaha NE 68117	402-331-5106	R	8*	<.1
335	PruGen Inc—Sean Lonergan	8714 E Vista Bonita Dr, Scottsdale AZ 85255	480-585-0122	R	7	<.1
336	Smart-Tek Solutions Inc—Brian Bonar	1100 Quail St Ste 100, Newport Beach CA 92660	858-798-1644	P	7	N/A
337	Imagenetix Inc—William P Spencer	10845 Rancho Bernardo, San Diego CA 92127	858-674-8455	P	7	<.1
338	Insmed Inc—Timothy Whitten	8720 Stony Point Pky S, Richmond VA 23235	804-565-3000	P	7	<.1
339	Lyne Laboratories Inc—Robert Crisafi	10 Burke Dr, Brockton MA 02301	508-583-8700	R	7*	.1
340	Ony Inc—Edmond A Egan	1576 Sweet Home Rd Ste, Amherst NY 14228	716-636-9096	R	6*	<.1
341	Professional Compounding Centers of America Inc—L David Sparks	9901 S Wilcrest Dr, Houston TX 77099	281-933-6948	R	6*	<.1
342	Tyson Nutraceutical Inc	3535 Lomita Blvd Unit, Torrance CA 90505	310-325-5600	R	6*	<.1
343	Lindi Skin—Lindy Snider	100 Four Falls Corpora, West Conshohocken PA 19428	610-649-3900	R	6*	<.1
344	Provista Life Sciences LLC—William Gartner	6225 N 24th St Ste 150, Phoenix AZ 85016	602-224-5500	R	6*	<.1
345	West Coast Laboratories Inc—Maurice Ovadia	116 E Alondra Blvd, Gardena CA 90248	310-532-6720	R	6*	.1
346	A and S Pharmaceutical Corp—Arnold Lewis	PO Box 2005, Bridgeport CT 06608	203-368-2538	R	6*	.1
347	BioSpecifics Technologies Corp—Thomas L Wegman	35 Wilbur St, Lynbrook NY 11563	516-593-7000	P	6	<.1
348	Molecular Insight Pharmaceuticals Inc—John Babich	160 2nd St, Cambridge MA 02142	617-492-5554	P	6	.1
349	Lobob Laboratories Inc—Robert Lohr	1440 Atteberry Ln, San Jose CA 95131	408-432-0580	R	6*	<.1
350	Alva/Amco Pharmacal Companies Inc—Jeffery Gerchenson	7711 N Merrimac Ave, Niles IL 60714	847-663-0700	R	5*	.1
351	Berkeley Nutritional Manufacturing Corp—Robert Matheson	1852 Rutan Dr, Livermore CA 94551	925-243-6300	R	5*	<.1
352	Biovest International Inc—Samuel Duffey Accentia BioPharmaceuticals Inc	324 S Hyde Park Ave St, Tampa FL 33606	813-864-2558	S	5*	<.1
353	Numark Laboratories Inc—Patrick Lonergan	164 Northfield Ave, Edison NJ 08837		R	5*	<.1
354	Acumed Pharmaceuticals Inc—Marc Lanser	20 Newbury St 5th Fl, Boston MA 02116	617-425-0200	S	5*	<.1
355	Ara Pharmaceuticals Inc—Marc Lanser	20 Newbury St 5th Fl, Boston MA 02116	617-425-0200	S	5*	<.1
356	Coda Pharmaceuticals Inc—Peter G Savas	239 South St, Hopkinton MA 01748	508-497-2360	S	5*	<.1
357	Neurobiologics Inc—Peter G Savas	239 Main St, Hopkinton MA 01748	508-497-2360	S	5*	<.1
358	Lexicon Pharmaceuticals Inc—Arthur T Sands	8800 Technology Forest, The Woodlands TX 77381	281-863-3000	P	5	.3
359	Phoenix Pharmaceuticals Inc—Jaw-Kang Chang	330 Beach Rd, Burlingame CA 94010	650-558-8898	R	5*	<.1
360	Silarx Pharmaceuticals Inc—Rohit Desai	PO Box 449, Spring Valley NY 10977	845-352-4020	R	5*	<.1
361	Elite Pharmaceuticals Inc—Jerry I Treppel	165 Ludlow Ave, Northvale NJ 07647	201-750-2646	P	5	<.1
362	Gebauer Co—David O'halloran	4444 E 153rd St, Cleveland OH 44128	216-581-3030	R	5*	<.1
363	General Research Laboratories—Alex Geczy	8900 Winnetka Ave, Northridge CA 91324	818-349-9911	R	5*	<.1
364	Helicos BioSciences Corp—Ivan Trifunovich	1 Kendall Sq Ste B2002, Cambridge MA 02139	617-264-1800	P	4	<.1
365	Edan Naturals LLC—Debi Wayda	PO Box 560, Wautoma WI 54982	920-787-3383	R	4*	<.1
366	Ajay Chemicals Inc—Alan Shipp	PO Box 127, Powder Springs GA 30127	770-943-6202	R	4*	<.1
367	Protherics Inc—Andrew Heath	5214 Maryland Way Ste, Brentwood TN 37027	615-327-1027	S	4*	.1
368	Randal Optimal Nutrients LLC—William Robotham	PO Box 7328, Santa Rosa CA 95407	707-528-1800	R	4*	<.1
369	Quality Formulation Laboratories Inc—Mohamed Desoky	110 Pennsylvania Ave, Paterson NJ 07503	973-977-8800	R	4*	<.1
370	Metabolic Maintenance Products Inc—Ed Fitzjarrell	68994 N Pine St, Sisters OR 97759	541-549-7800	R	4*	<.1
371	Twenty-First Century Laboratories Inc—Steve Snyder	2119 S Wilson St, Tempe AZ 85282	480-966-8201	R	4*	<.1
372	Dews Research LLC—Barbara Dews	PO Box 637, Mineral Wells TX 76068	940-325-0208	R	4*	<.1
373	Geron Corp—John A Scarlett	230 Constitution Dr, Menlo Park CA 94025	650-473-7700	P	4	.2
374	Hill Dermaceuticals Inc—Jerry Roth	2650 S Mellonville Ave, Sanford FL 32773	407-323-1887	R	4*	<.1
375	Mineral Resources International Inc—Bruce Anderson	PO Box 190, Roy UT 84067	801-731-7040	R	4*	<.1
376	Tec Laboratories Inc—Steven Smith	7100 Tec Labs Way Sw, Albany OR 97321	541-926-4577	R	3*	<.1
377	BioDelivery Sciences International Inc—Mark A Sirgo	801 Corporate Center D, Raleigh NC 27607	919-582-9050	P	3	<.1
378	Acura Pharmaceuticals Inc—Robert B Jones	616 N North Ct Ste 120, Palatine IL 60067	847-705-7709	P	3	<.1

Rank	Company Name—*Executive Officer*	Address, City, State, Zip	Phone	Type	Fin	Empls
379	Carolina Medical Products Co—*Henry Smith*	PO Box 147, Farmville NC 27828	252-753-7111	R	3*	<.1
380	BioNumerik Pharmaceuticals Inc—*Frederick H Hausheer*	8122 Datapoint Dr Ste, San Antonio TX 78229	210-614-1701	R	3*	<.1
381	Aderis Pharmaceuticals Inc	85 Main St, Hopkinton MA 01748	508-497-2300	R	3*	<.1
382	Pentech Pharmaceuticals Inc—*Al Hummel*	3315 W Algonquin Rd St, Rolling Meadows IL 60008	847-255-0303	R	3*	<.1
383	Thomas Laboratories Inc—*Steve Thomas*	9165 W Van Buren, Tolleson AZ 85353	623-936-8536	R	3*	<.1
384	Abela Pharmaceuticals Inc—*Colette Cozean*	21581 Midcrest Dr, Lake Forest CA 92630	949-855-2885	R	3*	<.1
385	airPharma—*Douglas R Dockhorn*	5370 College Blvd Ste, Overland Park KS 66211	913-498-0700	R	3*	<.1
386	Afton Scientific Corp—*Thomas Thorpe*	2030 Avon Ct Ste 1, Charlottesville VA 22902	434-979-3737	R	3*	<.1
387	Penick Corp—*Stuart Rose*	33 Industrial Park Rd, Newark NJ 07114	856-678-3601	R	3*	<.1
388	Cetylite Industries Inc—*Stanley Wachman*	9051 River Rd, Pennsauken NJ 08110	856-665-6111	R	3*	<.1
389	Acusphere Inc—*Sherri C Oberg*	99 Hayden Ave Ste 385, Lexington MA 02421	617-648-8800	P	3	.1
390	Daniella Koren Inc—*Daniella Koren*	160 Summit Ave, Montvale NJ 07645	201-391-6000	R	3*	<.1
391	Amerx Health Care Corp—*Justice W Anderson* Procyon Corp	1300 S Highland Ave, Clearwater FL 33756	727-443-0530	S	3	<.1
392	Cytokinetics Inc—*Robert Blum*	280 E Grand Ave, South San Francisco CA 94080	650-624-3000	P	3	.1
393	HealthSport Inc—*Kevin Taheri*	1620 Beacon Pl, Oxnard CA 93033	805-822-5090	P	3	<.1
394	Marina Biotech Inc—*J Michael French*	3830 Monte Villa Pky, Bothell WA 98021	425-908-3600	P	3	<.1
395	Achillion Pharmaceuticals Inc—*Michael D Kishbauch*	300 George St, New Haven CT 06511	203-624-7000	P	2	<.1
396	RIJ Pharmaceutical Corp—*Brij Gupta*	40 Commercial Ave, Middletown NY 10941	845-692-5799	R	2*	<.1
397	Welchdry Inc—*Dave Heide*	4270 Sunnyside Dr, Holland MI 49424	616-399-2711	R	2*	<.1
398	Omeros Corp—*Gregory O Demopulos*	1420 5th Ave Ste 2600, Seattle WA 98101	206-676-5000	P	2	.1
399	Pharmaceutical Innovations Inc—*Gilbert Buchalter*	897 Frelinghuysen Ave, Newark NJ 07114	973-242-2900	R	2*	<.1
400	Prima Yerba Inc—*John Jung*	740 Jefferson Ave, Ashland OR 97520	541-488-2228	R	2*	<.1
401	Diamond Drinks Inc—*Anthony Cenimo*	600 Railway St Unit 1, Williamsport PA 17701	570-322-2422	R	2*	<.1
402	AXM Pharma Inc—*Wang Wei Shi*	20955 Pathfinder Rd St, Diamond Bar CA 91765	909-843-6338	P	2	.2
403	Charlesson LLC—*Douglas Altschuler*	800 Research Pkwy Ste, Oklahoma City OK 73104	405-271-2552	R	2*	<.1
404	Wildlife Pharmaceuticals Inc—*Cobus Raath*	PO Box 2023, Fort Collins CO 80522	970-484-6267	R	2*	<.1
405	Nuun and Company Inc—*Dave Mutzel*	PO Box 20091, Seattle WA 98102	206-219-9237	R	2*	<.1
406	Allergy Laboratories Of Ohio—*Shelly Mullins*	623 E 11th Ave, Columbus OH 43211	614-291-7414	R	2*	<.1
407	Ari-Med Pharmaceuticals—*David Robertson*	1615 W University Dr S, Tempe AZ 85281	480-966-9802	R	2*	<.1
408	Uptime Sports Nutrition Medical Industries Inc—*Michael Scigliano*	PO Box 90659, Santa Barbara CA 93190		R	2*	<.1
409	Delmarva2000—*Charles Betyeman*	21 Shay Ln, Milton DE 19968	302-645-2226	R	2*	<.1
410	Soligenix Inc—*Christopher J Schaber*	29 Emmons Dr Ste C-10, Princeton NJ 08540	609-538-8200	P	2	<.1
411	Inhibitex Inc—*Russell H Plumb*	9005 Westside Pky, Alpharetta GA 30009	678-740-1100	P	2	<.1
412	AdvanSource Biomaterials Corp—*Michael F Adams*	229 Andover St, Wilmington MA 01887	978-657-0075	P	2	<.1
413	International Stem Cell Corp—*Andrey Semechkin*	5950 Priestly Dr, Carlsbad CA 92008	760-940-6383	P	2	.1
414	Optimer Pharmaceuticals Inc—*Pedro Lichtinger*	5355 Mira Sorrento Pl, San Diego CA 92121	858-909-0736	P	2	.1
415	Corcept Therapeutics Inc—*Joseph K Belanoff*	149 Commonwealth Dr, Menlo Park CA 94025	650-327-3270	P	2	<.1
416	Hogil Pharmaceutical Corp—*David Trager*	237 Mmaroneck Ave Ste, White Plains NY 10605	914-681-1800	R	1*	<.1
417	Somaxon Pharmaceuticals Inc—*Richard W Pascoe*	10935 Vista Sorrento P, San Diego CA 92130	858-876-6500	P	1	<.1
418	BioMarin Holdings Inc BioMarin Pharmaceutical Inc	105 Digital Dr, Novato CA 94949	415-884-6700	S	1*	.2
419	Orexigen Therapeutics Inc—*Michael Narachi*	3344 N Torrey Pines Ct, La Jolla CA 92037	858-436-8600	P	1	<.1
420	BioElectronics Corp—*Andrew J Whelan*	4539 Metropolitan Ct, Frederick MD 21704	301-874-4890	P	1	<.1
421	Access Business Group LLC—*Doug Devos*	PO Box 5940, Buena Park CA 90622	616-787-6767	S	1*	<.1
422	Predix Pharmaceuticals Inc—*Michael G Kauffman*	4 Maguire Rd, Lexington MA 02421	781-372-3260	R	1*	<.1
423	EpiCept Corp—*Jack V Talley*	777 Old Saw Mill River, Tarrytown NY 10591	914-606-3500	P	1	<.1
424	Brioschi Pharmaceutical International—*Patrick Duncan*	19-01 Pollitt Dr, Fair Lawn NJ 07410	201-796-4226	R	1*	<.1
425	At Last Naturals Inc—*Bruce Last*	401 Columbus Ave, Valhalla NY 10595		R	1*	<.1
426	Donell Inc—*Tod Kane*	PO Box 471, Bardstown KY 40004	502-331-0241	R	1*	<.1
427	Sporicidin International Inc—*Robert Schattner*	525 Locust Grove, Spartanburg SC 29303	864-503-8333	R	1*	<.1
428	Urigen NA Inc—*William J Garner MD*	1700 N Broadway, Walnut Creek CA 94596	925-280-2861	R	1*	<.1
429	Amplyx Pharmaceuticals Inc—*Elaine Heron*	548 Market St Ste 1258, San Francisco CA 94104		R	1*	<.1
430	Pharmasset Inc—*P Schaefer Price*	303-A College Rd E, Princeton NJ 08540	609-613-4100	P	1	.1
431	Helix BioMedix Inc—*R Stephen Beatty*	22118 20th Ave SE Ste, Bothell WA 98021	425-402-8400	P	1	<.1
432	Pharmacyclics Inc—*Robert W Duggan*	995 E Arques Ave, Sunnyvale CA 94085	408-774-0330	P	1	.1
433	Advanced Life Sciences Holdings Inc—*Michael T Flavin*	1440 Davey Rd, Woodridge IL 60517	630-739-6744	P	1	<.1
434	NeurogesX Inc—*Ronald Martell*	2215 Bridgepointe Pkwy, San Mateo CA 94404	650-358-3300	P	1	.1
435	NuPathe Inc—*Jane H Hollingsworth*	227 Washington St Ste, Conshohocken PA 19428	484-567-0130	P	1	<.1
436	Bionovo Inc—*Isaac Cohen*	5858 Horton St Ste 400, Emeryville CA 94608	510-601-2000	P	1	<.1
437	Gelstat Corp—*Gerald N Kieft*	3557 SW Corporate Pky, Palm City FL 34990	772-283-0020	P	1	<.1
438	Advanced Cell Technology Inc—*Gary Rabin*	PO Box 1707, Santa Monica CA 90406	310-576-0611	P	1	<.1
439	Catalyst Pharmaceutical Partners Inc—*Patrick J McEnany*	355 Alhambra Cir Ste 1, Coral Gables FL 33134	305-529-2522	P	1	<.1
440	Vitaminerals Inc—*Michael Gorman*	1815 Flower St, Glendale CA 91201	818-500-8718	R	<1*	<.1
441	Sunesis Pharmaceuticals Inc—*Daniel N Swisher Jr*	395 Oyster Point Blvd, South San Francisco CA 94080	650-266-3501	P	<1	<.1
442	Access Pharmaceuticals Inc—*Jeffrey B Davis*	2600 Stemmons Fwy Ste, Dallas TX 75207	214-905-5100	P	<1	<.1
443	Herborium Group Inc—*Agnes Olsvzewski*	3 Oak St, Teaneck NJ 07666	201-836-2424	P	<1	<.1
444	Radient Pharmaceuticals Corp—*Douglas MacLellan*	2492 Walnut Ave Ste 10, Tustin CA 92780	714-505-4461	P	<1	<.1
445	MannKind Corp—*Alfred E Mann*	28903 N Ave Paine, Valencia CA 91355	661-775-5300	P	<1	.4
446	Cadence Pharmaceuticals Inc—*Theodore R Schroeder*	12481 High Bluff Dr St, San Diego CA 92130	858-436-1400	P	<1	.2
447	OPKO Health Inc—*Phillip Frost*	4400 Biscayne Blvd, Miami FL 33137	305-575-4100	P	<1	.2
448	MAP Pharmaceuticals Inc—*Timothy S Nelson*	2400 Bayshore Pkwy Ste, Mountain View CA 94043	650-386-3100	P	<1	.1
449	Cell Therapeutics Inc—*James A Bianco*	501 Elliott Ave W Ste, Seattle WA 98119	206-282-7100	P	<1	.1
450	Endocyte Inc—*P Ron Ellis*	3000 Kent Ave Ste A1-1, West Lafayette IN 47906	765-463-1885	P	<1	.1
451	VIVUS Inc—*Leland F Wilson*	1172 Castro St, Mountain View CA 94040	650-934-5200	P	<1	<.1
452	Biodel Inc—*Errol De Souza*	100 Saw Mill Rd, Danbury CT 06810	203-796-5000	P	<1	<.1
453	Threshold Pharmaceuticals Inc—*Harold E Selick*	1300 Seaport Blvd Ste, Redwood City CA 94063	650-474-8200	P	<1	<.1
454	RXi Pharmaceuticals Corp—*Mark Ahn*	60 Prescott St, Worcester MA 01605	508-767-3861	P	<1	<.1
455	Anadys Pharmaceuticals Inc—*Steve Worland*	5871 Oberlin Dr Ste 20, San Diego CA 92121	858-530-3600	P	<1	<.1
456	Keryx Biopharmaceuticals Inc—*Rob Bentsur*	750 Lexington Ave 20th, New York NY 10022	212-531-5965	P	<1	<.1
457	Cardiovascular BioTherapeutics Inc—*Daniel C Montano*	1930 Village Center Ci, Las Vegas NV 89134	702-839-7200	P	<1	<.1
458	Adherex Technologies Inc *Rostislav Raykov*	PO Box 13628, Research Triangle Park NC 27709	919-636-4530	P	<1	<.1
459	Telik Inc—*Michael M Wick*	700 Hansen Way, Palo Alto CA 94304	650-845-7700	P	<1	<.1
460	AcelRx Pharmaceuticals Inc—*Richard King*	575 Chesapeake Dr, Redwood City CA 94063	650-216-3500	P	<1	<.1
461	Opexa Therapeutics Inc—*Neil K Warma*	2635 Technology Forest, The Woodlands TX 77381	281-775-0600	P	<1	<.1
462	MediciNova Inc—*Yuichi Iwaki*	4350 La Jolla Village, San Diego CA 92122	858-373-1500	P	<1	<.1
463	Aegerion Pharmaceuticals Inc—*Marc Beer*	101 Main St Ste 1850, Cambridge MA 02142	617-500-7867	P	<1	<.1
464	Celsion Corp—*Michael Tardugno*	10220-L Old Columbia R, Columbia MD 21046	410-290-5390	P	<1	<.1
465	Emisphere Technologies Inc—*Michael R Garone*	240 Cedar Knolls Rd, Cedar Knolls NJ 07927	973-532-8000	P	<1	<.1

Note: An asterisk (*) indicates an estimated financial figure. The company type code used is as follows: R = Private, P = Public, S = Private Subsidiary, B = Public Subsidiary, D = Division, J = Joint Venture, I = Investment Fund.

COMPANY RANKINGS BY SALES WITHIN 4-DIGIT SIC

Rank	Company Name—*Executive Officer*	Address, City, State, Zip	Phone	Type	Fin	Empls
466	Vyteris Holdings Inc—*Haro Hartounian*	13-01 Pollitt Dr, Fair Lawn NJ 07410	201-703-2299	P	<1	<.1
467	Neurologix Inc—*Adrian Adams*	1 Bridge Plz, Fort Lee NJ 07024	201-592-6451	P	<1	<.1
468	Biomoda Inc—*Maria Zannes*	609 Broadway NE, Albuquerque NM 87102	505-821-0875	P	<1	<.1
469	Raptor Pharmaceutical Corp—*Christopher M Starr*	9 Commercial Blvd Ste, Novato CA 94949	415-382-8111	P	<1	<.1
470	Harbor BioSciences Inc—*James M Frincke*	9191 Towne Centre Dr S, San Diego CA 92122	858-587-9333	P	<1	<.1
471	DARA Biosciences Inc—*Richard Franco*	8601 6 Forks Rd Ste 16, Raleigh NC 27615	919-872-5578	P	<1	<.1
472	MMRGlobal Inc—*Robert L Lorsch*	4401 Wilshire Blvd 2nd, Los Angeles CA 90010		P	<1	<.1
473	Poniard Pharmaceuticals Inc—*Ronald Martell*	750 Battery St Ste 330, San Francisco CA 94111	650-583-3774	P	<1	<.1
474	Aeolus Pharmaceuticals Inc—*John McManus*	26361 Crown Valley Pky, Mission Viejo CA 92691	949-481-9825	P	<1	<.1
475	Cobalis Corp—*Marty Marion*	16795 Von Karmann Ste, Irvine CA 92606	949-260-0123	P	<1	<.1
476	CorMedix Inc—*John C Houghton*	745 Rt 202-206 Ste 303, Bridgewater NJ 08807	908-517-9500	P	<1	<.1
477	Galectin Therapeutics Inc—*Peter Traber*	7 Wells Ave, Newton MA 02459	617-559-0033	P	<1	<.1
478	Northwest Biotherapeutics Inc—*Linda Bowers*	4800 Montgomery Ln Ste, Bethesda MD 20814	240-497-9024	P	<1	<.1
479	Provectus Pharmaceuticals Inc—*Craig Dees*	7327 Oak Ridge Hwy, Knoxville TN 37931		P	<1	<.1
480	Manhattan Pharmaceuticals Inc—*Douglas Abel*	48 Wall St Ste 1100, New York NY 10005	212-582-3950	P	<1	<.1
481	OncoVista Innovative Therapies Inc—*Alexander L Weis*	14785 Omicron Dr Ste 1, San Antonio TX 78245	210-677-6000	P	<1	<.1
482	SinoFresh HealthCare Inc—*David R Olund*	333 S Tamiami Trl Ste, Venice FL 34285	941-375-8174	P	<1	<.1
483	Pharmos Corp—*S Colin Neill*	99 Wood Ave S Ste 302, Iselin NJ 08830	732-452-9556	P	<1	<.1
484	Procyon Corp—*Regina W Anderson*	1300 S Highland Ave, Clearwater FL 33756	727-447-2998	P	<1	<.1
485	Kent International Holdings Inc—*Paul O Koether*	10911 Raven Ridge Rd S, Raleigh NC 27614	919-847-8710	B	<1	N/A
486	Tercica Inc—*John A Scarlett*	2000 Sierra Point Pkwy, Brisbane CA 94005	650-624-4900	S	N/A	.1
487	Lonza Viral—*J David Enloe Jr*	8066 El Rio St, Houston TX 77054	713-568-6190	R	N/A	<.1
488	CytoDyn Inc—*Kenneth J Van Ness*	110 Crenshaw Lake Rd, Lutz FL 33548		P	N/A	<.1
489	Ventrus Biosciences Inc—*Russell H Ellison*	99 Hudson St 5th Fl, New York NY 10013	646-706-5208	P	N/A	<.1
490	National Scent Co—*Victoria Dunn*	PO Box 382096, Germantown TN 38183	901-367-8388	R	N/A	<.1
491	CellCyte Genetics Corp—*John Fluke Jr*	14205 SE 36th StSte 10, Bellevue WA 98006	425-519-3775	P	N/A	N/A

TOTALS: SIC 2834 Pharmaceutical Preparations
Companies: 491

					428,291	821.3

2835 Diagnostic Substances

Rank	Company Name—*Executive Officer*	Address, City, State, Zip	Phone	Type	Fin	Empls
1	Genzyme General—*Henri Termeer*	500 Kendall St, Cambridge MA 02142	617-252-7500	S	32,000	N/A
2	Alere Inc—*Ron Zwanziger*	51 Sawyer Rd Ste 200, Waltham MA 02453	781-647-3900	P	1,683	14.5
3	IDEXX Laboratories Inc—*Jonathan W Ayers*	1 Idexx Dr, Westbrook ME 04092	207-856-0300	P	1,219	5.1
4	LifeScan Inc—*John Seffrin*	1000 Gibraltar Dr, Milpitas CA 95035	408-263-9789	S	695*	2.5
5	OSI Pharmaceuticals Inc—*Naoki Okamura*	41 Pinelawn Rd, Melville NY 11747	631-962-2000	B	428	.5
6	Quest Diagnostics Inc (San Juan Capistrano California)—*Surya Mohapatra*	33608 Ortega Hwy, San Juan Capistrano CA 92675	949-728-4000	S	419*	1.5
7	Genencor International Inc—*Tjerk de Ruiter*	925 Page Mill Rd, Palo Alto CA 94304	650-846-7500	S	410	1.3
8	Myriad Genetics Inc—*Peter D Meldrum*	320 Wakara Way, Salt Lake City UT 84108	801-584-3600	P	402	1.1
9	Immucor Inc—*Joshua H Levine*	PO Box 5625, Norcross GA 30091	770-441-2051	P	333	.8
10	Ista Pharmaceuticals Inc—*Vicente Anido Jr*	50 Technology Dr, Irvine CA 92618	949-788-6000	P	160	.3
11	BD Pharmingen Inc—*William Kozy*	10975 Torreyana Rd, San Diego CA 92121	858-812-8800	R	160*	.4
12	Meridian Bioscience Inc—*John Kraeutler*	3471 River Hills Dr, Cincinnati OH 45244	513-271-3700	P	160	.5
13	Human Genome Sciences Inc—*H Thomas Watkins*	14200 Shady Grove Rd, Rockville MD 20850	301-309-8504	P	157	1.1
14	Ge Healthcare Holdings Inc—*Daniel Peters*	3350 N Ridge Ave, Arlington Heights IL 60004	847-398-8400	S	155*	1.5
15	Quidel Corp—*Douglas Bryant*	10165 McKellar Ct, San Diego CA 92121	858-552-1100	P	113	.5
16	OraSure Technologies Inc—*Douglas A Michels*	220 E 1st St, Bethlehem PA 18015	610-882-1820	P	75	.2
17	Streck Inc—*Constance Ryan*	PO Box 45625, Omaha NE 68145	402-333-1982	R	70*	.3
18	AMAG Pharmaceuticals Inc—*Frank Thomas*	100 Hayden Ave, Lexington MA 02421	617-498-3300	P	66	.2
19	Monogram Biosciences Inc—*Steven M Anderson PhD*	345 Oyster Point Blvd, South San Francisco CA 94080	650-635-1100	S	62	.4
20	Scantibodies Laboratory Inc—*Thomas Cantor*	9336 Abraham Way, Santee CA 92071	619-258-9300	R	54*	.6
21	Syntron Bioresearch Inc—*Jin Lee*	2774 Loker Ave W, Carlsbad CA 92010	760-930-2200	R	49*	.3
22	Diagnostic Hybrids Inc—*David Scholl* Quidel Corp	1055 E State St Ste 10, Athens OH 45701	740-589-3300	S	45*	.2
23	SeraCare Life Sciences Inc—*Gregory A Gould*	37 Birch St, Milford MA 01757	508-244-6400	P	43	.2
24	Neogen Corp- Animal Safety Div and Life Sciences Div—*James Huerbert*	944 Nandino Blvd, Lexington KY 40511	859-254-1221	D	34*	.1
25	INOVA Diagnostics Inc—*Walter Binder*	9900 Old Grove Rd, San Diego CA 92131	858-586-9900	R	28*	.1
26	Bionostics Inc—*Jon Lang*	7 Jackson Rd, Devens MA 01434	978-772-7070	R	28*	.1
27	Athena Diagnostics Inc—*Robert E Flaherty*	Four Biotech Park 377, Worcester MA 01605	508-756-2886	S	27*	.1
28	BBI BioSeq Inc—*Mark Manak* SeraCare Life Sciences Inc	217 Perry Pky, Gaithersburg MD 20877	301-208-8100	S	25*	.1
29	BBI Biotech Research Laboratories Inc—*Mark Manak* SeraCare Life Sciences Inc	217 Perry Pky, Gaithersburg MD 20877	301-208-8100	S	25*	.1
30	Rules-Based Medicine Inc—*T Craig Benson*	3300 Duval Rd, Austin TX 78759	512-835-8026	R	25	.1
31	Enzo Therapeutics Inc—*Barry Weiner*	60 Executive Blvd, Farmingdale NY 11735	631-755-5500	S	21*	.2
32	Synbiotics Corp—*Paul R Hays*	12200 NW Ambassador Dr, Kansas City MO 64163	816-464-3500	R	19	.1
33	Gen-Probe Gti Diagnostics Inc—*Jim Tidey*	20925 Crossroads Cir, Waukesha WI 53186	262-754-1000	R	18*	.1
34	Cell Biosciences—*Tim Harkness*	3040 Oakmead Village D, Santa Clara CA 95051	408-510-5500	R	18	.1
35	Bion Enterprises Ltd—*Dennis Walczewski*	455 State St Ste 100, Des Plaines IL 60016	847-544-5044	R	18*	<.1
36	Immunomedics Inc—*Cynthia L Sullivan*	300 American Rd, Morris Plains NJ 07950	973-605-8200	P	15	.1
37	Hycor Biomedical Inc—*Bill Sullivan*	7272 Chapman Ave, Garden Grove CA 92841	714-933-3000	R	14*	.1
38	OncoGenex Pharmaceuticals Inc—*Scott Cormack*	1522 217th Pl SE Ste 1, Bothell WA 98021	425-686-1500	P	14	<.1
39	Peregrine Pharmaceuticals Inc—*Steven W King*	14282 Franklin Ave, Tustin CA 92780	714-508-6000	P	14	.2
40	Quantimetrix Corp—*Robert W Ban*	2005 Manhattan Beach B, Redondo Beach CA 90278	310-536-0006	R	12*	.1
41	Hitachi Chemical Diagnostics Inc	630 Clyde Ct, Mountain View CA 94043	650-961-5501	S	11*	.1
42	Ess Group Inc—*Ronald Kuprt*	78 Carranza Rd, Tabernacle NJ 08088	609-268-1200	R	11*	.1
43	Vicam LP—*Jack Radlo*	34 Maple St, Milford MA 01757		S	10*	<.1
44	Corgenix Inc—*Douglas Simpson* Corgenix Medical Corp	11575 Main St Ste 400, Broomfield CO 80020	303-457-4345	D	9*	<.1
45	Teco Diagnostics—*K Chen*	1268 N Lakeview Ave, Anaheim CA 92807	714-463-1101	R	9*	.1
46	Epoch BioSciences Inc—*William G Gerber*	21720 23rd Dr SE Ste 1, Bothell WA 98021	425-482-5555	D	9	<.1
47	Gbf Inc—*Danny Bowman*	PO Box 16128, High Point NC 27261	336-665-0205	R	8*	.1
48	National Diagnostics Inc—*Lisa Mirsky*	305 Patton Dr, Atlanta GA 30336	404-699-2121	S	8*	.1
49	Litmus Concepts Inc—*Caren L Mason* Quidel Corp	2981 Copper Rd, Santa Clara CA 95051	408-616-4300	S	8*	<.1
50	Corgenix Medical Corp—*Douglass T Simpson*	11575 Main St Ste 400, Broomfield CO 80020	303-457-4345	P	8	<.1
51	Worthington Biochemical Corp—*Von Worthington*	730 Vassar Ave, Lakewood NJ 08701	732-942-1660	R	7*	.1
52	Agdia Inc—*Baziel Vrient*	30380 County Rd 6, Elkhart IN 46514	574-264-2014	R	7*	.1
53	Zymequest Inc—*Douglas Clibourn*	100 Cummings Ctr Ste 4, Beverly MA 01915	978-232-8370	R	6*	<.1

Rank	Company Name—Executive Officer	Address, City, State, Zip	Phone	Type	Fin	Empls
54	Biolog Inc—Barry Bochner	21124 Cabot Blvd, Hayward CA 94545	510-785-2564	R	6*	<.1
55	International Immunology Corp—Shunsaku Shibota	25549 Adams Ave, Murrieta CA 92562	951-677-5629	R	6*	<.1
56	Hemagen Diagnostics Inc—William P Hales	9033 Red Branch Rd, Columbia MD 21045	443-367-5500	P	5	<.1
57	Ostex International Inc—Thomas A Bologna Alere Inc	2203 Airport Way S Ste, Seattle WA 98134	206-292-8082	S	5*	<.1
58	Bio/Data Corp—Eugene Messa	155 Gibraltar Rd, Horsham PA 19044	215-441-4000	R	5*	<.1
59	Midland Bioproducts Corp—Richard Jorgenson	PO Box 309, Boone IA 50036	515-432-5516	R	5*	<.1
60	Immucell Corp—Michael F Brigham	56 Evergreen Dr, Portland ME 04103	207-878-2770	P	4	<.1
61	Oncogene Science of Siemens Healthcare Diagnostics Inc	100 Acorn Park Dr, Cambridge MA 02140	617-492-3900	S	4*	<.1
62	Antibodies Inc—Richard Krogsrud	PO Box 1560, Davis CA 95617	530-758-4400	R	4*	<.1
63	American Biological Technologies Inc—Michael Schrage	940 Crossroads Blvd, Seguin TX 78155	830-372-1391	R	3*	<.1
64	Genemed Synthesis Inc—Masarrat Ali	6203 Woodlake Ctr, San Antonio TX 78244	210-745-3417	R	3*	<.1
65	Innominata—Fred Adler	15222 Ave Of Science, San Diego CA 92128	858-592-9300	R	3*	<.1
66	Valley Biomedical Products and Services Inc—Mario Romano	121 Industrial Dr, Winchester VA 22602	540-868-0800	R	2*	<.1
67	Interleukin Genetics Inc—Lewis H Bender	135 Beaver St, Waltham MA 02452	781-398-0700	R	2	N/A
68	Microbiologics Inc—Brad Goskowicz	217 Osseo Ave N, Saint Cloud MN 56303	320-253-1640	R	2*	.1
69	AutoGenomics Inc—Fareed Kureshy	2980 Scott St, Vista CA 92081	760-477-2251	R	2	.1
70	Anatech Ltd—Ada Feldman	1020 Harts Lake Rd, Battle Creek MI 49037	269-964-6450	R	2*	<.1
71	Chematics Inc—William Woenker	PO Box 293, North Webster IN 46555	574-834-2406	R	1*	<.1
72	BIODESIGN International—John Kraeutler	60 Industrial Park Rd, Saco ME 04072	207-283-6500	R	1*	<.1
73	Bio-Medical Products Corp—John Geppert	10 Halstead Rd, Mendham NJ 07945	973-543-7434	R	1*	<.1
74	SCOLR Pharma Inc—Stephen J Turner	19204 N Creek Pkwy Ste, Bothell WA 98011	425-368-1050	P	1	<.1
75	ARCA Biopharma Inc—Michael R Brostow	8001 Arista Pl Ste 200, Broomfield CO 80021	720-940-2100	P	<1	<.1
76	Bioheart Inc—Mike Tomas	13794 NW 4th St Ste 21, Sunrise FL 33325	954-835-1500	P	<1	<.1
77	Capsalus Corp—Steven M Grubner	2675 Paces Ferry Rd St, Atlanta GA 30339		P	<1	<.1
78	Ore Pharmaceutical Holdings Inc—Mark Gabrielson	1 Main St Ste 300, Cambridge MA 02142	617-649-2001	P	<1	<.1
79	Alliance Pharmaceutical Corp—Duane J Roth	4660 La Jolla Village, San Diego CA 92122	858-779-1458	P	<1	<.1

TOTALS: SIC 2835 Diagnostic Substances
Companies: 79   39,488   36.9

2836 Biological Products Except Diagnostic

Rank	Company Name—Executive Officer	Address, City, State, Zip	Phone	Type	Fin	Empls
1	Gilead Sciences Inc—John C Martin	333 Lakeside Dr, Foster City CA 94404	650-574-3000	P	7,949	4.0
2	Biogen Idec Inc—George A Scangos	133 Boston Post Rd, Weston MA 02493	781-464-2000	P	4,716	4.9
3	Genzyme Corp—Henri A Termeer	500 Kendall St, Cambridge MA 02142	617-252-7500	P	4,049	10.1
4	Charles River Laboratories International Inc—James C Foster	251 Ballardvale St, Wilmington MA 01887	781-222-6000	P	1,143	7.1
5	Integra LifeSciences Holdings Corp—Stuart M Essig	311 Enterprise Dr, Plainsboro NJ 08536	609-275-0500	P	780	3.4
6	ImClone Systems, Inc—Bernard Ehmer MD	33 ImClone Dr, Branchburg NJ 08876	908-243-9945	S	591	1.1
7	Martek Biosciences Corp—Peter A Nitze	6480 Dobbin Rd, Columbia MD 21045	410-740-0081	P	450	.6
8	PDL BioPharma Inc—John McLaughlin	932 Southwood Blvd, Incline Village NV 89451	650-454-1000	P	362	<.1
9	Techne Corp—Thomas E Oland	614 McKinley Pl NE, Minneapolis MN 55413	612-379-8854	P	290	.8
10	Gilead Palo Alto Inc—John Martin Gilead Sciences Inc	33 Lakeside Drive, Foster City CA 94404	650-574-3000	S	155	.6
11	MedImmune Vaccines Inc—Peter Greenleaf	319 N Bernardo Ave, Mountain View CA 94043	650-603-2000	S	114*	.5
12	Seattle Genetics Inc—Clay B Siegall	21823 30th Dr SE, Bothell WA 98021	425-527-4000	P	108	.3
13	Intervet Inc—Paul Casady	PO Box 318, Millsboro DE 19966	302-934-8051	S	103*	.5
14	NPS Pharmaceuticals Inc—Francois Nader	550 Hills Dr 3rd Fl, Bedminster NJ 07921	908-450-5300	P	102	.1
15	Enzon Pharmaceuticals Inc—Ana I Stancic	20 Kingsbridge Rd, Piscataway NJ 08854	732-980-4500	P	98	.1
16	United Biomedical Inc—Chang Yi Wang PhD	25 Davids Dr, Hauppauge NY 11788	631-273-2828	R	87*	.1
17	Boehringer Ingelheim Vetmedica Inc—George Heidgerken	2621 N Belt Hwy, Saint Joseph MO 64506	816-233-2571	S	70*	.6
18	Nutrition 21 Inc—Michael A Zeher	4 Manhattanville Rd, Purchase NY 10577	914-701-4500	P	67	<.1
19	Heska Corp—Robert B Grieve	3760 Rocky Mountain Av, Loveland CO 80538	970-493-7272	P	66	.3
20	PharMingen—Edward Ludwig	10975 Torreyana Rd, San Diego CA 92121	858-812-8800	S	61	N/A
21	PML Microbiologicals Inc	27120 SW 95th Ave, Wilsonville OR 97070		S	56*	.2
22	Embrex Inc—Randall L Marcuson	PO Box 13989, Research Triangle Park NC 27709	919-941-5185	S	53*	.3
23	Fujirebio Diagnostics Inc—Paul Touhey	201 Great Valley Pky, Malvern PA 19355	610-240-3800	S	46*	.1
24	Clontech Laboratories Inc—Kazuki Yamamoto	1290 Terra Bella Ave, Mountain View CA 94043	650-919-7300	S	43*	.2
25	Solazyme Inc—Jonathan S Wolfson	225 Gateway Blvd, South San Francisco CA 94080	650-780-4777	P	38	.1
26	Neurocrine Biosciences Inc—Kevin C Gorman	12780 El Camino Real, San Diego CA 92130	858-617-7600	P	34	.1
27	Micromet Inc—Christian Itin	6707 Democracy Blvd St, Bethesda MD 20817	240-752-1420	P	29	.2
28	GenoSpectra Inc—Frank Witney	6519 Dumbarton Cir, Fremont CA 94555	510-818-2600	R	28*	.2
29	Repligen Corp—Walter C Herlihy	41 Seyon St Bldg 1 Ste, Waltham MA 02453	781-250-0111	P	27	.1
30	Synageva BioPharma Corp—Sanj K Patel	128 Spring St Ste 520, Lexington MA 02421	781-357-9900	P	27	<.1
31	Biomune Co—Ronald Plylar	8906 Rosehill Rd, Shawnee Mission KS 66215	913-894-0230	S	26*	.1
32	ARIAD Pharmaceuticals Inc—Harvey J Berger	26 Landsdowne St, Cambridge MA 02139	617-494-0400	P	25	.1
33	Bachem Inc—Phillip Ottiger	3132 Kashiwa St, Torrance CA 90505	310-784-4440	R	24*	.1
34	Innovative Medical Device Solutions—Brady Shirley	13600 Heritage Pkwy St, Fort Worth TX 76177		R	22*	.1
35	ImmunoVision Inc—Giorgio D'Urso	1820 Ford Ave, Springdale AR 72764		S	20*	<.1
36	BioCryst Pharmaceuticals Inc—Jon P Stonehouse	2190 Parkway Lake Dr, Birmingham AL 35244	205-444-4600	P	20	.1
37	Irvine Scientific Sales Company Inc—Juanita Stark	2511 Daimler St, Santa Ana CA 92705	949-261-7800	R	20*	.1
38	Santa Cruz Biotechnology Inc—John Stephenson	2145 Delaware Ave, Santa Cruz CA 95060	831-457-3800	R	19*	.1
39	Mediatech Inc—James Deolden	13884 Park Ctr Rd, Herndon VA 20171	703-471-5955	S	17*	.1
40	Idera Pharmaceuticals Inc—Sudhir Agrawal	167 Sidney St, Cambridge MA 02139	617-679-5500	P	16	<.1
41	Curis Inc—Daniel R Passeri	4 Maguire Rd, Lexington MA 02421	617-503-6500	P	16	<.1
42	Colorado Serum Co—Joseph Huff	PO Box 16428, Denver CO 80216	303-295-7527	R	16*	.1
43	ZymoGenetics Inc—Douglas E Williams PhD	1201 Eastlake Ave E, Seattle WA 98102	206-442-6600	S	15	.3
44	Greer Laboratories Inc—John Roby	PO Box 800, Lenoir NC 28645	828-754-5327	R	15*	.2
45	Antigenics Inc (Lexington Massachusetts)—Garo H Armen Antigenics Inc	3 Forbes Rd, Lexington MA 02421	781-674-4400	S	15*	.1
46	AmpliPhi Biosciences—Edward Cappabianca	601 Union St Ste 4200, Seattle WA 98101	206-623-7612	P	12	<.1
47	Momenta Pharmaceuticals Inc—Craig A Wheeler	675 W Kendall St, Cambridge MA 02142	617-491-9700	P	12	.2
48	Quality Biological Inc—Sol Graham	PO Box 5781, Derwood MD 20855	301-840-9331	R	11*	.1
49	Titan Pharmaceuticals Inc—Sunil Bhonsle	400 Oyster Point Blvd, South San Francisco CA 94080	650-244-4990	P	10	<.1
50	BioPro Corp—William A Carter Hemispherx Biopharma Inc	1617 JFK Blvd 6th Fl, Philadelphia PA 19103	215-988-0080	S	9*	<.1
51	Vical Inc—Vijay B Samant	10390 Pacific Center C, San Diego CA 92121	858-646-1100	P	8	.1
52	Zeptometrix Corp—James Hengst	872 Main St, Buffalo NY 14202	716-882-0920	R	8*	.1
53	Alliant Healthcare Products—Bob Taylor	8850 M-89, Richland MI 49083	269-629-0300	D	8	<.1
54	Kirkegaard and Perry Labs Inc—Albert Perry	910 Clopper Rd Ste 150, Gaithersburg MD 20878	301-948-7755	R	7*	<.1
55	MaxCyte Inc—Douglas Doerfler	22 Firstfield Rd Ste 2, Gaithersburg MD 20878	301-944-1700	R	7*	<.1

Note: An asterisk (*) indicates an estimated financial figure. The company type code used is as follows: R = Private, P = Public, S = Private Subsidiary, B = Public Subsidiary, D = Division, J = Joint Venture, I = Investment Fund.

COMPANY RANKINGS BY SALES WITHIN 4-DIGIT SIC

Rank	Company Name—Executive Officer	Address, City, State, Zip	Phone	Type	Fin	Empls
56	Champions Oncology Inc—Joel Ackerman	855 N Wolfe St Ste 619, Baltimore MD 21205	410-369-0365	P	7	<.1
57	Myogen Inc—John Martin / Gilead Sciences Inc	7577 W 103rd Ave Ste 2, Westminster CO 80021	303-410-6666	S	6*	.1
58	Archemix Corp—Errol De Souza PhD	300 3rd St, Cambridge MA 02139	617-621-7700	R	6*	.1
59	IGI Laboratories Inc—Charles E Moore	PO Box 687, Buena NJ 08310	856-697-1441	P	6	<.1
60	Pel-Freez Arkansas LLC—Dennis Almond	219 N Arkansas St, Rogers AR 72756	479-636-4361	R	5*	.1
61	Cocalico Biologicals Inc—Jeanette Whitesell	PO Box 265, Reamstown PA 17567	717-336-1990	R	5*	<.1
62	NeoMPS Inc—Serge Plaue	9395 Cabot Dr, San Diego CA 92126	858-408-0808	R	5*	<.1
63	Maine Biotechnology Services Inc—Joseph Chandler	1037R Forest Ave, Portland ME 04103	207-797-5454	R	5*	<.1
64	Allergy Laboratories Inc—Rebecca Johnson	PO Box 348, Oklahoma City OK 73101	405-235-1451	R	5*	<.1
65	Protatek International Inc—Roger Headrick	2635 University Ave W, Saint Paul MN 55114	651-644-5391	R	4*	<.1
66	AmPharmCo—Jerry Payne	1401 Joel East Rd, Fort Worth TX 76140	817-293-6363	R	4*	<.1
67	BioTime Inc—Michael West	1301 Harbor Bay Pkwy, Alameda CA 94502	510-521-3390	P	4	<.1
68	EntreMed Inc—Cynthia Wong Hu	9640 Medical Center Dr, Rockville MD 20850	240-864-2600	P	4	<.1
69	Scripps Laboratories Inc—Simon Khoury	6838 Flanders Dr, San Diego CA 92121	858-546-5800	R	4*	<.1
70	Antigenics Inc—Garo H Armen PhD	3 Forbes Rd, Lexington MA 02421	781-674-4400	P	3	.1
71	GTC Biotherapeutics Inc—William Heiden	175 Crossing Blvd, Framingham MA 01702	508-620-9700	R	3	.1
72	Mml Diagnostics Packaging Inc—Dale Pestes	PO Box 458, Troutdale OR 97060	503-666-8398	R	3*	<.1
73	Biosante Pharmaceuticals—Stephen M Simes	111 Barclay Blvd, Lincolnshire IL 60069	847-478-0500	P	3	<.1
74	Immtech Pharmaceuticals Inc—Eric Sorkin	1 N End Ave, New York NY 10282	212-791-2911	P	2	<.1
75	Addison Biological Laboratory Inc—Bruce Addison	507 N Cleveland St, Fayette MO 65248	660-248-2215	R	2*	<.1
76	Biolex Therapeutics Inc—Jan Turek	158 Credle St, Pittsboro NC 27312	919-542-9901	R	2*	<.1
77	ExOxEmis Inc—Jackson Stephens	111 Ctr St Ste 1616, Little Rock AR 72201	501-375-0940	R	2*	<.1
78	Clearant Inc—Michael Bartlett	6001 Lexington Park, Orlando FL 32819	310-479-4570	P	2	<.1
79	StemCells Inc—Martin M McGlynn	7707 Gateway Blvd Ste, Newark CA 94560	510-456-4000	P	1	<.1
80	CEL-SCI Corp—Geert R Kersten	8229 Boone Blvd Ste 80, Vienna VA 22182	703-506-9460	P	1	<.1
81	Fibrocell Science Inc—David Pernock	405 Eagleview Blvd, Exton PA 19341	484-713-6000	P	1	<.1
82	Immuno-Dynamics Inc—Richard H Cockrum	1800 Dodge St, Fennimore WI 53809	608-822-4150	R	1*	<.1
83	Protide Pharmaceuticals Inc—Milo R Polovina	505 Oakwood Rd Ste 200, Lake Zurich IL 60047	847-726-3100	P	1	<.1
84	Nabi Biopharmaceuticals—Raafat EF Fahim	12276 Wilkins Ave, Rockville MD 20852	301-770-3099	P	<1	<.1
85	Aldagen Inc—Lyle A Hohnke	2810 Meridian Pkwy Ste, Durham NC 27713	919-484-2571	R	<1	<.1
86	Novavax Inc—Stanley C Erck	9920 Belward Campus Dr, Rockville MD 20850	240-268-2000	P	<1	.1
87	Cybrdi Inc—Yanbiao Bai	14804 Physicians Ln St, Rockville MD 20850	301-838-8966	R	<1	N/A
88	Oncothyreon Inc—Robert L Kirkman	2601 4th Ave Ste 500, Seattle WA 98121	206-801-2100	P	<1	<.1
89	Genta Inc—Raymond P Warrell Jr	200 Connell Dr, Berkeley Heights NJ 07922	908-286-9800	P	<1	<.1
90	Symbollon Pharmaceuticals Inc—Paul C Desjourdy	99 West St Ste J, Medfield MA 02052	508-242-7500	P	<1	<.1
91	Vitro Diagnostics Inc—James R Musick	4621 Technology Dr, Golden CO 80403	303-999-2130	P	<1	<.1
92	Discovery Laboratories Inc—W Thomas Amick	2600 Kelly Rd Ste100, Warrington PA 18976	215-488-9300	P	<1	.1
93	Chelsea Therapeutics International Ltd—Simon Pedder PhD	3530 Toringdon Way Ste, Charlotte NC 28277	704-341-1516	P	<1	<.1
94	Hemispherx Biopharma Inc—William A Carter	1617 JFK Blvd 6th Fl, Philadelphia PA 19103	215-988-0080	P	<1	<.1
95	BioAegean Corp William A Carter / Hemispherx Biopharma Inc	1617 JFK Blvd 6th Fl, Philadelphia PA 19103	215-988-0080	S	<1	<.1
96	Core BioTech Corp—William A Carter / Hemispherx Biopharma Inc	1617 JFK Blvd 6th Fl, Philadelphia PA 19103	215-988-0080	S	<1	<.1
97	OXiGENE Inc—Peter Langecker	701 Gateway Blvd Ste 2, South San Francisco CA 94080	650-635-7000	P	<1	<.1
98	TrovaGene Inc—Antonius Schuh	11055 Flintkote Ave St, San Diego CA 92121	858-217-4838	P	<1	<.1
99	Insys Therapeutics Inc—Michael L Babich	10220 S 51st St Ste 2, Phoenix AZ 85044	602-910-2617	P	<1	<.1
100	CytRx Corp—Steven A Kriegsman	11726 San Vicente Blvd, Los Angeles CA 90049	310-826-5648	P	<1	<.1
101	Repros Therapeutics Inc—Joseph P Podolski	2408 Timberloch Pl Ste, The Woodlands TX 77380	281-719-3400	P	<1	<.1
102	VIA Pharmaceuticals Inc—Lawrence K Cohen	750 Battery St Ste 330, San Francisco CA 94111	415-283-2200	P	<1	<.1
103	Tamir Biotechnology Inc—Charles Muniz	11 Deer Park Dr Ste 20, Monmouth Junction NJ 08852	732-823-1003	P	<1	<.1
104	CytoGenix Inc—Lex M Cowsert	3100 Wilcrest Dr Ste14, Houston TX 77042	713-789-0070	P	<1	<.1
105	La Jolla Pharmaceutical Co—Diedre Gillespie	4370 La Jolla Village, San Diego CA 92122	858-452-6600	P	<1	<.1
106	GeneThera Inc	3930 Youngfield St, Wheat Ridge CO 80033	303-463-6371	P	<1	<.1
107	Cadus Corp—David Blitz	767 5th Ave, New York NY 10153	212-702-4351	P	<1	N/A

TOTALS: SIC 2836 Biological Products Except Diagnostic
Companies: 107 — 22,217 — 40.2

2841 Soap & Other Detergents

Rank	Company Name—Executive Officer	Address, City, State, Zip	Phone	Type	Fin	Empls
1	Procter and Gamble Co—Robert A McDonald	1 Procter and Gamble P, Cincinnati OH 45202	513-983-1100	P	82,599	129.0
2	Astor Products Inc	PO Box 2366, Jacksonville FL 32203	904-783-5000	S	26,119*	130.0
3	Colgate-Palmolive Co—Ian M Cook	300 Park Ave, New York NY 10022	212-310-2330	P	15,564	39.2
4	Sun Products Corp—Jeffrey P Ansell	60 Danbury Rd, Wilton CT 06897	203-254-6700	R	11,401*	3.5
5	Unilever United States Inc	700 Sylvan Ave, Englewood Cliffs NJ 07632		S	8,000	22.0
6	Ecolab Inc—Douglas M Baker Jr	370 N Wabasha St, Saint Paul MN 55102	651-293-2233	P	6,090	26.5
7	Abernathy Co—Ray Abernathy	3800 Abernathy Dr, Texarkana AR 71854	870-774-5103	R	135*	.1
8	State Industrial Products Corp—Harold Uhrman	3100 Hamilton Ave, Cleveland OH 44114	216-861-7114	R	117*	1.1
9	Kik Custom Products Inc—Paul Cummings	1 W Hegeler Ln, Danville IL 61832	217-442-1400	R	97*	.9
10	Softsoap Enterprises Inc	300 Park Ave 8th Fl, New York NY 10022	212-310-2080	R	83*	.2
11	ABC Compounding Company Inc—Stephen Walker	PO Box 16247, Atlanta GA 30321	770-968-9222	R	71*	.1
12	Selig Chemical Industries	PO Box 43106, Atlanta GA 30336	404-691-9320	D	53*	.1
13	Piedmont Chemical Industries Inc—Fred Wilson	PO Box 2728, High Point NC 27261	336-885-5131	R	51*	.3
14	Original Bradford Soap Works Inc—Eric Olson	200 Providence St, West Warwick RI 02893	401-821-2141	R	44*	.4
15	JF Daley International Ltd—John Daley	4100 W 76th St, Chicago IL 60652	773-284-9189	R	35*	.3
16	Stearns Packaging Corp—John B Everitt	PO Box 3216, Madison WI 53704	608-246-5150	R	35*	.1
17	Valley Products Co—Kenneth Roberts	384 E Brooks Rd, Memphis TN 38109	901-396-9646	R	32*	.2
18	Cleaning Systems Inc—David Krause	PO Box 5606, De Pere WI 54115	920-337-2175	R	27*	<.1
19	Blue Cross Laboratories Inc	20950 Centre Pointe Pk, Santa Clarita CA 91350	661-255-0955	R	25*	.1
20	Bullen Midwest Inc—James Flanagan	900 E 103rd St Ste D, Chicago IL 60628	773-785-2300	R	24*	.1
21	Mt Hood Solutions Co—Tom Mulflur	14546 N Lombard St, Portland OR 97203	503-227-3505	R	23*	.1
22	Sani-Co Products—Gerald K Unick	PO Box 535, Agoura Hills CA 91376	818-706-2229	R	19*	<.1
23	Essential Industries Inc—Michael Wheeler	PO Box 12, Merton WI 53056	262-538-1122	R	18*	.1
24	Stone Soap Company Inc—Kenneth Stone	2000 Pontiac Dr, Sylvan Lake MI 48320	248-706-1000	R	18*	.1
25	Glissen Chemical Company Inc—Joseph Lehr	PO Box 190034, Brooklyn NY 11219	718-436-4200	R	15*	.1
26	Circle - Prosco Inc—Douglas Parker	401 N Gates Dr, Bloomington IN 47404	812-339-3653	P	14*	.1
27	Gurtler Chemicals Inc—William Gurtler	15475 La Salle St, South Holland IL 60473	708-331-2550	R	14*	.1
28	KO Manufacturing Inc—John Cunningham	PO Box 3574, Springfield MO 65808	417-866-8000	R	12*	.1
29	Stanson Corp—Robert Holuba	2 N Hackensack Ave, Kearny NJ 07032	973-344-8666	R	11*	.1
30	Ardex Laboratories Inc—Steve Goldman	2050 Byberry Rd, Philadelphia PA 19116	215-698-0500	R	11*	.1
31	Creative Aerosol Corp—James Mulligan	PO Box 118, Adelphia NJ 07710	732-431-7500	R	11*	<.1

Rank	Company Name—*Executive Officer*	Address, City, State, Zip	Phone	Type	Fin	Empls
32	Cul-Mac Industries Inc—*William Laughlin*	3720 Venoy Rd, Wayne MI 48184	734-728-9700	R	10*	.1
33	MD Stetson Company Inc—*Michael Glass*	PO Box 259, Randolph MA 02368	781-986-6161	R	10*	<.1
34	Concord Chemical Company Inc—*John Faucette*	1700 Federal St, Camden NJ 08105	856-966-1526	R	9*	<.1
35	Snee Chemical Co—*Linda Hartwell*	5565 Pepsi St, Harahan LA 70123	504-734-7633	R	7*	<.1
36	Mansfield-King Inc—*Charles Haywood*	6501 Julian Ave, Indianapolis IN 46219	317-788-0750	R	7	<.1
37	Certol International LLC—*Edward Cassinis*	6120 E 58th Ave, Commerce City CO 80022	303-799-9401	R	7*	<.1
38	Pharmacal Research Labs Inc—*Kenneth Shapiro*	PO Box 369, Naugatuck CT 06770	203-755-4908	R	7*	<.1
39	Abc Corp—*Gavin Morisada*	94-085 Leonui St, Waipahu HI 96797	808-671-2671	R	7*	<.1
40	R Square Products Inc—*Lowery Tillison*	2675 Monroe Dr, Gainesville GA 30507	770-536-5462	R	6*	<.1
41	Blachford Corp—*John Blachford*	401 Ctr Rd, Frankfort IL 60423	815-464-2100	R	5*	<.1
42	Sky Blue Industries Inc—*Steven Griffin*	PO Box 187, Ogden UT 84402	801-394-2808	R	5*	<.1
43	Cleanlook Chemical Corp—*Marcelo Rodriguez*	14939 Nw 27th Ave, Opa Locka FL 33054	305-687-1171	R	5*	<.1
44	C and H Chemical Inc—*Bill Cammack*	222 Starkey St, Saint Paul MN 55107	651-227-4343	R	4*	<.1
45	Value Products Inc—*Douglas Hall*	2128 Industrial Dr, Stockton CA 95206	209-983-4000	R	4*	<.1
46	Gent-L-Kleen Products Inc—*James Strickler*	3445 Board Rd, York PA 17406	717-767-6881	R	4*	<.1
47	Wepak Corp—*Robert Poffenbarger*	PO Box 36803, Charlotte NC 28236	704-334-5781	R	4*	<.1
48	America's Finest Products Corp—*Frank Kagarakis*	1639 9th St, Santa Monica CA 90404	310-450-6555	R	3*	<.1
49	National Purity Inc—*Sean Spillane*	6840 Shingle Creek Pkw, Minneapolis MN 55430	612-672-0022	R	3*	<.1
50	Exsl/Ultra Labs Inc—*Jon Tooper*	30921 Wiegman Ct, Hayward CA 94544	510-324-4567	R	3*	<.1
51	Dsm Industries Inc—*Scott Soble*	1340 E 289th St, Wickliffe OH 44092	440-585-1100	R	2*	<.1
52	Aldas LLC—*William G Ellis*	PO Box 45504, Little Rock AR 72214	501-565-2900	R	2*	<.1
53	Lerro Products Inc—*Dan Albanese*	PO Box 21840, Philadelphia PA 19146	215-732-9120	R	2*	<.1
54	Alconox Inc	30 Glenn St Ste 309, White Plains NY 10603	914-948-4040	R	2*	<.1
55	Unichem Corp—*Eugene Korey*	1201 W 37th St, Chicago IL 60609	773-376-8873	R	2*	<.1
56	Caravan Technologies Inc—*Christie Dolar*	3033 Bourke St, Detroit MI 48238	313-341-2551	R	1*	<.1
57	National Chemicals Inc—*L Charles*	PO Box 32, Winona MN 55987	507-454-5640	R	1*	<.1
58	Oneill Industries Inc—*Robert O'neill*	5101 Comly St Ste 1, Philadelphia PA 19135	215-333-5700	R	1*	<.1
59	Liquid Soap Products—*Douglas Glascock*	707 Sw 10th St, Blue Springs MO 64015.	816-228-9083	R	<1*	<.1

TOTALS: SIC 2841 Soap & Other Detergents
Companies: 59   150,888   355.4

2842 Polishes & Sanitation Goods

Rank	Company Name—*Executive Officer*	Address, City, State, Zip	Phone	Type	Fin	Empls
1	SC Johnson and Son Inc—*H Fisk Johnson*	1525 Howe St, Racine WI 53403	262-260-2000	R	8,750	12.0
2	Clorox Co—*Donald R Knauss*	1221 Broadway, Oakland CA 94612	510-271-7000	P	5,231	8.1
3	Church and Dwight Company Inc—*James R Craigie*	409 N Harrison St, Princeton NJ 08540	009-083-5900	P	2,749	3.5
4	Virginia Kik Inc—*David Cynamon*	PO Box 660, Salem VA 24153	540-389-5401	R	1,670*	.1
5	NCH Corp	PO Box 152170, Irving TX 75015	972-438-0211	R	688*	8.5
6	Zep Inc—*John K Morgan*	1310 Seaboard Industri, Atlanta GA 30318	404-355-3120	P	646	2.3
7	Arch Specialty Chemicals Inc—*Michael E Campbell*	70 Tyler Pl, South Plainfield NJ 07080	908-561-5200	S	597*	1.2
8	Turtle Wax Inc—*Denis J Healy Jr*	PO Box 247, Westmont IL 60559		R	484*	.9
9	Reckitt Benckiser LLC—*Rob Groot*	PO Box 225, Parsippany NJ 07054	973-404-2600	R	205*	1.6
10	Clorox International Co—*Warwick Every-Burns*	PO Box 24305, Oakland CA 94623	510-271-7000	R	147*	1.4
11	Rycoline Products LLC	PO Box 97043, Chicago IL 60690	773-775-6755	R	106*	.1
12	DuPont EKC Technology Inc—*John Odom*	2520 Barrington Ct, Hayward CA 94545	510-784-9105	S	77	.2
13	Oil-Dri Corporation Of Georgia—*Daniel Jaffee*	PO Box 200A, Ochlocknee GA 31773	229-574-5131	S	77*	.2
14	Claire Manufacturing Company Inc—*John Ferring*	1005 S Westgate Ave, Addison IL 60101	630-543-7600	R	75*	.1
15	Gojo Industries Inc—*Mark Lerner*	PO Box 991, Akron OH 44309	330-255-6000	R	69*	.6
16	Spartan Chemical Co (Toledo Ohio)—*Stephen H Swigart*	1110 Spartan Dr, Maumee OH 43537	419-531-5551	R	68*	.2
17	Faultless Starch/Bon Ami Co—*David Beaham*	1025 W 8th St, Kansas City MO 64101	816-842-1230	R	60*	.1
18	Hillyard Inc—*Bob Roth*	PO Box 909, Saint Joseph MO 64502	816-233-1321	R	55*	.2
19	Cookson Electronics Assembly Materials Group—*Dan Weaver*	4100 6th Ave, Altoona PA 16602	814-946-1611	D	54*	.1
20	Buckeye International Inc—*Kristopher Kosup*	2700 Wagner Pl, Maryland Heights MO 63043	314-291-1900	R	52*	.1
21	Tech Spray LP—*David Boysen*	PO Box 949, Amarillo TX 79105	806-372-8523	S	50*	.1
22	Absorption Corp—*Doug Ellis*	6960 Salashan Pky, Ferndale WA 98248	360-734-7415	S	47*	.1
23	Sunshine Makers Inc—*Bruce FaBrizio*	15922 Pacific Coast Hw, Huntington Beach CA 92649	562-795-6000	R	46*	.1
24	Canberra Corp—*R Yacko*	3610 Holland Sylvania, Toledo OH 43615	419-841-6616	R	41*	.2
25	Armor All/STP Products Co	PO Box 24305, Oakland CA 94623	510-271-7000	R	39	.1
26	Apollo Industries Inc—*Maria Callas*	1850 S Cobb Industrial, Smyrna GA 30082	770-433-0210	R	36*	.2
27	Gage Products Co—*Robert Jamrog*	821 Wanda Ave, Ferndale MI 48220	248-541-3824	R	36*	.1
28	Champion Packaging and Distribution Inc—*Thomas Pecora*	1840 Internationale Pk, Woodridge IL 60517	630-972-0100	R	34*	.2
29	Chemical Specialties Manufacturing Corp	901 N Newkirk St, Baltimore MD 21205	410-675-4800	S	34*	.1
30	R R Street and Company Inc—*L Beard*	184 Shuman Blvd Ste 15, Naperville IL 60563	630-416-4244	R	31*	.2
31	Magic American Corp	26901 Cannon Rd, Bedford Heights OH 44146		S	31*	.1
32	Car-Freshner Corp—*Richard Flechtner*	PO Box 719, Watertown NY 13601	315-788-6250	R	30*	.3
33	Momar Inc—*Julian Mohr*	1830 Ellsworth Industr, Atlanta GA 30318	404-355-4580	R	30*	.2
34	Aire-Master of America Inc—*Douglas McCauley*	PO Box 2310, Nixa MO 65714	417-725-2691	R	30*	.1
35	Dober Chemical Corp—*John Dobrez*	11230 Katherine Xing, Downers Grove IL 60517	630-410-7300	R	30*	.1
36	Hillyard Industries Inc—*Jim Carolus*	PO Box 909, Saint Joseph MO 64502	816-383-8333	R	29*	.2
37	Oil-Dri Production Co—*Daniel S Jaffee*	PO Box 476, Ripley MS 38663	662-837-9263	D	29*	.1
38	Connoisseurs Products Corp—*Douglas Dorfman*	17 Presidential Dr, Woburn MA 01801	781-932-3949	R	28*	.1
39	Ocean Bio-Chem Inc—*Peter G Dornau*	4041 SW 47th Ave, Fort Lauderdale FL 33314	954-587-6280	P	27	.1
40	Delta Foremost Chemical Corp—*Ronald Cooper*	PO Box 30310, Memphis TN 38130	901-363-4340	R	27*	.2
41	Goodwin Ammonia Co—*Tom Goodwin*	12102 Industry St, Garden Grove CA 92841	714-894-0531	R	27*	.2
42	Brulin and Company Inc—*Charles Pollnow*	PO Box 270, Indianapolis IN 46206	317-923-3211	R	25*	.2
43	Matchless Metal Polish—*Frank Ungari*	840 West 49th Place, Chicago IL 60609	773-924-1515	R	25*	.1
44	Penetone Corp—*Elwood Phares*	700 Gotham Pkwy Ste 2, Carlstadt NJ 07072	201-567-3000	R	24*	.1
45	Chemstation International Inc—*George Homan*	3400 Encrete Ln, Dayton OH 45439	937-294-8265	R	23*	<.1
46	Koster Keunen Manufacturing Inc—*John Koster*	PO Box 69, Watertown CT 06795	860-945-3333	R	23*	.1
47	Atco Manufacturing Co—*Jerry Tillem*	1401 Barclay Cir Se, Marietta GA 30060	770-424-7550	R	23*	.1
48	Anderson Chemical Co—*Terry Anderson*	PO Box 1041, Litchfield MN 55355	320-693-2477	R	22*	.1
49	Continental Manufacturing	305 Rock Industrial Pa, Bridgeton MO 63044		S	21	.1
50	Athea Laboratories Inc—*Thomas Jardins* Share Corp	PO Box 240014, Milwaukee WI 53224	414-354-6417	S	21*	.1
51	Misco Products Corp—*Steven Gable*	1048 Stinson Dr, Reading PA 19605	610-926-4106	R	21*	.1
52	Conklin Company Inc—*Charles Herbster*	PO Box 155, Shakopee MN 55379	952-445-6010	R	20*	.1
53	Intercon Chemical Co—*James Epstein*	1100 Central Industria, Saint Louis MO 63110	314-771-6600	R	20*	.1
54	Crescent Marketing Inc—*Richard Frazer*	PO Box 1500, North Collins NY 14111	716-337-0145	R	19*	.1
55	Continental Research Corp—*Thomas Epstein*	PO Box 15204, Saint Louis MO 63110		R	19*	.1
56	Midlab Inc—*Jorge Nieri*	232 Industrial Park Rd, Sweetwater TN 37874	423-337-3180	R	19*	.1

Note: An asterisk (*) indicates an estimated financial figure. The company type code used is as follows: R = Private, P = Public, S = Private Subsidiary, B = Public Subsidiary, D = Division, J = Joint Venture, I = Investment Fund.

COMPANY RANKINGS BY SALES WITHIN 4-DIGIT SIC

Rank	Company Name—Executive Officer	Address, City, State, Zip	Phone	Type	Fin	Empls
57	NYCO Products Co—Robert Stahurski	5332 Dansher Rd, Countryside IL 60525	708-579-8100	R	19*	<.1
58	Safeguard Chemical Corp—Poozant Piranian	411 Wales Ave, Bronx NY 10454	718-585-3170	R	17*	.1
59	Pro-Clean Of Arizona Inc—Richard Chiate	PO Box 18250, Phoenix AZ 85005	602-233-0457	R	17*	.1
60	Natural Gas Odorizing Inc	PO Box 1429, Baytown TX 77522	281-424-5568	S	17*	<.1
61	Questvapco Corp—Carl Hubble	12255 Fm 529 Rd, Houston TX 77041	713-896-8188	R	17*	.1
62	Morgan Gallacher Inc—David Smith	8707 Millergrove Dr, Santa Fe Springs CA 90670	562-695-1232	R	16*	<.1
63	Poloplaz—Mac Hogan	1 Paradise Park Rd, Jacksonville AR 72076	501-985-1172	R	16*	.1
64	National Products LLC	PO Box 1701, La Porte IN 46352	219-393-5536	R	16*	.1
65	Cpc Aeroscience Inc—Terry Colker	PO Box 667770, Pompano Beach FL 33066	954-974-5440	R	15*	.1
66	RPS Products Inc—Richard P Schuld	281 Keyes Ave, Hampshire IL 60140	847-683-3400	R	15*	.1
67	Premiere Packaging Inc—Mark Drolet	6220 Lehman Dr, Flint MI 48507	810-239-7650	R	15*	.1
68	Granitize Products Inc—Tony Raymondo	PO Box 2306, South Gate CA 90280	562-923-5438	R	14*	.1
69	Share Corp—Thomas Jardins	7821 N Faulkner Rd, Milwaukee WI 53224	414-355-4000	R	13*	.2
70	Shepard Brothers Inc—Ron Shepard	503 S Cypress St, La Habra CA 90631	562-697-1366	R	13*	.1
71	Sunburst Chemicals Inc—Robert Laughlin	220 W 86th St, Minneapolis MN 55420	952-884-3144	R	12*	.1
72	Adco Inc—Charles Van Dyne	PO Box 999, Sedalia MO 65302	660-826-3300	R	12*	.1
73	Microban Products Co—David Mayers	11400 Vanstory Dr, Huntersville NC 28078	704-875-0806	R	11*	.1
74	ECT Inc—Bruce Tassone	401 E 4th St Bldg 20, Bridgeport PA 19405	610-239-5120	R	11*	<.1
75	Vin-Dotco Inc	6970 Jonesboro Rd, Morrow GA 30260	770-968-9222	S	11*	<.1
76	Matchless Metal Polish Co—Frank Ungari	PO Box 88494, Chicago IL 60680	773-924-1515	R	11*	.1
77	Elco Laboratories Inc—Norman Elliott	2545 Palmer Ave, University Park IL 60484	708-534-3000	R	10*	.1
78	Milazzo Industries Inc—Joseph Milazzo	1609 River Rd, Pittston PA 18640	570-654-2433	R	10*	<.1
79	Reed Union Corp—Peter Goldman	875 N Michigan Ste 371, Chicago IL 60611	312-644-3200	R	10*	<.1
80	Delta Carbona LP—Tim Wells	376 Hollywood Ave Ste, Fairfield NJ 07004	973-808-6260	R	10*	<.1
81	Servaas Laboratories Inc—Paul Vass	5240 Walt Pl, Indianapolis IN 46254	317-636-7760	R	10*	<.1
82	Kyzen Corp—Kyle J Doyel	430 Harding Industrial, Nashville TN 37211	615-831-0888	P	10	<.1
83	Finger Lakes Chemicals Inc—Ewald Blatter	420 Saint Paul St, Rochester NY 14605	585-454-4760	R	10*	.1
84	Roebic Laboratories Inc—Stuart Bush	PO Box 927, Orange CT 06477	203-795-1283	R	10*	.1
85	Baf Industries—Otis Bell	1451 Edinger Ave Ste F, Tustin CA 92780	714-258-8055	R	9*	.1
86	Gulf Coast Chemical Inc—Jim Fusilier	PO Box 1810, Abbeville LA 70511	337-740-7414	R	9*	<.1
87	Mission Laboratories—Robert Rosenbaum	2433 Birkdale St, Los Angeles CA 90031	323-223-1405	R	9*	<.1
88	Rockland Corp (Tulsa Oklahoma)—Elmer Heinrich	12320 E Skelly Dr, Tulsa OK 74128	918-437-7310	R	9*	<.1
89	Kor-Chem Inc—John Fitzwater	PO Box 43163, Atlanta GA 30336	404-344-9580	R	9	<.1
90	Fukken Wax—Jim Schafter	9021 Gittins St, Commerce Township MI 48382		R	9*	<.1
91	Protect All Inc—Adam Huber	1910 E Via Burton St, Anaheim CA 92806	714-635-4491	R	9*	<.1
92	Surtec Inc—William Fields	1880 N Macarthur Dr, Tracy CA 95376	209-820-3700	R	9*	.1
93	Veltek Associates Inc—Arthur Vellutato	15 Lee Blvd, Malvern PA 19355	610-644-8335	R	8*	.1
94	Fresh Products Inc—Douglas Brown	4010 S Ave, Toledo OH 43615	419-531-9741	R	8*	.1
95	Metrotech Chemicals Inc—Joseph Gigler	2101 Wilkinson Blvd, Charlotte NC 28208	704-525-3600	R	8*	.1
96	Envirochem Inc—Deborah Gildersleeve	425 Whitehead Ave, South River NJ 08882	732-238-6700	R	8*	.1
97	Flo-Kem Inc—Thomas Cole	19402 S Susana Rd, Compton CA 90221	310-632-7124	R	8*	<.1
98	Detco Industries Inc—Edmond Elliot	PO Box 430, Conway AR 72033	501-329-6965	R	7*	.1
99	A and L Laboratories Inc—Roger Beers	1001 Glenwood Ave, Minneapolis MN 55405	612-374-9141	R	7*	<.1
100	Orange Sol Blending and Packaging Inc—Stephen Farnsworth	PO Box 306, Chandler AZ 85244	480-497-8822	R	7*	<.1
101	Omaha Compound Co—Todd Manvitz	2001 Nicholas St, Omaha NE 68102	402-346-7117	R	7*	<.1
102	Senoret Chemical Co—Thomas Kraatz	566 Leffingwell Ave, Saint Louis MO 63122	314-966-2394	R	7*	<.1
103	Duchem Industries Inc	370 N Wabasha St, St Paul MN 55102	651-292-2233	S	7*	<.1
104	Natural Chemistry Inc—Robert J Kulperger	40 Richards Ave 2nd Fl, Norwalk CT 06854	203-295-2300	R	7*	<.1
105	Andrea Aromatics Inc—Richard D'andrea	PO Box 3091, Princeton NJ 08543	609-695-7710	R	7*	<.1
106	Air-Scent International—Arnold Zlotnik	290 Alpha Dr 298, Pittsburgh PA 15238	412-252-2000	R	7*	<.1
107	Treatment Products Ltd—Charles Victor	4701 W Augusta Blvd, Chicago IL 60651	773-626-8888	R	7*	.1
108	Calwax LLC—Robert Weil	5367 Ayon Ave, Irwindale CA 91706	626-969-4334	R	7*	<.1
109	Whink Products Co—Steve Throssel	PO Box 230, Eldora IA 50627	641-939-2353	R	6*	.1
110	Peerless Materials Co—Louis Buty	PO Box 33228, Los Angeles CA 90033	323-266-0313	R	6*	<.1
111	Strahl and Pitsch Inc—William Deluca	PO Box 1098, West Babylon NY 11704	631-587-9000	R	6*	<.1
112	WJ Hagerty and Sons Limited Inc—Debra Hagerty	PO Box 1496, South Bend IN 46624	574-288-4991	R	6*	<.1
113	Harri Hoffmann Co—Lorraine Hoffmann	PO Box 510856, Milwaukee WI 53203	414-276-6190	R	6*	<.1
114	Alpha Chemical Services Inc—Mark Juckett	PO Box 431, Stoughton MA 02072	781-344-8688	R	6*	<.1
115	Pine Glow Products Inc—Robert Diehl	PO Box 429, Rolesville NC 27571	919-556-7787	R	6*	<.1
116	B and B Tritech Inc—William Brock	PO Box 660776, Miami Springs FL 33266	305-888-5247	R	5*	<.1
117	Crain Chemical Company Inc—Bob Queen	PO Box 540995, Dallas TX 75354	214-358-3301	R	5*	<.1
118	Empire Chemical Company Inc—Robert Cronyn	12821 S Figueroa St, Los Angeles CA 90061	310-715-6500	R	5*	<.1
119	Slide Products Inc—Jim Harms	PO Box 156, Wheeling IL 60090	847-541-7220	R	5*	<.1
120	Jiffy-Jr Products—Jan Adamczak	6870 Shingle Creek Pkw, Brooklyn Center MN 55430	763-560-1964	R	5*	<.1
121	Nilodor Inc—Les Mitson	PO Box 660, Bolivar OH 44612	330-874-1017	R	5*	<.1
122	PDQ Manufacturing Inc—Walter Drost	201 Victory Cir, Ellijay GA 30540	706-636-1848	R	5*	<.1
123	Paramount Chemical Specialties Inc—John Latta	PO Box 124, Redmond WA 98073	425-882-2673	R	5*	<.1
124	Abco Manufacturing Inc—Arnold Zlotnick	290-298 Alpha Dr, Pittsburgh PA 15238	412-252-2200	R	4*	.1
125	Handi-Clean Products Inc—Clark Bunting	PO Box 988, Greensboro NC 27402	336-292-3083	R	4*	<.1
126	Novus Inc—Keith Beveridge	12800 Hwy 13 S Ste 500, Savage MN 55378	952-944-8152	R	4*	<.1
127	ChemFree Corp—J Leland Strange	8 Meca Way, Norcross GA 30093	770-564-5580	S	4*	<.1
128	Biochem Systems Inc—William R Nath	PO Box 47610, Wichita KS 67201	316-838-4739	R	4*	<.1
129	Benchmark Inc—Richard Cook	PO Box 401588, Redford MI 48240	313-863-0900	S	4*	<.1
130	Fabritec International Corp—John Jordan	1157 Industrial Rd, Cold Spring KY 41076	859-781-8200	R	4*	<.1
131	Orchem Corp—Oscar Robertson	4293 Mulhauser Rd, Fairfield OH 45014	513-874-9700	R	4*	<.1
132	Big "d" Industries Inc—Donald Lees	PO Box 82219, Oklahoma City OK 73148	405-682-2541	R	4*	<.1
133	Chemclean Corp—Bernard Esquenet	13045 180th St, Jamaica NY 11434	718-525-4500	R	4*	<.1
134	Walex Products Company Inc—Bob Williams	PO Box 3785, Wilmington NC 28406	910-371-2242	R	4*	<.1
135	Flitz International Ltd—Peter Jentzsch	821 Mohr Ave, Waterford WI 53185	262-534-5898	R	4	<.1
136	Pci Inc—Charles Von Doersten	10800 Baur Blvd, Saint Louis MO 63132	314-872-9333	R	3*	<.1
137	Knapp Manufacturing Inc—Michael Knapp	5227 E Pine Ave, Fresno CA 93727	559-251-8254	S	3*	<.1
138	Chemco Corp—Paul Lewis	300 Canal St Ste 2, Lawrence MA 01840	978-687-9000	R	3*	<.1
139	Kuhn and Sons Inc—Richard Kuhn	210 S Morton Ave, Evansville IN 47713	812-424-8268	R	3*	<.1
140	Amodex Products Inc—Sylvia Fatse	PO Box 3332, Bridgeport CT 06605	203-335-1255	R	3*	<.1
141	Chemtron Inc—Blake Young	PO Box 383, Lorton VA 22199	703-550-7772	R	3*	<.1
142	Argo and Company Inc—Anne Sanders	PO Box 2747, Spartanburg SC 29304	864-583-9769	R	3*	<.1
143	Troy Chemical Industries Inc—Lee Imhof	PO Box 430, Burton OH 44021	440-834-4408	R	3*	<.1
144	Kinzua Environmental Inc—Bradley Waxman	1176 E 38th St, Cleveland OH 44114	216-881-4040	R	3*	<.1
145	JIT Packaging LLC—Michael Parnell	10 Gunnebo Dr, Lonoke AR 72086	501-676-2994	R	3*	<.1
146	Finney Company Inc—Allan Krysan	8075 215th St W, Lakeville MN 55044	952-469-6699	R	3*	<.1

Rank	Company Name—Executive Officer	Address, City, State, Zip	Phone	Type	Fin	Empls
147	Veridien Corp—Sheldon Fenton	1100 4th St N Ste 202-, St Petersburg FL 33701	727-576-1600	P	3	<.1
148	Rexford Rand Corp—Albert Ancel	PO Box 9005, Michigan City IN 46361	219-872-5561	R	2*	<.1
149	Capital Soap Products LLC—A Kretz	PO Box 357, Paterson NJ 07544	973-333-6100	R*	2*	<.1
150	King Research Inc—Bernard King	114 12th St, Brooklyn NY 11215	718-788-0122	R	2*	<.1
151	Paragon Household Products Inc—Raymond Creary	PO Box 2031, Wayne NJ 07474	973-591-0777	R	2*	<.1
152	Arrow Chemical Corp—Sherry Bernstein	28 Rider Pl, Freeport NY 11520	516-377-7770	R	2*	<.1
153	Quip Laboratories Inc—Tim Hidell	1500 Eastlawn Ave, Wilmington DE 19802	302-761-2600	R	2*	<.1
154	Dynasol Inc—Jacob Fleshel	330 Pine St, Canton MA 02021	781-821-8888	R	2*	<.1
155	Nwp Manufacturing Inc—John Werner	23546 Us Hwy 224, Alvada OH 44802	419-894-6871	R	2*	<.1
156	Dura Wax Co—Brian Schwerman	4101 W Albany St, Mchenry IL 60050	815-385-5000	R	2*	<.1
157	A J Funk and Co—Richard Lane	1471 Timber Dr, Elgin IL 60123	847-741-6760	R	2*	<.1
158	Shore Corp—Stuart Hammerschm	2917 Spruce Way, Pittsburgh PA 15201	412-471-3330	R	2*	<.1
159	Controlled Release Technologies Inc—Lynn Burkhart	1016 Industry Dr, Shelby NC 28152	704-487-0878	R	2*	<.1
160	Crucible Chemical Co—Robert Wilson	PO Box 6786, Greenville SC 29606	864-277-1284	R	2*	<.1
161	International Chemical Co—Donald Pelham	2628 N Mascher St 30, Philadelphia PA 19133	215-739-2313	R	2*	<.1
162	Qualitex Co—Harry Campagna	4248 N Elston Ave, Chicago IL 60618	773-463-6777	R	2*	<.1
163	Sanitek Products Inc—Robert Moseley	3959 Goodwin Ave, Los Angeles CA 90039	323-245-6781	R	2*	<.1
164	Angelus Shoe Polish Company Inc—Paul Angelus	PO Box 3066, Cerritos CA 90703	562-229-0521	R	1*	<.1
165	Walter G Legge Company Inc—Walter Wowtschuk	444 Central Ave, Peekskill NY 10566	914-737-5040	R	1*	<.1
166	Grav Company LLC—David Scheetz	PO Box 599, Sturgis MI 49091	269-651-5467	R	1*	<.1
167	Texas Nova-Chem Corp—Billy Self	1830 E Interstate 30 S, Rockwall TX 75087	972-771-1161	R	1*	<.1
168	Nuvite Chemical Compounds Corp—Clifford Lester	213 Freeman St 215, Brooklyn NY 11222	718-383-8351	R	1*	<.1
169	Apex Engineering Products Corp—Eric Ostermeier	1241 Shoreline Dr, Aurora IL 60504	630-820-8888	R	1*	<.1
170	Rooto Corp—Joon Moon	3505 W Grand River Ave, Howell MI 48855	517-546-8330	R	1*	<.1
171	Chemical Systems Inc—Kurt Criter	16401 E 33rd Dr Unit 3, Aurora CO 80011	303-371-7342	R	1*	<.1
172	Winfield Brooks Company Inc—Winnfield Perry	70 Connecticut St, Woburn MA 01801	781-933-5300	R	1*	<.1
173	Aztron Chemical Services Inc—Dennis Megarity	4530 New W Rd, Pasadena TX 77507	281-474-2227	R	1*	<.1
174	John Lincoln Co—Manfred Rice	172 Commercial St, Sunnyvale CA 94086	408-732-5120	R	1*	<.1
175	Unit Chemical Corp—Ray Chaplar	7360 Commercial Way, Henderson NV 89011	702-564-6454	R	1*	<.1
176	Orange-Mate Inc—Steve Estabrooks	PO Box 883, Waldport OR 97394	541-563-3290	R	1*	<.1
177	Huff Industries Inc—Bryan Huff	PO Box 2407, Corinth MS 38835	662-286-2408	R	1*	<.1
178	Edwards Creative Products Inc—Charles Cohen	910 Beechwood Ave, Cherry Hill NJ 08002	856-665-3200	R	1*	<.1
179	American Jetway Corp—Gordon Jones	34136 Myrtle St, Wayne MI 48184	734-721-5930	R	<1*	.1
180	Santeen Supply Co—Bernard Feltes	1321 7th St S, Hopkins MN 55343	952-935-4500	R	<1*	<.1

TOTALS: SIC 2842 Polishes & Sanitation Goods
Companies: 180 — 23,663 — 50.0

2843 Surface Active Agents

Rank	Company Name—Executive Officer	Address, City, State, Zip	Phone	Type	Fin	Empls
1	Stepan Co—F Quinn Stepan Jr	22 W Frontage Rd, Northfield IL 60093	847-446-7500	P	1,843	1.8
2	Pilot Chemical Corp—Paul Morrisroe	2744 E Kemper Rd, Cincinnati OH 45241	513-326-0600	R	126*	.2
3	Goulston Technologies Inc—Gordon Magee	PO Box 5025, Monroe NC 28111	704-289-6464	R	65*	.1
4	Lonmar Chomical Corp—J Price	PO Box 571, Dalton GA 30722	706-277-9505	R	18*	<.1
5	Nicca USA Inc—Masakazu Shimada	1044 S Nelson Dr, Fountain Inn SC 29644	864-862-1426	H	18*	<.1
6	Atlas Refinery Inc—Steven Schroeder	142 Lockwood St, Newark NJ 07105	973-589-2002	R	16*	<.1
7	Chemguard Inc—Roger Bower	204 S 6th Ave, Mansfield TX 76063	817-473-9964	R	14*	.1
8	Avatar Corp—Michael Shamie	500 Central Ave, University Park IL 60484	708-534-5511	R	10*	<.1
9	Pariser Industries Inc—Albert Pariser	91 Michigan Ave, Paterson NJ 07503	973-569-9090	R	8*	<.1
10	Cht R Beitlich Corp—Theodore Dickson	PO Box 240497, Charlotte NC 28224	704-523-4242	R	7*	<.1
11	Fiebing Company Inc—Richard Chase	PO Box 694, Milwaukee WI 53201	414-271-5011	R	6*	<.1
12	Surry Chemicals Inc—Sherman Shepherd	PO Box 1447, Mount Airy NC 27030	336-786-4607	R	5*	<.1
13	Justice Brothers Dist Company Inc—Edward Justice	2734 Huntington Dr, Duarte CA 91010	626-359-9174	R	5*	<.1
14	Berghausen Corp—Fritz Berghausen	4524 Este Ave, Cincinnati OH 45232	513-541-5631	R	4*	<.1
15	American Wax Inc—David Eudy	PO Box 508, Heath Springs SC 29058	803-273-9492	R	4*	<.1
16	Leatex Chemical Co—L Mcchesney	2722 N Hancock St, Philadelphia PA 19133	215-739-6324	R	4*	<.1
17	CNC International LP—Bruce Moger	PO Box 3000, Woonsocket RI 02895	401-769-6100	R	3*	<.1
18	Lindley Laboratories Inc—William Lindley	PO Box 341, Burlington NC 27216	336-449-7521	R	2*	<.1

TOTALS: SIC 2843 Surface Active Agents
Companies: 18 — 2,158 — 2.6

2844 Toilet Preparations

Rank	Company Name—Executive Officer	Address, City, State, Zip	Phone	Type	Fin	Empls
1	Avon Products Inc—Andrea Jung	1345 Ave of the Americ, New York NY 10105	212-282-5000	P	10,863	42.0
2	Estee Lauder Companies Inc—Fabrizio Freda	767 5th Ave, New York NY 10153	212-572-4200	P	7,796	31.2
3	L'Oreal USA Inc—Lyndsay Owen Jones	575 5th Ave, New York NY 10017	212-818-1500	S	7,295*	7.9
4	Coty Inc—Bernd Beetz	2 Park Ave, New York NY 10016	212-479-4300	R	3,500*	.5
5	Estee Lauder Inc—William P Lauder Estee Lauder Companies Inc	767 5th Ave, New York NY 10153	212-572-4200	S	2,899*	N/A
6	Maybelline New York—David Greenberg L'Oreal USA Inc	575 5th Ave 14th Fl, New York NY 10017	212-818-1500	S	1,867*	2.0
7	Revlon Holdings LLC—Howard Gittis Revlon Inc	237 Park Ave, New York NY 10017	212-527-4000	S	1,861	11.0
8	Alberto-Culver Co—V James Marino	2525 Armitage Ave, Melrose Park IL 60160	708-450-3000	S	1,597	2.6
9	Revlon Inc—Alan T Ennis	237 Park Ave, New York NY 10017	212-527-4000	B	1,381	5.2
10	Elizabeth Arden Inc—E Scott Beattie	2400 SW 145 Ave 2nd Fl, Miramar FL 33027	954-364-6900	P	1,176	2.3
11	Inter Parfums Inc—Jean Madar	551 5th Ave Ste 1500, New York NY 10176	212-983-2640	P	615	.3
12	Bare Escentuals—Leslie Blodgett	71 Stevenson St 22nd F, San Francisco CA 94105	415-489-5000	R	558	2.6
13	Pioneer Investment Management USA Inc—Daniel K Kingsbury	60 State St, Boston MA 02109	617-742-7825	S	528*	.6
14	Procter and Gamble Cosmetics	11050 York Rd, Hunt Valley MD 21030	410-785-7300	D	522*	1.5
15	Magnifique Parfumes and Cosmetics Inc—Michael W Katz	251 International Pkwy, Sunrise FL 33325	954-335-9100	S	500	.2
16	Den-Mat Corp—Robert Ibsen	PO Box 8999, Santa Maria CA 93456	805-922-8491	R	400*	.7
17	Dudley Products Inc—Ursula Dudley-Oglesby	1835 Eastchester Dr, High Point NC 27265	336-993-8800	R	351*	.4
18	Clairol Inc—Robert Matteucci	1 Blachley Rd, Stamford CT 06902	203-357-5000	S	350*	2.0
19	Matrix Essentials Inc	30601 Carter St, Solon OH 44139	440-248-3700	S	348	1.0
20	H2O Plus LP—Cindy Melk	845 W Madison St, Chicago IL 60607		R	186*	.2
21	Farouk Systems Inc—Shauky Gulamani	250 Pennbright Dr Ste, Houston TX 77090	281-876-2000	R	179*	.6
22	Sunstar Americas Inc—Tom Studney	4635 W Foster Ave, Chicago IL 60630	773-777-4000	S	179*	.6
23	Chanel Inc—Mike Allen	9 W 57th St Fl 44, New York NY 10019	212-688-5055	S	172*	1.5
24	Thibiant International Inc—Patrick Thibiant	20320 Prairie St, Chatsworth CA 91311	818-709-1345	R	170*	.5
25	Topiderm Inc—Burt Shaffer	5200 New Horizons Blvd, Amityville NY 11701	631-226-7979	R	154*	.3
26	Johnson and Johnson Consumer Products Co—SK D'Agostino	199 Grandview Rd, Skillman NJ 08558	908-874-1000	S	140*	.9

Note: An asterisk (*) indicates an estimated financial figure. The company type code used is as follows: R = Private, P = Public, S = Private Subsidiary, B = Public Subsidiary, D = Division, J = Joint Venture, I = Investment Fund.

COMPANY RANKINGS BY SALES WITHIN 4-DIGIT SIC

Rank	Company Name—*Executive Officer*	Address, City, State, Zip	Phone	Type	Fin	Empls
27	Parlux Fragrances Inc—*Frederick Purches*	5900 N Andrews Ave Ste, Fort Lauderdale FL 33309	954-316-9008	P	123	.1
28	Bonne Bell Inc—*Jess Bell Jr*	PO Box 770349, Lakewood OH 44107	216-221-0800	R	120*	.3
29	Bronner Brothers Inc—*Bernard Bronner*	2141 Powers Ferry Rd S, Marietta GA 30067	770-988-0015	R	113*	.5
30	Mana Products Inc—*Nikos Mouyiaris*	3202 Queens Blvd Fl 6, Long Island City NY 11101	718-361-2550	R	108*	1.0
31	Sebastian International Inc—*Claire Bruno*	PO Box 4111, Woodland Hills CA 91365	818-999-5112	R	105*	.4
32	Guerlain Inc—*Julia A Farrell*	19 E 57th St Ste 7, New York NY 10022	212-931-2400	S	103*	.1
33	Redken Laboratories Inc—*Paula Leporino* L'Oreal USA Inc	PO Box 832, Clark NJ 07066		D	99*	.4
34	Cosmolab Inc	1100 Garrett Pky, Lewisburg TN 37091	931-359-6253	R	87*	.3
35	Physicians Formula Holdings Inc—*Ingrid Jackel*	1055 W 8th St, Azusa CA 91702	626-334-3395	P	79	.2
36	Old 97 Co—*Lucille Murphy* Stephan Co	4829 E 7th Ave, Tampa FL 33605	813-248-5761	S	78*	.1
37	Kao Brands Co—*William Gentner*	2535 Spring Grove Ave, Cincinnati OH 45214	513-421-1400	R	75*	.6
38	Bijan Fragrances Inc—*Bijan Pakzad*	420 North Rodeo Dr, Beverly Hills CA 90210	310-273-6544	R	73*	.1
39	Quest International Fragrance—*Demi Thoman*	PO Box 901, Budd Lake NJ 07828	973-691-7100	D	70	.2
40	Soft Sheen-Carson L'Oreal USA Inc	575 5th Ave, New York NY 10017	212-818-1500	D	68	.4
41	Medicia Holdings LLC—*Dale Dvorak*	PO Box 1015, Dayton NJ 08810	732-438-3200	R	68*	<.1
42	Puretek Corp—*Barry Pressman*	1245 Aviation Pl, San Fernando CA 91340	818-898-2109	R	65*	.4
43	Gordon Laboratiories Inc	751 E Artesia Blvd, Carson CA 90746	310-327-5240	R	65*	.1
44	Pacific World Corp—*Joseph Fracassi*	25800 Commercentre Dr, Lake Forest CA 92630	949-598-2400	R	65*	.1
45	Northwest Cosmetic Labs LLC—*Allan Webb*	200 Technology Dr, Idaho Falls ID 83401	208-522-6723	R	61*	.1
46	Shiseido Cosmetics Ltd (Oakland New Jersey)—*Heidi Manheimer*	178 Bauer Dr, Oakland NJ 07436	201-337-3750	D	60*	.2
47	Sysco Guest Supply Inc—*Clifford W Stanley*	PO Box 902, Monmouth Junction NJ 08852	609-514-9696	S	55*	.2
48	Beauticontrol Inc—*Albert Bosch*	PO Box 815189, Dallas TX 75381	972-458-0601	S	54*	.3
49	Luster Products Inc—*Jory Luster*	1104 W 43rd St, Chicago IL 60609	773-579-1800	R	53*	.4
50	Deb USA Inc—*Bill Taylor*	1100 S Hwy 27, Stanley NC 28164	704-263-4240	R	50*	.1
51	CCA Industries Inc—*Dunnan D Edell*	200 Murray Hill Pky, East Rutherford NJ 07073	201-935-3232	P	49	.1
52	ET Browne Drug Company Inc—*Robert Neis*	PO Box 1613, Englewood Cliffs NJ 07632	201-894-9020	R	49*	.2
53	John Paul Mitchell Systems—*John Paul DeJoria*	PO Box 10597, Beverly Hills CA 90213	310-248-3888	R	48*	.1
54	Greyson International Inc—*Harvey Tauman*	1200 S Rogers Cir Ste, Boca Raton FL 33487		P	46	N/A
55	Denco Division Belcam—*David Bellm*	PO Box 38, Rouses Point NY 12979	518-297-3366	R	40*	.2
56	Orly International Inc—*Jeff Pink*	7710 Haskell Ave, Van Nuys CA 91406	818-994-1001	R	40*	.1
57	California Tan Inc—*Leslie Hartley*	6270 Corporate Dr, Indianapolis IN 46278		S	40*	.1
58	Rosa West Inc—*Norman Taver*	10639 Chandler Blvd, North Hollywood CA 91601	818-760-6655	R	40*	<.1
59	Schwan Cosmetics USA Inc—*Janet Alm*	21 Gordon Rd, Piscataway NJ 08854	732-777-6800	R	38*	.1
60	Inter Parfums USA LLC—*Jean Madar* Inter Parfums Inc	551 5th Ave, New York NY 10176	212-983-2640	S	37*	<.1
61	Belmay Inc—*Theodore Kesten*	200 Corporate Blvd S S, Yonkers NY 10701	914-376-1515	R	37*	.4
62	Levlad Inc—*Leo Wenstein*	9200 Mason Ave, Chatsworth CA 91311	818-882-2951	S	36*	.3
63	CBI Laboratories Inc—*Pam Busiek*	4201 Diplomacy Rd, Fort Worth TX 76155		R	35*	.1
64	Shield Packaging of California Inc—*George Bates*	5165 G St, Chino CA 91710	909-628-4707	R	34	<.1
65	Borghese Inc—*Georgette Mosbacheris*	10 E 34th St Fl 3, New York NY 10016	212-659-5318	R	30*	.2
66	Sun and Skin Care Research Inc—*Gary Deangelo*	851 Greensboro Rd, Cocoa FL 32926	321-633-4644	R	30*	.1
67	Aware Products LLC—*Liz Anguss*	9250 Mason Ave, Chatsworth CA 91311	818-206-6700	R	29*	.2
68	Rna Corp—*Muhammad Akhtar*	13750 Chatham St, Blue Island IL 60406	708-597-7777	R	29*	.2
69	Aroma Vera	5310 Beethoven St, Los Angeles CA 90066	310-574-6920	R	29*	.1
70	Tom's of Maine Inc—*Tom Chappell*	PO Box 710, Kennebunk ME 04043	207-985-2944	R	28*	.1
71	Hair Systems Inc—*William Covey*	PO Box 449, Englishtown NJ 07726	732-446-2202	R	28*	.2
72	220 Laboratories Inc—*Yoram Fishman*	2321 3rd St, Riverside CA 92507	951-683-2912	R	27*	.2
73	San-Mar Laboratories Inc—*Marvin Berkrot*	4 Warehouse Ln Ste 121, Elmsford NY 10523	914-592-3130	R	27*	.3
74	Faria Limited LLC—*Christine Lacoursiere*	170 Broad St, New London CT 06320	860-442-4451	R	26*	.1
75	Classic Cosmetics Inc—*Ida Csiszar*	9530 De Soto Ave, Chatsworth CA 91311	818-773-9042	R	26*	.2
76	Aromatic Technologies Inc—*Stuart Zlotnik*	140 Centennial Ave 100, Piscataway NJ 08854	732-393-7300	R	25*	.1
77	Beiersdorf Inc—*Bill Graham*	Wilton Corporate Crt 1, Wilton CT 06897	203-563-5800	S	24*	.1
78	Beaumont Products Inc—*Henry Picken*	1560 Big Shanty Dr Nw, Kennesaw GA 30144	770-514-9000	R	22*	.1
79	Bentley Laboratories LLC—*Brian Fitzpatrick*	111 Fieldcrest Ave, Edison NJ 08837	732-512-0200	R	22*	.1
80	Agilex Flavors and Fragrances—*Tom Lamb*	140 Centennial Ave, Piscataway NJ 08854		R	21*	.1
81	American Covers Inc—*Don Watkins*	675 W 14600 S, Riverton UT 84065	801-553-0600	R	20*	.1
82	Skinstore Inc—*James Steeb*	11344 Coloma Rd Ste 72, Gold River CA 95670	916-475-1464	R	20*	<.1
83	Aloette Cosmetics Inc—*Robert Cohen*	3715 Northside Pkwy NW, Atlanta GA 30327	678-444-2563	R	20*	<.1
84	Benefit Cosmetics Inc—*Jane A Ford*	685 Market St 7th Fl, San Francisco CA 94105	415-781-8153	R	20*	<.1
85	Fragrance Resources Inc—*Christoph Gerberding*	PO Box 4277, Clifton NJ 07012	973-777-2979	R	20*	.1
86	Dickinson Brands Inc (East Hampton Connecticut)	PO Box 149, East Hampton CT 06424	860-267-2279	D	19*	<.1
87	Stephan Co—*Frank F Ferola*	1850 W McNab Rd, Fort Lauderdale FL 33309	954-971-0600	P	19	.1
88	Heritage Store—*Thomas Johnson*	PO Box 444-WWW, Virginia Beach VA 23458	757-428-0500	R	18*	.1
89	Raani Corp—*Rashid Chaudary*	5202 W 70th Pl, Bedford Park IL 60638	708-496-8025	R	17*	.2
90	Parfums Givenchy Inc—*Pamela Baxter*	19 E 57th St, New York NY 10022	212-931-2600	R	17*	.1
91	Beautopia Inc—*David Kunin*	3939 E 46th St, Minneapolis MN 55406	612-729-6600	R	17*	<.1
92	Regency Cosmetics Inc—*Gary Rice*	1625 Lakes Pkwy Ste G, Lawrenceville GA 30043	770-623-2650	D	17*	<.1
93	DMIG Inc—*Myron Ferrall*	2763 Marquis Dr, Garland TX 75042	972-494-7477	R	16*	.1
94	Cosmetic Specialty Labs Inc—*Odus Hennessee*	PO Box 187, Lawton OK 73502	580-355-2182	R	16*	.1
95	Ladove Industries Inc—*Sheree Lacove*	PO Box 5169, Hialeah FL 33014	305-624-2456	R	15*	.1
96	Universal Beauty Products Inc—*Yong Park*	1200 Kirk St, Elk Grove Village IL 60007	847-787-0182	R	15*	<.1
97	Diversified Manufacturing Corp—*Rishikesh Motilall*	101 7th Ave, Newport MN 55055	651-458-8636	P	15*	.1
98	Scott's Liquid Gold Inc—*Mark E Goldstein*	PO Box 39S, Denver CO 80239		P	14	.1
99	Summit Laboratories Inc—*Clyde Hammond*	17010 Halsted St, Harvey IL 60426	708-333-2995	R	14*	.1
100	Set-N-Me-Free Aloe Vera Co—*Janet Heinrich*	19220 SE Stark St, Portland OR 97233	503-666-9661	R	13*	<.1
101	Chem Aid Inc—*Roy Reiner*	PO Box 843, Saddle Brook NJ 07663	201-843-3300	R	13*	.1
102	Robertet Fragrances Inc—*Christophe Maubert*	PO Box 650, Oakland NJ 07436	201-405-1000	R	12*	.1
103	Columbia Cosmetics Manufacturers Inc—*Rachel Rendel*	1661 Timothy Dr, San Leandro CA 94577	510-562-5900	R	12*	.1
104	Marilyn Miglin LP—*Marilyn Miglin*	112 E Oak St, Chicago IL 60611		R	12*	.1
105	Kiss My Face Corp—*Robert MacLeod*	PO Box 224, Gardiner NY 12525	845-255-0884	R	12*	<.1
106	Eqyss International Inc—*Dallas Van Kempen*	PO Box 130008, Carlsbad CA 92013	760-526-7469	R	12*	<.1
107	Fran Wilson Creative Cosmetics—*Fran Wilson*	411 Fifth Ave, New York NY 10016	212-447-0036	R	12*	<.1
108	Hydrox Chemical Company Inc—*Kappana Ramanandan*	825 Tollgate Rd Ste B, Elgin IL 60123	847-468-9400	R	12*	.1
109	Prime Enterprises Inc—*Mohamed Barakat*	16363 Nw 49th Ave, Hialeah FL 33014	305-625-4929	R	12*	.1
110	House Of Cheatham Inc—*Robert Bell*	1550 Roadhaven Dr, Stone Mountain GA 30083	770-414-7283	R	11*	.1
111	Sun Pharmaceuticals Corp—*Max Recone*	300 Nyala Farms Rd, Westport CT 06880	203-341-4000	S	11*	.1

Rank	Company Name—*Executive Officer*	Address, City, State, Zip	Phone	Type	Fin	Empls
112	J Strickland And Co—*Linda Clifton*	PO Box 1637, Olive Branch MS 38654	662-890-2306	R	11*	.1
113	Autumn-Harp Inc—*John Logan*	26 Thompson Dr, Essex Junction VT 05452	802-857-4600	R	11*	.1
114	Shaw Mudge and Co—*Grant Mudge*	PO Box 901, Budd Lake NJ 07828	203-925-5000	R	11*	.1
115	Person and Covey Inc—*Lorne Person*	PO Box 25018, Glendale CA 91221	818-240-1030	R	11*	.1
116	Kenra Ltd—*Diane Lines*	22 E Washington St Fl, Indianapolis IN 46204	317-356-6491	R	11*	.1
117	Sinful Colors Inc—*Paul Murphy*	10721 Tucker St, Beltsville MD 20705	301-937-6061	R	11*	.1
118	Davion Inc—*James Placa*	29 Riverside Ave Bldg, Newark NJ 07104	973-485-0793	R	10*	.1
119	Golden Sun Inc—*Al Rodriguez*	26529 Ruether Ave, Santa Clarita CA 91350	661-250-1111	R	10*	<.1
120	Nature's Formula Inc—*George Mitchell*	2120 Hutton Ste 500, Carrollton TX 75006	972-620-7990	R	10*	.1
121	All Season Nails Div—*Tony Cuccio*	29120 Ave Paine, Valencia CA 91355	661-257-7827	D	10*	<.1
122	Essie Cosmetics Ltd—*Esther Weingarten*	1919 37th St, Astoria NY 11105	718-726-5000	R	10*	.1
123	Body Shop (Wake Forest North Carolina)—*Peter Saunders*	5036 1 World Way, Wake Forest NC 27587	919-554-4900	S	9*	.1
124	Intarome Fragrance Corp—*Daniel Funsch*	370 Chestnut St, Norwood NJ 07648	201-767-8700	R	9*	.1
125	Lee Pharmaceuticals Inc—*Ron Lee*	1434 Santa Anita Ave, South El Monte CA 91733	626-442-3141	P	9	.1
126	Vege - Kurl Inc—*Eric Huffman*	412 W Cypress St, Glendale CA 91204	818-956-5582	R	8*	.1
127	Aubrey Organics Inc—*Aubrey Hampton*	4419 N Manhattan Ave, Tampa FL 33614	813-877-4186	R	8*	.1
128	Sinclair and Valentine Div—*Alida Stevens* Smith and Vandiver Corp	480 Airport Blvd, Watsonville CA 95076	831-722-9698	S	8*	.1
129	Smith and Vandiver Corp—*Alida Stevens*	480 Airport Blvd, Watsonville CA 95076	831-722-9526	R	8*	.1
130	Jessica Cosmetics International Inc—*Jessica Vartoughian*	13209 Saticoy St, North Hollywood CA 91605	818-759-1050	R	8*	.1
131	Noevir Inc—*Kazu Oide*	1095 SE Main St, Irvine CA 92614	949-660-1111	S	8*	<.1
132	ISP Sutton Laboratories—*Sunil Kumar*	PO Box 837, Chatham NJ 07928	973-635-1551	D	8*	<.1
133	Creative Laboratories Inc—*Dale Simmons*	1325 Eagandale Ct Ste, Saint Paul MN 55121	651-681-7740	R	8*	.1
134	Nextera Enterprises Inc—*Joseph J Millin*	14320 Arminta St, Panorama City CA 91402	818-902-5537	P	8	<.1
135	Nature's Cure Inc—*Amy Baker*	4096 Piedmont Ave Ste, Oakland CA 94611		R	8	<.1
136	O Grayson Co—*Van Stamey*	PO Box 278, Kannapolis NC 28082	704-932-6195	R	7*	.1
137	Tressa Inc—*Constance Barrett*	PO Box 75320, Cincinnati OH 45275	859-525-1300	R	7*	.1
138	Stylors Inc—*Michael Kersun*	640 W 41st St, Jacksonville FL 32206	904-765-4453	R	7*	.1
139	Bedoukian Research Inc—*Robert Bedoukian*	21 Finance Dr, Danbury CT 06810	203-830-4000	R	7*	<.1
140	Alcone Company Inc	5-45 49th Ave, Long Island City NY 11101	718-361-8373	R	7*	.1
141	Coughlan Products Corp—*Randolph Reynolds*	357 Hamburg Tpke, Wayne NJ 07470	973-904-1500	R	7*	.1
142	Alpine Aromatics International Inc—*John Yorey*	51 Ethel Rd W, Piscataway NJ 08854	732-572-5600	R	7*	<.1
143	Rudolph International Inc—*James Rudolph*	1150 Beacon St, Brea CA 92821	714-529-5696	R	6*	<.1
144	Trademark Cosmetic Inc—*David Ryngler*	3263 Trade Ctr Dr, Riverside CA 92507	951-683-2631	R	6*	<.1
145	J Stephen Scherer Inc—*John Scherer*	2850 Commerce Dr, Rochester Hills MI 48309	248-852-8500	R	6*	<.1
146	Custom HBC Corp—*Larry Wilhelm*	888 Industrial Blvd, Waconia MN 55387	952-442-8241	R	6*	<.1
147	International Beauty Products LLC—*Cathy Gonzales*	5850 Canoga Ave Ste 40, Woodland Hills CA 91367	818-999-1222	R	6*	<.1
148	Young E F Jr Manufacturing Co—*Charles Young*	425 26th Ave, Meridian MS 39301	601-693-1961	R	6*	<.1
149	Harrison Specialty Company Inc—*George Bates*	PO Box 190, Canton MA 02021	781-821-0400	R	5*	<.1
150	Aromatic Fusion—*Eric Albee*	3185 Tucker Rd, Bensalem PA 19020	215-244-1830	R	5	<.1
151	Central Solutions Inc—*Mark Nobrega*	PO Box 15276, Kansas City KS 66115	913-621-6542	R	5*	<.1
152	Cameo Inc—*E Ison*	PO Box 535, Toledo OH 43697	419-661-9611	R	5*	<.1
153	Mehron Inc—*Martin Melik*	100 Red Schoolhse Rd C, Chestnut Ridge NY 10977	845-426-1700	R	5*	<.1
154	Rachel Perry Inc—*Rachel Perry*	15140 Keswick St, Van Nuys CA 91405	818-374-3455	R	5*	<.1
155	International Flora Technologies Ltd—*James Brown*	291 E El Prado Ct, Chandler AZ 85225	480-545-7000	R	5*	<.1
156	Eoh Industries Inc—*Emmett Hickey*	1901 SE Pkwy, Arlington TX 76018	817-468-3181	R	5*	.1
157	Buds Cotton Inc—*Dewitt Paul*	1240 N Fee Ana St, Anaheim CA 92807	714-223-7800	R	5*	<.1
158	Tu-K Industries Inc—*Alpin Kaler*	5702 Firestone Pl, South Gate CA 90280	562-927-3365	R	5*	<.1
159	Natural Essentials Inc—*Gary Pellegrino*	PO Box 2095, Streetsboro OH 44241	330-562-8022	R	4*	<.1
160	Valjean Corp—*Richard Ferry*	1785 S Patrick Dr, Indian Harbour Beach FL 32937	321-773-2454	R	4*	<.1
161	Clintex Laboratories Inc—*Stephen Luster*	140 W 62nd St, Chicago IL 60621	773-493-9777	R	4*	<.1
162	Arizona Sun Products Inc—*Ellen Wallace*	14806 N 74th, Scottsdale AZ 85260	480-998-8861	R	4*	<.1
163	Essentiel Elements de la rue Verte—*Kathie DeVoe*	1535 E Naomi St, Indianapolis IN 46203	317-786-8037	S	4*	<.1
164	Good Home Co—*Christine Dimmick*	20 West 20th St Ste 60, New York NY 10011	212-352-1509	R	4*	<.1
165	Fantasia Industries Corp—*Paul Bogosian*	20 Park Pl, Paramus NJ 07652	201-261-7070	R	4*	<.1
166	Chuckles Inc—*Charles Frank*	PO Box 5126, Manchester NH 03108	603-669-4228	R	4*	<.1
167	Luzier Personalized Cosmetics Inc—*Kathleen Grissom*	7910 Troost Ave 12, Kansas City MO 64131		R	4*	<.1
168	Imperial Dax Co—*David Joy*	PO Box 10002, Fairfield NJ 07004	973-227-6105	R	4*	<.1
169	Sta Elements Inc—*Shaji Thomas*	7575 Kingspointe Pkwy, Orlando FL 32819	407-351-5656	R	3*	<.1
170	Base 10 Inc—*Matthew Papania*	PO Box 252, Kunia HI 96759	808-637-5620	R	3*	<.1
171	All Natural Botanicals Inc—*Andrew Rizzo*	15016 Ronnie Dr, Dade City FL 33523	352-567-4020	R	3*	<.1
172	Rozelle Inc—*Tom Basiliere*	PO Box 70, Westfield VT 05874	802-744-2270	R	3*	<.1
173	Brucci Limited Inc—*Murray Bober*	861 Nepperhan Ave, Yonkers NY 10703	914-965-0707	R	3*	.1
174	AR-EX Ltd—*Perry Blatt*	1282 Old Skokie Rd, Highland Park IL 60035	847-579-1408	R	3*	.1
175	Pedifix Footcare Co—*Ross Weale*	310 Guinea Rd, Brewster NY 10509	845-277-2850	R	3*	<.1
176	Gendarme Fragrances—*Topper Schroeder*	9071 Nemo St, West Hollywood CA 90069	310-281-3730	R	3*	<.1
177	Scientific Research Products Inc Stephan Co	1850 W McNab Rd, Fort Lauderdale FL 33309	954-971-0600	S	3*	<.1
178	Rocky Mountain Sunscreen Co—*David C Erickson*	14700 W 66th Pl Ste 7, Arvada CO 80004	303-940-9803	R	3*	<.1
179	Il Makiage Of 60th St Inc—*Sam Harkavi*	4549 Davis St, Long Island City NY 11101	718-361-3123	R	3*	<.1
180	CA Botana International Inc—*Dieter Kuster*	9365 Waples St Ste A, San Diego CA 92121	858-450-1717	R	3*	<.1
181	Lechler Laboratories Inc—*Martin Melik*	100 Red Schoolhse Rd C, Spring Valley NY 10977	845-426-6800	R	3*	<.1
182	Chemia Corp—*Norman Rees*	11558 Rock Island Ct, Maryland Heights MO 63043	314-567-0013	R	2*	<.1
183	Continental Aromatics—*Ira Schneider*	PO Box 567, Hawthorne NJ 07507	973-345-0200	R	2*	<.1
184	Keystone Laboratories Inc—*Melinda Menke*	PO Box 2026, Memphis TN 38101	901-774-8860	R	2*	<.1
185	Vienna Beauty Products Co—*Timothy Miller*	347 Leo St, Dayton OH 45404	937-228-7109	R	2*	<.1
186	Libby Laboratories Inc—*Susan Libby*	1700 6th St, Berkeley CA 94710	510-527-5400	R	2*	<.1
187	J Palazzolo Son Inc—*Joseph Palazzolo*	36 Lakeville Rd, New Hyde Park NY 11040	516-775-0220	R	2*	<.1
188	La Prairie Inc	680 5th Ave Fl 14, New York NY 10019	212-459-1600	R	2*	<.1
189	Amera Cosmetics Inc	6403 W Rio Grande Ave, Kennewick WA 99336	509-735-1531	R	2*	<.1
190	Jane Carter Solution—*Jane Carter*	45 S 17th St, East Orange NJ 07018		R	2*	<.1
191	Tepco Corp—*Don Lefevre*	PO Box 1160, Rapid City SD 57709	605-343-7200	R	2*	<.1
192	Alto Bella Hair Products Inc—*Dianne Altobelli*	14301 Burnsville Pkwy, Burnsville MN 55306	952-707-1900	S	2*	<.1
193	Idiom Press—*Robert Locher*	PO Box 1015, Merlin OR 97532	541-956-1297	R	2*	<.1
194	Elias Fragrances Inc—*Robert Elias*	999 E 46th St, Brooklyn NY 11203	718-693-6400	R	2*	<.1
195	Rowpar Pharmaceuticals Inc—*James Ratcliff*	16100 N Greenway Hayde, Scottsdale AZ 85260	480-948-6997	R	2*	<.1
196	Jensen's Inc—*Aksel Jensen*	PO Box 320, Shelbyville TN 37162	931-684-5021	R	1*	<.1
197	Carme Cosmeceutical Services Inc—*Frank Massino*	831 Latour Ct Ste A, Napa CA 94558	707-259-6220	R	1*	<.1
198	Peter Hantz Company Inc—*Jerry Johnson*	1840 E University Dr S, Tempe AZ 85281	480-967-6464	R	1*	<.1
199	Panama Jack Inc—*Jack Katz*	230 Ernestine St, Orlando FL 32801	407-843-8110	R	1*	<.1

Note: An asterisk (*) indicates an estimated financial figure. The company type code used is as follows: R = Private, P = Public, S = Private Subsidiary, B = Public Subsidiary, D = Division, J = Joint Venture, I = Investment Fund.

COMPANY RANKINGS BY SALES WITHIN 4-DIGIT SIC

Rank	Company Name—Executive Officer	Address, City, State, Zip	Phone	Type	Fin	Empls
200	Hogan Flavors and Fragrances Inc—Ray Hogan	130 E 18th St Frnt, New York NY 10003	212-598-4310	R	1*	<.1
201	Buty-Wave Products Co—Joseph Simon	7323 Beverly Blvd, Los Angeles CA 90036	323-936-2191	R	1*	<.1
202	Mercer Group Ltd/Baby Blanket—James Mercer	254 Hornbine Rd, Rehoboth MA 02769	508-679-1941	R	1*	<.1
203	Lucky Heart Cosmetics Inc—Tom Colturi	390 Mulberry St, Memphis TN 38103	901-526-7658	R	1*	<.1
204	International Abrasive Manufacturing Co—James George	1221 N Lakeview Ave, Anaheim CA 92807	714-779-9970	R	1*	<.1
205	Rubigo Cosmetics—Jules Schlesinger	PO Box 1026, Fair Lawn NJ 07410	973-636-6573	R	1*	<.1
206	Vellus Products Inc—Sharon Doherty	6442-44 Fiesta Dr, Columbus OH 43235	614-889-2391	R	1*	<.1
207	Hydron Technologies Inc—Richard Banakus	9843 18th St N Ste 150, Saint Petersburg FL 33716	727-342-5050	P	<1	<.1

TOTALS: SIC 2844 Toilet Preparations
Companies: 207

					49,422	134.0

2851 Paints & Allied Products

Rank	Company Name—Executive Officer	Address, City, State, Zip	Phone	Type	Fin	Empls
1	PPG Industries Inc—Charles E Bunch	1 PPG Pl, Pittsburgh PA 15122	412-434-3131	P	13,423	38.3
2	Sherwin-Williams Co—Christopher M Connor	101 W Prospect Ave, Cleveland OH 44115	216-566-2000	P	7,776	32.2
3	Valspar Corp—Gary E Hendrickson	PO Box 1461, Minneapolis MN 55440	612-851-7000	P	3,953	10.0
4	RPM International Inc—Frank C Sullivan	PO Box 777, Medina OH 44258	330-273-5090	P	3,382	9.0
5	Ferro Corp—James F Kirsch	6060 Parkland Blvd, Mayfield Heights OH 44124	216-875-5600	P	2,156	5.1
6	Akzo Nobel Coatings Inc—Hans Wijers	2031 Nelson Miller Pkw, Louisville KY 40223	502-254-0470	S	2,057*	2.8
7	ICI Paints North America	16651 W Sprague Rd, Strongsville OH 44136	440-297-7026	R	1,680*	6.0
8	Behr Process Corp—Jeff Filley	PO Box 1287, Santa Ana CA 92702	714-545-7101	S	1,630	.4
9	Benjamin Moore and Co—Denis S Abrams	101 Paragon Dr, Montvale NJ 07645	201-573-9600	S	966*	3.0
10	Spraylat Corp—Michael Borner	143 Sparks Ave, Pelham NY 10803	914-738-1600	R	402*	.3
11	Tremco Inc—Jeffrey Korach	3735 Green Rd, Beachwood OH 44122	216-292-5000	S	396*	1.9
	RPM International Inc					
12	Frazee Industries Inc—Elias Achar	PO Box 122471, San Diego CA 92112	858-626-3600	R	392*	.9
13	Muralo Company Inc—Jim Norton	PO Box 455, Bayonne NJ 07002		R	389*	.4
14	LMI Finishing Inc—Janice Loveless	2104 N 170th E Ave, Tulsa OK 74116	918-438-2122	S	255*	.8
15	Kelly-Moore Paint Company Inc—Steve Voe	PO Box 3016, San Carlos CA 94070	650-592-8337	R	240*	1.8
16	Dunn Edwards Corp—Ken Edwards	4885 E 52nd Pl, Los Angeles CA 90040	323-771-3330	R	208*	1.5
17	Guardsman Products Inc—Kate Bass	PO Box 1521, Grand Rapids MI 49501		S	202	1.0
	Valspar Corp					
18	Rentech Inc—D Hunt Ramsbottom	10877 Wilshire Blvd St, Los Angeles CA 90024	310-571-9800	P	180	.3
19	Parker Paint Manufacturing Company Inc—Ed Lanctot	PO Box 122590, San Diego CA 92112	253-473-1122	R	167*	.1
20	Miller Paint Company Inc—Steve Dearborn	12812 Ne Whitaker Way, Portland OR 97230	503-255-0190	R	158*	.2
21	Resinall Corp—Paul Pearce	PO Box 8149, Stamford CT 06905	252-585-1445	R	131*	.1
22	Tnemec Company Inc—Peter Cortelyou	6800 Corporate Dr, Kansas City MO 64120	816-483-3400	R	116*	.3
23	True Value Manufacturing Co—Lyle Lieberman	8600 W Bryn Mawr Ave, Chicago IL 60631		D	113*	.3
24	Plasti-Kote Company Inc—Gary Henderson	8724 W Higgins Rd Ste, Chicago IL 60631		S	94*	.3
	Valspar Corp					
25	Hirshfield's Inc—Hans Hirshfield	725 2nd Ave N, Minneapolis MN 55405	612-377-3910	R	93*	.5
26	Parks Corp—F Davidson	113 Olive St, Attleboro MA 02703	508-679-5938	R	89*	.1
27	Coronado Paint—James Wells	101 Paragon Dr, Montvale NJ 07645		R	89*	.2
28	Red Spot Paint and Varnish Company Inc—Kato Daisuke	PO Box 418, Evansville IN 47703	812-428-9100	R	80*	.5
29	Dryvit Systems Inc—Peter Balint	PO Box 1014, West Warwick RI 02893	401-822-4100	S	75*	.2
	RPM International Inc					
30	LaPolla Industries Inc—Douglas J Kramer	15402 Vantage Pky E St, Houston TX 77032	281-219-4700	P	71	.1
31	Premier Ink Systems Inc—Thomas Farmer	PO Box 670, Harrison OH 45030	513-367-2300	R	66*	.1
32	Deft Inc—Tony Desmond	17451 Von Karman Ave, Irvine CA 92614	949-474-0400	R	60*	.1
33	Samuel Cabot Inc	100 Hale St, Newburyport MA 01950	978-465-1900	S	58*	.1
	Valspar Corp					
34	Day-Glo Color Corp—Steve Demetriou	4515 Saint Clair Ave, Cleveland OH 44103	216-391-7070	S	57*	.2
	RPM International Inc					
35	Mohawk Finishing Products Inc—Frank C Sullivan	POBox 22000, Hickory NC 28603	828-261-0325	S	54	.2
	RPM International Inc					
36	Surface Protection Industries Inc—Robert Davidson	3360 E 14th St, Los Angeles CA 90023	323-269-9231	R	51*	.2
37	Rentech Development Corp—D Hunt Ramsbottom	1331 17th St Ste 720, Denver CO 80202	303-298-8008	S	51*	.1
	Rentech Inc					
38	Rentech Services Corp—D Hunt Ramsbottom	1331 17th St Ste 720, Denver CO 80202	303-298-8008	S	51*	.1
	Rentech Inc					
39	Color Wheel Paint Manufacturing Company Inc—Richard Strube	2814 Silver Star Rd, Orlando FL 32808	407-293-6810	R	48*	.2
40	Rodda Paint Co—Al Mordy	6107 N Marine Dr Ste 3, Portland OR 97203	503-521-4300	R	46*	.4
41	Npa Coatings Inc—Samuel Rhue	11110 Berea Rd Ste 2, Cleveland OH 44102	216-631-2002	R	45*	.2
42	Brewer Science Inc—Terry Brewer	2401 Brewer Dr, Rolla MO 65401	573-364-0300	R	44*	.3
43	Mobile Paint Manufacturing Company of Delaware Inc—Robert Williams	PO Box 717, Theodore AL 36590	251-443-6110	R	43*	.2
44	Valspar Industries USA Inc—William L Mansfield	PO Box 1461, Minneapolis MN 55440	612-851-7000	D	43	.1
	Valspar Corp					
45	California Products Corp—Peter Longo	150 Dascomb Rd, Andover MA 01810	978-623-9980	R	43*	.2
46	Watson-Standard Co—Henry Knox Watson III	PO Box 11250, Pittsburgh PA 15238	724-275-1000	R	41*	.2
47	United Gilsonite Laboratories—Thomas White	PO Box 70, Scranton PA 18501	570-344-1202	R	41*	.2
48	Berg Lacquer Inc—Sandra Berg	3150 E Pico Blvd, Los Angeles CA 90023	323-261-8114	R	40*	.2
49	Ennis Traffic Safety Solutions—Brad Ruiter	PO Box 1496, Los Angeles CA 90001	323-758-1147	R	37*	<.1
50	Cardinal Industrial Finishes Inc—Stanley Ekstrom	1329 Potrero Ave, South El Monte CA 91733	626-444-9274	R	37*	.2
51	General Coatings Technologies Inc—Michael Ghitelman	24 Woodward Ave, Ridgewood NY 11385	718-821-1232	R	34*	.1
52	Ennis Industries LLP—Amy Anderson	1509 S Kaufman St, Ennis TX 75119	214-874-7200	R	34*	.2
53	Aervoe Industries Inc—David Williams	P O Box 485, Gardnerville NV 89410	775-783-3100	R	33*	.1
54	Farrell-Calhoun Inc—John Ward	221 E Carolina Ave, Memphis TN 38126	901-526-2211	R	30*	.2
55	ECP Inc—Larry Bettendorf	11210 Katherines Cross, Woodridge IL 60517	630-754-4200	S	27*	<.1
56	G and W Enterprises Inc—W Gardner	1800 Park Pl Ave, Fort Worth TX 76110	817-926-6811	R	26*	.1
57	Cork Industries Inc—Frank Mcdonnell	500 Kaiser Dr, Folcroft PA 19032	610-522-9550	R	25*	.1
58	Seymour Of Sycamore Inc—Nancy Heatley	917 Crosby Ave, Sycamore IL 60178	815-895-9101	R	25*	.2
59	ITW American Safety Technologies—Norris Williamson	130 Commerce Dr, Montgomeryville PA 18936	215-855-8450	R	23	.1
60	Colorado Paint Co—Kevin Valis	4747 Holly St, Denver CO 80216	303-388-9265	R	22*	<.1
61	Truco Inc—Christopher Hoskins	4301 Train Ave, Cleveland OH 44113	216-631-1000	R	22*	<.1
62	Akron Paint and Varnish Inc—Dave Venarge	1390 Firestone Pkwy, Akron OH 44301		R	22*	.1
63	Hallman/Lindsay Paints Inc—Timothy Mielcarek	1717 N Bristol St, Sun Prairie WI 53590	608-834-8844	R	21*	.1
64	Flecto Company Inc—Frank C Sullivan	11 Hawthorn Pkwy, Vernon Hills IL 60061	847-367-7700	S	21*	.1
65	IVC Industrial Coatings Inc—Michael Mccracken	2831 N Industrial Park, Brazil IN 47834	317-636-4407	R	21*	.1
66	DecoArt Inc—Stanley Clifford	PO Box 386, Stanford KY 40484	606-365-3193	R	20*	.1

Rank	Company Name—*Executive Officer*	Address, City, State, Zip	Phone	Type	Fin	Empls
67	Matlab Inc—*Gayle Kurdian*	PO Box 2046, Asheboro NC 27204	336-629-4161	R	20*	.1
68	Red Spot Westland Inc—*Charles Storms* Red Spot Paint and Varnish Company Inc	550 Edwin St, Westland MI 48186	734-729-7400	S	19*	.1
69	Anchor Paint Manufacturing Co—*Roy Meade*	PO Box 1305, Tulsa OK 74101	918-836-4626	R	19*	.1
70	Matthews Paint Co PPG Industries Inc	760 Pittsburgh Dr, Delaware OH 43015	262-947-0700	S	19*	.1
71	Davis-Frost Inc—*Calvin Henning*	3416 Candlers Mountain, Lynchburg VA 24502	434-846-5277	R	18*	.1
72	US Paint Corp—*John Duchardt*	831 S 21st St, Saint Louis MO 63103	314-621-0525	R	18*	.1
73	Roberts Consolidated Industries Inc—*Lewis Gould*	1070 Mary Crest Rd, Henderson NV 89014		D	17*	.1
74	Palmer Paint Products Inc—*Beverly Geisler*	PO Box 1058, Troy MI 48099	248-588-4500	R	17*	.1
75	Gemini Coatings Inc—*David Warren*	PO Box 699, El Reno OK 73036	405-262-5710	R	17*	.1
76	United Paint And Chemical Corp—*John Piceu*	24671 Telegraph Rd, Southfield MI 48033	248-353-3035	R	16*	<.1
77	Strathmore Products Inc—*Eric Burr*	PO Box 151, Syracuse NY 13201	315-488-5401	R	16*	.1
78	Richards Paint Manufacturing Company Inc—*Eric Richard*	200 Paint St, Rockledge FL 32955	321-636-6200	R	16*	.1
79	Sem Products Inc—*Rick Menze*	1685 Overview Dr, Rock Hill SC 29730		R	16*	.1
80	Lymtal International Inc—*Francis Lymburner*	4150 S Lapeer Rd, Orion MI 48359	248-373-8100	R	16*	<.1
81	Coatings And Adhesives Corp—*Richard Pasin*	PO Box 1080, Leland NC 28451	910-371-3184	R	16*	.1
82	Ncp Coatings Inc—*Neil Hannewyk*	PO Box 307, Niles MI 49120	269-683-3377	R	16*	.1
83	Ultra Additives—*Arlene Kiste*	1455 Broad St Ste 3, Bloomfield NJ 07003	973-279-1306	R	15*	.1
84	Chemical Specialists And Development Inc—*Stephen Cooke*	PO Box 3087, Conroe TX 77305	936-228-0105	R	15*	.1
85	Ceram-Traz Corp—*Lyle Sommers*	PO Box 245, Osseo MN 55369	763-424-2044	R	14*	<.1
86	Specialty Coatings Co—*Seymour Neems*	2500 Delta Ln, Elk Grove Village IL 60007	847-766-3555	R	14*	.1
87	Rudd Company Inc—*Alan Park*	1141 Nw 50th St, Seattle WA 98107	206-789-1000	R	14*	.1
88	Pittsburgh Paints San Bernardino—*JE Dabbs* PPG Industries Inc	1595 E San Bernadino, San Bernardino CA 92408	909-478-3485	S	13*	.1
89	Federated Paint Manufacturing Company Inc—*John Bauchwitz*	5812 S Homan Ave, Chicago IL 60629	708-345-4848	R	13*	<.1
90	Universal Chemicals And Coatings Inc—*Daniel Chin*	1975 Fox Ln, Elgin IL 60123	847-931-1700	R	13*	.1
91	Atlas Putty Products Co—*David Payton*	8351 185th St, Tinley Park IL 60487	708-429-5858	R	12*	.1
92	Seaboard Asphalt Products Co—*Adrian Burger*	3601 Fairfield Rd, Baltimore MD 21226	410-355-0330	R	12*	<.1
93	Dudick Inc—*Thomas Dudick*	1818 Miller Pkwy, Streetsboro OH 44241	330-562-1970	R	11*	.1
94	Standard Tar Products Company Inc—*Edward F Chouinard*	2456 W Cornell St, Milwaukee WI 53209	414-873-7650	R	11*	<.1
95	Polibrid Coatings Inc—*George Ramirez*	6700 FM 802, Brownsville TX 78526	956-831-7818	R	11*	.1
96	H-I-S Paint Manufacturing Company Inc—*Joe Cox*	1801 W Reno Ave, Oklahoma City OK 73106	405-232-2077	R	10*	.1
97	Sterling Lacquer Manufacturing Co—*Leo Mitchell*	3150 Brannon Ave, Saint Louis MO 63139	314-776-4450	R	10*	.1
98	Chromatics Inc—*Dave Ely*	19 Francis J Clarke Ci, Bethel CT 06801	203-743-6868	R	10*	<.1
99	Kelley Technical Coatings Inc—*Nelson Auge*	PO Box 3726, Louisville KY 40201	502-636-2561	R	9*	<.1
100	National Coatings Inc—*James Hillhouse*	PO Box 1314, Galesburg IL 61402	309-342-4184	R	9*	.1
101	Prime Leather Finishes Co—*Terence Welch*	PO Box 550, Pewaukee WI 53072	262-691-1930	R	9*	<.1
102	Repcolite Paints Inc—*David Altena*	473 W 17th St, Holland MI 49423	616-396-1275	R	9*	.1
103	Delta Laboratories Inc—*Richard Pesola*	PO Box 2258, Ocala FL 34478	352-629-8101	R	8*	.1
104	Helen Inc—*Michael Allister*	6450 Hanna Lake Ave Se, Caledonia MI 49316	616-698-8102	R	8*	<.1
105	Us Polymers-Accurez LLC—*Mary Kalbfleisch*	300 E Primm St, Saint Louis MO 63111	314-638-1632	R	8*	<.1
106	Preserva-Products Inc—*Greg Riecks*	12860 Earhart Ave Ste, Auburn CA 95602	530-887-0177	R	8*	< 1
107	Carbit Paint Co—*James Westerman*	927 W Blackhawk St, Chicago IL 60642	312-280-2300	R	8*	.1
108	Axon Aerospace Inc—*Ivan Block*	307 Echelon Rd, Greenville SC 29605	864-299-2819	R	8*	<.1
109	Bennette Paint Manufacturing Company Inc—*Roger Neuharth*	PO Box 9088, Hampton VA 23670	757-838-7777	R	8*	.1
110	Davies-Imperial Coatings Inc—*Donn Davies*	PO Box 790, Hammond IN 46325	219-933-0877	R	7*	<.1
111	Prime Colorants Inc—*Endre Zongor*	PO Box 427, Franklin TN 37065	615-794-9551	R	7*	<.1
112	Gateway Paint and Chemical Co—*Harold Blumenfeld*	2929 Smallman St, Pittsburgh PA 15201	412-261-6642	R	7*	<.1
113	Steelcote Manufacturing Co—*John Milner*	5151 Natural Bridge, Saint Louis MO 63115	314-771-8053	R	7*	<.1
114	Davis Paint Co—*Kevin Ostby*	PO Box 7589, Kansas City MO 64116	816-471-4447	R	7*	<.1
115	Camger Coatings Systems Inc—*Daniel Iannuzzi*	364 Main St, Norfolk MA 02056	508-528-5787	R	7*	<.1
116	Triarch Industries Inc—*Bruce Wingate*	9550 W Wingfoot Rd Ste, Houston TX 77041	713-690-9977	R	7*	.1
117	Harrison Paint Co—*Patrick Lauber*	1329 Harrison Ave Sw, Canton OH 44706	330-455-5125	R	6*	<.1
118	Nu-Puttie Corp—*Steve Stefely*	PO Box 645, Maywood IL 60153	708-681-1040	R	6*	<.1
119	Crawford Laboratories Inc—*David Schmetterer*	4350 S Halsted St, Chicago IL 60609		R	6*	<.1
120	AIC Inc—*Vincent Sartorelli*	7 Martel Way, Georgetown MA 01833	978-352-4510	R	6*	<.1
121	Sampson Coatings Inc—*Mark Stewart*	PO Box 6625, Richmond VA 23230	804-359-5011	S	6*	.6
122	Chemcoat Inc—*James O'brien*	PO Box 188, Montoursville PA 17754	570-368-8631	R	6*	<.1
123	Crown Paint Co—*John Evans*	1801 W Sheridan Ave, Oklahoma City OK 73106	405-232-8580	R	6*	<.1
124	T C Dunham Paint Company Inc—*Isaac Schwartz*	581 Saw Mill River Rd, Yonkers NY 10701	914-969-4202	R	6*	<.1
125	Kalcor Coatings Company Inc—*Cori Zucker*	37721 Stevens Blvd, Willoughby OH 44094	440-946-4700	R	6*	<.1
126	John C Dolph Co—*Jack Hasson*	320 New Rd, Monmouth Junction NJ 08852	732-329-2333	R	6*	<.1
127	Cp Inc—*Glen Findley*	PO Box 1049, Connersville IN 47331	765-825-4111	R	5*	<.1
128	Northern Coating and Chemical—*Larry Melgary*	PO Box 456, Menominee MI 49858	906-863-2641	R	5*	<.1
129	Hurst Chemical Co—*Joanne Hirsh*	231 W Pedregosa St, Santa Barbara CA 93101		R	5*	<.1
130	John L Armitage and Co—*Norman Armitage*	545 National Dr, Gallatin TN 37066	615-452-6556	R	5*	<.1
131	Dampney Company Inc—*Raymond Pavlik*	85 Paris St, Everett MA 02149	617-389-2805	R	5*	<.1
132	Titan Coatings Inc—*Robert Hanna*	2025 Exchange Pl, Bessemer AL 35022	205-426-8149	R	5*	<.1
133	Patriot Paint LLC—*Linda Keller*	PO Box 1051, Portland IN 47371	260-726-6633	R	5*	<.1
134	Farwest Paint Manufacturing Co—*Paul Sheehan*	PO Box 68726, Seattle WA 98168	206-244-8844	R	5*	<.1
135	Hartin Paint and Filler Corp—*Richard Gottesman*	PO Box 116, Carlstadt NJ 07072	201-438-3300	R	5*	<.1
136	Simpson Coatings Group Inc—*Tim Simpson*	111 S Maple Ave, South San Francisco CA 94080	650-873-5990	R	5*	<.1
137	R J Mcglennon Company Inc—*Michael Mcglennon*	198 Utah St, San Francisco CA 94103	415-552-0311	R	5*	<.1
138	Polyurethane Products Corp—*Govind Lakshman*	100 W Interstate Rd, Addison IL 60101	630-543-6700	R	4*	<.1
139	Elpaco Coatings Corp—*Harold Peter*	PO Box 50256, Saint Louis MO 63105	574-295-3991	R	4*	<.1
140	VJ Dolan and Company Inc—*David Dolan*	1830 N Laramie Ave, Chicago IL 60639	773-237-0100	R	4*	<.1
141	Continental Coatings Inc—*Robert Wang*	10938 Beech Ave, Fontana CA 92337	909-355-1288	R	4*	<.1
142	Color Putty Company Inc—*Sheri Priewe*	PO Box 738, Monroe WI 53566	608-325-6033	R	4*	<.1
143	Cal-Western Paints—*Jerry Mulnix*	11748 Slauson Ave, Santa Fe Springs CA 90670	562-693-0872	R	4*	<.1
144	TJ Ronan Paint Corp—*Dennis Doran*	749 E 135th St, Bronx NY 10454	718-292-1100	R	4*	<.1
145	G J Nikolas and Company Inc—*George Nikolas*	2800 Washington Blvd, Bellwood IL 60104	708-544-0320	R	4*	<.1
146	M and M Manufacturing Inc—*Michael Murphy*	1120 Holstein Dr Ne, Pine City MN 55063	651-674-0007	R	4*	<.1
147	Performance Coatings Inc—*Barbara Newell*	PO Box 1569, Ukiah CA 95482	707-462-3023	P	4*	<.1
148	Columbia Paint Corp—*Richard Flowers*	PO Box 2888, Huntington WV 25728	304-529-3237	R	4*	<.1
149	Gillespie Coatings Inc—*Charles Kaplan*	211 Gum Springs Rd, Longview TX 75602	903-753-0393	R	4*	<.1
150	Mid-States Paint and Chemical Co—*Michael Meyers*	9315 Watson Industrial, Saint Louis MO 63126	314-961-6464	R	4*	<.1
151	Finishes Unlimited Inc—*Kenneth Burton*	PO Box 69, Sugar Grove IL 60554	630-466-4881	R	4*	<.1
152	Groco Paint Manufacturing Company Inc—*George Grogan*	PO Box 170790, Dallas TX 75217	972-286-7890	R	4*	<.1
153	Warlick Paint Company Inc—*Robert Lodgek*	PO Box 1508, Statesville NC 28687	704-873-2244	R	4*	<.1

Note: An asterisk (*) indicates an estimated financial figure. The company type code used is as follows: R = Private, P = Public, S = Private Subsidiary, B = Public Subsidiary, D = Division, J = Joint Venture, I = Investment Fund.

COMPANY RANKINGS BY SALES WITHIN 4-DIGIT SIC

Rank	Company Name—*Executive Officer*	Address, City, State, Zip	Phone	Type	Fin	Empls
154	Delta Industrial Coatings Inc—*Tuley Lynch*	PO Box 444, Arlington TN 38002	901-867-9000	R	4*	<.1
155	IVC Ti-Kromatic Industrial Coatings—*Michael Mccracken* IVC Industrial Coatings Inc	2492 Doswell Ave, Saint Paul MN 55108	651-644-4477	S	4*	<.1
156	Sheffield Bronze Paint Corp—*Mel Hart*	PO Box 19206, Cleveland OH 44119	216-481-8330	R	3*	<.1
157	Tennessee Technical Coatings Corp—*Brooks Hodges*	PO Box 1698, Lewisburg TN 37091	931-359-6666	R	3*	<.1
158	Kott Koatings Inc—*John Kott*	27161 Burbank St, Foothill Ranch CA 92610	949-770-5055	R	3*	<.1
159	Waterlox Coatings Corp—*John W Hawkins*	9808 Meech Ave, Cleveland OH 44105		R	3*	<.1
160	John P Nissen Jr Co—*John Nissen Jr*	PO Box 339, Glenside PA 19038	215-886-2025	R	3*	<.1
161	Del Technical Coatings Inc—*Sean Childers*	1801 W Reno Ave, Oklahoma City OK 73106	405-672-1431	R	3*	<.1
162	Scotch Paint Corp—*Charles Harg*	555 W 189th St, Gardena CA 90248	310-329-1259	R	3*	<.1
163	Watson Coatings Inc—*Gary Watson*	PO Box 35067, Saint Louis MO 63135	314-521-2000	R	3*	<.1
164	Swan Black Manufacturing Co—*Jeff Lichten*	4540 W Thomas St, Chicago IL 60651	773-227-3700	R	3*	<.1
165	Tenax Finishing Products Co—*James O'neill*	390 Adams St, Newark NJ 07114	973-589-9000	R	2*	<.1
166	Michigan Industrial Finishes Corp—*Norman Solomon*	29463 Shenandoah Dr, Farmington Hills MI 48331	248-553-7014	R	2*	<.1
167	Everseal International Sales Company Inc—*Justin D Miller*	33 Haynes Cir, Chicopee MA 01020	413-557-1570	R	2*	<.1
168	A-Line Products Corp—*Alger Laura*	2955 Bellevue St, Detroit MI 48207	313-571-8300	R	2*	<.1
169	Norfolk Corp—*Matthew Steele*	145 Enterprise Dr, Marshfield MA 02050	781-319-0400	R	2*	<.1
170	Jellico Chemical Company Inc—*Gene Lanning*	PO Box 11459, Louisville KY 40251	502-772-2547	R	2*	<.1
171	Industrial Nanotech Inc—*George Stuart Burchill*	1925 Trade Center Way, Naples FL 34109	239-254-0346	P	2	N/A
172	Anchor Coatings Of Leesburg Inc—*Gary Tutor*	2280 Talley Rd, Leesburg FL 34748	352-728-0777	R	2*	<.1
173	Union Chemical Industries Corp—*Richard Devick*	1320 Nw 23rd Ave, Fort Lauderdale FL 33311	954-581-6060	R	2*	<.1
174	CF Jameson and Company Inc—*Benjamin Jameson*	PO Box 5197, Haverhill MA 01835	978-374-4731	R	1*	<.1
175	Sterling Clark Lurton Corp—*Joseph Parker*	PO Box J, Malden MA 02148	781-322-0163	R	1*	<.1
176	Nelson Paint Company Of Oregon Inc—*Barbara Louys*	PO Box 2040, Iron Mountain MI 49802	906-774-5566	R	1*	<.1
177	Nesco Manufacturing Inc—*Lore Coultrap*	1510 W Drake Dr, Tempe AZ 85283	480-756-6675	R	1*	<.1
178	Rose's Quality Paints Inc—*Robert Walker*	PO Box 2658, West Columbia SC 29171	803-796-0324	R	<1*	<.1
179	Bradley Coatings Of Ga—*Regis Rumpf*	PO Box 130, Gordon GA 31031		R	<1*	<.1
180	Scott Paint Company Inc—*L Ramer*	7839 Fruitville Rd, Sarasota FL 34240	941-371-0015	R	N/A	<.1
181	Cee-Bee Aviation Products	2910 Harvard Ave, Cleveland OH 44105	216-441-4900	D	N/A	<.1

TOTALS: SIC 2851 Paints & Allied Products
Companies: 181

					43,167	128.2

2861 Gum & Wood Chemicals

Rank	Company Name—*Executive Officer*	Address, City, State, Zip	Phone	Type	Fin	Empls
1	Arch Wood Protection Inc—*Steve Wisnewski*	1955 Lake Park Dr Ste, Smyrna GA 30080	770-801-6600	S	109*	.2
2	Kop-Coat Company Inc—*Charles Pauli*	436 7th Ave, Pittsburgh PA 15219	412-227-2426	S	66*	.1
3	Sand Creek Energy LLC—*D Hunt Ramsbottom*	4150 E 60th Ave, Commerce City CO 80022	303-286-7233	S	6*	<.1
4	Mobile Rosin Oil Co—*Thomas Taylor*	PO Box 70107, Mobile AL 36670	251-476-4282	R	4*	<.1
5	T and R Chemicals Inc—*Fredo Arias*	PO Box 330, Clint TX 79836	915-851-2761	R	3*	<.1

TOTALS: SIC 2861 Gum & Wood Chemicals
Companies: 5

					188	.4

2865 Cyclic Crudes & Intermediates

Rank	Company Name—*Executive Officer*	Address, City, State, Zip	Phone	Type	Fin	Empls
1	Huntsman International LLC	500 Huntsman Way, Salt Lake City UT 84108	801-584-5700	S	6,503	5.7
2	Clover Technologies Group LLC—*Eric Martin*	2700 W Higgins Rd Ste, Hoffman Estates IL 60169	815-431-8100	R	165*	.5
3	Americhem Inc—*Richard Juve*	2000 Americhem Way, Cuyahoga Falls OH 44221	330-929-4213	R	74*	.6
4	Penn Color Inc—*Kevin Putman*	400 Old Dublin Pke, Doylestown PA 18901	215-345-6550	R	69*	.6
5	Vertellus Specialties Inc—*Richard Preziotti*	201 N Illinois St Ste, Indianapolis IN 46204	317-247-8141	R	63*	.5
6	Apollo Colors Inc—*David Klebine*	1401 Mound Rd, Rockdale IL 60436	815-741-2588	R	34*	.2
7	Standridge Color Corp—*Robert Standridge*	PO Box 1086, Social Circle GA 30025	770-464-3362	R	34*	.3
8	Cleveland Fp Inc—*Robert Searles*	12819 Coit Rd, Cleveland OH 44108	216-249-4900	R	32*	.1
9	Heucotech Limited A New Jersey LP—*June Dickenson*	99 Newbold Rd, Fairless Hills PA 19030	215-736-0712	R	28*	.1
10	Esco Company LLC—*Darrel Cardy*	1221 E Barney Ave, Muskegon MI 49444	231-726-3106	S	27*	.1
11	Greenville Colorants Inc—*Stephen Holland*	20 Linden Ave East, Jersey City NJ 07305	201-595-0200	R	23*	.1
12	Cardinal Cartridge Inc—*Lee Ferry*	20450 Plummer St, Chatsworth CA 91311	775-624-8135	R	23*	.2
13	National Plastics Color Inc—*Steven Sutherland*	PO Box 127, Valley Center KS 67147	316-755-1273	R	23*	.1
14	American Diagnostica Inc—*Richard Hart*	500 West Ave, Stamford CT 06902	203-602-7777	R	22*	<.1
15	Color Imaging Inc—*Jui-Kung Wang*	4350 Peachtree Industr, Norcross GA 30071	770-840-1090	R	21*	.1
16	Whittaker Clark and Daniels—*Theodore Hubbard*	1000 Coolidge St, South Plainfield NJ 07080	908-561-6100	R	18*	.1
17	Mesa Industries Inc—*Dennis Glaser*	230 N 48th Ave Ste 2, Phoenix AZ 85043	602-269-3199	R	17*	.1
18	Grant Industries Inc (Elmwood Park New Jersey)—*Tom Granatell*	125 Main Ave, Elmwood Park NJ 07407	201-791-6700	R	15*	<.1
19	Abbey Color Inc—*Roger Nielsen*	400 E Tioga St, Philadelphia PA 19134	215-739-9960	R	11*	<.1
20	Rite Systems Inc—*Manu Jogani*	625 Wegner Dr, West Chicago IL 60185	630-562-9700	S	11*	.1
21	General Press Colors Ltd—*Casimir Grabacki*	120 S Fairbank St, Addison IL 60101	630-543-7878	R	10*	.1
22	Arizona Oxides LLC	12519 W Butler Dr, El Mirage AZ 85335	623-935-9350	R	10*	<.1
23	Southern Indiana Properties Inc—*Carl L Chapman*	PO Box 209, Evansville IN 47702	812-491-4000	S	10*	.1
24	Hoover Color Corp—*Charles Hoover*	PO Box 218, Hiwassee VA 24347	540-980-7233	R	9*	.1
25	Styrene Products Inc—*Eldred Drescher*	5320 Fuller St, Schofield WI 54476	715-359-6600	R	6*	.1
26	Isochem Colors Inc—*William Whisenant*	138 Beeren St Ste 100, Clover SC 29710	803-325-7640	R	5*	<.1
27	Chem Service Inc—*Lyle Phifer*	PO Box 599, West Chester PA 19381	610-692-3026	R	4*	<.1
28	Color Science Inc—*Jocelyn Eubank*	1245 E Glenwood Pl, Santa Ana CA 92707	714-434-1033	S	3*	<.1
29	H and S Chemical Company Inc—*Damon Tang*	52 Van Dyke St 64, Wallington NJ 07057	201-939-8680	R	3*	<.1
30	Ashwell Label Dies Inc—*Wilfried Jeurink*	6545 44th St N Ste 400, Pinellas Park FL 33781	727-527-0098	R	2*	<.1
31	Key Tech Inc—*Patrick Ferguson*	128 Bay State Ave, Warwick RI 02888	401-732-7788	R	<1*	<.1

TOTALS: SIC 2865 Cyclic Crudes & Intermediates
Companies: 31

					7,275	9.7

2869 Industrial Organic Chemicals Nec

Rank	Company Name—*Executive Officer*	Address, City, State, Zip	Phone	Type	Fin	Empls
1	Bayer Corp—*Gregory S Babe*	100 Bayer Rd, Pittsburgh PA 15205	412-777-2000	S	9,786*	16.4
2	Lubrizol Corp—*James L Hambrick*	29400 Lakeland Blvd, Wickliffe OH 44092	440-943-4200	S	5,418	6.9
3	Sasol North America Inc—*Pat Brown*	PO Box 19029, Houston TX 77224	281-588-3000	R	5,333*	.6
4	Dow Corning Corp—*Robert D Hansen*	PO Box 994, Midland MI 48686	989-496-4000	R	4,940	10.0
5	Westlake Chemical Corp—*Albert Chao*	2801 Post Oak Blvd, Houston TX 77056	713-960-9111	P	3,620	1.8
6	International Flavors and Fragrances Inc—*Douglas D Tough*	521 W 57th St, New York NY 10019	212-765-5500	P	2,788	5.6
7	NewMarket Corp—*Thomas E Gottwald*	PO Box 2189, Richmond VA 23218	804-788-5000	P	2,150	1.6
8	Green Plains Renewable Energy Inc—*Todd Becker*	450 Regency Pky Ste 40, Omaha NE 68114	402-884-8700	P	2,133	.6
9	NutraSweet Kelco Co—*Craig Petray*	222 Merchandise Mart P, Chicago IL 60654	312-873-5000	S	1,512*	2.5
10	Sensient Technologies Corp—*Kenneth P Manning*	777 E Wisconsin Ave, Milwaukee WI 53202	414-271-6755	P	1,328	3.6
11	International Specialty Products Inc—*Sunil Kumar*	1361 Alps Rd, Wayne NJ 07470	973-628-4000	R	891*	3.0

Rank	Company Name—*Executive Officer*	Address, City, State, Zip	Phone	Type	Fin	Empls
12	Innospec Inc—*Patrick S Williams*	8375 S Willow St, Littleton CO 80124	303-792-5554	P	774	.9
13	Union Carbide Corp—*Patrick Gottschalk*	PO Box 4393, Houston TX 77210	281-966-2016	S	762*	2.4
14	Arizona Chemical Company Inc—*Kees Verhaar*	PO Box 550850, Jacksonville FL 32255	904-928-8700	R	715*	1.0
15	Texas Petrochemicals Holdings Inc—*Charles Shaver*	5151 San Felipe St Ste, Houston TX 77056	713-627-7474	R	600*	.4
16	ISP Chemical Products Inc	PO Box 37, Calvert City KY 42029	270-395-4169	S	578*	.5
17	ISP Chemicals Inc	PO Box 37, Calvert City KY 42029	270-395-4165	S	578*	.5
18	Buckman Laboratories Inc—*Jim Doan*	PO Box 80305, Memphis TN 38108	901-278-0330	R	500*	.4
19	Sigma-Aldrich Chemical Co—*Rod Kelley*	PO Box 355, Milwaukee WI 53201	414-438-3850	S	475*	.8
20	Elementis Specialties—*Bill French*	PO Box 700, Hightstown NJ 08520	609-443-2000	S	473*	.5
21	BioFuel Energy Corp—*Scott H Pearce*	1600 Broadway Ste 2200, Denver CO 80202	303-640-6500	P	453	.2
22	Symrise Inc—*Klaus Stanzl*	300 North St, Teterboro NJ 07608	201-288-3200	R	433*	.7
23	Merisant Worldwide Inc—*Paul Block*	33 N Dearborn St Ste 2, Chicago IL 60602	312-840-6000	R	265*	.4
24	Houghton International Inc—*William Macdonald*	PO Box 930, Valley Forge PA 19482	610-666-4000	R	205*	1.6
25	Givaudan Flavors And Fragrances Inc—*Stefan Giezandanner*	1199 Edison Dr, Cincinnati OH 45216	513-948-8000	S	168*	2.5
26	Clariant Corp—*Kenneth Golder*	PO Box 18278, Charlotte NC 28218	704-331-7000	R	162*	1.2
27	Muscatine Foods Corp—*G Kent*	1600 Oregon St, Muscatine IA 52761	563-264-4211	R	162*	1.8
28	Ethyl Corp—*Azfar Choudhury* NewMarket Corp	PO Box 2189, Richmond VA 23218	804-788-5000	S	155*	.2
29	SiVance LLC—*Craig Stafford*	PO Box 1466, Gainesville FL 32602	352-376-8246	R	130*	.1
30	Cumberland Packing Corp—*Jeffrey Eisenstadt*	2 Cumberland St, Brooklyn NY 11205	718-858-4200	R	111*	.4
31	First Chemical Corp—*Ellen Kullman*	PO Box 7005, Pascagoula MS 39568	228-762-0870	S	107*	.2
32	Detrex Corp—*Thomas E Mark*	PO Box 5111, Southfield MI 48086	248-358-5800	P	94	.2
33	Badger State Ethanol LLC—*Gary L Kramer*	PO Box 317, Monroe WI 53566	608-329-3900	R	92*	<.1
34	Hawkeye Renewables LLC—*Bruce Rastetter*	21050 140th St, Iowa Falls IA 50126	641-648-8910	R	89	.1
35	Emd Chemicals Inc—*Meiken Krebs*	480 S Democrat Rd, Gibbstown NJ 08027	856-423-6300	R	77*	.7
36	Alternative Petroleum—*Patrick Grimes*	280 Greg St Ste 20, Reno NV 89502	775-322-4605	R	65*	<.1
37	Alltech Inc—*Thomas Lyons*	3031 Catnip Hill Rd, Nicholasville KY 40356	859-885-9613	R	57*	.6
38	Chemtall Inc—*Peter Nichols*	PO Box 250, Riceboro GA 31323	912-884-3366	R	52*	.3
39	Verenium Corp—*James Levine*	55 Cambridge Pkwy 8th, Cambridge MA 02142	617-674-5300	P	52	.1
40	Vesta Intermediate Funding Inc—*Phillip Estes*	5400 W Franklin Dr, Franklin WI 53132	414-423-0550	R	51*	.3
41	Michelman Inc—*John Michelman*	9080 Shell Rd, Cincinnati OH 45236	513-793-7766	R	50*	.2
42	Chemico Systems Inc—*Leon Richardson*	50725 Richard W Blvd, Chesterfield MI 48051	248-723-3263	R	49*	<.1
43	Innospec Active Chemicals LLC—*David Shaffer*	510 W Grimes Ave, High Point NC 27260	336-882-3308	R	45*	<.1
44	Minnesota Energy Ethanol LP—*Robert Johansen*	PO Box 218, Buffalo Lake MN 55314	320-833-5939	R	44*	.1
45	Rockland Immunochemicals Inc—*Natalie Cappel*	PO Box 326, Gilbertsville PA 19525	610-369-1008	R	44*	<.1
46	3v Inc—*John Centioni*	PO Box 2810, Georgetown SC 29442	843-546-8556	R	43*	.5
47	Evonik Stockhausen LLC—*Reinhold Brand*	2401 Doyle St, Greensboro NC 27406	336-333-3500	R	42*	.4
48	Kemira Chemicals Inc—*Hannu Melarti*	1950 Vaughn Rd Nw Ste, Kennesaw GA 30144	770-436-1542	R	42*	.4
49	Bell Flavors And Fragrances Inc—*James Heinz*	500 Academy Dr, Northbrook IL 60062	847-291-8300	R	38*	.2
50	Troy Corp—*Daryl Smith*	PO Box 955, Florham Park NJ 07932	973-443-4200	R	37*	.4
51	Mane USA Inc—*Michel Mane*	60 Demarest Dr, Wayne NJ 07470	973-633-5533	S	33*	.2
52	Sachem Inc—*John Mooney*	821 Woodward St, Austin TX 78704	512-421-4900	R	30*	.3
53	Bluestar Silicones—*John Foley*	PO Box 11 674, Rock Hill SC 29731	803-329-5260	R	30	.1
54	American Gas Group	6055 Brent Dr, Toledo OH 43611	419-729-7732	S	28	.1
55	Research Corporation Technologies Inc—*Shaun A Kirkpatrick*	5210 E Williams Cir St, Tucson AZ 85711	520-748-4400	R	28*	<.1
56	Imperium Renewables Inc—*John Plaza*	1741 1st Ave S 2nd Fl, Seattle WA 98134	206-254-0203	R	28*	<.1
57	New Energy Corp—*Nathan Kimpel*	PO Box 2289, South Bend IN 46680	574-233-3116	R	28*	.1
58	Perstorp Polyols Inc—*David Wolf*	600 Matzinger Rd, Toledo OH 43612	419-729-5448	R	28*	.1
59	Ortec Inc—*David Brotherton*	PO Box 1469, Easley SC 29641	864-859-1471	R	27*	.2
60	Wessel Fragrances Inc—*Kenneth Wessel*	400 Sylvan Ave Ste 1, Englewood Cliffs NJ 07632	201-541-1119	S	26*	.1
61	Lindau Chemicals Inc—*Robert Robinson*	731 Rosewood Dr, Columbia SC 29201	803-799-6863	R	26*	<.1
62	Dodge Chemical Company Inc—*John Dodge*	165 Cambridgepark Dr, Cambridge MA 02140	617-661-0500	R	25*	.1
63	Cambridge Isotope Laboratories Inc—*Joel Bradley*	50 Frontage Rd, Andover MA 01810	978-749-8000	R	24*	.1
64	Boehme-Filatex Inc—*Rene Eckert*	209 Watlington Industr, Reidsville NC 27320	336-342-6631	R	24*	.1
65	Moses Lake Industries Inc—*Toshitsura Cho*	8248 Randolph Rd Ne, Moses Lake WA 98837	509-762-5336	R	23*	.1
66	Struktol Company Of America—*Gilbret Hamrick*	PO Box 1649, Stow OH 44224	330-928-5188	R	22*	.1
67	Elco Corp Detrex Corp	1000 Belt Line Ave, Cleveland OH 44109		S	21*	<.1
68	Lipo Chemicals Inc—*Louis Frischling*	207 19th Ave, Paterson NJ 07504	973-345-8600	R	21*	.1
69	Corsicana Technologies Inc—*Steven Lindley*	PO Box 1898, Corsicana TX 75151	903-874-9500	R	21*	.1
70	Marval Industries Inc—*Thomas Zimmerman*	315 Hoyt Ave, Mamaroneck NY 10543	914-381-2400	R	21*	.1
71	Arylessence Inc—*Steve Tanner*	1091 Lake Dr, Marietta GA 30066	770-924-3775	R	20*	.1
72	Cardolite Corp—*Anthony Stonis*	500 Doremus Ave, Newark NJ 07105	973-344-5015	R	20*	.1
73	Alps South Corp—*Aldo Laghi*	2895 42nd Ave N, Saint Petersburg FL 33714	727-528-8566	R	20*	.1
74	Oak-Bark Corp—*James Barker*	102 Orange St, Wilmington NC 28401	910-251-0234	R	20*	.1
75	Idq Operating Inc—*Michael Klein*	2901 W Kingsley Rd, Garland TX 75041	214-778-4600	R	19*	.1
76	National Enzyme Company Inc—*Anthony Collier*	15366 Us Hwy 160, Forsyth MO 65653	417-546-4796	R	19*	.1
77	Tedia Company Inc—*Hoon Choi*	1000 Tedia Way, Fairfield OH 45014	513-874-5340	R	18*	.1
78	Richland Research Corp—*David Smilovic*	3110 N 19th Ave Ste 22, Phoenix AZ 85015	602-230-0012	R	17*	.1
79	Spurrier Chemical Companies Inc—*Robert Spurrier*	PO Box 2812, Wichita KS 67201	316-265-9491	R	16*	.1
80	Wyoming Ethanol LLC—*Marianne Best*	PO Box 178, Torrington WY 82240	307-532-2449	R	16*	<.1
81	Synthetech Inc—*Gregory R Hahn*	1290 Industrial Way, Albany OR 97322	541-967-6575	S	15	.1
82	Comax Manufacturing Corp—*Peter Calabretta*	130 Baylis Rd, Melville NY 11747	631-249-0505	R	13*	.1
83	Sea Lion Inc—*Malcolm Colditz*	PO Box 1807, Texas City TX 77592	409-948-4351	R	12*	.1
84	Chippewa Valley Ethanol Company Lllp—*John Kent*	270 20th St Nw, Benson MN 56215	320-843-4813	R	12*	.1
85	Belle-Aire Fragrances Inc—*Donald Conover*	1600 Baskin Rd, Mundelein IL 60060	847-816-3500	R	12*	.1
86	Chemionics Corp—*Jeff Radler*	390 Munroe Falls Rd, Tallmadge OH 44278	330-733-8834	R	11*	<.1
87	Fontarome Chemical Inc—*Carl Sheeley*	4170 S Nevada St, Saint Francis WI 53235	414-744-3993	R	11*	<.1
88	Reclamation Technologies Inc—*Richard Marcus*	1100 Haskins Rd, Bowling Green OH 43402	419-867-8990	R	11*	<.1
89	Calhoun Plastics And Chemicals Inc—*Kenneth Parker*	PO Box 1295, Calhoun GA 30703	706-629-9077	R	10*	<.1
90	Corn Plus—*Rick Lunz*	711 6th Ave Se, Winnebago MN 56098	507-893-4747	R	10*	<.1
91	Aaper Alcohol And Chemical Co—*Gary Mcinerney*	PO Box 339, Shelbyville KY 40066	502-633-0650	R	10*	.1
92	Forth Technologies Inc—*John Lyle*	600 Bergman St, Louisville KY 40203	502-637-4553	R	10*	<.1
93	Polychem Dispersions Inc—*William Nichols*	16006 Industrial Pkwy, Middlefield OH 44062	440-632-0227	R	10*	<.1
94	Polyscientific Research And Development Corp—*John Caggiano*	70 Cleveland Ave, Bay Shore NY 11706	631-586-0400	R	9*	<.1
95	Zaclon Inc—*Jim Krimmel*	2981 Independence Rd, Cleveland OH 44115		R	9*	<.1
96	Associated Chemists Inc—*Steve Brown*	4401 Se Jhnson Creek B, Portland OR 97222	503-659-1708	R	9*	<.1
97	Nayak Aviation Corp—*Mike Mcwilliams*	1403 Northern Blvd, San Antonio TX 78216	210-824-7511	R	9*	<.1
98	Carrubba Inc—*Philip Carrubba*	70 Research Dr, Milford CT 06460	203-878-0605	R	9*	<.1

Note: An asterisk (*) indicates an estimated financial figure. The company type code used is as follows: R = Private, P = Public, S = Private Subsidiary, B = Public Subsidiary, D = Division, J = Joint Venture, I = Investment Fund.

COMPANY RANKINGS BY SALES WITHIN 4-DIGIT SIC

Rank	Company Name—Executive Officer	Address, City, State, Zip	Phone	Type	Fin	Empls
99	Cedar Concepts Corp—Linda Mcgill	4342 S Wolcott Ave, Chicago IL 60609	773-890-5790	R	8*	<.1
100	Hampford Research Inc—Clare Donahue	54 Veterans Blvd, Stratford CT 06615	203-375-1137	R	8*	<.1
101	Lacamas Laboratories Inc—Allen Erickson	PO Box 17659, Portland OR 97217	503-285-0360	R	7*	<.1
102	Imi Fabi LLC—Michelle Cortazzo	2nd Marshall St, Benwood WV 26031	304-233-0050	R	7*	<.1
103	Montana Limestone Co—Mike Jones	PO Box 166, Frannie WY 82423	406-764-2513	S	7*	<.1
104	Lipo Technologies Inc—Louis Frischling	800 Scholz Dr, Vandalia OH 45377	937-264-1222	R	6*	<.1
105	Heartland Corn Products—Perry Meyer	PO Box A, Winthrop MN 55396	507-647-5000	R	6*	<.1
106	Crown Delta Corp—Anthony Konopka	1550 Front St, Yorktown Heights NY 10598	914-245-8910	R	6*	<.1
107	Tobacco Technology Inc—Jeremy Cassels-Smith	600 Liberty Rd, Sykesville MD 21784	410-549-8800	R	6*	<.1
108	RSA Corp—Jan Anthony	36 Old Sherman Tpke, Danbury CT 06810	203-790-8100	R	6*	<.1
109	Alchem Limited Lllp—Kevin Rauser	PO Box 1728, Jamestown ND 58402	701-352-0602	R	5*	<.1
110	Bio-Energy Systems Inc—Phil Gaynor	1390 Us Hwy 2 W, Kalispell MT 59901	406-257-9111	R	5*	<.1
111	Aqua/Process Inc—Charles Staley	125 Southbelt Industri, Houston TX 77047	713-413-1216	R	5*	<.1
112	Hydrol Chemical Company Inc—H Haabestad	520 Commerce Dr Ste 2, Lansdowne PA 19050	610-622-3603	R	5*	<.1
113	Fujifilm Diosynth Biotechnologies—Stephen A Spearman	101 J Morris Commons L, Morrisville NC 27560	919-337-4477	R	5*	<.1
114	Sustainable Oils LLC—Scott Johnson s	214 Shepherd Trl, Bozeman MT 59718	406-522-8900	J	5*	<.1
115	Norquay Technology Inc—Robert Heldt	PO Box 468, Chester PA 19016	610-874-4330	R	5*	<.1
116	Chaska Chemical Company Inc—Sean Teske	12502 Xenwood Ave, Savage MN 55378	952-890-1820	R	4*	<.1
117	Frigid Fluid Co—Robert Yeazel	11631 W Grand Ave, Melrose Park IL 60164	708-836-1215	R	4*	<.1
118	J and M Laboratories Inc—Karen Mitzlaff	6533 Villa Spring Dr, Louisville KY 40291	502-290-3574	R	4*	<.1
119	Adron Inc—Louis Amaducci	PO Box 270, Boonton NJ 07005	973-334-1600	R	4*	<.1
120	Marlowe-Van Loan Corp—Paul Tharp	PO Box 1851, High Point NC 27261	336-886-7126	R	3*	<.1
121	Marnap Industries Inc—Dennis J Napora	225 French St, Buffalo NY 14211	716-897-1220	R	3*	<.1
122	New Generation Biofuels Holdings Inc—David Goebel	5850 Waterloo Rd Ste 1, Columbia MD 21045	410-480-8084	P	2	<.1
123	Terry Laboratories Inc—Rex Maughan	7005 Technology Dr, Melbourne FL 32904	321-259-1630	R	1*	<.1
124	Contronic Devices Inc—Robert Nibbe	15661 Producer Ln Ste, Huntington Beach CA 92649	714-897-2266	R	1*	<.1
125	Mead Technologies Inc—William James	PO Box 748, Rolla MO 65402	573-364-8844	R	1*	<.1
126	Krueger Enterprises—William Krueger	5057 American Legion R, Iowa City IA 52240	319-351-2808	R	1*	<.1
127	Specialty Organics Inc—Joseph Seruto	5263 4th St, Irwindale CA 91706	626-962-2008	R	<1*	<.1
128	PetroAlgae Inc—John S Scott	1901 S Harbor City Blv, Melbourne FL 32901	321-409-7970	P	<1	.1
129	Medical Chemical Corp—Emmanuel Didier	19430 Van Ness Ave, Torrance CA 90501	310-787-6800	R	<1	<.1
130	H Krevit And Company Inc—Thomas Ross	67 Welton St, New Haven CT 06511	203-772-3350	R	N/A	<.1
131	Aemetis Inc—Eric A McAfee	20400 Stevens Creek Bl, Cupertino CA 95014	408-213-0940	P	N/A	<.1

TOTALS: SIC 2869 Industrial Organic Chemicals Nec
Companies: 131

					49,787	78.1

2873 Nitrogenous Fertilizers

	Company Name—Executive Officer	Address, City, State, Zip	Phone	Type	Fin	Empls
1	Equistar Chemicals LP—Jim Gallogly	PO Box 2583, Houston TX 77252	713-652-7200	S	11,686	3.2
2	CF Industries Holdings Inc—Stephen R Wilson	4 Parkway N Ste 400, Deerfield IL 60015	847-405-2400	P	3,965	2.4
3	Scotts Miracle-Gro Co—James Hagedorn	14111 Scottslawn Rd, Marysville OH 43040	937-644-0011	P	2,836	6.3
4	Sun Gro Horticulture Inc—Mitchell J Weaver	15831 NE 8th St Ste 10, Bellevue WA 98008	425-641-7577	S	1,456*	.7
5	JR Simplot Minerals and Chemicals Group—Larry Hlobik	PO Box 27, Boise ID 83707	208-336-2110	S	460*	2.3
6	CVR Partners LP—Byron Kelley	2277 Plaza Dr Ste 500, Sugar Land TX 77479	281-207-3200	B	303	.1
7	South Dakota Wheat Growers Association—Dale Locken	PO Box 110, Aberdeen SD 57402	605-225-5500	R	238*	.3
8	Lykes Brothers Inc—John A Brabson	PO Box 1690, Tampa FL 33601	813-470-5000	R	92*	.3
9	Apache Nitrogen Products Inc—Robert Cashdollar	PO Box 700, Benson AZ 85602	520-720-2217	R	84*	.1
10	Senesac Inc—John Freeland	PO Box 592, Fowler IN 47944	765-884-1300	R	25*	<.1
11	Nutra-Flo Co—Eric Lohry	1919 Grand Ave, Sioux City IA 51106	712-277-2011	R	23*	.1
12	John Pryor Company Inc—Joe Wiley	PO Box 3650, Salinas CA 93902	831-422-5307	D	22*	.1
13	Green Valley Chemical Corp—Bernard Cox	PO Box 86, Creston IA 50801	641-782-7041	R	17*	<.1
14	Plantation Products LLC—Joseph Raffaele	202 S Washington St, Norton MA 02766	508-285-5800	R	16*	.1
15	Red Star Fertilizer Co—Paul Bernhard	17132 Hellman Ave, Corona CA 92880	909-597-4801	R	10*	.1
16	Fertrell Co—David Mattocks	PO Box 265, Bainbridge PA 17502	717-367-1566	R	10*	<.1
17	Houff's Feed And Fertilizer Company Inc—Neil Houff	97 Railside Dr, Weyers Cave VA 24486	540-234-9246	R	10*	<.1
18	Peak Minerals-Azomite Inc—William W Emerson	7406 NE 84th Terrace, Kansas City MO 64157	816-415-1919	R	6*	<.1
19	Winston Weaver Company Inc—Vernon Carlton	PO Box 17366, Winston Salem NC 27116	336-661-1495	R	6*	<.1
20	Tri-County Chemical Inc—H Melton	2441 Public Rd, Eldorado IL 62930	618-273-2071	R	5*	<.1
21	Fertilizer Corporation of America—David Christopherson	9380 SW 72 StB240, Miami FL 33173	305-595-6738	R	5*	<.1
22	Reed and Perrine Inc—Virginia Bulkowski	PO Box 100, Tennent NJ 07763	732-446-6363	R	5*	<.1
23	Gro-Power Inc—Brent Holden	15065 Telephone Ave, Chino CA 91710	909-393-3744	R	5*	<.1
24	Liquinox Co—Henry Garner	221 W Meats Ave, Orange CA 92865	714-637-6300	R	5*	<.1
25	Spray-N-Grow Inc—Bill Muskopf	PO Box 2137, Rockport TX 78382	361-790-9033	R	4*	<.1
26	Sustane Natural Fertilizer Inc—Craig Holden	PO Box 19, Cannon Falls MN 55009	507-263-3003	R	2*	<.1
27	Chamberlin and Barclay Inc—David Barclay	PO Box 416, Cranbury NJ 08512	609-655-0700	R	1*	<.1
28	Petrik Laboratories Inc—Valcav Petrik	109 Harter Ave, Woodland CA 95776	530-666-1157	R	1*	<.1

TOTALS: SIC 2873 Nitrogenous Fertilizers
Companies: 28

					21,296	16.2

2874 Phosphatic Fertilizers

	Company Name—Executive Officer	Address, City, State, Zip	Phone	Type	Fin	Empls
1	Mosaic Co—James T Prokopanko	Artria Corporate Ctr 3, Plymouth MN 55441	763-577-2700	P	9,938	7.7
2	Simplot Phosphates LLC—Darren Hurd	515 Hwy 430, Rock Springs WY 82901	307-382-1400	R	31*	.3
3	Howard Fertilizer and Chemical Company Inc—Robert Howard	PO Box 628202, Orlando FL 32862	407-855-1841	R	22*	.1
4	Mosaic Phosphates MP Inc Mosaic Co	PO Box 2000, Mulberry FL 33860	863-428-2500	S	21	.1
5	Advan LLC—Andy Lee	300 Colonial Center Pk, Roswell GA 30076	770-594-6363	R	15*	<.1
6	Pro-Boll Chemical and Fertilizer Company Inc—Don Raley	PO Box 804, Delhi LA 71232	318-878-2065	R	9*	<.1
7	Cytozyme Laboratories Inc—Steve Baughman	134 S 700 W, Salt Lake City UT 84104	801-533-9208	R	7*	<.1

TOTALS: SIC 2874 Phosphatic Fertilizers
Companies: 7

					10,043	8.3

2875 Fertilizers—Mixing Only

	Company Name—Executive Officer	Address, City, State, Zip	Phone	Type	Fin	Empls
1	Cherokee Nitrogen Holdings Inc—Jack E Golsen	PO Box 250, Cherokee AL 35616	256-359-7000	S	1,002*	1.3
2	Easy Gardener Products Ltd—Dick Grandy	PO Box 21025, Waco TX 76702	254-753-5353	R	220*	.2
3	American Plant Food Corp—Donald Ford	PO Box 584, Galena Park TX 77547	713-675-2231	R	168*	.1
4	Twin State Inc—R Tinsman	3541 E Kimberly Rd, Davenport IA 52807	563-359-3624	R	150*	.1
5	Central Missouri Agriservice LLC—Barb Berlin	PO Box 549, Marshall MO 65340	660-886-6976	R	112*	.1
6	Cedar Grove Composting Inc—Steve Banchero	7343 E Marginal Way S, Seattle WA 98108	206-832-3000	R	100*	.3
7	Farm Country Co-Op—Noel Frana	PO Box 1037, Pine Island MN 55963	507-356-8313	R	75*	.1
8	Frit Industries Inc—Shelton Allred	PO Box 1589, Ozark AL 36361	334-774-2515	R	75*	<.1
9	Douglass Fertilizer and Chemical Inc	800 Trafalgar Ct, Maitland FL 32751	407-682-6100	S	72*	.1

Rank	Company Name—*Executive Officer*	Address, City, State, Zip	Phone	Type	Fin	Empls
10	Pace International LLC—*George Lobisser*	1201 3rd Ave Ste 5450, Seattle WA 98101	206-331-4700	R	71*	.2
11	Brandt Consolidated Inc—*Rick Brandt*	2935 S Koke Mill Rd, Springfield IL 62711	217-547-5800	R	54*	.1
12	Kugler Oil Co—*John Kugler*	PO Box 1748, McCook NE 69001	308-345-2280	R	46*	.1
13	Voluntary Purchasing Group Inc	230 FM 87, Bonham TX 75418	903-583-5501	R	41*	.1
14	Harrell's Inc—*Jack Harrell*	PO Box 807, Lakeland FL 33802	863-687-2774	R	38*	.2
15	Growers Fertilizer Corp—*Brent Sutton*	PO Box 1407, Lake Alfred FL 33850	863-956-1101	R	31*	<.1
16	Growmark Fs LLC—*Paul Masula*	308 Ne Front St, Milford DE 19963	302-422-3001	R	29*	.3
17	Florida Potting Soils Inc—*Richard Fletcher*	6021 Beggs Rd, Orlando FL 32810	407-291-1676	S	26*	<.1
18	Hydro/Kirby Agri Services Inc—*Carroll Kirby*	PO Box 6277, Lancaster PA 17607	717-299-2541	R	26*	.1
19	Farmers Coop (Hanska Minnesota)—*Randall Rieke*	PO Box 6, Hanska MN 56041	507-439-6244	R	24*	.1
20	Whittier Fertilizer Co—*Robert Osborn*	PO Box 596, Pico Rivera CA 90660	562-699-3461	R	23*	.1
21	Wolfkill Feed and Fertilizer Corp—*Merritt Wolfkill*	PO Box 578, Monroe WA 98272	360-794-7065	R	23*	<.1
22	Joseph Enterprises Inc—*Joe Pedott*	425 California St Ste, San Francisco CA 94104	415-397-6992	R	19*	<.1
23	Specialty Fertilizer Products LLC—*J Larry Sanders*	11550 Ash Ste 220, Leawood KS 66211	913-956-7500	R	19*	<.1
24	Poole Chemical Company Inc—*Danny Poole*	PO Box 10, Texline TX 79087	806-362-4261	R	16*	.1
25	Graco Fertilizer Co—*Thomas Le Gette*	PO Box 89, Cairo GA 39828	229-377-1602	R	12*	.1
26	Romeo Packing Co—*Joe Romeo*	106 Princeton Ave, Half Moon Bay CA 94019	650-728-3393	R	11*	<.1
27	Chemical Dynamics Inc—*David Carson*	PO Box 486, Plant City FL 33564	813-752-4950	R	9*	<.1
28	Wheaton Dumont Cooperative Elevator Inc—*Vaugh Maudal*	6587 US Hwy 75, Wheaton MN 56296	320-563-8152	R	9*	<.1
29	Traylor Trucking Services—*Greg Traylor*	PO Box 69, Montgomery IN 47558	812-486-3285	R	9	<.1
30	Robert F Wiseman and Assoc Inc—*Robert Wiseman*	18375 Sw 260th St, Homestead FL 33031	305-247-8800	R	8*	<.1
31	Ag Services By Associated Tagline Corp—*Tom Erickson*	PO Box 1330, Salinas CA 93902	831-422-6452	R	6*	<.1
32	Banfe Products Inc—*Jerry Banfe*	145 Broadway, Westville NJ 08093	856-456-6300	R	6*	<.1
33	H and H Wood Recyclers Inc—*Richard Henker*	PO Box 1855, Battle Ground WA 98604	360-892-2805	R	5*	<.1
34	J R Peters Inc—*John Peters*	6656 Grant Way, Allentown PA 18106	610-395-7104	R	4*	<.1
35	Triad Energy Resources Inc—*Mike Daley*	204 Kerr Ave, Modesto CA 95354	209-527-0607	R	4*	<.1
36	Chastant Brothers Inc—*John Chastant*	PO Box 4507, Lafayette LA 70502	337-234-2351	R	4*	<.1
37	Webb Super-Gro Products Inc	30 Pennsylvania Ave, Mill Hall PA 17751	570-726-4525	R	3*	<.1
38	Permagreen Products Co—*Roxy Vendena*	5520 Harlan St, Arvada CO 80002	303-424-7291	R	2*	<.1
39	Egypt Farms Inc—*G Snyder*	PO Box 223, White Marsh MD 21162	410-335-3700	R	2*	<.1
40	Plant Foods Inc—*Robert Geary*	PO Box 1089, Vero Beach FL 32961	772-567-5741	R	2*	<.1
41	Canton Mills Inc—*David Bunky*	PO Box 97, Minnesota City MN 55959	507-689-2131	R	1*	<.1

TOTALS: SIC 2875 Fertilizers— Mixing Only

Companies: 41					2,554	4.1

2879 Agricultural Chemicals Nec

Rank	Company Name—*Executive Officer*	Address, City, State, Zip	Phone	Type	Fin	Empls
1	Monsanto Co—*Hugh Grant*	800 N Lindbergh Blvd, Saint Louis MO 63167	314-694-1000	P	11,822	20.6
2	FMC Corp—*Pierre Brondeau*	1735 Market St, Philadelphia PA 19103	215-299-6000	P	3,378	5.0
3	Albaugh Inc—*Dennis Albaugh*	1525 NE 36th St, Ankeny IA 50021	515-964-9444	R	1,100	.8
4	LESCO Inc—*Jeffrey L Rutherford*	1301 E 9th St Ste 1300, Cleveland OH 44114	216-706-9250	S	550*	1.1
5	Valent USA Corp—*Mike Donaldson*	1600 Riviera Ave Ste 2, Walnut Creek CA 94596		R	476*	.3
6	Cerexagri Inc—*Jeff Allison*	630 Freedom Business C, King of Prussia PA 19406	610-491-2800	R	444*	.6
7	American Vanguard Corp—*Eric G Wintemute*	4695 MacArthur Ct Ste, Newport Beach CA 92660	949-260-1200	P	230	.4
8	Wilco-Winfield LLC—*Douglas Hoffman*	PO Box 258, Mount Angel OR 97362	503-845-6122	R	222*	.5
9	Mycogen Corp—*Carlton J Eibl*	9330 Zionsville Rd, Indianapolis IN 46268		R	211	1.0
10	Alco Industries Inc—*T Lawrence Way*	820 Adams Ave Ste 130, Norristown PA 19403	610-666-0930	R	157*	<.1
11	Drexel Chemical Co—*Ben Johnson*	PO Box 13327, Memphis TN 38113	901-774-4370	R	102*	.2
12	Gowan Company LLC—*Juli Jessen*	PO Box 5569, Yuma AZ 85366	928-782-8844	R	62*	.1
13	Bell Laboratories Inc—*Steve Levy*	PO Box 8421, Madison WI 53708	608-241-0202	R	60*	.3
14	Amvac Chemical Corp—*Eric Wintemute* American Vanguard Corp	4100 E Washington Blvd, Los Angeles CA 90023	323-264-3910	S	55*	.2
15	Agrium Inc (Denver Colorado)	4582 S Ulster St Ste 1, Denver CO 80237	303-804-4400	S	47*	.1
16	Chem-Trol Inc—*Joe White*	PO Box 2343, Kansas City KS 66110	913-342-3006	R	36*	.1
17	West Agro Inc—*John Benjamin*	11100 N Congress Ave, Kansas City MO 64153	816-891-1600	R	36*	.2
18	Pbi-Gordon Corp—*Donald Chew*	PO Box 14090, Kansas City MO 64101	816-421-4070	R	34*	.3
19	Gowan Milling Company LLC	PO Box 5569, Yuma AZ 85366	928-344-1014	R	32*	.4
20	Dsm Neoresins Inc—*Larry Evans*	730 Main St, Wilmington MA 01887	978-658-6600	R	30*	.1
21	Sawyer Products Inc—*Kurt Avery*	PO Box 188, Safety Harbor FL 34695	727-725-1177	R	25*	<.1
22	Tender Corp—*Jason Cartwright*	106 Burndy Rd, Littleton NH 03561	603-444-5464	R	22*	.1
23	Mclaughlin Gormley King Co—*Steven Gullickson*	8810 10th Ave N, Minneapolis MN 55427	763-544-0341	R	22*	.1
24	Schirm USA Inc—*H Jones*	PO Box 237, Ennis TX 75120	972-878-4400	R	21*	.2
25	Agraquest Inc—*Marcus Smith*	1540 Drew Ave, Davis CA 95618	530-750-0150	R	21*	.2
26	James Varley and Sons LLC—*John Daley*	1200 Switzer Ave, Saint Louis MO 63147	314-383-4372	R	18*	.2
27	Cytozyme Inc—*Steve Baughman*	134 S 700 W, Salt Lake City UT 84104	801-533-9208	R	18*	<.1
28	Ap and G Company Inc—*Ilona Frisch*	170 53rd St, Brooklyn NY 11232	718-492-3648	R	17*	.1
29	Pro-Serve Of Memphis Inc—*William Sander*	PO Box 161059, Memphis TN 38186	901-332-7052	R	13*	.1
30	Lobel Chemical Corp—*Steve Lobel*	1556 Third Ave Ste 405, New York NY 10128	212-699-0060	R	13*	.1
31	Grow More Inc—*John Atwill*	15600 New Century Dr, Gardena CA 90248	310-515-1700	R	12*	.1
32	Pic Corp—*Allen Rubel*	1101 W Elizabeth Ave N, Linden NJ 07036		R	10*	<.1
33	Trece Corp—*Bill Lingren*	PO Box 129, Adair OK 74330	918-785-3061	R	8*	<.1
34	Precision Laboratories Inc—*Richard Wohlner*	1429 S Shields Dr, Waukegan IL 60085	847-596-3001	R	8*	<.1
35	Aquatrols Corporation Of America—*Tracy Jarman*	1273 Imperial Way, Paulsboro NJ 08066	856-537-6003	R	7*	<.1
36	Prentiss LLC—*Randall Canady*	200 Cascade Poi Ste 10, Cary NC 27513	919-610-1065	R	6*	<.1
37	Eastern Minerals Inc—*Alec Poitevint*	PO Box 1650, Bainbridge GA 39818	229-246-3396	R	6*	.1
38	Arr Maz Custom Chemicals—*Hank Waters*	4800 State Rd 60 E, Mulberry FL 33860	863-578-1206	R	5*	.1
39	WA Hammond Drierite Company Ltd—*Sandy Corbean*	PO Box 460, Xenia OH 45385	937-376-2927	R	5*	<.1
40	Bioworks Inc—*William Foster*	100 Rawson Rd Ste 205, Victor NY 14564		R	4*	<.1
41	Regal Chemical Co—*William King*	PO Box 900, Alpharetta GA 30009	770-475-4837	R	4*	<.1
42	Biofac Inc—*Malcolm Maedgen*	PO Box 87, Mathis TX 78368	361-547-3259	R	4*	<.1
43	Ishihara Corporation USA—*Marvin Hosokawa*	601 California St Ste, San Francisco CA 94108	415-421-8207	S	4*	<.1
44	IGENE Biotechnology Inc—*Stephen F Hiu*	9110 Red Branch Rd, Columbia MD 21045	410-997-2599	P	4	<.1
45	Converted Organics Inc—*Edward J Gildea*	137A Lewis Wharf, Boston MA 02110	617-624-0111	P	4	<.1
46	Cape Fear Chemicals Inc—*Henry Brice*	PO Box 095, Elizabethtown NC 28337	910-862-3139	R	3*	<.1
47	A To Z Drying—*Al Penfold*	PO Box 180, Osage IA 50461	641-732-5805	R	3*	.1
48	Bacon Products Company Inc—*Reed Bacon*	PO Box 22187, Chattanooga TN 37422	423-892-0414	R	3*	<.1
49	Summit Chemical Co—*Jonathan Cohen*	235 S Kresson St, Baltimore MD 21224	410-522-0661	R	2*	<.1
50	Fresh Mark Corp—*Michael Bowers*	12518 El Viento Rd, Clermont FL 34711	352-394-7746	R	2*	<.1
51	Walco Linck Co—*William L Burge*	PO Box 5643, Bellingham WA 98227		R	2*	<.1
52	Scott G Williams LLC—*Maximo Munoz*	2111 General Arts Rd N, Conyers GA 30012	770-761-4448	R	2*	<.1

Note: An asterisk (*) indicates an estimated financial figure. The company type code used is as follows: R = Private, P = Public, S = Private Subsidiary, B = Public Subsidiary, D = Division, J = Joint Venture, I = Investment Fund.

COMPANY RANKINGS BY SALES WITHIN 4-DIGIT SIC

Rank	Company Name—*Executive Officer*	Address, City, State, Zip	Phone	Type	Fin	Empls
53	Westbridge Research Group—*Tina Koenemann*	1260 Avenida Chelsea, Vista CA 92081	760-599-8855	R	1*	<.1
54	Seabright Laboratories	4026 Harlan St, Emeryville CA 94608	510-655-3126	R	1*	<.1
55	Copper-Brite Inc—*Alan Brite*	PO Box 50610, Santa Barbara CA 93150	805-565-1566	R	<1*	<.1
56	Bion Environmental Technologies Inc—*Mark A Smith*	9 E Park Ct, Old Bethpage NY 11804	212-758-6622	P	<1	<.1
57	American Soil Technologies Inc—*Carl P Ranno*	12224 Montague St, Pacoima CA 91331	818-899-4686	P	<1	<.1

TOTALS: SIC 2879 Agricultural Chemicals Nec
Companies: 57 — 19,382 — 33.7

2891 Adhesives & Sealants

Rank	Company Name—*Executive Officer*	Address, City, State, Zip	Phone	Type	Fin	Empls
1	Goodrich Corp—*Marshall O Larsen*	4 Coliseum Centre 2730, Charlotte NC 28217	704-423-7000	P	6,967	25.6
2	Avery Dennison Corp—*Dean A Scarborough*	PO Box 7090, Pasadena CA 91109	626-304-2000	P	6,513	32.1
3	Cytec Industries Inc—*Shane D Fleming*	5 Garret Mountain Plz, West Paterson NJ 07424	973-357-3100	P	3,073	5.5
4	Brady International Sales Inc—*Frank Jaehnert*	PO Box 571, Milwaukee WI 53201	414-438-6868	S	2,508*	5.0
5	Brady International Co—*Frank M Jaehnert*	PO Box 571, Milwaukee WI 53201	414-228-1411	S	1,944*	3.5
6	HB Fuller Co—*Jim Owens*	PO Box 64683, Saint Paul MN 55164	651-236-5900	P	1,558	3.5
7	Sud-Chemie Inc—*John A Ray*	PO Box 32370, Louisville KY 40232	502-634-7200	R	434*	.8
8	PRC-DeSoto International Inc—*Dennis Kovalsky*	PO Box 1800, Glendale CA 91209	818-240-2080	R	170*	1.0
9	Brady Identification Solutions—*Frank M Jaehnert*	PO Box 571, Milwaukee WI 53201		D	165*	.3
10	Custom Building Products Inc—*Thomas Peck*	13001 Seal Beach Blvd, Seal Beach CA 90740	562-598-8808	R	151*	1.2
11	Adhesives Research Inc—*George Stolakis*	PO Box 100, Glen Rock PA 17327	717-235-7979	R	114*	.5
12	Testor Corp—*Charles Miller*	440 Blackhawk Park Ave, Rockford IL 61104		S	100*	.3
13	Bemis Associates Inc—*Stephen Howard*	1 Bemis Way, Shirley MA 01464	978-425-6761	R	80*	.3
14	Brady Worldwide Inc—*Frank Jaehert*	PO Box 2131, Milwaukee WI 53201	414-228-1411	S	75*	.1
15	General Sealants Inc—*Bradley Boyle*	PO Box 3855, City Of Industry CA 91744	626-961-0211	R	73*	.1
16	Sermatech International Inc—*Jim Miller*	159 S Limerick Rd, Royersford PA 19468	610-474-1200	S	72*	.6
17	Diversified Chemical Technologies Inc—*George Hill*	15477 Woodrow Wilson S, Detroit MI 48238	313-867-5444	R	60*	.2
18	CFC International Inc—*Roger F Hruby*	500 State St, Chicago Heights IL 60411	708-891-3456	S	55*	.1
19	Sovereign Commercial Group Inc—*Robert Covalt*	710 Ohio St, Buffalo NY 14203	716-856-4910	R	55*	.3
20	Atlas Minerals and Chemicals Inc—*George Gabriel*	PO Box 38, Mertztown PA 19539	610-682-7171	R	51*	.1
21	Aabbitt Adhesives Inc—*Benjamin Sarmas*	2403 N Oakley Ave, Chicago IL 60647	773-227-2700	R	50*	.1
22	Henkel Loctite Corp—*Jeffrey C Piccolomini*	1 Dexter Dr, Seabrook NH 03874	603-474-5541	R	48*	.1
23	Dymax Corp—*A Bachmann*	318 Industrial Ln Ste, Torrington CT 06790	860-482-1010	R	46*	.1
24	ADCO Products Inc (Michigan City Michigan)	PO Box 457, Michigan Center MI 49254	517-764-0334	S	45*	.3
25	ITW Ramset/Red Head—*David Spear*	2171 Executive Dr, Addison IL 60101	630-350-0370	D	40*	.2
26	Tailored Chemical Products Inc—*E Temple*	PO Box 4186, Hickory NC 28603	828-322-6512	R	35*	.1
27	Robix America Inc—*Felix Furst*	7104 Cessna Dr, Greensboro NC 27409	336-668-9555	R	32*	.2
28	Super Glue Corp/Pacer Technology—*Richard S Kay*	9420 Santa Anita Ave, Rancho Cucamonga CA 91730	909-987-0550	R	32*	.2
29	Rectorseal Corp—*David Smith*	2601 Spenwick Dr, Houston TX 77055	713-263-8001	S	32*	.1
30	Red Devil Inc—*William Lee*	1437 S Boulder Ave Ste, Tulsa OK 74119	918-585-8111	R	31*	.1
31	Chemical Coatings Inc—*Ronald Rice*	PO Box 22000, Hickory NC 28603	828-261-0325	S	31*	.1
32	Cascades Sonoco Inc	1 N 2nd St, Hartsville SC 29550	843-339-6226	J	31	.1
33	Three Bond International Inc—*Ichiro Ukumori*	6184 Schumacher Park D, West Chester OH 45069	513-783-5250	R	31*	.2
34	Permabond International Corp—*Attilio Grossi*	20C World's Fair Dr, Somerset NJ 08873		R	30	.1
35	D and K Group Inc—*Karl Singer*	PO Box 1146, Elk Grove Village IL 60009	847-956-0160	R	29*	.2
36	ITW Plexus—*Peter Carbutt*	30 Endicott St, Danvers MA 01923	978-777-1100	D	29*	.1
37	Chemence Inc—*Hugh Cooke*	185 Bluegrass Valley P, Alpharetta GA 30005	770-664-6624	R	27*	.1
38	Devcon Ltd—*Chris Stevens*	30 Endicott St, Danvers MA 01923	978-777-1100	S	26*	.1
39	National Casein Co—*Hope Cook*	601 W 80th St, Chicago IL 60620	773-846-7300	R	26*	.1
40	Northwest Coatings Corp—*Jeffrey Holdsberg*	7221 S 10th St, Oak Creek WI 53154	414-762-3330	R	26*	.1
41	Adhesive Applications—*Michael Schaefer*	41 O'Neill St, Easthampton MA 01027	413-527-7120	R	26*	<.1
42	Holcim LP (Midlothian Texas)—*Patrick Dolberg*	1800 Dove Ln, Midlothian TX 76065	972-923-5800	R	25*	.2
43	Multiseal Inc—*Gary Rust*	4320 Hitch Peters Rd, Evansville IN 47711	812-428-3422	R	22*	.1
44	Sashco Inc—*Lester Burch*	10300 E 107th Pl, Brighton CO 80601	303-286-7271	R	20*	.1
45	Reynolds Co—*John Reynolds*	PO Box 1925, Greenville SC 29602	864-232-6791	R	20*	.1
46	UPACO Adhesives Div—*Robert Worthen*	3 E Spit Brook Rd, Nashua NH 03060	603-888-5443	D	20*	.1
47	Stahl (USA) Inc—*Huub Nanbeijerens*	13 Corwin St, Peabody MA 01960	978-531-0371	R	20*	.1
48	Adhesive Systems Inc—*Edward Koziol*	PO Box 518, Frankfort IL 60423	815-464-5606	R	19*	.1
49	Southern Grouts and Mortars Inc—*Ron Picou*	1502 Sw 2nd Pl, Pompano Beach FL 33069	954-943-2288	R	19*	.1
50	Sun Process Converting Inc—*Michael Moore*	1660 Kenneth Dr, Mount Prospect IL 60056	847-593-0447	R	17*	.1
51	Gulf States Asphalt Company LP—*Lynn Nance*	300 Christi Pl, South Houston TX 77587	713-941-4410	R	17*	.1
52	Adhesive Systems Inc (Detroit Michigan)—*George H Hill* Diversified Chemical Technologies Inc	14410 Woodrow Wilson S, Detroit MI 48238	313-865-4448	S	15	.1
53	Camie-Campbell Inc—*Vince Doder*	9225 Watson Industrial, Saint Louis MO 63126	314-968-3222	R	15*	<.1
54	Harper-Love Adhesives Corp—*Ronald Harper*	PO Box 410408, Charlotte NC 28241	704-588-1350	R	14*	.1
55	Geocel Corp—*Donald Krabill*	PO Box 398, Elkhart IN 46515	574-264-0645	R	14*	.1
56	Phillips Plating Corp—*William Baratka*	PO Box 72, Phillips WI 54555	715-339-3031	R	14*	.1
57	Adhesive Technologies Inc—*Peter Melendy*	3 Merrill Industrial D, Hampton NH 03842	603-926-1616	R	14*	.1
58	Hernon Manufacturing Inc—*Harry Arnon*	121 Tech Dr, Sanford FL 32771	407-322-4000	R	13*	<.1
59	Solar Compounds Corp—*Harry Bockus*	1201 W Blancke St, Linden NJ 07036	908-862-2813	R	13*	<.1
60	Epoxies Etc—*Michael Harrington*	21 Starline Way, Cranston RI 02921	401-946-5564	R	12*	<.1
61	Polymeric Systems Inc—*Theodore Flint*	PO Box 522, Elverson PA 19520	610-935-1180	R	11*	.1
62	Basic Adhesives Inc—*Yale Block*	60 Webro Rd, Clifton NJ 07012	973-614-9000	R	11	<.1
63	XL Adhesives LLC—*Joe Tuttolomondo*	4284 S Dixie Rd Sw, Resaca GA 30735	706-625-0025	R	10*	.1
64	Olympic Adhesives Inc—*John Murray*	670 Canton St, Norwood MA 02062	781-762-7550	R	10*	<.1
65	Ruscoe Co—*Paul Michalec*	PO Box 3858, Akron OH 44314	330-253-8148	R	10*	<.1
66	Q'so Inc—*Fred Arnoldt*	5117 NE Pkwy, Fort Worth TX 76106	817-232-2026	R	10*	.1
67	Z Technologies Corp—*Ellis Breskman*	26500 Capitol, Redford MI 48239	313-937-0710	R	10*	.1
68	Slocum Adhesives Corp—*Paul Brown*	PO Box 10294, Lynchburg VA 24506	434-847-5671	R	10*	<.1
69	International Coatings Company Inc—*Stephen Kahane*	13929 166th St, Cerritos CA 90703	562-926-1010	R	9*	.1
70	Manus-Products-Minnesota Inc—*Gary Grevillius*	866 Industrial Blvd, Waconia MN 55387	952-442-3323	R	9*	<.1
71	Super-Tek Products Inc—*John Garuti*	2544 Borough Pl, Woodside NY 11377	718-278-7900	R	9*	.1
72	Western American Inc—*Theo Newman*	1518 Taney St, Kansas City MO 64116	816-421-3000	R	9*	.1
73	Specialty Silicone Products Inc—*Daniel Natarelli*	Corporate Technology P, Ballston Spa NY 12020	518-885-8826	R	8*	<.1
74	Fox Industries Inc—*Michael Fox*	3100 Fallscliff Rd, Baltimore MD 21211	410-243-8856	R	8*	<.1
75	Egc Enterprises Inc—*Bernard Casamento*	140 Parker Ct, Chardon OH 44024	440-285-5835	R	8*	<.1
76	Marcus Paint Co—*Theresa Marcus*	235 E Market St, Louisville KY 40202	502-584-0303	R	8*	<.1
77	Eftec NA LLC—*Roslin Wilson*	23800 Research Dr, Farmington Hills MI 48335	248-471-6510	R	7*	<.1
78	Dela Inc—*Charles Abrams*	PO Box 8235, Haverhill MA 01835	978-372-7783	R	7*	<.1
79	Epoxy Technology Inc—*Frank Kulesza*	14 Fortune Dr, Billerica MA 01821	978-667-3805	R	7*	<.1
80	Helmitin Inc—*Larry Droski*	11110 Airport Rd, Olive Branch MS 38654	662-895-4565	R	6*	<.1

Rank	Company Name—*Executive Officer*	Address, City, State, Zip	Phone	Type	Fin	Empls
81	Therm-O-Web Inc—*Kenneth Glazer*	770 Glenn Ave, Wheeling IL 60090	847-520-5200	R	6*	<.1
82	Welco Manufacturing Co—*Milton Strader*	PO Box 12568, North Kansas City MO 64116	816-471-1788	R	6*	<.1
83	Industrial Floor Corp—*Fred J Coccagna*	261 Old York Rd Ste 61, Jenkintown PA 19046	215-886-1800	R	6*	<.1
84	Star Technology Inc—*Donn Starkey*	200 Executive Dr, Waterloo IN 46793	260-837-7833	R	6*	<.1
85	Precision Packing Corp—*Anthony Pappas*	2145 Centerwood Dr, Warren MI 48091	586-756-8700	R	6*	<.1
86	Southern Resin Inc—*E Temple*	PO Box 4186, Hickory NC 28603	336-475-1348	R	6*	<.1
87	Inland Inc—*Betty Field*	PO Box 644, Elizabethtown KY 42702	270-737-6757	R	6*	<.1
88	Shep Company LLC—*Craig Allard*	PO Box 385, Lawrence MA 01842	978-686-0632	R	6*	<.1
89	Lucas Products Corp—*Robert Urfer*	PO Box 6570, Toledo OH 43612	419-476-5992	R	5*	<.1
90	Magnolia Plastics Inc—*Richard Wells*	5547 Peachtree Industr, Chamblee GA 30341	770-451-2777	R	5*	<.1
91	Irontite By Kwik-Way—*Dave Parks*	9860 Baldwin Pl, El Monte CA 91731	626-443-0296	R	5*	<.1
92	Master Bond Inc—*James Brenner*	154 Hobart St, Hackensack NJ 07601	201-343-8983	R	4*	<.1
93	Clifton Adhesive Inc—*Robert Lefelar*	48 Burgess Pl, Wayne NJ 07470	973-694-0845	R	4*	<.1
94	Copps Industries Inc—*Patrick Copps*	10600 N Industrial Dr, Mequon WI 53092	262-238-1700	R	4*	<.1
95	Key Tech Corp—*Rosanne Cavanaugh*	1010 SE Everett Mall W, Everett WA 98208	425-347-3600	R	4*	<.1
96	Astro Chemical Company Inc—*Duane A Ball*	PO Box 1250, Ballston Lake NY 12019	518-399-5338	R	4*	<.1
97	Chemmasters Inc—*Daniel Schodowski*	300 Edwards St, Madison OH 44057	440-428-2105	R	4*	<.1
98	Fri Resins Corp—*Michael Harrington*	21 Starline Way, Cranston RI 02921	401-946-5564	R	4*	<.1
99	Metachem Resins Corp—*Herbert Spivack*	1505 Main St, West Warwick RI 02893	401-828-4550	R	4*	<.1
100	Advanced Adhesive Technologies Inc—*Gregory Wood*	419 S Glenwood Ave, Dalton GA 30721	706-226-0610	R	4*	<.1
101	Mid-West Industrial Chemical Co—*Robert Mc Kendry*	1509 Sublette Ave, Saint Louis MO 63110	314-781-5831	R	4*	<.1
102	Mace Adhesives And Coatings Company Inc—*James Gilloran*	PO Box 37, Dudley MA 01571	508-943-9052	R	4*	<.1
103	Bacon Industries Inc—*Richard Cass*	192 Pleasant St, Watertown MA 02472	617-926-2550	R	3*	<.1
104	Plcs Inc—*Howard Hardwick*	102 Gaither Dr Ste 1, Mount Laurel NJ 08054	856-722-1333	R	3*	<.1
105	Saf-T-Lok International Corp—*J Sherry*	300 Eisenhower Ln N, Lombard IL 60148	630-495-2001	R	3*	<.1
106	Mask-Off Company Inc—*Steven Sites*	345 W Maple Ave, Monrovia CA 91016	626-359-3261	R	3*	<.1
107	Evans Adhesive Corporation Ltd—*Dennis Julian*	925 Old Henderson Rd, Columbus OH 43220	614-451-2665	R	3*	<.1
108	Elektromek Inc—*Yale Block*	60 Webro Rd, Clifton NJ 07012	973-614-9000	R	2*	<.1
109	Norland Products Inc—*Robert Norland*	PO Box 637, Cranbury NJ 08512	609-395-1966	R	2*	<.1
110	Accrabond Corp—*Michael Reddoch*	PO Box 17945, Memphis TN 38187	662-895-4480	R	2*	<.1
111	Health Processes Inc—*Paul B O'Brien*	PO Box 423, Collbran CO 81624	970-487-3070	R	2*	<.1
112	Westech Seal Inc—*Mark Merritt*	PO Box 14610, Odessa TX 79768	432-367-1188	R	2*	<.1
113	Blair Adhesive Products—*Scott Heger*	11034 Lockport Pl, Santa Fe Springs CA 90670	562-946-6004	R	2*	<.1
114	Chemical Technology Inc—*Gerhard Weber*	13271 Mount Elliott St, Detroit MI 48212	313-893-4930	R	2*	<.1
115	Gluefast Company Inc—*Lester Mallet*	3535 Rte 66 Ste 1, Neptune NJ 07753	732-918-4600	R	2*	<.1
116	Master Mix Co—*Frederick Mccants*	612 S Mansfield St, Ypsilanti MI 48197	734-487-7870	R	2*	<.1
117	Dorn Equipment Corp—*Matthew Flynn*	27 Upham St, Melrose MA 02176	781-662-9300	R	2*	<.1
118	Adhesive Products Corp—*Sanford Hichman*	3020 W Carroll Ave, Chicago IL 60612	773-722-4583	R	1*	<.1
119	Bostik Inc(Wauwatosa Wisconsin)—*Bill Campbell*	11320 Watertown Plank, Wauwatosa WI 53226	414-774-2250	R	1*	<.1
120	ADM Tronics Unlimited Inc—*Andre DiMino*	224 Pegasus Ave, Northvale NJ 07647	201-767-6040	P	1	<.1
121	US Adhesives—*Jeff Niles*	1735 W Carroll Ave, Chicago IL 60612	312-829-7438	R	1*	<.1
122	Atwood Adhesives Inc—*Paul Shattuck*	945 S Doris St, Seattle WA 98108	206-762-7455	R	1*	<.1
123	RH Products Company Inc—*RN Derby*	PO Box 2301, Acton MA 01720	781-259-9464	R	1*	<.1
124	Skirges Corp	500 S 9th St, Lehighton PA 18235	610-377-4720	R	1*	<.1
125	Eastern Adhesives Inc—*Dale Craig*	PO Box 1106, Doylestown PA 18901	215-348-0119	R	1*	<.1
126	Manufacturers Resources Inc—*Patrick Reardon*	16320 W Glendale Dr, New Berlin WI 53151	262-827-2800	R	1*	<.1
127	Edwards and Cromwell Manufacturing Inc—*Pat Johnson*	11519 Investor Dr Ste, Baton Rouge LA 70809	225-292-3377	R	<1*	<.1
128	TEC Specialty Products Inc—*Michele Volpi* HB Fuller Co	315 S Hicks Rd, Palatine IL 60067	847-358-9500	S	N/A	3.1

TOTALS: SIC 2891 Adhesives & Sealants
Companies: 128

					25,568	89.9

2892 Explosives

Rank	Company Name—*Executive Officer*	Address, City, State, Zip	Phone	Type	Fin	Empls
1	Orica USA Inc—*Craig Elkinton*	33101 E Quincy Ave, Watkins CO 80137	303-268-5000	R	1,000*	.7
2	Ensign-Bickford Industries Inc—*Caleb White*	PO Box 7, Simsbury CT 06070	860-843-2000	R	179*	1.6
3	Austin Powder Co—*David Gleason*	25800 Science Park Dr, Cleveland OH 44122	216-464-2400	R	179*	1.2
4	Viking Explosives and Supply Inc—*DH Bednar*	4469 Hwy 5, Hibbing MN 55746	218-263-8845	R	52*	<.1
5	Accurate Energetic Systems LLC	5891 Hwy 230 W, Mc Ewen TN 37101	931-729-4207	R	13*	.1
6	Cartridge Actuated Devices Inc—*Jim Yeats*	51 Dwight Pl, Fairfield NJ 07004	973-575-1312	R	10*	<.1
7	Buckley Powder Co—*Daniel J Buckley*	42 Inverness Dr E Ste, Englewood CO 80112	303-790-7007	S	8	<.1
8	Hanley Industries Inc—*Gaynor Blake*	PO Box 1058, Alton IL 62002	618-465-8892	R	6*	<.1
9	Blastgard International Inc—*Michael J Gordon*	2451 McMullen Booth Rd, Clearwater FL 33759	727-592-9400	P	1	<.1

TOTALS: SIC 2892 Explosives
Companies: 9

					1,447	3.7

2893 Printing Ink

Rank	Company Name—*Executive Officer*	Address, City, State, Zip	Phone	Type	Fin	Empls
1	Sun Chemical Corp—*Rudi Linz*	35 Waterview Blvd, Parsippany NJ 07054	973-404-6000	S	4,439*	10.5
2	Kohl and Madden Inc—*Wes Lucas* Sun Chemical Corp	222 Bridge Pl S, Fort Lee NJ 07024		S	2,927*	10.0
3	Inx International Ink Co—*Rick Clendenning*	150 N Martingale Rd St, Schaumburg IL 60173	630-382-1800	R	296*	1.3
4	Wikoff Color Corp—*Geoffrey Peters*	1886 Merritt Rd, Fort Mill SC 29715	803-548-2210	R	239*	.5
5	Nazdar Co—*J Thrall*	8501 Hedge Ln Ter, Shawnee Mission KS 66227	913-422-1888	R	215*	.5
6	Flint Group North America Corp—*William Miller*	14909 N Beck Rd, Plymouth MI 48170	734-781-4600	R	160*	1.5
7	Coates Screen Inc—*Lyle Douthitt* Sun Chemical Corp	2445 Production Dr, Saint Charles IL 60174	630-513-5348	D	68*	.2
8	Printing Technology Inc—*Peter DeSalay*	21001 Nordhoff St, Chatsworth CA 91311		R	64*	.1
9	Braden-Sutphin Ink Co—*Jim Leitch*	3650 E 93rd St, Cleveland OH 44105	216-271-2300	R	53*	.3
10	Morway Corp—*D Scott Morrison*	4801 W 160th St, Cleveland OH 44135	216-267-4620	D	45*	.1
11	Siegwerk USA Inc—*Daniel Mcdowell*	3535 Sw 56th St, Des Moines IA 50321	515-471-2100	S	37*	.3
12	Sicpa Securink Corp—*James Bonhivert*	8000 Research Way, Springfield VA 22153	703-455-8050	R	36*	.1
13	Central Ink Corp—*Richard Breen*	1100 Harvester Rd, West Chicago IL 60185	630-231-6500	R	25*	.1
14	Environmental Inks and Coding—*David Lobes*	450 Wegner Dr, West Chicago IL 60185	630-231-7313	R	23*	.1
15	Hostmann Steinberg Inc—*Winfred Gleue*	6021 Fern Valley Rd, Louisville KY 40228	502-968-5961	R	21*	.2
16	Gans Ink And Supply Company Inc—*Jeff Koppelman*	PO Box 33806, Los Angeles CA 90033	323-264-2200	R	20*	.3
17	JM Fry Co—*James Hodges*	PO Box 7719, Richmond VA 23231	804-236-8100	R	17*	.1
18	Alden and Ott Printing Inks Co—*Thomas Alden*	616 E Brook Dr, Arlington Heights IL 60005	847-956-6830	R	17*	.1
19	Monarch Color Corp—*G West*	5327 Brookshire Blvd, Charlotte NC 28216	704-394-4626	R	15*	.1
20	Graphic Sciences Inc—*Gary McLean*	7515 NE Ambassador Pl, Portland OR 97220	503-460-0203	R	12*	.1
21	Cavalier Printing Ink Company Inc—*Samuel Johnson*	PO Box 24538, Richmond VA 23224	804-271-4214	R	8*	<.1

Note: An asterisk (*) indicates an estimated financial figure. The company type code used is as follows: R = Private, P = Public, S = Private Subsidiary, B = Public Subsidiary, D = Division, J = Joint Venture, I = Investment Fund.

COMPANY RANKINGS BY SALES WITHIN 4-DIGIT SIC

Rank	Company Name—Executive Officer	Address, City, State, Zip	Phone	Type	Fin	Empls
22	Quality Inks Inc—John Paterson	2327 E Jones Ave, Phoenix AZ 85040	602-268-4199	R	7*	<.1
23	Polymeric Imaging Inc—Don Sloan	117 E 14th Ave, Kansas City MO 64116	816-221-5567	R	7*	<.1
24	Keystone Printing Ink Co—Robert Chamness	PO Box 18508, Philadelphia PA 19129	215-228-8100	R	7*	<.1
25	Cabrun Ink Products Corp—Kenneth Reich	PO Box 4887, Philadelphia PA 19124	215-533-2990	R	7*	<.1
26	Midwest Ink Co—Frank Hannon	2701 S 12th Ave, Broadview IL 60155	708-345-7177	R	6*	<.1
27	Gotham Ink and Color Company Inc—William Olson	19 Holt Dr, Stony Point NY 10980	845-947-4000	R	6*	<.1
28	Kolorcure Corp—Brian Templeman	1180 Lyon Rd, Batavia IL 60510	630-879-9050	R	6*	<.1
29	Three Dimensional Chemical Corp—Christopher Dawe	PO Box 357, Danvers MA 01923	978-774-8595	R	6*	<.1
30	Tri-Century Corp—Mike Warner	385 S 31st St, Colorado Springs CO 80904	719-578-0506	R	6*	<.1
31	Bomark Inc—Herman Schowe	601 S 6th Ave, La Puente CA 91746	626-968-1666	R	5*	<.1
32	Ink Technology Corp—David Ringler	18320 Lanken Ave, Cleveland OH 44119	216-486-6720	R	5*	<.1
33	R A Kerley Ink Engineers Inc—John Whalen	PO Box 6009, Maywood IL 60155	708-344-1295	R	4*	<.1
34	POSitive Concepts—Lambert Thom	2021 N Glassell St, Orange CA 92865	714-490-5000	R	4*	<.1
35	Thrall Enterprises Inc—Jeff Thrall	8501 Hedge Ln Ter, Shawnee KS 66227	913-422-1888	R	3*	<.1
36	Hi-Tech Color Inc—Takashige Asai	1721 Midway Rd, Odenton MD 21113	410-551-9871	R	2*	<.1
37	Western Printing Ink Corp—Gary Burk	777 Tennessee St, San Francisco CA 94107	415-826-9333	R	2*	<.1
38	Ink Tech/Repeat-O-Type Manufacturing Corp—Whitney Keen	100 Huguenot Ave, Englewood NJ 07631	201-735-0232	R	2*	<.1
39	Kennedy Ink Company Inc—James Scott	5230 Wooster Pke, Cincinnati OH 45226	513-871-2515	R	2*	<.1
40	Ink Makers Inc—Kendrick Mills	6681 E 26th St, Commerce CA 90040	323-728-7500	R	2*	<.1
41	Uvexs Inc—Brent Puder	PO Box 64313, Sunnyvale CA 94088	408-734-4402	R	2*	<.1
42	Rhino Performance Products LLC	PO Box 967, Wake Forest NC 27588		R	1*	<.1
43	Media Sciences International Inc—Marc D Durand	8 Allerman Rd, Oakland NJ 07436	201-677-9311	P	<1	<.1

TOTALS: SIC 2893 Printing Ink
Companies: 43

					8,827	26.8

2895 Carbon Black

Rank	Company Name—Executive Officer	Address, City, State, Zip	Phone	Type	Fin	Empls
1	Cabot Corp—Patrick M Prevost	2 Seaport Ln Ste 1300, Boston MA 02210	617-345-0100	P	3,102	4.1
2	Sid Richardson Carbon and Gasoline Co—William Jones	201 Main St Ste 3000, Fort Worth TX 76102	817-390-8600	R	144*	.5
3	Columbian Chemicals Co—Kevin Boyle	1800 W Oak Commons Ct, Marietta GA 30062	770-792-9400	R	58*	1.3
4	Continental Carbon Co—Kim Pan	16850 Park Row, Houston TX 77084	281-647-3700	R	55*	.3
5	Solution Dispersions Inc—William Stoeppel	PO Box 8, Cynthiana KY 41031	859-234-8468	R	8*	<.1

TOTALS: SIC 2895 Carbon Black
Companies: 5

					3,367	6.2

2899 Chemical Preparations Nec

Rank	Company Name—Executive Officer	Address, City, State, Zip	Phone	Type	Fin	Empls
1	Kemira Water Solutions Inc—Jay Richey	316 Bartow Municipal A, Bartow FL 33830	863-533-5990	R	68,667*	.5
2	Innovene Inc—Ralph C Alexander	2600 S Shore Blvd, League City TX 77573	281-535-6600	S	17,937*	8.0
3	BASF Corp—Klaus Peter Lobbe	100 Campus Dr, Florham Park NJ 07932	973-245-6000	S	11,160	11.0
4	Huntsman Corp—Jon Huntsman Sr	10003 Woodloch Forest, The Woodlands TX 77380	281-719-6000	P	9,250	12.0
5	Momentive Specialty Chemicals Inc—Craig O Morrison	180 E Broad St, Columbus OH 43215	614-225-4000	S	4,818	6.0
6	Nalco Holding Co—J Erik Fyrwald	1601 W Diehl Rd, Naperville IL 60563	630-305-1000	S	4,251	12.4
7	Rockwood Holdings Inc—Seifi Ghasemi	100 Overlook Ctr, Princeton NJ 08540	609-514-0300	P	3,669	9.7
8	Diversey Inc—Edward F Lonergan	PO Box 902, Sturtevant WI 53177	262-631-4001	R	3,101	10.4
9	Wakefield Thermal Solutions Inc—Wayne Frerichs	33 Bridge St, Pelham NH 03076	603-635-2800	S	2,398*	.1
10	Solutia Inc—Jeffry N Quinn	575 Maryville Ctr Dr, Saint Louis MO 63141	314-674-1000	P	2,097	3.4
11	Grace Davison—Fred Festa	7500 Grace Dr, Columbia MD 21044	410-531-4000	D	1,802	3.7
12	Tronox Inc—Thomas J Casey	3301 NW 150th St, Oklahoma City OK 73134	405-775-5000	P	1,651	2.0
13	Arch Chemicals Inc—Michael E Campbell	PO Box 5204, Norwalk CT 06856	203-229-2900	S	1,377	2.5
14	Kronos Worldwide Inc—Steven Watson	5430 LBJ Fwy Ste 1700, Dallas TX 75240	972-233-1700	B	1,279	2.4
15	Arkema Inc—Bernard Roche	2000 Market St, Philadelphia PA 19103	215-419-7000	S	1,231*	2.0
16	Angstrom Technologies Inc—Tony Petrucci	7880 Foundation Dr, Florence KY 41042	859-282-0020	R	1,181*	<.1
17	Shipley Company LLC—Pierre R Brondeau	455 Forest St, Marlborough MA 01752	508-481-7950	S	1,129*	3.5
18	Noveon International Inc—Donald W Bogus	29400 Lakeland Blvd, Wickliffe OH 44092	216-447-5000	S	1,103*	2.7
19	Trans-Resources Inc—William Dowd	200 W 57th St, New York NY 10019	212-515-4100	R	1,045*	1.0
20	Sigma-Aldrich Biotechnology Holding Company Inc—Rakesh Sachdev	3050 Spruce St, Saint Louis MO 63103		S	811*	1.7
21	Sigma-Aldrich Lancaster Inc—Rakesh Sachdev	3050 Spruce St, Saint Louis MO 63103	314-771-5765	S	811*	1.7
22	Polypore International Inc—Robert B Toth	11430 N Community Hous, Charlotte NC 28277	704-587-8409	P	763	2.5
23	MacDermid Inc—Daniel Leever	1401 Blake St, Denver CO 80202	720-479-3060	CO	705*	2.5
24	Cognis Corporation USA	5051 Estecreek Rd, Cincinnati OH 45232	513-482-3000	S	698*	1.6
25	Pioneer Companies Inc	190 Carondelet Plaza S, Clayton MO 63105	314-480-1400	S	526	.6
26	Morton Salt—Mark Roberts	123 N Wacker Dr, Chicago IL 60606	312-807-2000	S	518*	2.9
27	Aventine Renewable Energy Holdings Inc—John Castle	5400 LBJ Fwy Ste 450, Dallas TX 75240	214-451-6750	P	448	.3
28	Rhodia Inc USA—James Harton	8 Cedar Brook Dr, Cranbury NJ 08512	609-860-4000	D	400*	1.6
29	WD-40 Co—Garry O Ridge	PO Box 80607, San Diego CA 92138	619-275-1400	P	336	.3
30	Pacific Ethanol Inc—Neil Koehler	400 Capitol Mall Ste 2, Sacramento CA 95814	916-403-2123	P	328	.1
31	Balchem Corp—Dino A Rossi	PO Box 600, New Hampton NY 10958	845-326-5600	P	292	.4
32	3form Inc—Talley Goodson	2300 S 2300 W Ste B, Salt Lake City UT 84119	801-649-2500	R	289*	.3
33	OMG Americas Inc—Beth Flemming	811 Sharon Dr, Westlake OH 44145	440-899-2950	S	289*	.2
34	United Laboratories Inc	320 37th Ave, St Charles IL 60174		R	269*	.3
35	KMG Chemicals Inc—J Neal Butler	9555 W Sam Houston Pkw, Houston TX 77099	713-600-3800	P	266	.3
36	AllChem Industries—Josh Feldstein	6010 NW 1st Pl, Gainesville FL 32607	352-378-9696	R	184*	.2
37	Cosmopolitan Chemical Co—Lisa Russo Metro Group Inc (Long Island City New York)	50-23 23rd St, Long Island City NY 11101	718-729-7200	D	173*	.1
38	KS North America Salt Holdings LLC	123 N Wacker Dr, Chicago IL 60606	312-807-2000	R	160*	2.9
39	Metro Group Inc (Long Island City New York)—Robert Seidman	50-23 23rd St, Long Island City NY 11101	718-729-7200	R	157*	.2
40	Hercules Chemical Company Inc—David Siegal	111 South St, Passaic NJ 07055	973-778-5000	R	156*	.1
41	Fiber Composites LLC—James Pryzbylinski	181 Random Dr, New London NC 28127	704-463-7120	R	150*	.4
42	Amyris Biotechnologies Inc—John Melo	5885 Hollis St Ste 100, Emeryville CA 94608	510-450-0761	P	147	.5
43	Flotek Industries Inc—John Chisholm	2930 W Sam Houston Pkwy, Houston TX 77043	713-849-9911	P	147	.3
44	Radiator Specialty Company Inc—John Huber	PO Box 34689, Charlotte NC 28234	704-688-2302	R	146*	.2
45	Hill Brothers Chemical Co—Ronald R Hill	1675 N Main St, Orange CA 92867	714-998-8800	R	137*	.1
46	PerkinElmer Life and Analytical Sciences Inc—Peter Coggins	549 Albany St, Boston MA 02118	203-925-4602	D	116	.4
47	Fritz Industries Inc—Dan Montgomery	PO Box 170040, Dallas TX 75217	972-285-5471	R	106*	.1
48	Boral Material Technologies Inc—Terry Peterson	45 NE Loop 410 Ste 700, San Antonio TX 78216	210-349-4069	S	105*	.3
49	Camco Manufacturing Inc—Donald Caine	121 Landmark Dr, Greensboro NC 27409	336-668-7661	R	101*	.3
50	De Nora Tech Inc—Paolo Dellacha	7590 Discovery Ln, Concord OH 44070	440-710-5300	S	100*	.4
51	Research Organics Inc—Rob Sternfeild	4353 E 49th St, Cleveland OH 44125	216-883-8025	R	97*	.1
52	Avantor Performance Materials Inc	3477 Corporate Pkwy St, Center Valley PA 18034	610-573-2600	S	91*	.5
53	Kinetics Systems Inc—Peter Maris	48400 Fremont Blvd, Fremont CA 94538	510-683-6000	R	82*	.2

Rank	Company Name—*Executive Officer*	Address, City, State, Zip	Phone	Type	Fin	Empls
54	Univertical Corp—*Wayne Walker*	203 Weatherhead St, Angola IN 46703	260-665-1500	R	78*	.1
55	ATI Wah Chang—*John Sims*	PO Box 460, Albany OR 97321	541-967-6977	S	72*	.5
56	Henkel Corp Surface Technologies Div—*Gerald Kohlsmith*	32100 Stephenson Hwy, Madison Heights MI 48071	248-583-9300	D	72*	.5
57	AMRESCO Inc (Solon Ohio)—*David Camiener*	PO Box 39098, Solon OH 44139	440-349-1313	R	71*	.2
58	Sigma-Genosys of Texas Inc—*Rakesh Sachdev*	1442 Lake Front Cir St, The Woodlands TX 77380	281-363-3693	S	67*	.1
59	Euclid Chemical Co—*Morrman Scott*	19218 Redwood Rd, Cleveland OH 44110	216-531-9222	S	64*	.2
60	Rust-Oleum Corp (Hagerstown Maryland)—*Tom Reed*	PO Box 1008, Hagerstown MD 21741	301-223-8500	S	64*	.2
61	Cambrex Charles City Inc—*Rosina Dixon*	1205 11th St, Charles City IA 50616	641-257-1000	S	63*	.2
62	Redmond Minerals Inc—*Rhett Roberts*	475 West 910 South, Heber UT 84032	435-529-7402	R	56*	.2
63	Reheis Inc—*Douglas McFarland*	235 Snyder Ave, Berkeley Heights NJ 07922	908-464-1500	S	55*	.3
64	Garratt-Callahan Co—*Jeffrey Garratt*	50 Ingold Rd, Burlingame CA 94010	650-689-6900	R	53*	.3
65	Crystal Incorporated - Pmc—*Paritosh Chakrabarti*	601 W 8th St, Lansdale PA 19446	215-368-1661	R	52*	.5
66	McGean Inc—*Dickson Whitney Jr*	2910 Harvard Ave, Cleveland OH 44105	216-441-4900	R	50*	.3
67	Uniqema—*Len Berlik*	1000 Uniqema Blvd, New Castle DE 19720	302-574-5000	S	48*	.2
68	Spray Products Corp—*Andrew Bastian*	PO Box 737, Norristown PA 19404	610-277-1010	R	47*	<.1
69	Gelita USA Inc—*Robert Mayberry*	PO Box 927, Sioux City IA 51102	712-943-5516	R	47*	.3
70	Technic Inc—*Al Antos*	PO Box 9650, Providence RI 02940	401-781-6100	R	46*	.4
71	JSR Microelectronics Inc—*Eric Johnson*	1280 N Mathilda Ave, Sunnyvale CA 94089	408-543-8800	R	46*	.1
72	Aqua Science Inc—*Daniel Smucker*	1601 Woodland Ave, Columbus OH 43219	614-252-5000	R	46*	<.1
73	E and A Industries Inc—*Al Hubbard*	101 W Ohio St Ste 1350, Indianapolis IN 46204	317-684-3150	R	45	.1
74	OMG Electronic Chemicals Inc—*Joseph Simeone*	400 Corporate Ct Ste A, S Plainfield NJ 07080	908-222-5800	S	44*	.1
75	Pavco Inc—*Scott Pavlish*	1935 John Crosland Jr, Charlotte NC 28208	704-496-6800	R	42*	<.1
76	Amerchol Corp—*Andrew Livreis*	PO Box 4051, Edison NJ 08818		S	40	.1
77	Bonide Products Inc—*James Wurz*	6301 Sutliff Rd, Oriskany NY 13424	315-736-8231	R	39*	.2
78	Intercit Inc—*Beverly Bateman*	1585 10th St S, Safety Harbor FL 34695	727-725-1678	R	39*	.1
79	Independent Ink Inc—*Barry Brucker*	13700 S Gramercy Pl, Gardena CA 90249	310-523-4657	R	38*	<.1
80	Zeolyst International—*John Lau*	280 Cedar Grove Rd, Conshohocken PA 19428	610-651-4621	R	37*	<.1
81	ITW Dymon—*Paul Taylor*	PO Box 340, Olathe KS 66051	913-829-6296	S	36*	.1
82	Magni Group Inc—*Timothy Berry*	390 Park St Ste 360, Birmingham MI 48009	248-647-4500	R	36*	.2
83	Technical Ordnance Inc—*David Price*	47600 180th St, Clear Lake SD 57226	952-446-1526	S	35*	.3
84	Power And Composite Technologies LLC	200 Wallins Corners Rd, Amsterdam NY 12010	518-843-6825	R	35*	.1
85	D-A Lubricant Company Inc—*Mikel Proteogere*	1340 W 29th St, Indianapolis IN 46208	317-923-5321	R	34*	.1
86	Liquidmetal Technologies Inc—*Thomas Steipp*	30452 Esperanza, Rancho Santa Margarita CA 92688	949-635-2100	P	33	<.1
87	ITW Chemtronics Inc—*Sue Max*	8125 Cobb Ctr Dr, Kennesaw GA 30152	770-424-4888	R	32*	.1
88	Whitmore Group *Roy Schworther*	PO Box 9300, Rockwall TX 75087	972-771-1000	S	32*	.1
89	Qualicaps Inc—*Herb Hugill*	6505 Franz Warner Pkwy, Whitsett NC 27377	336-449-3900	R	31*	.2
90	Westco Chemicals Inc	12551 Saticoy St S, North Hollywood CA 91605	818-255-3655	R	31*	<.1
91	PCC Chemax Inc—*Marsha Flrod*	30 Old Augusta Rd, Piedmont SC 29673	864-277-7000	S	31*	<.1
92	OpenWorks Cleaning Systems	4742 N 24th St Ste 300, Phoenix AZ 85016	602-224-0440	R	29*	.1
93	Evonik Rohmax USA Inc—*Gregory Bialy*	723 Electronic Dr Ste, Horsham PA 19044	215-706-5800	R	29*	.1
94	Strategic Diagnostics Inc—*Francis M DiNuzzo*	111 Pencader Dr, Newark DE 19702	302-456-6789	P	28	.2
95	Charm Sciences Inc—*Stanley E Charm*	659 Andover St, Lawrence MA 01843	978-687-9200	R	28*	.2
96	Emoral Inc—*Claude Bruell*	200 Theodore Conrad Dr, Jersey City NJ 07305	201-309-4500	R	25*	.1
97	Qualitek International Inc—*Phodi Han*	315 S Fairbank St, Addison IL 60101	630-628-8083	R	25*	.3
98	Polysciences Inc—*Michael Ott*	400 Valley Rd, Warrington PA 18976	215-343-6484	R	25*	.2
99	Orion Safety Products Corp—*David T McLaughlin*	PO Bos 1047, Easton MD 21601	410-822-0318	R	25*	.1
100	Liochem Inc—*Kazuhito Knakano*	2145 E Park Dr Ne, Conyers GA 30013	770-922-0800	R	24*	.1
101	Zinkan Enterprises Inc—*K Zinkan*	1919 Case Pkwy, Twinsburg OH 44087		R	24*	<.1
102	Teknol Inc—*Kent Behren*	PO Box 13387, Dayton OH 45413	937-890-6547	R	23*	.1
103	NovaCentrix—*Charles Munson*	200-B Parker Dr, Austin TX 78728	512-491-9500	R	23*	<.1
104	LM Scofield Co—*Phillip Arnold*	6533 Bandini Blvd, Commerce CA 90040	323-723-5285	R	22*	.1
105	Tanner Industries Inc—*Stephen B Tanner*	735 Davisville Rd, Southampton PA 18966	215-322-1238	R	22*	.1
106	Custom Chemicals Corp—*Robert Veilee*	30 Paul Kohner Pl, Elmwood Park NJ 07407	201-791-5100	R	22*	<.1
107	DiHydro Services Inc—*Danny Hutchins*	40833 Brentwood Dr, Sterling Heights MI 48310	586-978-0425	R	22*	<.1
108	Sunbelt Chemicals—*Mike Baily*	71 Hargrove Grade, Palm Coast FL 32137	386-446-4595	R	20*	.1
109	Kinpak Inc—*Anthony Hale*	2780 Gunter Park Dr E, Montgomery AL 36109	334-279-6550	S	20*	.1
110	Advanced Chemical Co—*Gerald Smith*	105 Bellows St, Warwick RI 02888	401-785-3434	R	20*	.1
111	Specified Technologies Inc—*Charbel Tagher*	210 Evans Way, Somerville NJ 08876	908-526-8000	R	20*	<.1
112	EvCo Research LLC—*Scott Seydel*	244 John B Brooks Rd, Pendergrass GA 30567	706-693-3154	R	20*	<.1
113	Eureka Chemical Co—*Genevieve Hess*	PO Box 2205, South San Francisco CA 94083	650-761-3536	R	20*	<.1
114	Deltech Corp—*Robert Elefante*	11911 Scenic Hwy, Baton Rouge LA 70807	225-775-0150	R	19*	.1
115	AgION Technologies LLC—*Paul C Ford*	60 Audubon Rd, Wakefield MA 01880	781-224-7101	R	19*	<.1
116	Harrell Industries Inc—*James Pugh*	2495 Commerce Dr, Rock Hill SC 29730	803-327-6335	R	19*	<.1
117	MPR Services Inc—*Kevin Boltz*	1201 FM 646, Dickinson TX 77539	281-337-7424	S	19*	<.1
118	TransChemical Inc—*William F Stovall Sr*	419 E De Soto Ave, Saint Louis MO 63147	314-231-6905	R	19*	<.1
119	Metal Coatings International Inc—*George Palek*	275 Industrial Pkwy, Chardon OH 44024	440-285-2231	R	19*	.1
120	Mace Security International Inc—*John J McCann*	240 Gibraltar Rd Ste 2, Horsham PA 19044	267-317-4009	P	18	.2
121	Distillata Co—*William Schroeder*	PO Box 93845, Cleveland OH 44101	216-771-2900	R	18*	.1
122	Midwest Industrial Supply Incorporated—*Robert Vitale*	PO Box 8431, Canton OH 44711	330-456-3121	R	18*	.1
123	Foseco Inc—*Lee Plutshack*	PO Box 81227, Cleveland OH 44181	440-826-4548	R	18*	.1
124	Anodes Nc Inc—*Peter Schorsch*	135 Old Boiling Spring, Shelby NC 28152	704-482-8200	R	17*	.1
125	Prosoco Inc—*Gerald Boyer*	3741 Greenway Cir, Lawrence KS 66046	785-865-4200	R	16*	.1
126	Kmco LP—*Lanice Adcox*	16503 Ramsey Rd, Crosby TX 77532	281-272-4100	R	16*	.1
127	Alexander Chemical Corp—*Gillman Leavitt*	1901 Butterfield Rd St, Downers Grove IL 60515	630-955-6050	R	16*	.1
128	Jessup Engineering Inc—*Ran Jessup*	2745 Bond St, Rochester Hills MI 48309	248-853-5600	R	16*	.1
129	Process Research Products—*Peter Horvath*	1013 Whitehead Rd Ext, Trenton NJ 08638	609-882-0400	D	16*	<.1
130	Applied Biochemists Inc Arch Chemicals Inc	W175N11163 Stonewood D, Germantown WI 53022		S	15	.1
131	Enthone-OMI Inc—*Nick Salmon*	350 Frontage Rd, West Haven CT 06516	203-934-8611	S	15*	.1
132	Bar's Products Inc—*Robert Mermuys*	PO Box 187, Holly MI 48442	248-634-8278	R	15*	<.1
133	Cudner and O'Connor Co—*David Knoll*	4035 W Kinzie St, Chicago IL 60624	773-826-0200	R	15*	<.1
134	Publicker Gasohol Inc	75 Rockefeller Plz 16t, New York NY 10019	212-265-7013	S	14*	<.1
135	Publicker Inc	75 Rockefeller Plz 16t, New York NY 10019	212-265-7013	S	14*	<.1
136	Sagrocry Inc	75 Rockefeller Plz 16t, New York NY 10019	212-265-7013	S	14*	<.1
137	Barclay Water Management Inc—*William Brett*	150 Coolidge Ave, Watertown MA 02472	617-926-3400	R	14*	.1
138	Insultech LLC—*Sheri Monroe*	3530 W Garry Ave, Santa Ana CA 92704	714-384-0506	R	13*	.1
139	Mitann Inc—*Charles Portier*	400 Jarvis Dr Ste A, Morgan Hill CA 95037	408-782-2500	R	13*	.1
140	Meyer Laboratory Inc—*Art Kurth*	2401 Nw Jefferson St, Blue Springs MO 64015	816-228-4433	R	13*	.1
141	NanoChem Solutions Inc—*Grace Fan*	6502 S Archer Rd, Bedford Park IL 60501	708-563-9200	D	12*	<.1
142	Optima Chemical Group LLC—*Glenda Mcdonald*	200 Willacooche Hwy, Douglas GA 31535	912-383-0533	R	11*	.1

Note: An asterisk (*) indicates an estimated financial figure. The company type code used is as follows: R = Private, P = Public, S = Private Subsidiary, B = Public Subsidiary, D = Division, J = Joint Venture, I = Investment Fund.

COMPANY RANKINGS BY SALES WITHIN 4-DIGIT SIC

Rank	Company Name—*Executive Officer*	Address, City, State, Zip	Phone	Type	Fin	Empls
143	American Radiolabeled Chemicals Inc—*Surendra Gupta*	101 Arc Dr, Saint Louis MO 63146	314-991-4545	R	11*	<.1
144	IBC Advanced Technologies—*Steven Izatt*	856 E Utah Valley Dr, American Fork UT 84003	801-763-8400	R	11*	<.1
145	Pennsylvania Brine Treatment Inc—*Paul Hart*	5148 US 322, Franklin PA 16323	814-437-3593	R	11*	<.1
146	Squid Ink Manufacturing Inc—*William Hoagland*	7041 Boone Ave N, Minneapolis MN 55428	763-795-8856	R	10*	.1
147	Jacam Chemicals LLC—*Charles Anderson*	PO Box 96, Sterling KS 67579	620-278-3355	R	10*	.1
148	Ecological Laboratories Inc—*Barry Richter*	PO Box 184, Malverne NY 11565	516-823-3441	R	10*	.1
149	Morgro Inc—*Delbert Davis*	145 W Central Ave, Salt Lake City UT 84107	801-266-1132	R	10*	<.1
150	Oil Chem Technologies—*Paul Berger*	12822 Park One Dr, Sugar Land TX 77478	281-240-0161	R	10*	<.1
151	Kustom Blending LLC—*Bonnie Helmig*	3 Carbon Way, Walton KY 41094	859-485-8600	R	10*	.1
152	Rbp Chemical Technology Inc—*Mark Kannenberg*	150 S 118th St, Milwaukee WI 53214	414-258-0911	R	10*	.1
153	Microchem Corp—*Donald Johnson*	90 Oak St, Newton MA 02464	617-965-5511	R	9*	.1
154	Relton Corp—*Craig Kinard*	PO Box 60019, Arcadia CA 91066	626-446-8201	R	9*	.1
155	Angus Chemical Co—*John Buckley*	1500 E Lake Cook Rd, Buffalo Grove IL 60089	847-215-8600	S	9*	<.1
156	Puritan Products Inc—*Louis DiRenzo*	2290 Ave A, Bethlehem PA 18017	610-866-4225	R	9*	<.1
157	Aqua Solutions Inc—*Thomas Bedford*	PO Box 70, Deer Park TX 77536	281-479-2569	R	9*	.1
158	Neutron Products Inc—*Jackson Ransohoff*	PO Box 68, Dickerson MD 20842	301-349-5001	R	9*	.1
159	Coventya Inc—*Eric Weyls*	4639 Van Epps Rd, Brooklyn Heights OH 44131	216-351-1500	R	8*	<.1
160	Pressure Chemical Co—*John Pannucci*	3419 Smallman St, Pittsburgh PA 15201	412-682-5882	R	8*	<.1
161	Crown Technology Inc—*Joseph Peterson*	PO Box 50426, Indianapolis IN 46250	317-845-0045	R	8*	<.1
162	Emerald Carolina Chemical LLC—*James Davis*	8309 Wilkinson Blvd, Charlotte NC 28214	704-393-0089	R	8*	.1
163	Performix Technologies—*Dwight Davis*	101 Tidewater Rd, Warren OH 44483	330-372-1781	S	8*	.1
164	Bpi Inc—*Joseph Quigley*	612 S Trenton Ave, Pittsburgh PA 15221	412-371-8554	R	8*	<.1
165	Bell Performance Inc—*Glen Williams*	1340 Bennett Dr, Longwood FL 32750	407-831-5021	R	8*	<.1
166	Altair Nanotechnologies Inc—*H Frank Gibbard*	204 Edison Way, Reno NV 89502	775-858-3744	P	8	.1
167	Labchem Inc—*Al Beranek*	200 William Pitt Way, Pittsburgh PA 15238	412-826-5230	R	8*	<.1
168	Power Service Products Inc—*Ed Kramer*	PO Box 1089, Weatherford TX 76086	817-599-9486	R	8*	<.1
169	Key Polymer Corp—*Robert Baker*	17 Shepard St, Lawrence MA 01843	978-683-9411	R	7*	<.1
170	Sos Products Company Inc—*William Pryor*	PO Box 47, East Greenville PA 18041	215-679-6262	R	7*	.1
171	StoneTech Professional Inc—*Kathy Hampton*	370 N Wiget Ln Ste 200, Walnut Creek CA 94598	925-295-9700	R	7*	<.1
172	Sunland Chemical and Research Corp—*S Dadone*	5447 San Fernando Rd W, Los Angeles CA 90039	818-244-9600	R	7*	<.1
173	Chemsol Inc	8423 Boettner Rd, Bridgewater MI 48115	734-429-0033	S	7*	<.1
174	Howell Mouldings LC—*Bryon Menoter*	201 Overland Park Pl, New Century KS 66031	913-782-0500	R	7*	<.1
175	Brand-Nu Laboratories Inc—*John Gorman*	PO Box 895, Meriden CT 06450	203-235-7989	R	7*	<.1
176	American Promotional Events Inc—*Terry Anderson*	5401 W Skelly Dr, Tulsa OK 74107	918-446-4441	R	6*	.1
177	Chem Arrow Corporation Intl—*AL Spalding*	PO Box 2366, Irwindale CA 91706	626-358-2255	R	6*	<.1
178	IBEX Chemicals Inc—*Glenn Keener*	PO Box 841209, Houston TX 77284	713-937-4533	R	6*	<.1
179	Montello Inc—*Allen Johnson*	6106 E 32nd Pl Ste 100, Tulsa OK 74135	918-665-1170	R	6*	<.1
180	Allied Pressroom Products Inc—*Richard Sures*	2040 Lee St, Hollywood FL 33020	954-923-9884	R	6*	<.1
181	L and M Construction Chemical Inc—*Greg Schwietz*	14851 Calhoun Rd, Omaha NE 68152	402-453-6600	R	6*	<.1
182	Aurora Specialty Chemistries Corp—*Harry Moyle*	PO Box 227, Lowell MI 49331	517-372-9121	R	6*	<.1
183	Kolene Corp—*Roger Shoemaker*	12090 Westwood St, Detroit MI 48223	313-273-9220	R	6*	<.1
184	Specialty Ink Company Inc—*Gary Werwa*	PO Box 778, Deer Park NY 11729	631-586-3666	R	5*	<.1
185	Roto Salt Company Inc—*Brett Oaks*	118 Monell St, Penn Yan NY 14527	315-536-3742	R	5*	<.1
186	Pace Products Inc (Overland Park Kansas)—*Mike McIntosh*	4510 W 89th St Ste 110, Prairie Village KS 66207	913-469-5588	R	5*	<.1
187	Blue Sun Biodiesel LLC—*Leigh Freeman*	3440 Young Field St St, Wheat Ridge CO 80033	303-865-7700	R	5*	<.1
188	Militec Inc—*Brad Giordani*	11828 Pika Dr, Waldorf MD 20602	301-893-3910	R	5*	<.1
189	Poly Sat Inc—*Darryl Manuel*	7240 State Rd, Philadelphia PA 19135	215-332-7700	R	5*	<.1
190	Luster-On Products Inc—*Paul Lane*	PO Box 90247, Springfield MA 01139	413-739-2541	R	5*	<.1
191	Fireworks By Grucci Inc—*Felix Grucci*	1 Grucci Ln, Brookhaven NY 11719	631-286-0088	R	5*	<.1
192	Flamemaster Corp—*Joseph Mazin*	PO Box 4510, Pacoima CA 91331	818-890-1401	P	5	<.1
193	Fusion Ceramics Inc—*Richard Hannon*	PO Box 127, Carrollton OH 44615	330-627-5821	R	5*	<.1
194	Gibson Laboratories LLC—*Bob Coborn*	1040 Manchester St, Lexington KY 40508	859-254-9500	R	5*	<.1
195	Apexical Inc—*Steven Baer*	1905 New Cut Rd, Spartanburg SC 29303	864-578-0030	R	5*	<.1
196	Benchmark Products Inc—*Blair Vandivier*	PO Box 68809, Indianapolis IN 46268	317-875-0051	R	5*	<.1
197	Cp Industries LLC—*Chris Sower*	560 N 500 W, Salt Lake City UT 84116	801-521-0313	R	5*	<.1
198	Fcc Acquisition LLC—*Norman Oliver*	4120 Hyde Park Blvd, Niagara Falls NY 14305	716-282-1399	R	4*	<.1
199	Comstar International Inc—*Steven Mella*	2045 128th St, College Point NY 11356	718-445-7900	R	4*	<.1
200	Aqua Smart Inc—*Jerry Grossblatt*	4445 Commerce Dr Sw A4, Atlanta GA 30336	404-696-4406	R	4*	<.1
201	Nox-Crete Manufacturing Inc—*Michael Linn*	PO Box 3764, Omaha NE 68103	402-341-2080	R	4*	<.1
202	Arrow-Magnolia International Inc—*David J Tippeconnic*	PO Box 59089, Dallas TX 75229	972-247-7111	R	4*	.1
203	Analab Inc—*Thomas Dreyer*	59 Davis Ave, Norwood MA 02062	781-769-8830	R	4*	<.1
204	Pristine Water Solutions Inc—*Vincent J Verdone*	1570 S Lakeside Dr, Waukegan IL 60085	847-689-1100	D	4*	<.1
205	Vanode Co	236 N Sunset Ave, City of Industry CA 91744	626-961-0387	R	4*	<.1
206	Johnson Manufacturing Company Inc—*Alan Gickler*	PO Box 96, Princeton IA 52768	563-289-5123	R	4*	<.1
207	Chem-Tex Laboratories Inc—*Michael Smith*	PO Box 5228, Concord NC 28027	704-795-9322	R	4*	<.1
208	Summit Brands—*Charlotte Simonis*	7201 Engle Rd, Fort Wayne IN 46804	260-483-2519	R	4*	<.1
209	Argent Chemical Laboratories Inc—*Elliott Lieberman*	8702 152nd Ave Ne, Redmond WA 98052	425-885-3777	R	4*	<.1
210	Bronz-Glow Technologies Inc—*Robert Haydu*	175 Bronz Glow Way, Saint Augustine FL 32095	904-825-0175	R	3*	<.1
211	Clinton Fireworks Inc—*David Collar*	PO Box 383, Clinton MO 64735	660-885-6961	R	3*	.1
212	Spacatomic Fireworks—*Lew Loyd*	PO Box 190, South Pittsburg TN 37380	423-837-7917	R	3*	<.1
213	T and L Specialty Company Inc—*Cecil Overton*	PO Box 2144, Tupelo MS 38803	662-842-8143	R	3*	<.1
214	Mer-Kote Products Inc	4125 E LaPalma Ave Ste, Anaheim CA 92807	714-778-2266	S	3*	<.1
215	Inksure Technologies Inc—*Tal Gilat*	589 5th Ave Ste 401, New York NY 10017	646-233-1454	P	3	<.1
216	Unelko Corp—*Steven Ohlhausen*	14641 N 74th St, Scottsdale AZ 85260	480-991-7272	R	3*	<.1
217	Guardian-Ipco Inc—*Cynthia Mitchell*	PO Box 380128, Birmingham AL 35238	205-991-5316	R	3*	<.1
218	Watcon Inc—*George Resnik*	2215 S Main St, South Bend IN 46613	574-287-3397	R	3*	<.1
219	Force Industries Inc—*James Mcbride*	28 Industrial Blvd, Paoli PA 19301	610-647-3575	R	2*	<.1
220	Blue Grass Chemical Specialties LLC—*Marsha Palaica*	895 Industrial Blvd, New Albany IN 47150	812-948-1115	R	2*	<.1
221	Kcc Corrosion Control Company Ltd—*Yasenia Arredondo*	4010 Trey Dr, Houston TX 77084	281-550-1199	R	2*	<.1
222	Atlantic Chemical And Equipment Co—*Keith Macrae*	PO Box 19697, Atlanta GA 30325	404-505-6626	R	2*	<.1
223	Wild Berry Incense Inc—*Mark Biales*	5475 College Corner Pk, Oxford OH 45056	513-523-8583	R	2*	<.1
224	Chem-Tech International Inc—*Robert Larsen*	400 Ternes Dr, Random Lake WI 53075	920-994-2299	R	2*	<.1
225	Cresset Chemical Company Inc—*George Baty*	PO Box 367, Weston OH 43569	419-669-2041	R	2*	<.1
226	Garden State Fireworks Inc—*Nunzio Santore*	PO Box 403, Millington NJ 07946	908-647-1086	R	2*	<.1
227	Zog Industries Inc	PO Box 1222, Carpinteria CA 93014	805-684-4139	R	2*	<.1
228	DGF Stoess Inc—*Charles Markham*	PO Box 927, Sioux City IA 51102	712-943-5516	R	2*	<.1
229	Shape Products—*Dan Daniel*	1127 57th Ave, Oakland CA 94621	510-534-1186	R	2*	<.1
230	Chemotex Protective Coatings Corp—*Kevin Wise*	15 Commerce Cir, Durham CT 06422	860-349-0144	R	2*	<.1
231	Premier Colors Inc—*Robert Neal*	100 Industrial Dr, Union SC 29379	864-427-0338	R	2*	<.1
232	Rusmar Inc—*J Butville*	216 Garfield Ave, West Chester PA 19380	610-436-4314	R	2*	<.1

Rank	Company Name—*Executive Officer*	Address, City, State, Zip	Phone	Type	Fin	Empls
233	Tuff-Kote Company Inc—*Britt Isham*	427 E Judd St, Woodstock IL 60098	815-338-2006	R	2*	<.1
234	Superior Flux and Manufacturing Co—*Yehuda Baskin*	6615 Parkland Blvd, Cleveland OH 44139	440-349-3000	R	2*	<.1
235	Cross Chemical Company Inc—*Mark Brown*	PO Box 09758, Detroit MI 48209	313-843-0600	R	2*	<.1
236	Skasol Inc—*David Marchman*	1696 W Grand Ave, Oakland CA 94607	510-839-1000	R	1*	<.1
237	Smc Technologies Inc—*Barbara Bowersox*	PO Box 18732, Oklahoma City OK 73154	405-737-3740	R	1*	<.1
238	Foamtech Corp—*Peter Popko*	1 Nursery Ln, Fitchburg MA 01420	978-343-4022	R	1*	<.1
239	Kenneth S Jarrell Inc—*Kenneth Jarrell*	PO Box 121, Mount Meigs AL 36057	334-215-7774	R	1*	<.1
240	Dell Marking Systems Inc—*Michael Grattan*	721 Wanda St, Ferndale MI 48220	248-547-7750	R	1*	<.1
241	Alken-Murray Corp—*Valerie Anne Edwards*	PO Box 718, Flint Hill VA 22627	540-636-1236	R	1*	<.1
242	Liquid Development Co—*Doug Hutchinson*	3748 E 91st St, Cleveland OH 44105	216-641-9366	R	1*	<.1
243	Nochar Inc—*Carl Gehlhausen*	8650 Commerce Park Pl, Indianapolis IN 46268	317-613-3046	R	1*	<.1
244	NoFire Technologies Inc—*Samuel Gotfried*	21 Industrial Ave, Upper Saddle River NJ 07458	201-818-1616	P	1	<.1
245	Snyder Manufacturing Corp—*Eric Snyder*	1541 W Cowles St, Long Beach CA 90813	562-432-2038	R	1*	<.1
246	Tanner Systems Inc—*John Watkins*	PO Box 488, Saint Joseph MN 56374	320-363-1800	R	1*	<.1
247	Stapleton Technologies Inc—*Phillip Stapleton*	1350 W 12th St, Long Beach CA 90813	562-437-0541	R	1*	<.1
248	BioLargo Inc—*Dennis Calvert*	PO Box 3950, Laguna Hills CA 92653	949-643-9540	P	<1	<.1

TOTALS: SIC 2899 Chemical Preparations Nec

	Companies: 248				152,540	131.0

2911 Petroleum Refining

Rank	Company Name—*Executive Officer*	Address, City, State, Zip	Phone	Type	Fin	Empls
1	Chevron Corp—*John S Watson*	6001 Bollinger Canyon, San Ramon CA 94583	925-842-1000	P	204,928	62.0
2	ConocoPhillips—*James J Mulva*	PO Box 2197, Houston TX 77252	281-293-1000	P	189,441	29.7
3	Valero Energy Corp—*William R Klesse*	PO Box 696000, San Antonio TX 78269	210-345-2000	P	82,233	20.3
4	Sunoco Inc—*Lynn L Elsenhans*	1735 Market St Ste LL, Philadelphia PA 19103	215-977-3000	P	37,264	10.2
5	Hess Corp—*John B Hess*	1185 Ave of the Americ, New York NY 10036	212-997-8500	P	33,862	13.8
6	Green Planet Group Inc—*Edmond L Lonergan*	14988 N 78th Way Ste 1, Scottsdale AZ 85260	480-222-6222	P	31,043	N/A
7	Shell Oil Co—*Marvin Odum*	PO Box 2463, Houston TX 77252	713-241-6161	S	26,943	N/A
8	Murphy Oil Corp—*David M Wood*	PO Box 7000, El Dorado AR 71731	870-862-6411	P	23,401	9.0
9	Marathon Ashland Petroleum LLC—*Gary R Heminger*	PO Box 1, Findlay OH 45839	419-422-2121	S	22,567*	22.7
10	Tesoro Corp—*Gregory J Goff*	19100 Ridgewood Pkwy, San Antonio TX 78259	210-626-6000	P	20,583	5.3
11	PDV America Inc	PO Box 4689, Houston TX 77210		S	18,458*	4.1
12	Chevron Products Company Inc—*John Watson*	6001 Bollinger Canyon, San Ramon CA 94583		R	15,300*	8.9
13	BP Chemicals Inc—*George Spindler*	150 W Warrenville Rd, Naperville IL 60563	630-420-5111	S	13,100	N/A
14	CITGO Petroleum Corp—*Alejandro Granado* PDV America Inc	PO Box 4689, Houston TX 77210	832-486-4000	S	10,428*	4.3
15	Western Refining Inc—*Jeff A Stevens*	123 W Mills Ave, El Paso TX 79901	915-534-1400	P	9,071	3.6
16	Sinclair Oil Corp—*Peter Johnson*	PO Box 30825, Salt Lake City UT 84130	801-524-2700	R	6,800*	7.0
17	Ashland Inc—*James J O'Brien*	PO Box 391, Covington KY 41012	859-815-3333	P	6,502	15.0
18	CVR Energy Inc—*John 'Jack' Lipinski*	2277 Plaza Dr Ste 500, Sugar Land TX 77479	281-207-3200	P	5,029	.8
19	Hunt Refining Co—*John Matson*	2200 Jack Warner Pkwy, Tuscaloosa AL 35401	205-391-3300	R	4,871*	1.1
20	Alon USA Energy Inc—*Paul Eisman*	7616 LBJ Fwy Ste 300, Dallas TX 75251	972-367-3600	B	4,031	2.8
21	Delek US Holdings Inc—*Ezra U Yemin*	7102 Commerce Way, Brentwood TN 37027	615-771-6701	P	3,756	3.4
22	Red Apple Group Inc—*John A Catsimatidis*	823 11th Ave, New York NY 10019	212-956-5803	H	3,630*	7.8
23	United Refining Co—*John A Catsimatidis*	PO Box 780, Warren PA 16365	814-723-1500	S	3,167	1.9
24	Chevron Phillips Chemical Company LLC—*Greg Garland*	10001 Six Pines Dr, The Woodlands TX 77380	832-813-4100	J	3,160*	5.3
25	Calumet Specialty Products Partners LP—*F William Grube*	2780 Waterfront Pkwy E, Indianapolis IN 46214	317-328-5660	P	3,135	.9
26	Enogex Products Corp—*Peter Delaney* Enogex Inc	PO Box 321, Oklahoma City OK 73101	405-525-7788	S	2,727*	.6
27	Ergon Inc—*Leslie B Lampton Sr*	PO Box 1639, Jackson MS 39215	601-933-3000	R	2,070*	3.0
28	Frontier Refining and Marketing Inc—*Paul Eisman*	4610 S Ulster St Ste 2, Denver CO 80237	303-714-0100	S	1,814*	.7
29	Crown Central Petroleum Corp—*Thomas L Owsley*	PO Box 1168, Baltimore MD 21203	410-539-7400	S	1,700*	2.6
30	CITGO Refining and Chemicals Inc—*Alejandro Granado* CITGO Petroleum Corp	1802 Nueces Bay Blvd, Corpus Christi TX 78407	361-844-4000	S	1,146*	.6
31	Ferrellgas Inc—*James E Ferrell*	1 Liberty Plz, Liberty MO 64068	816-792-1600	S	972*	3.5
32	Tesora Hawaii Corp—*Greg J Goff* Tesoro Corp	91-325 Komohana St, Kapolei HI 96707	808-547-3111	S	820*	1.2
33	Samson Investment Co—*Stacy Schusterman*	2 W 2nd St, Tulsa OK 74103	918-583-1791	R	570*	.6
34	Navajo Refining Co—*David Lamp*	501 E Main St, Artesia NM 88210	575-748-3311	S	554*	.4
35	Galaxie Corp (Jackson Mississippi)—*Mathew Holleman*	5170 Galaxie Dr, Jackson MS 39206	601-366-8414	R	519*	.1
36	Enogex Inc—*Peter B Delaney*	515 Central Park Dr St, Oklahoma City OK 73105	405-525-7788	S	507*	.6
37	Texas Oil and Chemical Company II Inc—*Nicholas N Carter* Arabian American Development Co	PO Box 1636, Silsbee TX 77656	409-385-1400	S	396*	.2
38	Chemoil Corp—*Clyde Michael Bandy*	4 Embarcadero Center 3, San Francisco CA 94111	415-268-2700	R	309*	<.1
39	Kern Oil and Refining Co—*Jacob Belin Jr*	7724 E Panama Ln, Bakersfield CA 93307	661-845-0761	R	282*	.1
40	International Group Inc—*Ross Reucassel*	PO Box 384, Wayne PA 19087	610-687-9030	R	279*	.4
41	Cross Oil Refining and Marketing Inc—*Don Neumeyr*	484 E 6th St, Smackover AR 71762	870-881-8700	R	265*	.1
42	American Shield Refining Co—*Hatem El-Khalidi* Arabian American Development Co	10830 N Central Expy S, Dallas TX 75231	214-692-7872	S	254*	.1
43	Flint Hills Resources LP—*Bradley J Razook*	PO Box 2917, Wichita KS 67201	316-828-3477	R	202*	.1
44	Buckeye Pipe Line Company LP—*William Shea*	PO Box 368, Emmaus PA 18049	484-232-4000	S	182*	.6
45	Total Petrochemicals USA Inc—*Bernard Claude*	PO Box 674411, Houston TX 77267	713-483-5000	R	165*	1.6
46	Arabian American Development Co—*Nicolas N Carter*	1600 Hwy 6 S Ste 240, Sugar Land TX 77478	409-385-8300	P	139	.1
47	PDVSA Services Inc—*Rafael Ramirez Carreno*	11490 Westheimer Rd St, Houston TX 77210	281-531-0004	R	101*	<.1
48	Tesoro Alaska Co—*Bruce Smith* Tesoro Corp	2700 Gambell Ste 500, Anchorage AK 99503	907-279-1526	S	75*	.5
49	Restore Inc	3000 NE 30th Pl Ste 20, Fort Lauderdale FL 33306	954-563-7001	R	61*	<.1
50	Red Star Oil Co—*Chester J Krala*	802 Purser Dr, Raleigh NC 27603	919-772-1944	R	41*	<.1
51	Motiva Enterprises LLC—*Robert W Pease*	700 Milam St, Houston TX 77002	713-277-8000	R	36	3.0
52	Octel America Inc—*Sarah Smith*	200 Executive Dr, Newark DE 19702	302-454-8100	R	29*	<.1
53	US Oil and Refining Co—*Robert Redd*	PO Box 2255, Tacoma WA 98401	253-383-1651	R	27*	.2
54	BG Products Inc—*Galen Myers*	PO Box 1282, Wichita KS 67201	316-265-2686	R	26*	.2
55	Ziegler Chemical and Mineral Corp—*Gordon Ziegler*	366 N Broadway Ste 210, Jericho NY 11753	516-681-9600	R	19*	.1
56	Beta Fluid Systems Inc—*Jeffrey Borg*	1209 Fwy Dr, Reidsville NC 27320	336-342-0306	R	18*	.1
57	Olds-Olympic Inc—*Forrest Bailey*	PO Box 180, Lynnwood WA 98046	425-778-1000	R	17*	<.1
58	Summit Lubricants Inc—*Ronald Krol*	PO Box 966, Batavia NY 14021	585-344-4301	R	8*	<.1
59	Sun Fab Industrial Contracting Inc—*Romeo Leija*	6248 Edgemere Blvd Ste, El Paso TX 79925	915-779-6991	R	8*	.1
60	Sound Refining Inc—*Troy Goodman*	PO Box 1372, Tacoma WA 98401	253-272-9348	R	4*	<.1
61	San Joaquin Refining Company Inc—*Majid Mojibi*	PO Box 5576, Bakersfield CA 93388	661-327-4257	R	4*	.1
62	Enterprise Products Operating LP	1100 Louisiana St, Houston TX 77002	713-880-6500	S	3*	.9

Note: An asterisk (*) indicates an estimated financial figure. The company type code used is as follows: R = Private, P = Public, S = Private Subsidiary, B = Public Subsidiary, D = Division, J = Joint Venture, I = Investment Fund.

COMPANY RANKINGS BY SALES WITHIN 4-DIGIT SIC

Rank	Company Name—*Executive Officer*	Address, City, State, Zip	Phone	Type	Fin	Empls
63	BP Prudhoe Bay Royalty Trust—*Mike Ulrich*	The Bank of New York M, Austin TX 78701	512-236-6565	P	1	N/A

TOTALS: SIC 2911 Petroleum Refining
Companies: 63 — — 799,051 262.3

2951 Asphalt Paving Mixtures & Blocks

Rank	Company Name—*Executive Officer*	Address, City, State, Zip	Phone	Type	Fin	Empls
1	Oldcastle Materials Inc—*Garry Higdem*	900 Ashwood Pkwy Ste 7, Atlanta GA 30338	770-522-5600	S	25,170*	1.5
2	Pike Industries Inc—*Randolph K Pike*	3 Eastgate Park Rd, Belmont NH 03220	603-527-5100	S	5,431*	1.3
3	Branscome Inc—*Stuart Patterson*	PO Drawer 5550, Williamsburg VA 23188	757-229-2504	R	1,255*	.3
4	Lane Construction Corp—*Robert E Alger*	90 Fieldstone Crt, Cheshire CT 06410	203-235-3351	R	882*	4.5
5	Tilcon Connecticut Inc—*Ciaran Brennan*	PO Box 1357, New Britain CT 06050	860-224-6005	S	359*	1.4
6	Suit-Kote Corp—*Frank Suits*	1911 Lorings Crossing, Cortland NY 13045	607-753-1100	R	250*	.7
7	Shelly Co—*Gail Thomas*	PO Box 611, Kent OH 44240	330-425-7861	R	156*	.1
8	APAC-Kansas Inc—*Max Breshears* Oldcastle Materials Inc	PO Box 23910, Overland Park KS 66283	913-814-6700	D	89*	.3
9	APAC-Carolina Inc Barrus Div—*Doug Black*	900 Ashwood Pkwy Ste 7, Atlanta GA 30338	770-522-5600	D	86*	.6
10	APAC-Southeast Inc—*Doug Black* Oldcastle Materials Inc	13101 Telecom Dr, Tampa FL 33637	813-973-2888	S	84*	.1
11	Vance Brothers Inc—*Mark Smith*	PO Box 300107, Kansas City MO 64130	816-923-4325	R	71*	.1
12	APAC-Tennessee Inc—*Nickolas R Haynes* Oldcastle Materials Inc	PO Box 13427, Memphis TN 38113	901-947-5600	S	64*	.3
13	McClinton-Anchor Div—*Lee S DuChanois*	PO Box 1367, Fayetteville AR 72702	479-587-3300	D	50*	.3
14	R A Cullinan and Son Inc—*Mike Cullinan*	PO Box 166, Tremont IL 61568	309-925-2711	R	50*	.3
15	APAC-Central Inc—*Doug Black* Oldcastle Materials Inc	PO Box 580670, Tulsa OK 74158	918-438-2020	D	50*	.1
16	Dustrol Inc—*Ted Dankert*	PO Box 309, Towanda KS 67144	316-536-2262	R	45*	.3
17	Atlantic Coast Asphalt Co—*John Stanton*	PO Box 40949, Jacksonville FL 32203	904-786-1020	D	37	.1
18	N B West Contracting Co—*Larry West*	2780 Mary Ave, Saint Louis MO 63144	314-962-3145	R	36*	.2
19	Pine Bluff Sand And Gravel Co—*W Scott Mc George*	PO Box 7008, Pine Bluff AR 71611	870-534-7120	R	34*	.3
20	WR Meadows Inc—*J F Dwyer*	PO Box 338, Hampshire IL 60140	847-214-2100	R	33*	.2
21	Peckham Industries Inc—*John Peckham*	20 Haarlem Ave Ste 200, White Plains NY 10603	914-949-2000	R	31*	.4
22	Brox Industries Inc—*Stephen Brox*	1471 Methuen St, Dracut MA 01826	978-454-9105	R	26*	.2
23	Peter Baker and Son Co—*Arthur Baker*	PO Box 187, Lake Bluff IL 60044	847-362-3663	R	26*	.2
24	Dunn Road Builders LLC—*Clifton Beckman Jr*	PO Box 6560, Laurel MS 39441	601-649-4111	S	23*	.1
25	Rlc Holding Company Inc—*Robert Cummins*	PO Box 748, Enid OK 73702	580-233-6000	R	23*	.2
26	Shelby Contracting Company Inc—*Jerry Chesser*	900 Conception Ave Nw, Huntsville AL 35801	256-533-4727	R	22*	.3
27	Ace Asphalt and Paving Co—*Andrew Wilson*	115 S Averill Ave, Flint MI 48506	810-238-1737	S	20*	.1
28	Eureka Stone Quarry Inc—*James Morrissey*	PO Box 249, Chalfont PA 18914	215-333-8000	R	17*	.1
29	Tex-Mastic International Inc—*Ron Palmer*	PO Box 210309, Dallas TX 75211	214-330-4605	R	15*	<.1
30	American Asphalt Paving Co—*Bernard Banks*	500 Chase Rd, Shavertown PA 18708	570-696-1181	R	14*	.1
31	Lorusso Corp—*Gerard Lorusso*	3 Belcher St, Plainville MA 02762	508-668-3100	R	14*	.1
32	A Colarusso And Son Inc—*Peter Colarusso*	PO Box 302, Hudson NY 12534	518-828-1531	R	13*	.1
33	J Lee Milligan Inc—*Doug Walterscheid*	PO Box 30188, Amarillo TX 79120	806-373-4386	R	13*	.1
34	South State Inc—*Chester Ottinger*	PO Box 68, Bridgeton NJ 08302	856-451-5300	R	10*	.1
35	Concrete Coring Co (Denver Colorado)—*Margaret Hainey*	4024 Jason St, Denver CO 80211	303-433-8818	R	10*	.1
36	Wille Brothers Company Concrete Div—*Curt Wille*	15800 S Lamon Ave, Oak Forest IL 60452	708-623-6026	D	10*	<.1
37	All-American Asphalt and Aggregates Inc—*Allan Henderson*	PO Box 2229, Corona CA 92879	951-736-7600	R	9*	.1
38	Wabash Asphalt Company Inc—*Charles Adams*	415 S Mulberry St, Mount Carmel IL 62863	618-263-3563	R	7*	.1
39	Rason Asphalt Inc—*Anthony Shakesby*	PO Box 530, Old Bethpage NY 11804	631-293-6210	R	7*	<.1
40	Mid-State Sand and Gravel Company Inc—*Bryan Bossier*	PO Box 7618, Alexandria LA 71306	318-427-1300	R	5*	.1
41	Oregon Asphaltic Paving Co—*Tony Urbanek*	PO Box 4810, Tualatin OR 97062	503-252-1497	S	5*	<.1
42	Highway Materials Inc—*Peter Paul*	PO Box 1667, Blue Bell PA 19422	610-832-8000	R	5*	<.1
43	Western Oil Spreading Services Inc—*Guy Tittlemier*	13812 A Better Way, Garden Grove CA 92843	714-638-4831	R	4*	<.1
44	Walter R Earle Corp—*Walter R Earle II*	PO Box 556, Farmingdale NJ 07727	732-308-1113	R	3*	<.1
45	Twin Lakes Quarrys Inc—*Jim King*	PO Box 705, Mountain Home AR 72654	870-425-4510	R	3*	<.1
46	Howell Asphalt Co—*Kenneth Ozier*	PO Box 1009, Mattoon IL 61938	217-234-8877	R	3*	<.1
47	Louis Marsch Inc—*Kirk Vocks*	PO Box 42, Morrisonville IL 62546	217-526-4423	R	3*	<.1
48	Sherwin Industries Inc—*Steven Schultz*	149 S Fox Run Ln, Byron IL 61010	815-234-8007	R	2*	<.1
49	Union Asphalt Inc—*Ron Root*	PO Box 1280, Santa Maria CA 93456	805-922-3551	R	2*	<.1
50	Paul H Rohe Company Inc—*Mork Richardson*	PO Box 67, Aurora IN 47001	812-926-1471	R	2*	<.1

TOTALS: SIC 2951 Asphalt Paving Mixtures & Blocks
Companies: 50 — — 34,576 15.4

2952 Asphalt Felts & Coatings

Rank	Company Name—*Executive Officer*	Address, City, State, Zip	Phone	Type	Fin	Empls
1	G-I Holdings Corp—*Alyssa Hall*	1361 Alps Rd, Wayne NJ 07470	973-628-3000	R	3,000	3.3
2	CertainTeed Corp—*Peter Duchowski*	PO Box 860, Valley Forge PA 19482	610-341-7000	S	2,300*	7.0
3	BFS Diversified Products LLC—*Mike Gorey*	250 W 96th St, Indianapolis IN 46260	317-575-7000	S	2,056*	1.3
4	Henry Co—*Brian C Strauss*	909 N Sepulveda Blvd S, El Segundo CA 90245	310-955-9200	R	867*	.6
5	Atlas Roofing Corp—*Kenneth Farrish*	2000 RiverEdge Pkwy NW, Atlanta GA 30328		R	415*	1.2
6	Interlock Industries Inc—*Jeff Mackin*	545 S 3rd St Ste 310, Louisville KY 40202	502-569-2007	R	371*	.1
7	Carlisle SynTec Inc—*John Altmeyer*	PO Box 7000, Carlisle PA 17013		S	320*	1.1
8	Carlisle Coatings and Waterproofing Inc—*Robert Stout*	900 Hensley Ln, Wylie TX 75098	972-442-6545	S	165*	.2
9	Century Industries Corp—*Don Brothers*	5331 State Rte 7, New Waterford OH 44445	330-457-2367	R	60*	.1
10	Sika Sarnafil Inc—*Brian Whelan*	100 Dan Rd, Canton MA 02021	781-828-5400	S	42*	.2
11	Lunday-Thagard Co—*Robert Roth*	PO Box 1519, South Gate CA 90280	562-928-7000	S	40*	.5
12	Fields Company LLC—*Sandy Mcarthur*	PO Box 687, Kent WA 98035	253-627-4098	R	37*	.1
13	Herbert Malarkey Roofing Co—*Michael Malarkey*	PO Box 17217, Portland OR 97217	503-283-1191	R	36*	.1
14	Pabco Roofing Products—*John Corbett*	1718 Thorne Rd, Tacoma WA 98421	253-272-0374	S	32*	.1
15	American Tar Co Fields Company LLC	2240 Taylor Way, Tacoma WA 98421	253-627-4098	S	29*	.1
16	Southwestern Petroleum Corp—*Robert Dickerson*	PO Box 961005, Fort Worth TX 76161	817-332-2336	R	22*	.2
17	Republic Powdered Metals Inc—*Frank C Sullivan*	2628 Pearl Rd, Medina OH 44256	330-225-3192	S	15*	.1
18	Karnak Corp—*James Hannah*	330 Central Ave, Clark NJ 07066	732-388-0300	R	14*	.1
19	Sunlife Systems International Inc—*Jerry Auten*	PO Box 12308, Charlotte NC 28220	704-527-2480	R	11*	.1
20	Monroe Iko Inc—*Henry Koschitzky*	120 Hay Rd, Wilmington DE 19809	302-764-3100	R	9*	.1
21	De Witt Products Co—*Donald Mcclellan*	5860 Plumer St, Detroit MI 48209	313-554-0575	R	7*	<.1
22	In-O-Vate Inc—*Richard Harpenau*	PO Box 46566, Cleveland OH 44146	216-581-7150	R	4*	<.1
23	Asphalt Cutbacks Inc—*Cleopatra Bizoukas*	3000 Gary Rd, East Chicago IN 46312	219-398-4230	R	1*	<.1
24	Emulsicoat Inc—*Fred Fehsenfeld*	705 E University Ave, Urbana IL 61802	217-344-7775	R	1*	<.1

TOTALS: SIC 2952 Asphalt Felts & Coatings
Companies: 24 — — 9,852 16.4

Rank	Company Name—*Executive Officer*	Address, City, State, Zip	Phone	Type	Fin	Empls
2992 Lubricating Oils & Greases						
1	Valvoline—*Samuel J Mitchell Jr*	PO Box 14000, Lexington KY 40512	859-357-7777	D	1,172*	.6
2	Warren Distribution Inc—*Robert Schlott*	727 S 13th St, Omaha NE 68102	402-341-9397	R	864*	.4
3	M-I LLC—*Don McKinsey*	5950 N Course Dr, Houston TX 77072	713-739-0222	S	644*	.3
4	Quaker Chemical Corp—*Michael F Barry*	1 Quaker Pk 901 Hector, Conshohocken PA 19428	610-832-4000	P	544	1.4
5	Fuchs Corp—*Steven Puffpaff*	17050 Lathrop Ave, Harvey IL 60426	708-333-8900	R	261*	.4
6	Windward Petroleum Inc—*Stephen Eldred*	1064 Goffs Falls Rd, Manchester NH 03103	603-222-2900	R	240*	.1
7	Jet-Lube Inc—*Greg Havelka*	4849 Homestead Rd Ste, Houston TX 77028	713-670-5700	S	143*	.1
8	De Menno-Kerdoon—*Bruce Menno*	9302 Garfield Ave, South Gate CA 90280	562-231-1550	R	113*	.1
9	Master Chemical Corp—*Joe Wright*	501 W Boundary St, Perrysburg OH 43551	419-874-7902	R	100*	.3
10	Whitmore Manufacturing Co—*Jeff Peterson*	930 Whitmore Dr, Rockwall TX 75087	972-771-1000	S	56	.1
11	Evergreen Oil Inc—*Russell Burbank*	2415 Campus Dr Ste 225, Irvine CA 92612	949-757-7770	R	49*	.2
12	Hangsterfers Laboratories Inc—*Ann Jones*	175 Ogden Rd, Mantua NJ 08051	856-468-0216	R	44*	<.1
13	Hagan Kennington Oil Company Inc—*Grady Kennington*	1405 Industrial Park, Gastonia NC 28052	704-865-9561	R	43*	<.1
14	Universal Lubricants LLC—*Donna Towell*	PO Box 2920, Wichita KS 67201	316-832-0151	R	41*	.2
15	GoldenWest Lubricants Inc	1937 Mount Vernon Ave, Pomona CA 91768		R	41*	<.1
16	International Refining and Manufacturing Co—*W Jeff Jeffery*	2117 Greenleaf St, Evanston IL 60202	847-864-0255	R	40*	.2
17	Primrose Oil Co—*Vicki Brin*	PO Box 29665, Dallas TX 75229	972-241-1100	R	36*	.3
18	Amsoil Inc—*Albert Amatuzio*	925 Tower Ave, Superior WI 54880	715-392-7101	R	35*	.2
19	Lubrication Technology Inc—*Christian Bame*	900 Mendelssohn Ave N, Golden Valley MN 55427	763-545-0707	R	34*	.1
20	LPS Laboratories Inc—*Jim Allen*	PO Box 105052, Tucker GA 30085	770-243-8800	S	33*	.1
21	Haynes Manufacturing Co—*Beth Kloos*	24142 Detroit Rd, Westlake OH 44145	440-871-2188	R	33*	<.1
22	Fiske Brothers Refining Company Inc—*Richard Mccluskey*	129 Lockwood St, Newark NJ 07105	973-589-9150	R	30*	.1
23	Lubricating Specialties Co—*Steve Milam*	8015 Paramount Blvd, Pico Rivera CA 90660	562-776-4000	R	29*	.2
24	CPI Engineering Services Inc—*Thomas Rajewski*	2300 James Savage Rd, Midland MI 48642	989-496-3780	S	25*	.1
25	Excelda Manufacturing Co—*William Lamarra*	12785 Emerson Dr, Brighton MI 48116	248-486-3800	R	25*	.2
26	Wallover Enterprises Inc—*George Marquis*	PO Box 361125, Strongsville OH 44136	440-238-9250	R	22*	.2
27	Yushiro Manufacturing America Inc—*Aisaku Ota*	PO Box 217, Shelbyville IN 46176	317-398-9862	R	21*	<.1
28	Texas Refinery Corp—*Jerry Hopkins*	PO Box 711, Fort Worth TX 76101	817-332-1161	R	18*	.1
29	Lowe Oil/Champion Brands—*David Lowe*	PO Box 645, Clinton MO 64735	660-885-8151	R	16*	.1
30	Acrotech Industries Inc—*Bruce Moncrieff*	5700 W Douglas Ave, Milwaukee WI 53218	414-464-7200	R	16*	<.1
31	Camco Chemical Co—*Richard Rolfes*	8150 Holton Dr, Florence KY 41042	859-727-3200	R	15*	.1
32	Sentinel Lubricants Inc—*Robert Chaban*	PO Box 694240, Miami FL 33269	305-625-6400	R	14*	.1
33	Bardahl Manufacturing Corp—*Hugh Mcniel*	PO Box 70607, Seattle WA 98127	206-783-4851	R	14*	<.1
34	Rock Valley Oil and Chemical Company Inc—*Roger Schramm*	1911 Windsor Rd, Loves Park IL 61111	815-654-2400	R	14*	.1
35	Lubrication Engineers Inc—*Scott Schwindaman*	300 Bailey Ave, Fort Worth TX 76107	817-834-6321	R	14*	.1
36	Oil Center Manufacturing Inc—*Robert Ahrabi*	PO Box 91510, Lafayette LA 70509	337-232-2496	R	13*	.1
37	JTM Products Inc—*Daniel Schodowski*	31025 Carter St, Solon OH 44139	440-287-2302	R	12*	<.1
38	76 Lubricants Co—*James Mulva*	600 N Dairy Ashford 2W, Houston TX 77079	619-234-0345	D	12*	<.1
39	Mid-State Chemical and Supply Corp—*Paul Bosler*	PO Box 18227, Indianapolis IN 46218	317-925-1407	R	7*	.1
40	Richards Apex Inc—*JH Richards III*	4202-24 Main St, Philadelphia PA 19127	215-487-1100	R	7*	.1
41	Dylon Industries Inc—*Robert Kowaleski*	7700 Clinton Rd, Brooklyn OH 44144	216-651-1300	R	7*	<.1
42	Cadillac Oil Co—*Roger Piceu*	13650 Helen St, Detroit MI 48212	313-305-0200	P	7*	<.1
43	Macdermid-Canning Ltd—*Mark Hollinger*	223 Brockman St, Pasadena TX 77506	713-472-5081	R	6*	<.1
44	Intercontinental Lubricants Corp—*David Miller*	993 Federal Rd, Brookfield CT 06804	203-775-1291	R	6*	<.1
45	Clc Lubricants Co—*Joseph O'brien*	PO Box 764, Geneva IL 60134	630-232-7900	R	5*	<.1
46	Berkebile Oil Company Inc—*Catherine Poorbaugh*	PO Box 715, Somerset PA 15501	814-443-1656	R	5*	<.1
47	Vestper Corp—*Roger Yamamoto*	2685 Airport Rd, Kinston NC 28504	252-522-4688	R	5*	.1
48	Battenfeld-American Inc—*John Bellanti*	1575 Clinton St, Buffalo NY 14206	716-822-8410	S	5*	<.1
49	WS Dodge Oil Company Inc—*Thomas J Downs*	3710 Fruitland Ave, Maywood CA 90270	323-583-3478	R	5*	<.1
50	Lubeco Inc—*Steven Rossi*	6859 Downey Ave, Long Beach CA 90805	562-602-1791	R	5*	<.1
51	Axel Plastics Research Laboratories Inc—*Jacob Axel*	PO Box 770855, Woodside NY 11377	718-672-8300	R	5*	<.1
52	Condat Corp—*Karen Mulvihill*	250 S Industrial Dr, Saline MI 48176	734-944-4994	R	5*	<.1
53	Etna Products Inc—*Isaac Tripp*	PO Box 23609, Chagrin Falls OH 44023	440-543-9845	R	4*	<.1
54	Tribology Inc—*William Krause*	35 Old Dock Rd, Yaphank NY 11980	631-345-3000	R	4*	<.1
55	Xentx Lubricants Inc—*Michael Dyson*	PO Box 266, Durant OK 74702	580-924-8834	R	3*	<.1
56	United Oil Company Inc—*Timothy Croke*	4405 E Baltimore St, Baltimore MD 21224	410-342-1200	R	3*	<.1
57	American Polywater Corp—*John Fee*	PO Box 53, Stillwater MN 55082	651-430-2270	R	3*	<.1
58	Functional Products Inc—*David Devore*	8282 Bavaria Dr E, Macedonia OH 44056	330-963-3060	R	3*	<.1
59	Monroe Fluid Technology Inc—*Mary Silloway*	PO Box 810, Hilton NY 14468	585-392-3434	R	3*	<.1
60	Famous Lubricants Inc—*Vaughn Hapeman*	124 W 47th St, Chicago IL 60609	773-268-2555	R	3*	<.1
61	Ore-Lube Corp—*Robert Silverstein*	20 Sawgrass Dr, Bellport NY 11713	631-205-9700	R	2*	<.1
62	Baums Castorine Company Inc—*Charles Mowry*	PO Box 230, Rome NY 13440	315-336-8154	R	2*	<.1
63	Armite Laboratories Inc—*Josh Walker*	1560 Superior Ave Ste, Costa Mesa CA 92627	949-646-9035	R	2*	<.1
64	Leahy-Wolf Co—*Keanan Leahy*	1724 W Armitage Ct, Addison IL 60101	708-432-0020	R	2*	<.1
65	United Oil Company Corp—*Charles Cross*	1800 N Franklin St, Pittsburgh PA 15233	412-231-1270	R	2*	<.1
66	Mullen Circle Brand Inc—*Kenneth Reed*	PO Box 8487, Northfield IL 60093	847-676-1880	R	1*	<.1
67	American Oil and Supply Co—*Stanley Ziemski*	22 Meridian Rd Ste 6, Eatontown NJ 07724	732-389-5514	R	1*	<.1
68	Renite Co- Lubrication Engineers—*Stephen Halliday*	PO Box 30830, Columbus OH 43230	614-253-5509	R	1*	<.1
69	BX-IR Corp—*Terry Craig*	375 Fentress Blvd, Daytona Beach FL 32114	386-271-7000	R	<1	<.1
TOTALS: SIC 2992 Lubricating Oils & Greases						
	Companies: 69				**4,993**	**7.5**
2999 Petroleum & Coal Products Nec						
1	Headwaters Inc—*Kirk A Benson*	10653 S River Front Pk, South Jordan UT 84095	801-984-9400	P	592	2.7
2	Great Lakes Carbon Corp—*James D McKenzie*	16945 Northchase Dr St, Houston TX 77060	281-775-4700	R	383*	.3
3	Renewable Energy Group Inc—*Jeffrey Stroburg*	PO Box 888, Ames IA 50010	515-239-8000	R	232*	.1
4	Blended Waxes Inc—*Paul Gereau*	PO Box 3044, Oshkosh WI 54903	920-236-8080	R	20*	<.1
5	Synthesis Energy Systems Inc—*Robert Rigdon*	Three Riverway Ste 300, Houston TX 77056	713-579-0600	P	10	.2
6	HRD Corp—*Abbas Hassan*	PO Box 450267, Houston TX 77245	713-721-9131	R	4*	<.1
7	Pellet America Corp—*Lee Robbert*	2601 W 2nd St, Appleton WI 54914	920-954-0466	R	3*	<.1
8	Changing World Technologies Inc—*Brian S Appel*	460 Hempstead Ave, West Hempstead NY 11552	516-486-0100	R	1*	<.1
TOTALS: SIC 2999 Petroleum & Coal Products Nec						
	Companies: 8				**1,246**	**3.4**
3011 Tires & Inner Tubes						
1	Continental Tire The Americas LLC—*Matthias Schonberg*	1830 Macmillan Park Dr, Fort Mill SC 29707	704-588-5895	R	21,429*	3.0
2	Goodyear Tire and Rubber Co—*Richard J Kramer*	1144 E Market St, Akron OH 44316	330-796-2121	P	18,832	72.0
3	Carlisle Tire and Wheel Co—*Fred Sutter*	25 Windham Blvd, Aiken SC 29805	803-643-2900	D	4,822*	.6

Note: An asterisk (*) indicates an estimated financial figure. The company type code used is as follows: R = Private, P = Public, S = Private Subsidiary, B = Public Subsidiary, D = Division, J = Joint Venture, I = Investment Fund.

COMPANY RANKINGS BY SALES WITHIN 4-DIGIT SIC

Rank	Company Name—*Executive Officer*	Address, City, State, Zip	Phone	Type	Fin	Empls
4	Cooper Tire and Rubber Co—*Roy V Armes*	PO Box 550, Findlay OH 45839	419-423-1321	P	3,927	12.9
5	Galaxy Tire and Wheel Inc—*Craig Steinke*	730 Eastern Ave, Malden MA 02148	781-321-3910	R	2,376*	2.5
6	Michelin North America Inc—*Michel Rollier*	PO Box 19001, Greenville SC 29602	864-458-5000	S	1,111	17.9
7	Bridgestone Americas Holding Inc—*Saul Solomon* Bridgestone Americas Inc	2905 N Hwy 61, Muscatine IA 52761	563-262-1400	S	930*	3.8
8	TAG Holdings LLC—*Joseph B Anderson Jr*	2075 W Big Beaver Rd S, Troy MI 48084	248-822-8056	R	500*	.3
9	Pirelli Tire North America—*Maurizio Sala*	PO Box 700, Rome GA 30162	706-368-5800	S	473*	1.0
10	Yokohama Tire Corp—*Norio Karashima*	601 S Acacia Ave, Fullerton CA 92831	714-870-3800	S	445*	1.2
11	Bridgestone Americas Inc—*Gary Garfield*	PO Box 140900, Nashville TN 37214		S	432*	50.0
12	Dunlop Tire—*James Galoppo* Goodyear Tire and Rubber Co	PO Box 1109, Amherst NY 14228	716-639-5200	S	320*	2.5
13	Titan Tire Corp—*Bill Campbell*	2345 E Market St, Des Moines IA 50317	515-265-9200	S	190*	.9
14	Yokohama Corporation Of North America—*Yasuo Tominaga*	601 S Acacia Ave, Fullerton CA 92831	714-870-3800	R	154*	2.1
15	Technical Rubber Company Inc—*Mike Chambers*	PO Box 486, Johnstown OH 43031	740-967-9015	R	40*	.6
16	Pirelli Tire Corp—*Marco Provera* Pirelli Tire North America	700 Industrial Dr, Lexington SC 29072		S	31*	.2
17	Superior Tire and Rubber Corp—*Henry Le Meur*	PO Box 308, Warren PA 16365	814-723-2370	R	26*	.1
18	Bandag Licensing Corp Bridgestone Americas Holding Inc	2500 E Thompson St, Long Beach CA 90805	562-531-3880	S	13*	.1
19	31 Inc—*Charles Muhs*	PO Box 278, Newcomerstown OH 43832	740-498-8324	R	11*	.1
20	Mclaren Industries Inc—*Richardson Doyle*	PO Box 7506, Torrance CA 90504	310-212-1333	R	6*	.1
21	Lone Star Wheel Components Inc—*Larry Coffey*	PO Box 531, Corsicana TX 75151	903-654-1132	R	4*	.1
22	Amerityre Corp—*Michael J Kapral Jr*	1501 Industrial Rd, Boulder City NV 89005	702-293-1930	P	4	<.1
23	Roll-Tech LLC—*Debbie English*	243 Performance Dr Se, Hickory NC 28602	828-431-4515	R	4*	<.1
24	BAS Recycling Inc—*Hratch Sarkis*	14050 Day St, Moreno Valley CA 92553	951-214-6590	R	3*	<.1
25	Presti Rubber Products Inc—*Duane Presti*	200 Hyde Park, Doylestown PA 18902	215-348-1888	R	2*	<.1
26	Marathon Industries Inc—*Jon Foster*	7925 S 196th St, Kent WA 98032	253-893-7014	R	2*	<.1
27	Automated Technology Equipment Consultants Inc—*Clyde Church*	815 E Tonto St, Phoenix AZ 85034	602-253-3921	R	2*	<.1
28	Titan Technologies Inc—*Ronald L Wilder*	3206 Candelaria Rd NE, Albuquerque NM 87107	505-884-0272	P	<1	<.1

TOTALS: SIC 3011 Tires & Inner Tubes
Companies: 28 — 56,087 — 171.9

3021 Rubber & Plastics Footwear

Rank	Company Name—*Executive Officer*	Address, City, State, Zip	Phone	Type	Fin	Empls
1	Skechers USA Inc—*Robert Greenberg*	228 Manhattan Beach Bl, Manhattan Beach CA 90266	310-318-3100	P	1,606	5.6
2	Deckers Outdoor Corp—*Angel Martinez*	495 S Fairview Ave Ste, Goleta CA 93117	805-967-7611	P	1,377	1.9
3	Crocs Inc—*John P McCarvel*	6328 Monarch Park Pl, Niwot CO 80503	303-848-7000	P	1,001	4.2
4	Totes-Isotoner Corp—*Douglas P Gernert*	9655 International Blv, Cincinnati OH 45246	513-682-8200	R	358*	1.1
5	LaCrosse Footwear Inc—*Joseph Schneider*	17634 NE Airport Way, Portland OR 97230	503-262-0110	P	131	.4
6	Jack Schwartz Shoes Inc—*Bernard Schwartz*	155 Ave of the America, New York NY 10013	212-691-4700	R	116*	.1
7	Meramec Group Inc—*Thomas Dieckhaus*	PO Box 279, Sullivan MO 63080	573-468-3101	R	33*	.3
8	Georgia Boot LLC	39 E Canal St, Nelsonville OH 45764	740-753-1951	D	10*	.1
9	Tingley Rubber Corp—*Paul Bolton*	PO Box 100, South Plainfield NJ 07080		R	9*	<.1
10	Sole Supports Inc—*Ed Glaser*	PO Box 400, Bon Aqua TN 37025	931-670-6111	R	4*	<.1
11	Principle Plastics—*David Hoyt*	PO Box 2408, Gardena CA 90247	310-532-3411	R	4*	<.1

TOTALS: SIC 3021 Rubber & Plastics Footwear
Companies: 11 — 4,649 — 13.8

3052 Rubber & Plastics Hose & Belting

Rank	Company Name—*Executive Officer*	Address, City, State, Zip	Phone	Type	Fin	Empls
1	Plastic Specialties And Technologies Inc—*Kenneth Baker*	101 Railroad Ave, Ridgefield NJ 07657	201-941-2900	R	7,224*	.2
2	Salisbury by Honeywell	101 E Crossroads Ste A, Bolingbrook IL 60440		S	265*	.2
3	Tti Floor Care North America Inc—*Chris Gurreri*	7005 Cochran Rd, Solon OH 44139	440-996-2000	R	159*	2.0
4	Continental Plastics Co—*Anthony Catenacci*	33525 Groesbeck Hwy, Fraser MI 48026	586-294-4600	R	108*	.5
5	Dynacraft	650 Milwaukee Ave N, Algona WA 98001	253-333-3000	D	106*	.2
6	Tigerflex Corp—*Seiji Shiga*	801 Estes Ave, Elk Grove Village IL 60007	847-640-8366	R	80*	1.1
7	Flexfab LLC—*Matt DeCamp*	1699 W M43 Hwy, Hastings MI 49058	269-945-2433	S	39*	.4
8	Contitech Thermopol LLC—*Greg Cloud*	9 Interstate Dr, Somersworth NH 03878	603-692-6300	R	30*	.2
9	Hitachi Cable Automotive Products USA Inc—*Ted Opsuka*	5300 Grant Line Rd, New Albany IN 47150	812-945-9011	R	26*	.4
10	Sperry and Rice Manufacturing Company LLC—*Bruce Croskey*	9146 Us Hwy 52, Brookville IN 47012	765-647-4141	R	20*	.3
11	Coilhose Pneumatics Inc—*Jack Burns*	19 Kimberly Rd, East Brunswick NJ 08816	732-390-8480	R	20*	.1
12	Chapin Watermatics Inc—*Narinder Gupta*	PO Box 490, Watertown NY 13601	315-782-1170	R	13*	.1
13	Mol Belting Systems Inc—*Edward Mol*	PO Box 141095, Grand Rapids MI 49514	616-453-2484	R	13*	.1
14	Key Fire Hose Corp—*Charles Genthner*	PO Box 7107, Dothan AL 36302	334-671-5532	R	12*	.1
15	Nephi Rubber Products Corp—*Terry Jones*	PO Box 140, Nephi UT 84648	435-623-1740	R	11*	.1
16	Freelin-Wade Co—*Marvin Aaron*	1730 Ne Miller St, Mcminnville OR 97128	503-434-5561	R	11*	.1
17	Wcco Belting Inc—*Thomas Shorma*	PO Box 1205, Wahpeton ND 58074	701-642-8787	R	10*	.1
18	North American Fire Hose Corp—*Michael Aubuchon*	PO Box 1968, Santa Maria CA 93456	805-922-7076	R	9*	.1
19	Flexmaster USA Inc—*Michael Jakobs*	5235 Ted St, Houston TX 77040	713-462-7694	R	9*	.1
20	Belt Corporation Of America Inc—*William Levensalor*	253 Castleberry Indust, Cumming GA 30040	770-887-9725	R	8*	.1
21	Crumb Rubber Technology Inc—*Mike Reali*	187-40 Hollis Ave, Hollis NY 11423	718-468-3988	R	8*	<.1
22	Atlanta Belting Co—*Ernest Key*	560 Edgewood Ave Ne, Atlanta GA 30312	404-688-1483	R	7*	<.1
23	Voss Belting and Specialty Co—*Richard Voss*	6965 N Hamlin Ave Ste, Lincolnwood IL 60712	847-673-8900	R	7*	<.1
24	Salem-Republic Rubber Co—*Drew Ney*	PO Box 339, Sebring OH 44672	330-938-9801	R	7*	<.1
25	Copper State Rubber Of Arizona Inc—*Robert Snider*	PO Box 14126, Phoenix AZ 85063	602-269-5927	R	7*	.1
26	Bridgestone Flowtech America—*Eric Tasso*	154 Industrial Loop S, Orange Park FL 32073	904-264-6841	R	6*	.1
27	Powell Electro Systems LLC	5 Briar Dr, West Grove PA 19390	610-869-8393	R	6*	<.1
28	Samar Company Inc—*William Selby*	PO Box 870, Stoughton MA 02072	781-341-0210	R	5*	<.1
29	Aarubco Rubber Company Inc—*Stephen Wharton*	PO Box 8028, Saddle Brook NJ 07663	973-772-8177	R	5*	<.1
30	Tektube Group LLC—*Kellly Posrina*	2925 State Rd, Croydon PA 19021	215-781-1700	R	5*	<.1
31	WF Lake Corp—*James Meyers*	PO Box 4214, Queensbury NY 12804	518-798-9934	R	3*	<.1
32	Harrison Hose And Tubing Inc—*James Logue*	PO Box 9386, Trenton NJ 08650	609-631-8804	R	3*	<.1
33	Technical Heaters Inc—*Bruce Jones*	710 Jessie St, San Fernando CA 91340	818-361-7185	R	3*	<.1
34	Couse and Bolten Co—*Michael F Nelson*	90 South St, Newark NJ 07114	973-344-6330	R	1*	<.1

TOTALS: SIC 3052 Rubber & Plastics Hose & Belting
Companies: 34 — 8,244 — 6.8

3053 Gaskets, Packing & Sealing Devices

Rank	Company Name—*Executive Officer*	Address, City, State, Zip	Phone	Type	Fin	Empls
1	Utex Industries Inc—*Michael Balas*	PO Box 79227, Houston TX 77279	713-467-1000	R	4,074*	.4
2	John Crane Sealol—*Bob Wasson* John Crane Inc	50 Sharpe Dr, Cranston RI 02920	401-463-8700	S	1,110	9.0

Rank	Company Name—*Executive Officer*	Address, City, State, Zip	Phone	Type	Fin	Empls
3	EnPro Industries Inc—*Stephen E MacAdam*	5605 Carnegie Blvd, Charlotte NC 28209	704-731-1500	P	865	3.6
4	Frenzelit Sealing Systems Inc—*Jerry Thorson*	16550 W Ryerson Rd, New Berlin WI 53151	262-786-5300	R	365*	.5
5	Garlock Sealing Technologies—*Stephen E Macadam* EnPro Industries Inc	1666 Division St, Palmyra NY 14522	315-597-4811	S	354*	1.5
6	GHX Industrial LLC—*Richard Harrison*	3440 S Sam Houston Pkw, Houston TX 77047	713-222-2231	R	178*	.2
7	Flexitallic Group Inc—*Dwight Beach*	6915 Hwy 225, Deer Park TX 77536	281-604-2400	R	164*	.2
8	A W Chesterton Co—*Richard Hoyle*	PO Box 4004, Woburn MA 01888	781-481-7000	R	88*	1.1
9	Dana Sealing Products	1945 Ohio St, Lisle IL 60532	630-271-0001	S	82*	.4
10	L and L Products Inc—*John Ligon*	PO Box 308, Romeo MI 48065	586-336-1600	R	58*	.8
11	John Crane Inc—*Bob Wasson*	6400 W Oakton St, Morton Grove IL 60053	847-967-2400	S	57*	.6
12	ITW Southland—*W James Farrell*	5700 Ward Ave, Virginia Beach VA 23455	757-543-5701	D	52	.5
13	Amesbury Group Inc—*Jon Petromelis*	57 Hunt Rd, Amesbury MA 01913	978-388-0581	R	52*	.7
14	Precix Inc—*Dave Slutz*	PO Box 6919, New Bedford MA 02742	508-998-4000	R	51*	.3
15	Stemco Inc—*Jon Cox*	PO Box 1989, Longview TX 75606	903-758-9981	S	42*	.3
16	Skf Polyseal Inc—*John Coleman*	1805 W 500 S, Salt Lake City UT 84104	801-973-9171	S	38*	.3
17	HSS Group—*Jeff Crouthamel*	426 W 4th St, San Pedro CA 90731	310-547-1181	R	31*	<.1
18	Forest City Technologies Inc—*John Cloud*	PO Box 86, Wellington OH 44090	440-647-2115	R	31*	.5
19	Tracewell Systems Inc—*Larry Tracewell*	567 Enterprise Dr, Westerville OH 43081	614-846-6175	R	28*	.2
20	Parco Inc—*Adam Burgener*	1801 S Archibald Ave, Ontario CA 91761	909-947-2200	R	27*	.2
21	Unique Fabricating Inc—*Douglas Stahl*	800 Standard Pkwy, Auburn Hills MI 48326	248-853-2333	R	25*	.4
22	Toyo Seal America Corp—*Toru Nishioka*	225 Mooresville Blvd, Mooresville NC 28115	704-660-9062	R	25*	.5
23	Excelsior Inc—*Kurt Johnson*	PO Box 970, Rockford IL 61105	815-987-2900	R	25*	<.1
24	Fast Group Houston Inc—*Leonard Casey*	8103 Rankin Rd, Humble TX 77396	281-446-6662	R	24*	.4
25	Accutrex Products Inc—*Martin Beichner*	112 Southpointe Blvd, Canonsburg PA 15317	724-746-4300	R	23*	.2
26	Corpus Christi Gasket/Fastener Inc—*David Massie*	PO Box 4074, Corpus Christi TX 78469	361-884-6366	R	21*	.1
27	Specification Rubber Products Inc—*S Smith*	PO Box 568, Alabaster AL 35007	205-663-2521	R	20*	.1
28	Foam Seal Inc—*Michael Sylvester*	PO Box 951130, Cleveland OH 44193	216-881-8111	R	20*	.1
29	Basic Rubber And Plastics Co—*David Smith*	8700 Boulder Ct, Walled Lake MI 48390	248-360-7400	R	20*	<.1
30	Eagleburgmann Industries LP—*Marcus Pillion*	10035 Brookriver Dr, Houston TX 77040	713-939-9515	S	20*	.2
31	Sur-Seal Gasket And Packing Co—*James Wilz*	6156 Wesselman Rd, Cincinnati OH 45248	513-574-8500	R	19*	.2
32	Produce Packaging Inc—*Gregory Fritz*	7501 Carnegie Ave, Cleveland OH 44103	216-391-6129	R	18*	.2
33	Hoosier Gasket Corp—*Argyle Jackson*	2400 Enterprise Park P, Indianapolis IN 46218	317-545-2000	R	18*	.2
34	Epg Inc—*Michael Orazen*	1780 Miller Pkwy, Streetsboro OH 44241	330-995-9725	R	18*	.1
35	Derby Cellular Products Inc—*Frank Osak*	PO Box 277, Derby CT 06418	203-735-4661	R	17*	.1
36	Bryant Rubber Corp—*Steven Bryant*	1112 Lomita Blvd, Harbor City CA 90710	310-530-2530	R	17*	.2
37	Cgr Products Inc—*Charles Keeley*	4655 Us Hwy 29 N, Greensboro NC 27405	336-621-4568	R	17*	.1
38	Concrete Sealants Inc—*Howard Wingert*	PO Box 176, New Carlisle OH 45344	937-845-8776	R	16*	.1
39	Xto Inc—*Donald Kreiger*	110 Wrentham Dr, Liverpool NY 13088	315-451-7807	R	16*	.1
40	Modern Silicone Technologies Inc—*Aron Grunfeld*	5777 Myerlake Cir, Clearwater FL 33760	727-507-9800	R	15*	.1
41	Plastomer Corp—*Walter Baughman*	37819 Schoolcraft Rd, Livonia MI 48150	734-464-0700	R	15*	.1
42	Rol Manufacturing Of America Inc—*Julian Haller*	1255 La Quinta Dr Ste, Orlando FL 32809		R	15*	.1
43	Gasket Engineering Company Inc—*Robert Comfort*	PO Box 320288, Kansas City MO 64132	816-363-8333	R	14*	.1
44	PI Components Corp	1951 Hwy 290 W, Brenham TX 77833	979-830-5400	S	13*	.1
45	Cooper Products Inc—*Thomas Gerber*	210 Fair St, Laconia NH 03246	603-524-3367	R	13*	.1
46	Seals-Eastern Inc—*Daniel Hertz*	PO Box 520, Red Bank NJ 07701	732-747-9200	R	13*	.2
47	Seal Science Inc—*Frederick Tuliper*	17131 Daimler St, Irvine CA 92614	949-253-3130	R	12*	.1
48	West Coast Gasket Co—*Louis Russell*	300 Ranger Ave, Brea CA 92821	714-869-0123	R	12*	.1
49	Vanguard Products Corp—*Robert Benn*	87 Newtown Rd, Danbury CT 06810	203-744-7265	R	12*	.1
50	Flexial Corp—*Richard Larsen*	PO Box 3105, Cookeville TN 38502	931-432-1853	R	12*	.1
51	Press Seal Gasket Corp—*James Skinner*	PO Box 10482, Fort Wayne IN 46852	260-436-0521	R	12*	.1
52	Action Fabricators Inc—*Jon Rudolph*	3760 E Paris Ave Se, Grand Rapids MI 49512	616-957-2032	R	10*	.1
53	Ohio Gasket And Shim Company Inc—*John Bader*	976 Evans Ave, Akron OH 44305	330-630-2030	R	10*	.1
54	Garlock Helicoflex Garlock Sealing Technologies	2770 The Blvd, Columbia SC 29209	803-783-1880	S	10*	.1
55	Cincinnati Gasket Packing and Manufacturing Inc—*Lawrence Uhlenbrock*	40 Illinois Ave, Cincinnati OH 45215	513-761-3458	R	10*	.1
56	Cri-Tech Inc—*Satoshi Doi*	85 Winter St, Hanover MA 02339	781-826-5600	R	10*	<.1
57	Precision Gasket Co—*Stephen Hanson*	5732 Lincoln Dr, Edina MN 55436	952-942-6711	R	9*	.1
58	Higbee Inc—*Lawrence Higbee*	PO Box 4882, Syracuse NY 13221	315-432-8021	R	9*	.1
59	Syna-Flex Rubber Products Company Inc—*Vernon Gibson*	1223 Cochran Ave, Talladega AL 35160	256-362-2431	R	8*	.1
60	Lti Flexible Products Inc—*Doug Bennet*	PO Box 13365, Spokane Valley WA 99213	509-922-4522	R	8*	.1
61	Pres-On Tape and Gasket Corp—*Henry Gianatasio*	21 W Factory Rd, Addison IL 60101	630-628-2255	R	8*	.1
62	International Star Corp—*E Schmidt*	52111 Sierra Dr, Chesterfield MI 48047	586-949-2200	R	8*	.1
63	Jade Engineered Plastic Inc—*Steve Holland*	121 Broadcommon Rd, Bristol RI 02809	401-253-4440	R	8*	<.1
64	Serra Manufacturing Corp—*Dominick Pellegrino*	PO Box 5684, Compton CA 90224	310-537-4560	R	8*	.1
65	Frank Lowe Rubber and Gasket Company Inc—*Ira Warren*	44 Ramsey Rd, Shirley NY 11967	631-777-2707	R	8*	<.1
66	Gsi Engine Management Group Inc—*Bob Killion*	7208 Weil Ave Stop 1, Saint Louis MO 63119	314-646-5300	R	7*	.1
67	Everseal Gasket Inc—*Ken Lane*	8309 Cole Pkwy, Shawnee Mission KS 66227	913-441-9232	R	7*	.1
68	Clark Seals LLC—*Jayson Zahn*	3824 S 79th E Ave, Tulsa OK 74145	918-664-0587	R	7*	.1
69	American Gasket Technologies Inc—*Nick Kalouris*	10 W Laura Dr, Addison IL 60101	630-543-1510	R	7*	<.1
70	Chambers Gasket and Manufacturing Co—*Margaret Holmberg*	4701 W Rice St, Chicago IL 60651	773-626-8800	R	6*	<.1
71	Seals Unlimited Inc—*Thad Fair*	23050 Nw Jacobson Rd, Hillsboro OR 97124	503-690-6644	R	6*	<.1
72	Tce/Turbo Components and Engineering Inc—*John Whalen*	8730 Meldrum Ln, Houston TX 77075	713-943-9100	R	6*	<.1
73	Newman Sanitary Gasket Company Inc—*David Newman*	PO Box 222, Lebanon OH 45036	513-932-7379	R	6*	<.1
74	Industrial Gasket And Supply Co—*William Hynes*	PO Box 4138, Torrance CA 90510	310-530-1771	R	6*	<.1
75	Gasket Resources Inc—*Gary Chappell*	PO Box 565, Exton PA 19341	610-363-5800	R	6*	.1
76	Mcpherson Manufacturing Corp—*James Mcpherson*	PO Box 1777, Hazlehurst GA 31539	912-375-5494	R	6*	<.1
77	Vellumoid Inc—*Peter Parseghian*	54 Rockdale St, Worcester MA 01606	508-853-2500	R	6*	<.1
78	Belcourt Corp—*Don Belcourt*	3100 W Park Dr, Burnsville MN 55306	952-894-0406	R	6*	<.1
79	Gasko Fabricated Products Co—*Gregory Nemecek*	4049 Ridge Rd, Medina OH 44256	330-239-1781	R	6*	<.1
80	Champion Hi-Tech Manufacturing Inc—*F Burton*	PO Box 262427, Houston TX 77207	713-644-2181	R	6*	<.1
81	James Walker Manufacturing Co—*Peter Needham*	PO Box 467, Glenwood IL 60425	708-754-4020	S	5*	<.1
82	Web Seal Inc—*John Hurley*	15 Oregon St, Rochester NY 14605	585-546-1320	R	5*	<.1
83	Midwest Sealing Products Inc—*Andrew Huggins*	1001 Commerce Ct, Buffalo Grove IL 60089	847-459-2202	R	5*	<.1
84	Southern Rubber Company Inc—*H Bowman*	2209 Patterson St, Greensboro NC 27407	336-299-2456	R	5*	<.1
85	Presscut Industries Inc—*James Swanson*	1730 Briercroft Ct, Carrollton TX 75006	972-389-0615	R	5*	<.1
86	Triad Precision Products Inc—*Jack Adkisson*	PO Box 3265, Tulsa OK 74101	918-584-3543	R	5*	<.1
87	Woodex Bearing Company Inc—*Glenn Irish*	216 Bay Point Rd, Georgetown ME 04548	207-371-2210	R	5*	<.1
88	G Gasket and Supply Inc—*Douglas Ginter*	PO Box 886, Waukesha WI 53187	262-549-8300	R	4*	<.1
89	Miles Rubber and Packing Co—*Larry Lempke*	9020 Dutton Dr, Twinsburg OH 44087	330-425-3888	R	4*	<.1

Note: An asterisk (*) indicates an estimated financial figure. The company type code used is as follows: R = Private, P = Public, S = Private Subsidiary, B = Public Subsidiary, D = Division, J = Joint Venture, I = Investment Fund.

COMPANY RANKINGS BY SALES WITHIN 4-DIGIT SIC

Rank	Company Name—*Executive Officer*	Address, City, State, Zip	Phone	Type	Fin	Empls
90	GFC Inc—*Bernadette Chrysler*	Quintin Rd, Olyphant PA 18447	570-587-4588	R	4*	<.1
91	DV Die Cutting Inc—*Richard Varney*	45 Prince St, Danvers MA 01923	978-777-0300	R	4*	<.1
92	Mercer Gasket And Shim—*Peter Taraborelli*	110 Benigno Blvd, Bellmawr NJ 08031	856-931-5000	R	4*	<.1
93	Texacone Co—*John Wheeler*	4111 Forney Rd, Mesquite TX 75149	972-288-4404	R	4*	<.1
94	Ciasons Industrial Inc—*Paul Hsieh*	1615 Boyd St, Santa Ana CA 92705	714-259-0838	R	4*	<.1
95	Spira Manufacturing Corp—*George Kunkel*	12721 Saticoy St S, North Hollywood CA 91605	818-764-8222	R	4*	<.1
96	Tfe Company Inc—*C Harvey*	PO Box 661, Brenham TX 77834	979-836-6111	R	4*	<.1
97	Akron Gasket and Packaging Enterprises Inc—*Carter Ray*	445 NE Ave, Tallmadge OH 44278	330-633-3742	R	4*	<.1
98	Advanced Sealing International LLC—*Jaynie Brown*	16384 Strain Rd, Baton Rouge LA 70816	225-272-2155	R	4*	<.1
99	REAL Seal Company Inc—*Patrick Tobin*	1971 Don Lee Pl, Escondido CA 92029	760-743-7263	R	4*	<.1
100	Blue Ridge Fabricators Inc—*Thomas Cox*	650 Industrial Dr, Elizabethton TN 37643	423-543-6151	R	4*	<.1
101	Chavers Gasket Corp—*Lloyd Chavers*	23325 Del Lago Dr, Laguna Hills CA 92653	949-472-8118	R	4*	<.1
102	Supreme Felt and Abrasives Inc—*David Mcneilly*	4425 James Pl, Melrose Park IL 60160	708-344-0134	R	4*	<.1
103	Grand Haven Gasket Co—*Kent Suchecki*	PO Box 671, Grand Haven MI 49417	616-842-7682	R	4*	<.1
104	Die Cut Technologies Inc—*Scott Flores*	10943 Leroy Dr, Northglenn CO 80233	303-452-4600	R	4*	<.1
105	T and M Rubber Inc—*Donald Acker*	PO Box 516, Goshen IN 46527	574-533-3173	R	3*	<.1
106	Phelps Industrial Products Inc—*Charles Phelps*	6300 Washington Blvd, Elkridge MD 21075	410-796-2222	R	3*	<.1
107	B G Peck Company Inc—*Stephen Greer*	50 Shepard St, Lawrence MA 01843	978-686-4181	R	3*	<.1
108	American Braiding and Manufacturing—*Gerald Bailey*	247 Old Tavern Rd, Howell NJ 07731	732-938-6333	R	3*	<.1
109	Conroe Plastics Molding Inc—*Brian Whirter*	1800 Orval Rd, Conroe TX 77301	936-539-2005	R	3*	<.1
110	Mariposa Corp—*Conover Able*	10893 Shadow Wood Dr, Houston TX 77043	713-222-0220	R	3*	<.1
111	Miami Valley Gasket Company Inc—*Robin Cunningham*	1222 E 3rd St, Dayton OH 45402	937-228-0781	R	3*	<.1
112	Slade Inc—*Ward Crosier*	181 Crawford Rd, Statesville NC 28625	704-873-1366	R	3*	<.1
113	Houston Manufacturing Specialty Company Inc—*Meg Mallay*	PO Box 24339, Houston TX 77229	713-675-7400	R	3*	<.1
114	Marsh C W Co—*Dave Utzinger*	PO Box 598, Muskegon MI 49443	231-722-3781	R	3*	<.1
115	Gasket and Seal Fabricators Inc—*Gerald Johnson*	1640 Sauget Industrial, East Saint Louis IL 62206	618-332-0425	R	3*	<.1
116	R and J Manufacturing Co—*Anabella Richardi*	3200 Martin Rd, Commerce Township MI 48390	248-669-2460	R	3*	<.1
117	Columbus Rubber and Gasket Co—*Billy Kerstetter*	PO Box 2206, Columbus MS 39704	662-328-9350	R	3*	<.1
118	Fluid Handling Components Inc—*Kris Holiman*	11225 Interstate 30, Little Rock AR 72209	501-455-4155	R	3*	<.1
119	Fibreflex Packing and Manufacturing Co—*Joseph Hofmann*	PO Box 4646, Philadelphia PA 19127	215-482-1490	R	3*	<.1
120	Metro Industries Inc—*Diana Simon*	4018 E 137th Ter, Grandview MO 64030	816-763-7277	R	3*	<.1
121	G F Cole Corp—*George Cole*	21735 S Western Ave, Torrance CA 90501	310-320-0601	R	3*	<.1
122	Darco Southern Inc—*David Durnovich*	PO Box 454, Independence VA 24348	276-773-2711	R	3*	<.1
123	Sealtec—*Charles Herrera*	120 Kendall Point Dr, Oswego IL 60543	630-692-0633	R	3*	<.1
124	Essential Sealing Products Inc—*Susan Pyle*	PO Box 23699, Chagrin Falls OH 44023	440-543-8108	R	3*	<.1
125	T and N Manufacturing Company Inc—*Nancy Whipple*	4345 Shiloh Church Rd, Davidson NC 28036	704-788-1418	R	2*	<.1
126	Zone Reed Industries Inc—*Scott Zone*	1615 N 25th St, Saint Louis MO 63106	314-436-5000	R	2*	<.1
127	Roettele Industries—*Mark Roettele*	15485 Dupont Ave, Chino CA 91710	909-606-8252	R	2*	<.1
128	Treaty City Industries Inc—*Mike Jones*	PO Box 39, Greenville OH 45331	937-548-9000	R	2*	<.1
129	Fairlane Industries Inc—*Raymond Ragland*	3868 Washington Blvd, Saint Louis MO 63108	314-531-9337	R	2*	<.1
130	Astroseal Products Manufacturing Corp—*Ronald Grass*	PO Box 617, Old Saybrook CT 06475	860-399-7916	R	2*	<.1
131	Hydrodyne-FPI Inc—*Jim Boyd*	3125 Damon Way, Burbank CA 91505	818-841-9667	R	2*	<.1
132	Reliable Products Inc—*Cherrian Easley*	PO Box 277, Lobelville TN 37097	931-593-2297	R	2*	<.1
133	Mechanical Rubber Products Co—*Cedric Glasper*	PO Box 593, Warwick NY 10990	845-986-2271	R	2*	<.1
134	Midwest Gasket Corp—*Robert Tobian*	PO Box 125, Milroy IN 46156	765-629-2221	R	2*	<.1
135	Champion Gasket and Rubber Inc—*Robin Dubuc*	3225 Haggerty Hwy, Commerce Township MI 48390	248-624-6140	R	2*	<.1
136	Comdaco Inc—*Donald Comley*	2000 N Jesse James Rd, Excelsior Springs MO 64024	816-637-6653	R	2*	<.1
137	Pacific States Felt and Manufacturing Company Inc—*Walter Perscheid*	PO Box 5024, Hayward CA 94540	510-783-0277	R	2*	<.1
138	Tides Marine Inc—*Jeff Strong*	3251A SW 13th Dr, Deerfield Beach FL 33442	954-420-0949	R	2*	<.1
139	Breiner Company Inc—*William Lucas*	259 Production Dr, Avon IN 46123	317-272-2521	R	2*	<.1
140	Flextron Industries Inc—*William Swan*	720 Mount Rd, Aston PA 19014	610-459-4600	R	2*	<.1
141	Rep Associates Inc—*Norman Ferber*	PO Box 161, Marlboro NJ 07746	732-591-1140	R	2*	<.1
142	Gaskets Inc—*Karen Mattacotti*	PO Box 398, Rio WI 53960	920-992-3137	R	2*	<.1
143	Quality Industrial Products Inc—*Larry Gilderoy*	21835 N 23rd Ave, Phoenix AZ 85027	602-861-2930	R	2*	<.1
144	Manufactured Rubber Products Co—*Edmond Furia*	4501 Tacony St, Philadelphia PA 19124	215-533-3600	R	2*	<.1
145	Poly-Tec Products Inc—*James Westhoff*	PO Box 1643, Tullytown PA 19007	215-547-3366	R	2*	<.1
146	SP M Inc—*Ronald Van Pelt*	PO Box 140, Spencer IA 51301	712-262-9313	R	1*	<.1
147	Material Fabricators Inc—*Neil Zuehlke*	PO Box 1818, Buellton CA 93427	805-686-5244	R	1*	<.1
148	Gindor Inc—*Ginny Nichols*	66101 Us Hwy 33, Goshen IN 46526	574-642-4004	R	1*	<.1

TOTALS: SIC 3053 Gaskets, Packing & Sealing Devices
Companies: 148

					8,704	28.4

3061 Mechanical Rubber Goods

Rank	Company Name—*Executive Officer*	Address, City, State, Zip	Phone	Type	Fin	Empls
1	Cooper-Standard Holdings Inc—*James S McElya*	39550 Orchard Hill Pl, Novi MI 48375	248-596-5900	P	1,405	19.0
2	Rex-Hide Inc—*Brad Hoeffner*	PO Box 4726, Tyler TX 75712	903-593-7387	R	663*	.3
3	Hutchinson Corp—*Jacques Maigne*	PO Box 1886, Grand Rapids MI 49501	616-459-4541	S	171*	.5
4	Lexington Rubber Group Inc	3565 Highland Park NW, North Canton OH 44720	330-305-1040	S	145*	.3
5	Hp Pelzer Automotive Systems Inc—*Wayne Robinson*	1175 Crooks Rd, Troy MI 48084	248-280-2500	R	115*	.6
6	Trelleborg YSH Inc—*Peter Nilsson*	400 Aylworth Ave, South Haven MI 49090	269-637-2116	S	94*	.8
7	Kirkhill-TA Co—*Brad Lawrence*	PO Box 1270, Brea CA 92822	714-529-4901	S	73*	.7
8	Trelleborg Automotive Molding Div—*Peter Nilsson* Trelleborg YSH Inc	102 Industrial Ave, Carmi IL 62821	618-382-2318	D	70*	.1
9	Creative Foam Corp—*Wayne Blessing*	300 N Alloy Dr, Fenton MI 48430	810-629-4149	R	67*	.6
10	Ettore Products Co—*Michael Smahlik*	2100 N Loop Rd, Alameda CA 94502		R	67*	.1
11	Mitchell Rubber Products Inc—*Mark Mitchell*	10220 San Sevaine Way, Mira Loma CA 91752	951-681-5655	R	50*	.4
12	Tepro Inc—*Takashi Tanabe*	590 Baxter Ln, Winchester TN 37398	931-967-5189	R	50*	.4
13	Pawling Corp—*Craig Busby*	157 Charles Colman Blv, Pawling NY 12564	845-855-1000	R	37*	.2
14	Rubbercraft Corporation Of California Ltd—*Eric Sanders*	3701 E Conant St, Long Beach CA 90808	562-354-2800	R	28*	.3
15	Griffith Rubber Mills—*Jennifer Chacon*	PO Box 10066, Portland OR 97296	503-226-6971	R	21*	.3
16	Microporous Products LP—*Gary Leonard*	596 Industrial Park Rd, Piney Flats TN 37686	423-538-7111	R	19*	.1
17	Clark Rubber Company Inc—*Gregory Clark*	PO Box 299, Mentor OH 44061	440-255-9793	R	17*	.1
18	Metso Paper USA Inc—*Jorma Eloranta*	987 Griffin Pond Rd, Clarks Summit PA 18411	570-587-5111	S	16	.2
19	Westland Technologies Inc—*Tom Halyburton*	107 S Riverside Dr, Modesto CA 95354	209-571-6400	R	16*	.1
20	DS Brown Company Inc—*Kirk Feuerbach*	PO Box 158, North Baltimore OH 45872	419-257-3561	S	11*	.2
21	Delta Rubber Co—*Roderick Baty*	PO Box 300, Danielson CT 06239	860-779-0300	S	11*	.1
22	Delford Industries Inc—*Robert Reach*	PO Box 863, Middletown NY 10940	845-342-3901	R	11*	.1
23	Elbex Corp—*Edward Bittle*	300 Martinel Dr, Kent OH 44240	330-673-3233	R	10*	.1
24	American Molded Products LLC—*Cindy Blackenburg*	51734 Filomena Dr, Utica MI 48315	586-247-5650	R	9*	<.1
25	Biltrite Corp—*Stanley Bernstein*	PO Box 9045, Waltham MA 02454	781-647-1700	R	8*	.1

Rank	Company Name—*Executive Officer*	Address, City, State, Zip	Phone	Type	Fin	Empls
26	Colonial Rubber Co—*Dale Fosnight*	PO Box 111, Ravenna OH 44266	330-296-2831	R	8*	.1
27	Omni Seals Inc—*Gary Lauritsen*	11031 Jersey Blvd Ste, Rancho Cucamonga CA 91730	909-946-0181	R	8*	.1
28	Pelmor Laboratories Inc—*E Ross*	401 Lafayette St, Newtown PA 18940	215-968-3334	R	8*	.1
29	Fmi Inc—*Scott Severson*	2382 United Ln, Elk Grove Village IL 60007	847-350-1535	S	7*	.1
30	Axil Corp—*Marc Sanders*	PO Box 98, South Plainfield NJ 07080	908-754-8100	R	7*	.1
31	Minor Rubber Company Inc—*David Humphreys*	49 Ackerman St, Bloomfield NJ 07003	973-338-6800	R	7*	.1
32	Ro-Lab American Rubber Company Inc—*Henry Wright*	PO Box 450, Tracy CA 95378	209-836-0965	R	7*	.1
33	Monmouth Rubber Corp—*John Bonforte*	75 Long Branch Ave, Long Branch NJ 07740	732-229-3444	R	6*	<.1
34	Envirotech Extrusion Inc—*Jerry Martin*	4810 Woodside Dr, Richmond IN 47374	765-966-8068	R	6*	.1
35	Tbmc Inc—*Philip Cohenca*	101 Pelham Davis Cir, Greenville SC 29615	864-288-9916	R	6*	.1
36	Kdl Precision Molding Corp—*David Wyckoff*	11381 Bradley Ave, Pacoima CA 91331	818-896-9899	R	6*	<.1
37	Denaka Partners LP—*Richard Balka*	PO Box 878, Trenton NJ 08605	609-394-1176	R	5*	<.1
38	EMT Industries Inc—*Thomas Taylor*	PO Box 443, Goshen IN 46527	574-533-1273	R	5*	.1
39	Dybrook Products Inc—*Diane Bumstead*	5232 Tod Ave Sw Ste 23, Warren OH 44481	330-392-7665	R	5*	<.1
40	Passaic Rubber Co—*John Mathey*	PO Box 505, Wayne NJ 07474	973-696-9500	R	5*	<.1
41	Associated Rubber Inc—*John Oldt*	PO Box 520, Quakertown PA 18951	215-536-2800	R	4*	<.1
42	Kismet Rubber Products Corp—*David Humphreys*	215 Industrial Blvd, Blue Ridge GA 30513	706-632-2261	R	4*	.1
43	Astro Molding Inc—*Werner Schon*	PO Box 429, Frenchtown NJ 08825	973-300-1508	R	4*	<.1
44	Southeastern Rubber Company Inc—*George Oxenreider*	PO Box 1, Felton GA 30140	770-646-3828	R	4*	<.1
45	Magna-Tex Inc—*Joyce Palmer*	2520 Ridgemar Ct, Louisville KY 40299	502-493-0558	R	4*	<.1
46	Columbia Rubber Mills Inc—*Leonard Sandness*	PO Box 220, Clackamas OR 97015	503-557-9919	R	4*	<.1
47	RD Rubber Technology Corp—*Walter Hopkins*	12870 Florence Ave, Santa Fe Springs CA 90670	562-941-4800	R	4*	<.1
48	M P Industries Inc—*Monroe Mirsky*	PO Box 130579, Tyler TX 75713	903-561-4232	R	4*	<.1
49	Ames Rubber Manufacturing Company Inc—*Tim Brown*	4516 Brazil St, Los Angeles CA 90039	818-240-9313	R	4*	<.1
50	Artemis Rubber Technology Inc—*Claudus Jaeger*	4175 Mulligan St, Longmont CO 80504	970-535-0554	R	4*	<.1
51	Winfield Rubber Manufacturing Company Inc—*Frank Hollingsworth*	PO Box 1768, Winfield AL 35594	205-487-3053	R	4*	<.1
52	Glazing Rubber Products Of Ga Inc—*Steve Sanvi*	71 Easy St, Dawsonville GA 30534	706-344-1462	R	4*	<.1
53	Polycraft Products Inc—*Thomas Landers*	5511 State Rte 128, Cleves OH 45002	513-353-3334	R	3*	<.1
54	Alloy Extrusion Co—*James Anthony*	4211 Karg Industrial P, Kent OH 44240	330-677-4946	R	3*	<.1
55	Jackson Flexible Products Inc—*Ronald K Jakubas*	7765 Clinton Rd, Jackson MI 49201	517-787-8877	R	3*	<.1
56	United Seal and Rubber Company Inc—*Virgil Alonso*	7025 Amwiler Industria, Atlanta GA 30360	770-729-8880	R	3*	<.1
57	Milligan Workshops Inc—*Sandra Milligan*	420 Industrial Pkwy, Bowling Green OH 43402	419-353-0099	R	3*	<.1
58	Bradco Rubber and Plastics Products Inc—*Brad Farrar*	11102 Kilrenny Ct, Louisville KY 40243	502-245-4081	R	2*	<.1
59	Esperanza Palms LLC—*J Vermudez*	31811 Industrial Park, Pinehurst TX 77362	281-252-8013	R	2*	<.1
60	R and R Rubber Molding Inc—*Richard Norman*	PO Box 3533, South El Monte CA 91733	626-575-8105	R	2*	<.1
61	Mark Industries Inc—*Billy Moore*	PO Box 261, Franklin LA 70538	337-828-4479	R	2*	<.1
62	Southern Plastics and Rubber Co—*Frank Noce*	565 Parque Dr. Ormond Beach FL 32174	386-672-1167	R	2*	<.1
63	Macdivitt Rubber Company LLC—*Jackie Bernot*	PO Box 129, Perry OH 44081	440-259-5937	R	2*	<.1
64	Kleen Polymers Inc—*John Marefka*	145 Rainbow St, Wadsworth OH 44281	330-336-4212	R	2*	<.1
65	Elk Grove Rubber and Plastic Company Inc—*Brian Lovitsch*	99 W Commercial Ave, Addison IL 60101	630-543-5656	R	1*	<.1
66	United Feed Screws Ltd—*Paul Norton*	PO Box 9433, Akron OH 44305	330-798-5532	R	1*	<.1
67	Fiberod	204 N Falcon, Oklahoma City OK 73127	405 780 1306	S	1*	<.1
68	Promed Molded Products Inc—*Wayne Kelly*	15600 Medina Rd, Plymouth MN 55447	763-559-3500	R	<1*	.2

TOTALS: SIC 3061 Mechanical Rubber Goods

Companies: 68					3,357	27.2

3069 Fabricated Rubber Products Nec

Rank	Company Name—*Executive Officer*	Address, City, State, Zip	Phone	Type	Fin	Empls
1	Virginia Harbor Services Inc—*Michael Harper*	PO Box 98, Clear Brook VA 22624	540-667-5191	R	6,331*	.1
2	Carlisle Companies Inc—*David A Roberts*	13925 Ballantyne Corpo, Charlotte NC 28277	704-501-1100	P	3,225	11.0
3	Omnova Solutions Inc—*Kevin M McMullen*	175 Ghent Rd, Fairlawn OH 44333	330-869-4200	P	1,201	2.3
4	West Pharmaceutical Services Inc—*Donald E Morel Jr*	101 Gordon Dr, Exton PA 19341	610-594-2900	P	1,192	6.3
5	Gleason Corporation and Precision Products—*Morton Kay*	10474 Santa Monica Blv, Los Angeles CA 90025	310-470-6001	R	716*	1.3
6	Firestone Building Products Co—*Tim Dunn*	250 W 96th St, Indianapolis IN 46260	317-575-7000	S	590*	1.3
7	Rubbermaid Home Products Div—*David R Lumley*	3320 W Market St, Fairlawn OH 44333	330-869-7100	D	479*	6.0
8	Rotation Dynamics Corp—*Thomas G Gilson*	8140 Cass Ave, Darien IL 60561	630-769-9700	R	338*	.6
9	Longwood Industries LLC—*Dana Waterman*	706 Green Valley Rd St, Greensboro NC 27408	336-272-3710	S	262*	.8
10	Oliver Rubber Co—*Larry Enders*	408 Telephone Ave, Asheboro NC 27205	864-458-6848	S	242*	.5
11	Frc Holding Corp—*John Finzer*	129 Rawls Rd, Des Plaines IL 60018	847-390-6200	R	238*	.1
12	Pacific Dunlop Investments (USA) Inc—*Doug Tough*	200 Schult Dr, Red Bank NJ 07701	732-345-5400	R	144*	3.0
13	Mission Rubber Company—*Walter Garrett* Mcp Industries Inc	PO Box 2349, Corona CA 92878		D	127*	.2
14	Duramax Inc—*Brad Stone*	PO Box 67, Middlefield OH 44062	440-632-1811	R	103*	.8
15	Mitchell Rubber Products Inc—*Ted Ballou*	491 Wilson Way, City Of Industry CA 91744	626-961-9711	R	88*	.2
16	RB Recycling Inc R-B Rubber Products Inc	8501 N Borthwick, Portland OR 97217	503-283-2261	S	85*	.2
17	Lexington Precision Corp—*Warren Delano*	3565 Highland Park St, North Canton OH 44720	330-305-1040	P	73	.5
18	Patch Rubber Co—*William Hodge*	100 Patch Rubber Rd, Weldon NC 27890	252-536-2574	S	72*	.2
19	T/CCI Manufacturing LLC—*Richard Demirjian*	2120 N 22nd St, Decatur IL 62526	217-422-0055	R	72*	.1
20	Plymouth Rubber Company Inc—*Sergio Pineiro*	275 Turnpike St Ste 31, Canton MA 02021	781-828-0220	R	66	.4
21	RCA Rubber Co—*Richard Reiss III*	PO Box 9240, Akron OH 44305	330-784-1291	R	65*	.2
22	Kraco Enterprises LLC—*John Goto*	505 E Euclid Ave, Compton CA 90222	310-639-0666	R	62*	.1
23	Industrial Rubber Products Inc—*Daniel O Burkes*	3516 E 13th Ave, Hibbing MN 55746	218-262-5211	R	58*	.1
24	Swarco America Inc—*Jon Sproul*	PO Box 89, Columbia TN 38402	931-388-5900	R	55*	.2
25	Paulstra Crc Corp—*Cedric Duclos*	PO Box 1886, Grand Rapids MI 49501	616-459-4541	R	51*	.7
26	CTI Industries Corp—*Howard W Schwan*	22160 N Pepper Rd, Lake Barrington IL 60010	847-382-1000	P	48	.4
27	O'neill Wetsuits LLC—*Pat O'neill*	PO Box 6300, Santa Cruz CA 95063	831-475-7500	R	47*	.2
28	American Roller Company LLC—*Chuck Tasch*	1440 13th Ave, Union Grove WI 53182	262-878-8665	R	44*	<.1
29	Boss Balloon Co—*Louis G Graziadio III*	221 W 1st St, Kewanee IL 61443	309-852-2131	S	43*	.1
30	Buckhorn Rubber Products Inc—*John Orr*	5151 Industrial Dr, Hannibal MO 63401	573-221-8933	R	42*	.3
31	Chicago Manifold Products Company Inc—*Richard Masters*	171 E Marquardt Dr, Wheeling IL 60090	847-459-6000	R	41*	.6
32	Fidelity Industries Inc—*Dvosia Rivkin*	559 State Rte 23, Wayne NJ 07470	973-696-9120	R	39*	.1
33	El Microcircuits—*Robert Else*	1651 Pohl Rd, Mankato MN 56001	507-345-5786	R	38*	.2
34	Duraco Inc—*Brett York*	7400 Industrial Dr, Forest Park IL 60130	708-488-1025	R	38*	.1
35	Watersaver Company Inc—*W Slifer*	PO Box 16465, Denver CO 80216	303-289-1818	R	37*	<.1
36	Quabaug Corp—*Kevin Donahue*	18 School St, North Brookfield MA 01535	508-867-7731	R	35*	.2
37	Pioneer National Latex Inc—*Lisa Bennett*	246 E 4th St, Ashland OH 44805	419-289-3300	R	34*	.6
38	Darnell-Rose—*Brent Bargar*	17915 Railroad St, City of Industry CA 91748	626-912-1688	R	34*	.1
39	Ames Rubber Corp—*Charles Roberts*	PO Box 15240, Newark NJ 07192	973-827-9101	R	33*	.2

Note: An asterisk (*) indicates an estimated financial figure. The company type code used is as follows: R = Private, P = Public, S = Private Subsidiary, B = Public Subsidiary, D = Division, J = Joint Venture, I = Investment Fund.

COMPANY RANKINGS BY SALES WITHIN 4-DIGIT SIC

Rank	Company Name—*Executive Officer*	Address, City, State, Zip	Phone	Type	Fin	Empls
40	Amtico International Inc—*Tyrone Johnson*	66 Perimeter Ctr E Ste, Atlanta GA 30346	404-267-1900	R	31*	.2
41	Allid-Baltic Rubber Inc dba Zhongding—*Allen R Myers*	PO Box 168, Strasburg OH 44680	330-878-7800	R	30*	.2
42	Polymer Enterprises Inc—*Donald Mateer*	4731 State Rte 30 Ste, Greensburg PA 15601	724-838-2340	R	29*	.7
43	Advanced Scientifics Inc—*Carl Martin*	163 Research Ln, Millersburg PA 17061	717-692-2104	R	29*	.2
44	Koneta/LRV—*John Kepler*	PO Box 150, Wapakoneta OH 45895	419-739-4200	S	28*	.2
45	Parker Hannifin Techseal Div	3025 W Croft Cir, Spartanburg SC 29302	864-573-7332	D	28*	.2
46	Vantage Industries LLC—*David S Haffner*	PO Box 43944, Atlanta GA 30336	404-691-9500	R	28*	.2
47	Clock Spring Co—*Shawn Laughlin*	621 Lockhaven Dr, Houston TX 77073	281-590-8491	R	28*	.1
48	Textileather Corp—*Robert Cristinzio*	3729 Twining St, Toledo OH 43608	419-729-3731	R	27*	.4
49	Rubber Enterprises Inc—*Mark Selleke*	2083 Reek Rd, Imlay City MI 48444	810-724-2400	R	27*	.2
50	Griswold Rubber Corp—*Mark O'Friel*	PO Box 638, Moosup CT 06354	860-564-3321	R	26*	.1
51	Lavelle Industries Inc—*Rhonda Sullivan*	665 McHenry St, Burlington WI 53105	262-763-2434	R	25*	.2
52	Hanna Rubber Co—*Connie Wodlinger*	1511 Baltimore Ave, Kansas City MO 64108	816-221-9600	R	25*	<.1
53	Pandel Inc	21 River Dr, Cartersville GA 30120	770-382-1034	S	25*	<.1
54	Universal Polymer and Rubber Ltd—*Joe Colebank*	PO Box 767, Middlefield OH 44062	440-632-1691	R	25*	.2
55	Mcp Industries Inc—*Walter Garrett*	PO Box 1839, Corona CA 92878	951-736-1881	R	24*	.4
56	Hygenic Corp—*Marshall Dahneke*	PO Box 1818, Akron OH 44309	330-633-8460	R	24*	.3
57	Martech Medical Products Inc—*David Markel*	1500 Delp Dr, Harleysville PA 19438	215-256-8833	R	23*	.2
58	Quality Products Inc—*Richard Drexler*	1250 Refugee Ln, Columbus OH 43207	614-228-0185	P	22	.1
59	Da-Pro Rubber Inc—*C Daubenberger*	PO Box 470175, Tulsa OK 74147	918-258-9386	R	21*	.3
60	Vulcan Corp—*Ed Ritter* Vulcan International Corp	1151 College St, Clarksville TN 37040	931-645-6431	S	21*	<.1
61	Ludlow Composites Corp—*Robert Moran*	2100 Commerce Dr, Fremont OH 43420	419-332-5531	R	21*	.2
62	Ier Fujikura Inc—*John Elsley*	8271 Bavaria Rd, Macedonia OH 44056	330-425-7121	R	21*	.2
63	Alliance Rubber Company Inc—*Bonnie Swayze*	PO Box 20950, Hot Springs AR 71903	501-262-2700	R	20*	.2
64	Mapa Professionel	100 Spontex Dr, Columbia TN 38401		R	20	.2
65	Custom Engineering Co—*David Tullio*	PO Box 10008, Erie PA 16514	814-898-2800	R	20*	.2
66	Rawcar Group LLC—*Sean Darling*	14241 N Fenton Rd, Fenton MI 48430	810-750-5300	R	20*	.2
67	Chestnut Ridge Foam Inc—*Larry Garrity*	PO Box 781, Latrobe PA 15650	724-537-9000	R	20*	.2
68	Gold Key Processing Inc—*Bob Toth*	14910 Madison Rd, Middlefield OH 44062	440-632-0901	R	20*	.2
69	SlipNot Metal Safety Flooring—*Marie Molnar*	2545 Beaufait St, Detroit MI 48207	313-923-0400	R	19*	<.1
70	Interstate Foam and Supply Inc—*Mark Webb*	PO Box 338, Conover NC 28613	828-459-9700	R	19*	.2
71	Female Health Co—*OB Parrish*	515 N State St Ste 222, Chicago IL 60610	312-595-9123	P	19	.1
72	Daicel Safety Systems America LLC—*Jan Perkins*	720 Old Liberty Church, Beaver Dam KY 42320	270-274-2600	R	18*	.3
73	Durable Products Inc—*Michael Dalton*	PO Box 826, Crossville TN 38557	931-484-3502	R	18*	.2
74	Flexan Corp—*Scott Severson*	6626 W Dakin St, Chicago IL 60634	773-685-6446	R	17*	.1
75	Finzer Roller Inc—*Thomas Ryan*	129 Rawls Rd, Des Plaines IL 60018	847-390-6200	R	17*	<.1
76	Acme-Machell Company Inc—*Robert Flatt*	2000 Airport Rd, Waukesha WI 53188	262-521-2870	R	16*	.1
77	Avalon Laboratories LLC—*Claudia Lepe*	2610 Homestead Pl, Rancho Dominguez CA 90220	310-761-8660	R	16*	.1
78	Mosites Rubber Company Inc—*Ray Garvey*	PO Box 2115, Fort Worth TX 76113	817-335-3451	R	16*	<.1
79	Good-West Rubber Corp—*Larry Sears*	8833 Industrial Ln, Rancho Cucamonga CA 91730	909-987-1774	R	16*	.1
80	Apple Rubber Products Inc—*Steven Apple*	310 Erie St, Lancaster NY 14086	716-684-6560	R	16*	.1
81	R E Darling Company Inc—*Gary Darling*	3749 N Romero Rd, Tucson AZ 85705	520-887-2400	R	16*	.1
82	American Phoenix Inc—*Clement Nelson*	800 Wisconsin St Unit, Eau Claire WI 54703	715-831-0966	R	16*	.2
83	Tennessee Mat Company Inc—*Elliot Greenberg*	199 Threet Industrial, Smyrna TN 37167	615-254-8381	R	15*	.1
84	Seal Master Corp—*Edward L Bittle*	368 Martinel Dr, Kent OH 44240	330-673-8410	R	15*	<.1
85	Vip Rubber Company Inc—*Howard Vipperman*	540 S Cypress St, La Habra CA 90631	562-905-3456	R	15*	.1
86	Karman Rubber Co—*David Mann*	2331 Copley Rd, Akron OH 44320	330-864-2161	R	15*	.1
87	Ritus Corp—*Tom Gebhardt*	7900 N 73rd St, Milwaukee WI 53223	414-586-3535	R	14*	.1
88	Hose Assemblies Inc—*Mat Veldman*	1906 E McKinley Ave, Mishawaka IN 46545	574-255-9774	R	14*	<.1
89	Reilly Foam Corp—*George Rule*	PO Box 465, Lafayette Hill PA 19444	610-834-1900	R	14*	.1
90	Proco Products Inc—*Edward Marchese*	PO Box 590, Stockton CA 95201	209-943-6088	R	14*	<.1
91	Robbins LLC—*Steve Saucier*	2306 S Wilson Dam Rd, Muscle Shoals AL 35661	256-383-5441	R	13*	.2
92	Classic Balloon Corp—*Les Barton*	1416 Upfield Dr, Carrollton TX 75006	972-242-2711	R	13*	.1
93	Duramax Marine LLC—*Richard Spangler* Duramax Inc	17990 Great Lakes Pkwy, Hiram OH 44234	440-834-5400	D	13*	.1
94	Protecto Wrap Co—*John Hopkins*	1955 S Cherokee St, Denver CO 80223	303-777-3001	R	13*	.1
95	Rahco Rubber Inc—*William Anton*	1633 Birchwood Ave, Des Plaines IL 60018	847-298-4200	R	13*	.1
96	Tmp Technologies Inc—*Jeffrey Dorn*	1200 Northland Ave, Buffalo NY 14215	716-895-6100	R	13*	.1
97	Holz Rubber Company Inc—*David Smith*	1129 S Sacramento St, Lodi CA 95240	209-368-7171	R	12*	.1
98	US Rubber Reclaiming Inc—*Don LaGrone*	PO Box 820165, Vicksburg MS 39182	601-636-7071	S	12*	.1
99	JDR Enterprises Inc—*John Kreikemeier*	292 S Main St Ste 200, Alpharetta GA 30009	770-442-1461	R	12*	<.1
100	R-B Rubber Products Inc—*Gregory J Divis*	904 NE 10th Ave, McMinnville OR 97128	503-472-4691	S	12	.1
101	Performance Polymer Technologies LLC—*Lonnie Wimberly*	8801 Washington Blvd S, Roseville CA 95678	916-677-1414	R	12*	.1
102	Ten Cate Enbi Inc (Shelbyville Indiana)—*Kevin Stephens*	1703 Mccall Dr, Shelbyville IN 46176	317-398-3267	R	12*	.1
103	Diacom Corp—*Scott Rafferty*	5 Howe Dr, Amherst NH 03031	603-880-1900	R	12*	.1
104	Lundell Manufacturing Corp—*Leroy Lundell*	PO Box 47396, Minneapolis MN 55447	763-559-4114	R	12*	.1
105	Star-Glo Industries LLC—*Dennis Assolina*	2 Carlton Ave, East Rutherford NJ 07073	201-939-6162	R	11*	.1
106	Roy Johnson Inc—*Roylene Slaughter*	PO Box 130, Clarksville AR 72830	479-754-6993	R	11*	.1
107	Jefferson Rubber Works Inc—*David Pentland*	17 Coppage Dr, Worcester MA 01603	508-791-3600	R	11*	.1
108	Hexpol Compounding Nc Inc—*Randy Simpson*	280 Crawford Rd, Statesville NC 28625	704-872-1585	R	11*	.1
109	7-Sigma Inc—*Kristian Wyrobek*	2843 26th Ave S, Minneapolis MN 55406	612-722-5358	R	11*	.1
110	Texre Inc—*Tom Kupke*	PO Box 6217, Tulsa OK 74148	918-425-5524	R	11*	.1
111	Cascade Gasket and Manufacturing Company Inc—*Franklin Terry*	8825 S 228th St, Kent WA 98031	253-854-1800	R	10*	.1
112	Rondy Inc—*Donald Rondy*	255 Wooster Rd N, Barberton OH 44203	330-745-9016	R	10*	.2
113	Precision Polymer Products Inc—*Joseph Voytilla*	815 S St, Pottstown PA 19464	610-326-0921	R	10*	.1
114	Rpp Corp—*Stephen Swensrud*	PO Box 847223, Boston MA 02284	978-689-2800	R	10*	.1
115	Molded Rubber and Plastic Corp—*Greg Riemer*	PO Box 246, Butler WI 53007	262-781-7122	R	10*	.1
116	Fiskars Royal Floor Mats—*Francis Kint*	197 Royal Dr SE, Calhoun GA 30701	706-629-9047	S	10*	.1
117	General Rubber Corp—*Lloyd Aanenson*	2201 E Ganley Rd, Tucson AZ 85706	520-889-2979	R	10*	.1
118	R and S Processing Company Inc—*Karen Kelly*	PO Box 2037, Paramount CA 90723	562-531-1403	R	10*	.1
119	Scougal Rubber Corp—*Tom Foley*	PO Box 80226, Seattle WA 98108	206-763-2650	R	10*	.1
120	Harwood Rubber Products Inc—*Richard Harwood*	1365 Orlen Ave, Cuyahoga Falls OH 44221	330-923-3256	R	10*	<.1
121	Polymerics Inc—*Joe Arhar*	2828 2nd St, Cuyahoga Falls OH 44221	330-928-2210	R	10*	.1
122	Custom Rubber Corp—*William Braun*	1274 E 55th St, Cleveland OH 44103	216-391-2928	R	10*	.1
123	Valley Rubber LLC—*Cronan Connell*	3899 Hwy 31 Sw, Falkville AL 35622	256-784-5231	R	10*	.1

Rank	Company Name—Executive Officer	Address, City, State, Zip	Phone	Type	Fin	Empls
124	Amazon Hose and Rubber Company Of Tampa Inc—Summer Rodman	1103 N 50th St, Tampa FL 33619	813-223-7554	R	10*	.1
125	Gayla Industries Inc—Douglas Phillips	PO Box 920800, Houston TX 77292	713-681-2411	R	10*	.1
126	Bedell-Kraus Flexographic And Pharmaceutical Rubber Inc—James Bedell	1350 Commerce Dr, Stow OH 44224	330-688-4881	R	10*	.1
127	Winslow Marine Products Corp—Steve Harvey	11700 Sw Winslow Dr, Lake Suzy FL 34269	941-613-6666	R	10*	.1
128	Armada Rubber Manufacturing Co—Lawerence Weymouth	PO Box 579, Armada MI 48005	586-784-9135	R	10*	.1
129	Valley Roller Company Inc—Mike Chase	N257 Stoney Brook Rd, Appleton WI 54915	920-733-1991	R	10*	.1
130	Rubber Industries Inc—Arthur Hatch	200 Cavanaugh Dr, Shakopee MN 55379	952-445-1320	R	9*	.1
131	Maple City Rubber Co—Jeffrey Tinker	PO Box 587, Norwalk OH 44857	419-668-8261	R	9*	.1
132	H and M Rubber Company Inc—James Moore	4200 Mogadore Rd, Kent OH 44240	330-678-3323	R	9*	.1
133	Corrosion Engineering Inc—Donald Dunn	PO Box 5670, Mesa AZ 85211	480-890-0505	R	9*	.2
134	Plastic and Metal Center Inc	23162 La Cadena Dr, Laguna Hills CA 92653	949-770-8230	R	9*	<.1
135	Renew Resources Inc—Charlie Baker	5121 Winnetka Ave N St, Minneapolis MN 55428	763-533-9200	R	9*	<.1
136	Mustang Survival Manufacturing Inc—Dwight Davies	PO Box 520, Elizabeth WV 26143	304-275-3306	R	9*	.1
137	Eutsler Technical Products Inc—M Borski	PO Box 920818, Houston TX 77292	713-686-8209	R	9*	<.1
138	Cascade Rubber Products Inc—Steven Byers	PO Box 10886, Portland OR 97296	503-248-1992	R	8*	.1
139	North American Latex Corp—Nelson Ellis	49 Industrial Park Dr, Sullivan IN 47882	812-268-6608	R	8*	.1
140	Great Lakes Rubber Co—Don Demallie	PO Box 930199, Wixom MI 48393	248-624-5710	S	8*	.1
141	Passport Carpets Inc—Marian Chilton	2301 Hwy 41 S Sw, Calhoun GA 30701	706-625-4165	R	8*	.1
142	AGI Rubber Co—Jeffrey Castaldo	PO Box 898, Bridgeport CT 06601	203-366-4318	R	8*	.1
143	Best Foam Inc—Tommy Thompson	PO Box 288, Sherman MS 38869	662-840-6700	R	8*	.1
144	Bumper Specialities Inc—Leon Braunstein	1607 Imperial Way, West Deptford NJ 08066	856-345-7650	R	8*	.1
145	Molded Dimensions Inc—Linda Katz	PO Box 364, Port Washington WI 53074	262-284-9455	R	8*	.1
146	Penn Foam Corp—Sandra Fromknecht	2625 Mitchell Ave, Allentown PA 18103	610-797-7500	R	8*	.1
147	Brp Manufacturing Co—Kendall House	PO Box 389, Lima OH 45802	419-228-4441	R	8*	.1
148	Standard Rubber Products Co—Larry Gualano	PO Box 797, Elk Grove Village IL 60009	847-593-5630	R	8*	<.1
149	Shaw Development LLC—Paul Bradley	25190 Bernwood Dr, Bonita Springs FL 34135	239-405-6100	R	8*	.1
150	WW Products Inc—Douglas Joseph	21801 Industrial Blvd, Rogers MN 55374	763-428-9119	R	8*	.1
151	Blair Rubber Co—David Jentzsch	5020 Panther Pkwy, Seville OH 44273	330-769-5583	R	8*	<.1
152	Durable Corp—Thomas Secor	PO Box 290, Norwalk OH 44857	419-668-8138	R	8*	.1
153	South Bend Modern Molding In—Charles Zimmerman	PO Box 850, Mishawaka IN 46546	574-255-0711	R	8*	.1
154	R Wales and Son LLC—Gary Wales	2665 N Flowing Wells R, Tucson AZ 85705	520-791-9001	R	7*	<.1
155	Universal Urethane Products Inc—Harry Conrad	PO Box 50617, Toledo OH 43605	419-693-7400	R	7*	.1
156	Aero Corp—Dale Mcbride	1200 W Bonodum Industr, Bridgeport WV 26330	304-842-1970	R	7*	.1
157	Southern Mold Builders—Carl Spruill	335 Industrial Dr, Mount Juliet TN 37122	615-758-2191	R	7*	.1
158	Polymeric Technology Inc—Patrick Tool	1900 Marina Blvd, San Leandro CA 94577	510-895-6001	R	7*	.1
159	Aero Rubber Company Inc—John Kasman	8100 185th St, Tinley Park IL 60487	708-430-4900	R	7*	<.1
160	Eagle Elastomer Inc—Regan Hale	PO Box 939, Cuyahoga Falls OH 44223	330-923-7070	R	6*	<.1
161	Polyvulc USA Inc—Fred Farrell	1645 Haining Rd, Vicksburg MS 39183	601-638-8040	R	6*	.1
162	Santa Fe Rubber Products Inc—William Krames	12306 Washington Blvd, Whittier CA 90606	562-693-2776	R	6*	.1
163	Lakeview Industries Inc—Lorretta Magnuson	1225 Lakeview Dr, Chaska MN 55318	952-368-3500	R	6*	<.1
164	Metro Moulded Parts Inc—Douglas Hajicek	PO Box 48130, Minneapolis MN 55448	763-757-0310	R	6*	<.1
165	United States Roller Works Inc—James Robers	1901 Elm Hill Pke, Nashville TN 37210	615-391-3300	R	6*	<.1
166	Aero Tec Laboratories Inc—Peter Regna	45 Spear Rd, Ramsey NJ 07446	201-825-1400	R	6*	.1
167	Plasticoid Company Inc—James Palinkas	249 W High St, Elkton MD 21921	410-398-2800	R	6*	.1
168	Vulcan International Corp—Benjamin Gettler	103 Foulk Rd Ste 202, Wilmington DE 19803	302-656-1950	P	6	.1
169	Biomedical Polymers Inc—John Fay	42 Linus Allain Ave, Gardner MA 01440	978-632-2555	R	6*	<.1
170	Dacon Industries Co—Darin Bay	10661 N Lombard St, Portland OR 97203	503-978-0801	R	6*	<.1
171	Hawthorne Rubber Manufacturing Inc—Michael Morton	PO Box 171, Hawthorne NJ 07507	973-427-3337	R	5*	.1
172	Prince Rubber and Plastics Company Inc—S Prince	137 Arthur St, Buffalo NY 14207	716-877-7400	R	5*	<.1
173	Act Technologies Inc—G Lyle	PO Box 279, Dalton GA 30722	706-226-6038	R	5*	<.1
174	Mullins Rubber Products Inc—William Mullins	PO Box 24830, Dayton OH 45424	937-233-4211	R	5*	<.1
175	Acutek Adhesive Specialties Inc—Jerry Muchin	540 N Oak St, Inglewood CA 90302	310-419-0567	R	5*	<.1
176	Jet Rubber Co—Thomas Smith	4457 Tallmadge Rd, Rootstown OH 44272	330-325-1821	R	5*	<.1
177	Bill Benetreu Co—Bill Benetreu	1635 N 30th St, Springfield OR 97478	541-747-2510	R	5*	<.1
178	Unicast Inc—Peter Molinaro	PO Box 4627, Easton PA 18043	610-559-9998	R	5*	.1
179	New England Foam Products LLC—Nick Elia	PO Box 583, Windsor CT 06095	860-524-0121	R	5*	<.1
180	Blakeman Industries Inc—Alan Blakeman	PO Box 1155, Euless TX 76039	817-267-4444	R	5*	<.1
181	Summit Rubber Company Inc—Patsy Singleton	PO Box 1054, Summerville SC 29484	843-875-4627	R	5*	<.1
182	Haydock Caster Co—Raymond Haydock	6220 Gross Point Rd, Niles IL 60714	708-387-3090	R	5*	<.1
183	Softseal Inc—Gary Anderson	104 May Dr, Harrison OH 45030	513-367-0028	R	5*	<.1
184	Treadway Industries LLC—Michele Luca	111 Weber Ave, Leesburg FL 34748	352-326-3313	R	5*	<.1
185	Aerofab Company Inc—Jules Bols	PO Box 20130, Ferndale MI 48220	248-542-0051	R	5*	<.1
186	Arc Equipment Inc—James Jennett	139 S Weber Dr, Chandler AZ 85226	480-961-0051	R	4*	<.1
187	Western Falcon Inc—Louis Russo	1304 Langham Creek Dr, Houston TX 77084	832-391-9454	R	4*	<.1
188	Indian Rubber Company Inc—Steven Crudup	440 W Fork Dr, Arlington TX 76012	817-265-6732	R	4*	<.1
189	Expanded Rubber Products Inc—Barbara Ney	PO Box 1070, Sanford ME 04073	207-324-8226	R	4*	<.1
190	Crushproof Tubing Co—Vance Kramer	100 North St, McComb OH 45858	419-293-2111	R	4*	<.1
191	Standard Rubber Products Inc—John Davis	PO Box 1157, Hanover MA 02339	781-878-2626	R	4*	<.1
192	Rubber Engineering And Development Company Inc—Mitch Watts	3000 Arrowhead Dr, Carson City NV 89706	775-882-3100	R	4*	<.1
193	Apex Marine Inc—Mark Dupuie	300 Woodside Dr, Saint Louis MI 48880	989-681-4300	R	4*	<.1
194	Stowe Woodward AG—Bertram Staudenmaier	51 Flex Way, Youngsville NC 27596	919-556-7235	S	4*	<.1
195	Packaging Materials Inc—Ronald Funk	PO Box 731, Cambridge OH 43725	740-432-6337	R	4*	<.1
196	Rol-Tec Inc—Matthew Umentum	1150 Glory Rd, Green Bay WI 54304	920-339-3150	R	4*	<.1
197	Fabsol LLC—Ernie Baker	277 Industrial Dr, Cadiz KY 42211	270-522-1070	R	4*	<.1
198	Manville Rubber Products Inc—Sophia Gajewski	1009 Kennedy Blvd, Manville NJ 08835	908-526-9111	R	4*	<.1
199	Cardinal Rubber Company Inc—Diane Mcconnell	939 Wooster Rd N, Barberton OH 44203	330-745-2191	R	4*	<.1
200	AME Corp—Ehren Dimitry	33 Jacksonville Rd Ste, Towaco NJ 07082	973-263-1700	R	4*	<.1
201	American Recycling Center Inc—Larry Fisher	655 Wabassee Dr, Owosso MI 48867	989-725-5100	R	4*	<.1
202	Allied Security Innovations Inc—Anthony Shupin	1709 Rte 34 Ste 2, Farmingdale NJ 07727	904-794-1111	P	4	<.1
203	Rubatex International LLC—Valerie Fitzgerald	906 Adams St, Bedford VA 24523	540-586-2611	R	4*	<.1
204	Stockton Rubber ManufacturingCoInc—Earl Wilson	PO Box 639, Linden CA 95236	209-887-1172	R	4*	<.1
205	Funsource Partners—Irma Christoffel	2301 Minimax St, Houston TX 77008	713-864-3412	R	4*	<.1
206	Guardian Manufacturing Co—Gene Lamoreaux	302 S Conwell Ave, Willard OH 44890	419-933-2711	R	4*	<.1
207	Bassco Foam Inc—Robert Bass	PO Box 2731, Tupelo MS 38803	662-842-4321	R	4*	<.1
208	Venango Machine Company Inc—David Tullio	PO Box 239, Wattsburg PA 16442	814-739-2211	R	4*	<.1
209	Lotridge Enterprises LLC	105 Dinsmore St, Botkins OH 45306	937-693-4611	R	3*	<.1
210	Tristan Rubber Molding Inc—Peter Fritz	6196 Dressler Rd Nw, Canton OH 44720	330-499-4055	R	3*	<.1

Note: An asterisk (*) indicates an estimated financial figure. The company type code used is as follows: R = Private, P = Public, S = Private Subsidiary, B = Public Subsidiary, D = Division, J = Joint Venture, I = Investment Fund.

COMPANY RANKINGS BY SALES WITHIN 4-DIGIT SIC

Rank	Company Name—Executive Officer	Address, City, State, Zip	Phone	Type	Fin	Empls
211	Hi Tech Profiles Inc—Raymond Quinlan	185 S Broad St Ste 301, Pawcatuck CT 06379	860-599-0500	R	3*	<.1
212	Acme Masking Company Inc—William Bailey	240 Production Dr, Avon IN 46123	317-272-6202	R	3*	<.1
213	Pacific Eagle USA Inc—Arthur Shih	9707 El Poche St Ste H, South El Monte CA 91733	626-455-0033	R	3*	<.1
214	California Gasket And Rubber Corp—Scott Franklin	533 Collins Ave, Orange CA 92867	714-202-8500	R	3*	<.1
215	Latitudes Inc—Andy Knouse	PO Box 39, Sullivan MO 63080	573-468-5564	R	3*	<.1
216	Pmr Precision Manufacturing and Rubber Company Inc—Sam Surh	8480 Red Oak Ave, Rancho Cucamonga CA 91730	909-989-9511	R	3*	<.1
217	Newby Rubber Inc—Kelly Newby	320 Industrial St, Bakersfield CA 93307	661-327-5137	R	3*	<.1
218	Vte Inc—Willem Roelof Van Tiel	PO Box 790, Pellston MI 49769	231-539-8000	R	3*	<.1
219	Precision Component and Machine Inc—Steve Chatteron	PO Box 580, Chesapeake OH 45619	740-867-6366	R	3*	<.1
220	Molded Products Inc—David Clonts	11524 E 58th St, Tulsa OK 74146	918-254-9061	R	3*	<.1
221	Linear Rubber Products Inc—John Lane	5416 46th St, Kenosha WI 53144	262-652-3912	R	3*	<.1
222	Triangle Rubber Company Inc—Thomas Barresi	50 Aero Rd, Bohemia NY 11716	631-589-9400	R	3*	<.1
223	Accurate Products Inc—Graham Satherlie	4645 N Ravenswood Ave, Chicago IL 60640	773-878-2200	R	3*	<.1
224	Kaswell and Company Inc—Norman J Kaswell	PO Box 549, Framingham MA 01704	508-879-1500	R	3*	<.1
225	Northern Prairie Polymers LLC—Donn Nystedt	20015 176th St Nw, Big Lake MN 55309	763-559-9061	R	3*	<.1
226	Qrp Inc—Duncan Casselman	PO Box 27466, Tucson AZ 85726	520-790-3533	R	3*	<.1
227	Cape Cod Doormats Of Distinction Inc—Dawn Stahl	105 Ferndoc St Ste E1, Hyannis MA 02601	508-790-0070	R	3*	<.1
228	Hydac Rubber Manufacturing—Jeanne Brown	PO Box 326, Smithton IL 62285	618-233-2129	R	3*	<.1
229	Minowitz Manufacturing Co—Paul Pereira	27941 Groesbeck Hwy, Roseville MI 48066	586-779-5940	R	3*	<.1
230	Republic Roller Corp—Gary Umphrey	PO Box 330, Three Rivers MI 49093	269-273-9591	R	3*	<.1
231	Rubber Specialties Inc—James Sifferle	8117 Pleasant Ave S, Minneapolis MN 55420	952-888-9225	R	3*	<.1
232	Die Cut Products Company Inc—Steve Comet	1801 E 30th St, Cleveland OH 44114	216-771-6994	R	3*	<.1
233	Gordon Rubber And Packing Company Inc—John Mazur	PO Box 298, Derby CT 06418	203-735-7441	R	3*	<.1
234	Keener Rubber Co—Richard Michelson	PO Box 2717, Alliance OH 44601	330-821-1880	R	3*	<.1
235	Schuyler Rubber Company Inc—Greg Armfield	16901 Wdnvl Red Rd Ne, Woodinville WA 98072	425-488-2255	R	3*	<.1
236	TL Sparton Enterprises Inc—James Little	3717 Clark Mill Rd, Norton OH 44203	330-745-6088	R	3*	<.1
237	Avon Custom Mixing Services Inc—Mark Chase	55 High St, Holbrook MA 02343	781-767-0511	R	3*	<.1
238	Schaeferrolls Inc—Bradley Moores	PO Box 697, Farmington NH 03835	603-335-1786	R	3*	<.1
239	Herbert Cooper Company Inc—Howard Cooper	PO Box 40, Genesee PA 16923	814-228-3417	R	3*	<.1
240	Superior Manufacturing Group - Europe Inc—John Wood	5655 W 73rd St, Chicago IL 60638	708-458-4600	R	3*	<.1
241	Rubber and Silicone Products Company Inc—Jeffery Dylla	PO Box 1215, Caldwell NJ 07007	973-227-2300	R	3*	<.1
242	Pacific Molding Inc—Mario Rueda	1612 Jenks Dr, Corona CA 92880	951-734-5210	R	2*	<.1
243	La Favorite Industries Inc—Thomas Mastin	33 Shady St, Paterson NJ 07524	973-279-1266	R	2*	<.1
244	Rti Recycled Technology Inc—Glen Baker	11800 Ne Sunny Acres L, Newberg OR 97132	503-691-5845	R	2*	<.1
245	Jedtco Corp—Nancy Siwik	5899 E Executive Dr, Westland MI 48185	734-326-3010	R	2*	<.1
246	Jvi Inc—James Voss	7131 N Ridgeway Ave, Lincolnwood IL 60712	847-675-1560	R	2*	<.1
247	Craftsman Foam Fabricators Inc—Olin Hill	196 Mason Way, Thomasville NC 27360	336-476-5655	R	2*	<.1
248	Central Rubber and Plastics Inc—Scott Salisbury	PO Box 821, Goshen IN 46527	574-534-6411	R	2*	<.1
249	Foam Products Inc—Karen Ippolito	360 Southern Blvd, Bronx NY 10454	718-292-4830	R	2*	<.1
250	Rubber and Plastic Applicators Inc—William Wells	PO Box 973, Satsuma AL 36572	251-452-0585	R	2*	<.1
251	M Trumbull A R S Inc—Michael Myhal	PO Box 4596, Youngstown OH 44515	330-270-9780	R	2*	<.1
252	American Pro-Mold Inc—Edward Steinkerchner	PO Box 325, Wadsworth OH 44282	330-336-4111	R	2*	<.1
253	Raydar Incorporated Of Ohio—Ray Mcintosh	1734 Wall Rd Ste B, Wadsworth OH 44281	330-334-6111	R	2*	<.1
254	Interdyne Inc—Antonin Slovacek	PO Box 165, Jonesville MI 49250	517-849-2281	R	2*	<.1
255	Bi-State Rubber Inc—Jeffery Franke	PO Box 608, Fenton MO 63026	636-349-2388	R	2*	<.1
256	Industrial Roller Co—George Linne	PO Box 329, Smithton IL 62285	618-234-0740	R	2*	<.1
257	Trexler Rubber Company Inc—Jack Schaefer	PO Box 667, Ravenna OH 44266	330-296-9677	R	2*	<.1
258	Inflatable Technology Corp—Richard G Fryburg	PO Box 2030, North Kingstown RI 02852	401-884-8801	R	2*	<.1
259	M and M Bumper Service Inc—Jerry Gonsulin	PO Box 237, Bourg LA 70343	985-594-4148	R	2*	<.1
260	Standard Washer and Mat Inc—Carl Eckblom	PO Box 368, Manchester CT 06045	860-643-5125	R	2*	<.1
261	Woodlawn Rubber Co—Kirk Heithaus	11268 Williamson Rd, Blue Ash OH 45241	513-489-1718	R	2*	<.1
262	Colorado Molded Products Co—C Scott Kayer	PO Box 1321, Englewood CO 80150	303-761-5801	R	2*	<.1
263	JL Schroth Company Inc—Richard R Davisson	24074 Gibson, Warren MI 48089	586-759-4240	R	2*	<.1
264	Airmec Inc—C Bacon	2102 Vanco Dr, Irving TX 75061	972-438-4015	R	2*	<.1
265	Inflation Systems Inc—Sandra Goldman	500 Ogden Ave, Mamaroneck NY 10543	914-381-8070	R	2*	<.1
266	P and E Rubber Processing Inc—Edmundo Bolanos	12247 Industrial Blvd, Victorville CA 92395	760-241-2643	R	2*	<.1
267	Boulder Blimp Co—Loni Gilfedder	505 Stacy Ct Ste A, Lafayette CO 80026	303-664-1122	R	2*	<.1
268	Rubber Developments Inc—Vernon Gidley	PO Box 782, Waverly IA 50677	319-352-5600	R	2*	<.1
269	Etec-Durawear Inc—Bryant Allen	2598 Alton Rd, Irondale AL 35210	205-833-1210	R	2*	<.1
270	Industrial Manufacturing Specialties Inc—Polan Willis	1268 Hwy 67 S, Decatur AL 35603	256-350-9334	R	2*	<.1
271	S And H Rubber Company Inc—Stephen Haney	1141 E Elm Ave, Fullerton CA 92831	714-525-0277	R	2*	<.1
272	Profile Rubber Corp—Lewis Winland	PO Box 299, Sharon Center OH 44274	330-239-1703	R	2*	<.1
273	Whitewater Manufacturing Inc—Glenn Lewman	724 Ort Ln, Merlin OR 97532	541-476-1344	R	2*	<.1
274	Enduro Rubber Co—Jerry Stuver	PO Box 752, Ravenna OH 44266	330-296-9603	R	1*	<.1
275	Arthur Asfar—Arthur Asfar	654 Bergen Blvd, Ridgefield NJ 07657	201-943-7650	R	1*	<.1
276	Reddaway Manufacturing Company Inc—Todd Walker	32 Euclid Ave, Newark NJ 07105	973-589-1410	R	1*	<.1
277	Davis Rubber Company Inc—Roger Davis	PO Box 3774, Little Rock AR 72203	501-374-1473	R	1*	<.1
278	Tulsa Rubber Co—Alan Grigg	PO Box 470692, Tulsa OK 74147	918-627-1371	R	1*	<.1
279	3-D Polymers—David Johnson	13026 S Normandie Ave, Gardena CA 90249	310-324-7694	R	1*	<.1
280	Arc Rubber Inc—Robert Johnson	100 Water St, Geneva OH 44041	440-466-4555	R	1*	<.1
281	Givens Marine Survival Service Co—Frank Perrino	550 Main Rd, Tiverton RI 02878	401-624-7900	R	1*	<.1
282	Tacki Mac Grips—Dave Kelley	22000 Northpark Dr, Humble TX 77339	281-358-6738	R	1*	<.1
283	Michael J Arnold and Co—Michael Arnold	1723 Eldridge Rd Ste E, Sugar Land TX 77478	281-494-0001	R	1*	<.1
284	International Dispensing Corp—Greg Abbott	1020 5th Ave 4th Fl, New York NY 10028	212-957-9330	R	<1	<.1
285	RPR Industries Inc—Robert Schnurr	PO Box 220, Grantsville WV 26147	304-354-7844	R	<1*	<.1
286	Ronsil Rubber Div—Carl E Reiss	PO Box 60, Blackstone VA 23824	434-292-1600	R	N/A	.1

TOTALS: SIC 3069 Fabricated Rubber Products Nec
Companies: 286   18,613   57.7

3081 Unsupported Plastics Film & Sheet

Rank	Company Name—Executive Officer	Address, City, State, Zip	Phone	Type	Fin	Empls
1	Tredegar Film Products - Lake Zurich LLC—Nancy M Taylor	351 Oakwood Rd, Lake Zurich IL 60047	847-438-2111	S	2,760*	1.0
2	Viskase Films Inc—Thomas D Davis	8205 S Cass Ave Ste 11, Darien IL 60561	630-874-0700	S	995*	1.5
3	Plastic Suppliers Inc—Theodore Riegert	2887 Johnstown Rd, Columbus OH 43219	614-471-9100	R	881*	.3
4	Flexcon Company Inc—Neil McDonough	1 Flexcon Industrial P, Spencer MA 01562	508-885-8200	R	730*	1.1
5	Sabic Polymershapes—Charlie Crew	11515 Vanstory Dr Ste, Huntersville NC 28078	704-948-5000	D	550*	2.2
6	GSE Lining Technology Inc (Houston Texas)—Mark C Arnold Gundle/SLT Environmental Inc	19103 Gundle Rd, Houston TX 77073	281-443-8564	S	550*	.9
7	Clopay Corp—Gary Abyad	8585 Duke Blvd, Mason OH 45040	513-770-4800	S	448*	3.0
8	Applied Extrusion Technologies Inc—Thomas Mohr	2751 Centerville Rd St, Wilmington DE 19808	302-326-5500	R	408*	.8

Rank	Company Name—*Executive Officer*	Address, City, State, Zip	Phone	Type	Fin	Empls
9	Gundle/SLT Environmental Inc—*Mark Arnold*	19103 Gundle Rd, Houston TX 77073	281-443-8564	S	252*	1.0
10	Interfilm Holdings Inc—*Andy Brewer*	PO Box 51128, Piedmont SC 29673	864-269-4690	R	237*	.2
11	Transilwrap Company Inc—*Herb Drower*	9201 W Belmont Ave, Franklin Park IL 60131	847-678-1800	R	236	.7
12	Scholle Corp—*Sohini Baxi*	19520 Jamboree Rd Ste, Irvine CA 92612	949-955-1750	R	167*	2.1
13	Poly-America LP—*Lacy Holt*	2000 W Marshall Dr, Grand Prairie TX 75051	972-337-7000	R	144*	1.8
14	Plastimayd Corp—*Todd Mulvaney*	PO Box 2320, Oregon City OR 97045	503-654-8502	R	139*	.2
15	Coast Converters Inc—*Bill Kauble*	12670 Paxton St, Pacoima CA 91331	818-890-7000	R	111*	.2
16	Clopay Plastic Products Co—*Gary Abyad* Clopay Corp	8585 Duke Blvd, Mason OH 45040	513-770-4800	S	99*	.2
17	Reflexite Corp—*Cecil Ursprung*	120 Darling Dr, Avon CT 06001	860-676-7100	R	93*	.5
18	Primex Plastics Corp—*Paul Bertsch*	1235 N F St, Richmond IN 47374	765-966-7774	R	88*	1.1
19	Inpro Corp—*Stephen Ziegler*	PO Box 406, Muskego WI 53150	262-679-9010	R	66*	.4
20	Formflex Inc—*Brent Thompson*	PO Box 218, Bloomingdale IN 47832	765-498-8900	R	64*	.1
21	Toray Plastics (America) Inc—*Richard Schloesser*	50 Belver Ave, North Kingstown RI 02852	401-294-4511	R	56*	.7
22	Glenroy Inc—*Richard Boss*	PO Box 534, Menomonee Falls WI 53052	262-255-4422	R	54*	.2
23	Abnote USA Inc—*Stuart Blank*	225 Rivermoor St, Boston MA 02132	617-325-9600	R	50*	.3
24	Winpak Films Inc—*Kevin Byers*	219 Andrews Pkwy, Senoia GA 30276	770-599-6656	R	47*	.2
25	Paragon Plastic Sheet Inc—*Ashley Wade*	PO Box 1024, Dequincy LA 70633	337-786-7022	R	46*	.1
26	Southwall Technologies Inc—*Dennis Capovilla*	3788 Fabian Way, Palo Alto CA 94303	650-798-1200	P	45	.1
27	CMS Gilbreth Packaging Systems—*Kevin H Kerchner*	3001 State Rd, Croydon PA 19021	215-785-3350	S	40	.2
28	Lucent Polymers Inc—*Kevin Kuhnash*	1700 Lynch Rd, Evansville IN 47711	812-421-2216	R	40*	.1
29	Bloomer Plastics Inc—*Neil Lundgren*	1710 N Industrial Dr, Bloomer WI 54724	715-568-5775	R	39*	.1
30	Flex Products Inc	2793 Northpoint Pky, Santa Rosa CA 95407	707-525-9200	S	38*	.2
31	Westlake Plastics Co	PO Box 127, Lenni PA 19052	610-459-1000	R	38*	.2
32	Bjk Industries Inc—*Brian Krein*	945 S 15th St, Louisville KY 40210	502-581-1800	R	37*	.1
33	Trm Manufacturing Inc—*Ted Moore*	PO Box 77520, Corona CA 92877	951-256-8550	R	36*	.2
34	Sheffield Plastics Inc—*Dennis Duff*	119 Salisbury Rd, Sheffield MA 01257	413-229-8711	S	34*	.2
35	Associated Bag Co—*Herbert Rubenstein*	400 W Boden St, Milwaukee WI 53207	414-769-1000	R	32*	.2
36	Kaneka High-Tech Materials Inc	6161 Underwood Rd, Pasadena TX 77507	281-474-7084	R	32*	.2
37	Mitsubishi Rayon America Inc—*H Sugao*	747 3rd Ave 19th Fl, New York NY 10017	212-223-3043	S	31*	<.1
38	Cadillac Products Packaging Co—*Robert Williams*	5800 Crooks Rd Ste 100, Troy MI 48098	248-879-5000	R	27*	.4
39	Cpi Scranton Inc—*Scott Harrison*	801 E Corey St, Scranton PA 18505	570-558-8000	S	27*	.4
40	Nexus Plastics Inc—*Marwan Sholakh*	PO Box 667, Hawthorne NJ 07507	973-427-3311	R	26*	.1
41	C E Shepherd Company LP—*C Shepherd*	2221 Canada Dry St, Houston TX 77023	713-924-4300	R	26*	.1
42	TM Poly-Film Inc—*K Morrison*	503 Gil Harbin Industr, Valdosta GA 31601	229-247-7734	R	25*	.2
43	Achilles USA Inc—*Hiroyuki Fuse*	1407 80th St Sw, Everett WA 98203	425-353-7000	R	25*	.2
44	All American Poly Corp—*Jack Klein*	PO Box 10148, New Brunswick NJ 08906	732-752-3200	R	23*	.3
45	Allen Extruders Inc—*Allen Angell*	1305 Lincoln Ave, Holland MI 49423	616-394-3810	R	23*	.1
46	Kw Plastics—*Stephanie Baker*	PO Box 707, Troy AL 36081	334-566-1563	R	22*	.3
47	Pacific Industries Inc—*James Roberson*	605 Satellite Blvd Nw, Suwanee GA 30024	678-638-9000	R	22*	.1
48	Midwest Canvas Corp—*Barry Handwerker*	4635 W Lake St, Chicago IL 60644	773-287-4400	R	21*	.3
49	Flex-O-Glass Inc—*Harold Warp*	4647 W Augusta Blvd St, Chicago IL 60651	773-261-5200	R	20*	.2
50	Danafilms Inc—*Sherman Olson*	PO Box 624, Westborough MA 01581	508-366-8884	R	19*	.1
51	Paragon Films Inc—*Michael Baab*	3500 W Tacoma St, Broken Arrow OK 74012	918-250-3456	R	19*	.1
52	Clear View Bag Company Inc—*William Romer*	PO Box 11160, Albany NY 12211	518-458-7153	R	19*	.2
53	Reef Industries Inc—*Troy Taylor*	9209 Almeda Genoa Rd, Houston TX 77075	713-507-4200	R	19*	.2
54	Bema Film Systems Inc—*Glen Galloway*	744 N Oaklawn Ave, Elmhurst IL 60126	630-279-7800	R	19*	.1
55	Petoskey Plastics Inc—*Paul Keiswetter*	4226 US 31 S, Petoskey MI 49770	231-347-2602	R	19*	.1
56	Multifilm Packaging Corp—*Olle Mannertorp*	1040 N Mclean Blvd, Elgin IL 60123	847-695-7600	R	19*	.1
57	ES Robbins Corp—*Edward Robbins*	2802 Avalon Ave, Muscle Shoals AL 35661	256-383-0124	R	18*	.2
58	Madico Inc—*Robert Connelly*	64 Industrial Pkwy, Woburn MA 01801	781-935-7850	R	18*	.1
59	Southern Film Extruders Inc—*Joe Martinez*	PO Box 2104, High Point NC 27261	336-885-8091	R	17*	.1
60	Mark Ronald Associates Inc—*Leslie Satz*	PO Box 776, Hillside NJ 07205	908-558-0011	R	17*	.1
61	Robbie Manufacturing Inc—*Irv Robinson*	10810 Mid America Dr, Shawnee Mission KS 66219	913-492-3400	R	17*	.1
62	Ppc Industries Inc—*Thomas Cowan*	10101 78th Ave, Pleasant Prairie WI 53158	262-947-0900	R	17*	.1
63	Goex Corp—*Joshua Gray*	PO Box 1507, Janesville WI 53547	608-754-3303	R	16*	.1
64	Sancap Liner Technology Inc—*Robert Stuhlmiller*	16125 Armour St Ne, Alliance OH 44601	330-821-1166	R	16*	.1
65	Package Development Industries Inc—*Charles Schwester*	100 Round Hill Dr Ste, Rockaway NJ 07866	973-983-8500	R	16*	.1
66	Tri Seal Holdings Inc—*F Smith*	900 Bradley Hill Rd, Blauvelt NY 10913	845-353-3300	R	16*	.1
67	King Plastic Corp—*Jeff King*	1100 N Toledo Blade Bl, North Port FL 34288	941-493-5502	R	16*	.1
68	Acton Technologies Inc—*Kevin Nelson*	PO Box 726, Pittston PA 18640	570-654-0612	R	16*	.1
69	LLC Shield Pack—*Graeme Mills*	411 Downing Pines Rd, West Monroe LA 71292	318-387-4743	R	16*	.1
70	Polyvinyl Films Inc—*John Baldwin*	PO Box 753, Sutton MA 01590	508-865-3558	R	15*	.1
71	Mid South Extrusion Inc—*Mark Anderson*	2015 Jackson St, Monroe LA 71202	318-322-7239	R	15*	.1
72	Maco Bag Corp—*J Miller*	412 Van Buren St, Newark NY 14513	315-226-1000	R	15*	.1
73	New England Extrusion Inc—*Cathy Bolhous*	18 Industrial Blvd, Turners Falls MA 01376	413-863-3171	R	15*	.1
74	Layfield Environmental Systems Corp—*Tom Rose*	851 Houser Way N Ste A, Renton WA 98057	619-562-1200	R	15*	.1
75	Allied Plastics Holdings LLC—*Nazy Louia*	3608 Review Ave, Long Island City NY 11101	718-729-5500	R	15*	.1
76	Vinyl Pak Inc—*Abe Bistritzky*	800 Snediker Ave, Brooklyn NY 11207	718-345-3200	R	14*	.1
77	Western Plastics Inc—*Thomas Cunningham*	PO Box 1636, Calhoun GA 30703	706-625-5260	R	14*	.1
78	Admiral Packaging Inc—*Harley Frank*	10 Admiral St, Providence RI 02908	401-274-7000	R	14*	.1
79	American Profol Inc—*Karl Schieferdecker*	4333 C St Sw, Cedar Rapids IA 52404	319-365-0599	R	14*	.1
80	Rexam Inc	4201 Congress St Ste 3, Charlotte NC 28209	704-551-1500	S	14*	.1
81	General Films Inc—*Tim Weikert*	645 S High St Ste 48, Covington OH 45318	937-473-2051	R	14*	.1
82	Hillside Plastics Corp—*Harold Kaufman*	PO Box 609, Hillside NJ 07205	973-923-2700	R	14*	.1
83	Louisiana Plastic Industries Inc—*Sidney Wilhite*	501 Downing Pines Rd, West Monroe LA 71292	318-388-4562	R	13*	.1
84	Summit Plastic Co—*Norman Belliveau*	PO Box 117, Tallmadge OH 44278	330-633-3668	R	13*	.1
85	Favorite Plastic Corp—*Hershey Friedman*	1465 Utica Ave, Brooklyn NY 11234	718-253-7000	R	12*	.1
86	Republic Plastics LP—*Gino Inman*	PO Box 707, Mc Queeney TX 78123	830-557-5574	R	12*	.1
87	Connor Sport Court International Inc—*Ronald Cerny*	939 S 700 W, Salt Lake City UT 84104	801-972-0260	R	12*	.1
88	Computer Designs Inc—*Scott Mckeever*	5235 W Coplay Rd, Whitehall PA 18052	610-261-2100	R	12*	.1
89	Europackaging LLC—*Arnold Raffel*	14 Garabedian Dr, Salem NH 03079	603-893-5351	R	12*	.1
90	Rowland Technologies Inc—*Stephen Dimugno*	320 Barnes Rd, Wallingford CT 06492	203-269-9500	R	12*	.1
91	Kimoto Tech Inc—*Yutaka Arita*	PO Box 1783, Cedartown GA 30125	770-748-2643	R	12*	.1
92	Fabpro Oriented Polymers Inc—*Jim Pilley*	PO Box 160454, Clearfield UT 84016	801-773-0914	S	11*	.1
93	Dallas Plastics Corp—*Dennis Pierce*	924 Dalworth Dr, Mesquite TX 75149	972-289-5500	R	11*	.1
94	Plastic Development Inc—*Alfred Elkin*	PO Box 19720, Johnston RI 02919	401-728-0010	R	10*	.1
95	Nuhart and Company Inc—*Alex Folkman*	PO Box 786, Deer Park NY 11729	718-383-8484	R	10*	.1
96	Pace Polyethylene Manufacturing Company Inc—*Stan Nathanson*	PO Box 385, Harrison NY 10528	914-381-3000	R	9*	.1

Note: An asterisk (*) indicates an estimated financial figure. The company type code used is as follows: R = Private, P = Public, S = Private Subsidiary, B = Public Subsidiary, D = Division, J = Joint Venture, I = Investment Fund.

COMPANY RANKINGS BY SALES WITHIN 4-DIGIT SIC

Rank	Company Name—*Executive Officer*	Address, City, State, Zip	Phone	Type	Fin	Empls
97	Tee Group Films Inc—*Thomas Malpass*	PO Box 425, Ladd IL 61329	815-894-2331	R	9*	.1
98	North Shore Strapping Inc—*Bridget Leneghan*	1400 Valley Belt Rd, Brooklyn Heights OH 44131	216-661-5200	R	9*	.1
99	Optimum Plastics Inc—*Robert Clemons*	1188 S Houk Rd, Delaware OH 43015	740-369-2770	R	9*	<.1
100	Daliah Plastics Corp—*Charles Gans*	PO Box 27, Asheboro NC 27204	336-629-0551	R	9*	.1
101	Polymask Corp—*George W Buckley*	PO Box 309, Conover NC 28613	828-465-3053	S	9*	.1
102	Montebello Plastics LLC—*Sue Ashton*	PO Box 2047, Montebello CA 90640	323-728-6814	R	9*	.1
103	Mpf Acquisitions Inc—*John Roggow*	PO Box 125, Martin MI 49070	269-672-5511	R	9*	<.1
104	Agru/America Inc—*Robert Johnson*	500 Garrison Rd, Georgetown SC 29440	843-546-0600	R	9*	<.1
105	B and F Plastics Inc—*Bruce Upchurch*	540 N 8th St, Richmond IN 47374	765-962-6125	R	8*	.1
106	Kayline Processing Inc—*Michael Lebwohl*	31 Coates St, Trenton NJ 08611	609-695-1449	R	8*	<.1
107	Lally-Pak Inc—*Henry Herbst*	1209 Central Ave, Hillside NJ 07205	908-351-4141	R	8*	.1
108	Unit Liner Co—*Alan Buck*	7901 N Kickapoo, Shawnee OK 74804	405-275-4600	R	8*	.1
109	Ncd Acquisition Inc—*Steve Robinson*	PO Box 2100, Santa Fe Springs CA 90670	562-447-1758	R	8*	.1
110	Innovative Plastics South Corp—*Jim Parrish*	2900 Old Franklin Rd, Antioch TN 37013	615-501-9100	S	8*	.1
111	Fresh-Pak Corp—*John Bazbaz*	16240 Port Nw Ste 300, Houston TX 77041	713-690-8742	R	8*	.1
112	Hi-Tech Plastics Inc—*Bernard Dahilin*	1700 Badger Rd, Kaukauna WI 54130	920-766-7432	R	8*	.1
113	Edco Supply Corp—*Carl Freyer*	323 36th St, Brooklyn NY 11232	718-788-8108	R	8*	.1
114	Zatec LLC—*Bruce Dias*	PO Box 588, North Dighton MA 02764	508-880-3388	R	8*	.1
115	Superior Plastics Extrusion Company Inc—*David Kingeter*	5 Highland Dr, Putnam CT 06260	860-963-1976	R	8*	.1
116	Kappus Plastic Company Inc—*Annette Gormly*	PO Box 151, Hampton NJ 08827	908-537-2288	R	7*	.1
117	Specialty Manufacturing Inc—*Jenny Ames*	6790 Nancy Ridge Dr, San Diego CA 92121	858-450-1591	R	7*	<.1
118	Western Summit Manufacturing Corp—*Donald Clark*	13290 Daum Dr, City Of Industry CA 91746	626-333-3333	R	7*	.1
119	American-Plastics Company Inc—*John Haug*	3606 Red Arrow Dr, Rhinelander WI 54501	715-369-9500	R	7*	.1
120	ATW Manufacturing Company Inc—*Tom Drew*	PO Box 7755, Eugene OR 97401	541-484-2111	R	7*	<.1
121	Wayne Pak Inc—*Ron Young*	214 Brace Ave, Elyria OH 44035	440-323-8744	R	7*	<.1
122	Azimuth Custom Extrusions LLC—*Don Ward*	1618 Lynch Rd, Evansville IN 47711	812-423-6180	R	7*	<.1
123	Manchester Packaging Co—*Charles Armistead*	PO Box 67, Saint James MO 65559	573-265-3569	R	7*	<.1
124	Formall Inc—*Mark Schappel*	3908 Fountain Valley D, Knoxville TN 37918	865-922-7514	R	6*	<.1
125	Ridout Plastics Co—*Elliott Rabin*	5535 Ruffin Rd, San Diego CA 92123	858-560-1551	R	6*	<.1
126	Creative Impressions Inc—*Marc Abbott*	7697 9th St, Buena Park CA 90621	714-521-4441	R	6*	<.1
127	Integra Plastics Inc—*Mick Green*	500 Se 12th St, Madison SD 57042	605-256-2666	R	6*	<.1
128	Rayven Inc—*Joe Heinemann*	431 Griggs St N, Saint Paul MN 55104	651-642-1112	R	6*	<.1
129	Highland Plastics Inc—*Stephen Simmons*	PO Box 99, Shepherd MI 48883	989-828-4400	R	6*	<.1
130	Dayton-Palmer Inc—*William Palmer*	3337 N Dixie Dr, Dayton OH 45414	937-279-9987	R	6*	<.1
131	Mrm Inc—*William Gregory*	102 Cabot St Ste 7, Holyoke MA 01040	413-533-7141	R	6*	.1
132	Zurn Pex Inc—*Alex Marini*	1900 W Hively Ave, Elkhart IN 46517	574-294-7541	R	6*	<.1
133	Shaant Industries Inc—*Khalid Khan*	PO Box 130, Dunkirk NY 14048	716-366-3654	R	5*	<.1
134	Poly Enterprises—*Al Provence*	230 E Pomona Ave, Monrovia CA 91016	626-358-5115	R	5*	<.1
135	Wbc Extrusion Products Inc—*Christian Ganser*	PO Box 700, Atkinson NH 03811	978-372-3300	R	5*	<.1
136	American Transparent Plastic Corp—*Emanuel Parnes*	PO Box 556, Edison NJ 08818	732-287-5555	R	5*	<.1
137	Blako Industries Inc—*Ed Long*	PO Box 179, Dunbridge OH 43414	419-833-4491	R	5*	<.1
138	Northwest Rubber Extruders Inc—*Susan Lucas*	PO Box 1541, Beaverton OR 97075	503-643-6878	R	5*	<.1
139	Barber-Webb Company Inc—*Donald Barber*	3833 E Medford St, Los Angeles CA 90063	323-264-4800	R	5*	.1
140	Commex Corp—*Edward Yau*	20408 Corsair Blvd, Hayward CA 94545	510-887-4000	R	5*	<.1
141	Comco Plastics Inc—*Morton French*	98 31 Jamaica Ave, Woodhaven NY 11421	718-849-9000	R	5*	<.1
142	Simplex Strip Doors Inc—*Duane Mckinnon*	14500 Miller Ave, Fontana CA 92336	909-429-0117	R	5*	<.1
143	W Plastics Inc—*Michael Cunningham*	41995 Remington Ave, Temecula CA 92590	951-695-1983	R	5*	<.1
144	Barnes Plastics Inc—*Charles Walker*	18903 Anelo Ave, Gardena CA 90248	323-321-2070	R	4*	<.1
145	Impex International Group LP—*Brenda Ellis*	2801 W Sam Houston Pkw, Houston TX 77043	281-416-4449	R	4*	<.1
146	National Plastek Inc—*Casey Dellen*	7050 Dutton Industrl P, Caledonia MI 49316	616-698-9559	R	4*	<.1
147	Architectural Polymers Inc—*Marshall Walters*	1220 Little Gap Rd, Palmerton PA 18071	610-824-3322	R	4*	<.1
148	D and B Plastics Inc—*Larry Fryklund*	706 Highland Court Dr, Fairmont MN 56031	507-235-5950	R	4*	<.1
149	Taylor Packaging Corp—*Glen Taylor*	925 Jeffco Executive D, Imperial MO 63052	636-464-0003	R	4*	<.1
150	Toner Plastics Inc—*Steven Graham*	699 Silver St, Agawam MA 01001	413-789-1300	R	4*	<.1
151	Specialized Plastics Inc—*Beverly Simmons*	567 Main St, Hudson MA 01749	978-562-9314	R	4*	<.1
152	Farber Trucking Corp—*Lewis Farber*	162 Hanse Ave, Freeport NY 11520	516-378-4860	R	3*	<.1
153	Speck Plastics Inc—*Walter Speck III*	PO Box 421, Nazareth PA 18064	610-759-1807	R	3*	<.1
154	Academy Acquisition Corp—*Patrick Rainey*	2609 Cruzen St, Nashville TN 37211	615-256-8623	R	3*	<.1
155	Strataglass LLC—*Carla Lissa*	2968 Ravenswood Rd Ste, Fort Lauderdale FL 33312	954-581-2221	R	3*	<.1
156	Traffic Works Inc—*Steve Josephson*	5720 Soto St, Huntington Park CA 90255	323-582-0616	R	3*	<.1
157	United Laminations Inc—*Herbert Perry*	1311 Lackawanna Ave, Mayfield PA 18433	570-876-1360	R	3*	<.1
158	Total Vinyl Products Inc—*Bill Kindness*	10750 Hi Tech Dr Ste B, Whitmore Lake MI 48189	734-485-7280	R	3*	<.1
159	Kings Film and Sheet Inc—*Forrest Weisburst*	PO Box 170144, Brooklyn NY 11217	718-624-7510	R	3*	<.1
160	Quality Extrusion Inc—*John Thro*	PO Box 3068, Mankato MN 56002	507-387-4131	R	3*	<.1
161	Transparent Protection Systems Inc—*Morton French*	6643 42nd Ter N, Riviera Beach FL 33407	561-840-9499	R	3*	<.1
162	Poly Films Inc—*Harry Currie*	1910 N Sooner Rd, Oklahoma City OK 73141	405-424-0050	R	3*	<.1
163	American Plastic Supply and Manufacturing Inc—*Bob Belzer*	4150 112th Ter N Ste E, Clearwater FL 33762	727-573-0636	R	3*	<.1
164	Mirwec Film Inc—*Y Yasui*	PO Box 2263, Bloomington IN 47402	812-331-7194	R	3*	<.1
165	Arlin Manufacturing Company Inc—*John Mitchell*	PO Box 222, Lowell MA 01853	978-454-9165	R	2*	<.1
166	Royal Plastics Corp—*Donald Marchese*	2840 Atlantic Ave Ste, Brooklyn NY 11207	718-647-7500	R	2*	<.1
167	New World Manufacturing Co—*Gerald Moore*	PO Box 248, Cloverdale CA 95425	707-894-5257	R	2*	<.1
168	Hinkle Manufacturing LLC—*Timothy Devos*	6340 Miller Rd, Dearborn MI 48126	313-584-0400	R	2*	<.1
169	Brandywine Investment Group Corp—*Robert Cahill*	11 Brookside Dr, Wilmington DE 19804	302-652-3686	R	2*	<.1
170	Homeland Vinyl Products Inc—*Randall Heath*	PO Box 170729, Birmingham AL 35217	205-854-3950	R	2*	.4
171	Midwest Urethane Inc—*Gordon Pendergrast*	6417 S 39th W Ave, Tulsa OK 74132	918-445-2277	R	1*	<.1
172	Brougham Corp—*Charles Wood*	9160 S Green St, Chicago IL 60620	773-233-6530	R	1*	<.1
173	FC Witt Associates Ltd—*Jacqueline Witt*	2211 El Anderson Blvd, Claremore OK 74017	918-342-0083	R	1*	<.1
174	Epv Plastics Corp—*Leonard Montione*	PO Box 660, Oxford MA 01540	508-987-2595	R	1*	<.1
175	Uni-Pixel Inc—*Reed J Killion*	8708 Technology Forest, The Woodlands TX 77381	281-825-4500	P	<1	<.1

TOTALS: SIC 3081 Unsupported Plastics Film & Sheet

Companies: 175					11,110	32.5

3082 Unsupported Plastics Profile Shapes

Rank	Company Name—*Executive Officer*	Address, City, State, Zip	Phone	Type	Fin	Empls
1	Teleflex Medical OEM—*Lori Connolly*	50 Plantation Dr, Jaffrey NH 03452	603-532-7706	S	154	.3
2	Rochling Engineering Plastics LP—*Lewis Carter*	903 Gastonia Tech Pkwy, Dallas NC 28034	704-922-7814	R	44*	.1
3	Conwed Plastics Inc—*Ian M Cumming*	1300 Godward St NE Ste, Minneapolis MN 55413	612-623-1700	S	31*	.3
4	Profile Plastics Inc—*Bryan Knowles*	1226 Prospect Ave SW, Canton OH 44706	330-452-7000	R	20*	<.1
5	Kelcourt Plastics Inc—*Patrick Mickle*	1000 Calle Recodo, San Clemente CA 92673	949-361-0774	R	16*	.1
6	Crane Materials International Limited Co—*John Irvine*	4501 Cir 75 Pkwy Se E5, Atlanta GA 30339	770-933-8166	R	15*	.1
7	Applied Plastics Company Inc—*Charles Klein*	7320 S 6th St, Oak Creek WI 53154	414-764-2900	R	12*	.1

Rank	Company Name—*Executive Officer*	Address, City, State, Zip	Phone	Type	Fin	Empls
8	Advanced Plastic Corp—*Harold Koenig*	3725 W Lunt Ave, Lincolnwood IL 60712	847-674-2070	R	12*	.1
9	United Plastics Corp—*Nick Antonnechia*	PO Box 807, Mount Airy NC 27030	336-786-2127	R	11*	.1
10	Reeves Extruded Products Inc—*Grady Reeves*	PO Box 457, Arvin CA 93203	661-854-5970	R	10*	.1
11	Insultab Inc—*Philip Cowen*	45 Industrial Pkwy, Woburn MA 01801	781-935-0800	R	10*	.1
12	Keystone Plastics Inc—*Marvin Naftal*	3451 S Clinton Ave, South Plainfield NJ 07080	908-561-1300	R	10*	.1
13	Cleveland Tubing Inc—*Catherine Boettner*	799 Industrial Dr Sw, Cleveland TN 37311	423-472-2554	R	10*	.1
14	Allstate Plastics Inc—*John Vaccaro*	237 Raritan St, South Amboy NJ 08879	732-721-4024	R	9*	.1
15	Double H Manufacturing Corporation Inc—*Joseph Harp*	2548 W 26th St, Marion IN 46953	765-664-9090	R	9*	.1
16	MTP Inc—*Joseph Kelley*	29797 Beck Rd, Wixom MI 48393	248-668-6269	R	8*	<.1
17	Processing And Packaging Supplies Co—*Bryan Russell*	700 S John Rodes Blvd, Melbourne FL 32904	321-723-2723	R	7*	.1
18	American Industrial Plastics Inc—*George Willis*	724 Fentress Blvd, Daytona Beach FL 32114	386-274-5335	R	6*	.1
19	Jabat Inc—*Russell Steele*	PO Box 38, Olney IL 62450	618-392-3010	R	6*	.1
20	Polytec Plastics Inc—*Karl Blum*	3730 Stern Ave, Saint Charles IL 60174	630-584-8282	R	6*	<.1
21	Ontario Plastics Inc—*Ralph Barnes*	2503 Dewey Ave, Rochester NY 14616	585-663-2644	R	6*	<.1
22	Plastic Services Inc—*Gary Monfre*	620 Cardinal Ln, Hartland WI 53029	262-369-5000	R	6*	<.1
23	Arista Tubes Inc—*Jeremy Paul*	201 Stinson Dr, Danville VA 24540	434-793-0660	R	5*	.1
24	Grayline Inc—*Milton Kuyers*	2101 Airport Rd, Waukesha WI 53188	262-542-4300	R	5*	.1
25	Ark-Plastics Products Inc—*Nueboch Vandermast*	PO Box 340, Flippin AR 72634	870-453-2343	R	5*	<.1
26	Kilder Corp—*John Sabatino*	7 Executive Park Dr, North Billerica MA 01862	978-663-8800	R	5*	<.1
27	C-K Plastics Inc—*Dianne Chitwood*	4530 Fyler Ave, Saint Louis MO 63116	314-353-0200	R	4*	<.1
28	Tiger Hawk Profiles—*Brad Buechler*	2803 W Grimes Ave, Fairfield IA 52556	641-472-6277	R	4*	<.1
29	Universal Plastics Inc—*William Brunelle*	7530 Tyler Blvd, Mentor OH 44060	440-942-7510	R	4*	<.1
30	Absolute Custom Extrusions Inc—*Barbara Cupertino*	3868 N Fratney St, Milwaukee WI 53212	414-332-8133	R	4*	<.1
31	Ber Plastic Corp—*Bernard Ewasko*	PO Box 2, Riverdale NJ 07457	973-839-2100	R	3*	<.1
32	Specialty Manufacturing Of Indiana Inc—*John Callis*	15412 Hwy 62, Charlestown IN 47111	812-256-4633	R	3*	<.1
33	Layman Plastics Corp—*C Layman*	1127 Tar Heel Rd, Charlotte NC 28208	704-394-1357	R	3*	<.1
34	Baumbach Engineering Company Inc—*Greg Baumbach*	640 National Ave, Mountain View CA 94043	650-968-0898	R	2*	<.1
35	Polymerex Medical Corp—*Yan-Ho Shu*	7358 Trade St, San Diego CA 92121	858-695-0765	R	2*	<.1
36	Great Lakes Plastics Company Inc—*Thomas Barzycki*	2371 Broadway St, Buffalo NY 14212	716-896-3100	R	2*	<.1
37	Certified Thermoplastics Inc—*Robert Duncan*	26381 Ferry Ct, Santa Clarita CA 91350	661-222-3006	R	2*	<.1
38	Norwe Inc—*Peter Weiner*	PO Box 2511, Canton OH 44720	330-497-8113	R	<1*	<.1

TOTALS: SIC 3082 Unsupported Plastics Profile Shapes
Companies: 38   473   2.3

3083 Laminated Plastics Plate & Sheet

Rank	Company Name—*Executive Officer*	Address, City, State, Zip	Phone	Type	Fin	Empls
1	Advanced Drainage Systems Inc—*Joseph Chlapaty*	PO Box 3000, Hilliard OH 43026	614-658-0050	R	1,200	4.0
2	Spartech Corp—*Victoria M Holt*	120 S Central Ave Ste, Clayton MO 63105	314-721-4242	P	1,102	2.5
3	Formica Corp—*Frank A Riddick III*	10155 Reading Rd, Cincinnati OH 45241		R	750	.4
4	General Binding Corp Film Products Div—*David Terhune*	775 Belden Ave, Addison IL 60101	630-543-7100	D	403*	1.0
5	STR Holdings Inc—*Dennis L Jilot*	1699 King St Ste 400, Enfield CT 06082	860-758-7300	P	372	2.2
6	Asahi Thermofil Inc	535 Madison Ave 33rd F, New York NY 10022	212-371-9900	S	347*	<.1
7	Nyloncraft Inc—*James M Krzwzenski*	616 W McKinley Ave, Mishawaka IN 46545	574-256-1521	S	273*	.7
8	Kloeckner Pentaplast of America Inc—*Michael F Tubridy*	PO Box 500, Gordonsville VA 22942	540-832-3600	S	237*	1.0
9	Creative Forming Inc—*Glen Yurjevich* Spartech Corp	PO Box 128, Ripon WI 54971	920-748-7285	S	221	.1
10	Pioneer Plastics Corp (Auburn Maine)—*Joe Deambrosio*	PO Box 1014, Auburn ME 04211	207-784-9111	S	202*	.5
11	Bunzl Extrusion	2500 North Winds Pkwy, Atlanta GA 30339	404-564-8560	D	150*	.9
12	Curwood Inc—*Thomaz Gruber*	PO Box 2968, Oshkosh WI 54904	920-303-7300	S	134*	1.9
13	Northern Contours Inc—*Mike Rone*	1355 Mendota Heights R, Saint Paul MN 55120	218-736-2973	R	50*	.5
14	Nelco Products Inc—*Margaret M Kendrick*	1411 E Orangethorpe Av, Fullerton CA 92831	714-879-4293	S	47*	.5
15	Hartson-Kennedy Cabinet Top Company Inc—*William Kennedy*	PO Box 3095, Marion IN 46953	765-668-8144	R	37*	.6
16	Lawson Mardon Thermaplate Corp—*Pete Mathias*	3033 E 16th St, Russellville AR 72802	479-880-8077	R	32*	.2
17	Baw Plastics Inc—*James Slovonic*	2148 Century Dr, Jefferson Hills PA 15025	412-384-3100	R	26*	.2
18	CUE Inc—*Joseph Scaletta*	11 Leonberg Rd, Cranberry Township PA 16066	724-772-5225	R	21*	.1
19	Mesa Fully Formed Inc—*Larry Cassaday*	1111 S Sirrine, Mesa AZ 85210	480-834-9331	R	19*	.4
20	Rotuba Extruders Inc—*Adam Bell*	1401 S Park Ave, Linden NJ 07036	908-486-1000	R	18*	.1
21	Bixby International Corp—*Daniel Rocconi*	1 Preble Rd, Newburyport MA 01950	978-462-4100	R	17*	.1
22	Composite Technologies of America—*Ron Cozean*	1331 S Chilicothe Rd, Aurora OH 44202	330-562-5201	R	15*	.1
23	Lamsco West Inc—*Gladden Baldwin*	PO Box 802050, Santa Clarita CA 91380	661-295-8620	S	15*	.1
24	Ameri-Kart Corp Ohio Div—*Debra Riser*	425 S Countyline St, Fostoria OH 44830	419-435-1811	D	15	.1
25	Enduris Extrusions Inc—*John Polidan*	7167 Old Kings Rd, Jacksonville FL 32219	904-378-1884	R	13*	.1
26	Betts USA Inc—*Thomas Lefevre*	PO Box 668, Florence KY 41022	859-342-8900	R	13*	.1
27	Maccourt Products Inc—*F Miner*	4881 Ironton St, Denver CO 80239	303-373-5411	R	13*	.1
28	Tpi Composites Inc—*Steven Lockard*	8501 N Scottsdale Rd, Scottsdale AZ 85253	480-305-8910	R	13*	.1
29	Flex Products LLC—*John Vigorigo*	PO Box 188, Carlstadt NJ 07072	201-933-3030	R	13*	.1
30	Plastics Research Corp—*Gene Gregory*	1400 S Campus Ave, Ontario CA 91761	909-391-2006	R	12*	.1
31	Oerlikon Optics USA Inc—*Mike Cusier*	16080 Table Mountain P, Golden CO 80403	303-273-9700	S	12*	.1
32	Anatomical Chart Co—*Jay Lippincott*	8221 Kimball Ave, Skokie IL 60076	847-679-4700	D	12	.1
33	General Plastics and Composites LP—*David Walstad*	5727 Ledbetter St, Houston TX 77087	713-644-1449	R	12*	.1
34	Panolam Industries International Inc—*Robert Muller*	20 Progress Dr, Shelton CT 06484	203-925-1556	R	12*	.1
35	Fiber Tech Industries Inc—*Harris Armstrong*	2000 Kenskill Ave, Wshngtn Ct Hs OH 43160	740-335-9400	R	12*	.1
36	Adept Corp—*David Williamson*	4601 N Susquehanna Trl, York PA 17406	717-266-3606	R	11*	.1
37	Royson's Corp—*Roy Ritchie*	40 Vanderhoof Ave, Rockaway NJ 07866	973-625-5570	R	11*	.1
38	South Tech Plastics Inc—*William Cohn*	PO Box 12705, New Bern NC 28561	252-638-4005	R	10*	.1
39	Plitek LLC—*Karl Hoffman*	69 Rawls Rd, Des Plaines IL 60018	847-827-6680	R	10*	.1
40	American Acrylic Corp—*Tom Ziegler*	400 Sheffield Ave, West Babylon NY 11704	631-422-2200	R	10*	<.1
41	Magee Plastics Co—*Marylou Magee*	303 Brush Creek Rd, Warrendale PA 15086	724-776-2220	R	10*	.1
42	Bruewer Woodwork Manufacturing Co—*Ralph Bruewer*	10000 Cilley Rd, Cleves OH 45002	513-353-3505	R	9*	.1
43	Pilgrim Badge and Label Corp—*Mark Abraham*	PO Box 317, Brockton MA 02303	508-436-6300	R	9*	.1
44	Bailey-Parks Urethane Inc—*Jeffrey Bailey*	184 Gilbert Ave, Memphis TN 38106	901-774-7930	R	8*	.1
45	Pacific Plastic Technology Inc—*Robert Sawyer*	9555 Hyssop Dr, Rancho Cucamonga CA 91730	909-987-4200	R	8*	.1
46	Atlas Fibre Co—*Mark Grusin*	3721 Chase Ave, Skokie IL 60076	847-674-1234	R	7*	.1
47	Southern Coating and Name Plates Inc—*Mark Osborne*	6200 Getty Dr, North Little Rock AR 72117	501-834-0100	R	7*	.1
48	Metplas Inc—*Russell Finsness*	3 Acee Dr, Natrona Heights PA 15065	724-295-1900	R	7*	.1
49	Tape Technologies Inc—*Arthur Wagner*	PO Box 56, Green Cove Springs FL 32043	904-284-0284	R	6*	<.1
50	Polyply Composites LLC—*Barry Lewellyn*	1540 Marion Ave, Grand Haven MI 49417	616-842-6330	R	6*	<.1
51	Repsco Inc—*Paul Bennett*	2950 Arkins Ct, Denver CO 80216	303-294-0364	R	6*	<.1
52	Sunrise Fiberglass Corp—*Byron Rieck*	PO Box 606, Wyoming MN 55092	651-462-5313	R	6*	<.1
53	Neptune Tech Services Inc—*Joseph Rocchi*	11657 Central Pkwy Ste, Jacksonville FL 32224	904-646-2700	R	6*	<.1

Note: An asterisk (*) indicates an estimated financial figure. The company type code used is as follows: R = Private, P = Public, S = Private Subsidiary, B = Public Subsidiary, D = Division, J = Joint Venture, I = Investment Fund.

COMPANY RANKINGS BY SALES WITHIN 4-DIGIT SIC

Rank	Company Name—Executive Officer	Address, City, State, Zip	Phone	Type	Fin	Empls
54	Panelgraphic Corp—Jane Ryan	PO Box 1265, Caldwell NJ 07007	973-227-1500	R	5*	<.1
55	Audioplex Technology Inc—Nancy Ingham	PO Box 440, Melvin Village NH 03850	603-544-8601	R	5*	<.1
56	Flex-Tech Hose and Tubing Inc—David Flint	1100 Civic Central Loo, San Marcos TX 78666	512-396-2667	R	5*	<.1
57	Advanced Displays In Plastic Inc—Diane Sullivan	500 N Raddant Rd, Batavia IL 60510	630-761-1711	R	5*	<.1
58	U S Plastics Inc—Wallace Norman	PO Box 152, Houston MS 38851	662-456-3726	R	4*	<.1
59	Swiss Productions Inc—Kenneth Putman	2801 Golf Course Dr, Ventura CA 93003	805-654-8525	R	4*	<.1
60	Alcat Inc—James Edwards	116 W Main St, Milford CT 06460	203-878-0648	R	4*	<.1
61	Custom Profiles Inc—Henry Sheffield	PO Box 279, Fitzgerald GA 31750	229-423-2929	R	4*	<.1
62	Dikeman Laminating Corp—Thomas Snyder	181 Sargeant Ave, Clifton NJ 07013	973-473-5696	R	4*	<.1
63	Ptm and W Industries Inc—Charles Owen	10640 Painter Ave, Santa Fe Springs CA 90670	562-946-4511	R	4*	<.1
64	Criterion Technology Inc—Christopher Mulvey	101 Mcintosh Pkwy, Thomaston GA 30286	706-647-5082	R	4*	<.1
65	Plastifab Inc—Rick Donnelly	1425 Palomares St, La Verne CA 91750	909-596-1927	R	4*	<.1
66	Proske Plastic Products Inc—Chester Walker	PO Box 231008, Houston TX 77223	713-926-9941	R	4*	<.1
67	Norva Plastics Inc—Howard Everton	PO Box 6226, Norfolk VA 23508	757-622-9281	R	4*	<.1
68	Franklin Fibre-Lamitex Corp—James Vachris	PO Box 1768, Wilmington DE 19899	302-652-3621	R	3*	<.1
69	Clear Vue Inc—David Desaulniers	905 Delaware St, Safety Harbor FL 34695	727-726-5386	R	3*	<.1
70	Patrick Custom Vinyl Industries—Todd Cleveland	107 W Franklin St, Elkhart IN 46516	574-294-7511	D	3*	<.1
71	Precision Trim Inc—John Cherney	PO Box 644, Boaz AL 35957	256-593-2346	R	3*	<.1
72	Port City Cabinet Works Inc—Frank Hvizdos	PO Box 15194, Houston TX 77220	713-673-7272	R	3*	<.1
73	International Laminating Corp—Raymond Horan	1712 Springfield St, Dayton OH 45403	937-254-8181	R	3*	<.1
74	Templex Inc—Chris Jones	PO Box 5648, High Point NC 27262	336-472-5933	R	3*	<.1
75	C-Thru Products Inc—Hilda Needleman	102 Sylvania Ave, Folsom PA 19033	610-586-1130	R	3*	<.1
76	Rulersmith Inc—Margaret Schafer	PO Box 253, Burlington WA 98233	360-707-2828	R	3*	<.1
77	Williams R Manufacturing Inc—Robert Williams	235 Industrial Rd, Butler KY 41006	859-472-2177	R	3*	<.1
78	Phillips Brothers Plastics Inc—James Phillips	17831 S Western Ave, Gardena CA 90248	310-532-8020	R	2*	<.1
79	D J Plastics Inc—Daniel Spence	PO Box 337, Folsom CA 95763	916-351-0161	R	2*	<.1
80	Industrial Molded Plastics Inc—Kelly Luli	PO Box 726, Kent OH 44240	330-673-1464	R	2*	<.1
81	Fax Plastics Inc—Francesco Dorigo	1205 Activity Dr, Vista CA 92081	760-599-6030	R	2*	<.1
82	Pro-Tect Computer Products Inc—Gil Workman	PO Box 1002, Centerville UT 84014	801-295-7739	R	2*	<.1
83	Credit Card Systems Inc—Peter Lazzari	180 Shepard Ave, Wheeling IL 60090	847-459-8320	R	2*	<.1
84	Protex Inc—Carol Botsolas	10500 47th St N, Clearwater FL 33762	727-573-4665	R	1*	<.1
85	World Manufacturing Inc—Michael Robinson	350 Fischer Ave Ste B, Costa Mesa CA 92626	714-662-3539	R	1*	<.1
86	Cross Industries Inc—John Lange	PO Box 344, Lilburn GA 30048	770-300-0002	R	1*	<.1
87	Mayon Plastics Inc—Ray Johnson	11595 K Tel Dr, Hopkins MN 55343	952-935-2187	R	1*	<.1
88	Ecomass Technologies—Robert Durkee	4101 Parkstone Heights, Austin TX 78746	512-306-0020	R	1*	<.1
89	Suncoast Identification Technologies Inc—Frank Savage	13300 S Cleveland Ave, Fort Myers FL 33907	239-277-9922	R	1*	<.1

TOTALS: SIC 3083 Laminated Plastics Plate & Sheet
Companies: 89   6,089   20.8

3084 Plastics Pipe

Rank	Company Name—Executive Officer	Address, City, State, Zip	Phone	Type	Fin	Empls
1	JM Eagle Company Inc—Walter W Wang	5200 W Century Blvd, Los Angeles CA 90045	973-535-1633	R	668*	.1
2	Varistar Corp—John Erickson	PO Box 496, Fergus Falls MN 56538	218-739-8200	S	582*	1.8
3	Sunburst Shutters Corp—Dix Jarman	4094 Ponderosa Way, Las Vegas NV 89118	702-870-4488	R	325*	.7
4	National Pipe and Plastics Inc—David Culbertson	3421 Old Vestal Rd, Vestal NY 13850	607-729-9381	R	256*	.3
5	Charlotte Pipe and Foundry Co—Roddey Dowd	PO Box 35430, Charlotte NC 28235	704-372-5030	R	141*	1.5
6	Georg Fischer LLC—Yves Serra	2882 Dow Ave, Tustin CA 92780	714-731-8800	D	82*	.1
7	Hancor Inc—Steven Anderson	PO Box 1047, Findlay OH 45839	419-422-6521	R	75*	1.0
8	Pipelife Jet Stream Inc—Alain Storet	PO Box 190, Siloam Springs AR 72761	479-524-5151	S	74*	.1
9	Silver-Line Plastics Corp—Ricky Silver	900 Riverside Dr, Asheville NC 28804	828-252-8755	R	72*	.2
10	Ameron Fiberglass Composite Pipe Div—Conway Beasley	9720 Cypresswood Rm 32, Houston TX 77070	832-912-8282	D	57*	.3
11	Cantex Inc—Hisayoshi Uno	301 Commerce St Ste 27, Fort Worth TX 76102	817-215-7000	R	50*	.7
12	Lamson Home Products—John B Schalze	25701 Science Park Dr, Cleveland OH 44122	216-464-3400	D	46*	.3
13	Accord Industries LLC—William Weir	4001 Forsyth Rd, Winter Park FL 32792	407-671-5200	S	40*	.1
14	Ershigs Inc—Eric Schumacher	PO Box 1707, Bellingham WA 98227	360-733-2620	R	32*	.3
15	Diamond Plastics Corp—John Britton	PO Box 1608, Grand Island NE 68802	308-384-4400	R	31*	.5
16	W Flying Plastics Inc—Doug Morris	PO Box 759, Glenville WV 26351	304-462-5779	R	29*	.1
17	WL Plastics Corp—Melissa Richardson	5880 Enterprise Dr Ste, Casper WY 82609	307-237-3261	R	28*	.2
18	Cresline Plastic Pipe Company Inc—Richard Schroeder	600 N Cross Pointe Blv, Evansville IN 47715	812-428-9300	R	27*	.4
19	Non Metallic Resources Inc—David Webster	PO Box 81303, Mobile AL 36689	251-633-3303	R	16*	.1
20	Vinyltech Corp—Steve Laskey Varistar Corp	201 S 61st Ave, Phoenix AZ 85043	602-233-0071	S	14*	.1
21	Conley Corp—Karen Greene	2795 E 91st St, Tulsa OK 74137	918-299-5051	R	14*	.1
22	NA Petroflex Ltd—Mitchell Shauf	PO Box 1356, Gainesville TX 76241	940-668-7283	R	13*	.1
23	Vanguard Industries Inc—John Fraser	831 N Vanguard St, Mcpherson KS 67460	620-241-6369	R	13*	.2
24	Endot Industries Inc—Jennifer Marin	60 Green Pond Rd, Rockaway NJ 07866	973-625-8500	R	11*	.1
25	Beetle Plastics LLC—Frank Knight	PO Box 1569, Ardmore OK 73402	580-389-5421	R	11*	<.1
26	Centennial Plastics Inc—G Konen	PO Box 329, Hastings NE 68902	402-462-2227	R	10*	.1
27	Sanderson Pipe Corp—Barry King	PO Box 700, Sanderson FL 32087	904-275-2833	R	10*	.1
28	Baughman Tile Company Inc—Gene Baughman	8516 Rr 137, Paulding OH 45879	419-399-3160	R	10*	.1
29	Rocky Mountain Colby Pipe Co—Steve Foote	5125 Race Ct Ste B, Denver CO 80216	303-295-3557	R	10*	<.1
30	Interstate Plastic Inc—Joyce Dougall	PO Box 398, Post Falls ID 83877	208-773-4538	R	10*	<.1
31	Crumpler Plastic Pipe Inc—John Crumpler	PO Box 2068, Roseboro NC 28382	910-525-4046	R	9*	.1
32	ISCO Industries LLC—James J Kirchdorfer	PO Box 4545, Louisville KY 40204	502-583-6591	R	9*	<.1
33	Sunbelt Innovative Plastics Inc—Linda Cousin	PO Box 5396, Slidell LA 70469	985-641-5660	R	8*	.1
34	Heritage Plastics South Inc—Charles Mccort	5128 W Hanna Ave, Tampa FL 33634	813-884-2525	R	8*	.1
35	Total Containment Inc—John R Wright Jr	10887 Portal Dr, Los Alamitos CA 90720	714-821-6570	R	8*	<.1
36	Popp Cement Tile Products Inc—Richard Popp	300 N Lilas Dr, Appleton WI 54914	920-734-2724	R	8*	.1
37	Industrial Fiberglass Specialties Inc—Theodore Morton	521 Kiser St, Dayton OH 45404	937-222-9000	R	7*	.1
38	Ocp Inc—Barry Ripper	PO Box 385, Titusville PA 16354	814-827-3661	R	7*	.1
39	Amalga Composites Inc—John De Luca	10600 W Mitchell St, Milwaukee WI 53214	414-453-9555	R	6*	.1
40	American Protectors Inc—C Seely	615 109th St, Arlington TX 76011	817-649-8843	R	6*	.1
41	Vinylplex Inc—G Baker	1800 E Atkinson Ave, Pittsburg KS 66762	620-231-8290	R	6*	<.1
42	Resin Systems Inc—Joseph Thomas	1586 Swisco Rd, Sulphur LA 70665	337-625-4541	R	6*	<.1
43	Tolloti Plastic Pipe Inc—Theodore Tolloti	PO Box 508, New Philadelphia OH 44663	330-364-6627	R	6*	<.1
44	Samson Plastic Pipe Inc—Gregory Anderson	PO Box 325, Samson AL 36477	334-898-7124	R	5*	<.1
45	Plastics Resources Inc—Jeffrey Hoggan	PO Box 3700, Logan UT 84323	435-753-7458	R	5*	<.1
46	Trenchless Pipe Company Inc—Donald Giannetti	3410 Bronze Ct, Shasta Lake CA 96019	530-275-9400	R	4*	<.1
47	Appalachian Piping Products Inc—Richard Burke	1152 Wv Hwy 5 E, Glenville WV 26351	304-462-5751	R	3*	<.1
48	Co-Ex Pipe Co—Dale Waldron	PO Box 3370, Midland TX 79702	432-263-0206	R	3*	<.1

Rank	Company Name—*Executive Officer*	Address, City, State, Zip	Phone	Type	Fin	Empls
49	Fusibond Piping Systems Inc—*Richard Krause*	2615 Curtiss St, Downers Grove IL 60515	630-969-4488	R	2*	<.1

TOTALS: SIC 3084 Plastics Pipe
Companies: 49 — 2,874 — 10.2

3085 Plastics Bottles

Rank	Company Name—*Executive Officer*	Address, City, State, Zip	Phone	Type	Fin	Empls
1	Graham Packaging Holdings Co—*Mark S Burgess*	2401 Pleasant Valley R, York PA 17402	717-849-8500	P	2,513	8.3
2	Plastic Container Corp—*Ron Rhoades*	PO Box 438, Champaign IL 61824	217-352-2722	R	1,875*	.1
3	Plastipak Packaging Inc—*Richard Darr*	41605 Ann Arbor Rd, Plymouth MI 48170	734-455-3600	S	839*	4.0
4	Consolidated Container Company LLC—*Jeffrey M Greene*	3101 Towercreek Pkwy S, Atlanta GA 30339	678-742-4600	R	706*	3.4
5	Constar International LLC—*Grant H Beard*	1100 Northbrook Dr Ste, Trevose PA 19053	215-552-3700	R	635	1.2
6	Southeastern Container Inc—*Tom Francis*	PO Box 909, Enka NC 28728	828-667-0101	R	500*	.8
7	Pretium Packaging LLC—*George Abd*	15450 S Outer Forty Dr, Chesterfield MO 63017	314-727-8200	S	144*	.8
8	Alpha Plastics Inc—*David Spence*	1555 Page Industrial B, Saint Louis MO 63132	314-427-4300	R	116*	.5
9	Luv N' Care Ltd—*Joseph Hakim*	PO Box 6050, Monroe LA 71211	318-388-4916	R	74*	.4
10	Encon Inc—*William Gaiser*	PO Box 13418, Dayton OH 45413	937-898-2603	R	59*	.1
11	IN ZONE Brands Inc—*Jim Scott*	2251 Corporate Plz Pky, Smyrna GA 30080	678-718-2000	R	43*	.1
12	Ring Container Technologies Inc—*Benjamin Livingston*	1 Industrial Park, Oakland TN 38060	901-466-7446	R	40*	.6
13	Poly-Tainer Inc—*Paul Strong*	450 W Los Angeles Ave, Simi Valley CA 93065	805-526-3424	R	39*	.3
14	Alpla Inc—*Helmut Scheffknecht*	289 Hwy 155 S, Mcdonough GA 30253	770-914-1407	S	35*	.3
15	Resilux America LLC—*Henry Carter*	265 John B Brooks Rd, Pendergrass GA 30567	706-693-7110	R	31*	.1
16	Blitz USA Inc—*John Elmburg*	404 26th Ave Nw, Miami OK 74354	918-540-1515	R	22*	.4
17	Brent River Packaging Corp—*Thomas Dolan*	208 Cougar Ct, Hillsborough NJ 08844	908-722-6021	R	22*	.1
18	Hillside Plastics Inc—*Peter Haas*	PO Box 490, Turners Falls MA 01376	413-863-2222	R	20*	.1
19	Schoeneck Containers Inc—*Paul Schoeneck*	2160 S 170th St, New Berlin WI 53151	262-786-9360	R	16*	.1
20	Altira Inc—*Ramon Poo*	3225 Nw 112th St, Miami FL 33167	305-687-8074	R	15*	.1
21	Plastic Technologies Of Vermont Inc—*Eugene Torvend*	PO Box 234, Shelburne VT 05482	802-658-6588	R	15*	.1
22	Plastic Industries Inc—*Nicholas Rende*	22324 Temescal Canyon, Corona CA 92883	951-277-4800	R	14*	.1
23	Kerr Group Inc	1706 Hempstead Rd, Lancaster PA 17601	717-299-6511	S	14*	.1
24	Suscon Inc—*Anthony Cenimo*	600 Railway St Unit 2, Williamsport PA 17701	570-326-2003	R	13*	.1
25	Apex Plastics Inc—*Sam Featherstone*	570 S Main St, Brookfield MO 64628	660-258-7283	R	12*	.1
26	Alpha Packaging (Ypsilanti Michigan)—*Dave Spence*	1236 Watson St, Ypsilanti MI 48198	734-481-1373	S	12*	.1
27	Colts Plastics Inc—*Charles Bentley*	PO Box 429, Dayville CT 06241	860-774-2301	R	11*	.2
28	Advance Plastics Unlimited Inc—*Abraham Kolker*	905 W 19th St, Hialeah FL 33010	305-885-6266	R	10*	.1
29	Midland Manufacturing Company Inc—*A Vriezelaar*	PO Box 899, Monroe IA 50170	641-259-2625	R	9*	.1
30	Weber International Packaging Company LLC—*Judith Lefebvre*	318 Cornelia St, Plattsburgh NY 12901	518-561-0202	R	8*	.1
31	Thomas Plastics Inc—*Roy Thomas*	4121 Stadium Dr, Fort Worth TX 76133	817-921-5275	R	8*	.1
32	Cardwell Containers Inc—*Ilsia Cardwell*	835 Herbert Rd, Cordova TN 38018	901-756-1474	R	7*	<.1
33	Abbott Industries Inc (Paterson New Jersey)—*Harold Sheck*	1 Morris St Ste 11, Paterson NJ 07501	973-345-1116	R	7*	<.1
34	Prime Industries LLP—*Debbie Fojtik*	PO Box 5, Schulenburg TX 78956	979-743-6577	R	6*	.1
35	Fulcrum Incorporated Of Minneapolis—*Samir Mehta*	3180 Spruce St, Saint Paul MN 55117	651-481-8601	R	6*	<.1
36	Triple Dot Corp—*Tony Tsai*	3302 S Susan St, Santa Ana CA 92704	714-241-0888	R	5*	<.1
37	Midwest Container And Industrial Supply Co—*Kent Meentemeyer*	PO Box 277, Barnhart MO 63012	636-464-7100	R	5*	<.1
38	Springdale Specialty Plastics Inc—*Mark Sever*	PO Box 296, Creighton PA 15030	724-274-4144	R	5*	.1
39	Container Options Inc—*Patricia Deleon*	1493 E San Bernardino, San Bernardino CA 92408	909-478-0045	R	5*	<.1
40	RN Fink Manufacturing Co—*Eric Fink*	PO Box 245, Williamston MI 48895	517-655-4351	R	4*	<.1
41	Keystone Containers LLC—*Norman Carr*	4201 Pottsville Pke St, Reading PA 19605	610-921-9175	R	3*	<.1
42	Roffe Container Inc—*David Thomas*	1802 2nd Ave N, Moorhead MN 56560	218-233-5145	R	3*	<.1
43	Plasticos Arco Iris Of San Antonio Inc—*Sergio Ramirez*	2819 Wdclffe St 100-10, San Antonio TX 78230	210-308-6500	R	3*	<.1
44	M and H Plastics Inc—*Dan Kliska*	485 Brooke Rd, Winchester VA 22603	540-504-0030	R	3*	<.1
45	Vanguard Manufacturing Inc—*Richard Meyersburg*	6831 Ruppsville Rd, Allentown PA 18106	610-481-0655	R	3*	<.1
46	Shapes Of Plastic Inc—*Lee Walker*	PO Box 68605, Seattle WA 98168	253-572-9323	R	3*	<.1
47	PCP Inc—*William Spencer*	13462 Brooks Dr, Baldwin Park CA 91706	626-813-6166	R	2*	<.1
48	Universal Container Company LLC	11805 State Rd 54, Odessa FL 33556	727-376-0036	R	1*	<.1
49	Midwest Plastics Company Inc—*David Cavaness*	PO Box 381, Cherryvale KS 67335	620-336-3611	R	1*	<.1

TOTALS: SIC 3085 Plastics Bottles
Companies: 49 — 7,939 — 23.2

3086 Plastics Foam Products

Rank	Company Name—*Executive Officer*	Address, City, State, Zip	Phone	Type	Fin	Empls
1	Dart Container Corp—*Robert Dart*	500 Hogsback Rd, Mason MI 48854	517-676-3800	R	1,540	5.8
2	Carpenter Co—*Stanley F Pauley*	5016 Monument Ave, Richmond VA 23230	804-359-0800	R	1,457*	5.9
3	Plastics Management Corp—*Philip Kamins*	PO Box 1367, Sun Valley CA 91353	818-896-1101	R	729*	4.0
4	Lifoam Industries LLC—*John Cantlin*	235 Schilling Cir Ste, Hunt Valley MD 21031	410-889-1023	R	567*	.5
5	Tegrant Corp—*Ron Leach*	1401 Pleasant St, Dekalb IL 60115	815-756-8451	R	225*	1.8
6	Nu-Foam Products Inc—*Charles Moeller* Ohio Decorative Products Inc	PO Box 5648, Chattanooga TN 37406	423-698-6911	S	213*	1.2
7	Barrette Outdoor Living Inc—*Jan Lembregts*	3200 Rbert T Longway B, Flint MI 48506	810-235-0400	R	162*	2.5
8	Fxi Holdings Inc—*John Cowles*	1400 N Providence Rd S, Media PA 19063	610-744-2300	R	141*	2.0
9	UFP Technologies Inc—*R Jeffrey Bailly*	172 E Main St, Georgetown MA 01833	978-352-2200	P	121	.6
10	Free-Flow Packaging International Inc—*Joe Nezwek*	1090 Mills Way, Redwood City CA 94063	650-261-5300	R	100*	.3
11	Ohio Decorative Products Inc—*Charles Moeller*	PO Box 126, Spencerville OH 45887	419-647-4191	R	95*	1.2
12	Convenience Products Inc	866 Horan Dr, Fenton MO 63026	636-349-5855	S	75*	.2
13	Outlook Label Systems Inc—*Glen Yurjevich*	1180 American Dr, Neenah WI 54956	920-722-7999	S	74*	.2
14	Rogers Foam Corp—*David Marotta*	20 Vernon St Ste 1, Somerville MA 02145	617-623-3010	R	68*	.5
15	General Packaging Corp—*James W Brown*	PO Box 832630, Richardson TX 75083	972-234-5499	R	68*	.2
16	Houston Foam Plastics Inc—*K Kurtz*	PO Box 1615, Houston TX 77251	713-224-3484	R	55*	.3
17	G and T Industries Inc—*Roland Grit*	1001 76th St Sw, Byron Center MI 49315	616-452-8611	R	42*	.2
18	Concote Corp—*Robert Hanton*	PO Box 3553, Coppell TX 75019	214-956-0077	R	42*	.3
19	Anchor Packaging Inc—*Jeffrey Wolff*	13515 Barrett Pky Dr S, Ballwin MO 63021	314-822-7800	R	40*	.5
20	Foam Fabricators Inc—*Warren Florkiewicz*	8722 E San Alberto Dr, Scottsdale AZ 85258	480-607-7330	R	36*	.5
21	Sekisui Voltek LLC—*Rob Demarco*	100 Shepard St, Lawrence MA 01843	978-685-2557	R	34*	.3
22	Allied Aerofoam Products LLC—*Alan Rash*	216 Kelsey Ln, Tampa FL 33619	813-626-0090	R	30*	.2
23	International Business Communications Inc—*Norman Kay*	1981 Marcus Ave Ste C1, New Hyde Park NY 11042	516-352-4505	R	29*	.3
24	Efp Corp—*Bill Flint*	PO Box 2368, Elkhart IN 46515	574-295-4690	R	27*	.2
25	United Industries Inc—*Don Ferm*	PO Box 715, Bentonville IN 72712	479-273-2924	R	27*	<.1
26	Frpc Liquidating Inc—*Frank Nold*	PO Box 525, New Castle IN 47362	765-521-2000	R	25*	.2
27	Rempac LLC—*Steven Dunay*	370 W Passaic St, Rochelle Park NJ 07662	973-881-8880	R	25*	.3
28	Plymouth Foam Inc—*David Bolland*	PO Box 407, Plymouth WI 53073	920-893-0535	R	24*	.2
29	Duerr Packaging Company Inc—*Samuel Duerr*	892 Steubenville Pke, Burgettstown PA 15021	724-947-1234	R	24*	.1

Note: An asterisk (*) indicates an estimated financial figure. The company type code used is as follows: R = Private, P = Public, S = Private Subsidiary, B = Public Subsidiary, D = Division, J = Joint Venture, I = Investment Fund.

COMPANY RANKINGS BY SALES WITHIN 4-DIGIT SIC

Rank	Company Name—Executive Officer	Address, City, State, Zip	Phone	Type	Fin	Empls
30	Eyelematic Manufacturing Company Inc—Henry Seebach	1 Seemar Rd, Watertown CT 06795	860-274-6791	R	24*	.4
31	Pak-Lite Inc—Tim LeClair Le Clair Industries Inc	PO Box 279, Grenada MS 38902	662-226-8183	D	23*	<.1
32	Foam Design Inc—Douglas Gradek	444 Transport Ct, Lexington KY 40511	859-231-7006	R	20*	.1
33	Leggett-Southwest Carpet—Felix E Wright	1050 S Dupont Ave, Ontario CA 91761	909-937-1010	R	20*	<.1
34	Concept Industries Inc—Shawn Eshragh	4950 Kraft Ave Se, Grand Rapids MI 49512	616-554-9000	R	20*	.2
35	Henry Products Inc—James Owen	302 S 23rd Ave, Phoenix AZ 85009	602-253-3191	R	18*	<.1
36	Texas Recreation Corp—Robert Scheurer	PO Box 539, Wichita Falls TX 76307	940-322-4463	R	18*	.2
37	Western Industries Corp—James Robertson	4249 Sw 29th St, Oklahoma City OK 73119	405-419-3100	R	17*	.1
38	General Pattern Company Inc—Dennis Reiland	3075 84th Ln Ne, Minneapolis MN 55449	763-780-3518	R	16*	.1
39	Falcon Foam—Lana Cooper	911 Industrial Dr, Perryville MO 63775	573-547-8388	D	16*	.1
40	Teach Enterprises Inc—Thomas Teach	PO Box 2207, Elkhart IN 46515	574-293-5547	R	16*	.2
41	General Plastics Manufacturing Co—Henry Schatz	PO Box 9097, Tacoma WA 98490	253-473-5000	R	15*	.1
42	Airtex Consumer Product Div—Lyman Smith	150 Industrial Park Rd, Cokato MN 55321		D	15*	.2
43	Woodbridge Foam Fabricating Inc—Robert Magee	1120 Judd Rd, Chattanooga TN 37406	423-622-8326	R	15*	.1
44	Foam Molders And Specialties—Daniel Doke	11110 Business Cir, Cerritos CA 90703	562-924-9173	R	14*	.1
45	Ward Process Inc—Russell Moody	311 Hopping Brook Rd, Holliston MA 01746	508-429-1165	R	14*	.1
46	Drew Foam Companies Inc—William Givens	1093 Hwy 278 E, Monticello AR 71655	870-367-6245	R	14*	.2
47	Minnesota Diversified Products Inc—Benjamin Sachs	PO Box 44, Rockford MN 55373	763-477-5854	R	14*	.1
48	Gdc Inc—Loretta Miller	PO Box 98, Goshen IN 46527	574-533-3128	R	13*	.1
49	Le Clair Industries Inc—Tim Clair	PO Box 279, Grenada MS 38902	662-226-8075	R	12*	.1
50	Advanced Materials Group Inc—Richard Brutocao	2364 Merritt Dr Ste A, Garland TX 75041	469-246-4100	R	12	.1
51	Gaska Tape Inc—Jack Smith	PO Box 1968, Elkhart IN 46515	574-294-5431	R	12*	.1
52	Carcoustics USA Inc—Larry Carlson	1400 Durant Dr, Howell MI 48843	517-548-6700	R	12*	.1
53	Form Plastics Co—James Pappas	3825 Stern Ave, Saint Charles IL 60174	630-443-1400	R	12*	.1
54	Orcon Industries Corp—Bruce Olson	8715 Lake Rd, Le Roy NY 14482	585-768-7000	R	11*	.1
55	Classic Packaging Co—Geraldine Pilla	PO Box 17109, Winston Salem NC 27116	336-922-4224	R	11*	.1
56	American Converters Inc—Steve Pasell	5360 Main St Ne, Minneapolis MN 55421	763-574-1044	R	11*	.1
57	Soundcoat Company Inc—Louis Nenninger	1 Burt Dr, Deer Park NY 11729	631-242-2200	R	11*	.1
58	Master Containers Inc—Clayton Lyons	200 Brickstone Sq Ste, Andover MA 01810		S	10*	.1
59	Polyfoam Corp—Henry Coz	PO Box 906, Northbridge MA 01534	508-234-6323	R	10*	.1
60	Pinta Foamtec Inc—Mark Frederick	2601 49th Ave N Ste 40, Minneapolis MN 55430	612-355-4200	R	10*	.1
61	Hibco Plastics Inc—Mark Pavlansky	PO Box 157, Yadkinville NC 27055	336-463-2391	R	10*	.1
62	Fomo Products Inc—Stefan Miczka	PO Box 1078, Norton OH 44203	330-753-4585	R	9*	.1
63	Shelter Enterprises Inc—Jeffory Myers	PO Box 618, Cohoes NY 12047	518-237-4100	R	9*	.1
64	Fagerdala USA - Lompoc Inc—John Ballinger	1017 W Central Ave, Lompoc CA 93436	805-735-5205	R	9*	.1
65	Zim's Bagging Co—Harry Zimmerman	PO Box 455, Kenova WV 25530	304-486-5651	R	9*	.1
66	Imperial Foam and Insulation Manufacturing Co—Robert Ahrens	2360 Old Tomoka Rd W, Ormond Beach FL 32174	386-673-4177	R	9*	.1
67	Trelleborg Offshore Boston Inc—Brian Mcsharry	290 Forbes Blvd, Mansfield MA 02048	774-719-1400	R	9*	.1
68	Volk Packaging Corp—Douglas Volk	PO Box 1011, Biddeford ME 04005	207-282-6151	R	8*	.1
69	RADVA Corp—Luther I Dickens	PO Box 2900, Radford VA 24143	540-731-3700	P	8	.1
70	Quality Foam Packaging Inc—Noel Castellon	31855 Corydon St, Lake Elsinore CA 92530	951-245-4429	R	8*	.1
71	Advanced Thermal Products Inc—Timothy Thompson	17365 Daimler St, Irvine CA 92614	949-468-3620	R	8*	<.1
72	Infinity Packaging—James Donoho	3131 Fernbrook Ln Ste, Plymouth MN 55447		R	8*	<.1
73	Waddington North America Inc—Mike Evans	50 E Rivercenter Blvd, Covington KY 41011	859-292-8028	S	8*	<.1
74	Perry Foam Products Inc—Scott Kempin	PO Box 6419, Lafayette IN 47903	765-474-3404	R	8*	.1
75	Foamcraft Inc—Jim Hensley	PO Box 2901, Tupelo MS 38803	662-844-2414	R	8*	<.1
76	Technicon Industries Inc—Tyler Keeley	4412 Republic Ct Nw, Concord NC 28027	704-788-1131	R	8*	<.1
77	Pacific Allied Products Ltd—Mike Bilby	91-110 Kaomi Loop, Kapolei HI 96707	808-682-2038	R	8*	.1
78	Foamworks Inc—Rick Bolles	PO Box 5208, Cleveland TN 37320	423-559-0509	R	7*	.1
79	Solution First Inc—Timothy Toole	PO Box 468, La Fayette GA 30728	706-638-5678	R	7*	.1
80	Northern Products Co—John Carmody	11536 S Central Ave, Alsip IL 60803	708-597-8501	R	7*	.1
81	Orlando Products Inc—Joseph Orlando	2639 Merchant Dr, Baltimore MD 21230	410-525-1502	R	7*	.1
82	Carolina Foam Inc—Jim Sipe	PO Box 369, Claremont NC 28610	828-459-1036	R	7*	.1
83	Fagerdala-Paclite Inc—John Ballinger	1300 S Parker St, Marine City MI 48039	810-765-8888	R	7*	.1
84	Hi-Line Plastics Inc—Galen Foule	801 E Hwy 56, Olathe KS 66061	913-782-3535	R	7*	.1
85	Lelanite Corp—Richard Perry	PO Box 160, Webster MA 01570	508-943-1968	R	7*	<.1
86	Ideal Foam LLC—Shine Brown	PO Box 563, Pontotoc MS 38863	662-489-2264	R	7*	.1
87	Epc Inc—James Carroll	2180 Bennett Rd, Philadelphia PA 19116	215-464-1440	R	7*	.1
88	Star Plastic Design—Dana Maltun	25914 President Ave, Harbor City CA 90710	310-530-7119	R	7*	.1
89	Key Packaging Company Inc—Earl Smith	7350 15th St E, Sarasota FL 34243	941-355-2728	R	7*	.1
90	Ocean Blue Inc—Mehdi Abbas	494 Commercial Rd, San Bernardino CA 92408	909-478-9910	R	6*	<.1
91	Elliott Company Of Indianapolis Inc—Bryan Elliott	9200 Zionsville Rd, Indianapolis IN 46268	317-291-1213	R	6*	<.1
92	Madison Polymeric Engineering Inc—Walter Maguire	965 W Main St, Branford CT 06405	203-488-2261	R	6*	<.1
93	Cushioneer Inc—Andrew Swift	1651 Pleasant St, Dekalb IL 60115	815-748-5505	R	6*	.1
94	Barber Packaging Co—David Barber	300 Industrial Park Rd, Bangor MA 49013	269-427-7995	R	6*	<.1
95	Benchmark Foam Inc—Tom Devine	401 Pheasant Ridge Dr, Watertown SD 57201	605-886-8084	R	6*	.1
96	Mvs Fulfillment Services Inc—Carl Beede	209 Flat Roof Mill Rd, Swanzey NH 03446	603-357-9690	R	6*	.1
97	Bud Wil Inc—M Williams	1170 N Red Gum St, Anaheim CA 92806	714-630-1242	R	6*	<.1
98	Packaging Specialists Incorporated Southwest—Patrick Coveney	602 S 54th Ave, Phoenix AZ 85043	602-269-5000	R	5*	<.1
99	RNC Industries Inc—Lawrence Clark	3105 Sweetwater Rd Ste, Lawrenceville GA 30044	770-368-8453	R	5*	<.1
100	Polar Industries Inc—David Lewis	PO Box 7075, Prospect CT 06712		R	5*	<.1
101	American Foam Corp—Aram Manouelian	61 John St, Johnston RI 02919	401-944-4990	R	5*	<.1
102	Big Sky Insulations Inc—Brad Huempfner	PO Box 838, Belgrade MT 59714	406-388-4146	R	5*	<.1
103	Advanced Foam Inc—James Conley	1745 W 134th St, Gardena CA 90249	310-515-0617	R	5*	<.1
104	Davis Core and Pad Company Inc—Joel Davis	PO Box 408, Cave Spring GA 30124	706-777-3364	R	5*	<.1
105	Diversified Packaging Inc—David Hoyt	2221 S Anne St, Santa Ana CA 92704	714-850-9316	R	5*	<.1
106	MH Stallman Company Inc—James Stallman	292 Charles St, Providence RI 02904	401-331-5129	R	5*	<.1
107	Styrotech Inc—John Stoddart	8800 Wyoming Ave N, Minneapolis MN 55445	763-425-4001	R	5*	<.1
108	Cook Brothers Insulation Inc—Andy Cook	1405 Saint Louis Ave, Kansas City MO 64101	816-421-6300	R	5*	<.1
109	Foam Fair Industries Inc—Alan Memmo	PO Box 304, Clifton Heights PA 19018	610-622-4665	R	5*	<.1
110	Hendren Plastics Inc—Jim Hendren	1607 Hwy 72 Se, Gravette AR 72736	479-787-6222	R	5*	<.1
111	Insulation Corporation Of America—Thomas Higgins	2571 Mitchell Ave, Allentown PA 18103	610-791-4200	R	4*	.1
112	Dependable Plastics and Pattern Inc—Harry Marquez	4900 Fulton Dr, Fairfield CA 94534	707-863-4900	R	4*	.1
113	Confortaire Inc—Mike Plyler	2133 S Veterans Blvd, Tupelo MS 38804	662-842-2966	R	4*	<.1
114	Gilman Corp—Richard Gilman	PO Box 68, Gilman CT 06336	860-887-7080	R	4*	<.1
115	Special Design Products Inc—Nancy Evanichko	500 Industrial Mile Rd, Columbus OH 43228	614-272-6700	R	4*	<.1
116	Diversified Foam Inc—Brent Matthews	PO Box 1358, Yadkinville NC 27055	336-463-5512	R	4*	<.1
117	Del-Tec Packaging Associates Inc—Richard Lackey	PO Box 6879, Greenville SC 29606	864-288-7390	R	4*	<.1

Rank	Company Name—Executive Officer	Address, City, State, Zip	Phone	Type	Fin	Empls
118	Thermal Foams/Syracuse Inc—John Jeffery	2101 Kenmore Ave, Buffalo NY 14207	716-874-6474	R	4*	<.1
119	Modern Polymers Inc—W Hilliard	PO Box 398, Cherryville NC 28021	704-435-5825	R	4*	<.1
120	Fitzpak Inc—Andrew Fitzsimmons	110 Melrich Rd Ste 2, Cranbury NJ 08512	609-860-0095	R	4*	<.1
121	Atlas Foam Products Inc—Jeff Naples	12836 Arroyo St, Sylmar CA 91342	818-837-3626	R	4*	<.1
122	American Foam Products Inc—Charles Luck	753 Liberty St, Painesville OH 44077	440-352-3434	R	4*	<.1
123	Foam Concepts Inc—Mark Villamaino	PO Box 410, Uxbridge MA 01569	508-278-7255	R	4*	<.1
124	Alaco Of Mississippi Inc—Sheila Singleton	PO Box 284, Ripley MS 38663	662-837-4041	R	4*	<.1
125	Snow Craft Company Inc—Kirk Guyton	PO Box 829, New Hyde Park NY 11040	516-739-1399	R	4*	<.1
126	Piedmont Foam Inc—Bob Patton	PO Box 394, Conover NC 28613	828-465-4106	R	4*	<.1
127	Kilmer Wagner And Wise Paper Company Inc—Frederic Wise	12751 Monarch St, Garden Grove CA 92841	714-892-3380	R	4*	<.1
128	Jones Holt Enterprises Inc—Robert Jones	13715 Topper Cir, San Antonio TX 78233	210-657-5917	R	4*	<.1
129	Ade Inc—Lewis Lofgren	1430 E 130th St, Chicago IL 60633	773-646-3400	R	4*	<.1
130	Deep River Fabricators Inc—Roy Luckenbach	PO Box 100, Franklinville NC 27248	336-824-8881	R	3*	<.1
131	Insul-Board Inc—Richard Estock	PO Box 8103, Erie PA 16505	814-833-7400	R	3*	<.1
132	Magna Manufacturing Inc—Paul Owens	PO Box 279, Fort Walton Beach FL 32549	850-243-1112	R	3*	<.1
133	Essco Geometric Inc—Stanley Safron	7140 Wellington Ct, Saint Louis MO 63143	314-678-0540	R	3*	<.1
134	Dura Foam Inc—Antony Fontana	6302 59th Ave, Maspeth NY 11378	718-894-2488	R	3*	<.1
135	Accessible Products Co—Walter Plummer	2122 W 5th Pl, Tempe AZ 85281	480-967-8888	R	3*	.1
136	Polly Knapp Pig Inc—Kenneth Knapp	1209 Hardy St, Houston TX 77020	713-222-0146	R	3*	<.1
137	Cpd Industries Inc—Carlos Hurtado	4665 State St, Montclair CA 91763	909-465-5596	R	3*	<.1
138	Engineered Packaging Inc—James Stout	1350 E Saint Louis St, Springfield MO 65802	417-831-0204	R	3*	<.1
139	Northwest Foam Products Inc—James Bartholome	2390 Rostron Cir, Twin Falls ID 83301	208-734-7426	R	3*	<.1
140	Foam Tec Products Inc—Bryant Rivard	410 Horizon Dr Ste 300, Suwanee GA 30024	678-380-6000	R	3*	<.1
141	Component Fabricators Inc—Ronald Bundy	PO Box 7628, High Point NC 27264	336-434-3316	R	3*	<.1
142	Insul-Bead Corp—Brent Cannon	PO Box 148, Gravette AR 72736	479-787-5991	R	3*	<.1
143	Tri-State Insulation Co—Vernon Joy	1003 Valley View Dr, Vermillion SD 57069	605-624-6405	R	3*	<.1
144	TruProtect—Mike McDonald	7012 Cedar, Lubbock TX 79404	806-281-9698	R	3*	<.1
145	Paragon Custom Plastics Inc—Mark Troder	PO Box 127, Bryan OH 43506	419-636-6060	R	3*	<.1
146	Ludwig Inc—Mark Ludwig	PO Box 450, Waldo AR 71770	870-693-5565	R	3*	<.1
147	Scottdel Cushion LLC	400 Church St, Swanton OH 43558	419-825-2341	R	3*	<.1
148	Tecnifoam Inc—Roger Funk	4400 Ball Rd Ne, Circle Pines MN 55014	763-537-7000	R	3*	<.1
149	Zebco Industries Inc—Kevin Stalter	211 N Columbus St, Lancaster OH 43130	740-654-4510	R	3*	<.1
150	Packaging Strategies Inc—Jeffrey Bell	PO Box 178, Phoenix MD 21131	410-547-7877	R	2*	<.1
151	Pierce Foam And Supply Inc—Calvin Pierce	PO Box 694, Booneville MS 38829	662-728-8070	R	2*	<.1
152	Grantco Manufacturing Inc—Patrick Grant	PO Box 104, Orland IN 46776	260-829-1155	R	2*	<.1
153	Texas Foam Inc—Thomas Forrest	1278 Hwy 71 W, Bastrop TX 78602	512-581-7500	R	2*	<.1
154	Wayne Manufacturing Industries LLC	13 Prescott Rd, Brentwood NH 03833	978-416-0899	R	2*	<.1
155	Hydrofera LLC	322 Main St, Willimantic CT 06226	860-456-0677	R	2*	<.1
156	Coast Packaging Inc—Barbara Fisler	PO Box 1459, Huntington Beach CA 92647	714-892-3626	R	2*	<.1
157	Tempo Plastic Co—Douglas Rogers	PO Box 431, Goshen CA 93227	559-651-7711	R	2*	<.1
158	Topper Plastics Inc—Patricia Beery	461 E Front St, Covina CA 91723	626-331-0561	R	2*	<.1
159	Foam Plastic Specialties Inc—Wayne Perry	1421 S Mcclintock Dr, Tempe AZ 85281	480-966-6889	R	2*	<.1
160	Gingerbread Trim Company Inc—Clif Campbell	PO Box 496200, Port Charlotte FL 33949	941-743-8556	R	2*	<.1
161	Lite-Form Technologies LLC—Sandy Boeshart	1950 W 29th St, South Sioux City NE 68776	402-241-4402	R	2*	<.1
162	Abi Packaging Inc—Roger Severson	1703 Union Rd, West Seneca NY 14224	716-677-2900	R	2*	<.1
163	Jetram Sales Inc—Charles Harris	PO Box 22109, Saint Louis MO 63116	636-326-3222	R	2*	<.1
164	Plasteel Corp—William Ohlsson	PO Box 555, Inkster MI 48141	313-562-5400	R	2*	<.1
165	Houston Foam Fabricators Inc—Lester Holder	1722 Hwy 8 E, Houston MS 38851	662-456-5875	R	2*	<.1
166	Inter Packing Inc—Jaime Cardenas	12315 Colony Ave, Chino CA 91710	909-465-5555	R	2*	<.1
167	Kidkusion Inc—Cindy Bowen	PO Box 1686, Washington NC 27889	252-946-7162	R	2*	<.1
168	Pedmic Converting Inc—William Mc Comb	PO Box 226, Croswell MI 48422	810-679-9600	R	2*	<.1
169	King And Company Inc—Bill Stone	PO Box 10, Clarksville AR 72830	479-754-6090	R	2*	<.1
170	Templock Enterprises LLC	1 N Calle Cesar Chavez, Santa Barbara CA 93103	805-962-3100	R	2*	<.1
171	Axion International Holdings Inc—Steve Silverman	180 South St Ste 104, New Providence NJ 07974	908-542-0888	P	2	<.1
172	Nu-Pak Solutions Inc—Herbert Bevelhymer	2850 Lincoln St, Norton Shores MI 49441	231-755-1662	R	1*	<.1
173	Kiva Container Corp—Claudia England	2700 E Regal Park Dr, Anaheim CA 92806	714-630-3850	R	1*	<.1
174	How-Mac Manufacturing Inc—Joel Howard	720 Puget Ave Ste A, Sedro Woolley WA 98284	360-855-2649	R	1*	<.1
175	Gladon Company Inc—John Haight	310 W Forest Hill Ave, Oak Creek WI 53154	414-766-2490	R	1*	<.1
176	Blue Feather Products Inc—Feather W King	165 Reiten Dr, Ashland OR 97520	541-482-5268	R	1*	<.1
177	Technifab Inc—John Cloud	1355 Chester Industria, Avon OH 44011	440-934-8324	R	1*	<.1
178	All Foam Products Co—Myrna Steinlauf	2546 Live Oak Ln, Buffalo Grove IL 60089	847-913-9341	R	1*	<.1
179	Roto-Plastics Corp—David Mulligan	PO Box 683, Adrian MI 49221	517-263-8981	R	N/A	.1

TOTALS: SIC 3086 Plastics Foam Products
Companies: 179

					7,074	37.9

3087 Custom Compound of Purchased Resins

Rank	Company Name—Executive Officer	Address, City, State, Zip	Phone	Type	Fin	Empls
1	A Schulman Inc—Joseph M Gingo	3550 W Market St, Akron OH 44333	330-666-3751	P	2,193	3.0
2	Teknor Apex Co—Jonathan Fain	PO Box 2290, Pawtucket RI 02861	401-725-8000	R	648*	2.1
3	Vi-Chem Corp—Len Slott	55 Cottage Grove St SW, Grand Rapids MI 49507	616-247-8501	R	318*	1.1
4	Sartomer Company Inc—Nicholas P Trainer	502 Thomas Jones Way, Exton PA 19341	610-363-4100	D	304*	.4
5	Miller Waste Mills Inc—Hugh Miller	PO Box 5439, Winona MN 55987	507-454-6900	R	47*	.7
6	Bayshore Industrial Inc—Steve Bartman	1300 McCabe Rd, La Porte TX 77571	281-867-3000	S	38*	.2
7	Washington Penn Plastic Company Inc—Robert Andy	450 Racetrack Rd, Washington PA 15301	724-228-1260	R	31*	.4
8	Ravago Manufacturing Americas LLC—Wayne Ballew	405 Parktower Rd, Manchester TN 37355	931-728-7009	R	23*	.3
9	Prime PVC Inc—Manoj Bhar	1400 N Washington St, Marion IN 46952	765-651-1546	R	20*	.1
10	J Meyer and Sons Inc—Daniel Ginty	PO Box 308, West Point PA 19486	215-699-7003	R	19*	.2
11	Mccann Plastics Inc—Michael Mccann	5600 Mayfair Rd, Canton OH 44720	330-499-1515	R	17*	.1
12	Heller Performance Polymers Inc—Herbert Heller	7227 W DOE Ave, Visalia CA 93291	559-651-2091	R	17*	.2
13	Advanced Polymer Compounding—Alan Coulson	400 Maple Ave Ste A, Carpentersville IL 60110	847-426-3350	D	15*	<.1
14	Modern Dispersions Inc—Janos Kozma	78 Marguerite Ave, Leominster MA 01453	978-534-3370	R	14*	.1
15	Rutland Plastic Technologies Inc—Dennis Gunson	10021 Rodney St, Pineville NC 28134	704-553-0046	R	13*	.1
16	Electric Cable Compounds Inc—Ida Fridland	108 Rado Dr, Naugatuck CT 06770	203-723-2590	R	12*	.1
17	Chemtrusion Inc—Ed Bourbonais	7115 Clinton Dr, Houston TX 77020	713-675-1616	R	11*	.1
18	Sylvin Technologies Inc—Jonathan Newman	PO Box 308, Denver PA 17517	717-336-2823	R	10*	<.1
19	Tyne Plastics LLC—Joseph Carrafa	PO Box 2000, Burlington CT 06013	860-673-7100	R	7*	<.1
20	Federal Plastics Corp—Peter Triano	715 S Ave E, Cranford NJ 07016	908-272-5800	R	6*	<.1
21	Tru-Contour Inc—Jim Srackangast	PO Box 28, Harrisburg PA 28075	704-455-8700	R	5*	<.1
22	Next Specialty Resins Inc—Abhay Prasad	PO Box 365, Addison MI 49220	517-547-4600	R	5*	<.1
23	Foam Supplies Inc—David Keske	4387 Rider Trl N, Earth City MO 63045	314-344-3330	R	4*	.1

Note: An asterisk (*) indicates an estimated financial figure. The company type code used is as follows: R = Private, P = Public, S = Private Subsidiary, B = Public Subsidiary, D = Division, J = Joint Venture, I = Investment Fund.

COMPANY RANKINGS BY SALES WITHIN 4-DIGIT SIC

Rank	Company Name—*Executive Officer*	Address, City, State, Zip	Phone	Type	Fin	Empls
24	Hayes-Ivy Manufacturing Inc—*Peter Knight*	PO Box 455, New Tripoli PA 18066	610-767-3865	R	4*	<.1
25	Portland Plastics Co—*Robert Tait*	PO Box 436, Portland MI 48875	517-647-4115	R	3*	<.1
26	Pyramid Plastics Inc—*Bill Tolleson*	PO Box 765, Hope AR 71802	870-777-5759	R	2*	<.1
27	Accra Industries Inc—*Ray Aumann*	586 Progressive Ln, South Beloit IL 61080	815-624-7849	R	2*	<.1

TOTALS: SIC 3087 Custom Compound of Purchased Resins
Companies: 27 — 3,785 — 9.2

3088 Plastics Plumbing Fixtures

Rank	Company Name—*Executive Officer*	Address, City, State, Zip	Phone	Type	Fin	Empls
1	Watkins Manufacturing Corp—*Steve Hammock*	1280 Park Center Dr, Vista CA 92083	760-598-6464	S	125*	1.1
2	Swan Corp—*Peter Warren*	515 Olive St Ste 1800, Saint Louis MO 63101	314-231-8148	R	40*	.3
3	L and M Laminates And Marble Inc—*Raymond St Cyr*	PO Box 2319, Phoenix AZ 85002	602-254-5629	R	29*	.3
4	Charloma Inc—*Charles Fink*	PO Box 367, Cherryvale KS 67335	620-336-2124	R	29*	.3
5	R W Lyall and Company Inc—*Jeffrey Lyall*	PO Box 2259, Corona CA 92878	951-270-1500	R	19*	.2
6	Frontline Manufacturing Inc—*Ray Doss*	PO Box 176, Leesburg IN 46538	574-453-2902	R	18*	.2
7	Onyx Collection Inc—*Robert Awerkamp*	PO Box 37, Belvue KS 66407	785-456-8604	R	17*	.2
8	Clarion Bathware Inc—*David Groner*	44 Amsler Ave, Shippenville PA 16254	814-226-5374	R	17*	.2
9	Carolina Classic Manufacturing Inc—*H Mccoy*	PO Box 159, Wilson NC 27894	252-237-9105	R	14*	.1
10	Royal SpA Corp—*Richard Bartlett*	2041 W Epler Ave, Indianapolis IN 46217	317-781-0828	R	14*	.1
11	Mr Tubs Inc—*J Henry*	670 N Price Rd, Sugar Hill GA 30518	770-271-8228	R	13*	.1
12	Lyons Industries Inc—*Lance Lyons*	PO Box 88, Dowagiac MI 49047	269-782-3404	R	13*	.1
13	Maax Hydro Swirl Manufacturing Co—*Placide Poulin*	2150 Division St, Bellingham WA 98226	360-734-0616	R	12*	.1
14	G K L Corp—*Kenneth Salach*	5 Greenwood Ave, Romeoville IL 60446	815-886-5900	R	11*	.1
15	Hydro Air Industries	450 Delta Ave, Brea CA 92821	714-257-9485	D	10	.1
16	Smith's Action Plastic Inc—*James Smith*	645 S Santa Fe St, Santa Ana CA 92705	714-836-4141	R	9*	.1
17	Jetta Corp—*Matt Peterson*	425 Centennial Blvd, Edmond OK 73013	405-340-6661	R	9*	.1
18	Proset Systems Inc—*Kenneth Cornwall*	1355 Capital Cir, Lawrenceville GA 30043	770-339-1782	R	7*	.1
19	Centoco Manufacturing Corp—*Anthony Tolodo*	PO Box 732, Mc Crory AR 72101	870-731-5454	R	6*	.1
20	Hydra Plastics Inc—*Ronald Clearwater*	PO Box 2140, Woodinville WA 98072	425-483-1877	R	6*	<.1
21	Re-Bath LLC—*Dave Sanders*	421 W Alameda Dr, Tempe AZ 85282	480-844-1575	S	6*	<.1
22	Water-Way Inc—*Bob Tiffin*	PO Box 418, Iuka MS 38852	662-423-0081	R	6*	<.1
23	Dal-Tex Specialty and Manufacturing Co—*Michael Knight*	1161 Ruggles St, Grand Prairie TX 75050	972-641-8444	R	6*	<.1
24	Premiere Plastics Inc—*John Metcalf*	PO Box 359, Pontotoc MS 38863	662-489-2007	R	5*	<.1
25	Luxury Bath Liners Inc—*Davis Glassberg*	1958 Brandon Ct, Glendale Heights IL 60139	630-295-9084	R	5*	<.1
26	Aqua Bath Company Inc—*William Dorris*	921 Cherokee Ave, Nashville TN 37207	615-227-0017	R	5*	<.1
27	American Acrylic and Injection Inc—*Kevin Wallace*	419 Welch Dr, Farmersville TX 75442	972-784-7759	R	4*	<.1
28	Fiberglass of Eatonton Inc—*Charles Scott*	PO Box 3992, Eatonton GA 31024	706-485-8327	R	4*	.1
29	Apollo Corp—*Adrian Sween*	PO Box 219, Somerset WI 54025	715-247-5625	R	4*	<.1
30	Viking Sink Company LLC—*Ronald Halvorson*	653 Tower Dr, Cadott WI 54727	715-289-3540	R	3*	<.1
31	Marble Lite Products Corp—*Nestor Perez*	9920 Nw 79th Ave, Hialeah FL 33016	305-557-8766	R	3*	<.1
32	Kfp Corp—*David Kusch*	PO Box 1196, Somerset PA 15501	814-443-9702	R	3*	<.1
33	JF Stouffer Co—*John Stotter*	2700 Atantic Blvd Ne, Canton OH 44705	330-453-8437	R	2*	<.1
34	Aries Acrylic Manufacturing Inc—*Larry Williams*	4176 E Interstate 30, Rockwall TX 75087	972-771-6286	R	2*	<.1
35	American Reinforced Plastics Inc—*Donald Jensen*	8209 Pacific Hwy E, Tacoma WA 98422	253-922-5808	R	1*	<.1
36	Composting Toilet Systems Inc	PO Box 1928, Newport WA 99156	509-447-3708	R	1*	<.1

TOTALS: SIC 3088 Plastics Plumbing Fixtures
Companies: 36 — 476 — 4.0

3089 Plastics Products Nec

Rank	Company Name—*Executive Officer*	Address, City, State, Zip	Phone	Type	Fin	Empls
1	Apex Medical Corp	PO Box 2526, Sioux Falls SD 57101	605-332-6689	R	12,203*	.1
2	Carlisle FoodService Products—*David Shannon*	PO Box 53006, Oklahoma City OK 73152	405-475-5600	S	11,250*	.5
3	Nypro Inc—*Ted Lapres*	101 Union St, Clinton MA 01510	978-365-9721	R	10,030*	17.0
4	Core Molding Technologies Inc—*Kevin L Barnett*	800 Manor Park Dr, Columbus OH 43228	614-870-5000	P	8,990	1.0
5	Cretex Companies Inc—*Lynn Schuler*	311 Lowell Ave Nw, Elk River MN 55330	763-441-2121	R	8,545*	1.7
6	Ropak Corp—*Greg Toft*	PO Box 8628, Fountain Valley CA 92728	714-845-2845	R	8,445*	1.1
7	Jarden Corp—*Martin E Franklin*	555 Theodore Fremd Ave, Rye NY 10580	914-967-9400	P	6,680	23.0
8	Berry Plastics Corp—*Jonathan ('Jon') Rich*	PO Box 959, Evansville IN 47706	812-424-2904	R	4,561	16.0
9	Silgan Holdings Inc—*Anthony J Allott*	4 Landmark Sq Ste 400, Stamford CT 06901	203-975-7110	P	3,509	8.7
10	ICO Inc—*John Knapp Jr*	1811 Bering Dr Ste 200, Houston TX 77057	713-351-4100	S	3,000	.8
11	Armstrong World Industries Inc—*Matthew J Espe*	PO Box 3001, Lancaster PA 17604	717-397-0611	P	2,860	9.1
12	Nordic Group of Companies Ltd—*William R Sauey*	414 Broadway Ste 200, Baraboo WI 53913	608-356-0136	R	2,706*	2.5
13	Tupperware Brands Corp—*EV (Rick) Goings*	PO Box 2353, Orlando FL 32802	407-826-5050	P	2,585	13.6
14	Vinylmax LLC—*James Doerger*	2921 McBride Ct, Hamilton OH 45011	513-772-2247	R	2,389*	.2
15	AptarGroup Inc—*Peter H Pfeiffer*	475 W Terra Cotta Ste, Crystal Lake IL 60014	815-477-0424	P	2,337	10.9
16	Superior Plastic LLC—*Norman Mackie*	417 E 2nd St, Rochester MI 48307	248-651-9311	S	2,313*	.2
17	Plastek Group—*Joseph J Prischak*	2425 W 23rd St, Erie PA 16506	814-878-4400	R	2,114*	2.0
18	Evanite Fiber Corp—*Frank Trombetta*	PO Box E, Corvallis OR 97339	541-753-1211	S	1,649*	.1
19	ENTEK International LLC—*Rob Keith*	250 Hansard Ave, Lebanon OR 97355	541-259-3901	R	1,519*	.2
20	Solo Cup Co—*Robert M Korzenski*	150 S Saunders Rd Ste, Lake Forest IL 60045	847-444-5000	R	1,503	6.8
21	Sigma Plastics Group—*Alfred Teo*	PO Box 808, Lyndhurst NJ 07071	201-507-9100	R	1,350*	5.0
22	Myers Industries International Inc Myers Industries Inc	1293 S Main St, Akron OH 44301	330-253-5592	S	1,303*	2.0
23	Xerxes Corp—*Venence Cote*	7901 Xerxes Ave S Ste, Minneapolis MN 55431	952-887-1890	S	1,237*	.3
24	United Plastics Group Inc—*Todd Dunn*	1420 Kesington Rd Ste, Oak Brook IL 60523	630-706-5500	R	1,206*	1.7
25	GPC Capital Corporation II	2401 Pleasant Valley, York PA 17402	717-849-8500	S	907*	4.1
26	Nalge Nunc International Corp—*Robert V Ahlgren*	75 Panorama Creek Dr, Rochester NY 14625	585-586-8800	S	843*	.9
27	AET Films—*Thomas Mohr*	2751 Centerville Rd St, Wilmington DE 19808	302-326-5500	D	825*	.1
28	Entegris Inc—*Gideon Argov*	3500 Lyman Blvd, Chaska MN 55318	952-556-4181	P	749	2.6
29	Myers Industries Inc—*John C Orr*	1293 S Main St, Akron OH 44301	330-253-5592	P	738	3.3
30	Saint-Gobain Performance Plastics—*John Crowe*	7301 Ovangewood Avenue, Garden Grove CA 92841		S	703*	4.8
31	Greene Tweed and Co—*Michael Delfiner*	2075 Detwiler Rd, Kulpsville PA 19443	215-256-9521	R	694*	1.2
32	Norandex Building Materials Distribution—*Brian Chambers*	300 Executive Pky W St, Hudson OH 44236	330-656-8800	S	650	3.2
33	Associated Materials LLC—*Michael J Caporale Jr*	3773 State Rd, Cuyahoga Falls OH 44223	330-922-2354	S	630*	2.6
34	Aptar Pharma—*Peter H Pfeiffer* AptarGroup Inc	250 N Rte 303, Congers NY 10920	845-639-3700	S	451	2.3
35	GenCorp Automotive—*Scott J Seymour*	PO Box 537012, Sacramento CA 95853	916-355-4000	S	385*	3.0
36	Hellermanntyton Corp—*James Campion*	7930 N Faulkner Rd, Milwaukee WI 53224	414-355-1130	R	380*	.3
37	Key Plastics—*B Edward Ewing*	21700 Haggerty Rd Ste, Northville MI 48167	248-449-6100	S	372*	5.0
38	The Brookside Group—*David D Buttolph*	80 Field Point Rd 3rd, Greenwich CT 06830	203-618-0202	R	361*	3.0
39	Ag-Bag International Ltd	PO Box 127, St Nazianz WI 54232	920-773-2121	S	353*	.1
40	Menasha Corp Thermotech Div—*John Bonham*	1302 S 5th St, Hopkins MN 55343	952-933-9400	D	345*	.7

Rank	Company Name—Executive Officer	Address, City, State, Zip	Phone	Type	Fin	Empls
41	Marley Cooling Technologies—Christopher Kearney	7401 W 129th St, Overland Park KS 66213	913-664-7400	S	344*	.5
42	ABTRE Inc American Biltrite Inc	57 River St, Wellesley Hills MA 02481	781-237-5655	S	326*	.5
43	Aimpar Inc American Biltrite Inc	57 River St, Wellesley Hills MA 02481	781-237-5655	S	326*	.5
44	American Biltrite Far East Inc American Biltrite Inc	57 River St, Wellesley Hills MA 02481	781-237-5655	S	326*	.5
45	American Biltrite Sales Corp American Biltrite Inc	57 River St, Wellesley Hills MA 02481	781-237-5655	S	326*	.5
46	Majestic Jewelry Inc American Biltrite Inc	57 River St, Wellesley Hills MA 02481	781-237-5655	S	326*	.5
47	Ocean State Jewelry Inc American Biltrite Inc	57 River St, Wellesley Hills MA 02481	781-237-5655	S	326*	.5
48	Carris Reels Inc—Michael Curran	49 Main Street, Proctor VT 05765	802-773-9111	R	316*	.6
49	Republic Packaging Corp—Charles Wood	9160 S Green St, Chicago IL 60620	773-233-6530	R	295*	.2
50	Arizona Archery Enterprises Inc—TJ Fisher	2781 Valley View Dr, Prescott Valley AZ 86314	928-772-9887	R	291*	<.1
51	Stull Closure Technologies—Gene Stull	17 Veronica Ave, Somerset NJ 08873	732-873-5000	R	285*	.3
52	Portola Packaging Inc	40 Shuman Blvd Ste 220, Naperville IL 60563		R	270*	1.2
53	Fabri-Kal Corp—R Kittredge	600 Plastics Pl, Kalamazoo MI 49001	269-385-5050	R	260*	.8
54	UFE Inc—Martin Kellogg	1850 S Greeley St, Stillwater MN 55082	651-351-4278	R	257*	.5
55	Cascade Engineering Inc—Frederick Keller	PO Box 888405, Grand Rapids MI 49588	616-975-4800	R	238*	1.1
56	Home Products International Inc—George E Hamilton	4501 W 47th St, Chicago IL 60632	773-890-1010	R	234*	1.3
57	Evco Plastics—Dale Evans	PO Box 497, De Forest WI 53532	608-846-6000	R	227*	.4
58	Sterilite Corp—David Stone	PO Box 8001, Townsend MA 01469	978-597-8702	R	226*	.1
59	Morton Industrial Group Inc—William D Morton	1021 W Birchwood St, Morton IL 61550	309-266-7176	R	223*	1.6
60	Silgan Plastics Corp—Alan Koblin Silgan Holdings Inc	PO Box 1080, Chesterfield MO 63006	314-542-9223	S	220*	1.8
61	Flambeau Corp—Jason C Souey Nordic Group of Companies Ltd	801 Lynn Ave, Baraboo WI 53913	608-356-5551	S	212*	3.0
62	Viskase Companies Inc—Thomas Davis	8205 S Cass Ave Ste 11, Darien IL 60561	630-874-0700	R	211*	1.6
63	M and Q Plastics Products Inc—David Carlin	1120 Welsh Rd Ste170, North Wales PA 19454	267-498-4000	R	202*	.4
64	American Biltrite Inc—Roger S Marcus	57 River St, Wellesley Hills MA 02481	781-237-6655	P	202	.6
65	Nyx Inc—Chain Sandhu	36111 Schoolcraft Rd, Livonia MI 48150	734-421-3850	R	200*	1.8
66	A and E Products Group LP—Phillip Williams	602 W Main St, Ringtown PA 17967		S	200*	1.2
67	South Corporation Packaging USA—Jim Sherbert	515 1st St, Peotone IL 60468	708-258-3211	D	200	1.2
68	Nifco LLC—John Kosik	8015 Dove Pky, Canal Winchester OH 43110	614-836-3808	R	199*	.4
69	JPS Industries Inc—Michael L Fulbright	55 Beattie Pl Ste 1510, Greenville SC 29601	864-239-3900	P	191	.6
70	Tech Group Inc—Harold Faig	14677 N 74th St, Scottsdale AZ 85260	480-281-4500	S	180*	1.5
71	Energy Absorption Systems Inc—Les Jezuit Quixote Corp	35 E Wacker Dr, Chicago IL 60601	312-467-6750	S	179*	.4
72	Buckhorn Inc—Joel Grant Myers Industries Inc	55 W TechneCenter Dr, Milford OH 45150	513-831-4402	S	167*	.3
73	Lacke Enterprises Inc—Richard Lacks	5460 Cascade Rd Se, Grand Rapids MI 49546	616-949-6570	R	164*	2.3
74	Cosmo Corp—Marc Gordon	30201 Aurora Rd, Cleveland OH 44139	440-498-7500	R	162*	.3
75	Tensar Corp—Don Meltzer	2500 Northwinds Pky St, Alpharetta GA 30009	770-344-2090	R	161*	.7
76	Safety 1st Inc—Michael Lerner	PO Box 2609, Columbus IN 47202		S	158	.3
77	Centro Inc—Brian Olesen	950 N Bend Dr, North Liberty IA 52317	319-626-3200	R	156*	.7
78	Titan Plastics Group—Greg Botner	PO Box 159, Stevensville MI 49127	269-429-3201	R	156*	.3
79	Bemis Manufacturing Company Inc—Richard Bemis	PO Box 901, Sheboygan Falls WI 53085	920-467-4621	R	155*	2.0
80	AGY Holding Corp—Doug Mattscheck	2556 Wagener Rd, Aiken SC 29801	803-648-8351	J	154*	1.5
81	Igloo Products Corp—James J Roberts	PO Box 19322, Houston TX 77224	713-584-6800	R	150*	1.5
82	CROWN Risdon—Stephen T Pearlman	PO Box 520, Naugatuck CT 06770	860-417-1100	S	150*	1.3
83	Variform Inc—John Wayne	PO Box 559, Kearney MO 64060	816-635-6400	S	150*	.6
84	First Years Inc	100 Technology Center, Stoughton MA 02072	781-341-6250	S	150*	.2
85	Techpack America Cosmetic Packaging Inc—Jean Imbert	595 Madison Ave Fl 10, New York NY 10022	212-371-5100	R	150*	2.2
86	AFC (Chatfield Minnesota)—G David Oakley Jr Strongwell Corp	1610 Hwy 52 S, Chatfield MN 55923	507-867-3479	D	149*	.9
87	Rochling Glastic Composites LP—Ludger Bartels	4321 Glenridge Rd, Cleveland OH 44121	216-406-0100	R	147*	.3
88	Simonton Holdings Inc—Samuel Ross	PO Box 1646, Parkersburg WV 26102	304-428-8261	R	142*	2.2
89	Congoleum Corp—Roger S Marcus	PO Box 3127, Mercerville NJ 08619	609-584-3000	R	136*	.5
90	C and M Fine Pack Inc—Mark Gomi	4162 Georgia Blvd, San Bernardino CA 92407	909-880-1781	R	134*	.3
91	Summit Polymers Inc—James H Haas	6715 S Sprinkle Rd, Portage MI 49002	269-324-9330	R	133*	2.0
92	Champion Opco LLC—Dennis Manes	12121 Champion Way, Cincinnati OH 45241	513-346-4600	R	133*	2.0
93	Adac Plastics Inc—Jim Teets	PO Box 888375, Grand Rapids MI 49588	616-957-0311	R	125*	.8
94	Plastic Products Company Inc—Marlene Messin	30355 Akerson St, Lindstrom MN 55045	651-257-5980	R	.125*	.8
95	Continental Structural Plastics Inc—Bruce Landino	755 W Big Beavr Rd Ste, Troy MI 48084	248-593-9500	R	120*	1.5
96	Volex Inc—James Stuart	1915 Tate Blvd Se Ste, Hickory NC 28602	828-485-4500	S	120*	1.9
97	Miniature Precision Components Inc—James Brost	820 Wisconsin St, Walworth WI 53184	262-275-5791	R	118*	1.7
98	Trienda LLC—Tom Dury	N7660 Industrial Rd, Portage WI 53901	608-742-5303	R	118*	.2
99	Intelicoat Products—Joe Lupone	28 Gaylord St, South Hadley MA 01075	413-536-7800	S	116*	.3
100	Bedford Reinforced Plastics—Brian E Stahl	264 Reynoldsdale Rd, Bedford PA 15522	814-623-8125	R	116*	.2
101	Protomold Company Inc—Larry Lukis	5540 Pioneer Creek Dr, Maple Plain MN 55359	763-479-3680	R	115*	.2
102	Sturgis Molded Products Co—Mark Weishaar	PO Box 246, Sturgis MI 49091	269-651-9381	R	115*	.2
103	Fibergrate Composite Structures Inc—Marshall Liverman	5151 Beltline Road Ste, Dallas TX 75254	972-250-1633	S	114*	.2
104	Polychem Systems—Pat Schuster Brentwood Industries Inc	621 Brentwood Dr, Reading PA 19611	484-651-1300	D	114*	.2
105	Great Pacific Enterprises (US) Inc—James Pattison	PO Box 727, Glens Falls NY 12801	518-798-9511	R	114*	2.0
106	Alliance Plastics Inc—Mike Conley	PO Box 7284, Erie PA 16510	814-899-7671	R	113*	.2
107	Eldon—Mark D Ketchum	2711 Washington Blvd, Oak Brook IL 60523		D	111*	.4
108	Sussex IM—Keith Everson	PO Box 902, Sussex WI 53089	262-246-8022	R	111*	.2
109	Doskocil Manufacturing Company Inc—Gary Kohlschmidt	PO Box 1246, Arlington TX 76004	817-467-5116	R	108*	.9
110	G and F Industries Inc—John Argitis	PO Box 515 - Rte 20, Sturbridge MA 01566	508-347-9132	R	108*	.2
111	Plastic Ingenuity Inc—Thomas Kuehn	1017 Park St, Cross Plains WI 53528	608-798-3071	R	108*	.5
112	Technimark LLC—Steve Hennen	PO Box 2068, Asheboro NC 27204	336-498-4171	R	102*	1.5
113	AMS Plastics Inc—Thomas Klein	1530 Hilton Head Rd St, El Cajon CA 92019	619-713-2000	R	100*	.4
114	National Diversified Sales Inc—Michael Gummeson	PO Box 339, Lindsay CA 93247	559-562-9888	R	97*	.5
115	Northern Pipe Products Inc—Wayne Voorhees	1302 39th St NW, Fargo ND 58102	701-282-7655	S	97	.1
116	Merrick Engineering Inc—Abraham Abdi	1275 Quarry St, Corona CA 92879	951-737-6040	R	96*	.6
117	Augusta Fiberglass Coatings Inc—John Boyd	86 Lake Cynthia Dr, Blackville SC 29817	803-284-2246	R	95*	.3
118	Davies Molding Co—Darran Smith	350 Kehoe Blvd, Carol Stream IL 60188	630-510-8188	R	95*	.1

Note: An asterisk (*) indicates an estimated financial figure. The company type code used is as follows: R = Private, P = Public, S = Private Subsidiary, B = Public Subsidiary, D = Division, J = Joint Venture, I = Investment Fund.

COMPANY RANKINGS BY SALES WITHIN 4-DIGIT SIC

Rank	Company Name—*Executive Officer*	Address, City, State, Zip	Phone	Type	Fin	Empls
119	Quixote Corp—*Bruce Reimer*	35 E Wacker Dr, Chicago IL 60601	312-467-6755	S	94	.5
120	Thermo-Serv Inc—*Jay Rigby*	3901 Pipestone Rd, Dallas TX 75212	214-631-0307	R	93*	.2
121	Hollywood Ribbon Industries Inc—*Jim Scott*	PO Box 63187, Los Angeles CA 90063	323-266-0670	R	92*	.2
122	ITW Deltar Tekfast—*David B Speer*	21555 S Harlem Ave, Frankfort IL 60423	708-720-2600	R	91*	.2
123	Jones Plastic And Engineering Company LLC—*Buster Coldwell*	2410 Plantside Dr, Louisville KY 40299	502-491-3785	R	88*	1.3
124	Composites Horizons Inc—*Jeffrey T Hynes*	1471 W Industrial Park, Covina CA 91722	626-331-0861	S	86*	.2
125	Triad Medical Disposables Inc/H and P Industries—*David Haertle*	700 W North Shore Dr, Hartland WI 53029	262-538-2890	R	86*	.2
126	Ck Technologies LLC—*Sharon Mayer* Cascade Engineering Inc	1701 Magda Dr, Montpelier OH 43543	419-485-1110	S	85*	.4
127	Wilkinson Industries LLC—*Michael Kocourek*	PO Box 490, Fort Calhoun NE 68023	402-468-5511	R	85*	.3
128	Kenro Inc—*David Carlisle*	200 Industrial Dr, Fredonia WI 53021	262-692-2411	S	85*	.2
129	Formed Plastics Inc—*Patrick Long*	207 Stonehinge Ln, Carle Place NY 11514	516-334-2300	R	85*	.1
130	Koller Craft Plastic Prouducts Div—*Al Koller III* Koller Enterprises Inc	PO Box 718, Fenton MO 63026	636-343-9220	D	84*	.2
131	Harvel Plastics Inc—*Earl E Wismer*	300 Kuebler Rd, Easton PA 18040	610-252-7355	S	84*	.1
132	Dickten Masch Plastics LLC—*Steven Dyer*	N44 W33341 Watertown P, Nashotah WI 53058	262-369-5555	R	81*	.3
133	Habasit Holding USA Inc	1101 California Ave St, Corona CA 92881	310-792-7204	R	80	.5
134	Jain Irrigation Inc—*Dave Abrams* Habasit Holding USA Inc	2060 E Francis St, Ontario CA 91761	909-395-5200	S	80*	.1
135	Gw Plastics Arizona Inc—*Benjamin Riehl* GW Plastics Inc	2901 E Valencia Rd, Tucson AZ 85706	520-294-9400	S	80*	.1
136	Blow Molded Specialties Inc—*David Carlsen*	PO Box 310, Foley MN 56329	320-968-7251	R	76*	.2
137	Whirley - DrinkWorks Inc—*Lincoln Sokolski* Whirley Industries Inc	618 4th Ave, Warren PA 16365	814-723-7600	S	76*	.4
138	Toledo Molding and Die Inc—*Donald Harbaugh*	PO Box 6760, Toledo OH 43612	419-470-3950	R	75*	1.0
139	Tg Missouri Corp—*Todd Huber*	2200 Plattin Rd, Perryville MO 63775	573-547-1041	S	72*	1.2
140	ENPAC Corp—*Doug Horner*	34355 Vokes Dr, Eastlake OH 44095		R	71	.1
141	Orbis Corp—*James Kotek*	PO Box 389, Oconomowoc WI 53066		D	68	.8
142	Packaging Plus LLC—*Richard Gordinier*	14450 Industry Cir, La Mirada CA 90638	714-522-5400	R	68*	.9
143	Rohrer Corp—*Scot Adkins*	PO Box 1009, Wadsworth OH 44282	330-335-1541	R	67*	.4
144	Nomaco Inc—*Claude Demby*	3006 Anaconda Rd, Tarboro NC 27886	919-269-6500	R	67*	.4
145	Mocap LLC—*Tammy Hovis*	409 Pky Dr, Park Hills MO 63601	314-543-4000	R	67*	.2
146	Cambro Manufacturing Company Inc—*Argyle Campbell*	PO Box 2000, Huntington Beach CA 92647	714-848-1555	R	63*	.9
147	Step2 Company LLC—*Ronald Mitchell*	10010 Aurora Hudson Rd, Streetsboro OH 44241	330-656-0440	R	63*	.9
148	Tenex Corp—*Albert Cheris*	1001 Green Bay Rd, Winnetka IL 60093	847-504-0400	R	63*	.5
149	Prent Corp—*Joseph Pregont*	PO Box 471, Janesville WI 53547	608-754-0276	R	62*	.5
150	Delta Consolidated Industries Inc—*H Lawrence Culp*	PO Box 1846, Jonesboro AR 72403		S	62*	.4
151	Moll Industries Inc—*Ron Embree*	13455 Noel Rd Ste 1310, Dallas TX 75240	972-383-8000	R	62*	.1
152	Dillen Products—*Chuck Beck* Myers Industries Inc	PO Box 738, Middlefield OH 44062	440-632-0230	S	60*	.5
153	Paragon Plastics Inc—*Mike Kio*	PO Box 100, Union SC 29379	864-427-0371	S	60*	.1
154	Reunion Industries Inc—*Kimball J Bradley*	11 Stanwix St Ste 1400, Pittsburgh PA 15222	412-281-2111	P	60	.3
155	Jet Plastica Industries Inc—*Jeff Dipasquale*	1100 Schwab Rd, Hatfield PA 19440	215-362-1501	R	59*	.6
156	Port Erie Plastics Inc—*John Johnson*	909 Troupe Rd, Harborcreek PA 16421	814-899-7602	R	59*	.6
157	Setco Inc—*Donald Parodi* Berry Plastics Corp	4875 E Hunter Ave, Anaheim CA 92807	714-777-5200	S	59*	.3
158	PI Inc—*Jeff Beene*	213 Dennis St, Athens TN 37303		R	58*	.4
159	Jones Zylon Co—*Todd Kohl*	PO Box 149, West Lafayette OH 43845	740-545-6341	R	58*	.1
160	Superior International Industries Inc—*Ray Derbecker*	1050 Columbia Dr, Carrollton GA 30117	770-832-6660	R	57*	.5
161	Hughes Supply Company of Thomasville Inc (Thomasville North Carolina)—*Jeff Hughes*	PO Box 1003, Thomasville NC 27361	336-475-8146	R	56*	.1
162	GI Plastek Wolfeboro—*Randy Herman*	5 Wickers Dr, Wolfeboro NH 03894	603-569-5100	R	55	.5
163	Tigerpoly Manufacturing Inc—*Seiji Shiga*	6231 Enterprise Pkwy, Grove City OH 43123	614-871-0045	R	54*	.4
164	Van Blarcom Closures Inc—*Vincent Scuderi*	156 Sandford St 170, Brooklyn NY 11205	718-855-3810	R	54*	.2
165	Pepro Enterprises Inc—*William Roberts*	4385 Garfield St, Ubly MI 48475	989-658-8557	R	53*	.5
166	Guttenberg Industries Inc—*Dave Kreul*	PO Box 190, Guttenberg IA 52052	563-252-3121	R	53*	.1
167	Porex Technologies Corp	500 Bohannon Rd, Fairburn GA 30213	770-964-1421	S	53*	.6
168	Precision Dynamics Corp—*Cecil Kost*	PO Box 9201, Sylmar CA 91392	818-897-1111	R	53*	.4
169	ABA-PGT Inc—*Samuel D Pierson*	P O Box 8270, Manchester CT 06040	860-649-4591	R	53*	.1
170	Rehau Inc—*Kathleen Saylor*	1501 Edwards Ferry Rd, Leesburg VA 20176	703-777-5255	R	53*	.8
171	Systex Products Corp—*Makoto Saito*	300 Buckner Rd, Battle Creek MI 49037	269-964-8800	R	52*	.2
172	ASK Plastics Inc—*Andrew D Vartanian*	9750 Ashton Rd, Philadelphia PA 19114	215-969-0800	R	52*	.1
173	TydenBrooks—*J Roessner*	227 North Route 303 Su, Congers NY 10920	845-353-3800	R	51*	.3
174	McVay Brothers Siding and Windows—*Michael McVay*	11420 E Montgomery Dr, Spokane WA 99206	509-928-4686	R	51*	<.1
175	Kalwall Corp—*Richard Keller*	PO Box 237, Manchester NH 03105	603-627-3861	R	50*	.5
176	Paragon Medical Inc—*Tobias Buck*	8 Matchett Dr, Pierceton IN 46562	574-594-2140	R	50*	.8
177	Attwood Corp—*Dirk Hyde*	1016 N Monroe St, Lowell MI 49331	616-897-9241	S	50*	.4
178	Strongwell Corp—*GDavid Oakley*	PO Box 580, Bristol VA 24203	276-645-8000	R	50*	.4
179	Oberthur Card Systems USA—*Philippe Geyres*	3150 E Ana St, Compton CA 90221	310-884-7900	S	50*	.3
180	Pretty Products LLC—*Jeffrey K Willis*	1513 Redding Dr, LaGrange GA 30240	706-884-1711	S	50*	.1
181	AMA Plastics—*Mark Atchinson*	350 W Rincon St, Corona CA 92880	951-734-5600	R	49*	.4
182	Normandy Industries Inc—*Robert Americus*	PO Box 38805, Pittsburgh PA 15238	412-826-1825	R	49*	.1
183	Polar Plastics Inc—*Andy Ave-Lallemant*	6959 N 55th St, Oakdale MN 55128	651-770-2925	R	49*	.1
184	Den Hartog Industries Inc—*John Den Hartog*	PO Box 425, Hospers IA 51238	712-752-8432	R	49*	.3
185	Rotonics Manufacturing Inc—*Sherman McKinniss*	17022 S Figueroa St, Gardena CA 90248	310-327-5401	R	48	.4
186	Plas-Tanks Industries Inc—*Mike Covey*	39 Standen Dr, Hamilton OH 45015	513-942-3800	R	47*	<.1
187	Tg Kentucky LLC—*Mark Tatum*	633 E Main St, Lebanon KY 40033	270-699-3300	S	47*	.9
188	Display Pack Inc—*Victor Hansen*	1340 Monroe Ave Nw Ste, Grand Rapids MI 49505	616-451-3061	R	47*	.8
189	B and S Plastics Inc—*William Spears*	2200 Sturgis Rd, Oxnard CA 93030	805-981-0262	R	47*	.7
190	United Plastic Fabricating Inc—*F Lingel*	165 Flagship Dr, North Andover MA 01845	978-975-4520	R	46*	.3
191	Perfecseal Inc—*Henry J Theisen*	PO Box 2968, Oshkosh WI 54903		D	46*	.2
192	New England Plastics Corp—*Robert Kearin*	308 Salem St, Woburn MA 01801	781-933-6004	R	46*	.1
193	Whirley Industries Inc—*Robert Sokolski*	PO Box 988, Warren PA 16365	814-723-7600	R	45*	.3
194	Custom Plastic Card Co—*Tony Gardner*	PO Box 4489, Deerfield Beach FL 33442	954-426-1331	R	45*	.1
195	Mars 2000 Inc—*Karl Krikorian*	40 Agnes St, Providence RI 02909	401-421-5275	R	44*	.9
196	Filtertek Inc—*David Atkinson*	PO Box 310, Hebron IL 60034	815-648-2416	S	44*	.9
197	Enplas USA Inc	1901 W Oak Cir, Marietta GA 30062	770-795-1100	R	44*	.1
198	Packerware LLC—*Roberto Buaron*	PO Box 219, Lawrence KS 66044	785-842-3000	R	44*	.4
199	Exotic Rubber and Plastics Corp—*Thomas Marino*	34700 Grand River Ave, Farmington Hills MI 48335	248-477-2122	R	43*	.1

Rank	Company Name—Executive Officer	Address, City, State, Zip	Phone	Type	Fin	Empls
200	NACO Industries Inc—W Michael Hopkins	395 W 1400 N, Logan UT 84341	435-753-8020	R	43*	.1
201	Rexam Closures and Containers—Graham Chipchase	3245 Kansas Rd, Evansville IN 47725	812-867-6671	D	42	.4
202	ITW Impro—Paul Sultenbach ITW Deltar Tekfast	9629 W 197th St, Mokena IL 60448	708-479-7200	D	42*	.3
203	Tessy Plastics Corp—Roland Beck	488 Rte 5 W, Elbridge NY 13060	315-689-3924	R	42*	.6
204	Dispoz-O Products Inc—Peter Iacovelli	PO Box 766, Fountain Inn SC 29644	864-862-4004	R	41*	.7
205	Mann-Hummel Automotive—Manfred Wolf	6400 S Sprinkle Rd, Portage MI 49002	269-329-3900	S	41*	.4
206	John D Brush and Company Inc—James Brush	900 Linden Ave, Rochester NY 14625	585-381-4900	R	41*	.6
207	Spotless Enterprises Inc—Peter Wilson	100 Motor Pkwy Ste 155, Hauppauge NY 11788	631-951-9000	R	41*	.7
208	Progressive Plastics Inc—A Busa	14801 Emery Ave, Cleveland OH 44135	216-252-5595	R	41*	.3
209	Bee Window Inc—George Faerber	1002 E 52nd St, Indianapolis IN 46205	317-283-8522	R	41*	.2
210	Plastican Inc—John Clementi	196 Industrial Rd, Leominster MA 01453	978-728-5000	R	41*	.6
211	Genova Products Inc—Donald Dinkgrave	PO Box 309, Davison MI 48423	810-744-4500	R	40*	.6
212	International Precision Components Corp—Michael Stolzman	28468 N Ballard Dr, Lake Forest IL 60045	847-234-1111	R	40*	.3
213	Gary Plastic Packaging Corp—Gary Hellinger	1340 Viele Ave, Bronx NY 10474	718-893-2200	R	40*	.4
214	Capsonic Group LLC	460 2nd St, Elgin IL 60123	847-888-7300	R	40*	.3
215	DecoGard Products Inc—Ronald Dadd	6696 Route405 Hwy, Muncy PA 17756	570-546-5941	D	40*	.3
216	Tenax Corp—Giovanni Capra	4800 E Monument St, Baltimore MD 21205	410-522-7000	R	40*	.1
217	Hobas Pipe USA Inc—Ed Kosurek	1413 E Richey Rd, Houston TX 77073	281-821-2200	R	38*	.1
218	Thermold Corp—Jeremy Schwimmer	7059 Harp Rd, Canastota NY 13032	315-697-3924	R	38*	.1
219	Jedlick Molding Corp—Mike Jedlick	8001 Swan Cir, La Palma CA 90623	323-753-5547	R	38*	<.1
220	Asahi/America Inc—Hidetoshi Hashimoto	PO Box 653, Malden MA 02148	781-321-5409	S	38	.1
221	PSC Fabricating Corp	1100 W Market St, Louisville KY 40251	502-625-7700	S	37*	.3
222	Viziflex Seels Inc	406 N Midland Ave, Saddle Brook NJ 07663		R	37*	<.1
223	Inline Plastics Corp—Thomas Orkisz	42 Canal St, Shelton CT 06484	203-924-5933	R	36*	.3
224	Lacks Enterprises Inc Plastic Plate Div—Richard Lacks Lacks Enterprises Inc	5460 Cascade Rd SE, Grand Rapids MI 49546	616-949-6570	D	36*	.3
225	Molecular Bio-Products Inc—Larry Scaramella	9880 Mesa Rim Rd, San Diego CA 92121	858-453-7551	S	36*	.3
226	Zeller Plastik Inc—Joe Pierce	1515 Franklin Blvd, Libertyville IL 60048	847-247-7900	S	36*	.3
227	W-L Molding Co—Al Mckeown	8212 Shaver Rd, Portage MI 49024	269-327-3075	R	36*	.7
228	Hedwin Corp—Randy Wolfinger	1600 Roland Heights Av, Baltimore MD 21211	410-467-8209	R	35*	.4
229	TSE Industries Inc—Robert R Klingel Sr	4370 112th Ter N, Clearwater FL 33762	727-573-7676	R	35*	.2
230	Modern Plastic Inc—Greg Lee	1393 S Santa Fe Dr, Denver CO 80223	303-761-1427	R	35*	.1
231	Vitec LLC—Anna Calderon	2627 Clark St, Detroit MI 48210	313-297-6676	R	35*	.3
232	Wna American Plastic Industries Inc—Mike Evans	5930 Quintus Loop, Chattanooga TN 37421	423-899-0929	R	35*	.3
233	Brentwood Industries Inc—Palle Rye	PO Box 605, Reading PA 19603	610-374-5109	R	34*	.5
234	Plastikon Industries Inc—Fred Soofer	688 Sandoval Way, Hayward CA 94544	510-400-1010	R	34*	.3
235	Maryland Plastics Inc—Allen Penrod	PO Box 472, Federalsburg MD 21632	410-754-5566	R	33*	.3
236	Adams Manufacturing Corp—William Adams	PO Box 1, Portersville PA 16051	724-368-8837	R	33*	.2
237	Univenture Inc—Ross O Youngs	13311 Industrial Pky, Marysville OH 43040	937-645-4600	R	33*	.2
238	Wausaukee Composites Inc—David Lisle	837 Cedar St, Wausaukee WI 54177	715-856-6321	R	33*	.3
239	Teel Plastics Inc—Jay Smith	1060 Teel Ct, Baraboo WI 53913	608-355-3080	R	33*	.3
240	Chem-Tainer Industries Inc—James Glen	361 Neptune Ave, West Babylon NY 11704	631-661-8300	R	32*	.3
241	Alltrista Industrial Plastics Co—Kyle DeJaeger Jarden Corp	8307 Ball Rd, Fort Smith AR 72908	501-646-8298	D	32*	.2
242	PRD Inc—John Passanisi	747 Washboard Rd, Springville IN 47462		R	32*	.2
243	Atlanta Nypro Inc—Brian Jones	1040 Cobb Industrial D, Marietta GA 30066	770-425-2704	R	31*	.2
244	Toter Inc—John Scott	PO Box 5338, Statesville NC 28687	704-872-8171	R	31*	.5
245	Chelsea Building Products Inc—Hans Spijkerman	565 Cedar Way, Oakmont PA 15139	412-826-8077	R	31*	.2
246	Polycon Industries Inc—Berle Blitstein	8919 Colorado St, Merrillville IN 46410	219-738-1000	R	31*	.3
247	Veka Inc—Joe Peilert	100 Veka Dr, Fombell PA 16123	724-452-1000	R	31*	.5
248	Polytop Corp—Steven Wilson	PO Box 68, Slatersville RI 02876	401-767-2400	R	30*	.3
249	Olsonite Inc—Peter Bemis	PO Box 901, Sheboygan Falls WI 53085	920-467-4621	R	30*	.5
250	Molding Corporation of America	10349 Noris Ave, Pacoima CA 91331	818-890-7877	R	30*	.3
251	Semco Plastic Co—Charles Voelkel	5301 Old Baumgartner R, Saint Louis MO 63129	314-487-4557	R	30*	.3
252	Agora Leather Products—Subash Dave	2101 28th St N, Saint Petersburg FL 33713	727-321-0707	R	30*	.2
253	Koller Enterprises Inc—Alois J Koller Jr	PO Box 718, Fenton MO 63026	636-343-9220	R	30*	.2
254	Gpk Products Inc—Spencer Hildre	1601 43rd St Nw, Fargo ND 58102	701-277-3225	R	30*	.1
255	D and B Industrial Group—Douglas Kinney	PO Box 822, Georgetown DE 19947	302-855-0585	R	30*	.1
256	Great Lakes Plastics Corp—George Kronschnabel	PO Box 600, Hancock MI 49930	906-482-3750	R	30*	.1
257	Fabrik Industries Inc—Seth Wagner	5213 Prime Pkwy, Mchenry IL 60050	815-385-9480	R	30*	.3
258	Suburban Plastics Co—W Baxter	340 Renner Dr, Elgin IL 60123	847-741-4900	R	29*	.5
259	Intec Group Inc—Steven Perlman	666 S Vermont St, Palatine IL 60067	847-358-0088	R	29*	.4
260	SKB Corp—Steven Kottman	434 W Levers Pl, Orange CA 92867	714-637-1252	R	29*	.4
261	Evans Manufacturing Inc—Alan Vaught	PO Box 5669, Garden Grove CA 92846	714-379-6100	R	29*	.3
262	International Container Systems—Fred Heptinstall	4343 Anchor Plaza Pky, Tampa FL 33634	813-287-8940	S	29*	<.1
263	Gadsden Coffee Company Inc—Angela Sam	109 6th Ave Nw, Attalla AL 35954	256-538-5439	R	29*	.3
264	Tec-Air Inc—Robert Mcmurtry	8075 Tec Air Ave, Willow Springs IL 60480	708-839-1400	R	29*	.3
265	Sabert Corp—Albert Salama	2288 Main St, Sayreville NJ 08872	732-952-2525	R	29*	.2
266	Ctp Carrera Inc—Mark Charbonneu	600 Depot St, Latrobe PA 15650	724-539-1833	R	29*	.2
267	Engineered Profiles LLC—Tim Tait	2141 Fairwood Ave, Columbus OH 43207	614-542-1155	R	29*	.3
268	Superior Engineered Products Corp—Gregory Faherty	1650 S Archibald Ave, Ontario CA 91761	909-930-1800	R	28*	.5
269	Dutchland Plastics Corp—Daven Claerbout	54 Enterprise Ct, Oostburg WI 53070	920-564-3633	R	28*	.4
270	Engineered Plastic Components Inc—Reza Kargarzadeh	1408 Zimmerman Dr, Grinnell IA 50112	641-236-3100	R	28*	.5
271	Poly-Seal Corp—Martin Imbler	1810 Portal St, Baltimore MD 21224	410-633-1990	R	28*	.5
272	Spirit Foodservice Inc—Donald Mc Cann	200 Brickstone Sq Ste, Andover MA 01810	978-964-1551	R	28*	.2
273	V-T Industries Inc—Douglas Clausen	1000 Industrial Park, Holstein IA 51025	712-368-4381	R	28*	.5
274	Industrial Molding Corp (Lubbock Texas)—Rock Baty	616 E Slaton Rd, Lubbock TX 79404	806-474-1000	S	28*	.4
275	Plastic Moldings Company LLC—Darrell East	2181 Grand Ave, Cincinnati OH 45214	513-921-5040	R	28*	.2
276	Intek Plastics Inc—John Penn	1000 Spiral Blvd, Hastings MN 55033	651-437-7700	R	28*	.2
277	Innovative Plastics Corp—Judith Hershaft	400 Rte 303, Orangeburg NY 10962	845-359-7500	R	28*	.2
278	IPEC—Joseph Giordano Silgan Holdings Inc	PO Box 5311, New Castle PA 16105	724-658-3004	S	28*	.2
279	Four Seasons Industries—Michael E Diskin	PO Box 31, Garrettsville OH 44231	330-527-4308	R	28*	.1
280	Polar Tech Industries Inc—Daniel Santeler	415 E Railroad Ave, Genoa IL 60135	815-784-9000	R	28*	.1
281	ITW Plastiglide Manufacturing Corp—Henry Swain	95 Commerce Dr, Somerset NJ 08873	732-873-5500	S	28*	<.1
282	GW Plastics Inc—Brenan Riehl	PO Box 56, Bethel VT 05032	802-234-9941	R	28*	.5
283	Icore International Inc—Ted Perdue	3780 Flightline Dr, Santa Rosa CA 95403	707-535-2750	R	28*	.2
284	Custom Plastics Inc—Peter Tisbo	1940 Lunt Ave, Elk Grove Village IL 60007	847-439-6770	R	27*	.2
285	Craftech Edm Corp—John Butler	2941 E La Jolla St, Anaheim CA 92806	714-630-8117	R	27*	.2

Note: An asterisk (*) indicates an estimated financial figure. The company type code used is as follows: R = Private, P = Public, S = Private Subsidiary, B = Public Subsidiary, D = Division, J = Joint Venture, I = Investment Fund.

COMPANY RANKINGS BY SALES WITHIN 4-DIGIT SIC

Rank	Company Name—Executive Officer	Address, City, State, Zip	Phone	Type	Fin	Empls
286	Minigrip/Zip-Pak—Jim Kohl	171 Rte 303, Orangeburg NY 10962		R	27*	.3
287	Falcon Plastics Inc—Jay Bender	PO Box 788, Brookings SD 57006	605-696-2500	R	27*	.3
288	Storopack Inc—Hermann Reichenecker	4758 Devitt Dr, Cincinnati OH 45246	513-874-0314	R	27*	.1
289	Ven-Tel Plastics Corp—Edward Venner	11311 74th St N, Largo FL 33773	727-546-7470	R	27*	.1
290	Delta Rexam Inc—Chris Rakhshan	106 Delta Pl, Hot Springs AR 71913	501-760-3000	S	27*	.5
291	BF Rich Company Inc—George Simmons	322 Ruthar Dr, Newark DE 19711	302-894-0498	R	27*	.2
292	Plastic Packaging Inc—Mark Coffey	PO Box 2029, Hickory NC 28603	828-328-2466	R	26*	.3
293	Plastic Dress-Up Co—Myron Funk	PO Box 3897, El Monte CA 91733	626-442-7711	R	26*	.5
294	Kennerley-Spratling Inc—Richard Spratling	2116 Farallon Dr, San Leandro CA 94577	510-351-8230	R	26*	.4
295	Formula Plastics Inc—Elias Mora	451 Tecate Rd Ste 2b, Tecate CA 91980	619-478-1056	R	26*	.4
296	Majors Plastics Inc—Tim Connell	10117 I St, Omaha NE 68127	402-331-1660	R	26*	.4
297	Willert Home Products Inc—William Willert	4044 Park Ave, Saint Louis MO 63110	314-772-2822	R	26*	.4
298	Jarden Plastic Solutions—Chuck Villa Alltrista Industrial Plastics Co	PO Box 2750, Greenville SC 29602	864-879-8100	D	26*	.3
299	Lenco Incorporated - Pmc—Paritosh Chakrabarti	PO Box 590, Waverly NE 68462	402-786-2000	R	26*	.2
300	ITW Space Bag—Steve Henn	7520 Airway Rd, San Diego CA 92154	619-671-9022	S	26*	<.1
301	Armand Manufacturing Inc—Richard De Heras	2399 Silver Wolf Dr, Henderson NV 89011	702-565-7500	R	26*	<.1
302	Royal Plastics Inc—Gary Connell	9410 Pineneedle Dr, Mentor OH 44060	440-352-1357	R	25*	.2
303	Plastic Enterprises Company Inc—Charles Koester	PO Box 248, Lees Summit MO 64063	816-246-8200	R	25*	.2
304	Syndicate Sales Inc—David Hendrickson	PO Box 756, Kokomo IN 46903	765-457-7277	R	25*	.4
305	Ras Industries Inc—William Creehan	12 Arentzen Blvd, Charleroi PA 15022	724-489-1111	R	25*	.3
306	Graber-Rogg Inc—Arthur Zampella	22 Jackson Dr, Cranford NJ 07016	908-272-4422	R	25*	.3
307	Dimex LLC—Jeff Amrine	28305 State Rte 7, Marietta OH 45750	740-374-3100	R	25*	.1
308	Vinylex Corp—Sam Reynolds	PO Box 7187, Knoxville TN 37921	865-690-2211	R	25*	.3
309	Landmark Plastic Corp—Robert Merzweiler	1331 Kelly Ave, Akron OH 44306	330-785-2200	R	25*	.2
310	Ventana USA—Mike Smith	6001 Enterprise Dr, Export PA 15632	724-325-3400	R	25*	.2
311	Hayward Industrial Products Inc—Robert Davis	620 Division St, Elizabeth NJ 07201	908-351-5400	R	25*	.5
312	Fremont Plastic Products Inc—Brian Beth	2101 Cedar St, Fremont OH 43420	419-332-6407	R	24*	.3
313	Comar Inc—Mike Ruggieri	1 Comar Pl, Buena NJ 08310	856-692-6100	R	24*	.4
314	Scientific Molding Corporation Ltd—Chetan Patel	330 Smc Dr, Somerset WI 54025	715-247-3500	R	24*	.2
315	Labcon North America—James Happ	3700 Lkeville Hwy Ste, Petaluma CA 94954	707-766-2100	R	24*	.2
316	Miles Fiberglass and Composites Inc—Lowell Miles	8855 Se Otty Rd, Portland OR 97086	503-775-7755	R	24*	.2
317	L T Hampel Corp—Lance Hampel	W194n11551 Mccormick D, Germantown WI 53022	262-255-4540	R	24*	.1
318	C and J Industries Inc—Dennis Frampton	PO Box 499, Meadville PA 16335	814-724-4950	R	24*	.4
319	Ashland Hardware Systems—Bob Bailey	790 W Commercial Ave, Lowell IN 46356	219-696-5950	D	24*	.2
320	North State Flexibles—Tim Mages	PO Box 5466, Greensboro NC 27435	336-292-9911	R	24*	.2
321	Selfix Inc—George Hamilton Home Products International Inc	4501 W 47th St, Chicago IL 60632	773-890-1010	S	24*	.2
322	ZERO Halliburton—Peter Marino	500 W 200 N, North Salt Lake UT 84054	732-393-7400	D	24*	.2
323	Meese Inc—Ronald Midili	535 N Midland Ave, Saddle Brook NJ 07663	201-796-4667	R	24*	.2
324	Vanguard Plastics Inc—William Seanor	PO Box 549, Mantua OH 44255	330-274-2855	S	24*	.2
325	Dimension Molding Corp—Michael Stiglianese	777 Annoreno Dr, Addison IL 60101	630-628-0777	R	24*	<.1
326	Red Ewald Inc—Mark Witte	PO Box 519, Karnes City TX 78118	830-780-3304	R	24*	<.1
327	Allied Moulded Products Inc—Walter Troder	222 N Union St, Bryan OH 43506	419-636-4217	R	24*	.2
328	D-W Tool Inc—Donald Wahlers	5830 State Hwy Y V, Jackson MO 63755	573-335-2400	R	24*	.2
329	Vermont Composites Inc—Patrick Wheeler	25 Performance Dr, Bennington VT 05201	802-442-9964	R	24*	.2
330	Fm Structural Plastic Technology Inc—Michael Watts	PO Box 1720, Rogers AR 72757	479-621-4674	R	23*	.3
331	Century Mold Company Inc—Ronald Ricotta	25 Vantage Point Dr, Rochester NY 14624	585-352-8600	R	23*	.2
332	LPS Industries Inc—Madeleine D Robinson	10 Caesar Pl, Moonachie NJ 07074	201-438-3515	R	23*	.2
333	Fiber Glass Industries Inc—Paul Lierheimer	69 Edson St, Amsterdam NY 12010	518-842-4000	R	23*	.1
334	Tasus Corp—Melanie Hart	300 N Daniels Way, Bloomington IN 47404	812-333-6500	R	23*	.1
335	Eptam Plastics Ltd—John Hollinger	2 Riverside Business P, Tilton NH 03276	603-286-8009	R	23*	.1
336	Forward Industries Inc—Brett M Johnson	3110 Main St Ste 400, Santa Monica CA 90405	310-526-3005	P	23	<.1
337	Rainsville Technology Inc—Akio Moramoto	189 Rti Dr, Rainsville AL 35986	256-638-9760	R	23*	.4
338	Genpak Southwest LP—Edward Fitts	505 E Cotton St, Carthage TX 75633	903-693-7151	R	23*	.2
339	Industrial Laminates/Norplex Inc—Thomas Merrell	PO Box 977, Postville IA 52162	563-864-7321	S	23*	.2
340	Nolato Contour—Barry Grant	660 Vandeberg St, Baldwin WI 54002	715-684-4614	R	23*	.2
341	Edge Plastics Inc—David Eckstein	449 Newman St, Mansfield OH 44902	419-522-6696	R	23*	.2
342	Invue Security Products Inc—James Sankey	15015 Lancaster Hwy, Charlotte NC 28277	704-752-6513	R	23*	.2
343	Precision Southeast Inc—Harry Ussery	PO Box 50610, Myrtle Beach SC 29579	843-347-4218	R	22*	.2
344	Advent Tool and Mold Inc—Kenneth Desrosiers	999 Ridgeway Ave, Rochester NY 14615	585-254-2000	R	22*	.1
345	Northwest Composites Inc—Joseph Moran	12810 State Ave, Marysville WA 98271	360-653-2211	R	22*	.4
346	Trimold LLC—DW Greenlee	PO Box 111, Circleville OH 43113	740-474-7591	S	22	.3
347	Iten Industries Inc—Peter Huggins	PO Box 2150, Ashtabula OH 44005	440-997-6134	R	22*	.2
348	Fiber Glass Systems LP—Merrill A Miller Jr	2700 W 65th St, Little Rock AR 72209	501-568-4010	S	22*	.2
349	Akro-Mils Corp—Bob Brady Myers Industries Inc	PO Box 989, Akron OH 44309	330-253-5592	D	22*	.2
350	Viwinco Inc—David Barnes	PO Box 499, Morgantown PA 19543	610-286-8884	R	22*	.2
351	Paulson Manufacturing Corp—Roy Paulson	46752 Rainbow Canyon R, Temecula CA 92592	951-676-2451	R	22*	.1
352	Polymer Corp (Rockland Massachusetts)—Frank Lessen	180 Pleasant St, Rockland MA 02370	781-871-4606	R	22*	.1
353	Blackmore Company Inc—Fred Blackmore	10800 Blackmore Ave, Belleville MI 48111	734-483-8661	R	22*	.1
354	Total Plastics Inc—Tom Garrett	2810 N Burdick St, Kalamazoo MI 49004	269-344-0009	S	22*	<.1
355	Crown Manufacturing Company Inc—Aziz Shariat	37625 Sycamore St, Newark CA 94560	510-742-8800	R	22*	<.1
356	Pool Cover Corp—Leeanan Pesta	390 Motor Pkwy, Hauppauge NY 11788	631-582-2626	S	22*	<.1
357	Century Manufacturing Inc—Gary Kemnitz	3351 N Webb Rd, Wichita KS 67226	316-636-5423	R	22*	.2
358	Mullinix Packages Inc—George Lueken	3511 Engle Rd, Fort Wayne IN 46809	260-747-3149	R	22*	.4
359	Transparent Container Company Inc—Daniel Greiwe	625 Thomas Dr, Bensenville IL 60106	708-449-8520	R	22*	.2
360	Kaysun Corp—Benjamin Harrison	5500 W Dr, Manitowoc WI 54220	920-682-6388	R	22*	.2
361	Continental Precision Corp—Prad Shah	230 Saint Nicholas Ave, South Plainfield NJ 07080	908-754-3030	R	22*	.2
362	Mold-Rite Plastics LLC—Brian Bauerbach	PO Box 160, Plattsburgh NY 12901	518-561-1812	R	21*	.4
363	New Thermo-Serv Ltd—James Hawadarden	3901 Pipestone Rd, Dallas TX 75212	214-631-0307	R	21*	.2
364	Upm Inc—Jason Dowling	13245 Los Angeles St, Baldwin Park CA 91706	626-962-4001	R	21*	.3
365	John W Lucas Specialty Manufacturers Inc—Alberto Silva	2410 Executive Dr, Indianapolis IN 46241	317-241-1111	R	21*	.2
366	Centron International Inc—Paul Brian	PO Box 490, Mineral Wells TX 76068	940-325-1341	S	21	.1
367	Meyer Plastics Inc—Ralph Meyer	5167 E 65th St, Indianapolis IN 46220	317-259-4311	R	21*	.1
368	Stonehouse Marketing Services LLC—Chris Lange	2039 Industrial Blvd, Norman OK 73069	405-360-5674	R	21*	.1
369	MarChem Pacific Inc—Marvin Wool	212 W Taft Ave, Orange CA 92865	314-921-2300	R	21*	<.1
370	R and R Technologies LLC—Allen Hobson	7560 E County Line Rd, Edinburgh IN 46124	812-526-2655	R	21*	<.1
371	Composite Engineering Inc—Amy Fournier	5381 Raley Blvd, Sacramento CA 95838	916-991-1990	R	21*	.4
372	Regency Plastics - Ubly Inc—William Roberts	4385 Garfield St, Ubly MI 48475	989-658-8504	R	21*	.5

Rank	Company Name—*Executive Officer*	Address, City, State, Zip	Phone	Type	Fin	Empls
373	Thomson Plastics Inc—*Jerry Harrison*	PO Box 1258, Thomson GA 30824	706-595-0658	R	21*	.4
374	Ironwood Plastics Inc—*Gordon Stephens*	1235 Wall St, Ironwood MI 49938	906-932-5025	R	21*	.2
375	Donnelly Custom Manufacturing Co—*Stan Donnelly*	105 Donovan Dr, Alexandria MN 56308	320-762-2396	R	21*	.2
376	Jatco Inc—*Paul Appelblom*	725 Zwissig Way, Union City CA 94587	510-487-0888	R	21*	.2
377	Mid-American Products Inc—*Travis Pearse*	PO Box 983, Jackson MI 49204	517-789-8116	R	21*	.3
378	Northland Aluminum Products Inc—*David Dalquist*	5005 Hwy 7, Minneapolis MN 55416	952-920-2888	R	21*	.3
379	Versatile Card Technology Inc—*Jack Hennessey*	5200 Thatcher Rd, Downers Grove IL 60515	630-852-5600	R	20*	.3
380	Schaefer Mold Inc—*Tom Limroth*	2358 Blue Smoke Ct N, Fort Worth TX 76105	817-534-7461	R	20*	.2
381	Vital Plastics Inc—*Terry Townsend*	680 Vandeberg St, Baldwin WI 54002	715-684-5300	R	20*	.2
382	Gkn Aerospace Transparency System—*James Dauw*	12122 Western Ave, Garden Grove CA 92841	714-893-7531	R	20*	.3
383	Cal-Mold Inc—*Erik Fleming*	3900 Hamner Ave, Mira Loma CA 91752	951-361-6400	R	20*	.2
384	Ferriot Inc—*Gordon Keeler*	PO Box 7670, Akron OH 44306	330-786-3000	R	20*	.2
385	Premix Inc—*Thomas Meola*	PO Box 281, North Kingsville OH 44068	440-224-2181	R	20*	.3
386	Sonoco Crellin Inc—*Harris DeLoach Jr*	87 Center St, Chatham NY 12037	518-392-2000	S	20*	.2
387	Tupperware US Inc—*Rick Goings* Tupperware Brands Corp	PO Box 2353, Orlando FL 32802	407-847-3111	S	20*	.2
388	Better Way Partners LLC—*Ellen Grewels*	70891 County Rd 23, New Paris IN 46553	574-831-3340	R	20*	.2
389	Charles Brewer E D M Inc—*Charles Brewer*	3630 E Miraloma Ave, Anaheim CA 92806	714-630-6810	R	20*	.2
390	BW Norton Manufacturing Company Inc—*Howard Norton*	20670 Corsair Blvd, Hayward CA 94545	510-786-1922	R	20*	.1
391	Reese Enterprises Inc—*Robert Ellingson*	PO Box 459, Rosemount MN 55068	651-423-1126	R	20*	.1
392	Innovative Molding—*Grahame Reid*	6775 Mckinley Ave, Sebastopol CA 95472	707-829-2666	R	20*	.1
393	Rolsafe International LLC—*Vernon Collins*	531 Se 20th Ct, Cape Coral FL 33990	239-458-9882	R	20*	.1
394	Rowmark Inc—*Duane E Jebbett*	PO Box 1605, Findlay OH 45840	419-425-8974	R	20*	.1
395	Bellen Container Corp—*Joseph Graziano Sr*	1460 Bowes Rd, Elgin IL 60123	847-741-5600	R	20*	<.1
396	Packnet Ltd—*Michael Nyberg*	2950 Lexington Ave S S, Eagan MN 55121	952-944-9124	R	20*	<.1
397	Paradigm Packaging East LLC—*Matt Marschhauser*	141 N 5th St, Saddle Brook NJ 07663	201-507-0900	R	20*	.3
398	Lakeland Tool And Engineering Inc—*Donald Gross*	2939 6th Ave, Anoka MN 55303	763-422-8866	R	20*	.2
399	Monoflo International Inc—*Henning Rader*	882 Baker Ln, Winchester VA 22603	540-665-1691	R	20*	.2
400	Pixley Richards Holding Inc—*Jonathan Soucy*	9 Collins Ave, Plymouth MA 02360	508-746-6082	R	20*	.2
401	Polymer Industries LLC—*Kapal Saigal*	PO Box 32, Henagar AL 35978	256-657-5197	R	20*	.2
402	Th Plastics Inc—*Patrick Haas*	PO Box 188, Mendon MI 49072	269-496-8495	R	19*	.3
403	Hoffer Plastics Corp—*William Hoffer*	500 N Collins St, South Elgin IL 60177	847-741-5740	R	19*	.3
404	Agape Plastics Inc—*Cindy Alt*	11474 1st Ave Nw, Grand Rapids MI 49534	616-735-4091	R	19*	.2
405	Reiss Industries LLC—*Dave Neitzel*	PO Box 524, Watertown WI 53094	920-261-7975	R	19*	.2
406	Iris USA Inc—*Akihiro Ohyama*	PO Box 581910, Pleasant Prairie WI 53158	262-612-1000	R	19*	.3
407	Robinson Industries Inc—*Ardis Robinson*	3051 W Curtis Rd, Coleman MI 48618	989-465-6111	R	19*	.2
408	Central Carolina Products Inc—*Carlos Diaz*	250 W Old Glencoe Rd, Burlington NC 27217	336-226-0005	R	19*	.2
409	Dixien LLC—*Tony Lewis*	PO Box 337, Forest Park GA 30298	404-366-7427	R	19*	.4
410	Venture Plastics Inc—*J Trapp*	PO Box 249, Newton Falls OH 44444	330-872-5774	R	19*	.2
411	Fawn Industries Inc—*John Franzone*	1920 Greenspring Dr St, Lutherville Timonium MD 21093	410-308-9200	R	19*	.3
412	Cpi Card Group - Colorado Inc—*Steve Montross*	10368 W Centennial Rd, Littleton CO 80127	303-973-9311	R	19*	.2
413	Cpi Card Group - Indiana Inc—*Steve Montross* Cpi Card Group - Colorado Inc	PO Box 10748, Fort Wayne IN 46853	260-424-4920	S	19*	.1
414	C and C Fiberglass Inc—*Cletis Miller*	3659 Destiny Dr, Bremen IN 46506	574-546-2868	R	19*	.1
415	Wright Plastic Products Company LLC—*Tom Arquette*	201 E Condensery Rd, Sheridan MI 48884	989-291-3211	R	19*	.1
416	Vinyl Window Technologies Inc—*Ronnie Brown*	PO Box 588, Paducah KY 42002	270-443-9622	R	19*	.2
417	Atrium Door And Window Company Of The Rockies—*Gregory Faherty*	12775 E 38th Ave Unit, Denver CO 80239	303-375-0570	R	19*	.2
418	Clairson Industries LLC—*Raymond Kaye*	2811 Ne 14th St, Ocala FL 34470	352-732-3244	R	19*	.1
419	Sur-Flo Plastics And Engineering Inc—*Mary Graff*	24358 Groesbeck Hwy, Warren MI 48089	586-773-0400	R	19*	.2
420	Natureworks LLC—*Marc Verbruggen*	PO Box 5830, Minneapolis MN 55440	952-742-0400	R	18*	.1
421	Aircom Manufacturing Inc—*Ronald Lyon*	PO Box 18054, Indianapolis IN 46218	317-545-5383	R	18*	.3
422	L F Manufacturing Inc—*C Johnston*	PO Box 578, Giddings TX 78942	979-542-8027	R	18*	.2
423	Vision Plastics Inc—*Ronald Stevens*	26000 Sw Pky Ctr Dr, Wilsonville OR 97070	503-685-9000	R	18*	.2
424	American Thermoplastic Extrusion Co—*Don Gellett*	4851 Nw 128th St Rd, Opa Locka FL 33054	305-769-9566	R	18*	.2
425	Gregory Holdings Inc—*Greg Vincent*	PO Box 247, Sharon Center OH 44274	330-239-0202	R	18*	.2
426	Pent Plastics Inc—*Charles Schrimper*	6928 N 400 E, Kendallville IN 46755	260-897-3775	R	18*	.1
427	Handgards Inc—*Robert Mclellan*	901 Hawkins Blvd, El Paso TX 79915	915-779-6606	R	18*	.3
428	Avedon Engineering Inc—*Ray Avedon*	PO Box 1018, Longmont CO 80502	303-772-2633	R	18*	.2
429	Ashley Industrial Molding Inc—*Rod Schoon*	PO Box 398, Ashley IN 46705	260-587-9155	R	18*	.2
430	Juno Inc—*David Novak* Cretex Companies Inc	1040 Lund Blvd, Anoka MN 55303	763-553-1312	S	18*	.2
431	Bhar Inc—*Norm Bhargava*	6509 Moeller Rd, Fort Wayne IN 46806	260-749-5168	R	18*	.2
432	Plaspros Inc—*David Georgi*	1143 Ridgeview Dr, Mchenry IL 60050	815-430-2300	R	18*	.2
433	Zippertubing Co—*Terry Plummer*	PO Box 61129, Los Angeles CA 90061	310-527-0488	R	18*	.2
434	Eagle Box Co—*Jay Hoffman*	1 Adams Blvd, Farmingdale NY 11735	631-249-6698	R	18*	<.1
435	Injectron Corp—*Lou Pollak*	PO Box 3012, Plainfield NJ 07063	908-753-1990	R	18*	.3
436	Action Products Co—*Martin Perry*	PO Box 170, Odessa MO 64076	816-633-5514	R	18*	.2
437	Gilkey Window Company Inc—*John Gilkey*	3625 Hauck Rd, Cincinnati OH 45241	513-769-4527	R	18*	.2
438	Stoffel Seals Corp—*Jerome Anderson*	PO Box 825, Nyack NY 10960	845-353-3800	R	18*	.3
439	Tervis Tumbler Co—*Laura Spencer*	201 Triple Diamond Blv, North Venice FL 34275	941-966-2114	R	18*	.3
440	General Pattern And Plastics Inc—*Dennis Reiland*	3075 84th Ln Ne, Minneapolis MN 55449	763-780-3518	R	18*	.2
441	Stelrema Corp—*William Gettig*	4055 E 250 N, Knox IN 46534	574-772-2103	R	18*	.2
442	Lsp Products Group Inc—*Rick Mejia*	3689 Arrowhead Dr, Carson City NV 89706	775-884-4242	R	18*	.2
443	Anna Young Assoc Ltd—*Carl Lombardi*	100 Doxsee Dr, Freeport NY 11520	516-546-4400	R	18*	.2
444	Reo Plastics Inc—*Carrie Sample*	11850 93rd Ave N, Maple Grove MN 55369	763-425-4171	R	18*	.1
445	Tray-Pak Corp—*Scott Myers*	PO Box 14804, Reading PA 19612	610-926-5800	R	17*	.3
446	United Window and Door Manufacturing Inc—*Howard Rose*	24-36 Fadem Rd, Springfield NJ 07081	973-912-0600	R	17*	.3
447	Dlh Industries Inc—*John Saxon*	2422 Leo Ave Sw, Canton OH 44706	330-478-2503	R	17*	.3
448	George Fischer Sloane Inc—*John Pregenzer*	7777 Sloane Dr, Little Rock AR 72176	501-490-7777	R	17*	.2
449	Automated Molding Corp—*Jerry Matausch*	40 E Verdugo Ave, Burbank CA 91502	818-972-5300	R	17*	.2
450	Basic Line Inc—*Yaffa Licari*	PO Box 1337, Perth Amboy NJ 08862	732-826-2000	R	17*	.2
451	J Co—*Douglas Jaques*	PO Box 1090, Mishawaka IN 46546	574-255-3169	R	17*	.1
452	OurPet's Co *Steven Tsengas*	1300 East St, Fairport Harbor OH 44077	440-354-6500	P	17	.1
453	Accu-Mold LLC—*Roger Hargens*	1711 Se Oralabor Rd, Ankeny IA 50021	515-964-5741	R	17*	.2
454	Kelch Corp—*Richard Bemis*	PO Box 901, Sheboygan Falls WI 53085		D	17*	.2
455	Atrion Medical Products	1426 Curt Francis Rd N, Arab AL 35016	256-586-1580	S	17*	.1
456	RTC Inc—*Mark F Nelson*	1777 Oakdale Ave, Saint Paul MN 55118	651-450-7400	R	17*	.1
457	Irathane Systems Co—*Daniel Burkes*	3516 E 13th Ave, Hibbing MN 55746	218-262-5211	R	17*	.1
458	ITW Hi-Cone Div—*Steve Henn*	1140 W Bryn Mawr Ave, Itasca IL 60143	630-438-5300	D	17*	.1

Note: An asterisk (*) indicates an estimated financial figure. The company type code used is as follows: R = Private, P = Public, S = Private Subsidiary, B = Public Subsidiary, D = Division, J = Joint Venture, I = Investment Fund.

COMPANY RANKINGS BY SALES WITHIN 4-DIGIT SIC

Rank	Company Name—Executive Officer	Address, City, State, Zip	Phone	Type	Fin	Empls
459	Polymer Corp—Robert Underwood	180 Pleasant St, Rockland MA 02370	781-871-4606	R	17*	.1
460	Holiday Housewares Inc—John Clementi	PO Box 868, Leominster MA 01453	978-840-3399	R	17*	.2
461	Henry Plastic Molding Inc—Edwin Henry	41703 Albrae St, Fremont CA 94538	510-490-7991	R	17*	.2
462	Pti Engineered Plastics Inc—Mark Rathbone	50900 Corporate Dr, Macomb MI 48044	586-263-5100	R	17*	.2
463	Accuma Corp—Francesca Inzernizzi	133 Fanjoy Rd, Statesville NC 28625	704-873-1488	R	17*	.1
464	Teraco Inc—Raymond Mcdowell	2080 Commerce Dr, Midland TX 79703	432-694-7736	R	17*	.2
465	Sajar Plastics Inc—Scott Simpson	15285 S State Ave, Middlefield OH 44062	440-632-5203	R	17*	.1
466	Grimm Industries Inc—Beatus Grimm	PO Box 924, Fairview PA 16415	814-474-2648	R	17*	.3
467	Injectronics Corp—Paul Nazzaro	1 Union St, Clinton MA 01510	978-368-8701	R	17*	.1
468	Klc Holdings Ltd—Lorne House	PO Box 9548, Yakima WA 98909	509-248-4770	R	16*	.3
469	Omico Inc—Roger Evans	PO Box 1405, Owensboro KY 42302	270-926-9981	R	16*	.1
470	Mar-Bal Inc—Scott Balogh	16930 Munn Rd, Chagrin Falls OH 44023	440-543-7526	R	16*	.4
471	Ajax - United Patterns and Molds Inc—Jonathan Chang	34585 7th St, Union City CA 94587	510-476-8000	R	16*	.1
472	Atp Manufacturing LLC	600 Putnam Pke Ste 8, Greenville RI 02828	401-765-8600	R	16*	.1
473	Industrial Netting Inc—Greg Frandsen	7681 Setzler Pkwy N, Brooklyn Park MN 55445	763-504-4360	R	16*	<.1
474	Syracuse Plastics LLC—Jennifer Heatherington	7400 Morgan Rd, Liverpool NY 13090	315-637-9881	R	16*	.2
475	Premier Technical Plastics Inc (Minden Louisiana)—Colleen McCalmont	118 Old Shreveport Rd, Minden LA 71055	318-377-8733	R	16*	.1
476	Belco Manufacturing Company Inc—Steve Macy	PO Box 210, Belton TX 76513	254-933-9000	R	16*	.2
477	Norco Injection Molding Inc—Jack Williams	PO Box 2528, Chino CA 91708	909-393-4000	R	16*	.2
478	Corpak MedSystems—Thomas Kuhn	100 Chaddick Dr, Wheeling IL 60090	847-403-3400	S	16	.1
479	Bulk Lift International Inc—Brian Kelly	1013 Tamarac Dr, Carpentersville IL 60110	847-428-6059	R	16*	.2
480	Crawford Industries LLC—Duane Bordon	1414 Crawford Dr, Crawfordsville IN 47933	765-359-2900	R	16*	.2
481	Custom Window Extrusions Inc—Angelo Laquatra	1 Contact Pl, Delmont PA 15626	724-468-4553	R	16*	.2
482	Vaupell Midwest Molding and Tooling—Annette Swartz	PO Box 188, Constantine MI 49042	269-435-8414	R	16*	.2
483	Epsilon Products Co—Philip Jardine	PO Box 432, Marcus Hook PA 19061	610-497-8850	J	16*	.1
484	Poly Vinyl Company Inc—Thomas Schnettler	PO Box 300, Sheboygan Falls WI 53085	920-467-4685	R	16*	.1
485	NewAge Industries Inc—Kenneth Baker	145 James Way, Southampton PA 18966	215-526-2300	R	16*	.1
486	B and P Plastics Inc—Bruce Brown	225 W 30th St, National City CA 91950	619-477-1893	R	16*	<.1
487	Sandee Plastic Extrusions—Bob Kunkel	10520 Waveland Ave, Franklin Park IL 60131	847-671-1335	R	16*	<.1
488	Z Microsystems Inc—Jack Wade	9820 Summers Ridge Rd, San Diego CA 92121	858-831-7000	R	16*	<.1
489	Zaca Inc—William Aisley	2630 Townsgate Rd, Westlake Village CA 91361	805-446-4460	R	16*	<.1
490	West Coast Plastics Inc—Javier Franco	10025 Shoemaker Ave, Santa Fe Springs CA 90670	562-777-8024	R	16*	<.1
491	Davis Tool Inc—Ron Davis	3740 Nw Aloclek Pl, Hillsboro OR 97124	503-648-0936	R	16*	.2
492	Fox Valley Molding Inc—Donald Haag	113 S Ctr St, Plano IL 60545	630-552-3176	R	16*	.2
493	Albar Industries Inc—Edward May	780 Whitney Dr, Lapeer MI 48446	810-667-0150	R	16*	.3
494	Williams Industries Inc—William Williams	PO Box 212, Shelbyville IN 46176	317-392-4701	R	16*	.2
495	American Window And Glass Inc—Patty Hertweck	2715 Lynch Rd, Evansville IN 47711	812-464-9400	R	16*	.1
496	Tribar Manufacturing LLC—Chuck Penner	2211 Grand Commerce Dr, Howell MI 48855	517-545-4200	R	16*	.1
497	Centrex Plastics LLC—Terrence Reinhart	PO Box 707, Findlay OH 45839	419-423-1213	R	15*	.1
498	Blackhawk Molding Company Inc—Douglas Hidding	PO Box 419, Addison IL 60101	630-543-3900	R	15*	.1
499	Concept Plastics Inc—Paul Saperstein	PO Box 847, High Point NC 27261	336-889-2001	R	15*	.2
500	Design and Molding Service Inc—Paul Maddalone	25 Howard St, Piscataway NJ 08854	732-752-0300	R	15*	.1
501	Jhj Investments Inc—Michael Illenberger	3800 N Milwaukee Ave, Chicago IL 60641	773-777-5050	R	15*	.1
502	M and M Industries Inc—Glenn Morris	316 Corporate Pl, Chattanooga TN 37419	423-821-3302	R	15*	.1
503	King Plastics Inc—Phillip Lathrum	PO Box 6229, Orange CA 92863	714-997-7540	R	15*	.1
504	C and N Packaging Inc—Christopher Young	105 Wyandanch Ave, Wyandanch NY 11798	631-491-1400	R	15*	.1
505	Ferguson Production Inc—Norlan Ferguson	2130 Industrial Dr, Mcpherson KS 67460	620-241-2400	R	15*	.1
506	Heyco Molded Products Inc—William Jemison	PO Box 517, Toms River NJ 08754	732-286-4336	R	15*	.1
507	Technipaq Inc—Philip Rosenburg	975 Lutter Dr, Crystal Lake IL 60014	815-477-1800	R	15*	.1
508	Radial Industries Inc—John Macho	3616 Noakes St, Los Angeles CA 90023	323-263-6991	R	15*	.1
509	Darling Industries Inc—Gary Darling	3749 N Romero Rd, Tucson AZ 85705	520-887-2400	R	15*	.1
510	National Hanger Company Inc—Michele Pilcher	PO Box 818, North Bennington VT 05257	802-447-1541	R	15*	.1
511	SFB Plastics Inc—David Long	PO Box 533, Wichita KS 67201	316-262-0409	R	15*	.1
512	Jessup Manufacturing Company Inc—Robert Jessup	PO Box 366, Mchenry IL 60051	815-385-6650	R	15*	.1
513	Neil Enterprises Inc—Neil Fine	450 Bunker Ct, Vernon Hills IL 60061	847-549-7627	R	15*	<.1
514	Cal-Mil Plastic Products Inc—John Callahan	4079 Calle Platino, Oceanside CA 92056	760-630-5100	R	15*	<.1
515	Lawrence Tool and Molding Co—Lloyd Lawrence	2050 W 7th Ave, Denver CO 80204	303-592-9548	R	15*	<.1
516	Crescent Industries Inc—Daryl Paules	70 E High St, New Freedom PA 17349	717-235-3844	R	15*	.2
517	Plastics Molding Co—Janet Hagy	4211 N Broadway, Saint Louis MO 63147	314-241-2479	R	15*	.1
518	Armstrong Mold Corp—John Armstrong	6910 Manlius Ctr Rd, East Syracuse NY 13057	315-437-1517	R	15*	.2
519	Inoac Packaging Group Inc—Ken Miwa	901 Nutter Dr, Bardstown KY 40004	502-348-5159	R	15*	.2
520	Mmi Engineered Solutions Inc—Thomas Connaughton	1715 Woodland Dr, Saline MI 48176	734-429-4664	R	15*	.1
521	Precision Molding Inc—Sarah Boles	5500 Roberts Matthews, Sparta TN 38583	931-738-8376	R	15*	.1
522	Ecm Plastics Inc—Wayne Marquis	53 Millbrook St Ste 2, Worcester MA 01606	508-756-0002	R	15*	.1
523	Bankier Companies Inc—Jack Bankier	6151 W Gross Point Rd, Niles IL 60714	847-647-6565	R	14*	.1
524	American Innotek Inc—Niki Kopenhaver	2320 Meyers Ave, Escondido CA 92029	760-741-6600	R	14*	.1
525	Jaco Manufacturing Co—Stephen Campbell	PO Box 619, Berea OH 44017	440-234-4000	R	14*	.1
526	United Southern Industries Inc—Joe Bennett	PO Box 469, Forest City NC 28043	828-245-6453	R	14*	.2
527	William H Harvey Co—John Harvey	4334 S 67th St, Omaha NE 68117	402-331-1175	R	14*	.2
528	Badger Plug Co—Dan Voissem	PO Box 199, Greenville WI 54942	920-757-7300	R	14*	.2
529	Confer Plastics Inc—Douglas Confer	97 Witmer Rd, North Tonawanda NY 14120	716-693-2056	R	14*	.1
530	Underwood Mold Company Inc—James Underwood	PO Box 1607, Woodstock GA 30188	770-926-2465	R	14*	.1
531	Precision Thermoplastic Components Inc—Randy Carter	PO Box 1296, Lima OH 45802	419-227-4500	R	14*	.1
532	Microdyne Plastics Inc—Ron Brown	1901 E Cooley Dr, Colton CA 92324	909-503-4010	R	14*	.1
533	Nupla Corp—Robert Perret	11912 Sheldon St, Sun Valley CA 91352	818-768-6800	R	14*	.1
534	Primera Plastics Inc—Noel Cuellar	3424 Production Ct, Zeeland MI 49464	616-748-6248	R	14*	.1
535	Zefon International—Russell Mantz	5350 SW 1st Ln, Ocala FL 34474	352-854-8080	R	14*	.1
536	Alco Plastics Inc—Daniel Conway	PO Box 447, Romeo MI 48065	586-752-4527	R	14*	.1
537	Y-Tex Corp—Jerry Payne	PO Box 1450, Cody WY 82414	307-587-5515	R	14*	.1
538	Greene Plastics Corp—Albert Seifert	PO Box 178, Hope Valley RI 02832	401-539-2432	R	14*	.1
539	Heinke Technology Inc—Sam Featherstone	5120 Nw 38th St, Lincoln NE 68524	402-470-2600	R	14*	.1
540	E and O Tool and Plastics Inc—Timothy Osterman	19178 Industrial Blvd, Elk River MN 55330	763-441-6100	R	14*	.1
541	Stanek E F And Associates Inc—Mark Davis	4565 Willow Pkwy, Cleveland OH 44125	216-341-7700	R	14*	.1
542	Jersey Plastic Molders Inc—Joseph Zazzara	149 Shaw Ave, Irvington NJ 07111	973-926-1800	R	14*	.1
543	New Berlin Plastics Inc—Jeffery Held	5725 S Westridge Dr, New Berlin WI 53151	262-784-3120	R	14*	.1
544	Fort Wayne Plastics Inc—Robb Robertson	510 Sumpter St, Fort Wayne IN 46804	260-432-2520	R	13*	.1
545	Macro Plastics Inc—Warren Mcdonald	2250 Huntington Dr, Fairfield CA 94533	707-437-1200	R	13*	.1
546	Flotation Tech LLC—Tim Cook	20 Morin St, Biddeford ME 04005	207-282-7749	R	13*	.1
547	Stephen Douglas Plastics Inc—Stewart Graff	PO Box 2775, Paterson NJ 07509	973-523-3030	R	13*	.1

Rank	Company Name—*Executive Officer*	Address, City, State, Zip	Phone	Type	Fin	Empls
548	Colonie Plastics Corp—*Paul Gurbatri*	188 Candlewood Rd, Bay Shore NY 11706	631-434-6969	R	13*	.1
549	Quaker Plastic Corp—*Donald Dahowski*	103 S Manor St, Mountville PA 17554	717-764-8585	R	13*	.1
550	Eger Products Inc—*Reva Eger*	1132 Ferris Rd, Amelia OH 45102	513-753-4200	R	13*	.1
551	Thompson Creek Window Co—*Rick Wuest*	PO Box 1440, Landover MD 20785		R	13*	.1
552	Midgard Inc—*Robert Brown*	1255 Nursery Rd, Green Lane PA 18054	215-536-3174	R	13*	.1
553	Seaway Manufacturing Corp—*Michael Goodrich*	2250 E 33rd St, Erie PA 16510	814-898-2255	R	13*	.1
554	Dreco Inc—*Christopher Draudt*	PO Box 39328, North Ridgeville OH 44039	440-327-6021	R	13*	.1
555	Plastic Molded Concepts Inc—*Larry Floyd*	PO Box 490, Eagle WI 53119	262-594-5050	R	13*	.1
556	Allegheny Plastics Inc—*Walter M Yost*	3 Ave A, Leetsdale PA 15056	412-749-0700	R	13*	.2
557	Tnt Plastic Molding Divison Of Artistic Plastics Inc—*Diane Mixson*	1700 E Via Burton, Anaheim CA 92806	714-490-1150	R	13*	.2
558	Wilson-Hurd Manufacturing Co—*Jim Mcintyre*	PO Box 8028, Wausau WI 54402	715-845-9221	R	13*	.1
559	Flexaust Company Inc—*Mike Harvey*	PO Box 4275, Warsaw IN 46581	574-267-7909	R	13*	.1
560	Spectrum Plastics Molding Resources Inc—*Pierre Dziubina*	401 Birmingham Blvd, Ansonia CT 06401	203-736-5200	S	13*	.1
561	Accent Plastics Inc—*Thomas Pridonoff*	1925 Elise Cir, Corona CA 92879	951-273-7777	R	13*	.1
562	Harrington Corp—*Michael Harrington*	PO Box 10335, Lynchburg VA 24506	434-845-7094	R	13*	.1
563	Oscoda Plastics Inc—*John Burt*	PO Box 189, Oscoda MI 48750	989-739-6900	R	13*	.1
564	QCH Inc—*Kenneth Chatterton*	230 Kendall Point Dr, Oswego IL 60543	630-820-5550	R	13*	.1
565	Topcraft Precision Molders Inc—*Pascual Musitano*	301 Ivyland Rd, Warminster PA 18974	215-441-4700	R	13*	.1
566	Qfc Plastics Inc—*Jeff Kelly*	PO Box 5313, Arlington TX 76005	817-649-7400	R	13*	.1
567	Molding International And Engineering Inc—*O Hughes*	42136 Avenida Alvarado, Temecula CA 92590	951-296-5010	R	13*	.1
568	Xten Industries LLC—*Paul Abrahams*	9600 55th St, Kenosha WI 53144	262-605-9000	R	13*	.1
569	Cortina Tool and Molding Co—*Michael Giannelli*	10706 Grand Ave Ste 1, Franklin Park IL 60131	847-455-2800	R	13*	.1
570	Cs Manufacturing Inc—*Tim Mabie*	299 W Cherry St, Cedar Springs MI 49319	616-696-2772	R	13*	.1
571	Cdf Corp—*Joseph Sullivan*	77 Industrial Park Rd, Plymouth MA 02360	508-747-5858	R	13*	.1
572	Centech Plastics Inc—*Gyongyi Varhegyi*	855 Touhy Ave, Elk Grove Village IL 60007	847-364-4433	R	13*	.1
573	Pinnacle Industrial Enterprises Inc—*Kevin Tearney*	PO Box 286, Bowling Green OH 43402	419-352-8688	R	13*	.1
574	Pioneer Plastics Corp—*Ralph Danesi*	3330 Massillon Rd, Akron OH 44312	330-896-2356	R	13*	.1
575	Anchor Tool And Plastics Inc—*Ronald Rogers*	8109 Lewis Rd, Minneapolis MN 55427	763-546-2401	R	13*	.1
576	Mercury Plastics Inc—*William Rowley*	PO Box 989, Middlefield OH 44062	440-632-5281	R	13*	.1
577	Olcott Plastics Inc—*Joseph Brodner*	95 N 17th St, Saint Charles IL 60174	630-584-0555	R	13*	.1
578	Master Molded Products Corp—*James Weinhart*	1000 Davis Rd, Elgin IL 60123	847-695-9700	R	13*	.1
579	Abtec Inc—*William Sinclair*	2570 Pearl Buck Rd, Bristol PA 19007	215-788-0950	R	13*	.1
580	Advanced Molding Technologies—*Kevin Kelly*	1425 Lake Ave, Woodstock IL 60098	815-334-3606	D	13*	.1
581	Rage Corp—*George Saliaris*	PO Box 159, Hilliard OH 43026	614-771-4771	R	13*	.1
582	W Kintz Plastics Inc—*Edwin Kintz*	165 Caverns Rd, Howes Cave NY 12092	518-296-8513	R	12*	.1
583	Joseph L Ertl Inc—*Joseph Ertl*	PO Box 327, Dyersville IA 52040	563-875-2436	R	12*	.1
584	Allianoe Carolina Tool and Mold Corp—*Dale Bizily*	PO Box 686, Arden NC 28704	828-684-7831	R	12*	.1
585	Dura Plastic Products Inc—*Hardy Rost*	PO Box 2097, Beaumont CA 92223	951-845-3161	R	12*	.1
586	Thorgren Tool and Molding Company Inc—*Robert Thorgren*	1100 Evans Ave, Valparaiso IN 46383	219-462-1801	R	12*	.1
587	WCP Inc—*Charles Neubauer*	17730 Crusader Ave, Cerritos CA 90703	562-653-9797	R	12*	.1
588	Action Windows Inc—*Felix Kotovnikov*	40 Progress Cir, Newington CT 06111	860-667-8451	R	12*	.1
589	Russell Plastics Technology Company Inc—*Alexandor Bozza*	521 W Hoffman Ave, Lindenhurst NY 11757	631-226-3700	R	12*	.1
590	Currier Plastics Inc—*John Currier*	101 Columbus St, Auburn NY 13021	315-255-1779	R	12*	.1
591	Clim-A-Tech Industries Inc—*J Perlich*	PO Box 221, Hopkins MN 55343	952-938-7649	R	12*	.1
592	Plasticraft Manufacturing Company Inc—*Edwin Ingram*	115 Plasticraft Dr, Albertville AL 35951	256-878-4105	R	12*	.2
593	Trim-Tex Inc—*Joseph Koenig*	3700 W Pratt Ave, Lincolnwood IL 60712	847-679-3000	R	12*	.1
594	Arthurmade Plastics Inc—*Kirk Marounian*	2131 Garfield Ave, Commerce CA 90040	323-888-1077	R	12*	.1
595	Surprise Plastics Inc—*Joseph Tancredi*	124 57th St, Brooklyn NY 11220	718-492-6355	R	12*	.1
596	Tri-Town Precision Plastics Inc—*Scott Goodspeed*	12 Bridge St, Deep River CT 06417	860-526-3200	R	12*	.1
597	Fenner Presision Inc—*Mike Thompson*	852 Kensington Ave, Buffalo NY 14215	716-833-6900	S	12*	.1
598	Design Molded Plastics Inc—*Jerry Honsaker*	8220 Bavaria Rd, Macedonia OH 44056	330-963-4400	R	12*	.1
599	Technical Precision Plastics Inc—*James Piermarini*	1405 Dogwood Way, Mebane NC 27302	919-563-9292	R	12*	.1
600	Bristol Fiberlite Industries Inc—*Rick Beets*	401 Goetz Ave, Santa Ana CA 92707	714-540-8950	R	12*	.1
601	Busse SJI Corp	124 N Columbus St, Randolph WI 53956	920-326-3131	S	12*	.1
602	Clairson Industries Corp—*Clo Kilkelly*	2811 NE 14th St, Ocala FL 34470	352-732-3244	R	12*	.1
603	Design Plastics Inc—*John Nepper Jr*	3550 Keystone Dr, Omaha NE 68134	402-572-7177	R	12*	.1
604	Greenbriar Scentex—*Steve Pridemore*	300 Greenbrier Rd, Summersville WV 26651	304-872-3000	D	12*	.1
605	Palmer Distributors Inc—*James Palmer*	23001 W Industrial Dr, Saint Clair Shores MI 48080	586-772-4225	R	12*	.1
606	Sunlite Plastics Inc—*Brant Stanford*	W194n11340 Mccormick D, Germantown WI 53022	262-253-0600	R	12*	.1
607	Three D Plastics Inc	430 N Varney St, Burbank CA 91502	323-849-1316	R	12*	.1
608	Plast-O-Foam LLC—*Lisa Antosh*	24061 Capital Blvd, Clinton Township MI 48036	586-307-3790	R	12*	.1
609	Duall Div	1550 Industrial Dr, Owosso MI 48867	989-725-8184	D	12*	.1
610	Global Polymer Industries Inc—*Todd Huntimer*	PO Box 339, Arlington SD 57212	605-983-5244	R	12*	.1
611	Performance Systematix Inc—*Karlis Vizulis*	5569 33rd St Se, Grand Rapids MI 49512	616-949-9090	R	12*	.1
612	Fiberglass Coatings Inc—*William Higman*	4301A 34th St N, Saint Petersburg FL 33714	727-327-8117	R	12*	<.1
613	Gulf Coast Plastics Inc—*Tom Coyrn*	9314 Princess Palm Ave, Tampa FL 33619	813-621-8098	S	12*	<.1
614	Rogers Manufacturing Co—*Vincent Bitel*	PO Box 155, Rockfall CT 06481	860-346-8648	R	12*	.1
615	E-S Plastic Products Inc—*Pete Keddie*	809 Mohr Ave, Waterford WI 53185	262-534-5555	R	12*	.1
616	Cobra Plastics Inc—*Kent Houser*	1244 Highland Rd E, Macedonia OH 44056	330-425-4260	R	12*	.1
617	W M Plastics Inc—*Chris Metz*	5151 Bolger Ct, Mchenry IL 60050	815-578-8888	R	12*	.1
618	Sandee Manufacturing Co—*Thomas Kunkel*	10520 Waveland Ave, Franklin Park IL 60131	847-671-1335	R	12*	<.1
619	Dimcogray Corp—*Michael Sieron*	900 Dimco Way, Dayton OH 45458	937-433-7600	R	12*	.1
620	Blue Star Plastics Inc—*Roger Storch*	801 Nandino Blvd, Lexington KY 40511	859-255-0714	R	12*	.1
621	Hi-Tech Mold and Tool Inc—*William Kristensen*	1 Technology Dr W, Pittsfield MA 01201	413-443-9184	R	12*	.1
622	Phillips Diversified Manufacturing Inc—*Russell Corum*	PO Box 250, Annville KY 40402	606-364-2750	R	12*	<.1
623	Spartek Inc—*Richard Kiedrowski*	PO Box 437, Sparta WI 54656	608-269-3154	R	12*	.2
624	Elgin Molded Plastics Inc—*Clarence Labar*	909 Grace St, Elgin IL 60120	847-931-2455	R	12*	.1
625	CAPS Inc—*James Kick*	13080 Hollenberg Dr, Bridgeton MO 63044	314-739-2002	R	12*	.1
626	Medway Plastics Corp—*Thomas Hutchinson*	2250 E Cherry Industri, Long Beach CA 90805	562-630-1175	R	12*	.1
627	Chemtech Plastics Inc—*Ragnar Korthase*	765 Church Rd, Elgin IL 60123	847-742-6800	R	12*	.1
628	Plastic Packaging Corp—*Susan Weiss*	PO Box 548, West Springfield MA 01090	413-785-1553	R	12*	.1
629	Gateway Plastics Inc—*Carl Vogel*	5650 W County Line Rd, Mequon WI 53092	262-242-2020	R	12*	.1
630	Mearthane Products Corp—*Kevin Redmond*	16 Western Industrial, Cranston RI 02921	401-946-4400	R	12*	.1
631	Pereles Brothers Inc—*Ted Muccio*	5840 N 60th St, Milwaukee WI 53218	414-463-1000	R	12*	.1
632	Plainfield Molding Inc—*Robert Aldi*	PO Box 265, Plainfield IL 60544	815-436-5671	R	12*	.1
633	Mdi Products LLC—*Carlos Chavarri*	10045 102nd Ter, Sebastian FL 32958	772-388-9892	R	11*	.1
634	Makray Manufacturing Company Inc—*Paul Makray*	4400 N Harlem Ave, Norridge IL 60706	708-456-7100	R	11*	.1
635	Dura-Cast Products Inc—*Bruce Orcutt*	16160 Hwy 27, Lake Wales FL 33859	863-638-3200	R	11*	.1
636	Trilogy Plastics Inc—*Stephen Osborn*	PO Box 2600, Alliance OH 44601	330-821-4700	R	11*	.1

Note: An asterisk (*) indicates an estimated financial figure. The company type code used is as follows: R = Private, P = Public, S = Private Subsidiary, B = Public Subsidiary, D = Division, J = Joint Venture, I = Investment Fund.

COMPANY RANKINGS BY SALES WITHIN 4-DIGIT SIC

Rank	Company Name—Executive Officer	Address, City, State, Zip	Phone	Type	Fin	Empls
637	Honeyware Inc—Tony Sheng	244 Dukes St, Kearny NJ 07032	201-997-5900	R	11*	.1
638	Akron Porcelain and Plastics Co—George Lewis	PO Box 15157, Akron OH 44314	330-745-2159	R	11*	.2
639	Jdr Engineering Consultants Inc—Dionisio Rodriguez	3122 Maple St, Santa Ana CA 92707	714-751-7084	R	11*	.1
640	Polyjohn Enterprises Corp—Edward Cooper	2500 Gaspar Ave, Whiting IN 46394		R	11*	.1
641	AK Industries Inc—John Sabo	PO Box 640, Plymouth IN 46563	574-936-6022	R	11*	.1
642	Mikros Engineering Inc—James Talmage	8755 Wyoming Ave N, Brooklyn Park MN 55445	763-424-4642	R	11*	.1
643	Trim-Lok Inc—Gary Whitener	PO Box 6180, Buena Park CA 90622	714-562-0500	R	11*	.1
644	Pacon Inc—Robert Austin	4249 Puente Ave, Baldwin Park CA 91706	626-814-4654	R	11*	.1
645	A and S Mold and Die Corp—Hugo Adlhoch	9705 Eton Ave, Chatsworth CA 91311	818-341-5393	R	11*	.1
646	Advanced Auto Trends Inc—Sandra Cornell	2230 Metamora Rd, Oxford MI 48371	248-628-6111	R	11*	.1
647	Garner Industries Inc—Philip Mullin	7201 N 98th St, Lincoln NE 68507	402-434-9100	R	11*	.1
648	Classic Mold Company Inc—Thomas Gebhardt	3800 Wesley Ter, Schiller Park IL 60176	847-671-7889	R	11*	.1
649	Intertech Plastics Inc—Noel Ginsburg	12850 E 40th Ave Unit, Denver CO 80239	303-371-4270	R	11*	.1
650	Plasticorp—Mike Tesar	24105 S Frampton Ave, Harbor City CA 90710	310-539-9530	R	11*	.2
651	Paradigm Packaging—Douglas E Ellis	141 N 5th St, Saddle Brook NJ 07663	201-909-3400	R	11*	.1
652	West Coast Vinyl Inc—James Keirstead	4023 S Orchard St, Tacoma WA 98466	253-565-4920	R	11*	.1
653	Newtown Manufacturing And Building Supply Corp—Carl Slocomb	247 Old River Rd, Wilkes Barre PA 18702	570-825-3675	R	11*	.1
654	Florida Custom Mold Inc—Michael Cave	1806 Gunn Hwy, Odessa FL 33556	813-343-5080	R	11*	.1
655	Bingham and Taylor Corp—Dennis Quinn	PO Box 939, Culpeper VA 22701	540-825-8334	R	11	.1
656	Remcon Plastics Inc—Peter Connors	208 Chestnut St, Reading PA 19602	610-376-2666	R	11*	.1
657	Lorentson Manufacturing Company Inc—Christian Sawyer	PO Box 932, Kokomo IN 46903	765-452-4425	R	11*	.1
658	Alabama Plastics Inc	PO Box 170748, Birmingham AL 35217	205-647-0700	S	11*	.1
659	Pinnacle Plastics Inc—Frank J Chiz	1513 Grimm Dr, Erie PA 16501	814-454-1007	S	11*	<.1
660	Industrial Pipe Fittings Inc—Robert Jones III	6020 Osborn St, Houston TX 77033	713-645-2858	R	11*	<.1
661	Tri-Star Plastics Inc—Eric Muller	1915 E Via Burton, Anaheim CA 92806	714-533-7360	R	11*	.1
662	Swimways Corp—Emanuel Arias	5816 Ward Ct, Virginia Beach VA 23455	757-440-1156	R	11*	.1
663	California Optical Corp—Fredric Grethel	30577 Huntwood Ave, Hayward CA 94544	510-487-8832	R	11*	.1
664	Madan Plastics Inc—Steven Skoler	PO Box 487, Cranford NJ 07016	908-276-8484	R	11*	.1
665	Jamestown Plastics Inc—Jay Baker	PO Box U, Brocton NY 14716	716-792-4144	R	11*	.1
666	Thombert Inc—Richard Davidson	316 E 7th St N, Newton IA 50208	641-792-4449	R	11*	.1
667	Klein Plastics Company LLC—Jay Bylsma	210 Rockford Park Dr N, Rockford MI 49341	616-863-9900	R	11*	.1
668	Eljobo Inc—Joel Glickman	2800 Sterling Dr, Hatfield PA 19440	215-822-5544	R	11*	.1
669	Stabilt America Inc—Stephen Adkins	285 Industrial Dr, Moscow TN 38057	901-877-3010	R	11*	.1
670	Edon Corp—Edwin Axel	1160 Easton Rd, Horsham PA 19044	215-672-8050	R	11*	.1
671	Cool-Pak LLC—Roy Thorsen	2601 Camino Del Sol, Oxnard CA 93030	805-981-2434	R	11*	.1
672	Deimling/Jeliho Plastics Inc—William Deimling	4010 Bach Buxton Rd, Amelia OH 45102	513-752-6653	R	11*	.1
673	Hanes Erie Inc—Thomas Hanes	7601 Klier Dr S, Fairview PA 16415	814-474-1999	R	11*	.1
674	Innovative Plastech Inc—Joanne Gustafson	1260 Kingsland Dr, Batavia IL 60510	630-232-1808	R	11*	.1
675	Uni-Sun Inc—Gary Watts	702 Ashland St, Houston TX 77007	713-869-8331	R	11*	.3
676	Bardot Plastics Inc—Joseph Boucher	PO Box 3369, Easton PA 18043	610-253-0600	R	11*	.1
677	D and M Custom Injection Moldings Corp—Steve Motisi	PO Box 158, Burlington IL 60109	847-683-2054	R	11*	.1
678	Available Plastics Inc—Steven Brown	5020 Beechmont Dr Ne, Huntsville AL 35811	256-859-4957	R	11*	.1
679	Industrial Fabrics Corp—Rolf Muehlenhaus	7160 Northland Cir N B, Minneapolis MN 55428	763-535-3220	R	11*	.1
680	Jet Plastics—Lee Johnson	941 N Eastern Ave, Los Angeles CA 90063	323-268-6706	R	11*	.1
681	Poly Flex Products Inc—Mark Kirchmer	34481 Industrial Rd, Livonia MI 48150	734-458-4194	R	11*	<.1
682	Bomatic Inc—Kjeld Hestehave	1841 E Acacia St, Ontario CA 91761	909-947-3900	R	11*	.1
683	Ims Gear Holding Inc—Clemens Rosenstiel	1234 Palmour Dr Ste B, Gainesville GA 30501	770-840-9600	R	11*	.1
684	Seville Flexpack Corp—Walter Yakich	PO Box 246, Oak Creek WI 53154	414-761-2751	R	11*	.1
685	Shur-Line Inc	8935 NorthPointe Execu, Huntersville NC 28078		S	11*	.1
686	United Comb and Novelty Corp—Edward Zephir	PO Box 358, Leominster MA 01453	978-537-2096	R	11*	.1
687	Astra Products Of Ohio Ltd	PO Box 848, Ravenna OH 44266	330-296-0112	R	11*	.1
688	Capco Plastics Inc—Richard Capuano	PO Box 9591, Providence RI 02940	401-272-3833	R	11*	.1
689	El Monte Plastics Company Inc—William Burlingham	2435 Strozier Ave, South El Monte CA 91733	626-442-0162	R	11*	.1
690	Illinois Valley Plastics Inc—Donald Tjarksen	300 N Cummings Ln, Washington IL 61571	309-444-8884	R	11*	.1
691	Universal Plastics Corp—Joseph Peters	75 Whiting Farms Rd, Holyoke MA 01040	413-592-4791	R	11*	.1
692	An-Cor Industrial Plastics Inc—Merrill Arthur	100 Melody Ln, North Tonawanda NY 14120	716-695-3141	R	11*	.1
693	Elgin Die Mold Co—John Sapiente	14n002 Prairie St, Pingree Grove IL 60140	847-464-0140	R	11*	.1
694	L B Plastics Inc—Harry Davis	PO Box 907, Mooresville NC 28115	704-663-1543	R	10*	.1
695	American Plastic Molding Corp—Floyd Coates	PO Box 480, Scottsburg IN 47170	812-752-7000	R	10*	.1
696	Comfort Line Inc—Richard La Valley	5500 Enterprise Blvd, Toledo OH 43612	419-729-8520	R	10*	.1
697	Component Plastics Inc—Joseph Valente	700 Tollgate Rd, Elgin IL 60123	847-695-9200	R	10*	.1
698	Impact Plastics Inc—Gerald O'connor	1070 S Industrial Dr A, Erwin TN 37650	423-743-3561	R	10*	.1
699	Iowa Rotocast Plastics Inc—Floyd Mount	PO Box 320, Decorah IA 52101	563-382-9636	R	10*	.1
700	Tech Molded Plastics Inc—Scott Hanaway	1045 French St, Meadville PA 16335	814-724-8222	R	10*	.1
701	Forte Product Solutions—Carl Dobrzeniecki	1601 Airpark Dr, Farmington MO 63640	573-760-1227	R	10*	.1
702	Accutech Packaging Inc—Richard Madigan	157 Green St, Foxboro MA 02035	508-543-3800	R	10*	.1
703	Minnesota Diversified Industries Inc—Peter Mcdermott	1700 Wynne Ave Ste 100, Saint Paul MN 55108	651-999-8200	R	10*	.2
704	Genesis Plastics And Engineering LLC—Karen Hawn	PO Box 228, Scottsburg IN 47170	812-752-6742	R	10*	.1
705	Portage Plastics Corp—David Bernard	PO Box 640, Portage WI 53901	608-745-1400	R	10*	.1
706	Erb Industries Inc—Sheila Eads	1 Safety Way, Woodstock GA 30188	770-926-7944	R	10*	.1
707	Commodore Plastics LLC—Lee Statt	26 Maple Ave, Bloomfield NY 14469	585-657-7777	R	10*	.1
708	Harkness Enterprises Inc—Stephanie Harkness Cretex Companies Inc	2840 Research Park Dr, Soquel CA 95073	831-462-1141	S	10*	.1
709	Rhino Inc—Richard Johanneck	411 Congress St W, Maple Lake MN 55358	320-963-5995	R	10*	.1
710	Teamvantage Molding LLC—Russ Meyer	22455 Everton Ave N, Forest Lake MN 55025	651-464-3900	R	10*	.1
711	PRA Co—Paul Aultman	1415 W Cedar St, Standish MI 48658	989-846-1029	R	10*	.1
712	Deluxe Plastics Inc—Charles Orth	220 Industrial Ave, Clintonville WI 54929	715-823-4200	R	10*	.1
713	Steinwall Properties LLC—Maureen Steinwall	1759 116th Ave Nw, Minneapolis MN 55448	763-767-7060	R	10*	.1
714	American Plastic Card Co—Jim Akbar	21550 Oxnard St Ste 30, Woodland Hills CA 91367	818-784-4224	R	10*	.1
715	Xcell International Corp—Raymond Henning	PO Box 452, Westmont IL 60559	630-323-0107	R	10*	.1
716	Topp Industries Inc—Kevin Birchmeyer	PO Box 420, Rochester IN 46975	574-223-3681	R	10*	.1
717	Cycles Inc—Chetan Patel Scientific Molding Corporation Ltd	32 Chocksett Rd, Sterling MA 01564	978-422-6800	S	10*	.1
718	Namsco Plastics Industries Inc—David Namey	100 Hunt Valley Rd, New Kensington PA 15068	724-339-3591	R	10*	.1
719	Royal Window Coverings (USA) LP—Gordon Case	900 Waltham Way, Mccarran NV 89434	775-343-7773	R	10*	.1
720	Hadlock Plastics LLC—Terry Morgan	110 N Eagle St, Geneva OH 44041	440-466-4876	R	10*	.1
721	Endura Plastics Inc—Mark Lillo	7955 Chardon Rd, Kirtland OH 44094	440-951-4466	R	10*	.1
722	Profile Plastics Inc—Stephen Murrill	65 Waukegan Rd, Lake Bluff IL 60044	847-604-5100	R	10*	.1
723	Continental Industries Inc—Levi Watson	4102 S 74th E Ave, Tulsa OK 74145	918-627-5210	D	10*	.2

Rank	Company Name—*Executive Officer*	Address, City, State, Zip	Phone	Type	Fin	Empls
724	B and R Plastics Inc—*Donald Welge*	4550 Kingston St, Denver CO 80239	303-373-0710	R	10*	.1
725	Par 4 Plastics Inc—*Joe Mcdaniel*	PO Box 385, Marion KY 42064	270-965-9141	R	10*	.1
726	Riverside Plastics Inc—*Thomas Gunn*	900 Washington St, Bonaparte IA 52620	319-592-3166	R	10*	.1
727	Supracor Systems Inc—*Curtis L Landi*	2050 Corporate Ct, San Jose CA 95131	408-432-1616	R	10*	.1
728	Williams Die and Mold Inc—*Clyde Williams*	6580 Jimmy Carter Blvd, Norcross GA 30071	770-613-0660	R	10*	.1
729	Microphor Inc—*Bill Kassling*	452 E Hill Rd, Willits CA 95490	707-459-5563	S	10*	.1
730	Daystar Inc—*Jean Goodman*	841 S 71st Ave, Phoenix AZ 85043	623-907-0081	R	10*	.1
731	ITW Thielex—*Henry Swain*	95 Commerce Dr, Somerset NJ 08873	732-873-5500	D	10*	.1
732	Kenway Corp—*Kenneth Priest*	681 Riverside Dr, Augusta ME 04330	207-623-8292	R	10*	.1
733	Rakar Inc—*Walter Pittman*	PO Box 2767, Oxnard CA 93034	805-487-2721	R	10*	.1
734	Forteq North America Inc—*Brune Bakke*	150 Park Centre Dr, West Henrietta NY 14586	585-427-9410	R	10*	.1
735	Unette Corp—*Joseph Hark*	1578 Sunjex Tpke Ste 4, Randolph NJ 07869	973-328-6800	R	10*	.1
736	Target Plastics Technology Corporation—*Ivan Racz*	400 Windy Point Dr, Glendale Heights IL 60139	630-545-1776	R	10*	.1
737	MerryWeather Foam Inc—*Robert G McCune*	11 Brown St, Barberton OH 44203	330-753-0353	R	10*	.1
738	AIA Plastics Inc—*Jim Donaldson*	290 E 56th Ave, Denver CO 80216	303-296-9696	R	10*	.1
739	Watertown Plastics Inc—*Jonathan Andrew*	PO Box 309, Watertown CT 06795	860-274-7535	R	10*	<.1
740	Stewart Industries Inc (Seattle Washington)—*Ralph Smith*	16 S Idaho St, Seattle WA 98134	206-652-9110	R	10*	<.1
741	Coon Manufacturing Inc—*Bill Coon*	PO Box 108, Spickard MO 64679	660-485-6299	R	10*	<.1
742	Acry Fab Inc—*Jeff Gunderson*	584 Progress Way, Sun Prairie WI 53590	608-837-0045	R	10*	<.1
743	TechniFoam Inc—*Todd Beaty*	514 Calvary Ave, Saint Louis MO 63147	314-421-4044	R	10*	<.1
744	Lesko Enterprises Inc—*John Lesko*	PO Box 71, Albion PA 16401	814-756-4030	R	10*	.1
745	Bur-Bak Plastics Corp—*Jerry Greene*	PO Box 669, Wilton NH 03086	603-654-2291	R	10*	.1
746	Weathergard Window Company Inc—*Albert Ben-Ezra*	14350 W 8 Mile Rd, Oak Park MI 48237	248-967-8822	R	10*	.1
747	Tailor Made Products Inc—*John Wilde*	101 Juneau St, Elroy WI 53929	608-462-8227	R	10*	.1
748	Dexas International Ltd—*Ellis Shamoon*	585 S Royal Ln Ste 200, Coppell TX 75019	469-635-8100	R	10*	.1
749	Lakone Co—*Bruce Rhoades*	1003 Aucutt Rd, Montgomery IL 60538	630-892-4251	R	10*	.1
750	Olsen Tool And Plastics Inc—*Robert Strom*	4060 Norex Dr, Chaska MN 55318	952-448-7892	R	10*	.1
751	American Plastics Group Inc—*Charles Hall*	715 W Park Rd, Union MO 63084	636-583-2583	R	10*	.1
752	C and K Plastics Inc—*Robert Carrier*	159 Liberty St, Metuchen NJ 08840	732-549-0011	R	10*	.1
753	Keco Inc—*Chris White*	8100 Sw 15th St, Oklahoma City OK 73128	405-745-2145	R	10*	.1
754	US Development Corp—*Jerold Ramsey*	900 W Main St, Kent OH 44240	330-673-6900	R	10*	.1
755	Vec Technology LLC—*Jacque Beck*	639 Keystone Rd, Greenville PA 16125	724-588-1000	R	10*	.1
756	Seemann Composites Inc—*William Seemann*	PO Box 3449, Gulfport MS 39505	228-314-8000	R	10*	.1
757	Polymer Process Development LLC—*Dianna Szymanski*	24201 Capital Blvd, Clinton Township MI 48036	586-464-6400	R	10*	.1
758	Metallized Products Inc—*Edward Alois*	PO Box 845563, Boston MA 02284	781-729-8300	R	10*	.1
759	Stone Plastics Inc—*Joseph Stone*	PO Box 1340, Cadiz KY 42211	270-522-6653	R	10*	.1
760	Tempco Products Co—*Steven Mcgahey*	PO Box 155, Robinson IL 62454	618-544-3175	R	10*	.1
761	Metro Plastics Technologies Inc—*Lindsey Hahn*	PO Box 1208, Noblesville IN 46061	317-776-0860	R	10*	.1
762	World Class Plastics Inc—*Steven Buchenroth*	7695 State Rte 708, Russells Point OH 43348	937-843-4927	R	10*	.1
763	Gregstrom Corp—*Jeffrey Didonato*	PO Box 609, Woburn MA 01801	781-935-6600	R	10*	.1
764	Advanced Window Corp—*Robert Gibes*	4935 W Le Moyne St, Chicago IL 60651	773-379-3500	R	10*	.1
765	Ab Plastics Inc—*Paul Farnor*	1000 S Industrial Dr, Erwin TN 37650	423-743-3123	R	10*	.1
766	Hub Plastics Inc—*Dennis Nielsen*	PO Box 350, Blacklick OH 43004	614-861-1791	R	10*	.1
767	Jacobson Plastics Inc—*Jeffrey Jacobson*	1401 Freeman Ave, Long Beach CA 90804	562-433-4911	R	10*	.1
768	Kastalon Inc—*R Dement*	4100 W 124th Pl, Alsip IL 60803	708-389-2210	R	10*	.1
769	Fairway Building Products LP—*Dale Adams*	PO Box 37, Mount Joy PA 17552	717-653-6777	R	10*	.1
770	Agri-Industrial Plastics Co—*Richard Smith*	PO Box 950, Fairfield IA 52556	641-472-4188	R	9*	.1
771	Algus Packaging Inc—*Arthur Gustafson*	PO Box 488, Dekalb IL 60115	815-756-1881	R	9*	.1
772	Mantex Corp—*Gary Yeomans*	PO Box 348, Metamora MI 48455	810-721-2100	R	9*	.1
773	Engineering Industries Inc—*Dean Vandeberg*	407 S Nine Mound Rd, Verona WI 53593	608-845-6569	R	9*	.1
774	21st Century Plastics Corp—*Greg Dobie*	PO Box 188, Potterville MI 48876	517-645-2695	R	9*	.1
775	Ironwood Industries Inc—*Robert Grala*	115 S Bradley Rd, Libertyville IL 60048	847-362-8681	R	9*	.1
776	Friedrichs and Rath Inc—*Stefan Rath*	105 Clemson Research B, Anderson SC 29625	864-624-1200	R	9*	.1
777	Mcm Composites LLC—*Karen Carstens*	1315 S 41st St, Manitowoc WI 54220	920-684-7800	R	9*	.1
778	Wrex Products Inc—*Jim Barnett*	25 Wrex Ct, Chico CA 95928	530-895-3838	R	9*	.1
779	Performance Engineered Products Inc—*Carl Dispenziere*	3270 Pomona Blvd, Pomona CA 91768	909-594-7487	R	9*	.1
780	Argee Corp—*Robert Goldman*	PO Box 710222, Santee CA 92072	619-449-5050	R	9*	.1
781	Magic Plastics Inc—*John Sarno*	25215 Ave Stanford, Santa Clarita CA 91355	661-257-4485	R	9*	.1
782	Superseal Manufacturing Company Inc—*Joseph Vespa*	PO Box 795, South Plainfield NJ 07080	908-561-5910	S	9*	.1
783	Productive Plastics Inc—*Harold Gilham*	103 W Park Dr, Mount Laurel NJ 08054	856-778-4300	R	9*	.1
784	Plastic Design International Inc—*Donald Bergeron*	111 Industrial Park Rd, Middletown CT 06457	860-632-2001	R	9*	.1
785	Plastic Enterprises Inc—*John Leonowich*	41520 Schadden Rd, Elyria OH 44035	440-324-3240	R	9*	<.1
786	Diamond Plastics Inc—*Kenneth Wessler*	PO Box 99, Dunkirk OH 45836	419-759-3838	R	9*	.1
787	East Coast Plastics Inc—*Nancy Gowan*	PO Box 8905, Michigan City IN 46361	772-429-1774	R	9*	.1
788	Innovend LLC—*Mario Guay*	30 Patriots Cir, Leominster MA 01453	978-534-5000	R	9*	.1
789	RL Holdings Inc—*Steven Linnemann*	9355 Le Saint Dr, Fairfield OH 45014	513-874-2800	R	9*	.1
790	Hycomp LLC—*Peter Molkenthin*	17960 Englewood Dr Ste, Cleveland OH 44130	440-234-2002	R	9*	.1
791	Joe Pietryka Inc—*Joseph Pietryka*	85 Charles Colman Blvd, Pawling NY 12564	845-855-1201	R	9*	.1
792	JSN Industries Inc—*Jim Nagel*	9700 Jeronimo Rd, Irvine CA 92618	949-458-0050	R	9*	.1
793	Lawrence Plastics Inc—*Matthew Cotter*	3250 E Oakley Park Rd, Commerce Township MI 48390	248-624-9292	R	9*	.1
794	Hayes Holdings Inc—*Norris Hayes*	PO Box 1665, Stafford TX 77497	281-565-8111	R	9*	.1
795	R P Industries Inc—*Tim Zimmerman*	311 Northland Blvd, Cincinnati OH 45246		D	9	.1
796	Midwest Plastic Engineering Inc—*Dennis Baker*	PO Box 320, Sturgis MI 49091	269-651-5223	R	9*	.1
797	Universal Protective Packaging Inc—*Rodney Rumberger*	61 Texaco Rd, Mechanicsburg PA 17050	717-766-1578	R	9*	.1
798	Polymer Conversions Inc—*Jack Bertsch*	5732 Big Tree Rd, Orchard Park NY 14127	716-662-8550	R	9*	.1
799	Printex Packaging Corp—*Joel Heller*	555 Raymond Dr, Central Islip NY 11749	631-234-4300	R	9*	.1
800	Tech Nh Inc—*Richard Grosky*	PO Box 476, Merrimack NH 03054	603-424-4404	R	9*	.1
801	LC Products LLC—*Ettore Barbatelli*	PO Box 570, Darien WI 53114	262-882-5633	R	9*	.1
802	Monogram International—*Vesiah Lee*	18840 US Hwy 19 N Rm 4, Clearwater FL 33764	727-536-1941	R	9*	<.1
803	Midwest Can Company and Container Specialties Inc	1950 N Mannheim Rd, Melrose Park IL 60160	708-615-1400	R	9*	<.1
804	Milwright Co—*Stephen Kurtz*	1450 Industrial Ave, Sebastopol CA 95472	707-823-1213	R	9*	<.1
805	Oak Ridge Products—*Conor O'Malley*	4612 Century Ct, McHenry IL 60050	815-363-4700	R	9*	<.1
806	THEM International Inc—*Michael Stokes*	1400 Battleground Ave, Greensboro NC 27408	336-855-7880	R	9*	<.1
807	Digger Specialties Inc—*Loren Graber*	PO Box 241, Bremen IN 46506	574-546-5999	R	9*	.1
808	Altec Engineering Inc—*Gary Robinson*	28274 County Rd 20, Elkhart IN 46517	574-293-1965	R	9*	.1
809	Foreman Tool and Mold Corp—*Richard Foreman*	3850 Swenson Ave, Saint Charles IL 60174	630-377-6389	R	9*	.1
810	Royal Outdoor Products Inc—*Dennis Yoder*	PO Box 360, Milford IN 46542	574-658-9442	R	9*	.1
811	Mc Pherson Plastics Inc—*Timothy Mc Pherson*	PO Box 58, Otsego MI 49078	269-694-9487	R	9*	.1
812	Vinylux Products Inc—*Ronald Nusbaum*	PO Box 8175, Akron OH 44320	330-753-4592	R	9*	.1
813	Arrowhead Plastic Engineering Inc—*Thomas Kishel*	2909 S Hoyt Ave, Muncie IN 47302	765-286-0533	R	9*	.1

Note: An asterisk (*) indicates an estimated financial figure. The company type code used is as follows: R = Private, P = Public, S = Private Subsidiary, B = Public Subsidiary, D = Division, J = Joint Venture, I = Investment Fund.

COMPANY RANKINGS BY SALES WITHIN 4-DIGIT SIC

Rank	Company Name—*Executive Officer*	Address, City, State, Zip	Phone	Type	Fin	Empls
814	Del and Wes Seapy Inc—*Mark Swanson*	208 S Garrard Blvd, Richmond CA 94801	510-236-6880	R	9*	.1
815	Associated Thermoforming Inc—*John Nix*	PO Box 479, Berthoud CO 80513	970-532-2000	R	9*	.1
816	Pf Technologies Inc—*Rudy Jaros*	3302 E Atlanta Ave, Phoenix AZ 85040	602-243-6293	R	9*	.1
817	Brisar Industries Inc—*Mark Cohen*	150 E 7th St, Paterson NJ 07524	973-278-2500	R	9*	.1
818	C-Thru Ruler Co—*Theodore Zachs*	PO Box B356, Bloomfield CT 06002	860-243-0303	R	9*	.1
819	Southern Tier Plastics Inc—*John Gwyn*	Kirkwood Industrial Pa, Binghamton NY 13902	607-723-2601	R	9*	.1
820	Kessler Containers Ltd—*Robert Kessler*	8544 Page Ave, Saint Louis MO 63114	314-429-5544	R	9*	.1
821	Plastic Molding Technology Inc—*Charles Sholtis*	12280 Rojas Dr Ste A, El Paso TX 79936	915-593-6922	R	9*	.1
822	Enjoy Plastics USA Inc—*Dae Lee*	2803 S Santa Fe Ave, Vernon CA 90058	323-581-1300	R	9*	<.1
823	Non-Metallic Components Inc—*Stuart Varner*	650 Northern Ct, Poynette WI 53955	608-635-7366	R	9*	.1
824	Sports Molding Inc—*Terry Greenman*	PO Box 160278, Clearfield UT 84016	801-776-4233	R	9*	.1
825	Hansen Plastics Corp—*David Watermann*	1270 Abbott Dr, Elgin IL 60123	847-741-4510	R	9*	.1
826	Discovery Plastics LLC	3607 28th Ave Ne, Miami OK 74354	918-540-2822	R	9*	.1
827	CIF Inc—*Kenneth Edgar*	4661 Giles Rd, Cleveland OH 44135	216-251-5200	R	9*	.1
828	Sanborn Plastics Corp—*P Sanborn*	PO Box 267, Chardon OH 44024	440-286-4122	R	9*	.1
829	Eikenberry and Associates Inc—*Michael Eikenberry*	PO Box 2676, Kokomo IN 46904	765-457-1166	R	9*	.1
830	P and S Products Inc—*Paul Heflin*	781 Enterprise Dr, Lexington KY 40510	859-231-0031	R	9*	<.1
831	Regenex Corp—*Dan Berent*	PO Box 608, West Middlesex PA 16159	724-528-5900	R	8*	.1
832	Vinylume Products Inc—*Jack White*	3745 Hendricks Rd, Youngstown OH 44515	330-799-2000	R	8*	.1
833	Conwed Corp—*Daniel Clark*	530 Gregory Ave Ne, Roanoke VA 24016	540-981-0362	R	8*	.1
834	SK Plastic Molding Inc—*Steven Streff*	PO Box 213, Monroe WI 53566	608-325-6004	R	8*	.1
835	Arthur Corp—*Charles Hensel*	1305 Huron Avery Rd, Huron OH 44839	419-433-7202	R	8*	.1
836	Whicker Asset Management LLC—*Cecil Herd*	PO Box 462105, Garland TX 75046	972-278-9700	R	8*	.1
837	C-K Composites Inc—*F Kozbelt*	361 Bridgeport Rd, Mount Pleasant PA 15666	724-547-4581	R	8*	.1
838	All West Plastics Inc—*Chris Navratil*	606 Drom Ct, Antioch IL 60002	847-395-8830	R	8*	.1
839	Debond Corp—*Donald Bond*	3720 W Washington St, Phoenix AZ 85009	602-269-7648	R	8*	.1
840	DK Manufacturing—*Daniel Keifer*	2118 Commerce St, Lancaster OH 43130	740-654-5566	R	8*	.1
841	Illinois Bottle Manufacturing Co—*Robert Klekauskas*	701 E Devon Ave, Elk Grove Village IL 60007	847-595-9000	R	8*	.1
842	Zemco Tool and Die—*John Zemaitis*	113 S W St, Williamstown PA 17098	717-647-7151	R	8*	.1
843	R and V Industries Inc—*Vincent Boragine*	PO Box 1106, Sanford ME 04073	207-324-5200	R	8*	.1
844	Fluortek Inc—*George Antoci*	12 Mcfadden Rd, Easton PA 18045	610-559-9000	R	8*	.1
845	Bright Enterprises Inc—*Stephen Bright*	4833 High Point Rd, Greensboro NC 27407	336-668-3636	R	8*	.1
846	Putnam Precision Molding Inc—*Robert Racchini*	11 Danco Rd, Putnam CT 06260	860-928-7911	S	8*	.1
847	Engineered Plastics Corp—*Deborah Bristoll*	W142n9078 Fountain Blv, Menomonee Falls WI 53051	262-251-9500	R	8*	.1
848	Decatur Plastic Products Inc—*John Kussman*	PO Box 1079, North Vernon IN 47265	812-346-5159	R	8*	.1
849	Connecticut Laminating Company Inc—*Henry Snow*	162 James St, New Haven CT 06513	203-787-2184	R	8*	.1
850	Flair Molded Plastics Inc—*James Peters*	2521 Lynch Rd, Evansville IN 47711	812-425-6155	R	8*	.1
851	Harry G Barr Co—*Larry Barr*	PO Box 10226, Fort Smith AR 72917	479-646-7891	R	8*	.1
852	Poly-Flex Inc—*Bill Lechner*	PO Box 943, Walworth WI 53184	262-275-2156	R	8*	.1
853	Plast-O-Matic Valves Inc—*George Drazinakis*	1384 Pompton Ave, Cedar Grove NJ 07009	973-256-3000	R	8*	.1
854	Allsafe Technologies Inc—*James Pokornowski*	290 Creekside Dr, Amherst NY 14228	716-691-0400	R	8*	.1
855	Global Plastics Inc—*J Spitznogle*	6739 Guion Rd, Indianapolis IN 46268	317-299-2345	R	8*	.1
856	Iso-Trude Inc—*Craig Januz*	1705 Eaton Dr, Grand Haven MI 49417	616-844-2888	R	8*	.1
857	Orange Products Inc—*Paul Sachdev*	1929 Vultee St, Allentown PA 18103	610-791-9711	R	8*	.1
858	Dordan Manufacturing Co—*Daniel Slavin*	2025 S Castle Rd, Woodstock IL 60098	815-334-0087	R	8*	.1
859	Hawkeye Molding Engineers Inc—*Bob Russell*	PO Box 216, Albia IA 52531	641-932-7851	R	8*	.1
860	Jenard Co—*Peter Siebert*	200 4th Ave N, Edgerton MN 56128	610-622-3600	R	8*	.1
861	Phil-Good Products Inc—*Peggy L Phillips*	3500 W Reno Ave, Oklahoma City OK 73107	405-942-5527	R	8*	.1
862	Vicas Manufacturing Company Inc—*Virginia Willoughby*	PO Box 36310, Cincinnati OH 45236	513-791-7741	R	8*	<.1
863	LW Reinhold Plastics Inc	8763 Crocker St, Los Angeles CA 90003	562-862-2714	R	8*	<.1
864	Rozzi Window Manufacturing Inc (Reading Pennsylvania)—*Mike Rozzi*	500 N 8th St, Reading PA 19601	610-373-3414	R	8*	<.1
865	Neodesha Plastics Inc—*Theodore Peitz*	PO Box 539, Neodesha KS 66757	620-325-3096	R	8*	.1
866	Paarlo Plastics Inc—*James Park*	PO Box 2556, Canton OH 44720	330-494-3798	R	8*	.1
867	Epp Team Inc—*Neal Elli*	500 Lee Rd Ste 400, Rochester NY 14606	585-454-4995	R	8*	.1
868	Accudyn Products Inc—*Margaret Bly*	2400 Yoder Dr, Erie PA 16506	814-833-7615	R	8*	.1
869	Fiberpro Inc—*Steve Welter*	2970 Luoyang Ave, La Crosse WI 54601	608-796-0800	R	8*	<.1
870	Injection Works Inc—*Christopher Rapacki*	104 Gaither Dr, Mount Laurel NJ 08054	856-802-6444	R	8*	<.1
871	R and D Molders Inc—*Gregory Brown*	107 Park Central Blvd, Georgetown TX 78626	512-763-3600	R	8*	.1
872	Scott Molders Inc—*Scott Yahner*	PO Box 645, Kent OH 44240	330-673-5777	R	8*	.1
873	Precise Plastics Inc—*Gregory Farrell*	7700 Middle Rd, Fairview PA 16415	814-474-5504	R	8*	.1
874	Sun Microstamping Technologies—*Bryan Clark*	14055 Us Hwy 19 N, Clearwater FL 33764	727-536-8822	R	8*	.1
875	Associated Plastics Corp—*Fred Wolber*	502 Eric Wolber Dr, Ada OH 45810	419-634-0460	R	8*	.1
876	Gessner Products Company Inc—*Edward Gessner*	PO Box 389, Ambler PA 19002	215-646-7667	R	8*	.1
877	Custom Molders Corp—*Joseph Caro*	160 Meister Ave Ste 1, Branchburg NJ 08876	908-218-7997	R	8*	.1
878	H P Manufacturing Company Inc—*John Melchiorre*	3705 Carnegie Ave, Cleveland OH 44115	216-361-6500	R	8*	.1
879	Fischer Mold Inc—*Robert Fischer*	393 Meyer Cir, Corona CA 92879	951-279-1140	R	8*	.1
880	Vision Technical Molding LLC—*Eric Hasel*	71 Utopia Rd, Manchester CT 06042	860-432-5902	R	8*	.1
881	Ron-Vik Inc—*James Greupner*	800 Colorado Ave S, Minneapolis MN 55416	763-545-0276	R	8*	.1
882	Hillsman Modular Molding Inc—*Rodney Hillsman*	189 Churchill Dr, Sparta TN 38583	931-837-9040	R	8*	.1
883	Canterbury Engineering Company Inc—*Vijay Anand*	1057 Vijay Dr, Atlanta GA 30341	770-458-4882	R	8*	.1
884	Petro Plastics Company Inc—*James Petrozziello*	PO Box 167, Garwood NJ 07027	908-789-1200	R	8*	.1
885	Desert Extrusion Corp—*Robert Phillips*	2737 E Chambers St, Phoenix AZ 85040	602-276-8009	R	8*	.1
886	Pinckney Molded Plastics Inc—*William Ash*	3970 Parsons Rd, Howell MI 48855	517-546-9900	R	8*	.1
887	Scott Industries Of Kentucky LLC—*Marco Maccaserri*	6701 Cane Run Rd, Louisville KY 40258	502-933-6060	R	8*	.1
888	Techatlantic Inc—*Jeffrey Hires*	114 New Park Dr, Berlin CT 06037	860-828-1504	R	8*	.1
889	WFC Company Inc—*John Roley*	PO Box 188, Southampton PA 18966	215-953-1260	R	8*	.1
890	Peerless Plastics Inc—*William Brummond*	PO Box 38, Farmington MN 55024	651-463-7147	R	8*	<.1
891	Austro Mold Inc—*Nathu Dandora*	3 Rutter St, Rochester NY 14606	585-458-1410	R	7*	.1
892	Cpi Binani Inc—*Ron Hawley*	PO Box 108, Winona MN 55987	507-452-2881	R	7*	.1
893	Recto Molded Products Inc—*Per Flem*	4425 Appleton St, Cincinnati OH 45209	513-871-5544	R	7*	.1
894	Custom Plastic Developments Inc—*Richard Hord*	2710 N John Young Pkwy, Kissimmee FL 34741	407-847-3054	R	7*	.1
895	Deb Of Findlay Inc—*Randy Grey*	1530 Harvard Ave, Findlay OH 45840	419-424-5250	R	7*	.1
896	Iso Plastics Corp—*Raul Silva*	160 E 1st St, Mount Vernon NY 10550	914-663-8300	R	7*	.1
897	Saginaw Bay Plastics Inc—*Warren Burke*	PO Box 507, Kawkawlin MI 48631	989-686-7860	R	7*	.1
898	Wisconsin Thermoset Molding Inc—*Duane Kreske*	900 E Vienna Ave, Milwaukee WI 53212	414-964-5200	R	7*	.1
899	Seagate Plastics Co—*Kevin Fink*	101 Park Dr, Waterville OH 43566	419-878-5010	R	7*	.1
900	Chocolate Delivery Systems Inc—*Timothy Thill*	85 River Rock Dr Ste 2, Buffalo NY 14207	716-854-6050	R	7*	.1
901	Strauss Engineering Company Inc—*Richard Strauss*	80 Tracey Rd, Huntingdon Valley PA 19006	215-947-1083	R	7*	.1
902	Value Plastics Inc—*Mike Rainsberger*	3325 Timberline Rd, Fort Collins CO 80525	970-223-8306	S	7*	<.1

Rank	Company Name—Executive Officer	Address, City, State, Zip	Phone	Type	Fin	Empls
903	Veltec Inc—Frank Vella	PO Box 788, Elkton MD 21922	410-392-2570	R	7*	.1
904	O'leary Brothers Signs and Awnings Inc—Daniel O'leary	PO Box 268, Bunkie LA 71322	318-346-2627	R	7*	.1
905	Luckmarr Plastics Inc—Luciano Pierobon	35735 Stanley Dr, Sterling Heights MI 48312	586-978-8498	R	7*	.1
906	Luetzow Industries LLP—Albert Luetzow	1105 Davis Ave, South Milwaukee WI 53172	414-762-0410	R	7*	.1
907	Apex Resource Technologies Inc—Don Rochelo	17 Downing Three Park, Pittsfield MA 01201	413-442-1414	R	7*	.1
908	Koba Corp—Joseph Koelmel	60 Baekeland Ave, Middlesex NJ 08846	732-469-0110	R	7*	.1
909	Pace Window And Door Corp—Steven Abramson	PO Box 24, Victor NY 14564	585-924-8350	R	7*	.1
910	Polyform US Ltd—Knut Beyer-Olsen	7030 S 224th St, Kent WA 98032	253-872-0300	R	7*	.1
911	Oregon Precision Industries Inc—Jim Borg	1680-B Irving Rd, Eugene OR 97402	541-461-5000	R	7*	.1
912	Cosmetic Specialties International LLC—Sheila Serbicki	PO Box 832, Oxnard CA 93032	805-487-6698	S	7*	.1
913	Tulox Plastics Corp—John Sciaudone	PO Box 984, Marion IN 46952	765-664-5155	R	7*	.1
914	General Plastics Inc—Robert Porsche	2609 W Mill Rd, Milwaukee WI 53209	414-351-1000	R	7*	.1
915	Mill Valley Molding Inc—Ralph Healy	15 W St, West Hatfield MA 01088	413-247-9313	R	7*	.1
916	Maryland Thermoform Corp—Jim Hall	2717 Wilmarco Ave, Baltimore MD 21223	410-947-5063	R	7*	.1
917	Fredman Bag Co—Timothy Fredman Jr	5801 W Bender Ct, Milwaukee WI 53218	414-462-9400	R	7*	.1
918	Hilco Plastics Products Company Inc—Matt Holwerda	4172 Danvers Ct SE, Grand Rapids MI 49512	616-957-1081	R	7*	.1
919	Schiffmayer Plastics Corp—Karl Schiffmayer	1201 Armstrong St, Algonquin IL 60102	847-658-8140	R	7*	.1
920	Fiber Pad Inc—Donald Law	PO Box 690660, Tulsa OK 74169	918-438-7430	R	7*	.1
921	Automation Plastics Corp—Harry Smith	150 Lena Dr, Aurora OH 44202	330-562-5148	R	7*	.1
922	Black River Plastics Inc—Faye Caballero	2611 16th St, Port Huron MI 48060	810-985-9730	R	7*	.1
923	Quintex Corp—Dorthea Christiansen	205 25th Ave S, Nampa ID 83686	208-467-1113	R	7*	.1
924	Western Case Inc—Martin Smetter	14351 Chambers Rd, Tustin CA 92780	714-838-8460	R	7*	.1
925	Flagship Converters Inc—E Davies	205 Shelter Rock Rd, Danbury CT 06810	203-792-0034	R	7*	.1
926	Terhorst Manufacturing Co—Brad Weber	PO Box 997, Minot ND 58702	701-852-0535	R	7*	.1
927	US Acrylic LLC—Anne Connel	1320 Harris Rd, Libertyville IL 60048	847-837-4800	R	7*	.1
928	Grand Traverse Plastics Corp—Chet Grant	5780 Moore Rd, Williamsburg MI 49690	231-267-5221	R	7*	.1
929	Perkasie Industries Corp—Adam Krisco	PO Box 179, Perkasie PA 18944	215-257-6581	R	7*	.1
930	Pittsfield Plastics Engineering Inc—Thomas Walker	PO Box 1246, Pittsfield MA 01202	413-442-0067	R	7*	.1
931	Plastinetics Inc—Edward J Batta	PO Box 322, Towaco NJ 07082	973-618-9090	R	7*	.1
932	Modern Molding Inc—Douglas Portman	796 7th St S, Delano MN 55328	763-972-6761	R	7*	<.1
933	Rolco Inc—Brian Olson	PO Box 8, Kasota MN 56050	507-931-4525	R	7*	<.1
934	Bo-Mer Pulaski LLC—Brian Colella	13 Pulaski St, Auburn NY 13021	315-252-7216	R	7*	<.1
935	Nation-Ruskin Inc—Ray C Adolf	206 Progress Dr, Montgomeryville PA 18936	267-654-4000	R	7*	<.1
936	Precision Fluorocarbon Inc—Howard Frank	9930 Fm 2920 Rd, Tomball TX 77375	281-351-4070	R	7*	<.1
937	Loose Plastics Inc—Scott C Loose	3132 Dale Rd, Beaverton MI 48612	989-435-9226	R	7*	<.1
938	Plastic Extruded Products Co—Edward Larsen	PO Box 206, Neshanic Station NJ 08853	908-688-1234	R	7*	.1
939	RTR Inc—Ted Novetzke	1020 International Dr, Fergus Falls MN 56537	218-739-9899	R	7*	.1
940	Marine Muffler Corp—Emery Sims	185 E 9th St, Apopka FL 32703	407-886-1144	R	7*	.1
941	Burco Molding Inc—Clovis Burrow	15015 Herriman Blvd, Noblesville IN 46060	317-773-5699	R	7*	.1
942	Wst Liq Corp—Wayne Thomas	8000 State Rd, Philadelphia PA 19136	215-335-0200	R	7*	.1
943	Crafted Plastics Inc—William Eastham	PO Box 327, Sheboygan WI 53082	920-457-5593	R	7*	.1
944	Jadra Inc—Jennifer Kaye	PO Box 38923, Sacramento CA 95838	916-921-3399	R	7*	.1
945	Versatile Distributors Inc—Joel Cuccio	80 Industrial Rd, Lodi NJ 07644	973-773-0550	R	7*	.1
946	Davalor Mold Corp—David Bernhardt	46480 Continental Dr, Chesterfield MI 48047	586-598-0100	R	7*	.1
947	Gamma2 Inc—Curtis Leland	3186 Lionshead Ave Ste, Carlsbad CA 92010	760-734-4003	R	7*	.1
948	Statistical Plastics Corp—Mark Sellers	W188n11707 Maple Rd, Germantown WI 53022	262-255-5790	R	7*	.1
949	Bkt Inc—Patrick Brandstatter	PO Box 895, Bridgman MI 49106	269-465-6404	R	7*	.1
950	Imperial Plastics Inc—Walter Staiger	80 Industrial St, Rittman OH 44270	330-927-5065	R	7*	.1
951	Instaset Corp—Douglas Burrell	PO Box 300, Anchorville MI 48004	586-725-0229	R	7*	.1
952	Performance Plastics Ltd—Peggy Delany	4435 Brownway Ave, Cincinnati OH 45209	513-321-8404	R	7*	<.1
953	Flextech Inc—James Monteiro	7300 W 27th St, Minneapolis MN 55426	952-345-0012	R	7*	<.1
954	Alsco Industries Inc—Allan Rieser	PO Box 1168, Sturbridge MA 01566	508-347-1199	R	7*	.1
955	Dimatic Die And Tool Co—Scott Drvol	PO Box 12037, Omaha NE 68112	402-571-7300	R	7*	.1
956	Nicolet Plastics Inc—Robert Macintosh	16685 State Rd 32, Mountain WI 54149	715-276-4200	R	7*	.1
957	Modern Mold and Tool Inc—David Pedrotti	1995 E St, Pittsfield MA 01201	413-443-1192	R	7*	.1
958	Production Plastics Corp—Daniel Lyons	400 N Progress Dr, Saukville WI 53080	262-375-0344	R	7*	.1
959	Tech-Way Industries Inc—Robin Parker	PO Box 517, Franklin OH 45005	937-746-1004	R	7*	.1
960	Bunzl Extrusion Philadelphia Inc—John Saxon	16 Progress Dr, Morrisville PA 19067	215-736-2553	R	7*	.1
961	Polycel Structural Foam Inc—Kurt Joerger	68 County Line Rd, Branchburg NJ 08876	908-722-5254	R	7*	.1
962	Amerimade Technology Inc—Todd Thomas	449 Mountain Vista Pkw, Livermore CA 94551	925-243-9090	R	7*	.1
963	World Plastic Extruders Inc—Charles Bierds	41 Park Ave, Rutherford NJ 07070	201-933-2915	R	7*	.1
964	Src Medical Inc—Roy Tinkham	263 Winter St, Hanover MA 02339	781-826-9100	R	7*	.1
965	Tankinetics Inc—William Schwarz	PO Box 1195, Harrison AR 72602	870-741-3626	R	7*	.1
966	Sunbelt Plastic Extrusions Inc—Wayne Williamson	949 Carl Vinson Pkwy, Centerville GA 31028	478-922-4028	R	7*	.1
967	Wadal Plastics Inc—Robert Lange	949 S Gibson St, Medford WI 54451	715-748-2227	R	7*	.1
968	Piller Plastics Inc—Jason Hannah	3925 Grant St, Washougal WA 98671	360-835-2103	R	7*	.1
969	Yoshino America Corp—Yataro Yoshino	2500 Palmer Ave, University Park IL 60484	708-534-1141	R	7*	<.1
970	Queen City Polymers Inc—James Powers	6101 Schumacher Park D, West Chester OH 45069	513-779-0990	R	7*	<.1
971	Winzeler Inc—John Winzeler	7355 W Wilson Ave, Chicago IL 60706	708-867-7971	R	7*	<.1
972	Pmw Products Inc—John Hallman	PO Box 25760, Raleigh NC 27611	919-779-4400	R	7*	.1
973	Vidon Plastics Inc—Donald Dube	PO Box 56, Lapeer MI 48446	810-667-0634	R	7*	.1
974	Aimet Technologies Inc—David Jackson	115 Legacy Crest Ct, Zebulon NC 27597	919-887-5205	R	7*	.1
975	Custom Resins Inc—Michael Warner	PO Box 740, Wayne NJ 07474	270-826-7641	S	7*	.1
976	Plastic Forming Company Inc—John Womer	20 S Bradley Rd, Woodbridge CT 06525	203-397-1338	R	7*	.1
977	Shelly Fisher—Melissa Keller	250 Wayne St, Mansfield OH 44902	419-524-8422	R	6*	.1
978	Fittings Inc—Lewis Graves	3300 Fisher Ave, Fort Worth TX 76111	817-332-3300	R	6*	.1
979	Pliant Plastics Corp—Thomas Devoursney	17000 Taft Rd, Spring Lake MI 49456	616-844-0300	R	6*	.1
980	Mold-Rite Inc—Gernot Hilse	PO Box 308, Woodinville WA 98072	425-483-2535	R	6*	.1
981	Tamshell Corp—John Hernandez	237 Glider Cir, Corona CA 92880	951-272-9395	R	6*	.1
982	Ki Industries Inc—David Goltermann	5540 Mcdermott Dr, Berkeley IL 60163	708-449-1990	R	6*	<.1
983	Fukuvi USA Inc—S Yagi	7631 Progress Ct, Dayton OH 45424	937-236-7288	R	6*	.1
984	Bloom Industries Inc—Ted Bloom	1052 Mahoney Ave Nw, Warren OH 44483	330-898-3878	R	6*	.1
985	Rotational Molding Technologies Inc—Dave Smith	67742 County Rd 23 Ste, New Paris IN 46553	574-831-6450	R	6*	.1
986	Omega Alpha Plastics Co—Michael Beladakis	1099 Touhy Ave, Elk Grove Village IL 60007	847-956-8777	R	6*	.1
987	Temple Tag Ii Ltd—Bill Mccoy	PO Box 369, Temple TX 76503	254-982-4212	R	6*	.1
988	P and P Industries Inc—Warren Pruis	14729 Spring Valley Rd, Morrison IL 61270	815-772-7618	R	6*	.1
989	Blackwell Plastics LP—Julie Rodriguze	5606 Cavanaugh St, Houston TX 77021	713-643-6577	R	6*	.1
990	Silicone Plastics Inc—Steve Miller	PO Box 438, Millville UT 84326	435-753-7307	R	6*	.1
991	Artek Inc—Dennis Dammeyer	PO Box 8975, Fort Wayne IN 46898	260-484-4222	R	6*	<.1
992	Modified Plastics Inc—Robert Estep	1240 E Glenwood Pl, Santa Ana CA 92707	714-546-4667	R	6*	<.1

Note: An asterisk (*) indicates an estimated financial figure. The company type code used is as follows: R = Private, P = Public, S = Private Subsidiary, B = Public Subsidiary, D = Division, J = Joint Venture, I = Investment Fund.

COMPANY RANKINGS BY SALES WITHIN 4-DIGIT SIC

Rank	Company Name—Executive Officer	Address, City, State, Zip	Phone	Type	Fin	Empls
993	Avon Plastic Products Inc—Edward Gorski	2890 Technology Dr, Rochester Hills MI 48309	248-852-1000	R	6*	.1
994	Resin Systems Corp—Daniel Prawdzik	62 Rte 101a Ste 1, Amherst NH 03031	603-673-1234	R	6*	.1
995	Continental Plastic Corp—Richard Alter	PO Box 902, Delavan WI 53115	262-728-4800	R	6*	.1
996	Innovative Components Inc—Mike O'connor	1050 National Pkwy, Schaumburg IL 60173	847-885-9050	R	6*	.1
997	Matrix Iv Inc—Raymond Wenk	610 E Judd St, Woodstock IL 60098	815-338-4500	R	6*	.1
998	Michael Brothers Inc—William Michael	2608 Spitfire Ln, Prescott AZ 86301	928-636-1010	R	6*	.1
999	Plastic Components Inc—Thomas Stark	9051 Nw 97th Ter, Medley FL 33178	305-885-0561	R	6*	<.1
1000	Plastics Design And Manufacturing Inc—Keith Giacchino	6284 S Nome Ct, Centennial CO 80111	303-768-8380	R	6*	.1
1001	Acm Plastic Products Inc—Maurice Walters	PO Box 580, Sturgis MI 49091	269-651-7888	R	6*	.1
1002	Racine Plastic Inc—Geoffrey Bergauer	3737 Douglas Ave, Racine WI 53402	262-639-2456	R	6*	.1
1003	Permalith Plastics LLC—Sidney Jacobs	6901 N Crescent Blvd, Pennsauken NJ 08110	856-488-8000	R	6*	.1
1004	Toolroom Express Inc—Richard Haddock	17 Chenango Bridge Rd, Binghamton NY 13901	607-723-5373	R	6*	.1
1005	Aggressive Industries Inc—Tom Berquist	8365 Sunset Rd Ne, Minneapolis MN 55432	763-786-8097	R	6*	.1
1006	American Integrity Corp—Dan Jaoudi	PO Box 999, Apple Valley CA 92307	760-247-1082	R	6*	.1
1007	Dunnage Engineering Inc—David Joseph	721 Advance St, Brighton MI 48116	810-229-9501	R	6*	.1
1008	Hy-Ten Die and Development Corp—Franz Fritsch	38 Powers St, Milford NH 03055	603-673-1611	R	6*	.1
1009	JG Plastics Group LLC—John Mack	335 Fischer Ave, Costa Mesa CA 92626	714-751-4266	R	6*	.1
1010	Kimberley Manufacturing Co—Julie Morrow	7510 Melrose Ln, Oklahoma City OK 73127	405-787-9797	R	6*	.1
1011	Harmony Systems And Service Inc—Edward Adams	PO Box 642, Piqua OH 45356	937-778-1082	R	6*	<.1
1012	Westec Plastics Corp	6757 Las Positas Rd St, Livermore CA 94551	925-454-3400	R	6*	.1
1013	Metrolina Plastics Inc—Conrad Sauer	PO Box 27366, Richmond VA 23261	804-359-5786	R	6*	.1
1014	Atco Plastics Inc—Ralph Schlenker	31 W Bacon St, Plainville MA 02762	508-695-3573	R	6*	.1
1015	Go Plastics LLC—Jan Evers	515 Brown Industrial P, Canton GA 30114	770-345-0535	R	6*	.1
1016	Master Window Systems Inc—Brian Brannick	2060 Defoor Hills Rd N, Atlanta GA 30318	404-355-5844	R	6*	.1
1017	Jackel Inc—Craig Nowicki	15314 Harrison Rd, Mishawaka IN 46544	574-256-5635	R	6*	.1
1018	Jule-Art Inc—Dave Grantham	PO Box 91748, Albuquerque NM 87199	505-344-8433	R	6*	.1
1019	Motor City Plastics Co—Keith Ruby	PO Box 144, Dundee MI 48131	734-529-2481	R	6*	.1
1020	Paramount Molded Products Inc—Robert Petrucci	1701 Nw 62nd St, Fort Lauderdale FL 33309	954-772-2333	R	6*	.1
1021	Pen-Cell Plastics Inc—Robert Schlegel	PO Box 8317, Rocky Mount NC 27804	252-467-2210	R	6*	.1
1022	Rolenn Manufacturing Inc—Thomas Accatino	2065 Roberta St, Riverside CA 92507	951-682-1185	R	6*	.1
1023	RT Plastics Inc—Joseph Frabizio	901 S 1st St, Las Vegas NV 89101	702-474-1112	R	6*	.1
1024	Vantage Associates Inc—Louis J Alpinieri	900 Civic Center Dr, National City CA 91950	619-477-6940	R	6*	.1
1025	Controlled Molding Inc—Raymond Mozes	3043 Perry Hwy, Hadley PA 16130	724-253-3550	R	6*	<.1
1026	GMI Composites Inc—Robert Brady	1355 W Sherman Blvd, Muskegon MI 49441		R	6*	<.1
1027	Lakeland Plastics Inc—Christopher Arendt	1550 Mccormick Blvd, Mundelein IL 60060	847-680-1550	R	6*	<.1
1028	Byron Originals Inc—Bruce Godbersen	PO Box 279, Ida Grove IA 51445	712-364-3165	R	6*	<.1
1029	Razzi Corp	1050 Branch Dr, Alpharetta GA 30004	770-475-2723	S	6*	<.1
1030	Allen Field Company Inc—Andrew Franzone	PO Box 3069, Farmingdale NY 11735	631-756-0810	R	6*	<.1
1031	It's Academic of Illinois Inc—Bruce Shapiro	707 Skokie Blvd Ste 45, Northbrook IL 60062	847-291-6882	R	6*	<.1
1032	ABltalia Inc—Roger S Marcus American Biltrite Inc	57 River St, Wellesley Hills MA 02481	781-237-6655	S	6*	<.1
1033	In House Media—Elaine Terbek-Kares	5750 Wilshire Blvd Ste, Los Angeles CA 90036	323-525-1700	R	6*	<.1
1034	Tallyho Plastics Inc—Jack Martinsen	1020 S Bolton St, Jacksonville TX 75766	903-586-2263	R	6*	.1
1035	Trc Manufacturing Inc—Terry Ross	15005 Enterprise Way, Middlefield OH 44062	440-834-0078	R	6*	.1
1036	D and W Awning And Window Co—David Wood	8068 E Ct St, Davison MI 48423	810-742-0340	R	6*	.1
1037	Inca Molded Products Inc—Jim Porter	6400 Louisiana Ave, Nashville TN 37209	615-350-7290	R	6*	.1
1038	K And C Plastics Inc—Kirt Wilbur	18 Crawford St, Leominster MA 01453	978-537-0605	R	6*	.1
1039	Macneill Engineering Company Inc—Harris Macneill	140 Locke Dr, Marlborough MA 01752	508-481-8830	R	6*	.1
1040	Uniphase Inc—Kenneth Maltas	425 38th Ave, Saint Charles IL 60174	630-584-4747	R	6*	.1
1041	Anaheim Custom Extruders Inc—William Czapar	4640 E La Palma Ave, Anaheim CA 92807	714-693-8508	R	6*	<.1
1042	TP Composites Inc—Ronald Taylor	8 Crozerville Rd, Aston PA 19014	610-358-9001	R	6*	<.1
1043	W and W Fiberglass Tank Co—Judd Wilson	8840 County Rd 10, Pampa TX 79065	806-669-1128	R	6*	.1
1044	Olympic Fiberglass Industries Inc—William Adams	PO Box 920, Rochester IN 46975	574-223-3101	R	6*	.1
1045	Gs Industries Of Bassett Ltd—Starlett Hedrick	85 Rosemont Rd, Bassett VA 24055	276-629-5317	R	6*	.1
1046	Cell-O-Core Co—David Nelson	PO Box 342, Sharon Center OH 44274	330-239-4370	R	6*	.1
1047	Continental Window and Glass Corp—Greg Sztejkowski	4311 W Belmont Ave, Chicago IL 60641	773-794-1600	R	6*	.1
1048	Crystal Die And Mold Inc—Mike Biangardi	5521 Meadowbrook Indus, Rolling Meadows IL 60008	847-658-6535	R	6*	.1
1049	Darter Plastics Inc—John Knutson	PO Box 278, Becker MN 55308	763-261-5000	R	6*	.1
1050	W K Hillquist Inc—Warren Hillquist	37 Executive Dr, Hudson NH 03051	603-595-7790	R	6*	.1
1051	Neo Pacific Holdings Inc—Steve Chan	14940 Calvert St, Van Nuys CA 91411	818-786-2900	R	6*	<.1
1052	American Window Products Inc—Thomas Gordon	10 Dunnell Ln Unit 1, Pawtucket RI 02860	401-722-6555	R	6*	Empls
1053	Delta Pacific Products Inc—Fred Betke	33170 Central Ave, Union City CA 94587	510-487-4411	R	6*	<.1
1054	Roma Tool and Plastics Inc—Milo Hennemann	107 Prospect Ave W, Almena WI 54805	715-357-3826	R	6*	<.1
1055	Plastruct Inc—John Wanderman Engineering Model Associates Inc	1020 Wallace Way, City Of Industry CA 91748	626-912-7017	S	6*	<.1
1056	Bud/Alan Plastics Inc—Alan Krenzer	3067 Old S 5, Camdenton MO 65020	573-346-6310	R	6*	.1
1057	Thermal Plastic Design Inc—John Meeham	1116 Pine St, Saint Croix Falls WI 54024	715-483-1841	R	6*	.1
1058	Cam Specialty Products Inc—James Campagna	11881 N Hwy 75, Willis TX 77378	936-890-0039	S	6*	.1
1059	Magna Visual Inc—William Cady	9400 Watson Rd, Saint Louis MO 63126	314-843-9000	R	6*	.1
1060	United Plastic Molders Inc—William Hoge	105 E Rankin St, Jackson MS 39201	601-353-3193	R	6*	.1
1061	Crisci Tool And Die Inc—Peter Crisci	32 Jungle Rd Ste 1, Leominster MA 01453	978-537-4102	R	6*	<.1
1062	Micron Molding Inc—Todd Johnson	101 American Blvd W, Minneapolis MN 55420	952-888-4468	R	6*	<.1
1063	Mountain Molding Ltd—Don Cheyne	14444 E I25 Frontage R, Longmont CO 80504	970-535-4777	R	6*	.1
1064	Enpac LLC	34355 Vokes Dr, Eastlake OH 44095	440-975-0070	R	6*	.1
1065	Parkway Plastics Inc—Edward Rowan	561 Stelton Rd, Piscataway NJ 08854	732-752-3636	R	6*	<.1
1066	Aroplax Corp—Steve Schoen	200 Chelsea Rd, Monticello MN 55362	763-295-5002	R	6*	<.1
1067	Baltimore Window Factory Inc—Pat Stout	8871 Citation Rd, Baltimore MD 21221	410-574-4750	R	6*	<.1
1068	Bloomdale Plastics Co—Phillip Gardner	PO Box 296, Bloomdale OH 44817	419-454-5135	R	6*	<.1
1069	Akron Polymer Products Inc—Gregory Anderson	PO Box 128, Mogadore OH 44260	330-628-5551	R	6*	<.1
1070	Viz Plastic Products Ltd—Vlasios Lymberis	210 Industrial Pkwy, Northvale NJ 07647	201-784-4442	R	6*	.1
1071	Spongex Foam Products LLC—Alfred Tortorra	PO Box 529, Shelton CT 06484	203-924-9335	R	6*	.1
1072	Alfred's Pictures Frames Inc—Pat Cochrane	1580 Sunflower Ave, Costa Mesa CA 92626	714-434-4838	R	6*	.1
1073	Innovative Plastic Solutions Inc—Ray Seward	1306 Governors Ct, Abingdon MD 21009	410-538-6886	R	6*	.1
1074	Micor Inc—Stephen Brushey	2855 Oxford Blvd, Allison Park PA 15101	412-487-1113	R	6*	<.1
1075	Rimnetics Inc—Walter Chew	433 Clyde Ave, Mountain View CA 94043	650-969-6590	S	6*	<.1
1076	Dawn Industries Inc—Duane Robertson	5055 W 58th Ave, Arvada CO 80002	303-296-4041	R	6*	<.1
1077	Patwin Plastics Inc—Thomas Hannon	2300 E Linden Ave, Linden NJ 07036	908-486-6600	R	6*	<.1
1078	Proulx Manufacturing Inc—Richard Proulx	11433 6th St, Rancho Cucamonga CA 91730	909-980-0662	R	6*	<.1
1079	Summit Plastic Molding Inc—Raymond Kalinowski	51340 Celeste, Shelby Township MI 48315	586-532-0027	R	6*	<.1
1080	Uniplast Industries Inc—A Goldman	PO Box 2367, South Hackensack NJ 07606	201-288-4540	R	6*	<.1

Rank	Company Name—*Executive Officer*	Address, City, State, Zip	Phone	Type	Fin	Empls
1081	York Imperial Plastics Inc—*Dennis Paulis*	718 Country Rd, York PA 17403	717-428-3939	R	6*	<.1
1082	H and N Manufacturing Inc—*Kurk Kendell*	PO Box 144, Dundee MI 48131	734-529-3952	R	5*	.1
1083	Maple Valley Plastics LLC	PO Box 130, Brown City MI 48416	810-346-3040	R	5*	.1
1084	New Process Fibre Co—*Henry Peters*	PO Box 2009, Greenwood DE 19950	302-349-4535	R	5*	.1
1085	Europlast Ltd—*Harald Zacharias*	PO Box 169, Endeavor WI 53930	608-587-2335	R	5*	.1
1086	Industrial Plastic Products Inc—*Veronika Thorne*	14025 Nw 58th Ct, Hialeah FL 33014	305-822-3223	R	5*	.1
1087	Ptc Enterprises Inc—*Bill Patton*	3047 County Rd K, Edon OH 43518	419-272-2524	R	5*	.1
1088	UFO Inc—*Efi Youavian*	2110 Belgrave Ave, Huntington Park CA 90255	323-588-6696	R	5*	.1
1089	Artistic Plastic And Fixtures Inc—*Donald Weatherby*	2214 Hwy 1187 Ste 1, Mansfield TX 76063	817-453-8810	R	5*	<.1
1090	Moldieco Plastic Products Inc—*Edwin Yuan*	PO Box 48, Fords NJ 08863	732-738-1400	R	5*	<.1
1091	Quashnick Tool Corp—*Robert Hampton*	401 S Main St, Lodi CA 95240	209-334-5283	R	5*	<.1
1092	RMI Nutron Plastics—*Sherman McKinniss* Rotonics Manufacturing Inc	230 Bartow Municipal A, Lakeland FL 33803	863-534-1786	D	5	<.1
1093	Norplex Inc—*Ralph Schley*	PO Box 814, Auburn WA 98071	253-735-3431	R	5*	<.1
1094	D and L Tooling And Plastics Inc—*Tommy Dement*	950 Se Loop 456, Jacksonville TX 75766	903-586-9894	R	5*	.1
1095	Epi 04 Inc—*Hilmar Skagfield*	5902 W Custer St, Manitowoc WI 54220	920-684-9650	R	5*	.1
1096	Ppp LLC—*Masataka Suzuki*	601 W Olympic Blvd, Montebello CA 90640	323-832-9627	R	5*	.1
1097	Hy Tech Forming Systems (USA) Inc—*Fred Himmelein*	2425 W Desert Cove Ave, Phoenix AZ 85029	602-944-1526	R	5*	<.1
1098	Abbott Plastics and Supply Co—*Roger Becknell*	3302 Lonergan Dr, Rockford IL 61109	815-874-8500	R	5*	<.1
1099	General Technologies Inc—*Felix Sorkin*	PO Box 1503, Stafford TX 77497	281-240-0550	R	5*	<.1
1100	Latrobe Associates Inc—*Alfred Crocker*	PO Box 29, Latrobe PA 15650	724-539-1612	R	5*	<.1
1101	Northland Plastics Inc—*John Zingsheim*	PO Box 290, Sheboygan WI 53082	920-458-0732	R	5*	<.1
1102	Moldtronics Inc—*Henry Schmidt*	703 Rogers St, Downers Grove IL 60515	630-968-7000	R	5*	<.1
1103	Armaly Sponge Co—*John Armaly*	PO Box 611, Walled Lake MI 48390	248-669-2100	R	5*	<.1
1104	Am-Source LLC—*John Madden*	PO Box 16330, Rumford RI 02916	401-431-4080	R	5*	.1
1105	Itouchless Housewares and Products Inc—*Fong Chan*	551 Foster City Blvd M, Foster City CA 94404	650-578-0578	R	5*	.1
1106	Mcmillan Fiberglass Stocks Inc—*Kelly Millan*	1638 W Knudsen Dr Ste, Phoenix AZ 85027	623-582-9635	R	5*	<.1
1107	Middlefield Plastics Inc—*John Fisher*	PO Box 708, Middlefield OH 44062	440-834-4638	R	5*	<.1
1108	Montville Plastics and Rubber Inc—*Don Hofstetter*	PO Box 527, Parkman OH 44080	440-548-3211	R	5*	<.1
1109	Vanguard Plastics Corp—*Lawrence Budnick*	100 Robert Porter Rd, Southington CT 06489	860-628-4736	R	5*	<.1
1110	Technical Coating International Inc—*Burt Moody*	150 Backhoe Rd Ne, Leland NC 28451	910-371-0860	R	5*	<.1
1111	Proto Plastics Inc—*Robert Bianco*	316 Park Ave, Tipp City OH 45371	937-667-8416	R	5*	<.1
1112	Distinctive Plastics Inc—*Timothy Curnutt*	1385 Decision St, Vista CA 92081	760-599-9100	R	5*	<.1
1113	Germanow-Simon Corp—*Andrew Germanow*	408 Saint Paul St, Rochester NY 14605	585-232-1440	R	5*	<.1
1114	Pac Strapping Products Inc—*Edwin Brownley*	307 National Rd, Exton PA 19341	610-363-8805	R	5*	<.1
1115	Petro Extrusion Technology Corp—*Robert Petrozziello*	PO Box 99, Garwood NJ 07027	908-789-3338	R	5*	<.1
1116	Total Quality Plastics Inc—*Bob Kearful*	PO Box 507, North Prairie WI 53153	262-392-2020	R	5*	<.1
1117	Retlaw Industries Inc—*Walter Eberhardt*	520 S Industrial Dr, Hartland WI 53029	262-367-2230	R	5*	.1
1118	Evco—*Don Evans*	9698 Shadowstone Way, Reno NV 89521	775-825-5655	R	5*	.1
1119	Fas Plastic Enterprises Inc—*Frank Mingione*	3408 W State Rd 56, Hanover IN 47243	812-265-2928	R	5*	.1
1120	Carolina Color Corp—*Matthew Barr*	PO Box 486, Salisbury NC 28145	704-637-7000	R	5*	.1
1121	Consolidated Models Inc—*Stephen Hasselbach*	222 Pepsi Way, Ayden NC 28513	252-746-2171	R	5*	.1
1122	TCI Vacuum Forming Company Inc—*John Vinka*	1620 Cambridge Dr, Elgin IL 60123	847-622-9100	R	5*	.1
1123	Precision Packaging Products Inc—*Kerry Kyle*	88 Nesbitt Dr, Holley NY 14470	585-638-8200	R	5*	.1
1124	Fielding Manufacturing Inc—*Steven Fielding*	780 Wellington Ave, Cranston RI 02910	401-461-0400	R	5*	<.1
1125	Aptimise Composites LLC—*Vern Shore*	8301 Clinton Park Dr, Fort Wayne IN 46825	260-484-3139	R	5*	<.1
1126	Inplex Custom Extruders LLC—*Mitchell Piecuch*	1663 S Mount Prospect, Des Plaines IL 60018	847-827-7046	R	5*	<.1
1127	Lexington Plastic Molding Co—*Forest Bush*	2029 Buck Ln, Lexington KY 40511	859-255-7077	R	5*	<.1
1128	Trend Plastics Inc—*Thomas Rendleman*	15665 S Keeler St, Olathe KS 66062	913-782-3080	R	5*	<.1
1129	Alladin Investments Inc—*Allen Vogel*	140 Industrial Dr, Surgoinsville TN 37873	423-345-2351	R	5*	.1
1130	Precision Custom Products Inc—*James Kerg Jr*	4590 County Rd 35 N, De Graff OH 43318		R	5*	.1
1131	Hood Manufacturing Inc—*Michael Hood*	2621 S Birch St, Santa Ana CA 92707	714-979-7681	R	5*	.1
1132	ADPI Enterprises Inc—*Steven Talis*	3621 B St Ste 3a, Philadelphia PA 19134	215-425-8866	R	5*	.1
1133	California Quality Plastics Inc—*Robert Kaplan*	2226 Castle Harbor Pla, Ontario CA 91761	909-930-5535	R	5*	.1
1134	K and R Products Inc—*Fred Vairetta*	PO Box 1178, Aptos CA 95001	831-426-6061	R	5*	.1
1135	Prototype and Plastic Mold Company Inc—*Victor DeJong*	35 Industrial Park Pl, Middletown CT 06457	860-632-2800	R	5*	.1
1136	TFI LLC—*Robert Biehler*	440 Oberlin Ave S, Lakewood NJ 08701	732-363-4818	R	5*	.1
1137	Air Check Manufacturing Company Inc—*John Mordenti*	876 Van Houten Ave, Clifton NJ 07013	973-473-7770	R	5*	<.1
1138	Excelsior Plastics Industries Inc—*Chris Bisbee*	201 S Mccleary Rd, Excelsior Springs MO 64024	816-637-4720	R	5*	<.1
1139	RPM Industries Inc—*Roger P Mueller*	26 Aurelius Ave, Auburn NY 13021	315-255-1105	R	5*	<.1
1140	Rps Construction Services Inc—*Michael Dunkeraley*	PO Box 255, Sharpsville PA 16150	724-962-9981	R	5*	<.1
1141	Thomas M Niland Co—*Thomas Niland*	320 N Clark Dr, El Paso TX 79905	915-779-1405	R	5*	<.1
1142	Smt LLC—*Monique Buchmann*	2768 Golfview Dr, Naperville IL 60563	630-961-3000	R	5*	<.1
1143	Sun State Plastics Inc—*Rick Dewees*	4045 Kevin St Nw, Canton OH 44720	330-494-5220	R	5*	<.1
1144	Americad Technology Corporat—*Mark Haslett*	PO Box 314, Norwood MA 02062	781-551-8220	R	5*	<.1
1145	Cmn Plastics Inc—*Mike Nelson*	4300 E Magnolia St Ste, Phoenix AZ 85034	602-437-4373	R	5*	<.1
1146	Harman Corp—*Jeff Harman*	PO Box 80665, Rochester MI 48308	248-651-4477	R	5*	<.1
1147	Hudson Extrusions Inc—*Marilyn Hansen*	PO Box 255, Hudson OH 44236	330-650-0524	R	5*	<.1
1148	S and W Plastics LLC—*David Goldstein*	1200 S Wanamaker Ave, Ontario CA 91761	909-390-0090	R	5*	<.1
1149	Tsi Plastics Inc—*Patrick Cready*	7705 Central Ave Ne, Minneapolis MN 55432	763-784-0240	R	5*	<.1
1150	Amatech/Polycel LLC—*David Amatangelo*	1460 Grimm Dr, Erie PA 16501	814-452-0010	S	5*	<.1
1151	Duo-Corp—*William Kinkade*	PO Box 313, North Lima OH 44452	330-549-2149	R	5*	<.1
1152	Jokari/US Inc—*Sam Ligon*	1220 Champion Cir Ste, Carrollton TX 75006	214-237-0625	R	5*	<.1
1153	Lucky Line Products Inc—*Bill Fleming*	7890 Dunbrook Rd, San Diego CA 92126		R	5*	<.1
1154	Phoenix Technology Ltd—*Zeljko Vesligaj*	PO Box 249, Burgaw NC 28425	910-259-6804	R	5*	<.1
1155	Polymer Instrumentation And Consulting Services Ltd—*Tim Hsu*	2215 High Tech Rd, State College PA 16803	814-357-5860	R	5*	<.1
1156	Total Plastic Services Inc—*Willy Solenthaler*	450 E Pima St Ste 2, Phoenix AZ 85004	602-252-6200	R	5*	<.1
1157	Vinyl Art Inc—*Robert Roy*	15300 28th Ave N, Minneapolis MN 55447	763-559-4443	R	5*	<.1
1158	West and Barker Inc—*Samuel Barker*	950 Summit Ave, Niles OH 44446	330-652-9923	R	5*	<.1
1159	Demtech Services Inc—*Dave Mclaury*	6414 Capitol Ave, Diamond Springs CA 95619	530-621-3200	R	5*	<.1
1160	Fluorolite Plastics Inc—*Greg Pink*	2 Central St, Framingham MA 01701	508-788-1200	R	5*	<.1
1161	Thrust Industries Inc—*Jim Stuteville*	10334 Hedden Rd, Evansville IN 47725	812-437-3643	R	5*	<.1
1162	Triton Products LLC—*Terry Palermo*	30700-D Carter St, Solon OH 44139	440-248-5480	R	5*	<.1
1163	Abimex LLC—*Roger S Marcus* American Biltrite Inc	57 River St Ste 302, Wellesley Hills MA 02481	781-237-6655	S	5*	<.1
1164	Unibox Enclosures Inc—*Sybill Jecker*	3620 Sacremento Dr Ste, San Luis Obispo CA 93401	805-785-0900	R	5*	<.1
1165	Apr Plastic Fabricating Inc—*Mark Allen*	2312 Cass St, Fort Wayne IN 46808	260-482-8523	R	5*	.1
1166	Ovadia Corp—*Joseph Ovadia*	101 E Main St Bldg 2, Little Falls NJ 07424	973-256-9200	R	5*	.1
1167	Plastic Reel Corporation Of America—*Ben Zuk*	PO Box 296, Park Ridge NJ 07656	201-933-5100	R	5*	.1

Note: An asterisk (*) indicates an estimated financial figure. The company type code used is as follows: R = Private, P = Public, S = Private Subsidiary, B = Public Subsidiary, D = Division, J = Joint Venture, I = Investment Fund.

COMPANY RANKINGS BY SALES WITHIN 4-DIGIT SIC

Rank	Company Name—Executive Officer	Address, City, State, Zip	Phone	Type	Fin	Empls
1168	International Hydraulics Inc—Charles Ridley	7638 Saint Clair Ave, Mentor OH 44060	440-951-7186	R	5*	<.1
1169	Curd Enterprises Inc—Deborah Herbert	476 Long Point Rd, Mount Pleasant SC 29464	843-881-0323	R	5*	<.1
1170	Engineered Plastics Of Pickwick Inc—Nancy Woods	PO Box 14, Pickwick Dam TN 38365	731-689-3138	R	5*	<.1
1171	LP Aero Plastics Inc—Thomas Frey	1086 Boquet Rd, Jeannette PA 15644	724-744-4448	R	5*	<.1
1172	Shinsei Corp—Toshino Mizuno	1001 Southpark Dr, Peachtree City GA 30269	770-487-2294	R	5*	<.1
1173	Tomken Plastic Technologies Inc—Randi Carmichael	4601 N Superior Dr, Muncie IN 47303	765-284-2472	R	5*	<.1
1174	Fred Knapp Engraving Company Inc—Jay Haertel	5102 Douglas Ave, Racine WI 53402	262-639-3941	R	5*	<.1
1175	Plasticards Inc—Kenneth Thompson	3711 Boettler Oaks Dr, Uniontown OH 44685	330-896-5555	R	5*	<.1
1176	Unipar Inc—Robert Parks	130 Royal St, Reedsville PA 17084	717-667-3354	R	5*	<.1
1177	Pro Window and Door Company Inc—Jim Draper	4113 Asher Ave, Little Rock AR 72204	501-663-3611	R	5*	<.1
1178	St Albans Window Manufacturing Inc—Burma Helm	2141 Maccorkle Ave, Saint Albans WV 25177	304-727-9363	R	5*	<.1
1179	Interpak Inc—Mark Shaw	7278 Justin Way, Mentor OH 44060	440-974-8999	R	5*	<.1
1180	Container Manufacturing Inc—J Jennings	PO Box 428, Middlesex NJ 08846	732-563-0100	R	5*	<.1
1181	Knightsbridge Plastics Inc—Dave Platt	3075 Osgood Ct, Fremont CA 94539	510-440-8444	R	5*	<.1
1182	Lee Plastics Inc—Leo Montagna	PO Box 39, Sterling MA 01564	978-422-7611	R	5*	<.1
1183	Precision Polymer Manufacturing Inc-Man—William Longjohn	3915 Ravine Rd, Kalamazoo MI 49006	269-344-2044	R	5*	<.1
1184	Geib Enterprises Ltd—Jeffrey Geib	PO Box 937, West Bend WI 53095	262-334-3030	R	5*	<.1
1185	J D Products Inc—John Denney	405 Commerce Ct, Saint Paul MN 55127	651-483-9166	R	5*	<.1
1186	Foremost Plastic Products Company Inc—Kenneth Muszynski	7834 W Grand Ave, Elmwood Park IL 60707	708-452-5300	R	5*	<.1
1187	Bentonville Plastics Inc—Terry Law	607 Sw A St, Bentonville AR 72712	479-273-7272	R	5*	<.1
1188	Cosmic Plastics Inc—Lillian Luh	28410 Industry Dr, Valencia CA 91355	661-257-3274	R	5*	<.1
1189	Echo Molding Inc—Dieter Hekler	911 Springfield Rd Ste, Union NJ 07083	908-688-0099	R	5*	<.1
1190	Proto - Plastics Inc—Frank Bianco	1100 Piedmont Dr, Troy MI 48083	248-689-2348	R	5*	<.1
1191	Permian Plastics Inc—Dale Emge	1477 Hoff Industrial C, O Fallon MO 63366	636-978-4655	R	5*	<.1
1192	Ultra Tech Extrustions Of Tennessee Inc—Harry Empting	150 Commercial Ln, Lake City TN 37769	865-426-2862	R	5*	<.1
1193	Accu-Form Polymers Inc—Pat Renfro	PO Box 445, Warsaw NC 28398	910-293-6961	R	5*	<.1
1194	Pine Hill Plastics Inc—Lonnie Capshaw	PO Box 202, Mcminnville TN 37111	931-934-3000	R	5*	<.1
1195	L and S Langco Properties LLC	34476 County Rd 347, Oran MO 63771	573-722-3392	R	5*	<.1
1196	Promex International Plastics Inc—Gilbert Anguiano	12860 San Fernando Rd, Sylmar CA 91342	818-367-5352	R	5*	<.1
1197	Advanced Fibermolding Inc—Dennis Webster	23773 14 Mile Rd, Leroy MI 49655	231-768-5177	R	5*	<.1
1198	Attbar Inc—John Barchek	5985 S 6th Way, Ridgefield WA 98642	360-887-3580	R	5*	<.1
1199	Kracor Inc—George Kraemer	5625 W Clinton Ave, Milwaukee WI 53223	414-355-6335	R	5*	<.1
1200	Marcon Marketing Concepts Inc—Randall Smith	101 W 10th Ave, Kansas City MO 64116	816-471-2327	R	5*	<.1
1201	Olan Plastics Inc—Olan Long	6550 Olan Dr, Canal Winchester OH 43110	614-834-6526	R	5*	<.1
1202	Wolverine Plastics Inc—Adam Hall	PO Box 160, Fombell PA 16123	724-758-8120	R	5*	<.1
1203	MC Molds Inc—Robert Palazzolo	125 Industrial Park Dr, Williamston MI 48895	517-655-5481	R	5*	<.1
1204	Volt Industrial Plastics Inc—Joseph Volltrauer	700 Hwy 202 W, Yellville AR 72687	870-449-8027	R	5*	.1
1205	Curtition LLC—Thomas Cerney	PO Box 367, Darien WI 53114	262-882-1233	R	5*	.1
1206	Quality Industries LLC—Tom Devaney	PO Box 340, Hartwell GA 30643	706-376-4793	R	5*	.1
1207	T-Plastech Corp—Greg Payne	PO Box 542, Englewood CO 80151	303-761-8263	R	5*	.1
1208	Modern Plastics Corp—Bernadette Murphy	152 Horton St, Wilkes Barre PA 18702	570-022-1124	R	5*	<.1
1209	Arbco Industries Inc—Gina Burkett	2040 Borland Rd, Export PA 15632	724-327-6300	R	5*	<.1
1210	Penn Plastics Inc—Raymond Pennoyer	381 Bishop Ave, Bridgeport CT 06610	203-334-2673	R	5*	<.1
1211	Aero-Med Molding Technologies Inc—Lawrence Saffran	50 Westfield Ave, Ansonia CT 06401	203-735-2331	R	5*	<.1
1212	Astar Inc—Sidney Moore	PO Box 3566, South Bend IN 46619	574-234-2137	R	5*	<.1
1213	D W Mack Company Inc—Dennis Mack	PO Box 1247, Monrovia CA 91017	626-969-1817	R	5*	<.1
1214	Wisconsin Plastic Products Inc—Edmund Gregoire	PO Box 580, Plymouth WI 53073	920-893-4500	R	5*	<.1
1215	Ohio Precision Molding Inc—Bruce Vereecken	122 E Tuscarawas Ave, Barberton OH 44203	330-745-9393	R	5*	<.1
1216	KHM Plastics Inc—Daniel Kloczkowski	4090 Ryan Rd Ste B, Gurnee IL 60031	847-249-4910	R	5*	<.1
1217	Welch Fluorocarbon Inc—Evan Welch	113 Crosby Rd Ste 10, Dover NH 03820	603-742-7070	R	5*	<.1
1218	All Plastics Molding Company Inc—Larry Byrd	PO Box 306, Addison TX 75001	972-239-2686	R	4*	.1
1219	Miu LLC	PO Box 2228, Issaquah WA 98027	206-605-0555	R	4*	<.1
1220	Phoenix Electric Manufacturing Co—Norberto Anselmi	3625 N Halsted St, Chicago IL 60613	773-477-8855	R	4*	<.1
1221	Ash Industries Inc—Hartie Spence	1330 W Willow St, Lafayette LA 70506	337-235-0977	R	4*	<.1
1222	Moldmaster Engineering Inc—Thomas Kushi	PO Box 1161, Pittsfield MA 01202	413-443-4406	R	4*	<.1
1223	Tech Medical Plastics Inc—James Piermarini	1403 Dogwood Way, Mebane NC 27302	919-563-9272	R	4*	<.1
1224	Granite State Plastics Inc—Stephen Getto	15 Tinker Ave, Londonderry NH 03053	603-669-6715	R	4*	<.1
1225	Maillis Strapping Systems USA Inc—Derek Laymon	404 Wall St, Fountain Inn SC 29644	864-601-1333	R	4*	<.1
1226	Par-Pak Inc—Sajjad Ebrahim	3450 Lang Rd, Houston TX 77092	713-686-6700	R	4*	<.1
1227	Engineered Composites Inc—Daniel Bolubash	55 Roberts Ave, Buffalo NY 14206	716-362-0295	R	4*	<.1
1228	Schoeller Arca Systems Inc—Robert Engle	5202 Old Orchard Rd St, Skokie IL 60077	847-410-1342	R	4*	<.1
1229	Manchester Molding And Manufacturing Co—Joseph Nadeau	96 Sheldon Rd, Manchester CT 06042	860-643-2141	R	4*	.1
1230	Accutec Systems Inc—Bob Krause	2121 Touhy Ave, Elk Grove Village IL 60007	847-956-6340	R	4*	.1
1231	Plastronics Interconnections Inc—Wayne Pfaff	2601 Texas Dr, Irving TX 75062	972-258-2580	R	4*	.1
1232	Durden Enterprises Ltd—John Durden	PO Box 909, Auburn GA 30011	770-963-0637	R	4*	<.1
1233	Carolina Plastics Inc—Ken Cobb	PO Box 969, West Union SC 29696	864-985-1501	R	4*	<.1
1234	Gmt Inc—Michelle Dubanowski	180 S Melrose Ave, Elgin IL 60123	847-697-8161	R	4*	<.1
1235	C-Plastics Inc—Chris Kostecki	12463 Cleveland St, Nunica MI 49448	616-837-7396	R	4*	<.1
1236	Life Of The Party LLC—Joanne Soltis	832 Ridgewood Ave Bldg, North Brunswick NJ 08902	732-828-0886	R	4*	<.1
1237	Van Norman Molding LLC—Jim Hager	9615 S 76th Ave, Oak Lawn IL 60455	708-430-4343	R	4*	<.1
1238	Medart Inc—Jeffrey Pierce	199 Clyde St, Ellwood City PA 16117	724-752-2900	R	4*	<.1
1239	Bardes Plastics Inc—Mary Strupp	5225 W Clinton Ave, Milwaukee WI 53223	414-354-5300	R	4*	<.1
1240	Syron Industries Inc—Robert Hyla	PO Box 126, Syracuse NY 13206	315-437-6133	R	4*	<.1
1241	Energy Composites Corp—Jamie Mancl	4400 Commerce Dr, Wisconsin Rapids WI 54494	715-421-2060	P	4	.1
1242	Ono Industries Inc—Carmine Petrozziello	PO Box 150, Ono PA 17077	717-865-6619	R	4*	<.1
1243	Eldora Plastics Inc—Jerrold Jenson	PO Box 127, Eldora IA 50627	641-858-2634	R	4*	<.1
1244	Holzmeyer Die And Mold Manufacturing Corp—Alan Holzmeyer	PO Box 610, Princeton IN 47670	812-386-6015	R	4*	<.1
1245	Resinart Corp—Gary Uecker	1621 Placentia Ave, Costa Mesa CA 92627	949-642-3665	R	4*	<.1
1246	North Canton Plastics Inc—John Kuebel	6658 Promway Ave Nw, Canton OH 44720	330-497-0071	R	4*	<.1
1247	Red Rib Inc—Richard Enders	4210 S 36th St, Phoenix AZ 85040	602-437-0136	R	4*	<.1
1248	Holbrook Tool and Molding Inc—Dale Barnard	PO Box 60, Meadville PA 16335	814-336-4113	R	4*	<.1
1249	Vantec Inc—W Van Wyhe	PO Box 847, Webster City IA 50595	515-832-3125	R	4*	<.1
1250	Century Molded Plastics Inc—Harry Lemanski	3120 W Lake Ave, Glenview IL 60026	847-729-3455	R	4*	<.1
1251	Larmco Windows Inc—Joe Talmon	8400 Sweet Valley Dr S, Cleveland OH 44125	216-525-0001	R	4*	<.1
1252	Midwest Insert Composite Moulding and Assembly Corp—Gi Patel	3940 Industrial Ave, Rolling Meadows IL 60008	847-818-8444	R	4*	<.1
1253	Reliable Caps LLC—George Murray	1001 W Hwy 56, Olathe KS 66061	913-764-2277	R	4*	<.1
1254	Trexel Inc—David Bernstein	45 6th Rd, Woburn MA 01801	781-932-0202	R	4*	<.1
1255	Cornell Concepts Corp—Stephen Cornell	13 Leonard St, Foxboro MA 02035	508-543-1483	R	4*	<.1
1256	Mastermolding Inc—Ray Steinhart	1715 Terry Dr, Joliet IL 60436	815-741-1230	R	4*	<.1

Rank	Company Name—*Executive Officer*	Address, City, State, Zip	Phone	Type	Fin	Empls
1257	Action Plastics Inc—*David Foss*	14720 Main St, Rogers MN 55374	763-428-4900	R	4*	<.1
1258	Bowsmith Inc—*Allan Smith*	PO Box 428, Exeter CA 93221	559-592-9485	R	4*	.1
1259	Robetex Inc—*Cary Talbot*	PO Box 1489, Rocky Face GA 30740	910-671-8787	R	4*	<.1
1260	Luttmann Precision Mold Inc—*William Luttmann*	1200 W Lafayette St, Sturgis MI 49091	269-651-1193	R	4*	<.1
1261	Advanced Plastiform Inc—*Chris Jolly*	535 Mack Todd Rd, Zebulon NC 27597	919-404-2080	R	4*	<.1
1262	D-Rep Plastics Inc—*Daniel Chalich*	720 Brooker Creek Blvd, Oldsmar FL 34677	727-573-7969	R	4*	<.1
1263	Mid-America Plastics Inc—*Dean Swanson*	700 Industrial Cir S, Shakopee MN 55379	952-445-7667	R	4*	<.1
1264	Excel Injection Molding Inc—*John Robinson*	977 Sullivan Dr, Hattiesburg MS 39401	601-544-6133	R	4*	<.1
1265	Jam Plastics Inc—*Joseph Mazzaferro*	22 Tucker Dr, Leominster MA 01453	978-537-2570	R	4*	<.1
1266	Hb Molding Inc—*Mark Hallam*	3001 Watterson Trl, Louisville KY 40299	502-261-1808	R	4*	<.1
1267	Techniform Industries Inc—*Clifford Robinette*	2107 Hayes Ave, Fremont OH 43420	419-332-8484	R	4*	<.1
1268	Inline Plastics Inc—*Kelly Orr*	1950 S Baker Ave, Ontario CA 91761	909-923-1033	R	4*	<.1
1269	Caprock Manufacturing Inc—*Ryan Provenzano*	2303 120th St, Lubbock TX 79423	806-745-6454	R	4*	.1
1270	Kevro Chemical Co—*Stefan Hershfield*	1680 E Market St, Akron OH 44305	330-794-9922	R	4*	.1
1271	Blue Ridge Industries Inc—*Mary Sarle*	PO Box 1847, Winchester VA 22604	540-662-3900	R	4*	.1
1272	Tower Tech Inc—*Robert C Brink*	PO Box 891810, Oklahoma City OK 73189	405-290-7788	R	4*	.1
1273	Cowan Plastics LLC	7 Starline Way, Cranston RI 02921	401-351-1400	R	4*	.1
1274	Mc Minnville Molding Company Inc—*Ricky Northcutt*	PO Box 765, Mcminnville TN 37111	931-473-5511	R	4*	.1
1275	Soroc Products Inc—*Dennis Cox*	4349 S Dort Hwy, Burton MI 48529	810-743-2660	R	4*	<.1
1276	Polymer Molding Inc—*John Sontag*	1655 W 20th St, Erie PA 16502	814-455-8085	R	4*	<.1
1277	Affinity Custom Molding Inc—*David Cook*	PO Box 9, Mendon MI 49072	269-496-8423	R	4*	<.1
1278	Billy Pugh Company Inc—*Paul W Liberato*	PO Box 802, Corpus Christi TX 78403	361-884-9351	R	4*	.1
1279	Sound Manufacturing Inc—*Chris Jensen*	PO Box 5097, Kent WA 98064	253-872-8007	R	4*	<.1
1280	Windstone Editions Inc—*John Alberti*	728 Sw Wake Robin Ave, Corvallis OR 97333	541-752-0404	R	4*	<.1
1281	Apogee Designs Ltd—*Robert Flesher*	101 Kane St, Baltimore MD 21224	410-633-6336	R	4*	<.1
1282	Pearce Plastics Inc—*Woodrow Pearce*	1309 Lincoln Ave, Pasadena CA 91103	626-797-8481	R	4*	<.1
1283	Addicks Engineering And Product Development Co—*Lyle Addicks*	6006 Shull St, Bell CA 90201	562-927-4711	R	4*	<.1
1284	Aero-Plastics Inc—*Mike Hammer*	903 Houser Way N, Renton WA 98055	425-226-3400	R	4*	<.1
1285	Bay City Window Co—*Devin Zimring*	2135 13th Ave N, Saint Petersburg FL 33713	727-323-5443	R	4*	<.1
1286	Beemak Plastics Inc—*Chris Braun*	16711 Knott Ave, La Mirada CA 90638	310-886-5880	S	4*	<.1
1287	C and E Plastics Inc—*Clifford Crighton*	2500 State Rte 168, Georgetown PA 15043	724-947-4949	R	4*	<.1
1288	R and D Plastics Inc—*R Weaver*	PO Box 219, Arden NC 28704	828-684-2692	R	4*	<.1
1289	Thermo-Fab Corp—*Thomas King*	76 Walker Rd, Shirley MA 01464	978-425-2311	R	4*	<.1
1290	Moore Fabrication Inc—*William Moore*	5645 Northdale St, Houston TX 77087	713-643-7477	R	4*	<.1
1291	Iowa Mold and Engineering Inc—*Bradley Cook*	401 3rd St, Belle Plaine IA 52208	319-444-2221	R	4*	<.1
1292	Elite Plastic Products Inc—*Robert Mandeville*	51476 Filomena Dr, Shelby Township MI 48315	586-247-5800	R	4*	<.1
1293	Liberty Packaging and Extruding Inc—*Bonnie Hudson*	3015 Supply Ave, Commerce CA 90040	323-722-5124	R	4*	<.1
1294	Raleigh Precision Products Inc—*Peter Smith*	131 Johnston Pkwy, Kenly NC 27542	919-284-9001	R	4*	<.1
1295	A and M Tool Molding Division Inc—*Fred Millar*	PO Box 1259, Arden NC 28704	828-687-0639	R	4*	<.1
1296	Continental Packaging Corp—*Andrew Krupsha*	PO Box 913, Berwick PA 18603	570-371-5777	R	4*	<.1
1297	Elkhart Cases Inc—*Dale D Fahlbeck*	57459 Dewitt St, Elkhart IN 46517	574-295-7700	R	4*	<.1
1298	Quadel Industries—*Eric Luckman*	PO Box 1047, Coos Bay OR 97420	541-269-7351	R	4*	<.1
1299	Retterbush Injection Molded Fiberglass Corp—*Bryan Retterbush*	PO Box 207, Piqua OH 45356	937-778-1936	R	4*	<.1
1300	Gatorhyde Protective Coatings Inc—*Orlin Emmons*	PO Box 323, Broken Arrow OK 74013	918-485-2835	R	4*	<.1
1301	Jerhel Plastics Inc—*Bob McLean*	63 Hook Rd, Bayonne NJ 07002	201-436-6662	R	4*	<.1
1302	Universal Pultrusions LLC—*Keith Jensen*	PO Box 1289, Marshall AR 72650	870-448-4406	R	4*	<.1
1303	Tex Trend Inc—*Gina Belcastro*	767 Kristy Ln, Wheeling IL 60090	847-215-6796	R	4*	.1
1304	Paramount Plastics Inc—*Rex Lim*	2810 Jeanwood Dr, Elkhart IN 46514	574-264-2143	R	4*	<.1
1305	Quality Custom Molding LLC—*Diane Armistead*	PO Box 1130, Linn MO 65051	573-897-4166	R	4*	<.1
1306	Columbine Plastics Corp—*William Leipold*	3195 Bluff St, Boulder CO 80301	303-442-0051	R	4*	<.1
1307	Quality Fencing and Supply—*Amos Lapp*	PO Box 185, New Holland PA 17557	717-355-7100	R	4*	<.1
1308	Assmann Corporation of America—*David Crager*	300 N Taylor Rd, Garrett IN 46738	260-357-3181	R	4*	<.1
1309	WJLS Inc—*Wesley Lawson*	PO Box 470651, Tulsa OK 74147	918-252-3636	R	4*	<.1
1310	Harrison Machine and Plastic Corp—*Bryson Swanda*	PO Box 1826, Hiram OH 44234	330-527-5641	R	4*	<.1
1311	Industrial Plastics And Machine Inc—*Carlo Cereda*	6829 S Choctaw Dr, Baton Rouge LA 70806	225-928-0113	R	4*	<.1
1312	M and A Plastics Inc—*Guillermo Morales*	11735 Sheldon St, Sun Valley CA 91352	818-768-0479	R	4*	<.1
1313	River City Products Inc—*Irene Gentry*	2735 W River Dr Nw, Grand Rapids MI 49544	616-365-0040	R	4*	<.1
1314	Walter Drake Inc—*James Mc Carthy*	PO Box 691, Holyoke MA 01041	413-536-5463	R	4*	<.1
1315	Extrudex LP—*Costel Lupoae*	310 Figgie Dr, Painesville OH 44077	440-352-7101	R	4*	.1
1316	Microsonic Inc—*Miklos Major*	PO Box 184, Ambridge PA 15003	724-266-9270	R	4*	<.1
1317	Just Plastics Inc—*Judy Eckstein*	PO Box 645, Galion OH 44833	419-468-5506	R	4*	<.1
1318	John L Perry Studio Inc—*John Perry*	300 Bernoulli Cir, Oxnard CA 93030	805-981-9665	R	4*	<.1
1319	Jifram Extrusions Inc—*Steven Fischer*	PO Box 121, Sheboygan Falls WI 53085	920-467-2477	R	4*	<.1
1320	Image Rotomolding Enterprises Inc—*James Wills*	PO Box 589, Troy AL 36081	218-828-3002	S	4*	<.1
1321	Mytex Polymers Us Corp—*Lawrence Smith*	1403 Port Rd, Jeffersonville IN 47130	812-280-2900	R	4*	<.1
1322	Sun Star Inc—*David Carrera*	4427 State Rte 982, Latrobe PA 15650	724-537-5990	R	4*	<.1
1323	Custom Craft Plastics—*Ken Silverman*	PO Box 6029, North Brunswick NJ 08902	732-843-3000	R	4*	.1
1324	Quality Profile Services Inc—*John True*	PO Box 256, Council Grove KS 66846	620-767-6757	R	4*	<.1
1325	Indiana Bottle Company Inc—*Dave Keener*	300 W Lovers Ln, Scottsburg IN 47170	812-752-8700	R	4*	<.1
1326	Accu-Mold and Tool Company Inc—*Mary Strohecker*	PO Box U, Halifax PA 17032	717-896-3937	R	4*	<.1
1327	Green Bay Plastics Inc—*Michael Hogan*	1028 N Ashland Ave, Green Bay WI 54303	920-435-3957	R	4*	<.1
1328	Balfor Industries Inc—*Donald Ballot*	4380 Bronx Blvd, Bronx NY 10466	718-994-9003	R	4*	<.1
1329	Kelly Company Inc—*J Kelly*	PO Box 830, Clinton MA 01510	978-368-8991	R	4*	<.1
1330	Nexpak Corp	29 New York Ave, Westbury NY 11590	516-333-8880	S	4	<.1
1331	Quality Plastics And Engineering Inc—*Rick Donati*	2507 Decio Dr, Elkhart IN 46514	574-262-1422	R	4*	<.1
1332	Calico Precision Molding LLC—*Teresa Gooding*	1211 Progress Rd, Fort Wayne IN 46808	260-484-4500	R	4*	<.1
1333	Good L Corp—*Phil Goodell*	PO Box 337, La Vergne TN 37086	615-793-7779	R	4*	<.1
1334	Sunbelt Plastics Tooling Inc—*John Anselmi*	PO Box 370, Frisco TX 75034	972-335-4100	R	4*	<.1
1335	Ci-Dell Plastics Inc—*Dan Trudell*	6301 W Executive Dr, Mequon WI 53092	262-512-4080	R	4*	<.1
1336	Plastic Designs Inc—*Steven Glazik*	1330 S Vermillion St, Paxton IL 60957	217-379-9214	R	4*	<.1
1337	Powertex Inc—*Stephen Podd*	1 Lincoln Blvd Ste 101, Rouses Point NY 12979	518-297-4000	R	4*	<.1
1338	Dana-Saad Co—*William Saad*	3808 N Sullivan Rd Ste, Spokane Valley WA 99216	509-924-6711	R	4*	<.1
1339	Drummond Industries Inc—*Matthew Gieser*	2616 N Cicero Ave, Chicago IL 60639	773-637-1264	R	4*	<.1
1340	Dynaco USA Inc—*Olivier Coune*	935 Campus Dr, Mundelein IL 60060	847-562-4910	R	4*	<.1
1341	Otto Enviornmental Systems Az LLC—*Paul Blair*	901 N Tweedy Rd, Eloy AZ 85131	520-466-3410	S	4*	<.1
1342	Select Plastics LLC—*Betty Rolland*	8800 S Fwy, Fort Worth TX 76140	817-595-3804	S	4*	<.1
1343	Poly-Foam Inc—*Robert Humboldt*	116 Pine St S, Lester Prairie MN 55354	320-395-2551	R	4*	.1
1344	J-Ron Inc—*Ronald Bugg*	PO Box 294, Henderson KY 42419	270-827-4953	R	4*	.1

Note: An asterisk (*) indicates an estimated financial figure. The company type code used is as follows: R = Private, P = Public, S = Private Subsidiary, B = Public Subsidiary, D = Division, J = Joint Venture, I = Investment Fund.

COMPANY RANKINGS BY SALES WITHIN 4-DIGIT SIC

Rank	Company Name—*Executive Officer*	Address, City, State, Zip	Phone	Type	Fin	Empls
1345	Elite Production Inc—*Beth Knutson*	PO Box 1134, Lakeville MN 55044	952-469-5454	R	4*	<.1
1346	Cornucopia Tool and Plastics Inc—*Larry Horn*	PO Box 1915, Paso Robles CA 93447	805-238-7660	R	4*	<.1
1347	Tag Plastics Inc—*Tommy Harwell*	PO Box 1389, Tracy City TN 37387	931-592-4888	R	4*	<.1
1348	Experimental Nylon Products Inc—*Charles Geisel*	PO Box 266, Osceola IN 46561	574-674-8747	R	4*	<.1
1349	Lima Plastics Inc—*Jose Caria*	56 Hillside Rd, Elizabeth NJ 07208	908-353-0138	R	4*	<.1
1350	Proto-Cast LLC—*Pam Beaton*	1460 Ben Franklin Hwy, Douglassville PA 19518	610-326-1723	R	4*	<.1
1351	Chippewa Plastics Inc—*Albert Rohe*	5843 100th Ave, Evart MI 49631	231-734-5517	R	4*	<.1
1352	Northern Precision Plastics Inc—*Bob Milnichuk*	6553 Revlon Dr, Belvidere IL 61008	815-544-8099	R	4*	<.1
1353	Perma-Graphics Inc—*James Vaughan*	2470 Schuetz Rd, Maryland Heights MO 63043	314-567-4624	R	4*	<.1
1354	Unit Pack Company Inc—*Ernest Loesser*	7 Lewis Rd, Cedar Grove NJ 07009	973-239-4112	R	4*	<.1
1355	Plastic-Craft Products Corp—*Mark Brecher*	PO Box 713, West Nyack NY 10994	845-358-3010	R	4*	<.1
1356	Aucilla Inc—*Paul Gonsoroski*	3333 N Kenmore St, South Bend IN 46628	574-234-9036	R	4*	<.1
1357	Han-Win Products Inc—*S Cherwin*	PO Box 4515, Aurora IL 60507	630-897-1591	R	4*	<.1
1358	J and L Custom Plastic Extrusions Inc—*Louis Salmon*	1532 Santa Anita Ave, South El Monte CA 91733	626-442-0711	R	4*	<.1
1359	King's Prosperity Industries LLC—*Rodolfo Carrizales*	PO Box 5344, Mcallen TX 78502	956-631-1115	R	4*	<.1
1360	Micro Mold Company Inc—*David Mead*	4820 Pittsburgh Ave, Erie PA 16509	814-838-3404	R	4*	<.1
1361	Mpr Plastics Inc—*Paul Doran*	1551 Scottsdale Ct Ste, Elgin IL 60123	847-468-9950	R	4*	<.1
1362	Plastex Industries Inc—*John Smotherman*	4050 S Ave, Toledo OH 43615	419-531-0189	R	4*	<.1
1363	Reliant Molding Inc—*David Diehl*	PO Box 300, Cranesville PA 16410	814-756-5522	R	4*	<.1
1364	Socomatic Inc—*Eileen Saccomonto*	534 Congress Cir N, Roselle IL 60172	630-539-4400	R	4*	<.1
1365	Advanced Polymer Technology—*Mark Hoofman*	3760 Marsh Rd, Madison WI 53718	608-838-8786	S	4	<.1
1366	Fibre Materials Corp—*Glenn Fellows*	40 Dupont St, Plainview NY 11803	516-349-1660	R	4*	<.1
1367	Plastic Monofil Company Ltd—*Calvert Kogan*	28 Industrial Dr, Milton VT 05468	802-893-1543	R	4*	<.1
1368	Delfin Design and Manufacturing Inc—*John Rief*	23301 Antonio Pkwy, Rcho Sta Marg CA 92688	949-888-4644	R	4*	<.1
1369	Plastikos Inc—*Timothy Katen* Micro Mold Company Inc	8165 Hawthorne Dr, Erie PA 16509	814-868-1656	S	4*	<.1
1370	Tri-Craft Inc—*Kathleen Byrnes*	17941 Englewood Dr, Cleveland OH 44130	440-826-1050	R	4*	<.1
1371	Selmax Corp—*Kenneth Mease*	PO Box 149, Selinsgrove PA 17870	570-374-2833	R	4*	<.1
1372	R-G-T Plastics Co—*Robert Drnek*	PO Box 8, Linesville PA 16424	814-683-2161	R	4*	<.1
1373	Regal Finishing Co—*Jim Kodis*	3927 Bessemer Rd, Coloma MI 49038	269-849-2963	R	3*	.1
1374	Knobby Krafters Inc—*Nicholas Nerney*	PO Box 300, Attleboro MA 02703	508-222-7272	R	3*	<.1
1375	Pier-Mac Plastics Inc—*Jim Hiester*	1000 N Morton St, Portland IN 47371	260-726-9844	R	3*	<.1
1376	Firelake Manufacturing LLC—*Douglas Bollman*	PO Box 388, Dassel MN 55325	320-275-3391	R	3*	<.1
1377	Texlon Plastics Corp—*Tony Beam*	PO Box 1284, Gastonia NC 28053	704-866-8785	R	3*	<.1
1378	Tunnell Hill Plastics Inc—*Steve Stone*	11636 Hwy 416 W, Corydon KY 42406	270-521-7912	R	3*	<.1
1379	Accurate Molded Products Inc—*Howard Devine*	459 Industrial Dr, Warwick RI 02886	401-739-2400	R	3*	<.1
1380	Gemini Plastic Enterprises Inc—*Richard Honstrater*	3574 Fruitland Ave, Maywood CA 90270	323-582-0901	R	3*	<.1
1381	Indiana Plastics Inc—*Jeff Kruis*	2221 Industrial Pkwy, Elkhart IN 46516	574-294-3253	R	3*	<.1
1382	Intrepid Molding Inc—*Mike Durkin*	1215 Karl Ct Ste 202, Wauconda IL 60084	847-526-9477	R	3*	<.1
1383	Mac Molding Company Inc—*Lance Loeffelman*	12814 Gravois Rd, Saint Louis MO 63127	314-849-0646	R	3*	<.1
1384	Rackow Polymers Corp—*Mario Rackow*	475 Thomas Dr, Bensenville IL 60106	630-766-6589	R	3*	<.1
1385	Technitool Inc—*Sal Russomanno*	1028 Industrial Dr, West Berlin NJ 08091	856-768-2707	R	3*	<.1
1386	Tri-Cities Manufacturing Inc—*William Behl*	PO Box 558, Tuscumbia AL 35674	256-381-3271	R	3*	<.1
1387	3m Automotive Woodville—*Mark Miller*	101 Trient Dr, Woodville WI 54028	715-698-2766	R	3*	<.1
1388	Akra Plastic Products Inc—*R Callaway*	1504 E Cedar St, Ontario CA 91761	909-930-1999	R	3*	<.1
1389	Indiana Vac-Form Inc—*Donald Robinson*	2030 N Boeing Rd, Warsaw IN 46582	574-269-1725	R	3*	<.1
1390	Mid-America Plastic Co—*Patricia Erdmann*	PO Box 667, Forreston IL 61030	815-938-3110	R	3*	<.1
1391	Bamar Plastics Inc—*Barry Lee*	1702 Robinson St, South Bend IN 46613	574-234-4066	R	3*	<.1
1392	Precision Marble Inc—*Tim Michaelbrink*	1102 Willow Creek Rd, Prescott AZ 86301	928-445-7642	R	3*	<.1
1393	Rjt Industries Inc—*Richard Kennel*	PO Box 4160, Woodbridge VA 22194	703-643-1510	R	3*	<.1
1394	Rotational Molding Of Utah Inc—*David Little*	1755 N 2000 W, Brigham City UT 84302	435-734-9920	R	3*	<.1
1395	Schlotter Precision Products Inc—*Frank Schlotter*	40 Indian Dr, Warminster PA 18974	215-354-3280	R	3*	<.1
1396	Sterling Molded Products Inc—*Steven Crescimanno*	9 17 Oliver Ave, Middletown NY 10940	845-344-4546	R	3*	<.1
1397	Thermo Plastic Tech Inc—*Tino Quintanilla*	1119 Morris Ave, Union NJ 07083	908-687-4833	R	3*	<.1
1398	Western Kentucky Plastics Inc—*James Baxter*	308 Dishman Ln, Bowling Green KY 42101	270-782-1881	R	3*	<.1
1399	Craig Technologies Inc—*Don Hollenbeck*	PO Box 180, Seaford DE 19973	302-628-9900	R	3*	<.1
1400	Canyon Plastics Inc—*Kirit Gajera*	28623 Industry Dr, Valencia CA 91355	661-257-4293	R	3*	<.1
1401	Terracon Corp—*Robert Jewett*	5 Boynton Rd, Holliston MA 01746	508-429-9950	MA	3*	<.1
1402	Newport Laminates Inc—*Brad Bollman*	3121 W Central Ave, Santa Ana CA 92704	714-545-8335	R	3*	<.1
1403	Quality Assured Plastics Inc—*Annette Crandall*	PO Box 888, Lawrence MI 49064	269-674-3888	R	3*	<.1
1404	Quality Thermoforming Inc—*Lidia Adams*	25 James P Murphy Indu, West Warwick RI 02893	401-823-5990	R	3*	<.1
1405	Techny Plastics Corp—*Roger Mann*	1919 Techny Rd, Northbrook IL 60062	847-498-2212	R	3*	<.1
1406	Hospital Disposables Inc—*Autrey De Busk*	104 Wheeler St, Portland TN 37148	615-325-9278	R	3*	<.1
1407	D Martone Industries Inc—*Frank Defino*	15060 Madison Rd, Middlefield OH 44062	440-632-5800	R	3*	<.1
1408	Fet Engineering Inc—*Takeshi Kitano*	903 Nutter Dr, Bardstown KY 40004	502-348-2130	R	3*	<.1
1409	Fibertech Corp—*John Wilson*	PO Box 8, Pendleton SC 29670	864-646-3800	R	3*	<.1
1410	Genesis Plastics Technologies Inc—*Randy Howe*	1226 E 18th St, Greeley CO 80631	970-356-3487	R	3*	<.1
1411	HN Lockwood Inc—*Daniel Lockwood*	PO Box 309, Mcarthur CA 96056	650-366-9557	R	3*	<.1
1412	Justin Tanks LLC—*Judith Holtzclaw*	21413 Cedar Creek Ave, Georgetown DE 19947	302-856-3521	R	3*	<.1
1413	Mack Prototype Corp—*Ric Perry*	424 Main St, Gardner MA 01440	978-632-3700	R	3*	<.1
1414	Plastics Dynamics Inc—*Rick Edris*	6004 S 190th St Ste 10, Kent WA 98032	206-762-2164	R	3*	<.1
1415	Tgs Plastics Inc—*Wesley Lawson*	PO Box 470651, Tulsa OK 74147	918-252-3636	R	3*	<.1
1416	Wilmington Fibre Specialty Co—*B Morris*	PO Box 192, New Castle DE 19720	302-328-7525	R	3*	<.1
1417	Brentwood Plastics Inc—*Sam Longstreth*	PO Box 440160, Saint Louis MO 63144	314-968-1135	R	3*	<.1
1418	Tri Tech Tool and Design Company Inc—*Arthur Weber*	30 Cherry St, South Bound Brook NJ 08880	732-469-5433	R	3*	<.1
1419	Rocal Corp—*Nick Calio*	150 Franklin Dr, Warrington PA 18976	215-343-2400	R	3*	<.1
1420	Scan Tool and Mold Inc—*John Gotch*	2 Trefoil Dr, Trumbull CT 06611	203-459-4950	R	3*	<.1
1421	Castino Corp—*Robert Castino*	16777 Wahrman St, Romulus MI 48174	734-941-7200	R	3*	<.1
1422	Scribner Engineering Inc—*Richard Scribner*	11455 Hydraulics Dr, Rancho Cordova CA 95742	916-638-1515	R	3*	<.1
1423	Techna Plastic Services Inc—*Stephen Barilla*	164 Seneca Rd, Lehighton PA 18235	570-386-2732	R	3*	<.1
1424	Research and Advanced Methods Industries Inc—*Diann Morris*	PO Box 47, Cisco TX 76437	254-442-1008	R	3*	<.1
1425	Swiss-Tex Inc—*Tom Mcdonough*	PO Box 9258, Greenville SC 29604	864-845-7541	R	3*	<.1
1426	Plastic Concept Inc—*Ronald Schulze*	15602 Container Ln, Huntington Beach CA 92649	714-895-4722	R	3*	<.1
1427	Southern Vinyle Window Manufacturing Inc—*Bill Gillespie*	PO Box 2, Liberty SC 29657	864-843-9966	R	3*	<.1
1428	C-Mold Inc—*Chuck Winkle*	175 Industrial Park Dr, Greenfield OH 45123	937-981-7797	R	3*	<.1
1429	GMR Technology Inc—*Ralph Giancola*	2131 Aetna Rd, Ashtabula OH 44004	440-992-6003	R	3*	<.1
1430	Pmp Composites Corp—*Peter Horvath*	572 Whitehead Rd Ste 1, Trenton NJ 08619	609-587-1188	R	3*	<.1
1431	Reel-Core Inc—*Greg Whalen*	PO Box 209, Waukon IA 52172	563-568-6307	R	3*	<.1
1432	Damron Corp—*Ronald Damper*	4433 W Ohio St, Chicago IL 60624	773-826-6000	R	3*	<.1
1433	Mohr Engineering Inc—*David Mcdowell*	PO Box 779, Brighton MI 48116	810-227-4598	R	3*	<.1

Rank	Company Name—*Executive Officer*	Address, City, State, Zip	Phone	Type	Fin	Empls
1434	MTM Molded Products Co—*Steve Minneman*	PO Box 13117, Dayton OH 45413	937-890-7461	R	3*	<.1
1435	Parker Industries Inc—*Bette Parker*	3585 Valley Dr, Pittsburgh PA 15234	412-561-6902	R	3*	<.1
1436	Plastic Dip Moldings Inc—*Ian Macknight*	PO Box 450, Plumsteadville PA 18949	215-766-2020	R	3*	<.1
1437	Koral Industries Inc—*Bob Christopher*	PO Box 1270, Ennis TX 75120	972-875-6555	R	3*	.1
1438	Sunrise Packaging Inc—*Mark Hector*	9937 Goodhue St NE, Blaine MN 55449	763-785-2505	R	3*	.1
1439	Jones Machine and Tool Inc—*Danny Jones*	14710 N Crossroad Nw, Fredericksburg IN 47120	812-364-4588	R	3*	<.1
1440	Ramtec Associates Inc—*Ralph Riehl*	3200 E Birch St Ste B, Brea CA 92821	714-996-7477	R	3*	<.1
1441	A and E Plastics Inc—*Maynard Ostrowski*	1620 Cambridge Dr, Elgin IL 60123	847-622-9200	R	3*	<.1
1442	Custom Service Plastics Inc—*Minoo Seifoddini*	1101 S Wells St, Lake Geneva WI 53147	262-248-9557	R	3*	<.1
1443	Form/Tec Plastics Inc—*William Shields*	PO Box 1672, Martinsville IN 46151	765-342-2300	R	3*	<.1
1444	RAM Inc (Cisco Texas)—*Diann Morris*	808 E 6th St, Cisco TX 76437	254-442-1008	R	3*	<.1
1445	Sterling Manufacturing Company Inc—*Dennis Wrzesinski*	PO Box 1205, South Lancaster MA 01561	978-368-8733	R	3*	<.1
1446	Precise Aerospace Manufacturing—*Ronnie Harwood*	224 Glider Cir, Corona CA 92880	951-898-0500	R	3*	<.1
1447	Applied Plastic Technology Inc—*Frank Beckerer*	169 Fremont St, Worcester MA 01603	508-752-5924	R	3*	<.1
1448	Buecomp Inc—*Nelfred Kimerline*	PO Box 467, Bucyrus OH 44820	419-284-3840	R	3*	<.1
1449	ETCO Specialty Products Inc—*Steve Thompson*	PO Box 346, Girard KS 66743	620-724-6463	R	3*	<.1
1450	Messenger Molding Inc—*Ronald Messenger*	7854 White Fir St, Reno NV 89523	775-747-7006	R	3*	<.1
1451	Billie-Ann Plastics Packing Corp—*William Rubinstein*	360 Troutman St, Brooklyn NY 11237	718-497-5555	R	3*	<.1
1452	Buckell Plastic Company Inc—*Brian Schell*	5 Industrial Park Rd, Lewistown PA 17044	717-242-3308	R	3*	<.1
1453	Kembric Manufacturing Corp—*Herman Brickman*	100 Franklin Dr, Torrington CT 06790	860-489-0458	R	3*	<.1
1454	LD Plastics Inc—*Charles Harlfinger*	1130 Pearl St, Brockton MA 02301	508-584-7651	R	3*	<.1
1455	Seal Reinforced Fiberglass Inc—*Patrick Kaler*	19 Bethpage Rd, Copiague NY 11726	631-842-2230	R	3*	<.1
1456	Shamrock Plastics Inc—*Mary Westphal*	PO Box 3530, Peoria IL 61612	309-243-7723	R	3*	<.1
1457	Kittyhawk Molding Company Inc—*Wilbur Wisecup*	10 Eagle Ct, Carlisle OH 45005	937-746-3663	R	3*	<.1
1458	River Valley Plastics Inc—*Harold Cracken*	27339 D I Dr, Elkhart IN 46514	574-262-5221	R	3*	<.1
1459	Edris Plastics Manufacturing Inc—*H Issagholian*	4560 Pacific Blvd, Vernon CA 90058	323-581-7000	R	3*	<.1
1460	Polyfab Plastics And Supply Inc—*Lowell Miller*	820 N Cedarbrook Ave, Springfield MO 65802	417-862-6512	R	3*	<.1
1461	Aline Components Inc—*Harry Davis*	PO Box 263, Kulpsville PA 19443	215-368-0300	R	3*	<.1
1462	Gibraltar Plastic Products Corp—*Harvey Jacobs*	15053 Ventura Blvd, Sherman Oaks CA 91403	818-385-0529	R	3*	<.1
1463	Master Plastics Inc—*Kurt Hashemian*	820 Eubanks Dr I, Vacaville CA 95688	707-451-3168	R	3*	<.1
1464	Mounted Memories Inc—*Mitch Adlestein*	5000 NW 108th Ave, Sunrise FL 33351	954-742-8544	S	3*	<.1
1465	Tru-Form Plastics Inc—*Doug Sahm*	17809 S Broadway, Gardena CA 90248	310-327-9444	R	3*	<.1
1466	C and R Molds Inc—*Randall Ohnemus*	PO Box 5644, Ventura CA 93005	805-658-7093	R	3*	<.1
1467	Horizon Plastics and Engineering Inc—*Michael Johnson*	PO Box 57, Osceola IN 46561	574-674-5443	R	3*	<.1
1468	Air Logistics Corp—*George Schirtzinger*	146 Railroad Ave, Monrovia CA 91016	626-256-1257	R	3*	<.1
1469	Nylacarb Corp—*Scott Cooley*	1725 98th Ave, Vero Beach FL 32966	772-569-5999	R	3	<.1
1470	Hosokawa Polymer Systems—*Doug Ort*	63 Fuller Way, Berlin CT 06037	860-828-0541	R	3*	<.1
1471	Anderson Die and Manufacturing Co—*George Anderson*	2425 Se Moores St, Milwaukie OR 97222	503-654-5629	R	3*	< 1
1472	Letourneau Plastics Inc—*Duane Le Tourneau*	PO Box 76, Oconto WI 54153	920-834-2777	R	3*	<.1
1473	Coverlay Manufacturing Inc—*Paul Cornwall*	4017 N Us Hwy 67, San Angelo TX 76905	325-659-4697	R	3*	<.1
1474	Holden Plastics Corp—*David True*	70 Fremont St, Worcester MA 01603	508-756-6241	R	3*	<.1
1475	Hagans Plastics Company Inc—*Dennis Hagan*	PO Box 153986, Irving TX 75015	972-790-9001	R	3*	<.1
1476	Adirondack Plastics And Recycling Inc—*John Aspland*	453 County Rte 45, Argyle NY 12809	518-638-8960	R	3*	<.1
1477	Edwards Fiberglass Inc—*Shane Edwards*	PO Box 1252, Sedalia MO 65302	660-826-3915	R	3*	<.1
1478	Jatal Inc—*Jack Lowrey*	4146 B Pl Nw, Auburn WA 98001	253-854-0034	R	3*	<.1
1479	Joslyn Manufacturing Co—*Charles Joslyn*	9400 Valley View Rd, Macedonia OH 44056	330-467-8111	R	3*	<.1
1480	Levic Plastics Inc—*Ronald Knight*	4003 E 137th Ter, Grandview MO 64030	816-761-8484	R	3*	<.1
1481	Proto-Mold Products Company Inc—*Graig Flintcraft*	1750 Commerce Dr, Piqua OH 45356	937-778-1959	R	3*	<.1
1482	Reeves Plastics LLC—*Frank Adamy*	507 Omalley Dr, Coopersville MI 49404	616-997-0777	R	3*	<.1
1483	Syntech Development And Manufacturing Inc—*Bob Hobbs*	13948 Mountain Ave, Chino CA 91710	909-465-5554	R	3*	<.1
1484	TW Currie Precision Tool Company Inc—*Thomas Currie*	1341 Vanguard Dr, Oxnard CA 93033	805-486-7800	R	3*	<.1
1485	Adventek Corp—*Kenneth Brandt*	10 Headley Pl, Levittown PA 19054	215-736-0961	R	3*	<.1
1486	Hall Manufacturing Corp—*Michael Goceljak*	297 Margaret King Ave, Ringwood NJ 07456	973-962-6022	R	3*	<.1
1487	Plasco Inc—*Ronald Schweller*	3075 Plainfield Rd, Kettering OH 45432	937-254-8444	R	3*	<.1
1488	Kel-Tech Plastics Inc—*Steven Keller*	3510 S Pine St, Tacoma WA 98409	253-472-9654	R	3*	<.1
1489	RW Wilson Inc—*Robert Wilson*	375 Joe Smith Rd, Bishop CA 93514	760-873-5600	R	3*	<.1
1490	Rim Manufacturing LLC—*Lisa Payne*	901 W Interstate 20, Weatherford TX 76087	817-599-6521	R	3*	<.1
1491	Sailing Specialties Inc—*Greig Parks*	43985 Commerce Ave, Hollywood MD 20636	301-373-2372	R	3*	<.1
1492	Industrial Thermoform Inc—*Keith Martinez*	PO Box 590, Cedar Hill TX 75106	972-299-5391	R	3*	<.1
1493	Graphic Tool Corp—*Richard Burman*	1211 Norwood Ave, Itasca IL 60143	630-250-9800	R	3*	<.1
1494	American Molding Technologies Inc—*Dimitri Poulos*	2350 Lunt Ave, Elk Grove Village IL 60007	847-437-6900	R	3*	<.1
1495	Anfinsen Plastic Moulding Company Inc—*Steve Ham*	445b Treasure Dr Unit, Oswego IL 60543	630-554-4100	R	3*	<.1
1496	Fabriform Plastics Inc—*Robert Parkes*	3300 Airport Way S, Seattle WA 98134	206-587-5303	R	3*	<.1
1497	Fiberglass Technologies Inc—*Scott Kennedy*	1610 Hanford St Ste P, Levittown PA 19057	215-943-4567	R	3*	<.1
1498	Krest Products Corp—*Richard Marzio*	PO Box 176, Leominster MA 01453	978-537-1244	R	3*	<.1
1499	Plastics Unlimited Inc—*Bruce Meihsner*	PO Box 26443, Milwaukee WI 53226	414-771-3834	R	3*	<.1
1500	Kinamor Inc—*John Romanik*	PO Box 100, Cheshire CT 06410	203-272-9800	R	3*	<.1
1501	Parsons Manufacturing Corp—*Alan Parsons*	1055 Obrien Dr, Menlo Park CA 94025	650-324-4726	R	3*	<.1
1502	Empire West Inc—*Richard Yonash*	PO Box 511, Graton CA 95444	707-823-1190	R	3*	<.1
1503	Greenleaf Industries Inc—*Earle Segrest*	310 Bussell Ferry Rd, Lenoir City TN 37771	865-988-5661	R	3*	<.1
1504	Lcs Precision Molding Inc—*Reed Hart*	119 2nd St S, Waterville MN 56096	507-362-8685	R	3*	<.1
1505	Advantage Plastics and Engineering Inc—*William Hamilton*	PO Box 18273, Louisville KY 40261	502-473-7331	R	3*	<.1
1506	Five Peaks Technology LLC—*Dave Bamberg*	1790 Sun Dolphin Rd, Muskegon MI 49444	231-830-8099	R	3*	<.1
1507	Ptm Inc—*Ron Peterson*	W6757 Abbey Rd, Onalaska WI 54650	608-783-7276	R	3*	<.1
1508	Bayhead Products Corp—*Elissa Moore*	173 Crosby Rd, Dover NH 03820	603-742-3000	R	3*	<.1
1509	ED Industries Inc—*Steve Brallier*	PO Box 620, Rogersville MO 65742	417-753-8000	R	3*	<.1
1510	Exton Inc—*Terry Truex*	PO Box 513, Goshen IN 46527	574-533-0447	R	3*	<.1
1511	Munot Plastics Inc—*Chandler Rees*	2935 W 17th St, Erie PA 16505	814-838-7721	R	3*	<.1
1512	Polytech Industries Inc—*Richard Walls*	PO Box 551, Geneva IL 60134	630-443-6030	R	3*	<.1
1513	Quad 4 Plastics Inc—*Fred Pletcher*	1840 Borneman Ave, Elkhart IN 46517	574-293-8660	R	3*	<.1
1514	Replication Unlimited LLC—*Nu Aguilera*	9200 Latty Ave, Hazelwood MO 63042	314-524-2040	R	3*	<.1
1515	Take-A-Ticket Inc—*Calvin Tigner*	130 Montgomery St Ne, Albany OR 97321	541-967-0433	R	3*	<.1
1516	Becher Engineering Inc—*Benjamin Becher*	721 Valley Rd, Menasha WI 54952	920-734-9035	R	3*	<.1
1517	Harkness Industries Inc—*Nancy Williams*	PO Box 764, Cheshire CT 06410	203-272-3219	R	3*	<.1
1518	Seaway Plastics Corp—*Alex Kindsvater*	PO Box 217, Marine City MI 48039	810-765-8864	R	3*	<.1
1519	Davric Plastic LLC—*Diane Bellio*	PO Box 1678, Crystal Lake IL 60039	815-459-3830	R	3*	<.1
1520	Salem Plastics Inc—*J Cousins*	700 Military Dr, Mountain Home AR 72653	870-895-4844	R	3*	<.1
1521	Atlantex Corporation Inc—*Ed Sisk*	221 Weaver St Ste 2, Fall River MA 02720	508-674-2445	R	3*	<.1
1522	Capco/Psa—*Zaven Berberian*	11125 Vanowen St, North Hollywood CA 91605	818-762-4276	R	3*	<.1
1523	Kepner Plastics Fabricators Inc—*Frank Meyers*	3131 Lomita Blvd, Torrance CA 90505	310-325-3162	R	3*	<.1

Note: An asterisk (*) indicates an estimated financial figure. The company type code used is as follows: R = Private, P = Public, S = Private Subsidiary, B = Public Subsidiary, D = Division, J = Joint Venture, I = Investment Fund.

COMPANY RANKINGS BY SALES WITHIN 4-DIGIT SIC

Rank	Company Name—Executive Officer	Address, City, State, Zip	Phone	Type	Fin	Empls
1524	Alpha Plastics Co—Donald Walczak	9315 Evergreen Blvd Nw, Minneapolis MN 55433	763-786-6940	R	3*	<.1
1525	Faro Industries Inc—Matthew Conville	340 Lyell Ave, Rochester NY 14606	585-647-6000	R	3*	<.1
1526	Gagne Associates Inc—Mary Holland	PO Box 487, Johnson City NY 13790	607-729-3366	R	3*	<.1
1527	Integrated Molding Solutions Inc—Terilynn Jones	6703 Theall Rd, Houston TX 77066	281-587-9996	R	3*	<.1
1528	Jos-Tech Inc—Bradford Joslyn	852 W Main St, Kent OH 44240	330-678-3260	R	3*	<.1
1529	Tom York Enterprises Inc—Juliet Oehler	2050 E 48th St, Vernon CA 90058	323-581-6194	R	3*	<.1
1530	Trans Form Plastics Corp—Tom Holloran	45 Prince St, Danvers MA 01923	978-777-1440	R	3*	<.1
1531	Coastal Windows Inc—Kurt Winner	94-533 Puahi St, Waipahu HI 96797	808-676-0529	R	3*	<.1
1532	Earmold Design Inc—Melvin Bloomgren	3424 E Lake St, Minneapolis MN 55406	612-721-5711	R	3*	<.1
1533	Flexi-Liner—Tait Eyre	3198 Factory Dr, Pomona CA 91768	909-594-6610	R	3*	<.1
1534	Gt Plastics Inc—Gary Thibault	4681 Industrial Row, Oscoda MI 48750	989-739-1112	R	3*	<.1
1535	Podnar Plastics Inc—Jack Podnar	1510 Mogadore Rd, Kent OH 44240	330-673-2255	R	3*	.1
1536	Oppenheim Plastics Company Inc—Florence Oppenheim	PO Box 310, Saddle River NJ 07458	201-995-9595	R	3*	<.1
1537	Milfoam Corp—Douglas Pfenninger	23 Marne St, Hamden CT 06514	203-248-8011	R	3*	<.1
1538	Ceng Plastic Inc—Greg Leighton	12729 Foothill Blvd, Sylmar CA 91342	818-837-3771	R	3*	<.1
1539	Cashion Thermoplastics Inc—Barbara Cashion	PO Box 400, Red Bay AL 35582	256-356-2017	R	3*	<.1
1540	Discraft Inc—James Kenner	29592 Beck Rd, Wixom MI 48393	248-624-2250	R	3*	<.1
1541	Eck Plastic Arts Inc—Robert Eck	87 Prospect Ave, Binghamton NY 13901	607-722-3227	R	3*	<.1
1542	Precision Plastic And Die Co—Benjamin Schwegman	205 Industrial Pkwy, Ithaca MI 48847	989-875-4191	R	3*	<.1
1543	Rex Plastics Inc—Rich Clark	12515 Ne 95th St, Vancouver WA 98682	360-892-0366	R	3*	<.1
1544	Somerset Plastics Inc—Edward Shapiro	1012 S Ctr Ave, Somerset PA 15501	814-445-8953	R	3*	<.1
1545	Suncoast Molders Inc—William Simmers	10760 76th Ct, Largo FL 33777	727-546-0041	R	3*	<.1
1546	Thermo Plastics Corp—John Boyer	PO Box 14275, Fort Worth TX 76117	817-281-9010	R	3*	<.1
1547	Valley Tool Inc—Cayce Washington	PO Box 663, Water Valley MS 38965	662-473-3066	R	3*	<.1
1548	Vinyl-Pro Inc—William Garceau	4449 Custer St, Manitowoc WI 54220	920-682-0240	R	3*	<.1
1549	Plan Tech Inc—David Stewart	7031 Shaker Rd Unit J, Loudon NH 03307	603-783-4767	R	3*	<.1
1550	Horsemen's Pride Inc—Rob Miavitz	10008 State Rte 43, Streetsboro OH 44241	330-626-5039	R	3*	<.1
1551	Kenson Plastics Inc—John Oleary	920 Brush Creek Rd, Warrendale PA 15086	724-776-6820	R	3*	<.1
1552	Orbit Plastics Corp—Thomas Feid	7 Fanaras Dr, Salisbury MA 01952	978-465-5300	R	3*	<.1
1553	Marco Molding Inc—Darraugh Brandon	6868 Homestretch Rd, Dayton OH 45414	937-890-7834	R	3*	<.1
1554	North American Plastics Ltd—Eero Hyvonen	349 E Industrial Park, Manchester NH 03109	603-644-1660	R	3*	<.1
1555	Pobco Inc—Stephen Johnson	99 Hope Ave, Worcester MA 01603	508-791-6376	R	3*	<.1
1556	Scientific Plastics Corp—Jeffrey Thiel	2271 2nd St N C, Saint Paul MN 55109	651-773-1822	R	3*	<.1
1557	Tabor Plastics Co—James Tabor	2817 Park Ave, Saint Louis MO 63104	314-773-6509	R	3*	<.1
1558	Ire-Tex Corp—Kurt Rozek	11035 Sw 11th St Ste 2, Beaverton OR 97005	503-924-5653	R	3*	<.1
1559	Vinyl Tech Window Systems Inc—Paul Baker	PO Box 331, Holly MI 48442	248-634-8900	R	3*	<.1
1560	Camden Industries Inc—Steve Greitzer	11658 Mcbean Dr, El Monte CA 91732	626-433-0405	R	3*	<.1
1561	Justand Plastics Inc—Michael Regan	250 Commerce Dr, Huntington IN 46750	260-356-5114	R	2*	<.1
1562	Molded Devices Inc—Brian Anderson	6918 Ed Perkic St, Riverside CA 92504	951-509-6918	R	2*	<.1
1563	Micalline Products Inc—Ernie William	PO Box 9385, Columbia SC 29290	803-783-5110	R	2*	<.1
1564	Escambia Molded Plastics Corp—Frank Powell	1660 W Roberts Rd, Pensacola FL 32523	850-937-2830	R	2*	<.1
1565	Abbacus Injection Molding Inc—Judith Beall	1248 Shappert Dr, Machesney Park IL 61115	815-637-9222	R	2*	<.1
1566	Kent Marine Inc—Mark Cavanaugh	5401 W Oakwood Park Dr, Franklin WI 53132	414-423-8544	R	2*	<.1
1567	Garfield Molding Company Inc—Charles Murray	10 Midland Ave, Wallington NJ 07057	973-777-5700	R	2*	<.1
1568	Waco Boom Company Ltd—Gwen Daugherty	PO Box 20667, Waco TX 76702	254-776-1695	R	2*	<.1
1569	Plastic Techniques Inc—Gossett Rae	PO Box 250, Goffstown NH 03045	603-645-6800	R	2*	<.1
1570	Cor-A-Vent Inc—Shirley Sells	PO Box 428, Mishawaka IN 46546	574-255-1910	R	2*	<.1
1571	Starbrook Industries Inc—Michael Huffman	325 S Hyatt St, Tipp City OH 45371	937-667-1151	R	2*	<.1
1572	DM Tool and Plastics Inc—Dennis Meyer	4140 State Rte 40 E, Lewisburg OH 45338	937-962-4140	R	2*	<.1
1573	Industrial Farm Tank Inc—Pyllis Yazel	10676 Township Rd 80, Lewistown OH 43333	937-843-2972	R	2*	<.1
1574	Jefferson Fiberglass Company Inc—Peter Vicari	1524 Macarthur Ave, Harvey LA 70058	504-347-6612	R	2*	<.1
1575	Morris Transparent Box Co—Alfred Morris	945 Warren Ave, East Providence RI 02914	401-438-6116	R	2*	<.1
1576	Polyform Inc—Jeff Pitt	317 Polymer Dr, Decatur TN 37322	423-334-9489	R	2*	<.1
1577	Wisconsin Tool and Mold Company Inc—Hans Lang	PO Box 318, Friendship WI 53934	608-339-7806	R	2*	<.1
1578	Connecticut Tool Company Inc—Philip Durand	6 Highland Dr, Putnam CT 06260	860-928-0565	R	2*	<.1
1579	Zordan Precision Tool Inc—Gerald Zordan	91 Technology Park Dr, Torrington CT 06790	860-482-8283	R	2*	<.1
1580	Wunder Mold Inc—William Martindale	4957 Allison Pkwy Ste, Vacaville CA 95688	707-448-2349	R	2*	<.1
1581	Classic Die Inc—Daniel Parmeter	610 Plymouth Ave Ne, Grand Rapids MI 49505	616-454-3760	R	2*	<.1
1582	Meridian Precision Inc—Bernard Kulkaski	PO Box 206, Pine Grove PA 17963	570-345-6600	R	2*	<.1
1583	Bbf Custom Products Inc—Brian Fitzgerald	10159 Sw Commerce Cir, Wilsonville OR 97070	503-691-1988	Type	2*	<.1
1584	Derby Molded Products Inc—Jim Janes	PO Box 396, Neenah WI 54957	920-725-1451	R	2*	<.1
1585	Netco Extruded Plastics Inc—Knut Schmiedeknecht	30 Tower St, Hudson MA 01749	978-562-3485	R	2*	<.1
1586	Pikes Peak Plastics Inc—Dave Anthony	4685 Northpark Dr, Colorado Springs CO 80918	719-531-5393	R	2*	<.1
1587	Plasti-Fab Inc—Richard Melin	2305 Hilton Rd, Ferndale MI 48220	248-543-1415	R	2*	<.1
1588	Niagara Fiberglass Inc—Stephen Gale	88 Okell St, Buffalo NY 14220	716-822-3921	R	2*	<.1
1589	Marlo Plastic Products Inc—Arthur Livingston	289 Hwy 33, Manalapan NJ 07726	732-792-1984	R	2*	<.1
1590	American Plastics Inc—Bart Richardson	15001 Mail Rte Rd, Little Rock AR 72206	501-888-7407	R	2*	<.1
1591	Ess Tec Inc—Larry Essenburg	3347 128th Ave, Holland MI 49424	616-394-0230	R	2*	<.1
1592	Jumbo Plastics Inc—Joe Ashey	PO Box 1447, Leominster MA 01453	978-537-7835	R	2*	<.1
1593	Haviland Plastic Products Co—Craig Stoller	PO Box 38, Haviland OH 45851	419-622-3110	R	2*	<.1
1594	Albert R Serviss—Albert Serviss	PO Box 5006, Kansas City KS 66119	913-621-1250	R	2*	<.1
1595	Carolina Color Corporation Of Ohio—Matt Barr	100 Colomet Dr, Delaware OH 43015	740-363-6622	R	2*	<.1
1596	Pioneer Custom Molding Inc—Terry Hendricks	PO Box 463, Pioneer OH 43554	419-737-3252	R	2*	<.1
1597	Q-Cast Inc—Les Finney	PO Box 230, Rochester PA 15074	724-728-7440	R	2*	<.1
1598	TA Tool and Molding Inc—Ludwig Konrad	185 Marine St, Farmingdale NY 11735	631-293-0172	R	2*	<.1
1599	Plasidyne Engineering and Manufacturing Inc—Dean Sutherland	PO Box 5578, Long Beach CA 90805	562-531-0510	R	2*	<.1
1600	Stiles Unlimited Inc—Barry Stiles	8820 Frey Rd, Houston TX 77034	281-489-4292	R	2*	<.1
1601	3 D Cam Inc—Gary Vassighi	9801 Variel Ave, Chatsworth CA 91311	818-773-8777	R	2*	<.1
1602	Wepco Plastics Inc—Waldo Parmelee	PO Box 182, Middlefield CT 06455	860-349-3407	R	2*	<.1
1603	Aztek Tool Company Inc—Stewart Swiss	180 Rodeo Dr, Edgewood NY 11717	631-243-1144	R	2*	<.1
1604	Fluoro-Plastics Inc—C Milner	3601 G St, Philadelphia PA 19134	215-425-5500	R	2*	<.1
1605	Frontline Mold Technology—Gary Nelsen	1030 Lutter Dr, Crystal Lake IL 60014	815-459-9422	R	2*	<.1
1606	Globe Plastics Inc—Nywood Wu	13477 12th St, Chino CA 91710	909-464-1520	R	2*	<.1
1607	Hoosier Pride Plastics—Mike Hoeppner	6120 Highview Dr, Fort Wayne IN 46818	260-497-7080	R	2*	<.1
1608	PDQ Plastics Inc—Barry Nathans	PO Box 1001, Bayonne NJ 07002	201-823-0270	R	2*	<.1
1609	Transparent Devices Inc—Abraham Gohari	853 Lawrence Dr, Newbury Park CA 91320	805-499-5000	R	2*	<.1
1610	Reny and Company Inc—Steve Raiken	4505 Littlejohn St, Baldwin Park CA 91706	626-962-3078	R	2*	<.1
1611	Seiler Plastics Corp—John Seiler	9750 Reavis Park Dr, Saint Louis MO 63123	314-815-3030	R	2*	<.1
1612	Precision Manufacturing And Assembly LLC	2240 Richard St, Dayton OH 45403	937-252-3507	R	2*	.1

Rank	Company Name—Executive Officer	Address, City, State, Zip	Phone	Type	Fin	Empls
1613	P and S Molded Products Inc—Jerry Stewart	700 S Keeneland Dr, Richmond KY 40475	859-624-1083	R	2*	<.1
1614	WM Gulliksen Manufacturing Company Inc—Chester Gillis	187 Gardner St, Boston MA 02132	617-323-5750	R	2*	<.1
1615	Colvin-Friedman LLC—Mitchell Friedman	PO Box 31, Springfield NJ 07081	973-376-4488	R	2*	<.1
1616	Reeves CoInc—Thomas Reeves	PO Box 719, Attleboro MA 02703	508-222-2877	R	2*	<.1
1617	Rimco Plastics Corp—Robert Reimsnyder	316 Colonial Dr, Horseheads NY 14845	607-739-3864	R	2*	<.1
1618	Summore Plastics Inc—Thomas Gerschman	2121 Logan St, Clearwater FL 33765	727-446-8573	R	2*	<.1
1619	Tech Tool Plastics Inc—John Wilson	7800 Skyline Park Dr, Fort Worth TX 76108	817-246-4694	R	2*	<.1
1620	American Handle Co—Beryle Goldman	7343 Edmund St, Philadelphia PA 19136	215-332-8000	R	2*	<.1
1621	Integrity Mold and Die Ltd—Kyle Thompson	PO Box 3109, Mount Vernon KY 40456	606-256-1947	R	2*	<.1
1622	Metro Custom Plastics Inc—Mike Havel	615 109th St, Arlington TX 76011	817-640-5646	R	2*	<.1
1623	Reube's Plastics Company Inc—Richard Reube	1001 W Orvilla Rd, Hatfield PA 19440	215-368-3010	R	2*	<.1
1624	Plastikos Corp—Richard Bates	PO Box 138, Batavia OH 45103	513-732-0961	R	2*	<.1
1625	Arc Plastics Inc—Richard Renaudo	14010 Shoemaker Ave, Norwalk CA 90650	562-802-3299	R	2*	<.1
1626	Bergauer Group Inc—Geoffrey Bergauer	3737 Douglas Ave, Racine WI 53402	262-639-2456	R	2*	<.1
1627	Deluxe Frame Company Inc—Paul Meloche	2275 N Opdyke Rd Ste D, Auburn Hills MI 48326	248-373-8811	R	2*	<.1
1628	Elm Industries Inc—George Martin	PO Box 717, West Springfield MA 01090	413-734-7762	R	2*	<.1
1629	Industrial Resin Recycling Inc—Patrick Cavanaugh	1480 Grand Oaks Dr, Howell MI 48843	517-548-4140	R	2*	<.1
1630	Mid-Continent Tool and Molding Inc—Kevin Godsey	7200 Ne Birmingham Rd, Randolph MO 64161	816-453-5000	R	2*	<.1
1631	Plastic Craft Inc—Mike Bauman	9649 Humboldt Ave S, Minneapolis MN 55431	952-884-9000	R	2*	<.1
1632	Plasto Tech International Inc—Jacqueline Khalaj	4 Autry, Irvine CA 92618	949-458-1880	R	2*	<.1
1633	Prototype Plastic Extrusion Company Inc—Jeffrey Wells	3637 131st Ave N, Clearwater FL 33762	727-572-0803	R	2*	<.1
1634	Upl International Inc—Jeffrey Scarpitti	2587 S Arlington Rd, Akron OH 44319	330-645-6873	R	2*	<.1
1635	Zivco Inc—Elliott Zivin	647 Clinton Ave, Bridgeport CT 06605	203-367-7900	R	2*	<.1
1636	Unipec Inc—Martin Berghers	678 Lofstrand Ln, Rockville MD 20850	301-762-9261	R	2*	<.1
1637	Accurate Mold Inc—Willard Miller	900 Chestnut Ave Ste G, Somerdale NJ 08083	856-784-8484	R	2*	<.1
1638	Imlay City Molded Products Corp—Charles Tesnow	593 S Cedar St, Imlay City MI 48444	810-721-9100	R	2*	<.1
1639	Texas Manufactured Marble Inc—Doyle Dittmar	PO Box 790, Columbus TX 78934	979-732-2382	R	2*	<.1
1640	Kent G Smith—Kent Smith	205 2nd Ave W, Bertha MN 56437	218-924-4024	R	2	<.1
1641	Network 1 Financial Group—Richard Hunt	2 Bridge Ave Ste 241, Red Bank NJ 07701		P	2	<.1
1642	Kathom Manufacturing Company Inc—Thomas Wells	661 Williams Ave, Hamilton OH 45015	513-868-8890	R	2*	<.1
1643	C-Tech Tool and Molding Inc—Clay Standler	4540 S Navajo St Unit, Englewood CO 80110	303-761-3505	R	2*	<.1
1644	Dexterous Mold And Tool Inc—Eugene Elpers	2535 Locust Creek Dr, Evansville IN 47720	812-422-8046	R	2*	<.1
1645	Fastcap LLC—Dawn Sessions	3725 Irongate Rd Ste 1, Bellingham WA 98226	360-752-2138	R	2*	<.1
1646	Federal Package Network Inc—Robert Chadfield	4044 Peavey Rd, Chaska MN 55318	952-448-7900	R	2*	<.1
1647	Great Plains Plastic Molding LLC—Dave Bodman	610 University Dr N, Fargo ND 58102	701-297-9685	R	2*	<.1
1648	Plastic Extrusion Technologies Ltd—William Spencer	PO Box 92, Middlefield OH 44062	440-632-5611	R	2*	<.1
1649	Sare Plastics Inc—Paul Sare	14600 Commerce St Ne, Alliance OH 44601	330-821-4299	R	2*	<.1
1650	Southwest Quality Molding Corp—Perry Estes	PO Box 439, Manvel TX 77578	281-643-4500	R	2*	<.1
1651	Tubro Company Inc—Harrison Gift	30 Council Rock Dr, Warminster PA 18974	215-322-4133	R	2*	<.1
1652	Valley Decorating Co—James Offen	2829 E Hamilton Ave, Fresno CA 93721	559-495-1100	R	2*	<.1
1653	Northeast Plastics Inc—Jean Leach	5a Del Carmine St, Wakefield MA 01880	781-245-5512	R	2*	<.1
1654	Willamette Plastics—Paul Dupont	1111 Nw 5th Pl, Canby OR 97013	503-266-6233	R	2*	<.1
1655	Eagle Manufacturing Corp—Brent Short	52113 Shelby Pkwy, Shelby Township MI 48315	586-323-0303	R	2*	<.1
1656	SCR Molding Inc—Carl Thompson	2340 Pomona Rd, Corona CA 92880	951-736-5490	R	2*	<.1
1657	Salem Technologies Inc—Robert Tribble	2580 Salem Point Ct, Winston Salem NC 27103	336-777-3652	R	2*	<.1
1658	Solo Cup Operating Corp—Robert Korzenski	150 Saunders Rd Ste 15, Lake Forest IL 60045	847-444-5000	R	2*	<.1
1659	Engineering Model Associates Inc—John Wanderman	1020 Wallace Way, City Of Industry CA 91748	626-912-7011	R	2*	<.1
1660	Wilmes Window Manufacturing Company Inc—Edward Wilmes	234 W 23rd St, Ferdinand IN 47532	812-367-1811	R	2*	.1
1661	Custom Assemblies Inc—Jack Peacock	PO Box 177, Pine Level NC 27568	919-202-8462	R	2*	<.1
1662	James Injection Molding Co—Martin Silovich	300 Pfingsten Rd, Northbrook IL 60062	847-564-3820	R	2*	<.1
1663	True Line Mold And Engineering Corp—Ray Adkins	12205 Hansen Rd, Hebron IL 60034	815-648-2739	R	2*	<.1
1664	Alloy Polymers Texas LP—Gene Siegmann	Hwy 287 and Fm2160 Ste, Latexo TX 75849	936-544-4043	R	2*	<.1
1665	Analytic Plastic Inc—John Bobko	1756 Winchester Rd, Bensalem PA 19020	215-638-7505	R	2*	<.1
1666	Diemold Machine Company Inc—Ulrich Boehnke	2350 Bruner Ln, Fort Myers FL 33912	239-482-1400	R	2*	<.1
1667	Micro Plastics Inc (Chatsworth California)—Wade Harb	801 E Mission Rd, San Marcos CA 92069	760-744-0125	D	2*	<.1
1668	Redi-Tag Corp—Karen Whistler	51 Century Blvd Ste 25, Nashville TN 37214		S	2*	<.1
1669	Bardes Products Inc—Peter Bardes	5245 W Clinton Ave, Milwaukee WI 53223	414-354-9000	R	2*	<.1
1670	Express Systems and Engineering Inc—Mike Arndt	PO Box 891258, Temecula CA 92589	951-461-1500	R	2*	<.1
1671	Jeco Plastic Products LLC—Craig Carson	PO Box 26, Plainfield IN 46168	317-839-4943	R	2*	<.1
1672	Hankamer Investments LP—Ronald Hankamer	2530 Old Louetta Loop, Spring TX 77388	281-355-7676	R	2*	<.1
1673	Pdq South Injection Technologies Inc—R Wallace	PO Box 549, Pageland SC 29728	843-672-3582	R	2*	<.1
1674	Ballqube Inc—Sally Rogers	12146 County Rd 4233 W, Cushing TX 75760	903-863-5600	R	2*	<.1
1675	Bob-Leon Plastics Inc—Patricia Crowder	5151 Franklin Blvd, Sacramento CA 95820	916-452-4063	R	2*	<.1
1676	Central California Container Manufacturing Inc—Reyes Morales	PO Box 848, Chowchilla CA 93610	559-665-7611	R	2*	<.1
1677	English's All Wood Homes Inc—Patsy English	PO Box 1137, Grifton NC 28530	252-524-5000	R	2*	<.1
1678	Fiberglass Engineering Co—James Morris	PO Box 117, Midland VA 22728	540-788-4800	R	2*	<.1
1679	Midstate Mold and Engineering—John Killian	20 Liberty Way, Franklin MA 02038	508-520-0011	R	2*	<.1
1680	Mortex Manufacturing Co—Ted Deason	1818 W Price St, Tucson AZ 85705	520-887-2631	R	2*	<.1
1681	Plasti Fab Inc—Marshall Sligar	6430 Wuliger Way Ste J, Fort Worth TX 76180	817-485-0156	R	2*	<.1
1682	Plastic Concepts Inc—Michael Thompson	PO Box 355, North Billerica MA 01862	978-663-7996	R	2*	<.1
1683	SLM Manufacturing Corp—Thomas Vajtay	PO Box 6722, Somerset NJ 08875	732-469-7500	R	2*	<.1
1684	South Bay Custom Plastic Extruders—Abraham Rafiee	PO Box 131195, San Diego CA 92170	619-544-0808	R	2*	<.1
1685	Vanderveer Industrial Plastics Inc—Mark Geiss	515 S Melrose St, Placentia CA 92870	714-579-7700	R	2*	<.1
1686	Vinylast Inc—Joseph Leary	1830 Swarthmore Ave St, Lakewood NJ 08701	732-367-7200	R	2*	<.1
1687	Hoschette Enterprises Inc—Timothy M Hoschette	820 NW 20th St, Faribault MN 55021	507-334-4376	R	2*	<.1
1688	Industrial Paper Tube Inc—Howard Kramer	1335 E Bay Ave, Bronx NY 10474	718-893-5000	R	2*	<.1
1689	Amplas Compounding Inc—Geraldine Beaupre	6675 Sterling Dr N, Sterling Heights MI 48312	586-795-2555	R	2*	<.1
1690	Ntp/Republic Clear Thru Corp—James Macarthy Walter Drake Inc	PO Box 2448, Holyoke MA 01041	413-493-6800	S	2*	<.1
1691	Reliable Plastic Seals Inc—Kathy Hubert	620 Fox Run Pkwy, Opelika AL 36801	334-742-0005	R	2*	<.1
1692	Polyfab Corp—Richard Gill	1705 Martin Ave, Sheboygan WI 53083	920-459-2525	R	2*	<.1
1693	Eagle Fastners Inc—Theresa Srock	185 Park Dr, Troy MI 48083	248-577-1441	R	2*	<.1
1694	New Market Plastics Inc—Kerry Hopkins	PO Box 57, New Market IN 47965	765-866-1276	R	2*	<.1
1695	Austin-Abbott Inc—Karl Nebarber	3616 Noakes St, Los Angeles CA 90023	323-263-6878	R	2*	<.1
1696	Erell Manufacturing Co—Randall Silton	7650 Austin Ave, Skokie IL 60077	847-663-8888	R	2*	<.1
1697	G-P Plastics Inc—Philip Cook	801 S Palm Ave, Alhambra CA 91803	626-289-9248	R	2*	<.1
1698	RM Reutlinger Inc—Max R Van Winlke	3480 Office Park Dr, Dayton OH 45439	937-298-3855	R	2*	<.1
1699	Selectech Inc—Thomas Ricciardelli	33 Wales Ave Ste F, Avon MA 02322	508-583-3200	R	2*	<.1
1700	Aero Thermic Shields—Steve Braun	PO Box 434, Buena Park CA 90621	714-523-0572	R	2*	<.1
1701	ASKA Co—Brett Ferguson	819 78th Ave SW, Tumwater WA 98501	360-753-4283	R	2*	<.1

Note: An asterisk (*) indicates an estimated financial figure. The company type code used is as follows: R = Private, P = Public, S = Private Subsidiary, B = Public Subsidiary, D = Division, J = Joint Venture, I = Investment Fund.

COMPANY RANKINGS BY SALES WITHIN 4-DIGIT SIC

Rank	Company Name—Executive Officer	Address, City, State, Zip	Phone	Type	Fin	Empls
1702	Mount Vernon Plastics Corp—Doug MacMurdo	276 Industrial Park Rd, Mount Vernon KY 40456	703-424-4079	R	2*	<.1
1703	P and M Technical Sales Co—Betty Mills	814 1st St, Indian Rocks Beach FL 33785	727-593-3248	R	2*	<.1
1704	Contemporary Design Plastics—Robert Brown	412 113th St, Arlington TX 76011	817-640-7539	R	2*	<.1
1705	Outsource Technologies Inc—Sylvester Klusczinski	1832 N Kenmore St, South Bend IN 46628	574-233-1303	R	2*	<.1
1706	Bangor Plastics Inc—Glenn Wokeck	PO Box 99, Bangor MI 49013	269-427-7971	R	2*	<.1
1707	Creative Plastics International Inc—Gerald Wurm	18163 Snider Rd, Jackson Center OH 45334	419-492-2648	R	2*	<.1
1708	Morgan Hill Plastics Inc—Chet Hudson	640 E Dunne Ave, Morgan Hill CA 95037	408-779-2118	R	2*	<.1
1709	Plas-Tix USA Inc—Glenn Layman	510 S Riverview Ave, Miamisburg OH 45342	937-866-3451	R	2*	<.1
1710	Sailor Equipment Inc—Terry Sailor	PO Box 309, Adrian MN 56110	507-483-2469	R	2*	<.1
1711	Hoffman Precision Plastics Inc—Robert Hoffman	548 Almonesson Rd, Blackwood NJ 08012	856-228-3550	R	2*	<.1
1712	Century Plastics And Engineering Inc—Peter Mangone	1224 Sherman Dr, Longmont CO 80501	303-678-3050	R	2*	<.1
1713	Quest Plastics Inc—James Bean	89 Commercial Blvd Ste, Torrington CT 06790	860-489-1404	R	2*	<.1
1714	Poly-Ject Inc—Larry Thibeault	8 Manhattan Dr, Amherst NH 03031	603-882-6570	R	2*	<.1
1715	Advantage Plastic Products Inc—Joel Beaudette	31 S Commercial St, Manchester NH 03101	603-629-9540	R	2*	<.1
1716	Plastic Injection Molders Of Arizona Inc—Bob Truxes	828 W 24th St, Tempe AZ 85282	480-966-8984	R	2*	<.1
1717	Consolidated Plastic Products Corp—Linda Dowdy-Lovines	PO Box 318, Bloomfield MO 63825	573-568-2196	R	2*	<.1
1718	Dimensional Plastics Corp—Sir Barnette	1074 E 27th St, Hialeah FL 33013	305-691-5961	R	2*	<.1
1719	Dynasauer Corp—Warren Sauer	3511 Tree Ct Industria, Saint Louis MO 63122	636-225-5358	R	2*	<.1
1720	Eclipse Products Inc—Joseph Pope	145 Authority Dr, Fitchburg MA 01420	978-343-8600	R	2*	<.1
1721	Four Star Plastics LLC	PO Box 1843, Aberdeen SD 57402	605-622-7000	R	2*	<.1
1722	Harrison Manufacturing LLC	PO Box 4901, Jackson MS 39296	601-362-7898	R	2*	<.1
1723	JCB Precision Tool And Mold Inc—Jim Bogucki	5460 Colorado Blvd, Commerce City CO 80022	303-292-4434	R	2*	<.1
1724	Mercury Plastics Corp—William Wright	989 Utica Ave 995, Brooklyn NY 11203	718-498-5400	R	2*	<.1
1725	Patents Pending Inc—Norman Carmen	12336 Conway Rd, Beltsville MD 20705	301-937-2900	R	2*	<.1
1726	Southern Manufacturing Company LLC—Randy Chette	PO Box 790, Groves TX 77619	409-962-4501	R	2*	<.1
1727	Tri-Tech Molded Products Inc—Robert Brown	PO Box 911, Mcminnville TN 37111	931-934-2040	R	2*	<.1
1728	Wilkerson Inc—Carson Wilkerson	718 E Emory Rd, Knoxville TN 37938	865-938-0854	R	2*	<.1
1729	Astrofoam Molding Company Inc—Steven Bevan	4117 Calle Tesoro, Camarillo CA 93012	805-482-7276	R	2*	<.1
1730	K and E Plastics Inc—Peter Broderson	361 S Rd, East Arlington VT 05252	802-375-0011	R	2*	<.1
1731	Summitt Molding and Engineering Inc—Charles Rothe	1671 Progress Rd, Madisonville KY 42431	270-821-2070	R	2*	<.1
1732	Mariplast North America Inc—Marco Bottari	365 Business Pkwy, Greer SC 29651	864-989-0560	R	2*	<.1
1733	Windsor Mold USA Inc—Keith Henry	PO Box 32523, Detroit MI 48232	956-787-8737	R	2*	<.1
1734	Cardxx Inc—Phil Worack	1555 W Thomas Ave, Englewood CO 80110	303-762-8570	R	2	<.1
1735	J and J Plastics Inc—Jerry Wyzgoski	3000 S 1st St, Clinton OH 44216	330-882-1211	R	2*	<.1
1736	Plastico Industries Inc—Louis Massei	PO Box 325, Springville CA 93265	616-304-6289	R	2*	<.1
1737	Comet Tool Company Inc—Frank Maatje	651 Lambs Rd, Pitman NJ 08071	856-256-1070	R	2*	<.1
1738	Addtronics Business Systems—Casey Cook	1722 S Glenstone Ave, Springfield MO 65804	417-883-7705	R	2*	<.1
1739	Faribault Manufacturing Co—Tim Hofchette	619 Park Ave Nw, Faribault MN 55021	507-334-4376	R	2*	<.1
1740	Stm Inc—Thomas Peterie	PO Box 38, Augusta KS 67010	316-775-2223	R	2*	<.1
1741	Brandywine Fibre Products Company Inc—Ben Campbell	424 Creamery Way, Exton PA 19341	610-363-6100	R	2*	<.1
1742	Bama Plastics Corp—Fred Frost	1400 Driving Range Rd, Cropwell AL 35054	205-525-4587	R	2*	<.1
1743	Branchcomb Inc—Gerald Branchcomb	9845 S Frankoma Rd Ste, Sapulpa OK 74066	918-224-8094	R	2*	<.1
1744	Mega Corp—A William Van Met	516 Morse Ave, Schaumburg IL 60193	847-985-1900	R	2*	<.1
1745	Pittsburgh Technologies Inc—David Namey	1035 Hunt Valley Cir, New Kensington PA 15068	724-339-0900	R	2*	<.1
1746	Universal Strapping Inc—Sol Oberlander	630 Corporate Way, Valley Cottage NY 10989	845-268-2500	R	2*	<.1
1747	Poly Tech Industries Inc—Jimmy Rabitsch	PO Box 349, Monticello GA 31064	706-468-2801	R	2*	<.1
1748	Fowler Products Inc—Mark Fowler	810 Colby Rd, Crestline OH 44827	419-683-4057	R	2*	<.1
1749	GreenMan Technologies Inc—Lyle Jensen	7 Kimball Ln Bldg A, Lynnfield MA 01940	781-224-2411	P	2	<.1
1750	Hopper Development Inc—Robert Hopper	PO Box 296, Logansport IN 46947	574-753-6621	R	2*	<.1
1751	Swenson Company Inc—Vic Swenson	PO Box 429, Frenchtown NJ 08825	908-707-9393	R	2*	<.1
1752	Advanced Plastic Molding Inc—Roy Bridges	15 Greg St, Sparks NV 89431	775-355-0333	R	2*	<.1
1753	Anderson Moulds Inc—Garry Anderson	3131 E Anita St, Stockton CA 95205	209-943-1145	R	2*	<.1
1754	Exothermic Molding Inc—Paul Steck	50 Lafayette Pl, Kenilworth NJ 07033	908-272-2299	R	2*	<.1
1755	Beaver State Plastics Inc—Andrew Hergert	4052 State Hwy 38, Drain OR 97435	541-836-2203	R	2*	<.1
1756	Cjk Manufacturing LLC	100 Boxart St, Rochester NY 14612	585-663-6370	R	2*	<.1
1757	Tropic Tool and Mold Inc—Robert Knoth	1420 Wagner Dr, Albertville AL 35950	256-593-3441	R	2*	<.1
1758	Frank Products Inc—John McMorrow	5400 Thorpe Rd, Belgrade MT 59714	406-388-6666	R	2*	<.1
1759	Princeton Case West Inc—Douglas Laggrenm	1444 W Mccoy Ln, Santa Maria CA 93455	805-928-8840	R	2*	<.1
1760	Reil Rock Products Inc—Larry Armstrong	PO Box 1030, Eufaula OK 74432	918-689-7791	R	2*	<.1
1761	Tire Tread Development Inc—Michael Sapp	1460 Martin Rd, Mogadore OH 44260	330-628-5666	R	2*	<.1
1762	JV Packaging Inc—Michael Roberts	230 Oconnor Dr, Elkhorn WI 53121	262-743-2040	R	2*	<.1
1763	Rochester Rotational Molding Inc—Marilyn Wade	PO Box 205, Rochester IN 46975	574-223-8844	R	2*	<.1
1764	Hoosier Fiberglass Industries Inc—Benjamin Tucker	PO Box 9625, Terre Haute IN 47808	812-232-5027	R	2*	<.1
1765	Leeann Plastics Inc—Gary Kirtley	300 Halfway Rd, Burr Oak MI 49030	269-489-5035	R	2*	<.1
1766	Jms Manufacturing Inc—Jose Sousa	198 Airport Rd, Fall River MA 02720	508-675-1141	R	2*	<.1
1767	Mentor Dynamics Limited Inc—Donald Watts	170 Penrod Ct Ste B, Glen Burnie MD 21061	410-760-6349	R	2*	<.1
1768	Permay Protypes and Composites Inc—James Johnson	W229n1855 Westwood Dr, Waukesha WI 53186	262-970-7350	R	2*	<.1
1769	Plas-Tech Molding And Design Inc—Dennis Berkey	7037b N Triplett St, Brimfield IN 46794	260-761-3006	R	2*	<.1
1770	R and E Tooling and Plastics Inc—Roger Dickey	PO Box 14156, Fort Worth TX 76117	817-834-2858	R	2*	<.1
1771	Valley Plastics Company Inc—David Thompson	399 Phillips Ave, Toledo OH 43612	419-666-2349	R	2*	<.1
1772	Wilco Molding Inc—Stanley Williams	2435 Rock Island Blvd, Maryland Heights MO 63043	314-872-9252	R	2*	<.1
1773	Pulse Plastics Products Inc—Alan Backelman	PO Box 1228, Bronx NY 10459	718-328-5224	R	2*	.1
1774	American Fiberglass Inc—James Donaldson	2533 W Cypress St, Phoenix AZ 85009	602-278-4505	R	2*	<.1
1775	Erwin Cole Enterprises Inc—Erwin Cole	1127 Haley Rd, Murfreesboro TN 37129	615-890-6139	R	2*	<.1
1776	Mccray Press—Demo Thenous	2710 State St, Saginaw MI 48602	989-792-8681	R	2*	<.1
1777	Cal-Tron Corp—Dan Pool	2290 Dixon Ln, Bishop CA 93514	760-873-8491	R	2*	<.1
1778	Case Princeton Company Inc—Steve Parker	1119 Morris Ave, Union NJ 07083	908-687-1750	R	2*	<.1
1779	House Of Plastics Unlimited Inc—John Davis	2580 S Orange Blossom, Orlando FL 32805	407-843-3290	R	2*	<.1
1780	Poly Fabricators Inc—William Polhemus	3876 S Eufaula Ave, Eufaula AL 36027	334-687-7055	R	2*	<.1
1781	Northern Tool Manufacturing Company Inc—George Frigo	170 Progress Ave, Springfield MA 01104	413-732-5549	R	2*	<.1
1782	Commercial Plastics Corp—Bruce Bruner	3414 4th Ave S, Seattle WA 98134	206-682-4832	R	2*	<.1
1783	GAIM Plastics Inc—Edward Glatt	789 Golf Ln, Bensenville IL 60106	630-350-9500	R	2*	<.1
1784	Berlekamp Plastics Inc—Ken Berlekamp	2587 County Rd 99, Fremont OH 43420	419-334-4481	R	2*	<.1
1785	Girardin Moulding Inc—Gaston Girardin	PO Box 577, Windsor Locks CT 06096	860-623-4486	R	2*	<.1
1786	Space Age Plastic Fabricators Inc—Arthur Barsky	4519 White Plains Rd, Bronx NY 10470	718-324-6677	R	2*	<.1
1787	Unifuse LLC—Robert Fried	2092 Rte 9g, Staatsburg NY 12580	845-889-4000	R	2*	<.1
1788	Tenn-Tex Plastics Inc—Richard Marsh	PO Box 550, Colfax NC 27235	336-931-1100	R	2*	<.1
1789	Industrial Plastics Of Minneapolis Inc—Joe Lucken	3328 Snelling Ave, Minneapolis MN 55406	612-721-6444	R	1*	<.1
1790	Brogan Manufacturing Inc—Michael Brogan	515 E Centralia St, Elkhorn WI 53121	262-723-6909	R	1*	<.1
1791	Dimensional Mold Engineering Inc—Michael Horton	1977 Rochester Industr, Rochester Hills MI 48309	248-651-7600	R	1*	<.1

Rank	Company Name—*Executive Officer*	Address, City, State, Zip	Phone	Type	Fin	Empls
1792	S Gager Industries Inc—*Forest Gager*	11436 Philips Hwy, Jacksonville FL 32256	904-268-6727	R	1*	<.1
1793	Hi-Tech Polymers Inc—*Larry Phippen*	7967 Crest Hills Dr, Loves Park IL 61111	815-282-2272	R	1*	<.1
1794	Poly Plastics Inc—*Andrew Michaletz*	3280 Park Dr, Owatonna MN 55060	507-451-8659	R	1*	<.1
1795	Protoco Enterprises LLC	PO Box 106, North Plains OR 97133	503-647-0082	R	1*	<.1
1796	Custom Pack Inc—*Frank Menichini*	650 Pennsylvania Dr, Exton PA 19341	610-321-2525	R	1*	<.1
1797	Lormac Plastics Inc—*Wayne Browning*	2225 Meyers Ave, Escondido CA 92029	760-745-9115	R	1*	<.1
1798	Plasmetex Industries—*Adolph Saupe*	1425 Linda Vista Dr, San Marcos CA 92078	760-744-8300	R	1*	<.1
1799	A and J Industries LLC—*Som Thepkaysone*	56 Industrial Dr, Uxbridge MA 01569	508-278-4531	R	1*	<.1
1800	Precision Plastics Inc—*Dennis Currie*	1405 Warford St, Memphis TN 38108	901-323-8668	R	1*	<.1
1801	Sonolite Plastics Corp—*Peter Lawrence*	10 Fernwood Lake Ave S, Gloucester MA 01930	978-281-0662	R	1*	<.1
1802	Valley Precision Plastics Corp—*Jon Lawlis* Del and Wes Seapy Inc	301 W Lone Cactus Dr, Phoenix AZ 85027	623-780-8722	S	1*	<.1
1803	Custom Fold Doors Inc—*Richard Weinberg*	110 W Ash Ave, Burbank CA 91502	323-849-3225	R	1*	<.1
1804	Multi-Plastics of New Mexico Inc—*Eric Hoover*	PO Box 605, Conneaut Lake PA 16316	575-526-5531	R	1*	<.1
1805	Polyfab Display Co—*Alvin Parker*	PO Box 4850, Woodbridge VA 22194	703-497-4577	R	1*	<.1
1806	Jc Plastics Inc—*Tracy Runnels*	1001 S Vista Ave, Independence MO 64056	816-796-3530	R	1*	<.1
1807	Leaf Terminator—*Tony Iannelli*	4111 Founders Blvd, Batavia OH 45103	513-797-0861	R	1*	<.1
1808	Palpac Industries Inc—*Danny Meyer*	PO Box 109, Ottawa OH 45875	419-523-3230	R	1*	<.1
1809	Anson Mold and Manufacturing Inc—*Harold Yannayon*	2012 E 33rd St, Erie PA 16510	814-452-3286	S	1*	<.1
1810	Polytech Molding Inc—*Steve Booth*	126 Industrial Park Rd, Prairie Grove AR 72753	479-846-2121	R	1*	<.1
1811	Teksun Inc—*David Meyer*	11368 W Olympic Blvd, Los Angeles CA 90064	310-479-0794	R	1*	<.1
1812	Micro Mold Plastics Inc—*Tom Haynes*	2314 Ludelle St, Fort Worth TX 76105	817-536-0930	R	1*	<.1
1813	Plastic Processors Inc—*Jackson Wetzel*	PO Box 508, Hamilton IN 46742	260-488-3999	R	1*	<.1
1814	Basque Plastics Corp—*Clifford Basque*	28 Jytek Park, Leominster MA 01453	978-537-5219	R	1*	<.1
1815	Comor Inc—*Robert Deets*	PO Box 248, Cochranton PA 16314	814-425-3943	R	1*	<.1
1816	Co-Tronics Inc—*Ronald Sink*	PO Box 1037, Logansport IN 46947	574-722-3850	R	1*	<.1
1817	General Tool Specialties Inc—*John Domici*	284 Sunnymeade Rd, Hillsborough NJ 08844	908-874-3040	R	1*	<.1
1818	Tetra Tool Co—*Thomas Newman*	1425 Industrial Dr, Erie PA 16505	814-833-6127	R	1*	<.1
1819	Altratek Plastics Inc—*Dan Kaven*	PO Box 1688, Longmont CO 80502	303-776-9722	R	1*	<.1
1820	Compact Mould East Inc—*Miguel Petrucci*	3737 Cook Blvd, Chesapeake VA 23323	757-487-9646	R	1*	<.1
1821	Newport Plastics Corp—*Lee Chamberlain*	630 Gilman Rd, Lyndonville VT 05851	802-626-4000	R	1*	<.1
1822	Jdi Mold And Tool LLC—*Debra Jurinak*	2510 Hiller Rdg, Johnsburg IL 60051	815-759-5640	R	1*	<.1
1823	Qube Corp—*William Mc Coy*	16722 W Park Cir Dr St, Chagrin Falls OH 44023	440-543-2393	R	1*	<.1
1824	Dike-O-Seal Inc—*Thomas Slepski*	3965 S Keeler Ave, Chicago IL 60632	773-254-3224	R	1*	<.1
1825	Meadville New Products Inc—*John Bainbridge*	PO Box 405, Meadville PA 16335	814-336-2174	R	1*	<.1
1826	A and M Engineering Plastics Inc—*Allen Caton*	10521 75th St, Largo FL 33777	727-541-4482	R	1*	<.1
1827	Engrave Inc—*Robert Polewski*	140 Industrial Dr, Lawrenceburg IN 47025	812-537-8693	R	1*	<.1
1828	Urethane Products Corp—*Elizabeth Thermos*	17842 Sampson Ln, Huntington Beach CA 92647	714-375-4982	R	1*	<.1
1829	Central Sierra Moldings Inc—*Jeffrey Hopwood*	20833 Mechanical Dr, Sonora CA 95370	209-532-5146	R	1*	<.1
1830	Annmar Industries Inc—*Mark Thornberg*	1171 N Hawk Cir, Anaheim CA 92807	714-630-5443	R	1*	<.1
1831	First Plastics Corp—*Edward Mazzaferro*	22 Jytek Rd, Leominster MA 01453	978-537-0367	R	1*	<.1
1832	Ricon Colors Inc—*Gerald Mcdonald*	675 Wegner Dr, West Chicago IL 60185	630-562-9000	R	1*	<.1
1833	American Building Components Inc—*Neil Richards*	401 N Heus St, Pensacola FL 32501	850-430-5999	R	1*	<.1
1834	Bittner Industries Inc—*William Bittner*	PO Box 10265, Prichard AL 36610	251-457-7671	R	1*	<.1
1835	Coastal Plastic Molding Inc—*Robert Wall*	735 County Rd 281, Alvin TX 77511	281-331-7909	R	1*	<.1
1836	East Iowa Plastics Inc—*Bret Kivell*	PO Box 350, Independence IA 50644	319-334-2552	R	1*	<.1
1837	Bermar Associates Inc—*Janet Roncelli*	PO Box 99430, Troy MI 48099	248-589-2460	R	1*	<.1
1838	Polymer Products LP—*Wayne Gilbert*	2613 Aviation Pkwy, Grand Prairie TX 75052	972-647-1000	R	1*	<.1
1839	Superior Window Manufacturing Inc—*Lou Lagrotteria*	470 Davidson Rd, Pittsburgh PA 15239	412-793-3500	R	1*	<.1
1840	Venture Precision Tool Inc—*Keith Foreman*	PO Box 262, Hummelstown PA 17036	717-566-6496	R	1*	<.1
1841	Omega Plastics Inc—*Jeff Kaczperski*	PO Box 898, Mount Clemens MI 48046	586-954-2100	R	1*	.1
1842	Ace Composites Inc—*Todd Hambrook*	PO Box 59, Olivehurst CA 95961	530-743-1885	R	1*	.1
1843	Philip's Plastics—*Philip Smid*	3801 E Roeser Rd Ste 1, Phoenix AZ 85040	602-470-1808	R	1*	<.1
1844	Better Plastics Inc—*Bill Messina Jr*	2206 N Main St, Kissimmee FL 34744	407-846-3127	R	1*	<.1
1845	Modern Alpha Plastics Inc—*Melvin Gross*	1026 S Powell Rd, Independence MO 64056	816-796-3800	R	1*	<.1
1846	Paco Plastics and Engineering Inc—*Greg Dowden*	8540 Dice Rd, Santa Fe Springs CA 90670	562-698-0916	R	1*	<.1
1847	Caulfield Associates Inc—*Anthony Caulfield*	Po Box 1448, Doylestown PA 18901	215-348-5565	R	1	<.1
1848	Nica Corp—*John Morrison*	6006 Shull St, Bell CA 90201	562-806-4755	R	1*	<.1
1849	Acramold Inc—*Dallas Trinkle*	1670 Distribution Dr, Burlington KY 41005	859-525-8811	R	1*	<.1
1850	Enflo Corp—*Robert Dalton*	PO Box 490, Bristol CT 06011	860-589-0014	R	1*	<.1
1851	Jesco Injection Molding Inc—*James Schoudel*	9513 S 500 W, Sandy UT 84070	801-255-2042	R	1*	<.1
1852	Raiford Printing Company Inc—*Lynn Henry*	PO Box 403, Vidalia GA 30475	912-537-7442	R	1*	<.1
1853	Cell Parts Manufacturing Co—*Valerie Door*	125 Prairie Lake Rd, East Dundee IL 60118	847-844-1115	R	1*	<.1
1854	Colonial Manufacturing LLC—*Patrick Bb*	1246 E Empire Ave, Benton Harbor MI 49022	269-926-1000	S	1*	<.1
1855	LBM Products Inc	10711 Chandler Blvd, N Hollywood CA 91601	818-769-5381	R	1*	<.1
1856	Alva-Tech Inc—*Philip Valenziano*	1208 Columbus Rd Ste G, Burlington Township NJ 08016	732-988-8225	R	1*	<.1
1857	C-Plex Inc—*David Howard*	PO Box 4363, West Columbia SC 29171	803-951-0628	R	1*	<.1
1858	Handley Industries Inc—*Robert Handley*	2101 Brooklyn Rd, Jackson MI 49203	517-787-8821	R	1*	<.1
1859	Prairie Plastics Inc—*Michael Wolfe*	PO Box 450, Sun Prairie WI 53590	608-834-9122	R	1*	<.1
1860	Pro Plastics Inc (Linden New Jersey)—*George Sieberight*	1190 Sylvan St, Linden NJ 07036	908-925-5555	R	1*	<.1
1861	Scientific Plastics Ltd—*Gabe Dickstein*	5854 Miami Lakes Dr E, Hialeah FL 33014	305-557-3737	R	1*	<.1
1862	Precision Mold Technologies Inc—*Enrique Dobrilla*	PO Box 667748, Miami FL 33166	305-594-1789	R	1*	<.1
1863	Rs Industries Inc—*Robert Snyder*	PO Box 1051, Monroe NC 28111	704-289-2734	R	1*	<.1
1864	Siltech Inc—*Dino J Longo*	1881 Trade Center Way, Naples FL 34109	239-593-7988	R	1*	<.1
1865	AVS Supply Inc—*William Doherty*	PO Box 35489, Phoenix AZ 85069	602-242-9207	R	1*	<.1
1866	Metapoint Partners LP—*Keith C Shaughnessy*	3 Centennial Dr, Peabody MA 01960	978-531-4444	R	1*	<.1
1867	Midland Technologies Inc—*Rick Dubay*	14800 James Rd, Rogers MN 55374	763-428-4229	R	1*	<.1
1868	Shaw-Clayton Corp—*Howard Shaw*	90 Montecito Rd, San Rafael CA 94901	415-453-1521	R	1*	<.1
1869	Plasticos Arco Iris Of San Antonio—*Junita Muniz*	4335 Vance Jackson Bld, San Antonio TX 78230		R	1*	<.1
1870	Acutek Inc—*Deborah Wagener*	2909 W 40 Hwy Ste A, Blue Springs MO 64015	816-228-7528	R	1*	<.1
1871	Phoenix Films Inc—*Ted Nitka*	PO Box 3816, Clearwater Beach FL 33767	727-446-0300	R	1*	<.1
1872	Mueller Plastics Corp—*William D O'Hagan*	8285 Tournament Dr Ste, Memphis TN 38125	901-753-3200	S	1	.1
1873	Absolute Quality Manufacturing Inc—*Duane Petersen*	401 Royalston Ave, Minneapolis MN 55405	612-372-3199	R	1*	<.1
1874	Plastic Assembly Corp—*Regis Magnus*	PO Box 632, Ayer MA 01432	978-772-4725	R	1*	<.1
1875	Heppner Molds Inc—*L Livingston*	1420 E 3rd Ave Ste 2, Post Falls ID 83854	208-773-4055	R	1*	<.1
1876	Patton Tool And Die Inc—*Dennis Patton*	7185 Baker Rd, Lexington MI 48450	810-359-5336	R	1*	<.1
1877	Hpi—*Tom Parisian*	1704 Colorado Ave, Santa Monica CA 90404	310-829-3449	R	1*	<.1
1878	Mod I Set Plastics Inc—*Wuyman Baker*	1105 Edgecliff Dr, Bedford TX 76022	817-267-2098	R	1*	<.1
1879	Hesco Inc—*Max Mogensen*	PO Box 386, Hagerstown MD 21741	301-739-5911	R	1*	<.1
1880	Tee Tool Inc—*George Paul*	PO Box 1147, Joplin MO 64802	417-623-5512	R	1*	<.1

Note: An asterisk (*) indicates an estimated financial figure. The company type code used is as follows: R = Private, P = Public, S = Private Subsidiary, B = Public Subsidiary, D = Division, J = Joint Venture, I = Investment Fund.

COMPANY RANKINGS BY SALES WITHIN 4-DIGIT SIC

Rank	Company Name—*Executive Officer*	Address, City, State, Zip	Phone	Type	Fin	Empls
1881	Molds And Plastic Machinery Inc—*Bruce Miller*	13145 Nw 47th Ave, Opa Locka FL 33054	305-828-3456	R	1*	<.1
1882	United Tool and Plastics Inc—*John Matherlee*	200 W 12th St, Waynesboro VA 22980	540-943-3434	R	1*	<.1
1883	Burnham Polymeric Inc—*Warren Burnham*	PO Box 317, Glens Falls NY 12801	518-792-1323	R	1*	<.1
1884	Sun Tech Industries—*Shannon Mackey*	41958 Hwy 2, Ravenna NE 68869	308-452-4044	R	1*	<.1
1885	Spaceage Synthetics Inc—*John Hertsgaard*	1402 39th St N Ste A, Fargo ND 58102	701-277-5631	R	1*	<.1
1886	Edinboro Molding Inc—*John Merritt*	25741 Fry Rd, Edinboro PA 16412	814-763-3770	R	1*	<.1
1887	Industrial Polymers Inc—*Labita Boddie*	3250 S Sam Houston Pkw, Houston TX 77047	713-943-8451	R	1*	<.1
1888	RH Murphy Company Inc—*Robert Murphy*	3 Howe Dr Ste 3, Amherst NH 03031	603-889-2255	R	1*	<.1
1889	Metabolix Inc—*Richard P Eno*	21 Erie St, Cambridge MA 02139	617-583-1700	P	1	.1
1890	Artmor Plastics Corp	PO Box 3187, Cumberland MD 21504	301-722-7440	R	1*	<.1
1891	Crystal-Like Plastics Co—*Robert Gayler*	2547 N Ontario St, Burbank CA 91504	818-846-1818	R	1*	<.1
1892	Exacta Plastics Inc—*Bill Schiffer*	9105 De Garmo Ave, Sun Valley CA 91352	818-768-1234	R	1*	<.1
1893	Ken Duncan Co—*Ken Duncan*	1078 E Edna Pl, Covina CA 91724	626-915-8827	R	1*	<.1
1894	Plastic Molding Development Inc—*Gary Kitts*	42400 Yearego Dr, Sterling Heights MI 48314	586-739-4500	R	1*	<.1
1895	Special Service Plastic Company Inc—*Doug Allison*	PO Box 38040, Charlotte NC 28278	704-587-0109	R	<1*	<.1
1896	Rabco Systems Inc—*Tab Cohen*	14786 Greenleaf Valley, Chesterfield MO 63017	636-537-0314	R	<1*	<.1
1897	Acorn Plastics Inc—*Donald Morris*	13818 Oaks Ave, Chino CA 91710	909-591-8461	R	<1*	<.1
1898	Pvc Industries Inc—*Louis Simonini*	107 Pierce Rd, Clifton Park NY 12065	518-877-8670	R	<1*	<.1
1899	Brown Co—*Patrick Brown*	Aileron Ave Ste N10102, Pensacola FL 32506	850-453-5426	R	<1*	<.1
1900	Genesis Molding Inc—*Kathleen Geisel*	55901 Currant Rd, Mishawaka IN 46545	574-256-9271	R	<1*	<.1
1901	Jlb Plastics Inc—*John Byrne*	County Hwy 49, Morris NY 13808	607-263-9786	R	<1*	<.1
1902	Lightwave Logic Inc—*James S Marcelli*	121 Continental Dr Ste, Newark DE 19713	302-356-2709	P	<1	3.6
1903	Vin-Tex Sealers Inc—*Eric Voller*	1447 W Ardmore Ave, Itasca IL 60143	630-773-1820	R	<1	<.1

TOTALS: SIC 3089 Plastics Products Nec
Companies: 1,903 — 147,491 — 393.3

3111 Leather Tanning & Finishing

Rank	Company Name—*Executive Officer*	Address, City, State, Zip	Phone	Type	Fin	Empls
1	Albert Trostel and Sons Co	330 E Kilbourn Ave Ste, Milwaukee WI 53202	414-223-1560	S	406*	3.5
2	SB Foot Tanning Co—*SB Foot III*	805 Bench St, Red Wing MN 55066	651-388-4731	R	172*	.3
3	Etienne Aigner Inc—*Tony Chang*	29 W 35th St, New York NY 10001		R	83*	.4
4	Robus Leather Corp—*Charles Spillman*	3333 Founders Rd, Indianapolis IN 46268	317-471-8686	S	35*	.1
5	Horween Leather Co—*Arnold Horween*	2015 N Elston Ave, Chicago IL 60614	773-772-2026	R	16*	.2
6	Wickett and Craig Of America Inc—*John Lee*	120 Cooper Rd, Grampian PA 16838	814-236-2220	R	11*	.1
7	Twin City Hide International Inc—*Guy Grove*	491 Malden St, South Saint Paul MN 55075	651-455-1511	R	7*	.1
8	Hermann Oak Leather Co—*Fredrick Hermann*	4050 N 1st St, Saint Louis MO 63147	314-421-1173	R	6*	.1
9	Tex Tan Western Leather Co—*Don Motsenbocker*	808 S US Hwy 77A, Yoakum TX 77995		R	5*	.1
10	Liberty Book And Bible Manufactures Inc—*Robert Horn*	901 E Maryland St, Indianapolis IN 46202	317-633-1450	R	4*	<.1
11	Wood and Hyde Leather Company Inc—*Randall Doerter*	PO Box 786, Gloversville NY 12078	518-725-7105	R	2*	<.1
12	Seton Company of Michigan—*Philip Kaltenbacher*	7001 Orchard Lake Rd S, West Bloomfield MI 48322	248-702-1440	R	N/A	4.5

TOTALS: SIC 3111 Leather Tanning & Finishing
Companies: 12 — 747 — 9.3

3131 Footwear Cut Stock

Rank	Company Name—*Executive Officer*	Address, City, State, Zip	Phone	Type	Fin	Empls
1	Vulcan Corp Rubber Products Div—*Ed Ritter*	PO Box 709, Clarksville TN 37041	931-645-6431	D	7*	.1
2	Leo F Maciver Company Inc—*Donald Maciver*	PO Box 2086, Brockton MA 02305	508-583-2501	R	2*	<.1

TOTALS: SIC 3131 Footwear Cut Stock
Companies: 2 — 9 — .1

3142 House Slippers

Rank	Company Name—*Executive Officer*	Address, City, State, Zip	Phone	Type	Fin	Empls
1	RG Barry Corp—*Greg A Tunney*	13405 Yarmouth Rd NW, Pickerington OH 43147	614-864-6400	P	130	.2
2	Barry of San Angelo—*Greg A Tunney* RG Barry Corp	3301 Barry Ave, San Angelo TX 76901	325-942-7664	D	11*	.1

TOTALS: SIC 3142 House Slippers
Companies: 2 — 141 — .2

3143 Men's Footwear Except Athletic

Rank	Company Name—*Executive Officer*	Address, City, State, Zip	Phone	Type	Fin	Empls
1	Timberland Co—*Patrick Frisk*	200 Domain Dr, Stratham NH 03885	603-772-9500	S	1,430	5.6
2	Vasque Outdoor Footwear Div—*Dave Murphy*	314 W Main St Ste 312, Red Wing MN 55066	651-388-6211	D	1,200*	2.0
3	Munro and Company Inc—*Don Munro*	PO Box 6048, Hot Springs AR 71902	501-262-6000	R	424*	2.5
4	K-Swiss Inc—*Steven Nichols*	31248 Oak Crest Dr, Westlake Village CA 91361	818-706-5100	P	268	.6
5	Weyco Group Inc—*Thomas W Florsheim Jr*	PO Box 1188, Milwaukee WI 53212	414-908-1600	P	229	.6
6	Lucchese Boot Company Inc—*Dough Kindy*	40 Walter Jones Blvd, El Paso TX 79906	915-778-8060	R	196*	.4
7	Dansko Inc—*Amanda C Cabot*	8 Federal Rd, West Grove PA 19390	610-869-8335	R	129*	.2
8	Justin Industries Inc—*Randy Watson*	PO Box 548, Fort Worth TX 76101	817-332-4385	S	96*	1.7
9	Belleville Shoe Manufacturing Co—*Eric Weidmann*	100 Premier Dr, Belleville IL 62220	618-233-5600	R	44*	.7
10	Allen-Edmonds Shoe Corp—*Mark Birmingham*	PO Box 998, Port Washington WI 53074	262-235-6000	R	36*	.6
11	PW Minor and Sons Inc—*Henry Minor III*	PO Box 678, Batavia NY 14021	585-343-1500	R	29*	.2
12	Lucchese Inc—*Doug Kindy*	40 Walter Jones Blvd, El Paso TX 79906	915-778-3066	R	24*	.4
13	Alden Shoe Company Inc—*Arthur Tarlow*	1 Taunton St, Middleboro MA 02346	508-947-3926	R	20*	.2
14	Belleville Shoe South Inc—*Eric Weidmann* Belleville Shoe Manufacturing Co	Hwy 1 S, De Witt AR 72042	870-946-3526	S	19*	.3
15	Weinbrenner Shoe Company Inc—*L Nienow*	108 S Polk St, Merrill WI 54452	715-536-5521	R	16*	.3
16	EJ Footwear Corp—*Gerald Cohn*	39 E Canal St, Nelsonville OH 45764	740-753-1951	S	7*	.1
17	GH Bass and Co—*Scott Orenstein*	PO Box 9431, South Portland ME 04116	207-791-4000	S	3*	<.1

TOTALS: SIC 3143 Men's Footwear Except Athletic
Companies: 17 — 4,170 — 16.3

3144 Women's Footwear Except Athletic

Rank	Company Name—*Executive Officer*	Address, City, State, Zip	Phone	Type	Fin	Empls
1	Steven Madden Ltd—*Edward Rosenfeld*	52-16 Barnett Ave, Long Island City NY 11104	718-446-1800	P	969	2.4
2	Arkansas Glass Container Corp—*Anthony Rampley*	PO Box 1717, Jonesboro AR 72403	870-932-4564	R	366*	.4
3	Penobscot Shoe Co—*Jim Reidman*	PO Box 545, Old Town ME 04468	207-827-4434	R	22	<.1
4	Nina Footwear Inc—*Scott Silverstein*	200 Park Ave S, New York NY 10003	212-399-2323	R	16*	.1
5	Magdesian Brothers Inc—*Wahram Magdesian*	730 S 5th Ave, City Of Industry CA 91746	626-330-3384	R	13*	.1
6	Dolphin Shoe Company Inc—*Edward Birnbaum*	3070 E 10th Ct, Hialeah FL 33013	305-836-0358	R	9*	.1
7	Abilene Boot Company Inc—*French Humphries*	841 S Ctr Ave, Somerset PA 15501	814-445-6545	R	4*	<.1

TOTALS: SIC 3144 Women's Footwear Except Athletic
Companies: 7 — 1,398 — 3.2

Rank	Company Name—*Executive Officer*	Address, City, State, Zip	Phone	Type	Fin	Empls
3149 Footwear Except Rubber Nec						
1	Nike Inc—*Mark Parker*	1 Bowerman Dr, Beaverton OR 97005	503-671-6453	P	20,862	38.0
2	Reebok International Ltd—*Paul Fireman*	1895 JW Foster Blvd, Canton MA 02021	781-401-5000	S	3,785	9.1
3	Brown Shoe Company Inc—*Ronald A Fromm*	PO Box 29, Saint Louis MO 63166	314-854-4000	P	2,504	13.4
4	SRCG/Ecom Inc—*David M Chamberlain* Stride Rite Corp	191 Spring St, Lexington MA 02420	617-824-6000	S	2,172*	2.5
5	Stride Rite Sourcing International Inc—*David M Chamberlain* Stride Rite Corp	191 Spring St, Lexington MA 02420	617-824-6000	S	2,172*	2.5
6	Tommy Hilfiger Footwear Inc—*David M Chamberlain* Stride Rite Corp	191 Spring St, Lexington MA 02420	617-824-6000	S	2,172*	2.5
7	New Balance Athletic Shoe Inc—*Robert T DeMartini*	20 Guest St, Boston MA 02135	617-783-4000	R	1,780	4.0
8	Wolverine World Wide Inc—*Blake W Krueger*	9341 Courtland Dr NE, Rockford MI 49351	616-866-5500	P	1,409	4.4
9	SR Holdings Inc (Lexington Massachusetts)—*David M Chamberlain* Stride Rite Corp	191 Spring St, Lexington MA 02420	617-824-6000	S	707	3.1
10	SRL Inc (Lexington Massachusetts)—*David M Chamberlain* Stride Rite Corp	191 Spring St, Lexington MA 02420	617-824-6000	S	707	3.1
11	SRR Inc (Lexington Massachusetts)—*David M Chamberlain* Stride Rite Corp	191 Spring St, Lexington MA 02420	617-824-6000	S	707	3.1
12	Stride Rite Corp	4200 S A St, Richmond IN 47374		S	707	3.1
13	Justin Brands	610 W Daggett, Fort Worth TX 76104	817-332-4385	S	678*	.9
14	Kenneth Cole Productions Inc—*Paul Blum*	603 W 50th St, New York NY 10019	212-265-1500	P	412	1.8
15	McRae Industries Inc—*D Gary McRae*	PO Box 1239, Mount Gilead NC 27306	910-439-6147	R	354*	.6
16	Rocky Brands Inc—*Mike Brooks*	39 E Canal St, Nelsonville OH 45764	740-753-1951	P	240	2.2
17	Converse Inc—*Betsy Flemming* Nike Inc	1 High St, North Andover MA 01845	978-983-3300	S	205*	.3
18	Cole-Haan Holdings Inc—*Kevin B Rollins* Nike Inc	1 Cole Haan Dr, Yarmouth ME 04096	207-846-2500	S	161*	.5
19	MUNROKids - Perfection Div—*Don Munro*	PO Box 6048, Hot Springs AR 71902	501-262-6000	D	152*	.4
20	Keds Corp—*Shawn Neville* Stride Rite Corp	4200 S A St, Richmond IN 47374		D	91*	.2
21	LA Gear Inc—*Scott Coble*	844 Miroga, Los Angeles CA 90049	310-889-3499	R	50*	<.1
22	Wellco Enterprises Inc	614 Mabry Hood Rd Ste, Knoxville TN 37932	865-392-9333	R	44*	.7
23	Heelys Inc—*Thomas C Hansen*	3200 Belmeade Dr Ste 1, Carrollton TX 75006	214-390-1831	P	30	<.1
24	Trimfoot Company LLC (Farmington Missouri)—*Larry Skaggs*	115 Trimfoot Ter, Farmington MO 63640	573-756-6616	R	30*	.1
25	Brooks Sports Inc—*Jim Weber*	19910 N Creek Pkwy Ste, Bothell WA 98011	425-488-3131	S	30*	.1
26	Propet USA Inc—*Jack Hawkins*	2415 W Valley Hwy N, Auburn WA 98001	253-854-7600	R	29*	.1
27	Nelson Sports Inc—*Young Chu*	12878 Florence Ave, Santa Fe Springs CA 90670	562-944-8081	R	4*	<.1
28	Badorf Shoe Company Inc—*Duane Gingerich*	1958 Auction Rd, Manheim PA 17545	717-653-0155	R	4*	<.1
29	Nfinity Products and Services Inc—*Tate Chalk*	201 17th St NW Ste 300, Atlanta GA 30363	404-870-3558	R	3*	<.1
30	Foot-So-Port (Oconomowoc Wisconsin)—*Linda Miller*	PO Box 247, Oconomowoc WI 53066	262-567-4416	R	2*	<.1
TOTALS: SIC 3149 Footwear Except Rubber Nec						
	Companies: 30				**42,203**	**96.9**
3151 Leather Gloves & Mittens						
1	Fownes Brothers and Company Inc—*Thomas Gluckman*	16 E 34th St Fl 5, New York NY 10016	212-683-0150	R	1,740*	2.2
2	Magid Glove and Safety Manufacturing Company LLC—*Matt Block*	2060 N Kolmar Ave, Chicago IL 60639	773-384-2070	R	26*	.4
3	Guard-Line Inc—*Dennis Stanley*	PO Box 1030, Atlanta TX 75551	903-796-4111	R	19*	.2
4	North American Fly Ltd—*Leland Christenson*	PO Box 99, Strum WI 54770	715-695-3533	R	9*	.1
5	Saranac Glove Co—*John Fabry*	PO Box 1477, Green Bay WI 54305	920-435-3737	R	6*	.1
TOTALS: SIC 3151 Leather Gloves & Mittens						
	Companies: 5				**1,800**	**2.9**
3161 Luggage						
1	Anvil Cases Inc—*Joe Calzone*	15730 Salt Lake Ave, City Of Industry CA 91745	626-968-4100	S	225*	.2
2	Yak Pak Inc	900 Broadway 3rd Fl, New York NY 10003	718-797-3671	R	50*	.5
3	Hartmann Inc—*David Herman*	200 Hartmann Dr, Lebanon TN 37087		S	26*	.2
4	Fish and Crown Ltd—*Bergljot Wathne*	42 W 39th St, New York NY 10018	212-707-9603	R	22*	.2
5	Tamrac Inc—*Jesselyn Cyr*	9240 Jordan Ave, Chatsworth CA 91311	818-407-9500	R	16*	.2
6	Commercial Sewing Inc—*Samuel Mazzarelli*	PO Box 1173, Torrington CT 06790	860-482-5509	R	14*	.1
7	Calzone Ltd—*Joseph Calzone*	225 Black Rock Ave, Bridgeport CT 06605	203-367-5766	R	13*	.1
8	Fieldtex Products Inc—*Sanford Abbey*	3055 Brghton Hnrtta Tl, Rochester NY 14623	585-427-2940	R	11*	.1
9	Mercury Luggage Manufacturing Co—*Andrew Pradella*	PO Box 47558, Jacksonville FL 32247	904-733-9595	R	11*	.1
10	Mulholland Brothers—*Jay Holland*	190 Napoleon St, San Francisco CA 94124	415-824-5995	R	11*	.1
11	Skyway Luggage Co—*Henry Kotkins Jr*	30 Wall St, Seattle WA 98121	206-256-1601	R	8*	.1
12	Case Design Corp—*Roger Ernst*	333 School Ln, Telford PA 18969	215-703-0130	R	8*	.1
13	Bee Electronics Inc—*Robert Lunn*	7440 Commercial Cir, Fort Pierce FL 34951	772-468-7477	R	8*	.1
14	Platt Luggage Inc—*Marc Platt*	4051 W 51st St, Chicago IL 60632	773-838-2000	R	6*	.1
15	American Leather Products—*John Caito*	530 Wellington Ave 22, Cranston RI 02910	401-273-0505	R	1*	<.1
TOTALS: SIC 3161 Luggage						
	Companies: 15				**430**	**2.1**
3171 Women's Handbags & Purses						
1	Koret Inc (New York New York)—*Michael Gordon*	101 W 55th St 11th Fl, New York NY 10019	212-581-8710	R	20	.2
2	Dooney and Bourke Inc—*Peter Dooney*	PO Box 841, Norwalk CT 06856	203-853-7515	R	17*	.1
3	AD Sutton and Sons Inc—*David Sutton*	20 W 33rd St 2nd Fl, New York NY 10001	212-695-7070	R	9*	.1
4	Stone Mountain Accessories Inc—*Kenneth Orr*	10 W 33rd St Ste 728, New York NY 10001		D	7*	<.1
5	Judith Leiber LLC—*Nicole Magann*	545 5th Ave Fl 8, New York NY 10017	212-736-4244	R	7*	.1
6	LANA MARKS Boutique—*Lana J Marks*	125 Worth Ave, Palm Beach FL 33480	561-655-3155	R	6*	<.1
7	Kalencom Corp—*Jeno Kalozdi*	740 Clouet St, New Orleans LA 70117	504-943-0123	R	4*	<.1
TOTALS: SIC 3171 Women's Handbags & Purses						
	Companies: 7				**70**	**.5**
3172 Personal Leather Goods Nec						
1	Coach Inc—*Lew Frankfort*	516 W 34th St, New York NY 10001	212-594-1850	P	4,159	15.0
2	Mundi-Westport Corp—*Kevin Ross*	PO Box 2002, Pinebrook NJ 07058	973-575-0110	R	58*	.1
3	Tandy Leather Company LP—*Jim Koerber*	1900 SE Loop 820 S, Fort Worth TX 76140	817-496-4874	S	50*	1.0

Note: An asterisk (*) indicates an estimated financial figure. The company type code used is as follows: R = Private, P = Public, S = Private Subsidiary, B = Public Subsidiary, D = Division, J = Joint Venture, I = Investment Fund.

COMPANY RANKINGS BY SALES WITHIN 4-DIGIT SIC

Rank	Company Name—Executive Officer	Address, City, State, Zip	Phone	Type	Fin	Empls
4	Sharif Designs Ltd—Sharif El Fouly	3412 36th Ave, Long Island City NY 11106	718-472-1100	R	20*	<.1
5	Wristbandfactorycom—Steve Hall	PO Box 5290, Benton City WA 99320		S	19*	<.1
6	Penthouse Manufacturing Company Inc—William Ostrower	225 Buffalo Ave, Freeport NY 11520	516-379-1300	R	18*	.4
7	Koszegi Industries Inc—Douglas W Sabra	1801 Green Rd Ste E, Pompano Beach FL 33068	954-419-9544	S	15*	<.1
8	Numaco Packaging LLC—Jita Tran	82 Boyd Ave, East Providence RI 02914	401-438-4952	R	12*	<.1
9	All Book Covers Arizona Inc—Ivan Fishman	1445 S Mcclintock Dr, Tempe AZ 85281	480-966-6283	S	11*	.1
10	Warner Jewelry Case Co—Marshall Weissman	1002 Sw Ard St, Lawton OK 73505	580-536-8885	R	9*	.2
11	Eric Scott Leathers Ltd—Ronald Coleman	PO Box 443, Sainte Genevieve MO 63670	573-883-7491	R	8*	.1
12	Valkyrie Company Inc—James Devaney	60 Fremont St, Worcester MA 01603	508-756-3633	R	5*	.1
13	LBU Inc—Jeffrey Mayer	217 Brook Ave, Passaic NJ 07055	973-773-4800	R	5*	<.1
14	Hugo Bosca Company Inc—Christopher Bosca	PO Box 777, Springfield OH 45501	937-323-5523	R	3*	<.1

TOTALS: SIC 3172 Personal Leather Goods Nec
Companies: 14 — 4,391 — 17.0

3199 Leather Goods Nec

Rank	Company Name—Executive Officer	Address, City, State, Zip	Phone	Type	Fin	Empls
1	Samsonite Corp—Marcello Bottoli	575 West St Ste 110, Mansfield MA 02048	508-851-1400	R	1,070*	5.0
2	Jaclyn Inc—Robert Chestnov	197 W Spring Valley Av, Maywood NJ 07607	201-909-6000	P	196	.2
3	Swank Inc—John A Tulin	90 Park Ave 13th Fl, New York NY 10016	212-867-2600	P	133	.3
4	Tandy Leather Factory Inc—Jon Thompson	1900 Southeast Lp 820, Fort Worth TX 76140	817-496-4414	P	60	.5
5	Action Inc—Don Motsenbocker	PO Box 8008, McKinney TX 75070	972-542-8700	R	28*	.5
6	John Tillman and Co—Blake Brown	1300 W Artesia Blvd, Compton CA 90220	310-764-0110	R	14*	.1
7	McGuire-Nicholas Company Inc—Dan Cabana	17280 N Green Mountain, San Antonio TX 78247	210-651-5288	D	13*	.2
8	Stebco Products Corp	33 Murray Hill Dr, Nanuet NY 10954		R	11	.1
9	Galco International Ltd—Richard Gallagher	2019 W Quail Ave, Phoenix AZ 85027	623-434-7070	R	7*	.1
10	Ariat International Inc—Elizabeth Cross	3242 Whipple Rd, Union City CA 94587	510-477-7000	R	7*	.1
11	Dabora Inc—David Howard	PO Box 1007, Shelbyville TN 37162	931-684-8123	R	6*	.1
12	Gould and Goodrich Inc—Robert Gould	709 E Mcneill St, Lillington NC 27546	910-893-2071	R	5*	.1
13	Sainberg and Company Inc—Jim Skinner	1270 Niagara St, Buffalo NY 14213	718-897-7000	S	5*	<.1
14	Lapco Manufacturing Inc—Freddie Triche	PO Box 2491, Morgan City LA 70381	985-385-5380	R	4*	<.1
15	Bray Manufacturing Company Inc—Tim Bray	225 E Saint Louis St, Pacific MO 63069	636-464-2700	R	3*	.1
16	Kane Manufacturing Company Inc—Michael N Kane	1101 NE 56th St, Des Moines IA 50327	515-262-3001	R	2*	<.1
17	Hunter Company Inc—James Holtzclaw	3300 W 71st Ave, Westminster CO 80030	303-427-4626	R	2*	<.1
18	Hamilton Animal Products LLC—Steve Lingo	331 Sw 57th Ave, Ocala FL 34474	352-690-9680	R	2*	<.1
19	Milcom Services Inc—Ursula Lemmens	1963 10th Ave N, Lake Worth FL 33461	561-588-9119	R	1*	<.1

TOTALS: SIC 3199 Leather Goods Nec
Companies: 19 — 1,568 — 7.2

3211 Flat Glass

Rank	Company Name—Executive Officer	Address, City, State, Zip	Phone	Type	Fin	Empls
1	Guardian Industries Corp—Russell J Ebeid	2300 Harmon Rd, Auburn Hills MI 48326	248-340-1800	R	4,661*	18.0
2	AGC America Inc—William Dankmyer	2201 Water Ridge Pkwy, Charlotte NC 20217	704-357-3631	R	2,514*	5.7
3	Libbey-Owens-Ford Co—Katsiyi Fujimoto	811 Madison Ave, Toledo OH 43604	419-247-3731	S	1,000*	7.0
4	Agc Flat Glass North America Inc—D Kennedy	PO Box 929, Kingsport TN 37662	404-446-4200	R	428*	5.3
5	Hartung Agalite Glass Co—Nick Sciola	17830 W Valley Hwy, Tukwila WA 98188	425-656-2626	R	333*	.4
6	Pilkington Holdings Inc—A Graham	PO Box 799, Toledo OH 43697	419-247-3731	R	324*	5.2
7	Oldcastle Glass Group	1331 W Sam Houston Pkw, Houston TX 77043	713-464-5611	S	267*	2.0
8	Gemtron Corp—Mark Delp	615 New Hwy 68, Sweetwater TN 37874	423-337-3522	R	99*	1.0
9	Tru Vue Inc—Jane Boyce	9400 W 55th St, McCook IL 60525	708-485-5080	S	29*	.2
10	Engineered Glass Products LLC—Cindy Maloney	2857 S Halsted St, Chicago IL 60608	312-326-4710	R	18*	.2
11	Abrisa Industrial Glass Inc—Jim Veler	PO Box 489, Santa Paula CA 93061	805-525-4902	R	16*	.1
12	Oldcastle Buildingenvelope Inc—Ted Hathaway	PO Box 18039, Hauppauge NY 11788	631-234-2200	S	16*	.1
13	Virginia Glass Products Corp—Christopher Beeler	PO Box 5431, Martinsville VA 24115	276-956-3131	S	14*	.2
14	Glasstech Inc—Mark Christman	995 4th St, Perrysburg OH 43551	419-661-9500	R	12*	.1
15	Bullseye Glass Co—Dan Schwoerer	3722 Se 21st Ave, Portland OR 97202	503-232-8887	R	10*	.1
16	Vogelin Optical Company Inc—Scott Pollock	PO Box 360, Norwood MN 55368	952-466-5516	R	3*	<.1
17	Blenko Glass Company Inc—William Blenko	PO Box 67, Milton WV 25541	304-743-9081	R	3*	.1
18	Northwestern Industries Inc—Yoshiyuki Fujii	2500 W Jameson St, Seattle WA 98199	206-285-3140	R	3*	<.1
19	Jobbers Inc—Dickson Ridgeway	2799 Hope Church Rd, Winston Salem NC 27127	336-768-3113	R	3*	<.1
20	North American Bullet Proof Inc—Stephen Rux	PO Box 628, Cibolo TX 78108	210-225-0982	R	3*	<.1
21	Igs Inc—John Gracia	916 E California Ave, Sunnyvale CA 94085	408-733-4621	R	2*	<.1
22	Paragon Optical Company Inc—Thaddeus Glembocki	658 S 7th St, Reading PA 19602	610-372-5056	R	1*	<.1
23	Fox Studios Inc—Clare Acheson	5901 N College Ave, Indianapolis IN 46220	317-253-0135	R	1*	<.1

TOTALS: SIC 3211 Flat Glass
Companies: 23 — 9,757 — 45.8

3221 Glass Containers

Rank	Company Name—Executive Officer	Address, City, State, Zip	Phone	Type	Fin	Empls
1	Owens-Illinois Inc—Albert PL Stroucken	1 Michael Owens Way, Perrysburg OH 43551	567-336-5000	P	6,633	24.0
2	Saint Gobain Container LLC—Joseph Grewe	PO Box 4200, Muncie IN 47307	765-741-7000	R	6,497*	.3
3	Ball Plastic Container Operations Div—David Hoover	10 Longs Peak Dr, Broomfield CO 80021	303-469-3131	S	790*	7.0
4	Anchor Glass Container Corp—James Fredlake	401 E Jackson St Ste 2, Tampa FL 33602	813-884-0000	D	764*	2.9
5	Piramal Glass - USA Inc—Niraj Tipre	401 Rte 73 N Ste 202, Marlton NJ 08053	856-293-6400	R	54*	.9
6	Leone Industries—Peter Leone	443 S E Ave, Bridgeton NJ 08302	856-455-2000	R	22*	.4
7	Penn Bottle and Supply Co—Keith Strope	710 E 3rd St, Essington PA 19029	610-521-6000	R	20*	.1
8	Wheaton Science Products Inc—Stephen R Drozdow	1501 N 10th St, Millville NJ 08332	856-825-1100	S	13*	.1
9	Jensen Scientific Products Inc—Steve Little	3773 Nw 126th Ave Ste, Coral Springs FL 33065	954-344-2006	R	4*	<.1
10	Acme Vial and Glass Company Inc—Debra Knowles	1601 Commerce Way, Paso Robles CA 93446	805-239-2666	R	3*	<.1
11	Pyromatics Corp—Andre Ezis	9321 Pineneedle Dr, Mentor OH 44060	440-352-3500	R	2*	<.1
12	Companion Star Memorials—Phyllis Janik	805 W Chicago Ave, Hinsdale IL 60521	630-561-1850	R	1*	<.1

TOTALS: SIC 3221 Glass Containers
Companies: 12 — 14,802 — 35.8

3229 Pressed & Blown Glass Nec

Rank	Company Name—Executive Officer	Address, City, State, Zip	Phone	Type	Fin	Empls
1	Libbey Inc—Stephanie A Streeter	PO Box 10060, Toledo OH 43699	419-325-2100	P	800	7.0
2	WKI Holding Company Inc—Joseph Mallof	5500 N Pearl St STE 40, Rosemont IL 60018	703-456-4700	R	515*	2.9
3	MacLean-Fogg Power Systems—Dominic DiFilippo	11411 Addison Ave, Franklin Park IL 60131	847-455-0014	S	200*	.3
4	Durand Glass Manufacturing Company Inc—Susan Saidman	901 S Wade Blvd, Millville NJ 08332	856-327-4800	S	75*	1.1
5	Dynasil Corporation of America—Steven Ruggieri	50 Hunt St, Watertown MA 02472	617-668-6855	P	47	.2
6	X-Cel Optical Co—Joseph Doescher	PO Box 420, Sauk Rapids MN 56379	320-251-8404	R	40*	.2
7	Steuben	667 Madison Ave, New York NY 10065	212-752-1441	S	34*	.2
8	Incom Inc—Anthony Detarando	294 Southbridge Rd, Charlton MA 01507	508-765-9151	R	27*	.2

Rank	Company Name—*Executive Officer*	Address, City, State, Zip	Phone	Type	Fin	Empls
9	Duck House Inc—*Mei Lien Chang*	4651 State St, Montclair CA 91763	909-628-0720	S	24*	<.1
10	Baron Glass Inc—*Ivan Morris*	1601 Diamond Springs R, Virginia Beach VA 23455	757-464-1131	R	23*	.3
11	United Lens Company Inc—*William Lannon*	259 Worcester St, Southbridge MA 01550	508-765-5421	R	22*	.2
12	Simon Pearce US Inc—*Simon Pearce*	109 Park Rd, Windsor VT 05089	802-674-6906	R	17*	.4
13	Fenton Art Glass Co—*George Fenton*	700 Elizabeth St, Williamstown WV 26187	304-375-6122	R	16*	.2
14	Neptune Communications LLC—*Donald Schroeder*	805 Broadway St Fl 3, Vancouver WA 98660	360-696-0983	R	14*	.2
15	West Coast Quartz Corp—*Johng Bae*	PO Box 14066, Fremont CA 94539	510-249-2160	R	13*	.1
16	United Process Inc—*Richard Mulcahy*	50 Almgren Dr, Agawam MA 01001	413-789-1770	R	13*	.1
17	Cat I Manufacturing Inc—*Robert Jaynes*	PO Box 208, South Elgin IL 60177	847-931-8986	R	11*	.1
18	Fiberoptics Technology Inc—*Keith Knowlton*	PO Box 286, Pomfret CT 06258	860-928-0443	R	11*	.1
19	Jeannette Shade And Novelty Co—*Kathleen Sarniak*	PO Box 99, Jeannette PA 15644	724-523-5567	R	9*	.1
20	Gillinder Brothers Inc—*Charles Gillinder*	PO Box 1007, Port Jervis NY 12771	845-856-5375	R	7*	.1
21	Leucos USA Inc	PO Box 7829, Edison NJ 08818	732-225-0010	R	7*	<.1
22	Optowaves Inc—*Chih-Ping Chung*	1982b Zanker Rd, San Jose CA 95112	408-441-1368	R	7*	.1
23	Allied Molded Products LLC—*Greg Miller*	PO Box 186, Palmetto FL 34220	941-723-3072	R	7*	.1
24	Fiberguide Industries Inc—*Theodore Rich*	1 Bay St Ste 1, Stirling NJ 07980	908-647-6601	R	7*	.1
25	Annieglass Inc—*Ann Morhauser*	310 Harvest Dr, Watsonville CA 95076	831-761-2041	R	6*	.1
26	Questar Corp (New Hope Pennsylvania)—*Earlene J Austin*	6204 Ingham Rd, New Hope PA 18938	215-862-5277	R	6*	<.1
27	Davis Lynch Glass Co—*R Lynch*	PO Box 4268, Morgantown WV 26504	304-599-2244	R	6*	.1
28	Performance Composites Inc—*Francis Hu*	1418 S Alameda St, Compton CA 90221	310-328-6661	R	6*	<.1
29	Appalachian Plastics Inc—*Betty Debusk*	PO Box 1044, Glade Spring VA 24340	276-429-2581	R	4*	<.1
30	John Krizay Inc—*William Stratton*	PO Box 974, Salem OH 44460	330-332-5607	R	3*	<.1
31	Ifiber Optix Inc—*Sanjeev Jaiswal*	51 Peters Canyon Rd, Irvine CA 92606	714-665-9796	R	3*	<.1
32	Alpha Precision Inc—*Kevin Brolsma*	PO Box 157, Yorkville IL 60560	630-553-7331	R	3*	<.1
33	Gould Technology LLC—*Beverly Hanna*	1121 Benfield Blvd Ste, Millersville MD 21108	410-987-5600	R	3*	<.1
34	Catamount Glassware Company Inc—*Alan Karyo*	309 County St, Bennington VT 05201	802-442-5438	R	2*	<.1
35	IDSI Products Of Georgia Inc—*Walter Nedriga*	PO Box 23208, Savannah GA 31403	912-234-5305	R	2*	<.1
36	United Silica Products Inc—*Lynn Kane*	3 Park Dr, Franklin NJ 07416	973-209-8854	R	2*	<.1
37	Hoya Corporation USA—*Hiroshi Suzuki*	3285 Scott Blvd, Santa Clara CA 95054	408-654-2200	R	2*	<.1
38	Pgc Acquisition LLC—*Tom Fiocco*	PO Box 515, Sagamore MA 02561	508-888-2344	R	1*	<.1
39	Industrial Fiberglass Inc—*Daryl Johnson*	1100 Main St, Melrose Park IL 60160	708-681-2707	R	1*	<.1
40	Canyon Materials Inc—*Chuck Wu*	6665 Nancy Ridge Dr, San Diego CA 92121	858-552-1188	R	1*	<.1
41	Glass Menagerie—*Anna McKinley*	105 S Vine St, O Fallon IL 62269	618-624-9926	R	1*	N/A
42	Commercial Optical Manufacturing Inc—*Kathy Runyon*	118 Bridge St, Huntington WV 25702	304-523-0193	R	1*	<.1
43	Optrand Inc—*Marek Wlodarczyk*	46155 Five Mile Rd, Plymouth MI 48170	734-451-3480	R	1*	<.1

TOTALS: SIC 3229 Pressed & Blown Glass Nec

					Fin	Empls
Companies: 43					1,999	14.6

3231 Products of Purchased Glass

Rank	Company Name—*Executive Officer*	Address, City, State, Zip	Phone	Type	Fin	Empls
1	Magna Mirrors Of America Inc—*James Brodie*	600 Wilshire Dr, Troy MI 48084	616-786-7000	S	4,607*	<.1
2	Benson Industries LLC—*Cami Cervantes*	1650 Nw Naito Pkwy Ste, Portland OR 97209	503-226-7611	R	2,085*	.6
3	Vitro America Inc—*Federico Sada*	PO Box 171173, Memphis TN 38187	901-767-7111	S	780*	3.0
4	Viracon/Curvlite Inc—*Don Pyatt* Apogee Enterprises Inc	800 Park Dr, Owatonna MN 55060	507-451-9555	S	697*	1.5
5	Harmon Auto Glass (Minneapolis Minnesota)—*Joseph T Deckman*	4000 Olson Memorial Hw, Minneapolis MN 55422		S	652*	3.0
6	Apogee Enterprises Inc—*Joseph S Puishys*	4400 W 78th St Ste 520, Minneapolis MN 55435	952-835-1874	P	583	3.6
7	Arc International North America (AINA)—*Susan Saideman*	901 S Wade Blvd, Millville NJ 08332		S	510*	4.2
8	PQ Corp—*William Sichko*	PO Box 840, Valley Forge PA 19482	610-651-4200	R	500*	1.6
9	CR Laurence Company Inc—*Donald E Friese*	PO Box 58923, Los Angeles CA 90058	323-588-1281	R	239*	.9
10	Viracon Georgia Inc—*Russell Huffer* Viracon Inc	8373 Zell Miller Pkwy, Statesboro GA 30458	912-871-3500	S	223*	.5
11	Viracon Inc—*Kelly Schuller* Apogee Enterprises Inc	PO Box 990, Owatonna MN 55060	507-451-9555	S	170	1.5
12	Gerresheimer Glass Inc—*Axel Herberg*	537 Crystal Ave, Vineland NJ 08360	856-692-3600	R	82*	1.2
13	Magna Mirrors North America LLC—*Mark Brushaber*	PO Box 96, Alto MI 49302	616-868-6122	S	77*	1.1
14	Naugatuck Glass Co	PO Box 71, Naugatuck CT 06770	203-729-4536	R	76*	.1
15	Lang-Mekra North America LLC—*Markus Reiter*	101 Tillessen Blvd, Ridgeway SC 29130	803-337-5264	R	60*	.3
16	Flex-O-Lite Inc—*Dave Gilchrist* Potters Industries Inc	50 Crestwood Executive, Saint Louis MO 63126		S	53*	.2
17	Larry Methvin Installations Inc—*Larry Methvin*	501 Kettering Dr, Ontario CA 91761	909-605-6468	R	51*	.4
18	Velvac Inc—*Jeff Porter*	2405 S Calhoun Rd, New Berlin WI 53151	262-786-0700	R	47*	.2
19	Schott North America Inc—*Gerry Fine*	555 Taxter Rd, Elmsford NY 10523	914-831-2200	S	47*	.1
20	Coastal Industries Inc—*William M Cobb*	PO Box 16091, Jacksonville FL 32245	904-642-3970	R	45*	.2
21	Radio Cap Company Inc—*Paul Laggy*	5335 Castroville Rd, San Antonio TX 78227	210-223-1115	R	44*	.8
22	Frank Fletcher Companies Ltd—*Frank Fletcher*	6301 Forbing Rd, Little Rock AR 72209	501-562-1000	R	34*	.2
23	Potters Industries Inc—*Scott Randolph*	PO Box 840, Valley Forge PA 19482	610-651-4700	R	33*	<.1
24	JE Berkowitz LP—*Tom Lynch*	PO Box 427, Pedricktown NJ 08067	856-456-7800	R	28*	.3
25	Coral Industries Inc—*Al Askew*	PO Box 40228, Tuscaloosa AL 35404	205-345-1013	R	27*	.2
26	Headwest Inc—*Louis Fideler*	15650 S Avalon Blvd, Compton CA 90220	310-532-5420	R	24*	.2
27	ShowerTek Inc—*Tom Christianson*	2775 Napa Valley Corpo, Napa CA 94558	707-224-1480	R	24*	<.1
28	Silverwood Products Inc—*Frank Fletcher* Frank Fletcher Companies Ltd	6301 Forbing Rd, Little Rock AR 72209	501-664-7416	S	22*	.2
29	Gardner Glass Products Inc—*Tommy Huskey*	PO Box 1570, North Wilkesboro NC 28659	336-651-9300	R	22*	.4
30	Christmas By Krebs Corp—*Eberhard Krebs*	3911 S Main St, Roswell NM 88203	575-624-2882	R	20*	.2
31	Pei Liquidation Co—*Robert Schneider*	700 Highland Rd E, Macedonia OH 44056	330-468-0700	R	19*	.2
32	Vacuum Process Technology Inc—*Ralph T Faber* Naugatuck Glass Co	70 Industrial Park Rd, Plymouth MA 02360	508-732-7200	S	19*	.1
33	Covega Corp—*Alex Cable*	10335 Guilford Rd, Jessup MD 20794	240-456-7100	R	19*	<.1
34	Oregon Glass Co—*Nick Sciola*	10450 Sw Ridder Rd, Wilsonville OR 97070	503-682-3846	R	19*	.2
35	Americana Art China Co—*James Puckett*	PO Box 310, Sebring OH 44672	330-938-6133	R	17*	<.1
36	J and B Manufacturing Corp—*Daniel Jaoudi*	2515 Industry St, Oceanside CA 92054	760-966-5800	R	17*	.2
37	Dacra Glass Inc—*Tom Hayth*	3333 N Commerce Dr, Muncie IN 47303	765-286-3855	S	15*	.1
38	Belletech Corp—*Arkaday Dorman*	PO Box 790, Bellefontaine OH 43311	937-599-3774	R	14*	.2
39	Virginia Mirror Company Inc—*Chris Beeler*	PO Box 5431, Martinsville VA 24115	276-632-9816	R	14*	.2
40	Ampac Enterprises Inc—*John Ham*	4621 192nd St E, Tacoma WA 98446	253-875-6900	R	13*	.2
41	Lenoir Mirror Co—*Drew Mayberry*	PO Box 1650, Lenoir NC 28645	828-728-3271	R	12*	.2
42	Swift Glass Company Inc—*Daniel Burke*	PO Box 879, Elmira NY 14902	607-733-7166	R	11*	.1
43	Accu-Glass LLC—*Clateo Castellini*	10765 Trenton Ave, Saint Louis MO 63132	314-423-0300	D	11*	.1

Note: An asterisk (*) indicates an estimated financial figure. The company type code used is as follows: R = Private, P = Public, S = Private Subsidiary, B = Public Subsidiary, D = Division, J = Joint Venture, I = Investment Fund.

COMPANY RANKINGS BY SALES WITHIN 4-DIGIT SIC

Rank	Company Name—*Executive Officer*	Address, City, State, Zip	Phone	Type	Fin	Empls
44	Flabeg Automotive Us Corp—*Charly Johnson*	851 3rd Ave, Brackenridge PA 15014	724-224-1800	R	10*	.1
45	Immco Diagnostics Inc—*William Maggio*	60 Pineview Dr, Buffalo NY 14228	716-691-0091	R	10*	.1
46	Elan Technology Inc—*P Argentinis*	PO Box 779, Midway GA 31320	912-880-3526	R	10*	.1
47	D and W Inc—*Anthony Warning*	941 Oak St, Elkhart IN 46514	574-264-9674	R	10*	.1
48	Thermoseal Industries LLC—*Kim Ciano*	400 Water St, Gloucester City NJ 08030	856-456-3109	R	9*	.1
49	Precision Electronic Glass Inc—*Phillip Rossi*	1013 Hendee Rd, Vineland NJ 08360	856-691-2234	R	8*	.1
50	Glass Dynamics Inc—*Robert Lankford*	8901 Us Hwy 220 Bus, Stoneville NC 27048	336-573-2393	R	7*	.1
51	Europtec USA Inc—*Kurt Ruefenacht*	423 Tuna St, Clarksburg WV 26301	304-624-7461	R	7*	.1
52	Blumcraft of Pittsburgh—*Myron Caplan*	460 Melwood Ave, Pittsburgh PA 15213	412-681-2400	R	7*	<.1
53	Janel Glass Company Inc—*David Utick*	2960 Marsh St, Los Angeles CA 90039	323-661-8621	R	6*	.1
54	Danny's Glass Inc—*Danny Edwards Sr*	112 Industry Dr, Yorktown VA 23693	757-867-8585	R	6*	.1
55	Andrews Glass Company Inc—*Dennis Courtney*	3740 N W Blvd, Vineland NJ 08360	856-692-4435	R	5*	<.1
56	Chemglass Inc—*Walter Surdam*	3800 N Mill Rd, Vineland NJ 08360	856-696-0014	R	5*	.2
57	Andrew Kolb and Son Ltd—*Claude Kolb*	728 E 136th St, Bronx NY 10454	212-684-2980	R	5*	.1
58	Techni-Glass Inc—*Pat Murphy*	916 Phipps Bend Rd, Surgoinsville TN 37873	423-345-4527	R	5*	.1
59	SWIBCO Inc—*John Pouleson*	4810 Venture Rd, Lisle IL 60532		R	5*	<.1
60	Standard Glass Corp—*James Huang*	14539 Marquardt Ave, Santa Fe Springs CA 90670	562-623-9822	R	5*	<.1
61	Francis L Freas Glass Works Inc—*Norma Ramey*	148 E 9th Ave, Conshohocken PA 19428	610-828-0430	R	3*	<.1
62	Golden Gate Glass and Mirror Company Inc—*Margaret Puent*	2011 Folsom St, San Francisco CA 94110	415-552-0220	R	3*	<.1
63	Bergin Glass Impressions Inc—*Michael Bergin*	2511 Napa Valley Ste, Napa CA 94558	707-224-0111	R	3*	<.1
64	Judson Studios—*Karen Judson*	200 S Ave 66, Los Angeles CA 90042	323-255-0131	R	2*	<.1
65	Dorothy C Thorpe LLC—*Gladys Alvarado*	12711 Ventura Blvd Ste, Studio City CA 91604	818-508-8100	R	2*	<.1
66	Midwest Tropical Inc—*Ken Burnett*	3420 W Touhy Ave, Lincolnwood IL 60712	847-679-6666	R	2*	<.1
67	Capri Industries Inc—*David Scalise*	PO Box 793, Morganton NC 28680	828-345-0216	R	2*	<.1
68	Klarmann Rulings Inc—*Christopher Wilmot*	480 Charles Bancroft H, Litchfield NH 03052	603-424-2401	R	1*	<.1
69	Fred Silver and Company Inc—*Martin Schlossberg*	1400 Broadway Fl 25, New York NY 10018	212-810-2800	R	1*	<.1
70	A-1 Shower Door Co—*Dennis Borm*	2019 S Ritchey St, Santa Ana CA 92705	714-258-3005	R	1*	<.1
71	Sabino Crystal Inc—*Richard Choucroun*	3701-3709 Main St, Houston TX 77002	713-528-5651	R	1*	<.1
72	Pressure Products Company Inc—*Peter Lalos*	4540 Washington St W, Charleston WV 25313	304-744-7871	R	1*	<.1
73	DB Kunz Inc—*Melinda Bowman*	PO Box 383, Bemidji MN 56619	218-751-4496	R	<1*	<.1
74	Pyraponic Industries Incorporated II	13435 S Main St Ste B, Los Angeles CA 90061	310-523-2225	R	N/A	<.1
75	Mika International Inc—*Jennifer Ma*	215 John Glenn Dr, Amherst NY 14228	716-854-1637	R	N/A	<.1

TOTALS: SIC 3231 Products of Purchased Glass
Companies: 75 — 12,202 — 29.5

3241 Cement—Hydraulic

Rank	Company Name—*Executive Officer*	Address, City, State, Zip	Phone	Type	Fin	Empls
1	Buzzi Unicem USA Inc—*Debbie Bahnick*	100 Brodhead Rd Ste 23, Bethlehem PA 18017	610-866-4400	R	37,669*	1.5
2	Ash Grove Cement Co—*Charles Sunderland*	PO Box 25900, Overland Park KS 66225	913-451-8900	R	11,846*	1.7
3	Lone Star Industries Inc—*Michael Clarke*	10401 N Meridian St St, Indianapolis IN 46290	317-706-3314	R	8,253*	.8
4	Holcim Inc—*Bernard Terver*	201 Jones Rd, Waltham MA 02451	781 647 2501	R	7,515*	2.2
5	Lafarge North America Inc—*Bruno Lafont*	12018 Sunrise Valley D, Reston VA 20191	703-480-3600	S	2,860*	10.9
6	Eagle Materials Inc—*Steven Rowley*	3811 Turtle Creek Blvd, Dallas TX 75219	214-432-2000	P	462	1.4
7	Capitol Aggregates Inc—*R Engberg*	PO Box 33240, San Antonio TX 78265	210-655-3010	R	404*	.5
8	California Portland Cement Co (Glendora California)—*Allen Hamblen*	PO Box 5025, Glendora CA 91740	626-852-6200	R	300*	.8
9	Lehigh Cement Company LLC—*Helmut Erhard*	7660 Imperial Way, Allentown PA 18195	610-366-4600	R	184*	2.2
10	Houston Cement Company LP—*Claudine Bhandari*	363 N Sam Houston Pkwy, Houston TX 77060	972-723-7274	R	163*	<.1
11	Giant Cement Holding Inc—*Duncan Gates*	320 Midland Pkwy Ste D, Summerville SC 29485	843-851-9898	S	156*	.8
12	Material Packaging Corp—*Steve Boyland*	PO Box B, Harrisonville MO 64701	816-380-4473	R	151*	2.5
13	Roanoke Cement Company LLC—*Aris Papadopoulos*	6071 Catawba Rd, Troutville VA 24175	540-992-1501	R	117*	.2
14	ESSROC Italcementi Group—*Jean Paul Meric*	3251 Bath Pike, Nazareth PA 18064	610-837-6725	S	86*	.1
15	Essroc Cement Corp—*Silvio Panseri*	3251 Bath Pke, Nazareth PA 18064	610-837-6725	R	83*	1.1
16	Keystone Cement Co—*Manuel Llop* Giant Cement Holding Inc	PO Box A, Bath PA 18014	610-837-1881	S	57*	.2
17	Aspen Masonry Inc—*James Griffen*	9241 4th St Nw, Albuquerque NM 87114	505-897-7099	R	30*	.3
18	Giant Cement Co—*Duncan Gage*	320 Midland Pkwy Ste D, Summerville SC 29485	843-851-9898	R	25*	.2
19	Heldenfels Enterprises Inc—*F Heldenfels*	5700 S Interstate 35, San Marcos TX 78666	512-396-2376	R	20*	.2
20	Cemex—*Gilberto Perez*	430 N Vineyard Ave Ste, Ontario CA 91764	909-974-5500	S	16*	.1
21	Cemex Cement Inc—*Lorenzo Zambrano*	920 Memorial City Way, Houston TX 77024	713-650-6200	S	15	N/A
22	Hercules Cement Company LP—*Jeffrey Lerch*	PO Box 69, Stockertown PA 18083	610-759-6300	R	14*	.1
23	Ash Grove Texas LP—*Todd Hinton*	PO Box 520, Midlothian TX 76065	972-723-2301	R	14*	.1
24	Sai Hydraulics Inc—*Mariano Pecorari*	168 E Ridge Rd Ste 106, Linwood PA 19061	610-497-0190	R	7*	<.1
25	Mutual-Target LLC—*Racquel Gates*	PO Box 2009, Bellevue WA 98009	425-452-2300	R	4*	<.1
26	Arizona Portland Cement Co—*James A Repman* California Portland Cement Co (Glendora California)	2400 N Central Ave Ste, Phoenix AZ 85004	602-271-0069	S	2*	<.1
27	TXI Riverside Cement Co	PO Box 51479, Ontario CA 91761	909-635-1800	S	1	N/A

TOTALS: SIC 3241 Cement—Hydraulic
Companies: 27 — 70,455 — 27.9

3251 Brick & Structural Clay Tile

Rank	Company Name—*Executive Officer*	Address, City, State, Zip	Phone	Type	Fin	Empls
1	Acme Brick Company Inc—*Dennis Knautz*	PO Box 425, Fort Worth TX 76101	817-332-4101	S	2,212*	2.6
2	First National Panel Company Inc—*Ricci D Null*	13290 Newlander Ave, Lindstrom MN 55045	651-314-4142	P	1,226	N/A
3	Redland Brick Inc—*Joseph Miles*	PO Box 160, Williamsport MD 21795	301-223-7700	R	197*	.3
4	Glen-Gery Corp—*Steve Matsick*	PO Box 7001, Reading PA 19610	610-374-4011	R	120*	.9
5	Praxair Surface Technologies Inc	39 Old Ridgebury Rd, Danbury CT 06810	317-240-2428	D	88*	.4
6	Robinson Brick Co—*Mark Stutz*	1845 W Dartmouth Ave, Englewood CO 80110	303-783-3000	R	35*	.6
7	Cherokee Brick and Tile Co—*Kenneth Sams*	PO Box 4567, Macon GA 31208	478-781-6800	R	32*	.3
8	Pine Hall Brick Company Inc—*W Steele*	PO Box 11044, Winston Salem NC 27116	336-721-7500	R	21*	.4
9	Jenkins Brick and Tile Company LLC—*Deborah Grier*	PO Box 91, Montgomery AL 36101	334-834-2210	R	19*	.3
10	Sioux City Brick and Tile Co—*Norman Mahoney*	PO Box 807, Sioux City IA 51102	712-258-6571	R	19*	.3
11	Old Virginia Brick Company Inc—*Cory Redifer*	PO Box 508, Salem VA 24153	540-389-2357	R	14*	.2
12	Tri-State Brick and Tile Company Inc—*Albert Baker*	PO Box 31768, Jackson MS 39286	601-981-1410	R	11*	.1
13	Lee Brick and Tile Co—*Don Perry*	PO Box 1027, Sanford NC 27331	919-774-4800	R	9*	.1
14	Stonehouse Building Products LLC—*Vince Suarace*	8025 Bluegrass Dr, Florence KY 41042	859-980-1040	R	8*	.1
15	Henry Brick Company Inc—*Ted Henry*	PO Box 850, Selma AL 36702	334-875-2600	R	7*	.1
16	Lawrenceville Brick Inc—*H Hays*	PO Box 45, Lawrenceville VA 23868	434-848-3151	R	7*	.1
17	American Pavers Consultants Inc—*Joseph Brito*	1251 Ne 48th St, Pompano Beach FL 33064	954-418-0000	R	6*	.1
18	Yankee Hill Brick Manufacturing Co—*David Murdock*	3705 S Coddington Ave, Lincoln NE 68522	402-477-6663	R	6*	.1
19	Potomac Valley Brick and Supply Co—*Alan Richardson*	PO Box 1309, Rockville MD 20849	240-499-2666	R	5*	.1

Rank	Company Name—*Executive Officer*	Address, City, State, Zip	Phone	Type	Fin	Empls
20	Acme Building Brands—*Dennis Knautz*	PO Box 425, Fort Worth TX 76107	817-332-4101	S	1*	2.9

TOTALS: SIC 3251 Brick & Structural Clay Tile
Companies: 20 ... 4,043 ... 9.6

3253 Ceramic Wall & Floor Tile

1	Dal-Tile International Inc—*Jacques Sardas*	PO Box 170130, Dallas TX 75217	214-398-1411	S	1,042*	8.0
2	American Marazzi Tile Inc—*Mauro Vandini*	359 Clay Rd, Mesquite TX 75182	972-226-0110	R	222*	.5
3	Florida Tile Industries Inc—*Emilio Mussini*	PO Box 447, Lakeland FL 33802	863-683-8936	S	144*	1.2
4	Summitville Tiles Inc—*David Johnson*	PO Box 73, Summitville OH 43962	330-223-1511	R	27*	.3
5	Florim USA Inc—*Giovanni Grossi*	300 International Blvd, Clarksville TN 37040	931-553-7548	R	21*	.4
6	Eleganza Tiles Inc—*Mike Darmawan*	3125 Coronado St, Anaheim CA 92806	714-224-1700	R	17*	<.1
7	Ironrock Capital Inc—*Guy Renkert*	PO Box 9240, Canton OH 44711	330-484-4887	R	12*	.1
8	Progressive Technology Inc—*Shannon Rogers*	4130 Citrus Ave Ste 17, Rocklin CA 95677	916-632-6715	R	5*	<.1
9	NEP Inc—*Dennis Rutledge*	810 E Saint Paul St, Litchfield MN 55355	320-693-7217	R	5*	<.1
10	Crossville Inc—*John Smith*	PO Box 1168, Crossville TN 38557	931-484-2110	R	4*	.3

TOTALS: SIC 3253 Ceramic Wall & Floor Tile
Companies: 10 ... 1,499 ... 10.7

3255 Clay Refractories

1	Riverside Clay Company Inc—*John Morris*	201 Truss Ferry Rd, Pell City AL 35128	205-338-3366	R	25*	.1
2	Bnz Materials Inc—*Kenneth Hunter*	6901 S Pierce St Ste 2, Littleton CO 80128	303-978-1199	R	20*	.2
3	Clay Endicott Products Co—*Ryan Parker*	PO Box 17, Fairbury NE 68352	402-729-3315	R	19*	.2
4	Universal Refractories Inc—*Walter Sylvester*	PO Box 97, Wampum PA 16157	724-535-4374	R	13*	.1
5	Commercial Brick Corp—*Bob Hartsock*	PO Box 1382, Wewoka OK 74884	405-257-6613	R	13*	.2
6	Diversified Thermal Solutions Inc—*B Grant Hunter*	4126 Delp St Ste 200, Memphis TN 38118	901-365-7650	P	11	N/A
7	Heater Specialists LLC—*T Haga*	PO Box 582707, Tulsa OK 74158	918-835-3126	R	11*	.1
8	Tyk America Inc—*Kenichi Sasaki*	301 Brickyard Rd, Clairton PA 15025	412-384-4259	R	11*	.1
9	Ncri Inc—*Thomas Shaffer*	3909 Station Rd, New Castle PA 16101	724-654-7711	R	9*	.1
10	Resco Products Inc—*Williams Brown*	2 Penn Center W Ste 43, Pittsburgh PA 15276	412-494-4491	R	8*	.1
11	Findlay Refractories Co—*Joe Hufnagel*	PO Box 517, Washington PA 15301	724-225-4400	R	7	.1
12	Vulcan Electric Co—*Michael Quick*	28 Endfield St, Porter ME 04068	207-625-3231	R	6*	.1
13	Holland Manufacturing Corp—*Kenneth Hoekstra*	PO Box 261, South Holland IL 60473	708-849-1000	R	5*	<.1
14	Owensboro Brick and Tile Co—*Nick Richard*	PO Box 907, Owensboro KY 42302	270-684-7268	R	5*	<.1
15	ITC Inc (Hunt Valley Maryland)—*Dennis Parker*	6 N Park Dr Ste 105, Hunt Valley MD 21030	410-825-2920	R	3*	<.1

TOTALS: SIC 3255 Clay Refractories
Companies: 15 ... 165 ... 1.3

3259 Structural Clay Products Nec

1	Pacific Clay Products Inc—*David Hollingsworth*	14741 Lake St, Lake Elsinore CA 92530	951-674-2131	R	70*	.2
2	Mission Clay Products Corp—*Owen Garrett*	PO Box 549, Corona CA 92878	951-277-4600	D	50*	.2
3	US Tile—*Barry Bridges*	909 W Railroad St, Corona CA 92882	951-737-0200	S	49*	.1
4	Hamilton Materials Inc—*Willis Hamilton*	345 W Meats Ave, Orange CA 92865	714-637-2770	R	21*	.2
5	Superior Clay Corp—*Elmer Mcclave*	PO Box 352, Uhrichsville OH 44683	740-922-4122	R	9*	.1
6	Clay Logan Products Co—*Richard Brandt*	PO Box 698, Logan OH 43138	740-385-2184	R	8*	.1
7	Coors Ceramicon Designs Inc—*Janet Comerford*	16000 Table Mountain P, Golden CO 80403	303-271-7000	R	7*	.1

TOTALS: SIC 3259 Structural Clay Products Nec
Companies: 7 ... 213 8

3261 Vitreous Plumbing Fixtures

1	Crane Plumbing LLC—*Jerry Vanhorn*	41 Cairns Rd, Mansfield OH 44903		R	168*	2.4
2	Globe Union Group Inc—*Dennis Dugas*	2500 Internationale Pk, Woodridge IL 60517	630-679-1420	R	153*	.2
3	Mansfield Plumbing Products LLC—*Adriana Bedoya*	PO Box 620, Perrysville OH 44864	419-938-5211	R	42*	.7
4	Cfpg Ltd—*Frank Feraco*	2500 International Pkw, Woodridge IL 60517	630-679-1420	R	38*	.7
5	A and J Washroom Accessories Inc—*Richard Rebusmen*	PO Box 4569, New Windsor NY 12553	845-562-3332	R	9*	.1
6	Peerless Pottery Inc—*John Bennett*	PO Box 5025, Rockport IN 47635	812-649-6430	R	1*	<.1

TOTALS: SIC 3261 Vitreous Plumbing Fixtures
Companies: 6 ... 411 ... 4.1

3262 Vitreous China Table & Kitchenware

1	Mikasa Inc—*Jeffrey Siegel*	12 Applegate Dr, Robbinsville NJ 08691		S	1,198*	3.4
2	MBI Inc—*Theodore R Stanley*	47 Richards Ave, Norwalk CT 06857	203-853-2000	R	400	.6
3	Windway Capital Corp—*Terry Kohler*	630 Riverfront Dr Ste, Sheboygan WI 53081	920-457-8600	R	138*	1.6
4	Decor Inc—*Richard Engel*	60 Cedar Ln, Englewood NJ 07631	201-569-1900	R	15*	.3
5	HF Coors China Co—*Dirck Schou*	1600 S Cherrybell Stra, Tucson AZ 85713	520-903-1010	D	4*	<.1
6	Racket Merchandise Co	713 Walnut St, Kansas City MO 64106	852-253-8106	R	3*	<.1

TOTALS: SIC 3262 Vitreous China Table & Kitchenware
Companies: 6 ... 1,758 ... 6.0

3263 Semivitreous Table & Kitchenware

1	Tag Trade Associates Group Ltd—*Karen Biedermann*	1730 W Wrightwood Ave, Chicago IL 60614	773-871-1300	R	28*	.1
2	Mackenzie-Childs LLC—*Lee Feldman*	107 Salem St, Union Springs NY 13160	315-364-7123	R	17*	.2
3	Zrike Co—*David G Zrike*	7 Fir Ct Door 2, Oakland NJ 07436	201-651-5158	R	14*	.1

TOTALS: SIC 3263 Semivitreous Table & Kitchenware
Companies: 3 ... 59 3

3264 Porcelain Electrical Supplies

1	Steward Inc—*Martin Rapp*	PO Box 510, Chattanooga TN 37401	423-867-4100	R	1,716*	.7
2	Hitachi Metals America Ltd—*Harry Tanaka*	2 Manhattanville Rd St, Purchase NY 10577	914-694-9200	R	161*	2.5
3	Cookson Precious Metals Div—*Stuart Daniels*	49 Pearl St, Attleboro MA 02703	774-203-1199	D	142*	2.3
4	NGK Ceramics USA Inc—*Shun Matsushita*	PO Box 390, Mooresville NC 28115	704-664-7000	S	113*	.4
5	Unifrax I LLC—*Garry Davies*	2351 Whirlpool St, Niagara Falls NY 14305	716-278-3800	R	74*	1.1
6	Porcelain Products Co—*Jonathan Whitmore*	981 Tyber Rd, Tiffin OH 44883	419-364-0113	R	40*	.4
7	Channel Industries Inc—*John Prizler*	839 Ward Dr, Santa Barbara CA 93111	805-967-0171	R	26*	.5
8	Lapp Insulators LLC—*John Hurshman*	130 Gilbert St, Le Roy NY 14482	585-768-6221	R	23*	.4
9	Du-Co Ceramics Co—*Reldon Cooper*	PO Box 568, Saxonburg PA 16056	724-352-1511	R	17*	.2
10	Locke Insulators Inc—*John Dippold*	2525 Insulator Dr, Baltimore MD 21230	410-347-1726	R	16*	.2
11	Hitachi Metals North Carolina Ltd—*Pat Barton*	1 Hitachi Metals Dr, China Grove NC 28023	704-855-2800	S	15*	.2

Note: An asterisk (*) indicates an estimated financial figure. The company type code used is as follows: R = Private, P = Public, S = Private Subsidiary, B = Public Subsidiary, D = Division, J = Joint Venture, I = Investment Fund.

COMPANY RANKINGS BY SALES WITHIN 4-DIGIT SIC

Rank	Company Name—*Executive Officer*	Address, City, State, Zip	Phone	Type	Fin	Empls
	Hitachi Metals America Ltd					
12	Victor Insulators Inc—*Andrew Schwalm*	280 Maple Ave, Victor NY 14564	585-924-2127	R	12*	.1
13	National Magnetics Group Inc—*Paul Oberbeck*	1210 Win Dr, Bethlehem PA 18017	610-867-7600	R	11*	.1
14	Tsc Pyroferric International Inc—*Tim Smith*	507 E Madison, Toledo IL 62468	847-249-4900	R	9*	.1
15	Reuel Inc—*Sue Davis*	PO Box 10561, Goldsboro NC 27532	919-734-0460	R	9*	.1
16	Metsch Refractories Inc—*Patricia Hays*	PO Box 268, Chester WV 26034	304-387-1067	R	8*	.1
17	V and S Clark Substations Inc—*Warren S Whitcomb*	3309 Hwy 31, Calera AL 35040	205-663-2411	R	7*	<.1
18	Ceramic Magnetics Inc—*Vernon Detlef*	16 Law Dr, Fairfield NJ 07004	973-227-4222	S	7*	.3
19	Ferronics Inc—*Timothy Reeder*	45 O Connor Rd, Fairport NY 14450	585-388-1020	R	4*	<.1
20	Maryland Lava Co—*Ernest Dinning*	PO Box 527, Bel Air MD 21014	410-838-4114	R	4*	.1
21	Permacor Inc—*Peter Tsoutsas*	9540 Tulley Ave, Oak Lawn IL 60453	708-422-3353	R	3*	<.1
22	Electro-Ceramic Industries—*Herbert Schlomann*	75 Kennedy St, Hackensack NJ 07601	201-342-2630	R	3*	<.1

TOTALS: SIC 3264 Porcelain Electrical Supplies
Companies: 22   2,418   9.8

3269 Pottery Products Nec

Rank	Company Name—*Executive Officer*	Address, City, State, Zip	Phone	Type	Fin	Empls
1	Lenox Corp—*Peter B Cameron*	PO Box 2006, Bristol PA 19007		R	452	2.1
2	Haeger Potteries—*Alexandra H Estes* Haeger Industries Inc	7 Maiden Ln, Dundee IL 60118		D	59*	.2
3	Haeger Industries Inc—*Alexandra Estes*	7 Maiden Ln, East Dundee IL 60118	847-426-3441	R	50*	.2
4	Eurokera North America Inc—*Bertrand Charpentier*	140 Southchase Blvd, Fountain Inn SC 29644	864-963-8082	R	28*	.1
5	Duncan Enterprises—*Larry Duncan*	5673 E Shields Ave, Fresno CA 93727	559-291-4444	R	24*	.2
6	CPS Technologies Corp—*Grant C Bennet*	PO Box 338, Chartley MA 02712	508-222-0614	P	21	.2
7	Selee Corp—*Ben Stocks*	700 Shepherd St, Hendersonville NC 28792	828-697-2411	R	20*	.2
8	Ferro Electronics Material Systems—*James F Kirsch*	6060 Parkland Blvd, Mayfield Heights OH 44124	216-875-5600	S	18*	.3
9	Marshall Pottery Inc—*Stefano Celletti*	PO Box 1839, Marshall TX 75671	903-927-5400	R	15*	.2
10	Hunter Manufacturing LLP—*Lesli Brosik*	201 W Loudon Ave, Lexington KY 40508	859-254-7573	R	13*	.1
11	Rowe Pottery Works Inc—*Justin Janisch*	404 England St, Cambridge WI 53523	608-423-3363	R	10*	.1
12	Bird Brain Inc—*Christine King*	52 E Cross St, Ypsilanti MI 48198	734-483-4536	R	9*	<.1
13	Gare Inc—*David Alaimo*	165 Rosemont St, Haverhill MA 01832	978-373-9131	R	6*	.1
14	General Porcelain Manufacturing Co—*Virginia Soltis*	PO Box 5005, Trenton NJ 08638	609-396-7588	R	6*	.1
15	Ceramo Company Inc—*Bernon Kasten*	PO Box 485, Jackson MO 63755	573-243-3138	R	5*	<.1
16	Co-Rect Products Inc—*Michael Pierce*	7105 Medicine Lake Rd, Minneapolis MN 55427	763-542-9200	R	4*	<.1
17	Ws Incorporated Of Manmouth—*Dong Chong*	521 W 6th Ave, Monmouth IL 61462	309-734-2161	R	3*	<.1
18	Art Klopfenstein Equipment Inc—*Jeffrey Penny*	PO Box 9057, Mansfield OH 44904	419-884-2900	R	<1*	<.1
19	C and L Manufacturing Enterprises Inc—*Thomas Lehnen*	2109 Holland St, Alton IL 62002	618-465-7623	R	<1*	<.1

TOTALS: SIC 3269 Pottery Products Nec
Companies: 19   743   4.1

3271 Concrete Block & Brick

Rank	Company Name—*Executive Officer*	Address, City, State, Zip	Phone	Type	Fin	Empls
1	Salina Concrete Products Inc—*Walter H Wulf Jr*	1100 W Ash St, Salina KS 67401	785-827-7281	S	588*	.6
2	EP Henry Corp—*JC Henry III*	PO Box 615, Woodbury NJ 08096	856-845-6200	R	224*	.3
3	Basalite Concrete Products LLC—*Scott Weber*	605 Industrial Blvd, Dixon CA 95620	707-678-1901	S	127*	.1
4	Old Castle Apg Northeast Inc—*Peter Kelly*	7920 Notes Dr, Manassas VA 20109	703-361-2777	R	125*	.4
5	Trenwyth Industries Inc—*Jay Toland* Old Castle Apg Northeast Inc	PO Box 438, Emigsville PA 17318	717-767-6868	S	64*	.2
6	Featherlite Building Products—*Edward Stout*	2801 E 3rd St, Amarillo TX 79104	806-373-6766	S	45	.3
7	County Materials Corp—*Tim Sonnentag*	PO Box 100, Marathon WI 54448	715-848-1365	R	38*	.6
8	Rcp Block and Brick Inc—*Michael Finch*	PO Box 579, Lemon Grove CA 91946	619-460-9101	R	32*	.3
9	Hanson Building Materials America-Hanson Brick and Tile—*Mike Donahue*	15720 John J Delaney D, Charlotte NC 28277	704-341-8750	S	24*	<.1
10	York Building Products Company Inc—*Robert Stewart*	PO Box 1708, York PA 17405	717-848-2831	R	24*	.2
11	RI Lampus Co—*DL Lampus*	PO Box 167, Springdale PA 15144	412-362-3800	R	18*	.1
12	JF Allen Co—*John Allen*	PO Box 2049, Buckhannon WV 26201	304-472-8890	R	18*	.4
13	Cranesville Block Company Inc—*John Tesiero*	1250 Riverfront Ctr, Amsterdam NY 12010	518-684-6000	R	15*	.2
14	Continental Cast Stone South Inc—*Dennis Bride*	22001 W 83rd St, Shawnee Mission KS 66227	913-422-7575	R	15*	.1
15	Lee Masonry Products Inc—*Carol Lee*	PO Box 3245, Bowling Green KY 42102	270-842-3472	R	13*	.1
16	Kirchner Block And Brick Inc—*Patrick Dubbert*	12901 St Charles Rock, Bridgeton MO 63044	314-291-3200	R	13*	.1
17	Basalite Div—*Scott Weber*	355 Greg St, Sparks NV 89431	775-358-1200	D	12*	.1
18	Amcon Block and Precast Inc—*David Pederson*	PO Box 546, Saint Cloud MN 56302	320-251-6030	R	10*	.1
19	Chandler Materials Co—*James Chandler*	5805 E 15th St, Tulsa OK 74112	918-836-9151	R	10*	.1
20	Higgins Brick Co—*Ronald Higgins*	PO Box 7000-167, Redondo Beach CA 90277		R	10*	.1
21	Valley View Industries HC Inc—*Howard Rynberk*	13834 Kostner Ave, Crestwood IL 60445	708-597-0885	R	7*	.1
22	Clifford Hampton Construction Inc—*Clifford Hampton*	1009 County Rd 172, Athens TN 37303	423-745-1352	R	5*	<.1
23	Orco Block Company Inc—*Richard Muth*	PO Box E, Stanton CA 90680	714-527-2239	R	1*	.2

TOTALS: SIC 3271 Concrete Block & Brick
Companies: 23   1,436   4.5

3272 Concrete Products Nec

Rank	Company Name—*Executive Officer*	Address, City, State, Zip	Phone	Type	Fin	Empls
1	Quikrete Companies Inc—*James Winchester*	3490 Piedmont Rd Ne, Atlanta GA 30305	404-634-9100	R	8,856*	3.8
2	Oldcastle Inc—*Mark Towe*	375 Northridge Rd Ste, Atlanta GA 30350	770-804-3363	S	6,373*	35.0
3	Oldcastle Precast Group—*Mark Schack* Oldcastle Inc	1002 15th St SW, Auburn WA 98001	253-833-2777	D	3,572*	5.0
4	Robertson's Ready Mix—*Dennis Troesh*	PO Box 3600, Corona CA 92878	951-685-2200	R	1,178*	1.4
5	Florida Rock Industries Inc—*Thompson Baker*	PO Box 4667, Jacksonville FL 32201	904-355-1781	S	1,081*	3.0
6	Wilbert Inc—*Greg Botener*	2913 Gardner Rd, Broadview IL 60155	708-865-1600	R	1,074*	1.2
7	American Concrete Products Inc US Concrete Inc	2925 Briarpark Dr Ste, Houston TX 77042	713-499-6200	S	790	2.9
8	Atlas-Tuck Concrete Inc—*Chris Okelly* US Concrete Inc	2112 W Bois D Arc, Duncan OK 73533		S	790	2.9
9	Beall Concrete Enterprises Inc US Concrete Inc	2925 Briarpark Dr Ste, Houston TX 77042	713-499-6200	S	790	2.9
10	Beall Industries Inc—*Eugene P Martineau* US Concrete Inc	2725 Premier St, Fort Worth TX 76111	817-831-3181	S	790	2.9
11	Beall Investment Corporation Inc US Concrete Inc	2925 Briarpark Dr Ste, Houston TX 77042	713-499-6299	S	790	2.9
12	Beall Management Inc US Concrete Inc	2925 Briar Park Dr Ste, Houston TX 77042	713-499-6200	S	790	2.9
13	Builder's Redi-Mix Inc	33469 W 14 Mile Rd, Farmington Hills MI 48331	517-372-9765	S	790	2.9

Rank	Company Name—Executive Officer	Address, City, State, Zip	Phone	Type	Fin	Empls
	US Concrete Inc					
14	BWB Inc—Jeff Spahr	3505 Auburn Rd, Auburn Hills MI 48321	248-788-8000	S	790	2.9
	US Concrete Inc					
15	Central Concrete Corp	755 Stockton Ave, San Jose CA 95126	408-293-6272	S	790	2.9
	US Concrete Inc					
16	Central Precast Concrete Inc—Larry Gielenfeldt	3049 Independence Dr S, Livermore CA 94551	925-960-8740	S	790	2.9
	US Concrete Inc					
17	Eastern Concrete Materials Inc—Michael Gentoso	475 Market St, Elmwood Park NJ 07407	201-797-7979	S	790	2.9
	US Concrete Inc					
18	Ready Mix Concrete Company of Knoxville—Eugene Martineau	1104 Springhill Rd, Knoxville TN 37914	865-524-3331	S	790	2.9
	US Concrete Inc					
19	Sierra Precast Inc—James C Felice	1 Live Oak Ave, Morgan Hill CA 95037	408-779-1000	S	790	2.9
	US Concrete Inc					
20	Smith Pre-Cast Inc—Michael W Harlan	2410 West Broadway Rd, Phoenix AZ 85041	602-268-0228	S	790*	2.9
	US Concrete Inc					
21	Superior Materials Inc—Jeff Spahr	3505 Auburn Rd, Auburn Hills MI 48321	248-788-8000	S	790	2.9
	US Concrete Inc					
22	Superior Concrete Materials Inc—Michael Harlan	2925 Briarpark Ste 105, Houston TX 77042	713-499-6200	S	701*	2.6
	US Concrete Inc					
23	Titan Concrete Industries Inc	2925 Briarpark Ste 105, Houston TX 77042	713-499-6200	S	701*	2.6
	US Concrete Inc					
24	USC Atlantic Inc—Michael Harlan	2925 Briarpark Ste 105, Houston TX 77042	713-499-6200	S	701*	2.6
	US Concrete Inc					
25	USC GP Inc	2925 Briarpark Ste 105, Houston TX 77042	713-499-6200	S	701*	2.6
	US Concrete Inc					
26	USC Limited Partnership Inc	2925 Briarpark Ste 105, Houston TX 77042	713-499-6200	S	701*	2.6
	US Concrete Inc					
27	USC Management Company LLC	2925 Briarpark Ste 105, Houston TX 77042	713-499-6200	S	701*	2.6
	US Concrete Inc					
28	USC Michigan Inc	2925 Briarpark Ste 105, Houston TX 77042	713-499-6200	S	701*	2.6
	US Concrete Inc					
29	Ameron International Corp—James S Marlen	245 S Los Robles Ave, Pasadena CA 91101	626-683-4000	P	503	2.8
30	US Concrete Inc—William J Sandbrook	2925 Briarpark Ste 105, Houston TX 77042	713-499-6200	P	456	2.0
31	Veneer Stone LP—Nicole Rex	1720 Couch Dr, Mckinney TX 75069	972-542-5701	R	350*	.2
32	RMC South Florida Inc—Richard Buckelew	5325 E State Rd 64, Bradenton FL 34208	941 748 1280	R	277*	.5
33	Unistress Corp—Perri Petricca	PO Box 1145, Pittsfield MA 01202	413-499-1441	S	262*	.3
34	Dura-Stress Inc—Wes Atkison	PO Box 490779, Leesburg FL 34749	352-787-1422	R	233*	.4
35	Coreslab Structures Inc (Marshall Missouri)	PO Box 996, Marshall MO 65340	660-886-3306	R	231*	.2
36	Adams Products Co—Colin Claimpett	333 N Green St Ste 201, Greensboro NC 27401	336-275-9114	S	177*	.3
	Oldcastle Inc					
37	Metromont Corp—Richard Pennell	PO Box 2486, Greenville SC 29602	864-295-0295	R	160*	.5
38	Sika Corp—Paul Schuler	201 Polito Ave, Lyndhurst NJ 07071		S	130	1.
39	Trap Rock Industries Inc—William Stavola	PO Box 419, Kingston NJ 08528	609-924-0300	R	120*	.6
40	Monier Lifetile LLC—Michael Penny	7575 Irvine Ctr Dr Ste, Irvine CA 92618	949-756-1605	S	101*	1.4
41	Tulsa Dynaspan Inc—Phil Rush	1601 E Houston St, Broken Arrow OK 74012	918-258-1549	S	100*	.2
42	Clark - Pacific Corp—Robert Clark	1980 S River Rd, West Sacramento CA 95691	916-371-0305	R	83*	.5
43	Columbia Machine Inc—Rick Goode	PO Box 8950, Vancouver WA 98668	360-694-1501	R	71*	.5
44	Premarc Corp—Daniel Marsh	7505 E M 71, Durand MI 48429	989-288-2661	R	63*	.2
45	Florida Engineered Construction Products Corpora—William Kardash	PO Box 24567, Tampa FL 33623	813-621-4641	R	54*	.4
46	Spancrete Machinery Corp—John Nagy	N16W23415 Stoneridge, Waukesha WI 53188	414-290-9000	R	53*	.7
47	Concrete Safety Systems LLC—James Milburn	9190 Old Rte 22, Bethel PA 19507	717-933-4107	R	47*	<.1
48	Foley Products Co—Frank Foley	PO Box 2447, Columbus GA 31902	706-563-7882	R	45*	.3
49	Gulf Coast Pre-Stress Inc—Mike Spruill	PO Box 825, Pass Christian MS 39571	228-452-9486	R	45*	.2
50	Finfrock Industries Inc—Robert Finfrock	PO Box 607754, Orlando FL 32860	407-293-4000	R	43*	.2
51	US Precast Corp—Alex De Bogory Jr	8351 NW 93rd St, Medley FL 33166	305-885-8471	R	38*	.3
52	Beatrice Concrete Co—Jamie Renshaw	400 Scott St, Beatrice NE 68310	402-223-4289	R	38*	.1
53	Centurion Products Inc—Tim Pardue	50 Van Buren St, Nashville TN 37208	615-256-6694	R	35*	.3
54	WG Block Co—Larry Wolfson	PO Box 280, Bettendorf IA 52722	563-823-2080	R	32*	.2
55	Spancrete Industries Inc—John Nagy	PO Box 828, Waukesha WI 53187	414-290-9000	S	32*	<.1
	Spancrete Machinery Corp					
56	Smith-Midland Corp—Rodney I Smith	PO Box 300, Midland VA 22728	540-439-3266	P	32	.1
57	Fabcon Inc—Michael Lejeune	6111 Hwy 13 W, Savage MN 55378	952-890-4444	R	31*	.3
58	Hanson Pressure Pipe Inc—Clifford Hahne	PO Box 569470, Dallas TX 75356	815-389-4800	R	30*	.5
59	Jensen Enterprises Inc—Donald Jensen	825 Steneri Way, Sparks NV 89431	775-352-2700	R	30*	.5
60	Blakeslee Prestress Inc—Mario Bertolini	PO Box 510, Branford CT 06405	203-481-5306	R	30*	.3
61	Gate Concrete Products Company Inc—Joseph Luke	402 Zoo Park Way, Jacksonville FL 32226	904-757-0860	R	28*	.3
62	Wausau Tile Inc—Brian Burelle	PO Box 1520, Wausau WI 54402	715-359-3121	R	28*	.3
63	Gage Brothers Concrete Products Inc—Tom Kelley	PO Box 1028, Sioux Falls SD 57101	605-336-1180	R	28*	.2
64	J W Peters Inc—Ken Burns	500 W Market St, Burlington WI 53105	262-763-2401	S	27*	.2
65	Bexar Concrete Works I Ltd—Marylyn House	PO Box 700250, San Antonio TX 78270	210-497-3773	R	27*	.2
66	RMX Holdings Inc—Bradley E Larson	4602 E Thomas Rd, Phoenix AZ 85018	602-249-5814	P	27	.2
67	United Precast Inc—John Ellis	PO Box 991, Mount Vernon OH 43050	740-393-1121	R	25*	.2
68	Isabel Bloom LLC—Cathy Nevins	736 Federal St Ste 210, Davenport IA 52803	563-333-2040	R	25*	.2
69	Stresscon Corp—David Bourgault	PO Box 15129, Colorado Springs CO 80935	719-390-5041	R	24*	.4
70	Dutchland Inc—Katie Kauffman	PO Box 549, Gap PA 17527	717-442-8282	R	23*	.1
71	Coreslab Structures Inc—Lou Franciosa	150 W Placentia Ave, Perris CA 92571	951-943-9119	R	23*	.2
72	Wareing Athon and Co—Merrell Athon	3355 W Alabama St Ste, Houston TX 77098	713-222-8804	R	21*	.4
73	Flexicore Of Texas—Joseph Phillips	PO Box 450049, Houston TX 77245	281-437-5700	R	21*	.2
74	Hanson Pipe and Precast—J Thomas Holton	300 E John Carpenter F, Irving TX 75062	972-653-5500	S	20	.2
75	A C Miller Concrete Products Inc—David Miller	PO Box 199, Spring City PA 19475	610-948-4600	R	20*	.2
76	Oldcastle Apg South Inc—Colin Clampett	PO Box 14489, Greensboro NC 27415	336-375-5656	R	19*	.2
77	Fort Miller Service Corp—John Hedbring	PO Box 98, Schuylerville NY 12871	518-695-5000	R	19*	.4
78	Terre Hill Silo Company Inc—A Martin	PO Box 10, Terre Hill PA 17581	717-445-3100	R	19*	.2
79	Creative Stone Manufacturing Inc—Melton Bacon	11191 Calabash Ave, Fontana CA 92337	909-357-8295	R	19*	.3
80	American Building Components Co (Nicholasville Kentucky)—AR Ginn	PO Box 310, Nicholasville KY 40356	859-887-4406	S	18*	<.1
81	Nitterhouse Concrete Products Inc—Mark Taylor	PO Box 2013, Chambersburg PA 17201	717-264-6154	R	18*	.2
82	Central Pre-Mix Prestress Co—Ron Schlerf	PO Box 3366, Spokane WA 99220	509-536-3300	S	17*	.2
83	Brooks Products Inc—Mike Heitman	1850 Parco Ave, Ontario CA 91761	909-947-7470	R	17*	<.1

Note: An asterisk (*) indicates an estimated financial figure. The company type code used is as follows: R = Private, P = Public, S = Private Subsidiary, B = Public Subsidiary, D = Division, J = Joint Venture, I = Investment Fund.

COMPANY RANKINGS BY SALES WITHIN 4-DIGIT SIC

Rank	Company Name—Executive Officer	Address, City, State, Zip	Phone	Type	Fin	Empls
84	Pre-Cast Specialties Inc—Fred Cianelli	1380 Ne 48th St, Pompano Beach FL 33064	954-781-4040	R	17*	.2
85	National Precast Inc—Nazzareno Piccinini	PO Box 48, Roseville MI 48066	586-294-6430	R	16*	.2
86	De Am-Ron Building Systems LLC—Greg Clark	PO Box 217, Owensboro KY 42302	270-684-6226	R	16*	.2
87	Csds LLC—Robert Lupold	301 Pleasant Dr, Dallas TX 75217	214-398-0999	R	16*	.2
88	East Texas Precast Co—James Harlow	PO Box 579, Waller TX 77484	281-463-0654	R	16*	.2
89	Texas Concrete Co—Paul Guthrie	PO Box 1070, Victoria TX 77902	361-573-9145	R	15	.2
90	Hamilton Form Company Ltd—Jonathan Daily	PO Box 99225, Fort Worth TX 76199	817-590-2111	R	15*	.1
91	Valley Building Supply Inc—Joseph Mullen	210 Stone Spring Rd, Harrisonburg VA 22801	540-434-6725	R	15*	.3
92	Seminole Precast Manufacturing Inc—Martin Neiswander	PO Box 531059, Debary FL 32753	386-668-7745	R	13*	.1
93	Lindsay Concrete Products Company Inc—Roland Lindsay	PO Box 578, Canal Fulton OH 44614	330-854-4511	R	12*	.1
94	Welch Brothers Inc—David Welch	PO Box 749, Elgin IL 60121	847-741-6134	R	12*	.1
95	Willis Construction CoInc—Lawrence Willis	2261 San Juan Hwy, San Juan Bautista CA 95045	831-623-2900	R	12*	.1
96	Rock-Tred Corp—Dan Moran	3415 Howard St, Skokie IL 60076	847-673-8200	R	12*	<.1
97	Guyer's Superior Walls—Steve Hunter	580 Schommer Dr, Hudson WI 54016	715-381-2500	R	12*	.1
98	Northern Concrete Pipe Inc—William Washabaugh	401 Kelton St, Bay City MI 48706	989-892-3545	R	12*	.1
99	Avila's Garden Art—Ralph Avila	14608 Merrill Ave, Fontana CA 92335	909-350-4546	R	12*	.1
100	J and R Slaw Inc—Robert Slaw	PO Box D, Bowmanstown PA 18030	610-852-2020	R	12*	.1
101	Advanced Cast Stone Inc—Eddie Lesok	115 Lee St, Fort Worth TX 76140	817-572-0018	R	12*	.1
102	Utility Vault Company Inc—Gary Venn Oldcastle Precast Group	PO Box 588, Auburn WA 98071	253-839-3500	D	12	.1
103	Royal Enterprise America Inc—Bill Makens	PO Box 430, Stacy MN 55079	651-462-2130	R	11*	.2
104	Conart Precast LLC—Tammy Teel	PO Box 335, Cobb GA 31735	229-853-5000	R	11*	.1
105	Cfs Forming Structure Company Inc—Vera Salvatore	21120 Milsa St, San Antonio TX 78256	210-698-9252	R	11*	.1
106	Structurecast—Brent Dezember	8261 Mccutchen Rd, Bakersfield CA 93311	661-833-4490	R	10*	.1
107	MBO Precast Inc—Jeff Opachinski	4 Marion Dr, Carver MA 02330	508-866-6900	R	10*	.1
108	Royal Concrete Pipe Inc—Bill Makens	PO Box 430, Stacy MN 55079	651-462-2130	R	10*	.1
109	Wilbert Funeral Services Inc—William Colson	PO Box 147, Forest Park IL 60130	708-865-1600	R	10*	.1
110	Manufactured Concrete Ltd—Carlos Cerna	6106 Fm 3009, Schertz TX 78154	210-690-1705	R	9*	.2
111	Lambert Corporation Florida—Steven Meyer	20 Coburn Ave, Orlando FL 32805	407-841-2940	R	9*	<.1
112	Fayblock Materials Inc—Richard Allen	PO Box 1867, Fayetteville NC 28302	910-323-9198	R	8*	.1
113	Murphy Wall Products International Inc—Joan Benton	2032 N Commerce St, Fort Worth TX 76164	817-626-1987	R	7*	.1
114	Calumet Flexicore Corp—Elizabeth Carlsson	24 Marble St, Hammond IN 46327	219-932-3340	R	7*	.1
115	Brown-Wilbert Inc—Chris Brown Wilbert Funeral Services Inc	2280 Hamline Ave N, Saint Paul MN 55113	651-631-1234	S	7*	.1
116	Stellar Materials Inc—Bernard Mintz	7777 Glades Rd Ste 200, Boca Raton FL 33434	561-330-9300	R	7*	<.1
117	Bomat Ltd—Jeffrey Deer	91-400 Komohana St, Kapolei HI 96707	808-673-2000	R	7*	<.1
118	Carolina Prestress Corporation Of Lake City Inc—Scott Askins	PO Box 160, Lake City SC 29560	843-394-3545	R	6*	<.1
119	Pretech Corp—William Bundschuh	8934 Woodend Rd, Kansas City KS 66111	913-441-4600	R	6*	<.1
120	Prestressed Casting Co—William Johnson	PO Box 3499, Springfield MO 65808	417-869-7350	R	6*	.1
121	American Fiberglass Products Inc—Greg Farris	PO Box 778, Double Springs AL 35553	205-489-3133	R	5*	.1
122	Mershon Concrete LLC—Randolph Mershon	PO Box 254, Bordentown NJ 08505	609-587-1346	R	5*	<.1
123	Dependable Bagging Company Inc—Bradley Simonson	264 Hord St, Harahan LA 70123	504-733-8650	R	4*	<.1
124	Texas Cement Products Inc—Richard Doty	PO Box 920726, Houston TX 77292	713-682-8411	R	4*	<.1
125	GMC Inc—Peter Terreri	1445 Ford Rd, Bensalem PA 19020	215-638-4400	R	3*	<.1
126	Greenbrier Valley Memorial Vault Company Inc—Arthur Baker	PO Box 188, Ronceverte WV 24970	304-647-4669	R	1*	<.1
127	Rolf Stone Inc—Philip Rolf	518 Hodge St, Newport KY 41071	859-581-9407	R	1*	<.1

TOTALS: SIC 3272 Concrete Products Nec
Companies: 127 43,764   134.9

3273 Ready-Mixed Concrete

Rank	Company Name—Executive Officer	Address, City, State, Zip	Phone	Type	Fin	Empls
1	Lyman-Richey Corp—Patrick Gorup	4315 Cuming St, Omaha NE 68131	402-558-2727	R	10,160*	.4
2	Kiewit Corp—Bruce Grewcock	3555 Farnam St, Omaha NE 68131	402-342-2052	S	10,000	N/A
3	Silver State Materials Corp—Steve Hill	4005 Dean Martin Dr, Las Vegas NV 89103	702-893-6557	R	8,300*	.1
4	JF Shea Company Inc—Peter Shea	655 Brea Canyon Rd, Walnut CA 91789	909-594-9500	R	2,355*	2.0
5	Transit Mix Concrete Co—Carl Herkind Continental Materials Corp	PO Box 1030, Colorado Springs CO 80901	719-475-0700	S	2,299*	.4
6	Springfield Ready Mix Co—Walter H Wulf Jr Monarch Cement Co	2836 W Division St, Springfield MO 65802	417-862-9203	S	2,134*	.6
7	Superior Ready Mix Concrete LP—Larry Cowne	1508 Mission Rd, Escondido CA 92029	760-745-0556	R	1,299*	.7
8	Rinker Materials Corp—David Clarke	6560 Langfield Rd Bldg, Houston TX 77092		R	1,089*	10.5
9	Shockey Precast Group—Don Cooper	PO Box 2530, Winchester VA 22604	540-667-7700	R	1,088*	.3
10	Lafarge Construction Materials (Albuquerque New Mexico)—Bruno Lafont	1500 N Renaissance Blv, Albuquerque NM 87107	505-343-7800	D	644*	.2
11	Concrete Materials Inc—Walter H Wulf Jr Monarch Cement Co	9900 W 75th St, Overland Park KS 66204	913-342-7700	S	643*	.6
12	APAC-Mississippi Inc—Doug Black	PO Box 24508, Jackson MS 39225	601-376-4000	D	563*	.4
13	Virginia Concrete Company Inc—Diggs Bishop	PO Box 666, Springfield VA 22151	703-354-7100	D	383	.2
14	Grand Rapids Gravel Co—Andrew Dykema	PO Box 9160, Grand Rapids MI 49509	616-538-9000	R	374*	.1
15	Wingra Stone Company Inc—Robert M Shea	PO Box 44284, Madison WI 53744		R	374*	.1
16	A Teichert and Son Inc—Judson T Riggs	3500 American River Dr, Sacramento CA 95864	916-484-3011	R	333*	2.5
17	Pennsy Supply Inc—Michael Lundin	1001 Paxton St, Harrisburg PA 17104	717-233-4511	D	304*	.5
18	Thomas Concrete of Georgia Inc—Johnny Senter	2500 Cumberland Pkwy S, Atlanta GA 30339	770-431-3300	R	299*	.7
19	Edw C Levy Co—Edward Levy	9300 Dix, Dearborn MI 48120	313-843-7200	R	294*	1.2
20	Prairie Material Sales Inc—Alan Oremus	PO Box 1123, Bridgeview IL 60455	708-458-0400	R	248*	1.5
21	JFShea CoInc—John Shea	PO Box 494519, Redding CA 96049	909-594-9500	R	157*	2.6
22	Mrm Holdings LLC—Jim Anderson	5745 N Scottsdale Rd S, Scottsdale AZ 85250	480-607-3999	R	143*	.2
23	Cemex Construction Materials LP—Gilberto Perez	840 Gessner Rd, Houston TX 77024	713-650-6200	R	143*	2.5
24	B and B Excavating Inc—Vaughn Pack	PO Box 1729 Drawer 249, Edwards CO 81632	970-926-3311	R	140*	<.1
25	Irving Materials Inc—Ronald Davis	8032 N State Rd 9, Greenfield IN 46140	317-326-3101	R	131*	2.0
26	Shelby Gravel Inc—Philip Haehl	PO Box 242, Shelbyville IN 46176	317-398-4485	R	128*	.2
27	Monarch Cement Co—Walter H Wulf Jr	PO Box 1000, Humboldt KS 66748	620-473-2222	P	121	.6
28	Continental Materials Corp—James G Gidwitz	200 S Wacker Dr Ste 40, Chicago IL 60606	312-541-7200	P	114	.6
29	Suzio York Hill—Leonardo Suzio	975 Westfield Rd, Meriden CT 06450	203-237-8421	R	84*	.1
30	Central Pre-Mix Concrete Co—Mark Murphy	PO Box 3366, Spokane WA 99220	509-534-6221	R	49*	.7
31	Monarch Cement of Iowa Inc—Jerry Green Monarch Cement Co	5200 Park Ave, Des Moines IA 50321	515-243-8176	S	45*	<.1
32	Antioch Building Materials Co—Susan Larsen	1375 California Ave, Pittsburg CA 94565	925-432-0171	R	42*	<.1
33	Cemex El Paso Inc—Bill Poole	1 Mckelligon Canyon Rd, El Paso TX 79930	915-565-4681	R	40*	.7
34	Eagle Precast Co—Bernd Scheifele	6087 W 5400 S, Salt Lake City UT 84110	801-966-1060	R	40*	.2
35	Island Ready-Mix Concrete Inc—Francis Kuhn	91-047 Hanua St, Kapolei HI 96707	808-682-1305	S	40*	<.1

Rank	Company Name—Executive Officer	Address, City, State, Zip	Phone	Type	Fin	Empls
36	High Grade Materials Co—James Sturrus	9266 Snows Lake Rd, Greenville MI 48838	616-754-5545	R	37*	.1
37	Kuhlman Corp (Toledo Ohio)—Tim Goligoski	1845 Indian Wood Cir, Maumee OH 43537	419-897-6000	R	35*	.2
38	Moraine Materials Co—George Kling Jr	1400 Commerce Center D, Franklin OH 45005	937-743-0650	R	35*	<.1
39	Ready-Mix Concrete Co (Rochester Minnesota)—Brandon Mc- Neil	412 2nd Ave NW, Rochester MN 55901	507-289-4023	R	34*	.1
40	County Concrete Corp—John Crimi	PO Box F, Kenvil NJ 07847	973-584-7122	R	31*	.1
41	Campbell Concrete and Materials LP—Scott Ducoff	105 E Boothe St, Cleveland TX 77327	281-592-5201	R	28*	.5
42	Illinois Cement Co—Wayne Emmer	1601 Rockwell Rd, La Salle IL 61301	815-224-2112	S	27*	.2
43	Mmc Materials Inc—Rodney Grogan	PO Box 2569, Madison MS 39130	601-898-4000	R	27*	.5
44	Consumers Concrete Corp—Stephen Thomas	PO Box 2229, Kalamazoo MI 49003	269-342-0136	R	27*	.5
45	Metro Ready Mix Concrete LLC—David Liles	1136 2nd Ave N, Nashville TN 37208	615-255-1900	R	25*	.2
46	Ozinga Illinois RMC Inc—Richard DeBoer	19001 S Old LaGrange R, Mokena IL 60448	708-326-4200	R	21*	.2
47	Central Concrete Supply Company Inc—Michael Harlan	755 Stockton Ave, San Jose CA 95126	408-293-6272	S	20*	.2
48	Chaney Enterprises LP—Patsy Bergquist	PO Box 548, Waldorf MD 20604	301-932-5000	R	20*	.4
49	Mcc Inc—Joseph Murphy	PO Box 1137, Appleton WI 54912	920-749-3360	R	18*	.3
50	Binggeli Rock Products Inc—Deanna Binggeli	PO Box 98, Heber City UT 84032	435-654-7480	R	18*	<.1
51	Ready Mixed Concrete Co—Ron Henley	PO Box 2290, Denver CO 80201	303-292-1771	R	17*	.2
52	Anderson Concrete Corp—Doug Anderson	PO Box 398, Columbus OH 43216	614-443-0123	R	16*	.2
53	Construction Dynamics Inc—John Silvi	355 Newbold Rd, Fairless Hills PA 19030	215-295-0777	R	16*	.1
54	Jones And Sons Inc—Darrell Jones	PO Box 2357, Washington IN 47501	812-254-4731	R	16*	.1
55	Medina Supply Co—Jerry Schwab	PO Box 400, Dover OH 44622	330-723-3681	R	15*	.3
56	Heck Enterprises Inc—Wallace Heck	5415 Choctaw Dr, Baton Rouge LA 70805	225-356-2481	R	15*	.2
57	Builder's Concrete and Supply Company Inc—Gus Nuckols	9170 E 131st St, Fishers IN 46038	317-570-6201	R	15*	.1
58	Carew Concrete and Supply Company Inc—Garrett Carew	1811 W Edgewood Dr, Grand Chute WI 54913	920-731-9771	R	14*	.1
59	Elmer Larson LLC—JS Larson	21218 Airport Rd, Sycamore IL 60178	815-895-4437	R	14*	.1
60	Coyote Gravel Products Inc—Anthony Villegas	PO Box 12275, Albuquerque NM 87195	505-877-3830	R	13*	.1
61	Hardaway Concrete Company Inc—Page Morris	PO Box 4128, Columbia SC 29240	803-254-4350	R	13*	.1
62	Gary Bale Redi-Mix Concrete Inc—William Bochman	16131 Construction Cir, Irvine CA 92606	949-786-9441	R	13*	.1
63	Kuert Concrete Inc—Stephen Fidler	3402 Lincoln Way W, South Bend IN 46628	574-232-9911	R	12*	.1
64	Michigan Foundation Company Inc—Raynold Schmick	PO Box 6349, Plymouth MI 48170	734-357-2119	R	12*	.1
65	Rockville Fuel And Feed Company Inc—James Ward	PO Box 1707, Rockville MD 20849	301-762-3988	R	12*	.1
66	Dayton Sand and Gravel Inc—Russell Keene	928 Goodwins Mills Rd, Dayton ME 04005	207-499-2306	R	12*	.1
67	Lrm Industries Inc—Stephen Glass	PO Box 4150, Lawrence KS 66046	785-843-1706	R	12*	.1
68	Dorsett Brothers Concrete Supply Inc—Bill Dorsett	PO Box 5766, Pasadena TX 77508	281-487-0264	R	11*	.1
69	Delaware Valley Concrete Company Inc—Mario Diliberto	PO Box 457, Hatboro PA 19040	215-675-8900	R	11*	.1
70	Arizona Materials LLC—Richard Hrubes	3636 S 43rd Ave, Phoenix AZ 85009	602-278-4444	R	11*	.1
71	St Henry Tile Company Inc—Robert Homan	PO Box 318, Saint Henry OH 45883	419-678-4168	R	11*	.1
72	Metro Products And Construction Inc—G Pleasant	PO Box 470, Fayetteville NC 28302	910-483-2525	R	10*	.1
73	Van Der Vaart Inc—Michael Harvey	PO Box 490, Sheboygan WI 53082	920-459-2400	R	10*	.1
74	Crider And Shockey Inc—James Shockey	PO Box 4099, Winchester VA 22604	540-665-3279	R	9*	.1
75	Jamo Inc—Thomas Peck	8850 Nw 79th Ave, Medley FL 33166	305-885-3444	S	9*	.1
76	Janesville Sand and Gravel Co—Goodwin Lyons	PO Box 427, Janesville WI 53547	608-754-7701	R	9*	.1
77	Seville Central Mix Corp—Peter Scalamandre	157 Albany Ave, Freeport NY 11520	516-868-3000	R	9*	.1
78	Buzzi Unicem Readymix LLC—Philip Palczer	1029 John A Denie Rd, Memphis TN 38134	901-386-8911	R	9*	.1
79	Metro Materials Inc—Perry Ferrell	2174 E Person Ave, Memphis TN 38114	901-324-3894	S	8*	.1
80	WF Saunders and Sons Inc—Sherman Saunders	PO Box A, Nedrow NY 13120	315-469-3217	R	8*	.1
81	Spragues' Rock And Sand Co—Michael Toland	230 Longden Ave, Irwindale CA 91706	626-445-2125	R	8*	.1
82	Atlas Concrete Batching Corp—Thomas Polsinelli	9511 147th Pl, Jamaica NY 11435	718-523-3000	R	8*	.1
83	Starvaggi Industries Inc—Donald Donell	401 Pennsylvania Ave, Weirton WV 26062	304-748-1400	R	8*	.1
84	Trenton Group Inc—G Albright	PO Box 156, Hanover PA 17331	717-637-2288	R	7*	<.1
85	Beaumont Concrete Co—Thomas L Daniel	13990 Apache Trl, Cabazon CA 92230	951-922-2611	R	7*	<.1
86	Windham Sand And Stone Inc—Martin Francis	PO Box 133, Willimantic CT 06226	860-643-5578	R	7*	.1
87	Barger And Son Construction Company Incorporated Charles W—Charles Barger	PO Box 778, Lexington VA 24450	540-463-2106	R	7*	.1
88	L Suzio Concrete Company Inc—Leonardo Suzio	PO Box 748, Meriden CT 06450	203-237-8421	R	7*	<.1
89	B Mayfield Mccraw And Brenda Mccraw—Mayfield Mccraw	PO Box 9, Telephone TX 75488	903-664-2332	R	6*	.1
90	Rosenfeld Concrete Corp—Jeanne-M Boylan	PO Box 9187, Boston MA 02114	508-473-7200	R	6*	<.1
91	Sadler Materials Corp	155 E 21st St, Jacksonville FL 32206	904-355-1761	R	5*	<.1
92	Canyon Country Enterprises Inc—Ben Curtis	PO Box 1367, Canyon Country CA 91386	661-251-2100	R	5*	<.1
93	Sakrete Inc—J Avril	5155 Fischer Ave, Cincinnati OH 45217	513-242-3644	R	4*	<.1
94	Prairie Ready Mix Inc—Blair Dillman	PO Box 210, Prairie Du Chien WI 53821	608-326-6471	R	4*	<.1
95	Fairbanks Sand And Gravel Inc—Mary Silvey	PO Box 70686, Fairbanks AK 99707	907-452-5336	R	3*	<.1
96	Transit Mix Concrete and Materials Co—Carl Campbell	PO Box 373, Ferris TX 75125	972-544-5900	S	3*	<.1
97	Adams Concrete Products Corp—David Adams	PO Box 2320, Pikeville KY 41502	606-432-2584	R	3*	<.1
98	General Material Co—Thomas Winter	13098 Gravois Rd, Saint Louis MO 63127	314-843-1400	R	3*	<.1
99	Flemington Block and Supply Inc—Frank Lentine	67 Hwy 31, Flemington NJ 08822	908-782-8548	R	2*	<.1
100	Prospect Concrete Inc—Donald Emich	PO Box 278, Landisville PA 17538	717-898-2277	R	2*	<.1
101	Calaveras-Standard Materials—David Vickers	PO Box 26240, Fresno CA 93729	559-277-7060	S	1*	.1
102	Mathews Ready-Mix Inc—Craig Callaway	PO Box 749, Marysville CA 95901	530-300-0093	S	1	<.1
103	Cadman Inc—Barry Irvine	PO Box 97038, Redmond WA 98073	425-868-1234	S	<1*	.4
104	Sherman Industries Inc—Frank Anderson	1400 Urban Ctr Dr Ste, Birmingham AL 35242	205-970-7500	S	<1*	<.1
105	Oldcastle Materials—Doug Black	900 Ashwood Pkwy Ste 7, Atlanta GA 30338	770-522-5600	S	N/A	17.5
106	Transit Mix of Pueblo Inc Continental Materials Corp	444 E Costilla St, Colorado Springs CO 80903	719-475-0700	S	N/A	.1

TOTALS: SIC 3273 Ready Mixed Concrete
Companies: 106   45,471   58.9

3274 Lime

Rank	Company Name—Executive Officer	Address, City, State, Zip	Phone	Type	Fin	Empls
1	Graymont Inc (Pleasant Gap Pennsylvania)—William Dodge	965 E College Ave, Pleasant Gap PA 16823	814-355-4761	R	92*	.2
2	Austin White Lime Co—Charlotte Allen	PO Box 9556, Austin TX 78766	512-255-3646	R	16*	.2
3	Rockydale Quarries Corp—Gordon Willis	PO Box 8425, Roanoke VA 24014	540-774-1696	R	9*	.1

TOTALS: SIC 3274 Lime
Companies: 3   117   .4

3275 Gypsum Products

Rank	Company Name—Executive Officer	Address, City, State, Zip	Phone	Type	Fin	Empls
1	James Hardie Transition Company Inc—Donald Manson	26300 La Alameda Ste 4, Mission Viejo CA 92691	949-348-1800	R	67,714*	1.3
2	USG Corp—James S Metcalf	550 W Adams St, Chicago IL 60661	312-436-4000	P	3,024	8.8
3	New NGC Inc—Thomas Nelson	2001 Rexford Rd, Charlotte NC 28211	704-365-7300	R	1,556*	2.8
4	United States Gypsum Co USG Corp	550 W Adams St, Chicago IL 60661	312-436-4000	S	455*	2.5

Note: An asterisk (*) indicates an estimated financial figure. The company type code used is as follows: R = Private, P = Public, S = Private Subsidiary, B = Public Subsidiary, D = Division, J = Joint Venture, I = Investment Fund.

COMPANY RANKINGS BY SALES WITHIN 4-DIGIT SIC

Rank	Company Name—*Executive Officer*	Address, City, State, Zip	Phone	Type	Fin	Empls
5	American Gypsum Co—*Lee Jones*	3811 Turtle Creek Blvd, Dallas TX 75219	214-530-5500	S	78*	.4
6	American Gypsum Marketing Co—*David Powers*	PO Box 199290, Dallas TX 75219	214-530-5500	S	42*	.1
7	Casting Designs Inc—*Jerry Bransom*	9320 Crowley Rd, Fort Worth TX 76134	817-551-7373	R	12*	.1
8	Maverick Design Inc—*Phyllis Stromberg*	PO Box 8036, Greenville TX 75404	903-454-8682	R	8*	.1
9	Doc Holliday Molds Inc—*Mark Denno*	128 Macarthur Ct, Nicholasville KY 40356	859-887-1427	R	4*	<.1

TOTALS: SIC 3275 Gypsum Products
Companies: 9 — 72,892 — 16.1

3281 Cut Stone & Stone Products

Rank	Company Name—*Executive Officer*	Address, City, State, Zip	Phone	Type	Fin	Empls
1	Rock of Ages Corp—*Donald Labonte* Swenson Granite Company LLC	560 Graniteville Rd, Graniteville VT 05654		S	46	.3
2	Cancos Tile Corp—*Robert Valva*	1085 Portion Rd, Farmingville NY 11738	631-736-0770	R	45*	.1
3	Rynone Manufacturing Corp—*Richard Rynone*	PO Box 128, Sayre PA 18840	570-888-5272	R	34*	.2
4	Halabi Inc—*Fadi Halabi*	2100 Huntington Dr, Fairfield CA 94533	707-402-1600	R	32*	.3
5	Swenson Granite Company LLC—*Kurt Swenson*	369 N State St, Concord NH 03301	603-225-4322	R	27*	.3
6	Top Master Inc—*Dan Richardson*	2844 Roe Ln, Kansas City KS 66103	913-492-3030	R	20*	.3
7	Carolina North Granite Corp—*Donald Shelton*	PO Box 151, Mount Airy NC 27030	336-786-5141	R	19*	.2
8	Imperial Marble Corp—*Richard Williams*	327 E Lasalle St, Somonauk IL 60552	815-498-2303	R	19*	.2
9	Dakota Granite Co—*Rick Dilts*	PO Box 1351, Milbank SD 57252	605-432-5580	R	14*	.1
10	K and K Langham Ltd—*Karen Icenhower*	11108 Bluff Bend Dr, Austin TX 78753	512-835-5100	R	14*	.1
11	Virginia Marble Manufacturers Inc—*Nancy Bridgforth*	PO Box 766, Kenbridge VA 23944	434-676-3204	R	13*	.3
12	Wienmar Inc—*Thomas Wienckowski*	1601 N La Fox St, South Elgin IL 60177	847-742-9222	R	13*	.1
13	GW Surfaces—*James Garver*	2432 Palma Dr, Ventura CA 93003	805-642-5004	R	13*	.2
14	Top South Inc—*Jerry Moore*	830 Pickens Industrial, Marietta GA 30062	770-422-4009	R	11*	.1
15	Environmental Stoneworks LLC	98 Pheasant Run Rd, Orwigsburg PA 17961	570-366-6460	R	11*	.1
16	Rockwood Quarry LLC—*Art Martinez*	PO Box 406, South Rockwood MI 48179	734-783-7415	R	10*	.1
17	Buechel Stone Corp—*Tim Buechel*	4399 N Hwy 175, Fond Du Lac WI 54937	920-849-9361	R	9*	.1
18	Granite Industries of Vermont Inc—*Glen Atherton*	PO Box 537, Barre VT 05641	802-479-2202	R	9*	<.1
19	Marble Products Inc—*Michael Feltus*	9410 Marbella Cv, Cordova TN 38018	901-386-6167	R	9*	.1
20	Bonanza Industries Inc—*Stephen Mitchell*	PO Box 801585, Houston TX 77280	713-466-3560	S	8*	.1
21	Vendura Industries Inc—*H Klotzbach*	1202 Femrite Dr, Monona WI 53716	608-223-9555	R	8*	.1
22	Bybee Stone Company Inc—*William Bybee*	PO Box 968, Bloomington IN 47402	812-876-2215	R	8*	.1
23	Sharcar Enterprises Inc—*Carl Schenewark*	PO Box 581710, Modesto CA 95358	209-531-2200	R	7*	.1
24	Carolina Stalite Company LP—*C Mc Glothin*	PO Box 1037, Salisbury NC 28145	704-637-1515	R	7*	.1
25	Evergreen Slate Company Inc—*Fred Whitridge*	PO Box 248, Granville NY 12832	518-642-2530	R	7*	.1
26	Waller Brothers Stone Company Inc—*Frank Waller*	PO Box 157, Mc Dermott OH 45652	740-259-2356	R	7*	<.1
27	Chantilly Crushed Stone Inc—*John Gudelsky*	PO Box 220112, Chantilly VA 20153	703-471-4461	R	6*	.1
28	United States Marble Inc—*John Bishop*	7839 Costabella Ave, Remus MI 49340	989-561-2293	R	6*	.1
29	Craig Baker Marble Company Inc—*Craig Baker*	PO Box 104, Barker TX 77413	281-492-2365	R	5*	.1
30	American Bluegrass Marble Inc—*J Payne*	1510 Algonquin Pkwy, Louieville KY 40210	502-634-4417	R	4*	.1
31	Tri-State Cut Stone Co—*Gary Murino*	10333 Vans Dr, Frankfort IL 60423	815-469-7550	R	4*	<.1
32	Alamo Marble Ltd—*Bill Sanders*	4931 Enterprise, San Antonio TX 78249	210-493-3711	R	4*	<.1
33	Southern Sand And Stone Inc—*Joseph Bonness*	9200 Collier Blvd, Naples FL 34114	239-775-0720	R	4*	<.1
34	Cleveland Granite and Marble LLC	4400 Carnegie Ave, Cleveland OH 44103	216-241-0220	R	3*	<.1
35	Quality Stone and Ready Mix Inc—*Kevin Holloway*	3260 N Preston Hwy, Shepherdsville KY 40165	502-955-6962	R	3*	<.1
36	Mini-Max Marble and Composites LLC—*Wayne Juang*	7421 Adrianne Pl, Bartlett TN 38133	901-386-6868	R	3*	<.1
37	New Mexico Travertine Inc—*Tim Lardner*	3700 Camino Del Llano, Belen NM 87002	505-864-6300	R	3*	<.1
38	Dixie Cultured Marble Company Inc—*Bobby Johnson*	37 W Park Cir, Birmingham AL 35211	205-942-3004	R	3*	<.1
39	Halcyon Marble Design Inc—*Scott Savage*	12337 E 1st St, Tulsa OK 74128	918-438-2333	R	3*	<.1
40	Standridge Granite Corp—*Deborah Deleon*	9437 Santa Fe Springs, Santa Fe Springs CA 90670	562-946-6334	R	3*	<.1
41	Pinta's Cultured Marble—*John Pinta*	5859 W 117th Pl, Alsip IL 60803	708-385-3360	R	3*	<.1
42	Midland Cut Stone Company Inc—*Cary Stapleton*	PO Box 1, Bloomington IN 47402	812-336-6189	R	3*	<.1
43	Tri City Marble Inc—*George Conly*	4724 Springside Ct, Allentown PA 18104	610-481-0177	R	3*	<.1
44	Midwest Marble Co—*Richard Mcmahon*	510 S Quincy Ave, Tulsa OK 74120	918-587-8193	R	3*	<.1
45	Sugar Loaf Quarries Inc—*Ed Reeves*	PO Box 469, Shady Point OK 74956	918-647-4244	R	2*	<.1
46	C and C Cast Polymers Inc—*Sidney Clements*	1555 W 200 S, Lindon UT 84042	801-796-8048	R	2*	<.1
47	International Trade Consultants Inc—*Lanley Cabell*	914 Adams Ave, Huntington WV 25704	304-529-1447	R	2*	<.1
48	Tarheel Marble Company Inc—*Richard Efird*	12445 Grey Commercial, Midland NC 28107	704-888-3470	R	2*	<.1
49	Marble Designs Inc—*Marvin Poulson*	PO Box 3786, Central Point OR 97502	541-664-1256	R	2*	<.1
50	Universal Slate Exports	1306 Norma Drive, Bloomington IL 61704	414-617-8552	R	2	<.1
51	Heritage Marble Of Ohio Inc—*Gene Daniels*	7086 Huntley Rd, Columbus OH 43229	614-436-1464	R	2*	<.1
52	Stonecraft Inc—*Ricciardi Jones*	10613 Lexington Dr, Knoxville TN 37932	865-966-3900	R	2*	<.1
53	Rainbow Cultured Marble—*Dale Boss*	1442 W 130th St, Brunswick OH 44212	330-225-3400	R	2*	<.1
54	Devido Ranier Stone Co	2619 New Butler Rd, New Castle PA 16101	724-658-8518	R	2*	<.1
55	Blue Ridge Quarries Inc—*Merle Andrews*	8487 Us 221 N, Marion NC 28752	828-756-4651	R	2*	<.1
56	Gold Star Marble Corp—*Trojan Tidwell*	16240 N I H 35, Austin TX 78728	512-251-2463	R	2*	<.1
57	Mcbride Stone Company Inc—*Oran Mcbride*	2340 Oneal Rd, Batesville AR 72501	870-793-7285	R	1*	<.1
58	Sioux Falls Monument Company Inc—*Donald Labonte* Rock of Ages Corp	4901 W 12th St, Sioux Falls SD 57106	605-339-3180	S	1*	<.1
59	Plattsburgh Quarry—*Todd Kempainen*	PO Box 825, Plattsburgh NY 12901	518-561-5200	R	1*	<.1
60	Pico Electrical Equipment Inc—*Gary Cogorno*	10640 Springdale Ave, Santa Fe Springs CA 90670	562-944-0626	R	<1*	<.1
61	American Marble Products Inc—*Daryl Sorensen*	2420 Main St, Conway SC 29526	843-248-0005	R	<1*	<.1

TOTALS: SIC 3281 Cut Stone & Stone Products
Companies: 61 — 509 — 4.6

3291 Abrasive Products

Rank	Company Name—*Executive Officer*	Address, City, State, Zip	Phone	Type	Fin	Empls
1	Washington Mills Tonawanda Inc—*Ron Campbell*	1000 E Niagara St, Tonawanda NY 14150	716-693-4550	R	1,972*	.5
2	Milacron Resin Abrasives Inc—*Dave Lawrence*	4165 Half Acre Rd, Batavia OH 45103	513-487-5000	S	115*	.3
3	Harsco Minerals—*Derek C Hathaway*	5000 Ritter Rd Ste 205, Mechanicsburg PA 17055	717-506-2071	D	68	.3
4	Radiac Abrasives Inc—*David Pryor*	PO Box 1410, Salem IL 62881	618-548-8348	S	26*	.5
5	Hermes Abrasives Limited A LP—*Glenn Hyatt*	PO Box 2389, Virginia Beach VA 23450	757-431-2353	R	23*	.2
6	Schaffner Manufacturing Company Inc—*James Schaffner*	21 Herron Ave, Pittsburgh PA 15202	412-761-9902	R	19*	.2
7	Klingspor Abrasives Inc—*Christoph Klingspor*	PO Box 2367, Hickory NC 28603	828-322-3030	R	17*	.3
8	United Abrasives Inc—*Eric Marziali*	PO Box 75, Willimantic CT 06226	860-456-7131	R	16*	.1
9	Glit-Microtron—*David J Feldman*	PO Box 709, Wrens GA 30833	314-739-8585	S	14*	.1
10	SDC Coatings Inc—*William A Gregg*	45 Parker Ste 100, Irvine CA 92618	714-939-8300	R	14*	<.1
11	VSM Abrasives Corp—*Brent Barton*	1012 E Wabash St, O Fallon MO 63366	636-272-7432	R	13*	.1
12	Uneeda Enterprizes Inc—*Bruce Fuchs*	PO Box 209, Spring Valley NY 10977	845-426-2800	R	11*	.1
13	Allison Abrasives Inc—*James Minteer*	PO Box 192, Lancaster KY 40444	859-792-7000	R	9*	.1

Rank	Company Name—Executive Officer	Address, City, State, Zip	Phone	Type	Fin	Empls
14	Chessco Industries Inc—Jeffrey Radler	1300 Post Rd E Ste 3, Westport CT 06880	203-255-2804	R	8*	.1
15	Imperial Industries Inc (Pompano Beach Florida)—Howard L Ehler Jr	3790 Park Central Blvd, Pompano Beach FL 33064	954-917-4114	P	8	<.1
16	Rex Cut Products Inc—Claude Gelinas	PO Box 2109, Fall River MA 02722	508-678-1985	R	7*	.1
17	Lexington Abrasives Inc—Robert Stuhlmiller	16123 Armour St Ne, Alliance OH 44601	330-821-3510	R	7*	.1
18	Dedeco International Sales Inc—Steven Antler	11617 State Rte 97, Long Eddy NY 12760	845-887-4840	R	7*	.1
19	Power and Industrial Services Corp—Lawrence Shekell	95 Washington St, Donora PA 15033	724-379-4477	R	6*	<.1
20	Kapp Technologies LP—Jim Buschy	2870 Wilderness Pl, Boulder CO 80301	303-447-1130	R	4*	<.1
21	LEXON Technologies Inc—James Park	14830 Desman Rd, La Mirada CA 90638	714-522-0260	P	4	<.1
22	Stan Sax Corp—David J Sax	101 S Waterman St, Detroit MI 48209	313-841-7170	R	4*	<.1
23	Davidson Mike Sand and Gravel LLC	PO Box 1530, Waldorf MD 20604	410-758-2618	R	4*	<.1
24	Sidley Diamond Tool Co—Michael Sidley	32320 Ford Rd, Garden City MI 48135	734-261-7970	R	3*	<.1
25	Leaders Manufacturing Inc—Bruce Torell	PO Box 1183, Willmar MN 56201	320-231-3897	R	3*	<.1
26	Advanced Cutting Systems Inc—Kevin Koenig	4030 Piper Dr, Fort Wayne IN 46809	260-423-3394	R	3*	<.1
27	Everett Industries Inc—William Everett	PO Box 2068, Warren OH 44484	330-372-3700	R	3*	<.1
28	Marshall Sample Laboratories Inc—James Sample	63 Park Ave, Lyndhurst NJ 07071	201-933-0570	R	2*	<.1
29	Belt Master Inc—Larry D Mohr	936 N Stadem Dr Ste 5, Tempe AZ 85281	480-921-3110	R	2*	<.1
30	Carbide Metals Inc—Dennis Gennaro	PO Box 7924, New Castle PA 16107	724-459-6355	R	2*	<.1
31	Shakespeare Machine Stamping Of Wisconsin Inc—Ronald Haarsma	2801 S Memorial Dr, Racine WI 53403	262-635-2449	R	1*	<.1
32	G and S Super Abrasives Inc—Paul Jordan	PO Box 461, Angola IN 46703	260-665-5562	R	1*	<.1

TOTALS: SIC 3291 Abrasive Products
Companies: 32 — 2,395 — 3.6

3292 Asbestos Products

1	GAF Materials Corp—Robert Tafaro	1361 Alps Rd, Wayne NJ 07470	973-628-3000	R	1,593*	3.3
2	Standco Industries Inc—L Mccann	PO Box 87, Houston TX 77001	713-224-6311	R	27*	.3
3	Proto Corp—Christos Botsolas	10500 47th St N, Clearwater FL 33762	727-573-4665	R	8*	.1

TOTALS: SIC 3292 Asbestos Products
Companies: 3 — 1,628 — 3.7

3295 Minerals—Ground or Treated

1	Superior Graphite Co—Edward Carney	10 S Riverside Plz Ste, Chicago IL 60606	312-559-2999	R	119*	.3
2	Luzenac America Inc	8051 E Maplewood Ave B, Greenwood Village CO 80111	303-713-5000	S	60*	.4
3	Multisorb Technologies Inc—James Renda	325 Harlem Rd, Buffalo NY 14224	716-824-8900	R	44*	.3
4	Aluchem Inc—Ronald Zapletal	1 Landy Ln, Cincinnati OH 45215	513-733-8519	R	27*	.1
5	Therm-O-Rock East Inc—Edward Dobkin	PO Box 429, New Eagle PA 15067	724-258-3670	R	24*	.1
6	American Art Clay Company Inc—Lester Sandoe	6060 Guion Rd, Indianapolis IN 46254	317-244-6871	R	20*	.1
7	Minnesota Mining and Manufacturing Company Industrial Mineral	3M Ctr, Saint Paul MN 55144		D	16*	.1
8	Grb Holdings Inc—David Gitridge	PO Box 173, Dayton OH 45404	937-236-3250	R	15*	.1
9	Seubert Excavators Inc—Nicholas Seubert	PO Box 57, Cottonwood ID 83522	208-962-3314	R	13*	< 1
10	Clay Laguna Co—Jonathan Brooks	14400 Lomitas Ave, City Of Industry CA 91746	626-330-0631	R	13*	.1
11	US Cosmetics Corp—Shigeru Kishida	PO Box 859, Dayville CT 06241	860-779-3990	R	13*	.1
12	Eugene Sand and Gravel Inc—KC Klosterman	PO Box 1067, Eugene OR 97440	541-683-6400	R	11*	.3
13	Hydraulic Press Brick Co—Tom Bennett	5505 W 74th St, Indianapolis IN 46268	317-290-1140	R	8*	.1
14	Quartz Scientific Inc—James Atwell	PO Box 1129, Fairport Harbor OH 44077	440-354-2186	R	7*	.1
15	Keystone Filler and Manufacturing Co—David Pfleegor	214 Railroad St, Muncy PA 17756	570-546-3148	R	7*	.1
16	Atlas Peat and Soil Inc—Brian Lulfs	9621 State Rd 7, Boynton Beach FL 33472	561-734-7300	R	5*	<.1
17	Virginia Vermiculite LLC—Todd Jancaitis	PO Box 70, Louisa VA 23093	540-967-2266	R	5*	<.1
18	Great Lakes Calcium Corp—Wesley Garner	PO Box 2236, Green Bay WI 54306	920-965-4200	R	4*	<.1
19	Industrial Quartz Corp—Richard Intihar	7552 Saint Clair Ave D, Mentor OH 44060	440-942-0909	R	3*	<.1
20	Norlite Corp—David Carabetta	PO Box 694, Cohoes NY 12047	518-235-0401	R	3*	.3
21	Southern Products Company Inc—Marshall Gilchrist	PO Box 189, Hoffman NC 28347	910-281-3189	R	2*	<.1
22	American Colloid Co—Gary Morrison	2870 Forbs Ave, Hoffman Estates IL 60192	847-851-1700	S	1	<.1

TOTALS: SIC 3295 Minerals— Ground or Treated
Companies: 22 — 418 — 2.7

3296 Mineral Wool

1	Owens Corning—Michael H Thaman	PO Box 10014, Toledo OH 43699	419-248-8000	P	4,997	15.0
2	Industrial Insulation Group LLC—Jim Tatman	2100 Line St, Brunswick GA 31520	912-264-6372	R	167*	.4
3	Scott Industries Inc—Scott Miller	PO Box 7, Henderson KY 42419	270-831-2037	R	54*	.1
4	Hi-Temperature Insulation Inc—Sieg Borck	4700 Calle Alto, Camarillo CA 93012	805-484-2774	R	50*	.4
5	Piqua Technologies Inc—Mitsuaki (Mitch) Kobayashi	PO Box 740, Piqua OH 45356	937-773-4820	R	48*	.2
6	Saint-Gobain BTI—Phil Harmon	1795 Baseline Rd, Grand Island NY 14072	716-775-3900	S	28*	.1
7	United States Mineral Products Company Inc—Giovanni Pacheco	41 Furnace St, Stanhope NJ 07874	973-347-1200	R	19*	.2
8	Thermafiber Inc—Steve Edris	3711 Mill St, Wabash IN 46992	260-563-2111	R	15*	.1
9	Silbrico Corp—Tom Mendius	6300 River Rd, Hodgkins IL 60525	708-354-3350	R	13*	.1
10	Supreme Insulation Inc—Kim Maty	4545 Emanuel Cleaver I, Kansas City MO 64130	816-861-8892	R	11*	.1
11	Anderson Products Inc—Lee Anderson	2500 17th St, Elkhart IN 46517	574-293-5574	R	10*	.1
12	Gordon Composites—Mike Gordon Jr	2350 Air Park Way, Montrose CO 81401	970-240-4460	R	10*	<.1
13	CA Schroeder Inc—Clifford Schroeder	1318 1st St, San Fernando CA 91340	818-365-9561	R	9*	.1
14	Eckel Industries Inc—Alan Eckel	155 Fawcett St, Cambridge MA 02138	617-491-3221	R	7*	.1
15	Ica Inc—Robert March	PO Box 436, South Plainfield NJ 07080	610-377-4120	R	7*	<.1
16	Rock Wool Manufacturing Co—Gerald Miller	PO Box 506, Leeds AL 35094	205-699-6121	R	7*	.1
17	Bigharn Insulation And Supply Company Inc—Robert Bryant	2816 Sw 3rd Ave, Fort Lauderdale FL 33315	954-522-2887	R	5*	<.1
18	Barrier Corp—Mark Dove	PO Box 23008, Tigard OR 97281	503-639-4192	R	5*	<.1
19	Dgp Inc—Steve Quade	PO Box 155, Marlette MI 48453	989-635-7531	R	5*	<.1
20	Extol Of Ohio Inc—Robin Degraff	208 Republic St, Norwalk OH 44857	419-668-2072	R	5*	<.1
21	E J Davis Co—Gregory Godbout	PO Box 326, North Haven CT 06473	203-239-5391	R	4*	<.1
22	UPF Corp—Jack Pfeffer	3747 Standard St, Bakersfield CA 93308	661-323-8227	R	4*	<.1
23	Custom Fiberglass Inc—Mark Dunbar	PO Box 70, Mills WY 82644	307-234-0744	R	4*	<.1

TOTALS: SIC 3296 Mineral Wool
Companies: 23 — 5,485 — 17.2

3297 Nonclay Refractories

1	Global Industrial Technologies Inc—Jon Allegretti Rhi Refractories Holding Co	400 Fairway Dr, Coraopolis PA 15108	412-375-6600	S	293*	4.3

Note: An asterisk (*) indicates an estimated financial figure. The company type code used is as follows: R = Private, P = Public, S = Private Subsidiary, B = Public Subsidiary, D = Division, J = Joint Venture, I = Investment Fund.

COMPANY RANKINGS BY SALES WITHIN 4-DIGIT SIC

Rank	Company Name—*Executive Officer*	Address, City, State, Zip	Phone	Type	Fin	Empls
2	ATI Firth Sterling	7300 Hwy 20 W, Huntsville AL 35806	256-837-1311	S	254*	.5
3	Rhi Refractories Holding Co—*Norbert Wittmann*	1105 N Market St Ste 1, Wilmington DE 19801	302-655-6497	R	161*	4.5
4	Allied Mineral Products Inc—*Jon Tabor*	2700 Scioto Pkwy, Columbus OH 43221	614-876-0244	R	85*	.3
5	Magneco/Metrel Inc—*Charles Connors*	223 W Interstate Rd, Addison IL 60101	630-543-6660	R	62*	.1
6	Rhi Monofrax Ltd—*Dalyl Clendenen*	1870 New York Ave, Falconer NY 14733	716-483-7200	S	60*	.3
7	BPI Inc (Pittsburgh Pennsylvania)—*Joseph Quigley*	612 S Trenton Ave, Pittsburgh PA 15221	412-371-8554	R	20*	<.1
8	Worldwide Refractories Inc—*William Brown*	PO Box 28, Tarentum PA 15084	724-224-8800	R	9*	.1
9	Minteq International Inc—*Han Schut*	35 Highland Ave, Bethlehem PA 18017	212-878-1831	S	8	<.1
10	Joy-Mark Inc—*J Lovejoy*	2121 E Norse Ave, Cudahy WI 53110	414-769-8155	R	7*	.1
11	Refractory Specialties Inc—*Richard Wilk*	230 W California Ave, Sebring OH 44672	330-938-2101	R	7*	<.1
12	Sauereisen Inc—*J Sauereisen*	160 Gamma Dr, Pittsburgh PA 15238	412-963-0303	R	5*	<.1
13	Hudco Industrial Products Inc—*Thomas Hudson*	3100 Morgan Rd, Bessemer AL 35022	205-424-2772	R	3*	<.1
14	Midwest Graphite Company Inc—*Ivanka Vidovich*	6101 W 31st St, Cicero IL 60804	708-780-7300	R	1*	<.1

TOTALS: SIC 3297 Nonclay Refractories
Companies: 14   975   10.3

3299 Nonmetallic Mineral Products Nec

Rank	Company Name—*Executive Officer*	Address, City, State, Zip	Phone	Type	Fin	Empls
1	ACM Holdings Corp—*David E Berges*	281 Tresser Blvd 2 Sta, Stamford CT 06901	203-969-0666	S	67,107*	4.1
2	Carbo Ceramics Inc—*Gary Kolstad*	575 N Dairy Ashford Rd, Houston TX 77079	281-921-6400	P	473	.8
3	Imperial Industries Inc—*Ed Creske*	PO Box 1685, Wausau WI 54402	715-359-0200	R	41*	.2
4	Kyocera Industrial Ceramics Corp (Mountain Home North Carolina)—*John Rigby*	PO Box 678, Mountain Home NC 28758	828-693-0241	S	16*	.2
5	Henri Studio Inc—*Mario Prosperi*	1250 Henri Dr, Wauconda IL 60084	847-526-5200	R	16*	.2
6	Plastrglas Inc—*Wallace Wilson*	PO Box 11038, Omaha NE 68111	402-455-0652	R	12*	.1
7	Fireline Inc—*Robert Wimer*	300 Andrews Ave, Youngstown OH 44505	330-743-1164	R	10*	.1
8	Industrial Converting Company Inc—*Chris Bender*	1841 Air Ln Dr, Nashville TN 37210	615-244-6700	R	8*	.1
9	Miller Studio Inc—*Jeffrey Miller*	PO Box 997, New Philadelphia OH 44663	330-339-1100	R	7*	.1
10	Accents Unlimited Inc—*Ron Creten*	5205 W Donges Bay Rd, Mequon WI 53092	262-242-5205	R	6*	.1
11	Insulation Specialties Of America Inc—*Monie Parker*	PO Box 10, Wanatah IN 46390	219-733-2502	R	4*	<.1
12	Crystex Composites LLC—*Joe Penkalski*	125 Clifton Blvd, Clifton NJ 07011	973-779-8866	R	4*	<.1
13	Aaa Architectural—*Richard Cary*	1751 12th St E, Palmetto FL 34221	941-729-2354	R	3*	<.1
14	Cetek Inc—*Fayiz Hilal*	19 Commerce St, Poughkeepsie NY 12603	845-452-3510	R	3*	<.1

TOTALS: SIC 3299 Nonmetallic Mineral Products Nec
Companies: 14   67,711   6.0

3312 Blast Furnaces & Steel Mills

Rank	Company Name—*Executive Officer*	Address, City, State, Zip	Phone	Type	Fin	Empls
1	United States Steel Corp—*John P Surma*	600 Grant St, Pittsburgh PA 15219	412-433-1121	P	17,374	42.0
2	Nucor Corp—*Daniel R DiMicco*	1915 Rexford Rd, Charlotte NC 28211	704-366-7000	P	15,845	20.5
3	Steel Dynamics Inc—*Mark Millett*	7575 W Jefferson Blvd, Fort Wayne IN 46804	260-969-3500	P	7,998	6.5
4	AK Steel Holding Corp—*James L Wainscott*	9227 Centre Pointe Dr, West Chester OH 45069	513-425-5000	P	6,468	6.6
5	MACSTEEL—*Raymond Jean*	1 Jackson Sq Ste 500, Jackson MI 49201	517-782-0415	S	6,184*	5.0
6	AK Steel Corp—*James L Wainscott* AK Steel Holding Corp	9227 Centre Pointe Dr, West Chester OH 45069	513-425-5000	S	5,890*	6.2
7	Allegheny Technologies Inc—*Richard J Harshman*	1000 Six PPG Pl, Pittsburgh PA 15222	412-394-2800	P	5,183	11.4
8	Gerdau AmeriSteel Corp—*Mario Longhi*	4221 W Boy Scout Blvd, Tampa FL 33607	813-286-8383	S	4,196	11.0
9	Oregon Steel Mills Inc—*Michael T Rehwinkel*	14400 N Rivergate Blvd, Portland OR 97203	503-286-9651	S	2,710*	2.8
10	Gkn Sinter Metals-Germantown Inc—*Greg Kern*	PO Box 1009, Germantown WI 53022	262-255-9050	R	2,053*	.5
11	Carpenter Technology Corp—*William A Wulfsohn*	PO Box 14662 Bldg L05, Reading PA 19612	610-208-2000	P	1,675	3.5
12	Walter Energy Inc—*Keith Calder*	4211 W Boy Scout Blvd, Tampa FL 33607	813-871-4811	P	1,588	2.1
13	Titan International Inc—*Maurice Taylor*	2701 Spruce St, Quincy IL 62301	217-228-6011	P	1,487	3.6
14	Precision Specialty Metals Inc	200 Old Wilson Bridge, Columbus OH 43085	323-475-3200	S	1,406	.2
15	Charter Manufacturing Company Inc—*John Mellowes*	PO Box 217, Thiensville WI 53092	262-243-4700	R	903*	1.1
16	California Steel Industries—*Vicente Wright*	PO Box 5080, Fontana CA 92334	909-350-6300	R	846*	1.0
17	Gibraltar Industries Inc—*Brian J Lipke*	PO Box 2028, Buffalo NY 14219	716-826-6500	P	767	2.2
18	Uss Posco Industries—*Robert Smith*	PO Box 471, Pittsburg CA 94565	925-439-6000	R	642*	.8
19	Arcelormittal Plate LLC—*Andrew Layser*	139 Modena Rd, Coatesville PA 19320	610-383-2000	R	638*	1.1
20	Texas Industries Inc—*Mel G Brekhus*	1341 W Mockingbird Ln, Dallas TX 75247	972-647-6700	P	622	2.0
21	LB Foster Co—*Stan L Hasselbusch*	415 Holiday Dr, Pittsburgh PA 15220	412-928-3431	P	475	.9
22	Carpenter Steel Div—*Gregory Pratt* Carpenter Technology Corp	PO Box 14662, Reading PA 19612	610-208-2000	D	470*	2.6
23	Keystone Consolidated Industries Inc—*David L Cheek*	5430 LBJ Fwy Ste 1740, Dallas TX 75240	972-458-0028	B	451	1.0
24	Allied Tube and Conduit Corp—*John P Williamson*	16100 S Lathrop Ave, Harvey IL 60426	708-339-1610	S	438*	3.1
25	Virginia Chaparral Inc—*Greg Bott*	25801 Hofheimer Way, Petersburg VA 23803	804-520-0286	R	355*	.4
26	Republic Engineered Products Inc—*Michael Houlihan*	2633 8th St NE, Canton OH 44704	330-438-5533	S	311*	.8
27	Bristol Metals LP—*Ron Braam*	PO Box 1589, Bristol TN 37621	423-989-4700	S	299*	.3
28	Union Electric Steel Corp—*Robert Carothers*	PO Box 465, Carnegie PA 15106	412-429-7655	S	277*	.4
29	Greenville Tube Co—*Harley Kaplan*	PO Box 389, Janesville WI 53547	608-531-3140	S	246*	.2
30	Indiana Nlmk Inc—*Paul Fiore*	6500 S Boundary Rd, Portage IN 46368	219-787-8200	R	200*	.4
31	Robinson Steel Company Inc—*Paul Labriola*	4303 Kennedy Ave, East Chicago IN 46312	219-398-4600	R	200*	.3
32	Universal Stainless and Alloy Products Inc—*Dennis M Oates*	600 Mayer St, Bridgeville PA 15017	412-257-7600	P	189	.5
33	Arkansas Steel Associates LLC—*Ginger Carlyle*	2803 Van Dyke Rd, Newport AR 72112	870-523-3693	R	157*	.2
34	Latrobe Specialty Steel Co—*B Christopher DiSantis*	2626 Ligonier St, Latrobe PA 15650	724-532-4530	R	156*	.1
35	Parthenon Metal Works Inc—*Karl VanBecelaerel*	PO Box 307, La Vergne TN 37086	615-793-6801	S	138*	.2
36	SMI Steel Alabama—*Mike Buckentin*	PO Box 321188, Birmingham AL 35232	205-592-8981	S	137*	.5
37	Vae Nortrak Inc—*Allan Tuningley*	3930 Valley E Industri, Birmingham AL 35217	205-854-2884	R	132*	.1
38	Eaton Metal Products Company LLC—*Timothy Travis*	PO Box 16405, Denver CO 80216	303-296-4800	R	125*	.2
39	Johnstown Wire Technologies Inc—*Walt Robertson*	124 Laurel Ave, Johnstown PA 15906	814-532-5600	R	120*	.3
40	Jersey Shore Steel Co—*John Schultz*	PO Box 5055, Jersey Shore PA 17740	570-398-0220	R	114*	.4
41	California Pellet Mill Co—*Carl Allis*	1114 E Wabash Ave, Crawfordsville IN 47933	765-362-2600	R	112*	1.0
42	SchmolzBickenbach USA—*Dan O'Donell*	365 Village Dr, Carol Stream IL 60188	630-682-3900	S	99*	.1
43	Heidtman Steel Products Inc—*Tim Berra*	2401 Front St, Toledo OH 43605	419-691-4646	R	99*	1.0
44	Cascade Steel Rolling Mills Inc—*Jeffery Dyck*	PO Box 687, Mcminnville OR 97128	503-472-4181	S	92*	.3
45	Sloss Industries Corp—*Kent Roberts* Walter Energy Inc	3500 35th Ave, Birmingham AL 35207	205-808-7806	S	88*	.4
46	Talley Metals Technology Inc—*Jerry Kershner*	205 Tabernacle Church, Mc Bee SC 29101	843-335-7540	R	85	.3
47	Chicago Heights Steel—*Frank Corral*	211 E Main St, Chicago Heights IL 60411	708-756-5648	R	76*	.2
48	Atlantic States Cast Iron Pipe Company Inc—*Dale Schemlzle*	183 Sitgreaves St, Phillipsburg NJ 08865	908-454-1161	R	69*	.3
49	Pennsylvania Industrial Heat Treaters Inc—*Joe Handwerger*	Elk County Industrial, Saint Marys PA 15857	814-781-6262	R	66*	.1
50	Southeast Texas Industries Inc—*Paul Spence*	PO Box 1449, Buna TX 77612	409-994-3570	R	66*	.9
51	Clingan Steel Inc—*Tom Bolin*	2525 Arthur Ave, Elk Grove Village IL 60007	847-228-6200	R	64*	.1

Rank	Company Name—*Executive Officer*	Address, City, State, Zip	Phone	Type	Fin	Empls
52	Tonawanda Coke Corp—*James Crane*	PO Box 5007, Tonawanda NY 14151	716-876-6222	R	61*	.1
53	Arcelormittal Steelton LLC—*Richard Westermeier*	215 S Front St, Steelton PA 17113	717-986-2000	R	54*	.6
54	Harbor Metal Treating Co—*Mile Wellham*	800 S Fair Ave, Benton Harbor MI 49022	269-925-6581	R	50*	.1
55	Berg Steel Pipe Corp—*Dave Delie*	PO Box 59209, Panama City FL 32412	850-769-2273	R	43*	.3
56	Ovako North America Inc—*Mikael G Wiel*	1096 Assembly Dr Ste 3, Fort Mill SC 29708	803-802-1500	S	42	.3
57	Elderlee Inc—*Basil Shorb*	PO Box 10, Oaks Corners NY 14518	717-843-0021	R	40*	.3
58	Win-Holt Equipment Corp—*Jonathan Holtz*	141 Eileen Way, Syosset NY 11791	516-222-0335	R	38*	.3
59	Friedman Industries Inc—*William E Crow*	4001 Homestead Rd, Houston TX 77028		P	37	.1
60	Vinton Arcelormittal Inc—*Rangasswamy Kesavan*	PO Box 12843, El Paso TX 79913	915-886-2000	R	35*	.5
61	Bjerke Forgings Inc—*Dale Bjerke*	PO Box 250, Allen Park MI 48101	313-382-2600	R	34*	.6
62	Seymour Tubing Inc—*Yoshi Shirakawa*	1515 E 4th St Rd, Seymour IN 47274	812-523-3638	R	32*	.4
63	Phillips Manufacturing And Tower Co—*Angela Phillip*	PO Box 125, Shelby OH 44875	419-347-1720	R	31*	.1
64	ShapedWire—*David Hoffner*	30000 Solon Rd, Solon OH 44139	440-248-7600	D	30*	.1
65	Lortz Manufacturing Co—*Charles W Lortz Jr*	4042 Patton Way, Bakersfield CA 93308	661-587-2020	R	30*	.1
66	Steel Ventures LLC—*Annellee Donnelly*	555 Poyntz Ave Ste 122, Manhattan KS 66502	785-587-5100	R	29*	.1
67	Shenango Inc—*Andrew Aloe*	200 Neville Rd Ste 8, Pittsburgh PA 15225	412-771-4400	R	29*	.2
68	Ellwood Quality Steels Co—*Robert Rumcik*	700 Moravia St Ste 7, New Castle PA 16101	724-658-6502	R	28*	.2
69	JSW Steel (USA) Inc—*Rajiv Garg*	5200 E Mckinney Rd Ste, Baytown TX 77523	281-383-2525	R	27*	.4
70	Amg Industries Corp—*Allan Goldstein*	2 Robinson Plz Ste 350, Pittsburgh PA 15205	412-331-0770	R	27*	.3
71	North Star Bluescope Steel LLC—*Barb Fournier*	6767 County Rd 9, Delta OH 43515	419-822-2200	R	27*	.3
72	Dakota Systems Inc—*John Thomas*	1057 Broadway Rd, Dracut MA 01826	978-275-0600	R	26*	.1
73	Basden Steel And Erection Inc—*Bruce Basden*	PO Box 1061, Burleson TX 76097	817-295-6100	R	26*	.2
74	Die-Tech Industries Inc—*Thomas Wysoczynski*	102 Automation Dr, Carrollton GA 30117	770-836-1042	R	25*	.1
75	J J Ryan Corp—*Ronald Fontanella*	PO Box 39, Plantsville CT 06479	860-628-0393	R	25*	.2
76	Northland Process Piping Inc—*Dan Tramm*	1662 320th Ave, Isle MN 56342	320-679-2119	R	24*	.1
77	Mcdonald Steel Corp—*A Egnot*	PO Box 416, Mc Donald OH 44437	330-530-9118	R	21*	.2
78	Gerdau Ameristeel Perth Amboy Inc—*Robert Bullard*	225 Elm St, Perth Amboy NJ 08861	732-442-1600	R	20*	.3
79	Erie Coke Corp—*James Crane*	PO Box 6180, Erie PA 16512	814-454-0177	R	19*	.1
80	Southwest Steel Casting Co—*Harry Phillips*	600 Foundry Dr, Longview TX 75604	903-759-3946	R	19*	.3
81	W Silver Inc—*Mark Fenenbock*	PO Box 12904, El Paso TX 79913	915-886-3553	R	18*	.1
82	Oakley Industries Inc—*Gary Oakley*	3211 W Bear Creek Dr, Englewood CO 80110	303-761-1835	R	18*	.1
83	United Performance Metals—*Thomas Kennard*	3475 Symmes Rd, Hamilton OH 45015	513-860-6500	R	17*	.1
84	Danlin Industries Corp—*Roger Floyd*	PO Box 307, Thomas OK 73669	580-661-3248	R	16*	.1
85	HMK Enterprises Inc—*Steven Karol*	750 Marrett Rd, Lexington MA 02421	781-891-6660	R	16*	<.1
86	Southern Source Inc—*Rufus Mcpeak*	454 Swanson Dr, Dresden TN 38225	731-364-3070	R	16*	.2
87	Sandmeyer Steel Co—*Ronald Sandmeyer*	1 Sandmeyer Ln, Philadelphia PA 19116	215-464-7100	R	14*	.2
88	Ultra Aluminum Manufacturing Inc—*Russell Springborn*	2124 Grand Commerce Dr, Howell MI 48855	517-548-6755	R	14*	.1
89	Superior Forge and Steel Corp—*James Markovitz*	1820 Mcclain Rd, Lima OH 45804	419-222-4412	R	14*	.1
90	Middletown Tube Works Inc—*Angela Phillips*	2201 Trine St, Middletown OH 45044	800-841-4207	R	14*	.1
91	Ski Prime Equipment Services Inc—*Mitch Long*	2880 N Hwy 360 Ste 200, Grand Prairie TX 75050	469-733-1540	R	13*	.1
92	O and K American Corp—*Kazuta Oku*	4630 W 55th St, Chicago IL 60632	773-767-2500	R	11*	.1
93	Plymouth Steel Corp—*John Quay*	22700 Nagel St, Warren MI 48089	586-755-5800	R	11*	.1
94	Thyssenkrupp AST USA Inc—*Debbie Bradford*	2275 Half Day Rd Ste 3, Bannockburn IL 60015	847 317 1400	R	9*	<.1
95	Jaquith Industries Inc—*D Jaquith*	PO Box 780, Syracuse NY 13205	315-478-5700	R	9*	.1
96	JL Houston Company Inc—*Ronald Houston*	208 Craig St, Hopkins MO 64461	660-778-3393	R	9*	.1
97	Majac Inc—*Dave Hegan*	PO Box 382, East Chicago IN 46312	219-397-5489	R	9*	<.1
98	Quality Cryogenics Of Atlanta LLC—*Mike Dewey*	425 Gennett Dr, Jasper GA 30143	706-692-6167	S	9*	<.1
99	Ftt Manufacturing Inc—*Gary Kone*	112 Riverside Dr, Geneseo NY 14454	585-243-0300	R	8*	.1
100	Precision Tube Inc—*Mark Gentry*	1025 Fortune Dr, Richmond KY 40475	859-623-5595	R	8*	.1
101	Hi-Tech Wire Inc—*Bill Hemmelgarn*	631 E Washington St, Saint Henry OH 45883	419-678-8376	R	7*	.1
102	Tubacex Inc—*Alvaro Videgain*	5430 Brystone Dr, Houston TX 77041	713-856-2700	R	7*	<.1
103	I and M Machine and Fabrication Corp—*Thomas Leinen*	401 S 3rd St, Saint Joseph MO 64501	816-233-6841	R	7*	<.1
104	Air-Cure Acquisitions Corp—*Michael Harris*	8501 Evergreen Blvd Nw, Minneapolis MN 55433	763-717-0707	R	7*	<.1
105	Lee Controls Inc—*Alan Haveson*	PO Box 365, Middlesex NJ 08846	732-752-5200	R	7*	<.1
106	Vanam Tool And Engineering Inc—*Ivan Russell*	5025 Se Easton Rd, Saint Joseph MO 64507	816-233-6622	R	6*	<.1
107	Bullet Guard Corp—*Sharon Durst*	3963 Commerce Dr, West Sacramento CA 95691	916-373-0402	R	6*	<.1
108	Shawmut Metal Products Inc—*Kevin Kelly*	PO Box 543, Swansea MA 02777	508-379-0803	R	6*	<.1
109	Modern Custom Fabrication Inc—*James Gray*	PO Box 11925, Fresno CA 93775	559-264-4741	R	6*	<.1
110	Manufactured Component Parts Ltd—*A Schill*	PO Box 70256, Houston TX 77270	713-880-0590	R	5*	<.1
111	R and D Engineering Incorporated Of Earlham—*Rodney Ramsey*	690 N Chestnut Ave, Earlham IA 50072	515-758-2262	R	5*	<.1
112	C and F Forge Co—*Thomas Herbstritt*	9100 Parklane Ave, Franklin Park IL 60131	847-455-6609	R	4*	<.1
113	Signs and Shapes International Inc—*Lee Bowen*	2320 Paul St, Omaha NE 68102	402-331-3181	R	4*	<.1
114	Barclay Machine Inc—*Jeff Cushman*	PO Box 299, Salem OH 44460	330-337-9541	R	4*	<.1
115	Minnesota Tool and Die Works Inc—*Keith Sherer*	6220 Mckinley St Nw, Anoka MN 55303	763-323-0145	R	4*	<.1
116	WH Fetzer and Sons Manufacturing Inc—*William Fetzer*	PO Box 45, Plymouth OH 44865	419-687-8237	R	4*	<.1
117	Scientific Fabrication Service Inc—*Robert Sprunk*	PO Box 504, Plaquemine LA 70765	225-687-8209	R	3*	<.1
118	Cmi-Promex Inc—*Wayne Ligato*	7 Benjamin Green Rd, Pedricktown NJ 08067	856-351-1000	R	3*	<.1
119	Hooley Inc—*Wilie Rucker*	PO Box 19370, New Orleans LA 70179	504-482-3619	R	3*	<.1
120	McHone Industries Inc—*Arnold McHone*	PO Box 69, Salamanca NY 14779	716-945-3380	R	3*	<.1
121	Holt Tool and Machine Inc—*Leo Hoenighausen*	2909 Middlefield Rd, Redwood City CA 94063	650-364-2547	R	3*	<.1
122	Nifty-Bar Inc—*Grant Gillette*	450 Whitney Rd, Penfield NY 14526	585-381-0450	R	3*	<.1
123	Harvard Coil Processing Inc—*Eileen Jacobs*	5400 Harvard Ave, Cleveland OH 44105	216-883-6366	R	3*	<.1
124	Millinocket Fabrication And Machine Inc—*Frederick Lewis*	432 Katahdin Ave, Millinocket ME 04462	207-723-9733	R	2*	<.1
125	River Valley Machine Inc—*Lyle Kollar*	PO Box 54, Allegan MI 49010	269-673-8070	R	2*	<.1
126	Buschman Corp—*Thomas Buschman*	4100 Payne Ave Ste 1, Cleveland OH 44103	216-431-6633	R	2*	<.1
127	Poly Profiles Technology Corp—*Jerry Levingston*	3 Industrial Dr, Steelville MO 65565	573-775-3301	R	2*	<.1
128	Electric Metal Fab Inc—*Amanda Chittum*	4889 Helmsburg Rd, Nashville IN 47448	812-988-9353	R	2*	<.1
129	Martino Industries Inc—*Thomas Bieneman*	1751 W 10th St, Riviera Beach FL 33404	561-844-5200	R	2*	<.1
130	Dyer Industries Inc—*Glenn Dyer*	PO Box 207, Bunola PA 15020	724-258-3400	R	2*	<.1
131	Ashby Manufacturing Company Inc—*Manus O'donnell*	12 Leonberg Rd, Cranberry Township PA 16066	724-776-5566	R	2*	<.1
132	Collins Machine and Tool Company Inc—*Mike Collins*	924 Myatt Industrial D, Madison TN 37115	615-860-2846	R	2*	<.1
133	Ph Tool—*Phil Herman*	4406 Bethlehem Pke, Telford PA 18969	215-822-1933	R	1*	<.1
134	City Industrial Tool and Die Inc—*Steve Kuljis*	25524 Frampton Ave, Harbor City CA 90710	310-530-1234	R	1*	<.1
135	Wiesen Edm Inc—*Jeff Wiesen*	8630 Storey Rd, Belding MI 48809	616-794-9870	R	1*	<.1
136	Expert Coating Company Inc—*Erik Klimek*	2855 Marlin Ct Nw, Grand Rapids MI 49534	616-453-8261	R	1*	<.1
137	Cnc Prose Inc—*Greg Martin*	1261 S Redwood Rd Ste, Salt Lake City UT 84104	801-973-0800	R	1*	<.1

TOTALS: SIC 3312 Blast Furnaces & Steel Mills
Companies: 137

91,689   157.4

Note: An asterisk (*) indicates an estimated financial figure. The company type code used is as follows: R = Private, P = Public, S = Private Subsidiary, B = Public Subsidiary, D = Division, J = Joint Venture, I = Investment Fund.

COMPANY RANKINGS BY SALES WITHIN 4-DIGIT SIC

Rank	Company Name—*Executive Officer*	Address, City, State, Zip	Phone	Type	Fin	Empls
3313 Electrometallurgical Products						
1	Metallurg Inc—*Heinz Schimmelbusch*	435 Devon Park Dr Bldg, Wayne PA 19087	610-293-2501	S	3,513*	.9
2	Elkem Metals Inc—*Geir Kvernmo*	PO Box 266, Pittsburgh PA 15230	412-299-7200	R	889*	.3
3	Special Metals Corp—*Joseph Snowden*	4317 Middle Settlement, New Hartford NY 13413	315-798-2900	S	729	3.2
4	Globe Specialty Metals Inc—*Jeff Bradley*	250 W 34th St Ste 4125, New York NY 10119	212-798-8122	P	642	1.2
5	Spinnaker Industries Inc—*Maurice Lattanzio*	4846 Jennings Ln, Louisville KY 40218		R	357*	.1
6	Grosfillex Inc	230 Old W Penn Ave, Robesonia PA 19551	610-693-5835	R	50*	.2
7	American Flux and Metal—*Rod Werner*	PO Box 74, Winslow NJ 08095	609-561-7500	R	4*	<.1
8	New England Alloys—*Chris Salvadore*	24 Althea St, Providence RI 02907	401-331-6158	R	<1*	<.1

TOTALS: SIC 3313 Electrometallurgical Products
Companies: 8   6,184   5.8

Rank	Company Name—*Executive Officer*	Address, City, State, Zip	Phone	Type	Fin	Empls
3315 Steel Wire & Related Products						
1	Johnson Steel and Wire Corp—*John Work*	110 Industrial Park Dr, Clarksdale MS 38614	662-627-7853	R	699*	.1
2	Sherman Wire	428 Gibbons Rd, Sherman TX 75091	903-893-0191	D	460*	.1
3	Bekaert Corp—*David Best*	3200 W Market St Ste 3, Fairlawn OH 44333	330-867-3325	R	209*	1.9
4	Draka Cableteq USA Corp—*Joe Dixon*	22 Joseph E Warner Blv, North Dighton MA 02764	508-822-5444	S	170*	.9
5	South Bay Cable	PO Box 67, Idyllwild CA 92549	951-659-2183	R	130*	1.3
6	National-Standard Co—*Frank Hagan*	1631 Lake St, Niles MI 49120	616-683-8100	S	110*	.6
7	BCS Industries LLC—*Joseph A Higdon*	1175 Harbor Ave, Memphis TN 38113	901-946-1005	R	75*	.2
8	Loos and Company Inc—*William Loos*	PO Box 98, Pomfret CT 06258	860-928-7981	R	71*	.4
9	WW Cross Industries Inc—*Tom Trudeau*	2510 Allen Ave SE, Canton OH 44707	330-588-8400	R	67*	<.1
10	Southwestern Wire Inc—*David Weinand*	PO Box Cc, Norman OK 73070	405-447-6900	R	43*	.1
11	Fort Wayne Metals Research Products Corp—*Scott Glaze*	PO Box 9040, Fort Wayne IN 46899	260-747-4154	R	40*	.5
12	Tappan Wire and Cable Inc—*Darren Krych*	100 Bradley Pkwy, Blauvelt NY 10913	845-353-9000	R	40*	.2
13	American Spring Wire Corp—*Timothy Selhorst*	26300 Miles Rd, Cleveland OH 44146	216-292-4620	R	38*	.4
14	Davis Wire Corp—*Jim Hillebrandt*	PO Box 2145, Irwindale CA 91706	626-969-7651	R	34*	.4
15	Taubensee Steel and Wire Co—*Dale Taubensee*	600 Diens Dr, Wheeling IL 60090	847-459-5100	R	34*	.2
16	Hamrock Inc—*Stephen Hamrock*	12521 Los Nietos Rd, Santa Fe Springs CA 90670	562-944-0255	R	34*	.3
17	Knox Enterprises Inc—*Paul K Kelly*	33 Riverside Ave 5th F, Westport CT 06880	203-226-6408	R	27*	.1
18	Awp Industries Inc—*Craig Chamberlin*	616 Industrial Park, Frankfort KY 40601	502-695-0070	R	25*	.1
19	Tokusen USA Inc—*Ken Nagai*	PO Box 1150, Conway AR 72033	501-327-6800	R	24*	.3
20	Mid-South Wire Company Inc—*John Johnson*	1070 Visco Dr, Nashville TN 37210	615-743-2500	R	23*	.1
21	G and D LLC—*David Pollock*	5000 Independence St, Arvada CO 80002	303-424-7300	R	22*	.1
22	Marwas Steel Co—*Jeffrey Pfeiffer*	18 Mount Pleasant Rd, Scottdale PA 15683	724-887-8090	R	18*	.1
23	Wiretech Inc—*William Hillpot*	6440 Canning St, Commerce CA 90040	323-722-4933	R	17*	.1
24	Iowa Steel and Wire Co—*Craig Moore*	PO Box 156, Centerville IA 52544	641-856-6300	R	14*	.1
25	Torpedo Specialty Wire Inc—*Loren Ota*	1115 Instrument Dr, Rocky Mount NC 27804	252-977-3900	R	12*	.1
26	Inwesco Inc—*David Morris*	746 N Coney Ave, Azusa CA 91702	626-334-9304	R	12*	.1
27	Npi Solutions Inc—*Kevin Andersen*	721 Charcot Ave, San Jose CA 95131	408-944-9178	R	12*	.1
28	Lynn Electronics Corp	154 Railroad Dr, Ivyland PA 18974	215-355-8200	R	11*	.2
29	Fox Valley Steel and Wire—*James Monroe*	PO Box 130, Hortonville WI 54944	920-779-4544	S	10*	.1
30	Idaho Laboratories Corp—*Katz Nukaya*	2101 Hemmert Ave, Idaho Falls ID 83401	208-522-0055	R	10*	.1
31	Northwest Regulator Supply Inc—*Alan Melton*	5061 N Lagoon Ave, Portland OR 97217	503-235-1038	R	6*	<.1
32	Ametco Manufacturing Corp—*Steve Mitrovich*	PO Box 1210, Willoughby OH 44096	440-951-4300	R	6*	<.1
33	Murphy Industries Inc—*Theodore Murphy*	1650 Cascade Dr, Marion OH 43302	740-387-7890	R	5*	<.1
34	Miraco Inc—*Joseph Roberts*	102 Maple St, Manchester NH 03103	603-665-9449	R	4*	<.1
35	Metal Resource Solutions—*Rich Tereba*	7770 W Chester Rd Ste, West Chester OH 45069	513-874-7630	R	3*	<.1
36	Pneu Fast Inc—*Edward Chester*	2200 Greenleaf St, Evanston IL 60202	847-866-8180	R	2*	<.1
37	United Microwave Products Inc—*Edwin Jacobs*	22129 S Vermont Ave, Torrance CA 90502	310-320-1244	R	2*	<.1
38	Sheltered Workshop For Disabled Inc—*Dennis Donovan*	PO Box 310, Binghamton NY 13902	607-722-2364	R	2*	.2
39	Precision Wire Components—*Jeff Hall*	10230 SW Spokane Ct, Tualatin OR 97062	503-691-2027	R	N/A	.4

TOTALS: SIC 3315 Steel Wire & Related Products
Companies: 39   2,516   10.0

Rank	Company Name—*Executive Officer*	Address, City, State, Zip	Phone	Type	Fin	Empls
3316 Cold-Finishing of Steel Shapes						
1	Worthington Industries Inc—*John P McConnell*	200 Old Wilson Bridge, Columbus OH 43085	614-438-3210	P	2,443	8.4
2	Esmark Inc—*David A Luptak*	2500 Euclid Ave, Chicago Heights IL 60411	708-756-0400	R	978*	.8
3	Steel Technologies Inc—*Michael J Carroll*	PO Box 43339, Louisville KY 40253	502-245-2110	S	876*	1.0
4	GKN Sinter Metals Inc—*Andy Reynolds Smith*	3300 University Dr, Auburn Hills MI 48326	248-371-0800	S	720*	7.2
5	Thomas Steel Strip Corp—*Dennis Wist*	400 Delaware Ave NW, Warren OH 44485	330-841-6429	S	472*	.4
6	Ice Industries Inc—*Howard Ice*	3810 Herr Rd, Sylvania OH 43560	419-842-3600	R	267*	.2
7	Michgian Seamless Tube LLC—*Russell W Maier*	400 McMunn St, South Lyon MI 48178	248-486-0210	S	179*	.1
8	Cmc Steel Inc—*Marvin Selig*	PO Box 1046, Dallas TX 75221	214-689-4300	R	143*	1.8
9	Worthington Specialty Processing—*John McConnell*	PO Box 1068, Jackson MI 49204	517-789-0200	J	140*	.1
10	North American Stainless General Partnership—*Anil Yadav*	6870 Us Hwy 42 E, Ghent KY 41045	502-347-6000	R	98*	1.2
11	Spectro Alloys Corp—*Greg Palen*	13220 Doyle Path E, Rosemount MN 55068	651-437-2815	R	84*	.1
12	Wells Manufacturing Co (Woodstock Illinois)—*Tom Wells*	2100 W Lake Shore Dr, Woodstock IL 60098	815-338-3900	R	70*	.4
13	Feroleto Steel Company Inc—*Harold Wood*	PO Box 3344, Bridgeport CT 06605	203-366-3263	R	54*	.1
14	Blue Ridge Metals Corp—*Isao Yoshida*	PO Box 189, Fletcher NC 28732	828-974-9226	R	50*	.1
15	Service Center Metals LLC—*Scott Kelley*	5850 Quality Way, Prince George VA 23875		R	45*	<.1
16	Coil Clip Inc—*L Douglas Lippert*	90 Gilland Cir, Boaz AL 35956	256-593-8158	S	41*	<.1
17	Calstrip Steel Corp—*Thomas Nelis*	7140 Bandini Blvd, Commerce CA 90040	323-726-1345	R	40*	.1
18	Corey Steel Co—*Paul Darling*	PO Box 5137, Chicago IL 60680	708-735-8000	R	38*	.2
19	Theis Precision Steel Corp—*Viola Hallman*	300 Broad St, Bristol CT 06010	860-589-5511	R	33*	.2
20	Precision Industries Inc—*Jack Milhollan*	PO Box 711, Washington PA 15301	724-222-2100	R	27*	.1
21	Ohio River Metal Services Inc—*Shirley Ohta*	5150 Loop Rd, Jeffersonville IN 47130	812-282-4770	R	21*	.1
22	Nelsen Steel And Wire LP—*C Nelsen*	9400 Belmont Ave, Franklin Park IL 60131	847-671-9700	R	19*	.1
23	Maurice Pincoffs Company Inc—*John Griffin*	PO Box 920919, Houston TX 77292	713-681-5461	R	19*	<.1
24	Hercules Drawn Steel Corp—*Mark Goodman*	38901 Amrhein Rd, Livonia MI 48150	734-464-4454	R	18*	.1
25	Spectra LMP LLC—*Michael Guthrie*	6501 Lynch Rd, Detroit MI 48234	313-571-2100	R	18*	.2
26	Universal Metal Service Corp—*Mark Ruder*	16655 S Canal St, South Holland IL 60473	708-596-2700	R	18*	.2
27	Bcs Cuyahoga LLC—*Roger Hurley*	5800 Sterling Ave, Maple Heights OH 44137	440-248-0290	R	17*	.1
28	Blair Strip Steel Co—*Bruce Kinney*	PO Box 7159, New Castle PA 16107	724-658-2611	R	14*	.1
29	Mid-State Industries Operating Inc—*Kevin Corley*	908 Bob King Dr, Arcola IL 61910	217-268-3900	R	13*	.1
30	Enduro Industries LLC—*Henry Crute*	PO Box 509, Hannibal MO 63401	573-248-2084	R	12*	.1
31	Bar Technologies LLC—*Fred Parkar*	500 Fluid Power Dr, Geneva IL 60134	630-208-7000	R	5*	<.1

TOTALS: SIC 3316 Cold Finishing of Steel Shapes
Companies: 31   6,974   23.8

Rank	Company Name—*Executive Officer*	Address, City, State, Zip	Phone	Type	Fin	Empls
3317 Steel Pipe & Tubes						
1	Bellville Tube Company LP—*John P Surma*	PO Box 220, Bellville TX 77418	979-865-9111	S	9,683*	2.4
2	Environmental Holdings Inc—*John P Surma*	PO Box 803546, Dallas TX 75380	972-770-6401	S	9,683*	2.4
3	Lone Star Logistics Inc—*John P Surma*	PO Box 803546, Dallas TX 75380	972-386-3981	S	9,683*	2.4
4	Lone Star Steel International LP—*Rhys J Best*	PO Box 803546, Dallas TX 75380	972-386-3981	S	9,683*	2.4
5	US Steel- Bellville Operations Div—*John P Surma*	PO Box 220, Bellville TX 77418	979-865-9111	S	9,683*	2.4
6	Zinklahoma Inc—*John P Surma*	PO Box 803546, Dallas TX 75380	972-770-6401	S	9,683*	2.4
	Environmental Holdings Inc					
7	John Maneely Co—*Barry Zekelman*	3201 Enterprise Pkwy S, Beachwood OH 44122	216-910-3700	S	2,757*	1.5
8	US Steel (Houston Texas)—*John P Surma*	650 N Sam Houston Pkwy, Houston TX 77060	713-993-3101	S	2,160*	2.7
9	Superior Group Inc—*William G Warden III*	One Tower Bridge 100 F, West Conshohocken PA 19428	610-397-2040	R	750	3.4
10	Copperweld BiMetallics LLC—*Li Fu*	254 Cotton Mill Rd, Fayetteville TN 37334	931-433-7177	S	732*	3.0
11	Handy and Harman Tube Company Inc—*John Coates*	12244 Willow Grove Rd, Camden DE 19934	302-697-9521	D	496*	.2
12	Webco Industries Inc—*Dana Weber*	PO Box 100, Sand Springs OK 74063	918-245-2211	P	466	.9
13	Stupp Corp—*Chuck King*	12555 Ronaldson Rd, Baton Rouge LA 70807	225-775-8800	D	449*	.3
14	Northwest Pipe Co—*Richard A Roman*	5721 SE Columbia Way S, Vancouver WA 98661	360-397-6250	P	387	1.2
15	Wheatland Tube Co—*Peter S Dooner III*	700 S Dock St, Sharon PA 16146		S	340*	1.7
	John Maneely Co					
16	Pittsburgh Tube Co—*Peter Whiting*	6051 Wallace Rd Ext, Wexford PA 15090	412-299-7900	R	289*	1.7
17	MicroGroup Inc—*William Bergen*	7 Industrial Park Rd, Medway MA 02053	508-533-4925	R	278*	.1
18	Arcelormittal Tubular Products USA Corp—*Jerome Granboulan*	4 Gateway Ctr Ste 2105, Pittsburgh PA 15222	412-263-3200	R	225*	2.3
19	Southland Tube Inc—*John Montgomery*	3525 Richard Arringt, Birmingham AL 35234	205-251-1884	S	180*	.3
20	Synalloy Corp—*Craig C Bram*	PO Box 5627, Spartanburg SC 29304	864-585-3605	P	151	.4
21	Troxel Co—*Bobby Rowlett*	PO Box 276, Moscow TN 38057	901-877-6875	R	136*	.5
22	Western Tube and Conduit Corp	PO Box 2720, Long Beach CA 90801	310-537-6300	R	133*	.3
23	Hanna Steel Corp—*Phyllis Paramore*	PO Box 558, Fairfield AL 35064	205-780-1111	R	118*	.4
24	Plymouth Tube Co—*Donald Van Pelt*	29w 150 Warrenville Rd, Warrenville IL 60555	630-393-3550	R	97*	1.0
25	Kellogg Brown and Root Inc	PO Box 9807, Houston TX 77213	713-753-2000	S	75*	1.0
26	Felker Brothers Corp—*Thomas Henke*	22 N Chestnut Ave, Marshfield WI 54449	715-384-3121	R	69*	.3
27	Metal-Matic Inc—*Thomas Bliss*	629 2nd St Se, Minneapolis MN 55414	612-378-0411	R	56*	.6
28	Outokumpu Stainless Pipe Inc—*Tom Kern*	1101 N Main St, Wildwood FL 34785	352-748-1313	R	55*	.1
29	Superior Tube Company Inc—*Anthony Jost*	3900 Germantown Pke, Collegeville PA 19426	610-489-5200	R	55*	.2
30	Bull Moose Tube Co—*John Meyer*	1819 Clarkson Rd Ste 1, Chesterfield MO 63017	636-537-2600	S	53*	.5
31	Noble-Met LLC—*John Trinchere*	200 S Yorkshire St, Salem VA 24153	540-389-7860	R	51*	.2
32	Naylor Pipe Co—*John Czulno*	1230 E 92nd St, Chicago IL 60619	773-721-9400	R	49*	.2
33	Hannibal Industries Inc—*Blanton Bartlett*	3851 S Santa Fe Ave, Vernon CA 90058	323-588-4261	R	47*	.3
34	Independence Tube Corp—*Rick Werner*	6226 W 74th St, Chicago IL 60638	708-496-0380	R	45*	.2
35	Tubular Products Co—*Charles Brown*	PO Box 170100, Birmingham AL 35217	205-856-1300	R	41*	.2
36	V and M Star LP—*Kunibert Martin*	8603 Sheldon Rd, Houston TX 77049	281-456-6000	R	40*	.6
37	Leavitt Tube Company LLC—*Su Honda*	1717 W 115th St, Chicago IL 60643	773-239-7700	R	40*	.5
38	Salem Tube Inc—*Rufino Orce*	951 4th St, Greenville PA 16125	724-646-4301	R	36*	.1
39	Lock Joint Tube LLC—*Gerald Lerman*	515 W Ireland Rd, South Bend IN 46614	574-299-5327	R	34*	.2
40	Western Pneumatic Tube Company LLC	835 6th St S, Kirkland WA 98033	425-822-8271	R	34*	.1
41	LeFiell Manufacturing Co—*George Ray*	13700 Firestone Blvd, Santa Fe Springs CA 90670		R	32*	.1
42	Markin Tubing LP—*Barton P Dambra*	One Markin Ln, Wyoming NY 14591	585-495-6211	R	25*	.2
43	Tex-Tube Co—*Dan Keffer*	PO Box 55710, Houston TX 77255	713-686-4351	R	24*	.2
44	Jackson Tube Service Inc—*Robert Jackson*	PO Box 1650, Piqua OH 45356	937-773-8550	R	23*	.2
45	Camp-Hill Corp—*Robert Campana*	PO Box 3128, McKeesport PA 15134	412-675-5580	R	23*	.2
46	Sterling Pipe and Tube Inc—*Fred Shelar*	5335 Enterprise Blvd, Toledo OH 43612	419-729-9756	R	21*	.1
47	Welded Tube Of Canada Inc—*Barry Sonshine*	6401 Rogers Rd Ste A, Delta OH 43515	419-822-3333	R	21*	.4
48	Tube Methods Inc—*Gary Johnson*	PO Box 460, Bridgeport PA 19405	610-279-7700	R	18*	.1
49	Vest Inc—*Iwaki Sugimoto*	PO Box 58827, Los Angeles CA 90058	323-581-8823	R	17*	.1
50	Phoenix Tube Company Inc—*Anthony Reale*	1185 Win Dr, Bethlehem PA 18017	610-865-5337	R	17*	.1
51	California Steel And Tube—*Michael Hoffman*	16049 Stephens St, City Of Industry CA 91745	626-968-5511	R	15*	.1
52	Bock Industries Inc—*John Meyer*	PO Box 1037, Elkhart IN 46515	574-295-8070	S	13*	.1
	Bull Moose Tube Co					
53	Caporal Industries Ltd—*William Murphy*	PO Box 1728, Stephenville TX 76401	254-965-5162	R	13*	.1
54	Roscoe Moss Manufacturing Co—*Robert Vanvaler*	PO Box 31064, Los Angeles CA 90031	323-263-4111	R	13*	.1
55	Valley Metals LLC—*Don Rediker*	PO Box 85402, San Diego CA 92186	858-513-1300	S	11*	<.1
	Western Pneumatic Tube Company LLC					
56	K-Tube Corp—*Greg May*	13400 Kirkham Way, Poway CA 92064	858-513-9229	S	8*	.1
57	Angstrom USA LLC—*Kumar Amm*	26980 Trlley Industral, Taylor MI 48180	313-295-0100	R	8*	<.1
58	Bendco/Bending and Coiling Co—*James Friery*	PO Box 3384, Pasadena TX 77501	713-473-1557	R	7*	<.1
59	K and K Supply Inc—*Roy Kimbal*	PO Box 578, Conroe TX 77305	936-539-2210	R	6*	<.1
60	NitroSteel Div—*Lee Petzel*	9955 80th Ave, Pleasant Prairie WI 53158	262-947-0441	D	4*	<.1
61	Welding Apparatus Co—*Brant Terzic*	1668 N Ada St, Chicago IL 60642	773-252-7670	R	3*	<.1
62	Tubetech Inc—*Stephen Oliphant*	PO Box 470, East Palestine OH 44413	330-426-9476	R	2*	<.1
TOTALS: SIC 3317 Steel Pipe & Tubes						
	Companies: 62				69,345	43.8
3321 Gray & Ductile Iron Foundries						
1	Neenah Foundry Co—*Robert E Ostendorf Jr*	PO Box 729, Neenah WI 54957		R	3,106*	3.0
2	Amsted Industries Inc—*W Robert Reum*	2 Prudential Plaza 180, Chicago IL 60601	312-645-1700	R	2,800*	9.2
3	American Cast Iron Pipe Co—*Van L Richey*	PO Box 2727, Birmingham AL 35202	205-325-7701	R	778*	3.0
4	Nfc Castings Inc—*Robert Ostendorf*	PO Box 729, Neenah WI 54957	920-725-7000	S	634*	1.9
5	Grede Holdings LLC—*Douglas J Grimm*	4000 Town Center Ste50, Southfield MI 48075	248-440-9500	R	616*	5.1
6	Grede Foundries Inc—*Doug Grimm*	PO Box 26499, Milwaukee WI 53226	414-257-3600	R	506*	4.5
7	US Foundry and Manufacturing Corp—*Alex DeBogory Jr*	8351 NW 93rd St, Medley FL 33166		R	187*	.2
8	ATTC Manufacturing Inc—*Mr Uesugi*	10455 State Rd 37, Tell City IN 47586	812-547-5060	S	176*	.2
9	Metso Minerals Industries Inc—*Mike Phillips*	20965 Crossroads Cir, Waukesha WI 53186	262-717-2500	R	139*	1.5
10	Dexter Apache Holdings Inc—*Patrick Albregts*	PO Box 7901, Fairfield IA 52556	641-472-5131	R	133*	.8
11	Anaco Inc	1001 El Camino Ave, Corona CA 92879	951-372-2732	R	128*	.1
12	Taylor and Fenn Co—*Edgar Dutler Jr*	22 Deerfield Rd, Windsor CT 06095	860-249-7531	R	99*	.2
13	Maddox Foundry and Machine Works Inc—*Monte Marchant*	PO Drawer 7, Archer FL 32618	352-495-2121	R	96*	.1
14	Ward Manufacturing LLC—*Arthur Guidi*	PO Box 9, Blossburg PA 16912	570-638-2100	S	83*	1.1
15	RH Sheppard Company Inc—*Peter Sheppard*	PO Box 877, Hanover PA 17331	717-637-3751	R	61*	1.0
16	Brillion Iron Works Inc	200 Park Ave, Brillion WI 54110	920-756-6450	S	60*	.4
17	Anbakam Metals LLC—*Sivakumar Balasubramaniam*	1200 Tices Ln Ste 201, East Brunswick NJ 08816	732-710-4360	R	48*	.1

Note: An asterisk (*) indicates an estimated financial figure. The company type code used is as follows: R = Private, P = Public, S = Private Subsidiary, B = Public Subsidiary, D = Division, J = Joint Venture, I = Investment Fund.

COMPANY RANKINGS BY SALES WITHIN 4-DIGIT SIC

Rank	Company Name—*Executive Officer*	Address, City, State, Zip	Phone	Type	Fin	Empls
18	Dalton Corporation Kendallville Manufacturing Facility—*Joseph Derita*	200 W Ohio St, Kendallville IN 46755	260-347-6360	R	44*	.3
19	Grede Wisconsin Subsidiaries LLC—*Frederick Sommer*	242 S Pearl St, Berlin WI 54923	920-361-2220	R	36*	.3
20	Osco Industries Inc—*John Burke*	PO Box 1388, Portsmouth OH 45662	740-354-3183	R	35*	.4
21	Baker Manufacturing Company LLC—*Donald Wesdell*	133 Enterprise St, Evansville WI 53536	608-882-5100	R	33*	.2
22	AB and I—*Allan Boscacci*	7825 San Leandro St, Oakland CA 94621	510-632-3467	R	33*	.2
23	Frazier and Frazier Industries Inc—*Charles Frazier*	PO Box 279, Coolidge TX 76635	254-786-2293	R	32*	.3
24	Bremen Castings Inc—*James Brown*	PO Box 129, Bremen IN 46506	574-546-2411	R	32*	.2
25	Strohwig Industries Inc—*Wolfgang Strohwig*	PO Box 38, Richfield WI 53076	262-628-4477	R	29*	.2
26	Benton Foundry Inc—*Fritz Hall*	5297 State Rte 487, Benton PA 17814	570-925-6711	R	29*	.3
27	Intat Precision Inc—*Donald Carson*	PO Box 488, Rushville IN 46173	765-932-5323	R	29*	.4
28	Ebaa Iron Inc—*Earl Bradley*	PO Box 877, Eastland TX 76448	254-629-1737	R	24*	.4
29	Jensen International Inc—*J Jensen*	PO Box 1509, Coffeyville KS 67337	620-251-5700	R	24*	.2
30	Great Lakes Castings Corp—*Robert Killips*	800 N Washington Ave, Ludington MI 49431	231-843-2501	R	23*	.3
31	Motorcasting Inc—*Joseph Kemfton*	1323 S 65th St, Milwaukee WI 53214	414-476-1434	R	23*	.2
32	Quality Castings Co—*Anthony Yonto*	PO Box 58, Orrville OH 44667	330-682-6010	R	23*	.3
33	Atlas Foundry Company Inc—*James Gartland*	601 N Henderson Ave, Marion IN 46952	765-662-2525	R	22*	.1
34	Willman Industries Inc—*Clayton Willman*	PO Box 487, Cedar Grove WI 53013	920-668-8526	R	22*	.2
35	Paragon Metals Inc—*Michael Smith*	14120 Balntyn Corp Pl, Charlotte NC 28277	980-235-1400	R	21*	.3
36	Ellwood Engineered Casting Co—*Kevin Handerhan*	7158 Hubbard Masury Rd, Hubbard OH 44425	330-534-8668	R	21*	.1
37	ATI Casting Service—*David Neal*	PO Box 488, LaPorte IN 46350	219-362-1000	S	18*	.2
38	Badger Foundry Co—*Angus Callender*	PO Box 1306, Winona MN 55987	507-452-5760	R	18*	.2
39	Castalloy Corp—*John Braatz*	PO Box 827, Waukesha WI 53187	262-547-0070	R	18*	.2
40	Rolls Technology Inc—*Thomas Adams*	400 Railroad Ave, Avonmore PA 15618	724-697-4533	R	17*	.4
41	Harrison Ironworks LLC	1612 Aqua Vista Dr, Lawrenceburg IN 47025	812-537-2737	R	17*	.2
42	Gartland Foundry Company Inc—*William Grimes*	PO Box 2008, Terre Haute IN 47802	812-232-0226	R	16*	.1
43	Russell Pipe and Foundry Co—*Cecil L Walton*	1500 Hwy 22 W, Alexander City AL 35010	256-234-2514	R	15	.1
44	Kirsh Foundry Inc—*James Kirsh*	125 Rowell St, Beaver Dam WI 53916	920-887-0395	R	14*	.1
45	Manchester Metals LLC—*Kevin Weaver*	205 Wabash Rd, North Manchester IN 46962	260-982-2191	R	13*	.1
46	D and L Foundry Inc—*John Leftwich*	PO Box 1319, Moses Lake WA 98837	509-765-7952	R	12*	.1
47	Prospect Foundry Inc—*John Gerszewski*	1225 NE Winter St, Minneapolis MN 55413	612-331-9282	S	12*	.1
48	Hamburg Manufacturing Inc—*David Pendergast*	PO Box 147, Hamburg PA 19526	610-562-2203	R	12*	.1
49	Thyssenkrupp Waupaca Inc—*Gary Gigante*	PO Box 249, Waupaca WI 54981	715-258-6611	R	12*	.1
50	Betz Industries Inc—*Karl Betz*	2121 Bristol Ave Nw, Grand Rapids MI 49504	616-453-4429	R	11*	.1
51	T and B Foundry Co—*Edward Pruc*	2469 E 71st St, Cleveland OH 44104	216-391-4200	R	11*	.1
52	Kent Foundry Co—*Gerald Poorman*	PO Box 187, Greenville MI 48838	616-754-1100	R	10*	<.1
53	Hodge Foundry—*Joe Simko*	PO Box 550, Greenville PA 16125	724-588-4100	R	10*	.1
54	Anaconda Foundry Fabrication Company Inc—*Jim Liebetrau*	1015 E 6th St, Anaconda MT 59711	406-563-8494	R	9*	.1
55	Pier Foundry and Pattern Shop Inc—*Randall Grilz*	51 State St, Saint Paul MN 55107	651-222-4461	R	8*	.1
56	Unicast Co—*Louis Monaco*	241 N Washington St, Boyertown PA 19512	610-367-0155	R	8*	.1
57	Harris Industries Inc—*H Smith*	PO Box 4199, Longview TX 75606	903-759-4485	R	7*	.1
58	Clay And Bailey Manufacturing Co—*Ronald Borst*	6401 E 40th St, Kansas City MO 64129	816-924-3900	R	7*	.1
59	Warsaw Foundry Company Inc—*William Petro*	PO Box 227, Warsaw IN 46581	574-267-8772	R	6*	.1
60	Bentonville Casting Co—*Chris Hines*	PO Box 1109, Bentonville AR 72712	479-273-7723	R	6*	.1
61	Campbell Foundry Co—*Christopher Campbell*	800 Bergen St, Harrison NJ 07029	973-483-5480	R	6*	<.1
62	Col-Pump Company Inc—*Thomas Bowker*	131 E Railroad St, Columbiana OH 44408	330-482-3381	R	6*	.1
63	Jacobs Manufacturing Co—*H Jacobs*	311 Edmonds Ave, Bridgeport AL 35740	256-495-2261	R	5*	.1
64	Bloomfield Foundry Inc—*Monica Ausdal*	PO Box 200, Bloomfield IA 52537	641-664-2191	R	4*	.1
65	Plymouth Foundry Inc—*Sam Schlosser*	PO Box 537, Plymouth IN 46563	574-936-2106	R	4*	<.1
66	Clearfield Machine Company Inc—*Douglas Gallaher*	520 S 3rd St, Clearfield PA 16830	814-765-6544	R	3*	<.1
67	Thompson Gundrilling Inc—*Michael Thompson*	13840 Saticoy St, Van Nuys CA 91402	818-781-7776	R	3*	<.1
68	Mabry Foundry Company Inc—*Brian Shoaf*	PO Box 21777, Beaumont TX 77720	409-842-2223	R	2*	<.1
69	St Marys Foundry Inc—*Angela Molaskey*	405 E South St, Saint Marys OH 45885	419-394-3346	R	2*	<.1
70	Oneida Foundries Inc—*John Albanse*	559 Fitch St, Oneida NY 13421	315-363-4570	R	2*	<.1
71	Progressive Foundry Inc—*Dallas Vankirk*	PO Box 338, Perry IA 50220	515-465-5697	R	N/A	.1

TOTALS: SIC 3321 Gray & Ductile Iron Foundries
Companies: 71

					10,507	40.0

3322 Malleable Iron Foundries

Rank	Company Name—*Executive Officer*	Address, City, State, Zip	Phone	Type	Fin	Empls
1	Dotson Company Inc—*Dennis Dotson*	200 W Rock St, Mankato MN 56001	507-345-5018	R	17*	.1
2	Paxton-Mitchell Co—*Al Campbell*	2614 Martha St, Omaha NE 68105	402-345-6767	R	15*	.1
3	A Moresi Foundry Inc—*L Bergeron*	PO Box 512, Jeanerette LA 70544	337-276-4533	R	1*	<.1

TOTALS: SIC 3322 Malleable Iron Foundries
Companies: 3

					34	.2

3324 Steel Investment Foundries

Rank	Company Name—*Executive Officer*	Address, City, State, Zip	Phone	Type	Fin	Empls
1	Precision Castparts Corp—*Mark Donegan*	4650 SW Macadam Ave St, Portland OR 97239	503-417-4800	P	6,220	18.3
2	Northern Precision Casting Co—*Jeffrey Giovannetti*	300 Interchange N, Lake Geneva WI 53147	262-248-4461	R	462*	.1
3	Precision Castparts Corp Structurals Div—*Ross Lienhart* Precision Castparts Corp	4650 SW Macadam Ave St, Portland OR 97239	503-417-4850	S	318*	2.7
4	Alcoa Howmet—*Raymond Mitchell*	1 Misco Dr, Whitehall MI 49461	231-894-5686	D	240*	2.0
5	Esco Turbine Technologies - Syracuse Inc—*John O'neil*	901 E Genesee St, Chittenango NY 13037	315-687-0014	S	26*	.4
6	Cast Parts Inc—*Steve Clodfelter*	4200 Valley Blvd, Walnut CA 91789	909-595-2252	R	26*	.4
7	Miller Castings Inc—*Ralph Miller*	2503 Pacific Park Dr, Whittier CA 90601	562-695-0461	R	23*	.3
8	Post Precision Castings Inc—*John Post*	PO Box A, Strausstown PA 19559	610-488-1011	R	23*	.2
9	Aero Metals Inc—*James Fleming*	1201 E Lincolnway, La Porte IN 46350	219-326-1976	R	22*	.3
10	Bescast Inc—*Lee Watson*	4602 E 355th St, Willoughby OH 44094	440-946-5300	R	19*	.2
11	Kovatch Castings Inc—*Frank Kovatch*	3743 Tabs Dr, Uniontown OH 44685	330-896-9944	R	15*	.2
12	Consolidated Casting Corp—*Richard Grant*	1501 S I-45, Hutchins TX 75141	972-225-7305	R	14*	.2
13	Pennsylvania Precision Cast Parts Inc—*Richard Miller*	PO Box 1429, Lebanon PA 17042	717-273-3338	R	13*	.1
14	Engineered Precision Casting Co—*Walter Dubovick*	952 Palmer Ave, Middletown NJ 07748	732-671-2424	R	12*	.1
15	Harbor Castings Inc—*C Lynham*	4321 Strausser St Nw, Canton OH 44720	330-499-7178	R	10*	.1
16	American Aerospace Technical Castings Inc—*Patti Bredengerd*	2950 W Catalina Dr, Phoenix AZ 85017	602-268-1467	R	10*	.1
17	T Cast Holdings LLC—*David Jaeger*	640 S Cherry St, Myerstown PA 17067	717-866-9009	R	9*	.1
18	Sure Cast Inc—*William Wurster*	PO Box 930, Burnet TX 78611	512-756-6500	R	8*	.1
19	RLM Industries Inc—*Louis Verville*	PO Box 505, Oxford MI 48371	248-628-5103	R	8*	.1
20	Chain Industries Inc—*James Chain*	51035 Grand River Ave, Wixom MI 48393	248-348-7722	R	6*	<.1
21	Wolf Technologies LLC—*Gregory Wolf*	PO Box 185, Douglassville PA 19518	610-385-6091	R	5*	<.1
22	Shear Tool Inc—*Charles Lange*	5763 Dixie Hwy, Saginaw MI 48601	989-777-0110	S	4*	<.1
23	Ruger Investment Castings Div—*William Ruger Jr*	411 Sunapee St, Newport NH 03773	603-863-2000	D	4	N/A

Rank	Company Name—*Executive Officer*	Address, City, State, Zip	Phone	Type	Fin	Empls
24	Parrten Products Inc—*Howard Parrett*	6650 La Contenta Rd, Yucca Valley CA 92284	760-365-5536	R	2*	<.1

TOTALS: SIC 3324 Steel Investment Foundries
Companies: 24 — 7,499 — 25.9

3325 Steel Foundries Nec

Rank	Company Name—*Executive Officer*	Address, City, State, Zip	Phone	Type	Fin	Empls
1	Standard Steel and Wire—*Dennis D Hack*	2450 W Hubbard St, Chicago IL 60612	312-226-6100	R	2,275*	<.1
2	Intermet Corp—*Steve Lake*	301 Commerce St Ste 29, Fort Worth TX 76102	817-348-9190	R	837	5.3
3	Bradken—*Brian Hodges*	PO Box 188, Atchison KS 66002	816-270-0700	S	388	3.0
4	Park Corp (Cleveland Ohio)—*Joe Adams*	6200 Riverside Dr, Cleveland OH 44135	216-267-4870	R	271*	3.2
5	Wollaston Alloys Inc—*Steve Clodfelter*	205 Wood Rd, Braintree MA 02184	781-848-3333	R	208*	.2
6	E2 Acquisition Corp—*Craig Bouchard*	1430 Sparrows Point Bl, Sparrows Point MD 21219	410-388-3000	R	168*	2.5
7	Bradken Inc—*Jeff Brentano*	12200 N Ambassador Dr, Kansas City MO 64163	816-270-0700	R	155*	2.0
8	Ervin Industries Inc—*John Pearson*	PO Box 1168, Ann Arbor MI 48108	734-769-4600	R	120*	.4
9	Bradken Inc—*Steven Gear*	3021 S Wilkeson St, Tacoma WA 98409	253-475-4600	R	105*	.5
10	Shultz Steel Co—*Stephen W Shultz*	5321 Firestone Blvd, South Gate CA 90280	323-564-3281	R	71*	.5
11	Harrison Steel Castings Co—*Wade Harrison*	PO Box 60, Attica IN 47918	765-762-2481	R	65*	.9
12	American Steel LLC—*Craig Schwartz*	PO Box 10086, Portland OR 97296	503-226-1511	S	65*	.3
13	Columbus Steel Castings Co—*Rick Mavrakis*	2211 Parsons Ave, Columbus OH 43207	614-444-2121	R	62*	.8
14	Varicast Inc—*Dan Swartz*	866 N Columbia Blvd, Portland OR 97217	503-821-8100	R	47*	.3
15	Consolidated Fabrication And Constructors Inc—*Ronald Spork*	3851 Ellsworth St, Gary IN 46408	219-884-6150	R	42*	.3
16	Winsert Inc—*Trisha Dickinson*	PO Box 198, Marinette WI 54143	715-732-1703	R	40*	.1
17	Hensley Industries Inc—*H Kuribayashi*	PO Box 29779, Dallas TX 75229	972-241-2321	R	38*	.5
18	Me Global Inc—*David Delozier*	3901 University Ave Ne, Minneapolis MN 55421	763-788-1651	R	36*	.2
19	Huron Casting Inc—*Leroy Wurst*	PO Box 679, Pigeon MI 48755	989-453-3933	R	32*	.5
20	Carondelet Foundry Co—*EJ Kubick*	8600 Commercial Blvd, Pevely MO 63070	636-479-4499	D	30*	.2
21	Sandusky International Inc—*Edward Ryan*	615 W Market St, Sandusky OH 44870	419-626-5340	S	28*	.2
22	Maynard Steel Casting Company Inc—*Michael Wabiszewski*	2856 S 27th St, Milwaukee WI 53215	414-385-6500	R	27*	.2
23	Frog Switch And Manufacturing Co—*James Folk*	600 E High St, Carlisle PA 17013	717-243-2454	R	27*	.2
24	Alcon Industries Inc—*John Cracken*	7990 Baker Ave, Cleveland OH 44102	216-961-1100	R	26*	.2
25	Waukesha Foundry Inc—*Barry Kerwin*	1300 Lincoln Ave, Waukesha WI 53186	262-542-0741	R	25*	.2
26	Sivyer Steel Corp—*Arthur Gibeaut*	225 33rd St, Bettendorf IA 52722	563-355-1811	R	24*	.3
27	Dameron Alloy Foundries—*John Dameron*	PO Box 8000, Compton CA 90224	310-631-5165	R	21*	.1
28	Duraloy Technologies Inc—*Vincent Schiavoni*	120 Bridge St, Scottdale PA 15683	724-887-5100	R	18*	.1
29	Spuncast Inc—*Don Payne*	PO Box 521, Watertown WI 53094		R	18*	.1
30	Omaha Steel Castings Co—*Phillip Teggart*	4601 Farnam St, Omaha NE 68132	402-558-6000	H	16*	.2
31	Rmf Steel Products Co—*John Robertson*	4417 E 119th St, Grandview MO 64030	816-765-4101	R	15*	.1
32	Korff Holdings LLC—*Pam Brooks*	310 E Euclid Ave, Salem OH 44460	330-332-1566	R	13*	.1
33	General Plug and Manufacturing Co *Kevin J Flanigan*	PO Box 26, Grafton OH 44044	440-926-2411	R	12*	.1
34	H and H Steel Fabricators Inc—*Brian Harris*	PO Box 95, Springtown TX 76082	817-677-5490	R	12	.1
35	Steeltech Ltd—*Gary Salerno*	1251 Phillips Ave Sw, Grand Rapids MI 49507	616-243-7920	R	11*	.1
36	Bay Cast Inc—*Max Holman*	PO Box 126, Bay City MI 48707	989-892-0511	R	11*	.1
37	Southern Alloy Corp—*Billy Bobbitt*	PO Box 1168, Sylacauga AL 35150	256-245-5237	R	8*	.1
38	Utah Fabrication Inc—*Roger Peterson*	1485 James Way, Tooele UT 84074	435-843-8317	R	7*	.1
39	Sfi Gray Steel Ltd—*Terry Culberth*	3511 W 12th St, Houston TX 77008	713-864-6450	R	7*	.1
40	Bernier Cast Metals—*David Bernier*	2626 Hess St, Saginaw MI 48601	989-754-7571	R	5	<.1
41	Idaho Falls Foundry and Machine Company Inc—*Ted Ballard*	PO Box 2267, Idaho Falls ID 83403	208-522-7412	R	3*	<.1
42	Colonial Processing Inc—*Steven Gove*	1930 S 6th St, Camden NJ 08104	856-966-3313	R	2*	<.1
43	McConway and Torley Group—*Pat Wallace*	109 48th St, Pittsburgh PA 15201	412-682-4700	S	<1	.6

TOTALS: SIC 3325 Steel Foundries Nec
Companies: 43 — 5,389 — 24.6

3331 Primary Copper

Rank	Company Name—*Executive Officer*	Address, City, State, Zip	Phone	Type	Fin	Empls
1	Silver Bell Mining LLC—*Mark Kalmi*	25000 W Avra Valley Rd, Marana AZ 85653	520-682-2420	S	284*	.1
2	China Direct Industries Inc—*James Wang*	431 Fairway Dr Ste 200, Deerfield Beach FL 33441	954-363-7333	P	188	1.6
3	CSG Direct Inc—*Michael Hemphill*	640 Maestro Dr No 107, Reno NV 89511	775-852-9777	R	4	<.1

TOTALS: SIC 3331 Primary Copper
Companies: 3 — 476 — 1.8

3334 Primary Aluminum

Rank	Company Name—*Executive Officer*	Address, City, State, Zip	Phone	Type	Fin	Empls
1	Alcoa Inc—*Klaus Kleinfeld*	201 Isabella St, Pittsburgh PA 15212	412-553-4545	P	21,013	59.0
2	3a Composites USA Inc—*Brendan Cooper*	PO Box 507, Benton KY 42025	704-658-3500	R	2,080*	1.3
3	Connell LP—*Frank Doyle*	1 International Pl 31s, Boston MA 02110	617-391-5577	R	1,428*	2.0
4	Kaiser Aluminum Corp—*Jack A Hockema* MAXXAM Inc	27422 Portola Pkwy Ste, Foothill Ranch CA 92610	949-614-1740	B	1,301	2.6
5	Noranda Aluminum Holding Corp—*Layle K Smith*	801 Crescent Centre Dr, Franklin TN 37067	615-771-5700	P	1,295	2.4
6	Century Aluminum Co—*Logan W Kruger*	2511 Garden Rd Bldg A, Monterey CA 93940	831-642-9300	P	1,169	1.3
7	Norsk Hydro Americas Inc—*Eivind Reiten*	100 N Tampa St Ste 335, Tampa FL 33602	813-222-5700	S	1,012*	2.4
8	Goldendale Aluminum Co—*Brett Wilcox*	85 John Day Dam Rd, Goldendale WA 98620	509-778-5811	R	453*	.7
9	Ormet Corp—*Mike Tanchuk*	PO Box 176, Hannibal OH 43931	724-483-1381	R	419*	2.0
10	Intalco Aluminum Corp—*Alain JP Belda* Alcoa Inc	PO Box 937, Ferndale WA 98248	360-384-7061	S	189*	.7
11	MAXXAM Inc—*Charles E Hurwitz*	1330 Post Oak Blvd Ste, Houston TX 77056	713-975-7600	R	84	.2
12	Southwire Co NSA Div—*Stuart Thorn*	1987 State Rte 271 N, Hawesville KY 42348	270-927-6971	D	41*	.3
13	Modern Equipment Company Inc (Port Washington Wisconsin)—*Jim Wenistorfer*	369 W Western Ave, Port Washington WI 53074	262-284-9431	S	25*	.1
14	Columbia Falls Aluminum Company LLC—*Starr Macdonald*	2000 Aluminum Dr, Columbia Falls MT 59912	406-892-8400	R	18*	.2
15	Kkt Inc—*David Lamson*	31251 Industrial Rd, Livonia MI 48150	734-425-5330	R	7*	<.1
16	Dantherm Air Handling Inc—*Kristian Askegaard*	4260 Orchard Park Blvd, Spartanburg SC 29303	864-595-9800	S	5*	<.1
17	Maurice and Maurice Engineering Inc—*Glen Maurice*	17579 Mesa St Ste B4, Hesperia CA 92345	760-949-5151	R	3*	<.1

TOTALS: SIC 3334 Primary Aluminum
Companies: 17 — 30,543 — 75.1

3339 Primary Nonferrous Metals Nec

Rank	Company Name—*Executive Officer*	Address, City, State, Zip	Phone	Type	Fin	Empls
1	Momentive Performance Materials Inc—*Craig O Morrison*	22 Corporate Woods, Albany NY 12211	518-533-4600	S	6,000	10.0
2	Shin-Etsu Handotai America Inc—*Tomio Shibata*	PO Box 8965, Vancouver WA 98668	360-883-7000	S	1,850*	.7
3	Sanders Lead Company Inc—*Wiley Sanders*	PO Box 707, Troy AL 36081	334-566-1563	R	542*	.4
4	Starck H C Inc—*Andreas Meier*	45 Industrial Pl, Newton Highlands MA 02461	617-630-5800	D	522*	.4
5	Horsehead Holding Corp—*James M Hensler*	4955 Steubenville Pike, Pittsburgh PA 15205	724-774-1020	B	382	1.1

Note: An asterisk (*) indicates an estimated financial figure. The company type code used is as follows: R = Private, P = Public, S = Private Subsidiary, B = Public Subsidiary, D = Division, J = Joint Venture, I = Investment Fund.

COMPANY RANKINGS BY SALES WITHIN 4-DIGIT SIC

Rank	Company Name—*Executive Officer*	Address, City, State, Zip	Phone	Type	Fin	Empls
6	Rec Advanced Silicon Materials LLC—*Mike Carden*	119140 Rick Jones Way, Butte MT 59750	406-496-9898	S	245*	.7
7	Century Aluminum of West Virginia Inc—*Craig Davis*	PO Box 98, Ravenswood WV 26164	304-273-6000	S	162*	.6
8	Silterra Malaysia Sdn Bhd—*Kamarulzaman M Zin*	2880 Zanker Rd Ste 207, San Jose CA 95134	408-530-0888	R	150	N/A
9	Louis Padnos Iron and Metal Co—*Jeffrey S Padnos*	PO Box 1979, Holland MI 49422	616-396-6521	R	123*	.4
10	Strategic Minerals Corp—*Heinrich Enslin*	4285 Malvern Rd, Hot Springs AR 71901	501-262-1270	R	108*	.4
11	Ati Titanium LLC—*Scott Mcdaniel*	PO Box 460, Albany OR 97321	541-926-4211	R	102*	1.2
12	Cabot Supermetals	PO Box 1608, Boyertown PA 19512	610-367-1500	D	80*	.4
13	Johnson Matthey Inc Precious Metals Div—*Don D Lockhart*	1401 King Rd, West Chester PA 19380	610-648-8000	D	57*	.2
14	Argen Corp—*Bertram Woolf*	5855 Oberlin Dr, San Diego CA 92121	858-455-7900	R	39*	.3
15	I Schumann and Co—*Michael Schumann*	22500 Alexander Rd, Bedford OH 44146	440-439-2300	R	35*	.1
16	Semco Enterprises Inc—*Tom Seminoff*	475 S Wilson Way, City of Industry CA 91744	626-333-2237	R	23*	<.1
17	Mitsubishi Polycrystalline Silicon America Corp—*Akira Seino*	7800 Mitsubishi Ln, Theodore AL 36582	251-443-6440	R	19*	.1
18	Sipi Metals Corp—*Marion Cameron*	1720 N Elston Ave, Chicago IL 60642	773-276-0070	R	18*	.1
19	United States Antimony Corp—*John C Lawrence*	PO Box 643, Thompson Falls MT 59873	406-827-3523	P	7	<.1
20	Virginia Semiconductor Inc—*Thomas Digges*	1501 Powhatan St, Fredericksburg VA 22401	540-373-2900	R	3*	<.1
21	InterGroup International Ltd—*Neil Gloger*	1111 E 200th St, Euclid OH 44117	216-862-9289	R	3*	<.1
22	Amorphous Materials Inc—*Ray Hilton*	3130 Benton St, Garland TX 75042	972-494-5624	R	2*	<.1
23	BEM Services Inc—*Gordon Havnett*	17876 St Clair Ave, Cleveland OH 44110	216-486-4200	S	1*	<.1
24	Brush International Inc—*Mark M Comerford*	17876 St Clair Ave, Cleveland OH 44110	216-486-4200	S	1*	<.1

TOTALS: SIC 3339 Primary Nonferrous Metals Nec
Companies: 24   10,474   17.2

3341 Secondary Nonferrous Metals

Rank	Company Name—*Executive Officer*	Address, City, State, Zip	Phone	Type	Fin	Empls
1	Aleris International Inc—*Steven J Demetriou*	25825 Science Park Dr, Beachwood OH 44122	216-910-3400	S	5,990	8.8
2	Titanium Metals Corp—*Bobby O'Brien*	5430 LBJ Fwy Ste 1700, Dallas TX 75240	972-934-5300	P	1,045	2.8
3	Kester Solder Div—*Roger Savage*	800 W Thorndale Ave, Itasca IL 60143	630-616-4000	S	830*	2.5
4	RSR Corp—*Robert E Finn*	2777 N Stemmons Fwy St, Dallas TX 75207	214-631-6070	R	633*	.6
5	Metalico Inc—*Carlos E Aguero*	186 N Ave E, Cranford NJ 07016	908-497-9610	P	553	.8
6	Haynes International Inc—*Mark M Comerford*	PO Box 9013, Kokomo IN 46904	765-456-6000	P	543	1.1
7	Bonnell Aluminum—*Duncan Crowdis*	PO Box 428, Newnan GA 30264	770-253-2020	S	263*	1.0
8	Matthey Johnson Inc—*N Carson*	435 Devon Park Dr Ste, Wayne PA 19087	610-971-3000	R	169*	1.7
9	David H Fell and Company Inc—*Lawrence Fell*	PO Box 910952, Los Angeles CA 90091	323-722-9992	R	149*	<.1
10	Colonial Metals Co—*David Serls*	217 Linden St, Columbia PA 17512	717-684-2311	R	110*	.1
11	Audubon Metals LLC—*James Muehlbauer*	PO Box 14, Henderson KY 42419	270-830-6622	R	87*	.2
12	Tst Inc—*Andrew Stein*	11601 Etiwanda Ave, Fontana CA 92337	951-685-2155	R	86*	.3
13	Mervis Industries Inc—*Adam Mervis*	PO Box 827, Danville IL 61834	217-442-5300	R	83*	.3
14	Pease and Curren Inc—*Francis Curren*	75 Pennsylvania Ave, Warwick RI 02888	401-739-6350	R	83*	<.1
15	Galt Alloys Inc—*Dawne S Hickton*	1550 Marietta Ave SE, Canton OH 44707	330-453-2118	S	74*	.1
16	Cannon Muskegon Corp—*Joseph Snowden*	PO Box 506, Muskegon MI 49443	231-755-1681	R	66*	.2
17	Trialco Inc—*Jay Armstrong*	900 E 14th St Ste 1, Chicago Heights IL 60411	708-757-4200	R	50*	.1
18	International Metals Reclamation Company Inc—*Mark To-maszewski*	1 Inmetco Dr, Ellwood City PA 16117	724-758-2800	S	48*	.1
19	Metalor USA Refining Corp—*Michael Mooiman*	PO Box 255, North Attleboro MA 02761	508-699-8800	R	46*	.2
20	Heraeus Metal Processing LLC—*Peter Buehler*	13429 Alondra Blvd, Santa Fe Springs CA 90670	562-921-7464	R	32*	.4
21	Canfield Technologies Inc—*Robert McIntire*	1 Crossman Rd, Sayreville NJ 08872	732-316-2100	R	31*	.1
22	Mid-Carolina Steel and Recycling Company Inc—*Fred Seidenberg*	PO Box 3764, Columbia SC 29230	803-786-9888	R	24*	<.1
23	Ansam Metals Corp—*Benjamin Zager*	PO Box 3408, Baltimore MD 21225	410-355-8220	R	24*	.1
24	Interamerican Zinc Inc—*Steven J Demetriou* Aleris International Inc	245 N Fillmore Rd, Coldwater MI 49036	517-279-1011	S	24*	.1
25	Loveman Steel Corp—*Ralph Loveman*	PO Box 46430, Bedford Heights OH 44146	440-232-6200	R	16*	.1
26	Hoover and Strong Inc—*Torrance Hoover*	10700 Trade Rd, Richmond VA 23236	804-794-3700	R	16*	.1
27	Charleston Steel And Metal Co—*Samuel Steinberg*	PO Box 814, Charleston SC 29402	843-722-7278	R	14*	.1
28	Newell Recycling Of San Antonio LP—*Natalee Newell*	PO Box 830808, San Antonio TX 78283	210-227-3141	R	14*	.1
29	Imperial Zinc Corp—*Mark Spellman*	1031 E 103rd St, Chicago IL 60628	773-264-5900	R	12*	.1
30	Oakwood Industries Inc—*David Nagusky*	7250 Division St, Cleveland OH 44146	440-232-8700	R	10*	.1
31	Babbitting Service Inc—*Kristoffer Farrar*	PO Box 1051, Belvidere IL 61008	847-841-8008	R	9*	.1
32	US Bronze Foundry And Machine Inc—*Dan Higham*	18649 Brake Shoe Rd, Meadville PA 16335	814-337-4234	R	8*	.1
33	Continental Aluminum Corp—*William Altgilbers*	29201 Milford Rd, New Hudson MI 48165	248-437-1001	R	8*	.1
34	Manufacturing Sciences Corp—*Dave Brown*	804 S Illinois Ave, Oak Ridge TN 37830	865-481-0455	R	6*	.1
35	Western Scrap Processing Company Inc—*Tchad Robinson*	3315 Drennan Industria, Colorado Springs CO 80910	719-390-7986	R	4*	<.1
36	Eutectic Engineering Company Inc—*Charles Baer*	6350 E Davison St, Detroit MI 48212	313-892-2248	R	4*	<.1
37	Futura Corp (Boise Idaho)—*Brent S Lloyd*	PO Box 7968, Boise ID 83707	208-336-0150	R	3*	<.1
38	WJ Bullock Inc—*William Bullock*	PO Box 539, Fairfield AL 35064	205-788-6586	R	2*	<.1
39	Conway Detroit Corp—*D Conway*	34635 Nova Dr, Clinton Township MI 48035	586-791-2000	R	2*	<.1
40	Lee Metals Inc—*Donald Feigert*	PO Box 141, Coraopolis PA 15108	412-331-8630	R	1*	<.1
41	Rotometals Inc—*Gary Hora*	865 Estabrook St, San Leandro CA 94577	510-346-4770	R	1*	<.1

TOTALS: SIC 3341 Secondary Nonferrous Metals
Companies: 41   11,171   22.2

3351 Copper Rolling & Drawing

Rank	Company Name—*Executive Officer*	Address, City, State, Zip	Phone	Type	Fin	Empls
1	Encore Wire Corp—*Daniel L Jones*	1329 Millwood Rd, McKinney TX 75069	972-562-9473	P	1,180	.9
2	Mueller Copper Tube Company Inc	PO Box 849, Fulton MS 38843	662-862-2181	S	1,169	4.8
3	CMC Howell Metal—*Jim Forkovitch*	PO Box 218, New Market VA 22844	540-740-4700	S	873*	.3
4	Wolverine Tube Inc—*Harold M Karp*	2100 Market St NE, Decatur AL 35601	256-353-1310	P	816	1.4
5	Dover Diversified Inc—*William W Spurgeon*	3005 Highland Pky Ste, Downers Grove IL 60515	630-541-1540	S	781*	4.0
6	GT Technologies—*William F Redmond Jr*	5815 Executive Dr, Westland MI 48185	734-467-8371	S	398	N/A
7	Global Brass And Copper Inc—*John Walker* Global Brass And Copper Holdings Inc	427 N Shamrock St, East Alton IL 62024	618-258-5000	S	173*	2.0
8	Gbc Metals LLC—*Mary Crockett* Global Brass And Copper Inc	427 N Shamrock St, East Alton IL 62024	618-258-2350	S	171*	2.0
9	Global Brass And Copper Holdings Inc—*John Walker*	427 N Shamrock St, East Alton IL 62024	618-258-2350	S	160*	2.0
10	Actelis Networks Inc—*Vivek Ragavan*	6150 Stevenson Blvd, Fremont CA 94538	510-545-1045	R	113*	<.1
11	Ems Engineered Materials Solutions LLC—*Paul Duffuy*	39 Perry Ave, Attleboro MA 02703	508-342-2100	R	105*	.4
12	Chase Brass and Copper Company LLC—*Devin Denner*	PO Box 152, Montpelier OH 43543	419-485-3193	R	86*	.3
13	Deutsche Nickel America Inc—*Paul Parsons*	70 Industrial Rd, Cumberland RI 02864	401-334-4800	R	83*	<.1
14	Electric Materials Co—*Douglas Winner*	PO Box 390, North East PA 16428	814-725-9621	R	60*	.3
15	Ansonia Copper and Brass Inc—*Raymond McGee*	725 Bank St, Waterbury CT 06708	203-732-6600	R	59*	.2
16	National Copper and Smelting Company Inc—*Thomas Fox*	3333 Stanwood Blvd Ne, Huntsville AL 35811	256-859-4510	R	44*	.5
17	Wieland Copper Products LLC—*Dawn Cardinal*	PO Box 160, Pine Hall NC 27042	336-445-4500	R	36*	.5

Rank	Company Name—*Executive Officer*	Address, City, State, Zip	Phone	Type	Fin	Empls
18	Spectra-Strip Cable Products—*Mike Carbray*	720 Sherman Ave, Hamden CT 06514	203-281-3200	D	32*	<.1
19	American Tubing Inc—*Charles Lewis*	2191 Ford Ave, Springdale AR 72764	479-756-1291	R	30*	.5
20	Luvata Buffalo Inc—*Raymond Mercer*	PO Box 981, Buffalo NY 14240	716-879-6700	R	29*	.3
21	Alan Wire Co—*Alan Keenan*	830 S W St, Sikeston MO 63801	573-471-9548	R	20*	.2
22	Nehring Electrical Works Co—*Raymond Hott*	PO Box 965, Dekalb IL 60115	815-756-2741	R	19*	.1
23	Wieland Metals Inc—*Werner Traa*	567 Northgate Pkwy, Wheeling IL 60090	847-537-3990	R	16*	.1
24	Metal Forming Industries Inc—*James Staley*	PO Box 203, Russellville IN 46175	765-435-3091	R	3*	<.1

TOTALS: SIC 3351 Copper Rolling & Drawing
Companies: 24 — — — — **6,456** **20.8**

3353 Aluminum Sheet, Plate & Foil

Rank	Company Name—*Executive Officer*	Address, City, State, Zip	Phone	Type	Fin	Empls
1	Lonza Inc (Allendale New Jersey)—*Stephen Kutzer*	90 Boroline Rd, Allendale NJ 07401	201-316-9200	S	20,806*	8.3
2	Kaiser Aluminum and Chemical Corp—*Jack A Hockema*	5847 San Felipe Ste 25, Houston TX 77057	713-273-9566	S	1,928*	7.8
3	Wise Metals Group LLC—*David F D'Addario*	857 Elkridge Landing R, Linthicum Heights MD 21090	410-636-6500	R	986	N/A
4	Century Kentucky Inc—*Logan W Kruger*	1627 State Hwy 271 N, Hawesville KY 42348	270-685-2493	S	921*	.8
5	JW Aluminum Co—*Don Kessing*	PO Box 29419-05, Charleston SC 29419	843-572-1100	S	912*	.8
6	Nichols Aluminum—*Raymond A Jean*	PO Box 3808, Davenport IA 52808	563-324-2121	D	158*	.2
7	Jupiter Aluminum Corp—*Dietrich Gross*	1745 165th St, Hammond IN 46320	219-932-3322	R	32*	.2
8	United Aluminum Corp—*John Lapides*	PO Box 215, North Haven CT 06473	203-239-5881	R	22*	.1
9	Becromal Of America Inc—*Robert Glenn*	350 J D Yrnell Industr, Clinton TN 37716	865-457-8914	R	19*	<.1
10	Kroy Industries Inc—*Kenneth Nordlund*	PO Box 309, York NE 68467	402-362-6651	R	14*	.1
11	Quanex Corporation Chatsworth Group—*Raymond Jean*	7942 N 3350 E Rd, Chatsworth IL 60921	815-635-3171	D	12*	.2
12	Republic Foil-Garmco USA—*Tony Ellis*	55 Triangle St, Danbury CT 06810	203-743-2731	S	9*	<.1
13	Voyager Aluminum Inc—*Gary Suckow*	PO Box 566, Brandon MN 56315	320-834-4940	R	6*	<.1
14	Alcan Foil Products Div—*Philip Martens*	1513 Redding Dr, LaGrange GA 30240	706-812-2000	R	4*	<.1
15	Sea Converting Inc—*Paula Johnson*	895 Sivert Dr, Wood Dale IL 60191	630-694-9178	R	1*	<.1

TOTALS: SIC 3353 Aluminum Sheet, Plate & Foil
Companies: 15 — — — — **25,830** **18.5**

3354 Aluminum Extruded Products

Rank	Company Name—*Executive Officer*	Address, City, State, Zip	Phone	Type	Fin	Empls
1	Indalex Inc—*Timothy RJ Stubbs*	75 Tristate Internatio, Mundelein IL 60060	847-810-3000	S	1,843*	3.4
2	Bon L Campo LP *Tredegar Corp*	902 Gladys St, El Campo TX 77437	979-543-0600	S	1,249*	3.1
3	Bon L Holdings Corp—*Nancy M Taylor* *Tredegar Corp*	1100 Boulders Pkwy, Richmond VA 23225		S	1,209*	3.0
4	Bon L Manufacturing Company of Virginia—*Nancy M Taylor* *Tredegar Corp*	1100 Boulders Pkwy, Richmond VA 23225		S	1,209*	3.0
5	Sapa Extrusions	PO Box 187, Cressona PA 17929	570-385-5000	S	810*	1.5
6	Tredegar Corp—*Nancy Taylor*	1100 Boulders Pkwy, Richmond VA 23225	804-330-1000	P	798	2.2
7	Tecnocap LLC	1701 Wheeling Ave, Glen Dale WV 26038	304-845-3402	R	421*	.4
8	William L Bonnell Company Inc—*Duncan Crowdis* *Tredegar Corp*	PO Box 428, Newnan GA 30264	770-253-2020	S	330*	1.0
9	Tifton Aluminum Company Inc—*Mike Delf*	PO Box 88, Tifton GA 31793	912-382-7380	R	175	N/A
10	Cardinal Aluminum Co—*William Edwards*	PO Box 19987, Louisville KY 40259	502-969-9302	R	93*	.5
11	Brazeway Inc—*Stephanie Boyse*	2711 E Maumee St, Adrian MI 49221	517-265-2121	R	92*	1.2
12	Sapa Profiles Inc—*John Noordwijk*	PO Box 11263, Portland OR 97211	503-802-3000	R	80*	.8
13	Keymark Corp—*William Keller*	PO Box 626, Fonda NY 12068	518-853-3421	R	68*	.9
14	Franklin Aluminum Company Inc—*Jack Falcon*	PO Box 266, Franklin GA 30217	706-675-3341	R	60*	.9
15	Loxcreen Company Inc—*John Parrish*	PO Box 4004, West Columbia SC 29171	803-822-8200	R	58*	.7
16	Indalex Aluminum Solutions—*Matt Zundel*	18111 Railroad St, City of Industry CA 91748		D	51	.3
17	Hydro Aluminum Rockledge Inc—*Dennis J Herron*	100 Gus Hipp Blvd, Rockledge FL 32955	321-636-8147	S	50*	.3
18	Custom Aluminum Products Inc—*John Castoro*	414 Division St, South Elgin IL 60177	847-717-5000	R	44*	.4
19	Afco Industries Inc—*James Waters*	PO Box 5085, Alexandria LA 71307	318-448-1651	R	42*	.4
20	General Extrusions Inc—*Michael Schuler*	PO Box 3460, Youngstown OH 44513	330-783-0270	R	41*	.3
21	Light Metals Corp—*George Boylan*	PO Box 902, Grand Rapids MI 49509	616-538-3030	R	39*	.3
22	Magnode Corp—*Arthur Bidwell*	400 E State St, Trenton OH 45067	513-988-6351	R	36*	.2
23	Florida Extruders International Inc—*Joel Lehman*	2540 Jewett Ln, Sanford FL 32771	407-323-3300	R	31*	.4
24	Sierra Aluminum Co—*William Hunter*	2345 Fleetwood Dr, Riverside CA 92509	951-781-7800	R	31*	.2
25	Wing Enterprises Inc—*Ryan Moss*	PO Box 3100, Springville UT 84663	801-491-7621	R	30*	.2
26	Star Extruded Shapes Inc—*Kenneth George*	PO Box 553, Canfield OH 44406	330-533-9863	R	29*	.2
27	Gordon Aluminum Industries Inc—*Alfred Gordon*	1000 Mason St, Schofield WI 54476	715-359-6101	R	27*	.4
28	Astro Shapes Inc—*Paul Cene*	65 Main St, Struthers OH 44471	330-755-1414	R	26*	.3
29	Metals USA Building Products SouthEast Inc—*Bill Bowen*	7815 American Way, Groveland FL 34736	352-787-7766	S	25	.2
30	Patrick Industries Inc Patrick Metals Div—*Red Wiedner*	5020 Lincolnway E, Mishawaka IN 46544	574-255-9692	D	25*	.2
31	Aerolite Extrusion Co—*Thomas Hutch*	4605 Lake Park Rd, Youngstown OH 44512	330-782-1127	R	16*	.1
32	Aluminum Extruded Shapes Inc—*Robert Hoeweler*	10549 Reading Rd, Cincinnati OH 45241	513-563-2205	R	15*	.1
33	Vari-Wall Tube Specialists Inc—*Randall Alexoff*	PO Box 340, Columbiana OH 44408	330-482-0000	R	14*	.1
34	Ashe Industries Inc—*Stan Ashe*	4505 Transport Dr, Tampa FL 33605	813-247-2743	R	14*	<.1
35	Pries Enterprises Inc—*Merle Mcmahon*	701 17th St Se, Independence IA 50644	319-334-7068	R	14*	.1
36	American Aluminum Extrusions of Ohio LLC—*Jennifer Hudnell*	4416 Louisville St Ne, Canton OH 44705	330-458-0300	R	13*	.1
37	Anaheim Extrusion Company Inc—*Pam Silverstein*	PO Box 6380, Anaheim CA 92816	714-630-3111	S	13*	.1
38	Southern Metals Company Inc—*J Dill*	PO Box 471, Sheffield AL 35660	256-383-3261	R	12*	.1
39	Taber Extrusions LLC—*William Wetmore*	915 S Elmira Ave, Russellville AR 72802	479-968-1021	R	12*	.1
40	Hydro Aluminum North America	999 Corporate Blvd Ste, Linthicum Heights MD 21090		S	9*	.1
41	Tower Extrusions Ltd	PO Box 218, Olney TX 76374	940-564-5681	R	9*	.1
42	Midamerica Holdings Corp—*Bill Witherspoon*	4925 Aluminum Dr, Indianapolis IN 46218	317-545-1221	R	9*	<.1
43	Central Aluminum Company LLC—*Steve White*	2045 Broehm Rd, Columbus OH 43207	614-491-5700	R	8*	.1
44	Alexandria Acquisition Company LLC—*Bibiana Mariono*	PO Box 678307, Dallas TX 75267	972-721-7174	R	5*	.1
45	Fabricated Metals LLC—*Thomas Diebold*	PO Box 9535, Louisville KY 40209	502-363-2625	R	5*	.1
46	Decor Products Inc—*Jeffrey Townsend*	PO Box 320, Wausaukee WI 54177	715-856-5101	R	3*	.1
47	Parker Tooling and Design Inc—*Doug Parker*	2563 3 Mile Rd Nw, Grand Rapids MI 49534	616-791-1080	R	2*	<.1
48	80/20 Inc—*Donald Wood*	1701 S 400 E, Columbia City IN 46725	260-248-8030	R	<1*	.3

TOTALS: SIC 3354 Aluminum Extruded Products
Companies: 48 — — — — **9,193** **28.2**

3355 Aluminum Rolling & Drawing Nec

Rank	Company Name—*Executive Officer*	Address, City, State, Zip	Phone	Type	Fin	Empls
1	Euramax Holdings Inc—*Mitchell Lewis*	5445 Triangle Pkwy Ste, Norcross GA 30092	770-449-7066	R	812*	2.2
2	Alcan Cable Div—*Ian Hewett*	3 Ravinia Dr Ste 1600, Atlanta GA 30346	770-394-9886	D	200*	.8
3	Golden Aluminum Company Inc—*Ron Toma*	14555 Old Crpus Chrsti, Elmendorf TX 78112	210-635-6000	R	150*	.4

Note: An asterisk (*) indicates an estimated financial figure. The company type code used is as follows: R = Private, P = Public, S = Private Subsidiary, B = Public Subsidiary, D = Division, J = Joint Venture, I = Investment Fund.

COMPANY RANKINGS BY SALES WITHIN 4-DIGIT SIC

Rank	Company Name—Executive Officer	Address, City, State, Zip	Phone	Type	Fin	Empls
4	Arcadia Inc—James Schladen	2301 E Vernon Ave, Vernon CA 90058	323-269-7300	R	30*	.4
5	L T C Roll and Engineering Co—Andrew Ligda	23500 John Gorsuch Dr, Clinton Township MI 48036	586-465-1023	R	25*	.2
6	Alcotec Wire Corp—Tom Svaboda	2750 Aero Park Dr, Traverse City MI 49686	231-941-4111	R	19*	.1
7	Joseph Freedman Company Inc—John Freedman	115 Stevens St, Springfield MA 01104	413-781-4444	R	17*	.1
8	Temcor—Charles Miller	879 W 190th St Ste 110, Gardena CA 90248	310-523-2322	R	16*	.1
9	Pro-Fab Inc (Bosque Farms New Mexico)—Martha Swinney	1040 Bosque Farms Blvd, Bosque Farms NM 87068	505-869-2222	R	12*	<.1
10	Advanced Industries Inc—Charles Wesonig	PO Box 350, Odessa MO 64076	816-230-4064	R	10*	.1
11	Met-Al Inc—Robert Lee	1349 23rd St, Racine WI 53403	262-637-9858	R	6*	<.1

TOTALS: SIC 3355 Aluminum Rolling & Drawing Nec
Companies: 11 1,296 4.4

3356 Nonferrous Rolling & Drawing Nec

Rank	Company Name—Executive Officer	Address, City, State, Zip	Phone	Type	Fin	Empls
1	Extrusion Technology Corporation of America RTI International Metals Inc	7600 S Santa Fe Bldg C, Houston TX 77061	713-641-6010	S	2,635*	1.9
2	RTi Energy Systems Inc Manufacturing Facility—Dawne Hickton RTI International Metals Inc	7211 Spring Cypress Rd, Spring TX 77379	281-379-4289	S	2,428*	1.8
3	RTI Fabrications LP—Dawne Hickton RTI International Metals Inc	7373 Hunt Ave, Garden Grove CA 92841	713-641-6010	S	2,428*	1.8
4	Mueller Industries Inc—Gregory L Christopher	8285 Tournament Dr Ste, Memphis TN 38125	901-753-3200	P	2,418	3.8
5	RTI Niles—Dawne Hickton RTI International Metals Inc	1000 Warren Ave, Niles OH 44446	330-544-7633	S	1,924*	1.8
6	RTI CT—Dawne Hickton RTI International Metals Inc	827 Marshall Phelps Rd, Windsor CT 06095	860-688-8393	S	1,678*	1.8
7	New Century Metals Southeast Inc—Dawne Hickton RTI International Metals Inc	7373 Hunt Ave, Garden Grove CA 92841	714-677-6760	S	1,677*	1.2
8	RTI Energy Systems Inc Business Offices—Dawne Hickton RTI International Metals Inc	9720 Cypresswood Dr St, Houston TX 77070	281-379-4289	S	1,675*	1.2
9	RTI Energy Systems Manufacturing Facility—Dawne Hickton RTI International Metals Inc	7211 Spring Cypress Rd, Spring TX 77379	281-379-4289	S	1,675*	1.2
10	RTI Fabrication and Distribution Inc—Dawne Hickton RTI International Metals Inc	7600 Santa Fe Bldg C, Houston TX 77061	713-641-6010	S	1,665*	1.2
11	RTI St Louis Inc—Dawne Hickton RTI International Metals Inc	950 Franklin St, Sullivan MO 63080	573-468-3176	S	1,665*	1.2
12	Metaldyne Corp—Thomoas A Amato	47603 Halyard Dr, Plymouth MI 48170	734-207-6200	S	919*	3.9
13	RTI International Metals Inc—Dawne S Hickton	1550 Coraopolis Height, Coraopolis PA 15108	412-893-0051	P	530	1.7
14	UMC Acquisition Corp—Dominick Baione	9151 Imperial Hwy, Downey CA 90242	562-886-1750	R	456*	.3
15	Steelscape Inc—Miguel Alvarez	222 W Kalama River Rd, Kalama WA 98625	360-673-8200	S	198*	.2
16	Inco United States Inc—Richard Guido	Park 80 W Plz Ii, Saddle Brook NJ 07663	416-361-7669	R	166*	2.4
17	Piper Impact Inc—Jeff Petry	PO Box 726, New Albany MS 38652	662-538-6500	S	163	.9
18	Titanium Fabrication Corp—Brent Willey	110 Lehigh Dr, Fairfield NJ 07004	973-227-5300	R	140*	.1
19	Farrell Duferco Corp—Benedict Sciortino	15 Roemer Blvd, Farrell PA 16121	724-983-6464	R	47*	.5
20	Swepco Tube LLC—Phil Lehr	PO Box 1899, Clifton NJ 07015	973-778-3000	R	41*	.1
21	Jarden Zinc Products Inc—Al Giles	PO Box 1890, Greeneville TN 37744	423-639-8111	R	39*	.3
22	Gulf Chemical And Metallurgical Corp—William Deering	PO Box 2290, Freeport TX 77542	979-233-7882	R	34*	.1
23	Leach and Garner Co—Edwin Leach	PO Box 358, Attleboro MA 02703	508-695-7800	R	29*	.4
24	Sigmund Cohn Corporation Of California—Thomas Cohn	121 S Columbus Ave, Mount Vernon NY 10553	914-664-5300	R	27*	.1
25	D and W Enterprises—Carl Woodworth	211 Lakerim Ct, Lake Placid FL 33852	863-699-6384	R	22*	<.1
26	Platt Brothers and Co—James Behuniak	PO Box 1030, Waterbury CT 06721	203-753-4194	R	22*	.1
27	Big River Zinc Corp—George Obeldobel	2401 Mississippi Ave, East Saint Louis IL 62201	618-274-5000	R	21*	.3
28	Magnesium Elektron North America Inc—Chris Barnes	PO Box 258, Madison IL 62060	618-452-5190	R	16*	.1
29	Driver-Harris Co—Frank L Driver IV	200 Madison Ave, Convent Station NJ 07961	973-267-8100	R	13	.1
30	P Kay Metal Supply—Larry Kay	2448 E 25th St, Los Angeles CA 90058	323-585-5058	R	10*	<.1
31	Southern Metals Co—Robert Helbein	PO Box 668923, Charlotte NC 28266	704-394-3161	R	9*	.1
32	SET Enterprises Inc (Warren Michigan)—Sid E Taylor	30500 Van Dyke Ave Ste, Warren MI 48093	586-573-3600	R	9*	<.1
33	Midland Industries Inc—Laurence Spector	1424 N Halsted St, Chicago IL 60642		R	9*	<.1
34	Carbide Technologies Inc—Theresa Monks	18101 Malyn Blvd, Fraser MI 48026	586-296-5200	R	8*	.1
35	Union City Filament Corp—Joseph Celia	PO Box 777, Ridgefield NJ 07657	201-945-3366	R	6*	<.1
36	Interspace Battery Inc—Donald Godber	2009 W San Bernardino, West Covina CA 91790	626-813-1234	R	5*	<.1
37	Kearny Smelting and Refining Corp—Francine Rothschild	936 Harrison Ave Ste 5, Kearny NJ 07032	201-991-7276	R	3*	<.1
38	Vermont American Corp Multi-Metals Div—Gene Cowley	715 E Gray St, Louisville KY 40202		S	2*	<.1
39	Ames Metal Products Co—Lewis Edelstein	4323 S Western Blvd, Chicago IL 60609	773-523-3230	R	2*	<.1

TOTALS: SIC 3356 Nonferrous Rolling & Drawing Nec
Companies: 39 24,810 30.6

3357 Nonferrous Wiredrawing & Insulating

Rank	Company Name—Executive Officer	Address, City, State, Zip	Phone	Type	Fin	Empls
1	Corning Inc—Wendell P Weeks	1 Riverfront Plz, Corning NY 14831	607-974-9000	P	6,632	26.2
2	General Cable Corp—Gregory B Kenny	4 Tesseneer Dr, Highland Heights KY 41076	859-572-8000	P	5,867	12.0
3	Southwire Co—Stuart Thorn	PO Box 1000, Carrollton GA 30112	770-832-4242	R	4,600*	4.0
4	Andrew Corp	2700 Ellis Rd, Joliet IL 60433	708-236-6600	S	2,195*	11.0
5	Belden Inc—John S Stroup	7733 Forsyth Blvd Ste, Saint Louis MO 63105	314-854-8000	P	1,617	6.6
6	International Wire Group Inc—Rodney D Kent	12 Masonic Ave, Camden NY 13316	315-245-3800	P	693	1.6
7	Handy and Harman Ltd—Glenn M Kassan	1133 Westchester Ave S, White Plains NY 10604	914-461-1300	P	582	1.9
8	American Fiber Systems Inc—Dave Rusin	100 Meridian Ctr Ste 3, Rochester NY 14618		S	501*	.2
9	Accellent Corp—Donald Spence	PO Box 26992, Collegeville PA 19426	610-489-0300	S	472*	1.3
10	AboveNet Inc—William G LaPerch	360 Hamilton Ave, White Plains NY 10601	914-421-6700	P	410	.7
11	Nexans Berk-Tek Electronics Cable—Frederic Vincent	PO Box 909, Elm City NC 27822	252-236-4311	R	376*	.2
12	Sensors Unlimited Inc—Ed Hart	3490 Rte 1 Bldg 12, Princeton NJ 08540	609-520-0610	S	294*	.1
13	Olympic Manufacturing Group Inc—Hubert McGovern Handy and Harman Ltd	153 Bowles Rd, Agawam MA 01001		S	291*	.3
14	Temp-Flex Cable Inc—Raymond Baril	26 Milford Rd, South Grafton MA 01560	508-839-5987	R	253*	.1
15	TA Pelsue Co—Brad Pelsue	2500 S Tejon St, Englewood CO 80110	303-936-7432	R	199*	.1
16	Ofs Brightwave LLC—Patrice Dubois	2000 NE Expy, Norcross GA 30071	770-798-3000	R	164*	2.3
17	Tyco Electronics Integrated Cable Systems LLC—Wayne Stiles	PO Box 479, Portsmouth NH 03802	603-436-6100	R	129*	.4
18	Source Photonics—Near Margalit	20550 Nordhoff St, Chatsworth CA 91311	818-773-9044	R	124	1.6
19	Alpine Group Inc—Steven S Elbaum	1 Meadowlands Plz, East Rutherford NJ 07073	201-549-4400	P	124	.4
20	Wire Technologies Inc International Wire Group Inc	833 Legner St, Bremen IN 46506	574-546-4680	S	105*	.1
21	Okonite Company Inc—A Coppola	PO Box 340, Ramsey NJ 07446	201-825-0300	R	103*	1.0
22	Aetna Insulated Wire Co—Walt Smith	1537 Air Rail Ave, Virginia Beach VA 23455		R	96*	.3

Rank	Company Name—*Executive Officer*	Address, City, State, Zip	Phone	Type	Fin	Empls
23	ADVA Optical Networking—*Brian L Protiva*	140 E Ridgewood Ave St, Paramus NJ 07652		R	93	N/A
24	AFC Cable Systems Inc—*Bob Tereira*	272 Duchaine Blvd, New Bedford MA 02745	508-998-1131	S	76*	1.3
25	New England Wire Technologies Corp—*Richard Johns*	PO Box 264, Lisbon NH 03585	603-838-6625	R	75*	.6
26	Horizon Music Inc—*Dale Williams*	3581 Larch Ln, Jackson MO 63755	573-651-6500	R	74*	.3
27	Optical Cable Corp—*Neil D Wilkin Jr*	5290 Concourse Dr, Roanoke VA 24019	540-265-0690	P	73	.3
28	Del City Wire Company Inc—*Robert Arzbaecher*	2101 W Camden Rd, Milwaukee WI 53209	414-247-5531	R	66*	.1
29	Monster Cable Products Inc—*Noel Lee*	455 Valley Dr, Brisbane CA 94005	415-840-2000	R	64*	.7
30	LGC Wireless Inc—*Ian Sugarbroad*	2540 Junction Ave, San Jose CA 95134	408-952-2400	S	58*	.1
31	Belden Wire and Cable Co—*John S Stroup* Belden Inc	PO Box 1980, Richmond IN 47375	765-983-5200	S	56*	.3
32	Wyre-Wynd Southwire Co	77 Anthony St, Jewett City CT 06351	860-376-2516	D	52*	.2
33	Amphenol Interconnect Products Corp—*Martin Loeffler*	20 Valley St, Endicott NY 13760	607-754-4444	S	50*	.2
34	Champlain Cable Corp—*Richard Hall*	175 Hercules Dr, Colchester VT 05446	802-655-2121	S	48*	.3
35	Draka Cableteq USA Inc—*Joseph Dickson*	PO Box 347, Schuylkill Haven PA 17972	570-385-4381	S	44*	.2
36	Ortronics Inc—*John Selldorf*	125 Eugene Oneill Dr, New London CT 06320	860-445-3800	R	43*	.3
37	Gehr Industries Inc—*Norbert Gehr*	7400 E Slauson Ave, Commerce CA 90040	323-728-5558	R	37*	.3
38	Chromatic Technologies Inc	20 Forge Park, Franklin MA 02038	508-541-7100	S	37*	.1
39	Therm-O-Link Inc—*David Campbell*	10513 Freedom St, Garrettsville OH 44231	330-527-2124	R	34*	.2
40	Monroe Cable Company Inc—*Yitzchok Wieder*	14 Commercial Ave, Middletown NY 10941	845-692-2800	R	33*	.1
41	Trilogy Communications Inc—*Grace Lee*	2910 Hwy 80 E, Pearl MS 39208	601-932-4461	R	32*	.2
42	Kalas Manufacturing Inc—*Richard Witwer*	PO Box 328, Denver PA 17517	717-336-5575	R	26*	.3
43	Multi-Plex Inc—*Won Tsang*	5000 Hadley Rd, South Plainfield NJ 07080	908-757-8817	R	25*	.3
44	National Wire and Cable Corp—*James Wiley*	PO Box 31307, Los Angeles CA 90031	323-225-5611	R	25*	.3
45	A-1 Wire Tech Inc—*Steve Winnell*	4550 Kishwaukee St, Rockford IL 61109	815-226-0477	S	24*	.1
46	Radix Wire Co—*R Vermerris*	26000 Lakeland Blvd, Cleveland OH 44132	216-731-9191	R	19*	.1
47	Madison Cable Corp—*Tom Lynch*	125 Goddard Memorial D, Worcester MA 01603	508-752-2884	R	18*	.1
48	Aved Electronics Inc—*Ralph Santosuosso*	95 Billerica Ave, North Billerica MA 01862	978-453-6393	R	17*	.1
49	Specialty Cable Corp—*Carl Shanahan*	PO Box 50, Wallingford CT 06492	203-265-7126	R	14*	.1
50	Quabbin Wire and Cable Company Inc—*Paul Engel*	10 Maple St, Ware MA 01082	413-967-3117	R	13*	.1
51	Cordset Designs Inc—*Steven Peltz*	PO Box 650, Pink Hill NC 28572	252-568-4001	R	12*	.1
52	Global Technologies Inc—*Stan Lichenstein*	81 E Jefryn Blvd Ste D, Deer Park NY 11729	631-351-6100	R	11*	.1
53	Ripley Co—*Sean Powell*	46 Nooks Hill Rd, Cromwell CT 06416	860-635-2200	R	10	.1
54	Us Conec Ltd—*Bill Blubaugh*	PO Box 2306, Hickory NC 28603	828-323-8883	R	10*	.1
55	Steelflex Electro Corp—*Philip Rine*	145 S 13th St, Lindenhurst NY 11757	631-226-4466	R	9*	.1
56	Xponet Inc—*Don Barber*	20 Elberta Rd, Painesville OH 44077	440-354-6617	R	8*	.1
57	CCX Corp—*Tom Hanchin*	1399 Horizon Ave, Lafayette CO 80026	303-666-5206	R	8	<.1
58	V-Tron Electronics Corp—*Douglas Goblin*	10 Venus Way, Attleboro MA 02703	508-761-9100	R	8*	.1
59	Times Fiber Communications Inc—*Zach Raley*	PO Box 384, Wallingford CT 06492	203-265-8500	D	8*	<.1
60	Cicoil LLC—*Jim Alderson*	24960 Ave Tibbitts, Valencia CA 91355	661-295-1295	R	8*	.1
61	Pasternack Enterprises Inc—*Chuck Becker*	PO Box 16759, Irvine CA 92623		R	7*	<.1
62	CE Precision Assemblies Inc—*Susan Ross*	6849 W Frye Rd, Chandler AZ 85226	480-940-0740	R	7*	<.1
63	Prime Wire and Cable Inc—*John Shieh*	280 Machlin Ct, Walnut CA 91789	909-718-5271	R	7*	.1
64	General Wire Products Inc—*Thomas Andrews*	425 Shrewsbury St, Worcester MA 01604	508-752-8260	R	7*	<.1
65	US Pioneer LLC—*Seth Lapidus*	PO Box 472065, Tulsa OK 74147	918-359-5200	R	6*	<.1
66	Bridgeport Insulated Wire Co—*Christopher Pelletier*	PO Box 5217, Bridgeport CT 06610	203-333-3191	R	6*	<.1
67	Nexxus Lighting Inc—*Michael Bauer*	124 Floyd Smith Dr Ste, Charlotte NC 28262	704-405-0416	P	5	<.1
68	Caton Connector Corp—*Daniel Galambos*	26 Wapping Rd Ste 1, Kingston MA 02364	781-585-4315	R	5*	<.1
69	Wire Technology Corp—*Rachel Mendoza*	PO Box 1608, South Gate CA 90280	323-564-6894	R	5*	<.1
70	Optimum Fiberoptics Inc—*Francis Megan*	6655 Amberton Dr Ste N, Elkridge MD 21075	410-379-0084	R	4*	<.1
71	Fiberoptic Systems Inc—*Sanford Stark*	60 Moreland Rd Ste A, Simi Valley CA 93065	805-583-2088	R	4*	<.1
72	Stonewall Cable Inc—*Jeffrey Emery*	126 Hawkensen Dr, Rumney NH 03266	603-536-1601	R	4*	.1
73	Micro Computer Cable Company Inc	6739 Cypress, Romulus MI 48174	734-946-9700	R	3*	<.1
74	Omnitronics LLC—*F Briggs Carr*	6573 Cochran Road Ste, Solon OH 44139	440-349-4900	R	3*	<.1
75	Flexco Microwave Inc—*William Pote*	PO Box 115, Port Murray NJ 07865	908-835-1720	R	3*	<.1
76	Integrated Cable Solutions Inc	5905 Johns Rd Ste 101, Tampa FL 33634	813-769-5740	R	2*	<.1
77	Ecm Electronics—*Martin Biles*	111 Industrial Way Ste, Belmont CA 94002	650-593-1077	R	2*	<.1
78	Blake Wire and Cable Corp—*Robert Weiner*	16134 Runnymede St, Van Nuys CA 91406	818-781-8300	R	1*	<.1
79	Cable Assemblies Inc—*Donald Boulard*	13 Columbia Dr Unit 17, Amherst NH 03031	603-889-4090	R	1*	<.1
80	Brim Electronics Inc—*Barry Danziger*	PO Box 336, Fair Lawn NJ 07410	201-796-2886	R	1*	<.1
81	Phoenix Cable Inc—*William Maryan*	10801 N 24th Ave Ste 1, Phoenix AZ 85029	602-870-8870	R	1*	<.1
82	SI Tech Inc—*Ramesh Sheth*	PO Box 609, Geneva IL 60134	630-761-3640	R	1*	<.1
83	Coleman Cable Systems Inc—*Gary Yetman*	1530 Shields Dr, Waukegan IL 60085	847-672-2300	P	1	1.1
84	Fairhill Cable Products Inc—*Shelia Hoffman*	PO Box 189, Norristown PA 19404	484-322-0810	R	<1*	<.1
85	A-G Devices Of Colorado Inc—*Richard Schaefer*	9595 Hwy 65, Austin CO 81410	970-835-4800	R	<1*	<.1
86	Camdel Metals Corp—*John Coates* Handy and Harman Ltd	12244 Willow Grove, Camden DE 19934	302-697-9521	S	N/A	.1

TOTALS: SIC 3357 Nonferrous Wiredrawing & Insulating

	Companies: 86				27,230	81.9

3363 Aluminum Die-Castings

Rank	Company Name—*Executive Officer*	Address, City, State, Zip	Phone	Type	Fin	Empls
1	J L French LLC—*Kevin Claereaut*	PO Box 1024, Sheboygan WI 53082	920-458-7724	R	4,204*	.7
2	Lynchburg Foundry Co—*Gary F Ruff*	620 Court St, Lynchburg VA 24504	434-528-8200	S	1,898*	5.3
3	General Aluminum Manufacturing Co—*Gary McLaughlin*	6065 Parkland Blvd, Cleveland OH 44124	440-947-2000	R	308*	.8
4	Gibbs Die Casting Corp—*Steven Church*	369 Community Dr, Henderson KY 42420	270-827-1801	R	210*	1.3
5	Tuthill Vaccums And Blowers Systems—*John Ermold*	4840 W Kearney St, Springfield MO 65803	417-865-8715	R	160*	2.0
6	Contech Metal Forge—*John Blystone*	21177 Hilltop St, Southfield MI 48033	248-351-1051	D	150	.8
7	Twin City Die Castings Co—*Douglas Harmon*	1070 33rd Ave Se, Minneapolis MN 55414	651-645-3611	R	93*	.3
8	Leggett and Platt Office Components	1430 Sherman Ct, High Point NC 27260	336-885-4000	D	72*	.6
9	Spartan Light Metal Products Inc—*Don Jubel*	510 E Mcclurken Ave, Sparta IL 62286	618-443-4346	R	65*	.6
10	Diversified Machine Milwaukee LLC—*Bruce Swift*	28059 Center Oaks Ct, Wixom WI 48393	248-277-4400	R	62*	.5
11	Albany-Chicago Company LLC—*Joseph Aperi*	8200 100th St, Pleasant Prairie WI 53158	262-947-7600	R	60*	.3
12	RCM Industries Inc (Franklin Park Illinois)—*Robert C Marconi*	3021 Cullerton Dr, Franklin Park IL 60131	847-455-1950	R	56*	.5
13	Walker Die Casting Inc—*John Walker*	PO Box 1189, Lewisburg TN 37091	931-359-6206	R	55*	.6
14	Le Sueur Inc—*Mark Mueller*	PO Box 149, Le Sueur MN 56058	507-665-6204	R	43*	.6
15	Madison-Kipp Corp—*Robert Johnston*	PO Box 8043, Madison WI 53708	608-244-3511	R	41*	.5
16	Trace Die Cast Inc—*Lowell Guthrie*	140 Graham Ave, Bowling Green KY 42101	270-781-0049	R	34*	.5
17	Stroh Die Casting Company Inc—*Michael Stroh*	11123 W Burleigh St, Milwaukee WI 53222	414-771-7100	R	33*	.2
18	Empire Die Casting Company Inc—*Richard Rogel*	635 Highland Rd E, Macedonia OH 44056	330-467-0750	R	30*	.2

Note: An asterisk (*) indicates an estimated financial figure. The company type code used is as follows: R = Private, P = Public, S = Private Subsidiary, B = Public Subsidiary, D = Division, J = Joint Venture, I = Investment Fund.

COMPANY RANKINGS BY SALES WITHIN 4-DIGIT SIC

Rank	Company Name—*Executive Officer*	Address, City, State, Zip	Phone	Type	Fin	Empls
19	Eck Industries Inc—*Philip Eck*	PO Box 967, Manitowoc WI 54221	920-682-4618	R	30*	.4
20	C and H Die Casting Inc—*Charles Hinkle*	PO Box 1170, Temple TX 76503	254-938-2541	R	26	.4
21	Cambridge Tool and Manufacturing Inc—*Jason Allen*	67 Faulkner St, North Billerica MA 01862	978-667-8400	S	25*	.3
22	Ahresty Wilmington Corp—*Kenichi Nonaka*	2627 S S St, Wilmington OH 45177	937-382-6112	R	25*	.4
23	Alloy Die Casting Co—*Eric Sanders*	6550 Caballero Blvd, Buena Park CA 90620	714-521-9800	R	24*	.4
24	Consolidated Precision Products—*Steve Clodfelter*	4200 W Valley Blvd, Pomona CA 91769	909-595-2252	R	23*	.2
25	Hoffmann Die Cast Corp—*Michael Oros*	229 Kerth St, Saint Joseph MI 49085	269-983-1102	R	22*	.2
26	Yoder Industries Inc—*Ron Zeverka*	2520 Needmore Rd, Dayton OH 45414	937-278-5769	R	22*	.1
27	Cascade Die Casting Group Inc—*Phil Torchil*	7441 Division Ave S St, Grand Rapids MI 49548	616-281-1660	S	20*	.2
28	Quad Cast Inc—*Andrew Debrey*	3800 River Dr, Moline IL 61265	309-762-7346	R	20*	.2
29	Adc Diecasting LLC—*Wayne Heiman*	1720 S Wolf Rd, Wheeling IL 60090	847-541-3030	R	18*	.1
30	Chicago White Metal Casting Inc—*Eric Treiber*	649 N Rte 83, Bensenville IL 60106	630-595-4424	R	17*	.1
31	Yoder Die Casting—*Michael Stolle*	727 Kiser St, Dayton OH 45404	937-222-6734	R	17*	.2
32	Sanders Industries Co—*Eric Sanders*	6550 Caballero Blvd, Buena Park CA 90620	714-562-2930	R	17*	.1
33	Abeco Die Casting Inc—*Ray Brooks*	PO Box 2697, Lewisburg TN 37091	931-359-4287	R	15*	.1
34	Intermet Stevensville	301 Commerce St Ste 29, Fort Worth TX 76102	817-348-9190	S	13	.1
35	Acme Alliance LLC—*Cheryl Lebron*	3610 Commercial Ave, Northbrook IL 60062	847-272-9520	R	13*	.1
36	Bardane Manufacturing Co—*Neil Horvick*	PO Box 70, Jermyn PA 18433	570-876-4844	R	12*	.1
37	Great Lakes Die Cast Corp—*Con Nolan*	701 W Laketon Ave, Muskegon MI 49441	231-726-4002	R	10*	.1
38	Mdh Acquisition LLC—*Greg Maley*	3315 Haseley Dr, Niagara Falls NY 14304	716-297-0652	R	9*	.1
39	G and S Foundry and Manufacturing Co—*Charles Wasem*	210 Kaskaskia Dr, Red Bud IL 62278	618-282-4114	R	9*	.1
40	G and M Die Casting Company Inc—*Mark Hirsh*	284 Richert Rd, Wood Dale IL 60191	630-595-2340	R	8*	.1
41	Technical Die-Casting Inc—*Bernie Merchlewitz*	8910 W Main St, Winona MN 55987	507-689-2194	R	8*	.1
42	Aluminum Die Casting Company Inc—*Steven Bennett*	10775 San Sevaine Way, Mira Loma CA 91752	951-681-3900	R	7*	.1
43	Sks Die Casting And Machining Inc—*Jerome Keating*	1849 Oak St, Alameda CA 94501	510-523-2541	R	7*	.1
44	Premier Die Casting Co—*Leonard Cordaro*	1177 Rahway Ave, Avenel NJ 07001	732-634-3000	R	7*	.1
45	T and L Foundry Inc—*Bill Covington*	PO Box 279, Glenpool OK 74033	918-322-3310	R	6*	.1
46	Rangers Die Casting Co—*Larry Larson*	PO Box 127, Lynwood CA 90262	310-764-1800	R	6*	<.1
47	Diamond Casting And Machine Company Inc—*Gerald Letendre*	PO Box 420, Hollis NH 03049	603-465-2263	R	5*	<.1
48	Phb Inc—*William Hilbert*	7900 W Ridge Rd, Fairview PA 16415	814-474-5511	R	4*	.7
49	Kitchen-Quip Inc—*Stephen Sparling*	PO Box 548, Waterloo IN 46793	260-837-8311	R	4*	<.1
50	Kearney's Aluminum Foundry Inc—*Victor Kearney*	PO Box 2926, Fresno CA 93745	559-233-2591	R	3*	<.1
51	Latrobe Foundry Machine and Supply Co—*Sally Shirey*	PO Box 431, Latrobe PA 15650	724-537-3341	R	2*	<.1
52	B Tech—*Jeff Branch*	PO Box 465323, Lawrenceville GA 30042	770-972-4289	R	1*	<.1
53	Thresher Industries Inc—*Tom Flessner*	13400 Hanford-Armona R, Hanford CA 93230	559-585-3400	P	<1	N/A

TOTALS: SIC 3363 Aluminum Die-Castings
Companies: 53   **8,031   21.5**

3364 Nonferrous Die-Castings Except Aluminum

Rank	Company Name—*Executive Officer*	Address, City, State, Zip	Phone	Type	Fin	Empls
1	Matthews International Corp—*Joseph C Bartolacci*	2 North Shore Ctr, Pittsburgh PA 15212	412-442-8200	P	899	5.3
2	Matthews International Corp Bronze Div—*David Decarlo* Matthews International Corp	1315 W Liberty Ave, Pittsburgh PA 15226	412-571-5500	D	105*	.3
3	TCH Industries Inc—*Jim Terlizzi*	7441 S Division, Grand Rapids MI 49548	616-942-0505	R	36*	.3
4	Precision Metalsmiths Inc—*David Dolata*	1081 E 200th St, Cleveland OH 44117	216-481-8900	R	33*	.2
5	Del Mar Industries—*Douglas Taylor*	12901 S Western Ave, Gardena CA 90249	323-321-0600	R	31*	.2
6	Consolidated Industries Inc—*John Wilbur*	677 Mixville Rd, Cheshire CT 06410	203-272-5371	R	30*	.1
7	Magnesium Products Of America Inc—*Erick Showalter*	2001 Industrial Dr, Eaton Rapids MI 48827	517-663-2700	R	29*	.4
8	Alpha Technology Corp—*Stephen Sweda*	PO Box 168, Howell MI 48844	517-546-9700	R	28*	.2
9	Premier Tool and Die Cast Corp—*Paul Brancaleon*	PO Box 210, Berrien Springs MI 49103	269-471-7715	R	22*	.3
10	Premier Tooling and Manufacturing Inc—*Janda Heister*	PO Box 12, Peosta IA 52068	563-557-7006	R	21*	.1
11	General Die Casters Inc—*James Mathias*	2150 Highland Rd, Twinsburg OH 44087	330-657-2300	R	20*	.2
12	Aurora Metals Division LLC—*James Pearson*	1995 Greenfield Ave, Montgomery IL 60538	630-844-4900	R	19*	.1
13	Lansco Die Casting Inc—*Ron Garland*	900 Glenneyre St, Laguna Beach CA 92651	626-961-3441	R	18*	.2
14	Quality Metal Finishing Co—*Matthew Bortoli*	PO Box 922, Byron IL 61010	815-234-2711	R	18*	.1
15	Production Castings Inc—*Alan Loeffelman*	1410 W Lark Industrial, Fenton MO 63026	636-677-3364	R	17*	.1
16	Cast Products Inc—*Ron Paquet*	4200 N Nordica Ave, Norridge IL 60706	708-457-1500	R	15*	.1
17	Port City Metal Products Inc—*Bruce Essex*	1985 E Laketon Ave, Muskegon MI 49442	231-777-3941	R	11*	.1
18	Berkley Machine Works and Foundry Company Inc—*Kelly Jones*	PO Box 4566, Norfolk VA 23523	757-545-3561	R	9*	.1
19	Inventix Manufacturing LLC—*Paul Menzel*	N60w16350 Kohler Ln, Menomonee Falls WI 53051	262-252-4488	R	9*	.1
20	Wear-Tek Inc—*Bill Reynolds*	8021 W Hwy 2, Spokane WA 99224	509-747-4139	R	7*	.1
21	Custom Metal Crafters Inc—*Daniel Bourget*	815 N Mountain Rd, Newington CT 06111	860-953-4210	R	6*	.1
22	Dura-Cast Inc—*Hinton Hall*	PO Box 311287, Enterprise AL 36331	334-347-2076	R	6*	.1
23	Wichita Falls Manufacturing Inc—*Richard Jeter*	PO Box 5326, Wichita Falls TX 76307	940-322-4491	R	5*	.1
24	Micro Industries Inc—*Lance Robinson*	PO Box 400, Rock Falls IL 61071	815-625-8000	R	5*	.1
25	Ryder-Heil Bronze Inc—*Herbert Kleine*	PO Box 647, Bucyrus OH 44820	419-562-2841	R	5*	<.1
26	Metallurgical Products Co—*Michael Goodman*	PO Box 598, West Chester PA 19381	610-696-6770	R	3*	<.1
27	Kenalloy Foundry Manufacturing Company Inc—*Mike Hrevus*	9735 Gravois Rd Ste R, Saint Louis MO 63123	314-544-1707	R	3*	<.1
28	Proto-Cast Inc—*William Covington*	2699 John Daly St, Inkster MI 48141	313-565-5400	R	2*	<.1
29	Allied Die Casting Corp—*Michael Albanese*	3923 W W Ave, Mchenry IL 60050	815-385-9330	R	2*	<.1
30	Mag-Tec Casting Corp—*Allen Schroeder*	2411 Research Dr, Jackson MI 49203	517-789-8505	R	2*	<.1
31	Fall River Tool and Die Company Inc—*OA Fontaine*	PO Box 4070 Flint Sta, Fall River MA 02723	508-674-4621	R	2*	<.1
32	Sdc Inc—*Jerome Graeser*	945 Franklin St, Sullivan MO 63080	573-468-3107	R	1*	<.1
33	Rvs and Co—*Roger Scungio*	387 George Waterman Rd, Johnston RI 02919	401-231-8200	R	1*	<.1

TOTALS: SIC 3364 Nonferrous Die-Castings Except Aluminum
Companies: 33   **1,418   8.9**

3365 Aluminum Foundries

Rank	Company Name—*Executive Officer*	Address, City, State, Zip	Phone	Type	Fin	Empls
1	Fort Wayne Foundry Corp—*Byron Cole*	4912 Lima Rd, Fort Wayne IN 46808	260-483-0382	R	2,433*	1.0
2	Mirro/Calphalon—*Mark Ketchum*	Ampoint Industrial Par, Perrysburg OH 43551	419-666-8700	D	300	2.0
3	Aluminum Shapes LLC—*Steve Grabell*	9000 River Rd, Delair NJ 08110	856-662-5500	R	113*	.8
4	Milestone Metals Inc—*Ram Gurunathan*	12587 Fair Lakes Cir S, Fairfax VA 22033	703-222-0074	R	34	<.1
5	Galvotec Alloys Inc—*Rogelio Garza*	6712 S 36th St, Mcallen TX 78503	956-630-3500	R	31*	.1
6	Michigan Wheel Corp—*William Lowen*	1501 Buchanan Ave SW, Grand Rapids MI 49507	616-452-6941	R	26*	.2
7	Gupta Permold Corp—*Lakshmi Gupta*	234 Lott Rd, Pittsburgh PA 15235	412-397-7410	R	25*	.2
8	Cast Technologies Inc—*Clay Canterbury*	PO Box 959, Peoria IL 61653	309-676-2157	R	25*	.1
9	Sawbrook Steel Castings Co—*Michael Beyersdorfer*	PO Box 15527, Cincinnati OH 45215	513-554-1700	R	24*	.2
10	Morris Bean and Co—*Edward Myers*	777 E Hyde Rd, Yellow Springs OH 45387	937-767-7301	R	24*	.2
11	Le Claire Manufacturing Co—*Robert Zimmerman*	PO Box 1344, Bettendorf IA 52722	563-332-6550	R	23*	.1
12	Ampco Metal Inc—*Ronn Page*	1117 E Algonquin Rd, Arlington Heights IL 60005	847-437-6000	R	23*	.2

Rank	Company Name—*Executive Officer*	Address, City, State, Zip	Phone	Type	Fin	Empls
13	Denison Industries Inc—*Chris Norch*	PO Box 1459, Denison TX 75021	903-786-6500	R	21*	.2
14	Ross Aluminum Castings LLC—*Michael Balazs*	PO Box 609, Sidney OH 45365	937-492-4134	R	19*	.3
15	Tazewell Machine Works Inc—*Mack Cakora*	PO Box 895, Pekin IL 61555	309-347-3181	R	17*	.1
16	Uni-Cast Inc—*Henri Fine*	11 Industrial Dr, Londonderry NH 03053	603-625-5761	R	16*	.1
17	Magparts—*Richard Emerson*	1545 W Roosevelt St, Azusa CA 91702	626-334-7897	R	15*	.2
18	Ohio Aluminum Industries Inc—*John Blemaster*	4840 Warner Rd, Cleveland OH 44125	216-641-8865	R	15*	.1
19	Taylor Metalworks Inc—*Peter Taylor*	3925 California Rd, Orchard Park NY 14127	716-662-3113	R	14*	.1
20	Atlantic Casting and Engineering Corp—*James Binns*	PO Box 4016, Clifton NJ 07012	973-779-2450	R	13*	.1
21	Pride Cast Metals Inc—*Thomas Hamm*	2737 Colerain Ave, Cincinnati OH 45225	513-541-1295	R	13*	.1
22	Littler Diecast Corp—*John Littler*	PO Box 96, Albany IN 47320	765-789-4456	R	13*	.1
23	Wer Corp—*William Rita*	PO Box 2197, Reading PA 19608	610-678-8023	R	12*	.1
24	Nu-Cast Inc—*D Donald Mc Kitte*	29 Grenier Field Rd, Londonderry NH 03053	603-432-1600	R	11*	.1
25	Viking Tool and Gage Inc—*Brian Burns*	11160 State Hwy 18, Conneaut Lake PA 16316	814-382-8691	R	11*	.1
26	Dundee Castings Co—*Edgar Crawley*	500 Ypsilanti St, Dundee MI 48131	734-529-2455	R	10*	.1
27	Cast Products Inc (Athens Alabama)	PO Box 1202, Athens AL 35612	256-233-1500	R	10*	.1
28	Dolphin Inc—*John Solheim*	PO Box 6514, Phoenix AZ 85005	602-272-6747	R	9*	.1
29	Buddy Bar Casting Corp—*Edward Barksdale*	PO Box 2667, Downey CA 90242	562-861-9664	R	9*	.1
30	Bronze Craft Corp—*James Bernard*	PO Box 788, Nashua NH 03061	603-883-7747	R	9*	.1
31	Lakeland Mold Co—*John Newhouse*	1021 Madison St, Brainerd MN 56401	218-828-0110	R	7*	.1
32	Mansfield Brass and Aluminum Corp—*Lynn Bierly-Edmonds*	636 S Ctr St, New Washington OH 44854	419-492-2154	R	7*	.1
33	Skrl Die Casting Inc—*Sandra Szuch*	34580 Lakeland Blvd, Willoughby OH 44095	440-946-7200	R	7*	.1
34	Alabama Copper Bronze Company Inc—*Johnny Aycock*	1501 Red Hollow Rd, Birmingham AL 35215	205-856-3737	R	6*	<.1
35	MA Harrison Manufacturing Company Inc—*James A Harrison*	PO Box 38, Birmingham OH 44816	440-965-4306	R	5*	.1
36	Portage Casting and Mold Inc—*Dennis Griep*	2901 Portage Rd, Portage WI 53901	608-742-7137	R	5*	<.1
37	Carson Industries Inc—*Harry Carson*	189 Foreman Rd, Freeport PA 16229	724-295-5147	R	5*	.1
38	Hegedus Aluminum Industries Inc—*Glenn Davis*	PO Box 1067, Oil City PA 16301	814-676-5635	R	4*	.1
39	S and H Products Inc—*Steve Larson*	5891 Nolan St Ste A, Arvada CO 80003	303-422-5781	R	4*	<.1
40	Texas Metal Casting Co—*Don Smith*	PO Box 3259, Lufkin TX 75903	936-639-1131	R	4*	<.1
41	Rotocast Technologies Inc—*Edward Kissel*	1900 Englewood Ave, Akron OH 44312	330-798-9091	R	3*	<.1
42	Aluminum Components Ent Corp—*Darrell Bradfish*	5602 Jamar St, Schofield WI 54476	715-241-8711	R	3*	<.1
43	Alloy Casting Company Inc—*Jon Graw*	PO Box 800008, Mesquite TX 75180	972-286-2368	R	3*	<.1
44	Hauser Foundry Inc—*Robert Hauser*	1025 Joseph St, Shreveport LA 71107	318-222-6631	R	3*	<.1
45	Phoenix Casting and Machining Inc—*Edwin Loutzenheiser*	906 Juniata Ave, Juniata NE 68955	402-751-2135	R	2*	<.1
46	Airfoils Impellers Corp—*Dennis Anderholm*	PO Box 9966, College Station TX 77842	979-822-6418	R	2*	<.1
47	Corbett Steeves Pattern Works Inc—*John Steeves*	80 Lowell St, Rochester NY 14605	585-546-7109	R	2*	<.1
48	Foley Pattern Company Inc—*Ellen Stahly*	PO Box 150, Auburn IN 46706	260-925-4113	R	2*	<.1
49	Gray Mold Company Inc—*Keith Gray*	1308 Meador Ave Ste C6, Bellingham WA 98229	360-671-5711	R	2*	<.1
50	Quality Match Plate Co—*James Dittrioh*	4211 State Rte 534, Southington OH 44470	330-009-2402	R	1*	<.1
51	Palmer Engineered Products Inc—*Jack Palmer*	PO Box 1593, Springfield OH 45501	937-322-1481	R	1*	<.1
52	Ultron—*Reinhold Grassl*	1345 Cota Ave, Long Beach CA 90813	562-437-3567	R	<1*	<.1

TOTALS: SIC 3365 Aluminum Foundries
Companies: 52   **3,395**   **8.2**

3366 Copper Foundries

Rank	Company Name—*Executive Officer*	Address, City, State, Zip	Phone	Type	Fin	Empls
1	Pmx Industries Inc—*S Kim*	5300 Willow Creek Dr S, Cedar Rapids IA 52404	319-368-7700	R	35*	.4
2	Orion Corp—*Timothy Reece*	PO Box 84, Grafton WI 53024	262-377-2210	R	32*	.2
3	All American Products Co—*Art Benyasri*	PO Box 190, San Fernando CA 91341	818-361-0059	R	25*	.1
4	Lee Brass Co—*Robert Heath*	1800 Golden Springs Rd, Anniston AL 36207	256-831-2501	S	23*	.3
5	Magnolia Metal Corp—*Adam Koslosky*	PO Box 34370, Omaha NE 68134	402-455-8760	R	20*	.1
6	Burnstein Von Seelen Precision Castings Corp—*Daniel Burnstein*	608 Carwellyn Rd, Abbeville SC 29620	864-366-2527	R	18*	.1
7	Johnson Brass and Machine Foundry Inc—*Lance Johnson*	PO Box 219, Saukville WI 53080	262-377-9440	R	15*	.1
8	Excal Inc—*Don Harper*	PO Box 3030, Mills WY 82644	307-237-0920	R	12*	.1
9	Falcon Foundry Co—*Gary Slaven*	PO Box 301, Lowellville OH 44436	330-536-6221	R	12*	.1
10	MetalTek International—*Robert Smickley*	905 E St Paul Ave, Waukesha WI 53188	262-544-7700	R	11*	.1
11	Fleetwood Continental Inc—*David Forster*	19451 S Susana Rd, Compton CA 90221	310-609-1477	R	10*	.1
12	Sound Propeller Services Inc—*Clifford Burns*	7916 8th Ave S, Seattle WA 98108	206-788-4202	R	9*	<.1
13	Becotek Manufacturing Inc—*Ronald Bellottie*	1305 Oberlin Ave, Lorain OH 44052	440-245-6826	R	9*	.1
14	ARK -Ramos Foundry And Manufacturing Co—*Beatrice Ramos*	PO Box 26388, Oklahoma City OK 73126	405-235-5505	R	6*	.1
15	Mcneil Industries Inc—*Randall Mcneil*	835 Richmond Rd, Painesville OH 44077	440-721-0400	R	6*	<.1
16	Galaxy Die And Engineering Inc—*Jawahar Saini*	24910 Ave Tibbitts, Valencia CA 91355	661-775-9301	R	3*	<.1
17	Advance Bronze Inc—*David Propost*	PO Box 280, Lodi OH 44254	330-948-1231	R	3*	.1
18	Argos Inc—*Steven Roy*	397 Rte 312, Brewster NY 10509	845-278-2454	R	2*	<.1
19	Eureka Electrical Products Inc—*James Meehl*	PO Box 230, North East PA 16428	814-725-9638	R	2*	<.1
20	Duluth Brass Manufacturing Inc—*John Holt*	2301 Commonwealth Ave, Duluth MN 55808	218-626-2564	R	2*	<.1
21	Conejo Industries Inc—*Peter Jorgensen*	996 Lawrence Dr Ste 31, Newbury Park CA 91320	805-498-6761	R	1*	<.1

TOTALS: SIC 3366 Copper Foundries
Companies: 21   **255**   **2.0**

3369 Nonferrous Foundries Nec

Rank	Company Name—*Executive Officer*	Address, City, State, Zip	Phone	Type	Fin	Empls
1	Superior Essex Inc—*Stephen M Carter*	6120 Powers Ferry Rd S, Atlanta GA 30339	770-657-6000	S	2,993*	4.5
2	Broadwind Energy Inc—*Peter C Duprey*	47 E Chicago Ave Ste 3, Naperville IL 60540	630-637-0315	P	137	.9
3	Bodine Aluminum Inc	2100 Walton Rd, Saint Louis MO 63114	314-423-8200	S	94*	.3
4	Pacific Steel Casting Co—*Horst Emmerichs*	1333 2nd St, Berkeley CA 94710	510-525-9200	R	75*	.6
5	Wisconsin Aluminum Foundry Company Inc—*Kory Brockman*	PO Box 246, Manitowoc WI 54221	920-682-8286	R	65*	.4
6	Deco Products Co—*Chris Storlie*	506 Sanford St, Decorah IA 52101	563-382-4264	R	62*	.2
7	Gamco Products Co—*Richard Manoogian*	1105 5th St, Henderson KY 42420	270-826-9573	S	59*	.5
8	Kaydon Ring and Seal Inc—*James O'Leary*	PO Box 626, Baltimore MD 21203	410-547-7700	S	35*	.3
9	Akron Foundry Co—*George Ostich*	PO Box 27028, Akron OH 44319	330-745-3101	R	33*	.2
10	Magotteaux Inc—*Bernard Goblet*	PO Box 518, Pulaski TN 38478	931-363-7471	R	31*	.5
11	Selmet Inc—*Gordon Allen*	PO Box 689, Albany OR 97321	541-926-7731	R	29*	.2
12	Jet Engineering Inc—*Matt Rudd*	5212 Aurelius Rd, Lansing MI 48911	517-882-4311	R	26*	.3
13	Tampa Brass And Aluminum Corporation—*Chris Leto*	8511 Florida Mining Bl, Tampa FL 33634	813-885-6064	R	18*	.1
14	Piad Precision Casting Corp—*Holger Schweisthal*	112 Industrial Park Rd, Greensburg PA 15601	724-838-5500	R	15*	.1
15	United Titanium Inc—*C Reardon*	3450 Old Airport Rd, Wooster OH 44691	330-264-2111	R	14*	.1
16	Francis Manufacturing Co—*William Francis*	PO Box 400, Russia OH 45363	937-526-4551	R	13*	.1
17	Halex Co—*Brent Elliott*	23901 Aurora Rd, Bedford Heights OH 44146	440-439-2223	D	12*	.1
18	CL Dews and Sons Foundry And Machinery Company Inc—*Thomas Dews*	PO Box 1647, Hattiesburg MS 39403	601-582-4427	R	10*	.1

Note: An asterisk (*) indicates an estimated financial figure. The company type code used is as follows: R = Private, P = Public, S = Private Subsidiary, B = Public Subsidiary, D = Division, J = Joint Venture, I = Investment Fund.

COMPANY RANKINGS BY SALES WITHIN 4-DIGIT SIC

Rank	Company Name—Executive Officer	Address, City, State, Zip	Phone	Type	Fin	Empls
19	Ridco Casting Co—Stanley Cohen	6 Beverage Hill Ave, Pawtucket RI 02860	401-724-0400	R	10*	.1
20	Pankl Aerospace Systems—Sonja Zierhut	16615 Edwards Rd, Cerritos CA 90703	562-207-6300	R	10*	.1
21	Fenico Precision Castings Inc—Don Tomeo	7805 Madison St, Paramount CA 90723	562-634-5000	R	8*	.1
22	Wemco Casting LLC	20 Jules Ct Ste 2, Bohemia NY 11716	631-563-8050	R	8*	.1
23	Miller Industrial Products Inc—William Miller	801 Water St, Jackson MI 49203	517-783-2756	R	7*	.1
24	Excelity—Shaun Tan	11127 Dora St, Sun Valley CA 91352	818-767-1000	R	5*	.1
25	CMH Manufacturing Co—Charles Hall	1320 Harvard St, Lubbock TX 79403	806-744-8003	R	5*	<.1
26	Schunk Inex Corporation Inc—Mike Kaspryzk	9229 Olean Rd, Holland NY 14080	716-537-2270	S	5*	<.1
27	J Walter Miller Co—Milton Morgan	411 E Chestnut St, Lancaster PA 17602	717-392-7428	R	5*	<.1
28	Stegman Tool Company Inc—Robert Begeny	1985 Ring Dr, Troy MI 48083	248-588-4634	R	5*	<.1
29	Microweld Engineering Inc—Robert Lloyd	7451 Oakmeadows Dr, Worthington OH 43085	614-847-9410	R	4*	<.1
30	Ken-Dec Inc—CL Moeller	PO Box 129, Horse Cave KY 42749	270-786-2111	R	4*	<.1
31	High-Tech Industries Of Holland Inc—David Tenbrink	3269 John F Donnelly D, Holland MI 49424	616-399-5430	R	3*	<.1
32	Grosse Tool And Machine Co—Douglas Mack	23080 Groesbeck Hwy, Warren MI 48089	586-773-6770	R	2*	<.1
33	Precision Technology Corp—Michael Ochoa	18640 59th Dr Ne, Arlington WA 98223	360-403-0254	R	2*	<.1
34	High-Tec Machining Center Inc—Dugar Strickland	1223 Airport Rd, Jefferson GA 30549	706-367-5137	R	1*	<.1

TOTALS: SIC 3369 Nonferrous Foundries Nec
Companies: 34   3,805   10.1

3398 Metal Heat Treating

Rank	Company Name—Executive Officer	Address, City, State, Zip	Phone	Type	Fin	Empls
1	Wall Colmonoy Corp—Craig Johnson	101 West Girard, Madison Heights MI 48071	248-585-6400	R	336*	.4
2	Metal Improvement Company LLC—Wendy Butterfield	80 E Rte 4 Ste 310, Paramus NJ 07652	201-843-7800	R	163*	1.8
3	Metal Improvement Company Inc—Martin Benante	80 Route 4 East Rm 310, Paramus NJ 07652	201-843-7800	S	92*	1.0
4	Donsco Inc—Arthur Mann	PO Box 2001, Wrightsville PA 17368	717-252-1561	R	43*	.5
5	FP M LLC—Patrick Regan	1501 Lively Blvd, Elk Grove Village IL 60007	847-952-5221	R	37*	.3
6	Wec Carolina Energy Solutions LLC—Richard Bryant	244 E Mount Gallant Rd, Rock Hill SC 29730	803-980-3060	R	30*	.3
7	Amac Enterprises Inc—Constantine Chimples	5909 W 130th St, Cleveland OH 44130	216-362-1880	R	17*	.1
8	Metals Technology Corp—Ed Vandyck	120 N Schmale Rd, Carol Stream IL 60188	630-221-2500	R	15*	.1
9	Milastar Corp—Dennis Stevermer	7317 W Lake St, Minneapolis MN 55426	952-929-4774	R	14*	.1
10	Industrial Steel Treating Co—Timothy Levy	PO Box 98, Jackson MI 49204	517-787-6312	R	12*	.1
11	Rex Heat Treat—John Rex	PO Box 270, Lansdale PA 19446	215-855-1131	R	11*	.1
12	Northlake Steel Corp—William Bissett	5455 Wegman Dr, Valley City OH 44280	330-220-7717	R	11*	.1
13	Super Steel Treating Inc—Terence Farrar	6227 Rinke Ave, Warren MI 48091	586-755-9140	R	9*	.1
14	Horizon Steel Treating Inc—Joseph Lebar	231 Jandus Rd, Cary IL 60013	847-639-4030	R	8*	.1
15	American Steel Treating Inc—Roy Waits	525 W 6th St, Perrysburg OH 43551	419-874-2044	R	7*	.1
16	Electro Seal Corp—Robert Dragani	PO Box 46, Bourbon IN 46504	574-342-2105	R	6*	<.1
17	Gerdau Macsteel Atmosphere Annealing Inc—Sanjeev Deshpande	209 W Mount Hope Ave, Lansing MI 48910	517-485-5090	S	5*	<.1
18	United-County Industries Corp—William Nartowt	PO Box 330, Millbury MA 01527	508-865-5885	R	5*	<.1
19	Metal Prep Gary D Noobit	501 N Greenwood St, Houston TX 77011	713-921-7997	D	4*	<.1
20	Applied Process Inc—John Keough	12238 Newburgh Rd, Livonia MI 48150	734-464-2030	R	3*	<.1
21	LC Miller Co—Dolores Naimy	717 Monterey Pass Rd, Monterey Park CA 91754	323-268-3611	R	3*	<.1
22	Donovan Heat Treating Company Inc—Jeffrey Uhlenburg	7399 Tulip St, Philadelphia PA 19136	215-335-2200	R	3*	<.1
23	Kinton Carbide Inc—Charles Rankin	3000 Venture Ct, Export PA 15632	724-327-3141	R	2*	<.1
24	Certified Heat Treating Inc—Joseph Biehn	PO Box 354, Dayton OH 45409	937-866-0245	R	2*	<.1
25	300 Below Inc—Pete Paulin	2999 E Pky Dr, Decatur IL 62526	217-423-3070	R	2*	<.1
26	Thermet Inc—Paul Mikna	203 Travis Ln, Waukesha WI 53189	262-544-9800	R	2*	<.1

TOTALS: SIC 3398 Metal Heat Treating
Companies: 26   841   5.1

3399 Primary Metal Products Nec

Rank	Company Name—Executive Officer	Address, City, State, Zip	Phone	Type	Fin	Empls
1	Wellman Products Group—Ronald Wenberg	6180 Cochran Rd, Solon OH 44139	440-528-4000	S	699*	.3
2	US Bronze Powders Inc—K Ramsey	PO Box 31, Flemington NJ 08822	908-782-5464	R	574*	.3
3	Insteel Industries Inc—Howard O Woltz III	1373 Boggs Dr, Mount Airy NC 27030	336-786-2141	P	337	.7
4	Pyrotek Inc—Allan Roy	9503 E Montgomery Ave, Spokane WA 99206	509-926-6212	R	225*	1.5
5	Dynamic Materials Corp—Yvon P Cariou	5405 Spine Rd, Boulder CO 80301	303-665-5700	B	155	.4
6	Abbott Ball Company Inc—Craig Bond	PO Box 330100, West Hartford CT 06133	860-236-5901	R	142*	.1
7	Duo-Fast Corp	888 Forest Edge Dr, Vernon Hills IL 60061	847-634-1900	S	136*	.9
8	Acupowder International LLC—Shannon Warren	901 Lehigh Ave, Union NJ 07083	908-851-4500	R	110*	.1
9	Vacumet Corp (Franklin Massachusetts)—Leon Gianneschi	24 Forge Pky, Franklin MA 02038	508-541-7700	R	105*	.3
10	Keystone Powdered Metal Co—Conrad Kogovsek	251 State St, Saint Marys PA 15857	814-781-1591	R	57*	.8
11	Symmco Inc—John Bean	PO Box F, Sykesville PA 15865	814-894-2461	R	49*	.1
12	Alpha Sintered Metals—Joanne Ryan	95 Mason Run Rd, Ridgway PA 15853	814-773-3191	S	29*	.2
13	Capstan Industries Inc—Chris Doughty	10 Cushing Dr, Wrentham MA 02093	508-384-3100	R	27*	.2
14	Reade Advanced Materials—Charles Reade	PO Drawer 15039, East Providence RI 02915	401-433-7000	R	24*	.1
15	Clarion Sintered Metals Inc—Howard Peterson	3472 Montmorenci Rd, Ridgway PA 15853	814-773-3124	R	20*	.2
16	St Marys Carbon Company Inc—Jerome Lanzel	259 Eberl St, Saint Marys PA 15857	814-781-7333	R	19*	.3
17	Homogeneous Metals Inc—Mark Hewko	PO Box 294, Clayville NY 13322	315-839-5421	S	18*	.1
18	Chemalloy Company Inc—Anthony Demos	PO Box 350, Bryn Mawr PA 19010	610-527-3700	R	17*	.1
19	Toyal America Inc—Hiro Kosuge	1717 N Naper Blvd Ste, Naperville IL 60563	630-505-2160	R	14*	.1
20	Hoover Precision Products Inc—Eric Sturdy	PO Box 899, Cumming GA 30028	770-889-9223	R	13*	1.3
21	Micro Metals Inc—Scott Edwards	PO Box 669, Jamestown TN 38556	931-879-9946	R	13*	.1
22	PRL Inc—Janis Herschkowitz	PO Box 142, Cornwall PA 17016	717-273-2470	R	13*	.1
23	Dynametal Technologies Inc—Robert Nolan	400 N Dupree Ave, Brownsville TN 38012	731-772-3780	R	10*	.1
24	O Alpine Pressed Metals Inc—Elliot Archer	310 Tanner St, Ridgway PA 15853	814-776-2141	R	10*	.1
25	Nanophase Technologies Corp—Jess A Jankowski	1319 Marquette Dr, Romeoville IL 60446	630-771-6700	P	10	<.1
26	Gould Electronics Inc—Keiji Katagiri	125 N Price Rd, Chandler AZ 85224	480-732-9857	R	8*	.1
27	Hpm Industries Inc—Richard Pfingstler	PO Box P, Du Bois PA 15801	814-371-4800	R	8*	.1
28	American Metal Fibers Inc—Robert Carlson	13420 Rockland Rd, Lake Bluff IL 60044	847-362-2634	R	7*	.1
29	Micro Surface Engineer Inc—Eugene Gleason	1550 E Slauson Ave, Los Angeles CA 90011	323-582-7348	R	6*	.1
30	Rebco Inc—Kenneth Huey	650 Brandy Camp Rd, Kersey PA 15846	814-885-8035	R	6*	.1
31	Elcam Tool and Die Inc—Edward Anderson	479 Buena Vista Hwy, Wilcox PA 15870	814-929-5831	R	3*	<.1
32	Particle Size Technology Inc—James Perry	1930 Kumry Rd, Quakertown PA 18951	215-529-9771	R	3*	<.1
33	United Welding And Manufacturing Co—Gerald Grant	PO Box 100225, Cudahy WI 53110	414-744-1530	R	3*	<.1
34	US Aluminum Inc—K Ramsey	408 Us Hwy 202, Flemington NJ 08822	908-782-5454	R	3*	<.1
35	Cameron Diversified Products Inc—Edward Anderson Elcam Tool and Die Inc	479 Buena Vista Hwy, Wilcox PA 15870	814-929-5834	S	2*	<.1
36	Clendenin Brothers Inc—John Corckran	4309 Erdman Ave, Baltimore MD 21213	410-327-4500	R	2*	.1
37	Eastern Sintered Alloys Inc—John Sterbank	PO Box 708, Saint Marys PA 15857	440-356-5552	R	2*	.3

Rank	Company Name—*Executive Officer*	Address, City, State, Zip	Phone	Type	Fin	Empls
38	B and B Tool And Die Inc—*Gary Brown*	5878 Beechwood Rd, Emporium PA 15834	814-486-5355	R	1*	<.1

TOTALS: SIC 3399 Primary Metal Products Nec
Companies: 38   2,879   9.3

3411 Metal Cans

Rank	Company Name—*Executive Officer*	Address, City, State, Zip	Phone	Type	Fin	Empls
1	Novelis Inc—*Philip Martens*	3399 Peachtree Rd NE S, Atlanta GA 30326	416-814-4200	S	11,246	12.7
2	Crown Holdings Inc (Philadelphia Pennsylvania)—*John W Conway*	1 Crown Way, Philadelphia PA 19154	215-698-5100	P	7,941	20.5
3	Ball Corp—*John A Hayes*	10 Longs Peak Dr, Broomfield CO 80021	303-469-3131	P	7,630	8.9
4	Crown Cork and Seal Company Inc—*John W Conway* Crown Holdings Inc (Philadelphia Pennsylvania)	1 Crown Way, Philadelphia PA 19154	215-698-5100	S	5,773*	24.1
5	BWAY Holding Co—*Kenneth M Roessler*	8607 Roberts Dr Ste 25, Atlanta GA 30350	770-645-4800	S	904	2.7
6	Phoenix Coca-Cola Bottling Co—*John F Brock*	PO Box 20008, Phoenix AZ 85036	480-831-0400	D	410*	1.0
7	Amtrol Inc—*Larry T Guillemette*	1400 Division Rd, West Warwick RI 02893	401-884-6300	R	287*	1.7
8	ITW Sexton—*Edward W Sexton Jr*	3101 Sexton Rd, Decatur AL 35603	256-355-5850	D	134*	.2
9	Zero Manufacturing Inc—*Dan Leininger*	500 W 200 N, North Salt Lake UT 84054	801-298-5900	S	123*	.3
10	All American Containers Inc—*Remedios Diaz-Oliver*	9330 NW 110th Ave, Miami FL 33178	305-887-0797	R	110*	.2
11	Independent Can Co—*Richard Huether*	PO Box 370, Belcamp MD 21017	410-272-0090	R	45*	.2
12	Eagle Manufacturing Co—*Joseph Eddy*	2400 Charles St, Wellsburg WV 26070	304-737-3171	R	41*	.2
13	Can Corporation Of America Inc—*Ronald Moreau*	326 June Ave, Blandon PA 19510	610-926-3044	R	27*	.2
14	Exal Corp—*Delfin Gibert*	1 Performance Pl, Youngstown OH 44502	330-744-2267	R	25*	.4
15	Ccl Container Corp—*Eric Frantz*	1 Llodio Dr, Hermitage PA 16148	724-981-4420	R	22*	.2
16	Conco Inc—*Robert Pope*	PO Box 19076, Louisville KY 40259	502-969-1333	R	16*	.1
17	Phoenix Container Inc—*Ken Sokoloff*	1202 Airport Rd, North Brunswick NJ 08902	732-247-6700	R	15*	.1
18	Brakewell Steel Fabricators Inc—*Dan Doyle*	55 Leone Ln, Chester NY 10918	845-469-9131	R	7*	<.1
19	Container Products Corp—*Constance Johnston*	PO Box 3767, Wilmington NC 28406	910-392-6100	R	3*	<.1

TOTALS: SIC 3411 Metal Cans
Companies: 19   34,759   73.7

3412 Metal Barrels, Drums & Pails

Rank	Company Name—*Executive Officer*	Address, City, State, Zip	Phone	Type	Fin	Empls
1	Hoover Materials Handling Group Inc—*Donald W Young*	2135 Highway 6 S, Houston TX 77077		R	287*	.4
2	Berenfield Containers Inc—*Leonard Berenfield*	PO Box 350, Mason OH 45040	513-398-1300	R	100*	.3
3	Spartanburg Stainless Products Inc—*Steven Sthies*	PO Box 3488, Spartanburg SC 29304	864-699-3200	R	36*	.6
4	Consolidated Container Co (Minneapolis Minnesota)—*J Phillip Dworsky*	109 27th Ave NE, Minneapolis MN 55418	612-781-0923	R	35*	.1
5	Container Research Corp—*Ron Schlegel*	PO Box 159, Glen Riddle Lima PA 19037	610-459-2160	R	29*	.3
6	Columbus Qcb Inc—*Edward Paul*	PO Box 535, Blacklick OH 43004	614-864-1900	R	19*	.4
7	Queen City Barrel Co—*Edward Paul*	1937 S St, Cincinnati OH 45204	513-921-8811	R	17*	.4
8	Repair Industries Of Michigan Inc—*Todd Schorer*	6501 E Mcnichols Rd, Detroit MI 48212	313-365-5300	R	11*	.1
9	Syme Inc—*Robert Syme*	300 Lake Rd, Medina OH 44256	330-723-6000	R	5*	.1
10	Slickbar Products Corp—*Stephen J Reilly*	18 Beach St, Seymour CT 06483	203-888-7700	R	4*	<.1
11	Justrite Manufacturing Company LLC—*Rich Alsager*	2454 E Dempster St, Des Plaines IL 60016	847-298-9250	3	4*	<.1

TOTALS: SIC 3412 Metal Barrels, Drums & Pails
Companies: 11   547   2.5

3421 Cutlery

Rank	Company Name—*Executive Officer*	Address, City, State, Zip	Phone	Type	Fin	Empls
1	Gillette Co—*Alan G Lafley*	PO Box 720, Boston MA 02217	617-421-7000	S	10,477	28.7
2	Kenwood Silver Company Inc—*James E Joseph*	PO Box 1, Oneida NY 13421	315-361-3800	S	3,586*	2.9
3	World Kitchen LLC—*Joseph Mallof*	1200 South Antrim Way, Greencastle PA 17225		R	1,326*	2.9
4	Lifetime Brands Inc—*Jeffrey Siegel*	1000 Stewart Ave, Garden City NY 11530	516-683-6000	P	443	1.0
5	M Kamenstein Corp Lifetime Brands Inc	1 Merrick Ave, Westbury NY 11590	516-683-6000	S	308	1.0
6	Personna American Safety Razor Co—*James D Murphy*	240 Cedar Knolls Rd St, Cedar Knolls NJ 07927	973-753-3000	R	254*	2.0
7	WR Case and Sons Cutlery Co—*William Russell*	PO Box 4000, Bradford PA 16701	814-368-4123	S	156*	.4
8	Schick Wilkinson Sword—*Joseph Lynch*	10 Leighton Rd, Milford CT 06460	203-882-2100	S	97*	.6
9	Kai USA Ltd—*Koji Endo*	18600 Sw Teton Ave, Tualatin OR 97062	503-682-1966	R	41*	.1
10	Robinson Knife Manufacturing Co	PO Box 550, Buffalo NY 14225	716-685-6300	R	32*	.3
11	Buck Knives Inc—*Charles Buck*	660 S Lochsa St, Post Falls ID 83854	208-262-0500	R	30*	.3
12	Benchmade Knife Company Inc—*Lester Asis*	300 S Beavercreek Rd, Oregon City OR 97045	503-655-6004	R	15*	.1
13	Emerson Knives Inc—*Ernest Emerson*	1234 254th st, Harbor City CA 90710	310-212-7455	R	13*	<.1
14	Mega Manufacturing Inc—*Robert Green*	PO Box 457, Hutchinson KS 67504	620-663-1127	R	12*	.1
15	Lamson and Goodnow Manufacturing Co—*J Anderson*	PO Box 449, Shelburne Falls MA 01370	413-774-9830	R	12*	.1
16	Midwest Tool And Cutlery Co—*Stephen Deter*	PO Box 160, Sturgis MI 49091	269-651-2476	R	9*	.1
17	Queen Cutlery Co—*Bob Breton*	PO Box 408, Titusville PA 16354	814-827-3673	S	7*	.1
18	Speco Inc—*Craig Hess*	3946 Willow St, Schiller Park IL 60176	847-678-4240	R	7*	<.1
19	Spyderco Inc—*Sal Glesser*	PO Box 800, Golden CO 80402	303-279-8383	R	6*	<.1
20	Delaware Diamond Knives Inc—*Joseph Tabeling*	3825 Lancaster Pke Ste, Wilmington DE 19805	302-999-7476	R	3*	<.1
21	Donahue Industries Inc—*Judith Donahue*	5 Industrial Dr, Shrewsbury MA 01545	508-845-6501	R	2*	<.1

TOTALS: SIC 3421 Cutlery
Companies: 21   16,836   40.7

3423 Hand & Edge Tools Nec

Rank	Company Name—*Executive Officer*	Address, City, State, Zip	Phone	Type	Fin	Empls
1	Stanley Black and Decker Inc—*John F Lundgren*	1000 Stanley Dr, New Britain CT 06053	860-225-5111	P	8,410	36.7
2	Snap-On Inc—*Nicholas T Pinchuk*	PO Box 1410, Kenosha WI 53141	262-656-5200	P	2,854*	11.5
3	Danaher Tool Group—*H Lawrence Culp*	125 Powder Forest Dr, Weatogue CT 06089	860-843-7300	S	1,380*	4.7
4	Oregon Cutting Systems Group—*Jim Oscermanc*	PO Box 22127, Portland OR 97269	503-653-4692	D	674*	1.0
5	Matco Tools Corp—*Thomas Willis*	4403 Allen Rd, Stow OH 44224	330-929-4949	S	467*	.5
6	Stanley Hand Tools—*Jeffrey Ansell* Stanley Black and Decker Inc	480 Myrtle St, New Britain CT 06053	860-225-5111	D	276*	.3
7	QEP Company Inc—*Lewis Gould*	1001 Broken Sound Pky, Boca Raton FL 33487	561-994-5550	P	238	.4
8	Hutchinson-Mayrath—*Cliff Williams*	PO Box 629, Clay Center KS 67432	785-632-2161	P	227*	.3
9	Ames True Temper—*Richard Dell*	PO Box 8859, Camp Hill PA 17001	717 737 1500	S	200*	1.6
10	Acorn Products Inc (Columbus Ohio)—*A Corydon Meyer*	PO Box 1930, Columbus OH 43216	614-222-4400	R	91	.5
11	Klein Tools Inc—*Thomas Klein*	PO Box 1418, Lincolnshire IL 60069	847-821-5500	R	71*	1.0
12	Stanley Mechanics Tools—*John F Lundgren* Stanley Black and Decker Inc	1000 Stanley Dr, New Britain CT 06053	860-225-5111	S	69*	.5
13	Mac Tools Inc—*John Aden* Stanley Black and Decker Inc	505 N Cleveland Ave St, Westerville OH 43082		S	67*	.6
14	Acme United Corp—*Walter C Johnsen*	60 Round Hill Rd, Fairfield CT 06824	203-254-6060	P	63	.1

Note: An asterisk (*) indicates an estimated financial figure. The company type code used is as follows: R = Private, P = Public, S = Private Subsidiary, B = Public Subsidiary, D = Division, J = Joint Venture, I = Investment Fund.

COMPANY RANKINGS BY SALES WITHIN 4-DIGIT SIC

Rank	Company Name—Executive Officer	Address, City, State, Zip	Phone	Type	Fin	Empls
15	Corona Clipper Inc—Stephen Erickson	22440 Temescal Canyon, Corona CA 92883	951-737-6515	R	60*	.1
16	Herschel-Adams Inc—Ronald Robinson	1301 N 14th St, Indianola IA 50125	515-961-7481	S	59*	.2
17	Warner Manufacturing Co—Gerald Ranallo	13435 Industrial Pk Bl, Plymouth MN 55441	763-559-4740	R	54*	.1
18	Apex-Cooper Tools Div—Kirk Hachigian	PO Box 952, Dayton OH 45401	937-222-7871	D	44*	.4
19	Empire Level Manufacturing Corp—Jenni Becker	PO Box 800, Mukwonago WI 53149	262-368-2000	R	37*	.3
20	Channellock Inc—William De Arment	PO Box 519, Meadville PA 16335	814-724-8700	R	36*	.4
21	General Tools and Instruments—Gerald Weinstein	80 White St, New York NY 10013	212-431-6100	R	35*	<.1
22	Hyde Group Inc—Richard Hardy	PO Box 1875, Southbridge MA 01550	508-764-4344	R	33*	.5
23	Magna Industrial Tools Div—Manfred Seitz	1001 W Park Rd, Elizabethtown KY 42701	270-737-3311	D	31*	.3
24	Walter Meier Inc—Robert Romano	427 New Sanford Rd, La Vergne TN 37086	615-793-8900	R	30*	.3
25	Greenlee Textron Inc—Barclay Olsen	4411 Boeing Dr, Rockford IL 61109	815-397-7070	S	27*	.1
26	A and E Inc—John Lang	PO Box 1616, Racine WI 53401	262-554-2300	R	25*	.2
27	Estwing Manufacturing Company Inc—Robert Youngren	2647 8th St, Rockford IL 61109	815-397-9521	R	23*	.4
28	Seymour Manufacturing Company Inc—Berl Grant	PO Box 248, Seymour IN 47274	812-522-2900	R	22*	.2
29	Douglas Quikut—Warren E Buffett	PO Box 29, Walnut Ridge AR 72476		D	22*	.1
30	Malco Products Inc—Paul Keymer	PO Box 400, Annandale MN 55302	320-274-8246	R	21*	.2
31	Lisle Corp—William Lisle	PO Box 89, Clarinda IA 51632	712-542-5101	R	20*	.2
32	Johnson Level and Tool Manufacturing Company Inc—William Johnson	6333 W Donges Bay Rd, Mequon WI 53092	262-242-1161	R	20*	.2
33	Rigid Products	14100 Old Gordonsville, Orange VA 22960	540-672-5150	D	20*	.2
34	Fletcher Terry Co—Terry Fletcher	65 Spring Ln, Farmington CT 06032	860-677-7331	R	20*	.1
35	Wright Tool Co—Terry Taylor	PO Box 512, Barberton OH 44203	330-848-0600	R	19*	.2
36	Kraft Tool Co—Ronald Meyer	PO Box 860230, Shawnee Mission KS 66286	913-422-4848	R	19*	.2
37	Allway Tools Inc—Howard Soled	PO Box 777, Bronx NY 10462	718-792-3636	R	18*	.2
38	Mr Long-Arm Inc—Dere Newman	PO Box 377, Greenwood MO 64034	816-537-6777	R	17*	.1
39	Daniels Manufacturing Corp—George Daniels	PO Box 593872, Orlando FL 32859	407-855-6161	R	17*	.2
40	C S Osborne And Co—R Osborne	125 Jersey St, Harrison NJ 07029	973-483-3232	R	16*	.1
41	Everhard Products Inc—James Anderson	1016 9th St Sw, Canton OH 44707	330-453-7786	R	16*	.1
42	Stride Tool Inc—Lori Northrup	30333 Emerald Valley P, Glenwillow OH 44139	440-247-4600	R	15*	.2
43	Summit Tool Co—H Pendleton	PO Box 9320, Akron OH 44305	330-535-7177	R	15*	.1
44	Pull'r Holding Company LLC—Judy Roberts	1000 Greenleaf St, Elk Grove Village IL 60007	224-366-2500	R	15*	<.1
45	Mayhew Steel Products Inc—John Lawless	199 Industrial Blvd, Turners Falls MA 01376	413-863-4860	R	15*	.1
46	Hastings Fiber Glass Products Inc—Larry Baum	PO Box 218, Hastings MI 49058	269-945-9541	R	12*	.1
47	Bon Tool Co—Carl Bongiovanni	4430 Gibsonia Rd, Gibsonia PA 15044	724-443-7080	R	10*	.1
48	Chase Dan Taxidermy Supply Company Incorporated—Daniel Chase	13599 Blackwater Rd, Baker LA 70714	225-261-3795	R	9*	.1
49	Dalen Products Inc—David Caldwell	700 Dalen Ln, Knoxville TN 37932	865-966-3256	R	9*	.1
50	Sheyenne Tooling And Manufacturing Inc—Patricia Broten	PO Box 647, Cooperstown ND 58425	701-797-2700	R	8*	.1
51	Lee Precision Inc—John Lee	4275 Hwy U, Hartford WI 53027	262-673-3075	R	8*	.1
52	Lancaster Knives Inc—Scott Cant	165 Ct St, Lancaster NY 14086	716-603-5050	R	6*	<.1
53	Tamco Inc—Alan Citron	PO Box 371, Monongahela PA 15063	724-258-6622	R	6*	.1
54	Everwear Inc—Tom Wood	401 Stag Industrial Bl, Lake Saint Louis MO 63367	636-625-1551	R	6*	<.1
55	Augerscope Inc—Lawrence Irwin	640 Jessie St, San Fernando CA 91340	818-367-2227	R	6*	<.1
56	Rostra Tool Co—Richard Steiner	30 E Industrial Rd, Branford CT 06405	203-488-8665	R	6*	<.1
57	Superion—Alton Choiniere	1285 S Patton St, Xenia OH 45385	937-374-0033	R	5*	<.1
58	Swing-A-Way Products LLC—Mary Underwood	4100 Beck Ave, Saint Louis MO 63116	314-773-1487	S	5*	.1
59	Electric Eel Manufacturing Company Inc—C Hale	PO Box 419, Springfield OH 45501	937-323-4644	R	5*	<.1
60	Products Engineering Corp—Martin Luboviski	2645 Maricopa St, Torrance CA 90503	310-787-4500	R	4*	.1
61	Connectool Inc—Steven Erickson	2559 Turkey Creek Rd, Oilville VA 23129	804-459-3224	R	4*	<.1
62	Caretree Systems Inc—Gebhard Keny	PO Box 250, Hilliard OH 43026	614-861-7775	R	4*	<.1
63	New England Die Cutting Inc—Kimberly Abare	42 Newark St, Haverhill MA 01832	978-374-0789	R	4*	<.1
64	Xuron Corp—Frank Brown	62 Industrial Park Rd, Saco ME 04072	207-283-1401	R	4*	<.1
65	Craftsman Cutting Dies Inc—Thomas Hughes	1055 E Discovery Ln, Anaheim CA 92801	714-776-8995	R	3*	<.1
66	Diamond Lach Inc—Horst Lach	4350 Airwest Dr Se Off, Grand Rapids MI 49512	616-698-0101	R	3*	<.1
67	EMT Ohio Knife and Grinding Co	219 Annadale St, Akron OH 44304	330-773-6646	R	3*	<.1
68	Swanson's Die Company Inc—William Swanson	141 Queen City Ave, Manchester NH 03101	603-623-3832	R	3*	<.1
69	Gartech Manufacturing Co—Janet Garrett	PO Box 186, Litchfield IL 62056	217-324-6527	R	3*	<.1
70	Precision Part Systems Of Winston-Salem Inc—Nick Doumas	PO Box 5565, Winston Salem NC 27113	336-723-5210	R	3*	<.1
71	Seekonk Manufacturing Company Inc—Frederick Dobras	87 Perrin Ave, Seekonk MA 02771	508-761-8284	R	2*	<.1
72	Cows Locomotive Manufacturing Co—Richard Wiand	32052 Edward Ave, Madison Heights MI 48071	248-583-7150	R	2*	<.1
73	M W Bevins Co—Richard Bevins	9903 E 54th St, Tulsa OK 74146	918-627-1273	R	2*	<.1
74	National Knife Company Inc—Jerome Oconnor	17135 Amber Dr, Cleveland OH 44111	216-671-8596	R	2*	<.1
75	Electroline Corp—Robert Erbrick	6182 Easton Rd, Pipersville PA 18947	215-766-2229	R	2*	<.1
76	Desert Cutting Tools Inc—Richard Driver	2643 N 37th Dr, Phoenix AZ 85009	602-269-7783	R	2*	<.1
77	Seatek Company Inc—Lucien Ducret	392 Pacific St, Stamford CT 06902	203-324-0067	R	2*	<.1
78	Thexton Manufacturing Co—Brian Tichy	6539 Cecilia Cir, Minneapolis MN 55439	952-831-4171	R	2*	<.1
79	Pelletizer Knives Inc—Michael Tofte	9703 Telge Rd, Houston TX 77095	281-859-4492	R	2*	<.1
80	Harrington Tools Inc—Eugene Harrington	6895 Speedway Blvd, Las Vegas NV 89115	702-413-6524	R	1*	<.1
81	Archer Tool Co—O Archer	PO Box 209, Keytesville MO 65261	660-288-3257	R	1*	<.1
82	American Power Pull Corp—Edward Kraemer	PO Box 109, Wauseon OH 43567	419-335-7050	R	1*	<.1
83	Plumb-It Inc—Paul Semler	3045 N Dodge Blvd, Tucson AZ 85716	520-881-5777	R	1*	<.1
84	Telephone Tools Of Georgia Inc—Rebecca Johnson	PO Box 1240, Cartersville GA 30120	770-386-3239	R	1*	<.1
85	C-H Tool and Die—David Davison	PO Box 889, Mount Vernon OH 43050	740-397-7214	R	<1*	<.1

TOTALS: SIC 3423 Hand & Edge Tools Nec
Companies: 85

					16,069	67.3

3425 Saw Blades & Handsaws

Rank	Company Name—Executive Officer	Address, City, State, Zip	Phone	Type	Fin	Empls
1	Robert Bosch Tool Corp—Timothy Shea	1961 Bishop Ln Ste 102, Louisville KY 40218	502-625-2050	S	968*	.2
2	Simonds International Corp—Raymond J Martino	PO Box 500, Fitchburg MA 01420	978-424-0100	R	286*	.4
3	Blount Inc Oregon Cutting Systems Div	PO Box 22127, Portland OR 97269	503-653-8881	D	135*	1.0
4	MK Morse Co—Jim Batchelder	PO Box 8677, Canton OH 44711	330-453-8187	R	116*	.4
5	Marvel Manufacturing Company Inc—John Petek	3501 Marvel Dr, Oshkosh WI 54902	920-236-7200	R	25*	.2
6	Pacific Saw And Knife Co—James Ruthven	PO Box 82155, Portland OR 97282	503-234-9501	R	17*	.2
7	Carlton Co—Russ German	PO Box 68309, Portland OR 97268	503-659-8911	R	14*	.1
8	Contour Saws Inc—Michael Wilkie	1217 E Thacker St, Des Plaines IL 60016	847-824-1146	R	14*	.1
9	Lie-Nielsen Toolworks Inc—Thomas Lie-Nielsen	PO Box 9, Warren ME 04864		R	10*	.1
10	Diamond Hoffman Products Inc—Steve Palovchik	121 Cedar St, Punxsutawney PA 15767	814-938-7600	R	10*	<.1
11	Western Saw Manufacturers Inc—Kraig Baron	3200 Camino Del Sol, Oxnard CA 93030	805-981-0999	R	7*	.1
12	Carbide Processors Inc—Thomas Walz	3847 S Union Ave, Tacoma WA 98409	253-476-1338	R	4*	<.1
13	Texas Diamond Tools Inc—Bill Bridwell	805 Hilbig Rd, Conroe TX 77301	936-756-0646	R	2*	<.1

Rank	Company Name—*Executive Officer*	Address, City, State, Zip	Phone	Type	Fin	Empls
14	Supreme Saw and Service Co—*Gregory Muntean*	3820 W 128th Pl, Alsip IL 60803	708-396-1125	R	<1*	<.1

TOTALS: SIC 3425 Saw Blades & Handsaws
Companies: 14   1,609   2.8

3429 Hardware Nec

Rank	Company Name—*Executive Officer*	Address, City, State, Zip	Phone	Type	Fin	Empls
1	Crosby Group LLC—*Larry Postelwait*	PO Box 3128, Tulsa OK 74101	918-834-4611	R	111,046*	.7
2	Tkk USA Inc—*Jaime Valle*	2550 Golf Rd Ste 800, Rolling Meadows IL 60008	847-439-7821	R	15,993*	.2
3	Avis Industrial Corp—*Leland Boren*	PO Box 548, Upland IN 46989	765-998-8100	R	4,155*	1.1
4	Johnson Controls Interiors—*Stephen Roell*	49200 Halyard Dr, Plymouth MI 48170	734-254-5000	S	1,286*	2.5
5	American Auto Accessories Inc—*Henry Hsu*	35-06 Leavitt St Unit, Flushing NY 11354	718-886-6600	R	800*	1.3
6	Simpson Strong-Tie Company Inc—*Tom Fitzmyers*	PO Box 10789, Pleasanton CA 94588	925-560-9000	S	475*	2.0
7	MW Industries Inc—*Dan Sebastian*	101 Godfrey St, Logansport IN 46947	574-722-8242	R	448*	.9
8	Gem Industries Inc—*M Rolla*	PO Box 610, Toccoa GA 30577	706-886-8431	R	405*	.7
9	Schlage Lock Co—*Herbert Henkel*	3899 Hancock Expy, Colorado Springs CO 80911	719-896-3000	S	397*	.8
10	Hearth and Home Technologies Inc—*Brad Determan*	1915 W Saunders St, Mount Pleasant IA 52641		S	369	2.8
11	Accuride International Inc—*Scott Jordan*	PO Box 2597, Calexico CA 92232	562-903-0200	S	264*	2.0
12	LS Starrett Co—*Douglas A Starrett*	121 Crescent St, Athol MA 01331	978-249-3551	P	245	2.0
13	Valcor Inc—*Robert Singer*	5430 Lyndon B Johnson, Dallas TX 75240	972-233-1700	S	198*	.1
14	De-Sta-Co Industries—*Dan Peretz*	PO Box 2800, Troy MI 48007	248-397-6700	S	193*	.8
15	United Steel Products Co—*Robert Brunson*	703 Rogers Dr, Montgomery MN 56069	507-364-7333	S	159*	.6
16	Hurd Corp—*Leland Boren* Avis Industrial Corp	PO Box 548, Upland IN 46989	423-787-8800	S	149*	1.1
17	CompX International Inc—*David A Bowers*	5430 LBJ Fwy Ste 1700, Dallas TX 75240	972-448-1400	B	139	.8
18	HBD Industries Inc	1301 W Sandusky Ave, Bellefontaine OH 43311	937-593-5010	R	132*	.3
19	Eastern Co (Naugatuck Connecticut)—*Leonard F Leganza*	PO Box 460, Naugatuck CT 06770	203-729-2255	P	130	.6
20	Ideal Clamp Products Inc—*Mike Reese*	8150 Tridon Dr, Smyrna TN 37167	615-459-5800	S	130*	.2
21	Best Access Systems—*John Lundgren*	PO Box 50444, Indianapolis IN 46250	317-849-2250	S	115*	1.1
22	Lodge Manufacturing Co—*Bob Kellermann*	PO Box 380, South Pittsburg TN 37380	423-837-7181	R	115*	.2
23	Prime-Line Products Co—*Richard Crowther*	26950 San Bernadino Av, Redlands CA 92374	909-887-8118	R	109*	.3
24	Barbour Corp—*Richard Hynes*	55 Meadowbrook Dr, Milford NH 03055	603-673-1313	R	103*	.2
25	ITW Bee Leitzke—*Jerry Dewitz*	2000 Industrial Rd, Iron Ridge WI 53035	920-625-2342	R	103*	.2
26	Everburn Manufacturing Inc—*Ajay Gupta*	454 Fairman Rd, Lexington KY 40511	859-231-6492	R	88*	.1
27	Rev-A-Shelf Company LLC—*J Jones*	PO Box 99585, Louisville KY 40269	502-499-5835	S	88*	1.3
28	Akron Brass Co—*Dan Peters*	PO Dox 86, Woootor OH 44691	330-264-5678	D	87*	.2
29	Master Lock Co—*John Heppner*	PO Box 100367, Milwaukee WI 53210	414-444-2800	S	86	.7
30	Falcon Lock—*Mark Hester*	2315 Briargate Pkwy St, Colorado Springs CO 80920		S	76*	.2
31	M/A/R/C Research—*Merrill Dubrow*	1660 N Westridge Cir, Irving TX 75038	972-506-3400	S	72*	1.0
32	Raymarine Inc—*Dave Bimschleger*	21 Manchester St, Merrimack NH 03054	603-881-5200	R	72*	.6
33	Yale Security Inc—*Thanasis Molokotos*	1902 Airport Rd, Monroe NC 28110	704-283-2101	R	71*	1.1
34	Glynn-Johnson Corp	2720 Tobey Dr, Indianapolis IN 46219		S	70*	.7
35	Anchor Coupling Inc—*Douglas Oberhelman*	5520 13th St, Menominee MI 49858	906-863-2672	S	70*	.2
36	Kaba Ilco Corp—*Frank Belflower*	PO Box 2027, Rocky Mount NC 27802	252-446-3321	R	69*	1.3
37	Chicago Hardware and Fixture Co—*Thomas Herbstritt Jr*	9100 Parklane Ave, Franklin Park IL 60131	847-455-6609	R	67*	.1
38	Rolls-Royce Naval Marine—*Jim Guyette*	110 Norfolk St, Walpole MA 02081	508-668-9610	D	63*	.3
39	Nucor Fastener Div—*Tom Miller*	PO Box 6100, Saint Joe IN 46785	260-337-1600	D	52*	.2
40	AnchorPad Security Inc—*Jim McGovern*	5576 Corporate Ave, Cypress CA 90630	714-827-8888	R	51*	.1
41	Innov-X Systems—*Toshihiko Okubo*	100 Sylvan Rd Ste 500, Woburn MA 01801	781-938-5005	R	51*	.1
42	R G Ray Corp—*Daniel Mitrano*	900 Busch Pkwy, Buffalo Grove IL 60089	847-459-5900	R	46*	.4
43	Portland Willamette	6800 NE 59th Pl, Portland OR 97206	503-288-7511	R	44*	.1
44	Sargent Manufacturing Co—*Douglas Bell*	PO Box 9725, New Haven CT 06536	203-562-2151	R	43*	.7
45	Woodstream Corp—*Harry Whaley*	PO Box 327, Lititz PA 17543	717-626-2125	S	43*	.2
46	Holmes-Hally Industries Inc—*Richard Holmes*	PO Box 22113, Los Angeles CA 90022		S	42*	.1
47	C Hager and Sons Hinge Manufacturing Co—*August Hager*	139 Victor St, Saint Louis MO 63104	314-772-4400	R	38*	.6
48	National Cabinet Lock—*David Bowers* CompX International Inc	PO Box 200, Mauldin SC 29662	864-297-6655	S	36	.3
49	Payson Casters Inc—*Harold Sullivan III*	2323 Delaney Rd, Gurnee IL 60031	847-336-6200	R	35*	.1
50	Voss Industries Inc—*Daniel Sedor*	2168 W 25th St, Cleveland OH 44113	210-771-7655	R	31*	.3
51	Aluma-Form Inc—*Fred Newman*	PO Box 18555, Memphis TN 38181	901-362-0100	R	31*	.2
52	Universal Metal Products Inc—*Hugh Seaholm*	PO Box 130, Wickliffe OH 44092	440-943-3040	R	31*	.3
53	J K Pulley Company Inc—*Leonard Koch*	3805 Bates St, Saint Louis MO 63116	314-481-2900	R	30*	<.1
54	Allfast Fastening Systems Inc—*James Randall*	PO Box 3166, City Of Industry CA 91744	626-968-9388	R	30*	.3
55	Peerless Industries Inc—*Walter Snodell*	2300 White Oak Cir, Aurora IL 60502	630-375-5100	R	28*	.5
56	Perko Inc—*Frederick Perkins*	16490 Nw 13th Ave, Miami FL 33169	305-621-7525	R	27*	.5
57	Shur-Co LLC—*Terry Tennant*	PO Box 713, Yankton SD 57078	605-665-6000	R	27*	.2
58	Hudson Lock LLC—*Robert Kay*	81 Apsley St, Hudson MA 01749	978-562-3481	R	27*	.2
59	AdelWiggins Group—*W Nicholas Howley*	5000 Triggs St, Los Angeles CA 90022	323-269-9181	D	26*	.1
60	Travers Tool Company Inc—*Bruce Zolot*	PO Box 541550, Flushing NY 11354	718-886-7200	R	26*	.1
61	A and G Machine Inc—*Abe Mathew*	1231 37th St Nw, Auburn WA 98001	253-887-8433	R	25*	.1
62	Trimark Corp—*Dan Huffman*	PO Box 350, New Hampton IA 50659	641-394-3188	R	25*	.3
63	Weiser Lock Corp—*John F Lundgren*	19701 Da Vinci, Lake Forest CA 92610		S	24*	.1
64	Jonathan Engineered Solutions Corp—*Michael Berneth*	410 Exchange Ste 200, Irvine CA 92602	714-665-4400	R	23*	.4
65	BAND-IT-IDEX Inc	4799 Dahlia St, Denver CO 80216	303-320-4555	S	22*	.3
66	Oetiker Inc	PO Box 217, Marlette MI 48453	989-635-3621	S	22*	.1
67	Rockford Process Control Inc—*Patrick Derry*	2020 7th St, Rockford IL 61104	815-966-2000	R	22*	.2
68	Blum Inc—*Karl Ruedisser*	7733 Old Plank Rd, Stanley NC 28164	704-827-1345	S	22*	.4
69	Marinco—*Tim McDonnell*	N85 W12545 Westbrook C, Menomonee Falls WI 53051	262-293-1700	S	21	.2
70	Amtex Inc—*Curt Campbell*	1500 Kingsview Dr, Lebanon OH 45036	513-932-9319	R	21*	.1
71	Heckethorn Manufacturing Co—*Jon Walter*	2005 Forrest St, Dyersburg TN 38024	731-285-3310	R	20*	.2
72	Task Force Tips Inc—*Stewart Mcmillan*	3701 Innovation Way, Valparaiso IN 46383	219-462-6161	R	20*	.2
73	Renovator's Supply Inc—*Claude Jeanloz*	Renovators Old Ml, Millers Falls MA 01349	413-423-3300	R	20*	.1
74	Rotor Clip Company Inc—*Robert Slass*	187 Davidson Ave, Somerset NJ 08873	732-469-7333	R	20*	.3
75	Adams Rite Manufacturing Co—*Dick Kreidel*	260 W Santa Fe St, Pomona CA 91767	909-632-2300	R	19*	.4
76	Aerial Machine and Tool Corp—*John Marcaccio*	PO Box 222, Vesta VA 24177	276-952-2006	R	19*	.2
77	Shepherd Caster Corp—*Dennis Jones*	203 Kerth St, Saint Joseph MI 49085	269-983-7351	R	19*	.1
78	LE Johnson Products Inc—*Larry Johnson*	2100 Sterling Ave, Elkhart IN 46516	574-293-5664	R	19*	.2
79	Triangle Brass Manufacturing Company Inc—*Martin Simon*	PO Box 23277, Los Angeles CA 90023	323-262-4191	R	17*	.2
80	Arrow Tru-Line Inc—*David Shaffer*	2211 S Defiance St, Archbold OH 43502	419-446-2785	R	17*	.2
81	Component Hardware Group Inc—*John Vresics*	PO Box 2020, Lakewood NJ 08701	732-363-4700	R	17*	<.1
82	Blaser Die Casting Co—*P Foley*	PO Box 80286, Seattle WA 98108	206-767-7800	R	17*	.3

Note: An asterisk (*) indicates an estimated financial figure. The company type code used is as follows: R = Private, P = Public, S = Private Subsidiary, B = Public Subsidiary, D = Division, J = Joint Venture, I = Investment Fund.

COMPANY RANKINGS BY SALES WITHIN 4-DIGIT SIC

Rank	Company Name—Executive Officer	Address, City, State, Zip	Phone	Type	Fin	Empls
83	Weber-Knapp Co—Rex Mccray	441 Chandler St, Jamestown NY 14701	716-484-9135	R	16*	.2
84	Agm Container Controls Inc—Howard Stewart	PO Box 40020, Tucson AZ 85717	520-881-2130	R	16*	.1
85	Adjustable Clamp Co—Daniel Holman	404 N Armour St, Chicago IL 60642	312-666-0640	R	15*	.2
86	Acme Manufacturing Company Inc—L Broderick	4661 Monaco St, Denver CO 80216	303-355-2344	R	14*	.1
87	Garelick Manufacturing Co—Kenneth Garelick	PO Box 8, Saint Paul Park MN 55071	651-459-9795	R	14*	.1
88	International Engineering and Manufacturing Inc—Robert Musselman	PO Box 316, Edenville MI 48620	989-689-4911	R	13*	.1
89	Albion Industries Inc—Scott Chahalis	800 N Clark St, Albion MI 49224	517-629-9441	R	13*	.1
90	Crown Metal Manufacturing Co—Richard Ernest	765 S State Rte 83, Elmhurst IL 60126	630-279-9800	R	13*	.1
91	Accurate Products Manufacturing Corp—Robert Stippich	PO Box 255, Waukesha WI 53187	262-542-8166	R	13*	.1
92	Driv-Lok Inc—Gary Seegers	1140 Park Ave, Sycamore IL 60178	815-895-8161	R	12*	.1
93	Swoboda Inc—Christoph Hirt	4108 52nd St Se, Grand Rapids MI 49512	616-554-6161	R	12*	.1
94	Jrl Ventures Inc—Robert Long	2443 Sw Pine Island Rd, Cape Coral FL 33991	239-283-0800	R	12*	.1
95	Felix Thomson Co—Mike Verucchi	PO Box 10387, Fort Smith AR 72917	479-646-7321	R	12*	.1
96	Unistrut Corp—Glen Noble	4205 Elizabeth, Wayne MI 48184		D	12*	<.1
97	Saturn Fasteners Inc—Raymond Barker	425 S Varney St, Burbank CA 91502	818-846-7145	R	12*	.1
98	Rockwood Manufacturing Co—William Gurzenda	PO Box 79, Rockwood PA 15557	814-926-2026	R	11*	.1
99	Cascaded Purchase Holdings Inc—J Miller	68 Etna Rd, Lebanon NH 03766	603-448-1090	R	11*	.1
100	Clampco Products Inc—James Venner	1743 Wall Rd, Wadsworth OH 44281	330-336-8857	R	11*	.1
101	Fort Lock Corp—Jay Fine	715 Ctr St, Grayslake IL 60030	847-752-2500	R	11*	.2
102	John Sterling Corp—John Sterling	PO Box 469, Richmond IL 60071	815-678-2031	R	11*	.1
103	Crain Cutter Company Inc—Millard Crain	1155 Wrigley Way, Milpitas CA 95035	408-946-6100	R	10*	.1
104	DMEInc—Michael Moore	14001 Marquardt Ave, Santa Fe Springs CA 90670	562-921-0464	R	9*	.1
105	Brammall Inc—Steve Trent	409 Hoosier Dr, Angola IN 46703	260-665-3176	R	9*	.1
106	Ultra-Mek Inc—D Hoffman	PO Box 518, Denton NC 27239	336-859-4552	R	9*	.1
107	Countrywide Hardware Inc—Chris Klieforth	10333 Windhorst Rd, Tampa FL 33619	813-988-2628	S	9*	<.1
108	Gater Industries Inc—Kevin Mallory	4400 Dell Range Blvd, Cheyenne WY 82009	307-635-4166	R	9*	.1
109	Parts Unlimited Inc—Rollo Fox	2801 Interior Way, La Grange KY 40031	502-425-3766	R	8*	.1
110	Group Industries Inc—Martin Tiernan	PO Box 25409, Cleveland OH 44125	216-271-0702	R	8*	.1
111	Batesville Products Inc—Richard Weber	434 Margaret St, Lawrenceburg IN 47025	812-537-2275	R	7*	.1
112	Collier-Keyworth Inc—David Haffner	PO Box 1109, Liberty NC 27298	336-622-0121	S	7*	<.1
113	Royal Lock Corp—Larry Freck	301 W Hintz Rd, Wheeling IL 60090	847-537-1800	D	7*	<.1
	Eastern Co (Naugatuck Connecticut)					
114	US Ring Binder LP—Mark Nold	6800 Arsenal St, Saint Louis MO 63139	314-645-7880	R	7*	.1
115	Sebewaing Tool And Engineering Co—Bernard Hoeh	PO Box 685, Sebewaing MI 48759	989-883-2000	R	6*	.1
116	R and H Manufacturing Inc—Alan Pollock	PO Box 1492, Kingston PA 18704	570-288-6648	R	6*	<.1
117	Syraco Products Inc—Fred Honnold	1054 S Clinton St, Syracuse NY 13202	315-476-5306	R	5*	<.1
118	James Ippolito and Company Of Connecticut Inc—Gerald Cavallo	1069 Connecticut Ave, Bridgeport CT 06607	203-366-3840	R	5*	<.1
119	S Parker Hardware Manufacturing Corp—Chuck Silberman	PO Box 9882, Englewood NJ 07631	201-569-1600	R	5*	<.1
120	Dynamic Machine and Fabrication Corp—James Stewart	3845 E Winslow Ave, Phoenix AZ 85040	602-437-0339	R	5*	<.1
121	Wind Corp—Patrick Wind	14 Finance Dr, Danbury CT 06810	203-778-1001	R	5*	<.1
122	Zephyr Lock LLC—Patrick Wind	14 Finance Dr, Danbury CT 06810	203-743-2976	R	5*	<.1
123	HK Precision Parts Inc—Hans Kocher	2039 9th Ave, Ronkonkoma NY 11779	631-738-2925	R	5*	<.1
124	Wesanco Inc—Andrew Shyer	14870 Desman Rd, La Mirada CA 90638	714-739-4989	R	5*	<.1
125	New Richmond Industries Inc—Richard Simma	905 N Knowles Ave, New Richmond WI 54017	715-246-6571	R	5*	.1
126	Radio Component Corp—Jeff Marberblatt	161 Eastern Ave, Lynn MA 01902	781-592-3070	R	4*	<.1
127	Progressive Machine Die Inc—Julius Feitl	8406 Bavaria Dr E, Macedonia OH 44056	330-405-6600	R	4*	<.1
128	Tog Manufacturing Company Inc—Craig Miller	1454 S State St, North Adams MA 01247	413-664-6711	R	4*	<.1
129	Kaba Mas LLC—Frank Belflower	749 W Short St, Lexington KY 40508	859-253-4744	R	4*	<.1
130	Birmingham Rubber And Gasket Company Inc—Chris Wilder	PO Box 26230, Birmingham AL 35260	205-942-2541	R	4*	<.1
131	Franklin Manufacturing Corp—Lawrence Franklin	300 Smith St, Farmingdale NY 11735		S	4*	<.1
	Countrywide Hardware Inc					
132	Wartian Lock Co	20525 E Nine Mile Rd, Saint Clair Shores MI 48080	586-777-2244	R	4*	<.1
133	West Manufacturing—David West	910 Eldridge Dr, Hagerstown MD 21740	301-797-4479	R	4*	<.1
134	Colorado WaterJet Co—Dan Nibbelink	5186 Longs Peak Rd Uni, Berthoud CO 80513	970-532-5404	R	4*	<.1
135	Ball and Ball LLP—John Muuge	463 W Lincoln Hwy, Exton PA 19341	610-363-7330	R	4*	<.1
136	A and B Tube Benders Inc—Joseph Rea	13465 E 9 Mile Rd, Warren MI 48089	586-773-0440	R	3*	<.1
137	Brawn Mixer Inc—Jerry Fleishman	3389 128th Ave, Holland MI 49424	616-399-5600	R	3	<.1
138	Plant Equipment Company Inc—Lee MacDonald	PO Box 3157, Rock Island IL 61204	309-786-3369	R	3*	<.1
139	TECHNALOCK Computer Security—Connie Rhoades	PO Box 920, Ozark MO 65721	417-868-8711	R	3*	<.1
140	Illinois Fibre Specialty Company Inc—Casimir Kasper	4301 S Western Blvd, Chicago IL 60609	773-376-1122	R	3*	<.1
141	Hartford Aircraft Products Inc—James Griffin	94 Old Poquonock Rd, Bloomfield CT 06002	860-242-8228	R	3*	<.1
142	Byco Plastics Inc—Robert Tapscott	PO Box 729, Decatur AL 35602	256-355-2544	R	3*	<.1
143	Velter Products Inc—Eric Keller	22 N 27th St, Harrisburg PA 17103	717-234-4262	R	3*	<.1
144	Baron Manufacturing Company LLC—Robert Mckinney	1200 W Capitol Dr, Addison IL 60101	630-628-9110	R	2*	<.1
145	WW Patterson Co—David Grapes	870 Riversea Rd, Pittsburgh PA 15233	412-322-2012	R	2*	<.1
146	Carr Lane Roemheld Manufacturing Co—Earl Walker	16345 Westwoods Bus Pa, Ellisville MO 63021	636-386-8022	R	2*	<.1
147	E V M Inc—Keith Bruder	PO Box 153, Two Rivers WI 54241	920-793-4467	R	2*	<.1
148	H Neuman and Co—Todd Miller	10524 United Pkwy, Schiller Park IL 60176	847-671-5885	S	2*	<.1
	Cascaded Purchase Holdings Inc					
149	Vitsur Industries Inc—John Vitsur	130 Evernia St Ste 3, Jupiter FL 33458	561-744-1290	R	2*	<.1
150	Rem Products Inc—Chuck Lipscomb	3830 E 40th St, Tucson AZ 85713	520-747-1939	R	2*	<.1
151	Solid-Scope Machining Company Inc—Patsy Rhinehart	17925 Adria Maru Ln, Carson CA 90746	310-523-2366	R	2*	<.1
152	Bourdon Forge Company Inc—Peter Bourdon	99 Tuttle Rd, Middletown CT 06457	860-632-2740	R	2*	.1
153	Detmar Corp—George Wrigley	PO Box 8098, Detroit MI 48208	313-831-1155	R	2*	<.1
154	Ultra-Fab Products Inc—Darryl Searer	57985 State Rd 19, Elkhart IN 46517	574-294-7571	R	1*	<.1
155	Engineered Inserts and Systems Inc—Teri Cook	PO Box 610, Watertown CT 06795	860-274-3628	R	1*	<.1
156	Franks Cane and Rush Supply Inc—Mike Frank	7252 Heil Ave, Huntington Beach CA 92647	714-847-0707	R	1*	<.1
157	Domino Engineering Corp—Lawrence Peterson	PO Box 376, Taylorville IL 62568	217-824-9441	R	1*	<.1
158	Southco Inc—Brian McNeal	PO Box 0116, Concordville PA 19331	610-459-4000	R	N/A	.5

TOTALS: SIC 3429 Hardware Nec

Companies: 158					140,380	45.3

3431 Metal Sanitary Ware

Rank	Company Name—Executive Officer	Address, City, State, Zip	Phone	Type	Fin	Empls
1	Elkay Manufacturing Co—Tim Jahnke	2222 Camden Ct, Oak Brook IL 60523	630-574-8484	R	522*	4.0
2	MAAX SpA Industries Corp—Paul Golden	9224 73rd Ave N, Minneapolis MN 55428		S	376	2.1
3	Mag Aerospace Industries Inc—Mike Rozenblatt	PO Box 11189, Carson CA 90749	310-884-7000	R	31*	.4
4	Bootz Manufacturing Co—Pete Socio	PO Box 18010, Evansville IN 47719	812-423-5401	R	16*	.1
5	American Shower and Bath Corp—Chris Yankowicz	540 Glen Ave, Moorestown NJ 08057	856-235-7700	S	16*	.1

Rank	Company Name—*Executive Officer*	Address, City, State, Zip	Phone	Type	Fin	Empls
6	Liners Direct Inc—*Jess Connor*	401 S Gary Ave Ste 1, Roselle IL 60172	630-227-1737	R	15*	<.1
7	Hydro Systems Inc—*Scott Steinhardt*	29132 Ave Paine, Valencia CA 91355	661-775-0686	R	13*	.1
8	Poly Portables Inc—*Kathryn Crafton*	99 Crafton Dr, Dahlonega GA 30533	706-864-3776	R	10*	.1
9	Just Manufacturing Company Inc—*Paul Just*	9233 King St, Franklin Park IL 60131	847-678-5150	R	9*	.2
10	Accent Marble Company Inc—*Paul Gutierrez*	210 W Helms Rd, Houston TX 77037	281-448-3696	R	9*	.1
11	Josam Co—*Caswell Holloway*	PO Box T, Michigan City IN 46361	219-872-5531	R	7*	.1

TOTALS: SIC 3431 Metal Sanitary Ware
Companies: 11   1,024   7.4

3432 Plumbing Fixtures Fittings & Trim

Rank	Company Name—*Executive Officer*	Address, City, State, Zip	Phone	Type	Fin	Empls
1	Masco Corp—*Timothy Wadhams*	21001 Van Born Rd, Taylor MI 48180	313-274-7400	P	7,592	32.5
2	Fortune Brands Home and Hardware Inc—*Bruce A Carbonari*	520 Lake Cook Rd, Deerfield IL 60015	847-484-4400	S	5,678*	8.6
3	Kohler Co—*Herbert V Kohler Jr*	444 Highland Dr, Kohler WI 53044	920-457-4441	R	4,333*	25.0
4	American Standard Inc Plumbing Div—*Fred Poses*	PO Box 6820, Piscataway NJ 08855	732-980-3000	D	3,323*	12.0
5	Jacuzzi Brands Inc—*Thomas Koos*	13925 City Center Dr S, Chino Hills CA 91709	909-247-2920	S	1,202	4.5
6	AY McDonald Industries Inc—*Michael B McDonald*	PO Box 508, Dubuque IA 52004	563-583-7311	R	130*	.7
7	Parker Hannifin Corp Brass Products Div—*Todd Keeler*	300 Parker Dr, Otsego MI 49078	269-694-9411	D	104*	.6
8	Davis-Ulmer Sprinkler Company Inc—*R Steven Ulmer*	One Commerce Dr, Amherst NY 14228	716-691-3200	R	76*	.2
9	Bobrick Washroom Equipment Inc—*Mark Louchheim*	11611 Hart St, North Hollywood CA 91605	818-764-1000	R	61*	.2
10	Price Pfister Inc—*James T Caudill*	19701 Da Vinci, Lake Forest CA 92610	949-672-4000	S	55*	.4
11	Symmons Industries Inc—*William OKeeffe*	31 Brooks Dr, Braintree MA 02184	781-848-2250	R	54*	.3
12	Zurn Plumbing Products Group—*Bob Carter*	1801 Pittsburgh Ave, Erie PA 16502	814-455-0921	R	52*	.3
13	Delta Faucet Co—*Keith Allman* Masco Corp	PO Box 40980, Indianapolis IN 46240	317-848-1812	D	48*	.4
14	Starline Manufacturing Company Inc—*Keith Kramer* Chicago Faucet Co	6060 W Douglas Ave, Milwaukee WI 53218	414-358-4060	S	40*	.2
15	Anderson Copper and Brass Co—*Steve Anton*	4325 Frontage Rd, Oak Forest IL 60452	708-535-9030	S	37*	.1
16	Alson's Corp—*Timothy Wadhams* Masco Corp	PO Box 282, Hillsdale MI 49242	517-439-1411	S	35*	.2
17	Keeney Manufacturing Company Inc—*R Holden*	PO Box 310159, Newington CT 06131	860-666-3342	R	31*	.5
18	Jay R Smith Manufacturing Co—*Jay L Smith*	PO Box 3237, Montgomery AL 36109	334-277-8520	R	30*	.4
19	AY McDonald Manufacturing Co—*Michael Mcdonald* AY McDonald Industries Inc	PO Box 508, Dubuque IA 52004	563-583-7311	S	28*	.4
20	T and S Brass and Bronze Works Inc—*Claude Thiesen*	PO Box 1088, Travelers Rest SC 29690		R	27*	.2
21	Zurn Wilkins—*Chris Conners*	1747 Commerce Way, Paso Robles CA 93446		R	26	.2
22	American Granby Inc—*John Lowe*	7652 Morgan Rd, Liverpool NY 13090	315-451-1100	R	25*	.1
23	Chicago Faucet Co—*Andreas Nowak*	2100 Clearwater Dr, Des Plaines IL 60018	847-803-5000	R	25*	.4
24	Brass-Craft Manufacturing Co—*Don Woody* Masco Corp	39600 Orchard Hill Pl, Novi MI 48375	248-305-6000	S	24*	.2
25	Fernco Inc—*Christoper Cooper*	300 S Dayton St, Davison MI 48423	810-653-9626	R	16*	.2
26	Speakman Co—*Rodman Ward*	PO Box 191, Wilmington DE 19899	302-764-7100	R	12*	.1
27	Water Saver Faucet Co—*Steven Kersten*	701 W Erie St, Chicago IL 60654	312-666-5500	R	12*	.1
28	Danfoss Haqo Inc—*Phil Emond*	1120 Globe Ave, Mountainside NJ 07092	908-232-8687	R	11*	.1
29	Northwest Automated Machining Inc—*Chuck Perrott*	7021 Ne 79th Ct, Portland OR 97218	503-252-7742	R	11*	<.1
30	Bead Industries Inc—*Kenneth Bryant*	11 Cascade Blvd, Milford CT 06460	203-301-0270	R	11*	.1
31	Telsco Industries Inc—*Mike Mason*	3301 W Kingsley Rd, Garland TX 75041	972-278-6131	R	10*	.1
32	K-Rain Manufacturing Corp—*Carl Kah*	1640 Australian Ave, Riviera Beach FL 33404	561-844-1002	R	8*	.1
33	Fisher Manufacturing Company Inc—*Ray Fisher*	PO Box 60, Tulare CA 93275	559-685-5200	R	5*	<.1
34	Guardian Equipment Inc—*Steven Kersten*	1140 N N Branch St, Chicago IL 60642	312-447-8100	R	3*	<.1
35	Kraft Hardware Inc	315 E 62nd St, New York NY 10065	212-838-2214	R	3*	<.1
36	American Beverage Equipment Company Inc—*James Testori*	27560 Groesbeck Hwy, Roseville MI 48066	586-773-0094	R	2*	<.1
37	Grace Composites LLC—*Jeff Foster*	351 Ruth Rd, Lonoke AR 72086	501-676-9505	R	1*	<.1

TOTALS: SIC 3432 Plumbing Fixtures Fittings & Trim
Companies: 37   23,141   89.2

3433 Heating Equipment Except Electric

Rank	Company Name—*Executive Officer*	Address, City, State, Zip	Phone	Type	Fin	Empls
1	Lennox Industries Inc (Richardson Texas)—*Robert Schjerven*	PO Box 799900, Dallas TX 75379	972-497-5000	S	880	3.7
2	ALSTOM Power Inc—*E Bysiek*	3020 Truax Rd, Wellsville NY 14895	585-593-2700	S	191*	.6
3	Roberts-Gordon LLC—*Sylvester Jezidrowski*	PO Box 44, Buffalo NY 14240	716-852-4400	R	140*	.4
4	WaterFurnace Renewable Energy—*Thomas F Huntington*	9000 Conservation Way, Fort Wayne IN 46809	260-478-5667	P	138	.3
5	Bradford White Corp—*Nicholas Giuffre*	725 Talamore Dr, Ambler PA 19002	215-641-9400	R	95*	1.2
6	Bmc Holdings Inc—*Michael Lehman*	PO Box 607, Bryan OH 43506	419-636-1194	R	79*	.4
7	Bloom Engineering Company Inc—*Christopher Armitage*	5460 Horning Rd, Pittsburgh PA 15236	412-653-3500	R	73*	.1
8	Westcast Inc—*John E Reed*	260 N Elm St, Westfield MA 01085	413-562-9631	S	67*	.3
9	Air System Components LP—*Terry O'Halloran*	605 Shiloh, Plano TX 75074	972-212-4888	S	42*	.1
10	General Thermodynamics	4700 Ironwood Dr, Franklin WI 53132	414-761-4500	D	42*	.1
11	Taco Inc—*John White*	1160 Cranston St, Cranston RI 02920	401-942-8000	R	36*	.5
12	Williams Comfort Products—*Warren Shoulders*	250 W Laurel St, Colton CA 92324	909-825-0993	S	35*	.3
13	Magic Aire—*Ron Duncan*	501 Galveston St, Wichita Falls TX 76301	940-397-2100	S	34*	.3
14	Eclipse Inc—*Douglas Perks*	1665 Elmwood Rd, Rockford IL 61103	815-877-3031	R	33*	.5
15	Solaria Corp—*Daniel Shugar*	46420 Fremont Blvd, Fremont CA 94538	510-270-2500	R	33*	.1
16	TRad North America Inc—*Yoshitaka Momose*	PO Box 2300, Hopkinsville KY 42241	270-885-9116	R	33*	.6
17	Power Flame Inc—*William Wiener*	PO Box 974, Parsons KS 67357	620-421-0480	R	33*	.2
18	Ecr International Inc—*Timothy Reed*	PO Box 4729, Utica NY 13504	315-797-1310	R	32*	.5
19	Detroit Stoker Co—*Mark Eleniewski*	PO Box 732, Monroe MI 48161	734-241-9500	S	31*	.3
20	Thermal Solutions Products LLC—*Chris Drew*	PO Box 3244, Lancaster PA 17605	717-239-7642	S	30*	.1
21	Slant/Fin Corp—*Adam Dubin*	PO Box 416, Greenvale NY 11548	516-484-2600	R	29*	.1
22	Kyocera Solar Inc—*Steven C Hill*	7812 E Acoma, Scottsdale AZ 85260	480-948-8003	S	28*	.1
23	Fives North American Combustion Inc—*J Paisley*	4455 E 71st St, Cleveland OH 44105	216-271-6000	R	28*	.4
24	Tocco Inc—*Tom Illencik*	1745 Overland Ave, Warren OH 44483		D	27	.1
25	Marathon Heater LLC—*Mike Wrob*	HCR 3 Box 86E, Del Rio TX 78840	830-775-1417	R	27*	.1
26	Coen Company Inc—*Earl Schnell*	951 Mariners Island Bl, San Mateo CA 94404	650-522-2100	R	27*	.3
27	Beckett Gas Inc—*Morrison Carter*	PO Box 4037, Elyria OH 44036	440-327-3141	R	26*	.2
28	Wayne Combustion Systems—*Larry Davis*	801 Glasgow Ave, Fort Wayne IN 46803	260-425-9200	S	26*	.1
29	Tulsa Heaters Inc—*Mat Loveless*	1350 S Boulder Ave Ste, Tulsa OK 74119	918-582-9918	R	25*	<.1
30	Electro-Flex Heat Inc—*Carlos Cardenas*	PO Box 88, Bloomfield CT 06002	860-242-6287	D	23*	.1
31	ITW BGK Finishing Systems—*Mark Rekucki*	4131 Pheasant Ridge Dr, Minneapolis MN 55449	763-784-0466	R	20*	.1
32	Monessen Hearth Systems Co—*Dave Barett*	149 Cleveland Dr, Paris KY 40361	859-987-0740	R	19*	.4
33	Sure Heat Manufacturing Inc—*Mike Mulberry*	1861 W Oak Pkwy, Marietta GA 30062	770-422-8008	R	19*	.2

Note: An asterisk (*) indicates an estimated financial figure. The company type code used is as follows: R = Private, P = Public, S = Private Subsidiary, B = Public Subsidiary, D = Division, J = Joint Venture, I = Investment Fund.

COMPANY RANKINGS BY SALES WITHIN 4-DIGIT SIC

Rank	Company Name—Executive Officer	Address, City, State, Zip	Phone	Type	Fin	Empls
34	Zeeco Inc—Darton Zink	22151 E 91st St S, Broken Arrow OK 74014	918-258-8551	R	18*	.4
35	Beckett Air Inc—Daniel Mobert	PO Box 1236, Elyria OH 44036	440-327-9999	R	17*	.2
36	Boyertown Foundry Co—Richard Riggs	PO Box 443, New Berlinville PA 19545	610-473-1000	R	17*	.1
37	L B White Company Inc—Anthony Wilson	W6636 L B White Rd, Onalaska WI 54650	608-783-5691	R	15*	.1
38	FAFCO Inc—Robert Leckinger	435 Otterson Dr, Chico CA 95928	530-332-2100	R	15*	.1
39	Scheu Manufacturing Co—Allyn Scheu	PO Box 250, Upland CA 91785	909-982-8933	R	13*	.1
40	Indiana Heat Transfer Corp—Daniel B Altman	500 W Harrison St, Plymouth IN 46563	574-936-3171	R	12*	.2
41	Berry Metal Co—George Koenig	2408 Evans City Rd, Harmony PA 16037	724-452-8040	R	12*	.1
42	Newpoint Thermal—Greg Jacobi	PO Box 2408, Atlanta GA 30301	404-446-4610	R	12*	<.1
43	SLR Contracting and Service Company Inc—Sundra L Ryce	260 Michigan Ave No 1, Buffalo NY 14203	716-896-8148	R	11*	<.1
44	Carlin Combustion Technology Inc—Russell Phelon	70 Maple St, East Longmeadow MA 01028	413-525-7700	R	10*	.1
45	New Buck Corp—Robert Bailey	PO Box 69, Spruce Pine NC 28777	828-765-6144	R	10*	.1
46	General Machine Corp—John C Clauss	301 S 4th St, Emmaus PA 18049	610-967-3550	S	10*	.1
47	Parker Boiler Co—Sid Danehauer	5930 Bandini Blvd, Los Angeles CA 90040	323-727-9800	R	9*	.1
48	Westinghouse Solar Inc—Barry Cinnamon	1475 S Bascom Ave Ste, Campbell CA 95008	408-402-9400	P	9	<.1
49	Hussong Manufacturing Company Inc—Jim Hussong	PO Box 577, Lakefield MN 56150	507-662-6641	R	9*	.1
50	Sid Harvey Industries Inc—Sidney W Harvey	605 Locust St, Garden City NY 11530	516-745-9200	R	7*	.1
51	Taitem Engineering—Ian Shapiro	110 S Albany St, Ithaca NY 14850	607-277-1118	R	7*	<.1
52	Detroit Radiant Products Company Inc—Joseph Wortman	21400 Hoover Rd, Warren MI 48089	586-756-0950	R	6*	<.1
53	Enerco Technical Products Inc—Allen Haire	PO Box 6660, Cleveland OH 44101	216-916-3000	R	6*	<.1
54	Paragon Airheater Technologies—Chris Turner	23143 Temescal Canyon, Corona CA 92883	951-277-8035	R	6*	<.1
55	Refrigeration Research Inc—Edward Bottum	PO Box 869, Brighton MI 48116	810-227-1151	R	6*	.1
56	Hastings Hvac Inc—Jerry Juggert	3606 Yost Ave, Hastings NE 68901	402-463-9821	R	5*	<.1
57	Sgm Company Inc—Patrick Gerboth	9060 Tyler Blvd, Mentor OH 44060	440-255-1190	R	4*	<.1
58	Embassy Industries Inc—Robert Ramistella	315 Oser Ave, Hauppauge NY 11788	631-694-1800	S	4*	<.1
59	Solterra Renewable Technologies Inc—Stephen Squires	7700 S River Pky, Tempe AZ 85284	214-701-8779	S	4*	<.1
60	Aldrico Inc—Fred Howard	PO Box 97, Wyoming IL 61491	309-695-2311	R	3*	<.1
61	Enercon Systems Inc—David Hoecke	PO Box 4030, Elyria OH 44036	440-323-7080	R	3*	<.1
62	Gc Aero Inc—Jim Cowherd	21143 Hawthorne Blvd, Torrance CA 90503	310-539-7600	R	3*	<.1
63	Manown Engineering Company Inc—Darwin Gilmore	PO Box 937, Bonifay FL 32425	850-547-9336	R	1*	<.1
64	New Yorker Boiler Company Inc—Elaine Phillips	PO Box 10, Hatfield PA 19440	215-855-8055	R	<1*	<.1
65	Entech Solar Inc—David Gelbaum	13301 Park Vista Blvd, Fort Worth TX 76177	817-224-3600	P	<1	<.1
66	Solarattic Inc—Edward Palmer	15548 95th Cir Ne, Elk River MN 55330	763-441-3440	R	<1*	<.1

TOTALS: SIC 3433 Heating Equipment Except Electric
Companies: 66

					2,663	15.1

3441 Fabricated Structural Metal

Rank	Company Name—Executive Officer	Address, City, State, Zip	Phone	Type	Fin	Empls
1	Tyco Electronics Corp—Tom Lynch	1050 Westlakes Dr, Berwyn PA 19312	610-893-9800	R	18,056*	.4
2	Valmont Industries Inc—Mogens C Bay	1 Valmont Plz, Omaha NE 68154	402-963-1000	P	2,662	9.5
3	Silgan Containers Corp—Anthony J Allott	21800 Oxnard St Ste 60, Woodland Hills CA 91367	818-348-3700	S	1,648*	5.0
4	High Industries Inc—Jeffrey D Smith	PO Box 10008, Lancaster PA 17605	717-293-4444	R	1,284*	2.5
5	Carolina Steel Corp—W Reeves	PO Box 20888, Greensboro NC 27420	336-275-9711	R	1,054*	.5
6	Cives Steel Co—Raymond Phillips	1825 Old Alabama Rd St, Roswell GA 30076	770-993-4424	R	381*	.8
7	DMI Industries Inc—Stefan Nilsson	PO Box 938, West Fargo ND 58078	701-282-6959	S	346*	.7
8	Middle Atlantic Products Inc—Robert J Schluter	300 Fairfield Rd, Fairfield NJ 07004	973-839-1011	R	314*	.5
9	John S Frey Enterprises—John S Frey	1900 E 64th St, Los Angeles CA 90001	323-583-4061	R	308*	.6
10	CCC Group Inc—Dennis Huebner	PO Box 200350, San Antonio TX 78220	210-661-4251	R	250*	2.5
11	Gulf Island Fabrication Inc—Kerry J Chauvin	PO Box 310, Houma LA 70361	985-872-2100	P	248	1.3
12	Riggs Industries Inc—C Daniel Riggs	PO Box 96, Boswell PA 15531	814-629-5621	R	239*	.5
13	PDM Bridge LLC—John Grzybowski	PO Box 1545, Eau Claire WI 54702	715-835-2800	D	235*	.6
14	Eastern Shipbuilding Group Inc—Brian D'isernia	2200 Nelson Ave, Panama City FL 32401	850-763-1900	R	196*	.6
15	Hirschfeld Steel Group LP—Dennis Hirschfeld	112 W 29th St, San Angelo TX 76903	325-486-4201	R	175*	.4
16	CMC Steel Group—Phil Seidenberger	PO Box 911, Seguin TX 78156	830-372-8200	S	173*	.8
17	Frazier Industrial Company Inc—William Mascharka	91 Fairview Ave, Long Valley NJ 07853	908-876-3001	R	169*	.6
18	Dietrich Industries Inc—Edmund Ponko	PO Box 68, Blairsville PA 15717		R	156*	1.7
19	Stupp Bridge Co—Kenneth J Kubacki	PO Box 6600, Saint Louis MO 63125	314-638-5000	R	152*	.6
20	Sulzer Chemtech USA Inc—Mauricio Bannwart	8505 E N Belt, Humble TX 77396	281-441-5200	R	151*	.2
21	B and B ARMR Corp—Paul Matthews	2009 Chenault Dr Ste 1, Carrollton TX 75006	972-385-7899	S	145*	.3
22	Economy Forms Corp—AL Jennings	1800 NE Broadway Ave, Des Moines IA 50313	515-313-4350	R	144*	1.0
23	Nucor-Yamato Steel Co—Doug Jellison	PO Box 1228, Blytheville AR 72316	870-762-5500	S	137*	1.0
24	Owen Industries Inc—John Sunderman	PO Box 1085, Omaha NE 68101	712-347-5500	R	134*	.4
25	Structural Steel Services Inc—Tommy Dulaney	PO Box 2929, Meridian MS 39302	601-483-5381	R	104*	.3
26	Oregon Iron Works Inc—Robert Beal	9700 Se Lawnfield Rd, Clackamas OR 97015	503-653-6300	R	99*	.4
27	Mid America Steel Inc—George Cook	PO Box 2807, Fargo ND 58108	701-232-8831	R	74*	.1
28	Le Jeune Steel Co—Jim Torborg	PO Box 19070, Minneapolis MN 55419	612-861-3321	R	73*	.1
29	Southern Fabricators Inc (Memphis Tennessee)—Greg Langston	4768 Hungerford Rd, Memphis TN 38118	901-363-1571	R	72*	.7
30	Safety Steel Service Inc—Clyde Selig	PO Box 2298, Victoria TX 77902	361-575-4561	S	69*	.2
31	Warren Fabricating Corp—Eric Rebhan	PO Box 1032, Warren OH 44482	330-847-0596	R	64*	.2
32	Merrill Iron and Steel Inc—Roger E Hinner	PO Box 110, Schofield WI 54476	715-355-8924	R	62*	.3
33	Orizon Industries Inc—Curtis Jones	7007 Fm 362 Rd, Brookshire TX 77423	281-375-7700	R	61*	.3
34	Cf and I Steel LP—Rob Simon	PO Box 316, Pueblo CO 81002	719-561-6000	S	61*	.7
35	Steel LLC—Blake Hoskisson	PO Box 845, Scottdale GA 30079	404-292-7373	R	60*	.1
36	Cleveland Track Material Inc—William Willoughby	PO Box 603160, Cleveland OH 44103	216-641-4000	R	58*	.4
37	Roscoe Steel And Culvert Co—James Roscoe	1501 S 30th St W, Billings MT 59102	406-869-2631	R	55*	.2
38	Carbis Inc—Samuel Cramer	PO Box 6229, Florence SC 29502		R	50*	.3
39	Cauttrell Enterprises Inc—Charles Cauttrell	7618 N Broadway, Saint Louis MO 63147	314-385-4270	R	49*	.1
40	Gayle Manufacturing Company Inc—Andrew Stoll	PO Box 1365, Woodland CA 95776	530-662-0284	R	47*	.1
41	Valley Joist/Western Div—Kim James Valley Joist Inc	PO Box 2170, Fernley NV 89408	775-575-7337	S	47*	.2
42	Magnolia Steel Company Inc—Christopher Crowe	PO Box 5007, Meridian MS 39302	601-693-4301	R	43*	.1
43	Petersen Inc—Jon Ballantyne	1527 N 2000 W, Ogden UT 84404	801-732-2000	R	42*	.4
44	Senior Flexonics Inc	2400 Longhorn Industri, New Braunfels TX 78130	830-629-8080	S	42	.3
45	Williams Industries Inc (Manassas Virginia)—Frank Williams III	PO Box 1770, Manassas VA 20108	703-335-7800	P	42	.5
46	Mechanical Products Manufacturing Company LLC	3880 Grace St, New Boston OH 45662	740-259-6444	R	41*	.3
47	Steel Service Corp—Lawrence Cox	PO Box 321425, Jackson MS 39232	601-939-9222	R	40*	.2
48	ArcRon—Craig Seifert	PO Box 700, Menomonee Falls WI 53052	262-255-4150	R	40*	.1
49	Delong's Inc—F De Long	PO Box 479, Jefferson City MO 65102	573-635-6121	R	39*	.2
50	Steel-King Industries Inc—Robert White	2700 Chamber St, Stevens Point WI 54481	715-341-3120	R	39*	.3
51	Lynchburg Steel and Specialty Company Inc—Glen Chambers	PO Box 158, Monroe VA 24574	434-929-0951	R	39*	.1

Rank	Company Name—*Executive Officer*	Address, City, State, Zip	Phone	Type	Fin	Empls
52	Qualico Steel Company Inc—*John Downs*	PO Box 149, Webb AL 36376	334-793-1290	R	39*	.3
53	Met-Con Inc—*Billy Sheffield*	PO Box 236129, Cocoa FL 32923	321-632-4880	R	38*	.2
54	Liphart Steel Company Inc—*E Jennings*	PO Box 6326, Richmond VA 23230	804-355-7481	R	38*	.1
55	USF Fabrication Inc—*Alexander Bogory*	3200 W 84th St, Hialeah FL 33018	305-556-1661	R	38*	.5
56	Precision Machine And Manufacturing Company LLC—*Tony Caudill*	500 Industrial Rd, Grove OK 74344	918-786-9094	R	38*	.2
57	Metals USA (Wilmington North Carolina)—*Lourenco Concalves*	2925 US Hwy 421 N, Wilmington NC 28401	910-763-6237	D	37*	.2
58	Superior Steel Inc—*Mark Munday*	5277 N National Dr, Knoxville TN 37914	865-522-0253	R	37*	.3
59	Bratton Corp—*Robert Long*	2801 E 85th St, Kansas City MO 64132	816-363-1014	R	37*	.2
60	Boman and Kemp Manufacturing Inc—*Jeff Kemp*	PO Box 9725, Ogden UT 84409	801-731-0615	R	37*	.1
61	M-E-C Co—*David M Parker*	PO Box 330, Neodesha KS 66757	620-325-2673	R	36*	.2
62	Erico International Corp—*William Roj*	31700 Solon Rd, Solon OH 44139	440-349-2630	R	35*	.4
63	Craft Machine Works Inc—*Dannie Schrum*	2102 48th St, Hampton VA 23661	757-380-8615	R	35*	.2
64	Delcor USA Inc—*James Walsh*	PO Box 520, Channelview TX 77530	713-461-6200	R	34*	.3
65	SMI Companies Inc—*Benny Splane*	1456 Hwy 317 S, Centerville LA 70522	337-836-9894	R	30*	.1
66	Geiger and Peters Inc—*James Colzani*	PO Box 33807, Indianapolis IN 46203	317-359-9521	R	29*	.1
67	Cameron Manufacturing and Design Inc—*Ronald Johnson*	PO Box 478, Horseheads NY 14845	607-739-3606	R	29*	.2
68	Lyndon Steel LP—*David Collins*	1947 Union Cross Rd, Winston Salem NC 27107	336-785-0848	R	29*	.2
69	Signal Metal Industries Inc—*Ryan Robinson*	PO Box 171178, Irving TX 75017	972-438-1022	R	27*	.2
70	S and H Steel Company Inc—*Gail Sherwood*	PO Box 1267, Gilbert AZ 85299	480-926-6062	R	27*	.2
71	Wotco—*Steve Shellenberger*	PO Box 250, Casper WY 82602	307-235-1591	R	26*	.2
72	Mesco Building Solutions	PO Box 93629, Southlake TX 76092		S	26*	.2
73	New Millennium Building Systems—*Gary Heasley*	7575 W Jefferson Ave, Fort Wayne IN 46804	260-969-3500	S	26	.2
74	Drilling Structures International Inc—*Phillip Rivera*	2431 Kelly Ln, Houston TX 77066	281-880-8833	R	25*	.2
75	West Coast Wire and Steel Inc—*William Stalberger*	PO Box 52027, Riverside CA 92517	951-683-7252	R	25*	.1
76	Vestal Manufacturing Enterprises Inc—*Dave Dugan*	PO Box 420, Sweetwater TN 37874	423-337-6125	R	25*	.2
77	Spi/Mobile Pulley Works Inc—*William Prine*	PO Box 50010, Mobile AL 36605	251-653-0606	R	25*	.2
78	Mertz Inc—*Steve Ballinger*	PO Box 150, Ponca City OK 74602	580-762-5646	R	25*	.2
79	Cives Steel Co Mid Atlantic Div—*Ashley Twining* Cives Steel Co	PO Box 2778, Winchester VA 22604	540-667-3480	D	25*	.2
80	Mil Ltd—*Rodney Wade*	9119 Weedy Ln, Houston TX 77093	713-691-5200	R	24*	.1
81	Hercules Steel Company Inc—*Louis Jourden*	PO Drawer 35208, Fayetteville NC 28303	910-488-5110	R	23*	.1
82	Fabarc Steel Supply Inc—*Gene Heathcock*	PO Box 7280, Oxford AL 36203	256-831-8770	R	23*	.3
83	J and G Steel Corp—*James Pharr*	PO Box 1208, Sapulpa OK 74067	918-227-3131	R	22*	.2
84	Clestra Hauserman Inc—*James Hackett*	PO Box 906, Doylestown PA 18901	267-880-3700	S	22	.2
85	Indiana Bridge Midwest Steel Inc—*Christian Klink*	1810 S Macedonia Ave, Muncie IN 47302	765-288-1985	R	22*	.1
86	Zimkor LLC—*Willie Clark*	PO Box 1006, Littleton CO 80160	303-791-1333	R	22*	.1
87	S and G Manufacturing Group LLC—*Gerry Riendeau*	4830 NW Pkwy, Hilliard OH 43026	614-334-3600	R	22*	.1
88	Jesse Engineering Co—*Jeff Gellert*	1840 Marine View Dr, Tacoma WA 98422	253-922-7433	R	22*	.2
89	Helmark Steel Inc—*John O'brien*	PO Box 487, Wilmington DE 19899	302-652-3341	R	21*	.2
90	Grain Belt Supply Company Inc—*Marc Wingo*	PO Box 615, Salina KS 67402	785-827-4491	P	21*	.1
91	United Steel Inc—*Kenneth Corneau*	164 School St, East Hartford CT 06108	860-289-2323	R	21*	.1
92	Sippel Company Inc—*John Sippel*	2100 Georgetown Dr Ste, Sewickley PA 15143	724-266-9800	R	21*	.1
93	Mason Corp—*Russell Chambliss*	PO Box 59226, Birmingham AL 35259	205-942-4100	R	21*	.2
94	Bennett Manufacturing Company Inc—*Steven Yellen*	13315 Railroad St, Alden NY 14004	716-937-9161	R	21*	.2
95	Lee's Imperial Welding Inc—*Gary Lee*	3300 Edison Way, Fremont CA 94538	510-657-4900	R	20*	.2
96	Express Metal Fabricators Inc—*Terry Cowan*	9490 E Hwy 412, Locust Grove OK 74352	918-479-8700	R	20*	.3
97	Palmer Steel Supplies Inc—*James Thompson*	PO Box 10, Mcallen TX 78505	956-686-6575	R	20*	.2
98	Bohn And Dawson Inc—*Steven Hurster*	3500 Tree Ct, Saint Louis MO 63122	636-225-5011	R	20*	.2
99	Laurel Machine And Foundry Co—*Patrick Mulloy*	PO Box 1049, Laurel MS 39441	601-428-0541	R	20*	.1
100	Fort Worth Tower Company Inc—*Fred Moore*	PO Box 8597, Fort Worth TX 76124	817-255-3060	R	20*	.1
101	ABW Technologies Inc—*James Anderson*	6720 191st Pl Ne, Arlington WA 98223	360-618-4400	R	19*	.1
102	Bell Steel Co—*Randall Bell*	PO Box 12109, Pensacola FL 32591	850-432-1545	R	19*	.1
103	Alfab Inc—*David L Knight*	PO Box 26, Smithville WV 26845	304-477-3356	R	19*	.1
104	Shepard Steel Company Inc—*George Beckerman*	110 Meadow St, Hartford CT 06114	860-525-4446	R	19*	.1
105	Midwest Metal Products Co—*G Urban*	800 66th Ave Sw, Cedar Rapids IA 52404	319-366-6264	R	18*	.1
106	Schenectady Steel Company Inc—*Anthony Tebano*	18 Mariaville Rd, Schenectady NY 12306	518-355-3220	R	18*	.1
107	Crown Products Company Inc—*Peter Tuggle*	6390 Philips Hwy, Jacksonville FL 32216	904-737-7144	R	18*	.2
108	Quincy Joist—*Sam Mahdavi*	520 S Virginia St, Quincy FL 32351	850-875-1075	S	18*	.1
109	Decimet Sales Inc—*Joseph Hines*	14200 James Rd, Rogers MN 55374	763-428-4321	R	18*	Empls
110	E and H Steel Corp—*Robert Thomas*	PO Box 1170, Midland City AL 36350	334-983-5636	R	18*	<.1
111	Shaw SSS Fabricators Inc	PO Box 1268, Baton Rouge LA 70821	225-749-3165	S	17*	.1
112	George Steel Fabricating Inc—*John George*	1207 S US Rte 42, Lebanon OH 45000	513-932-2887	R	17*	<.1
113	Henderson Steel Corp—*Roger C Henderson*	PO Box 580, Meridian MS 39302	601-484-3000	R	17*	<.1
114	Valley Joist Inc—*Frederick Steele*	PO Box 680718, Fort Payne AL 35968	256-845-2330	R	17*	.1
115	Novel Iron Works Inc—*Thomas Heaney*	250 Ocean Rd, Greenland NH 03840	603-436-7950	R	16*	.1
116	Vance Metal Fabricators Inc—*Joe Hennessy*	PO Box 191, Geneva NY 14456	315-789-5626	R	16*	.1
117	Ameron Pole Products Div—*John Marlin*	1020 B St, Fillmore CA 93015	805-524-0223	D	16*	.1
118	Pkm Steel Service Inc—*Frieda Weis*	PO Box 920, Salina KS 67402	785-827-3638	R	16*	.1
119	Steffes Corp—*Joe Rothschiller*	3050 Hwy 22 N, Dickinson ND 58601	701-483-5400	R	16*	.1
120	Quality Manufacturing Corp—*Tom Koehn*	4300 Nw Urbandale Dr, Des Moines IA 50322	515-331-4300	R	16*	.1
121	Wasco Products Inc—*Christian Magnuson*	PO Box 559, Wells ME 04090	207-216-4500	R	16*	.1
122	Michelman-Cancelliere Iron Works Inc—*John Cancelliere*	PO Box 20431, Lehigh Valley PA 18002	610-837-9914	R	15*	.1
123	Brilex Industries Inc—*Brian Benyo*	PO Box 749, Youngstown OH 44501	330-744-1114	R	15*	.1
124	Zimmerman Metals Inc—*Mark Zimmerman*	201 E 58th Ave, Denver CO 80216	303-294-0180	R	15*	.1
125	Anco Engineering Inc—*Lucian Leszczynski*	217 Long Hill Cross Rd, Shelton CT 06484	203-925-9235	R	14*	.1
126	Southern Iron Works Inc—*Theodore Shaw*	PO Box 188, Springfield VA 22150	703-354-5500	R	14*	.1
127	Shioleno Metal Products Inc—*Tony Shioleno*	1715 Peyco Dr N, Arlington TX 76001	817-465-9361	R	14*	.1
128	Wildeck—*Keith Pignolet*	PO Box 89, Waukesha WI 53187	262-549-4000	R	14*	.1
129	Walters Metal Fabrication Inc—*Laurence Dittmeier*	PO Box 1245, Granite City IL 62040	618-931-5551	R	14*	.1
130	VT Hatler Marine—*William E Skinner*	P O Box 1328, Pascagoula MS 39568	228-696-6888	R	14*	.1
131	Quality Machine And Welding Company Inc—*John Roth*	PO Box 27345, Knoxville TN 37927	865-524-2162	R	14*	.1
132	Breitinger Co—*Milo Breitinger*	595 Oakenwaldt St, Mansfield OH 44905	419-526-4255	R	14*	.1
133	Campbellsville Industries Inc—*Wilbur Cox*	PO Box 278, Campbellsville KY 42719	270-465-8135	R	14*	.1
134	Midstate Steel Inc—*B Slocumb*	PO Box 28, Macon GA 31202	478-741-4598	R	14*	.1
135	Chicago Metal Rolled Products Co—*George Wendt*	3715 S Rockwell St, Chicago IL 60632	773-523-5757	R	14*	.1
136	Richards Sheet Metal Works Inc—*Stephen Richards*	2680 Industrial Dr, Ogden UT 84401	801-621-3341	R	13*	.1
137	Davis Iron Works Inc—*Joe Williams*	224 N Hewitt Dr, Hewitt TX 76643	254-666-1000	R	13*	.1
138	Pivot Corp—*Bobby Spruiell*	PO Box 1515, Rowlett TX 75030	972-475-4747	R	13*	.1
139	Du Fresne Manufacturing Company Inc—*Robert Fresne*	1380 County Rd E E, Saint Paul MN 55110	651-483-8130	R	13*	.1

Note: An asterisk (*) indicates an estimated financial figure. The company type code used is as follows: R = Private, P = Public, S = Private Subsidiary, B = Public Subsidiary, D = Division, J = Joint Venture, I = Investment Fund.

COMPANY RANKINGS BY SALES WITHIN 4-DIGIT SIC

Rank	Company Name—Executive Officer	Address, City, State, Zip	Phone	Type	Fin	Empls
140	Superior Iron Works Inc—Gary Hall	45034 Underwood Ln Ste, Sterling VA 20166	703-471-5500	R	13*	.1
141	Doherty Steel Inc—Dennis Doherty	PO Box 428, Paola KS 66071	913-557-9200	R	13*	.1
142	Smci Inc—Mike Grammer	PO Box 7120, Lakeland FL 33807	863-644-8432	R	13*	.1
143	Builders Steel Co—Ronald Bruce	601 E 12th Ave, North Kansas City MO 64116	816-471-1626	R	13*	.1
144	Arnold Steel Company Inc—Felix Pflaster	79 Randolph Rd, Howell NJ 07731	732-363-1079	R	13*	.1
145	Conservatek Industries Inc—Dave Abbott	PO Box 1678, Conroe TX 77305	936-539-1747	R	12*	.1
146	Sargent Metal Fabricators Inc—James Sargent	PO Box 2705, Anderson SC 29622	864-226-0063	R	12*	.1
147	Seismic Energy Products LP—Rob Myers	518 Progress Way, Athens TX 75751	903-675-8571	R	12*	.1
148	Tucker's Machine and Steel Service Inc—B Tucker	PO Box 492810, Leesburg FL 34749	352-787-3157	R	12*	.1
149	Clinch River LLC—Stephen Patterson	521 Claypool Hill Mall, Cedar Bluff VA 24609	276-963-5271	R	12*	.1
150	Farris Fab and Machine Inc—Corwin Farris	1941 Bess Town Rd, Bessemer City NC 28016	704-629-4879	R	12*	.1
151	Munich Welding Company Inc—Paul Ernstberger	211 Eastern Blvd, Jeffersonville IN 47130	812-282-0488	R	12*	.1
152	Loudon Steel Inc—Gregg Loudon	PO Box 312, Millington MI 48746	989-871-9353	R	12*	.1
153	Smede-Son Steel And Supply Company Inc—Albert Huyser	12584 Inkster Rd, Redford MI 48239	313-937-8300	R	12*	.1
154	Southeastern Steel Co—Juanita Bulloch	PO Box 989, Florence SC 29503	843-662-5236	R	11*	.1
155	Almet Inc—James Greim	PO Box 346, New Haven IN 46774	260-493-1556	R	11*	.1
156	M-C Fabrication Inc—Don Mitchell	15612 S Keeler Ter, Olathe KS 66062	913-764-5454	R	11*	.1
157	Wahlcometroflex Inc—John Powell	29 Lexington St, Lewiston ME 04240	207-784-2338	R	11*	.1
158	Egger Steel Co—Burke Blackman	PO Box 2698, Sioux Falls SD 57101	605-336-2490	R	11*	.1
159	American Iron Works Inc—Savvas Savopoulos	5010 Inwood St, Hyattsville MD 20781	301-277-8444	R	11*	.1
160	J R Hoe and Sons—Harry Hoe	PO Box 1737, Middlesboro KY 40965	606-248-5560	R	11*	<.1
161	L and M Steel Company Inc—Lester Maxey	PO Box 200242, San Antonio TX 78220	210-661-4241	R	11*	<.1
162	Ozark Steel Fabricators Inc—Robert Laut	1 Ozark Steel Dr, Farmington MO 63640	573-756-5741	R	11*	.1
163	Towe Iron Works Inc—David Towe	PO Box 51690, Knoxville TN 37950	865-546-5131	R	11*	.1
164	K and K Iron Works Inc—Karl Kulhanek	5100 Lawndale Ave Ste, Mc Cook IL 60525	708-924-0000	R	11*	.1
165	Jer-Co Industries Inc—Jerry Rush	14302 S 442 Rd, Locust Grove OK 74352	918-598-3430	R	11*	.1
166	International Bridge and Iron Co—Joseph Bachta	90 Day St, Newington CT 06111	860-953-6550	R	11*	.1
167	Turchan Technologies Group Inc—Jahr Turchan	12825 Ford Rd, Dearborn MI 48126	313-581-0043	R	10*	.1
168	Capitol Steel Corp—Timmy Distefano	PO Box 66636, Baton Rouge LA 70896	225-356-4631	D	10*	.1
169	CMC Rebar Georgia—Joseph Alvardo CMC Steel Group	PO Box 368, Lawrenceville GA 30046	770-963-6251	S	10*	.1
170	Gerlinger Foundry And Machine Works Inc—Fred Gerlinger	1527 Sacramento St, Redding CA 96001	530-243-1053	R	10*	.1
171	Gulf Tool Corp—Paul Robinson	8470 Gulf Beach Hwy, Pensacola FL 32507		R	10*	<.1
172	Carver Machine Works Inc—Lindsey Crisp	129 Christian Svc Camp, Washington NC 27889	252-975-3101	R	10*	.1
173	Gooder-Henrichsen Company Inc—Tom Ryan	2900 State St, Chicago Heights IL 60411	708-757-5030	R	10*	.1
174	Steven-Sharon Corp—Jayson Levy	7701 Harborside Dr, Galveston TX 77554	409-744-4538	R	10*	<.1
175	Commercial Metal Fabricators Company Inc—Patrick Dakin	150 Commerce Park Dr, Dayton OH 45404	937-233-4911	R	9*	.1
176	Communication Steel Inc—Eddie Perkins	900 E 69th St, Cleveland OH 44103	216-881-4600	R	9*	.1
177	St George Steel Fabrication—Mike Housley	1301 E 700 N, Saint George UT 84770	435-673-4856	R	9*	.1
178	R and R Erectors Inc—Richard Harvey	8427 Hixson Pke, Hixson TN 37343	423-842-3444	R	9*	.1
179	Topper and Griggs Inc—Dave Ward	PO Box L, Plainville CT 06062	860-747-5737	R	9*	<.1
180	Bristol Steel and Conveyor Corp—Raymond Oliver	4416 N State Rd, Davison MI 48423	810-658-9510	R	9*	.1
181	Quality Fab and Mechanical LLC—Tammy Baker	PO Box 339, Saint Rose LA 70087	504-469-1272	R	9*	.1
182	Advanced Machining and Tool Inc—Elsie Walker	1616 N Beckley St, Lancaster TX 75134	972-228-1987	R	8*	.1
183	Highview Custom Fabricating Inc—Joseph Wojkiewicz	PO Box 11416, Green Bay WI 54307	920-869-1900	R	8*	.1
184	Innovated Machine and Tool Company Inc—Dwight Bryant	250 Picketts Line, Newport News VA 23603	757-887-2181	R	8*	.1
185	Eip Manufacturing LLC—Kathy Krapfl	PO Box 336, Earlville IA 52041	563-923-7315	R	8*	.1
186	Heil Environmental Industries Ltd	PO Box 8676, Chattanooga TN 37414	423-899-9100	S	8*	.1
187	Jones and Brown Company Inc—Ronald L Krol	145 N Swift Rd, Addison IL 60101	630-543-0300	R	8*	<.1
188	Selkey Manufacturing Co—Tony Selkey	13170 Lindblom Rd, Baraga MI 49908	906-353-7104	R	7*	<.1
189	C-N-D Industries Inc—Clyde Shetler	4520 Southway St Sw, Canton OH 44706	330-478-8811	R	7*	<.1
190	Rjglobal Wika LLC—Robert Aus	10910 W Sam Huston Pkw, Houston TX 77064	281-897-9222	R	7*	<.1
191	Leatherwood Manufacturing Inc—Michael Leatherwood	4355 Dorchester Rd, North Charleston SC 29405	843-744-4500	R	7*	<.1
192	Chesapeake Machine Co—C Sims	210 S Janney St, Baltimore MD 21224	410-327-3350	R	7*	<.1
193	Endres Manufacturing Co—Kenneth Ballweg	PO Box 217, Waunakee WI 53597	608-849-4143	R	7*	<.1
194	Johnson System Inc—Kathleen Johnson	18999 US Hwy 27 N, Marshall MI 49068	269-781-9000	R	7*	<.1
195	Wayron LLC—Karen Askin	PO Box 1059, Longview WA 98632	360-425-8600	R	7*	<.1
196	Magnum Construction Services Inc—Donald Arroyo	PO Box 4076, Slidell LA 70459	985-649-2135	R	7*	<.1
197	Schuler Manufacturing—Kevin Schuler	PO Box 37282, Louisville KY 40233	502-637-4700	R	7*	<.1
198	Denios Inc—Brian Pahl	1152 Industrial Blvd, Louisville KY 40219	502-933-7272	R	7*	<.1
199	Merrill Equipment Co—T Rudolph	2209 Sturdevant St, Merrill WI 54452	715-536-2471	R	6*	<.1
200	Accu-Fab And Construction Inc—Paul Bosarge	5313 Mirror Lake Rd, Moss Point MS 39562	228-475-0082	R	6*	<.1
201	Industrial Metal Fabricators Inc—Lynn White	PO Box 453, Greeneville TN 37744	423-639-6141	R	6*	.1
202	Eilers Machine and Welding Inc—Anne Eilers	PO Box 517, Lexington NE 68850	308-324-3751	R	6*	<.1
203	Bickers Metal Products Inc—Robert Graff	PO Box 648, Miamitown OH 45041	513-353-4000	R	6*	.1
204	Broadway Metal Works Inc—Mark Showalter	PO Box 125, Broadway VA 22815	540-896-7027	R	6*	.1
205	B and K Installations Inc—William Berzowski	246 Sw 4th Ave, Homestead FL 33030	305-245-6968	R	6*	<.1
206	Tri City Steel and Fabricating Inc—Barbara Luther	PO Box 733, Pharr TX 78577	956-787-0663	R	6*	<.1
207	Jet Industries Inc—Elizabeth Twardowski	6025 S Oak Park Ave, Chicago IL 60638	773-586-8900	R	6*	<.1
208	Stahl Equipment Inc—Norbert Stahl	PO Box 130, Chandler IN 47610	812-925-3341	R	6*	<.1
209	Builders Steel Company Inc—Lauri Noble	1924 S 49th W Ave, Tulsa OK 74107	918-583-1191	R	6*	<.1
210	Best Equipment Technologies Inc—David Miller	PO Box 429, Poplarville MS 39470	601-795-2208	R	6*	<.1
211	Gavan Graham Electrical Products Corp—Norman Cummerson	751 Rahway Ave, Union NJ 07083	908-729-9000	R	6*	<.1
212	A J Weller Corp—Thomas Edwards	PO Box 17566, Shreveport LA 71138	318-925-1010	R	6*	<.1
213	Kiczan Manufacturing Inc—Ken Kiczan	3916 Crooked Run Rd, North Versailles PA 15137	412-678-0980	R	5*	<.1
214	Arnold Fabricating And Machine Inc—Kenny Arnold	3333 Reynoldsburg Rd, Camden TN 38320	731-584-3601	R	5*	<.1
215	Welfab Inc—Bruce Martin	100 Rangeway Rd, North Billerica MA 01862	978-667-0180	R	5*	<.1
216	Equipment Roundup and Manufacturing Inc—Douglas Beattie	1109 Ne 146th St, Vancouver WA 98685	360-576-1171	R	5*	<.1
217	JHR Inc—Richard Faulkner	2132 Railroad Ave, Anchorage AK 99501	907-276-4303	R	5*	<.1
218	Performance Fabricating LLC—Mike Cronin	PO Box 560, Howell MI 48844	517-545-5559	R	5*	<.1
219	Liberty Industries LC	2855 Hwy 261, Newburgh IN 47630	812-853-0595	R	5*	<.1
220	Maxwell Welding And Machine Inc—Gary Maxwell	11 Starck Dr, Burgettstown PA 15021	724-729-3160	R	5*	<.1
221	Memphis Wire and Iron Works Inc—James Stafford	PO Box 13183, Memphis TN 38113	901-775-0107	R	5*	<.1
222	W and K Steel LLC	98 Antisbury St, Braddock PA 15104	412-271-1620	R	5*	<.1
223	Terminal Manufacturing Company LLC	707 Gilman St, Berkeley CA 94710	510-526-3071	R	5*	<.1
224	Ability Engineering Technology Inc—Michael Morgan	16140 Vincennes Ave, South Holland IL 60473	708-331-0025	R	5*	<.1
225	Paul W Marino Gages Inc—Paul Marino	21300 Mac Arthur Blvd, Warren MI 48089	586-759-2400	R	5*	<.1
226	Fabricon Inc—Carl Knutsen	4860 5th St Hwy, Temple PA 19560	610-921-0203	R	5*	<.1
227	Jem Engineering and Manufacturing Company Inc—James Janosky	PO Box 571421, Tulsa OK 74157	918-446-4517	R	5*	<.1

Rank	Company Name—*Executive Officer*	Address, City, State, Zip	Phone	Type	Fin	Empls
228	Corcoran Sawtelle and Rosprim Inc—*Terry Kwast*	542 Otis Ave, Corcoran CA 93212	559-992-2117	R	4*	<.1
229	Broome Welding Co—*Herbert Broome*	7909 Bayside Ave, Galveston TX 77554	409-744-0407	R	4*	<.4
230	CB and I SERVICES Inc—*Gerald Glen*	14105 S Rte 59, Plainfield IL 60544	815-439-6000	S	4*	.4
231	Esparza's Welding And Machine Shop Inc—*Tiberio Esparza*	PO Box 2189, El Centro CA 92244	760-337-0020	R	4*	.1
232	Kilroy Structural Steel Co—*Nick Dorony*	8500 Union Ave, Cleveland OH 44105	216-883-3000	S	4*	<.1
233	Summa Holdings Inc—*James Benenson Jr*	6950 S Edgerton Rd, Brecksville OH 44141	440-838-4700	R	4*	<.1
234	Moore's Pump and Services Inc—*Andrew Cormier*	105 Derrick Rd, Broussard LA 70518	337-837-2794	R	4*	<.1
235	Schuff Steel Management—*Scott Schuff*	619 N Cooper Rd, Gilbert AZ 85233	480-892-7509	S	4*	<.1
236	Andrews Metal Works Inc—*Harry Walters*	PO Box 13, Andrews SC 29510	843-264-3545	R	4*	<.1
237	United Fabricating Inc—*Camille Sushel*	PO Box 726, Claysville PA 15323	724-663-5891	R	4*	<.1
238	Hays Fabricating and Welding Inc—*Clayton Hays*	633 E Leffel Ln, Springfield OH 45505	937-325-0031	R	4*	<.1
239	Alabama Converter Corporation Inc—*Paul Sides*	PO Box 740056, Tuscumbia AL 35674	256-381-5293	R	4*	<.1
240	Mofab Inc—*Max Hains*	1415 Fairview St, Anderson IN 46016	765-649-5577	R	4*	<.1
241	Adc Custom LLC—*Michael Kross*	5311 Fuller St, Schofield WI 54476	715-359-8338	R	4*	<.1
242	Florig R and J Industrial Company Inc—*Robert Florig*	910 Brook Rd, Conshohocken PA 19428	610-825-6655	R	4*	<.1
243	Pemco-Naval Engineering Works Inc—*Bobby Green*	3614 Frederic St, Pascagoula MS 39567	228-769-7081	R	4*	<.1
244	Adrian Tool Corp—*G Pickle*	360 Mulzer Ave, Adrian MI 49221	517-263-6530	R	4*	<.1
245	T and L Manufacturing Corp—*Dorothy Wagner*	PO Box 790, Aurora IL 60507	630-898-7100	R	4*	<.1
246	Century Steel Products Inc—*Joel Gundersheimer*	45034 Underwood Ln Ste, Sterling VA 20166	703-471-7606	R	3*	<.1
247	Mansfield Structural And Erecting Co—*Richard Gash*	PO Box 427, Mansfield OH 44901	419-522-5911	R	3*	<.1
248	Bedford Crane LLC—*Jospeh Elliott*	PO Box 668, Bedford IN 47421	812-275-4411	R	3*	<.1
249	Contract Steel Sales Inc—*Larry Bunden*	895 Airport Rd, Rockingham NC 28379	910-582-4026	R	3*	<.1
250	Schrupp Industries Inc—*Ken Kirk*	PO Box 330, Parker PA 16049	724-399-2938	R	3*	<.1
251	Atlantic Metal Products Inc—*Raymond Campbell*	PO Box 10, Topping VA 23169	804-758-4915	R	3*	<.1
252	Evans Steel Service Inc—*Pat Evans*	PO Box 2419, West Columbia SC 29171	803-955-9278	R	3*	<.1
253	B W Byrd Metal Fabricators Inc—*Billy Byrd*	PO Box 5435, Knoxville TN 37928	865-687-0343	R	3*	<.1
254	Jarrett Welding Company Inc—*Sam Pruitt*	954 Goodyear Blvd, Danville VA 24541	434-793-3717	R	3*	<.1
255	Kalamazoo Steel Processing Inc—*Darren Draves*	6450 Valley Industrial, Kalamazoo MI 49009	269-344-9778	R	3*	<.1
256	Marketech International Inc—*Beth Juran*	192 Otto St, Port Townsend WA 98368	360-379-6707	R	3*	<.1
257	Marion Metal Products Inc—*Tom Brubaker*	401 N Henderson Ave, Marion IN 46952	765-662-8333	R	3*	<.1
258	Custom Metal Inc—*Warren Henner*	PO Box 4488, Eatonton GA 31024	706-485-6178	R	3*	<.1
259	Leman Machine Co—*Stuart Leman*	PO Box 269, Portage PA 15946	814-736-9696	R	3*	<.1
260	Lake Road Welding Co—*Donald Morgan*	PO Box 4711, Wichita Falls TX 76308	940-692-4988	R	3*	<.1
261	Goyal Industries Inc—*Prakash Goyal*	382 Park Ave E, Mansfield OH 44905	419-522-7099	R	3*	<.1
262	Lake Co—*John Lake*	PO Box 2248, Bakersfield CA 93303	661-399-9131	R	3*	<.1
263	Lilly Machinery Inc—*Roy Lilly*	PO Box 130655, Tyler TX 75713	903-561-6733	R	3*	<.1
264	Davis Machine Works Of Opelika Inc—*Tom Rickles*	PO Box 2154, Opelika AL 36803	334-745-3548	R	3*	<.1
265	Overbilt Trailer Co—*William Schiffmacher*	PO Box 272, Drumright OK 74030	918-352-4474	R	3*	<.1
266	Ashley Welding and Machine Co—*Mitchell Byrd*	PO Box 383, Edenton NC 27932	252-482-3321	R	2*	<.1
267	Partin Management Inc—*Bruce Partin*	PO Box 23147, Houston TX 77228	281-458-0152	R	2*	<.1
268	Progressive Machine Inc—*Joseph Alvarez*	318 E B Cir, Pasco WA 99301	509-547-4062	R	2*	<.1
269	Scully Metal Fabrication—*Shane Scully*	1015 Stevenville Rd, Morgan City LA 70380	985-385-6509	R	2*	<.1
270	Loos Machine Shop Inc—*Dennis Baumgartner*	205 W Washington St, Colby WI 54421	715-223-2844	R	2*	<.1
271	Metwood Inc—*Robert M Callahan*	819 Naff Rd, Boones Mill VA 24065	540-334-4294	P	2	<.1
272	Pabst Enterprises Equipment Co—*Robert Verkouille*	676 Pennsylvania Ave, Elizabeth NJ 07201	908-353-2880	R	2*	<.1
273	Chickasha Manufacturing Company Inc—*Larry Lewis*	5501 Hwy 81 S, Chickasha OK 73018	405-224-5200	R	2*	<.1
274	Consumers Inc—*David Eck*	PO Box 1870, Manitowoc WI 54221	920-682-4613	S	2*	<.1
275	Sonrise Metal—*Todd Abrams*	171 N Ethel Ave, Hawthorne NJ 07506	973-423-4717	R	2*	<.1
276	Elbex Industrial Supplies LLC—*Stan Bialek*	1101 W Lincoln St, Phoenix AZ 85007	602-253-7360	R	2*	<.1
277	Rance Industries Inc—*John Rance*	PO Box 325, Columbiana OH 44408	330-482-1745	R	2*	<.1
278	Mellies Products Inc—*Jim Mellies*	PO Box 64, Morganville KS 67468	785-926-4331	R	2*	<.1
279	Busch Industries Inc—*John Busch*	900 E Paris Ave SE Ste, Grand Rapids MI 49546	616-957-3737	R	2*	<.1
280	Bgrs Inc—*Frank Cmajdalka*	10440 Windfern Rd Ste, Houston TX 77064	281-890-6862	R	2*	<.1
281	A Engineering and Fabrication Inc—*David Arno*	PO Box 470, Grand Rapids OH 43522	419-832-0748	R	2*	<.1
282	Interstate Equipment Corp—*James Vogel*	929 Park Ave, Pittsburgh PA 15234	412-563-5556	R	2*	<.1
283	Elliott Bay Metal Fabricating Inc—*Chris Michaelsen*	12108 Mukilteo Speedwa, Mukilteo WA 98275	425-788-5297	R	2*	<.1
284	Central States Fabricating Corp—*Michael Cocanower*	2720 17th St, Elkhart IN 46517	574-293-8691	R	1*	<.1
285	Brandywine Valley Fabricators Inc—*John Crane*	PO Box 111, Coatesville PA 19320	610-384-7440	R	1*	<.1
286	Prometco Inc—*Phillip Proctor*	7429 W Bostian Rd, Woodinville WA 98072	425-486-0759	R	1*	<.1
287	Creative Fabrication Inc—*George Chatham*	PO Box 637, Hartwell GA 30643	706-376-7874	R	1*	<.1
288	Coanda Intakes LLC—*Kevin Toler*	401 Barnstaple Dr, Daniels WV 25832	304-767-5055	R	1*	<.1
289	Clayton Industries Inc—*James Clayton*	315 4th St N, Birmingham AL 35204	205-715-2000	R	1*	<.1
290	Hi-Tech Machining LLC—*Gina Bade*	1481 Doss Rd, Concord VA 24538	434-993-3256	R	1*	<.1
291	JR Lukeman and Associates Inc—*John Lukeman*	3017 Hemingford Ln, Oklahoma City OK 73120	405-842-6548	R	<1*	<.1
292	Washington Ornamental Iron Works—*Joe Cochran*	17926 S Broadway, Gardena CA 90247	310-327-8660	R	N/A	.3

TOTALS: SIC 3441 Fabricated Structural Metal
Companies: 292   33,114   59.4

3442 Metal Doors, Sash & Trim

Rank	Company Name—*Executive Officer*	Address, City, State, Zip	Phone	Type	Fin	Empls
1	Overhead Door Corp—*Dennis Stone*	2501 S State Hwy Ste 2, Lewisville TX 75067	469-549-7100	R	12,266*	2.5
2	Quanex Building Products Corp—*David D Petratis*	1900 W Loop S Ste 1500, Houston TX 77027	713-961-4600	P	848	2.3
3	Hrh Door Corp—*Willis Mullet*	1 Door Dr, Mount Hope OH 44660	850-474-9890	R	738*	2.5
4	Alside Inc	PO Box 2010, Akron OH 44309		D	670*	3.0
5	Drew Industries Inc—*Fredric M Zinn*	200 Mamaroneck Ave, White Plains NY 10601	914-428-9098	P	573	3.0
6	Windsor Republic Doors—*Mike Taylor*	155 Republic Dr, Mc Kenzie TN 38201	731-352-3383	R	514*	1.2
7	Hehr International Inc—*David Utick*	PO Box 39160, Los Angeles CA 90039	323-663-1261	R	512*	1.0
8	Therma-Tru Corp—*Dave Randich*	1750 Indian Wood Cir, Maumee OH 43537	419-891-7400	S	491*	.1
9	Curries—*Jerry N Currie*	1502 12th St NW, Mason City IA 50401	641-423-1334	R	396*	1.0
10	Robertson-Ceco Corp—*John Scarbrough*	PO Box 911, Columbus MS 39703	662-243-6400	S	286	1.5
11	International Architectural Group LLC—*Ronald Rudy*	PO Box 6, Monterey Park CA 91754	323-264-1670	R	281	1.6
12	Pgt Industries Inc—*Rodney Hershberger*	PO Box 1529, Nokomis FL 34274	941-480-1600	R	278*	1.0
13	Alenco Holding Corp—*Lynn Morstadt*	615 W Carson St, Bryan TX 77801	979-779-1051	R	270*	.9
14	Philips Products Inc—*Dennis Ruben*	PO Box 2327, Elkhart IN 46515	574-296-0000	S	200	2.2
15	Three Rivers Aluminum—*Robert P Randall*	71 Progress Ave, Cranberry Township PA 16066	724-776-7000	R	200*	2.0
16	PGT Inc—*Rodney Hershberger*	1070 Technology Dr, North Venice FL 34275	941-480-1600	P	176	1.2
17	Sanwa USA Inc—*Brian Bolton*	4020 Mcewen Rd Ste 118, Dallas TX 75244	972-503-3031	R	172*	3.4
18	Homeshield—*David D Petratis* Quanex Building Products Corp	311 W Coleman St, Rice Lake WI 54868	715-234-9061	D	147*	.4
19	Eagle Window and Door Inc—*David Beeken*	PO Box 1072, Dubuque IA 52004	563-556-2270	S	142*	.4

Note: An asterisk (*) indicates an estimated financial figure. The company type code used is as follows: R = Private, P = Public, S = Private Subsidiary, B = Public Subsidiary, D = Division, J = Joint Venture, I = Investment Fund.

COMPANY RANKINGS BY SALES WITHIN 4-DIGIT SIC

Rank	Company Name—Executive Officer	Address, City, State, Zip	Phone	Type	Fin	Empls
20	Nishikawa Standard Co—Mike Talaga	207 S W St, Auburn IN 46706	260-925-0700	S	138*	1.5
21	Soft-Lite LLC—Roy Anderson	10250 Phillip Pkwy, Streetsboro OH 44241	330-528-3400	R	138*	.3
22	Steelcraft Manufacturing Co—Chris Mosby	9017 Blue Ash Rd, Cincinnati OH 45242	513-745-6400	D	119*	1.0
23	Wausau Window and Wall Systems—Russ Huffer	7800 International Dr, Wausau WI 54401	715-845-2161	D	119*	1.0
24	MI Windows And Doors—Peter DeSoto	PO Box 370, Gratz PA 17030	717-365-2500	R	104*	1.0
25	Larson Manufacturing Company Of South Dakota Inc—Dale Larson	2333 Eastbrook Dr, Brookings SD 57006	605-692-6115	R	102*	1.0
26	Eggers Industries Inc Neenah Div—Jay Streu	164 N Lake St, Neenah WI 54956	920-722-6444	D	102*	.2
27	Thermwell Products Company Inc—David Gerstein	420 State Rt 17, Mahwah NJ 07430	201-684-4400	R	94*	.7
28	Peachtree Doors and Windows Inc—Bob MacDonald	880 Southview Dr, Mosinee WI 54455		R	89*	.6
29	International Window Corp (Hayward California)—Cornelius C Vanderstar International Window Corp	30526 San Antonio St, Hayward CA 94544	510-487-1122	S	88*	.2
30	Thermal Windows Inc—Dennis Lane	12805 E 31st St, Tulsa OK 74146	918-663-7580	R	83*	.2
31	West Window Corp—WE Giesler	PO Box 3071, Martinsville VA 24115	276-638-2394	R	71*	.2
32	Garage Door Group Inc—Richard Brenner	3800 Greenway Cir, Lawrence KS 66046	785-865-5500	R	68*	.5
33	ABC Window Co—Brian Ruttencutter	PO Box 4210, Ontario CA 91761	909-391-6491	R	64*	.2
34	Champion Window Inc—Gregory Faherty	PO Box 680705, Houston TX 77268	281-440-7000	R	61*	1.1
35	Viking Aluminum Products Inc—Morris Trachten	33 John St, New Britain CT 06051	860-225-6478	R	60*	.5
36	Folding Shutter Corp—Gary Hemstreet	7089 Hemstreet Pl, West Palm Beach FL 33413	561-683-4811	R	59*	.2
37	Kasson and Keller Inc—William Keller	PO Box 777, Fonda NY 12068	518-853-3421	R	56*	.9
38	M-D Building Products Inc—Loren Plotkin	PO Box 25188, Oklahoma City OK 73125	405-528-4411	R	55*	.6
39	Balance Systems Inc—Rich Koopman	517 E 52nd St N, Sioux Falls SD 57104	605-339-3115	S	55*	.4
40	Empire Pacific Windows Corp—Justin Kent	PO Box 4210, Tualatin OR 97062	503-692-6167	R	51*	.3
41	Thermal Industries Inc—David Rascoe	5450 2nd Ave, Pittsburgh PA 15207	412-395-1900	R	50*	.3
42	Crystal Window and Door Systems Ltd—Steven Chen	31-10 Whitestone Expy, Flushing NY 11354	718-961-7300	R	48*	.4
43	International Extrusion Corp—Cornelius Vanderstar International Architectural Group LLC	202 Singleton Dr, Waxahachie TX 75165	972-937-7032	S	47*	.3
44	Pemko Manufacturing Co—Phil Goossens	4226 Transport St, Ventura CA 93003	805-642-2600	R	45*	.3
45	ASI Technologies Inc (Milwaukee Wisconsin)—Jesse Watzka	5848 N 95th Ct, Milwaukee WI 53225	414-464-6200	R	45*	.1
46	Kawneer Company Inc—Glenn Morrison	555 Guthridge Ct, Norcross GA 30092	770-449-5555	S	44*	.1
47	Lausell Aluminum Jalousies Inc—Janette Ojeda	PO Box 938, Bayamon PR 00960	787-798-7610	R	43*	.7
48	Western Window Systems—Jeff Miller	5621 S 25th St, Phoenix AZ 85040	602-268-1300	R	43*	.1
49	Amsco Windows—Bart Naylor	PO Box 25368, Salt Lake City UT 84125	801-972-6444	R	43*	.6
50	General Aluminum Company Of Texas—Chris Rix	PO Box 819022, Dallas TX 75381	972-242-5271	R	43*	.6
51	International Window Corp—John P Cunningham International Architectural Group LLC	5625 E Firestone Blvd, South Gate CA 90280	562-928-6411	S	36	.3
52	Peerless Products Inc—Bill Osbern	PO Box 431, Fort Scott KS 66701	620-223-4610	R	35*	.5
53	International Window-Arizona Inc International Architectural Group LLC	2500 E Chambers St, Phoenix AZ 85040		S	34*	.1
54	Hormann LLC—Frank Weber	5050 Baseline Rd, Montgomery IL 60538	630-859-3000	R	33*	.3
55	Columbia Manufacturing Corp—Lawrence Goodman	14400 S San Pedro St, Gardena CA 90248	310-327-9300	R	32*	.2
56	Quaker Window Products Co—Marguerite Knoll	PO Box 128, Freeburg MO 65035	573-744-5211	R	32*	.5
57	Desco Corp—Arnold Siemer	150 E Campus View Blvd, Columbus OH 43235	614-888-8855	R	31*	.3
58	Dunbarton Corp—Oscar Hughes	PO Box 8577, Dothan AL 36304	334-794-0661	R	31*	.2
59	National Guard Products Inc—C Smith	PO Box 753430, Memphis TN 38175	901-795-6900	R	31*	.2
60	Cornell Iron Works Inc—Andrew Cornell	24 Elmwood Ave, Mountain Top PA 18707	570-474-6773	R	28*	.4
61	Janus International Corp—David Curtis	PO Box 567, Temple GA 30179	770-562-2850	R	27*	.4
62	Door Components Inc—Robert Briggs	7980 Redwood Ave, Fontana CA 92336	909-770-5700	R	27*	.2
63	Northeast Building Products Corp—Alan Levin	4280 Aramingo Ave, Philadelphia PA 19124	215-535-7110	R	26*	.2
64	Winco Manufacturing Inc—John Herman	6200 Maple Ave, Saint Louis MO 63130	314-725-8088	R	26*	.2
65	Cookson Co—Bob Cookson	2417 S 50th Ave, Phoenix AZ 85043	602-272-4244	R	26	.3
66	Nofziger Door Sales Inc—Edward Nofziger	320 Sycamore St, Wauseon OH 43567	419-337-9900	R	26*	.2
67	Moss Supply Co—Robert Moss	PO Box 26338, Charlotte NC 28221	704-596-8717	R	25*	.4
68	Thermo-Twin Industries Inc—Joseph Palermo	1155 Allegheny Ave, Oakmont PA 15139	412-826-1000	R	24*	.2
69	Windowmaster Products—Ron Walker	1111 Pioneer Way, El Cajon CA 92020	619-588-1144	R	24*	.4
70	Pease Industies Inc—Leonard Cavens	7100 Dixie Hwy, Fairfield OH 45014	513-870-3600	R	23*	.4
71	Public Supply Co—Bob Bennett	PO Box 60486, Oklahoma City OK 73146	405-272-9621	R	23*	.2
72	Mid-America Door Co—John Earnest	1001 W Hartford Ave, Ponca City OK 74601	580-765-9994	R	21*	.2
73	Champion Aluminum Corp—Anthony Muraco	140 Eileen Way, Syosset NY 11791	516-921-6200	R	21*	.1
74	Rolladen Inc—Robert Hoffman	550 Ansin Blvd, Hallandale Beach FL 33009	954-921-1522	R	21*	.2
75	Allmetal Inc—Philip Collin	PO Box 850, Bensenville IL 60106	630-250-8090	R	20*	.2
76	ARC One LLC—James Schechter	1350 NW 74th St, Miami FL 33147	305-691-1500	R	20*	.2
77	Mesker Door Inc—Dave Johnson	3440 Stanwood Blvd Ne, Huntsville AL 35811	256-851-6670	R	20*	.2
78	Eliason Corp—Jason Doezema	9229 Shaver Rd, Portage MI 49024	269-327-7003	R	20*	.2
79	A J Manufacturing Inc—Todd Carlson	1217 Oak St, Bloomer WI 54724	715-568-2204	R	20*	.2
80	Yale Ogron Windows and Doors—Manny Valladares	8130 Nw 74th Ave, Medley FL 33166	305-887-2646	R	19*	.3
81	Jamison Door Co—John Williams	PO Box 70, Hagerstown MD 21741	301-733-3100	R	19*	.1
82	Jones Paint And Glass Inc—Merlynn Jones	PO Box 1403, Provo UT 84603	801-374-6711	R	19*	.2
83	Ankmar LLC—Angus Lewis	4600 Kansas Ave, Kansas City KS 66106	913-621-7000	R	19*	.1
84	Best Built Inc—Terry Rowley	PO Box 10444, Yakima WA 98909	509-248-4462	R	19*	.3
85	Special-Lite Inc—Kevin Hanley	PO Box 6, Decatur MI 49045	269-423-7068	R	18*	.1
86	Habersham Metal Products Company Inc—James Stapleton	264 Stapleton Rd, Cornelia GA 30531	706-778-2212	R	18*	.2
87	Benchmark Doors—Bill Henshaw	PO Box 7387, Fredericksburg VA 22404	540-898-5700	R	17*	.4
88	Columbia Extrusion Corp—Charles Bricker	1200 E Washington St, Rockwall TX 75087	972-771-5362	R	16*	.2
89	Lif Industries Inc—Joseph Gallo	5 Harbor Park Dr Ste 1, Port Washington NY 11050	516-390-6800	R	16*	.1
90	Don Young Company Inc—Don Young	PO Box 560608, Dallas TX 75356	214-630-0934	R	15*	.1
91	Karp Associates Inc—Gerry Gorman	5454 43rd St, Maspeth NY 11378	718-784-2105	R	15*	.1
92	Hopes Windows Inc—Randall Manitta	PO Box 580, Jamestown NY 14702	716-665-5124	R	15*	.2
93	Peelle Co—HE Peelle III	373 Nesconset Hwy #311, Hauppauge NY 11788	905-846-4545	R	15*	.1
94	Dor-O-Matic Inc—Mike Murray	2720 Tobey Dr, Indianapolis IN 46219		S	15*	.1
95	United States Aluminum Corp International Architectural Group LLC	767 Monterey Pass Rd, Monterey Park CA 91754	323-264-1670	S	15	.1
96	Atmos Corp—Raymond Bjerrum	4385 W Shaw Ave, Fresno CA 93722	559-275-3200	R	15*	.1
97	Northern Building Products Inc—Robert Pecorella	111 Central Ave, Teterboro NJ 07608	201-943-6400	R	15*	.1
98	Interstate Window Corp—Robert Salzer	345 Crooked Hill Rd St, Brentwood NY 11717	631-231-0800	R	14*	.1
99	Columbia Glass and Windows—Arnie Mears	1600 North Jackson, Kansas City MO 64120	816-241-5800	R	14*	<.1
100	Mayfair Window and Door Company LP—Paul Calaway	PO Box 26338, Charlotte NC 28221	337-233-2470	R	14*	.1
101	Lang Exterior Inc—Eugene Lang	2323 W 59th St, Chicago IL 60636	773-737-4500	R	14*	.1
102	Rosati Windows LLC—Dave Keplar	4200 Roberts Rd, Columbus OH 43228	614-777-4806	R	14*	.1

Rank	Company Name—*Executive Officer*	Address, City, State, Zip	Phone	Type	Fin	Empls
103	Lockheed Window Corp—*Jeffrey Kosiver*	PO Box 166, Pascoag RI 02859	401-568-3061	R	13*	.1
104	Window Technology Inc—*Robert Berger*	PO Box 480, Monett MO 65708	417-235-7821	R	13*	.1
105	Home Guard Industries Inc—*Brian Barbieri*	PO Box 39, Grabill IN 46741	260-627-6060	R	13*	.1
106	Winchester Industries Inc—*George Yuhasz*	PO Box 160, Saltsburg PA 15681	724-639-3551	R	13*	.1
107	Miami Wall Systems Inc—*Lawrence Johnson*	PO Box 28109, Hialeah FL 33002	305-888-2300	R	12*	.1
108	Taylor Building Products Inc—*Nick Cangialosi*	PO Box 457, West Branch MI 48661	989-345-5110	R	12*	.1
109	Haas Door Co—*Edward Nofziger*	320 Sycamore St, Wauseon OH 43567	419-337-9900	R	12*	.2
110	Custom Window Systems Inc—*John Cwik*	1900 Sw 44th Ave, Ocala FL 34474	352-368-6922	R	12*	.3
111	Delafontaine Industries—*Robert Delafontaine*	202 Decalb Ave, Wilmington DE 19804	302-993-0220	R	11*	.2
112	Benchmark Sales Agency Inc—*Richard Gann*	2727 S Santa Fe Dr, Englewood CO 80110	303-722-0822	R	11*	.1
113	Tug River Armature and Machine Company Inc—*Thomas Sheppard*	PO Box 770, Williamson WV 25661	304-235-5370	R	11*	.1
114	Stiles Custom Metal Inc—*David Stiles*	1885 Kinser Rd, Ceres CA 95307	209-538-3667	R	10*	.1
115	Blomberg Building Materials Inc—*J Collier*	PO Box 22485, Sacramento CA 95822	916-428-8060	R	10*	.1
116	Coastal Plain Ventures LLC—*Regina Scott*	PO Box 313, Swainsboro GA 30401	706-413-3806	R	9*	.1
117	Hayfield Window and Door Co—*Richard Rouhoff*	PO Box 25, Hayfield MN 55940	507-477-3224	R	9*	.1
118	Ceco Door Products—*Larry Denbrock*	9159 Telecom Dr, Milan TN 38358	731-686-8345	S	9*	<.1
119	Comprehensive Manufacturing Services LLC—*Rick Bleckler*	3044 Lambdin Ave, Saint Louis MO 63115	314-533-5700	R	8*	.1
120	Diamond Windows and Doors Manufacturing Inc—*Yu Tseng*	99 E Cottage St, Dorchester MA 02125	617-282-1688	R	8*	<.1
121	Samuels Glass Co—*Jenni Haverda*	PO Box 12775, San Antonio TX 78212	210-227-2481	R	8*	.1
122	Radco Exteriors Inc—*Peter Bell*	2800 Industrial Pkwy, Santa Maria CA 93455	805-925-2614	R	7*	.1
123	M-B Products Inc—*Robert Breihan*	2005 Mcdaniel Dr Ste 1, Carrollton TX 75006	214-638-6525	R	6*	.1
124	Capitol Aluminum and Glass Corp—*Gail Coe*	1276 W Main St, Bellevue OH 44811	419-483-7050	R	6*	<.1
125	Active Window Products—*Michael Schoenfeld*	PO Box 39125, Los Angeles CA 90039	323-245-5185	R	5*	.1
126	Kaufmann Window and Door Corp—*Daniel Padilla*	PO Box 15146, Detroit MI 48215	313-893-9500	R	5*	<.1
127	Fentech Inc—*R Mirau*	1510 N 5th St, Superior WI 54880	715-392-9500	R	5*	<.1
128	Armaclad Inc—*Nick Turano*	4422 W 46th St, Chicago IL 60632	773-446-7800	D	5*	<.1
129	Hormann Flexon LLC—*Bevan Amy*	Ave C Bldg 20a, Leetsdale PA 15056	412-749-0400	R	5*	<.1
130	Slate Security Systems Inc—*Channing Woodard*	PO Box 789, Hartselle AL 35640	256-773-3017	R	4*	<.1
131	Impact Precious Wood Inc	5701A NW 74th Ave, Miami FL 33166	786-222-0427	R	4*	<.1
132	Marathon Manufacturing Inc—*Roy Hall*	110 W Laura Dr, Addison IL 60101	630-543-6262	R	4*	<.1
133	Ajax Window Corp—*Jason Blyveis*	625 Century Ave Sw, Grand Rapids MI 49503	616-459-3463	R	3*	<.1
134	Pal Manufacturing Corp—*Laurel Marneris*	250 Duffy Ave Unit B, Hicksville NY 11801	516-937-3771	R	3*	<.1
135	Polyshot Corp—*Douglas Hepler*	75 Lucius Gordon Dr, West Henrietta NY 14586	585-292-5010	R	2*	<.1
136	Champion Window Company Of Kansas City Inc—*Don Seabaugh*	7920 Marshall Dr, Lenexa KS 66214	913-541-8282	S	2*	<.1
137	West Virginia Glass Company Inc—*Rhonda Smilek*	235 Rural Acres Dr, Beckley WV 25801	304-252-6343	R	2*	<.1
138	General Window Corp—*Rick Johnson* International Architectural Group LLC	30526 San Antonio St, Hayward CA 94544	510-487-1122	S	1*	.1
139	United States Aluminum Corporation - Texas—*Rick Thornton* International Architectural Group LLC	5910 West by Northwest, Houston TX 77040	713-462-1766	S	1*	<.1
140	Dominion Building Products Inc—*Tom Granitz*	6949 Fairbanks N Houst, Houston TX 77040	713-466-6790	S	N/A	<.1

TOTALS: SIC 3442 Metal Doors, Sash & Trim
Companies: 140 — 22,795 — 60.2

3443 Fabricated Plate Work—Boiler Shops

Rank	Company Name—*Executive Officer*	Address, City, State, Zip	Phone	Type	Fin	Empls
1	McDermott International Inc—*Steven M Johnson*	757 N Eldridge Pky, Houston TX 77079	281-870-5000	P	3,445	13.5
2	Williams Enterprise of Georgia Inc—*Phil Tordhio*	1285 Hawthorne, Smyrna GA 30080	770-436-1596	R	1,478*	.6
3	Foster Wheeler Energy Corp—*Raymond Milkovich*	Perryville Corporate P, Clinton NJ 08809	908-730-4000	S	1,252*	1.5
4	TriMas Corp—*David Wathen*	39400 Woodward Ave Ste, Bloomfield Hills MI 48304	248-631-5450	B	1,084	4.1
5	Babcock and Wilcox Co—*Brandon C Bethards* McDermott International Inc	13024 Ballantyne Corpo, Charlotte NC 28277	434-522-6000	S	1,080*	10.8
6	Nooter Corp—*Ross Osiek*	PO Box 66514, Saint Louis MO 63166	314-421-7750	R	682*	1.0
7	Chicago Bridge and Iron Co—*Gerald M Glenn*	2103 Research Forest D, The Woodlands TX 77380	832-513-1000	S	675	5.7
8	Chart Industries Inc—*Samuel F Thomas*	1 Infinity Corporate C, Garfield Heights OH 44125	440-753-1490	P	556	3.0
9	Southern Heat Exchanger Corp—*Bill Laganke*	PO Box 1850, Tuscaloosa AL 35403	205-345-5335	R	289*	.2
10	Roberts Company Inc—*D Chris Bailey*	PO Box 1109, Winterville NC 28590	252-355-9353	R	261*	.4
11	Thermasys Corp—*Paul Schmitz*	2776 Gunter Park Dr E, Montgomery AL 36109	334-244-9240	R	261*	.4
12	Des Champs Technologies Inc—*Nicholas Des Champs*	225 S Magnolia Ave, Buena Vista VA 24416	540-291-1111	R	253*	.3
13	CEI Enterprises Inc—*Mike Bremmer*	245 Woodward Rd SE, Albuquerque NM 87102	505-842-5556	S	238*	.1
14	Atco Rubber Products Inc—*Ramesh Bhatia*	7101 Atco Dr, Fort Worth TX 76118	817-595-2894	R	225*	1.2
15	Feldmeier Equipment Inc—*John Feldmeier*	PO Box 474, Syracuse NY 13211	315-454-8608	R	210*	.4
16	Burnham Holdings Inc—*Albert Morrison III*	PO Box 3245, Lancaster PA 17604	717-390-7800	P	190	1.0
17	Diamond Power International Inc—*Eileen Competti*	2600 E Main St, Lancaster OH 43130	740-687-6500	S	189*	.3
18	Hudson Products Corp—*Grady Walker*	PO Box 20029, Sugar Land TX 77496	281-275-8100	R	183*	.1
19	Besicorp Development Company LLC—*David Kulik*	1151 Flatbush Rd, Kingston NY 12401	845-336-7700	R	145	.1
20	Paul Mueller Co—*David T Moore*	PO Box 828, Springfield MO 65801	417-575-9000	P	130	.7
21	Braden Construction Services Inc—*Gene Schockemeal*	5199 N Mingo Rd, Tulsa OK 74117	918-272-5371	S	112*	.2
22	Koch-Glitsch LP	4111 E 37th St N, Wichita KS 67220	316-828-5110	R	98*	.9
23	Evapco Inc—*Wilson Bradley*	5151 Allendale Ln, Taneytown MD 21787	410-756-2600	R	93*	1.1
24	Weil-McLain—*John Way*	500 Blaine St, Michigan City IN 46360	219-879-6561	S	89*	.7
25	Manchester Tank and Equipment Company Inc—*Larry Whitehead*	1000 Corporate Centre, Franklin TN 37067	615-370-3833	S	88*	1.1
26	Small Parts Inc—*John Barnes*	PO Box 7002, Logansport IN 46947	574-753-6323	R	85*	.7
27	Ohmstede Inc—*Frank MacInnis*	895 N Main St, Beaumont TX 77701	409-833-6375	S	84	.6
28	Enerfab Inc—*Wendell R Bell*	4955 Spring Grove Ave, Cincinnati OH 45232	513-641-0500	R	84*	.3
29	Consolidated Fabricators Corp—*Michael Melideo*	14620 Arminta St, Van Nuys CA 91402	818-901-1005	R	81*	.4
30	Deltak LLC—*Jeff Davis*	13330 12TH Ave N, Plymouth MN 55441	763-557-7440	S	73*	.1
31	Caldwell Tanks Inc—*Bernard Fineman*	PO Box 35770, Louisville KY 40232	502-964-3361	R	72*	.5
32	Koch Heat Transfer Co—*John R Rosso*	12602 FM 529, Houston TX 77041	713-466-3535	S	71*	.4
33	American Tank and Fabricating Co—*Michael Ripich*	12314 Elmwood Ave, Cleveland OH 44111	216-252-1500	R	66*	.2
34	Mid-State Machine and Fabricating Corp—*Harold Kersey*	2730 Mine Mill Rd, Lakeland FL 33801	863-665-6233	R	56*	.1
35	Taylor Forge Engineered Systems Inc—*Michael Kilkenny*	208 N Iron St, Paola KS 66071	913-294-5331	R	54*	.3
36	Industrial Container Services LLC—*Michael Osborne*	PO Box 2067, Montebello CA 90640	323-724-8500	R	52*	.7
37	Harsco Industrial Air-X-Changers—*Rick Ketchum*	5215 Arkansas Rd, Catoosa OK 74015	918-619-8000	D	51*	.4
38	Aggregate Plant Products Co—*Ronald Walchek* Conner Steel Products Inc	PO Box 1198, San Antonio TX 78294	210-333-1111	S	50*	.1
39	Superior Holding Inc—*John Murphy*	PO Box 1527, Hutchinson KS 67504	620-662-6693	R	50*	.1
40	Sivalls Inc—*C Sivalls*	PO Box 2792, Odessa TX 79760	432-337-3571	R	47*	.2

Note: An asterisk (*) indicates an estimated financial figure. The company type code used is as follows: R = Private, P = Public, S = Private Subsidiary, B = Public Subsidiary, D = Division, J = Joint Venture, I = Investment Fund.

COMPANY RANKINGS BY SALES WITHIN 4-DIGIT SIC

Rank	Company Name—*Executive Officer*	Address, City, State, Zip	Phone	Type	Fin	Empls
41	Hughes-Anderson Heat Exchangers Inc—*Monte Stewart*	1001 N Fulton Ave, Tulsa OK 74115	918-836-1681	R	46*	.1
42	Young Touchstone Co	PO Box 7568, Jackson TN 38302	731-265-2238	S	45*	.4
43	Process Equipment and Service Company Inc—*Kyle Rhodes*	PO Box 929, Farmington NM 87499	505-327-2222	R	41*	.3
44	Precision Custom Components LLC—*Mark Sealover*	PO Box 15101, York PA 17405	717-848-1126	R	41*	.3
45	Pfaudler Inc—*Peter C Wallace*	PO Box 23600, Rochester NY 14692	585-235-1000	S	40*	.4
46	Augsburg Fortress Publishers—*Beth Lewis*	PO Box 1209, Minneapolis MN 55440	612-330-3300	R	40*	.2
47	Dynasteel Corp—*James Russell*	PO Box 27640, Memphis TN 38167	901-358-6231	R	40*	.3
48	Pittsburg Tank and Tower Company Inc—*William Johnston*	PO Box 913, Henderson KY 42419	270-826-9000	R	38*	.4
49	Royal Oak Industries Inc—*Daniel Carroll*	PO Box 127, Lake Orion MI 48361	248-340-9200	R	38*	.4
50	Conner Steel Products Inc—*Joseph Fiamingo*	PO Box 3287, San Angelo TX 76902	325-655-8225	R	38*	.3
51	Super Steel LLC—*Dali Lezic*	7900 W Tower Ave, Milwaukee WI 53223	414-355-4800	R	37*	.3
52	Diamond Power Specialty Co Diamond Power International Inc	PO Box 415, Lancaster OH 43130	740-687-6500	D	37*	.5
53	Flsmidth Krebs Inc—*Douglas Schlepp*	5505 W Gillette Rd, Tucson AZ 85743	520-744-8200	R	36*	.2
54	Laron Inc—*Glenn Thoroughman*	4255 N Santa Fe Dr, Kingman AZ 86401	928-757-8424	R	36*	.3
55	Contech Construction Products Inc—*Ronald C Keating*	9025 Centre Pointe Dr, West Chester OH 45069	513-645-7000	S	36*	.2
56	Taylor-Wharton—*Robert Corbin*	4075 Hamilton Blvd, Theodore AL 36582	251-443-8680	S	36	.3
57	Permian Tank and Manufacturing Inc—*Glen Womack*	PO Box 4456, Odessa TX 79760	432-333-4591	R	36*	.3
58	Beall Trailers Of Montana Inc—*Jerry Beall*	PO Box 2543, Billings MT 59103	406-252-7163	S	35*	.3
59	Whitcraft LLC—*Gary Bowne*	PO Box 128, Eastford CT 06242	860-974-0786	R	35*	.3
60	Chart Heat Exchangers—*Samuel Thomas* Chart Industries Inc	2191 Ward Ave, La Crosse WI 54601	608-787-3333	D	35*	.3
61	Nebraska Boiler Co—*Tom Lehman*	6940 Cornhusker Hwy, Lincoln NE 68507	402-434-2000	R	35*	.3
62	Mitternight Boiler Works Inc—*Walter Mcrae*	PO Box 489, Satsuma AL 36572	251-675-2550	R	35*	.2
63	Fabcorp Inc—*Marianne Hohman*	6951 W Little York Rd, Houston TX 77040	713-466-3962	R	34*	.2
64	D and S ManufacturingCoInc—*Michael Dougherty*	PO Box 279, Black River Falls WI 54615	715-284-5376	R	33*	.2
65	Aerofin Corp—*David L Corell*	PO Box 10819, Lynchburg VA 24506	434-845-7081	S	32*	.3
66	Thermal Transfer Products Ltd—*Paul Schmitz* Thermasys Corp	5215 21st St, Racine WI 53406	262-554-8330	S	32	.3
67	Indeck Power Equipment Co—*Gerald R Forsythe*	1111 Willis Ave, Wheeling IL 60090	847-541-8300	R	32*	.1
68	Phoenix Fabricators and Erectors Inc—*Jeffery Short*	PO Box 34410, Indianapolis IN 46234	317-271-7002	R	32*	.2
69	Hurst Boiler and Welding Company Inc—*Clifton Hurst*	PO Box 530, Coolidge GA 31738	229-346-3545	R	31*	.3
70	Tomco2 Equipment Co—*John Toepke*	3340 Rosebud Rd, Loganville GA 30052	770-979-8000	R	31*	.1
71	Pax LLC—*Victor Phillips*	39386 Babin Rd, Gonzales LA 70737	225-644-6885	R	30*	.2
72	Arrow Tank and Engineering Co—*John Haskins*	650 N Emerson St, Cambridge MN 55008	763-689-3360	R	30*	.2
73	Sentry Equipment Corp—*Mike Farrell*	PO Box 127, Oconomowoc WI 53066	262-567-7256	R	30*	.1
74	Certified Stainless Service Inc—*Grant Smith*	PO Box 100, Ceres CA 95307	209-537-4747	R	30*	.1
75	Lee Industries Inc—*Robert W Montler*	PO Box 687, Philipsburg PA 16866	814-342-0461	R	29*	.2
76	Peerless Heater Co—*Robert E Fish*	PO Box 388, Boyertown PA 19512	610-367-2153	R	29*	.2
77	Tranter PHE Inc	PO Box 2289, Wichita Falls TX 76307	940-723-7125	S	29*	.2
78	Helgesen Industries Inc—*Keith Trafton*	7261 Hwy 60, Hartford WI 53027	262-673-4444	R	29*	.4
79	Freeport Welding And Fabricating Inc—*Roy Yates*	PO Box 2076, Freeport TX 77542	979-233-0121	R	28*	.1
80	Streator Industrial Handling Inc—*Paul Walker*	1705 N Shabbona St, Streator IL 61364	815-672-0551	R	28*	.4
81	Tankcraft Corp—*Robert Fettig*	N2900 Foundry Rd, Darien WI 53114	262-882-2500	R	28*	.2
82	Hahn and Clay—*Don Sheffield*	PO Box 15521, Houston TX 77220	713-672-1671	R	27*	.2
83	Wayne Metals LLC—*Rick Rogers*	400 E Logan St, Markle IN 46770	260-758-3121	R	27*	.2
84	Central Maintenance And Welding Inc—*Conrad Varnum*	2620 E Keysville Rd, Lithia FL 33547	813-737-1402	R	26*	.4
85	Cooler Master USA Inc	4820 Schaeffer Ave, Chino CA 91710	909-673-9880	S	26*	.1
86	Mississippi Tank Company Inc—*Robert Tatum*	PO Box 1391, Hattiesburg MS 39403	601-264-1800	R	26*	.2
87	Bigbee Steel And Tank Company Inc—*Mike Vanlenten*	4535 Elizabethtown Rd, Manheim PA 17545	717-664-0600	R	25*	.2
88	API Heat Transfer Inc—*Joe Cordosi*	2777 Walden Ave, Buffalo NY 14225	716-684-6700	S	25	.2
89	Holman Boiler Works Inc—*John Campolo*	1956 Singleton Blvd, Dallas TX 75212	214-637-0020	R	25*	.2
90	Psf Industries Inc—*Jeff Brown*	PO Box 3747, Seattle WA 98124	206-622-1252	R	25*	.2
91	Burgess-Manning Inc—*Warren G Martin* Nitram Energy Inc	50 Cobham Dr, Orchard Park NY 14127	716-662-6540	S	24*	.3
92	Goodhart Sons Inc—*Gary Goodhart*	PO Box 10308, Lancaster PA 17605	717-656-2404	R	24*	.2
93	Fiberdome Inc—*Richard Wollin*	865 Stony Rd, Lake Mills WI 53551	920-648-8376	R	23*	.2
94	Silvan Industries Inc—*Barry Berquist*	PO Box 767, Marinette WI 54143	715-735-9311	S	23*	.3
95	Rocky Mountain Fabrication Inc—*Randy Guest*	PO Box 16409, Salt Lake City UT 84116	801-596-2400	R	23*	.3
96	Stainless Fabrication Inc—*Michael Pyle*	PO Box 1127, Springfield MO 65801	417-865-5696	R	23*	.1
97	Benicia Fabrication and Machine Inc—*Dennis Rose*	101 E Channel Rd, Benicia CA 94510	707-745-8111	R	22*	.2
98	Custom Seating Inc—*Charles Gresham*	341 S 41st St E, Muskogee OK 74403	918-682-4400	R	22*	.2
99	Mark Steel Corp—*James Vemich*	PO Box 16006, Salt Lake City UT 84116	801-521-0670	R	22*	.2
100	Steel Tank and Fabricating Co—*Richard Harding*	4545 Clawson Tank Dr, Clarkston MI 48346	248-625-8700	R	21*	.2
101	Energy Exchanger Co—*JeanAnn Brinley*	1844 N Garnett Rd, Tulsa OK 74116	918-437-3000	R	21*	.1
102	NexGen Fueling Inc—*Tom Carey* Chart Industries Inc	3505 County Rd 42 W, Burnsville MN 55306	952-882-5000	D	21*	<.1
103	Ottenweller Company Inc—*Michael Ottenweller*	3011 Congressional Pkw, Fort Wayne IN 46808	260-484-3166	R	21*	.1
104	Pasadena Tank Corp—*Robert Block*	15915 Jacintoport Blvd, Houston TX 77015	281-457-3996	R	21*	.1
105	Kennedy Tank and Manufacturing Company Inc—*Patrick Kennedy*	PO Box 47070, Indianapolis IN 46247	317-787-1311	R	21*	.1
106	Cust-O-Fab Inc—*Berry Keeler*	8888 W 21st St, Sand Springs OK 74063	918-245-6685	R	20*	.2
107	DC I Inc—*Jeffrey Keller*	PO Box 1227, Saint Cloud MN 56302	320-252-8200	R	20*	.3
108	Bath Fitter Tennessee Inc—*Brian Cotton*	102 Evergreen Dr, Springfield TN 37172	615-612-2940	R	20*	.2
109	Charles Ross and Son Co—*Richard Ross*	PO Box 12308, Hauppauge NY 11788	631-234-0500	R	20*	.1
110	La Grange Products Inc—*Lynn Blue*	PO Box 658, Fremont IN 46737	260-495-3025	R	19*	.1
111	General Welding Works Inc—*Graham Webb*	PO Box 925749, Houston TX 77292	713-869-6401	R	18*	.1
112	Rentech Boiler Services Inc—*David Hunter*	PO Box 3295, Abilene TX 79604	325-672-2900	R	18*	.1
113	Highland Tank And Manufacturing Co—*Michael Vanlenten*	PO Box 338, Stoystown PA 15563	814-893-5701	R	18*	.1
114	Bryan Steam LLC—*Thomas May*	783 Chili Ave, Peru IN 46970	765-473-6651	R	18*	.1
115	Hammersmith Manufacturing and Sales Inc—*Edward Hammer-smith*	401 Central Ave, Horton KS 66439	785-486-2121	R	18*	<.1
116	Rumar Manufacturing Corp—*Frances Laufenberg*	PO Box 193, Mayville WI 53050	920-387-2104	R	17*	.1
117	Smithco Engineering Inc—*Judith Smith*	PO Box 571330, Tulsa OK 74157	918-446-4406	R	17*	.1
118	Fisher Tank Co—*Michael Szelak*	3131 W 4th St, Chester PA 19013	610-494-7200	R	17*	.1
119	Metalforms Manufacturing Inc—*David Hearn*	PO Box 20118, Beaumont TX 77720	409-842-1626	R	17*	.1
120	Mgs Inc—*Andrew Gehman*	178 Muddy Creek Church, Denver PA 17517	717-336-7528	R	16*	.1
121	Cmi-Schneible Co—*William Goetz*	714 N Saginaw St, Holly MI 48442	248-634-8211	R	16*	.2
122	Associated Rack Corp—*William L Faulman*	1245 16th St, Vero Beach FL 32960	772-567-4771	R	16*	.1

Rank	Company Name—*Executive Officer*	Address, City, State, Zip	Phone	Type	Fin	Empls
123	Chattanooga Boiler and Tank Company Inc Williams Enterprise of Georgia Inc	PO Box 110, Chattanooga TN 37401	423-266-7118	S	16*	.1
124	Lewis Steel Works Inc—*Bryan Lewis*	PO Box 338, Wrens GA 30833	706-547-6561	R	15*	.1
125	James Machine Works Inc—*Joe Reljac*	1521 Adams St, Monroe LA 71201	318-322-6104	R	15*	.1
126	Tobul Accumulator Inc—*James Tobul*	186 Accumulator St, Bamberg SC 29003	803-245-5111	R	15*	.1
127	Jindal Pipes USA Inc—*Indresh Batra*	5200 E Mckinney Rd Ste, Baytown TX 77523	281-383-3300	R	15*	.2
128	Rocky Mountain Welding and Fabricating Inc—*Lawrence De-roest*	PO Box 397, Pleasant Grove UT 84062	801-785-5990	R	15*	.1
129	A L Eastmond and Sons Inc—*Leon Eastmond*	1175 Leggett Ave, Bronx NY 10474	718-378-3000	R	14*	.1
130	American Grinding and Machine Co—*Greg Leonard*	2000 N Mango Ave, Chicago IL 60639	773-889-4343	R	14*	.1
131	X-Mark/CDT—*John S Stroup*	2001 N Main St, Washington PA 15301	724-228-7373	S	14*	.1
132	L and M Fabrication And Machine Inc—*Bruce Lack*	PO Box 124, Bath PA 18014	610-837-1848	R	14*	.1
133	Turbotec Products Inc—*Sunil Raina*	651 Day Hill Rd, Windsor CT 06095	860-731-4200	S	14*	.1
134	Helser Industries Inc—*Max Helser*	PO Box 1569, Tualatin OR 97062	503-692-6909	R	14*	.1
135	Rockett Inc—*John Mcgregor*	PO Box 6066, Jackson MS 39288	601-939-2471	R	14*	.1
136	Rudco Products Inc—*Robert Rudolph*	PO Box 705, Vineland NJ 08362	856-691-0800	R	13*	.1
137	Continental Fabricators Inc—*Thomas Fournie*	5601 W Park Ave, Saint Louis MO 63110	314-781-6300	R	13*	.1
138	Rds Manufacturing Inc—*Joseph Roberts*	PO Box 1908, Perry FL 32348	850-584-6898	R	13*	.1
139	Hayden Products LLC—*Jon Perry*	1531 Pomona Rd, Corona CA 92880	951-736-2600	R	13*	.1
140	MP Husky Corp—*Mike Pollard*	PO Box 16749, Greenville SC 29606	864-234-4800	R	12*	.1
141	Potts Welding and Boiler Repair—*Dennis Dakin*	1901 Ogletown Rd, Newark DE 19711	302-453-2550	R	12*	.1
142	Structural Composites Industries—*Harry Goussetis*	336 Enterprise Pl, Pomona CA 91768	909-594-7777	S	12*	.1
143	J T Cullen Company Inc—*Eric Johnson*	PO Box 311, Fulton IL 61252	815-589-2412	R	12*	.1
144	Kanawha Manufacturing Co—*William Davis*	PO Box 1786, Charleston WV 25326	304-342-6127	R	12*	.1
145	Joseph Oat Corp—*Martin Kaplan*	2500 Broadway Drawer 1, Camden NJ 08104	856-541-2900	R	11*	.1
146	Roy E Hanson Jr Manufacturing—*Johnathan Goss*	PO Box 30507, Los Angeles CA 90030	213-747-7514	R	11*	.1
147	Kbk Industries LLC—*William Baalman*	Rr Ste 2 Box 3, Rush Center KS 67575	785-372-4331	R	11*	.1
148	Sauder Custom Fabrication Inc—*Dale Davis*	PO Box 1158, Emporia KS 66801	620-342-2550	R	11*	.1
149	Johnston Boiler Co—*R Black*	PO Box 300, Ferrysburg MI 49409	616-842-5050	R	11*	.1
150	Zak Inc—*Douglas Zak*	1 Tibbits Ave, Green Island NY 12183	518-273-3912	R	10*	.1
151	Erm Thermal Technologies Inc—*Christopher Cutaia*	6377 Dean Pkwy, Ontario NY 14519	585-265-0330	R	10*	.1
152	Hart Heat Transfer Products Inc—*John Hart*	8226 Kerr St, Houston TX 77029	713-675-9848	R	10*	.1
153	Winbco Tank Co—*John Travlos*	PO Box 618, Ottumwa IA 52501	641-683-1855	R	10*	.5
154	Baker's Waste Equipment Inc—*Rick Raynes*	3679 Cook Rd, Valdese NC 28690	828-879-8222	R	10*	.1
155	JBL International Inc—*James Reigel*	PO Box 369, Marshfield WI 54449	715-384-3158	R	10*	.1
156	Erie Engineered Products Inc—*Barry Newman*	908 Niagara Falls Blvd, North Tonawanda NY 14120	716-694-2020	R	10*	.1
157	Youngberg Industries Inc—*Thomas Larson*	6863 Indy Dr, Belvidere IL 61008	815-544-2177	R	10*	.1
158	Par-Kan Co—*Steve Parker*	2915 W 900 S, Silver Lake IN 46982	260-352-2141	R	9*	.1
159	Service Machine And Welding Company Inc—*Jeffrey Layne*	PO Box 2083, Ashland VA 23005	804-798-1381	R	9*	.1
160	Fulton Boiler Works Inc—*Ronald Palm*	PO Box 257, Pulaski NY 13142	315-298-5121	R	9*	.1
161	Gaspar's Inc—*Gary Gaspar*	1545 Whipple Ave Sw, Canton OH 44710	330-479-9366	R	9*	.1
162	Quality Fabrication and Machine Works Inc—*Dale Dryden*	3631 E Us Hwy 90, Lake City FL 32055	386-755-0220	R	8*	.1
163	Offonhauser Co—*Robert Dillard*	PO Box 230068, Houston TX 77223	713-928-2981	R	8*	.1
164	Avon Engineered Fabrications Inc—*Michael Hamner*	1200 Martin Luther, Picayune MS 39466	601-799-1217	R	0*	.1
165	Wichita Steel Fabricators Inc—*Jim L Smith*	3400 N Broadway St, Wichita KS 67219	316-838-3301	R	8*	.1
166	Alfa Laval Inc—*Mark Larsen*	5400 International Tra, Richmond VA 23231	804-222-5300	S	8*	.1
167	IS Parts International Inc—*Stephen Abernathy*	3603 N Mill Rd, Vineland NJ 08360	856-691-2203	R	8*	.1
168	Stephens Pneumatics Inc—*Stan Stophens*	147 County Rd 4840, Haslet TX 76052	817-636-9004	R	8*	.1
169	Fabrication Associates Inc—*William Little*	PO Box 25326, Charlotte NC 28229	704-535-8050	R	8*	.1
170	Titan Fabricators Inc—*Michael Horn*	PO Box 927, Owensboro KY 42302	270-686-7436	R	7*	.1
171	Clark Machine Corp—*Dan Hefner*	1000 Todds Ln, Baltimore MD 21237	410-687-3020	R	7*	.1
172	San-I-Pak Pacific Inc—*John Hall*	PO Box 1183, Tracy CA 95378	209-836-2310	R	7*	.1
173	Nitram Energy Inc—*Robert M Sherman*	50 Cobham Dr, Orchard Park NY 14127	716-662-6540	R	7*	.1
174	American Industrial Plant Services Inc—*Wesley Babin*	12423 Jim Babin Rd, Saint Amant LA 70774	225-647-6786	R	7*	.1
175	Peninsular Inc—*Brent Paterson*	27650 Groesbeck Hwy, Roseville MI 48066	586-775-7211	R	7*	.1
176	Clawson Tank Co—*Terrance Groh*	4545 Clawson Tank Dr, Clarkston MI 48346	248-625-8700	R	7*	<.1
177	General Industries Inc—*John Wiggins*	PO Box 1279, Goldsboro NC 27533	919-751-1791	R	6*	<.1
178	DM Manufacturing Inc—*Donald Myers*	2750 Kennedy Dr, Beloit WI 53511	608-362-2095	R	6*	.1
179	De Jong Manufacturing Inc—*Bonnie De Jong*	PO Box 515, New Sharon IA 50207	641-637-4455	R	6*	.1
180	Dixie Poly-Drum Corp—*Pete Hamiker*	PO Box 597, Yemassee SC 29945	843-589-6660	R	6*	<.1
181	Combustion Associates Inc—*Mukund Kavia*	555 Monica Cir, Corona CA 92880	951-272-6999	R	6*	<.1
182	Custom Biogenic Systems Inc—*John Brothers*	150 Shaffer Dr, Romeo MI 48065	586-331-2600	R	6*	<.1
183	Penn Iron Works Inc—*Stylianos Philippides*	PO Box 6858, Wyomissing PA 19610	610-777-7656	R	6*	<.1
184	Harliss Specialties Corp—*John Harkobusic*	PO Box R, Irwin PA 15642	724-863-0321	R	5*	<.1
185	Twin Oaks Industries Inc—*Timothy Ochs*	PO Box 1723, Salina KS 67402	785-827-4839	R	5*	<.1
186	Klein Products Of Kansas Inc—*Scott Klein*	3904 Liberty Bell Rd, Fort Scott KS 66701	620-223-0340	R	5*	<.1
187	Air Power Systems Company Inc—*Larry Mocha*	PO Box 470948, Tulsa OK 74147	918-622-5600	R	5*	<.1
188	Russell James Engineering Works Inc—*David Hahn*	9 Dewar St, Dorchester MA 02125	617-265-2240	R	5*	<.1
189	Hensley Fabricating and Equipment Company Inc—*Gregory Hensley*	17624 State Rd 331, Tippecanoe IN 46570	574-498-6514	R	5*	<.1
190	Geo Knight and Company Inc—*Chesterton Knight*	52 Perkins St, Brockton MA 02302	508-588-0186	R	5*	<.1
191	Allister Fabricating Inc—*Gregory Sieckert*	PO Box 316, Lannon WI 53046	262-251-3540	R	5*	<.1
192	Cleveland Steel Specialty Company Inc—*Robert Ehrhardt*	26001 Richmond Rd, Cleveland OH 44146	216-464-9400	R	5*	<.1
193	Superior Fabricators Inc—*L Bergeron*	PO Box 539, Baldwin LA 70514	337-923-7271	R	4*	<.1
194	Alloy Hardfacing And Engineering Co—*Mark Aulik*	20425 Johnson Memorial, Jordan MN 55352	952-492-5569	R	4*	<.1
195	Southeastern Machine and Welding Company Inc—*R Edens*	PO Box 3383, Wilmington NC 28406	910-791-6661	R	4*	<.1
196	G2k Corp—*Kirby Gray*	190 S Union Blvd, Lakewood CO 80228	303-988-6450	R	4*	<.1
197	Western Pennsylvania Steel Fabricating Inc—*Fredric Defiore*	550 Honey Bee Ln, New Castle PA 16105	724-658-8575	R	4*	<.1
198	Quikcut Inc—*Mark Webb*	4630 Allen Martin Dr, Fort Wayne IN 46806	260-447-3880	R	4*	<.1
199	Rus Industries Inc—*Alice Carlson*	PO Box 256, Niagara Falls NY 14305	716-284-7828	R	4*	<.1
200	Matrix Service Mid-Continent Inc—*Michael Bradley*	6945 Crabb Rd, Temperance MI 48182	734-847-4605	S	4*	<.1
201	Able Fab Co—*William Demott*	18 Mileed Way, Avenel NJ 07001	732-396-0600	R	4*	<.1
202	Southern Tank and Manufacturing Company Inc—*Patrick Kennedy*	PO Box 2066, Owensboro KY 42302	270-684-2321	R	4*	<.1
203	Samson Metal And Machine Inc—*Barak Samson*	PO Box 1586, Lakeland FL 33802	863-665-6151	R	4*	<.1
204	Polytank Inc—*Richard Johanneck*	62824 250th St, Litchfield MN 55355	320-693-8370	R	4*	<.1
205	Therma-Flow Inc—*Edwin Hill*	PO Box 416, Watertown MA 02471	617-924-3877	R	4*	<.1
206	Schwabel Fabricating Company Inc—*Gerald Schwabel*	349 Sawyer Ave, Tonawanda NY 14150	716-876-2086	R	4*	<.1
207	Barber Welding And Manufacturing Co—*C Barber*	7171 Scout Ave, Bell CA 90201	562-928-2570	R	4*	<.1
208	Industrial Container Inc—*David Tito*	6671 French Rd, Detroit MI 48213	313-923-8778	R	4*	<.1

Note: An asterisk (*) indicates an estimated financial figure. The company type code used is as follows: R = Private, P = Public, S = Private Subsidiary, B = Public Subsidiary, D = Division, J = Joint Venture, I = Investment Fund.

COMPANY RANKINGS BY SALES WITHIN 4-DIGIT SIC

Rank	Company Name—*Executive Officer*	Address, City, State, Zip	Phone	Type	Fin	Empls
209	RPI Of Indiana Inc—*Adrienne Cooper*	PO Box 38, Holmesville OH 44633	330-279-2421	R	3*	<.1
210	Illinois Fabricators Inc—*Jackie Hawker*	265 S Kinzie Ave, Bradley IL 60915	815-939-3551	R	3*	<.1
211	Industrial Alloy Fabricators LLC—*Gary Booth*	1501 Valley Rd, Richmond VA 23222	804-321-3333	R	3*	<.1
212	Hydraulic Specialists Inc—*Dale Burkholder*	PO Box 500, Midvale OH 44653	740-922-3343	R	3*	<.1
213	Dry Coolers Inc—*Brian Russell*	3232 Adventure Ln, Oxford MI 48371	248-969-3400	R	3*	<.1
214	Valiant Products Inc—*Robert English*	PO Box 405, Lakeland FL 33802	863-688-7998	R	3*	<.1
215	Texas Pipe Fabricators Inc—*Joe Fleck*	709 High Starr Dr, Corpus Christi TX 78408	361-882-5541	R	3*	.1
216	Valco Plastics Inc—*Frank Valacak*	14505 S Main St, Gardena CA 90248	310-532-1988	R	3*	<.1
217	WW Metal Products Inc—*Randal Walker*	1226 N Fm 2148, Texarkana TX 75501	903-838-4329	R	3*	<.1
218	Massman Enterprises Inc—*C Clugston*	1314 N Wheeling Ave, Tulsa OK 74110	918-583-9129	R	3*	<.1
219	Yardarm Marine Products Inc—*Paul Delk*	2100 Hancel Pkwy, Mooresville IN 46158	317-831-4950	R	3*	<.1
220	Modern Welding Company Of Texas Inc—*John Jones*	PO Box 85, Rhome TX 76078	817-636-2215	S	3*	<.1
221	Acme Mechanical Contractors Inc—*Tom Broadbent*	612 Volunteer Pkwy, Manchester TN 37355	931-728-5115	R	3*	<.1
222	Rotary Airlock LLC—*Jill Near*	707 E 17th St, Rock Falls IL 61071	815-626-0388	R	3*	<.1
223	Geo Heat Exchangers LLC—*Bo Bienvenu*	PO Box 750, Saint Gabriel LA 70776	225-642-8900	R	2*	.1
224	John R Robinson Inc—*Frank Cunningham*	3805 30th St, Long Island City NY 11101	718-786-6088	R	2*	<.1
225	Massie Manufacturing Inc—*Peter Massie*	PO Box 339, Baraga MI 49908	906-353-6381	R	2*	<.1
226	Vitta Corp—*Aloyzas Petrikas*	7 Trowbridge Dr, Bethel CT 06801	203-790-8155	R	2*	<.1
227	Quest Manufacturing Inc—*John Lichter*	2503 Spring Ridge Dr, Spring Grove IL 60081	815-675-2442	R	2*	.1
228	Precision Grinding Inc—*William J Cabaniss Jr*	PO Box 19925, Birmingham AL 35219	205-942-2491	R	2*	<.1
229	Custom Cylinders International Inc—*Grover Taylor*	PO Box 4242, Winchester KY 40392	859-744-5544	R	2*	<.1
230	Sharon Manufacturing Inc—*John Beres*	PO Box 119, Sharon Center OH 44274	330-239-1561	R	2*	<.1
231	Enterprise Sales Inc—*Scott Wilson*	540 Se 9th Ave, Ontario OR 97914	541-889-5541	R	2*	<.1
232	Precision Cryogenic Systems Inc—*Roy Larrison*	7804 Rockville Rd, Indianapolis IN 46214	317-273-2800	R	2*	<.1
233	Waste Quip Inc—*Roger Oukrop*	33710 Oakville Rd Sw, Albany OR 97321	541-926-5578	R	1*	<.1
234	Atlas Metal Working Corp—*Nick Peros*	PO Box 1216, Hudson NY 12534	518-828-4170	R	1*	<.1
235	Biobubble Inc—*Chuck Spengler*	3024 W Prospect Rd, Fort Collins CO 80526	970-224-4262	R	1*	<.1
236	Design Integrated Technology Inc—*Stephen Andrews*	100 E Franklin St, Warrenton VA 20186	540-349-9425	R	1*	<.1
237	Scientific Alloys Corp—*Wayne Connelly*	5 Troast Ct, Clifton NJ 07011	973-478-8323	R	1*	<.1
238	Pressure-Tech Inc—*Craig Walck*	PO Box 430, Greencastle PA 17225	717-597-1868	R	1*	<.1
239	EF Britten and Company Inc—*Richard Stokes*	22 S Ave W, Cranford NJ 07016	908-276-4800	R	1*	<.1
240	Excel Plating Technology Inc—*Vickie Gouker*	328 E Pima St Bldg 5, Phoenix AZ 85004	480-940-1805	R	1*	<.1
241	Sidehill Copper Works Inc—*Andrew Fynan*	12 Port Access Rd Ste, Erie PA 16507	814-451-0400	R	1*	<.1
242	Stainless Fabricators Inc—*Angelo Begovich*	PO Box 424, Belle Chasse LA 70037	504-392-2011	R	1*	<.1
243	Hydrogen Components Inc—*Frank Lynch*	27 Hi Meadow Dr, Bailey CO 80421	303-791-7972	R	1*	<.1
244	H and H Engineering Company Inc—*Joseph Helfrich*	6 Pine St, Methuen MA 01844	978-682-0567	R	1*	<.1
245	Stainless Metals Inc—*Fred Meier*	4349 10th St Fl 1, Long Island City NY 11101	718-784-1454	R	1*	<.1
246	Skye International Inc—*Perry D Logan*	7756 E Greenway Rd, Scottsdale AZ 85260	480-993-2300	P	<1	<.1

TOTALS: SIC 3443 Fabricated Plate Work—Boiler Shops
Companies: 246

					17,370	77.6

3444 Sheet Metal Work

Rank	Company Name—*Executive Officer*	Address, City, State, Zip	Phone	Type	Fin	Empls
1	Louis Berkman Co—*Louis Berkman*	PO Box 820, Steubenville OH 43952	740-283-3722	R	1,050*	.5
2	Maysteel LLC—*Kim Harter*	PO Box 1240, Menomonee Falls WI 53052	262-251-1632	R	823*	.2
3	HM White Holding Company Inc—*Bill White*	12855 Burt Rd, Detroit MI 48223	313-531-8477	R	404*	.1
4	Alcoa—*George E Bergeron*	PO Box 40, Magnolia AR 71754	870-234-4260	S	324*	.8
5	Owens Corning Fabricating Solutions—*David Brown*	PO Box 1366, Elkhart IN 46515	574-522-8473	D	207	.8
6	Amerimax Home Products Inc—*Dudley Rowe*	PO Box 4515, Lancaster PA 17604	717-299-3711	S	135*	.4
7	A Zahner Co—*L William Zahner*	1400 E 9th St, Kansas City MO 64106	816-474-8882	R	110*	.2
8	RTI Tradco Inc—*Leonard Stanley*	1701 W Main St, Washington MO 63090	636-239-7816	S	103*	.2
9	Snappy Air Distribution Products—*Edward J Trainor*	1011 11th Ave SE, Detroit Lakes MN 56501	218-847-9258	D	84*	.3
10	Allmet Building Products LP—*Val Jacklyn*	227 S Town E Blvd, Mesquite TX 75149	714-529-0407	S	83	.1
11	Parker Hannifin Corp Chomerics Div—*Heinz Droxner*	77 Dragon Ct, Woburn MA 01801	781-935-4850	D	74	.6
12	Western Industries Inc—*Tom Hall*	1st and B St Strother, Winfield KS 67156	620-221-9464	R	67*	.6
13	American Products LLC—*Steve Smith*	597 Evergreen Rd, Strafford MO 65757	417-736-2135	R	66*	.1
14	Berger Brothers Co—*Michael Berger* Berger Building Products Inc	805 Pennsylvania Blvd, Feasterville PA 19053	215-355-1200	S	58*	.3
15	Dee Zee Inc—*Ronald Shivers*	PO Box 3090, Des Moines IA 50316		S	56*	.5
16	Thybar Corp—*William Evitt*	913 S Kay Ave, Addison IL 60101	630-543-5300	R	55*	.1
17	LI Building Products Inc—*Bill Collins*	1361 Alps Rd, Wayne NJ 07470	973-628-3000	R	53*	.5
18	Hooper Corporation—*Fred Davie*	PO Box 7455, Madison WI 53707	608-249-0451	R	50*	.4
19	Captive-Aire Systems Inc—*Robert Luddy*	4641 Paragon Park Rd S, Raleigh NC 27616	919-882-2410	R	49*	.6
20	Berridge Manufacturing Company Inc—*Joel Jesse*	6515 Fratt Rd, San Antonio TX 78218	210-650-3050	R	48*	.2
21	Motek-Team Industries Inc—*David Ricke*	625 2nd Ave SE, Cambridge MN 55008	763-689-1333	S	46*	.2
22	Berger Building Products Inc—*David Stewart*	805 Pennsylvania Blvd, Feasterville Trevose PA 19053	215-355-1200	S	45*	.2
23	Western Forms Inc—*Ronald Ward*	6200 Equitable Rd, Kansas City MO 64120		R	45*	.3
24	California Expanded Metal Products Co—*Raymond Poliquin*	263 N Covina Ln, City Of Industry CA 91746	626-369-3564	R	44*	.3
25	Arizona Precision Sheet Metal Inc—*John Thul*	2140 W Pinnacle Peak R, Phoenix AZ 85027	623-516-3700	R	43*	.3
26	Metal-Fab Inc—*Steve Hughbanks*	PO Box 1138, Wichita KS 67201	316-943-2351	R	43*	.3
27	Highway Safety Corp—*Frank Luszcz*	PO Box 358, Glastonbury CT 06033	860-633-9445	R	43*	.1
28	Allentown Inc—*Michael Coiro*	PO Box 698, Allentown NJ 08501	609-259-7951	R	42*	.3
29	Englert Inc—*Debra Harnett*	1200 Amboy Ave, Perth Amboy NJ 08861	732-826-8614	R	40*	.3
30	Kogok Corp—*Jeffrey Kogok*	4011a Penn Belt Pl, District Heights MD 20747	301-736-5300	R	39*	.3
31	Tenere Inc—*John Kamakian*	700 Kelly Ave, Dresser WI 54009	715-755-2158	R	39*	.2
32	Mccorvey Sheet Metal Works LP—*Kristal Crites*	8610 Wallisville Rd, Houston TX 77029	713-672-7545	R	38*	.3
33	ACME Manufacturing Company Inc (Philadelphia Pennsylvania)—*Roger Fix*	7601 State Rd, Philadelphia PA 19136	215-338-2850	D	38*	.5
34	Fabrication Concepts Corp—*David Smith*	1800 E Saint Andrew Pl, Santa Ana CA 92705	714-881-2000	R	37*	.3
35	Cobra Metal Works Inc—*Anton Hirsch*	1140 Jansen Dr, Elgin IL 60123	847-214-8400	R	36*	.3
36	Arrow United Industries—*Earl Lewis Jr*	PO Box 69, Wyalusing PA 18853	570-746-1888	D	36*	.1
37	HPMNC Inc	1780 Rohrerstown Rd, Lancaster PA 17601	717-569-7061	D	36*	.1
38	Melanson Company Inc—*Robert Therrien*	PO Box 523, Keene NH 03431	603-352-4232	R	36*	.3
39	Semco Duct And Acoustical Products Inc—*William Thurman*	1800 E Pointe Dr, Columbia MO 65201	573-443-1481	R	35*	.5
40	Rollex Corp—*James Brittingham*	800 Chase Ave, Elk Grove Village IL 60007	847-437-3000	R	35*	.4
41	Trend Technologies LLC—*Hernan Arriaga*	4626 Eucalyptus Ave, Chino CA 91710	909-597-7861	R	34*	.5
42	Airtronics Metal Products Inc—*John Richardson*	1991 Senter Rd, San Jose CA 95112	408-977-7800	R	33*	.2
43	American Fabricators Inc—*Milton Grief*	PO Box 111025, Nashville TN 37222	615-834-8700	R	33*	.2
44	Wriglesworth and Willock Metal Fab Inc—*James Wriglesworth*	9510 Se Main St, Portland OR 97222	503-513-0590	R	32*	.1
45	Consolidated Systems Inc—*G Rogers*	PO Box 1756, Columbia SC 29202	803-771-7920	R	32*	.4
46	Nelson Air Device Corp—*Nelson Blitz*	4628 54th Ave, Maspeth NY 11378	718-729-3801	R	32*	.2
47	Caid Industries Inc—*William Assenmacher*	PO Box 26945, Tucson AZ 85726	520-294-3126	R	30*	.2

Rank	Company Name—Executive Officer	Address, City, State, Zip	Phone	Type	Fin	Empls
48	Stonhard Inc	1000 E Park Ave, Maple Shade NJ 08052		S	30*	.1
49	Daviess County Metal Sales Inc—John Lengacher	9929 E Us Hwy 50, Cannelburg IN 47519	812-486-4299	R	30*	.1
50	Nsa Industries LLC—Ed Bailey	PO Box 54, Lyndonville VT 05851	802-748-5007	R	29*	.3
51	Modern Tool Inc—Barry Larson	1200 Northdale Blvd Nw, Minneapolis MN 55448	763-754-7337	R	28*	.2
52	Kice Industries Inc—Thomas Kice	5500 Mill Heights Dr, Park City KS 67219	316-744-7151	R	28*	.2
53	Mid-Lakes Distributing Co—Mike Hollub	1029 W Adams St 37, Chicago IL 60607	312-733-1033	R	27*	.1
54	Micro Metl Corp—Gerald Schultz	3035 N Shadeland Ave S, Indianapolis IN 46226	317-524-5400	R	27*	.3
55	Klauer Manufacturing Company Inc—William Klauer	PO Box 59, Dubuque IA 52004	563-582-7201	R	27*	.2
56	Metal Trades Inc—Russell Corbin	PO Box 129, Hollywood SC 29449	843-889-6442	R	27*	.2
57	Juniper Elbow Company Inc—Jesse Wiener	PO Box 790148, Middle Village NY 11379	718-326-2546	R	26*	.3
58	Billy Penn Corp	PO Box 37982, Jacksonville FL 32236		R	26*	.3
59	Excelsior Manufacturing and Supply Corp—John Brady	1999 N Ruby St, Melrose Park IL 60160	708-344-1802	R	26*	.2
60	Cody Company Inc—Steve Stephens	PO Box 1320, Ennis TX 75120	972-875-5884	R	25*	.2
61	Acro Industries Inc—Joseph Noto	554 Colfax St, Rochester NY 14606	585-254-3661	R	25*	.2
62	Louisville Tin and Stove Co—Richard Mudd	PO Box 2767, Louisville KY 40201	502-589-5380	R	25*	.1
63	Global Finishing Solutions LLC—Jonathan Barrick	PO Box 250, Osseo WI 54758	715-597-3168	R	25*	.4
64	ABB Incorporated Automation Technologies Div	1250 Brown Rd, Auburn Hills MI 48326	248-391-9000	D	24*	.2
65	Special Products and Manufacturing Inc—Robert Grand-Lienard	2625 Discovery Blvd, Rockwall TX 75032	972-771-8851	R	24*	.2
66	Lomanco Inc—Chris Grimes	PO Box 519, Jacksonville AR 72078	501-982-6511	R	24*	.2
67	Gallagher-Kaiser Corp—Robert Kaiser	13710 Mount Elliott St, Detroit MI 48212	313-368-3100	R	24*	.2
68	Cupples' J and J Company Inc—James Cupples	PO Box 458, Jackson TN 38302	731-424-3621	R	23*	.2
69	LE Schwartz and Son Inc—Melvin Kruger	279 Reid St, Macon GA 31206	478-745-6563	R	23*	.3
70	Ampp Inc—Joseph Young	400 F St, Perrysburg OH 43551	419-666-4747	S	23*	.2
71	Salsbury Industries Mailboxes—Dennis Fraher	1010 E 62nd St, Los Angeles CA 90001	323-846-6700	R	23*	.2
72	Appleton Supply Company Inc—Brent Listin	1905 W Haskell St, Appleton WI 54914	920-738-4242	S	21*	.1
73	Montana Metal Products LLC—Pat Dombek	25 E Howard St, Des Plaines IL 60018	847-803-6600	R	20*	.1
74	American Aluminum Co—Robert Brucker	230 Sheffield St, Mountainside NJ 07092	908-998-2592	R	20*	.1
75	Mid-Park Inc—G Bernard	PO Box 326, Leitchfield KY 42755	270-259-3152	R	20*	.1
76	Metalworking Group—Mike Schmitt	9070 Pippin Rd, Cincinnati OH 45251	513-521-4114	R	20*	.1
77	Harford Systems Inc—George Gabriel	PO Box 700, Aberdeen MD 21001	410-272-3400	R	20*	.2
78	Midwest Products And Engineering Inc—Dennis Wenger	10597 W Glenbrook Ct, Milwaukee WI 53224	414-355-0310	R	19*	.1
79	Mc Daniel Metals Inc—William Daniel	1318 Buschong St, Houston TX 77039	281-987-8400	R	18*	.1
80	Triumph Fabrications-Shelbyville—Don Kendall	850 Elston Dr, Shelbyville IN 46176	317-398-6684	S	18*	.2
81	Royal Metal Products Inc—John Crider	100 Royal Way, Temple GA 30179	678-563-0003	R	18*	.2
82	Gerome Manufacturing Co—Henry Gerome	PO Box 1089, Uniontown PA 15401	724-438-8544	R	18*	.1
83	Impulse Manufacturing Inc—Ronald Baysden	55 Impulse Industrial, Dawsonville GA 30534	706-216-1700	R	17*	.1
84	Endicott Precision Inc—Ronald Oliveira	1328-30 Campville Rd, Endicott NY 13760	607-754-7076	R	17*	.1
85	Lambro Industries Inc—Shivraj Anand	PO Box 367, Amityville NY 11701	631-842-8088	R	17*	.1
86	Miller Co—Richard Archambault	275 Pratt St, Meriden CT 06450	203-235-4474	D	17*	.1
87	Pepco Manufacturing Co—John Kennedy	PO Box 160, Somerdale NJ 08083	856-783-3700	R	17*	.1
88	Engines Inc—Carl Grover	PO Box 428, South Point OH 45680	304-743-1581	R	17*	.1
89	Landmark Manufacturing Corp—Donald Critten	28100 Quick Ave, Gallatin MO 64640	660-663-2185	R	16*	.2
90	Jones Metal Products Inc—Peter Jones	3201 3rd Ave, Mankato MN 56001	507-625-4436	R	16*	.1
91	Amf Anaheim LLC	2100 E Orangewood Ave, Anaheim CA 92806	714-363-9206	R	16*	.1
92	Precise Industries Inc—Terry Wells	610 Neptune Ave, Brea CA 92821	714-482-2333	R	16*	.1
93	AW Mercer Inc—John Meade	PO Box 508, Boyertown PA 19512	610-367-8460	R	16*	.1
94	Gary Metal Manufacturing LLC	2700 E 5th Ave, Gary IN 46402	219-885-3232	R	16*	.1
95	Qualex Manufacturing LC—Gary Everman	PO Box 807, Georgetown KY 40324	502-803-6040	R	16*	.1
96	PAS U Inc—Donald Palumbo	PO Box 1109, Bonita CA 91908	619-421-1151	R	16*	.1
97	California Chassis Inc—Michael Doyle	3356 E La Palma Ave, Anaheim CA 92806	714-666-8511	R	16*	.1
98	Gardner Manufacturing Co—John Jones	PO Box 147, Horicon WI 53032	920-485-4303	R	16*	.1
99	Exact Inc—W Allen	PO Box 61087, Jacksonville FL 32236	904-783-6640	R	15*	.1
100	Cinfab LLC—Bern Chouteau	5240 Lester Rd, Cincinnati OH 45213	513-396-6100	R	15*	.1
101	Ducommun AeroStructures Inc—Paul J Burton	2 Flint Mine Rd, Coxsackie NY 12051	518-731-4600	S	15*	.1
102	Dawson Metal Company Inc—David Dawson	PO Box 278, Jamestown NY 14702	716-664-3815	R	15*	.1
103	Oreco Duct Systems Inc—Robert Havai	PO Box 1460, Baldwin Park CA 91706	626-337-8832	R	15*	.1
104	Pickwick Co—Walter Corey	4200 Thomas Dr Sw, Cedar Rapids IA 52404	319-393-7443	R	15*	.1
105	Arthur B Myr Industries Inc—Hugh Marshke	39635 I94 S Service Dr, Belleville MI 48111	734-941-2200	R	15*	.1
106	Ventcon Inc—Todd Hill	500 Enterprise Dr, Allen Park MI 48101	313-336-4000	R	14*	.1
107	A and E Manufacturing Company Inc—Erick Ast	2110 Hartel Ave, Levittown PA 19057	215-943-9460	R	14*	.1
108	Genesis Inc—William Stringfellow	301 Central Ave, Roselle IL 60172	630-894-6634	R	14*	.1
109	Elite Manufacturing Technologies Inc—James Conlon	333 Munroe Dr, Bloomingdale IL 60108	630-351-5757	R	14*	.1
110	Linde Process Plants Inc—Steven Bertone	6100 S Yale Ave Ste 12, Tulsa OK 74136	918-477-1200	R	14*	.1
111	Aero-Data Metal Crafters Inc—Robert Luca	2085 5th Ave, Ronkonkoma NY 11779	631-471-7733	R	14*	.1
112	Dewys Manufacturing Inc—Jon Dewys	15300 8th Ave, Marne MI 49435	616-677-5281	R	14*	.1
113	Quality Fabricator's Inc—Tom Lovelace	1035 W Fullerton Ave, Addison IL 60101	630-543-0540	R	14*	.1
114	Gauthier Industries Inc—Michael Jensen	PO Box 6700, Rochester MN 55903	507-289-0731	R	14*	.1
115	United Metal Products Inc—Steve Kinkel	1920 E Encanto Dr, Tempe AZ 85281	480-968-9550	R	14*	.1
116	Icon Metalcraft Inc—Silvia Mclain	940 Dillon Dr, Wood Dale IL 60191	630-766-5600	R	13*	.1
117	Geater Machining And Manufacturing Co—Jerry Bitterman	901 12th St Ne, Independence IA 50644	319-334-6026	R	13*	.1
118	Electrorack Products Co—R Shew	1443 S Sunkist St, Anaheim CA 92806	714-776-5420	R	13*	.1
119	Quality Fabrication—Pradeep Kumar	9631 Irondale Ave, Chatsworth CA 91311	818-709-8505	R	13*	.1
120	Baldauf Enterprises Inc—Harold Baldauf	1321 S Valley Ctr Dr, Bay City MI 48706	989-686-0350	R	13*	.1
121	Computer Metal Products Corp—Jim Visage	370 E Easy St, Simi Valley CA 93065	805-520-6966	R	13*	.1
122	Metalcraft Technologies Inc—David Grant	498 N 2774 W, Cedar City UT 84721	435-586-3871	R	13*	.1
123	Advanced Metal Components Inc—Doug Brown	PO Box 1327, Swainsboro GA 30401	478-237-8994	R	12*	.1
124	Stoll Metalcraft Inc—Gunter Stoll	24808 Anza Dr, Valencia CA 91355	661-295-0401	R	12*	.1
125	Eastern Sheet Metal Inc—William Stout	8959 Blue Ash Rd, Blue Ash OH 45242	513-793-3440	R	12*	.1
126	Girtz Industries Inc—David Girtz	5262 N E Shafer Dr, Monticello IN 47960	574-278-7510	R	12*	.1
127	Household Utilities Inc—Kurtis Bell	10 E Park Ave, Kiel WI 53042	920-894-2233	R	12*	.1
128	Blackstone Business Enterprises Inc—Daniel Black	100 Blackstone Ave, Jamestown NY 14701	716-665-5410	R	12*	.2
129	Dallas A C Horn and Company Inc—Doug Horn	1269 Majesty Dr, Dallas TX 75247	214-630-3311	R	12*	.1
130	Ruskin Co—Tom Edwards	3900 Dr Greaves Rd, Grandview MO 64030	816-761-7476	S	12*	.1
131	Clark Metal Products Co—Dave Clark	100 Serrell Dr, Blairsville PA 15717	724-459-7550	R	12*	.1
132	Laptalo Enterprises Inc—Jakov Laptalo	2360 Zanker Rd, San Jose CA 95131	408-727-6633	R	12*	.1
133	M and S Industrial Metal Fabricators Inc—Jay Buzzard	5 Commercial Rd, Huntington IN 46750	260-356-0300	R	12*	.1
134	Irving Tool and Manufacturing Company Inc—Harold Stringer	PO Box 461586, Garland TX 75046	972-926-4000	R	12*	.1
135	GTR Manufacturing Corp—James Craig	1 Jonathan Dr, Brockton MA 02301	508-588-3240	R	12*	.1
136	Epic Metals Corp—Donald Landis	11 Talbot Ave, Braddock PA 15104	412-351-3913	R	12*	.1

Note: An asterisk (*) indicates an estimated financial figure. The company type code used is as follows: R = Private, P = Public, S = Private Subsidiary, B = Public Subsidiary, D = Division, J = Joint Venture, I = Investment Fund.

COMPANY RANKINGS BY SALES WITHIN 4-DIGIT SIC

Rank	Company Name—*Executive Officer*	Address, City, State, Zip	Phone	Type	Fin	Empls
137	Industrial Metal Products Company Inc—*Evelyn Hurlbut*	15 Merchant St, Sharon MA 02067	781-536-5132	R	12*	.1
138	Mac Cal Co—*Renee Hall*	1754 Junction Ave Ste, San Jose CA 95112	408-441-1435	R	12*	.1
139	Metal Works Inc—*Frederick Pierce*	24 Industrial Dr, Londonderry NH 03053	603-669-6180	R	12*	.1
140	Greene Technologies Inc—*Carol Rosenkrantz*	PO Box 616, Greene NY 13778	607-656-4166	R	11*	.1
141	Endicott Machine and Tool CoInc—*Patricia Marconi*	101 Delaware Ave, Endicott NY 13760	607-754-7111	R	11*	.1
142	Air Conditioning Products Co—*Philip Mebus*	30350 Ecorse Rd, Romulus MI 48174	734-326-0050	R	11*	.1
143	California Precision Products Inc—*Joe Bean*	6790 Flanders Dr, San Diego CA 92121	858-638-7300	R	11*	.1
144	EK Machine Company Inc—*Gary Errthum*	PO Box 57, Fall River WI 53932	920-484-3700	R	11*	.1
145	Classic Sheet Metal Inc—*Jack Lococo*	1065 Sesame St, Franklin Park IL 60131	630-694-0300	R	11*	.1
146	Metaltech Industries Inc—*Bill Hickey*	20 S Bowen St, Longmont CO 80501	303-651-1953	R	11*	.1
147	Service Metal Fabricators Inc—*Edgar Roesch*	1708 Endeavor Dr, Williamsburg VA 23185	757-887-3500	R	11*	.1
148	Spacesonics Inc—*Ignacio Palomarez*	266 Industrial Rd, San Carlos CA 94070	650-610-0999	R	11*	.1
149	Mech-Tronics Corp—*Eugene Demuro*	1635 N 25th Ave, Melrose Park IL 60160	708-344-9823	R	11*	.1
150	H and F Manufacturing Company Inc—*Richard Farniok*	8949 Zachary Ln N, Maple Grove MN 55369	763-493-5606	R	11*	.1
151	Wyoming Machine Inc—*Traci Tapani*	PO Box 180, Stacy MN 55079	651-462-4156	R	11*	.1
152	Safe-Air Of Illinois Inc—*Frank Ruiz*	1855 S 54th Ave, Cicero IL 60804	708-652-9100	R	11*	.1
153	AL Garey and Associates Inc—*Alan Garey*	2640 N Powerline Rd, Pompano Beach FL 33069	954-975-7992	R	11*	.1
154	Signature Skylights LLC—*Sherri Herbertz*	101 Linel Dr, Mooresville IN 46158	317-831-5314	R	10*	.1
155	Murray's Sheet Metal Company Inc—*Chris Campbell*	3112 7th St, Parkersburg WV 26104	304-422-5431	R	10*	.2
156	Coy Industries Inc—*Michael Coy*	2970 E Maria St, East Rancho Dominguez CA 90221	310-603-2970	R	10*	.1
157	Morris Sheet Metal Corp—*James Morris*	PO Box 8007, Fort Wayne IN 46898	260-497-1300	R	10*	.1
158	H and M Metals LLC—*Amos Chamberlin*	PO Box 969, Amherst NH 03031	603-889-8320	R	10*	.1
159	Hamilton Precision Metals—*Mike Stub*	1780 Rohrerstown Rd, Lancaster PA 17601	717-569-7061	S	10*	.1
160	Super Sky Products Inc—*James Roesing*	10301 N Enterprise Dr, Mequon WI 53092	262-242-2000	S	10*	.1
161	Craftsman Custom Metals LLC—*Eric Siegal*	3838 N River Rd, Schiller Park IL 60176	847-655-0040	R	10*	.1
162	Voss Manufacturing Inc—*Rita Kammerer*	2345 Lockport Rd, Sanborn NY 14132	716-731-5062	R	10*	.1
163	Concise Industries Inc—*Fred Rieble*	1101 Estes Ave, Elk Grove Village IL 60007	847-439-4550	R	10*	.1
164	Lapin Sheet Metal Co—*Ronald Lapin*	3825 Gardenia Ave, Orlando FL 32839	407-423-9897	R	10*	.1
165	Dj Acquisition Management Corp—*Donald Cornwell*	6364 Dean Pkwy, Ontario NY 14519	585-265-3000	R	10*	.1
166	Cmi Champion LLC—*Anne Fox*	6021 N Galena Rd, Peoria IL 61614	309-685-1031	R	9*	.1
167	Data Matique Properties LP—*C Theis*	2110 Sherwin St, Garland TX 75041	972-272-3446	R	9*	.1
168	Pemberton Fabricators Inc—*Robert Murnan*	PO Box 157, Rancocas NJ 08073	609-267-0922	R	9*	<.1
169	A and B Precision Metals Inc—*Orval Arnett*	13715 Mount Anderson S, Reno NV 89506	775-323-2546	R	9*	.1
170	Anco Products Inc—*Ray Plagens Jr*	2500 S 17th St, Elkhart IN 46517	574-293-5574	S	9*	.1
171	Kal Tool And Die Company Inc—*Allan Liwush*	657 Basket Rd, Webster NY 14580	585-265-4310	R	9*	.1
172	Southern Fabricators Inc—*Kenneth Carpenter*	PO Box 97, Polkton NC 28135	704-272-7615	R	9*	.1
173	Ag Machining and Industries Inc—*Arliss Gelwick*	4607 S Windermere St, Englewood CO 80110	303-783-0081	R	8*	.1
174	Quality Fabrication and Design Inc—*Alex Pier*	955 Freeport Pkwy Ste, Coppell TX 75019	972-304-3266	R	8*	.1
175	Jack A Farrior Inc—*Jack Farrior*	PO Box 839, Farmville NC 27828	252-753-2020	R	8*	.1
176	Electro-Space Fabricators Inc—*William Straccia*	300 W High St, Topton PA 19562	610-682-7181	R	8*	.1
177	Metalcraft Enterprises Inc	202 Industrial Dr, New Haven MO 63068	573-237-3016	S	8*	.1
178	Delta Metals Incorporated—*Benjamin Wells*	PO Box 1706, Savannah GA 31402	912-234-8201	R	8*	.2
179	Semifab Inc—*Glenn Roberson*	5853 Rue Ferrari Rm 20, San Jose CA 95138	408-754-8510	R	8*	.1
180	Mack Hils Inc—*Mack Hils*	PO Box 856, Moberly MO 65270	660-263-7444	R	8*	.1
181	Mjm Manufacturing Inc—*Michael Mijares*	PO Box 5427, Hialeah FL 33014	305-620-2020	R	8*	.1
182	Kentuckiana Curb Company Inc—*Al Fiorini*	2716 Grassland Dr, Louisville KY 40299	502-491-9880	R	8*	.1
183	Metalfab Inc—*William Westdyk*	PO Box 9, Vernon NJ 07462	973-764-2000	R	8*	<.1
184	American Metal Fab Inc—*John Crowell*	55515 Franklin Dr, Three Rivers MI 49093	269-279-5108	R	7*	.1
185	Industrial Ventilation Inc—*Frank Bushman*	723 E Karcher Rd, Nampa ID 83687	208-463-6305	R	7*	.1
186	Cianbro Corp—*Malcolm Cianchette*	PO Box 1000, Pittsfield ME 04967	207-487-3311	R	7*	.1
187	Andrews Laser Works Corp—*David Schneider*	100 Andrews Way, Wilder KY 41071	859-292-8881	R	7*	.1
188	Corry Contract Inc—*Douglas Kafferlin*	21 Maple Ave, Corry PA 16407	814-665-8221	R	7*	.1
189	Detronic Industries Inc—*James Carne*	PO Box 608, Sterling Heights MI 48311	586-977-5660	R	7*	.1
190	Precision Metal Industries Inc—*Gregory Wilson*	1408 Sw 8th St, Pompano Beach FL 33069	954-942-6303	R	7*	.1
191	Independent Sheet Metal Company Inc—*Edward Rebeneck*	PO Box 649, Hawthorne NJ 07507	973-423-1150	R	7*	.1
192	Westport Precision LLC—*John Delvecchio*	280 Hathaway Dr, Stratford CT 06615	203-378-2175	R	7*	.1
193	Kelly Fabricators Corp—*Jeffery Deye*	PO Box 39126, Louisville KY 40233	502-964-5407	R	7*	.1
194	Metro-Fabricating LLC—*Dan Boyd*	1650 Tech Dr, Bay City MI 48706	989-667-8100	R	7*	.1
195	Mitchell Metal Products Inc—*Dewitte Belk*	PO Box 789, Kosciusko MS 39090	662-289-7110	R	7*	.1
196	San Diego Precision Machining Inc—*William Matteson*	9375 Ruffin Ct, San Diego CA 92123	858-499-0379	R	7*	.1
197	Jamestown Advanced Products Corp—*Wendi Lodestro*	2855 Girts Rd, Jamestown NY 14701	716-483-3406	R	7*	<.1
198	Bmg of Kansas Inc—*Joe Brenneman*	PO Box 698, Hesston KS 67062	620-327-4038	R	7*	.1
199	Alcoa Building Products Inc—*John Wayne*	1590 Omega Dr, Pittsburgh PA 15205	937-497-7008	S	6*	<.1
200	Hart Design and Manufacturing—*John Adams*	1940 Radisson St, Green Bay WI 54302	920-468-5927	R	6*	<.1
201	Recoating-West Inc—*Brian Hope*	6200 Angelo Ct, Loomis CA 95650	916-652-8290	R	6*	<.1
202	Westfield Sheet Metal Works Inc—*Campbell Johnstone*	PO Box 128, Kenilworth NJ 07033	908-276-5500	R	6*	<.1
203	Qmf Metal and Electronic Solutions Inc—*Tina Rierson*	324 Berry Garden Rd, Kernersville NC 27284	336-996-5570	R	6*	.1
204	A G Miller Company Inc—*Frederick Miller*	53 Batavia St, Springfield MA 01109	413-732-9297	R	6*	<.1
205	Castle Industries Incorporated Of California—*Jerry Valliere*	601 S Dupont Ave, Ontario CA 91761	909-390-0899	S	5*	<.1
206	COW Industries Inc—*John Burns*	1875 Progress Ave, Columbus OH 43207	614-443-6537	R	5*	<.1
207	Taylor Metal Works and Pipe Company Inc—*Thomas Taylor*	215 W Hwy 365, Port Arthur TX 77640	409-736-3555	R	5*	.1
208	Specialty Tool and Machine Company Inc—*David Weyler*	3331 Gilmore Industria, Louisville KY 40213	502-969-8609	R	5*	.1
209	G B Manufacturing Co—*Nelson Reyes*	PO Box 8, Delta OH 43515	419-822-5323	R	5*	.1
210	Fabrication Services Inc—*Robert Oleson*	1902 E 22nd St, Little Rock AR 72206	501-375-6581	R	5*	<.1
211	Missouri Equipment Co—*Gregory Klapp*	2222 N 9th St, Saint Louis MO 63102	314-621-0144	R	5*	<.1
212	Weaver and Sons Inc—*Dyron Overton*	1200 Ward Ave, Talladega AL 35160	256-362-3614	R	5*	<.1
213	Fashion Inc—*Lonnie King*	PO Box 1050, Ottawa KS 66067	785-242-8111	R	5*	<.1
214	Precision Machine and Metal Fabrication Inc—*C Michael*	PO Box 7006, Tupelo MS 38802	662-844-4606	R	5*	<.1
215	Helmick Corp—*Louis Helmick*	PO Box 71, Fairmont WV 26555	304-366-3520	R	5*	.1
216	New Mexico Metal Systems LLC—*Mark Martinez*	PO Box 91630, Albuquerque NM 87199	505-343-9230	R	5*	<.1
217	Holbrook Manufacturing Inc—*Avis Holbrook*	PO Box 95, Franklin IN 46131	317-736-9387	R	5*	<.1
218	Vicart Precision Fabricators Inc—*Arthur Handshy*	4101 Leap Rd, Hilliard OH 43026	614-771-0080	R	5*	<.1
219	OEM Sales Inc—*Edward Giannantonio*	3 Lattimore Ct, Freehold NJ 07728	732-780-5167	R	5*	<.1
220	Excel Machine and Fabrication Inc—*Joseph Johnson*	1230 Ridgely St, Baltimore MD 21230	410-576-9480	R	4*	<.1
221	Western Systems and Fabrication Inc—*Mark Choate*	911 N Thierman Rd, Spokane Valley WA 99212	509-922-1300	R	4*	<.1
222	O and A Manufacturing Inc—*Fred Salzmann*	503 S Nine Mound Rd, Verona WI 53593	608-845-8190	R	4*	<.1
223	AJ Oster West Inc—*Richard Berg*	275 W Natick Rd Ste 50, Warwick RI 02886	401-736-2600	S	4*	<.1
224	B-C-D Metal Products Inc—*Karin Carlson*	PO Box 667, Malden MA 02148	781-397-9922	R	4*	<.1
225	William Smith Enterprises Inc—*John Ryzewic*	PO Box 127, Coopers Mills ME 04341	207-549-3103	R	4*	<.1
226	HLH Inc—*Bruce Guyette*	50 Optical Ave, Keene NH 03431	603-352-1667	R	4*	<.1

Rank	Company Name—*Executive Officer*	Address, City, State, Zip	Phone	Type	Fin	Empls
227	D and R Specialties Inc—*Raymond Pasket*	7400 Fm 1774 Rd, Navasota TX 77868	936-873-2947	R	4*	<.1
228	Alloy Welding Corp—*John Troccoli*	2033 Janice Ave, Melrose Park IL 60160	708-345-6756	R	4*	<.1
229	Keystone Custom Fabricators Inc—*Bret Holden*	108 Atlantic Ave, Elizabeth PA 15037	412-384-9131	R	4*	<.1
230	Darby Metalworks Inc—*Steven Darby*	PO Box 73, Anderson SC 29622	864-225-6906	R	4*	<.1
231	Precision Products Machine and Fab Inc—*Jewell Miles*	PO Box 819, Hazlehurst GA 31539	912-375-9159	R	4*	<.1
232	Valley Precision Metal Product—*Howard Vermillion*	27771 Ave Hopkins, Santa Clarita CA 91355	661-607-0100	R	4*	<.1
233	Versatile Manufacturing Inc—*Dick Ulrich*	4021 Ne 5th Ter, Oakland Park FL 33334	954-561-8083	R	4*	<.1
234	Span-O-Matic Inc—*Wolfgang Arnold*	825 Columbia St, Brea CA 92821	714-256-4700	R	4*	.1
235	Progressive Tool And Manufacturing Co—*Wendell Zwart*	PO Box 668, Pine Island MN 55963	507-356-8345	R	4*	<.1
236	Multimetal Products Corp—*Kenneth Marsch*	3965 Grove Ave, Gurnee IL 60031	847-662-9110	R	4*	<.1
237	West Coast Fab Inc—*Thomas Nelson*	700 S 32nd St, Richmond CA 94804	510-529-0177	R	4*	<.1
238	Universal Metalcraft Inc—*Donald Haines*	4215 W 750 N, Decatur IN 46733	260-547-4457	R	3*	<.1
239	A and C Welding Inc—*Carl Lamancusa*	80 Cuyahoga Falls Indu, Peninsula OH 44264	330-762-4777	R	3*	<.1
240	Ed-K Machine Inc—*Edward Krug*	6400 Falls Rd, Baltimore MD 21209	410-823-1683	R	3*	<.1
241	Rayco Burial Products Inc—*Geza Dala*	1601 Raymond Ave, Monrovia CA 91016	626-357-1996	R	3*	<.1
242	L and L Industries Inc—*Bobby Lowery*	500 Industrial Dr Ne, White GA 30184	770-382-2861	R	3*	<.1
243	Excalibur Machine And Sheet Metal Inc—*John Gonzales*	208 W Buchanan St Ste, Colorado Springs CO 80907	719-520-5404	R	3*	<.1
244	Suppliers To Wholesalers Inc—*Charles Witherspoon*	PO Box 31548, Charlotte NC 28231	704-375-7406	R	3*	<.1
245	Vlj Inc—*Vicki Lewis*	116 Regency Dr, Wylie TX 75098	972-442-4673	R	3*	<.1
246	B-R-O-T Inc—*Kenneth Ott*	4730 Briar Rd, Cleveland OH 44135	216-267-5335	R	3*	<.1
247	Parks Metal Products Inc—*Loren Parks*	PO Box 5669, Beaverton OR 97006	503-591-7272	R	3*	<.1
248	American Precision Inc—*Keith Archambeau*	20615 Plummer St, Chatsworth CA 91311	818-718-6110	R	3*	<.1
249	Noel Systems Inc—*Frank Borgsmiller*	8310 Shell Rd Ste 106, Richmond VA 23237	804-743-8108	R	3*	<.1
250	Air Duct Systems Manufacturing Co—*Mahmood Khawaja*	1309 Ashland St, Houston TX 77008	713-869-6500	R	3*	<.1
251	Merit Ends Inc—*Spencer Brog*	620 Clark Ave, Pittsburg CA 94565	925-432-6900	R	3*	<.1
252	Metal Forms Corp—*Thomas Miller*	3334 N Booth St, Milwaukee WI 53212	414-964-4550	R	3*	<.1
253	Apahouser Inc—*Glenn Prouty*	40 Hayes Memorial Dr, Marlborough MA 01752	508-786-0309	R	3*	.1
254	Polaris Manufacturing Inc—*Michael Bontatibus*	103 Cedar Ave, Marysville WA 98270	360-653-7676	R	3*	<.1
255	Alan Manufacturing Inc—*Richard Bluestone*	PO Box 24875, Cleveland OH 44124	330-262-8077	R	3*	<.1
256	Kustom Machine Inc—*Nancy Janneck*	PO Box 146, Oakes ND 58474	701-742-3188	R	3*	<.1
257	Crown Products Inc—*David Carr*	177 Newport Dr Ste A, San Marcos CA 92069	760-471-1188	R	3*	<.1
258	Johnson-Nash Metal Products Inc—*Craig Johnson*	9265 Seward Rd, Fairfield OH 45014	513-874-7022	R	3*	<.1
259	RedyRef Division-Dawnex Industries Inc—*William Pymm*	38-61 11th St, Long Island City NY 11101	718-784-3690	D	3*	<.1
260	Jenfab Inc—*Phillip Bowen*	1201 Commerce Ctr Dr, Covington VA 24426	540-862-4200	R	3*	<.1
261	Buhrt Engineering and Construction Inc—*Dennis Buhrt*	27 E 250 N, Warsaw IN 46582	574-267-3720	R	3*	<.1
262	Gieske Custom Metal Fabricators Inc—*Cliff Anderson*	PO Box 414116, Kansas City MO 64141	816-471-2300	R	3*	<.1
263	Imco Inc—*A Davis*	858 N Lenola Rd Bldg 1, Moorestown NJ 08057	856-235-7540	R	3*	<.1
264	M-Pact Corp—*Toul Ramberg*	4090 94th Ln Ne, Minneapolis MN 55449	763-428-8280	R	3*	<.1
265	Copp Industrial Manufacturing Inc—*Larry Marvin*	2837 Metropolitan Pl, Pomona CA 91767	909-593-7448	R	3*	<.1
266	General Aviation and Electronics Manufacturing Company Inc—*John Baker*	PO Box 2245, South Hackensack NJ 07606	201-487-1700	R	3*	<.1
267	Zomeworks Corp—*Stephen Baer*	PO Box 25805, Albuquerque NM 87125	505-242-5354	R	3*	<.1
268	Lafayette Quality Products Inc—*Ron Kuntz*	PO Box 5827, Lafayette IN 47903	765-447-3106	R	3*	<.1
269	Samuel Clark—*Samuel Clark*	PO Box 119, New Albany OH 43054	614-855-2263	R	3*	<.1
270	Buww Coverings Inc—*Phil Zeilinger*	4462 Boeing Dr, Rockford IL 61109	815-962-2899	R	3*	<.1
271	Fab-Tech Inc—*Kevin Teerec*	12 N 25th St, Van Buren AR 72956	479-474-1788	R	3*	<.1
272	Pathfinder Industries Inc—*Marsha Ives*	117 N 3rd St, Fulton NY 13069	315-593-2483	R	3*	<.1
273	Pico Metal Products Inc—*Gary Cogorno*	10640 Springdale Ave, Santa Fe Springs CA 90670	562-944-0626	R	3*	<.1
274	Loyal Manufacturing Corp—*Ronald Lambert*	1121 S Shortridge Rd, Indianapolis IN 46239	317-359-3185	R	2*	<.1
275	De La Torre Sheet Metal Manufacturing Company Inc—*David De La Torre*	4081 Shilling Way, Dallas TX 75237	214-330-8334	R	2*	<.1
276	Cabletek Wiring Products Inc—*Stan Leonowigh*	1150 Taylor St, Elyria OH 44035	440-365-3889	R	2*	<.1
277	Lime Engineering Inc—*Edward Ruminski*	16840 Joleen Way Ste F, Morgan Hill CA 95037	408-779-5800	R	2*	<.1
278	Biltrite Metal Products Inc—*Linda Thomas*	PO Box 97, Leland IL 60531	815-495-2211	R	2*	<.1
279	RPS Engineering Inc—*Richard Stanis*	PO Box 5186, Elgin IL 60121	847-931-1950	R	2*	<.1
280	R and D Precision Inc—*William Harkness*	63 N Cherry St Ste 1, Wallingford CT 06492	203-284-3396	R	2*	<.1
281	Vista Manufacturing Co—*Dick Gredell*	1307 Central Ave, Kansas City KS 66102	913-342-4939	R	2*	<.1
282	Dye Sheet Metal Products Inc—*William Greene*	467 Hull Rd, Athens GA 30601	706-548-1101	R	2*	<.1
283	R F Higginbotham Inc—*Robert Higginbotham*	8723 N Lamar Blvd, Austin TX 78753	512-836-9654	R	2*	<.1
284	Scamardo Metal Fabricators Inc—*Charles Scamardo*	422 S 9th St, Fort Smith AR 72901	479-783-1162	R	2*	<.1
285	Roar Industries Inc—*Guile Wood*	120 Jeffrey Ave, Holliston MA 01746	508-429-5952	R	2*	<.1
286	Trola-Dyne Inc—*Robert Kirkhoff*	7 Interchange Pl, York PA 17406	717-840-1770	R	2*	<.1
287	Lund Equipment Company Inc—*John Skeel*	PO Box 213, Bath OH 44210	330-659-4800	R	2*	<.1
288	Adler Norco Inc—*Leonard Degand*	2222 Commonwealth Ave, North Chicago IL 60064	847-473-3600	R	2*	<.1
289	Pro-Fab Metals Inc—*Mark Wetton*	139 Franklin Rd, Russellville KY 42276	270-726-2381	R	2*	<.1
290	Orion Industries—*John Theisen*	33926 9th Ave S, Federal Way WA 98003	253-661-7805	R	2*	.1
291	California Hydroforming Company Inc—*David Bonafede*	850 Lawson St, City Of Industry CA 91748	626-912-0036	R	2*	<.1
292	Master Metal Products Co—*Lee Henderson*	495 Emory St, San Jose CA 95110	408-275-1210	R	2*	<.1
293	Modern Metalcraft Inc—*John Peak*	1257 E Wackerly Rd, Midland MI 48642	989-835-3291	R	2*	<.1
294	Empire Ventilation Equipment Company Inc—*George Taylor*	35 39 Vernon Blvd, Long Island City NY 11106	718-728-2143	R	2*	<.1
295	Ajax Metal Products Inc—*Ronald Ohm*	PO Box 240057, Milwaukee WI 53224	262-242-7373	R	1*	<.1
296	Meyers Sheet Metal Box Inc—*James Liang*	447 10th St, San Francisco CA 94103	415-431-9934	R	1*	<.1
297	Johnson Industrial Sheet Metal Inc—*Curtiss Johnson*	PO Box 15859, Sacramento CA 95852	916-927-8244	R	1*	<.1
298	Custom and Precision Products Inc—*Diamante Dente*	PO Box 5446, Hamden CT 06518	203-281-0818	R	1*	<.1
299	Southland Precision Inc—*Larry Graves*	5525 Hwy 431 S, Brownsboro AL 35741	256-533-0910	R	1*	<.1
300	Stowers Manufacturing Company Inc—*Danny Stowers*	PO Box A, Gadsden AL 35904	256-547-8647	R	1*	<.1
301	RWE Inc—*Eric Whittenburg*	PO Box 431, Putnam CT 06260	860-928-1199	R	1*	<.1
302	North Industries Inc—*James North*	PO Box 16326, Seattle WA 98116	206-767-4422	R	<1*	<.1
303	Southeastern Machine and Tool Inc—*Susan Rothecker*	7300 ACC Blvd, Raleigh NC 27617	919-782-4804	R	N/A	.2

TOTALS: SIC 3444 Sheet Metal Work
	Companies: 303				7,414	34.5

3446 Architectural Metal Work

Rank	Company Name—*Executive Officer*	Address, City, State, Zip	Phone	Type	Fin	Empls
1	Harsco Corp—*Salvatore D Fazzolari*	350 Poplar Church Rd, Camp Hill PA 17011	717-763-7064	P	3,303	19.7
2	Brand Energy and Infrastructure Services LLC—*Paul T Wood*	1325 Cobb Internationl, Kennesaw GA 30144	678-285-1400	R	723*	2.5
3	Chicago Metallic Corp—*Sandra Wilson*	4849 S Austin Ave, Chicago IL 60638	708-563-4600	R	524*	1.1
4	City Store Gates Manufacturing Corp—*Vincent R Greco Sr*	15-20 129th St, College Point NY 11356		R	200*	.6
5	Bleacher Sales Co—*William Gilbreath*	PO Box 8508, Houston TX 77249	713-869-3491	R	198*	.7
6	Hart and Cooley Inc—*Bernard Roy*	5030 Corporate Exchang, Grand Rapids MI 49512	616-656-8200	S	154	2.0

Note: An asterisk (*) indicates an estimated financial figure. The company type code used is as follows: R = Private, P = Public, S = Private Subsidiary, B = Public Subsidiary, D = Division, J = Joint Venture, I = Investment Fund.

COMPANY RANKINGS BY SALES WITHIN 4-DIGIT SIC

Rank	Company Name—*Executive Officer*	Address, City, State, Zip	Phone	Type	Fin	Empls
7	Patent Construction Systems—*Robert Safier* Harsco Corp	1 Mack Centre Dr, Paramus NJ 07652	201-261-5600	D	77*	.7
8	Forms And Surfaces Inc—*J Flannery*	30 Pine St, Pittsburgh PA 15223	412-781-9003	R	60*	.3
9	Spider Staging Corp—*Scott Fine*	365 Upland Dr, Seattle WA 98188	206-574-0292	D	56*	.3
10	Ameristar Fence Products Inc—*Edward Gibbs*	1555 N Mingo Rd, Tulsa OK 74116	918-835-0898	R	46*	.6
11	Tecnico Corp—*Michael Torrech*	831 Industrial Ave, Chesapeake VA 23324	757-545-4013	R	39*	.6
12	Tarter Gate Wood Products Inc—*Donald Tarter*	PO Box 10, Dunnville KY 42528	606-787-7455	R	38*	.6
13	Bil-Jax Inc—*Jeff Ott*	125 Taylor Pkwy, Archbold OH 43502	419-445-8915	R	38*	.2
14	Jerith Manufacturing Company Inc—*Bruce Schwartz*	14400 Mcnulty Rd, Philadelphia PA 19154	215-676-4068	R	33*	.2
15	Hayes Retail Services LLC—*David Culliton*	7700 N Hayes Dr, Park City KS 67147	316-838-8000	R	30*	.2
16	Ohio Gratings Inc—*John Bartley*	PO Box 80489, Canton OH 44708	330-477-6707	R	29*	.2
17	Klemp Corp (Chicago Illinois)—*Robert Van Geertry*	1115 E 5000 N Rd, Bourbonnais IL 60914	815-932-1200	R	28*	.2
18	Metpar Corp—*John Fallarino*	PO Box 1873, Westbury NY 11590	516-333-2600	R	25*	.2
19	Swanton Welding and Machining Company Inc—*Norman Zeiter*	407 Broadway Ave, Swanton OH 43558	419-826-4816	R	25*	.2
20	Ecolite Manufacturing Co—*Ron Caferro*	PO Box 11366, Spokane Valley WA 99211	509-922-8888	R	24*	.2
21	Won-Door Corp—*Ronald Smart*	1865 S 3480 W, Salt Lake City UT 84104	801-973-7500	R	24*	.2
22	Standard Steel Specialty Co—*Robert E Conley*	PO Box 20, Beaver Falls PA 15010	724-846-7600	S	22*	.1
23	Lane Supply Inc—*Ronnie Jones*	120 Fairview St, Arlington TX 76010	817-261-9116	R	18*	.1
24	Dixie Metal Products Inc—*J Schnorr*	442 Sw 54th Ct, Ocala FL 34474	352-873-2554	R	18*	.1
25	Morton Manufacturing Co—*William Morton*	700 Liberty Dr, Libertyville IL 60048	847-362-5400	R	17*	.1
26	Lawrence Metal Products Inc—*Jeremy Williman*	PO Box 400, Bay Shore NY 11706	631-666-0300	R	16*	.1
27	Bennington Iron Works Inc—*Curtis Morin*	PO Box 798, Bennington VT 05201	802-442-3145	R	15*	.1
28	Miscellaneous Metals Inc—*Kenneth Mc Combs*	PO Box 3818, Frederick MD 21705	301-695-8820	R	14*	.1
29	MM Systems Corp—*Mike Attaway*	PO Box 98, Pendergrass GA 30567	706-824-7500	R	14*	.1
30	Lavi Industries—*Gavriel Lavi*	27810 Ave Hopkins, Valencia CA 91355	661-219-3131	R	13*	.1
31	Livers Bronze Co—*Richard Livers*	4621 E 75th Ter, Kansas City MO 64132	816-300-2828	R	13*	.1
32	Manufab Inc—*Walter Morton*	129 E 3rd St, Kenner LA 70062	504-466-2368	R	13*	.1
33	Airflex Industrial Inc—*Jonathan Fogelman*	965 Conklin St, Farmingdale NY 11735	631-752-1219	R	13*	.1
34	Airolite Company LLC—*Bill Lampkin*	PO Box 410, Schofield WI 54476	740-373-7676	R	12*	.1
35	Wooster Products Inc—*G Arora*	PO Box 6005, Wooster OH 44691	330-264-2844	R	12*	.1
36	Shoemaker Manufacturing Co—*Jerry Hein*	104 N Montgomery Ave, Cle Elum WA 98922	509-674-4414	R	10*	.1
37	Metallic Products Corp—*Daryl Wendt*	7777 Hollister St, Houston TX 77040	713-856-9696	R	9*	.1
38	Thompson Fabricating LLC—*Spencer Turner*	PO Box 170160, Birmingham AL 35217	205-841-0441	R	8*	.1
39	Safespan Inc—*Lambros Apostolopoulos*	252 Fillmore Ave, Tonawanda NY 14150	716-694-1100	R	8*	.1
40	Universal Manufacturing Corp—*Robert Carbeau*	PO Box 220, Zelienople PA 16063	724-452-8300	R	8*	.1
41	Ryan Iron Works Inc—*Howard Shea*	PO Box 159, Raynham MA 02767	508-822-8001	R	8*	.1
42	Stairways Inc—*John Anderson*	4166 Pinemont Dr, Houston TX 77018	713-680-3110	R	6*	.1
43	Wifco Steel Products Inc—*Fred Ade*	PO Box 1325, Hutchinson KS 67504	620-543-2827	R	6*	<.1
44	S and S Welding Inc—*Thomas Stucke*	PO Box 1505, Kent WA 98035	253-872-3833	R	5*	<.1
45	Mack Iron Works Company Inc—*John Bacon*	124 Warren St, Sandusky OH 44870	419-626-6225	R	5*	<.1
46	Overly Manufacturing Co—*Timothy Reese*	PO Box 70, Greensburg PA 15601	724-834-7300	R	4*	<.1
47	Kesclo Financial Inc—*Charles Close*	150 W 6th St Ste 205, San Pedro CA 90731	310-604-8420	R	4*	<.1
48	Sky Climber LLC	1800 Pittsburgh Dr, Delaware OH 43015	740-203-3900	R	4*	<.1
49	Automated Equipment Co—*Jerry Alahadeff*	10847 E Marginal Way S, Tukwila WA 98168	206-767-9080	R	4*	<.1
50	H and H Farm Products Manufacturing Inc—*Leamon Havens*	1951 Jones St, Bolivar MO 65613	417-777-6636	R	3*	<.1
51	Delta Ironworks—*Marcy Charleworth*	PO Box 10580, Salinas CA 93912	831 663 1190	D	2*	<.1

TOTALS: SIC 3446 Architectural Metal Work

Companies: 51					5,974	33.4

3448 Prefabricated Metal Buildings

Rank	Company Name—*Executive Officer*	Address, City, State, Zip	Phone	Type	Fin	Empls
1	Kingspan Insulated Panels North America Inc—*Russell Shiels*	725 Summerhill Dr, Deland FL 32724	386-626-6789	R	4,496*	.4
2	Mid-West Steel Building Co—*Ed Kohutek* NCI Building Systems Inc	PO Box 40220, Houston TX 77240	713-466-7788	D	2,011*	3.6
3	NCI Building Systems Inc—*Norman C Chambers*	PO Box 692055, Houston TX 77269	281-897-7788	P	960	3.6
4	Butler Manufacturing Co—*Patrick Finan*	PO Box 419917, Kansas City MO 64141	816-968-3000	S	796*	4.3
5	Dyson-Kissner-Moran Corp—*Robert R Dyson*	565 5th Ave 4th Fl, New York NY 10017	212-661-4600	R	767	4.5
6	American Buildings Co—*Larry Hughes*	PO Box 698, Eufaula AL 36072	334-687-2032	R	441*	2.9
7	Mcelroy Metal Mill Inc—*Ian Mcelroy*	PO Box 1148, Shreveport LA 71163	318-747-8000	R	420*	.8
8	Schult Homes Corp	221 US Hwy 20, Middlebury IN 46540	574-825-5881	S	348	2.6
9	Whirlwind Holding Company Inc—*Jack Sturdivant*	PO Box 75280, Houston TX 77234	713-946-7140	R	160*	.4
10	Robertson-Ceco Ii Corp—*Norman Chambers*	10943 N Sam Houston Pk, Houston TX 77064	281-897-7788	R	141*	1.7
11	Four Seasons Solar Products LLC—*Patrick Marron*	5005 Veterans Memorial, Holbrook NY 11741	631-563-4000	R	122*	.2
12	Arrow Shed LLC—*Barbara Capo*	PO Box 928, Wayne NJ 07474	973-696-6900	R	100*	.4
13	Miller Building Systems Inc—*Rick J Bedell*	PO Box 1283, Elkhart IN 46515	574-295-2114	S	71	.5
14	Satellite Industries Inc—*Todd Hilde*	2530 Xenium Ln N Ste 1, Minneapolis MN 55441	763-553-1900	R	65*	.1
15	Metal Sales Manufacturing Corp	545 S 3rd St Ste 200, Louisville KY 40202	502-855-4300	S	63*	.2
16	A and S Building Systems LP—*Denny McDeavitt* NCI Building Systems Inc	PO Box 53, Caryville TN 37714	865-426-2141	D	46*	.3
17	Delta Scientific Corp—*Harry D Dickinson*	40355 Delta Ln, Palmdale CA 93551	661-575-1100	R	43*	.2
18	United Structures Of America Inc—*F Drake*	PO Box 60069, Houston TX 77205	281-442-8247	R	42*	.6
19	Trachte Building Systems Inc—*Jim Mastrangelo*	314 Wilburn Rd, Sun Prairie WI 53590	608-837-7899	R	35*	.2
20	Aci Building Systems Inc—*W Watkins*	PO Box 1316, Batesville MS 38606	662-563-4574	R	28*	.2
21	Protect Controls Inc—*Don Davis*	303 Little York Rd, Houston TX 77076	713-691-5183	R	25*	.1
22	Dean Steel Buildings Inc—*Charles Dean*	2929 Industrial Ave, Fort Myers FL 33901	239-334-1051	R	25*	.1
23	Industrial Acoustics Company Inc—*Kenneth Delasho*	1160 Commerce Ave, Bronx NY 10462	718-931-8000	R	24*	.2
24	Trident Building Systems Inc—*Carl Petrat*	2812 Tallevast Rd, Sarasota FL 34243	941-755-7073	R	24*	.2
25	Jack Walters And Sons Corp—*Bruce Lindsey*	PO Box 388, Allenton WI 53002	262-629-5521	R	24*	.2
26	Temo Inc—*Giovanni Vitale*	20400 Hall Rd, Clinton Township MI 48038	586-286-0410	R	24*	.2
27	Burley Corp—*David Davenport*	754 N Burleson Blvd, Burleson TX 76028	817-295-1128	R	23*	.5
28	Mueller Inc—*David Davenport* Burley Corp	1913 Hutchins Ave, Ballinger TX 76821	325-365-3555	S	22*	.4
29	Rom Acquisition Corp—*Jeff Hupke*	6800 E 163rd St, Belton MO 64012	816-318-8000	R	21*	.1
30	Betco Inc—*Sam Sabri*	PO Box 1650, Statesville NC 28687	704-872-2999	R	17*	.1
31	Ruffin Building Systems Inc—*Shelton Ruffin*	6914 Hwy 2, Oak Grove LA 71263	318-428-2305	R	16*	.1
32	Porter Corp—*William Porter*	4240 136th Ave, Holland MI 49424	616-399-1963	R	16*	.1
33	Coeur D'alene Builders Supply Inc—*Fabian Andres*	655 W Clayton Ave, Coeur D Alene ID 83815	208-667-6481	R	14*	.1
34	Mcgee Corp—*Richard Mc Gee*	PO Box 1375, Matthews NC 28106	704-882-1500	R	14*	.1
35	Smithbilt Industries Inc—*Donald Smith*	1061 Us Hwy 92 W, Auburndale FL 33823	863-665-3767	R	13*	.1
36	Huskey Truss and Building Supply Inc—*James Huskey*	PO Box 682023, Franklin TN 37068	615-791-0100	R	13*	.1
37	Goldin Metals Inc—*Alan Goldin*	12440 Seaway Rd Ste 1, Gulfport MS 39503	228-896-6216	R	13*	.1

Rank	Company Name—*Executive Officer*	Address, City, State, Zip	Phone	Type	Fin	Empls
38	John L Conley Inc—*Tom Conley*	4344 Mission Blvd, Montclair CA 91763	909-627-0981	R	12*	.1
39	Bigbee Steel Buildings Inc—*Roy Rudolph*	PO Box 2314, Muscle Shoals AL 35662	256-383-7322	R	12*	.1
40	Bebco Industries Inc—*B Baucom*	PO Box 128, Hitchcock TX 77563	409-935-5743	R	12*	.1
41	Lark Builders Inc—*Robert Moore*	PO Box 629, Vidalia GA 30475	912-538-1888	R	12*	.1
42	Chief Industries Inc—*Robert Eihusen*	PO Box 2078, Grand Island NE 68802	308-389-7200	R	10*	1.6
43	Tj Truss Corp—*James White*	PO Box 13823, Fort Pierce FL 34979	772-466-3388	R	10*	.1
44	Porta-Fab Corp—*Wayne McGee*	PO Box 1084, Chesterfield MO 63006	636-537-5555	R	9*	.1
45	Coast To Coast Carports Inc—*Venancio Torres*	PO Box 100, Knoxville AR 72845	208-436-3157	R	7*	.1
46	Heritage Manufacturing Inc—*Rod Tompkins*	PO Box 37, Wayne NE 68787	402-375-4770	R	7*	.1
47	Akerue Industries LLC—*Richard Wiesek*	90 Mcmillen Rd, Antioch IL 60002	847-395-3300	R	7*	.1
48	Acoustical Solutions Inc—*Michael Binns*	2420 Grenoble Rd, Richmond VA 23294	804-346-8350	R	7*	<.1
49	Precision Quincy Corp—*John Guanci*	1625 W Lake Shore Dr, Woodstock IL 60098	815-338-2675	R	6*	.1
50	AFC Finishing Systems—*Carl Hagan*	250 Airport Pkwy, Oroville CA 95965	530-533-8907	R	5*	<.1
51	True Precision Machining LLC—*Win Walstad*	601 Pine Ave Ste A, Goleta CA 93117	805-964-4545	R	4*	<.1
52	T and S Equipment Co—*Ralph Trine*	PO Box 496, Angola IN 46703	260-665-9521	R	4*	.3
53	Belden Plastics Inc—*John Johnson*	2582 Long Lake Rd, Saint Paul MN 55113	651-636-1330	R	3*	<.1
54	Dade Engineering Corp—*Joanne Goodstein*	558 W 18th St, Hialeah FL 33010	305-885-2766	R	2*	<.1

TOTALS: SIC 3448 Prefabricated Metal Buildings
Companies: 54   11,609   32.9

3449 Miscellaneous Metal Work

Rank	Company Name—*Executive Officer*	Address, City, State, Zip	Phone	Type	Fin	Empls
1	Manufacturers Industrial Group LLC—*Andre L Gist*	659 Natchez Trace Dr, Lexington TN 38351	731-967-0001	R	180*	.9
2	Barker Steel LLC—*Susan Durand*	55 Sumner St, Milford MA 01757	508-473-8484	R	50*	.6
3	TechPrecision Corp—*James C Molianaro*	1 Bella Dr, Westminster MA 01473	978-874-0591	P	32	.2
4	Howard Finishing LLC—*Keith Avallone*	32565 Dequindre Rd, Madison Heights MI 48071	248-588-9050	R	28*	.2
5	Millennium Steel Services LLC—*Henry Jackson*	300 E 350S, Princeton IN 47670	812-385-1122	R	27*	.1
6	United Fixtures Holdings—*Dan Wilson*	4300 Quality Dr, South Bend IN 46628		R	26*	.1
7	Baker Metal Products Inc—*Robert Baker*	PO Box 59445, Dallas TX 75229	972-241-3553	R	21*	.2
8	Midwest Roll Forming and Manufacturing Inc—*Gary Schuster*	1 Ghean Arnolt Dr, Pierceton IN 46562	574-594-2100	R	20*	.1
9	CMC Rebar Florida—*Joseph Alvardo*	PO Box 6716, Jacksonville FL 32236	904-781-4780	D	18*	.1
10	Brougher Inc—*Wade Brougher*	8881 Hempstead Rd, Houston TX 77008	713-869-7577	R	15*	.1
11	Water Works Manufacturing LLC—*Melanie Bias*	500 Cleveland St S, Cambridge MN 55008	763-689-4800	R	15*	.1
12	Haydon Corp—*Doug Hillman*	415 Hamburg Tpke Ste 1, Wayne NJ 07470	973-904-0800	R	15*	.1
13	Western Metal Lath—*Antelo Gentile*	6510 General Rd, Riverside CA 92509	951-360-3500	R	13*	.1
14	GMF Industries Inc—*Vincent Norman*	PO Box 6688, Lakeland FL 33807	863-646-5081	R	13*	.1
15	2ls Inc—*Gary W Burchill*	75 West St, Walpole MA 02081	508-850-7520	R	11*	<.1
16	Midwest Curtainwalls Inc—*Donald Kelly*	5171 Grant Ave, Cleveland OH 44125	216-641-7900	R	11*	.1
17	Harris/Arizona Rebar Inc—*Darell Brodhead*	PO Box 6472, Phoenix AZ 85005	602-254-0091	R	10*	.1
18	Ecological Services International Inc—*F Seales*	41786 Fm 510, Los Fresnos TX 78566	956-233-4609	R	10*	.1
19	Chadco Enterprises—*Chad Williams*	2075 47th St, Sarasota FL 34234	941-351-2776	R	9*	.1
20	CMC Rebar Carolinas—*Joseph Alvardo*	2105 S Beltline Blvd, Columbia SC 29201	803-254-4660	D	8*	<.1
21	Unitron Products Inc—*Daniel Ilich*	905 Brush Ave, Bronx NY 10465	718-863-7000	R	7*	<.1
22	Las Cruces Machine Manufacturing And Engineering Inc—*Kari Mitchell*	6000 S Main St Ste B, Mesilla Park NM 88047	575-526-1411	R	6*	.1
23	Complex Fabricators Inc—*Rick Brewer*	1620 Awl Cir, Salt Lake City UT 84104	801-355-2830	R	6*	<.1
24	Custom Rollforming Corp—*David Bradbury*	PO Box 698, Moundridge KS 67107	620-345-2821	S	6*	<.1
25	Southern Enterprises Of Southeast Louisiana Inc—*David Barron*	PO Box 1916, Ponchatoula LA 70454	985-386-2053	R	4*	<.1
26	Fallline Corp—*Erik York*	4625 Aircenter Cir, Reno NV 89502	775-827-6400	R	4*	<.1
27	Wayne Steel Supply Inc—*David Seybert*	7707 Freedom Way, Fort Wayne IN 46818	260-489-6249	R	4*	<.1
28	Mid Florida Steel Corp—*Dale Coxwell*	870 Cidco Rd, Cocoa FL 32926	321-632-8228	R	4*	<.1
29	Advanced Waterjet Cutting Inc—*Clif Gibson*	2825 Reward Ln, Dallas TX 75220	214-358-2194	R	3*	<.1
30	Csc Inc—*William Thorndike*	PO Box 1588, Medford OR 97501	541-779-1970	R	3*	.1
31	C and S Engineering Inc—*Alfred Cavallo*	956 Old Colony Rd, Meriden CT 06451	203-235-5727	R	3*	<.1
32	US Manufacturing Inc—*Loran Balvanze*	1707 21st St, Eldora IA 50627	641-939-7476	R	3*	<.1
33	Hygrade Precision Technologies Inc—*John Salce*	329 Cooke St, Plainville CT 06062	860-747-5773	R	3*	<.1
34	Richards-Klein Sheet Metal Fabricators Inc—*Ronald Richards*	3116 Millers Ln, Louisville KY 40216	502-772-7600	R	2*	<.1
35	Grippe Machining And Manufacturing Co—*Salvatore Militello*	15642 Common Rd, Roseville MI 48066	586-778-3150	R	2*	<.1
36	Intricate Grinding And Machine Specialties Inc—*Brenda Amaya*	1081 S Gateway Blvd, Norton Shores MI 49441	231-798-2154	R	2*	<.1
37	A and S Fabricating Co—*Henry Sonner*	PO Box 160, Livermore KY 42352	270-278-2371	R	2*	<.1
38	Metal Technology Of Indiana Inc—*Donna Hoyt*	810 Hendricks Dr, Lebanon IN 46052	765-482-1100	R	2*	<.1
39	Rollform Of Jamestown Inc—*Edward Ruttenberg*	181 Blackstone Ave, Jamestown NY 14701	716-665-5310	R	2*	<.1
40	Nucon Inc—*Donald Jones*	PO Box 1928, Leland NC 28451	910-371-9383	R	1*	<.1
41	Ulti-Mate Highway Products Inc—*Steven Ellsworth*	PO Box 7, Stanton CA 90680	714-527-2261	R	<1*	<.1

TOTALS: SIC 3449 Miscellaneous Metal Work
Companies: 41   600   3.8

3451 Screw Machine Products

Rank	Company Name—*Executive Officer*	Address, City, State, Zip	Phone	Type	Fin	Empls
1	Ashley F Ward Inc—*Terry Bien*	7490 Easy St, Mason OH 45040	513-398-1414	R	235*	.3
2	Curtis Screw Company LLC—*Paul Hojnacki*	50 Thielman Dr, Buffalo NY 14206	716-885-0110	R	90*	.5
3	Iseli Co—*Carey Luiting*	402 N Main St, Walworth WI 53184	262-275-2108	S	88*	.1
4	Supreme Machined Products Company Inc—*Gregory Olson*	18686 172nd Ave, Spring Lake MI 49456	616-842-6550	R	46*	.3
5	Melling Tool Co—*Mark Melling*	PO Box 1188, Jackson MI 49204	517-787-8172	R	44*	.7
6	Huron Inc—*Robert Bales*	6554 Lakeshore Rd, Lexington MI 48450	810-359-5344	R	43*	.5
7	Greystone Of Lincoln Inc—*John Maconi*	7 Wellington Rd, Lincoln RI 02865	401-333-0444	R	40*	.3
8	Defiance Precision Products	1125 Precision Way, Defiance OH 43512	419-782-8955	S	40*	.3
9	Mitchel and Scott Machine Company Inc—*Brett Pheffer*	1841 Ludlow Ave, Indianapolis IN 46201	317-639-5331	R	35*	.3
10	C Thorrez Industries Inc—*Camiel Thorrez*	4909 W Michigan Ave, Jackson MI 49201	517-750-3160	R	30	.2
11	Standby Screw Machine Products Co—*Sal Caroniti*	1122 W Bagley Rd, Berea OH 44017	440-243-8200	R	24*	.4
12	Alpha Grainger Manufacturing Inc—*Jacob Grainger*	20 Discovery Way, Franklin MA 02038	508-520-4005	R	23*	.1
13	Quality Control Corp—*Richard Michalek*	7315 W Wilson Ave, Chicago IL 60706	708-887-5400	R	23*	.2
14	Security Signals Inc—*Susan Lee*	PO Box 910, Cordova TN 38088	901-754-7228	R	22*	.1
15	Manth-Brownell Inc—*Wesley Skinner*	1120 Fyler Rd, Kirkville NY 13082	315-687-7263	R	20*	.2
16	Accurate Screwmachine Corp—*Daniel Sebastian*	PO Box 10095, Fairfield NJ 07004	973-244-9200	R	20*	.1
17	Onyx Industries Inc—*Vladimir Reil*	25311 Normandie Ave, Harbor City CA 90710	310-539-8830	R	20*	.2
18	Herker Industries Inc—*Edward Nunemaker*	N57w13760 Carmen Ave, Menomonee Falls WI 53051	262-781-8270	R	20*	.2
19	Mkm Machine Tool Company Inc—*Robert Moore*	PO Box 2307, Clarksville IN 47131	812-282-6627	R	19*	.2
20	Alger Manufacturing LLC—*Carl Boyd*	724 S Bon View Ave, Ontario CA 91761	909-986-4591	R	19*	.2
21	Sorenson Engineering Inc—*Paul Sewell*	32032 Dunlap Blvd, Yucaipa CA 92399	909-795-2434	R	19*	.2

Note: An asterisk (*) indicates an estimated financial figure. The company type code used is as follows: R = Private, P = Public, S = Private Subsidiary, B = Public Subsidiary, D = Division, J = Joint Venture, I = Investment Fund.

COMPANY RANKINGS BY SALES WITHIN 4-DIGIT SIC

Rank	Company Name—*Executive Officer*	Address, City, State, Zip	Phone	Type	Fin	Empls
22	Charleston Metal Products Inc—*G Tucker*	350 Grant St, Waterloo IN 46793	260-837-8211	R	19*	.1
23	Metal Seal and Products Inc—*Alan Pirnat*	4323 Hamann Pkwy, Willoughby OH 44094	440-946-8500	R	18*	.2
24	Dawlen Corp—*Faith F Small*	PO Box 884, Jackson MI 49204	517-787-2200	R	18*	.1
25	Swagelok Hy-Level Co—*Peter Rebar*	15400 Foltz Pkwy, Strongsville OH 44149	440-572-1540	R	18*	.3
26	Master Automatic Machine Company Inc—*Mark Evasic*	40485 Schoolcraft Rd, Plymouth MI 48170	734-414-0500	R	17*	.3
27	John J Steuby Co—*John Steuby*	6002 N Lindbergh Blvd, Hazelwood MO 63042	314-895-1000	R	17*	.2
28	V-S Industries Inc—*John Schietert*	900 Chaddick Dr, Wheeling IL 60090	847-520-1800	R	17*	.2
29	Nook Industries Inc—*Chirstopher Nook*	4950 E 49th St, Cleveland OH 44125	216-271-7186	R	17*	.2
30	Sbs Industries Inc—*Darwin James*	1843 N 106th E Ave, Tulsa OK 74116	918-836-7756	R	15*	.2
31	CSM Manufacturing Corp—*William Fleury*	24650 N Industrial Dr, Farmington Hills MI 48335	248-471-0700	R	15*	.1
32	Microbest Inc—*Steven Griffin*	670 Captain Neville Dr, Waterbury CT 06705	203-597-0355	R	15*	.1
33	R and B Grinding Company Inc—*Raymond Biddle*	1900 Clark St, Racine WI 53403	262-634-5538	R	15*	.1
34	Summit Machine Inc—*Todd Bauerfeind*	561 Shoreview Park Rd, Shoreview MN 55126	651-773-3200	R	15*	<.1
35	Tomz Corp—*Zbignew Matulaniec*	47 Episcopal Rd, Berlin CT 06037	860-829-0670	R	15*	.1
36	General Automation Inc—*Ed Gajewski*	3300 Oakton St, Skokie IL 60076	847-676-4004	R	15*	.1
37	Mercury Manufacturing Co—*Fred May*	1212 Grove St, Wyandotte MI 48192	734-285-5150	R	14*	.1
38	Enoch Manufacturing Co—*Thomas Aitchison*	PO Box 98, Clackamas OR 97015	503-659-2660	R	14*	.1
39	Swiss-Tech LLC—*John Jones*	PO Box 326, Delavan WI 53115	262-728-6363	R	14*	.1
40	Lutco Bearings Inc—*John Stowe*	677 Cambridge St Ste 1, Worcester MA 01610	508-756-6296	R	13*	.1
41	T and L Automatics Inc—*Thomas Hassett*	770 Emerson St, Rochester NY 14613	585-647-3717	R	13*	.1
42	Torco Inc—*Robert Torras*	PO Box 4070, Marietta GA 30061	770-427-3704	R	13*	.1
43	Bracalente Manufacturing Co—*Thomas Bracalente*	PO Box 570, Trumbauersville PA 18970	215-536-3077	R	12*	.2
44	World Class Manufacturing Group Inc—*Darold Paisar*	1101 S Pine St, Weyauwega WI 54983	920-867-2527	R	11*	.1
45	Classic Turning Inc—*Philip Curtis*	2500 W Argyle St, Jackson MI 49202	517-764-1335	R	11*	.1
46	Devon Precision Industries Inc—*Yvon Desaulniers*	PO Box 6555, Wolcott CT 06716	203-879-1437	R	11*	.2
47	DuPage Machine Products Inc—*David R Knuepfer*	311 Longview Dr, Bloomingdale IL 60108	630-690-5400	R	11*	.1
48	Gits Manufacturing Co—*Avee Poston*	1739 Commerce Rd, Creston IA 50801	641-782-2105	S	11*	.1
49	Elyria Manufacturing Corp—*Jeffrey Ohlemacher*	PO Box 479, Elyria OH 44036	440-365-4171	R	11*	.1
50	Meaden Precision Machined Products Co—*Thomas Meaden*	16W210 83rd St, Burr Ridge IL 60527	630-655-0888	R	11*	.1
51	X-L-Engineering Corp—*Paul Prikos*	6150 W Mulford St, Niles IL 60714	847-965-3030	R	11*	.1
52	Precisionform Inc—*William Kopetz*	148 W Airport Rd, Lititz PA 17543	717-560-7610	R	11*	.1
53	Anderson Precision Inc—*Steven Godfrey*	20 Livingston Ave, Jamestown NY 14701	716-484-1148	R	11*	.1
54	Hmp Industries Inc—*Einar Gudjohnsen*	4 Hershey Dr, Ansonia CT 06401	203-734-3301	R	11*	.1
55	Corlett-Turner Co—*Jesse Massengill*	2500 104th Ave, Zeeland MI 49464	616-772-9082	R	11*	.1
56	Galgon Industries Inc—*Manfred Galgon*	37399 Centralmont Pl, Fremont CA 94536	510-792-8211	R	11*	.1
57	Kadon Precision Machining Inc—*Jeffrey Franklin*	3744 Publishers Dr, Rockford IL 61109	815-874-5850	R	10*	.1
58	Rima Manufacturing Company Inc—*Edward Engle*	3850 Munson Hwy, Hudson MI 49247	517-448-8921	R	10*	.1
59	Slabe Machine Products Co—*Edward Slabe*	4659 Hamann Pkwy, Willoughby OH 44094	440-946-6555	R	10*	.1
60	RM Precision Of Neveda Inc—*Roy Mendoza*	10624 S Eastern Ave St, Henderson NV 89052	702-617-1111	R	10*	.1
61	TI Machine Inc—*Thanh Ly*	14272 Commerce Dr, Garden Grove CA 92843	714-554-8809	R	10*	.1
62	Abel Holdings Inc—*Edward Abel*	4442 Douglas Ave, Racine WI 53402	262-639-2211	R	10*	.1
63	Jewel Vallorbs Co—*Jeanette Steudler*	PO Box 958, Lancaster PA 17608	717-392-3978	R	10*	.2
64	Yankee Hill Machine Company Inc—*James Graham*	20 Ladd Ave Ste 1, Florence MA 01062	413-584-1400	R	9*	.1
65	Jessen Manufacturing Company Inc—*John Jessen*	PO Box 549, Elkhart IN 46515	574-295-3836	R	9*	.1
66	Mantel Machine Products Inc—*Alvin Mantel*	PO Box 325, Menomonee Falls WI 53052	262-255-6780	R	9*	.1
67	Valley Machining Co—*Joe Vantol*	PO Box 155, Rock Valley IA 51247	712-476-2828	R	9*	.1
68	Winegar Inc—*Timothy Wenzel*	1209 State St S, Waseca MN 56093	507-835-3495	R	9*	.1
69	Micron Manufacturing Inc—*Mark Zupan*	186 Commerce Dr, Lagrange OH 44050	440-355-4200	R	8*	.1
70	Anderson Automatics Inc—*Douglas Anderson*	6401 Welcome Ave N, Minneapolis MN 55429	763-533-2206	R	8*	.1
71	Northwest Swiss-Matic Inc—*G Lee Martin*	8400 89th Ave N, Minneapolis MN 55445	763-544-4222	R	8*	.1
72	Barton Precision Components LLC—*David Froemming*	PO Box 1060, West Bend WI 53095	262-334-5583	R	8*	.1
73	Precision Turned Components Corp—*Scot Jones*	331 Farnum Pke, Smithfield RI 02917	401-232-3377	R	8*	.1
74	Krist Krenz Machine Inc—*Richard Krenz*	9801 York Alpha Dr, North Royalton OH 44133	440-237-1800	R	8*	.1
75	AS Pindel Corp—*Marc Pindel*	2505 S 170th St, New Berlin WI 53151	262-786-2550	R	8*	.1
76	S and S Screw Machine Company LLC—*J Battle*	1500 Mcminnville Hwy, Sparta TN 38583	931-738-3631	R	8*	.1
77	Dabko Industries Inc—*Robert Dabkowski*	PO Box 9308, Bristol CT 06011	860-589-0756	R	7*	.1
78	Screwmatics Of South Carolina Inc—*Thomas Hogge*	PO Box 355, Pageland SC 29728	843-672-3213	R	7*	.1
79	Richard H Bird and Company Inc—*Carl Cunningham*	PO Box 540569, Waltham MA 02454	781-894-0160	R	7*	<.1
80	Valley Tool and Die Inc—*Adolf Eisenloeffel*	10020 York Theta Dr, North Royalton OH 44133	440-237-0160	R	7*	.1
81	General Automatic Machine Products Company Inc—*Tracy Mc-cullough*	266 Industrial Dr, Hillsdale MI 49242	517-437-6000	R	7*	.1
82	Holt Products Co—*Thomas Hunt*	PO Box 99, Holt MI 48842	517-699-2111	R	6*	.1
83	Hanel Corp—*Mark Strehlow*	16600 W Ryerson Rd, New Berlin WI 53151	262-784-3131	R	6*	.1
84	Pohlman Inc—*Harold Studt*	140 Long Rd, Chesterfield MO 63005	636-537-1909	R	6*	.1
85	Northern Indiana Manufacturing Inc—*Robert Dragani*	PO Box 46, Bourbon IN 46504	574-342-2105	R	6*	<.1
86	Roberts Automatic Products Inc—*W Roberts*	880 Lake Dr, Chanhassen MN 55317	952-949-1000	R	6*	<.1
87	Cox Manufacturing Co—*William Cox*	5500 N Loop 1604 E, San Antonio TX 78247	210-657-7731	R	6*	.1
88	Lakeshore Fittings Inc—*Albert Hoffman*	1865 Industrial Dr, Grand Haven MI 49417	616-846-5090	R	6*	.1
89	Champion Fasteners Inc—*Aldo Magazzeni*	707 Smithville Rd, Lumberton NJ 08048	609-267-5222	R	6*	<.1
90	Fettes Manufacturing Co—*James Mckown*	5400 Gatewood Dr, Sterling Heights MI 48310	586-939-8500	R	5*	<.1
91	Automatic Products Company Inc—*Joel Gregory*	5858 S 194th St, Kent WA 98032	253-872-0203	R	5*	<.1
92	Bystrom Brothers Inc—*Vivian Freund*	2200 Snelling Ave, Minneapolis MN 55404	612-721-7511	R	5*	.1
93	MK Chambers Co—*Gerald Chambers*	2251 Johnson Mill Rd, North Branch MI 48461	810-688-3750	R	5*	.1
94	Imperial Metal Products Co—*Jeff Dean*	835 Hall St Sw, Grand Rapids MI 49503	616-452-1700	R	5*	<.1
95	AT and G Co—*Fred Bononi*	7545 N Hagerty Rd, Canton MI 48187	734-737-9200	R	5*	.1
96	Abel Automatics Inc—*Andrew Madoff*	165 N Aviador St, Camarillo CA 93010	805-484-8789	R	5*	<.1
97	Liberty Research Company Inc—*Derrick Perkins*	PO Box 7338, Rochester NH 03839	603-332-2730	R	5*	<.1
98	Obars Machine And Tool Co—*Gregory Obarski*	115 N Westwood Ave, Toledo OH 43607	419-535-6307	R	5*	<.1
99	FC Phillips Inc—*Craig Snow*	471 Washington St, Stoughton MA 02072	781-344-9400	R	5*	.1
100	United Scientific Inc—*Stan Monson*	15 Yorkton Ct, Saint Paul MN 55117	651-483-1500	R	5*	<.1
101	Efficient Machine Products Corp—*Ted Imbrogno*	12133 Alameda Dr, Strongsville OH 44149	440-268-0205	R	5*	<.1
102	Guthrie Machine Works Inc—*Charles Perry*	3101 Verona Ave, Buford GA 30518	770-831-5551	R	5*	<.1
103	Amco Products Inc—*Joseph Raby*	PO Box 292860, Dayton OH 45429	937-433-7982	R	4*	<.1
104	Vandeventer Manufacturing Company Inc—*Ronald Link*	PO Box 249, Batavia IL 60510	630-879-3842	R	4*	<.1
105	Precision Plus Inc—*Phil Reader*	PO Box 168, Elkhorn WI 53121	262-743-1700	R	4*	<.1
106	Process Screw Products Inc—*William Hammer*	PO Box 545, Shannon IL 61078	815-864-2220	R	4*	<.1
107	Bront Machining Inc—*Gary Warlaumont*	529 Hunter Ave, Dayton OH 45404	937-228-4551	R	4*	<.1
108	Janesco Inc—*James Janes*	PO Box 262, Oshkosh WI 54903	920-231-5580	R	4*	<.1
109	Davison-Rite Products Co—*Arthur Krol*	12921 Stark Rd, Livonia MI 48150	734-513-0505	R	4*	<.1
110	Brada Manufacturing Inc—*W Hamilton*	PO Box 7614, Warwick RI 02887	401-739-3774	R	4*	<.1

Rank	Company Name—*Executive Officer*	Address, City, State, Zip	Phone	Type	Fin	Empls
111	Selflock Screw Products Company Inc—*Daniel Kuhns*	114 Marcy St, East Syracuse NY 13057	315-437-3367	R	4*	<.1
112	Aaa Industries Inc—*Mark Yessian*	24500 Capitol, Redford MI 48239	313-255-0420	R	3*	<.1
113	Lenz Inc—*John Lenz*	3301 Klepinger Rd, Dayton OH 45406	937-277-9364	R	3*	<.1
114	Weber Manufacturing and Supplies Inc—*L Prost*	304 Triple Diamond Blv, North Venice FL 34275	941-488-5185	R	3*	<.1
115	Anpec Industries Inc—*Douglas Allen*	PO Box 539, Pecatonica IL 61063	815-239-2303	R	3*	<.1
116	Edgewater Manufacturing Company Inc—*Robert Fischbein*	91 Woodland Ave, Westwood NJ 07675	201-664-0022	R	3*	<.1
117	Freedom Manufacturing Inc—*Robert Baker*	5320 6 Mile Ct NW, Comstock Park MI 49321	616-647-9200	R	3*	<.1
118	Marvel Screw Machine Products Inc—*David Perriello*	58 Lafayette St, Waterbury CT 06708	203-756-7058	R	3*	<.1
119	A and A Machine and Development Company Inc—*Arlene Hymovitz*	16625 Gramercy Pl, Gardena CA 90247	310-532-7706	R	3*	<.1
120	St Joe Tool Co—*Henry Braddock*	PO Box 578, Bridgman MI 49106	269-426-4300	R	3*	<.1
121	Spartan Manufacturing Co—*R Horton*	7081 Patterson Dr, Garden Grove CA 92841	714-894-1955	R	3*	<.1
122	Universal Screw Products Inc—*Homer Evensen*	20421 Earl St, Torrance CA 90503	310-371-1170	R	3*	<.1
123	JC Gibbons Manufacturing Inc—*Jerry Gibbons*	35055 Glendale St, Livonia MI 48150	734-266-5544	R	3*	<.1
124	Anwright Corp—*Lloyd Anderson*	PO Box 330940, Pacoima CA 91333	818-896-2465	R	2*	<.1
125	Worley Machine Enterprises Inc—*Donald Worley*	PO Box 80, Woolwine VA 24185	276-930-2695	R	2*	<.1
126	RT and T Machining Inc—*F Thompson*	8195 Tyler Blvd Ste 56, Mentor OH 44060	440-974-8479	R	2*	<.1
127	Precision Feedscrews Inc—*James Fagan*	PO Box 7357, New Castle PA 16107	724-654-9676	R	2*	<.1
128	Sperry Automatics Company Inc—*Charles Pugliese*	PO Box 717, Naugatuck CT 06770	203-729-4589	R	2*	<.1
129	Integrity Manufacturing Corp—*Richard Halderman*	PO Box 312, Dayton OH 45404	937-233-6792	R	2*	<.1
130	Wiscon Products Inc—*Rolfe Christensen*	5022 Douglas Ave, Racine WI 53402	262-639-2272	R	2*	<.1
131	Industrial Machine and Engineering Co—*Valeria Peti*	1807 W Elizabeth Ave, Linden NJ 07036	908-862-8874	R	2*	<.1
132	Peterson and Co—*Leo Peterson*	PO Box 408, Inkster MI 48141	313-562-4444	R	2*	<.1
133	Williams Machine And Tool Company Inc—*Wanda Williams*	PO Box 188, Galena KS 66739	620-783-5184	R	2*	<.1
134	Nebraska Machine Products Inc—*Ron Rosso*	9370 N 45th St, Omaha NE 68152	402-455-0128	R	2*	<.1
135	American Shaft Co—*Joanne Nordlof*	PO Box 5906, Rockford IL 61125	815-229-5130	R	2*	<.1
136	Swiss American Screw Products Inc—*Roland Leist*	5740 S Sheldon Rd, Canton MI 48188	734-397-1600	R	2*	<.1
137	Stockbridge Manufacturing Co—*Albert Thorrez*	PO Box 189, Stockbridge MI 49285	517-851-7865	R	2*	<.1
138	Profile Grinding Inc—*Karen Homer*	4593 Spring Rd, Cleveland OH 44131	216-351-0600	R	2*	<.1
139	J and J Machine Products Company Inc—*Stephanie Dougherty*	12734 Inkster Rd, Redford MI 48239	313-534-8024	R	2*	<.1
140	L A Martin Co—*Paul Martin*	14400 Henn St, Dearborn MI 48126	313-581-3444	R	2*	<.1
141	Bmp Industries LLC—*Ron Hibbard*	PO Box 57, Birmingham OH 44816	440-965-4041	R	2*	<.1
142	Epco Products Inc—*Fredric Aichele*	PO Box 9250, Fort Wayne IN 46899	260-747-8888	R	2*	<.1
143	Micromatic Screw Products Inc—*Harold Burke*	825 Carroll Ave, Jackson MI 49202	517-787-3666	R	2*	<.1
144	Troy International Products Inc—*Michael Durant*	21850 Wyoming Pl, Oak Park MI 48237	248-548-8646	R	2*	<.1
145	Lakeview Precision Machining Inc—*Debra Sommers*	751 Schneider Dr, South Elgin IL 60177	847-742-7170	R	2*	<.1
146	Abbott Products Inc—*Fred Smith*	1617 Fern Valley Rd, Yadkinville NC 27055	336-463-3135	R	2*	<.1
147	Fostermation Inc—*Susan Ritchey*	200 Valleyview Dr, Meadville PA 16335	814-336-6211	R	2*	<.1
148	Arrow Specialties Inc—*Patricia Luter*	1695 S Hanley Rd, Saint Louis MO 63144	314-645-3665	R	1*	<.1
149	Globe Electronic Hardware Inc—*Caroline Dennehy*	PO Box 770727, Woodside NY 11377	718-457-0303	R	1*	<.1
150	Vineburg Machining Inc—*Gerd Poppinga*	25 Brown Dr, Carson City NV 89706	775-246-4336	R	1*	<.1
151	Demco Products Inc—*Robert Dempster*	4644 W 92nd St, Oak Lawn IL 60453	708-636-6240	R	1*	<.1
152	Ernst Timing Screw Co—*Suzanne Cannon*	1534 Bridgewater Rd, Bensalem PA 19020	215-639-1438	R	1*	<.1
153	R/C Machining Company Inc—*Brent Cochran*	440 15th St Se, Glenwood MN 56334	320-634-4461	R	1*	<.1
154	Borneman and Peterson Inc—*Roger Blevins*	1810 Remell St, Flint MI 48503	810-744-1890	R	1*	<.1
155	Princeton Industrial Products Inc—*Sue Schreiber*	2119 Stonington Ave, Hoffman Estates IL 60169	847-839-8500	R	1*	<.1

TOTALS: SIC 3451 Screw Machine Products
Companies: 155

					1,851	14.0

3452 Bolts, Nuts, Rivets & Washers

Rank	Company Name—*Executive Officer*	Address, City, State, Zip	Phone	Type	Fin	Empls
1	Illinois Tool Works Inc—*David B Speer*	3600 W Lake Ave, Glenview IL 60026	847-724-7500	P	15,870	61.0
2	Stanley-Bostitch Inc—*John F Lundgren*	Briggs Dr, East Greenwich RI 02818		D	2,997*	2.5
3	ACCO Brands Corp—*Robert J Keller*	300 Tower Pkwy, Lincolnshire IL 60069	847-541-9500	P	1,318	3.8
4	SPS Technologies LLC—*John Thompson*	301 Highland Ave, Jenkintown PA 19046	215-572-3000	S	830	5.9
5	Supply Technologies LLC	6065 Parkland Blvd, Cleveland OH 44124	440-947-2100	S	489*	1.5
6	Huck International Inc	PO Box 27207, Tucson AZ 85726	520-519-7400	S	373*	2.5
7	MacLean-Fogg Co—*Barry L MacLean*	1000 Allanson Rd, Mundelein IL 60060	847-566-0010	R	348*	2.3
8	Captive Fasteners Corp	19 Thornton Rd, Oakland NJ 07436	201-337-6800	R	322*	.3
9	John Wagner Associates Inc—*Jack Kroll*	14801 Willard Rd Ste 7, Chantilly VA 20151	703-631-8770	R	292*	.3
10	Penn Engineering and Manufacturing Corp—*Mark Petty*	PO Box 1000, Danboro PA 18916	215-766-8853	R	230*	1.3
11	Elco Fastening Systems LLC—*Timothy Weir*	840 W Long Lake Rd Ste, Troy MI 48098	248-879-8660	R	166*	2.5
12	Ohio Nut and Bolt Co—*Patrick Finnegam* Fastener Industries Inc	5250 West 164th St, Brook Park OH 44142	216-267-2240	D	137*	.1
13	Tinnerman Palnut Engineered Products LLC—*Joseph R Ponteri*	1060 W 130th St, Brunswick OH 44212	330-220-5100	S	133*	.6
14	H and L Tool Company Inc Chicago Rivet and Machine Co	32701 Dequindre Rd, Madison Heights MI 48071	248-585-7474	S	123*	.1
15	CWR Manufacturing Co—*James A Murphy*	PO Box 2669, Syracuse NY 13220	315-437-1032	R	102*	.1
16	Mnp Corp—*Thomas Klein*	PO Box 189002, Utica MI 48318	586-254-1320	R	95*	1.0
17	Dexter Fastener Technologies Inc—*Mike Frazier*	2110 Bishop Cir E, Dexter MI 48130	734-426-5200	R	88*	.2
18	Stafast Products Inc—*Donald S Selle*	505 Lake Shore Blvd, Painesville OH 44077	440-357-5546	R	80*	.1
19	Huck International Inc Aerospace Div Huck International Inc	3724 E Columbia St, Tucson AZ 85714	520-519-7400	D	67*	.2
20	Limitorque Corp—*Mark A Blinn*	PO Box 11318, Lynchburg VA 24506	434-528-4400	S	65*	.3
21	Federal Screw Works—*Thomas ZurSchmiede*	20229 Nine Mile Rd, Saint Clair Shores MI 48080	586-443-4200	P	56	.2
22	Arnold Engineering Co—*Charles W Grigg*	300 N West St, Marengo IL 60152	815-568-2000	S	50*	.2
23	Greenville Metals Inc—*Charles W Grigg* SPS Technologies LLC	99 Crestview Dr Ext, Transfer PA 16154	724-646-0654	S	50*	.2
24	Edward W Daniel Co—*Charles W Smith*	11700 Harvard Ave, Cleveland OH 44105	216-295-2750	R	37*	.1
25	MS Aerospace Inc—*Michel Szostak*	13928 Balboa Blvd, Sylmar CA 91342	818-833-9095	R	34*	.3
26	Monogram Aerospace Fasteners Inc—*Gregg Anderson*	3423 S Garfield Ave, Los Angeles CA 90040	323-722-4760	R	34*	.3
27	Accurate Threaded Fasteners Inc—*Don Surber*	3550 W Pratt Ave, Lincolnwood IL 60712	847-677-1300	R	33*	.3
28	B and G Manufacturing Company Inc—*William Edmonds*	PO Box 904, Hatfield PA 19440	215-822-1925	R	32*	.2
29	B and D Threadrolling—*Dennis Doyle*	36820 Van Born Rd, Wayne MI 48184	734-728-7070	R	30*	.1
30	Birmingham Fastener and Supply—*Howard Tinney*	PO Box 10323, Birmingham AL 35202	205-595-3511	R	29*	.2
31	Chicago Rivet and Machine Co—*John A Morrissey*	PO Box 3061, Naperville IL 60566	630-357-8500	P	29	.2
32	Kamax LP—*Joseph Sobczynski*	500 W Long Lake Rd, Troy MI 48098	248-879-0200	R	28*	.4
33	Semblex Corp—*Charles Cunningham*	199 W Diversey Ave, Elmhurst IL 60126	630-833-2880	R	27*	.2
34	ITW Fastex—*David Hauner*	195 E Algonquin Rd, Des Plaines IL 60016	847-299-2222	R	27*	.2

Note: An asterisk (*) indicates an estimated financial figure. The company type code used is as follows: R = Private, P = Public, S = Private Subsidiary, B = Public Subsidiary, D = Division, J = Joint Venture, I = Investment Fund.

COMPANY RANKINGS BY SALES WITHIN 4-DIGIT SIC

Rank	Company Name—*Executive Officer*	Address, City, State, Zip	Phone	Type	Fin	Empls
35	SPS Technologies Waterford Co—*Donald Stockton* SPS Technologies LLC	5331 Dixie Hwy, Waterford MI 48329	248-623-0800	S	27	.2
36	Fastco Industries Inc—*Bruce Tap*	PO Box 141427, Grand Rapids MI 49514	616-453-5428	R	25*	.1
37	Fixture Hardware Manufacturing Corp—*Ken Weiss*	4116 First Ave, Brooklyn NY 11232	718-499-9422	R	25*	<.1
38	Nd Industries Inc—*Richard Wallace*	1000 N Crooks Rd, Clawson MI 48017	248-655-2520	R	25*	.4
39	Edwin B Stimpson Company Inc—*Howard Rau*	1515 Sw 13th Ct, Pompano Beach FL 33069	954-946-3500	R	25*	.4
40	Nelson Stud Welding Inc—*Ken Caratelli*	PO Box 4019, Elyria OH 44036	440-329-0400	R	24*	.4
41	Maclean Vehicle Systems—*Pat Garlow*	3200 W 14 Mile Rd, Royal Oak MI 48073	248-280-0880	R	23*	.2
42	Valley-Todeco Inc—*Jim Cotello*	PO Box 9205, Sylmar CA 91392	818-367-2261	S	23*	.1
43	Southern Imperial Inc—*Stanley Valiulis*	1400 Eddy Ave, Rockford IL 61103	815-877-7041	R	23*	.2
44	Polygon Co—*Jim Shobert*	PO Box 176, Walkerton IN 46574	574-586-3145	R	22*	.3
45	Cold Heading Co—*James Joliet*	21777 Hoover Rd, Warren MI 48089	586-497-7000	R	21*	.3
46	Altenloh Brinck and Company Inc—*Brian Roth*	2105 County Rd 12c, Bryan OH 43506	419-636-6715	R	21*	.1
47	Decker Manufacturing Corp—*BL Konkle*	703 N Clark St, Albion MI 49224	517-629-3955	R	20*	.1
48	Anchor Bolt and Screw Co—*Pat Henriksen*	1100 Davis Rd, Elgin IL 60123	847-841-7000	R	20*	.1
49	First Lexington Corp—*Robert Bennet*	14275 Midway Rd, Addison TX 75001	972-934-1212	R	19*	.1
50	Murray Corp	260 Schilling Cir, Hunt Valley MD 21031	410-771-0380	R	18	.1
51	MacLean Maynard LLC—*Barry MacLean* Maclean Vehicle Systems	50855 E Russell Schmid, Chesterfield MI 48051	248-853-2525	S	18*	.1
52	Spirol International Corp—*Jeffrey Koehl*	30 Rock Ave, Danielson CT 06239	860-774-8571	R	18*	.3
53	Prestige Stamping Inc—*Robert Rink*	PO Box 1086, Warren MI 48090	586-773-2700	R	17*	.1
54	Acme Screw Co—*William Roche*	PO Box 906, Wheaton IL 60187	630-665-2200	R	16*	.1
55	Consolidated Metal Products Inc—*Hugh Gallagher*	1028 Depot St, Cincinnati OH 45204	513-251-2624	R	16*	.1
56	Boker's Inc—*Amy Kersey*	3104 Snelling Ave, Minneapolis MN 55406	612-729-9365	R	16*	.1
57	Fabristeel Products Inc—*Rex Ogg*	22100 Trolley Industri, Taylor MI 48180	313-299-8500	R	14*	.1
58	Industrial Nut Corp—*J William Springer*	1425 Tiffin Ave, Sandusky OH 44870	419-625-8543	R	14*	.1
59	Washers Inc—*Nicholas Strumbos*	33375 Glendale St, Livonia MI 48150	734-523-1000	R	14*	.1
60	Header Products Inc—*Michael Mc Manus*	PO Box 74188, Romulus MI 48174	734-941-2220	R	14*	.2
61	John Hassall Inc—*Theodore Smith*	609 Cantiague Rock Rd, Westbury NY 11590	516-334-6200	R	14*	.1
62	Hindley Manufacturing Company Inc—*Charles Hindley*	PO Box 38, Cumberland RI 02864	401-722-2550	R	14*	.1
63	Unytite Inc—*Jun Hashimoto*	1 Unytite Dr, Peru IL 61354	815-224-2221	R	13*	.1
64	Slidematic Industries Inc—*Randy Baker*	1303 Samuelson Rd, Rockford IL 61109	815-986-0500	R	12*	.1
65	Haydon Kerk Motion Solutions Inc—*John Norris*	1 Kerk Dr, Hollis NH 03049	603-465-7227	R	12*	.1
66	Specialty Screw Corp—*Russell Johansson*	PO Box 5003, Rockford IL 61125	815-969-4100	R	11*	.1
67	Superior Washer and Gasket Corp—*Allan Lippolis*	PO Box 5407, Hauppauge NY 11788	631-273-8282	R	11*	.1
68	Lyn-Tron Inc—*Donald Lynn*	6001 S Thomas Mallen R, Spokane WA 99224	509-456-4545	R	11*	.1
69	Anderson Manufacturing Company Inc—*Roy Anderson*	PO Box 158, Bristol WI 53104	262-857-7056	R	10*	<.1
70	AAA Aircraft Supply LLC—*Robert L Darbelnet* SPS Technologies LLC	68 Shaker Rd, Enfield CT 06082	860-749-1116	S	10*	<.1
71	Rex Realty Co—*Harold Kalich*	10541 E Ute St, Tulsa OK 74116	918-693-8121	R	9*	.1
72	Stanley Fastening Systems LP Stanley-Bostitch Inc	125 Circuit Dr, North Kingstown RI 02852		D	9*	.1
73	Hexagon Industries Inc—*Stephen Jackson*	1135 Ivanhoe Rd, Cleveland OH 44110	216-249-0200	R	9*	.1
74	Allstar Fasteners Inc—*Allan Vodicka*	PO Box 866, Elk Grove Village IL 60009	847-640-7827	R	8*	.1
75	Better Engineering Manufacturing Inc—*Keith Hiss*	8361 Town Ctr Ct, Baltimore MD 21236	410-931-0000	R	8*	.1
76	Portland Bolt and Manufacturing Company Inc—*Jonathan Todd*	PO Box 2866, Portland OR 97208	503-227-5488	R	7*	<.1
77	Keystone Screw Corp—*George Hanny*	535 Davisville Rd, Willow Grove PA 19090	215-657-7100	R	6*	.1
78	Brainard Rivet Co—*JF Volpe*	PO Box 30, Girard OH 44420	330-545-4931	R	5*	<.1
79	Fastener Industries Inc—*Patrick Finnegan*	1 Berea Commons Ste 20, Berea OH 44017	440-243-0034	R	5*	<.1
80	J T D Stamping Company Inc—*Giovanni Bianco*	403 Wyandanch Ave, West Babylon NY 11704	631-643-4144	R	5*	<.1
81	Gage Bilt Inc—*Bruce Godfrey*	44766 Centre Ct, Clinton Township MI 48038	586-226-1500	R	4*	<.1
82	Anillo Industries Inc—*Kurt Koch*	PO Box 5586, Orange CA 92863	714-637-7000	R	4*	<.1
83	Orlotronics Corp—*Steve Shankin*	401 E 4th St Ste 7, Bridgeport PA 19405	610-239-8200	R	4*	<.1
84	Vermat Corp—*Allenby Matthews*	2101 S Hathaway St, Santa Ana CA 92705	714-540-2846	R	4*	<.1
85	Steel City Bolt and Screw LLC—*Fred Mathis*	PO Box 1747, Birmingham AL 35201	205-942-4567	R	4*	<.1
86	General Plastex Inc—*Renee Hershberger*	35 Stuver Pl, Barberton OH 44203	330-745-7775	R	3*	<.1
87	Skach Manufacturing Company Inc—*Will Shineflug*	950 Anita Ave, Antioch IL 60002	847-395-3560	R	3*	<.1
88	Greer Stop Nut Inc—*Mark Christman* SPS Technologies LLC	481 McNally Dr, Nashville TN 37211	615-832-8375	D	2	.1
89	Kre Inc—*Richard Hendershot*	4010 E 116th St, Cleveland OH 44105	216-883-1600	R	2*	<.1
90	JB Booth And Co—*John Mowry*	PO Box 98, Zelienople PA 16063	724-452-8400	R	1*	<.1
91	California Swiss Machine Inc—*Clarence Kersey*	2640 S Shannon St, Santa Ana CA 92704	714-545-9481	R	1*	<.1
92	Modular Systems Inc—*Montgomery Welch*	PO Box 399, Fruitport MI 49415	231-865-3167	R	1*	<.1
93	Ivan Extruders Company Inc—*Keith Sigfreud*	2404 Pickle Rd, Akron OH 44312	330-644-7400	R	<1*	<.1

TOTALS: SIC 3452 Bolts, Nuts, Rivets & Washers
Companies: 93

					25,360	95.6

3462 Iron & Steel Forgings

Rank	Company Name—*Executive Officer*	Address, City, State, Zip	Phone	Type	Fin	Empls
1	Greenbrier Rail Services—*Rick Turner*	1200 Corporate Dr, Birmingham AL 35242	205-991-0384	R	4,062*	4.5
2	Elwood Group Inc—*David E Barensfeld*	PO Box 790, Ellwood City PA 16117	724-752-3680	R	1,815*	1.8
3	Park-Ohio Holdings Corp—*Edward F Crawford*	6065 Parkland Blvd, Cleveland OH 44124	440-947-2000	P	814	3.2
4	Colfor Manufacturing Inc	3255 Alliance Rd NW, Malvern OH 44644	330-863-0404	S	652*	.7
5	Walker Forge Inc—*Willard Walker*	222 E Erie St Ste 300, Milwaukee WI 53202	414-223-2000	R	588*	.3
6	Thermal Structures Inc—*Vaughn Barnes*	2362 Railroad St, Corona CA 92880	951-736-9911	S	412	.3
7	Colfor Manufacturing Inc Forging Div—*Thomas Szymanski* Colfor Manufacturing Inc	PO Box 485, Malvern OH 44644	330-868-1700	D	311*	.7
8	Carlisle Industrial Friction—*Sam Johnson*	1441 Holland St, Logansport IN 46947	574-753-6391	D	255*	.3
9	Laclede Chain Manufacturing Co—*James Riley*	1549 Fenpark Dr, Fenton MO 63026	636-680-2320	R	249*	.3
10	Riverside Engineering—*Bart Mitchell*	121 Interpark Blvd Ste, San Antonio TX 78216	210-227-9090	D	161*	.3
11	Scot Forge Co—*John Cain*	8001 Winn Rd, Spring Grove IL 60081	847-587-1000	R	143*	.5
12	Markovitz Enterprises Inc—*James C Markovitz*	PO Box 7027, New Castle PA 16107		R	106*	.1
13	Meadville Forging Co—*James Martin* Keller Group Inc	PO Box 459, Meadville PA 16335	814-332-8200	S	100*	.4
14	Keller Group Inc—*J Keller*	1 Northfield Plz, Northfield IL 60093	847-446-7550	R	80*	.4
15	Forged Metals Inc—*Armand Lauzon*	10685 Beech Ave, Fontana CA 92337	909-350-9260	R	75*	.4
16	Bonney Forge Corp—*John Leone*	PO Box 330, Mount Union PA 17066	814-542-2545	R	60*	.3
17	Moro Corp—*David W Menard*	994 Old Eagle School R, Wayne PA 19087	484-367-0300	P	58	.1
18	Canton Drop Forge Inc—*Bradly Ahbe*	4575 Southway St Sw, Canton OH 44706	330-477-4511	R	56*	.3
19	Pacific Forge Inc—*Ron Browne*	10641 Etiwanda Ave, Fontana CA 92337	909-390-0701	S	49*	<.1

Rank	Company Name—*Executive Officer*	Address, City, State, Zip	Phone	Type	Fin	Empls
20	JM Ahle Company Inc—*John Ahle* Moro Corp	PO Box 282, South River NJ 08882	732-238-1700	S	43*	.1
21	Letts Industries Inc—*Charles E Letts Jr*	1111 Bellevue St D, Detroit MI 48207	313-579-1100	R	42*	.3
22	Portland Forge—*Patrick W Bennett*	PO Box 905, Portland IN 47371	260-726-8121	S	42*	.3
23	Metal Forming and Coining Corp—*Thomas Wienrich*	1007 Illinois Ave, Maumee OH 43537	419-893-8748	R	40*	.1
24	T and W Forge Inc—*Joe Schatz*	562 W Ely St, Alliance OH 44601	330-821-5740	R	40*	.1
25	Mercer Forge Corp—*James Ackerman*	PO Box 272, Mercer PA 16137	724-662-2750	R	37*	.2
26	Pennsylvania Machine Works Inc—*Ronald Lafferty*	PO Box 2170, Boothwyn PA 19061	610-497-3300	R	36*	.3
27	Presrite Corp—*Chris Carman*	3665 E 78th St, Cleveland OH 44105	216-441-5990	R	33*	.4
28	Dayton Forging And Heat Treating Co—*Eric Wilson*	PO Box 1629, Dayton OH 45401	937-253-4126	R	30*	.1
29	Kervick Enterprises Inc—*Robert B Kervick*	40 Rockdale St, Worcester MA 01606	508-853-4500	R	29*	.2
30	Komtek Inc—*Robert Kervick* Kervick Enterprises Inc	40 Rockdale St, Worcester MA 01606	508-853-4500	D	29*	.2
31	Mid-West Forge Corp—*Paul Gum*	17301 Saint Clair Ave, Cleveland OH 44110	216-481-3030	R	28*	.2
32	Reell Precision Manufacturing Corp—*Kyle Smith*	1259 Willow Lake Blvd, Saint Paul MN 55110	651-484-2447	R	28*	.1
33	Weldbend Corp—*James Coulas*	6600 S Harlem Ave, Argo IL 60501	773-582-3500	R	27*	.2
34	Drives LLC—*Norm Adell*	901 19th Ave, Fulton IL 61252	815-589-2211	R	27*	.4
35	Midland Forge	101 50th Ave SW, Cedar Rapids IA 52404	319-362-1111	D	26*	.2
36	Erie Forge And Steel Inc—*Charles Novelli*	1341 W 16th St, Erie PA 16502	814-452-2300	R	25*	.1
37	Trinity Forge Inc—*Dennis Withers*	947 Trinity Dr, Mansfield TX 76063	817-473-1515	R	25*	.2
38	Cornell Forge Co—*William Brewer*	6666 W 66th St, Chicago IL 60638	708-458-1582	R	24*	.1
39	Brad Foote Gear Works Inc—*Daniel E Schueller*	1309 S Cicero Ave, Cicero IL 60804	708-652-7700	S	22*	.1
40	Machine Tool and Gear Inc—*David Segal*	1021 N Shiawassee, Corunna MI 48817	989-743-3936	S	21*	.2
41	Unit Drop Forge Company Inc—*Godfrey Sullivan*	PO Box 340350, Milwaukee WI 53234	414-545-3000	R	18*	.1
42	Berkeley Forge and Tool Inc—*Peter Bierwith*	1331 Eastshore Hwy, Berkeley CA 94710	510-526-5034	R	18*	.1
43	Ken Forging Inc—*Richard Kovach*	PO Box 277, Jefferson OH 44047	440-993-8091	R	17*	.1
44	Trenton Forging Co—*David Moxlow*	5523 Hoover St, Trenton MI 48183	734-675-1620	R	16*	.1
45	Core Pipe Products Inc—*Steve Romanelli*	170 Tubeway Dr, Carol Stream IL 60188	630-690-7000	R	16*	.1
46	Charles E Larson and Sons Inc—*Donald C Larson*	2645-65 N Keeler Ave, Chicago IL 60639	773-772-9700	R	16	.1
47	Ellwood Texas Forge LP—*Michael Henthorne*	PO Box 1477, Houston TX 77251	713-434-5100	R	15*	.1
48	Ferrotherm Corp—*Haakon Egeland*	4758 Warner Rd Ste 1, Cleveland OH 44125	216-883-9350	R	14*	.1
49	Mckay Acquisition Inc—*William Mckay*	2735 Hickory Grove Rd, Davenport IA 52804	563-391-1300	R	14*	.1
50	Ohio Metal Technologies Inc—*Akira Nagata*	470 John Alford Pkwy, Hebron OH 43025	740-928-8288	R	13*	.1
51	Net Forge Inc—*Robert Stevens*	PO Box 2007, Columbus IN 47202	812-342-5527	R	12*	.1
52	Norforge And Machining Inc—*Patricia Hayes*	195 N Dean St, Bushnell IL 61422	309-772-3124	R	12*	.1
53	Churon Co	300 Livley Ave, Norcross GA 30071	770-676-0731	R	11*	<.1
54	Phoenix Forging Company Inc—*John Rodgers*	800 Front St, Catasauqua PA 18032	610-264-2861	R	11*	.1
55	Riley Gear Corp—*Thomas Lowry*	1 Precision Dr, Saint Augustine FL 32092	904-829-5652	R	11*	.1
56	Missouri Forge Inc—*Michael Wicklund*	PO Box 397, Doniphan MO 63935	573-996-7177	R	10*	.1
57	M and N Alloy Cast Products Inc—*Honald Minor*	PO Box 1349, Sylacauga AL 35150	256-245-2627	R	9*	.1
58	Moline Forge Inc—*Thomas Getz*	4101 4th Ave, Moline IL 61265	309-762-5506	R	9*	.1
59	Secs Inc—*Vincent Giagni*	550 S Columbus Ave, Mount Vernon NY 10550	914-667-5600	R	8*	.1
60	Solmet Technologies Inc—*Joseph Haller*	2716 Shepler Ch Ave Sw, Canton OH 44706	330-455-4328	R	8*	.1
61	A and A Industries Inc—*Aurelian Mardiros*	320 Jubilee Dr, Peabody MA 01960	978-977-9800	P	7*	<.1
62	Highway Machine Company Inc—*Robert Smith*	3010 S Old Us Hwy 41, Princeton IN 47670	812-385-3639	R	7*	<.1
63	Expert Forge and Machine Inc—*Simon Ormarod*	PO Box 860, York SC 29745	803-684-3133	R	7*	<.1
64	Modern Drop Forge Co—*Gregory Heim*	PO Box 429, Blue Island IL 60406	708-388-1806	R	6*	.6
65	Riverside Spline and Gear Inc—*Wayne Forest*	PO Box 340, Marine City MI 48039	810-765-8302	R	5*	<.1
66	Volvo Motor Graders Inc—*Andres Larsson*	8844 Mount Holly Rd, Charlotte NC 28214	704-392-7307	R	5*	<.1
67	Premier Gear and Machine Works Inc—*Russel Cole*	1700 Nw Thurman St, Portland OR 97209	503-227-3514	R	5*	<.1
68	Ductilic Inc—*David Hwang*	14109 Orange Ave, Paramount CA 90723	562-634-1088	R	5*	<.1
69	Vi-Star Gear Company Inc—*Thomas Redfield*	7312 Jefferson St, Paramount CA 90723	323-774-3750	R	5*	<.1
70	Oliver Gear Inc—*Samuel Haines*	1120 Niagara St, Buffalo NY 14213	716-885-1080	R	5*	<.1
71	Southeastern Forge Inc—*A Stout*	PO Box 12068, Columbus GA 31917	706-685-8080	R	4*	<.1
72	Lampin Corp—*Rick Mongeau*	PO Box 327, Uxbridge MA 01569	508-278-2422	R	4*	<.1
73	Ketchie-Houston Inc—*Robert Ketchie*	201 Winecoff School Rd, Concord NC 28027	704-786-5101	R	3*	<.1
74	Orbix Corp—*Robert N Posey*	4450 S Hwy 6, Clifton TX 76634	254-675-8651	R	3*	.1
75	Leonardi Manufacturing Company Inc—*Ezio Leonardi Sr*	2728 Erie Dr, Weedsport NY 13166	315-834-6611	R	3*	<.1
76	American Hollow Boring Co—*Don Woodin*	PO Box 338, Erie PA 16512	814-452-3664	R	1*	<.1
77	OEM Industries Inc—*Edward Steiner*	PO Box 210427, Dallas TX 75211	214-330-7271	R	1*	<.1
78	Ken Elliott Company Inc—*Kent Elliot*	3704 Riehl Ln, Godfrey IL 62035	618-466-8200	R	<1*	<.1

TOTALS: SIC 3462 Iron & Steel Forgings
Companies: 78   11,033   21.4

3463 Nonferrous Forgings

Rank	Company Name—*Executive Officer*	Address, City, State, Zip	Phone	Type	Fin	Empls
1	Sypris Technologies Inc—*Paul G Larouchelle*	2820 W Broadway, Louisville KY 40211	502-774-6011	S	1,583*	2.6
2	Bharat Forge America Inc—*Stu McGowen*	2807 S Martin Luther K, Lansing MI 48910	517-393-5300	S	882*	.2
3	Wyman-Gordon Co—*Dave Gruber*	PO Box 8001, North Grafton MA 01536	508-839-4441	S	730*	3.4
4	Aluminum Precision Products Inc—*Dan Mcmahon*	3333 W Warner Ave, Santa Ana CA 92704	714-546-8125	R	115*	.9
5	Fansteel Inc—*Curtis J Zamec II*	570 Lake Cook Road Ste, Deerfield IL 60015	847-689-4900	R	80	.7
6	Brass Aluminum Forging Ent—*Kim Weishan*	PO Box 20760, Ferndale MI 48220	248-542-9258	R	55*	<.1
7	Westport Axle Corp—*Alexander Leyen*	12740 Westport Rd Ste, Louisville KY 40245	502-425-2103	R	46*	.2
8	Weber Metals Inc—*Rick Creet*	PO Box 318, Paramount CA 90723	562-602-0260	R	41*	.3
9	Plansee USA LLC—*Markus Mueller*	115 Constitution Blvd, Franklin MA 02038	508-553-3800	R	37*	.3
10	Cleveland Hardware And Forging Co—*William Hoban*	3270 E 79th St, Cleveland OH 44104	216-641-5200	R	28*	.2
11	Smiths Tubular Systems-Laconia Inc—*Ann York*	93 Lexington Dr, Laconia NH 03246	603-524-2064	R	21*	.3
12	Continental Forge Company Inc—*Charles E Haueisen*	412 E El Segundo Blvd, Compton CA 90222	310-603-1014	R	21*	.2
13	Anchor-Harvey Components LLC—*Tom Lefaivre*	600 W Lamm Rd, Freeport IL 61032	815-235-4400	R	17*	.1
14	Maass Flanges Corp—*Michael Maass*	6202 Lumberdale Rd, Houston TX 77092	713-329-5500	R	16*	.1
15	Non-Ferrous Extrusion and Scrap Metals Inc—*Norman Feil*	8410 Hempstead Rd, Houston TX 77008	713-869-9551	R	15*	.1
16	Hammond and Irving Inc—*James Taylor*	254 N St, Auburn NY 13021	315-253-6265	R	15*	.1
17	Vulcan Global Manufacturing Solutions Inc—*Charles Yanke*	1400 W Pierce St, Milwaukee WI 53204	414-645-2040	S	12*	.1
18	National Flange and Fitting Co—*Alois Keilers*	PO Box 924149, Houston TX 77292	713-688-2515	R	11*	.1
19	Aero Propulsion Support Inc—*Allan Slattery*	108 May Dr Ste A, Harrison OH 45030	513-367-9452	R	8*	<.1
20	Voss Engineering Inc—*Richard Voss*	6965 N Hamlin Ave Ste, Lincolnwood IL 60712	847-673-8900	R	6*	<.1
21	Dynamic Isolation Systems Inc—*Robert Betschart*	885 Denmark Dr Ste 101, Sparks NV 89434	775-359-3333	R	6*	<.1
22	Sierra Alloys Co—*Joe Augustyn*	5467 Ayon Ave, Irwindale CA 91706	626-969-6711	R	6*	<.1
23	OBBCO Consolidated Industries Inc—*John Holdridge*	PO Box 7178, Odessa TX 79760	432-337-5341	R	4*	<.1
24	Bakton Enterprises—*Diane Baker*	12450 Whittier Blvd, Whittier CA 90602	562-696-2326	R	3*	<.1

Note: An asterisk (*) indicates an estimated financial figure. The company type code used is as follows: R = Private, P = Public, S = Private Subsidiary, B = Public Subsidiary, D = Division, J = Joint Venture, I = Investment Fund.

COMPANY RANKINGS BY SALES WITHIN 4-DIGIT SIC

Rank	Company Name—*Executive Officer*	Address, City, State, Zip	Phone	Type	Fin	Empls
25	Earthquake Protection Systems Inc—*Victor Zayas*	451 Azuar Ave Bldg 759, Vallejo CA 94592	707-644-5993	R	<1*	<.1

TOTALS: SIC 3463 Nonferrous Forgings
Companies: 25

					3,757	10.1

3465 Automotive Stampings

Rank	Company Name—*Executive Officer*	Address, City, State, Zip	Phone	Type	Fin	Empls
1	Select International Corp—*Robert Whited*	PO Box 887, Dayton OH 45401	937-233-9191	R	5,257*	.4
2	Tower International Inc—*Mark Malcolm*	17672 N Laurel Park Dr, Livonia MI 48152	248-675-6000	P	2,406	7.8
3	Benteler Automotive Corp North American Div—*Walter Frankiewicz*	2650 N Opdyke Rd Bldg, Auburn Hills MI 48326	248-364-7190	D	335*	1.8
4	Northern Stamping Co—*Matthew Friedman*	6600 Chapek Pkwy, Cleveland OH 44125	216-883-8888	R	317*	1.7
5	Jsj Corp—*Philip Taylor*	700 Robbins Rd, Grand Haven MI 49417	616-842-6350	R	289*	2.6
6	Pridgeon and Clay Inc—*Donald Clay*	50 Cottage Grove St Sw, Grand Rapids MI 49507	616-241-5675	R	221*	.6
7	Tower Automotive Operations USA I LLC—*Dev Kapadia*	17672 Laurel Pk Dr 400, Livonia MI 48152	248-675-6000	R	178*	2.3
8	Guelph Tool Sales Inc—*Robert Ireland*	24150 Gibson Dr, Warren MI 48089	586-755-3333	S	168*	.9
9	Challenge Manufacturing Co—*Bruce Vor Broker*	3079 3 Mile Rd Nw, Grand Rapids MI 49534	616-735-6500	R	95*	1.2
10	Gill Industries Inc—*Rita Williams*	5271 Plainfield Ave Ne, Grand Rapids MI 49525	616-559-2700	R	88*	.7
11	Pk USA Inc—*Hirosige Kakudo*	600 Northridge Dr, Shelbyville IN 46176	317-398-6909	R	76*	.4
12	Stanco Metal Products Inc—*Warren Stansberry*	PO Box 307, Grand Haven MI 49417	616-842-5000	R	66*	.2
13	Ogihara America Corp—*Tokio Ogihara*	1480 Mcpherson Park Dr, Howell MI 48843	517-548-4900	R	62*	.9
14	Dongwon Autopart Technology Alabama LLC—*Bo Byeon*	12970 Montgomery Hwy, Luverne AL 36049	334-537-5000	R	59*	.2
15	Yorozu Automotive Tennessee Inc—*Yusuke Kawada*	395 Mt View Industrial, Morrison TN 37357	931-668-7700	R	56*	.3
16	Hatch Stamping Co—*Daniel Craig*	635 E Industrial Dr, Chelsea MI 48118	734-475-8628	R	50*	.2
17	Sfi Of Tennessee LLC—*Frank Trusty*	4768 Hungerford Rd, Memphis TN 38118	901-363-1571	R	45*	.2
18	Traer Manufacturing—*Stan Oaks*	PO Box 56, Traer IA 50675	319-478-8818	R	44*	.1
19	Arcelormittal Tailored Blanks Americas Corp—*Joe Neri*	PO Box 939, Pioneer OH 43554	419-737-3180	R	42*	.1
20	Spartanburg Automotive Steel Inc—*John Byers*	PO Box 6428, Spartanburg SC 29304	864-585-5211	R	41*	.6
21	Guardian Automotive—*Jim Davis*	2300 Harmon Rd, Auburn Hills MI 48326	248-340-1800	D	39*	.2
22	Wellington Industries Inc—*Marvin Tyghem*	39555 S I 94 S Service, Belleville MI 48111	734-942-1060	R	34*	.3
23	Advance Engineering Co—*George Helms*	12025 Dixie, Redford MI 48239	313-537-3500	R	31*	.3
24	Anchor Tool and Die Co—*Frederick Pfaff*	11830 Brookpark Rd, Cleveland OH 44130	216-362-1850	R	30*	.3
25	Ki (USA) Corp—*H Kanno*	501 Mayde Rd, Berea KY 40403	859-986-1420	R	29*	.2
26	A J Rose Manufacturing Co—*Daniel Pritchard*	38000 Chester Rd, Avon OH 44011	440-934-7700	R	27*	.4
27	BAE Industries Inc—*Jessee Lopez*	26020 Sherwood Ave, Warren MI 48091	586-754-3000	R	27*	.3
28	Global Advanced Products LLC—*Mark Schlump*	30707 Commerce Blvd, Chesterfield MI 48051	586-749-6800	R	26*	.1
29	Unipres USA Inc—*M Nakazato*	PO Box 799, Portland TN 37148	615-325-7311	R	25*	.4
30	Oakwood Metal Fabricating Co—*Richard Audi*	1100 Oakwood Blvd, Dearborn MI 48124	313-561-7740	R	25*	.4
31	Heritage Products Inc—*Norihede Moriya*	2000 Smith Ave, Crawfordsville IN 47933	765-364-9002	R	24*	.2
32	Logghe Stamping Co—*Mark Schettler*	16711 Thirteen Mile Rd, Fraser MI 48026	586-293-2250	R	23*	.1
33	Lenawee Stamping Corp—*Allan Power*	1200 E Chicago Blvd, Tecumseh MI 49286	517-423-2400	S	22*	.3
34	Motor City Stampings Inc—*Judith Kucway*	47783 Gratiot Ave, Chesterfield MI 48051	586-949-8420	R	22*	.3
35	Wrena LLC—*Michael Tanner*	265 Lightner Rd, Tipp City OH 45371	937-667-4403	R	22*	.2
36	Compressorworks Inc—*Stanley Davidow*	3609 Pipestone Rd, Dallas TX 75212		R	21*	.1
37	Kyoho Manufacturing California—*Shigenori Hamada*	2222 S Sinclair Ave, Stockton CA 95215	209-941-6200	R	21*	.2
38	Su-Dan Co—*Dennis Keat*	1853 Rochester Industr, Rochester Hills MI 48309	248-651-6035	R	20*	.3
39	Concord Tool And Manufacturing Inc—*Mark Dichtel*	118 N Groesbeck Hwy St, Mount Clemens MI 48043	586-465-6537	R	20*	.2
40	Wico Metal Products Company Inc—*Richard Drodie*	23500 Sherwood Ave, Warren MI 48091	586-755-9600	R	19*	.2
41	Iroquois Industries Inc—*Leo Deutschmann*	25101 Groesbeck Hwy, Warren MI 48089	586-771-5734	R	19*	.1
42	Gestamp South Carolina LLC—*Oliver Wackenhut*	1 Lsp Dr, Union SC 29379	864-466-3960	R	18*	.2
43	Amg Industries Inc—*David Meelroy*	200 Commerce Dr, Mount Vernon OH 43050	740-397-4044	R	17*	.1
44	Traverse City Products Inc—*Herman Thomas*	501 Hughes Dr, Traverse City MI 49696	231-946-4414	R	16*	.1
45	Unipres Southeast USA Inc—*Enisuke Tsuchiya*	1001 Fountain Dr, Forest MS 39074	601-469-0234	R	16*	.2
46	Grant Industries Inc—*Robert Grant*	33415 Groesbeck Hwy, Fraser MI 48026	586-293-9200	R	16*	.1
47	D and N Bending Corp—*Brian Murray*	101 E Pond Dr, Romeo MI 48065	586-752-5511	R	16*	.1
48	E and G Classics Inc—*David Eash*	8910 Mcgaw Ct, Columbia MD 21045	410-381-4900	R	15*	.1
49	Chiyoda USA Corp—*Michihiro Oe*	PO Box 494, Greencastle IN 46135	765-653-9098	R	15*	.2
50	Perfection Spring and Stamping Corp—*David Kahn*	PO Box 275, Mount Prospect IL 60056	847-437-3900	R	15*	.1
51	Truarc Company LLC	187 Davidson Ave, Somerset NJ 08873	908-859-4266	D	14*	<.1
52	New Center Stamping Inc—*Ronald Hall*	950 E Milwaukee St, Detroit MI 48211	313-872-1722	R	13*	.1
53	Ohio Stamping and Machine LLC—*Daniel Mcgregor*	PO Box 1846, Springfield OH 45501	937-322-3880	R	13*	.1
54	Inalfa/Ssi Roof Systems LLC—*Dave Odlewski*	12500 E 9 Mile Rd, Warren MI 48089	586-758-6620	R	13*	.1
55	E and W Enterprises Of Powell Inc—*Wayne Brumfield*	2601 Enon Rd, Enon OH 45323	937-864-7305	R	12*	.1
56	Superior Cam Inc—*John Basso*	31240 Stephenson Hwy, Madison Heights MI 48071	248-588-1100	R	12*	.1
57	Utica Metal Products Inc—*Charles Fields*	1526 Lincoln Ave, Utica NY 13502	315-732-6163	R	12*	.1
58	Bopp-Busch Manufacturing Co—*Robert Busch*	PO Box 589, Au Gres MI 48703	989-876-7121	R	10*	.1
59	K and K Stamping Co—*Joseph Koch*	23015 W Industrial Dr, Saint Clair Shores MI 48080	586-443-7900	R	8*	.1
60	Auto Metal Craft Inc—*Patrick Woody*	12741 Capital St, Oak Park MI 48237	248-398-2600	R	8*	<.1
61	Stamco Industries Inc—*William Sopko*	26650 Lakeland Blvd, Cleveland OH 44132	216-731-9333	R	7*	<.1
62	Sakaiya Company Of America Ltd—*Akira Sakaitani*	901 Highview Dr, Webberville MI 48892	517-521-5633	R	7*	<.1
63	Unique Tool and Manufacturing Company Inc—*Daniel Althaus*	100 Reed Dr, Temperance MI 48182	734-850-1050	R	6*	<.1
64	Exact-Tool and Die Inc—*Frank Chesek*	5425 W 140th St, Cleveland OH 44142	216-676-9140	R	6*	<.1
65	Kirmin Die and Tool Inc—*Tom Mulanka*	36360 Ecorse Rd, Romulus MI 48174	734-722-9210	R	5*	<.1
66	Dettmer Mold Inc—*Ernie Dettmer*	3150 Scott Dr, Columbus IN 47201	812-378-0247	R	5*	<.1
67	Style Craft Prototype Inc—*Michael Muszynski*	1820 Brinston Dr, Troy MI 48083	248-619-9048	R	4*	<.1
68	Ada Metal Products Inc—*Peter Barkules*	7120 N Capitol Dr, Lincolnwood IL 60712	847-673-1190	R	4*	<.1
69	Deluxe Stamping And Die Co—*Theresia Nowak*	PO Box 730, Troy MI 48099	586-264-9400	R	4*	<.1
70	Versatube Corp—*Eugene Goodman*	4755 Rochester Rd Ste, Troy MI 48085	248-689-7373	R	1*	<.1
71	Aaron Inc—*Thomas Dempsey*	33674 Kelly Rd, Clinton Township MI 48035	586-791-0320	R	1*	<.1

TOTALS: SIC 3465 Automotive Stampings
Companies: 71

					10,727	30.3

3466 Crowns & Closures

Rank	Company Name—*Executive Officer*	Address, City, State, Zip	Phone	Type	Fin	Empls
1	Orca Inc—*Gregory Goguen*	199 Whiting St Ste 5, New Britain CT 06051	860-223-4180	R	5*	<.1

3469 Metal Stampings Nec

Rank	Company Name—*Executive Officer*	Address, City, State, Zip	Phone	Type	Fin	Empls
1	Meyer Corp—*Robert Rae*	1 Meyer Plz, Vallejo CA 94590		R	1,973*	5.0
2	Tang Industries Inc—*Cyrus Tang*	8960 Spanish Ridge Ave, Las Vegas NV 89148	702-734-3700	R	1,688*	3.6
3	Elixir Industries—*Christopher Sahm*	24800 Chrisanta Dr Ste, Mission Viejo CA 92691	949-860-5000	R	1,587*	.7
4	Materion Corp—*Richard Hipple*	6070 Parkland Blvd, Mayfield Heights OH 44124	216-486-4200	P	1,302	2.5
5	Closure Systems International	6625 Network Way Ste 2, Indianapolis IN 46278		S	980*	3.0
6	Shiloh Industries Inc—*Theodore K Zampetis*	880 Steel Dr, Valley City OH 44280	330-558-2600	P	518	1.3

Rank	Company Name—*Executive Officer*	Address, City, State, Zip	Phone	Type	Fin	Empls
7	ATI Ladish LLC—*Gary Vroman*	5481 S Packard Ave, Cudahy WI 53110	414-747-2611	S	470	1.3
8	American Trim LLC—*Jeffrey Hawk*	1005 W Grand Ave, Lima OH 45801	419-739-4349	R	230*	1.5
9	Regal Ware Inc—*Jeffrey A Reigle*	1675 Reigle Dr, Kewaskum WI 53040	262-626-2121	R	220*	.5
10	Defiance Metal Products Co—*Jon Zachrich*	PO Box 447, Defiance OH 43512	419-784-5332	R	211*	1.7
11	Rittal Corp—*Arnold Buescher*	1 Rittal Pl, Springfield OH 45504	937-399-0500	R	210*	.7
12	Shiloh Industries Wellington Stamping—*Theodore Zampetis* Shiloh Industries Inc	350 Maple St, Wellington OH 44090	440-647-2100	S	177	N/A
13	Tempel Steel Co—*Tim Taylor*	5500 N Wolcott Ave, Chicago IL 60640	773-250-8000	R	175*	1.9
14	Midwest Stamping Inc—*Ronald L Thompson*	3455 Briarfield Blvd S, Maumee OH 43537	419-724-6970	R	155*	.6
15	Mayville Engineering Company Inc—*Robert Kamphuis*	715 S St, Mayville WI 53050	920-387-4500	R	154*	.7
16	MPI International Inc—*Karl A Pfister*	21177 Hilltop St, Southfield MI 48033	248-351-1030	S	152*	1.0
17	Precision Flooring Solutions Inc	140 Etowah Trace, Fayetteville GA 30214	678-817-5404	R	127	1.3
18	Ysk Corp—*Seith Tokairin*	1 Colomet Rd, Chillicothe OH 45601	740-775-9752	R	100*	.3
19	Oberg Industries Inc—*Robert Wagner*	PO Box 368, Freeport PA 16229	724-295-2121	R	99*	.7
20	Block And Company Inc—*Gregory Carlson*	PO Box 1995 Momentum P, Chicago IL 60689	847-537-7200	R	97*	.3
21	Vulcan Inc—*Robert W Lee*	PO Box 1850, Foley AL 36536	251-943-7000	R	96*	.3
22	Interplex Industries Inc—*Jack Seidler*	14-34 110 St Ste 301, College Point NY 11356	718-961-6212	R	96*	.2
23	Trans-Matic Manufacturing Co—*Patrick Thompson*	300 E 48th St, Holland MI 49423	616-820-2500	R	94*	.3
24	Northern Engraving Corp—*P Gelatt*	PO Box 377, Fort Mccoy WI 54656	608-269-6911	R	82*	1.2
25	Gill Industires Inc—*Rita Woodruff*	5271 Plainfield Ave NE, Grand Rapids MI 49525	616-559-2700	R	79*	.6
26	Heyco Metals Inc—*Michael Jemison*	1069 Stinson Dr, Reading PA 19605	610-926-4131	R	75*	.1
27	ITW Highland—*Gilles Boehm*	1240 Wolcott St, Waterbury CT 06705	203-574-3200	S	70*	.2
28	Parkview Metal Products Inc—*Nels Leutwiler*	1275 Ensell Rd, Lake Zurich IL 60047	847-540-2323	R	70*	.5
29	Truelove and MacLean Inc—*Richard Bouffard*	PO Box 4700, Waterbury CT 06704	860-274-9600	R	62*	.2
30	Copco Inc	2240 W 75th St, Woodridge IL 60517		D	60*	.6
31	Harvey Vogel Manufacturing Co—*Bob Verhey*	425 Weir Dr, Woodbury MN 55125	651-739-7373	R	58*	.2
32	ITW Drawform	500 Fairview Rd, Zeeland MI 49464	616-772-1910	R	57*	.3
33	Yarema Die and Engineering Co—*George W Lukowski*	300 Minnesota Dr, Troy MI 48083	248-585-2830	R	55*	.1
34	Fic America Corp—*Akira Ohama*	485 E Lies Rd, Carol Stream IL 60188	630-871-7609	R	53*	.7
35	Stack On Products Co—*John W Lynn*	PO Box 489, Wauconda IL 60084	847-526-1611	R	48*	.2
36	Solar Group Inc—*Cliff Tucker*	PO Box 525, Taylorsville MS 39168		S	47*	.2
37	Deflecta-Shield Accessories Inc—*Jim Coffield*	7225 N State Rd 9, Howe IN 46746	260-562-3511	R	47*	.4
38	Pax Machine Works Inc—*Mike Pax*	PO Box 338, Celina OH 45822	419-586-2337	R	44*	.2
39	ER Wagner Manufacturing Company Inc—*Frank Sterner*	4611 N 32nd St, Milwaukee WI 53209	414-871-5080	R	42*	.3
40	R and R Products Inc—*Tom Rogers*	3334 E Milber St, Tucson AZ 85714	520-889-3593	R	41*	.3
41	Connecticut Spring And Stamping Corp—*William Stevenson*	PO Box 40000, Hartford CT 06151	860-677-1341	R	40*	.3
42	Principal Manufacturing Corp—*Paul Barnett*	2800 S 19th Ave, Broadview IL 60155	708-865-7500	R	40*	.3
43	Wedge Products Inc—*Anthony Defino*	2181 Enterprise Pkwy, Twinsburg OH 44087	330-425-0099	R	39*	.3
44	Stewart EFI Texas LLC—*Bernie Rosselli*	27 Leigh Fisher Blvd, El Paso TX 79906	915-775-2558	R	36*	.3
45	Atlantic Tool and Die Company Inc—*Frank Mehwald*	19963 Progress Dr, Strongsville OH 44149	440-238-6931	R	36*	.5
46	Clairon Metals Corp—*Drew Link*	11194 Alcovy Rd, Covington GA 30014	770-786-9681	R	35*	.3
47	Self Industries Inc—*J Mcdowell*	3491 Mary Taylor Rd, Birmingham AL 35235	205-655-3284	R	35*	.1
48	Buhrke Industries LLC—*Robert Nollomann*	511 W Algonquin Rd, Arlington Heights IL 60005	847-981-7550	R	34*	.5
49	Alinabal Inc—*Sam Bergami*	28 Woodmont Rd, Milford CT 06460	203-877-3241	R	33*	.3
50	Precision Tool Die And Machine Company Inc—*Tom Hudson*	6901 Preston Hwy, Louisville KY 40219	502-479-0800	R	33*	.2
51	Cly-Del Manufacturing Co—*Robert Garthwait*	PO Box 1367, Waterbury CT 06721	203-574-2100	R	33*	.2
52	Enprotech Mechanical Services Inc—*Albert E Fountain*	2200 Olds Ave, Lansing MI 48915	517-372-0950	S	32*	.3
53	F and B Manufacturing Co—*Elizabeth Kepuraitis*	4316 N 39th Ave, Phoenix AZ 85019	602-272-3900	R	32*	.1
54	Wisconsin Tool and Stamping Co—*Peter K Ewert*	9521 Ainslie St, Schiller Park IL 60176	847-678-7573	R	31*	.2
55	Metal Flow Corp—*Robert Knittel*	11694 James St, Holland MI 49424	616-392-7976	R	31*	.1
56	Tech-Etch Inc—*George Keeler*	45 Aldrin Rd, Plymouth MA 02360	508-747-0300	R	30*	.5
57	Clow Stamping Co—*Reginal Clow*	23103 County Rd 3, Merrifield MN 56465	218-765-3111	R	30*	.3
58	Midwest Instrument Company Inc—*R Falk*	PO Box 80, Hartland WI 53029	262-367-4421	R	28*	.2
59	Sacoma International Inc—*Tom Thornburg*	955 S Walnut, Edinburgh IN 46124	812-526-5600	R	28*	.1
60	Millennium Industries Corp—*Gary Vollmar*	925 N Main St, Ligonier IN 46767	260-894-3163	R	27*	.4
61	Norlen Inc—*Thomas Suthers*	PO Box 200, Schofield WI 54476	715-359-0506	R	27*	.1
62	LH Stamping Corp—*Bruce Emerick*	4708 Clubview Dr, Fort Wayne IN 46804	260-432-9372	R	27*	.1
63	Trident Precision Manufacturing Inc—*Nicholas Juskiw*	734 Salt Rd, Webster NY 14580	585-265-2010	R	26*	.1
64	Laird Technologies—*Martin L Rapp*	3481 Rider Trail S, Earth City MO 63045	314-344-9300	S	26*	.2
65	Amtekco Industries Inc—*John Mccormick*	1205 Refugee Rd, Columbus OH 43207	614-449-7057	R	26*	.2
66	Fraen Corp—*Charles Fuller*	80 New Crossing Rd, Reading MA 01867	781-942-2223	R	25*	.2
67	Diamond Manufacturing Co—*Charles Flack*	PO Box 4174, Wyoming PA 18644	570-693-0300	R	25*	.2
68	Wisco Industries Inc—*Gary Kjellstrom*	PO Box 10, Oregon WI 53575	608-835-3106	R	25*	.2
69	Walker Corp—*Bruce Walker*	1555 S Vintage Ave, Ontario CA 91761	909-390-4300	R	25*	.2
70	Component Engineers Inc—*Ronald Hansen*	108 N Plains Industria, Wallingford CT 06492	203-269-0557	R	25*	.1
71	Center Industries Corp—*Robert Jackson*	2505 S Custer Ave, Wichita KS 67217	316-942-8255	R	25*	.3
72	Rockford Toolcraft Inc—*Gerald Busse*	766 Research Pkwy, Rockford IL 61109	815-398-5507	R	24*	.2
73	Muza Metal Products LLC—*Thomas Muza*	PO Box 707, Oshkosh WI 54903	920-236-3535	R	24*	.2
74	Jagemann Stamping Co—*Thomas Jagemann*	PO Box 217, Manitowoc WI 54221	920-682-4633	R	24*	.2
75	Oakland Stamping LLC—*Scott Jones*	1200 Woodland St, Detroit MI 48211	734-397-6300	R	24*	.3
76	Wozniak Industries Inc—*Michael Wozniak*	2 Mid America Plz Ste, Oakbrook Terrace IL 60181	630-954-3400	R	23*	.2
77	Pennant Moldings Inc—*Kurt Walterhouse*	PO Box 188, Sabina OH 45169	937-584-5411	R	23*	.2
78	Brunk Industries Inc—*Lars Brunk*	PO Box 310, Lake Geneva WI 53147	262-248-8873	R	22*	.2
79	Hobson and Motzer Inc—*Bruce Dworak*	PO Box 427, Durham CT 06422	860-349-1756	R	22*	.2
80	Bermo Inc—*Daniel Berdass*	4501 Ball Rd Ne, Circle Pines MN 55014	763-786-7676	R	21*	.3
81	Feintool US Operations Inc—*Richard Surico*	11280 Cornell Park Dr, Blue Ash OH 45242	513-247-0110	R	21*	.2
82	Contico Manufacturing—*Dave Rahilly*	305 Rock Industrial Pa, Bridgeton MO 63044		D	21	.2
83	Jm Consolidated Industries LLC—*Chris Wood*	PO Box 460, Lawrenceburg TN 38464	931-762-9403	R	21*	.4
84	Premium Allied Tool Inc—*James Hines*	PO Box 1598, Owensboro KY 42302	270-729-4242	R	20*	.3
85	Erdle Perforating Holdings Inc—*Frank Pfau*	PO Box 31568, Rochester NY 14603	585-247-4700	R	20*	.1
86	Bi-Link Metal Specialties Inc—*David Myers*	391 Glen Ellyn Rd, Bloomingdale IL 60108	630-858-5900	R	20*	.2
87	Pinnacle Precision Sheet Metal Corp—*David Oddo*	3431 E La Palma Ave, Anaheim CA 92806	714-632-7910	R	20*	.2
88	Rome Tool and Die Company Inc—*Jimmie Dudley*	113 Hemlock St Sw, Rome GA 30161	706-234-6743	R	20*	.1
89	Gasser and Sons Inc—*Richard Gasser*	440 Moreland Rd, Commack NY 11725	631-543-6600	R	19*	.1
90	Quality Perforating Inc—*Bob Farber*	166 Dundaff St, Carbondale PA 18407	570-282-4344	R	19*	.1
91	Taylor Metal Products Co—*Richard Taylor*	700 Springmill St, Mansfield OH 44903	419-522-0751	R	19*	.2
92	Mursix Corp—*Todd Murray*	PO Box 591, Muncie IN 47308	765-282-2221	R	19*	.1
93	D and D Tooling And Manufacturing Inc—*William Diedrick*	500 Territorial Dr, Bolingbrook IL 60440	630-759-0015	R	19*	.2
94	Quaker Manufacturing Corp—*Christopher Smith*	PO Box 449, Salem OH 44460	330-337-6883	R	19*	.2
95	Experi-Metal Inc—*Valiena Allison*	6385 Wall St, Sterling Heights MI 48312	586-977-7800	R	18*	.1

Note: An asterisk (*) indicates an estimated financial figure. The company type code used is as follows: R = Private, P = Public, S = Private Subsidiary, B = Public Subsidiary, D = Division, J = Joint Venture, I = Investment Fund.

COMPANY RANKINGS BY SALES WITHIN 4-DIGIT SIC

Rank	Company Name—*Executive Officer*	Address, City, State, Zip	Phone	Type	Fin	Empls
96	Market Forge Industries Inc—*David Zappala*	35 Garvey St, Everett MA 02149	617-387-4100	R	18*	.1
97	Austin Tri-Hawk Automotive Inc—*Toshitsugu Kikuchi*	PO Box 40, Austin IN 47102	812-794-0062	R	18*	.2
98	National Manufacturing Company Inc—*Robert Staudinger*	12 River Rd, Chatham NJ 07928	973-635-8846	R	18*	.2
99	Kerns Manufacturing Corp—*Louis Srybnik*	3714 29th St, Long Island City NY 11101	718-784-4044	R	18*	.1
100	Durham Manufacturing Co—*Richard Patterson*	PO Box 230, Durham CT 06422	860-349-3427	R	17*	.1
101	Triton Industries Inc—*Brenton Wortell*	1020 N Kolmar Ave, Chicago IL 60651	773-384-3700	R	17*	.2
102	Schaller Corp—*Albert Schaller*	49495 Gratiot Ave, Chesterfield MI 48051	586-949-6000	R	17*	.1
103	Wauconda Tool and Engineering Company Inc—*Chuck Burnside*	821 W Algonquin Rd, Algonquin IL 60102	847-658-4588	R	17*	.1
104	Ataco Steel Products Corp—*Richard Reichertz*	PO Box 270, Cedarburg WI 53012	262-377-3000	R	17*	.1
105	Kenmode Tool And Engineering Inc—*Werner Moders*	820 W Algonquin Rd, Algonquin IL 60102	847-658-5041	R	17*	.1
106	Radar Industries Inc—*David Zmyslowski*	27101 Groesbeck Hwy, Warren MI 48089	586-779-0300	R	17*	.1
107	Jd Norman Industries Inc—*Justin Norman*	787 W Belden Ave, Addison IL 60101	630-458-3700	R	16*	.1
108	Christopher Tool and Manufacturing Co—*Patrick Christopher*	30500 Carter St Frnt, Cleveland OH 44139	440-248-8080	R	16*	.1
109	Dubuque Stamping and Manufacturing Inc—*David Spahn*	PO Box 798, Dubuque IA 52004	563-583-5716	R	16*	.1
110	Triangle Industries Inc—*Roger Stoick*	2930 Anthony Ln, Minneapolis MN 55418	612-638-1330	R	16*	.1
111	American Pan Co—*Gilbert Bundy*	PO Box 628, Urbana OH 43078	937-652-3232	R	16*	.1
112	Rago and Son Inc—*Anne Rago*	PO Box 7309, Oakland CA 94601	510-536-5700	R	16*	.1
113	WLS Stamping Co—*Daniel Cronin*	3292 E 80th St, Cleveland OH 44104	216-271-5100	R	15*	.1
114	Assurance Manufacturing Company Inc—*Herb Lindberg*	9010 Evergreen Blvd Nw, Minneapolis MN 55433	763-780-4252	R	15*	.1
115	Kinney Tool And Die Inc—*Gerald Henk*	2024 Kinney Ave Nw, Grand Rapids MI 49534	616-453-0901	R	15*	.1
116	Intri-Plex Technologies Inc—*Lawney Falloon*	751 S Kellogg Ave, Goleta CA 93117	805-683-3414	R	15*	.1
117	Roesch Inc—*Pauline Voges*	PO Box 328, Belleville IL 62222	618-233-2760	R	15*	.1
118	Nina Enterprises—*Tony Difiglio*	1350 S Leavitt St, Chicago IL 60608	312-733-6400	R	15*	.2
119	Cleveland Die and Manufacturing Co—*Juan Chahda*	20303 1st Ave, Middleburg Heights OH 44130	440-243-3404	R	15*	.1
120	Capital Industries Inc—*Ronald Taylor*	PO Box 80983, Seattle WA 98108	206-762-8585	R	15*	.1
121	Roll-Offs Of America Inc—*Daniel Hankey*	PO Box 727, Durant OK 74702	580-924-6355	R	15*	.1
122	Btd Manufacturing Inc—*Jody Fledderman*	177 Six Pine Ranch Rd, Batesville IN 47006	812-934-5616	R	15*	.5
123	Fulton Industries Inc—*Glenn Badenhop*	PO Box 377, Wauseon OH 43567	419-335-3015	R	15*	.1
124	Morgal Machine Tool Co—*James Mc Gregor*	PO Box 1103, Springfield OH 45501	937-325-5561	R	15*	.1
125	Varbros Corp—*Joseph Dunn*	16025 Brookpark Rd, Cleveland OH 44142	216-267-5200	R	15*	.1
126	Bud Industries Inc—*Blair Haas*	4605 E 355th St, Willoughby OH 44094	440-946-3200	R	15*	.1
127	Microprecision Inc—*Joseph Moser*	PO Box 327, Delavan WI 53115	262-728-5262	R	15*	.1
128	Royal Die and Stamping Company Inc—*Henrik Freitag*	949 E Green St, Bensenville IL 60106	630-766-2685	R	15*	.1
129	LH Carbide Corp—*Bruce Emerick*	4420 Clubview Dr, Fort Wayne IN 46804	260-432-5563	R	15*	.1
130	Allied Tool and Die Company LLC—*Alan Burnett*	3807 S 7th St, Phoenix AZ 85040	602-276-2439	R	15*	.1
131	Auer Precision Stamping Inc—*Brent Bollong*	1050 W Birchwood Ave, Mesa AZ 85210	480-834-4637	R	14*	.1
132	Barco Stamping Co—*Thomas Mullally*	1095 Carolina Dr, West Chicago IL 60185	630-293-5155	R	14*	.1
133	Buferd Company Inc—*Richard Buferd*	PO Box 462321, Garland TX 75046	972-272-9502	R	14*	.1
134	Willie Washer Manufacturing Co—*William Neumann*	2101 Greenleaf Ave, Elk Grove Village IL 60007	847-956-1344	R	14*	.1
135	Ferguson Perforating and Wire Company Inc—*Bruce Ferguson*	PO Box 2038, Providence RI 02905	401-941-8876	R	14*	.1
136	New England Manufacturing Group Inc—*Kurt Maurer*	PO Box 564, Orange CT 06477	203-799-8800	R	14*	.1
137	Maynard Inc—*Joe Maynard*	1324 W Van Asche Dr, Fayetteville AR 72704	479-443-6677	R	14*	.1
138	SEMX Corp—*Gary Holcomb* Coining Inc	15 Mercedes Dr, Montvale NJ 07645	201-791-4020	S	14	.1
139	Coinco Inc—*James Cokley*	PO Box 248, Cochranton PA 16314	814-425-7407	R	14*	.1
140	P-K Tool and Manufacturing Co—*Thomas Kaiser*	4700 W Le Moyne St, Chicago IL 60651	773-235-4700	R	13*	.1
141	Alton Manufacturing Inc—*Andrew Chornobil*	825 Lee Rd, Rochester NY 14606	585-458-2600	R	13*	.1
142	Tempco Manufacturing Co—*Daniel Cronen*	2475 Hwy 55, Saint Paul MN 55120	651-452-1441	R	13*	.1
143	Guarantee Specialties Inc—*Ed Pages*	9401 Carr Ave, Cleveland OH 44108	216-451-9744	R	13*	.1
144	Tenibac-Graphion Inc—*John Gusmano*	35155 Automation Dr, Clinton Township MI 48035	586-792-0150	R	13*	.1
145	Wolverine Metal Stamping Inc—*Eric Jackson*	3600 Tennis Ct, Saint Joseph MI 49085	269-429-6600	R	13*	.1
146	Durex Inc—*Robert Denholtz*	5 Stahuber Ave, Union NJ 07083	908-688-0800	R	13*	.1
147	Meriden Manufacturing Inc—*Lester Maloney*	PO Box 694, Meriden CT 06450	203-237-7481	R	13*	.1
148	Niles Manufacturing and Finishing Inc—*Robert Hendricks*	465 Walnut St, Niles OH 44446	330-544-0402	R	13*	.1
149	Triad Metal Products Co—*Patricia Basista*	12990 Snow Rd, Cleveland OH 44130	216-676-6505	R	13*	.1
150	Ken-Tron Manufacturing Inc—*Robert Hudson*	PO Box 21250, Owensboro KY 42304	270-684-0431	R	13*	.1
151	Odm Tool and Manufacturing Company Inc—*Carl Michaelsen*	9550 Joliet Rd, Hodgkins IL 60525	708-485-6130	R	12*	.1
152	Quality Tool and Stamping Company Inc—*Edward Kuznar*	2642 Mcilwraith St, Muskegon MI 49444	231-733-2538	R	12*	.1
153	Lsa United Inc—*Richard Gessner*	2310 W 78th St, Chicago IL 60620	773-476-2700	R	12*	.1
154	Precision Machine Of Savannah Inc—*Hugh Kesler*	8 Telfair Pl, Savannah GA 31415	912-234-1107	R	12*	.1
155	Manor Tool And Manufacturing Company Inc—*Thomas Simeone*	9200 Ivanhoe St, Schiller Park IL 60176	847-678-2020	R	12*	.1
156	Falstrom Co—*Clifford Lindholm*	PO Box 118, Passaic NJ 07055	973-777-0013	R	12*	.1
157	Medalcraft Mint Inc—*Ron Chimenti*	PO Box 10267, Green Bay WI 54307	920-499-4249	R	12*	.1
158	American Metalcraft Inc—*David Kahn*	2074 George St, Melrose Park IL 60160	708-345-1177	R	12*	.1
159	Eclipse Manufacturing Co—*David Arndt*	PO Box 788, Sheboygan WI 53082	920-457-2311	R	12*	.1
160	Mckey Perforating Company Inc—*Jean Mckey*	PO Box 510206, New Berlin WI 53151	262-786-2700	R	12*	.1
161	Eyelet Design Inc—*Robert Hughes*	PO Box 808, Waterbury CT 06720	203-754-4141	R	12*	.1
162	Lgs Technologies LP—*Wallace Arnold*	PO Box 763039, Dallas TX 75376	972-224-9201	R	12*	.1
163	Hamlin Steel Products LLC—*Harry Mason*	2741 Wingate Ave, Akron OH 44314	330-753-7791	R	12*	.1
164	Aluminum Blanking Company Inc—*Marvin Hole*	360 W Sheffield Ave, Pontiac MI 48340	248-338-4422	R	12*	.1
165	Fayette Tool and Engineering Inc—*Gary Adams*	PO Box 716, Connersville IN 47331	765-825-7518	R	11*	.1
166	Preferred Tool and Die Inc—*Michael Fortin*	30 Forest Pkwy, Shelton CT 06484	203-925-8525	R	11*	.1
167	Big Rapids Products Inc—*John Chaput*	1313 Maple St, Big Rapids MI 49307	231-796-3593	R	11*	.1
168	Amclo Group Inc—*William Harkins*	2750 Grand Ave, Cleveland OH 44104	216-791-8400	R	11*	.1
169	Blase Manufacturing Co—*John Blase*	60 Watson Blvd Ste 3, Stratford CT 06615	203-375-5646	R	11*	.1
170	Florida Metal Services Inc—*John Jones*	6951 108th Ave, Largo FL 33777	727-541-6441	R	11*	.1
171	New Can Company Inc—*Thomas Houston*	PO Box 421, Holbrook MA 02343	781-767-1650	R	11*	.1
172	Seastrom Manufacturing Company Inc—*Robert Seastrom*	456 Seastrom St, Twin Falls ID 83301	208-737-4300	R	11*	.1
173	Bayloff Stamped Products Kinsman Inc—*Richard Bayer*	8091 State Rte 5, Kinsman OH 44428	330-876-4511	R	11*	.1
174	Alfred Manufacturing Co—*Greg Alfred*	4398 Elati St, Denver CO 80216	303-433-6385	R	11*	.1
175	Goshen Stamping Company Inc—*Gerald Trolz*	1025 S 10th St, Goshen IN 46526	574-533-4108	R	11*	.1
176	Evans Tool and Die Inc—*Leonard Evans*	157 N Salem Rd Ne, Conyers GA 30013	770-922-3480	R	11*	.1
177	Paris Metal Products LLC—*Randy Kolter*	13571 Il Hwy 133, Paris IL 61944	217-465-6321	R	11*	.1
178	Keystone Friction Hinge Co—*Edward Hannan*	PO Box 5087, Williamsport PA 17702	570-323-9479	R	11*	.1
179	Lamination Specialties Corp—*Albert Delighter*	235 N Artesian Ave, Chicago IL 60612	312-243-2181	R	11*	.1
180	Technical Metals Inc—*Gerald Hoffman*	PO Box 140, Fairbury IL 61739	815-692-4643	R	10*	.1
181	Houston Bazz Co—*Javier Castro*	12700 Western Ave, Garden Grove CA 92841	714-898-2666	R	10*	.1
182	Alwin Manufacturing Company Inc—*Donald Krueger*	PO Box 2126, Green Bay WI 54306	920-499-1424	R	10*	.1

Rank	Company Name—Executive Officer	Address, City, State, Zip	Phone	Type	Fin	Empls
183	Htt Inc—Greg Noble	PO Box 126, Sheboygan Falls WI 53085	920-467-0599	R	10*	.1
184	Art Materials Service Inc—Joseph Eichert	625 Joyce Kilmer Ave, New Brunswick NJ 08901	732-545-8888	R	10*	.1
185	Pentaflex Inc—Robert Buroker	4981 Gateway Blvd, Springfield OH 45502	937-325-5551	R	10*	.1
186	Intometal Inc—Joe Kennedy	3340 N 33rd St, Lincoln NE 68504	402-466-2571	R	10*	.1
187	Alcore Inc—Dave Cross	1502 Quarry Dr, Edgewood MD 21040	410-676-7100	S	10*	.1
188	Oregon Aero Inc—Michael Dennis	34020 Skyway Dr, Scappoose OR 97056	503-543-7399	R	10*	.1
189	Spring Stanley And Stamping Corp—Ronald Banas	5050 W Foster Ave, Chicago IL 60630	773-777-2600	R	10*	.1
190	Die-Matic Corp—Louie Zeitler	201 Eastview Dr, Brooklyn Heights OH 44131	216-749-4656	R	10*	.1
191	Premier Pan Company Inc—John Bundy	33 Mcgovern Blvd, Glenwillard PA 15046	724-457-4220	R	10*	.1
192	Dow Screw Products Inc—Michael Ruwitch	3810 Paule Ave, Saint Louis MO 63125	314-638-5100	R	10*	.1
193	Imperial Stamping Corp—John Conner	4801 Middlebury St, Elkhart IN 46516	574-294-3780	R	10*	.1
194	Coining Inc—Gary Holcomb	PO Box 875, Saddle Brook NJ 07663	201-791-4020	R	10*	.1
195	Interplex Engineered Products Inc—Steven Feinstein	54 Venus Way, Attleboro MA 02703	508-399-6810	R	10*	.1
196	Middleville Tool and Die Company Inc—Gary Middleton	1900 Patterson Rd, Middleville MI 49333	269-795-3646	R	10*	.1
197	Buckeye Stamping Co—Ken Tumblison	555 Marion Rd, Columbus OH 43207	614-445-8433	R	9*	.1
198	Chicago Turnrite Company Inc—Raymond Carlson	4459 W Lake St, Chicago IL 60624	773-626-8404	R	9*	.1
199	Brodeur Machine Company Business Trust—Mark Brodeur	62 Wood St, New Bedford MA 02745	508-995-2662	R	9*	.1
200	Design Standards Corp—Laurence Crainich	PO Box 1620, Charlestown NH 03603	603-826-7744	R	9*	.1
201	Hpl Stampings Inc—Roger Hedberg	425 Enterprise Pkwy, Lake Zurich IL 60047	847-540-1400	R	9*	.1
202	Com-Corp Industries Inc—Thomas Stanciu	7601 Bittern Ave, Cleveland OH 44103	216-431-6266	R	9*	.1
203	Schott Metal Products Co—Samuel Schott	2225 Lee Dr, Akron OH 44306	330-773-7873	R	9*	.1
204	Melrose Nameplate and Label Co—Chris Somers	26575 Corporate Ave, Hayward CA 94545	510-732-3100	R	9*	<.1
205	Emf Company Inc—J Tignor	PO Box 560345, Dallas TX 75356	214-350-6848	R	9*	.1
206	Talan Products Inc—Steve Peplin	18800 Cochran Ave, Cleveland OH 44110	216-458-0170	R	9*	.1
207	Spacecraft Machine Products Inc—Lloyd Leavitt	1521 N Placentia Ave, Anaheim CA 92806	714-502-0274	R	9*	.1
208	Kreider Corp—Aristides Gianakopoulas	2000 S Yellow Springs, Springfield OH 45506	937-390-0463	R	9*	.1
209	Sjoberg Tool And Manufacturing Corp—Emmett Sjoberg	535 S Industrial Dr, Hartland WI 53029	262-367-4469	R	9*	.1
210	Atlas Tool and Die Works Inc—Daniel Mottl	PO Box 32, Lyons IL 60534	708-442-1661	R	9*	.1
211	Commercial Kitchens Inc—David Calfee	2320 Peyton Rd, Houston TX 77032	281-442-8001	R	8*	.1
212	O And G Spring And Wire Form Specialty Co—Richard Gregg	4500 W Division St, Chicago IL 60651	773-772-9331	R	8*	.1
213	Inland Tool Co—Mark Hughes	PO Box 137, Mount Pulaski IL 62548	217-792-3206	R	8*	.1
214	Koester Metals Inc—Gary Koester	1441 Quality Dr, Defiance OH 43512	419-782-2595	R	8*	.1
215	P and G Steel Products Company Inc—David Ponkow	54 Gruner Rd, Buffalo NY 14227	716-896-7900	R	8*	.1
216	Edmar Manufacturing Inc—Edward Shidler	526 E 64th St, Holland MI 49423	616-392-7184	R	8*	.1
217	Ramcel Engineering Co—Rocco Palmi	2926 Macarthur Blvd, Northbrook IL 60062	847-272-6980	R	8*	.1
218	S and W Manufacturing Company Inc—William Burr	216 Evergreen Ave, Bensenville IL 60106	630-595-5044	R	8*	<.1
219	Albest Metal Stamping Corp—Alexander Fischer	1 Kent Ave, Brooklyn NY 11249	718-388-6000	R	8*	.1
220	Norwood Marking Systems—Bhavin Dave	2538 Wisconsin Ave, Downers Grove IL 60515	630-968-0646	R	8*	.1
221	Metcom Inc—Loren Aschbrenner	PO Box 49065, Cookeville TN 38506	931-526-8412	R	8*	.1
222	Micro Contacts Inc—G Tucci	62 Alpha Plz, Hicksville NY 11801	516-433-4830	R	8*	.1
223	Lake Air Metal Stamping LLC—Greg Paul	7709 Winpark Dr, Minneapolis MN 55427	763-546-0994	R	8*	.1
224	All-Tech Machine and Engineering Inc—Richard Gale	2700 Prune Ave, Fremont CA 94539	510-353-2000	R	8*	<.1
225	Wisconsin Metal Products Co—John Janes	1807 De Koven Ave, Racine WI 53403	262-633-6301	R	7*	<.1
226	Banner Metals Group Inc—John O'brien	1308 Holly Ave, Columbus OH 43212	614-291-3105	R	7*	<.1
227	Allied Metal Spinning Corp—Arlene Saunders	1290 Viele Ave, Bronx NY 10474	718-893-3300	R	7*	.1
228	KS Of West Virginia Company Ltd—Fumiyuki Hioki	PO Box 86, Ravenswood WV 26164	304-273-5500	R	7*	.1
229	Leader Tech Inc—Dario Negrini	12420 Race Track Rd, Tampa FL 33626	813-855-6921	S	7*	.1
230	Roberts Tool and Die Co—Rick Grell	PO Box 527, Chillicothe MO 64601	660-646-5950	R	7*	.1
231	Brainerd Industries Inc—Gregory Finch	680 Precision Ct, Miamisburg OH 45342	937-228-0488	R	7*	.1
232	Premier Prototype Inc—Jim Elmhirst	7775 18 1/2 Mile Rd, Sterling Heights MI 48314	586-323-6114	R	7*	.1
233	Genco Stamping And Manufacturing Co—Robert Moore	2001 Genco Dr, Cookeville TN 38506	931-528-5574	R	7*	.1
234	Toledo Metal Spinning Co—Kenneth Fankhauser	1819 Clinton St, Toledo OH 43607	419-535-5931	R	7*	<.1
235	Jonesville Tool and Manufacturing LLC—Jeremy Pann	PO Box 4364, Jackson MI 49204	517-849-2923	R	7*	<.1
236	Seljan Tool Company Inc—Scott Seljan	PO Box 158, Lake Mills WI 53551	920-648-3402	R	7*	.1
237	G and Z Chaddick Inc—David Gill	541 Chaddick Dr, Wheeling IL 60090	847-215-2300	R	7*	<.1
238	Charles A Rogers Enterprises Inc—Charles Rogers	PO Box 627, Victor NY 14564	585-924-6400	R	7*	<.1
239	Columbia Metal Spinning Co—Fred Haberkamp	4351 N Normandy Ave, Chicago IL 60634	773-685-2800	R	7*	<.1
240	Orick Tool And Die Co—Paul Orick	614 E Kiracofe Ave, Elida OH 45807	419-331-0600	R	7*	.1
241	Taylor Press Products Co—James Taylor	13675 N Ih 35, Jarrell TX 76537	512-746-5556	R	7*	.1
242	Ecp Corp—Steven Began	1305 Chester Industria, Avon OH 44011	440-934-0444	R	7*	<.1
243	Tro Manufacturing Company Inc—Laddie Sanda	PO Box 528, Franklin Park IL 60131	847-455-3755	R	7*	<.1
244	United Standard Industries Inc—Sherwin Feldstein	2062 Lehigh Ave, Glenview IL 60026	847-724-0350	R	6*	.1
245	Mrg Tool And Die Corp—Mike Gramse	1100 Cannon Cir, Faribault MN 55021	507-334-1847	R	6*	.1
246	Stever-Locke Industries Inc—Elaine Davin	179 N Main St, Honeoye Falls NY 14472	585-624-3450	R	6*	.1
247	All Southern Fabricators Inc—Manuel Santana	PO Box 658, Pinellas Park FL 33780	727-573-4846	R	6*	<.1
248	Ro-Banks Tool and Manufacturing Co—Robert Banks	PO Box 968, Wahpeton ND 58074	701-642-2671	R	6*	.1
249	Kopykake Enterprises Inc—Gerald Mayer	3699 W 240th St, Torrance CA 90505	310-373-8906	R	6*	<.1
250	Precision Tool and Stamping Inc—Tart Lee	PO Box 615, Clinton NC 28329	910-592-0174	R	6*	<.1
251	DD Wire Company Inc—Dorsey D Wire	4335 Temple City Blvd, Temple City CA 91780	626-442-0459	R	6*	<.1
252	Allen Machine Products Inc—Peter Allen	120 Ricefield Ln Ste 1, Hauppauge NY 11788	631-630-8800	R	6*	.1
253	Hill Manufacturing Co—Marion Hill	PO Box 241, Wauseon OH 43567	419-335-5006	R	6*	.1
254	Belmet Products Inc—Donald Bady	PO Box 229029, Brooklyn NY 11222	718-782-3554	R	6*	.1
255	Decco Graphics Inc—Harry Line	24411 Frampton Ave, Harbor City CA 90710	310-534-2861	R	6*	<.1
256	Precision Photo-Fab Inc—Dennis Switzer	4020 Jeffrey Blvd, Buffalo NY 14219	716-821-9393	R	6*	<.1
257	Richmond Industries Inc—Norbert Allmenger	4460 Hamann Pkwy, Willoughby OH 44094	440-942-6060	R	6*	<.1
258	Talent Tool and Die Inc—Thanh Pham	777 Berea Industrial P, Berea OH 44017	440-239-8777	R	6*	<.1
259	Kaga (USA) Inc—Masaaki Nozaki	2620 S Susan St, Santa Ana CA 92704	714-540-2697	R	6*	<.1
260	Prikos and Becker Tool Co—William Becker	8109 Lawndale Ave, Skokie IL 60076	847-675-3910	R	6*	<.1
261	Jackson Precision Industries Inc—John Ziemba	1900 Cooper St, Jackson MI 49202	517-782-8103	R	6*	<.1
262	Kuester Tool and Die Inc—Stanley Musholt	PO Box 3583, Quincy IL 62305	217-223-1955	R	5*	<.1
263	Herd Manufacturing Inc—Erich Rock	9227 Clinton Rd, Cleveland OH 44144	216-651-4221	R	5*	<.1
264	Lookout Valley Tool and Machine Inc—Jerry Walls	2923 Gordon Rd, Chattanooga TN 37419	423-825-5203	R	5*	<.1
265	Lyons Tool and Die Co—William Lyons	185 Research Pkwy, Meriden CT 06450	203-238-2689	R	5*	<.1
266	Ceramco Inc—Terry Link	PO Box 7265, Charlotte NC 28241	704-588-3121	R	5*	<.1
267	Kitcor Corp—William Kitchen	9959 Glenoaks Blvd, Sun Valley CA 91352	818-767-4800	R	5*	<.1
268	Chase Manufacturing—Bryan Anderson	PO Box 37, Corry PA 16407	814-664-9069	R	5*	<.1
269	Penrose Machining Inc—Eugene Penrose	2810 E Us Hwy 30, Grand Island NE 68801	308-381-7391	R	5*	<.1
270	Top Tool Co—Elizabeth Abraham	3100 84th Ln Ne Ste C, Minneapolis MN 55449	763-786-0030	R	5*	<.1
271	Nielsen Sessions—Dick Sim	11 Beckwith Ave, Binghamton NY 13901	607-772-0404	S	5*	<.1
272	Simplomatic Manufacturing Co—David Hahn	816 N Kostner Ave, Chicago IL 60651	773-342-7757	R	5*	<.1
273	Uei Inc—Greg Usher	2771 W River Dr Nw, Grand Rapids MI 49544	616-361-6093	R	5*	<.1

Note: An asterisk (*) indicates an estimated financial figure. The company type code used is as follows: R = Private, P = Public, S = Private Subsidiary, B = Public Subsidiary, D = Division, J = Joint Venture, I = Investment Fund.

COMPANY RANKINGS BY SALES WITHIN 4-DIGIT SIC

Rank	Company Name—Executive Officer	Address, City, State, Zip	Phone	Type	Fin	Empls
274	BEC Systems Inc—Earl Bulgier	100 Christopher Ln, Harleysville PA 19438	215-256-3100	R	5*	<.1
275	Branch Manufacturing Co—Delmer Fairbanks	PO Box 68, North Branch MN 55056	651-674-4441	R	5*	.1
276	Ace Stamping and Machine Company Inc—Ronald Haarsma	2801 S Memorial Dr, Racine WI 53403	262-637-7946	R	5*	<.1
277	Leefson Tool and Die Co—Richard Leefson	850 Henderson Blvd, Folcroft PA 19032	610-461-7772	R	5*	<.1
278	Industrial Gasket Inc—Albert Gray	PO Box 760, Mustang OK 73064	405-376-9393	R	5*	<.1
279	Superior Metal Products Inc—Henry Mathes	PO Box 490, Greeneville TN 37744	423-257-2154	R	5*	.1
280	Marco Manufacturing Company Inc—Anthony Simiriglio	1701 15 S 26th St 15, Philadelphia PA 19145	215-463-2332	R	5*	<.1
281	Cotter Machine Company Inc—Gregory Cotter	PO Box 249, West Wareham MA 02576	508-291-7400	R	5*	<.1
282	Perrysburg Machine And Tool Inc—Lawrence Van Vlerah	PO Box 1595, Maumee OH 43537	419-874-3146	R	5*	<.1
283	Stripmatic Products Inc—William Adler	1501 Abbey Ave, Cleveland OH 44113	216-241-7143	R	5*	<.1
284	Acrontos Manufacturing Inc—Ngoc Hoang	1641 E Saint Gertrude, Santa Ana CA 92705	714-850-9133	R	5*	<.1
285	Highwood Die and Engineering Inc—Marilyn Miller	1353 Highwood Blvd, Pontiac MI 48340	248-338-1807	R	5*	<.1
286	Mcminnville Tool and Die Inc—Myers Hand	PO Box 8245, Mcminnville TN 37111	931-473-8464	R	4*	<.1
287	Branko Perforating Fwd Inc—Herb Watts	PO Box 55, Bristol WI 53104	262-857-2389	R	4*	<.1
288	Dalla's Machine Inc—James Palu	4410 Park View Dr, Schnecksville PA 18078	610-799-2800	R	4*	<.1
289	Action Tool and Manufacturing Inc—Troy Gay	5573 Sandy Hollow Rd, Rockford IL 61109	815-874-5775	R	4*	<.1
290	Globe Technologies Corp—Norman Van Wormer	PO Box 1070, Standish MI 48658	989-846-9591	R	4*	<.1
291	Square Stamping Manufacturing Corp—David Allen	PO Box 207, Barneveld NY 13304	315-896-2641	R	4*	<.1
292	Sundstrom Pressed Steel Co—Richard Sundstrom	8030 S S Chicago Ave, Chicago IL 60617	773-721-2237	R	4*	<.1
293	Twinplex Manufacturing Co—Kenneth Floyd	840 Lively Blvd, Wood Dale IL 60191	630-595-2040	R	4*	<.1
294	Northland Machine Inc—Marvin Gustafson	35234 Us Hwy 2, Grand Rapids MN 55744	218-328-6479	R	4*	<.1
295	Spindustries LLC—Ellen Rogers	1301 La Salle St, Lake Geneva WI 53147	262-248-6601	R	4*	<.1
296	Intrepid Machine Inc—Tim Tabor	2305 Circuit Way, Brooksville FL 34604	352-540-9919	R	4*	<.1
297	Cumberland Tool and Die Inc—Kenneth Brown	6 Brenneman Cir, Mechanicsburg PA 17050	717-691-1125	R	4*	<.1
298	Rockford Co—Joseph Klinck	1827 Broadway, Rockford IL 61104	815-397-2677	R	4*	<.1
299	Bryant's Precision M F G Corp—Brenda Bryant	PO Box 2844, Vero Beach FL 32961	772-569-2319	R	4*	<.1
300	Abbott Tool Inc—Arthur Stange	405 Dura Ave, Toledo OH 43612	419-476-6742	R	4*	<.1
301	A and M Tool C Inc—Dieter Ade	450 Chaddick Dr, Wheeling IL 60090	847-215-8140	R	4*	<.1
302	Dupree and Phillips Enterprises Inc—Duval Campbell	3160 Marjan Dr, Atlanta GA 30340	770-452-0445	R	4*	<.1
303	Pocasset Machine Corp—Barry Kent	PO Box 3088, Pocasset MA 02559	508-563-5572	R	4*	<.1
304	R-Bo Company Inc—Larry Rigterink	150 W Washington Ave, Zeeland MI 49464	616-748-9733	R	4*	<.1
305	Amity Die and Stamping Co—Lyn Westphal	13870 W Polo Trl Dr, Lake Forest IL 60045	847-680-6600	R	4*	<.1
306	Gemel Precision Tool Inc—Klaus Gehlert	31 Industrial Dr, Warminster PA 18974	215-355-9052	R	4*	<.1
307	P O Mcintire Co—James Goglin	4727 E 355th St, Willoughby OH 44094	440-269-1848	R	4*	<.1
308	American Standard Co—Nathaniel Florian	157 Water St, Southington CT 06489	860-628-9643	R	4*	<.1
309	Formco Metal Products Inc—Peter Weiss	556 Clayton Ct, Wood Dale IL 60191	630-766-4441	R	4*	<.1
310	H and O Tool and Die Inc—Bobby Oliver	620 W Cheatham St, Union City TN 38261	731-885-2001	R	4*	<.1
311	Archer Manufacturing Corp—Joseph Sekula	4439 S Knox Ave, Chicago IL 60632	773-585-7181	R	4*	<.1
312	New Bremen Machine and Tool Co—Joan Leffel	705 Kuenzel Dr, New Bremen OH 45869	419-629-3295	R	4*	<.1
313	G and M Company Inc—William Markle	PO Box 4009, Reading PA 19606	610-779-7812	R	4*	<.1
314	Durivage Pattern and Manufacturing Company Inc—Gary Durivage	PO Box 337, Williston OH 43468	419-836-8655	R	3*	<.1
315	Cap and Seal Co—Thomas Brown	1591 Fleetwood Dr, Elgin IL 60123	847-741-3101	R	3*	<.1
316	German Machine and Assembly Inc—Scott Boheen	10 Excel Dr, Rochester NY 14621	585-467-5351	R	3*	<.1
317	Mastercraft Engineering Inc—James Haswell	323 Southwell Blvd, Tifton GA 31794	229-386-1858	R	3*	<.1
318	Carter Manufacturing Company Inc—John Scholz	55 Anderson Ave, Moonachie NJ 07074	201-935-0770	R	3*	<.1
319	Heb Manufacturing Company Inc—Bonnie Kennedy	PO Box 188, Chelsea VT 05038	802-685-4821	R	3*	<.1
320	Atlas Stamping and Manufacturing Corp—Kenneth Prigodich	729 N Mountain Rd, Newington CT 06111	860-947-2027	R	3*	<.1
321	Co-Planar Inc—James Moody	PO Box 1115, Denville NJ 07834	973-625-3500	R	3*	<.1
322	Creative Design And Machine Inc—Cliff Broderick	197 Stone Castle Rd, Rock Tavern NY 12575	845-778-9001	R	3*	<.1
323	Stuebing Automatic Machine Company Inc—William Hoffman	10400 Taconic Ter, Cincinnati OH 45215	513-771-8028	R	3*	<.1
324	Chiptec Inc—Lloyd Mc Call	708 State Docks Rd, Decatur AL 35601	256-350-1797	R	3*	.1
325	Paramount Tool LLC—George Fabnetts	473 Pleasant St, Fall River MA 02721	508-672-0852	R	3*	<.1
326	Cc Coating and Machine Inc—Mark Rider	PO Box 4244, Corpus Christi TX 78469	361-884-9753	R	3*	<.1
327	Domeny Tool and Stamping Co—Marge Domeny	354 Hollow Hill Rd, Wauconda IL 60084	847-526-5700	R	3*	<.1
328	National Wire and Metal Technologies Inc—Bump Hedman	200 Harrison St Ste 10, Jamestown NY 14701	716-661-9180	R	3*	<.1
329	Bridgeport Tool and Stamping Corp—Julius Kish	35 Burr Ct, Bridgeport CT 06605	203-336-2501	R	3*	<.1
330	Valley Tool and Die Stampings Inc—Norman Miller	PO Box 6, Lake Cicott IN 46942	574-722-4566	R	3*	<.1
331	Manufacturers Service Inc—Carl Jordan	11440 Brookpark Rd, Cleveland OH 44130	216-267-3771	R	3*	<.1
332	Independent Stamping Inc—William Nester	12025 Zelis Rd, Cleveland OH 44135	216-251-3500	R	3*	<.1
333	Astro Tool and Die Company Inc—Elmer Lorenzen	5201 S Whitnall Ave, Cudahy WI 53110	414-483-0343	R	3*	<.1
334	Barber Electric Manufacturing Company Inc—Norman Langelier	30 Chestnut St, North Attleboro MA 02760	508-699-4872	R	3*	<.1
335	Gentzler Tool and Die Corp—Geraldine Gentzler	PO Box 158, Green OH 44232	330-896-1941	R	3*	<.1
336	Spaceage Tool and Manufacturing Inc—Thomas Dearmin	611 N Park St, Saint Ansgar IA 50472	641-713-2055	R	3*	<.1
337	Cicero Plastic Products Inc—George Driggers	121 Anton Dr, Romeoville IL 60446	815-886-9522	R	3*	<.1
338	Sgjb Business Holdings Inc—Bob Baker	450 Apollo Dr, Circle Pines MN 55014	651-784-4240	R	3*	<.1
339	Stromberg Tool and Machine Company Inc—Paul Stromberg	PO Box 578, Sterling MA 01564	978-422-8178	R	3*	<.1
340	Howland Machine Corp—Bruce Dewey	947 Summit Ave, Niles OH 44446	330-544-4029	R	3*	<.1
341	Rj Stuckel Company Inc—Robert Stuckel	211 Seegers Ave, Elk Grove Village IL 60007	847-593-7220	R	3*	<.1
342	Eugenio's Sheet Metal Inc—Eugenio Lozano	2151 Maple Privado, Ontario CA 91761	909-923-2002	R	2*	<.1
343	Eastman-Booth Inc—Ralph Hinkle	4101 W Commercial St, Harrison AR 72601	870-741-1000	R	2*	<.1
344	Impulse Packaging Inc—Deborah Meyers	55 Pawtucket Ave Ste D, Rumford RI 02916	401-434-5588	R	2*	<.1
345	Jordan Manufacturing Co—Steven Johnson	PO Box 130, Belding MI 48809	616-794-0900	R	2*	<.1
346	Maudlin and Son Manufacturing Inc—Earl T Maudlin	PO Box 699, Kemah TX 77565	281-334-7566	R	2*	<.1
347	Quality Die Set Corp—Jerry Shank	PO Box 157, Flora IN 46929	574-967-4411	R	2*	<.1
348	Hub Manufacturing Company Inc—Gerald Benda	1212 N Central Park Av, Chicago IL 60651	773-252-1373	R	2*	<.1
349	Tool Specialties Co—William P Rauch	128 Ford Ln, Hazelwood MO 63042	314-731-3270	R	2*	<.1
350	Freeport Screen and Stamping Inc—Stan Papot	31 Hanse Ave, Freeport NY 11520	516-379-0330	R	2*	<.1
351	K and E Manufacturing Co—Laurence Kopek	PO Box 841, Lees Summit MO 64063	816-525-3777	R	2*	<.1
352	Vulcan Tool Company Inc—Anton Heldmann	1080 Garden State Rd S, Union NJ 07083	908-686-0550	R	2*	<.1
353	Great Lakes Pressed Steel Corp—Timothy Nichols	1400 Niagara St, Buffalo NY 14213	716-885-4037	R	2*	<.1
354	TMU Inc—Robert Bartle	910 Shunpike Rd Ste A, Cape May NJ 08204	609-884-7656	R	2*	<.1
355	Cheek Engineering and Stamping—Chris Huff	14341 Franklin Ave, Tustin CA 92780	714-832-9480	R	2*	<.1
356	Continental Business Enterprises Inc—Louis Trolli	7311 Northfield Rd, Cleveland OH 44146	440-439-4400	R	2*	<.1
357	Middco Tool and Equipment Inc—Kevin Middaugh	PO Box 11978, Spokane Valley WA 99211	509-535-1701	R	2*	<.1
358	Sossner Tool Corp—Neil Friedman	180 Judge Don Lewis Bl, Elizabethton TN 37643	423-543-4001	R	2*	<.1
359	Bandel Manufacturing Inc—Edward Finley	PO Box 39346, Los Angeles CA 90039	323-245-4747	R	2*	<.1
360	Tech-Med Inc—Gary White	1080 E 222nd St, Euclid OH 44117	216-486-0900	R	2*	<.1
361	Eagle Precision Products LLC—Rick Greene	13800 Progress Pkwy St, North Royalton OH 44133	440-582-9393	R	2*	<.1

Rank	Company Name—*Executive Officer*	Address, City, State, Zip	Phone	Type	Fin	Empls
362	Compac Development Corp—*Peter Rao*	1460 N Clinton Ave O15, Bay Shore NY 11706	631-585-3400	R	2*	<.1
363	WT Pettit and Sons Company Inc—*Francis Poe*	1670 Keefer Rd, Girard OH 44420	330-539-6100	R	2*	<.1
364	Die-Matic Tool Company Inc—*James Gaston*	PO Box 620, Meridianville AL 35759	256-828-3429	R	1*	<.1
365	Magnolia Tool and Manufacturing Company Inc—*Dallas Crory*	PO Box 426, Ridgeland MS 39158	601-856-4333	R	1*	<.1
366	Progressive Die and Stamping Inc—*Ben Perron*	PO Box 49195, Cookeville TN 38506	931-537-6528	R	1*	<.1
367	United Tool and Die Company Inc—*Scott Fallo*	98 Eames St, Wilmington MA 01887	978-658-5500	R	1*	<.1
368	Sos Engineering Inc—*David Suchecki*	1901 Hayes St, Grand Haven MI 49417	616-846-5767	R	1*	<.1
369	Derita Precision Machine Company Inc—*Dennis Butts*	PO Box 645, Paw Creek NC 28130	704-392-7285	R	1*	<.1
370	Galaxy Manufacturing Inc—*Kevin Lettire*	PO Box 1153, Santa Clara CA 95052	408-654-4583	R	1*	<.1
371	Brandt Precision Machining Inc—*Duane Brandt*	11116 N Lamar Blvd Uni, Austin TX 78753	512-339-7251	R	1*	<.1
372	Built-Rite Manufacturing Inc—*Robert Weiser*	PO Box 338, Conger MN 56020	507-265-3235	R	1*	<.1
373	Precision Concepts Inc—*Vince Marino*	2701 Boulder Park Ct, Winston Salem NC 27101		R	1*	.1
374	Hi-Tech Inc—*John Lavin*	11 Sunnyside Ave, Johnston RI 02919	401-331-0781	R	1*	<.1
375	Van Reenen Tool and Die Inc—*Richard Reenen*	PO Box 10256, Rochester NY 14610	585-288-6000	R	1*	<.1
376	Brooks Precision Machining Inc—*Charles Brooks*	4 Kidder Rd, Chelmsford MA 01824	978-256-7477	R	1*	<.1
377	Kwikprint Manufacturing Company Inc—*Jay Cann*	4868 Victor St, Jacksonville FL 32207	904-737-3755	R	1*	<.1
378	Stephens Precision Inc—*Franklin Stephens*	293 Industrial Dr, Bradford VT 05033	802-222-9600	R	1*	<.1
379	Electro Optics Manufacturing Inc—*Kathryn Chambers*	4459 13th St, Wyandotte MI 48192	734-283-3000	R	1*	<.1
380	Plasticrest Products Inc—*Robert Pauley*	4519 W Harrison St, Chicago IL 60624	773-826-2163	R	1*	<.1
381	Us Machine And Tool—*Jim Gillentine*	PO Box 3121, Muncie IN 47307	765-282-2724	R	1*	<.1
382	Brw Tool Inc—*Ray Barber*	PO Box 417, Saint Marys OH 45885	419-394-3371	R	1*	<.1
383	Nowak Products Inc—*Gary Nowak*	101 Rockwell Rd, Newington CT 06111	860-666-9685	R	1*	<.1
384	Arco Metals Inc—*William Brigman*	3546 Old York Rd, Baltimore MD 21218	410-235-7977	R	1*	<.1
385	Wonderfoil Inc—*Richard Russell*	4790 Crittenden Dr Ste, Louisville KY 40209	502-368-5380	R	1*	<.1
386	Kennley Corp—*Ken Guthrie*	8808b Metro Ct, Richmond VA 23237	804-275-9088	R	<1*	<.1
387	Sharp Technologies Inc—*Jeffrey Sharp*	615 Berry Ave, Bellevue KY 41073	859-431-5389	R	<1*	<.1

TOTALS: SIC 3469 Metal Stampings Nec

	Companies: 387				15,518	64.0

3471 Plating & Polishing

Rank	Company Name—*Executive Officer*	Address, City, State, Zip	Phone	Type	Fin	Empls
1	Spectrum Industries Inc (Grand Rapids Michigan)—*Keith Bassett*	700 Wealthy St SW, Grand Rapids MI 49504	616-451-0784	R	156*	.4
2	Hytek Finishes Co—*Cliff Johnson*	8127 S 216th St, Kent WA 98032	253-872-7160	S	138*	.3
3	International Metals and Chemicals Group—*David Verien*	135 Old Boiling Spring, Shelby NC 28152	704-482-8200	R	105*	.2
4	Pioneer Metal Finishing LLC—*Robert Pyle*	PO Box 28440, Green Bay WI 54324	920-499-6996	R	102*	.7
5	Industrial Polishing Services Inc	9465 Customhouse Plz, San Diego CA 92154	619-661-1691	R	60*	1.8
6	Linetec Co—*Rick Marshall*	725 S 75th Ave, Wausau WI 54401	715-843-4100	S	44	.5
7	Flat Rock Metal Inc—*Keith King*	PO Box 1090, Flat Rock MI 48134	734-782-4454	R	40*	.7
8	Southwest United Industries Inc—*W Emery*	422 S Saint Louis Ave, Tulsa OK 74120	918-587-4161	R	38*	.2
9	Automated Wheel—*Gregory Hadgis*	8525 Clinton Rd, Brooklyn OH 44144	216-651-9022	R	34*	.4
10	Bowers Manufacturing Co—*Jon Bowers*	6565 S Sprinkle Rd, Portage MI 49002	269-323-2565	R	31*	.3
11	Anomatic Corp—*William Rusch*	1650 Tamarack Rd, Newark OH 43055	740-522-2203	R	29*	.5
12	Empire Hard Chrome Inc—*William Horne*	1615 S Kostner Ave, Chicago IL 60623	773-762-3156	R	27*	.3
13	AACOA Inc—*Dan Formsma*	2005 Mayflower Rd, Niles MI 49120	269-697-6063	R	26*,	.2
14	Precision Roll Grinders Inc—*James Manley*	6356 Chapmans Rd, Allentown PA 18106	610-395-6966	R	25*	.2
15	Plating Technology Inc—*Dennis Goldman*	PO Box 06236, Columbus OH 43206	614-228-2325	R	24*	.2
16	Quaker City Plating and Silversmith A California LP—*Chuck Wolitski*	PO Box 2406, Whittier CA 90610	562-309-8560	R	22*	.2
17	Tanury Industries Inc—*Michael Akkaoui*	6 New England Way, Lincoln RI 02865	401-333-9400	H	21*	.2
18	Lincoln Industries Inc—*Marc Baron*	600 W E St, Lincoln NE 68522	402-475-3671	R	21*	.3
19	Induplate Inc—*Everett Fernald*	1 Greystone Ave Ste 1, North Providence RI 02911	401-231-5770	R	20*	.2
20	Embee Inc—*John Dahlberg*	PO Box 15705, Santa Ana CA 92735	714-546-9842	R	20*	.4
21	Aluminum Coil Anodizing Corp—*Ronald Rusch*	501 E Lake St, Streamwood IL 60107	630-837-4000	R	20*	.2
22	Innovative Certified Technical Plating LLC—*Deena Leonard*	160 83rd Ave Ne Ste 10, Minneapolis MN 55432	763-717-7016	R	20*	.2
23	Roll Coater Inc—*Bob O'Neal*	8440 Woodfield Crossin, Indianapolis IN 46240	317-462-7761	S	19	.2
24	Electro Chemical Finishing Co—*Terry Vollmer*	2610 Remico St Sw, Grand Rapids MI 49519	616-531-0670	R	19*	.2
25	Arlington Plating Co—*Marvin Gollob*	PO Box 974, Palatine IL 60078	847-359-1490	R	19*	.2
26	Sigma Plating Company Inc—*Jeffrey Sharp*	4000 Valley Blvd Ste 1, Walnut CA 91789	626-965-2561	R	18*	.2
27	Paulo Products Co—*Benjamin Rassieur*	5620 W Park Ave, Saint Louis MO 63110	314-647-7500	R	17*	.3
28	Apollo Plating Inc—*Jim Grimes Sr*	15765 Sturgeon St, Roseville MI 48066	810-777-0070	R	17*	.1
29	Lorin Industries Inc—*Robert Kersman*	PO Box 766, Muskegon MI 49443	231-722-1631	R	16*	.1
30	Metal Surfaces Inc—*Bob Ledterman*	PO Box 5001, Bell Gardens CA 90202	562-927-1331	R	16*	.2
31	Mueller Corp—*Glen Mueller*	530 Spring St, East Bridgewater MA 02333	508-583-2800	R	16*	.2
32	General Super Plating Company Inc—*Thomas Gerhardt*	5762 Celi Dr, East Syracuse NY 13057	315-446-2264	R	15*	.1
33	Allied Finishing Inc—*Bruce Stone*	PO Box 3728, Grand Rapids MI 49501	616-698-7550	R	15*	.2
34	Gene's Plating Works Inc—*Harry Levy*	3498 E 14th St, Los Angeles CA 90023	323-269-8748	R	15*	.2
35	Triumph Processing Inc—*Peter J LaBarbera*	2605 Industry Way, Lynwood CA 90262	323-563-1338	S	14*	.1
36	Belmont Plating Works Inc—*Mark Toni*	9145 King St, Franklin Park IL 60131	847-678-0200	R	14*	.1
37	United Plating Inc—*Michael Fann*	PO Box 2046, Huntsville AL 35804	256-852-8700	R	13*	.1
38	Park Nameplate Company Inc—*William Hand*	27 Production Dr, Dover NH 03820	603-749-7600	R	13*	.1
39	East Side Plating Inc—*Gary Rehnberg*	8400 Se 26th Pl, Portland OR 97202	503-654-3774	R	13*	.1
40	All Metals Processing Of San Diego Inc—*Stephen Sellwood*	8401 Standustrial St, Stanton CA 90680	714-828-8238	R	13*	.1
41	Nex-Tech Processing Inc—*Tom Gibbons*	1702 S Knight St, Wichita KS 67213	316-943-0731	R	12*	.1
42	Industrial Hard Chrome Ltd—*C Therkildsen*	501 Fluid Power Dr, Geneva IL 60134	630-208-7000	R	12*	.1
43	Ihc Inc—*Jeffrey Pernick*	12400 Burt Rd, Detroit MI 48228	313-535-3210	R	12*	.1
44	Nico Products Inc—*Kirk Lindgren*	2929 1st Ave S, Minneapolis MN 55408	612-822-2185	R	11*	.1
45	Springco Metal Coating—*Paul W Springer*	12500 Elmwood Ave, Cleveland OH 44111	216-941-0020	R	11*	.2
46	Master Finish Co—*Dale Mulder*	PO Box 7505, Grand Rapids MI 49510	616-245-1228	R	11*	.1
47	Seidel Inc—*Michael Ritzenhoff*	2223 Thomaston Ave, Waterbury CT 06704	203-757-7349	R	11*	.1
48	Acme Galvanizing Inc—*Edward Weiss*	PO Box 340050, Milwaukee WI 53234	414-645-3250	R	11*	.1
49	Professional Plating Inc—*Robert Endries*	705 Northway Dr, Brillion WI 54110	920-756-2153	R	11*	.1
50	Light Metals Coloring Company Inc—*Richard Fleet*	270 Spring St, Southington CT 06489	860-621-0145	R	11*	.1
51	Erieview Metal Treating Company Inc—*Alex Kappos*	4465 Johnston Pkwy, Cleveland OH 44128	216-663-1780	R	11*	.1
52	Swd Inc—*Richard Delawder*	910 S Stiles Dr, Addison IL 60101	630-543-3003	R	10*	.1
53	General Metal Finishing Company Inc—*Robert Palos*	42 Frank Mossberg Dr, Attleboro MA 02703	508-222-9683	R	10*	.1
54	Highland Plating Co—*Max Faeth*	PO Box 38941, Los Angeles CA 90038	323-850-1020	R	10*	.1
55	Metco Treating And Development Co—*John Glass*	2001 S Kilbourn Ave, Chicago IL 60623	773-277-1600	R	10*	.1
56	MPC Plating Inc—*Albert Walcutt*	1859 E 63rd St, Cleveland OH 44103	216-881-7220	R	10*	.1
57	Summit Corporation Of America—*Harry Scoble*	1430 Waterbury Rd, Thomaston CT 06787	860-283-4391	R	10*	.1

Note: An asterisk (*) indicates an estimated financial figure. The company type code used is as follows: R = Private, P = Public, S = Private Subsidiary, B = Public Subsidiary, D = Division, J = Joint Venture, I = Investment Fund.

COMPANY RANKINGS BY SALES WITHIN 4-DIGIT SIC

Rank	Company Name—Executive Officer	Address, City, State, Zip	Phone	Type	Fin	Empls
58	SIFCO Selective Plating	5708 E Schaaf Rd, Cleveland OH 44131	216-524-0099	S	10*	<.1
59	Precision Finishing Inc—John Bell	708 Lawn Ave, Sellersville PA 18960	215-257-6862	R	10*	<.1
60	Librandi Machine Shop Inc—Thomas Librandi	93 Airport Dr, Middletown PA 17057	717-944-9442	R	10*	.1
61	Aluminum Finishing Of Georgia Corp—Ken Sigsbury	PO Box 509, Adel GA 31620	229-896-4531	R	10*	.1
62	Avtec Finishing Systems Inc—Mark Hockley	9101 Science Ctr Dr, Minneapolis MN 55428	763-533-4822	R	10*	.1
63	Cooperative Plating Co—Kenneth Rosenblum	271 Snelling Ave N, Saint Paul MN 55104	651-645-0787	R	10*	.1
64	Flexible Controls Corp—Thomas Melita	17450 Filer St, Detroit MI 48212	313-368-3630	R	10*	.1
65	Gleco Plating Inc—Jeff Fodge	2220 Grisham Dr, Rowlett TX 75088	972-475-4300	R	9*	.1
66	Eastern Plating Inc—Michael Mullaney	371 Chemwood Dr, Newport TN 37821	423-623-0062	R	9*	.1
67	Modern Plating Corp—James Stenberg	PO Box 838, Freeport IL 61032	815-235-3111	R	9*	.1
68	Barry Avenue Plating Company Inc—Chuck Kearsley	2210 Barry Ave, Los Angeles CA 90064	310-478-0078	R	9*	.1
69	Asko Processing Inc—David Kelly	434 N 35th St, Seattle WA 98103	206-634-2080	R	9*	.1
70	Quality Rolling And Deburring Company Inc—George Capra	135 S Main St Ste 3, Thomaston CT 06787	860-283-0271	R	9*	.1
71	Blough Inc—Arthur Blough	9885 Centerline Rd, Lowell MI 49331	616-897-8407	R	8*	.1
72	Lustre-Cal Nameplate Corp—Clydene Hohenrieder	PO Box 439, Lodi CA 95241	209-370-1600	R	8*	.1
73	Gatto Industrial Platers Inc—George Gatto	4620 W Roosevelt Rd, Chicago IL 60644	773-287-0100	R	8*	.1
74	Foremost Manufacturing Company Inc—Herbert Schiller	941 Ball Ave, Union NJ 07083	908-687-4646	R	8*	.1
75	Ultramet—Andrew Duffy	12173 Montague St, Pacoima CA 91331	818-899-0236	R	8*	.1
76	Ai Industries LLC—Charles Botti	1709 E Bayshore Rd Ste, Redwood City CA 94063	650-366-8855	R	7*	.1
77	Coastal Coatings Inc—Bob Spears	PO Box 13190, San Diego CA 92170	619-702-5267	R	7*	.1
78	Precious Plate Inc—David Hurst	2124 Liberty Dr, Niagara Falls NY 14304	716-283-0690	R	7*	.1
79	Jagemann Plating Co—Scott Jagemann	PO Box 1447, Manitowoc WI 54221	920-682-6883	R	7*	.1
80	Possehl Connector Services—Ronald Papesh	445 Bryant Blvd, Rock Hill SC 29732	803-366-8316	D	7*	.1
81	Plateco Inc—Gerald Schweich	1375 Industrial St, Reedsburg WI 53959	608-524-8241	R	7*	.1
82	Briteline Extrusions Inc—Kenneth Kabine	575 Beech Hill Rd, Summerville SC 29485	843-873-4410	R	7*	.1
83	Production Plating Inc—Patrick Keating	4412 Russell Rd, Mukilteo WA 98275	425-347-4635	R	6*	.1
84	Opti-Forms Inc—Clint Tinker	42310 Winchester Rd, Temecula CA 92590	951-296-1300	R	6*	.1
85	Nu-Lustre Finishing Corp—Robert Mansour	1 Magnolia St, Providence RI 02909	401-521-7800	R	6*	.1
86	Marsh Plating Corp—Matthew Marsh	103 N Grove St, Ypsilanti MI 48198	734-483-5767	R	6*	.1
87	Sms Moderns Hard Chrome LLC—Charles Nicholl	12880 E 9 Mile Rd, Warren MI 48089	586-445-0330	R	6*	.1
88	Erie Plating Co—David Briggs	656 W 12th St, Erie PA 16501	814-453-7531	R	6*	.1
89	Winterville Machine Works Inc—John Carroll	PO Box 520, Winterville NC 28590	252-756-2130	R	6*	.1
90	Blitz Manufacturing Company Inc—Howard Sturm	PO Box 846, Jeffersonville IN 47131	812-284-2548	R	6*	.1
91	Hadronics Inc—Michael Green	4570 Steel Pl, Cincinnati OH 45209	513-321-9350	R	6*	.1
92	CP Auto Products Inc—Tom Longo	3901 Medford St, Los Angeles CA 90063	323-266-3850	R	5*	.1
93	South Holland Metal Finishing Company Inc—Robert Meagher	26100 S Whiting Way, Monee IL 60449	708-235-0842	R	5*	.1
94	Kenwal Pickling LLC—Debraah Martell	8223 W Warren Ave, Dearborn MI 48126	313-739-1040	R	5*	.1
95	Wisconsin Plating Works Inc—Robert Toeppe	PO Box 1813, Racine WI 53401	262-631-6120	R	5*	.1
96	Signal Plating Inc—Eugene Nowell	1608 Camden St, Chattanooga TN 37406	423-624-9018	R	5*	.1
97	Modern Aluminum Fabricators Inc—Frank Sigsbury	PO Box 408, North Adams MA 01247	413-664-9876	R	5*	.1
98	Surtronics Inc—Angela Stanley	PO Box 33459, Raleigh NC 27636	919-834-8027	R	5*	<.1
99	Power Engineering Co—Richard Lilienthal	2525 S Delaware St, Denver CO 80223	303-777-8782	R	5*	<.1
100	C and R Plating Corp—Bob Burger	PO Box 247, Columbia City IN 46725	260-248-8148	R	4*	<.1
101	Medina Plating Corp—Shawn Ritchie	940 Lafayette Rd, Medina OH 44256	330-725-4155	R	4*	<.1
102	PM Testing Laboratory Inc—Patrick Murphie	3921 Pacific Hwy E, Fife WA 98424	253-922-1321	R	4*	<.1
103	Delta Plating Inc—Gregory Kalikas	2125 Harrison Ave Sw, Canton OH 44706	330-452-2300	R	4*	<.1
104	Chromium Industries Inc—Peter Heidengren	4645 W Chicago Ave, Chicago IL 60651	773-287-3716	R	4*	<.1
105	Cal-Tron Plating Inc—Carl Troncale	11919 Rivera Rd, Santa Fe Springs CA 90670	562-945-1181	R	4*	.1
106	Rocklin Manufacturing Co—James Rocklin	110 S Jennings St, Sioux City IA 51101	712-255-7957	R	4*	<.1
107	L and J Of New England Inc—Duncan Leith	15 Sagamore Rd Ste 2, Worcester MA 01605	508-756-8080	R	4*	<.1
108	General Grinding Inc—Michael Bardon	801 51st Ave, Oakland CA 94601	510-261-5557	R	4*	<.1
109	Plateronics Processing Inc—Joseph Roter	9164 Independence Ave, Chatsworth CA 91311	818-341-2191	R	3*	<.1
110	Reliable Plating and Polishing Company Inc—James Bourdeau	80 Bishop Ave, Bridgeport CT 06607	203-366-5261	R	3*	<.1
111	SL Surface Technologies—James Taylor	1416 S 6th St, Camden NJ 08104	856-966-9707	R	3*	<.1
112	Poeton Max Power Inc—Josh Larkosh	7841 Morrison St, Morrisonville WI 53571	608-842-0680	S	3*	<.1
113	Maracle Industrial Finishing Company Inc—Thomas Maracle	39 Commercial St, Webster NY 14580	585-872-5100	R	3*	<.1
114	Michigan Mold Inc—Larry Bittner	PO Box 705, Coloma MI 49038	269-468-3346	R	2*	<.1
115	Ics Inc—Larry Rickner	210 N Elder St, Mcpherson KS 67460	620-241-1194	R	2*	<.1
116	Hardcoat Inc—Kenneth Heroux	7300 W Lake St, Minneapolis MN 55426	952-935-5715	R	2*	<.1
117	Koller Industries Inc—David Koller	1099 County Rd B, Niagara WI 54151	715-589-2604	R	2*	<.1
118	MATCOR Inc—William Schutt	301 Airport Blvd, Doylestown PA 18902	215-348-2974	R	2*	<.1
119	Providence Metallizing Company Inc—Richard Sugarman	51 Fairlawn Ave, Pawtucket RI 02860	401-722-5300	R	2*	<.1
120	Ultrasil Corp—John Dancovich	3527 Breakwater Ave, Hayward CA 94545	510-266-3700	R	2*	<.1
121	Raf Acquisition Co—John Mckay	11288 Alameda Dr, Strongsville OH 44149	440-572-5999	R	2*	<.1
122	Hand Industries Inc—Terry Hand	315 S Hand Ave, Warsaw IN 46580	574-267-3525	R	1*	<.1
123	Del's Plating Industries Corp—Bill Lee	8736 Schumacher Ln, Houston TX 77063	713-785-4955	R	1*	<.1
124	Polco Metal Finishing Inc—Zbigniew Kulig	4703 W Electric Ave, Milwaukee WI 53219	414-649-9230	R	1*	<.1
125	RA Heller Co—Steve Heller	10530 Chester Rd, Cincinnati OH 45215	513-771-6100	R	1*	<.1
126	Molectrics—William Demand	4008 E 89th St, Cleveland OH 44105	216-641-0090	R	1*	<.1
127	Brooktronics Engineering Corp—Chris Helwig	28231 Ave Crocker Ste, Santa Clarita CA 91355	661-294-1195	R	1*	<.1
128	Gold Effects Inc—Daniel Mclaughlin	13100 56th Ct Ste 701, Clearwater FL 33760	727-573-1990	R	1*	<.1
129	Metal Finishing Equipment Company Inc—Gary Lauderdale	8000 S Spoede Ln, Warrenton MO 63383	636-456-1974	R	<1*	<.1

TOTALS: SIC 3471 Plating & Polishing
Companies: 129 — 1,864 — 17.2

3479 Metal Coating & Allied Services

Rank	Company Name—Executive Officer	Address, City, State, Zip	Phone	Type	Fin	Empls
1	ICO Global Services Inc—A John Knapp Jr	1811 Bering Dr Ste 200, Houston TX 77057	713-351-4100	S	380*	.9
2	Metokote Corp—DeWayne Pinkstaff	1340 Neubrecht Rd, Lima OH 45801	419-996-7800	R	364*	1.0
3	Crown Group Inc—William P Baer	2111 Walter P Reuther, Warren MI 48091	586-575-9800	R	362*	1.0
4	Things Remembered Inc—Michael Anthony	5500 Avion Park Dr, Highland Heights OH 44143	440-473-2000	S	320*	4.0
5	Precoat Metals—Gerard M Dombek	1310 Papin St 3rd Fl, Saint Louis MO 63103	314-436-7010	S	191*	.7
6	Engineered Materials and Solutions Group Inc—Cliff Nastas Material Sciences Corp	2200 E Pratt Blvd, Elk Grove Village IL 60007	847-439-2210	S	189*	.6
7	Acheson Colloids Co—Gino Mariani	1600 Washington Ave, Port Huron MI 48060	810-984-5581	S	165*	.9
8	Material Sciences Corp—Clifford D Nastas	2200 E Pratt Blvd, Elk Grove Village IL 60007	847-439-2210	P	138	.3
9	DuPont Powder Coatings USA Inc—Ellen J Kullman	9800 Genard Rd, Houston TX 77041	713-939-4000	S	104*	.5
10	T-L Irrigation Co—Leroy Thom	PO Box 1047, Hastings NE 68902	402-462-4128	R	78*	.3
11	I/N Kote LLP—Gary Asperen	30755 Edison Rd, New Carlisle IN 46552	574-654-1000	R	38*	.3
12	Northern Metal Products—Larry Lautt	6601 Ridgewood Rd, Saint Cloud MN 56303	320-252-3442	R	35*	.2
13	Shawcor Pipe Protection LLC—Kathy Blankenhorn	3838 N Sam Houston Pkw, Houston TX 77032	281-886-2350	R	34*	.3

Rank	Company Name—*Executive Officer*	Address, City, State, Zip	Phone	Type	Fin	Empls
14	Sharon Coating LLC—*Thomas Burke*	277 N Sharpsville Ave, Sharon PA 16146	724-981-3545	R	33*	.2
15	Downey Investments Inc—*Bernard Downey*	2125 Gardner Rd, Broadview IL 60155	708-345-8000	R	31*	.3
16	Voigt and Schweitzer LLC—*Werner Niehaus*	1000 Buckeye Park Rd, Columbus OH 43207	614-449-8281	R	31*	.3
17	Hughes Brothers Inc—*John Hughes*	210 N 13th St, Seward NE 68434	402-643-2991	R	31*	.3
18	Womble Company Inc—*Alice Womble*	12821 Industrial Rd, Houston TX 77015	713-636-8707	R	30*	.5
19	Carboline Co—*Dick Wilson*	2150 Schuetz Rd, Saint Louis MO 63146	314-644-1000	S	29*	.1
20	Texas Electric Cooperatives Inc Treating Div	1122 Colorado St 24th, Austin TX 78701	512-454-0311	D	29*	.1
21	American Metals Corp—*William Foote*	1000 Crocker Rd, Westlake OH 44145	440-871-8200	S	27*	.1
22	Commercial Steel Treating Corp—*Scott Hoensheid*	PO Box 908, Troy MI 48099	248-588-3300	R	26*	.2
23	TCI Powder Coatings—*Frank C Sullivan*	PO Box 13, Ellaville GA 31806	229-937-5411	S	23*	.1
24	Specialty Coating Systems Inc—*Derry Bush*	7645 Woodland Dr, Indianapolis IN 46278	317-244-1200	R	23*	.4
25	Techno-Coat Inc—*Ike Wege*	861 E 40th St, Holland MI 49423	616-396-6446	R	22*	.1
26	Metallics Inc—*Doug Dale*	PO Box 99, Onalaska WI 54650	608-781-5200	R	21*	.2
27	Andover Healthcare Inc—*Thomas Murphy*	9 Fanaras Dr, Salisbury MA 01952	978-465-0044	R	21*	.2
28	Powder Cote Ii Inc—*Eric Trott*	PO Box 368, Mount Clemens MI 48046	586-463-7040	R	21*	.2
29	Aps-Materials Inc—*Michael Wilson*	PO Box 1106, Dayton OH 45401	937-278-6547	R	21*	.1
30	Witt Industries Inc—*Tim Harris*	4454 Steel Pl, Cincinnati OH 45209	513-871-5700	R	20*	.2
31	Eastern Etching and Manufacturing Co—*Gary Spooner*	Foot Of Grape St, Chicopee MA 01013	413-594-6601	R	17*	.2
32	Galvan Industries Inc—*Laurens Willard*	PO Box 369, Harrisburg NC 28075	704-455-5102	R	17*	.1
33	United Galvanizing Inc—*Harold Kahla*	PO Box 40207, Houston TX 77240	713-466-4161	R	16*	.2
34	Double Eagle Steel Coating Co—*Bill Boege*	3000 Miller Rd, Dearborn MI 48120	313-203-9800	R	16*	.1
35	Metal Coaters—*Lonnie Carroll*	951 Prisock Rd, Jackson MS 39212	601-373-0374	D	15*	.1
36	KJ Quinn and Company Inc—*Lee Quinn Jr*	34 Folly Mill Rd, Seabrook NH 03874	603-474-5753	R	15*	<.1
37	Calibre Inc—*Jonathan Reno*	2395 Dakota Dr, Grafton WI 53024	262-375-4671	R	14*	.1
38	Erler Industries Inc—*J Erler*	418 Stockwell St, North Vernon IN 47265	812-346-4421	R	14*	.2
39	Double G Coatings Company LP—*Samuel Moore*	1096 Mendell Davis Dr, Jackson MS 39272	601-371-3460	J	14*	.1
40	Certified Enameling Inc—*Glenn Zlegel*	3342 Emery St, Los Angeles CA 90023	323-264-4403	R	14*	.1
41	White Engineering Surfaces Corp—*Diane Nyland*	1 Pheasant Run, Newtown PA 18940	215-968-5021	R	14*	.1
42	Acme Finishing Company Inc—*Dennis Walters*	1595 Oakton St, Elk Grove Village IL 60007	847-640-7890	R	11*	.1
43	Alpha Coatings Inc—*Terence White*	1100 N Main St, Fostoria OH 44830	419-435-5111	R	10*	.1
44	Teknicote Inc—*Steve Dolan*	2 Titus St Unit 2, Cumberland RI 02864	401-724-2230	R	10*	.1
45	General Magnaplate Corp—*Wayne Cromwell*	1331 W Edgar Rd, Linden NJ 07036	908-862-6200	R	10*	.1
46	Chemart Co—*Richard Beaupre*	15 New England Way, Lincoln RI 02865	401-333-9200	R	10*	.1
47	Transco Products Inc—*Edward Wolbert*	55 E Jackson Blvd Ste, Chicago IL 60604	312-427-2818	R	10*	.1
48	St Louis Metallizing Co—*Joseph Stricker*	4123 Sarpy Ave, Saint Louis MO 63110	314-531-5253	S	10*	.1
49	Production Engineering Corp—*Michael Albers*	3515 Marshall St Ne, Minneapolis MN 55418	612-788-9123	R	9*	.1
50	Metal Cladding Inc—*A Robb*	230 S Niagara St, Lockport NY 14094	716-434-5513	R	9*	.1
51	Metal Coatings Corp—*Tim Mullen*	PO Box 630407, Houston TX 77263	713-977-0123	R	9*	.1
52	Straits Steel And Wire Co—*Paul Kara*	PO Box 589, Ludington MI 49431	231-843-3416	R	9*	.1
53	Winona Powder Coating Inc—*Jamie Visker*	PO Box 527, Mentone IN 46539	574-353-7346	R	9*	.1
54	Southwest Galvanizing Inc—*Wanda Wright*	PO Box 24188, Houston TX 77229	713-675-0921	R	8*	.2
55	EDLON Inc—*Tim Hull*	PO Box 667, Avondale PA 19311	610-268-3101	S	8*	.1
56	Turbocare Gas Turbine Services—*Scott Nichols*	11241 Gemini Ln, Dallas TX 75229	972-484-5252	S	8*	.1
57	Boyko Metal Finishing Company Inc—*John Boyko*	100 Poinier St, Newark NJ 07114	973-623-4264	R	7*	.1
58	Tiodize Company Inc—*Thomas Adams*	5858 Engineer Dr, Huntington Beach CA 92649	714-898-4377	R	6*	.1
59	Duncan Galvanizing Corp—*Abby Brooks*	69 Norman St Ste 2, Everett MA 02149	617-389-8440	R	6*	.1
60	Crest Coating Inc—*Michael Erickson*	1361 S Allec St, Anaheim CA 92805	714-635-7090	R	6*	.1
61	Para Tech Coating Inc—*Jeffrey Stewart*	35 Argonaut, Aliso Viejo CA 92656	949-855-8010	R	6*	.1
62	Imprex Inc—*Thomas Juday*	PO Box 270558, Milwaukee WI 53227	414-321-9300	R	6*	.1
63	Royston Laboratories—*Doug Zuberer*	128 1st St, Pittsburgh PA 15238	412-828-1500	S	5	<.1
64	Associated Finishing Inc—*William Klammer*	320 Mallard Ln, Mankato MN 56001	507-345-5861	R	5*	.1
65	Servitech Industries Inc—*Kevin Cradduck*	550 Brick Church Park, Nashville TN 37207	615-227-9899	R	5*	.1
66	Decc Company Inc—*Fred Mellema*	1266 Wallen Ave Sw, Grand Rapids MI 49507	616-245-0431	R	5*	.1
67	Donwell Co—*Tracey Sherman*	PO Box 906, Manchester CT 06045	860-649-5375	R	5*	<.1
68	Chemi-Graphic Inc—*Paul Pohl*	PO Box 410, Ludlow MA 01056	413-589-0151	R	5*	.1
69	Engineered Products and Services Inc—*Kissak Sarajian*	4221 Courtney Rd, Franksville WI 53126	262-835-0782	R	5*	.1
70	D and D Industrial Coatings Inc—*Jeff D'acquisto*	1640 Racine St, Racine WI 53403	262-637-0686	R	5*	.1
71	Eb Pipe Coating Inc—*Hans Sack*	PO Box 59770, Panama City FL 32412	850-763-0244	S	5*	<.1
72	Metallizing Service Company Inc—*David Gollob*	11 Cody St, Hartford CT 06110	860-953-1144	R	5*	<.1
73	E and R Powder Coatings Inc—*Mark Clausius*	3729 W 49th St, Chicago IL 60632	773-523-9510	R	5*	<.1
74	Worldclass Processing Corp—*Daniel Magee*	21 Century Dr, Ambridge PA 15003	724-251-9000	R	5*	<.1
75	R Mar Coat—*John Parkinson*	E Hwy 80, Grand Saline TX 75140	903-962-7573	R	4*	.1
76	Applied Graphics Inc—*Barbara Burnim*	61 Hunt Rd, Amesbury MA 01913	978-388-5300	R	4*	.1
77	C L Smith Industrial Co—*Clarence Smith*	PO Box 841155, Kansas City MO 64184	636-296-1036	R	4*	.1
78	Craddock Finishing Corp—*Marc Craddock*	PO Box 269, Evansville IN 47702	812-429-1369	R	4*	.1
79	Air Touch Powder Coating Inc—*Frank Kubat*	14489 Industry Cir, La Mirada CA 90638	714-228-2900	R	4*	.1
80	Dempsey Industries Inc—*John Dempsey*	802 N 4th St, Miamisburg OH 45342	937-866-2345	R	4*	<.1
81	Grothe Industrial Coating—*Melvin Grothe*	23095 Yupon, Porter TX 77365	281-354-1574	R	4*	<.1
82	Beamalloy Technologies LLC—*Arnold H Deutchman*	8270 Estates Pkwy, Plain City OH 43064	614-873-4529	R	4*	<.1
83	Foothill Workshop For The Handicapped Inc—*James Hall*	789 N Fair Oaks Ave, Pasadena CA 91103	626-449-0218	R	4*	.2
84	Newcut Inc—*Chester Poplaski*	PO Box 66, Newark NY 14513	315-331-7680	R	4*	<.1
85	Toefco Engineering Inc—*Arthur Mcelwee*	1220 N 14th St, Niles MI 49120	269-683-0188	R	3*	<.1
86	Industrial Nameplate Inc—*J Stitzer*	29 Indian Dr, Warminster PA 18974	215-322-1111	R	3*	<.1
87	Gulf Coast Galvanizing Inc—*Tim Carroll*	PO Box 325, Citronelle AL 36522	251-866-2873	S	3*	<.1
88	Hanson Porcelain Company Inc	PO Box 10608, Lynchburg VA 24506	434-845-9091	R	3*	<.1
89	Thermal Designs Inc—*Gardner Baldwin*	5352 Prudence Dr, Houston TX 77045	713-433-8110	R	3*	<.1
90	Economic Plastic Coating Inc—*Christos Marinos*	2080 N 15th Ave, Melrose Park IL 60160	708-343-2216	R	3*	<.1
91	Wisconsin Engraving Company Inc—*Chris Kambouris*	2435 S 170th St, New Berlin WI 53151	262-786-4521	R	3*	<.1
92	Plasfinco Inc—*Kenton Rousch*	PO Box 372, North Vernon IN 47265	812-346-3900	R	3*	<.1
93	High Tech Elastomers Inc—*James Back*	885 Scholz Dr, Vandalia OH 45377	937-236-6575	R	3*	<.1
94	Technigraphics Of Maryland Inc—*Gilbert Hooper*	350 Clubhouse Rd Ste 2, Hunt Valley MD 21031	410-584-9500	R	3*	<.1
95	Plasti Dip International Inc—*Scott Haasl*	3920 Pheasant Ridge Dr, Minneapolis MN 55449	763-785-2156	R	3*	<.1
96	Socco Plastic Coating Co—*Peter Smits*	11251 Jersey Blvd, Rancho Cucamonga CA 91730	909-987-4753	R	3*	<.1
97	De Nora North America Inc—*Lucieno Iacopepti*	100 7th Ave Ste 300, Chardon OH 44024	440-285-0300	R	2*	<.1
98	Bilsons Industries Inc—*Eric Pfleger*	2733 W Carmen Ave, Milwaukee WI 53209	414-464-4870	R	2*	<.1
99	Southwest Impreglon R Inc—*Greg Butler*	15014 Lee Rd, Humble TX 77396	281-441-2000	R	2*	<.1
100	Rapid Finishing Corp—*Barbara O'halloran*	43 Simon St, Nashua NH 03060	603-889-4234	R	2*	<.1
101	Slipmate Co—*Steve Matecki*	1693 Todd Farm Dr, Elgin IL 60123	847-289-9200	R	2*	<.1
102	Pcm Products Inc—*Liv Richards*	PO Box 5399, Titusville FL 32783	321-267-7500	R	2*	<.1
103	Innovative Coatings Inc—*George Maravelias*	24 Jayar Rd, Medway MA 02053	508-533-6101	R	2*	<.1

Note: An asterisk (*) indicates an estimated financial figure. The company type code used is as follows: R = Private, P = Public, S = Private Subsidiary, B = Public Subsidiary, D = Division, J = Joint Venture, I = Investment Fund.

COMPANY RANKINGS BY SALES WITHIN 4-DIGIT SIC

Rank	Company Name—*Executive Officer*	Address, City, State, Zip	Phone	Type	Fin	Empls
104	LR Powder Coats Div	4730 NW 128th St, Opa Locka FL 33054	305-685-8231	D	2*	<.1
105	Pearson Engineering Corp—*Colleen Trost*	2505 Loma Ave, El Monte CA 91733	626-442-7436	R	2*	<.1
106	Cactus Coatings Inc—*Mick Eminger*	463 28 1/2 Rd Ste A, Grand Junction CO 81501	970-241-3011	R	2*	<.1
107	Cametoid Technologies Inc—*John Adams*	150 Colonial Rd, Manchester CT 06042	860-646-4667	R	2*	<.1
108	Eemus Manufacturing Corp—*Gitte Simionian*	11111 Rush St, South El Monte CA 91733	626-443-8841	R	2*	<.1
109	Electrostatic Coating Technologies Corp—*Rocco Francoline*	1265 John Fitch Blvd, South Windsor CT 06074	860-610-9097	R	1*	<.1
110	GB Embossing Inc—*Steven Jossart*	1260 Ashwaubenon St, Green Bay WI 54304	920-339-9019	R	1*	<.1
111	Rust-Oleum Corp (Tulsa Oklahoma)—*Todd Garr*	1326 W 37th Pl, Tulsa OK 74107	918-446-6399	S	1*	<.1
112	Commercial Enameling Co—*Mark Hurray*	1310 E Borchard Ave, Santa Ana CA 92705	714-656-1950	R	1*	<.1
113	Scientific Coating Labs—*Richard Rennolds*	350 Martin Ave, Santa Clara CA 95050	408-727-3296	R	1*	<.1
114	Carlisle Plastics Company Inc—*Cynthia Clay*	PO Box 146, New Carlisle OH 45344	937-845-9411	R	1*	<.1
115	Matthews International Corp (Searcy Arkansas)—*David M Kelley*	501 Lincoln St, Searcy AR 72143	501-268-3504	S	N/A	.2

TOTALS: SIC 3479 Metal Coating & Allied Services
Companies: 115   **3,344**   **19.2**

3482 Small Arms Ammunition

Rank	Company Name—*Executive Officer*	Address, City, State, Zip	Phone	Type	Fin	Empls
1	Alliant Lake City Small Caliber Ammunition Company LLC—*Karen Davies*	PO Box 1000, Independence MO 64051	816-796-7101	S	747*	3.0
2	Day and Zimmermann Inc Lone Star Div—*Michael Yoh*	Hwy 82 W, Texarkana TX 75505	903-255-2801	D	110*	.4
3	Federal Cartridge Co—*Gerald Bersett*	900 Ehlen Dr, Anoka MN 55303	763-323-2300	S	100*	1.0
4	Hornady Manufacturing Co—*Steve Hornady*	PO Box 1848, Grand Island NE 68802	308-382-1390	R	19*	.2
5	First Defense International—*Jude Aluce*	24040 Camino Del Ave A, Dana Point CA 92629	949-366-6444	R	17*	.4
6	Nosler Inc—*Robert Nosler*	PO Box 671, Bend OR 97709	541-382-3921	R	14*	.1

TOTALS: SIC 3482 Small Arms Ammunition
Companies: 6   **1,007**   **5.0**

3483 Ammunition Except for Small Arms

Rank	Company Name—*Executive Officer*	Address, City, State, Zip	Phone	Type	Fin	Empls
1	General Dynamics Ordnance And Tactical Systems Inc—*Michael Wilson*	11399 16th Ct N Ste 20, Saint Petersburg FL 33716	727-578-8100	R	163*	2.3
2	Day and Zimmermann Inc Kansas Div—*Michael Yoh*	23018 Rooks Rd Ste A, Parsons KS 67357	620-421-7400	D	58*	.3
3	Medico Industries Inc—*Tom Medico*	1500 Hwy 315 Ste 1, Wilkes Barre PA 18711	570-825-7711	R	45*	.3
4	Action Manufacturing Company Inc—*Arthur Mattia*	100 E Erie Ave, Philadelphia PA 19134	215-739-6400	R	32*	.3
5	Delfasco Inc—*Philip Kadlecek*	PO Box 725, Greeneville TN 37744	423-639-6191	R	6*	.1
6	Cesaroni Technology Inc—*Anthony Cesaroni*	1144 Tallevast Rd Ste, Sarasota FL 34243	941-360-3100	R	5*	<.1

TOTALS: SIC 3483 Ammunition Except for Small Arms
Companies: 6   **309**   **3.2**

3484 Small Arms

Rank	Company Name—*Executive Officer*	Address, City, State, Zip	Phone	Type	Fin	Empls
1	Modern Muzzleloading Inc—*James Beene*	213 Dennis St, Athens TN 37303		R	2,951*	.1
2	Freedom Group Inc—*David Huffman*	870 Remington Dr, Madison NC 27025	336-548-8700	R	878*	3.0
3	CIC International Ltd—*Satiris G Fassoulis*	PO Box 533 Old Chelsea, New York NY 10011	212-213-0089	R	773	.7
4	Colt's Manufacturing Company LLC—*William Keys*	PO Box 1868, Hartford CT 06144	860-236-6311	R	412*	.5
5	Smith and Wesson Holding Corp—*P James Debney*	2100 Roosevelt Ave, Springfield MA 01104	413-781-8300	P	392	1.5
6	Smith and Wesson Corp Smith and Wesson Holding Corp	PO Box 2208, Springfield MA 01102		S	296*	1.0
7	Winchester Repeating Arms—*Charles Guevremont*	275 Winchester Ave, Morgan UT 84050	801-876-2711	R	250*	3.0
8	Remington Arms Company LLC—*Loretta Bailey*	PO Box 700, Madison NC 27025	336-548-8700	R	168*	2.3
9	Savage Sports Corp—*Albert Kasper*	100 Springdale Rd, Westfield MA 01085	413-568-7001	R	150*	.4
10	Michaels of Oregon Co	9200 Cody, Overland Park KS 66214		S	111*	.3
11	Savage Arms Inc—*Albert Kasper*	100 Springdale Rd Ste, Westfield MA 01085	413-568-7001	R	109*	.4
12	Colt Defense Inc—*William M Keyes*	PO Box 118, Hartford CT 06141	860-232-4489	R	69*	.4
13	OF Mossberg and Sons Inc—*A Iver Mossberg*	PO Box 497, North Haven CT 06473	203-230-5300	R	55*	.6
14	Benjamin Sheridan Corp—*Ken D'Arcy* Crosman Corp	PO Box 308, East Bloomfield NY 14443	585-657-6161	S	29*	.3
15	Fn Manufacturing LLC—*Jean Vanderstraeten*	PO Box 24257, Columbia SC 29224	803-736-0522	R	23*	.4
16	Burris Company Inc—*Jukka Koponen*	PO Box 1899, Greeley CO 80632	970-356-1670	R	20*	.1
17	Crosman Corp—*Ken D'Arcy*	PO Box 308, East Bloomfield NY 14443	585-657-6161	R	18*	.3
18	Springfield Inc—*Tom Reese*	420 W Main St, Geneseo IL 61254	309-944-5631	R	16*	.2
19	Glock Inc—*Gaston Glock*	PO Box 369, Smyrna GA 30081	770-432-1202	R	11*	.1
20	Daisy Manufacturing Company Inc—*Ray Hobbs*	PO Box 220, Rogers AR 72757	479-636-1200	R	8*	<.1
21	Weatherby Inc—*Ed Weatherby*	1605 Commerce Way, Paso Robles CA 93446	805-227-2600	R	7*	<.1
22	KW Thompson Tool Company Inc—*Gregg Ritz*	PO Box 5002, Rochester NH 03866	603-332-2333	R	5*	.1
23	C Products LLC—*Michelle Favale*	30 Elmwood Ct, Newington CT 06111	860-953-5007	R	4*	<.1
24	Redding-Hunter Inc—*Richard Beebe*	1089 Starr Rd, Cortland NY 13045	607-753-3331	R	3*	<.1
25	Browning Arms Co—*Charles Guevremont*	1 Browning Pl, Morgan UT 84050	801-876-2711	S	<1	.2

TOTALS: SIC 3484 Small Arms
Companies: 25   **6,759**   **15.7**

3489 Ordnance & Accessories Nec

Rank	Company Name—*Executive Officer*	Address, City, State, Zip	Phone	Type	Fin	Empls
1	Alliant Defense LLC Alliant Holdings LLC	7480 Flying Cloud Dr, Eden Prairie MN 55344	952-351-3000	S	6,444*	18.0
2	Alliant Holdings LLC—*Daniel Murphy* Alliant Techsystems Inc	7480 Flying Cloud Dr, Eden Prairie MN 55344	952-351-3000	S	6,086*	17.0
3	Alliant Techsystems Inc—*Mark W DeYoung*	7480 Flying Cloud Dr, Eden Prairie MN 55344	952-351-3000	P	4,842	15.0
4	Alliant Ammunition and Powder Company LLC—*Daniel Murphy* Alliant Techsystems Inc	Rte 114 PO Box 1, Radford VA 24143	540-639-7631	S	1,680*	5.0
5	ATK Space Systems Alliant Holdings LLC	PO Box 98, Magna UT 84044	801-251-5911	S	1,450*	4.1
6	Blount International Inc—*Joshua L Collins*	PO Box 22127, Portland OR 97269	503-653-8881	P	612	3.6
7	National Presto Industries Inc—*Maryjo Cohen*	3925 N Hastings Way, Eau Claire WI 54703	715-839-2121	P	431	1.1
8	Advanced Space Systems—*David Thompson*	21839 Atlantic Blvd, Dulles VA 20166	703-406-5000	D	361*	1.1
9	Sturm Ruger and Company Inc—*Michael O Fifer*	1 Lacey Pl, Southport CT 06890	603-865-2442	P	329	1.2
10	Lockheed Martin Missiles and Fire Control	459 John F Kennedy Dr, Archbald PA 18403	570-803-2300	D	299*	.7
11	Pacific Scientific Energetic Materials Co—*Kenyon Pixpy*	7073 W Willis Rd, Chandler AZ 85226	480-763-3000	S	22*	.3
12	Gayston Corp—*Mark Stone*	200 S Pioneer Blvd, Springboro OH 45066	937-746-8500	R	18*	.3
13	Dse Inc—*Dae Shin*	5201 S Westshore Blvd, Tampa FL 33611	813-831-0750	R	16*	.1
14	Systems 3 Inc—*Craig Berland*	1515 W 17th St, Tempe AZ 85281	480-894-2581	R	14*	.1
15	R Streau Laboratory Inc—*Wayne Hanson*	N8265 Medley Rd, Spooner WI 54801	715-635-2777	R	10*	.1

Rank	Company Name—*Executive Officer*	Address, City, State, Zip	Phone	Type	Fin	Empls
16	Alloy Surfaces Company Inc—*John Lafemina*	121 N Commerce Dr, Aston PA 19014	610-497-7979	R	9*	.1
17	Dewey Electronics Corp—*John HD Dewey*	27 Muller Rd, Oakland NJ 07436	201-337-4700	P	8	<.1
18	Pyrotechnic Specialties Inc—*David Karlson*	1661 Juniper Creek Rd, Byron GA 31008	478-956-5400	R	6*	.1
19	Fraser Manufacturing Corp—*Joseph Wilhelm*	PO Box 296, Lexington MI 48450	810-359-5338	R	4*	<.1
20	Choate Machine and Tool Company Inc—*Garth Choate*	PO Box 218, Bald Knob AR 72010	501-724-6193	R	3*	<.1
21	United States Fire Arms Manufacturing Co—*Douglas Donnelly*	445 Ledyard St Ste 453, Hartford CT 06114	860-724-1152	R	2*	<.1
22	Superior Signal Company LLC	PO Box 96, Spotswood NJ 08884	732-251-0800	R	1*	<.1
23	Allied Defense Group Inc—*John G Meyer*	120 E Baltimore St Ste, Baltimore MD 21202	703-847-5268	P	<1	N/A

TOTALS: SIC 3489 Ordnance & Accessories Nec
Companies: 23

					22,646	67.8

3491 Industrial Valves

Rank	Company Name—*Executive Officer*	Address, City, State, Zip	Phone	Type	Fin	Empls
1	Mueller Water Products Inc—*Gregory E Hyland*	1200 Abernathy Rd NE S, Atlanta GA 30328	770-206-4200	P	1,339	4.8
2	ASCO—*Jean Pierre*	50-60 Hanover Rd, Florham Park NJ 07932	973-966-2000	D	1,169*	1.0
3	CIRCOR International Inc—*Bill Higgins*	25 Corporate Dr Ste 13, Burlington MA 01803	781-270-1200	P	822	3.4
4	Velan Valve Corp—*Adolph Velan*	94 Ave C, Williston VT 05495	802-863-2561	R	466*	.2
5	Spence Engineering Company Inc—*David A Bloss Sr* CIRCOR International Inc	PO Box 230, Walden NY 12586	845-778-5566	S	329*	.2
6	Tyco Valves and Controls Inc—*Patrick Decker*	10707 Clay Rd, Houston TX 77041	713-986-4665	S	244*	1.5
7	Engineered Controls International LLC—*Gary Boone*	PO Box 247, Elon College NC 27244	336-449-7707	R	232*	.9
8	Mogas Industries Inc—*Matt Mogas*	PO Box 11529, Houston TX 77293	281-449-0291	R	150*	.3
9	Flowserve Fcd Corp—*Lew Kling*	1350 N Mountain Spring, Springville UT 84663	801-489-8611	R	149*	2.0
10	Waterous Co—*Donald Haugen*	125 Hardman Ave S, South Saint Paul MN 55075	651-450-5000	R	141*	2.0
11	Ge Oil and Gas Pressure Control LP—*Leonard Schluns*	PO Box 82, Houston TX 77001	832-325-4200	R	107*	1.5
12	Control Components Inc—*Mike Senens-Slanagan*	22591 Avenida Empresa, Rcho Sta Marg CA 92688	949-858-1877	R	68*	.9
13	Red Valve Company Inc—*George Raftis*	PO Box 548, Carnegie PA 15106	412-279-0044	R	59*	.2
14	Rodney Hunt Company Inc—*John Kemp*	46 Mill St, Orange MA 01364	978-544-2511	R	50*	.2
15	Henry Technologies Inc—*Michael Giordano*	655 3rd St Ste 100, Beloit WI 53511	608-361-4400	R	40*	.5
16	US Para Plate Corp—*David A Bloss Sr* CIRCOR International Inc	1100 Page St, Bristol VA 24201	276-591-4837	D	37*	.3
17	Armstrong International Inc—*David Armstrong*	816 Maple St, Three Rivers MI 49093	269-273-1415	R	31*	.3
18	Conval Inc—*Frank Siver*	PO Box 1049, Somers CT 06071	860-749-0761	R	31*	.1
19	Beta International Inc—*Bryan Leavitt*	8303 Millet St, Houston TX 77012	713-921-3600	R	31*	<.1
20	Cashco Inc—*Phillip Rogers*	PO Box 6, Ellsworth KS 67439	785-472-4461	R	30*	.3
21	Koontz-Wagner Holdings LLC—*Michael Pound*	3801 Voorde Dr, South Bend IN 46628	574-232-2051	R	28*	.4
22	SH Leggitt Co—*Don Leggitt*	1000 Civic Ctr Loop, San Marcos TX 78666	512-396-0707	R	27*	.5
23	Standard Machine and Manufacturing Company Inc—*Jeremy Deutsch*	10014 Big Bend Rd, Saint Louis MO 63122	314-966-4500	R	26*	.2
24	Ortloff Engineers Ltd—*John Wilkinson*	415 W Wall Ave, Midland TX 79701	432-685-0277	R	26*	<.1
25	Weir Valves and Controls USA Inc—*William Fath*	29 Old Right Rd, Ipswich MA 01938	978-744-5690	R	23*	.2
26	Continental Disc Corp—*David Brown*	3160 W Heartland Dr, Liberty MO 64068	816-792-1500	R	23*	.4
27	Hoerbiger Corporation Of America Inc—*Hannes Hunschofsky*	3350 Gateway Dr, Pompano Beach FL 33069	954-974-5700	R	22*	.3
28	Meggitt Inc (North Hollywood California)—*Ken Guss*	12838 Saticoy St, North Hollywood CA 91605	818-765-8160	R	20*	.3
29	Kennedy Industries Inc—*Stephen Sadler*	PO Box 809, Milford MI 48381	248-684-1200	R	20*	.1
30	Fabco-Air Inc—*William Schmidt*	PO Box 5159, Gainesville FL 32627	352-373-3578	R	17*	.1
31	Iva LLC—*Arthur Brennes*	12880 Moya Blvd, Reno NV 89506	775-359-4442	R	17*	.1
32	Peter Paul Electronics Company Inc—*Paul Mangiafico*	PO Box 1180, New Britain CT 06050	860-229-4884	R	16*	.1
33	Richards Industries Inc—*Bruce Broxterman*	3170 Wasson Rd, Cincinnati OH 45209	513-533-5600	R	16*	.1
34	Transpo Trading Inc—*Frank Oropeza*	3063 Mercy Dr, Orlando FL 32808	407-298-4563	R	15*	.1
35	Controls Corporation Of America—*Sander Dukas*	1501 Harpers Rd, Virginia Beach VA 23454	757-422-8330	R	15*	.1
36	United Brass Works Inc—*Michael Berkelhammer*	714 S Main St, Randleman NC 27317	336-498-2661	R	15*	.2
37	Val-Matic Valve And Manufacturing Corp—*Patricia Nuter*	905 S Riverside Dr, Elmhurst IL 60126	630-941-7600	R	15*	.1
38	Enterprise Brass Works Corp	3760 Marsh Rd, Madison WI 53718	608-838-8786	S	15*	.1
39	Legris Inc	7205 E Hampton Ave, Mesa AZ 85209	480-830-0216	S	15*	.1
40	Primore Inc—*Robert Price*	PO Box 605, Adrian MI 49221	517-265-6168	R	13*	.1
41	American Products Company Inc—*Richard Picut*	610 Rahway Ave, Union NJ 07083	908-687-4100	R	13*	.1
42	Norriseal—*Jerry Sanderlin*	11122 W Little York, Houston TX 77041	713-466-3552	D	13*	.1
43	Burkert Contromatic Corp—*Harm Stratman*	2572 White Rd, Irvine CA 92614	949-223-3100	R	13*	.1
44	Groth Corp—*David Brown* Continental Disc Corp	PO Box 840160, Kansas City MO 64184	281-295-6800	S	11*	.1
45	Olson Technologies Inc—*James Olson*	160 W Walnut St, Allentown PA 18102	610-770-1100	R	10*	<.1
46	FCKingston Co—*Joe Taormina*	23201 Normandie Ave, Torrance CA 90501	310-326-8287	R	9*	.1
47	Fetterolf Corp—*Paul Holloway*	PO Box 103, Skippack PA 19474	610-584-1500	R	8*	<.1
48	Zimmermann and Jansen Inc—*James W Adams*	PO Box 3365, Humble TX 77347	281-446-8000	S	8*	.1
49	Akron Steel Fabricators Co—*David Poling*	3291 Manchester Rd, Akron OH 44319	330-644-0616	R	8*	.1
50	Gemu Valves Inc—*Gerhard Braunberger*	3800 Camp Creek Pkwy S, Atlanta GA 30331	678-553-3400	R	7*	<.1
51	Quality Controls Inc—*Edmond Young*	200 Tilton Rd, Northfield NH 03276	603-286-3321	R	7*	<.1
52	Portersville Valve Co—*Robert Pozzuto*	PO Box 89, Portersville PA 16051	724-368-8725	R	6*	<.1
53	Ecorse Machinery Sales and Rebuilders Inc—*Joseph Magyar*	75 Southfield Rd, Ecorse MI 48229	313-383-2100	R	4*	<.1
54	Shan-Rod Inc—*Dave Hatala*	PO Box 380, Berlin Heights OH 44814	419-588-2066	R	4*	<.1
55	J and S Machine and Valve Inc—*Verla Smith*	PO Box 152, Nowata OK 74048	918-273-1582	R	2*	<.1
56	Alta Robbins Inc—*Greg Wilson*	110 S 1200 W, Lindon UT 84042	801-785-1114	R	2*	<.1
57	Louisiana Valves and Machine Works Inc—*Wayne Marchand*	PO Box 12, Port Allen LA 70767	225-344-1445	R	1*	<.1
58	Sherwood—*Bill Corbin*	2200 N Main St, Washington PA 15301	724-225-8000	S	N/A	.5

TOTALS: SIC 3491 Industrial Valves
Companies: 58

					6,036	25.4

3492 Fluid Power Valves & Hose Fittings

Rank	Company Name—*Executive Officer*	Address, City, State, Zip	Phone	Type	Fin	Empls
1	Dvcc Inc—*Richard Goodall*	800 High St, Chestertown MD 21620	410-778-2000	R	548*	1.3
2	Parker Hannifin Corp Tube Fittings Div—*Jerry Brown*	3885 Gateway Blvd, Columbus OH 43228	614-279-7070	D	214*	.7
3	Husco International Inc—*Austin Ramirez*	PO Box 257, Waukesha WI 53187	262-513-4200	R	200*	1.0
4	Barksdale Inc—*Ian Dodd*	PO Box 58843, Los Angeles CA 90058	323-589-6181	S	157*	.2
5	Young and Franklin Inc—*Dudley Johnson*	942 Old Liverpool Rd, Liverpool NY 13088	315-457-3110	R	144*	.2
6	Cross Manufacturing Inc—*John Cross*	11011 King St Ste 210, Overland Park KS 66210	913-451-1233	R	110*	.3
7	Parker Hannifin Corp Hose Products Div—*Don Washkewicz*	30240 Lakeland Blvd, Wickliffe OH 44092	440-943-5700	D	100*	1.2
8	Hydraforce Inc—*James Brizzolara*	500 Barclay Blvd, Lincolnshire IL 60069	847-793-2300	R	38*	.5
9	Delta Power Co—*John Fulton*	PO Box 5906, Rockford IL 61125	815-397-6628	R	35*	.1
10	Air-Way Manufacturing Company Inc—*Charles Blank*	586 N Main St, Ollvet MI 49076	269-749-2161	R	30*	.3
11	Humphrey Products Co—*Robert Humphrey*	PO Box 2008, Kalamazoo MI 49003	269-381-5500	R	28*	.4

Note: An asterisk (*) indicates an estimated financial figure. The company type code used is as follows: R = Private, P = Public, S = Private Subsidiary, B = Public Subsidiary, D = Division, J = Joint Venture, I = Investment Fund.

COMPANY RANKINGS BY SALES WITHIN 4-DIGIT SIC

Rank	Company Name—*Executive Officer*	Address, City, State, Zip	Phone	Type	Fin	Empls
12	SPX Valves and Controls—*Howie Wynn*	250 Riverside Ave N, Sartell MN 56377	320-259-2000	D	27*	.3
13	Parker-Hannifin Corp Fluid Control Div	147 W Hoy Rd, Madison MS 39110	601-856-4123	D	27	.2
14	Griswold Industries—*Martin Pickett*	PO Box 1325, Newport Beach CA 92659	949-722-4800	R	26*	.4
15	Purolator Facet Inc—*Richard Von Drehle*	8439 Triad Dr, Greensboro NC 27409	336-668-4444	S	26*	.2
16	Micro Pneumatic Logic Inc—*Gerald Tucci*	2901 Gateway Dr, Pompano Beach FL 33069	954-973-6166	R	17*	.1
17	James Jones Co	1470 S Vintage Ave, Ontario CA 91761		S	16	.1
18	Cc Daman Products Company Inc—*Larry Davis*	1811 N Home St, Mishawaka IN 46545	574-259-7841	R	15*	.1
19	Versa Products Company Inc—*Karl Larsson*	22 Spring Valley Rd, Paramus NJ 07652	201-843-2400	R	15*	.1
20	Fluid Line Products Inc—*John Hetzer*	PO Box 1000, Willoughby OH 44096	440-946-9470	R	13*	.1
21	Ripley Industries Inc—*Kelley Bonawitz*	PO Box 245, Adamsville TN 38310	731-632-3328	R	9*	.1
22	Faber Enterprises Inc—*Ronald Spencer*	6606 Variel Ave, Canoga Park CA 91303	818-999-1300	R	9*	.1
23	Kinemotive Corp—*Arthur Szeglin*	222 Central Ave Ste 1, Farmingdale NY 11735	631-249-6440	R	9*	.1
24	Spiral Industries Inc—*James Linfield*	1572 N Old Us 23, Howell MI 48843	810-632-6300	R	8*	.1
25	B W B Controls Inc—*Faye Warren*	PO Box 670, Houma LA 70361	985-876-4117	R	5*	<.1
26	Cline Hose and Hydraulics LLC—*John Lathan*	PO Box 3477, Greenville SC 29602	864-233-7104	R	5*	<.1
27	Sinecera Inc—*Lisa Miller*	5137 Elton St, Baldwin Park CA 91706	626-962-1087	R	5*	<.1
28	Mid-Atlantic Manufacturing And Hydraulics Inc—*Tom Dewitt*	708 Milk Plant Rd, Rural Retreat VA 24368	276-686-5000	R	4*	<.1
29	Ohio Hydraulics Inc—*Dianne Farwick*	2510 E Sharon Rd Ste 1, Cincinnati OH 45241	513-771-2590	R	4*	<.1
30	Quad City Hose—*J Zespy*	2844 W 72nd St, Davenport IA 52806	563-386-8936	R	4*	<.1
31	Kobold Instruments Inc—*Klaus Kobold*	1801 Pky View Dr, Pittsburgh PA 15205	412-788-2830	R	3*	<.1
32	Birmingham Hydraulics Inc—*Thomas Lyon*	1675 E Maple Rd, Troy MI 48083	248-689-2400	R	3*	<.1
33	Dayni Controls Manufacturing Co—*Clifton Burwell*	18414 Eddy St, Northridge CA 91325	818-349-8367	R	3*	<.1
34	Quality Machining And Manufacturing Inc—*Dale Dreher*	270 State Rte 18, Sherwood OH 43556	419-899-2543	R	2*	<.1
35	HLR Controls Inc—*Julien Roy*	124 Banks Ave, Lafayette LA 70506	337-233-7380	R	2*	<.1
36	Enfield Technologies LLC—*Ed Howe*	35 Nutmeg Dr Ste 11, Trumbull CT 06611	203-375-3100	R	1*	<.1
37	New Jersey Meter Co—*Anthony Abbate*	1 Hazel St, Woodland Park NJ 07424	973-345-6200	S	1*	<.1
38	Kidd Pipeline and Specialties Inc—*Billy Davis*	14826 Yarberry St, Houston TX 77039	281-442-0270	R	<1*	<.1
39	Mac Valves Inc—*Robert Neff*	PO Box 111, Wixom MI 48393	248-624-7700	R	N/A	,9

TOTALS: SIC 3492 Fluid Power Valves & Hose Fittings
Companies: 39   1,863   9.4

3493 Steel Springs Except Wire

Rank	Company Name—*Executive Officer*	Address, City, State, Zip	Phone	Type	Fin	Empls
1	Tuthill Transport Technologies—*Greg Rocque*	1205 Industrial Park D, Mount Vernon MO 65712	417-466-2178	S	95*	.4
2	Spring Napoleon Works Inc—*Robert Shram*	PO Box 160, Archbold OH 43502	419-445-1010	R	43*	.2
3	Automatic Spring Products Corp—*Steven Moreland*	803 Taylor Ave, Grand Haven MI 49417	616-842-7800	R	31*	.2
4	Betts Spring Co—*William Betts*	2843 S Maple Ave, Fresno CA 93725	559-498-3304	R	28*	.2
5	Smalley Steel Ring Co—*Charles Greenhill*	555 Oakwood Rd, Lake Zurich IL 60047	847-719-5900	R	25*	.2
6	Union Spring and Manufacturing Corp—*Ray Beacha*	4268 N Pke Ste 1, Monroeville PA 15146	412-843-5900	R	21*	.1
7	Spring Draco Manufacturing Co—*Barry Drager*	7042 Long Dr, Houston TX 77087	713-645-4973	R	15*	.2
8	Haven Steel Products Inc—*Marlon Cohn*	PO Box 430, Haven KS 67543	620-465-2573	R	14*	.1
9	Spring Exacto Corp—*Greg Heitz*	PO Box 24, Grafton WI 53024	262-377-3970	R	13*	.2
10	Barber Manufacturing Company Inc—*Jeff W Barber*	PO Box 2454, Anderson IN 46018	765-643-6905	R	11*	.1
11	Quality Spring/Togo Inc—*Mark Katayama*	355 Jay St, Coldwater MI 49036	517-278-2391	R	10*	.1
12	Gemco Manufacturing Company Inc—*Mark DiVenere*	555 W Queen St, Southington CT 06489	860-628-5529	R	6*	<.1
13	Spring Novi Inc—*Gerald Johnson*	7735 Boardwalk Rd, Brighton MI 48116	248-486-4220	R	5*	<.1
14	Spring Fourslide And Stamping Inc—*Arthur Funk*	PO Box 839, Bristol CT 06011	860-583-1688	R	3*	<.1
15	Temper Corp—*John Rode*	PO Box 1127, Fonda NY 12068	518-853-3467	R	2*	<.1

TOTALS: SIC 3493 Steel Springs Except Wire
Companies: 15   322   2.0

3494 Valves & Pipe Fittings Nec

Rank	Company Name—*Executive Officer*	Address, City, State, Zip	Phone	Type	Fin	Empls
1	Crane Co—*Eric C Fast*	100 First Stamford Pl, Stamford CT 06902	203-363-7300	P	2,546	10.5
2	Synalloy Metals Inc—*Ron Braam*	390 Bristol Metals Rd, Bristol TN 37621	423-989-4700	S	2,012*	.4
3	Watts Water Technologies Inc—*David Coghlan*	815 Chestnut St, North Andover MA 01845	978-688-1811	P	1,437	5.8
4	Dresser Inc—*John P Ryan*	15455 Dallas Pkwy, Addison TX 75001	972-361-9800	S	1,410*	6.3
5	Swagelok Co—*Arthur F Anton*	29500 Solon Rd, Solon OH 44139	440-248-4600	R	1,333*	4.0
6	Parker Hannifin Corp Skinner Valve Div	95 Edgewood Ave, New Britain CT 06051	860-827-2300	D	1,138*	.3
7	Henry Pratt Co—*Steve Sharp*	401 S Highland Ave, Aurora IL 60506	630-844-4000	S	688*	.2
8	LASCO Fittings Inc	PO Box 116, Brownsville TN 38012	731-772-3180	S	463*	.5
9	Fresno Valves and Castings Inc—*OR Showalter Jr*	PO Box 40, Selma CA 93662	559-834-2511	R	367*	.2
10	KF Industries Inc—*Paul M Coppinger*	1500 SE 89th St, Oklahoma City OK 73149	405-631-1533	D	255*	.4
11	Victaulic Co—*John Malloy*	PO Box 31, Easton PA 18044	610-559-3300	R	248*	3.0
12	Fluidmaster Inc—*Adolf Schoepe*	30800 Rancho Viejo Rd, San Juan Capistrano CA 92675	949-728-2000	R	200*	.5
13	KF Sales Corp—*Bill Higgins*	25 Corporate Dr Ste130, Burlington MA 01803	781-270-1200	S	175*	.1
14	Fisher Controls International Inc	PO Box 190, Marshalltown IA 50158	641-754-3011	S	173*	2.0
15	Xomox Corp—*Tom Pozda* Crane Co	4444 Cooper Rd, Cincinnati OH 45242	513-745-6000	S	145	2.5
16	Shaw Alloy Piping Products Co—*JM Bernhard*	PO Box 7368, Shreveport LA 71137	318-674-9860	S	127*	.2
17	Orbit Irrigation Products Inc—*Kent Ericksen*	PO Box 328, Bountiful UT 84011	801-299-5555	R	78*	.5
18	ITT Industries Inc Engineered Valves Div—*Robert L Ayers*	PO Box 6164, Lancaster PA 17607	717-509-2200	D	60	.3
19	CIRCOR IP Holding Co—*Bill Higgins*	25 Corporate Dr Ste 13, Burlington MA 01803	781-270-1200	S	57*	<.1
20	Snap-Tite Inc—*John Clark*	8325 Hessinger Dr, Erie PA 16509	814-838-5700	R	56*	.7
21	Sloan Valve Co—*Charles Allen*	10500 Seymour Ave, Franklin Park IL 60131	847-671-4300	R	48*	.6
22	Balon Corp—*Phil Scaramucci*	3245 S Hattie Ave, Oklahoma City OK 73129	405-677-3321	R	48*	.7
23	Allen-Sherman-Hoff—*Steve Scott*	PO Box 3006, Malvern PA 19355	610-647-9900	D	45*	.2
24	OPW Fueling Components—*David Crouse*	PO Box 405003, Cincinnati OH 45240	513-870-3100	D	40*	.3
25	Parker Hannifin Corporation Refrigerating Specialties—*Paul Bishop*	2445 S 25th Ave, Broadview IL 60155	708-681-6300	D	38*	<.1
26	Valex Corp—*Daniel A Mangan*	6080 Leland St, Ventura CA 93003	805-658-0944	S	37*	.2
27	Microflex Inc—*Josif Atanasoski*	1800 N Us Hwy 1, Ormond Beach FL 32174	386-677-8100	R	35*	.2
28	Leslie Controls Inc—*Roland Robichaud*	12501 Telecom Dr, Tampa FL 33637	813-978-1000	D	32*	.3
29	Metso Automation USA Inc	44 Bearfoot Dr, Northborough MA 01532	508-852-0200	S	32*	.3
30	Pacific Valves—*Eric C Fast*	3201 Walnut Ave, Signal Hill CA 90755	562-426-2531	R	32*	.3
31	Curtiss-Wright Flow Control Corp—*David J Linton*	2941 Fairview Park Dr, Falls Church VA 22042	703-286-2000	S	32*	.2
32	Milwaukee Valve Company Inc—*Richard Giannini*	16550 W Stratton Dr, New Berlin WI 53151	262-432-2800	R	30*	.5
33	Hunt Valve Company Inc—*Gerald Bogner*	1913 E State St, Salem OH 44460	330-337-9535	R	29*	.2
34	Betts Industries Inc—*Rodney Betts*	PO Box 888, Warren PA 16365	814-723-1250	R	27*	.2
35	Clark-Reliance Corp—*Dennis Pesek*	16633 Foltz Pkwy, Strongsville OH 44149	440-572-1500	R	26*	.2
36	Dresser Piping Specialties—*Barry Glickman* Dresser Inc	41 Fisher Ave, Bradford PA 16701	814-362-9200	D	26*	.2

Rank	Company Name—*Executive Officer*	Address, City, State, Zip	Phone	Type	Fin	Empls
37	Halkey-Roberts Corp—*David Battat*	2700 Halkey-Roberts Pl, Saint Petersburg FL 33716	425-951-6200	S	26*	.2
38	Romac Industries Inc—*James Larkin*	21919 20th Ave Se Ste, Bothell WA 98021		R	23*	.3
39	Flotech Inc—*Richard Bazar*	PO Box 3824, Jacksonville FL 32206	904-358-1849	R	23*	.1
40	Parker Hannifin Corp Instrumentation Valve Div—*John R Greco*	2651 AL Hwy 21 N, Jacksonville AL 36265	256-435-2130	D	20*	.2
41	Specialty Manufacturing Co—*Dan Keown*	5858 Centerville Rd, Saint Paul MN 55127	651-653-0599	R	20*	.1
42	Ssp Fittings Corp—*Raymond King*	8250 Boyle Pkwy, Twinsburg OH 44087	330-425-4250	R	19*	.2
43	Nelson Irrigation Corp—*Barton Nelson*	848 Airport Rd, Walla Walla WA 99362	509-525-7660	R	18*	.2
44	L and J Technologies Inc—*Lou Jannotta*	5911 Butterfield Rd, Hillside IL 60162	708-236-6000	R	18*	.1
45	Nor-Cal Products Inc—*Craig Hill*	PO Box 518, Yreka CA 96097	530-842-4457	R	18*	.2
46	Ames Company Inc Watts Water Technologies Inc	1427 N Market Blvd Ste, Sacramento CA 95834	916-928-0123	S	17*	.1
47	Wm Steinen Manufacturing Co—*William Steinen*	29 E Halsey Rd, Parsippany NJ 07054	973-887-6400	R	17*	.2
48	Dynamic Products Inc—*Ronald Lindquist*	16520 Peninsula St, Houston TX 77015	281-457-3500	R	16*	.1
49	Cameron Valves and Measurement Group	3250 Briar Park Dr Ste, Houston TX 77042	281-499-8511	D	16*	.1
50	Allenair Corp—*Ron Buttner*	255 E 2nd St, Mineola NY 11501	516-747-5450	S	15*	.2
51	Hajoca—*Richard J Klau*	PO Box 668, Alexandria VA 22314	703-548-7600	D	15*	.1
52	A and N Corp—*David Vaudreuil*	707 Sw 19th Ave, Williston FL 32696	352-528-4100	R	14*	.1
53	PBM Inc—*Stuart Zarembo*	1070 Sandy Hill Rd, Irwin PA 15642	724-863-0550	R	14*	.1
54	Carpenter and Paterson Inc—*Donald R Paterson*	225 Merrimac St, Woburn MA 01801	781-935-7036	R	14*	.1
55	Ameriflex Inc—*David Lawrence*	2390 Railroad St, Corona CA 92880	951-737-5557	R	13*	.1
56	Sweco Fab Inc—*Durga Agrawal*	PO Box 34546, Houston TX 77234	713-731-0030	R	13*	.4
57	Legend Valve and Fitting Inc—*David Hickman*	51245 Filomena Dr, Shelby Township MI 48315	586-566-7400	R	13*	.1
58	Automatic Machine Products Sales Co—*John Holden*	400 Constitution Dr, Taunton MA 02780	508-822-4226	R	13*	.1
59	American Valve Inc—*Frederick Guterman*	PO Box 35229, Greensboro NC 27425	336-668-0554	R	12*	.1
60	Jm Fittings LLC—*Barb Satterfield*	PO Box 11324, Fort Wayne IN 46857	260-747-9200	R	11*	.1
61	Taylor Forge Stainless Inc—*Michael Kearney*	PO Box 610, Somerville NJ 08876	908-722-1313	R	11*	.1
62	Performance Pipe Div—*David Morgan*	5085 W Park Blvd Ste 5, Plano TX 75093		D	11*	.1
63	Vac-U-Max—*Stevens Pendleton*	69 William St, Belleville NJ 07109	973-759-4600	R	11*	.1
64	Campbell Manufacturing Inc—*Emery W Davis*	PO Box 207, Bechtelsville PA 19505	610-367-2107	R	10*	.1
65	Tate Andale Inc—*William Tate*	1941 Lansdowne Rd, Baltimore MD 21227	410-247-8700	R	8*	.1
66	Engineered Sales Inc—*Warren Hoffner*	18 Progress Pkwy, Maryland Heights MO 63043	314-878-4500	D	6*	<.1
67	Gibson Products LP—*Chris Gibson*	5691 Surrey Sq St, Houston TX 77017	713-941-4890	R	6*	<.1
68	JH Robotics Inc—*John Hartman*	109 Main St, Johnson City NY 13790	607-729-3758	R	6*	<.1
69	Soileau Industries Inc—*Chad Soileau*	800 Nw Railroad Ave, Ville Platte LA 70586	337-363-2519	R	5*	<.1
70	American Energy Services Inc—*Patrick S Elliott*	7224 Lawndale, Houston TX 77012	713-928-5311	R	5	<.1
71	Steuby Manufacturing Co—*Thomas Steuby*	PO Box 1023, Ballwin MO 63022	636-394-2300	R	5*	<.1
72	Rubberfab Gasket And Molding Inc—*Bob Dupont*	PO Box 626, Andover NJ 07821	973-579-2959	R	4*	<.1
73	Micromold Products Inc—*Arthur Lukach*	200 Corporate Blvd S S, Yonkers NY 10701	914-969-2850	R	3*	<.1
74	Sims Pump Valve Company Inc—*John Kozel*	1314 Park Ave, Hoboken NJ 07030	201-792-0600	R	3*	<.1
75	Kraissl Company Inc—*Richard Michel*	PO Box 2363, South Hackensack NJ 07606	201-342-0008	R	3*	<.1
76	Oceco Inc—*Richard Borer*	PO Box 159, Tiffin OH 44883	419-447 0016	R	2*	<.1
77	Weather Tec Corp—*William Rogers*	5645 E Clinton Ave, Fresno CA 93727	559-291-5555	R	2*	<.1
78	Goodman Main Stopper Manufacturing Company Inc—*Joseph Petrone*	523 Atlantic Ave, Brooklyn NY 11217	718-875-5140	R	2*	<.1

TOTALS: SIC 3494 Valves & Pipe Fittings Nec

Companies: 78					14,024	46.8

3495 Wire Springs

1	Associated Spring—*Richard P McCorry*	18 Main St, Bristol CT 06010		D	279*	2.0
2	Mid-West Spring and Stamping—*Michael B Curran*	1404 Joliet Rd Ste C, Romeoville IL 60446	574-353-7611	R	216*	.5
3	Peterson American Co—*Pete Peterson*	21200 Telegraph Rd, Southfield MI 48034	248-799-5400	R	100*	1.0
4	Hyson Products—*Regis Minerd* Associated Spring	10367 Brecksville Rd, Brecksville OH 44141	440-526-5900	D	70*	.5
5	Connor Formed Metal Products—*Robert Sloss*	1301 Shoreway Rd Ste 3, Belmont CA 94002	650-591-2026	R	32	.2
6	Twist Inc—*Joe Wright*	PO Box 177, Jamestown OH 45335	937-675-9581	R	25*	.3
7	Caldwell Manufacturing Co—*Edward Boucher*	PO Box 92891, Rochester NY 14692	585-352-3790	R	25*	.4
8	Mapes Piano String Co—*William Schaff*	PO Box 700, Elizabethton TN 37644	423-543-3195	R	24*	.2
9	Bal Seal Engineering Inc—*Rob Jostedt*	19650 Pauling, Foothill Ranch CA 92610	949-460-2100	R	24*	.4
10	Ark Technologies Inc—*Al Kabeshita*	3655 Ohio Ave, Saint Charles IL 60174	630-377-8855	R	24*	.1
11	Lewis Spring and Manufacturing	7500 N Natchez Ave, Niles IL 60714	847-647-2200	R	23*	.1
12	Lee Spring Co—*Albert Mangles*	140 58th St Unit 3C, Brooklyn NY 11220		R	20*	.2
13	Spring Rowley and Stamping Corp—*Stanley Bitel*	PO Box 276, Bristol CT 06011	860-582-8175	R	19*	.2
14	Spring Mid-Continent Co—*Donald Langhi*	PO Box 649, Hopkinsville KY 42241	270-885-8433	R	19*	.2
15	Spring Suhm Works Inc—*Russell Morgan*	2710 Mckinney St, Houston TX 77003	713-224-9293	R	17*	.1
16	Winamac Coil Spring Inc—*Joseph Pesaresi*	PO Box 278, Kewanna IN 46939	574-653-2186	R	16*	.2
17	R and L Spring Co—*Scott Forsythe*	1097 Geneva Pkwy N, Lake Geneva WI 53147	262-249-7854	R	16*	.1
18	Kern-Liebers USA Inc—*Lothar Bauerle*	PO Box 396, Holland OH 43528	419-865-2437	R	13*	.1
19	Peck Spring Corp—*John Everett*	89 Whiting St, Plainville CT 06062	860-747-5715	R	11*	.1
20	International Spring Co—*Joseph Goldberg*	7901 Nagle Ave, Morton Grove IL 60053	847-470-8170	R	11*	.1
21	Barnes Group LLC—*Gregory F Milzcik*	PO Box 489, Bristol CT 06011	860-583-7070	S	11*	.1
22	Spring Micromatic And Stamping Company Inc—*Theodore Prociuk*	9325 King St, Franklin Park IL 60131	847-671-6600	R	11*	.1
23	Cook Spring Company Inc—*Randall Cook*	233 Sarasota Center Bl, Sarasota FL 34240	941-377-5766	R	9*	.1
24	Orlando Spring Corp—*Paul Orlando*	11131 Winners Cir, Los Alamitos CA 90720	562-594-8411	R	5*	<.1
25	Wire Products Company Inc—*E Kennedy*	14601 Industrial Pkwy, Cleveland OH 44135	216-267-0777	R	5*	.2
26	Aero Spring and Manufacturing Company Inc—*Craig Roth*	3325 E Wier Ave, Phoenix AZ 85040	602-243-4329	R	4*	<.1
27	Lone Star Industrial Corporation Of Texas—*Ralph Navar*	PO Box 26911, El Paso TX 79926	915-779-7255	R	2*	<.1
28	Pullman Manufacturing Corp—*William Palmer*	77 Commerce Dr, Rochester NY 14623	585-334-1350	R	<1*	<.1

TOTALS: SIC 3495 Wire Springs

Companies: 28					1,030	7.3

3496 Miscellaneous Fabricated Wire Products

1	Keystone Steel and Wire Co—*David Cheek*	7000 SW Adams St, Peoria IL 61641	309-697-7020	S	828*	1.5
2	Ivy Steel and Wire—*Liz Potts* MMI Products Inc	400 N Sam Houston Pkwy, Houston TX 77020	281-876-0080	D	808*	1.0
3	Suzuki Garphyttan Corp—*Jay C Longbottom*	4404 Nimitz Pky, South Bend IN 46628	574-232-8800	D	525*	.4
4	MMI Products Inc	400 N Sam Houston Pky, Houston TX 77060		R	445*	2.5
5	Adrian Steel Co—*David Pilmore*	906 James St, Adrian MI 49221	517-265-6194	R	238*	.5
6	Allied Locke Industries Inc—*William Crowson*	1088 Corregidor Rd Gre, Dixon IL 61021	815-288-1471	R	219*	.4

Note: An asterisk (*) indicates an estimated financial figure. The company type code used is as follows: R = Private, P = Public, S = Private Subsidiary, B = Public Subsidiary, D = Division, J = Joint Venture, I = Investment Fund.

COMPANY RANKINGS BY SALES WITHIN 4-DIGIT SIC

Rank	Company Name—Executive Officer	Address, City, State, Zip	Phone	Type	Fin	Empls
7	Phelps Dodge International—Mathias Sandoval	806 Douglas Rd Ste 800, Coral Gables FL 33134	305-648-8000	S	170*	1.3
8	Abbott Industries Inc—Leonard Grossman	9525 149th St, Jamaica NY 11435	718-291-0880	R	156*	.4
9	Wireco Worldgroup Inc—Ira Glazer	12200 N Ambassador Dr, Kansas City MO 64163	816-270-4700	R	141*	2.0
10	Insteel Wire Products Co	1373 Boggs Dr, Mount Airy NC 27030	336-786-2141	S	135*	.5
11	Phifer Inc—Beverly Phifer	PO Box 1700, Tuscaloosa AL 35403	205-345-2120	R	74*	1.0
12	Atlantic Teleconnect Inc—Richard O Galbeirath	2529 Commerce Pkwy, North Port FL 34286		R	62*	.1
13	Gr Spring and Stamping Inc—James Zawacki	706 Bond Ave Nw, Grand Rapids MI 49503	616-453-4491	R	50*	.3
14	Webster Industries Inc—Fred Spurck	325 Hall St, Tiffin OH 44883	419-447-8232	R	50*	.3
15	West Penn Wire (Washington Pennsylvania)—Bob Speed	2833 W Chestnut St, Washington PA 15301		D	46*	.1
16	Peerless Chain Co—Gil King	PO Box 5349, Winona MN 55987		R	45*	.3
17	Western Wire Works Inc—Zanley Galton	3950 Nw Saint Helens R, Portland OR 97210	503-222-1644	R	41*	.3
18	Wayne Wire Cloth Products Inc—Michael Brown	PO Box 550, Kalkaska MI 49646	231-258-9187	R	40*	.4
19	International Staple and Machine Co—Farhad Gerannayeh	PO Box 629, Butler PA 16002		R	40*	.2
20	M and B Hangers Co—Milton Magnus III	8575 Parkway Dr, Leeds AL 35094		R	40*	.2
21	Rapid Manufacturing A California LP—Melanie Cobb	1044 W Grove Ave, Orange CA 92865	714-974-2432	R	37*	.2
22	Neptco Inc—Gaetano Marini	PO Box 2323, Pawtucket RI 02861	401-722-5500	R	37*	.5
23	Alpha Wire Co—John Valentine	711 Lidgerwood Ave, Elizabeth NJ 07202	908-925-8000	R	36*	.2
24	Enterprise Products Inc—Ron Spicer	6846 Suva St, Bell Gardens CA 90201	562-927-2515	R	36*	<.1
25	Rochester Corp—Gary Hyde	751 Old Brandy Rd, Culpeper VA 22701	540-825-2111	S	35	.4
26	Display Source Design and Factory Ltd—Randy Norrell	11218 Limestone Dr, Mesquite TX 75180	972-288-7471	R	33*	.3
27	Southern Steel and Wire Company Inc—Paul Kara	PO Box 6537, Fort Smith AR 72906	479-646-1651	R	32*	.3
28	Charter Automotive—John Mellowes	7850 N 81 St, Milwaukee WI 53223	414-365-5000	D	32	.2
29	Masonry Reinforcing Corporation Of America—Ralph Johnson	PO Box 240988, Charlotte NC 28224	704-525-5554	R	31*	.3
30	Unarco Industries—Ken Bush	400 SE 15th St, Wagoner OK 74467	918-485-9531	S	30*	.3
31	Wireway/Husky Corp—Ron Young	PO Box 645, Denver NC 28037	704-483-1900	R	30*	.2
32	Schulte Corp—John Kokenge	3100 E Kemper Rd Ste A, Cincinnati OH 45241	513-489-9300	R	28*	.2
33	Top-Shelf Fixtures LLC—Sheila Boutt	PO Box 2470, Chino CA 91708	909-627-7423	R	27*	.2
34	Cable Manufacturing and Assembly Inc—Robert Clegg	PO Box 409, Bolivar OH 44612	330-874-2900	R	26*	.3
35	Lift-All Company Inc	1909 McFarland Dr, Landisville PA 17538	717-898-6615	R	26*	.2
36	Metex Corp—Greg Vongas	970 New Durham Rd, Edison NJ 08817	732-287-0800	S	25*	.2
37	Mount Joy Wire Corp—Thomas D Duff	1000 E Main St, Mount Joy PA 17552	717-653-1461	R	25*	.1
38	Apache Hose and Belting Company Inc—Tom Pientok	PO Box 1719, Cedar Rapids IA 52406	319-365-0471	R	25*	.2
39	Lodan Electronics Inc—Raymond Kedzior	3311 N Kennicott Ave, Arlington Heights IL 60004	847-398-5311	R	25*	.2
40	Argo Products Co—George Goldstein	3500 Goodfellow Blvd, Saint Louis MO 63120	314-385-1803	R	23*	.2
41	Michigan Rod Products	1326 Grand Oaks Dr, Howell MI 48843	517-552-9812	R	23*	.1
42	Southwest Wire Rope Inc—Mitch Hausman	1902 Federal Rd, Houston TX 77015	713-453-8518	S	22*	<.1
43	United Wire Hanger Corp—Lawrence Goldman	PO Box 2367, South Hackensack NJ 07606	201-288-4540	R	21*	.1
44	Chemprene Inc—John Nicoletti	PO Box 471, Beacon NY 12508	845-831-2800	R	21*	.2
45	Carl Stahl Sava Industries Inc—Zdenek Fremund	PO Box 30, Riverdale NJ 07457	973-835-0882	R	20*	.1
46	Sumitomo Electric Wintec America Inc—Masaharu Kurata	909 Industrial Dr, Edmonton KY 42129	270-432-2233	R	20*	.1
47	Tote Cart Co—Paul Mills	1802 Preston St, Rockford IL 61102	815-963-3414	R	19*	.2
48	Orscheln Products LLC—William Orschelin	PO Box 280, Moberly MO 65270	660-263-4377	R	17*	.3
49	Cooperative Bright Inc—Charles Bright	803 W Seale St, Nacogdoches TX 75964	936-564-8378	R	17*	.2
50	Cove Four-Slide and Stamping Corp—Barry Jaffee	PO Box 272, Freeport NY 11520	516-379-4232	R	16*	.1
51	Oklahoma Steel and Wire Company Inc—Beverly Moore	PO Box 220, Madill OK 73446	580-795-7311	H	16*	.3
52	Roytec Industries Inc—George Koebel	306 Bell Park Dr, Woodstock GA 30188	770-926-5470	R	16*	.1
53	Fick Alloy Wire Inc—Eric Fisk	PO Box 26, Hawthorne NJ 07507	973-427-7550	R	15*	.1
54	Northern Wire LLC—Chris Marschner	PO Box 545, Merrill WI 54452	715-536-9551	R	14*	.1
55	Franklin Display Group—George Mutert	PO Box 127, Belvidere IL 61008	815-544-6676	R	14*	.1
56	Keats Manufacturing Co—Wade Keats	PO Box 526, Wheeling IL 60090	847-520-1133	R	14*	.1
57	Wire Belt Company Of America Inc—David Greer	154 Harvey Rd, Londonderry NH 03053	603-644-2500	R	14*	.1
58	Fortress Forms—Richard Clemins	2225 S 170th St, New Berlin WI 53151	262-797-7520	Berlin	13*	.1
59	Riverdale Mills Corp—James Knott	PO Box 200, Northbridge MA 01534	508-234-8715	R	12*	.1
60	Precision Wire Products Inc—John Ondrasick	6150 Sheila St, Commerce CA 90040	323-890-9100	R	12*	.3
61	Cook Technologies Inc—Thomas Panzarella	PO Box 129, Green Lane PA 18054	215-234-4535	R	12*	.1
62	Amanda Bent Bolt Co—Donald Gruschow	PO Box 1027, Logan OH 43138	740-385-9380	R	12*	.1
63	Park Manufacturing Corp—Dennis Kleven	555 Garfield St S, Cambridge MN 55008	763-552-2000	R	11*	.1
64	Miller Wire Works Inc—Robin Battles	PO Box 610280, Birmingham AL 35261	205-592-0341	R	10*	.1
65	National Wire Fabric Inc—Ric Drehle	PO Box 159, Star City AR 71667	870-628-4201	R	10*	.1
66	Mid-West Wire Products Inc—Richard Geralds	800 Woodward Hts, Ferndale MI 48220	248-399-5100	R	10*	.1
67	Royal Wire Products Inc—William Peshina	13450 York Delta Dr, North Royalton OH 44133	440-237-8787	R	10*	.1
68	Pentwater Wire Products Inc—Jay Petter	PO Box 947, Pentwater MI 49449	231-869-6911	R	9*	.1
69	Merrill Manufacturing Corp—Richard Taylor	PO Box 566, Merrill WI 54452	715-536-5533	R	9*	.1
70	Main Robert A and Sons Holding Company Inc—Robert Main	PO Box 159, Wyckoff NJ 07481	201-447-3700	R	9*	.2
71	Premier Manufacturing Corporation—Paul Kara	12117 Bennington Ave, Cleveland OH 44135	216-941-9700	R	8*	.2
72	Sinclair International Co—David Sinclair	85 Blvd, Queensbury NY 12804	518-747-2803	R	8*	.1
73	Bay State Cable Ties LLC—Stephen Dalton	5680 John Givens Rd, Crestview FL 32539		R	8*	.1
74	Ashley Sling Inc—Greg Ashley	PO Box 44413, Atlanta GA 30336	404-691-2604	R	7*	.1
75	Lafayette Wire Products Inc—Sam Newton	PO Box 4552, Lafayette IN 47903	765-474-7896	R	7*	.1
76	Process Specialties Inc—Edward Morris	1660 W Linne Rd Ste A, Tracy CA 95377	209-832-1344	R	7*	<.1
77	Midwest Wire Products LLC—Sally Beisner	PO Box 770, Sturgeon Bay WI 54235	920-743-6591	R	7*	.1
78	Safeguard Products Inc—Willis Kurtz	PO Box 8, New Holland PA 17557	717-354-4586	R	7*	.1
79	J and L Wire Cloth LLC—Patricia Goldammer	268 Water St W, Saint Paul MN 55107		R	7*	<.1
80	Cpi Wirecloth and Screens Inc—Glenn Lillie	PO Box 1710, Pearland TX 77588	281-485-2300	R	6*	.1
81	Spring Wesco Co—Martha Quezada	4501 S Knox Ave, Chicago IL 60632	773-838-3350	R	6*	.1
82	Wire Mesh Products Inc—Rich Riva	PO Box 1988, York PA 17405	717-848-3620	R	6*	.1
83	Cargill Steel and Wire Div—Joseph Lea	21 Waterway Ave Ste 52, The Woodlands TX 77380	281-298-0320	D	6*	<.1
84	Wire Products Manufacturing Corp—Roger Dupke	PO Box 407, Merrill WI 54452	715-536-7144	R	6*	.1
85	Form Cut Industries Inc—Charles Alberto	195 Mount Pleasant Ave, Newark NJ 07104	973-483-5154	R	6*	<.1
86	Donner Industries Inc—Joseph Glamos	PO Box 46, Hugo MN 55038	651-429-0890	R	6*	<.1
87	United States Alumoweld Company LLC—Sarah King	115 Usac Dr, Duncan SC 29334	864-848-1901	R	6*	<.1
88	B and J Wire Inc—Josephine Soltysiak	1919 S Fairfield Ave, Chicago IL 60608	773-927-9473	R	5*	<.1
89	Custom Wire Industries Inc—Jeffery Delaney	S83w18787 Saturn Dr, Muskego WI 53150	262-679-9700	R	5*	<.1
90	General Cage LLC—David Cook	PO Box 104, Elwood IN 46036	765-552-5039	R	5*	<.1
91	Glamos Wire Products Company Inc—Joseph Glamos	PO Box 46, Hugo MN 55038	651-429-5386	R	5*	<.1
92	Duecker Rubber Service Inc—Bill Duecker	PO Box 35163, Houston TX 77235	713-433-1272	R	5*	<.1
93	Cor-Met Inc—J Kiilunen	12500 Grand River Rd, Brighton MI 48116	810-227-3257	R	4*	<.1
94	Friendship Trap Company Inc—J Bartlett	570 Cushing Rd, Friendship ME 04547	207-354-2545	R	4*	<.1
95	Ejay Filtration Inc—Jerry Green	PO Box 5268, Riverside CA 92517	951-683-0805	R	4*	<.1
96	US Rubber Corp—Peter Chen	PO Box 520, Conroe TX 77305	936-756-1977	R	4*	<.1

Rank	Company Name—*Executive Officer*	Address, City, State, Zip	Phone	Type	Fin	Empls
97	Mathews Wire Inc—*Mike Mathews*	654 W Morrison St, Frankfort IN 46041	765-659-3542	R	3*	<.1
98	Anrod Screen Cylinder Co—*Gregory Biddinger*	PO Box 117, Cass City MI 48726	989-872-2101	R	3*	<.1
99	Jackburn Manufacturing Inc—*Paul Kelly*	PO Box 166, Girard PA 16417	814-774-3573	R	3*	<.1
100	Bergen Cable Technology LLC—*Richard Anders*	343 Kaplan Dr, Fairfield NJ 07004	973-276-9596	D	3*	<.1
101	Apex Conveyor Manufacturing LLC—*Robert Lowery*	PO Box 812, Murrieta CA 92564	951-304-7808	R	3*	<.1
102	Communication Cable Co—*Paul Black*	140 Quaker Ln, Malvern PA 19355	610-644-1900	R	3*	<.1
103	Lee Jensen Sales Company Inc—*James Jensen*	101 W Terra Cotta Ave, Crystal Lake IL 60014	815-459-0929	R	3*	<.1
104	Beaden Screen Inc—*William O'connor*	PO Box 199, Croswell MI 48422	810-679-3119	R	3*	<.1
105	Aero Assemblies Inc—*Anthony Winick*	12012 12th Ave S, Burnsville MN 55337	952-894-5552	R	2*	<.1
106	Electronic Cabling and Assembly Inc—*Maryann Nitchmann*	PO Box 746, Charlottesville VA 22902	434-293-2593	R	2*	<.1
107	Apco Products—*Morton Reich*	PO Box 236, Essex CT 06426	860-767-2108	R	2*	<.1
108	O/K Machinery Corp—*Owen Kellett*	73 Bartlett St, Marlborough MA 01752	508-303-8286	R	2*	<.1
109	Bel Mar Wire Products Inc—*Anastase Marinos*	2343 N Damen Ave, Chicago IL 60647	773-342-3800	R	2*	<.1
110	Netsource Inc—*Thor Swanson*	25 W St, Bolton CT 06043	860-649-6000	R	2*	<.1
111	Marshall Manufacturing Inc—*Richard Marshall*	PO Box 190, Atlantic VA 23303	757-824-4061	R	2*	<.1
112	Life Saver Pool Fence Systems Inc—*Robert Lupton*	1085 Sw 15th Ave Ste 3, Delray Beach FL 33444	561-272-8242	R	2*	<.1
113	KIO Kables Inc—*Bruce Scott*	2525 W 10th St, Antioch CA 94509	925-778-7500	R	2*	<.1
114	Advanced Cable Connection Inc—*Richard Schemitsch*	PO Box 8097, Tampa FL 33674	813-978-0101	R	2*	<.1
115	Datapro International Inc—*Jim Sherman*	1144 Nw 52nd St, Seattle WA 98107	206-782-5259	R	2*	<.1
116	Nax Products Inc—*Richard Knaack*	1501 W Diggins St, Harvard IL 60033	815-943-3400	R	2*	<.1
117	Roy I Kaufman Inc—*Martin Kaufman*	1672 Marion Uppr Sndsk, Marion OH 43302	740-382-0643	R	2*	<.1
118	R-Tronics LLC—*Joan Burth*	222 Erie Blvd E, Rome NY 13440	315-337-7574	R	1*	<.1
119	Redco Audio Inc—*David Berliner*	1701 Stratford Ave, Stratford CT 06615	203-502-7600	R	1*	<.1
120	Protopac Inc—*Hugh Langin*	120 Echo Lake Rd, Watertown CT 06795	860-274-6796	R	1*	<.1
121	Hawkeye Of Iowa Ltd—*Don Schmidgall*	PO Box 9, Mediapolis IA 52637	319-394-3197	R	<1*	<.1
122	Law Enforcement Supply Inc—*Gerald Carter*	10920 64th Ave, Allendale MI 49401	616-895-7875	R	<1*	<.1
123	Micro Wire Forms Inc—*Terry Elliot*	998 Josiane Ct Ste 105, Altamonte Springs FL 32701	407-331-6652	R	<1*	<.1
124	Computer Cable Makers Inc—*Richard Buch*	819 Striker Ave Ste 6, Sacramento CA 95834	916-921-2243	R	<1*	<.1

TOTALS: SIC 3496 Miscellaneous Fabricated Wire Products
Companies: 124   5,392   23.7

3497 Metal Foil & Leaf

Rank	Company Name—*Executive Officer*	Address, City, State, Zip	Phone	Type	Fin	Empls
1	Hfa Inc—*Norton Sarnoff*	135 E Hintz Rd, Wheeling IL 60090	847-520-1000	R	400*	.7
2	Oracle Flexible Packaging—*Scott Dickman*	220 E Polo Rd, Winston-Salem NC 27105	336-777-5000	D	300*	1.2
3	International Converter Inc	17153 Industrial Hwy, Caldwell OH 43724		S	143*	.2
4	Durable Inc—*Scott Anders*	750 Northgate Pkwy, Wheeling IL 60090	847-541-4400	R	93*	.8
5	Revere Industries LLC—*David Charles*	838 N Delsea Dr, Clayton NJ 08312	856-881-3600	R	67*	1.0
6	Api Foils Inc—*David Walton*	329 New Brunswick Ave, Rahway NJ 07065	732-382-6800	R	19*	.2
7	Chicago Metallic Products Inc—*Mark Faber*	800 Ela Rd, Lake Zurich IL 60047	847-438-2171	R	18*	.3
8	Graphic Specialties Inc—*Dale Hutchins*	2350 Breton Industrial, Grand Rapids MI 49508	616-247-0060	R	3*	<.1
9	Yates Foil USA Inc—*Craig Yates*	PO Box 43627, Philadelphia PA 19106	856-467-6668	R	1*	<.1
10	Crown Roll Leaf Inc—*Margaret Waitts*	PO Box 2305, Clifton NJ 07015	973-742-4000	R	<1*	.3

TOTALS: SIC 3497 Metal Foil & Leaf
Companies: 10   1,044   4.7

3498 Fabricated Pipe & Fittings

Rank	Company Name—*Executive Officer*	Address, City, State, Zip	Phone	Type	Fin	Empls
1	Shaw Group Inc—*J M Bernhard Jr*	4171 Essen Ln, Baton Rouge LA 70809	225-932-2500	P	5,938	27.0
2	Edgen Murray Ltd—*Dan J O'Leary*	18444 Highland Rd, Baton Rouge LA 70809		R	1,097*	.3
3	United States Pipe and Foundry Co—*Paul Ciolino*	PO Box 10406, Birmingham AL 35202		S	985*	2.5
4	Lone Star Steel Co	PO Box 803546, Dallas TX 75380	972-386-3981	S	425*	1.5
5	Spitzer Industries Inc—*Cullen Spitzer*	11250 Tanner Rd, Houston TX 77041	713-466-1518	R	337*	.9
6	NIBCO Inc—*Rex Martin*	1516 Middlebury St, Elkhart IN 46516	574-295-3000	R	292*	3.0
7	Trinity—*Tim Wallace*	2525 Stemmons Fwy, Dallas TX 75207	214-631-4420	S	248*	.8
8	Sunland Fabricating Inc—*Brian Bodin*	30103 Sunland Dr, Walker LA 70785	225-667-1000	R	228*	.6
9	Pioneer Pipe Inc—*David Archer*	2021 Hanna Rd, Marietta OH 45750	740-376-2400	R	209*	.5
10	Premier Pipe LLC—*Ron Dewan*	654 N Sam Houston Pkwy, Houston TX 77060	832-300-8100	R	184*	.1
11	TI Automotive - North America—*William Kozyra*	1272 Doris Rd, Auburn Hills MI 48326	248-494-5000	J	166*	.4
12	Mueller Brass Co—*Gregory L Christopher*	PO Box 5021, Port Huron MI 48061	810-987-7770	S	151*	.4
13	Performance Contractors Inc—*Art Favre*	9901 Pecue Ln, Baton Rouge LA 70810	225-751-4156	R	109*	1.5
14	Hofmann Industries Inc—*Stephen P Owens*	PO Box 2147, Sinking Spring PA 19608	610-678-8051	R	104*	.3
15	AAON Coil Products Inc—*Scott Asbjornson*	203 Gum Springs Rd, Longview TX 75602	903-236-4403	S	90*	.7
16	Team Industries Inc—*John Panetti*	PO Box 350, Kaukauna WI 54130	920-766-7977	R	77*	.3
17	Indiana Tube Corp—*John Whitenack*	2100 Lexington Ave, Evansville IN 47720	812-424-9028	S	76*	.2
18	Morton Industries LLC—*Gary Rickert*	70 Commerce Dr, Morton IL 61550	309-263-2590	R	58*	.4
19	Precision Tube Co—*William D O'Hagan*	287 Wissahickon Ave, North Wales PA 19454	215-699-5801	D	51*	.1
20	Triplex Inc	1122 Kress St, Houston TX 77020	713-672-9911	R	48*	.1
21	Elster Perfection Corp—*Bary O'Connell*	436 N Eagle St, Geneva OH 44041	440-428-1171	S	39*	.3
22	Word Industries Pipe Fabricators Inc—*James Bernhard Jr* Shaw Group Inc	4140 S Galveston Ave, Tulsa OK 74107	918-446-8184	S	38	.3
23	Deublin Co—*Ronald Kelner*	2050 Norman Dr, Waukegan IL 60085	847-689-8600	R	38*	.6
24	Scott Process Systems Inc—*Thomas Bach*	1160 Sunnyside St Sw S, Hartville OH 44632	330-877-2350	R	33*	.3
25	Blissfield Manufacturing Co—*Patrick Farver*	626 Depot St, Blissfield MI 49228	517-486-2121	R	33*	.3
26	Universal Tube Inc—*William Henson*	2607 Bond St, Rochester Hills MI 48309	248-853-5100	R	31*	.3
27	Pegasus Manufacturing Inc (Middletown Connecticut)—*Todd DiPentima*	422 Timber Ridge Rd, Middletown CT 06457	860-635-8811	R	30*	.1
28	Texas Steel Conversion Inc—*Brian Binau*	3101 Holmes Rd, Houston TX 77051	713-733-6013	R	28*	.5
29	Tube Specialties Company Inc—*Richard Weyhrich*	PO Box 20608, Portland OR 97294	503-618-8823	R	28*	.4
30	Controls Southeast Inc—*Fred Stubblefield*	PO Box 7500, Charlotte NC 28241	704-588-3030	R	27*	.2
31	Advanced Tubing Technology Inc—*Hal Mulveney*	150 Intercraft Dr, Statesville NC 28625	704-924-7020	R	26*	.3
32	Curtis Products Inc—*David Heckaman*	228 E Bronson St, South Bend IN 46601	574-289-4891	R	26*	.2
33	Riker Products Inc—*Gary Frye*	PO Box 6976, Toledo OH 43612	419-729-1626	R	25*	.3
34	Whitley Products Inc—*Jim Ciar*	493 S Cir Dr W, Warsaw IN 46580	574-267-7114	R	25*	.2
35	PC Campana Inc—*David Campana*	1374 E 28th St, Lorain OH 44055	440-246-6500	R	21*	.1
36	Tube Forgings Of America Inc—*Jay Zidell*	5200 Nw Front Ave, Portland OR 97210	503-228-8691	R	21*	.2
37	Boccard Pipe Fabricators Inc—*Bruno Boccard*	2500 Galveston Rd, Houston TX 77017	713-643-0681	R	20*	.2
38	Vam-Usa—*Pierre Frentzel*	19210 E Hardy Rd, Houston TX 77073	281-821-5510	R	20*	.2
39	Reynolds Cycling LLC—*Joe Pagett*	3392 W 8600 S, West Jordan UT 84088	801-565-8003	R	20*	.2
40	Accrotool Inc—*William Phillips*	401 Hunt Valley Rd, New Kensington PA 15068	724-339-3560	R	19*	.2
41	Custom Alloy Corp—*Adam Ambielli*	3 Washington Ave Ste 5, High Bridge NJ 08829	908-638-6200	R	17*	.2

Note: An asterisk (*) indicates an estimated financial figure. The company type code used is as follows: R = Private, P = Public, S = Private Subsidiary, B = Public Subsidiary, D = Division, J = Joint Venture, I = Investment Fund.

COMPANY RANKINGS BY SALES WITHIN 4-DIGIT SIC

Rank	Company Name—Executive Officer	Address, City, State, Zip	Phone	Type	Fin	Empls
42	Global Tube Form Partners LLC	3405 Engle Rd, Fort Wayne IN 46809	260-478-2363	R	17*	.2
43	Kraftube Inc—Kevin Kinnally	925 E Church Ave, Reed City MI 49677	231-832-5562	S	16*	.1
44	Cobey Inc—John Obey	1 Ship Canal Pkwy, Buffalo NY 14218	716-362-9550	R	15*	.1
45	Rovanco Piping Systems Inc—Larry Stonitsch	20535 Se Frontage Rd, Joliet IL 60431	815-741-6700	R	15*	.1
46	Leonhardt Manufacturing Company Inc—Robert Jacobs	800 High St, Hanover PA 17331	717-632-4150	R	15*	.1
47	Bendtec Inc—Robert Meierhoff	PO Box 457, Duluth MN 55801	218-722-0205	R	13*	.1
48	Phs Industries Inc—Wayne Mansfield	434 Latigue Rd, Westwego LA 70094	504-431-7722	R	13*	.1
49	Dynamic Lighting Inc—Bradley Somers	5220 Shank Rd, Pearland TX 77581	281-997-5400	S	13*	.1
50	Bauer Welding And Metal Fabricators Inc—Douglas Bauer	2159 Mustang Dr, Saint Paul MN 55112	763-786-6025	R	13*	.1
51	Tube Fab/Roman Engineering Company Inc—Thomas Redman	1715 M 68, Afton MI 49705	231-238-9366	R	13*	.2
52	Shelby Enterprises Inc—Curt Howell	70701 Powell Rd, Bruce Twp MI 48065	586-752-4552	R	13*	.1
53	Hydro Tube Enterprises Inc—Mike Prokop	137 Artino St, Oberlin OH 44074	440-774-1022	R	12*	.1
54	Peoria Tube Forming Corp—Rodger Butler	1331 Spring Bay Rd, East Peoria IL 61611	309-822-0274	R	12*	.1
55	Apex Piping Systems Inc—Ronald Sabbato	302 Falco Dr, Wilmington DE 19804	302-995-6136	R	11*	.1
56	Spinco Metal Products Inc—C Straubing	1 Country Club Dr, Newark NY 14513	315-331-6285	R	11*	.1
57	Woodmack Products Inc—Gilman Mc Millan	11430 White Rock Rd, Rancho Cordova CA 95742	916-853-6150	R	10*	.1
58	Seal Tite LLC—Michael Kelley	120 Moore Rd, Hillsboro OH 45133	937-393-4268	R	10*	.1
59	Diversified Plant Services LLC—Ken Mathewes	14004 S Hwy 288b, Angleton TX 77515	979-848-8900	R	10*	.1
60	Esterle Mold and Machine Company Inc—Richard Esterle	1539 Commerce Dr, Stow OH 44224	330-686-1685	R	8*	.1
61	Engineering Tube Specialties Inc—Valerie Oldenburg	85 Myron St, Ortonville MI 48462	248-627-2871	R	8*	.1
62	Hollaender Manufacturing Co—Robert Hollaender	10285 Wayne Ave, Cincinnati OH 45215	513-772-8800	R	8*	.1
63	BL Harroun And Son Inc—Willard Harroun	1018 Staples Ave, Kalamazoo MI 49007	269-345-8657	R	8*	.1
64	Flexible Metal Inc—Donald Heye	2467 Mountain Industri, Tucker GA 30084	770-493-1100	S	8*	.1
65	Quality Pipe Products Inc—Erwin Melton	PO Box 667, New Boston MI 48164	734-374-5100	R	7*	.1
66	Texas Arai	8204 Fairbanks N Houst, Houston TX 77064	713-937-1800	S	7	.4
67	Parts And Machinery Company Inc—Robert Neal	PO Box 841, Union SC 29379	864-429-3648	R	6*	<.1
68	CS Precision Manufacturing Inc—Scott James	140028 Lockwood Rd, Gering NE 69341	308-436-2099	R	6*	<.1
69	New England Union Company Inc—Glen Petit	PO Box 70, West Warwick RI 02893	401-821-0800	R	6*	<.1
70	Industrial Plastic Systems Inc—Barron Burhans	PO Box 6280, Lakeland FL 33807	863-646-8551	R	6*	<.1
71	Foster Manufacturing Company Inc—Daniel Nowlin	2324 W Battlefield St, Springfield MO 65807	417-881-6600	R	6*	<.1
72	G and J Steel and Tubing—John Tursky	406 Roycefield Rd, Hillsborough NJ 08844	908-526-4445	R	6*	<.1
73	Rexarc International Inc—Robert Moyer	PO Box 7, West Alexandria OH 45381	937-839-4604	R	6*	<.1
74	Selling Precision Inc—William Calcagno	264 Marshall Hill Rd, West Milford NJ 07480	973-728-1214	R	5*	<.1
75	J and L Manufacturing Company Inc—James Dominique	PO Box 189, Marshall MI 49068	269-789-1507	R	5*	<.1
76	High Performance Tube Inc—John Odonnell	792 Chimney Rock Rd St, Martinsville NJ 08836	732-469-1861	R	4*	<.1
77	Vindee Industries Inc—Robert Carthy	965 Lambrecht Dr, Frankfort IL 60423	815-469-3300	R	4*	<.1
78	Leroy Plastics Inc—Keith Truax	15 Lent Ave, Le Roy NY 14482	585-768-8158	R	4*	<.1
79	Pittsburgh Tubular Shafting Inc—Thomas Boffo	PO Box 149, Rochester PA 15074	724-774-7212	R	2*	<.1
80	Jettron Products Inc—Edward Balzarotti	PO Box 337, East Hanover NJ 07936	973-887-0571	R	2*	<.1
81	Huth Manufacturing Corp—Joseph Becker	PO Box 270467, Hartford WI 53027	262-673-9440	S	2*	<.1
82	Bendco Corp—Darrell Smith	1625 E Easton St, Tulsa OK 74120	918-583-1566	R	2*	<.1
83	Aaa Technology And Specialties Company Inc—Reid Mcnally	6219 Brittmoore Rd, Houston TX 77041	713-849-3366	R	2*	<.1
84	Tube Forming and Machin Inc—Jerome Orefice	4614 Industrial Row, Oscoda MI 48750	989-739-3323	R	2*	<.1
85	Rps Shenandoah Inc—Diane Ratcliffe	211 E 4th St, Front Royal VA 22630	540-635-2131	R	1*	<.1
86	Houston Elbow and Nipple Company Inc—Richard Honeycutt	PO Box 230301, Houston TX 77223	713-225-2257	R	1*	<.1

TOTALS: SIC 3498 Fabricated Pipe & Fittings
Companies: 86   11,795   50.0

3499 Fabricated Metal Products Nec

Rank	Company Name—Executive Officer	Address, City, State, Zip	Phone	Type	Fin	Empls
1	United Components Inc—Bruce Zorich	14601 Hwy 41 N, Evansville IN 47725	812-867-4156	S	885*	6.8
2	Commercial Vehicle Group Inc—Mervin Dunn	7800 Walton Pkwy, New Albany OH 43054	614-289-5360	P	832	5.4
3	Precision Parts International LLC—Michael Bryant	2129 Austin Ave, Rochester Hills MI 48309	248-724-7282	R	644*	1.2
4	Specialty Bar Products Co—Ann Harvey	200 Martha St, Blairsville PA 15717	724-459-7500	R	345*	.3
5	Ulbrich Stainless Steels and Special Metals Inc—Chris Ulbrich	57 Dodge Ave, North Haven CT 06473	203-239-4481	R	331*	.6
6	Metal Building Compnents Inc—Wayne Dickinson	PO Box 38217, Houston TX 77238	281-445-8555	D	280*	.3
7	Raytech Corp—Larry W Singleton	4 Corporate Dr Ste 295, Shelton CT 06484	203-925-8023	R	227	1.7
8	Burgess-Norton Manufacturing Co—Brett Vasseur	737 Peyton St, Geneva IL 60134	630-232-4100	S	199*	.9
9	Signode Packaging Systems—Suvit Woravisitwongse	800 Corporate Woods Pk, Vernon Hills IL 60061		S	188*	1.3
10	Sun Hydraulics Corp—Allen J Carlson	1500 W University Pkwy, Sarasota FL 34243	941-362-1200	P	151	.6
11	Roll Forming Corp—Ray Leathers	1070 Brooks Industrial, Shelbyville KY 40065	502-633-4437	S	108*	.2
12	Atek Manufacturing LLC—Jim Bartel	PO Box 403, Brainerd MN 56401	218-829-4719	R	107*	.2
13	Kurt Manufacturing Company Inc—William Kuban	5280 Main St Ne, Minneapolis MN 55421	763-572-1500	R	81*	.4
14	Crown Electrical Services and Automation Inc—Bradley Hendrickson	5960 Southport Rd, Portage IN 46368	219-762-0700	R	81*	.1
15	United Capital Corp—Attilio F Petrocelli	9 Park Pl, Great Neck NY 11021	516-466-6464	P	81	.5
16	Thomas and Skinner Inc—Vernon Detlef	PO Box 150, Indianapolis IN 46206	317-923-2501	R	74*	.5
17	Mid-American Precision Products LLC—Randy Lepper	PO Box 1444, Joplin MO 64802	417-623-2285	R	69*	.1
18	Spraying Systems Co—James Bramsen	PO Box 7900, Wheaton IL 60187	630-665-5000	R	68*	.9
19	Louisville Ladder Group LLC—Carlos Marino	7765 National Turnpike, Louisville KY 40214	502-636-2811	R	65	.3
20	Bunting Magnetics Co—Robert Bunting Sr	PO Box 468, Newton KS 67114	316-284-2020	R	57*	.1
21	MMG Corp—John W Newman	271 Rte 46 West, Fairfield NJ 07004	973-227-2176	S	55*	.1
22	Innovex Ltd	3033 Campus Dr Ste E18, Plymouth MN 55441	763-383-4000	S	53*	2.0
23	United Industries Inc (Beloit Wisconsin)—Greg Sturicz	1546 Henry Ave, Beloit WI 53511	608-365-8891	R	53	.3
24	Scherping Systems Inc—Tim High	PO Box 10, Winsted MN 55395	320-485-4401	S	53*	.3
25	Medeco Security Locks Inc—Tom Kaika	PO Box 3075, Salem VA 24153	540-380-5000	R	45*	.3
26	Onity—Bob Aquilino	2232 Northmont Pkwy, Duluth GA 30096	770-497-3949	R	45*	.2
27	Cannon Safe Inc—Aaron Baker	19949 Kendall Dr, San Bernardino CA 92407	909-382-0303	R	43*	.5
28	A and A Manufacturing Company Inc—James D O'Rourke	2300 S Calhoun Rd, New Berlin WI 53151	262-786-1500	S	39	.3
29	Summit Packaging Systems Inc—Gordon Gilroy	PO Box 5304, Manchester NH 03108	603-669-5410	R	38*	.5
30	Steel Craft Corporation of Hartford—Gene Wendorff	105 Steel Craft Dr, Hartford WI 53027	262-673-6770	R	37*	.3
31	Gleason Reel Corp	PO Box 26, Mayville WI 53050	920-387-4120	S	37*	.2
32	Global Industries Inc (Grand Island Nebraska)—Jack Henry	2928 E Hwy 30, Grand Island NE 68801	308-384-9320	R	36*	.1
33	Tosoh Smd Inc—Marten Blazic	3600 Gantz Rd, Grove City OH 43123	614-875-7912	R	35*	.3
34	Wincraft Inc—John Killen	PO Box 888, Winona MN 55987	507-454-5510	R	34*	.6
35	Pentadyne Power Corp—Mark McGough	20750 Lassen St, Chatsworth CA 91311	818-350-0370	R	32*	.1
36	American Security Products Co—Dave Lazier	11925 Pacific Ave, Fontana CA 92337	951-685-9680	R	31*	.1
37	Aluminum Ladder Co—Samuel Cramer	PO Box 5329, Florence SC 29502	843-662-2595	R	30*	.3
38	Chapin Manufacturing Inc—James Campbell	PO Box 549, Batavia NY 14021	585-343-3140	R	29*	.2
39	International Packaging Corp—John Kilmartin	PO Box 427, Pawtucket RI 02862	401-724-1600	R	27*	.5
40	Samuel Strapping Systems Inc—Robert Hickey	1401 Davey Rd Ste 300, Woodridge IL 60517	630-783-8900	R	27*	.4

Rank	Company Name—*Executive Officer*	Address, City, State, Zip	Phone	Type	Fin	Empls
41	Magnet LLC—*Tricia Piontek*	PO Box 605, Washington MO 63090	636-239-5661	R	26*	.4
42	Magnum Magnetics Corp—*Allen Love*	801 Masonic Park Rd, Marietta OH 45750	740-373-7770	R	25*	.2
43	Flinchbaugh Engineering Inc—*Mike Lehman*	4387 Run Way, York PA 17406	717-755-1900	R	25*	.2
44	Metalworks Inc—*Thomas Paine*	902 4th St, Ludington MI 49431	231-845-5136	R	25*	.2
45	Gorell Enterprises Inc—*Wayne Gorrell*	1380 Wayne Ave, Indiana PA 15701	724-465-1800	R	24*	.3
46	Bishop-Wisecarver Corp—*Pamela Wisecarver-Kan*	2104 Martin Way, Pittsburg CA 94565	925-439-8272	R	23*	.1
47	Reelcraft Industries Inc—*Walt Sterniman*	2842 E Business 30, Columbia City IN 46725	260-248-8188	R	20*	.2
48	Arland Tool and Manufacturing Inc—*William Gagnon*	PO Box 207, Sturbridge MA 01566	508-347-3368	R	20*	.1
49	Art Cathedral Metal Company Inc—*Leo Tracey*	PO Box 6146, Providence RI 02940	401-273-7200	R	19*	.2
50	Base Manufacturing Inc—*Steve South*	PO Box 586, Monroe GA 30655	770-207-0002	R	19*	.1
51	Gregory Industries Inc—*T Gregory*	PO Box 80508, Canton OH 44708	330-477-4800	R	18*	.1
52	Palmer International Inc—*Kevin Palmer*	PO Box 315, Skippack PA 19474	610-584-4241	R	18*	.1
53	Magnet Sales and Manufacturing Company Inc—*Anil Nanji*	11248 Playa Ct, Culver City CA 90230	310-391-7213	R	17*	.1
54	Linett Company Inc—*Fred Schwartz*	390 Fountain St, Pittsburgh PA 15238	412-826-8531	R	17*	.1
55	Jewel Case Corp—*Therese Eisen*	110 Dupont Dr, Providence RI 02907	401-943-1400	R	17*	.3
56	Schafer Gear Works Inc—*Bipin Doshi*	4701 Nimtz Pkwy, South Bend IN 46628	574-234-4116	R	17*	.1
57	October Company Inc—*H Schaefer*	51 Ferry St, Easthampton MA 01027	413-527-9380	R	16*	.2
58	Delavan Spray LLC—*Marshall Larsen*	2730 W Tyvola Rd, Charlotte NC 28217	704-423-7000	S	16*	.2
59	Charles W Weaver Manufacturing Company Inc—*Timothy Horner*	3101 Justin Rd, Flower Mound TX 75028	972-539-1537	R	16*	.3
60	Tooling and Equipment International Corp—*Wendell Doolin*	12550 Tech Ctr Dr, Livonia MI 48150	734-522-1422	R	15*	.1
61	Industrial Gasket and Shim Company Inc—*Kaye Desch*	PO Box 368, Meadow Lands PA 15347	724-222-5800	R	15*	.1
62	Iowa Laser Technology Inc—*Mark Baldwin*	7100 Chancellor Dr, Cedar Falls IA 50613	319-266-3561	R	14*	.1
63	Inland Marine Industries Inc—*Stan Sutton*	3245 Depot Rd, Hayward CA 94545	510-785-8555	R	14*	.1
64	Coxwells Inc—*Donald Cox*	6720 S Clementine Ct, Tempe AZ 85283	480-820-6396	R	13*	.1
65	Tread Corp—*John Frye*	PO Box 13207, Roanoke VA 24032	540-982-6881	R	13*	.1
66	Magnetic Component Engineering Inc—*Linda Montgomerie*	2830 Lomita Blvd, Torrance CA 90505	310-784-3100	R	13*	.1
67	Drugstore-Direct Inc—*Todd Cohen*	2525 State Rd, Bensalem PA 19020	215-788-0600	R	12*	.1
68	Psm Industries Inc—*Craig Paullin*	14000 Avalon Blvd, Los Angeles CA 90061	310-715-9800	R	12*	.1
69	New England Sterling Inc—*Richard Blackinton*	49 Pearl St, Attleboro MA 02703	508-222-5551	R	12*	.1
70	Bete Fog Nozzle Inc—*Matthew Bete*	50 Greenfield St, Greenfield MA 01301	413-772-0846	R	12*	.1
71	Flexmag Industries Inc—*Jim McNerney*	107 Industry Rd, Marietta OH 45750	740-374-8024	S	12*	.1
72	Trendler Inc—*Andreas Gfesser*	4540 W 51st St, Chicago IL 60632	773-284-6600	R	12*	.1
73	Berkshire Investments LLC—*J Massa*	1601 S 54th Ave, Cicero IL 60804	708-656-7900	R	12*	.1
74	Husky Corp—*Grenville Sutcliffe*	2325 Husky Way, Pacific MO 63069	636-257-3073	R	12*	.1
75	Graphik Dimensions Ltd—*Lauri Feinsod*	2103 Brentwood St, High Point NC 27263	336-887-3700	R	11*	.1
76	Jebco Inc—*James Barrow*	405 Mayfield Rd, Warrenton GA 30828	706-465-3378	R	11*	.1
77	Tropar Trophy Manufacturing Company Inc—*Peter Ilaria*	5 Vreeland Rd, Florham Park NJ 07932	973-822-2400	R	11*	.1
78	Planter Inc—*Steven Kite*	1820 N Major Ave, Chicago IL 60639	773-637-7777	R	11*	.1
79	Sani-Matic Inc—*Ted Lingard*	PO Box 8662, Madison WI 53708	608-222-2399	R	10*	.1
80	Quickpartscom Inc—*Ron L Hollis*	301 N Perimeter Center, Atlanta GA 30346	770-901-3200	R	10*	<.1
81	Quadrant Solutions Inc—*Christopher Moore*	800 E Main St, Louisville KY 40206	502-589-9650	R	10*	<.1
82	Fort Knox Security Products Inc—*Thomas James*	993 Industrial Park Rd, Orem UT 84057	801-224-7233	R	10*	.1
83	Shickel Corp—*Helen Shickel*	115 Dry River Rd, Bridgewater VA 22812	540-828-2530	R	9*	.1
84	Dimar Manufacturing Corp—*Gregory Fry*	PO Box 597, Clarence NY 14031	716-759-0351	R	9*	.1
85	Supreme Products Inc—*Pat Hood*	PO Box 154308, Waco TX 76715	254-799-4941	R	9*	<.1
86	Saunders Manufacturing Company Inc—*John Rosmarin*	65 Nickerson Hill Rd, Readfield ME 04355	207-685-3385	R	9*	.1
87	Rivers Metal Products Inc—*Todd Rivers*	3100 N 38th St, Lincoln NE 68504	402-466-2329	R	8*	.1
88	Ramsey Products Corp—*William Hall*	PO Box 668827, Charlotte NC 28266	704-394-0322	R	8*	.1
89	Grand Transformers Inc—*Jerry Retzlaff*	PO Box 799, Grand Haven MI 49417	616-842-5430	R	7*	.1
90	Watson Grinding and Manufacturing Co—*John Watson*	4525 Gessner, Houston TX 77041	713-466-3053	R	7*	.1
91	Tru-Stone Technologies—*Carol Schwinn*	PO Box 430, Waite Park MN 56387	320-251-7171	S	7*	.1
92	Bassett Industries Inc—*David Milks*	2119 Sanatoga Station, Pottstown PA 19464	610-327-1200	R	7*	<.1
93	Bankers Security Safe and Vault Co—*Keith Anderberg*	9909 E 56th St, Raytown MO 64133	816-358-0883	R	7*	<.1
94	International Machinery Sales Inc—*David Earl*	1282 Camp Creek Rd, Lancaster SC 29720	803-286-5875	R	6*	.1
95	Dcg-Pmi Inc—*Gerald Palanzo*	9 Trowbridge Dr, Bethel CT 06801	203-743-5525	R	6*	<.1
96	Hyper Alloys Inc—*Pamela Neumann-Liedke*	29153 Groesbeck Hwy, Roseville MI 48066	586-772-0571	R	6*	<.1
97	Kay Home Products Inc—*Jack Murray*	90 McMillen Rd, Antioch IL 60002		R	6*	.1
98	Sonoco Products Baker Div—*John Linville*	PO Box 668, Hartselle AL 35640	256-773-6581	D	6*	.1
99	Colby Metal Inc—*Leonard Nemschoff*	PO Box 466, Colby WI 54421	715-223-2334	R	6*	.1
100	Thieman Stamping Co—*Thomas Thieman*	PO Box 45, New Bremen OH 45869	419-629-2612	R	6*	.1
101	Exair Corp—*Hoy Sweeney*	PO Box 766, Cincinnati OH 45201	513-671-3322	R	6*	<.1
102	Ohio Magnetics Inc—*Randy Greely*	5400 Dunham Rd, Maple Heights OH 44137	216 662-8484	R	6*	<.1
103	JH Smith Company Inc—*Kenneth Sittig*	330 Chapman St, Greenfield MA 01301	413-772-0191	R	5*	.1
104	Arrow Tool and Stamping Company Inc—*David Parker*	4548 W Mitchell St, Milwaukee WI 53214	414-383-5710	R	5*	<.1
105	Cummings Holdings LLC—*David Cummings*	3003 Ryan Rd, New Haven IN 46774	260-493-4405	R	5*	<.1
106	Torqmaster Inc—*Garrett Bebell*	200 Harvard Ave, Stamford CT 06902	203-326-5945	R	5*	<.1
107	Tuttle Aluminum and Bronze Inc—*Quinn Tuttle*	120 Shadow Lawn Dr, Fishers IN 46038	317-842-2420	R	5*	.1
108	California Metal and Supply Inc—*Kenneth Lee*	10450 Pioneer Blvd Ste, Santa Fe Springs CA 90670		R	5*	<.1
109	Power Engineering and Manufacturing Ltd—*Saul Herscovici*	PO Box 4055, Waterloo IA 50704	319-232-2311	R	5*	<.1
110	Gem Manufacturing Inc—*Kevin Gottschalk*	PO Box 247, Bristol WI 53104	262-857-7274	R	5*	<.1
111	Deltec Inc—*Chris Dugle*	4230 Grissom Dr, Batavia OH 45103	513-732-0800	R	4*	<.1
112	Strong Built Inc—*Ken Killen*	PO Box 157, Waterproof LA 71375	318-749-3303	R	4*	<.1
113	Cryomagnetics Inc—*Michael Coffey*	1006 Alvin Weinberg Dr, Oak Ridge TN 37830	865-482-9551	R	4*	<.1
114	Duo-Safety Ladder Corp—*Phillip Schwab*	513 W 9th Ave, Oshkosh WI 54902	920-231-2740	R	4*	<.1
115	Smith McDonald Corp—*Bill Breeser*	1270 Niagara St, Buffalo NY 14213	716-362-8960	R	4*	<.1
116	Calumet Industries Inc (Calumet Oklahoma)—*Roger Fee*	14005 W Hwy 66, Calumet OK 73014	405-262-2263	R	4*	<.1
117	Unique Lamps By K W Bertschinger Inc—*Ken Bertschinger*	3730 Industry Ave, Lakewood CA 90712	562-427-4885	R	4*	<.1
118	Wedlake Fabricating Inc—*Brian Wedlake*	6041 N Yorktown Ave, Tulsa OK 74130	918-428-1641	R	4*	<.1
119	Kraftware Corp—*D Grant*	270 Cox St, Roselle NJ 07203	908-259-8883	R	3*	<.1
120	AZ Industries Inc—*Jim Adam*	PO Box 539, Ash Flat AR 72513		R	3	<.1
121	Vibro Dynamics Corp—*Ada Young*	2443 Braga Dr, Broadview IL 60155	708-345-2050	R	3*	<.1
122	Criterion Bell and Specialty Inc—*Abraham Damast*	4312 2nd Ave, Brooklyn NY 11232	718-788-2600	R	3*	<.1
123	Airpot Corp—*Mark Gaberman*	35 Lois St, Norwalk CT 06851	203-846-2021	R	3*	<.1
124	Tran-Tec Corp—*Robert Powers*	PO Box 1044, Columbus NE 68602	402-564-2748	R	2*	<.1
125	Greenfield Amermac Inc	3451 S 40th St, Phoenix AZ 85040	602-437-5020	R	2*	<.1
126	Precision Metal Form Div—*Dan Davis*	12 Cork Hill Rd, Franklin NJ 07416	973-827-9111	D	2*	<.1
127	All-States Equipment Inc—*Dale White*	RR Box 166, Memphis MO 63555	660-465-8572	R	2*	<.1
128	Artistic Accent Inc—*Vincent Rullo*	900 Carolina Ave, Chester WV 26034	304-387-3226	R	2*	<.1
129	Oxford General Industries Inc—*Louis Voegeli*	PO Box 7033, Prospect CT 06712	203-758-4467	R	2*	<.1

Note: An asterisk (*) indicates an estimated financial figure. The company type code used is as follows: R = Private, P = Public, S = Private Subsidiary, B = Public Subsidiary, D = Division, J = Joint Venture, I = Investment Fund.

COMPANY RANKINGS BY SALES WITHIN 4-DIGIT SIC

Rank	Company Name—*Executive Officer*	Address, City, State, Zip	Phone	Type	Fin	Empls
130	Custom Coils Inc—*Tom Quinn*	1045a Shary Cir A, Concord CA 94518	925-680-0688	R	2*	<.1
131	Advanced Design Products Inc—*William Fauntleroy*	2919 Industrial Park D, Finksburg MD 21048	410-833-8814	R	2*	<.1
132	C D Sparling Co—*Torbett Guenther*	498 Farmer St, Plymouth MI 48170	734-455-3121	R	1*	<.1
133	Ronard Industries Inc—*Leonard Olken*	PO Box 708, Michigan City IN 46361	219-874-4801	R	1*	<.1
134	Haewa Corp—*Arno Mueller*	3764 Peachtree Crest D, Duluth GA 30097	770-921-3272	R	1*	<.1
135	Thermodynetics Inc—*Robert A Lerman*	651 Day Hill Rd, Windsor CT 06095	860-683-2005	P	1	<.1
136	Jerome Remien Corp—*Jerome Remien*	409 Busse Rd, Elk Grove Village IL 60007	847-806-0888	R	1*	<.1

TOTALS: SIC 3499 Fabricated Metal Products Nec
Companies: 136   6,549   37.2

3511 Turbines & Turbine Generator Sets

Rank	Company Name—*Executive Officer*	Address, City, State, Zip	Phone	Type	Fin	Empls
1	General Electric Company Power Systems—*James Cash*	4200 Wildwood Pkwy, Atlanta GA 30339	770-859-6000	D	152,000*	N/A
2	Solar Turbines Inc—*Stephen A Gosselin*	PO Box 85376, San Diego CA 92186	619-544-5000	S	13,091*	5.5
3	Jason Inc—*David C Westgate*	411 E Wisconsin Ave St, Milwaukee WI 53202	414-277-9300	R	2,919*	3.5
4	Briggs and Stratton Corp—*Todd J Teske*	PO Box 702, Milwaukee WI 53201	414-259-5333	P	2,110	6.7
5	Rolls-Royce Energy Systems Inc—*John Rishton*	105 N Sandusky St, Mount Vernon OH 43050	740-393-8888	S	2,080*	1.0
6	Sequa Corp—*Armand F Lauzon Jr*	3000 Bayport Dr Ste 88, Tampa FL 33607	813-434-4522	S	2,030	9.4
7	Elliott Overseas Corp—*Tony Casillo*	901 N Fourth St, Jeannette PA 15644	724-527-2811	S	2,023*	2.0
8	Babcock Power Inc—*Michael LeClair*	55 Ferncraft Rd Ste 21, Danvers MA 01923	978-646-3300	R	1,152*	1.4
9	Vestas Americas—*Martha Wyrsch*	1881 SW Naito Pkwy Ste, Portland OR 97201	503-327-2000	S	870*	.1
10	Tuthill Corp—*James G Tuthill*	8500 S Madison St, Burr Ridge IL 60527	630-382-4900	R	437*	2.4
11	Revak Turbomachinery Services—*Lynn Revak*	PO Box 1645, La Porte TX 77572	281-474-4458	R	186*	.1
12	Voith Hydro Inc—*Kevin Frank*	PO Box 712, York PA 17405	717-792-7000	R	179*	.6
13	Ge Wind Energy LLC	13000 Jameson Rd, Tehachapi CA 93561	661-823-6700	R	153*	1.7
14	Cooper Turbocompressor Inc—*Sheldon Erikson*	PO Box 209, Buffalo NY 14225	716-896-6600	S	130	.5
15	Capstone Turbine Corp—*Darren R Jamison*	21211 Nordhoff St, Chatsworth CA 91311	818-734-5300	P	82	.2
16	LM Wind Power (USA) Inc—*Roland Sunden*	PO Box 5637, Grand Forks ND 58206	701-780-9910	R	79*	.9
17	Chromalloy Castings Tampa Corp—*Martin Weinstein*	7030 Anderson Rd, Tampa FL 33634	813-885-4781	S	51*	.2
18	Alturdyne—*Frank Verbeke*	660 Steel St, El Cajon CA 92020	619-440-5531	R	51*	.1
19	Turbocare Inc—*Donald Clews*	2140 Westover Rd, Chicopee MA 01022	413-593-0500	S	50*	.7
20	Stork H and E Turbo Blading Inc—*John Slocum*	PO Box 177, Ithaca NY 14851	607-277-4968	R	41*	.2
21	Katana Summit LLC—*Christopher Mosley*	1600 E 29th Ave, Columbus NE 68601	402-563-9318	R	22*	.2
22	American Hydro Corp—*Selim Chacour*	PO Box 3628, York PA 17402	717-755-5300	S	21*	.1
23	Baker Energy—*Bradley Mallory*	785 Greens Pky Ste 100, Houston TX 77067	281-579-7850	S	18*	.1
24	Arcturus Marine Systems—*D Hallerberg*	517 Martin Ave A, Rohnert Park CA 94928	707-586-3155	R	17*	.1
25	Richton Farms—*Stewart Cramer*	28 Pond View Dr, Scarborough ME 04074	207-883-7424	R	17*	.1
26	Hardie-Tynes Company Inc—*Earnest Wright*	PO Box 12166, Birmingham AL 35202	205-252-5191	R	15*	.1
27	Tech Development Inc—*Ron Albrecht*	PO Box 13557, Dayton OH 45413	937-898-9600	R	12*	.1
28	Precision Aerospace LLC—*Barbara Mcgee*	3011 W Windsor Ave, Phoenix AZ 85009	602-352-8658	R	9*	<.1
29	Btec Turbines LP—*Manfred Leong*	16730 Jacintoport Blvd, Houston TX 77015	281-864-9122	R	8*	.1
30	R and D Dynamics Corp—*Giri Agrawal*	49 W Dudley Town Rd, Bloomfield CT 06002	860-726-1204	R	6*	<.1
31	Steam Turbine Alternative Resources—*Tammy Flaherty*	PO Box 862, Marion OH 43301	740-387-5535	R	6*	<.1
32	Hoerbiger Automotive Comfort Systems Inc—*Gerhard Schoell*	284 Enterprise Dr, Auburn AL 36830	334-321-2292	R	5*	<.1
33	Mi-Tech Inc—*William Totten*	PO Box 62499, North Charleston SC 29419	843-553-2743	R	5*	<.1
34	Entegrity Wind Systems Inc—*James Heath*	4855 Riverbend Rd Ste, Boulder CO 80301	303-440-8799	R	5*	<.1
35	Alessi Manufacturing Corp—*Richard Alossi*	19 Jackson Ave, Collingdale PA 19023	610-586-4200	R	4*	<.1
36	Lkm Industries Inc—*Salvatore Colucciello*	44 6th Rd, Woburn MA 01801	781-935-9210	R	3*	<.1
37	Trireme Manufacturing Company Inc—*John Tsiplakis*	245 Boston St, Topsfield MA 01983	978-887-2132	R	3*	<.1
38	Advance Hydraulics Inc—*Andy Frailing*	3073 S Chase Ave, Milwaukee WI 53207	414-481-1545	R	3*	<.1
39	Symtech Corporation International—*Richard Perera*	25700 N I 45 Ste 105, Spring TX 77386	281-419-3912	R	3*	<.1
40	Plant Wind Turbine Group—*William Plant*	44575 Antelope Dr, Bennett CO 80102	303-375-7821	R	3*	<.1
41	Corfu Machine Inc—*David Johnson*	1977 Genesee St, Corfu NY 14036	585-599-4691	R	2*	<.1
42	Newton Manufacturing Co—*Noel Cook*	4249 Delemere Blvd, Royal Oak MI 48073	248-549-9600	R	2*	<.1
43	Turbo City Inc—*Tom Miller*	1137 W Katella Ave, Orange CA 92867	714-639-4933	R	2*	<.1
44	Coates International Ltd—*George J Coates*	2100 Hwy 34 and Ridgew, Wall Township NJ 07719	732-449-7717	P	1	<.1
45	Moya Terra Aqua Inc—*Ronald Taylor*	PO Box 706, Cheyenne WY 82003	307-772-0200	R	1*	<.1

TOTALS: SIC 3511 Turbines & Turbine Generator Sets
Companies: 45   179,904   38.3

3519 Internal Combustion Engines Nec

Rank	Company Name—*Executive Officer*	Address, City, State, Zip	Phone	Type	Fin	Empls
1	Cummins Inc—*N Thomas Linebarger*	PO Box 3005, Columbus IN 47202	812-377-5000	P	13,226	39.2
2	Caterpillar Inc Engines Div—*Joshua Smith*	100 NE Adams, Peoria IL 61629	309-675-1000	D	3,950*	8.0
3	Electro-Motive Diesel Inc—*John Hamilton*	9301 W 55 St, La Grange IL 60525		R	2,177*	3.3
4	Detroit Diesel Overseas Distribution Corp Detroit Diesel Corp	13400 W Outer Dr, Detroit MI 48239	313-592-5000	S	853*	2.6
5	Detroit Diesel Corp—*Henning Oeltjenbruns*	13400 W Outer Dr, Detroit MI 48239	313-592-5000	S	608*	1.7
6	Deere Power Systems Group—*Samuel R Allen*	PO Box 5100, Waterloo IA 50704	319-292-5643	D	271*	1.0
7	Cummins Power Systems LLC—*Brian Ford* Cummins Inc	2727 Ford Rd, Bristol PA 19007	215-785-6005	S	199*	.6
8	Mercury Marine Group—*Pat Mackey*	PO Box 1939, Fond du Lac WI 54936	920-929-5040	D	178*	.6
9	Engineered Machined Products Inc—*Brian Larche*	PO Box 1246, Escanaba MI 49829	906-786-8404	R	120*	.5
10	Asmo North Carolina Inc—*Yutaka Kuroyanagi*	470 Crawford Rd, Statesville NC 28625	704-878-6663	R	101*	1.3
11	Pratt and Whitney Power Systems—*Peter Christman*	400 Main St, East Hartford CT 06108	860-565-4321	S	54	.2
12	Penn Detroit Diesel Allison LLC—*Gerald Tiffan*	8330 State Rd, Philadelphia PA 19136	215-335-0500	R	38*	.4
13	Gale Banks Engineering—*Gale Banks*	546 S Duggan Ave, Azusa CA 91702	626-969-9600	R	29*	.2
14	Interstate Bearing Technology Inc	2601 American Blvd E, Bloomington MN 55425	952-854-0836	S	20*	.1
15	Bully Dog Technologies LLC—*Ellen Rupp*	2839 Hwy 39, American Falls ID 83211		R	20*	<.1
16	Hy-Production Inc—*Mathew Roach*	6000 Grafton Rd, Valley City OH 44280	330-273-2400	R	17*	.1
17	Western Diesel Services Inc—*John Costello*	1100 Research Blvd, Saint Louis MO 63132	314-868-8620	R	16*	<.1
18	Indian Motorcycle Corp—*Scott Wine*	116 Battleground Rd, Kings Mountain NC 28086	704-937-7333	S	15*	<.1
19	Industrial Parts Depot LLC—*Mike Wu*	23231 Normandie Ave, Torrance CA 90501	310-530-1900	R	14*	<.1
20	Crusader Engines—*Chester Janssens* Pleasurecraft Marine Engine Co	40580 Vandyke Blvd, Sterling Heights MI 48312	586-977-0100	S	12*	<.1
21	Diesel Exchange Inc—*Steven Hendrick*	3811 E Kearney St, Springfield MO 65803	417-831-5600	R	11*	.1
22	Pleasurecraft Marine Engine Co—*John Thurman*	PO Box 369, Little Mountain SC 29075	803-345-1337	R	10*	.1
23	Cameron	1333 W Loop S, Houston TX 77027	713-513-3300	D	8*	<.1
24	Cdi Electronics Inc—*Ray Anders*	111 Commerce Cir, Madison AL 35758	256-772-3829	R	7*	<.1
25	Jasper Penske Engines—*Scott Miller*	4361 Motorsports Dr Sw, Concord NC 28027	704-788-8996	R	6*	<.1
26	Indmar Products Company Inc—*Richard Rowe*	5400 Old Millington Rd, Millington TN 38053	901-353-9930	R	5*	.1
27	Chemequip Sales Inc—*Jeanie Menke*	1004 Swartz Rd, Akron OH 44319	330-724-5526	R	4*	<.1

Rank	Company Name—*Executive Officer*	Address, City, State, Zip	Phone	Type	Fin	Empls
28	P and S Diesel Service Inc—*Charlotte Sierra*	17 Louisana St, Westwego LA 70094	504-341-1606	R	4*	<.1
29	United Auto Parts Inc—*Jerry Livingston*	14801 W Kellogg St, Wichita KS 67235	316-721-6868	R	4*	<.1
30	Diesel Products Inc—*Ed Wegner*	13150 Leadwell St, North Hollywood CA 91605	818-764-2506	R	4*	<.1
31	Tom Daenen Inc—*Tom Daenen*	PO Box 86, Hitchcock TX 77563	409-978-2132	R	4*	<.1
32	North American Marine Jet Inc—*Leonard Hill*	PO Box 1232, Benton AR 72018	501-778-4151	R	2*	<.1
33	Bruckner Truck Sales - Tye—*Ben Bruckner*	PO Box 397, Tye TX 79563	325-692-8400	R	2*	<.1
34	Nissan Industrial Engine Manufacturing—*Koichiro Anraku*	PO Box 116, Marengo IL 60152	815-568-0214	R	2*	<.1
35	Oil Purification Systems Inc—*Greg Slawson*	2176 Thomaston Ave, Waterbury CT 06704		R	2*	<.1
36	Amw Cuyuna Engine Company Inc—*J Stonebreaker*	8 Schein Loop, Beaufort SC 29906	843-846-2167	R	2*	<.1
37	Enduro Products Inc—*Michie White*	2964 Irving Blvd, Dallas TX 75247	214-630-4006	R	2*	<.1
38	Engine Lab Of Tampa Inc—*Susan Deegan*	201 S 78th St, Tampa FL 33619	813-630-2422	R	1*	<.1
39	Gem Remotes Inc—*Jim Muth*	356 Capri Blvd, Naples FL 34113	239-642-0873	R	1*	<.1
40	Energy Conversions Inc—*Scott Jensen*	6411 Pacific Hwy E, Fife WA 98424	253-922-6670	R	1*	<.1

TOTALS: SIC 3519 Internal Combustion Engines Nec
Companies: 40

					21,999	60.7

3523 Farm Machinery & Equipment

Rank	Company Name—*Executive Officer*	Address, City, State, Zip	Phone	Type	Fin	Empls
1	Deere and Co—*Samuel R Allen*	1 John Deere Pl, Moline IL 61265	309-765-8000	P	26,005	55.7
2	AGCO Corp—*Martin H Richenhagen*	4205 River Green Pkwy, Duluth GA 30096	770-813-9200	P	6,897	14.3
3	New Holland North America Inc—*Roland Sunden*	PO Box 1895, New Holland PA 17557	717-355-1121	S	702*	1.7
4	Blount Inc—*Joshua Collins*	PO Box 22127, Portland OR 97269	503-653-4692	S	602*	3.1
5	CTB International Corp—*Victor A Mancinelli*	PO Box 2000, Milford IN 46542	574-658-4191	S	589*	1.1
6	Brock Manufacturing—*Warren E Buffett* CTB International Corp	PO Box 2000, Milford IN 46542	574-658-4191	S	552*	1.0
7	Chore-Time/Brock International—*Warren E Buffett* CTB International Corp	PO Box 2000, Milford IN 46542	574-658-9293	S	552*	1.0
8	Chore-Time Egg Production Systems—*Warren E Buffett* CTB International Corp	PO Box 2000, Milford IN 46542	574-658-4101	S	552*	1.0
9	Chore-Time Poultry Production Systems—*Warren E Buffett* CTB International Corp	PO Box 2000, Milford IN 46542	574-658-4101	S	552*	1.0
10	Alamo Group Inc (Seguin Texas)—*Ronald A Robinson*	1627 E Walnut St, Seguin TX 78155	830-379-1480	P	525	2.3
11	Lindsay Corp—*Richard W Parod*	2222 N 111th St, Omaha NE 68164	402-829-6800	P	479	1.0
12	Gehl Power Products Inc—*William Gehl*	900 Ferdig St, Yankton SD 57078	605-665-6500	S	415*	.7
13	Applegate Livestock Equipment Inc—*Aaron Applegate*	PO Box 68, Saratoga IN 47382	765-964-4631	R	214*	.1
14	John Deere/Des Moines Works—*Samuel Allen* Deere and Co	PO Box 1595, Des Moines IA 50306	515-289-1350	D	194	N/A
15	Alamo Group Inc USA—*Ronald A Robinson* Alamo Group Inc (Seguin Texas)	1627 E Walnut, Seguin TX 78155	830-379-1480	S	181*	.3
16	Crary Industries—*Chuck Crary*	PO Box 849, West Fargo ND 58078	701-282-5520	R	169*	.2
17	Sunflower Manufacturing Co—*Ron Harris* AGCO Corp	3154 Hallie Tr, Beloit KS 67420	785-738-2261	D	166*	.3
18	Bobcat Co	PO Box 6000, West Fargo ND 58078	701-241-8700	S	154*	.8
19	Rain Bird Sprinkler Manufacturing Corp—*Tony LaFetra*	1000 W Sirerra Madre A, Azusa CA 91702	626-812-3400	R	131*	.3
20	Kuhn North America Inc—*Thierry Krier*	PO Box 167, Brodhead WI 53520	608-897-2131	S	126*	.6
21	Xylem Flowtronex—*Roger Vowell*	10661 Newkirk St, Dallas TX 75220	469-221-1200	R	98*	.2
22	Hog Slat Inc—*William Herring*	PO Box 300, Newton Grove NC 28366	910-594-0219	R	91*	.7
23	J and M Manufacturing Company Inc—*Michael Grieshop*	PO Box 547, Fort Recovery OH 45846	419-375-2376	R	90*	.2
24	John Deere Reman - Springfield LLC	4500 E Mustard Way, Springfield MO 65803	417-829-2000	R	87*	.2
25	CrustBuster/Speed King Inc—*Donald Hornung*	PO Box 1438, Dodge City KS 67801	620-227-7106	R	80*	.2
26	CNH Goodfield	PO Box 65, Goodfield IL 61742	309-965-2233	D	69*	.4
27	Rome Plow Co—*Danny Dumey*	PO Box 48, Cedartown GA 30125	770-748-4450	R	62*	.1
28	Travis Pattern and Foundry Inc—*Travis Garske*	PO Box 6325, Spokane WA 99217	509-466-3545	R	60*	.2
29	Crary Co—*Keith J Nilson*	PO Box 849, West Fargo ND 58078	701-282-5520	R	59*	.2
30	Taylor-Dunn Corp—*Arthur J Goodwin*	2114 W Ball Rd, Anaheim CA 92804	714-956-4040	R	54*	.1
31	Miller Manufacturing Co (South Saint Paul Minnesota)—*Tom Botten*	2910 Waters Rd Ste 150, Eagan MN 55121	651-928-5100	R	53*	.1
32	Heartland Equipment Inc—*JD Underwood*	PO Box 1050, Wynne AR 72396	870-238-1234	R	46*	.1
33	Sukup Manufacturing Co—*Charles Sukup*	PO Box 677, Sheffield IA 50475	641-892-4222	R	45*	.3
34	Wil-Rich LLC—*Kurt Muehler*	PO Box 1030, Wahpeton ND 58074	701-642-2621	R	45*	.2
35	AO Smith Engineered Storage Products Co—*Richard W Enners*	345 Harvestore Dr, Dekalb IL 60115	815-756-1551	D	41*	.2
36	Lor-AL Products Inc—*AE McQuinn*	202 Industrial Park, Jackson MN 56143		R	39*	.2
37	Amerequip Corp—*Michael Festge*	PO Box 36, Kiel WI 53042	920 894-7063	R	35*	.2
38	Priefert Manufacturing Company Inc—*William Priefert*	PO Box 1540, Mount Pleasant TX 75456	903-572-1741	R	34*	.5
39	Cpm Acquisition Corp—*Ted Waitman*	2975 Airline Cir, Waterloo IA 50703	319-232-8444	R	34*	.2
40	Spudnik Equipment Company LLC—*Michael Bamberger*	PO Box 1045, Blackfoot ID 83221	208-785-0480	R	33*	.2
41	Earthmaster—*Ronald A Robinson* Alamo Group Inc USA	1020 S Sangamon Ave, Gibson City IL 60936	217-784-4261	S	33*	.1
42	Bou-Matic LLC	PO Box 8050, Madison WI 53708	608-222-3484	R	31*	.3
43	Sudenga Industries Inc—*Larry Kruse*	PO Box 8, George IA 51237	712-475-3301	R	31*	.2
44	Miller St Nazianz Inc—*John W Miller*	PO Box 127, Saint Nazianz WI 54232	920-773-2121	R	30*	.2
45	Manitou North America Inc—*Serge Bosche*	PO Box 21386, Waco TX 76702	254-799-0232	S	30*	.1
46	Tiger Corp—*Ronald A Robinson* Alamo Group Inc USA	3301 N Louise Ave, Sioux Falls SD 57107		S	30*	.1
47	Alamo Group SMC Inc—*Shawn T Cleary* Alamo Group Inc USA	300 E 60th St N, Sioux Falls SD 57104	605-336-3628	S	30*	<.1
48	Hcc Inc—*Donald Bickel*	PO Box 952, Mendota IL 61342	815-539-9371	R	30*	.2
49	Philadelphia Tramrail Enterprises Inc—*Mike Savage*	2207 E Ontario St, Philadelphia PA 19134	215-533-5100	R	30*	.2
50	Powder River Livestock Handling—*Randy Thompson*	PO Box 50758, Provo UT 84603	801-374-2983	R	29*	.2
51	Hagie Manufacturing Co—*John Hagie*	PO Box 273, Clarion IA 50525	515-532-2861	R	29*	.1
52	Oxbo International Corp—*Gary Stich*	7275 Batavia Byron Rd, Byron NY 14422	585-548-2665	R	29*	.2
53	Art's-Way Manufacturing Company Inc—*Carrie L Majeski*	PO Box 288, Armstrong IA 50514	712-864-3131	P	28	.1
54	RM King Co—*Drake King*	315 N Marks Ave, Fresno CA 93706	559-266-0258	R	27*	<.1
55	Osborne Industries Inc—*Stan Thibault*	PO Box 388, Osborne KS 67473	785-346-2192	R	26*	.1
56	RM Wade and Co—*Edward Newbegin*	PO Box 23666, Portland OR 97281	503-641-1865	R	24*	.1
57	Durand-Wayland Inc—*Bob Collins*	101 Durand Rd, Lagrange GA 30241	706-882-8161	R	24*	.2
58	HD Hudson Manufacturing Co—*R Hudson*	500 N Michigan Ave Ste, Chicago IL 60611	312-644-2830	R	23*	.2
59	Pierce Corp—*Cecil Rock*	PO Box 458, Junction City OR 97448	541-998-0300	R	23*	.1
60	Diamond Automations Inc—*Douglas Mack*	23400 Haggerty Rd, Farmington Hills MI 48335	248-476-7100	R	23*	.1

Note: An asterisk (*) indicates an estimated financial figure. The company type code used is as follows: R = Private, P = Public, S = Private Subsidiary, B = Public Subsidiary, D = Division, J = Joint Venture, I = Investment Fund.

COMPANY RANKINGS BY SALES WITHIN 4-DIGIT SIC

Rank	Company Name—Executive Officer	Address, City, State, Zip	Phone	Type	Fin	Empls
61	Netafim Irrigation Inc—Igal Aisenberg	5470 E Home Ave, Fresno CA 93727	559-453-6800	R	23*	.2
62	Evans Mactavish Agricraft Inc—Donald Evans	PO Box 3408, Wilson NC 27895	252-243-4006	R	22*	.1
63	Storm Management Inc—Guy E Marge	23223 Normandie Ave, Torrance CA 90501	310-534-5232	R	22*	.2
64	Al-Jon Manufacturing LLC—Kendig Kneen	15075 Al-jon Ave, Ottumwa IA 52501	641-682-4506	R	21*	.1
65	Kbh Corp—Buddy Bass	395 Anderson Blvd, Clarksdale MS 38614	662-624-5471	R	21*	.2
66	Kondex Corp—Scott Moon	1500 Technology Dr, Lomira WI 53048	920-269-4100	R	21*	.2
67	Loftness Specialized Farm Equipment Inc—Gloria Nelson	PO Box 337, Hector MN 55342	320-848-6266	R	21*	.1
68	Industrial Iron Works Inc—Billy Adams	PO Box 628, De Witt AR 72042	870-946-2494	R	20*	.2
69	Yargus Manufacturing Inc—Larry Yargus	PO Box 238, Marshall IL 62441	217-826-6352	R	20*	.1
70	Soo Tractor Sweeprake Co—Allen Mahaney	PO Box 1283, Sioux City IA 51102	712-252-4373	R	20*	.1
71	Egging Co—Ted Egging	12145 Rd 38, Gurley NE 69141	308-884-2233	R	19*	.2
72	Noffsinger Manufacturing Company Inc—Robert Noffsinger	PO Box 1150, Greeley CO 80632	970-352-0463	R	19*	.1
73	Chick Master Incubator Co—Robert Holzer	PO Box 704, Medina OH 44258	330-722-5591	R	19*	.1
74	Kmw Ltd—Michael Bender	PO Box 327, Sterling KS 67579	620-278-3641	R	17*	.1
75	Val-Co Pax Inc—Frederick Steudler	PO Box 117, Coldwater OH 45828	419-678-8731	R	17*	.1
76	Patz Sales Inc—Darrell Patz	PO Box 7, Pound WI 54161	920-897-2251	R	16*	.1
77	Nichols Tillage Tools Inc—R Nichols	312 Hereford St, Sterling CO 80751	970-522-8676	R	16*	.1
78	Taylor Manufacturing Inc—Ron Taylor	PO Box 518, Elizabethtown NC 28337		R	16*	.1
79	Game Equipment LLC	3322 Hwy 308, Napoleonville LA 70390	985-369-9292	R	16*	<.1
80	NatureForm Hatchery Systems Inc—Harold Warren	925 N Ocean St, Jacksonville FL 32202	904-358-0355	R	16*	<.1
81	Meyer Manufacturing Corp—Donald Meyer	PO Box 405, Dorchester WI 54425	715-654-5132	R	16*	.1
82	Root-Lowell Manufacturing Co—Tony Asselta	PO Box 289, Lowell MI 49331	616-897-9211	R	15*	.1
83	Hydro Engineering Inc—Austin Huffman	PO Box 300, Norwood MN 55368	952-467-3100	R	15*	<.1
84	Automatic Equipment Manufacturing Co—Jay Hesse	1 Mill Rd, Pender NE 68047	402-385-3051	R	15*	.2
85	EVH Manufacturing Company LLC	4895 Red Bluff Rd, Loris SC 29569	843-756-2555	S	15*	.1
86	Rears Manufacturing Co—Michael Rears	PO Box 23510, Eugene OR 97402	541-688-1002	R	15*	<.1
87	Northwestern Plastics Ltd—Sam West	1731 N Roosevelt Ave S, Burlington IA 52601	319-754-4000	R	14*	.1
88	Edstrom Industries Inc—William Edstrom	819 Bakke Ave, Waterford WI 53185	262-534-5181	R	14*	.1
89	Star Forge Inc—Clarence Johnson	1801 S Ihm Blvd, Freeport IL 61032	815-235-7750	R	14*	.1
90	Gvm Inc—Mark Anderson	PO Box 358, Biglerville PA 17307	717-677-6197	R	14*	.1
91	Extru-Tech Inc—La Wenger	PO Box 8, Sabetha KS 66534	785-284-2153	S	14*	.1
92	Hy-Capacity Inc—Steve Olson	PO Box 156, Humboldt IA 50548	515-332-2125	R	13*	.1
93	Kejr Inc—Melvin Kejr	1835 Wall St, Salina KS 67401	785-825-1842	R	13*	.1
94	King Kutter Inc—James Fraley	PO Box 1200, Winfield AL 35594	205-487-3202	R	13*	.1
95	Miskin Scraper Works Inc—Mark Miskin	PO Box 218, Ucon ID 83454	208-522-2139	R	13*	.1
96	Howse Implement Company Inc—Ben Howse	PO Box 86, Laurel MS 39441	601-428-0841	R	13*	.1
97	Mathews Co—Lawrence Antos	PO Box 70, Crystal Lake IL 60039	815-459-2210	R	13*	.1
98	Van Doren Sales Inc—Bret Pittsinger	PO Box 1746, Wenatchee WA 98807	509-886-1837	R	13*	.1
99	Flory Industries—Howard Flory	PO Box 908, Salida CA 95368	209-545-1167	R	13*	.1
100	Big Dutchman Inc—Clovis Rayzel	PO Box 1017, Holland MI 49422	616-392-5981	R	13*	.1
101	Gary W Clem Inc—Gary Clem	99 M Ave, Nevada IA 50201	515-382-3506	R	12*	.1
102	Conrad-American Inc—Marvin Bricker	PO Box 2000, Houghton IA 52631	319-469-4111	R	12*	.1
103	Wylie and Son Inc—Scot Wylie	PO Box 100, Petersburg TX 79250	806-667-3566	R	12*	.1
104	Kirby Manufacturing Inc—Richard Kirby	PO Box 989, Merced CA 95341	209-723-0778	R	12*	.1
105	Shivvers Manufacturing Inc—Carl Shivvers	614 W English St, Corydon IA 50060	641 872-1005	R	12*	.1
106	Schlagel Inc—Chris Schlagel	491 Emerson St N, Cambridge MN 55008	763-689-5991	R	11*	.1
107	Orchard Machinery Corp—Don Mayo	2700 Colusa Hwy, Yuba City CA 95993	530-673-2822	R	11*	.1
108	Femco Inc—Rodney Borman	1132 W 1st St, Mcpherson KS 67460	620-241-5119	R	10*	.1
109	Federal Manufacturing Co—Otis Cobb	PO Box 04215, Milwaukee WI 53204	414-384-3200	R	10*	.1
110	Harriston-Mayo LLC—Dan Dunnigan	PO Box 378, Minto ND 58261	701-248-3286	R	10*	.1
111	KWMI Manufacturing—Eddie Warner	26264 US Hwy 98, Elberta AL 36530	251-986-7900	R	10*	<.1
112	J and D Sales Incorporated Of Eau Claire Wisconsin—Don Redetzke	6200 Us Hwy 12, Eau Claire WI 54701	715-834-1439	R	10*	.1
113	Korvan Industries Inc—Herb Korthuis	270 Birch Bay Lynden R, Lynden WA 98264	360-354-1500	R	10*	.1
114	Ziggity Systems Inc—Dale Hostetler	PO Box 1169, Middlebury IN 46540	574-825-5849	R	10*	<.1
115	Westendorf Manufacturing Company Inc—Neal Westendorf	PO Box 29, Onawa IA 51040	712-423-2762	R	9*	.1
116	Honeyville Metal Inc—Mark Hochstetler	4200 S 900 W, Topeka IN 46571	260-593-2266	R	9*	.1
117	Miraco—Carter Thomson	PO Box 686, Grinnell IA 50112	641-236-5822	D	9*	.1
118	Wasco Hardfacing Co—Robin Messick	PO Box 2395, Fresno CA 93745	559-485-5860	R	9*	.1
119	Bushnell Illinois Tank Co—Ernest Schuld	PO Box 179, Bushnell IL 61422	309-772-9471	R	9*	.1
120	Dig Corp—David Levy	1210 Activity Dr, Vista CA 92081	760-727-0914	R	9*	.1
121	Liberty Inc—Darlaine Champaigne	451 Hwy 9, Waterville KS 66548	785-363-2552	R	9*	.1
122	Doyle Equipment Manufacturing Co—Monty Doyle	PO Box 3024, Quincy IL 62305	217-222-1592	R	8*	.1
123	Lee E Norris Construction and Grain Company Inc—Dan Norris	7930 N 700 E, Tippecanoe IN 46570	574-353-7855	R	8*	<.1
124	L Double Inc—Chris Hunsaker	PO Box 597, American Falls ID 83211	208-226-5592	R	8*	.1
125	Wiese Industries Inc—Deanna Smith	PO Box 39, Perry IA 50220	515-465-9854	R	8*	.1
126	Graetz Manufacturing Inc—Alton Graetz	W11094 State Hwy 64, Pound WI 54161	920-897-4041	R	8*	.1
127	Brock Grain Systems—Bill Crosby CTB International Corp	1750 W State Rd 28, Frankfort IN 46041	765-654-8517	D	8*	.1
128	Laidig Inc—Jonathon Laidig	14535 Dragoon Trl, Mishawaka IN 46544	574-256-0204	R	8*	.1
129	Ranco Fertiservice Inc—Paul Krile	PO Box 329, Sioux Rapids IA 50585	712-283-2525	R	8*	.1
130	Honiron Corp—Jacob Giardina	PO Box 620, Jeanerette LA 70544	337-276-6314	R	8*	.1
131	Laird Manufacturing LLC	531 S State Hwy 59, Merced CA 95341	209-722-4145	R	8*	.1
132	Ag Spray Equipment Inc—David Barbee	1100 New Industry Ln, Hopkinsville KY 42240	270-886-0296	R	8*	.1
133	Remlinger Manufacturing Company Inc—John Remlinger	PO Box 299, Kalida OH 45853	419-532-3647	R	8*	<.1
134	Brown Manufacturing Co—William Brown	6001 E Hwy 27, Ozark AL 36360	334-795-6603	R	8*	.1
135	Agritek Industries Inc—Larry Kooiker	4211 Hallacy Dr, Holland MI 49424	616-786-9200	R	7*	.1
136	Pik Rite Inc—Elvin Stoltzfus	60 Pik Rite Ln, Lewisburg PA 17837	570-523-8174	R	7*	<.1
137	Earthway Products Inc—Ken Pickett	PO Box 547, Bristol IN 46507	574-848-7491	R	7*	.1
138	Utility Tool and Trailer Inc—Joe Weiland	PO Box 360, Clintonville WI 54929	715-823-3167	R	7*	.1
139	Rowse Hydraulic Rakes Company Inc—Ron Rowse	84504 State Hwy 11, Burwell NE 68823	308-348-2276	R	7*	<.1
140	Thurston Manufacturing Co—Wayne Jensen	PO Box 218, Thurston NE 68062	402-385-3041	R	7*	.1
141	Aweta-Autoline Inc—Art Lopez	23243 Clayton Ave, Reedley CA 93654	559-638-5432	R	7*	.1
142	Berg Equipment Corp—Vernon Berg	PO Box 507, Marshfield WI 54449	715-384-2151	R	7*	.1
143	Tanner Equipment Corp—David Tanner	221 Airport Rd, Blackfoot ID 83221	208-785-1450	R	7*	<.1
144	Bazooka-Farmstar Inc—Ronald Stutsman	PO Box 869, Washington IA 52353	319-653-5080	R	7*	<.1
145	River Valley Manufacturing Inc—Delon Jones	976 E Main St, Burley ID 83318	208-678-0855	R	7*	<.1
146	Hatfield Manufacturing Inc—David Hatfield	1823 Shoestring Rd, Gooding ID 83330	208-934-5182	R	6*	.1
147	Hawkline Nevada LLC—Brian Brooks	200 Front St, Mount Orab OH 45154	937-444-4295	R	6*	.1
148	Bdp Industries Inc—Carl Fronhofer	PO Box 118, Greenwich NY 12834	518-695-6851	R	6*	<.1

Rank	Company Name—Executive Officer	Address, City, State, Zip	Phone	Type	Fin	Empls
149	Terog Manufacturing Co—Tom Rogus	PO Box 587, Stephen MN 56757	218-478-3395	R	6*	<.1
150	Unist Inc—Wallace Boelkins	4134 36th St Se, Grand Rapids MI 49512	616-949-0853	R	6*	<.1
151	Fast Distributing Inc—Verlyn Fast	54859 County Rd 44, Mountain Lake MN 56159	507-427-3861	R	6*	<.1
152	Hitchcock Inc—Duane Hitchcock	49994 Us Hwy 24, Burlington CO 80807	719-346-8488	R	6*	<.1
153	RHS Inc—Rick Heiniger	2021 Iowa, Hiawatha KS 66434	785-742-2949	R	6*	<.1
154	Lyon Technologies Inc—Thomas Daly	1690 Brandywine Ave St, Chula Vista CA 91911	619-216-3400	R	6*	<.1
155	MDS Manufacturing Inc—Steven Hohn	1301 S Sd Hwy 37, Parkston SD 57366	605-928-7951	R	6*	.1
156	Shintone USA Inc—Yasuhiko Miyake	5380 Rafe Banks Dr Ste, Flowery Branch GA 30542	770-965-2460	R	6*	<.1
157	Wildcat Manufacturing Company Inc—Pat Dooey	PO Box 1100, Freeman SD 57029	605-925-4512	R	6*	<.1
158	Schuette Manufacturing And Steel Sales Inc—Donald Schuette	5028 State Hwy 42, Manitowoc WI 54220	920-758-2491	R	6*	<.1
159	Dramm Corporation Of Manitowoc—Kurt Dramm	PO Box 1960, Manitowoc WI 54221	920-684-0227	R	5*	<.1
160	Haines Equipment Inc—Patricia Haines	20 Carrington St, Avoca NY 14809	607-566-8531	R	5*	.1
161	Forsberg's Inc—Denny Bakke	PO Box 510, Thief River Falls MN 56701	218-681-1927	R	5*	<.1
162	Bentley Instruments Inc—Bent Lyder	4004 Peavey Rd, Chaska MN 55318	952-448-7600	R	5*	<.1
163	C W Mill Equipment Company Inc—Tim Wenger	PO Box 246, Sabetha KS 66534	785-284-3454	R	5*	<.1
164	G Q F Manufacturing Company Inc—R Mcgehee	PO Box 1552, Savannah GA 31402	912-236-0651	R	5*	<.1
165	B and H Manufacturing Inc—Randy Newman	141 County Rd 34E, Jackson MN 56143	507-847-2802	R	5*	<.1
166	Amco Manufacturing Inc—Thomas Peaster	PO Box 1107, Yazoo City MS 39194	662-746-4464	R	5*	<.1
167	Et Works LLC—Tracy Kincaid	2201 Hancel Pkwy, Mooresville IN 46158	317-834-4500	R	5*	<.1
168	Bigbee Metal Manufacturing Company Inc—Darrell Harp	PO Box 147, Tremont MS 38876	662-652-3374	R	5*	.1
169	Domries Enterprises Inc—Bernard Domries	12281 Rd 29, Madera CA 93638	559-673-9143	R	5*	<.1
170	E-Z Trail Inc—Abe Kuhns	PO Box 168, Arthur IL 61911	217-543-3471	R	5*	<.1
171	Hastings Equity Grain Bin Manufacturing Co—W Langford	PO Box 1007, Hastings NE 68902	402-462-2189	R	5*	<.1
172	Taylor Pittsburgh Co—Phillip Fraley King Kutter Inc	PO Box 1866, Athens TN 37371	423-745-3110	S	5*	<.1
173	Kringstad Ironworks Inc—Bernie Kringstad	406 Tower St, Park River ND 58270	701-284-6194	R	4*	<.1
174	Monroe-Tufline Manufacturing Company Inc—Sid Perkins	PO Box 186, Columbus MS 39703	662-328-8347	R	4*	<.1
175	Union Iron Inc—Robert Curry	PO Box 1038, Decatur IL 62525	217-429-5148	R	4*	<.1
176	Pamco Inc—Dennis Palmer	PO Box 298, Oskaloosa IA 52577	641-672-2576	R	4*	<.1
177	American Farm Implement And Specialty Company Inc—William Decker	PO Box 89, Janesville WI 53547	608-755-5466	R	4*	<.1
178	Thorp Equipment Inc—Roy Lato	N14160 County Rd M, Thorp WI 54771	715-669-5050	R	4*	.1
179	Maxijet Inc—Susan Thayer	PO Box 1849, Dundee FL 33838	863-439-3667	R	4*	<.1
180	Cal-Coast Dairy Systems Inc—Lon Baptista	PO Box 737, Turlock CA 95381	209-634-9026	R	4*	<.1
181	Kelderman Manufacturing Inc—Gary Kelderman	2686 Hwy 92, Oskaloosa IA 52577	641-673-0468	R	4*	.1
182	Richway Industries Ltd—Richard Borglum	PO Box 508, Janesville IA 50647	319-987-2976	R	4*	<.1
183	Dempster Industries Inc—Wallace Davis	PO Box 848, Beatrice NE 68310	402-223-4026	R	4*	<.1
184	Ag-Industrial Manufacturing—Claude Brown	PO Box 53, Lodi CA 95241	209-369-1994	R	4*	<.1
185	Warrior Manufacturing LLC—Paul Soukup	PO Box 8, Hutchinson MN 55350	320-587-5505	R	4*	<.1
186	Seedburo Equipment Co—Tom Runyon	2293 South Mt Prospect, Des Plaines IL 60018	312-738-3700	R	4*	<.1
187	Betterbee-Meadery Inc—Bob Stevens	8 Meader Rd, Greenwich NY 12834	518-692-9669	R	4*	<.1
188	Diamond Blue Manufacturing Company Inc—Ken Johnson	3709 Old Hwy 99 S, Mount Vernon WA 98273	360-428-1744	R	4*	<.1
189	Jerry Jamoe Trailers Inc—Jerry James	PO Box 163, Sikeston MO 63801	573-471-6057	R	4*	<.1
190	Claude Perry Co—Jeff Weaver	500 S Valley Mills Dr, Waco TX 70711	254-756-2139	R	4*	<.1
191	Newton Crouch Inc—J Crouch	PO Box 17, Griffin GA 30224	770-227-1234	R	4*	<.1
192	Titan West Inc—Dave Smerchek	PO Box 8, Linn KS 66953	785-348-5660	R	4*	<.1
193	Westheffer Company Inc—Samih Staitieh	PO Box 363, Lawrence KS 66044	785-843-1633	R	4*	<.1
194	American International Manufacturing Co—David Neilson	1230 Fortna Ave, Woodland CA 95776	530-666-2446	R	4*	<.1
195	Lowry Manufacturing Co—John Dahlseng	PO Box 121, Lowry MN 56349	320-283-5450	R	4*	<.1
196	Mechanical Transplanter Company LLC—Daniel Timmer	1150 Central Ave, Holland MI 49423	616-396-8738	R	4*	<.1
197	Vittetoe Slat Flooring Inc—David Vittetoe	2112 Keokuk Washington, Keota IA 52248	641-636-2259	R	4*	<.1
198	Crippen Manufacturing Co—Jim Gascho	PO Box 128, Alma MI 48801	989-681-4323	R	4*	<.1
199	T G Schmeiser Company Inc—Andrew Cummings	PO Box 1047, Fresno CA 93714	559-268-8128	R	4*	<.1
200	Harvest Moon Hay LLC	9097 River Rd, Wittenberg WI 54499	715-454-6201	R	4*	<.1
201	Warren and Baerg Manufacturing Inc—Randy Baerg	39950 Rd 108, Dinuba CA 93618	559-591-6790	R	4*	<.1
202	Tarter Industries Inc—David Tarter	750 N Wllace Wlknson B, Liberty KY 42539	606-787-8298	R	3*	<.1
203	Bei International LLC—Sarah Walden	1375 Kalamazoo St, South Haven MI 49090	269-637-8541	R	3*	<.1
204	Kamper Fabrication Inc—Richard Kamper	PO Box 177, Ripon CA 95366	209-599-7137	R	3*	<.1
205	Tebben Enterprises Inc—Michael Tebben	10009 Hwy 7 Se, Clara City MN 56222	320-847-3512	R	3*	<.1
206	Steiner Tractor Parts Inc—David Steiner	PO Box 449, Lennon MI 48449	810-621-3000	R	3*	<.1
207	Gearn Industries Inc—Gary Gearn	PO Box 993, Hereford TX 79045	806-357-2222	R	3*	<.1
208	Eagle Group Ii Ltd—Roy Ferguson	8384 Peck Rd, Greenville MI 48838	616-754-7777	R	3*	<.1
209	Bloom Inc—Mark Collett	1443 220th St, Independence IA 50644	319-827-1139	R	3*	<.1
210	Classen Manufacturing Inc—Larry Classen	PO Box 2401, Norfolk NE 68702	402-371-2294	R	3*	<.1
211	Creamer Metal Products Inc—Karen Peters	PO Box 27, London OH 43140	740-852-1752	R	3*	<.1
212	Hawkes Manufacturing Inc—Kevin Pierce	PO Box 14111, Grand Forks ND 58208	218-773-4247	R	3*	<.1
213	Kilby E D Manufacturing and Farming Inc—Edward Kilby	286 W Evans Reimer Rd, Gridley CA 95948	530-846-5625	R	3*	<.1
214	B W Implement Co—John Blair	PO Box 758, Buttonwillow CA 93206	661-764-5254	R	3*	<.1
215	Agile Manufacturing LLC	1242 Arizona Ave, Larchwood IA 51241	712-477-2795	R	3*	<.1
216	Natureform Inc—Harold Warren	925 N Ocean St, Jacksonville FL 32202	904-358-0355	R	3*	<.1
217	Crescent Equipment Company Inc—Revis Barrow	PO Box 155, Crescent GA 31304	912-832-4425	R	3*	<.1
218	American-Iowa Manufacturing Inc—Mark Simon	PO Box 757, Cascade IA 52033	563-852-7397	R	3*	<.1
219	Ada Enterprises Inc—Thomas Stensrud	PO Box 77, Northwood IA 50459	641-324-1093	R	3*	<.1
220	Reddick Equipment Company Inc—C Graves	PO Box 71, Williamston NC 27892	252-792-1191	R	3*	<.1
221	Pacific Macadamia Nuts Corp—Arnold Tengan	PO Box 1716, Hilo HI 96721	808-935-0543	R	3*	<.1
222	First Products Inc—Don Jones	164 Oakridge Church Rd, Tifton GA 31794	229-382-4768	R	3*	<.1
223	Sund Manufacturing Company Inc—Paul Sund	PO Box 79, Newburg ND 58762	701-272-6161	R	3*	<.1
224	Ashley Brooks—Bob Taylor	PO Box 8, Bethel OH 45106	513-734-3980	R	3*	<.1
225	Delta Technology Corp—Lorne Libin	1602 Townhurst Dr, Houston TX 77043	713-464-7407	R	3*	<.1
226	Dpc Inc—Blair Underhill	PO Box 149, Delphi IN 46923	765-564-3752	R	3*	<.1
227	Gandy Co—Dale Gandrud	PO Box 528, Owatonna MN 55060	507-451-5430	R	3*	<.1
228	Savage Equipment Inc—Basil Savage	400 Industrial Rd, Madill OK 73446	580-795-3395	R	3*	<.1
229	Fred Clayton and Sons Inc—Fred Clayton	79 Ralph Rd, Imperial CA 92251	760-355-1074	R	3*	<.1
230	Olson Irrigation Systems—Donald Olson	PO Box 711570, Santee CA 92072	619-562-3100	R	3*	<.1
231	CU Stoltzfus Manufacturing Inc—Gary Lake	PO Box 527, Morgantown PA 19543	610-286-5146	R	3*	<.1
232	Rhinehart Development Corp—Phillip Rhinehart	5345 County Rd 68, Spencerville IN 46788	260-238-4442	R	3*	<.1
233	Lane and Sons Inc—Thomas Lane	211 Industrial Dr, Ruckersville VA 22968	434-985-9969	R	3*	<.1
234	Cronkhite Industries Inc—Cynthia Cronkhite	2212 Kickapoo Dr, Danville IL 61832	217-443-3700	R	3*	<.1
235	Newhouse Manufacturing Company Inc—Marinus Newhouse	1048 Nw 6th St, Redmond OR 97756	541-548-1055	R	3*	<.1
236	Atlas Manufacturing Inc—Darrell Harp	51 Dow Dr, Tremont MS 38876	662-652-3900	R	3*	<.1

Note: An asterisk (*) indicates an estimated financial figure. The company type code used is as follows: R = Private, P = Public, S = Private Subsidiary, B = Public Subsidiary, D = Division, J = Joint Venture, I = Investment Fund.

COMPANY RANKINGS BY SALES WITHIN 4-DIGIT SIC

Rank	Company Name—Executive Officer	Address, City, State, Zip	Phone	Type	Fin	Empls
237	R-Tech Feeders Inc—Jeffrey Richards	5292 American Rd, Rockford IL 61109	815-874-2990	R	3*	<.1
238	Holland Transplanter Company Inc—Howard Poll	PO Box 1527, Holland MI 49422	616-392-3579	R	3*	<.1
239	Blade Runner Farms Inc—David Doguet	802 Howard Rd, Poteet TX 78065	830-276-4455	R	2*	<.1
240	Hipro Manufacturing Inc—Clifford Stan	1909 E 1800 N Rd, Watseka IL 60970	815-432-5271	R	2*	<.1
241	Dspc Co—John Gazley	3939 S Central Ave, Rockford IL 61102	815-997-1116	R	2*	<.1
242	Escofab Inc—Ellis Beachy	171 Industrial Dr, Atmore AL 36502	251-368-1261	R	2*	<.1
243	Earley Tractor Inc—Mike Earley	PO Box 736, Cameron MO 64429	816-632-7277	R	2*	<.1
244	Bradford Built Inc—Brad Portenier	1803 Industrial Park D, Washington KS 66968	785-325-3300	R	2*	<.1
245	Agri Machinery and Parts Inc—Gillian Dobes	3489 All American Blvd, Orlando FL 32810	407-299-1592	R	2*	<.1
246	Van's Equipment Company Inc—Calvin Vlake	PO Box 3157, Moultrie GA 31776	229-985-1101	R	2*	<.1
247	Leeway Inc—Charles Leonard	7396 Hwy 44, Star ID 83669	208-286-7707	R	2*	<.1
248	Luffland Industries Inc—John Luff	PO Box 228, Bates City MO 64011	816-625-4022	R	2*	<.1
249	Neelco Industries Inc—Robert Martin	420 Shearer Blvd, Cocoa FL 32922	321-632-5303	R	2*	<.1
250	Broyhill Inc—Craig Broyhill	PO Box 475, Dakota City NE 68731	402-987-3412	R	2*	<.1
251	University Transplant Program—Steven Gensick	1725 W Harrison St Ste, Chicago IL 60612	312-942-4252	R	2*	<.1
252	Walluski Western Ltd—Steve Cullen	PO Box 642, Astoria OR 97103	503-325-5187	R	2*	<.1
253	Cox Richard Manufacturing Co—Richard Cox	PO Box 387, Carrollton MO 64633	660-542-0967	R	2*	<.1
254	GT Manufacturing Inc—Dennis M Pedersen	PO Box 525, Clay Center KS 67432	785-632-2151	R	2*	<.1
255	Kennco Manufacturing Inc—Robin Knowles	PO Box 1149, Ruskin FL 33575	813-645-2591	R	2	<.1
256	Ronald Wetherell Inc—Ronald Wetherell	407 W Grace St, Cleghorn IA 51014	712-436-2266	R	2*	<.1
257	Agri-Products Inc—Don Freeman	PO Box 542, York NE 68467	402-362-5500	R	2*	<.1
258	Freeland Industries Inc—James Van Epps	PO Box 59, Portage WI 53901	608-742-2189	R	2*	<.1
259	Tri County Feed And Grain Inc—Allan Burbach	PO Box 128, Randolph NE 68771	402-337-0260	R	2*	<.1
260	Pearson's Inc—Jack Johnston	PO Box 268, Thedford NE 69166	308-645-2231	R	2*	<.1
261	Ag Engineering and Development Inc—Thayne Wiser	1515 E 7th Ave, Kennewick WA 99337	509-582-8900	R	2*	<.1
262	Johnson Farm Machinery Company Inc—Howard Johnson	PO Box 1237, Woodland CA 95776	530-662-1788	R	2*	<.1
263	Donahue Corp—James Donahue	PO Box 126, Durham KS 67438	620-732-2665	R	2*	<.1
264	Ross Manufacturing Company Inc—Glenda Autry	9415 Hwy 54 W, Brownsville TN 38012	731-772-0567	R	2*	<.1
265	Strobel Industries Inc—Dwight Strobel	PO Box 255, Clarks NE 68628	308-548-2254	R	2*	<.1
266	Nth Inc—Clinton Nesseth	PO Box 136, Barron WI 54812	715-537-9207	R	2*	<.1
267	Southern Equipment Manufacturing Inc—Donald Humphreys	2371 White Oak Valley, Cleveland TN 37312	423-479-9939	R	2*	<.1
268	Bel-Air Turf Products LLC	PO Box 188, Leeds AL 35094	205-699-4870	R	2*	<.1
269	Shore Liquidations Inc—Fred Seeber	1112 Enterprise, Rantoul IL 61866	217-892-2544	R	2*	<.1
270	Durabilt Industries Inc—Jerry Nelson	1810 Airport Rd, Pocahontas AR 72455	870-892-4501	R	1*	<.1
271	Intraco Inc—Gary Hall	PO Box 148, Oskaloosa IA 52577	641-673-8451	R	1*	<.1
272	Roadrunner Manufacturing Company Inc—Brian Heavey	PO Box 371, Manteca CA 95336	209-823-5261	R	1*	<.1
273	JT Marketing Ltd—John Tackett	PO Box 2667, Mesa AZ 85214	480-829-0412	R	1*	<.1
274	Agri Business International Inc—Philip Saunders	PO Box 909, Villa Rica GA 30180	770-459-4401	R	1*	<.1
275	Hagan Electronics Inc—James Hagan	9290 Prototype Dr, Reno NV 89521	775-853-5100	R	1*	<.1
276	Whitfield R A Manufacturing Company Inc—James Whitfield	PO Box 948, Mableton GA 30126	770-948-1212	R	1*	<.1
277	Fogmaster Corp—Thomas Latta	1051 Sw 30th Ave, Deerfield Beach FL 33442	954-481-9975	R	1*	<.1
278	Bee Trailers Inc—Bobby Harrell	524 Harrell Rd, Climax GA 39834	229-246-2052	R	1*	<.1
279	Speer Cushion Co—Debra Dusenbury	431 S Interocean Ave, Holyoke CO 80734	970-854-2911	R	1*	<.1
280	Gamet Manufacturing Co—Mark Olson Seedburo Equipment Co	698 Prior Ave North, Saint Paul MN 55104	651-647-5410	D	1*	<.1
281	Howard Price Turf Equipment Inc—Howard Price	18155 Edison Ave, Chesterfield MO 63005	636-532-7000	R	1*	<.1
282	Sweoney Enterprises Inc—Zachary Sweeney	321 Waring Welfare Rd, Boerne TX 78006	830-537-4631	R	1*	<.1
283	Hayden Manufacturing Company Inc—Beverly Jacques	50 Carver Rd, West Wareham MA 02576	508-295-0497	R	1*	<.1
284	Express Scale Parts Inc—Carla Mattson	6873 Martindale Rd, Shawnee Mission KS 66218	913-441-4787	R	1*	<.1
285	Field Gymmy Inc—Dennis Nienberg	PO Box 121, Ottawa OH 45875	419-538-6511	R	1*	<.1
286	International A I—Bradley Blume	7909 S Fairfax Rd, Bloomington IN 47401	812-824-2473	R	1*	<.1
287	Sinca Industries Inc—Doug Stevens	PO Box 1247, Norfolk NE 68702	402-371-1400	R	<1*	<.1
288	AG Systems Inc (Hutchinson Minnesota)—Craig Lenz	1180 State Hwy 7 E, Hutchinson MN 55350	320-587-4030	R	N/A	.1

TOTALS: SIC 3523 Farm Machinery & Equipment
  Companies: 288   42,966   104.4

3524 Lawn & Garden Equipment

Rank	Company Name—Executive Officer	Address, City, State, Zip	Phone	Type	Fin	Empls
1	Toro Co—Michael J Hoffman	8111 Lyndale Ave S, Bloomington MN 55420	952-888-8801	P	1,884	4.6
2	MTD Products Inc—Curtis E Moll	PO Box 368022, Cleveland OH 44136	330-225-2600	R	1,030*	6.8
3	Douglas Dynamics Inc—James Janik	7777 N 73rd St, Milwaukee WI 53223	414-354-2310	R	180	.5
4	Mtd Southwest Inc—Phil Clouse	9235 S Mckemy St, Tempe AZ 85284	480-961-1002	R	169*	.7
5	Snapper Inc—James Wier	PO Box 702, Milwaukee WI 53201		S	167*	1.0
6	Textron Turf Care and Specialty Products—Phil Tralies	1721 Packard Ave, Racine WI 53403	262-637-6711	R	135*	.9
7	Exmark Manufacturing Company Inc—Mark Stinson Toro Co	PO Box 808, Beatrice NE 68310	402-223-6300	D	121*	.7
8	Magic Circle Corp—Arthur Evans	6302 E County Rd 100 N, Coatesville IN 46121	765-246-6845	R	70*	.2
9	Turf Products LLC—Frederick N Zeytoonjian	PO Box 1200, Enfield CT 06083	860-763-3581	R	68*	.2
10	Scott's Co—Jim Hadeon	252 Ladder Ln, Carrollton KY 41008	502-732-8141	R	56*	1.0
11	Commercial Turf Products Ltd—Ed Zsemdik	1777 Miller Pkwy, Streetsboro OH 44241	330-995-7000	R	40*	.2
12	Tuff Torq Corp—Shigenori Sakikawa	5943 Commerce Blvd, Morristown TN 37814	423-585-1980	R	35*	.3
13	Walker Manufacturing Co (Fort Collins Colorado)—Bob Walker	5925 E Harmony Rd, Fort Collins CO 80528	970-221-5614	R	29*	.1
14	Swisher Mower and Machine Company Inc—Wayne Swisher	1602 Corporate Dr, Warrensburg MO 64093	660-747-8183	R	29*	.4
15	McLane Manufacturing Inc—Elmer Malchow	P O Box 438, Paramount CA 90723	562-633-8158	R	28*	.1
16	Precision Products Inc—Mort Kay	316 Limit St, Lincoln IL 62656	217-735-1590	R	25*	.2
17	John Deere Southeast Engineering Center—Samuel R Allen	PO Box 7047, Charlotte NC 28241	704-588-3200	S	21*	.2
18	Wright Manufacturing Inc—William Wright	4600 Wedgewood Blvd St, Frederick MD 21703	301-360-9810	R	18*	.1
19	PECO Inc—Peter Cook	PO Box 1197, Arden NC 28704	828-684-1234	R	12*	.1
20	AeroGrow International Inc—Jack J Walker	6075 Longbow Dr Ste 20, Boulder CO 80301	303-444-7755	P	11	<.1
21	Smithco West Inc—Donald Smith	PO Box 487, Cameron WI 54822	715-458-4192	R	10*	<.1
22	Future Products Inc—Don Lenz	2100 Minnesota Ave, Benson MN 56215	320-843-4614	R	8*	.1
23	Mbtm Limited Inc—Jack Lapinski	503 Mall Ct Ste 310, Lansing MI 48912	517-333-0383	R	8*	.1
24	Whirltronics—Steve Thul	208 Centennial Dr, Buffalo MN 55313	763-682-1716	R	8*	.1
25	Erskine Attachments Inc—Todd Olson	PO Box 1083, Alexandria MN 56308	218-687-4045	R	7*	<.1
26	Novae Corp—Steven P Bermes	1 Novae Pkwy, Markle IN 46770	260-758-9838	R	7*	<.1
27	Maxim Holding Company Inc—Albert Easom	PO Box 110, Sebastopol MS 39359	601-625-7471	R	6*	.1
28	Rotating Engineered Products Inc—Jim Hene	2405 Murphy Blvd, Gainesville GA 30504	770-538-0020	R	6*	<.1
29	Superior Cedar Products Inc—Dwaine Mellen	PO Box 38, Carney MI 49812	906-639-2132	R	5*	<.1
30	Palmor Products Inc—Stanley Morton	5225 Serum Plant Rd, Thorntown IN 46071	765-436-2496	R	4*	<.1
31	Big John Tree Transplanter Manufacturing Inc—Charles Blankenship	PO Box 960, Heber Springs AR 72543	501-362-8161	R	4*	<.1

Rank	Company Name—Executive Officer	Address, City, State, Zip	Phone	Type	Fin	Empls
32	Ingersoll Tractor Co—Nicholas Nikazmerad	70 Ingersol Dr, Portland ME 04103	207-878-5353	R	4*	<.1
33	Encore Manufacturing Company Inc—Douglas Tegtmeier	PO Box 888, Beatrice NE 68310	402-228-4255	R	3*	<.1
34	Easy Lawn Inc—Robert Lisle	9599 Nantcke Bus Pk Dr, Greenwood DE 19950	302-815-6500	R	3*	<.1
35	Sarlo Power Mowers Inc—Arnold Sarlo	PO Box 1169, Fort Myers FL 33902	239-332-1955	R	3*	<.1
36	Southern Green Inc—Harry Knight	4391 Mac Byrnes Rd, Ethel LA 70730	225-683-0802	R	2*	<.1
37	Mo-Trim Inc—Jack Cartner	PO Box 850, Cambridge OH 43725	740-439-2725	R	2*	<.1
38	K-W Manufacturing Co—Donald Molstad	800 S Marion Rd, Sioux Falls SD 57106	605-336-6032	R	2*	<.1
39	Precision Small Engine Co—Andrew Masciarella	2510 Nw 16th Ln, Pompano Beach FL 33064	954-974-1960	R	2*	<.1
40	Northwest Tiller's Inc—Todd Marquis	3715 W Washington Ave, Yakima WA 98903	509-575-1950	S	2*	<.1
41	Fair Manufacturing Inc—Walter Fair	PO Box 306, Menno SD 57045	605-387-2389	R	1*	<.1
42	Vermont Ware Inc—Dale Dawson	399 Barber Rd, Saint George VT 05495	802-482-4426	R	1*	<.1

TOTALS: SIC 3524 Lawn & Garden Equipment
Companies: 42   4,225   18.8

3531 Construction Machinery

Rank	Company Name—Executive Officer	Address, City, State, Zip	Phone	Type	Fin	Empls
1	Manitowoc Company Inc—Glen E Tellock	2400 S 44th St, Manitowoc WI 54220	920-684-4410	P	3,652	12.9
2	Grace Davison Discovery Sciences—Fred Festa	2051 Waukegan Rd, Deerfield IL 60015	847-948-8600	R	3,265*	6.3
3	JLG Industries Inc—Craig Paylor	1 Jlg Dr, McConnellsburg PA 17233	717-485-5161	S	2,289*	4.1
4	Astec Industries Inc—J Don Brock PhD	1725 Shepherd Rd, Chattanooga TN 37421	423-899-5898	P	956	1.1
5	Tulsa Winch Group—Steve Oden	PO Box 1130, Jenks OK 74037	918-298-8300	D	854	.2
6	Heico Holding Inc—Michael Heisley	2626 Warrenville Rd St, Downers Grove IL 60515	630-353-5000	R	680*	6.8
7	Komatsu America International Co—David W Grzelak	1701 W Golf Rd, Rolling Meadows IL 60008	847-437-5800	S	634*	4.6
8	Grove Worldwide LLC Manitowoc Company Inc	PO Box 21, Shady Grove PA 17256	717-597-8121	S	628*	2.7
9	Gardner Asphalt Inc—Raymond Hyer	PO Box 5449, Tampa FL 33675	813-248-2101	R	574*	.5
10	Link-Belt Construction Equipment Company LP Lllp—Chuck Martz	PO Box 13600, Lexington KY 40583	859-263-5200	R	570*	.8
11	Columbus McKinnon Corp—Timothy T Tevens	140 John James Audubon, Amherst NY 14228	716-689-5400	P	524	2.5
12	JCB Inc—John Patterson	2000 Bamford Blvd, Pooler GA 31322	912-447-2000	R	501*	.3
13	Vermeer Manufacturing Company Inc—Mary Andringa	PO Box 200, Pella IA 50219	641-628-3141	R	500*	2.1
14	McNeilus Companies Inc—Micheal Wuest	524 County Rd 34 E, Dodge Center MN 55927	507-374-6321	S	485*	1.0
15	Dayton Superior Corp—Eric R Zimmerman	1125 Byers Rd, Miamisburg OH 45342	937-866-0711	R	476	1.4
16	Schwing America Inc—Brian Hazelton	5900 Centerville Rd, Saint Paul MN 55127	651-429-0999	R	472*	.6
17	Cooper Crouse-Hinds LLC—Kirk Hachigian	PO Box 4999, Syracuse NY 13221	315-477-5531	S	460*	2.3
18	ED Etnyre and Co—Tom Brown	1333 S Daysville Rd, Oregon IL 61061	815-732-2116	R	337*	.4
19	Roadtec Inc—Jeff Richmond Astec Industries Inc	PO Box 180515, Chattanooga TN 37405	423-265-0600	S	313*	.3
20	Caterpillar Paving Products Inc—James McReynolds	PO Box 1362, Minneapolis MN 55440	763-425-4100	S	295*	.6
21	CMI Terex Corp—Don Anderson	PO Box 1985, Oklahoma City OK 73101	405-787-6020	S	228	1.7
22	Equipment Technology Inc—Jim Neuberger	341 NW 122nd St, Oklahoma City OK 73114	405-748-3841	R	189*	.2
23	Er Equipment Inc—Eileen Teissonniere	PO Box 150, Mercedita PR 00715	787-841-2743	R	178*	3.5
24	Pettibone LLC—El Roskovensky Heico Holding Inc	2626 Warrenville Rd St, Downers Grove IL 60515	630-353-5000	S	174*	2.3
25	Wacker Neuson Corp—Christopher Barnard	N92w15000 Anthony Ave, Menomonee Falls WI 53051	262-255-0500	R	172*	.6
26	Volvo Road Machinery Inc—Pat Olney	1 Volvo Dr, Asheville NC 28803	828-650-2000	R	164*	2.0
27	Genie Manufacturing Inc—Robert Wilkerson	PO Box 97030, Redmond WA 98073		S	160*	1.8
28	Compaction America Inc—Robert Patterson	2000 Kentville Rd, Kewanee IL 61443	309-853-3571	D	158*	.5
29	Altec Industries Inc—Lee Styslinger	PO Box 10264, Birmingham AL 35202	205-991-7733	R	150*	1.5
30	Deere-Hitachi Construction Machinery Corp—Al Seeba	PO Box 1187, Kernersville NC 27285	336-996-8100	J	149*	.7
31	Blaw-Knox Construction Equipment—Herbert Henkel	750 Broadway Ave E, Mattoon IL 61938	217-234-8811	S	133	.6
32	Ditch Whitch—Ed Malzahn	PO Box 66, Perry OK 73077	580-336-4402	R	132*	1.2
33	ASV Distribution Inc—Ronald Defeo	PO Box 5160, Grand Rapids MN 55744	218-327-3434	S	114*	.3
34	Process Equipment Inc—James A Woods	PO Box 1607, Pelham AL 35124	205-663-5330	R	106*	.2
35	Dynapac	PO Box 462288, Garland TX 75046	972-496-7400	S	83*	.1
36	H and L Tooth Co—Richard Launder	PO Box 48, Owasso OK 74055	918-272-0951	R	81*	.1
37	Telsmith Inc—Rick Patek Astec Industries Inc	PO Box 539, Mequon WI 53092	262-242-6600	S	77*	.4
38	Godbersen-Smith Construction Company Inc—Gary Godbersen	PO Box 151, Ida Grove IA 51445	712-364-3347	R	75*	.5
39	Volvo Construction Equipment North America Inc—Dennis Eagan	1 Volvo Dr, Asheville NC 28803	828-650-2000	S	68*	.1
40	Braden Carco Gearmatic Winch Div—Mark Pigott	Po Box 547, Broken Arrow OK 74013	918-251-8511	D	66*	.3
41	Cedarapids Inc	909 17th St NE, Cedar Rapids IA 52402	319-363-3511	S	66*	.1
42	General Asphalt Company Inc—Robert Lopez	PO Box 522306, Miami FL 33152	305-592-3480	R	60*	.2
43	Gencor Industries Inc—EJ Elliott	5201 N Orange Blossom, Orlando FL 32810	407-290-6000	P	60	.3
44	Pubco Corp—Robert H Kanner	3830 Kelley Ave, Cleveland OH 44114	216-881-5380	R	55	.3
45	Stanley Hydraulic Tools—Bill Bray	3810 SE Naef Rd, Milwaukie OR 97267	503-652-7583	D	55*	.3
46	Terex Mining	PO Box 998, Sherman TX 75091	903-337-4140	S	53*	.1
47	M-B Companies Inc—Terry Cosgrove	PO Box 200, New Holstein WI 53061	920-898-1560	R	53*	.1
48	Thrustmaster Of Texas Inc—Joseph Bekker	PO Box 840189, Houston TX 77284	713-937-6295	R	44*	.2
49	JLG Manufacturing LLC JLG Industries Inc	220 Success Dr, McConnellsburg PA 17233	717-485-5161	S	43*	.1
50	Carpenter Group—Bernie Martin	222 Napolean St, San Francisco CA 94124	415-285-1954	R	42*	.1
51	Hensley Attachments—H Kuribayashi	800 S 5th St, Mansfield TX 76063	817-477-3167	S	38*	.1
52	Hitachi Construction Machinery Corp (Kernersville North Carolina) Deere-Hitachi Construction Machinery Corp	PO Box 1187, Kernersville NC 27285	281-821-2400	D	38*	.1
53	Stone Construction Equipment Inc—Lynne Woodworth	PO Box 150, Honeoye NY 14471	585-229-5141	R	36*	.2
54	Nordco Inc—Bruce Boczkiewicz	245 W Forest Hill Ave, Oak Creek WI 53154	414-766-2180	S	36*	.2
55	Trencor Inc Astec Industries Inc	1725 Shepherd Rd, Chattanooga TN 37421	423-899-5898	D	35	.2
56	Precision Sure-Lock—Bob Van Noord	704 W Simonds Rd, Dallas TX 75159	972-287-2390	S	33*	.1
57	Pacal LLC—Ervin F Kamm	PO Box 64432, Saint Paul MN 55164	651-631-1111	R	32*	.2
58	Bid-Well Corp—Fred Bidwell CMI Terex Corp	PO Box 97, Canton SD 57013	605-987-2603	D	32*	.1
59	Plasser American Corp—Joseph Neuhofer	PO Box 5464, Chesapeake VA 23324	757-543-3526	R	32*	.2
60	Caron Compactor Co—Jim Caron	1204 Ullrey Ave, Escalon CA 95320	209-838-2062	R	28*	<.1
61	Allied Systems Co—Lewis Rlnk	21433 Sw Oregon St, Sherwood OR 97140	503-625-2560	R	28*	.3
62	Cemen Tech Inc—Gary Ruble	1700 N 14th St, Indianola IA 50125	515-961-7407	R	28*	.1

Note: An asterisk (*) indicates an estimated financial figure. The company type code used is as follows: R = Private, P = Public, S = Private Subsidiary, B = Public Subsidiary, D = Division, J = Joint Venture, I = Investment Fund.

COMPANY RANKINGS BY SALES WITHIN 4-DIGIT SIC

Rank	Company Name—Executive Officer	Address, City, State, Zip	Phone	Type	Fin	Empls
63	Edison Control Corp—Alan J Kastelic	PO Box 308, Port Washington WI 53074	262-284-7800	R	27*	.1
64	Polyclutch—Gerald Shaff	457 State St, North Haven CT 06473	203-248-6397	D	27*	.1
65	Midwest International Standard Products Incorporated Intermidwest Ltd—Ron Pair	105 Stover Rd, Charlevoix MI 49720	231-547-4000	R	27*	<.1
66	Dp Manufacturing Inc—Steve Oden	PO Box 1130, Jenks OK 74037	918-250-2450	R	26*	.2
67	Weldall Manufacturing Inc—David Bahl	2001 S Prairie Ave, Waukesha WI 53189	262-544-1155	R	25*	.1
68	Dynacon Inc—James Stasny	831 Industrial Blvd, Bryan TX 77803	979-823-2690	R	25*	.1
69	Fabco Inc—Jon Ballinger	PO Box 673, Findlay OH 45839	419-422-4533	R	25*	.1
70	Bucyrus Blades Inc—Tim Myers	260 E Beal Ave, Bucyrus OH 44820	419-562-6015	S	25*	.2
71	Johnson Crushers International Inc—Jeff Elliott Astec Industries Inc	86470 Franklin Blvd, Eugene OR 97405	541-736-1400	S	24*	.2
72	Kress Corp—Rita Kress	227 W Illinois St, Brimfield IL 61517	309-446-3395	R	24*	.2
73	Protection Services Inc—Douglas Danko	635 Lucknow Rd, Harrisburg PA 17110	717-236-9307	R	23*	.3
74	Kewaunee Fabrications LLC—John Robillard	520 N Main St, Kewaunee WI 54216	920-388-2000	S	22*	.2
75	Western Products (Milwaukee Wisconsin)	PO Box 245038, Milwaukee WI 53224	414-354-2310	D	22*	.2
76	Mixer Systems Inc—William Boles	PO Box 10, Pewaukee WI 53072	262-691-3100	R	22*	.1
77	Asphalt Drum Mixers Inc—Wayne Boyd	1 Adm Pkwy, Huntertown IN 46748	260-637-5729	R	20*	.1
78	Efficiency Production Inc—Kenneth Forsberg	685 Hull Rd, Mason MI 48854	517-676-8800	R	20*	.1
79	Werk-Brau Co—Paul Ballinger	PO Box 545, Findlay OH 45839	419-422-2912	R	19*	.1
80	Tmf Center Inc—Andy Meter	300 W Washington St, Williamsport IN 47993	765-762-1000	R	18*	.3
81	Good Earth Tools Inc—Keith Williams	PO Box 66, Crystal City MO 63019	636-937-3330	R	18*	.1
82	Griswold Machine And Engineering Inc—Don Sepeta	PO Box 98, Union City MI 49094	517-741-4471	R	18*	.1
83	General Equipment Co—Dennis Von Ruden	PO Box 334, Owatonna MN 55060	507-451-5510	R	18*	<.1
84	Robertson Transformer Co—William Bryant	13611 Thornton Rd, Blue Island IL 60406	708-388-2315	R	18*	.1
85	Vt Leeboy Inc—Calvin Majeskie	500 Lincoln County, Lincolnton NC 28092	704-966-3300	S	17*	.1
86	MIC Industries Inc—Michael Ansari	11911 Freedom Dr Ste 1, Reston VA 20190	703-318-1900	R	17*	.1
87	Air-Flo Manufacturing Company Inc—Charles Musso	PO Box 289, Prattsburgh NY 14873	607-522-3574	R	16*	.1
88	Distribution Support Service Inc—Steven Albanese	1860 Commonwealth Ave, Boston MA 02135	617-232-1234	R	16*	.2
89	Highway Equipment Co—Rocky Shephard	PO Box 241, Des Moines IA 50301	319-363-8281	R	16*	.1
90	LeTourneau Sales and Service Co—Lowry Wood	6393 S Campbell Ave, Tucson AZ 85706	520-294-6600	D	16*	<.1
91	Allen Engineering Corp—Jay Allen	PO Box 819, Paragould AR 72451	870-236-7751	R	16*	.1
92	Erie Strayer Co—Robert Strayer	PO Box 1031, Erie PA 16512	814-456-7001	R	15*	.1
93	General Machine Products Company Inc—William Pfundt	3111 Old Lincoln Hwy, Feasterville Trevose PA 19053	215-357-5500	R	15*	.1
94	Elliott Equipment Co—James Glazer	4427 S 76th Cir, Omaha NE 68127	402-592-4500	R	15*	.1
95	Panther Products Corp—Steve Jones	2501 Anaconda Rd, Harrisonville MO 64701	816-884-4444	R	15*	.1
96	Valk Manufacturing Co—Ted Valk	PO Box 428, New Kingstown PA 17072	717-766-0711	R	14*	.1
97	Rockland Inc—Daniel Shaffer	152 Weber Ln, Bedford PA 15522	814-623-1115	R	14*	.1
98	Omni Rail Products Inc—Kevin Hines	3911 W Dayton St, McHenry IL 60050	815-344-3100	R	14	.1
99	Sauber Manufacturing Co—Charles Sauber	10 N Sauber Rd, Virgil IL 60151	630-365-6600	R	13*	.1
100	Weldco-Beales Manufacturing Corp—Doug Schindel	1850 Marine View Dr, Tacoma WA 98422	253-383-0180	R	13*	<.1
101	Pioneer Manufacturing Co—Doug Schattinger	4529 Industrial Pkwy, Cleveland OH 44135	216-671-5500	R	13*	.2
102	Bradley Lifting Corp—Thomas Thole	1030 Elm St, York PA 17403	717-848-3121	S	13*	<.1
103	Superwinch LLC—James Allen	45 Danco Rd, Putnam CT 06260	860-928-7787	R	13*	.1
104	Amadas Industries Inc—James Adams	PO Box 1833, Suffolk VA 23439	757-539-0231	R	12*	.1
105	Lowe Manufacturing Company Inc—Richard Lowe	PO Box 275, Readstown WI 54652	608-538-4000	R	12*	.1
106	Northshore Manufacturing Inc—John Anderson	530 Recycle Ctr Dr, Two Harbors MN 55616	218-834-5555	R	12*	.1
107	KR Komarek Inc—Richard Komarek	548 Clayton Ct, Wood Dale IL 60191	847-956-0060	R	12*	<.1
108	Pro-Tec Equipment Inc—Don Septa	PO Box 130, Charlotte MI 48813	517-541-0303	R	12*	.1
109	Goff Inc—Keith Yerby	PO Box 1607, Seminole OK 74818	405-382-6900	R	12*	<.1
110	Gundlach Equipment Corp—Mark Kohler	PO Box 385, Belleville IL 62222	618-233-7223	R	12*	.1
111	Asphalt Zipper Inc—Terry Hanson	310 W 700 S, Pleasant Grove UT 84062	801-785-0706	R	12*	.1
112	Rexcon LLC—Adam Komornicki	2841 Whiting Rd, Burlington WI 53105	414-351-7000	R	11*	.1
113	Vibco Inc—Ted Wadensten	PO Box 8, Wyoming RI 02898	401-539-2392	R	11*	.1
114	Front Range Precast Concrete	5439 N Foothills Hwy, Boulder CO 80302	303-442-3207	R	11*	<.1
115	Gradall Co—Jim Waitzman Jr JLG Industries Inc	309 Hamric Dr W, Oxford AL 36203	256-831-2440	S	11*	<.1
116	Equipment Development Company Inc—William Harding	100 Thomas Johnson Dr, Frederick MD 21702	301-663-1600	R	11*	.1
117	Calder Brothers Corp—Glen Calder	250 E Warehouse Ct, Taylors SC 29687	864-244-4800	R	11*	.1
118	Friesen's Inc—Brett Friesen	PO Box 889, Detroit Lakes MN 56502	218-844-4437	R	10*	.1
119	Aerial Lift Of Connecticut Inc—Ernest Depiero	PO Box 66, Milford CT 06460	203-878-0694	R	10*	<.1
120	Fulghum Industries Inc—Heyward Wells	PO Box 909, Wadley GA 30477	478-252-5223	R	10*	.1
121	Bonnell Industries Inc—Joseph Bonnell	1385 Franklin Grove Rd, Dixon IL 61021	815-284-3819	R	9*	<.1
122	Broderson Manufacturing Corp—Gaylen Sprecker	PO Box 14770, Shawnee Mission KS 66285	913-888-0606	R	9*	.1
123	Ringwood Co—Charles Nodus	6715 W 73rd St, Bedford Park IL 60638	708-458-6000	R	9*	.1
124	Akkerman Inc—Maynard Akkerman	58256 266th St, Brownsdale MN 55918	507-567-2261	R	9*	.1
125	Seaberg Industries Inc—Craig Kinzer	8301 42nd St W, Rock Island IL 61201	309-787-9494	R	8*	.1
126	American Urethane Inc—Jude Masters	1905 Betson Ct, Odenton MD 21113	410-672-2100	R	8*	.1
127	Guntert and Zimmerman Const Division Inc—Ronald Guntert	222 E 4th St, Ripon CA 95366	209-599-0066	R	8*	.1
128	Acrowood Corp—Farhang Javid	PO Box 1028, Everett WA 98206	425-258-3555	R	8*	.1
129	Gledhill Road Machinery Co—Michael Rarick	PO Box 567, Galion OH 44833	419-468-4400	R	8*	.1
130	Shelby Industries LLC—Herman Brown	175 Mcdaniels Rd, Shelbyville KY 40065	502-633-2040	R	8*	.1
131	Morpac Industries Inc—Heidi Morgan	117 Frontage Rd N Ste, Pacific WA 98047	253-735-8922	R	8*	<.1
132	Altec Hiline LLC	PO Box 16288, Duluth MN 55816	218-722-9200	R	8*	.1
133	Bear Cat Manufacturing Inc—F Hill	3650 N Sabin Brown Rd, Wickenburg AZ 85390	928-684-7851	R	8*	<.1
134	Mack Manufacturing Inc—Charles Mc Elderry	PO Box 1559, Theodore AL 36590	251-653-9999	R	7*	.1
135	Pemberton Inc—Todd Pemberton	PO Box 521000, Longwood FL 32752	407-831-6688	R	7*	.1
136	Diamond Black Blade Co—Franklin Brenner	234 E O St, Colton CA 92324	909-825-4017	R	7*	<.1
137	Bay Shore Systems Inc—William Minatre	14206 N Ohio St, Rathdrum ID 83858	208-687-3311	R	7*	<.1
138	Layton Manufacturing Co—John Layton	672 Murlark Ave Nw, Salem OR 97304	503-585-4888	R	7*	.1
139	Entoleter LLC—Robert Wentzel	251 Welton St, Hamden CT 06517	203-787-3575	S	7*	<.1
140	Ameri-Tech Equipment Co—Larry Spence	PO Box 2888, Casper WY 82602	307-234-9921	R	7*	<.1
141	M-B-W Inc—Frank Multerer	PO Box 440, Slinger WI 53086	262-644-5234	R	7*	.1
142	Jwb Manufacturing Inc—John Bell	PO Box 727, Cedar Rapids IA 52406	319-365-3655	R	7*	.1
143	Empire Bucket Inc—Joseph Pertz	1360 Livingstone Rd, Hudson WI 54016	715-386-2930	R	7*	.1
144	Forestry Equipment Of Va Inc—Louis Denaples	12660 E Lynchburg Sale, Forest VA 24551	434-525-2929	R	7*	.1
145	Vulcan Company Inc—Alexander Clark	PO Box 36, Hingham MA 02043	781-337-5970	R	7*	.1
146	Pulva Corp—Edward Ferree	PO Box 427, Saxonburg PA 16056	724-898-3000	R	7*	.1
147	Kalco Machine and Manufacturing Co—David Kulbeth	2524 Sheppard Access R, Wichita Falls TX 76306	940-761-1060	R	7*	<.1
148	Jensen Mixers International Inc—Louis Jensen	PO Box 470368, Tulsa OK 74147	918-627-5770	R	6*	<.1
149	Stephens Manufacturing Company Inc—Murray Stephens	PO Box 488, Tompkinsville KY 42167	270-487-6774	R	6*	<.1

Rank	Company Name—Executive Officer	Address, City, State, Zip	Phone	Type	Fin	Empls
150	Universal Truck Equipment Inc—Eugene Dubiel	N15921 Schubert Rd, Galesville WI 54630	608-539-4600	R	6*	<.1
151	Safe-T-Shore—Frank Franks	375 E Comstock Dr, Chandler AZ 85225	480-838-5329	R	6*	.1
152	Dur-A-Lift Inc—Larry Kruse	PO Box 31, George IA 51237	712-475-2804	R	6*	.1
153	Construction Equipment Manufacturing Company Inc—Carla Perry	RR 3 Box 14, Olney TX 76374	940-564-5855	R	6*	<.1
154	Kawasaki Heavy Industries (USA) Inc—Takeshi Teranishi	2140 Barrett Park Dr N, Kennesaw GA 30144	770-499-7000	S	6*	<.1
155	Harper Air Tool Co—Harry Gilmore	4915 Pacific Blvd, Vernon CA 90058	323-589-8171	R	6*	<.1
156	American Road Machinery Co—Nicholas Ballas	401 Bridge St, Minerva OH 44657	330-868-7724	R	6*	<.1
157	Oztec Industries Inc—Fred Oswald	65 Channel Dr, Port Washington NY 11050	516-883-8857	R	6*	<.1
158	Diamond Manufacturing Inc—Ronnie Cochran	2801 S Mkokippi Ave St, Atoka OK 74525	580-889-6202	R	6*	.1
159	Custom Machine Manufacturer LLC	4111 Technology Dr, South Bend IN 46628	574-251-0292	R	6*	<.1
160	Cityscapes International Inc—James Cullinan	4200 Lyman Ct, Hilliard OH 43026	614-850-2540	R	6*	<.1
161	Flink Co—Mike Supergan	502 N Vermillion St, Streator IL 61364	815-673-4321	R	6*	.1
162	Port Industries Inc—Kevin Shimp	802 Industrial Rd, Palmyra MO 63461	573-769-3338	R	6*	<.1
163	Tink Inc—Robert Du Bose	2361 Durham Dayton Hwy, Durham CA 95938	530-895-0897	R	5*	<.1
164	Hood Equipment Inc—Eileen Hood	PO Box 307, Iron River WI 54847	715-372-4222	R	5*	<.1
165	Barbco Inc—James Barbera	PO Box 30189, Canton OH 44730	330-488-9400	R	5*	<.1
166	Buck Equipment Inc—Dennis Hamilton	1720 Feddern Ave, Grove City OH 43123	614-539-3039	R	5*	<.1
167	Nj Transportation Bd Mst	455 Us Hwy 202-206, Bedminster NJ 07921	908-234-2132	R	5*	.1
168	Zimmerman Industries Inc—Jerry Stoner	196 Wabash Rd, Ephrata PA 17522	717-733-6166	R	5*	<.1
169	Marion Mixers Inc—Douglas Grunder	PO Box 286, Marion IA 52302	319-377-6371	R	5*	<.1
170	Witbro Inc—Gina Ashjian	959 Clovis Ave, Clovis CA 93612	559-222-7325	R	5*	<.1
171	Pro-Tech Manufacturing and Distribution Inc—Michael Weagley	711 West Ave, Rochester NY 14611		R	5*	.1
172	Somatex Inc—Laurie Ferland	PO Box 487, Pittsfield ME 04967	207-487-6141	R	5*	<.1
173	Asphalt Equipment Company Inc—Michael Shurtz	13333 Us Hwy 24 W, Fort Wayne IN 46814	260-672-3422	R	5*	<.1
174	Meadowbrook Machine and Tool Inc—Harold Jordan	PO Box 685, Toccoa GA 30577	706-779-3327	R	5*	<.1
175	Asphalt Equipment and Service Co—John Ferris	1531 20th St Nw, Auburn WA 98001	253-939-4150	R	5*	<.1
176	Cleasby Manufacturing Company Inc—John Cleasby	PO Box 24132, San Francisco CA 94124	415-822-6565	R	5*	<.1
177	Drillco National Group Inc—Patrick Lacey	PO Box 2182, Long Island City NY 11102	718-726-9801	R	4*	<.1
178	Maxon Industries Inc—William Maxon	3204 W Mill Rd, Milwaukee WI 53209	414-351-4000	R	4*	<.1
179	Dymax Inc—Clark Balderson	PO Box 297, Wamego KS 66547	785-456-2081	R	4*	<.1
180	Fleming Manufacturing Company Inc—Dan Curlee	PO Box 789, Saint James MO 65559	573-885-3311	R	4*	<.1
181	Mid-America Manufacturing Company Inc—John Craft	PO Box 2278, Jonesboro AR 72402	870-972-8080	R	4*	<.1
182	Concord Road Equipment Manufacturing Inc—Glen Warfield	PO Box 772, Painesville OH 44077	440-357-5344	R	4*	<.1
183	Kenco Engineering Inc—David Lutz	PO Box 1467, Roseville CA 95678	916-782-8494	R	4*	<.1
184	Indco Inc—James Sims	PO Box 589, New Albany IN 47151	812-945-4383	R	4*	<.1
185	Kelley Manufacturing Corp—David M Kelley	61501 Bremen Hwy, Mishawaka IN 46544	574-255-4746	R	4*	<.1
186	SIMCO Drilling Equipment—Doug Hamilton	PO Box 448, Osceola IA 50213	641-342-2166	R	4*	<.1
187	Custom Welding and Metal Fabricating—Carmela Mick	701 Julep Rd, Waite Park MN 56387	320-251-1306	R	4*	<.1
188	Wagman Metal Products Inc—George Wagman	400 S Albemarle St, York PA 17403	717-854-2120	R	4*	<.1
189	Miller Formless Company Inc—Charles Miller	PO Box 250, Mchenry IL 60051	815-385-7700	R	4*	<.1
190	H D Industries Inc—Harold Dillingham	PO Box 8250, Jacksonville TX 75766	903-586-6126	R	4*	<.1
191	Quik Manufacturing Co—Steve Schmidt	18071 Mount Washington, Fountain Valley CA 92708	714-754-0337	R	4*	<.1
192	Bc Pavers Inc—Brian Crooks	PO Box 3401, Renton WA 98056	206-679-5804	R	4*	<.1
193	Minnich Manufacturing Company Inc—James Minnich	PO Box 367, Mansfield OH 44901	419-524-1000	R	4*	<.1
194	Sarott Construction Co—Scott Griffiths	3133 Morgan Territory, Clayton CA 94517	925-672-7220	R	3*	<.1
195	D and E Manufacturing Inc—Edna Smith	2936 S Live Oak Dr, Moncks Corner SC 29461	843-761-5588	R	3*	<.1
196	Aaron Engineered Process Equipment Inc—David Swirley	735 E Green St, Bensenville IL 60106	630-350-2200	S	3*	<.1
197	Maimin Technology Group Inc—Lance Khubchandani	227 Ambrogio Dr Ste B, Gurnee IL 60031	847-263-8200	R	3*	<.1
198	K-Ter Imagineering Inc—Roger Gubbels	8600 Ne Underground Dr, Kansas City MO 64161	816-453-6551	R	3*	<.1
199	Cme Arma Inc—Katherine Yasgar	4500 Nw 36th Ave, Miami FL 33142	305-633-1524	R	3*	<.1
200	Dyna-Fab Corp—Robert Rew	PO Box 538, West Lebanon IN 47991	765-893-4423	R	3*	<.1
201	Uflex USA Inc—Anna Gai	6442 Parkland Dr, Sarasota FL 34243	941-351-2628	R	3*	<.1
202	Future-All Inc—Charles King	PO Box 528, Carnegie PA 15106	412-279-2670	R	3*	<.1
203	Syltone Marine Inc—Graham Killarney	9111 Jackrabbit Rd, Houston TX 77095	281-856-1300	R	3*	<.1
204	Ground Hog Inc—Edward Carlson	PO Box 290, San Bernardino CA 92402	909-478-5700	R	3*	<.1
205	Stepp Manufacturing Company Inc—Shane Stepp	12335 River Rd, North Branch MN 55056	651-674-4491	R	3*	<.1
206	Floyd Concrete Inc—Shera Floyd	42 Telfair Pl, Savannah GA 31415	912-231-1334	R	3*	<.1
207	Jones Heavy Equipment Products Inc—Gordon Jones	PO Box 55007, Portland OR 97238	503-256-5852	R	3*	<.1
208	Keystone Engineering and Manufacturing Corp—Chester Latham	9786 E County Rd 200 N, Avon IN 46123	317-271-6192	R	3*	<.1
209	Schutte Pulverizer Company Inc—Thomas Warne	PO Box 546, Buffalo NY 14240	716-855-1555	R	3*	<.1
210	Bobcat Co/Apl—Crystal Stram	2649 Internationale Pk, Woodridge IL 60517	701-241-8719	R	3*	<.1
211	Lorenz Manufacturing Co—Donn Lorenz	PO Box 127, Benson MN 56215	320-843-3210	R	3*	<.1
212	Cammond Industries Inc—Dave Hammond	902 Arlington Ctr Ste, Ada OK 74820	580-332-9300	R	3*	<.1
213	Root Spring Scraper Co—Frederick Root	527 W N St, Kalamazoo MI 49007	269-382-2025	R	3*	<.1
214	Garlinghouse Brothers Inc—Roland Garlinghouse	PO Box 1078, Heber Springs AR 72543	501-362-8171	R	3*	<.1
215	Lemac Corp—Frank Coleman	22909 Airpark Dr, Petersburg VA 23803	804-862-8481	R	3*	<.1
216	District 5 Road and Public Works Commission Of St Landry Parish—Ronald Buschel	PO Box 86, Lebeau LA 71345	337-585-6637	R	3*	<.1
217	Zigler Power Systems—Curt Bailey	8050 Hwy 101 E, Shakopee MN 55379	952-887-4530	R	3*	<.1
218	Schumacher Manufacturing Inc—Nell Schumacher	498 8 Mile Rd, Remus MI 49340	989-561-2280	R	3*	<.1
219	Rugg Manufacturing Company Inc—Stephen Peck	105 Newton St, Greenfield MA 01301	413-773-5471	R	2*	<.1
220	Hadley-Keeney Chipping Inc—Kelly Hadley	Hc 76 Box 232, Eagletown OK 74734	580-835-2645	R	2*	<.1
221	Transport Cranes LLC	2050 Constitution Ave, Hartford WI 53027	262-670-6100	R	2*	<.1
222	Mixmor Inc—Mike Namara	3131 Casitas Ave, Los Angeles CA 90039	323-664-1941	R	2*	<.1
223	Reinco Inc—Erich Reinecker	PO Box 512, Plainfield NJ 07061	908-755-0921	R	2*	<.1
224	Miller Curber Company LLC—James Rochette	4020 Simon Rd, Youngstown OH 44512	330-782-8081	R	2*	<.1
225	Jewell Hudgens Inc—Tom Billingsley	PO Box 3626, Lufkin TX 75903	936-632-6691	R	2*	<.1
226	Wtc Machinery LLC—Rick Baas	W1222 Linden Rd, Ixonia WI 53036	262-567-3993	R	2*	<.1
227	GHM Industries Inc—Paul Jankovic	100a Sturbridge Rd, Charlton MA 01507	508-248-3941	R	2*	<.1
228	Dandy Digger And Supply Inc—James Mahon	244 W State Rte 4, Cathlamet WA 98612	360-795-3617	R	2*	<.1
229	Mac Stripers Inc—Forrest Marcato	PO Box 211089, Montgomery AL 36121	334-244-7865	R	2*	<.1
230	Wicker Machine Co—Allen Wicker	PO Box 338, Hollandale MS 38748	662-827-5434	R	2*	<.1
231	Harig Products Inc—Denny Zummer	PO Box 46965, Mount Clemens MI 48046	847-695-1000	R	1*	<.1
232	Schamas Manufacturing CoInc—William Schaeffler	6356 N Irwindale Ave, Irwindale CA 91702	626-334-6870	R	1*	<.1
233	HC Davis Sons' Manufacturing Company Inc—Thomas Mcpherson	PO Box 395, Bonner Springs KS 66012	913-422-3000	R	1*	<.1
234	Hamernik-Harrod Inc—William Harrod	3061 103rd Ln Ne Ste 2, Minneapolis MN 55449	763-786-4020	R	1*	<.1
235	Kelly's Directional Inc—Ada Grimes	3240 Olympic St, Springfield OR 97478	541-746-5200	R	1*	<.1

Note: An asterisk (*) indicates an estimated financial figure. The company type code used is as follows: R = Private, P = Public, S = Private Subsidiary, B = Public Subsidiary, D = Division, J = Joint Venture, I = Investment Fund.

COMPANY RANKINGS BY SALES WITHIN 4-DIGIT SIC

Rank	Company Name—*Executive Officer*	Address, City, State, Zip	Phone	Type	Fin	Empls
236	Combotronics Inc—*John Kerr*	2800 Lock And Dam Rd, Inola OK 74036	918-543-3300	R	1*	<.1
237	Bromma Inc—*Terry Howell*	4400 Bn Frnkln Blvd 20, Durham NC 27704	919-471-4000	R	1*	<.1
238	Ark Seal International—*Jessie Aragon*	14100 E 35th Pl, Aurora CO 80011	303-934-7772	R	1*	<.1
239	T And M Engineering and Manufacturing Inc—*Thomas Kubes*	PO Box 464, Faribault MN 55021	507-334-6437	R	1*	<.1
240	Ultra Safety Systems Inc—*Robert Mergenthaler*	1601 Hill Ave Ste C, West Palm Beach FL 33407	561-845-1086	R	1*	<.1
241	Overbuilt Paving and Mining Inc—*Scott Rink*	550 Nevada Ave Sw, Huron SD 57350	605-352-1412	R	<1*	<.1
242	Hug Manufacturing Corp—*John Hug*	PO Box 667, Norwalk OH 44857	419-668-5086	R	<1*	<.1
243	Acs Northwest Inc—*Joseph Zeno*	19602 60th Ave Ne, Arlington WA 98223	360-474-1940	R	<1*	<.1
244	Hansen Fabrication—*John Gunnarsson*	4254 23rd Ave W, Seattle WA 98199	206-283-9181	R	<1*	<.1

TOTALS: SIC 3531 Construction Machinery
Companies: 244 — 23,554 — 82.9

3532 Mining Machinery

Rank	Company Name—*Executive Officer*	Address, City, State, Zip	Phone	Type	Fin	Empls
1	Joy Global Inc—*Michael W Sutherlin*	PO Box 554, Milwaukee WI 53201	414-319-8500	P	3,524	11.9
2	Metso Minerals Inc—*Matti Kahkonen*	20965 Crossroads Cir, Waukesha WI 53186	262-717-2500	S	922*	1.5
3	Joy Mining Machinery—*Edward Doheny* Joy Global Inc	177 Thorn Hill Rd, Warrendale PA 15086	724-779-4500	D	865*	4.5
4	Oldenburg Group Inc—*Wayne C Oldenburg*	1717 W Civic Dr, Glendale WI 53209	414-977-1717	R	600*	1.0
5	Esco Corp—*Cal Collins*	PO Box 10123, Portland OR 97296	503-228-2141	R	545*	5.2
6	Victory Of West Virginia Inc—*Wayne H Stanley*	PO Box 2648, Fairmont WV 26555	304-363-4100	R	287*	.4
7	LeTourneau Inc—*Thomas Burke*	PO Box 2307, Longview TX 75606	903-237-7000	S	286*	1.3
8	P and H Mining Equipment Inc—*Robert Hale* Joy Global Inc	PO Box 310, Milwaukee WI 53201	414-671-4400	S	272*	.9
9	Liebherr Mining Equipment Co—*Ron Jacobson*	4100 Chestnut Ave, Newport News VA 23605	757-245-5251	R	195*	.4
10	Caterpillar Work Tools Inc—*James Owens*	PO Box 6, Wamego KS 66547	785-456-2224	S	52*	.3
11	Brunner and Lay Inc—*Fred Brunner*	PO Box 1190, Springdale AR 72765	479-756-0880	R	50*	.3
12	Townley Engineering And Manufacturing Company Inc—*J Townley*	PO Box 221, Candler FL 32111	352-687-3001	R	49*	.3
13	Tabor Machine Co—*Bryan Walker*	1176 Shelter Rd, Princeton WV 24739	304-327-2431	R	43*	.6
14	Sandvik Mining and Construction USA LLC—*Bill Baker*	13500 Nw County Rd 235, Alachua FL 32615	386-462-4100	S	39*	.3
15	Stock Equipment Co—*Christopher Kearney*	16490 Chillicothe Rd, Chagrin Falls OH 44023	440-543-6000	S	32*	.2
16	Atlas Copco CMT USA Inc—*Jim Levitt*	3700 E 68th Ave, Commerce City CO 80022	303-287-8822	S	30*	.1
17	Mclanahan Corp—*George Sidney*	PO Box 229, Hollidaysburg PA 16648	814-695-9807	R	28*	.3
18	Sandvik Tamrock USA Inc—*Caroline Jones*	345 Patton Dr SW, Atlanta GA 30336	404-589-3800	S	25*	.2
19	Keene Engineering Company Inc—*Jerry Keene*	20201 Bahama St, Chatsworth CA 91311		R	22*	<.1
20	Durex Products Inc—*Ronald Martin*	PO Box 354, Luck WI 54853	715-472-2111	R	21*	.2
21	Screen Machine Industries Inc—*Steven Cohen*	PO Box 423, Etna OH 43018	740-927-3464	R	20*	.1
22	Rimpull Corp—*Richard Davis*	PO Box 748, Olathe KS 66051	913-782-4000	R	19*	.2
23	Vira Corp—*Diane Gabriel*	PO Box 100586, Cudahy WI 53110	414-744-2565	R	19*	.1
24	Numa Tool Co—*Ralph Leonard*	PO Box 348, Thompson CT 06277	860-923-9551	R	16*	.1
25	Rockmore International Inc—*Cyrus Eghdami*	10065 Sw Commerce Cir, Wilsonville OR 97070	503-682-1001	R	16*	.1
26	Shumar's Welding and Machine Service Inc—*Eli Shumar*	414 Stone Church Rd, Grindstone PA 15442	724-246-8095	R	16*	.1
27	Polydeck Screen Corp—*Peter Freissle*	1790 Dewberry Rd, Spartanburg SC 29307	864-579-4594	R	16*	.1
28	Fairchild Equipment And Supply Co—*Myrleen Fairchild*	PO Box 300, Glen Lyn VA 24093	540-726-2380	R	15*	.1
29	Williams Patent Crusher and Pulverizer Company Inc—*Robert Williams*	813 Montgomery St, Saint Louis MO 63102	314-621-3348	R	15*	.1
30	Conn-Weld Industries Inc—*James Connolly*	PO Box 5329, Princeton WV 24740	304-487-1421	R	14*	.1
31	A L Lee Corp—*Leonard Urtso*	PO Box 99, Lester WV 25865	304-934-5361	R	13*	.1
32	Mcsweeney's Inc—*L Joe Mc Sweeney*	PO Box 7995, Huntington WV 25779	740-894-3353	R	13*	.1
33	Aggregate Machinery Inc—*Roger Jensen*	PO Box 17160, Salem OR 97305	503-390-6284	R	12*	.1
34	Brookville Locomotive Inc—*Dalph Mcneil*	PO Box 130, Brookville PA 15825	814-849-2000	R	10*	.1
35	Norris Screen And Manufacturing LLC—*Carl Arney*	21405 Gvrnor G C Pery, Tazewell VA 24651	276-988-8901	R	10*	<.1
36	Factory Company International Inc—*Christopher Wood*	PO Box 7287, Spokane WA 99207	509-252-9290	R	9*	<.1
37	Petitto Mine Equipment Inc—*Angelo Petitto Jr*	PO Box 1586, Morgantown WV 26507	304-292-3936	R	8*	<.1
38	Schoeller-Bleckmann Energy Services LLC—*Donald Cross*	PO Box 492, Broussard LA 70518	337-837-2030	R	8*	.1
39	Elenburg Exploration Inc	1910 N Loop Ave, Casper WY 82602	307-235-8609	S	7*	.1
40	Damascus Equipment LLC—*Charles Phillips*	PO Box 610, Abingdon VA 24212	276-676-2376	R	7*	<.1
41	Brydet Development—*Julie Pepper*	PO Box 199, Conesville OH 43811	740-623-0455	R	7*	.1
42	Munson Machinery Company Inc—*B Divine*	210 Seward Ave, Utica NY 13502	315-797-0090	R	7*	<.1
43	Wilmot Engineering Co—*K Glenn Cole*	183 South St Ste2, Freeland PA 18224	570-636-5871	R	6*	<.1
44	Gill Rock Drill Company Inc—*James Gill*	903 Cornwall Rd 905, Lebanon PA 17042	717-272-3861	R	6*	<.1
45	Appalachian Mine Sales Inc—*Allen Morefield*	PO Box 534, Tazewell VA 24651	276-988-2581	R	6*	<.1
46	Centrifugal Services Inc—*Dale Martin*	5595 Hwy 34 N, Raleigh IL 62977	618-268-4850	R	6*	<.1
47	Hartman-Fabco Inc—*Robert Duniec*	1415 Lake Lansing Rd, Lansing MI 48912	517-485-9493	R	5*	<.1
48	Acker Drill Company Inc—*Wyane Wise*	PO Box 830, Scranton PA 18501	570-586-2061	R	5*	<.1
49	Carr Tool Co—*Patricia Blum*	575 Security Dr, Fairfield OH 45014	513-825-2900	R	5*	<.1
50	Ramco Construction Tools Inc—*David Blackburn*	21213 76th Ave S, Kent WA 98032	253-796-3051	R	5*	<.1
51	Drilling Supply And Manufacturing Inc—*Stanley Martin*	7301 Hwy 183 S, Austin TX 78744	512-243-1986	R	4*	<.1
52	Matrix Drilling Products Co—*Kent Peters*	PO Box 2036, Lewisburg TN 37091	931-359-6564	R	4*	<.1
53	Wsb Inc—*Dan Wright*	2209 Anderson Rd, Opelika AL 36801	334-749-3377	R	4*	<.1
54	2828 Clinton Inc—*Michael Valore*	2828 Clinton Ave, Cleveland OH 44113	216-241-7157	R	4*	<.1
55	Bowdil Co—*Robert Morrow*	2030 Industrial Pl Se, Canton OH 44707	330-456-7176	R	4*	<.1
56	Reed International—*Wendell Reed*	PO Box 178, Hickman CA 95323	209-874-2357	R	4*	<.1
57	Peters Equipment Inc—*Wayne Ramsey*	PO Box 1050, Bluefield VA 24605	276-322-5451	R	4*	<.1
58	American Mine Research Inc—*Robert Graf*	PO Box 234, Rocky Gap VA 24366	276-928-1712	R	4*	<.1
59	Tema Systems Inc—*Mike Mullins*	7806 Redsky Dr, Cincinnati OH 45249	513-489-7811	R	4*	<.1
60	Davey Kent Inc—*J Myers*	PO Box 400, Kent OH 44240	330-673-5400	R	4*	<.1
61	Null's Machine and Manufacturing Inc—*Robert Null*	PO Box 9336, Huntington WV 25704	304-523-3459	R	3*	<.1
62	Drillco Equipment Company Inc—*Nick Lacey*	3452 11th St, Long Island City NY 11106	718-777-5986	R	3*	<.1
63	Lawrence Brothers Inc—*James Lawrence*	PO Box 737, Bluefield VA 24605	276-322-4988	R	3*	<.1
64	Mid-Western Machinery Company Inc—*Gregg Beechwood*	PO Box 458, Joplin MO 64802	417-624-2400	R	3*	<.1
65	Young's Machine Co—*Gary Young*	PO Box 489, Monticello UT 84535	435-587-2292	R	3*	<.1
66	Consolidated Metal Services Inc—*Robert Fry*	PO Box 568, Chattanooga TN 37401	423-265-1123	R	3*	<.1
67	Frontier Fabricating LLC—*Becky Dick*	15704 Hwy14, Sterling CO 80751	970-522-0916	R	3*	<.1
68	Border City Tool And Manufacturing Co—*Don Rothburn*	23325 Blackstone Ave, Warren MI 48089	586-758-5574	R	3*	<.1
69	Caprock Oil Tools Inc—*Glenn Gault*	2951 Marina Bay Dr, League City TX 77573	281-485-4777	R	3*	<.1
70	National Fab And Machine Inc—*George Devenney*	PO Box 231, North East PA 16428	814-725-9611	R	3*	<.1
71	Angelo Nieto Inc—*Greg Nieto*	PO Box 95, Peckville PA 18452	570-489-6761	R	3*	<.1
72	Montgomery Industries International Inc—*Robert Montgomery*	PO Box 3687, Jacksonville FL 32206	904-355-5671	R	3*	<.1
73	Eastern Machine and Conveyor Inc—*Richard Clark*	PO Box 742, Donora PA 15033	724-379-4701	R	2*	<.1

Rank	Company Name—*Executive Officer*	Address, City, State, Zip	Phone	Type	Fin	Empls
74	Lawson M Whiting Inc—*Jay Whiting*	PO Box 617, Macedon NY 14502	315-986-3064	R	2*	<.1
75	Asbury Machine Corp—*Gary Hayes*	PO Box 416, Tonkawa OK 74653	580-628-3416	R	2*	<.1
76	Scheirer Machine Company Inc—*Marlene Scheirer*	3200 Industrial Blvd, Bethel Park PA 15102	412-833-6500	R	2*	<.1
77	Carol Tabor—*Carol Tabor*	4900 Memco Ln, Racine WI 53404	262-639-2420	R	2*	<.1
78	Crisp Manufacturing Company Inc—*Paul Crisp*	PO Box 396, Rural Retreat VA 24368	276-686-4131	R	1*	<.1
79	Salem Tool Inc—*Laird Orr*	PO Box 760, London KY 40743	606-528-2963	R	1*	<.1
80	Mefcor Inc—*Charlene Hurt*	PO Box 818, Bluefield VA 24605	276-322-5021	R	1*	<.1
81	International Process Equipment Company Inc—*Ronald Miller*	9300 N Rte 130, Pennsauken NJ 08110	856-665-4007	R	1*	<.1
82	Lufkin Industries Inc Oil Field Div	601 S Raguet St, Lufkin TX 75904	936-634-2211	D	N/A	2.7

TOTALS: SIC 3532 Mining Machinery
Companies: 82   8,294   35.1

3533 Oil & Gas Field Machinery

Rank	Company Name—*Executive Officer*	Address, City, State, Zip	Phone	Type	Fin	Empls
1	Baker Hughes Inc—*Chad C Deaton*	2929 Allen Pkwy Ste 21, Houston TX 77019	713-439-8600	P	14,414	53.1
2	National Oilwell Varco Inc—*Merrill A Miller Jr*	7909 Parkwood Circle D, Houston TX 77036	713-375-3700	P	12,156	41.0
3	Smith International Inc—*John Kennedy*	16740 Hardy St, Houston TX 77032	281-443-3370	S	8,219	21.9
4	Cameron International Corp—*Jack B Moore*	1333 W Loop S Ste 1700, Houston TX 77027	713-513-3300	P	6,135	19.5
5	FMC Technologies Inc—*John T Gremp*	1803 Gears Rd, Houston TX 77067	281-591-4000	P	4,126	11.5
6	Psp Industries Inc—*Michael Senneway*	9885 Doerr Ln, Schertz TX 78154	210-651-9595	R	3,493*	.5
7	Oil States International Inc—*Cindy B Taylor*	3 Allen Ctr 333 Clay S, Houston TX 77002	713-652-0582	P	3,479	7.9
8	Baker Hughes INTEQ—*Chad C Deaton* Baker Hughes Inc	2929 Allan Pkwy, Houston TX 77019	713-625-4200	D	3,141*	5.0
9	SPM Flow Control Inc—*Steve Noon*	7601 Wyatt Dr, Fort Worth TX 76108	817-246-2461	S	2,273*	.3
10	Weatherford Completion and Oilfield Systems	7587 Hwy 75 S, Huntsville TX 77340	936-295-0080	D	1,433*	2.0
11	Baker Oil Tools—*Chad Deaton* Baker Hughes Inc	PO Box 40129, Houston TX 77240	713-466-1322	D	1,167*	7.0
12	Newpark Resources Inc—*Paul L Howes*	2700 Research Forest D, The Woodlands TX 77381	281-362-6800	P	958	2.1
13	Oil States Industries Inc—*Douglas E Swanson* Oil States International Inc	PO Box 670, Arlington TX 76004	817-548-4200	S	893*	1.3
14	Cameron Drilling and Production Systems—*John Carne* Cameron International Corp	PO Box 1212, Houston TX 77251	713-939-2211	D	850	5.9
15	Dril-Quip Inc—*Blake T DeBerry*	13550 Hempstead Hwy, Houston TX 77040	713-939-7711	P	601	2.2
16	Hydril Co	302 McCarty Dr, Houston TX 77029	713-670-3500	S	503	1.8
17	TD Williamson Inc—*D Bruce Brinkley*	6120 S Yale Ste 1700, Tulsa OK 74136	918-447-5001	R	457*	1.4
18	Owen Oil Tools Inc—*Jeff West*	PO Box 568, Garland TX 75044	817-551-0540	S	348*	.5
19	Frigoscandia Inc—*Charles Cannon* FMC Technologies Inc	400 Highpoint Dr, Chalfont PA 18914	215-822-4600	S	304*	.4
20	J-W Operating Co—*H Westerman*	PO Box 226406, Dallas TX 75222	972-233-8191	R	220*	.7
21	T-3 Energy Services Inc—*Steven Krablin*	117 Rosewood St, Bowie TX 76230	940-872-1400	D	219	.6
22	Loadcraft Industries Ltd—*Terry McIver*	PO Box 1429, Brady TX 76825	325-597-2911	R	202*	.3
23	Boots and Coots International Well Control Inc—*Jerry L Winchester*	7908 N Sam Houston Pkw, Houston TX 77064	281-931-8884	S	195	.7
24	Hydra-Rig Inc National Oilwell Varco Inc	1020 Everman Pkwy, Fort Worth TX 76140	817-985-5000	S	163*	.2
25	Hydril USA Distribution LLC—*Charles Chauvier*	PO Box 60458, Houston TX 77205	281-449-2000	R	162*	1.7
26	Weatherford Oil Country Manufacturing	300 W Stanley Ave, Ventura CA 93001	805-643-1200	S	135*	.2
27	KBA Engineering LLC—*Rick Jones*	2157 Mohawk St, Bakersfield CA 93308	661-323-0487	R	102*	.2
28	Production Management Industries LLC—*Donald P Mehrtens*	PO Box 2692, Morgan City LA 70381	985-631-3837	S	80*	.8
29	Worldwide Oilfield Machine Inc—*Sudhir Puranik*	11809 Canemont St, Houston TX 77035	713-729-9200	R	67*	.2
30	Derrick Corp—*James Derrick*	590 Duke Rd, Buffalo NY 14225	716-683-9010	R	67*	.7
31	Tam International Inc—*Bently Sanford*	4620 Southerland Rd, Houston TX 77092	713-462-7617	R	60*	.4
32	Tiw Corp—*Stephen Pearce*	PO Box 35729, Houston TX 77235	713-729-2110	R	56*	.4
33	Global Energy Services Inc—*Byron Dunn*	11616 N Galayda St, Houston TX 77086	281-447-9000	R	50*	.6
34	Gougler Industries Inc—*Larry Wittensoldner*	PO Box 807, Kent OH 44240	330-673-5821	R	42*	.1
35	Control Flow Inc—*William Laird*	PO Box 40788, Houston TX 77240	281-890-8300	R	41*	.1
36	Bolt Technology Corp—*Raymond M Soto*	4 Duke Pl, Norwalk CT 06854	203-853-0700	P	39	.2
37	Harbison-Fischer Inc—*Charles Fischer*	901 N Crowley Rd, Crowley TX 76036	817-297-2211	R	36*	.5
38	Greenline Industries—*Donn Tice*	2425 Larkspur Landing, Larkspur CA 94939		R	35	<.1
39	Bilco Tools Inc—*William Coyle*	PO Box 9064, Houma LA 70361	985-851-2240	R	34*	.1
40	Davis-Lynch Inc—*Carl Davis*	2357 Garden Rd, Pearland TX 77581	281-485-8301	R	33*	.2
41	Wood Group ESP—*Allister G Langlands*	17420 Katy Fwy Ste 300, Houston TX 77094	281-828-3500	S	31*	.2
42	Collier Well Equipment and Supply Inc—*Doug Drughal*	3310 Columbus Rd, Wooster OH 44691	330-345-3968	R	31*	<.1
43	Watson-Hopper Inc—*Charley Smith*	PO Box 10, Hobbs NM 88241	575-397-2411	R	29*	<.1
44	Schramm Inc—*Edward Breiner*	800 E Virginia Ave Ste, West Chester PA 19380	610-696-2500	R	28*	.2
45	Balmoral Group International Inc—*Mike Aigkenhit*	1902 Rankin Rd, Houston TX 77073	281-774-2600	S	27*	.2
46	Rush Sales Co—*Jerry Rush*	PO Box 2488, Odessa TX 79760	432-337-2397	R	22*	.1
47	En-Fab Inc—*Chandra Tripathy*	PO Box 21361, Houston TX 77226	713-225-4913	R	22*	.1
48	Honeywell Enraf	2000 Northfield Ct, Roswell GA 30076	770-475-1900	S	21*	<.1
49	Seaboard International Inc—*J Joy*	PO Box 450989, Houston TX 77245	713-644-3535	R	19*	.1
50	Faith Manufacturing Company Inc—*Norman Webster*	406 Atascocita Rd, Humble TX 77396	281-441-9595	R	18*	.1
51	Frederick's Machine and Tool Shop Inc—*James Frederick*	3903 2nd St Ara, New Iberia LA 70560	337-367-9943	R	16*	.1
52	Eckel Manufacturing Company Inc—*Terry Eckel*	PO Box 1375, Odessa TX 79760	432-362-4336	R	16*	.1
53	Upco Inc—*William Ridenour*	PO Box 725, Claremore OK 74018	918-342-1270	R	15*	.1
54	Smi Manufacturing Inc—*Jerome Sqweres*	13312 E Hardy Rd, Houston TX 77039	281-449-0345	R	14*	.1
55	Kmt International Inc—*Boris Melamed*	39271 Mssion Blvd Ste, Fremont CA 94539	510-713-1400	R	14*	<.1
56	Q B Johnson Manufacturing Inc—*Lory Johnson*	PO Box 890120, Oklahoma City OK 73189	405-677-6676	R	14*	.1
57	Oem Components Inc—*John Morvant*	14535 Chrisman Rd, Houston TX 77039	281-449-6258	R	13*	.1
58	Southern Technology and Services Inc—*Bryan Bunn*	PO Box 9129, Houma LA 70361	985-851-5474	R	13*	.1
59	Kem-Tron Technologies Inc—*Jai Mehta*	10050 Cash Rd, Stafford TX 77477	281-261-5778	R	11*	.1
60	Rampp Co—*Mark Fulton*	PO Box 608, Marietta OH 45750	740-373-7886	R	11*	.1
61	Synergy Industries LP—*Walt Coram*	12963 Oak Grove Rd S, Burleson TX 76028	817-295-1161	R	11*	.1
62	Woolslayer Companies Inc—*Thomas Wingerter*	PO Box 216, Tulsa OK 74101	918-523-9191	R	11*	.1
63	Mingo Manufacturing Inc—*Terry Ingle*	PO Box 30, Owasso OK 74055	918-272-1151	R	10*	<.1
64	Reamco Inc—*Brent Milam*	1149 Smede Hwy, Broussard LA 70518	337-364-9244	R	10*	<.1
65	Dawson Enterprises—*Harry Dawson*	PO Box 6039, Long Beach CA 90806	562-424-8564	R	10*	.1
66	Hutchison Hayes Separation Inc—*Michael Dunson*	PO Box 2965, Houston TX 77252	713-455-9600	R	9*	.1
67	Double-E Inc—*James Wilson*	1261 Profit Dr, Dallas TX 75247	214-631-2290	R	9*	.1
68	Downhole Stabilization Inc—*James Calanchinl*	PO Box 2467, Bakersfield CA 93303	661-631-1044	R	8*	.1
69	Specialty Supply LP—*Jason Pope*	12920 Cypress N Housto, Cypress TX 77429	281-970-8444	R	8*	.1

Note: An asterisk (*) indicates an estimated financial figure. The company type code used is as follows: R = Private, P = Public, S = Private Subsidiary, B = Public Subsidiary, D = Division, J = Joint Venture, I = Investment Fund.

COMPANY RANKINGS BY SALES WITHIN 4-DIGIT SIC

Rank	Company Name—*Executive Officer*	Address, City, State, Zip	Phone	Type	Fin	Empls
70	Tucker Technologies Inc—*Wayne Tucker*	12607 E 60th St, Tulsa OK 74146	918-252-5416	R	8*	.1
71	Sargent Pipe Company Inc—*Mike Whitesel*	PO Box 627, Broken Bow NE 68822	308-872-6477	R	8*	<.1
72	Petrex Inc—*Brian Lacour*	PO Box 37, Harvey LA 70059	504-341-2700	R	8*	.1
73	Industrial Rubber Inc—*Paul Chaney*	PO Box 95389, Oklahoma City OK 73143	405-632-9783	R	8*	.1
74	Resource Production Co—*Brad Walls*	PO Box 3076, Farmington NM 87499	505-325-7927	R	8*	.1
75	Maass Midwest Manufacturing Inc—*John Surinak*	PO Box 547, Huntley IL 60142	847-669-5135	R	8*	.1
76	New Tech Systems Inc—*Patrick Hanlon*	PO Box 60276, Midland TX 79711	432-561-5393	R	8*	.1
77	Radoil Inc—*Benton Baugh*	12251 Fm 529 Rd Ste A, Houston TX 77041	713-937-4494	R	7*	<.1
78	Jjw Interests Inc—*James Woodcock*	PO Box 4185, Midland TX 79704	432-697-2292	R	7*	<.1
79	Gemstar Inc—*Peggy Glover*	PO Box 12376, Odessa TX 79768	432-362-2315	R	7*	<.1
80	Hydraulic Power Technology-Texas Inc—*Ramadan Ismail*	18109 Foust Dr, Buda TX 78610	512-295-4234	R	7*	<.1
81	Downing Wellhead Equipment Inc—*Gene Downing*	8528 SW 2nd St, Oklahoma City OK 73128	405-789-8182	R	6*	.1
82	WEDGE Group Inc—*James Tidwell*	PO Box 130688, Houston TX 77219	713-739-6500	R	6*	.1
83	Spectrum Batteries Inc—*Jim Dutchak*	6910 Sprigg St, Fulshear TX 77441	281-533-9596	R	6*	<.1
84	Petroleum Elastomers Inc—*Michael Ward*	757 Kenrick Dr Ste 112, Houston TX 77060	281-591-1500	R	6*	<.1
85	Stratco Inc—*Diane Graham*	14821 N 73rd St, Scottsdale AZ 85260	480-991-0450	R	6	<.1
86	Hmc Instrument and Machine Works Ltd—*Eugene Chung*	2325 Blalock Rd, Houston TX 77080	713-468-1426	R	6*	<.1
87	Tools International Corp—*John Boulanger*	PO Box 52323, Lafayette LA 70505	337-837-9261	R	6*	<.1
88	Industrial Vehicles International Inc—*James Bird*	6737 E 12th St, Tulsa OK 74112	918-836-6516	R	6*	<.1
89	Godwin Craig Inc—*Joseph Adams*	PO Box 525, New Waverly TX 77358	936-344-6115	R	5*	<.1
90	Fogle Manufacturing Services LP—*Allen Fogle*	PO Box 1309, Stafford TX 77497	281-495-1828	R	5*	<.1
91	D and L Manufacturing Inc—*Lee Eslicker*	PO Box 52220, Tulsa OK 74152	918-587-3504	R	5*	<.1
92	Double Life Corp—*Phillip Banta*	200 N Rockwell Ave, Oklahoma City OK 73127	405-789-7867	R	5*	<.1
93	Midco Fabricators Inc—*J Valentine*	3110 W Noble Ave, Guthrie OK 73044	405-282-6667	R	5*	<.1
94	Chandler Manufacturing Inc—*Ronald Chandler*	PO Box 4684, Wichita Falls TX 76308	940-763-1528	R	5*	<.1
95	Mathey Dearman Inc—*Donald Lockhart*	PO Box 472110, Tulsa OK 74147	918-447-1288	R	5*	<.1
96	Testers Inc—*Herbert Hailey*	PO Box 83437, Oklahoma City OK 73148	405-235-7446	R	5*	<.1
97	Team Oil Tools LLC—*Lance Gardner*	PO Box 470126, Tulsa OK 74147	918-461-8104	R	5*	<.1
98	JW Manufacturing Inc—*Jim Lewis* J-W Operating Co	1701 Texoma Dr, Sherman TX 75090	903-892-0561	S	5*	<.1
99	Production Facilities Equipment Company Inc—*Paul Carr*	28010 Fm 2978 Rd, Magnolia TX 77354	281-356-1107	R	4*	<.1
100	Hasco Manufacturing Co—*B Borden*	PO Box 505, Sapulpa OK 74067	918-224-0816	R	4*	<.1
101	Global Oil Tools Inc—*Wilford Barnhill*	PO Box 3580, Houma LA 70361	985-868-3404	R	4*	<.1
102	Saxon Industries Inc—*Warren Dale*	932 W 20th St, Houston TX 77008	713-869-6939	R	4*	<.1
103	Mills Machine Company Inc—*Charles Mills*	PO Box 1514, Shawnee OK 74802	405-273-4900	R	4*	<.1
104	Ortco Inc—*Carole Newton*	PO Box 94127, Oklahoma City OK 73143	405-670-2803	R	4*	<.1
105	Engineering Technology Inc—*Jack Earls*	5555 E 71st St Ste 810, Tulsa OK 74136	918-492-0508	R	4*	<.1
106	Jt Oilfield Manufacturing Company Inc—*Tom Mooney*	PO Box 750459, Houston TX 77275	713-947-7006	R	4*	<.1
107	Productioneered Products Co—*Phil Rummell*	PO Box 7734, The Woodlands TX 77387	281-364-1086	R	4*	<.1
108	Paramount Pumps and Supplies Inc—*Mark Burris*	PO Box 607, Iola KS 66749	620-365-7255	R	4*	<.1
109	Consolidated Pressure Control LLLP—*James Kuchenbrod*	7614 Bluff Point Dr, Houston TX 77086	281-893-5900	R	4*	<.1
110	Electronic Data Devices Co—*Robert Williams*	PO Box 12128, Odessa TX 79768	432-366-8699	R	3*	<.1
111	Epley Enterprises Inc—*Michael Epley*	PO Box 60226, San Angelo TX 76906	325-651-8811	R	3*	<.1
112	L-K Industries Inc—*Joseph Hugghins*	PO Box 230305, Houston TX 77223	713-926-2623	R	3*	<.1
113	Puradyn Filter Technologies Inc—*Joseph V Vittoria*	2017 High Ridge Rd, Boynton Beach FL 33426	561-547-9499	P	3	<.1
114	Conrad Machine Inc—*Jim Conrad*	1627 E 27th Ter, Pittsburg KS 66762	620-231-9458	R	3*	<.1
115	Wellhead Control Products—*Ray Hunt*	PO Box 1283, Bellaire TX 77402	713-475-2283	R	3*	<.1
116	Mitco Industries Inc—*Larry Mitchell*	2235 S Vista Ave, Bloomington CA 92316	909-877-0800	R	3*	<.1
117	Markco Machine Works Inc—*Mark Taliaserro*	PO Box 12165, Odessa TX 79768	432-362-8921	R	3*	<.1
118	Spectra Engineering Inc—*Donald Bennett*	825 W 68th St, Odessa TX 79764	432-367-8413	R	2*	<.1
119	Penn Machine Inc—*Jeff Hall*	8513 Sw 2nd St, Oklahoma City OK 73128	405-789-0084	R	2*	<.1
120	Standard Machine Works Inc—*Edlar Blanton*	PO Box 15335, Houston TX 77220	713-673-1111	R	2*	<.1
121	Drillmec Inc—*Brando Ballerini*	PO Box 2534, Conroe TX 77305	281-885-0777	R	2*	<.1
122	LJ Machine Works Inc—*Lonnie Jones*	5510 Lawndale St, Houston TX 77023	713-928-5786	R	2*	<.1
123	M Company Ltd	1175 State Rte 19, Chickasha OK 73018	405-224-5779	R	2*	<.1
124	Orange Pump and Valve Inc—*Mona Broussard*	606 Border St, Orange TX 77630	409-883-6415	R	2*	<.1
125	Pipeline Equipment Inc—*Jack Lollis*	8403 S 89th West Ave, Tulsa OK 74131	918-224-4144	R	2*	<.1
126	Rama Fabrication Inc—*Ronald Rains*	PO Box 7346, Odessa TX 79760	432-362-9291	R	2*	<.1
127	H and S Company Inc—*Kurtis Hoelscher*	7219 Harris Rd, Celina OH 45822	419-394-4444	R	2*	<.1
128	Hdi Instruments LLC—*Carl Azbell*	4130 Directors Row, Houston TX 77092	713-688-8555	R	2*	<.1
129	Filtration Technology Corp—*John Hampton*	5175 Ashley Ct, Houston TX 77041	713-849-0849	R	2*	.1
130	D and W Wireline Inc—*Jack Highfaw*	PO Box 40, Scott LA 70583	337-237-3990	R	2*	<.1
131	International Equipment Distributors—*Robert Burton*	2561 S 1560 W, Woods Cross UT 84087	801-295-3835	R	1*	<.1
132	Atlas Instrument Supply Company Inc—*Thomas Jacobs*	4802 Renies Ct Ste A, Needville TX 77461	713-697-0510	R	1*	<.1
133	Laney Machine Inc—*J Laney*	PO Box 1299, Humble TX 77347	281-987-2511	R	1*	<.1
134	Comanche Bit Service Inc—*Jimmy Diehl*	2 Miles N Hwy 81, Comanche OK 73529	580-439-6424	R	1*	<.1
135	Cuming Corp—*Larry Parkenson*	225 Bodwell St, Avon MA 02322	508-580-2660	R	<1*	<.1
136	G S F Plastics Corp—*Tom Lankford*	12035 Proctor St, Houston TX 77038	281-820-4801	R	<1*	<.1

TOTALS: SIC 3533 Oil & Gas Field Machinery
Companies: 136   67,736   198.4

3534 Elevators & Moving Stairways

Rank	Company Name—*Executive Officer*	Address, City, State, Zip	Phone	Type	Fin	Empls
1	United Technologies Corp—*Louis R Chenevert*	United Technologies Bl, Hartford CT 06103	860-728-7000	P	54,326	208.0
2	Otis Elevator Co—*Didier Michaud Daniel* United Technologies Corp	10 Farm Springs Rd, Farmington CT 06032	860-676-6000	S	4,976*	64.0
3	ThyssenKrupp Elevator—*Ulrich Albrecht-Frueh*	2591 Dallas Pkwy Ste 6, Frisco TX 75034		R	2,700	13.0
4	Ricon Corp	7900 Nelson Rd, Panorama City CA 91402	818-267-3000	S	502*	.3
5	Electronic Micro Systems Inc—*Michael Byrn*	125 Ricefield Ln, Hauppauge NY 11788	631-864-3699	S	162*	.2
6	Janus Elevator Products Inc—*Mike Byrne*	125 Ricefield Ln, Hauppauge NY 11788	631-864-3699	S	88*	.1
7	Essick Air Products Inc—*Kim Stafford*	5800 Murray St, Little Rock AR 72209	501-562-1094	R	87*	.4
8	Bagby Elevator Company Inc—*Arthur Bagby*	PO Box 320919, Birmingham AL 35232	205-591-4245	R	52*	.2
9	Motion Control Engineering Inc—*Javad Rahimian*	11380 White Rock Rd, Rancho Cordova CA 95742	916-463-9200	R	32*	.4
10	Minnesota Elevator Inc—*John Romnes*	19336 607th Ave, Mankato MN 56001	507-245-3060	R	29*	.2
11	Hollister-Whitney Elevator Corp—*Bud Briscoe*	PO Box 4025, Quincy IL 62305	217-222-0466	R	28*	.2
12	Gunderlin Limited Inc—*Jay Bass*	3625 E 11th Ave, Hialeah FL 33013	305-696-6071	R	19*	.1
13	Harmar Summit LLC—*Julie Hunter*	18505 E 163rd St, Greenwood MO 64034	816-537-0661	R	17*	<.1
14	Long Elevator And Machine Company Inc—*Patrick Long*	PO Box 500, Riverton IL 62561	217-629-9648	R	16*	.1
15	Elevator Research and ManufacturingCo—*Frank Park*	1417 Elwood St, Los Angeles CA 90021	213-746-1914	R	16*	.1
16	Bay State Elevator Company Inc—*Harold Potts*	PO Box 910, Agawam MA 01001	413-786-7000	R	14*	.1
17	Elevator Equipment Corp—*Abe Salehpour*	PO Box 39714, Los Angeles CA 90039	323-245-0147	R	13*	.1

Rank	Company Name—*Executive Officer*	Address, City, State, Zip	Phone	Type	Fin	Empls
18	CEC Elevator Cab Corp—*Carlos Vanga*	540 Manida St, Bronx NY 10474	718-328-3632	R	11*	.1
19	Quality Elevator Products Inc—*Joe Kawa*	7760 N Merrimac Ave, Niles IL 60714	847-581-0085	R	10*	<.1
20	National Elevator Cab and Door Corp—*Harold Friedman*	5315 37th Ave, Woodside NY 11377	718-478-5900	R	9*	.1
21	Inclinator Company Of America—*Melvyn Bowman*	PO Box 1557, Harrisburg PA 17105	717-939-8420	R	9*	.1
22	Eastern Elevator Service and Sales—*Bradley Westover*	PO Box 158, Windber PA 15963	814-467-8350	R	7*	.1
23	Gms Elevator Services Inc—*G Simpkins*	446 W Arrow Hwy Ste 30, San Dimas CA 91773	909-599-3904	R	6*	<.1
24	Elevator Cable and Supply Co—*Kenneth Sullivan*	2741 S 21st Ave, Broadview IL 60155	708-338-9700	R	6*	<.1
25	Versalift East Inc—*Keith Joseph*	2706 Brodhead Rd, Bethlehem PA 18020	610-866-1400	R	4*	<.1
26	Mitsubishi Elevator Co—*Kenichiro Yamanishi*	5665 Plz Dr, Cypress CA 90630	714-220-4700	S	4*	<.1
27	Benko Products Inc—*John Benko*	5350 Evergreen Pkwy, Sheffield Village OH 44054	440-934-2180	R	4*	<.1
28	Regency Elevator Products Corp—*John Bramer*	870 Mount Prospect Ave, Newark NJ 07104	973-481-1400	R	4*	<.1
29	K-Tech International Inc—*Samuel Massameno*	56 Ella Grasso Ave, Torrington CT 06790	860-489-9399	R	3*	<.1
30	Elevator Enterances Of NY Inc—*Thomas Aveni*	15 Jane St, Paterson NJ 07522	973-790-9100	R	3*	<.1
31	Tyler Cole Enterprises Inc—*Jonathan Heffer*	2394 W Currahee St, Toccoa GA 30577	706-886-2121	R	2*	<.1
32	Elevator Components Company USA—*Michael Richmon*	1725 Arlington Rd Ste, Richmond VA 23230	804-421-4091	R	1*	<.1

TOTALS: SIC 3534 Elevators & Moving Stairways
Companies: 32   63,158   288.0

3535 Conveyors & Conveying Equipment

Rank	Company Name—*Executive Officer*	Address, City, State, Zip	Phone	Type	Fin	Empls
1	Jervis B Webb Co—*Dina Salehi*	34375 W 12 Mile Rd, Farmington Hills MI 48331	248-553-1000	R	4,740*	.9
2	AmBec Inc	8020 Forsyth Blvd, St Louis MO 63105	314-862-8000	D	1,258*	.2
3	Cannon Equipment Inc—*Chuck Gruber*	15100 Business Pky, Rosemount MN 55068	651-322-6300	R	445*	.3
4	Kuka Welding Systems and Robot Corp—*Larry Drake*	6600 Center Dr, Sterling Heights MI 48312	586-795-2000	R	209*	.4
5	Translogic Corp—*Charles Kegley*	10825 E 47th Ave, Denver CO 80239	303-371-7770	R	128*	.3
6	Fleetwoodgoldcowyard Inc—*Phillip Ostapowicz*	1305 Lakeview Dr, Romeoville IL 60446	630-759-6800	R	117*	.5
7	J Richards Industries—*Larry Webber*	PO Box 1040, Holland OH 43528	419-866-8000	R	105*	.2
8	G and T Conveyor Company Inc—*Michael Malkowski*	476 Southridge Industr, Tavares FL 32778	352-343-1500	R	105*	1.1
9	Nkc Of America Inc—*Hideo Nagasawa*	1584 E Brooks Rd, Memphis TN 38116	901-396-5353	R	81*	.2
10	United Conveyor Corp—*Douglas S Basler*	2100 Norman Dr S, Waukegan IL 60085	847-473-5900	R	80*	.2
11	Eagle Crusher Company Inc—*Susanne Cobey*	PO Box 537, Galion OH 44833	419-468-2288	R	72*	.2
12	Fki Logistex Automation Inc—*John Westendorf*	10045 International Bl, Cincinnati OH 45246	513-874-0788	R	61*	.7
13	Hytrol Conveyor Company Inc—*Gregg Goodner*	2020 Hytrol St, Jonesboro AR 72401	870-935-3700	R	58*	.8
14	Key Handlings System Inc—*William Stefan*	137 W Commercial Ave, Moonachie NJ 07074	201-933-9333	R	56*	.2
15	Allor Manufacturing Inc—*Fred M Allor*	PO Box 1540, Brighton MI 48116	248-486-4500	R	54*	.1
16	MAC Equipment Inc—*Gary Cavey*	7901 NW 107th Ter, Kansas City MO 64153	816-891-9300	S	52*	.3
17	ThyssenKrupp Robins Inc—*Sheta Ramsis*	6400 S Fiddles Green C, Greenwood Village CO 80111	303-770-0808	S	52*	.1
18	Intralox LLC—*James Lapeyre*	PO Box 50699, New Orleans LA 70150	504-733-0463	R	50*	.6
19	W and H Systems Inc—*Don Betman*	120 Asia Pl, Carlstadt NJ 07072	201-933-7840	R	47*	.1
20	Mayfran International Inc—*Dennis Kriesen*	PO Box 43038, Cleveland OH 44143	440-461-4100	R	45*	.3
21	Carrier Vibrating Equipment Inc—*Brian Trudel*	PO Box 37070, Louisville KY 40233	502-969-3171	R	42*	.1
22	Heyl and Patterson Inc—*John Edelman*	PO Box 36, Pittsburgh PA 15230	412-788-9810	R	42*	.1
23	Dynamic Air Inc—*James Steele*	1125 Willow Lake Blvd, Saint Paul MN 55110	651-484-2900	R	41*	.3
24	INTERROLL Corp—*Kim Byriel*	3000 Corporate Dr, Wilmington NC 28405	910-799-1100	S	40*	.3
25	Automotion Inc—*Merle Davis*	11000 Lavergne Ave, Oak Lawn IL 60453	708-229-3700	R	40*	.2
26	Overhead Conveyor Co—*Thomas Woodbeck*	1330 Hilton Rd, Ferndale MI 48220	248-547-3800	R	35*	.1
27	Arrowhead Conveyor Corp—*Tom Young*	PO Box 2408, Oshkosh WI 54903	920-235-5562	R	34*	.2
28	Western Pneumatics Inc—*Richard Nicol*	PO Box 21340, Eugene OR 97402	541-461-2600	R	32*	.2
29	Gammerler US Corp—*Clay Bruneman*	431 Lakeview Ct Ste B, Mount Prospect IL 60056	941-465-4400	R	32*	.1
30	Automated Conveyor Systems Inc—*Charles Doty*	3850 Southland Dr, West Memphis AR 72301	870-732-5050	R	31*	.2
31	Sentry Equipment Erectors Inc—*Adam Vinoskey*	13150 E Lynchburg Sale, Forest VA 24551	434-525-0769	R	31*	.2
32	Sdi Industries Inc—*Mary Adams*	13000 Pierce St, Pacoima CA 91331	818-890-6002	R	29*	.2
33	Webb-Stiles Co—*Donald Stiles*	PO Box 464, Valley City OH 44280	330-225-7761	R	27*	.2
34	Premier Pneumatics Inc	PO Box 17, Salina KS 67402	785-825-1611	S	24*	.1
35	Fred D Pfening Co—*Fred Pfening*	1075 W 5th Ave, Columbus OH 43212	614-294-5361	R	24*	<.1
36	Shick Tube-Veyor Corp—*Joseph Ungashick*	4346 Clary Blvd, Kansas City MO 64130	816-861-7224	R	23*	.2
37	Cyclonaire Corp—*Don Baker*	PO Box 366, York NE 68467	402-362-2000	R	23*	<.1
38	Highland Engineering Inc—*Ralph Beebe*	1153 Grand Oaks Dr, Howell MI 48843	517-548-4372	R	23*	.1
39	Clayton H Landis Company Inc—*James Landis*	476 Meetinghouse Rd, Souderton PA 18964	215-723-7284	R	23*	.2
40	Witron Integrated Logistics Inc—*Karl Hoegen*	3721 N Ventura Dr Ste, Arlington Heights IL 60004	847-385-6000	R	22*	.2
41	Pevco Systems International Inc—*Fred Valerino Jr*	1401 Tangier Dr, Middle River MD 21220	410-931-8800	R	22*	<.1
42	Saginaw Products Corp—*Nicolaos Rapanos*	68 Williamson St, Saginaw MI 48601	989-753-1411	R	22*	.2
43	C and M Conveyor Inc—*Jeff Smeathers*	4598 State Rd 37, Mitchell IN 47446	812-849-5647	R	21*	.2
44	Screw Conveyor Corp—*Garry Abraham*	700 Hoffman St, Hammond IN 46327	219-931-1450	R	21*	.1
45	Diversified Conveyors Inc—*Elizabeth Phillips*	3160 Directors Row, Memphis TN 38131	901-396-5370	R	21*	<.1
46	Chantland-Pvs Co—*Jim Nickleson*	PO Box 69, Humboldt IA 50548	515-332-4040	R	19*	.2
47	Rotec Industries Inc—*Alan Ledger*	270 Industrial Dr, Hampshire IL 60140	847-683-1809	R	19*	.1
48	Roach Manufacturing Corp—*Gay Roach*	PO Box 1310, Trumann AR 72472	870-483-7631	R	19*	.3
49	American Pulverizer Co—*Chris Griesedieck*	1319 Macklind Ave, Saint Louis MO 63110	314-781-6100	R	18*	.1
50	Smalley Manufactring Company Inc—*Dale Roberto*	10640 Dutchtown Rd, Knoxville TN 37932	865-966-5866	R	18*	.1
51	Boneal Inc—*Oliver Gannon*	PO Box 49, Means KY 40346	606-768-3620	R	18*	.1
52	Southern Systems Inc—*Leon Linton*	4101 Viscount Ave, Memphis TN 38118	901-362-7340	R	17*	.1
53	Dairy Conveyor Corp—*Gary Freudenberg*	PO Box 411, Brewster NY 10509	845-278-7878	R	17*	.1
54	Kws Manufacturing Company Ltd—*Mark Osborn*	3041 Conveyor Dr, Burleson TX 76028	817-295-2247	R	17*	.1
55	Itoh Denki USA Inc—*Kazuo Itoh*	135 Stewart Rd, Hanover Township PA 18706	570-820-8811	R	17*	<.1
56	Rapat Corp—*Thomas Sparrow*	919 Odonnel St, Hawley MN 56549	218-483-3344	R	17*	.1
57	W Meyer William And Sons Inc—*William Meyer*	1700 Franklin Blvd, Libertyville IL 60048	847-918-0111	R	17*	.1
58	Garvey Corp—*William Garvey*	208 S Rte 73, Hammonton NJ 08037	609-561-2450	R	16*	.1
59	Systec Corp—*Richard Harris*	10010 Conveyor Dr, Indianapolis IN 46235	317-890-9230	R	15*	.1
60	Evana Tool and Engineering Inc—*William Phillips*	5825 Old Boonville Hwy, Evansville IN 47715	812-479-8246	R	15*	.1
61	Versa Handling Co	12995 Hillview, Detroit MI 48227	313-491-0500	R	15*	<.1
62	Lewco Inc—*Ronald Guerra*	706 Ln St, Sandusky OH 44870	419-625-4014	R	15*	.1
63	R/K Belting Specialties Inc—*James Reilly*	PO Box 18520, Erlanger KY 41018	859-525-2358	R	14*	.1
64	Designed Conveyor Systems Inc—*David Belt*	1886 Gen George Patton, Franklin TN 37067	615-377-9774	R	14*	.1
65	Nol-Tec Systems Inc—*Vern Hudalla*	425 Apollo Dr, Circle Pines MN 55014	651-780-8600	R	13*	.1
66	Multi-Conveyor LLC—*Dennis Orseske*	PO Box 10, Winneconne WI 54986	920-582-7960	R	13*	.1
67	Ingalls Conveyors Inc—*Bill Ingalls*	140 E Whittier Blvd, Montebello CA 90640	323-837-9900	R	13*	<.1
68	Cinetic Sorting Corp—*Thomas Barry*	PO Box 17167, Louisville KY 40217	502-636-1414	R	12*	.1
69	Carman Industries Inc—*C Hyslop*	PO Box 579, Jeffersonville IN 47131	812-288-4700	R	12*	.1
70	Smoot Co—*Lewis Ribich*	1250 Seminary St, Kansas City KS 66103	913-362-1710	D	12*	.1

Note: An asterisk (*) indicates an estimated financial figure. The company type code used is as follows: R = Private, P = Public, S = Private Subsidiary, B = Public Subsidiary, D = Division, J = Joint Venture, I = Investment Fund.

COMPANY RANKINGS BY SALES WITHIN 4-DIGIT SIC

Rank	Company Name—Executive Officer	Address, City, State, Zip	Phone	Type	Fin	Empls
71	NCC Automated Systems Inc—Kevin Mauger	255 Schoolhouse Rd, Souderton PA 18964	215-721-1900	R	12*	<.1
72	Shuttleworth Inc—Carol Shuttleworth	10 Commercial Rd, Huntington IN 46750	260-356-8500	R	12*	.1
73	US Conveyor Technologies Manufacturing Inc—Kent Graves	30000 Illinois Rte 9, Mackinaw IL 61755	309-359-4088	R	12*	<.1
74	Conveyor Technologies Of Sanford NC Inc—Tim Pilson	5313 Womack Rd, Sanford NC 27330	919-776-7227	R	12*	.1
75	Unex Manufacturing Inc—Brian Neuwirth	50 Progress Pl, Jackson NJ 08527	732-982-2800	R	12*	.1
76	Stockton Tri-Industries Inc—Fred Wells	PO Box 6097, Stockton CA 95206	209-948-9701	R	12*	.1
77	JR Custom Metal Products Inc—Patricia Koehler	2237 S W St Ct, Wichita KS 67213	316-263-1318	R	12*	.1
78	Meyer Industries Inc—Eugene Teeter	PO Box 5460, San Antonio TX 78201	210-736-1811	R	11*	.1
79	Conveyor Eng and Manufacturing Co—Joseph Cone	1345 76th Ave Sw, Cedar Rapids IA 52404	319-364-5600	R	11*	.1
80	Sterling Blower Co—David Snowman	135 Vista Centre Dr, Forest VA 24551	434-316-5310	R	11*	.1
81	Century Conveyor Service Inc—Ronald Ferrara	4 Gladys Ct, Edison NJ 08817	732-248-4900	R	11*	<.1
82	Can Lines Engineering Inc—Keenan Koplien	PO Box 7039, Downey CA 90241	562-861-2996	R	11*	<.1
83	Irwin Car and Equipment Inc—William Baker	PO Box 409, Irwin PA 15642	724-864-8900	R	11*	.1
84	Hansen Manufacturing Corp—Gary Anderson	5100 W 12th St, Sioux Falls SD 57107	605-332-3200	R	11*	.1
85	KFT Inc—Ronald Eubanks	726 Mehring Way, Cincinnati OH 45203	513-241-5910	R	11*	.1
86	Ralphs-Pugh Company Inc—William Pugh	3931 Oregon St, Benicia CA 94510	707-745-6363	R	11*	.1
87	Altron Automation Inc—Ronald Mcnees	3523 Highland Dr, Hudsonville MI 49426	616-669-7711	R	10*	.1
88	Pride Conveyance Systems Inc—Shannon Pride	1781 Shelton Dr, Hollister CA 95023	831-637-1787	R	10*	.1
89	Advanced Manufacturing Technology For Bottles Inc—Thomas Ingraham	3920 Patton Ave, Loveland CO 80538	970-612-0315	R	10*	.1
90	Padgett Manufacturing Inc—Arthur Fowler	2915 62nd Ave E, Bradenton FL 34203	941-756-8566	R	10*	.1
91	Essmueller Co—William Mc Lean	PO Box 1966, Laurel MS 39441	601-649-2400	R	10*	.1
92	Aggregates Equipment Inc—D Stairs	PO Box 39, Leola PA 17540	717-656-2131	R	10*	<.1
93	Tsubaki Conveyor Of America Inc—Hirokazu Iba	138 Davis St, Portland TN 37148	615-325-9221	R	10*	.1
94	Alba Manufacturing Inc—Tom Moon	8950 Seward Rd, Fairfield OH 45011	513-874-0551	R	10*	.1
95	Pack Air Inc—Randy Carry	449 S Green Bay Rd, Neenah WI 54956	920-727-3000	R	10*	.1
96	Continntal Screw Conveyor Corp—Terry Adcock	4343 Easton Rd, Saint Joseph MO 64503	816-233-1800	R	10*	.1
97	Waconia Manufacturing Inc—Gary Burau	33 E 8th St, Waconia MN 55387	952-442-4450	R	9*	.1
98	Hohl Machine And Conveyor Company Inc—Richard Milazzo	1580 Niagara St, Buffalo NY 14213	716-882-7210	R	9*	.1
99	Le Fiell Co—Baldwin S Schmidt	5601 Echo Ave, Reno NV 89506	775-677-5300	R	9*	<.1
100	Custom Metal Designs Inc—Steven Grimes	PO Box 783037, Winter Garden FL 34778	407-656-7771	R	9*	.1
101	Dcl Inc—Reinhard Matye	PO Box 125, Charlevoix MI 49720	231-547-5600	R	9*	.1
102	Continental Steel And Conveyor Co—Robert Bisbee	1600 Dora St, Kansas City MO 64106	816-471-7200	R	9*	.1
103	Bonntech International Inc—Martin Bonneson	1700 Division St, New London WI 54961	920-982-4030	R	9*	.1
104	Wilkie Brothers Conveyors Inc—Robert Wilkie	PO Box 219, Marysville MI 48040	810-364-4820	R	9*	.1
105	Automation and Modular Components Inc—Richard Shore	10301 Enterprise Dr, Davisburg MI 48350	248-922-4740	R	8*	.1
106	Divine Engineering Inc—Jared Hills	PO Box 1345, Cedar Rapids IA 52406	319-365-0564	R	8*	<.1
107	Container Handling Systems Corp—John Nalbach	621 E Plainfield Rd, Countryside IL 60525	708-482-9900	R	8*	<.1
108	Ohio Blow Pipe Co—Edward Fakeris	446 E 131st St, Cleveland OH 44108	216-681-7379	R	8*	.1
109	Con-Vey/Keystone Inc—Donald Goeckner	PO Box 1399, Roseburg OR 97470	541-672-5506	R	8*	.1
110	Allied Uniking Corporation Inc—Kenneth Anderson	4750 Cromwell Ave, Memphis TN 38118	901-365-7240	R	8*	.1
111	Clinton Machine Inc—Terry Loznak	PO Box 617, Ovid MI 48866	989-834-2235	R	8*	.1
112	Jorgensen Conveyors Inc—Chuck D'amico	10303 N Baehr Rd, Mequon WI 53092	262-242-3089	R	8*	.1
113	Rbt Services Inc—William Hart	218 Corporate Dr, Elizabethtown KY 42701	270-763-6649	R	8*	<.1
114	Industrial Screw Conveyors Inc—Ralph Jones	4133 Conveyor Dr, Burleson TX 76028	817-641-0691	R	7*	<.1
115	Titan Industries Inc—Dan Baumbach	735 Industrial Loop Rd, New London WI 54961	920-982-6600	R	7*	<.1
116	Rapid Industries Inc—Mary Sheets	PO Box 19259, Louisville KY 40259	502-968-3645	R	7*	.1
117	Uhrden Inc—Kenneth Cook	PO Box 705, Sugarcreek OH 44681	330-852-2411	R	7*	<.1
118	Capway Systems Inc—Pieter Capelleveen	725 Vogelsong Rd, York PA 17404	717-843-0003	R	7*	<.1
119	Metro Automation Inc—John Crossno	PO Box 168223, Irving TX 75016	972-659-1600	R	7*	<.1
120	Sweet Manufacturing Co—Alicia Sweet-Hupp	PO Box 1086, Springfield OH 45501	937-325-1511	R	7*	.1
121	Whirl-Air-Flow Corp—Edward Mueller	20055 177th St Nw, Big Lake MN 55309	763-262-1200	R	7*	<.1
122	Steel Master LLC—Julie Wood	2171 Excelsior Dr, Oxford MI 48371	248-969-9900	R	7*	<.1
123	Morrison Timing Screw Company Inc—Nick Wilson	335 W 194th St, Glenwood IL 60425	708-756-6660	R	7*	<.1
124	Vibra Screw Inc—Eugene Wahl	PO Box 229, Totowa NJ 07511	973-256-7410	R	7*	<.1
125	Douglas Manufacturing Company Inc—P Ross	300 Industrial Park Dr, Pell City AL 35125	205-884-1200	R	7*	<.1
126	North Mississippi Conveyor Company Inc—Darrick Vanderford	PO Box 1375, Oxford MS 38655	662-236-1000	R	7*	.1
127	Boston Dynamics Inc—Marc Raibert	78 4th Ave, Waltham MA 02451	617-868-5600	R	7*	<.1
128	K and K Mine Products Inc—Ed Kokolis	PO Box 160, Indiana PA 15701	724-463-5000	R	6*	.1
129	Action Equipment Company Inc—Andrew Laveine	PO Box 3100, Newberg OR 97132	503-537-1111	R	6*	<.1
130	Prime Conveyor Inc—James Robinson	8903 Louisiana St, Merrillville IN 46410	219-736-1994	R	6*	<.1
131	Rees-Memphis Inc—Richard Cowan	PO Box 13225, Memphis TN 38113	901-774-8830	R	6*	<.1
132	Shingle Belting—Renwick Keating	420 Drew Ct, King of Prussia PA 19406	610-239-6667	R	6*	<.1
133	Gough Econ Inc—David Risley	PO Box 668583, Charlotte NC 28266	704-399-4501	R	6*	<.1
134	Metzgar Conveyor Company Inc—D Richard Metzgar	901 Metzgar Dr, Comstock Park MI 49321	616-784-0930	R	6*	<.1
135	B W Sinclair Inc—Bobby Sinclair	PO Box 1111, Wichita Falls TX 76307	940-766-2556	R	6*	<.1
136	Vibra-Pro Company Inc—John O Roisum	PO Box 9227, Boise ID 83707	208-362-5548	R	6*	<.1
137	Communications Conveyor Company Inc—James Paul	PO Box 1718, Lake Dallas TX 75065	940-498-1850	R	6*	<.1
138	Master Solutions Inc—David Lutz	PO Box 4444, Carlisle PA 17013	717-243-6849	R	6*	<.1
139	Sardee Corporation Of California—Steve Sarovich	2731 E Myrtle St, Stockton CA 95205	209-466-1526	R	6*	<.1
140	Tuttle Inc—Gary Tuttle	110 Page St, Friend NE 68359	402-947-9391	R	6*	<.1
141	Air Conveying Corp—Richard Johnson	2196 E Person Ave, Memphis TN 38114	901-454-5016	R	6*	<.1
142	Icb LLC—Iris Chasteen	PO Box 7648, Charlotte NC 28241	704-333-3377	R	6*	<.1
143	Gudel Inc—Jeff Stadler	4881 Runway Blvd, Ann Arbor MI 48108	734-214-0000	R	6*	<.1
144	Tecnetics Industries Inc—John Madgett	1811 Buerkle Rd, Saint Paul MN 55110	651-777-4780	R	6*	<.1
145	Automated Systems Inc—Bruce Claycomb	2400 Commercial Dr, Auburn Hills MI 48326	248-373-5600	R	5*	<.1
146	Grob Systems Inc—Ralf Bronnenmeier	1070 Navajo Dr, Bluffton OH 45817	419-358-9015	R	5*	.2
147	Creative Ergonomic Systems Inc—Gerald Vanneste	6301 Hughes Dr, Sterling Heights MI 48312	586-939-9939	R	5*	<.1
148	Fabacraft Inc—William Sieber	201 Grandin Rd, Maineville OH 45039	513-677-0500	R	5*	<.1
149	Sager Metal Strip Company LLC—Kay Frank	100 Boone Dr, Michigan City IN 46360	219-874-3609	R	5*	<.1
150	Hostar International Inc—Claudia Berg	15000 Cross Creek Pkwy, Newbury OH 44065	440-564-7400	R	5*	<.1
151	American Conveyor Corp—Valdi Freidman	1819 Flushing Ave, Ridgewood NY 11385	718-386-0480	R	5*	<.1
152	James Eagen Sons Co—James Golden	PO Box 4097, Wyoming PA 18644	570-693-2100	R	5*	<.1
153	Ashtech Corp—Gerald Deroy	PO Box 24129, Cleveland OH 44124	440-646-9911	R	5*	<.1
154	Hoover Conveyor and Fabrication Corp—Jerry Hoover	262 Industrial Park Rd, Meyersdale PA 15552	814-634-5431	R	5*	<.1
155	Mid-States Corp—Donald Bartolini	3245 Holeman Ave, S Chicago Hts IL 60411	708-754-1760	R	5*	<.1
156	B and R Sheet Metal Inc—Bob Wheat	29495 W Enid Rd, Eugene OR 97402	541-688-2536	R	5*	<.1
157	Ranger Conveying and Supply Company Inc—Brent Singer	4701 Clinton Dr, Houston TX 77020	713-671-0004	R	5*	<.1
158	Dynapace Acquisition LLC—Bell Patterson	PO Box 7, Palatine IL 60078	847-398-5757	R	5*	<.1
159	Alliance Industrial Corp—Gary Garner	208 Tomahawk Industria, Lynchburg VA 24502	434-239-2641	R	5*	<.1

Rank	Company Name—*Executive Officer*	Address, City, State, Zip	Phone	Type	Fin	Empls
160	Austin-Mac Inc—*George Austin*	PO Box 3746, Seattle WA 98124	206-624-7066	R	5*	<.1
161	Cross Brothers Company Inc—*Thomas Pavone*	3353 Brghton Hnrtta Tl, Rochester NY 14623	585-427-7850	R	4*	<.1
162	National Conveyors Company Inc—*Donald Brant*	33 Nicholson Rd, East Granby CT 06026	860-653-0374	R	4*	<.1
163	Wilson Manufacturing And Design Inc—*Raymond Miller*	1011 E Main St, Cecilia KY 42724	270-862-3265	R	4*	<.1
164	Eagle Pneumatic Inc—*Karl Kondolf*	3902 Industry Blvd, Lakeland FL 33811	863-644-4870	R	4*	<.1
165	Hosch Company LP—*Randy Gardner*	1002 International Dr, Oakdale PA 15071	724-695-3002	R	4*	<.1
166	Sandusky Fabricating and Sales Inc—*Timothy Shenigo*	2000 Superior St, Sandusky OH 44870	419-626-4465	R	4*	<.1
167	Traycon Manufacturing Company Inc—*August Pisto*	555 Barell Ave, Carlstadt NJ 07072	201-939-5555	R	4*	<.1
168	Spectrum Automation Co—*Richard Zimmerman*	34447 Schoolcraft Rd, Livonia MI 48150	734-522-2160	R	4*	<.1
169	Barrington Automation Ltd—*Al Mueller*	9116 Virginia Rd, Lake In The Hills IL 60156	847-458-0900	R	4*	<.1
170	Heco-Pacific Manufacturing Inc—*Malik Alarab*	1510 Pacific St, Union City CA 94587	510-487-1155	R	4*	<.1
171	Global Manufacturing Inc—*Catherine Janosky*	PO Box 3824, Little Rock AR 72203	501-374-7416	R	4*	<.1
172	Laros Equipment Company Inc—*George Laure*	8278 Shaver Rd, Portage MI 49024	269-323-1441	R	4*	<.1
173	National Conveyor Corp—*Jared Ufland*	2250 Yates Ave, Commerce CA 90040	323-725-0355	R	4*	<.1
174	Rebsco Inc—*Tyeis Baker-Baumann*	PO Box 423, Greenville OH 45331	937-548-2246	R	4*	<.1
175	Flexoveyor Industries Inc—*David Huddleston*	3795 Paris St Unit D, Denver CO 80239	303-375-0200	R	4*	<.1
176	Deamco Corp—*Nick Kanian*	6520 E Washington Blvd, Commerce CA 90040	323-890-1190	R	3*	<.1
177	Macawber Engineering Inc—*Michael Crawley*	1829 Clydesdale St, Maryville TN 37801	865-984-5286	R	3*	<.1
178	D and D Products Inc—*Jane Dauffenbach*	PO Box 215, North Prairie WI 53153	262-392-2162	R	3*	<.1
179	Pacific Conveyor Systems Inc—*Leo Blair*	1535 E Edinger Ave, Santa Ana CA 92705	714-557-7420	R	3*	<.1
180	Jayhawk Millwright and Erectors Company Inc—*Phillip Heavelow*	811 S Coy St, Kansas City KS 66105	913-371-5212	R	3*	<.1
181	American Ultraviolet West Inc—*Meredith Stines*	23555 Telo Ave, Torrance CA 90505	310-784-2930	R	3*	<.1
182	Tekno Inc—*Tom Clopton*	1 Wall St, Cave City KY 42127	270-773-4181	R	3*	<.1
183	Tarlton C and T Company Inc—*Curtis Tarlton*	967 Lehigh Ave, Union NJ 07083	908-964-9400	R	3*	.1
184	Uni-Pak Corp—*Jeff Coutant*	PO Box 522168, Longwood FL 32752	407-830-9300	R	3*	<.1
185	Keenline Conveyor Systems Inc—*David Kersztyn*	1936 Chase Dr, Omro WI 54963	920-685-0365	D	3*	<.1
186	Kinergy Corp—*George Dumbaugh*	7310 Grade Ln, Louisville KY 40219	502-366-5685	R	3	<.1
187	Riley Equipment Inc—*Charles Riley*	PO Box 435, Vincennes IN 47591	812-886-5500	R	3*	<.1
188	Frazier and Son LP—*Joan Frazier*	PO Box 2847, Conroe TX 77305	936-494-4040	R	3*	<.1
189	Beaumont Birch Co	PO Box 3006, Malvern PA 19355	610-647-9900	S	3*	<.1
190	American Iron-Steel Manufacturing Company Inc—*Geff Gutmann*	757 Whispering Meadows, Ballwin MO 63021	314-645-5819	R	3*	<.1
191	International Material Handling Equipment Ltd—*Jim Carter*	PO Box 87, Oskaloosa IA 52577	641-673-4781	R	3*	<.1
192	Innovative Handling and Metalfab LLC—*Tom Curry*	7755 Sylvania Ave, Sylvania OH 43560	419-882-7480	R	3*	<.1
193	Transcon Inc—*John Musial*	PO Box 29, Mentor OH 44061	440-255-7600	R	3*	<.1
194	Sst Conveyor Components Inc—*Winfield Scott*	154 Commerce Dr, Loveland OH 45140	513-583-5500	R	3*	<.1
195	Flo-Pro Systems Inc—*Charles Hall*	415 4th St W, Milan IL 61264	309-787-9868	R	3*	<.1
196	Dean Research Corp—*George Vetter*	8100 Nw 97th Ter, Kansas City MO 64153	816-891-7800	R	3*	<.1
197	Duplex Mill and Manufacturing Co—*Eric Wise*	PO Box 1266, Springfield OH 45501	937-325-5555	R	3*	<.1
198	Industrial Service And Installation Inc—*Steven Smith*	PO Box 436, Emigsville PA 17318	717 767-1129	R	2*	.1
199	Airtube Service Company LLC—*Mark Walters*	4 Newport Dr Ste B, Forest Hill MD 21050	410-893-1020	R	2*	<.1
200	Dpcc LLC	10241 W Main St, Kalamazoo MI 49009	269-375-9455	R	2*	<.1
201	Tmp Acquisition Inc—*John Beir*	400 Riverside Ave, Torrington CT 06790	860-482-8566	R	2*	<.1
202	Kornylak Corp—*Thomas Kornylak*	400 Heaton St, Hamilton OH 45011	513-863-1277	R	2*	<.1
203	Mid-South Conveying Inc—*Rick Reid*	PO Box 1209, Collierville TN 38027	901-853-5335	R	2*	<.1
204	Rigs Sheet Metal—*Yury Anguiano*	14501 Joanbridge St, Baldwin Park CA 91706	626-813-6621	R	2*	<.1
205	CSS International Corp—*Herbert V Coulston*	PO Box 19560, Philadelphia PA 19124	215-533-6110	R	2*	<.1
206	Mill Power Inc—*Dale Tompkins*	3141 Sw High Desert Dr, Prineville OR 97754	541-447-1100	R	2*	<.1
207	Smock Materials Handling Company Inc—*William Smock*	3420 Park Davis Cir, Indianapolis IN 46235	317-890-3200	R	2*	<.1
208	S2F Engineering Inc—*Steve Dobson*	324 Sherman St, Blissfield MI 49228	517-486-5737	R	2*	<.1
209	Tec Engineering Corp—*Maurice Minardi*	31 Town Forest Rd, Oxford MA 01540	508-987-0231	R	2*	<.1
210	Serpentix Conveyor Corp—*Mark Alldredge*	9085 Marshall Ct, Westminster CO 80031	303-430-8427	R	2*	<.1
211	Continental Crane and Service—*Edward Dungan*	33681 Groesbeck Hwy, Fraser MI 48026	586-294-7900	R	2*	<.1
212	Oakes Equipment Company Inc—*Robert Stachowicz*	9761 York Alpha Dr, North Royalton OH 44133	440-237-2010	R	2*	<.1
213	Hovair Systems Inc—*Gus Hart*	6912 S 220th St Bldg 3, Kent WA 98032	253-872-0405	R	2*	<.1
214	Arkansas Independent Millwrights—*Teresa Bradley*	830 Hwy 240, Morrilton AR 72110	501-354-0184	R	2*	<.1
215	Jantec Inc—*Ronald Sommerfield*	1777 Northern Star Dr, Traverse City MI 49696	231-941-4339	R	2*	<.1
216	Vertical Systems International LLC—*Daniel Quinn*	PO Box 176490, Covington KY 41017	859-485-9650	R	2*	<.1
217	Feedall Inc—*Roger Winslow*	38379 Pelton Rd, Willoughby OH 44094	440-942-8100	R	2*	<.1
218	Colombo Sales and Engineering Inc—*Harry Colombo*	2321 Wolcott St, Ferndale MI 48220	248-547-2820	R	1*	<.1
219	Process Automation Technologies Inc—*Bruce Campbell*	132 Buckeye Cove Rd, Swannanoa NC 28778	828-298-1055	R	1*	<.1
220	Custom Conveyor Inc—*James Stapp*	4858 E State Rd 46, Greensburg IN 47240	812-663-2023	R	1*	<.1
221	Erie Manufacturing Inc—*Phil Dosso*	1520 Centennial Blvd, Bartow FL 33830	863-534-3743	R	1*	<.1
222	Felco Industries Ltd—*John Felton*	PO Box 16750, Missoula MT 59808	406-728-9103	R	1*	<.1
223	Gardner Machinery Corp—*Richard Gardner*	PO Box 33818, Charlotte NC 28233	704-372-3890	R	1*	<.1
224	Dover Conveyor and Equipment Co—*Joseph J Coniglio*	PO Box 300, Midvale OH 44653	740-922-9390	R	1*	<.1
225	Bmco Industries Inc—*Bruno Pironio*	159 Frances Ave, Cranston RI 02910	401-781-6884	R	1*	<.1
226	Chip Systems International—*Jeff Dudley*	10953 Norscott St, Scotts MI 49088	269-626-8000	R	1*	<.1
227	Production Systems Inc—*Michael Anderson*	850 Mountain Industria, Marietta GA 30060	770-424-9784	R	1*	<.1
228	New Castle Company Inc—*Dennis Alduk*	3812 Wilmington Rd, New Castle PA 16105	724-658-4516	R	1*	<.1
229	Dyna Veyor Inc—*Beverly Ayre*	10 Hudson St, Newark NJ 07103	973-484-1119	R	1*	<.1
230	Conveying Industries Inc—*David Huddleston*	3795 Paris St Unit D, Denver CO 80239	303-373-2035	R	1*	<.1
231	Creative Systems Inc—*A Wiles*	3068 Ashley Dr, Edgewood KY 41017	859-341-0026	R	1*	<.1
232	Bel-Fab Co—*Patrick Bellows*	PO Box 786, Rogersville TN 37857	423-235-4163	R	<1*	<.1
233	Ledow Company Inc—*Leon Downing*	PO Box 527, Akron OH 44309	330-376-7297	R	<1*	<.1
234	QC Industries LLC—*Dave Endres*	4057 Clough Woods Dr, Batavia OH 45103	513-753-6000	R	<1*	<.1
235	Thoreson McCosh Inc—*David Klatt*	1885 Thunderbird St, Troy MI 48084	248-362-0960	R	N/A	.1

TOTALS: SIC 3535 Conveyors & Conveying Equipment

Companies: 235					9,803	19.3

3536 Hoists, Cranes & Monorails

Rank	Company Name—*Executive Officer*	Address, City, State, Zip	Phone	Type	Fin	Empls
1	Demag Cranes and Components Corp—*John Paxton*	PO Box 39245, Cleveland OH 44139	440-248-2400	R	168*	.4
2	Morris Material Handling Inc—*Fabio Fiorino*	PO Box M2015, Milwaukee WI 53201	414-764-6200	R	107*	1.0
3	Applied Hydraulic Systems Inc—*Robert Nelson*	311 Industrial Ave C, Houma LA 70363	985-851-5600	S	79*	.1
4	Harsh International Inc—*Robert Brown*	600 Oak Ave, Eaton CO 80615	970-454-2291	R	78*	.1
5	Iowa Mold Tooling Company Inc—*Steve Fairbanks*	500 W US Highway 18, Garner IA 50438	641-923-3711	S	60*	.4
6	Crane Equipment and Service Inc—*Tim Tivens*	16615 E Admiral Pl Ste, Tulsa OK 74116	918-437-2562	D	60*	.1
7	Konecranes Americas Inc—*Steve Kosir*	7300 Chippewa Blvd, Houston TX 77086	281-445-2225	S	56*	.1

Note: An asterisk (*) indicates an estimated financial figure. The company type code used is as follows: R = Private, P = Public, S = Private Subsidiary, B = Public Subsidiary, D = Division, J = Joint Venture, I = Investment Fund.

COMPANY RANKINGS BY SALES WITHIN 4-DIGIT SIC

Rank	Company Name—*Executive Officer*	Address, City, State, Zip	Phone	Type	Fin	Empls
8	American Handling Systems Inc—*Mike Olson*	191 N Rush Lake Rd, Laurens IA 50554	712-841-4548	R	52*	.1
9	American Crane and Equipment—*Oddvar Norheim*	531 Old Swede Rd, Douglassville PA 19518	610-385-6061	R	52*	.1
10	Hydralift AmClyde Inc—*Robert E Cook*	240 Plato Blvd E, Saint Paul MN 55107	651-293-4646	S	45*	.3
11	Proserv Crane and Equipment Inc—*Neal Wilson*	PO Box 670965, Houston TX 77267	281-405-9048	R	45*	.1
12	Gorbel Inc—*David Reh*	PO Box 593, Fishers NY 14453	585-924-6262	R	37*	.3
13	Gunnebo Corporation U S A—*William Shenloogian*	1240 N Harvard Ave, Tulsa OK 74115	918-832-8933	R	33*	.2
14	Whiting Corp—*Jeffrey Kahn*	26000 S Whiting Way, Monee IL 60449	708-587-2100	R	31*	.2
15	Sunstream Corp—*Ken Hey*	22149 68th Ave S, Kent WA 98032	253-395-0500	R	30*	<.1
16	Deuer Manufacturing Inc—*Marvin H Sauner*	PO Box 4014, Dayton OH 45401	937-254-3812	R	30	.2
17	Deshazo Crane Company LLC—*Guy Mitchell Lll*	PO Box 1450, Alabaster AL 35007	205-664-2006	R	23*	.2
18	Marine Travelift Inc—*Steve Pfeifer*	PO Box 66, Sturgeon Bay WI 54235	920-743-6202	R	23*	.1
19	American Crane Corp	202 Raleigh St, Wilmington NC 28412	910-395-8500	S	22*	.2
20	Zenar Corp—*John Maiwald*	PO Box 107, Oak Creek WI 53154	414-764-1800	R	20*	.1
21	Foley Material Handling Company Inc—*Dale Foley*	PO Box 289, Ashland VA 23005	804-798-1343	R	19*	.1
22	Frost Inc—*Charles Frost*	2900 Northridge Dr NW, Grand Rapids MI 49544	616-453-7781	R	17*	.1
23	Detroit Hoist and Crane Company LLC—*Chuck Melder*	6650 Sterling Dr N, Sterling Heights MI 48312	586-268-2600	R	15*	<.1
24	Battery Handling Systems Inc—*William Huber*	PO Box 28990, Saint Louis MO 63132	314-423-7091	R	14*	.1
25	Nai Cranes LLC—*Bernadette Groves*	80 Holton St, Woburn MA 01801	781-897-4100	R	13*	.1
26	American Crane And Hoist Corp—*Arthur Leon*	1234 Washington St, Boston MA 02118	617-482-8383	R	13*	.1
27	Hi-Tide Sales Inc—*Donald Wood*	4050 Selvitz Rd, Fort Pierce FL 34981	772-461-4660	R	10*	.1
28	Westmont Industries—*Diane Henderson*	10805 Painter Ave, Santa Fe Springs CA 90670	562-275-7067	R	9*	.1
29	Omi Crane Systems Inc—*Mike Bunnel*	PO Box 1719, Rockwall TX 75087	972-636-8000	R	7*	.1
30	Reimann and Georger Corp—*E Von Dungen*	PO Box 681, Buffalo NY 14240	716-895-1156	R	7*	.1
31	Wolverine Crane and Service Inc—*Rich Kelps*	2557 Thornwood St Sw, Grand Rapids MI 49519	616-538-4870	R	7*	<.1
32	Emh Inc—*Edis Hazne*	550 Crane Dr, Valley City OH 44280	330-220-8600	R	6*	<.1
33	Trambeam Corp—*Ronald Weiskircher*	PO Box 211, Attalla AL 35954	256-538-9983	R	6*	<.1
34	Contrx Industries Inc—*Ronald Phillips*	1377 Kimberly Dr, Neenah WI 54956	920-722-0101	R	6*	<.1
35	Quality Boat Lifts Inc—*Charles Sargent*	7600 Alico Rd Ste 12, Fort Myers FL 33912	239-432-9110	R	6*	<.1
36	Hy-H Manufacturing Company Inc—*Ed Willis*	915 W Blue Starr Dr, Claremore OK 74017	918-341-6811	R	6*	<.1
37	Letellier Material Handling Equipment Inc—*Ronald Letellier*	16650 State St, South Holland IL 60473	708-339-0545	R	6*	<.1
38	Overhead Material Handling Inc—*Mike Obermeier*	7747 S 6th St, Oak Creek WI 53154	414-768-9090	R	6*	<.1
39	Electro Lift Inc—*David Erenstoft*	PO Box 827, Clifton NJ 07015	973-778-5127	R	5*	<.1
40	Production Equipment Co—*Rebecca Davis*	401 Liberty St, Meriden CT 06450	203-235-5795	R	4*	<.1
41	Equipment Fabricators Inc—*Michael Olsen*	655 Cidco Rd, Cocoa FL 32926	321-632-0990	R	4*	<.1
42	Ace Boat Lifts LLC—*Glen Kinley*	2211 Tamiami Trl S, Venice FL 34293	941-493-8100	R	4*	<.1
43	Lincoln Precision Machining Co—*David Hallen*	PO Box 458, North Grafton MA 01536	508-839-2175	R	3*	<.1
44	Lithibar Matik Inc—*Larry Dutkiewicz*	13521 Quality Dr, Holland MI 49424	616-399-5215	S	3*	<.1
45	Mobile Equipment Co—*Evelyn Stanfill*	3610 Gilmore Ave, Bakersfield CA 93308	661-327-8476	R	3*	<.1
46	Yale Industrial Products Inc—*Timothy Tevens*	140 John James Audubon, Amherst NY 14228	716-689-5400	S	3*	<.1
47	Imm Survivor Inc—*George Becker*	17030 Alico Ctr Rd, Fort Myers FL 33967	239-454-7020	R	3*	<.1
48	Cms-Crane Manufacturing and Service—*Dave Corbett*	PO Box 510820, New Berlin WI 53151	262-785-4440	R	3*	<.1
49	Milwaukee International Inc—*Arthur Pascuzzi*	10250 Sw N Dakota St, Tigard OR 97223	503-639-8891	R	2*	<.1
50	General Crane And Hoist Inc—*Gary Russell*	PO Box 1059, Richmond Hill GA 31324	912-756-2872	R	2*	<.1
51	TG Industries Inc—*Terry Luscombe*	PO Box 109, Armstrong IA 50514	712-864-3737	R	2*	<.1
52	BE Wallace Products Corp—*Sherry De Carville*	71 N Bacton Hill Rd, Malvern PA 19355	610-647-1400	R	2*	<.1
53	Washington Equipment Manufacturing Company Inc—*John Rouse*	PO Box 3703, Spokane WA 99220	509-244-4773	R	2*	<.1
54	North Pacific Crane Company LLC—*Virginia English*	10734 Lake City Way Ne, Seattle WA 98125	206-361-7064	R	1*	<.1
55	East Coast Hoist Inc—*Theodore Harrison*	105 Keystone Dr, Telford PA 18969	215-257-0155	R	1*	.1
56	Manitowoc Cranes Inc	PO Box 70, Manitowoc WI 54221	920-684-6621	D	N/A	N/A

TOTALS: SIC 3536 Hoists, Cranes & Monorails
Companies: 56 — 1,270 — 5.9

3537 Industrial Trucks & Tractors

Rank	Company Name—*Executive Officer*	Address, City, State, Zip	Phone	Type	Fin	Empls
1	Caterpillar Inc—*Douglas R Oberhelman*	100 NE Adams St, Peoria IL 61629	309-675-1000	P	42,588	104.5
2	NACCO Industries Inc—*Alfred M Rankin Jr*	5875 Landerbrook Dr St, Cleveland OH 44124	440-449-9600	P	3,331	8.9
3	Volvo Trucks North America Inc—*Dennis Slagle*	PO Box 26115, Greensboro NC 27402	336-393-2000	S	1,737*	5.0
4	CC Industries Inc—*William H Crown*	222 N LaSalle St 8th F, Chicago IL 60601	312-855-4000	S	1,560*	6.0
5	Crown Equipment Corp—*James F Dicke III*	44 S Washington St, New Bremen OH 45869	419-629-2311	R	1,049*	7.6
6	Telair International Inc—*Hector Plaza*	4175 Guardian St, Simi Valley CA 93063	805-306-8066	S	911*	.2
7	Cascade Corp—*Robert C Warren Jr*	2201 NE 201st Ave, Fairview OR 97024	503-669-6300	P	410	1.8
8	West Bend Mutual Insurance Co—*Kevin Steiner*	1900 S 18th Ave, West Bend WI 53095	262-334-5571	R	395*	1.0
9	Dexter Axle—*William Jones*	PO Box 250, Elkhart IN 46515	574-295-7888	S	299*	1.7
10	Heil Trailer International—*Andy Fincher*	5741 Cornelison Rd Ste, Chattanooga TN 37411	423-499-1300	S	258*	1.5
11	JCM Industries Inc—*Ronald Collins*	PO Box 1220, Nash TX 75569	903-832-2581	R	182*	.1
12	Linde Material Handling North America Corp—*Brain Butler*	PO Box 2400, Summerville SC 29484	843-875-8000	R	167*	.2
13	Raymond Corp (Greene New York)—*James L Malvaso*	22 S Canal St, Greene NY 13778	607-656-2311	R	148*	1.0
14	Gradall Industries Inc—*Mike Haberman*	406 Mill Ave SW, New Philadelphia OH 44663	330-339-2211	R	141*	.7
15	Toyota Material Handling USA Inc—*Jeff Rufener*	PO Box 17419, Irvine CA 92623		S	122*	.7
16	Mitsubishi Caterpillar Forklift America Inc—*Hideaki Ninomiya*	2121 W Sam Houston Pkw, Houston TX 77043	713-365-1000	R	98*	1.1
17	Angus Industries Inc—*Robert Kluver*	PO Box 610, Watertown SD 57201	605-886-5681	R	82*	1.0
18	Taylor Machine Works Inc—*William Taylor*	650 N Church Ave, Louisville MS 39339	662-773-3421	R	70*	.8
19	Knight Industries and Associates Inc—*James Zaguroli*	1140 Centre Rd, Auburn Hills MI 48326	248-377-4950	R	66*	.2
20	Landoll Corp—*Dan Caffrey*	PO Box 111, Marysville KS 66508	785-562-5381	R	56*	.5
21	Henderson Products Inc—*Mart Ward*	PO Box 40, Manchester IA 52057	563-927-2828	R	55*	.3
22	NACCO Materials Handling Group—*Michael Brogan* NACCO Industries Inc	4000 Blue Lake Rd, Fairview OR 97024	503-721-6000	S	43	.3
23	Ancra International LLC—*Steve Frediani*	4880 W Rosecrans Ave, Hawthorne CA 90250	310-973-5000	S	41*	.3
24	TC/American Monorail Inc (Saint Michael Minnesota)—*Jerry Lague*	12070 43rd St NE, Saint Michael MN 55376	763-497-7000	R	38*	.3
25	Southworth International Group Inc—*Lewis Cabot*	PO Box 1380, Portland ME 04104	207-878-0700	R	36*	.3
26	Valley Craft Products Inc—*Mike Fiterman*	2001 S Hwy 61, Lake City MN 55041	651-345-3386	S	36*	.2
27	Autoquip Corp—*Joe Robillard*	PO Box 1058, Guthrie OK 73044	405-282-5200	S	35*	.1
28	Mustang Manufacturing Company Inc—*William Gehl*	1880 Austin Rd, Owatonna MN 55060	507-451-7112	S	34*	.2
29	Perry Slingsby Systems Inc	10642 W Little York St, Houston TX 77041	713-329-8230	S	33*	.1
30	Otto Industries North America Inc—*Luc Mueller*	PO Box 410251, Charlotte NC 28241	704-588-9191	R	32*	.4
31	Harper Trucks Inc—*Phillip Ruffin*	PO Box 12330, Wichita KS 67277	316-942-1381	R	31*	.2
32	Wasp Inc—*Merle Wagner*	PO Box 249, Glenwood MN 56334	320-634-5126	R	31*	.2
33	Western Securities Company of Delaware—*Richard Johnson*	PO Box 12278, Omaha NE 68112	402-341-4939	R	30*	.2
34	Global Ground Support LLC—*Richard Smith*	540 E Hwy 56, Olathe KS 66061	913-780-0300	S	28*	.2

Rank	Company Name—*Executive Officer*	Address, City, State, Zip	Phone	Type	Fin	Empls
35	Taylor-Dunn Manufacturing Co—*Arthur Goodwin*	2114 W Ball Rd, Anaheim CA 92804	714-956-4040	R	25*	.2
36	Cargotec Solutions LLC—*Jorma Tirkkonen*	415 E Dundee St, Ottawa KS 66067	785-242-2200	R	23*	.4
37	Waltco Lift Corp—*Michael Militello*	PO Box 354, Tallmadge OH 44278	330-633-9191	R	22*	.2
38	United Rentals Aerial	226 McEvoy St, San Jose CA 95126	408-269-4989	D	21	.1
39	Wesco Industrial Products Inc—*Allen Apter*	PO Box 47, Lansdale PA 19446	215-699-7031	R	21*	.2
40	Harlo Corp—*Mary Crooks*	PO Box 129, Grandville MI 49468	616-538-0550	R	20*	.1
41	Goldco Industries Inc—*Richard Vandermeer*	5605 Goldco Dr, Loveland CO 80538	970-663-4770	R	20*	.1
42	Atap Inc—*Henry Washburn*	PO Box 98, Eastaboga AL 36260	256-362-2221	R	20*	.1
43	Hoist Liftruck Manufacturing Inc—*Martin Flaska*	6499 W 65th St, Bedford Park IL 60638	708-458-2200	R	19*	.1
44	ECOA Industrial Products Inc—*Steve Konop*	7700 NW 74th Ave, Medley FL 33166		R	19*	<.1
45	Bpr-Rico Manufacturing Inc—*David Mueller*	691 W Liberty St, Medina OH 44256	330-723-4050	R	16*	.1
46	Kandi Kountry Express Ltd—*Brian Weseman*	61381 Us Hwy 12, Litchfield MN 55355	320-693-7900	R	16*	.1
47	Pettibone/Traverse Lift LLC—*Pete Negro*	1100 S Superior Ave, Baraga MI 49908	906-353-6611	S	15*	.1
48	Garsite TSR Inc—*Steven Paul*	539 S 10 St, Kansas City KS 66105	913-342-5600	R	14*	.1
49	Princeton Delivery System—*Bill Pohl*	8170 Dove Pkwy, Canal Winchester OH 43110	614-834-5000	R	14*	.1
50	Magline Inc—*Michael Kirby*	1205 W Cedar St, Standish MI 48658	989-879-2411	R	13*	.1
51	Gapvax Inc—*Gary Pobrosky*	575 Central Ave, Johnstown PA 15902	814-535-6766	R	12*	.1
52	Nmc/Wollard Inc—*John Steingart*	2021 Truax Blvd, Eau Claire WI 54703	715-835-3151	R	12*	.1
53	Harlo Products Corp—*Mary Crooks* Harlo Corp	PO Box 129, Grandville MI 49468	616-538-0550	S	12*	.1
54	Tiger Manufacturing Corp—*C Schwark* Taylor-Dunn Manufacturing Co	PO Box 1340, Lees Summit MO 64063	816-525-3900	S	11*	.1
55	Southworth Products Corp—*Brian McNamara* Southworth International Group Inc	PO Box 1380, Portland ME 04104	207-878-0700	S	10*	.1
56	Kawasaki Construction	2140 Barrett Park Dr S, Kennesaw GA 30144	770-499-7000	D	10*	.1
57	Wiggins Lift Company Inc—*Mike Wiggins*	PO Box 5187, Oxnard CA 93031	805-485-7821	R	9*	.1
58	Kalamar Industries USA Inc—*Gilbert Pilz*	1301 Cherokee Trce, White Oak TX 75693	903-759-5490	R	9*	.1
59	Sfi Acquisition Inc—*Charles Peltz*	30550 W 8 Mile Rd, Farmington Hills MI 48336	248-471-1500	R	9*	.1
60	Shanafelt Manufacturing Co—*Leo Kovachic*	PO Box 7040, Canton OH 44705	330-455-0315	R	9*	.1
61	Fairbanks Co—*Robert Lahre*	PO Box 1871, Rome GA 30162	706-234-6701	R	9*	.1
62	Indiana Toyoshima Inc—*Yoshi Tanave*	735 Saint Paul St, Indianapolis IN 46203	317-638-3511	R	9*	<.1
63	Molded Plastic Industries Inc—*Frank Phillips*	PO Box 70, Holt MI 48842	517-694-7434	R	9*	.1
64	Brennan Equipment And Manufacturing Inc—*John Brennan*	730 Central Ave, University Park IL 60484	708-534-5500	R	9*	.1
65	Royal Tractor Company Inc—*Thomas Hardwick*	109 Overland Park Pl, New Century KS 66031	913-782-2598	R	9*	.1
66	Lift Moore Inc—*Herb Koenig*	7810 Pinemont Dr, Houston TX 77040	713-688-5533	R	8*	<.1
67	Phelps Industries Inc—*Ivo Phelps*	PO Box 1093, Little Rock AR 72203	501-375-1141	R	8*	.1
68	Master Engineering Inc—*Richard Eschman*	PO Box 705, Shepherdsville KY 40165	502-955-8299	R	8*	.1
69	Quality Corp—*Kenton Ensor*	PO Box 246, Littleton CO 80160	303-777-6608	R	8*	<.1
70	Clyde Machines Inc—*Sallie Boer*	PO Box 194, Glenwood MN 56334	320-634-4504	R	8*	.1
71	Columbia/Okura LLC—*Brian Hutton*	301 Grove St Ste A, Vancouver WA 98661	360-735-1952	R	8*	<.1
72	Alum-A-Lift Inc—*Stanley Bressner*	7909 Bankhead Hwy, Winston GA 30187	770-489-0328	R	8*	.1
73	Rightline Equipment Inc—*Jerry Hamlik*	PO Box 130, Rainier OR 97048	503-556-1761	R	8*	.1
74	Starlite Trailers Inc—*Nim Pope*	15251 S Hwy 66, Claremore OK 74017	918-341-6615	R	7*	.1
75	Pioneer Manufacturing Inc—*Randy Kozak*	PO Box 338, Spring Hill TN 37174	931-486-2296	R	7*	<.1
76	Overland Tank Inc—*Jerry Rush*	PO Box 2080, Abilene TX 79604	325-673-7132	R	6*	<.1
77	EZ- Dumper—*Nick Turano*	PO Box 70, Waynesboro PA 17268	717-762-1303	R	6*	<.1
78	General Aviation Industries Inc—*Paul Mauldin*	415 Jones Rd, Weatherford TX 76088	817-598-4848	R	6*	<.1
79	General Transervice Inc—*Michael Wilkinson*	140 Stewart Huston Dr, Coatesville PA 19320	610-857-1900	R	6*	<.1
80	Hoist Equipment Company Inc—*Nicholas Gambatesa*	26161 Cannon Rd, Bedford OH 44146	440 232-0300	R	5*	<.1
81	Stilson/Die-Draulic—*Jeff Smith*	15935 Sturgeon St, Roseville MI 48066	586-778-1100	S	5	<.1
82	Yale Materials Handling Corp—*Donald Chance* NACCO Industries Inc	1400 Sullivan Dr, Greenville NC 27834	252-758-9253	S	5	<.1
83	Stertil Alm Corp—*Douglas Grunnet*	200 Benchmark Industri, Streator IL 61364	815-673-5546	R	5*	<.1
84	Rush Gold Inc—*Glenn Hyneman*	920 Stone Hill Rd, Denver PA 17517	717-738-1849	R	5*	<.1
85	Peterbilt Motors Co	1700 Woodbrook St, Denton TX 76205	940-591-4000	S	4	2.0
86	Stevens Appliance Truck Co—*William Stevens*	PO Box 897, Augusta GA 30903	706-798-8535	R	4*	<.1
87	Ite LLC—*Eric Pearson*	140 Manley St, Brockton MA 02301	508-313-5600	R	4*	<.1
88	Mcculloch Industries Inc—*Stephen Mccullough*	PO Box 222, Kenton OH 43326	419-673-0767	R	4*	<.1
89	Meto Corp—*Helmut Habicht*	556 Commerce St, Franklin Lakes NJ 07417	201-405-0311	R	4*	<.1
90	Paiute Trailers—*Kevin Neil*	1680 S 550 W, Salina UT 84654	435-529-2285	R	4*	<.1
91	H Holcomb and Son Welding and Machine Works Inc—*Kevin Holcomb*	PO Box 586, Anna IL 62906	618-833-4411	R	3*	<.1
92	Multi-Shifter Inc—*John Pratt*	PO Box 38310, Charlotte NC 28278	704-588-9011	R	3*	<.1
93	Basiloid Products Corp—*Eric Lane*	312 N E St, Elnora IN 47529	812-692-5511	R	3*	<.1
94	Wesley International Corp—*Robert Fisher*	3680 Chestnut St, Scottdale GA 30079	404-292-7441	R	3*	<.1
95	Doughlety Equipment Company Inc—*Michael Doughlety*	10223 Timber Ridge Dr, Ashland VA 23005	804-550-1017	R	3*	<.1
96	Koke Inc—*Richard Koke*	582 Queensbury Ave, Queensbury NY 12804	518-793-6767	R	3*	<.1
97	Air Technical Industries Inc—*Pero Novak*	PO Box 149, Mentor OH 44061	440-951-5191	R	3*	<.1
98	Twin Mills Timber and Tie Company Inc—*Fred Wilson*	3268 State Hwy 37, West Frankfort IL 62896	618-932-3662	R	3*	<.1
99	Chicago Pallet Service Inc—*Leo Rodriguez*	PO Box 426, Maywood IL 60153	708-344-7874	R	3*	<.1
100	Rock-Built Inc—*Rock Ferrone*	1000 Rock Point Blvd, Tarentum PA 15084	724-265-1130	R	3*	<.1
101	Atlantic Engineer Products LLC	PO Box 639, Kinderhook NY 12106	518-822-1800	R	3*	<.1
102	Leebaw Manufacturing Company Inc—*Kenneth George*	PO Box 553, Canfield OH 44406	330-533-3368	R	2*	<.1
103	Gillingham-Best Inc—*Thomas Best*	17305 E Euclid Ave, Spokane Valley WA 99216	509-928-5463	R	2*	<.1
104	Converto Manufacturing Company Inc—*Jeff France*	220 S 3rd St, Cambridge City IN 47327	765-478-3205	R	2*	<.1
105	Saturn Overhead Equipment LLC—*Vania Kaleva*	10 Main St, Newark NJ 07105	973-465-0224	R	2*	<.1
106	Glenwood Manufacturing Co—*Robert Graef*	1209 Koa Dr, Forked River NJ 08731	609-693-6417	R	2*	<.1
107	Viking Lifts Inc—*Harry Oates*	125 Commerce Dr, Enterprise AL 36330	334-347-8500	R	2*	<.1
108	Pallet Repair Systems Inc—*Carolyn Williams*	2 Eastgate Dr, Jacksonville IL 62650	217-291-0009	R	2*	<.1
109	Vermette Machine Company Inc—*Joseph Geisen*	7 143rd St, Hammond IN 46327	219-931-5406	R	2*	<.1
110	Galfab Inc—*Donald Galbreath*	PO Box 39, Winamac IN 46996	574-946-7767	R	2*	.1
111	Bondfire Co—*Lawrence Bond*	PO Box 106, Bailey MI 49303	231-834-5696	R	2*	<.1
112	Control Design and Manufacturing Inc—*Dale Kintgen*	2626 S Zuni St, Englewood CO 80110	303-922-7902	R	2*	<.1
113	Kalyn/Siebert Heil Trailer International	PO Box 1078, Gatesville TX 76528		S	1	.1
114	Brown Bear Corp—*Stan Brown*	PO Box 29, Corning IA 50841	641-322-4220	R	1*	<.1
115	Monroe Table Co—*Ken Meyer*	316 N Walnut St, Colfax IA 50054	515-674-3511	R	1	<.1
116	Envirokare Tech Inc—*Nicholas Pappas*	5836 S Pecos Rd, Las Vegas NV 89120	702-315-0447	R	1	<.1

Note: An asterisk (*) indicates an estimated financial figure. The company type code used is as follows: R = Private, P = Public, S = Private Subsidiary, B = Public Subsidiary, D = Division, J = Joint Venture, I = Investment Fund.

COMPANY RANKINGS BY SALES WITHIN 4-DIGIT SIC

Rank	Company Name—*Executive Officer*	Address, City, State, Zip	Phone	Type	Fin	Empls
117	Ldc Industries Inc—*Jim Dowsett*	1201 7th St, East Moline IL 61244	309-752-1345	R	<1*	<.1

TOTALS: SIC 3537 Industrial Trucks & Tractors
Companies: 117 ... 54,826 ... 153.9

3541 Machine Tools—Metal Cutting Types

Rank	Company Name—*Executive Officer*	Address, City, State, Zip	Phone	Type	Fin	Empls
1	Kennametal Inc (Latrobe Pennsylvania)—*Carlos M Cardoso*	PO Box 231, Latrobe PA 15650		P	2,404	11.6
2	MAG Industrial Automation Systems—*Dan Janka*	6015 Center Dr, Sterling Heights MI 48312	586-446-7000	R	930*	3.5
3	Giddings and Lewis Machine Tools LLC—*Steve Peterson*	PO Box 590, Fond du Lac WI 54936	920-921-9400	R	757*	.4
4	PR Hoffman Machine Products Inc	1517 Commerce Ave, Carlisle PA 17015	717-243-9900	S	568*	<.1
5	Haas Automation Inc—*Gene Haas*	2800 Sturgis Rd, Oxnard CA 93030	805-278-1800	R	409*	1.0
6	Mazak Corp—*Brian Papke*	PO Box 970, Florence KY 41022	859-342-1222	R	355*	.8
7	Gleason Corp (Rochester New York)—*John J Perrotti*	PO Box 22970, Rochester NY 14692	585-473-1000	R	350*	2.6
8	Thermadyne Holdings Corp—*Paul D Melnuk*	16052 Swingley Ridge R, Chesterfield MO 63017	636-728-3000	R	348	1.8
9	Summit Machine Tool—*Steve Golsen* Summit Machine Tool Manufacturing Corp	PO Box 1402, Oklahoma City OK 73101	405-235-2075	S	332*	1.3
10	Summit Machine Tool Manufacturing Corp—*Steve Golsen*	PO Box 1402, Oklahoma City OK 73101	405-235-2075	S	332*	1.3
11	Makino Inc—*Donald Lane*	7680 Innovation Way, Mason OH 45040	513-573-7200	R	274*	.4
12	Hardinge Inc—*Richard L Simons*	PO Box 1507, Elmira NY 14902	607-734-2281	P	257	1.2
13	Valenite Inc—*Walter Brooks*	1675 E Whitcomb, Madison Heights MI 48071	248-733-6980	R	217*	.8
14	Branson Ultrasonics Corp—*Ed Boone*	PO Box 1961, Danbury CT 06813	203-796-0400	S	150*	1.5
15	Manan Tool and Manufacturing Inc—*Laurie Hektor*	241 W Palatine Rd, Wheeling IL 60090	847-637-3333	R	84*	1.1
16	Brubaker Tool Corp—*Robert C McKee*	200 Front St, Millersburg PA 17061		S	81*	.3
17	Peddinghaus Corp—*Carl Peddinghaus*	300 N Washington Ave, Bradley IL 60915	815-937-3800	R	80*	.3
18	Fadal Machining Centers LLC—*Peter Mosher*	20701 Plummer St, Chatsworth CA 91311	818-407-1400	R	63*	.3
19	Loc Performance Products Inc—*Victor Vojcek*	13505 N Haggerty Rd, Plymouth MI 48170	734-453-2300	R	59*	.2
20	Hypertherm Inc—*Richard Couch*	PO Box 5010, Hanover NH 03755	603-643-3441	R	59*	.7
21	AK Allen Inc—*AK Allen*	PO Box 350, Mineola NY 11501	516-747-5450	R	56*	.2
22	Gleason Cutting Tools Corp—*Stuart Piper* Gleason Corp (Rochester New York)	1351 Windsor Rd, Loves Park IL 61111	815-877-8900	D	42*	.3
23	New York Twist Drill Inc	PO Box 368, South Beloit IL 61080		D	42*	.2
24	Cogsdill Tool Products Inc—*Don Mitchell*	PO Box 7007, Camden SC 29021	803-438-4000	R	38*	.2
25	IMPCO Machine Tools—*Dave Houghton*	PO Box 10156, Lansing MI 48901	517-484-9411	R	38*	.2
26	Continental Machines Inc—*M Johnson*	5505 W 123rd St, Savage MN 55378	952-890-3300	S	37*	.3
27	Toyoda Machinery USA Inc—*Howard Michael*	316 W University Dr, Arlington Heights IL 60004	847-253-0340	R	37*	.1
28	Tri Tool Inc—*George Wernette*	3041 Sunrise Blvd, Rancho Cordova CA 95742	916-288-6100	R	36*	.2
29	Faxon Machining Inc—*Barry Faxon*	11101 Adwood Dr, Cincinnati OH 45240	513-851-4644	R	35*	.2
30	Thielenhaus Microfinish Corp—*J Thielenhaus*	42925 W 9 Mile Rd, Novi MI 48375	248-349-9450	R	33*	.3
31	Mosey Manufacturing Company Inc—*George Mosey*	1700 N F St, Richmond IN 47374	765-983-8800	R	33*	.5
32	MC Machinery Systems Inc—*Tetsuji Koike*	1500 Michael Dr, Wood Dale IL 60191	630-860-4210	R	32*	.2
33	Moore Land Company Inc—*Newman Marsilius* Pmt Group Inc	PO Box 4088, Bridgeport CT 06607	203-366-3224	S	30*	.2
34	Brinkman Products Inc—*Andrew Laniak*	167 Ames St, Rochester NY 14611	585-235-4545	R	28*	.4
35	Robbins Co (Solon Ohio)—*Lok Home*	29100 Hall St Ste 100, Solon OH 44139	440-248-3303	R	27*	.1
36	PMC - Colinet Inc	29100 Lakeland Blvd, Wickliffe OH 44092	440-943-3300	S	25*	.1
37	Republic Drill/Apt Corp—*Hy Ash*	8405 Nw 66th St, Miami FL 33166	305-592-7775	R	25*	.2
38	Engis Corp—*Stephen Griffin*	105 W Hintz Rd, Wheeling IL 60090	847-808-9400	R	25*	.2
39	US Group Inc—*Paul Simon*	20580 Hoover Rd, Detroit MI 48205	313-526-8300	R	22*	.2
40	Woodlawn Manufacturing Ltd—*Wanda Cameron*	PO Box 788, Marshall TX 75671	903-938-1882	R	20*	.1
41	Southwestern Industries Inc—*Richard Leonhard*	PO Box 9066, Compton CA 90224	310-608-4422	R	20*	.1
42	Forge Welkin LLC—*Dan Larson*	PO Box 2207, Wilsonville OR 97070	503-682-0991	R	20*	<.1
43	Precise Tool and Manufacturing Inc—*John Gizzi*	9 Coldwater Cres, Rochester NY 14624	585-247-0700	R	20*	.1
44	American Augers Inc—*James Pfeiffer*	PO Box 814, West Salem OH 44287	419-869-7107	S	19*	.1
45	Pmt Group Inc—*Newman Marsilius*	800 Union Ave, Bridgeport CT 06607	203-367-8675	R	19*	.3
46	Tool-Flo Manufacturing Inc—*Dennis Flolo*	7803 Hansen Rd, Houston TX 77061	713-941-1080	R	19*	.1
47	CIVCO Medical Instruments Co—*Charles R Klasson*	102 1st St S, Kalona IA 52247	319-656-4447	S	18*	.1
48	Hetran Inc—*Helmut Oertmann*	70 Pinedale Industrial, Orwigsburg PA 17961	570-366-1411	R	18*	.1
49	Jarvis Cutting Tools Inc—*Marshall Jarvis*	100 Jarvis Ave, Rochester NH 03868	603-332-9000	R	17*	.1
50	Simmons Machine Tool Corp—*John Naumann*	1700 Broadway, Menands NY 12204	518-462-5431	R	16*	.1
51	Weldon Tool Co—*William Coyle* Brubaker Tool Corp	200 Front St, Millersburg PA 17061		S	15	.3
52	Saginaw Machine Systems Inc—*Gary Rottman*	800 N Hamilton St, Saginaw MI 48602	989-758-5587	R	15*	.2
53	Masters Machine Co—*Richard Masters*	PO Box 16, Round Pond ME 04564	207-529-5191	R	15*	.1
54	Hammond Machinery Inc—*Robert Hammond*	1600 Douglas Ave, Kalamazoo MI 49007	269-345-7151	R	14*	.1
55	Climax Portable Machine Tools Inc—*Geoff Gilmore*	PO Box 1210, Newberg OR 97132	503-538-2185	S	14*	.1
56	Drake Corp—*James Braunecker*	916 Jeffco Executive D, Imperial MO 63052	636-464-5070	R	14*	.1
57	Wright-K Technology Inc—*John Sivey*	2025 E Genesee Ave, Saginaw MI 48601	989-752-3103	R	13*	.1
58	Wisconsin Knife Works Inc—*Bruce Swing*	2505 Kennedy Dr, Beloit WI 53511	608-363-7888	R	13*	.1
59	Hem Inc—*Douglas Harris*	PO Box 1148, Pryor OK 74362	918-825-1000	R	12*	.2
60	Picut Manufacturing Co—*Frederick Picut*	140 Mount Bethel Rd, Warren NJ 07059	908-754-1333	R	12*	.1
61	Kingsbury Corp—*Iris Mitropoulis*	80 Laurel St, Keene NH 03431	603-352-5212	R	12*	.1
62	Cinetic Landis Corp—*James Herrman*	16778 Halfway Blvd, Hagerstown MD 21740	301-797-3400	S	12*	.1
63	Betty Machine Company Inc—*John Zobl*	324 Free Hill Rd, Hendersonville TN 37075	615-826-6004	R	12*	.1
64	Barth Industries Company LP—*Robert Tracy*	12650 Brookpark Rd, Cleveland OH 44130	216-267-1950	R	12*	.1
65	S and S Machinery Corp—*Simon Srybnik*	140 53rd St, Brooklyn NY 11232	718-492-7400	R	11*	.1
66	Nagel Precision Inc—*Peter Nagel*	288 Dino Dr, Ann Arbor MI 48103	734-426-5650	R	11*	.1
67	Vertex Diamond Tool Co—*Tony Pontone*	940 Cienega Ave, San Dimas CA 91773	909-599-1129	R	11*	<.1
68	Tarus Products Inc—*Douglas Greig*	38100 Commerce Dr, Sterling Heights MI 48312	586-977-1400	R	10*	.1
69	Bahco North America	PO Box 7577, Columbus GA 31908		S	10*	.1
70	Keo Cutters Inc—*Chuck Curtiss*	PO Box 717, Warren MI 48090	586-771-2050	R	10*	.1
71	Jewell Tool Technology—*Robert Jewell*	PO Box 388, Bettendorf IA 52722	563-355-5010	R	10	.1
72	Edgetek Machine Corp—*Graham Dewhurst*	17 Talcott Notch Rd St, Farmington CT 06032	860-409-7722	S	10*	<.1
73	Bourn and Koch Inc—*Timothy Helle*	2500 Kishwaukee St, Rockford IL 61104	815-965-4013	R	10*	.1
74	Cajun Cutters Inc—*Thomas Aston*	PO Box 447, Bourg LA 70343	985-868-2112	R	10*	.1
75	Edge Manufacturing Inc—*John Wightman*	1120 Mason Cir S, Pevely MO 63070	636-224-0004	R	10*	.1
76	American National Carbide Co—*D Stroud*	915 S Cherry St, Tomball TX 77375	281-351-7165	R	9*	.1
77	Raymath Co—*James Ruef*	2323 W State Rte 55, Troy OH 45373	937-335-1860	R	9*	.1
78	Amamco Tool and Supply Company Inc—*Elizabeth Gilpin*	PO Box 200, Greer SC 29652	864-877-0919	R	9*	.1
79	Kaufman Manufacturing Co—*Robert Kaufman*	PO Box 1056, Manitowoc WI 54221	920-684-6641	R	9*	.1
80	Gnb Corp—*W Ellison*	3200 Dwight Rd Ste 100, Elk Grove CA 95758	916-395-3003	R	9*	.1
81	Grob Inc—*Steven Vandyck*	1731 10th Ave, Grafton WI 53024	262-377-1400	R	8*	<.1

Rank	Company Name—*Executive Officer*	Address, City, State, Zip	Phone	Type	Fin	Empls
82	Royal Master Grinders Inc—*John Memmelaar*	PO Box 630, Oakland NJ 07436	201-337-8500	R	8*	.1
83	Union Process Inc—*Arno Szegvari*	1925 Akron Peninsula R, Akron OH 44313	330-929-3333	R	8*	<.1
84	Barnes International Inc—*David Gollob*	PO Box 1203, Rockford IL 61105	815-964-8661	R	8*	.1
85	Sunshine Fifty Inc—*Duane Rose*	609 St Jean St, Detroit MI 48214	313-821-0671	R	8*	<.1
86	Best Carbide Cutting Tools Inc—*Salvador Nunez*	1454 W 135th St, Gardena CA 90249	310-464-8050	R	8*	.1
87	Rottler Manufacturing Co—*Andrew Rottler*	8029 S 200th St, Kent WA 98032	253-872-7050	R	7*	.1
88	Data Flute CNC Inc—*Dave Pelizzon*	9 Betnr Industrial Dr, Pittsfield MA 01201	413-447-7662	D	7*	<.1
89	Drake Manufacturing Services—*Jim Vosmik*	4371 N Leavitt Rd, Warren OH 44485	330-847-7291	R	7*	<.1
90	Rockford-Ettco Procunier—*Larry Bull*	304 Winston Creek Pkwy, Lakeland FL 33810	863-688-0071	S	7*	<.1
91	Lucas Precision Machine Tool Group—*Paul Mandelbaum*	13020 St Claire Ave, Cleveland OH 44108	216-451-5588	R	7*	<.1
92	C and B Machinery Co—*Joseph Parker*	12001 Globe St, Livonia MI 48150	734-462-0600	R	7*	<.1
93	Crankshaft Machine Co—*Craig Little*	PO Box 1127, Jackson MI 49204	517-787-3791	S	7*	.1
94	Immagetech Inc—*Wayne Oettinger*	1009 Pineville Rd, Chattanooga TN 37405	423-267-0456	R	6*	<.1
95	Normac Inc—*Raymond Bodie*	PO Box 69, Arden NC 28704	828-209-9000	R	6*	.1
96	Kirsan Engineering Inc—*Jp Droppleman*	8201 100th St, Pleasant Prairie WI 53158	262-658-1860	R	6*	.1
97	Kays Engineering Inc—*Edward Kays*	900 Industrial Dr, Marshall MO 65340	660-886-9929	R	6*	.1
98	Yankee Corp—*James Bryce*	125 Yankee Park Rd, Fairfax VT 05454	802-527-0177	R	6*	.1
99	Ellis Manufacturing Company Inc—*Bobby Ellis*	PO Box 930219, Verona WI 53593	608-845-6472	R	6*	<.1
100	Kitamura Machinery of USA Inc—*Greg Knox*	78 E Century Dr, Wheeling IL 60090	847-520-7755	R	6*	<.1
101	B and O Saws Inc—*Jason Kohn*	PO Box 26, Belding MI 48809	616-794-7297	R	6*	<.1
102	Huron Tool and Engineering Co—*Neil Rogers*	635 Liberty St, Bad Axe MI 48413	989-269-9927	R	6*	.1
103	Nrl and Associates Inc—*James Smith*	112 Log Canoe Cir, Stevensville MD 21666	410-643-4063	R	6*	<.1
104	Downey Grinding Co—*Larry Sequeira*	PO Box 583, Downey CA 90241	562-803-5556	R	6*	.1
105	Royberg Inc—*Maya Royberg*	315 N Park Dr, San Antonio TX 78216	210-525-0094	R	6*	.1
106	Shields Enterprises Inc—*Deann Dutro*	8740 Avenida Costa Bla, San Diego CA 92154	619-276-9100	R	6*	.1
107	Zwack Inc—*Frank Zwack*	PO Box 100, Stephentown NY 12168	518-733-5135	R	6*	.1
108	Universal-Automatic Corp—*Kenneth Klancnik*	2064 Mannheim Rd, Des Plaines IL 60018	847-296-6181	R	6*	<.1
109	Lester Detterbeck Enterprises Ltd—*Lester Detterbeck*	3390 E Us Hwy 2, Iron River MI 49935	906-265-5121	R	6*	.1
110	Milwaukee Broach Company Inc—*Michael De Bakker*	N52 W 13821 N Park Dr, Menomonee Falls WI 53051	262-781-7644	R	6*	<.1
111	Grind-All Corp—*Henry Matousek*	1113 Industrial Pkwy N, Brunswick OH 44212	330-220-1600	R	5*	<.1
112	Tank Truck Service and Sales Inc—*James Lawler*	25150 Dequindre Rd, Warren MI 48091	586-757-6500	R	5*	<.1
113	Industrial Applications International Inc—*Herman Bronstein*	3901 Hamilton Ave, Cleveland OH 44114	216-721-1333	R	5*	<.1
114	Custom Machines Inc—*Dean Clenathen*	1441 Enterprise Ave, Adrian MI 49221	517-265-5759	R	5*	<.1
115	Moon Cutter Company Inc—*Eleanor Moon*	2969 State St, Hamden CT 06517	203-230-3670	R	5*	<.1
116	Usach Technologies Inc—*Giacomo Antonini*	1524 Davis Rd, Elgin IL 60123	847-888-0148	R	5*	<.1
117	Cable West Inc—*Donald Nichols*	276 Preuit Rd, Wheatland WY 82201	307-322-9214	R	5*	.1
118	Ramdy Corp—*Allen Thornberg*	PO Box 834, Watertown CT 06795	860-274-3713	R	5*	<.1
119	Hole Specialists Inc—*Larry Robinson*	27950 Commercial Park, Tomball TX 77375	281-290-7770	R	5*	<.1
120	WJ Savage Company Inc—*Chuck Corallo*	31 Commerce St, East Haven CT 06512	203-468-4100	R	5*	<.1
121	Agi-Vr/Wesson Inc—*Tom Fliss*	2673 Ne 9th Ave, Cape Coral FL 33909	239-573-5132	R	5*	<.1
122	Jet Pulverizer Company Inc—*Edwin Fay*	PO Box 212, Palmyra NJ 08065	856-235-5554	R	5*	<.1
123	Grayson Tool Co—*Alvan Lux*	PO Box 26, Minden NE 68959	308-832-2613	R	5*	<.1
124	Banister Tool Inc—*Ray Banister*	PO Box 7769, Round Rock TX 78683	512-258-8351	R	5*	<.1
125	Supfina Machine Company Inc—*Andrew Corsini*	181 Circuit Dr, North Kingstown RI 02852	401-294-6600	R	5*	<.1
126	Abc Boring Company Inc—*Dave Duhaime*	30600 Ryan Rd, Warren MI 48092	586-751-2580	R	5*	<.1
127	Decker Precision Machining Inc—*Randy Decker*	PO Box 9, Peosta IA 52068	563-582-3242	R	5*	<.1
128	Commonwealth Tool And Machine Inc—*Robin Parker*	PO Box 120, Stamping Ground KY 40379	502-535-4430	R	5*	<.1
129	Rock Tool and Machine Company Inc—*Robert Oak*	46145 Five Mile Rd, Plymouth MI 48170	734-455-9840	R	5*	<.1
130	Uni-Hydro Inc—*James Dvorak*	310 Gemini Ave E, Cosmos MN 56228	320-877-7284	R	4*	<.1
131	American Broach and Machine Company Inc—*Ken Nemec*	575 S Mansfield St, Ypsilanti MI 48197	734-961-0300	R	4*	.1
132	Machined Products Co—*Gerard Gammache*	PO Box 10428, Lancaster PA 17605	717-299-3757	R	4*	<.1
133	Glebar Company Inc—*Frederick Schumacher*	PO Box 623, Franklin Lakes NJ 07417	201-337-1500	R	4*	<.1
134	Dcm Tech Ii Inc—*Daniel Arnold*	PO Box 1304, Winona MN 55987	507-452-4043	R	4*	<.1
135	Professional Tool Grinding Company Inc—*Carmen Tropeano*	18 Plymouth Dr, South Easton MA 02375	508-230-3535	R	4*	<.1
136	Technidrill Systems Inc—*Jim Kent*	429 Portage Blvd, Kent OH 44240	330-678-9980	R	4*	<.1
137	New Unison Corp—*David Swider*	1601 Wanda St, Ferndale MI 48220	248-544-9500	R	4*	<.1
138	Systems Unlimited Inc—*David Hanna*	PO Box 529, Coldwater MI 49036	517-279-8407	R	4*	<.1
139	Monarch Lathes LP—*Harry Camp* Lucas Precision Machine Tool Group	PO Box 4609, Sidney OH 45365	937-492-4111	S	4*	<.1
140	Phoenix Inc—*Robert Fuller*	257 Pine St, Seekonk MA 02771	508-399-7100	R	4*	<.1
141	Vulcan Engineering Co—*Bruce Mcmellon*	PO Box 307, Helena AL 35080	205-663-0732	R	4*	<.1
142	Quality Metal Products Inc—*Alan Recce*	PO Box R, Dallas PA 18612	570-333-4248	R	4*	<.1
143	Foothills Machining Inc—*Bob Stewart*	2502 Walhalla Hwy, Pickens SC 29671	864-868-0994	R	4*	<.1
144	Petty Machine and Tool Inc—*Bobby Petty*	4035 Morrill Rd, Jackson MI 49201	517-782-9355	R	4*	<.1
145	W and G Machine Works Inc—*Wayne Carroll*	PO Box 5159, Pasadena TX 77508	713-475-1111	R	4*	<.1
146	Diversified Precision Products Inc—*Stephen Lazaroff*	PO Box 488, Spring Arbor MI 49283	517-750-2310	R	4*	<.1
147	Wire Cut Company Inc—*Milton Thomas*	6750 Caballero Blvd, Buena Park CA 90620	714-994-1170	R	4*	<.1
148	Electro Arc Manufacturing Co—*Harold Stark*	161 Enterprise Dr, Ann Arbor MI 48103	734-761-5400	R	4*	<.1
149	Cincinnati Gilbert Machine Tool Company LLC—*Paul Lamping*	3366 Beekman St, Cincinnati OH 45223	513-541-4815	R	4*	<.1
150	Levan Enterprises Inc—*Peter Levan*	4585 Allen Rd, Stow OH 44224	330-923-9797	R	4*	<.1
151	L and L Machine Tool Inc—*Leroy Lajeunesse*	PO Box 807, Grand Blanc MI 48480	810-695-3970	R	4*	<.1
152	Lexington Cutter Inc—*Paul Enander*	2951 63rd Ave E, Bradenton FL 34203	941-739-2726	R	4*	<.1
153	Design Engineering Management Co—*Scott Baylor*	810 E Adams St, New London IA 52645	319-367-2282	R	4*	<.1
154	Viking Tool Co—*Ole Severson*	PO Box 808, Shelton CT 06484	203-929-1457	R	3*	<.1
155	U S Equipment Co—*George Simon*	20580 Hoover St, Detroit MI 48205	313-526-8300	R	3*	<.1
156	Klh Industries Inc—*Kenneth Heins*	N117w18607 Fulton Dr, Germantown WI 53022	262-253-4990	R	3*	<.1
157	Technox Machine and Manufacturing Inc—*Sham Shirsat*	2619 N Normandy Ave, Chicago IL 60707	773-745-6800	R	3*	<.1
158	Clark Machine Tool And Die Inc—*Ray Clark*	1314 Shun Pke, Nicholasville KY 40356	859-885-9488	R	3*	<.1
159	Modern Machine Tool Co—*Gregory Walker*	2005 Losey Ave, Jackson MI 49203	517-788-9120	R	3*	<.1
160	Bcl Manufacturing Inc—*William Sipko*	161 Bello Dr, Windber PA 15963	814-467-8225	R	3*	<.1
161	A and P Tool Inc—*Pat Weidenhamer*	605 Industrial Dr, Hicksville OH 43526	419-542-6681	R	3*	<.1
162	Mason Machinings Inc—*Leslie Mason*	1015 Jaybird Rd, Morristown TN 37814	423-586-2555	R	3*	<.1
163	Moore Production Tool Specialties Inc—*Richard Moore*	37531 Grand River Ave, Farmington MI 48335	248-476-1200	R	3*	<.1
164	Roderick Arms And Tool Corp—*Harold Schelin*	PO Box 38, Monett MO 65708	417-235-7801	R	3*	<.1
165	American Specialty Grinding Company Inc—*Raymond Fontaine*	904 Sheridan St, Chicopee MA 01022	413-593-5216	R	3*	<.1
166	Marsh Aviation Co—*Floyd Stilwell*	5060 E Falcon Dr, Mesa AZ 85215	480-832-3770	R	3*	<.1
167	Seneca Falls Machine Tool Company Inc—*Attila Libertiny*	314 Fall St, Seneca Falls NY 13148	315-568-5804	R	3*	<.1
168	International Tool Machines Of Florida Inc—*Karl Giebmanns*	5 Industry Dr, Palm Coast FL 32137	386-446-0500	R	3*	<.1
169	Active Manufacturing Corp—*Jeff Braak*	17127 Hickory St, Spring Lake MI 49456	616-842-0800	R	3*	<.1
170	Ty Miles Inc—*Steve Mueller*	9855 Derby Ln, Westchester IL 60154	708-344-5480	R	3*	<.1

Note: An asterisk (*) indicates an estimated financial figure. The company type code used is as follows: R = Private, P = Public, S = Private Subsidiary, B = Public Subsidiary, D = Division, J = Joint Venture, I = Investment Fund.

COMPANY RANKINGS BY SALES WITHIN 4-DIGIT SIC

Rank	Company Name—*Executive Officer*	Address, City, State, Zip	Phone	Type	Fin	Empls
171	Watkins Manufacturing Inc—*Friedhelm Greulich*	10565 Medallion Dr, Cincinnati OH 45241	513-563-0440	R	3*	<.1
172	Dynatorch Inc—*Walter Tyler*	3530 Starnes Dr, Paducah KY 42003	270-442-0560	R	3*	<.1
173	PrintersEdge—*George M Rogers*	4965 Mahoning Ave, Warren OH 44483	330-372-2232	R	3*	<.1
174	United States Machine Tools Corp—*James Duquette*	70 Horizon Dr, Bristol CT 06010	860-953-8306	R	3*	<.1
175	Madison Cutting Tools Inc—*Lars Floderus*	485 Narragansett Park, Pawtucket RI 02861	401-333-0400	R	3*	<.1
176	Vern's Machine Company Inc—*Al Visingard*	4929 Steel Point Rd, Marion NY 14505	315-926-4223	R	3*	<.1
177	Advanced Tooling Inc—*Lisa Pankratz*	PO Box 218, Mount Calvary WI 53057	920-753-2420	R	3*	<.1
178	Migatron Precision Products Inc—*Ronald Edwards*	PO Box 100, Oscoda MI 48750	989-739-1439	R	3*	<.1
179	Cdp Diamond Products Inc—*William Dillon*	PO Box 51727, Livonia MI 48151	734-591-1041	R	3*	<.1
180	Liberty Tool Inc—*Chris Maier*	43110 Merrill Rd, Sterling Heights MI 48314	586-726-2449	R	3*	<.1
181	Posa-Cut Corp—*Kevin Brien*	23600 Haggerty Rd, Farmington Hills MI 48335	248-474-5620	R	3*	<.1
182	Chas G Allen Co—*David Krupp*	25 Williamsville Rd, Barre MA 01005	978-355-2911	R	3*	<.1
183	Heeco Associates And Equipment Company Inc—*Edward Mihalcin*	PO Box 9279, Tampa FL 33674	813-886-7584	R	3*	<.1
184	National Jet Company Inc—*R Griffith*	10 Cupler Dr, Cumberland MD 21502	301-729-2300	R	3*	<.1
185	John Deere Parts Distribution Center	PO Box 8808, Moline IL 61266	309-756-1355	R	3*	<.1
186	Kha Kenney Products Inc—*Kenny Kha*	18386 Mount Langley St, Fountain Valley CA 92708	714-963-2114	R	3*	<.1
187	Workrite Machine and Tool Inc—*Charles Hagan*	6319 Discount Dr, Fort Wayne IN 46818	260-489-4778	R	3*	<.1
188	Herdeman Corp—*Henry Herdeman*	5429 S Buckhorn Ave, Cudahy WI 53110	414-481-8550	R	3*	<.1
189	Kiene Diesel Accessories Inc—*John Craychee*	325 S Fairbank St, Addison IL 60101	630-543-5950	R	3*	<.1
190	Metlsaw Systems Inc—*Lisa Kvech*	2950 Bay Vista Ct Ste, Benicia CA 94510	707-746-6200	R	3*	<.1
191	Petron Automation Inc—*Michael Petro*	PO Box 399, Watertown CT 06795	860-274-9091	R	3*	<.1
192	Action Tool Service Inc—*Larry Franklin*	2202 Mingee Dr, Hampton VA 23661	757-838-4555	R	3*	<.1
193	Midstates Tool and Die And Engineering Inc—*Michael Masten*	3407 Cooper Dr, Elkhart IN 46514	574-264-3521	R	2*	<.1
194	Amar Precision Corp—*Michael Ratynets*	24749 Ave Rockefeller, Valencia CA 91355	661-775-0600	R	2*	<.1
195	Grindal Co—*Norman Spooner*	1551 Industrial Dr, Itasca IL 60143	630-250-8950	R	2*	<.1
196	Grt Utilicorp Inc—*Rod Zimmermen*	9268 Ashland Rd, Wooster OH 44691	330-264-8444	R	2*	<.1
197	High Point Precision Products Inc—*Charles Stipo*	1 1st St, Sussex NJ 07461	973-875-6229	R	2*	<.1
198	Hypneumat Inc—*Thomas Short*	5900 W Franklin Dr, Franklin WI 53132	414-423-7400	R	2*	<.1
199	Illinois Broaching Co—*Thomas Kelly*	4200 Grace St, Schiller Park IL 60176	847-678-3080	R	2*	<.1
200	Omega Consolidated Corp—*Martin Hunte*	101 Heinz St, Hilton NY 14468	585-392-9262	R	2*	<.1
201	Berg Tool Inc—*Michael Bergmann*	56253 Precision Dr, Chesterfield MI 48051	586-646-7100	R	2*	<.1
202	Brown Equipment Manufacturing Company Inc—*Neil Brown*	PO Box 32214, Charlotte NC 28232	704-921-4644	R	2*	<.1
203	Lahm-Trosper Inc—*James Trosper*	PO Box 336, Dayton OH 45401	937-252-8791	R	2*	<.1
204	Punch Tech—*Richard Zenow*	2701 Busha Hwy, Marysville MI 48040	810-364-4811	R	2*	<.1
205	Ohio Broach and Machine Co—*Charles Van De Motter*	35264 Topps Industrial, Willoughby OH 44094	440-946-1040	R	2*	<.1
206	Competetive Carbide Inc—*Tom Cirino*	9332 Pinecone Dr, Mentor OH 44060	440-350-9393	R	2*	<.1
207	Chart Tech Tool Inc—*Eugene Crompton*	PO Box 477, Tipp City OH 45371	937-667-3543	R	2*	<.1
208	Conway Machine Inc—*Marti Davis*	192 Commerce Rd, Conway AR 72032	501-327-1311	R	2*	<.1
209	GF Goodman and Son Inc—*William Rumble*	PO Box 2909, Warminster PA 18974	215-672-8810	R	2*	<.1
210	Torin Products Inc—*Tom Bernstein*	2455 16th Ave, Columbus NE 68601	402-564-1261	R	2*	<.1
211	King Tool Co—*Robert King*	1338 Cox Ave, Erlanger KY 41018	859-525-1799	R	2*	<.1
212	Star Machine and Tool Co—*Morris Wisti*	215 6th St Se, Minneapolis MN 55414	612-378-3232	R	2*	<.1
213	A and H Tool Engineering Corp—*Jerry Donley*	17109 Edwards Rd, Cerritos CA 90703	562-623-9717	R	2*	<.1
214	JGS Precision Tool Manufacturing LLC—*Kenneth Humbert*	60819 Selander Rd, Coos Bay OR 97420	541-267-4331	R	2*	<.1
215	Scheer Bay LP—*Michael Boyce*	3503 N Euclid Ave, Bay City MI 48706	989-671-9630	R	2*	<.1
216	Bor-It Manufacturing Inc—*Michael Albers*	PO Box 789, Ashland OH 44805	419-289-6639	R	2*	<.1
217	Farwest Aircraft Inc—*Jay Marshall*	PO Box 1889, Milton WA 98354	253-927-4321	R	2*	<.1
218	Hms Industries Inc—*John Hornock*	1256 Rte 22 Hwy W, Blairsville PA 15717	724-459-5090	R	2*	<.1
219	Lorik Tool Inc—*Roger Gosselin*	2003 Liberty Ave, Lawrenceburg TN 38464	931-762-3495	R	2*	<.1
220	Prototype and Production Co—*Lana Raskin*	546 Quail Hollow Dr, Wheeling IL 60090	847-419-1553	R	2*	<.1
221	Waber Tool and Engineering Company Inc—*Heidi Waber*	1335 Ravine Rd, Kalamazoo MI 49004	269-342-0765	R	2*	<.1
222	Koyo Machinery USA Inc—*Dan Geddes*	14878 Galleon Ct, Plymouth MI 48170	734-454-4107	S	2*	<.1
223	Ronshare Inc—*Ronald Weber*	PO Box 565, South Lyon MI 48178	734-591-1021	R	2*	<.1
224	Rytan Inc—*Riley Sopko*	455 Maple Ave, Torrance CA 90503	310-328-6553	R	2*	<.1
225	Sjogren Industries Inc—*Carl Sjogren*	982 Southbridge St, Worcester MA 01610	508-987-3206	R	2*	<.1
226	Ieppert Machine Tool and Screw Products Inc—*John Ieppert*	1807 W Outer Hwy 61, Moscow Mills MO 63362	636-366-4433	R	2*	<.1
227	Kasper Machine Co—*Raffeale Ghilardi*	29275 Stephenson Hwy, Madison Heights MI 48071	248-547-3150	R	2*	<.1
228	Lortone Inc—*Doug Guthrie*	12130 Cyrus Way, Mukilteo WA 98275	425-493-1600	R	2*	<.1
229	Production Tool and Grinding Inc—*Michael Miller*	PO Box 440, Orange MA 01364	978-544-8206	R	2*	<.1
230	Southern California Carbide—*Harjeet Singh*	12216 Thatcher Ct, Poway CA 92064	858-513-7777	R	2*	<.1
231	Kingston Machine Tool Inc—*Daniel Lin*	5421 Business Dr, Huntington Beach CA 92649	714-894-1648	R	2*	<.1
232	Sheffield Cutting Equipment	4561 Mission Gorge Pl, San Diego CA 92120	619-280-0278	R	2	<.1
233	Orange Coast Rebuilding—*Jerry Remick*	4616 E La Palma Ave, Anaheim CA 92807	714-777-5900	R	2*	<.1
234	Cdm Machine Co—*Calvin Davidson*	24450 Capitol, Redford MI 48239	313-538-9100	R	2*	<.1
235	Rockford Drill Head Inc—*Larry Bull*	PO Box 5744, Rockford IL 61125	815-874-9421	R	2*	<.1
236	Versatility Tool Works And Manufacturing Company Inc—*Edward Freimuth*	11532 S Mayfield Ave, Alsip IL 60803	708-389-8909	R	2*	<.1
237	US Tool and Cutter Co—*David Price*	PO Box 9050, Farmington Hills MI 48333	248-553-7745	R	2*	<.1
238	Hyper Tool Co—*Morton Mc Clennan*	16829 Park Cir Dr, Chagrin Falls OH 44023	440-543-5151	R	2*	<.1
239	Bertsche Engineering Corp—*Richard Bertsche*	711 Dartmouth Ln, Buffalo Grove IL 60089	847-537-8757	R	2*	<.1
240	Fortune Champion Corp—*Gregg Hetzinger*	PO Box 849, Houghton Lake MI 48629	989-422-6130	R	2*	<.1
241	Kevil Tool and Die Inc—*Paul Owen*	PO Box 190, Kevil KY 42053	270-462-2178	R	2*	<.1
242	Emporium Specialties Company Inc—*Marvin Deupree*	PO Box 65, Austin PA 16720	814-647-8661	R	2*	.1
243	J-C-R Tech Inc—*Rick Carmean*	PO Box 65, Blanchester OH 45107	937-783-2296	R	2*	<.1
244	Production Threaded Parts Co—*Ralph Deshetsky*	PO Box 320, North Branch MI 48461	810-688-3053	R	2*	<.1
245	Tri-Turn Technologies—*J Banbury*	6200 Riverside Dr Ste, Cleveland OH 44135	216-265-7444	R	2*	<.1
246	HB Rouse and Co—*John Knoll*	1101 W Diggins St, Harvard IL 60033	815-943-4426	R	1*	<.1
247	Huff Carbide Tool Inc—*Earl Huff*	6541 Industrial Ave, Port Richey FL 34668	727-848-4001	R	1*	<.1
248	Apex Broaching Systems Inc—*Leonard Bantleon*	22862 Hoover Rd, Warren MI 48089	586-758-2626	R	1*	<.1
249	Libert Machine Corp—*Thomas Libert*	324 N Roosevelt St Frn, Green Bay WI 54301	920-432-2408	R	1*	<.1
250	Laser Tool Company Inc—*Faye Duquette*	98 N Main St, Thomaston CT 06787	860-283-8284	R	1*	<.1
251	Cutting Tool Innovations Inc—*Gohei Osawa*	759 Industrial Dr, Bensenville IL 60106	630-595-0700	S	1*	<.1
252	Pierce Inc—*Danny Pierce*	16 Industrial Blvd, Greenbrier AR 72058	501-679-2828	R	1*	<.1
253	P and E Machine Company Inc—*Derek Eudy*	2003 Ln St, Kannapolis NC 28083	704-933-0160	R	1*	<.1
254	Advanced Machine Design Company Inc—*Reiner Moelbert*	45 Roberts Ave, Buffalo NY 14206	716-826-2000	R	1*	<.1
255	Amada Wasino America Inc	2324 Palmer Dr, Schaumburg IL 60173	847-285-4800	S	1*	<.1
256	Rogers Manufacturing Inc—*Leah Gillespie*	PO Box 518, Mineral Wells TX 76068	940-325-7806	R	1*	<.1
257	General Broach Co—*S David Graham*	307 Salisbury St, Morenci MI 49256	517-458-7555	R	1*	<.1
258	Bos Machine Tool Services Inc—*Charles Bos*	PO Box 96, Hillsdale IL 61257	309-658-2223	R	1*	<.1
259	Infra Corp—*Bryan Mcgraw*	PO Box 300997, Drayton Plains MI 48330	248-623-0400	R	1*	<.1

Rank	Company Name—*Executive Officer*	Address, City, State, Zip	Phone	Type	Fin	Empls
260	Blue Valley Machine And Manufacturing Co—*Dale Johnston*	6832 E Truman Rd, Kansas City MO 64126	816-231-1480	R	1*	<.1
261	DG Industries—*David Gillanders*	226 Viking Ave, Brea CA 92821	714-990-3787	R	1*	<.1
262	Pro Precision Inc—*Robert Proszkowski*	23250 Sherwood Ave, Warren MI 48091	586-757-7755	R	1*	<.1
263	H and M Pipe Beveling Machine Co—*Margaret Stallard*	311 E 3rd St, Tulsa OK 74120	918-582-9984	R	1*	<.1
264	Koro Industries Inc—*John Korosec*	PO Box 244, Osseo MN 55369	763-425-5247	R	1*	<.1
265	Oliver Of Adrian Inc—*Neal Garrison*	PO Box 189, Adrian MI 49221	517-263-2132	R	1*	<.1
266	Eiger Machinery Inc—*Dave Peterson*	888 E Belvidere Rd Ste, Grayslake IL 60030	847-548-0044	R	1*	<.1
267	Schienke Electric and Machine Services Inc—*David Schienke*	120 Mclean, Bruce Twp MI 48065	586-752-5454	R	1*	<.1
268	Jamieson Manufacturing Company Inc—*Scott Jamieson*	PO Box 966, Torrington CT 06790	860-482-6543	R	1*	<.1
269	Lavallee And Ide Inc—*Nancy Ballard*	110 W Canal St, Winooski VT 05404	802-655-1870	R	1*	<.1
270	Leavitt Machine Co—*David Coolidge*	24 E River St, Orange MA 01364	978-544-2751	R	1*	<.1
271	Mataco—*Jeff Bubb*	2861 E Royalton Rd, Broadview Heights OH 44147	440-546-8355	R	<1*	<.1
272	Henry Tools Inc—*Richard Henry*	498 S Belvoir Blvd, Cleveland OH 44121	216-291-1011	R	<1*	<.1
273	Automation Associates Inc—*William Moyer*	1605 Dundee Ave Ste E, Elgin IL 60120	847-255-4500	R	<1*	<.1
274	Martin Aircraft Tool Co—*Frank Negri*	PO Box 8097, Fountain Valley CA 92728	714-962-6641	R	<1*	<.1
275	Mardon Manufacturing Co—*Donald Thurston*	237r Main St, Rowley MA 01969	978-948-2285	R	<1*	<.1
276	NATCO/Carlton—*Eugene Sizelove* Lucas Precision Machine Tool Group	PO Box 1758, Richmond IN 47375	765-962-6511	S	N/A	<.1

TOTALS: SIC 3541 Machine Tools—Metal Cutting Types
Companies: 276   9,925   44.4

3542 Machine Tools—Metal Forming Types

Rank	Company Name—*Executive Officer*	Address, City, State, Zip	Phone	Type	Fin	Empls
1	Ingersoll Machine Tools Inc—*George H Dorkhom*	707 Fulton Ave, Rockford IL 61103	815-987-6000	S	400	2.5
2	Trumpf Inc—*Rolf Biekert*	111 Hyde Rd, Farmington CT 06032	860-255-6000	S	229*	.6
3	Minster Machine Co—*John Winch*	PO Box 120, Minster OH 45865	419-628-2331	R	91*	.6
4	Bradbury Company Inc—*David Cox*	PO Box 667, Moundridge KS 67107	620-345-6394	R	80*	.5
5	National Machinery LLC—*Robert Loy*	PO Box 747, Tiffin OH 44883	419-447-5211	R	56*	.4
6	SPX Precision Components—*Ron Felix*	300 Fenn Rd, Newington CT 06111	860-666-2471	S	50	.3
7	Strippit Inc—*John Lesebbre*	12975 Clarence Ctr Rd, Akron NY 14001	716-542-4511	R	44*	.3
8	General Electro-Mechanical Corp—*Thomas H Speller Jr*	100 Gemcor Dr, West Seneca NY 14224	716-674-9300	R	41*	.1
9	Anderson-Cook Inc—*Matthew Richey*	44785 Macomb Industria, Clinton Township MI 48036	586-954-0700	R	40*	.3
10	Magnetic Metals Corp—*Frank Raneiro*	1900 Hayes Ave, Camden NJ 08105	856-964-7842	R	38*	.3
11	WA Whitney Co—*Gary Geller*	PO Box 1206, Rockford IL 61105	815-964-6771	S	33*	.2
12	Gasbarre Products Inc—*Thomas Gasbarre*	PO Box 1011, Du Bois PA 15801	814-371-3015	R	31*	.2
13	Mate Precision Tooling Inc—*Dean Sundquist*	1295 Lund Blvd, Anoka MN 55303	763-421-0230	R	28*	.4
14	Gemcor Ii LLC—*David Pritchard*	100 Gemcor Dr, West Seneca NY 14224	716-674-9300	R	25*	.1
15	Roper Whitney Of Rockford Inc—*David Casazza*	2833 Huffman Blvd, Rockford IL 61103	815-962-3011	R	22*	.2
16	Williams White And Co—*Sunder Subbaroyan*	600 River Dr, Moline IL 61265	309-797-7650	R	20*	.1
17	American Gfm Corp—*Robert Kralowetz*	1200 Cavalier Blvd, Chesapeake VA 23323	757-487-2442	R	19*	.2
18	Cyril Bath Co—*Michael Zimmer*	1610 Airport Rd, Monroe NC 28110	704-289-8531	R	19*	<.1
19	HPM Division Taylor's Industrial Services LLC—*Charles Clark*	820 W Marion Rd, Mount Gilead OH 43338	419-946-0222	R	19*	.2
20	QPI Multipress Inc—*Barney Raye*	1250 Refugee Ln, Columbus OH 43207	614-228-0185	S	19*	<.1
21	Wysong and Miles Company Inc—*Russell Hall*	PO Box 21168, Greensboro NC 27420	336-621-3960	R	17*	.1
22	Erie Press Systems Inc—*Gary Lunger*	PO Box 4061, Erie PA 16512	814-455-3941	R	17*	.1
23	Clark Granco Inc—*Lawrence Difatta*	7298 Storey Rd, Belding MI 48809	616-794-2600	R	17*	.1
24	Wabash Metal Products Inc—*Bruce Freeman*	PO Box 298, Wabash IN 46992	260-563-1184	S	16*	.1
25	Stolle Machinery Company LLC—*Julian Candia*	6949 S Potomac St, Centennial CO 80112	303-708-9044	R	16*	.1
26	Schmiede Corp—*Brad Ferrell*	PO Box 1630, Tullahoma TN 37388	931-455-4801	R	15*	.1
27	Wallner Tooling/Expac Inc—*Michael Wallner*	9160 Hyssop Dr, Rancho Cucamonga CA 91730	909-481-8800	R	14*	.1
28	Geo T Schmidt Inc—*Neal O'connor*	6151 W Howard St, Niles IL 60714	847-647-7117	R	14*	.1
29	Miller Tool and Die Co—*Philip Miller*	829 Belden Rd, Jackson MI 49203	517-782-0347	R	14*	<.1
30	Galland Henning Nopak Inc—*Daniel Steele*	1025 S 40th St, Milwaukee WI 53215	414-645-6000	R	13*	.1
31	Hi-Tech Tool Industries Inc—*Arno Rabin*	6701 Ctr Dr, Sterling Heights MI 48312	586-826-8346	R	13*	<.1
32	Amada Manufacturing America Inc—*Tokuro Takohara*	14646 Northam St, La Mirada CA 90638	714-670-6472	R	12*	.1
33	Daugherty Tool And Die Inc—*Timothy Beringer*	325 Industry Rd, Buena Vista PA 15018	412-754-0200	R	11*	.1
34	Phoenix Process Equipment Company Inc—*Gary L Drake*	2402 Watterson Trl, Louisville KY 40299	502-499-6198	R	11*	<.1
35	Hf Rubber Machinery Inc—*Andreas Limper*	PO Box 8250, Topeka KS 66608	785-235-2336	R	11*	.1
36	Logemann Brothers Co—*Carl Dieterle*	3150 W Burleigh St, Milwaukee WI 53210	414-445-2700	R	11*	.1
37	Edmunds Manufacturing Co—*Robert F Edmunds Jr*	45 Spring Ln, Farmington CT 06034	860-677-2813	R	10*	.1
38	Ajax Manufacturing Co—*Charlie Grout*	29100 Lakeland Blvd, Wickliffe OH 44092	440-295-0244	S	10*	.1
39	Gtm Energy Partners LLC—*Nikey Robert*	442 County Rd 464, Flat Rock AL 35966	256-632-2267	R	10*	.1
40	Standard Industrial Corp—*Terry Hays*	1115 Hwy 49 S, Clarksdale MS 38614	662-624-2436	R	9*	.1
41	Universal Punch Corp—*Kenneth Williams*	PO Box 26879, Santa Ana CA 92799	714-556-4488	R	9*	.1
42	First Tool Corp—*Robert Davis*	612 Linden Ave, Dayton OH 45403	937-254-6197	R	8*	.1
43	Bruderer Machinery Inc—*Alois Rupp*	1200 Hendricks Causewa, Ridgefield NJ 07657	201-941-2121	R	8*	<.1
44	Littell International Inc—*Sterling Stevenson*	1211 Tower Rd, Schaumburg IL 60173	630-622-4700	R	7*	<.1
45	Carando Machine Works Inc—*Edwin Cain*	PO Box 1167, Stockton CA 95201	209-948-6500	R	7*	<.1
46	Cloos Robotic Welding Inc—*Hartmut Boegel*	911 Albion Ave, Schaumburg IL 60193	847-923-9988	R	7*	<.1
47	Pacific Press Technologies Inc—*Michael Stein*	714 N Walnut St, Mount Carmel IL 62863	618-262-8666	R	7*	<.1
48	Presses Inc—*William Ramsey*	5360 W 73rd St, Bedford Park IL 60638	708-496-7450	R	6*	<.1
49	Solidscape Inc—*Michael Varanka*	316 Daniel Webster Hwy, Merrimack NH 03054	603-429-9700	R	6*	.1
50	Tools For Bending Inc—*Eric Stange*	194 W Dakota Ave, Denver CO 80223	303-777-7170	R	6*	.1
51	Vermont Machine Tool Corp—*Craig Barrett*	65 Pearl St, Springfield VT 05156	802-885-4521	R	6*	<.1
52	Rogers Industrial Products Inc—*John Cole*	532 S Main St, Akron OH 44311	330-535-3331	R	6*	<.1
53	Rafter Equipment Corp—*Walter Krenz*	12430 Alameda Dr, Strongsville OH 44149	440-572-3700	R	5*	<.1
54	Die-Matic LLC—*Nike Nykamp*	4309 Aldrich Ave Sw, Grand Rapids MI 49509	616-531-0060	R	5*	<.1
55	Atlantagrotnes Machine Co—*Carl Grotnes*	305 Selig Dr Sw, Atlanta GA 30336	404-691-0471	R	5*	<.1
56	Fdc Machine Repair Inc—*Fred Censo*	5585 Venture Dr, Cleveland OH 44130	216-362-1082	R	5*	<.1
57	Northern Extrusion Tooling—*William Berry*	PO Box 662, Yankton SD 57078	605-665-3603	R	5*	<.1
58	Mathy Machine Inc—*Jay Mathy*	9315 Wheatlands Rd, Santee CA 92071	619-448-0404	R	5*	<.1
59	Brandtjen and Kluge Inc—*Henry Brandtjen*	539 Blanding Woods Rd, Saint Croix Falls WI 54024	715-483-3265	R	5*	<.1
60	Knudson Manufacturing Inc—*Gary Knudson*	10401 W 120th Ave, Broomfield CO 80021	303-469-2101	R	5*	<.1
61	Amega Tool Works Inc—*Jerry Rawlinson*	29 Frj Dr, Longview TX 75602	903-753-7203	R	5*	<.1
62	Krofam Inc—*Jerry Crutch*	PO Box 850, Philip SD 57567	605-859-2542	R	4*	.1
63	Brake Roller Company Inc—*Jack Budrow*	PO Box 460, Battle Creek MI 49016	269-965-2371	R	4*	<.1
64	Form Roll Die Corp—*Mildred Mason*	217 Stafford St, Worcester MA 01603	508-755-2010	R	4*	<.1
65	Tecre Company Inc—*Ben Braunberger*	W5747 Lost Arrow Rd, Fond Du Lac WI 54937	920-922-9168	R	4*	<.1
66	Roll Former Corp—*Phil Altomare*	140 Independence Ln, Chalfont PA 18914	215-997-2511	R	4*	<.1
67	Unique Tool and Bending Inc—*Eston Martin*	2312 Centennial Cir, Gainesville GA 30504	770-503-0963	R	4*	<.1

Note: An asterisk (*) indicates an estimated financial figure. The company type code used is as follows: R = Private, P = Public, S = Private Subsidiary, B = Public Subsidiary, D = Division, J = Joint Venture, I = Investment Fund.

COMPANY RANKINGS BY SALES WITHIN 4-DIGIT SIC

Rank	Company Name—*Executive Officer*	Address, City, State, Zip	Phone	Type	Fin	Empls
68	Midwest Tool Inc—*Les Scheurich*	3637 Enterprise Ave, Joplin MO 64801	417-623-6872	R	4*	<.1
69	Webb Corp—*Richard Bentley*	402 E Broadway St, Webb City MO 64870	417-673-4646	R	4*	<.1
70	George A Mitchell Co—*George Mitchell*	PO Box 3727, Youngstown OH 44513	330-758-5777	R	4*	<.1
71	Joshua LLC—*Jean Federici*	90 Hamilton St, New Haven CT 06511	203-624-0080	R	4*	<.1
72	THT Presses Inc—*Mike Thieman*	7475 Webster St, Dayton OH 45414	937-898-2012	R	4*	<.1
73	Ecenbarger Inc—*Gary Ecenbarger*	1036 Saint Marys Ave, Fort Wayne IN 46808	260-424-4834	R	4*	<.1
74	Dmt Workholding Inc—*Lawrence Wagner*	PO Box 210, Slinger WI 53086	262-644-5000	R	4*	<.1
75	Aberdeen Machine Tool Inc—*Steve Hilton*	2903 Industrial Ave, Aberdeen SD 57401	605-225-8030	R	4*	<.1
76	Bohl Machine and Tool Company Inc—*Theodore Bohl*	4405 78th Ave, Milan IL 61264	309-799-5122	R	3*	<.1
77	Developmental Industries Inc—*Lawrence Rider*	915 Hwy 45, Corinth MS 38834	662-287-6626	R	3*	<.1
78	Grover Machine Co—*Jean Micouleau*	207 Prospect Ave, Saint Louis MO 63122	314-965-6808	R	3*	<.1
79	Jam Industries Inc—*Eric Johnson*	1580 Emerson St, Rochester NY 14606	585-458-9830	R	3*	<.1
80	Betenbender Manufacturing Inc—*Glen Betenbender*	PO Box 140, Coggon IA 52218	319-435-2378	R	3*	<.1
81	Erie M and P Company Inc—*John Nowak*	PO Box 6349, Erie PA 16512	814-454-1581	R	3*	<.1
82	Mor-Tech Design Inc—*David Morin*	44249 Phoenix Dr, Sterling Heights MI 48314	586-254-7982	R	3*	<.1
83	Savage Engineering Inc—*Daniel Wolbert*	4855 Chaincraft Rd, Garfield Heights OH 44125	216-587-2885	R	3*	<.1
84	Precision Industries Corp—*Sue Ellen Mc Kinnel*	PO Box 1923, Elkhart IN 46515	574-522-2626	R	3*	<.1
85	Texas Extrusion Service Inc—*Sharon Kores*	PO Box 2807, Spring TX 77383	281-350-2288	R	3*	<.1
86	National Sheet Metal Machines Inc—*Jim Smith*	PO Box 72, Smartt TN 37378	931-668-3643	R	3*	<.1
87	Delta Machine and Tool Inc—*Norbert Ruppert*	1501 Lexington Ave, Deland FL 32724	386-738-2204	R	3*	<.1
88	First Header Die Inc—*Mark Gritzmacher*	1313 Anvil Rd, Machesney Park IL 61115	815-282-5161	R	3*	<.1
89	West Coast-Accudyne Inc—*George Schofhauser*	PO Box 2159, Bell CA 90202	562-927-2546	R	3*	<.1
90	Flagler Corp—*Harley Flagler*	56513 Precision Dr, Chesterfield MI 48051	586-749-6300	R	3*	<.1
91	Moran Tools—*Max Moran*	PO Box 1141, Vista CA 92085	760-801-3570	R	3*	<.1
92	Greenerd Press and Machine Company Inc—*Donald Moodie*	PO Box 886, Nashua NH 03061	603-889-4101	R	3*	<.1
93	Rock River Tool And Die Inc—*James Wright*	PO Box 706, Rock Falls IL 61071	815-625-8957	R	2*	<.1
94	Mjc Engineering And Technology Inc—*Carl Lorentzen*	15701 Container Ln, Huntington Beach CA 92649	714-890-0618	R	2*	<.1
95	Riteway Brake Dies Inc—*Richard Bernecker*	7440 W 100th Pl, Bridgeview IL 60455	708-430-0795	R	2*	<.1
96	Down East Machine and Engineering Inc—*Keith Beaule*	26 Maple St, Mechanic Falls ME 04256	207-345-8111	R	2*	<.1
97	Air-Hydraulics Co—*Tom Moore*	6074 Baumgartner Indus, Saint Louis MO 63129	314-487-9100	R	2*	<.1
98	Rempco Inc—*Thomas Harris*	PO Box 1020, Cadillac MI 49601	231-775-0108	R	2*	<.1
99	Air-Hydraulics Inc—*Joseph Miller*	PO Box 831, Jackson MI 49204	517-787-9444	R	2*	<.1
100	Tetrahedron Associates Inc—*Angela Deane*	PO Box 710157, San Diego CA 92171	619-661-0552	R	2*	<.1
101	Barrel Reconditioning Industries Inc—*Jay Ahern*	10500 Ideal Ave S, Cottage Grove MN 55016	651-458-3466	R	2*	<.1
102	Precision Service Motor Inc—*Kevin Zierke*	121 W Fullerton Ave, Addison IL 60101	630-628-9900	R	2*	<.1
103	Loomis Products Co—*Karl Kahlefeld*	5500 Emilie Rd, Levittown PA 19057	215-547-2121	R	2*	<.1
104	A and A Magnetics Inc—*Jeffrey Arnold*	PO Box 1427, Woodstock IL 60098	815-338-6054	R	2*	<.1
105	Die-Quip Corp—*Thomas Maxwell*	5360 Enterprise Blvd, Bethel Park PA 15102	412-833-1662	R	2*	<.1
106	Dynamic Equipment Corp—*Roy Marburger*	PO Box 46, Allison Park PA 15101	724-449-4620	R	2*	<.1
107	Ferguson Equipment Inc—*Melvin Burdue*	25170 Edison Rd, South Bend IN 46628	574-234-4303	R	1*	<.1
108	Salvo Tool and Engineering Company Inc—*Bruce Bedker*	PO Box 129, Brown City MI 48416	810-346-2727	R	1*	<.1
109	Magma Engineering Co—*Robert Clausen*	PO Box 161, Queen Creek AZ 85142	480-987-3301	R	1*	<.1
110	Mchal Corp—*Danny Toothman*	PO Box 1587, Fairmont WV 26555	304-363-6900	R	1*	<.1
111	Capitol Technologies Inc—*Johann Hess*	30257 Redfield St, Niles MI 49120	269-683-4182	R	1*	<.1
112	Rotex Punch Company Inc—*Ronald Rose*	PO Box 2017, San Leandro CA 94577	510-357-3600	R	1*	<.1
113	Fabriweld Corp—*Christopher Price*	360 Eastpark Dr, Norwalk OH 44857	419-668-3358	R	1*	<.1
114	Racine Federated Inc—*Dave Perkins*	8635 Washington Ave, Racine WI 53406	262-639-6770	R	1*	<.1
115	ECS Manufacturing Inc—*Eugene J Pian*	554 N State Rd, Briarcliff Manor NY 10510	914-273-1400	R	1*	<.1
116	Bendco Machine and Tool Company Inc—*Kenneth Wolaver*	PO Box 6, Minster OH 45865	419-628-3802	R	1*	<.1
117	Calx Inc—*Thomas Mc Donough*	440 Lynnway, Lynn MA 01905	781-599-7400	R	1*	<.1
118	Eitel Presses Inc—*Ronald Schildge*	PO Box 130, Orwigsburg PA 17961	570-366-0585	R	1*	<.1
119	Tiegel Manufacturing Co—*Ralph Tiegel*	PO Box 830, Belmont CA 94002	650-593-7881	R	<1*	<.1

TOTALS: SIC 3542 Machine Tools—Metal Forming Types
    Companies: 119

					1,837	10.7

3543 Industrial Patterns

Rank	Company Name—*Executive Officer*	Address, City, State, Zip	Phone	Type	Fin	Empls
1	Vaupell Inc	1144 Northwest 53rd St, Seattle WA 98107	206-784-9050	S	76	.5
2	Air Power Dynamics LLC	7350 Corporate Blvd, Mentor OH 44060	440-701-2100	R	25*	.2
3	Mid-City Foundry Co—*Richard Wieland*	PO Box 04696, Milwaukee WI 53204	414-645-0840	R	22*	.2
4	Anderson Global Inc—*John Mc Intyre*	500 W Sherman Blvd, Muskegon MI 49444	231-733-2164	R	19*	.1
5	Midwest Patterns Inc—*Thomas Tushaus*	4901 N 12th St, Quincy IL 62305	217-228-6900	R	14*	.1
6	Jay Enn Corp—*Burton Kirsten*	33943 Dequindre Rd, Troy MI 48083	248-588-2393	R	12*	.1
7	Plas-Mac Corp—*Jonathon Petrenchik*	30250 Carter St, Solon OH 44139	440-349-2750	R	10*	.1
8	Humtown Pattern Co—*Mark Moncha*	PO Box 367, Columbiana OH 44408	330-482-5555	R	10*	.1
9	Smith Brothers Tool Co—*Hodges Smith*	50600 Corporate Dr, Shelby Township MI 48315	586-726-5756	R	10*	.1
10	Metro Technologies Ltd—*Alfred Hook*	1462 E Big Beaver Rd, Troy MI 48083	248-528-9240	R	9*	.1
11	Griffin Industries Corp—*Jonathan Krouth*	PO Box 347, Suamico WI 54173	920-434-4440	R	9*	.1
12	Kenona Industries Inc—*Nat Rich*	3044 Wilson Dr Nw, Grand Rapids MI 49534	616-735-6228	R	9*	.1
13	B and H Pattern Inc—*Lloyd Herwig*	3240 W Highview Dr, Appleton WI 54914	920-731-3861	R	9*	.1
14	Mill Masters Inc—*William Panthofer*	PO Box 7566, Jackson TN 38302	731-668-5558	R	8*	.1
15	Sentury Raider Pattern Shop—*Curt Nelson*	1201 D I Dr, Elkhart IN 46514	574-264-5800	R	7*	.1
16	HI Industries Inc—*Dennis Kocian*	PO Box 673, Brenham TX 77834	979-836-2661	R	7*	.1
17	Winona Production Services Inc—*Perrin Rondeau*	1025 E King St, Winona MN 55987	507-452-0228	R	7*	.1
18	Bender Foundry Service Inc—*William Bender*	1410 E Sadc Ave, Sigourney IA 52591	641-622-2046	R	7*	.1
19	Cobra Patterns and Models Inc—*Eric Myers*	32303 Howard Ave, Madison Heights MI 48071	248-588-2669	R	7*	.1
20	Perfect Patterns Inc—*Scott Gauerke*	2221 E Pensar Dr, Appleton WI 54911	920-734-6643	R	6*	<.1
21	Production Pattern—*Tom Wilson*	560 Solon Rd, Bedford OH 44146	440-439-3243	R	6*	<.1
22	Dependable Pattern Works Inc—*Thomas Mattson*	737 Se Market St, Portland OR 97214	503-239-5464	R	6*	<.1
23	Ravenna Pattern and Manufacturing Inc—*Dennis Emery*	PO Box 219, Ravenna MI 49451	231-853-2264	R	6*	<.1
24	Advantage Industries Inc—*William Bos*	2196 Port Sheldon St, Jenison MI 49428	616-669-2400	R	6*	<.1
25	Muncie Casting Corp—*Wayne Vest*	PO Box 2328, Muncie IN 47307	765-288-2611	R	6*	<.1
26	Diversified Pattern and Engineering Company Inc—*James Parker*	PO Box 230, Avilla IN 46710	260-897-3771	R	5*	<.1
27	Model Pattern Company Inc—*Joseph Schlatter*	8499 Centre Industrial, Byron Center MI 49315	616-878-9710	R	5*	<.1
28	DC Pattern And Tooling Inc—*Kurt Grigg*	4450 Sunset Pke, Chambersburg PA 17201	717-267-2748	R	5*	<.1
29	Cascade Pattern Company Inc—*Charles Petek*	519 Ternes Ln, Elyria OH 44035	440-323-4300	R	5*	<.1
30	Briggs Industries Inc—*Elmer Briggs*	PO Box 160, New Baltimore MI 48047	586-749-5191	R	4*	<.1
31	National Pattern Inc—*C Larson*	5900 Sherman Rd, Saginaw MI 48604	989-755-6274	R	4*	<.1
32	Colonial Patterns Inc—*Martin Meluch*	920 Overholt Rd, Kent OH 44240	330-673-6475	R	4*	<.1
33	Maumee Pattern Company Inc—*H Neuman*	1019 Hazelwood St, Toledo OH 43605	419-693-4968	R	4*	<.1

Rank	Company Name—Executive Officer	Address, City, State, Zip	Phone	Type	Fin	Empls
34	Northbend Pattern Works Inc—Dale Ziegler	PO Box 160, Harrison OH 45030	812-637-3000	R	4*	<.1
35	Cas Tech Inc—James O'sullivan	PO Box 14204, Milwaukee WI 53214	414-476-1230	R	4*	<.1
36	Craft Pattern and Mold Inc—Tony Cremeres	1410 County Rd 90 Ste, Maple Plain MN 55359	763-479-1969	R	4*	<.1
37	Seaway Pattern Manufacturing Inc—Richard Johnston	5749 Angola Rd, Toledo OH 43615	419-865-5724	R	4*	<.1
38	J P Pattern Inc—John Puhl	5038 N 125th St, Butler WI 53007	262-781-2040	R	4*	<.1
39	Quality Model and Pattern Co—Ed Doyle	2663 Elmridge Dr Nw, Grand Rapids MI 49534	616-791-1156	R	3*	<.1
40	Al-Cast Mold and Pattern Inc—Thomas Haglund	15720 Lincoln St Ne, Anoka MN 55304	763-434-4471	R	3*	<.1
41	Green Bay Pattern Inc—Chris Wurzer	1026 Centennial St, Green Bay WI 54304	920-336-5764	R	3*	<.1
42	Bespro Pattern Inc—John Basso	6101 Product Dr, Sterling Heights MI 48312	586-268-6970	R	3*	<.1
43	U S Pattern Company Inc—Louis Trautman	PO Box 220, Richmond MI 48062	586-727-2896	R	3*	<.1
44	Husite Engineering Company Inc—Larry Huston	364 Minnesota Dr, Troy MI 48083	248-588-0337	R	3*	<.1
45	Paragon Pattern And Manufacturing Co—Larry Dorato	PO Box 4187, Muskegon MI 49444	231-733-1582	R	3*	.1
46	Latrobe Pattern Co—Chris Adams	523 Lloyd Ave, Latrobe PA 15650	724-539-9753	R	3*	<.1
47	Technical Methods Inc—Stephen Nelson	20777 Kensington Blvd, Lakeville MN 55044	952-469-2185	R	2*	<.1
48	Cunningham Pattern And Engineering Inc—Joseph Cunningham	PO Box 854, Columbus IN 47202	812-379-9571	R	2*	<.1
49	Central Pattern Co—Mark Petersen	PO Box 10, Hazelwood MO 63042	314-524-3626	R	2*	<.1
50	Manitowoc Pattern And Manufacturing Co—Daniel Place	4315 Expo Dr, Manitowoc WI 54220	920-682-1912	R	2*	<.1
51	Baseline Tool Company Inc—Clayton Morr	8458 N Baseline Rd, Wawaka IN 46794	260-761-4932	R	2*	<.1
52	Willamette Pattern Works—Ken Kaster	2336 Se 9th Ave, Portland OR 97214	503-232-0793	R	2*	<.1
53	Richard W Blatt Pattern Shop Inc—Richard Blatt	760 Meckville Rd, Fredericksburg PA 17026	717-933-5633	R	1*	<.1
54	K and P Pattern Company Inc—Frank Massen	333 Rock Island Ave, Waterloo IA 50701	319-235-6411	R	1*	<.1

TOTALS: SIC 3543 Industrial Patterns
Companies: 54   405   3.0

3544 Special Dies, Tools, Jigs & Fixtures

Rank	Company Name—Executive Officer	Address, City, State, Zip	Phone	Type	Fin	Empls
1	A Finkl and Sons Co—Joseph Curci	2011 N Southport Ave, Chicago IL 60614	773-975-2510	R	140*	.4
2	Lempco Industries Inc—Richard Myles	6779 Engle Rd Ste A, Cleveland OH 44130	216-475-2400	R	117*	.2
3	BTD Manufacturing Inc—Richard Whittier	1111 13th Ave SE, Detroit Lakes MN 56501	218-847-4446	S	111*	.5
4	Penn United Technologies Inc—William Jones	PO Box 399, Saxonburg PA 16056	724-352-1507	R	84*	.5
5	AJL Manufacturing Corp—Geoff Buell	100 Holleder Pkwy, Rochester NY 14615	585-254-1128	R	66*	.2
6	C and A Tool Engineering Inc—Richard Conrow	PO Box 94, Churubusco IN 46723	260-693-2167	R	65*	.5
7	Elizabeth Carbide Die Company Inc—R Pagliari	PO Box 95, Mckeesport PA 15135	412-751-3000	R	63*	.4
8	Griffiths Holding Corp—Kenneth Griffiths	2717 Niagara Ln N, Minneapolis MN 55447	763-557-8935	R	62*	.7
9	Danly Die Set Div	PO Box 99897, Chicago IL 60696	708-780-5800	D	60	.6
10	Jergens Inc—Jack Schron	15700 S Waterloo Rd, Cleveland OH 44110	216-486-2100	R	57*	.3
11	Dayton Progress Corp—Alan Shaffer	PO Box 39, Dayton OH 45405	937-859-5111	S	50*	.5
12	Quality Mold Inc (Akron Ohio)—Steve Zoumberakis	2200 Massillon Rd, Akron OH 44312	330-645-6653	R	50*	.2
13	Xaloy Inc—Ron Auletta	PO Box 7359, New Castle PA 16107	724-656-5600	R	48*	.6
14	Taylor Turning Inc—Russell Taylor	29632 W Tech Dr, Wixom MI 48393	248-960-7920	R	41*	<.1
15	Dynacast Inc—Simon Newman	14045 Ballantyne Corpo, Charlotte NC 28277	704-927-2788	R	40*	.8
16	Quality Metalcraft Inc—Michael Chetcuti	33355 Glendale St, Livonia MI 48150	734-261-6700	R	40*	.3
17	R and D Tool and Engineering Co—Ivan Drienik	1009 Se Browning Ave, Lees Summit MO 64081	816-525-0353	R	39*	.3
18	Superior Die Set Corp—Casimir Janiszewski	900 W Drexel Ave, Oak Creek WI 53154	414-764-4900	R	30*	.4
19	Composidie Inc—L Wohlin	1295 State Rte 380, Apollo PA 15613	724-727-3466	R	36*	.5
20	Extrusion Dies Industries LLC—Bill Kinderman	911 Kurth Rd, Chippewa Falls WI 54729	715-726-1201	R	33*	.3
21	Roto-Die Company Inc—Melvin Stanley	800 Howerton Ln, Eureka MO 63025	636-587-3600	R	32*	.5
22	Gonzalez Production Systems Inc—Gary Gonzales	29401 Stephenson Hwy, Madison Heights MI 48071	248-745-1200	R	32*	.2
23	Tom Smith Industries Inc—Annette Smith	500 Smith Dr, Clayton OH 45315	937-832-1555	R	30*	.2
24	Ross Mould Inc—Larry Ross	259 S College St, Washington PA 15301	724-222-7006	R	29*	.4
25	Trojan Inc—Danny Duzyk	198 Trojan St, Mount Sterling KY 40353	859-498-0526	R	29*	.1
26	Hi-Tech Mold and Engineering Inc—Robert Schulte	2775 Commerce Dr, Rochester Hills MI 48309	248-852-6600	R	29*	.2
27	Howmet TMP Corp—Ray Mitchell	3960 S Marginal Rd, Cleveland OH 44114	216-391-3885	S	28*	.2
28	Mid-South Extrusion Die Company Inc—Terry Cockburn	PO Box 2369, Muscle Shoals AL 35662	256-381-3620	R	28*	.2
29	Delta Tooling Co—Peter Mozer	1350 Harmon Rd, Auburn Hills MI 48326	248-391-6800	R	26*	.2
30	American Tool and Mold Inc—Demetre Loulourgas	1700 Sunshine Dr, Clearwater FL 33765	727-447-7377	R	26*	.2
31	E-T-M Enterprises I Inc—David Mohnke	920 N Clinton St, Grand Ledge MI 48837	517-627-8461	R	26*	.2
32	Triangle Tool Corp—Le Roy Luther	8609 W Port Ave, Milwaukee WI 53224	414-357-7117	R	25*	.2
33	T and T Tool Inc—Steve Sundeen	PO Box 118, Spooner WI 54801	715-635-8421	R	24*	.2
34	Cast-Rite Corp—Donald Haan	515 E Airline Way, Gardena CA 90248	310-532-2080	R	24*	.1
35	Mistequay Group Ltd—James Shinners	PO Box 1367, Saginaw MI 48605	989-752-7700	R	24*	.2
36	Drt Manufacturing Co—Gary Van Gundy	618 Greenmount Blvd, Dayton OH 45419	937-298-7391	R	24*	.2
37	Ontario Die Company Of America—Gary Levene	2735 20th St, Port Huron MI 48060	810-987-5060	R	23*	.2
38	Precision Grinding and Manufacturing Corp—Michael Hockenberger	1305 Emerson St, Rochester NY 14606	585-458-4300	R	23*	.2
39	General Carbide Corp—Mona Pappafava	1151 Garden St, Greensburg PA 15601	724-836-3000	R	23*	.2
40	Hammill Manufacturing Co—John Hamill	PO Box 1450, Maumee OH 43537	419-476-0789	R	23*	.2
41	Mold Masters Intl Inc—Shana Cichon	7500 Clover Ave, Mentor OH 44060	440-953-0220	R	22*	.2
42	Futuramic Tool and Engineering Company Inc—Robert Warner	24680 Gibson Dr, Warren MI 48089	586-758-2200	R	22*	.1
43	Carbidie Corp—Carlos Cardoso	PO Box 509, Irwin PA 15642	724-864-5900	D	22*	.1
44	Engineered Plastics Inc—Kurt M Duska	PO Box 410, Lake City PA 16423	814-774-2970	R	22*	.1
45	Walker Tool and Die Inc—Bob Borgeld	2411 Walker Rd NW, Grand Rapids MI 49544	616-453-5471	R	22*	.1
46	Zanesville Mould Div	PO Box 2340, Zanesville OH 43702	740-452-2743	D	22*	.1
47	Paragon Die and Engineering Co—Dave Muir	5225 33rd St Se, Grand Rapids MI 49512	616-949-2220	R	22*	.1
48	Proper Polymers-Anderson Inc—Geoff O'brien	101 Clemson Research B, Anderson SC 29625	586-779-8787	R	22*	.3
49	Hoppe Technologies Inc—Eric Hagopian	107 First Ave, Chicopee MA 01020	413-592-9213	R	21*	.1
50	Jasco Tools Inc—Gene Baldino	PO Box 60497, Rochester NY 14606	585-254-7000	R	21*	.2
51	Royal Oak Boring—Dan Carroll	PO Box 127, Lake Orion MI 48361	248-340-9200	D	21*	.1
52	Central Extrusion Die Company Inc—Gary Cockburn	PO Box 2850, Muscle Shoals AL 35662	256-381-8262	R	21*	.2
53	Commercial Tool and Die Inc—Doug Bouwman	5351 Rusche Dr Nw, Comstock Park MI 49321	616-785-8100	R	21*	.1
54	Fastek Products Inc—David Gard	515 Noid St, Canton SD 57013	605-987-4361	S	20*	.1
55	Carr Lane Manufacturing Company Inc—Earl Walker	PO Box 191970, Saint Louis MO 63119	314-647-6200	R	20*	.1
56	Stauble Machine and Tool Company Inc—Brad Armbruster	PO Box 787, Shelbyville KY 40066	502-451-7060	R	19*	.2
57	Greenville Tool and Die Co—Dale Hartway	PO Box 310, Greenville MI 48838	616-754-5693	R	19*	.1
58	Carlson Tool and Manufacturing Corp—Jerome Edquist	PO Box 85, Cedarburg WI 53012	262-377-2020	R	19*	.1
59	Chem-Cast Ltd—Carrie Kiser	1009 Lynch Rd, Danville IL 61834	217-443-5532	R	18*	.1
60	Big 3 Precision Products Inc—Alan Scheidt	PO Box A, Centralia IL 62801	618-533-3251	R	18*	.1
61	Emery Corp—Beverley Emery	PO Box 1104, Morganton NC 28680	828-433-1536	R	18*	.1
62	Modern Tools Inc—John A Nardone	PO Box 2996, Woburn MA 01888	781-438-3211	R	17	.1

Note: An asterisk (*) indicates an estimated financial figure. The company type code used is as follows: R = Private, P = Public, S = Private Subsidiary, B = Public Subsidiary, D = Division, J = Joint Venture, I = Investment Fund.

COMPANY RANKINGS BY SALES WITHIN 4-DIGIT SIC

Rank	Company Name—Executive Officer	Address, City, State, Zip	Phone	Type	Fin	Empls
63	Fischer Tool and Die Corp—Michael Fischer	7155 Industrial Dr, Temperance MI 48182	734-847-4788	R	17*	.1
64	Porter Precision Products Co—John Cipriani	2734 Banning Rd, Cincinnati OH 45239	513-923-3777	R	17*	.1
65	Advanced Tooling Systems Inc—Drew Boresma	1166 7 Mile Rd Nw, Comstock Park MI 49321	616-784-7513	R	16*	.1
66	Tella Tool and Manufacturing Co—Daniel Provenzano	1015 N Ridge Ave Ste 1, Lombard IL 60148	630-495-0545	R	16*	.1
67	Decatur Mold Tool And Engineering Inc—Richard Apsley	PO Box 387, North Vernon IN 47265	812-346-5188	R	16*	.1
68	Parmatech Corp—Brian McBride	2221 Pine View Way, Petaluma CA 94954	707-778-2266	R	16*	.1
69	Best Cutting Die Co—Edward Porento	8080 Mccormick Blvd, Skokie IL 60076	847-675-5522	R	16*	.1
70	Apple Steel Rule Die Company Inc—Barbara Wambold	7817 W Clinton Ave, Milwaukee WI 53223	414-353-2444	R	15*	.1
71	May Tool And Mold Company Inc—Ernest May	2922 Wheeling Ave, Kansas City MO 64129	816-923-6262	R	15*	.1
72	Bronson and Bratton Inc—Mark Bronson	220 Shore Dr, Burr Ridge IL 60527	630-986-1815	R	15*	.1
73	Mt Acquisitions LLC—Cam Cadarean	51400 Bellestri Ct, Shelby Township MI 48315	586-580-6900	R	15*	.1
74	Frimo Inc—Hans Bayer	50685 Century Ct, Wixom MI 48393	248-668-3160	R	15*	.1
75	Industrial Molds Inc—Jack Peterson	5175 27th Ave, Rockford IL 61109	815-397-2971	R	15*	.1
76	Cks Tool and Engineering Inc—William Roberts	700 E Soper Rd, Bad Axe MI 48413	989-269-9702	R	15*	.1
77	JB Tool Die and Engineering Company Inc—David Bear	1509 Dividend Rd, Fort Wayne IN 46808	260-483-9586	R	15*	.1
78	B and H Toolworks Inc—Sammy Hammons	1785 Lancaster Rd, Richmond KY 40475	859-624-2458	R	15*	.1
79	Woodburn Diamond Die Company Inc—Rex Farver	PO Box 155, Woodburn IN 46797	260-632-4217	R	15*	.1
80	Fox Valley Tool and Die Inc—John Tetzlaff	PO Box 380, Kaukauna WI 54130	920-766-9455	R	14*	.2
81	Avis Roto-Die Co—Avo Askanian	PO Box 65617, Los Angeles CA 90065	323-255-7070	R	14*	.1
82	Hi-Tech Mold And Tool LLC—Gerald Cox	PO Box 197349, Louisville KY 40259	502-969-0492	R	14*	.1
83	F and S Tool Inc—Michael Faulkner	2300 Powell Ave, Erie PA 16506	814-838-7991	R	14*	.1
84	Interplex Nas Inc—Jack Seidler	1434 110th St Apt 4a, College Point NY 11356	718-961-6757	R	14*	.1
85	G H Tool and Mold Inc—Gerard Hellebusch	28 Chamber Dr, Washington MO 63090	636-390-2424	R	14*	.1
86	Progressive Molding Of Bolivar Inc—Garry Martin	10882 Fort Laurens Rd, Bolivar OH 44612	330-874-3000	R	13*	.1
87	Edro Engineering Inc—Eric Henn	20500 Carrey Rd, Walnut CA 91789	909-594-5751	R	13*	.1
88	Rand Machine Products Inc—Herman Ruhlman	PO Box 72, Falconer NY 14733	716-665-5217	R	13*	.1
89	Rapid Die and Engineering Inc—James Jones	PO Box 66201, Roseville MI 48066	616-241-5406	R	13*	.1
90	Silicone Products and Technology—Patrick Smith	4471 Walden Ave, Lancaster NY 14086	716-681-8222	S	13*	.1
91	Advance Mold and Manufacturing Inc—Douglas Schneider	71 Utopia Rd, Manchester CT 06042	860-432-5887	R	13*	.1
92	Sipco Inc	PO Box 725, Meadville PA 16335	814-724-2243	R	13*	.1
93	Tech Mold Inc—William Kushmaul	1735 W 10th St, Tempe AZ 85281	480-968-8691	R	13*	.1
94	Creative Techniques Inc—Gary Mooneyham	200 Northpointe Dr, Orion MI 48359	248-373-3050	R	13*	.1
95	Ameriken Die Supply Inc—Dale Kengott	618 N Edgewood Ave, Wood Dale IL 60191	630-766-6226	R	13*	.1
96	Msi Mold Builders Southeast Inc—Roger Klouda	12300 6th St Sw, Cedar Rapids IA 52404	319-848-7001	R	12*	.1
97	Chelar Tool and Die Inc—Malcolm Katt	11 N Florida Ave, Belleville IL 62221	618-234-6550	R	12*	.1
98	Wilson Manufacturing Co—Matthew Wilson	4725 Green Park Rd, Saint Louis MO 63123	314-416-8900	R	12*	.1
99	Mol-Son Inc—Ronald Molitor	53196 N Main St, Mattawan MI 49071	269-668-3377	R	12*	.1
100	American Die Technology Inc—Wayne Stollenwerk	3870 Lakefield Dr, Suwanee GA 30024	770-623-6111	R	12*	.1
101	Tri-V Tool and Manufacturing Co—Dave Vyhlidal	13434 Centech Rd, Omaha NE 68138	402-895-9000	R	12*	.1
102	Special Tool and Engineering Inc—Andre Special	33910 James J Pompo Dr, Fraser MI 48026	586-285-5900	R	12*	.1
103	K-Fab Inc—Martin Koch	PO Box 345, Berwick PA 18603	570-759-1247	R	12*	.1
104	EFM Corp—James Eversole	1480 14th St, Columbus IN 47201	812-372-4421	R	12*	.1
105	Norstar Aluminum Molds Inc—Sandy Scaccia	PO Box 991, Cedarburg WI 53012	262-375-5600	R	12*	.1
106	Ford Tool and Machining Inc—Thomas Chustak	PO Box 2211, Loves Park IL 61131	815-633-5727	R	12*	.1
107	Galaxy Tool Corp—Larry Payne	PO Box 531, Winfield KS 67156	620-221-6262	R	12*	.1
108	K and S Tool Die and Manufacturing Inc—Thomas Klusken	PO Box 308, Ixonia WI 53036	920-261-4663	R	12*	.1
109	Mantz Automation Inc—Denise Mantz	1630 Innovation Way, Hartford WI 53027	262-673-7560	R	12*	.1
110	Oxbow Machine Products Inc—John Tiano	12777 Merriman Rd, Livonia MI 48150	734-422-7730	R	12*	.1
111	Metal Products Inc—Alan Tetzlaff	1201 N Perkins St, Appleton WI 54914	920-739-6511	R	12*	.1
112	Standard Tool and Die Inc—Mark Lehmann	PO Box 608, Stevensville MI 49127	269-465-6004	R	12*	.1
113	Midwest Mold and Texture Corp—Katsumi Kawaguchi	4270 Armstrong Blvd, Batavia OH 45103	513-732-1300	R	11*	<.1
114	American Tooling Center Inc—John Basso	4111 Mount Hope Rd, Grass Lake MI 49240	517-522-8411	R	11*	.1
115	Lane Punch Corp—William Porter	281 Ln Pkwy, Salisbury NC 28146	704-633-3900	R	11*	.1
116	Custom Tool And Manufacturing Co—Rodney Cunningham	1031 Industry Rd, Lawrenceburg KY 40342	502-839-9541	R	11*	.1
117	Hess Engineering Inc—Dave Thomson	2950 Redfield Rd, Niles MI 49120	269-683-4182	S	11*	.1
118	Triangle Dies And Supplies Inc—Joseph Marovich	1436 Louis Bork Dr, Batavia IL 60510	630-454-3200	R	11*	.1
119	Davis Tool and Die Company Inc—Donald Davis	888 Bolger Ct, Fenton MO 63026	636-343-0828	R	11*	.1
120	MS Willett Inc—Jim Lekin	220 Cockeysville Rd, Cockeysville MD 21030	410-771-0460	R	11*	.1
121	X-Cel Tooling Inc—Bruce Becker	PO Box 338, Iron Ridge WI 53035	920-387-2780	R	11	.1
122	Genca Corp—Prem Anand	9600 18th St N, Saint Petersburg FL 33716	727-524-3622	R	11*	<.1
123	Reliance Tool and Manufacturing—Paul Knowlton	900 N State St, Elgin IL 60123	847-695-1234	R	11*	<.1
124	Kilroy Co—Paul Cardinale	9470 Pinecone Dr, Mentor OH 44060	440-951-8700	R	11*	.1
125	Exco Extrusion Dies Inc—Bryan Robbins	56617 N Bay Dr, Chesterfield MI 48051	586-749-5400	R	11*	.1
126	Decatur Wire Die LLC—Dave Hoover	PO Box 187, Decatur IN 46733	260-728-9272	R	11*	.1
127	Grace Engineering Corp—Louis Grace	34775 Potter St, Memphis MI 48041	810-392-2181	R	11*	.1
128	Reddog Industries Inc—William Hilbert	2012 E 33rd St, Erie PA 16510	814-898-4321	R	10*	.1
129	Marquette Tool and Die Co—Don Freber	3185 S Kingshighway Bl, Saint Louis MO 63139	314-771-8509	R	10*	.1
130	Die-Tech Inc—Randy Bassham	4504 Helton Dr, Florence AL 35630	256-764-7077	R	10*	.1
131	Century Die Co—Dennis Maloy	215 N Stone St, Fremont OH 43420	419-332-2693	R	10*	.1
132	Mueller Machine and Tool Company LLC—Sharon Mueller	5932 Jackson Ave, Saint Louis MO 63134	314-522-8080	R	10*	.1
133	Komarnicki Tool and Die Co—Joseph Komarnicki	29650 Pky, Roseville MI 48066	586-776-9300	R	10*	.1
134	Hodge Tool Company Inc—Edward Hodgen	2831 Old Tree Dr, Lancaster PA 17603	717-393-5543	R	10*	<.1
135	Phinney Tool and Die Company Inc—Harold Whistler	PO Box 270, Medina NY 14103	585-798-3000	R	10*	<.1
136	Standard Die and Fabricating Inc—Douglas Menzies	12980 Wayne Rd, Livonia MI 48150	734-422-4430	R	10*	.1
137	Ram Tool Inc—Roy Kannenberg	PO Box 656, Grafton WI 53024	262-375-3036	R	10*	.1
138	Clifty Engineering And Tool Company Inc—Robert Hughes	2949 Clifty Dr, Madison IN 47250	812-273-3272	R	10*	.1
139	Century Tool and Gage Co—Michael Cummings	200 S Alloy Dr, Fenton MI 48430	810-629-0784	R	10*	.1
140	Dentech Inc—Martin Berndt	PO Box 339, Brownstown PA 17508	717-656-0400	R	10*	<.1
141	S-K Mold and Tool Co—Samuel Kingrey	955 N 3rd St, Tipp City OH 45371	937-667-2428	R	9*	.1
142	Tools Inc—Brian Snyder	PO Box 910, Sussex WI 53089	262-246-3400	R	9*	.1
143	Riviera Tool LLC	5460 Executive Pkwy Se, Grand Rapids MI 49512	616-698-2100	R	9*	.1
144	Arc Industries Inc—Dennis Sjodin	2020 Hammond Dr, Schaumburg IL 60173	847-303-5005	R	9*	.1
145	Stillwater Technologies Inc—William Lukens	1040 S Dorset Rd, Troy OH 45373	937-440-2500	R	9*	.1
146	Kentucky Electronics Inc—Kenneth J Best Sr	PO Box 447, Portland TN 37148	615-325-4127	R	9*	.1
147	Comet Die and Engraving Co—Terence Donlin	909 N Larch Ave, Elmhurst IL 60126	630-833-5600	R	9*	.1
148	Model Die and Mold Inc—Gordan Brown	3859 Roger B Chaffee B, Grand Rapids MI 49548	616-243-6996	R	9*	.1
149	Tennessee Tool And Engineering Inc—Larry Palmer	735 Emory Valley Rd, Oak Ridge TN 37830	865-483-6334	R	9*	.1
150	Custom Tooling Systems Inc—John Bouwkamp	3331 80th Ave, Zeeland MI 49464	616-748-9880	R	9*	.1
151	Romeo Technologies Inc—Mark Suddon	101 Mclean, Bruce Twp MI 48065	586-336-5015	R	9*	.1
152	Danko Arlington Inc—John Danko	4800 E Wabash Ave, Baltimore MD 21215	410-664-8930	R	9*	.1

Rank	Company Name—*Executive Officer*	Address, City, State, Zip	Phone	Type	Fin	Empls
153	Xli Corp—*Peter Schott*	55 Vanguard Pkwy, Rochester NY 14606	585-436-2250	R	9*	.1
154	American Plastic Products Inc—*Roupen Yegavian*	9243 Glenoaks Blvd, Sun Valley CA 91352	818-504-1073	R	9*	.1
155	Gruber Tool and Die Inc—*David Gruber*	2605 E Progress Dr, West Bend WI 53095	262-338-8197	R	9*	.1
156	Moldex Tool and Design Corp—*Brian Shorey*	823 Bessemer St, Meadville PA 16335	814-337-3190	R	9*	.1
157	Allstate Tool And Die Inc—*Paul Held*	15 Coldwater Cres, Rochester NY 14624	585-426-0400	R	9*	.1
158	D P Tool and Machine Inc—*Peter Phillips*	5638 Tec Dr, Avon NY 14414	585-226-3200	R	9*	.1
159	Ambrit Engineering Corp—*John Mattimoe*	2640 Halladay St, Santa Ana CA 92705	714-557-1074	R	9*	.1
160	Cameron Tool Corp—*John Pettinger*	1800 Bassett St, Lansing MI 48915	517-487-3671	R	9*	.1
161	Madison Tool And Die Inc—*Terry Sparks*	3000 Michigan Rd, Madison IN 47250	812-273-2250	R	9*	.1
162	Cambridge Tool and Die Corp—*Thomas Russell*	PO Box 1104, Cambridge OH 43725	740-432-7328	R	9*	.1
163	United Tool And Engineering Co—*Rodney Meade*	4095 Prairie Hill Rd, South Beloit IL 61080	815-389-3021	R	9*	.1
164	Reuther Mold and Manufacturing Company Inc—*Karl Reuther*	1225 Munroe Falls Ave, Cuyahoga Falls OH 44221	330-923-5266	R	9*	.1
165	Converting Technology Inc—*John Norgard*	1557 Carmen Dr, Elk Grove Village IL 60007	847-290-0590	R	9*	.1
166	Seaway Plastics Engineering Inc—*Tim Smock*	PO Box 927, Port Richey FL 34673	727-845-3235	R	8*	.1
167	Fairway Injection Molding Systems Inc—*Eric Henn*	20109 Paseo Del Prado, Walnut CA 91789	909-595-2201	R	8*	.1
168	Quala Die Inc—*Dennis Schatz*	1250 Brusselles St, Saint Marys PA 15857	814-781-6280	R	8*	.1
169	Broadway Companies Inc—*William Gaiser*	PO Box 13418, Dayton OH 45413	937-890-1888	R	8*	.1
170	Cole Tool and Die Co—*Alan Cole*	PO Box 187, Mansfield OH 44901	419-522-1272	R	8*	.1
171	Prestige Mold Inc—*Donna Pursell*	11040 Tacoma Dr, Rancho Cucamonga CA 91730	909-980-6600	R	8*	.1
172	Cavaform International LLC—*Tom Spencer*	2700 72nd St N, Saint Petersburg FL 33710	727-384-3676	R	8*	.1
173	R J Zeman Tool and Manufacturing Company Inc—*Robert Zeman*	W228 N 575 Westmound D, Waukesha WI 53186	262-549-4400	R	8*	.1
174	Ever Ready Pin and Manufacturing Inc—*Steve Liphart*	5560 International Dr, Rockford IL 61109	815-874-4949	R	8*	.1
175	Elkhart Pattern Works Inc—*Richard Hilde*	1500 W Hively Ave, Elkhart IN 46517	574-293-5090	R	8*	.1
176	Mold-Base Industries Inc—*Jay Ebersole*	7501 Derry St, Harrisburg PA 17111	717-564-7960	R	8*	.1
177	Hi-Craft Engineering Inc—*Bill Duke*	33105 Kelly Rd, Fraser MI 48026	586-293-0551	R	8*	.1
178	Northwest Tool and Die Company Inc—*Anthony Chopp*	2980 3 Mile Rd NW, Grand Rapids MI 49544	616-453-8286	R	8*	.1
179	Accede Mold and Tool Company Inc—*Alton Fox*	1125 Lexington Ave, Rochester NY 14606	585-254-6490	R	8*	.1
180	Mastercraft Mold Inc—*Arle Rawlings*	3301 W Vernon Ave, Phoenix AZ 85009	602-484-4520	R	8*	.1
181	A J R Industries Inc—*Alan Wojtowicz*	117 Gordon St, Elk Grove Village IL 60007	847-439-0380	R	8*	<.1
182	Preferred Industries Inc—*Charles Kott*	11 Ash Dr, Kimball MI 48074	810-364-4090	R	8*	<.1
183	Helfer Tool Co—*Ben Helfer*	3030 Oak St, Santa Ana CA 92707	714-557-2733	R	8*	<.1
184	Bermer Tool and Die Inc—*John Szugda*	PO Box 159, Southbridge MA 01550	508-764-2521	R	8*	.1
185	Apex Mold and Engineering Inc—*Ryang Hong*	36458 Bagdad Dr, Sterling Heights MI 48312	586-979-8900	R	8*	.1
186	Heise Industries Inc—*Brooks Heise*	196 Commerce St, East Berlin CT 06023	860-828-6538	R	8*	.1
187	Vaughn Manufacturing Company Inc—*Orville Vaughn*	PO Box 70217, Nashville TN 37207	615-262-5775	R	8*	.1
188	Paramount Die Company Inc—*Richard Sarver*	1206 Belmar Dr, Belcamp MD 21017	410-272-4600	R	8*	.1
189	FH Uelner Precision Tools and Dies Inc—*Thomas Uelner*	4545 Futuro Ct, Dubuque IA 52002	563-583-5125	R	8*	.1
190	Lenhardt Tool And Die Co—*Jack Lenhardt*	PO Box 279, Alton IL 62002	618-462-1075	R	8*	.1
191	Cobra Tool and Die Inc—*Daniel Mcknight*	39115 Warren Rd, Westland MI 48185	734-710-0010	R	8*	.1
192	Metco Manufacturing Company Inc—*Bruce Kanter*	PO Box 375, Holicong PA 18928	215-343-1993	R	8*	.1
193	Wentworth Mold Incorporated Central USA Div—*Walter Kuskowski*	852 Scholz Dr, Vandalia OH 45377	937-898-8460	R	8*	.1
194	Toolcraft Products Inc—*Mark Klug*	PO Box 482, Dayton OH 45401	937-223-8271	R	8*	.1
195	Youngstown Tool and Die Company Inc—*Lawrence Stanislav*	1261 Poland Ave, Youngstown OH 44502	330-747-4464	R	8*	.1
196	Acro Tool and Die Co—*T Thompson*	325 Morgan Ave, Akron OH 44311	330-773-5173	R	8*	.1
197	Pacific West Coast Dies Inc—*Thomas Mason*	401 N Walnut Rd, Turlock CA 95380	209-664-1402	R	8*	.1
198	Easom Automation Systems Inc—*Reg Kelley*	32471 Industrial Dr, Madison Heights MI 48071	248-307-0650	R	8*	.1
199	Dieco Manufacturing Inc—*Robert Buchanan*	15715 E Pine St, Tulsa OK 74116	018-438-2193	R	7*	.1
200	Dynamic Tool and Design Inc—*John Lau*	W133n5180 Campbell Dr, Menomonee Falls WI 53051	262-783-6340	R	7*	.1
201	Chicago Mold Engineering Company Inc—*Richard Laverty*	615 Stetson Ave, Saint Charles IL 60174	630-584-1311	R	7*	.1
202	Mid-Ohio Products Inc—*Richard Coleman*	4329 Reynolds Dr, Hilliard OH 43026	614-771-2795	R	7*	.1
203	Trucut Inc—*David Gano*	PO Box 338, Sebring OH 44672	330-938-9806	R	7*	.1
204	F and G Tool And Die Co—*Jeff Johnson*	3024 Dryden Rd, Moraine OH 45439	937-294-1405	R	7*	.1
205	Clarion Technology Center—*Mike Muller*	6719 Pine Ridge Ct SW, Jenison MI 49428	616-669-6800	R	7	.1
206	Idea Tooling and Engineering Inc—*Peter Janner*	20601 Annalee Ave, Carson CA 90746	310-608-7488	R	7*	.1
207	Dixie Tool and Die Company Inc—*Harold Weaver*	PO Box 327, Gadsden AL 35902	256-442-3220	R	7*	.1
208	Lincoln Mold and Die Corp—*Edward Drozd*	225 E 1st Ave, Roselle NJ 07203	908-241-3344	R	7*	.1
209	Versevo Inc—*Terry Moon*	1055 Cottonwood Ave St, Hartland WI 53029	262-369-8210	R	7*	.1
210	Marion Mold and Tool Inc—*Karl Kalber*	PO Box 967, Marion VA 24354	276-783-6101	R	7*	<.1
211	Quality Rubber Manufacturing Company Inc—*L Lorenzo*	PO Box 709, Hendersonville NC 28793	828-696-2000	R	7*	.1
212	Stm Manufacturing Inc—*Roger Blauwkamp*	494 E 64th St, Holland MI 49423	616-392-4656	R	7*	.1
213	Wisconsin Metal Parts Inc—*Daniel Erschen*	N4 W 22450 Bluemound R, Waukesha WI 53186	262-524-9100	R	7*	.1
214	Dekalb Tool and Die Inc—*John Brown*	PO Box 121, Tucker GA 30085	770-938-5605	R	7*	.1
215	Willer Tool Corp—*James Willer*	W225n16683 Cedar Park, Jackson WI 53037	262-677-6000	R	7*	.1
216	Enterprise Tool and Die LLC—*Doug Groom*	PO Box 439, Grandville MI 49468	616-538-0920	R	7*	.1
217	Sharp Model Co—*Roger Walker*	70745 Powell Rd, Bruce Twp MI 48065	586-752-3099	R	7*	.1
218	Southeastern Tool And Die Inc—*Gary Pinson*	PO Box 297, Greenbrier TN 37073	615-643-4591	R	7*	.1
219	H And K Tool And Machine Company Inc—*Stanley Elias*	125 Pke Cir, Huntingdon Valley PA 19006	215-322-0380	R	7*	.1
220	Omega Tool Inc—*John Weber*	N93w14430 Whittaker Wa, Menomonee Falls WI 53051	262-255-0205	R	7*	<.1
221	Hughes Brothers Aircrafters Inc—*Susan Hughes*	11010 Garfield Pl, South Gate CA 90280	323-773-4541	R	7*	.1
222	Monarch Tool and Die Co—*Stanley Kabat*	862 Industrial Dr, Elmhurst IL 60126	630-530-8886	R	7*	.1
223	Datum Industries LLC—*Craig Broucek*	4740 44th St Se, Grand Rapids MI 49512	616-977-1995	R	7*	.1
224	Ovidon Manufacturing LLC—*Dave Marshall*	1200 Grand Oaks Dr, Howell MI 48843	517-548-4005	R	7*	.1
225	Bradrock Molding Inc—*Edward Lapinski*	75 Bradrock Dr, Des Plaines IL 60018	847-299-8151	R	7*	.1
226	Lupaul Industries Inc—*J Smith*	1911 S Cooper St, Jackson MI 49203	517-789-7779	R	7*	.1
227	Future Mold Corp—*Melvin Otto*	215 S Webber St, Farwell MI 48622	989-588-9948	R	7*	.1
228	Guill Tool and Engineering Company Inc—*A Guillemette*	20 Pke St, West Warwick RI 02893	401-828-7600	R	7*	.1
229	Vicount Industries Inc—*Philip Padula*	24704 Hathaway St, Farmington Hills MI 48335	248-471-5071	R	7*	.1
230	Jonco Die Co—*John Gordon*	5201 Program Ave, Saint Paul MN 55112	763-783-9300	R	7*	.1
231	Wagner Die Supply—*Ellsworth Knutson*	2041 Elm Ct, Ontario CA 91761	909-947-3044	D	7*	<.1
232	Kdi Technologies Inc—*Bruce Krouskop*	2206 Pine Ridge Dr Sw, Jenison MI 49428	616-667-1600	R	7*	.1
233	Leader Tool Company Inc—*Allen Gunn*	PO Box 66, Harbor Beach MI 48441	989-479-3281	R	7*	.1
234	Pace Punches Inc—*Edward Pepper*	297 Goddard, Irvine CA 92618	949-428-2750	R	7*	.1
235	J H Benedict Company Inc—*Robert Jones*	3211 N Main St, East Peoria IL 61611	309-694-3111	R	7*	.1
236	Brogdon Tool and Die Inc—*Nick Ruitenberg*	PO Box 306, Blue Springs MO 64013	816-229-1171	R	7*	<.1
237	Toolroom Inc—*Karl Krupp*	PO Box 329, Owensville MO 65066	573-437-4154	R	7*	.1
238	Adena Tool Corp—*Gary Gundy*	4201 Little York Rd, Dayton OH 45414	937-890-8428	R	7*	.1
239	Dieco Inc—*John Zaiger*	PO Box 6331, Arlington TX 76005	817-608-9856	R	7*	.1
240	4-M Industries Inc—*Christopher Marsh*	35300 Glendale St, Livonia MI 48150	734-762-7200	R	7*	.1

Note: An asterisk (*) indicates an estimated financial figure. The company type code used is as follows: R = Private, P = Public, S = Private Subsidiary, B = Public Subsidiary, D = Division, J = Joint Venture, I = Investment Fund.

COMPANY RANKINGS BY SALES WITHIN 4-DIGIT SIC

Rank	Company Name—*Executive Officer*	Address, City, State, Zip	Phone	Type	Fin	Empls
241	Planet Tool and Gear Inc—*Donald Grassmuck*	315 S Cool Springs Rd, O Fallon MO 63366	636-379-9800	R	7*	.1
242	Esteves-Dwd LLC	1921 Patterson St, Decatur IN 46733	260-728-9272	R	7*	.1
243	Jamison Steel Rule Die Inc—*James Jamison*	PO Box 447, Murfreesboro TN 37133	615-893-5234	R	7*	.1
244	Catalina Tool and Mold Inc—*Scott Kelley*	11200 E Cmino Del Sahu, Tucson AZ 85749	520-746-0105	R	7*	.1
245	Peak Industries Company Inc—*James Kostaroff*	5320 Oakman Blvd, Dearborn MI 48126	313-846-8666	R	7*	.1
246	Alaark Tooling and Automation Inc—*Mark Koenig*	4336 Gateway Dr, Sheboygan WI 53081	920-452-8231	R	7*	.1
247	Cs Tool Engineering Inc—*Don Mabie*	PO Box K210, Cedar Springs MI 49319	616-696-0940	R	7*	.1
248	Starn Tool and Manufacturing Co—*William Starn*	PO Box 209, Meadville PA 16335	814-724-1057	R	6*	.1
249	T and W Tool and Die Corp—*Herbert Trute*	21770 Wyoming Pl, Oak Park MI 48237	248-548-5400	R	6*	.1
250	United Western Industries Inc—*L Simmons*	3515 N Hazel Ave, Fresno CA 93722	559-226-7236	R	6*	<.1
251	Everett Pattern and Manufacturing Inc—*Eric Johnson*	PO Box 930, Middleton MA 01949	978-777-4575	R	6*	<.1
252	A and M Tool and Die Company Inc—*Alvino Aliberti*	PO Box 400, Southbridge MA 01550	508-764-3241	R	6*	<.1
253	Cdm Tool and Manufacturing Company Inc—*Brian Priestaf*	749 N Wacker Dr, Hartford WI 53027	262-673-5620	R	6*	<.1
254	King Industrial Corp—*Mark King*	PO Box 372, Seymour IN 47274	812-522-3261	R	6*	.1
255	O Keller Tool Engineering Co—*Barry La Chance*	PO Box 510327, Livonia MI 48151	734-425-4500	R	6*	.1
256	Matrix Tooling Inc—*Paul Ziegenhorn*	949 Aec Dr, Wood Dale IL 60191	630-595-6144	R	6*	.1
257	True Industries Inc—*Dan Brown*	PO Box 769, Ravenna OH 44266	330-296-4342	R	6*	.1
258	Bernal Inc—*Luigi Pessarelli*	2960 Technology Dr, Rochester Hills MI 48309	248-299-3600	R	6*	<.1
259	M-1 Tool Works Inc—*Martin Ryba*	1419 S Belden St, Mchenry IL 60050	815-344-1275	R	6*	.1
260	Tool-All Inc—*John Farrell*	2053 E 30th St, Erie PA 16510	814-898-3917	R	6*	.1
261	Designs For Tomorrow Inc—*Judy Harris*	2401 Schuetz Rd, Maryland Heights MO 63043	314-432-5566	R	6*	.1
262	Mathias Die Company Inc—*Thomas Mathias*	391 Malden St, South Saint Paul MN 55075	651-451-0105	R	6*	.1
263	Bennett Metal Products Inc—*James Bennett*	PO Box 34, Mount Vernon IL 62864	618-244-1911	R	6*	.1
264	American Tool and Engineering Inc—*Dennis Hobson*	102 Industrial Pkwy, Greene IA 50636	641-816-4921	R	6*	.1
265	Plastic Mold Technologies Inc—*Gary Proos*	PO Box 8025, Grand Rapids MI 49518	616-698-9810	R	6*	.1
266	Precision Punch Corp—*Robert Peterson*	304 Christian Ln, Berlin CT 06037	860-229-9902	R	6*	.1
267	Automation Tool and Die Inc—*William Bennett*	2867 Nationwide Pkwy, Brunswick OH 44212	330-225-8336	R	6*	<.1
268	Lasercam LLC—*Kathy Midgley*	1039 Hoyt Ave, Ridgefield NJ 07657	201-941-1262	R	6*	<.1
269	Tmd Machining Inc—*Thomas Darby*	PO Box 342, Plainwell MI 49080	269-685-3091	R	6*	<.1
270	Tool Ventures International—*J Reesor*	3695 44th St SE, Kentwood MI 49512	616-532-4800	R	6*	<.1
271	Northern Machine Tool Co—*Stephen Olsen*	761 Alberta Ave, Norton Shores MI 49441	231-755-1603	R	6*	<.1
272	Sirois Tool Company Inc—*Marc Begin*	169 White Oak Dr, Berlin CT 06037	860-828-5327	R	6*	<.1
273	Enmark Tool Co—*Gary Enmark*	PO Box 217, Fraser MI 48026	586-293-2797	R	6*	<.1
274	Viking Tool and Engineering Inc—*Warren Hutchins*	PO Box 278, Whitehall MI 49461	231-893-0031	R	6*	<.1
275	Diamond Tool and Die Co—*Ellene Fertal*	33220 Lakeland Blvd, Eastlake OH 44095	216-481-0808	R	6*	<.1
276	Multi-Precision Detail Inc—*Michael Dean*	2635 Paldan Dr, Auburn Hills MI 48326	248-373-3330	R	6*	<.1
277	Pollington Machine Tool Inc—*Claude Pollington*	20669 30th Ave, Marion MI 49665	231-743-2003	R	6*	<.1
278	Ultra Punch Of Dayton Inc—*John Stickel*	3980 Benner Rd, Miamisburg OH 45342	937-859-4644	R	6*	.1
279	Magor Mold Inc—*Wolfgang Buhler*	420 S Lone Hill Ave, San Dimas CA 91773	909-592-3663	R	6*	<.1
280	Apex Tool Works Inc—*William Collins*	3200 Tollview Dr, Rolling Meadows IL 60008	847-394-5810	R	6*	<.1
281	Edco Inc—*Jan Tesar*	5244 Enterprise Blvd S, Toledo OH 43612	419-726-1595	R	6*	<.1
282	Forge Die and Tool Corp—*Eric Kchikian*	31800 W 8 Mile Rd, Farmington Hills MI 48336	248-477-0020	R	6*	<.1
283	Applied Composites Engineering Inc—*Leigh Sargent*	705 S Girls School Rd, Indianapolis IN 46231	317-243-4225	R	6*	<.1
284	Mayer Tool and Engineering Inc—*John Mayer*	PO Box 8, Sturgis MI 49091	269-651-1428	R	6*	.1
285	United Die Company Inc—*John Kontra*	199 Devon Ter, Kearny NJ 07032	201-997-0250	R	6*	.1
286	Big 3 Precision Mold Services LLC—*Larry Barresi*	PO Box A, Centralia IL 62801	856-293-1400	R	6*	<.1
287	Grw Technologies Inc—*Rosemarie Suehner*	4460 44th St Se Ste B, Grand Rapids MI 49512	616-575-8119	R	6*	<.1
288	Precision Boring Co—*Gerald Decker*	24400 Maplehurst Dr, Clinton Township MI 48036	586-463-3900	R	6*	<.1
289	Armin Tool And Manufacturing Co—*Paul Stoll*	1500 N La Fox St, South Elgin IL 60177	847-742-1864	R	6*	.1
290	Mccurdy Tool and Machining Co—*F Mccurdy*	1912 Krupke Rd, Caledonia IL 61011	815-765-2117	R	6*	.1
291	Modified Technologies Inc—*Charles Russell*	6500 Bethuy Rd, Ira MI 48023	586-725-0448	R	6*	<.1
292	Crowley Tool Co—*E Crowley*	190 Molly Walton Dr, Hendersonville TN 37075	615-824-5594	R	6*	<.1
293	Precision Mold Base Corp—*William Horst*	2405 W Geneva Dr, Tempe AZ 85282	602-431-8131	R	6*	<.1
294	B and B Tool and Die Company Inc—*Kurt Jones*	624 S Jefferson St, Muncie IN 47305	765-288-7668	R	6*	<.1
295	Express Tool and Die Co—*Paul Varady*	5900 Schooner St, Belleville MI 48111	734-485-5900	R	6*	<.1
296	Federal Tool and Engineering LLC—*Robert Beverung*	N52 W 5338 Portland Rd, Cedarburg WI 53012	262-377-7070	R	6*	<.1
297	Glen Carbide Inc—*Edward Fawcett*	PO Box 498, Carnegie PA 15106	412-279-7500	R	6*	<.1
298	Swan Engineering and Machine Co—*David Weigle*	2611 State St, Bettendorf IA 52722	563-355-2671	R	6*	<.1
299	Plastic Engineering and Technical Services Inc—*Patrick Tooman*	4141 Luella Ln, Auburn Hills MI 48326	248-373-0800	R	6*	<.1
300	Tnt-Edm Inc—*Thomas Mullen*	47689 E Anchor Ct, Plymouth MI 48170	734-459-1700	R	6*	<.1
301	Canadian Engineering and Tool Company Limited Inc—*Donald Tregenza*	2265 S Cameron Blvd, Windsor CA 95492	313-961-2165	R	6*	.1
302	Auto Craft Tool and Die Co—*Michael Duvernay*	1800 Fruit St, Clay MI 48001	810-794-4929	R	6*	.1
303	Exxene Corp—*Lili Karsh*	PO Box 81203, Corpus Christi TX 78468	361-991-8391	R	6*	.1
304	Fermer Precision Inc—*Stewart Bunce*	114 Johnson Rd, Ilion NY 13357	315-822-6371	R	6*	.1
305	Linden Mold And Tool Corp—*Vincent Illuzzi*	PO Box C, Rahway NJ 07065	732-381-1411	R	6*	<.1
306	Republic Die and Tool Co—*John Lasko*	45000 Van Born Rd, Belleville MI 48111	734-699-3400	R	5*	<.1
307	Lawrence Mold And Tool Corp—*George Lesenskyj*	1412 Ohio Ave, Lawrenceville NJ 08648	609-392-5422	R	5*	<.1
308	Cambron Engineering Inc—*Stephen Sheppard*	3800 Wilder Rd, Bay City MI 48706	989-684-5890	R	5*	<.1
309	Hoosier Tool and Die Company Inc—*Mark Foster*	2860 N National Rd, Columbus IN 47201	812-376-8286	R	5*	<.1
310	Bay Products Inc—*Thomas Bayagich*	17800 15 Mile Rd, Fraser MI 48026	586-296-1880	R	5*	<.1
311	Delco Corp—*Fred Kungl*	3300 Massillon Rd, Akron OH 44312	330-896-4220	R	5*	<.1
312	Die-Tech And Engineering Inc—*William Berry*	4620 Herman Ave Sw, Grand Rapids MI 49509	616-530-9030	R	5*	<.1
313	MC Ward Inc—*Mark Ward*	4100 Griswold Rd, Port Huron MI 48060	810-982-9720	R	5*	.1
314	North Hartland Tool Corp—*John Mullen*	PO Box 38, North Hartland VT 05052	802-295-3196	R	5*	<.1
315	Jolico/J-B Tool Inc—*Patricia Wieland*	4325 22 Mile Rd, Shelby Township MI 48317	586-739-5555	R	5*	<.1
316	Kw Inc—*William Kennedy*	325 W Main St, Birdsboro PA 19508	610-582-8735	R	5*	<.1
317	Superior Mold and Die Co—*Richard Yamokoski*	449 N Main St, Munroe Falls OH 44262	330-688-8251	R	5*	<.1
318	Franchino Mold and Engineering Co—*Richard Franchino*	5867 W Grand River Ave, Lansing MI 48906	517-321-5609	R	5*	<.1
319	Alpha Carb Enterprises Inc—*Louis Leibert*	691 Hyde Park Rd, Leechburg PA 15656	724-845-2500	R	5*	.1
320	Maloney Tool and Mold Inc—*Edward Maloney*	PO Box 379, Meadville PA 16335	814-337-8407	R	5*	.1
321	X-L Machine Company Inc—*James King*	20481 M 60, Three Rivers MI 49093	269-279-5128	R	5*	<.1
322	Capital Tool Co—*Richard Crane*	1110 Brookpark Rd, Cleveland OH 44109	216-661-5750	R	5*	<.1
323	Simpsons Enterprises Inc—*James Simpson*	55255 Franklin Dr, Three Rivers MI 49093	269-279-7237	R	5*	<.1
324	Apollo Tool Inc—*Fritz Menke*	PO Box 305, Westfield WI 53964	608-296-2112	R	5*	<.1
325	Psk Steel Corp—*Jerry Kinast*	PO Box 308, Hubbard OH 44425	330-759-1251	R	5*	<.1
326	Hamilton Mold and Machine Company Inc—*Dale Fleming*	25016 Lakeland Blvd, Cleveland OH 44132	216-732-8200	R	5*	<.1
327	Rhinestahl Corp—*Heinz Moeller*	PO Box 21339, Georgetown OH 45121	513-489-1317	R	5*	<.1
328	Alcona Tool and Machine Inc—*Monty Kruttlin*	PO Box 340, Lincoln MI 48742	989-736-8151	R	5*	.1

Rank	Company Name—*Executive Officer*	Address, City, State, Zip	Phone	Type	Fin	Empls
329	R and D Manufacturing Inc—*Ken Owens*	7009 Industrial Park R, Mount Pleasant TN 38474	931-379-5805	R	5*	<.1
330	Dramco Tool Company Inc—*Bill Koch*	502 Claude Rd, Grand Island NE 68803	308-382-5251	R	5*	<.1
331	United Tool and Engineering Inc—*Richard Penn*	337 Campbell St, Mishawaka IN 46544	574-259-1953	R	5*	<.1
332	Kennebec Technologies—*Charles Johnson*	150 Church Hill Rd, Augusta ME 04330	207-626-0188	R	5*	<.1
333	Mach Mold Inc—*William Mach*	360 Urbandale Ave, Benton Harbor MI 49022	269-925-2044	R	5*	<.1
334	Schrey and Sons Mold Company Inc—*Walter Schrey*	24735 Ave Rockefeller, Valencia CA 91355	661-294-2260	R	5*	<.1
335	Bel-Kur Inc—*Jeffery Kuhr*	7297 Express Rd, Temperance MI 48182	734-847-0651	R	5*	<.1
336	Fiber-Tech Inc—*J Rogers*	4155 Courtney Rd, Franksville WI 53126	262-835-1300	R	5*	<.1
337	Herbert Machine Works Inc—*Mathias Walter*	850 Moe Dr, Akron OH 44310	330-929-4297	R	5*	<.1
338	L and H Mold and Engineering Inc—*Stan Hillary*	2031 Del Rio Way, Ontario CA 91761	909-930-1550	R	5*	<.1
339	Ready Molds Inc—*Lawrence Nussio*	32645 Folsom Rd, Farmington Hills MI 48336	248-474-4007	R	5*	<.1
340	CPC of Vermont Inc—*Michael Funk*	PO Box 706, Middlebury VT 05753	802-388-6381	R	5*	.1
341	Tech Tool and Molded Plastics—*Scott Hanaway*	1045 French St, Meadville PA 16335	814-724-8222	R	5*	.1
342	Pivot Punch Corp—*Robert King*	6550 Campbell Blvd, Lockport NY 14094	716-625-8000	R	5*	.1
343	Header Die And Tool Inc—*Thomas Derry*	PO Box 5846, Rockford IL 61125	815-397-0123	R	5*	.1
344	Hellebusch Tool and Die Inc—*Walter Hellebusch*	4 Southlink Dr, Washington MO 63090	636-239-7543	R	5*	.1
345	Imperial Wire Die Inc—*Marion Aiello*	256 E 3rd St, Mount Vernon NY 10553	914-699-1112	R	5*	.1
346	P and R Industries Inc—*Lawrence Coyle*	1524 Clinton Ave N, Rochester NY 14621	585-266-6725	R	5*	.1
347	Ameritek Lasercut Dies Inc—*Bill Hicks*	122 S Walnut Cir, Greensboro NC 27409	336-292-1165	R	5*	<.1
348	Chirch Global Manufacturing LLC—*Franz Osterhues*	1150 Ridgeview Dr, Mchenry IL 60050	815-385-5600	R	5*	<.1
349	Peterson Jig and Fixture Inc—*David Schuiling*	301 Rockford Park Dr N, Rockford MI 49341	616-866-8296	R	5*	<.1
350	Homeyer Tool and Die Co—*Herb Homeyer*	PO Box 247, Marthasville MO 63357	636-433-2244	R	5*	<.1
351	Hommer Tool/Manufacturing Inc—*James Hommer*	311 W University Dr, Arlington Heights IL 60004	847-394-3355	R	5*	<.1
352	Caliber Mold And Machine Inc—*Jack Thornton*	PO Box 847, Athens OH 45701	330-633-8171	R	5*	<.1
353	Carroll Tool And Die Co—*Thomas Plotzke*	46650 Erb Dr, Macomb MI 48042	586-949-7670	R	5*	<.1
354	Janler Corp—*Carol Ebel*	6545 N Avondale Ave, Chicago IL 60631	773-774-0166	R	5*	<.1
355	Precise Rotary Die Inc—*Ray Barak*	9250 Ivanhoe St, Schiller Park IL 60176	847-678-0001	R	5*	<.1
356	Reich Tool and Design Inc—*Fred Reich*	W175n5750 Technology D, Menomonee Falls WI 53051	262-252-3440	R	5*	<.1
357	Rpm Carbide Die Inc—*Eric Metcalfe*	PO Box 278, Arcadia OH 44804	419-894-6426	R	5*	<.1
358	Mauston Tool Corp—*Jeff Schwab*	1015 Parker Dr, Mauston WI 53948	608-847-5162	R	5*	<.1
359	AM Tool and Die—*Alan Mortenson*	1000 Carnegie St, Rolling Meadows IL 60008	847-398-7530	R	5*	<.1
360	St Mary's Tool and Die Inc—*Craig White*	504 Floral Ave, Troy OH 45373	937-335-8540	R	5*	<.1
361	Numerics Unlimited Inc—*Wayne Atkins*	1700 Dalton Dr, New Carlisle OH 45344	937-849-0100	R	5*	<.1
362	Radial Manufacturing Inc—*Paul G Keefe*	3543 N Martens Ave, Franklin Park IL 60131	847-678-5808	R	5*	<.1
363	Gadsden Tool Inc—*Jimmy Hill*	PO Box 979, Gadsden AL 35902	256-442-8777	R	5*	.1
364	Aggressive Tooling Inc—*Richard Jones*	608 Industrial Park Dr, Greenville MI 48838	616-754-1404	R	5*	<.1
365	Kent Mold And Manufacturing Co—*Paul Ferder*	1190 W Main St, Kent OH 44240	330-673-3469	R	5*	<.1
366	Pyper Tool and Engineering Inc—*Jeff Pyper*	3003 Wilson Dr Nw, Grand Rapids MI 49534	616-791-9788	R	5*	<.1
367	Wolverine Carbide and Tool Inc—*Derek Stevens*	15300 Martin Rd, Roseville MI 48066	586-772-1298	R	5*	<.1
368	Master Precision Products Inc—*Stephen Drake*	PO Box 190, Greenville MI 48838	616-754-5483	R	5*	<.1
369	New England Mold Sterling Inc—*Jeffrey Barhoff*	PO Box 495, Shrewsbury MA 01545	978-422-8050	R	5*	<.1
370	Oak Burr Tool Inc—*Brian Mcconnell*	PO Box 338, Sturgis MI 49091	269-651-9393	R	5*	.3
371	Hill Machinery Co—*Donald Bos*	4585 Danvers Dr Se, Grand Rapids MI 49512	616-940-2800	R	5*	<.1
372	Ultra Precision Inc—*Frank Paz*	PO Box E, Freeport PA 16229	724-205-6161	R	5*	<.1
373	Reber Machine and Tool Company Inc—*Neil Reber*	PO Box 2403, Muncie IN 47307	765-288-0297	R	5*	<.1
374	Tibor Inc—*Ted Juracsik*	255 N Congress Ave, Delray Beach FL 33445	561-272-0770	R	5*	<.1
375	Producto Dieco Corp—*Newman Marsilius*	5835 Harper Rd, Cleveland OH 44139	440-542-0000	S	5*	<.1
376	Action Rotary Die Inc—*Scott Curtin*	1208 W National Ave, Addison IL 60101	630-628-6830	R	5*	<.1
377	Steeplechase Tool and Die Inc—*Michael Baird*	9307 Howard City Edmor, Lakeview MI 48850	989-352-5544	R	5*	<.1
378	Excel Tool And Manufacturing Inc—*Karin Kelter*	14344 W 96th Ter, Lenexa KS 66215	913-894-6415	R	5*	<.1
379	Royal Diversified Products Inc—*Roger Ellin*	PO Box 444, Warren RI 02885	401-245-6900	R	5*	.1
380	Electro Magnetic Products Inc—*Gordon Mason*	355 Crider Ave, Moorestown NJ 08057	856-235-3011	R	5*	<.1
381	JK Tool and Die Inc—*Celesta Kiebler*	321 N Washington Rd, Apollo PA 15613	724-727-2490	R	5*	<.1
382	Precision Die Technologies Inc—*John Frieburger*	4716 Speedway Dr, Fort Wayne IN 46825	260-482-5001	R	5*	<.1
383	Accu Die and Mold Inc—*Daniel Reifschneider*	7473 Red Arrow Hwy, Stevensville MI 49127	269-465-4020	R	5*	<.1
384	Pro-Mold Inc—*Walter Schaub*	55 Chancellor Dr, Roselle IL 60172	630-893-3594	R	5*	<.1
385	Mike Alexander Dies Inc—*Mike Alexander*	1134 W Kentucky St, Louisville KY 40210	502-515-2777	R	5*	<.1
386	Trutron Corp—*Lisa Kingsley*	274 Executive Dr, Troy MI 48083	248-583-9166	R	5*	<.1
387	Regal Mold and Die—*Gary Rheude*	25208 Leer Dr, Elkhart IN 46514	574-262-4110	R	5*	<.1
388	Miller Tool and Die Company Inc—*Nancy Trott*	PO Box 233, Mayville WI 53050	920-387-4040	R	5*	<.1
389	Homestead Tool And Machine Inc—*Bernard Robinson*	2618 Coolidge Rd, Coleman MI 48618	989-465-6182	R	4*	.1
390	East Pattern and Model Corp—*Warren Kellogg*	41 Saginaw Dr, Rochester NY 14623	585-461-3240	R	4*	<.1
391	Greiner Extrusion Us Inc—*James Hess*	PO Box 556, Meadville PA 16335	814-333-2060	R	4*	<.1
392	Accu Laser Technologies Inc—*David Hrycaj*	21 Father Devalles Blv, Fall River MA 02723	508-674-0294	R	4*	<.1
393	Niron Inc—*Glen Nieberle*	20541 Earlgate St, Walnut CA 91789	909-598-1526	R	4*	<.1
394	Vitols Tool and Machine Corp—*Robert Vitols*	10082 Sandmeyer Ln, Philadelphia PA 19116	215-464-8240	R	4*	<.1
395	Wolverine Tool and Engineering Co—*Bill Fish*	5641 W River Dr Ne, Belmont MI 49306	616-785-9796	R	4*	<.1
396	Kastler and Reichlin Inc—*James Kastler*	710 Taylor St, Elyria OH 44035	440-322-0970	R	4*	.1
397	Nanlee Tooling Inc—*Anderson Moore*	2920 Kreitzer Rd, Dayton OH 45439	937-434-3133	R	4*	<.1
398	Howard Tool Company Inc—*Marty Arsenault*	547 Odlin Rd, Bangor ME 04401	207-942-1203	R	4*	<.1
399	Temco Tool Company Inc—*Norman Gagne*	PO Box 5031, Manchester NH 03108	603-622-6989	R	4*	<.1
400	Rsk Tool Inc—*Ronald Kohagura*	410 W Carob St, Compton CA 90220	310-537-3302	R	4*	<.1
401	Superior Tool and Machining Co—*Bruce Hanson*	8700 Monticello Ln N, Maple Grove MN 55369	763-425-2540	R	4*	<.1
402	US Steel Rule Dies Inc—*David Reynolds*	13030 Alondra Blvd, Cerritos CA 90703	562-207-1424	R	4*	<.1
403	Northeast Tire Molds Inc—*Stephanie Sipe*	159 Opportunity Pkwy, Akron OH 44307	330-376-6107	R	4*	<.1
404	Actco Tool and Manufacturing Co—*Rob Gruber*	PO Box 675, Meadville PA 16335	814-336-4235	R	4*	<.1
405	Hermetic Coil Company Inc—*David Barton*	PO Box 219, Bicknell IN 47512	812-735-2400	R	4*	<.1
406	Industrial Machining Services Inc—*John Puthoff*	PO Box 228, Fort Loramie OH 45845	937-295-2022	R	4*	<.1
407	Mc Afee Tool and Die Inc—*Gary Afee*	1717 Boettler Rd, Uniontown OH 44685	330-896-9555	R	4*	<.1
408	Bodine Tool and Machine Company Inc—*William Lauth*	1273 N Church St Ste 1, Moorestown NJ 08057	856-234-7800	R	4*	<.1
409	O and R Precision Grinding Inc—*Tony Oswalt*	5315 W 900 S, Geneva IN 46740	260-368-9394	R	4*	<.1
410	Bennett Die and Tool Inc—*Jim Millen*	130 Wygant Rd, Horseheads NY 14845	607-739-3871	R	4*	<.1
411	Concours Mold Alabama Inc—*Mark Googin*	651 24th St Sw, Cullman AL 35055	256-255-1100	R	4*	<.1
412	Anka Tool and Die Inc—*Agnes Karl*	150 Wells Ave, Congers NY 10920	845-268-4116	R	4*	<.1
413	Concrete Mold Corp—*Bradley Gardner*	2121 E Del Amo Blvd, Compton CA 90220	310-537-5171	S	4*	<.1
414	Connecticut Die Cutting Services Inc—*Robert Bessette*	440 Chase River Rd, Waterbury CT 06704	203-756-6591	R	4*	<.1
415	Gma Tooling—*Gerald Adasavage*	110 Pke Cir, Huntingdon Valley PA 19006	215-355-3105	R	4*	<.1
416	H-E Tool and Manufacturing Company Inc—*Pauline Hamin*	800 Industrial Hwy Uni, Cinnaminson NJ 08077	856-303-8787	R	4*	<.1
417	Midwest Tool and Die Corp—*Victor Felger*	327 Ley Rd, Fort Wayne IN 46825	260-483-4282	R	4*	<.1
418	Suburban Tool and Die Company Inc—*David Mc Guire*	4940 Pacific Ave, Erie PA 16506	814-833-4882	R	4*	<.1

Note: An asterisk (*) indicates an estimated financial figure. The company type code used is as follows: R = Private, P = Public, S = Private Subsidiary, B = Public Subsidiary, D = Division, J = Joint Venture, I = Investment Fund.

COMPANY RANKINGS BY SALES WITHIN 4-DIGIT SIC

Rank	Company Name—*Executive Officer*	Address, City, State, Zip	Phone	Type	Fin	Empls
419	Basilius Inc—*Scott Basilius*	4338 S Ave, Toledo OH 43615	419-536-5810	R	4*	<.1
420	Dollins Tool Inc—*Jan Klestinec*	PO Box 170, Independence MO 64051	816-252-3093	R	4*	<.1
421	Radian Precision Inc—*David Tate*	32853 Edward Ave, Madison Heights MI 48071	248-616-6112	R	4*	<.1
422	Southwest Mold Inc—*Brian Anderson*	740 W Knox Rd, Tempe AZ 85284	480-785-9100	R	4*	<.1
423	MR Mold and Engineering Corp—*Richard Finnie*	2700 E Imperial Hwy St, Brea CA 92821	714-996-5511	R	4*	.1
424	Excel Tool Inc—*Richard Elmore*	2020 1st Ave, Seymour IN 47274	812-522-6880	R	4*	.1
425	A and O Mold And Eng Inc—*Douglas Northup*	301 N 4th St, Vicksburg MI 49097	269-649-0600	R	4*	<.1
426	QME Inc—*James Florian*	PO Box 285, Baroda MI 49101	269-422-2137	R	4*	<.1
427	Fort Wayne Mold and Engineering Inc—*Richard Schmidt*	4501 Earth Dr, Fort Wayne IN 46809	260-747-9168	R	4*	<.1
428	Schoitz Engineering Inc—*Ed Jensen*	PO Box 546, Waterloo IA 50704	319-234-6615	R	4*	<.1
429	Abbottstown Industries Inc—*James Lewis*	W Fleet St, Abbottstown PA 17301	717-259-0112	R	4*	<.1
430	Accurate Steel Rule Cutting Die Inc—*Scott Cason*	6994 Rogers Lake Rd, Lithonia GA 30058	770-484-0273	R	4*	<.1
431	Arkansas Tool and Die Inc—*Wayne Pavan*	PO Box 2036, North Little Rock AR 72115	501-374-6972	R	4*	<.1
432	Baxter Machine and Tool Co—*Larry Baxter*	103 N Horton St, Jackson MI 49202	517-782-2808	R	4*	<.1
433	Chenango Valley Technologies Inc—*Lloyd Baker*	PO Box 1038, Sherburne NY 13460	607-674-4115	R	4*	<.1
434	Mac Machine and Metal Works Inc—*John Malone*	PO Box 609, Connersville IN 47331	765-825-4121	R	4*	<.1
435	Forster Tool and Manufacturing Company Inc—*Maureen Forster*	1135 Industrial Dr, Bensenville IL 60106	630-616-8177	R	4*	<.1
436	Savage Ventures Inc—*Mark Krosney*	1702 Se Village Green, Port Saint Lucie FL 34952	772-335-5655	R	4*	<.1
437	Pacific Tool Inc—*Frank Garbarino*	15235 Ne 92nd St, Redmond WA 98052	425-882-1970	R	4*	<.1
438	Circle Mold Inc—*Edward Siciliano*	PO Box 513, Tallmadge OH 44278	330-633-7017	R	4*	<.1
439	Industrial Custom Products Inc—*Herb Houndt*	2801 37th Ave Ne, Minneapolis MN 55421	612-781-2255	R	4*	<.1
440	Lonero Engineering Company Inc—*Vincent Lonero*	PO Box 935, Troy MI 48099	248-689-9120	R	4*	<.1
441	New Tech Industries Inc—*Joanne Bigelow*	7911 44th Ave W, Mukilteo WA 98275	425-778-1200	R	4*	<.1
442	Springfield Tool And Die Inc—*Thomas Aldridge*	PO Box 6787, Greenville SC 29606	864-877-9666	R	4*	<.1
443	Alpha Mold West Inc—*Dane Whittington*	7005 W 116th Ave, Broomfield CO 80020	303-465-1701	R	4*	<.1
444	Innovative Mold Inc—*George Kasper*	12500 31 Mile Rd, Washington MI 48095	586-752-2996	R	4*	<.1
445	Precision Pattern Inc (Tacoma Washington)—*Brian Retzloff*	2620 E G St, Tacoma WA 98421	253-572-4333	S	4*	<.1
446	Precision Tool and Die of Ponca City Inc—*Greg Neisen*	2200 N Ash St, Ponca City OK 74601	580-762-2421	R	4*	<.1
447	Progress Tool and Stamping Inc—*Brian Westerheide*	PO Box 53, Minster OH 45865	419-628-2384	R	4*	<.1
448	Fancort Industries Inc—*Ronald Corey*	PO Box 565, Caldwell NJ 07007	973-575-0610	R	4*	<.1
449	Duo-Tec Tool Co—*Orville Hanken*	8550 Revere Ln N, Maple Grove MN 55369	763-425-5005	R	4*	<.1
450	Fitco—*George Fischer*	1211 W Acacia Ave Ste, Hemet CA 92543	951-652-4858	R	4*	.1
451	Central Ky Tool and Engineering Corp—*Willam Mattingly*	645 Metts Dr, Lebanon KY 40033	270-692-4556	R	4*	<.1
452	Withers Tool Die and Manufacturing Co—*William Adams*	1238 Veterans Memorial, Mableton GA 30126	770-948-2544	R	4*	<.1
453	Michiana Plastics Inc—*James Orszulak*	1702 E 7th St, Mishawaka IN 46544	574-259-6262	R	4*	<.1
454	Oakley Die and Mold Company Inc—*Ernest Petrinowitsch*	7595 Innovation Way, Mason OH 45040	513-754-8500	R	4*	<.1
455	JM Mold South Inc—*David Bowers*	807 Sheffield Rd, Easley SC 29642	864-855-0450	R	4*	<.1
456	Palma Tool and Die Company Inc—*William Tate*	40 Ward Rd, Lancaster NY 14086	716-681-4464	R	4*	<.1
457	Chicago Roll Company Inc—*Cathleen Focht*	970 N Lombard Rd, Lombard IL 60148	630-627-8888	R	4*	<.1
458	International Cutting Die Inc—*Kevin Mchenry*	2045 N 15th Ave, Melrose Park IL 60160	708-343-3333	R	4*	<.1
459	Snider Mold Company Inc—*Timothy Mieritz*	6303 W Industrial Dr, Mequon WI 53092	262-242-0870	R	4*	<.1
460	Mayville Die and Tool Inc—*Greg Krapfl*	PO Box 113, Mayville WI 53050	920-387-3500	R	4*	<.1
461	Mold Craft Inc—*Peter Manship*	PO Box 458, Willernie MN 55090	651-426-3216	R	4*	<.1
462	Met-L-Tec LLC—*Juanita Stubleski*	7193 Sulier Dr, Temperance MI 48182	734-847-7004	R	4*	<.1
463	Jimdi Plastics Inc—*Richard Schrotenboer*	5375 Edgeway Dr, Allendale MI 49401	616-895-7766	R	4*	<.1
464	PDQ Tool and Stamping Co—*Thomas Miller*	14901 Greenwood Rd, Dolton IL 60419	708-841-3000	R	4*	<.1
465	Southbridge Tool and Manufacturing Inc—*Peter Didonato*	181 Southbridge Rd, Dudley MA 01571	508-764-2779	R	4*	<.1
466	Trademark Die and Engineering Inc—*Michael O'keefe*	8060 Graphic Dr Ne Uni, Belmont MI 49306	616-863-6660	R	4*	<.1
467	Ptc-In-Liquidation Inc—*Thomas Kapusta*	PO Box 659, Saegertown PA 16433	814-763-2000	R	4*	<.1
468	Colonial Mold Inc—*Richard Roberts*	44479 Reynolds Dr, Clinton Township MI 48036	586-469-4944	R	4*	<.1
469	Matchless Machine and Tool Company Inc—*Gerald Etter*	PO Box 1733, Martinsville IN 46151	765-342-4550	R	4*	<.1
470	Northwest Tool And Manufacturing Company Inc—*Matthew Brill*	2200 N 4th Ave, Wausau WI 54401	715-675-7424	R	4*	<.1
471	Advanced Mold and Tooling Inc—*Peter Grassl*	769 Trabold Rd, Rochester NY 14624	585-426-2110	R	4*	<.1
472	Custom Tool and Design Inc—*Jeffrey Mertz*	4962 Pittsburgh Ave, Erie PA 16509	814-838-9777	R	4*	<.1
473	D Maldari and Sons Inc—*Chris Maldari*	PO Box 150541, Brooklyn NY 11215	718-499-3555	R	4*	<.1
474	Estee Mold and Die Inc—*Bruce Hackett*	1467 Stanley Ave, Dayton OH 45404	937-224-7853	R	4*	<.1
475	Kreis Tool and Manufacturing Company Inc—*E Kreis*	1615 Cambridge Dr, Elgin IL 60123	847-289-3700	R	4*	<.1
476	Pronto Tool and Die Company Inc—*Michael Silvestri*	50 Remington Blvd, Ronkonkoma NY 11779	631-981-8920	R	4*	<.1
477	Windy City Cutting Die Inc—*John Rzeszot*	104 Foster Ave, Bensenville IL 60106	630-521-9410	R	4*	<.1
478	Wright Engineered Plastics Inc—*Barbara Roberts*	3225 Regional Pkwy, Santa Rosa CA 95403	707-575-1218	R	4*	.1
479	Oliphant Tool Co—*William Oliphant*	15652 Chemical Ln, Huntington Beach CA 92649	714-903-6336	R	4*	<.1
480	Superior Engineering Company Inc—*A Johnson*	39374 Grand Ave, North Branch MN 55056	651-674-4427	R	4*	<.1
481	Tri-Star Engineering Inc—*Robert Lindstrom*	2455 Pan Am Blvd, Elk Grove Village IL 60007	847-595-3377	R	4*	<.1
482	AW Die Engraving Inc—*Arnold Werdin*	8550 Roland St, Buena Park CA 90621	714-521-0842	R	4*	<.1
483	Bradley-Thompson Tool Co—*Michael Huard*	22108 W 8 Mile Rd, Southfield MI 48033	248-352-1466	R	4*	<.1
484	Centennial Technologies Inc—*James Hammis*	1335 Agricola Dr, Saginaw MI 48604	989-752-6167	R	4*	<.1
485	Frizzelle and Parsons Die Sinking Co—*Richard Parsons*	6602 John Deere Rd, Moline IL 61265	309-796-1030	R	4*	<.1
486	Glaze Tool And Engineering Inc—*E Glaze*	PO Box 267, New Haven IN 46774	260-493-4557	R	4*	<.1
487	L and Z Tool And Engineering Inc—*Thomas Lamarca*	1691 Rte 22, Watchung NJ 07069	908-322-2220	R	4*	<.1
488	Snapp Tool and Die Inc—*Gregory Snapp*	10885 Dyer St Ste A, El Paso TX 79934	915-821-2046	R	4*	<.1
489	Specialties Steel Rule Dies Inc—*John Nagy*	PO Box 33, Windsor NJ 08561	609-443-9200	R	4*	<.1
490	Henze Machine And Tool Company LLC—*Judith Canning*	PO Box 250358, Franklin MI 48025	248-588-5620	R	4*	<.1
491	Superior Jig Inc—*John Morrissey*	1540 N Orangethorpe Wa, Anaheim CA 92801	714-525-4777	R	4*	<.1
492	Custom Tool And Die Co—*Harry Reinhardt*	7059 Red Arrow Hwy, Stevensville MI 49127	269-465-9130	R	4*	<.1
493	Multi Tool Inc—*Eric Hoover*	PO Box 605, Conneaut Lake PA 16316	814-763-6664	R	4*	<.1
494	Frankfort Manufacturing Inc—*Donald Surber*	1105 Main St, Frankfort MI 49635	231-352-7551	R	4*	<.1
495	Jamesway Tool And Die Inc—*James Rozeboom*	401 120th Ave, Holland MI 49424	616-396-3731	R	4*	<.1
496	All Five Tool Company Inc—*Joseph Panella*	70 Enterprise Dr Ste 2, Bristol CT 06010	860-583-1691	R	4*	<.1
497	Fremar Industries Inc—*Marcus Bauman*	2808 Westway Dr, Brunswick OH 44212	330-220-3700	R	4*	<.1
498	P Tool and Die Company Inc—*Thomas Allen*	PO Box 369, North Chili NY 14514	585-889-1340	R	4*	<.1
499	Pelco Tool and Mold Inc—*Richard Truhlar*	181 Exchange Blvd, Glendale Heights IL 60139	630-871-1010	R	4*	<.1
500	Valley Header Die Inc—*Norland Bolen*	6833 Irene Rd, Belvidere IL 61008	815-544-2169	R	4*	<.1
501	New Jersey Tool And Die Co—*Anton Kemps*	800 Colfax Ave, Kenilworth NJ 07033	908-245-0020	R	4*	<.1
502	Advance Engineering and Manufacturing Co—*Robert Vance*	1 Vance Dr, O Fallon MO 63366	636-281-8444	R	4*	<.1
503	Mac-Mold Base Inc—*Michael Gustavus*	14921 32 Mile Rd, Bruce Twp MI 48065	586-752-1956	R	4*	<.1
504	Precision Process Corp—*Vladimir Moskin*	780 Bonnie Ln, Elk Grove Village IL 60007	847-952-8088	R	4*	<.1
505	Topaz Tool and Die Inc—*Charles Carter*	1617 Marilyn Ave, Dayton OH 45420	937-252-8084	R	4*	<.1
506	Industrial Machine Service Inc—*Michael Prichard*	110 Industrial Rd, Alexandria TN 37012	615-529-2145	R	4*	<.1
507	Schmald Tool and Die Inc—*Laurie Moncrieff*	G4206 S Saginaw St, Burton MI 48529	810-743-1600	R	3*	<.1

Rank	Company Name—*Executive Officer*	Address, City, State, Zip	Phone	Type	Fin	Empls
508	Capitol Tool and Die LP—*Jeff Hickey*	PO Box 326, Madison TN 37116	615-868-8372	R	3*	<.1
509	Encompass Tool and Machine Inc—*Paul Maples*	PO Box 531, Winfield KS 67156	580-762-5800	R	3*	<.1
510	Monticello Tool And Die Inc—*Danny Morgan*	PO Box 148, Monticello KY 42633	606-348-8104	R	3*	<.1
511	Quality Mold Shop Inc—*Karen Bouldin*	4247 Smithville Hwy, Mcminnville TN 37110	931-668-3876	R	3*	<.1
512	B and D Precision Tools Inc—*Heliodoro Duran*	2367 W 8th Ln, Hialeah FL 33010	305-885-1583	R	3*	<.1
513	Alliance Industries Inc—*Todd Sangster*	15721 Leone Dr Ste A, Macomb MI 48042	586-781-5160	R	3*	<.1
514	Custom Design Inc—*Tim Bickings*	4481 Commercial Ave, Portage MI 49002	269-323-8561	R	3*	<.1
515	Roth-Williams Industries Inc—*Patricia Williams*	34335 Groesbeck Hwy, Clinton Township MI 48035	586-792-0090	R	3*	<.1
516	Southeastern Tool Company Inc—*Donald Cheeks*	PO Box 481, Aiken SC 29802	803-649-4127	R	3*	<.1
517	Vinyltech Inc—*Rick Amato*	PO Box 127, North Jackson OH 44451	330-538-0369	R	3*	<.1
518	Action Tool and Machine Inc—*San Miyamoto*	5976 Ford Ct, Brighton MI 48116	810-229-6300	R	3*	<.1
519	Allright Tool Company Inc—*Frances Whittington*	PO Box 320261, Birmingham AL 35232	205-591-1468	R	3*	<.1
520	Argus Corp—*Fred Ransford*	12540 Beech Daly Rd, Redford MI 48239	313-937-2900	R	3*	<.1
521	Preferred Tool and Die Company Inc—*Timothy Launiere*	5400 W River Dr Ne, Comstock Park MI 49321	616-784-6789	R	3*	.1
522	Versatile Mold and Design Inc—*Franklyn Heusser*	PO Box 158, Rutledge GA 30663	706-557-8397	R	3*	<.1
523	Bestech Tool Corp—*Mike Korneli*	1605 Corporate Ctr Dr, West Bend WI 53095	262-338-6312	R	3*	<.1
524	Corydon Machine and Tool Company Inc—*Steven Yahraus*	615 Quarry Rd Nw, Corydon IN 47112	812-738-3107	R	3*	<.1
525	Zin-Tech Inc—*Joseph Zingaro*	1416 Union Ave, Pennsauken NJ 08110	856-661-0900	R	3*	<.1
526	Cleveland Steel Tool Co—*Mark Dawson*	474 E 105th St, Cleveland OH 44108	216-681-7400	R	3*	<.1
527	Tooling Science Inc—*Edwin Kelly*	9424 Deerwood Ln N, Maple Grove MN 55369	763-425-6001	R	3*	<.1
528	Dauntless Industries Inc—*George Payton*	806 N Grand Ave, Covina CA 91724	626-966-4494	R	3*	<.1
529	Northland Tool and Die Inc—*Richard Cossin*	10399 Northland Dr Ne, Rockford MI 49341	616-866-4451	R	3*	<.1
530	Arrow Diversified Tooling Inc—*David Trench*	PO Box 508, Ellington CT 06029	860-872-9072	R	3*	<.1
531	Jordan Tool Corp—*Donna Pilarski*	11801 Commerce St, Warren MI 48089	586-755-6700	R	3*	<.1
532	Mcx Inc—*Pam Dutton*	1315 Oregon Ave, Klamath Falls OR 97601	541-884-4004	R	3*	<.1
533	Machine Tek Systems Inc—*Tim Paul*	PO Box 187, Garrettsville OH 44231	330-527-4450	R	3*	<.1
534	Concept Molds Inc—*Jim Northup*	12273 N Us Hwy 131, Schoolcraft MI 49087	269-679-2100	R	3*	<.1
535	Precise Tool and Die Inc—*Jeff Swartzlander*	1711 Piper Rd, Leechburg PA 15656	724-845-1285	R	3*	<.1
536	Ranger Tool and Die Co—*John Kuhnle*	317 S Westervelt Rd, Saginaw MI 48604	989-754-1403	R	3*	<.1
537	Tipco Punch Inc—*Jack Pickins*	6 Rowe Ct, Hamilton OH 45015	513-874-9140	R	3*	<.1
538	Voisard Tool Service—*Eugene Voisard*	PO Box 276, Russia OH 45363	937-526-5451	R	3*	<.1
539	Laser Tool Inc—*Thomas Hilburn*	PO Box 728, Saegertown PA 16433	814-763-2032	R	3*	<.1
540	Pen Ro Mold And Tool Inc—*Rick Arena*	343 Pecks Rd Ste 5, Pittsfield MA 01201	413-499-0464	R	3*	<.1
541	Rapid Mold Solutions Inc—*Damian Kuzmin*	4820 Pacific Ave, Erie PA 16506	814-833-2721	R	3*	<.1
542	Superior Tool and Die Co—*Roy Hershberger*	2325 S Nappanee St, Elkhart IN 46517	574-293-2591	R	3*	<.1
543	Midwest Tool and Engineering Co—*Robert Cammerer*	112 Webster St, Dayton OH 45402	937-224-0756	R	3*	<.1
544	Praet Tool and Engineering Inc—*Alan Praet*	51214 Industrial Dr, Macomb MI 48042	586-677-3800	R	3*	<.1
545	Whip City Tool and Die Corp—*Raymond Salois*	PO Box 99, Southwick MA 01077	413-569-5528	R	3*	<.1
546	Suruga USA Corp—*Masayuki Takaya*	40 S Addison Rd Ste 30, Addison IL 60101	630-628-4000	R	3*	<.1
547	Maco Tool and Engineering Inc—*Steve Hiner*	210 Spring St, Saint Johns MI 48879	989-224-6723	R	3*	<.1
548	Tri-R Dies Inc—*Benjamin Morucci*	556 Bev Rd, Youngstown OH 44512	330-758-8050	R	3*	<.1
549	Compacting Tooling Inc—*Kenneth Lasica*	PO Box 89, Mckeesport PA 15135	412-751-3535	R	3*	<.1
550	Helm Corp—*Norman Helm*	1403 Technogly Way, Morristown TN 37813	423-581-1703	R	3*	<.1
551	AJ Tool Company Inc—*Albert Jubeck*	3026 Beechwood Industr, Hubertus WI 53033	262-628-4445	R	3*	<.1
552	American Die Corp—*Steve Bartolomucci*	6860 Holland Rd, Clay MI 48001	810-794-4080	R	3*	<.1
553	J A English Ii Inc—*Jae English*	11495 Sorrento Valley, San Diego CA 92121	858-455-0371	R	3*	<.1
554	Maq Investments Group Inc—*Daniel Ziadi*	4600 Nw 128th St, Opa Locka FL 33054	305-691-1468	R	3*	<.1
555	RA Serafini Inc—*Robert Serafini*	PO Box 6100, Gastonia NC 28056	704-864-6763	R	3*	<.1
556	Shield Pattern Works Inc—*Glen Frischmon*	1740 99th Ln Ne, Minneapolis MN 55449	763-784-3920	R	3*	<.1
557	Indiana Southern Mold Corp—*Angela Grindstaff*	PO Box 119, North Vernon IN 47265	812-346-2622	R	3*	<.1
558	Banner Mold and Die Company Inc—*James De Felice*	251 Florence St, Leominster MA 01453	978-534-6558	R	3*	<.1
559	Old Hickory Tool and Die LP—*Annette Wilson*	3135 Pleasant Grove Rd, White House TN 37188	615-672-3318	R	3*	<.1
560	Preferred Tool Inc—*Larry Bryant*	2710 Montgomery Dr, Seymour IN 47274	812-524-7033	R	3*	<.1
561	Data Technology Inc—*David H Buckley*	260 Fordham Rd, Wilmington MA 01887	978-694-0055	R	3*	<.1
562	Rainbow Tool And Machine Company Inc—*James Martin*	PO Box 7067, Rainbow City AL 35906	256-442-3888	R	3*	<.1
563	Ken-Bar Tool and Engineering I—*Richard Smith*	3121 S Walnut St, Muncie IN 47302	765-284-4408	R	3*	<.1
564	Adko Inc—*Joe Adkison*	6901 Jenny Lind Rd, Fort Smith AR 72908	479-646-2533	R	3*	<.1
565	A F and G Company Inc—*Harry Cann*	3908 Frankford Ave, Philadelphia PA 19124	215-533-6400	R	3*	<.1
566	Danielson Tool and Die—*Ronald Hill*	9924 E Jackson Ave, Spokane Valley WA 99206	509-924-5734	R	3*	<.1
567	Horizon Die Company Inc—*Daniel Badovinac*	160 Windsor Dr, East Dundee IL 60118	847-426-8558	R	3*	<.1
568	Schulze Tool Co—*Bruce Goin*	1032 S Vista Ave, Independence MO 64056	816-257-1414	R	3*	<.1
560	Netstal Machinery Inc—*Michael Sansocy*	57 Jackson Rd, Devens MA 01434	978-772-5100	R	3*	<.1
570	Del-Tool Company Inc—*Doug Brinker*	640 Commerce Ave, Baraboo WI 53913	608-356-7726	R	3*	<.1
571	Artech Diversified Inc—*Mark Shabadash*	3821 Hawthorn Ct, Waukegan IL 60087	847-249-7718	R	3*	<.1
572	A and C Mold Company Inc—*Andrew Mendala*	3870 Swenson Ave, Saint Charles IL 60174	630-587-0177	R	3*	<.1
573	Accuchrome Tool and Mold Inc—*James Sides*	240 Rock Crusher Rd, Asheboro NC 27203	336-626-2552	R	3*	<.1
574	Bemcore Tool Inc—*Bill Merritt*	6161 Rip Rap Rd, Dayton OH 45424	937-233-0135	R	3*	<.1
575	Crum Manufacturing Inc—*Ernest Crum*	PO Box 28, Waterville OH 43566	419-878-9779	R	3*	<.1
576	J and L Tool Company Inc—*Leonard Rossicone*	368 N Cherry St Ext, Wallingford CT 06492	203-265-6237	R	3*	<.1
577	Kent Machine Inc—*Zane Kennedy*	8677 S State Rd 9, Pendleton IN 46064	765-778-7777	R	3*	<.1
578	Schaller Tool and Die Co—*Steven Shaller*	49505 Gratiot Ave, Chesterfield MI 48051	586-949-5500	R	3*	<.1
579	Tri Star Tool and Machine Inc—*Michael Fischer*	W245n5474 S Corporate, Sussex WI 53089	262-820-1859	R	3*	<.1
580	Union Tool and Mold Company Inc—*Anthony Arrighi*	220 Rutgers St, Maplewood NJ 07040	973-763-6611	R	3*	<.1
581	Portsmouth Tool and Die Corp—*Jerry Miller*	807 Florida Ave, Portsmouth VA 23707	757-393-0034	S	3*	<.1
582	Swan Industries Inc—*Helmut Kramer*	10975 Lin Valle Dr, Saint Louis MO 63123	314-894-5678	R	3*	<.1
583	Falcon Tool Company Inc—*Debra Hummert*	7500 Hub Pkwy, Cleveland OH 44125	216-328-0300	R	3*	<.1
584	Tucker Technology Inc—*Mike Reusing*	PO Box 66, Tucker GA 30085	770-938-6662	R	3*	<.1
585	Excel Pattern Works Inc—*Roland Gauvin*	7020 Chase Rd, Dearborn MI 48126	313-581-1150	R	3*	<.1
586	Progressive Tool Co—*Carl Meyer*	PO Box 4060, Waterloo IA 50704	319-234-6619	R	3*	<.1
587	AA Precisioneering Inc—*Pat Abbondanza*	PO Box 84, Meadville PA 16335	814-724-6668	R	3*	<.1
588	Aries Inc—*Joseph Anthony*	326 Carpenter St, Providence RI 02909	401-331-7738	R	3*	<.1
589	G and F Tool Products—*George Goodnoe*	7127 5 Point Hwy, Eaton Rapids MI 48827	517-663-3646	R	3*	<.1
590	Versatool and Die Machining and Engineering Inc—*Donald Baker*	2890 Kennedy Dr, Beloit WI 53511	608-365-3621	R	3*	<.1
591	Hytech Tool and Design Co—*Bernard Pelkowski*	12076 Edinboro Rd, Edinboro PA 16412	814-734-6000	R	3*	<.1
592	Champion Die Inc—*Robert Champion*	5510 W River Dr Ne, Comstock Park MI 49321	616-784-2397	R	3*	<.1
593	Dec Tool Corp—*Jeff Decore*	2651 Dukane Dr, Saint Charles IL 60174	630-513-9883	R	3*	<.1
594	Parr-Green Mold and Machine Co—*Terry Green*	9107 Pleasantwood Ave, Canton OH 44720	330-499-4913	R	3*	<.1
595	Westosha Tool Company Inc—*Betty Seltz*	PO Box 6, Bristol WI 53104	262-857-7866	R	3*	<.1
596	CG Automation And Fixture Inc—*Doug Bouwman*	5352 Rusche Dr Nw, Comstock Park MI 49321	616-785-5400	R	3*	<.1

Note: An asterisk (*) indicates an estimated financial figure. The company type code used is as follows: R = Private, P = Public, S = Private Subsidiary, B = Public Subsidiary, D = Division, J = Joint Venture, I = Investment Fund.

COMPANY RANKINGS BY SALES WITHIN 4-DIGIT SIC

Rank	Company Name—Executive Officer	Address, City, State, Zip	Phone	Type	Fin	Empls
597	Dickerson Tool and Engineering LLC	1020 S Mitchell Ave, Chillicothe MO 64601	660-646-3378	R	3*	<.1
598	Sterling Die and Engineering Inc—Chester Wisniewski	15767 Claire Ct, Macomb MI 48042	586-677-0707	R	3*	<.1
599	Tw Stamping and Tool Inc—Terry Warren	PO Box 176, Winona TX 75792	903-877-2353	R	3*	<.1
600	Milwaukee Punch Corp—Russel Lee Superior Die Set Corp	PO Box 313, Greendale WI 53129	414-421-8482	S	3*	<.1
601	Diamond Tool And Engineering—Kent Smith	PO Box 97, Bertha MN 56437	218-924-4024	R	3*	<.1
602	Scori Mold And Engineering Inc—Robert Lammon	PO Box 575, Centreville MI 49032	269-467-7200	R	3*	<.1
603	Jus Rite Engineering Inc—David Bratton	56977 Elk Ct, Elkhart IN 46516	574-522-9600	R	3*	<.1
604	Matheson Higgins Congress Press Inc—Jay Smith	166 New Boston St, Woburn MA 01801	781-935-6400	R	3*	<.1
605	Imperial Tool Inc—James Olson	15195 Freeland Ave N, Hugo MN 55038	651-429-2418	R	3*	<.1
606	Marten Models and Molds Inc—Steve Marten	18291 Mike C Ct, Fraser MI 48026	586-293-2260	R	3*	<.1
607	Hoffman Tool and Die Inc—Jerry Hoffman	PO Box 257, Fairbury IL 61739	815-692-2628	R	3*	<.1
608	John J Adams Die Corp—Richard Adams	PO Box 157, Worcester MA 01613	508-757-3894	R	3*	<.1
609	Penco Tool LLC—James Cufr	PO Box 429, Ashtabula OH 44005	440-998-1116	R	3*	<.1
610	Wrentham Tool Products—Robert Croteau	155 Farm St, Bellingham MA 02019	508-966-2332	R	3*	<.1
611	E-Lite Tool and Manufacturing Co—Scott Jones	122 Industrial Dr, Belleville IL 62220	618-236-1580	R	3*	<.1
612	Jim Dresslar Inc—John Pinney	390 E Old Plank Rd, Bargersville IN 46106	317-422-5147	R	3*	<.1
613	JCS Tool and Manufacturing Company Inc—Roger Felske	193 N Powell Rd, Essexville MI 48732	989-892-8975	R	3*	<.1
614	Alpha Star Tool and Mold Inc—John Thurow	11 Burdent Dr, Crystal Lake IL 60014	815-455-2802	R	3*	<.1
615	Ward Mclaughlin and Co—John Richard	1 Wardcraft Dr, Spring Arbor MI 49283	517-750-9100	R	3*	<.1
616	Alliance Pattern Inc—Larry Sibbing	2560 Kindustry Park Rd, Keokuk IA 52632	319-524-2624	R	3*	<.1
617	Paravis Industries Inc—Glenn Charest	1597 Atlantic Blvd, Auburn Hills MI 48326	248-393-2300	R	3*	<.1
618	Ultra-Sonic Extrusion Dies Inc—David Schoenegge	34863 Groesbeck Hwy, Clinton Township MI 48035	586-791-8550	R	3*	<.1
619	Production Mold Inc—John Mc Intyre	PO Box 35007, Phoenix AZ 85069	602-278-8722	R	3*	<.1
620	Orycon Control Technology Inc—Salvatore Benenati	3407 Rose Ave, Ocean NJ 07712	732-922-2400	R	3*	<.1
621	Standard Precision Manufacturing—Christopher Repko	13617 Broadway Dr, Meadville PA 16335	814-724-1202	R	3*	<.1
622	Abco Tool and Die Inc—David Bourque	PO Box 458, Hyannis MA 02601	508-771-3225	R	3*	<.1
623	Ledford Engineering Company Inc—Lowell Ledford	200 Prospect Pl Sw, Cedar Rapids IA 52404	319-363-0211	R	3*	<.1
624	Northwest Tool and Machine Inc—Kent Pickett	1014 Hurst Rd, Jackson MI 49201	517-750-1332	R	3*	<.1
625	Perm Industries Inc—Lee Milazzo	PO Box 660, Saint John IN 46373	219-365-5002	R	3*	<.1
626	Sturgis Tool And Die Inc—Robert Zimmerman	PO Box 368, Sturgis MI 49091	269-651-5435	R	3*	<.1
627	Tekcast Industries Inc—Len Schaer	12 Potter Ave, New Rochelle NY 10801	914-576-0222	R	3*	<.1
628	Wire Cut E D M Inc—Ken Hill	PO Box 59429, Dallas TX 75229	972-247-5777	R	3*	<.1
629	Davis and Pierce Die Service Inc—Eugene Pierce	6602 Royal St Ste A, Pleasant Valley MO 64068	816-781-7757	R	3*	<.1
630	Polyurethane Molding Industries Inc—William Ober	100 Founders Dr, Woonsocket RI 02895	401-765-6700	R	3*	<.1
631	Computer Plastics—Wayne Harshbarger	1914 National Ave, Hayward CA 94545	510-785-3600	R	3*	<.1
632	Sipper Products Inc—Rick Maddox	PO Box 2947, Corona CA 92878	951-735-7026	R	3*	<.1
633	Delux Industries Inc—William Schindler	1187 Burch Dr, Evansville IN 47725	812-867-7485	R	3*	<.1
634	Linwood Tool Company Inc—Matt Copus	PO Box 69, Linwood MI 48634	989-697-4403	R	3*	<.1
635	Midwest Machining Inc—Phillip Allor	526 Omalley Dr, Coopersville MI 49404	616-837-9721	R	3*	<.1
636	Olympian Tool LLC—Todd Deitrich	604 N Us Hwy 27, Saint Johns MI 48879	989-224-4817	R	3*	<.1
637	Choice Mold Components Inc—James Humes	44347 Reynolds Dr, Clinton Township MI 48036	586-783-5600	R	3*	<.1
638	Cliffco Stands Inc—Steve Garrison	397 Starbuck Rd, Wilmington OH 45177	937-382-3700	R	3*	<.1
639	JM Kusch Inc—Jeffrey Kusch	PO Box 1337, Bay City MI 48706	989-684-8820	R	3*	<.1
640	Truskill Machining Inc—Walt Kimberlin	1000 Alvin Weinberg Dr, Oak Ridge TN 37830	865-483-1957	R	3*	<.1
641	Tech Ridge Inc—Stephen Comeau	PO Box 4001, Chelmsford MA 01824	978-256-5741	R	3*	<.1
642	Gottschall Tool and Die Inc—Danny Beegle	14028 W Middletown Rd, Salem OH 44460	330-332-1544	R	3*	<.1
643	Lincoln Tool and Die Inc—John Rich	PO Box 357, Stanford KY 40484	606-365-3101	R	3*	<.1
644	M Curry Corp—Richard Curry	PO Box 269, Bridgeport MI 48722	989-777-7950	R	3*	<.1
645	Apex Mold and Die Corp—Harald Zacharias	PO Box 169, Endeavor WI 53930	608-587-2333	R	3*	<.1
646	Cj Enterprises—Chuck Boyles	11530 Western Ave, Stanton CA 90680	714-898-8558	R	3*	<.1
647	Diemaster Machine and Tool LLC—Jim Burton	PO Box 409, Portland TN 37148	615-325-9288	R	3*	<.1
648	Elite Mold and Engineering Inc—Robert Mandeville	51548 Filomena Dr, Shelby Township MI 48315	586-314-4000	R	3*	<.1
649	Johnson Forging Equipment—Neil Johnson	12660 Mansfield St, Detroit MI 48227	313-838-9628	R	3*	<.1
650	Mar-Vel Tool Company Inc—John Glaser	858 Hall Ave, Dayton OH 45404	937-223-2137	R	3*	<.1
651	Samuel Stamping Technologies LLC—Tony Demarco	1760 Broadway Rd, Hermitage PA 16148	724-981-5042	R	3*	<.1
652	Stellar Mold and Tool Inc—Arden Vikre	20850 W Gale Ave, Galesville WI 54630	608-582-4118	R	3*	<.1
653	Shannon Precision LLC—Kathy Williams	2033 Fall River Rd, Leoma TN 38468	931-762-9228	R	3*	<.1
654	Conley Casting Supply Corp—Arthur Francis	124 Maple St, Warwick RI 02888	401-785-9500	R	3*	<.1
655	Evansville Tool and Die Inc—Jack Droste	4900 N Saint Joseph Av, Evansville IN 47720	812-422-7101	R	3*	<.1
656	New Ulm Precision Tool Inc—Dan Mckeowm	PO Box 517, New Ulm MN 56073	507-233-2900	R	3*	<.1
657	Seabrook Plastics Inc—Serge Cousins	1869 Lindberg Dr, Norton Shores MI 49441	231-759-8820	R	3*	<.1
658	KAM Tool and Die Inc—William Alford	530 N Industrial Dr, Zebulon NC 27597	919-269-5099	R	3*	<.1
659	IE and E Industries Inc—Ron Webber	111 E 10 Mile Rd, Madison Heights MI 48071	248-544-8181	R	3*	<.1
660	Pedavena Mould And Die Company Inc—Steve Scardenzan	1535 W 130th St, Gardena CA 90249	310-327-2814	R	3*	<.1
661	Precision Masking Inc—Diane Lavoy	721 Lavoy Rd, Erie MI 48133	734-848-4200	R	3*	<.1
662	Schneider and Marquard Inc—Michael O'shea	PO Box 39, Newton NJ 07860	973-383-2200	R	3*	<.1
663	Tolerance Tool and Engineering Ltd—Gerard Fiorentino	20541 Glendale St, Detroit MI 48223	313-592-4011	R	3*	<.1
664	Tools and Production Inc—Michael Lamberti	4924 Encinita Ave, Temple City CA 91780	626-286-0213	R	3*	<.1
665	US Machine and Tool LLC—Phil Kelley	150 Shamrock Industria, Tyrone GA 30290	770-487-2015	R	3*	<.1
666	Co-Ex Plastic Tooling, Inc—Roger Smith	Rr 3 Box 51, Milton WV 25541	304-743-4024	R	3*	<.1
667	Gemco Of Port Lavaca Inc—Jurhee Ivy	6611 Lone Tree Rd N, Victoria TX 77905	361-570-6611	R	2*	<.1
668	Great Southwest Tool Co—Andres Gutierrez	1220 Barranca Dr Ste 1, El Paso TX 79935	915-594-7804	R	2*	<.1
669	Monarch Products Corp—Gene Mercarelli	PO Box 118, Minerva OH 44657	330-868-7717	R	2*	<.1
670	H and H Mold And Tooling Co—Clayton Herman	PO Box 1209, Fairfield IA 52556	641-472-7300	R	2*	<.1
671	Quad City Engineering Company Inc—Roger Dolleslager	PO Box 377, East Moline IL 61244	309-755-9762	R	2*	<.1
672	West Michigan Tool and Die Co—Jerry Jackson	1007 Nickerson Ave, Benton Harbor MI 49022	269-925-0900	R	2*	<.1
673	Diamond Die Inc—Richard Sweeting	6691 N Sidney Pl, Milwaukee WI 53209	414-355-7788	R	2*	<.1
674	Dyer Tool and Die Inc—Mark Dyer	379 S Long Hollow Rd, Maryville TN 37801	865-983-7593	R	2*	<.1
675	Front Range Tooling Inc—Scott Sullivan	7700 Miller Dr, Longmont CO 80504	303-776-2295	R	2*	<.1
676	J F Schroeder Company Inc—John Schroeder	2616 S Clearbrook Dr, Arlington Heights IL 60005	847-357-8600	R	2*	<.1
677	Kwik Tech Inc—Thomas Sondey	35150 Beattie Dr, Sterling Heights MI 48312	586-268-6201	R	2*	<.1
678	Precision Mold and Engineering Inc—David Loehr	13143 E 9 Mile Rd, Warren MI 48089	586-774-2330	R	2*	<.1
679	Withers Corp—Kathleen Withers	23801 Mound Rd, Warren MI 48091	586-758-2750	R	2*	<.1
680	Kent Tool And Die Inc—Steve Ellis	50605 Richard W Blvd, Chesterfield MI 48051	586-949-6600	R	2*	<.1
681	Master Tool and Die Inc—Wayne Renfro	117 Regional Park Dr, Kingsport TN 37660	423-349-4949	R	2*	<.1
682	Pennco Tool and Die Inc—Philip Passilla	99 Mead Ave, Meadville PA 16335	814-336-5035	R	2*	<.1
683	Tennessee Precision Inc—Steven Reynolds	109 Candy St, Greenbrier TN 37073	615-643-4065	R	2*	<.1
684	Novi Die and Engineering Co—Earl Wedemeyer	50450 Wing Dr, Shelby Township MI 48315	586-566-6390	R	2*	<.1
685	Tru-Tex International Corp—Ruth Henn	11050 Southland Rd, Cincinnati OH 45240	513-825-8844	R	2*	<.1

Rank	Company Name—*Executive Officer*	Address, City, State, Zip	Phone	Type	Fin	Empls
686	Cavalla Inc—*Arthur Pisani*	111 Union St, Hackensack NJ 07601	201-343-3338	R	2*	<.1
687	Dcd Technologies Inc—*Dave Hodgson*	17920 S Waterloo Rd, Cleveland OH 44119	216-481-0056	R	2*	<.1
688	Helm Tool Company Inc—*Helmut Mueller*	1290 Brummel Ave, Elk Grove Village IL 60007	847-364-0855	R	2*	<.1
689	Mill Tool And Manufacturing Corp—*James Winget*	PO Box 637, Kewaskum WI 53040	262-334-7833	R	2*	<.1
690	Millennium Die Group Inc—*Richard Sweeting*	PO Box 128, Three Rivers MA 01080	413-283-3500	R	2*	<.1
691	Moldcraft Inc—*John Chase*	240 Gould Ave, Depew NY 14043	716-684-1126	R	2*	<.1
692	Sohacki Industries Inc—*Thomas Sohacki*	185 Cumberland Park Dr, Saint Augustine FL 32095	904-826-0130	R	2*	<.1
693	Stellar Forge Products Inc—*Diran Arslanian*	13050 Inkster Rd, Redford MI 48239	313-535-7631	R	2*	<.1
694	Talbar Inc—*Thomas Parks*	PO Box 401, Meadville PA 16335	814-337-8400	R	2*	<.1
695	Trinity Tools Inc—*Mitchell Banas*	261 Main St, North Tonawanda NY 14120	716-694-1111	R	2*	<.1
696	Wire Shop Inc—*John Ferguson*	5959 Pinecone Dr, Mentor OH 44060	440-354-6842	R	2*	<.1
697	Midwest Press Brake Dies Inc—*Anton Berger*	7520 W 100th Pl, Bridgeview IL 60455	708-598-3860	R	2*	<.1
698	RJW Manufacturing Inc—*Carolyn Weatherford*	PO Box 1103, Athens AL 35612	256-232-6751	R	2*	<.1
699	Douglas Machine And Engineering Company Inc—*Arthur Hite*	PO Box 3528, Davenport IA 52808	563-324-0611	R	2*	<.1
700	Cgs Machine and Tool Inc—*Stephen Allen*	2750 Griffin Dr, Bowling Green KY 42101	270-783-3589	R	2*	<.1
701	Northern Precision Inc—*Ralph Diemond*	PO Box 189, Lincoln MI 48742	989-736-6322	R	2*	<.1
702	Aggressive Engineering Corp—*John Bridges*	1235 N Knollwood Cir, Anaheim CA 92801	714-995-8313	R	2*	<.1
703	Allied Steel Rule Dies Inc—*Falco Desiderio*	1125 Brookside Ave Ste, Indianapolis IN 46202	317-634-9835	R	2*	<.1
704	Hilton Tool Company Inc—*Mitch Furrow*	PO Box 217, Clackamas OR 97015	503-657-9312	R	2*	<.1
705	Jatco Machine and Tool Company Inc—*Richard Salle*	4429 Ohio River Blvd, Pittsburgh PA 15202	412-761-4344	R	2*	<.1
706	Kiger Brothers Machine Tool and Die Works Inc—*Gary Kiger*	609 Carby Rd, Houston TX 77037	281-447-1315	R	2*	<.1
707	Matrex Mold And Tool Inc—*John Matson*	PO Box 262, Portage WI 53901	608-742-6565	R	2*	<.1
708	Miami Valley Punch and Manufacturing Inc—*Kamlesh Trivedi*	3425 Successful Way, Dayton OH 45414	937-237-0533	R	2*	<.1
709	Momentum Industries Inc—*Dean Sharick*	100 Woodside Dr, Saint Louis MI 48880	989-681-5735	R	2*	<.1
710	Norwalk Precast Molds Inc—*Jan Graves*	PO Box 293, Norwalk OH 44857	419-668-1639	R	2*	<.1
711	RBKTool and Die—*John Alcamo*	PO Box B, Modesto CA 95352	209-521-2282	R	2*	<.1
712	Rol-Flo Engineering Inc—*Randall Orlomoski*	85a Tom Harvey Rd, Westerly RI 02891	401-596-0060	R	2*	<.1
713	Somerset Plastics Company Inc—*Clifford White*	PO Box 8446, Berlin CT 06037	860-635-1601	R	2*	<.1
714	American Tool and Machining Company Inc—*Mark Miller*	1910 Benton St, Searcy AR 72143	501-268-7011	R	2*	<.1
715	Four-Way Tool And Die Inc—*Lawrence Erickson*	239 Indusco Ct, Troy MI 48083	248-585-8255	R	2*	<.1
716	Fame Tool and Manufacturing Company Inc—*Helen Snyder*	5340 Hetzell St, Cincinnati OH 45227	513-271-6387	R	2*	<.1
717	South Bend Form Tool Company Inc—*Herb Eggers*	408 W Indiana Ave, South Bend IN 46613	574-289-2441	R	2*	<.1
718	Macdonald Carbide Co—*Amy Donald*	4510 Littlejohn St, Baldwin Park CA 91706	626-960-4034	R	2*	<.1
719	Total Support Tooling Inc—*Joe Wilson*	508 Wilhite St, Florence AL 35630	256-767-1406	R	2*	<.1
720	Abc Die Cutting And Embossing Inc—*Kim Moravec*	6363 E 38th Ave, Denver CO 80207	303-333-1212	R	2*	<.1
721	Artisan Tool and Die Inc—*H Mansfield*	3805 W State Rd 28, Muncie IN 47303	765-288-6653	R	2*	<.1
722	Ck Manufacturing Inc—*Brian Kaltner*	8 Gardner Rd, Fairfield NJ 07004	973-808-3500	R	2*	<.1
723	Creative Precision Inc—*Allen Kiesel*	PO Box 1378, Linwood PA 19061	610-364-1500	R	2*	<.1
724	Ken Die Cutting Supplies Inc—*Byran Kengott*	2280 Conestoga Dr, Carson City NV 89706	775-882-4453	R	2*	<.1
725	Knise and Krick Inc—*John Extrom*	PO Box 6508, Syracuse NY 13217	315-422-3516	R	2*	<.1
726	Maddox Industries Inc—*Steve Maddox*	PO Box 190, Bronson MI 49028	517-369-8665	R	2*	<.1
727	Marlan Tool Inc—*Marlan Jones*	13385 Denny Rd, Meadville PA 16335	814-382-2744	R	2*	<.1
728	Roscoe Tool and Manufacturing Inc—*Edward Forsling*	5339 Stern Dr, Roscoe IL 61073	815-633-8808	R	2*	<.1
729	Technical Precision Inc—*Gregory Carone*	PO Box 98, Hadley PA 16130	724-253-2800	R	2*	<.1
730	Industrial Tool and Die Corp—*Charles Coughlin*	2201 Lexington Rd, Evansville IN 47720	812-424-9971	R	2*	<.1
731	Varbros Tool And Die Company Inc—*Ernest Vargo*	16025 Brookpark Rd, Cleveland OH 44142	216-267-5200	R	2*	.1
732	Bell Tool Inc—*Ronald Belyk*	24200 Link Rd, Southfield MI 48034	248-352-4760	R	2*	<.1
733	North Tool And Manufacturing Co—*Cynthia Blake*	17140 E 10 Mile Rd, Eastpointe MI 48021	586-776-6680	R	2*	<.1
734	Quality Mould Inc—*David A Danko*	110 Dill Ln Bldg 2, Latrobe PA 15650	724-532-3678	R	2*	<.1
735	Charles Meisner Inc—*Charles Meisner*	201 Sierra Pl Ste A, Upland CA 91786	909-946-6766	R	2*	<.1
736	Lenard Tool and Machine Inc—*Leonard Schilz*	4480 S Nicholson Ave, Saint Francis WI 53235	414-483-7620	R	2*	<.1
737	Master Workholding Inc—*Mike Powell*	PO Box 2845, Morganton NC 28680	828-437-0011	R	2*	<.1
738	Portland Pattern Inc—*Peter Roska*	2305 Nw 30th Ave, Portland OR 97210	503-224-9276	R	2*	<.1
739	Draeving Machine Tool Inc—*Judith Draeving*	2710 Prairie Ave, Beloit WI 53511	608-365-6014	R	2*	<.1
740	Sure Tool and Manufacturing Company Inc—*Jerrald Kuriger*	429 Winston Ave, Dayton OH 45403	937-253-9111	R	2*	<.1
741	Vishion Tool And Machine Co—*James Vishion*	3344 Greenwood Blvd, Saint Louis MO 63143	314-781-6631	R	2*	<.1
742	Ace Tooling Inc—*Thomas Whaling*	1188 E Broadway Ave, Norton Shores MI 49444	231-733-1913	R	2*	<.1
743	Bra-Vor Tool and Die Company Inc—*Scott Devore*	11189 Murray Rd, Meadville PA 16335	814-724-1557	R	2*	<.1
744	Busy Bee Tooling—*Robert Phillips*	1620 S Marigold Ave, Ontario CA 91761	909-947-8712	R	2*	<.1
745	Doutt Tool Inc—*Dennis Doutt*	21879 Gravel Run Rd, Venango PA 16440	814-398-2989	R	2*	<.1
746	Ken-Tronics Inc—*Maxine Hoexter*	527 Andalusia Rd, Milan IL 61264	309-787-4918	R	2*	<.1
747	Modern Die Systems Inc—*Daniel Neuendorf*	1104 N J St, Elwood IN 46036	765-552-3145	R	2*	<.1
748	Muthig Industries Inc—*Bruce Muthig*	33 E Larsen Dr, Fond du Lac WI 54937	920-922-9814	R	2*	<.1
749	Parris Tool and Die Co—*Paul Parris III*	847 Springfield Hwy, Goodlettsville TN 37072	615-859-0288	R	2*	<.1
750	Perfection Tool Co—*Limous Buckelew*	PO Box 1096, Hendersonville TN 37077	615-824-4341	R	2*	<.1
751	Tnr Machine Inc—*Norman Watson*	2050 W Dowling Rd, Dowling MI 49050	269-623-2827	R	2*	<.1
752	Triplet Tool And Die Company Inc—*Gary Turpin*	8039 Burch Park Dr, Evansville IN 47725	812-867-2494	R	2*	<.1
753	WR Sharples Company Inc—*Daniel Sharples*	211 John Dietsch Sq, North Attleboro MA 02763	508-695-5656	R	2*	<.1
754	Advanced Mold Technology Inc—*Greg Mitchell*	398 Cliffwood Park St, Brea CA 92821	714-990-0144	R	2*	<.1
755	Arro Tool and Die Inc—*James Lindell*	4687 Gleason Rd, Lakewood NY 14750	716-763-6203	R	2*	<.1
756	Fehrman Tool and Die Inc—*Delbert Fehrman*	8824 Clay Pke, Byesville OH 43723	740-685-2637	R	2*	<.1
757	H and M Machining Inc—*David Glaza*	29625 Pky, Roseville MI 48066	586-778-5028	R	2*	<.1
758	Lasercutting Services Inc—*Steve Schroder*	4101 40th St Se Ste 7, Grand Rapids MI 49512	616-975-2000	R	2*	<.1
759	Lion Tool and Die Co—*Leonard Doerrfeld*	PO Box 7066, Algonquin IL 60102	847-658-8898	R	2*	<.1
760	Raloid Tool Company Inc—*Ronald Brownell*	PO Box 551, Mechanicville NY 12118	518-664-4261	R	2*	<.1
761	Value Tool and Engineering Inc—*Steven Hartz*	2629 Foundation Dr, South Bend IN 46628	574-246-1913	R	2*	<.1
762	Westwood Machine and Tool Co—*David Hurless*	1703 Westwood Dr, Sterling IL 61081	815-626-5090	R	2*	<.1
763	Constellation Mold Inc—*Donald Kappert*	4825 Hitch Peters Rd, Evansville IN 47711	812-424-5338	R	2*	<.1
764	Fidelity Tool and Mold Ltd—*James Vassar*	1885 Suncast Ln, Batavia IL 60510	630-879-2300	R	2*	<.1
765	King Machine And Tool Co—*William Kapper*	1237 Sanders Ave Sw, Massillon OH 44647	330-833-7217	R	2*	<.1
766	TIB Inc—*James Jim Barnhill*	9525 Pathway St, Santee CA 92071	619-562-3071	R	2*	<.1
767	Blandford Machine and Tool Company Inc—*David Blandford*	5604 Fern Valley Rd, Louisville KY 40228	502-964-3375	R	2*	<.1
768	Gemini Tool and Manufacturing—*Paul Keefe*	3541 Martens St, Franklin Park IL 60131	847-678-5000	R	2*	<.1
769	Danly IEM—*Roy Verstraete*	3650 S Derenzy Rd, Bellaire MI 49615	248-489-7816	R	2*	<.1
770	Illinois Mold Builders Inc—*Paul Makray*	250 Jamie Ln, Wauconda IL 60084	847-526-0400	R	2*	<.1
771	JD Tool and Machine Company Inc—*Donna Coulter*	12321 Sampson St Ste D, Riverside CA 92503	951-371-6653	R	2*	<.1
772	Kuhn Tool and Die Co—*Kenneth Kuhn*	PO Box 574, Meadville PA 16335	814-336-2123	R	2*	<.1
773	Northern Illinois Mold Corp—*Bruce Niggemann*	11200 E Main St, Huntley IL 60142	847-669-2100	R	2*	<.1
774	Precision Industries Inc (Flint Michigan)—*Jeff Swanson*	3002 E Court St, Flint MI 48506	810-239-5816	R	2*	<.1
775	Tool Automation Enterprises Corp—*John Kut*	1516 175th St, East Hazel Crest IL 60429	708-799-6847	R	2*	<.1

Note: An asterisk (*) indicates an estimated financial figure. The company type code used is as follows: R = Private, P = Public, S = Private Subsidiary, B = Public Subsidiary, D = Division, J = Joint Venture, I = Investment Fund.

COMPANY RANKINGS BY SALES WITHIN 4-DIGIT SIC

Rank	Company Name—*Executive Officer*	Address, City, State, Zip	Phone	Type	Fin	Empls
776	George Hansen and Company Inc—*Bill Hansen*	50 W Laua Dr, Addison IL 60101	630-628-8700	R	2*	<.1
777	Acme Carbide Die Inc—*Allen Schmitt*	6202 E Executive Dr, Westland MI 48185	734-722-2303	R	2*	<.1
778	Parkway Steel Rule Cutting Dies Inc—*Mark Venhorst*	1912 Woodside Ave, Bedford VA 24523	540-586-4948	R	2*	<.1
779	Barron Metal Products Inc—*Richard Cleary*	286 Nepperhan Ave, Yonkers NY 10701	914-965-1232	R	2*	<.1
780	Trimline Die Corp—*Rick Fargo*	421 Commerce Dr E, Lagrange OH 44050	440-355-6900	R	2*	<.1
781	Celco Tool and Engineering Inc—*John Cielak*	9300 Bernice Ave, Schiller Park IL 60176	847-671-2520	R	2*	<.1
782	Qualitek Engineering and Manufacturing Inc—*Duane Devereaux*	2455 Louisiana Ave N, Minneapolis MN 55427	763-544-9507	R	2*	<.1
783	Pederson Tool and Design Inc—*Ben Pederson*	700 Lund Blvd, Anoka MN 55303	763-421-0355	R	2*	<.1
784	Accurate Tool and Manufacturing Corp—*Charles Dobes*	6139 W Ogden Ave, Cicero IL 60804	708-652-4266	R	2*	<.1
785	Industrial Standard Tooling Inc—*Virgil Plum*	PO Box 1842, Waterloo IA 50704	319-235-9200	R	2*	<.1
786	Chesapeake Leather Works Inc—*R Wherry*	5850 Bayside Ct, Buford GA 30518	770-932-2838	R	2*	<.1
787	Luick Quality Gage and Tool Inc—*Robert Nottingham*	PO Box 2608, Muncie IN 47307	765-288-1818	R	2*	<.1
788	K-K Tool And Design Inc—*Jim Blake*	PO Box 456, Markle IN 46770	260-758-2940	R	2*	<.1
789	Westgood Manufacturing Co—*Edna Westerman*	15211 E 11 Mile Rd, Roseville MI 48066	586-771-3970	R	2*	<.1
790	Gromax Precision Die and Manufacturing Inc—*Guntis Aulis*	W185n11474 Whitney Dr, Germantown WI 53022	262-255-0223	R	2*	<.1
791	Lancaster Metal Products Inc—*Max Giles*	520 Slocum St, Lancaster OH 43130	740-653-3421	R	2*	<.1
792	Neu Dynamics Corp—*Kevin Hartsow*	110 Steam Whistle Dr, Warminster PA 18974	215-355-2460	R	2*	<.1
793	Borke Mold Specialist Inc—*Fritz Borke*	9541 Glades Dr, Hamilton OH 45011	513-870-8000	R	2*	<.1
794	Imperial Punch and Manufacturing—*Bruce Keirn*	2016 23rd Ave, Rockford IL 61104	815-226-8200	R	2*	<.1
795	Mdf Tool Corp—*John Bunjevac*	10166 Royalton Rd, North Royalton OH 44133	440-237-2277	R	2*	<.1
796	Rowley Tool Corp—*Byron Hill*	PO Box 247, Green Lake WI 54941	920-294-6520	R	2*	<.1
797	Toolcraft LLC—*Mary Winscott*	2620 Adams Ctr Rd, Fort Wayne IN 46803	260-749-0454	R	2*	<.1
798	Boyle Inc—*James Boyle*	82 Main St Ste A, Freeport PA 16229	724-295-2420	R	2*	<.1
799	Space Machine Company Inc—*William MAI*	6714 Whitestone Rd, Baltimore MD 21207	410-298-1065	R	2*	<.1
800	Lunar Tool and Mold Inc—*Friedrich Hoffman*	9860 York Alpha Dr, North Royalton OH 44133	440-237-2141	R	2*	<.1
801	Master Precision Tool Corp—*Douglas Wolfe*	7362 19 Mile Rd, Sterling Heights MI 48314	586-739-3240	R	2*	<.1
802	BA Die Mold Inc—*Alan Petrucci*	3685 Prairie Lake Ct, Aurora IL 60504	630-978-4747	R	2*	<.1
803	Cobb Tool Inc—*Mike Edmonds*	5886 Dodgen Rd Sw, Mableton GA 30126	770-948-3775	R	2*	<.1
804	Janesville Tool and Manufacturing Inc—*Chris Roach*	PO Box 67, Milton WI 53563	608-868-4711	R	2*	<.1
805	B and B Precision Tool Co—*Robert Kaydo*	PO Box 1540, Ashtabula OH 44005	440-998-0775	R	2*	<.1
806	Rochester Stampings Inc—*L Hicks*	400 Trade Ct, Rochester NY 14624	585-467-5241	R	2*	<.1
807	T and S Die Cutting—*James Good*	13301 Alondra Blvd, Santa Fe Springs CA 90670	562-802-1731	R	2*	<.1
808	JM Mold Inc—*Robert Scheer*	1707 Commerce Dr, Piqua OH 45356	937-778-0077	R	2*	<.1
809	Kensen Tool and Die Inc—*Louis Kenyeri*	9200 Parklane Ave, Franklin Park IL 60131	847-455-0150	R	2*	<.1
810	Western Supplies Co—*Roger Altvater*	PO Box 7916, Saint Louis MO 63106	314-531-0100	R	2*	<.1
811	Centaur Tool and Die Inc—*Paul Faykosh*	2019 Wood Bridge Blvd, Bowling Green OH 43402	419-352-7704	R	2*	<.1
812	RJD Machine Products Inc—*Richard Roslowski*	1424 Heath Ave, Ewing NJ 08638	609-392-1515	R	2*	<.1
813	Book Tool Company Inc—*Bernie Brown*	300 Security Dr, Fairfield OH 45014	513-870-9622	R	2*	<.1
814	Pace Machine and Tool Inc—*Richard Dirr*	1425 Commerce Ln, Jupiter FL 33458	561-747-5444	R	2*	<.1
815	U S Machine and Tool Inc—*Christopher Deroo*	732 Old Salem Rd, Murfreesboro TN 37129	615-893-8984	R	2*	<.1
816	Universal Tooling Corp—*Warren Piazza*	PO Box 364, Gerry NY 14740	716-985-4691	R	2*	<.1
817	Van Wert Machine Inc—*Jesse Hitchcock*	PO Box 40, Delphos OH 45833	419-692-6836	R	2*	<.1
818	Maya Gage Co—*Kim Beier*	20770 Parker St, Farmington Hills MI 48336	248-471-0820	R	2*	<.1
819	Stanco Tool and Die Inc—*Robert Simonelli*	PO Box 490, Southbridge MA 01550	508-764-2594	R	2*	<.1
820	Mendoza Tool—*Antonio Mendoza*	155 Talzada Fresno, Los Angeles CA 90032	323-256-2648	R	2*	<.1
821	A and D Plastics Inc—*Gerald Jagacki*	1255 S Mill St, Plymouth MI 48170	734-455-2255	R	2*	<.1
822	American Mold Service—*S Wright*	9623 Grossmont Summit, La Mesa CA 91941	619-461-3616	R	2*	<.1
823	Cole's Machine Service Inc—*Kenneth Cole*	201 W Rising St, Davison MI 48423	810-658-5373	R	2*	<.1
824	Paragon Molds Corp—*Daniel Smoger*	33997 Riviera, Fraser MI 48026	586-294-7630	R	2*	<.1
825	Custom Tool And Die Inc—*William Woratyla*	2970 Old Tree Dr, Lancaster PA 17603	717-397-2542	R	2*	<.1
826	Century Tool Company Inc—*Joseph Simonelli*	PO Box 314, Thompson CT 06277	860-923-9523	R	2*	<.1
827	Rolleigh Inc—*Michael Clark*	PO Box 419, Reading MI 49274	517-283-3811	R	2*	<.1
828	Frew Mill Die Crafts Inc—*Charles Lee Mc Combs*	311 W Grant St, New Castle PA 16101	724-658-9026	R	2*	<.1
829	Arnim Tool Inc—*Kingston Arnim*	2204 Joe Field Rd, Dallas TX 75229	972-247-0802	R	2*	<.1
830	Coil Stamping Inc—*Edward Kiss*	1340 Lincoln Ave Ste 1, Holbrook NY 11741	631-588-3040	R	2*	<.1
831	JW Molding Inc—*Ralf Wolters*	2523 Calcite Cir, Newbury Park CA 91320	805-499-2682	R	2*	<.1
832	Kipe Molds Inc—*George Kipe*	340 E Crowther Ave, Placentia CA 92870	714-572-9576	R	2*	<.1
833	MGR Molds Inc—*Robert Walter*	6450 Cotter Ave, Sterling Heights MI 48314	586-254-6020	R	2*	<.1
834	Mmd Mountain Mold And Die Inc—*Joe Crisp*	127 River Bend Dr, Sevierville TN 37876	865-428-3611	R	2*	<.1
835	Reef Tool and Gage Co—*E Langtry*	44800 Macomb Industria, Clinton Township MI 48036	586-468-3000	R	2*	<.1
836	Reliance Tool and Engineering LLC—*Stanley Anderson*	1779 Scherer Pkwy, Saint Charles MO 63303	636-947-7011	R	2*	<.1
837	Ameri-Tool Industries Inc—*Burl Smith*	PO Box 1809, Albany OR 97321	541-926-8647	R	2*	<.1
838	C and E Tooling Inc—*Glenn Cole*	2560 W Brooks Ave Ste, North Las Vegas NV 89032	702-736-2958	R	2*	<.1
839	Spark Technologies Inc—*Dennis Smail*	150 Railroad St, Schenley PA 15682	724-295-3860	R	2*	<.1
840	C and T Engineering Inc—*Richard Troxell*	322 Thompson Rd, Seymour IN 47274	812-522-5854	R	2*	<.1
841	Gaging Technologies Inc—*Nikolas Galinac*	3000 Spring Industrial, Powder Springs GA 30127	770-943-0555	R	2*	<.1
842	Parker Precision Products—*Quincy Lucarello*	PO Box 579, Orange NJ 07051	973-678-8450	R	1*	<.1
843	Arrow Tool Die and Machine Company Inc—*Richard Comly*	2065 Bennett Rd, Philadelphia PA 19116	215-676-1300	R	1*	<.1
844	Brown's Tool and Mold Company Inc—*William Brown*	PO Box 2342, Opelika AL 36803	334-745-4911	R	1*	<.1
845	Contract Design Inc—*Rudy Tschida*	8399 Coral Sea St Ne, Minneapolis MN 55449	763-786-8563	R	1*	<.1
846	Hipsher Tool and Die Inc—*James Hipsher*	1593 S State Rd 115, Wabash IN 46992	260-563-4143	R	1*	<.1
847	Kennedy and Bowden Machine Company Inc—*D Kennedy*	1229 Heil Quaker Blvd, La Vergne TN 37086	615-793-6653	R	1*	<.1
848	Alpha Industries Inc—*Charles Cottrill*	3650 N 126th St, Brookfield WI 53005	262-783-6204	R	1*	<.1
849	Clifford H Jones Inc—*Phillip Jones*	608 Young St, Tonawanda NY 14150	716-693-2444	R	1*	<.1
850	Knight Tool Works Inc—*Richard Peterson*	365 Industrial Dr, South Elgin IL 60177	847-289-0005	R	1*	<.1
851	Creative Paradise Inc—*Stephanie O'toole*	PO Box 734, Goddard KS 67052	316-794-8621	R	1*	<.1
852	Edge-Rite Tools Inc—*John Kaput*	7700 Exchange St, Cleveland OH 44125	216-642-0966	R	1*	<.1
853	Emerson Industries LLC—*Bill Maculan*	721 N Yale Ave, Villa Park IL 60181	630-279-0920	R	1*	<.1
854	Lowry Tool and Die Inc—*Robert Lowry*	986 Salem Pkwy, Salem OH 44460	330-332-1722	R	1*	<.1
855	Pi Tape Corp—*Harold Phillips*	344 N Vinewood St, Escondido CA 92029	760-746-9830	R	1*	<.1
856	Rockstedt Tool and Die Inc—*Josef Schuessler*	2974 Interstate Pkwy, Brunswick OH 44212	330-273-9000	R	1*	<.1
857	Specialty Tool and Die Company Inc—*Gordon Riley*	1614 Rank Pky Ct, Kokomo IN 46901	765-452-9209	R	1*	<.1
858	Die-Mension Corp—*Karen Thompson*	3020 Nationwide Pkwy, Brunswick OH 44212	330-273-5872	R	1*	<.1
859	Metric Design and Manufacturing Inc—*Gunther Unruh*	217 E Hacienda Ave, Campbell CA 95008	408-378-4544	R	1*	<.1
860	Guyer Die Company Inc—*Donald Guyer*	PO Box 1382, Corona CA 92878	714-449-9219	R	1*	<.1
861	Omni Tool Inc—*Steve Zamboki*	2710 Boulder Park Ct, Winston Salem NC 27101	336-724-5152	R	1*	<.1
862	K and K Inc—*Kirk Blank*	28440 Glenview Dr, Elkhart IN 46514	574-266-8040	R	1*	<.1
863	Williams Tooling and Manufacturing Inc—*Jerry Williams*	PO Box 7, Dorr MI 49323	616-681-2093	R	1*	<.1
864	Area Tool and Manufacturing Inc—*John Wehrle*	PO Box 1409, Meadville PA 16335	814-724-3166	R	1*	<.1

Rank	Company Name—*Executive Officer*	Address, City, State, Zip	Phone	Type	Fin	Empls
865	Brownsville Products Inc—*Rolando Gonzalez*	3320 E 14th St, Brownsville TX 78521	956-982-0910	R	1*	<.1
866	Maes Tool and Die Company Inc—*Joseph Maes*	1074 Toro Dr, Jackson MI 49201	517-750-3131	R	1*	<.1
867	Ram Tool Company Inc—*Jerry Dobrianski*	6013 Ontario Cir, Morristown TN 37814	423-587-1923	R	1*	<.1
868	Nelson Tool Corp—*Michael Nelson*	388 N County Line Rd, Sunbury OH 43074	740-965-1894	R	1*	<.1
869	Williams Steel Rule Die Company Inc—*Jeff Jazbec*	PO Box 43518, Cleveland OH 44143	216-431-3231	R	1*	<.1
870	Walker Tool and Machine Co—*Tarry Beard*	7700 Ponderosa Rd, Perrysburg OH 43551	419-661-8000	R	1*	<.1
871	K Mold And Engineering Inc—*Kenneth Kasner*	PO Box 96, Granger IN 46530	574-272-5858	R	1*	<.1
872	TM Machine and Tool Inc—*Judith Manders*	521 Mel Simon Dr, Toledo OH 43612	419-478-0310	R	1*	<.1
873	Dixon Tool and Die Inc—*Phyllis Dixon*	PO Box 188, Tyrone PA 16686	814-684-0266	R	1*	<.1
874	Finney Impression Die Corporation Of Greenwood—*Dana Finney*	1502 Hwy 246 S, Greenwood SC 29646	864-942-0345	R	1*	<.1
875	D and D Production Inc—*Scott Kather*	2500 Williams Dr, Waterford MI 48328	248-334-2112	R	1*	<.1
876	Letsch Manufacturing Inc—*Donald Mainland*	1925 Roosevelt Ave, Racine WI 53406	262-554-6900	R	1*	<.1
877	Neudecker Manufacturing Of Indiana Inc—*Evelyn Brosch*	2230 E State Rd 32, Winchester IN 47394	765-584-1669	R	1*	<.1
878	Sancliff Inc—*William Drumm*	PO Box 2444, Worcester MA 01613	508-795-0747	R	1*	<.1
879	Naugler Mold and Engineering Inc—*James Curtin*	60 Dunham Rd, Beverly MA 01915	978-922-5634	R	1*	<.1
880	Carroll Industrial Molds Inc—*Craig Dusing*	PO Box 429, Milledgeville IL 61051	815-225-7250	R	1*	<.1
881	Northeast Carbide Inc—*William Lyons*	525 W Queen St, Southington CT 06489	860-621-0118	R	1*	<.1
882	D and S Mold and Tool Co—*Tom Stark*	PO Box 540, Marinette WI 54143	715-732-0504	R	1*	<.1
883	Jenco Metal Products Inc—*Gregory Jensen*	1690 W Imperial Ct, Mount Prospect IL 60056	847-956-0550	R	1*	<.1
884	Lyons Tool and Engineering Inc—*Mary Lyons*	13720 E 9 Mile Rd, Warren MI 48089	586-776-6302	R	1*	<.1
885	Empire Machine Co—*Lazell Davis*	2710 S 3rd St, Niles MI 49120	269-684-3713	R	1*	<.1
886	Imperial Tool and Plastics Corp—*Leonard Niemiec*	7020 Industrial Loop, Greendale WI 53129	414-421-2884	R	1*	<.1
887	Center Line Mold and Tool Inc—*Scott Bringle*	703 S Eisenhower Dr, Edinburgh IN 46124	812-526-0970	R	1*	<.1
888	Diamond Die And Mold Co—*Joann Hinds*	35401 Groesbeck Hwy, Clinton Township MI 48035	586-791-0700	R	1*	<.1
889	P D Q Tooling Inc—*Brian Bailey*	940 Grnock Buena Vista, McKeesport PA 15135	412-751-2214	R	1*	<.1
890	Boothe Inc—*George Boothe*	2520 Christopher Lake, Saint Louis MO 63129	314-846-8112	R	1*	<.1
891	Creative Mold Company LLC—*Anne Lafontaine*	2 Gendron Dr Unit 1, Lewiston ME 04240	207-784-9126	R	1*	<.1
892	Press Brake Tooling Corp—*Govind Lakshman*	102 W Interstate Rd, Addison IL 60101	630-543-6702	R	1*	<.1
893	Ultra-Carbide Grinding Corp—*Albert Block*	971 Oakton St, Elk Grove Village IL 60007	847-956-0332	R	1*	<.1
894	Beck Tool Inc—*Patrick Beck*	25741 Fry Rd, Edinboro PA 16412	814-734-8513	R	1*	<.1
895	Perfection Mold and Machine Co—*Jack Bailey*	2057 E Aurora Rd Ste H, Twinsburg OH 44087	330-784-5435	R	1*	<.1
896	Altman Manufacturing Company Inc—*Paul Altman*	1990 Ohio St, Lisle IL 60532	630-963-0031	R	1*	<.1
897	Enterprise Tool and Die Company Inc—*Robert Schweikert*	4940 Schaaf Ln, Cleveland OH 44131	216-351-1300	R	1*	<.1
898	Mercury Tool And Engineering Co—*Harry Christiansen*	3815 Jefferson St Ne, Minneapolis MN 55421	763-788-9678	R	1*	<.1
899	St Marys Tool and Die Company Inc—*George Gausman*	PO Box 14, Saint Marys PA 15857	814-834-7420	R	1*	<.1
900	Brownsville Quality Tool and Design Inc—*Anthony Nehrt*	1408 E State Rd 250, Brownstown IN 47220	812-358-4593	R	1*	<.1
901	Saturn Tool and Die Co—*Jacques Benoit*	2920 Janet Dr, Waterloo IA 50703	319-232-5325	R	1*	<.1
902	Toman Tool Corp—*Anthony Rubasch*	PO Box 72, Viroqua WI 54665	608-637-3900	R	1*	<.1
903	Abbott Tool And Die Inc—*Tom Abbott*	920 Lone Star Dr, O Fallon MO 63366	636-240-2723	R	1*	<.1
904	Ajax Tool Inc—*William Osterholt*	2828 Commercial Rd, Fort Wayne IN 46809	260-747-7482	P	1*	<.1
905	Vulcan Tool Co—*Dan Kuchenbuch*	730 Lorain Ave, Dayton OH 45410	937-253-6194	R	1*	<.1
906	Mesick Precision Co—*Karl Stovens*	PO Box 421970, Del Rio TX 78842	616-885-1204	R	1*	<.1
907	Bonney-Vehslage Tool Co—*Ramsay Vehslage*	61 New Jersy Railrd 2n, Newark NJ 07105	973-580-6075	R	1*	<.1
908	Ballek Die Mold Inc—*Stefan Ballek*	2125 Stonington Ave, Hoffman Estates IL 60169	847-885-2300	R	1*	<.1
909	Varco Precision Products Co—*Donald Vartoogian*	26935 W 7 Mile Rd, Redford MI 48240	313-538-4300	R	1*	<.1
910	Harbor Patterns—*Donald Cox*	3271 Sausalito St, Los Alamitos CA 90720	562-596-1616	R	1*	<.1
911	Erva Tool and Die Co—*Erwin Heyek*	3100 W Grand Ave, Chicago IL 60622	773-533-7806	R	1*	<.1
912	Graham Tech Inc—*Mark Graham*	237 S Franklin St, Cochranton PA 16314	814-425-7953	R	<1*	<.1
913	FJ Weidner Inc—*John Weidner*	34 Tyler St Ext, East Haven CT 06512	203-469-4202	R	<1*	<.1
914	Croney Enterprises Inc—*Howard Croney*	5032 Fm 901, Whitesboro TX 76273	903-564-6053	R	<1*	<.1
915	Xcel Mold And Machine Inc—*Bruce Cain*	7661 Freedom Ave Nw, Canton OH 44720	330-499-8450	R	<1*	<.1

TOTALS: SIC 3544 Special Dies, Tools, Jigs & Fixtures
Companies: 915   6,123   47.8

3545 Machine Tool Accessories

Rank	Company Name—*Executive Officer*	Address, City, State, Zip	Phone	Type	Fin	Empls
1	Carl Zeiss Industrial Metrology LLC—*Gregory Lee*	6250 Sycamore Ln N, Maple Grove MN 55369	763-744-2400	R	8,840*	.3
2	Rosemount Inc—*Michael Train*	8200 Market Blvd, Chanhassen MN 55317	952-906-8888	S	1,220*	10.0
3	MSC Industrial Supply Co	75 Maxess Rd, Melville NY 11747	516-812-2000	D	841*	3.0
4	Teledyne Hastings Instruments Div—*Aldo Pichelli*	PO Box 1436, Hampton VA 23661	757-723-6531	D	573	.1
5	ATI Metalworking Products—*David M Hogan*	1 Teledyne Pl, La Vergne TN 37086	615-641-4200	S	402*	1.0
6	Regal-Beloit Flight Services Inc—*Henry W Knueppel*	200 State St, Beloit WI 53511		S	275*	1.0
7	Hughes Christensen Co	9110 Grogans Mill Rd, The Woodlands TX 77380	281-363-6000	D	270*	1.6
8	Kyocera Tycom North America—*Scott Yardley*	3565 Cadillac Ave, Costa Mesa CA 92626	714-428-3600	S	108*	.4
9	Ridge Tool Co—*Fred Pond*	PO Box 4023, Elyria OH 44036	440-323-5581	S	100*	1.0
10	Cleveland Twist Drill Co—*Paul Jones*	12985 Snow Rd, Cleveland OH 44130	216-265-3300	R	75	1.1
11	Cole Carbide Industries Inc—*John Cole*	24703 Ryan Rd, Warren MI 48091	586-757-8700	R	73*	.1
12	Brown and Sharpe Manufacturing Co—*William Gruber*	250 Circuit Dr, North Kingstown RI 02852	401-886-2000	R	73*	1.3
13	Triumph Twist Drill Company Inc—*Arthur Beck*	PO Box 9000, Crystal Lake IL 60039	815-459-6250	R	60*	.5
14	Industrial Motion Control LLC—*Bill Crusey*	1444 S Wolf Rd, Wheeling IL 60090	847-459-5200	R	55*	.2
15	Fastcut Tool Corp—*Bill Coyle*	200 Front St, Millersburg PA 17061	717-692-8232	S	52*	.1
16	Messer Cutting Systems Inc—*Gary Norville*	PO Box 290, Menomonee Falls WI 53052	262-255-5520	R	45*	.2
17	Mid State Machine Products—*Alan Dorval*	83 Verti Dr, Winslow ME 04901	207-873-6136	S	44*	.1
18	Prince Industries Inc—*Mark Miller*	745 N Gary Ave, Carol Stream IL 60188	630-588-0088	R	44*	.3
19	Precision Aerospace Inc—*Jack Hillman*	88 Cogwheel Ln, Seymour CT 06483	203-888-3022	R	38*	<.1
20	N C Industries Inc—*Roger Bollier*	200 John James Audbn 2, Buffalo NY 14228	716-689-8400	R	36*	.5
21	Stadco Corp—*Ben Nazarian*	1931 N Broadway, Los Angeles CA 90031	323-227-8888	R	35*	.2
22	Anchor Lamina America Inc—*Roy Verstraete*	PO Box 2540, Farmington Hills MI 48333	248-489-9122	R	35*	.2
23	Allied Machine and Engineering Corp—*William Stokey*	PO Box 36, Dover OH 44622	330-343-4283	R	34*	.3
24	Ingersoll Cutting Tool Co—*Charles Elder*	845 S Lyford Rd, Rockford IL 61108	815-387-6600	R	33*	.5
25	Fori Automation Inc—*Bernd Koerner*	50955 Wing Dr, Shelby Township MI 48315	586-247-2336	R	31*	.2
26	Regal Cutting Tools Inc—*Ho Song*	5330 E Rockton Rd, Roscoe IL 61073	815-389-3461	R	30*	.2
27	Pb Holdings Inc—*Brian Manley*	3063 Philmont Ave, Huntingdon Valley PA 19006	215-947-3333	R	30*	.2
28	Detroit Tool and Engineering Co—*John Schott*	441 W Elm St, Lebanon MO 65536	417-532-2141	D	29*	.3
29	Rollway Bearing International Ltd—*Bill Eames*	PO Box 4827, Syracuse NY 13221		S	29*	.2
30	Minnesota Twist Drill Inc—*Scott Allison*	PO Box 312, Chisholm MN 55719	218-254-3362	R	29*	.1
31	Excellon Automation Co—*David Balsbough*	20001 S Rancho Way, Rancho Dominguez CA 90220	310-668-7700	S	27*	.3
32	Votaw Precision Technologies Inc—*Scott G Wallace*	13153 Lakeland Rd, Santa Fe Springs CA 90670	562-944-0661	R	27*	.1
33	Tivoly Inc—*Josepf Wiseman*	434 Baxter Ave, Derby Line VT 05830	802-873-3106	R	26*	.2

Note: An asterisk (*) indicates an estimated financial figure. The company type code used is as follows: R = Private, P = Public, S = Private Subsidiary, B = Public Subsidiary, D = Division, J = Joint Venture, I = Investment Fund.

COMPANY RANKINGS BY SALES WITHIN 4-DIGIT SIC

Rank	Company Name—*Executive Officer*	Address, City, State, Zip	Phone	Type	Fin	Empls
34	Detroit Tool Metal Products—*Tom Kowall*	PO Box 512, Lebanon MO 65536	417-532-2142	R	26*	.2
35	Kennametal Inc—*Carlos M Cardoso*	1600 Technology Way, Latrobe PA 15650	724-539-5000	D	25*	.3
36	CITCO Diamond and CBN Products—*Michael Sweeney*	PO Box 84, Chardon OH 44024	440-285-9181	R	25*	.2
37	Greenleaf Corp—*Walter Greenleaf*	PO Box 1040, Saegertown PA 16433	814-763-2915	R	25*	.4
38	Total Component Solutions Corp—*Verlyn Mulder*	PO Box 178, Rock Valley IA 51247	712-476-5315	R	25*	.2
39	North American Tool Corp—*Roger Taylor*	PO Box 116, South Beloit IL 61080	815-389-2300	R	24*	.2
40	Dff Corp—*Ernest Denby*	PO Box 285, Agawam MA 01001	413-786-8880	R	24*	.2
41	Global Tooling Systems Inc—*Randal Bellestri*	16445 23 Mile Rd, Macomb MI 48042	586-726-0500	S	24*	.2
42	Guhring Inc—*Peter Haenle*	PO Box 643, Brookfield WI 53008	262-784-6730	R	22*	.3
43	Indiana Tool and Manufacturing Company Inc—*Donald Neidig*	PO Box 399, Plymouth IN 46563	574-936-2112	R	21*	.2
44	Viking Drill and Tool Inc—*Dennis Nyhus*	PO Box 65278, Saint Paul MN 55165	651-227-8911	R	21*	.2
45	Vermont Precision Tools Inc—*Monica Greene*	PO Box 182, Swanton VT 05488	802-868-4246	R	21*	.1
46	Balax Inc—*Tom McClure*	PO Box 96, North Lake WI 53064	262-966-2355	R	20*	.1
47	United Drill Bushing Corp—*Dale Bethke*	PO Box 4250, Downey CA 90241	562-803-1521	R	20*	.2
48	SL Fusco Inc—*Eric Rosen*	1966 E Via Arado, Rancho Dominguez CA 90220	310-868-1010	R	19*	.1
49	Glassline Corp—*Tom Ziems*	PO Box 147, Perrysburg OH 43552	419-666-5942	R	18*	.1
50	OS Walker Company Inc—*Peter Bartran*	20 Rockdale St, Worcester MA 01606	508-853-3232	R	18*	.2
51	Central Rolled Thread Die Co—*Earl Nowicke*	16 Research Park Dr, Saint Charles MO 63304	636-939-9797	R	18*	.2
52	Double E Company LLC—*Mark Fortin*	319 Manley St Ste 301, West Bridgewater MA 02379	508-588-8099	R	18*	.1
53	Fullerton Tool Company Inc—*Morgan Curry*	PO Box 2008, Saginaw MI 48605	989-799-4550	R	18*	.1
54	ITW Workholding Group—*Chris Brown*	2155 Traversefield Dr, Traverse City MI 49686	231-947-5755	S	17*	.1
55	Peterson Tool Company Inc—*Nancy Peterson*	PO Box 100830, Nashville TN 37224	615-242-7341	R	17*	.1
56	Wisconsin Machine Tool Corporation Inc—*Patrick Cherone*	3225 Gateway Rd Ste 10, Brookfield WI 53045	262-317-3048	R	17*	.1
57	Michigan Drill Corp—*Richard Kandarian*	PO Box 7012, Troy MI 48007	248-689-5050	R	16*	.1
58	Vista Metals Inc—*William Riley*	1024 E Smithfield St, Mckeesport PA 15135	412-751-4600	R	16*	.1
59	Cjt Koolcarb Inc—*Terry Loveless*	PO Box 5941, Carol Stream IL 60197	630-690-5933	R	16*	.1
60	Intra Corp—*John Battista*	885 Manufacturers Dr, Westland MI 48186	734-326-7030	R	16*	.1
61	Wetmore Tool And Engineering Co—*Phil Kurtz*	5091 G St, Chino CA 91710	909-364-1000	R	15*	.1
62	Setco Sales Co—*Jeffrey Clark*	5880 Hillside Ave, Cincinnati OH 45233	513-941-5110	R	15*	.1
63	Star Metal Products Company Inc—*John Murray*	30405 Clemens Rd, Westlake OH 44145	440-899-7000	R	15*	.1
64	Quality Carbide Tool Inc—*Gohei Osawa*	759 Industrial Dr, Bensenville IL 60106	630-274-4200	S	14*	.1
65	G and G Manufacturing Co—*Roxann Tucker*	PO Box 12086, Omaha NE 68112	402-453-9595	R	14*	.1
66	Vektek Inc—*J Gray*	PO Box 625, Emporia KS 66801	620-342-7637	R	14*	.1
67	James Tool Machine and Engineering Inc—*Bud Toner*	130 Reep Dr, Morganton NC 28655	828-584-8722	R	14*	.1
68	Southwick and Meister Inc—*Ernest Meister*	PO Box 725, Meriden CT 06450	203-237-0000	R	13*	.1
69	Tawas Tool Company Inc—*Brad Lawton*	756 Aulerich Rd, East Tawas MI 48730	989-362-6121	R	12*	.1
70	Zephyr Manufacturing Company Inc—*Bernard Kersulis*	PO Box 759, Inglewood CA 90307	310-410-4907	R	12*	.1
71	AG Davis Gage and Engineering Co—*Edwin Chapman*	6533 Sims Dr, Sterling Heights MI 48313	586-977-9000	R	12*	.1
72	Invo Spline Inc—*Vincent Spica*	2357 E 9 Mile Rd, Warren MI 48091	586-757-8840	R	12*	.1
73	Imco Carbide Tool Inc—*Perry Osburn*	28170 Cedar Park Blvd, Perrysburg OH 43551	419-661-6313	R	11*	.1
74	Perry Technology Corp—*Lansford Perry*	PO Box 21, New Hartford CT 06057	860-738-2525	R	11*	.1
75	Mclaughlin Group Inc—*David Gasmovic*	2006 Perimeter Rd, Greenville SC 29605	864-277-5870	R	11*	.1
76	Hannibal Carbide Tool Inc—*Paul Enander*	PO Box 954, Hannibal MO 63401	573-221-2775	R	11*	.1
77	Mechanical Development Company Inc—*John Powell*	PO Box 190, Salem VA 24153	540-389-9395	R	11*	.1
78	Empire Tool Company Inc—*Brad Roe*	PO Box 547, Memphis MI 48041	810-392-2101	R	11*	.1
79	Mapal Inc—*Lutz Grossmann*	4032 Dove Rd, Port Huron MI 48060	810-364-8020	R	11*	.1
80	Thaler Machine Co—*William Thaler*	PO Box 430, Springboro OH 45066	937-550-2400	R	11*	.1
81	Cline Tool And Service Co—*Jim Long*	PO Box 866, Newton IA 50208	641-792-7081	R	11*	.1
82	Specialties Tool Co—*Lee Hiler*	PO Box 127, Sparta MI 49345	616-887-1714	R	10*	.1
83	S and S Tool And Machine Co—*Charles Siegel*	PO Box 23267, Louisville KY 40223	502-245-3481	R	10*	.1
84	Alvord-Polk Inc—*Ronald Boyer*	PO Box 97, Millersburg PA 17061	717-692-2128	R	10*	.1
85	Branick Industries Inc—*Duane E Brasch*	PO Box 1937, Fargo ND 58107	701-281-8888	R	10*	.1
86	Sbmc Solutions LLC	2960 Copper Rd, Santa Clara CA 95051	408-732-3200	R	10*	.1
87	Pan American Tool Corp—*Bert Leon*	5990 NW 31st Ave, Fort Lauderdale FL 33309	954-735-8665	R	10*	<.1
88	Accu-Cut Diamond Tool Company Inc—*Christine Domanski*	4229 N Nordica Ave, Norridge IL 60706	708-457-8800	R	10*	<.1
89	American Hofmann Corp—*Stephen Norris*	PO Box 10369, Lynchburg VA 24506	434-522-0300	R	10*	.1
90	Micro 100 Tool Corp—*Dale Newberry*	1410 E Pine Ave, Meridian ID 83642	208-888-7310	R	10*	.1
91	Ats Workholding Inc—*William Murphy*	30222 Esperanza, Rcho Sta Marg CA 92688	949-888-1744	R	10*	.1
92	Schenck Trebel Corp—*Bertram Dittmar*	535 Acorn St, Deer Park NY 11729	631-242-4010	R	10*	.1
93	K and G Manufacturing Co—*Thomas Gerbig*	PO Box 187, Faribault MN 55021	507-334-5501	R	10*	.1
94	Command Tooling Systems LLC—*Robert Roubenstahl*	13931 Sunfish Lake Blv, Anoka MN 55303	763-576-6910	R	9*	.1
95	Witco Inc—*Georgina Witt*	6401 Bricker Rd, Greenwood MI 48006	810-387-4231	R	9*	.1
96	J-Lenco Inc—*Edward Murphy*	PO Box 346, La Rue OH 43332	740-499-2260	R	9*	.1
97	M and S Precision Machine Inc—*Larry Fair*	900 E Randall St, Greensburg IN 47240	812-663-3870	R	9*	.1
98	Te-Co Manufacturing LLC—*Tim Lindemuth*	109 Quinter Farm Rd, Union OH 45322	937-836-0961	R	8*	.1
99	Will-Mor Engineering Company Inc—*Fran Roman*	153 Batchelder Rd, Seabrook NH 03874	603-474-8971	R	8*	.1
100	Menlo Tool Company Inc—*Lawrence Osburn* Imco Carbide Tool Inc	22760 Dequindre Rd, Warren MI 48091	586-756-6010	S	8*	.1
101	Melin Tool Company Inc—*Mike Wochna*	5565 Venture Dr Ste C, Cleveland OH 44130	216-362-4200	R	8*	.1
102	Sesco Products Group Inc—*John Coe*	40549 Brentwood Dr, Sterling Heights MI 48310	586-979-4400	R	8*	.1
103	Stewart Tool Co—*Richard Stewart*	3647 Omec Cir, Rancho Cordova CA 95742	916-635-8321	R	8*	.1
104	Ultra-Dex Inc—*Mark Birchmeier*	7162 Sheridan Rd, Flushing MI 48433	810-638-5388	R	8*	.1
105	Chick Workholding Solutions Inc—*George Swann*	500 Keystone Dr, Warrendale PA 15086	724-772-1644	R	8*	.1
106	Comet Tool Inc—*Hans Wiesmayer*	880 Nicholas Blvd, Elk Grove Village IL 60007	847-956-0126	R	8*	.1
107	Jerhen Industries Inc—*Roger Jerie*	5052 28th Ave, Rockford IL 61109	815-397-0400	R	8*	.1
108	Morgood Tools Inc—*Doug Meier*	PO Box 24997, Rochester NY 14624	585-436-8828	R	7*	.1
109	Pioneer Broach Co—*Gary Ezor*	6434 Telegraph Rd, Commerce CA 90040	323-728-1263	R	7*	.1
110	D and R Products Company Inc—*Richard Newman*	PO Box 718, Hudson MA 01749	978-562-4137	R	7*	.1
111	Logan Graphic Products Inc—*Malcolm Logan*	1100 Brown St, Wauconda IL 60084	847-526-5515	R	7*	.1
112	Rockford Systems Inc—*Richard Provi*	PO Box 5525, Rockford IL 61125	815-874-7891	R	7*	.1
113	American Drill Bushing Co	5740 Hunt Rd, Valdosta GA 31606	229-253-8928	R	7*	<.1
114	ChipBLASTER Inc—*Greg Antoun*	13605 S Mosiertown Rd, Meadville PA 16335	814-724-6278	R	7*	<.1
115	Lavelle Machine and Tool Company Inc—*Edwin Lavelle*	PO Box 1558, Westford MA 01886	978-692-8825	R	7*	<.1
116	H E Morse Co—*Christopher Wysong*	455 Douglas Ave, Holland MI 49424	616-396-4604	R	7*	.1
117	Mastercut Tool Corp—*Michael Shaluly*	PO Box 902, Safety Harbor FL 34695	727-726-5336	R	7*	.1
118	Saw Misenheimer and Tool Inc—*Judy Misenheimer*	PO Box 1163, Morristown TN 37816	423-587-4300	R	7*	.1
119	Gage Assembly Co—*Daniel Plodzeen*	3771 W Morse Ave, Lincolnwood IL 60712	847-679-5180	R	7*	.1
120	Xactra Technologies Inc—*David Binn*	9 Marway Cir, Rochester NY 14624	585-426-2030	R	7*	.1
121	CJ Winter Machine Technologies Inc—*Robert Brinkman*	167 Ames St, Rochester NY 14611	585-429-5000	R	7*	<.1
122	Riten Industries Inc—*Andrew Lachelt*	PO Box 340, Wshngtn Ct Hs OH 43160	740-335-5353	R	7*	<.1

Rank	Company Name—*Executive Officer*	Address, City, State, Zip	Phone	Type	Fin	Empls
123	WF Meyers Company Inc—*Kenneth Barnes*	PO Box 426, Bedford IN 47421	812-275-4485	R	6*	.1
124	Lindar Corp—*Thomas Haglin*	7789 Hastings Rd, Baxter MN 56425	218-829-3457	R	6*	.1
125	Toolcraft Incorporated Of North Carolina—*Ray Porter*	1877 Rutherford Rd, Marion NC 28752	828-659-7379	R	6*	.1
126	L Hardy Company Inc—*Norman Monks*	PO Box 30277, Worcester MA 01603	508-756-1511	R	6*	.1
127	Royal Machine And Tool Corp—*Richard Ruscio*	PO Box Y, Berlin CT 06037	860-828-6555	R	6*	.1
128	J and J Carbide and Tool Inc—*John Pavlopoulos*	5656 W 120th St, Alsip IL 60803	708-489-0300	R	6*	.1
129	Omni-X USA Inc—*Alexandr Slouka*	2751 W Mansfield Ave, Englewood CO 80110	303-789-3575	R	6*	.1
130	Ceratizit - Michigan Corp—*David Carter*	11350 Stephens Rd, Warren MI 48089	586-759-2280	R	6*	<.1
131	Reiff and Nestor Co—*Patrick Savage*	PO Box 147, Lykens PA 17048	717-453-7113	R	6*	.1
132	Bates Technologies Inc—*Travis Rhoden*	9059 Technology Ln, Fishers IN 46038	317-841-2400	D	6*	.1
133	Spartan Carbide Inc—*Mark Maron*	34110 Riviera Dr, Fraser MI 48026	586-285-9786	R	6*	.1
134	Knight Carbide Corp—*Bruce Kyle*	48665 Structural Dr, Chesterfield MI 48051	586-598-4888	R	6*	.1
135	Swanson Tool Manufacturing Inc—*Kenneth Swanson*	PO Box 330318, West Hartford CT 06133	860-953-1641	R	6*	.1
136	Stress-Tek Inc—*Keith Reichow*	5920 S 194th St, Kent WA 98032	253-872-1910	R	6*	<.1
137	Vortex Tool Company Inc—*Ron Serwa*	5605 E Jelinek Ave, Schofield WI 54476	715-355-7707	R	6*	<.1
138	Stelron Components Inc—*James Beezer*	1495 Macarthur Blvd, Mahwah NJ 07430	201-529-5450	R	6*	<.1
139	South Shore Tool and Die Inc—*Larry Keene*	PO Box 235, Baroda MI 49101	269-422-2606	R	6*	<.1
140	Severance Tool Industries Inc—*John Pease*	PO Box 1866, Saginaw MI 48605	989-777-5500	R	6*	<.1
141	Fielding Manufacturing Zinc Diecasting Inc—*Steven Fielding*	780 Wellington Ave, Cranston RI 02910	401-461-0400	R	5*	.1
142	B and A Manufacturing Co—*Norman Schmotzer*	3665 E Industrial Way, Riviera Beach FL 33404	561-848-8648	R	5*	<.1
143	Guardian Manufacturing Corp—*Melvin Stevens*	12193 Levan Rd, Livonia MI 48150	734-591-1454	R	5*	.1
144	Mc Pherson Industrial Corp—*Keith Pherson*	PO Box 496, Romeo MI 48065	586-752-5555	R	5*	.1
145	Elmhirst Industries Inc—*John Elmhirst*	7630 19 Mile Rd, Sterling Heights MI 48314	586-731-8663	R	5*	.1
146	Quality Tech Tool Inc—*Zoran Denic*	759 Industrial Dr, Bensenville IL 60106	847-690-9643	R	5*	<.1
147	Chardon Tool and Supply Company Inc—*Judith Fankdoner*	PO Box 291, Chardon OH 44024	440-286-6440	R	5*	<.1
148	Lovejoy Tool Company Inc—*Douglas Priestley*	PO Box 949, Springfield VT 05156	802-885-2194	R	5*	.1
149	Laydon Enterprises Inc—*John Laydon*	PO Box 459, Iron Mountain MI 49801	906-774-0284	R	5*	.1
150	Peachtree Tooling Corp—*Arnold Cochran*	PO Box 201, Braselton GA 30517	770-867-9090	R	5*	<.1
151	Imex Diamond Tools And Segments Inc—*Massoud Besharat*	PO Box 7, Elberton GA 30635	706-213-1318	R	5*	.1
152	Van Keuren—*Thomas Nixon*	470 Old Evans Rd, Evans GA 30809		S	5*	.1
153	Southeast Broach Company LLC	1420 Nw 65th Ave, Plantation FL 33313	954-584-0960	R	5*	<.1
154	Delta GearInc—*Bob Sakuta*	36251 Schoolcraft, Livonia MI 48150	734-525-8000	R	5*	<.1
155	Fall Machine Company Inc—*Richard Fall*	10 Willand Dr, Somersworth NH 03878	603-750-7100	R	5*	<.1
156	Hydra-Lock Corp—*Eugene Andre*	25000 Joy Blvd, Mount Clemens MI 48043	586-783-5007	R	5*	<.1
157	Micro Centric Corp—*Nicholas Fink*	25 S Terminal Dr, Plainview NY 11803	516-349-7220	R	5*	<.1
158	Craig Tools Inc—*William Cleveland*	PO Box 747, El Segundo CA 90245	310-414-5707	R	5*	<.1
159	Wel-Co Diamond Tool Corp—*Georgia Welch*	PO Box 1767, Oldsmar FL 34677	813-854-2638	R	5*	<.1
160	Machine Sciences Corp—*Brian Mccabe*	PO Box 969, Wilsonville OR 97070	503-682-9980	R	5*	<.1
161	Microtool And Instrument Inc—*Jennifer Leach*	1401 Brickell Ave Fl 5, Miami FL 33131	305-358-7770	R	5*	<.1
162	Velmex Inc—*Mitchel Evans*	7550 State Rte 5 And 2, Bloomfield NY 14469	585-657-6151	R	5*	<.1
163	Continental Diamond Tool Corp—*Ray Viggiano*	PO Box 126, New Haven IN 46774	200-493-1294	P	5*	<.1
164	Advance Products Corp—*David Kraklau*	2527 N M 63, Benton Harbor MI 49022	269-849-1000	R	5*	<.1
165	Bruce Diamond Corp—*Steven Puleston*	1231 County St, Attleboro MA 02703	508-222-3755	R	5*	<.1
166	Criterion Machine Works—*Gary Vanderpol*	765 W 16th St, Costa Mesa CA 92627	949-631-5444	R	5*	<.1
167	Fotofabrication Corp—*Jamie Howton*	3758 W Belmont Ave, Chicago IL 60618	773-463-6211	R	5*	<.1
168	Spie Tool Co—*Mabel Khoshaba*	1350 Wright Blvd, Schaumburg IL 60193	847-891-6556	R	5*	<.1
169	Global CNC Industries Ltd—*Helen Stassinos*	11865 Globe St, Livonia MI 48150	734-464-1920	R	5*	<.1
170	Lotec Inc—*Gary Renaud*	PO Box 596, Elkhart IN 46515	574-294-1506	R	5*	.1
171	Carbro Corp—*Ed Plano*	PO Box 278, Lawndale CA 90260	310-643-8400	R	5*	<.1
172	Dundick Corp—*Len Pernecky*	4616 W 20th St, Cicero IL 60804	708-656-6363	R	5*	<.1
173	Ostrem Tool Company Inc—*Heath Bolds*	PO Box 845, Lyman SC 29365	864-879-7451	R	5*	<.1
174	Counterbalance Corp—*Timothy Howard*	PO Box 2185, Doylestown PA 18901	215-957-9260	R	5*	<.1
175	Edmik Inc—*Haydee Knill*	3850 Grove Ave, Gurnee IL 60031	847-263-0460	R	5*	<.1
176	Machining and Fabricating Inc—*James Gielghem*	30546 Groesbeck Hwy, Roseville MI 48066	586-773-9288	R	5*	<.1
177	Pennoyer-Dodge Co—*Hazel Dodge*	6650 San Fernando Rd, Glendale CA 91201	818-547-2100	R	5*	<.1
178	H and R Manufacturing And Supply Inc—*Harvey Hivnor*	12400 Rose Rd, Willis TX 77378	936-856-5529	R	5*	<.1
179	Rts Cutting Tools Inc—*Michael Disser*	24100 Capital Blvd, Clinton Township MI 48036	586-954-1900	R	5*	<.1
180	Rainbow Enterprises Inc—*Bill Harris*	108 Chelsea Rd, Monticello MN 55362	763-295-1100	R	5*	<.1
181	Damen Carbide Tool Company Inc—*Jakob Bachmeier*	344 Beinoris Dr, Wood Dale IL 60191	630-766-7875	R	5*	<.1
182	Maurice S Dessau Company Inc—*Richard Dessau*	15-01 Pollitt Dr Ste 1, Fair Lawn NJ 07410	201-791-2005	R	4*	<.1
183	Dorian Tool International Inc—*Enrico Giannetti*	615 County Rd 219, East Bernard TX 77435	979-282-2861	R	4*	<.1
184	Progress Machine and Tool Inc—*Lance Norris*	1155 Judson Rd, Norton Shores MI 49456	231-798-3410	R	4*	<.1
185	Precision Spring and Stamping Corp—*Sean Mchugh*	22617 85th Pl S, Kent WA 98031	253-852-6911	R	4*	<.1
186	Johnson Gage Co—*Lowell Johnson*	534 Cottage Grove Rd, Bloomfield CT 06002	860-242-5541	R	4*	<.1
187	Rbi Manufacturing Inc—*Scott Fuhrman*	PO Box 250, Sharpsburg NC 27878	252-977-6764	R	4*	<.1
188	Nanney and Son Inc—*Tim Nanney*	205 E Air Depot Rd, Glencoe AL 35905	256-492-2910	R	4*	<.1
189	Contour Tool Inc—*Paul Reichlin*	38830 Taylor Pkwy, Elyria OH 44035	440-365-7333	R	4*	<.1
190	Marion Tool and Die Inc—*Tim Marion*	1126 W Us Hwy 40, West Terre Haute IN 47885	812-533-9800	R	4*	<.1
191	Retco Tool Company Inc—*John Cade*	9030 Viscount Row, Dallas TX 75247	214-358-5039	R	4*	<.1
192	S-T Industries Inc—*Margaret Smith*	PO Box 517, Saint James MN 56081	507-375-3211	R	4*	<.1
193	Motors and Controls International Inc—*Lester Tjelmeland*	1440 N Burton Pl, Anaheim CA 92806	714-956-0480	R	4*	<.1
194	Product Design And Development Inc—*Michael Brezler*	2603 Keyway Dr, York PA 17402	717-741-4844	R	4*	<.1
195	Kingsford Broach and Tool Inc—*Raymond Schultz*	PO Box 2277, Kingsford MI 49802	906-774-4917	R	4*	<.1
196	Disston Precision Inc—*Joseph Lukes*	6795 State Rd, Philadelphia PA 19135	215-338-1200	R	4*	<.1
197	Dura-Mill Inc—*Richard Walrath*	16 Stonebreak Rd, Ballston Spa NY 12020	518-899-2255	R	4*	<.1
198	Astra Associates Incorporated dba Mid-West Instrument—*Frederick Lueck*	6500 Dobry Dr, Sterling Heights MI 48314	586-254-6500	R	4*	.1
199	Unique Tool And Manufacturing Company Inc—*Jimmy Scott*	PO Box 909, Randleman NC 27317	336-498-2614	R	4*	<.1
200	Johnson Carbide Products Inc—*James Foulds*	1422 S 25th St, Saginaw MI 48601	989-754-7496	R	4*	<.1
201	Methods Tooling and Manufacturing Inc—*Keith Michaels*	PO Box 400, Mount Marion NY 12456	845-246-7100	R	4*	<.1
202	Huron Tool and Cutter Grinding Company Inc—*James Cosenza*	2045 Wellwood Ave, Farmingdale NY 11735	631-420-7000	R	4*	<.1
203	Miller Broach Inc—*Jeffrey Miller*	14510 Bryce Rd, Capac MI 48014	810-395-8810	R	4*	<.1
204	Mp Tool and Engineering Company Inc—*Longine Morawski*	PO Box 631, Roseville MI 48066	586-772-7730	R	4*	<.1
205	Dijet Inc—*Keiichiro Izumi*	45807 Helm St, Plymouth MI 48170	734-454-9100	R	4*	<.1
206	A and H Industries Inc—*Frederick Hoffman*	837 S Railroad St, Myerstown PA 17067	717-866-7591	R	4*	<.1
207	Benny Gage Inc—*Benny Dorenzo*	41260 Joy Rd, Plymouth MI 48170	734-455-3080	R	4*	<.1
208	Prototype Products Inc—*Jeffrey Mark*	13225 Industrial Pk Bl, Minneapolis MN 55441	763-557-0995	R	4*	<.1
209	United States Drill Head Co *J Nymberg*	5298 River Rd, Cincinnati OH 45233	513-941-0300	R	4*	<.1
210	Lapointe Hudson Broach Company Inc—*Gary Ezor*	569 Main St, Hudson MA 01749	978-562-7943	R	4*	<.1

Note: An asterisk (*) indicates an estimated financial figure. The company type code used is as follows: R = Private, P = Public, S = Private Subsidiary, B = Public Subsidiary, D = Division, J = Joint Venture, I = Investment Fund.

COMPANY RANKINGS BY SALES WITHIN 4-DIGIT SIC

Rank	Company Name—Executive Officer	Address, City, State, Zip	Phone	Type	Fin	Empls
211	Pompano Precision Products Inc—George Spirio	1100 Sw 12th Ave, Pompano Beach FL 33069	954-946-6059	R	4*	<.1
212	Belden Tools Inc—Perry Sainati	2500 Braga Dr, Broadview IL 60155	708-344-4600	R	4*	<.1
213	Positrol Inc—David Weber	3890 Virginia Ave, Cincinnati OH 45227	513-272-0500	R	4*	<.1
214	R and A Tool and Engineering Co—Richard Raymond	39127 Ford Rd, Westland MI 48185	734-981-2000	R	4*	<.1
215	Northeastern Water Jet Inc—Leonard Porte	4 Willow St, Amsterdam NY 12010	518-843-4988	R	4*	<.1
216	Mincon Rockdrills USA Inc—Mike Jones	PO Box 189, Benton IL 62812	618-435-3404	R	4*	<.1
217	Jennison Precision Machine Inc—Thomas Jennison	PO Box 861, Carnegie PA 15106	412-279-3007	R	4*	<.1
218	Valley Grinding Service and Supply Inc—Joseph Solberg	PO Box 246, Little Chute WI 54140	920-788-9131	R	4*	<.1
219	Deweyl Tool Company Inc—William Cline	959 Transport Way, Petaluma CA 94954	707-765-5779	R	4*	<.1
220	RI Carbide Tool Co—John Lombari	339 Farnum Pke, Smithfield RI 02917	401-231-1020	R	4*	<.1
221	Rock River Tool Inc—Robert Enander	2953 63rd Ave E, Bradenton FL 34203	941-753-6343	R	4*	<.1
222	Alden Tool Company Inc—Charles Muravnick	199 New Park Dr, Berlin CT 06037	860-828-3557	R	4*	<.1
223	British Precision Inc—Ralph Naylor	20 Sequin Dr, Glastonbury CT 06033	860-633-3343	R	4*	<.1
224	Kabelschlepp America Inc—Stephan Achs	7100 W Marcia Rd, Milwaukee WI 53223	414-354-1994	R	4*	<.1
225	Milwaukee Machinetool Corp—Michael Batzler	8803 W Fond Du Lac Ave, Milwaukee WI 53225	414-578-8699	R	4*	<.1
226	Productive Solutions Inc—Lewis Krueger	PO Box 618, Neenah WI 54957	920-751-1555	R	4*	<.1
227	Rite Way Industries Inc—David Embry	4201 Reas Ln, New Albany IN 47150	812-206-8665	R	4*	<.1
228	East Side Machine Inc—Paul Derleth	625 Phillips Rd, Webster NY 14580	585-265-4560	R	4*	<.1
229	Diomex Inc—Bob Pensec	PO Box 175, Chesterfield MI 46017	765-378-6976	R	4*	<.1
230	Patriot Machining and Maintenance Services Inc—Phillip Hubbell	512 Linden Ave, Franklin OH 45005	937-746-2117	R	4*	<.1
231	Ohio Metal Working Products Company Inc—Paul Ernenwein	PO Box 7069, Canton OH 44705	330-453-8438	R	4*	<.1
232	Starlite Industries Inc—Jay Rosenbluth	PO Box 990, Bryn Mawr PA 19010	610-527-1300	R	4*	<.1
233	MG Machining—Matt Grundman	904 State St, Bedford IA 50833	712-523-2840	R	4*	<.1
234	Bocra Industries Inc—Kirk Boswell	140 Batchelder Rd, Seabrook NH 03874	603-474-3598	R	4*	<.1
235	Drewco Corp—Ann Pettibone	3745 Nicholson Rd, Franksville WI 53126	262-886-5050	R	4*	<.1
236	Joint Production Technology Inc—Robert Peuterbaugh	15381 Hallmark Ct, Macomb MI 48042	586-786-0080	R	4*	<.1
237	E P Heller Co—August Daub	PO Box 26, Madison NJ 07940	973-377-2878	R	4*	<.1
238	Hoosier Spline Broach Corp—Gilbert Larison	PO Box 538, Kokomo IN 46903	765-452-8273	R	4*	<.1
239	Gus Pech Manufacturing Company Inc—Cris Collins	PO Box 96, Le Mars IA 51031	712-546-4145	R	4*	<.1
240	Bechert Brothers Manufacturing Company Inc—James Bechert	PO Box 9067, Bristol CT 06011	860-583-7734	R	3*	<.1
241	Huron Machine Products Inc—Harold Lindemann	228 Sw 21st Ter, Fort Lauderdale FL 33312	954-587-4541	R	3*	<.1
242	TM Smith Tool International Corp—Gerald Norton	PO Box 1065, Mount Clemens MI 48046	586-468-1465	R	3*	<.1
243	Innex Industries Inc—Luka Gakovic	6 Marway Dr, Rochester NY 14624	585-247-3575	R	3*	<.1
244	Wit-Son Carbide Tool Inc—Douglas Barrett	PO Box 339, East Jordan MI 49727	231-536-2247	R	3*	<.1
245	Aloris Tool Co—Rich Roslowski	PO Box 1529, Clifton NJ 07015	973-772-1201	R	3*	<.1
246	Ferguson Tools Inc—William Ferguson	103 Industrial Dr, Edgerton OH 43517	419-298-2327	R	3*	<.1
247	Thermocarbon Inc—John Boucher	PO Box 181220, Casselberry FL 32718	407-834-7800	R	3*	<.1
248	Walter's Precision Service Inc—Walter Scurei	229 S River Dr, Tempe AZ 85281	480-968-1834	R	3*	<.1
249	Pdc Machines Inc—Syed Afzal	PO Box 2733, Warminster PA 18974	215-443-9442	R	3*	<.1
250	Tosco - Tool Specialty Co—Jerry Tetzlaff	PO Box 512157, Los Angeles CA 90051	323-232-3561	R	3*	<.1
251	Troyke Manufacturing Co—Bernard Froehlich	PO Box 62327, Cincinnati OH 45262	513-769-4242	R	3*	<.1
252	Pennsylvania Tool And Gages Inc—Kathleen Glover	16906 Pennsylvania Tl, Meadville PA 16335	814-336-3136	R	3*	<.1
253	Shape-Master Tool Co—Donald Spolum	PO Box 520, Kirkland IL 60146	815-522-6186	R	3*	<.1
254	Osborn Products Inc—Roy Osborn	1127 W Melinda Ln, Phoenix AZ 85027	623-587-0335	R	3*	<.1
255	Somma Tool Co—Eric Somma	109 Scott Rd, Waterbury CT 06705	203-753-2114	R	3*	<.1
256	A and B Machine Inc—Robert Alexander	PO Box 540, Sidney OH 45365	937-492-8662	R	3*	<.1
257	RJS Tool and Gage Co—Richard Stamp	1081 S Eton St, Birmingham MI 48009	248-642-8620	R	3*	<.1
258	Sterling Manufacturing and Engineering Inc—Kenneth Davis	7539 19 Mile Rd, Sterling Heights MI 48314	586-254-5310	R	3*	<.1
259	Western Gage Corp—Donald Moors	3316 Maya Linda Ste A, Camarillo CA 93012	805-445-1410	R	3*	<.1
260	Tungsten Industries Inc—James Cordovano	PO Box 909, Travelers Rest SC 29690	864-834-2323	R	3*	<.1
261	Rock Valley Tool LLC—Sue Church	54 Oneil St, Easthampton MA 01027	413-527-2350	R	3*	<.1
262	Accurate Machine and Tool Corp—Martin Folgmann	PO Box 519, Madison AL 35758	256-461-8063	R	3*	<.1
263	Cams Inc	5546 Elmwood Ct, Indianapolis IN 46203	317-418-8531	R	3*	<.1
264	Force Flow—Mark Nelson	2430 Stanwell Dr Ste 1, Concord CA 94520	925-686-2231	R	3*	<.1
265	Di-Coat Corp—Zigmund Grutza	42900 W 9 Mile Rd, Novi MI 48375	248-349-1211	R	3*	<.1
266	Gauging Systems Inc—Alan Westmoreland	PO Box 680, Sugar Land TX 77487	281-980-3999	R	3*	<.1
267	Precision Gage and Tool Co—Gwen Waltz	375 Gargrave Rd, Dayton OH 45449	937-866-9666	R	3*	<.1
268	Accuratus Ceramic Corp—Raymond Tsao	35 Howard St, Phillipsburg NJ 08865	908-213-7070	R	3*	<.1
269	Dumont Company LLC—Peter Elliott	PO Box 469, Greenfield MA 01302	413-773-3675	R	3*	<.1
270	Turbine Tool and Gage Inc—Audrey Murtland	PO Box 3334, Livonia MI 48151	734-427-2270	R	3*	<.1
271	Steelcraft Tool Company Inc—James Glaser	12930 Wayne Rd, Livonia MI 48150	734-522-7130	R	3*	<.1
272	Egli Machine Company Inc—Denis Egli	240 State Hwy 7, Sidney NY 13838	607-563-3663	R	3*	<.1
273	Wolverine Broach Company Inc—Bernard Aude	41200 Executive Dr, Harrison Township MI 48045	586-468-4445	R	3*	<.1
274	Warren Broach and Machine Corp—Donald Mahon	6541 Diplomat Dr, Sterling Heights MI 48314	586-254-7080	R	3*	<.1
275	Bar-Lo Carbon Products Inc—Barry Flowers	PO Box 10031, Fairfield NJ 07004	973-227-2717	R	3*	<.1
276	Martel Tool Corp—Steven Martel	5831 Pelham Rd, Allen Park MI 48101	313-278-2420	R	3*	<.1
277	Active Machine and Tool Co—August Van Dam	PO Box 199, Jenison MI 49429	616-662-9730	R	3*	<.1
278	Elenco Carbide Tool Corp—Douglas Baumann	PO Box 273, Plymouth WI 53073	920-893-6311	R	3*	<.1
279	Precision Masters Inc—William Cleeland	4935 28th Ave, Rockford IL 61109	815-397-3894	R	3*	<.1
280	Global Engineering Inc—Mark Koerner	50685 Rizzo Dr, Shelby Township MI 48315	586-247-7303	R	3*	<.1
281	Ligi Tool and Engineering Inc—Domenic Mucciacciaro	3220 Sw 15th St, Deerfield Beach FL 33442	954-332-2921	R	3*	<.1
282	B and B Precision Manufacturing Inc—Desmond Beck	PO Box 279, Avon NY 14414	585-226-6226	R	3*	<.1
283	Carbide Probes Inc—Dan Shellabarger	1328 Research Park Dr, Beavercreek OH 45432	937-429-9123	R	3*	<.1
284	Lovejoy Chaplet Corp—Peter Mcguire	PO Box 66, Hoosick Falls NY 12090	518-686-5232	R	3*	<.1
285	Alpha Manufacturing Company Inc—Robert Ballington	PO Box 2809, West Columbia SC 29171	803-739-4500	R	3*	<.1
286	Atlantic Tooling And Fabricating Company Inc—Larry Lyerly	PO Box 15124, Quinby SC 29506	843-662-7379	R	3*	<.1
287	Sharp Tool Service Inc—Richard Schirripa	2927 Nationwide Pkwy, Brunswick OH 44212	330-273-4144	R	3*	<.1
288	Midwest Cutting Tools Inc—Charles Wright	833 W College Ave, Waukesha WI 53186	262-896-0883	R	3*	<.1
289	Powerhold Inc—R Spooner	PO Box 447, Middlefield CT 06455	860-349-1044	R	3*	<.1
290	Sandar Industries Inc—Peter Rodriguez	PO Box 330106, Atlantic Beach FL 32233	904-246-4309	R	3*	<.1
291	EC Kitzel and Sons Inc—Allan Kitzel	4775 Manufacturing Ave, Cleveland OH 44135	216-267-6850	R	3*	<.1
292	B and T Tool and Engineering Inc—William Meras	PO Box 62253, Phoenix AZ 85082	602-267-1481	R	3*	<.1
293	Collis Toolholder Corp—Paul Gassman	PO Box 140, Camanche IA 52730	563-259-2454	R	3*	<.1
294	Advanced Superabrasives Inc—Attila Szucs	PO Box 1390, Mars Hill NC 28754	828-689-3200	R	3*	<.1
295	RL Schmitt Company Inc—Paul Schmitt	34506 Glendale St, Livonia MI 48150	734-525-9310	R	3*	<.1
296	Zyvex Instruments LLC—Randy Schussler	1321 N Plano Rd, Richardson TX 75081	972-792-1625	R	3*	<.1
297	F Tinker and Sons Company Inc—Regis Synan	5665 Butler St, Pittsburgh PA 15201	412-781-3553	R	3*	<.1
298	Mark Tool and Die Company Inc—George Vidu	4360 Haggerty Hwy, Commerce Township MI 48390	248-363-1567	R	3*	<.1
299	Toolmasters LLC—John Nelson	PO Box 1611, Rockford IL 61110	815-968-0961	R	3*	<.1

Rank	Company Name—*Executive Officer*	Address, City, State, Zip	Phone	Type	Fin	Empls
300	Big W Industries Inc—*C Nickloy*	200 S 5th St, Kansas City KS 66101	913-321-2112	R	3*	<.1
301	Turmatic Systems Inc—*Bruno Schmitter*	11600 Adie Rd, Maryland Heights MO 63043	314-993-0600	R	3*	<.1
302	I and G Tool Company Inc—*Sigfried Charow*	51528 Industrial Dr, New Baltimore MI 48047	586-777-7690	R	3*	<.1
303	Workblades Inc—*Edward Bard*	21535 Groesbeck Hwy, Warren MI 48089	586-778-0060	R	3*	<.1
304	PMI Phoenix Metallurgical Inc—*Donald Cooper*	183 Yew St, East Douglas MA 01516	508-476-7375	R	3*	<.1
305	BCI Collet Inc—*Richard Baruk*	PO Box 85718, Westland MI 48185	734-326-1222	R	3*	<.1
306	Jade Tool Inc—*John Korson*	891 Duell Rd, Traverse City MI 49686	231-946-7710	R	3*	<.1
307	Layke Tool and Manufacturing Company Inc—*Douglas Sheets*	PO Box 438, Meadville PA 16335	814-333-1169	R	3*	<.1
308	Tool Fabrication Corp—*Jeff Hesse*	PO Box 26248, Milwaukee WI 53226	414-453-5030	R	3*	<.1
309	Michigan Spline Gage Company Inc—*Bernard Hagen*	PO Box 69, Hazel Park MI 48030	248-544-7303	R	3*	<.1
310	Southern Carbide Specialists Inc—*Stan Weiss*	PO Box 879, Quitman GA 31643	229-263-8927	R	2*	<.1
311	Loughmiller Machine Tool and Design—*Jason Loughmiller*	12851 E 150 N, Loogootee IN 47553	812-295-3903	R	2*	<.1
312	H and P Tool Company Inc—*George Peters*	PO Box 486, Richmond IN 47375	765-962-4505	R	2*	<.1
313	Admiral Broach Company Inc—*Patrick Considine*	21391 Carlo Dr, Clinton Township MI 48038	586-468-8411	R	2*	<.1
314	Chucks Stace-Allen Inc—*Marcia Grimes*	PO Box 21216, Indianapolis IN 46221	317-632-2401	R	2*	<.1
315	Novatech Inc—*John Popovich*	190 Gruner Rd, Cheektowaga NY 14227	716-892-6682	R	2*	<.1
316	Reed Tool and Die Inc—*David Reed*	1643 Pleasant Valley R, Mount Pleasant PA 15666	724-547-3500	R	2*	<.1
317	Schlitter Tool Inc—*Jeanne Schlitters*	27450 Gloede Dr, Warren MI 48088	586-771-5700	R	2*	<.1
318	Arlyn Tool and Manufacturing Company Inc—*Edwin Einwich*	3515 Airway Dr Ste 206, Reno NV 89511	775-852-4600	R	2*	<.1
319	Harig Manufacturing Corp—*Theodore Eckert*	5757 W Howard St, Niles IL 60714	847-647-9500	R	2*	<.1
320	Coordinate Machine Co—*Shirley Luschen*	59 Congress Cir W, Roselle IL 60172	630-894-9880	R	2*	<.1
321	Associated Broach Corp—*Malcolm Davis*	7481 Research Dr, Almont MI 48003	810-798-9112	R	2*	<.1
322	Mid-West Feeder Inc—*Cindy Gustasson*	601 E Pleasant St, Belvidere IL 61008	815-544-2994	R	2*	<.1
323	T M Electronics Inc—*Richard Small*	45 Main St, Boylston MA 01505	508-869-6400	R	2*	<.1
324	Custom Feeder Company Of Rockford—*James Stamm*	6207 Material Ave Ste, Loves Park IL 61111	815-654-2444	R	2*	<.1
325	Form Tools Inc—*Mark Eriksson*	12900 Hwy 55, Minneapolis MN 55441	763-559-7170	R	2*	<.1
326	George Ford and Sons Inc—*George Ford*	900 E Mermaid Ln, Glenside PA 19038	215-233-5200	R	2*	<.1
327	Pacific Tool and Gauge—*Dave Kiss*	PO Box 2549, White City OR 97503	541-826-5808	R	2*	<.1
328	Sev-Cal Tool Inc—*James Severance*	3231 Halladay St, Santa Ana CA 92705	714-549-2211	R	2*	<.1
329	VIP Tooling Inc—*Paul Nolting*	739 E Franklin St, Shelbyville IN 46176	317-398-0753	R	2*	<.1
330	W L Fuller Inc—*Gary Fuller*	PO Box 8767, Warwick RI 02888	401-467-2900	R	2*	<.1
331	Entek Corp—*Ladd Adams*	3106 Broce Dr, Norman OK 73072	405-364-5588	R	2*	<.1
332	Tj Grinding Inc—*Michael Winters*	W241s3970 Rockwood Cir, Waukesha WI 53189	262-549-6885	R	2*	<.1
333	DC Morrison Company Inc—*Henry Reder*	PO Box 12586, Covington KY 41012	859-581-7511	R	2*	<.1
334	Whitney Tool Company Inc—*Linda Flynn*	PO Box 545, Bedford IN 47421	812-275-4491	R	2*	<.1
335	Atwood Tool and Machine Inc—*Blair Atwood*	PO Box 609, Chenango Bridge NY 13745	607-648-6543	R	2*	<.1
336	Caro Carbide Corp—*Richard Cieszkowski*	553 Robbins Dr, Troy MI 48083	248-588-4252	R	2*	<.1
337	Elk Lake Tool Co—*Jerald Rives*	PO Box 79, Elk Rapids MI 49629	231-264-5616	R	2*	<.1
338	Quality Assurance International Corp—*Dominic Persichini*	36010 Industrial Rd, Livonia MI 48150	734-591-0134	R	2*	<.1
339	Z-Patch Inc—*Greg Sprehe*	PO Box 3220, Carbondale IL 62902	618-529-2431	R	2*	<.1
340	Wedge-Mill Tool Inc—*John Yaros*	7771 Kensington Ct, Brighton MI 48116	248-486-6400	R	2*	<.1
341	Carbide Products Inc—*Danny Strippelhoff*	PO Box 550, Georgetown KY 40324	502-863-2340	R	2*	<.1
342	Abrasive Diamond Tool Company Inc—*Thomas Lucas*	PO Box 71278, Madison Heights MI 48071	248-588-4800	R	2*	<.1
343	Anson Machine Works Inc—*R Garris*	PO Box 269, Peachland NC 28133	704-272-7657	R	2*	<.1
344	Consolidated Carbide Ltd—*John Walgren*	1929 Commander Dr, Lake Havasu City AZ 86403	928-453-8181	R	2*	<.1
345	Micro Tool Service Inc—*Gus Leis*	PO Box 227, New Lebanon OH 45345	937-835-5621	R	2*	<.1
346	Monaghan and Associates Inc—*Scott Monaghan*	PO Box 1165, Dayton OH 45401	937-253-7706	R	2*	<.1
347	Rota File Corp—*Don Nevin*	PO Box 678, Syosset NY 11791	516-496-7200	R	2*	<.1
348	Stanhope Tool Inc—*Brian Fish*	395 W Girard Ave, Madison Heights MI 48071	248-585-5711	H	2*	<.1
349	Logansport Machine Company Inc—*Gordon Duerr*	PO Box 7006, Logansport IN 46947	574-753-3104	R	2*	<.1
350	Master-Cut Tool Co—*Kenneth Saxe*	PO Box 510595, Livonia MI 48151	734-525-9305	R	2*	<.1
351	ME Neuber Industrial Diamonds Company Inc—*Ralph Annese*	10 B St, Burlington MA 01803	781-273-5656	R	2*	<.1
352	Burris Machine Company Inc—*Jerry Sellers*	PO Box 2858, Hickory NC 28603	828-322-6914	R	2*	<.1
353	Century Tool And Design Inc—*Michael Aldi*	PO Box 545, Milldale CT 06467	860-621-6748	R	2*	<.1
354	Stapels Manufacturing LLC	2612 Elliott Dr, Troy MI 48083	248-577-5570	R	2*	<.1
355	Dikar Tool Company Inc—*Robert Forsyth*	PO Box 916, Novi MI 48376	248-348-0010	R	2*	<.1
356	Kon-Suit Inc—*Ken Kopka*	6 Birch St, Hudson NH 03051	603-882-7464	R	2*	<.1
357	Lumco Manufacturing Co—*Patrick Gleason*	2027 Mitchell Lake Rd, Lum MI 48412	810-724-0582	R	2*	<.1
358	Rusach International Inc—*Hans Sachs*	5230 Park Emerson Dr L, Indianapolis IN 46203	317-638-0298	R	2*	<.1
359	Maverick Tool Company Inc—*John Woodward*	211 Beeline Dr Ste 5, Bensenville IL 60106	630-766-2313	R	2*	<.1
360	North American Carbide Of Missouri Inc—*Bernard Nothstine*	PO Box 160, Jonesburg MO 63351	636-488-5416	R	2*	<.1
361	Precision Tool Inc—*Percy Haines*	PO Box 189, Vermontville MI 49096	517-726-1060	R	2*	<.1
362	Southanchor Manufacturing LLC	PO Box 3613, El Paso TX 79923	915-533-8879	R	2*	<.1
363	Carbide Grinding Company Inc—*Kevin Cranker*	W226n735 Eastmound Dr, Waukesha WI 53186	262-549-5940	R	2*	<.1
364	Maro Precision Tool Co—*Laurence Rothenberg*	12400 Merriman Rd, Livonia MI 48150	734-261-3100	R	2*	<.1
365	Proto-Cutter Inc—*Peter Alber*	1555 Hwy 75 E Ste 1, Freeport IL 61032	815-232-2300	R	2*	<.1
366	P and P Manufacturing Company Inc—*Jon Kirsch*	260 Mccormick Dr, Lapeer MI 48446	810-667-2712	R	2*	<.1
367	Precision Tool Company Inc—*David Reck*	2839 Henry St, Muskegon MI 49441	231-733-0811	R	2*	<.1
368	US Avionics Inc—*Manu Sdez*	30 Arbor St, Hartford CT 06106	860-233-7185	R	2*	<.1
369	Ajax Industries Inc—*David De Matteo*	575 N Hague Ave, Columbus OH 43204	614-272-6944	R	2*	<.1
370	Comtorgage Corp—*Pauline Brodeur*	PO Box 1217, Slatersville RI 02876	401-765-0900	R	2*	<.1
371	Crv Lancaster—*Pat Lancaster*	455 N Artesian Ave, Chicago IL 60612	312-738-4750	R	2*	<.1
372	Dependable Gage and Tool Co—*Leigh Smith*	15321 W 11 Mile Rd, Oak Park MI 48237	248-545-2100	R	2*	<.1
373	Shouse Tool Inc—*Virgil Shouse*	290 N Alloy Dr, Fenton MI 48430	810-629-0391	R	2*	<.1
374	Apollo Tool and Engineering Inc—*Mike Hartley*	3020 Wilson Dr Nw, Grand Rapids MI 49534	616-735-4934	R	2*	<.1
375	Moehrle Inc—*Milton Stemen*	1081 E N Territorial R, Whitmore Lake MI 48189	734-761-2000	R	2*	<.1
376	Precision Cutter and Tool Co—*Rob Baker*	PO Box 1666, Lebanon MO 65536	417-532-7729	R	2*	<.1
377	Cap Collet and Tool Company Inc—*John Potter*	4082 6th St, Wyandotte MI 48192	734-283-4040	R	2*	<.1
378	Uhrichsville Carbide Inc—*Bob Septer*	410 N Water St, Uhrichsville OH 44683	740-922-9197	R	2*	<.1
379	DC Lites Co—*Jack Jeter*	10740 Goodnight Ln, Dallas TX 75220	972-556-0260	R	2*	<.1
380	Quality Grinding Company Inc—*Tom Brice*	6800 Caballero Blvd, Buena Park CA 90620	714-228-2100	R	2*	<.1
381	Marena Industries Inc—*Teodoro Marena*	433 School St, East Hartford CT 06108	860-528-9701	R	2*	<.1
382	Madill Carbide Inc—*Dennis Morris*	1504 E Waterman St, Wichita KS 67211	316-263-9285	R	2*	<.1
383	Norman Tool Inc—*John Norman*	15415 Old State Rd, Evansville IN 47725	812-867-3496	R	2*	<.1
384	Aggressive Tool and Machine Company Inc—*Sarah Sharpe*	6000 Industrial Hts Dr, Knoxville TN 37909	865-588-6551	R	2*	<.1
385	Dillon Manufacturing Inc—*Joseph Shouvlin*	2115 Progress Rd, Springfield OH 45505	937-325-8482	R	2*	<.1
386	Meyer Gage Company Inc—*John Meyer*	230 Burnham St, South Windsor CT 06074	860-528-6526	R	2*	<.1
387	Special Drill And Reamer Corp—*Michael Obloy*	PO Box 71105, Madison Heights MI 48071	248-588-5333	R	2*	<.1
388	Canto Tool Corp—*Dale Cummings*	PO Box 533, Meadville PA 16335	814-724-2865	R	2*	<.1
389	Quality Machine Inc—*Gary Cicale*	31 Kingston Rd, Plaistow NH 03865	603-382-2334	R	2*	<.1

Note: An asterisk (*) indicates an estimated financial figure. The company type code used is as follows: R = Private, P = Public, S = Private Subsidiary, B = Public Subsidiary, D = Division, J = Joint Venture, I = Investment Fund.

COMPANY RANKINGS BY SALES WITHIN 4-DIGIT SIC

Rank	Company Name—*Executive Officer*	Address, City, State, Zip	Phone	Type	Fin	Empls
390	Tooltech Machinery Inc—*Robert Trottier*	PO Box 543, Oxford MI 48371	248-628-1813	R	2*	<.1
391	Triangle Broach Co—*Gary Hanton*	18404 Fitzpatrick St, Detroit MI 48228	313-838-2150	R	2*	<.1
392	Tool Service Company Inc—*Bruce Bellard*	34150 Riviera, Fraser MI 48026	586-296-2500	R	2*	<.1
393	GAL Gage Co—*Goodwin Lycan*	PO Box 218, Stevensville MI 49127	269-465-5750	R	2*	<.1
394	Kent Demolition Tool—*Jeff Crane*	711 Lake St, Kent OH 44240	330-673-5826	R	2*	<.1
395	Hanlo Gauges and Engineering Co—*Barbara Williams*	34403 Glendale St, Livonia MI 48150	734-422-4224	R	2*	<.1
396	Form Tool Technology Inc—*Michael Robbins*	5174 Commerce Dr, York PA 17408	717-792-3626	R	1*	<.1
397	Aw Carbide Fabricators Inc—*Dennis Wegner*	33891 Doreka, Fraser MI 48026	586-294-1850	R	1*	<.1
398	Midland Precision Machining Inc—*Ed Walimaa*	4043 W Kitty Hawk Ste, Chandler AZ 85226	480-777-5740	R	1*	<.1
399	Circle Broach Company Inc—*Robert Duquette*	38358 Abruzzi Dr, Westland MI 48185	734-722-9221	R	1*	<.1
400	Harrington Tool Co—*Fred Harrington*	PO Box 280, Ludington MI 49431	231-843-3445	R	1*	<.1
401	Titan Tool Co—*Brian McKean*	PO Box 220, Fairview PA 16415	814-474-1583	R	1*	<.1
402	Mueller Gages Co—*Rhett Mueller*	PO Box 310, San Gabriel CA 91778	626-287-2911	R	1*	<.1
403	Custom Carbide Corp—*Paul St Louis*	572 Saint James Ave, Springfield MA 01109	413-732-7470	R	1*	<.1
404	Gage Rite Products Inc—*Art Jadach*	356 Executive Dr, Troy MI 48083	248-588-7796	R	1*	<.1
405	Fore Tool Co—*Kent Nelson*	300 E Park St, Mundelein IL 60060	847-949-5844	R	1*	<.1
406	Reif Carbide Tool Company Inc—*Fred Reif*	PO Box 862, Warren MI 48090	586-754-1890	R	1*	<.1
407	Kermitool Inc—*Kermit Hoke*	401 Manor St, York PA 17401	717-846-8665	R	1*	<.1
408	Acme Grooving Tool Co—*Michael Nyeste*	15330 Dale St, Detroit MI 48223	313-532-4522	R	1*	<.1
409	Park Enterprises Of Rochester Inc—*Rob Brunskill*	226 Jay St, Rochester NY 14608	585-546-4200	R	1*	.2
410	Rietech Global LLC—*Kathy Ritter*	3700 Singer Blvd Ne St, Albuquerque NM 87109	505-299-6623	R	1*	<.1
411	Cross Tool and Manufacturing—*Eric Stone*	1000 E Butler Ave Ste, Flagstaff AZ 86001	928-779-4218	R	1*	<.1
412	Gross Machine Inc—*Bruce Gross*	1760 Costner Dr Ste 1, Warrington PA 18976	215-491-7077	R	1*	<.1
413	Vogform Tool and Die Company Inc—*John Vogel*	56 Doty Cir, West Springfield MA 01089	413-737-6947	R	1*	<.1
414	Jepson Precision Tool Inc—*Daniel Jepson*	10524 Crosby Cir, Cranesville PA 16410	814-756-5639	R	1*	<.1
415	Leverwood Machine Works Inc—*Patrick Lever*	282 N Park St, Dallastown PA 17313	717-246-4105	R	1*	<.1
416	Contract Manufacturing Services Inc—*John Lloyd*	12164 Severn Way, Riverside CA 92503	951-520-8267	R	1*	<.1
417	Owosso Automation Inc—*Ernie Rivers*	1650 E S St 488, Owosso MI 48867	989-725-8804	R	1*	<.1
418	Trusted Tool Manufacturing Inc—*John Martin*	8075 Old Us 23, Fenton MI 48430	810-750-6000	R	1*	<.1
419	Harroun Enterprises Inc—*Hugh Harroun*	1111 Fenway Cir, Fenton MI 48430	810-629-9885	R	1*	<.1
420	New England Tap Corp	200 Front St, Millersburg PA 17061	508-543-2596	S	1*	N/A
421	JE Wood Co—*Brian Fish*	395 W Girard Ave, Madison Heights MI 48071	248-585-5711	R	1*	<.1
422	H E Long Co—*Michael Long*	PO Box 197, Morrow OH 45152	513-899-2610	R	1*	<.1
423	Holly Pipe Corp—*Jerry Nugent*	1978 Atchfalaya Rvr Hw, Breaux Bridge LA 70517	337-228-1128	R	1*	<.1
424	E-Z Burr Tool Co—*William Robinson*	41180 Joy Rd, Plymouth MI 48170	734-459-5310	R	1*	<.1
425	Active Grinding and Manufacturing Co—*Richard Pevitts*	1800 Parkes Dr, Broadview IL 60155	708-344-0510	R	1*	<.1
426	Morgan Precision Instruments LLC—*George Koberlein*	3375 Miller Park Rd, Akron OH 44312	330-896-0846	R	1*	<.1
427	Euclid Machine and Manufacturing Company Inc—*Robert Kluba*	29030 Northline Rd, Romulus MI 48174	734-941-1080	R	1*	<.1
428	Cedarberg Industries Inc—*John Cedarberg*	1960 Seneca Rd, Saint Paul MN 55122	651-452-5012	R	1*	<.1
429	International Carbide Corp—*Bruce Mackey*	305 Creek St Ne B, Yelm WA 98597	360-458-1603	R	1*	<.1
430	Dynacut Inc—*Robert Platt*	PO Box 156, Springtown PA 18081	610-346-7386	R	1*	<.1
431	LC Smith Co—*Francis Fife*	196 Morgan Ave, Elyria OH 44035	440-327-1251	R	1*	<.1
432	Brunswick Instrument Inc—*Kelvin Palmer*	6150 W Mulford St, Niles IL 60714	847-965-9191	R	1*	<.1
433	Brothers Precision Tool Co—*Joe Brooks*	310 S Broome St, Albemarle NC 28001	704-982-566/	R	<1*	<.1
434	Spence Industries Inc—*Charles Dillon*	23888 Dequindre Rd, Warren MI 48091	586-758-3800	R	<1*	<.1
435	Thinking Tools LLC	PO Box 1606, Palmer Lake CO 80133	719-488-9640	R	<1*	<.1

TOTALS: SIC 3545 Machine Tool Accessories

	Companies: 435				15,706	43.1

3546 Power-Driven Handtools

Rank	Company Name—*Executive Officer*	Address, City, State, Zip	Phone	Type	Fin	Empls
1	Danaher Corp—*H Lawrence Culp Jr*	2200 Pennsylvania Ave, Washington DC 20037	202-828-0850	P	13,203	48.2
2	Black and Decker Corp—*Nolan D Archibald*	701 E Joppa Rd, Towson MD 21286	410-716-3900	S	4,775	19.9
3	Senco Products Inc—*Ben Johansen*	4270 Ivy Pointe Blvd, Cincinnati OH 45245	513-388-2000	R	405	2.0
4	Williams Tool Company Inc—*Dan Stubblefield*	PO Box 180310, Fort Smith AR 72918	479-646-8866	S	111	.1
5	Sioux Tools Inc—*Mark Pozzoni*	PO Box 1596, Murphy NC 28906	828-835-9765	S	100*	.5
6	Dynabrade Inc—*Walter Welsch*	8989 Sheridan Dr, Clarence NY 14031	716-631-0100	R	51*	.2
7	P and F Industries Inc—*Richard A Horowitz*	445 Broadhollow Rd, Melville NY 11747	631-694-9800	P	51	.1
8	Stanley Assembly Technologies—*Allen Powell*	5335 Avion Park Dr, Cleveland OH 44143	440-461-5500	D	45	.2
9	Ingersoll-Rand Company Productivity Solutions—*Michael W Lamach*	PO Box 1776, Annandale NJ 08801	908-238-7000	D	41*	.1
10	Diamond Mk Products Inc—*Robert Delahaut*	PO Box 2803, Torrance CA 90509	310-539-5221	R	34*	.2
11	Jefferson City Tool Co—*Bob Folerth*	6530 Poe Ave, Dayton OH 45414	937-898-6070	S	23*	.1
12	Shopsmith Woodworking Centers Limited Co—*Bob Folerth*	6530 Poe Ave, Dayton OH 45414	937-898-6070	S	23*	.1
13	Shopsmith Woodworking Promotions Inc—*Bob Folerth*	6530 Poe Ave, Dayton OH 45414	937-898-6070	S	23*	.1
14	Jore Corp—*Frank Tiegs*	34837 Innovation Dr, Ronan MT 59864	406-528-4350	S	18*	.2
15	Ryobi Technologies Inc—*Jeffrey Dils*	PO Box 1207, Anderson SC 29622	864-226-6511	R	17*	.3
16	Diamond Z Trailer Inc—*Steve Peel*	11299 Bass Ln, Caldwell ID 83605	208-585-2929	R	16*	.1
17	Ardisam Inc—*Mark Ruppel*	PO Box 666, Cumberland WI 54829	715-822-2415	R	15*	.1
18	Zircon Corp—*John Stauss*	1580 Dell Ave, Campbell CA 95008	408-866-8600	R	12*	.1
19	Thomas C Wilson Inc—*Charles Hanley*	2111 44th Ave, Long Island City NY 11101	718-729-3360	R	11*	.1
20	George Jue Manufacturing Company Inc—*George Jue*	8140 Rosecrans Ave, Paramount CA 90723	562-634-8180	R	9*	.1
21	Merrick Machine Co—*Richard Merrick*	PO Box 188, Alda NE 68810	308-384-1780	R	8*	.1
22	S and G Tool Aid Corp—*George Gering*	43 E Alpine St, Newark NJ 07114	973-824-7730	R	7*	.1
23	Miracle Tools America LLC—*Mark Bawden*	PO Box 3628, Davenport IA 52808	563-391-6220	R	7*	<.1
24	Florida Pneumatic Manufacturing Corp—*Bart Swank* P and F Industries Inc	851 Jupiter Park Ln, Jupiter FL 33458	561-744-9500	S	7*	<.1
25	Diedrich Drill Inc—*Thomas Ledonne*	5 Fisher St, La Porte IN 46350	219-326-7788	R	7*	<.1
26	Guardair Corp—*Thomas Tremblay*	54 2nd Ave, Chicopee MA 01020	413-594-4400	R	6*	<.1
27	AWB Industries Inc—*Desmond Lynch*	PO Box 370, Oscoda MI 48750	989-739-1447	R	6*	<.1
28	T C Service Co—*Edgar Henry*	38285 Pelton Rd, Willoughby OH 44094	440-954-7500	R	6*	<.1
29	Jiffy Air Tool Inc—*Jack Pettit*	PO Box 2222, Carson City NV 89702	775-883-1072	R	5*	<.1
30	Century Drill and Tool Company Inc—*Donald Long*	PO Box 5216, De Pere WI 54115	920-339-8700	R	5*	<.1
31	National Detroit Inc—*Roger Hoffman*	PO Box 2285, Loves Park IL 61131	815-877-4041	R	5*	<.1
32	Zagar Inc—*John Zagar*	24000 Lakeland Blvd, Euclid OH 44132	216-731-0500	R	5*	<.1
33	Gch Tool Group Inc—*Dennis Nicholas*	13265 E 8 Mile Rd, Warren MI 48089	586-777-6250	R	5*	<.1
34	Lemco Tool Corp—*Michael Miller*	1850 Metzger Ave, Cogan Station PA 17728	570-494-0620	R	4*	<.1
35	Meritool LLC—*Darryl Bates*	PO Box 745, Ellicottville NY 14731	716-699-6005	R	4*	<.1
36	WHO Manufacturing Company Inc—*Jon Littler*	PO Box 1153, Lamar CO 81052	719-336-7433	R	3*	<.1
37	Simonds Inc—*Joan Logee*	PO Box 100, Southbridge MA 01550	508-764-3235	R	3*	<.1

Rank	Company Name—*Executive Officer*	Address, City, State, Zip	Phone	Type	Fin	Empls
38	Feldmann Engineering and Manufacturing Company Inc—*Clifford Feldmann*	520 Forest Ave, Sheboygan Falls WI 53085	920-467-6167	R	3*	<.1
39	Bayou Outdoor Equipment—*Jim Allen*	489 Valparaiso Pkwy, Valparaiso FL 32580	850-729-2711	R	3*	<.1
40	Iceskate Conditioning Equipment Co—*Sid Broadbent*	5265 W Quarles Dr, Littleton CO 80128	303-979-3800	R	2*	<.1
41	Welliver and Sons Inc—*Barry Welliver*	1540 New Milford Schoo, Rockford IL 61109	815-874-2400	R	2*	<.1
42	National Band Saw Co—*Harley Frank*	PO Box 800190, Santa Clarita CA 91380	661-294-9552	R	2*	<.1
43	American Pneumatic Tool Inc	9949 Tabor Pl, Santa Fe Springs CA 90670	562-204-1555	R	2*	<.1
44	Regis Delta Tools Inc—*Thomas Deadman*	3315 Industrial 25th S, Fort Pierce FL 34946	772-465-4302	R	2*	<.1
45	Cyclo Manufacturing Co—*Robert Johnson*	7085 W Belmont Dr, Littleton CO 80123	720-981-1647	R	2*	<.1
46	Warwood Tool Co—*Robert Burke*	PO Box 6357, Wheeling WV 26003	304-277-1414	R	1*	<.1
47	Diamond Tech Inc—*John Ward*	PO Box 756, Rocklin CA 95677	916-624-1118	R	1*	<.1
48	Pneutek Inc—*Harry Haytayan*	17 Friars Dr Ste D, Hudson NH 03051	603-883-1660	R	1*	<.1
49	Clifford Gage—*Clifford Gage*	PO Box 107, Fort Edward NY 12828	518-747-7850	R	<1*	<.1

TOTALS: SIC 3546 Power Driven Handtools
Companies: 49

					19,093	73.6

3547 Rolling Mill Machinery

Rank	Company Name—*Executive Officer*	Address, City, State, Zip	Phone	Type	Fin	Empls
1	RB and W Manufacturing LLC	10080 Wellman Rd, Streetsboro OH 44241	234-380-8540	S	6,375*	.1
2	New Tech Machinery Corp—*Lawrence Coben*	1300 40th St, Denver CO 80205	303-294-0538	R	38*	<.1
3	Yoder Manufacturing Co—*Darrin Muchnicki*	4899 Commerce Pkwy, Cleveland OH 44128	216-292-4460	S	31*	.2
4	Formtek Metal Forming Inc—*Joe Mayer*	4899 Commerce Pkwy, Cleveland OH 44128	216-292-6300	R	29*	.2
5	Intergrated Industrial Systems Inc—*John Herbst*	475 Main St, Yalesville CT 06492	203-265-5684	R	23*	.2
6	Bud Red Industries Inc—*Kalin Liefer*	200 B And E Industrial, Red Bud IL 62278	618-282-3801	R	20*	.1
7	T and H Lemont—*John Hillis*	5118 Dansher Rd, Countryside IL 60525	708-482-1800	S	14*	.1
8	Perfecto Industries Inc—*Kevin Roberts*	1567 Calkins Dr, Gaylord MI 49735	989-732-2941	R	13*	.1
9	Fives Bronx Inc—*Richard Jeschelnig*	8817 Pleasantwood Ave, North Canton OH 44720	330-244-1960	R	12*	.1
10	Addison Machine Engineering Inc—*Gerald Brunken*	1301 Industrial St, Reedsburg WI 53959	608-524-6454	R	10*	<.1
11	Tru-Tech Tool and Machinery Corp—*Max Baauw*	1030 S Gateway Blvd, Muskegon MI 49441	231-798-7237	R	10	<.1
12	Dalton Industries LLC—*Mark Marcol*	PO Box 300888, Drayton Plains MI 48330	248-673-0755	R	9*	.1
13	Bonell Manufacturing Co—*Thomas Okleshen*	13521 S Halsted St Fl, Riverdale IL 60827	708-849-1770	R	7*	<.1
14	Circle Machine Rolls Inc—*Peter Kuhlmann*	PO Box 9, Sebring OH 44672	330-938-9010	R	4*	<.1
15	Winchester Precision Technologies Ltd—*Barry Bordner*	41 Hildreth St, Winchester NH 03470	603-239-6326	R	3*	<.1
16	Gega Corp—*Horst Lotz*	4853 Campbells Run Rd, Pittsburgh PA 15205	412-787-2832	R	3*	<.1
17	Laneko Roll Form Inc—*Ernest Pfeiffer*	3003 Unionville Pke, Hatfield PA 19440	215-822-1930	R	3*	<.1
18	Konrad Corp—*Ken Konrad*	1421 Hanley Rd, Hudson WI 54016	715-386-4200	R	3*	<.1
19	Chartwell Metal Fabricating Inc—*Allean Johnson*	PO Box 2270, Youngstown OH 44504	330-746-4628	R	2*	<.1
20	George L Kovacs—*George Kovacs*	1810 W Business Ctr Dr, Orange CA 92867	714-538-8026	R	2*	<.1
21	Roller Equipment Manufacturing Company Inc—*J Armstrong*	13903 Norby Rd, Grandview MO 64030	816-966-8717	R	2*	<.1
22	Mill Assist Services Inc—*Denis Gloede*	141 N Farmer St, Otsego MI 49078	269-692-3211	R	2*	<.1
23	Grinding Equipment And Machinery Company Inc—*James Johnson*	15 S Worthington St, Youngstown OH 44502	330-747-2313	R	2*	<.1
24	Western Technologies Inc *Russell Patterson*	4404 S Maybelle Ave, Tulsa OK 74107	918-712-2406	R	2*	<.1
25	Konrad Marine Inc—*Ken Konrad*	1421 Hanley Rd, Hudson WI 54016	715-386-4203	R	1*	<.1
26	Indemax Inc—*Alphonse Infurna*	1 Industrial Dr, Vernon NJ 07462	973-209-2424	R	1*	<.1

TOTALS: SIC 3547 Rolling Mill Machinery
Companies: 26

					6,620	1.4

3548 Welding Apparatus

Rank	Company Name—*Executive Officer*	Address, City, State, Zip	Phone	Type	Fin	Empls
1	Stoody Co—*Ron Grim*	5557 Nashville Rd, Bowling Green KY 42101	270-781-9777	S	1,537*	3.0
2	Thermadyne Industries Inc	16052 Swingley Ridge R, Chesterfield MO 63017	636-728-3000	S	1,530*	3.0
3	Thermal Dynamics Corp	82 Benning St, West Lebanon NH 03784	603-298-5711	S	1,530*	3.0
4	Progressive Tool and Industries Co/ Wisne Design—*Robert Stoutenburg*	21000 Telegraph Rd, Southfield MI 48034	248-353-8888	D	733*	5.5
5	Western Enterprises—*Warren E Buffett*	875 Bassett Rd, Westlake OH 44145		S	385*	.6
6	Airgas Intermountain Inc—*Max Hooper*	4810 Vasquez Blvd, Denver CO 80216	303-370-7800	S	292*	.5
7	Deloro Stellite Company Inc—*Andy Caffyn*	1201 Eisenhower Dr N, Goshen IN 46526	574-534-2585	S	153*	1.2
8	Miller Electric Manufacturing Co—*Michael Weller*	PO Box 1079, Appleton WI 54912	920-734-9821	R	145*	1.5
9	Comau Pico Holdings Corp—*Luca Savi*	21000 Telegraph Rd, Southfield MI 48033	248-353-8888	R	142*	1.5
10	Bernard Weldcraft and Plazcraft Products—*David B Speer*	PO Box 667, Beecher IL 60401	708-946-2281	R	70*	.1
11	Aquilex WSI	2225 Skyland Ct, Norcross GA 30071	770-452-0005	S	50*	.3
12	Miyachi Unitek Corp	1820 S Myrtle Ave, Monrovia CA 91016	626-303-5676	S	43*	.1
13	Uniweld Products Inc—*David Pearl*	PO Box 8427, Fort Lauderdale FL 33310	954-584-2000	R	43*	.3
14	Paslin Co—*Charles Pasque*	25411 Ryan Rd, Warren MI 48091	586-758-0200	R	41*	.5
15	Forney Industries Inc—*Steve Anderson*	PO Box 563, Fort Collins CO 80521	970-482-7271	R	38*	.5
16	Manufacturing Technology Inc—*Robert Adams*	1702 W Washington St, South Bend IN 46628	574-233-9490	R	36*	.1
17	Wolf Robotics Inc—*Doug Rhoda*	4600 Innovation Dr, Fort Collins CO 80525	970-225-7600	R	34*	.1
18	Smith Equipment	2601 Lockheed Ave, Watertown SD 57201	605-882-3200	S	33*	.2
19	BernzOmatic—*Ken Goodgame*	92 Grant St, Wilmington OH 45177	585-798-4949	D	28*	.2
20	Thermatool Corp—*Micheal Nallen*	31 Commerce St, East Haven CT 06512	203-468-4100	S	22*	.1
21	Weldmation Inc—*Earl Kansier*	31720 Stephenson Hwy, Madison Heights MI 48071	248-585-0010	R	21*	.2
22	Taylor - Winfield Corp—*Roger Bacon*	PO Box 477, Brookfield OH 44403	330-448-4464	R	19*	.1
23	American Torch Tip Co—*John Walters*	6212 29th St E, Bradenton FL 34203	941-753-7557	R	17*	.2
24	C and G Systems Inc—*Oliver Osterhues*	320 East Main street, Lake Zurich IL 60047	847-816-9700	R	16*	<.1
25	M K Products Inc—*Douglas Kensrue*	16882 Armstrong Ave, Irvine CA 92606	949-863-1234	R	15*	.1
26	Weld Tooling Corp—*Herbert Cable*	161 Hillpointe Dr, Canonsburg PA 15317	412-331-1776	R	14*	.1
27	Aro Welding Technologies Inc—*Pierre Barthelemy*	48500 Structural Dr, Chesterfield MI 48051	586-949-9353	S	14*	.1
28	Goss Inc—*Jacqueline Goss*	PO Box 57, Glenshaw PA 15116	412-486-6100	R	13*	.1
29	Ultra Sonic Seal Co—*Mark Caldwell*	53 Church Hill Rd, Newtown CT 06470	203-270-4600	D	12*	.1
30	Melton Machine and Control Co—*Randy Folkmann*	6350 Bluff Rd, Washington MO 63090	636-239-7765	R	12*	.1
31	STI Electronics Inc—*David Raby*	261 Palmer Rd, Madison AL 35758	256-461-9191	R	11*	<.1
32	Magnatech LLC	PO Box 260, East Granby CT 06026	860-653-2573	R	11*	.1
33	Ace Production Technologies Inc—*Alan Cable*	3010 N First St, Spokane Valley WA 99216	509-924-4898	R	10*	<.1
34	Weldlogic Inc—*Robert Elizarraz*	2550 Azurite Cir, Newbury Park CA 91320	805-498-4004	R	10*	.1
35	Electron Beam Technologies Inc—*Paul Wlos*	1275 Harvard Dr, Kankakee IL 60901	815-935-2211	R	10*	.1
36	Banner Welder Inc—*John Waldron*	PO Box 1008, Germantown WI 53022	262-253-2900	R	10*	.1
37	Air-Vac Engineering Company Inc—*Clifford Lasto*	PO Box 216, Seymour CT 06483	203-888-9900	R	9*	.1
38	Automation International Inc—*Larry Moss*	1020 Bahls St, Danville IL 61832	217-446-9500	R	9*	.1
39	Pandjiris Inc—*Robert Mann*	PO Box 790100, Saint Louis MO 63179	314-776-6893	R	8*	.1
40	Miller Electric Manufacturing—*Mike Weller*	PO Box 1079, Appleton WI 54912	920-734-9821	S	8*	.1

Note: An asterisk (*) indicates an estimated financial figure. The company type code used is as follows: R = Private, P = Public, S = Private Subsidiary, B = Public Subsidiary, D = Division, J = Joint Venture, I = Investment Fund.

COMPANY RANKINGS BY SALES WITHIN 4-DIGIT SIC

Rank	Company Name—Executive Officer	Address, City, State, Zip	Phone	Type	Fin	Empls
41	Technical Devices Co—Douglas Winther	560 Alaska Ave, Torrance CA 90503	310-618-8437	R	8*	<.1
42	Greenville Metal Works Inc—Tom Norris	PO Box 4484, Greenville MS 38704	662-335-8510	R	8*	.1
43	Miller Weldmaster Corp—Scott Miller	4220 Alabama Ave Sw, Navarre OH 44662	330-833-6739	R	8*	<.1
44	Maitlen and Benson Inc—Kem Gallagher	PO Box 4146, Long Beach CA 90804	562-597-5594	R	8*	<.1
45	Welding Alloys (USA) Inc—Dominic Stekly	8535 Dixie Hwy, Florence KY 41042	859-525-0165	R	7*	<.1
46	Tri-State Industries Inc—Donald Keller	4923 Columbia Ave, Hammond IN 46327	219-933-1710	R	7*	.1
47	COMETALS—Eli Skornicki	2050 Center Ave Ste 25, Fort Lee NJ 07024	201-302-0888	D	7*	<.1
48	Grossel Tool Co—Kurt Kowal	34190 Doreka, Fraser MI 48026	586-294-3660	R	7*	.1
49	J W Holdings Inc—Dennis Madden	2530 Thornwood St Sw A, Grand Rapids MI 49519	616-530-9889	R	7*	<.1
50	Dynaflux Inc—Larry Pogue	241 Brown Farm Rd Sw, Cartersville GA 30120	770-382-8843	R	6*	<.1
51	Alexander Binzel Corp—John Kaylor	650 Medimmune Ct Ste 1, Frederick MD 21703	301-846-4196	R	6*	.1
52	NL C Inc—David Hoelscher	PO Box 348, Jackson MO 63755	573-243-3141	R	6*	.1
53	Janda Company Inc—Janet White	1275 Railroad St, Corona CA 92882	951-734-1935	R	6*	<.1
54	Howard G Hinz Company Inc—David Hinz	9930 S Franklin Dr, Franklin WI 53132	414-421-8890	R	6*	<.1
55	Cadi Company Inc—Rocco Capozzi	PO Box 1127, Naugatuck CT 06770	203-729-1111	R	5*	<.1
56	Preston-Eastin Inc—Dennis George	PO Box 582288, Tulsa OK 74158	918-834-5591	R	5*	<.1
57	Sonic And Thermal Technologies Inc—Robert Bishop	84 Research Dr, Milford CT 06460	203-878-9321	R	4*	<.1
58	Polaris Electronics Corp—Jim Kay	630 S Rogers Rd, Olathe KS 66062	913-764-5210	R	4*	<.1
59	Ssco Manufacturing Inc—Victor Miller	1245 30th St, San Diego CA 92154	619-628-1022	R	3*	<.1
60	Waltex Inc—Koichi Kimura	12111 Chandler Dr, Walton KY 41094	859-485-8550	R	3*	<.1
61	Emabond Solutions LLC—Earl Casey	49 Walnut St Ste 2, Norwood NJ 07648	201-767-7400	R	3*	<.1
62	Resistance Welding Solutions Inc—Edward Onny	1090 Lousons Rd, Union NJ 07083	908-964-9100	R	3*	<.1
63	Sommer Products Company Inc—Robert Franzwa	7100 S Adams St Ste 2, Bartonville IL 61607	309-697-1216	R	3*	<.1
64	Novastar Technologies Inc—Peretz Shiloh	PO Box 1044, Huntingdon Valley PA 19006	215-947-4700	R	3*	<.1
65	Bancroft Corp—Kavern Magee	21550 Doral Rd, Waukesha WI 53186	262-786-1880	R	3*	<.1
66	Sikama International Inc—Sigurd Wathne	PO Box 40298, Santa Barbara CA 93140	805-962-1000	R	2*	<.1
67	EF Technologies Inc—William Groft	119b Sandy Dr, Newark DE 19713	302-451-1088	R	1*	<.1
68	Lincoln Electric Co	22801 St Clair Ave, Cleveland OH 44117	216-481-8100	S	N/A	9.0

TOTALS: SIC 3548 Welding Apparatus

Companies: 68					7,270	33.7

3549 Metalworking Machinery Nec

Rank	Company Name—Executive Officer	Address, City, State, Zip	Phone	Type	Fin	Empls
1	Lincoln Electric Holdings Inc—John M Stropki	22801 St Clair Ave, Cleveland OH 44117	216-481-8100	P	2,695	9.9
2	Palomar Technologies Inc—Bruce W Hueners	2728 Loker Ave W, Carlsbad CA 92010	760-931-3600	R	120	.5
3	Sunnen Products Co—Matt Kreider	7910 Manchester Rd, Saint Louis MO 63143	314-781-2100	R	73*	.7
4	Wright Industries Inc—David Takes	PO Box 17914, Nashville TN 37217	615-361-6600	R	45*	.3
5	Assembly and Test Worldwide Inc	313 Mound St, Dayton OH 45402	937-586-5500	R	40*	.2
6	Herr-Voss—Kip Mostowy	PO Box AB, Callery PA 16024	724-538-3180	D	40*	.2
7	Delta Brands Inc—Samuel Savariego	2204 Century Ctr Blvd, Irving TX 75062	972-438-7150	R	28*	.1
8	Cooper-Weymouth Peterson	76 Hinckley Rd, Clinton ME 04927	207-426-2351	D	27	.2
9	WSI Industries Inc—Michael J Pudil	213 Chelsea Rd, Monticello MN 55362	763-295-9202	P	25	.1
10	JR Automation Technologies LLC—Joel Cooper	13365 Tyler St, Holland MI 49424	616-399-2168	R	21*	.2
11	Automatic Feed Co—Kim Beck	476 E Riverview Ave, Napoleon OH 43545	419-592-0050	R	20*	.1
12	Bardons and Oliver Inc—Heath Oliver	5800 Harper Rd, Solon OH 44139	440-498-5800	R	20*	.1
13	Rwc Inc—William Perlberg	PO Box 920, Bay City MI 48707	989-684-4030	R	20*	.1
14	Bartell Machinery Systems LLC—Mike Afanan	6321 Elmer Hill Rd, Rome NY 13440	315-336-7600	S	19*	.2
15	Merrill Tool and Machine Inc—Jeff Merrill	21659 W Gratiot Rd, Merrill MI 48637	989-643-7981	D	19*	.1
16	Clemco Industries Corp—Arnie Sallaverry	1 Cable Car Dr, Washington MO 63090	636-239-0300	R	18*	.1
17	Golden States Engineering Inc—Alexandra Rostovski	15338 Garfield Ave, Paramount CA 90723	562-634-3125	R	17*	.1
18	Entrust Tool and Design Company Inc—Anthony Fettig	N58w14630 Shawn Cir, Menomonee Falls WI 53051	262-252-3802	R	16*	<.1
19	Schenck Rotec Corp—Bertram Dittmar	2469 Executive Hills D, Auburn Hills MI 48326	248-377-2100	R	15*	<.1
20	TA Systems Inc—Tim Gale	1842 Rochester Industr, Rochester Hills MI 48309	248-656-5150	R	15*	.1
21	Starting USA Corp—Allen Redfearn	1676 Rowe Pkwy, Poplar Bluff MO 63901	573-686-9430	R	14*	.1
22	Artos Engineering Co—John Olsen	21605 Gateway Ct, Brookfield WI 53045	262-252-8350	R	14*	.1
23	P/A Industries Inc—Jerome Finn	522 Cottage Grove Rd B, Bloomfield CT 06002	860-243-8306	R	13*	.1
24	Rowe Machinery and Manufacturing Co—Bob Evans	76 Hinckley Rd, Clinton ME 04927	207-426-2351	D	13*	.1
25	HMS Products Co—Dave Sofy	1200 E Big Beaver Rd, Troy MI 48083	248-689-8120	R	13*	.1
26	Dane Systems LLC—Stephen Klotz	7275 Red Arrow Hwy, Stevensville MI 49127	269-465-3263	R	13*	.1
27	Auto/Con Corp—Ronald Matheson	18901 15 Mile Rd, Clinton Township MI 48035	586-791-7474	R	13*	.1
28	ADS Machinery Corp—Dale C Minton	PO Box 1027, Warren OH 44482	330-399-3601	R	12*	.1
29	MGS Manufacturing Inc—Robert Johnson	PO Box 4259, Rome NY 13442	315-337-3350	R	11*	.1
30	Lomar Machine and Tool Co—James Geisman	PO Box 128, Horton MI 49246	517-563-8136	R	10*	.1
31	Metro Machine and Engineering Corp—Robert Midness	8001 Wallace Rd, Eden Prairie MN 55344	952-937-2800	R	10*	.1
32	Norwood Marketing Systems—W James Farrell	2538 Wisconsin Ave, Downers Grove IL 60515	630-968-0646	D	10*	.1
33	Ameritec Machining Inc—Richard Walter	2210 270th St, New Hampton IA 50659	641-394-4993	R	9*	<.1
34	Tennsmith Inc—Douglas Smith	6926 Smithville Hwy, Mcminnville TN 37110	931-934-2211	R	9*	.1
35	Hahn Manufacturing Co—Robert Hahn	5332 Hamilton Ave, Cleveland OH 44114	216-391-9300	R	9*	.1
36	Lapmaster International LLC—Brian Nelson	501 W Algonquin Rd, Mount Prospect IL 60056	224-659-7104	R	9*	.1
37	Rockford Manufacturing Group Inc—Timothy J Taylor	14343 Industrial Pkwy, South Beloit IL 61080	815-624-2500	R	9*	.1
38	Marland Mold Inc—John Barmack	12 Betnr Industrial Dr, Pittsfield MA 01201	413-443-4481	R	9*	.1
39	Amber Engineering And Manufacturing Co—Sigismund Paul	2400 Brickvale Dr, Elk Grove Village IL 60007	847-595-6966	R	9*	.1
40	Braner USA Inc—Douglas Matsunaga	9301 W Bernice St, Schiller Park IL 60176	847-671-6210	R	9*	.1
41	Guardian Metal Sales Inc—William Bohnen	PO Box 1298, Morton Grove IL 60053	847-967-7400	R	8*	<.1
42	M2 Global Technology Ltd—Bill Blessing	5714 Epsilon, San Antonio TX 78249	210-561-4800	R	8*	.1
43	Tarpon Automation and Design Co—Robert Legeret	26692 Groesbeck Hwy, Warren MI 48089	586-774-8020	R	8*	.1
44	Semtorq Inc—Joseph Seme	PO Box 895, Aurora OH 44202	330-995-7676	R	7*	.1
45	Joseph Machine Company Inc—Joseph Pigliacampo	PO Box 121, Dillsburg PA 17019	717-432-3442	R	7*	<.1
46	Edwards Manufacturing Co—Kim Hanson	PO Box 166, Albert Lea MN 56007	507-373-8206	R	7*	<.1
47	Alliance Innovative Manufacturing Inc—Richard St John	1 Alliance Dr, Lackawanna NY 14218	716-822-1626	R	7	<.1
48	Tannewitz Inc—Morry Pysarchik	794 Chicago Dr, Jenison MI 49428	616-457-5999	R	7*	<.1
49	Wand Special Equipment and Design Company Inc—William Anderson	1029 Green Bay Rd, Highland Park IL 60035	847-433-0231	R	7*	.1
50	Bmci Inc—Scott Barsotti	PO Box 510, Mira Loma CA 91752	626-602-2000	R	7*	<.1
51	Broomfield Laboratories Inc—Thomas Broomfield	PO Box 157, Bolton MA 01740	978-368-0931	R	6*	<.1
52	Columbia Marking Tools Inc—Michelle Krembel	27430 Luckino Dr, Chesterfield MI 48047	586-949-8400	R	6*	<.1
53	Industrial Concepts Inc—Tim Taylor	106 Supply Ct, Georgetown KY 40324	502-868-7638	R	6*	<.1
54	Todd Industries Inc—Gerald Boehnlein	7300 Northfield Rd Ste, Cleveland OH 44146	440-439-2900	R	6*	<.1
55	Almco Inc—Richard Rocklin	507 W Front St, Albert Lea MN 56007	507-377-2102	S	6*	<.1
56	Mark One Corp—Francis Kestler	517 Alpine Rd, Gaylord MI 49735	989-731-3800	R	6*	.1
57	Van-Mark Products Corp—Jeff Cleave	24145 Industrial Park, Farmington Hills MI 48335	248-478-1200	R	6*	<.1

Rank	Company Name—*Executive Officer*	Address, City, State, Zip	Phone	Type	Fin	Empls
58	Tulsa Power LLC—*Mike Spence*	913 N Wheeling Ave, Tulsa OK 74110	918-584-1000	R	6*	<.1
59	R And D Tool Inc—*Loren Esch*	PO Box 228, Lake Villa IL 60046	847-395-3330	R	6*	<.1
60	Avans Machine Inc—*Jeff Avans*	25490 Al Hwy 79, Scottsboro AL 35768	256-587-6071	R	6*	<.1
61	Kalt Manufacturing Co—*Joseph Kalt*	36700 Sugar Ridge Rd, North Ridgeville OH 44039	440-327-2102	R	5*	<.1
62	Weber Electric Manufacturing Co—*Salvatore Munaco*	2465 23 Mile Rd, Shelby Township MI 48316	586-323-9000	R	5*	<.1
63	Spen-Tech Machine Engineering Corp—*Troy Spence*	2475 E Judd Rd, Burton MI 48529	810-743-4010	R	5*	.1
64	Urgent Design and Manufacturing Inc—*Douglas Peterson*	3142 John Conley Dr, Lapeer MI 48446	810-245-1300	R	5*	<.1
65	Assembly Automation Industries—*Francis Frost*	1849 Business Ctr Dr, Duarte CA 91010	626-303-2777	R	5*	<.1
66	Eubanks Engineering Co—*David Eubanks*	3022 Inland Empire Blv, Ontario CA 91764	909-483-2456	R	5*	<.1
67	Entec Composite Machines Inc—*Robert Murdock*	2975 S 300 W, Salt Lake City UT 84115	801-486-8721	S	5*	<.1
68	Mold-A-Matic Corp—*Siro Vergari*	147 River St, Oneonta NY 13820	607-433-2121	R	5*	<.1
69	Air Way Automation Inc—*Robert Toms*	PO Box 563, Grayling MI 49738	989-348-5176	R	5*	<.1
70	Weber and Scher Manufacturing Company Inc—*J Scher*	PO Box 366, Lebanon NJ 08833	908-236-8484	R	5*	<.1
71	Abacus Automation Inc—*Donald Alvarado*	264 Shields Dr, Bennington VT 05201	802-442-3662	R	5*	<.1
72	Allied Tool And Machine Co—*Fred Becker*	PO Box 1407, Saginaw MI 48605	989-755-5384	R	4*	<.1
73	Research Automation Inc—*Steve Arbizzani*	601 W New York St Frnt, Aurora IL 60506	630-897-1220	R	4*	<.1
74	Omega Automation Inc—*Marybeth Krystofik*	2850 Needmore Rd, Dayton OH 45414	937-277-2929	R	4*	.1
75	Six Sigma Inc—*Owen Thompson*	2811 Watterson Trl, Louisville KY 40299	502-267-6555	R	4*	<.1
76	Accurite Industries Inc—*Kirko Mickovski*	51047 Oro Dr, Shelby Township MI 48315	586-247-0060	R	4*	<.1
77	Custom Rollform Products Inc—*Larry Slavik*	3991 Green Park Rd, Saint Louis MO 63125	314-894-3903	R	4*	<.1
78	Jovil Manufacturing Company Inc—*Bruno Tropeano*	10 Precision Rd, Danbury CT 06810	203-792-6700	R	4*	<.1
79	Schmidt Feintechnik Corp—*Daniel Baumann*	PO Box 1410, Cranberry Township PA 16066	724-772-4600	S	4*	<.1
80	Amacoil Inc	PO Box 2228, Aston PA 19014	610-485-8300	R	4*	<.1
81	Cardinal Machine Co—*Brian Pennington*	860 Tacoma Ct, Clio MI 48420	810-686-1190	R	4*	<.1
82	Feed-Lease Corp—*John Stretten*	2600 Crooks Rd, Rochester Hills MI 48309	248-852-6660	R	4*	<.1
83	Tristar Systems Corp—*Ahmad Akrami*	6250 Joyce Dr, Arvada CO 80403	303-420-3525	R	4*	<.1
84	Gorecki Manufacturing Inc—*Benedict Gorecki*	560 8th St Ne, Milaca MN 56353	320-983-3171	R	4*	<.1
85	Pro-Tech Machine Inc—*David Currie*	3085 Joyce St, Burton MI 48529	810-743-1854	R	4*	<.1
86	Wright Machine Tool Company Inc—*Duncan Mclean*	365 Palmer Ave, Cottage Grove OR 97424	541-942-3712	R	4*	<.1
87	Crossridge Precision Inc—*Joseph Hall*	121 Flint Rd, Oak Ridge TN 37830	865-482-1704	R	4*	<.1
88	Novi Precision Products Inc—*Ronald Karaisz*	11777 Grand River Rd, Brighton MI 48116	810-227-1024	R	4*	<.1
89	Southern Engineering and Automation Inc—*D Macgregor*	1827 Industrial Blvd, Tarpon Springs FL 34689	727-939-1922	R	3*	<.1
90	Sterling Handling Systems Inc—*Tom Miller*	3334 N Booth St, Milwaukee WI 53212	414-228-7728	R	3*	<.1
91	S and H Engineering Inc—*Stephen Smith*	248 Mill Rd, Chelmsford MA 01824	978-256-7231	R	3*	<.1
92	Readco Kurimoto LLC—*Dana Grim*	460 Grim Ln, York PA 17406	717-848-2801	R	3*	<.1
93	Accu-Fab Inc (Ithaca New York)—*Gary Wojcik*	232 Cherry St, Ithaca NY 14850	607-273-3706	R	3*	<.1
94	Leonard Machine Tool Systems Inc—*Leonard Bantleon*	22800 Hoover Rd, Warren MI 48089	586-757-8040	R	3*	<.1
95	Automec Inc—*James Ofria*	82 Calvary St, Waltham MA 02453	781-893-3403	R	3*	<.1
96	Carpenter Manufacturing CoInc—*Thomas Carpenter*	PO Box 188, Manlius NY 13104	315-682-9176	R	3*	<.1
97	Engineered Fabrication Inc—*Horst Klein*	PO Box 383, Watkinsville GA 30677	706-769-6757	R	3*	<.1
98	Filmtec Inc—*John Hollingsworth*	1120 Sandusky St, Fostoria OH 44830	419-435-7504	R	3*	<.1
99	Gatco Inc—*Mark Sulkowski*	42330 Ann Arbor Rd E, Plymouth MI 48170	734-453-2295	R	3*	<.1
100	Miami Industrial Supply And Manufacturing Inc—*Curtis Jurgensmeyer*	7251 S Hwy 69a, Miami OK 74354	918-542-6317	R	3*	<.1
101	Custom Machine and Design Inc—*Jeff Kiser*	7220 Hwy 544, Myrtle Beach SC 29588	843-236-5800	R	3*	<.1
102	Knoxville Stamping And Assembly LLC—*Karen Brown*	PO Box 6169, Maryville TN 37802	865-273-2100	R	3*	<.1
103	Unidox Corporation of Western NY—*Arthur Crater*	2416 N Main St, Warsaw NY 14569	585-786-3170	R	2*	<.1
104	Manufacturing Solutions And Technologies LLC—*Linda Vohs*	46909 W Rd, Wixom MI 48393	248-896-0000	R	2*	<.1
105	Newport Cutter Grinding Company Inc—*Jeff Duncan*	2305 56th St, Hampton VA 23661	757-838-3224	R	2*	<.1
106	Design Tool Inc—*Wayne Oram*	1607 Norfolk Pl Sw, Conover NC 28613	828-328-6414	R	2*	<.1
107	Precision Tool and Engineering Of Gainesville Inc—*Bette Thibault*	2709 Ne 20th Way, Gainesville FL 32609	352-376-2533	R	2*	<.1
108	Becker Inc—*Donald Becker*	PO Box 1258, Kenosha WI 53141	715-359-6133	R	2*	<.1
109	Gorman Machine Corp—*Kenneth Gorman*	7 Burke Dr, Brockton MA 02301	508-588-2900	R	2*	<.1
110	Design Technologies and Manufacturing Co—*D Meredith*	2000 Corporate Dr, Troy OH 45373	937-335-1950	R	2*	<.1
111	Haeger Inc—*Wouter Kleizen*	811 Wakefield Dr Ste B, Oakdale CA 95361	209-848-4000	R	2*	<.1
112	De Mott Technologies Corp—*Robert Lieberman*	14556 Raymer St, Van Nuys CA 91405	818-988-4975	R	2*	<.1
113	Steimer And Company Inc—*John Steimer*	157 E 7 Stars Rd, Phoenixville PA 19460	610-933-7450	R	2*	<.1
114	Qc Manufacturing Co—*Gwen Newton*	1101 State Hwy 31 W, Kilgore TX 75662	903-983-1921	R	2*	<.1
115	Assembly Specialists Inc—*Jason Ball*	8030 S Willow St Unit, Manchester NH 03103	603-624-9563	R	2*	<.1
116	Automation Specialists Inc—*Mitch Weener*	12555 Superior Ct, Holland MI 49424	616-738-8288	R	2*	<.1
117	Shuster-Mettler Corp—*Dennis Polio*	485 Ella T Grasso Blvd, New Haven CT 06519	203-562-3178	R	2*	<.1
118	Alva Allen Industries—*Alva Allen*	PO Box 427, Clinton MO 64735	660-885-3331	R	2*	<.1
119	Grinding And Polishing Machinery Corp—*Larry Hardin*	2801 Tobey Dr, Indianapolis IN 46219	317-898-0750	R	2*	<.1
120	Western Machine Works Inc—*R Schmitz*	652 E 11th St, Tacoma WA 98421	253-627-6538	R	2*	<.1
121	Hy-Tech Machining Systems LLC—*Doug Brannies*	PO Box 3223, Anderson IN 46018	765-649-6852	R	1*	<.1
122	Accra-Wire Controls Inc—*Johnnie Jones*	10891 Northland Dr NE, Rockford MI 49341	616-866-3434	R	1	<.1
123	Spati Industries Inc—*Joseph Berberich*	10 Kenner St, Ludlow KY 41016	859-291-1404	R	1*	<.1
124	Assembly and Automation Technologies Inc—*Peter Maclaren*	9 Presidential Way Ste, Woburn MA 01801	978-692-1801	R	1*	<.1
125	Coastal Bend Tooling and Automation—*Richard Reinhart*	4234 Beacon St, Corpus Christi TX 78405	361-883-0376	R	1*	<.1
126	Borlaug Systems Inc—*Bob Schumacher*	2555 Bing Miller Ln, Urbana IA 52345	319-443-3172	R	1*	<.1
127	Conklin Equipment Company Inc—*Richard Markano*	584 Industrial Way, Fallbrook CA 92028	760-728-6146	R	1*	<.1
128	Carlson Engineering and ManufacturingInc—*Cliff Carlson*	425 W Allen Ave Ste 10, San Dimas CA 91773	909-599-8087	R	<1*	<.1

TOTALS: SIC 3549 Metalworking Machinery Nec
Companies: 128   3,845   17.2

3552 Textile Machinery						
1	Saurer Holding Inc—*Peter Kern*	1575 W 124th Ave, Denver CO 80234	303-457-1234	S	5,857*	.2
2	Singer Sewing Co—*Stephen H Goodman*	PO Box 7017, La Vergne TN 37086	615-213-0880	R	66*	.1
3	Tuftco Corp—*Steve Frost*	2318 S Holtzclaw Ave, Chattanooga TN 37408	423-698-8601	R	30*	.2
4	Gtp Greenville Inc—*James Thomas*	PO Box 1867, Greenville SC 29602	864-288-5475	R	27*	.2
5	Hollingsworth John D On Wheels Inc—*Carl Martin*	PO Box 516, Greenville SC 29602	864-297-1000	R	25*	.4
6	Washex Inc—*Bob Montgomery*	2815 Barge Lane, Dallas TX 75212	214-630-4517	S	24*	.2
7	Kusters Corp—*Ken Kruse*	PO Box 6128, Spartanburg SC 29304	864-576-0660	R	24*	.1
8	A B Carter Inc—*Richard Craig*	PO Box 518, Gastonia NC 28053	704-865-1201	R	19*	.1
9	Card-Monroe Corp—*Charles Monroe*	PO Box 639, Hixson TN 37343	423-842-3312	R	18*	.1
10	Morrison Textile Machinery Co—*John White*	6044 Lancaster Hwy, Fort Lawn SC 29714	803-872-4401	R	15*	.1
11	Tuftco Finishing Systems Inc—*Bobby Cresswell*	PO Box 704, Dalton GA 30722	706-277-1110	R	13*	.1
12	Tufting Machine Company Inc—*Spencer Wright*	1731 Kimberly Park Dr, Dalton GA 30720	706-278-1857	R	12*	.1

Note: An asterisk (*) indicates an estimated financial figure. The company type code used is as follows: R = Private, P = Public, S = Private Subsidiary, B = Public Subsidiary, D = Division, J = Joint Venture, I = Investment Fund.

COMPANY RANKINGS BY SALES WITHIN 4-DIGIT SIC

Rank	Company Name—Executive Officer	Address, City, State, Zip	Phone	Type	Fin	Empls
13	Saber Industries Inc—Robert Stevenson	779 Washington St, Buffalo NY 14203	716-856-2200	R	12*	<.1
14	American Trutzschler Inc—Kurt Scholler	PO Box 669228, Charlotte NC 28266	704-399-4521	R	11*	.1
15	Monarch Knitting Machinery Corp—Bruce Pernick	PO Box 5009, Monroe NC 28111	704-291-3300	R	11*	.1
16	Tran Tek Automation Corp—John Wenden	2470 N Aero Park Ct, Traverse City MI 49686	231-946-6270	R	11*	.1
17	Mayer Wildman Industries Inc—Peter Mayer	PO Box 1466, Orangeburg SC 29116	803-536-3500	R	10*	.1
18	Hills Inc—Arnold Wilkie	7785 Ellis Rd, Melbourne FL 32904	321-724-2370	R	10*	.1
19	Precision Machine Products Inc—Robert Blalock	PO Box 1576, Gastonia NC 28053	704-865-8507	R	10*	.1
20	Abm International Inc—Neal Schwarzberger	PO Box 132679, The Woodlands TX 77393	281-443-4440	R	8*	.1
21	Bowman-Hollis Manufacturing Company Inc—Tom Bowman	PO Box 19249, Charlotte NC 28219	704-374-1500	R	8*	.1
22	Morrison Berkshire Inc—Jim S White Morrison Textile Machinery Co	PO Box 958, North Adams MA 01247	413-663-6501	S	7*	<.1
23	Lawson-Hemphill Inc—Avishai Nevel	7 Winfield Rd, Providence RI 02906	401-272-9038	R	7*	<.1
24	Westerly Inc—James Burton	17 E Meadow Ave, Robesonia PA 19551	610-693-8866	R	7*	.1
25	Palmetto Loom Reed Co—William Richardson	PO Box 8517, Greenville SC 29604	864-277-8585	R	7*	.1
26	Belmont Textile Machinery Co—Walter Rhyne	PO Box 568, Mount Holly NC 28120	704-827-5836	R	6*	<.1
27	Premtec—E Smith	PO Box 399, China Grove NC 28023	704-857-0121	R	6*	.1
28	Catbridge Machinery LLC—William Christman	222 New Rd Ste 1, Parsippany NJ 07054	973-808-0029	R	6*	<.1
29	Surface Engineering Specialties Inc—Richard Peattie	919 Hamlin Ct, Sunnyvale CA 94089	408-734-8810	R	5*	<.1
30	Machined Metals Company Inc—Joseph Colen	PO Box 909, Norristown PA 19404	610-272-1600	R	5*	<.1
31	Sherrill Industries Inc—Rick Hargis	110 Durkee Ln, Dallas NC 28034	704-922-7871	R	5*	<.1
32	Jbm Fibers Inc—John Cowen	4695 Towerwood Dr, Brownsville TX 78521	956-831-8533	R	4*	<.1
33	Stewarts Of America Inc—Brian Leach	PO Box 1058, Simpsonville SC 29681	864-967-7085	R	4*	<.1
34	Martin Screen Prints Inc—William Martin	3490 E Virginia Beach, Norfolk VA 23502	757-855-5416	R	4*	<.1
35	Barudan America Inc—Ted Yamaue	29500 Fountain Pkwy, Solon OH 44139	440-248-8770	R	4*	<.1
36	Roberts Tool Co—Allen Roberts	PO Box 400, Tecumseh MI 49286	517-423-6691	R	4*	<.1
37	Birch Brothers Southern Inc—Steven Birch	PO Box 70, Waxhaw NC 28173	704-843-2111	R	3*	<.1
38	Louis P Batson Co—Caroline Stewart	PO Box 3978, Greenville SC 29608	864-242-5262	R	3*	<.1
39	Stretch Devices Inc—Don Newman	3401 I St Ste 1, Philadelphia PA 19134	215-739-3000	R	3*	<.1
40	B and J Machinery Company Inc—Dan Cobble	122 York St, Dalton GA 30721	706-259-4841	R	3*	<.1
41	Fletcher Industries Inc—John Taws	1485 Central Dr, Southern Pines NC 28387	910-692-7133	R	3*	<.1
42	J B Gury Manufacturing Co—Harold Gaebe	10270 Page IndustrialB, Saint Louis MO 63132	314-427-1600	R	3*	<.1
43	Systematic Automation Inc—Joseph Gilberti	20 Executive Dr, Farmington CT 06032	860-677-6400	R	3*	<.1
44	Eastlex Machine Corp—Volker Schmidt	2170 Christian Rd, Lexington KY 40509	859-254-1388	R	3*	<.1
45	Karg Corp—Michael Karg	PO Box 197, Tallmadge OH 44278	330-633-4916	R	3*	<.1
46	Biax-Fiberfilm Corp—Doug Brown	N992 Quality Dr Ste B, Greenville WI 54942	920-757-9000	R	3*	<.1
47	Myers Quality Machine Company Inc—Bobby Myers	PO Box 546, Randleman NC 27317	336-498-4187	R	2*	<.1
48	T and W Textile Machinery Inc—Timothy Spicer	PO Box 237, Clover SC 29710	803-222-7181	R	2*	<.1
49	J and P Enterprises Of The Carolinas Inc—C Greene	5640 Galligher Dr, Gastonia NC 28052	704-861-1867	R	2*	<.1
50	Rome Machine and Foundry Co—Albert Berry	PO Box 1425, Rome GA 30162	706-234-6763	R	2*	<.1
51	Cliff Hix Engineering Inc—Cliff Hix	PO Box 21, Pittsburg KS 66762	620-232-3000	R	2*	<.1
52	Carolina Loom Reed Company Inc—Ernest Mcfetters	PO Box 22111, Greensboro NC 27420	336-274-7631	R	2*	<.1
53	Tandematic Inc—William Young	2730 Cnnons Campground, Spartanburg SC 29307	864-579-3050	R	2*	<.1
54	Lang Ligon and Company Inc—Lang Ligon	PO Box 5578, Greenville SC 29606	864-288-7993	R	2*	<.1
55	Mohawk Valley Knitting Machinery—Joseph Firsching	PO Box 120, New York Mills NY 13417	315-736-3038	R	2*	<.1
56	Liberty Reed Company Inc—Ted Wagner	PO Box 788, Drayton SC 29333	864-585 8292	R	2*	<.1
57	Waring Products Inc—Mitchell Crow	PO Box 916, Resaca GA 30735	706-602-7442	R	1*	<.1
58	Textile Parts And Machine Company Inc—John Stewart	PO Box 12305, Gastonia NC 28052	704-865-8564	R	1*	<.1
59	Wis Seaming Equipment Inc—Christian Freid	907 N Triangle Dr, Ponderay ID 83852	208-263-0307	R	1*	<.1
60	Alandale Industries Inc—Don Trexler	PO Box 804, Troy NC 27371	910-576-1291	R	1*	<.1
61	Becmar Corp—Arthur Proctor	PO Box 396, Fremont MI 49412	616-675-7479	R	1*	<.1
62	Dbh Attachments Inc—Dean Hunt	PO Box 734, Adamsville TN 38310	731-632-0532	R	1*	<.1
63	MDM Inc—Ronald Meyers	PO Box 4339, Archdale NC 27263	336-861-6666	R	1*	<.1

TOTALS: SIC 3552 Textile Machinery

Companies: 63					6,357	3.5

3553 Woodworking Machinery

Rank	Company Name—Executive Officer	Address, City, State, Zip	Phone	Type	Fin	Empls
1	SCM Group USA Inc—John Gangone	2475 Satellite Blvd, Duluth GA 30096	770-813-8818	R	1,587*	3.8
2	Accu Systems Inc—Mel Hatch	1810 W 5000 S, Salt Lake City UT 84129	801-965-1900	R	1,396*	<.1
3	Unique Machine and Tool Co—Kenny Moffatt	4232 E Magnolia St, Phoenix AZ 85034	602-470-1911	R	86*	<.1
4	Diehl Machines Inc—Robert Rozman	PO Box 465, Wabash IN 46992	260-563-2102	R	41*	.1
5	Newman Machine Company Inc—Frank York	2949 Lees Chapel Rd, Browns Summit NC 27214	336-273-8261	R	41*	.1
6	Globe Machine Manufacturing Co—Calvin Bamford	PO Box 2274, Tacoma WA 98401	253-383-2584	R	40*	.3
7	Wood-Mizer Products Inc—Jeffrey Laskowski	8180 W 10th St, Indianapolis IN 46214	317-271-1542	R	29*	.4
8	Nicholson Manufacturing Company Inc—Scott Howell	200 S Orcas St, Seattle WA 98108	206-682-2752	R	22*	.2
9	Morris Industrial Corp—James Williamson	PO Box 249, Saraland AL 36571	251-675-4636	R	18*	.1
10	Kval Inc—Jerry Kvalheim	825 Petaluma Blvd S, Petaluma CA 94952	707-762-4363	R	17*	.1
11	Precision Husky Corp—Bob Smith	PO Box 507, Leeds AL 35094	205-640-5181	R	14*	.1
12	Salem Equipment Inc—Lewis Judson	PO Box 1030, Sherwood OR 97140	503-581-8411	R	14*	.1
13	Timesavers Inc—Gregory Larson	11123 89th Ave N, Maple Grove MN 55369	763-488-6600	R	12*	.1
14	Sherline Products Inc—Joseph Martin	3235 Executive Ridge, Vista CA 92081	760-727-5857	R	11*	<.1
15	Rp Fletcher Machine Company Inc—Richard Piselli	4305 E Us Hwy 64, Lexington NC 27292	336-249-6101	R	10*	.1
16	Price LogPro—James Harper	314 Reynolds Rd Bldg 3, Malvern AR 72104	501-844-4260	R	10*	.1
17	Burelbach Industries Corp—Calvin Bamford	PO Box 2274, Tacoma WA 98401	503-623-8102	R	10*	.1
18	Pendu Manufacturing Inc—Marlin Hurst	718 N Shirk Rd, New Holland PA 17557	717-354-4348	R	9*	.1
19	Ellington Industrial Supply Inc—Michael Mcnail	PO Box 128, Ellington MO 63638	573-663-7711	R	8*	.1
20	West Coast Industrial Systems Inc—Blane Belveal	1995 W Airway Rd, Lebanon OR 97355	541-451-6677	R	8*	.1
21	Viking Engineering and Development Inc—Mark Stevens	5750 Main St Ne, Minneapolis MN 55432	763-571-2400	R	7*	.1
22	Coxline Inc—Robert Boyle	2829 N Burdick St, Kalamazoo MI 49004	269-345-1132	R	7*	.1
23	Mereen-Johnson Machine Co—Harry Miller	4401 Lyndale Ave N, Minneapolis MN 55412	612-529-7791	R	7*	.1
24	Northwood Industrial Machinery Inc—Behrouz Alizadeh	11610 Commonwealth Dr, Louisville KY 40299	502-267-5504	R	6*	.1
25	Brewco Inc—Clarence Brewer	PO Box 150, Central City KY 42330	270-754-5847	R	6*	.1
26	Dubois Machine Company Inc—James Arvin	PO Box 470, Jasper IN 47547	812-482-3644	R	6*	.1
27	Pistorius Machine Company Inc—Robert Pistorius	1785 Express Dr N, Hauppauge NY 11788	631-582-6278	R	6*	.1
28	Black Brothers Co—James Carroll	501 9th Ave, Mendota IL 61342	815-539-7451	R	6*	.1
29	Froedge Machine And Supply Company Inc—Wendall Froedge	317 Radio Station Rd, Tompkinsville KY 42167	270-487-5891	R	6*	.1
30	Hmc Corp—Peter Taylor	284 Maple St, Hopkinton NH 03229	603-746-4691	R	5*	.1
31	Barr-Mullin Inc—Sandy Mullin	2506 Yonkers Rd, Raleigh NC 27604	919-833-3334	R	5*	.1
32	Yates-American Machine Company Inc—Darrell Borghi	PO Box 958, Beloit WI 53512	608-364-0333	R	5*	.1
33	Stapling Machines Inc—Wade Howle	41 Pine St Ste 101, Rockaway NJ 07866	973-627-4400	R	5*	<.1
34	Braid Sales And Marketing Inc—Fred Braid	320 N Dr, Melbourne FL 32934	321-752-8180	R	5*	.1

Rank	Company Name—*Executive Officer*	Address, City, State, Zip	Phone	Type	Fin	Empls
35	Ultimizer's Inc—*Leroy Cothrell*	28380 Se Stone Rd, Boring OR 97009	503-663-7263	R	5*	<.1
36	Rayco Industries Inc—*Ray Poston*	1502 Valley Rd, Richmond VA 23222	804-321-7111	R	4*	<.1
37	Kimwood Corp—*Kristan Woodard*	PO Box 97, Cottage Grove OR 97424	541-942-4401	R	4*	<.1
38	Voorwood Co—*Adam Britton*	PO Box 1127, Anderson CA 96007	530-365-3311	R	4*	<.1
39	Schuon Manufacturing Company Inc—*Robert Schuon*	PO Box 1565, Hayden ID 83835	208-664-3836	R	4*	<.1
40	James L Taylor Manufacturing Co—*Michael Burdis*	108 128 Parker Ave, Poughkeepsie NY 12601	845-452-3780	R	4*	<.1
41	L and L Machinery Inc—*Peter Nemeth*	5901 W Hwy 22, Crestwood KY 40014	502-241-1502	R	4*	<.1
42	Kasco Manufacturing Company Inc—*P Kaster*	170 W 600 N, Shelbyville IN 46176	317-398-4636	R	3*	<.1
43	Stringer Industries Inc—*George Stringer*	PO Box 450, Tylertown MS 39667	601-876-3376	R	3*	.1
44	Evans Machinery Inc—*Robert Perez*	PO Box 1406, Glendale AZ 85311	623-934-7294	R	3*	<.1
45	Cooper Machine Company Inc—*Robert Cooper*	PO Box 550, Wadley GA 30477	478-252-5885	R	3*	<.1
46	Toolco Industrial Corp—*James Braswell*	PO Box 996, Marion NC 28752	828-652-2273	R	3*	<.1
47	Meadows Mills Inc—*Robert Hege*	PO Box 1288, North Wilkesboro NC 28659	336-838-2282	R	3*	<.1
48	Accu-Router Inc—*Todd Herzog*	634 Mt View Industrial, Morrison TN 37357	931-668-7127	R	2*	<.1
49	Merritt Machinery LLC—*John Boyer*	10 Simonds St, Lockport NY 14094	716-434-5558	R	2*	<.1
50	Gbn Machine and Engineering Corp—*Raj Nainani*	17073 Bull Church Rd, Woodford VA 22580	804-448-2033	R	2*	<.1
51	Calvert Manufacturing Inc—*Dana Tucker*	245 N St, Longwood FL 32750	407-331-5522	R	2*	<.1
52	Readwood Inc—*Charles Read*	PO Box 80, Milwaukee WI 53201	414-933-7000	R	2*	<.1
53	Sawmill Hydraulics—*Verle Helle*	23522 W Farmington Rd, Farmington IL 61531	309-245-2448	R	2*	<.1
54	Alain's Originals In Wood Inc—*Ann Virlouvet*	423 S 8th St, La Porte TX 77571	281-470-8666	R	2*	<.1
55	Alexander Dodds Co—*Brian Campbell*	3000 Walkent Dr Nw, Grand Rapids MI 49544	616-784-6000	R	2*	<.1
56	Premier Furniture Manufacturing Inc—*Terry Poter*	PO Box 1686, Hartselle AL 35640	256-751-1520	R	2*	<.1
57	Mobile Manufacturing Co—*Ronald Harriman*	PO Box 250, Troutdale OR 97060	503-666-5593	R	1*	<.1
58	Industrial Research and Engineering Inc—*John Coats*	PO Box 2892, Portland OR 97208	503-288-5816	R	1*	<.1
59	LA Weaver Company Inc—*Rick Weaver*	1108 S 37th St, Kansas City KS 66106	913-831-1800	R	1*	<.1
60	Ligna Machinery Inc—*H Wilson*	PO Box 4098, Burlington NC 27215	336-584-0030	R	1*	<.1
61	Automated Lumber Handling Inc—*William Dugger*	PO Box 796, Lenoir NC 28645	828-754-4662	R	1*	<.1
62	Otb Machinery Inc—*Kevin Arvin*	4601 Jamesford Dr, Jamestown NC 27282	336-323-1035	R	1*	<.1
63	Rawlings Manufacturing Inc—*John Rawlings*	1780 Idaho St, Missoula MT 59801	406-728-6182	R	1*	<.1
64	Rose Machinery Inc—*Ray Rose*	61543 American Loop, Bend OR 97702	541-388-2015	R	<1*	<.1
65	Workrite Inc—*Robert Meyer*	1315 S Flower St, Burbank CA 91502	818-241-3682	R	<1*	<.1

TOTALS: SIC 3553 Woodworking Machinery
Companies: 65   3,535   7.0

3554 Paper Industries Machinery

Rank	Company Name—*Executive Officer*	Address, City, State, Zip	Phone	Type	Fin	Empls
1	Kadant Inc—*Jonathan Painter*	1 Technology Park Dr, Westford MA 01886	978-776-2000	P	270	1.6
2	Voith Paper Inc—*Robert Gallo*	PO Box 2337, Appleton WI 54911	920-731-7724	R	85*	1.0
3	Curt G Joa Inc—*Donald Lammers*	PO Box 903, Sheboygan Falls WI 53085	920-467-6136	R	51*	.3
4	Metso Power—*David King*	3430 Toringdon Way Ste, Charlotte NC 28277	704-541-1453	R	36*	.2
5	Martin George M Co—*Robert Morgan*	PO Box 8464, Oakland CA 94662	510-652-2200	R	32*	.1
6	Paper Machinery Corp—*Donald Baumgartner*	PO Box 240100, Milwaukee WI 53224	414-354-8050	R	31*	.2
7	Asc Machine Tools Inc—*Ray Griff*	PO Box 11619, Spokane Valley WA 99211	509-534-6600	R	28*	.2
8	Kadant Solutions—*William Rainville* Kadant Inc	35 Sword St, Auburn MA 01501	508-791-8171	D	23	.2
9	Sun Automation Inc—*Pat Oconnor*	66 Loveton Cir, Sparks Glencoe MD 21152	410-472-2900	R	23*	.1
10	Lasermax Roll Systems Inc—*William Carroll*	53 3rd Ave, Burlington MA 01803	781-229-2266	R	22*	.2
11	Weber H G and Company Inc—*John Koehn*	PO Box 196, Kiel WI 53042	920-894-2221	R	21*	.1
12	J and L Fiber Services Inc—*Fred Schillinger*	809 Phillip Dr, Waukesha WI 53186	262-544-1890	S	19*	.1
13	J J Plank Corp—*David Plank*	PO Box 1955, Appleton WI 54912	920-733-4479	R	16*	.1
14	Sure-Feed Engineering Inc—*Todd Werner*	12050 49th St N, Clearwater FL 33762	727-571-3330	R	16*	.1
15	Challenge Machinery Co—*Larry Ritsema*	6125 Norton Ctr Dr, Norton Shores MI 49441	231-799-8484	R	16*	<.1
16	Crathern Machinery Group Inc—*Larry Pitsch*	PO Box 1180, Manchester NH 03105	603-314-0444	R	15*	.1
17	Kirk-Rudy Inc—*Harry Kirk*	125 Lorraine Pkwy, Woodstock GA 30188	770-427-4203	R	14*	.1
18	Geo M Martin Co—*Robert A Morgan*	PO Box 8464, Oakland CA 94662	510-652-2200	R	13*	.1
19	Industrial Engraving and Manufacturing Corp—*Joseph Kaufmann*	5324 Kunesh Rd, Pulaski WI 54162	920-865-7304	R	13*	.1
20	Security Engineered Machinery Company Inc—*Andrew Kelleher*	PO Box 1045, Westborough MA 01581	508-366-1488	R	12*	<.1
21	Elsner Engineering Works Inc—*Frank Elsner*	PO Box 66, Hanover PA 17331	717-637-5991	R	10*	.1
22	Anthony-Ross Co—*Gary Kopka*	5600 SW Arctic Dr Ste, Beaverton OR 97005	503-641-0545	S	9*	.1
23	Corrugated Replacements Inc—*Robert Lee*	PO Box 2809, Blairsville GA 30514	706-781-6650	R	9*	.1
24	Keene Technology Inc—*Mark Spain*	14357 Commercial Pkwy, South Beloit IL 61080	815-624-8989	R	9*	.1
25	Motor Martco LLC—*Richard Bach*	3350 Yankee Rd, Middletown OH 45044	513-424-5307	R	9*	.1
26	Peerless Machine and Tool Corp—*Jeffrey Carson*	PO Box 385, Marion IN 46952	765-662-2586	R	8*	.1
27	L E Sauer Machine Co—*Warren Sauer*	3535 Tree Ct Indus, Saint Louis MO 63122	636-225-5358	R	8*	.1
28	FL Smithe Machine Company Inc—*Edgar A Smithe Jr*	Old Rte 220 N, Duncansville PA 16635	814-695-5521	R	8*	.1
29	Montague Industries Inc—*Judith Pierce*	15 Rastallis St, Turners Falls MA 01376	413-863-4301	R	8*	.1
30	Jennerjahn Machine Inc—*Brian Jennerjahn*	PO Box 379, Matthews IN 46957	765-998-2733	R	8*	.1
31	GG C Inc—*Orval Gould*	PO Box 15546, Santa Ana CA 92735	714-835-0541	R	8*	.1
32	Johnston Dandy Co—*Robert Johnston*	PO Box 670, Lincoln ME 04457	207-794-6571	R	8*	.1
33	Maxson Automatic Machinery Co—*Joseph Matthews*	70 Airport Rd, Westerly RI 02891	401-596-0162	R	7*	.1
34	Essco Inc—*Joseph Korte*	PO Box 10297, Green Bay WI 54307	920-494-3480	R	7*	.1
35	Universal Precision Products Inc—*Jon Munson*	1480 Industrial Pkwy, Akron OH 44310	330-633-6128	R	7*	<.1
36	Moen Industries—*Carl Moen*	12333 Los Nietos Rd, Santa Fe Springs CA 90670	562-946-6381	R	6*	.1
37	Ashe Converting Equipment—*Barbara Godbold*	23 Marlboro Rd, Brattleboro VT 05301	802-254-0200	R	5*	.1
38	Acumeter Laboratories Inc—*Mark Westin*	2976 Cleveland Ave N, Saint Paul MN 55113	651-765-9686	R	5*	<.1
39	Cranston Machinery Company Inc—*Albert Cranston*	2251 Se Oak Grove Blvd, Oak Grove OR 97267	503-654-7751	R	5*	<.1
40	Agnati America Inc—*Manfred Hagin*	371 Gees Mill Business, Conyers GA 30013	770-922-5870	R	5*	<.1
41	Holyoke Machine Co—*James Sagalyn*	PO Box 988, Holyoke MA 01041	413-534-5612	R	5*	<.1
42	Converting Machines Inc—*Todd Macdonald*	PO Box 55187, Portland OR 97238	503-286-4646	R	5*	<.1
43	Ouachita Machine Works Inc—*Jimmy Dulaney*	120 N Hilton St, West Monroe LA 71291	318-396-1468	R	5*	<.1
44	Rosenthal Manufacturing Company Inc—*Lorelei Rosenthal*	1840 Janke Dr, Northbrook IL 60062	847-714-0404	R	5*	<.1
45	Cline Acquisition Corp—*Robert Buchanan*	5210 Edwards Rd, Taylors SC 29687	864-235-6371	R	4*	<.1
46	Unique Products LLC	8650 Yermoland Dr, El Paso TX 79907	915-592-8051	R	4*	<.1
47	Forthmann Machines Inc—*Fred Forthmann*	1495 Macarthur Blvd, Mahwah NJ 07430	201-818-1221	R	4*	<.1
48	Absolute Investments Inc—*Joseph Kasperski*	1393 W Jeffrey Dr, Addison IL 60101	630-495-0077	R	4*	<.1
49	Uff Machine Co—*Richard Clure*	30741 Duck Puddle Rd, Kennedyville MD 21645	410-648-6768	R	3*	<.1
50	Craft Industrial Inc—*David Schrum*	2300 58th St, Hampton VA 23661	757-825-1195	R	3*	<.1
51	Haire Machine Corp—*Douglas Muller*	PO Box 11030, Merrillville IN 46411	219-947-4545	R	3*	<.1

Note: An asterisk (*) indicates an estimated financial figure. The company type code used is as follows: R = Private, P = Public, S = Private Subsidiary, B = Public Subsidiary, D = Division, J = Joint Venture, I = Investment Fund.

COMPANY RANKINGS BY SALES WITHIN 4-DIGIT SIC

Rank	Company Name—*Executive Officer*	Address, City, State, Zip	Phone	Type	Fin	Empls
52	Profold Inc—*John Pinchin*	PO Box 780929, Sebastian FL 32978	772-589-0063	R	3*	<.1
53	John Eppler Machine Works Inc—*Helen Schnabl*	9150 State Rd, Philadelphia PA 19136	215-624-3400	R	3*	<.1
54	Paco Winders Manufacturing Inc—*Steven Kiss*	2040 Bennett Rd, Philadelphia PA 19116	215-637-6265	R	3*	<.1
55	Bolton-Emerson Americas Inc—*Sandra Krug*	PO Box 569, Lawrence MA 01842	978-686-3961	R	3*	<.1
56	Standard Paper Box Machine Company Inc—*Bruce Adams*	347 Coster St Fl 2, Bronx NY 10474	718-328-3300	R	2*	<.1
57	Scm Container Machinery Inc—*Jean Chevalier*	PO Box 405, Agawam MA 01001	413-786-3366	R	2*	<.1
58	Miami Machine Corp—*Michael Mc Neil*	PO Box 145, Overpeck OH 45055	513-863-6707	R	2*	<.1
59	Brown Machine Works and Supply Inc—*Shelia Brown*	PO Box 879, Alexander City AL 35011	256-234-7491	R	2*	<.1
60	Dovey Corp—*Kay Reed*	PO Box 2249, Anderson IN 46018	765-649-2576	R	2*	<.1
61	C And W Die Inc—*Tommy Cooper*	6300 Brookville Rd Bld, Indianapolis IN 46219	317-352-1000	R	2*	<.1
62	Bfmc LLC—*Hamel Emilienne*	PO Box 127, Berlin NH 03570	603-752-4550	R	2*	<.1
63	Thomas M Leonard Inc—*Tom Leonard*	543 N 5th St, Garland TX 75040	972-271-4295	R	2*	<.1
64	Culmac Inc—*Archie Cullen*	PO Box 151, Geneseo IL 61254	309-944-6494	R	1*	<.1
65	Pioneer Point Corp—*John Pickell*	PO Box 727, Heber Springs AR 72543	870-536-1113	R	1*	<.1
66	Ibs Of America Corp—*Heins Bartelmass*	3732 Profit Way, Chesapeake VA 23323	757-485-4210	R	1*	<.1
67	Gilbert and Nash Company Inc—*Dan Brooks*	1100 Prospect Ln, Kaukauna WI 54130	920-759-2700	R	1*	<.1
68	Advent Machine Tool Inc—*Jim Saladino*	70 Toledo St, Farmingdale NY 11735	631-420-1548	R	1*	<.1
69	Kadant GranTek Inc—*Michael Devic* Kadant Inc	607 Liberty St, Green Bay WI 54304	920-435-5200	S	1*	<.1

TOTALS: SIC 3554 Paper Industries Machinery
Companies: 69   982   6.7

3555 Printing Trades Machinery

Rank	Company Name—*Executive Officer*	Address, City, State, Zip	Phone	Type	Fin	Empls
1	Agfa Corp (Ridgefield Park New Jersey)—*Jo Cornu*	611 River Dr Ste 3, Elmwood Park NJ 07407	201-440-2500	S	1,300*	4.5
2	Goss International Corp—*Jochen Meissner*	3 Territorial Ct, Bolingbrook IL 60440	630-755-9300	R	1,112*	4.0
3	Heidelberg USA Inc—*James P Dunn*	1000 Gutenberg Dr NW, Kennesaw GA 30144	770-419-6591	S	771*	.9
4	MacDermid Graphic Arts Inc—*Anthony Agostini*	5210 Phillip Lee Dr, Atlanta GA 30336	404-696-4565	S	546*	1.0
5	Ricoh Americas Corp—*Katsumi Yoshida*	5 Dedrick Pl, West Caldwell NJ 07006	973-882-2000	R	402*	.6
6	Baldwin Technology Company Inc—*Mark T Becker*	2 Trap Falls Rd Ste 40, Shelton CT 06484	203-402-1000	P	161	.5
7	MAN Roland Inc—*Vincent Lapinski*	800 E Oak Hill Dr, Westmont IL 60559	630-920-2000	S	151*	.1
8	Presstek Inc—*Ronald T Cardone*	55 Executive Dr, Hudson NH 03051	603-595-7000	P	129	.5
9	MEGTEC Systems Inc—*Mohit Uberoi*	PO Box 5030, De Pere WI 54115		S	68*	.8
10	Asahi Tec America Corp—*Yasunori Hagita*	1767 Sheridan St, Richmond IN 47374	765-962-8399	R	48*	<.1
11	Delphax Technologies Inc—*Dieter P Schilling*	6100 W 110th St, Bloomington MN 55438	952-939-9000	R	45	.3
12	Baldwin Kansa Corp—*Jerry Waddell*	3700 Oakes Dr, Emporia KS 66801	620-343-6700	R	35*	.1
13	ATS Systems—*John Boland*	30222 Esperanza, Rancho Santa Margarita CA 92688	949-888-1744	R	35*	.1
14	Mark/Trece Inc—*Richard Godfrey*	2001 Stockton Rd, Joppa MD 21085	410-879-0060	R	26*	.2
15	Altair Corp—*Garry Brainin*	350 Barclay Blvd, Lincolnshire IL 60069	847-634-9540	R	23*	.4
16	Fisher Graphic Industries A California Corp—*Phillip Saunders*	1137 Graphics Dr, Modesto CA 95351	209-577-0181	R	23*	.4
17	Web Printing Controls Company Inc—*Herman Gnuechtel*	23872 N Kelsey Rd, Lake Barrington IL 60010	847-382-7970	R	22*	.2
18	Harper Corporation Of America—*Madelene Crawford*	PO Box 38490, Charlotte NC 28278	704-588-3371	R	17*	.1
19	Halm Industries Company Inc—*Stephen Lyon*	180 Glen Head Rd, Glen Head NY 11545	516-676-6700	R	17*	.1
20	Nilpeter USA Inc—*Andrew Colletta*	11550 Goldcoast Dr, Cincinnati OH 45249	513-489-4400	R	17*	.1
21	Scheffer Inc—*Bruce Scheffer*	1565 E 91st Ave, Merrillville IN 46410	219-736-6200	R	16*	.1
22	Bmp America Inc—*Peter Milicia*	11625 Maple Ridge Rd, Medina NY 14103	585-798-0950	R	16*	.1
23	Xitron Inc—*Mark Fisenschenk*	781 Avis Dr Ste 200, Ann Arbor MI 48108	734-913-8080	R	16*	<.1
24	Manugraph Dgm Inc—*Brian Bine*	PO Box 573, Elizabethville PA 17023	717-362-3243	R	15*	.1
25	Kase Equipment Corp—*Partick Hawkins*	7400 Hub Pkwy, Cleveland OH 44125	216-642-9040	R	14*	.1
26	Gem Gravure Company Inc—*David Gemelli*	PO Box 1158, Hanover MA 02339	781-878-0456	R	14*	.1
27	Glunz and Jensen K and F Inc—*Thomas Kocsis*	12633 Industrial Park, Granger IN 46530	574-272-9950	R	14*	.1
28	Kgp Group Inc—*Gregory Burger*	1103 Stanley Dr, Euless TX 76040	817-354-0766	R	13*	.1
29	Lederle Machine Co—*Debbie Lederle*	PO Box 426, Pacific MO 63069	636-271-7200	R	13*	.1
30	Irotas Manufacturing Company Inc—*William Kiser*	393 Pearce Industrial, Shelbyville KY 40065	502-633-6402	R	13*	<.1
31	Southern Illinois Machinery Company Inc—*John Newsome*	6903 E 1600th Ave, Shumway IL 62461	217-868-5431	R	12*	.1
32	Numerical Concepts Inc—*Donald Jones*	4040 1st Pkwy, Terre Haute IN 47804	812-466-5261	R	12*	.1
33	Fine Line Graphics Inc—*James Toles*	PO Box 17370, Smithfield RI 02917	401-854-8300	R	12*	.1
34	Polyurethane Engineering Techniques Company Inc—*Russell Smith*	28041 N Bradley Rd, Lake Forest IL 60045	847-362-1820	R	12*	.1
35	Butler Automatic Inc—*Andrew Butler*	41 Leona Dr, Middleboro MA 02346	508-923-0544	R	12*	.1
36	North American Cerutti Corp—*Giancarlo Cerutti*	15800 W Overland Dr, New Berlin WI 53151	262-827-3800	R	12*	.1
37	Castlereagh Printcraft Inc—*James Vollaro*	PO Box 9062, Freeport NY 11520	516-379-2122	R	11*	.1
38	Printing Research Corp—*Howard Moore*	10954 Shady Trl, Dallas TX 75220	214-353-9000	R	10*	.1
39	Therm-O-Type Corp—*Ted Van Pelt*	PO Box 998, Nokomis FL 34274	941-488-0123	R	9	.1
40	Mark Bst-Pro Inc—*Kristian Juenke*	650 W Grand Ave Ste 30, Elmhurst IL 60126	630-833-9900	R	9*	<.1
41	Hodgins Engraving Company Inc—*Robert Hodgins*	3817 W Main St, Batavia NY 14020	585-343-4444	R	9*	.1
42	Web Press Corp—*Brian Haun*	701 East D St, Tacoma WA 98421	253-620-4747	R	9	.1
43	Precision Rubber Plate Company Inc—*Lawrence Green*	5620 Elmwood Ave, Indianapolis IN 46203	317-783-3226	R	8*	.1
44	Printex Inc—*James Cheng*	12113 Kirkham Rd, Poway CA 92064	858-513-2418	R	8*	.1
45	Baldwin Asia Pacific Corp—*Gerald Mathe* Baldwin Technology Company Inc	2 Trap Falls Rd, Shelton CT 06484	203-402-1000	S	8*	<.1
46	Tensor Group Inc—*Martin Hozjan*	10351 Rising Ct, Woodridge IL 60517	630-739-9600	R	8*	.1
47	Mosstype Holding Corp—*Lester Moss*	150 Franklin Tpke, Waldwick NJ 07463	201-444-8000	R	7*	.1
48	Robertson Equipment Company Inc—*Charles Robertson*	1301 S Maiden Ln, Joplin MO 64801	417-781-3702	R	7*	.1
49	Plastic Card Systems Inc—*Robert P Axline*	31 Pierce St, Northboro MA 01532	508-351-6210	R	7*	.1
50	Practical Automation Inc—*Samuel Bergami*	PO Box 3028, Milford CT 06460	203-882-5640	R	7*	.1
51	Western Printing Machinery Co—*Paul Kaponek*	9229 Ivanhoe St, Schiller Park IL 60176	847-678-1740	R	7*	<.1
52	Lith-O-Roll Corp—*Rita Sepe*	PO Box 5328, El Monte CA 91734	626-579-0340	R	7*	.1
53	Litho Tech Inc—*Irvin Platt*	2020 N 22nd Ave, Phoenix AZ 85009	602-254-2427	R	7*	<.1
54	F P Rosback Co—*Larry Bowman*	125 Hawthorne Ave, Saint Joseph MI 49085	269-983-2582	R	7*	.1
55	Irotas Manufacturing Company LLC	PO Box 277, Shelbyville KY 40066	502-633-6402	R	7*	.1
56	Apexx Omni-Graphics Inc—*Larry Peters*	5829 64th St, Maspeth NY 11378	718-326-3330	R	7*	.1
57	Capco Machinery Systems Inc—*Edward West*	PO Box 11945, Roanoke VA 24022	540-977-0404	R	7*	.1
58	TruColor Visions Systems Inc—*James Doerr*	1603 Whitesville Rd, LaGrange GA 30240	706-845-6970	R	6*	<.1
59	Milara Inc—*Krassy Petkov*	4 Marc Rd, Medway MA 02053	508-533-5322	R	6*	<.1
60	Midwest Graphics Inc—*Michael Lalonde*	5550 Elmwood Ct, Indianapolis IN 46203	317-780-4600	R	6*	.1
61	Roskam Automatic Machinery LLC—*Mervin Roskam*	PO Box 1000, Pinson AL 35126	205-520-0000	R	6*	.1
62	Press-A-Print International LLC—*Judy Bramer*	1463 Commerce Way, Idaho Falls ID 83401	208-523-7620	R	6*	<.1
63	Tresu Royse Inc—*Mark Hischer*	8517 Directors Row, Dallas TX 75247	214-631-2844	R	6*	.1
64	Laserequipment Inc—*Darrel Ochs*	9301 W 53rd St, Shawnee Mission KS 66203	913-362-9600	R	6*	<.1
65	SI Industries Inc—*James Marciniak*	PO Box 490203, Minneapolis MN 55449	763-784-1430	R	5*	<.1

Rank	Company Name—*Executive Officer*	Address, City, State, Zip	Phone	Type	Fin	Empls
66	Roller Service Corp—*James Veacock*	23 Mcmillan Way, Newark DE 19713	302-737-5000	R	5*	<.1
67	Imperial Rubber Products Inc—*Ronald Hill*	5691 Gates St, Chino CA 91710	909-393-0528	R	5*	<.1
68	Indemnity Company of California—*Walter Crowell*	17780 Fitch Ste 200, Irvine CA 92614		R	5*	<.1
69	RW Hartnett Co—*Andrea Boyce*	2055 Bennett Rd, Philadelphia PA 19116	215-969-9190	R	5*	<.1
70	Automated Systems Technology Inc—*Chester Moore*	PO Box 2795, Eagle River WI 54521	715-477-1320	R	5*	<.1
71	B Bunch Company Inc—*Ben Bunch*	9619 N 21st Dr, Phoenix AZ 85021	602-997-6452	R	5*	<.1
72	Perretta Graphics Corp—*Lawrence Perretta*	46 Violet Ave, Poughkeepsie NY 12601	845-473-0550	R	5*	<.1
73	Advance Graphics Equipment Of York Inc—*Dennis Snyder*	4700 Raycom Rd, Dover PA 17315	717-292-9183	R	5*	<.1
74	Renz America Company Inc—*Peter Renz*	92 Almgren Dr, Agawam MA 01001	413-789-7700	R	5*	<.1
75	Laser Recharge Inc—*Dan Rees*	3324 N San Marcos Pl, Chandler AZ 85225	480-829-6725	R	5*	<.1
76	EC Shaw Co—*Joseph Grome*	1242 Mehring Way, Cincinnati OH 45203	513-721-6334	R	5*	<.1
77	Banner Moulded Products—*Michael Randazzo*	3050 River Rd, River Grove IL 60171	773-625-4313	R	4*	<.1
78	KC Photo Engraving Co—*Michael Curley*	5600 Ayala Ave, Irwindale CA 91706	626-795-4127	R	4*	<.1
79	Super Web Inc—*Marcel Edelstein*	97 Lamar St, West Babylon NY 11704	631-643-9100	R	4*	<.1
80	Legend Industries Inc—*Larry Hines*	PO Box 743, Effingham IL 62401	217-342-3918	R	4*	<.1
81	Ackley Machine Corp—*E Ackley*	1273 N Church St Ste 1, Moorestown NJ 08057	856-234-3626	R	4*	<.1
82	Zenith Rollers LLC—*Sashi Ravada*	764 NW 57th Ct, Fort Lauderdale FL 33309	954-493-6484	R	4*	<.1
83	Machtronic Products Company Inc—*Thomas Morrow*	PO Box 217, Minong WI 54859	715-466-2244	R	4*	<.1
84	D and K Custom Machine Design Inc—*Karl Singer*	PO Box 1146, Elk Grove Village IL 60009	847-956-4757	S	4*	<.1
85	Townsend Industries Inc—*John Jorgensen*	PO Box 97, Altoona IA 50009	515-967-4261	R	4*	<.1
86	Desco Equipment Corp—*Leo Henry*	1903 Case Pkwy, Twinsburg OH 44087	330-405-1581	R	4*	<.1
87	Printer's Repair Parts Inc—*Nikki Calhoun*	2706 Edgington St Unit, Franklin Park IL 60131	847-288-9000	R	4*	<.1
88	Stevens Technology LLC—*Richard Stevens*	5700 E Belknap St, Fort Worth TX 76117	817-831-3911	P	3	N/A
89	Box Dies Manufacturing Inc—*Ralph Huepler*	55 Contant Ave, Lodi NJ 07644	973-772-5088	R	3*	<.1
90	Austrian Machine Corp—*Marjorie Kern*	25 Stamp Farm Rd, Cranston RI 02921	401-946-4090	R	3*	<.1
91	Perfecta USA—*Paul Myer*	5505 S Franklin Rd, Indianapolis IN 46239	317-862-7371	R	3*	<.1
92	Cc1 Inc—*Richard Lewis*	200 International Dr S, Portsmouth NH 03801	603-319-2000	R	3*	<.1
93	Flexoplate Inc—*Thomas Bock*	6504 Corporate Dr, Blue Ash OH 45242	513-489-0433	R	3*	<.1
94	Draiswerke Inc—*Gisbert Schall*	40 Whitney Rd, Mahwah NJ 07430	201-847-0600	R	3*	<.1
95	Affiliated Manufacturers Inc—*Tam Atkinson*	PO Box 429, Frenchtown NJ 08825	908-722-7100	R	3*	<.1
96	Para Plate and Plastics Company Inc—*Robert Clapp*	15910 Shoemaker Ave, Cerritos CA 90703	562-404-3434	R	3*	<.1
97	Packaging Graphics Inc—*Eileen Koff*	PO Box 160, West Berlin NJ 08091	856-767-9000	R	3*	<.1
98	Allied Graphics Inc—*Bayless Guenther*	PO Box 1902, Memphis TN 38101	901-774-5502	R	3*	<.1
99	Xenetech Global Inc—*Guy Barone*	12139 Airline Hwy, Baton Rouge LA 70817	225-752-0225	R	3*	<.1
100	Van Pelt Equipment Inc—*Christopher Van Pelt*	PO Box 1487, Nokomis FL 34274	941-485-7496	R	3*	<.1
101	AT Information Products Inc—*Roger Angrick*	575 Corporate Dr Ste 4, Mahwah NJ 07430	201-529-0202	R	3*	<.1
102	Johnson B W Manufacturing Company Inc—*Richard Mertens*	PO Box 1282, Joplin MO 64802	417-623-2570	R	3*	<.1
103	Count Numbering Machine Inc—*Irwin Wertheimer*	2128 Vineyard Ave, Escondido CA 92029	760-489-1400	R	3*	<.1
104	CTS Technical Resources Inc—*C Collins*	408 S 2nd St, Cedartown GA 30125	770-748-3497	R	3*	<.1
105	Autoroll Print Technologies LLC—*Mike Dissel*	PO Box 488, West Newbury MA 01985	978-777-2160	R	3*	<.1
106	Si Roller—*Rick Marciniak*	PO Box 742, Watertown WI 53094	920-262-1817	R	3*	<.1
107	Bay Classifieds Inc—*Steve Marini*	10950 Bigge St, San Leandro CA 94577	510-420-8498	R	2*	<.1
108	Poly Plate Inc—*Steve Gardner*	1102 Myers Pkwy, Ashland OH 44805	419-289-7763	R	2*	<.1
109	FT Group Inc—*Thomas Wortley*	220 High St, Franklin OH 45005	937-746-6430	R	2*	<.1
110	WR Chesnut Engineering Inc—*Richard Chesnut*	14 Spielman Rd, Fairfield NJ 07004	973-227-6995	R	2*	<.1
111	In-Line Labeling Equipment Inc—*Greg Brandon*	7282 Spa Rd, North Charleston SC 29418	843-569-2530	R	2*	<.1
112	Cincinnati Precision Plate Inc—*William Painer*	9185 Le Saint Dr, Fairfield OH 45014	513-874-6922	R	2*	<.1
113	Dms Inc—*David Polkinghorne*	570 Telser Rd Sto A, Lake Zurich IL 60047	847-726-2828	R	2*	<.1
114	Unique Coupons Inc—*C Witt*	2836 Corporate Pkwy, Algonquin IL 60102	847-540-1200	R	2*	<.1
115	Prim Hall Enterprises Inc—*John Prim*	11 Spellman Rd, Plattsburgh NY 12901	518-561-7408	R	2*	<.1
116	Brackett Inc—*Michael Murray*	PO Box 19306, Topeka KS 66619	785-862-2205	R	2*	<.1
117	Allison Systems Corp—*Thomas Allison*	220 Adams St, Riverside NJ 08075	856-461-9111	R	2*	<.1
118	Pic Manufacturing Inc—*Michael Camp*	PO Box 665, Paso Robles CA 93447	805-238-5451	R	2*	<.1
119	Tooling Research Inc—*Milton Florest*	PO Box 306, Walpole MA 02081	508-668-1950	R	2*	<.1
120	Teca-Print USA Corp—*Jean-Louis Dubuit*	10 Cook St Ste 2, Billerica MA 01821	978-667-8655	R	2*	<.1
121	Roconex Corp—*Ty Spear*	20 Marybill Dr S, Troy OH 45373	937-339-2616	R	2*	<.1
122	Smith RPM Corp—*Janette Schumm*	15019 W 95th St, Shawnee Mission KS 66215	913-888-0695	R	2*	<.1
123	Carter Screen Inc—*Scott Carter*	PO Box 978, Galion OH 44833	734-261-1900	R	1*	<.1
124	Fenimore Manufacturing Inc—*Steve Smith*	PO Box 1287, Chickasha OK 73023	405-224-2637	R	1*	<.1
125	National Direct Dataflow—*Ann Zimmerman*	71 Fuller Rd Ste 6, Albany NY 12205	518-462-2226	R	1*	<.1
126	EL Harley Inc—*Richard Harley*	3715 Fiscal Ct, West Palm Beach FL 33404	561-841-9887	R	1*	<.1
127	Bisco International Inc—*Michael Rizzo*	543 Granville Ave, Hillside IL 60162	708-544-6308	R	1*	<.1
128	Arcaine Technology—*Anthony Caine*	960 Neilson St, Albany CA 94706	510-527-9859	R	1*	<.1
129	Flexo Tech Inc—*Lee Lightfoot*	2333 Executive Dr, Garland TX 75041	972-926-0749	R	1*	<.1
130	Howard Imprinting Machine Company Inc—*James Wrobbel*	PO Box 15027, Tampa FL 33684	813-884-2398	R	1*	<.1
131	Alpha Printing Inc—*Joseph Tucker*	PO Box 11458, Alexandria VA 22312	703-321-2071	R	<1*	<.1

TOTALS: SIC 3555 Printing Trades Machinery
Companies: 131   5,565   19.0

3556 Food Products Machinery

Rank	Company Name—*Executive Officer*	Address, City, State, Zip	Phone	Type	Fin	Empls
1	ITW Food Equipment Group LLC—*Harold Smith*	701 S Ridge Ave, Troy OH 45373	937-332-3000	S	1,081*	10.0
2	APV Americas—*Haluk Drougan*	105 Crosspoint Pky, Getzville NY 14068	716-692-3000	S	521*	2.5
3	Middleby Marshall Inc—*Selim A Bassoul*	1400 Toastmaster Dr, Elgin IL 60120	847-741-3300	R	135	.8
4	Buhler Inc—*Rene Steiner*	PO Box 9497, Minneapolis MN 55440	763-847-9900	R	129*	.2
5	Key Technology Inc—*David M Camp*	150 Avery St, Walla Walla WA 99362	509-529-2161	P	116	.6
6	TurboChef Technologies Inc—*James K Price*	6 Concourse Pky Ste 19, Atlanta GA 30328	678-987-1700	S	105*	.3
7	Baker Perkins Inc APV Americas	3223 Kraft Ave SE, Grand Rapids MI 49512	616-784-3111	S	75	.1
8	Atlas Pacific Engineering Co—*Erik Teranchi*	PO Box 500, Pueblo CO 81002	719-948-3040	R	46*	.3
9	GS Blodgett Corp—*Gary Mick*	44 Lakeside Ave, Burlington VT 05401	802-658-6600	S	44*	.1
10	N Wasserstrom and Sons Inc—*Alan Wasserstrom*	2300 Lockbourne Rd, Columbus OH 43207	614-228-5550	R	44*	.5
11	Emi Industries LLC—*Scott Lybbert*	1316 Tech Blvd, Tampa FL 33619	813-626-3166	R	40*	.3
12	Relco LLC—*Loren Corle*	PO Box 1689, Willmar MN 56201	320-231-2210	R	40*	.1
13	Crown Iron Works—*Cliff Anderson*	PO Box 1364, Minneapolis MN 55440	651-639-8900	S	40*	.1
14	Pitco Frialator Inc—*Selim A Bassoul*	PO Box 501, Concord NH 03302	603-225-6684	S	38*	.3
15	Khs USA Inc—*Mark Arrant*	PO Box 1508, Waukesha WI 53187	262-797-7200	R	34*	.4
16	Wenger Manufacturing Inc—*Lavon Wenger*	PO Box 130, Sabetha KS 66534	785-284-2133	R	33*	.3
17	Marel Stork Poultry Processing Inc—*Kenneth Falls*	PO Box 1258, Gainesville GA 30503	770-532-7041	R	33*	.3
18	Triangle Package Machinery Co—*Robert Muskat*	6655 W Diversey Ave, Chicago IL 60707	773-889-0200	R	32*	.2

Note: An asterisk (*) indicates an estimated financial figure. The company type code used is as follows: R = Private, P = Public, S = Private Subsidiary, B = Public Subsidiary, D = Division, J = Joint Venture, I = Investment Fund.

COMPANY RANKINGS BY SALES WITHIN 4-DIGIT SIC

Rank	Company Name—Executive Officer	Address, City, State, Zip	Phone	Type	Fin	Empls
19	Robot-Coupe Incorporated USA—Jay Williams	PO Box 16625, Jackson MS 39236	601-898-8411	R	32*	<.1
20	Primedge Inc—Ivo Cozzini	PO Box 46489, Chicago IL 60646	773-478-9700	R	32*	.2
21	Lawrence Equipment Inc—John Lawrence	2034 Peck Rd, El Monte CA 91733	626-442-2894	R	32*	.2
22	Weiler And Company Inc—Mel Cohen	1116 E Main St, Whitewater WI 53190	262-473-5254	R	31*	.2
23	Urschel Laboratories Inc—Robert Urschel	PO Box 2200, Valparaiso IN 46384	219-464-4811	R	29*	.3
24	Little Kentucky Smokehouse LLC—Linda Baird	400 T Frank Wathen Rd, Uniontown KY 42461	270-822-4350	R	28*	.1
25	Meyer Co—H Meyer	13700 Broadway Ave, Cleveland OH 44125	216-587-3400	R	28*	.2
26	Abec Inc—Scott Pickering	3998 Schelden Cir, Bethlehem PA 18017	610-861-4666	R	27*	.2
27	Heat and Control Inc—Andrew Caridis	21121 Cabot Blvd, Hayward CA 94545	510-259-0500	R	27*	.2
28	Crescent Metal Products Inc—Clifford Baggott	5925 Heisley Rd, Mentor OH 44060	440-350-1100	R	27*	.2
29	AMF Bakery Systems—Ken Newsome	2115 W Laburnum Ave, Richmond VA 23227	804-355-7961	S	26*	.1
30	Par-Way Tryson Co—Mandy Hanson	107 Bolte Ln, Saint Clair MO 63077	636-629-4545	R	26*	.1
31	Custom Metalcraft Inc—Dwayne Holden	PO Box 10587, Springfield MO 65808	417-862-0707	R	25*	.2
32	Belshaw Adamatic Group—Roger A Faw	814 44th St NW Ste 103, Auburn WA 98001	206-322-5474	R	25*	.2
33	APW/Wyott—Hylton Jones	729 3rd Ave, Dallas TX 75226	214-421-7366	R	24*	.3
34	Apache Stainless Equipment Corp—Patrick Albregts	PO Box 538, Beaver Dam WI 53916	920-356-9900	S	24*	.2
35	Gem Equipment Of Oregon Inc—Edward Mc Kenney	PO Box 359, Woodburn OR 97071	503-982-9902	R	23*	.2
36	HC Duke and Son Inc—Jino Cocchi	2116 8th Ave, East Moline IL 61244	309-755-4553	R	23*	.2
37	Dunkley International Inc—Richard Bogard	1910 Lake St, Kalamazoo MI 49001	269-343-5583	S	21*	.1
38	Idaho Steel Products Inc—Lynn Bradshaw	255 E Anderson St, Idaho Falls ID 83401	208-522-1275	R	21*	.1
39	Casa Herrera Inc—Ron Meade	2655 Pine St, Pomona CA 91767	909-392-3930	R	21*	.1
40	New Age Industrial Corporation Inc—Larry Nelson	PO Box 520, Norton KS 67654	785-877-5121	R	21*	.1
41	Brown International Corp—Charlie Gagliano	PO Box 713, Winter Haven FL 33882	863-299-2111	R	20*	.2
42	Bakers Pride Oven Company Inc—Hylton Jonas	30 Pine St, New Rochelle NY 10801	914-576-0200	R	20*	.2
43	Eirich Machines Inc—Paul Eirich	4033 Ryan Rd, Gurnee IL 60031	847-336-2444	R	20*	.1
44	Anderson International Corp—Len Trocano	6200 Harvard Ave, Cleveland OH 44105	216-641-1112	R	20*	.1
45	Fitzpatrick Industries Inc—Scott Paterson	832 N Industrial Dr, Elmhurst IL 60126	630-530-3333	R	20*	.1
46	Magna Machine Co—Scott Kramer	11180 Southland Rd, Cincinnati OH 45240	513-851-6900	R	18*	.1
47	Marel Seattle Inc—Henrik Rasmussen	2001 W Garfield St, Seattle WA 98119	206-781-1827	R	18*	.1
48	Giles Enterprises Inc—David Byrd	PO Box 210247, Montgomery AL 36121	334-272-1457	R	18*	.1
49	Jarvis Products Corp—Vincent Volpe	33 Anderson Rd, Middletown CT 06457	860-347-7271	R	18*	.1
50	Fabco Equipment Company Inc—Rocky Frazier	PO Box 754, Albertville AL 35950	256-878-5010	R	17*	.1
51	Baader Food Processing Machinery Inc—Shawn Nicholas	PO Box 15300, Kansas City KS 66115	913-621-3366	R	16*	.1
52	Wood Stone Corp—Keith Carpenter	1801 W Bakerview Rd, Bellingham WA 98226	360-650-1111	R	16*	.1
53	Reading Pretzel Systems—E Groff	380 Old W Penn Ave, Robesonia PA 19551	610-693-5816	R	16*	.1
54	Marlen International Inc—Nikola Vajda	9202 Barton St, Overland Park KS 66214		R	16*	.1
55	J C Ford Co—Thomas Ruhe	901 Leslie St, La Habra CA 90631	714-871-7361	R	15*	.1
56	Peerless Machinery Corp—Robert Zielsdorf	PO Box 769, Sidney OH 45365	937-492-4158	S	15*	.2
57	Stewart Systems Inc—Nand Kumar	808 Stewart Dr, Plano TX 75074	972-422-5808	R	15*	.1
58	Great Western Manufacturing Company Inc—James Schroeder	PO Box 149, Leavenworth KS 66048	913-682-2291	R	14*	.1
59	Vita Buona Inc—Paul Infranco	1 S Industrial Blvd, Bridgeton NJ 08302	856-453-7972	R	14*	.1
60	Hill and Sons LLC—Sam Ferguson	211 Hogan Pond Ln, Ball Ground GA 30107	770-735-4199	R	13*	.1
61	Burford Corp—Fred Springer	11284 Hwy 74, Maysville OK 73057	405-867-4467	R	13*	.1
62	Biro Manufacturing Company Inc—Richard Biro	1114 W Main St, Marblehead OH 43440	419-798-4451	R	13*	.1
63	Kysor Panel Inc—Junior Burnside	PO Box 14248, Fort Worth TX 76117	817-281-5121	R	12*	.2
64	Moline Machinery Ltd—Gary Moline	PO Box 16308, Duluth MN 55816	218-624-5734	R	12*	.1
65	Revent Inc—Daniel Lago	100 Ethel Rd W, Piscataway NJ 08854	732-777-9433	R	12*	<.1
66	Avure Technologies LLC—Todd Winders	22408 66th Ave S, Kent WA 98032	253-981-6350	R	12*	.1
67	FMC Food Technology—Pierre Brondeau	PO Box 5710, Riverside CA 92517	951-222-2300	D	11	.1
68	Matfer Bourgeat Inc—Pierre Pirisot	16300 Stagg St, Van Nuys CA 91406	818-782-0792	R	11*	.1
69	Maddox Metal Works Inc—Samuel Maddox	4116 Bronze Way, Dallas TX 75237	214-333-2311	R	11*	.1
70	R and D Manufacturing Company Inc—Tom Peterson	PO Box 3393, Gainesville GA 30503	770-532-9161	R	11*	.1
71	Brewmatic Co—Roy Farmer	PO Box 2959, Torrance CA 90509	310-787-5444	S	11*	.1
72	Archibald Frozen Desserts—Ed Meyer	990 Progress Blvd, New Albany IN 47150	812-941-8267	R	11*	<.1
73	Wolftec Inc—Ralf Ludwig	20 Kieffer Ln, Kingston NY 12401	845-340-9727	R	11*	.1
74	Lematic Inc—Dale Le Crone	2410 W Main St, Jackson MI 49203	517-787-3301	R	11*	.1
75	Desu Machinery Corp—Martin Golden	PO Box 245, Depew NY 14043	716-681-5798	R	11*	.1
76	Custom Powder Systems LLC—Ron Gielow	2715 N Airport Commerc, Springfield MO 65803	417-868-8002	R	10*	.1
77	Food Craft Inc—Helge Fillipsen	4225 Sw Kirklawn Ave, Topeka KS 66609	785-267-9400	R	10*	.1
78	Hayes and Stolz Industrial Manufacturing—BJ Masters	3521 Hemphill St, Fort Worth TX 76110	817-926-3391	R	10*	.1
79	Foodtools—Martin Grano	315 Laguna St, Santa Barbara CA 93101	805-962-8383	R	10*	<.1
80	C E Rogers Co—Howard Rogers	PO Box 118, Mora MN 55051	320-679-2172	R	10*	<.1
81	Continental Distilling Corp	75 Rockefeller Plz 16t, New York NY 10019	212-265-7013	S	10*	<.1
82	Remco Industries International Inc—Roman Moretth	3290 Ne 33rd St, Fort Lauderdale FL 33308	954-462-0000	R	10*	<.1
83	Piper Products Inc—Tony Sweeney	300 S 84th Ave, Wausau WI 54401	715-842-2724	R	10*	.1
84	Billington Welding and Manufacturing Inc—Francis Billington	PO Box 4460, Modesto CA 95352	209-526-9312	R	10*	.1
85	Univex Corp—John Tsiakos	3 Old Rockingham Rd, Salem NH 03079	603-893-6191	R	10*	.1
86	Pro Sales Inc—Gregory Wood	4230 B St Nw, Auburn WA 98001	253-852-6046	R	10*	.1
87	Kuhl Corp—Henry Kuhl	PO Box 26, Flemington NJ 08822	908-782-5696	R	9*	.1
88	Vendome Copper and Brass Works Inc—Thomas Sherman	729 Franklin St, Louisville KY 40202	502-587-1930	R	9*	.1
89	Southbend—John Perrucio	1100 Old Honeycutt Rd, Fuquay Varina NC 27526	919-762-1000	D	9*	.1
90	A and K Development Co—Ronald L Anderson	410 Chambers St, Eugene OR 97402	541-686-0012	R	9*	.1
91	Vincent Corp—Robert Johnston	2810 E 5th Ave, Tampa FL 33605	813-248-2650	R	9*	.1
92	Kossuth Fabricators Inc—Sharon Schiltz	PO Box 130, Algona IA 50511	515-295-7265	R	9*	<.1
93	Dahmes Stainless Inc—Forrest Dahmes	524 Industrial Ave, New London MN 56273	320-354-5711	R	9*	<.1
94	American Food Equipment Company Inc—Michael Botto	21040 Forbes Ave, Hayward CA 94545	510-783-0255	R	9*	.1
95	OHI Co—Thomas Hubbard	PO Box 622, Stockton CA 95201	209-466-8921	R	9*	.1
96	Wrh Holdings LLC—Mike Fowler	PO Box 757, Gainesville GA 30503	770-536-3611	R	9*	.1
97	Cvp Systems Inc—Wes Bork	2518 Wisconsin Ave, Downers Grove IL 60515	630-852-1190	R	9*	.1
98	Shaffer Manufacturing Corp—Mark Geise	PO Box 64, Urbana OH 43078	937-492-4142	S	9*	.1
99	Waltz Brothers Inc—Larry Waltz	10 W Waltz Dr, Wheeling IL 60090	847-520-1122	R	9*	<.1
100	Kusel Equipment Co—David Smith	PO Box 87, Watertown WI 53094	920-261-4112	R	8*	.1
101	Designer's Choice Stainless Iv Inc—Alan Wasserstrom N Wasserstrom and Sons Inc	7620 W Olive Ave, Peoria AZ 85345	623-878-7900	S	8*	.1
102	Caddy Corporation Of America—Craig Cohen	PO Box 345, Bridgeport NJ 08014	856-467-4222	R	8*	.1
103	FPEC Corporation A California Corp—Alan Davison	13623 Pumice St, Santa Fe Springs CA 90670	562-802-3727	R	8*	<.1
104	Rbm Conveyor Systems Inc—Roobik Kureghian	1570 W Mission Blvd, Pomona CA 91766	909-620-1333	R	8*	.1
105	Commercial Manufacturing—Larry Hagopian	PO Box 947, Fresno CA 93714	559-237-1855	R	8*	.1
106	C H Babb Company Inc—Charles Foran	445 Paramount Dr, Raynham MA 02767	508-977-0600	R	8*	<.1
107	Nimco Corp—Larry Bachner	PO Box 320, Crystal Lake IL 60039	815-459-4200	R	8*	.1

Rank	Company Name—*Executive Officer*	Address, City, State, Zip	Phone	Type	Fin	Empls
108	Stanford Bettendorf Inc—*John Stanford*	PO Box 790, Salem IL 62881	618-548-3555	R	8*	.1
109	Buflovak LLC—*Dave Bielecki*	750 E Ferry St, Buffalo NY 14211	716-895-2100	R	8*	<.1
110	Blentech Corp—*Darrell Horn*	PO Box 3109, Rohnert Park CA 94927	707-523-5949	R	7*	<.1
111	M and E Manufacturing Company Inc—*Jeff Weinberger*	PO Box 1548, Kingston NY 12402	845-331-2110	R	7*	<.1
112	Carruthers Equipment Co—*Gary Wygal*	441 30th St, Astoria OR 97103	503-861-2273	R	7*	<.1
113	Acadian Fine Foods LLC—*Lance Roberie*	329 S Main St, Church Point LA 70525	337-684-3045	R	6*	.1
114	Tri-Pak Machinery Inc—*David Fitzgerald*	PO Box 1228, Harlingen TX 78551	956-423-5140	R	6*	.1
115	Carver Inc—*Steve Marbut*	PO Box 4259, Savannah GA 31407	912-447-9000	S	6*	<.1
116	Hughes Company Incorporated Of Columbus—*Jefferey Powell*	1200 W James St, Columbus WI 53925	920-623-2000	R	6*	<.1
117	Superior-Lidgerwood-Mundy Corp—*S Phillips*	PO Box 39, Superior WI 54880	715-394-4444	R	6*	<.1
118	Lifestyle Foods Inc—*Jason Bro*	600 N Hartley St Ste 1, York PA 17404	717-718-5423	R	6*	<.1
119	Kb Systems Inc—*Karl Brunner*	PO Box 229, Bangor PA 18013	610-588-7788	R	6*	<.1
120	Automated Process Equipment Corp—*Kendall Wilcox*	1201 4th Ave, Lake Odessa MI 48849	616-374-1000	R	5*	<.1
121	Coastline Equipment Inc—*Kurt Lunde*	2235 E Bakerview Rd, Bellingham WA 98226	360-734-8509	R	5*	<.1
122	Savage Brothers Co—*M Floreani*	1125 Lunt Ave, Elk Grove Village IL 60007	847-981-3000	R	5*	<.1
123	Union Standard Equipment Co—*Andrew Greenberg*	801-825 E 141st St, Bronx NY 10454	718-585-0200	R	5*	.1
124	Del Packaging Ltd—*Loretta Mylius*	18113 Telge Rd, Cypress TX 77429	281-653-0099	R	5*	<.1
125	Tech-Mark Inc—*Gildo Martini*	PO Box 1569, Clackamas OR 97015	503-655-6117	R	5*	<.1
126	Sort-Rite International Inc—*Willam Capt*	PO Box 1805, Harlingen TX 78551	956-423-2427	R	5*	<.1
127	American Extrusion International Corp—*Richard Warner*	498 Prairie Hill Rd, South Beloit IL 61080	815-624-6616	R	5*	<.1
128	Gea Intec LLC	4319 S Alston Ave Ste, Durham NC 27713	919-433-0131	S	5*	<.1
129	Grove Dale Corp—*Stephanie Mattos*	1501 Stone Creek Dr, San Jose CA 95132	408-251-7220	R	5*	<.1
130	A-One Manufacturing LLC—*Debbie Denney*	549 Evergreen Rd, Strafford MO 65757	417-736-2195	R	5*	<.1
131	Atwood Corp—*Edward Mentz*	14151 Irving Ave, Dolton IL 60419	708-841-0959	R	4*	<.1
132	Unitherm Food Systems Inc—*David Howard*	502 Industrial Rd, Bristow OK 74010	918-367-0197	R	4*	<.1
133	Potential Design Inc—*William Tjerrild*	4185 E Jefferson Ave, Fresno CA 93725	559-834-5361	R	4*	<.1
134	Sidney Manufacturing Company Inc—*Jon Baker*	PO Box 380, Sidney OH 45365	937-492-4154	R	4*	<.1
135	Starflex Corp—*Michael Wilson*	204 Turner Rd, Jonesboro GA 30236	770-471-2111	R	4*	<.1
136	Food Design Inc—*Joseph Mistretta*	PO Box 2449, Wilsonville OR 97070	503-685-5030	R	4*	<.1
137	Cookshack Inc—*Stuart Powell*	2304 N Ash St, Ponca City OK 74601	580-765-3669	R	4*	<.1
138	F and S Engraving Inc—*James Fromm*	1620 W Central Rd, Mount Prospect IL 60056	847-870-8400	R	4*	<.1
139	SE C Inc—*Juanita Simmons*	PO Box 546, Dallas GA 30132	770-445-6085	R	4*	<.1
140	Odenberg Inc—*Robert Hunter*	4038 Seaport Blvd, West Sacramento CA 95691	916-371-0700	R	4*	<.1
141	Reed Oven Co—*Kathryn Davies*	PO Box 33414, Kansas City MO 64120	816-842-7446	R	4*	<.1
142	CMI Equipment and Engineering Co—*Althea Mathwig*	41663 170th St, Glencoe MN 55336	320-864-5894	R	4*	<.1
143	Gregor Jonsson Associates Inc—*Frank Heurich*	13822 W Laurel Dr, Lake Forest IL 60045	847-247-4200	R	4*	<.1
144	Hot Food Boxes Inc—*John Schirico*	PO Box 1089, Mooresville IN 46158	773-533-5912	R	4*	<.1
145	Machine Building Specialties Inc—*Dennis Conaway*	1977 Blake Ave, Los Angeles CA 90039	323-666-8340	R	4*	<.1
146	Nothum Manufacturing Co—*Robert Nothum*	631 S Kansas Ave, Springfield MO 65802	417-831-2816	R	4*	<.1
147	Pisces Fish Machinery Inc—*Trevor Wastell*	PO Box 189, Wells MI 49894	906-789-1636	R	4*	<.1
148	Alliance Products LLC—*Francisco Bonilla*	820 Esther Ln, Murfreesboro TN 37129	615-895-5333	R	4*	<.1
149	Packers Manufacturing Inc—*Dwight Plumley*	30467 Rd 158, Visalia CA 93292	559-732-4886	R	3*	<.1
150	M W Waldrop Co—*Wayne Waldrop*	8125 Kempwood Dr, Houston TX 77055	713-337-5600	R	3*	<.1
151	Frost Engineering Inc—*Charles Frost*	3408 Beekman St, Cincinnati OH 45223	513-541-6330	R	3*	<.1
152	ET Oakes Corp—*W Oakes*	686 Old Willets Path, Hauppauge NY 11788	631-232-0002	R	3*	<.1
153	Emi Inc—*James Donkin*	4 Heritage Park Rd, Clinton CT 06413	860-669-1199	R	3*	<.1
154	Dairy-Tek Industries Inc—*Richard Smith*	PO Box 1330, Pomona CA 91769	909-623-3174	R	3*	<.1
155	Weidenmiller Co—*Charles Fortner*	1464 Industrial Dr, Itasca IL 60143	630-250-2500	R	3*	<.1
156	Goodnature Products Inc—*Dale E Wettlaufer*	3860 California Rd, Orchard Park NY 14127	716-855-3325	R	3*	<.1
157	More Than Bread Inc—*Giuseppe Consarino*	5755 Spring Mountain R, Las Vegas NV 89146	702-253-5686	R	3*	<.1
158	G J Olney Inc—*G Olney*	PO Box 280, Westerville NY 13486	315-827-4208	R	3*	<.1
159	L and W Equipment Inc—*Roger Pugh*	210 Kerr Ave, Poteau OK 74953	918-647-5101	R	3*	<.1
160	H Putsch and Co—*Carl Christian*	PO Box 5128, Asheville NC 28813	828-684-0671	S	3*	<.1
161	Ripon Manufacturing Co—*Glenn Navarro*	652 S Stockton Ave, Ripon CA 95366	209-599-2148	R	3*	<.1
162	Skipper Rota Corp—*C Fitch*	PO Box 219, South Holland IL 60473	708-331-0660	R	3*	<.1
163	Norvell Company Inc—*Alan Hale*	4002 Liberty Bell Rd, Fort Scott KS 66701	620-223-3110	R	3*	<.1
164	Mc Brady Engineering Inc—*William Brady*	PO Box 2549, Joliet IL 60434	815-744-8900	R	2*	<.1
165	Dorado Seafood Inc—*Andre Alba*	211 W Orange Grove Ave, Burbank CA 91502	818-843-6100	R	2*	<.1
166	Cobatco Inc—*Donald Stephens*	1215 Ne Adams St, Peoria IL 61603	309-676-2663	R	2*	<.1
167	Towne Machine Tool Co—*Clinton Towne*	PO Box 685, Danville IL 61834	217-442-4910	R	2*	<.1
168	Flodin Inc—*John Flodin*	13624 N Frontage Rd E, Moses Lake WA 98837	509-766-2996	R	2*	<.1
169	Midwest B R D Inc—*Duane Corkill*	11731 Sw 49th St, Topeka KS 66610	785-256-6054	R	2*	<.1
170	Lowe Industries Inc—*Jim Schmitt*	PO Box 626, Marion IA 52302	319-447-9724	R	2*	<.1
171	Ralph W Cook—*Ralph Cook*	PO Box 1073, Dunedin FL 34697	727-796-1367	R	2*	<.1
172	Custom Systems Inc—*Robert Stanford*	PO Box 1738, Granite City IL 62040	314-355-4575	R	2*	<.1
173	Mmyb Inc—*Martin Weibye*	PO Box 341, Parkers Prairie MN 56361	218-338-5000	R	2*	<.1
174	NA Bar Inc—*Ramlakhan Boodram*	PO Box 6599, Champaign IL 61826	217-687-4810	R	2*	<.1
175	Empire Metal Manufacturing Inc—*Pam Iannone*	305 Tremont St, Rochester NY 14608	585-436-2870	R	2*	<.1
176	Versaco Manufacturing Inc—*Alan Owens*	550 E Luchessa Ave, Gilroy CA 95020	408-848-2880	R	2*	<.1
177	Shaver Specialty Co Inc—*George Shaver*	20608 Earl St, Torrance CA 90503	310-370-6941	R	2*	<.1
178	Wemco Inc—*Brandon Goodwin*	11721 S Austin Ave, Alsip IL 60803	708-388-1980	R	2*	<.1
179	Unified Brands—*Eddie Adkins*	1055 Mendell Davis Dr, Jackson MS 39212	601-372-3903	S	1	.5
180	General Machinery Corp—*Michael Horwitz*	PO Box 717, Sheboygan WI 53082	920-458-2189	R	1*	<.1
181	AB Mclauchlan Company Inc—*John Layton*	PO Box 12006, Salem OR 97309	503-363-8611	R	1*	<.1
182	Women's Bean Project—*Tamra Ryan*	3201 Curtis St, Denver CO 80205	303-292-1919	R	1*	<.1
183	Garroutte Inc—*Eugene Teeter*	151 Kearney St, Watsonville CA 95076	831-722-2487	R	1*	.1
184	LH Corp—*Clemens Claparede*	4945 Stepp Pl, Dublin VA 24084	540-674-8803	R	1*	<.1
185	Food Instrument Corp—*Richard Kudlich*	PO Box 66, Federalsburg MD 21632	410-754-5714	R	1*	<.1
186	Cook And Beals Inc—*Patrick Kuehl*	PO Box 220, Loup City NE 68853	308-745-0154	R	1*	<.1
187	Spiral-Matic Inc—*Daniel Mc Phail*	7772 Park Pl, Brighton MI 48116	248-486-5080	R	1*	<.1
188	Dantco Corp—*Michael Antuono*	9 Oak St, Paterson NJ 07501	973-278-8776	R	1*	<.1
189	MD Holdings LLC—*Lynn Haddix*	PO Box 1089, Mooresville IN 46158	317-831-7030	R	1*	<.1

TOTALS: SIC 3556 Food Products Machinery
Companies: 189

					4,247	27.9

3559 Special Industry Machinery Nec

Rank	Company Name—*Executive Officer*	Address, City, State, Zip	Phone	Type	Fin	Empls
1	Dover Corp—*Robert A Livingston*	3005 Highland Pkwy Ste, Downers Grove IL 60515	630-541-1540	P	7,133	32.0
2	Lam Research Corp—*Martin Anstice*	PO Box 5010, Fremont CA 94536	510-572-0200	P	2,134	3.2
3	Fluid Management Operations LLC—*Andrew K Silvernail* Fluid Management Inc	1023 Wheeling Rd, Wheeling IL 60090	847-537-0880	S	1,935*	4.3
4	FM Delaware Inc—*Andrew K Silvernail*	1023 Wheeling Rd, Wheeling IL 60090	847-537-0880	S	1,935*	4.3

Note: An asterisk (*) indicates an estimated financial figure. The company type code used is as follows: R = Private, P = Public, S = Private Subsidiary, B = Public Subsidiary, D = Division, J = Joint Venture, I = Investment Fund.

COMPANY RANKINGS BY SALES WITHIN 4-DIGIT SIC

Rank	Company Name—*Executive Officer*	Address, City, State, Zip	Phone	Type	Fin	Empls
	Fluid Management Inc					
5	Knight LLC—*George Noa*	20531 Crescent Bay Dr, Lake Forest CA 92630	949-595-4800	S	1,889*	4.2
	Fluid Management Inc					
6	GE Infrastructure Water and Process Technologies—*George Oliver*	4636 Somerton Rd, Trevose PA 19053	215-355-3300	S	1,769*	4.0
7	Novellus Systems Inc—*Richard S Hill*	4000 N First St, San Jose CA 95134	408-943-9700	P	1,353	2.9
8	ASM Lithography Holding Inc—*Eric Meurice*	8555 S River Pkwy, Tempe AZ 85284	480-383-4422	S	1,022*	2.5
9	Veeco Instruments Inc—*John R Peeler*	Terminal Dr, Plainview NY 11803	516-677-0200	P	979	.9
10	Varian Semiconductor Equipment Associates Inc—*Gary Dickerson*	35 Dory Rd, Gloucester MA 01930	978-282-2000	S	832	1.5
11	FEI Co—*Don R Kania*	5350 NE Dawson Creek D, Hillsboro OR 97124	503-726-7500	P	826	2.0
12	MI 2009 Inc—*Dennis Smith*	4165 Half Acre Rd, Batavia OH 45103	513-487-5000	R	808	3.4
13	Brooks Automation Inc—*Stephen S Schwartz*	15 Elizabeth Dr, Chelmsford MA 01824	978-262-2400	P	688	1.4
14	SPX Corporation Kent Moore—*Christopher Kearney*	13515 Ballantyne Corpo, Charlotte NC 28277	704-752-4400	D	606*	4.0
15	Cymer Inc—*Bob Akins*	17075 Thornmint Ct, San Diego CA 92127	858-385-7300	P	594	1.1
16	Gerber Scientific Inc—*Marc T Giles*	24 Industrial Park Rd, Tolland CT 06084	860-870-2890	S	463	1.8
17	Crossing Automation Inc—*Aaron Tachibana*	46897 Bayside Pkwy, Fremont CA 94538	510-661-5000	R	457	1.0
18	Fanuc Robotics America Corp—*Richard Schneider*	3900 W Hamlin Rd, Rochester Hills MI 48309	248-377-7000	R	445*	1.1
19	Universal Instruments Corp—*Gerhard Meese*	PO Box 825, Binghamton NY 13902	607-779-7522	S	389*	1.1
20	Tokyo Electron America Inc—*Barry Mayer*	PO Box 17200, Austin TX 78760	512-424-1000	R	372*	1.0
21	Toppan Photomasks Inc—*David S Murray*	400 Texas Ave, Round Rock TX 78664	512-310-6500	S	354	1.6
22	GE Ionics Inc—*Douglas R Brown*	4636 Somerton Rd, Trevose PA 19053	215-355-3300	S	347	2.4
23	Axcelis Technologies Inc—*Mary G Puma*	108 Cherry Hill Dr, Beverly MA 01915	978-787-4000	P	275	.4
24	Amtech Systems Inc—*Jong S Whang*	131 S Clark Dr, Tempe AZ 85281	480-967-5146	P	247	.4
25	Gerber Scientific Products Inc—*Rod Larson*	83 Gerber Rd, South Windsor CT 06074	860-644-1551	S	214*	.4
	Gerber Scientific Inc					
26	Emcore Corp—*Hong Q Hou PhD*	10420 Research Rd SE B, Albuquerque NM 87123	505-332-5000	P	201	1.0
27	SGE Inc—*Earnest Dawes*	2007 Kramer Ln, Austin TX 78758	512-837-7190	S	195*	.4
28	Celerity Group Inc—*Timmothy Harris*	2645 Zanker Rd Ste 101, San Jose CA 95134	408-935-4500	S	190*	1.1
29	Mattson Technology Inc—*David L Dutton*	47131 Bayside Pkwy, Fremont CA 94538		P	185	.4
30	Welex Inc—*Wayne B Lewis*	1600 Union Meeting Rd, Blue Bell PA 19422	215-542-8000	R	168*	.1
31	FSI International Inc Surface Conditioning Div—*Donald Mitchell*	3455 Lyman Blvd, Chaska MN 55318	952-448-5440	D	166*	.9
	FSI International Inc					
32	American Bio Tech Inc—*John G Laurenson Jr*	3223 Harbor Dr Ste 411, Saint Augustine FL 32084	904-825-1500	R	151*	1.0
33	Katy Industries Inc—*David J Feldman*	305 Rock Industrial Pa, Bridgeton MO 63044	314-656-4321	P	141	.6
34	Ultratech Inc—*Arthur W Zafiropoulo*	3050 Zanker Rd, San Jose CA 95134	408-321-8835	P	141	.3
35	Semitool Inc—*Raymon F Thompson*	655 W Reserve Dr, Kalispell MT 59901	406-752-2107	S	139	.8
36	Conair Group Inc—*Chris Keller*	200 W Kensinger Dr, Cranberry Township PA 16066	724-584-5500	R	122*	.6
37	Wagstaff Inc—*Bill Wagstaff*	3910 N Flora Rd, Spokane WA 99216	509-922-1404	R	111*	.3
38	Electroglas Foreign Sales Corp—*Thomas M Rohrs*	30974 Santana St, Hayward CA 94544	408-528-3000	S	104*	.3
	EG Systems LLC					
39	FSI International Inc—*Donald S Mitchell*	3455 Lyman Blvd, Chaska MN 55318	952-448-5440	P	97	.4
40	Design Systems Inc	38799 W Twelve Mile Rd, Farmington Hills MI 48331	248-489-4300	R	94	.3
41	Global Equipment Company Inc	11 Harbor Park Dr, Port Washington NY 11050	516-625-6200	S	93*	.3
42	Industrial Dynamics Company Ltd—*Steve Calhoun*	PO Box 2945, Torrance CA 90509	310-325-5633	R	93*	.2
43	Americast Metal Products Inc—*Michael Lloyd*	4725 Winfield Rd, Houston TX 77039	281-449-3007	R	88*	.1
44	Electroglas International Inc	30974 Santana St, Hayward CA 94544	408-528-3000	S	85*	.2
	EG Systems LLC					
45	Advanced Semiconductor Materials America—*Charles D del Prado*	3440 E University Dr, Phoenix AZ 85034	602-470-5700	S	83*	.5
46	Intevac Inc—*Kevin Fairbairn*	3560 Bassett St, Santa Clara CA 95054	408-986-9888	P	83	.4
47	BTU International Inc—*Paul J Van der Wansem*	23 Esquire Rd, North Billerica MA 01862	978-667-4111	P	82	.4
48	Akrion Inc—*James S Molinaro*	6330 Hedgewood Dr, Allentown PA 18106	610-391-9200	R	80*	.3
49	Spire Corp—*Roger G Little*	1 Patriots Park, Bedford MA 01730	781-275-6000	P	80	.2
50	FLSmidth Inc—*Jorgen Huno Rasmussen*	2040 Ave C, Bethlehem PA 18017	610-264-6011	S	79*	.1
51	Uniloy Milacron Inc—*Dave Skala*	5550 Occidental Hwy St, Tecumseh MI 49286	517-424-8756	S	75	.5
	MI 2009 Inc					
52	Nikon Precision Inc—*Takao Naito*	1399 Shoreway Rd, Belmont CA 94002	650-508-4674	S	71*	.3
53	Hunter Engineering Co—*Stephen F Brauer*	11250 Hunter Dr, Bridgeton MO 63044	314-731-3020	R	68*	.5
54	Materion Technical Materials Inc—*Al Lubrano*	5 Wellington Rd, Lincoln RI 02865	401-333-1700	S	68	.2
55	Midwestern Industries Inc—*Barbara Sylvester*	PO Box 810, Massillon OH 44648	330-837-4203	R	66*	.1
56	Lucas-Milhaupt Inc—*Phillip Maliet*	5656 S Pennsylvania Av, Cudahy WI 53110	414-769-6000	D	66*	.1
57	Besser Co—*Kevin Curtis*	801 Johnson St, Alpena MI 49707	989-354-4111	R	61*	.8
58	Adept Technology Inc—*John Dulchinos*	5960 Inglewood Dr, Pleasanton CA 94588	925-245-3400	P	58	.2
59	Genus Inc—*William WR Elder*	1139 Karlstad Dr, Sunnyvale CA 94089	408-747-7120	S	57*	.2
60	Datron Dynamics Inc—*Bill King*	115 Emerson Rd, Milford NH 03055	603-672-8890	R	56*	.1
61	ADT Engineering and Machine—*Dan Minor*	PO Box 647, Au Gres MI 48703	989-876-7161	R	54*	.1
62	Arbin Corp—*John Zhang*	762 Peach Creek Cut Of, College Station TX 77845	979-690-2751	R	52*	.1
63	Jacobs Applied Technology Inc—*Craig L Martin*	PO Box 63125, Charleston SC 29419	843-824-1100	S	50*	.3
64	Decision Systems Inc—*Peter Voss*	2935 Woodcliff Dr Nw, Canton OH 44718	330-456-7600	R	49*	.2
65	Small Precision Tools Inc—*Bob Whitlock*	1330 Clegg St, Petaluma CA 94954	707-765-4545	S	49*	.2
66	Mcelroy Manufacturing Inc—*Arthur Mcelroy*	PO Box 580550, Tulsa OK 74158	918-831-9214	R	48*	.3
67	Energy Recovery Inc—*Thomas S Rooney Jr*	1717 Doolittle Dr, San Leandro CA 94577	510-483-7370	P	46	.1
68	Essex Industries Inc—*Keith Guller*	7700 Gravois Rd, Saint Louis MO 63123	314-832-4500	R	46*	.3
69	EG Systems LLC—*Raj Kaul*	30974 Santana St, Hayward CA 94544	408-528-3000	P	45	.2
70	Tks Industrial Co—*Masami Denawa*	901 Tower Dr Ste 150, Troy MI 48098	248-786-5000	R	43*	.1
71	Burke E Porter Machinery Co—*Andrew Murch*	730 Plymouth Ave NE, Grand Rapids MI 49505	616-234-1200	R	43*	.2
72	Orcon Corp—*Hollis Bascom*	1570 Atlantic St, Union City CA 94587	510-489-8100	R	41*	.3
73	Wellons Inc—*Martin Nye*	2525 W Firestone Ln, Vancouver WA 98660	360-750-3500	R	39*	.4
74	SAES Pure Gas Inc—*Tim Johnson*	4175 Santa Fe Rd, San Luis Obispo CA 93401	805-541-9299	S	37*	.1
75	Able Builders Equipment—*Stanford Freedman*	7475 NW 63rd St, Miami FL 33166	305-592-5940	R	36*	.1
76	Nachi Robotic Systems Inc—*Y Takeuchi*	22285 Roethel Dr, Novi MI 48375	248-305-6545	S	34*	.1
77	Fluid Management Inc	1023 Wheeling Rd, Wheeling IL 60090	847-537-0880	D	33*	.2
78	Brunner-Hildebrand Lumber Dry Kiln Co—*Rein Juergen*	125 Belle Forest Cir S, Nashville TN 37221	615-662-0745	R	30*	.2
79	White Industries LLC—*Charles Abbott*	309 Exchange Ave, Conway AR 72032		S	30*	.1
80	Lummus Corp—*Stephen Marbut*	PO Box 4259, Savannah GA 31407	912-447-9000	R	29*	.2
81	Morrison Brothers Co—*Charles Glab*	PO Box 238, Dubuque IA 52004	563-583-5701	R	29*	.1
82	Kobelco Stewart Bolling Inc—*Atsushi Shigeno*	1600 Terex Rd, Hudson OH 44236	330-655-3111	R	28*	.1

Rank	Company Name—*Executive Officer*	Address, City, State, Zip	Phone	Type	Fin	Empls
83	United Silicone Inc	4471 Walden Ave, Lancaster NY 14086	716-681-8222	S	28*	.1
84	Custom Machine Inc—*Carl Pasciuto*	30 Nashua St, Woburn MA 01801	781-935-4940	R	27*	.1
85	ITT Water and Wastewater USA Inc	14125 S Bridge Cir, Charlotte NC 28273	704-409-9700	S	25*	.1
86	Jim Coleman Co—*Jim Coleman*	5842 W 34th St, Houston TX 77092	713-683-9878	R	25*	.1
87	American Metal Wash Inc—*Steven Nourie*	360 Euclid Ave, Canonsburg PA 15317	724-746-4203	R	25*	N/A
88	Natoli Engineering Company Inc—*Carmelo Natoli*	PO Box Dept XX 66971, Saint Louis MO 63160	636-926-8900	R	25*	.2
89	Tom Richards Inc—*Tom Richards*	PO Box 660, Mentor OH 44061	440-974-1300	R	24*	.2
90	Mcneil and Nrm Intl Inc—*F Yared*	96 E Crosier St, Akron OH 44311	330-253-2525	R	23*	.2
91	Materials Transportation Co—*William Jones*	PO Box 1358, Temple TX 76503	254-298-2900	R	23*	.2
92	Sartorius Stedim Systems Inc—*Mary Lavin*	5 Orville Dr Ste 200, Bohemia NY 11716	631-588-2737	R	23*	.1
93	Continental Eagle Corp—*Roger Fermon*	PO Box 1000, Prattville AL 36067	334-365-8811	R	23*	.2
94	Hantronix Inc—*Wayne Choi*	10080 Bubb Rd, Cupertino CA 95014	408-522-1100	R	22*	<.1
95	J C Steele And Sons Inc—*David Steele*	PO Box 1834, Statesville NC 28687	704-872-3681	R	22*	.1
96	Chemineer Inc—*John Fenic*	PO Box 1123, Dayton OH 45401		S	22*	.2
97	Contact Systems Inc—*John Pompea*	50 Miry Brook Rd, Danbury CT 06810	203-743-3837	R	21*	.1
98	Pantograms Manufacturing Co—*John Colman*	4537 S Dale Mabry Hwy, Tampa FL 33611	813-839-5697	R	21*	.1
99	Rhetech Inc—*Vince McGinty* Semitool Inc	416 S 4th St, Coopersburg PA 18036	610-282-0105	S	21*	.1
100	Smith and Richardson Manufacturing Company Inc—*Phil Cowen*	PO Box 589, Geneva IL 60134	630-232-2581	R	21*	<.1
101	Stellar Industries Inc—*David Zrostlik*	PO Box 169, Garner IA 50438	641-923-3741	R	21*	.2
102	Greystone Logistics Inc—*Warren F Kruger*	1613 E 15th St, Tulsa OK 74120		P	21	.1
103	Acme Cryogenics Inc—*Frank Hartzell*	PO Box 445, Allentown PA 18105	610-791-7909	R	20*	.1
104	Gardner Cryogenics—*Gary T Strobl*	2136 City Line Rd, Bethlehem PA 18017	610-264-4523	D	20*	.2
105	Chart Cryogenic Components—*Samuel Thomas*	1 Infinity Corporate C, Garfield Heights OH 44125	440-753-1490	D	20*	.1
106	Bell Equipment Co—*James Bell*	78 Northpointe Dr, Lake Orion MI 48359	248-370-0000	R	20*	<.1
107	Ged Integrated Solutions Inc—*William Weaver*	9280 Dutton Dr, Twinsburg OH 44087	330-963-5401	R	20*	.1
108	Mei LLC—*Dan Cappello*	3838 Western Way Ne, Albany OR 97321	541-917-3626	R	20*	.2
109	Engel Machinery Inc—*Walter Jungwirth*	3740 Board Rd, York PA 17406	717-764-6818	R	19*	.1
110	Surface Mount Technology Corp—*Christopher Sumnicht*	5660 Technology Cir, Appleton WI 54914	920-954-8324	R	19*	.1
111	Kiefel Inc—*Bob Hawkins*	475 Washington St, Wrentham MA 02093	508-384-1200	S	19*	<.1
112	Thomas Engineering Inc—*Joseph Kingsley*	575 W Central Rd, Hoffman Estates IL 60192	847-358-5800	R	18*	.1
113	Hexco International—*Ross Brown*	25720 Jefferson Ave, Murrieta CA 92562	951-696-7840	R	18*	.1
114	Shredding Systems Inc—*Thomas Garnier*	9760 SW Freeman Dr, Wilsonville OR 97070	503-682-3633	R	18*	.1
115	Hennessy Industries Inc—*Tim Gilmore*	PO Box 3002, La Vergne TN 37086	615-641-7533	S	18*	.1
116	Cannon USA Inc—*Paolo Spinelli*	1235 Freedom Rd, Cranberry Township PA 16066	724-772-5600	R	18*	.1
117	Maida Development Co—*Edward Maida*	PO Box 3529, Hampton VA 23663	757-723-0785	R	18*	.2
118	Burton Industries Inc (Goodrich Michigan)—*David J Yanniello*	PO Box 279, Goodrich MI 48438	810-636-2215	R	17*	.1
119	RCBS Operations—*Allan Jernigan*	605 Oro Dam Blvd, Oroville CA 95965	530-533-5191	R	17*	.1
120	Really Innovations LLC—*Really Nolen*	605 Townsend Rd, Cocoa FL 32926	321-631-2414	R	17*	<.1
121	Billco Manufacturing Inc—*William Billinger*	100 Halstead Blvd, Zelienople PA 16063	724-452-7390	R	17*	.1
122	Cp Manufacturing Inc—*Robert Davis*	1300 Wilson Ave, National City CA 91950	619-477-3175	R	17*	.1
123	CVD Equipment Corp—*Leonard A Rosenbaum*	1860 Smithtown Ave, Ronkonkoma NY 11779	631-981-7081	P	16	.1
124	Solid State Equipment Corp—*Richard Richardson*	185 Gibraltar Rd, Horsham PA 19044	215-328-0700	R	16*	.1
125	Lyman Products Corp—*J Thompson*	475 Smith St, Middletown CT 06457	860-632-2020	R	16*	.1
126	Intertec Corp—*Fred Paulsen*	PO Box 2927, Toledo OH 43606	419-537-9711	R	16*	.2
127	FLAVORx Inc—*Kenneth L Kramm*	9475 Gerwig Ln, Columbia MD 21046		R	16*	.1
128	New Logic Research Inc—*Gregory Johnson*	1295 67th St, Emeryville CA 94608	510-655-7305	R	16*	.1
129	Midbrook Inc—*Joanne Houghton*	PO Box 867, Jackson MI 49204	517-787-3481	R	16*	.1
130	Vacuum Barrier Corp—*Russell Blanton*	PO Box 529, Woburn MA 01801	781-933-3570	R	16*	<.1
131	Eckhart and Associates—*Richard Girth*	16185 National Pkwy, Lansing MI 48906	517-321-7700	R	16*	<.1
132	S and H Metal Works and Manufacturing Inc—*Oliver Shadden*	2501 E Dubuque, Lubbock TX 79401		R	16*	<.1
133	Grenzebach Corp—*Stefan Grenzebach*	10 Herring Rd, Newnan GA 30265	770-253-4980	R	15*	.1
134	Union Special LLC	1 Union Special Plz, Huntley IL 60142	847-669-5101	R	15*	.1
135	Wirtz Manufacturing Company Inc—*John Wirtz*	PO Box 5006, Port Huron MI 48061	810-987-4700	R	15*	.1
136	Granutech-Saturn Systems Corp—*Glen E Newton*	201 E Shady Grove Rd, Grand Prairie TX 75050	972-790-7800	R	15*	.1
137	Huntington Mechanical Laboratories Inc—*Tom Frantz*	310 Colfax Ave, Grass Valley CA 95945	650-964-3323	R	15*	<.1
138	DuBois Equipment Company Inc—*Jim Arvin*	PO Box 749, Jasper IN 47547	812-482-3644	R	15*	<.1
139	Lanco Assembly Systems Inc—*Thomas Zack*	12 Thomas Dr, Westbrook ME 04092	207-773-2060	R	15*	.1
140	Aceco Precision Industrial Knives—*Raleigh Jensen*	4419 S Federal Way, Boise ID 83716	208-343-7712	R	15*	.1
141	Hunter Automated Machinery Corp—*William Hunter*	2222 Hammond Dr, Schaumburg IL 60196	847-397-5110	R	15*	.1
142	B and P Process Equipment And Systems LLC—*Robert Naglick*	1000 Hess Ave, Saginaw MI 48601	989-757-1300	R	14*	.1
143	Giffin Inc—*Donald Giffin*	1900 Brown Rd, Auburn Hills MI 48326	248-340-0726	R	14*	.1
144	CRC-Evans Pipeline International Inc—*M Timothy Carey*	20445 State Hwy 249 St, Houston TX 77070	832-249-3100	S	14*	.1
145	Scott Equipment Co—*Richard Lucas*	605 4th Ave Nw, New Prague MN 56071	952-758-2591	R	14*	.1
146	PRAB Inc—*Ned Thompson*	PO Box 2121, Kalamazoo MI 49003	269-382-8200	R	14*	.1
147	Kw Products Inc—*David Parks*	500 57th St, Marion IA 52302	319-377-9421	R	14*	.1
148	M E Baker Co—*Stephen Roiter*	945 Concord St, Framingham MA 01701	508-620-5304	R	14*	.1
149	Artisan Industries Inc—*Richard Giberti*	73 Pond St, Waltham MA 02451	781-893-6800	R	13*	.1
150	Con-Syst-Int Group Inc—*Lewis Bodner*	14200 Frazho Rd, Warren MI 48089	586-779-7914	R	13*	.1
151	Shopsmith Inc—*John R Folkerth*	6530 Poe Ave, Dayton OH 45414	937-898-6070	R	13*	.1
152	Walton-Stout Inc—*Joe Walton*	6863 Chapman Rd, Lithonia GA 30058	770-482-4613	R	13*	.1
153	Ultrablend LLC—*Spencer Berg*	1440 Westernghse Blvd, Charlotte NC 28273	704-504-8969	R	13*	<.1
154	Lci Corporation International—*Lacey Hayes*	PO Box 16348, Charlotte NC 28297	704-394-8341	R	13*	.1
155	Tnt Steel Industries Inc—*Adam Auld*	1555 Hwy 75 E, Freeport IL 61032	815-233-0022	R	13*	.1
156	Starco Enterprises Inc—*Jerry Ulrich*	3137 E 26th St, Vernon CA 90058	323-266-7111	R	12*	.1
157	Anderson Tool and Engineering Company Inc—*Ted Fiock*	PO Box 1158, Anderson IN 46015	765-643-6691	R	12*	.1
158	Hockmeyer Equipment Corp—*Herman Hockmeyer*	610 Supor Blvd Ste 1, Harrison NJ 07029	973-482-0225	R	12*	.1
159	R and B Plastics Machinery LLC—*Ray Crandle*	1605 Woodland Dr, Saline MI 48176	734-429-9421	R	12*	.1
160	J and S Industrial Machine Products Inc—*Nancy Colyer*	123 Oakdale Ave, Toledo OH 43605	419-691-1380	R	12*	.1
161	French Oil Mill Machinery Co—*Daniel French*	PO Box 920, Piqua OH 45356	937-773-3420	R	12*	.1
162	Thermwood Corp—*Kenneth J Susnjara*	PO Box 436, Dale IN 47523	812-937-4476	P	11	.2
163	Gaston Electronics LLC—*Richard Knorr*	PO Box 308, Stanley NC 28164	704-822-5001	R	11*	.1
164	Tompkins Metal Finishing Inc—*Allen Tompkins*	6 Apollo Dr, Batavia NY 14020	585-344-2600	R	11*	.1
165	Boride Products—*Carlos Cardoso*	2879 Aero Park Dr, Traverse City MI 49686	231-946-2100	D	11*	.1
166	Ganzcorp Investments Inc—*Dean Ganzhorn*	2300 Pinnacle Pkwy, Twinsburg OH 44087	330-963-5400	R	11*	.1
167	Ozonia North America Inc—*Anthony Dusovic*	600 Willow Tree Rd, Leonia NJ 07605	201-676-2525	R	11*	.1
168	Hause Machines Inc—*James Fruchey*	PO Box 229, Montpelier OH 43543	419-485-3158	R	11*	.1
169	Peaker Services Inc—*Ian Bradbury*	8080 Kensington Ct, Brighton MI 48116	248-437-4174	R	11*	<.1

Note: An asterisk (*) indicates an estimated financial figure. The company type code used is as follows: R = Private, P = Public, S = Private Subsidiary, B = Public Subsidiary, D = Division, J = Joint Venture, I = Investment Fund.

COMPANY RANKINGS BY SALES WITHIN 4-DIGIT SIC

Rank	Company Name—Executive Officer	Address, City, State, Zip	Phone	Type	Fin	Empls
170	AZO Inc—Robert Moore	PO Box 181070, Memphis TN 38181	901-794-9480	R	11*	<.1
171	Rao Design International Inc—Rao Murukurthy	9451 Ainslie St, Schiller Park IL 60176	847-671-6182	R	11*	.1
172	Polyumac Inc—Mariella Vazquez	1060 E 30th St, Hialeah FL 33013	305-691-9093	R	11*	.1
173	Processing Technologies Inc—Dana Hanson	2655 White Oak Cir, Aurora IL 60502	630-585-5800	R	11*	.1
174	American Maplan Corp—Kurt Waldhauer	PO Box 832, Mcpherson KS 67460	620-241-6843	R	10*	.1
175	Service Engineering Inc—Ryan Jennings	PO Box 5001, Greenfield IN 46140	317-467-2000	R	10*	.1
176	Sebright Products Inc—Brent Sebright	PO Box 296, Hopkins MI 49328	269-793-7183	R	10	.1
177	ELVO Div—Sigrid Fuchs	140 Kisco Ave, Mount Kisco NY 10549	914-241-7080	D	10*	.1
178	Trion Technology—Randy Crockett	2131 Sunnydale Blvd, Clearwater FL 33765	727-461-1888	R	10*	.1
179	Dac International Inc—James Drain	6390 Rose Ln, Carpinteria CA 93013	805-684-8307	R	10*	<.1
180	Saf-Tee Siping and Grooving Inc—Wesley Sprunk	3451 S 40th St, Phoenix AZ 85040	602-437-5020	R	10*	<.1
181	Application Engineering Inc—Peter Mosher	1310 Kalamazoo St, South Haven MI 49090	269-639-7229	R	10*	<.1
182	Mannhardt Inc—John Williams	511 Broadway St Ste 1, Sheboygan Falls WI 53085	920-467-1027	R	10*	.1
183	Ube Machinery Inc—Mitsuhiro Kawamura	5700 S State Rd, Ann Arbor MI 48108	734-741-7000	R	10*	.1
184	Black Clawson-Sano Inc—Jan Ivey	8798 Honeycomb Path, Cicero NY 13039	315-598-7121	R	10*	.1
185	Technifab Products Inc—Noel Short	PO Box 315, Brazil IN 47834	812-442-0520	R	10*	.1
186	Cps Color Equipment Inc—Daniel Bush	7295 Westwinds Blvd Nw, Concord NC 28027	704-588-8408	R	9*	.1
187	Franklin Miller Inc—William Galanty	60 Okner Pkwy, Livingston NJ 07039	973-535-9200	R	9*	.1
188	Curtis Dyna-Fog Ltd—Conrad McGinnis	PO Box 297, Westfield IN 46074	317-896-2561	R	9*	.1
189	Pro Quip Inc—Harry Abraham	850 Highland Rd E, Macedonia OH 44056	330-468-1850	R	9*	.1
190	Cryomech Inc—Peter Gifford	113 Falso Dr, Syracuse NY 13211	315-455-2555	R	9*	.1
191	Alliance Winding Equipment Inc—Keith Moser	3939 Vanguard Dr, Fort Wayne IN 46809	260-478-2200	R	9*	.1
192	Zed Industries Inc—Peter Zelnick	PO Box 458, Vandalia OH 45377	937-667-8407	R	9*	.1
193	Autec Inc—Thomas Hobby	2500 W Front St, Statesville NC 28677	704-871-9141	R	9*	.1
194	Micafil Inc—Scott Kroencke	5079 Kitridge Rd, Dayton OH 45424	937-233-0233	S	9*	.1
195	Mac Engineering And Equipment Company Inc—Al Levin	2775 Meadowbrook Rd, Benton Harbor MI 49022	269-925-3295	R	9*	.1
196	Industrial Tool Inc—Richard C Lueck	9210 52nd Ave N, Minneapolis MN 55428	763-533-7244	R	9	<.1
197	Compu Graphics—Mark Crownover	120 Albright Way Ste C, Los Gatos CA 95032	408-341-1600	S	9*	<.1
198	Links Medical Products Inc—Thomas Buckley	9247 Research Dr, Irvine CA 92618	949-753-0001	R	9*	<.1
199	Swanson Systems Inc—Douglas Swanson	PO Box 1217, Erie PA 16512	814-453-5841	R	9*	<.1
200	Imtec Acculine Inc—Paul Mendes	49036 Milmont Dr, Fremont CA 94538	510-770-1800	R	9*	<.1
201	Encap Technologies Inc—Griffith Neal	666 S Vermont St, Palatine IL 60067	847-548-0600	R	9*	.1
202	Golden By-Products Inc—James Barstow	PO Box 1, Ballico CA 95303	209-668-4855	R	9*	.1
203	Royal Design and Manufacturing Inc—Rodney Paulick	32401 Stephenson Hwy, Madison Heights MI 48071	248-588-0110	R	9*	.1
204	Findlay Machine Tool Inc—Joseph Kirk	PO Box 1562, Findlay OH 45839	419-422-0768	R	9*	.1
205	Cosmodyne LLC—Frank Andrews	3010 Old Ranch Pkwy St, Seal Beach CA 90740	562-795-5990	R	9*	.1
206	Jomar Corp—William Petrino	PO Box 1020, Pleasantville NJ 08232	609-646-8000	R	9*	.1
207	Foremost Machine Builders Inc—Marlene Heydenreich	PO Box 10155, Fairfield NJ 07004	973-227-0700	R	8*	.1
208	Dedoes Industries Inc—Nancy Amberger	1060 W W Maple Rd, Walled Lake MI 48390	248-624-7710	R	8*	.1
209	March Plasma Systems Inc—Peter F Bierhuis	2470 Bates Ave, Concord CA 94520	925-827-1240	S	8*	.1
210	Carl Herrmann Associates—Richard Roth	4201 Business Ctr Dr, Fremont CA 94538	510-683-8554	R	8*	<.1
211	Industrial Tools Inc—Donald Murphy	1111 S Rose Ave, Oxnard CA 93033	805-483-1111	R	8*	.1
212	Herr Industrial Inc—Timothy Herr	PO Box 5249, Lancaster PA 17606	717-569-6619	R	8*	.1
213	Designetics Inc—Craig Williams	1624 Eber Rd, Holland OH 43528	419-866-0700	R	8*	.1
214	Sweed Machinery Inc—Scott Ashpole	PO Box 228, Gold Hill OR 97525	541-855-1512	R	8*	.1
215	Blackstone Ultrasonics Inc—Tim Piazza	PO Box 220, Jamestown NY 14702	716-665-2340	R	8*	.1
216	Noah Precision LLC—Pete Adams	2501 SE Columbia Way S, Vancouver WA 98661	360-993-1395	S	8*	.1
217	Pfeiffer Vacuum Inc—Wolfgang Dondorf	24 Trafalgar Sq, Nashua NH 03063	603-578-6500	S	8*	.1
218	Pillar Technologies Inc—Mark Stoll	PO Box 110, Hartland WI 53029	262-912-7200	D	8*	.1
219	American Baler Co—Dave Kowaleski	800 E Center St, Bellevue OH 44811	419-483-5790	R	8*	<.1
220	Myers Engineering Inc—Gary Myers	8376 Salt Lake Ave, Bell CA 90201	323-560-4723	R	8*	<.1
221	Spadone Hypex Inc—John C Spadone	45 Banner Dr, Milford CT 06460	203-877-1041	S	8*	<.1
222	Straub Design Co—Dennis Schuette	2238 Florida Ave S, Minneapolis MN 55426	952-546-6686	R	8*	<.1
223	LOI Inc—William Wolfe	100 Corporate Center D, Coraopolis PA 15108	412-262-2240	S	8*	<.1
224	Capital Machine Company Inc—William L Koss	2801 Roosevelt Ave, Indianapolis IN 46218	317-638-6661	R	8*	.1
225	Windfield Alloy Inc—Eric Ttlen	2 Rte 111 Ste 2, Atkinson NH 03811	603-329-1230	R	8*	.1
226	MGB Engineering Company Inc—Michael Beladakis	1099 Touhy Ave, Elk Grove Village IL 60007	847-956-7444	R	7*	.1
227	Kirby Lester LLC—Mark Collier	13700 W Irma Lee Ct, Lake Forest IL 60045	847-984-3377	R	7*	<.1
228	Wyko Inc—Woody Linkous	PO Box 130, Greenback TN 37742	865-856-2317	R	7*	.1
229	Fountain Industries Co—Riger Sherping	922 E 14th St, Albert Lea MN 56007	507-373-2351	R	7*	.1
230	Ro-Search Inc	614 Mabry Hood Rd Ste, Knoxville TN 37932		S	7*	<.1
231	Toledo Automated Concepts—Kent Delventhal	619 S Church St, Clyde OH 43410	419-547-0547	R	7*	<.1
232	Fab Fours Bumpers—Greg Higgs	1312 Camp Creek Rd, Lancaster SC 29720	803-416-1100	R	7*	<.1
233	Dynatronix Inc—Dennis Malecek	462 Griffin Blvd, Amery WI 54001	715-268-8118	R	7*	.1
234	Monco Products Inc—Tom Monson	7562 Acacia Ave, Garden Grove CA 92841	714-891-2788	R	7*	.1
235	Maac Machinery Company Inc—Paul Alongi	590 Tower Blvd, Carol Stream IL 60188	630-665-1700	R	7*	.1
236	Latex Equipment Sales and Service Inc—Michael Brown	PO Box 2086, Dalton GA 30722	706-278-0272	R	7*	.1
237	Bargo Engineering Inc—Charles Goforth	PO Box 226, Fayetteville AR 72702	479-442-7711	R	7*	<.1
238	General Machine CoOf New Jersey—Robert Zangara	301 Smalley Ave, Middlesex NJ 08846	732-752-7900	R	7*	<.1
239	Wise Machine Company Inc—Robert Garrard	244 S Cliff St, Butler PA 16001	724-287-2705	R	7*	<.1
240	Aot Inc—Katie Magoteaux	4800 Gateway Blvd, Springfield OH 45502	937-323-9669	R	7*	.1
241	Carl Strutz and Company Inc—Carl Strutz	PO Box 509, Mars PA 16046	724-625-1501	R	7*	.1
242	Linden Industries Inc—Peter Tilgner	137 Ascot Pkwy, Cuyahoga Falls OH 44223	330-928-4064	R	7*	<.1
243	Ecircuits LLC—Richard Limbach	2305 Nw Jeffferson St, Blue Springs MO 64015	816-224-6611	R	7*	<.1
244	John W Kennedy Company Inc—Joanne Kennedy	408 E Montpelier Rd, Montpelier VT 05602	802-224-9020	R	6*	.1
245	General Fabrications Corp—Chester Boraski	PO Box 2461, Sandusky OH 44871	419-625-6055	R	6*	<.1
246	Conforming Matrix Corp—Rick Howell	6255 Suder Ave, Toledo OH 43611	419-729-3777	R	6*	<.1
247	Jensen Fabricating Engineers Inc—Kurt Jensen	555 Wethersfield Rd, Berlin CT 06037	860-828-6516	R	6*	<.1
248	Mc Clean-Anderson Inc—Herbert Liedtke	PO Box 20, Schofield WI 54476	715-355-3006	R	6*	<.1
249	Rocheleau Tool And Die Company Inc—Steven Rocheleau	117 Industrial Rd, Fitchburg MA 01420	978-345-1723	R	6*	<.1
250	Soligen Inc—Yehoram Uziel Soligen Technologies Inc	6849 Woodley Ave, Van Nuys CA 91406	818-285-0692	S	6*	.1
251	Eden Cryogenics LLC—Angie Dimasso	8500 Rausch Dr, Plain City OH 43064	614-873-3949	R	6*	<.1
252	Creative Automation Co—Jack Engel	11641 Pendleton St, Sun Valley CA 91352	818-767-6220	R	6*	<.1
253	Vhc Ltd—Steven Smith	PO Box 310, Winchester IN 47394	765-584-2101	R	6*	<.1
254	PlastiVac Inc—Martin Eichenberger	PO Box 5543, Charlotte NC 28299	704-334-4728	R	6*	<.1
255	MGI Electronics LLC—Diane Butler	1203 W Geneva Dr, Tempe AZ 85282	480-967-8011	R	6*	<.1
256	Technical Glass Products Inc—Jim Horvath	881 Callendar Blvd, Painesville OH 44077	440-639-6399	R	6*	<.1
257	Multiple Systems Inc—Preston Montgomery	PO Box 15025, Amarillo TX 79105	806-373-7073	R	6*	<.1
258	Quantum Engineered Products Inc—Joseph Kozora	438 Saxonburg Blvd, Saxonburg PA 16056	724-352-5100	R	6*	<.1

Rank	Company Name—*Executive Officer*	Address, City, State, Zip	Phone	Type	Fin	Empls
259	Miller Mold Co—*Robert Piesko*	3320 Bay Rd, Saginaw MI 48603	989-793-8881	R	6*	<.1
260	Ranger Automation Systems Inc—*Fidel Ramos*	820 Boston Tpke, Shrewsbury MA 01545	508-842-6500	R	6*	<.1
261	Witte Company Inc—*Richard Witte*	PO Box 47, Washington NJ 07882	908-689-6500	R	6*	<.1
262	Maren Engineering Corp—*Derek Simons*	111 W Taft Dr, South Holland IL 60473	708-333-6250	R	6*	<.1
263	Advanced Illumination Inc—*William Thrailkill*	24 Peavine Dr, Rochester VT 05767	802-767-3830	R	6*	<.1
264	New Gencoat Inc—*Robert Williams*	N53w24900 S Corporate, Sussex WI 53089	262-695-7226	R	5*	<.1
265	Rdn Manufacturing Company Inc—*Robert Decoursey*	160 Covington Dr, Bloomingdale IL 60108	630-893-4500	R	5*	<.1
266	Youngstown Plastic Tooling and Machinery Inc—*Donald Liga*	1209 Velma Ct, Youngstown OH 44512	330-782-7222	R	5*	<.1
267	LS Industries Inc—*Linda Weir-Enegren*	PO Box 1442, Wichita KS 67201	316-265-7997	R	5*	<.1
268	Reynolds Tech Fabricators Inc—*Joan Reynolds*	6895 Kinne St, East Syracuse NY 13057	315-437-0532	R	5*	<.1
269	Soligen Technologies Inc—*Yehoram Uziel*	1356 N Santiago Ave, Santa Ana CA 92701	818-285-0692	R	5*	<.1
270	Acme Manufacturing Co (Auburn Hills Michigan)—*GA Carlson III*	4240 N Atlantic Blvd, Auburn Hills MI 48326	248-393-7300	R	5*	.1
271	Dover Highperformance Plastics Inc—*Mary Schwab*	140 Williams Dr Nw, Dover OH 44622	330-343-3477	R	5*	<.1
272	Can and Bottle Systems Inc—*Bill Janner*	2525 Se Stubb St, Milwaukie OR 97222	503-236-8817	R	5*	<.1
273	Comco Inc—*Neil Weightman*	2151 N Lincoln St, Burbank CA 91504	818-841-5500	R	5*	<.1
274	Equipment Merchants International Inc—*Gerald Senk*	PO Box 94725, Cleveland OH 44101	216-651-6700	R	5*	<.1
275	Schold Machine Corp—*Jerome Tippett*	7201 W 64th Pl, Bedford Park IL 60638	708-458-3788	R	5*	<.1
276	Jaygo Inc—*John Hayday*	675 Rahway Ave, Union NJ 07083	908-688-3600	R	5*	<.1
277	Sturtevant Inc—*W Sturtevant English Jr*	348 Circuit St, Hanover MA 02339	781-829-6501	R	5*	<.1
278	TP Tools and Equipment—*Robert Zwicker*	PO Box 649, Canfield OH 44406	330-533-3384	R	5*	<.1
279	Ashby Cross Company Inc—*Wayne Sturtevant*	28 Parker St, Newburyport MA 01950	978-463-0202	R	5*	<.1
280	Rasirc Inc—*Jeffrey Spiegelman*	11760 Sorrento Valley, San Diego CA 92121	858-259-1220	R	5*	<.1
281	Durable Manufacturing Co—*Ed Sowin*	232 Evergreen Ave, Bensenville IL 60106	630-766-0398	R	5*	<.1
282	Southeastern Installation Inc—*Dan Mathews*	PO Box I, Lexington NC 27293	336-357-7146	R	5*	.1
283	Rti Technologies Inc—*Jeffrey Bmurphy*	PO Box 3099, York PA 17402	717-840-0678	R	5*	<.1
284	Corrotec Inc—*David Stratton*	1125 W N St, Springfield OH 45504	937-325-3585	R	5*	<.1
285	W G Benjey Inc—*Michael Ableidinger*	2293 Werth Rd, Alpena MI 49707	989-356-1433	R	5*	<.1
286	Rubber City Machinery Corp—*George Sobieraj*	PO Box 2043, Akron OH 44309	330-434-3500	R	5*	<.1
287	Powell Fabrication and Manufacturing Inc—*Duane Powell*	740 E Monroe Rd, Saint Louis MI 48880	989-681-2158	R	5*	<.1
288	Modern Machinery Of Beaverton Inc—*Thomas Pohlman*	PO Box 423, Beaverton MI 48612	989-435-9071	R	5*	<.1
289	Summit Foundry Systems Inc—*Richard Meyer*	2100 Wayne Haven St, Fort Wayne IN 46803	260-749-7740	R	5*	<.1
290	Belke Manufacturing Company Inc—*W Faulman*	5810 N NW Hwy, Chicago IL 60631	773-467-0420	R	5*	<.1
291	PKG Equipment Inc—*Stephen Pontarelli*	367 Paul Rd, Rochester NY 14624	585-436-4650	R	5*	<.1
292	Rubicon Express—*Ryan Wallace*	3290 Monier Cir Ste 10, Rancho Cordova CA 95742	916-858-8575	R	4*	<.1
293	Alturnamats Inc—*Janet Aaron*	701 E Spring St Unit 9, Titusville PA 16354	814-827-8884	R	4*	<.1
294	Engineered Production Equipment Inc—*Bob Reischl*	8461 Lake St, Omaha NE 68134	402-399-8282	R	4*	<.1
295	Crossley Economy Company Inc—*Dennis Garrett*	PO Box 510, East Palestine OH 44413	330-426-9486	R	4*	<.1
296	FP Developments Inc—*Frederick Pfleger*	402 S Main St, Williamstown NJ 08094	856-875-7100	R	4*	<.1
297	Cjj Inc—*Charles Beaton*	PO Box 480, Detroit Lakes MN 56502	218-847-2608	R	4*	<.1
298	Accurate Machine Products Corp—*Kenneth Gough*	710 W Walnut St, Johnson City TN 37604	423-928-8134	R	4*	.1
299	Autotool Inc—*Bassam Homsi*	8150 Business Way, Plain City OH 43064	614-733-0222	R	4*	<.1
300	United Plastics Machinery Inc—*Ronald Roberts*	131 S Whitford Rd, Exton PA 19341	610-363-0990	R	4*	<.1
301	RSI Co—*Steve Sords*	12911 Taft Ave, Cleveland OH 44108	216-451-9300	R	4*	<.1
302	Eidschun Engineering Inc—*Charles Eidschun*	5181 113th Ave N, Clearwater FL 33760	727-572-9867	R	4*	<.1
303	Lumenyte International Corp—*Peter Costigan*	74 Icon St, Foothill Ranch CA 92610	949-829-5200	R	4*	<.1
304	Rapid Granulator Inc—*Kirk Winstoad*	200 W Kensinger Dr Ste, Cranberry Township PA 16066	724-584-5220	R	4*	<.1
305	Cryogenic Systems Equipment Inc—*Brian Sink*	2363 136th St, Blue Island IL 60406	708-385-4216	R	4*	<.1
306	Athena Brands Inc	PO Box 398, Gardnerville NV 89410	775-703-3100	R	4*	<.1
307	Bishamon Industries Corp—*Wataru Sugiura*	5651 E Francis St, Ontario CA 91761	909-390-0055	R	4*	<.1
308	Ultrasonic Systems Inc—*Drew Erickson*	135 Ward Hill Ave, Haverhill MA 01835	978-521-0095	R	4*	<.1
309	Shar Systems Inc—*Gregory Long*	PO Box 9196, Fort Wayne IN 46899	260-432-5312	R	4*	<.1
310	International Inventory Management LLC—*Daryll Gauthier*	PO Box 943, Elon NC 27244	336-584-4777	R	4*	<.1
311	Snugl Div—*Tom Willingham*	1498 Kleppe Ln, Sparks NV 89431	775-359-4200	D	4*	<.1
312	Future Cure Inc—*Tom Beck*	2 W Mountain Rd, Ridgefield CT 06877		R	4*	<.1
313	Melanie Machine Co—*Arnold M Kay*	4371 E 49th St, Vernon CA 90058	323-586-2090	R	4*	<.1
314	Quest Corp—*Ronald Powell*	PO Box 5668, Pine Bluff AR 71611	870-534-6411	R	4*	<.1
315	Expert Semiconductor Technology Inc—*Jonathan George*	PO Box 66508, Scotts Valley CA 95067	831-439-9300	R	4*	<.1
316	Process Development Corp—*Cliff Blacke*	6060 Milo Rd, Dayton OH 45414	937-890-3388	R	4*	<.1
317	Industrial Design and Fabrication Inc—*Charles Phy*	PO Box 317, Mc Ewen TN 37101	931-582-8844	R	4*	<.1
318	Mitchell Machine Inc—*John Mitchell*	PO Box 90128, Springfield MA 01139	413-739-9693	R	4*	<.1
319	Ecozone Inc—*Ronald Barnes*	2610 6th St Sw, Huntsville AL 35805	256-539-4570	R	4*	<.1
320	MM Industries Inc—*Barbara Maroscher*	PO Box 720, Salem OH 44460	330-332-4958	R	4*	<.1
321	Dynocom Industries Inc—*Bill Pitts*	2447 Riverbend W Dr, Fort Worth TX 76118	817-284-8844	R	4*	<.1
322	Ultrablend Systems Inc—*Carlos Salas*	1440 Westernghse Blvd, Charlotte NC 28273	704-504-8969	R	4*	<.1
323	CDL Technology Inc—*George Holmes*	511 S Vista Ave Ste A, Addison IL 60101	630-543-5240	R	4*	<.1
324	Dinsmore Manufacturing Company Inc—*Charlotte Duke*	PO Box 267, Salem MA 01970	978-744-1005	R	3*	<.1
325	US Molding Machinery Company Inc—*Zac Cohen*	38294 Pelton Rd, Willoughby OH 44094	440-918-1701	R	3*	<.1
326	Poor and Co—*Gene Poor*	2029 Wood Bridge Blvd, Bowling Green OH 43402	419-352-2101	R	3*	<.1
327	Wilmington Machinery Inc—*Russell Labelle*	PO Box 7308, Wilmington NC 28406	910-452-5090	R	3*	<.1
328	Chemical Safety Technology Inc—*Lincoln Bejan*	2461 Autumnvale Dr, San Jose CA 95131	408-263-0984	R	3*	<.1
329	Granutec Inc—*Merritt Tetreault*	PO Box 537, East Douglas MA 01516	508-476-3801	R	3*	<.1
330	Norcimbus F Crawford Iv Inc—*John Wheeler*	3451 E Harbour Dr, Phoenix AZ 85034	602-437-8500	R	3*	<.1
331	W Schmidt Karl and Associates Inc—*Karl Schmidt*	3900 E 68th Ave, Commerce City CO 80022	303-287-7400	R	3*	<.1
332	James Morris—*James Morris*	6697 Airport Rd, Hamilton NY 13346	315-824-8519	R	3*	<.1
333	Zook Enterprises LLC—*Alan Kohta*	PO Box 419, Chagrin Falls OH 44022	440-543-1010	R	3*	<.1
334	Paydata Inc—*Jon Rocca*	70 Midwest Dr, Pacific MO 63069	636-271-1391	R	3*	<.1
335	Stemmerich Inc—*Colleen Weber*	PO Box 2708, Saint Louis MO 63116	314-832-7726	R	3*	<.1
336	Digital Matrix Corp—*Alex Greenspan*	92 Madison Ave, Hempstead NY 11550	516-481-7990	R	3*	<.1
337	Whitney and Son Inc—*Daniel Whitney*	95 Kelly Ave, Fitchburg MA 01420	978-343-6353	R	3*	<.1
338	Reliable Welding and Machine Work Inc—*Helga Liccardo*	2008 Union Tpke, North Bergen NJ 07047	201-865-2850	R	3*	<.1
339	Boston Matthews Inc—*Colin Brookes*	57 Oak St, Norwood NJ 07648	201-767-7111	R	3*	<.1
340	Murko Machinery and Die A Ykk USA Inc—*Morris Mendlowitz*	3238 62nd St, Woodside NY 11377	718-728-4428	R	3*	<.1
341	American and Schoen Machinery Co—*Ed Skoniecki*	100 Cummings Ctr Ste 1, Beverly MA 01915	978-524-0168	R	3*	<.1
342	Optical Works Corp—*James Coburn*	PO Box 1686, Muskogee OK 74402	918-682-1806	R	3*	<.1
343	Interlab Inc—*Liviu Marian*	3 Precision Rd, Danbury CT 06810	203-748-5624	R	3*	<.1
344	Better Process Services—*Gary Bettcher*	3942 Valley Ave Ste J, Pleasanton CA 94566	925-461-1200	R	3	<.1
345	Esc Control Electronics LLC	77 Windsor Pl Ste 18, Central Islip NY 11722	631-467-5328	R	3*	<.1
346	Hmt Manufacturing Inc—*Burton Bucher*	2323 Commonwealth Ave, North Chicago IL 60064	847-473-2310	R	3*	<.1
347	Vulcan Machinery Corp—*David Jacobs*	20 N Case Ave, Akron OH 44305	330-376-6025	R	3*	<.1

Note: An asterisk (*) indicates an estimated financial figure. The company type code used is as follows: R = Private, P = Public, S = Private Subsidiary, B = Public Subsidiary, D = Division, J = Joint Venture, I = Investment Fund.

COMPANY RANKINGS BY SALES WITHIN 4-DIGIT SIC

Rank	Company Name—*Executive Officer*	Address, City, State, Zip	Phone	Type	Fin	Empls
348	Lectro Engineering Co—*R Williams*	1643 Lotsie Blvd, Saint Louis MO 63132	314-567-3100	R	3*	<.1
349	Clinton Industries Inc—*Harry Klein*	207 Redneck Ave, Little Ferry NJ 07643	201-440-0400	R	3*	<.1
350	Mushield Company Inc—*David Grilli*	PO Box 5045, Manchester NH 03108	603-666-4433	R	3*	<.1
351	BH Bunn Co—*John R Bunn*	2730 Drane Field Rd, Lakeland FL 33811	863-647-1555	R	3*	<.1
352	Modular Process Technology Corp—*Meiying Forney*	2233 Paragon Dr, San Jose CA 95131	408-325-8640	R	3*	<.1
353	Century Design Inc—*Robert Basso*	3635 Afton Rd, San Diego CA 92123	858-292-1212	R	3*	<.1
354	Shellenberger Gregg Inc—*Ken Freisleben*	6333 N Teutonia Ave, Milwaukee WI 53209	414-352-2700	R	3*	<.1
355	Precision Instrumentation Co—*Linda Stevens*	13413 Benson Ave, Chino CA 91710	909-590-0408	R	3*	<.1
356	Ward Technologies Inc—*Howard Ward*	1065 E Lehi Rd, Mesa AZ 85203	602-418-0824	R	3*	<.1
357	Ameri-Shred Corp—*Donna Steffan*	PO Box 68, Alpena MI 49707	989-354-6121	R	3*	<.1
358	Desco Inc—*George Gambini*	1240 Howard St, Elk Grove Village IL 60007	847-439-2130	R	3*	<.1
359	JH Bender Equipment Co—*John H Bender*	9507 Santa Fe Springs, Santa Fe Springs CA 90670	562-781-1055	R	3*	<.1
360	USNI Tech LLC—*Kazuo Otomo*	818 Terminal Rd, Lansing MI 48906	517-321-4055	R	3*	<.1
361	S Howes Inc—*Wayne Mertz*	25 Howard St, Silver Creek NY 14136	716-934-2611	R	3*	<.1
362	Global Procurement Solutions Inc—*Scott Aoki*	6375 S Pecos Rd Ste 22, Las Vegas NV 89120	702-933-3454	R	3*	<.1
363	Hall Dielectric Machinery Company Inc—*William Hall*	420 Bryant Blvd, Rock Hill SC 29732	803-324-0202	R	3*	<.1
364	Edward Segal Inc—*David Segal*	PO Box 429, Thomaston CT 06787	860-283-5821	R	3*	<.1
365	Thermoplastics Company Inc—*G Murphy*	24 Woodward St, Worcester MA 01610	508-754-4668	R	3*	<.1
366	Industrial Machine Manufacturing Inc—*Marvin Garrett*	8140 Virginia Pine Ct, Richmond VA 23237	804-271-6979	R	3*	<.1
367	Sonicron Systems Corp—*Ronald Cecchini*	PO Box 38, Westfield MA 01086	413-562-5218	R	3*	<.1
368	Manetek Inc—*F Leblanc*	PO Box 39, Broussard LA 70518	337-837-2921	R	3*	<.1
369	Rucker and Kolls Inc—*Arlen Chou*	1054 Yosemite Dr, Milpitas CA 95035	408-934-9875	R	3*	<.1
370	Advanced Ventures In Technology Inc—*Albert Petersen*	1120 N Shaw Rd, Gladwin MI 48624	989-426-1351	R	3*	<.1
371	Honey Creek Machine LLC	1537 W Harlan Dr, Terre Haute IN 47802	812-299-5255	R	3*	<.1
372	Starkey Machinery Inc—*James Starkey*	PO Box 207, Galion OH 44833	419-468-2560	R	3*	<.1
373	Alphatest Corp—*Patrick Tarzwell*	PO Box 1791, Shelton WA 98584	360-462-0201	R	3*	<.1
374	Jaco Racing Products Inc—*Jack Rimer*	600 Shenandoah Ave, Elkton VA 22827	540-298-0446	R	3*	<.1
375	Kiln Drying Systems and Components Inc—*Robert Girardi*	PO Box 643, Arden NC 28704	828-891-8115	R	3*	<.1
376	Nickerson Machinery Company Inc—*John Lesha* MI 2009 Inc	PO Box 213, Accord MA 02018	781-740-0500	S	3	<.1
377	T Ultra Equipment Co—*John Flaagan*	41980 Christy St, Fremont CA 94538	510-440-3900	R	3*	<.1
378	Inland Star Distribution Cente	4505 Commerce Blvd S, Mobile AL 36619	334-408-4000	R	2*	<.1
379	Hardwood Line Manufacturing Co—*Anton Lazaro*	4045 N Elston Ave, Chicago IL 60618	773-463-2600	R	2*	<.1
380	Lord Ga'y Foundry Enterprises Inc—*Daniel Gaylord*	PO Box 1863, Independence MO 64055	816-833-4575	R	2*	<.1
381	Superior Dry Kilns Inc—*Brett Bollinger*	PO Box 1586, Lenoir NC 28645	828-754-7001	R	2*	<.1
382	Swanson's Repair Inc—*Jeff Swanson*	PO Box 188, Detroit Lakes MN 56502	218-847-2157	R	2*	<.1
383	Greco Brothers Inc—*Ralph Greco*	1 Greco Ln, Providence RI 02909	401-421-9306	R	2*	<.1
384	United Engineered Tooling Inc—*Dietrich Heyde*	2382 Cass Rd, Traverse City MI 49684	231-947-3650	R	2*	<.1
385	American Commerce Solutions Inc—*Daniel L Hefner*	PO Box 269, Bartow FL 33831	863-533-0326	P	2	<.1
386	Ideal Manufacturing and Sales Corp—*Steven Bethke*	4607 Dovetail Dr, Madison WI 53704	608-241-1118	R	2*	<.1
387	Ensign Equipment Inc—*David Pulver*	12523 Superior Ct, Holland MI 49424	616-738-9000	R	2*	<.1
388	R and B Machinery Corp—*James Broman*	400 Kennedy Rd Ste 3, Buffalo NY 14227	716-894-3332	R	2*	<.1
389	Glastar Corp—*Lorie Mitchell*	20721 Marilla St, Chatsworth CA 91311	818-341-0301	R	2*	<.1
390	J Pollard Staley—*Pollard Staley*	PO Box 203, Russellville IN 46175	765-435-3091	R	2*	<.1
391	Puritan Industries Inc—*Andrew Papanek*	PO Box 186, Collinsville CT 06022	860-693-0791	R	2*	<.1
392	Medelco Inc—*Elaine Robinson*	54 Washburn St, Bridgeport CT 06605	203-275-8070	R	2*	<.1
393	Singleton Corp—*Raymund Singleton*	3280 W 67th Pl, Cleveland OH 44102	216-651-7800	R	2*	<.1
394	Ultron Systems Inc—*Aki Egerer*	5105 Maureen Ln, Moorpark CA 93021	805-529-1485	R	2*	<.1
395	Aramco Inc—*Robert Brauer*	PO Box 1169, Ozark AL 36361	334-774-6485	R	2*	<.1
396	E and C Manufacturing Company Inc—*Peter Ujvagi*	225 Miami St, Toledo OH 43605	419-693-4781	R	2*	<.1
397	Micro-Precision Inc—*John Wiggins*	PO Box 714, Sunapee NH 03782	603-763-2394	R	2*	<.1
398	Tilton Rack and Basket Co—*Joe Tilton*	66 Passaic Ave, Fairfield NJ 07004	973-226-6010	R	2*	<.1
399	International Machine Technology Inc—*Ron Dyle*	952 Alice St, Waycross GA 31501	912-285-1168	R	2	<.1
400	Alto Precision Inc—*David Owen*	6534 Clay Ave SW, Grand Rapids MI 49548	616-698-8088	R	2*	<.1
401	Day-Tec Tool and Manufacturing Inc—*Gerald Whitehead*	4900 Lyons Rd, Miamisburg OH 45342	937-847-0022	R	2*	<.1
402	Advanced Design Industries Inc—*Michael Winiasz*	4686 French Creek Rd, Sheffield Village OH 44054	440-277-4141	R	2*	<.1
403	Iowa Engineered Processes Corp—*Ed Larson*	513 17th St Se, Independence IA 50644	319-334-7274	R	2*	<.1
404	Eagle Sales and Service Inc—*Ed Barnhill*	PO Box 2114, Fort Pierce FL 34954	772-465-7100	R	2*	<.1
405	WFP Inc—*James Woody*	Rr 1 Box 106, Buckhannon WV 26201	304-472-4400	R	2*	<.1
406	Andela Products Ltd—*Cynthia Andela*	493 State Rte 28, Richfield Springs NY 13439	315-858-0055	R	2*	<.1
407	Loma Automation Technologies Inc—*Brian Martin*	PO Box 905, Louisville KY 40201	502-583-4200	R	2*	<.1
408	MPG Services and Sales Inc—*Frank Parker*	526 FM 286, Hillsboro TX 76645	254-582-9249	R	2*	<.1
409	Progressive Design and Machine—*Robert Kutz*	PO Box 1006, Lancaster PA 17605	717-393-0478	R	2*	<.1
410	Monark Equipment Technologies Co—*Steven Clark*	PO Box 335, Auburn MI 48611	989-662-7250	R	2	<.1
411	Semiconductor Equipment Corp—*Donald Moore*	5154 Goldman Ave, Moorpark CA 93021	805-529-2293	R	2*	<.1
412	3DT LLC—*Morten Jorgensen*	N114W18850 Clinton Dr, Germantown WI 53022	262-253-6700	R	2*	<.1
413	Custom Metal Fabricators Inc—*J Dean Johnson*	PO Box 98, Richmond VA 23218	804-271-6094	R	2*	<.1
414	TCI Mobility Inc—*Hannes M Charen*	PO Box 939, Gastonia NC 28053	704-867-8331	R	2*	<.1
415	Auto-Systems and Service Inc—*Jimmy Harris*	PO Box 1180, Ramseur NC 27316	336-824-3580	R	2*	<.1
416	Americhem Engineering Services—*Wallace Myers*	3430 E Broadway Rd, Phoenix AZ 85040	602-437-1188	R	2*	<.1
417	Afcon Products Inc—*John Chayka*	PO Box 206, Bethany CT 06524	203-393-9301	R	2	<.1
418	Campbell-Randall Leather Machine Corp	401 Irvine St, Yoakum TX 77995	361-293-7015	R	2*	<.1
419	Coggins-Welborn Machine Inc—*Lynn Welborn*	PO Box 919, Trinity NC 27370	336-882-2712	R	2*	<.1
420	Exeter Machine Company Inc—*Ed Sadler*	309 S Water St, Lomira WI 53048	920-269-4376	R	2*	<.1
421	Jackson Machinery Inc—*Robert Jackson*	3830 Hwy H, Port Washington WI 53074	262-284-1066	R	2*	<.1
422	USA X-Tractions Inc—*Ronald Wadle*	Rt 4 Box 215, Navasota TX 77868	936-825-4728	R	2*	<.1
423	H and G Industries International—*Peggy Gerich*	17 Affonso Dr, Carson City NV 89706	775-246-3031	R	2*	<.1
424	Hyperflo LLC—*Charlotte Frederick*	1301 West Geneva Dr, Tempe AZ 85282	480-813-1110	R	2*	<.1
425	Randcastle Extrusion Systems Inc—*Keith Luker*	220 Little Falls Rd St, Cedar Grove NJ 07009	973-239-1150	R	2*	<.1
426	Seawolf Design Inc—*Wolfgang Unger*	PO Box 250, Edgewater FL 32132	386-428-4722	R	2*	<.1
427	ACS Technologies Corp—*Dave Corey*	11046 Little Elm Rd, Farmington AR 72730	479-846-2403	R	2*	<.1
428	Hines Flask Co—*Leo L Kovachic*	5906 W Center Rd, Linesville PA 16424	814-683-4420	R	2*	<.1
429	Naiad Of New Hampshire Inc—*Christopher Klinck*	11 Gibson Rd, Hillsborough NH 03244	603-464-4622	R	2*	<.1
430	Summit Equipment Inc—*D Hissong*	3621 W Riverbend Ave, Post Falls ID 83854	208-773-3885	R	2*	<.1
431	Mss Inc—*Robert Davis* Cp Manufacturing Inc	3738 Keystone Ave, Nashville TN 37211	615-781-2669	S	2*	<.1
432	Penntech Machinery Corp—*Ger Smit*	103 Steam Whistle Dr, Warminster PA 18974	215-396-2200	R	2*	<.1
433	NC Carpet Binding and Equipment Corp—*Mark Caplan*	858 Summer Ave, Newark NJ 07104	973-481-3500	R	2*	<.1
434	Scott Office Systems LLC—*Garry Davis*	600 Newbern Rd, Dublin VA 24084	204-697-7913	R	2*	<.1
435	Plastics Extrusion Machinery Inc—*Hal Wright*	PO Box 1285, Mcpherson KS 67460	620-241-3873	R	2*	<.1

Rank	Company Name—Executive Officer	Address, City, State, Zip	Phone	Type	Fin	Empls
436	Miller's Feeding Solutions Inc—Larry Miller	10721 75th St, Largo FL 33777	727-541-5763	R	2*	<.1
437	Plastic Molded Technologies Inc—Michael Ladney	PO Box 183190, Utica MI 48318	586-532-5400	R	2*	<.1
438	RP Gatta Inc—Raymond Gatta	435 Gentry Dr, Aurora OH 44202	330-562-2288	R	2*	<.1
439	Woodman Agitator Inc—James Bielozer	1404 Lear Industrial P, Avon OH 44011	440-937-9865	R	2*	<.1
440	Feeding Concepts Inc—John Graham	15235 Herriman Blvd, Noblesville IN 46060	317-773-2040	R	2*	<.1
441	Hi-Lite Machine Company Inc—Ben Beaird	2014 N 44th St, Sheboygan WI 53083	920-452-0861	R	2*	<.1
442	Gaither Tool Co—Richard Brahler	21 Harold Cox Dr, Jacksonville IL 62650	217-245-0545	R	2*	<.1
443	Tennessee Sewing Machine Attachment Company Inc—Robert Galya	PO Box 188, White Bluff TN 37187	615-797-3144	R	2*	<.1
444	International Cryogenics Inc—Donna Jung	4040 Championship Dr, Indianapolis IN 46268	317-297-4777	R	2*	<.1
445	Pekay Machine and Engineering Company Inc—Jules Parisi	2520 W Lake St, Chicago IL 60612	312-829-5530	R	2*	<.1
446	Tooltex Inc—Paul Spurgeon	6160 Seeds Rd, Grove City OH 43123	614-539-3222	R	2*	<.1
447	Flight Microwave Corp—Rolf Kich	410 S Douglas St, El Segundo CA 90245	310-607-9819	R	2*	<.1
448	Tru Square Metal Products Inc—Albert Thumler	PO Box 585, Auburn WA 98071	253-833-2310	R	2*	<.1
449	Carlson Tool and Machine Co—John Carlson	2300 Gary Ln, Geneva IL 60134	630-232-2460	R	2*	<.1
450	Omsac Inc—Ralph Newman	1700 Jasper St Ste F, Aurora CO 80011	303-364-7786	R	2*	<.1
451	Cox Machine Company Inc—Douglas Cox	2336 Concord Hwy, Monroe NC 28110	704-296-0118	R	2*	<.1
452	Kansmackers Manufacturing Inc—Nick Yono	1510 N Grand River Ave, Lansing MI 48906	517-374-8807	R	2*	<.1
453	Lamco Machine Tool Inc—Lois Fowler	PO Box 2357, Morehead City NC 28557	252-247-4360	R	2*	<.1
454	Crank Works Inc—Phil Shafer	5245 S Kyrene Rd Ste 3, Tempe AZ 85283	480-897-1746	R	2*	<.1
455	Gary Lyells Inc—Gary Lyells	766 W 2nd St, Ogden UT 84404	801-334-7000	R	2*	<.1
456	Sterling Systems Sales Corp—Jerome Schultz	3745 Stern Ave, Saint Charles IL 60174	630-584-3580	R	2*	<.1
457	Berner Industries Inc—Rolf Berner	PO Box 8228, New Castle PA 16107	724-924-9240	R	1*	<.1
458	Engineered Treatment Systems LLC	PO Box 392, Beaver Dam WI 53916	920-885-4628	R	1*	<.1
459	Component Manufacturing and Design Inc—Edward Crist	PO Box 845, Brunswick OH 44212	330-225-8080	R	1*	<.1
460	Lundell Enterprises Inc—Steve Lundell	5134 Hwy 3, Cherokee IA 51012	712-225-5181	R	1*	<.1
461	Milhous Control Co—John Milhous	PO Box 1080, Amherst VA 24521	434-946-5302	R	1*	<.1
462	Waterways Inc—Edwood Wood	PO Box 220, Waterboro ME 04087	207-247-4008	R	1*	<.1
463	Rch Associates Inc—Robert Hoelsch	4115 Business Ctr Dr, Fremont CA 94538	510-657-7846	R	1*	<.1
464	Northstar Equipment Inc—Rhonda Elliott	1341 W 1st St, Cheney WA 99004	509-235-9200	R	1*	<.1
465	Scharch Manufacturing Inc—Dan Scharch	10325 County Rd 120 C, Salida CO 81201	719-539-7242	R	1*	<.1
466	Azego Technology Services Inc (Ramsey New Jersey)—Robert Gallagher	628 Swan St, Ramsey NJ 07446	201-327-7500	R	1*	<.1
467	Scanner Technologies Corp—Paul Crawford	125 Main St Ste 270, Minneapolis MN 55414	612-676-1436	P	1	<.1
468	Machine and Environmental Products Inc—Connie Boria	1301 E 84th St S, Wichita KS 67233	316-788-3615	R	1*	.2
469	Empire Abo Gas Plant—Dave Harris	PO Box 70, Artesia NM 88211	575-677-2192	R	1*	<.1
470	Fremont Flask Co—Carl Yeager	PO Box 594, Fremont OH 43420	419-332-2231	R	1*	<.1
471	Jordan Equipment Supply Corp—Shirley Jordan	15270 Flight Path Dr, Brooksville FL 34604	352-754-1117	R	1*	<.1
472	Curtin-Hebert Company Inc—James Curtin	11 Forest St, Gloversville NY 12078	518-725-7157	R	1*	<.1
473	Quantum Mold and Engineering LLC—Donna Rossan	35700 Stanley Dr, Sterling Heights MI 48312	586-276-0100	R	1*	<.1
474	Ultra-Kool Inc—Albert Hartman	PO Box 458, Gilbertsville PA 19525	610-367-2019	R	1*	<.1
475	Arbe Machinery Inc—Artin Karakaya	54 Allen Blvd, Farmingdale NY 11735	631-756-2477	R	1*	<.1
476	Hydropro Inc—William Hendershaw	990 W 15th St, Riviera Beach FL 33404	561-848-6788	R	1*	<.1
477	Technical Machine Products Inc—Daniel French French Oil Mill Machinery Co	5500 Walworth Ave, Cleveland OH 44102	216-281-9500	S	1*	<.1
478	L and L Engineering and Manufacturing Inc—Leslie Rockwood	34303 Industrial Rd, Livonia MI 48150	734-522-9252	R	1*	<.1
479	Finishing Equipment Inc—Winston Sabatka	8725 209th St W Apt 21, Lakeville MN 55044	952-469-3086	R	1*	<.1
480	Stephen A Manoogian Inc—Stephen Manoogian	12 Industrial Pkwy, Johnstown NY 12095	518-762-2525	R	1*	<.1
481	Scientific Process and Research—Ron Klein	1254 State Rte 27, North Brunswick NJ 08902	732-046-3477	R	1*	<.1
482	Broncorp Manufacturing Company Inc—Gary Caldwell	5957 Broadway, Denver CO 80216	303-296-8362	R	1*	<.1
483	High Frequency Technology Company Inc—Andrew Amabile	172 Brook Ave Ste D, Deer Park NY 11729	631-242-3020	R	1*	<.1
484	Innovative Plastic Machinery—Abe Kauffman	5252 Southway St Sw, Canton OH 44706	330-478-1825	R	1*	<.1
485	Naegle's Industrial Leather Machinery Co—Connie Naegle	401 Irvine St, Yoakum TX 77995	361-293-7015	R	1*	<.1
486	Broco Products Inc—Barry Brown	18624 Syracuse Ave, Cleveland OH 44110	216-531-0880	R	1*	<.1
487	Symtech Corp—Robert Griesenauer	524 Transport Dr, Lees Summit MO 64081	816-525-9263	R	1*	<.1
488	FSI International Inc Microlithography Div—John Walker FSI International Inc	600 Millenium Dr, Allen TX 75013	972-643-2000	D	1*	.1
489	East Tech Inc—Frank Alford	116 Lincoln Ave, Marion AR 72364	870-732-1166	R	1*	<.1
490	Steinert Industries Inc—John Steinert	1507 Franklin Ave, Kent OH 44240	330-678-0028	R	1*	<.1
491	RAG Tooling Co—Michael Grimstad	PO Box 86, Salem OH 44460	330-337-3126	R	1*	<.1
492	ICM Inc—Tracy Polley	11936 Front St, Norwalk CA 90650	562-869-3004	R	1*	<.1
493	Castec Inc—Ronald Parker	1462 Delberts Dr, Monongahela PA 15063	724-258-8700	R	1*	<.1
494	Mechanized Enterprises Inc—George Hansel	1021 N Grove St, Anaheim CA 92806	714-630-5512	R	1*	<.1
495	R and R Loopers Inc—Mac Carson	PO Box 4125, Dalton GA 30719	706-278-1635	R	1*	<.1
496	Tranoco Inc—Charles F Travis	PO Box 267, Travelers Rest SC 29690	864-246-2481	R	1*	<.1
497	Va-Tran Systems Inc—James Sloan	677 Anita St Ste A, Chula Vista CA 91911	619-423-4555	R	1*	<.1
498	American Manufacturing and Equipment Inc—Albert Penter	4990 Factory Dr, Fairfield OH 45014	513-829-2248	R	1*	<.1
499	Covington Engineering Corp—Dan Drouault	715 W Colton Ave, Redlands CA 92374	909-793-6636	R	1*	<.1
500	Grapar Inc—Harold Parslow	25133 Flanders Ave, Warren MI 48089	586-773-5356	R	1*	<.1
501	International Molding Machine Co—Tyrrell Eichler	PO Box 1366, La Grange Park IL 60526	708-354-1380	R	1*	<.1
502	Axic Inc—Frank Bazzarre	493 Gianni St, Santa Clara CA 95054	408-980-0240	R	1*	<.1
503	GII Solutions Inc—George Fletcher	PO Box 428, Central SC 29630	864-639-6605	R	1*	<.1
504	Marvel Photo Inc—Anthony Perrault	PO Box 2464, Tulsa OK 74101	918-836-0741	R	1*	<.1
505	Web Systems Inc—George Zuments	PO Box 6443, Broomfield CO 80021	303-440-4868	R	1*	<.1
506	C3 Design Innovations—Robert J Sclabassi	362 W 6100 S, Salt Lake City UT 84107	801-281-1331	R	1*	<.1
507	Global Kitting Systems Co—Ulrich Wettstein	10518 Hufford Ranch Rd, Whitmore CA 96096	530-472-3697	R	1*	<.1
508	JC Nabity Lithography Systems—Joe Nabity	PO Box 5354, Bozeman MT 59717	406-587-0848	R	1*	<.1
509	Chuck Bivens Services Inc—Chuck Bivens	PO Box 9590, Fort Wayne IN 46899	260-747-6195	R	1*	<.1
510	Simmonsteen Inc—Charles Simmons	2608 SW Dr, New Iberia LA 70560	337-364-3416	R	1*	<.1
511	Tri Technologies Inc—Audrey Dyer	1300 Lafayette Ave, Middletown OH 45044	513-422-1300	R	1*	<.1
512	Emp Industries Inc—Ed Pentz	109-111 Industrial Dr, Warminster PA 18974	215-357-5333	R	1*	<.1
513	Machine World Inc—Cindy Briceno	3985 Eastside Rd Ste 9, Redding CA 96001	530-246-1911	R	1*	<.1
514	Rk Inc—Ed Prell	6962 State Rte 17, West Plains MO 65775	417-256-9225	R	1*	<.1
515	Mactavish Machine Manufacturing Co—Donald Evans	7429 Whitepine Rd, Richmond VA 23237	804-264-6109	R	1*	<.1
516	Accu-Turn Tool Company Inc—Richard Antoszewski	1049 William Flynn Hwy, Glenshaw PA 15116	412-492-7270	R	1*	<.1
517	Advanced International Technology LLC—Margaret Yount	9909 Hibert St Ste A, San Diego CA 92131	858-566-2945	R	1*	<.1
518	IG Brenner Inc—Robert Fitzgerald	32 E N St, Newark OH 43055	740-345-8845	R	1*	<.1
519	Litton Engineering Laboratories—Charles Litton	PO Box 950, Grass Valley CA 95945	530-273-6176	R	1*	<.1
520	Therma-Kleen Inc—Andrew Heller	10212 S Mandel St Ste, Plainfield IL 60585	630-718-0212	R	1*	<.1
521	Polydyne Inc—Jim Sorenson	16725 Columbia River H, Clatskanie OR 97016	503-656-4733	R	1*	<.1

Note: An asterisk (*) indicates an estimated financial figure. The company type code used is as follows: R = Private, P = Public, S = Private Subsidiary, B = Public Subsidiary, D = Division, J = Joint Venture, I = Investment Fund.

COMPANY RANKINGS BY SALES WITHIN 4-DIGIT SIC

Rank	Company Name—Executive Officer	Address, City, State, Zip	Phone	Type	Fin	Empls
522	Polymer Recovery Systems Inc—John Ayres	945 Short St, Eau Claire WI 54701	715-835-3233	R	1*	<.1
523	Surface Blasting Systems LLC—Gerald Gurney	7300 Division Ave S, Grand Rapids MI 49548	616-532-4950	R	1*	<.1
524	Midwest Mixing Inc—Robert Smith	5630 Pleasant Blvd, Chicago Ridge IL 60415	708-422-8100	R	1*	<.1
525	Wafer Process Systems Inc—Douglas Caldwell	3641 Charter Park Dr, San Jose CA 95136	408-445-3010	R	1*	<.1
526	Morgan Industries Inc—Charles Land	3311 E 59th St, Long Beach CA 90805	562-634-4074	R	1*	<.1
527	Electro-Optical Systems Inc—William Pinkston	1288 Valley Forge Rd S, Phoenixville PA 19460	610-935-5838	R	1*	<.1
528	Glass Components Inc—Terry Wymer	PO Box 537, Winchester IN 47394	765-584-6225	R	1*	<.1
529	Jet Process Corp—Richard Hart	57 Dodge Ave, North Haven CT 06473	203-985-6000	R	1*	<.1
530	J-Mar Metal Fabricating Company Inc—John Marricone	PO Box 160, Croydon PA 19021	215-785-6521	R	1*	<.1
531	Inlustra Technologies Inc—Benjamin Haskell	5385 Hollister Ave Ste, Santa Barbara CA 93111	805-504-4639	R	1*	<.1
532	Automated Blasting Systems Inc—Michael Economos	46 Schwier Rd, South Windsor CT 06074	860-528-5525	R	1*	<.1
533	Summit Manufacturing Corp—Paul Cotter	248 Pine St, Pawtucket RI 02860	401-723-6272	R	1*	<.1
534	Vibcon Corp—Dennis Haskett	PO Box 542, Arcadia IN 46030	317-984-3543	R	1*	<.1
535	Nordcast Inc—Jean Cote	16201 Clinton St, Harvey IL 60426	708-339-0033	R	1*	<.1
536	Glass Technology Inc—Dan Wanstrath	434 Turner Dr Ste 6, Durango CO 81303	970-247-9374	R	1*	<.1
537	J and M Associates—Jim Jablonsky	1610 Hedgewood Rd, Hatfield PA 19440	215-368-6822	R	1*	<.1
538	Parking Products Inc—Holger Niebisch	2517 Wyandotte Rd Ste, Willow Grove PA 19090	215-657-7500	R	1*	<.1
539	Generation Tool Inc—Michael Rotter	307 Manufacturers Dr, Westland MI 48186	734-641-6937	R	1*	<.1
540	Gryphon Corp—Robert Baumbach	12417 Foothill Blvd, Sylmar CA 91342	818-890-7770	R	1*	<.1
541	Poly Products Inc—Walter Senney	777 E 82nd St, Cleveland OH 44103	216-391-7659	R	1*	<.1
542	Automate Tech Inc—John Devries	4711 126th Ave N Ste J, Clearwater FL 33762	727-572-7474	R	1*	<.1
543	Kalamazoo Packaging Systems Inc—Charles Rencurrel	PO Box 88141, Grand Rapids MI 49518	616-534-2600	R	1*	<.1
544	Metalink Corp—Martin Pawloski	325 E Elliot Rd Ste 23, Chandler AZ 85225	480-926-0797	R	1*	<.1
545	Plastixs LLC	151 Memorial Dr Ste H, Shrewsbury MA 01545	508-842-1606	R	1*	<.1
546	Rapid Electroplating Process Inc—Richard Rapids	2901 W Soffel Ave, Melrose Park IL 60160	708-344-2504	R	1*	<.1
547	Mullen Testers	939 Chicopee St, Chicopee MA 01013	413-536-1311	S	1	<.1
548	General Air Corp—David Sagi	9254 Deering Ave Ste A, Chatsworth CA 91311	818-718-8955	R	1*	<.1
549	Universal Magnetics Inc—George Ravell	5555 Amy School Rd, Howard City MI 49329	231-937-5555	R	1*	<.1
550	Ader Inc—Gary Pollack	6549 Nw 99th Ave, Tamarac FL 33321	954-722-6849	R	1*	<.1
551	American Meta's Pack Company Inc—Dai Vu	1185 Park Ctr Dr Ste C, Vista CA 92081	760-734-1680	R	1*	<.1
552	Size Reduction Specialists Corp—Don Maynard	3510 W Rd, East Lansing MI 48823	517-333-2605	R	1*	<.1
553	West Code—Skip Kinyon	1372 Enterprise Dr, West Chester PA 19380	610-696-7420	R	1*	<.1
554	Collins Craft Corp—Ken Collins	2309 Sandifer Blvd, Westminster SC 29693	864-647-9198	R	1*	<.1
555	DH Melton Company Inc—Douglas Melton	1221 E Del Rio Dr, Tempe AZ 85282	480-967-6218	R	1*	<.1
556	Miniature Plastic Molding LLC—George Hockett	1111 N Washington St, Wichita KS 67214	316-264-2827	R	1*	<.1
557	Omco Group Ltd—Richard Roy	445 Mckenzie Rd, Mukwonago WI 53149	262-363-6626	R	1*	<.1
558	Datco Manufacturing—Michael Datus	2070 Barney Rd Ste A, Anderson CA 96007	530-365-6885	R	1*	<.1
559	Garb-Oil and Power Corp—John Rossi	5248 Pinemont Dr Ste C, Murray UT 84123	801-738-1355	P	1	<.1
560	Hycon Inc—Eero Hyvonen	349 E Industrial Park, Manchester NH 03109	603-644-1414	R	1*	<.1
561	Juice Manufacturing Inc—Thomas Thompson	PO Box 233, Fountain Inn SC 29644	864-862-3218	R	1*	<.1
562	M and K Industrial Sewing—Kirk Durbin	RR 4 Box 1109, Piedmont MO 63957	573-223-2151	R	<1*	<.1
563	New Vista Corp—Jack Wickham	900 N Macon St Ste D, Baltimore MD 21205	410-342-3820	R	<1*	<.1
564	Kevko Race And Manufacturing Inc—Kevin Kollofski	915 N Orient St, Fairmont MN 56031	507-238-9633	R	<1*	<.1
565	Tri-Tool Inc—Don Masterson	7809 Baumgart Rd, Evansville IN 47725	812-867-3506	R	<1*	<.1
566	General Plastics Machines Inc—Bob Elder	2828 Kauffman Ave, Vancouver WA 98660	360-694-8836	R	<1*	<.1
567	Bradford Neal Machinery Inc—James Skinner	PO Box 1237, Middlefield OH 44062	440-632-1393	R	<1*	<.1
568	Liberty Manufacturing—Louis Francioli	5620 48th Dr Ne, Marysville WA 98270	360-659-0387	R	<1*	<.1
569	Advanced Tooling—Scott Dase	PO Box 670, Ashville AL 35953	205-594-5353	R	<1*	<.1
570	Electroprep Corp—George Morones	PO Box 110614, Campbell CA 95011	408-727-7505	R	<1*	<.1
571	Ozone Company Inc—Bill Better	PO Box 845, Aberdeen ID 83210	208-397-3033	R	<1*	<.1
572	Genesis Development Inc—Craig Stauffer	1128 S Sage Ct, Sunnyvale CA 94087	408-746-0875	R	<1*	<.1
573	YK International Inc—Yuzo Kojima	10104 Russwill Ln, Union KY 41091	859-384-3126	R	<1*	<.1
574	Sea-Ro Inc—Janine Babich	1209 Tangelo Isle, Fort Lauderdale FL 33315	954-527-5282	R	<1*	<.1
575	Hess Technologies Inc—Paul Hess	PO Box 2877, Springfield OH 45501	937-322-0198	R	<1*	<.1
576	Deer Corp—Allan Hansen	11034 Bailey Rd, Cornelius NC 28031	704-896-7535	R	<1*	<.1
577	Criterion Machinery Inc—Rose Prescott	7655 Hub Pkwy Ste 201, Cleveland OH 44125	216-573-0311	R	<1*	<.1
578	Edge Industries Inc—Richard Hungerford	2887 3 Mile Rd Nw, Grand Rapids MI 49534	616-453-5458	R	<1*	<.1
579	Powertech Equipment Inc—Lon Pinaire	PO Box 15442, Evansville IN 47716	812-477-9276	R	<1*	<.1
580	Amistar Corp—Bobby L Watson	1269 Linda Vista, San Marcos CA 92078	760-471-1700	P	<1	<.1
581	Profile Technologies Inc—Richard Palmer	2 Park Ave Ste 201, Manhasset NY 11030	516-365-1909	P	<1	<.1
582	Russell Crosby—Russell Crosby	PO Box 514, Oakham MA 01068	508-882-3841	R	<1*	<.1
583	Seamtek Inc—Kim Benefield	PO Box 1866, Sandpoint ID 83864	208-265-9499	R	<1*	<.1
584	Tirex Corp—John L Threshie Jr	1771 Post Rd E, Westport CT 06880	203-292-6922	P	<1	<.1
585	Ck Enterprises—Carl Kingsley	PO Box 93665, Phoenix AZ 85070	813-962-1846	R	<1*	<.1
586	Jerry F Hawkins—Jerry Hawkins	22525 Benjamin St, Saint Clair Shores MI 48081	586-775-5490	R	<1*	<.1
587	Plating Engineering—John Ritzenphaler	415 Piccadilly Pl Apt, San Bruno CA 94066	650-952-8066	R	<1*	<.1
588	Roy M Mcdougal—Roy Mcdougal	7412 Humboldt Ave N, Minneapolis MN 55444	763-561-3424	R	<1*	<.1
589	Tegal Corp—Thomas R Mika	PO Box 6020, Petaluma CA 94954	707-763-5600	P	<1	<.1

TOTALS: SIC 3559 Special Industry Machinery Nec
Companies: 589   35,561   118.6

3561 Pumps & Pumping Equipment

Rank	Company Name—Executive Officer	Address, City, State, Zip	Phone	Type	Fin	Empls
1	FAST and Fluid Management SRL—Andrew K Silvernail	1023 Wheeling Rd, Wheeling IL 60090	847-537-0880	S	42,499*	4.2
2	Wright Pump Inc—Lawrence D Kingsley IDEX Corp	S84 W18693 Enterprise, Muskego WI 53150	262-679-8000	S	42,488*	4.2
3	Depco Pump Company Inc—Kevin Griffith	PO Box 6820, Clearwater FL 33758	727-446-1656	R	23,868*	<.1
4	Envirotech Pumpsystems Inc—James Board	PO Box 209, Salt Lake City UT 84110	801-359-8731	R	8,538*	.5
5	EMSAR Ventures Inc	125 Access Rd, Stratford CT 06615	203-377-8100	S	4,818*	.5
6	Seaquist Closures LLC—Peter H Pfeiffer	711 Fox St, Mukwonago WI 53149	262-363-7191	S	4,628*	.5
7	Dover Resources Inc—Robert A Livingston	3005 Highland Pky Ste, Downers Grove IL 60515	630-541-1540	S	4,446*	26.6
8	Flowserve Corp—James O Rollans	5215 N O'Connor Blvd S, Irving TX 75039	972-443-6500	P	4,032	15.0
9	Beckett Corp—Wingate Sung	3250 N Skyway Circle D, Irving TX 75038	972-871-8000	S	2,818*	.3
10	ACD LLC—Ross M Brown	2321 Pullman St, Santa Ana CA 92705	949-261-7533	R	2,572*	.1
11	ITT - Goulds Pumps—Paul Baldetti	240 Fall St, Seneca Falls NY 13148	315-568-2811	D	2,367*	.4
12	Red Jacket Pumps	125 Powder Forest Dr, Simsbury CT 06089	860-651-2700	D	2,305*	.2
13	Hydromatic Pump Myers F E Co	1101 Myers Pky, Ashland OH 44805	419-289-1144	S	2,000	10.0
14	Hypro Corp	375 5th Ave NW, New Brighton MN 55112	651-766-6300	S	1,998*	.1
15	Weir Floway Inc—Barry Cockerham	PO Box 164, Fresno CA 93707	559-442-4000	S	1,943*	.2
16	IDEX Corp—Andrew Silvernail	630 Dundee Rd, Northbrook IL 60062	847-498-7070	P	1,838	6.8

Rank	Company Name—Executive Officer	Address, City, State, Zip	Phone	Type	Fin	Empls
17	Conergy Inc—Anthony Fotopoulos	2460 W 26th Ave Ste 28, Denver CO 80211		R	1,606*	1.7
18	ClydeUnion Pumps Co	4600 W Dickman Rd, Battle Creek MI 49037	269-966-4600	S	1,352*	.2
19	Goodrich Fuel and Utility Systems—Brian Smith	104 Otis St, Rome NY 13441	315-838-1200	D	1,223*	.2
20	Lufkin Industries Inc—Jay F Glick	PO Box 849, Lufkin TX 75902	936-634-2211	P	932	4.0
21	Robbins and Myers Inc—Peter C Wallace	51 Plum St Ste 260, Dayton OH 45440	937-458-6600	P	821	3.4
22	WICOR Inc—Randall J Hogan	626 E Wisconsin Ave, Milwaukee WI 53202	414-291-7076	S	750	3.5
23	Colfax Corp—Clay H Kiefaber	8170 Maple Lawn Blvd S, Fulton MD 20759	301-323-9000	P	693	1.5
24	Buffalo Pumps Inc—Charles Kistner Ampco-Pittsburgh Corp	874 Oliver St, North Tonawanda NY 14120	716-693-1850	D	623*	.1
25	Procon Products—Roger Fix	869 Seven Oaks Blvd St, Smyrna TN 37167	615-355-8000	S	516*	.1
26	Puronics Inc	5775 Las Positas Rd, Livermore CA 94551	925-456-7000	R	391*	.1
27	Beach-Russ Co—CA Beach	544 Union Ave, Brooklyn NY 11211	718-388-4090	R	362*	<.1
28	Ampco-Pittsburgh Corp—Robert A Paul	600 Grant St Ste 4600, Pittsburgh PA 15219	412-456-4400	P	327	1.2
29	Sta-Rite Industries Inc—James Donnelly	293 Wright St, Delavan WI 53115		S	300*	1.8
30	Gorman-Rupp Co—Jeffrey S Gorman	PO Box 1217, Mansfield OH 44901	419-755-1011	P	297	1.1
31	Roy E Roth Co—Peter Roth	PO Box 4330, Rock Island IL 61204	309-787-1791	R	242*	<.1
32	Valley Power Systems Inc—Sam Hill	425 S Hacienda Blvd, City of Industry CA 91745	626-333-1243	S	177*	.6
33	Pump Star Inc—Soubhi Naddaf	PO Box 872, Enid OK 73702	580-548-2723	R	168*	.9
34	Ampco UES Sub Inc—Robert Paul	600 Grant St Ste 4600, Pittsburgh PA 15219	412-456-4400	S	164*	<.1
35	Zoeller Pump Company—John Zoeller	PO Box 16347, Louisville KY 40256	502-778-2731	R	138*	.3
36	Sterling Fluid Systems LLC (Indianapolis Indiana)—Dean Douglas	PO Box 7026, Indianapolis IN 46207	317-925-9661	R	125*	.4
37	Sundyne Corp—Phil Ruffner	14845 W 64th Ave, Arvada CO 80007	303-425-0800	S	118*	.7
38	ARO Corp—Hub Hinkle	PO Box 151, Bryan OH 43506	419-636-4242	D	111*	.8
39	Myers F E Co	1101 Myers Pkwy, Ashland OH 44805	419-289-1144	D	101*	.6
40	Transdigm Inc—Raymond Laubenthal	1301 E 9th St Ste 3710, Cleveland OH 44114	216-706-2939	R	99*	1.1
41	ITT Industries Inc Bell and Gossett Div—Pat DePalma	8200 N Austin Ave, Morton Grove IL 60053	847-966-3700	S	89	.8
42	Wilden Pump and Engineering Company Inc—Denny Buskirk	22069 Van Buren St, Grand Terrace CA 92313	909-422-1730	S	68*	.2
43	Patterson Pump Co—Albert Huber Gorman-Rupp Co	PO Box 790, Toccoa GA 30577	706-886-2101	S	61*	.4
44	Viking Pump Inc—Jason Struthers IDEX Corp	PO Box 8, Cedar Falls IA 50613	319-266-1741	S	60*	.5
45	Little Giant Pump Co—Norman Heidebrecht	PO Box 12010, Oklahoma City OK 73157	405-947-2511	S	55*	.5
46	Lawrence Pumps Inc—Paul Reddick	371 Market St, Lawrence MA 01843	978-682-5248	R	55*	.1
47	Aptar—Francesco Mascitelli	125 Access Rd, Stratford CT 06615	203-377-8100	S	51*	.3
48	Pulsafeeder Inc—Paul Beldham IDEX Corp	2883 Brighton-Henriett, Rochester NY 14623	585-292-8000	S	51*	.3
49	Sulzer Process Pumps Inc (Easley South Carolina)—Alan Crawford	PO Box 2069, Easley SC 29641	864-855-9090	R	50*	.1
50	SHURflo LLC—Russ Phillips WICOR Inc	5900 Katella Ave, Cypress CA 90630	562-795-5200	S	47*	.4
51	Thompson Pump And Manufacturing Company Inc—William Thompson	PO Box 291370, Port Orange FL 32129	386-767-7310	R	41*	.3
52	Gast Manufacturing Inc IDEX Corp	PO Box 97, Benton Harbor MI 49023	269-926-6171	D	40*	.6
53	Environment One Corp—George A Earle	2773 Balltown Rd, Niskayuna NY 12309	518-346-6161	S	39*	.2
54	Baxa Corp—Greg Baldwin	9540 S Maroon Cir Ste, Englewood CO 80112	303-690-4204	R	35*	.5
55	Roper Pump Co—Walt Stadnisky	PO Box 269, Commerce GA 30529	706-335-5551	S	35*	.2
56	Ebara International Corp—Joel Madison	350 Salomon Cir, Sparks NV 89434	775-356-2796	R	35*	.2
57	Aurora Pump	800 Airport Rd, North Aurora IL 60542	630-859-7000	S	34*	.2
58	Fairbanks Morse Pump Corp—Christopher Kearney	PO Box 6999, Kansas City KS 66106	913-371-5000	S	34*	.2
59	Milton Roy Co—Jean-Claude Pharamond	201 Ivyland Rd, Ivyland PA 18974	215-441-0800	S	34*	.2
60	SPX Fluid Power	5885 11th St, Rockford IL 61109	815-874-5556	D	34	.2
61	Mwi Corp—Dana Eller	201 N Federal Hwy Ste, Deerfield Beach FL 33441	954-426-1500	R	34*	.2
62	Morgantown Machine and Hydraulics Inc—Robert Gluth	437 Goshen Rd, Morgantown WV 26508	304-296-8371	R	33*	.4
63	Putzmeister America Inc—Dave Adams	1733 90th St, Sturtevant WI 53177	262-886-3200	R	31*	.4
64	New Era Ohio LLC—David Duthie	520 W Mulberry St, Bryan OH 43506	419-633-1616	R	30*	.2
65	Haskel International Inc—Jean-Claude Pharamond	100 E Graham Pl, Burbank CA 91502	818-843-4000	R	30*	.2
66	Dean Pump Div—Gennaro D'Alterio	PO Box 68172, Indianapolis IN 46268	317-293-2930	D	30*	<.1
67	Otec Inc—William Pielop	PO Box 1849, Houston TX 77251	713-692-3532	R	29*	.2
68	Frac Tech Services LLC—Dan Wilks	16858 Interstate 20, Cisco TX 76437	817-850-1008	R	28*	.2
69	Warren Rupp Inc—Dennis K Williams IDEX Corp	PO Box 1568, Mansfield OH 44901	419-524-8388	S	27	.2
70	Iwaki Walchem Corp—Ronald Yates Iwaki America Inc	5 Boynton Rd, Holliston MA 01746	508-429-1440	S	27*	.1
71	Sihi Pumps Inc—Janet Astins	PO Box 460, Grand Island NY 14072	716-773-6450	R	25*	.1
72	Diversified Dynamics Corp—William Bruggeman	1681 94th Ln Ne, Minneapolis MN 55449	763-780-5440	R	22*	.2
73	Oteco Inc—William Pielop Otec Inc	PO Box 1849, Houston TX 77251	713-695-3693	S	21*	.2
74	Systecon Inc—Terrence Moses	6121 Schumacher Park D, West Chester OH 45069	513-777-7722	R	21*	.1
75	Gorman-Rupp Industries—Micheal Hill Gorman-Rupp Co	180 Hines Ave, Bellville OH 44813	419-886-3001	S	20	.1
76	Blackmer Flow Technologies—Carmine Bosco Dover Resources Inc	1809 Century Ave SW, Grand Rapids MI 49503	616-241-1611	D	20*	.3
77	Engineered Fluid Inc—William Goodspeed	PO Box 723, Centralia IL 62801	618-533-1351	R	19*	.1
78	Cs and P Technologies LP—Kennis Baskin	PO Box 130, Cypress TX 77410	713-467-0869	R	19*	.1
79	Cornell Pump Co—Jeff Markham	16261 SE 130th Ave, Clackamas OR 97015	503-653-0330	S	17*	.1
80	Newport News Industrial—Mike Marlow	182 Enterprise Dr, Newport News VA 23603	757-380-7053	D	17*	.1
81	Parker Industries Inc (Bohemia New York)—Bruce Cowley	1650 Sycamore Ave, Bohemia NY 11716	631-567-1000	R	17*	<.1
82	Yeomans Chicago Corp—John Kelly	3905 Enterprise Ct, Aurora IL 60504	630-236-5500	R	16*	.1
83	Autoform Tool and Manufacturing Inc—Robert Jacoby	PO Box 988, Fremont IN 46737	260-495-9641	R	16*	.1
84	ACD Inc—Carl Hennison	2321 S Pullman St, Santa Ana CA 92705	949-261-7533	S	16*	.1
85	Weil Pump Company Inc	PO Box 887, Cedarburg WI 53012	262-377-1399	R	16*	.1
86	Versa-Matic Tool Inc—William Versaw IDEX Corp	PO Box 1568, Mansfield OH 44901	419-526-7296	S	16	<.1
87	A R Wilfley and Sons Inc—Michael Wilfley	PO Box 2330, Denver CO 80201	303-779-1777	R	16*	.1
88	Aqua-Flo LLC—Dirk Caudill	PO Box 77100, Corona CA 92877	909-591-7453	R	16*	.1
89	Industrial Filter and Pump Manufacturing Co—James F Zievers	5900 W Ogden Ave, Cicero IL 60804	708-656-7800	R	15*	.1
90	Weir Lewis Pumps—Bob Braun	8625 Grant Rd, Saint Louis MO 63123	314-843-4437	S	15*	.1
91	QED Environmental Systems Inc—Michael Cross	PO Box 3726, Ann Arbor MI 48106	734-995-2547	H	15*	.1

Note: An asterisk (*) indicates an estimated financial figure. The company type code used is as follows: R = Private, P = Public, S = Private Subsidiary, B = Public Subsidiary, D = Division, J = Joint Venture, I = Investment Fund.

COMPANY RANKINGS BY SALES WITHIN 4-DIGIT SIC

Rank	Company Name—*Executive Officer*	Address, City, State, Zip	Phone	Type	Fin	Empls
92	Larkin Products LLC—*Wallace Tipsword*	PO Box 3644, Tulsa OK 74101	918-584-3475	R	15*	<.1
93	Coffin Turbo Pump Inc—*Kevin Powers*	326 S Dean St, Englewood NJ 07631	201-568-4700	R	14*	.1
94	March Manufacturing Inc—*Fred Zimmermann*	1819 Pickwick Ln, Glenview IL 60026	847-729-5300	R	14*	.1
95	Afton Pumps Inc—*Michael Derr*	PO Box 9426, Houston TX 77261	713-923-9731	R	14*	.1
96	Carver Pump Co—*Roy Carver*	2415 Park Ave, Muscatine IA 52761	563-263-3410	R	13*	.1
97	MP Pumps Inc—*Greg Peabody*	34800 Bennett Dr, Fraser MI 48026	586-293-8240	S	13*	.1
98	Holland Pump Manufacturing Inc—*William Blodgett*	7312 Westport Pl, West Palm Beach FL 33413	561-697-3333	R	13*	.1
99	Wanner Engineering Inc—*Joseph Grewe*	1204 Chestnut Ave, Minneapolis MN 55403	612-332-5681	R	13*	.1
100	Superior Manufacturing and Hydraulics Inc—*David Buck*	4225 Hwy 90 E, Broussard LA 70518	337-837-8847	R	12*	.1
101	Standard Industrial Manufacturing Partners Ltd—*Donna Ross*	920 W 2nd St, Odessa TX 79763	432-332-5955	R	12*	<.1
102	T and T Pump Company Inc—*Donnie Tucker*	Rt 8 PO Box 343, Fairmont WV 26555	304-366-1300	R	11*	.1
103	Vaughan Company Inc—*Dale Vaughan*	364 Monte Elma Rd, Montesano WA 98563	360-249-4042	R	11*	.1
104	Franklin Fueling Systems—*Don Kenney*	3760 Marsh Rd, Madison WI 53718	608-838-8786	D	11	.1
105	Liberty Pumps Inc—*Charles Cook*	7000 Appletree Ave, Bergen NY 14416	585-494-1817	R	11*	.1
106	Hayward Tyler Inc—*Vince Conte*	PO Box 680, Colchester VT 05446	802-655-4444	R	10*	.1
107	Finish Thompson Inc—*Kasey Bose*	921 Greengarden Rd, Erie PA 16501	814-455-4478	R	10*	<.1
108	Mjw Inc—*Michael Curry*	1328 W Slauson Ave, Los Angeles CA 90044	323-778-8900	R	9*	.1
109	Whitten Pumps Inc—*Fred Whitten*	502 County Line Rd, Delano CA 93215	661-725-0250	R	9*	.1
110	Iwaki America Inc—*Ronald Yates*	5 Boynton Rd, Holliston MA 01746	508-429-1110	R	9*	.1
111	Graymills Corp—*Gerald N Shields*	3705 N Lincoln Ave, Chicago IL 60613	773-477-4100	R	9*	.1
112	Beckson Manufacturing Inc—*Frank Sbeckerer*	PO Box 3336, Bridgeport CT 06605	203-366-3644	R	9*	.1
113	Georgia Hydraulic Cylinder Inc—*Joe Bajjani*	260 The Blfs, Austell GA 30168	678-355-2240	R	9*	.1
114	Vertical Turbine Specialists Inc—*Douglas Allen*	1802 E 50th St Unit 10, Lubbock TX 79404	806-743-5555	R	8*	.1
115	Cascade Pump Co—*Tom Summerfield*	PO Box 2767, Santa Fe Springs CA 90670	562-946-1414	R	8*	.1
116	Roth Pump Co Roy E Roth Co	PO Box 4330, Rock Island IL 61204	309-787-1791	S	8*	.1
117	Houston Grinding and Manufacturing Co—*Brian Lattimer*	3544 W 12th St, Houston TX 77008	713-869-3573	R	8*	.1
118	REDA Pumping Systems—*Andrew Gould*	12131 Industry St, Garden Grove CA 92841	714-379-7332	S	8*	.1
119	Trebor International—*Donald Paris* IDEX Corp	8100 S 1300 W, West Jordan UT 84088	801-561-0303	D	8*	.1
120	Fessler Machine Co—*Charles Fessler*	105 Mcknight Park Dr S, Pittsburgh PA 15237	412-367-3663	R	8*	.1
121	BFI Pump Inc—*James Shaffer*	6320 Cunningham Rd, Houston TX 77041	713-937-9001	R	8*	.1
122	Canariis Corp—*Garry John*	7905 Eagle Palm Dr, Riverview FL 33578	813-621-8643	R	7*	.1
123	Flickinger Industries Inc—*Ronald Flickinger*	1801 Carlton Ave, Fort Wayne IN 46802	260-432-4527	R	7*	<.1
124	Smart Pumps Inc—*J Jernigan*	675 Jarvis Dr Ste A, Morgan Hill CA 95037	408-776-3035	R	7*	<.1
125	Price Pump Manufacturing Co—*Robert Piazza*	21775 8th St E, Sonoma CA 95476	707-938-8441	R	7*	<.1
126	Ivek Corp—*Mark Tanny*	10 Fairbanks Rd, North Springfield VT 05150	802-886-2238	R	6*	<.1
127	Stenner Sales Inc—*Timothy Ware*	3174 Desalvo Rd, Jacksonville FL 32246	904-641-1666	R	6*	<.1
128	Vanton Pump and Equipment Corp—*Gerald Lewis*	201 Sweetland Ave Ste, Hillside NJ 07205	908-688-4216	R	6*	<.1
129	Federal Pump Corp—*John Marr*	1144 Utica Ave, Brooklyn NY 11203	718-451-2000	R	6*	<.1
130	Industrial Parts Specialties—*Will Ganley*	630 Lot Rd, Port Allen LA 70767	225-408-7500	R	6*	.1
131	SAES Getters USA Inc—*Patrick J Glennon*	1122 E Cheyenne Mounta, Colorado Springs CO 80906	719-576-3200	S	6*	<.1
132	Discflo Corp—*Max Gurth*	10850 Hartley Rd, Santee CA 92071	619-596-3181	R	6*	<.1
133	Thrush Company Inc—*Julius Marburger*	PO Box 228, Peru IN 46970	765-472-3351	R	6*	<.1
134	Bowie Industries Inc—*Larry Birch*	PO Box 931, Bowie TX 76230	940-872-1106	R	5*	<.1
135	Pump Engineering Inc—*Robert Oklejas*	1004 W Hurd Rd, Monroe MI 48162	734-242-1772	R	5*	<.1
136	Tri-State Coating And Machine Company Inc—*David Thompson*	PO Box 296, Salt Rock WV 25559	304-736-7733	R	5*	<.1
137	Dubric Industries Inc—*Charles Brickey*	PO Box 43, Comstock Park MI 49321	616-784-6355	R	5*	<.1
138	Giant Industries Inc (Toledo Ohio)—*Ed Simon*	PO Box 3187, Toledo OH 43607	419-531-4600	R	5*	<.1
139	D and D Machine and Hydraulics Inc—*W Harlan*	10945 Metro Pkwy, Fort Myers FL 33966	239-275-7177	R	5*	<.1
140	Murzan Inc—*Alberto Bazan*	2909 Langford Rd Ste A, Norcross GA 30071	770-448-0583	R	5*	<.1
141	Tramco Pump Co—*John Obermaier*	1500 W Adams St, Chicago IL 60607	312-243-5800	R	5*	<.1
142	Huber Inc—*Kevin Hays*	PO Box 10459, New Orleans LA 70181	504-733-0900	R	4*	<.1
143	Hydrolec Limited Inc—*Kim Kawasaki*	5050 Stepp Ave, Jacksonville FL 32216	904-730-3766	R	4*	<.1
144	Foley's Pump Service Inc—*James Foley*	30 Miry Brook Rd, Danbury CT 06810	203-792-2236	R	4*	<.1
145	Unitra Inc—*Nami Sukun*	12601 Exchange Dr Ste, Stafford TX 77477	281-240-1500	R	4*	<.1
146	Anniston Pump Shop Inc—*Margaret Turner*	PO Box 1198, Anniston AL 36202	256-820-2980	R	4*	<.1
147	Srs Crisafulli Inc—*Richard Memhard*	1610 Crisafulli Dr, Glendive MT 59330	406-365-3392	R	4*	<.1
148	Eastern Industrial Products Inc—*Tobias Koch*	830 Tryens Rd, Aston PA 19014	610-459-1212	R	4*	<.1
149	Ace Pump Corp—*Roy Bell*	PO Box 13187, Memphis TN 38113	901-948-8514	R	4*	<.1
150	Kerr Machine Co—*Eddie Nowell*	PO Box 735, Sulphur OK 73086	580-622-4207	R	4*	<.1
151	Northeast Equipment Inc—*Carl Bjornson*	44 Probber Ln, Fall River MA 02720	508-324-1409	R	4*	<.1
152	Fisonic Corp—*Robert Kremer*	94 Greenwich St, New York NY 10006	212-732-3777	R	4*	<.1
153	Pearce Foundry Inc—*Charles Walker*	PO Box 66, Prairieville LA 70769	225-673-6188	R	4*	<.1
154	Spray Force Manufacturing Inc—*Bryan Thompson*	2880 N Larkin Ave, Fresno CA 93727	559-291-3300	R	4*	<.1
155	Fluid Automation Inc—*Lance Daby*	PO Box 930302, Wixom MI 48393	248-912-1970	R	4*	<.1
156	Hydr-O-Dynamic Corp—*Juan Guzman*	5860 La Costa Canyon C, Las Vegas NV 89139	702-367-7727	R	4*	<.1
157	Advanced Machine Works Inc—*Ervin Hendricks*	PO Box 1020, Easley SC 29641	864-859-0380	R	4*	<.1
158	Sharpe Mixers Inc—*Jay Dinnison*	PO Box 3906, Seattle WA 98124	206-767-5660	R	4*	<.1
159	R S Corcoran Co—*William Kramer*	500 N Vine St, New Lenox IL 60451	815-485-2156	R	4*	<.1
160	Onyx Water Products Inc—*Margaret King*	11601 Mitchell Bend Ct, Granbury TX 76048	817-573-2012	R	3*	<.1
161	Gecko Alliance—*David Stokes*	PO Box 77100, Corona CA 92877	951-667-2000	R	3*	<.1
162	Texco Trim Inc—*Bryan Snoek*	PO Box 8616, Houston TX 77249	713-861-1892	R	3*	.1
163	Hawk Of South Carolina Inc—*Bobbie Hawkins*	4 New Cir Rd, Travelers Rest SC 29690	864-834-7212	R	3*	<.1
164	Bsm Pump Corp—*Thomas Ruthman*	180 Frenchtown Rd, North Kingstown RI 02852	401-471-6350	R	3*	<.1
165	Rife Hydraulic Engine Manufacturing Co—*N Gupta*	PO Box 95, Nanticoke PA 18634	570-740-1100	R	3*	<.1
166	Armstrong Machine Company Inc—*Cliff Porter*	201 Sw 7th St, Pocahontas IA 50574	712-335-4131	R	3*	<.1
167	A and F Machine Products Co—*Fred Helwig*	454 Geiger St, Berea OH 44017	440-243-0040	R	3*	<.1
168	Hannmann Machinery Systems Inc—*Ralph Hannmann*	1 Horne Dr, Folcroft PA 19032	610-583-6900	R	3*	<.1
169	Trusty Warns Inc—*Karl Niedermeyer*	320 E Irving Park Rd, Wood Dale IL 60191	630-766-9015	R	3*	<.1
170	Cook Pump Co—*John Carmack*	1400 W 12th St, Coffeyville KS 67337	620-251-0880	R	3*	<.1
171	Irrigation Machine and Supply Inc—*William Young*	PO Box 5932, Lubbock TX 79408	806-747-3443	R	3*	<.1
172	Ketcham Pump Company Inc—*Stuart Hruska*	3420 64th St, Woodside NY 11377	718-457-0800	R	2*	<.1
173	Smith Precision Products Co—*Walter Smith*	PO Box 276, Newbury Park CA 91319	805-498-6616	R	2*	<.1
174	Hugo Vogelsang Machinenbau Gmbh—*Russell Boring*	PO Box 751, Ravenna OH 44266	330-296-3820	R	2*	<.1
175	Acme Dynamics Inc—*Joseph Murphy*	PO Box 1780, Plant City FL 33564	813-752-3137	R	2*	<.1
176	Trench and Marine Pump Company Inc—*Herman Azia*	PO Box 543, Bronx NY 10456	212-423-9098	R	2*	<.1
177	Action Pump Co—*Robert Barrett*	170 Chicago St, Cary IL 60013	847-516-3636	R	2*	<.1
178	Park Engineering Inc—*Ed Swan*	9227 Parklane Ave, Franklin Park IL 60131	847-455-1424	R	2*	<.1

Rank	Company Name—*Executive Officer*	Address, City, State, Zip	Phone	Type	Fin	Empls
179	Motion Controls—*Brad Engstrand*	1174 Western Dr, Hartford WI 53027	262-673-9255	R	1*	<.1
180	Micropump Inc—*Lawrence D Kingsley* IDEX Corp	1402 NE 136th Ave, Vancouver WA 98684	360-253-2008	S	1*	4.3
181	Waterra U S A Inc—*John Mcadam*	4252 Spring Creek Ln B, Bellingham WA 98226	360-738-3366	R	1*	<.1
182	Metropolitan Industries Inc—*John Kochan*	37 Forestwood Dr, Romeoville IL 60446	815-886-9200	R	<1*	<.1

TOTALS: SIC 3561 Pumps & Pumping Equipment
Companies: 182   166,969   112.6

3562 Ball & Roller Bearings

Rank	Company Name—*Executive Officer*	Address, City, State, Zip	Phone	Type	Fin	Empls
1	Schaeffler Group USA Inc—*Bruce Warmbold*	308 Springhill Farm Rd, Fort Mill SC 29715	803-548-8500	R	7,964*	3.2
2	Timken Co—*James W Griffith*	1835 Dueber Ave SW, Canton OH 44706	330-438-3000	P	5,170	21.0
3	Brenco Inc—*Rolando Madrazo*	PO Box 389, Petersburg VA 23804	804-732-0202	S	1,635*	.6
4	MRC Bearings—*Paul Aube* SKF USA Inc	402 Chandler St, Jamestown NY 14701	716-661-2600	S	1,012*	1.6
5	Kaydon Corp—*James O'Leary*	315 E Eisenhower Pkwy, Ann Arbor MI 48108	734-747-7025	P	460	2.3
6	Virginia Industries Inc—*Laura Grondin*	1022 Elm St, Rocky Hill CT 06067	860-571-3602	R	453*	.2
7	NN Inc—*Roderick R Baty*	2000 Waters Edge Dr St, Johnson City TN 37604	423-743-9151	P	365	1.8
8	RBC Bearings Inc—*Michael J Hartnett*	1 Tribology Ctr 102 Wi, Oxford CT 06478	203-267-7001	P	336	2.0
9	Emerson Power Transmission	PO Box 687, Maysville KY 41056	606-564-2011	S	160*	1.1
10	General Bearing Corp—*David L Gussack*	44 High St, West Nyack NY 10994	845-358-6000	P	158	1.0
11	Timken Aerospace and Super Precision Bearings - MPB Div—*Richard Breunich* Timken Co	7 Optical Ave, Keene NH 03431	603-352-0310	S	91*	.6
12	Networks Electronic Corp—*Tamara Christen*	9750 DeSoto Ave, Chatsworth CA 91311	818-341-0440	R	73*	.1
13	Kamatics Corp—*Paul Kuhn*	PO Box 1, Bloomfield CT 06002	860-243-7100	S	66*	.5
14	Tridan Intl—*Brian Campbell* Kaydon Corp	130 N Jackson St, Danville IL 61832	217-443-3592	S	55*	.1
15	Barden Corp—*Peter Enright* Schaeffler Group USA Inc	PO Box 2449, Danbury CT 06813	203-744-2211	S	54*	.6
16	Ntn-Bower Corp—*Yasunori Terada*	707 Bower Rd, Macomb IL 61455	309-837-0440	R	54*	.8
17	NTN Bearing Corporation of America—*Peter Eich*	PO Box 7604, Mount Prospect IL 60056	847-298-7500	S	52*	.4
18	American NTN Bearing Manufacturing Corp—*Dan Milanovic*	9515 Winona Ave, Schiller Park IL 60176	847-671-5450	S	50*	.1
19	Carolina Forge Company LLC—*Carol Owens*	PO Box 370, Wilson NC 27894	252-237-8181	R	34*	.1
20	SKF USA Inc—*Sten Malmstrom*	PO Box 352, Lansdale PA 19446	267-436-6000	S	32*	.2
21	Bearing Service Company of Pennsylvania—*William Banks*	630 Alpha Dr RIDC Park, Pittsburgh PA 15238	412-963-7710	R	25*	.2
22	Rotek Inc—*Mike Drobik*	PO Box 312, Aurora OH 44202	330-562-4000	R	24*	.3
23	Standard Locknut LLC—*Randy Carter*	PO Box 780, Westfield IN 46074	317-867-0100	R	22*	.2
24	Fag Bearings Corp—*Dieter Kuetemeier*	PO Box 1933, Danbury CT 06813	203-790-5474	S	22*	.3
25	Industrial Tectonics Inc—*Mike Purchase* Kaydon Corp	7222 W Huron River Dr, Dexter MI 48130	734-426-4681	S	20*	<.1
26	Tente Casters Inc—*Bradford Hood*	2266 S Park Dr, Hebron KY 41048	859-586-5558	R	18*	.1
27	Rexnord Industries Inc—*Todd Adams*	7601 Rockville Rd, Indianapolis IN 46214	317-273-5500	R	17*	.1
28	Divine Brothers Co—*B Divine*	200 Seward Ave, Utica NY 13502	315-797-0470	R	14*	.1
29	National Bearings Inc—*Jessica H May*	1596 Manheim Pike, Lancaster PA 17601	717-569-0485	S	12*	.1
30	Winsted Precision Ball Co—*Charles Alicandro* Barden Corp	159 Colebrook River Rd, Winsted CT 06098	860-379-7558	D	12*	.1
31	Randall Bearings Inc—*Kent Morgan*	PO Box 1258, Lima OH 45802	419-223-1075	R	12*	.1
32	Schatz Bearing Corp—*Stephen Pomeroy*	10 Fairview Ave, Poughkeepsie NY 12601	845-452-6000	R	11*	.1
33	Advanced Green Components LLC—*Lisa Norwood*	4005 Corporate Dr, Winchester KY 40391	859-737-6000	R	11*	.1
34	Oiles America Corp	4510 Enterprise Dr NW, Concord NC 28027	734-414-7400	S	10*	.1
35	Oconomowoc Manufacturing Corp—*Donald Sydow*	PO Box 436, Oconomowoc WI 53066	262-567-8383	R	8*	.1
36	Jpm Of Mississippi Inc—*William Taber*	PO Box 1446, Hattiesburg MS 39404	601-544-9950	R	6*	<.1
37	Del-Tron Precision Inc—*Ralph Mcintosh*	5 Trowbridge Dr, Bethel CT 06801	203-778-2727	R	6*	.1
38	American Metal Bearing Co—*Mike Tornberg*	7191 Acacia Ave, Garden Grove CA 92841	714-892-5527	R	6*	<.1
39	Roll Master Corp—*Sandy Tucker*	7432 Ranger Way, Fort Worth TX 76133	817-292-4319	R	3*	.1
40	S/N Precision Enterprises Inc—*Augustine Sperrazza*	145 Jordan Rd Ste 1, Troy NY 12180	518-283-8002	R	3*	<.1
41	Miller Bearing Company Inc—*Donald Miller*	420 Portage Blvd, Kent OH 44240	330-678-8844	R	3*	<.1
42	Mb Holdings Inc—*Robert Matthews*	10385 Drummond Rd, Philadelphia PA 19154	215-739-6880	R	3*	<.1
43	Keystone North Inc—*Karen Russel*	310 S Main St, Mansfield PA 16933	570-662-3882	R	3*	<.1

TOTALS: SIC 3562 Ball & Roller Bearings
Companies: 43   18,544   40.2

3563 Air & Gas Compressors

Rank	Company Name—*Executive Officer*	Address, City, State, Zip	Phone	Type	Fin	Empls
1	Gardner Denver Inc—*Barry L Pennypacker*	1800 Gardner Expy, Quincy IL 62305	217-222-5400	P	2,371	6.8
2	Dresser-Rand Group Inc—*Vincent R Volpe Jr*	10205 Westheimer Rd W, Houston TX 77042	713-354-6100	B	2,312	7.5
3	Edwards Ltd—*Matthew Taylor*	301 Ballardvale St, Wilmington MA 01887	978-658-5410	S	1,303*	3.0
4	Ariel Corp (Mount Vernon Ohio)—*Karen Buchwald Wright*	35 Blackjack Rd, Mount Vernon OH 43050	740-397-0311	R	985*	.7
5	Bristol Compressors International Inc—*Chris Robinson*	15185 Industrial Park, Bristol VA 24202	276-466-4121	S	483*	2.5
6	Elliott Co—*Antonio Casillo*	901 N 4th St, Jeannette PA 15644	724-527-2811	R	475*	1.3
7	Thomas Industries Inc—*Jim Beckner* Gardner Denver Inc	211 Industrial Ct, Wabasha MN 55981	651-565-3395	S	410	2.2
8	Arrow Pneumatics Inc	2111 W 21st St, Broadview IL 60155	708-343-9595	R	404*	.1
9	Scroll Technologies—*Jorgen Clausen*	1 Scroll Dr, Arkadelphia AR 71923	870-246-0700	S	383*	.4
10	Sullair Corp—*Stephen Oswald*	3700 E Michigan Blvd, Michigan City IN 46360	219-879-5451	S	140*	.7
11	BeaconMedaes—*Jim Papkas*	1800 Overview Dr, Rock Hill SC 29730	803-817-5600	R	96*	.1
12	Graham Corp—*James R Lines*	PO Box 719, Batavia NY 14021	585-343-2216	P	74	.3
13	Oxy-Dry Corp—*Martin Haver*	1210 N Swift Rd, Addison IL 60101	630-595-3651	S	72*	.1
14	Wagner Spray Tech Corp—*Richard Swenson*	PO Box 9362, Minneapolis MN 55440	763-553-7000	R	68*	.3
15	Oerlikon USA Holding Inc—*James Brissenden*	5700 Mellon Rd, Export PA 15632	724-327-5700	S	59*	.8
16	Compressed Air Systems Inc—*Brint Waring*	9303 Stannum St, Tampa FL 33619	813-626-8177	R	56*	<.1
17	Mitsubishi Heavy Industries Climate Control Inc	1200 N Mitsubishi Pkwy, Franklin IN 46131	317-346-5000	R	41*	.4
18	Gssc Inc—*Thomas Hedger*	5148 113th Ave N, Clearwater FL 33760	727-573-2955	R	41*	.1
19	Saylor-Beall Manufacturing Co—*Bruce Mc Fee*	PO Box 40, Saint Johns MI 48879	989-224-2371	S	36*	.3
20	Quincy Compressor Div—*John Thompson*	PO Box C2, Quincy IL 62305	217-222-7700	D	34*	.5
21	Riley Industrial Services Inc—*G Sonny Riley*	PO Box 2014, Farmington NM 87499	505-327-4947	R	34*	.2
22	Champion Air Compressors Gardner Denver Inc	1800 Gardner Expy, Quincy IL 62305		S	33*	.2
23	Sullivan-Palatek Inc—*Bruce Mcfee*	1201 W Us Hwy 20, Michigan City IN 46360	219-874-2497	S	32*	.1
24	Bauer Compressors Inc—*Jan Dobeneck*	1328 Azalea Garden Rd, Norfolk VA 23502	757-855-6006	R	27*	.2

Note: An asterisk (*) indicates an estimated financial figure. The company type code used is as follows: R = Private, P = Public, S = Private Subsidiary, B = Public Subsidiary, D = Division, J = Joint Venture, I = Investment Fund.

COMPANY RANKINGS BY SALES WITHIN 4-DIGIT SIC

Rank	Company Name—*Executive Officer*	Address, City, State, Zip	Phone	Type	Fin	Empls
25	Fountainhead Group Inc—*John Romano*	23 Garden St, New York Mills NY 13417	315-736-0037	R	27*	.2
26	Curtis-Toledo Inc—*K Carpenter*	1905 Kienlen Ave, Saint Louis MO 63133	314-383-1300	R	25*	.2
27	Zeks Air Drier Corp	1302 Goshen Pky, West Chester PA 19380	610-692-9100	R	24*	.1
28	Dresser-Rand LLC—*Yogesh Joshi*	West8 Tower 10205 West, Houston TX 77042	713-354-6100	R	18*	.2
29	Belco Industries Inc (Belding Michigan)—*Michael Kohn*	9138 West Belding Rd, Belding MI 48809	616-794-0410	R	15*	.1
30	Atlas Copco Hurricane LLC	1015 Hurricane Rd, Franklin IN 46131	317-736-3800	D	14*	.1
31	Sterwart and Stevenson—*Michael Grimes*	1000 Louisiana Ste 590, Houston TX 77002	713-751-2600	S	14*	<.1
32	Kobelco Compressors (America) Inc—*Kevin Neill*	3000 Hammond Ave, Elkhart IN 46516	574-295-3145	R	13*	.1
33	Thomas Energy Systems Inc—*Vince Thomas*	PO Box 471453, Tulsa OK 74147	918-665-0031	R	12*	<.1
34	Boss Industries Inc—*Patrick Wilkins*	1761 Genesis Dr, La Porte IN 46350	219-324-7776	R	9*	<.1
35	Total Compression and Measurement Systems LP—*Steve Evans*	PO Box 11211, Midland TX 79702	432-563-7999	R	9*	.1
36	Heartland Enterprises Ltd—*Dave Campbell*	1039 Kerr Rd, Fredericksburg TX 78624	830-997-9434	R	9*	<.1
37	Associate Engineering Corp—*Timothy Kelley*	PO Box 346, Hustisford WI 53034	920-349-3281	R	9*	.1
38	Precision Plus Vacuum Parts Inc—*Tina Kalley*	2055 Niagara Falls Blv, Niagara Falls NY 14304	716-297-2039	S	7*	.1
39	General Air Products Inc—*Robert Fremont*	PO Box 1387, West Chester PA 19380	610-363-5624	R	7*	<.1
40	Universal Air Products Corp—*Kurt Kondas*	1135 Lance Rd, Norfolk VA 23502	757-461-0077	R	6*	<.1
41	Mako Compressors LLC—*Becky Dreier*	100 Gardner Park, Peachtree City GA 30269		R	6*	.1
42	Eagle Compressors Inc—*Peter Nielsen*	3003 Thurston Ave, Greensboro NC 27406	336-398-8000	S	5*	<.1
43	Hydro-Pac Inc—*Walter Robertson*	PO Box 921, Fairview PA 16415	814-474-1511	R	5*	<.1
44	CM Automotive Systems Inc—*Chander Mittal*	120 Commerce Way, Walnut CA 91789	909-869-7912	R	5*	<.1
45	Potemkin Industries Inc—*Horst Krajenski*	8043 Columbus Rd, Mount Vernon OH 43050	740-397-4888	R	4*	<.1
46	Aavolyn Corp—*Lynn Farrell*	PO Box 1097, Millville NJ 08332	856-327-8040	R	4*	<.1
47	Deco Tools Inc—*Mike Bollenbacher*	1541 Coining Dr, Toledo OH 43612	419-476-9321	R	4*	<.1
48	Milwaukee Sprayer Manufacturing Company Inc—*Alan Rohrick*	N90w14337 Commerce Dr, Menomonee Falls WI 53051	262-437-0330	R	3*	<.1
49	Brama Inc—*Dennis Blong*	5855 Kopetsky Dr Ste I, Indianapolis IN 46217	317-786-7770	R	3*	<.1
50	ITW Poly Craft Systems	195 Internationale Blv, Glendale Heights IL 60139	630-237-5000	D	3*	<.1
51	Aci Services Inc—*Debbie Johnson*	125 Steubenville Ave, Cambridge OH 43725	740-435-0240	R	3*	<.1
52	Lone Star Compressor Corp—*Keith Feaster*	1100 Louisiana St, South Houston TX 77587	713-947-9975	R	3*	<.1
53	Orion Machinery Company Ltd—*Thomas Latsos*	150 S Van Brunt St, Englewood NJ 07631	201-569-3220	R	3*	<.1
54	Vaccon Company Inc—*Richard Ferri*	9 Industrial Park Rd, Medway MA 02053	508-359-7200	R	2*	<.1
55	Price Compressor Company Inc—*Billy Price*	7752 Braniff St, Houston TX 77061	713-649-6050	R	2*	<.1
56	Auburn Vacuum Forming Company Inc—*Paul Hickey*	PO Box 489, Auburn NY 13021	315-253-2440	R	2*	<.1
57	Hydro-Test Products Inc—*Douglas Sagar*	85 Hudson Rd, Stow MA 01775	978-897-4647	R	2*	<.1
58	NEAC Compressor Service USA Inc—*David M Pryer*	191 Howard St, Franklin PA 16323	814-437-3711	S	2*	<.1
59	Compressed Air Concepts—*Mark Hana*	16207 Camenita Rd, Cerritos CA 90703	310-537-1350	R	2*	<.1
60	Tepro Vacuum Products Inc—*Patricia Michaels*	9285 Luna Dr, Saint Cloud FL 34773	407-957-5974	R	1*	<.1
61	Ventura Poole Inc—*Henry Poole*	PO Box 5023, Oxnard CA 93031	805-981-1784	R	1*	<.1
62	Trusco Manufacturing Company Inc—*Brad Harris*	545 Nw 68th Ave, Ocala FL 34482	352-237-0311	R	1*	<.1

TOTALS: SIC 3563 Air & Gas Compressors
Companies: 62   **10,251**   **30.6**

3564 Blowers & Fans

Rank	Company Name—*Executive Officer*	Address, City, State, Zip	Phone	Type	Fin	Empls
1	Donaldson Company Inc—*William M Cook*	PO Box 1299, Minneapolis MN 55440	952-887-3131	P	2,294	13.0
2	Broan-Nutone LLC—*David L Pringle*	PO Box 270140, Hartford WI 53027	262-673-4340	S	896*	3.2
3	Purolator Air Filtration—*Jeff Tumm*	100 River Ridge Cir, Jeffersonville IN 47130	502-969-2304	S	886*	6.7
4	Spencer Turbine Co—*Robert Rayve*	600 Day Hill Rd, Windsor CT 06095	860-688-8361	R	296*	2.1
5	Flanders Filters Inc—*Harry L Smith Jr* Flanders Corp	531 Flanders Filters R, Washington NC 27889	252-946-8081	S	269*	.3
6	Flanders Corp—*Harry L Smith Jr*	531 Flanders Filters R, Washington NC 27889		P	244	2.1
7	Midwesco Filter Resources Inc—*David Unger*	7720 N Lehigh Ave, Niles IL 60714	847-966-1000	P	219	1.1
8	Simpson Dura-Vent—*Brooks Sherman*	PO Box 1510, Vacaville CA 95696	707-446-1786	S	204*	.2
9	BHA Group Holdings Inc—*James E Lund*	8800 E 63rd St Ste 500, Raytown MO 64133	816-356-8480	S	179	1.0
10	Air Vent Inc—*Cliff Tucker*	4117 Pinnacle Point Rd, Dallas TX 75211	214-630-7377	S	155*	.1
11	Venturedyne Ltd	600 College Ave, Pewaukee WI 53072	262-691-9900	R	147*	1.3
12	CECO Environmental Corp—*Jeffrey Lang*	4625 Red Bank Rd Ste 2, Cincinnati OH 45227	513-458-2600	P	141	.6
13	United Air Specialists Inc—*Rich Larson*	4440 Creek Rd, Cincinnati OH 45242	513-891-0400	S	135*	.2
14	Clarcor Air Filtration Products Inc	100 River Ridge Cir, Jeffersonville IN 47130	502-969-2304	S	117*	1.0
15	General Resource Corp—*Tim Masterman*	5909 Baker Rd, Minnetonka MN 55345	952-933-4774	R	112*	.2
16	Lau Industries Inc—*Tom Edwards*	4509 Springfield St, Dayton OH 45431	937-476-6500	S	95*	1.1
17	TBDN Tennessee Co—*Tokuja Yamauchi*	PO Box 1887, Jackson TN 38302	731-421-4800	J	91*	.4
18	Met-Pro Corp—*Raymond J De Hont*	PO Box 144, Harleysville PA 19438	215-723-6751	P	89	.3
19	Fuel Tech Inc—*Douglas G Bailey*	27601 Bella Vista Pky, Warrenville IL 60555	630-845-4500	P	82	.2
20	Loren Cook Co—*Steve Burney*	PO Box 4047, Springfield MO 65808	417-869-6474	R	78*	.9
21	Hilliard Corp—*Nelson Blink*	PO Box 866, Elmira NY 14902	607-733-7121	R	74*	.4
22	Buffalo Air Handling Co—*William Phelps*	467 Zane Snead Dr, Amherst VA 24521	434-946-7455	S	68*	.5
23	Acme Engineering and Manufacturing Corp—*Lee Buddrus*	PO Box 978, Muskogee OK 74402	918-682-7791	R	59*	.5
24	Robinson Fans Inc—*Carl Staible*	PO Box 100, Zelienople PA 16063	724-452-6121	R	46*	.3
25	Met-Pro Corp Systems Div—*Paul A Tetley* Met-Pro Corp	PO Box 144, Harleysville PA 19438	215-723-9300	D	41	<.1
26	Aerotech Inc (Lansing Michigan)—*Robert Mitchell*	4215 Legion Dr, Mason MI 48854	517-676-7070	S	38*	.2
27	Shawndra Products Inc—*Gerald Henry*	PO Box 488, Lima NY 14485	585-624-4500	R	38*	<.1
28	Epcon Industrial Systems Inc—*Aziz Jamaluddin*	PO Box 7060, The Woodlands TX 77385	936-273-3300	R	36*	<.1
29	Schaefer Ventilation Equipment	PO Box 460, Sauk Rapids MN 56379	320-251-8696	R	35*	<.1
30	Revcor Inc—*John Reichwein*	251 Edwards Ave, Carpentersville IL 60110	847-428-4411	R	35*	.5
31	Pneumatic Products Corp	4647 SW 40th Ave, Ocala FL 34474	352-873-5793	S	34*	.3
32	Strobic Air Corp—*William Kacin* Met-Pro Corp	PO Box 144, Harleysville PA 19438	215-723-4700	S	34*	.1
33	American Fan Co—*John Morrissette*	2933 Symmes Rd, Fairfield OH 45014	513-874-2400	R	31*	.2
34	Guzzler Manufacturing Inc—*Robert D Welding*	1621 S Illinois St, Streator IL 61364	815-627-3171	S	27*	.2
35	Atlas Copco Mafi-Trench Company LLC—*James Reilly*	3037 Industrial Pkwy, Santa Maria CA 93455	805-928-5757	R	26*	.2
36	Anemostat—*David Chipman*	PO Box 4938, Carson CA 90749	310-835-7500	S	24*	.1
37	Soler and Palau - USA—*Patrick Williams*	6393 Powers Ave, Jacksonville FL 32217	904-731-4711	R	24*	.2
38	Mott Corp—*Roger Klene*	84 Spring Ln, Farmington CT 06032	860-747-6333	R	23*	.2
39	Mcgill Corp—*James Mcgill*	1 Mission Park, Groveport OH 43125	614-829-1200	R	23*	.4
40	Delta T Corp—*James Smith*	PO Box 11307, Lexington KY 40575	859-233-1271	R	22*	.2
41	Glasfloss Industries Inc—*Scott Lange*	2168 Commerce St, Lancaster OH 43130	740-687-1100	R	22*	.3
42	Hauck Manufacturing Co—*Michael Shay*	PO Box 90, Lebanon PA 17042	717-272-3051	R	22*	.2
43	Airflow Products Company Inc—*Roy Boswell*	100 Oak Tree Dr, Selma NC 27576	919-975-0240	R	20*	.2
44	Ventamatic Ltd—*Bernard Berman*	PO Box 728, Mineral Wells TX 76068	940-325-7887	R	20*	.1

Rank	Company Name—Executive Officer	Address, City, State, Zip	Phone	Type	Fin	Empls
45	Wahlco Inc—Alonso Munoz	2722 S Fairview St, Santa Ana CA 92704	714-979-7300	R	20	.1
46	Adwest Technologies Inc—Craig Bayer	1175 North Van Horne W, Anaheim CA 92806	714-632-9801	R	20*	<.1
47	Universal Air Filter Co—Todd Deibel	PO Box 5006, East Saint Louis IL 62206	618-271-7300	R	19*	<.1
48	Ventline	902 S Division St, Bristol IN 46507	574-848-4491	S	19*	.2
49	RGF Environmental Group—Ronald G Fink	3875 Fiscal Ct, West Palm Beach FL 33404	561-848-1826	R	19*	.1
50	Air Filter Sales and Service-Denver Inc—Jason Boyd	134 Yuma St, Denver CO 80223	303-777-2603	R	18*	<.1
51	Tri-Dim Filter Corp—John Stanley	93 Industrial Dr, Louisa VA 23093	540-967-2600	R	17*	.2
52	Filters-NowCom Inc—Ronald Allen	9800 I65 Service Rd N, Creola AL 36525	251-342-5004	R	16*	.1
53	Wems Inc—Ronald Hood	PO Box 528, Hawthorne CA 90251	310-644-0251	R	16*	.1
54	Breidert Air Products Inc—Patrick Williams	6393 Powers Ave, Jacksonville FL 32217	904-731-4711	R	15*	.1
55	Aircon Corp—Fred Edmaiston	PO Box 80446, Memphis TN 38108	901-452-0230	R	15*	.1
56	Lifetime Industries Inc—Jim Lattimore	2130 Memphis Depot Pkw, Memphis TN 38114	901-362-5690	R	14*	.1
57	Viron International Corp—Gary Gregoricka	505 N Hintz Rd, Owosso MI 48867	989-723-8255	R	14*	.1
58	Gaylord Industries Inc—Aaron Zell	10900 SW Avery St, Tualatin OR 97062	503-691-2010	D	13*	.1
59	Renewaire LLC—Leotta Dye	4510 Helgesen Dr, Madison WI 53718	608-221-4499	R	13*	.1
60	Precipitator Services Group Inc—Carl Nidiffer	PO Box 339, Elizabethton TN 37644	423-543-7331	R	13*	.1
61	Blocksom and Co—Andrew Swan	PO Box 2007, Michigan City IN 46361	219-874-3231	R	12*	.1
62	Lott Enterprises Inc—T Lott	PO Box 9519, Greenwood MS 38930	662-453-0034	R	12*	.2
63	Solberg Manufacturing Inc—Charles Solberg	1151 Ardmore Ave, Itasca IL 60143	630-773-1363	D	12*	.1
64	Iap Inc—Robert Theis	PO Box 56, Phillips WI 54555	715-339-3024	R	11*	.1
65	Henderson Engineering Company Inc—Terry Henderson	95 N Main St, Sandwich IL 60548	815-786-9471	R	10*	.1
66	Sly Inc—T Kurz	8300 Dow Cir Ste 100, Strongsville OH 44136	440-891-3200	R	10*	.1
67	Custom Filter LLC—Dave Fuller	401 Hankes Ave, Aurora IL 60505	630-906-2100	R	10*	.1
68	Tjernlund Products Inc—Robert Tjernlund	1601 9th St, Saint Paul MN 55110	651-426-2993	R	10*	<.1
69	R P Fedder Corp—John Helm	740 Driving Park Ave B, Rochester NY 14613	585-288-1600	R	10*	<.1
70	Fan Group Inc—Ric Pawloski American Fan Co	1701 Terminal Rd Ste 2, Niles MI 49120	269-683-1150	S	10*	.1
71	Airjet Inc—David Leiter	PO Box 1247, Elkhart IN 46515	574-262-4511	R	10*	.1
72	Austin Air Systems Ltd—Richard Taylor	500 Elk St, Buffalo NY 14210	716-856-3704	R	10*	.1
73	Bruning And Federle Manufacturing Co—Thomas Bass	PO Box 5547, Statesville NC 28687	704-873-7237	R	10*	.1
74	Tri-Mer Corp—John Pardell	PO Box 730, Owosso MI 48867	989-723-7838	R	9*	.1
75	Illinois Blower Inc—Tyler Barth	750 Industrial Dr Ste, Cary IL 60013	847-639-5500	R	9*	<.1
76	Pangborn Corp—Ken Dickson	4630 Coates Dr, Fairburn GA 30213	404-665-5700	R	9*	.1
77	March Johnson Systems Inc—Thomas Connell	220 Railroad Dr, Warminster PA 18974	215-364-2500	R	9*	<.1
78	Blowers Inc—William Croft	6650 S Narragansett Av, Chicago IL 60638	708-594-1800	R	9*	.1
79	Greenlees Filter LLC—Carl Myslinski	7550 Industrial Dr, Forest Park IL 60130	708-366-3256	R	8*	.1
80	Vanegas Enterprises Inc—Gary Vanegas	10090 Bunsen Way, Louisville KY 40299	502-491-3553	R	8*	.1
81	Pneumech Systems Manufacturing LLC—Butch Knox	201 Pneu Mechanical Dr, Statesville NC 28625	704-873-2475	R	8*	.1
82	North American Filter Corp—Steve Taylor	200 W Shore Blvd, Newark NY 14513	315-331-7000	R	8*	.1
83	Patterson Fan Company Inc—Vance Patterson	1120 Northpoint Blvd, Blythewood SC 29016	803-691-4750	R	8*	.1
84	Berner International Corp—Georgia Berner	111 Progress Ave, New Castle PA 16101	724-658-3551	R	8*	.1
85	Air Quality Engineering Inc—Heidi Oas	7140 Northland Dr N, Minneapolis MN 55428	763-531-9823	R	7*	.1
86	Krebbs Inc—Ron Krebs	PO Box 390, Falls City NE 68355	402-245-2325	R	7*	.1
87	B and B Technology Inc—Anthony Dimicelli	8282 Warren Rd, Houston TX 77040	713-896-0901	R	7*	<.1
88	Pfm Inc—Joe Haddan	PO Box 190718, Little Rock AR 72219	501-568-5550	R	7*	.1
89	Dynamic Air Engineering Inc—Sharon Morrison	620 E Dyer Rd, Santa Ana CA 92705	714-540-1000	R	7*	<.1
90	Aero Filter Inc—Gerald Festian	1604 E Avis Dr, Madison Heights MI 48071	248-837-4100	R	7*	<.1
91	Transweb LLC—Ogale Kumar	1473 W Forest Grove Rd, Vineland NJ 08360	856-205-1313	R	7*	.1
92	Aircon Filter Sales and Service Co—Leon Schwartz	437 Green St, Philadelphia PA 19123	215-922-5222	R	7*	<.1
93	Dust Free LP—Cathy Gibbs	PO Box 519, Royse City TX 75189	972-635-9565	R	7*	<.1
94	Car - Mon Products Inc—Fred Imming	1225 Davis Rd, Elgin IL 60123	847-695-9000	R	7*	.1
95	Westport Environmental Systems LP—John Olinger	251 Forge Rd, Westport MA 02790	508-636-8811	R	7*	.1
96	Viskon-Aire Corp—Henry Zenzie	410 Winfield Ave, Salisbury MD 21801	410-543-8802	R	7*	<.1
97	Holming Co—Robert Holming	6900 N Teutonia Ave, Milwaukee WI 53209	414-352-3250	R	7*	<.1
98	Sonic Air Systems Inc—Daniel Vanderpyl	1050 Beacon St, Brea CA 92821	714-255-0124	R	7*	<.1
99	Standard Filter Corp—Tobey Wiik	5928 Balfour Ct, Carlsbad CA 92008	760-929-8559	R	6*	<.1
100	Andrews Filter And Supply Corp—Wallace Andrews	2309 Coolidge Ave, Orlando FL 32804	407-423-3310	R	6*	<.1
101	Nuventix Inc—Jim Balthazar	4635 Boston Ln, Austin TX 78735	512-382-8100	R	6*	<.1
102	PureChoice Inc—Bryan Reichel	11481 Rupp Dr, Burnsville MN 55337	952-985-0500	R	6*	<.1
103	Hood Depot International Inc—Donald Lubowicki	710 S Powerline Rd Ste, Deerfield Beach FL 33442	954-570-9860	R	6*	<.1
104	Stoltcr And Brinck Inc—Gerry Koch	201 Sales Ave, Harrison OH 45030	513-367-9300	R	6*	<.1
105	Clean Air Products Co—Kevin Weist	8605 Wyoming Ave N, Minneapolis MN 55445	763-425-9122	R	5*	<.1
106	P Feiner and Sons Inc—Gerson Feiner	PO Box 356, Bogota NJ 07603	201-488-1600	R	5*	<.1
107	Multi-Wing America Inc—James Crowley	PO Box 425, Burton OH 44021	440-834-9400	R	5*	<.1
108	Tigg Corp—Georgiana Riley	1 Willow Ave, Oakdale PA 15071	724-703-3020	R	5*	<.1
109	Tri Bms LLC—John Kolcun	PO Box 937, Royersford PA 19468	610-495-9700	R	5*	<.1
110	Sy-Klone Co—James Moredock	PO Box 550859, Jacksonville FL 32255	904-448-6563	R	5*	<.1
111	Skuttle Manufacturing Co—David Powers	101 Margaret St, Marietta OH 45750	740-373-9169	R	5*	<.1
112	Beakley Enterprises Inc—Deryl Beakley	PO Box 908, Crowley TX 76036	817-783-5600	R	5*	<.1
113	Envirco Corp—Paul Christiansen	101 McNeil Rd, Sanford NC 27330	919-775-2201	R	5*	<.1
114	Beltran Associates Inc—Michael Beltran	1133 E 35th St Ste 1, Brooklyn NY 11210	718-338-3311	R	5*	<.1
115	Airflo Cooling Technologies LLC—Mike Rush	728 S Wheeling Ave, Tulsa OK 74104	918-585-5638	R	5*	<.1
116	Viking Packaging Machinery Inc—Rocky Marquis	PO Box 9039, Yakima WA 98909	509-452-7143	R	5*	<.1
117	D-Mark Inc—James Kasmark	25712 Dhondt Ct, Chesterfield MI 48051	586-949-3610	R	5*	<.1
118	Raydot Systems LLC—Karen Larson	145 Jackson Ave Sw, Cokato MN 55321	320-286-2103	R	5*	<.1
119	JetAir Technologies LLC—William Anderson	1884 Eastman Ave, Ventura CA 93003	805-654-7000	R	5	<.1
120	Ron Pair Enterprises Inc—Ronald Pair	PO Box 438, Charlevoix MI 49720	231-547-4000	R	4*	<.1
121	Kennedy Gustafson And Cole Inc—Edward Cole	100 White Oak Dr, Berlin CT 06037	860-828-3762	R	4*	<.1
122	Kch Services Inc—Ken Hankinson	PO Box 1287, Forest City NC 28043	828-245-9836	R	4*	<.1
123	Excelsior Blower Systems Inc—William Montgomery	PO Box 15126, Reading PA 19612	610-921-9558	R	4*	<.1
124	Bioclimatic Inc—Stephen Zitin	600 Delran Pkwy Ste D, Delran NJ 08075	856-764-4300	R	4*	<.1
125	Royal Hand Equity Corp—Horice Robinson	1489 W Warm Springs Rd, Henderson NV 89014	702-966-8336	R	4*	.1
126	Met-Pro Corp Keystone Filter Div—Lewis E Osterhoudt Met-Pro Corp	2385 N Penn Rd, Hatfield PA 19440	215-822-1963	D	4*	<.1
127	Euramco Safety Inc—Wayne Allen	2746 Via Orange Way, Spring Valley CA 91978	619-670-9590	R	4*	<.1
128	Thermtech Inc—William Hedges	PO Box 5318, Kingwood TX 77325	281-359-7555	R	4*	<.1
129	United Air Filter Co—William Kinney	PO Box 34215, Charlotte NC 28234	704-334-5311	R	4*	<.1
130	Seneca Consolidated Industries Corp—C Harple	PO Box 429, Tiffin OH 44883	419-447-1282	R	4*	<.1
131	Aget Manufacturing Co—Ray Wakefield	PO Box 248, Adrian MI 49221	517-263-5781	R	4*	<.1
132	American Environmental Systems Inc—James Yehl	PO Box 17580, Boulder CO 80308	303-449-3670	R	4*	<.1

Note: An asterisk (*) indicates an estimated financial figure. The company type code used is as follows: R = Private, P = Public, S = Private Subsidiary, B = Public Subsidiary, D = Division, J = Joint Venture, I = Investment Fund.

COMPANY RANKINGS BY SALES WITHIN 4-DIGIT SIC

Rank	Company Name—*Executive Officer*	Address, City, State, Zip	Phone	Type	Fin	Empls
133	Insulation Technology Corp—*Rex Deitesfeld*	PO Box 579, Frederick CO 80530	303-833-6644	R	4*	<.1
134	Jan-Air Inc—*Mark Sattersten*	PO Box J, Richmond IL 60071	815-678-4516	R	4*	<.1
135	Tiernan Aeration Inc—*Mike Tiernan*	PO Box 7588, Amarillo TX 79114	806-372-4051	R	4*	<.1
136	Energenics Corp—*John Hutterly*	1470 Don St, Naples FL 34104	239-643-1711	R	3*	<.1
137	Krenz and Company Inc—*Rod Petersen*	PO Box 187, Germantown WI 53022	262-255-2310	R	3*	<.1
138	Jordan Technologies Inc—*Mark Jordan*	PO Box 118, Fisherville KY 40023	502-267-8344	R	3*	<.1
139	Universal Blower Pac Inc—*Ray Fiechter*	440 Park 32 W Dr, Noblesville IN 46062	317-773-7256	R	3*	<.1
140	Scrubair Systems Inc—*Thomas O'connor*	1250 Rose Rd, Lake Zurich IL 60047	847-550-8061	R	3*	<.1
141	Midwest Air Products Company Inc—*Rick Whiteherse*	PO Box 5319, Traverse City MI 49696	231-941-5865	R	3*	<.1
142	Oem Corp—*Randy Shupert*	3660 Benner Rd, Miamisburg OH 45342	937-859-7492	R	3*	<.1
143	Worldwide Technology Inc—*Edward Contreras*	PO Box 1693, Oldsmar FL 34677	813-855-2443	R	3*	<.1
144	Central Blower Company Inc—*David Petersen*	211 S 7th Ave, City Of Industry CA 91746	626-330-3182	R	2*	<.1
145	Western Professional Group Inc—*Robert Good*	6607 E Yosemite Ave, Orange CA 92867	714-628-0732	R	2*	<.1
146	Gremarco Industries Inc—*Gregory Deotte*	131 E Main St, West Brookfield MA 01585	508-867-5244	R	2*	<.1
147	Walsh Manufacturing Corp—*Frank Walsh*	13825 Triskett Rd, Cleveland OH 44111	216-251-6400	R	2*	<.1
148	Florence Filter Corp—*Erica Anhood*	530 W Manville St, Compton CA 90220	310-637-1137	R	2*	<.1
149	Aran Laboratories—*Conrad Mir*	3574 Melrose Dr Unit E, Wooster OH 44691	330-262-3460	R	2*	<.1
150	Andreae Team Inc—*Robert Andreae*	PO Box 2538, Ardmore OK 73402	580-223-9334	R	2*	<.1
151	Breezemaker Fan Company Inc—*Ron Myers*	PO Box 483, Odessa FL 33556	813-248-5552	R	2*	<.1
152	Agri Ventilation Systems LLC	PO Box 40, Dayton VA 22821	540-879-9864	R	2*	<.1
153	Unisorb Corp—*Larry Thomas*	PO Box 388, South Houston TX 77587	713-943-3753	R	2*	<.1
154	Complete Filtration Inc—*Kenneth Matheis*	PO Box 65, Lake Orion MI 48361	248-693-0500	R	2*	<.1
155	Beverly Pacific Company Inc—*David Ullrich*	PO Box 609, Redmond OR 97756	541-548-0810	R	2*	<.1
156	Modec Inc—*Brian Kalamanka*	4725 Oakland St, Denver CO 80239	303-373-2696	R	2*	<.1
157	Filter Services International—*Roger Guess*	2001 Reliance Pkwy Ste, Bedford TX 76021	817-571-4004	R	2*	<.1
158	Air Craftsman Inc—*Ken Hodges*	617 N Greensboro St, Lexington NC 27292	336-248-5777	R	2*	<.1
159	Airsan Corp—*Arlin Ratajczak*	4554 W Woolworth Ave, Milwaukee WI 53218	414-353-5800	R	1*	<.1
160	Jkh Services Inc—*Jhon Kane*	1109 N New Hope Rd, Raleigh NC 27610	919-231-8596	R	1*	<.1
161	Aeropulse LLC—*Virginia Barrett*	1746 Winchester Rd Fl, Bensalem PA 19020	215-245-7554	R	1*	<.1
162	Airmax International Inc—*Jack Balon*	PO Box 5206, Manchester NH 03108	603-434-2407	R	1*	<.1
163	Tekquest Industries Corp—*Carl Bailey*	4275 Church St, Sanford FL 32771	407-324-5887	R	1*	<.1
164	Entech Environmental Systems Inc—*S Oglesby*	703 Bascomb Commercial, Woodstock GA 30189	770-592-2106	R	1*	<.1
165	Troy Manufacturing New York Inc—*Salvatore Yacuzzo*	59 Lake St, Le Roy NY 14482	585-768-8170	R	1*	<.1
166	American Wholesale Supply Inc—*Gary Maria*	1120 E Chestnut Ave, Santa Ana CA 92701	714-834-0770	R	1*	<.1
167	Saum Enterprises Inc—*David Saum*	5613 Leesburg Pke Ste, Falls Church VA 22041	703-820-7696	R	<1*	<.1
168	Clyde Bergemann EEC—*Greg Golub*	7380 Coca-Cola Dr, Hanover MD 21076	410-368-7000	S	N/A	.1

TOTALS: SIC 3564 Blowers & Fans
Companies: 168

					8,369	46.1

3565 Packaging Machinery

Rank	Company Name—*Executive Officer*	Address, City, State, Zip	Phone	Type	Fin	Empls
1	Cozzoli Machine Co—*Frank Cozzoli*	50 Schoolhouse Rd, Somerset NJ 08873	732-564-0400	R	900*	.1
2	Krones Inc—*Holger Beckmann*	9600 S 58th St, Franklin WI 53132	414-409-4000	R	364*	.4
3	KHS-Bartelt—*Mike Brancato*	5501 N Washington Blvd, Sarasota FL 34243	941-359-4000	R	251*	.6
4	Sumitomo Heavy Industries (USA) Inc—*Ron Smith*	4200 Holland Blvd, Chesapeake VA 23322	757-485-3355	S	150*	.3
5	Evergreen Packaging Equipment	2400 6th St SW, Cedar Rapids IA 52404	319-399-3200	S	143*	.4
6	Disc Makers (Pennsauken New Jersey)—*Tony van Veen*	7905 N Rte 130, Pennsauken NJ 08110	856-663-9030	S	116*	.3
7	Bosch Packaging Technology Inc—*Robert Lawhon*	869 S Knowles Ave, New Richmond WI 54017	715-246-6511	R	105*	.3
8	Douglas Machine Inc—*Rick Paulsen*	3404 Iowa St, Alexandria MN 56308	320-763-6587	R	94*	.5
9	Loveshaw Corp—*Winton Loveland*	PO Box 83, South Canaan PA 18459	570-937-4921	S	92*	.2
10	SWF Cos—*Ed Suarez*	1949 E Manning Ave, Reedley CA 93654	559-638-8484	D	75*	.2
11	Hayssen Inc—*Robert Chapman*	225 Spartangreen Blvd, Duncan SC 29334	864-486-4000	R	73*	.3
12	LantechCom LLC—*Steve Clifford*	11000 Bluegrass Pkwy, Louisville KY 40299	502-267-4200	R	63*	.4
13	Angelus Sanitary Can Machine Co—*Maury Koeberle*	4900 Pacific Blvd, Los Angeles CA 90058	323-583-2171	R	56*	.5
14	Bosch Packaging Technology—*Don DeMorett*	8700 Wyoming Ave N, Minneapolis MN 55445	763-424-4700	D	55*	.2
15	Pneumatic Scale Corp—*Robert Chapman*	10 Ascot Pkwy, Cuyahoga Falls OH 44223	330-923-0491	R	47*	.3
16	Standard-Knapp Inc—*Mike Weaver*	63 Pickering St, Portland CT 06480	860-342-1100	R	46*	.1
17	Klikwood Corp—*William Crist*	5224 Snapfinger Woods, Decatur GA 30035	770-981-5200	R	44*	.3
18	Conair Corporate Office and Technology Centre—*Chris Keller*	200 W Kensinger Dr, Cranberry Township PA 16066	724-584-5500	R	42*	.1
19	Arpac LP—*Richard Allegretti*	PO Box 88497, Chicago IL 60680	847-678-4001	R	40*	.3
20	Winpak Portion Packaging Inc—*Thomas Herlihy*	828a Newtown Yardley R, Newtown PA 18940	267-685-8200	R	40*	.2
21	R A Jones and Company Inc—*Gordon Bonfield*	2701 Crescent Springs, Covington KY 41017	859-341-0400	R	37*	.4
22	MorphiusDisc Manufacturing—*David Andler*	100 E 23rd St, Baltimore MD 21218	410-662-0112	R	37*	.1
23	Packaging Technologies Inc—*Barry Shoulders*	PO Box 3848, Davenport IA 52808	563-391-1100	R	35*	.2
24	Accraply Inc—*Gregory Tschida*	PO Box 95635, Chicago IL 60694	763-557-1313	R	35*	.1
25	Hunkar Technologies Inc—*Eric Thiemann*	2106 Florence Ave Ste, Cincinnati OH 45206	513-272-1010	R	33*	.1
26	Great Lakes LLC—*Angela Tillander* Arpac LP	9511 River St, Schiller Park IL 60176	847-678-3668	S	32*	.2
27	US DigitalMedia—*Chris Pignotti*	1929 W Lone Cactus Dr, Phoenix AZ 85027	623-587-4900	R	32*	.1
28	Acma USA Inc	501 Southlake Blvd, Richmond VA 23236	804-794-9777	D	31*	.2
29	Hudson-Sharp Machine Co—*Kim Davis*	PO Box 19038, Green Bay WI 54307	920-494-4571	R	29*	.2
30	Woodman Company Inc—*Curt Kuhr* Klikwood Corp	5224 Snapfinger Woods, Decatur GA 30035	770-981-5200	S	27*	.2
31	Martin Automatic Inc—*Roger Cederholm*	1661 Northrock Ct, Rockford IL 61103	815-654-4800	R	26*	.2
32	Nercon Eng and Manufacturing Inc—*James Nerenhausen*	PO Box 2288, Oshkosh WI 54903	920-233-3268	R	25*	.2
33	RA Pearson Company Inc—*Michael A Senske*	8120 W Sunset Hwy, Spokane WA 99224	509-838-6226	R	23*	.2
34	Flexicell Inc—*Hans DeKoning*	10463 Wilden Dr, Ashland VA 23005	804-550-7300	R	23*	.1
35	Flexicon Corp—*David Gill*	2400 Emrick Blvd, Bethlehem PA 18020	610-814-2400	R	22*	.1
36	Heisler Industries Inc—*Richard Heisler*	224 Passaic Ave, Fairfield NJ 07004	973-227-6300	R	21*	.1
37	B and H Manufacturing Company Inc—*Lyn Bright*	PO Box 247, Ceres CA 95307	209-537-5785	R	21*	.2
38	Pmi Cartoning Inc—*Branko Tisma*	850 Pratt Blvd, Elk Grove Village IL 60007	847-437-1427	R	19*	.1
39	Brenton LLC—*Mark Anderson*	4750 County Rd 13 Ne, Alexandria MN 56308	320-852-7705	R	19*	.1
40	AGI Media—*Gene Kelly*	5055 Wilshire Blvd Ste, Los Angeles CA 90036	323-937-0220	R	19*	.1
41	Elopak Inc—*Robert Gillis*	30000 S Hill Rd, New Hudson MI 48165	248-486-4600	R	18*	.1
42	ATMI Packaging Inc—*Doug Neugold*	10851 Louisiana Ave S, Bloomington MN 55438	952-942-0855	S	18*	.1
43	Aylward Enterprises Inc—*Luke Northwood*	401 Industrial Dr, New Bern NC 28562	252-633-5757	R	16*	.1
44	Lacerta Group Inc—*Ali Lotfi*	360 Forbes Blvd, Mansfield MA 02048	508-339-3312	R	16*	<.1
45	Mgs Machine Corp—*Richard Bahr*	9900 85th Ave N, Maple Grove MN 55369	763-425-8808	R	15*	.1
46	Heat Seal LLC—*R Skalsky*	4580 E 71st St, Cleveland OH 44125	216-341-2022	R	15*	.1
47	Formost Fuji Corp—*Norm Formo*	PO Box 359, Woodinville WA 98072	425-483-9090	R	15*	<.1
48	Premier Packaging Corp	PO Box 352, Victor NY 14564	585-924-8460	R	15*	<.1

Rank	Company Name—Executive Officer	Address, City, State, Zip	Phone	Type	Fin	Empls
49	United Bakery Equipment Company Inc—Frank Bastasch	15815 W 110th St, Lenexa KS 66219	913-541-8700	R	15*	.1
50	Maf Industries Inc—Thomas Blanc	PO Box 218, Traver CA 93673	559-897-2905	R	15*	.1
51	Shibuya Hoppmann Corp—Mark Flanagan	13129 Airpark Dr Ste 1, Elkwood VA 22718	540-829-2564	R	14*	.1
52	Weiler Engineering Inc—Gerhard Weiler	1395 Gateway Dr, Elgin IL 60124	847-697-4900	R	14*	.1
53	Osgood Industries Inc—Martin Mueller	601 Burbank Rd, Oldsmar FL 34677	813-855-7337	R	14*	.1
54	Raque Food Systems LLC—Ken Simpson	PO Box 99594, Louisville KY 40269	502-267-9641	R	14*	.1
55	Busse Brothers Inc—Thomas Young	124 N Columbus St, Randolph WI 53956	920-326-3131	R	13*	.1
56	Haumiller Engineering Co—Russ Holmer	445 Renner Dr, Elgin IL 60123	847-695-9111	R	13*	.1
57	All-Fill Corp—Richard Edginton	418 Creamery Way, Exton PA 19341	610-524-7350	R	13*	.1
58	Clamco Corp	775 Berea Industrial P, Berea OH 44017	216-267-1911	R	13*	<.1
59	Jescorp Inc—John Sanfilippo	1900 Pratt Blvd, Elk Grove Village IL 60007	847-378-1200	S	12*	.1
60	Lane Winpak Inc—Ted Torrens	998 S Sierra Way, San Bernardino CA 92408	909-885-0715	R	12*	.1
61	Emhart Glass Manufacturing Inc—Glen Long	13075 Us Hwy 19 N, Clearwater FL 33764	727-669-9999	R	12*	.1
62	Kisters Kayat Inc—Andrew Neagle	5501 N Washington Blvd, Sarasota FL 34243	941-359-4000	S	12*	.1
63	Ossid LLC—Carol Causeway	PO Box 1968, Rocky Mount NC 27802	252-446-6177	R	11*	.1
64	Tetra Pak Americas Inc—Nick Shreiber	1221 Brickell Ave Ste, Miami FL 33131	305-416-2460	D	11*	.1
65	Dyco Inc—Peter Yohe	6951 Naus Way, Bloomsburg PA 17815	570-752-2757	R	11*	.1
66	Enquatics Inc—Nicholas Nigrelli	16024 County Rd X, Kiel WI 53042	920-693-3161	R	11*	.1
67	General Plasma Inc—John Madocks	546 E 25th St, Tucson AZ 85713	520-882-5100	R	11*	.1
68	Prototype Equipment Corp—James Goodman	1081 S Northpoint Blvd, Waukegan IL 60085	847-596-9000	R	10*	.1
69	Highlight Industries Inc—Kurt Riemenschneider	2694 Prairie St Sw, Grand Rapids MI 49519	616-531-2464	R	10*	.1
70	Omega Design Corp—Glen Siegele	211 Philips Rd, Exton PA 19341	610-363-6555	R	10*	.1
71	Accutek Packaging Equipment Co—Edward Chocholek	1399 Specialty Dr, Vista CA 92081	760-734-4177	R	10*	<.1
72	Precision Powerhouse—Daniel Piepho	2155 Niagara Ln N, Plymouth MN 55447	763-449-5500	S	10*	<.1
73	Traco Manufacturing Inc—John Palica	PO Box 1065, Orem UT 84059	801-225-8040	R	10*	.1
74	Stork Fabricators Inc—Robert Stork	PO Box 185, Washington MO 63090	636-239-7424	R	10*	.1
75	Now Disc—Brian Powell	3875 S American Way, Idaho Falls ID 83402	208-552-1720	R	9*	<.1
76	Roberts Polypro Inc—Roy Tetreault	5416 Wyoming Ave, Charlotte NC 28273	704-588-1794	R	9*	.1
77	Matrix Packaging Machinery Inc—Marc Willden	650 N Dekora Woods Blv, Saukville WI 53080	262-268-8300	R	9*	.1
78	Econocorp Inc—Wayne Goldberg	72 Pacella Park Dr, Randolph MA 02368	781-986-7500	R	9*	.1
79	Dayton Systems Group Inc—Henry Bachmann	3003 S Tech Blvd, Miamisburg OH 45342	937-885-5665	R	8*	.1
80	Kodiak Cartoners Inc—Casandra Tanney	2550 S E Ave Ste 101, Fresno CA 93706	559-266-4844	R	8*	.1
81	Polypack Inc—Alain Cerf	3301 Gateway Centre Bl, Pinellas Park FL 33782	727-578-5000	R	8*	.1
82	Universal Labeling Systems Inc—L Hall	3501 8th Ave S, Saint Petersburg FL 33711	727-327-2123	R	8*	.1
83	RED Stamp Inc—Bruce Boer	PO Box 9967, Wyoming MI 49509	616-878-7771	R	8*	<.1
84	Advanced Digital Media—Patricia Ratner	9144 Deering Ave, Chatsworth CA 91311	818-882-3095	R	8*	.1
85	Pdc International Corp—Anatole Konstantin	PO Box 492, Norwalk CT 06856	203-853-1516	R	8*	.1
86	Lock Inspection Systems Inc—David Garnett	207 Authority Dr, Fitchburg MA 01420	978-343-3716	R	8*	.1
87	OKL Can Line Inc—Al Omernick	11235 Sebring Dr, Cincinnati OH 45240	513-825-1655	R	8*	.1
88	Kabar Manufacturing Corp—Bruce Kee	140 Schmitt Blvd, Farmingdale NY 11735	631-694-6857	S	7*	<.1
89	National Instrument LLC—Bob Downs	4119 Fordleigh Rd, Baltimore MD 21215	410-764-0900	R	7*	<.1
90	E-Pak Machinery Inc—Ronald Sarto	1535 S State Rd 39, La Porte IN 46350	219-393-5541	R	7*	<.1
91	Princeton Disc Corp—Avi Itzhakov	1913 Atlantic ASve, Manasquan NJ 08736	732-892-5655	R	7*	<.1
92	Dove Enterprises—Larry Adams	4520 Hudson Dr, Stow OH 44224	330-928-9160	R	7*	<.1
93	Massman Automation Designs LLC—Scott Nelson	1010 E Lake St, Villard MN 56385	320-554-3611	R	7*	<.1
94	Quadrel Inc—Lon Deckard	7670 Jenther Dr, Mentor OH 44060	440-602-4700	R	7*	<.1
95	Farason Corp—Joseph Hurley	735 Fox Chase Ste 110, Coatesville PA 19320	610-383-6224	R	7*	<.1
96	Whallon Machinery Inc—Leslie Smith	PO Box 429, Royal Center IN 46978	574-643-9561	R	7*	.1
97	Ropak Manufacturing Company Inc—Ralph Matthews	1019 Cedar Lake Rd Se, Decatur AL 35603	256-350-4241	R	7*	.1
98	Taylor Products Company Inc—Lewis Ribich	2205 Jothi Ave, Parsons KS 67357	620-421-5550	R	7*	.1
99	Wayne Automation Corp—A Johnson	605 General Wash Ave, Norristown PA 19403	610-630-8900	R	7*	.1
100	Spee-Dee Packaging Machinery Inc—James Navin	1360 Grandview Pkwy, Sturtevant WI 53177	262-886-4402	R	6*	<.1
101	M and O Perry Industries Inc—Joseph Osterhaus	412 N Smith Ave, Corona CA 92880	951-734-9838	R	6*	<.1
102	Pace Packaging Corp—Kenneth Regula	3 Sperry Rd, Fairfield NJ 07004	973-227-1040	R	6*	<.1
103	New England Machinery Inc—Judith Nickse	PO Box 20299, Bradenton FL 34204	941-755-5550	R	6*	<.1
104	Packaging Automation Corp—David Chase	2725 Hwy 55, Saint Paul MN 55121	651-456-0003	R	6*	<.1
105	Per-Fil Industries Inc—Shari Boellmann	PO Box 9, Riverside NJ 08075	856-461-5700	R	6*	<.1
106	Royle Printing Co—Chris D Carpenter	745 S Bird St, Sun Prairie WI 53590	608-837-5161	R	6*	<.1
107	Scandia Packaging Machinery Co—Wilhelm Bronander	15 Industrial Rd, Fairfield NJ 07004	973-473-6100	R	6*	<.1
108	Palace Packaging Machines Inc—Paul Taraschi	4102 Edges Mill Rd, Downingtown PA 19335	610-873-7252	R	6*	<.1
109	Axon LLC—Andy Perry	3080 Bsnenc Pk Dr Ste, Raleigh NC 27610	919-772-8383	R	5*	<.1
110	Volckening Inc—Frederick Schneider	6700 3rd Ave, Brooklyn NY 11220	718-836-4000	R	5*	<.1
111	Ctm Integration Inc—Thomas Rumsey	PO Box 589, Salem OH 44460	330-332-1800	R	5*	<.1
112	Doyen Medipharm Inc—Martin Beriswill	4030 S Pipkin RdSte 10, Lakeland FL 33811	863-683-6335	S	5*	.1
113	Reactive Resin Products Co—Jeff Freiburger	327 5th St, Perrysburg OH 43551	419-666-6119	R	5*	<.1
114	John R Nalbach Engineering Company Inc—John Nalbach	621 E Plainfield Rd, Countryside IL 60525	708-579-9100	R	5*	<.1
115	Dubuit of America Inc—Micheal Taylor	70 Monaco Dr, Roselle IL 60172	630-894-9500	R	5*	<.1
116	Valley Litho Supply—Walter Babineau	1047 Haugen Ave, Rice Lake WI 54868		R	5*	<.1
117	Miconvi Properties Inc—Michael Connelly	4711 E 355th St, Willoughby OH 44094	440-954-3500	R	5*	<.1
118	Hannan Products Corp—Henry Jenkins	220 N Smith Ave, Corona CA 92880	951-735-1587	R	5*	<.1
119	Batching Systems Inc—Donald Wooldridge	50 Jibsail Dr, Prince Frederick MD 20678	410-414-8111	R	5*	<.1
120	Marq Packaging Systems Inc—Rocky Marquis	PO Box 9063, Yakima WA 98909	509-966-4300	R	5*	<.1
121	Oden Corp—Iver Phallen	199 Fire Tower Dr, Tonawanda NY 14150	716-874-3000	R	5*	<.1
122	Greener Corp—Theodore Wojtech	4 Helmly St, Bayville NJ 08721	732-341-3880	R	5*	<.1
123	W E Plemons Machinery Services Inc—William Plemons	PO Box 787, Parlier CA 93648	559-834-1744	R	4*	<.1
124	Southern Packaging Machinery Corp—David Raska	PO Box 349197, Homestead FL 33034	305-245-3045	R	4*	<.1
125	Anderson-Martin Machine Co—Frank Anderson	PO Box 145, Fort Smith AR 72902	479-646-8946	R	4*	<.1
126	Ctc International Inc—Erwin Herbert	PO Box 1137, West Caldwell NJ 07007	973-228-2300	R	4*	<.1
127	Dubhouse—Michael Pardo	404 SE 15th St, Fort Lauderdale FL 33316	954-524-3658	R	4*	<.1
128	Spectrum Digital Services LLC—Russell S Gnant	600 Northshore Dr, Hartland WI 53029	262-369-1577	R	4*	<.1
129	DVD/Works—Jeff Starfield	93 Park St, Beverly MA 01915	978-922-4990	R	4*	<.1
130	Packaging Systems International Inc—Michael Lott	4990 Acoma St, Denver CO 80216	303-296-4445	R	4*	<.1
131	Rockford Packaging Systems Inc—Adrienne Murphy	1715 Northrock Ct, Rockford IL 61103	815-877-0212	R	4*	<.1
132	Thermoforming Systems LLC	1601 W Pine St, Union Gap WA 98903	509-454-4578	R	4*	<.1
133	Food Equipment Manufacturing Corp—Robert Sauer	22201 Aurora Rd, Bedford Heights OH 44146	216-663-1208	R	4*	<.1
134	Hartness Visy Automation LLC—Cindy Fruth	PO Box 26509, Greenville SC 29616	864-213-1767	R	4*	<.1
135	Ouellette Machinery Systems Inc—Joseph Ouellette	1761 Chase Dr, Fenton MO 63026	636-343-7200	R	4*	<.1
136	Clements Industries—Alan Clements	50 Ruta Ct, South Hackensack NJ 07606	201-440-5500	R	4*	<.1
137	Compacker Systems LLC—Jane Bower	PO Box 2026, Davenport IA 52809	563-391-2751	R	4*	<.1
138	Terco Inc—Dennis Ahrens	459 Camden Dr, Bloomingdale IL 60108	630-894-8828	R	4*	<.1

Note: An asterisk (*) indicates an estimated financial figure. The company type code used is as follows: R = Private, P = Public, S = Private Subsidiary, B = Public Subsidiary, D = Division, J = Joint Venture, I = Investment Fund.

COMPANY RANKINGS BY SALES WITHIN 4-DIGIT SIC

Rank	Company Name—*Executive Officer*	Address, City, State, Zip	Phone	Type	Fin	Empls
139	Allpac Inc—*Lawrence Lakey*	810 Buffalo Springs Dr, Prosper TX 75078	972-347-2286	R	3*	<.1
140	Exact Packaging Inc—*Randy Cotteleer*	1145 E Wellspring Rd, New Freedom PA 17349	717-235-8345	R	3*	<.1
141	Park Air Corp—*Jerald Goldman*	204 Ct St, Brockton MA 02302	508-584-3440	R	3*	<.1
142	Circle Packaging Machinery Inc—*John Dykema*	2020 American Blvd, De Pere WI 54115	920-983-3420	R	3*	<.1
143	Potdevin Machine Co—*Robert Potdevin*	PO Box 1409, Caldwell NJ 07007	973-227-8828	R	3*	<.1
144	Zygot Automation Inc—*Youssef Hennes*	2525 W Evans Ave Ste 3, Denver CO 80219	303-922-7344	R	3*	<.1
145	Custom Equipment Design Inc—*Sandra Decrane*	PO Box 4807, Monroe LA 71211	318-345-2222	R	3*	<.1
146	General Packaging Equipment Co—*Robert Kelly*	6048 Westview Dr, Houston TX 77055	713-686-4331	R	3*	<.1
147	Translab Inc—*Ed Newcomb*	5408 3m Dr Ste A, Menomonie WI 54751	715-235-1111	R	3*	<.1
148	Michael Pace Interactive—*Michael A Pace*	628 Vernon Ave Studio, Venice CA 90291	310-450-1280	R	3*	<.1
149	AJM Shrink Wrap Co—*Jed Jelincic*	1664 Delta Ct, Hayward CA 94544	510-357-7791	R	3*	<.1
150	Multi-Media Duplication Inc—*Gerry Rasch*	4132 Shoreline Dr Ste, Earth City MO 63045	314-291-7800	R	3*	<.1
151	Prodo-Pak Corp—*John Mueller*	PO Box 363, Garfield NJ 07026	973-772-4500	R	3*	<.1
152	Burghof Engineering and Manufacturing Co—*Kaspar Kammerer*	16051 Deerfield Pkwy S, Lincolnshire IL 60069	847-634-0737	R	3*	<.1
153	Petty Machine Company Inc—*Larry Petty*	PO Box 1888, Gastonia NC 28053	704-864-3254	R	3*	<.1
154	Audion Automation Ltd—*Ian Oroura*	1533 Crescent Dr Ste 1, Carrollton TX 75006	972-389-0777	R	3*	<.1
155	M and S Automated Feeding Systems Inc—*Mark Grinager*	1194 Cliff Rd E, Burnsville MN 55337	952-894-3263	R	3*	<.1
156	Filler Specialties Inc—*Norman Slagh*	440 100th Ave, Zeeland MI 49464	616-772-9235	R	2*	<.1
157	Metro Weighing and Automation Inc—*Tim Harrison*	7641 Holland Rd, Taylor MI 48180	313-299-9600	R	2*	<.1
158	Wrabacon Inc—*Bob Nelson*	PO Box 7, Oakland ME 04963	207-465-2068	R	2*	<.1
159	American Packaging Machinery Inc—*Tadiya Peric*	2550 S Eastwood Dr, Woodstock IL 60098	815-337-8580	R	2*	<.1
160	Geiger Tool and Manufacturing Company Inc—*James Nogrady*	50 Liberty St, Passaic NJ 07055	973-777-2136	R	2*	<.1
161	Wild Horse Industrial Corp—*G Murray*	640 Airpark Rd Ste A, Napa CA 94558	707-265-6801	R	2*	<.1
162	C M Ambrose Co—*John Bowman*	2919 Fulton St, Everett WA 98201	425-317-9818	R	2*	<.1
163	Digital Media Automation Inc—*Wally Willemse*	12815 Stone Canyon Rd, Poway CA 92064	858-673-8505	R	2*	<.1
164	Partner Pak Inc—*Paul Appelbaun*	5770 Research Dr, Huntington Beach CA 92649	714-799-7879	R	2*	<.1
165	RGB Productions Inc—*Greg Bollin*	1678 Lance Pointe Rd, Maumee OH 43537	419-891-2120	R	2*	<.1
166	Saint Media Inc—*John St Martin*	212 Sudbury St, Marlborough MA 01752	508-229-8063	R	2*	<.1
167	Groove House Records—*Bryan Kelley*	5029 Serrania Ave, Woodland Hills CA 91364		R	2*	<.1
168	A E Randles Company Inc—*Patrick Randles*	4617 S 3rd Ave, Tucson AZ 85714	520-889-7533	R	2*	<.1
169	George Gordon Associates Inc—*Donald Belanger*	12 Continental Blvd, Merrimack NH 03054	603-424-5204	R	2*	<.1
170	Lepel Corp—*Aver Guez*	W227n937 Westmound Dr, Waukesha WI 53186	262-782-0450	R	2*	<.1
171	Deitz Company Inc—*Steven Deitz*	PO Box 1108, Wall NJ 07719	732-681-0200	R	2*	<.1
172	Rose Packaging and Design—*Rob Rose*	PO Box 3316, Basalt CO 81621	970-927-6515	R	2*	<.1
173	Wozniak Machinery Co—*Craig Wozniak*	906 Riverstone Way, Woodstock GA 30188	770-924-0806	R	2*	<.1
174	Ihly Industries Inc—*Eugen Ihly*	2191 W Cornell Ave, Englewood CO 80110	303-761-6624	R	2*	<.1
175	Laub Engineering Corp—*Edward Hunt*	13547 Excelsior Dr, Norwalk CA 90650	562-802-9591	R	1*	<.1
176	Peerless Pattern Works Inc—*William Bonner*	3325 Nw Yeon Ave, Portland OR 97210	503-227-6561	R	1*	<.1
177	Qc Electronics Inc—*Kenneth Klein*	1635 La Dawn Dr, Portage WI 53901	608-742-1661	R	1*	<.1
178	Seal-A-Tron Corp—*Werner Duemmer*	3815 Se Naef Rd, Portland OR 97267	503-652-5200	R	1*	<.1
179	Wrap-Ade Machine Company Inc—*Robert Mc Closky*	180 Brighton Rd Ste B, Clifton NJ 07012	973-773-6150	R	1*	<.1
180	Action Packaging Automation Inc—*John Wojnicki*	PO Box 190, Roosevelt NJ 08555	609-448-9210	R	1*	<.1
181	Pack-Rite Machines	3026 Phillips Ave, Racine WI 53403	262-635-6966	D	1	<.1
182	Viking Machine And Design Inc—*Donald Lindgren*	1408 Viking Ln, De Pere WI 54115	920-336-1190	R	1*	<.1
183	Package Machinery Company Inc—*Katherine Putnam*	380 Union St Ste 58, West Springfield MA 01089	413-732-4000	R	1*	<.1
184	Weldotron Inc—*David Olsen*	300 Bryant Ln, Woodbury TN 37190	615-563-6318	R	1*	<.1
185	Digital Disc Manufacturing Inc	PO Box 714, Kenilworth NJ 07033	908-591-7686	R	1*	<.1
186	Digital Wave Technologies Inc—*James Horigan*	1800 Byberry Rd Bldg 9, Huntington Valley PA 19006	215-544-1200	R	1*	<.1
187	Rainbow Packaging Inc—*Susan Schmidt*	1352 W Indigo Dr, Chandler AZ 85248	480-821-8626	R	1*	<.1
188	Purchasing Services Limited Inc—*Tracey Vernier*	602 Industrial St, Mascoutah IL 62258	618-566-8100	R	1*	<.1
189	Nestech Machine Systems Inc—*Steve Foldesi*	PO Box 462, Hinesburg VT 05461	802-482-4575	R	1*	<.1
190	Mgl International Inc—*M Griebat*	230 Leonard St, Lewisville TX 75057	972-221-3555	R	1*	<.1
191	Madgar Genis Corp—*Normand Madgar*	131 Snyder Ave, Barberton OH 44203	330-848-6950	R	1*	<.1
192	Eagle Automation Inc—*Larry Salter*	PO Box 1018, Sterling IL 61081	815-625-1858	R	1*	<.1
193	Kaps-All Packaging Systems Inc—*Kenneth Herzog*	200 Mill Rd, Riverhead NY 11901	631-727-0300	R	1*	<.1

TOTALS: SIC 3565 Packaging Machinery
Companies: 193

					4,261	14.2

3566 Speed Changers, Drives & Gears

Rank	Company Name—*Executive Officer*	Address, City, State, Zip	Phone	Type	Fin	Empls
1	Twin Disc SouthEast Inc—*Michael E Batten* Twin Disc Inc	11700 NW 101 Rd Ste 19, Medley FL 33178	305-885-0707	S	5,317*	.9
2	Horsburgh and Scott Co—*Christopher Kete*	5114 Hamilton Ave, Cleveland OH 44114	216-431-3900	R	477*	.6
3	Twin Disc Inc—*Michael E Batten*	1328 Racine St, Racine WI 53403	262-638-4000	P	310	.9
4	Falk Corp—*Dave Doerr*	1600 Pumphrey Ave, Auburn AL 36832		S	238	1.4
5	Triumph Gear Systems—*Pat Coward*	PO Box 680910, Park City UT 84068	435-649-1900	S	172*	.3
6	SEW-Eurodrive Inc—*Juergen Blickle*	1275 Old Spartanburg H, Lyman SC 29365	864-439-7537	S	66	.5
7	Milwaukee Gear Company Inc—*Richard Fullington*	5150 N Port Washington, Milwaukee WI 53217	414-962-3532	R	41*	.3
8	Hub City Inc—*Henry W Knueppel*	PO Box 1089, Aberdeen SD 57402	605-225-0360	S	40*	.3
9	Bunting Bearings LLC—*Thomas Kwiatkowski*	PO Box 729, Holland OH 43528	419-866-7000	R	36*	.2
10	Columbia Gear Corp—*Dana Lynch*	530 County Rd 50, Avon MN 56310	320-356-7301	R	32*	.4
11	Ac Technology Corp—*Allen Ottoson*	630 Douglas St, Uxbridge MA 01569	508-278-9100	R	30*	.4
12	Koellmann Gear Corp—*Michael Rasovic*	PO Box 101, Waldwick NJ 07463	201-447-0200	R	28*	.3
13	Nord Gear Corp—*Terry Schadeberg*	PO Box 367, Waunakee WI 53597	608-849-7300	R	27*	.2
14	AMI Arc Machines Inc—*David Sherrington*	10500 Orbital Way, Pacoima CA 91331	818-896-9556	R	25*	.3
15	Precipart Corp—*John Walter*	90 Finn Ct, Farmingdale NY 11735	631-694-3100	R	23*	.1
16	Overton Gear and Tool Corp—*Louis Ertel*	530 Westgate Dr, Addison IL 60101	630-543-9570	R	23*	.2
17	Grove Gear—*Mike Manna*	1524 15th Ave, Union Grove WI 53182	262-878-1221	D	23	.2
18	Gear Works Seattle Inc—*Roland Ramberg*	PO Box 80886, Seattle WA 98108	206-762-3333	R	21*	.1
19	Chicago Gear - D O James Corp—*Wayne Wellman*	2823 W Fulton St, Chicago IL 60612	773-638-0508	R	17*	.1
20	Cleveland Gear Company Inc—*Dana Lynch*	PO Box 70100t, Cleveland OH 44190	216-641-9000	R	14*	.1
21	Superior Gearbox Co—*Richard Carr*	PO Box 645, Stockton MO 65785	417-276-5191	R	13*	.1
22	American Autogard Corp—*Derek Gold*	5173 26th Ave, Rockford IL 61109	815-229-3190	R	13*	.1
23	Zero-Max Inc—*Douglas Moore*	13200 6th Ave N, Minneapolis MN 55441	763-546-4300	R	11*	.1
24	Quad Plus LLC—*Carol Nuffelen*	1921 Cherry Hill Rd, Joliet IL 60433	815-740-0860	R	11*	.1
25	Sterling Electric Inc—*Raymond Helton*	7997 Allison Ave, Indianapolis IN 46268	317-872-0471	R	10*	.1
26	Steward Machine Company Inc—*Whitney Debardeleben*	PO Box 11008, Birmingham AL 35202	205-841-6461	R	9*	.1
27	De'ran Gear Inc—*Douglas Randolph*	9405 N County Rd 2000, Lubbock TX 79415	806-746-6926	R	7*	.1
28	St Louis Gear Company Inc—*Daniel Hodges*	PO Box 880, Keokuk IA 52632	319-524-5042	R	7*	.1
29	Reliance Gear Corp—*Leroy Maros*	205 W Factory Rd, Addison IL 60101	630-543-6640	R	7*	.1

Rank	Company Name—*Executive Officer*	Address, City, State, Zip	Phone	Type	Fin	Empls
30	Productigear Inc—*Richard Wieker*	1900 W 34th St, Chicago IL 60608	773-847-4505	R	7*	<.1
31	Acme Gear Company Inc—*Joseph Gelles*	PO Box 779, Englewood NJ 07631	201-568-2245	R	6*	.1
32	Process Industries Consortium Llc—*Jeff Monger*	3860 River Rd, Schiller Park IL 60176	847-671-1631	R	6*	.1
33	Circle Gear and Machine Company Inc—*Albert Knez*	1501 S 55th Ct, Cicero IL 60804	708-652-1000	R	6*	<.1
34	Stahl Gear and Machine Co—*Herman Bronstein*	3901 Hamilton Ave, Cleveland OH 44114	216-431-2820	R	5*	.1
35	Walter Machine Company Inc—*Donald Chatrnuck*	PO Box 7700, Jersey City NJ 07307	201-656-5654	R	4*	<.1
36	ASI Technologies Inc—*Barney Berlinger Jr*	209 Progress Dr, Montgomeryville PA 18936	215-661-1002	R	4*	<.1
37	Raycar Tool and Machine Co—*Dan Schwartz*	4884 Stenstrom Rd, Rockford IL 61109	815-874-3948	R	3*	<.1
38	Buffalo Gear Inc—*Daniel Szczygiel*	3635 Lockport Rd, Sanborn NY 14132	716-731-2100	R	3*	<.1
39	Engelhardt Gear Co—*Armin Engelhardt*	2526 American Ln, Elk Grove Village IL 60007	847-766-7070	R	3*	<.1
40	Toledo Gearmotor Co—*John S Toth*	5459 Roan Rd, Sylvania OH 43560	419-885-3769	R	2*	<.1
41	Hadley Gear Manufacturing Co—*John Davey*	4444 W Roosevelt Rd, Chicago IL 60624	773-722-1030	R	2*	<.1
42	Great Lakes Hydraulics Inc—*Arthur Apkarian*	4170 36th St Se, Grand Rapids MI 49512	616-949-8844	R	2*	<.1
43	Std Precision Gear and Instrument Inc—*James Manning*	318 Manley St Ste 5, West Bridgewater MA 02379	508-580-0035	R	1*	<.1
44	Charles Bond Co—*Charles Bond*	PO Box 105, Christiana PA 17509	610-593-5171	R	1*	<.1

TOTALS: SIC 3566 Speed Changers, Drives & Gears
Companies: 44   7,101   8.6

3567 Industrial Furnaces & Ovens

Rank	Company Name—*Executive Officer*	Address, City, State, Zip	Phone	Type	Fin	Empls
1	Nordyne Inc—*David Lagrand*	8000 Phoenix Pkwy, O Fallon MO 63368	636-561-7300	S	377*	1.8
2	Petro-Chem Development Company Inc—*Stephen T Limpe*	122 E 42nd St Ste 2308, New York NY 10168	212-455-6500	S	101*	.3
3	Indel Inc—*Henry M Rowen*	PO Box 157, Rancocas NJ 08073	609-267-9000	R	67*	.2
4	Chromalox Inc—*Scott Dysert*	103 Gamma Dr Ext, Pittsburgh PA 15238	412-967-3940	S	53	.2
5	Tpi Corp—*Robert Henry*	PO Box 4973, Johnson City TN 37602	423-477-4131	R	45*	.6
6	Johnson Gas Appliance Co—*Stephen O'donnell*	520 E Ave Nw, Cedar Rapids IA 52405	319-365-5267	R	37*	.1
7	George Koch Sons LLC—*Robert L Koch*	10 S 11th Ave, Evansville IN 47712	812-465-9600	S	36*	.2
8	I Cerco Inc—*Byron Anderson*	453 W Mcconkey St, Shreve OH 44676	330-567-2145	R	30*	.3
9	Ebner Furnaces Inc—*Peter Ebner*	224 Quadral Dr, Wadsworth OH 44281	330-335-1600	R	28*	.1
10	Tempco Electric Heater Corp—*Fermin Adames*	607 N Central Ave, Wood Dale IL 60191	630-350-2252	R	27*	.3
11	Seco Warwick Corp—*Keith Boeckenhauer*	PO Box 908, Meadville PA 16335	814-332-8400	R	26*	.1
12	Callidus Technologies LLC—*Doyle Bishop*	7130 S Lewis Ste 335, Tulsa OK 74136	918-496-7599	D	25*	.2
13	Durex International Corp—*Edward Hinz*	190 Detroit St, Cary IL 60013	847-639-5600	R	24*	.2
14	Wolverine Proctor	121 Proctor Ln, Lexington NC 27292	336-248-5181	S	24*	.2
15	Sierra Therm Production Furnaces Inc—*Thomas Stewart*	200 Westridge Dr, Watsonville CA 95076	831-763-0113	R	24*	.1
16	Consarc Corp—*William Marino*	PO Box 156, Rancocas NJ 08073	609-267-8000	R	23*	.2
17	Thermo Fisher Scientific LLC	81 Wyman St, Waltham MA 02451	781-622-1000	S	22*	.2
18	Matthews Cremation Div—*Paul F Rahill*	2045 Sprint Blvd, Apopka FL 32703	407-886-5533	S	21*	.1
19	Electric Furnace Co—*Phillip Greenisen*	435 W Wilson St, Salem OH 44460	330-332-4661	R	21*	.4
20	Surface Combustion Inc—*William Bernard*	PO Box 428, Maumee OH 43537	419-891-7150	R	20*	.1
21	International Thermal Systems LLC—*Linda Erie*	4697 W Greenfield Ave, Milwaukee WI 53214	414-672-7700	R	20*	.1
22	Centorr-Vacuum Industries Inc—*William Nareski*	55 Northeastern Blvd S, Nashua NH 03062	603-595-7233	R	20*	<.1
23	Retech Systems LLC—*Leroy Leland*	100 Henry Station Rd, Ukiah CA 95482		R	19*	.1
24	Jhawar Industries Inc—*Suresh Jhawar*	525 Klug Cir, Corona CA 92880	951-340-4646	R	19*	<.1
25	Selas Fluid Processing Corp—*John McDermott*	5 Sentry Pkwy E Ste 20, Blue Bell PA 19422	610-804-0300	D	18*	.1
26	Vitronics Soltec Corp—*Aaron Saxton*	2 Marin Way, Stratham NH 03885	603-772-7778	S	18*	.1
27	Engineered Ceramics—*Robert Simpson*	PO Box 365, Gilberts IL 60136	847-428-4455	R	16*	<.1
28	Harper International Corp—*Charles Miller*	100 W Drullard Ave Ste, Lancaster NY 14086	716-684-7400	R	16*	.1
29	Grieve Corp—*Pat Calabrese*	500 Hart Rd, Round Lake IL 60073	847-546-8225	R	16*	.1
30	Therma-Tron-X Inc—*Bradley Andreae*	1155 S Neenah Ave, Sturgeon Bay WI 54235	920-743-6568	R	15*	.1
31	Cambridge Engineering Inc—*John Kramer*	PO Box 1010, Chesterfield MO 63006	636-532-2233	R	15*	.1
32	Bethlehem Corp—*Alan H Silverstein*	25th and Lennox St, Easton PA 18045	610-258-7111	R	15*	.1
33	Afc-Holcroft LLC—*Mike Boutsikaris*	49630 Pontiac Trl, Wixom MI 48393	248-624-8191	R	14*	.1
34	Heatron Inc—*Michael Keenan*	3000 Wilson Ave, Leavenworth KS 66048	913-651-4420	R	14*	.1
35	Rama Corp—*Pepper Renshaw*	600 W Esplanade Ave, San Jacinto CA 92583	951-654-7351	R	13*	.1
36	GC Broach Co—*George C Broach*	7667 E 46th Pl, Tulsa OK 74145	918-664-7420	R	13*	.1
37	Omega Heater Company Inc—*Alfred Gaudio*	2059 9th Ave, Ronkonkoma NY 11779	631-588-8820	R	12*	.1
38	Consolidated Engineering Company Inc—*Scott Crafton*	1971 Mccollum Pkwy Nw, Kennesaw GA 30144	770-422-5100	R	12*	.1
39	Kaufman Engineered Systems Inc—*Charles Kaufman*	1260 Waterville Monclo, Waterville OH 43566	419-878-9727	R	12*	.1
40	Industrial Heater Corp—*Ted Mcgwire*	30 Knotter Dr, Cheshire CT 06410	203-250-0500	R	12*	.1
41	Rogers Engineering And Manufacturing Company Inc—*William Rogers*	112 S Ctr St, Cambridge City IN 47327	765-478-5444	R	12*	.1
42	Quench Press Specialists Inc—*James Duncan*	204 Woodwind Ct, Spartanburg SC 29302	864-576-3502	R	11*	<.1
43	Centrifugal and Mechanical Industries—*Antone Sebastiao*	201 President St, Saint Louis MO 63118	314-776-2848	S	10*	.1
44	Therm-Tec Inc—*Dean Robbins*	PO Box 1105, Tualatin OR 97062	503-625-7575	R	10*	<.1
45	CM Furnaces Inc—*David Neill*	103 Dewey St, Bloomfield NJ 07003	973-338-6500	R	9*	<.1
46	Conceptronic Inc—*Eric Seekins*	1860 Smithtown Ave, Ronkonkoma NY 11779	631-981-7081	S	9*	<.1
47	Thermal Equipment Corp—*Lee Courtney*	2030 E University Dr, Rancho Dominguez CA 90220	310-328-6600	D	9	.1
48	Moorhead Machinery and Boiler Co—*Jon A Schmoeckel*	3477 University Ave NE, Minneapolis MN 55418	612-789-3541	R	8*	.1
49	Furnace Technologies Inc—*Tim Fisher*	1070 Disher Dr, Waterville OH 43566	419-878-2100	R	8*	.1
50	Hix Corp—*Bruce Huelat*	1201 E 27th Ter, Pittsburg KS 66762	620-231-8568	R	8*	.1
51	B and L Cremation Systems Inc—*Steve Looker*	7205 114th Ave, Largo FL 33773	727-541-4666	R	8*	<.1
52	Core Furnace Systems Corp—*Dominic Faccone*	100 Corporate Center D, Coraopolis PA 15108	412-262-2240	D	8	<.1
53	M H Detrick Co—*R Pena*	9400 Bormet Dr Ste 10, Mokena IL 60448	708-479-5085	R	8*	<.1
54	Solaronics Inc—*Richard Rush*	PO Box 80217, Rochester MI 48308	248-651-5333	R	8*	<.1
55	Cosmos Electronic Machine Corp—*Kenneth Arutt*	140 Schmitt Blvd, Farmingdale NY 11735	631-249-2535	R	7*	<.1
56	CA Litzler Company Inc—*Matthew Litzler*	4800 W 160th St, Cleveland OH 44135	216-676-8020	R	7*	<.1
57	Benchmark Thermal Corp—*Gil Mathew*	PO Box 1799, Grass Valley CA 95945	530-477-5011	R	7*	.1
58	Skutt Ceramic Products Inc—*James Skutt*	6441 Se Johnsn Creek B, Portland OR 97206	503-774-6000	R	7*	<.1
59	Williams Industrial Service Inc—*Robert Williams*	2120 Wood Bridge Blvd, Bowling Green OH 43402	419-353-2120	R	7*	<.1
60	Ds Fibertech Corp—*Duong Nguyen*	11015 Mission Park Ct, Santee CA 92071	619-562-7001	R	7*	<.1
61	Heatrex Inc—*Frederick O'polka*	PO Box 515, Meadville PA 16335	814-724-1800	R	7*	.1
62	Procedyne Corp—*Thomas Parr*	11 Industrial Dr, New Brunswick NJ 08901	732-249-8347	R	6*	<.1
63	Vacuum Furnace Systems Corp—*James Kellogg*	1946 E Cherry Ln, Souderton PA 18964	215-723-4623	R	6*	<.1
64	Steelman Industries Inc—*Richard Fraser*	PO Box 1461, Kilgore TX 75663	903-984-3061	R	6*	<.1
65	TM Vacuum Products—*Fred Stuffer*	PO Box 2248, Cinnaminson NJ 08077	856-829-2000	R	6*	<.1
66	Aztec Machinery Co—*David Rattner*	PO Box 2069, Warminster PA 18974	215-672-2600	R	6*	<.1
67	Contour Hardening Inc—*John Storm*	8401 NW Blvd, Indianapolis IN 46278	317-876-1530	R	6*	<.1
68	Glenro Inc—*Gary Denend*	PO Box 3052, Paterson NJ 07509	973-279-5900	R	5*	<.1
69	Dalton Electric Heating Company Inc—*Thomas Shields*	28 Hayward St, Ipswich MA 01938	978-356-9844	R	5*	.1

Note: An asterisk (*) indicates an estimated financial figure. The company type code used is as follows: R = Private, P = Public, S = Private Subsidiary, B = Public Subsidiary, D = Division, J = Joint Venture, I = Investment Fund.

COMPANY RANKINGS BY SALES WITHIN 4-DIGIT SIC

Rank	Company Name—Executive Officer	Address, City, State, Zip	Phone	Type	Fin	Empls
70	Armil/Cfs Inc—Walter Parduhn	PO Box 114, South Holland IL 60473	708-339-6810	R	5*	<.1
71	Flynn Burner Corp—Jullian Modzelesky	PO Box 431, New Rochelle NY 10802	914-636-1320	R	5*	<.1
72	Infratrol Manufacturing Corp—Steven Onsager	2500 S 162nd St, New Berlin WI 53151	262-797-8140	R	5*	<.1
73	Dri-Air Industries Inc—Charles Sears	PO Box 1020, East Windsor CT 06088	860-627-5110	R	5*	<.1
74	Solar Products Inc—David Eck	228 Wanaque Ave, Pompton Lakes NJ 07442	973-835-6581	R	5*	<.1
75	Saturn Machine And Welding Company Inc—Billy Baird	PO Box 69, Sturgis KY 42459	270-333-2104	R	5*	<.1
76	Thorpe Technologies Inc—John Allen	449 W Allen Ave Ste 11, San Dimas CA 91773	562-903-8230	R	5*	<.1
77	Radiant Energy Systems Inc—Sarvejit Narang	175 N Ethel Ave, Hawthorne NJ 07506	973-423-5220	R	5*	<.1
78	National Element Inc—Lauren Best	7939 Lochlin Dr, Brighton MI 48116	248-486-1810	R	4*	<.1
79	Lakeway Manufacturing Inc—Jack Kenning	PO Box 486, Huron OH 44839	419-433-3030	R	4*	<.1
80	Zion Industries Inc—Bob Puls	6229 Grafton Rd, Valley City OH 44280	330-483-4650	R	4*	.1
81	Kleenair Products Co—Robert Oeck	14230 Se 98th Ct, Clackamas OR 97015	503-653-6925	R	4*	<.1
82	Boyertown Furnace Co—John Meade	PO Box 100, Boyertown PA 19512	610-369-1450	R	4*	<.1
83	Advanced Combustion Systems Inc—Michael Milnes	1999 Alpine Way, Bellingham WA 98226	360-676-6005	R	3*	<.1
84	Furnace Builders Inc—Norman Miller	PO Box 1376, Dayton OH 45401	270-685-9911	R	3*	<.1
85	Wyssmont Company Inc—Edward Weisselberg	1470 Bergen Blvd, Fort Lee NJ 07024	201-947-4600	R	3*	<.1
86	Argus International Inc—Bernard Costello	PO Box 559, Ringoes NJ 08551	609-466-1677	R	3*	<.1
87	Upton Industries Inc—William Minoletti	30435 Groesbeck Hwy St, Roseville MI 48066	586-771-1200	R	3*	<.1
88	Cci Thermal Technologies Indiana Inc—David Boyle	PO Box 146, Greensburg IN 47240	812-663-4141	R	3*	<.1
89	Industrial Combustion Engineers Inc—Leonard Nowak	7000 W 21st Ave, Gary IN 46406	219-949-5066	R	3*	<.1
90	Wellington Development Corp—Carl Hayes	800 Wellington Ave, Cranston RI 02910	401-467-5201	R	3*	<.1
91	Glo-Quartz Electric Heater Company Inc—George Strokes	PO Box 358, Mentor OH 44061	440-255-9701	R	3*	<.1
92	Marsden Inc—Thomas Smith	1675 Hylton Rd, Pennsauken NJ 08110	856-663-2227	R	3*	<.1
93	Bbc Industries Inc—Ronald Vinyard	5 Capper Dr, Pacific MO 63069	636-343-5600	R	3*	<.1
94	Circle Industrial Manufacturing Corp—Ronald La Forest	1613 W El Segundo Blvd, Compton CA 90222	310-638-5101	R	3*	<.1
95	E H Inc—David Wade	PO Box D, Allegan MI 49010	269-673-6456	R	3*	<.1
96	Heater Designs Inc—Tom Odendahl	2211 S Vista Ave, Bloomington CA 92316	909-421-0971	R	3*	<.1
97	Thermal Process Construction Company Inc—Al Gupta	19 Engineers Ln, Farmingdale NY 11735	631-293-6400	R	3*	<.1
98	Prime Heat Inc—Herb Boekamp	1844 Friendship Dr Ste, El Cajon CA 92020	619-449-6623	R	2*	<.1
99	Catalytic Products Intnlinc—Dennis Lincoln	980 Ensell Rd, Lake Zurich IL 60047	847-438-0334	R	2*	<.1
100	Lambda Technologies Inc—Richard Garard	860 Aviation Pkwy Ste, Morrisville NC 27560	919-462-1919	R	2*	<.1
101	Induction Technology Corp—Michael Dicken	9924 Rancho Rd, Adelanto CA 92301	760-246-7333	R	2*	<.1
102	O'Brien and Gere Manufacturing—Terry Brown	547 E Genesee St, Fayetteville NY 13066	315-637-2234	S	2*	<.1
103	Lucifer Furnaces Inc—Larry Jones	2048 Bunnell Rd, Warrington PA 18976	215-343-0411	R	2*	<.1
104	L and L Special Furnace Company Inc—Gregory Lewicki	PO Box 2129, Aston PA 19014	610-459-9216	R	2*	<.1
105	Fast Heat Inc—Tim Stojka	776 N Oaklawn Ave, Elmhurst IL 60126	630-359-6300	R	2*	<.1
106	Air and Process Systems Inc—Michael Tackney	PO Box 15622, Baton Rouge LA 70895		R	2*	<.1
107	Bel Thermal Units Inc—Bill Brown	4810 Nw 35th Ave, Miami FL 33142	954-566-0043	R	2*	<.1
108	Custom Electric Manufacturing Co—Robert Edwards	48941 W Rd, Wixom MI 48393	248-305-7700	R	2*	<.1
109	Bixby Energy Systems Inc—Melanie Bonnie	6893 139th Ln Nw, Anoka MN 55303	763-404-7800	R	2*	<.1
110	Hed International Inc—James Dennis	PO Box 246, Ringoes NJ 08551	609-466-1900	R	2*	<.1
111	Ajax Electric Co—John Barry	60 Tomlinson Rd, Huntingdon Valley PA 19006	215-947-8500	R	2*	<.1
112	Delta Manufacturing Company Inc—Richard Houskeeper	PO Box 9889, Tulsa OK 74157	918-224-6755	R	2*	<.1
113	Heat Sensor Technologie LLC	601 Norgal Dr Ste A, Lebanon OH 45036	513-228-0481	R	2*	<.1
114	Trent Inc—L Silverthorn	201 Leverington Ave, Philadelphia PA 19127	215-482-5000	R	1*	<.1
115	Microdry Inc—Peter Nemeth	5901 W Hwy 22, Crestwood KY 40014	502-241-8933	R	1*	<.1
116	Uas Automation Systems Inc—Larry Mcgurk	3413 Lake Breeze Dr, Orlando FL 32808	407-294-8551	R	1*	<.1
117	Capital Induction Inc—Larry Misner	6505 Diplomat Dr, Sterling Heights MI 48314	586-254-2740	R	1*	<.1
118	Industrial Furnace Interiors Inc—Clyde Bennett	43551 Utica Rd, Sterling Heights MI 48314	586-726-2388	R	1*	<.1
119	Degenfelder John—John Degenfelder	350 Sw Wake Robin Ave, Corvallis OR 97333	541-758-8133	R	1*	<.1
120	Evenheat Kiln Inc—John Watson	PO Box 399, Caseville MI 48725	989-856-2281	R	1*	<.1
121	IVI Corp—George Mackertich	265 Oak St, Pembroke MA 02359	781-826-3195	R	1*	<.1
122	Sheler Corp—Gary Burnash	37885 Commerce Dr, Sterling Heights MI 48312	586-979-8560	R	1*	<.1
123	Sivon Manufacturers Co—Charlotte Kieffer	3131 Perry Park Rd, Perry OH 44081	440-259-5505	R	<1*	<.1
124	Bickley Inc—Genaro Cueva	550 State Rd, Bensalem PA 19020	215-638-4500	R	<1*	<.1
125	Flame Treating Systems—Mark Sirrine	715 E Geer St Ste A4, Durham NC 27701	919-956-5208	R	<1*	<.1
126	Rupp Air Management—Jeff Fels	101 N Industrial Pkwy, West Union IA 52175	563-422-8894	R	<1*	<.1

TOTALS: SIC 3567 Industrial Furnaces & Ovens
Companies: 126

					1,702	9.9

3568 Power Transmission Equipment Nec

Rank	Company Name—Executive Officer	Address, City, State, Zip	Phone	Type	Fin	Empls
1	Rail Bearing Service Inc—James Griffith	PO Box 6932, Canton OH 44706	330-438-3000	S	5,200	N/A
2	RBS Global Inc—Todd A Adams	4701 Greenfield Ave, Milwaukee WI 53214		S	1,700	6.2
3	Sauer-Danfoss Co USA—Sven Ruder	2800 East 13th St, Ames IA 50010	515-239-6000	S	1,600	6.0
4	US Tsubaki Inc—Yoshi Kitayama	301 E Marquardt Dr, Wheeling IL 60090	847-459-9500	S	644*	1.0
5	Neapco Components LLC—Dum Benhauer	PO Box 399, Pottstown PA 19464	610-323-6000	R	600*	2.2
6	Ameridrives International LLC—Cristy Ray-Beardsley	1680 Cornell Rd, Green Bay WI 54313	920-593-2444	R	283*	3.4
7	Waukesha Bearings Corp—Ronald L Hoffman	W231 N2811 Roundy Cir, Pewaukee WI 53072	262-506-3000	S	245*	.6
8	Peer Bearing Co—Laurence Spungen	2200 Norman Dr S, Waukegan IL 60085	847-578-1000	R	200*	.6
9	Jeffrey Chain LP—Marylou Mauney	2307 Maden Dr, Morristown TN 37813	423-586-1951	S	155*	.3
10	Kop-Flex Inc—Dale Skoch	PO Box 1696, Baltimore MD 21203	410-768-2000	S	143*	.4
11	Glacier Garlock Bearings—Bernd Fischer	PO Box 189, Thorofare NJ 08086	856-848-3200	S	124*	.3
12	Alto Products Corp—David Landa	PO Box 1088, Atmore AL 36504	251-368-7777	R	123*	.3
13	Ntn Driveshaft Inc—Nobuo Satoh	8251 S International D, Columbus IN 47201	812-342-7000	R	81*	1.0
14	Xtek Inc—Kyle Seymour	11451 Reading Rd, Cincinnati OH 45241	513-733-7800	R	71*	.3
15	Eaton Corp Airflex Div	9919 Clinton Rd, Cleveland OH 44144	216-281-2211	D	67*	.2
16	Funk Manufacturing Co—Robert Chopp	PO Box 251-3400, Coffeyville KS 67337	620-251-3400	S	63*	.5
17	Magnetic Power Systems Inc—Bruce Ryan	PO Box 26508, Oklahoma City OK 73126	405-755-1600	R	56*	.7
18	Arens Controls Company LLC—John Saunders	3602 N Kennicott Ave, Arlington Heights IL 60004	847-844-4700	R	50*	.1
19	Lovejoy Inc—Michael Hennessy	2655 Wisconsin Ave, Downers Grove IL 60515	630-852-0500	R	45*	.3
20	Kingsbury Inc—Woods Brown	10385 Drummond Rd, Philadelphia PA 19154	215-824-4000	R	44*	.3
21	Bison Gear and Engineering Corp—Martin Swarbrick	3850 Ohio Ave, Saint Charles IL 60174	630-377-4327	R	37*	.2
22	Ringfeder Corp—Carl Fenstermacher	PO Box 691, Westwood NJ 07675	201-666-3320	R	36*	.1
23	Elkhart Products Corp—Dale A Dieckbernd	PO Box 1008, Elkhart IN 46515	574-264-3181	S	35*	.3
24	Aurora Bearing Co—Charles Richard	901 Aucutt Rd, Montgomery IL 60538	630-859-2030	R	35*	.3
25	Hyspan Precision Products Inc—Donald Heye	1685 Brandywine Ave, Chula Vista CA 91911	619-421-1355	R	34*	.2
26	Sargent Controls and Aerospace—Ronald Hoffman	5675 W Burlingame Rd, Tucson AZ 85743	520-744-1000	D	27*	.2
27	SS White Technologies Inc—Rahul Shukla	151 Old New Brunswick, Piscataway NJ 08854	732-752-8300	R	27*	.2
28	Regal-Beloit Corp Durst Div—Henry Knueppel	PO Box 298, Beloit WI 53512	608-365-2563	D	25*	.2
29	Weasler Engineering Inc—James Hawkins	PO Box 558, West Bend WI 53095	262-338-2161	R	22*	.2

Rank	Company Name—*Executive Officer*	Address, City, State, Zip	Phone	Type	Fin	Empls
30	Morris Coupling Co—*Howard Pollock*	2240 W 15th St, Erie PA 16505	814-459-1741	R	20*	.1
31	DuPont Vespel Parts and Shapes—*Ellen J Kullman*	6200 Hillcrest Dr, Valley View OH 44125	216-901-3600	S	20*	.2
32	Beere Precision Products—*Dick Beere*	4915 21st St, Racine WI 53406	262-632-0472	S	19*	.1
33	E C Styberg Engineering Co—*Ernest Styberg*	PO Box 788, Racine WI 53401	262-637-9301	R	19*	.2
34	WM Berg Inc—*Kelly Keller*	PO Box 100558, Cudahy WI 53110	414-747-5800	R	18*	.1
35	Linn Gear Co—*Gill Hartl*	PO Box 397, Lebanon OR 97355	541-259-1211	R	18*	.1
36	Dynamic Sealing Technologies Inc—*Jeffrey Meister*	13829 Jay St Nw, Anoka MN 55304	763-786-3758	R	16*	.1
37	Renold Inc—*Thomas Murrer*	100 Bourne St, Westfield NY 14787	716-326-3121	R	15*	.1
38	Helical Products Company Inc—*Herbert Merrell*	PO Box 1069, Santa Maria CA 93456	805-928-3851	R	14*	.1
39	Dfb Holdings Inc—*Tim Steele*	PO Box 45, Seville OH 44273	330-769-2071	R	10*	.1
40	Climax Metal Products Co—*Gerald Wheaton*	30202 Lakeland Blvd, Wickliffe OH 44092	440-585-0300	R	10*	.1
41	Ball Screws and Actuators Company Inc	3616 Snell Ave, San Jose CA 95136	408-629-1132	S	9*	.1
42	Force Control Industries Inc—*James Besl*	3660 Dixie Hwy, Fairfield OH 45014	513-868-0900	R	9*	.1
43	American Solar Electric—*Sean Seitz*	3008 N Civic Ctr Plz, Scottsdale AZ 85251	480-994-1440	R	9*	.1
44	Hayes Manufacturing Inc—*Raymond Hayes*	PO Box 220, Fife Lake MI 49633	231-879-3372	R	8*	<.1
45	Clutchco International Inc—*Mike Killion*	PO Box 1089, Humble TX 77347	281-446-1297	R	8*	.1
46	Art Technologies Inc—*Carl Pfirrmann*	3795 Symmes Rd, Hamilton OH 45015	513-942-8800	R	8*	.1
47	American-Metric Corp—*John Bettger*	52 Metric Rd, Laurens SC 29360	864-876-2011	R	8*	.1
48	North American Clutch Corp—*Jeffrey Hargarten*	PO Box 090228, Milwaukee WI 53209	414-267-4000	R	8*	.1
49	Nim-Cor Inc—*Edgar Smith*	PO Box 330, Nashua NH 03061	603-889-2153	R	7*	.1
50	Whittet-Higgins Co—*Andrew Brown*	PO Box 8, Central Falls RI 02863	401-728-0700	R	7*	.1
51	Jackson Wheeler Metals Service Inc—*Eric Aitkin*	270 Georgia Ave, Brooklyn NY 11207	718-342-5000	R	7*	.1
52	Barnes Industries Inc—*Glen Barnes*	PO Box 71543, Madison Heights MI 48071	248-541-2333	R	7*	.1
53	Carlson Company Inc—*William Spangler*	PO Box 2822, Wichita KS 67201	316-744-0481	R	7*	.1
54	Great Lakes Industry Inc—*Larry Schultz*	1927 Wildwood Ave, Jackson MI 49202	517-784-3153	R	7*	<.1
55	Carlyle Johnson Machine Company LLC—*Brian Gamache*	PO Box 9546, Bolton CT 06043	860-643-1531	R	6*	<.1
56	Belt Technologies Inc—*Alan Wosky*	11 Bowles Rd, Agawam MA 01001	413-786-9922	R	6*	<.1
57	Missouri Pressed Metals Inc—*Rand Bankovich*	PO Box 1544, Sedalia MO 65302	660-827-3460	R	6*	.1
58	Milwaukee Bearing and Machining Inc—*Kenneth Chybowski*	W134 N5235 Campbell Dr, Menomonee Falls WI 53051	262-783-1100	R	6*	.1
59	Gear Products Inc—*Bill Alford*	1111 N 161st E Ave, Tulsa OK 74116	918-234-3044	S	6*	.1
60	Liston Manufacturing Inc—*Theodore Pyrak*	PO Box 178, North Tonawanda NY 14120	716-695-2111	R	6*	.1
61	Triangle Manufacturing Co—*Jack Sullivan*	PO Box 1070, Oshkosh WI 54903	920-235-3710	R	6*	<.1
62	Ebo Group Inc—*David Heidenreich*	PO Box 305, Sharon Center OH 44274	330-239-4933	R	6*	<.1
63	Kmc Inc—*Fouad Zeidan*	20 Technology Way, West Greenwich RI 02817	401-392-1900	R	6*	<.1
64	American Sleeve Bearing LLC—*Richard Toney*	1 Spring St, Stafford Springs CT 06076	860-684-8060	R	5*	<.1
65	System Components Inc—*Eugen Gawreliuk*	1635 Stieve Dr, South Haven MI 49090	269-637-2191	R	5*	<.1
66	Valiant Industries Inc—*Thomas Williams*	6525 Ctr Dr, Sterling Heights MI 48312	586-826-3500	R	5*	<.1
67	Craft Steel Products Inc—*Steven Snyder*	1048 Ken O Sha Industr, Grand Rapids MI 49508	616-247-1090	R	5*	<.1
68	Curtis Universal Joint Company Inc—*Richard Hartmann*	PO Box 70038, Springfield MA 01107	413-737-0281	R	5*	<.1
69	P and F Machining Inc—*Patsy Pawlak*	17171 113th Ave N Ste, Maple Grove MN 55369	763-428-3100	R	5*	<.1
70	Logan Clutch Corp—*Madelon Logan*	28855 Ranney Pkwy, Cleveland OH 44145	440-808-4258	R	5*	<.1
71	Bh North America Corp—*Stephen Wilkins*	20155 Ellipse, Foothill Ranch CA 92610	949-206-0330	R	4*	<.1
72	Orlandi Gear Company Inc—*Michael Schiavi*	6566 Sterling Dr S, Sterling Heights MI 48312	586-264-6700	R	4*	<.1
73	Wadler Manufacturing Company Inc—*Stephen Wade*	1909 E 12th St, Galena KS 66739	620-783-1355	R	4*	<.1
74	American Mact Inc—*Phil Hampton*	5400 Cedar Crest St, Houston TX 77087	713-643-4321	R	4*	<.1
75	Mill Sprocket and Machinery Corp—*Kevin Gielich*	3539 Commercial Ave, Springfield OR 97478	541-746-8817	R	4*	<.1
76	Machine Components Corp—*Joseph Kaplan*	70 Newtown Rd, Plainview NY 11803	516-694-7222	R	4*	<.1
77	Stromag Inc—*James Albrecht*	PO Box 41250, Dayton OH 45441	937-433-3882	R	4*	<.1
78	Masterline Design and Manufacturing—*Kathleen Pomaville*	41580 Production Dr, Harrison Township MI 48045	586-463-5888	R	4*	<.1
79	Drive Source International Inc—*David Fenton*	PO Box 361, Sturtevant WI 53177	262-554-7977	R	4*	<.1
80	ATR Sales Inc—*Jerry Hauck*	110 E Garry Ave, Santa Ana CA 92707	714-432-8411	R	3*	<.1
81	Rocom Corp—*Hollis Jewell*	5957 Engineer Dr, Huntington Beach CA 92649	714-891-9922	R	3*	<.1
82	Andantex U S A Inc—*Michael Munn*	1705 Valley Rd, Ocean NJ 07712	732-493-2812	R	3*	<.1
83	Fusion Babbitting Company Inc—*John Povlich*	4540 W Burnham St, Milwaukee WI 53219	414-645-5800	R	3*	<.1
84	Sprocket Specialties—*Jeff Gentry*	6251 Lincoln Blvd, Oroville CA 95966	530-533-0802	R	3*	<.1
85	Baker Inc—*Lisa Baker*	9804 E Saginaw Rd, Haslett MI 48840	517-339-3835	R	3*	<.1
86	Agricultural Distributing Inc—*Joe Heidrick*	1535 Case Pl, Woodland CA 95776	530-662-0558	R	3*	<.1
87	Pyramid Inc—*Susan Fortune*	522 N 9th Ave E, Newton IA 50208	641-792-2405	R	2*	<.1
88	Torrey Hills Technologies LLC—*Ken Kuang*	6370 Lusk Blvd Ste F11, San Diego CA 92121	858-558-6666	R	2*	<.1
89	Aql Quality Arson Test Labs—*Doug Kocher*	25599 Sw 95th Ave Ste, Wilsonville OR 97070	503-682-3193	R	2*	<.1
90	Ryle Manufacturing Co—*James Ryle*	PO Box 5347, Wichita Falls TX 76307	940-767-4354	R	2*	<.1
91	Hamil Holding Company Inc—*Lonnie Hamil*	PO Box 13377, Odessa TX 79768	432-362-0494	R	1*	<.1
92	Wells Compression Inc—*Frank Pickett*	PO Box 4377, Odessa TX 79760	432-363-8111	R	1*	<.1

TOTALS: SIC 3568 Power Transmission Equipment Nec
    Companies: 92   12,215   29.5

3569 General Industrial Machinery Nec

Rank	Company Name—*Executive Officer*	Address, City, State, Zip	Phone	Type	Fin	Empls
1	ABB Flexible Automation Inc—*Silas Nichols*	1250 Brown Rd, Auburn Hills MI 48326	248-391-9000	S	9,600*	1.2
2	Pall Corp—*Eric Krasnoff*	25 Harbor Park Dr, Port Washington NY 11050	516-484-5400	P	2,741	10.9
3	Enterprises International Inc—*David Lamb*	PO Box 293, Hoquiam WA 98550	360-533-6222	R	2,258*	.3
4	Trelleborg Sealing Solutions Americas—*Tim Callison*	10220 SW Greenburg Rd, Portland OR 97223	260-749-9631	S	2,250*	1.0
5	Veritec Technologies Inc—*Ed Campbell* Nordson Corp	11475 Lakefield Dr, Duluth GA 30097		S	2,167*	4.1
6	Nordson Corp—*Michael F Hilton*	28601 Clemens Rd, Westlake OH 44145	440-892-1580	P	1,233	4.1
7	TB Wood's Corp—*Carl R Christenson* Altra Holdings Inc	440 N 5th Ave, Chambersburg PA 17201	717-264-7161	S	1,085*	.8
8	Altra Holdings Inc—*Carl R Christenson*	300 Granite St Ste 201, Braintree MA 02184	781-917-0600	P	675	3.5
9	iRobot Inc—*Colin M Angle*	8 Crosby Dr, Bedford MA 01730	781-430-3000	P	466	.6
10	3M Purification Inc—*Chris O'Connor*	400 Research Pky, Meriden CT 06450	203-237-5541	S	352*	2.2
11	Veeder-Root Co—*Brian Burnett*	PO Box 2003, Simsbury CT 06070	860-651-2700	S	282*	.6
12	Lincoln Industrial Corp—*Bart Aitken*	1 Lincoln Way, Saint Louis MO 63120	314-679-4200	S	236*	.4
13	Flow International Corp—*Charles Brown*	23500 64th Ave S, Kent WA 98032	253-850-3500	P	217	.6
14	GE Osmonics Inc—*Jeff Garwood*	5951 Clearwater Dr, Minnetonka MN 55343		S	204*	1.3
15	Balcrank Products Inc	115 Reems Creek Rd, Weaverville NC 28787		R	154*	.1
16	Viking Corp—*Kevin Ortyl*	210 N Industrial Park, Hastings MI 49058	269-945-9501	R	142*	.3
17	Johnson Screens	1950 Old Hwy 8 NW, New Brighton MN 55112	651-636-3900	R	141*	.3
18	Tyco Fire Products LP—*Robert Budziak*	1400 Pennbrook Pkwy, Lansdale PA 19446	215-362-0700	S	126*	1.2
19	Nammo Talley—*Steve Wegener*	PO Box 34299, Mesa AZ 85277	480-898-2200	S	122*	.3
20	PMFG Inc—*Peter J Burlage*	14651 N Dallas Pky Ste, Dallas TX 75254	214-357-6181	P	122	.4

Note: An asterisk (*) indicates an estimated financial figure. The company type code used is as follows: R = Private, P = Public, S = Private Subsidiary, B = Public Subsidiary, D = Division, J = Joint Venture, I = Investment Fund.

COMPANY RANKINGS BY SALES WITHIN 4-DIGIT SIC

Rank	Company Name—Executive Officer	Address, City, State, Zip	Phone	Type	Fin	Empls
21	Lindgren RF Enclosures Inc (Glendale Heights Illinois)—VL Rickey	400 High Grove Blvd, Glendale Heights IL 60139	630-307-7200	S	120*	.8
22	E-ONE—Mark Gastafin	1601 SW 37 Ave, Ocala FL 34474	352-237-1122	D	117*	.8
23	Class 1—Dave Guynn	607 NW 27th Ave, Ocala FL 34475	352-629-5020	S	114*	.2
24	Reliable Automatic Sprinkler Company Inc—Frank Fee	103 Fairview Pk Dr Ste, Elmsford NY 10523	914-829-2042	R	113*	1.2
25	Riley Power Inc—Angelos Kokkinos	PO Box 15040, Worcester MA 01615	508-852-7100	R	106*	.5
26	Central Sprinkler Corp	1400 Pennbrook Pkwy, Lansdale PA 19446	215-362-0700	S	99*	.7
27	Alstom Power Conversion—Shoun Kerbaugh	610 Epsilon Dr, Pittsburgh PA 15238	412-967-0765	S	93*	.2
28	Hirotec America Inc—Katsutoshi Uno	4567 Glenmeade Ln, Auburn Hills MI 48326	248-836-5100	R	90*	.3
29	Peerless Manufacturing Co—Peter J Burlage PMFG Inc	PO Box 540667, Dallas TX 75354	214-357-6181	S	89*	.3
30	Clear Edge Filtration Inc—Rick Drehle	4563 Jordan Rd, Skaneateles Falls NY 13153	315-685-3466	R	78*	.2
31	MTS Medication Technologies Inc—Todd E Siegel	2003 Gandy Blvd N Ste, Saint Petersburg FL 33702	727-576-6311	R	76	.3
32	Columbus Industries Inc—Jeffrey Pontius	PO Box 257, Ashville OH 43103	740-983-2552	R	72*	.9
33	Parker Hannifin Hydraulic Pump Div—Ken Theiss	14249 Industrial Pky, Marysville OH 43040	937-644-3915	D	60*	.3
34	Hankison International	1000 Philadelphia St, Canonsburg PA 15317	724-745-1555	R	58*	.5
35	Alfa Laval Inc (Warminster Pennsylvania)—Lars Renstrom	955 Mearns Rd, Warminster PA 18974	215-443-4000	S	56*	.7
36	Facilitec Corp—Daryl Mirza	2410 Vantage Dr, Elgin IL 60124		S	56*	.4
37	Filmtec Corp—Ian Barbour	5230 W 73rd St, Edina MN 55439	952-897-4200	S	53	.4
38	Graham Engineering Corp—Steve Wood Graham Companies Inc	1203 Eden Rd, York PA 17402	717-848-3755	S	53*	.1
39	IMI Norgren Inc—JD Johnson	5400 S Delaware St, Littleton CO 80120	303-794-2611	S	52*	.9
40	Genmark Automation—Victor Sales	1201 Cadillac Ct, Milpitas CA 95035	408-678-8500	R	47*	.3
41	Everpure LLC—Michael Madsen	1040 Muirfield Dr, Hanover Park IL 60133	630-307-3000	S	44*	.3
42	Hannay Reels Inc—Roger Hannay	553 State Rte 143, Westerlo NY 12193	518-797-3791	R	43*	.1
43	E L Pruitt Co—John Pruitt	PO Box 3306, Springfield IL 62708	217-789-0966	R	42*	.1
44	American Fire Protection Group Inc—Jerry Morrison	PO Box 3154, Little Rock AR 72203	501-490-2181	R	42*	.3
45	Mi-T-M Corp—A Spiegel	PO Box 50, Peosta IA 52068	563-556-7484	R	41*	.3
46	Clayton Manufacturing Co—William Clayton	17477 Hurley St, City Of Industry CA 91744	626-435-1200	R	40*	.3
47	Koch Membrane Systems Inc—David Koch	850 Main St, Wilmington MA 01887	978-657-4250	R	40*	.5
48	RDI Group—Curtis N Maas	1025 W Thorndale Ave, Itasca IL 60143	630-773-2500	R	34*	.2
49	Yaskawa Electric America Inc—Gen Kudo	2121 Norman Dr S, Waukegan IL 60085	847-887-7000	S	33*	.3
50	Brockman Enterprises—Ralph W Brockman	2812 Armand St, Monroe LA 71201	318-388-2341	R	33*	.2
51	Mountain States Automation—Martyn Sutton	2740 S Vallejo St, Englewood CO 80110	303-781-9450	R	33*	<.1
52	Blackhawk Automatic Sprinklers Inc—Robert Fontanini	525 E 18th St, Cedar Falls IA 50613	319-232-7721	R	32*	.1
53	Cognex Distribution Corp	1 Vision Dr, Natick MA 01760	508-650-3000	S	30*	.1
54	Pittsfield Products Inc—Theodore Fosdick	PO Box 1027, Ann Arbor MI 48106	734-665-3771	R	27*	.1
55	Magnatech Engineering Inc—Bill Graveman	1204 Tonganoxie Rd, Tonganoxie KS 66086	913-845-3553	R	27*	.1
56	Global Equipment Marketing Inc—Marshall L Gralnick	PO Box 810483, Boca Raton FL 33481	561-750-8662	R	27*	<.1
57	D L Martin Co—Daniel Fisher	25 Harbaugh Dr, Mercersburg PA 17236	717-328-2141	R	26*	.2
58	Bardex Corp—Dennis Graney	6338 Lindmar Dr, Goleta CA 93117	805-964-7747	R	26*	.1
59	National Filter Media Corp—John Eugster	691 N 400 W, Salt Lake City UT 84103	801-363-6736	R	26*	.3
60	United Fabricants Strainrite Corp—Alan Lapoint	PO Box 1970, Auburn ME 04211	207-777-3100	R	25*	.1
61	Crane Environmental—Don Borden	2650 Eisenhower Ave St, Trooper PA 19403	610-631-7700	S	24*	.1
62	Ats Systems Oregon Inc—Klaus Woerner	2121 Ne Jack London St, Corvallis OR 97330	541-758-3329	R	23*	.3
63	Gray Manufacturing Company Inc—Joseph Gray	PO Box 728, Saint Joseph MO 64502	816-233-6121	R	23*	.2
64	Delta Tau Data Systems Incorporated Of California—Tom Zirnite	21314 Lassen St, Chatsworth CA 91311	818-998-2095	R	23*	.1
65	J and J Manufacturing Co—James Hayes	PO Box 6295, Beaumont TX 77725	409-833-8951	R	22*	<.1
66	Industrial Maintenance Welding and Machining Company Inc—Gene Berchem	PO Box 385, Kingsbury IN 46345	219-393-5531	R	21*	.2
67	Ldi Industries Inc—Gus Lukas	PO Box 1810, Manitowoc WI 54221	920-682-6877	R	21*	.2
68	Belvac Production Machinery Inc—Robert A Livingston	237 Graves Mill Rd, Lynchburg VA 24502	434-239-0358	D	21*	.1
69	Air Relief Inc—Ross J Centanni	PO Box 311, Mayfield KY 42066	270-247-0203	S	21*	.1
70	Taylor Devices Inc—Douglas P Taylor	90 Taylor Dr, North Tonawanda NY 14120	716-694-0800	P	21	.1
71	Kaydon Custom Filtration Corp (LaGrange Georgia)—Brian P Campbell	1571 Lukken Industrial, LaGrange GA 30240	706-884-3041	D	20*	.1
72	Webber Metal Products Inc—James Webber	PO Box 10, Cascade IA 52033	563-852-7122	R	20*	.2
73	Ozzie's Pipeline Padder Inc—Robert Dunston	7102 W Sherman St, Phoenix AZ 85043	480-585-9400	R	20*	.1
74	Netzsch Inc—Thomas Netzsch	119 Pickering Way, Exton PA 19341	610-363-8010	S	19*	.1
75	Kongsberg Power Product Systems I Inc—Jim Ryan	PO Box 588, Willis TX 77378	240-310-1100	R	19*	.2
76	Kmi Systems Inc—Kevin Coursin	4704 3 Oaks Rd, Crystal Lake IL 60014	815-459-5255	R	19*	<.1
77	Challenger Lifts Inc—Milo Bryant	PO Box 3944, Louisville KY 40201	502-625-0700	R	18*	.1
78	Mikron Corp (Denver Colorado)	562 Sable Blvd, Aurora CO 80011	303-364-5222	D	18*	<.1
79	Monroe Environmental Corp—Gary Pashaian	PO Box 806, Monroe MI 48161	734-242-7654	R	18*	<.1
80	Joyce/Dayton Corp—Tim Gockel	PO Box 1630, Dayton OH 45401	937-294-6261	R	17*	.1
81	ITW Dynatec—David B Speer	31 Volunteer Dr, Hendersonville TN 37075	615-824-3634	R	17*	.1
82	Advance Management Corp—Frank Lawson	1530 Glen Ave Ste 1, Moorestown NJ 08057	856-608-7878	R	17*	.1
83	SystemOne Technologies Inc—Paul I Mansur	8305 NW 27th St Ste 10, Miami FL 33122	305-593-8015	R	17*	<.1
84	Automation Tool Co—William Curran	PO Box 2649, Cookeville TN 38502	931-528-5417	R	17*	.1
85	Abco Automation Inc—Brad Kemmerer	6202 Technology Dr, Browns Summit NC 27214	336-375-6400	R	17*	.1
86	Hydac Technology Corp—Matthias Mueller	PO Box 22050, Lehigh Valley PA 18002	610-266-0100	R	16*	.1
87	Kane Manufacturing Corp—Peter Scannell	515 N Fraley St, Kane PA 16735	814-837-6464	R	16*	.1
88	Kawasaki Robotics Inc (Wixom Michigan)—Mike Miyamoto	28140 Lakeview Dr, Wixom MI 48393	248-446-4100	S	16*	.1
89	Pacific Consolidated Industries LLC—Jeff Appel	12201 Magnolia Ave, Riverside CA 92503	951-479-0860	R	15*	.1
90	Progressive Surface Inc—Lewis Kuiken	4695 Danvers Dr Se Ste, Grand Rapids MI 49512	616-957-0871	R	15*	.1
91	Psb Industries Inc—Mark Mccain	PO Box 1318, Erie PA 16512	814-452-4536	R	15*	.1
92	Astec Mobile Screens Inc—Tim Gonigam	2704 W LaFevre Rd, Sterling IL 61081	815-626-6374	S	15*	.1
93	Environtronics—Jens Schaefer	3881 N Greenbrooke Dr, Grand Rapids MI 49512	616-554-5020	R	15*	.1
94	Clarus Technologies LLC—Karl Thomas	2015 Alpine Way Ste A, Bellingham WA 98226	360-671-1514	S	15*	.1
95	Paratech Inc—Peter Nielsen	PO Box 1000, Frankfort IL 60423	815-469-3911	R	14*	.1
96	Glacier Bay Technology—Derek Kaufman	2930 Faber St, Union City CA 94587	510-437-9100	R	14	.1
97	Schroeder Industries LLC—Phil Applegate Hydac Technology Corp	580 W Park Rd, Leetsdale PA 15056	724-318-1100	S	14*	.1
98	Heller Industries Inc—David Heller	4 Vreeland Rd Ste 1, Florham Park NJ 07932	973-377-6800	R	14*	.1
99	Steamist Inc—Jeffrey Noll	25 E Union Ave Ste 1, East Rutherford NJ 07073	201-933-5800	R	14*	<.1
100	Amatrol Inc—Don Perkins	2400 Centennial Blvd, Jeffersonville IN 47130	812-288-8285	R	14*	.1
101	Mann and Hummel Advanced Filtration Concepts Inc—Brian Pahl	7070 International Dr, Louisville KY 40258	502-935-9333	R	13*	.1
102	Empire Abrasive Equipment Company LP—Anthony Martin	2101 Cabot Blvd W, Langhorne PA 19047	215-752-8800	R	13*	.1

Rank	Company Name—*Executive Officer*	Address, City, State, Zip	Phone	Type	Fin	Empls
103	Rimrock Corp—*Bob Archer*	1700 Jetway Blvd, Columbus OH 43219	614-471-5926	R	13*	.1
104	Sussman-Automatic Corp—*Charles Monteverdi*	4320 34th St, Long Island City NY 11101	718-937-4500	R	13*	.1
105	Wasser Filtration Inc—*Sean Duby*	2418 Cypress Way, Fullerton CA 92831	714-525-0630	R	12*	.1
106	Midwest Filtration Co—*Johnny Chua*	9775 International Blv, Cincinnati OH 45246	513-874-6510	R	12*	.1
107	Advent Design Corp—*Tom Lawton*	Canal St and Jefferson, Bristol PA 19007	215-781-0500	R	12*	.1
108	Day Carter International Inc—*Paul Ernst*	500 73rd Ave Ne Ste 10, Minneapolis MN 55432	763-571-1000	R	12*	.1
109	American Lifts Corp—*Clay Brinson*	PO Box 1058, Guthrie OK 73044	405-282-5200	R	12*	.1
110	Keltec Inc—*Edward Kaiser*	2300 E Enterprise Pkwy, Twinsburg OH 44087	330-425-3100	R	12*	.1
111	Trico Corp—*Robert Jung*	1235 Hickory St, Pewaukee WI 53072	262-691-9336	R	12*	.1
112	Globe Fire Sprinkler Corp—*Robert Worthington*	4077 Airpark Dr, Standish MI 48658	989-846-4583	R	12*	.1
113	Production Design Services Inc—*John Schultz*	401 Fame Rd, Dayton OH 45449	937-866-3377	R	12*	.1
114	Ziamatic Corp—*Mike Ziaylek*	PO Box 337, Yardley PA 19067	215-493-3618	R	12*	<.1
115	Graham Companies Inc—*Libertz Wolfgang*	1203 Eden Rd, York PA 17402	717-848-3755	R	11*	.1
116	International Baler Corp—*Roger Griffin*	5400 Rio Grande Ave, Jacksonville FL 32254	904-358-3812	P	11	.1
117	CECO Filters Inc—*Matt Lee*	PO Box 683, Conshohocken PA 19428	610-825-8585	D	11*	.1
118	American Compaction Equipment Inc—*Mike Shoemaker*	32981 Calle Perfecto, San Juan Capistrano CA 92675	949-661-2921	S	11*	<.1
119	Kmt Robotic Solutions Inc—*Kevin Mcmanus*	1255 Harmon Rd, Auburn Hills MI 48326	248-829-2800	R	11*	.1
120	Gatlin Group Inc—*Jeff Gatlin*	PO Box 1156, Brookhaven MS 39602	601-833-9475	R	11*	.1
121	Harmony Enterprises Inc—*Steve Cremer*	704 Main Ave N, Harmony MN 55939	507-886-6666	R	11*	.1
122	Oil-Rite Corp—*Donald Gruett*	PO Box 1207, Manitowoc WI 54221	920-682-6173	R	10*	.1
123	Intertech Development Co—*Jacques Hoffmann*	7401 Linder Ave, Skokie IL 60077	847-679-3377	R	10*	.1
124	Diamond Machine Werks Inc—*Siegfried Weiler*	2445 E Oakton St, Arlington Heights IL 60005	847-437-0665	R	10*	.1
125	Guyson Corporation Of U S A—*Steve Byrnes*	13 Grande Blvd, Saratoga Springs NY 12866	518-587-7894	R	10*	.1
126	Marvel Engineering Co—*Forest Niccum*	2085 N Hawthorne Ave, Melrose Park IL 60160	708-343-4090	R	10*	.1
127	Precision Automation Company Inc—*G Rexon*	PO Box 18, Haddonfield NJ 08033	856-428-7400	R	10*	.1
128	Filter Belts Inc—*Frederick Best*	12 Winada Dr, Winthrop ME 04364	207-377-2626	R	10*	.1
129	Rosedale Products Inc—*Nils Rosaen*	PO Box 1085, Ann Arbor MI 48106	734-665-8201	R	9*	.1
130	Innotek Corp—*Denny Burns*	9140 Zachary Ln N, Maple Grove MN 55369	763-493-2810	R	9*	.1
131	American Felt and Filter Company Inc—*Wilson Pryne*	361 Walsh Ave, New Windsor NY 12553	845-561-3560	R	9*	.1
132	Tool North Inc—*Kenneth Berg*	2475 N Aero Park Ct, Traverse City MI 49686	231-941-1150	R	9*	<.1
133	Progressive Recovery Inc—*Daniel Marks*	700 Industrial Dr, Dupo IL 62239	618-286-5000	R	9*	.1
134	Belco Technologies Corp—*Kevin Gilman*	9 Entin Rd, Parsippany NJ 07054	973-884-4700	R	9*	<.1
135	Dudley C Jackson Inc—*Ken Jackson*	PO Box 261, Helena AL 35080	205-663-2611	R	9*	<.1
136	Master Pneumatic-Detroit Inc—*Wendy Goscenski*	6701 18 Mile Rd, Sterling Heights MI 48314	586-254-1000	R	9*	.1
137	Star Automation Inc—*Kenji Shiotani*	N90w14401 Commerce Dr, Menomonee Falls WI 53051	262-253-3550	R	9*	.1
138	Nutro Corp—*Jochen Grocke*	11515 Alameda Dr, Strongsville OH 44149	440-572-3800	R	9*	.1
139	Rhba Acquisitions LLC	PO Box 566, Shreve OH 44676	330-567-2903	R	8*	.1
140	Fisher-Klosterman Inc—*William Heumann*	822 S 15th St, Louisville KY 40210	502-572-4000	R	8*	.1
141	Central Research Laboratories—*Lawton Cain*	3965 Pepin Ave, Red Wing MN 55066	651-388-3565	S	8	.1
142	Filter Tech Inc—*Ahmad Hindi*	PO Box 527, Manlius NY 13104	315-682-8815	R	8*	<.1
143	West Bond Inc—*John Price*	1551 S Harris Ct, Anaheim CA 92806	714-978-1551	R	8*	<.1
144	Schleuniger Inc—*Michael Rizzo*	87 Colin Dr, Manchester NH 03103	603-668-8117	R	8*	.1
145	Steel and Alloy Utility Products Inc—*Nathan Gallo*	110 Ohio Ave, Mc Donald OH 44437	330-530-2220	R	8*	.1
146	J-I-T Distributing Inc—*Stephen Johnson*	4111 Technology Dr, South Bend IN 46628	574-251-0292	R	8*	.1
147	New 9 Inc—*Peter Cordes*	1411 Michigan St Ne, Grand Rapids MI 49503	616-459-8274	R	7*	.1
148	Stavo Industries Inc—*George Vogel*	PO Box 3449, Kingston NY 12402	845-331-4552	R	7*	.1
149	Ats Sortimat USA LLC—*Hans Baumtrog*	5655 Meadowhrook Indus, Rolling Meadows IL 60008	847-925-1234	R	7*	.1
150	Waste Processing Equipment Inc—*Bill Traylor*	PO Box 1047, Rainsville AL 35986	256-638-6355	R	7*	.1
151	H/A Industries Inc—*Gordon Pesola*	5510 Gatewood Dr, Sterling Heights MI 48310	586-939-0550	R	7*	<.1
152	Larsen's Manufacturing Co—*Dave Fudge*	7421 Commerce Ln Ne, Minneapolis MN 55432	763-571-1181	R	6*	.1
153	Dee-Blast Corp—*Michael Johnson*	PO Box 517, Stevensville MI 49127	269-428-2400	R	6*	<.1
154	Industrial Filter Manufacturers Inc—*Michael Bartholome*	10244 Hedden Rd, Evansville IN 47725	812-867-4730	R	6*	<.1
155	Komax Systems Rockford Inc—*William Hoff*	1321 Capital Dr, Rockford IL 61109	815-229-3800	R	6*	<.1
156	Remtec Engineering—*Keith Rosnell*	10148 Commerce Park Dr, Cincinnati OH 45246	513-860-4299	R	6*	<.1
157	Lectrodryer LLC—*Douglas Morris*	PO Box 2500, Richmond KY 40476	859-624-2091	R	6*	<.1
158	Oxegen Generating Systems Intl—*Joseph McMahon*	814 Wurlitzer Dr, North Tonawanda NY 14120	716-564-5165	S	6*	<.1
159	Automation Devices Inc—*Larry Smith*	7050 W Ridge Rd, Fairview PA 16415	814-474-5561	R	6*	<.1
160	Hammonds Technical Services Inc—*Carl Hammonds*	910 Rankin Rd, Houston TX 77073	281-999-2900	R	6*	<.1
161	Flexible Automation Inc—*Edward Osterholzer*	3387 E Bristol Rd, Burton MI 48529	810-742-8540	R	6*	<.1
162	Nova Fire Protection Inc—*Michael Evans*	304 41st St Sw, Fargo ND 58103	701-282-0268	R	6*	<.1
163	Wartrom Machine Systems Inc—*Terry Ward*	22786 Patmore Dr, Clinton Township MI 48036	586-469-1915	R	5*	<.1
164	Chemco Manufacturing Company Inc—*Rand Schweizer*	515 Huehl Rd, Northbrook IL 60062	847-480-7700	R	5*	<.1
165	Gas Equipment Engineering Corp—*Tony Dellavolpe*	1240 Oronoque Rd, Milford CT 06461	203-874-6786	R	5*	<.1
166	Air Cryo Inc—*Galal Badr*	190 Boundary Rd, Marlboro NJ 07746	732-780-0220	R	5*	<.1
167	Filtration Systems Inc—*Doug Bayerlein*	W229n591 Foster Ct, Waukesha WI 53186	262-548-6210	R	5*	<.1
168	ITW Ransburg Electrostatic Systems	320 Phillips Ave, Toledo OH 43612	419-470-2000	R	5*	<.1
169	Smico Manufacturing Company Inc—*Eric Heald*	500 N Macarthur Blvd, Oklahoma City OK 73127	405-946-1461	R	5*	<.1
170	Change Parts Inc—*Ronald Sarto*	185 S Jebavy Dr, Ludington MI 49431	231-845-5107	R	5*	<.1
171	Happijac Intellemax Co—*Martin Rassmussen*	505 N Kays Dr, Kaysville UT 84037	801-546-8899	R	5*	<.1
172	Summit Filter Corp—*James Shahidi*	PO Box 427, Union NJ 07083	908-687-3500	R	5*	<.1
173	Mmlj Inc—*G Lecompte*	5711 Sehurmier Rd, Houston TX 77048	713-869-2227	R	5*	<.1
174	Age Logistics Corp—*Roger Mcmullin*	730 E Cypress Ave, Monrovia CA 91016	626-243-5253	R	5*	<.1
175	Oil Process Systems Inc—*Bernard Friedman*	602 Tacoma St, Allentown PA 18109	610-437-4618	R	5*	<.1
176	Barebo Inc—*Christopher Barebo*	3840 Main Rd E, Emmaus PA 18049	610-965-6019	R	5*	<.1
177	Russell's Technical Products Inc—*Gary Molenaar*	1883 Russel Ct, Holland MI 49423	616-392-3161	R	5*	<.1
178	Algas-Sdi International LLC—*Flemming Ethelfeld*	151 S Michigan St, Seattle WA 98108	206-789-5410	R	5*	<.1
179	Hot Melt Technologies Inc—*Bryan Tanury*	PO Box 80067, Rochester MI 48308	248-853-2011	R	5*	<.1
180	Smith Grover Manufacturing Corp—*Arlene Meeker*	PO Box 986, Montebello CA 90640	323-724-3444	R	5*	<.1
181	Applied Home Healthcare Equipment Inc—*David Marquard*	28825 Ranney Pkwy, Westlake OH 44145	440-716-9962	R	4*	<.1
182	Nu-Era Holdings Inc—*Patrick Nichols*	PO Box 409, Algonac MI 48001	810-794-4935	R	4*	<.1
183	Holmatro Inc—*William Swayne*	505 Mccormick Dr, Glen Burnie MD 21061	410-768-9662	R	4*	<.1
184	Rennco Automation Systems Inc—*Mike Owens*	971 Hamilton Dr, Holland OH 43528	419-861-2340	R	4*	<.1
185	James W Mcclellan and Associates Inc—*James Mcclellan*	70 Tirrell Hill Rd, Bedford NH 03110	603-644-2369	R	4*	<.1
186	Deschner Corp—*Joe Alessi*	3211 W Harvard St, Santa Ana CA 92704	714-557-1261	R	4*	<.1
187	Sierra Machinery Inc—*Krestine Corbin*	PO Box 435, Reno NV 89504	775-358-6721	R	4*	<.1
188	Simplex Manufacturing Co—*Steven Daniels*	13340 Ne Whitaker Way, Portland OR 97230	503-257-3511	R	4*	<.1
189	Crawford Sprinkler Co—*Frank McKinnon*	PO Box 1430, Hickory NC 28603	828-327-4116	R	4*	.1
190	Schmitt Measurement Systems—*Wayne Case*	2765 NW Nicolai St, Portland OR 97210	503-227-7908	S	4*	<.1
191	Creative Automation Inc—*Bernard Walter*	709 James L Hart Parkw, Ypsilanti MI 48197	734-879-2210	R	4*	<.1
192	Electro-Hydraulic Automation Inc—*Jim Kaas*	PO Box 10495, Cedar Rapids IA 52410	319-395-0005	R	4*	<.1

Note: An asterisk (*) indicates an estimated financial figure. The company type code used is as follows: R = Private, P = Public, S = Private Subsidiary, B = Public Subsidiary, D = Division, J = Joint Venture, I = Investment Fund.

COMPANY RANKINGS BY SALES WITHIN 4-DIGIT SIC

Rank	Company Name—Executive Officer	Address, City, State, Zip	Phone	Type	Fin	Empls
193	Duro Manufacturing Inc—David Motte	3505 Arrowhead Dr, Carson City NV 89706	775-687-8866	R	4*	<.1
194	Duperon Corp—Terry Duperon	515 N Wash Ave Ste 101, Saginaw MI 48607	989-754-8800	R	4*	<.1
195	WO Hickok Manufacturing Co—Peter Hickok	900 Cumberland St, Harrisburg PA 17103	717-234-8041	R	4*	<.1
196	Intersource Recovery Systems Inc—William Nemedi	1470 S 8th St, Kalamazoo MI 49009	269-375-5100	R	4*	<.1
197	Fireblast 451 Inc—Richard Egelin	545 Monica Cir, Corona CA 92880	951-277-8319	R	4*	<.1
198	Matrix Separation LLC—Jared Barlow	6000 Century Oaks Dr, Chattanooga TN 37416	423-267-2397	R	4*	<.1
199	Clark Sprinkler Fabrication Of In Inc—Carol Kurtz	PO Box 8918, Fort Wayne IN 46898	260-484-9619	R	4*	<.1
200	Delta Pure Filtration Corp—J Furbee	11011 Richardson Rd, Ashland VA 23005	804-798-2888	R	4*	<.1
201	Amkus Inc—Margaret Weigand	2700 Wisconsin Ave, Downers Grove IL 60515	630-515-1800	R	4*	<.1
202	Us Motion Inc—Lee Norman	PO Box 828, Liberty Lake WA 99019	509-924-9777	R	4*	<.1
203	Sparkler Group Inc—James Reneau	PO Box 19, Conroe TX 77305	936-756-4471	R	3*	<.1
204	Beam On Technology Corp—Rajoo Venkat	2318 Calle De Luna, Santa Clara CA 95054	408-982-0161	R	3*	<.1
205	Carolina Fire Protection Inc—Jeffrey Dunn	PO Box 250, Dunn NC 28335	910-892-1700	R	3*	<.1
206	Automatic Feeder Company Inc—Jack Verhasselt	921 Albion Ave, Schaumburg IL 60193	847-534-2300	R	3*	<.1
207	Royal Filter Manufacturing Co—Glenn Mcnatt	4327 S 4th St, Chickasha OK 73018	405-224-0229	R	3*	<.1
208	Comnav Engineering Inc—Martin Geesaman	987 Riverside St, Portland ME 04103	207-797-4588	R	3*	<.1
209	J and R Engineering Company Inc—Kevin Johnston	PO Box 447, Mukwonago WI 53149	262-363-9660	R	3*	<.1
210	Universal Fire Protection Ltd—Richard Loveless	PO Box 5326, Aurora IL 60507	630-499-0803	R	3*	<.1
211	Wire Tech Inc—Kenneth Rodgers	3441 W Highview Dr, Appleton WI 54914	920-993-5580	R	3*	<.1
212	East Chicago Machine Tool Sales Corp—Cornel Raab	980 Crown Ct, Crown Point IN 46307	219-663-4525	R	3*	<.1
213	Shamrock Engineering Inc—David Dunn	1325 E Virginia St, Evansville IN 47711	812-867-0009	R	3*	<.1
214	Tinny Corp—Robert Leconche	100 Bradley St, Middletown CT 06457	860-854-6121	R	3*	<.1
215	Webber Manufacturing Company Inc—David Lovett	PO Box 19449, Indianapolis IN 46219	317-357-8681	R	3*	<.1
216	International Filter Manufacturing Corp—Cecilia Ewing	PO Box 549, Litchfield IL 62056	217-324-2303	R	3*	<.1
217	Trinity Tool Co—Katherine Boyle	PO Box 98, Fraser MI 48026	586-296-5900	R	3*	<.1
218	Vibracraft Inc—Daniel Baumann	PO Box 157, South Beloit IL 61080	815-316-4000	R	3*	<.1
219	Dellinger Enterprises Ltd—Larry Dellinger	PO Box 627, Belmont NC 28012	704-825-9687	R	3*	<.1
220	Filter Factory Inc—Jerry Paulin	PO Box 122, Yuma AZ 85366	928-627-5500	R	3*	<.1
221	Star Systems Filtration Div—Paul Webb	100 W 4th St, Elmira NY 14901	607-733-7121	S	3*	<.1
222	Wittemann Company LLC—Bill Geiger	1 Industry Dr Ste A, Palm Coast FL 32137	386-445-4200	S	3	<.1
223	Barrett Technology Inc—William Townsend	625 Mt Auburn St, Cambridge MA 02138	617-252-9000	R	3*	<.1
224	Electro Steam Generator Corp—Barbara Akens	PO Box 438, Rancocas NJ 08073	609-288-9071	S	3*	<.1
225	Mefiag Div—Robert P Replogle	1550 Industrial Dr, Owosso MI 48867	989-725-8184	D	3*	<.1
226	Rolf Koerner LLC—Phil Lail	610-B Minuet Ln Ste 14, Charlotte NC 28217	704-714-8866	S	3*	<.1
227	Wlm Enterprises Inc—Wayne Mediamolle	5630 Powell St, Harahan LA 70123	504-733-3235	R	3*	<.1
228	Bay Area Industrial Filtration Inc—Thomas Schneider	PO Box 2071, San Leandro CA 94577	510-562-6373	R	3*	<.1
229	Concep Machine Company Inc—Jefferey Fischer	1800 Holste Rd, Northbrook IL 60062	847-498-9740	R	3*	<.1
230	Par Nuclear Inc—William Burns	899 Hwy 96 W, Saint Paul MN 55126	651-484-7261	R	3*	<.1
231	Madison Fire Protection LLC	360 W 31st St Rm 1000, New York NY 10001	516-616-6464	R	3*	<.1
232	FEC Inc—Yuji Shiroi	51341 Celeste, Shelby Township MI 48315	586-580-2536	R	3*	<.1
233	Polley Inc—Tracy Polley	PO Box 305, Norwalk CA 90651	562-868-9861	R	3*	<.1
234	Independent Machine Co—Jack Lucia	2 Stewart Pl, Fairfield NJ 07004	973-882-0060	R	3*	<.1
235	Roberts Fire Protection Inc—Ruben Roberts	PO Box 2161, Smyrna GA 30081	678-842-0202	R	3*	<.1
236	Microphoto Inc—Richard Wade	30499 Edison Dr, Roseville MI 48066	586-772-1999	R	3*	<.1
237	Filter Fab—Tracy Allen	7218 Canal St, Houston TX 77011	713-433-5621	R	3*	<.1
238	Oil Skimmers Inc—William Townsend	PO Box 33092, North Royalton OH 44133	440-237-4600	R	3*	<.1
239	Bek Systems Inc—Paul Englram	PO Box 769, Oak Park IL 60303	630-268-0880	R	3*	<.1
240	Mcfadden Machine and Manufacturing Co—Robert Hlusko	160 Hill Rd, Blairsville PA 15717	724-459-9278	R	3*	<.1
241	Sterling-Detroit Co—Herman Canner	5060 Delemere Ave, Royal Oak MI 48073	248-280-3500	R	3*	<.1
242	Automated Industrial Machine Inc—Andrew Lewis	347 Farnum Pke, Smithfield RI 02917	401-232-1710	R	3*	<.1
243	Medtech Automation LLC—Peter Georgelos	68 Acton St, West Haven CT 06516	203-932-6406	R	2*	<.1
244	Como Industrial Equipment Inc—Douglas Schade	PO Box 1671, Janesville WI 53547	608-756-3838	R	2*	<.1
245	Magnum Fabrications Inc—Kenneth Broussard	6648 Gulfway Dr, Port Arthur TX 77642	409-963-0161	R	2*	<.1
246	Sidco Filter Corp—Sidney Cutt	58 N Ave, Manchester NY 14504	585-289-3100	R	2*	<.1
247	Universal Filters Inc—Jerrold Kolton	1207 Main St Ste A, Asbury Park NJ 07712	732-774-8555	R	2*	<.1
248	Sims Machine and Controls Inc—Robert Jones	15538 Aviation Loop Dr, Brooksville FL 34604	352-799-2405	R	2*	<.1
249	Bmi Automation Inc—Henry Burns	2580 S Brannon Stand R, Dothan AL 36305	334-793-7086	R	2*	<.1
250	Process Pressure Vessels—James Reneau	PO Box 19, Conroe TX 77305	936-756-4824	R	2*	<.1
251	Albarrie Technical Fabrics Inc—Reginald Driscoll	PO Box 1226, Lewiston ME 04243	207-786-0424	R	2*	<.1
252	Shupeco LLC—Stephen Pitkin	3715 Collins Ln, Louisville KY 40245	502-267-1807	R	2*	<.1
253	Urethane Roller Specialist Inc—Jeff Glassner	PO Box 566, Eureka MO 63025	636-938-5351	R	2*	<.1
254	Hook Industrial Sales Inc—Thomas Hook	PO Box 9177, Fort Wayne IN 46899	260-432-9441	R	2*	.1
255	Barbron Corp—James Hart	8720 Dixie Hwy, Ira MI 48023	586-716-3530	R	2*	<.1
256	White's Bridge Tooling Inc—Peter Odland	PO Box 8, Lowell MI 49331	616-897-4151	R	2*	<.1
257	Stainless Design Concepts Ltd—Kevin Collins	1117 Kings Hwy, Saugerties NY 12477	845-246-3631	D	2*	<.1
258	A and J Automation Inc—Jerry Duda	21356 Carlo Dr, Clinton Township MI 48038	586-468-7555	R	2*	<.1
259	Coopermatics Inc—Cullen Cooper	PO Box 450, Northampton PA 18067	610-262-7700	R	2*	<.1
260	Doran Precision Inc	76 N Georges Hill Rd, Southbury CT 06488	203-262-8200	R	2*	<.1
261	CeraMem Separations Inc—Bruce Bishop	12 Clematis Ave, Waltham MA 02453	781-899-4495	S	2	<.1
262	Richard Dudgeon Inc—Allen Haight	1565 Railroad Ave, Bridgeport CT 06605	203-336-4459	R	2*	<.1
263	Filtra-Systems Manufacturing Co—Jack Bratten	190 Spicer Dr, Gordonsville TN 38563	615-683-8261	R	2*	<.1
264	Hoffmann Filter Corp—Georg Hoffmann	7627 Kensington Ct, Brighton MI 48116	248-486-8430	R	2*	<.1
265	Essex Brass Corp—David Nagel	PO Box 629, Warren MI 48090	586-757-8200	R	2*	<.1
266	Marmac Co—Gary Walthall	PO Box 157, Xenia OH 45385	937-372-8093	R	2*	<.1
267	Rosenmund Inc—Don Doyle	9110 Forsyth Park Dr, Charlotte NC 28273	704-587-0440	R	2*	<.1
268	Scientific Motion LLC	4400 N Scottsdale Rd S, Scottsdale AZ 85251	602-308-4801	R	2*	<.1
269	Ruemelin Manufacturing Company Inc—Charles Ruemelin	330 E Kilbourn Ave Ste, Milwaukee WI 53202	414-962-6500	R	2*	<.1
270	Abrasive Blast Systems Inc—Karyl Ford	PO Box 307, Abilene KS 67410	785-263-3786	R	2*	<.1
271	J R Schneider Company Inc—Donna Block	849 Jackson St, Benicia CA 94510	707-745-0404	R	2*	<.1
272	Vapor Blast Manufacturing Co—Kevin Scherbarth	3025 W Atkinson Ave, Milwaukee WI 53209	414-871-6500	R	2*	<.1
273	Allen Filters Inc—Katherine Allen	PO Box 747, Springfield MO 65801	417-865-2844	R	2*	<.1
274	C and D Skilled Robotics Inc—Gastone Trecco	4780 S 23rd St, Beaumont TX 77705	409-840-5252	R	1*	<.1
275	Harvey S Freeman—Harvey Freeman	PO Box 251685, West Bloomfield MI 48325	248-852-2222	R	1*	<.1
276	Service Tectonics Sales Inc—Stephen Dalton	2827 Treat St, Adrian MI 49221	517-263-0758	R	1*	<.1
277	Micro-Filtration Inc—John Welker	3309 John Conley Dr, Lapeer MI 48446	810-667-3600	R	1*	<.1
278	Jenzano Inc—John Jenzano	820 Oak St, Port Orange FL 32127	386-761-4474	R	1*	<.1
279	Enviro-Clear Company Inc—J Muldowney	152 Cregar Rd, High Bridge NJ 08829	908-638-5507	R	1*	<.1
280	New Idea Inc—Joe Carter	1115 Race St, Plattsmouth NE 68048	402-296-3915	R	1*	<.1
281	Filter Fabrics Inc—Nancy Graw	814 E Jefferson St, Goshen IN 46528	574-533-3114	R	1*	<.1
282	Programmable Control Service Inc—Phil Fraley	6900 Blacks Rd Sw, Pataskala OH 43062	740-927-0744	R	1*	<.1

Rank	Company Name—*Executive Officer*	Address, City, State, Zip	Phone	Type	Fin	Empls
283	Texas Spectrum Electronic Inc—*Paul Zimmer*	120 Regency Dr, Wylie TX 75098	972-296-3699	R	1*	<.1
284	Croll-Reynolds Engineering Company Inc—*Samuel W Croll III*	6 Campus Dr, Parsippany NJ 07054	908-232-4200	R	1*	<.1
285	Wayne Products Inc—*Richard Segermark*	PO Box 788, Malvern PA 19355	610-251-0933	R	1*	<.1
286	Filtration Specialties Inc—*Mike Swink* CECO Filters Inc	4225 Sandy Bay Dr, Virginia Beach VA 23455	757-363-9818	D	1*	<.1
287	Meissner Filtration Products Inc—*Christopher Meissner*	4181 Calle Tesoro, Camarillo CA 93012	805-388-9911	R	1*	<.1
288	Elaine Inc—*Elaine Abbate*	PO Box 300, Paterson NJ 07543	973-345-6200	R	1*	<.1
289	Brooks CNC Services—*Scott Brooks*	PO Box 6223, Anaheim CA 92816	714-632-1300	R	1*	<.1
290	Radford Manufacturing Inc—*Troy Radford*	1800 Duval St, Fort Worth TX 76104	817-536-7706	R	1*	<.1
291	Cimco Technologies LLC—*Dave Fluharty*	PO Box 715, Newark OH 43058	740-763-0991	R	1*	<.1
292	Process Innovations Inc—*Robert Crow*	PO Box 25, Fowler OH 44418	330-856-5192	R	1*	<.1
293	Federal Assembly Inc—*Chris Holley*	115 S Hall St, Princeton IN 47670	812-386-7062	R	1*	.1
294	Pro Techmation Inc—*Don Meyer*	PO Box 1769, Crystal Lake IL 60039	815-459-5909	R	1*	<.1
295	Doms Inc—*Mark Stevens*	940 Anita Ave, Antioch IL 60002	847-838-6723	R	1*	<.1
296	Al T Inc—*Mike Phelps*	3000 Sw 42nd Ave, Palm City FL 34990	772-287-9280	R	1*	<.1
297	Edjean Technical Services Inc—*Douglas Heidenreich*	22036 Fairgrounds Rd, Wellington OH 44090	440-647-3300	R	1*	<.1
298	K-Com—*Peter Krieger*	PO Box 82, Randolph OH 44265	330-325-2110	R	<1*	<.1
299	Pulsonics Inc—*Stevens Pendleton*	PO Box 578, Belleville NJ 07109	973-759-4025	R	<1*	<.1
300	Quality Filters Inc—*David Husak*	PO Box 129, Dexter MI 48130	734-668-0211	R	<1*	<.1
301	Steve Rosenquist LLC—*Steve Rosenquist*	PO Box 1162, Wilkesboro NC 28697	336-262-5595	R	<1	<.1
302	Peregrine Industries Inc—*Richard Rubin*	40 Wall St 28th Fl, New York NY 10005	212-400-7198	P	<1	<.1
303	Rival Technologies Inc—*Peter G Matthews*	375 N Stephanie St Ste, Henderson NV 89014		P	<1	N/A
304	Frymaster Corp—*Gene Baugh*	8700 Line Avenue, Shreveport LA 71106	318-865-1711	S	N/A	N/A

TOTALS: SIC 3569 General Industrial Machinery Nec
Companies: 304

					28,510	58.6

3571 Electronic Computers

Rank	Company Name—*Executive Officer*	Address, City, State, Zip	Phone	Type	Fin	Empls
1	Hewlett-Packard Co—*Meg Whitman*	PO Box 10301, Palo Alto CA 94303	650-857-1501	P	127,245	349.6
2	Apple Inc—*Arthur Levinson*	1 Infinite Loop, Cupertino CA 95014	408-996-1010	P	108,249	60.4
3	International Business Machines Corp—*Samuel J Palmisano*	1 New Orchard Rd, Armonk NY 10504	914-499-1900	P	99,870	426.8
4	Siemens IT Solutions and Services Inc—*Thierry Breton*	101 Merritt 7, Norwalk CT 06851	203-642-2300	S	39,634*	43.0
5	Lenovo Group Ltd—*Yuanqing Yang*	1009 Think Pl, Morrisville NC 27560		P	21,594	27.0
6	SYNNEX Corp—*Kevin M Murai*	44201 Nobel Dr, Fremont CA 94538	510-656-3333	P	8,614	7.5
7	Acer America Corp—*Rudi Schmidleithner*	333 W San Carlos St Rm, San Jose CA 95110	408-533-7700	S	5,833*	5.0
8	Unisys Corp—*J Edward Coleman*	801 Lakeview Dr Ste 10, Blue Bell PA 19422	215-986-4011	P	3,854	22.7
9	Gateway Inc—*Richard Snyder*	7565 Irvine Center Dr, Irvine CA 92618	949-471-7000	S	3,513*	1.5
10	Teradata Corp—*Michael F Koehler*	10000 Innovation Dr, Miamisburg OH 45342	937-242-4030	P	1,936	7.4
11	Sony Electronics/Info Technology—*Ryoji Chubachi*	1730 N First St, San Jose CA 95112	408-352-4000	S	1,328*	2.1
12	Creative Labs Inc—*Craig McHugh*	1523 Cimmaron Pl, Stillwater OK 74075	408-428-6600	S	1,224	N/A
13	MA LABS Inc—*Abraham Ma*	2075 N Capitol Ave, San Jose CA 95132	408-941-0808	R	1,072*	1.0
14	Super Micro Computer Inc—*Charles Liang*	980 Rock Ave, San Jose CA 95131	408-503-8000	P	943	.5
15	Silicon Graphics International Corp—*Ronald D Verdoorn*	46600 Landing Pkwy, Fremont CA 94538	510-933-8300	P	630	1.5
16	Epson America Inc—*John Lang*	3840 Kilroy Airport Wa, Long Beach CA 90806	562-981-3840	S	453*	.7
17	Cognex Corp—*Robert Willett*	1 Vision Dr, Natick MA 01760	508-650-3000	P	322	.9
18	PC Mall Gov Inc—*Humberto Pujais*	7421 Gateway Ct, Manassas VA 20109	703-594-8100	S	246*	.2
19	Cray Inc—*Peter J Ungaro*	901 5th Ave Ste 1000, Seattle WA 98164	206-701-2000	P	236	.9
20	Omnicell Inc—*Randall A Lipps*	1201 Charleston Rd, Mountain View CA 94043	650-251-6100	P	222	.8
21	Gerber Technology Inc—*John Hancock*	24 Industrial Park Rd, Tolland CT 06084	860-871-8082	S	196*	1.2
22	Hynix Semiconductor America Inc	3101 N 1st St, San Jose CA 95134	408-232-8000	S	185*	1.2
23	AAEON Technology Inc—*Yung-Shun Chuang*	3 Crown Plz, Hazlet NJ 07730	732-203-9300	R	173*	.3
24	Bull Data Systems Inc—*Gervais Pellissier*	285 Billerica Rd Ste 2, Chelmsford MA 01824	978-294-6000	R	147*	2.2
25	RadiSys Communications Platform Div—*Mike Dagenais*	5435 NE Dawson Creek D, Hillsboro OR 97124	503-615-1100	D	145*	.6
26	Vocollect Inc—*Joe Pajer*	703 Rodi Rd, Pittsburgh PA 15235	412-829-8145	R	129*	.3
27	Crestron Electronics Inc—*George Feldstein*	15 Volvo Dr, Rockleigh NJ 07647	201-767-3400	R	128*	1.3
28	ABS Computer Technologies Inc	18045 Rowland St, City of Industry CA 91748	626-271-1580	R	110*	.2
29	Endeca Technologies Inc—*Steve Papa*	101 Main St, Cambridge MA 02142	617-674-6000	R	108	.1
30	Radix Corp—*Dave Wakefield*	846 N Mart-Way Ct, Olathe KS 66061	913-754-5228	D	99*	.2
31	Boundless Technologies Inc	1916 State Rte 96, Phelps NY 14532	315-548-6189	S	98*	.3
32	Fargo Electronics Inc—*David M Sullivan*	6533 Flying Cloud Dr, Eden Prairie MN 55344	952-941-9470	S	81*	.2
33	CCS-Inc—*Marty Muscatello*	105 Industrial Dr, Christiansburg VA 24073	540-382-4234	R	68*	.1
34	Ineoquest Technologies Inc—*Marc Todd*	170 Forbes Blvd, Mansfield MA 02048	508-339-2497	R	67*	.1
35	Concurrent Computer Corp—*Dan Mondor*	4375 River Green Pky S, Duluth GA 30096	678-258-4000	P	67	.3
36	Root Group Inc—*Bill Calderwood*	1790 30th St Ste 140, Boulder CO 80301	303-447-8093	R	64*	<.1
37	XATA Corp—*Jay Coughlan*	965 Prairie Ctr Dr, Eden Prairie MN 55344	952-707-5600	P	63	.2
38	Sceptre Technologies Inc—*Richard L Knowles*	16800 E Gale Ave, City of Industry CA 91745		R	63*	.1
39	Egenera Inc—*Pete Manca*	80 Central St, Boxborough MA 01719	978-206-6300	R	53*	.3
40	GENTEK Media Group—*Gene Szeto*	5678 E Concours Ave, Ontario CA 91764	909-476-3818	R	48*	.1
41	Gamma Tech Computer Corp—*Steven Gau*	48303 Fremont Blvd, Fremont CA 94538	510-492-0828	S	47*	.1
42	Dfi Technologies LLC—*Albert Chien*	PO Box 340759, Sacramento CA 95834	916-568-1234	R	46*	.1
43	Golden Star Technology Inc—*Alice Wang*	13043 166th St, Cerritos CA 90703	562-345-8700	R	43*	.1
44	Hard Drives Northwest Inc—*Hugh Stewart*	14315 NE 20th St, Bellevue WA 98007	425-644-6474	R	42*	.1
45	Amax Engineering Corp—*Jerry KC Shih*	1565 Reliance Way, Fremont CA 94539	510-651-8886	R	41*	.3
46	Tangent Computer Inc—*Doug Monsour*	191 Airport Blvd, Burlingame CA 94010	650-342-9388	R	41*	.1
47	Transource Services Corp—*Li-Yu Ting*	2405 W Utopia Rd, Phoenix AZ 85027	623-879-8882	R	39*	<.1
48	Daisy Data Displays Inc—*David Shefet*	2850 Lewisberry Rd, York Haven PA 17370	717-932-9999	R	38*	.1
49	CSS Laboratories Inc—*Siew Yeung*	1641 McGaw Ave, Irvine CA 92614	949-852-8161	R	36*	.1
50	Exacq Technologies Inc—*David Underwood*	11955 Exit Five Pky Bl, Fishers IN 46037	317-845-5710	R	34*	.1
51	Omron Systems LLC	55 E Commerce Dr, Schaumburg IL 60173	847-843-0515	S	33*	<.1
52	Venkel Corp—*Anil Venkatrao*	5900 Shepherd Mountain, Austin TX 78730	512-794-0081	R	32*	.1
53	Microboards Technology Inc—*Yoshihito Kumakura*	8150 Mallory Ct, Chanhassen MN 55317	952-556-1600	R	32*	.1
54	Syn-Tech Systems Inc—*Doug Dunlap*	PO Box 5258, Tallahassee FL 32314	850-878-2558	R	32*	.2
55	Collabraspace Inc—*Ray Schwemmer*	180 Admiral Cochrane D, Annapolis MD 21401	410-224-4343	R	31*	.1
56	MS Engineering Inc	10601 S De Anza Blvd, Cupertino CA 95014	408-257-4249	R	31*	<.1
57	PerifiTech of Ohio Inc—*Robert Kuchta*	23108 Felch St Ste 201, Cleveland OH 44128	216-332-0655	R	30*	.1
58	Micon Computer Co	13608 Merriman Rd, Livonia MI 48150	734-261-3828	R	29*	<.1
59	Bytespeed LLC—*Jason Redfield*	3131 24th Ave S, Moorhead MN 56560	218-227-0445	R	27*	<.1
60	Micro Express Inc—*Jay Jordan*	8 Hammond Dr Ste 105, Irvine CA 92618	949-460-9911	R	25	.1
61	Keydata International Inc—*George Wu*	201 Circle Dr N Ste 10, Piscataway NJ 08854	732-868-0588	R	25*	<.1
62	Resilience Corp—*Sean Scott*	7502 Connelley Dr Ste, Hanover MD 21076	617-245-0512	R	24*	<.1

Note: An asterisk (*) indicates an estimated financial figure. The company type code used is as follows: R = Private, P = Public, S = Private Subsidiary, B = Public Subsidiary, D = Division, J = Joint Venture, I = Investment Fund.

COMPANY RANKINGS BY SALES WITHIN 4-DIGIT SIC

Rank	Company Name—*Executive Officer*	Address, City, State, Zip	Phone	Type	Fin	Empls
63	Clearcube Technology Inc—*Liz Buchanan*	8834 N Capital Of Texa, Austin TX 78759	512-652-3500	R	22*	.2
64	Jetta International Inc—*David Su*	51 Stouts Ln Ste 5, Monmouth Junction NJ 08852	732-329-9651	R	22*	<.1
65	Trex Enterprises Corp—*Kenneth Tang*	10455 Pacific Ctr Ct, San Diego CA 92121	858-646-5300	R	22*	.2
66	XKL LLC—*Leonard Bosack*	12020 113th Ave NE Ste, Kirkland WA 98034	425-869-9050	R	21*	<.1
67	Edge World—*Carl Everett*	5405 Alton Pky Ste 5A-, Irvine CA 92604	949-654-9200	R	21*	<.1
68	Data Limited Inc—*Bryan Wesolek*	PO Box 761, La Porte IN 46352	219-362-1809	R	20*	.1
69	SYS International Inc—*William Yen*	5300 Orange Ave Rm 127, Cypress CA 90630	714-228-1856	R	20*	<.1
70	Granite Microsystems Inc—*Daniel Armbrust*	10202 N Enterprise Dr, Mequon WI 53092	262-242-8800	R	20*	.1
71	Shuttle Computer Group Inc—*Jack Wang*	17068 Evergreen Pl, City Of Industry CA 91745	626-820-9000	R	19*	<.1
72	Topcoder Inc—*Robert Hughes*	95 Glastonbury Blvd, Glastonbury CT 06033	860-633-5540	R	19	.1
73	Logixml Inc—*Brett Jackson*	7900 Westpark Dr T107, Mclean VA 22102	703-752-9700	R	19*	<.1
74	ProStar Computer Inc—*Terry Wang*	837 S Lawson St, City of Industry CA 91748	626-839-6472	R	19*	<.1
75	Hertell Enterprises Inc—*Jeff Hertell*	2329 W Division St, Springfield MO 65802	417-862-6752	R	18*	<.1
76	Winsystems Inc—*Jerry Winfield*	PO Box 121361, Arlington TX 76012	817-274-7553	R	18*	.1
77	Parallax Inc—*Charles Gracey*	599 Menlo Dr Ste 100, Rocklin CA 95765	916-624-8333	R	18*	<.1
78	Polywell Computers Inc—*Sam Chu*	1461 San Mateo Ave, South San Francisco CA 94080		R	18	.1
79	Panasonic Personal Computer Co—*Rance Poehier*	50 Meadowland Pkwy, Secaucus NJ 07094	201-348-7000	S	17*	.1
80	River Run Computers Inc—*Paul T Riedl Jr*	2320 W Camden Rd, Glendale WI 53209	414-228-7474	R	17*	<.1
81	L-3 Communications Global Network Solutions—*Michael T Strianese*	1519 Grundy's Ln, Bristol PA 19007	215-957-3719	S	16*	.1
82	InfoGOLD Corp—*Adriaan van Wyk*	1830 Houret Ct, Milpitas CA 95035	408-945-2296	R	16*	<.1
83	American Reliance Inc—*Edward Chen*	3445 Fletcher Ave, El Monte CA 91731	626-443-6818	R	16*	.1
84	Efacec Acs Inc—*Jose Barbosa*	PO Box 922548, Norcross GA 30010	770-446-8854	R	15*	.1
85	Win Enterprises Inc—*Chiman Patel*	300 Willow St S, North Andover MA 01845	978-688-2000	R	15*	.2
86	Flytech Technology Inc (Fremont California)—*Thomas Lam*	47825 Warm Springs Blv, Fremont CA 94539	510-257-5180	S	15*	<.1
87	XMultiple Technologies—*Alan Pocrass*	1060 Los Angeles Ave, Simi Valley CA 93065	805-579-1100	R	15*	<.1
88	Versalogic Corp—*Leonard Crane*	4211 W 11th Ave, Eugene OR 97402	541-485-8575	R	14*	.1
89	Socket Mobile Inc—*Kevin J Mills*	39700 Eureka Dr, Newark CA 94560	510-933-3000	P	14	.1
90	Corvallis MicroTechnology Inc	413 SW Jefferson Ave, Corvallis OR 97333	541-752-5456	R	13*	.1
91	Technology Advancement Group Inc—*James S McEwan*	22355 TAG Way, Dulles VA 20166	703-406-3000	R	13*	.1
92	Broadax Systems Inc	17539 E Rowland St, City of Industry CA 91748	626-964-2600	R	13*	<.1
93	Micro Symplex Inc—*Theo Soumilas*	1202 E Maryland Ave St, Phoenix AZ 85014	602-244-0080	R	13*	<.1
94	Computer Technology Link Corp—*David Kim*	3460 NW Industrial St, Portland OR 97210	503-646-3733	R	12*	.1
95	Image Microsystems Inc—*Alex Abadi*	6301 Chalet Dr, Commerce CA 90040	562-776-3333	R	12*	<.1
96	Reason Computer Inc—*Bruno Bonnell*	901 E Cliff Rd Ste 101, Burnsville MN 55337	952-229-2060	R	11*	<.1
97	Applied Dynamics International Inc—*Scott James*	3800 Stone School Rd, Ann Arbor MI 48108	734-973-1300	R	10*	.1
98	Comark Corp—*Steve Schott*	93 West St, Medfield MA 02052	508-359-8161	R	10*	.1
99	Koutech Systems Inc—*Jeff Tang*	15308 E Valley Blvd, City of Industry CA 91746	626-369-9600	S	10*	<.1
100	Alpha Research and Technology Inc—*Deann Kerr*	1107 Investment Blvd, El Dorado Hills CA 95762	916-431-9340	R	9*	.1
101	Advanced Programs Inc—*Steve Rice*	7125 Riverwood Dr Ste, Columbia MD 21046	410-312-5800	R	9*	.1
102	JLT Mobile Computers Inc—*Todd Einck*	7450 S Priest Dr, Tempe AZ 85283	480-705-4200	S	9*	<.1
103	Nematron—*Greg Chander*	5840 Interface Dr, Ann Arbor MI 48103	734-214-2000	R	9	<.1
104	Western Computer—*Tom Bardos*	351 Candelaria Rd, Oxnard CA 93030	805-581-5020	R	7*	.1
105	Nortech Engineering Inc—*Robert Davis*	10 Commerce Way Ste E, Norton MA 02766	508-285-7831	R	7*	<.1
106	Contec Microelectronics USA Inc	1294 Lawrence Station, Sunnyvale CA 94089	408-400-8700	S	7*	<.1
107	CyberResearch Inc—*Robert C Molloy*	25 Business Park Dr, Branford CT 06405	203-643-5000	R	7*	<.1
108	KnowledgeBroker Inc—*Brad Stanley*	PO Box 17097, Reno NV 89511	626-441-0702	R	7*	<.1
109	Lightfleet Corp—*John Peers*	PO Box 87998, Vancouver WA 98687	360-816-5700	R	7*	<.1
110	Probe-Logic Inc—*Hon Cheng*	1885 Lundy Ave Ste 101, San Jose CA 95131	408-416-0777	R	7*	.1
111	Midern Computer Inc—*Shooing Yuan*	18005 Cortney Ct, City Of Industry CA 91748	626-964-8682	R	6*	.1
112	Two Technologies Inc—*David Young*	419 Sargon Way Ste A, Horsham PA 19044	215-441-5305	R	6*	<.1
113	Digital Dynamics Inc—*James Jerde*	5 Victor Sq, Scotts Valley CA 95066	831-438-4444	R	6*	.1
114	STA Inc—*Charles Phyle*	4150 Grange Hall Rd, Holly MI 48442	248-328-5000	R	6*	.1
115	Modular Information Systems—*Lisa Corbett*	2303 Camino Ramon Ste, San Ramon CA 94583	925-244-5930	R	6*	<.1
116	Solflower Computer Inc—*Kim Vu*	3337 Kifer Rd, Santa Clara CA 95051	408-733-8100	R	6*	<.1
117	Revonate Manufacturing LLC	4697 Crossroads Park D, Liverpool NY 13088	315-433-1160	R	6*	.1
118	Phytec America LLC—*Venessa Harper*	203 Parfitt Way Sw, Bainbridge Island WA 98110	206-780-9047	R	5*	<.1
119	Blue Star Marketing Inc—*Sanjay Syal*	4660 Churchill St, Saint Paul MN 55126	651-766-2800	R	5*	<.1
120	Cypress Creation Inc—*Sammy Sze*	44368 S Grimmer Blvd, Fremont CA 94538	510-668-1330	R	5*	<.1
121	GW Micro Inc—*Paul Silva*	725 Airport N Office P, Fort Wayne IN 46825	260-489-3671	R	5*	<.1
122	Centercomm Corp—*Kiem Le*	6720 Cobra Way, San Diego CA 92121	858-677-5575	R	5*	<.1
123	Ancol—*Ann Quirk*	860 Bradford Ave, Westfield NJ 07090	908-233-8907	R	5*	<.1
124	Dpa Labs Inc—*Douglas Young*	2251 Ward Ave Ste B, Simi Valley CA 93065	805-581-9200	R	5*	.1
125	Tri-L Data Systems Inc—*Matthew Lau*	94-409 Puko St Ste 100, Waipahu HI 96797	808-671-5133	R	5*	<.1
126	Creative Vision Technologies Inc—*Tom Henderson*	2950 Xenium Ln N Ste 1, Plymouth MN 55441	763-478-6446	R	5*	<.1
127	Cyclone Microsystems Inc—*Joel Zackin*	370 James St Ste 203, New Haven CT 06513	203-786-5536	R	4*	<.1
128	Datacom Systems Inc—*Sam Lanzafane*	9 Adler Dr, East Syracuse NY 13057	315-463-9541	R	4*	<.1
129	Manutronics Co—*Nobuyuki Horita*	48501 Warm Springs Blv, Fremont CA 94539	510-651-7540	R	4*	<.1
130	Src Computers LLC—*Jon Huppenthal*	4240 N Nevada Ave, Colorado Springs CO 80907	719-262-0213	R	4*	<.1
131	ColorWare Inc—*Justin Cisewski*	2050 W 4th St, Winona MN 55987	507-474-6567	R	4*	<.1
132	TEK Industries Inc	48 Hockanum Blvd, Vernon CT 06066	860-870-0001	R	4*	<.1
133	ATS Computers Inc	8250 Vickers St Ste B, San Diego CA 92111	858-279-1305	R	4*	<.1
134	Dynatem Inc—*Michael Horan*	23263 Madero Ste C, Mission Viejo CA 92691	949-855-3235	R	4*	<.1
135	Macrotron Systems Inc—*Gordon Ting*	44235 Nobel Dr, Fremont CA 94538	510-683-9600	R	4*	<.1
136	MobileDemand—*Matt Miller*	1350 Boyson Rd Bldg B, Hiawatha IA 52233	319-363-4121	R	4*	<.1
137	All-City Computers Inc—*Keith Grim*	1221 Avenida Acaso Ste, Camarillo CA 93012	805-388-8557	S	4*	<.1
138	Alacron Inc—*Joseph Sgro*	71 Spit Brook Rd Ste 2, Nashua NH 03060	603-891-2750	R	4*	<.1
139	Acme Portable Machines Inc—*James Cheng*	1330 Mountain View Cir, Azusa CA 91702	626-610-1888	R	4*	<.1
140	Aw Sheepscot Holding Company Inc—*Roger Tambling*	8809 Industrial Dr, Franksville WI 53126	262-884-9800	R	4*	<.1
141	Tri Map International Inc—*Lee Jensen*	111 Val Dervin Pkwy, Stockton CA 95206	209-234-0100	R	3*	<.1
142	ASA Engineering Inc—*Art Afshar*	8 Hammond Ste 105, Irvine CA 92618	949-460-9911	R	3*	<.1
143	Compudyne Inc—*Thomas Vidovic*	1524 E 37th St, Hibbing MN 55746	218-263-3624	R	3*	<.1
144	Computer Conversions Corp—*Stephen Renard*	6 Dunton Ct, East Northport NY 11731	631-261-3300	R	3*	<.1
145	Mercury Computer System Inc—*Lance Turner*	1815 Aston Ave Ste 107, Carlsbad CA 92008	760-494-9600	R	3*	<.1
146	Space Computer Corp—*Wiliam Kendall*	12121 Wilshire Blvd St, Los Angeles CA 90025	310-481-6000	R	3*	<.1
147	Foxconn Assembly LLC—*Teresa Hsu*	8807 Fallbrook Dr, Houston TX 77064	281-668-1668	R	3*	<.1
148	Greco Systems Inc	448 N Hwy 89 Ste E, Chino Valley AZ 86323		D	3*	<.1
149	Logistix Inc—*Frank Morrisroe*	8207 North 59th Ave, Glendale AZ 85302	623-772-8121	R	3*	<.1
150	Praim Inc—*Robert Fitzer*	16 Gleasondale Rd, Stow MA 01775	978-631-0408	S	3*	<.1
151	Ultraview Corp—*Joel Libove*	808 Gilman St, Berkeley CA 94710	925-253-2960	R	3*	<.1

Rank	Company Name—*Executive Officer*	Address, City, State, Zip	Phone	Type	Fin	Empls
152	MaxVision Corp—*Bruce Imsand*	495 Production Ave, Madison AL 35758	256-772-3058	R	3*	<.1
153	Yang-Ming International Corp—*Betty Shou*	595 Yorbita Rd, La Puente CA 91744	626-956-0100	R	3*	<.1
154	Flight Systems Inc—*Robert Shaffner*	505 Fishing Creek Rd, Lewisberry PA 17339	717-932-9900	R	3*	<.1
155	Argon Corp—*Moshe Albaum*	343 Great Neck Rd, Great Neck NY 11021	516-487-5314	R	3*	<.1
156	Hardcore Computer Inc—*Allen Berning*	2717 Hwy 14 W Ste D, Rochester MN 55901	507-285-0101	R	3*	<.1
157	Repcor—*Ken Wisz*	1 Light Sky Ct Ste 4, Sacramento CA 95828	916-386-2233	R	3*	<.1
158	Reed Manufacturing and Services—*Alejandro Estrada*	2200 N Yarbrough Dr B2, El Paso TX 79925	915-309-7487	R	3*	<.1
159	Amtek Electronic Inc—*Kathryn Yuen*	1150 N 5th St, San Jose CA 95112	408-971-8787	R	3*	<.1
160	Silverstone Technology—*Ai Cheng*	13626 Monte Vista Ave, Chino CA 91710	909-465-9596	R	3*	<.1
161	J and N Computer Services Inc—*Nancy Jacobsen*	1387 Fairport Rd Ste 9, Fairport NY 14450	585-388-8780	R	3*	<.1
162	Freedom USA Inc—*Alex Sonis*	1750 Highland Rd Ste 4, Twinsburg OH 44087	216-503-6363	R	2*	<.1
163	Pci Procal Inc—*Maureen Bolda*	PO Box 115, Alpena MI 49707	989-358-7070	R	2*	<.1
164	Agm Electronics Inc—*James Lenhart*	PO Box 32227, Tucson AZ 85751	520-722-1000	R	2*	<.1
165	HMW Enterprises Inc—*Mike Wutz*	PO Box 309, Waynesboro PA 17268	717-765-4690	R	2*	<.1
166	Micro-Smart Systems Inc—*Otis Anderson*	5355 Anderson Rd, Houston TX 77053	713-433-2277	R	2*	<.1
167	Rackmaster Systems Inc—*Patrick Buhl*	5244 Valley Industrial, Shakopee MN 55379	952-233-9820	R	2*	<.1
168	Recortec Inc—*Lester H Lee*	1620-A Berryessa Rd, San Jose CA 95133	408-928-1480	R	2*	<.1
169	SIA Computer Corp—*Bruce Bohuslav*	W3679 McDonald Rd, Lake Geneva WI 53147	262-249-8543	R	2*	<.1
170	Apex Embedded Systems—*Michael Ihm*	116 Owen Rd, Monona WI 53716	608-256-0767	R	2*	<.1
171	John Tse Computers—*John Tse*	1141 W Minster, Los Angeles CA 90032	323-225-3361	R	2*	<.1
172	Cygnus Labs LLC—*Marvin Shafer*	1612 E Erda Way, Erda UT 84074	435-882-0609	R	2*	<.1
173	Qualtronic Devices Inc—*Peter Ferentinos*	130 Oakside Dr, Smithtown NY 11787	631-360-0859	R	2*	<.1
174	Micro Computer Analysts Inc—*Eric Lakes*	128 Southland Dr, Lexington KY 40503	859-275-1228	R	2*	<.1
175	N and L Instruments Inc—*John Walz*	90 13th Ave Unit 1, Ronkonkoma NY 11779	631-471-4000	R	2*	<.1
176	Centent Co—*August Freimanis*	3879 S Main St, Santa Ana CA 92707	714-979-6491	R	2*	<.1
177	Unitek Technology Inc—*Yubo Ho*	2037 Pointe Ave, Ontario CA 91761	909-930-5700	R	2*	<.1
178	Comtech Micro System Inc—*Robert Wang*	3026 Javier Rd, Fairfax VA 22031	703-560-3500	R	2*	<.1
179	SteelCloud Inc—*Brian H Hajost*	20110 Ashbrook Pl Ste, Ashburn VA 20147	703-674-5500	P	2	<.1
180	Vpc Computers Inc—*Ali Khalaj*	2651 W Woodland Dr, Anaheim CA 92801	714-995-1276	R	2*	<.1
181	Marspec-Abernaqui-America Corp—*George Denoncourt*	PO Box 631, North Hampton NH 03862	603-964-4063	R	1*	<.1
182	Ilis Inc—*Bob Ilis*	1 Righter Pkwy Ste 160, Wilmington DE 19803	302-654-3000	R	1*	<.1
183	Duratab Corp—*Mark Burns*	145 Loganberry Dr, Abington MA 02351	508-944-3818	R	1*	<.1
184	Display Edge Technology Inc—*Ronald Earley*	2650 Indian Ripple Rd, Beavercreek OH 45440	937-320-9225	R	1*	<.1
185	Pjrs Technology—*Rich Sanders*	7793 Pine Island Way, West Palm Beach FL 33411	561-659-1004	R	1*	<.1
186	PST Computers Inc—*Patrick Guertin*	2808 N Federal Hwy, Fort Lauderdale FL 33306	954-561-9766	R	1*	<.1
187	Data-Pac Mailing Systems Corp—*Richard Yankloski*	1217 Bay Rd Ste 12, Webster NY 14580	585-671-0210	R	1*	<.1
188	Inducomp Corp—*John Weldon*	1265 Jefferson St, Pacific MO 63069	636-257-2111	R	1*	<.1
189	New Tech Texas Inc—*Ron Diu*	PO Box 202170, Austin TX 78720	512-250-0001	R	1*	<.1
190	Ldg Electronics Inc—*Jennifer Kincaid*	PO Box 48, Saint Leonard MD 20685	410-586-2177	R	1*	<.1
191	Psitech Inc—*John Kerr*	18368 Bandilier Cir, Fountain Valley CA 92708	714-964-7818	R	1*	<.1
192	Joint Technologies Ltd—*Nigel Cheatle*	1046 Calle Recodo Ste, San Clemente CA 92673	949-361-1158	R	1*	<.1
193	CAD/CAM Integration Inc—*Joe Lewis*	76 Winn St, Woburn MA 01801	781-933-9500	R	1	<.1
194	Cyberware Inc—*David Addleman*	2110 Del Monte Ave, Monterey CA 93940	831-657-1450	R	1*	<.1
195	Brick Computer Co—*David Dion*	80 Turnpike Rd, Ipswich MA 01938	978-356-1229	R	1*	<.1
196	Omni Flow Computers Inc—*Alan L McCartney*	12620 W Airport Blvd S, Sugar Land TX 77478	281-240-6161	R	1*	<.1
197	Phoenix Kiosk LLC	1155 W Rio Salado Pkwy, Tempe AZ 85281	480-505-5742	R	1*	<.1
198	VIC Hi-Tech Corp *Mackey McDonald*	17908 La Salle Ave, Gardena CA 90248	310-715-9182	R	1*	<.1
199	Imperial Computer Corp—*George Chang*	318 S San Gabriel Blvd, San Gabriel CA 91776	626-285-1256	R	1*	<.1
200	Integrated Business and Industrial Systems Inc—*Daljeet Singh*	6842 NW 20th Ave, Fort Lauderdale FL 33309	954-978-9225	R	1*	<.1
201	RuggedNotebookscom—*Alan Shad*	1574 N Batavia St Ste, Orange CA 92867	714-998-1828	R	1*	<.1
202	Advanced Business Systems Inc—*Steve Burger*	5630 Silverado Way Ste, Anchorage AK 99518	907-562-5505	R	1*	<.1
203	Lanford Manufacturing Corporation Inc—*Mark Mccrill*	43 Merrimack St, Lawrence MA 01843	978-557-0240	R	1*	<.1
204	Link Depot Corp—*Jung Ting*	491 Yorbita Rd, La Puente CA 91744	626-581-8887	R	1*	<.1
205	Evercase USA Inc—*Mike Chen*	1925 Lundy Ave, San Jose CA 95131	408-894-9003	R	1*	<.1
206	Scidyne—*Mark Durgin*	649 School St, Pembroke MA 02359	781-293-3059	R	1*	<.1
207	National Datacomputer Inc—*Bruna Bucacci*	900 Middlesex Tpke Bld, Billerica MA 01821	978-663-7677	P	1	<.1
208	Aurora Computer Systems Inc—*Kathleen Freidhoff*	151 Freidhoff Ln, Johnstown PA 15902	814-539-9777	R	1*	<.1
209	Axper Corp—*Tony WEI*	3761 Grove Ave, Palo Alto CA 94303	650-565-8420	R	1*	<.1
210	Martinez Electronics—*Lupita Woodcock*	PO Box 21447, Long Beach CA 90801	562-595-5462	R	1*	<.1
211	Abi—*Benny Ngo*	233 E Weddell Dr Ste G, Sunnyvale CA 94089	408-946-8710	R	1*	<.1
212	Broussard Iron Works and Welding Inc—*Troy Broussard*	2702 N Herpin Ave, Kaplan LA 70548	337-643-6515	R	1*	<.1
213	Cape Setups LLC—*Diane Mailloux*	1611 Main St, West Barnstable MA 02668	508-477-6444	R	1*	<.1
214	Dax Systems Inc—*Ernie Kaminaris*	343 New Rd Ste 4, Parsippany NJ 07054	973-227-8111	R	1*	<.1
215	Performance Imaging Corp—*Wolfan Ermel*	5392 Leon St, Oceanside CA 92057	760-721-2925	R	1*	<.1
216	Comp-U-Build Computers Inc—*Brian Itskin*	45 S Maine St, Fallon NV 89406	775-423-8229	R	1*	<.1
217	Pro-Active Technology Marketing Inc—*Gei-Jon Pao*	715 W Katella Ave, Anaheim CA 92802	714-533-7835	R	1*	<.1
218	Anysolv Technologies Inc—*Tyrone Adams*	10451 Mill Run Cir, Owings Mills MD 21117	410-654-3312	R	1*	<.1
219	Comped—*John Young*	36956 County Rd 14, Belgrade MN 56312	320-987-3535	R	1*	<.1
220	Falcon Ridge Technologies LLC	1255 Euclid Ave Ste 50, Cleveland OH 44115	216-674-1649	R	1*	<.1
221	Bahia 21 Corp—*Serge Montacq*	2275 Res Blvd Ste 500, Rockville MD 20850	301-296-4333	R	<1*	<.1
222	Compuzoo—*Ruth Gottenbos*	20214 Delight St, Canyon Country CA 91351	661-298-0982	R	<1*	<.1
223	Jena Band of Choctaw Indians	1052 Chinaha Hina St, Trout LA 71371	318-992-2717	R	<1*	<.1
224	Micro Basics Co—*Kelly Binning*	1815 Broadway, Denison IA 51442	712-263-3495	R	<1*	<.1
225	Business Network Technology Inc—*Robert Wang*	2901 E Miraloma Ave St, Anaheim CA 92806	714-666-1848	R	<1*	<.1
226	Custom Computers and Software Inc—*Martin Juhl*	PO Box 310, Sherburn MN 56171	507-764-7022	R	<1*	<.1
227	M and S Computer Products Inc—*Marcia Posen*	505 Liberty St, Boonton NJ 07005	973-263-9041	R	<1*	<.1
228	Rugid Computer Inc—*Don Bedlington*	9730 Lathrop Industria, Olympia WA 98512	360-866-4492	R	<1*	<.1
229	Terra Comp Technology—*Terry Silvester*	449 4th St Nw, Barberton OH 44203	330-745-8912	R	<1*	<.1
230	Alea Systems Inc—*Umberto Cettomai*	10810 Guilford Rd Ste, Annapolis Junction MD 20701	301-776-3754	R	<1*	<.1
231	Jli Electronics Inc—*Mark Strong*	PO Box 7, Harleysville PA 19438	215-256-3200	R	<1*	<.1
232	Voyager Computer Corp—*Mildred Palm*	2253 Camino Rey, Fullerton CA 92833	714-526-0626	R	<1*	<.1
233	ABS Data Systems Inc—*Heidi Schevker*	12445 Picrus St Ste 10, San Diego CA 92129	858-484-1096	R	<1*	<.1
234	Ricavision International Inc—*Max Li*	4540 Campus Dr Ste 108, Newport Beach CA 92660	949-252-5356	R	<1*	<.1
235	Gerald Welch—*Gerald Welch*	9562 W Wesley Dr, Lakewood CO 80227	303-716-0880	R	<1*	<.1
236	Luna Labs—*Clyde Calcote*	3018 Silver Springs Ln, Richardson TX 75082	972-238-1339	R	<1*	<.1
237	Measurements Technology Inc—*Michael Duggan*	4240 Loch Highland Pkw, Roswell GA 30075	770-587-2222	R	<1*	<.1
238	Mr Sign Inc—*Ronald Gengoult*	350 Mountain Ave Ste 1, Middlesex NJ 08846	732-560-0606	R	<1*	<.1
239	Rudy's Dad Inc—*Marc Robinette*	207 Ter Ave, San Rafael CA 94901	415-459-0362	R	<1*	<.1
240	Arbus Inc—*Anthony Swanic*	5720 Hedgeford Ct, Las Vegas NV 89120	702-736-9334	R	<1*	<.1
241	Ortek Data Systems Inc—*James Strelchun*	10445 SW Canyon Rd Ste, Beaverton OR 97005	503-626-0475	R	<1*	<.1

Note: An asterisk (*) indicates an estimated financial figure. The company type code used is as follows: R = Private, P = Public, S = Private Subsidiary, B = Public Subsidiary, D = Division, J = Joint Venture, I = Investment Fund.

COMPANY RANKINGS BY SALES WITHIN 4-DIGIT SIC

Rank	Company Name—*Executive Officer*	Address, City, State, Zip	Phone	Type	Fin	Empls
242	Omnidyne Corp—*Lou Levy*	14 Connor Ln, Deer Park NY 11729	631-789-3600	R	<1*	<.1
243	A2z Computers Inc—*George Faint*	PO Box 5633, Dothan AL 36302	334-677-3469	R	<1*	<.1
244	Jorway Corp—*Timothy Radway*	223 Wall St Ste 156, Huntington NY 11743	631-351-1203	R	<1*	<.1
245	Zoltech Corp—*Les Lazar*	16009 Arminta St, Van Nuys CA 91406	818-780-1800	R	<1*	<.1
246	Kolias and Co—*Diane Kolias*	214 Musconetcong River, Washington NJ 07882	908-689-9499	R	<1*	<.1
247	Mean Machine Computers—*Christopher Carlson*	1422 Whitestown Rd Ext, Prospect PA 16052	724-865-9823	R	<1*	<.1
248	Mechling Computers and Communications Networking—*Curt Mechling*	1200 E Main St, Ashland OH 44805	419-281-4555	R	<1*	<.1
249	Test And Repair Services—*Dave Andersen*	3529 Old Conejo Rd Ste, Newbury Park CA 91320	805-499-7010	R	<1*	<.1
250	Home Computer Support—*Francis Dabarera*	311 Warren St, Waltham MA 02453	781-894-8381	R	<1*	<.1
251	R Tech Systems—*Robert Tetzlaff*	980 Sw Alcora Dr, Pullman WA 99163	509-334-9433	R	<1*	<.1
252	Osec Robotics Inc—*Irene Liu*	1387 Dillon Way, Superior CO 80027	720-304-2754	R	N/A	<.1

TOTALS: SIC 3571 Electronic Computers
Companies: 252   430,839   974.7

3572 Computer Storage Devices

Rank	Company Name—*Executive Officer*	Address, City, State, Zip	Phone	Type	Fin	Empls
1	EMC Corp—*Paul T Dacier*	176 South St, Hopkinton MA 01748	508-435-1000	P	17,015	48.5
2	Hitachi Global Storage Technologies—*Steve Milligan*	3403 Yerba Buena Rd, San Jose CA 95135	408-717-5000	J	13,500*	30.0
3	Western Digital Corp—*John F Coyne*	3355 Michelson Dr Ste, Irvine CA 92612	949-672-7000	P	9,526	65.4
4	Hitachi Data Systems Corp—*Jack Domme*	750 Central Expy, Santa Clara CA 95050	408-970-1000	S	5,293*	5.4
5	NetApp Inc—*Tom Georgens*	495 E Java Dr, Sunnyvale CA 94089	408-822-6000	P	5,123	10.2
6	SanDisk Corp—*Sanjay Mehrotra*	601 McCarthy Blvd, Milpitas CA 95035	408-801-1000	P	4,827	3.5
7	SMART Modular Technologies Inc—*Iain MacKenzie*	39870 Eureka Dr, Newark CA 94560	510-623-1231	P	703	1.2
8	Wintec Industries Inc—*Shi Hui (Sue) Jeng*	675 Sycamore Dr, Milpitas CA 95035	408-856-0500	R	686*	.2
9	Quantum Corp—*Jon Gacek*	1650 Technology Dr Ste, San Jose CA 95110	408-944-4000	P	627	1.8
10	Cray Federal Inc—*Peter J Ungaro*	901 5th Ave Ste 1000, Seattle WA 98164	206-701-2000	S	577*	.9
11	Blue Coat Systems Inc—*Brian M NeSmith*	420 N Mary Ave, Sunnyvale CA 94085	408-220-2200	P	487	1.3
12	LSI Logic Storage Systems Inc—*Abhi Talwalkar*	1621 Barber Ln, Milpitas CA 95035	408-433-8000	S	427	.9
13	STEC Inc—*Manouch Moshayedi*	3001 Daimler St, Santa Ana CA 92705	949-476-1180	P	308	1.0
14	Promise Technology Inc—*James Lee*	580 Cottonwood Dr, Milpitas CA 95035	408-228-1400	R	279*	.5
15	Dot Hill Systems Corp—*Dana Kammersgard*	1351 S Sunset St, Longmont CO 80501	303-845-3200	P	239	.3
16	3PAR Inc—*David C Scott*	4209 Technology Dr, Fremont CA 94538	510-413-5999	S	194	.7
17	Plextor LLC	42000 Christy St, Fremont CA 94538	510-824-9695	S	165*	.1
18	LaCie USA Ltd—*Scott Phillips*	22985 NW Evergreen Pky, Hillsboro OR 97124	503-844-4500	S	117*	.2
19	Softchoice Optimus Solutions Inc—*David McDonald*	22 Technology Park S, Norcross GA 30092	770-447-1951	R	83*	.2
20	DataDirect Networks Inc—*Alex Bouzari*	9351 Deering Ave, Chatsworth CA 91311	818-700-7600	R	79*	.1
21	Hitachi America Ltd Computer Div—*Kazuo Furukawa*	1000 Marina Blvd, Brisbane CA 94005	650-589-8300	D	72*	.3
22	ClubMac Inc—*Frank F Khulusi*	2555 W 190th St, Torrance CA 90504	949-768-8114	D	67*	.2
23	Transpower Technologies Inc	980 Sandhill Rd Ste 10, Reno NV 89521	775-852-0140	S	61*	2.2
24	Alliance Peripheral Systems Inc—*Philippe Spruch* LaCie USA Ltd	22985 NW Evergreen Pkw, Hillsboro OR 97124	503-844-4500	S	61*	.1
25	LaserCard Corp—*Robert DeVincenzi*	1875 N Shoreline Blvd, Mountain View CA 94043	650-969-4428	S	59	.2
26	Innovative Micro Technology Inc—*John S Foster*	75 Robin Hill Rd, Santa Barbara CA 93117	805-681-2800	R	56*	.1
27	Ampex Data System Corp—*D Gordon Strickland*	500 Broadway, Redwood City CA 94063	650-367-2011	S	53*	.1
28	Dataram Corp—*John H Freeman*	777 Alexander Rd Ste 1, Princeton NJ 08540	609-799-0071	P	47	.1
29	Xtera Communications Inc—*John Hopper*	500 W Bethany Dr Ste 1, Allen TX 75013	972-649-5000	R	38*	.4
30	Fusion-Io Inc—*David Flynn*	2855 E Cottonwood Pkwy, Salt Lake City UT 84121	801-424-5500	R	36*	.4
31	Pillar Data Systems Inc—*Michael Workman*	2840 Junction Ave, San Jose CA 95134	408-503-4000	R	36*	.4
32	TechWorks Inc	4030 W Braker Ln Ste 1, Austin TX 78759		R	34*	<.1
33	Atp Electronics Inc—*Tim Hsieh*	750 N Mary Ave, Sunnyvale CA 94085	408-732-5000	R	33*	.1
34	TEAC America Inc Data Storage Products Div—*Koichiro Nakamura*	PO Box 750, Montebello CA 90640	323-726-0303	D	31*	.1
35	MicroNet Technology Inc	20525 Manhattan Pl, Torrance CA 90501	310-320-7272	R	31*	.1
36	Rorke Data Inc—*Joe Swanson*	7626 Golden Triangle D, Eden Prairie MN 55344	952-829-0300	S	30*	.1
37	Spectra Logic Corp—*Nathan C Thompson*	6285 Lookout Rd, Boulder CO 80301	303-449-6400	R	29*	.3
38	Contemporary Cybernetics Group Inc—*Maria Lennman*	111 Cybernetics Way, Yorktown VA 23693	757-833-9000	R	28*	.1
39	Sharp Microelectronics Group—*John Marck*	5700 NW Pacific Rim Bl, Camas WA 98607	360-834-2500	S	27*	.1
40	Adtron Corp—*Bob Benkendorf* SMART Modular Technologies Inc	4415 E Cotten Center B, Phoenix AZ 85040	602-735-0300	S	26*	<.1
41	IMC Networks Corp—*Jerry Roby*	19772 Pauling, Foothill Ranch CA 92610	949-465-3000	R	25*	.1
42	CMS Peripherals Inc—*Frank Salmon*	12 Mauchly Unit E, Irvine CA 92618	714-424-5520	R	25*	.1
43	Perceptics LLC—*John Dalton*	9737 Cogdill Rd Ste 20, Knoxville TN 37932	865-966-9200	R	17*	.1
44	Appro International Inc—*Daniel Kim*	446 S Abbott Ave, Milpitas CA 95035	408-941-8100	R	15*	.1
45	Cambex Foreign Sales Corp—*Joseph F Kruy* Cambex Corp	115 Flanders Rd, Westborough MA 01581	508-983-1200	S	14	<.1
46	Alanco Technologies Inc—*Robert R Kauffman*	7950 E Acoma Dr Ste 11, Scottsdale AZ 85260	480-607-1010	P	14	<.1
47	Excel Meridian Data Inc	4418 Sunbelt Dr, Addison TX 75001	972-980-7098	S	12*	<.1
48	Micro Design International Inc	45 Skyline Dr Ste 1017, Lake Mary FL 32746	407-472-6000	R	12*	<.1
49	Winchester Systems Inc—*Joel Leider*	101 Billerica Ave Bldg, Billerica MA 01862	781-265-0200	R	11*	<.1
50	Glyph Technologies Inc—*Mike Driscoll*	3736 Kellogg Rd, Cortland NY 13045	607-275-0345	S	11*	<.1
51	Digi-Data Corp—*Dennis Cindrich*	7165 Columbia Gateway, Columbia MD 21046	410-730-6880	R	10*	.1
52	Onset Computer Corp—*Justin Testa*	PO Box 3450, Pocasset MA 02559	508-759-9500	R	10*	.1
53	Gim Electronics Corp—*Mark Douenias*	270 Duffy Ave Ste H, Hicksville NY 11801	516-942-3382	R	10*	<.1
54	Nexsan Technologies Inc—*Philip Black*	555 St Charles Dr Ste, Thousand Oaks CA 91360	818-715-9111	R	8*	<.1
55	IceWEB Storage Corp—*John R Tibbitts* IceWeb Inc	22900 Shaw Rd Ste 111, Sterling VA 20166	571-287-2380	S	8*	<.1
56	ComSquared Systems Inc	5125 Peachtree Industr, Norcross GA 30092	770-734-5300	S	7*	.1
57	CSSI Systems—*Denny Maetzold*	1870 Lake Dr W, Chanhassen MN 55317	612-949-0053	R	6*	.1
58	Bering Technology Inc—*Jay Franz*	591 W Hamilton Ave Ste, Campbell CA 95008	408-364-6500	R	6*	<.1
59	Tape Laboratories Inc—*Brian Ignatin*	5301 Beethoven St Ste2, Los Angeles CA 90066	310-577-1700	S	6*	<.1
60	Accurite Technologies Inc—*Brad Baker*	46712 Fremont Blvd, Fremont CA 94538	510-668-4980	R	6*	<.1
61	Seek Systems Inc—*Terry McFadden*	19501 144th Ave NE Ste, Woodinville WA 98072	425-806-7335	R	6*	<.1
62	Diverse Logistics Inc—*Jon Klotz*	2651 Dow, Tustin CA 92780	714-508-1040	R	6*	<.1
63	I/OMagic Corp—*Tony Shahbaz*	4 Marconi, Irvine CA 92618	949-707-4800	P	6	<.1
64	Gst Inc—*David Breisacher*	3419 Via Lido Ste 164, Newport Beach CA 92663		R	5*	.1
65	Todd Enterprises Systems Inc	747 Middle Neck Rd Ste, Great Neck NY 11024	516-773-8087	R	5*	<.1
66	Solid Data Systems Inc—*Wade Truma*	3542 Bassett St, Santa Clara CA 95054	408-845-5700	R	5*	<.1
67	Memtec Corp—*Dennis Garboski*	68 Stiles Rd Ste D, Salem NH 03079	603-893-8080	R	4*	<.1
68	Diamond Systems Corp—*Jonathan Miller*	555 Ellis St, Mountain View CA 94043	650-810-2500	R	4	<.1
69	Kintronics Inc—*Bob Mesnik*	500 Executive Blvd Ste, Ossining NY 10562	914-944-3425	R	4*	<.1

Rank	Company Name—*Executive Officer*	Address, City, State, Zip	Phone	Type	Fin	Empls
70	Citek Inc	1953 N Main St, Garden Grove CA 92842	714-283-8668	R	4*	<.1
71	Rank Technology Corp—*Fred Barez*	1190 Miraloma Way Ste, Sunnyvale CA 94085	408-737-1488	R	4*	<.1
72	Conduant Corp—*Kenneth R Owens*	1501 S Sunset St Ste C, Longmont CO 80501	303-485-2721	R	3*	<.1
73	Akiwa Technology Inc—*Bill Lin*	13317 166th St, Cerritos CA 90703	562-483-6767	R	3*	<.1
74	M and R Technologies Inc (Dayton Ohio)—*Mark Miller*	2445 E River Rd, Dayton OH 45439	937-294-1983	R	3*	<.1
75	Dualcor Technologies Inc—*Tim Glass*	1 Embarcadero Ctr Ste, San Francisco CA 94111	831-684-2457	R	3*	<.1
76	Compucable Corp—*Sharon Lcharna*	459 Wald, Irvine CA 92618	949-341-0888	R	3*	<.1
77	IceWeb Inc—*John R Signorello*	PO Box 617, Sterling VA 20166	571-287-2380	P	3	<.1
78	Allstar Microelectronics Inc—*James Chiang*	30191 Avendia De Las, Rancho Santa Margarita CA 92688	949-546-0888	R	3*	<.1
79	Rising Edge Technologies Inc—*Michael Schutte*	500 Huntmar Park Dr St, Herndon VA 20170	703-471-8108	R	3*	<.1
80	Cambex Corp—*Joseph F Kruy*	337 Turnpike Rd, Southboro MA 01772	508-281-0209	P	2	<.1
81	Dinamica Inc—*Michael Bavel*	10808 Fallstone Rd Ste, Houston TX 77099	281-564-5100	R	2*	<.1
82	Summatec Computer Corp—*Glen W Goglia*	1441 LaLoma Dr, San Marcos CA 92078		R	2	<.1
83	Jmr Electronics Inc—*Josef Rabinovitz*	8968 Fullbright Ave, Chatsworth CA 91311	818-993-4801	R	2*	<.1
84	Nikon Americas Inc—*Michio Kariya*	1300 Walt Whitman Rd, Melville NY 11747	631-547-4200	S	2*	<.1
85	Storage Engine Inc—*Gregg M Azcuy*	1 Sheila Dr, Tinton Falls NJ 07724	732-747-6995	R	2*	<.1
86	MP Tapes Inc—*Peter Groel*	1233 Sherman Dr, Longmont CO 80501	303-774-6361	R	2*	<.1
87	Aurora Research Company Inc—*Donna Barbetta*	200 Munsonhurst Rd Ste, Franklin NJ 07416	973-827-8055	R	2*	<.1
88	Computer and Control Solutions Inc—*Rokneddin Alavi*	1856 Buford Hwy Ste 10, Duluth GA 30097	770-491-1131	R	2*	<.1
89	Athana International Inc—*Wolfgang Arnold*	1624 240th St, Harbor City CA 90710	310-539-7280	R	1*	<.1
90	Microdrive Corp—*Ephraim Moya*	8325 Denise Ln Ste G, Canoga Park CA 91304	818-700-1200	R	1*	<.1
91	Refly Of Miami Inc—*Oscar Molina*	7360 Nw 35th St, Miami FL 33122	305-716-8800	R	1*	<.1
92	Vanguard Rugged Storage LLC	6525 Gunpark Dr Ste 37, Boulder CO 80301	303-527-3003	R	1*	<.1
93	Service Storage International Inc—*Craig Budreo*	38316 Airport Pkwy, Willoughby OH 44094	440-951-7579	R	1*	<.1
94	Removable Media Solutions Inc—*Mary Lusi*	3235 Sunrise Blvd Ste, Rancho Cordova CA 95742	916-858-3300	R	1*	<.1
95	Chi Corp—*Diane Thome*	5265 Naiman Pky, Cleveland OH 44139	440-498-2300	R	1*	<.1
96	Luna Imaging Inc—*Marlo Lee*	2702 Media Center Dr, Los Angeles CA 90065		R	1*	<.1
97	Creative Micro Designs Inc—*Charles Christianson*	PO Box 646, East Longmeadow MA 01028	413-525-0023	R	1*	<.1
98	Inter-Tech Corp—*Dick Roemer*	PO Box 32100, Phoenix AZ 85064	480-945-0085	R	1	<.1
99	Arraid Inc—*Norm Boudreau*	9414 E San Salvador Dr, Scottsdale AZ 85258	480-699-3047	R	1*	<.1
100	Nelson's Vegetable Storage Systems Inc—*Holly Nelson*	PO Box 215, Plainfield WI 54966	715-335-6660	R	1*	<.1
101	Tri Magnetics Corp—*Moon Hahn*	PO Box 7939, Fresno CA 93747	559-251-3331	R	1*	<.1
102	Memory Storage Devices—*Ross Estep*	121 Interpark Blvd Ste, San Antonio TX 78216	210-496-3689	R	1*	<.1
103	Primearray Systems Inc—*Willard Rice*	12 Michigan Dr, Natick MA 01760	508-653-6250	R	1*	<.1
104	Ps Solutions Inc—*Jacqueline Green*	411 Interchange St, Mckinney TX 75071	972-548-8080	R	1*	<.1
105	Teresa Rhoades—*Teresa Rhoades*	PO Box 4357, Clearwater FL 33758	727-442-7604	R	<1*	<.1
106	Imaging Resource Associates Inc—*Deborah Capps*	2708 College Farm Rd, Mooresboro NC 28114	828-684-1302	R	<1*	<.1
107	Shining Technology Inc—*Chris Wang*	10533 Progress Way Ste, Cypress CA 90630	714-761-9598	R	N/A	.1

TOTALS: SIC 3572 Computer Storage Devices
Companies: 107   61,452   179.5

3575 Computer Terminals

Rank	Company Name—*Executive Officer*	Address, City, State, Zip	Phone	Type	Fin	Empls
1	webOS Global Business Unit—*Stephen DeWitt*	950 W Maude Ave, Sunnyvale CA 94085	408-617-7000	S	736	.9
2	Wyse Technology Inc—*Tarkan Maner*	3471 N 1st St, San Jose CA 95134	408-473-1200	R	221*	.9
3	Fluitec International LLC	PO Box 579, Rutledge GA 30663		R	174*	<.1
4	Canvys—*Wendy Diddell*	PO Box 393, LaFox IL 60147	508-460-5400	D	45	.1
5	Crystal Group Inc—*Scott Kongable*	850 Kacena Rd, Hiawatha IA 52233	319-378-1636	R	36*	.1
6	Optoma Technology Inc	3178 Laurelview Ct, Fremont CA 94500	510-897-8600	R	33	<.1
7	Envision Peripherals Inc—*Alec Chan*	47490 Seabridge Dr, Fremont CA 94538	510-770-9988	R	29*	<.1
8	Intersystems USA Inc—*Nimrod Halfon*	12650 E Briarwood Ave, Centennial CO 80112	303-858-1000	R	28*	.1
9	Ultimate Technology Corp—*Samuel J Villanti*	100 Rawson Rd, Victor NY 14564	585-924-9500	R	26*	.1
10	Gre-America Inc—*Teruo Takahashi*	425 Harbor Blvd Ste B, Belmont CA 94002	650-591-1400	R	25*	.4
11	Linx Data Terminals Inc—*John Hallmark*	1501 10th St Ste 110, Plano TX 75074	972-964-7090	R	22*	<.1
12	Milwaukee PC Incorporated A Wisconsin Corp—*Jim Petr*	6013 W Bluemound Rd, Milwaukee WI 53213	414-258-2275	R	20*	.1
13	Kristel LP—*Lorraine Chmielewski*	555 Kirk Rd, Saint Charles IL 60174	630-443-1290	R	17*	.1
14	Wind Energy America Inc—*Melvin E Wentz*	12100 Singletree Ln, Eden Prairie MN 55344	952-746-1234	P	16	N/A
15	Addonics Technologies Corp—*Victor Wu*	1918 Junction Ave, San Jose CA 95131	408-573-8580	R	15*	<.1
16	Passur Aerospace Inc—*James T Barry*	1 Landmark Sq Ste 1900, Stamford CT 06901	203-622-4086	P	14	<.1
17	Expedition Networks Ltd—*Richard Favara*	8600 Aqueduct Ave, North Hills CA 91343	818-830-6006	R	11*	<.1
18	Digitron Electronics	7801 E Telegraph RdSte, Montebello CA 90640	323-887-0777	R	10*	<.1
19	TeleVideo Inc—*K Philip Hwang*	2562 Seaboard Ave, San Jose CA 95131	408-954-8333	R	8*	<.1
20	Bartizan Data Systems LLC—*Lew Hoff*	217 Riverdale Ave, Yonkers NY 10705	914-965-7977	R	7*	.1
21	Electronic Monitoring Systems—*Fiona Walters*	30201 Aventura, Rcho Sta Marg CA 92688	949-635-1600	R	7*	<.1
22	New England Keyboard Inc—*David Myers*	1 Princeton Rd Ste 1, Fitchburg MA 01420	978-345-8332	R	6*	.1
23	Likom Caseworks USA Inc—*Kim Chow*	17890 Castleton St Ste, City Of Industry CA 91748	626-854-2029	R	6*	.1
24	Transparent Products Inc—*John Mcvay*	28064 Ave Stanford E, Valencia CA 91355	661-294-9787	R	6*	<.1
25	Portable Warehouse Corp—*Kenny Le*	1247 N Lakeview Ave St, Anaheim CA 92807	714-701-1830	R	5*	<.1
26	Behemoth Corp—*Luanne Edelman*	202 Reynolds Ave, League City TX 77573	281-332-4798	R	5*	<.1
27	3k Computers LLC	PO Box 480416, Delray Beach FL 33448	561-470-6089	R	5*	.1
28	CSI Keyboards Inc—*Peter Castner*	56 Pulaski St Unit 1, Peabody MA 01960	978-532-8181	R	4*	<.1
29	Esprit Systems Inc—*Jason Barnes*	1684 Decoto Rd Ste 306, Union City CA 94587	510-394-1998	R	4*	<.1
30	Posiflex Business Machines Inc—*Owen Chen*	30689 Huntwood Ave, Hayward CA 94544	510-429-7097	R	4*	<.1
31	Sgb Enterprises Inc—*William Blowers*	24844 Anza Dr Unit Ab, Valencia CA 91355	661-294-8306	R	3*	<.1
32	Les Faerber—*Les Faerber*	1146 N Mesa Dr Ste 276, Mesa AZ 85201	602-370-7877	R	3*	<.1
33	Dynics Inc—*Edward Gatt*	4330 Varsity Dr, Ann Arbor MI 48108	734-677-6100	R	3*	<.1
34	All Technics Products Inc—*David Wu*	216 Gates Rd, Little Ferry NJ 07643	201-440-2225	R	3*	<.1
35	Rice Integration LLC—*Brian Rice*	1251 N Lynwood Dr, Anaheim CA 92807	714-432-6630	R	3*	<.1
36	Ezenia! Inc—*Khoa D Nguyen*	14 Celina Ave Ste 17, Nashua NH 03063	603-589-7600	P	3	<.1
37	Ocp Group Inc—*Tracy Sommer*	7130 Engineer Rd, San Diego CA 92111	858-279-7400	R	3*	<.1
38	Westport Research Associates Inc—*Don Cartner*	7001 Blue Ridge Blvd, Raytown MO 64133	816-358-8990	R	3*	<.1
39	Martech Computers—*Marvin Tedjamulia*	5235 Cottage Farm Rd, Alpharetta GA 30022	770-418-0101	R	2*	<.1
40	JCCConnectnet	7825 Langwood Dr, Indianapolis IN 46268	317-879-9049	R	2*	<.1
41	Technology Alternatives Corp—*Candy Lechter*	1950 NE 208 Ter, Miami FL 33179	305-933-2026	R	2*	<.1
42	Custom Board Design Ltd—*Tony Marasco*	609 Rte 109 Ste 2b, West Babylon NY 11704	631-884-2700	R	2*	<.1
43	Argyll Technology Inc—*Robert Burnes*	24216 Michigan Ave, Dearborn MI 48124	313-359-0900	R	2*	<.1
44	Caltron Industries Inc—*Jim Wang*	4120 Clipper Ct, Fremont CA 94538	510-440-1800	R	2*	<.1
45	RGB Display Corp—*William Laughlin*	22525 Kingston Ln, Grass Valley CA 95949	530-268-2222	R	1*	<.1
46	Cybernetic Micro Systems Inc—*Edwin Klingman*	3000 Hwy 84, San Gregorio CA 94074	650-726-3000	R	1*	<.1
47	eRoomSystem Technologies Inc—*David A Gestetner*	1072 Madison Ave, Lakewood NJ 08701	732-730-0116	P	1	<.1

Note: An asterisk (*) indicates an estimated financial figure. The company type code used is as follows: R = Private, P = Public, S = Private Subsidiary, B = Public Subsidiary, D = Division, J = Joint Venture, I = Investment Fund.

COMPANY RANKINGS BY SALES WITHIN 4-DIGIT SIC

Rank	Company Name—Executive Officer	Address, City, State, Zip	Phone	Type	Fin	Empls
48	Advanced Digital Research Inc—Dennis Childs	1813 E Dyer Rd Ste 410, Santa Ana CA 92705	949-252-1055	R	1*	<.1
49	Peak Computer Services Inc—Matthew Hyatt	2905 Premiere Pkwy Ste, Duluth GA 30097	770-441-2520	R	1*	<.1
50	Informer Computer Systems Inc—Wilfred R Little	12711 Western Ave, Garden Grove CA 92841	714-891-1112	R	1*	<.1
51	Actuality Systems Inc—Michael Goldstein	1337 Massachusetts Ave, Arlington MA 02476	781-541-6036	R	1*	<.1
52	Data Check Video Inc—Darrell Bevan	5148 N Commerce Ave St, Moorpark CA 93021	805-517-1907	R	1*	<.1
53	Synctronics—Michael Sinclair	PO Box 91226, San Diego CA 92169	619-275-3525	R	1*	<.1
54	Current Computers LLC—Ashley Kuehl	62 Maxwell, Irvine CA 92618	949-425-9700	R	1*	<.1
55	Stanford Electronics Manufacturing and Sales—Ann Klieves	915 Berry Rd, Brodnax VA 23920	434-676-6630	R	1*	<.1
56	Assured Computing Technologies Inc—Frank Pivonka	19 Harvey Rd Unit 15-4, Bedford NH 03110	603-627-8728	R	1*	<.1
57	Netinlink—Edward Chan	345 Paseo Tesoro, Walnut CA 91789	909-468-1750	R	<1*	<.1
58	Tri Star Cnc Services LLC	2314 N Grandview Blvd, Waukesha WI 53188	262-547-1742	R	<1*	<.1
59	Portable Computer Systems LLC	20360 Channing Ln, Yorba Linda CA 92887	714-777-4289	R	<1*	<.1
60	PC City—Larry Viccho	3400 State Rte 35 Ste, Hazlet NJ 07730	732-203-1640	R	<1*	<.1
61	Durasys Corp—George Perrine	107 Silver St, Dover NH 03820	603-742-7363	R	<1*	<.1
62	Iicon Technology LLC	PO Box 434, Ashland OR 97520	541-488-7958	R	<1*	<.1
63	In Touch Systems—Jerry Crouch	11 Westview Rd, Spring Valley NY 10977	845-354-7431	R	<1*	<.1

TOTALS: SIC 3575 Computer Terminals
Companies: 63 — Fin 1,589 — Empls 3.8

3577 Computer Peripheral Equipment Nec

Rank	Company Name—Executive Officer	Address, City, State, Zip	Phone	Type	Fin	Empls
1	Cisco Systems Inc—John T Chambers	170 W Tasman Dr, San Jose CA 95134	408-526-4000	P	43,218	71.8
2	Alps Electric—Masataka Kataoka	910 E Hamilton Ave Ste, Campbell CA 95008	408-361-6400	R	22,987*	38.5
3	RISO Inc—Fumiya Tomiyama	300 Rosewood Dr Ste 21, Danvers MA 01923	978-777-7377	R	13,721*	.4
4	Lexmark International Inc—Paul Rooke	740 W New Circle Rd, Lexington KY 40550	859-232-2000	P	4,173	13.3
5	NVIDIA Corp—Jen-Hsun Huang	2701 San Tomas Expwy, Santa Clara CA 95050	408-486-2000	P	3,534	4.2
6	MATCO Group Inc—Kenneth Elliott	320 N Jensen Rd, Vestal NY 13850	607-729-4921	R	3,335*	5.6
7	Pearson Assessments—John Harnett	5601 Green Valley Dr, Bloomington MN 55437		S	3,252*	6.0
8	Kyocera Mita America Inc—Katsumi Komaguchi	PO Box 40008, Fairfield NJ 07004	973-808-8444	S	3,124*	14.7
9	Brocade Communications Systems Inc—Michael Klayko	130 Holger Way, San Jose CA 95134	408-333-8000	P	2,147	4.5
10	Newegg Inc—Fred Chang	9997 Rose Hill Rd, Whittier CA 90601	626-271-9700	R	2,113*	2.0
11	Northstar Systems Inc—Bob Thunell	8351 Elm Ave Ste 103, Rancho Cucamonga CA 91730	909-483-9900	R	2,104*	3.5
12	Scanport Inc	938 Radecki Ct, Rowland Heights CA 91748	310-687-5767	R	2,026*	<.1
13	Embedded Communications Computing—Jay Geldmacher	2900 S Diablo Way, Tempe AZ 85282	602-438-5720	S	1,732*	1.5
14	Videojet Technologies Inc—Matt Trerotola	1500 Mittel Blvd, Wood Dale IL 60191	630-860-7300	S	1,712*	2.6
15	Oki Data Americas Inc—Takabumi Asahi	2000 Bishops Gate Blvd, Mount Laurel NJ 08054	856-235-2600	S	1,641	.4
16	Peripheral Dynamics Inc—Lawrence Hyer	5150 Campus Dr, Plymouth Meeting PA 19462	610-825-7090	R	1,437*	.1
17	Media Sciences Inc—Michael W Levin	8 Allerman Rd, Oakland NJ 07436	201-677-9311	S	1,311*	.1
18	HID Global Corp—Denis Hebert	15370 Barranca Pky, Irvine CA 92618	949-732-2000	S	1,177*	2.0
19	F5 Networks Inc—John McAdam	401 Elliott Ave W, Seattle WA 98119	206-272-5555	P	1,152	2.5
20	Coburn Technologies Inc—Alex Incera	55 Gerber Rd, South Windsor CT 06074	860-648-6600	S	1,148*	1.9
21	Black Box Corp—Terry Blakemore	1000 Park Dr, Lawrence PA 15055	724-746-5500	P	1,068	4.4
22	Zebra Technologies Corp—Anders Gustafsson	475 Half Day Rd Ste 50, Lincolnshire IL 60069	847-634-6700	P	983	2.5
23	Hyperdata—KC Lou	372 S Lemon Ave, Walnut CA 91789	909-839-1985	R	907*	<.1
24	Intermec Inc—Patrick J Byrne	6001 36th Ave W, Everett WA 98203	425-348-2600	P	848	2.3
25	Intermec Technologies Corp—Patrick J Byrne / Intermec Inc	6001 36th Ave W, Everett WA 98203	425-348-2600	S	825*	2.7
26	Riverbed Technology Inc—Jerry M Kennelly	199 Fremont St, San Francisco CA 94105	415-247-8800	P	727	1.6
27	OPTIA—Hok S Yau / United Computer Products Company Inc	1883 E Pleasant Valley, Altoona PA 16602	814-943-1133	D	669*	<.1
28	Avocent Corp—Michael J Borman	4991 Corporate Dr, Huntsville AL 35805	256-430-4000	S	657	1.1
29	Logitech Inc—Guerrino DeLuca	6505 Kaiser Dr, Fremont CA 94555	510-795-8500	S	637*	2.6
30	Compix Media Inc	26 Edelman, Irvine CA 92618	949-585-0055	R	616*	<.1
31	Synaptics Inc—Rick Bergman	3120 Scott Blvd Ste 13, Santa Clara CA 95054	408-454-5100	P	599	.7
32	QLogic Corp—Simon Biddiscombe	26650 Aliso Viejo Pky, Aliso Viejo CA 92656	949-389-6000	P	597	1.1
33	Electronics For Imaging Inc—Guy Gecht	303 Velocity Way, Foster City CA 94404	650-357-3500	P	592	2.1
34	Belkin Corp—Chester Pipkin	12045 E Waterfront Dr, Playa Vista CA 90094	310-751-5100	R	589*	1.0
35	NMB Inc (Chatsworth California)—Myron Jones	9730 Independence Ave, Chatsworth CA 91311	818-341-3355	S	588*	1.0
36	Cisco-Linksys LLC—Charles H Giancarlo / Cisco Systems Inc	121 Theory Dr, Irvine CA 92617	949-823-3000	D	564*	.4
37	CTX Technologies Inc—Jim Chen	16728 E Gale Ave, City of Industry CA 91745	626-363-9328	R	550	.1
38	NMB Technologies Corp / NMB Inc (Chatsworth California)	9730 Independence Ave, Chatsworth CA 91311	818-341-3355	S	536*	.3
39	Honeywell Scanning and Mobility—Darius Adamczyk	PO Box 208, Skaneateles Falls NY 13153	315-554-6000	S	524*	5.5
40	Modem Express Inc—Mavis Yang	115 Thomas Park Dr, Monticello MN 55362	763-295-8205	R	522*	<.1
41	Airgain—Pertti Visuri	1930 Palomar Point Way, Carlsbad CA 92008	760-579-0200	R	503*	<.1
42	ViewSonic Corp—James Chu	381 Brea Canyon Rd, Walnut CA 91789	909-444-8888	R	487*	.8
43	Empire Resources Inc—Nathan Kahn	1 Parker Plz 400 Kelby, Fort Lee NJ 07024	201-944-2200	P	465	.1
44	Oce Printing Systems USA Inc—Joseph D Skrzypczak	5600 Broken Sound Blvd, Boca Raton FL 33487		S	461*	.9
45	TallyGenicom LP—Stan Bikulege	4500 Daly Dr Ste 100, Chantilly VA 20151	703-633-8700	R	453	1.5
46	Emulex Corp—Jim McCluney	3333 Susan St, Costa Mesa CA 92626	714-662-5600	P	453	1.0
47	Zebra Technology of Camarillo—Anders Gustafsson / Zebra Technologies Corp	1001 Flynn Rd, Camarillo CA 93012	805-579-1800	D	399	1.7
48	Continuous Computing Corp—Mike Dagenais	9450 Carroll Park Dr, San Diego CA 92121	858-882-8800	R	360*	.3
49	Enterasys Networks Inc—Chris Crowell	50 Minuteman Rd, Andover MA 01810	978-684-1000	R	357	1.2
50	BancTec Inc—J Coley Clark	2701 E Grauwyler Rd, Irving TX 75061	972-821-4000	S	356*	2.6
51	Macase Industrial Corp—Herman Lin	4187 Pleasant Hill Rd, Duluth GA 30096	678-417-6470	R	353*	.6
52	BVM Associates—Mike Lucyk	151-1 W Industry Ct, Deer Park NY 11729	631-254-6220	R	353*	<.1
53	Pace Micro Technology—John Dyson	3701 FAU Blvd Ste 200, Boca Raton FL 33431	561-995-6000	S	351*	.6
54	Allied Telesyn International Corp—Takayoshi Oshima	19800 N Creek Pkwy Ste, Bothell WA 98011		S	350*	1.2
55	STMicroelectronics—C Ferro	1310 Electronics Dr, Carrollton TX 75006	972-466-6000	D	346*	1.5
56	Genesys Telecommunications Laboratories Inc—Paul Serge	2001 Junipero Serra Bl, Daly City CA 94014		S	342*	1.8
57	Novatel Wireless Inc—Peter V Leparulo	9645 Scranton Rd Ste 2, San Diego CA 92121	858-812-3400	P	339	.5
58	Smartronix Inc—M Arshed Javaid	44150 Smartronix Way, Hollywood MD 20636	301-373-6000	P	337*	.5
59	Extreme Networks Inc—Oscar Rodriguez	3585 Monroe St, Santa Clara CA 95051	408-579-2800	P	334	.7
60	RAD Data Communications Inc—Uri Zilberman	900 Corporate Dr, Mahwah NJ 07430	201-529-1100	S	329*	.5
61	Corsair Components Inc—Andrew Paul	46221 Landing Pkwy, Fremont CA 94538	510-657-8747	R	326	.4
62	KingMax Micro Technology Inc—Joe Liu	132 S 6th Ave, La Puente CA 91746		R	325*	.6
63	RSA Security Inc—Arthur W Coviello Jr	174 Middlesex Tpk, Bedford MA 01730	781-515-5000	S	310	1.3
64	Acme Packet Inc—Andrew Ory	100 Crosby Dr, Bedford MA 01730	781-328-4400	P	307	.2
65	Lasergraphics Inc—Stefan Demetrescu	20 Ada, Irvine CA 92618	949-753-8282	R	302*	.5

Rank	Company Name—*Executive Officer*	Address, City, State, Zip	Phone	Type	Fin	Empls
66	Aware Electronics Corp	PO Box 4299, Wilmington DE 19807	302-655-3800	R	288*	<.1
67	Continental Resources Inc (Bedford Massachusetts)—*Mary Nardella*	PO Box 9137, Bedford MA 01730	781-275-0850	R	276*	.4
68	LSI Logic Broadband Entertainment Div—*Abhi Y Talwalker*	1621 Barber Ln, Milpitas CA 95035		S	265*	1.1
69	Nokia Inc—*Stephen Elop*	102 Corporate Pk Dr, White Plains NY 10604	914-368-0400	S	264*	3.0
70	Avision Labs Inc	6815 Mowry Ave, Newark CA 94560	510-739-2369	S	258*	.5
71	InFocus Corp—*Robert G O'Malley*	13190 SW 68th Pkwy Ste, Portland OR 97223	503-207-4700	R	256	.3
72	Key Tronic Corp—*Craig D Gates*	PO Box 14687, Spokane WA 99214	509-928-8000	P	254	2.0
73	Skullcandy Inc—*Jeremy Andrus*	1441 W Ute Blvd Ste 25, Park City UT 84098	435-940-1545	P	233*	.1
74	D-Link Systems Inc—*Tony Tsao*	17595 Mt Herrmann, Fountain Valley CA 92708	714-885-6000	S	225*	.2
75	Sicon International—*Russ Wirtala*	2031 O'Toole Ave, San Jose CA 95131	408-954-9880	R	220*	.4
76	Stork Veco International Inc—*D Joustra*	15 A St Ste 2, Burlington MA 01803	781-425-6050	S	216*	<.1
77	Speedline Technologies—*Scott Koizumi*	16 Forge Park, Franklin MA 02038	508-520-0083	S	211*	1.0
78	Metrologic Instruments Inc	90 Coles Rd, Blackwood NJ 08012	856-228-8100	S	211	1.4
79	Scantron Corp—*William D Hansen*	1313 Lone Oak Rd, Eagan MN 55121	651-683-6000	S	208	1.1
80	GWC Technology Inc—*Timothy Burland*	365 Cloverleaf Dr Ste, Baldwin Park CA 91706	626-820-0665	S	200*	1.2
81	Elo TouchSystems Inc—*Mark Mendenhal*	301 Constitution Dr, Menlo Park CA 94025	650-361-4800	S	200*	.5
82	eForce Inc—*Nat Natraj*	1669 2 Hollenbeck Ave, Sunnyvale CA 94087	650-587-3866	R	199*	.4
83	2Wire Inc—*Pasquale Romano*	1704 Automation Pky, San Jose CA 95131	408-428-9500	R	186*	.3
84	Ricoh Printing Solutions	2390A Ward Ave, Simi Valley CA 93065	805-578-4000	R	180*	1.2
85	Epson Portland Inc—*David Graham*	3950 NW Aloclek Pl, Hillsboro OR 97124	503-645-1118	S	179*	.3
86	Genband Inc—*Pablo Gargiulo*	2801 Network Blvd STe, Frisco TX 75034	972-521-5800	R	178*	.3
87	Ruggedtronics Inc—*Don Parker*	24711 Redlands Blvd St, Loma Linda CA 92354	909-796-5374	R	176*	<.1
88	Kofax Image Products Inc—*Rick Murphy*	15211 Laguna Canyon Rd, Irvine CA 92618		S	166*	.4
89	Epic Technologies LLC—*Scott Smith*	200 Bluegrass Dr E, Norwalk OH 44857	419-668-8117	R	166*	1.8
90	Geo Space LP	7007 Pinemont Dr, Houston TX 77040	713-986-4444	S	162*	.3
91	US Epson Inc—*John Lang*	3840 Kilroy Airport Wa, Long Beach CA 90806	562-981-3840	R	158*	2.2
92	Stratasys Inc—*S Scott Crump*	7665 Commerce Way, Eden Prairie MN 55344	952-937-3000	P	156	.4
93	CABLExpress Corp—*William Pomeroy*	PO Box 4799, Syracuse NY 13221	315-476-3000	R	155*	.3
94	Banta Global Turnkey Ltd—*Thomas Quinlan*	6315 W By NW Blvd, Houston TX 77040	713-354-1300	R	153*	2.5
95	Minolta-QMS Inc—*Yoshikatsu Ota*	2070 Schillinger Rd S, Mobile AL 36695		S	151*	.9
96	Delta Products Corp (Fremont California)—*M S Chen*	4405 Cushing Pkwy, Fremont CA 94538	510-668-5100	S	150*	.3
97	World Wide Packets Inc—*Gary W Smith*	115 N Sullivan Rd, Spokane Valley WA 99037	509-242-9000	S	147*	.2
98	Acer American Holdings Corp—*Rudi Schmidleither*	333 W San Carlos St St, San Jose CA 95110	408-533-7700	R	141*	1.7
99	Lasercard Systems Corp—*Robert T Devincenzi*	1875 N Shoreline Blvd, Mountain View CA 94043	650-969-4428	S	139*	.2
100	Mustek Inc—*David Wang*	14751 Franklin Ave Uni, Tustin CA 92780	949-790-3800	R	134*	.1
101	Printronix Inc—*Robert A Kleist*	PO Box 19559, Irvine CA 92623	714-368-2300	R	128	.7
102	GTCO CalComp Inc—*Bill Kautter*	7125 Riverwood Dr, Columbia MD 21046	410-381-6688	R	120*	.2
103	American Traffic Solutions Inc—*James D Tuton*	7681 E Gray Rd, Scottsdale AZ 85260	480-443-7000	R	119*	.2
104	Sequoia Voting Systems—*Jack A Blaine*	717 17th St Ste 310, Denver CO 80202		R	119*	.2
105	Extron Electronics—*Andrew Edwards*	1230 S Lewis St, Anaheim CA 92805	714-491-1500	R	117*	.2
106	Echelon Corp—*Ron Sege*	550 Meridian Ave, San Jose CA 95126	408-938-5200	P	111	.3
107	Xante Corp—*Robert C Ross Jr*	2800 Dauphin St Ste 10, Mobile AL 36606	251-473-6502	R	108*	.2
108	Image Projections West Inc—*Kedar Morarka*	14135 E 42nd Ave Ste 4, Denver CO 80239	303-570-9477	R	107*	.2
109	Datamax Oneill—*Paul Sindoni*	4501 Pky Commerce Blvd, Orlando FL 32808	407-578-8007	S	106*	.5
110	thePlatform Inc—*Ian Blaine*	3101 Western Ave Ste 3, Seattle WA 98121	206-436-7900	R	94*	.1
111	ENCAD Inc—*Terry Vandewarkor*	6059 Cornerstone Ct W, San Diego CA 92121	858-452-0882	S	94	.4
112	Microscan Systems Inc—*Dennis Kaill*	700 SW 39th St Ste 100, Renton WA 98057	425-226-5700	S	92*	.2
113	Rimage Corp—*Sherman L Black*	7725 Washington Ave S, Minneapolis MN 55439	952-944-8144	P	80	.2
114	ID TECH Inc (Fullerton California)	10721 Walker St, Cypress CA 90630	714-761-6388	R	87*	.1
115	Cyber Power Systems Inc—*Robert Danese*	4241 12th Ave E Rm 400, Shakopee MN 55379	952-403-9500	R	86*	.3
116	Eurotech Inc—*Robert Olsen*	10260 Old Columbia Rd, Columbia MD 21046	301-490-4007	R	86*	.1
117	Identive Group Inc—*Ayman S Ashour*	1900-B Carnegie Ave Bl, Santa Ana CA 92705	949-250-8888	P	85	.4
118	SCM Microsystems—*Manfred Mueller* Identive Group Inc	1900-B Carnegie Ave, Santa Ana CA 92705	949-250-8888	D	85	.4
119	Occam Networks Inc—*Bob Howard-Anderson*	6868 Cortona Dr, Santa Barbara CA 93117	805-692-2900	S	84	.2
120	Physical Optics Corp—*Joanna Jannson*	20600 Gramercy Pl Bldg, Torrance CA 90501	310-320-3088	R	83*	.2
121	Microtek Lab Inc—*Mary Whitlock*	9960 Bell Ranch DrSte, Santa Fe Springs CA 90670	310-687-5800	R	82	.2
122	Hawking Technologies—*Frank Lin*	35 Hammond Ste 150, Irvine CA 92618	949-206-6900	R	78*	.1
123	SICK Inc—*Alberto Bertomeu*	6900 W 110th St, Minneapolis MN 55438	952-941-6780	S	77*	.1
124	3M Touch Systems—*Chris Colbert*	501 Griffin Brook Park, Methuen MA 01844	978-659-9000	S	77*	.1
125	Lynn Products Inc—*Hsinyu Lin*	2645 W 237th St, Torrance CA 90505	310-530-5966	R	77*	1.0
126	Edimax Computer Co—*Danny Awhang*	10807 NW 29Th St Ste 1, Miami FL 33172	786-845-8099	R	75*	.3
127	Visiontek Products LLC—*Michael Innes*	105 Prairie Lake Dr, East Dundee IL 60118	224-836-3900	R	75*	.1
128	Steel Excel Inc—*John Quicke*	691 S Milpitas Blvd, Milpitas CA 95035	408-945-8600	P	74	.2
129	Astro-Med Inc—*Everett V Pizzuti*	600 E Greenwich Ave, West Warwick RI 02893	401-828-4000	P	71	.4
130	Overland Storage Inc—*Eric Kelly*	9112 Spectrum Center B, San Diego CA 92123	858-571-5555	P	70	.2
131	Teledyne Electronic Technology—*Aldo Pichelli*	1049 Camino Dos Rios, Thousand Oaks CA 91360	805-373-4545	D	68*	.3
132	Scientific Solutions Inc	9323 Hamilton, Mentor OH 44060	440-357-1400	R	68*	.1
133	Kiosk Information Systems—*Rick Malone*	346 S Arthur Ave, Louisville CO 80027	303-466-5471	R	66*	.1
134	Mack Technologies Inc—*John Kovach*	27 Carlisle Rd, Westford MA 01886	978-392-5500	R	65*	.7
135	Comair Rotron Inc—*Peter Howard*	2675 Customhouse Ct, San Diego CA 92154	619-661-6688	R	65*	1.0
136	Micro Solutions Enterprises Inc—*Avi Wazana*	8201 Woodley Ave, Van Nuys CA 91406	818-407-7500	R	65*	.4
137	NIKSUN Inc—*Parag Pruthi*	100 Nassau Park Blvd, Princeton NJ 08540	609-936-9999	R	65*	.1
138	TransAct Technologies Inc—*Bart C Shuldman*	1 Hamden Ctr 2319 Whit, Hamden CT 06518	203-859-6800	P	63	.1
139	Advanced Input Devices Inc	600 W Wilbur Ave, Coeur D Alene ID 83815		S	62*	.3
140	Sundog Interative—*Brent Teiken*	2000 44th St SW 6th Fl, Fargo ND 58103	701-235-5525	R	62*	.1
141	Multi-Tech Systems Inc—*Patricia Sharma*	2205 Woodale Dr, Mounds View MN 55112	763-785-3500	R	61*	.2
142	Network Equipment Technologies Inc—*C Nicholas Keating Jr*	6900 Paseo Padre Pkwy, Fremont CA 94555	510-713-7300	P	60	.2
143	Datalux Corp—*Gary Davis*	155 Aviation Dr, Winchester VA 22602	540-662-1500	R	60*	.1
144	Voyetra Turtle Beach Inc—*Carmine Bonanno*	150 Clearbrook Rd, Elmsford NY 10523	914-345-2255	R	60*	.1
145	Digitran Div	9654 Hermosa, Rancho Cucamonga CA 91730	909-581-0855	S	60*	.1
146	Themis Computer—*Bill Kehretf*	47200 Bayside Pkwy, Fremont CA 94538	510-252-0870	R	59*	.1
147	Elitegroup Computer Systems	44259 Nobel Ave, Fremont CA 94538	510-226-7333	R	57*	.2
148	Alliance Distributors Holding Inc—*Jay Gelman*	1160 Commerce Ave, Bronx NY 10462	718-536-2248	P	57	<.1
149	Digital Image Design Inc—*Bradford Paley*	170 Claremont Ave Ste, New York NY 10027	212-343-2442	R	57*	<.1
150	ECRM Inc—*Richard Black*	554 Clark Rd, Tewksbury MA 01876	978-851-0207	R	56*	.2
151	Data I/O International Inc	6464 185th Ave NE, Redmond WA 98052	425-881-6444	S	56*	.1
152	IOGEAR—*Stamson Yates*	19641 Da Vinci, Foothill Ranch CA 92610	949-453-8782	R	55*	.1
153	NETsilicon Inc	411 Waverley Oaks Rd S, Waltham MA 02452	781-647-1234	S	54*	.1

Note: An asterisk (*) indicates an estimated financial figure. The company type code used is as follows: R = Private, P = Public, S = Private Subsidiary, B = Public Subsidiary, D = Division, J = Joint Venture, I = Investment Fund.

COMPANY RANKINGS BY SALES WITHIN 4-DIGIT SIC

Rank	Company Name—*Executive Officer*	Address, City, State, Zip	Phone	Type	Fin	Empls
154	MPI Tech Inc—*Les Silver*	450 W Broad St Ste 216, Falls Church VA 22046	703-531-1940	S	51*	.1
155	Spyrus Inc—*Tom Dickens*	1860 Hartog Dr, San Jose CA 95131	408-392-9131	R	50*	.1
156	Bluesocket Inc—*Mads Lillelund*	52 2nd Ave, Burlington MA 01803	781-328-0888	S	50*	.1
157	Lantronix Inc—*Kurt F Busch*	167 Technology Dr, Irvine CA 92618	949-453-3990	P	49	.1
158	PSi Printer Systems International—*Adrian Zameir*	250 East Dr Ste E, Melbourne FL 32904	321-254-1946	S	49*	.2
159	Otter Products LLC—*Daniel Raymond*	1 Old Town Sq Ste 303, Fort Collins CO 80524	970-493-8446	R	49*	.1
160	Miltope Group Inc—*Thomas R Dickinson*	3800 Richardson Rd S, Hope Hull AL 36043	334-284-8665	S	49	.2
161	Intelligent Systems Software Inc	98 Spit Brook Rd, Nashua NH 03062	603-882-5200	S	47*	.1
162	Diversified Technology Group Inc—*Robert McIntyre*	1720 Starkey Rd, Largo FL 33771	727-812-5000	R	45*	.1
163	General Micro Systems Inc—*Benjamin K Sharfi*	3 Tulare Dr, Aliso Viejo CA 92656	949-986-9137	R	45*	.1
164	Tervela—*Eric Schnadig*	174 Hudson St 2nd Fl, New York NY 10013	646-586-4220	R	45*	.1
165	One Stop Media Shop—*Bill Connard*	349 N Hwy 101, Solana Beach CA 92075		R	44*	.1
166	Symbolic Displays—*Candy Suits*	1917 Saint Andrew Pl E, Santa Ana CA 92705	714-258-2811	R	44*	.1
167	iGo Inc—*Michael D Heil*	17800 N Perimeter Dr S, Scottsdale AZ 85255	480-596-0061	P	43	.1
168	Hauppauge Digital Inc—*Kenneth H Plotkin*	91 Cabot Ct, Hauppauge NY 11788	631-434-1600	P	42	.1
169	NOMADICS ICX	1024 S Innovation Way, Stillwater OK 74074	405-372-9535	S	42*	.1
170	Radio Frequency Systems—*Jorg Sellner*	200 Pondview Dr, Meriden CT 06450	203-630-3311	R	41*	.5
171	Valor Computerized Systems Inc—*Don Hoz*	30211 Avenida de las B, Rancho Santa Margarita CA 92688	949-586-5969	R	41*	.2
172	Vericept Corp—*Robert J McCullen*	555 17th St Ste 1500, Denver CO 80202	303-798-1568	R	41*	.1
173	Printek Inc—*Julie Payovich*	1517 Townline Rd, Benton Harbor MI 49022	269-925-3200	R	41*	.1
174	Trident Systems Inc—*Nick Karanglen*	10201 Fairfax Blvd Ste, Fairfax VA 22030	703-273-1012	R	41*	.1
175	Cadmus Micro Inc—*Derek Ma*	1840 S Carlos Ave, Ontario CA 91761	909-947-3333	R	40*	.1
176	Mextel Inc—*Vedran Skulic*	159 Beeline Dr, Bensenville IL 60106	630-595-4146	R	40*	.1
177	Accu-Sort Systems Inc—*Greg Branning*	511 School House Rd, Telford PA 18969	215-723-0981	S	39*	.4
178	Pivot3 Inc—*Rich Bravman*	6605 Cypresswood Dr, Spring TX 77379	281-516-6000	R	39*	.1
179	Myricom Inc—*Nanette Boden*	325 N Santa Anita Ave, Arcadia CA 91006	626-821-5555	R	39*	.1
180	KIP America Inc—*Sherman Sawtele*	39575 13 Mile Rd, Novi MI 48377	248-474-2900	S	38*	.1
181	CH Products—*Frank Meyers*	970 Park Ctr Dr, Vista CA 92081	760-598-2518	R	37*	.2
182	L-3 Communications Systems and Imagery Div—*Michael Strianese*	PO Box 550, Melbourne FL 32902	321-727-0660	S	37*	.2
183	GCC Technologies Inc—*Kevin Curran*	209 Burlington Rd Ste, Bedford MA 01730	781-275-5800	R	37*	.1
184	TouchNet Information Systems Inc—*Daniel Toughey*	15520 College Blvd, Lenexa KS 66219	913-599-6699	R	36*	.1
185	Airbiquity Inc—*Kamyar Moinzadeh*	1011 Western Ave Ste 6, Seattle WA 98104	206-219-2700	R	36*	.1
186	AVST—*Hardy Myers*	27042 Towne Centre Dr, Foothill Ranch CA 92610	949-699-2300	R	36*	.1
187	Fujifilm Recording Media Manufacturing USA Inc—*Terry Takahashi*	45 Crosby Dr, Bedford MA 01730	781-271-4400	R	36*	.3
188	SATO America Inc—*Kazuo Matsuyama*	10350A Nations Ford Rd, Charlotte NC 28273	704-644-1650	R	35*	.1
189	Marburg Technology Inc—*Margelus Burga*	304 Turquoise St, Milpitas CA 95035	408-262-8400	R	35*	.2
190	Data Device Corp—*Clifford Lane*	105 Wilbur Pl, Bohemia NY 11716	631-567-5600	R	34*	.4
191	Centon Electronics Inc—*Gene Miscione*	15 Argonaut, Aliso Viejo CA 92656	949-855-9111	R	33*	.1
192	SensAble Technologies Inc—*Curt Rawley*	15 Consititution Way, Woburn MA 01801	781-937-8315	R	33*	.1
193	Numonics Corp—*Alfred Basilicato*	PO Box 1005, Montgomeryville PA 18936	215-362-2766	R	32*	.1
194	Addmaster Corp—*John Clary*	PO Box 5016, Monrovia CA 91017	626-358-2395	R	32*	.1
195	Hunter Digital Ltd—*Aaron H Sones*	8726 S Sepulveda Blvd, Los Angeles CA 90045	310-598-6167	R	32*	.1
196	Fuji Hi-Tech Inc—*Minoru Yamamoto*	47520 Westinghouse Dr, Fremont CA 94539	510-651-0811	R	32*	<.1
197	Immersion Corp—*Victor Viegas*	801 Fox Ln, San Jose CA 95131	408-467-1900	P	31	.1
198	Cambridge Technology Inc—*Red Aylward*	25 Hartwell Ave, Lexington MA 02421	781-541-1600	S	31*	.1
199	Sonnet Technologies Inc—*Robert L Farnsworth*	8 Autry, Irvine CA 92618	949-587-3500	R	31*	.1
200	Teledyne Interconnect Devices	9855 Carroll Canyon Rd, San Diego CA 92131		D	31*	.1
201	Z Corp—*John M Kawola*	32 Second Ave, Burlington MA 01803	781-852-5005	R	30*	.2
202	FOCUS Enhancements Inc—*Brett A Moyer*	931 Benecia Ave, Sunnyvale CA 94085	650-230-2400	R	30*	.1
203	Microtech Systems—*Corwin Nichols*	1164 Triton Dr, Foster City CA 94404	650-596-1900	R	30*	.1
204	Schooner Information Technology Inc—*Jerry Rudisin*	501 Macara Ave Ste 101, Sunnyvale CA 94085	408-773-7500	R	30*	.1
205	Starbak Communications Inc—*Tom Racca*	35 Corporate Dr 4th Fl, Burlington MA 01803	781-736-1200	R	30*	.1
206	Election Systems and Software Inc—*Aldo Tesi*	11208 John Galt Blvd, Omaha NE 68137	402-593-0101	R	29*	.4
207	Scan-Optics LLC—*Thomas Rice*	169 Progress Dr, Manchester CT 06042	860-645-7878	S	29*	.2
208	Champion Solutions Group Inc—*Chris Pyle*	791 Park Of Commerce B, Boca Raton FL 33487	561-997-2900	R	29*	.1
209	IntelliTools Inc—*Arjan Khalsa*	4185 Salazar Way, Frederick CO 80504	303-651-2829	S	29*	.1
210	Logitech Product Group—*Christopher Sopko*	24766 Detroit Rd, Westlake OH 44145	440-871-0071	R	29*	.1
211	SMDK Inc—*Michael S Battaglia*	27499 Riverview Center, Bonita Springs FL 34134	239-425-4000	R	29	N/A
212	Atalla Corp	10555 Ridgeview Ct, Cupertino CA 95014		S	28*	.1
213	Payformance Corp—*Dwayne McAfee*	7751 Belfort Pkwy Ste, Jacksonville FL 32256	904-997-6777	R	28*	.1
214	Performance Technologies Inc (Rochester New York)—*John Slusser*	205 Indigo Creek Dr, Rochester NY 14626	585-256-0200	P	28	.2
215	Datasouth Computer Corp—*Michael Cummings*	5033 Sirona Dr Ste 800, Charlotte NC 28273		R	27*	.1
216	Clarity Visual Systems	1195 NW Compton Dr, Beaverton OR 97006	503-748-1100	D	27*	.1
217	Visara Inc—*Kenneth A Bloom* MATCO Group Inc	2700 Gateway Center Bl, Morrisville NC 27560	919-882-0200	D	27*	.1
218	SYSCON International Inc PlantStar Div—*Townsend Thomes*	1108 High St, South Bend IN 46601	574-232-3900	D	27*	<.1
219	Think Computer Products—*Bill Hojreh*	16812 Hale Ave, Irvine CA 92606	949-833-3222	R	27*	<.1
220	ITOCHU Technology Inc—*Shinichi Uemura*	3945 Freedom Cir Ste 3, Santa Clara CA 95054	408-727-8810	S	27*	<.1
221	Unimark Inc—*James Mackin* Microcom Corp	9818 Pflumm Rd, Lenexa KS 66215	913-649-2424	S	27*	<.1
222	DNE Technologies Inc—*William Gill Jr*	PO Box 30, Wallingford CT 06492	203-265-7151	S	26*	.1
223	Wave Systems Corp—*Steven K Sprague*	480 Pleasant St, Lee MA 01238	413-243-1600	P	26	.1
224	Primera Technology Inc—*Bob Cummins*	2 Carlson Pkwy N Ste 3, Plymouth MN 55447		R	26*	<.1
225	Power Systems and Controls Inc—*Thomas J Delano*	3206 Lanvale Ave, Richmond VA 23230	804-355-2803	R	26*	<.1
226	Preh Electronics Inc—*Bob Nelson*	590 Telser Rd Unit B, Lake Zurich IL 60047	847-438-4000	S	26*	<.1
227	ATTO Technology Inc—*Timothy J Klein*	155 CrossPoint Pky, Amherst NY 14068	716-691-1999	R	25*	.1
228	ProMax Systems Inc (Irvine California)—*Jess Hartmann*	18241 McDurmott W Ste, Irvine CA 92614		R	25*	<.1
229	Attune Systems—*Alan Kessler*	3255 Scott Blvd Ste 2-, Santa Clara CA 95054	408-855-1015	R	24*	<.1
230	Mechdyne Corp—*Christopher Clover*	11 E Church St Ste 400, Marshalltown IA 50158	641-754-4649	R	23*	.1
231	Ems Aviation Inc—*John Jarrell*	121 Whittendale Dr, Moorestown NJ 08057	856-234-5020	R	22*	.1
232	Specialties Research Inc—*Ron Huang*	19433 San Jose Ave, City of Industry CA 91748	909-598-6988	R	22*	<.1
233	Ceiva Logic Inc—*Dean Schiller*	214 E Magnolia Blvd, Burbank CA 91502	818-562-3105	R	22*	<.1
234	LightPointe Communications Inc—*Heinz A Willebrand*	10140 Barnes Canyon Rd, San Diego CA 92121	858-834-4083	R	22*	<.1
235	Microboards Technology LLC—*Mitch Akman*	PO Box 846, Chanhassen MN 55317	952-556-1600	R	22*	<.1
236	Xplore Technologies Corporation of America—*Mark Holleran*	14000 Summit Dr Ste 90, Austin TX 78728	512-336-7797	R	22	N/A
237	Telemechanics Inc—*Harry Prival*	55 Post Ave, Westbury NY 11590		R	21*	.1
238	Pertech Resources Inc—*Kevin Kershisnik*	860 College View Dr, Riverton WY 82501	307-856-4821	R	21*	<.1

Rank	Company Name—*Executive Officer*	Address, City, State, Zip	Phone	Type	Fin	Empls
239	Rose Electronics—*Dave Rahvar*	10707 Stancliff Rd, Houston TX 77099	281-933-7673	R	20*	.1
240	Barr Systems Inc—*Tony Barr*	4500 NW 27th Ave, Gainesville FL 32606	352-491-3100	R	20*	.1
241	Imaging Business Machines LLC—*Derrick Murphy*	2750 Crestwood Blvd, Birmingham AL 35210	205-439-7100	R	20*	.1
242	Heartland Micorpayments—*Ron Farmer*	2115 Chapman Rd Ste 15, Chattanooga TN 37421	423-894-6177	S	20*	<.1
243	NCE Storage Solutions—*Jim Raven*	1866 Friendship Dr, El Cajon CA 92020	619-212-3000	D	20*	<.1
244	Aztech Labs Inc—*Hong Yew Mun*	4005 Clipper Ct, Fremont CA 94538	510-683-9800	D	20*	<.1
245	Avistar Communications Corp—*Bob Kirk*	1875 S Grant St 10th F, San Mateo CA 94402	650-525-3300	P	20	.1
246	Media 100 Inc—*Boris Yamnitsky*	25 Thompson PL 4th Fl, Boston MA 02210	508-573-5100	D	19	.1
247	Boca Systems Inc—*Joseph Gross*	1065 S Rogers Cir, Boca Raton FL 33487	561-998-9600	R	19*	.1
248	Kirtas Technologies Inc—*Lotfi Belkhir*	7620 Omnitech Pl, Victor NY 14564	585-924-2420	R	19*	.1
249	Sealevel Systems Inc—*Tom OHanlan*	PO Box 830, Liberty SC 29657	864-843-4343	R	19*	<.1
250	Interphase Corp—*Gregory B Kalush*	2901 N Dallas Pkwy Ste, Plano TX 75093	214-654-5000	P	18	.1
251	Surgient Inc—*Tim Lucas*	8303 MoPac Ste C300, Austin TX 78759	512-241-4600	S	18*	.2
252	Fischer International Systems Corp—*Rene Bacherman*	5801 Pelican Bay Blvd, Naples FL 34108	239-643-1500	R	18*	.1
253	Intelligent Instrumentation Inc—*Rick Daniel*	3000 E Valencia Rd Ste, Tucson AZ 85706		S	18*	.1
254	Vicom Systems Inc—*Sam Tam*	3200 Bridge Pky, Redwood City CA 94065	650-241-3302	R	18*	.1
255	Anzac Computer Equipment Corp—*Richard Hamilton-Gibbs*	PO Box 2524, Manteca CA 95336	209-518-3276	R	18*	<.1
256	Communications Specialties Inc—*John Lopinto*	55 Cabot Ct, Hauppauge NY 11788	631-273-0404	R	18*	<.1
257	Digital Peripheral Solutions Inc—*Priti Sharma*	8015 E Crystal Dr, Anaheim CA 92807	714-998-3440	R	18*	<.1
258	Image Access Inc—*Ted Webb*	543 NW 77th St, Boca Raton FL 33487	561-995-8334	R	18*	<.1
259	Lumidigm Inc—*Robert M Harbour*	801 University Blvd SE, Albuquerque NM 87106	505-272-7084	R	18*	<.1
260	Dataco DeRex Inc—*Lee Pearlmutter*	9001 Lenexa Dr, Overland Park KS 66215	913-438-2444	R	18*	<.1
261	Vidar Systems Corp—*John E Hart*	365 Herndon Pkwy, Herndon VA 20170	703-471-7070	R	17*	.1
262	Control Module Inc—*Jana Moak*	89 Phoenix Ave, Enfield CT 06082	860-745-2433	R	17*	<.1
263	Thomas Engineering Co—*Kent Mishler*	7024 Northland Dr, Minneapolis MN 55428	763-533-1501	R	17*	<.1
264	Amazing! Smart Card Technologies Inc Chazak Value Corp	75 Rockefeller Plz 16t, New York NY 10019	212-265-7013	S	17*	<.1
265	Ethertronics Inc—*Laurent Desclos*	9605 Scranton Rd Ste 3, San Diego CA 92121	858-550-3820	R	17*	<.1
266	Telebyte—*Kenneth S Schneider*	355 Marcus Blvd, Hauppauge NY 11788	631-423-3232	R	17*	<.1
267	Galil Motion Control Inc—*Jacob Tal*	270 Technology Way, Rocklin CA 95765	916-626-0101	R	17*	<.1
268	ABV Electronics Inc—*Kunhamed Bicha*	1200 Northbrook Pkwy S, Suwanee GA 30024	770-408-0470	R	17*	.1
269	Znyx Networks Inc—*Connie Austin*	48421 Milmont Dr, Fremont CA 94538	510-249-0800	R	17*	.1
270	Aot Electronics Inc—*Omar Turbi*	22981 Mill Creek Dr, Laguna Hills CA 92653	949-852-9999	R	16*	.1
271	EFI Georgia—*Michael E Kohlsdorf* Electronics For Imaging Inc	1300 Oakbrook Dr, Norcross GA 30093	770-448-9008	S	16*	.1
272	Dynamics Research Corp Metrigraphics Div—*James Regan*	60 Concord St, Wilmington MA 01887	978-658-6100	D	16	.1
273	PC Power and Cooling Inc	5995 Avenida Encinas, Carlsbad CA 92008	760-931-5700	S	16*	.1
274	Biopac Systems Inc—*Alan Macy*	42 Aero Camino, Goleta CA 93117	805-685-0066	R	16*	<.1
275	Absec USA Inc Chazak Value Corp	75 Rockefeller Plz 16t, New York NY 10019	212-265-7013	S	16*	<.1
276	AESP Inc—*Slav Stein*	16295 NW 13th Ave Ste, Miami FL 33169	305-944-7710	R	16	.1
277	Industrial Electronic Engineers Inc—*Richard Pleasant*	7740 Lemona Ave, Van Nuys CA 91405	818-787-0311	R	16*	.1
278	Crossroads Systems Inc—*Robert C Sims*	11000 N Mo Pac Expy, Austin TX 78759	512-349-0300	P	15	.1
279	Corner Products Co—*Rick Hsu*	17110 Armstrong Ave, Irvine CA 92614	949-231-5000	R	15*	.1
280	GarrettCom Inc—*Frank Madren*	47823 Westinghouse Dr, Fremont CA 94539	510-438-9071	R	15*	.1
281	Initio Corp—*Kenneth Wu*	2050 Ringwood Ave, San Jose CA 95131	408-943-3189	R	15	<.1
282	Sumitomo Electric USA Inc—*Masayoshi Matsumoto*	360 Lexington Ave 24th, New York NY 10017	212-490-6620	S	15*	<.1
283	Enabling Technologies Co—*Tony Schenk*	1601 NE Braille Pl, Jensen Beach FL 34957	772-225-3687	R	15*	.1
284	Guide Technology Inc—*Oren Rajuan*	616 National Ave, Mountain View CA 94043	408-733-6555	R	15*	<.1
285	Micro Accessories Inc—*Peter McHale*	6086 Stewart Ave, Fremont CA 94538	510-226-6310	R	15*	<.1
286	Xybernaut Corp—*Dewayne Adams*	12701 Fair Lakes Cir S, Fairfax VA 22033	703-631-6925	R	15	.1
287	TRENDware International Inc—*Haung Pei*	20675 Manhattan Pl, Torrance CA 90501	310-961-5500	R	14*	.1
288	Blackwold Inc Chazak Value Corp	75 Rockefeller Plz 16t, New York NY 10019	212-265-7013	S	14*	<.1
289	Boxsterview Inc Chazak Value Corp	75 Rockefeller Plz 16t, New York NY 10019	212-265-7013	S	14*	<.1
290	Redwold Inc Chazak Value Corp	75 Rockefeller Plz 16t, New York NY 10019	212-265-7013	S	14*	<.1
291	Candelis—*Alex Razmjoo*	18821 Bardeen Av, Irvine CA 92612	949-852-1000	R	14*	<.1
292	ITAC Systems Inc—*Don Bynum*	3113 Benton St, Garland TX 75042	972-494-3073	R	14*	.1
293	Hidden Valley Electronics Inc—*James Ballus*	2060 Main St Ste 1, Apalachin NY 13732	607-625-5888	R	14*	.1
294	Seiko Instruments USA Inc Business and Home Office Products Div	2990 Lomita Blvd, Torrance CA 90505	310-517-7700	D	13*	<.1
295	Tharo Systems Inc—*Tom Thatcher*	PO Box 798, Brunswick OH 44212	330-273-4408	R	13*	<.1
296	IKEY Industrial Peripherals—*Steve Meyerp*	PO Box 49182, Austin TX 78765	512-837-0283	R	13*	<.1
297	Champion Systems Corp—*Ming Lac*	5 Division St, Warwick RI 02818	401-885-7828	R	13*	<.1
298	Itc Systems—*Campbell Richardson*	800 Fee Fee Rd, Maryland Heights MO 63043	314-872-7772	R	13*	.1
299	Grace Manufacturing Inc—*Christopher Grace*	614 State Rd 247, Russellville AR 72802	479-968-5455	R	12*	.1
300	Racore Technology Corp—*James Snow*	4125 S 6000 W, West Valley City UT 84128	801-963-5112	S	12*	.1
301	CTC Parker Automation—*Bob Bond*	50 W TechneCenter Dr, Milford OH 45150	513-831-2340	D	12*	.1
302	L-com Inc—*Edward Caselden*	45 Beechwood Dr, North Andover MA 01845	978-682-6936	R	12*	.1
303	Bp Microsystems Management LLC—*Julie Long*	5373 W Sam Houston Pkw, Houston TX 77041	713-688-4600	R	12*	.1
304	Compsee Inc—*Billy Graham*	PO Box 1305, Gig Harbor WA 98335	253-851-6500	S	12*	.1
305	AMT Datasouth Corp—*Joe Eichberger*	803 Camarillo Springs, Camarillo CA 93012	805-388-5799	R	12*	.1
306	Screen (USA) Inc—*Mike Fox*	5110 Tollview Dr, Rolling Meadows IL 60008	847-870-7400	S	12*	<.1
307	Contour Design Inc—*Steve Wang*	10 Industrial Dr, Windham NH 03087	603-462-6678	R	12*	<.1
308	TouchSystems Inc—*Eric Anderson*	220 Tradesmen Dr, Hutto TX 78634	512-846-2424	R	12*	<.1
309	Data Translation Inc—*Fred Molinari*	100 Locke Dr, Marlboro MA 01752	508-481-3700	R	12	.1
310	Se-Kure Controls Inc—*Roger J Leyden*	3714 Runge St, Franklin Park IL 60131	847-288-1111	R	11*	.2
311	Vela Research LP—*Scott Cooper*	5540 Rio Vista Dr, Clearwater FL 33760	727-507-5300	R	11*	.1
312	RTD Embedded Technologies Inc—*John Hazel*	PO Box 906, State College PA 16804	814-234-8087	R	11*	.1
313	Gd California Inc—*Ethan Plotkin*	1799 Portola Ave Ste 1, Livermore CA 94551	925-456-9900	R	11*	<.1
314	American Microsystems Ltd—*Mike Kearby*	2190 Regal Pkwy, Euless TX 76040	817-571-9015	R	11*	<.1
315	Alpha Telecom Incorporated USA—*Sid Sung*	2674 N First St 101, San Jose CA 95134	408-895-1800	R	11*	<.1
316	SW Electronics and Manufacturing Corp—*Carl Szczepkowski*	1215 N Church St, Moorestown NJ 08057	856-222-9900	R	10*	.1
317	Atronix Sales Inc—*Peter Schofield*	780 Boston Rd Ste 4, Billerica MA 01821	978-313-2500	R	10*	.1
318	Mitek Systems Inc—*James B De Bello*	8911 Balboa Ave Ste B, San Diego CA 92123	858-503-7810	P	10	.1
319	Packing Inc—*Homy Panahi*	580 E Corporate Dr, Meridian ID 83642	208-884-4900	R	10*	.1
320	Kelly Computer Systems Inc—*Larry Kelly*	1060 La Avenida St, Mountain View CA 94043	650-960-1010	R	10*	<.1
321	Dymo Corp—*Phil Damiano*	44 Commerce Rd, Stamford CT 06902	203-355-9000	R	10*	.1

Note: An asterisk (*) indicates an estimated financial figure. The company type code used is as follows: R = Private, P = Public, S = Private Subsidiary, B = Public Subsidiary, D = Division, J = Joint Venture, I = Investment Fund.

COMPANY RANKINGS BY SALES WITHIN 4-DIGIT SIC

Rank	Company Name—Executive Officer	Address, City, State, Zip	Phone	Type	Fin	Empls
322	Activar Technical Products Group—Jon L Reissner	700 Industrial Circle, Shakopee MN 55379	952-935-6921	P	10	.1
323	RGB Spectrum—Robert Marcus	950 Marina Village Pkw, Alameda CA 94501	510-814-7000	R	10*	<.1
324	Spartanics Ltd—Thomas Kleeman	3605 Edison Pl, Rolling Meadows IL 60008	847-394-5700	R	10*	<.1
325	Maxxar Corp—Robert Chencinski	455 Winding Brook Dr, Glastonbury CT 06033	860-652-3155	S	10	<.1
326	Command Communications Inc—William C Mcclure	14510 E Fremont Ave, Centennial CO 80112	303-792-0890	R	10*	<.1
327	Worth Data Inc—Hall Worthington	623 Swift St, Santa Cruz CA 95060	831-458-9938	R	10*	<.1
328	Aboutgolf Ltd—Robert Ryan	352 Tomahawk Dr, Maumee OH 43537	419-482-9095	R	10*	<.1
329	PI Engineering Inc	101 Innovation Pky Ste, Williamston MI 48895	517-655-5523	R	10*	<.1
330	Circle Inc—Lee Ashby	2125 Wright Ave C12, La Verne CA 91750	909-392-7564	R	10*	<.1
331	Inside Out Networks	115 Wild Basin Rd S St, Austin TX 78746	512-306-0600	S	10*	<.1
332	CMS Technologies—John Austermann III	36528 Grand River Ave, Farmington Hills MI 48335	248-478-4400	R	10*	<.1
333	WorkRite Ergonomic Accessories Inc—Todd Hauge	1450 Technology Ln, Petaluma CA 94954		R	10	.1
334	AITech International—Michae lJ Chen	1288 Kifer Road Ste 20, Sunnyvale CA 94086	408-991-9699	R	9*	.1
335	Microcom Corp—Jim Larson	8220 Green Meadows Dr, Lewis Center OH 43035	740-548-6262	R	9*	<.1
336	Topaz Systems Inc—Anthony Zank	650 Cochran St Ste 6, Simi Valley CA 93065	805-520-8282	R	9*	<.1
337	GATR Technologies—Paul Gierow	11506 Gilleland Rd, Huntsville AL 35803	256-382-1334	R	9*	<.1
338	MagicRAM Inc	3540 Wilshire Blvd Ste, Los Angeles CA 90010	213-380-5555	R	9*	<.1
339	Polychromix Inc—Brian Mitchell	30 Upton Dr, Wilmington MA 01887	978-284-6000	R	9*	<.1
340	Antex Electronics Corp—David C Antrim	19160 Van Ness Ave, Torrance CA 90501	310-532-3092	R	9*	<.1
341	CTI Electronics Corp—Peter Mikan	110 Old South Ave, Stratford CT 06615	203-386-9779	R	9*	<.1
342	Blue Wave Micro—Keith Andrews	26895 Aliso Creek Rd S, Aliso Viejo CA 92656	949-297-3877	R	9*	.1
343	Silicom Inc (Mahwah New Jersey)—Shaike Orbach	6 Forest Ave, Paramus NJ 07652	201-843-1175	S	9*	<.1
344	Leica Geosystems Hds LLC—Daniel Dykhuis	4550 Norris Canyon Rd, San Ramon CA 94583	925-790-2300	R	9*	.1
345	Amag Technology Inc—Robert Sawyer	20701 Manhattan Pl, Torrance CA 90501	310-518-2380	R	9*	<.1
346	Intercard Inc—Ray Sherrod	1884 Lacklnd Hl Pkwy S, Saint Louis MO 63146	314-275-8066	R	8*	.1
347	Dawar Technologies Inc—Carl Snyder	1016 N Lincoln Ave, Pittsburgh PA 15233	412-322-9900	R	8*	.1
348	Interlink Electronics Inc—Steven N Bronson	546 Flynn Rd, Camarillo CA 93012	805-484-8855	P	8	.2
349	Westrex International	25 Denby Rd, Boston MA 02134	617-254-1200	R	8*	<.1
350	Foresight Imaging LLC—Mark Mariotti	1 Executive Dr Ste 102, Chelmsford MA 01824	978-458-4624	R	8*	<.1
351	Ampro ADLINK Technology America Inc—Jim Liu	5215 Hellyer Ave Ste11, San Jose CA 95138	408-360-0200	S	8*	<.1
352	Adesso Inc—Stan Harfenist	160 Commerce Way, Walnut CA 91789	909-839-2929	R	8*	<.1
353	Rosenberger Cds LLC—Paul Smith	1100 Professional Dr, Plano TX 75074	972-423-8991	R	8*	<.1
354	APCON Inc—Richard Rauch	9255 SW Pioneer Ct, Wilsonville OR 97070	503-682-4050	R	7*	.1
355	Videx Inc—Paul Davis	1105 NE Cir Blvd, Corvallis OR 97330	541-758-0521	R	7	.1
356	Measurement Computing Corp—Ben Bailey	10 Commerce Blvd, Norton MA 02766	508-946-5100	S	7*	.1
357	Datalogic Inc—Darrell Owen	3000 Earhart Ct Ste 13, Hebron KY 41048	859-689-7000	S	7*	<.1
358	Connector Resources Unlimited Inc—Jon Johnson	1000 SE Tech Ctr Dr St, Vancouver WA 98683	360-816-1772	R	7*	<.1
359	Cobra Systems Inc—Matt Erickson	3521 E Enterprise Dr, Anaheim CA 92807	714-688-7999	R	7*	<.1
360	Barix Technology Inc—Andy Stankiewicz	553 Hayward Ave N Ste, Oakdale MN 55128		S	7*	<.1
361	Datadesk Technologies Inc—Bob Jacobs	PO Box 4627, Rollingbay WA 98061	206-842-5480	R	7*	<.1
362	DiscBurn	2668 Patton Rd, Roseville MN 55113	612-782-8200	R	7*	<.1
363	I-Concepts Inc—Ed Hayden	705 Misty Hollow Dr, Maple Glen PA 19002	215-412-9270	R	7*	<.1
364	Wholesale Tape and Supply Co—Michael Salley	2841 Hickory Valley Rd, Chattanooga TN 37421	423-894-9427	R	7*	<.1
365	Neotec Graphic International Inc	2721 N Towne Ave, Pomona CA 91767	909-626-9889	R	7*	.1
366	Southland Technologies Inc—Kimberly Goodwin	PO Box 830, Sylvester GA 31791	229-777-7907	R	7*	.1
367	Contemporary Control Systems Inc—George Thomas	2431 Curtiss St, Downers Grove IL 60515	630-963-7070	R	7*	<.1
368	Pro Tech Computer Supply Inc—Glenn Nicholson	PO Box 67, Sterling CT 06377	860-564-1150	R	7*	<.1
369	Singer Data Products Inc—Theodore Singer	790 Maple Ln, Bensenville IL 60106	630-860-6500	R	7*	.1
370	Titan Power Inc—Andrew Berney	4640 E Elwood St Ste 6, Phoenix AZ 85040	480-968-3191	R	6*	.1
371	Bestek Manufacturing Inc—Frank Dang	2150 Del Franco St, San Jose CA 95131	408-321-8834	R	6*	.1
372	Pacific Image Electronics Inc	367 Van Ness Way Ste 6, Torrance CA 90501	310-618-8100	D	6*	.1
373	Anacom General Corp—Daniel S Haines	1240 S Claudina St, Anaheim CA 92805	714-774-8484	R	6*	.1
374	Antec Inc—Andrew Lee	47900 Fremont Blvd, Fremont CA 94538	510-770-1200	R	6*	.1
375	Microstar Laboratories Inc—Neil Fenichel	2265 116th Ave NE, Bellevue WA 98004	425-453-2345	R	6*	<.1
376	Quatech Inc—Steven Runkle	5675 Hudson Industrial, Hudson OH 44236	330-655-9000	S	6*	.1
377	Unicom Electric Inc—Jeffrey Lo	908 Canada Ct, City of Industry CA 91748	626-964-7873	R	6*	<.1
378	Data Systems Hardware Inc—Gregory Rayburn	6594 Commerce Ct, Warrenton VA 20187	703-737-7914	S	6*	<.1
379	Ponica Industrial Company Ltd—Joseph Chien	125 Klug Cir, Corona CA 92880	951-371-5781	R	6*	<.1
380	Variant Microsystems	4128 Business Center D, Fremont CA 94538	510-440-2870	R	6*	<.1
381	Shaffstall Corp—Evert L Shaffstall	8531 Bash St, Indianapolis IN 46250	317-842-2077	R	6	<.1
382	Danpex Corp—Mike Lee	2528 Qume Dr Ste B, San Jose CA 95131	408-573-1788	R	6*	<.1
383	Lighthorse Technologies Inc—Michael Held	9511 Ridgehaven Ct Ste, San Diego CA 92123	858-292-8876	R	6*	<.1
384	Video Transfer Inc—Karl Renwanz	115 Drummer St, Brookline MA 02446	617-487-6200	R	6*	<.1
385	Nextus Inc—Klaus Bollman	101 Halmar Cove, Georgetown TX 78628	512-869-1018	R	6*	<.1
386	Alpha and Omega Computer Corp—Thomas Lee	624 S Hambledon Ave, City of Industry CA 91744	626-330-9833	R	6*	<.1
387	Applied Integration Corp—Frederick Pingal	3930 W New York Dr, Tucson AZ 85745	520-743-3095	R	6*	<.1
388	Boulder Innovation Group—Ivan Faul	4824 Sterling Dr Sterl, Boulder CO 80301	303-447-0248	R	6*	<.1
389	Graftek Imaging—Giuseppe Zima	8900 Shoal Creek Blvd, Austin TX 78757	512-416-1099	R	6*	<.1
390	Lasonic Electronics Corp—Hong-Xi Chen	15759 Tapia St, Irwindale CA 91706	626-480-1218	R	6*	<.1
391	Master Recording Supply Inc—Blair LaGrandeur	510 E Goetz Ave, Santa Ana CA 92707	714-556-6700	R	6*	<.1
392	N-trig Inc—Eyal Leibovitz	3409 Executive Center, Austin TX 78731	512-351-8111	R	6*	<.1
393	PressOK Entertainment Inc—Ryan Morel	710 2nd Ave Ste 411, Seattle WA 98104	206-332-1749	R	6*	<.1
394	Wireless Computing Inc—Martin Phillips	3703 Peak Lookout, Austin TX 78737	512-263-2205	R	6*	<.1
395	Glowa Manufacturing Inc—Jerry Glowa	6 Emma St, Binghamton NY 13905	607-770-0811	R	6*	<.1
396	Encore Networks Inc—Peter Madsen	3800 Concorde Pkwy Ste, Chantilly VA 20151	703-318-7750	R	6*	<.1
397	Intrusion Inc—G Ward Paxton	1101 E Arapaho Rd Ste, Richardson TX 75081	972-234-6400	P	6	<.1
398	Vinatekco Corp—Thanh Nguyen	1070 S Milpitas Blvd, Milpitas CA 95035	408-263-2816	R	5*	<.1
399	Advanced Tracking Technologies Inc—Paul Glass	PO Box 168, Sugar Land TX 77487		R	5*	<.1
400	Kamel Peripherals Inc—Michael Vangie	25 S St Ste C, Hopkinton MA 01748	508-435-7771	R	5*	<.1
401	Allen Datagraph Systems Inc—Michael Elliott	56 Kendall Pond Rd, Derry NH 03038	603-216-6344	R	5*	<.1
402	Cables To Go Inc—Michael Shane	3555 Kettering Blvd, Moraine OH 45439	937-224-8646	R	5*	.1
403	Moxa Americas Inc—Ben Chen	3001 Enterprise St Ste, Brea CA 92821	714-528-6777	R	5*	<.1
404	Kantek Inc—Herman Kappel	3460a Hampton Rd, Oceanside NY 11572	516-594-4600	R	5*	<.1
405	Altek Corp—Doug Cameron	12210 Plum Orchard Dr, Silver Spring MD 20904	301-572-2555	R	5*	<.1
406	Control Vision Corp—Jay Humbard	PO Box 596, Pittsburg KS 66762	620-231-6647	R	5*	<.1
407	Computerwise Inc—Curtis Wood	302 N Winchester, Olathe KS 66062	913-829-0600	R	5*	<.1
408	Genovation Inc—Max Rahim	17741 Mitchell N, Irvine CA 92614	949-833-3355	R	5*	<.1
409	Signature Engraving Systems Inc—Christopher Parent	120 Whiting Farms Rd, Holyoke MA 01040	413-533-7500	R	5*	<.1
410	VisionShape Inc—Reynolds Bish / Peripheral Dynamics Inc	1830 E Miraloma Ave St, Placentia CA 92870	610-825-7090	S	5*	<.1

Rank	Company Name—*Executive Officer*	Address, City, State, Zip	Phone	Type	Fin	Empls
411	Visix Inc—*Edward Matthews*	230 Scientific Dr Ste, Norcross GA 30092	770-446-1416	R	5	<.1
412	TriSquare Inc	6855 Lyons Technology, Coconut Creek FL 33073	954-421-4004	R	5*	<.1
413	Interface Electronics Inc—*Chuck Singer*	3680 Burnette Park Dr, Suwanee GA 30024	770-623-1066	R	5*	<.1
414	Jantek Electronics Inc—*Danny Jan*	4820 Arden Dr, Temple City CA 91780	626-350-4198	R	5*	<.1
415	REYcomp Inc—*George Rey*	2525 Dalworth St, Grand Prairie TX 75050	972-606-4600	R	5	<.1
416	Pretec—*David Chow*	43289 Osgood Rd, Fremont CA 94539	510-249-9055	R	5*	<.1
417	Spur Support Services LLC—*Ray Lorenzo*	907 S Owyhee St, Boise ID 83705	208-377-0001	R	5*	<.1
418	All Pro Solutions Inc—*Tibi Czentye*	1351 E Black St, Rock Hill SC 29730	803-980-4141	R	5*	<.1
419	Axes Technologies Inc—*Vineet Nayyar*	2140 Lake Park Blvd St, Richardson TX 75080	972-991-2800	R	5*	<.1
420	Printer Friends Inc—*Jimmie Moglia*	14250 NW Science Park, Portland OR 97229	503-626-2291	R	5*	<.1
421	Rena Systems Inc—*Mark Burns*	PO Box 1069, Oaks PA 19456	610-650-9170	S	5*	<.1
422	Video Network Services Inc—*Edward E Weston*	75 Calvert St, Harrison NY 10528	914-964-1427	R	5*	<.1
423	Data Research and Applications Inc—*Jeffrey R Dobson*	10425 Cogdill Rd Ste 4, Knoxville TN 37932	865-671-4474	R	5*	<.1
424	United Computer Products Company Inc—*Danny Yau*	1883 E Pleasant Valley, Altoona PA 16602	814-943-1133	R	5*	<.1
425	American Digital Corp—*Ken Bruner*	3030 W Salt Creek Ln S, Arlington Heights IL 60005	847-637-5209	R	5*	<.1
426	Princeton Technology Inc—*Nasir Javed*	1691 Browning, Irvine CA 92606	949-851-7776	R	4*	<.1
427	Mission Technology Group Inc—*Randy Jones*	9918 Via Pasar, San Diego CA 92126	858-530-2511	R	4*	<.1
428	IX Systems—*Mike Lauth*	2490 Kruse Dr, San Jose CA 95131	408-943-4100	R	4*	<.1
429	Maverick International Inc—*Randy Braa*	1500 Industry St Ste 2, Everett WA 98203	425-355-7474	R	4*	<.1
430	Apricorn—*Paul Brown*	12191 Kirkham Rd, Poway CA 92064	858-513-2000	R	4*	<.1
431	LandAirSea Systems Inc—*Robert Wagner*	2040 Dillard Ct, Woodstock IL 60098	847-462-8100	R	4	<.1
432	Wintriss Engineering Corp—*Vic Wintriss*	9965 Carroll Canyon Rd, San Diego CA 92123	858-550-7300	R	4*	.1
433	Acuprint Technology Inc—*Richard Love*	5973 Avenida Encinas S, Carlsbad CA 92008	760-929-4808	R	4*	<.1
434	Metrofuser LLC—*Eric Katz*	263 Cox St, Roselle NJ 07203	908-245-2100	R	4*	<.1
435	Photo Sciences Inc—*Kyle Stogsdill*	2542 W 237th St, Torrance CA 90505	310-784-7460	R	4*	<.1
436	ACCES I/O Products Inc	10623 Roselle St, San Diego CA 92121	858-550-9559	R	4*	<.1
437	Intelligent Computer Solutions Inc (Chatsworth California)—*Gonen Ravid*	9350 Eton Ave, Chatsworth CA 91311	818-998-5805	R	4*	<.1
438	Nordco Rail Services and Inspection Technologies—*Patrick Graham*	241 Ethan Allen Hwy, Ridgefield CT 06877	203-438-9696	S	4*	<.1
439	Cirque Corp—*Richard Clasen*	2463 S 3850 W Ste A, Salt Lake City UT 84120	801-467-1100	S	4*	<.1
440	Gyration Inc—*Thomas Quinn*	12950 Saratoga Ave, Saratoga CA 95070	408-973-7070	S	4*	<.1
441	Opticon—*Paul Aiello*	2220 Lind Ave SW Ste 1, Renton WA 98057	425-651-2120	R	4*	<.1
442	Chesapeake Systems Inc—*Mark R Dent*	3000 Chestnut Ave Ste, Baltimore MD 21211	410-243-1023	R	4*	<.1
443	ACDNet Inc—*Kevin Schoen*	1800 N Grand River Ave, Lansing MI 48906	517-999-9999	R	4*	<.1
444	TSC America Inc—*Arthur Wang*	125 Mercury Cir, Pomona CA 91768	909-468-0100	S	4*	<.1
445	Electro-Optical Products Corp—*Ziva Tuchman*	PO Box 650441, Fresh Meadows NY 11365	718-456-6000	R	4*	<.1
446	Neuron Electronics Inc—*Luke Yen*	8541 Wellsford Pl Ste, Santa Fe Springs CA 90670	562-946-1322	R	4*	<.1
447	Reach Technology Inc—*Jonathon More*	4575 Cushing Pk W, Fremont CA 94538	510-770-1417	R	4*	<.1
448	ZBA Inc (Hillsborough New Jersey)—*Vivian Han*	94 Old Camplain Rd, Hillsborough NJ 08844	908-359-2070	R	4*	<.1
449	Advanced Barcode Technology Inc—*Charles Bibas*	46 Schenck Ave Apt 3l, Great Neck NY 11021	516-829-2135	R	4*	<.1
450	Swp Inc—*Wayne Pigmon*	PO Box 1400, Morristown TN 37816	423-586-7632	R	4*	<.1
451	Prophecy Technology LLC—*Paul Goodson*	339 Cheryl Ln, Walnut CA 91789	909-598-7998	R	4*	<.1
452	Portable Systems Solutions Inc—*David Schultze*	PO Box 5047, Scottsdale AZ 85261	480-760-9007	R	3*	<.1
453	Chazak Value Corp—*Joseph Sarachek*	One Rockefeller Plz 16, New York NY 10020	212-651-3302	R	3	<.1
454	World Wide Acquisitions and Sales Inc—*Sal Frazzitta*	3300 Keller St Ste 201, Santa Clara CA 95054	408-943-9055	R	3*	<.1
455	Source Communications LLP—*William Voss*	2260 Industrial Ln, Broomfield CO 80020	303-466-8925	R	3*	<.1
456	Fushan Enterprises—*Juijung Lin*	44040 Fremont Blvd, Fremont CA 94538	510-226-0888	R	3*	<.1
457	Datametrics Corp—*Carl Stella*	940 Enchanted Way Ste, Simi Valley CA 93065	805-577-9710	D	3	<.1
458	Florida Digital Inc—*Lisa Beeman*	9240 Babcock St SE, Palm Bay FL 32909	321-952-2842	R	3*	<.1
459	Video Products Inc—*Carl Jagatich*	1275 Danner Dr, Aurora OH 44202	330-562-7070	R	3*	.1
460	Fernqvist Labeling Solutions	2544 Leghorn St, Mountain View CA 94043	650-428-0330	R	3*	<.1
461	Parwan Electronics Corp—*Suraj P Tschand*	1230 Hwy 34, Aberdeen NJ 07747	732-290-1900	R	3*	<.1
462	Somat Corp—*Jim Kirk*	702 W Killarney St, Urbana IL 61801	217-328-5359	R	3*	<.1
463	Polhemus Inc—*Al Rodgers*	PO Box 560, Colchester VT 05446	802-655-3159	R	3*	<.1
464	DataHand Systems Inc—*James A Cole*	3044 N 33rd Ave, Phoenix AZ 85017	602-233-6000	R	3*	<.1
465	BOSaNOVA Inc—*Israel Gal*	2012 W Lone Cactus Dr, Phoenix AZ 85027	623-516-0029	S	3*	<.1
466	Bravo Communications Inc	1310 Tully Rd Ste 107, San Jose CA 95122	408-297-8700	R	3*	<.1
467	Covid Inc—*Tommy Norris*	1723 W 4th St, Tempe AZ 85281	480-966-2221	R	3	<.1
468	alfaQuest Technology—*Dennis E Nierman*	2100 Golf Rd, Rolling Meadows IL 60008	847-427-8800	R	3*	<.1
469	Contek International Corp—*John Chen*	93 Cherry St, New Canaan CT 06840	203-972-1377	R	3*	<.1
470	Fakespace Systems Inc—*Carol Leaman* Mechdyne Corp	11 E Church St 4th Fl, Marshalltown IA 50158	641-754-4649	S	3	<.1
471	Printer Works Inc—*Stephen Roberts*	39980 Eureka Dr, Newark CA 94560	510-670-2700	R	3*	<.1
472	Rancho Technology Inc	9155 Archibald Ave Ste, Rancho Cucamonga CA 91730	909-987-3966	R	3*	<.1
473	Control Technology Inc—*Todd Ferguson*	7608 N Hudson Ave, Oklahoma City OK 73116	405-840-3163	R	3*	<.1
474	RJS Systems International—*Randy Eisenbach* Printronix Inc	PO Box 19559, Irvine CA 92623	714-368-2300	D	3*	<.1
475	Scion Corp—*Tod Weinberg*	82 Wormans Mill Ct Ste, Frederick MD 21701	301-695-7870	R	3*	<.1
476	C Sys Labs Inc—*William Smith*	3030 Thorntree Dr Ste, Chico CA 95973	530-894-7954	R	3*	<.1
477	Cactus Computer Inc—*Jake Smith*	1120 Metrocrest Dr Ste, Carrollton TX 75006	972-416-0525	R	3*	<.1
478	Engineering Solutions Inc (Tukwila Washington)	6300 Southcenter Blvd, Tukwila WA 98188	206-241-9395	R	3*	<.1
479	ErgonomiXX Inc (Kensington Maryland)—*Alan H Grant*	2813 University Blvd W, Kensington MD 20895	301-933-3747	R	3*	<.1
480	Kalglo Electronics Company Inc	5911 Colony Dr, Bethlehem PA 18017	610-837-0700	R	3*	<.1
481	Themenaps LLC—*Barbara Cannington*	417 9th Ave W, Ashland WI 54806	715-682-1080	R	3*	<.1
482	Biomagnetic Research Inc—*Robert T McKusick*	9025 S Kellner Canyon, Globe AZ 85501	928-425-5051	R	3*	<.1
483	Data Pure LLC—*Brian New*	914 2nd St Bldg 2 Unit, Berthoud CO 80513	970-532-4608	R	3*	<.1
484	Santa Fe Systems Inc—*Larry Peterson*	PO Box 39, Tesuque NM 87574	505-424-1954	R	3*	<.1
485	Plexon Inc—*Harvey Wiggins*	6500 Greenville Ave St, Dallas TX 75206	214-369-4957	R	3*	<.1
486	Reliable Electronics Of Mt Vernon Inc—*Jay Friedman*	519 S 5th Ave Ste 6, Mount Vernon NY 10550	914-668-4440	R	3*	<.1
487	Bi Ra Systems Inc—*William Biswell*	2410 Midtown Pl Ne Ste, Albuquerque NM 87107	505-881-8887	R	3*	<.1
488	Quantronix Inc—*Clark Skeen*	PO Box 929, Farmington UT 84025	801-451-7000	R	3*	<.1
489	Gulton Inc—*Om Srivastava*	116 Corporate Blvd Ste, South Plainfield NJ 07080	908-791-4622	R	3*	<.1
490	Input/Output Technology Inc—*Ted Drapala*	28303 Industry Dr, Valencia CA 91355	661-257-1000	R	3*	<.1
491	Lektron Inc—*James Chapman*	2106 Hwy 31 Nw, Hartselle AL 35640	256-751-0981	R	3*	<.1
492	Cadco Program And Machine Inc—*Joan Klopfenstein*	1716 Scherer Pkwy, Saint Charles MO 63303	636-946-6700	R	3*	<.1
493	Seamark International LLC—*Linda Jinnings*	16 Celina Ave Unit 5, Nashua NH 03063	603-546-0100	R	3*	<.1
494	Bcc Distribution Inc—*Jon Newman*	12815 Premier Ctr Ct, Plymouth MI 48170	734-737-9300	R	3*	<.1
495	Thales Computers Inc—*Richard Goodell*	3100 Spring Forest Rd, Raleigh NC 27616	919-231-8000	R	3*	<.1
496	Digital Outpost Inc—*Brian Douglass*	2772 Loker Ave W, Carlsbad CA 92010	760-431-3575	R	3*	<.1

Note: An asterisk (*) indicates an estimated financial figure. The company type code used is as follows: R = Private, P = Public, S = Private Subsidiary, B = Public Subsidiary, D = Division, J = Joint Venture, I = Investment Fund.

COMPANY RANKINGS BY SALES WITHIN 4-DIGIT SIC

Rank	Company Name—Executive Officer	Address, City, State, Zip	Phone	Type	Fin	Empls
497	Cardlogix—Bruce Ross	16 Hughes Ste 100, Irvine CA 92618	949-380-1312	R	3*	<.1
498	Elesys Inc—Michael Covert	236 E Caribbean Dr, Sunnyvale CA 94089	408-747-0233	R	3*	<.1
499	I/O Concepts Inc—Michael Millspaugh	2125 112th Ave Ne Fl 2, Bellevue WA 98004	425-450-0650	S	3*	<.1
500	Center For Tribology Inc—Norm Gitis	1717 Dell Ave, Campbell CA 95008	408-376-4040	R	2*	<.1
501	Dataq Instruments—John Bowers	241 Springside Dr, Akron OH 44333	330-668-1444	R	2*	<.1
502	Prologic Engineering Inc—Kathy Maricle	3979 Hammer Dr Ste B, Bellingham WA 98226	360-734-9825	R	2	<.1
503	Byte Brothers Inc—Darrell Igelmund	7003 132nd Pl Se, Newcastle WA 98059	425-917-8380	R	2*	<.1
504	Micro Connectors Inc—Charlie Lin	2700 Mccone Ave, Hayward CA 94545	510-266-0299	R	2*	<.1
505	SmsmemoryCom—Sal Scuderi	370 Laurelwood Rd Ste, Santa Clara CA 95054	408-492-9770	R	2*	<.1
506	Nexsys Electronics Corp—Peter Killcommons	667 Folsom St Fl 2, San Francisco CA 94107	415-541-9980	R	2*	<.1
507	Convenience Electronics Inc—J Harry Lum	2306 Vondron Rd, Madison WI 53718	608-273-4856	R	2*	<.1
508	KEYTEC Inc—Brian Sun	520 Shepherd Dr, Garland TX 75042	972-272-7555	R	2*	<.1
509	Synergistics Inc	16 Tech Cir, Natick MA 01760	508-655-1340	R	2*	<.1
510	WideBand Corp—Joseph R Billings	401 W Grand St, Gallatin MO 64640	660-663-3000	R	2*	<.1
511	Quist International Inc—Mindi Rosenquist	1350 Mnscture Ring Ste, Dallas TX 75207	214-420-1980	R	2*	<.1
512	Image Graphics Inc—Patrick Grosso	917 Bridgeport Av, Shelton CT 06484	203-926-0100	R	2*	<.1
513	Touchstone Technology Inc—Eric Snavely	350 Mile Crossing Blvd, Rochester NY 14624	585-458-2690	R	2*	<.1
514	Modular Industrial Solutions Inc—William Carey	1729 Little Orchard St, San Jose CA 95125	408-971-0910	R	2*	<.1
515	Cybertech Inc—Ronald Schmidt	935 Horsham Rd Ste 1, Horsham PA 19044	215-957-6220	R	2*	<.1
516	EPIX Inc—Howard M Dreizen	381 Lexington Dr, Buffalo Grove IL 60089	847-465-1818	R	2*	<.1
517	GBT Inc—James Liao	17358 Railroad St, City of Industry CA 91748	626-854-9338	S	2*	<.1
518	Lemoine Multinational Technologies Inc—Yigal Ziv	3170 Martin Rd, Walled Lake MI 48390	248-960-5989	R	2*	<.1
519	Mega Communication Technologies Inc—Robert Morgan	4380-C Viewridge Ave, San Diego CA 92123	858-268-0525	R	2*	<.1
520	Nutfield Technology Inc—Robert Milkowski	1 Wall St Ste 13, Hudson NH 03051	603-893-6200	R	2*	<.1
521	Two Day Corp—Robert Wilczewski	326 Broadacres Ave, Riverton WY 82501	307-856-7541	R	2*	<.1
522	Heart-Smart Chicken Inc—James Campbell	23042 N 15th Ln, Phoenix AZ 85027	623-780-0015	R	2*	<.1
523	Fawkes Engineering LLC	1012 Oak Ln, Escondido CA 92029	760-737-9240	R	2*	<.1
524	Video Associates Labs Inc—Randy Feingersh	2201 Denton Dr Ste 109, Austin TX 78758	512-491-7091	R	2*	<.1
525	Axonix Corp—Douglas Kihm	3785 S 700 E, Salt Lake City UT 84106	801-685-0900	R	2*	<.1
526	Factory Systems LLC—John Flint	3790 Fernandina Rd Ste, Columbia SC 29210	803-754-0090	R	2*	<.1
527	IC Engineering Inc—Robert E Glaser	PO Box 321, Owings Mills MD 21117	410-363-8748	R	2*	<.1
528	ICS Electronics	7034 Commerce Cir, Pleasanton CA 94588	925-416-1000	R	2*	<.1
529	Kinesis Corp—William Hargreaves	22121 17th Ave SE Ste, Bothell WA 98021	425-402-8100	R	2*	<.1
530	Printerm Datascribe Inc	300 International Dr S, Williamsville NY 14221	716-635-0797	R	2*	<.1
531	Secure-It Inc	140 Denslow Rd, East Longmeadow MA 01028	413-525-7039	R	2*	<.1
532	Font Bureau Inc—Sam Burlo	50 Melcher St Ste 2, Boston MA 02210	617-423-8770	R	2*	<.1
533	Applied Data Sciences Inc—Tom Crandell	PO Box 814209, Dallas TX 75381	972-620-8530	R	2*	<.1
534	Forvus Research Inc—Carl McLawhorn	PO Box 1261, Knightdale NC 27545	919-954-0063	R	2*	<.1
535	Infogrip Inc (Ventura California)—Liza Jacobs	1899 E Main St, Ventura CA 93001	805-652-0770	R	2*	<.1
536	Metapo Inc—Fred Yang	2380-D Qume Dr, San Jose CA 95131	408-943-9308	R	2*	<.1
537	SunMax Corp—Vincent Chang	9550 Flair Dr, El Monte CA 91731	626-607-6076	R	2*	<.1
538	Taneum Computer Products Inc—Steve Grand	PO Box 6178, Kent WA 98064	425-251-0711	R	2*	<.1
539	Synergystex International Inc—Richard Winbrenner	PO Box 798, Brunswick OH 44212	330-225-3112	R	2*	<.1
540	Automated Vision LLC—Reddiar S Anbalagan	1111 Deming Way, Madison WI 53717	608-836-9393	R	2*	<.1
541	3DTV Corp—Michael Starks	1863 Pioneer Pky E Ste, Springfield OR 97477	415-680-1678	R	2*	<.1
542	Berkshire Products Inc—Simon Machell	PO Box 2819, Cumming GA 30028	770-271-0088	R	2*	<.1
543	Kidtech Inc	101 Buckhaven Ct, Apex NC 27502	919-387-6088	R	2*	<.1
544	Lane Telecommunications Incorporated - Little Rock—John Hughes	3 Innwood Cir, Little Rock AR 72211	501-227-6637	R	2*	<.1
545	Troll Touch—Nick Durso	25345 Ave Stanford Ste, Valencia CA 91355	661-998-8533	R	2*	<.1
546	ACECAD Inc—Todd Waldman	PO Box 1071, Monterey CA 93942	831-655-1900	R	2*	<.1
547	MAS Systems—Lynn Nguyen	9702 Bolsa Ave Ste 36, Westminster CA 92683	714-775-8116	R	2*	<.1
548	Pakedge Device and Software Inc—Victor Pak	1163 Triton Dr, Foster City CA 94404	650-385-8700	R	2*	<.1
549	Unitrend Inc—Conrad AH Jelinger	4665 W Bancroft St, Toledo OH 43615	419-536-2090	R	2*	<.1
550	Touch Screens Inc—Scott C Tippetts	4830 Lawrenceville Hwy, Lilburn GA 30047	770-921-8436	S	2*	<.1
551	Gb Marketing Inc—Thomas Gust	200 N Fairway Dr Ste 2, Vernon Hills IL 60061	847-367-0101	R	2*	<.1
552	Signatec Inc—Thomas Hunt	359 San Miguel Dr Ste, Newport Beach CA 92660	949-729-1084	R	2*	<.1
553	Beall Technologies Inc—Purnendu Chatterjee	200 Meadowlands Pkwy, Secaucus NJ 07094	201-689-2130	R	2*	<.1
554	Intradyn Inc—Gary Doan	3285 Northwood Cir Ste, Saint Paul MN 55121	651-203-4600	R	2*	<.1
555	Kurdex Corp—Bijan Pourmand	343 Gibraltar Dr, Sunnyvale CA 94089	408-734-8181	R	2*	<.1
556	Griffith Electrical Control Systems Inc—Ed Griffith	491 Conklin Rd, Chenango Forks NY 13746	607-648-9059	R	2*	<.1
557	Microstore Inc—Ed Loewe	PO Box 125, Le Sueur MN 56058	507-665-3284	R	2*	<.1
558	Interaction Systems Inc—Michael Marino	PO Box 838, Lynnfield MA 01940	781-932-3088	R	2*	<.1
559	X2 Digital Wireless Systems Inc—Guy Coker	PO Box 1255, Rocklin CA 95677	916-779-1040	R	2*	<.1
560	Atlaz International Ltd—Loretta Zalta	298 Lawrence Ave Unit, Lawrence NY 11559	516-239-1854	R	2*	<.1
561	Micromint Inc—Frank Cerasoli	115 Timberlachen Cir S, Lake Mary FL 32746	407-262-0066	R	2*	<.1
562	Audience Voting Inc—Jeff Roache	6074 E Brainerd Rd, Chattanooga TN 37421	423-296-0798	R	2*	<.1
563	Instrumentation Technology Systems—Don Janess	19360 Business Ctr Dr, Northridge CA 91324	818-886-2034	R	1*	<.1
564	Parallel Systems Corp—Paul Schmitt	118 Tenney St, Georgetown MA 01833	978-352-7100	R	1*	<.1
565	Circuit Spectrum Inc—Zaven Tashjian	1759 S Main St Ste 124, Milpitas CA 95035	408-946-8484	R	1*	<.1
566	Cal Blen Electronic Industries Inc—Rod Staehlin	44 Jefryn Blvd Ste H, Deer Park NY 11729	631-242-6243	R	1*	<.1
567	Aries Research Inc—Lawrence Kou	46750 Fremont Blvd Ste, Fremont CA 94538	510-413-0288	R	1*	<.1
568	Ashby Industries Inc—H Ashby	9500 Westgate Rd Ste 2, Oklahoma City OK 73162	405-722-1705	R	1*	<.1
569	Newnex Technology Corp—Sam Liu	3041 Olcott St, Santa Clara CA 95054	408-986-9988	R	1*	<.1
570	Scan Technology Inc—Paul Flowers	10305 Nw 4th Pl, Gainesville FL 32607	352-332-2093	R	1*	<.1
571	Blastronix Inc—David Barnes	PO Box 369, Murphys CA 95247	209-795-0738	R	1*	<.1
572	Connect Tech International LLC	PO Box 2415, Flagstaff AZ 86003	928-527-4662	R	1*	<.1
573	Label Vision Systems Inc—Tim Lydell	101 Auburn Ct, Peachtree City GA 30269	770-487-6414	R	1*	<.1
574	Reliable Communications Inc—Robert Henkel	PO Box 640, Angels Camp CA 95222	209-736-0421	R	1*	<.1
575	Printworx Inc—David Willmon	921 Cleveland Ave Nw, Huntsville AL 35801	256-704-7772	R	1*	<.1
576	Prism Software Corp—E Ted Daniels	15500-C Rockfield Blvd, Irvine CA 92618	949-855-3100	P	1	<.1
577	Ghi Systems Inc—George Henderson	916 N Western Ave Ste, San Pedro CA 90732	310-548-6544	R	1*	<.1
578	Toye Corp—Gordon Morris	PO Box 3997, Chatsworth CA 91313	818-882-4000	R	1*	<.1
579	TS Microtech Inc—Steve Heung	17109 Gale Ave, City Of Industry CA 91745	626-839-8998	R	1*	<.1
580	Precision Display Technologies Corp—Jonathan Garman	4635 Longley Ln Ste 10, Reno NV 89502	775-825-4488	R	1*	<.1
581	Adder Corp—Adrian Dickens	29 Water St Ste 202, Newburyport MA 01950	978-499-2105	R	1*	<.1
582	Tek Resource Service Corp—David Peterson	2964 W Lake Rd, Cazenovia NY 13035	315-655-3352	R	1*	<.1
583	Constantine Engineering Labs Co—John Constantine	8660 Red Oak Ave, Rancho Cucamonga CA 91730	909-481-4648	R	1*	<.1
584	CopyTele Inc—Denis Krusos	900 Walt Whitman Rd, Melville NY 11747	631-549-5900	P	1	<.1
585	Phase One Inc (Northport New York)—Jacob Struckmann	200 Broadhollow Rd Ste, Melville NY 11747	631-547-8900	S	1*	<.1

Rank	Company Name—Executive Officer	Address, City, State, Zip	Phone	Type	Fin	Empls
586	Sedona GeoServices Inc—David R Vey	1003 W 9th Ave 2nd Fl, King of Prussia PA 19406	610-337-8400	S	1*	<.1
587	Star Panel Technologies Inc—Brian Dolinar	9200 Se Sunnybrook Blv, Clackamas OR 97015	503-654-6216	R	1*	<.1
588	William Ho—William Ho	40760 Encyclopedia Cir, Fremont CA 94538	510-226-9089	R	1*	<.1
589	Comfort Keyboard Company Inc	5215 W Clinton St, Milwaukee WI 53223	414-434-1022	R	1*	<.1
590	Assmann Electronics Inc—Frank Walter	1840 W Drake Dr Ste 10, Tempe AZ 85283	480-897-7001	S	1*	<.1
591	Bow Industries Of Virginia Inc—Dale Whysong	10349 Balls Ford Rd, Manassas VA 20109	703-361-7704	R	1*	<.1
592	Vista Imaging Inc—Christopher Dopp	521 Taylor Way, San Carlos CA 94070	650-802-9685	R	1*	<.1
593	Xijet Corp—Philip Black	8 Lunar Dr Ste 3, New Haven CT 06525	203-397-2800	R	1*	<.1
594	Fox Network Systems	7968 Arjons Dr Ste 103, San Diego CA 92126	858-689-8350	R	1*	<.1
595	Webster Computer Corp—David Webster	3300 N Palm Aire Dr St, Pompano Beach FL 33069	954-283-8958	R	1*	<.1
596	Dunamis Inc—Ben Satterfield	950 Herrington Rd Ste, Lawrenceville GA 30044	770-279-1144	R	1*	<.1
597	Lawson Labs Inc—Thomas Lawson	3217 Phoenixville Pike, Malvern PA 19355	610-725-8800	R	1*	<.1
598	Sakor Technologies Inc—Randal Beattie	2855 Jolly Rd, Okemos MI 48864	517-332-7256	R	1*	<.1
599	Smart Cable Co—Peter Dean	7403 Lakewood Dr W Ste, Lakewood WA 98499	253-474-9967	R	1*	<.1
600	Digital Communications Technologies LLC—Mario Bueno	5201 Blue Lagoon Dr 81, Miami FL 33126	305-718-3336	R	1*	<.1
601	GMM Research Corp—Luis Taveras	5557 E Santa Ana Canyo, Anaheim Hills CA 92807	714-632-0196	R	1*	<.1
602	Peripheral Manufacturing Inc—Ron Carboy	4775 Paris St Ste A, Denver CO 80239	303-371-8651	R	1*	<.1
603	Forward Pay Systems Inc—Verne Severson	9531 W 78th St Ste 245, Eden Prairie MN 55344	952-941-8188	R	1*	<.1
604	Power Print Digital Fabric Construction—Mike Curtiss	828 W Ahwanee Ave, Sunnyvale CA 94089	408-745-6300	R	1*	<.1
605	Waters Network Systems LLC	7401 Metro Blvd Ste 56, Edina MN 55439	952-831-5604	R	1*	<.1
606	Langan Products Inc—Leon Langan	2660 California St, San Francisco CA 94115	415-567-8089	R	1*	<.1
607	SecurTech Co—Robert C Perry	14865 SW 74th Ave Ste, Tigard OR 97224	503-372-6794	R	1*	<.1
608	Tahoma Technology Inc—Glen Bradburn	2819 Elliott Ave Ste 2, Seattle WA 98121	206-728-6465	R	1*	<.1
609	Fametech America Inc—Rex Liang	12343 Hymeadow Dr Ste, Austin TX 78750	512-331-4656	S	1*	<.1
610	Tanasi Products	PO Box 27, Friendsville TN 37737	865-995-1201	R	1*	<.1
611	Wiltec Inc—Robert E Conti	116 S Kerr Ave, Wilmington NC 28403	910-763-8400	R	1*	<.1
612	Advanced Storage Concepts Inc—William J Casey	2200 Market St Ste 810, Galveston TX 77550	409-762-0604	R	1*	<.1
613	CSA—Steve Riker	405 Vernon Way, El Cajon CA 92020	619-593-2663	R	1*	<.1
614	Navman Wireless—TJ Chung	2701 Patriot Blvd Ste, Glenview IL 60026	847-832-2367	R	1*	<.1
615	Value Computer Accessories Inc—Jennifer Deglopper	3215 Golf Rd, Delafield WI 53018	262-650-2222	R	1*	<.1
616	RC Systems Inc—Randy Carlstrom	1609 England Ave, Everett WA 98203	425-355-3800	R	1*	<.1
617	Ridgefield Acquisition Corp—Steven N Bronson	225 NE Mizner Blvd Ste, Boca Raton FL 33432	561-362-5385	P	1	<.1
618	Communication Intelligence Corp—Philip S Sassower	275 Shoreline Dr Ste 5, Redwood City CA 94065	650-802-7888	P	1	<.1
619	Reallm Technologies Corp—Walter Wojciechowski	2 Mason Ct, Lindenwold NJ 08021	856-627-3584	R	1*	<.1
620	T and T Computer Products Inc—Sue Mount	PO Box 14010, Tulsa OK 74159	918-742-1816	R	1*	<.1
621	Top Microsystems Corp—Bora Kim	3261 Keller St, Santa Clara CA 95054	408-980-9813	R	1*	<.1
622	Boss Inc—Kerry Hartley	120 S Main St Ste A, Milford MI 48381	248-685-7171	R	1*	<.1
623	J2 International Inc—Jack Jaw	660 S Jefferson St Ste, Placentia CA 92870	714-666-8886	R	1*	<.1
624	Tigertronics—John Olson	PO Box 2490, Grants Pass OR 97528	541-474-6700	R	1*	<.1
625	Cim Bar Code Technology Inc—William Dempsey	PO Box 537, Lincolnshire IL 60069	847-559-9776	R	1*	<.1
626	Euro Tech Corp—Dolf Schroeder	9615 E Tom Tom Dr, Parker CO 80138	720-851-8800	R	1*	<.1
627	Wehrli and Associates Inc—Craig Wehrli	7 Upland Dr, Valhalla NY 10595	914-948-7941	R	1*	<.1
628	Future Tech Procurement Solutions Inc—Tracey Venero	2465 Centreville Rd St, Herndon VA 20171	703-879-6701	R	1*	<.1
629	Link Computer Graphics Inc—Hung-Wei Yeh	17a Daniel Rd E, Fairfield NJ 07004	973-808-8990	R	1*	<.1
630	Decitek Corp—Heng Seng	PO Box 930, Westborough MA 01581	508-366-1011	R	1*	<.1
631	Duplication Systems Inc—Gene Klawetter	129 S Madison Ave, Loveland CO 80537	970-292-5995	R	1*	<.1
632	Dancraft Enterprises—Dan Rumsey	5520 W 118th Pl, Inglewood CA 90304	310-643-8782	R	1*	<.1
633	Pda Panache Corp—Paul Schiller	PO Box 577, Bellport NY 11713	631-776-0523	R	1*	<.1
634	Talaris Systems Inc—Calvin E Burgart	PO Box 22926, San Diego CA 92196	858-539-1542	R	1	<.1
635	Ontarget Technologies LLC—Ryan Duffner	615 7th Ave N, Birmingham AL 35203	205-222-7926	R	1*	<.1
636	Control Logic Corp—Randy Holdredge	2533 State Hwy 80, West Burlington NJ 13482	607-965-6423	R	1*	<.1
637	Raac Technologies Inc—David Franke	219 N Milwaukee St Ste, Milwaukee WI 53202	414-277-1889	R	1*	<.1
638	FirewiredirectCom Inc—Roy Stocker	PO Box 160007, Austin TX 78716	512-302-0012	R	1*	<.1
639	International Bar Code Systems Inc—Joseph Mizla	160 Oak St Ste 1a, Glastonbury CT 06033	860-659-9660	R	1*	<.1
640	Rainforest Industry—Paul Middlesworth	847 W San Marcos Blvd, San Marcos CA 92078	760-744-4315	R	1*	<.1
641	Aprotek Inc—Paul Johnson	9323 W Evans Creek Rd, Rogue River OR 97537	541-582-2120	R	1*	<.1
642	BG Instruments Inc—David Wright	13607 E Trent Ave, Spokane Valley WA 99216	509-893-9881	R	1*	<.1
643	Resource Data Management—Clarence Mcgill	PO Box 17639, Dayton OH 45417	513-769-3912	R	1*	<.1
644	NetSpan Corp	5757 Alpha Rd Rm 110, Dallas TX 75240	972-690-8844	R	1	<.1
645	T G's Supply And Support LLC	13001 Armadillo Dr, Guthrie OK 73044	405-586-9228	R	1*	<.1
646	Advance Computer Solutions Inc—Fred Ward	12311 Old Pomerado Rd, Poway CA 92064	858-748-6800	R	1*	<.1
647	Nemonix Engineering Inc—Daniel Bumbarger	56 Hudson St Ste 2, Northborough MA 01532		R	1*	<.1
648	Tyler Martin Company Inc—Rex Price	PO Box 282, Marysville KS 66508	785-562-2276	R	<1*	<.1
649	Fulcrum Design—Thomas Longton	PO Box 104, Bennington VT 05201	802-442-6441	R	<1*	<.1
650	Bedford Products Corp—H Allen	PO Box 469, Bedford VA 24523	540-586-4100	R	<1*	<.1
651	Novint Technologies Inc—Tom Anderson	PO Box 66956, Albuquerque NM 87193		P	<1	<.1
652	Custom Sensors Inc—Michael Mac Master	30 York St Ste 1, Auburn NY 13021	315-252-3741	R	<1*	<.1
653	Timeout Devices Inc—Jim Daniel	2718 Covert Rd, Glenview IL 60025	847-729-6543	R	<1*	<.1
654	Astrocom Corp—Ronald B Thomas	950 Xenium Ln N Ste 10, Minneapolis MN 55441	763-694-9949	R	<1*	<.1
655	BCD Associates Inc—Mary Wills	2800 NW 36th St Ste 22, Oklahoma City OK 73112		R	<1*	<.1
656	Dtsystems Inc—Frank Nicorera	18302 Hghwods Prsrve P, Tampa FL 33647	813-632-3456	R	<1*	<.1
657	Quartech Corp—Perry Muckenthaler	15923 Angelo Dr, Macomb MI 48042	586-781-0373	R	<1*	<.1
658	Avisio Inc (Riverside California)—Amro Albanna	871 Marlborough Ave St, Riverside CA 92507	951-786-9474	P	<1	<.1
659	ICC Worldwide Inc—Rich Lauer	2906 Alex McKay Pl, Sarasota FL 34240	949-200-7569	P	<1	<.1
660	New Innovations Inc—Gary Rucker	PO Box 944, La Fayette GA 30728	706-638-9998	R	<1*	<.1
661	Compucover Inc—James Garrett	PO Box 972, Defuniak Springs FL 32435	850-835-4671	R	<1*	<.1
662	Logicom Systems—Dave Westerveld	17615 Iroquois Trce, Tinley Park IL 60477	708-429-6340	R	<1*	<.1
663	Measurement Research Inc—Simon Harrison	12840 Bradley Ave, Sylmar CA 91342	818-837-3456	R	<1*	<.1
664	Superior Software Systems Inc—Alfred Carter	3224 S Main St, Salisbury NC 28147	704-636-7748	R	<1*	<.1
665	Electronic Energy Control Inc—Bert Brundage	14960 Maple Ridge Rd, Milford Center OH 43045	937-349-6000	R	<1*	<.1
666	Software Integrators Inc—Joseph Mccarthy	255 Comfort Ln, Bozeman MT 59718	406-586-8866	R	<1*	<.1
667	Fascinating Electronics Inc—Ronald Jackson	925 Sw 83rd Ave, Portland OR 97225	503-292-4785	R	<1*	<.1
668	Hawk Systems Inc—Michael Diamant	2385 NW Executive Cent, Boca Raton FL 33431	561-962-2885	P	<1	<.1
669	Ignition Media—James Howard	637 Parkside Dr, Lexington KY 40505	859-299-8259	R	<1*	<.1
670	Optwise Corp—William Fisher	200 Estrella Rd, Fremont CA 94539	510-573-1686	R	<1*	<.1
671	Speed I/O Technologies—Steve Pham	8551 Amy Ave, Garden Grove CA 92841	714-539-6194	R	<1*	<.1
672	Cosine Communications Inc—Terry R Gibson	61 E Main St Ste B, Los Gatos CA 95030	408-399-6490	R	<1	N/A
673	Order-Matic Corp—Bill Cunningham	PO Box 25463, Oklahoma City OK 73125	405-672-1487	R	N/A	.2
674	Heights-USA—Tim Philburn	1445 Lower Ferry Rd, Ewing NJ 08628	609-530-1300	D	N/A	<.1
675	Mind Path Technologies Inc InFocus Corp	27700 SW Pky Ave, Wilsonville OR 97070	503-685-8888	S	N/A	<.1

Note: An asterisk (*) indicates an estimated financial figure. The company type code used is as follows: R = Private, P = Public, S = Private Subsidiary, B = Public Subsidiary, D = Division, J = Joint Venture, I = Investment Fund.

COMPANY RANKINGS BY SALES WITHIN 4-DIGIT SIC

Rank	Company Name—*Executive Officer*	Address, City, State, Zip	Phone	Type	Fin	Empls
676	MIDlator Systems—*Ron Perry*	PO Box 6065, San Diego CA 92166	619-223-9000	R	N/A	<.1

TOTALS: SIC 3577 Computer Peripheral Equipment Nec
Companies: 676 | | | | | 156,227 | 284.8

3578 Calculating & Accounting Equipment

Rank	Company Name—*Executive Officer*	Address, City, State, Zip	Phone	Type	Fin	Empls
1	National Cash Register Co—*John G Bruno*	3097 Satellite Blvd, Duluth GA 30096	937-445-1936	P	5,443	23.5
2	Diebold Inc—*Thomas W Swidarski*	PO Box 3077, North Canton OH 44720	330-490-4000	P	2,836	16.5
3	Hypercom Corp—*Albert Liu*	8888 E Raintree Dr Ste, Scottsdale AZ 85260	480-642-5000	S	407	1.4
4	PAR Technology Corp—*John W Sammon Jr*	8383 Seneca Tpke, New Hartford NY 13413	315-738-0600	P	240	1.5
5	Aristocrat Technologies Inc—*Nick Khin*	7230 Amigo St, Las Vegas NV 89119	702-270-1000	S	212*	.5
6	ParTech Inc—*Rick Franklin* PAR Technology Corp	8383 Seneca Tpk, New Hartford NY 13413	315-738-0600	D	126*	.4
7	VeriFone Inc—*Douglas G Bergeron*	2099 Gateay Pl Ste 600, San Jose CA 95110	408-232-7800	S	121*	.9
8	Triton Systems of Delaware LLC—*Daryl Cornell*	21405 B St, Long Beach MS 39560	228-575-3100	R	71*	.2
9	Comdata Corp Merchant Services Div—*Steve Stevenson*	5301 Maryland Way, Brentwood TN 37027	615-370-7000	D	50*	.1
10	Greenwald Industries—*Leonard Samela*	212 Middlesex Ave, Chester CT 06412	860-526-0800	D	48*	.1
11	Mei Inc—*Michael Hayes*	1301 Wilson Dr, West Chester PA 19380	610-430-2700	R	42*	.5
12	Cormark Inc—*Tom Conway*	1701 Winthrop Dr, Des Plaines IL 60018	847-364-5900	R	30*	.4
13	Csi Acquisition Corp—*Albin Tiley*	645 W 200 N, North Salt Lake UT 84054	801-936-8082	R	21*	.2
14	Real-Time Data Management Services Inc—*Ernest Sammons*	5400 Robin Hood Rd, Norfolk VA 23513	757-855-2750	R	20*	.1
15	Act Acquisitions LLC—*Davidoff LLC*	5341 Mount View Rd, Antioch TN 37013		R	17*	.2
16	Alpha Technology Inc—*Dennis Tate*	PO Box 5408, Anderson SC 29623	864-225-7245	R	17*	.1
17	USA Technologies Inc—*Stephen P Herbert*	100 Deerfield Ln Ste 1, Malvern PA 19355	610-989-0340	P	16	<.1
18	Advanced Data Services Inc—*Billie F Attaway Jr*	401 W Coleman Blvd Ste, Mount Pleasant SC 29464	843-852-3031	R	12*	<.1
19	Datacap Systems Inc—*Terry Zeigler*	100 New Britain Blvd, Chalfont PA 18914	215-997-8989	R	10*	.1
20	American Changer Corp—*Harry Steinbok*	1400 Nw 65th Pl, Fort Lauderdale FL 33309	954-917-3009	R	9*	.1
21	Mintronix Inc—*Robert Lee*	5251 Verdugo Way Ste J, Camarillo CA 93012	805-482-1298	R	7*	<.1
22	International Lottery and Totalizator Systems Inc—*Jeffrey Johnson*	2310 Cousteau Ct, Vista CA 92081	760-598-1655	B	6	<.1
23	Nextran Industries Inc—*Tony Park*	PO Box 628, Edgewater NJ 07020	201-498-0707	R	5*	.1
24	Calculated Industries Inc—*Steve Kennedy*	4840 Hytech Dr, Carson City NV 89706	775-885-4900	R	5*	.1
25	Auto-Gas Systems Inc—*G Nicholson*	PO Box 6957, Abilene TX 79608	325-676-3150	R	5*	<.1
26	MacSema Inc—*Don Rowden*	62971 Plateau Dr Ste 4, Bend OR 97701	541-389-1122	R	5*	<.1
27	Bellatrix Systems Inc—*Thomas Ellsberg*	1015 Sw Emkay Dr, Bend OR 97702	541-382-2208	R	5*	<.1
28	Logic Controls Inc—*Jackson Lum*	355 Denton Ave, New Hyde Park NY 11040	516-248-0400	R	5*	<.1
29	Advanced Retail Management Systems Inc—*Bruce Klepper*	8100 Suthpark Way Ste, Littleton CO 80120	303-738-1800	R	5*	<.1
30	Demoteller Systems Inc—*Terilee East*	1212 Royal Pkwy, Euless TX 76040	817-494-9300	R	4*	<.1
31	Sierra National Corp—*Fred Forbes*	8790 Cuyamaca St Ste G, Santee CA 92071	619-258-8200	R	4*	<.1
32	Innovonics Inc	PO Box 41517, Phoenix AZ 85080	602-906-1000	R	4*	<.1
33	Cambridge Ohio Production and Assembly Corp—*Mike Arent*	1521 Morton Ave, Cambridge OH 43725	740-432-6383	R	4*	<.1
34	Access Pos LLC—*Brad O'malley*	990 Lone Oak Rd Ste 10, Eagan MN 55121	651-209-3140	R	3*	<.1
35	Automated Financial Technologies LLC—*Rafael Gutierrez*	1240 Pa St Ne Ste D, Albuquerque NM 87110	505-881-2486	R	3*	<.1
36	Klopp International Inc—*Rick Nelson*	PO Box 985, Oldsmar FL 34677	813-855-6789	R	3*	<.1
37	Internatational Point Of Sale—*Joshua Zizmor*	555 Cedar Ln Ste 7, Teaneck NJ 07666	201-928-0222	R	3*	<.1
38	Ja Max Machine Company Inc—*Jack Maxted*	PO Box 328, Roland IA 50236	515-388-4900	R	2*	<.1
39	Valpar International Corp—*Paul Swartz*	PO Box 5767, Tucson AZ 85703	520-293-1510	R	2*	<.1
40	Emf Corp—*James Kraft*	PO Box 9, Monroe WA 98272	360-794-9885	R	2*	<.1
41	Preimer Atms Inc—*Miguel Espaillat*	2700 N 29th Ave Ste 20, Hollywood FL 33020	954-923-8033	R	1*	<.1
42	Peregrin Technologies Inc—*Samuel Bosch*	1225 Nw Murray Rd Ste, Portland OR 97229	503-690-1111	R	1*	<.1
43	Varametrix Corp—*David Pierce*	490 Laurel Ln, Stateline NV 89449	775-588-0356	R	1*	<.1
44	Global Investment Management Inc—*Mehdi Daemi*	10835 Santa Monica Blv, Los Angeles CA 90025	310-446-8190	R	1*	<.1
45	Money Systems Technology—*Adil Said*	3522 Dividend Dr, Garland TX 75042	972-272-3262	R	1*	<.1
46	Dtech Pos LLC—*Mark Kirchner*	3920 E Patrick Ln 4, Las Vegas NV 89120	702-269-4135	R	<1*	<.1
47	Hoover Business Systems LLC	1187 Township Rd 753, Ashland OH 44805	419-281-8487	R	N/A	<.1

TOTALS: SIC 3578 Calculating & Accounting Equipment
Companies: 47 | | | | | 9,831 | 47.1

3579 Office Machines Nec

Rank	Company Name—*Executive Officer*	Address, City, State, Zip	Phone	Type	Fin	Empls
1	Canon USA Inc—*Joe Adachi*	1 Canon Plz, Lake Success NY 11042	516-328-5000	S	13,328	11.0
2	Pitney Bowes Inc—*Murray D Martin*	1 Elmcroft Rd, Stamford CT 06926	203-356-5000	P	5,425	30.7
3	Harris Corp—*Thomas A Dattilo*	1025 W NASA Blvd, Melbourne FL 32919		P	5,206	15.8
4	Oce-USA Inc	5450 N Cumberland Ave, Chicago IL 60656	773-714-8500	S	3,671*	3.1
5	Fellowes Inc—*James Fellowes*	1789 Norwood Ave, Itasca IL 60143	630-893-1600	R	1,112*	2.7
6	Ricoh Electronics Inc—*Yoshinori Yamashita*	1100 Valencia Ave, Tustin CA 92780	714-566-2500	R	250	1.0
7	Streamfeeder LLC—*Mitch Speicher*	315 27th Ave NE, Minneapolis MN 55418	763-502-0000	R	223*	.1
8	Digi International Inc—*Joseph T Dunsmore*	11001 Bren Rd E, Minnetonka MN 55343	952-912-3444	P	204	.7
9	Toshiba America Information Systems Inc—*Mark Simons*	PO Box 19724, Irvine CA 92623	949-583-3000	S	167*	1.0
10	Neopost USA—*Dennis LeStrange*	478 Wheelers Farms Rd, Milford CT 06461	203-301-3442	D	130*	.9
11	Brother Industries (USA) Inc—*Toru Uchibayashi*	7819 N Brother Blvd, Bartlett TN 38133	901-377-7777	R	101*	1.2
12	Cummins-Allison Corp—*Douglas Mennie*	PO Box 339, Mount Prospect IL 60056	847-299-9550	R	86*	.9
13	Atlantic Zeiser Co—*Walter Klingler*	15 Patton Dr W, Caldwell NJ 07006	973-228-0800	R	75*	.3
14	Franklin Electronic Publishers Inc—*Barry J Lipsky*	1 Franklin Plz, Burlington NJ 08016	609-386-2500	R	46	.1
15	American Thermoform Corp	1758 Brackett St, La Verne CA 91750	909-593-6711	R	45*	<.1
16	Smith Corona Corp—*Martin Wilson*	3830 Kelley Ave, Cleveland OH 44114		S	44*	.1
17	Amano Cincinnati Inc—*Osamu Okagaki*	140 Harrison Ave, Roseland NJ 07068	973-403-1900	S	39*	.3
18	Varitronic Systems Inc—*David Grey*	2355 Polaris Ln N Ste, Plymouth MN 55447	763-536-6400	D	38*	.3
19	Gunther International Ltd—*Marc I Perkins*	1 Winnenden Rd, Norwich CT 06360	860-823-1427	R	34*	.2
20	C P Bourg Inc—*Christian Bourg*	50 Samuel Barnet Blvd, New Bedford MA 02745	508-998-2171	R	23*	.1
21	Newbold Corp—*Robert Scott*	450 Weaver St, Rocky Mount VA 24151	540-489-4400	R	21*	.2
22	incjet Inc Gunther International Ltd	1 Winnenden Rd, Norwich CT 06360	860-823-3090	S	20*	.1
23	Automecha International Ltd—*Kenneth St John*	PO Box 660, Oxford NY 13830	607-843-2235	R	20*	<.1
24	Parker Powis Inc—*Kevin Parker*	775 Heinz Ave, Berkeley CA 94710	510-848-2463	R	19*	.1
25	Heidelberg/Baumfolder Corp—*Ulrik Nygaard*	PO Box 728, Sidney OH 45365	937-492-1281	D	19*	.1
26	Silgan Closures—*Glenn Paulson*	1140 31st St, Downers Grove IL 60515	630-515-8383	S	18*	.1
27	ID Technology LLC	2051 Franklin Dr, Fort Worth TX 76106	817-626-7779	D	15*	.1
28	Doar Communications Inc—*Paul Neale*	170 Earle Ave, Lynbrook NY 11563	516-823-4000	R	13*	.2
29	Buckeye Business Products Inc—*Robert H Kanner* Kroy LLC	3830 Kelley Ave, Cleveland OH 44114		D	13*	.1

Rank	Company Name—*Executive Officer*	Address, City, State, Zip	Phone	Type	Fin	Empls
30	John Christian Company Inc—*James Decker*	PO Box 3137, Center Line MI 48015	586-757-5005	R	13*	.1
31	Lathem Time Corp—*Bill Lathem*	200 Selig Dr SW, Atlanta GA 30336		R	12*	.2
32	Rapidprint—*Donald Bidwell Sr*	2055 S Main St, Middletown CT 06457	860-346-9283	D	12*	.1
33	Kroy LLC	3830 Kelley Ave, Cleveland OH 44114	216-426-5600	S	11*	.1
34	Agissar Corp—*James Foley*	526 Benton St, Stratford CT 06615	203-375-8662	R	9*	<.1
35	Sonexis Inc—*Giorgio Coraluppi*	300 Seco Rd, Monroeville PA 15146	978-640-2000	R	7*	<.1
36	Pyramid Technologies LLC—*Luann Buono*	45 Gracey Ave, Meriden CT 06451	203-238-0550	R	7*	.1
37	Energy Saving Products And Sales Corp—*Richard Lamothe*	PO Box 2037, Burlington CT 06013	860-675-6443	R	7*	.1
38	Paymaster Technologies Inc—*Bob Kooper*	61 Garlisch Dr, Elk Grove Village IL 60007	847-758-1234	R	6*	<.1
39	R-Tas Systems Inc—*Jerry Delaney*	31 Union Ave, Sudbury MA 01776		R	5*	<.1
40	Astro Machine Corp—*George Selak*	630 Lively Blvd, Elk Grove Village IL 60007	847-364-6363	R	5*	<.1
41	Hedman Company Inc—*John Lindberg*	189 Gordon St, Elk Grove Village IL 60007	847-718-6500	R	4*	<.1
42	GBR Systems Corp—*Terry Carpenter*	12 Inspiration Ln, Chester CT 06412	860-526-9561	R	4*	<.1
43	Atrix International Inc—*Steve Riedel*	1350 Larc Industrial B, Burnsville MN 55337	952-894-6154	R	4*	<.1
44	Office Systems Inc—*Bruce DeVoss*	2701 Grand Ave, Galesburg IL 61401	309-343-6137	R	4*	<.1
45	Card Technology Corp—*Bryan Hills*	10925 Bren Rd E, Minnetonka MN 55343	952-912-9400	R	3*	<.1
46	Inscerco Manufacturing Inc—*Robert Kruk*	4621 138th St, Crestwood IL 60445	708-597-8777	R	3*	<.1
47	Lynde-Ordway Company Inc—*Thomas Ordway*	PO Box 8709, Fountain Valley CA 92728	714-957-1311	R	3*	<.1
48	Male LLC—*Donald Smith*	3899 Produce Rd Ste 11, Louisville KY 40218	502-966-4141	R	2*	<.1
49	Staplex Company Inc—*James Cussani*	777 5th Ave, Brooklyn NY 11232	718-768-3333	R	2*	<.1
50	International Roll-Call Corp—*William Schaeffer*	8346 Old Richfood Rd C, Mechanicsville VA 23116	804-519-4429	R	2*	<.1
51	Addressing Machines and Supply Company Inc	940 Virginia Ave, Indianapolis IN 46203	317-633-0530	R	2*	<.1
52	Kliewer Knife Co—*Robert Kliewer*	8400 Secura Way, Santa Fe Springs CA 90670	562-696-4912	R	2*	<.1
53	Microfilm Products Co	266 Germonds Rd, West Nyack NY 10994	845-371-3700	R	2*	<.1
54	United American Election Supply Inc—*Edward Oday*	PO Box 769, Blythewood SC 29016	803-333-8001	R	2*	<.1
55	Americlock Inc—*Alan Endrouais*	560 Cool Dell Ct, Ballwin MO 63021	636-527-2277	R	2*	<.1
56	Election Data Direct Inc—*Randall Rattray*	PO Box 302021, Escondido CA 92030	760-751-9900	R	2*	<.1
57	REG Inc—*Robert Gilmartin*	2020 Jefferson St, Houston TX 77003	713-237-1120	R	1*	<.1
58	Tritek Technologies Inc—*James Malatesta*	103 E Bridle Path, Hockessin DE 19707	302-239-1638	R	1*	<.1
59	Force Manufacturing Inc—*John Roccoforte*	PO Box 746, Apex NC 27502	919-362-9200	R	1*	<.1
60	Cylix Inc—*Cyril Bell*	3045 Regal Dr, Alcoa TN 37701	865-681-5921	R	1*	<.1
61	Industrial Electronic Service Ltd—*Jim Staffan*	325 Industry Dr, Carlisle OH 45005	937-746-9750	R	1*	<.1
62	National Time Recording Equipment Company Inc—*Stanley Akivis*	64 Reade St Fl 2, New York NY 10007	212-227-3310	R	1*	<.1
63	Vital Presentation Concepts Inc—*Paul Clements*	PO Box 21247, Saint Paul MN 55121	651-322-4500	R	1*	<.1
64	MC Mieth Manufacturing Inc—*Greg Feldman*	PO Box 291129, Port Orange FL 32129	386-767-3494	R	1*	<.1
65	Dynetics Engineering Corp—*Jeffery Hill*	515 Bond St, Lincolnshire IL 60069	847-541-7300	R	1*	<.1
66	Hagan Business Machines Of Butler Inc—*Rick Mcdeavitt*	1773 N Main St Ext, Butler PA 16001	724-287-8777	R	1*	<.1
67	Impact Devices Inc—*Ken Roy*	929 E Central Ave, Dayton OH 45449	937-866-9996	R	1*	<.1
68	Applied Computer Engineering—*John Emigh*	980 N State St, La Verkin UT 84745	435-635-5998	R	1*	<.1
69	Roover's Inc—*Nancy Andrasko*	125 Butler Dr, Hazleton PA 18201	570-455-7548	R	1*	<.1
70	Metro Copier Service—*Richard Whiten*	PO Box 369, Newborn GA 30056	770-761-4059	R	<1*	<.1
71	Exactbind West—*Tom Carpenter*	20331 Lake Forest Dr C, Lake Forest CA 92630	949-349-0094	R	<1*	<.1
72	Chauncey Wings Sons Inc—*Donald Wing*	PO Box 420, Marion MA 02738	413-772-6611	R	<1*	<.1
73	Moffett Precision Products Inc—*Daniel Moffett*	10596 W Twin Lake Rd, Hayward WI 54843	715-462-3353	R	<1*	<.1

TOTALS: SIC 3579 Office Machines Nec
Companies: 73   30,552   72.3

3581 Automatic Vending Machines

Rank	Company Name—*Executive Officer*	Address, City, State, Zip	Phone	Type	Fin	Empls
1	Royal Vendors Inc—*Chuck Millbum*	426 Industrial Blvd, Kearneysville WV 25430	304-728-7056	R	84*	1.2
2	SerVend/ Multiplex	2100 Future Dr, Sellersburg IN 47172		D	35	.3
3	Hotel Outsource Management International Inc—*Daniel Cohen*	80 Wall St Ste 815, New York NY 10005	212-344-1600	P	33	<.1
4	Custom Food Group—*Margaret Hoffman*	1903 Anson Rd, Dallas TX 75235	214-631-7040	R	31*	.3
5	A and A Global Industries—*Edward Kovens*	PO Box 5618, Timonium MD 21094	410-252-1020	R	18*	.2
6	GFI Genfare—*Kim Green*	751 Pratt Blvd, Elk Grove Village IL 60007	847-593-8855	S	14*	.1
7	Bev-O-Matic Vending Co—*Leslie Frank*	127 E 7th Ave, Homestead PA 15120	412-461-6400	R	10*	.1
8	Partec Inc—*Brian Poklacki*	9301 Belmont Ave, Franklin Park IL 60131	847-678-9520	R	9*	.1
9	International Carbonic Inc—*Craig Williams*	16630 Koala Rd, Adelanto CA 92301	760-246-3900	R	9*	.1
10	Hamilton Manufacturing Corp—*Robin Ritz*	1026 Hamilton Dr, Holland OH 43528	419-867-4858	R	8*	.1
11	Northwestern Corp—*Richard Bolen*	PO Box 490, Morris IL 60450	815-942-1300	R	6*	.1
12	Savamco Manufacturing Inc—*Bill Kreitz*	PO Box 190, Mcgregor MN 55760	218-768-2015	R	5*	.1
13	Automation Dynamics LLC—*Mike Frankeberger*	605 N High St, Independence MO 64050	816-461-8989	R	4*	<.1
14	Midwest Vending Inc—*Wayne Doyle*	11750 Millpond Ave, Burnsville MN 55337	952-707-1990	R	3*	<.1
15	Ok Manufacturing—*Jeff Ostler*	2340 S 900 W, Salt Lake City UT 84119	801-974-9116	R	3*	<.1
16	Air Serv South West—*Kirk Wall*	6180 S Eastern Ave, Commerce CA 90040	323-721-0660	R	2*	<.1
17	Oak Manufacturing Company Inc—*James Hinton*	2120 E 25th St, Los Angeles CA 90058	323-581-8087	R	2*	<.1
18	Library Automation Technologies—*Oleg Boyarsky*	2 E Atlantic Ave, Somerdale NJ 08083	856-566-4121	R	2*	<.1
19	Monarch Coin And Security Inc—*Stephanie Hall*	1512 Russell St, Covington KY 41011	859-261-4421	R	1*	<.1
20	Pop N Go Inc—*Melvin Wyman*	12429 E Putnam St, Whittier CA 90602	562-945-9351	P	<1	<.1

TOTALS: SIC 3581 Automatic Vending Machines
Companies: 20   278   2.6

3582 Commercial Laundry Equipment

Rank	Company Name—*Executive Officer*	Address, City, State, Zip	Phone	Type	Fin	Empls
1	Alliance Laundry Systems LLC—*Thomas F L'Esperance*	PO Box 990, Ripon WI 54971	920-748-3121	R	317	N/A
2	American Dryer Corp—*Dennis Slutsky*	88 Currant Rd, Fall River MA 02720	508-678-9000	R	47*	.3
3	Pellerin Milnor Corp—*James Pellerin*	PO Box 400, Kenner LA 70063	504-467-9591	R	46*	.6
4	Chicago Dryer Co—*Bruce Johnson*	2200 N Pulaski Rd, Chicago IL 60639	773-235-4430	R	20*	.1
5	Kemco Systems Inc—*Carroll Gorrell*	11500 47th St N, Clearwater FL 33762	727-573-2323	R	13*	.1
6	Hoyt Corp—*Steven Rooney*	251 Forge Rd, Westport MA 02790	508-636-8811	R	13*	.1
7	Unipress Corp—*Peter Hamlin*	3501 Queen Palm Dr, Tampa FL 33619	813-623-3731	R	11*	.1
8	Forenta LP—*Leland White*	PO Box 607, Morristown TN 37815	423-586-5370	R	10*	.1
9	Ellis Corp—*Victoria Fesmire*	1400 W Bryn Mawr Ave, Itasca IL 60143	630-250-9222	R	9*	.1
10	CMV Sharper Finish—*Craig R Roberts*	4500 W Augusta Blvd, Chicago IL 60651	773-276-4800	R	9*	.1
11	Judge's Inc—*Wayne Herzog*	2150 Maple Dr, Plover WI 54467	715-343-1769	R	6*	<.1
12	General Automatic Transfer Co—*Dan Guirl*	100 Lrkin Williams Ind, Fenton MO 63026	636-343-6370	R	6*	<.1
13	Lavatec Inc—*Samir Tadros*	300 Great Hill Rd, Naugatuck CT 06770	203-723-1122	R	6*	<.1
14	Resillo Press Pad Co—*Leo Pearl*	6950 N Central Park Av, Lincolnwood IL 60712	847-674-2170	R	5*	<.1
15	Automated Finishing Inc—*John Deede*	N60 W14521 Kaul Ave, Menomonee Falls WI 53051	262-252-4646	R	5*	<.1
16	Equipment Distributors International Co—*Mark Jacobs*	1753 Blake Ave, Los Angeles CA 90031	323-660-1635	R	5*	<.1

Note: An asterisk (*) indicates an estimated financial figure. The company type code used is as follows: R = Private, P = Public, S = Private Subsidiary, B = Public Subsidiary, D = Division, J = Joint Venture, I = Investment Fund.

COMPANY RANKINGS BY SALES WITHIN 4-DIGIT SIC

Rank	Company Name—*Executive Officer*	Address, City, State, Zip	Phone	Type	Fin	Empls
17	Edro Corp—*Edward Kirejczyk*	PO Box 308, East Berlin CT 06023	860-828-0311	R	5*	<.1
18	Fairfield Laundry Machinery Corp—*Raymond Hall*	5 Montesano Rd Ste 1, Fairfield NJ 07004	973-575-4330	R	3*	<.1
19	Hunt Design and Manufacturing Inc—*Ronald Hunt*	2581 Us Hwy 231, Arab AL 35016	256-586-2519	R	3*	<.1
20	Southern L and R Maintenance Inc—*Shirley Rose*	218 Rose Rd, Rainbow City AL 35906	256-413-7702	R	2*	<.1
21	Finishing Systems Corp—*David Gidman*	770 E Broadway St, Fortville IN 46040	317-485-6988	R	1*	<.1
22	Talley Machinery Corp—*William Tingue*	7009 Cessna Dr, Greensboro NC 27409	336-664-0012	R	1*	<.1

TOTALS: SIC 3582 Commercial Laundry Equipment
Companies: 22   543   1.7

3585 Refrigeration & Heating Equipment

Rank	Company Name—*Executive Officer*	Address, City, State, Zip	Phone	Type	Fin	Empls
1	Cornelius IMI Inc—*Tim Hubbard*	101 Broadway St W Ste, Osseo MN 55369	763-488-8200	R	26,720*	2.0
2	American Standard Inc—*Fredrick Poses* Trane Inc	PO Box 6820, Piscataway NJ 08855	732-980-3000	S	7,614*	67.0
3	TLD (USA) Inc—*Antonine Maguin*	812 Bloomfield.Ave, Windsor CT 06095	860-602-3400	R	7,475*	.3
4	Hussmann Corp—*Dennis Gibson*	12999 St Charles Rock, Bridgeton MO 63044	314-291-2000	S	4,623*	8.0
5	York International Corp—*C David Myers*	PO Box 1592, York PA 17405	717-771-7890	S	4,510	23.2
6	Marley-Wylain Co—*Christopher J Kearney*	13515 Ballantyne Corpo, Charlotte NC 28277	704-752-4400	S	4,372*	23.8
7	Thermo King Corp—*R Frank Campbell*	314 W 90th St, Minneapolis MN 55420	952-887-2200	S	3,937*	4.2
8	Carrier Corp—*Geraud Darnis*	1 Carrier Pl, Farmington CT 06032		S	3,852*	4.3
9	Lennox International Inc—*Todd M Bluedorn*	2140 Lake Park Blvd, Richardson TX 75080	972-497-5000	P	3,304	12.4
10	Goodman Global Inc—*David L Swift*	2550 North Loop W Ste, Houston TX 77092	713-861-2500	S	1,795	4.9
11	DRS Sustainment Systems Inc—*Mark S Newman*	201 Evans Ln, Saint Louis MO 63121	314-553-4000	S	1,736*	5.7
12	Formtek Inc (Westfield Massachusetts)—*John E Reed* Mestek Inc	260 N Elm St, Westfield MA 01085	413-568-9571	S	1,530*	2.6
13	Kysor Warren Corp—*Jim Laycock*	5201 Transport Blvd, Columbus GA 31907	706-568-1514	S	1,245	7.2
14	Pace Industries Inc—*N Yamahuchi*	405 Lexington Ave, New York NY 10174	212-916-8199	R	1,100	5.0
15	Rheem Manufacturing Co—*JR Jones*	1100 Abernathy Rd Ste, Atlanta GA 30328	770-351-3000	S	1,000*	5.0
16	Tecumseh Products Co—*Jim Wainright*	1136 Oak Valley Dr, Ann Arbor MI 48108	734-585-9500	P	934	8.6
17	McQuay International—*Michael Schwartz*	13600 Industrial Park, Minneapolis MN 55441	763-553-5330	S	838*	5.0
18	Middleby Corp—*Selim A Bassoul*	1400 Toastmaster Dr, Elgin IL 60120	847-741-3300	P	719	2.1
19	Standex International Corp—*Roger L Fix*	11 Keewaydin Dr, Salem NH 03079	603-893-9701	P	634	4.0
20	International Comfort Products Carrier Corp	PO Box 128, Lewisburg TN 37091		S	571*	2.4
21	Beverage-Air Corp—*Philippo Berti*	3779 Champion Blvd, Winston-Salem NC 27105	336-245-6400	D	504*	.7
22	Hill Phoenix Inc—*Ralph Coppola*	1003 Sigman Rd, Conyers GA 30013	770-285-3264	S	494*	.6
23	Lan-Leasing Inc—*Chris Hughes* Lancer Corp	6655 Lancer Blvd, San Antonio TX 78219	210-310-7000	S	386*	.7
24	Mestek Inc—*John E Reed*	260 N Elm St, Westfield MA 01085	413-568-9571	R	372*	2.6
25	Michigan Automotive Compressor Inc—*Yuji Ishizaki*	2400 N Dearing Rd, Parma MI 49269	517-622-7000	R	348*	.6
26	Mammoth Inc—*David J Huntley*	13200 Pioneer Trail St, Eden Prairie MN 55347	952-358-6600	S	299*	.4
27	AAON Inc—*Norman H Asbjornson*	2425 S Yukon Ave, Tulsa OK 74107	918-583-2266	P	245	1.4
28	Leer Inc—*Patrick Albregts*	PO Box 206, New Lisbon WI 53950	608-562-3161	S	201*	.2
29	Heatcraft Inc—*Rudy Hartanto* Lennox International Inc	2175 W Park Pl Blvd, Stone Mountain GA 30087	770-465-5600	S	200*	1.0
30	AEC Inc—*Thomas Breslin*	1100 E Wdfield Rd Ste, Schaumburg IL 60173	630-595-1060	S	200*	.8
31	Krack Corp	1300 N Arlington Heigh, Itasca IL 60143	630-629-7500	S	199*	.3
32	Williams Furnace Co	250 W Laurel St, Colton CA 92324	909-825-0993	S	187*	.2
33	Carrier Refrigeration—*Geraud Darnis* Carrier Corp	1 Carrier Pl, Farmington CT 06034	860-674-3000	D	175*	.3
34	American Combustion Industries Inc—*Tim Curlin*	3520 Bladensburg Rd, Brentwood MD 20722	301-779-3400	R	173*	.2
35	Russell—*Earl Adams*	221 S Berry St, Brea CA 92821	714-529-1935	S	160	1.2
36	Lancer Corp—*Christopher D Hughes*	PO Box 131425, San Antonio TX 78219	210-310-7000	R	157*	1.5
37	International Cold Storage Co—*Kevin Larkey* Carrier Corp	215 E 13th, Andover KS 67002	316-733-4088	S	125*	.2
38	Sanden Of America Inc—*Kazuhiko Arai*	601 Sanden Blvd, Wylie TX 75098	972-442-8400	R	122*	2.0
39	Federal Industries—*John Minahan* Standex International Corp	215 Federal Ave, Belleville WI 53508		D	113*	.2
40	A-1 Components Inc	PO Box 1325, O Fallon MO 63366		R	105*	.4
41	Enviro Systems Inc—*Craig Froelich*	12037 N Hwy 99, Seminole OK 74868	405-382-0731	R	96*	.1
42	Lennox Industries Inc (Stuttgart Arkansas)—*Todd M Bluedorn*	PO Box 799900, Dallas TX 75379	972-497-5000	D	92*	1.0
43	U S Natural Resources Inc Friedrich Air Conditioning Div—*Richard Ward*	8000 NE Pkwy Dr Ste 10, Vancouver WA 98662	360-892-2650	R	84*	.8
44	JB Industries Inc—*Jeff Cherif*	PO Box 1180, Aurora IL 60507	630-851-9444	R	84*	.1
45	Airxcel Inc—*Melvin Adams*	PO Box 4020, Wichita KS 67204	316-832-3400	R	79*	.9
46	Allied Air Enterprises—*Robert E Schjerven* Lennox International Inc	215 Metropolitan Dr, West Columbia SC 29170	803-738-4000	S	77*	.4
47	Ware Inc—*Richard Ware*	4005 Produce Rd, Louisville KY 40218	502-968-2211	R	74*	.1
48	Scotsman Ice Systems—*Mark McClanahan* Manitowoc Foodservice	775 Corporate Woods Pk, Vernon Hills IL 60061	847-215-4500	S	71*	.1
49	Climate Master Inc—*Steve Golsen*	7300 SW 44th St, Oklahoma City OK 73179	405-745-6000	S	70*	.4
50	Manitowoc Ice Inc—*Lee Wichlacz*	PO Box 1720, Manitowoc WI 54221	920-682-0161	S	64*	.3
51	Water Services of America Inc	2018 S 1st St, Milwaukee WI 53207	414-481-4120	R	61*	.2
52	Cryoquip Inc—*Ross Brown*	25720 Jefferson Ave, Murrieta CA 92562	951-677-2060	R	60*	.1
53	Gateway Industrial Power Inc—*John Wagner*	921 Fournie Ln, Collinsville IL 62234	618-345-0123	R	58*	.1
54	Energy Labs Inc—*Reza Irani*	9651 Airway Rd Ste E, San Diego CA 92154	619-671-0100	R	56*	.6
55	Rae Corp—*Eric Swank*	PO Box 1206, Pryor OK 74362	918-825-7222	R	50*	.3
56	True Manufacturing Company Inc—*Steven Trulaske*	2001 E Terra Ln, O Fallon MO 63366	636-240-2400	R	48*	.5
57	Johnson Truck Bodies Inc—*Ron Ricci*	215 E Allen St, Rice Lake WI 54868	715-234-7071	S	48*	.3
58	Micro Matic USA Inc—*Peter Muzzonigro*	19791 Bahama St, Northridge CA 91324	818-882-8012	R	47*	.1
59	Vilter Manufacturing LLC—*Ron Prebish*	PO Box 8904, Cudahy WI 53110	414-744-0111	R	46*	.3
60	Danfoss LLC—*Lawrence Pairitz*	11655 Crossroads Cir, Baltimore MD 21220	410-931-8250	R	44*	.5
61	Nor-Lake Inc—*Charles Dullea*	727 2nd St, Hudson WI 54016	715-386-2323	R	43*	.3
62	Gea Fes Inc—*John Ansbro*	PO Box 2306, York PA 17405	717-767-6411	R	43*	.3
63	Kolpak Inc—*Gary Hainley* Manitowoc Foodservice	2915 Tennessee Ave, Parsons TN 38363	731-847-5328	S	42*	.2
64	Bally Refrigerated Boxes Inc—*Michael Coyle*	135 Little Nine Rd, Morehead City NC 28557	252-240-2829	R	42*	.2
65	Kysor Panel Systems Inc—*David Frase* Scotsman Ice Systems	PO Box 14248, Fort Worth TX 76117	817-281-5121	S	41*	.2
66	ATCO Products Inc—*John Clarke*	PO Box 430, Ferris TX 75125	989-463-9200	S	41*	.2
67	Airtex Manufacturing LLP—*Robert Gregory*	PO Box 650, De Soto KS 66018	913-583-3181	R	40*	.3

Rank	Company Name—*Executive Officer*	Address, City, State, Zip	Phone	Type	Fin	Empls
68	Modine Climate Systems Inc—*Thomas A Burke*	1500 DeKoven Ave, Racine WI 53403	262-636-1200	D	39*	.2
69	Ice-O-Matic—*Kevin Fink* Manitowoc Foodservice	11100 E 45th Ave, Denver CO 80239	303-371-3737	S	36*	.2
70	Farnam Custom Products—*Neil Farnam*	PO Box 1377, Arden NC 28704	828-684-3766	S	36*	.1
71	Dyne Duro Corp—*Randall Hinden*	PO Box 9117, Bay Shore NY 11706	631-249-9000	R	36*	.2
72	Marlow Industries Inc—*Barry Nickerson*	10451 Vista Park Rd, Dallas TX 75238	214-340-4900	S	34	.2
73	Trans/Air Manufacturing Corp—*James Prock*	PO Box 70, Dallastown PA 17313	717-246-2627	R	34*	.2
74	Zero Zone Inc—*Jack Van Der Ploeg*	110 N Oakridge Dr, North Prairie WI 53153		R	32*	.2
75	Hdt Ep Inc—*Vince Nardy*	5455 N River Rd W, Geneva OH 44041	440-466-6640	R	31*	.2
76	Dial Manufacturing Inc—*Duane Johnston*	25 S 51st Ave, Phoenix AZ 85043	602-278-1100	R	31*	<.1
77	Governair Corp—*George Halko*	4841 N Sewell, Oklahoma City OK 73118	405-525-6546	S	31*	.2
78	Alma Products Co—*Alan Galtan*	2000 Michigan Ave, Alma MI 48801	989-463-1151	R	30*	.2
79	Bcll Inc—*Pat Mcmahon*	PO Box 478, Keosauqua IA 52565	319-293-3777	R	30*	.5
80	Dimplex Thermal Solutions—*Ola Wettergren*	2625 Emerald Dr, Kalamazoo MI 49001	269-349-6800	D	30	.2
81	Afe Victory Inc—*Richard Babboni*	110 Woodcrest Rd, Cherry Hill NJ 08003	856-428-4200	R	30*	.1
82	Warren Technology Inc—*Winfield Kelley*	PO Box 5347, Hialeah FL 33014	305-556-6933	R	30*	.2
83	Frigid Coil/Frick Inc York International Corp	13711 Freeway Dr, Santa Fe Springs CA 90670	815-288-3859	S	29*	.2
84	Multi-Flow Dispensers LP—*Bernard Gottlieb*	1434 County Line Rd, Huntingdon Valley PA 19006	215-322-1800	R	29*	.2
85	DWD International LLC—*Gerald Scott*	PO Box 42026, Houston TX 77242	713-683-8321	R	28*	.1
86	Follett Corp—*Steven Follett*	801 Church Ln, Easton PA 18040	610-252-7301	R	28*	.2
87	Seasons-4 Inc—*Lewis Watford*	4500 Industrial Access, Douglasville GA 30134	770-489-0716	R	27*	.2
88	Huntair Inc—*Dave Benson*	11555 Sw Myslony St, Tualatin OR 97062	503-639-0113	R	26*	.3
89	Koch Filter Corp—*David Cook*	625 W Hill St, Louisville KY 40208	502-634-4796	R	26*	.2
90	Carrier Transicold AC Industries—*Geraud Darnis* Carrier Corp	715 Willow Springs Ln, York PA 17406	717-767-6531	D	26	.1
91	Behr Climate Systems Inc—*Hans-Joachim Lange*	5020 Augusta Dr, Fort Worth TX 76106	817-624-7273	R	26*	.4
92	International Environmental Corp—*Dennis Kloster*	PO Box 2598, Oklahoma City OK 73101	405-605-5000	S	25*	.5
93	Kairak Innovation Inc—*Mark Curran*	500 S State College Bl, Fullerton CA 92831	714-870-8661	R	24*	.1
94	Sealed Unit Parts Company Inc—*Chris Mancuso*	PO Box 21, Allenwood NJ 08720	732-223-6644	R	22*	.1
95	Compu-Aire Inc—*Balbir Narang*	8167 Byron Rd, Whittier CA 90606	562-945-8971	R	22*	.1
96	Doucette Industries Inc—*John E Lebo*	20 Leigh Dr, York PA 17406	717-845-8746	R	22*	<.1
97	Cooling and Applied Technology Inc—*Michael Miller*	PO Box 1279, Russellville AR 72811	479-890-3433	R	21*	.2
98	Mid-South Industries Inc—*M Mclaughlin*	PO Box 989, Laurel MS 39441	601-649-4600	R	21*	.2
99	Temp-Air Inc—*Jim Korn*	3700 W Preserve Blvd, Burnsville MN 55337		R	21*	.1
100	PoolPak Inc—*Robert Paley*	PO Box 3331, York PA 17402	717-757-2648	R	21*	.1
101	Great Lakes Air Products Inc—*Patricia Larson*	5861 Commerce Dr, Westland MI 48185	734-326-7080	R	21*	<.1
102	Tomita Electric Corp—*Masaaki Yamanoi*	180 Otay Lakes Rd Ste, Bonita CA 91902	619-470-7790	R	21*	.3
103	Storflex Fixture Corp—*Ralph Santell*	392 Pulteney St, Corning NY 14830	607-962-2137	R	21*	.2
104	Snoke Special Products Company Inc—*W Snoke*	PO Box 1958, Jacksonville TX 75766	903-586-3618	R	20*	.2
105	Danfoss Chatleff LLC—*Jennifer Hill*	PO Box 1350, Buda TX 78610	512-295-2217	R	20*	.2
106	Advanced Aerospace—*Steve Flowers*	10781 Forbes Ave, Garden Grove CA 92843	714-265-6200	R	19*	.2
107	Recreational Vehicle Products Inc—*Gregg Guinn*	PO Box 4020, Wichita KS 67204	316-832-3400	R	19*	.2
108	Amerikooler Inc—*Renato Alonso*	575 E 10th Ave, Hialeah FL 33010	305-884-8384	R	18*	.1
109	ProAir LLC—*Dennis Mitchell*	28731 County Rd 6, Elkhart IN 46514	574-264-5494	R	18*	.1
110	Kooltronic Inc—*Anne Freedman*	30 Pennington Hopewell, Pennington NJ 08534	609-466-3400	R	17*	.1
111	Imperial Manufacturing Ice Cold Coolers Inc—*Richard Schermerhorn*	2271 Ne 194th Ave, Portland OR 97230	503-665-5539	R	16*	.1
112	Packless Metal Hose Inc—*L Zifferer*	PO Box 20668, Waco TX 76702	254-666-7700	R	16*	.1
113	Whalen Co—*Ronald Wanner*	PO Box 1390, Easton MD 21601	410-822-9200	R	16*	.1
114	American Panel Corp—*Danny Duncan*	5800 SE 78th St, Ocala FL 34472	352-245-7055	R	15*	.1
115	Marc Climatic Controls Inc—*John Kinsel*	PO Box 218309, Houston TX 77218	713-464-8587	R	15*	.1
116	La Rosa Refrigeration and Equipment—*Sebastian Grillo*	19191 Filer, Detroit MI 48234	313-368-6620	R	15*	<.1
117	Harris Environmental Systems Inc—*Alexander Murray*	11 Connector Rd, Andover MA 01810	978-475-0104	R	15*	.1
118	Niagara Blower Co—*Peter Demakos*	673 Ontario St, Buffalo NY 14207	716-875-2000	R	14*	.1
119	Ellis and Watts International LLC—*David Dirksen*	4400 Glen Willow Lake, Batavia OH 45103	513-752-9000	R	14*	.1
120	General Filters Inc—*John Redner*	43800 Grand River Ave, Novi MI 48375	248-476-5100	R	13*	.1
121	FMC Foodtech Northfield—*Charles Cannon*	1700 Cannon Rd, Northfield MN 55057	507-645-9546	D	13*	.1
122	Miyama USA Inc—*Mark Koeberlein*	7081 International Dr, Louisville KY 40258	502-933-4100	R	13*	.1
123	Food Warming Equipment Company Inc—*Deron Lichte*	PO Box 1001, Crystal Lake IL 60039	815-459-7500	R	13*	.1
124	Arctic Industries Inc—*Donald Goodstein*	9731 Nw 114th Way, Medley FL 33178	305-883-5581	R	13*	.1
125	Poolpak International—*Robert Paley*	3491 Industrial Hwy, York PA 17402	717-757-2648	R	12*	.1
126	United Coolair Corp—*Neil Tucker*	PO Box 5085, York PA 17405	717-843-4311	R	12*	.1
127	Rapid Engineering LLC—*Robert Long*	1100 7 Mile Rd Nw, Comstock Park MI 49321	616-784-0500	R	12*	.1
128	Mee Industries Inc—*Thomas Mee*	16021 Adelante St, Irwindale CA 91702	626-359-4550	R	12*	.1
129	Airtherm LLC—*MP O'Rourke* Mestek Inc	260 N Elm St, Westfield MA 01085	413-568-9571	D	12*	.1
130	R-Cold Inc—*Michael Mulcahy*	5060 Eucalyptus Ave, Chino CA 91710	909-517-1877	R	12*	.1
131	Vintage Air Inc—*Jack Chisenhall*	18865 Goll St, San Antonio TX 78266	210-654-7171	R	12*	.1
132	Tmp Manufacturing Company Inc—*William Carr*	PO Box 269, Hyde PA 16843	814-765-9615	R	11*	.1
133	Concepts And Designs Inc—*Tom Peterson*	PO Box 288, Owatonna MN 55060	507-451-2198	R	11*	.1
134	Thermo Products LLC—*Dale Bowman*	PO Box 217, North Judson IN 46366	574-896-2133	R	11*	.1
135	Diversified Heat Transfer Inc—*Norman Goldberg*	1710 Flushing Ave Ste, Ridgewood NY 11385	718-386-6666	R	10*	.1
136	Penn Refrigeration Service Corp—*Albert Finarelli*	PO Box 1261, Wilkes Barre PA 18703	570-825-5666	R	10*	.1
137	Weather-Rite LLC—*Darryl Wicklund*	616 N 5th St, Minneapolis MN 55401	612-338-1401	R	10*	.1
138	Banner Equipment Co—*James Groh*	1370 Bungalow Rd, Morris IL 60450	815-941-9600	R	10*	<.1
139	Lintern Corp—*Richard Lintern*	PO Box 90, Mentor OH 44061	440-255-9333	R	10*	<.1
140	Budzar Industries Inc—*David Young*	38241 Willoughby Pkwy, Willoughby OH 44094	440-918-0505	R	9*	.1
141	Bankcrafters Inc—*Daniel Bernheim*	12 E Oregon Ave, Philadelphia PA 19148	215-467-3700	R	9*	.1
142	AirPro Holdings Inc—*Arnie Gartman*	3918 US Hwy 80 E, Mesquite TX 75149	972-288-8888	R	9*	.1
143	Dole Refrigerating Cos—*John Cook*	1420 Higgs Rd, Lewisburg TN 37091	931-359-6211	R	9*	<.1
144	Ultra-Cool Corp—*Cleon Merrill*	1901 Bell Ave Ste 2, Des Moines IA 50315	515-243-7509	R	9*	.1
145	Carroll Coolers Inc—*Steve Dolezel*	PO Box 671, Carroll IA 51401	712-792-6834	R	8*	.1
146	Hartford Compressors Inc—*Jeff Albright*	179 S St, West Hartford CT 06110	860-249-8671	R	8*	<.1
147	McQuay of Georgia LLP—*Fred Ashby* McQuay International	2660 Holcomb Bridge Rd, Alpharetta GA 30022	770-674-9100	S	8*	<.1
148	Kimre Inc—*Micheal Simons*	PO Box 571240, Miami FL 33257	305-233-4249	R	8*	<.1
149	Insource Tech Inc—*Ken Manz*	12124 Rd 111, Paulding OH 45879	419-399-3600	R	8*	<.1
150	Haakon Industries Inc—*Robert Hole*	1633 W 1st St, Cheney WA 99004	509-235-6801	R	8*	.1
151	First Call Installation—*Alan Sanchez*	13150 S Clckamas River, Oregon City OR 97045	503-557-0230	R	7*	.1

Note: An asterisk (*) indicates an estimated financial figure. The company type code used is as follows: R = Private, P = Public, S = Private Subsidiary, B = Public Subsidiary, D = Division, J = Joint Venture, I = Investment Fund.

COMPANY RANKINGS BY SALES WITHIN 4-DIGIT SIC

Rank	Company Name—Executive Officer	Address, City, State, Zip	Phone	Type	Fin	Empls
152	Heat Controller Inc—Don Peck	1900 Wellworth Ave, Jackson MI 49203	517-787-2100	R	7*	.1
153	Three Star Refrigeration Engineering Inc—James Pak	21720 S Wilmington Ave, Long Beach CA 90810	310-851-8901	R	7*	.1
154	Contract Manufacturers Inc—Robert Burch	PO Box 2034, Tyler TX 75710	903-597-8297	R	7*	<.1
155	Demartino Fixture Company Inc—Dominick Demartino	920 S Colony Rd, Wallingford CT 06492	203-269-3971	R	7*	<.1
156	Electro Impulse Laboratory Inc—Mark Rubin	PO Box 278, Neptune NJ 07754	732-776-5800	R	7*	<.1
157	Seaward Products Corp—Frank Butler	3721 Capitol Ave, City Of Industry CA 90601	562-699-7997	R	7*	.1
158	Air Engineers Inc—John Kinsel	PO Box 218309, Houston TX 77218	281-492-1786	R	7*	<.1
159	Titan Air Inc—Gregory Hageness	PO Box 717, Osseo WI 54758	715-597-2050	R	6*	<.1
160	Maine Market Refrigeration LLC	98 Morris Springer Rd, Fayette ME 04349	207-685-3504	R	6*	<.1
161	Bry-Air Inc—Mel Meyers	10793 E State Rte 37, Sunbury OH 43074	740-965-2974	R	6*	<.1
162	Salof Refrigeration Company Inc—George Salof	5141 Ih 35 S, New Braunfels TX 78132	830-625-1613	R	6*	<.1
163	Filtrine Manufacturing Co	15 Kit St, Keene NH 03431	603-352-5500	R	6*	.1
164	Colmac Coil Manufacturing Inc—Bruce Nelson	PO Box 571, Colville WA 99114	509-684-2595	R	6*	.1
165	Nance International Inc—R Nance	PO Box 1547, Beaumont TX 77704	409-838-6127	R	6*	<.1
166	Advanced Beverage Solutions Inc—Patrick Titreny	100 N Gary Ste C, Roselle IL 60172		R	6*	<.1
167	Terra Innova Investments Inc—Matt Pearson	158 W 4640 S, Salt Lake City UT 84107	801-269-1530	R	6*	<.1
168	Bassamaire Sales LLC—Hugh Baxley	26881 Cannon Rd, Cleveland OH 44146	440-439-1200	R	6*	<.1
169	Fisen Corp—Chris Beggs	6871 Dtton IndustrialP, Caledonia MI 49316	616-698-7279	R	6*	<.1
170	S and S Refrigeration Corp—Michael Williams	9435 Sorensen Ave, Santa Fe Springs CA 90670	562-944-1969	R	6*	<.1
171	Chudnow Manufacturing Company Inc—Richard Cohen	PO Box 10, Oceanside NY 11572	516-593-4222	R	5*	<.1
172	Mc Cormack Manufacturing Company Inc—Gary Montgomery	PO Box 1727, Lake Oswego OR 97035	503-639-2137	R	5*	<.1
173	Hydro - Temperature Corp—Mike Jones	PO Box 566, Pocahontas AR 72455	870-892-8343	R	5*	<.1
174	American Insulated Panel Company Inc—John Lynch	75 John Hancock Rd, Taunton MA 02780	508-823-7003	R	5*	<.1
175	Louisville Cooler Manufacturing Co—James Kinser	7635 National Tpke Ste, Louisville KY 40214	502-363-1692	R	5*	<.1
176	Five Star Manufacturing Co—F Kjellgren	1004 Central Ave W, Springfield TN 37172	615-382-5099	R	5*	.1
177	Crown Acquisition LLC—Dave O'neil	1224 S Main St, Bluffton IN 46714	260-824-2630	R	5*	<.1
178	Jls Building Services LLC	PO Box 1846, Chillicothe OH 45601	740-779-2019	R	5*	<.1
179	Alton/Aztec—William Coad Mestek Inc	4830 Transport Dr, Dallas TX 75247	214-638-6010	D	5*	<.1
180	Kdindustries Inc—Leonard Kosar	1525 E Lake Rd, Erie PA 16511	814-453-6761	R	5*	<.1
181	PS Acquisition Company Corp—Phillip Smith	3317 Durham Dr, Raleigh NC 27603	919-772-8820	R	5*	<.1
182	H A Phillips and Co—Michael Ryan	1612 Louise Dr, South Elgin IL 60177	847-289-0050	R	5*	<.1
183	Eic Solutions Inc—Bruce Blackway	1825 Stout Dr, Warminster PA 18974	215-443-5190	R	5*	<.1
184	C Nelson Manufacturing Co—Kelly Smith	265 N Lake Winds Pkwy, Oak Harbor OH 43449	419-898-3305	R	5*	<.1
185	Powers Equipment Company Inc—Bruce Powers	105 Steamboat Dr, Warminster PA 18974	215-675-9220	R	5*	<.1
186	B and D Manufacturing Inc—Dallas Warnke	901 9th St, Scranton IA 51462	712-652-3424	R	4*	<.1
187	Vista Solutions Inc—Peggy Thodos	281 Keyes Ave, Hampshire IL 60140	847-683-1205	R	4*	<.1
188	Karma Inc—Jim Pound	PO Box 433, Watertown WI 53094	920-261-1424	R	4*	<.1
189	Flinn and Dreffein Engineering Co—J Balaz	3520 Commercial Ave, Northbrook IL 60062	847-272-6370	R	4*	<.1
190	Cospolich Inc—Mark Whitfield	PO Box 1206, Destrehan LA 70047	985-725-0222	R	4*	.1
191	Klinge Corp—Henrich Klinge	4075 E Market St, York PA 17402	717-840-4500	R	4*	<.1
192	Tisdale Air Conditioning and Heating Co—Lloyd Tisdale	PO Box 2728, Conroe TX 77305	936-856-1500	R	4*	<.1
193	Pure Humidifier Co—Willard Martin	141 Jonathan Blvd N, Chaska MN 55318	952-368-9335	R	4*	<.1
194	Coil Company Inc—Thomas Jacobs	3223 Phoenixville Pke, Malvern PA 19355	610-251-0257	R	4*	<.1
195	Cps Products Inc—Ed Jeffers	1010 E 31st St, Hialeah FL 33013	305-835-2832	R	4*	<.1
196	Artic-Temperature Inc—Calvin Gatlin	2015 W Main, Prague OK 74864	405-567-1960	R	4*	<.1
197	Danhard Inc—Gerhard Dankowski	3839 Dilido Rd, Dallas TX 75228	214-328-8541	R	4*	<.1
198	California Controlled Atmosphere—Ray Kliewer	39138 Rd 56, Dinuba CA 93618	559-591-8874	R	4*	<.1
199	Annex Manufacturing LLC	15 Depew Ave, Lyons NY 14489	315-946-0100	R	4*	<.1
200	Hydro-Thrift Corp—T Heston	PO Box 1037, Massillon OH 44648	330-837-5141	R	4*	<.1
201	Advance Energy Technologies Inc—David O'hanlon	1 Solar Dr, Clifton Park NY 12065	518-371-2140	R	4*	<.1
202	Cooling Technology Inc—Pratap Oza	PO Box 560369, Charlotte NC 28256	704-596-4109	R	4*	<.1
203	Turbo Refrigeration LLC—E Beard	PO Box 396, Denton TX 76202	940-387-4301	R	4*	<.1
204	Pioneer Air Systems Inc—Sam Basseen	210 Flat Fork Rd, Wartburg TN 37887	423-346-6693	R	4*	<.1
205	Arctic Star Refrigeration Manufacturing Co—James Dunnagan	3540 W Pioneer Pkwy, Pantego TX 76013	817-274-1396	R	4*	<.1
206	Hartwell Corp—John Gouveia	4210 N Sullinger Ave, Tucson AZ 85705	520-888-1100	R	4*	<.1
207	Mainstream Engineering Corp—Robert Scaringe	200 Yellow Pl, Rockledge FL 32955	321-631-3550	R	4*	<.1
208	Mgr Equipment Corp—Gerald Ross	22 Gates Ave, Inwood NY 11096	516-239-3030	R	3*	<.1
209	Loop Tech International Ltd—Ralph Cadwallader	2928 State Hwy 19, Huntsville TX 77320	936-295-7038	R	3*	<.1
210	Custom Coolers LLC—Beth Hines	5609 Azle Ave, Fort Worth TX 76114	817-626-3737	R	3*	<.1
211	Air/Tak Inc—Donald Burk	107 W Main St, Worthington PA 16262	724-297-3416	R	3*	<.1
212	200 Park Inc—Pat Occhicone	PO Box 717, Newberry SC 29108	803-321-1891	R	3*	<.1
213	Marc Refrigeration Manufacturing Inc—Hyman Widelitz	7453 Nw 32nd Ave, Miami FL 33147	305-691-0500	R	3*	<.1
214	Holiday Ice Inc—Ray Armstrong	PO Box 520606, Longwood FL 32752	407-831-2077	R	3*	<.1
215	Perfection Equipment Inc—Sanford Hahn	4259 Lee Ave, Gurnee IL 60031	847-244-7200	R	3*	<.1
216	Klimaire Products Inc—Iltekin Korkmaz	7909 Nw 54th St, Doral FL 33166	305-593-8358	R	3*	<.1
217	Southern Stainless Equipment—Larry Rouse	1400 Hopeman Pkwy, Waynesboro VA 22980	540-943-8000	D	3*	.1
218	Redi Controls Inc—Dan Albertson	755 E Main St, Greenwood IN 46143	317-865-4130	R	3*	<.1
219	American Environ Inc—Robert Powell	PO Box 560744, Dallas TX 75356	214-634-1744	R	3*	<.1
220	Aircorps Inc—Kieth Steiner	3300 Airport Rd, Boulder CO 80301	303-440-4075	R	3*	<.1
221	Texas Furnace LLC—Michael Barbhouse	PO Box 40008, Houston TX 77240	713-466-1504	R	3*	<.1
222	Mermaid Manufacturing Of Southwest Florida Inc—William Banfield	2651 Park Windsor Dr S, Fort Myers FL 33901	239-418-0535	R	3*	<.1
223	Combustion Research Corp—Winifred Johnson	2516 Leach Rd, Rochester Hills MI 48309	248-852-3611	R	3*	<.1
224	Southeast Cooler Corp—Steve Krieger	1520 Westfork Dr Ste H, Lithia Springs GA 30122	770-941-6703	R	3*	<.1
225	Banner Engineering and Sales Inc—Joseph Day	PO Box 1372, Saginaw MI 48605	989-755-0583	R	3*	<.1
226	Haskris Company Inc—Daniel Falotico	100 Kelly St, Elk Grove Village IL 60007	847-956-6420	R	3*	<.1
227	Forma-Kool Manufacturing Inc—Andrew Tassopoulos	46880 Continental Dr, Chesterfield MI 48047	586-949-4813	R	3*	<.1
228	Transit Air Inc—Dhruv Sharma	27 Bank St, Hornell NY 14843	607-324-7860	R	3*	<.1
229	Custom Controls Co—Timothy Rodwell	PO Box 16668, Houston TX 77222	713-666-3258	R	3*	<.1
230	Tithe Corp—Lisa Ambrose	1809 Bayard St, Baltimore MD 21230	410-625-7545	R	3*	<.1
231	Adams Manufacturing Co—Marty Schonberger	9545 Granger Rd, Cleveland OH 44125	216-587-6801	R	3*	<.1
232	Scientemp Corp—Howard Tenniswood	3565 S Adrian Hwy, Adrian MI 49221	517-263-6020	R	3*	<.1
233	Mydax Inc—Richard Frankel	12260 Shale Ridge Ln S, Auburn CA 95602	530-888-6662	R	3*	<.1
234	Air Solutions Heating And Cooling Inc—Billy Quillen	4725 Hwy Ave, Jacksonville FL 32254	904-221-2704	R	2*	<.1
235	Refrigeration Engineered Systems Inc—Juan Hernandez	7215 Nw 36th Ave, Miami FL 33147	305-836-6900	R	2*	<.1
236	Transarctic Of North Carolina Inc—Michael Marlin	5270 Glenola Industria, High Point NC 27263	336-861-6116	R	2*	<.1
237	Sticker Corp—Douglas Reighart	37877 Elm St, Willoughby OH 44094	440-946-2100	R	2*	<.1
238	American Moistening Company Inc—James Alexander	PO Box 1066, Pineville NC 28134	704-889-7281	R	2*	<.1
239	Davidon Industries Inc—Donald Dinuccio	205 Hallene Rd Unit 31, Warwick RI 02886	401-737-8380	R	2*	<.1

Rank	Company Name—*Executive Officer*	Address, City, State, Zip	Phone	Type	Fin	Empls
240	James D Nall Company Inc—*James Nall*	1050 E 9th St, Hialeah FL 33010	305-884-8363	R	2*	<.1
241	Layton Manufacturing Corp—*Steve Layton*	864 E 52nd St, Brooklyn NY 11203	347-663-9043	R	2*	<.1
242	Coldvault LLC—*Ryan Kuehne*	PO Box 1690, Henderson TX 75653	903-657-2377	R	2*	<.1
243	Fire From Ice Ventures LLC—*Brain Tomazic*	7555 Tyler Blvd Ste 7, Mentor OH 44060	440-946-2700	R	1*	<.1
244	Buenger Enterprises—*F Buenger*	PO Box 5286, Oxnard CA 93031	805-985-5828	R	1*	<.1
245	Dienes Apparatus Inc—*Dan Miller*	PO Box 549, Pineville NC 28134	704-525-3770	R	1*	<.1
246	Air Water International Corp—*Michael J Zwebner*	407 Lincoln Rd Ste 304, Miami FL 33139	305-672-6344	R	1	<.1
247	Biloff Manufacturing Company Inc—*Arlis Biloff*	PO Box 206, New Lisbon WI 53950	661-746-3976	R	1*	<.1
248	Brainerd Compressor Rebuilders Inc—*James Barton*	3034 Sandbrook St, Memphis TN 38116	901-396-4051	R	1*	<.1
249	American Hydrotherm Corp—*Rajat Shah*	1103 Drummond Office P, Newark DE 19711		R	1*	<.1
250	OPM Services Inc—*Kent Oyler*	657 S Hurstbourne Pkwy, Louisville KY 40222	502-499-1126	R	1*	<.1
251	Ztech—*Michael Kuhlmann*	11460 Sunrise Gold Cir, Rancho Cordova CA 95742	916-635-7484	R	1*	<.1
252	Wag Corp—*John Denton*	386 Hwy 6 W, Tupelo MS 38801	662-844-8478	R	1*	<.1
253	Oz Technology Inc—*Gary Lindgren*	509 E 14th Ave, Post Falls ID 83854	208-687-7000	R	1*	<.1
254	Bepco Inc—*Steve Winters*	PO Box 24159, Winston Salem NC 27114	336-760-0740	R	<1*	<.1
255	Sunroc Corp—*Anthony Salamone*	60 Starlifter Ave, Dover DE 19901	302-678-7800	S	<1	.3
256	Trane Inc—*Frederic M Poses*	1 Centennial Ave, Piscataway NJ 08855	732-652-7100	S	N/A	29.0
257	Manitowoc Foodservice—*Jim Weaks*	2227 Welbilt Blvd, New Port Richey FL 34655	727-375-7010	D	N/A	N/A

TOTALS: SIC 3585 Refrigeration & Heating Equipment
Companies: 257 — 86,848 — 264.3

3586 Measuring & Dispensing Pumps

Rank	Company Name—*Executive Officer*	Address, City, State, Zip	Phone	Type	Fin	Empls
1	Liquid Controls LLC—*Andrew K Silvernail*	105 Albrecht Dr, Lake Bluff IL 60044	847-295-1050	S	11,215*	4.2
2	Graco Minnesota Inc—*Patrick J McHale* Graco Inc	PO Box 1441, Minneapolis MN 55440	612-623-6000	S	5,326*	1.8
3	Nordson EFD—*Jeff Pembroke*	40 Catamore Blvd, East Providence RI 02914	401-434-1680	S	972*	.3
4	Graco Inc—*Patrick J McHale*	PO Box 1441, Minneapolis MN 55440	612-623-6000	P	895	2.3
5	Taylor Co (Rockton Illinois)—*Clark Wangaard*	750 N Blackhawk Blvd, Rockton IL 61072	815-624-8333	R	362*	1.0
6	Bulman Products Inc—*Joseph Bullman*	1650 McReynolds NW, Grand Rapids MI 49504	616-363-4416	R	124*	.1
7	Dresser Wayne—*Neil H Thomas*	3814 Jarrett Way, Austin TX 78728	512-388-8311	S	96*	.5
8	Nordson Asymtek—*John P Byers*	2747 Loker Ave W, Carlsbad CA 92010	760-431-1919	S	77*	.4
9	Great Plains Industries Inc—*Grant Nutter*	PO Box 8901, Wichita KS 67208	316-686-7361	R	42*	.3
10	Berg Company LLC—*Jeff Barsness*	PO Box 7065, Madison WI 53707	608-221-4281	R	32*	.5
11	Valco Cincinnati Inc—*Richard Santefort*	PO Box 465619, Cincinnati OH 45246	513-874-6550	R	32*	.2
12	Clayton Corp—*Byron Lapin*	866 Horan Dr, Fenton MO 63026	636-349-5333	R	29*	.2
13	O'Day Equipment Inc—*Jim O'Day*	PO Box 2706, Fargo ND 58108	701-282-9260	R	16*	.1
14	Natural Fuels Company LLC—*Chad Lindholm*	3020 Old Ranch Pkwy, Seal Beach CA 90740	562-493-2804	R	11*	.1
15	Fluid Dynamics Inc	PO Box 576, Lansdale PA 19446	215-699-8700	S	4*	<.1
16	Tucs Equipment Inc—*Marty Tucs*	755 S Old Hwy 18, Princeton MN 55371	763-631-8827	R	3*	<.1
17	Fluid Management Systems Inc—*Hamid Shirkhan*	580 Pleasant St, Watertown MA 02472	781-891-6522	R	3*	<.1
18	HE Anderson Company Inc—*Herbert Anderson*	PO Box 1006, Muskogee OK 74402	918-687-4426	R	3*	<.1
19	Suntec Industries Inc—*Lucient Goldaorto*	PO Box 5000, Glasgow KY 42142	270-651-7116	R	3*	<.1
20	SCA Schucker Company LP—*Dori Blackledge*	46805 Magellan Dr, Novi MI 48077	248-669-3399	R	3*	<.1
21	Sensing Systems Corp—*Laverne Wallace*	PO Box 50180, New Bedford MA 02745	508-992-0872	R	2*	<.1
22	Meters Inc—*Douglas Duncan*	PO Box 2109, Cartersville GA 30120	770-386-0080	R	1*	<.1

TOTALS: SIC 3586 Measuring & Dispensing Pumps
Companies: 22 — 19,249 — 12.0

3589 Service Industry Machinery Nec

Rank	Company Name—*Executive Officer*	Address, City, State, Zip	Phone	Type	Fin	Empls
1	Infilco Degremont Inc—*Shyam Bhan*	PO Box 71390, Richmond VA 23255	804-756-7600	S	10,000	.3
2	Culligan International Co	9399 W Higgins Rd Ste, Rosemont IL 60018	847-430-2800	R	4,469*	5.0
3	Actuant Corp—*Robert C Arzbaecher*	PO Box 3241, Milwaukee WI 53201	262-290-1500	P	1,445	6.2
4	Scott Fetzer Co—*Robert McBride*	28800 Clemens Rd, Westlake OH 44145	440-892-0300	R	935*	14.5
5	Tennant Co—*Chris H Killingstad*	PO Box 1452, Minneapolis MN 55440	763-540-1200	P	754	2.9
6	Hydranautics Inc—*Upen Bharwada*	401 Jones Rd, Oceanside CA 92054	760-901-2500	S	396*	.2
7	Aladdin Temp-Rite LLC—*James Clapper*	250 E Main St, Hendersonville TN 37075	615-537-3600	S	352*	.2
8	US Filter Wheelabrator Corp—*Dave Foster*	1606 Executive Dr, LaGrange GA 30241	706-884-6884	R	307*	.3
9	Pall Life Sciences Div—*Eric Krasnoff*	600 S Wagner Rd, Ann Arbor MI 48103	734-665-0651	S	287*	.3
10	Pure Cycle Corp—*Mark W Harding*	1490 Lafayette St Ste, Denver CO 80218	303-292-3456	P	282	<.1
11	Oreck Corp—*Doug Cahill*	565 Marriott Dr Ste 30, Nashville TN 37214	615-316-5800	R	237*	1.0
12	Jackson MSC Inc	PO Box 1060, Barbourville KY 40906		S	206*	.2
13	Bissell Homecare Inc—*Mark Bissell*	PO Box 3606, Grand Rapids MI 49501	616-453-4451	R	162*	.5
14	Imperial Commercial Cooking Equipment—*Peter Spenuzza*	1128 Sherborn St, Corona CA 92879	951-281-1830	R	137*	.2
15	Ultra Pure Water Technologies Inc—*Daniel LeBlanc*	PO Box 91105, Lafayette LA 70509	337-233-7317	R	132*	1.1
16	Westech Engineering Inc—*Steven Brewster*	3625 S W Temple, Salt Lake City UT 84115	801-265-1000	R	108*	.4
17	Cleaver-Brooks Inc—*P Goggins*	PO Box 421, Milwaukee WI 53201	414-359-0600	R	100*	1.0
18	Shop Vac Corp—*David Grill*	PO Box 3307, Williamsport PA 17701	570-326-0502	R	89*	.5
19	Alto-Shaam Inc—*Karen Hansen*	PO Box 450, Menomonee Falls WI 53052	262-251-3800	R	85*	.3
20	Marathon Equipment Co—*Gordon Shaw*	PO Box 1798, Vernon AL 35592	205-695-9105	S	75*	.6
21	APTwater Inc—*David Stanton*	3333 Vincent Rd Ste 22, Pleasant Hill CA 94523	925-977-1811	R	70*	<.1
22	Pentair Pool Products	10951 W Los Angeles Av, Moorpark CA 93021		D	62*	.3
23	Dayton Water Systems—*Bill Miller*	430 Leo St, Dayton OH 45404	937-461-5900	R	59*	<.1
24	Crest Ultrasonics Inc—*Michael Goodson*	PO Box 7266, Trenton NJ 08628		R	50*	1.0
25	Coffin World Water Systems—*Robert Elders*	1732 McGaw Ave, Irvine CA 92614	949-222-5777	S	47*	<.1
26	Nss Enterprises Inc—*Mark Bevington*	3115 Frenchmens Rd, Toledo OH 43607	419-531-2121	R	47*	.2
27	Ryko Manufacturing Co—*Tom Carleton*	PO Box 38, Grimes IA 50111	515-986-3700	R	45*	.5
28	The Filta Group Inc—*Victor Clewes*	7075 Kingspointe Pkwy, Orlando FL 32819	407-996-5550	R	44*	<.1
29	Clack Corp—*Richard Clack*	4462 Duraform Ln, Windsor WI 53598	608-846-3010	R	43*	.3
30	JV Manufacturing Inc—*Chris Weiser*	PO Box 229, Springdale AR 72765	479-751-7320	R	41*	.2
31	Smith and Loveless Inc—*Frank Rebori*	14040 Santa Fe Trl Dr, Shawnee Mission KS 66215	913-888-5201	R	41*	.3
32	Aquatech International Corp—*VN Sharma*	1 Four Coins Dr, Canonsburg PA 15317	724-746-5300	R	40	.2
33	Polaris Pool Holdings Corp—*Eric Kownacki*	2620 Commerce Way, Vista CA 92081	760-599-9600	R	40*	.3
34	Wolf Range Co—*Brian Harris*	10405 Westlake Dr, Charlotte NC 28273		S	38*	.3
35	ITW DeVilbiss	195 Internationale Blv, Glendale Heights IL 60139		R	38*	<.1
36	Lincoln Food Service Products—*Charlie Kingdon*	1111 North Hadley Rd, Fort Wayne IN 46804	260-459-8200	S	35*	.3
37	Metal Masters Food Service Equipment Company Inc—*Larry McAllister*	100 Industrial Blvd, Clayton DE 19938	302-653-3000	R	34*	.5
38	Minuteman International Inc—*Rudi Gutmann*	111 S Rohlwing Rd, Addison IL 60101	630-627-6900	S	34*	.2
39	Merco/Savory Inc—*Alan Isenogle*	PO Box 1229, Fort Wayne IN 46801	260-459-8200	S	33*	.4

Note: An asterisk (*) indicates an estimated financial figure. The company type code used is as follows: R = Private, P = Public, S = Private Subsidiary, B = Public Subsidiary, D = Division, J = Joint Venture, I = Investment Fund.

COMPANY RANKINGS BY SALES WITHIN 4-DIGIT SIC

Rank	Company Name—*Executive Officer*	Address, City, State, Zip	Phone	Type	Fin	Empls
40	Belanger Inc—*L Belanger*	PO Box 5470, Northville MI 48167	248-349-7010	R	32*	.2
41	Kegel Company Inc—*John Davis*	1951 Longleaf Blvd, Lake Wales FL 33859	863-734-0200	R	32*	.2
42	Powerain Systems Inc—*Stephen Kerr*	1 Enterprise Dr, Tower MN 55790	218-753-5312	R	32*	<.1
43	Advanced Containment Systems Inc—*Phil Dunne*	8720 Lambright Rd, Houston TX 77075	713-987-0336	R	31*	.2
44	United Service Equipment Co—*John Abbott*	869 Seven Oaks Ste 140, Smyrna TN 37167		S	31*	.2
45	Hatco Corp—*David Rolston*	PO Box 340500, Milwaukee WI 53234	414-671-6350	R	30*	.4
46	H and K Dallas Inc—*Nole Coler*	PO Box 180729, Dallas TX 75218	214-821-2740	R	30*	.2
47	Environmental Dynamics Inc—*Randall Chann*	5601 Paris Rd, Columbia MO 65202	573-474-9456	R	30*	.1
48	America Shredding—*Kevin Duncomed*	6565 Smith Ave, Newark CA 94560	510-477-3444	R	30*	.1
49	Advance Food Service Company Inc—*Daniel Schwartz*	200 Heartland Blvd, Edgewood NY 11717	631-242-4800	R	27*	.2
50	Glastender Inc—*Jon Hall*	5400 N Michigan Rd, Saginaw MI 48604	989-752-4275	R	27*	.2
51	Winston Industries LLC—*Ernestine Carpenter*	2345 Carton Dr, Louisville KY 40299	502-495-5400	R	27*	.2
52	Hoffland Environmental Inc—*Robert Hoffland*	10391 Silver Springs R, Conroe TX 77303	936-856-4515	R	27*	<.1
53	Low Temperature Industries Inc—*William Casey*	PO Box 795, Jonesboro GA 30237	770-478-8803	R	27*	.2
54	Food Equipment Technologies Co—*Zbigniew Lassota*	600 Rose Rd, Lake Zurich IL 60047	847-719-3000	R	26*	.2
55	Waste Solutions Group	50 Square Dr Ste 200, Victor NY 14564	585-421-3500	S	26*	.1
56	Meurer Research Inc—*Charles Meurer*	6270 Joyce Dr, Golden CO 80403	303-279-8373	R	26*	<.1
57	Omnipure Filter Company Inc—*Roger Reid*	1904 Industrial Way, Caldwell ID 83605	208-454-2597	R	25*	.2
58	Chemical Methods Associates Inc—*Fred Palmer*	12700 Knott St, Garden Grove CA 92841	714-898-8781	R	25*	.1
59	William R Hague Inc—*Robert Hague*	PO Box 298, Groveport OH 43125	614-836-2115	R	24*	.1
60	Grindmaster Corp—*Micheal Tinsley*	PO Box 35020, Louisville KY 40232	502-425-4776	R	24*	.3
61	Farley Group Inc—*John Daley*	4550 Jackson St, Denver CO 80216	303-355-3566	R	24*	.1
62	Watts Premier Inc—*Patrick S O'Keefe*	8716 W Ludlow Dr Ste 1, Peoria AZ 85381	480-675-7995	S	24*	<.1
63	Ashbrook Simon-Hartley Operations LP—*Robert Williams*	PO Box 974343, Dallas TX 75397	281-449-0322	R	23*	.2
64	Cloud Company Inc—*Greg Boege*	4120 A Horizon Ln, San Luis Obispo CA 93401	805-549-8093	R	23*	<.1
65	Thorne Electric Co—*Kim Thorne*	PO Box 321, Wheaton IL 60189	630-668-4853	R	23*	<.1
66	JE Grote Company Inc—*Bob Grote*	1160 Gahanna Pkwy, Columbus OH 43230	614-868-8414	R	22*	.2
67	R-V Industries Inc	584 Poplar Rd, Honey Brook PA 19344	610-273-2457	R	22*	.3
68	Mechanical Equipment Company Inc—*George Gsell*	13189 Hwy 190, Covington LA 70433	985-249-5500	R	21*	.2
69	Dri-Eaz Products Inc—*William Bruders*	15180 Josh Wilson Rd, Burlington WA 98233	360-757-7776	R	20*	.1
70	Komar Industries Inc—*Larry Koenig*	4425 Marketing Pl, Groveport OH 43125	614-836-2366	R	19*	.1
71	W Hall Ford Co—*Ford Hall*	PO Box 2110, Richmond KY 40476	859-624-1077	R	18*	<.1
72	New Aqua LLC—*Gail Mason*	7785 E Us Hwy 36, Avon IN 46123	317-272-3000	R	17*	.1
73	H-O-H Water Technology Inc—*Thomas Hutchison*	PO Box 487, Palatine IL 60078	847-358-7400	R	17*	.1
74	Marlo Incorporated Of Racine Wisconsin—*Michael Glines*	PO Box 44170, Racine WI 53404	262-681-1300	R	17*	.1
75	Montague Co—*Thomas Whalen*	PO Box 4954, Hayward CA 94540	510-785-8822	R	17*	.1
76	D and S Car Wash Equipment Co—*Jon Jansky*	4200 Brandi Ln, High Ridge MO 63049	636-677-3442	R	16*	.1
77	Schlueter Co—*Bradley Losching*	PO Box 548, Janesville WI 53547	608-755-5444	R	16*	<.1
78	Ginsan Industries Inc—*Sigrid Valk*	3611 3 Mile Rd Nw, Grand Rapids MI 49534	616-791-8100	R	15*	.1
79	Auto Butler Inc—*Keith Schleeter*	4701 Humboldt Ave N, Minneapolis MN 55430	612-529-3345	R	15*	.1
80	Galesburg Manufacturing Co—*Steve Apsey*	PO Box 710, Galesburg IL 61402	309-342-3173	R	15*	.1
81	Von Schrader Co—*Earnie Middleton*	1600 Junction Ave, Racine WI 53403	262-634-1956	R	15*	.1
82	Project Services Group Inc—*Mark Boswell*	911 Maryland Dr, Irving TX 75061	972-812-7370	R	15*	.1
83	Selecto Inc—*Ehud Levy*	3980 Lakefield Ct, Suwanee GA 30024	678-475-0799	R	15*	.1
84	Aquafine Corp—*Michael Murphy*	29010 Ave Paine, Valencia CA 91355	661-257-4770	R	15*	.1
85	Harmsco Inc—*Harold Harms*	PO Box 14066, North Palm Beach FL 33408	561-848-9628	R	14*	.1
86	Schreiber LLC—*Fred Dew*	100 Schreiber Dr, Trussville AL 35173	205-655-7466	R	14*	.1
87	J F Duncan Industries Inc—*Johnny Wong*	9301 Stewart And Gray, Downey CA 90241	562-862-4269	R	14*	.1
88	Proteam Inc—*Matthew Wood*	PO Box 7385, Boise ID 83707	208-377-9555	R	14*	.1
89	Server Products Inc—*Paul Wickesberg*	PO Box 98, Richfield WI 53076	262-628-5600	R	14*	.1
90	Vanaire Inc—*Richard Vande Vusse*	840 Clark Dr, Gladstone MI 49837	906-428-4656	R	14*	.1
91	Sewer Equipment Company Of America—*Daniel O'brien*	2111 Chestnut Ave Ste, Glenview IL 60025	847-729-3316	R	13*	.1
92	Alkota Cleaning Systems Inc—*Gary Scott*	PO Box 288, Alcester SD 57001	605-934-2222	R	13*	.1
93	Its Engineered Systems Inc—*John Ladd*	6818 Fm 2855 Rd, Katy TX 77493	281-371-3333	R	13*	.1
94	Standard Casing Company Inc—*Michael Koss*	165 Chubb Ave, Lyndhurst NJ 07071	201-434-6300	R	13	.1
95	American Manufacturing and Machine Inc—*Don Buckner*	27137 S Hwy 33, Okahumpka FL 34762	352-728-5445	R	13*	<.1
96	Powerboss Inc—*Steve Liew*	175 Anderson St, Aberdeen NC 28315	910-944-2105	R	13*	.1
97	Pioneer/Eclipse Corp—*Byron Snyder*	PO Box 909, Sparta NC 28675	336-372-8080	S	13*	.1
98	Hydro Tek Systems Inc—*John Koen*	2353 Almond Ave, Redlands CA 92374	909-799-9222	R	13*	.1
99	Paddock Pool Equipment Company Inc—*Paul Nigro*	PO Box 11676, Rock Hill SC 29731	803-324-1111	R	13*	.1
100	Advanced Precision Manufacturing Inc—*Tadeusz Kozlowski*	2301 Estes Ave, Elk Grove Village IL 60007	847-981-9800	R	13*	.1
101	Wedeco Uv Technologies Inc—*John Marrino*	14125 S Bridge Cir, Charlotte NC 28273	704-716-7600	R	12*	.1
102	Tonka Equipment Co—*Thomas Davis*	13305 Water Tower Cir, Minneapolis MN 55441	763-559-2837	R	12*	.1
103	Blue Desert International Inc—*Christopher Kuttig*	510 N Sheridan St Ste, Corona CA 92880	951-273-7575	R	12*	.1
104	Nieco Corp—*Edward Baker*	7950 Cameron Dr, Windsor CA 95492	707-284-7100	R	12*	.1
105	US Jetting LLC—*Catrina Hendrick*	850 Mcfarland Pkwy, Alpharetta GA 30004	770-740-9917	R	12*	<.1
106	Rps Corp—*Sean Goff*	PO Box 368, Racine WI 53401	262-681-3583	R	12*	.1
107	Aero Manufacturing Company Inc—*Wayne Phillips*	PO Box 1250, Clifton NJ 07012	973-473-5300	R	12*	.1
108	J Ii Inc—*Ben Israel*	PO Box 496, Highland Park IL 60035	847-432-8979	R	11*	.1
109	Blako Inc—*Erik Vilen*	1228 W Capitol Dr, Addison IL 60101	630-532-5021	R	11*	.1
110	Aaladin Industries Inc—*Patrick Wingen*	32584 477th Ave, Elk Point SD 57025	605-356-3325	R	11*	.1
111	Gardner Denver Water Jetting Systems Inc—*Ross Centanni*	1800 Gardner Expy, Quincy IL 62305	217-222-5400	D	11*	.1
112	Sun Water Systems Inc—*Charles Strand*	6310 Midway Rd, Haltom City TX 76117	817-536-5250	R	11*	<.1
113	Excell Technologies International Corp—*Leonard Graziano*	1110 Industrial Blvd, Sugar Land TX 77478	281-240-6770	R	11*	.1
114	N/S Corp—*G Ennis*	235 W Florence Ave, Inglewood CA 90301	310-412-7074	R	11*	.1
115	Aero-Mod Inc—*John Mcnellis*	7927 E Us Hwy 24, Manhattan KS 66502	785-537-4995	R	10*	<.1
116	Whiting Systems Inc—*Donel Whiting*	9000 Hwy 5 N, Alexander AR 72002	501-847-9031	R	10*	.1
117	Stero Co—*Lin Sensenig*	3200 Lakeville Hwy, Petaluma CA 94954	707-762-0071	D	10	.1
118	Trisep Corp—*Peter Knappe*	6325 Lindmar Dr, Goleta CA 93117	805-964-8003	R	10*	.1
119	Insinger Machine Co—*Robert Cantor*	6245 State Rd, Philadelphia PA 19135	215-624-4800	R	10*	.1
120	Yardney Water Management Systems Inc—*Kenneth Phillips*	6666 Box Springs Blvd, Riverside CA 92507	951-656-6716	R	10*	<.1
121	Jim Myers and Sons Inc—*David Myers*	PO Box 240038, Charlotte NC 28224	704-554-8397	R	10*	<.1
122	Aeromix Systems Inc—*Peter Gross*	7135 Madison Ave W, Minneapolis MN 55427	763-746-8400	R	10*	<.1
123	Hellenbrand Inc—*Jeff Hellenbrand*	404 Moravian Valley Rd, Waunakee WI 53597	608-849-3050	R	10*	.1
124	Hydro Service and Supplies Inc—*Dave Currin*	PO Box 12197, Durham NC 27709	919-544-3744	R	10*	.1
125	Hungerford and Terry Inc—*Alan Davis*	PO Box 650, Clayton NJ 08312	856-881-3200	R	10*	.1
126	Pronto Products Co—*William Parrott*	11765 Goldring Rd, Arcadia CA 91006	626-358-5718	R	9*	.1
127	JL Wingert Co—*Tommy Thomas*	PO Box 6207, Garden Grove CA 92846	714-379-5519	R	9*	.1
128	Atlantic Ultraviolet Corp—*Hilary Boehme*	375 Marcus Blvd, Hauppauge NY 11788	631-273-0500	R	9*	<.1
129	Salvajor Co—*George Hohl*	4530 E 75th Ter, Kansas City MO 64132	816-363-1030	R	9*	.1

Rank	Company Name—*Executive Officer*	Address, City, State, Zip	Phone	Type	Fin	Empls
130	Miox Corp—*Carlos Perea*	5601 Balloon Fiesta Pk, Albuquerque NM 87113	505-343-0090	R	9*	.1
131	Ovivo USA LLC—*Jim Porteous*	2404 Rutland Dr, Austin TX 78758	512-834-6000	R	9*	<.1
132	Ecological Tanks Inc—*George Johnson*	2247 Hwy 151, Downsville LA 71234	318-644-0397	R	9*	<.1
133	Fab Wright Inc—*James Wright*	13912 Enterprise Dr, Garden Grove CA 92843	714-554-5544	R	9*	.1
134	Axeon Water Technologies—*Augustin Pavel*	541 Industrial Way Ste, Fallbrook CA 92028	760-723-5417	R	9*	.1
135	Marberry Machine Inc—*Redgie Marberry*	6210 Cunningham Rd, Houston TX 77041	713-466-9666	R	9*	.1
136	D R Sperry and Co—*David Murray*	623 Rathbone Ave, Aurora IL 60506	630-892-4361	R	9*	.1
137	Norwalk Wastewater Equipment Co—*Gregory Graves*	PO Box 410, Norwalk OH 44857	419-668-4471	R	9*	.1
138	Qmp Inc—*Freddy Vidal*	9837 Glenoaks Blvd, Sun Valley CA 91352	818-252-4771	R	8*	.1
139	U-Tech Environmental Manufacturing Supply Inc—*Alison Dresang*	W137n5560 Williams Pl, Menomonee Falls WI 53051	262-783-6666	R	8*	.1
140	Nedland Industries Inc—*Sam Jacobsen*	PO Box 217, Ridgeland WI 54763	715-949-1982	R	8*	.1
141	Kelmax Equipment	11230 Harland Dr NE, Covington GA 30014	678-823-4001	D	8*	.1
142	Serfilco Ltd—*Jack H Berg*	2900 MacArthur Blvd, Northbrook IL 60062	847-509-2900	R	8*	.1
143	Vector Technologies Ltd—*Stephen Schoenberger*	6820 N 43rd St, Milwaukee WI 53209	414-247-7100	R	8*	<.1
144	Stoneage Inc—*Kerry Petranek*	PO Box 2907, Durango CO 81302	970-259-2869	R	8*	.1
145	Saf T Cart Inc—*James Walker*	PO Box 1869, Clarksdale MS 38614	662-624-6492	R	8*	.1
146	Bestech Inc—*Gary Barr*	442 S Dixie Hwy E, Pompano Beach FL 33060	954-785-4550	R	8*	.1
147	Water Resources International Inc—*Lowell Foletta*	2800 E Chambers St Ste, Phoenix AZ 85040	602-268-2580	R	8*	.1
148	Brite-O-Matic Manufacturing Inc—*Lynne Mohr*	527 W Algonquin Rd, Arlington Heights IL 60005	847-956-1100	R	7*	.1
149	Esd Waste 2 Water Inc—*Jon Houchens*	495 Oak Rd, Ocala FL 34472	352-680-0400	R	7*	.1
150	Envirodyne Systems Inc—*Laurence Sheker*	75 Zimmerman Dr, Camp Hill PA 17011	717-763-0500	R	7*	<.1
151	Jri Holdings Inc—*James Jones*	1339 N Cedarbrook Ave, Springfield MO 65802	417-866-8855	R	7*	<.1
152	Mytee Products Inc—*John Barbera*	13655 Stowe Dr, Poway CA 92064	858-679-1191	R	7*	.1
153	Great Lakes International Inc—*Robert Faas*	1905 Kearney Ave, Racine WI 53403	262-634-2386	R	7*	.1
154	B B Robertson Co—*Mike Robertson*	PO Box 970, Marion IL 62959	618-997-9348	R	7*	<.1
155	Aqua Treatment Services Inc—*David Rishell*	194 Hempt Rd, Mechanicsburg PA 17050	717-697-4998	R	7*	<.1
156	Wittco Foodservice Equipment Inc—*Steve Jensen*	7737 N 81st St, Milwaukee WI 53223	414-354-3080	R	7*	<.1
157	Adamation Inc (Newton Massachusetts)—*Alan Adam*	7039 E Slauson Ave, Commerce CA 90040		R	7*	<.1
158	A La Cart Inc—*Wade Moyer*	9771 Southern Pine Blv, Charlotte NC 28273		R	7*	<.1
159	Allegheny-Wagner Industries Inc—*John Wagner*	PO Box 80, Delmont PA 15626	724-468-4300	R	7*	<.1
160	Jenny Products Inc—*Peter Leiss*	850 N Pleasant Ave, Somerset PA 15501	814-445-3400	R	7*	.1
161	Douglas Machines Corp—*David Ward*	2101 Calumet St, Clearwater FL 33765	727-461-3477	R	7*	<.1
162	Pleatco LLC—*John Antretter*	28 Garvies Point Rd, Glen Cove NY 11542	516-609-0200	R	7*	<.1
163	Shredfast Mobile Data Destruction Inc—*Dave Rajewski*	PO Box 1180, Airway Heights WA 99001	509-244-7076	R	7*	<.1
164	Lds Vacuum Products Inc—*Carl Russo*	773 Big Tree Dr, Longwood FL 32750	407-862-4643	R	7*	<.1
165	Sioux Corp—*John Finger*	1 Sioux Plz, Beresford SD 57004	605-763-3333	R	6*	<.1
166	Aeration Industries International Inc—*Daniel Durda*	PO Box 59144, Minneapolis MN 55459	952-448-6789	R	6*	<.1
167	Hydration Technology Innovations LLC—*Robert Salter*	PO Box 1027, Albany OR 97321	541-917-3335	R	6*	<.1
168	Paragon Water Systems Inc—*George Lutich*	14001 63rd Way N, Clearwater FL 33760	727-538-4704	R	6*	<.1
169	General Ecology Inc—*Richard Williams*	151 Sheree Blvd, Exton PA 19341	610-363-7900	R	6*	<.1
170	S Morantz Inc—*Stan Morantz*	9984 Gantry Rd, Philadelphia PA 19115	215-969-0266	R	6*	<.1
171	GE Mobile Water	4740 Bronze Way, Dallas TX 75236	214-339-2135	S	6*	<.1
172	Timbucktoo Manufacturing Inc—*Kyu Lee*	1633 W 134th St, Gardena CA 90249	310-323-1134	R	6*	<.1
173	Paragon International Inc—*David Swegle*	PO Box 560, Nevada IA 50201	515-382-8000	R	6*	<.1
174	Shred-Pac Inc—*Dennis Pool*	2982 Jefferson Rd, Hopkins MI 49328	269-793-3232	R	5*	<.1
175	Jero Manufacturing Inc—*John Pingleton*	PO Box 472033, Tulsa OK 74147	918-628-0230	R	5*	<.1
176	Enting Water Conditioning Inc—*Mel Enting*	3211 Dryden Rd Frnt Fr, Moraine OH 45439	937-294-5100	R	5*	<.1
177	Blower Application Company Inc—*Michael Young*	PO Box 279, Germantown WI 53022	262-255-5580	R	5*	<.1
178	Power Container Corp—*Chris Nimo*	33 Schoolhouse Rd Ste, Somerset NJ 08873	732-560-3655	R	5*	<.1
179	Dupure International Inc—*Stuart Tillman*	11321 Windfern Rd Ste, Houston TX 77064	281-890-7900	R	5*	.1
180	Hydro-Blast Inc—*Bruce Bosch*	10250 SE Mather Rd, Clackamas OR 97015	503-496-1100	R	5*	<.1
181	Arch Environmental Equipment—*Rick Archer*	PO Box 1760, Paducah KY 42002	270-898-6821	R	5*	<.1
182	Click Industries Inc—*Ronald Click*	PO Box 279, Arlington TN 38002	901-867-7854	R	5*	<.1
183	Atlantic Filter Corp—*James Wakem*	3112 45th St, West Palm Beach FL 33407	561-683-0101	R	5*	<.1
184	Texas Shines Inc—*Chris Lovelace*	17301 Bell N Dr, Schertz TX 78154	210-651-1151	R	5*	<.1
185	Shamrock Pipe Tools Inc—*Barbara Schweitzer*	PO Box 15588, Baton Rouge LA 70895	225-275-7696	R	5*	<.1
186	Stormtech LLC	20 Beaver Rd, Wethersfield CT 06109	860-529-8188	R	5*	<.1
187	Chlorinators Inc—*Diane Haskett*	PO Box 1518, Stuart FL 34995	772-288-4854	R	5*	<.1
188	Gorlitz Sewer and Drain Inc—*Gerd Kruger*	10132 Norwalk Blvd, Santa Fe Springs CA 90670	562-944-3060	R	5*	<.1
189	Lima Sheet Metal Machine and Manufacturing Inc—*Michael Emerick*	1001 Bowman Rd, Lima OH 45804	419-229-1161	R	4*	<.1
190	Key High Vacuum Products Inc—*Anthony Kozyrski*	36 Southern Blvd, Nesconset NY 11767	631-360-3970	R	4*	<.1
191	Neptune-Benson Inc—*Barry Gertz*	6 Jefferson Dr, Coventry RI 02816	401-821-2200	R	4*	<.1
192	Clearstream Wastewater Systems Inc—*Jerry Mckinney*	PO Box 7568, Beaumont TX 77726	409-755-1500	R	4*	<.1
193	Barone Inc—*Frank Barone*	5879 W 58th Ave, Arvada CO 80002	303-424-4497	R	4*	<.1
194	Manson Meads Complex	2799 Griffith Rd, Winston Salem NC 27103	336-659-4300	R	4*	.1
195	DPL Enterprises Inc—*Richard Papaleo*	3868 E Post Rd, Las Vegas NV 89120	702-454-5515	R	4*	<.1
196	CONTECH Stormwater Solutions Inc—*Ronald C Keating*	9025 Centre Pt Dr, West Chester OH 45069		S	4*	<.1
197	Robert Yick Company Inc—*Joseph Yick*	261 Bay Shore Blvd, San Francisco CA 94124	415-282-9707	R	4*	<.1
198	United Fabricators Inc—*Jerry Bollin*	PO Box 471, Fort Smith AR 72902	479-782-9169	R	4*	<.1
199	Adf Systems Ltd—*Louis Fontana*	PO Box 278, Humboldt IA 50548	515-332-5400	R	4*	<.1
200	Sono-Tek Inc—*Christopher Coccio*	2012 Rte 9 W, Milton NY 12547	845-795-2020	S	4*	<.1
201	Avw Equipment Company Inc—*Milovan Vidakovich*	105 S 9th Ave, Maywood IL 60153	708-343-7738	R	4*	<.1
202	Farleys Inc—*Bob Farley*	PO Box 1209, Siloam Springs AR 72761	479-524-9594	R	4*	<.1
203	Clean Line Inc—*John Donaldson*	746 Selby Ave, Saint Paul MN 55104	651-222-1738	R	4*	<.1
204	Clements National Co—*Reginald Barrett*	6650 S Narragansett Av, Chicago IL 60638	708-594-5890	R	4*	<.1
205	AquaTec Inc—*J Johnson*	1235 Shappert Dr, Machesney Park IL 61115	815-654-1500	R	4*	<.1
206	AgWater Technologies Inc—*David Frackelton*	P O Box 2355, Harrisonburg VA 22801	540-434-4921	R	4*	<.1
207	Cromaglass Corp—*Allan Young*	PO Box 3215, Williamsport PA 17701	570-326-3396	R	4*	<.1
208	American Engineering Services Inc—*Mo Malki*	9203 King Palm Dr Ste, Tampa FL 33619	813-621-3932	R	4*	<.1
209	Coffee Inns Of America LLC—*Mary Jungling*	3730 E Southern Ave, Phoenix AZ 85040	602-438-8286	R	4*	<.1
210	LVO Manufacturing Inc—*Lambert Olst*	PO Box 188, Rock Rapids IA 51246	712-472-3734	R	4*	<.1
211	Com Pac Filtration Inc—*Dean Atkinson*	PO Box 40071, Jacksonville FL 32203	904-356-4003	R	4*	<.1
212	Water Tec International Inc—*Richard Grave*	PO Box 31775, Tucson AZ 85751	520-790-3222	R	4*	<.1
213	Alliance Manufacturing Inc—*Jeffery Brouchoud*	PO Box 2006, Fond Du Lac WI 54936	920-922-8100	R	4*	<.1
214	Hickory Industries Inc—*Steven Maroti*	4900 W Side Ave, North Bergen NJ 07047	201-223-0050	R	4*	<.1
215	Multi-Pak Corp—*Phil Cahill*	180 Atlantic St, Hackensack NJ 07601	201-342-7474	R	4*	<.1
216	Thermodyne Food Service Products Inc—*Vincent Tippmann*	4418 New Haven Ave, Fort Wayne IN 46803	260-428-2535	R	4*	<.1
217	Telemetry And Process Controls Inc—*Tom Edison*	11320 Upper 33rd St N, Lake Elmo MN 55042	651-430-0435	R	4*	<.1

Note: An asterisk (*) indicates an estimated financial figure. The company type code used is as follows: R = Private, P = Public, S = Private Subsidiary, B = Public Subsidiary, D = Division, J = Joint Venture, I = Investment Fund.

COMPANY RANKINGS BY SALES WITHIN 4-DIGIT SIC

Rank	Company Name—*Executive Officer*	Address, City, State, Zip	Phone	Type	Fin	Empls
218	SDP Manufacturing Inc—*Stanley Pitman*	PO Box 44, Albany IN 47320	765-789-6213	R	4*	<.1
219	Nimbus Water Systems—*Anthony Capone*	41840 Mcalby Ct Ste A, Murrieta CA 92562	951-894-2800	R	3*	<.1
220	Royce Rolls Ringer Company Inc—*Charles Royce*	PO Box 1831, Grand Rapids MI 49501	616-361-9266	R	3*	<.1
221	Enviro-Systems Corp—*David Jackson*	PO Box 50938, Mesa AZ 85208	480-946-3566	R	3*	<.1
222	Geerpres Inc—*Michael Gluhanich*	PO Box 658, Muskegon MI 49443	231-773-3211	R	3*	<.1
223	Osmosis Technology Inc—*Mike Joulakian*	6900 Hermosa Cir, Buena Park CA 90620	714-670-9303	R	3*	<.1
224	FRC Environmental Inc—*Lonnie Finley*	568 Tommy Aaron Dr, Gainesville GA 30506	770-536-2107	R	3*	<.1
225	Mcintyre Softwater Service—*James Intyre*	1014 N Bridge St, Linden MI 48451	810-735-7444	R	3*	<.1
226	Waterplay Manufacturing Inc—*Jill White*	487 Reginald Ln, Collegeville PA 19426	610-489-4595	R	3*	<.1
227	IAS National Inc—*Michael Flaxman*	95 W Hills Rd, Huntington Station NY 11746	631-423-6900	R	3*	<.1
228	Aztec Products Inc—*Whit Beverly*	201 Commerce Dr, Montgomeryville PA 18936	215-393-4700	R	3*	<.1
229	Aquathin Corp—*Alfred Lipshultz*	950 S Andrews Ave, Pompano Beach FL 33069	954-781-7777	R	3*	<.1
230	Aerospace America Inc—*Murray Sutherland*	PO Box 189, Bay City MI 48707	989-684-2121	R	3*	<.1
231	Aqualogic Inc—*Anthony Papa*	30 Devine St, North Haven CT 06473	203-248-8959	R	3*	<.1
232	International Waterjet Parts Inc—*Greg Emerson*	1299 A St SE, Ephrata WA 98823	509-754-3284	R	3*	<.1
233	Three G Enterprises Inc—*Mike Scholz*	220 77th Ave Ne, Minneapolis MN 55432	763-571-3000	R	3*	<.1
234	Max Endura Inc—*Gregory Winter*	PO Box 205, Alpena MI 49707	989-356-1593	R	3*	<.1
235	Harben Inc—*Shaun Virgo*	PO Box 2250, Cumming GA 30028	770-889-9535	R	3*	<.1
236	Pro Equipment Company Inc—*Randy Travis*	PO Box 441, Benton KY 42025	270-527-1366	R	3*	<.1
237	Cooktek Inc—*Robert E Wolters Jr*	156 N Jefferson St Ste, Chicago IL 60661	312-563-9600	S	3	.1
238	Wilmington Public Treatment Sw	407 Hilton Rd, Wilmington NC 28401	910-343-3690	R	2*	<.1
239	Dayton Utilities—*Janette Hoffert*	PO Box 1699, Dayton NV 89403	775-246-6220	R	2*	<.1
240	SES Industries Inc—*R Moorman*	5568 Bowens Mill Rd, Douglas GA 31533	912-383-9477	R	2*	<.1
241	Jerry's Iron Works Inc—*Herman Kaptein*	PO Box 334, Duvall WA 98019	425-788-1467	R	2*	<.1
242	Corbett Enterprises Inc—*Bill Corbett*	1300 Woodswether Rd, Kansas City MO 64105	816-421-5080	R	2*	<.1
243	Kinetico Quality Water Systems—*Doug Snell*	3880 Pendleton Way Ste, Indianapolis IN 46226	317-542-8888	R	2*	<.1
244	Proto-Vest Inc—*Lucian Mc Elroy*	7400 N Glen Harbor Blv, Glendale AZ 85307	623-872-8300	R	2*	<.1
245	Custom Applied Technology Corp—*Howard Taylor*	2361 Whitfield Park Av, Sarasota FL 34243	941-751-5656	R	2*	<.1
246	Continental Equipment Corp—*Fred Felder*	PO Box 18662, Milwaukee WI 53218	414-463-0500	R	2*	<.1
247	Rankin-Delux Inc—*L Vasan*	12862 Florence Ave, Santa Fe Springs CA 90670	562-944-7076	R	2*	<.1
248	Media Blast and Abrasive Inc—*Ronald Storer*	591 Apollo St, Brea CA 92821	714-257-0484	R	2*	<.1
249	Economy Tank Co—*William Setterstrom*	99 Winfield Rd, Saint Albans WV 25177	304-727-4338	R	2*	<.1
250	Delta Fabricators Inc—*Gary Myers*	5863 Raytown Rd, Raytown MO 64133	816-737-1230	R	2*	<.1
251	Nunnery-Freeman Inc—*Gary Freeman*	PO Box 332, Henderson NC 27536	252-438-3149	R	2*	.1
252	Ozotech Inc—*Stephen Christiansen*	2401 E Oberlin Rd, Yreka CA 96097	530-842-4189	R	2*	<.1
253	Allied Industrial Distributors Inc—*Donald Clyde*	1102 E Cherry St, Vermillion SD 57069	605-624-2685	R	1*	<.1
254	Safe Systems Inc—*Glenn Seaverns*	18420 68th Ave S Ste 2, Kent WA 98032	425-251-8662	R	1*	<.1
255	Process Engineered Equipment Co—*Larry Green*	PO Box 9549, Corpus Christi TX 78469	361-289-8891	R	1*	<.1
256	Eco Safe Systems USA Inc—*Michael Elliot*	7306 Coldwater Canyon, North Hollywood CA 91605	818-602-5742	R	1*	<.1
257	Western Water Products Inc—*Daniel Robey*	6060 Enterprise Dr, Diamond Springs CA 95619	530-621-0255	R	1*	<.1
258	Arcoa Industries LLC	24338 El Toro Rd, Laguna Woods CA 92637	949-492-7000	R	1*	<.1
259	Sonford Samplers Inc—*Gary Glenna*	8287 214th St W, Lakeville MN 55044	952-469-4832	R	1*	<.1
260	Water Technology Of Pensacola—*William Boesch*	3000 W Nine Mile Rd, Pensacola FL 32534	850-477-4789	R	1*	<.1
261	Resys Inc—*Brian Maheu*	4560 Ridge Dr Ne, Salem OR 97301	503-393-8000	R	1*	<.1
262	Fresh Squeezed Water Inc—*Al Lozier*	6917 Martindale Rd, Shawnee KS 66218	913-441-0870	R	1*	<.1
263	Econocraft Worldwide Manufacturing Inc—*Shlomo Malki*	56 Worth St Frnt Unit, Yonkers NY 10701	914-966-2280	R	1*	<.1
264	Cairns Manufacturing Inc—*Paul Cairns*	4929 Nw 18th St, Oklahoma City OK 73127	405-947-1350	R	1*	<.1
265	Industrial Paper Shredders Inc—*Deanna Thomas*	PO Box 218, North Lima OH 44452	330-332-0024	R	1*	<.1
266	Rank Industries Inc—*Jules Marcogliese*	330 Warren Way, Arcadia CA 91007	626-574-9409	R	1*	<.1
267	Scale Watcher North America Inc—*Jan De Baat Doelman*	345 Lincoln St, Oxford PA 19363	610-932-6888	R	<1*	<.1
268	Triad Industries Inc—*David Burk*	PO Box 3674, Cleburne TX 76033	817-202-9989	R	<1*	<.1
269	Oztec Business Machines Inc—*Fred Oswald*	65 Channel Dr, Port Washington NY 11050	516-944-5007	R	<1*	<.1
270	Thomas Green LLC—*Terry Groff*	7802 Moller Rd, Indianapolis IN 46268	317-337-0000	R	<1*	<.1
271	Budd Built-In Vacuum Cleaners—*Bernard Schwartz*	445 W Main St Ste 4, Wyckoff NJ 07481	201-891-3010	R	<1*	<.1
272	PureSafe Water Systems Inc—*Leslie J Kessler*	25 Fairchild Ave Ste 2, Plainview NY 11803	516-208-8250	P	<1	<.1

TOTALS: SIC 3589 Service Industry Machinery Nec
Companies: 272   23,567   52.3

3592 Carburetors, Pistons, Rings & Valves

Rank	Company Name—*Executive Officer*	Address, City, State, Zip	Phone	Type	Fin	Empls
1	Sauer-Danfoss Inc—*Sven Ruder*	2800 E 13th St, Ames IA 50010	515-239-6000	P	1,641	6.0
2	Walbro Corp—*Franklin Bauchiero*	6242 Garfield St, Cass City MI 48726	989-872-2131	S	678	5.4
3	ITT Industries Inc Aerospace Controls Div—*Bob Briggs*	28150 Industry Dr, Valencia CA 91355	661-295-4000	D	360*	.4
4	Celina Aluminum Precision Technology Inc—*Kenichi Kinoshita*	7059 Staeger Rd, Celina OH 45822	419-586-2278	R	200*	.5
5	Tyde Group Worldwide LLC	5700 Crooks Rd Ste 207, Troy MI 48098	248-879-7656	R	146*	2.1
6	United Engine and Machine Co—*Dan Mondragon*	1040 Corbett St, Carson City NV 89706	775-882-7790	R	129*	.1
7	Walker Products—*Michael Weaver*	14291 Commerce Dr, Garden Grove CA 92843	714-554-5151	R	116*	.3
8	Karl Schmidt Unisia Inc—*Donald Cameron*	1731 Industrial Pkwy N, Marinette WI 54143	715-732-0181	R	67*	.9
9	L E Jones Co—*Peter Vennema*	1200 34th Ave, Menominee MI 49858	906-863-4411	R	50*	.4
10	Performance Motorsports Inc	7201 Industrial Park B, Mentor OH 44060		S	47*	.3
11	Dexter Automatic Products Co—*Scott Adle*	2500 Bishop Cir E, Dexter MI 48130	734-426-8900	R	26*	.2
12	Helio Precision Products Inc—*John Salamone*	601 N Skokie Hwy Ste B, Lake Bluff IL 60044	847-473-1300	R	24*	.2
13	Tomco Auto Products Inc—*Victor Moss*	PO Box 15478, Los Angeles CA 90015	323-268-4830	R	21*	.4
14	Westlock Controls Corp—*Russ Chorniak*	280 N Midland Ave Ste, Saddle Brook NJ 07663	201-794-7650	S	18*	.1
15	Cook Compression	PO Box 1038, Louisville KY 40201		D	14*	.2
16	Wesco Valve and Manufacturing Co—*Stanley Baker*	PO Box J, Marshall TX 75671	903-938-9241	R	11*	.1
17	Pacific Piston Ring Company Inc—*Forest Shannon*	PO Box 987, Culver City CA 90232	310-836-3322	R	11*	.1
18	France Compressor Products Div—*Tony Geoffredi*	4100 Greenbriar, Stafford TX 77477	281-207-4600	D	9*	.1
19	CP Pistons LLC—*Barry Calvert*	1902 McGaw Ave, Irvine CA 92614	949-567-9000	R	8*	.1
20	United Carburetor Inc—*Robert Portman*	5050 W Lawrence Ave, Chicago IL 60630	773-777-1223	R	8*	.1
21	Hydro Fitting Manufacturing Corp—*Seth Schwartz*	PO Box 1558, Covina CA 91722	626-967-5151	R	6*	<.1
22	Rtr Industries LLC—*Craig Marger*	1360 N Jefferson St, Anaheim CA 92807	714-996-0050	R	6*	<.1
23	Ross Racing Pistons—*Ken Roble*	625 S Douglas St, El Segundo CA 90245	310-536-0100	R	4*	<.1
24	Tor CA M Industries Inc—*Frank Pisino*	2160 E Cherry Industri, Long Beach CA 90805	562-531-8463	R	4*	<.1
25	Noel Burt—*Noel Burt*	661 Garcia Ave, Pittsburg CA 94565	925-439-7030	R	4*	<.1
26	Spectrum Associates Inc—*Richard Meisenheimer*	PO Box 470, Milford CT 06460	203-878-4618	R	3*	<.1
27	Greg-Co Piston Rings Inc—*Kerri Hill*	4407 Ne 28th St, Fort Worth TX 76117	817-831-0253	R	3*	<.1
28	FBS Corp—*Kurt Dannehl*	PO Box 2348, Kearney NE 68848	308-233-3040	R	2*	<.1
29	Dual Dynamics Inc—*Scott Kuck*	PO Box 80436, Lincoln NE 68501	402-441-4300	R	2*	<.1
30	Mizpah Precision Manufacturing—*David Steinhorst*	PO Box 22, Mizpah MN 56660	218-897-5922	R	1*	<.1

TOTALS: SIC 3592 Carburetors, Pistons, Rings & Valves
Companies: 30   3,617   18.1

Rank	Company Name—*Executive Officer*	Address, City, State, Zip	Phone	Type	Fin	Empls
3593 Fluid Power Cylinders & Actuators						
1	Parker Hannifin Corp—*Donald E Washkewicz*	6035 Parkland Blvd, Cleveland OH 44124	216-896-3000	P	12,346	58.4
2	Custom Hoists Inc—*Rick Paul*	PO Box 98, Ashland OH 44805	419-368-4721	D	487*	.1
3	PHD Inc—*Joseph Oberlin*	PO Box 9070, Fort Wayne IN 46899	260-747-6151	R	218*	.3
4	Hyco International Inc—*Ronald C Whitaker*	100 Galleria Pkwy Ste, Atlanta GA 30339	770-980-1935	R	189	1.2
5	Hol-Mac Corp—*Charles Holder*	PO Box 349, Bay Springs MS 39422	601-764-4121	R	75*	.3
6	Emerson Process Management Bettis Div	PO Box 508, Waller TX 77484	281-727-5300	D	69*	.6
7	Parker Hannifin Corp Pneumatic Div—*Donald E Washkewicz* Parker Hannifin Corp	8876 E M-89, Richland MI 49083	269-629-5000	D	36*	.3
8	Tol-O-Matic Inc—*William Toles*	3800 County Rd 116, Hamel MN 55340	763-478-8000	R	31*	.2
9	Indian Head Industries Inc—*Ronald Parker*	8530 Cliff Cameron Dr, Charlotte NC 28269	704-547-7411	R	31*	.4
10	RHM Fluid Power Inc—*William W Tulloch III*	375 Manufacturers Dr, Westland MI 48186	734-326-5400	R	27*	.1
11	Helac Corp—*Dean Weyer*	225 Battersby Ave, Enumclaw WA 98022	360-825-1601	R	26*	.2
12	Suspa Inc—*Guido Wey*	3970 Roger B Chaffee M, Grand Rapids MI 49548	616-241-4200	R	25*	.2
13	Jarp Industries Inc—*John Kraft*	PO Box 923, Wausau WI 54402	715-359-4241	R	24*	.2
14	HSI Corp—*Orland Stanford*	PO Box 706, Bay Springs MS 39422	601-764-4131	R	22*	<.1
15	Ligon Industries LLC—*John McMahon Jr*	1927 1st Ave N Fl 5, Birmingham AL 35203	205-322-3302	R	18*	.1
16	Parker Hannifin Corp Cylinder Div—*Donald E Washkewicz* Parker Hannifin Corp	500 S Wolf Rd, Des Plaines IL 60016	847-298-2400	D	16*	.1
17	Milwaukee Cylinder—*Frank Meiland*	PO Box 498, Cudahy WI 53110	414-769-9700	S	15*	.1
18	Hydratech LLC—*Craig Braun*	PO Box 12344, Fresno CA 93777	559-233-0876	R	14*	.1
19	Dadco Inc—*Michael Diebolt*	43850 Plymouth Oaks Bl, Plymouth MI 48170	734-207-1100	R	14*	.1
20	Ramrod Industries LLC—*Tim Brumb*	800 S Monroe St, Spencer WI 54479	715-659-4996	R	13*	.1
21	Columbus Hydraulics Co—*John Cimpl*	PO Box 250, Columbus NE 68602	402-564-8544	R	13*	.1
22	Blac Inc—*Judyann Oshita*	195 W Spangler Ave Ste, Elmhurst IL 60126	630-279-6400	R	13*	.1
23	Yates Industries Inc—*William Yates*	23050 E Industrial Dr, Saint Clair Shores MI 48080	586-778-7680	R	12*	.1
24	General Engineering Company Of Virginia—*John Owens*	PO Box 549, Abingdon VA 24212	276-628-6068	R	12*	.1
25	Great Bend Industries	8701 6th St, Great Bend KS 67530	620-792-4368	D	12*	.1
26	West Craft Manufacturing Inc—*Gerald West*	PO Box 596, Alto TX 75925	936-858-4426	R	12*	<.1
27	Carter Machine Company Inc—*Andrea Carter*	820 Edward St, Galion OH 44833	419-468-3530	R	11*	.1
28	Bobalee Inc—*Richard Smith*	PO Box 151, Ida Grove IA 51445	712-845-4554	S	11*	.2
29	Alliance Remanufacturing Inc—*Roger Tarno*	450 E Luzerne St, Philadelphia PA 19124	215-425-7779	R	11*	.1
30	Motion Systems Corp—*William Wolf*	600 Industrial Way W, Eatontown NJ 07724	732-222-1800	R	11*	.1
31	V and P Hydraulic Products LLC—*Melissa Harvey*	1700 Pittsburgh Dr, Delaware OH 43015	740-203-3600	R	10*	.1
32	Positech Corp—*Mike Olson*	191 N Rush Lake Rd, Laurens IA 50554	712-841-4548	D	9*	.1
33	Temple Machine Shop Inc—*Stewart Fettig*	1401 N 14th St, Temple TX 76501	254-774-8099	R	9*	.1
34	Jit Industries Inc—*Ginger Mccomb*	2201 Hwy 31 Sw, Hartselle AL 35640	256-751-2548	R	8*	.1
35	Elliott Kenneth Co—*Kent Elliott*	3704 Riehl Ln, Godfrey IL 62035	618-466-8200	R	7*	<.1
36	Turlock Machine Works—*Vivian Manha*	1240 S 1st St, Turlock CA 95380	209-632-2275	R	6*	<.1
37	Purakal Cylinders Inc—*Thomas Philip*	PO Box 22038, Eugene OR 97402	541-345-4199	R	6*	<.1
38	Hader-Seitz Inc—*Wayne Hader*	PO Box 510260, New Berlin WI 53151	262-641-6000	R	6*	.1
39	Southern Hydraulic Cylinder Inc—*Jeff Zabo*	3020 Lee Hwy, Athens TN 37303	423-744-8988	R	6*	.1
40	Zaytran Inc—*Theodore Zajac*	PO Box 1660, Elyria OH 44036	440-324-2811	R	5*	<.1
41	R and J Cylinder and Machine Inc—*Ronald Sandy*	2155 Progress St, Dover OH 44622	330-364-8263	R	5*	<.1
42	Garrod Hydraulics Inc—*Wesley Garrod*	1050 Locust Point Rd, York PA 17406	717-767-6429	R	5*	<.1
43	Cunningham Manufacturing Co—*Scott Ericksen*	318 S Webster St, Seattle WA 98108	206-767-3713	R	4*	<.1
44	Hydraulic Component Services Inc—*John Greenwood*	1760 S Springdale Rd, New Berlin WI 53146	262-549-1760	R	4*	<.1
45	Kerry Company Inc—*John Keegan*	PO Box 51, Allison Park PA 15101	412-486-3388	R	3*	<.1
46	R and M Fluid Power Inc—*Robert Gustafson*	7953 Southern Blvd, Youngstown OH 44512	330-758-2766	R	3*	<.1
47	Lehigh Fluid Power Inc—*Francis Mcgonigle*	1413 Rte 179, Lambertville NJ 08530	609-397-8594	R	3*	<.1
48	Midway Manufacturing Inc—*Daniel Woolard*	PO Box 251, Kinsley KS 67547	620-659-3631	R	2*	<.1
49	Kubik Inc—*Philip Kubik*	247 Minnesota Dr, Troy MI 48083	248-585-7031	R	2*	<.1
50	WC Branham Inc—*W Branham*	398 Troy St, River Falls WI 54022	715-426-2000	R	2*	<.1
51	Advance Automation Co—*Joseph Hanley*	3526 N Elston Ave, Chicago IL 60618	773-539-7633	R	2*	<.1
52	Springville Manufacturing Company Inc—*Daniel Schmauss*	PO Box 367, Springville NY 14141	716-592-4957	R	2*	<.1
53	Duramaster Cylinders—*Joseph Greene*	5688 W Crenshaw St, Tampa FL 33634	813-882-0040	R	2*	<.1
54	Chicago Cylinders Corp—*Albert Winterle*	3145 W Columbus Ave, Chicago IL 60652	773-476-0440	R	2*	<.1
55	Greenco Manufacturing Corp—*Joseph Green*	5688 W Crenshaw St Frn, Tampa FL 33634	813-882-4400	R	1*	<.1
56	Hunger Hydraulics Cc Ltd—*Walter Hunger*	PO Box 377, Rossford OH 43460	419-666-4510	R	1*	<.1
57	Catching Hydraulics Company Ltd—*Inderjit Sundal*	1733 N 25th Ave, Melrose Park IL 60160	708-344-2334	R	1*	<.1
58	Products for Automation—*Jerry Klimowicz*	N 118 W 18251 Bunsen D, Germantown WI 53022	262-250-4410	R	1*	<.1

TOTALS: SIC 3593 Fluid Power Cylinders & Actuators
Companies: 58   13,930   64.9

Rank	Company Name—*Executive Officer*	Address, City, State, Zip	Phone	Type	Fin	Empls
3594 Fluid Power Pumps & Motors						
1	Oilgear Co—*David A Zuege*	2300 S 51st St, Milwaukee WI 53219	414-327-1700	R	1,888*	.8
2	ITT Industries Inc Fluid Technology Div—*Gretchen W McClain*	1133 Westchester Ave, White Plains NY 10604	914-641-2000	D	1,833	N/A
3	Paul-Munroe Enertech—*Stan Miller*	2950 E Birch St, Brea CA 92821	714-528-2301	S	232*	.1
4	Bosch Rexroth Corp/Mobile Hydraulics—*Manfred Hann*	PO Box 25407, Lehigh Valley PA 18002	610-694-8300	D	200*	.5
5	Best Equipment Co—*Al Jones*	8885 Monroe Rd, Houston TX 77061	713-956-2002	R	200*	.2
6	Bosch Rexroth Corp—*Berend Bracht*	5150 Prairie Stone Pkw, Hoffman Estates IL 60192	847-645-3600	R	200*	2.0
7	Pacific Power Tech LLC—*Gregory E Abel*	18977 NE Portal Way, Portland OR 97230	503-667-9222	R	142*	.1
8	Applied Energy Company LLC—*Claude Badgett*	1205 Venture Court Sui, Carrollton TX 75006	214-355-4200	R	122*	.1
9	Sulzer Pumps Inc (Brookshire Texas)—*Cesar Montenegro*	PO Box 10247, Portland OR 97296	281-934-6014	R	43*	.6
10	Mechanical Tool and Engineering Company Inc—*Richard Nordlof*	PO Box 5906, Rockford IL 61125	815-397-4701	R	41*	.3
11	ITT Industries Inc Flojet Div—*Nick Kendall-Jones*	666 E Eyer Rd, Santa Ana CA 92705	949-859-4945	S	37*	.3
12	Bucher Hydraulics Inc—*Dan Vaughan*	1363 Michigan St Ne, Grand Rapids MI 49503	616-458-1306	R	29*	.2
13	Guyan International Inc—*Patrick Farrell*	PO Box 2068, Streetsboro OH 44241	330-626-2801	R	19*	.1
14	White Drive Products Inc—*Charles Maddux*	PO Box 1127, Hopkinsville KY 42241	270-887-2100	R	19*	.2
15	Power Gear—*Marty Palmer*	1217 E 7th St, Mishawaka IN 46544	574-254-5265	S	16*	.1
16	Crissair Inc—*Linda Bradley*	38905 10th St E, Palmdale CA 93550	661-273-5411	R	16*	.1
17	Attica Hydraulic Exchange Corp—*William Wildner*	48175 Gratiot Ave, Chesterfield MI 48051	586-949-4240	R	15*	.1
18	Western Hydrostatics Inc—*Doug Felton*	1956 Keats Dr, Riverside CA 92501	951-784-2133	R	8*	.1
19	Edwards Engineering Corp—*Don West*	1773 Westborough Dr, Katy TX 77449	713-849-6825	R	8*	<.1
20	Predator Systems Inc—*Thomas Quinly*	600 Psi Dr, Boca Raton FL 33431	561-394-9991	S	6*	<.1
21	Flint Hydrostatics Inc—*Craig Fionup*	PO Box 18367, Memphis TN 38181	901-794-2462	R	6*	<.1
22	Brock Equipment Co—*Marvin Richer*	PO Box 218, Crystal Lake IL 60039	815-459-4210	R	6*	<.1

Note: An asterisk (*) indicates an estimated financial figure. The company type code used is as follows: R = Private, P = Public, S = Private Subsidiary, B = Public Subsidiary, D = Division, J = Joint Venture, I = Investment Fund.

COMPANY RANKINGS BY SALES WITHIN 4-DIGIT SIC

Rank	Company Name—Executive Officer	Address, City, State, Zip	Phone	Type	Fin	Empls
23	Bernell Hydraulics Inc—Rhonda Garness	PO Box 417, Rancho Cucamonga CA 91739	909-899-1751	R	5*	<.1
24	Hyvair Corp—Kenneth Vairin	31341 Friendship Dr, Magnolia TX 77355	281-259-7768	R	5*	<.1
25	Hadady Machining Company Inc—Peter Lanman	16730 Chicago Ave, Lansing IL 60438	708-474-0876	R	4*	<.1
26	Hartmann Controls Inc—Don Bethke	604 Progress Dr, Hartland WI 53029	262-367-4299	R	3*	<.1
27	Pmc Liquiflo Equipment Company Inc—Richard Picut	443 N Ave, Garwood NJ 07027	908-518-0666	R	3*	<.1
28	Hydraulic Systems Inc—John Day	1505 E High St, Jackson MI 49203	517-787-7818	R	3*	<.1
29	Rda Corp—Robert Arnett	2113 Seabrook Cir, Seabrook TX 77586	281-474-2881	R	3*	<.1
30	Schultz Machine Company Inc—James Schultz	PO Box 1998, Fairmont WV 26555	304-363-4964	R	2*	<.1
31	Hydroacoustics Inc—Michael Czora	999 Lehigh Station Rd, Henrietta NY 14467	585-359-1000	R	2*	<.1
32	Vertiflo Pump Company Inc—Phil Eldridge	7807 Redsky Dr, Cincinnati OH 45249	513-530-0888	R	2*	<.1
33	Matthews Marine Systems Inc—Robert Troudt	4734 N Albina Ave, Portland OR 97217	503-288-7493	R	<1*	<.1

TOTALS: SIC 3594 Fluid Power Pumps & Motors
Companies: 33   5,118   6.0

3596 Scales & Balances Except Laboratory

Rank	Company Name—Executive Officer	Address, City, State, Zip	Phone	Type	Fin	Empls
1	Alpha Scale Company Inc—Steve Riendeau	980A Quaker Hwy, Uxbridge MA 01569	508-278-8002	R	1,572*	<.1
2	Mettler-Toledo Inc—Ollivier Fillol	1900 Polaris Pkwy, Columbus OH 43240	614-438-4511	S	1,304	8.5
3	Fairbanks Scales Inc—Richard Norden	821 Locust St, Kansas City MO 64106	816-471-0231	R	1,040*	.6
4	Cardinal Scale Manufacturing Co—David Perry	PO Box 151, Webb City MO 64870	417-673-4631	R	69*	.6
5	Thermo Ramsey	81 Wyman St, Waltham MA 02451	781-622-1000	S	56*	.2
6	E Rowe Foundry and Machine Co—Ellen Norton	PO Box 130, Martinsville IL 62442	217-382-4135	R	23*	.1
7	Measurement Systems Intl Inc—Ron Wenzel	14240 Interurban Ave S, Seattle WA 98168	206-433-0199	R	15*	<.1
8	Intercomp Co—William Kroll	3839 County Rd 116, Medina MN 55340	763-476-2531	R	13*	.1
9	Digi-Star LLC—Grant Ihrke	W5527 State Rd 106, Fort Atkinson WI 53538	920-563-1400	R	13*	.1
10	Drafto Corp—Peter Wassmer	PO Box 158, Cochranton PA 16314	814-425-7445	R	8*	.1
11	General Electrodynamics Corp—George Lindberg	PO Box 550089, Arlington TX 76015	817-572-0366	R	7*	<.1
12	Doran Scales Inc—William Podl	1315 Paramount Pkwy, Batavia IL 60510	630-879-1200	R	6*	<.1
13	Unibridge Systems Inc—Joe Hamilton	RR 1 Box 8, Knowles OK 73844	580-934-3211	R	6*	.1
14	Scales Unlimited Inc—Robert Luna	196 W 280 S, Jerome ID 83338	208-324-7490	R	6*	<.1
15	Totalcomp Inc—Rudolph J Kolaci	99 Reagent Lane, Fair Lawn NJ 07410	201-797-2718	R	4*	<.1
16	Weightech Inc—Steve Tull	PO Box 769, Waldron AR 72958	479-637-4182	R	4*	<.1
17	Jonel Engineering—John Lawson	PO Box 798, Fullerton CA 92836	714-879-2360	R	3*	<.1
18	Mos International Inc—Barrett Fait	3198 Airport Loop Dr S, Costa Mesa CA 92626	714-754-7841	R	3*	<.1
19	Sterling Scale Co—E Dixon	20955 Boening Dr, Southfield MI 48075	248-358-0590	R	3*	<.1
20	Circuits and Systems Inc—Arnold Gordon	59 2nd St, East Rockaway NY 11518	516-593-4301	R	3*	<.1
21	Jer-Mac Industries Inc—Kenneth Mc Daniel	2385 Liberty Ave, Vermilion OH 44089	440-967-5630	R	3*	<.1
22	Cambridge Scale Works Inc—Jennette Cantrell	PO Box 670, Honey Brook PA 19344	610-273-7040	R	3*	<.1
23	Lectro Tek Services Inc—Jim Tarrant	PO Box 2161, Wenatchee WA 98807	509-663-2891	R	2*	<.1
24	Spinks Scale Company Inc—Michael Standridge	1690 Hwy 155 S, Mcdonough GA 30253	770-914-6600	R	2*	<.1
25	Lts Scale Corp—Kenneth Filing	1500 Enterprise Pkwy, Twinsburg OH 44087	330-425-3092	R	1*	<.1
26	Morrison Weighing Systems Inc—Donald Morrison	PO Box 860, Milan IL 61264	309-799-7311	R	1*	<.1
27	Scaletron Industries Ltd—Edward Dougherty	PO Box 365, Plumsteadville PA 18949	215-766-2670	R	1*	<.1
28	Vishay Precision Group	PO Box 1484, Cumberland MD 21502	301-722-5900	D	1	<.1
29	Sooner Scale Inc—Steve Mcfadden	PO Box 82386, Oklahoma City OK 73148	405-236-3566	R	1*	<.1

TOTALS: SIC 3596 Scales & Balances Except Laboratory
Companies: 29   4,170   10.7

3599 Industrial Machinery Nec

Rank	Company Name—Executive Officer	Address, City, State, Zip	Phone	Type	Fin	Empls
1	Kelco Industries Inc—Kevin Kelly	9210 Country Club Rd, Woodstock IL 60098	815-338-5521	R	9,220*	.8
2	4Front Engineered Solutions Inc—Keith Moore	1612 Hutton Dr Ste 140, Carrollton TX 75006	972-466-0707	R	2,608*	.7
3	Moog Inc—Robert T Brady	Jamison Rd, East Aurora NY 14052	716-652-2000	P	2,331	10.3
4	Marvin Group—Jerry Friedman	261 W Beach Ave, Inglewood CA 90302	310-674-5030	R	2,162*	.5
5	Curtiss-Wright Corp—Martin R Benante	10 Waterview Blvd 2nd, Parsippany NJ 07054	973-541-3700	P	2,054	8.9
6	GE Water and Process Technologies—Heiner Markoff	4636 Somerton Rd, Trevose PA 19053	215-355-3300	S	1,146*	8.0
7	HyPex Inc—James E Hasson	1000 Industrial Blvd, Southampton PA 18966	215-322-0545	R	792*	.2
8	Phillips Corp—Allan Phillips	7390 Coca Cola Dr, Hanover MD 21076	410-564-2929	R	744*	.2
9	SencorpWhite Inc—Richard Paolino	400 Kidds Hill Rd, Hyannis MA 02601	508-771-9400	R	673*	.3
10	Triumph Structures - Kansas City—David Soper	4020 E 138th St, Grandview MO 64030	816-763-8600	S	613*	.1
11	Davco Manufacturing Corp—Mark Bara	PO Box 487, Saline MI 48176	734-429-5665	R	434*	.1
12	Overton and Sons Tool and Die Co—Ron Overton	PO Box 69, Mooresville IN 46158	317-831-4542	R	433*	.1
13	Tss Technologies Inc—Brent Nichols	8800 Global Way, West Chester OH 45069	513-772-7000	R	305*	.4
14	Grand Traverse Machine Co—Michael Alfonso	PO Box 948, Traverse City MI 49685	231-946-8006	R	279*	.1
15	Pall Aeropower Corp—Lawrence D Kingsley	10540 Ridge Rd, New Port Richey FL 34654	727-849-9999	S	271*	.5
16	Senior Operations LLC—Hong Spanek	300 E Devon Ave, Bartlett IL 60103	630-837-1811	S	253*	2.5
17	Atscott Manufacturing Company Inc—John Norris	1150 Holstein Dr, Pine City MN 55063	320-629-2501	R	237*	.1
18	Systems Electro Coating LLC—William Cooley	253 Old Jackson Rd, Madison MS 39110	601-407-2340	R	235*	.1
19	Ronson Machine and Manufacturing—Terry Carver	3000 S Jackson Dr, Independence MO 64057	816-373-2720	R	217*	.1
20	KV F-Quad Corp—Michael Crotty	PO Box 795, East Moline IL 61244	309-755-1101	R	199*	.1
21	Advanced Cutting Systems Corp—William Sulosky	891 Centennial Dr, Windber PA 15963	814-467-0822	R	198*	.1
22	Dern Trophy Corp—Ron Spohn	6225 Frost Rd, Westerville OH 43082	614-895-3260	R	197*	.1
23	Valley Perforating Co—Mike Dover	3201 Gulf St, Bakersfield CA 93308	661-324-4964	R	197*	.1
24	Schaefers Enterprise Of Wolf Lake Inc	PO Box 136, Wolf Lake IL 62998	618-833-5498	R	190*	<.1
25	Federal Hose Manufacturing—Craig Cassady	25 Florence Ave, Painesville OH 44077	440-352-8927	R	186*	.1
26	Domaille Engineering Inc—Nancy Domaille	7100 Dresser Dr NE, Rochester MN 55906	507-281-0275	R	181*	<.1
27	Ace Machine and Metal Sales Co—Steven Gnyp	629 Cornelia Ct, Cleveland TN 37217	615-361-7548	R	173*	<.1
28	Stark Industrial Inc—Ray Wilkof	PO Box 3030, North Canton OH 44720	330-966-8108	R	166*	.1
29	Trico Nonferrous Metal Products Inc—Peter Pritz	2309 Wyandotte Rd, Willow Grove PA 19090	215-659-2673	R	164*	<.1
30	Flanco Gasket and Manufacturing Co—Bill Flanary	PO Box 96768, Oklahoma City OK 73143	405-672-7893	R	159*	<.1
31	G and L Precision Die Cutting—Loren Alberico	1766 Junction Ave, San Jose CA 95112	408-453-9400	R	157*	.1
32	Zamperla Inc	49 Fanny Rd, Boonton NJ 07005	973-334-8133	R	154*	<.1
33	Meta Manufacturing Corp—David McSwain	8901 Blue Ash Rd, Cincinnati OH 45242	513-793-6382	R	153*	<.1
34	Micronics Inc—Barry Hibble	200 West Rd, Portsmouth NH 03801	603-433-1299	R	147*	<.1
35	Tennessee Cummins Mid-South LLC—Ben Strafuss	PO Box 3080, Memphis TN 38173	901-577-0600	S	143*	.6
36	Hartzell Manufacturing Company Inc—David Vickroy	PO Box 808, Miamisburg OH 45343	937-859-5955	R	138*	<.1
37	Crown Machine Inc—Daniel J Glavin	2707 N Main St, Rockford IL 61103	815-877-7700	R	130*	<.1
38	Mastercraft Tool and Machine Co—Steve Lassy	100 Newell St, Southington CT 06489	860-628-5551	R	129*	<.1
39	Carolina Tractor/CAT—Edward Weisiger jr	PO Box 1095, Charlotte NC 28201	704-596-6700	R	127*	.7
40	Dana Corp Plumley Div—Roger J Wood	100 Plumley Dr, Paris TN 38242	731-642-5582	J	123*	1.5
41	Main Tool and Manufacturing Co—Samual Jefferson	7800 Beech St NE, Fridley MN 55432	763-571-1772	R	119*	<.1
42	JK Manufacturing Co—Jozef Koniecko	7301 W 66th St, Bedford Park IL 60638	708-563-2500	R	95*	<.1

Rank	Company Name—*Executive Officer*	Address, City, State, Zip	Phone	Type	Fin	Empls
43	Major Die and Engineering Co—*James Fett Jr*	1352 Industrial Dr, Itasca IL 60143	630-773-3444	R	95*	<.1
44	Keller Technology Corp—*Michael Keller*	PO Box 103, Buffalo NY 14217	716-693-3840	R	90*	.3
45	Remmele Engineering Inc—*Richard Pogue*	10 Old Hwy 8 SW, New Brighton MN 55112	651-635-4100	S	88*	.5
46	Fm Industries Inc—*David Miller*	221 E Warren Ave, Fremont CA 94539	510-668-1900	R	80*	.1
47	Triumph Engines - Tempe—*Elizabeth Rakestraw*	2015 W Alameda Dr, Tempe AZ 85282	602-438-8760	S	79*	.3
48	Angstrom Precision Metals—*Joe Harden*	8229 Tyler Blvd, Mentor OH 44060	440-255-6700	I	77*	.3
49	Maynard Precision Inc—*Amin Khoury*	wwwbeaerospacecom, Vista CA 92083	760-599-1130	S	75*	<.1
50	Parker Hannifin Corp Racor Div—*Brian Hook*	PO Box 3208, Modesto CA 95353	209-521-7860	D	74*	.6
51	WEDCO Technology Inc—*John Knapp*	1811 Bering Dr Ste 200, Houston TX 77057	713-351-4100	S	72*	.8
52	Flexfab Horizons International Inc—*Matt DeCamp*	1699 W M-43 Hwy, Hastings MI 49058	269-945-3533	R	69*	.5
53	Knust-Sbo Ltd—*David Prickett*	PO Box 631329, Houston TX 77263	713-785-1060	R	69*	.2
54	Innovance Inc—*Mike Larson*	505 W Front St, Albert Lea MN 56007	507-377-8910	R	67*	.3
55	L and H Industrial Inc—*Mike Wandler*	913 L and J Ct, Gillette WY 82718	307-682-7238	R	66*	.3
56	Hvac Mechanical Services Of Texas Ltd—*Richard Hunton*	10555 Westpark Dr, Houston TX 77042	713-266-3900	S	59*	.3
57	Morbark Inc—*Lon Morey*	PO Box 1000, Winn MI 48896	989-866-2381	R	58*	.6
58	K and B Machine Works LLC—*Kenneth Wood*	2186 Grand Caillou Rd, Houma LA 70363	985-868-6730	R	57*	.4
59	Colonna's Shipyard Inc—*Tom Godfrey*	400 E Indian River Rd, Norfolk VA 23523	757-545-2414	R	56*	.5
60	Delafield Corp—*Nik Ray*	1520 Flower Ave, Duarte CA 91010	626-303-0740	R	50*	.2
61	Will-Burt Co—*Jeffrey Evans*	PO Box 900, Orrville OH 44667	330-682-7015	R	50*	.3
62	Omega Flex Inc—*Kevin R Hoben*	451 Creamery Way, Exton PA 19341	610-524-7272	B	47	.1
63	General Products Delaware Corp—*Dave Rawl*	1411 Wohlert St, Angola IN 46703	260-668-1487	R	47*	.3
64	Timken Boring Specialties LLC—*Donna Fick*	PO Box 90246, Houston TX 77290	281-449-0319	R	46*	.1
65	Stainless Foundry and Engineering Inc—*Daniel Brockington*	5150 N 35th St, Milwaukee WI 53209	414-462-7400	R	46*	.3
66	Alex Products Inc—*Dave Deylen*	PO Box 326, Ridgeville Corners OH 43555	419-267-5240	R	45*	.6
67	Godwin-Sbo LP—*Ron Hultquist*	28825 Katy Brookshire, Katy TX 77494	281-371-5400	R	45*	.2
68	Line Craft Tool Co—*Jack Amstadt*	10 W North Ave, Lombard IL 60148	630-932-1182	R	45*	.2
69	Acme Industries Inc—*Warren Young*	1325 Pratt Blvd, Elk Grove Village IL 60007	847-296-3346	R	45*	.1
70	National Machine Co—*Peter Piglia*	4880 Hudson Dr, Stow OH 44224	330-688-6494	R	43*	.3
71	Aaa Sales and Engineering Inc—*Michael Mazur*	1120 W Northbranch Dr, Oak Creek WI 53154	414-764-2700	R	43*	.2
72	Integral Automation Inc—*Lou Wroblewski*	16W 171 Shore Ct, Burr Ridge IL 60527	630-654-4300	R	43*	<.1
73	Atlas Technologies Inc—*Bill Rogner*	201 S Alloy Dr, Fenton MI 48430	810-629-6663	R	40*	.2
74	Triumph Gear Systems - Macomb Inc—*Carla Bowman*	15375 23 Mile Rd, Macomb MI 48042	586-781-2800	S	38*	.4
75	Process Equipment Company Of Tipp City—*Michael Haaren*	6555 S State Rte 202, Tipp City OH 45371	937-667-4451	R	38*	.1
76	EFA Technologies Inc	2701 Del Paso Rd Ste 1, Sacramento CA 95835	916-443-8842	R	38*	<.1
77	Hypro Inc—*Robert Schildt*	PO Box 370, Waterford WI 53185	262-534-5141	R	38*	.5
78	Al-Be Industries Inc—*Donald J Shaw*	4230 Artesia Ave, Fullerton CA 92833	714-523-4646	R	37*	<.1
79	K and D Co	7850 Gloria Ave, Van Nuys CA 91406	818-782-5150	R	37*	<.1
80	Floturn Inc—*R Glutting*	4236 Thunderbird Ln, Fairfield OH 45014	513-860-8040	R	37*	.3
81	Acutec Precision Machining Inc—*Robert Smith*	16891 State Hwy 198, Saegertown PA 16433	814-763-3214	R	36*	.2
82	Allied Chucker And Engineering Co—*William Schomer*	3529 Scheele Dr, Jackson MI 49202	517-787-1370	R	36*	.2
83	Ace Precision Machining Corp—*Paul Erdmann*	977 Blue Ribbon Cir N, Oconomowoc WI 53066	262-252-4003	R	36*	.3
84	Calvary Design Team Inc—*Mark Chaney*	45 Hendrix Rd, West Henrietta NY 14586	585-321-5055	R	36*	.1
85	Nex-Tech Aerospace Inc—*Thomas Gibbons*	4201 S 119th St W, Wichita KS 67215	316-522-5426	R	35*	.2
86	Dearborn Precision Tubular Products Inc—*Bill Findeisen*	PO Box 126, Fryeburg ME 04037	207-935-2171	R	35*	.3
87	American Wire Tie Inc—*James Smith*	PO Box 696, North Collins NY 14111	716-337-2412	R	33*	.1
88	Springfield Remanufacturing Corp—*Ryan Stack*	650 N Broadview Pl, Springfield MO 65802	417-862-3501	R	33*	.3
89	Metalex Manufacturing Inc—*Werner Kummorlo*	5750 Cornell Rd, Blue Ash OH 45242	513-489-0507	R	32*	.1
90	Abrasive-Form Inc—*Ken Kummer*	454 Scott Dr, Bloomingdale IL 60108	630-893-7800	R	32*	.2
91	D-Velco Manufacturing Of Arizona Inc—*John Maris*	401 S 36th St, Phoenix AZ 85034	602-275-4406	R	32*	.2
92	Funtastic Shows Inc—*Ron Burback*	3407 SE 108th Ave, Portland OR 97266	503-761-0989	R	32*	<.1
93	General Tool Co—*William Kramer*	101 Landy Ln, Cincinnati OH 45215	513-733-5500	R	32*	.3
94	K and M Machine-Fabricating Inc—*Michael Loughlin*	PO Box 218, Cassopolis MI 49031	269-445-2495	R	32*	.3
95	Norman Noble Inc—*Lawrence Noble*	1650 Collamer Ave, Cleveland OH 44110	216-761-2133	R	31*	.4
96	Magnetic Instruments Corp—*Nelson Byman*	1801 Industrial Blvd, Brenham TX 77833	979-836-4481	R	31*	.5
97	Patz Corp—*Darrell Patz*	PO Box 7, Pound WI 54161	920-897-2251	D	31*	.3
98	J L Haley Enterprises—*James Haley*	3510 Luyung Dr, Rancho Cordova CA 95742	916-631-6375	R	31*	.1
99	P and H Manufacturing Co—*Earl Peifer*	PO Box 349, Shelbyville IL 62565	217-774-2123	R	31*	.3
100	Wausau Equipment Company Inc—*Rodney Winter*	1905 S Moorland Rd, New Berlin WI 53151	262-784-6066	R	30*	.1
101	Team Industries Park Rapids - DI Inc—*David Ricke*	501 Industrial Park Rd, Park Rapids MN 56470	218-732-4666	S	30*	.1
102	Process Fab Inc—*Tim Dumbauld*	15644 Clanton Cir, Santa Fe Springs CA 90670	562-921-1979	R	30*	.2
103	Hebeler Corp—*Ken Snyder*	2000 Military Rd, Tonawanda NY 14150	716-873-9300	R	28*	.2
104	Nationwide Precision Products	200 Tech Park Dr, Rochester NY 14623	585-697-5469	S	28*	.3
105	Vermont Aerospace Manufacturing Inc—*Sheryl Cota*	PO Box 1148, Lyndonville VT 05851	802-748-8705	R	28*	.2
106	Pioneer Products Inc—*F Beere*	PO Box 1348, Racine WI 53401	262-633-6304	R	28*	.1
107	Erika Record LLC—*Max Oehler*	37 Atlantic Way, Clifton NJ 07012	973-614-8500	S	28*	<.1
108	Hamill Manufacturing Co—*Jeffrey Kelly*	500 Pleasant Valley Rd, Trafford PA 15085	724-744-2131	R	27*	.1
109	Hader Industries Inc—*Wayne K Hader*	Box 510260, New Berlin WI 53151	262-641-5310	R	27*	.1
110	Rms Co—*Lee Zachman*	8600 Evergreen Blvd Nw, Minneapolis MN 55433	763-786-1520	S	27*	.4
111	Perfekta Inc—*Julian Guerra*	480 E 21st St N, Wichita KS 67214	316-263-2056	R	27*	.2
112	Parsons Company Inc—*Robert Parsons*	1386 State Rte 117, Roanoke IL 61561	309-467-9100	R	27*	.2
113	Busche Enterprise Division Inc—*Nick Busche*	PO Box 77, Albion IN 46701	260-636-7030	R	26*	.4
114	Weldmac Manufacturing Co—*Marshall Rugg*	1533 N Johnson Ave, El Cajon CA 92020	619-440-2300	R	26*	.1
115	Atlas Machine And Supply Inc—*Richard Gimmel*	7000 Global Dr, Louisville KY 40258	502-584-7262	R	26*	.2
116	Advanced Filtration Systems Inc—*Nickolas Priadka*	3206 Farber Dr, Champaign IL 61822	217-351-3073	R	26*	.2
117	Bayless Engineering and Manufacturing Inc—*Earl Bayless*	26100 Avenue Hall, Valencia CA 91355	661-257-3373	R	26*	.1
118	Industrial Piping Inc—*Michael Jones*	PO Box 518, Pineville NC 28134	704-588-1100	R	25*	.2
119	Creed-Monarch Inc—*Richard Creed*	PO Box 550, New Britain CT 06050	860-225-7884	R	25*	.4
120	Thomas Instrument and Machine Co—*Thomas R Blackburn*	PO Box 999, Brookshire TX 77423	281-375-6300	R	25*	.2
121	Fort Walton Machining Inc—*Greg Britton*	43 Jet Dr Nw, Fort Walton Beach FL 32548	850-244-9095	R	24*	.2
122	Machinists Inc—*Hugh Bossier*	7600 5th Ave S, Seattle WA 98108	206-736-0990	R	24*	.2
123	LAI International—*Stewart Cramer*	1110 Business Pkwy S, Westminster MD 21157	410-857-0770	S	24*	.1
124	Machining Corporation of America—*Peter Bilinovich*	PO Box 345, Barberton OH 44203	330-745-4408	R	24*	.3
125	Skyway Precision Inc—*Bill Bonnell*	41225 Plymouth Rd, Plymouth MI 48170	734-454-3550	R	24*	.2
126	NEW Industries Inc—*Christopher Moore*	905 S Neenah Ave, Sturgeon Bay WI 54235	920-743-8575	R	23*	.2
127	Tower Industries Inc—*Tom Stull*	2951 E La Palma Ave, Anaheim CA 92806	714-630-6981	R	23*	.2
128	Custom Air Products and Services Inc—*John Boger*	35 Southbelt Industria, Houston TX 77047	713-460-9009	R	23*	.2
129	D and S Machine Service Inc—*Russel Nowak*	412 4th St, Luxemburg WI 54217	920-845-5425	R	23*	.1
130	Machine Specialties Inc—*Robert Simmons*	6511 Franz Warner Pkwy, Whitsett NC 27377	336-603-1919	R	23*	.2
131	Furmanite America Inc	101 Old Underwood Rd S, La Porte TX 77571	281-842-5100	D	23*	.3
132	Dudek and Bock Spring Manufacturing Co—*John Dudek*	5100 W Roosevelt Rd, Chicago IL 60644	773-379-4100	R	23*	.2

Note: An asterisk (*) indicates an estimated financial figure. The company type code used is as follows: R = Private, P = Public, S = Private Subsidiary, B = Public Subsidiary, D = Division, J = Joint Venture, I = Investment Fund.

COMPANY RANKINGS BY SALES WITHIN 4-DIGIT SIC

Rank	Company Name—*Executive Officer*	Address, City, State, Zip	Phone	Type	Fin	Empls
133	Karlee Co—*Jo Brumit*	PO Box 461207, Garland TX 75046	972-272-0628	R	23*	.3
134	Nfm/Welding Engineers Inc—*Phillip Roberson*	577 Oberlin Ave Sw, Massillon OH 44647	330-837-3868	R	23*	.2
135	Verhoff Machine and Welding Inc—*Edward Verhoff*	7300 Rd 18, Continental OH 45831	419-596-3202	R	23*	.1
136	Michigan Production Machining Inc—*Donald West*	16700 23 Mile Rd, Macomb MI 48044	586-228-9700	R	22*	.3
137	Metem Corp—*Steven Goldthwaite*	700 Parsippany Rd, Parsippany NJ 07054	973-887-6635	R	22*	.2
138	Huestis Industrial—*Krishnan Suthanthiran*	68 Buttonwood St, Bristol RI 02809	401-253-5500	R	22*	.2
139	Aero Design and Manufacturing Inc—*Michael Holnes*	3409 E Wood St, Phoenix AZ 85040	602-437-8080	R	22*	.1
140	Westbrook Manufacturing Inc—*Robert Mays*	600 N Irwin St, Dayton OH 45403	937-254-2004	R	22*	.2
141	Dakota Tube Inc—*John Steinbauer*	221 Airport Dr, Watertown SD 57201	605-882-2156	R	22*	.2
142	Alin Machining Company Inc—*Manny Gandhi*	3131 W Soffel Ave, Melrose Park IL 60160	708-345-8600	R	21*	.2
143	Superior Companies Inc—*J Judd*	101 N Johnstone Ave, Bartlesville OK 74003	918-336-5075	R	21*	.2
144	General Dynamics Robotic Systems Inc—*Philip Cory*	1234 Tech Ct, Westminster MD 21157	410-876-9200	S	21*	.3
145	Mennie Machine Co—*Hubert Mennie*	PO Box 110, Mark IL 61340	815-339-2226	R	21*	.2
146	Illinois Machine and Tool Works LLC—*Laurie Hanson*	1961 Edgewater Dr, Pekin IL 61554	309-382-3045	R	21*	.2
147	M Cubed Technologies Inc—*Joseph Hochreiter*	921 Main St, Monroe CT 06468	203-452-2333	R	21*	.2
148	Bachman Machine Co—*Jerry Coleman*	4321 N Broadway, Saint Louis MO 63147	314-231-4221	R	21*	.1
149	RAM Aircraft Corp—*Horst Schoen*	PO Box 5219, Waco TX 76708	254-752-8381	R	21*	.1
150	King Tool Co—*Charles G Tullis*	PO Box 150128, Longview TX 75615	903-759-4478	R	21*	.1
151	Olson Industries Inc—*Ted Olson*	PO Box 880, Atkinson NE 68713	402-925-5090	R	21*	.1
152	Sieger Engineering Inc—*Leonard Mezhvinsky*	148 Beacon St, South San Francisco CA 94080	650-583-5345	R	20*	.3
153	UMC Inc—*Don Tomann*	500 Chelsea Rd, Monticello MN 55362	763-271-5200	R	20*	.2
154	Ixmation Inc—*Martin Pfister*	31 Presidential Dr, Roselle IL 60172	630-351-3000	R	20*	.2
155	B and C Machine Company LLC—*Joe Cralik*	PO Box 345, Barberton OH 44203	330-745-4013	R	20*	.3
156	Chance Rides Manufacturing Inc—*Richard Chance*	PO Box 12328, Wichita KS 67277	316-942-7411	R	20*	.1
157	Walden's Division—*Randy Baskins*	3030 N Erie Ave, Tulsa OK 74115	918-836-6317	D	20*	.1
158	McCue Corp—*David McCue*	35 Congress St Ste 150, Salem MA 01970	978-741-8500	R	20*	.1
159	Production Engineering Inc—*James Jansen*	2400 Enterprise St, Jackson MI 49203	517-788-6800	R	20*	.1
160	Toth Industries Inc—*Richard Toth*	5102 Enterprise Blvd, Toledo OH 43612	419-729-4669	R	20*	.1
161	Active Grinding Inc—*Joe Le May*	871 S Rose Pl, Anaheim CA 92805	714-772-7610	R	20*	<.1
162	G and B Specialties Inc—*Lewis Griffiths*	PO Box 305, Berwick PA 18603	570-752-5901	R	20*	.2
163	Micro Instrument Corp—*John Pfeffer*	PO Box 60619, Rochester NY 14606	585-458-3150	R	20*	.2
164	Hi-Tek Manufacturing Inc—*Cletis Jackson*	6050 Hi Tek Ct, Mason OH 45040	513-459-1094	R	19*	.2
165	Martinez And Turek Inc—*Larry Tribe*	300 S Cedar Ave, Rialto CA 92376	909-820-6800	R	19*	.1
166	Medplast West Berlin Inc—*Robert Piccoli*	225 Old Egg Harbor Rd, West Berlin NJ 08091	856-753-7600	R	19*	.2
167	Clyde Bergemann Inc—*Hans Schwade*	4015 Presidential Pkwy, Atlanta GA 30340	770-557-3600	R	19*	.1
168	Vickers Engineering Inc—*Matthew Tyler*	PO Box 346, New Troy MI 49119	269-426-8545	R	19*	.1
169	Farrar Corp—*Joe Farrar*	PO Box 8, Norwich KS 67118	785-537-7733	R	19*	.3
170	Commercial Honing LLC—*Valerie Woodburn*	2997 Progress St, Dover OH 44622	330-343-8896	R	19*	.2
171	Classic Wire Cut Company Inc—*Brett Bannerman*	28210 Constellation Rd, Valencia CA 91355	661-257-0558	R	19*	.1
172	Best Tool And Manufacturing Company Inc—*Roland Mayer*	3515 Ne 33rd Ter, Kansas City MO 64117	816-454-4000	R	19*	.1
173	Quality Manufacturing Company Inc—*James Barker*	PO Box 616, Winchester KY 40392	859-744-0420	R	18*	.3
174	Midstate Manufacturing Company Inc—*Curtis Pitman*	750 W 3rd St, Galesburg IL 61401	309-342-9555	R	18*	.2
175	True-Tech Corp—*Doug Hill*	4050 Technology Pl, Fremont CA 94538	510-353-1000	R	18*	.1
176	Boston Centerless Inc—*Steven Tamasi*	11 Presidential Way, Woburn MA 01801	781-994-5000	R	18*	.1
177	Daco Inc—*Kenneth Lindgren*	609 Airport Rd, North Aurora IL 60542	630-897-8797	R	18*	.1
178	General Grind and Machine Inc—*Mark Rieri*	PO Box 168, Aledo IL 61231	309-582-5959	R	18*	.2
179	Jonaco Machine Inc—*Rick Green*	3990 Peavey Rd, Chaska MN 55318	952-448-5544	R	18*	.1
180	Piper Plastics Inc—*Randall White*	PO Box 536, Mundelein IL 60060	847-367-0110	R	18*	.1
181	Max Daetwyler Inc—*Ralph Daetwyler*	13420 Reese Blvd W, Huntersville NC 28078	704-875-1200	R	18*	.1
182	Denco Manufacturing Inc—*Mark Cooper*	2300 S 179th St, New Berlin WI 53146	262-782-2322	R	18*	.1
183	Veridiam Medical—*Andrew Gale*	4645 North Ave, Oceanside CA 92056	760-941-1702	R	18*	.1
184	Forward Technology Industries Inc—*J Goodson*	260 Jenks Ave Sw, Cokato MN 55321	320-286-2578	R	18*	.1
185	Allied Welding Inc—*Terry Nelson*	PO Box 410, Chillicothe IL 61523	309-274-6227	R	18*	.1
186	Onamac Industries Inc—*Jim Loveall*	11504 Airport Rd Bldg, Everett WA 98204	425-743-6676	R	18*	.1
187	Fletcher Machine Inc—*Terry Hurst*	19537 Us Hwy 6, Weston OH 43569	419-669-2063	R	18*	.2
188	Highland Machine and Screw Products Co—*Edwin Frisse*	700 5th St, Highland IL 62249	618-654-2103	R	18*	.1
189	Metalcraft Of Mayville Se Inc—*C Neal*	PO Box 151, Mayville WI 53050	336-544-7500	R	17*	.2
190	D and H Manufacturing Co—*Angelo Grestoni*	49235 Milmont Dr, Fremont CA 94538	510-770-5100	R	17*	.1
191	Skee Ball Inc—*Joseph Sladek*	121 Liberty Ln, Chalfont PA 18914	215-997-8900	R	17*	.1
192	Micro-Tronics Inc—*Robert Marusiak*	2905 S Potter Dr, Tempe AZ 85282	602-437-8995	R	17*	.1
193	New Dimensions Precision Machining Inc—*Nancy Halwix*	6614 S Union Rd, Union IL 60180	815-923-8300	R	17*	.1
194	Advance Manufacturing Company Inc—*Anthony Amanti*	PO Box 726, Westfield MA 01086	413-568-2411	R	17*	.2
195	Rochester Gear Inc—*John Aldridge*	9900 Main St, Clifford MI 48727	989-761-7521	S	17*	.2
196	Accurate Metal Machining Inc—*John Racic*	882 Callendar Blvd, Painesville OH 44077	440-350-8225	R	17*	.1
197	Rsb Transmissions NA Inc—*Sanjay Chadda*	PO Box 68, Homer MI 49245	517-568-4171	R	17*	.1
198	Gremada Industries Inc—*Steven Walker*	PO Box 715, West Fargo ND 58078	701-356-0184	R	17*	.1
199	Automatic Products Corp—*Gary Tedford*	2735 Forest Ln, Garland TX 75042	972-272-6422	R	17*	.1
200	Whitworth Tool Inc—*Kenny Whitworth*	PO Box 759, Hardinsburg KY 40143	270-756-0098	R	17*	.2
201	Arlington Machine and Tool Co—*Sue Blanck*	90 New Dutch Ln, Fairfield NJ 07004	973-276-1377	R	17*	.1
202	H M Dunn Company LP—*Beverly Davis*	3301 House Anderson Rd, Euless TX 76040	817-283-3722	R	16*	.1
203	Urban Manufacturing Inc—*Sandor Urbanchek*	1288 Hickory St, Pewaukee WI 53072	262-691-2455	R	16*	.1
204	Barnard Manufacturing Company Inc—*Gary Barnard*	PO Box 10, Saint Johns MI 48879	989-224-1070	R	16*	.1
205	AB Heller Inc—*James Heller*	PO Box 640, Milford MI 48381	248-685-9500	R	16*	.1
206	Brazonics Inc—*Mike Mastergeorge*	94 Tide Mill Rd, Hampton NH 03842	603-926-5700	R	16*	.1
207	Boley Tool and Machine Works Inc—*Warren Boley*	1044 Spring Bay Rd, East Peoria IL 61611	309-694-2722	R	16*	.1
208	Damar Machine Co—*M Kroon*	PO Box 9, Monroe WA 98272	360-794-4448	S	16*	.1
209	Tibor Machine Products Inc—*Mark Lindermulder*	7400 W 100th Pl, Bridgeview IL 60455	708-499-3700	R	16*	.1
210	Glunt Industries Inc—*Dennis Glunt*	319 N River Rd Nw, Warren OH 44483	330-399-7585	R	16*	.1
211	Turbocam Inc—*Marian Noronha*	PO Box 830, Barrington NH 03825	603-905-0220	R	16*	.1
212	Wilco Machine and Fab Inc—*Kris Boles*	PO Box 48, Marlow OK 73055	580-658-6993	R	16*	.1
213	Precision Defense Services Inc—*Robert Perkins*	1 Quality Way, Irwin PA 15642	724-863-1100	R	16*	.1
214	Kay Manufacturing Co—*Steven Pelke*	602 State St, Calumet City IL 60409	708-862-6800	R	16*	.1
215	Sussek Machine Corp—*Christopher Sussek*	PO Box 98, Waterloo WI 53594	920-478-2126	R	16*	.1
216	Petersen Precision Engineering LLC—*Gary Dutton*	611 Broadway St, Redwood City CA 94063	650-365-4373	R	15*	.1
217	Norotos Inc—*Ronald Soto*	201 E Alton Ave, Santa Ana CA 92707	714-662-3113	R	15*	.1
218	Lebanon Tool Company Inc—*Janis Herschkowitz*	PO Box 29, Lebanon PA 17042	717-273-3711	S	15*	.1
219	Best Metal Products Company Inc—*David Faasse*	3570 Raleigh Ave Se, Grand Rapids MI 49512	616-942-7141	R	15*	.1
220	Biddle Precision Components Inc—*Brian Myers*	701 S Main St, Sheridan IN 46069	317-758-4451	R	15*	.2
221	Bellwright Industries Inc—*Kenneth Waterlander*	10186 Bellwright Rd, Summerville SC 29483	843-871-5030	R	15*	.1
222	East End Welding Co—*John Susong*	357 Tallmadge Rd, Kent OH 44240	330-677-6000	R	15*	.1

Rank	Company Name—*Executive Officer*	Address, City, State, Zip	Phone	Type	Fin	Empls
223	Process Manufacturing Company Inc—*Frank Chrisco*	5800 W 68th St, Tulsa OK 74131	918-445-0909	R	15*	.1
224	Delta Industrial Service Inc—*Dave Schiebout*	11501 Eagle St NW, Minneapolis MN 55448	763-755-7744	R	15*	.1
225	MotorVac Technologies Inc—*Mark J Hallsman*	1431 S Village Way, Santa Ana CA 92705	714-558-4822	R	15*	.1
226	Republic-Lagun Machine Tool Co—*Olaf Tessarzyk*	PO Box 5328, Carson CA 90745	310-518-1100	R	15*	.1
227	Bob's Space Racers Inc—*Robert Cassata*	427 15th St, Daytona Beach FL 32117	386-677-0761	R	15*	.1
228	Tri-Tube Inc—*Arthur Porter*	14378 Enterprise Rd, Abingdon VA 24210	276-628-5932	R	15*	.1
229	Kocsis Brothers Machine Co—*Louis Kocsis*	11755 S Austin Ave, Alsip IL 60803	708-597-8110	R	15*	.1
230	Prattville Machine And Tool Company Inc—*John Russo*	240 Jubilee Dr Fl 2, Peabody MA 01960	978-538-5229	R	15*	.1
231	A Trace Matic Corp—*Thorsten Wienss*	1570 Commerce Ave, Brookfield WI 53045	262-797-7300	R	15*	.1
232	Lavigne Manufacturing Inc—*David Lavigne*	15 Western Industrial, Cranston RI 02921	401-943-9292	R	14*	.1
233	1660 Group LLC—*Deb Fischer*	1660 Lake Dr W, Chanhassen MN 55317	952-937-1000	R	14*	<.1
234	Precise Products Corp—*Darrell Freitag*	1201 Plymouth Ave N, Minneapolis MN 55411	612-522-2141	R	14*	.1
235	Advanced Machine and Engineering Company Inc—*Dietmar Goellner*	2500 Latham St, Rockford IL 61103	815-962-6076	R	14*	.1
236	Precision Machine And Supply Inc—*Daniel Wenstrom*	PO Box 1539, Lewiston ID 83501	208-746-2621	R	14*	.1
237	Advanced Machine and Tool Corp—*Frederick Burke*	3706 Transportation Dr, Fort Wayne IN 46818	260-489-3572	R	14*	.1
238	Tri-State Machine Inc—*Walter Moskey*	PO Box 6566, Wheeling WV 26003	304-234-0170	R	14*	.1
239	Service Guide Inc—*Grant Oakes*	3605 Warren Meadville, Cortland OH 44410	330-637-6060	R	14*	.1
240	Panek Precision Products Co—*Gregg Panek*	455 Academy Dr, Northbrook IL 60062	847-291-9755	R	14*	.1
241	PMSD Inc—*Daniel Olesen*	950 George St, Santa Clara CA 95054	408-988-5235	R	14*	.1
242	Duro-Life Corp—*Marshall Wells*	2401 Huntington Dr N, Algonquin IL 60102	847-854-1044	S	14*	.1
243	Youngers And Sons Manufacturing Company Inc—*Wayne Youngers*	19223 W K 42, Viola KS 67149	620-545-7133	R	14*	.1
244	Simpson Technologies Corp—*Henry Dienst*	751 Shoreline Dr, Aurora IL 60504	630-978-0044	R	14*	.1
245	Niedwick Machine Co—*Ted Niedwick*	1928 W Business Ctr Dr, Orange CA 92867	714-771-9999	R	14*	<.1
246	Renco Machine Company Inc—*Donald Renard*	1421 Eastman Ave, Green Bay WI 54302	920-448-8000	R	14*	.1
247	Pyramid Precision Machine Inc—*Robert Taylor*	6721 Cobra Way, San Diego CA 92121	858-642-0713	R	14*	.1
248	Cad Enterprises Inc—*Arvin Loudermilk*	302 N 52nd Ave, Phoenix AZ 85043	602-278-4407	R	14*	.1
249	Fabricated Metals Co—*David Pingel*	2121 Landmeier Rd, Elk Grove Village IL 60007	847-718-1300	R	14*	.1
250	FMH Corp—*Hangup Moon*	17072 Daimler St, Irvine CA 92614	714-751-1000	R	14*	.1
251	Stanley Machining and Tool Corp—*Stanley Trzaska*	425 Maple Ave, Carpentersville IL 60110	847-426-4560	R	14*	.1
252	CNC Machine Products Inc—*Greg Scheurich*	PO Box 2701, Joplin MO 64803	417-782-2627	R	14*	.1
253	Hunt and Hunt Ltd—*David Hunt*	PO Box 262325, Houston TX 77207	713-413-2500	R	14*	.1
254	Walco Tool and Engineering Corp—*David Walsh*	18954 Airport Rd, Romeoville IL 60446	815-834-0225	R	14*	.1
255	G R Manufacturing Inc—*William Fyfe*	PO Box 380, Trussville AL 35173	205-655-8001	R	14*	.1
256	Power Repair Service Inc—*James Power*	314 Mcbride Ln, Corpus Christi TX 78408	361-289-1471	R	14*	.1
257	Cutting Dynamics Inc—*William Carson*	980 Jaycox Rd, Avon OH 44011	440-249-4150	R	14*	.1
258	In-Place Machining Company Inc—*Jonathan Eder*	3811 N Holton St, Milwaukee WI 53212	414-562-2000	R	14*	.1
259	Standard Jig Boring Service LLC—*David Stuller*	3360 Miller Park Rd, Akron OH 44312	330-896-9530	R	14*	.1
260	Nc Dynamics Inc—*Lyle Scott*	3401 E 69th St, Long Beach CA 90805	562-634-7392	R	14*	.1
261	Triple/S Dynamics Inc—*James Sullivan*	PO Box 151027, Dallas TX 75315	214-828-8600	R	13*	.1
262	Magnum Tool Company Inc—*Ricky Campbell*	615 Wooten Rd Ste 150, Colorado Springs CO 80915	719-590-7575	R	13*	.1
263	South Side Machine Works Inc—*James Jost*	3761 Eiler St, Saint Louis MO 63116	314-481-7171	R	13*	.1
264	Anderson Machining Service Inc—*Susan Anderson*	211 Collins Rd, Jefferson WI 53549	920-674-6003	R	13*	.1
265	David Price Metal Service Inc—*Christopher Price*	360 Eastpark Dr, Norwalk OH 44857	419-663-0279	R	13*	.1
266	H and S Swansons' Tool Co—*James Swanson*	9000 68th St N, Pinellas Park FL 33782	727-541-3575	R	13*	.1
267	Metalcut Products Inc—*David Wait*	1024 Michigan Ave, South Milwaukee WI 53172	414-762-6480	R	13*	.1
268	Mid Valley Industries LLC—*Chris Bos*	1161 Dolanglade St, Kaukauna WI 54130	920-759-0314	R	13*	.1
269	Era Industries Inc—*Paul Podedworny*	10103 Pacific Ave, Franklin Park IL 60131	847-678-6617	R	13*	.1
270	Len Industries Inc—*Leonard Len*	815 Rice St, Leslie MI 49251	517-589-8241	R	13*	.2
271	Leiss Tool and Die Co—*Peter Leiss*	801 N Pleasant Ave, Somerset PA 15501	814-444-1444	R	13*	.1
272	McNally Industries Inc—*Tom Brunts*	PO Box 129, Grantsburg WI 54840	715-463-8300	R	13*	.1
273	Casey Machine Company Inc—*Ronald Radziwon*	74 Ward Rd, Lancaster NY 14086	716-651-0150	R	13*	.1
274	Creative Machining Technologies Inc—*William Hayes*	3560 5th Ave, East Moline IL 61244	309-755-7700	R	13*	.1
275	Crown Parts and Machine Inc—*Paul Hatzell*	1733 Hwy 87 E, Billings MT 59101	406-252-6682	R	13	.1
276	Mac Machine Company Inc—*George Nab*	7209 Rutherford Rd, Baltimore MD 21244	410-944-6171	R	13*	.1
277	American Drilling Co—*Wayne Tatum*	15118 Grevillea Ave, Lawndale CA 90260	310-970-1010	R	13*	.1
278	Seabrook International LLC—*Paul Barck*	15 Woodworkers Way, Seabrook NH 03874	603-474-1919	R	13*	.1
279	Dial Precision Inc—*Earl Wolleson*	17235 Darwin Ave, Hesperia CA 92345	760-947-3557	R	13*	.1
280	Kenlee Precision Corp—*Kenneth Lewis*	1701 Inverness Ave, Baltimore MD 21230	410-525-3800	R	13*	.1
281	Coffeyville Sektam Inc—*Steve Cornell*	509 Cline Rd, Coffeyville KS 67337	620-251-3880	R	13*	.1
282	Sonfarrel Inc—*Frank Powers*	3000 E La Jolla St 301, Anaheim CA 92806	714-630-7280	R	13*	.1
283	Western Cnc Inc—*Danny Ashcraft*	1001 Park Ctr Dr, Vista CA 92081	760-597-7000	R	13*	.1
284	Powill Manufacturing and Engineering Inc—*James Buchanan*	21039 N 27th Ave, Phoenix AZ 85027	623-780-4100	R	13*	.1
285	Latva Machine Inc—*Mitchell Latva*	744 John Stark Hwy, Newport NH 03773	603-863-5155	R	13*	.1
286	Usm Precision Products Inc—*Donald Nettis*	2002 Joseph Lloyd Pkwy, Willoughby OH 44094	440-975-8600	R	13*	.1
287	Dynamic Tool Company Inc—*John Thompson*	1421 Vanderbilt Dr, El Paso TX 79935	915-598-2330	R	13*	.1
288	Sterling Engineering Corp—*John Lavieri*	PO Box 559, Winsted CT 06098	860-379-3366	R	13*	.1
289	Southern Manufacturing Technologies Inc—*Roy Sweatman*	5910 Johns Rd, Tampa FL 33634	813-888-8151	R	13*	.1
290	Specialized Products Ltd—*Wayne Oestreich*	200 Summer St, Clintonville WI 54929	715-823-3727	R	13*	.1
291	Delta Mold Inc—*Eric Mozer*	9415 Stockport Pl, Charlotte NC 28273	704-588-6600	R	13*	.1
292	Thorud Inc—*Steven Thorud*	10501 Hampshire Ave S, Minneapolis MN 55438	952-996-9020	R	13*	.1
293	Greno Industries Inc—*Robert Golden*	PO Box 542, Schenectady NY 12301	518-393-4195	R	13*	.1
294	Arwood Machine Corp—*Michael Munday*	95 Parker St Ste 4, Newburyport MA 01950	978-463-3777	R	12*	.1
295	Karder Machine Co—*Daniel Abraham*	PO Box 549, Akron OH 44309	330-535-7826	R	12*	.1
296	Kemp Manufacturing Co—*Hylee Kemp*	4310 N Voss St, Peoria IL 61616	309-682-7292	R	12*	.1
297	B and D Industrial And Mining Services Inc—*Charles Bishop*	200 18th Ave Sw, Jasper AL 35501	205-221-4950	R	12*	.1
298	Wolfe Industrial Inc—*Armer Wolfe*	1512 Jp Hennessy Dr, La Vergne TN 37086	615-641-6964	R	12*	.1
299	Wright Metal Products Inc—*Clyde Edwards*	PO Box 609, Simpsonville SC 29681	864-688-6540	R	12*	.1
300	Steelville Manufacturing Co—*Dennis Bell*	PO Box 919, Steelville MO 65565	573-775-2977	R	12*	.1
301	Faustel Inc—*Milton Kuyers*	W194n11301 Mccormick D, Germantown WI 53022	262-253-3333	R	12*	.1
302	Fairlawn Tool and Die Co—*Kathleen Barber*	1900 Hanover Pke, Hampstead MD 21074	410-374-1100	R	12*	.1
303	FK Instrument Company Inc—*Alfred Klopter*	2134 Sunnydale Blvd, Clearwater FL 33765	727-461-6060	R	12*	.1
304	Alloy Carbide Co—*Walter Mccaine*	PO Box 5368, Houston TX 77262	713-923-2700	R	12*	.1
305	B-W Grinding Service Inc—*William Hargrave*	5807 Nunn St, Houston TX 77087	713-641-0888	R	12*	.1
306	RW Raddatz Inc—*Robert W Raddatz*	280 SW 12th Ave, Deerfield Beach FL 33442	954-480-9327	R	12*	<.1
307	Howestemco Inc—*Robert Maloof*	50 Earls Way, Franklin MA 02038	508-528-6500	R	12*	.1
308	Rds Manufacturing Inc—*Roy Sturgeon*	4217 W Seattle St, Broken Arrow OK 74012	918-459-5100	R	12*	.1
309	Adcor Industries Inc—*Jimmy Stavrakis*	234 S Haven St, Baltimore MD 21224	410-327-3083	R	12*	.1
310	Ross Machine Company Inc—*Thomas Ross*	4605 Compass Point Rd, Belcamp MD 21017	410-575-6100	R	12*	<.1

Note: An asterisk (*) indicates an estimated financial figure. The company type code used is as follows: R = Private, P = Public, S = Private Subsidiary, B = Public Subsidiary, D = Division, J = Joint Venture, I = Investment Fund.

COMPANY RANKINGS BY SALES WITHIN 4-DIGIT SIC

Rank	Company Name—Executive Officer	Address, City, State, Zip	Phone	Type	Fin	Empls
311	Lindquist Machine Corp—Mark Kaiser	610 Baeten Rd, Green Bay WI 54304	920-713-4100	R	12*	.1
312	Wolfe And Swickard Machine Company Inc—Samuel Swickard	1344 S Tibbs Ave, Indianapolis IN 46241	317-241-2589	R	12*	.1
313	Texas Honing Inc—Robert Steele	1710 Mykawa Rd, Pearland TX 77581	281-485-8339	R	12*	.1
314	True Position Technologies Inc—Allen Sumian	24900 Ave Stanford, Valencia CA 91355	661-294-0030	R	12*	.1
315	Isthmus Engineering and Manufacturing Coop—Pete Daubner	4035 Owl Creek Dr, Madison WI 53718	608-222-9000	R	12*	<.1
316	Mid-Continent Engineering Inc—Sanders Marvin	405 35th Ave Ne Ste 1, Minneapolis MN 55418	612-781-0260	R	12*	.1
317	Kimastle Corp—Kirk Gilewski	28291 Kehrig St, Chesterfield MI 48047	586-949-2355	R	12*	.1
318	O and F Machine Products Co—Cleetus Pattyson	PO Box 1363, Joplin MO 64802	417-623-7476	R	12*	.1
319	RK Manufacturing Corporation Of Connecticut—Donna Krebs	34 Executive Dr Ste 1, Danbury CT 06810	203-797-8700	R	12*	.1
320	Darko Precision Inc—Dardo Simunic	470 Gianni St, Santa Clara CA 95054	408-988-6133	R	12*	.1
321	Morgan Bronze Products Inc—Leonard Harder	367 Hollow Hill Rd, Wauconda IL 60084	847-526-6000	R	12*	.1
322	Hanard Machine Inc—Frank Kirsch	859 7th St Nw, Salem OR 97304	503-364-3952	R	11*	.1
323	Sycamore Precision Machine Inc—Ernest Hirn	334 E 1st St Ste 1, Genoa IL 60135	815-784-5151	R	11*	.1
324	Ohlinger Industries Inc—Henry Ohlinger	PO Box 42268, Phoenix AZ 85080	602-285-0911	R	11*	.1
325	Versatech Inc—Richard Versaw	PO Box 608, Export PA 15632	724-327-8324	R	11*	.1
326	Stewart Manufacturing Company Inc—Patrick Stewart	1620 W Knudsen Dr, Phoenix AZ 85027	623-582-2261	R	11*	.1
327	Spm Industries Inc—Frank Bellisario	2455 E 10 Mile Rd, Warren MI 48091	586-758-1100	R	11*	.1
328	Forsythe And Dowis Rides Inc—Victor Wisdom	3758 County Rd 237, Merino CO 80741	970-522-7515	R	11*	.1
329	Knappe and Koester Inc—Claus Knappe	18 Bradco St, Keene NH 03431	603-355-1166	R	11*	.1
330	Industrial Sales and Manufacturing Inc—James Rutkowski	2609 W 12th St, Erie PA 16505	814-833-9876	R	11*	.1
331	Smart Machine Technologies Inc—Mark Gibb	PO Box 4828, Martinsville VA 24115	276-632-9853	R	11*	.1
332	Aero Precision Products Inc—Paul Fournier	14000 Nw 19th Ave, Opa Locka FL 33054	305-688-2565	R	11*	.1
333	Baumann Engineering Inc—Fred Baumann	212 S Cambridge Ave, Claremont CA 91711	909-621-4181	R	11*	.1
334	Ahaus Tool and Engineering Inc—Kevin Ahaus	PO Box 280, Richmond IN 47375	765-962-3571	R	11*	.1
335	Tram-Tek Inc—Jacqueline Cowin	3035 E Chambers St, Phoenix AZ 85040	602-305-8100	R	11*	.1
336	Soleras Ltd—Dean Plaisted	PO Box 1867, Biddeford ME 04005	207-282-5699	R	11*	.1
337	Fluid Energy Processing and Equipment Company Inc—Patricia Stephanoff	4300 Bethlehem Pke, Telford PA 18969	215-368-2510	R	11*	.1
338	JWD Machine Inc—John Dupea	7215 45th St Ct E, Fife WA 98424	253-922-3806	R	11*	.1
339	Gillette Machine and Tool Company Inc—Gary A Masse	955 Millstead Way, Rochester NY 14624	585-436-0058	S	11*	.1
340	North East Machine and Tool Co—William Stokes	PO Box 248, Janesville IA 50647	319-987-2003	R	11*	.1
341	Hill Engineering Inc—Don Hill	373 Randy Rd, Carol Stream IL 60188	630-834-4430	S	11*	.1
342	Kennedy Machine and Tool Inc—Joyce Kennedy	8201 N State Rd 9, Alexandria IN 46001	765-724-2225	R	11*	.1
343	Full Vision Inc—Peter Benson	3017 Full Vision Dr, Newton KS 67114	316-283-3344	R	11*	.1
344	Norbert Industries Inc—Kevin Johnston	PO Box 1324, Sterling Heights MI 48311	586-977-9200	R	11*	.1
345	Precision Manufacturing Group LLC—Benjamin Giess	501 Little Falls Rd, Cedar Grove NJ 07009	973-785-4630	R	11*	<.1
346	All Diameter Grinding Inc—Marvin Goodwin	725 N Main St, Orange CA 92868	714-744-1200	R	11*	<.1
347	Donson Machine Co—Joseph Bettinardi	12416 S Kedvale Ave, Alsip IL 60803	708-388-0880	R	11*	.1
348	Richardson Manufacturing Co—John Richardson	2209 Old Jacksonville, Springfield IL 62704	217-546-2249	R	11*	.1
349	Consulting Engineering And Development Services Inc—Steven Meyer	78 S End Plz, New Milford CT 06776	860-350-4027	R	11*	.1
350	Vectron Inc—Robert Pustay	201 Perry Ct, Elyria OH 44035	440-323-3369	R	11*	.1
351	Yanke Machine Shop Inc—Winda Yanke	PO Box 5405, Boise ID 83705	208-342-8901	R	11*	.1
352	Component Specialty Inc—Bruce Carter	412 N State St, Elgin IL 60123	847-742-4400	R	11*	.1
353	Contract Industrial Tooling Inc—Kim Wuertemberger	2351 Production Ct, Richmond IN 47374	765-966-1134	R	11*	.1
354	Butler Tool Inc—Gene Liebl	4731 N 125th St, Butler WI 53007	262-781-9505	R	.11*	<.1
355	Mackay Manufacturing Inc—Mike Mackay	PO Box 11278, Spokane Valley WA 99211	509-922-7742	R	11*	.1
356	Ryan Manufacturing Inc—Mark Kruncos	6606 Machmueller St, Schofield WI 54476	715-359-2565	R	11*	.1
357	Stellar Precision Components Ltd—Lori Allbright	1201 Rankin Ave, Jeannette PA 15644	724-523-5559	R	11*	.1
358	Harbor Tool Manufacturing Inc—John Stratta	8300 185th St, Tinley Park IL 60487	708-614-6400	R	11*	.1
359	Fredon Corp—Roger Sustar	7911 Enterprise Dr, Mentor OH 44060	440-951-5200	R	11*	.1
360	Logan Machine Co—Mark Schoenbaechler	1405 Home Ave, Akron OH 44310	330-633-6163	R	11*	.1
361	Precision Innovations Inc—Cherylanne Marx	PO Box 726, Germantown WI 53022	262-255-6116	R	10*	.1
362	Computer Assisted Manufacturing Technology Corp—Lance Young	8710 Research Dr, Irvine CA 92618	949-263-8911	R	10*	.1
363	East Texas Machine Works Inc—Neil Swisher	PO Box 150488, Longview TX 75615	903-759-9796	R	10*	.1
364	Tru-Flex Real Estate Holdings Inc—Win Thomas	PO Box 247, West Lebanon IN 47991	765-893-4403	R	10*	.1
365	Breaux Machine Works LP—Dena Chamber	PO Box 152, Tomball TX 77377	281-351-4042	R	10*	.1
366	Stewart Manufacturing LLC—Linda Laviolette	PO Box 219, Hermansville MI 49847	906-498-7600	R	10*	.1
367	Elite Cnc Machining Inc—S Hooper	12395 Belcher Rd S, Largo FL 33773	727-571-1068	R	10*	.1
368	A To Z Machine Company Inc—Dale Skovera	2701 E Winslow Ave, Appleton WI 54911	920-993-0640	R	10*	.1
369	Turnamatic Machine Inc—Kala Arguello	1725 Jay Ell Dr, Richardson TX 75081	972-235-1923	R	10*	.1
370	United Machine Works Inc—Herbert Brown	1716 Nc 903 N Hwy, Greenville NC 27834	252-752-7434	R	10*	.1
371	Ace Machine Shop Inc—Pedro Gallinucci	11200 Wright Rd, Lynwood CA 90262	310-608-2277	R	10*	.1
372	B-Tec Solutions Inc—John Brenner	913 Cedar Ave, Croydon PA 19021	215-785-2400	R	10*	.1
373	Harrison Mullane Inc—George Mullane	10938 Lucerne St, Houston TX 77016	281-449-4846	R	10*	.1
374	Sterling Machinery Inc—Robert Martin	PO Box 1407, Mena AR 71953	479-394-4248	R	10*	.1
375	Industrial Engineering Inc—Harry Laffkas	4430 Tielker Rd, Fort Wayne IN 46809	260-478-1514	R	10*	.1
376	W L Doffing Co—Keith Byers	PO Box 35997, Houston TX 77235	713-433-3643	R	10*	.1
377	Stanley Engineering Company Inc—Ken Stanley	6721 Baymeadow Dr, Glen Burnie MD 21060	410-787-0150	R	10*	.1
378	Swissline Products Inc—David Chenevert	23 Ashton Park Way Uni, Cumberland RI 02864	401-333-8888	R	10*	.1
379	Nelson-Rose Inc—Debbie Kuntze	185 Vallecitos De Oro, San Marcos CA 92069	760-744-7400	R	10*	.1
380	JCM Engineering Corp—Carlo Moyano	2690 E Cedar St, Ontario CA 91761	909-923-3730	R	10*	.1
381	Conner Brothers Machine Company Inc—Bobby Conner	PO Box 2809, Gastonia NC 28053	704-864-6084	R	10*	.1
382	Little Rock Tool Service Inc—Jerry Victory	PO Box 192207, Little Rock AR 72219	501-888-2457	R	10*	.1
383	Amg Inc—Pat Ferguson	PO Box 4321, Lynchburg VA 24502	434-385-7525	R	10*	.1
384	Telcon LLC—Kevin Kummerlen	1677 Miller Pkwy, Streetsboro OH 44241	330-562-5566	R	10*	.1
385	TM Industries Inc—Rosemarie Fischer	PO Box 278, East Berlin CT 06023	860-828-0344	R	10*	.1
386	Vescio Threading Co—Robert Vescio	14002 Anson Ave, Santa Fe Springs CA 90670	562-802-1868	R	10*	.1
387	SC Manufacturing Inc—Lee Combs	380 Kennedy Rd, Akron OH 44305	330-784-3151	R	10*	.1
388	Triplett Machine Inc—Douglas Triplett	1374 Phelps Junction R, Phelps NY 14532	315-548-3198	R	10*	.1
389	Aero Chip Inc—Solomon Gavrila	14333 S Figueroa St, Gardena CA 90248	310-329-8600	R	10*	.1
390	Bo/Gar Enterprises Inc—Andy Dwyer	401 S Main Ave, Wyoming IL 61491	309-695-2025	R	10*	.1
391	Bob Inc—Thomas Gearou	8740 49th Ave N, Minneapolis MN 55428	763-533-2261	R	10*	.1
392	Artcraft Fabricators Inc—Robert Twine	PO Box 546, Portsmouth VA 23705	757-399-7777	R	10*	<.1
393	Elcon Inc (San Jose California)—JE (Mollie) Dayo	1009 Timothy Dr, San Jose CA 95133	408-292-7800	R	10*	<.1
394	Sandray Precision Grinding Co—J Sanders	632 Grable St, Rockford IL 61109	815-226-0660	R	10*	<.1
395	Comet Automation Systems Inc—Tom Rajkovich	2220 W Dorothy Ln, Dayton OH 45439	937-296-9166	R	10*	<.1
396	Calmax Technology—George Marcinkowski	3491 Lafayette St, Santa Clara CA 95054	408-748-8660	R	10*	.1
397	Little Enterprises Inc—Scott Little	31 Locust St, Ipswich MA 01938	978-356-7422	R	10*	.1

Rank	Company Name—*Executive Officer*	Address, City, State, Zip	Phone	Type	Fin	Empls
398	Aranda Tooling Inc—*Pedro Aranda*	15301 Springdale St, Huntington Beach CA 92649	714-379-6565	R	10*	.1
399	Blue Mountain Machine Inc—*Phillip Myers*	725 State Rd, Lehighton PA 18235	610-377-4690	R	10*	.1
400	EF Precision Inc—*Ernest Farabella*	2301 Computer Rd Ste A, Willow Grove PA 19090	215-784-0861	R	10*	.1
401	Jayna Inc—*Damaroo Shah*	15 Marybill Dr S, Troy OH 45373	937-335-8922	R	10*	.1
402	O-S Inc—*Roger Downum*	1011 Pecten Ct, Milpitas CA 95035	408-946-5890	R	10*	.1
403	A-1 Jay's Machining Inc—*James Machathio*	2228 Oakland Rd, San Jose CA 95131	408-262-1845	R	10*	.1
404	Lowell Inc—*Patrick Lilja*	9425 83rd Ave N, Minneapolis MN 55445	763-425-3355	R	10*	.1
405	Mid-America Machining Inc—*Robert Berry*	11530 Brooklyn Rd, Brooklyn MI 49230	517-592-8988	R	10*	.1
406	Sparton Technology Corp—*Victor Breton*	8 Hampshire Dr, Hudson NH 03051	603-880-3692	R	10*	.1
407	Mitchum-Schaefer Inc—*Steven Schaefer*	4901 W Raymond St, Indianapolis IN 46241	317-546-4081	R	10*	.1
408	York-Seaway Industrial Products Inc—*Rick York*	PO Box 408, Lake City PA 16423	814-774-7080	R	10*	.1
409	Harris and Bruno Machine Colnc—*Nick Bruno*	8555 Washington Blvd, Roseville CA 95678	916-781-7676	R	10*	.1
410	ET Precision Optics Inc—*Thomas Eckler*	33 Curlew St, Rochester NY 14606	585-254-2560	R	10*	.1
411	Titan Machine Products Inc—*Mark Acker*	600 County Rd, Westbrook ME 04092	207-775-0011	R	10*	.1
412	Starke Machine Co—*Dennis Starke*	2109 Brennan Ave, Fort Worth TX 76106	817-625-6821	R	10*	.1
413	C and C Machining Inc—*Galen Cowan*	22233 230th Ave, Centerville IA 52544	641-856-8288	R	10*	.1
414	Lewis Machine and Tool Co—*Karl Lewis*	1305 11th St W, Milan IL 61264	309-787-7151	R	10*	.1
415	Master Metal Machining Inc—*Brian Pyszka*	4520 S Burnett Dr, South Bend IN 46614	574-299-0222	R	10*	.1
416	United Grinding And Machine Co—*Allan Pfabe*	2315 Ellis Ave Ne, Canton OH 44705	330-453-7402	R	10*	.1
417	Laurel Machine Inc—*John Novak*	PO Box 133, Mount Braddock PA 15465	724-438-8661	R	10*	.1
418	Wendon Company Inc—*Julius Bogdan*	17 Irving Ave, Stamford CT 06902	203-348-6271	R	10*	<.1
419	D and E Machining Ltd—*Jean Reizer*	150 Industrial Dr, Corry PA 16407	814-664-3531	R	10*	<.1
420	Mouldagraph Corp—*Dennis Moulder*	PO Box 99, Nitro WV 25143	304-759-2150	R	9*	.1
421	J and M Machine Products Inc—*Joseph Rahrig*	1821 Manor Dr, Norton Shores MI 49441	231-755-1622	R	9*	.1
422	May Foundry and Machine Co—*Mark May*	PO Box 396, Salt Lake City UT 84110	801-531-8931	R	9*	.1
423	D and G Machine Products Inc—*Duane Gushee*	50 Eisenhower Dr, Westbrook ME 04092	207-854-1500	R	9*	.1
424	Roth Manufacturing Corp—*Klaus Bauer*	81 E Washburn St, New London OH 44851	419-929-1554	S	9*	.1
425	Oil Capital Valve Co—*Britt Radford*	7400 E 42nd Pl, Tulsa OK 74145	918-627-2474	R	9*	.1
426	Elk River Machine Co—*James Barthel*	828 4th St Nw, Elk River MN 55330	763-441-1581	S	9*	.1
427	Paramount Precision Products Inc—*Sheila Rossmann*	15255 W 11 Mile Rd, Oak Park MI 48237	248-543-2100	R	9*	.1
428	Koester Corp—*Michael Koester*	1650 Commerce Dr, Napoleon OH 43545	419-599-0291	R	9*	.1
429	RAM Inc—*Richard Mount*	11125 Yankee St Ste A, Dayton OH 45458	937-885-7700	R	9*	.1
430	Babbitt Bearings Inc—*Charles Wart*	734 Burnet Ave, Syracuse NY 13203	315-479-6603	R	9*	.1
431	Columbia Machine Works Inc—*James Langsdon*	PO Box 1018, Columbia TN 38402	931-388-6202	R	9*	.1
432	Piedmont Precision Machine Company Inc—*William Gentry*	PO Box 10309, Danville VA 24543	434-793-0677	R	9*	.1
433	Orient Machining and Welding Inc—*Andrzej Plewa*	14501 Wood St Ste A, Dixmoor IL 60426	708-371-3500	R	9*	.1
434	Metric Manufacturing Company Inc—*Charles Thomas*	PO Box 226, Lowell MI 49331	616-897-5959	R	9*	.1
435	Grover Gundrilling Inc—*Garth Grover*	PO Box 711, Norway ME 04268	207-743-7051	R	9*	.1
436	Rocon Manufacturing Corp—*Roland Paul*	PO Box 60710, Rochester NY 14606	585-436-8189	R	9*	<.1
437	Davis Boat Works Inc—*Ira Trocki*	PO Box 702, Egg Harbor NJ 08215	609-965-3877	R	9*	.1
438	Apex Machine Tool Co—*Rock Mortel*	1790 New Britain Ave, Farmington CT 06032	860-677-2884	D	9*	.1
439	Central Illinois Manufacturing Co—*James Ayers*	201 N Champaign St, Bement IL 61813	217-678-2511	R	9*	.1
440	Elliott Machine Shop Inc—*AV Elliott*	5495 Level Acres Dr, Macon GA 31217	478-745-0279	R	9*	.1
441	Royster's Machine Shop LLC—*Ben Berry*	PO Box 1199, Henderson KY 42419	270-826-3396	R	9*	.1
442	Wauseon Machine And Manufacturing Inc—*Russell Dominique*	995 Enterprise Ave, Wauseon OH 43567	419-337-0940	R	9*	.1
443	Addison Precision Manufacturing Corp—*Robert Champagne*	PO Box 15393, Rochester NY 14615	585-254-1386	R	9*	.1
444	Reno Machine Company Inc—*Mark Occhialini*	170 Pane Rd, Newington CT 06111	860-666-5641	R	9*	.1
445	Khuu's Inc—*Peter Khuu*	171 Commercial St, Sunnyvale CA 04086	408-522-8000	R	9*	.1
446	South Bay Solutions Inc—*Adam Drewniany*	4019 Transport St, Palo Alto CA 94303	650-843-1800	R	9*	.1
447	Aztalan Engineering Inc—*James Brey*	PO Box 739, Lake Mills WI 53551	920-648-3411	R	9*	.1
448	Barton Manufacturing—*Greg Mason*	1395 S Taylorville Rd, Decatur IL 62521	217-428-0711	R	9*	<.1
449	Kahlenberg Industries Inc—*Steve Kahlenberg*	PO Box 358, Two Rivers WI 54241	920-793-4507	R	9*	<.1
450	Tooling Specialists Inc—*Theodore Prettiman*	PO Box 828, Latrobe PA 15650	724-539-2534	R	9*	.1
451	Three M Holding Company Inc—*Michael Medwid*	8155 Richardson Rd, Commerce Township MI 48390	248-363-1555	R	9*	.1
452	Hoosier Plastic Fabrication Inc—*Robert Simms*	PO Box 78926, Corona CA 92877	951-272-3070	R	9*	.1
453	A and E Grinding Inc—*Alan Rogowski*	1000 W Pelton Dr, Oak Creek WI 53154	414-766-1180	R	9*	.1
454	A and G Manufacturing Company Inc—*Arvin Shifley*	PO Box 935, Galion OH 44833	419-468-7433	R	9*	.1
455	Screwmatic Inc—*Louis Zimmerli*	PO Box 518, Azusa CA 91702	626-334-7831	R	9*	.1
456	Modern Packaging Inc—*Syed Hossain*	505 Acorn St, Deer Park NY 11729	631-595-2437	R	9*	.1
457	Acm Machining Inc—*Alfred Balbach*	11390 Gold Dredge Way, Rancho Cordova CA 95742	916-852-8600	R	9*	.1
458	Industrial Welding and Supply Co—*Roger Stump*	PO Box 1169, Sterling CO 80751	970-522-2206	R	9	.1
459	Burgess Speciality Fabrication Inc—*William Burgess*	8222 Fawndale Ln, Houston TX 77040	713-462-0293	R	9*	.1
460	Komax Corp—*Jim Sopp*	1100 Corporate Grove D, Buffalo Grove IL 60089	847-537-6640	R	9*	.1
461	Kirby Engine Systems Inc—*Bill Lvey*	PO Box 1537, Houston TX 77251	713-435-1000	S	9	N/A
462	Central Valley Machine Inc—*Jerry Wursten*	1886 N 100 E, North Logan UT 84341	435-752-0934	R	9*	.1
463	Baton Rouge Machine Works Inc—*Glenn Rivette*	12612 Ronaldson Rd, Baton Rouge LA 70807	225-775-2542	R	9*	.1
464	Applied Industrial Machining Inc—*Robert Gilson*	1930 Se 29th St, Oklahoma City OK 73129	405-672-2222	R	9*	.1
465	Ideal Machine and Manufacturing Inc—*Leo Long*	PO Box 11152, Tacoma WA 98411	253-475-3464	R	9*	.1
466	Micro Machine Company LLC—*Diana Lanning*	2429 N Burdick St, Kalamazoo MI 49007	269-388-2440	R	9*	.1
467	Davlan Engineering Inc—*H Lamont*	3644 Scarlet Oak Blvd, Saint Louis MO 63122	636-225-5310	R	9*	.1
468	Haig Precision Manufacturing Corp—*Daniel Sarkisian*	186 Gilman Ave, Campbell CA 95008	408-378-4920	R	9*	.1
469	C and S Machine Products Inc—*Joseph Saratore*	215 Post Rd, Buchanan MI 49107	269-695-6859	R	9*	<.1
470	Begneaud Manufacturing Inc—*Donald Begneaud*	PO Box 62949, Lafayette LA 70596	337-237-5069	R	8*	.1
471	Cleveland Jsm Inc—*Dave Holm*	11792 Alameda Dr, Strongsville OH 44149	440-876-3050	R	8*	.1
472	Wilsey Tool Company Inc—*Timothy Wilsey*	PO Box 699, Quakertown PA 18951	215-538-0800	R	8*	.1
473	Anver Corp—*Franck Vernooy*	36 Parmenter Rd, Hudson MA 01749	978-568-0221	R	8*	.1
474	Tomenson Machine Works Inc—*Scott Roake*	3945 Stern Ave, Saint Charles IL 60174	630-377-7670	R	8*	.1
475	Tsm Corp—*Thomas Pryor*	1175 N Opdyke Rd, Auburn Hills MI 48326	248-276-4700	R	8*	.1
476	Wilcox Machine Co—*George Schofhauser*	PO Box 2159, Bell CA 90202	562-927-5353	R	8*	.1
477	Whitehall Products LLC—*Jim Holz*	8786 Water St, Montague MI 49437	231-894-2688	R	8*	.1
478	Commerce Grinding Management Inc—*Joe Lodor*	600 W Commerce St, Dallas TX 75208	214-651-1977	R	8*	.1
479	Clark Manufacturing Co—*Robert Milliron*	2485 Aero Park Dr, Traverse City MI 49686	231-946-5110	R	8*	.1
480	Continental Machine Tool Company Inc—*Tadeusz Malkowski*	533 John Downey Dr, New Britain CT 06051	860-223-2896	R	8*	.1
481	P and N Machine Company Inc—*Patrick Napier*	12450 Windfern Rd, Houston TX 77064	281-469-9140	R	8*	.1
482	Mkt Innovations—*Mike Kenney*	2900a Saturn St Ste A, Brea CA 92821	714-524-7668	R	8*	.1
483	Wright Machine and Tool Company Inc—*Frank Wright*	101 Jims Branch Rd, Swannanoa NC 28778	828-298-8440	R	8*	.1
484	Denny Machine Company Inc—*Frank Deni*	PO Box 863, Buffalo NY 14240	716-873-6865	R	8*	.1
485	Saturn Machine Inc—*Salvador Soliz*	PO Box 1276, Brookshire TX 77423	281-391-7800	R	8*	.1
486	Montague Tool And Manufacturing Co—*Jim Montague*	11533 Liberty St Ste 3, Clio MI 48420	810-686-0000	R	8*	.1
487	Byran Company Inc—*Janell Dunagan*	18092 Redondo Cir, Huntington Beach CA 92648	714-841-9808	R	8*	.1

Note: An asterisk (*) indicates an estimated financial figure. The company type code used is as follows: R = Private, P = Public, S = Private Subsidiary, B = Public Subsidiary, D = Division, J = Joint Venture, I = Investment Fund.

COMPANY RANKINGS BY SALES WITHIN 4-DIGIT SIC

Rank	Company Name—*Executive Officer*	Address, City, State, Zip	Phone	Type	Fin	Empls
488	CR Machine Company Inc—*Gary Rigoli*	13 Alexander Rd Ste 5a, Billerica MA 01821	978-663-3989	R	8*	.1
489	Production Saw and Machine Co—*James Vancalbergh*	9091 S Meridian Rd, Clarklake MI 49234	517-529-4014	R	8*	.1
490	Crystal Lake Grinders—*Glenwood O'dell*	PO Box 846, North Fork CA 93643	559-297-0737	R	8*	.1
491	Thomas/Euclid Industries Inc—*Bill Thomas*	PO Box 33459, Indianapolis IN 46203	317-783-7171	R	8*	.1
492	Washington County Machine Shop Inc—*Tony Veal*	1003 S Harris St, Sandersville GA 31082	478-552-2046	R	8*	.1
493	Alexandria Pro-Fab Company Inc—*Donald Wilkins*	8210 State Hwy 29 N, Alexandria MN 56308	320-852-7918	R	8*	.1
494	Magnat-Fairview Inc—*Mike Heroux*	1102 Sheridan St, Chicopee MA 01022	413-593-5742	R	8*	.1
495	Smoky Mountain Machining Inc—*Paul Mckinney*	PO Box 6173, Asheville NC 28816	828-665-1193	R	8*	.1
496	C D and N Manufacturing Inc—*James Crosby*	5904 Jetxamine St Ste, Houston TX 77081	713-667-8021	R	8*	.1
497	National Bulk Equipment Inc—*Joe Reed*	12838 Stainless Dr, Holland MI 49424	616-399-2220	R	8*	.1
498	Penn Manufacturing Industries Inc—*Nand Todi*	506 Stump Rd, Montgomeryville PA 18936	215-362-1217	R	8*	.1
499	Raloid Corp—*Ramon Jadra*	PO Box 338, Reisterstown MD 21136	410-833-2272	R	8*	.1
500	Delta Machining Inc—*Wannis Parris*	2361 Reum Rd, Niles MI 49120	269-683-7775	R	8*	.1
501	RA Zweig Inc—*Arie Zweig*	2500 Ravine Way, Glenview IL 60025	847-832-9001	R	8*	.1
502	Midwest Industries and Development Ltd—*Jeffrey Bremyer*	1125 W 1st St, Mcpherson KS 67460	620-241-5996	R	8*	.1
503	Langham Creek Machine Works Inc—*Mary Boyle*	4408 Joyce Blvd Ste D, Houston TX 77084	281-550-9587	R	8*	.1
504	Plouse Machine Shop Inc—*Kermit Seitz*	4510 Paxton St, Harrisburg PA 17111	717-558-8530	R	8*	.1
505	Milton Vermont Sheet Metal Inc—*Yancy Martell*	103 Gonyeau Rd, Milton VT 05468	802-893-1581	R	8*	.1
506	Colleen and Herb Enterprises Inc—*Colleen Schmidt*	801 Boggs Ave, Fremont CA 94539	510-226-6083	R	8*	.1
507	GE Mathis Co—*Craig Mathis*	6100 S Oak Park Ave, Chicago IL 60638	773-586-3800	R	8*	.1
508	Krueger Bearings Inc—*Terry Krueger*	8811 W Dean Rd, Milwaukee WI 53224	414-357-7292	R	8*	.1
509	Q-E Manufacturing Company Inc—*Kathy Stauder*	PO Box 525, New Berlin PA 17855	570-966-1017	R	8*	.1
510	Treske Precision Machining Inc—*Gustav Treske*	14140 Sw Galbreath Dr, Sherwood OR 97140	503-625-2821	R	8*	.1
511	IMT Precision Inc—*Tim Ilario*	31902 Hayman St, Hayward CA 94544	510-324-8926	R	8*	.1
512	Metals Fabrication Company Inc—*Todd Weaver*	PO Box 19266, Spokane WA 99219	509-244-2909	R	8*	.1
513	Ace Machine and Fabrication Inc—*James Glasgow*	PO Box 1577, Broussard LA 70518	337-369-6100	R	8*	.1
514	Universal Machine and Engineering Corp—*Rick Francis Jr*	645 Old Reading Pke, Stowe PA 19464	610-323-1810	R	8*	.1
515	Quantech Machining Inc—*Riad Hussein*	24911 Ave Stnford Ste, Santa Clarita CA 91355	661-775-3990	R	8*	<.1
516	FH Ayer Manufacturing Co—*Bob DeBolt*	PO Box 247, Chicago Heights IL 60412	708-755-0550	R	8*	<.1
517	Five Star Systems Inc—*Donald Carman*	51341 Celeste, Shelby Township MI 48315	586-850-0055	R	8*	<.1
518	Malmberg Engineering Inc—*Beverly Ginestra*	550 Commerce Way, Livermore CA 94551	925-606-6500	R	8*	<.1
519	Diamond Tool And Die Inc—*Darrell Holt*	508 29th Ave, Oakland CA 94601	510-534-7050	R	8*	<.1
520	Frank's Welding Company Inc—*Frank Mari*	PO Box 129, Crystal Lake IL 60039	708-343-7800	R	8*	<.1
521	Lake Engineering Inc—*Steven Magnuson*	PO Box 787, Long Lake MN 55356	952-473-5485	R	8*	<.1
522	Paragon Technologies Inc—*Leonard Yurkovic*	600 Kuebler Rd, Easton PA 18040	610-252-3205	P	8	<.1
523	Penco Precision—*Glynn Pennington*	15251 Boyle Ave, Fontana CA 92337	909-349-2892	R	8*	<.1
524	Cinex Inc—*Gary Smith*	2641 Cummins St, Cincinnati OH 45225	513-921-2825	R	8*	.1
525	Gett Industries Ltd—*Patricia Edwards*	7307 50th St, Milan IL 61264	309-799-5131	R	8*	.1
526	Dow Precision Hydraulics Inc—*Richard Dow*	1835 Wright Ave, La Verne CA 91750	909-596-6602	R	8*	.1
527	F H Peterson Machine Corp—*Stanley Urban*	PO Box 617, Stoughton MA 02072	781-341-4930	R	8*	.1
528	Neosho Trompler Inc—*Christina Trompler*	580 S Industrial Dr St, Hartland WI 53029	262-367-5600	R	8*	.1
529	P and W Quality Machines Inc—*Mike Parnell*	707 S Hwy 67, Cedar Hill TX 75104	972-299-0500	R	8*	.1
530	Instrument Development Inc—*Kevin Sinnett*	820 Swan Dr, Mukwonago WI 53149	262-363-7307	R	8*	.1
531	Triangle Precision Industries Inc—*Gerald Schriml*	1650 Delco Park Dr, Dayton OH 45420	937-299-6776	R	8*	.1
532	Bakersfield Machine Company Inc—*John Meyer*	PO Box 122, Bakersfield CA 93302	661-393-8441	R	8*	.1
533	Two Harbors Machine Shop Inc—*David Coolidge*	611 2nd Ave, Two Harbors MN 55616	218-834-5118	R	8*	.1
534	Machining Programming Manufacturing Inc—*Stuart Stevenson*	2100 S W St, Wichita KS 67213	316-945-1227	R	8*	.1
535	Kuhn Industries Inc—*Randy Kuhn*	PO Box 2547, Wichita Falls TX 76307	940-592-0095	R	8*	.1
536	Precision Machine Inc—*Buel Alexander*	PO Box 2753, Paducah KY 42002	270-443-8444	R	8*	.1
537	HR Edgar Machining and Fabricating Inc—*Harry Edgar*	931 Merwin Rd, New Kensington PA 15068	724-339-6694	R	8*	.1
538	Tj Machine and Tool Ltd—*Tommy Wright*	700 W Main St, Azle TX 76020	817-444-5548	R	8*	.1
539	Chipmatic Tool and Machine Inc—*Michael Detzel*	PO Box 87, Elmore OH 43416	419-862-2737	R	8*	.1
540	AAA Mine Service Inc—*Donald Farler*	18 Mountain View Dr, Hazard KY 41701	606-439-3328	R	8*	.1
541	Quality Machine and Tool Works Inc—*William Ehrensberger*	1201 Michigan Ave, Columbus IN 47201	812-379-2660	R	8*	.1
542	Thomas L Snarey and Associates Inc—*Thomas Snarey*	513 N Dixie Hwy, Monroe MI 48162	734-241-8474	R	8*	.1
543	Kooima Co—*John Kooima*	PO Box 156, Rock Valley IA 51247	712-476-5600	R	8*	.1
544	Aerostar Aerospace Manufacturing Inc—*Brandon Mcdermott*	20825 N 25th Pl, Phoenix AZ 85050	602-861-1145	R	8*	.1
545	Alt's Tool and Machine Inc—*Dean Alt*	10926 Woodside Ave N, Santee CA 92071	619-562-6653	R	8*	.1
546	Milan's Machining and Manufacturing Company Inc—*Milan Pecharich*	1301 S Laramie Ave, Cicero IL 60804	708-780-6600	R	8*	.1
547	Uni-Tek LLC	1030 N 53rd Ave, Phoenix AZ 85043	602-272-2601	R	8*	.1
548	Swebco Manufacturing Inc—*Kirk Schwebke*	7909 Burden Rd, Machesney Park IL 61115	815-636-7160	R	8*	<.1
549	Contine Corp—*Constance Ellrich*	1820 Nagle Rd, Erie PA 16510	814-899-0006	R	8*	<.1
550	Arnette Pattern Company Inc—*Gary Zimmer*	3203 Missouri Ave, Granite City IL 62040	618-451-7700	R	8*	.1
551	Fab Masters Company Inc—*Ronald Troxell*	PO Box 278, Marcellus MI 49067	269-646-5315	R	8*	.1
552	Rheaco Inc—*Ron Jensen*	PO Box 530702, Grand Prairie TX 75053	972-264-0368	S	8*	.1
553	Mark's Machine Company Inc—*Mark Pratka*	PO Box 1596, El Campo TX 77437	979-543-9204	R	8*	.1
554	R L Best Co—*Richard Best*	824 Bev Rd, Youngstown OH 44512	330-758-8601	R	8*	.1
555	Multax Corp—*Don Bigger*	PO Box 266, Morton IL 61550	309-266-9765	R	8*	.1
556	Illiana Machine and Manufacturing Corp—*Tito Mattera*	19700 97th Ave, Mokena IL 60448	708-479-1333	R	8*	.1
557	Earth Tool Company LLC—*Brian Metcalf*	PO Box 3, Oconomowoc WI 53066	262-567-8833	R	8*	.1
558	Custom Engineering Inc—*James Mc Cormick*	PO Box 320, Clay KY 42404	270-664-6207	R	8*	<.1
559	Accurate Technology Manufacturing—*John Dukanovic*	930 Thompson Pl, Sunnyvale CA 94085	408-733-4344	R	7*	.1
560	Stanfordville Machine and Manufacturing Company Inc—*John Johnsen*	PO Box B, Stanfordville NY 12581	845-868-2266	R	7*	.1
561	G and G Manufacturing Co—*Kurt Gleich*	4015 Red Bank Rd, Cincinnati OH 45227	513-271-2901	R	7*	.1
562	Mendell Machine And Manufacturing Inc—*Bryan Bartz*	21463 Grenada Ave, Lakeville MN 55044	952-469-5500	R	7*	.1
563	Northwest Machining and Manufacturing Inc—*Guy Gage*	1957 E Lanark St, Meridian ID 83642	208-888-5334	R	7*	.1
564	Penflex Corp—*Robert Barker*	105 Industrial Dr, Gilbertsville PA 19525	610-367-2260	R	7*	.1
565	Swiss-Micron Inc—*Kurt Sollberger*	22361 Gilberto Ste A, Rcho Sta Marg CA 92688	949-589-0430	R	7*	<.1
566	Premier Fabrication Inc—*Bruce Hohulin*	PO Box 36, Congerville IL 61729	309-448-2338	R	7*	.1
567	Minimatics Inc—*Walter Chew*	433 Clyde Ave, Mountain View CA 94043	650-969-5630	R	7*	.1
568	Ase Industries Inc—*Joseph Lepera*	23850 Pinewood St, Warren MI 48091	586-754-7480	R	7*	.1
569	DL Horton Enterprises Inc—*Douglass Horton*	12705 Daphne Ave, Hawthorne CA 90250	323-777-5003	R	7*	.1
570	Sumatech Inc—*Christopher Steg*	PO Box 252, White Marsh MD 21162	410-335-2929	R	7*	.1
571	Perbix Machine Company Inc—*James Dudley*	7130 Sandburg Rd, Minneapolis MN 55427	763-546-7122	R	7*	.1
572	Metalcraft Mining Equipment Rebuilders Inc—*Harley Mcclung*	PO Box 58, Fenwick WV 26202	304-846-2678	R	7*	<.1
573	Mod Tech Industries Inc—*James Lacy*	PO Box 701, Shawano WI 54166	715-524-4510	R	7*	.1
574	Aeromet Industries Inc—*Fred Wahlberg*	739 S Arbogast St, Griffith IN 46319	219-924-7442	R	7*	.1
575	Owens Precision Inc—*John Owens*	5966 Morgan Mill Rd, Carson City NV 89701	775-883-4690	R	7*	.1

Rank	Company Name—*Executive Officer*	Address, City, State, Zip	Phone	Type	Fin	Empls
576	Sotek Inc—*John Maurer*	3590 Jeffrey Blvd, Blasdell NY 14219	716-821-5961	R	7*	.1
577	Gurecky Manufacturing Service Inc—*Joe Gurecky*	2420 3rd St, Rosenberg TX 77471	281-342-5926	R	7*	.1
578	Z and L Machining Inc—*John Lemm*	3140 Central Ave, Waukegan IL 60085	847-623-9500	R	7*	.1
579	Rable Machine Inc—*Scott Carter*	PO Box 1583, Mansfield OH 44901	419-525-2255	R	7*	.1
580	Krendl Machine Company Inc—*John Krendl*	1201 Spencerville Rd, Delphos OH 45833	419-692-3060	R	7*	.1
581	Adron Tool Corp—*Brian Hagmayer*	PO Box 960, Menomonee Falls WI 53051	262-255-4433	R	7*	.1
582	Atlantis Equipment Corp—*Louis Schroeter*	16941 Ny 22, Stephentown NY 12168	518-733-5910	R	7*	.1
583	Micro Precision Corp—*Michael Peck*	200 Centerville Rd, Lancaster PA 17603	717-393-4100	R	7*	.1
584	Ray Machine Inc—*Nathu Dandora*	12 Lynbrook Rd, Baltimore MD 21220	410-686-6955	R	7*	.1
585	AM Precision Machine Inc—*Margaret Kozlowski Van H*	170 Lively Blvd, Elk Grove Village IL 60007	847-439-9955	R	7*	.1
586	Thul Machine Works—*Lawrence Thul*	PO Box 2794, Plainfield NJ 07062	908-754-3800	R	7*	.1
587	J Horst Manufacturing Co—*Roland Horst*	PO Box 507, Dalton OH 44618	330-828-2216	R	7*	.1
588	Jh Industries Inc—*John Hallack*	1981 E Aurora Rd, Twinsburg OH 44087	330-963-4105	R	7*	.1
589	Leader Engineering-Fabrication Inc—*Charles Leader*	PO Box 670, Napoleon OH 43545	419-592-0008	R	7*	<.1
590	McNeal Enterprises Inc—*Deanna Godfrey*	2031 Ringwood Ave, San Jose CA 95131	408-922-7290	R	7*	<.1
591	Ralph E Ames Machine Works—*Michael Ames*	2255 Dominguez Way, Torrance CA 90501	310-320-2637	R	7*	<.1
592	Trans-Tec Machine Ltd—*George Ritchey*	6320 Ridgemont St, Houston TX 77087	713-643-9114	R	7*	<.1
593	CNC Precision Machining Inc—*Tom Spaman*	5247 6 Mile Ct Nw, Comstock Park MI 49321	616-785-6030	R	7*	<.1
594	Gage Pattern and Model Inc—*Werner Schulte*	32070 Townley St, Madison Heights MI 48071	248-585-2476	R	7*	<.1
595	Interscope Manufacturing Inc—*John Brill*	2901 Carmody Blvd, Middletown OH 45042	513-423-8866	R	7*	<.1
596	Robert C Weisheit Company Inc—*Robert Weisheit*	1011 Sesame St, Franklin Park IL 60131	630-766-1213	R	7*	<.1
597	Rolled Threads Unlimited LLC—*Sherry Bigel*	1404 Pearl St, Waukesha WI 53186	262-547-6160	R	7*	<.1
598	Wm C Anderson Inc—*Charles Anderson*	1743 Anderson Blvd, Hebron KY 41048	859-689-4085	R	7*	<.1
599	Inland Lakes Machine Inc—*Carl Kuhn*	314 Haynes St, Cadillac MI 49601	231-775-6543	R	7*	<.1
600	KB Tooling and Manufacturing Co	8630 Tamarack Ave, Sun Valley CA 91352	818-504-9491	R	7*	<.1
601	Liberty Technologies—*Lionel W Trebilcock*	840 McClurg Rd, Youngstown OH 44512	330-729-2120	S	7*	<.1
602	Teton Machine Co—*Andy Oyervides*	1805 NE 10th Ave, Payette ID 83661	208-642-9344	R	7*	<.1
603	Kittatinny Manufacturing Services Inc—*Rick Fleming*	PO Box 39, Shippensburg PA 17257	717-530-1242	R	7*	<.1
604	Jewett Machine Manufacturing Company Incorporated Bryce D—*Bryce Jewett*	2901 Maury St, Richmond VA 23224	804-233-9873	R	7*	.1
605	Daca Machine and Tool Company Inc—*Phillip Pecaut*	PO Box 10, Dutzow MO 63342	636-433-5590	R	7*	.1
606	Hartman Enterprises Inc—*Bob Sweep*	PO Box 360, Oneida NY 13421	315-363-7300	R	7*	.1
607	Toolkraft Inc—*William Zbikowski*	7500 Commerce Ln Ne, Minneapolis MN 55432	763-571-7400	R	7*	.1
608	Fluke Metal Products Inc—*Robert Fluke*	10223 Woodinville Dr, Bothell WA 98011	425-485-9666	R	7*	.1
609	Flexible Concepts Inc—*Beth Gerstbauer*	1620 Middlebury St, Elkhart IN 46516	574-296-0941	R	7*	.1
610	Tomi Engineering Inc—*Michael Falbo*	414 E Alton Ave, Santa Ana CA 92707	714-556-1474	R	7*	.1
611	Automated Systems Of Tacoma LLC—*Don Hoban*	4110 S Washington St, Tacoma WA 98409	253-475-0200	R	7*	.1
612	Contract Machining and Manufacturing Company Inc—*Fred Lawson*	2425 Over Dr, Lexington KY 40511	859-253-9700	R	7*	.1
613	Sterling Machine Company Inc—*Gregory Caravella*	4 Peerless Way, Enfield CT 06082	860-741-2546	R	7*	.1
614	Western Screw Products Inc—*Lester Kovats*	11770 Slauson Ave, Santa Fe Springs CA 90670	562-698-5793	R	7*	.1
615	Ka-Wood Gear and Machine Co—*Joseph Kloka*	32500 Industrial Dr, Madison Heights MI 48071	248-585-8870	R	7*	<.1
616	B and B Machine and Grinding Service Corp—*Richard Bergquist*	303 W Evans Ave, Denver CO 80223	303-744-2751	R	7*	<.1
617	Kentucky Machine and Engineering Inc—*Chappel Allen*	PO Box 619, Cadiz KY 42211	270-522-6061	R	7*	.1
618	North Fast Precision Inc—*Bruce Benoit*	PO Box 7, Saint Johnsbury VT 05819	802-748-1440	R	7*	.1
619	Normandy Machine Company Inc—*Richard Garrott*	815 E Cherry St, Troy MO 63379	636-528-8913	R	7*	.1
620	Gross Mechanical Laboratories Inc—*Donald Gross*	7240 Standard Dr, Hanover MD 21076	410-712-4242	R	7*	.1
621	B and B Pipe And Tool Co—*Robert Braly*	3035 Walnut Ave, Long Beach CA 90807	562-424-0704	R	7*	.1
622	Kenwell Corp—*Roger Horning*	PO Box 207, Fulton NY 13069	315-592-4263	R	7*	.1
623	Elmco Engineering Inc—*Robert Behrens*	6107 Churchman Byp, Indianapolis IN 46203	317-788-4114	R	7*	.1
624	Framingham Welding and Engineering Corp—*Gertrude Sebastian*	PO Box 112, Framingham MA 01704	508-875-3563	R	7*	.1
625	H and B Tool and Engineering Co—*Janice Proll*	PO Box 717, South Windsor CT 06074	860-528-9341	R	7*	.1
626	Machintek Co—*Roger Hasler*	3721 Port Union Rd, Fairfield OH 45014	513-942-4500	R	7*	.1
627	Melkes Machine Inc—*Isabelle Melkesian*	9928 Hayward Way, South El Monte CA 91733	626-448-5062	R	7*	.1
628	Olson And Olson Inc—*Jon Olson*	PO Box 402, Chambersburg PA 17201	717-263-8170	R	7*	.1
629	Streich Brothers Inc—*Wayne Streich*	1650 Marine View Dr Ma, Tacoma WA 98422	253-383-1491	R	7*	.1
630	Vr Industries Inc—*Joseph Oakes*	333 Strawberry Field R, Warwick RI 02886	401-732-6800	R	7*	.1
631	A and E Machine Shop Inc—*Earl Alexander*	PO Box 190, Lone Star TX 75668	903-656-3485	R	7*	<.1
632	Thermo Craft Engineering Corp—*Ralph Faia*	701 Western Ave, Lynn MA 01905	781-599-4023	R	7*	<.1
633	Numerical Productions Inc—*Sheila Elliott*	3901 S Arlington Ave, Indianapolis IN 46203	317-783-1362	R	7*	.1
634	Tw Design And Manufacturing LLC—*Vicky Hamele*	PO Box 310, Montello WI 53949	608-297-9000	R	7*	.1
635	Advanced Machine And Tool Inc—*Lloyd Riley*	3900 Selvitz Rd, Fort Pierce FL 34981	772-465-6546	R	7*	.1
636	K and A Precision Machine Inc—*Arie Zweig*	2500 Ravine Way, Glenview IL 60025	847-832-9001	R	7*	.1
637	Racine Metal-Fab Ltd—*Margaret Madson*	2137 Roosevelt Ave, Racine WI 53406	262-554-1140	R	7*	.1
638	Amfan Corp—*Dennis Williams*	3443 Morse Dr, Dallas TX 75236	214-638-2451	R	7*	.1
639	Folsom Tool and Mold Corp—*Neal Ellixson*	12 Mount Pleasant Rd, Aston PA 19014	610-358-5030	R	7*	.1
640	Mono Engineering Corp—*Siamak Moini*	20977 Knapp St, Chatsworth CA 91311	818-772-4998	R	7*	.1
641	Owens Industries Inc—*Krishna Adusumilli*	7815 S 6th St, Oak Creek WI 53154	414-764-1212	R	7*	.1
642	Specialties Technologies Inc—*Richard Schneider*	51455 Schoenherr Rd, Shelby Township MI 48315	586-726-0000	R	7*	.1
643	Tecton Industries Inc—*Bruce Tamisiea*	PO Box 877, Spencer IA 51301	712-262-4116	R	7*	.1
644	Baum Machine Inc—*Roger Baum*	N253 Stoney Brook Rd, Appleton WI 54915	920-738-6613	R	7*	.1
645	Tampa Bay Machining Inc—*Jeff Kefauver*	13601 Mccormick Dr, Tampa FL 33626	813-855-5768	R	7*	.1
646	Chicago Grinding and Machine Co—*Leonard Kreplin*	1950 N 15th Ave, Melrose Park IL 60160	708-681-4010	R	7*	<.1
647	Dynamic Flowform Corp—*Venanzioro Fonte*	12 Suburban Park Dr, Billerica MA 01821	978-667-0202	R	7*	<.1
648	DCG Machine Inc—*David Grotheim*	1001 Cherokee Trce, White Oak TX 75693	903-297-2053	R	7*	<.1
649	Ripley Precision Inc—*Terry Abby*	501 Cr Rd, Walnut MS 38683	662-223-5339	R	7*	.1
650	Semicon Products Manufacturing Inc—*Alvin Sather*	300 Park Central Blvd, Georgetown TX 78626	512-930-0201	R	7*	.1
651	JC Industrial Manufacturing Corp—*Pedro Amador*	5700 Nw 32nd Ct, Miami FL 33142	305-634-5280	R	7*	.1
652	Eastwood Enterprises Inc—*Paul Levi*	PO Box 219, Highland Park IL 60035	847-940-4008	R	7*	.1
653	CV Tool Company Inc—*Carmine Votino*	44 Robert Porter Rd, Southington CT 06489	860-621-0494	R	7*	.1
654	Dearborn Inc—*Kenneth Dearborn*	678 Front St, Berea OH 44017	440-234-1353	R	7*	.1
655	J Newell Corp—*Jeff Newell*	PO Box 477, Arlington WA 98223	360-435-8955	R	7*	.1
656	Vertec Tool Inc—*Dennis Chambon*	1123 Elkton Dr, Colorado Springs CO 80907	719-598-6300	R	7*	.1
657	Lukas Machine Inc—*Brenda Lukas*	707 S Riverside Dr, Seattle WA 98108	206-763-9282	R	7*	<.1
658	Subcon Tool/Accutool Machine Group Inc—*John Murosky*	5301 Iroquois Ave, Erie PA 16511	814-456-7797	R	7*	<.1
659	P R Machine Works Inc—*Mark Romanchuk*	1825 Nussbaum Pkwy, Ontario OH 44906	419-529-5748	R	7*	<.1
660	Ammcon Corp—*Cathy Grow*	21450 Nw W Union Rd, Hillsboro OR 97124	503-645-5206	R	7*	<.1
661	Nekoosa Corp—*Theodore Olson*	PO Box 129, Nekoosa WI 54457	715-886-3800	R	7*	<.1

Note: An asterisk (*) indicates an estimated financial figure. The company type code used is as follows: R = Private, P = Public, S = Private Subsidiary, B = Public Subsidiary, D = Division, J = Joint Venture, I = Investment Fund.

COMPANY RANKINGS BY SALES WITHIN 4-DIGIT SIC

Rank	Company Name—*Executive Officer*	Address, City, State, Zip	Phone	Type	Fin	Empls
662	Tolerance Masters Inc—*Verne Pherson*	4444 Ball Rd Ne, Circle Pines MN 55014	763-717-9845	R	7*	<.1
663	Lee Precision Machine Shop Inc—*Gin Johnson*	26182 Us Hwy 72, Athens AL 35613	256-233-3131	R	7*	<.1
664	Centerline Manufacturing Ltd—*Tim Rueder*	5711 Campbell Rd, Houston TX 77041	713-329-9070	R	7*	<.1
665	B-K Manufacturing Company Inc—*Yvonne Kelley*	100 Technology Park, Arab AL 35016	256-753-2252	R	7*	<.1
666	Superior Machine Inc—*Kevin Loon*	31 B Ave W, Albia IA 52531	641-932-5999	R	6*	.1
667	Atlas Machining and Welding Inc—*Harold Keeney*	777 Smith Ln, Northampton PA 18067	610-262-1374	R	6*	.1
668	Fraser Grinding Co—*Rudolf Lipski*	34235 Riviera, Fraser MI 48026	586-293-6060	R	6*	.1
669	Metro Metal and Design Inc—*Kenneth Troutman*	200 Beltway Blvd, Matthews NC 28104	704-882-4550	R	6*	.1
670	Prime Products Inc—*Andy Bolovil*	307 E Dunn St, Converse IN 46919	979-743-6555	R	6*	.1
671	Special Fab and Machine Inc—*Avalon Potts*	PO Box 808, Linwood NC 27299	336-956-2121	R	6*	.1
672	K and A Machine And Tool Inc—*Karl Fridd*	PO Box 1173, Jackson MI 49204	517-750-9244	R	6*	<.1
673	Millennium Machining LLC—*Catrina Fox*	3265 Blue Heron Dr, Macedon NY 14502	315-986-2121	R	6*	.1
674	H and H Manufacturing Company Inc—*Thomas Tomei*	2 Horne Dr, Folcroft PA 19032	610-532-8100	R	6*	.1
675	Clean Machine Inc—*Ken Curry*	6162 S 350 W, Salt Lake City UT 84107	801-261-4206	R	6*	.1
676	Chrisman Sales And Services Inc—*Mark Chrisman*	7399 Beatline Rd, Long Beach MS 39560	228-864-6293	R	6*	.1
677	Essex Engineering Inc—*James Munro*	PO Box 328, Lynn MA 01905	781-595-2114	R	6*	.1
678	HMC Products Inc—*Ralph Kreissler*	5196 27th Ave, Rockford IL 61109	815-397-9145	R	6*	.1
679	Werco Manufacturing Inc—*Jon Werthen*	415 E Houston St, Broken Arrow OK 74012	918-251-6880	R	6*	.1
680	Voith Paper Rolls West Inc—*Greg Graso*	PO Box 846, Springfield OR 97477	541-726-5014	R	6*	<.1
681	Astro Machine Works Inc—*Eric Blow*	PO Box 328, Ephrata PA 17522	717-738-4281	R	6*	<.1
682	Helm Precision Ltd—*Hugh Helm*	2426 E Washington St, Phoenix AZ 85034	602-275-2122	R	6*	.1
683	Viper Northwest Inc—*Guy Lude*	1216 Jackson St Se, Albany OR 97322	541-928-2529	R	6*	<.1
684	Knox Machine Company Inc—*Richard Maxcy*	PO Box 68, Warren ME 04864	207-273-2296	R	6*	.1
685	J and A Manufacturing Inc—*David Johnson*	PO Box 472309, Garland TX 75047	972-494-5552	R	6*	.1
686	Cliflex Bellows Corp—*Patricia George*	45 W 3rd St, Boston MA 02127	617-268-5774	R	6*	.1
687	Kelsch Machine Corp—*Bruce Kiesling*	1328 County Rd Pb, Belleville WI 53508	608-845-7090	R	6*	.1
688	Northeast Quality Services LLC—*Betty Soboflai*	701 Middle St, Middletown CT 06457	860-632-7242	R	6*	.1
689	Southeastern Industrial Inc—*James Hutto*	PO Box 12188, Rock Hill SC 29731	803-327-3171	R	6*	.1
690	Thompson Machine Company Inc—*Tim Drenning*	1128 N 4th Ave, Altoona PA 16601	814-941-4982	R	6*	.1
691	Tvt Die Casting and Manufacturing Inc—*Thomas Thiel*	7330 Sw Landmark Ln, Portland OR 97224	503-639-3850	R	6*	.1
692	Wabel Tool Co—*Jenny Hornback*	1020 E Eldorado St, Decatur IL 62521	217-429-3656	R	6*	.1
693	Robrad Tool and Engineering Inc—*Felix Gottwald*	564 E Juanita Ave Ste, Mesa AZ 85204	480-892-2529	R	6*	<.1
694	Aero-K—*Robert Krusic*	10764 Lower Azusa Rd, El Monte CA 91731	626-350-5125	R	6*	<.1
695	Ansco Machine Co—*Michael Sterling*	60 Cuyhoga Fls Industr, Peninsula OH 44264	330-929-8181	R	6*	<.1
696	Aphelion Precision Technologies Corp—*Jane Black*	5 W Waltz Dr, Wheeling IL 60090	847-215-7285	R	6*	<.1
697	High-Tech Machine and Tool Inc—*Robert Moores*	177 Riverneck Rd, Chelmsford MA 01824	978-256-1600	R	6*	<.1
698	Owens Design Inc—*John Apgar*	47427 Fremont Blvd, Fremont CA 94538	510-659-1800	R	6*	<.1
699	Production Tool Companies LLC—*Stanley Malec*	1229 E 74th St, Chicago IL 60619	773-288-4400	R	6*	<.1
700	Century Tool Inc—*Gerald Korpela*	21495 147th Ave N, Rogers MN 55374	763-428-2168	R	6*	<.1
701	Industrial Welders and Machinists Inc—*Donald Abernethy*	PO Box 16720, Duluth MN 55816	218-628-1011	R	6*	<.1
702	Bgs Industries LP—*Bob Burke*	PO Box 272922, Houston TX 77277	281-970-4118	R	6*	<.1
703	K-M Machine Company Inc—*Kelly Kellam*	201 Mccaskill St, Biscoe NC 27209	910-428-2368	R	6*	.1
704	Beatty Machine and Manufacturing Co—*William Beatty*	940 150th St, Hammond IN 46327	219-931-3000	R	6*	.1
705	Oak Ridge Tool - Engineering Inc—*Terry Mullins*	PO Box 4458, Oak Ridge TN 37831	865-482-1061	R	6*	.1
706	A and M Industries Inc—*Frank Migliaczo*	35590 Groesbeck Hwy, Clinton Township MI 48035	586-791-5610	R	6*	.1
707	Arnold Tool and Die Co—*Thomas Mckay*	48200 Structural Dr, Chesterfield MI 48051	586-598-0099	R	6*	.1
708	Glenridge Machine Co—*Gerald Negrelli*	4610 Beidler Rd, Willoughby OH 44094	440-975-1055	R	6*	.1
709	Huffman Welding and Machine Inc—*Mike Huffman*	6224 Ave O, Fort Madison IA 52627	319-372-7232	R	6*	.1
710	Plant Machine Works Inc—*Thomas Barber*	PO Box 74090, Baton Rouge LA 70874	225-775-7163	R	6*	.1
711	Awerkamp Machine Co—*William Awerkamp*	237 N 7th St, Quincy IL 62301	217-222-3480	R	6*	<.1
712	Custom Machining Services Inc—*Jack Thompson*	326 N County Rd 400 E, Valparaiso IN 46383	219-462-6128	R	6*	<.1
713	Loveridge Machine and Tool Inc—*Dennis Loveridge*	4097 S W Temple, Salt Lake City UT 84107	801-262-1414	R	6*	<.1
714	Ran-Shel Inc—*Gerald Karp*	5585 Gatewood Dr, Sterling Heights MI 48310	586-268-2300	R	6*	<.1
715	JT Fennell Company Inc—*James Fennell*	PO Box 337, Chillicothe IL 61523	309-274-2145	R	6*	.1
716	Modern Equipment Company Inc—*Jim Winistorfer*	PO Box 993, Port Washington WI 53074	262-284-9431	R	6*	.1
717	Cutting Edge Machine And Tool Inc—*David Berkey*	PO Box 128, New Paris IN 46553	574-831-5464	R	6*	.1
718	Acro Machining Inc—*Dan Edmonds*	PO Box 3187, Arlington WA 98223	360-653-1492	R	6*	.1
719	Grand Valley Manufacturing Co—*David Ewing*	701 E Spring St, Titusville PA 16354	814-827-2707	R	6*	.1
720	Gulf South Machine Inc—*Walerij Holak*	PO Box 730, Ponchatoula LA 70454	985-386-9401	R	6*	.1
721	Modern Machine Shop Inc—*Danny Garcia*	PO Box 1969, Laredo TX 78044	956-722-4656	R	6*	.1
722	Nelson Numeric Inc—*G Nelson*	1750 W 96th St, Minneapolis MN 55431	952-829-7337	R	6*	.1
723	YS Manufacturing Inc—*Wei Yang*	5 Regents Ct, Kennett Square PA 19348	610-444-4832	R	6*	.1
724	AMG Engineering and Machining Inc—*Ted Gary*	PO Box 681245, Indianapolis IN 46268	317-329-4000	R	6*	.1
725	Senga Engineering Inc—*Roy Jones*	1525 E Warner Ave, Santa Ana CA 92705	714-549-8011	R	6*	<.1
726	A and D Precision Machining Inc—*David Dreifort*	4165 Bus Ctr Dr, Fremont CA 94538	510-657-6781	R	6*	<.1
727	Choice Precision Machine Inc—*Thomas Gunkel*	4380 Commerce Dr, Whitehall PA 18052	610-502-1111	R	6*	<.1
728	F M Machine Co—*Robert Christian*	1114 Triplett Blvd, Akron OH 44306	330-773-8237	R	6*	<.1
729	Ivarson Inc—*Lennart Ivarson*	3100 W Green Tree Rd, Milwaukee WI 53209	414-351-0700	R	6*	<.1
730	Niedwick Corp—*Theodore Niedwick*	1928 W Business Ctr Dr, Orange CA 92867	714-771-9999	R	6*	<.1
731	Tin-Mar Inc—*Tina Mcelwee*	70 Shields Rd, Huntsville AL 35811	256-859-1212	R	6*	<.1
732	Antron Engineering and Machine Company Inc—*Anthony De-nietolis*	PO Box 619, Bellingham MA 02019	508-966-2803	R	6*	<.1
733	Colonial Machine and Tool Company Inc—*Harry Masiello*	5 Salvas Ave, Coventry RI 02816	401-826-1883	R	6*	<.1
734	Norman Scott Company Inc—*Robert Becker*	126 29th St Dr Se, Cedar Rapids IA 52403	319-363-8561	R	6*	<.1
735	Hunt Jrt Inc—*James Hunt*	1107 W Geneva Dr, Tempe AZ 85282	480-968-5928	R	6*	<.1
736	M S --Action Machining Corp—*Norman Stengel*	4061 W Dayton St, Mchenry IL 60050	815-344-3770	R	6*	<.1
737	Advance Industrial Machine A Wisconsin LP—*Luke Boort*	W6335 Design Dr, Greenville WI 54942	920-757-6786	R	6*	<.1
738	Hanagriff's Machine Shop Inc—*Charles Hanagriff*	8728 Hwy 182, Centerville LA 70522	337-836-9954	R	6*	<.1
739	International Precision Machining—*Dan Meyer*	PO Box 309, Waite Park MN 56387	320-656-1241	R	6*	<.1
740	Olson Machining Inc—*John Olson*	1804 Holian Dr, Spring Grove IL 60081	815-675-2900	R	6*	<.1
741	Research Inc—*Brad Yopp*	7128 Shady Oak Rd, Eden Prairie MN 55344	952-949-9009	S	6*	<.1
742	Bundy Manufacturing Inc—*James Bundy*	507 S Douglas St, El Segundo CA 90245	323-772-3273	R	6*	<.1
743	JM Die Co—*John Morawa*	466 Meyer Rd, Bensenville IL 60106	630-616-7776	R	6*	<.1
744	S and J Precision Inc—*Sheila Wallace*	4239 Earnings Way, New Albany IN 47150	812-944-9368	R	6*	<.1
745	Welz Tool Machine and Boring Company Inc—*Zef Vuljevic*	11952 Hubbard St, Livonia MI 48150	734-425-3920	R	6*	<.1
746	Bison Engineering Co—*Neil Thompson*	6980 Cherry Ave, Long Beach CA 90805	562-408-1525	R	6*	<.1
747	EM Smith and Co—*Jack Cook*	826 W Detweiller Dr, Peoria IL 61615	309-691-6812	R	6*	<.1
748	Ickler Bearing and Machine Company Inc—*Todd Mc Gonagle*	2832 S 1st St, Saint Cloud MN 56301	320-251-8282	R	6*	<.1
749	Synehi Castings Inc—*Shirley Gaines*	PO Box 49113, Greenwood SC 29646	864-229-5927	R	6*	<.1
750	Twin City Mold Engineering Co—*Steve Icard*	PO Box 268, Waconia MN 55387	952-442-4501	R	6*	<.1

Rank	Company Name—*Executive Officer*	Address, City, State, Zip	Phone	Type	Fin	Empls
751	H and H Machine Service LLC—*Tommy Ladewig*	PO Box 162, Brenham TX 77834	979-836-2599	R	6*	<.1
752	B and B Machine and Tool Inc—*James Benton*	3406 Orange Ave Ne, Roanoke VA 24012	540-344-6820	R	6*	.1
753	Brooks Machine Company Inc—*Ronnie Erwin*	1116 New Hwy 7, Columbia TN 38401	931-388-2978	R	6*	.1
754	Equipment Parts Inc—*William Jarchow*	PO Box 1156, Belmont NC 28012	704-827-7545	R	6*	.1
755	Precisionmatics Company Inc—*Laslo Pustay*	PO Box 250, West Winfield NY 13491	315-822-6324	R	6*	.1
756	Houston Dynamic Service Inc—*Clayton Lau*	8150 Lawndale St, Houston TX 77012	713-928-6200	R	6*	<.1
757	R M Industries Inc—*Mike Roller*	PO Box 485, Purdy MO 65734	417-442-3277	R	6*	<.1
758	C-B-Gear and Machine Inc—*Jack Nowlin*	PO Box 111278, Houston TX 77293	281-449-0777	R	6*	<.1
759	Bic Manufacturing Inc—*David Carr*	26420 Cntury Corners P, Euclid OH 44132	216-531-9393	R	6*	<.1
760	Gentry Machine Works Inc—*Thomas Gentry*	5110 Transport Blvd, Columbus GA 31907	706-569-1899	R	6*	<.1
761	Bissinger And Stein Inc—*Philip Stein*	PO Box 316, Kulpsville PA 19443	215-256-1122	R	6*	<.1
762	Riggins Engineering Inc—*Joe Grossnickle*	13932 Saticoy St, Van Nuys CA 91402	818-782-7010	R	6*	<.1
763	Pre-Mach Inc—*Barry Klinedinst*	4365 Run Way, York PA 17406	717-757-5685	R	6*	<.1
764	Aitkin Iron Works Inc—*Jeffrey Chatelle*	301 Bunker Hill Dr, Aitkin MN 56431	218-927-2400	R	6*	.1
765	Bronco Manufacturing Inc—*Johnny Bradley*	PO Box 8, Anna TX 75409	972-924-4576	R	6*	.1
766	Auto-Turn Manufacturing Inc—*Garry Shotton*	9800 S 219th E Ave, Broken Arrow OK 74014	918-451-4511	R	6*	.1
767	Goetsch's Welding and Machine Inc—*Kevin Goetsch*	9480 S County Rd K, Merrill WI 54452	715-536-2658	R	6*	.1
768	Nmp Inc—*Kenneth Nowak*	6170 Norton Ctr Dr, Norton Shores MI 49441	231-798-8851	R	6*	.1
769	Starting Line Products Inc—*Jim Fairchild*	743 E Iona Rd, Idaho Falls ID 83401	208-529-0244	R	6*	.1
770	ARE Manufacturing Inc—*Alvin Elbert*	518 Wilsonville Rd, Newberg OR 97132	503-538-0350	R	6*	<.1
771	Micro-Mechanical Inc—*Takehiko Hayashi*	PO Box 229, Ipswich MA 01938	978-356-2966	R	6*	<.1
772	Oemmcco Inc—*Patricia Dihel*	9606 58th Pl, Kenosha WI 53144	262-605-1170	R	6*	<.1
773	American Drilling Inc—*Jim Shanahan*	625 Glenn Ave, Wheeling IL 60090	847-850-5090	R	6*	<.1
774	Chamberlain Machine Inc—*Robert Boynton*	PO Box 847, Walpole NH 03608	603-756-2560	R	6*	<.1
775	Fortune Manufacturing Inc—*Henry David*	PO Box 307, Sun Valley CA 91353	909-591-1547	R	6*	<.1
776	Midwest Precision Tool and Die Inc—*Burdell Coy*	2000 E 54th St N, Sioux Falls SD 57104	605-373-1160	R	6*	<.1
777	Numerical Control Support Inc—*Gary Dobbins*	21945 W 83rd St, Shawnee Mission KS 66227	913-441-3500	R	6*	<.1
778	Polytec Products Corp—*John Parissenti*	1190 Obrien Dr, Menlo Park CA 94025	650-322-7555	R	6*	<.1
779	Schwartz Machine Co—*Kenneth Sabo*	4441 E 8 Mile Rd, Warren MI 48091	586-756-2300	R	6*	<.1
780	Form Grind Corp—*Ernest Treichler*	30062 Aventura, Rcho Sta Marg CA 92688	949-858-7000	R	6*	<.1
781	Gaum Inc—*Robert Gaum*	PO Box 485, Trenton NJ 08691	609-586-0132	R	6*	<.1
782	Khs Corp—*Katharina Schwemlein*	2693 Philmont Ave Rear, Huntingdon Valley PA 19006	215-947-4010	R	6*	<.1
783	Lincoln Machine Inc—*Robert Lichtenberg*	PO Box 29798, Lincoln NE 68529	402-434-9140	R	6*	.1
784	Snavely's Machine and Manufacturing Company Inc—*James Snavely*	1070 Industrial Pkwy, Peru IN 46970	765-473-8395	R	6*	.1
785	A1 Technologies Inc—*Bruce Ray*	7022 Alondra Blvd, Paramount CA 90723	562-408-1808	R	6*	<.1
786	Laser Fabrication and Machine Company Inc—*Alvin Thacker*	PO Box 709, Alexandria AL 36250	256-892-1600	R	6*	<.1
787	Wsi Machine and Supply LLC—*Larry Lewis*	PO Box 6390, Farmington NM 87499	505-326-0308	R	6*	<.1
788	B and Z Manufacturing Company Inc—*Dennis Kimball*	1478 Seareel Ln, San Jose CA 95131	408-943-1117	R	6*	<.1
789	Advance Manufacturing Corp—*Herman Bredenbeck*	6800 Madison Ave, Cleveland OH 44102	216-961-9191	R	6*	<.1
790	Bestweld Inc—*Rod Bayard*	40 Robinson St, Pottstown PA 19464	610-718-9700	R	6*	<.1
791	New Era Converting Machinery Inc—*Frank Lembo*	PO Box 377, Hawthorne NJ 07507	973-345-3939	R	6*	<.1
792	Metal Technologies Of Murfreesboro Inc—*Ray Felton*	314 W Broad St, Murfreesboro NC 27855	252-398-4041	R	6*	.1
793	Xact Wire Edm Corp—*John Dora*	N8w22399 Johnson Dr, Waukesha WI 53186	262-549-9005	R	6*	.1
794	Energy Machine Inc—*Brian Meiers*	100 Commerce Dr, Mount Vernon OH 43050	740-397-1155	R	6*	.1
795	L W Schneider Inc—*Lloyd Schneider*	1180 N 6th St, Princeton IL 61356	815-875-3835	R	6*	.1
796	Prompton Tool Inc—*Martin Rollison*	120 Sunrise Ave Ste 2, Honesdale PA 18431	570-253-4141	R	6*	.1
797	Reid Products Inc—*Kevin Reid*	21430 Waalew Rd, Apple Valley CA 92307	760-240-1355	R	6*	<.1
798	M and W Manufacturing Company Inc—*Daniel Musil*	809 58th Ave Ct Sw, Cedar Rapids IA 52404	319-362-8030	R	6*	<.1
799	Midwest Screw Products Inc—*Steven Horn*	3501 48th Ave N, Minneapolis MN 55429	763-533-4666	R	6*	<.1
800	Rb Machine Works Inc—*Roger Bethune*	PO Box 218, Humble TX 77347	281-446-1414	R	6*	<.1
801	M and H Engineering Company Inc—*Martin Martens*	183 Newbury St Ste 1, Danvers MA 01923	978-777-1222	R	6*	<.1
802	Vulcan Machine Inc—*James Williams*	1217 Tech Blvd, Tampa FL 33619	813-664-0032	R	6*	<.1
803	Whistler Machine Works Inc—*John Gormandy*	3036 W Turner Rd, Whistler AL 36612	251-452-0070	R	6*	<.1
804	Axis Welding and Machine Works Inc—*George Smith*	PO Box 95, Axis AL 36505	251-675-1130	R	6*	<.1
805	Chris Aire Corp—*Christopher Jones*	4057 Sapphire Dr, Encino CA 91436	818-783-3088	R	6*	.1
806	Hone Tree Company Inc—*Lee Malloy*	PO Box 988, Clovis NM 88102	575-769-2211	R	6*	.1
807	Milltech Manufacturing Co—*Robert Black*	537 Easy St, Garland TX 75042	972-276-1786	R	6*	.1
808	Graham Research Inc—*John Huston*	13305 Industrial Pk Bl, Minneapolis MN 55441	763-553-1339	R	6*	.1
809	Brewton Iron Works Inc—*Earl Wilson*	PO Box 1228, Brewton AL 36427	251-867-3603	R	6*	.1
810	Noremac Manufacturing Corp—*Janice Connelly*	PO Box 867, Westborough MA 01581	508-366-8822	R	6*	.1
811	I Auman Machine Co—*Timothy Auman*	1525 Joel Dr, Lebanon PA 17046	717-273-6748	R	6*	<.1
812	Innovative Machine Specialists Inc—*Anthony Martin*	1907 Laemle Ave, Marshfield WI 54449	715-389-1511	R	6*	<.1
813	Knighten Machine And Service Inc—*William Knighten*	PO Box 12587, Odessa TX 79768	432-362-0468	R	6*	<.1
814	Turn-Tech Inc—*Murray Jaeger*	32007 Industrial Park, Pinehurst TX 77362	281-356-1290	R	6*	<.1
815	Woods Precision Products Inc—*Jerry Fidler*	PO Box 74, Owasso OK 74055	918-371-1810	R	6*	<.1
816	Wordingham Machine Company Inc—*Alok Kapoor*	580 Fishers Station Dr, Victor NY 14564	585-924-2294	R	6*	<.1
817	Guico Machine Works Inc—*Dave Guidry*	1170 Destrehan Ave, Harvey LA 70058	504-340-7111	R	6*	<.1
818	Rite Engineering Co—*Richard Hennig*	8719 Industrial Dr, Franksville WI 53126	262-884-0133	R	6*	<.1
819	Walerko Tool And Engineering Corp—*Edward Walerko*	1935 W Lusher Ave, Elkhart IN 46517	574-295-2233	R	6*	<.1
820	B and G Machine Inc—*John Bianchi*	PO Box 80483, Seattle WA 98108	206-767-3130	R	6*	<.1
821	Centerpoint ManufacturingCoInc—*John Rotunno*	2617 N San Fernando Bl, Burbank CA 91504	818-842-2147	R	6*	<.1
822	Reynolds Machine Company Inc—*Wilbur Reynolds*	PO Box 77, Muskego WI 53150	262-679-6666	R	6*	<.1
823	Molnar Engineering Inc—*Lee Molnar*	20731 Marilla St, Chatsworth CA 91311	818-993-3495	R	6*	<.1
824	Mcmillan's Mechanical and Machine Company Inc—*R Mc Millan*	PO Box 7661, Shreveport LA 71137	318-226-8835	R	5*	.1
825	Time Machine Inc—*Jeffrey Latchaw*	1746 Pittsburgh Rd, Polk PA 16342	814-432-5281	R	5*	<.1
826	F N Smith Corp—*Fred Smith*	PO Box 179, Oregon IL 61061	815-732-2171	R	5*	<.1
827	Gates Machine and Fabrication Inc—*Gary Gates*	8025 Jethro Ln, San Antonio TX 78266	210-651-6567	R	5*	<.1
828	Two M Precision Company Inc—*Mate Brkic*	1747 Joseph Lloyd Pkwy, Willoughby OH 44094	440-946-2120	R	5*	<.1
829	All-American Engineering and Manufacturing Inc—*Dale Roberts*	1519 Johnson Ferry Rd, White Bear Lake MN 55110	651-483-4140	R	5*	<.1
830	Bothe Associates Inc—*Cathryn Bothe*	6901 46th St, Kenosha WI 53144	262-656-1860	R	5*	<.1
831	C E Machine Company Inc—*Brian Eck*	1741 S Hoover Ct, Wichita KS 67209	316-942-0411	R	5*	<.1
832	Knowlton Machine Co—*Normand Trudel*	PO Box 190, Gorham ME 04038	207-854-8471	R	5*	<.1
833	Quality Machine Engineering Inc—*Rudy Hirschnitz*	5600 Skylane Blvd, Santa Rosa CA 95403	707-528-1900	R	5*	<.1
834	2m Oilfield Group Inc—*Douglas Miller*	PO Box 550, Lydia LA 70569	337-365-5555	R	5*	<.1
835	Riverside Machine and Automation Inc—*Jerry Giesler*	1240 N Genoa Clay Ctr, Genoa OH 43430	419-855-8308	R	5*	<.1
836	Akron Special Machinery Inc—*David Poling*	2740 Cory Ave, Akron OH 44314	330-753-1077	R	5*	.1
837	Glenn Tool Inc—*David Glenn*	5940 Nw 5th St, Oklahoma City OK 73127	405-789-2190	R	5*	.1

Note: An asterisk (*) indicates an estimated financial figure. The company type code used is as follows: R = Private, P = Public, S = Private Subsidiary, B = Public Subsidiary, D = Division, J = Joint Venture, I = Investment Fund.

COMPANY RANKINGS BY SALES WITHIN 4-DIGIT SIC

Rank	Company Name—*Executive Officer*	Address, City, State, Zip	Phone	Type	Fin	Empls
838	Acra Grinding Company Inc—*Nancy Dybowski*	40597 Brentwood Dr, Sterling Heights MI 48310	586-979-5900	R	5*	.1
839	Testa Machine Company Inc—*Richard Lounder*	PO Box 416, Slovan PA 15078	724-947-9397	R	5*	<.1
840	Jordan Machinery Corp—*Byron Jordan*	512 S 5th St, Milwaukee WI 53204	414-272-0828	R	5*	<.1
841	Source Fluid Power Inc—*Gary Miller*	331 Lake Hazeltine Dr, Chaska MN 55318	952-448-4440	R	5*	<.1
842	Emc Global Technologies Inc—*Jay Johnson*	130 Penn Am Dr, Quakertown PA 18951	215-340-0650	R	5*	<.1
843	Goldstar Machine and Tool Limited Co—*Ari Arendt*	PO Box 618186, Orlando FL 32861	407-843-5537	R	5*	<.1
844	Continental Machining Co—*David Denison*	6824 Washington St Ne, Albuquerque NM 87109	505-345-2483	R	5*	<.1
845	Richardson Place LLC—*Susan Richardson*	PO Box 2158, Dearborn MI 48123	313-562-5550	R	5*	<.1
846	All-Type Welding And Fabrication Inc—*Mike Distaulo*	7690 Bond St, Cleveland OH 44139	440-439-3990	R	5*	<.1
847	Bogue Machine Company Inc—*Mark Bogue*	7401 Edith Blvd Ne, Albuquerque NM 87113	505-344-9988	R	5*	<.1
848	Metem International Corp—*Steven Goldthwaite*	404 Union Blvd, Allentown PA 18109	610-770-1881	R	5*	<.1
849	Midaco Corp—*Michael Cayley*	2000 Touhy Ave, Elk Grove Village IL 60007	847-593-8420	R	5*	<.1
850	Sample Machining Inc—*Beverly Bleicher*	220 N Jersey St, Dayton OH 45403	937-258-3338	R	5*	<.1
851	Lincoln Tool and Machine Corp—*James Ferrechia*	PO Box 443, Hudson MA 01749	978-567-9993	R	5*	<.1
852	Tsw Industries Inc—*Tich Wan*	14960 Foltz Pkwy, Strongsville OH 44149	440-572-7200	R	5*	<.1
853	Customer Metal Fabrication Inc—*Richard Sparapani*	PO Box 669, Iron Mountain MI 49801	906-774-3216	R	5*	.1
854	Form Centerless Grinding Inc—*Alan Rose*	1 Kenwood Cir, Franklin MA 02038	508-520-0900	R	5*	.1
855	Atlantic Precision Inc—*Timothy Ritter*	600 Nw Peacock Blvd St, Port Saint Lucie FL 34986	772-878-7583	R	5*	<.1
856	Kronenberger Manufacturing Corp—*Gunter Kronenberger*	115 Despatch Dr, East Rochester NY 14445	585-385-2340	R	5*	<.1
857	Quality Machine Co—*Baily Marsh*	PO Box 878, Bridgeport WV 26330	304-842-6229	R	5*	<.1
858	Ideal Products Inc—*Gerald Meyers*	PO Box 2254, Oshkosh WI 54903	920-231-3540	R	5*	<.1
859	Lentros Engineering Inc—*Peter Lentros*	280 Eliot St, Ashland MA 01721	508-881-1160	R	5*	<.1
860	Saliga Machine Company Inc—*Michael Saliga*	10 Bonazzoli Ave, Hudson MA 01749	978-562-7959	R	5*	<.1
861	Ssi Manufacturing Technologies Corp—*Gary Hutchison*	675 Emmett St, Bristol CT 06010	860-589-8004	R	5*	<.1
862	Ultimate Machining and Engineering Inc—*John Kulczuga*	14015 S Van Dyke Rd, Plainfield IL 60544	815-439-8361	R	5*	<.1
863	Wesco Machine Products Inc—*Leonard Mueller*	S84 W 18569 Enterprise, Muskego WI 53150	262-679-4799	R	5*	<.1
864	Apex Bolt and Machine Co—*Michael Petree*	5324 Enterprise Blvd, Toledo OH 43612	419-729-3741	R	5*	<.1
865	Honeycutt Machine Inc—*Mike Luitgaarden*	12402 Evergreen Dr, Mukilteo WA 98275	425-745-1775	R	5*	<.1
866	Rockford Burrall Machine Company Inc—*Raymond Smith*	4520 Shepherd Trl, Rockford IL 61103	815-877-7428	R	5*	<.1
867	Electro-Mechanical Specialties Inc—*Andrew Meikle*	3913 Hawkins Ave, Sanford NC 27330	919-774-7827	R	5*	<.1
868	Lloyd E Hennessey Jr—*Lloyd Hennessey*	7200 Alexander St, Gilroy CA 95020	408-842-8437	R	5*	<.1
869	Lycro Products Company Inc—*Gregory Schoen*	PO Box 571, Wakarusa IN 46573	574-862-4981	R	5*	<.1
870	Midway Grinding Inc—*Jerry Malachowski*	1451 Lunt Ave, Elk Grove Village IL 60007	847-439-7424	R	5*	<.1
871	Clark's Guns And Ammo Inc—*Bobby Clark*	636 Profit St, Azle TX 76020	817-444-2533	R	5*	<.1
872	Connecticut Coining Inc—*Gregory Marciano*	10 Trowbridge Dr, Bethel CT 06801	203-743-3861	R	5*	<.1
873	Ardel Engineering and Manufacturing Inc—*Frank Pichelman*	9335 Science Ctr Dr, Minneapolis MN 55428	763-533-5324	R	5*	<.1
874	D and B Machining Inc—*Rui Duarte*	53 John St, Cumberland RI 02864	401-726-2347	R	5*	<.1
875	D S Anthony and Sons Inc—*Steven Fraunhofer*	1235 W Laurel, San Antonio TX 78201	210-734-5121	R	5*	<.1
876	E R Smith Associates Inc—*Frank Andaloro*	83 Tom Harvey Rd, Westerly RI 02891	401-348-4000	R	5*	<.1
877	Eme Technologies Inc—*Walter Nguyen*	PO Box 61926, Sunnyvale CA 94088	408-720-8817	R	5*	<.1
878	Erie Industries Inc—*Wendy Patrick*	810 E Cambourne St, Ferndale MI 48220	248-547-6393	R	5*	<.1
879	Mikim Industries Inc—*Michael Loiacono*	30 W Jefryn Blvd Ste 2, Deer Park NY 11729	631-586-2344	R	5*	<.1
880	Precision Products Of Asheville Inc—*Shannon Herren*	PO Box 1047, Arden NC 28704	828-684-4207	R	5*	<.1
881	Ptr Manufacturing Inc—*Sai La*	33390 Transit Ave, Union City CA 94587	510-477-9654	R	5*	<.1
882	Bizal Manufacturing Inc—*Michael Bizal*	7880 Ranchers Rd Ne, Minneapolis MN 55432	763-571-4030	R	5*	<.1
883	Machine And Fabrication Industries LLC—*Karen Epley*	7032 S 196th St, Kent WA 98032	253-395-3630	R	5*	<.1
884	Cummins Engine Company Incorporated Engineering Test Services—*Jim Kelly*	4500 Leeds Ave Ste 201, North Charleston SC 29405	843-745-1620	D	5*	.1
885	Astralloy Steel Products Inc	PO Box 170974, Birmingham AL 35217	205-853-0300	D	5*	.1
886	Preferred Machine and Tool Products Corp—*Rod Rumer*	7337 S Mason, Bedford Park IL 60638	708-594-6600	D	5*	.1
887	Southern Machine and Fabrication Company Inc—*Michael Stephens*	18 Commerce Dr, Cartersville GA 30120	770-386-0194	R	5*	.1
888	Buckeye Machine and Fabricators Inc—*D'Marshall*	610 E Lima St, Forest OH 45843	419-273-2521	R	5*	.1
889	Delva Tool and Machine—*Stephen Voellinger*	PO Box 2249, Cinnaminson NJ 08077	856-786-8700	R	5*	.1
890	Metal Cutting Service Inc—*David Viel*	16233 E Gale Ave, City of Industry CA 91745	626-968-4764	R	5*	.1
891	OP Schuman and Sons Inc—*William T Schuman*	2001 County Line Rd, Warrington PA 18976	215-343-1530	R	5*	.1
892	Shareway Industries Inc—*Donald Shumway*	2526 E St NE, Auburn WA 98002		R	5*	.1
893	Sun Engineering Inc—*Walter Williams*	950 Marquette Rd, Lake Station IN 46405	219-962-1191	R	5*	.1
894	Protum Inc—*Linda Mobley*	14192 Fir St Ste 100, Oregon City OR 97045	503-657-3858	R	5*	<.1
895	Baity Screw Products Inc—*Richard Pace*	PO Box 1367, Chickasha OK 73023	405-222-1520	R	5*	<.1
896	Industrial Specialty Company Inc—*Darrell Dapprich*	PO Box 3262, Montgomery AL 36109	334-277-2224	R	5*	<.1
897	Bennett Machine And Fabricating Inc—*Dean Martin*	103 Chamber Dr, Anamosa IA 52205	319-462-5944	R	5*	<.1
898	Elliott Manufacturing Company Inc—*Richard Allbritton*	PO Box 11277, Fresno CA 93772	559-233-6235	R	5*	<.1
899	Hampton Machine Shop Inc—*James Wilson*	900 39th St, Newport News VA 23607	757-380-8500	R	5*	<.1
900	Majestic Manufacturing Inc—*Paul Kudler*	PO Box 128, New Waterford OH 44445	330-457-2447	R	5*	<.1
901	Service Machine Specialties Inc—*Brett Soileau*	1519 Aymond St, Eunice LA 70535	337-457-8712	R	5*	<.1
902	Weldfit Corp—*Steven Maddan*	4135 Dayco St, Houston TX 77092	713-460-3700	R	5*	<.1
903	A and R Engineering Company Inc—*Murat Sehidoglu*	1053 E Bedmar St, Carson CA 90746	310-603-9060	R	5*	<.1
904	Gulf Machine Shop Inc—*Lloyd Smith*	PO Box 16779, Lake Charles LA 70616	337-436-9411	R	5*	<.1
905	Aerospec Inc—*Stephen Marinella*	505 E Alamo Dr, Chandler AZ 85225	480-892-7195	R	5*	<.1
906	Boyer Machine and Tool Company Inc—*William Boyer*	PO Box 422, Columbus IN 47202	812-379-9581	R	5*	<.1
907	United Tool and Mold Inc—*Scott Phipps*	2809 Greenville Hwy, Easley SC 29640	864-859-8300	R	5*	<.1
908	Alltech Manufacturing Ltd—*Laura Bellar*	1477 Industrial Pkwy, Akron OH 44310	330-633-1095	R	5*	<.1
909	C and C Acquisition Corp—*Craig Cook*	15215 Chatfield Ave, Cleveland OH 44111	216-252-0372	R	5*	<.1
910	General Machine Works Company Inc—*Eugene Wood*	13 W 1st St, Spencer IA 51301	712-262-3738	R	5*	<.1
911	H and H Technologies Inc—*Henry Kleitsch*	10 Colt Ct, Ronkonkoma NY 11779	631-567-3526	R	5*	<.1
912	Petersen Machine Company Inc—*Michael Maitland* Pioneer Products Inc	PO Box 1348, Racine WI 53401	262-637-9501	S	5*	<.1
913	Samax Precision Inc—*Vicki Murray*	926 W Evelyn Ave, Sunnyvale CA 94086	408-245-9555	R	5*	<.1
914	Tuffer Manufacturing Company Inc—*Cathy Kim*	163 E Liberty Ave, Anaheim CA 92801	714-526-3077	R	5*	<.1
915	Westwood Precision Inc—*Gordon Nisbet*	7509 Hardeson Rd, Everett WA 98203	425-742-7011	R	5*	<.1
916	Trj Inc—*Dale Bradley*	8900 Forum Way, Fort Worth TX 76140	817-568-1600	R	5*	<.1
917	Allied Engineering And Production Corp—*Sharon Miller*	PO Box 1230, Alameda CA 94501	510-522-1500	R	5*	<.1
918	Global Tool and Manufacturing Co—*Joseph Tracey*	1990 Berwyck Ave, Dayton OH 45414	937-275-0617	R	5*	<.1
919	Industrial Machine and Engineering Co—*Dan Connor*	1716 N 9th St, Monett MO 65708	417-235-3053	R	5*	<.1
920	Modyne Machining and Manufacturing Inc—*Heather Higgins*	2482 S 3270 W, Salt Lake City UT 84119	801-973-0093	R	5*	<.1
921	Precise Tool and Die Company Inc—*Steve Hunyadi*	PO Box 1055, Willoughby OH 44096	440-951-9173	R	5*	<.1
922	Riverside Machine Company Inc—*Martin Whited*	PO Box 5301, Chattanooga TN 37406	423-698-4597	R	5*	<.1
923	Fleck Machine Company Inc—*David Fleck*	7177 Ridge Rd, Hanover MD 21076	410-859-5775	R	5*	<.1
924	WS Anderson Associates Inc—*Ricard Shea*	303 Washington St 313, Auburn MA 01501	508-832-5550	R	5*	<.1

Rank	Company Name—*Executive Officer*	Address, City, State, Zip	Phone	Type	Fin	Empls
925	Foltz Machine Inc—*Edward Welshenbaugh*	2030 Allen Ave Se, Canton OH 44707	330-453-9235	R	5*	<.1
926	Triangle Engineering Corp—*Douglas Staten*	2206 Production Dr, Indianapolis IN 46241	317-243-8549	R	5*	<.1
927	Fusion Systems Inc—*Craig Zoberis*	7035 High Grove Blvd, Burr Ridge IL 60527	630-323-4115	R	5*	<.1
928	Hirsch Machine Inc—*Robert Hirsch*	164 Commercial St, Sunnyvale CA 94086	408-738-8844	R	5*	<.1
929	Donal Machine Inc—*John Bergstedt*	PO Box 750637, Petaluma CA 94975	707-763-6625	R	5*	<.1
930	Dixon Automatic Tool Inc—*Paul Dixon*	2300 23rd Ave, Rockford IL 61104	815-226-3000	R	5*	<.1
931	Jakes Machining and Rebuilding Service Inc—*Jacob Krippelz*	131 2nd St, Aurora IL 60506	630-892-3291	R	5*	<.1
932	Redco Machine Shop Inc—*Steve Lee*	PO Box 866, Bedford VA 24523	540-586-3545	R	5*	<.1
933	Collins Instrument Company Inc—*Roger Collins*	PO Box 938, Angleton TX 77516	979-849-8266	R	5*	<.1
934	Bradley Pulverizer Co—*James Fronheiser*	PO Box 1318, Allentown PA 18105	610-434-5191	R	5*	<.1
935	PURE Bioscience Inc—*Michael L Krall*	1725 Gillespie Way, El Cajon CA 92020	619-596-8600	P	5	<.1
936	Lawruk Machine and Tool Company Inc—*Michael Frederick*	PO Box 1825, Altoona PA 16603	814-943-6136	R	5*	<.1
937	Broadalbin Manufacturing Corp—*James Stark*	PO Box 398, Broadalbin NY 12025	518-883-5313	R	5*	<.1
938	Versatile Engineering Corp—*Adolph Weiss*	1559 W 135th St, Gardena CA 90249	310-532-6044	R	5*	<.1
939	JE Hoffman and Co—*Joseph Hoffman*	739 N Lake St, Mundelein IL 60060	847-566-6800	R	5*	<.1
940	United Drilling Co—*Pedro Araona*	11807 3/4 Slauson Ave, Santa Fe Springs CA 90670	562-945-8833	R	5*	<.1
941	Ala Wai Marine Ltd—*Shigeru Matsui*	1651 Ala Moana Blvd, Honolulu HI 96815	808-946-4213	R	5*	<.1
942	MediNiche Inc—*Samuel J Alioto*	167 Lamp & Lantern Vil, Chesterfield MO 63017	314-542-9539	R	5*	<.1
943	Bw Manufacturing Company Inc—*Gary Weed*	111 Enterprise Dr, Bristol CT 06010	860-584-9303	R	5*	.1
944	Mull Machine Co—*W Mull*	PO Box 6561, Wheeling WV 26003	304-233-3369	R	5*	.1
945	Bms Manufacturing Company Inc—*William Meehan*	2857 County Line Rd, Watkins Glen NY 14891	607-535-2426	R	5*	<.1
946	Magna Machine and Tool Company Inc—*Eugene Weaver*	3722 N Messick Rd, New Castle IN 47362	765-766-5388	R	5*	<.1
947	Diversified Machining Inc—*Joseph Marshall*	PO Box 180, Forest Hill MD 21050	410-879-1400	R	5*	<.1
948	Mittler Corp—*Mike Mittler*	PO Box 110, Foristell MO 63348	636-745-7757	R	5*	<.1
949	Pk3 Group Inc—*Peter Mendes*	PO Box 1086, Sterling MA 01564	978-422-4481	R	5*	<.1
950	A and B Manufacturing Company Inc—*Thomas Bothwell*	1019 E Summit St, Crown Point IN 46307	219-663-4540	R	5*	<.1
951	Jewett Automation Inc—*Bryce Jewett*	2501 Mechanicsville Tp, Richmond VA 23223	804-344-8101	R	5*	<.1
952	Mercier Tool and Die Company Inc—*John Mercier*	PO Box 6120, Canton OH 44706	330-454-9119	R	5*	<.1
953	Valley Machine Shop Inc—*Victor Dalosto*	12221 164th Ave SE, Renton WA 98059	425-226-5040	R	5*	<.1
954	Valley Tool and ManufacturingCoInc—*Fred Brenda*	PO Box 220, Hughson CA 95326	209-883-4093	R	5*	<.1
955	Custom Production Grinding Inc—*Robert Marx*	N56 W13500 Silver Spg, Menomonee Falls WI 53051	262-783-5770	R	5*	<.1
956	Mike Kenney Tool Inc—*Mike Kenney*	2900 Saturn St Ste A, Brea CA 92821	714-524-7668	R	5*	<.1
957	Excel Manufacturing Inc—*Walt Halliday*	24820 Ave Tibbitts, Valencia CA 91355	661-257-1900	R	5*	<.1
958	Supreme Manufacturing Co—*Louis Spizziri*	1755 E Birchwood Ave, Des Plaines IL 60018	847-297-8212	R	5*	<.1
959	Fabritek Company Inc—*Robert Hahn*	416 Battaile Dr, Winchester VA 22601	540-662-9095	R	5*	<.1
960	Octa Inc—*Robert Adams*	PO Box 217, Buckner KY 40010	502-222-8985	R	5*	<.1
961	Precision Shapes Inc—*Joseph Metzger*	PO Box 5099, Titusville FL 32783	321-269-2555	R	5*	<.1
962	Sulzer Machine and Manufacturing Inc—*Gary Sulzer*	2475 Spring Brook Rd, Mosinee WI 54455	715-443-2569	R	5*	<.1
963	Jet Machine Works Inc—*Mark Reneau*	1107 Aldine Mail Rd, Houston TX 77039	281-449-0046	R	5*	<.1
964	Oneida Tool Corp—*John Darnbrook*	12700 Inkster Rd, Redford MI 48239	313-537-0770	R	5*	<.1
965	Beta Industries Inc—*William Walcott*	2860 Culver Ave, Dayton OH 45429	937-299-7385	R	5*	<.1
966	Charles Machine Inc—*C Miller*	1557 Limestone Rd, Summerville PA 15864	814-379-3706	R	5*	<.1
967	Plastic Distributors and Fabricators Inc—*David Cummings*	419 River St, Haverhill MA 01832	978-374-0300	R	5*	<.1
968	RW Machine and Tool Inc—*Alan Wilbur*	7944 State Rte 44, Ravenna OH 44266	330-298-5211	R	5*	<.1
969	G and J Machine Shop Inc—*Michael Jones*	PO Box 941, High Point NC 27261	336-668-0996	R	5*	<.1
970	Alco Machine Company Inc—*David Mcalpin*	PO Box 170430, Birmingham AL 35217	205-323-4593	R	5*	<.1
971	Compatible Manufacturing Inc—*Tim Miller*	386 Laurelwood Rd, Santa Clara CA 95054	408-982-9580	R	5*	<.1
972	Leese and Company Inc—*Christian Klanica*	PO Box 610, Greensburg PA 15601	724-834-5810	R	5*	<.1
973	Prescott Aerospace Inc—*Michael Dailey*	6600 E 6th St, Prescott Valley AZ 86314	928-772-7605	R	5*	<.1
974	Trivak Inc—*Paul Novak*	280 Howard St, Lowell MA 01852	978-453-7123	R	5*	<.1
975	Sunbelt Machine Works—*C Scantlin*	13411 Redfish Ln, Stafford TX 77477	281-499-0051	R	5*	<.1
976	Perfection Machine And Tool Works A California Corp—*Alfred Hix*	1568 E 22nd St, Los Angeles CA 90011	213-749-5095	R	5*	.
977	Rebb Industries Inc—*Richard Jacobson*	1617 Fern Valley Rd, Yadkinville NC 27055	336-463-2311	R	5*	.1
978	Specialty Design and Manufacturing Company Inc—*Craig Knabb*	PO Box 4039, Reading PA 19606	610-779-1357	R	5*	.1
979	T and K Specialty Products Inc—*William Thery*	1501 9th St, Racine WI 53403	262-634-7744	R	5*	.1
980	Quantex Instrument Co—*Clifford Price*	PO Box 520, Crockett TX 75835	936-544-5732	R	5*	<.1
981	Automotive Servicenter Inc—*Susan Blavatt*	5563 Suffield Ct, Columbia MD 21044	410-730-6517	R	5*	<.1
982	Daleo Machining Inc—*Sharon Daleo*	PO Box 632, Platteville WI 53818	608-348-2207	R	5*	<.1
983	Mitchell Manufacturing LLC	3150 W Havens Ave, Mitchell SD 57301	605-996-1121	R	5*	<.1
984	Service Machine and Supply Inc—*Harlan Denais*	1828 Denais Rd, Duson LA 70529	337-216-1000	R	5*	<.1
985	Eastlake Machine Products Inc—*Ivan Saric*	1956 Joseph Lloyd Pkwy, Willoughby OH 44094	440-953-1014	R	5*	<.1
986	Eaton Fabricating Company Inc—*Ray Roach*	1009 Mcalpin Ct, Grafton OH 44044	440-926-3121	R	5*	<.1
987	Canfield Machine and Tool LLC—*Debra Canfield*	121 Howard Rd, Fulton NY 13069	315-593-8062	R	5*	<.1
988	Butler and Cook Inc—*John Koprovic*	7900 Ball Rd, Fort Smith AR 72908	479-783-6962	R	5*	<.1
989	International Machining Inc—*John Strobel*	2885 Nationwide Pkwy, Brunswick OH 44212	330-225-1963	R	5*	<.1
990	Machining Concepts Inc—*Wayne Beebout*	PO Box 334, Cedarburg WI 53012	262-375-9007	R	5*	<.1
991	Mission Tool and ManufacturingCoInc—*Gary Smith*	3440 Arden Rd, Hayward CA 94545	510-782-8383	R	5*	<.1
992	Valley Machine Tool Company Inc—*Larry Wilson*	9773 Morrow Cozaddale, Morrow OH 45152	513-899-2737	R	5*	<.1
993	Ver-Mac Industries Inc—*Dennis Mcelroy*	100 Progress Dr, Mount Vernon OH 43050	740-397-3939	R	5*	<.1
994	Toolcraft Company Inc—*Kathleen Rogers*	W194n11092 Kleinmann D, Germantown WI 53022	262-250-7640	R	5*	<.1
995	Ely Company Inc—*Walter Senff*	3046 Kashiwa St, Torrance CA 90505	310-539-5831	R	5*	<.1
996	Big B Manufacturing Inc—*Russell Blyler*	17 Municipal Rd, Klingerstown PA 17941	570-648-2084	R	5*	<.1
997	Valley Tool And Machine Company Inc—*Charles Rogers*	111 Explorer St, Pomona CA 91768	909-595-2205	R	5*	<.1
998	Joma Machine Company Inc—*Wilhelm Moser*	5 Front St, Mohnton PA 19540	610-775-3323	R	5*	<.1
999	Aci Industries Inc—*William Nell*	851 N Progress Dr, Saukville WI 53080	262-268-2837	R	5*	<.1
1000	Crane Research and Engineering Company Inc—*Dannie Schrum*	PO Box 9009, Hampton VA 23670	757-826-1707	R	5*	<.1
1001	Gtr Enterprises Inc—*Martin Randant*	6352 Corte Del Abeto E, Carlsbad CA 92011	760-931-1192	R	5*	<.1
1002	Odat Machine Inc—*Richard Pratt*	20 Sanford Dr, Gorham ME 04038	207-854-2455	R	5*	<.1
1003	Eagle Tool and Design Inc—*Mike Tschida*	7979 Central Ave Ne, Minneapolis MN 55432	763-784-7400	R	5*	<.1
1004	Sunset Manufacturing Co—*James Warren*	PO Box 308, Tualatin OR 97062	503-692-1900	R	5*	<.1
1005	Cassavant Machining Inc—*Joe Cassavant*	3641 E La Salle St, Phoenix AZ 85040	602-437-4005	R	5*	<.1
1006	Innovative Machine Corp—*James Nielsen*	PO Box 9908, Birmingham AL 35220	205-856-4100	R	5*	<.1
1007	Peninsula Iron Works—*James Johnson*	PO Box 83067, Portland OR 97283	503-286-4461	R	5*	<.1
1008	Gki Inc—*Olaf Klutke*	6204 Factory Rd, Crystal Lake IL 60014	815-459-2330	R	5*	<.1
1009	Harrington Machine And Tool Company Inc—*Tom Harrington*	1027 Chestnut St, Franklin PA 16323	814-432-7339	R	5*	<.1
1010	Damar Tool and Manufacturing Inc—*Steve Omlmar*	18240 Rialto St, Melvindale MI 48122	313-383-9480	R	5*	<.1
1011	TGG Inc—*George King*	PO Box 366, Middleton MA 01949	978-777-5010	R	5*	<.1

Note: An asterisk (*) indicates an estimated financial figure. The company type code used is as follows: R = Private, P = Public, S = Private Subsidiary, B = Public Subsidiary, D = Division, J = Joint Venture, I = Investment Fund.

COMPANY RANKINGS BY SALES WITHIN 4-DIGIT SIC

Rank	Company Name—Executive Officer	Address, City, State, Zip	Phone	Type	Fin	Empls
1012	Mcm Corporation Of Oneida—Charles Mcbroom	385 One Industrial Pk, Oneida TN 37841	423-569-9232	R	5*	<.1
1013	Fortville Feeders Inc—Michael Crouse	PO Box 70, Fortville IN 46040	317-485-5195	R	5*	<.1
1014	Perfecto Tool and Engineering Company Inc—Stephen Skaggs	PO Box 2039, Anderson IN 46018	765-644-2821	R	5*	<.1
1015	Quality Products and Machine LLC—Alison Lail	4600 Westinghouse Blvd, Charlotte NC 28273	704-504-3330	R	5*	<.1
1016	Spyco Industries Inc—John Spytek	7029 High Grove Blvd, Burr Ridge IL 60527	630-655-5900	R	5*	<.1
1017	Valley Mine Service Inc—Danny Gibson	PO Box 57, Speedwell TN 37870	423-869-3155	R	5*	<.1
1018	Wolverine Carbide Die Co—Gus Stavropoulos	2613 Industrial Row Dr, Troy MI 48084	248-280-0300	R	5*	<.1
1019	Aer-Dan Precision—Steve Morton	1458 Seareel Pl, San Jose CA 95131	408-954-8704	R	5*	<.1
1020	NET and Die Inc—Richard Shatrau	PO Box 240, Fulton NY 13069	315-592-4311	R	5*	<.1
1021	Funtastic Factory Inc—Ross Andrizzi	12405 Telegraph Rd, Santa Fe Springs CA 90670	562-777-1140	R	5*	<.1
1022	Metal-Flex Welded Bellows Inc—Barrie Hume	149 Lakemont Rd, Newport VT 05855	802-334-5550	R	5*	<.1
1023	Suburban Manufacturing Co—Richard Grice	1924 E 337th St, Eastlake OH 44095	440-953-2024	R	5*	<.1
1024	Weaver Machine and Tool Company Inc—Caroline Weaver	44 York St, Auburn NY 13021	315-253-4422	R	5*	<.1
1025	Aerodynamic Engineering Inc—Alfred Mayer	15495 Graham St, Huntington Beach CA 92649	714-891-2651	R	5*	<.1
1026	Lake Country Cnc Machining Inc—Lawrence Line	513 6th St Ne, Long Prairie MN 56347	320-732-3454	R	5*	<.1
1027	Machining Center Inc—Jerry Isbell	5959 Ford Ct, Brighton MI 48116	810-229-9208	R	5*	<.1
1028	Metal-Tech Manufacturing Inc—Karen Herrington	1445 S 18th St, Clinton IA 52732	563-242-3481	R	5*	<.1
1029	Schram Enterprises Inc—Mark Schram	5017 W Lake St, Melrose Park IL 60160	708-345-2252	R	5*	<.1
1030	Schwartz Industries Inc—Thomas Hammond	6909 E 11 Mile Rd, Warren MI 48092	586-759-1777	R	5*	<.1
1031	Techni-Products Inc—Margery Morehardt	PO Box 215, East Longmeadow MA 01028	413-525-6321	R	5*	<.1
1032	Triad Tool and Die Company Inc—William Wichelhaus	9 Commerce St, Somerville NJ 08876	908-534-1784	R	5*	<.1
1033	Stevens Manufacturing Company Inc—Stephen Fogler	PO Box 3041, Milford CT 06460	203-878-2328	R	5*	<.1
1034	JL Rushing Machine Shop Inc—Leon Rushing	PO Box 609, White Oak TX 75693	903-759-6000	R	5*	<.1
1035	Jwf Industries Inc—Brandall Wright	PO Box 82, Trussville AL 35173	205-655-7738	R	5*	<.1
1036	Foranne Manufacturing Inc—Victor Gentile	83 Steam Whistle Dr, Warminster PA 18974	215-357-4650	R	5*	<.1
1037	J and C Industries Inc—Christopher Zanellis	PO Box 2390, Seabrook NH 03874	603-474-9589	R	5*	<.1
1038	Fims Manufacturing Corp—Sergio Facchini	162 Central Ave, Rochelle Park NJ 07662	201-845-7088	R	5*	<.1
1039	Michigan Rebuild And Automation Inc—Timothy Galloway	760 Herring Rd, Litchfield MI 49252	517-542-6000	R	5*	<.1
1040	Mercury Tool And Machine Inc—Jack Peck	PO Box 5190, Waco TX 76708	254-752-1639	R	4*	.1
1041	Kings Welding And Fabricating Inc—Glen King	5259 Bane Rd Ne, Mechanicstown OH 44651	330-738-3592	R	4*	<.1
1042	Woodlan Tool And Machine Company Inc—Patrick Boylan	PO Box 7211, Portland ME 04112	802-463-4597	R	4*	<.1
1043	Charl Industries Inc—Richard Coronato	225 Engineers Rd, Hauppauge NY 11788	631-234-0100	R	4*	<.1
1044	Dial-X Automated Equipment Inc—Michael Katz	3903 S State Rd 9, Albion IN 46701	260-636-7588	R	4*	<.1
1045	Industrial Machine Work Inc—Ann Howell	PO Box 762, Flomaton AL 36441	251-296-2096	R	4*	<.1
1046	Machine Builders and Design Inc—Daryl Mims	806 N Post Rd, Shelby NC 28150	704-482-3456	R	4*	<.1
1047	Central State Enterprises Inc—Donald Kuenzli	1331 Freese Works Pl, Galion OH 44833	419-468-8191	R	4*	<.1
1048	Kovacs Machine And Tool Company Inc—Allen Cuccaro	50 N Plains Industrial, Wallingford CT 06492	203-269-4949	R	4*	<.1
1049	Machine Products Co—Robert Appenzeller	5660 Webster St, Dayton OH 45414	937-890-6600	R	4*	<.1
1050	Middleton Machining and Welding Inc—Scott Difiore	7629 Donna Dr, Middleton WI 53562	608-831-6807	R	4*	<.1
1051	Shop Acquisitions LLC—Jeff Smith	6989 Lindsay Dr, Mentor OH 44060	440-266-7700	R	4*	<.1
1052	Vinyl Technologies Inc—Dirk Burrowes	195 Industrial Rd, Fitchburg MA 01420	978-342-9800	R	4*	<.1
1053	M and K Engineering Inc—Henry Bernardo	66 Concord St, North Reading MA 01864	978-276-1973	R	4*	<.1
1054	Central Dynamic Manufacturing Inc—Sheryl Mc Coy	PO Box 679, Mansfield TX 76063	817-473-3899	R	4*	<.1
1055	Qsi Automation Inc—Phillip Munk	4585 S State Rd 9-57, Churubusco IN 46723	260-693-1500	R	4*	<.1
1056	Weld-Fab Manufacturing Corp—Art Hahn	180 James St, Slinger WI 53086	262-644-4131	R	4*	<.1
1057	Husa Accurate Machine Works Inc—Hugo Sapien	830 Dorchester St, Houston TX 77022	713-691-0685	R	4*	<.1
1058	Aljo Precision Products Inc—John Adelmann	205 Sweet Hollow Rd, Old Bethpage NY 11804	516-420-4419	R	4*	<.1
1059	Arc Manufacturing Company Inc—Stephen Feuchter	1651 Loretta Ave, Feasterville Trevose PA 19053	215-355-8500	R	4*	<.1
1060	Cheetah Precision Inc—Manfred Niedernhoefer	55 Mounds St Ne, Saint Paul MN 55112	651-633-4566	R	4*	<.1
1061	Disco Machine and Manufacturing Inc—Zbigniew Brzostowski	7327 W Agatite Ave, Norridge IL 60706	708-456-0835	R	4*	<.1
1062	Horizon Carbide Tool Inc—Carrie Fetter	2404 S Industrial Pk A, Tempe AZ 85282	480-968-0957	R	4*	<.1
1063	Limerick Machine Company Inc—Jackie Harrington	PO Box 534, Limerick ME 04048	207-793-2288	R	4*	<.1
1064	Mike's Micro Parts Inc—Robert Oganesian	1901 Potrero Ave, South El Monte CA 91733	626-443-0675	R	4*	<.1
1065	Pacific Perforating Inc—Troy Ducharme	25090 Hwy 33, Fellows CA 93224	661-768-9224	R	4*	<.1
1066	Standard Bellows Co—Stanley Tkacz	375 Ella Grasso Tpke, Windsor Locks CT 06096	860-623-2307	R	4*	<.1
1067	W C Machine and Tool Inc—Walter Moulten	3100 N San Marcos Pl, Chandler AZ 85225	480-507-4620	R	4*	<.1
1068	Wagner Machine Inc—Michael Wagner	5151 Wooster Rd W, Norton OH 44203	330-706-0700	R	4*	<.1
1069	Plainville Machine Works Inc—Henning Frederiksen	PO Box 1508, Plainville MA 02762	508-699-7575	R	4*	<.1
1070	Price Products Inc—John Price	106 State Pl, Escondido CA 92029	760-745-5602	R	4*	<.1
1071	Serrano Industries Inc—Hoberto Serrano	9922 Tabor Pl, Santa Fe Springs CA 90670	562-777-8180	R	4*	<.1
1072	Global Machine Works Inc—Brad Stuczynski	19130 59th Dr Ne, Arlington WA 98223	360-403-8432	R	4*	<.1
1073	Suburban Machine Company Inc—Brad Barger	301 Chelsea Rd, Monticello MN 55362	763-295-5635	R	4*	<.1
1074	Tapemation Machining Inc—Phyllis Erickson	13 Janis Way, Scotts Valley CA 95066	831-438-3069	R	4*	<.1
1075	Reliance Industries Inc—Devandra Desai	PO Box 1146, Stafford TX 77497	281-499-9926	R	4*	<.1
1076	Tmx Engineering/Manufacturing Crp—Gus Toubia	2141 S Standard Ave, Santa Ana CA 92707	714-641-5884	R	4*	.1
1077	Digital Machining Systems LLC—Ruth Collins	929 Ridge Rd, Duson LA 70529	337-984-6013	R	4*	.1
1078	Reed's Precision Machine Inc—Shawn Bindrup	844 W 400 N, Logan UT 84321	435-753-6370	R	4*	<.1
1079	G and G Grinding and Machine Inc—Lee Graske	PO Box 12236, Omaha NE 68112	402-453-9595	R	4*	<.1
1080	Globe Machine Company And Metal Fabricators Inc—Judy Godfrey	PO Box 885, Canton GA 30169	770-345-5551	R	4*	<.1
1081	Highland Machine Tool Inc—James Bezy	PO Box 156, Floyds Knobs IN 47119	812-923-8884	R	4*	<.1
1082	Todd Grinding Co—James Todd	PO Box 580, Dryden MI 48428	810-796-3656	R	4*	<.1
1083	Valley Precision Inc—Daniel Drumheller	501 Delaware Ave, Waynesboro VA 22980	540-942-3346	R	4*	<.1
1084	Elite Tool LLC—Brenda Moore	1011 Industrial Ct, Moscow Mills MO 63362	636-366-4145	R	4*	<.1
1085	Chapter 2 Inc—Timothy Johnston	PO Box 128, Lake Mills WI 53551	920-648-8125	R	4*	<.1
1086	Craig Instruments Ltd—Ronald Buchtien	6333 Guhn Rd, Houston TX 77040	713-690-6904	R	4*	<.1
1087	Midland Wellhead Inc—Keith Morgan	40 E Industrial Loop, Midland TX 79701	432-682-0856	R	4*	<.1
1088	Tessa Precision Products Inc—Paul Battaglia	850 Callendar Blvd, Painesville OH 44077	440-392-3470	R	4*	<.1
1089	Cameron Machine Shop—Wilburn Cameron	404 N Bowser Rd, Richardson TX 75081	972-235-8876	R	4*	<.1
1090	Chase Machine Company Inc—Steve Sheldon	324 Washington St, West Warwick RI 02893	401-821-8879	R	4*	<.1
1091	Eagle Bridge Machine and Tool Inc—Robert Farrara	135 State Rte 67, Eagle Bridge NY 12057	518-686-4541	R	4*	<.1
1092	Edhard Corp—Edgar Bars	279 Blau Rd, Hackettstown NJ 07840	908-850-8444	R	4*	<.1
1093	HW Nicholson Welding And Manufacturing Inc—Russell Coking	375 Larimer Trl, Apollo PA 15613	724-727-3461	R	4*	<.1
1094	Millrite Machine Inc—Robert Valcourt	587 Southampton Rd, Westfield MA 01085	413-562-9212	R	4*	<.1
1095	Ok Machine and Manufacturing Inc—Glenn Strobel	2522 N Columbia Pl, Tulsa OK 74110	918-838-1300	R	4*	<.1
1096	Scientific Tool Inc—William Faltz	596 Middletown Rd, New Stanton PA 15672	724-446-9311	R	4*	<.1
1097	Truform Machine Inc—Frank Phillips	2510 Precision St, Jackson MI 49202	517-782-8523	R	4*	<.1
1098	Byrtech Custom Machine Works Inc—Robby Byrd	PO Box 4768, Greenville SC 29608	864-242-9946	R	4*	<.1
1099	Baker-Hill Industries Inc—William Ricci	3850 Nw 118th Ave, Coral Springs FL 33065	954-752-3090	R	4*	<.1
1100	Cardish Machine Works Inc—Eugene Cardish	7 Elm St, Watervliet NY 12189	518-273-1713	R	4*	<.1

Rank	Company Name—*Executive Officer*	Address, City, State, Zip	Phone	Type	Fin	Empls
1101	Dynamic Enterprises Inc—*Mildred Sudduth*	10015 Greenleaf Ave, Santa Fe Springs CA 90670	562-944-0271	R	4*	<.1
1102	Turk Manufacturing Inc—*Dennis Turk*	1500 Ne 48th Ave, Hillsboro OR 97124	503-681-3093	R	4*	<.1
1103	Ace Manufacturing Co—*Linda Fullbeck*	5031 Winton Rd, Cincinnati OH 45232	513-541-2490	R	4*	<.1
1104	Ponderosa Industries Inc—*John Moyski*	3821 Steele St Ste E, Denver CO 80205	303-298-1801	R	4*	<.1
1105	Painted Feather Precision LLC—*Mary Wiedner*	8401 73rd Ave N Ste 56, Minneapolis MN 55428	763-537-6466	R	4*	<.1
1106	Pattison Precision Products Inc—*Raymond Pattison*	701 N 15th St, Broken Arrow OK 74012	918-251-9967	R	4*	<.1
1107	El Camino Machine and Welding LLC	296 El Camino Real S, Salinas CA 93901	831-758-8309	R	4*	<.1
1108	Uintah Machine And Manufacturing Co—*John Skewes*	PO Box 8, Duchesne UT 84021	435-738-2453	R	4*	<.1
1109	Machinewell Inc—*Wayne Kehler*	PO Box 157, Grygla MN 56727	218-294-6101	R	4*	.1
1110	Maclean Precision Machine Company Inc—*Allan Maclean*	PO Box 70, Madison NH 03849	603-367-9011	R	4*	<.1
1111	Decherts Machine Shop Inc—*William Herr*	PO Box 272, Palmyra PA 17078	717-838-1326	R	4*	<.1
1112	Gloucester Associates Inc—*Byrom Atwood*	PO Box 477, Barre VT 05641	802-479-1088	R	4*	<.1
1113	Jorgensen Tool and Stamping Inc—*Richard Jorgensen*	23 Fruite St, Belmont NH 03220	603-524-5813	R	4*	<.1
1114	Machine Craft Of San Diego Inc—*Chinta Sawh*	9822 Waples St, San Diego CA 92121	858-642-0509	R	4*	<.1
1115	NJ Precision Technologies Inc—*Robert Tarantino*	1081 Bristol Rd, Mountainside NJ 07092	908-232-8847	R	4*	<.1
1116	Sematco Inc—*Jack Kearney*	275 Eastpark Dr, Roanoke VA 24019	540-977-3200	R	4*	<.1
1117	American Quality Manufacturing Inc—*Mark Dzurisin*	3519 Kishwaukee St Ste, Rockford IL 61109	815-226-9301	R	4*	<.1
1118	Dillon Precision Inc—*Bradford Dillon*	3870 Dividend Dr, Shingle Springs CA 95682	530-672-6794	R	4*	<.1
1119	Valent Aerostructures - St Louis Inc—*Bruce Breckenridge*	2280 Chaffee Dr A, Saint Louis MO 63146	314-699-9072	R	4*	<.1
1120	Elliot Tool Inc—*Tim Lappe*	4400 Gustine Ave, Saint Louis MO 63116	314-652-6939	R	4*	<.1
1121	Precision Machining Services Inc—*Eric Kleinschmidt*	PO Box 13631, Dayton OH 45413	937-222-4608	R	4*	<.1
1122	Wilshire Precision Products Inc—*Thomas Lewis*	7353 Hinds Ave, North Hollywood CA 91605	818-765-4571	R	4*	<.1
1123	Garabedian Brothers Inc—*Joseph Garabedian*	PO Box 2455, Fresno CA 93745	559-268-5014	R	4*	<.1
1124	SRP M Inc—*Mark Steinmeyer*	30300 Bruce Industrial, Cleveland OH 44139	440-248-8440	R	4*	<.1
1125	Haulette Manufacturing Inc—*Fred Kremer*	8271 Us Rte 127, Celina OH 45822	419-586-1717	R	4*	.1
1126	Bowe Machine Co—*Simon Bowe*	PO Box 1570, Bettendorf IA 52722	563-355-4777	R	4*	.1
1127	Eran Engineering Inc—*Timothy Consalvi*	2672 Dow Ave, Tustin CA 92780	714-543-2966	S	4*	.1
1128	LA Gauge Company Inc	7440 San Fernando Rd, Sun Valley CA 91352	818-767-7193	D	4*	.1
1129	Metal Essence Inc—*Al Stimac*	930 Britt Ct Ste 124, Altamonte Springs FL 32701	407-478-8480	R	4*	.1
1130	Salco Inc—*Robert Salvatore*	5955 Sheridan Blvd, Arvada CO 80003	303-423-2012	R	4*	.1
1131	R L Lewis Industries Inc—*Tracy Williams*	14215 Towerline Rd, Pekin IL 61554	309-353-7670	R	4*	<.1
1132	Aero Space Tooling and Machining—*Rolf Salm*	PO Box 25606, Salt Lake City UT 84125	801-972-1279	R	4*	<.1
1133	Barrel Service Co—*WJ Bramble*	105 S Pacific St, San Marcos CA 92078	760-744-2122	R	4*	<.1
1134	Creative Design and Machining Inc—*William Toman*	PO Box 773, Clarks Summit PA 18411	570-587-3077	R	4*	<.1
1135	EA Quirin Machine Shop Inc—*Edmund Quirin*	PO Box 98, Saint Clair PA 17970	570-429-0590	R	4*	<.1
1136	H and E Cutter Grinding Inc—*Michael Morgan*	6251 Industrial Ave N, Connersville IN 47331	765-825-0541	R	4*	<.1
1137	Mid South Machine Inc—*Ronald Semar*	PO Box 720, Broussard LA 70518	337-837-1669	R	4*	<.1
1138	Quality Machine Works Inc—*Daniel Louque*	32838 La 642 N, Paulina LA 70763	225-869-9809	R	4*	<.1
1139	Schroeder Tool and Die Corp—*Steve Schroeder*	25448 Cumberland Ln, Calabasas CA 91302	818-786-9360	R	4*	<.1
1140	Western Precision Aero—*Ed McKenna*	11600 Monarch St, Garden Grove CA 92841	714-893-7999	S	4*	<.1
1141	Fisher Products LLC—*Michael Shorts*	1320 W 22nd Pl, Tulsa OK 74107	918-582-2204	R	4*	<.1
1142	Grindco Inc—*Adam Bellar*	PO Box 819, Chesterton IN 46304	219-763-6130	R	4*	<.1
1143	MRS Machining Company Inc—*Nancy Guse*	PO Box 24, Augusta WI 54722	715-286-2448	R	4*	<.1
1144	Associated Welding and Machine Works Inc—*Steve Coleman*	19555 Sw 129th Ave, Tualatin OR 97062	503-091-1818	R	4*	<.1
1145	Putnam Machine Products Inc—*Glenna Bartholomew*	35 Cecil Dr, Coldwater MI 49036	517-278-2364	R	4*	<.1
1146	Aremac Associates Inc—*Scott Sher*	2004 S Myrtle Ave, Monrovia CA 91016	626-303-8795	R	4*	<.1
1147	D and R Machine Co—*Paul Redante*	1330 Industrial Blvd, Southampton PA 18966	215-526-2080	R	4*	<.1
1148	Daman Industrial Services Inc—*Allan Stipp*	PO Box 486, East Brady PA 16028	724-526-5714	R	4*	<.1
1149	Dimension Machine Tool Inc—*Hans Lohr*	24750 21 Mile Rd, Macomb MI 48042	586-786-9023	R	4*	<.1
1150	Layke Inc—*Ernest J Apodaca*	3330 W Osborn Rd, Phoenix AZ 85017	602-272-2654	R	4*	<.1
1151	Macton Corp—*David Perkins*	116 Willenbrock Rd, Oxford CT 06478	203-267-1500	R	4	<.1
1152	Murko Machinery and Die Corp—*Morris Mendlowitz*	32-38 62nd St, Woodside NY 11377	718-728-4427	R	4*	<.1
1153	Sanco Industries Inc—*Kevin Appenzeller*	1819 S Calhoun St, Fort Wayne IN 46802	260-426-6281	R	4*	<.1
1154	Cason Engineering Inc—*Brad Cason*	4789 Golden Foothill P, El Dorado Hills CA 95762	916-939-9311	R	4*	<.1
1155	GNW Machine Inc—*James Wahlstrand*	2289 E Cedar St Ste 10, Hugo MN 55038	651-426-8708	R	4*	<.1
1156	Haberman Machine Inc—*John Ness*	6290 Hwy 36 Blvd N, Saint Paul MN 55128	651-777-4511	R	4*	<.1
1157	C Wright's Machine Tool Inc—*Charles Wright*	12293 Fm 2879, Diana TX 75640	903-777-2344	R	4*	<.1
1158	Colorado Precision Machining Inc—*Donald Salvatori*	6452 Fig St Unit F, Arvada CO 80004	303-467-3835	R	4*	<.1
1159	D and B Machine Inc—*Betty Frostad*	1855 61st St, Sarasota FL 34243	941-355-8002	R	4*	<.1
1160	Frantz Machine Products Inc—*Donald Frantz*	1785 S Johnson Rd, New Berlin WI 53146	262-544-5611	R	4*	<.1
1161	High Precision Grinding and Machining Inc—*Keith Brawner*	1130 Pioneer Way, El Cajon CA 92020	619-440-0303	R	4*	<.1
1162	Kercher Machine Works Inc—*Edwin Kercher*	920 Mechanic St, Lebanon PA 17046	717-273-2111	R	4*	<.1
1163	Montalvo Corp—*Margaret Montalvo*	50 Hutcherson Dr, Gorham ME 04038	207-856-2501	R	4*	<.1
1164	Precision Technologies Inc—*Walter Subsick*	PO Box 610, Tyngsboro MA 01879	978-649-8715	R	4*	<.1
1165	Purcell Co—*Milton Purcell*	PO Box 440, Hershey PA 17033	717-838-5611	R	4*	<.1
1166	SSD Control Technology Inc—*Steve Estes*	1801 S Main St, South Bend IN 46613	574-289-5942	R	4*	<.1
1167	Standard Machine Inc—*Jim Dopoulos*	1952 W 93rd St, Cleveland OH 44102	216-631-4440	R	4*	<.1
1168	A-Z Manufacturing Inc—*Ann Lukas*	200 Briggs Ave, Costa Mesa CA 92626	714-444-4446	R	4*	<.1
1169	Falcon Precision Industries Inc—*Albert Antoni*	PO Box 337, Wauconda IL 60084	847-487-9000	R	4*	<.1
1170	J and L Precision Machine Company Inc—*John Lack*	102 N Commerce Way, Bethlehem PA 18017	610-691-8411	R	4*	<.1
1171	Kitch Engineering Inc—*Steven Kitching*	12455 Branford St Ste, Pacoima CA 91331	818-897-7133	R	4*	<.1
1172	M and R Precision Machining Inc—*Richard Beinhauer*	680 Lively Blvd, Elk Grove Village IL 60007	847-364-1050	R	4*	<.1
1173	McBride and Shoff Inc—*Cliff Shoff*	PO Box 739, Metamora IL 61548	309-367-4193	R	4*	<.1
1174	Ohio Machine and Manufacturing Company Inc—*Lou T Fike*	1623 E Nadeau St, Los Angeles CA 90001	323-588-8257	R	4*	<.1
1175	Precision Metal Works Inc—*Tony Singleton*	PO Box 9261, Montgomery AL 36108	334-265-1678	R	4*	<.1
1176	Sinn-Tech Inc—*Andrew Sinn*	48 Gleam St, West Babylon NY 11704	631-643-1171	R	4*	<.1
1177	Watts Machining Inc—*Doug Watts*	2339 Calle Del Mundo, Santa Clara CA 95054	408-654-9300	R	4*	<.1
1178	Aerodyne Industries LLC—*Angelita Trepanier*	8737 N 77th Dr, Peoria AZ 85345	623-878-6800	R	4*	<.1
1179	Endyn Manufacturing Inc—*Tracy Little*	PO Box 18312, San Antonio TX 78218	210-655-6046	R	4*	<.1
1180	Zet-Tek Precision Machining—*Dan Zettler*	1315 N Brasher St, Anaheim CA 92807	714-777-8770	R	4*	<.1
1181	Griffin Automation Inc—*Jerry Biblack*	PO Box 347, West Seneca NY 14224	716-674-2300	R	4*	<.1
1182	Pleasanton Tool and Manufacturing Inc—*Chester Thomas*	1181 Quarry Ln Ste 450, Pleasanton CA 94566	925-426-0500	R	4*	<.1
1183	R and D Custom Machine and Tool Inc—*David Skomer*	5961 American Rd E, Toledo OH 43612	419-727-1700	R	4*	<.1
1184	Terrell Manufacturing Inc—*George Roth*	19444 Progress Dr, Strongsville OH 44149	440-238-5445	R	4*	<.1
1185	Performance Pattern and Machine Inc—*Tom Herman*	2421 Sw Adams St, Peoria IL 61602	309-676-0907	R	4*	<.1
1186	Blair Machine and Tool Inc—*Grover Blair*	8665 Philips Hwy, Jacksonville FL 32256	904-731-4377	R	4*	<.1
1187	Bless Precision Tool Inc—*Howard Bless*	80 Pacific Dr, Quakertown PA 18951	215-536-7836	R	4*	<.1
1188	HKK Machining Co—*Duane King*	1201 Oak St, West Unity OH 43570	419-924-5116	R	4*	<.1
1189	Precise Machine and Manufacturing Inc—*Danny Fancher*	PO Box 217, Cassville MO 65625	417-847-3405	R	4*	<.1
1190	United Machine Shop Inc—*Kevin Copeland*	PO Box 588, Kilgore TX 75663	903-984-0218	R	4*	<.1

Note: An asterisk (*) indicates an estimated financial figure. The company type code used is as follows: R = Private, P = Public, S = Private Subsidiary, B = Public Subsidiary, D = Division, J = Joint Venture, I = Investment Fund.

COMPANY RANKINGS BY SALES WITHIN 4-DIGIT SIC

Rank	Company Name—*Executive Officer*	Address, City, State, Zip	Phone	Type	Fin	Empls
1191	Axion Corp—*Beth Latifi*	317 Nick Fitcheard Rd, Huntsville AL 35806	256-851-9770	R	4*	<.1
1192	UltraTech International Inc—*Tad Heyman*	11542 Davis Creek Ct, Jacksonville FL 32256	904-292-1611	R	4*	<.1
1193	Berglin Corp—*Scott Berglin*	15 Orondo Ave, East Wenatchee WA 98802	509-888-8880	R	4*	<.1
1194	Jerry Roberts Machine Co—*John Jeska*	3309 Labore Rd, Saint Paul MN 55110	651-481-0139	R	4*	<.1
1195	Veloxion Inc—*Steven Robinson*	1 Industrial Dr, Pelham NH 03076	603-889-6871	R	4*	<.1
1196	MaxTorque LLC—*Patrick West*	14 Businss Park Rd, Limerick ME 04048	207-793-2289	R	4*	<.1
1197	Advance Synthetic Products Inc—*Roger Whited*	8104 Edgewater Ave, Rosedale MD 21237	410-780-4616	R	4*	<.1
1198	G and G Industrial Corp—*George Liu*	148 Haddon Ave, Haddon Township NJ 08108	856-858-7766	R	4*	<.1
1199	Bridgeways—*Donna Konicki*	5801 23rd Dr W Ste 104, Everett WA 98203	425-513-8213	R	4*	.1
1200	Ainslie Corp—*Eric Sandquist*	610 Harland St, Milton MA 02186	781-848-0850	R	4*	.1
1201	Spm Corp—*Samuel Hopp*	73 Holton St Ste 1, Woburn MA 01801	781-721-5450	R	4*	<.1
1202	Trotwood Corp—*Bruce Flora*	11 N Broadway St, Trotwood OH 45426	937-854-3047	R	4*	<.1
1203	Jaco Engineering—*H Meagher*	879 S E St, Anaheim CA 92805	714-991-1680	R	4*	<.1
1204	Montgomery Machine and Fabrication Inc—*Carry Montgomery*	PO Box 247, Jackson OH 45640	740-286-2863	R	4*	<.1
1205	Partco Inc—*J Mackie Langloi*	PO Box 40083, Baton Rouge LA 70835	225-272-3767	R	4*	<.1
1206	Penn Cigar Machines Inc—*Niranjan Gupta*	PO Box 149, Nanticoke PA 18634	570-740-1112	R	4*	<.1
1207	Progressive Tool Company Inc—*Gordon Markoff*	3221 Lawndale St, Endwell NY 13760	607-748-8294	R	4*	<.1
1208	Dupont Tool and Machine Co—*Vincent Bryk*	311 Elm St, Dupont PA 18641	570-655-1728	R	4*	<.1
1209	Maverick Precision Manufacturing Ltd—*Walt Coram*	13604 Almeda School Rd, Houston TX 77047	713-433-3756	R	4*	<.1
1210	C and A Machine And Repair Service Inc—*Lloyd Parrent*	6227 Nyoka St, Houston TX 77041	713-937-3426	R	4*	<.1
1211	Florida Metallizing Service Inc—*Thomas Crews*	PO Box 585, Mulberry FL 33860	863-425-1143	R	4*	<.1
1212	J B Manufacturing Inc—*John Anderson*	PO Box 318, Tallmadge OH 44278	330-676-9744	R	4*	<.1
1213	PM Armor Inc—*Wilson Mirza*	237 E Prospect Ave, Mount Prospect IL 60056	847-797-9940	R	4*	<.1
1214	Rose Machine and Tool LLC—*Louie Gaither*	290 Industrial Rd N, Covington TN 38019	901-476-2202	R	4*	<.1
1215	Accura Precision Inc—*Peter Matkovic*	PO Box 1840, Cupertino CA 95015	408-988-7633	R	4*	<.1
1216	Bonnot Co—*George Bain*	1520 Corporate Woods P, Uniontown OH 44685	330-896-6544	R	4*	<.1
1217	Jbk Manufacturing LLC—*James Pearson*	2127 Troy St, Dayton OH 45404	937-233-8300	R	4*	<.1
1218	Lee's Grinding Inc—*Nick Papanikolaou*	PO Box 360169, Strongsville OH 44136	440-572-4610	R	4*	<.1
1219	Metalore Inc—*Kenneth Hill*	750 S Douglas St, El Segundo CA 90245	310-643-0360	R	4*	<.1
1220	Pamco Machine Works Inc—*James Wilkinson*	9359 Feron Blvd, Rancho Cucamonga CA 91730	909-941-7260	R	4*	<.1
1221	Precision Component Industries LLC—*Sandy Stransky*	5325 Southway St Sw, Canton OH 44706	330-477-6287	R	4*	<.1
1222	Ronlo Engineering Ltd—*Ronnie Lowe*	955 Flynn Rd, Camarillo CA 93012	805-388-3227	R	4*	<.1
1223	Sonoma Precision Manufacturing Co—*Robert Levinson*	3055 Wiljan Ct, Santa Rosa CA 95407	707-576-1550	R	4*	<.1
1224	Tape Master Tool Co—*Ronald Galli*	900 Rochester Rd, Troy MI 48083	248-616-8880	R	4*	<.1
1225	Valley Machine Works Inc—*Lawrence Johnsen*	701 W Jackson St, Phoenix AZ 85007	602-254-4173	R	4*	<.1
1226	Windsor Beach Technologies Inc—*Robert Macyko*	7321 Klier Dr, Fairview PA 16415	814-474-4900	R	4*	<.1
1227	Wonder Machine Services Inc—*George Woyansky*	35340 Avon Commerce Pk, Avon OH 44011	440-937-7500	R	4*	<.1
1228	Tree City Tool and Engineering Company Inc—*Steve Simmonds*	1954 N Montgomery Rd, Greensburg IN 47240	812-663-4196	R	4*	<.1
1229	Northern Precision Products Inc—*Mary Nagengast*	PO Box 202, Leroy MI 49655	231-768-4435	R	4*	<.1
1230	Line Precision Inc—*Stanley Clarke*	31666 W 8 Mile Rd, Farmington Hills MI 48336	248-474-5280	R	4*	<.1
1231	Melching Machine Inc—*Ted Melching*	1630 Baker Dr, Ossian IN 46777	260-622-4315	R	4*	<.1
1232	Northwest Manufacturing Company Inc—*Randall Smitheal*	9553 Clay Rd, Houston TX 77080	713-460-2323	R	4*	<.1
1233	Pelham Machine and Tool Inc—*Bobby Ellison*	PO Box 423, Pelham AL 35124	205-663-0566	R	4*	<.1
1234	Trade Line Fabricating Inc—*James Klem*	22422 State Line Rd, Lawrenceburg IN 47025	812-637-1444	R	4*	<.1
1235	Z and Z Machine Products Inc—*Franciszek Kumosz*	1225 14th St, Racine WI 53403	262-637-4933	R	4*	<.1
1236	Noble Tool Corp—*Thomas Biegel*	1535 Stanley Ave, Dayton OH 45404	937-461-4040	R	4*	<.1
1237	Telco Machine and Manufacturing Inc—*Neil David*	3957 N Normandy Ave, Chicago IL 60634	773-725-4441	R	4*	<.1
1238	Able Tool Company Inc—*Daniel Brammell*	13160 Rte 993, Trafford PA 15085	724-863-2508	R	4*	<.1
1239	Aertech Machining and Manufacturing Inc—*Michael Macchia*	2903 W Michigan Ave, Jackson MI 49202	517-782-4644	R	4³	<.1
1240	Brevard Robotics Inc—*George Kellgren*	PO Box 236651, Cocoa FL 32923	321-637-0367	R	4*	<.1
1241	Cigas Machine Shop Inc—*Craig Cigas*	1245 Manor Rd, Coatesville PA 19320	610-384-5239	R	4*	<.1
1242	Forge Precision Co—*Van Kchikian*	31800 W 8 Mile Rd, Farmington Hills MI 48336	248-478-4040	R	4*	<.1
1243	H and J Tool and Die Company Inc—*Joseph Hauger*	1565 Ocean Ave, Bohemia NY 11716	631-589-7500	R	4*	<.1
1244	Jerpbak-Bayless Company Inc—*Jeffrey Jerpbak*	PO Box 39157, Solon OH 44139	440-248-5387	R	4*	<.1
1245	JV Precision Machine Co—*Josef Visinski*	71 Cogwheel Ln, Seymour CT 06483	203-888-0748	R	4*	<.1
1246	Kuntz Manufacturing Company Inc—*Roger Kuntz*	PO Box 2517, Laguna Hills CA 92654	714-540-7370	R	4*	<.1
1247	L F M Enterprises Inc—*Dennis Laporte*	33256 Kelly Rd, Clinton Township MI 48035	586-792-7220	R	4*	<.1
1248	Park Engineering And Manufacturing Co—*Joanna Tenney*	6430 Roland St, Buena Park CA 90621	714-521-4660	R	4*	<.1
1249	R A Industries LLC—*Mike Dowse*	3207 W Pendleton Ave, Santa Ana CA 92704	714-557-2322	R	4*	<.1
1250	Ruoff and Sons Inc—*Steve Ruoff*	PO Box 320, Runnemede NJ 08078	856-931-2064	R	4*	<.1
1251	Sloan Industries Inc—*Henry Slowinski*	1550 N Michael Dr, Wood Dale IL 60191	630-350-1614	R	4*	<.1
1252	Urschel Manufacturing Inc—*Scott Urschel*	7442 E Butherus Dr, Scottsdale AZ 85260	480-951-9029	R	4*	<.1
1253	Vanderhulst Associates Inc—*Hank Vanderhulst*	3300 Victor Ct, Santa Clara CA 95054	408-727-1313	R	4*	<.1
1254	Vangura Tool Inc—*Dave Evanchak*	PO Box 300, Clairton PA 15025	412-233-6401	R	4*	<.1
1255	Bendon Gear and Machine Inc—*S Belezos*	100 Weymouth St Ste A1, Rockland MA 02370	781-878-8100	R	4*	<.1
1256	Moore-Addison Co—*Jim Holland*	518 W Factory Rd, Addison IL 60101	630-543-6744	R	4*	<.1
1257	NICO Machine Inc—*Quinton Smith*	2656 N 37th Dr, Phoenix AZ 85009	602-352-1808	R	4*	<.1
1258	Lange Precision Inc—*Gregory Lange*	1106 E Elm Ave, Fullerton CA 92831	714-870-5420	R	4*	<.1
1259	Parameters Industries Inc—*Richard Schwichtenberg*	900 W Sunset Dr, Waukesha WI 53189	262-549-3448	R	4*	<.1
1260	Costa Precision Manufacturing Corp—*Edward Zielinski*	PO Box 990, Claremont NH 03743	603-542-5229	R	4*	<.1
1261	Texas Toolmakers Inc—*John Bishop*	11411 E Coker Loop, San Antonio TX 78216	210-494-3651	R	4*	<.1
1262	Accraline Inc—*Richard Cormican*	1420 W Bike St, Bremen IN 46506	574-546-3484	R	4*	<.1
1263	Arnold-Gonsalves Inc—*Manuel Gonsalves*	5731 Chino Ave, Chino CA 91710	909-465-1579	R	4*	<.1
1264	Bachman Tool and Die Co—*Eugene Bachman*	PO Box 189, Independence IA 50644	319-334-6004	R	4*	<.1
1265	Imperial Machine Company Inc—*Larry Russell*	PO Box 12506, Gastonia NC 28052	704-739-8038	R	4*	<.1
1266	M Rodrigue and Son Inc—*Francis Rodrigue*	2239 Hwy 20, Vacherie LA 70090	225-265-4284	R	4*	<.1
1267	Morton and Company Inc—*David Morton*	11 Eames St, Wilmington MA 01887	978-657-7726	R	4*	<.1
1268	Mechanical Designs Of Virginia Inc—*Wayne Gilley*	PO Box 280, Patrick Springs VA 24133	276-694-7442	R	4*	<.1
1269	Oskaloosa Manufacturing Inc—*Carol Snowbarger*	PO Box 216, Oskaloosa IA 52577	641-672-2539	R	4*	<.1
1270	C and S Machine and Manufacturing Corp—*John Yuda*	3832 Fitzgerald Rd, Louisville KY 40216	502-778-4479	R	4*	<.1
1271	Biwal Manufacturing Company Inc—*Joseph Mrocka*	48 Industrial St W, Clifton NJ 07012	973-778-0105	R	4*	<.1
1272	Chick Machine Company Inc—*James Chick*	118 Chick Ln, Butler PA 16002	724-352-3330	R	4*	<.1
1273	Csm Manufacturing Co—*Fred Hatfield*	505 8th St Se, Loveland CO 80537	970-667-6122	R	4*	<.1
1274	Duke Manufacturing Inc—*Jeff Newmark*	38205 Western Pkwy, Willoughby OH 44094	440-942-6537	R	4*	<.1
1275	Frey and Weiss Precision Machining Inc—*Ernie Pabon*	384 Beinoris Dr, Wood Dale IL 60191	630-595-9073	R	4*	<.1
1276	K-M-S Industries Inc—*Gerald Korman*	6880 Lake Abrams Dr, Cleveland OH 44130	440-891-1577	R	4*	<.1
1277	Prescott Precision Die Inc—*Cliff O'brien*	3231 Tower Rd Ste B, Prescott AZ 86305	928-778-3774	R	4*	<.1
1278	Proto Space Engineering Inc—*Linda Dabbs*	2214 Loma Ave, South El Monte CA 91733	626-442-8273	R	4*	<.1
1279	Rem-Tech Inc—*Linda Werth*	5872 N Government Way, Dalton Gardens ID 83815	208-762-9202	R	4*	<.1

Rank	Company Name—*Executive Officer*	Address, City, State, Zip	Phone	Type	Fin	Empls
1280	S and S Engineering LLC—*Glen Lacher*	7703 Commerce Way, Eden Prairie MN 55344	952-937-2027	R	4*	<.1
1281	Toolbold Corp—*Harry Eisengrein*	5330 Commerce Pkwy W, Cleveland OH 44130	216-676-9840	R	4*	<.1
1282	Trv Inc—*Peter Kolaric*	4860 E 345th St, Willoughby OH 44094	440-951-7722	R	4*	<.1
1283	Dial Machine Inc—*Malcolm Anderberg*	PO Box 5246, Rockford IL 61125	815-397-6660	R	4*	<.1
1284	Neumeier Engineering Inc—*Heinz Neumeier*	22610 88th Ave S Ste D, Kent WA 98031	253-854-3635	R	4*	<.1
1285	Oregon Industrial Repair Inc—*John Gall*	PO Box 1053, Salem OR 97308	503-399-1926	R	4*	<.1
1286	A and D Precision Manufacturing Inc—*Dan Wiegel*	4751 E Hunter Ave, Anaheim CA 92807	714-779-2714	R	4*	<.1
1287	Rozal Industries Inc—*Brian Casio*	151 Marine St, Farmingdale NY 11735	631-420-4277	R	4*	<.1
1288	Industrial Plating and Grinding Inc—*Eugene Shima*	PO Box 7193, Sheridan WY 82801	307-674-4431	R	4*	<.1
1289	Racoh Products Inc—*Nancy Housler*	1751 Rich Valley Rd, Emporium PA 15834	814-486-3288	R	4*	<.1
1290	Squaglia Manufacturing—*Pat Pellizzari*	275 Polaris Ave, Mountain View CA 94043	650-965-9644	R	4*	<.1
1291	Aaseby Industrial Machining Inc—*Vern Aaseby*	301 6th St S, Wahpeton ND 58075	701-642-8820	R	4*	<.1
1292	FA Tech Corp—*Michael Michimi*	9065 Sutton Pl, Hamilton OH 45011	513-942-1920	R	4*	<.1
1293	Jarrett Machine Co—*Robert Jarrett*	PO Box 436, Bradford PA 16701	814-362-2755	R	4*	<.1
1294	Lakeside Manufacturing Co—*Lawrence Holben*	4999 Advance Way, Stevensville MI 49127	269-429-6193	R	4*	<.1
1295	U P Machine and Engineering Co—*Cal Land*	PO Box 400, Powers MI 49874	906-497-5278	R	4*	<.1
1296	Coleman Machine Works Inc—*Gene Coleman*	N1597 Us Hwy 41, Menominee MI 49858	906-863-8945	R	4*	<.1
1297	A-1 Production Inc—*Mary Snyder*	5809 E Leighty Rd, Kendallville IN 46755	260-347-0960	R	4*	<.1
1298	G and G Machine and Maintenance Inc—*Mike Grantham*	1709 N Wayside Dr, Houston TX 77020	713-673-4235	R	4*	<.1
1299	Union Tool Corp—*Michael Simpson*	PO Box 935, Warsaw IN 46581	574-267-3211	R	4*	<.1
1300	A and A Machine Company Inc—*Andrew Schlotter*	1085 Industrial Blvd, Southampton PA 18966	215-355-8330	R	4*	<.1
1301	Aero Components Inc—*Danny Odom*	535 Se 82nd St, Oklahoma City OK 73149	405-631-6644	R	4*	<.1
1302	Aerospace Inc—*John Cattell*	PO Box 385, Grass Lake MI 49240	517-522-8448	R	4*	<.1
1303	Allon Industries Inc—*Doug Debellis*	12200 Dorsett Rd, Maryland Heights MO 63043	314-434-5800	R	4*	<.1
1304	American Linc Corp—*D Hoover*	159 Wolfpack Rd, Gastonia NC 28056	704-861-9242	R	4*	<.1
1305	Badge Machine Products Inc—*Gail Flugel*	2491 Brickyard Rd, Canandaigua NY 14424	585-394-0330	R	4*	<.1
1306	Bell Machine Company Inc—*Jewel Bell*	PO Box 7799, Shreveport LA 71137	318-227-2515	R	4*	<.1
1307	Central Industrial Supply Inc—*Timothy Bragg*	PO Box 210, Montevallo AL 35115	205-665-4516	R	4*	<.1
1308	Central Machining and Pump Repair Inc—*Curtis Latendresse*	4127 Burdick Expy E, Minot ND 58701	701-852-2405	R	4*	<.1
1309	Lebanon Machine and Manufacturing Company Inc—*William Sprecher*	PO Box 1066, Lebanon PA 17042	717-274-3636	R	4*	<.1
1310	Oakdale Precision Inc—*Scott Justesen*	7022 6th St N, Oakdale MN 55128	651-730-7700	R	4*	<.1
1311	Pyle Machine Company Inc—*Eldon Pyle*	4201 Clay Ave, Fort Worth TX 76117	817-485-6011	R	4*	<.1
1312	Schneider's Manufacturing Inc—*Nick Schneider*	11122 Penrose St, Sun Valley CA 91352	818-771-0082	R	4*	<.1
1313	Southeastern Machining and Field Service Inc—*John Treitmaier*	500 Lincoln Ave, Lancaster OH 43130	740-689-1147	R	4*	<.1
1314	Flex-Hose Company Inc—*Philip Argersinger*	6801 Crossbow Dr, East Syracuse NY 13057	315-437-1611	R	4*	<.1
1315	Honematic Machine Corp—*Joseph Cusimano*	PO Box 1100, Boylston MA 01505	508-869-2131	R	4*	<.1
1316	LAB Equipment Inc—*William Noonan*	1549 Ardmore Ave, Itasca IL 60143	630-595-4288	R	4*	<.1
1317	Makjohn LLC—*B Gardner*	PO Box 27875, Salt Lake City UT 84127	801-972-5570	R	4*	<.1
1318	Production Machining Of Alma Inc—*Raymond Cull*	6595 N Jerome Rd, Alma MI 48801	989-463-1495	R	4*	<.1
1319	Numerical Precision Inc—*Egon Jaeggin*	2200 Foster Ave, Wheeling IL 60090	847-394-3610	R	4*	<.1
1320	Mitchell and Son Inc—*Dale Pollet*	1580 Chelsea Ave, Memphis TN 38108	901-276-5432	R	4*	<.1
1321	Blue Grass Manufacturing Company Of Lexington Inc—*Donald Bundy*	1454 Jingle Bell Ln, Lexington KY 40509	859-233-7445	R	4*	1
1322	Southern California Technical Arts Inc—*John Robson*	370 E Crowther Ave, Placentia CA 92870	714-524-2626	R	4*	<.1
1323	Grand Rapids Metaltek Inc—*Paul Bultinck*	2860 Marlin Ct Nw, Grand Rapids MI 49534	616-791-2373	R	4*	<.1
1324	Alpha Lehigh Tool and Machine Company Inc—*William Green*	41 Industrial Rd, Alpha NJ 08865	908-454-6481	R	4*	<.1
1325	G and G Machine Technologies LLC—*Robert Atkins*	2506 Fair Rd, Sidney OH 45365	937-492-8565	R	4*	<.1
1326	Odawara Automation Inc—*Takayuki Tsugawa*	4805 S County Rd 25a, Tipp City OH 45371	937-667-8433	R	4*	<.1
1327	Guzman's Machine Works Inc—*Janice Gauzman*	PO Box 554, Lutcher LA 70071	225-869-3542	R	4*	<.1
1328	Omnitec Precision Manufacturing Inc—*Eric Kawano*	435 Queens Ln, San Jose CA 95112	408-437-9056	R	4*	<.1
1329	Questech Services Corp—*Robert Chapman*	2201 Executive Dr, Garland TX 75041	972-278-8006	R	4*	<.1
1330	American Welding And Engineering LLC—*Bruce Amborn*	6001 S Pennsylvania Av, Cudahy WI 53110	414-769-8500	R	4*	<.1
1331	Brewer Machine and Manufacturing Inc—*Darren Brewer*	1501 Miller Ave, Shelbyville IN 46176	317-398-3505	R	4*	<.1
1332	D and G Machine Company Inc—*Donald White*	PO Box 31, Mannington WV 26582	304-986-1020	R	4*	<.1
1333	Dexco Company Inc—*Joseph Michael*	PO Box 4235, Burlington NC 27215	336-584-0260	R	4*	<.1
1334	Diamondback Steel Company Inc—*Keith Wright*	419 S Cherokee St, Muskogee OK 74403	918-686-6340	R	4*	<.1
1335	LL Brown Inc—*Lawrence Brown*	348 Sample Bridge Rd, Enola PA 17025	717-766-1885	R	4*	<.1
1336	Rapid Product Solutions Inc—*Max Gerdts*	2240 Celsius Ave Ste D, Oxnard CA 93030	805-485-7234	R	4*	<.1
1337	Rochester Machine Corp—*Jeffrey Bruce*	PO Box 94, New Brighton PA 15066	724-843-7820	R	4*	<.1
1338	Thomas Precision Machining Inc—*Donn Thomas*	3278 S Main St, Rice Lake WI 54868	715-234-8827	R	4*	<.1
1339	Urania Engineering Company Inc—*Joseph Zoba*	198 S Poplar St, Hazleton PA 18201	570-455-7531	R	4*	<.1
1340	Applied Plastic Machining Inc—*Donald Riddle*	PO Box 42413, Portland OR 97242	503-232-5056	R	4*	<.1
1341	Auto-Swage Products Inc—*David Brenton*	726 River Rd, Shelton CT 06484	203-929-1401	R	4*	<.1
1342	Admiral Engineering and Manufacturing Co—*David Schlosser*	21609 N 14th Ave, Phoenix AZ 85027	623-869-9257	R	4*	<.1
1343	Alkab Contract Manufacturing Inc—*William Kabazie*	843 Industrial Blvd, New Kensington PA 15068	724-335-7050	R	4*	<.1
1344	Big Bear Oil Field Services Inc—*Terry Stahl*	PO Box 1555, Levelland TX 79336	806-229-6129	R	4*	<.1
1345	J Stadler Machine Inc—*Jimmy Stadler*	PO Box 2505, Oshkosh WI 54903	920-235-2907	R	4*	<.1
1346	Ohio Camshaft Inc—*John Hiler*	8333 Boyle Pkwy, Twinsburg OH 44087	330-425-4900	R	4*	<.1
1347	Allen-Mitchell and Co—*Tom Mitchell*	515 V St Ne, Washington DC 20002	202-526-8989	R	4*	<.1
1348	Heritage Carbide Inc—*Ronnie Tipton*	1591 N Main St, Orange CA 92867	714-974-6377	R	4*	<.1
1349	Plasma-Tec Inc—*Laurence Wysong*	7500 Clyde Park Ave Sw, Byron Center MI 49315	616-455-2593	R	4*	<.1
1350	Specialties Engineering Company Inc—*Gregory Viksman*	13754 Saticoy St, Van Nuys CA 91402	818-780-3045	R	4*	<.1
1351	Scs Machine and Fabricating Inc—*Mike Chirpich*	6847 Signat Dr, Houston TX 77041	713-466-0550	R	4*	<.1
1352	Skild Manufacturing Inc—*Alison Graunke*	160 Bond St Fl 1, Elk Grove Village IL 60007	847-437-1717	R	4*	<.1
1353	H and S Tool And Engineering Inc—*Karl Hetzler*	777 Airport Rd, Fall River MA 02720	508-672-6509	R	4*	<.1
1354	Orion Tool Die and Machine Co—*William Lange*	1400 16th St, Orion IL 61273	309-526-3303	R	4*	<.1
1355	Lunquist Manufacturing Corp—*Donald Lunquist*	5681 11th St, Rockford IL 61109	815-874-2437	R	4*	<.1
1356	Metal-Tech Inc—*Hugh Hood*	265 Airport Rd, New Castle DE 19720	302-322-7770	R	4*	<.1
1357	Pauli Systems Inc—*Robert Pauli*	1820 Walters Ct, Fairfield CA 94533	707-429-2434	R	4*	<.1
1358	Valtec Hydraulics Inc—*Richard Valleroy*	1100 Pershall Rd, Saint Louis MO 63137	314-867-1100	R	4*	<.1
1359	Western Industrial Tooling Inc—*Ernst Buchmayer*	14511 Ne 87th St, Redmond WA 98052	425-883-6644	R	4*	<.1
1360	Micro Lapping and Grinding Company Inc—*Ray Robaugh*	12320 Plz Dr, Cleveland OH 44130	216-267-6500	R	3*	<.1
1361	Gibson Machine Co—*A Kellar*	PO Box 2226, Gastonia NC 28053	704-922-3155	R	3*	<.1
1362	Reardon Machine Company Inc—*Joseph Reardon*	5015 Se Hwy 169, Saint Joseph MO 64507	816-279-0906	R	3*	<.1
1363	Leelanau Industries Inc—*George Kausler*	PO Box 4120, Traverse City MI 49685	231-947-0372	R	3*	<.1
1364	AC Tool and Machine Company Inc—*Friedrich Schwartz*	W185n11424 Whitney Dr, Germantown WI 53022	262-255-1552	R	3*	<.1
1365	Braswell Precision Inc—*James Braswell*	2406 Peppermill Dr, Glen Burnie MD 21061	410-761-3366	R	3*	<.1
1366	Covington Machine And Welding Inc—*Donald Covington*	2015 Renard Ct, Annapolis MD 21401	410-841-6868	R	3*	<.1

Note: An asterisk (*) indicates an estimated financial figure. The company type code used is as follows: R = Private, P = Public, S = Private Subsidiary, B = Public Subsidiary, D = Division, J = Joint Venture, I = Investment Fund.

COMPANY RANKINGS BY SALES WITHIN 4-DIGIT SIC

Rank	Company Name—*Executive Officer*	Address, City, State, Zip	Phone	Type	Fin	Empls
1367	DC Industries Inc—*Dennis Clark*	200 Ida St, Waterloo IA 50701	319-234-1075	R	3*	<.1
1368	Farzati Manufacturing Corp—*Frank Farzati*	125 Theobold Ave Ste 2, Greensburg PA 15601	724-836-3508	R	3*	<.1
1369	Fluets Corp—*Ray Fluet*	260 Pennsylvania Ave, Hillside NJ 07205	908-353-5229	R	3*	<.1
1370	Lowrance Machine Shop Inc—*Ronald Lowrance*	13510 E Hardy Rd, Houston TX 77039	281-449-6524	R	3*	<.1
1371	Macon Machine Inc—*B Slocumb*	PO Box 1096, Macon GA 31202	478-743-4466	R	3*	<.1
1372	Master Precision Machining Inc—*Richard Rossi*	2199 Ronald St, Santa Clara CA 95050	408-727-0185	R	3*	<.1
1373	Mrl Manufacturing Inc—*Lynn West*	465 Griffin Blvd, Amery WI 54001	715-268-2681	R	3*	<.1
1374	Portable Machine Works Inc—*Guy Harrell*	PO Box 3032, Prairieville LA 70769	225-673-5940	R	3*	<.1
1375	Storage Machine—*Jim Stout*	481 Gianni St, Santa Clara CA 95054	408-988-8582	R	3*	<.1
1376	N and N Machine Inc—*E Newton*	2950 Wayne Sullivan Dr, Paducah KY 42003	270-442-7988	R	3*	<.1
1377	Alvellan Inc—*Sean Mclellan*	1030 Shary Ct, Concord CA 94518	925-689-2421	R	3*	<.1
1378	Ceramic Tech Inc—*Kanu Gandhi*	46211 Research Ave, Fremont CA 94539	510-252-8500	R	3*	<.1
1379	Keller Engineering Inc—*Kathy Keller*	3203 Kashiwa St, Torrance CA 90505	310-326-2205	R	3*	<.1
1380	Northeast Manufacturing Company Inc—*Chris Lobdell*	35 Spencer St, Stoneham MA 02180	781-438-3022	R	3*	<.1
1381	John W Heaton Inc—*Charles Heaton*	PO Box 2203, Aiken SC 29802	803-649-6582	R	3*	<.1
1382	Reliable Tool and Die Inc—*Russell Vecsey*	435 Woodmont Rd, Milford CT 06460	203-877-3264	R	3*	<.1
1383	Ace Precision Industries Inc—*Jerry Wolf*	925 Moe Dr, Akron OH 44310	330-633-8523	R	3*	<.1
1384	Frentzel Products Inc—*Thomas Frentzel*	125 W Melvina St, Milwaukee WI 53212	414-962-2448	R	3*	<.1
1385	Kempsmith Machine Company Inc—*Robert Burris*	PO Box 14336, Milwaukee WI 53214	414-256-8160	R	3*	<.1
1386	Vector Tool and Manufacturing Inc—*Jim Harwood*	206 Dundas Rd, Monticello MN 55362	763-295-0909	R	3*	<.1
1387	Hardy Machine Inc—*William Hardy*	2326 N Penn Rd, Hatfield PA 19440	215-822-9359	R	3*	<.1
1388	J D Cousins Inc—*Gregory Pauly*	667 Tifft St, Buffalo NY 14220	716-824-1098	R	3*	<.1
1389	Meteor Supply Inc—*William Brunell*	PO Box 129, Southampton PA 18966	215-426-9000	R	3*	<.1
1390	Tri-Way Manufacturing Inc—*John Burke*	15363 E 12 Mile Rd, Roseville MI 48066	586-776-0700	R	3*	<.1
1391	Capcon International Inc—*Mario Irizarry*	120 Craft Ave, Inwood NY 11096	516-371-5600	R	3*	<.1
1392	Dixie Precision Inc—*John Oliver*	4137 Lewisburg Rd, Birmingham AL 35207	205-841-8400	R	3*	<.1
1393	Irwin Automation Inc—*Jason Taylor*	715 Cleveland St, Greensburg PA 15601	724-834-7160	R	3*	<.1
1394	Royalty Investments LLC	2476 E Us Hwy 50, Seymour IN 47274	812-358-3534	R	3*	<.1
1395	Hawkeye Tool And Die Inc—*Lyle Michaels*	PO Box 547, Jesup IA 50648	319-827-3838	R	3*	<.1
1396	About Time Machining Inc—*Craig Langiewicz*	7271 Commerce Cir W, Minneapolis MN 55432	763-571-6123	R	3*	<.1
1397	Balancing Company Inc—*Donald Belcher*	PO Box 490, Vandalia OH 45377	937-898-9111	R	3*	<.1
1398	C and C Machine Inc—*H Craig*	PO Box 2317, La Crosse WI 54602	608-784-4427	R	3*	<.1
1399	AF Machine Inc—*Kevin Whidder*	2911 Apache Dr, Plover WI 54467	715-341-7663	R	3*	<.1
1400	Bar S Machine Inc—*Robert Schaible*	2575 N Us Hwy 89 A, Chino Valley AZ 86323	928-636-2115	R	3*	<.1
1401	Beloit Special Machining Company Inc—*John Jensen*	1504 6th St, Beloit WI 53511	608-365-0147	R	3*	<.1
1402	Hi-Tec Machine Corp—*Russell Wysong*	295 Carson St Ste B, Marion NC 28752	828-659-1655	R	3*	<.1
1403	Lagoe-Oswego Corp—*David Falk*	45 E 12th St, Oswego NY 13126	315-343-3160	R	3*	<.1
1404	Spectralytics Inc—*Gary Oberg*	PO Box L, Dassel MN 55325	320-275-2118	R	3*	<.1
1405	Unas Grinding Corp—*John Orzech*	PO Box 280535, East Hartford CT 06128	860-289-1538	R	3*	<.1
1406	Vero Machine Industries Inc—*Robert Beaucher*	5400 85th St, Vero Beach FL 32967	772-589-5808	R	3*	<.1
1407	Windham Machine Company Inc—*Jack Swendsen*	PO Box 96, South Windham CT 06266	860-423-4575	R	3*	<.1
1408	Mid America Machine Inc—*Paul Crowell*	PO Box 483, Mayfield KY 42066	270-247-6909	R	3*	<.1
1409	Asteroid Grinding Co—*Sheryl Decoteau*	2190 S Wolf Rd, Des Plaines IL 60018	847-298-8109	R	3*	<.1
1410	Custom Machine and Tool Inc—*David Andrews*	PO Box 507, Graham NC 27253	336-226-1643	R	3*	<.1
1411	International Machine and Tool Inc—*Henry Meador*	PO Box 2378, Hendersonville TN 37077	615-824-6635	R	3*	<.1
1412	Astro Tool and Machine Company Inc—*Gary Price*	PO Box 1264, Rahway NJ 07065	732-382-2454	R	3*	<.1
1413	Hanel Storage Systems LP—*Scott Katzenell*	121 Industry Dr, Pittsburgh PA 15275	412-787-3444	R	3*	<.1
1414	Robmar Precision Manufacturing Inc—*Greg Doss*	38189 Abruzzi Dr, Westland MI 48185	734-326-2664	R	3*	<.1
1415	Able Tool Corp—*Daniel Hayes*	617 N Wayne Ave, Cincinnati OH 45215	513-733-8989	R	3*	<.1
1416	American Machining and Welding Inc—*Stanley Sieczka*	6009 S New England Ave, Chicago IL 60638	773-586-2585	R	3*	<.1
1417	D and L Machine Company Inc—*Richard Gingo*	1029 Arlington Cir, Akron OH 44306	330-785-0781	R	3*	<.1
1418	Grain Valley Tool and Manufacturing Company Inc—*Norbert Apel*	PO Box 170, Oak Grove MO 64075	816-690-8202	R	3*	<.1
1419	Sei Manufacturing Inc—*Kyu Shin*	171 Nick Fitcheard Rd, Huntsville AL 35806	256-858-8085	R	3*	<.1
1420	Vandeventer Machine Works Corp—*Mark Hoff*	1446 S Vandeventer Ave, Saint Louis MO 63110	314-652-0742	R	3*	<.1
1421	Midwest Laser Systems Inc—*William Hunter*	1101 Commerce Pkwy, Findlay OH 45840	419-424-0062	R	3*	<.1
1422	Levan Machine Company Inc—*Brian Levan*	3417 Pricetown Rd, Fleetwood PA 19522	610-944-7455	R	3*	<.1
1423	Industrial Products And Services Inc—*Harry Wallace*	PO Box 460, Hartsville SC 29551	843-332-6131	R	3*	<.1
1424	Ryeco Inc—*Roger Kemman*	2549 Park Ave, Beloit WI 53511	608-362-7007	R	3*	<.1
1425	Mertz Enterprises Inc—*Robert Mertz*	PO Box 548, Webster City IA 50595	515-832-2832	R	3*	<.1
1426	Mid Kansas Machine Inc—*Doug Schulz*	PO Box 560, Mcpherson KS 67460	620-241-2959	R	3*	<.1
1427	Alliance Dynamic Group Inc—*Jerzy Gorko*	16222 S Maple Ave, Gardena CA 90248	310-538-4644	R	3*	<.1
1428	MG Machine Inc—*Merle Galessi*	PO Box 620, Belton MO 64012	816-331-8886	R	3*	<.1
1429	Modern Machine Co—*Gary Emede*	1111 S Water St, Bay City MI 48708	989-895-8563	R	3*	<.1
1430	Nedmac Inc—*Jim Tilbury*	5410 International Pkw, Minneapolis MN 55428	763-537-8435	R	3*	<.1
1431	Ohio Roll Grinding Inc—*James Robinson*	PO Box 7099, Canton OH 44705	330-453-1884	R	3*	<.1
1432	Swiss Technologies Inc—*Jay Crippen*	2502 Quality Ln, Knoxville TN 37931	865-560-1011	R	3*	<.1
1433	Babbitt Bearing Company Inc—*Stanley Sinn*	1170 N 5th St, San Jose CA 95112	408-298-1101	C	3*	<.1
1434	Brown Industries Inc—*Larry Brown*	2307 Indiana Ave, Kansas City MO 64127	816-231-2454	R	3*	<.1
1435	Desert Sky Machining Inc—*Chris Studzinski*	1236 Quarry Ln Ste 104, Pleasanton CA 94566	925-426-0400	R	3*	<.1
1436	E B Bronson and Company Inc—*James Bronson*	PO Box 267, Blue Island IL 60406	708-385-3600	R	3*	<.1
1437	Edwin J Mckenica and Sons Inc—*Richard Mckenica*	1200 Clinton St, Buffalo NY 14206	716-823-4646	R	3*	<.1
1438	Ferry Machine Corp—*Louis Ferretti*	75 Industrial Ave, Little Ferry NJ 07643	201-641-9191	R	3*	<.1
1439	Micro Manufacturing Inc—*Donald Jolliffe*	6900 Dutton Industry P, Caledonia MI 49316	616-554-9200	R	3*	<.1
1440	Premier Gear and Machining Inc—*William Murphy*	PO Box 2799, Corona CA 92878	951-278-5505	R	3*	<.1
1441	Pva Tepla America Inc—*Bill Marsh*	251 Corporate Ter St, Corona CA 92879	951-371-2500	R	3*	<.1
1442	Quadrant Tool And Manufacturing Co—*Kenneth Kraemer*	1720 W Irving Park Rd, Schaumburg IL 60193	847-352-6977	R	3*	<.1
1443	R and R Machine Industries Inc—*Roland Legare*	PO Box 119, Slatersville RI 02876	401-766-2505	R	3*	<.1
1444	Royersford Foundry And Machine Company Inc—*Kurt Deisher*	PO Box 190, Royersford PA 19468	610-935-7200	R	3*	<.1
1445	Victory Industries Inc—*Ronald Walczak*	990 S Oakwood, Detroit MI 48217	313-841-0264	R	3*	<.1
1446	Qualitum Inc—*James Barber*	9081 Le Saint Dr, Fairfield OH 45014	513-868-3333	R	3*	<.1
1447	Indtool Inc—*David Phillips*	412 Bradley St, Burlington NC 27215	336-226-4923	R	3*	<.1
1448	Medlin and Son Engineering Service Inc—*George Medlin*	12484 Whittier Blvd, Whittier CA 90602	562-464-5889	R	3*	.1
1449	El Campo Machine and Repair Inc—*David Pratka*	RR 1 Box 300, El Campo TX 77437	979-543-9663	R	3*	<.1
1450	M and F Gauge and Specialty Company Inc—*Jack Matthaei*	PO Box 693, Brownwood TX 76804	325-643-2655	R	3*	<.1
1451	Sembol Systems Inc—*Jon Manning*	100 Industrial Dr, Richmond KY 40475	859-624-1200	R	3*	<.1
1452	Touchdown Machining Inc—*Michael Moore*	432 S Mapleton St, Columbus IN 47201	812-378-0300	R	3*	<.1
1453	Limited Industries Inc—*C Duncan*	14310 E Back Rd, Lewistown IL 61542	309-547-3251	R	3*	<.1
1454	Milan's Machine Shop and Welding Service Inc—*Milan Baranek*	8052 Nw 56th St, Doral FL 33166	305-592-2447	R	3*	<.1

Rank	Company Name—*Executive Officer*	Address, City, State, Zip	Phone	Type	Fin	Empls
1455	Tape Machining Corp—*Rubin Littmann*	2222 S Calhoun Rd, New Berlin WI 53151	262-782-7070	R	3*	<.1
1456	Mafco Inc—*Joe Weber*	PO Box 1058, Rogers AR 72757	479-631-0404	R	3*	<.1
1457	Nu-Star Inc—*Scott Lorch*	1425 Stagecoach Rd, Shakopee MN 55379	952-445-8295	R	3*	<.1
1458	Dalane Machining Inc—*Dale Baird*	13530 Wright Cir, Tampa FL 33626	813-854-5905	R	3*	<.1
1459	J F Burns Machine Company Inc—*Donald Burns*	4583 School Rd S, Export PA 15632	724-327-2870	R	3*	<.1
1460	Metal Research Inc—*Sam Wolford*	PO Box 338, Guntersville AL 35976	256-582-2362	R	3*	<.1
1461	Polcraft Inc—*Andrew Filipowicz*	930 Rincon Cir, San Jose CA 95131	408-955-0101	R	3*	<.1
1462	Precision Forms Inc—*William Sulski*	97 Decker Rd, Butler NJ 07405	973-838-3800	R	3*	<.1
1463	R and L Enterprises Inc—*Robert Rand*	1955 S Mary St, Fresno CA 93721	559-233-1608	R	3*	<.1
1464	2-M Manufacturing Co—*Mirko Cukelj*	34560 Lakeland Blvd, Eastlake OH 44095	440-269-1270	R	3*	<.1
1465	Billet Industries Inc—*Keith Billet*	247 Campbell Rd, York PA 17402	717-804-0280	R	3*	<.1
1466	Dso Manufacturing Company Inc—*Carl Leo*	390 John Downey Dr, New Britain CT 06051	860-224-2641	R	3*	<.1
1467	Pinnacle Converting Equipment Inc—*Bob Hillebrand*	1720 Toal St, Charlotte NC 28206	704-376-3855	R	3*	<.1
1468	Production Tool and Manufacturing Co—*Troy Peterson*	16240 Sw 72nd Ave, Portland OR 97224	503-598-0393	R	3*	<.1
1469	R-P Screw Machine Products Inc—*Karen Braidwood*	421 Rowland Ave, Santa Ana CA 92707	714-557-6620	R	3*	<.1
1470	Southworth Tool and Gage Company Inc—*John Kolcun*	PO Box 641, Saegertown PA 16433	814-763-5453	R	3*	<.1
1471	Strom Manufacturing—*William Strom*	5285 Ne Elam Young Pkw, Hillsboro OR 97124	503-648-7131	R	3*	<.1
1472	Swissway Inc—*Gerard Cavalier*	123 W Hills Rd, Huntington Station NY 11746	631-351-5350	R	3*	<.1
1473	Nickson's Machine Shop Inc—*Dennis Leal*	PO Box 5200, Santa Maria CA 93456	805-925-2525	R	3*	<.1
1474	Ultra Specialty Holdings Inc—*Hans Scheel*	1360 Howard St, Elk Grove Village IL 60007	847-437-8110	R	3*	<.1
1475	C-Axis Inc—*Jeffrey Haley*	800 Tower Dr, Hamel MN 55340	763-478-8982	R	3*	<.1
1476	Dakota Engineering Inc—*Alan Jones*	2851 N Webster Ave, Indianapolis IN 46219	317-546-8460	R	3*	<.1
1477	United Precision Machine and Engineering Co—*Floyd Childs*	2380 S 3600 W, Salt Lake City UT 84119	801-972-3890	R	3*	<.1
1478	Schult Engineering—*Andrew Kusek*	PO Box 225, Princeton IA 52768	563-289-5808	R	3*	.1
1479	Habco Tool And Development Company Inc—*Steven Sanders*	7725 Metric Dr, Mentor OH 44060	440-255-8122	R	3*	<.1
1480	IMCO Inc (Moorestown New Jersey)—*A Ross Davis*	858 N Lenola Rd, Moorestown NJ 08057	856-235-7540	R	3*	<.1
1481	Twin City EDM Inc—*Robert Lindell*	7940 Ranchers Rd Ne, Minneapolis MN 55432	763-783-7808	R	3*	<.1
1482	CA Foy Machine Co—*Chip Foy*	PO Box 706, Kings Mountain NC 28086	704-734-4833	R	3*	<.1
1483	Albert E Erickson Co—*Donald Erickson*	1111 Honeyspot Rd Ste, Stratford CT 06615	203-386-8931	R	3*	<.1
1484	Bowman Tool and Machining Inc—*William Bowman*	660 37th St NW, Rochester MN 55901	507-286-1400	R	3*	<.1
1485	Collins Machine and Manufacturing Inc—*Dabney Collins*	5461 Western Ave, Boulder CO 80301	303-449-6912	R	3*	<.1
1486	Comstock Industries Inc—*Richard Comstock*	23 Foundry Ave, Meredith NH 03253	603-279-7045	R	3*	<.1
1487	Precision Machined Products Div—*Andy Newcomb*	1017 Smithfield Dr, Fort Collins CO 80524	970-482-7676	D	3*	<.1
1488	Linmark Machine Products Inc—*Lee Abbonizio*	PO Box 408, Union MO 63084	636-583-8984	R	3*	<.1
1489	Springer Thomas W Inc—*Thomas Springer*	227 Buttonwood Rd, Landenberg PA 19350	610-274-8400	R	3*	<.1
1490	Andrew Tool and Machining Company Inc—*Bruce Hanson*	15300 28th Ave N Ste A, Minneapolis MN 55447	763-559-0402	R	3*	<.1
1491	Cave Manufacturing Inc—*Jim Hayssen*	22 Browne Ct Unit 104, Brattleboro VT 05301	802-257-9253	R	3*	<.1
1492	Famco Enterprises Inc—*Patrick Cormack*	PO Box 143, Port Allen LA 70767	225-749-2871	R	3*	<.1
1493	Hanchett Manufacturing—*Don Selfridge*	906 N State St, Big Rapids MI 49307	231-796-7678	R	3*	<.1
1494	Pinnacle Manufacturing Company Inc—*Thomas Stanley*	5310 S 32nd St Ste 2, Phoenix AZ 85040	602-276-0100	R	3*	<.1
1495	Reed Instrument Company Inc—*Alan Reed*	PO Box 19462, Houston TX 77224	713-464-5431	R	3*	<.1
1496	Sims Machinery Company Inc—*Lynn Duncan*	PO Box 446, Lanett AL 36863	334-576-2101	R	3*	<.1
1497	Lyons Machine Tool Company Inc—*Kevin Lyons*	5115 Crescent Technica, Saint Augustine FL 32086	904-797-1550	R	3*	<.1
1498	Palmer Machine Company Inc—*Michael Palmer*	PO Box 358, Conway NH 03818	603-447-2069	R	3*	<.1
1499	Bent River Machine Inc—*Norela Harrington*	951 Rio Torcido, Clarkdale AZ 86324	928-634-7568	R	3*	<.1
1500	Ewart-Ohlson Machine Company Inc—*Brian Ewart*	PO Box 359, Cuyahoga Falls OH 44222	330-928-2171	R	3*	<.1
1501	South-Side Machine Shop Inc—*Henry Elrod*	PO Box 3426, Paducah KY 42002	270-442-6107	R	3*	<.1
1502	Alabama Dynamics Inc—*Malcolm Ernest*	PO Box 1630, Calera AL 35040	205-668-0708	R	3*	<.1
1503	Allied Machine Inc—*Kenneth Cronk*	11171 Spruce Ave, Grant MI 49327	231-834-0050	R	3*	<.1
1504	Bnb Manufacturing Company Inc—*Bernardino Nanni*	PO Box 556, Winsted CT 06098	860-379-0783	R	3*	<.1
1505	Burtree Inc—*Cyrus Massoudi*	13513 Sherman Way, Van Nuys CA 91405	818-786-4276	R	3*	<.1
1506	Lunar Tool LLC—*Randy Travers*	4600 Shaw Ave, Saint Louis MO 63110	314-772-8900	R	3*	<.1
1507	Roe Machine Inc—*Willard Strain*	PO Box 531, West Frankfort IL 62896	618-937-2509	R	3*	<.1
1508	Stephens Machine Inc—*Gregory Stephens*	1600 Dodge St, Kokomo IN 46902	765-459-4017	R	3*	<.1
1509	Avon Broach and Production Company LLC—*George Buhaj*	PO Box 80310, Rochester MI 48308	248-651-9321	R	3*	<.1
1510	Chrome Machine—*Bernie Thomas*	PO Box 299, Bushland TX 79012	806-358-3636	R	3*	<.1
1511	Custom Micro Machining—*Tao Chou*	707 Brown Rd, Fremont CA 94539	510-651-9434	R	3*	<.1
1512	Houston North Machine Inc—*Karl Johnson*	PO Box 1647, Tomball TX 77377	281-351-8108	R	3*	<.1
1513	M and F Machine and Tool Inc—*Mark Milano*	7355 Sulier Dr, Temperance MI 48182	734-847-0571	R	3*	<.1
1514	Mecpro Inc—*Son Ho*	980 George St, Santa Clara CA 95054	408-727-9757	R	3*	<.1
1515	Richmond Machine Co—*Lee Richmond*	1528 Travis Dr, Montpelier OH 43543	419-485-3134	R	3*	<.1
1516	Bauman Machine Inc—*Mark Mccarty*	PO Box 526, Wheatland OK 73097	405-745-3484	R	3*	<.1
1517	Bay Tech Industries Inc—*Robert Bourassa*	14500 McCormick Dr, Tampa FL 33626	813-854-1774	R	3*	<.1
1518	Blue Ridge Tool and Machine Company Inc—*Chris Tollison*	PO Box 1507, Easley SC 29641	864-859-4758	R	3*	<.1
1519	Cam Industries Inc—*Charles Mc Gough III*	215 Philadelphia St, Hanover PA 17331	717-637-5988	R	3*	<.1
1520	Certified Metals Services—*Lawrence Brooks* Metal Services Group	4848 Azusa Canyon Rd, Irwindale CA 91706	626-813-1180	D	3*	<.1
1521	Columbia Grinding Inc—*Richard Lussier*	7411 S 10th St, Oak Creek WI 53154	414-762-7320	R	3*	<.1
1522	Crane Hill Machine Inc—*Marshall Royalty*	2476 E Us Hwy 50, Seymour IN 47274	812-358-3534	R	3*	<.1
1523	Cte California Tool and Engineering Inc—*Rocky Lowstetter*	7417 Orangewood Dr, Riverside CA 92504	951-358-1111	R	3*	<.1
1524	Excello Tool Engineering and Manufacturing Co—*Michael Zahornacky*	37 Warfield St, Milford CT 06461	203-878-4073	R	3*	<.1
1525	Global Inc—*Joseph Kirst*	PO Box 24, Somerset PA 15501	814-445-9671	R	3*	<.1
1526	Hummel Machine and Tool Co—*Charles Hummel*	580 Davis Ave, Kearny NJ 07032	201-991-5200	R	3*	<.1
1527	Miller Machine Inc—*Chuck Miller*	353 Industrial Way, Fallbrook CA 92028	760-723-9446	R	3*	<.1
1528	Portland Precision Manufacturing—*Gene Bensene*	16327 NE Cameron Blvd, Portland OR 97230	503-253-6700	R	3*	<.1
1529	Progress Machine Inc—*Kenneth Arceneaux*	PO Box 883, Morgan City LA 70381	985-631-2141	R	3*	<.1
1530	Schmid Tool and Engineering Corp—*Heidi Leahy*	930 N Villa Ave, Villa Park IL 60181	630-333-1733	R	3*	<.1
1531	Slim Haney Inc—*Newton Box*	5615 N Mingo Rd, Tulsa OK 74117	918-274-1082	R	3*	<.1
1532	Thistle Foundry and Machine Company Inc—*J Kelly*	101 Thistle St, Bluefield VA 24605	276-326-1196	R	3*	<.1
1533	TRP Machine Inc—*Patrick Price*	35 Davinci Dr Ste B, Bohemia NY 11716	631-567-9620	R	3*	<.1
1534	Vermes Machine Company Inc—*Erwin Vermes*	351 Crider Ave, Moorestown NJ 08057	856-642-9300	R	3*	<.1
1535	Watford Industry Inc—*Harold Watford*	PO Box 760, Kingstree SC 29556	843-382-8611	R	3*	<.1
1536	Webco Machine Products Inc—*Douglas Luks*	7800 Exchange Rd, Cleveland OH 44125	216-524-6210	R	3*	<.1
1537	Kimberly Machine Inc—*Kary Laursen*	12822 Joy St, Garden Grove CA 92840	714-539-0151	R	3*	<.1
1538	Shackelford Machine Shop—*Carl Shackelford*	PO Box 670, Clearwater KS 67026	620-584-6418	R	3*	<.1
1539	Tri-Kris Co—*William Carling*	PO Box 785, Lansdale PA 19446	215-855-5183	R	3*	<.1
1540	William J Labb Sons Inc—*Olga Wallace*	4617 Milnor St, Philadelphia PA 19137	215-289-4515	R	3*	<.1
1541	JM Schmidt Precision Tool Company Inc—*Robert Harple*	1035 Saunders Ln, West Chester PA 19380	610-436-5010	R	3*	<.1
1542	Linda Tool and Die Corp—*Michael Marino*	163 Dwight St, Brooklyn NY 11231	718-522-2066	R	3*	<.1

Note: An asterisk (*) indicates an estimated financial figure. The company type code used is as follows: R = Private, P = Public, S = Private Subsidiary, B = Public Subsidiary, D = Division, J = Joint Venture, I = Investment Fund.

COMPANY RANKINGS BY SALES WITHIN 4-DIGIT SIC

Rank	Company Name—*Executive Officer*	Address, City, State, Zip	Phone	Type	Fin	Empls
1543	Tru Manufacturing Corp—*Angela Mastropietro*	40 Oak St, Norwood NJ 07648	201-768-4050	R	3*	<.1
1544	Concentric Industries Inc—*Thomas Lingle*	720 Lavoy Rd, Erie MI 48133	734-848-5133	R	3*	<.1
1545	Hicks Machine Inc—*Randall Hicks*	PO Box 445, Walpole NH 03608	603-756-4132	R	3*	<.1
1546	Joka Industries Inc—*Deepali Ghai*	65 Knickerbocker Ave A, Bohemia NY 11716	631-589-0444	R	3*	<.1
1547	Bayfab Metals Inc—*Susan Miranda*	870 Doolittle Dr, San Leandro CA 94577	510-568-8950	R	3*	<.1
1548	General Weldments Inc—*Robert Potter*	PO Box 508, Irwin PA 15642	724-744-2105	R	3*	<.1
1549	International Tool Inc—*Travis Steinfeld*	N15811 Klein Ln, Trempealeau WI 54661	608-539-2220	R	3*	<.1
1550	Lincoln Park Boring Co	28089 Wick Rd, Romulus MI 48174	734-946-8300	R	3*	<.1
1551	Mechanical Device Co—*Daniel Sperry*	2005 General Electric, Bloomington IL 61704	309-663-2843	R	3*	<.1
1552	Sunset Industries Inc—*Tony Hauptman*	1272 E 286th St, Cleveland OH 44132	216-731-8131	R	3*	<.1
1553	Unitech Tool and Machine Inc—*Ramin Lak*	3025 Stender Way, Santa Clara CA 95054	408-566-0333	R	3*	<.1
1554	Devin Manufacturing Inc—*Bill Devin*	40 Edward St, Arcade NY 14009	585-496-5770	R	3*	<.1
1555	Cavallo and Cavallo Inc—*Thomas Kearns*	14955 Hilton Dr, Fontana CA 92336	909-428-6994	R	3*	<.1
1556	Alro Machine Tool And Die Company Inc—*Ronald Young*	593 W Hoffman Ave, Lindenhurst NY 11757	631-226-5020	R	3*	<.1
1557	HT Machine Company Inc—*Howard Tryba*	15 Town Forest Rd, Webster MA 01570	508-949-1105	R	3*	<.1
1558	King Tool and Die Inc—*Larry King*	971 Division St, Adrian MI 49221	517-265-2741	R	3*	<.1
1559	Puskar Precision Machining Co—*Asim Puskar*	1610 Cambridge Dr, Elgin IL 60123	847-888-2929	R	3*	<.1
1560	Trojon Gear Inc—*Charles Smith*	418 San Jose St, Dayton OH 45403	937-254-1737	R	3*	<.1
1561	American Manufacturing Network Inc—*Sandip Desai*	16525 Sherman Way Ste, Van Nuys CA 91406	818-786-1113	R	3*	<.1
1562	Stone Mountain Tool Inc—*David Duke*	480 Gees Mill Business, Conyers GA 30013	770-929-0166	R	3*	<.1
1563	JR Machine Company LLC—*Joe Reyes*	13245 Florence Ave, Santa Fe Springs CA 90670	562-903-9477	R	3*	<.1
1564	Component Parts Machine Company Inc—*Don Sanders*	PO Box 7514, Fort Worth TX 76111	817-834-7202	R	3*	<.1
1565	Paramont Machine Company Inc—*Paul Cipar*	963 Commercial Ave Se, New Philadelphia OH 44663	330-339-3489	R	3*	<.1
1566	Artcraft Machine And Tool Corp—*Ruth Benek*	PO Box 156, Langhorne PA 19047	215-757-7753	R	3*	<.1
1567	B and K Machine Products Inc—*Gary Plankenhorn*	PO Box 187, South Haven MI 49090	269-637-3001	R	3*	<.1
1568	Bowen Machine Company Inc—*Stuart Bowen*	3421 Fairview Dr, Gastonia NC 28052	704-629-9111	R	3*	<.1
1569	Carbaugh Tool Company Inc—*Arnold Carbaugh*	126 Philo Rd W, Elmira NY 14903	607-739-3293	R	3*	<.1
1570	Edmore Tool and Grinding Inc—*Vic Johnson*	4255 E Howard City Edm, Edmore MI 48829	989-427-3790	R	3*	<.1
1571	Detailed Machining Inc—*John Bertsch*	2490 Ross St, Sidney OH 45365	937-492-1264	R	3*	<.1
1572	Arrow Machining Company Inc—*Joseph Shipp*	PO Box 768, Marysville WA 98270	360-659-0342	R	3*	<.1
1573	Sherman Corp—*Helen Sherman*	955 W Hyde Park Blvd, Inglewood CA 90302	323-678-7857	R	3*	<.1
1574	Apple Machine and Supply Co—*James Turner*	PO Box 68, Fort Pierce FL 34954	772-466-9353	R	3*	<.1
1575	Baum Precision Machining Inc—*William Baum*	5136 Applebutter Rd, Pipersville PA 18947	215-766-3066	R	3*	<.1
1576	Advanced Machining and Fabricating Inc—*Steve Shortess*	11212 E 112th St N, Owasso OK 74055	918-664-5410	R	3*	<.1
1577	Banner Machine Company Inc—*Paul Buckmaster*	3224 S Hi Lo Cir Ne, Huntsville AL 35811	256-533-1470	R	3*	<.1
1578	Beaumac Company Inc—*William Beaucher*	382 Suncook Valley Hwy, Epsom NH 03234	603-736-9321	R	3*	<.1
1579	Donham Craft Inc—*Tom Sellers*	2332 E Grauwyler Rd, Irving TX 75061	972-438-2251	R	3*	<.1
1580	Extrusion Punch and Tool Inc—*Roger Michels*	2326 Alger Dr, Troy MI 48083	248-689-3300	R	3*	<.1
1581	Job Dave's Shop Inc—*Susan Schulteis*	865 Cleveland Ave, Hartford WI 53027	262-673-4321	R	3*	<.1
1582	Kutzner Manufacturing Company Inc—*Jo Kutzner*	3255 Meetinghouse Rd, Telford PA 18969	215-721-1712	R	3*	<.1
1583	Precision Machine and Welding Inc—*Bob Cutshall*	175 Holder Rd, Afton TN 37616	423-638-9000	R	3*	<.1
1584	Precision Manufacturing And Engineering Company Inc—*John Helfrick*	3155 Buchanan Trl W, Greencastle PA 17225	717-597-2165	R	3*	<.1
1585	Precision Screw Machine Products Inc—*Joseph Moreshead*	PO Box 1944, Biddeford ME 04005	207-283-0121	R	3*	<.1
1586	Seeley Machine Inc—*Craig Seeley*	75 Big Boom Rd, Queensbury NY 12804	518-798-9510	R	3*	<.1
1587	Swiss Screw Products Inc—*Sung Hwang*	339 Mathew St, Santa Clara CA 95050	408-748-8400	R	3*	<.1
1588	Wilson Tool Corp—*Virginia Wilson*	2401 20th St, Rockford IL 61104	815-226-0147	R	3*	<.1
1589	Criterion Tool And Die Co—*Tanya Disalvo*	5349 W 161st St, Cleveland OH 44142	216-267-1733	R	3*	<.1
1590	Dimension Enterprises Inc—*Ray Menard*	14308 Mead St, Longmont CO 80504	970-535-0546	R	3*	<.1
1591	Extreme Precision Screw Products Inc—*Mark Blevins*	1838 Remell St, Flint MI 48503	810-744-1980	R	3*	<.1
1592	Kaskaskia Tool And Machine Inc—*Roy Albert*	107 S Benton St, New Athens IL 62264	618-475-3301	R	3*	<.1
1593	C and T Machining Inc—*John Carmack*	12991 Buchanan Trl W, Mercersburg PA 17236	717-328-9572	R	3*	<.1
1594	D and N Precision Inc—*Norm Dreyer*	727 Calle Artis, San Jose CA 95131	408-321-8400	R	3*	<.1
1595	Mica Tool and Manufacturing Inc—*Frank Concotelli*	730 Perkins Dr, Mukwonago WI 53149	262-363-9363	R	3*	<.1
1596	Oem Press Systems Inc—*John Copp*	311 S Highland Ave, Fullerton CA 92832	714-449-7500	R	3*	<.1
1597	Gibbs Machine Company Inc—*H Gibbs*	2012 Fairfax Rd, Greensboro NC 27407	336-856-1907	R	3*	<.1
1598	LRG Corp—*Lewis Gainfort*	PO Box 490, Jeannette PA 15644	724-523-3131	R	3*	<.1
1599	Unimatic Inc—*Elizabeth Conlin*	3501 Raleigh Ave, Minneapolis MN 55416	952-922-7744	R	3*	<.1
1600	Davis Manufacturing Co—*James Davis*	3990 S Windermere St, Englewood CO 80110	303-762-0550	R	3*	<.1
1601	Foxboro Industries Inc—*Jim Hackstedt*	603 W Flottmann Rd, Gerald MO 63037	573-764-4224	R	3*	<.1
1602	Marble Machine Inc—*Joseph Marble*	21204 Rileysburg Rd, Danville IL 61834	217-431-3014	R	3*	<.1
1603	General Machine Service Inc—*Stephen Slachta*	494 E Morley Dr, Saginaw MI 48601	989-752-5161	R	3*	<.1
1604	Turn Tech Inc—*Leonard Johnson*	33901 Riviera, Fraser MI 48026	586-415-8090	R	3*	<.1
1605	Cummins Manufacturing Inc—*Robert Cummins*	PO Box 465, Tipton IA 52772	563-886-2255	R	3*	<.1
1606	G and E Machine Works Inc—*Steven Graves*	2988 S Blvd, Brewton AL 36426	251-867-3207	R	3*	<.1
1607	Bay City Shovels Inc—*Peter Kaiser*	PO Box 169, Au Gres MI 48703	989-876-8121	R	3*	<.1
1608	Demco Manufacturing Inc—*Charles Schmidt*	PO Box 757, Diboll TX 75941	936-829-4771	R	3*	<.1
1609	Carolina Precision Components Inc—*Randy Walker*	4181 Us Hwy 321a, Granite Falls NC 28630	828-879-3936	R	3*	<.1
1610	Acme Machine Co—*Bertyl Carlson*	2901 Fremont Ave S, Minneapolis MN 55408	612-827-3571	R	3*	<.1
1611	Auglaize-Erie Machine—*Tom Slife*	PO Box 72, New Bremen OH 45869	419-629-2068	R	3*	<.1
1612	B and R Machine Inc—*Gerald Renaud*	305a Moody St Ste A, Ludlow MA 01056	413-547-2920	R	3*	<.1
1613	Bohr Precision Machining Inc—*Ilene Bohr*	W194n11160 Kleinmann D, Germantown WI 53022	262-251-0761	R	3*	<.1
1614	Bolero Industries Inc—*Daniel Imasdounian*	11850 Burke St, Santa Fe Springs CA 90670	562-693-3000	R	3*	<.1
1615	Carson Manufacturing Inc—*Ed Capps*	5001 Grumman Dr, Carson City NV 89706	775-883-3366	R	3*	<.1
1616	Clark Industries Inc—*Jack Schulz*	816 Callan St, Monett MO 65708	417-235-7182	R	3*	<.1
1617	Component Engineering Inc—*Patrick Panella*	1610 Independence Ave, Hartford WI 53027	262-673-0511	R	3*	<.1
1618	Cornett Machine Shop Inc—*Ira Cornett*	1635 S Hwy 27, Somerset KY 42501	606-678-5163	R	3*	<.1
1619	Courser Inc—*Daniel Herman*	802 County Rd 64 Ste 1, Elmira NY 14903	607-739-3861	R	3*	<.1
1620	GG Premier Precision Inc—*Glenn Grozich*	500 Shawmut Ave, La Grange Park IL 60526	708-588-1234	R	3*	<.1
1621	Johnson Tool and Manufacturing Inc—*Raymond Johnson*	6 H Putnam Rd, Charlton MA 01507	508-248-3125	R	3*	<.1
1622	Precision Metalcrafters Inc—*Frank Falconi*	17 Filbert St, Williamstown NJ 08094	856-629-1020	R	3*	<.1
1623	Speedwell Machine Works Inc—*Amos Benfield*	1301 Crowders Creek Rd, Gastonia NC 28052	704-866-7418	R	3*	<.1
1624	Taurus Tool and Engineering Inc—*William Buntin*	5101 W County Rd 400 S, Muncie IN 47302	765-282-2090	R	3*	<.1
1625	Unique Machine Shop Inc—*Perry Head*	PO Box 7, Oglesby TX 76561	254-456-2972	R	3*	<.1
1626	Dave Hunter Company LLC	PO Box 1716, Albany OR 97321	541-926-5238	R	3*	<.1
1627	Gen-El-Mec Associates Inc—*Dean Constix*	PO Box 3364, Bridgeport CT 06605	203-333-0565	R	3*	<.1
1628	Knighton's Automotive Machine Shop Inc—*Brian Knighton*	PO Box 25087, Albuquerque NM 87125	505-247-0257	R	3*	<.1
1629	Niagara Precision Inc—*Roger Hood*	233 Market St, Lockport NY 14094	716-439-0956	R	3*	<.1
1630	Semco Machine Corp—*Fred Holmes*	5 Kenneth Miner Dr, Wrentham MA 02093	508-384-8303	R	3*	<.1
1631	Triad Machine Inc—*H Wetmore*	PO Box 208, Roebuck SC 29376	864-574-4530	R	3*	<.1

Rank	Company Name—*Executive Officer*	Address, City, State, Zip	Phone	Type	Fin	Empls
1632	Varney Manufacturing Inc—*Gary Varney*	2026 Lars Way, Medford OR 97501	541-608-0144	R	3*	<.1
1633	Connelly Machine Works—*Ray Connelly*	420 N Terminal St, Santa Ana CA 92701	714-558-6855	R	3*	<.1
1634	D And D Manufacturing LLC—*Melissa Spiridigliozzi*	49 Mitchell Rd, Ipswich MA 01938	978-356-9188	R	3*	<.1
1635	GSP Precision Inc—*George Gottardi*	2915 Floyd St, Burbank CA 91504	818-845-2212	R	3*	<.1
1636	Paul Machine Corp—*Barry Feldman*	161 Tower Dr Ste B, Burr Ridge IL 60527	630-734-1800	R	3*	<.1
1637	Total Manufacturing Company Inc—*Robert Wisen*	PO Box 5053, Mentor OH 44061	440-946-0211	R	3*	<.1
1638	Machine Experience and Design Inc—*David Bobbitt*	2964 Phillip Ave, Clovis CA 93612	559-291-7710	R	3*	<.1
1639	S and B Machine Inc—*James Stadt*	820 Blackburn Dr, Mobile AL 36608	251-633-4443	R	3*	<.1
1640	Reliance Machine Company Inc—*Richard Cardemon*	4605 S Walnut St, Muncie IN 47302	765-284-0151	R	3*	<.1
1641	Packer Metal Works Inc—*Edward Packer*	11301 Electron Dr, Louisville KY 40299	502-297-6506	R	3*	.1
1642	Arrow Screw Products Inc—*Robert Vine*	941 W Mccoy Ln, Santa Maria CA 93455	805-928-2269	R	3*	<.1
1643	Cdk Enterprises LLC—*Robin Camilleri*	16601 E 13 Mile Rd, Fraser MI 48026	586-296-9300	R	3*	<.1
1644	Grindley Manufacturing Inc—*John Grindley*	1989 Blake Ave, Los Angeles CA 90039	323-665-5781	R	3*	<.1
1645	C And F Machinery Corp—*Francis Santos*	91-060 Hanua St, Kapolei HI 96707	808-682-1541	R	3*	<.1
1646	Honomach Inc—*Jean Fennimore* C And F Machinery Corp	91-060 Hanua St, Kapolei HI 96707	808-682-5701	S	3*	<.1
1647	Bmw Precision Machining Inc—*Richard Blakely*	2379 Industry St, Oceanside CA 92054	760-439-6813	R	3*	<.1
1648	Engineering Design and Development Inc—*Eric Jenkins*	1001 W Jefferson St, Morton IL 61550	309-266-6298	R	3*	<.1
1649	Lamm's Machine Inc—*Jeffrey Lamm*	3216 Berger St, Allentown PA 18103	610-797-2023	R	3*	<.1
1650	Machine Tool Engineering Inc—*Sarah George*	PO Box 94, Charles City IA 50616	641-228-4524	R	3*	<.1
1651	V Brothers Machine Co—*Damjan Vujanovic*	4900 W 16th St, Cicero IL 60804	708-652-0062	R	3*	<.1
1652	Fraser Fab And Machine Inc—*David Hartig*	1696 Star Batt Dr, Rochester Hills MI 48309	248-852-9050	R	3*	<.1
1653	Gischel Mechanical Service Company Inc—*James Gischel*	7605 Energy Pkwy, Baltimore MD 21226	410-360-0800	R	3*	<.1
1654	Sks Machine Inc—*David Serafin*	2610 Industrial St, Wisconsin Rapids WI 54495	715-421-1900	R	3*	<.1
1655	Imco Industrial Machine Corp—*Steve Higgins*	PO Box 943, Crown Point IN 46308	219-663-6100	R	3*	<.1
1656	J H and H Management Inc—*Helun Chahda*	3811 W 150th St, Cleveland OH 44111	216-252-0430	R	3*	<.1
1657	Modern Industries Inc—*Gregory Senn*	6610 Metta Ave, Cleveland OH 44103	216-432-2855	R	3*	<.1
1658	Precision Bearing and Machine Inc—*Jack Robinson*	PO Box 6051, Spartanburg SC 29304	864-576-5355	R	3*	<.1
1659	Smt Machine and Tool Inc—*Russel Styczynski*	1325 Cornell Rd, Green Bay WI 54313	920-434-3272	R	3*	<.1
1660	T D M Corp—*Edgar Ramsey*	PO Box 277, Fletcher NC 28732	828-684-9818	R	3*	<.1
1661	Accurate Tool and Die Inc—*Jeffrey Salvatore*	16 Leon Pl, Stamford CT 06902	203-967-1200	R	3*	<.1
1662	Aluminum Fabricators Inc—*George Mansfield*	PO Box 270350, Kansas City MO 64127	816-231-8888	R	3*	<.1
1663	Esterline and Sons Manufacturing Co—*Dale Esterline*	6508 Old Clifton Rd, Springfield OH 45502	937-265-5278	R	3*	<.1
1664	General Machine-Diecron Inc—*C Gwyn*	3131 Hwy 41, Griffin GA 30224	770-228-6200	R	3*	<.1
1665	Kennedy Machine and Manufacturing Inc—*Hubert Kennedy*	11152 Shady Trl, Dallas TX 75229	972-241-7610	R	3*	<.1
1666	Lagonda Machine Inc—*Donald Greene*	2410 Park Ave, Washington PA 15301	724-222-2710	R	3*	<.1
1667	Machine Power Inc—*David Kvamme*	PO Box 1312, Mankato MN 56002	507-387-5846	R	3*	<.1
1668	Micron Machine Co—*John Conley*	12530 Stowe Dr, Poway CA 92064	858-486-5900	R	3*	<.1
1660	Trec Industries Inc—*James Trecokas*	4713 Spring Rd, Cleveland OH 44131	216-741-4114	R	3*	<.1
1670	Ace Metal Kraft Company Inc—*Richard Zega*	815 Mobrido Ave, Woodland Park NJ 07424	973-278-6605	R	3*	<.1
1671	Cascade Precision Inc—*Michael Hall*	PO Box 567, Boring OR 97009	503-663-9508	R	3*	<.1
1672	Ace Industries Inc—*Su Yi*	738 Design Ct Ste 302, Chula Vista CA 91911	619-482-2700	R	3*	<.1
1673	Desco Manufacturing Company Inc—*Ralph Fabian*	30081 Comercio, Rcho Sta Marg CA 92688	949-858-7400	R	3*	<.1
1674	Precision Tool And Machine Co—*John Haydt*	1698 Stairville Rd, Mountain Top PA 18707	570-800-3920	R	3*	<.1
1675	Staub Machine Company Inc—*Anthony Staub*	206 Lake St, Hamburg NY 14075	716-649-4211	R	3*	<.1
1676	Zircon Precision Products Inc—*Bruce Treichler*	818 W 24th St, Tempe AZ 85282	480-967-8688	R	3*	<.1
1677	Proficient Machining Co—*Kenneth Putman*	7522 Tyler Blvd Unit B, Mentor OH 44060	440-942-4942	R	3*	<.1
1678	Alpine Precision LLC—*Michael Barsoian*	3 Executive Park Dr St, North Billerica MA 01862	978-667-6333	R	3*	<.1
1679	Circle Boring and Machine Co—*Glen Ekberg*	3161 Forest View Rd, Rockford IL 61109	815-398-4150	R	3*	<.1
1680	Southwest Industrial Services Inc—*Michael Goold*	2413 Whitmore St, Fort Worth TX 76107	817-332-6481	R	3*	<.1
1681	Tabco Machines Inc—*Todd Benson*	1114 N Ave T, Lubbock TX 79415	806-749-5649	R	3*	<.1
1682	Bausch Advanced Technologies Inc—*Luann Tarvin*	115 Nod Rd, Clinton CT 06413	860-669-7380	R	3*	<.1
1683	Southland CNC Inc—*Keith Armour*	5691 Duncan Bridge Rd, Cornelia GA 30531	706-778-0369	R	3*	<.1
1684	Accuturn Corp—*Iggy Araujo*	6510 Box Springs Blvd, Riverside CA 92507	951-656-6621	R	3*	<.1
1685	B and D Machine Inc—*Scott Ulfers*	1102 1st St Ne, Buffalo MN 55313	763-682-0500	R	3*	<.1
1686	Bell Engineering Inc—*Richard Bell*	735 S Outer Dr, Saginaw MI 48601	989-753-3127	R	3*	<.1
1687	Cct Plastics Inc—*Greg Mince*	804 Port America Pl St, Grapevine TX 76051	817-410-1222	R	3*	<.1
1688	Clarklake Machine Inc—*Michael De Karske*	9451 S Meridian Rd, Clarklake MI 49234	517-529-9454	R	3*	<.1
1689	Frazier-Simplex Machine Co—*John Frazier*	1720 N Main St, Washington PA 15301	724-222-5700	R	3*	<.1
1690	Holmes Tool and Engineering Inc—*Alois Bunz*	PO Box 95, Bonifay FL 32425	850-547-4418	R	3*	<.1
1691	Kasper Industries Inc—*Tim Kasper*	356 Expy Ct, Gaylord MI 49735	989-705-1177	R	3*	<.1
1692	Millipart Inc—*Scot Jamlson*	412 W Carter Dr, Glendora CA 91740	626-963-4101	R	3*	<.1
1693	Pushman Manufacturing Company Inc—*Michael Pushman*	1044 Grant St, Fenton MI 48430	810-629-9688	R	3*	<.1
1694	Quality Precision Inc—*Michael Varin*	31159 San Benito St, Hayward CA 94544	510-475-4244	R	3*	<.1
1695	Spaulding Machine Company Inc—*Lucile Brettrager*	5366 E Rd, Saginaw MI 48601	989-777-0694	R	3*	<.1
1696	Williams Tool Inc—*Ray Williams*	PO Box 430, Chadwicks NY 13319	315-737-7226	R	3*	<.1
1697	WJ Roberts Company Inc—*William Roberts*	PO Box 1146, Saugus MA 01906	781-233-8176	R	3*	<.1
1698	Astro-Craft Inc—*Otto Dschida*	7509 Spring Grove Rd, Spring Grove IL 60081	815-675-1500	R	3*	<.1
1699	Matrix Tool and Machine Inc—*Richard Wilson*	7870 Division Dr, Mentor OH 44060	440-255-0300	R	3*	<.1
1700	Southwestern Precision Company Inc—*James Trull*	1916 W 144th St, Gardena CA 90249	310-324-1141	R	3*	<.1
1701	Clinkenbeard and Associates Inc—*Ronald Gustafson*	577 Grable St, Rockford IL 61109	815-226-0291	R	3*	<.1
1702	Raybar Inc—*Robert Susen*	303 N Progress Dr, Saukville WI 53080	262-377-0666	R	3*	<.1
1703	Richards Machine Tool Company Inc—*Dennis Richards*	3753 Walden Ave, Lancaster NY 14086	716-683-3380	R	3*	<.1
1704	Berran Industrial Group Inc—*Randy Adair*	PO Box 3205, Kent OH 44240	330-673-4722	R	3*	<.1
1705	D and H Machine Service Inc—*Brian Hillard*	4903 Shady Rd, Strawberry Plains TN 37871	865-933-7310	R	3*	<.1
1706	Elliott Precision Products Inc—*Steve Elliott*	16309 E Latimer St, Tulsa OK 74116	918-234-4001	R	3*	<.1
1707	Farrow Machine and Manufacturing Company Inc—*Sid Farrow*	419 Duncan Perry Rd St, Arlington TX 76011	817-633-4686	R	3*	<.1
1708	Hubbard Tool And Die Corp—*Eric Hubbard*	Rome Industrial Ctr St, Rome NY 13440	315-337-7840	R	3*	<.1
1709	JBAT Inc—*John Schallenhammer*	28 Coles Ave, Cherry Hill NJ 08002	856-667-7307	R	3*	<.1
1710	Mid-South Machine and Welding Company Inc—*Thomas Young*	PO Box 1405, Jackson TN 38302	731-422-4919	R	3*	<.1
1711	Neal Perschke—*Neal Perschke*	N8109 State Rd 33, Beaver Dam WI 53916	920-885-3591	R	3*	<.1
1712	Ultra-Tech Inc—*Pat Chapman*	3003 Power Dr, Kansas City KS 66106	913-262-7009	R	3*	<.1
1713	American Punch Company Inc—*Robert Olson*	1655 Century Corners P, Euclid OH 44132	216-731-4501	R	3*	<.1
1714	Industrial Engineering Co—*Alois Kosch*	2070 E 32nd Ave, Columbus NE 68601	402-564-1383	R	3*	<.1
1715	Integrated Production Systems Inc—*Don Jackson*	2750 113th St Ste 100, Grand Prairie TX 75050	972-988-0900	R	3*	<.1
1716	Lancaster Metals Science Corp—*Ralph Ludewig*	826 N Queen St, Lancaster PA 17603	717-299-9709	R	3*	<.1
1717	Tobin Machining Inc—*Thomas Tobin*	PO Box 1009, Fond Du Lac WI 54936	920-921-9110	R	3*	<.1
1718	A and J Precision Sheetmetal Inc—*Amrik Atwal*	1161 N 4th St, San Jose CA 95112	408-885-9134	R	3*	<.1
1719	Allied Machine Tool and Design Inc—*Walter Bates*	4050 Ne 9th Ave, Oakland Park FL 33334	954-561-3474	R	3*	<.1

Note: An asterisk (*) indicates an estimated financial figure. The company type code used is as follows: R = Private, P = Public, S = Private Subsidiary, B = Public Subsidiary, D = Division, J = Joint Venture, I = Investment Fund.

COMPANY RANKINGS BY SALES WITHIN 4-DIGIT SIC

Rank	Company Name—*Executive Officer*	Address, City, State, Zip	Phone	Type	Fin	Empls
1720	Bitzer Products Co—*Raymond Coopman*	2714 S 9th Ave, Broadview IL 60155	708-345-0795	R	3*	<.1
1721	Carolina Laser Cutting Inc—*Bruce Cromes*	4400 S Holden Rd, Greensboro NC 27406	336-292-1474	R	3*	<.1
1722	Casemer Tool and Machine Inc—*Amy Reed*	2765 Metamora Rd, Oxford MI 48371	248-628-4807	R	3*	<.1
1723	ENR General Machining Co—*Eugene Szydlo*	PO Box 32168, Chicago IL 60632	773-523-2944	R	3*	<.1
1724	KSDInc—*Robert Anderson*	161 W Lincoln St, Banning CA 92220	951-849-7669	R	3*	<.1
1725	Martinic Engineering Inc—*Tony Martinic*	10932 Chestnut Ave, Stanton CA 90680	714-527-8988	R	3*	<.1
1726	Mid-City Precision Inc—*Steve Carlson*	7430 Oxford St, Minneapolis MN 55426	952-933-2501	R	3*	<.1
1727	Morton Machining LLC—*Chuck Hudspath*	701 Flint Ave, Morton IL 61550	309-266-6551	R	3*	<.1
1728	Quest Fabrication Corp—*Jim Meter*	435 Preston Ct, Livermore CA 94551	925-455-1155	R	3*	<.1
1729	Sobot Tool and Manufacturing Co—*Steven Sobot*	3975 Commercial Ave, Northbrook IL 60062	847-480-0560	R	3*	<.1
1730	Sportsman Manufacturing Co—*Greg Schaefer*	5495 E 69th Ave, Commerce City CO 80022	303-287-2125	R	3*	<.1
1731	Bonal Technologies Inc—*Thomas E Hebel*	1300 N Campbell Rd, Royal Oak MI 48067	248-582-0900	S	3	<.1
1732	Trucast Inc—*Raymond Newcomb*	4382 Hamann Pkwy, Willoughby OH 44094	440-942-4923	R	3*	.1
1733	Alexander's Machine and Maintenance Service Company Inc—*Ron Alexander*	3700 N Commerce St, Fort Worth TX 76106	817-625-4175	R	3*	<.1
1734	Majestic Tool And Machine Inc—*Walter Krueger*	18035 Rockside Rd, Bedford OH 44146	440-439-6549	R	3*	<.1
1735	CAM Machine Inc—*Douglas Macy*	513 S Springfield St, Saint Paris OH 43072	937-663-5000	R	3*	<.1
1736	Kopis Machine Company Inc—*Floyd Kopis*	PO Box 187, Addison IL 60101	630-543-4138	R	3*	<.1
1737	Cf Metals LLC—*Cathy Lancaster*	3860 River Rd, Schiller Park IL 60176	847-671-1631	R	3*	<.1
1738	Albert Webster Engineering Co—*Michael Webster*	PO Box 758, Sterling Heights MI 48311	586-777-0116	R	3*	<.1
1739	D Mills Grinding and Machining Company Inc—*Anthony Puccio*	6131 Quail Valley Ct, Riverside CA 92507	951-697-6847	R	3*	<.1
1740	HH Arnold Company Inc—*John Arnold*	PO Box 526, Rockland MA 02370	781-878-0346	R	3*	<.1
1741	New World Machining Inc—*Marvin Elsten*	2799 Aiello Dr, San Jose CA 95111	408-227-3810	R	3*	<.1
1742	Omega Precision—*Joseph Venegas*	13040 Telegraph Rd, Santa Fe Springs CA 90670	562-946-2491	R	3*	<.1
1743	Spencer-Harris Of Arkansas Inc—*George Black*	PO Box 579, Magnolia AR 71754	870-234-3264	R	3*	<.1
1744	Sullivan Manufacturing Corp—*Brian Sullivan*	10201 N Enterprise Dr, Mequon WI 53092	262-242-5560	R	3*	<.1
1745	Ter Precision Machining Inc—*Edward Cech*	306 Mathew St, Santa Clara CA 95050	408-986-9920	R	3*	<.1
1746	Warwick Machine and Tool Company Inc—*Brian Shank*	1917 Mcfarland Dr, Landisville PA 17538	717-892-6814	R	3*	<.1
1747	American Babbitt Bearing Inc—*William White*	PO Box 3069, Huntington WV 25702	304-523-5700	R	3*	<.1
1748	Ed Dang's Machine Works Inc—*Edward Dang*	1804 Democrat St, Honolulu HI 96819	808-847-1581	R	3*	<.1
1749	Medway Tool Corp—*Tom Drake*	2100 Corporate Dr, Troy OH 45373	937-335-7717	R	3*	<.1
1750	Bibey Machine Company Inc—*Ronald Bibey*	642 S Spring St, Greensboro NC 27406	336-275-9421	R	3*	<.1
1751	Data Machine Inc—*Harry Miller*	PO Box 409, Adamsburg PA 15611	724-864-4370	R	3*	<.1
1752	Edwards Machining Inc—*Scott Penrod*	2335 Research Dr, Jackson MI 49203	517-782-2568	R	3*	<.1
1753	Pump Arts Inc—*James Stevens*	PO Box 750725, Houston TX 77275	713-946-0500	R	3*	<.1
1754	Scandia Manufacturing Company Inc—*Evan Krometis*	480 Brunswick St, Baltimore MD 21223	410-233-5050	R	3*	<.1
1755	Victory Tool Inc—*Sheldon Halberg*	1151 Mckinley St, Anoka MN 55303	763-323-8877	R	3*	<.1
1756	Wisconsin Industrial Machine Service Inc—*Dan Rich*	21500 Doral Rd, Waukesha WI 53186	262-784-2300	R	3*	<.1
1757	C Machine Company Inc—*Kevin Dickison*	7980 Ranchers Rd Ne, Minneapolis MN 55432	763-785-2056	R	3*	<.1
1758	EC Machining Inc—*Edward Czorniak*	8267 S 86th Ct, Oak Lawn IL 60458	708-496-0116	R	3*	<.1
1759	Hawk Tool And Machine Inc—*George Hawkins*	PO Box 930351, Wixom MI 48393	248-349-0121	R	3*	<.1
1760	Machine Products Company Inc—*Michael Harris*	PO Box 577, Gadsden AL 35902	256-538-9991	R	3*	<.1
1761	Smith's Machine And Grinding Inc—*Scott Ogden*	203 E Battle Creek St, Galesburg MI 49053	269-665-4231	R	3*	<.1
1762	Sunshine Filters Of Pinellas Inc—*Fred Cooklin*	12415 73rd Ct, Largo FL 33773	727-530-3884	R	3*	<.1
1763	Adom Engineering Inc—*John Moda*	131 Avco Rd, Haverhill MA 01835	978-372-7757	R	3*	<.1
1764	AJ Tuck Co—*Alvin Tuck*	PO Box 215, Brookfield CT 06804	203-775-1234	R	3*	<.1
1765	American Tool Co—*Richard Mc Cally*	623 Washington Hwy, Lincoln RI 02865	401-333-0111	R	3*	<.1
1766	B and C Machining Inc—*Jim Leibrand*	108 N Wiggs St, Griffith IN 46319	219-924-5411	R	3*	<.1
1767	Brickham Machining Company Inc—*Mark Brickham*	PO Box 257, Oshkosh WI 54903	920-231-7676	R	3*	<.1
1768	Clifford Manufacturing Company Inc—*Arthur Clifford*	5631 Raytown Rd, Raytown MO 64133	816-358-4291	R	3*	<.1
1769	J-K Tool Company Inc—*Joseph Kowal*	41 Russo Cir, Agawam MA 01001	413-789-0613	R	3*	<.1
1770	Lemke Industrial Machine Inc—*Donald Lemke*	1204 County Rd Nn, Marathon WI 54448	715-842-3221	R	3*	<.1
1771	P and L Machine Company Inc—*Kenneth Mckelvie*	168 Ayer Rd Unit 4, Littleton MA 01460	978-486-9626	R	3*	<.1
1772	Precision Specialists Inc—*Richard Dove*	1004 Industrial Dr Ste, West Berlin NJ 08091	856-768-5990	R	3*	<.1
1773	RJ Corbus Inc—*Lorri Zimmer*	3551 Victor St, Santa Clara CA 95054	408-970-9661	R	3*	<.1
1774	Stanley Industries Inc—*Jay Cusick*	19120 Cranwood Pkwy, Cleveland OH 44128	216-475-4000	R	3*	<.1
1775	Stuart Steel Protection Corp—*Gordon Stuart*	PO Box 476, South Bound Brook NJ 08880	732-469-5544	R	3*	<.1
1776	System's South Inc—*Jay Vaughan*	422 Hwy 418, Fountain Inn SC 29644	864-862-9777	R	3*	<.1
1777	Tampa Machine Products Inc—*James Lyngholm*	PO Box 2152, Oldsmar FL 34677	813-854-3332	R	3*	<.1
1778	Tangent Machine and Tool Corp—*Joseph Scafidi*	108 Gazza Blvd, Farmingdale NY 11735	631-249-3088	R	3*	<.1
1779	Three Daughters Corp—*Richard Allen*	5005 County Rd 29, Auburn IN 46706	260-925-2128	R	3*	<.1
1780	Ushers Machine And Tool Company Inc—*Joseph Hopeck*	180 Ushers Rd, Round Lake NY 12151	518-877-5501	R	3*	<.1
1781	Vector Engineering And Manufacturing Corp—*Daryl Sullivan*	17506 Chicago Ave, Lansing IL 60438	708-474-3900	R	3*	<.1
1782	West Machine Products Inc—*Robert Szwaya*	606 Long Lake Dr, Round Lake IL 60073	847-740-2404	R	3*	<.1
1783	Royalton Manufacturing Inc—*Kenneth Wesner*	PO Box 33190, Cleveland OH 44133	440-237-2233	R	3*	<.1
1784	Z and Z Manufacturing Inc—*Tom Zovko*	4765 E 355th St, Willoughby OH 44094	440-953-2800	R	3*	<.1
1785	Creative Tool and Machining Inc—*Dana Herr*	4010 Middle Rd, Columbus IN 47203	812-378-3562	R	3*	<.1
1786	Mile-Hi Machine Inc—*George Szabo*	6395 W 56th Ave, Arvada CO 80002	303-425-0760	R	3*	<.1
1787	Dwyer Enterprises Inc—*Kenneth Dwyer*	PO Box 295, Neosho MO 64850	417-451-5222	R	3*	<.1
1788	Degood Dimensional Concepts Inc—*Scott Degood*	7815 N State Rd 13, North Webster IN 46555	574-834-5437	R	3*	<.1
1789	C and F Machine Corp—*Julian Kuta*	176 Covington Dr, Bloomingdale IL 60108	630-924-0300	R	3*	<.1
1790	Highline Portafab Inc—*Wendell Malmberg*	20105 Broadway Ave, Snohomish WA 98296	425-486-8031	R	3*	<.1
1791	Multi-Machining Company Inc—*Tony Linduff*	701 Business Way, Wylie TX 75098	972-429-6111	R	2*	<.1
1792	Columbus Engineering Inc—*Burdett Noblitt*	6600 S 50 W, Columbus IN 47201	812-342-1231	R	2*	<.1
1793	Crush Master Grinding Corp—*Sherman Durousseau*	755 Penarth Ave, Walnut CA 91789	909-595-2249	R	2*	<.1
1794	Granite Mountain Design Inc—*Kurt Wilkinson*	11500 E Santa Fe Loop, Dewey AZ 86327	928-775-2553	R	2*	<.1
1795	Mercury Machining Company Inc—*Dale Macarthy*	PO Box 1364, Pensacola FL 32591	850-433-5017	R	2*	<.1
1796	Northwind Industries Inc—*Garry Patla*	15500 Commerce Park Dr, Cleveland OH 44142	216-433-0666	R	2*	<.1
1797	Har-Son Manufacturing Inc—*R Harris*	7 Palmer St, Gowanda NY 14070	716-532-2641	R	2*	<.1
1798	Mega Tool and Manufacturing Corp—*Craig Spencer*	1023 Caton Ave, Elmira NY 14904	607-734-5057	R	2*	<.1
1799	Metal-Line Corp—*Joe Balaskovitz*	237 Renaissance Dr, Manistee MI 49660	231-723-7041	R	2*	<.1
1800	Orc-O Tool and Machine Inc—*Roger Watson*	701 S Prairie St, Cuba MO 65453	573-885-4286	R	2*	<.1
1801	Quality Aircraft Tooling Inc—*Benny Mccleskey*	1048 King Industrial D, Marietta GA 30062	770-429-8157	R	2*	<.1
1802	Robinson-Latva Company LLP—*Dana Persells*	PO Box 1235, Alexander City AL 35011	256-329-8481	R	2*	<.1
1803	D and G Manufacturing Inc—*David Dallapiazza*	107 Jennifer Ln, Eden WI 53019	920-477-3609	R	2*	<.1
1804	Digital Machine Company Inc—*Gregory Schmitt*	1055 Louis Dr Ste B, Warminster PA 18974	215-672-6454	R	2*	<.1
1805	Lamb's Machine Works Inc—*James Lamb*	296 E Mallory Ave, Memphis TN 38109	901-775-0663	R	2*	<.1
1806	CNC Industries Inc—*J Morgan*	PO Box 1667, Fairmont WV 26555	304-366-8262	R	2*	<.1
1807	General Machine Inc—*Joseph Kreher*	6038 Schiermeier Rd, Freeburg IL 62243	618-234-1919	R	2*	<.1
1808	International Precision Inc—*Ron Brendel*	PO Box 4839, Chatsworth CA 91313	818-882-3933	R	2*	<.1

Rank	Company Name—*Executive Officer*	Address, City, State, Zip	Phone	Type	Fin	Empls
1809	Quality Fabrication Inc—*Dale Holt*	555 Brown Ln, Madisonville KY 42431	270-824-9791	R	2*	<.1
1810	Radke Machine and Tool Inc—*Donald Radke*	603 Ne 4th St, Hubbard TX 76648	254-576-2513	R	2*	<.1
1811	Toolex Inc—*Marcel Carrascosa*	7570 Morley St, Houston TX 77061	713-644-8071	R	2*	<.1
1812	Beamaco LLC—*Mike Lodel*	PO Box 97, Manitowoc WI 54221	920-686-2326	R	2*	<.1
1813	Fulton Tool Company Inc—*Bruce Phelps*	802 W Broadway Ste 1, Fulton NY 13069	315-598-2900	R	2*	<.1
1814	J Brisbois Tool Sales and Service Inc—*Michael Brisbois*	15040 Cleat St, Plymouth MI 48170	734-455-1144	R	2*	<.1
1815	Monks Manufacturing Company Inc—*Ian Monks*	1 Upton Dr, Wilmington MA 01887	978-657-8282	R	2*	<.1
1816	S and D Machine and Tool Inc—*Warren Daniels*	1404 Old Oxford Hwy, Durham NC 27704	919-479-8433	R	2*	<.1
1817	Tdl Tool Inc—*Steve Mangan*	1296 S Patton St, Xenia OH 45385	937-374-0055	R	2*	<.1
1818	Alfa Machine and Tool Company Inc—*Gary Serio*	19 Just Rd, Fairfield NJ 07004	973-227-1962	R	2*	<.1
1819	Apollo Precision Machining Inc—*Joe Mankowski*	4085 Ralph Jones Dr, South Bend IN 46628	574-271-1197	R	2*	<.1
1820	B and B Tool Co—*Kent Akerman*	5005 27th Ave, Rockford IL 61109	815-229-5792	R	2*	<.1
1821	B and S Machine Tool Inc—*Bart Blackwell*	PO Box 1141, Aiken SC 29802	803-648-1826	R	2*	<.1
1822	Beckman Machine Inc—*Mary Lynch*	PO Box 37655, Cincinnati OH 45222	513-242-2700	R	2*	<.1
1823	Classic Precision Inc—*Lawrence Waligorski*	48009 Anna Ct, Wixom MI 48393	248-349-8811	R	2*	<.1
1824	Deland Manufacturing Inc—*Dennis Wygocki*	50674 Central Industri, Shelby Township MI 48315	586-323-2350	R	2*	<.1
1825	Don's Machine Shop Inc—*Donald Eifert*	777 Ash St, West Pittston PA 18643	570-655-1950	R	2*	<.1
1826	Dynamic Jig Grinding Corp—*John Eckhout*	1000 Livernois Rd, Troy MI 48083	248-589-3110	R	2*	<.1
1827	Epic Machine Inc—*Michael Parker*	201 Industrial Way Ste, Fenton MI 48430	810-629-9400	R	2*	<.1
1828	Farmer Mold And Machine Works Inc—*James Gilmour*	3101 46th Ave N, Saint Petersburg FL 33714	727-522-0515	R	2*	<.1
1829	Giordano Inc—*Michael Giordano*	840 Mill Rd, Bensalem PA 19020	215-639-7650	R	2*	<.1
1830	Guide Engineering LLC—*Steve Armey*	5505 Distribution Dr, Fort Wayne IN 46825	260-483-1153	R	2*	<.1
1831	Hartzell Machine Works Inc—*Richard Hartzell*	3354 Market St, Aston PA 19014	610-485-3502	R	2*	<.1
1832	Hoefner Corp—*Gerald Hoefner*	9722 Rush St, South El Monte CA 91733	626-443-3258	R	2*	<.1
1833	Krisalis Inc—*William Kannenberg*	28216 Industrial Blvd, Hayward CA 94545	510-786-0858	R	2*	<.1
1834	Master Machining Inc—*James Carter*	410 Hermitage Rd, Castle Hayne NC 28429	910-675-3660	R	2*	<.1
1835	North Carolina Manufacturing Inc—*Ray Mayo*	100 Industry Ct, Goldsboro NC 27530	919-734-1115	R	2*	<.1
1836	Pace Machine Tool Inc—*Linda Hobbel*	1144 Rig St, Commerce Township MI 48390	248-960-9903	R	2*	<.1
1837	Precision Machining Sheet Metal Inc—*Eric Olsen*	2250 N Forbes Blvd Ste, Tucson AZ 85745	520-622-0050	R	2*	<.1
1838	Quality Contour Inc—*Brian Bernloehr*	21323 Heywood Ave, Lakeville MN 55044	952-985-5050	R	2*	<.1
1839	Sienko Precision LLC—*Teresa Laskoc*	10102 Sussex Ln, Houston TX 77041	713-462-7482	R	2*	<.1
1840	Standley Brothers Machine Company Inc—*John Standley*	PO Box 85, Beverly MA 01915	978-927-0278	R	2*	<.1
1841	Tool Technology Corp—*James Reid*	PO Box 937, Inman SC 29349	864-472-1867	R	2*	<.1
1842	Unique Machine Co—*Robert Barndt*	131 Commerce Dr, Montgomeryville PA 18936	215-368-8550	R	2*	<.1
1843	Wildridge Machine LLC—*Judy Johnson*	163 Bud Crockett Dr, Lexington TN 38351	731-967-4900	R	2*	<.1
1844	Highland Tool Company Inc—*Donald Boulia*	20 Simon St, Nashua NH 03060	603-882-6907	R	2*	<.1
1845	Utec Metals Inc—*Thomas Best*	17305 E Euclid Ave, Spokane Valley WA 99216	509-922-1832	R	2*	<.1
1846	Gli-Dex Sales Corp—*James Gerace*	855 Wurlitzer Dr, North Tonawanda NY 14120	716-692-6501	R	2*	<.1
1847	Spartan Precision Machining Corp—*George Pappas*	9 Niagara Ave, Freeport NY 11520	516-546-5171	R	2*	<.1
1848	John Prosock Machine Inc—*John Prosock*	2250 Trumbauersville R, Quakertown PA 18951	215-804-0321	R	2*	<.1
1849	Riddle Machine Co—*Jack Riddle*	12951 Sunnyside Pl, Santa Fe Springs CA 90670	714-549-0357	R	2*	<.1
1850	Hartig Industries Inc—*Stephen Hartig*	682 E Lincoln Ave, Columbus OH 43229	614-885-6029	R	2*	<.1
1851	Qtm Inc—*Richard Peck*	300 Stevens Ave, Oldsmar FL 34677	813-891-1300	R	2*	<.1
1852	Oilco Machine Shop Inc—*Russell Mire*	1323 Eraste Landry Rd, Lafayette LA 70506	337-234-8508	R	2*	<.1
1853	Pioneer Precision Products Inc—*Marian Rozycki*	PO Box 396, Berlin CT 06037	860-828-5838	R	2*	<.1
1854	Tombigbee Tooling Inc—*Dewayne Thornton*	PO Box 280, Mantachie MS 38855	662-282-4273	R	2*	<.1
1855	White-Brook Inc—*Thomas Dinger*	1 Sylvania St, Brookville PA 15825	814-849-8441	R	2*	<.1
1856	Ellis Tool and Machine Inc—*David Ellis*	PO Box 710, Tom Bean TX 75489	903-546-6540	R	2*	<.1
1857	Precision Results Manufacturing Inc—*Kent Paulson*	210 17th St Sw, Jamestown ND 58401	701-252-0875	R	2*	<.1
1858	RW Machine Inc—*Richard Wyman*	PO Box 670348, Houston TX 77267	281-784-1600	R	2*	<.1
1859	Appalachian Machine Inc—*Jerry Jones*	PO Box 1507, Dublin VA 24084	540-674-1914	R	2*	<.1
1860	Integrity Saw and Tool Inc—*Paul Reetz*	507 W Rolling Meadows, Fond Du Lac WI 54937	920-923-4474	R	2*	<.1
1861	Linear Measurement Instruments Corp—*Ernest Booker*	101 N Alloy Dr Ste B, Fenton MI 48430	810-714-5811	R	2*	<.1
1862	Nebraska Welding Ltd—*Alan Wear*	13600 Giles Rd, Omaha NE 68138	402-895-6500	R	2*	<.1
1863	Albertson and Hein Inc—*Jim Hein*	3617 Walker St, Wichita KS 67213	316-943-7441	R	2*	<.1
1864	B and H Technical Ceramics—*Gunther Horn*	390 Industrial Rd, San Carlos CA 94070	650-637-1171	R	2*	<.1
1865	Cape Haze Investments Ltd—*Chris Allender*	10159 Sw Commerce Cir, Wilsonville OR 97070	503-582-0405	R	2*	<.1
1866	Cmmc Machine Inc—*Michael Rowland*	2081 Hayter St, North Charleston SC 29405	843-554-0993	R	2*	<.1
1867	Creative Machine Co—*Gordon Boring*	50140 Pontiac Trl, Wixom MI 48393	248-669-4230	R	2*	<.1
1868	Ecm Photo Tooling Inc—*Howard Lewis*	58157 Charlotte Ave, Elkhart IN 46517	574-295-0189	R	2*	<.1
1869	Fitech Inc—*Thomas Fitzgerald*	2031 Tryon Rd, Michigan City IN 46360	219-879-4177	R	2*	<.1
1870	Fox Valley Machining Company Inc—*Joseph Kawa*	198 Poplar Pl, North Aurora IL 60542	630-859-0700	R	2*	<.1
1871	Horton Machine And Custom Design Inc—*Gary Horton*	PO Box 489, Heath Springs SC 29058	803-273-3595	R	2*	<.1
1872	Industrial Machine And Fabrication Inc—*James Bennett*	PO Box 181242, Memphis TN 38181	901-365-1400	R	2*	<.1
1873	JIMachine Company Inc—*Ila Piel*	9720 Distribution Ave, San Diego CA 92121	858-695-1787	R	2*	<.1
1874	Johnson Pattern and Machine Works Inc—*Esther Johnson*	350 W Marquette St, Ottawa IL 61350	815-433-2775	R	2*	<.1
1875	L and M Machine Inc—*Ann Moran*	PO Box 6041, Chelsea MA 02150	617-389-3069	R	2*	<.1
1876	Magee Machine And Manufacturing Inc—*Michael Magee*	3535 Executive Blvd, Mesquite TX 75149	972-285-2554	R	2*	<.1
1877	Magna Tool Inc—*Bob Melton*	5594 Market Pl, Cypress CA 90630	714-826-2500	R	2*	<.1
1878	Mardinly Enterprises LLC—*Anna Weir*	701 Pky, Broomall PA 19008	610-544-9490	R	2*	<.1
1879	Material Transfer And Storage Inc—*Scott Nyhof*	PO Box 218, Allegan MI 49010	269-673-2125	R	2*	<.1
1880	Nikolic Industries Inc—*Martha Nikolic*	43252 Merrill Rd, Sterling Heights MI 48314	586-254-4810	R	2*	<.1
1881	North East Cutting Die Corp—*Mark Geller*	PO Box 6858, Portsmouth NH 03802	603-436-8952	R	2*	<.1
1882	Performex Machining Co—*Joseph Iffla*	963 Terminal Way, San Carlos CA 94070	650-595-2228	R	2*	<.1
1883	Pettey Machine Works Inc—*Bill Pettey*	PO Box 729, Trinity AL 35673	256-355-0085	R	2*	<.1
1884	Reymond Products International Inc—*Greg Dean*	PO Box 202, Midvale OH 44653	330-339-3583	R	2*	<.1
1885	T and M Machining Inc—*Mario Mangone*	331 Irving Dr, Oxnard CA 93030	805-983-6716	R	2*	<.1
1886	Tri-C Machine Corp—*Clyde Lamar*	520 Harbor Blvd, West Sacramento CA 95691	916-371-8090	R	2*	<.1
1887	W Haut Specialty Company Inc—*John Haut*	N56 W13664 Silver Spg, Menomonee Falls WI 53051	262-790-0425	R	2*	<.1
1888	William Kenyon and Sons Inc—*William Clark*	90 Ethel Rd W, Piscataway NJ 08854	732-985-8980	R	2*	<.1
1889	Williams Machine Works Inc—*David Hicks*	PO Box 8640, Moss Point MS 39562	228-475-7651	R	2*	<.1
1890	Micro Precision Of Texas Inc—*Greg Hummel*	PO Box 40146, Houston TX 77240	713-462-7599	R	2*	<.1
1891	CH Grinding Inc—*Ernest Treichler*	30062 Aventura, Rcho Sta Marg CA 92688	949-858-4613	R	2*	<.1
1892	Sellner Manufacturing Co—*Erin Ward*	515 Fowler St, Faribault MN 55021	507-334-5584	R	2*	<.1
1893	S and S Welding Company Inc—*Tom Young*	416 35th Ave Ne Ste 1, Minneapolis MN 55418	612-788-2001	R	2*	<.1
1894	Boulevard Machine and Gear Inc—*Susan Kasa*	785 Page Blvd, Springfield MA 01104	413-788-6466	R	2*	<.1
1895	Wheeler Industries Inc—*Loyde Wheeler*	1118 N Howe Rd, Spokane Valley WA 99212	509-534-4556	R	2*	<.1
1896	Custom Machine Works Inc—*Ralph Magouirk*	PO Box 245, West Monroe LA 71294	318-325-6844	R	2*	<.1
1897	Moral's Precision Machine Manufacturing Company Inc—*William Moral*	PO Box 1457, Florence SC 29503	843-395-0982	R	2*	<.1

Note: An asterisk (*) indicates an estimated financial figure. The company type code used is as follows: R = Private, P = Public, S = Private Subsidiary, B = Public Subsidiary, D = Division, J = Joint Venture, I = Investment Fund.

COMPANY RANKINGS BY SALES WITHIN 4-DIGIT SIC

Rank	Company Name—Executive Officer	Address, City, State, Zip	Phone	Type	Fin	Empls
1898	Steel Products Corporation of Akron—*William Welsh*	1699 Commerce Dr, Stow OH 44224	330-688-6633	R	2*	<.1
1899	Bellwether Inc—*Robert Jenkins*	PO Box 190, Mcdonough GA 30253	770-957-6651	R	2*	<.1
1900	Alliance Machine Tool Company Inc—*Janet Margerum*	524 Baxter Ave, Louisville KY 40204	502-587-6224	R	2*	<.1
1901	Aqua Tool LLC	32360 Edward Ave Ste 1, Madison Heights MI 48071	248-307-1984	R	2*	<.1
1902	Daven Industries Inc—*Lou Lever*	5 Just Rd, Fairfield NJ 07004	973-808-8848	R	2*	<.1
1903	Evden Enterprises Inc—*Dennis Grath*	2000 Wellmar Dr, Ukiah CA 95482	707-462-0375	R	2*	<.1
1904	Global Manufacturing Of Acadiana Inc—*Mike Klipstein*	PO Box 80534, Lafayette LA 70598	337-237-1727	R	2*	<.1
1905	Globe Products Inc—*James Kroencke*	5051 Kitridge Rd, Dayton OH 45424	937-233-0233	R	2*	<.1
1906	Grimm Mold and Die Company Inc—*Timothy Grimm*	PO Box 218, Rolling Prairie IN 46371	219-778-4211	R	2*	<.1
1907	H G Steinmetz Machine Works Inc—*John Michelotti*	2 Turnage Ln, Bethel CT 06801	203-327-0118	R	2*	<.1
1908	Holland Manufacturing Inc—*Willard Holland*	6851 51st St, Kenosha WI 53144	262-654-5300	R	2*	<.1
1909	Horst Equipment Repair Inc—*Karen Thibado*	PO Box 1224, Pell City AL 35125	205-338-4763	R	2*	<.1
1910	J and R Machine Works—*Jesse Alvarado*	45420 60th St W, Lancaster CA 93536	661-945-8826	R	2*	<.1
1911	Jorgensen Machining Corp—*James Jorgensen*	15601 W Lincoln Ave, New Berlin WI 53151	262-786-1070	R	2*	<.1
1912	JR Higgins Associates LLC—*Stanley Crowell*	898 Main St, Acton MA 01720	978-266-1200	R	2*	<.1
1913	K and S Machine Manufacturing Inc—*Temothy Cho*	2586 Seaboard Ave, San Jose CA 95131	408-526-1123	R	2*	<.1
1914	Leach's Industrial Service Inc—*Mary Leach*	2508 Industrial Ct, Grand Junction CO 81505	970-242-3813	R	2*	<.1
1915	Linear and Metric Co—*Leonard Galvin*	PO Box 233, Londonderry NH 03053	603-432-1700	R	2*	<.1
1916	Norfolk Machine And Welding Inc—*Bobby Mallard*	1019 W 41st St, Norfolk VA 23508	757-489-0330	R	2*	<.1
1917	Sherman Machine Inc—*Richard Harris*	PO Box 102, Sherman TX 75091	903-892-2889	R	2*	<.1
1918	Sollami Co—*Phillip Sollami*	PO Box 627, Herrin IL 62948	618-988-1521	R	2*	<.1
1919	Millennium Three LLC—*Rich Mcnett*	PO Box 775, Platteville WI 53818	608-348-5045	R	2*	<.1
1920	Ragsdale Industries Inc—*Mark Woelfel*	3870 S Kalamath St, Englewood CO 80110	303-781-8234	R	2*	<.1
1921	H T Specialty Inc—*Russel Thiel*	70 Bermar Park, Rochester NY 14624	585-458-4060	R	2*	<.1
1922	Fullenkamp Machine and Manufacturing Inc—*Richard Fullenkamp*	1507 N Meridian St, Portland IN 47371	260-726-8345	R	2*	<.1
1923	Crumpler's Machine and Welding Service Inc—*James Crumpler*	PO Box 848, Bridge City TX 77611	409-735-5356	R	2*	<.1
1924	Crystal Welding Inc—*Michelle Labrosse*	17601 113th Ave N, Maple Grove MN 55369	763-428-8281	R	2*	<.1
1925	Gardner Products Co—*Robert Gardner*	20530 Plummer St, Chatsworth CA 91311	818-998-8181	R	2*	<.1
1926	R And L Machine Shop Inc—*Kenneth Roth*	2900 Yadkin Rd, Chesapeake VA 23323	757-487-8879	R	2*	<.1
1927	Milko Tool and Die Inc—*Dennis Miller*	2405 N 11th St Ste A, Omaha NE 68110	402-345-2923	R	2*	<.1
1928	Trepanning Specialty A California Corp—*Donald Laughlin*	16201 Illinois Ave, Paramount CA 90723	562-633-8110	R	2*	<.1
1929	RWK Tool Inc—*William Buggie*	200 Corporate Row, Cromwell CT 06416	860-635-0116	R	2*	<.1
1930	Turning Inc—*Kristin Kooiker*	13820 Industrial Pk Bl, Plymouth MN 55441	763-450-7990	R	2*	<.1
1931	A To Z Machining Service LLC—*Sharon Tows*	PO Box 2586, Ponca City OK 74602	580-765-1306	R	2*	<.1
1932	Lee-Lynn Machining Inc—*Bradley Murrell*	2200 Concrete Rd, Carlisle KY 40311	859-289-4402	R	2*	<.1
1933	Mountaineer Manufacturing Inc—*Robert Gilliam*	PO Box 488, Smithers WV 25186	304-442-2454	R	2*	<.1
1934	Prentice Machine Works JR—*William Hogan*	7325 Ne 55th Ave, Portland OR 97218	503-285-1718	R	2*	<.1
1935	Advanced Components Manufacturing—*Craig Corey*	1415 N Carolan Ave 2, Burlingame CA 94010	650-344-6272	R	2*	<.1
1936	Aircraft Cylinders Of America Inc—*Rama Palepu*	1006 E Independence St, Tulsa OK 74106	918-582-1785	R	2*	<.1
1937	Consolidated Hinge And Manufactured Products—*Karl Herbst*	1150b Dell Ave, Campbell CA 95008	408-379-6550	R	2*	<.1
1938	GL Tool and Manufacturing Company Inc—*Gerhard Liepold*	26 Okner Pkwy, Livingston NJ 07039	973-740-0001	R	2*	<.1
1939	Harbor Island Machine Works Inc—*Michael Defaccio*	3431 11th Ave Sw, Seattle WA 98134	206-682-7637	R	2*	<.1
1940	Headco Machine Works Inc (Keokukk Iowa)—*Frank Timble*	2666 Kindustry Park Rd, Keokuk IA 52632	319-524-1804	R	2*	<.1
1941	M and W Engineering Inc—*Frank Marsh*	3880 Dividend Dr Ste 1, Shingle Springs CA 95682	530-676-7185	R	2*	<.1
1942	Maverick Machine Tool—*Jim Dominique*	PO Box 647, Marshall MI 49068	269-789-1617	R	2*	<.1
1943	Mc Bride's Research and Machine Inc—*Rex Bride*	1345 E Glendale Ave, Sparks NV 89431	775-358-0201	R	2*	<.1
1944	MI Inc—*Steve Orand*	2007 Lamar Dr, Round Rock TX 78664	512-244-3676	R	2*	<.1
1945	Neptune Machine Inc—*Nicholas Karkas*	521 Carroll St, Brooklyn NY 11215	718-852-4100	R	2*	<.1
1946	Sattler Companies Inc—*David Sattler*	PO Box 306, Sharon Center OH 44274	330-239-2552	R	2*	<.1
1947	Southfield Machining Services Inc—*Jackie Souther*	5659 Southfield Dr, Flowery Branch GA 30542	770-965-2570	R	2*	<.1
1948	Stamler Rfi—*Gerald Stamler*	828 S 17th St, Louisville KY 40210	502-585-1520	R	2*	<.1
1949	T Precision Machining Inc—*Tom Finger*	123 Lyman St, Asheville NC 28801	828-250-0993	R	2*	<.1
1950	Winchester Tool LLC—*Scott Cole* Fabritek Company Inc	110a Industrial Dr, Winchester VA 22602	540-869-1150	S	2*	<.1
1951	Commercial Machine Inc—*Robert Jones*	2706 Rady St, Richmond VA 23222	804-329-5405	R	2*	<.1
1952	York Precision Inc—*Robert Mc Cutcheon*	6531 Charlotte Hwy, York SC 29745	803-831-7395	R	2*	<.1
1953	Tarheel Tooling and Precision Machining Inc—*Bobby Pilkington*	PO Box 1063, Smithfield NC 27577	919-965-6160	R	2*	<.1
1954	Giles and Ransome Inc—*Wayne Bromley*	2975 Galloway Rd, Bensalem PA 19020	215-639-4300	R	2*	.6
1955	Bartley Machine and Manufacturing Company Inc—*Richard Bartley*	35 Water St, Amesbury MA 01913	978-388-0085	R	2*	.1
1956	Strong Forge and Fabrication LLC—*Debbie Buchinger*	PO Box 803, Batavia NY 14021	585-343-5251	R	2*	<.1
1957	Ebert Machine Company Inc—*Joel Ebert*	2177 S State Rd 19, Peru IN 46970	765-473-3728	R	2*	<.1
1958	Britt Metal Processing Inc—*Juan Vega*	15800 NW 49th Ave, Miami FL 33014	305-621-5200	R	2*	<.1
1959	Rincon Engineering Corp—*Roger Hugo*	6325 Carpinteria Ave, Carpinteria CA 93013	805-684-4144	R	2*	<.1
1960	R and R Tool Manufacturing Inc—*Mike Rollins*	PO Box 397, La Porte IN 46352	219-325-9222	R	2*	<.1
1961	E and R Machine Inc—*Garry Sauls*	PO Box 499, Lockport NY 14095	716-434-6639	R	2*	<.1
1962	Eastside Machine Company Inc	PO Box 2426, Fargo ND 58108	701-235-3626	R	2*	<.1
1963	Gasdorf Tool And Machine Company Inc—*Richard Rapp*	PO Box 1194, Lima OH 45802	419-227-0103	R	2*	<.1
1964	JIT Tool and Die Inc—*Robert Beimel*	7294 Rt 219, Brockport PA 15823	814-265-0257	R	2*	<.1
1965	Marshall Manufacturing Co (Minneapolis Minnesota)—*John Timmersman*	3820 Chandler Dr, Minneapolis MN 55421		R	2*	
1966	Sroka Industries Inc—*John Sroka*	PO Box 360047, Strongsville OH 44136	440-572-2811	R	2*	<.1
1967	Wartburg Tool and Die Inc—*John Dagley*	1738 Knoxville Hwy, Wartburg TN 37887	423-346-6427	R	2*	<.1
1968	JB Tool and Die Company Inc—*Frank Tabone*	629 Main St, Westbury NY 11590	516-333-1480	R	2*	<.1
1969	UPI Of Alabama Inc—*Shirley Miller*	PO Box 14100, Mexico Beach FL 32410	334-702-8720	R	2*	<.1
1970	R P N Inc—*George Haggard*	PO Box 3099, Morristown TN 37815	423-586-8663	R	2*	<.1
1971	Regal Machine and Engineering Inc—*Val Darie*	5200 E 60th St, Maywood CA 90270	323-773-7462	R	2*	<.1
1972	Caudell's Machine and Tooling Inc—*Bobby Caudell*	PO Box 220, Homer GA 30547	706-335-5895	R	2*	<.1
1973	A-1 Machine Inc—*Roger Shay*	PO Box 185, Farmington NM 87499	505-327-9572	R	2*	<.1
1974	Brackett And Cochran Manufacturing Inc—*Neil Brackett*	5 Corporate Pkwy, Goose Creek SC 29445	843-553-2021	R	2*	<.1
1975	C And H Tooling Inc—*Kevin Creasmen*	95 Fairmont Rd, Candler NC 28715	828-667-0575	R	2*	<.1
1976	Christy Industries Inc (Fraser Michigan)—*Mark Judkins*	18320 Malyn Blvd, Fraser MI 48026	586-293-8800	R	2*	<.1
1977	Eastern Science Company Inc—*Richard Alfoni*	PO Box 774, Rowley MA 01969	978-948-7300	R	2*	<.1
1978	Ethylene Atlantic Corp—*Michael Johnston*	PO Box 430, Swedesboro NJ 08085	856-467-0010	R	2*	<.1
1979	JFK Machine Inc—*Joel Kowalski*	2201 Park St, Muskegon MI 49444	231-739-9165	R	2*	<.1
1980	Lyn-Weld Company Inc—*Joan Bilbow*	633 Fellows Ave, Wilkes Barre PA 18706	570-823-0049	R	2*	<.1
1981	Parkway-Kew Corp—*Eugene Klein*	2095 Excelsior Ave, North Brunswick NJ 08902	732-398-2100	R	2*	<.1
1982	Rendas Tool and Die Inc—*Laszlo Rendas*	PO Box 49, Martinsville NJ 08836	732-469-4670	R	2*	<.1

Rank	Company Name—*Executive Officer*	Address, City, State, Zip	Phone	Type	Fin	Empls
1983	Sandberg Enterprises Inc—*Robert Sandberg*	PO Box 779, Chepachet RI 02814	401-568-1602	R	2*	<.1
1984	American Precision Manufacturing LLC—*Leigh Dawid*	26 Beaver St Ste 1, Ansonia CT 06401	203-734-1800	R	2*	<.1
1985	Erickson Corp—*Don Erickson*	PO Box 527, Du Bois PA 15801	814-371-4350	R	2*	<.1
1986	Maritec Corp—*R Daly*	PO Box 5497, Greenville SC 29606	864-277-7782	R	2*	<.1
1987	Sims Machining—*Lynn Sims*	3506 Sardis Hwy, Timmonsville SC 29161	843-346-4891	R	2*	<.1
1988	Unity Tool Inc—*Ronald Van Essen*	11660 Troy Ln, Dayton MN 55369	763-428-9888	R	2*	<.1
1989	Parker Industries Inc (Connelly Springs North Carolina)—*Jeff Parker*	4867 Rhoney Rd, Connellys Springs NC 28612	828-437-7779	R	2*	<.1
1990	Peacock Industries Inc—*Kit Bull*	254 S M 37, Baldwin MI 49304	231-745-4609	R	2*	<.1
1991	Brown Machine Works Inc—*Kenneth Brown*	8459 Wards Rd, Rustburg VA 24588	434-821-5008	R	2*	<.1
1992	Remarque Manufacturing Corp—*Joseph Panholzer*	35 Research Dr, Hampton VA 23666	757-766-3535	R	2*	<.1
1993	Vanpro Inc—*Gene Alstine*	725 3rd Ave SE, Cambridge MN 55008	763-689-1559	R	2*	<.1
1994	Apex Tool and Manufacturing Inc—*Bill Hodgson*	2306 N New York Ave, Evansville IN 47711	812-425-8121	R	2*	<.1
1995	Catoe's Welding and Fabrication Inc—*Jimmy Catoe*	PO Box 12014, Rock Hill SC 29731	803-324-8500	R	2*	<.1
1996	Econo Machine Inc—*Bernard Dick*	220 W 14th St, Chanute KS 66720	620-431-3303	R	2*	<.1
1997	Tri-Tech Engineering Inc—*Mark Circo*	3663 11th St, Wyandotte MI 48192	734-283-3700	R	2*	<.1
1998	Vanco Tool Inc—*Bo Sheiverick*	PO Box 807, Chardon OH 44024	440-286-2007	R	2*	<.1
1999	Accurate Industrial Machining Inc—*Jerome Bricker*	35 W Jefryn Blvd Ste 2, Deer Park NY 11729	631-242-0566	R	2*	<.1
2000	Action Precision Products Inc—*Linda Heisler*	100 E N Ave, Pioneer OH 43554	419-737-2348	R	2*	<.1
2001	Amwell Machine and Fabrication Inc—*Harold Burt*	450 Crile Rd, Washington PA 15301	724-229-0750	R	2*	<.1
2002	ATC Inc—*Karin Riedel*	4077 Calle Tesoro, Camarillo CA 93012	805-482-1280	R	2*	<.1
2003	Barron Machine and Fabrication Inc—*Connie Sherrod*	PO Box 395, Fairfield AL 35064	205-781-5010	R	2*	<.1
2004	Byford Machine-Tool Inc—*Robert Hoffmann*	PO Box 646, Valley Mills TX 76689	254-932-6111	R	2*	<.1
2005	CAD Cut Inc—*R Ward Osgood*	PO Box 856, Marblehead MA 01945	802-223-4055	R	2*	<.1
2006	Conner Engineering Inc—*Robert Olson*	21200 Carlo Dr, Clinton Township MI 48038	586-465-9590	R	2*	<.1
2007	Davies Precision Machining Inc—*Pearl Davies*	2400 Colebrook Rd, Lebanon PA 17042	717-273-5495	R	2*	<.1
2008	Dynak Inc—*Bob Vorndran*	33 Saginaw Dr, Rochester NY 14623	585-271-2255	R	2*	<.1
2009	G and G Products LLC	282 River St, Springvale ME 04083	207-490-2729	R	2*	<.1
2010	Gilson Machine and Tool Company Inc—*William Gilson*	529 Freedom Dr, Napoleon OH 43545	419-592-2911	R	2*	<.1
2011	Grinding Specialists Inc—*Dennis Johnson*	38310 Abruzzi Dr, Westland MI 48185	734-729-1775	R	2*	<.1
2012	Jack C Drees Grinding Company Inc—*Jack Drees*	11815 Vose St B, North Hollywood CA 91605	818-764-8301	R	2*	<.1
2013	Lane Tool and Manufacturing Company Inc—*Edward Arnicri*	800 Schneider Dr, South Elgin IL 60177	847-622-1506	R	2*	<.1
2014	Langa Tool and Machine Inc—*William Langa*	36430 Reading Ave Ste, Willoughby OH 44094	440-953-1130	R	2*	<1
2015	Larson Systems Inc—*David Larson*	10073 Baltimore St Ne, Minneapolis MN 55449	763-780-2131	R	2*	<.1
2016	Latham-Hall Corp—*Gary Dellinger*	5003 Ball Park Rd, Thomasville NC 27360	336-475-9723	R	2*	<.1
2017	Liddy's Machine Shop Inc—*Ted Gollnick*	825 Dora St, Jacksonville FL 32204	904-354-0134	R	2*	<.1
2018	Mikel Machine Inc—*R Quarles*	24792 Ford Rd, Porter TX 77365	281-354-2750	R	2*	<.1
2019	Owens Steel and Machine Works Inc—*William Owens*	PO Box 412, Myrtle Beach SC 29578	843-448-5050	R	2*	<.1
2020	Production Machining Inc—*Larry Bossier*	PO Box 80505, Seattle WA 98108	206-763-0840	R	2*	<.1
2021	Quenneville Enterprises Inc—*Ed Quenneville*	3261 Edward Ave, Santa Clara CA 95054	408-988-3228	R	2*	<.1
2022	Rassey Industries Inc—*Louis N Rassey*	50375 Central Industri, Shelby Township MI 48315	586-803-9500	R	2*	<.1
2023	Romar Machine and Tool Co—*Robert Thum*	521 Commerce St, Franklin Lakes NJ 07417	201-337-7111	R	2*	<.1
2024	Ronald L Jordan Co—*Ronald Jordan*	4271 Magnolia St, Pearland TX 77584	281-485-6626	R	2*	<.1
2025	Tech-Max Machine Inc—*Richard Malek*	1170 W Ardmore Ave, Itasca IL 60143	603-875-0054	R	2*	<.1
2026	Aiw-Alton Inc—*Valmiki Hoffberg*	PO Box 130, Windsor CT 06095	860-683-0731	R	2*	<.1
2027	Fleming Metal Fabricators—*Wade Fleming*	2810 S Tanager Ave, Los Angeles CA 90040	323-723-8203	R	2*	<.1
2028	Gain Industries Inc—*Jennifer Toetz*	9720 S 54th St, Franklin WI 53132	414-421-4500	R	2*	<.1
2029	General Machine Shop Inc—*Kenneth Hinehart*	6000 Columbia Park Rd, Hyattsville MD 20785	301-773-5050	R	2*	<.1
2030	Kms Machine Works Inc—*Charles Cronin*	447 Winthrop St, Taunton MA 02780	508-822-3151	R	2*	<.1
2031	VW Broaching Services—*Russell Roschman*	3250 W Lake St, Chicago IL 60624	773-533-9000	R	2*	<.1
2032	AAM-RO Corp—*Richard Carey*	3110 S 26th Ave, Broadview IL 60155	708-343-5543	R	2*	<.1
2033	Bristol Tool And Die Inc—*Brian Price*	17992 Commerce Dr, Bristol IN 46507	574-848-5354	R	2*	<.1
2034	Fenbar Pricision Machinists Inc—*Leonard Vallender*	633 Commerce St, Thornwood NY 10594	914-769-5506	R	2*	<.1
2035	Gvs Technologies LLC—*Jorge Leon*	21744 Beck Dr, Elkhart IN 46516	574-293-0974	R	2*	<.1
2036	Machine Center Inc—*James Mc Laughlin*	4344 Bridgeton Industr, Bridgeton MO 63044	314-739-3181	R	2*	<.1
2037	Nelgo Industries Inc—*Peter Goethel*	598 Airport Rd, Oceanside CA 92058	760-433-6434	R	2*	<.1
2038	Slater Precision Cutting Tool Manufacturing Inc—*Thomas Slater*	4712 68th Ave, Kenosha WI 53144	262-658-8626	R	2*	<.1
2039	A and A Machine And Welding LLC—*Patty Sanders*	135 Reed Rd, Jasper AL 35504	205-384-9436	R	2*	<.1
2040	Cunningham Engineering Inc—*Thomas Cunningham*	9 Electronics Ave, Danvers MA 01923	978-774-4169	R	2*	<.1
2041	Snyder Machine Company Inc—*Henry Snyder*	190 Walnut St, Saugus MA 01906	781-233-2080	R	2*	<.1
2042	Tri-State Electric And Machine Co—*Rod Vellenoweth*	1702 Wheeling Ave, Glen Dale WV 26038	304-845-4540	R	2*	<.1
2043	J and M Machine Inc—*John Stoneback*	1234 High St, Fairport Harbor OH 44077	440-357-1234	R	2*	<.1
2044	Metal Services Group	41690 Ivy St Ste C, Murrieta CA 92562	626-813-1180	R	2*	<.1
2045	Product Manufacturing Inc—*Delbert Remmen*	PO Box 190, Sherwood OR 97140	503-625-6196	R	2*	<.1
2046	Pro-Met Machining Inc—*Francis Parsons*	2441 Nw Eleven Mile Av, Gresham OR 97030	503-666-3510	R	2*	<.1
2047	Surface Manufacturing Inc—*Lee Baker*	2025 Airpark Ct Ste 10, Auburn CA 95602	530-235-6583	R	2*	<.1
2048	Boos Products Inc—*Bill Jewell*	20416 Kaiser Rd, Gregory MI 48137	734-498-2207	R	2*	<.1
2049	Container Machinery Incorporated - Versatile Machining Inc—*Bill Stevens*	4116 Cockrell Ave, Fort Worth TX 76133	817-589-2172	R	2*	<.1
2050	Core Assemblies Inc—*Cory Navoy*	21 Meadowbrook Ln Unit, Gilford NH 03249	603-293-0270	R	2*	<.1
2051	Ed Stiglic—*Ed Stiglic*	1125 Linda Vista Dr St, San Marcos CA 92078	760-744-7239	R	2*	<.1
2052	Mountain Precision Tool Company Inc—*Steven Drumheller*	451 Industrial Park Rd, Blacksburg VA 24060	540-552-0178	R	2*	<.1
2053	Valco Precision Works Inc—*Leo Valerio*	6131 Maywood Ave, Huntington Park CA 90255	323-582-6355	R	2*	<.1
2054	Vaportek Inc—*John D Bryson Jr*	W226N6339 Village Dr, Sussex WI 53089	262-246-5060	R	2*	<.1
2055	Pneumatic Systems Company Inc—*Rick Belew*	225 Sterling St, Jackson TN 38301	731-422-1999	R	2*	<.1
2056	H and M Machine Shop Inc—*Todd Horstman*	24656 State Rte 189, Fort Jennings OH 45844	419-453-3414	R	2*	<.1
2057	Motion Machine Co—*Danny Walters*	524 Mccormick Dr, Lapeer MI 48446	810-664-9901	R	2*	<.1
2058	PV Tool Company Inc—*Jeanne Valentini*	4910 Pineview Cir, Delray Beach FL 33445	516-333-8055	R	2*	<.1
2059	Dynasty Hydraulic/Machine Ltd—*Patricia Ryan*	PO Box 310, Glen Daniel WV 25844	304-934-7986	R	2*	<.1
2060	Membrane System Specialists Inc—*Gregory W Pesko*	PO Box 998, Wisconsin Rapids WI 54494	715-421-2333	R	2*	<.1
2061	Eckert Enterprises Ltd—*Frank Eckert*	6631 S Dateland Dr, Tempe AZ 85283	480-820-0380	R	2*	<.1
2062	DD Youells Machining Inc—*Daniel D Youells*	4529 Bethlehem Pike, Telford PA 18969	215-257-4109	R	2*	<.1
2063	Six-B Manufacturing Company Inc—*Dean Ballard*	PO Box 72, Wahoo NE 68066	402-443-4651	R	2*	<.1
2064	Taurus Numeric Tool Inc—*Mike Pudil*	213 Chelsea Rd, Monticello MN 55362	763-295-9202	S	2	.1
2065	Cerbaco Ltd—*Alan Flash*	809 Harrison St, Frenchtown NJ 08825	908-996-1333	R	2*	<.1
2066	North Country Engineering Inc—*Jean Clark*	106 John Taplin Rd, Derby VT 05829	802-766-5396	R	2*	<.1
2067	JW Appley And Son Inc—*Doug Jennings*	13215 38th St N, Clearwater FL 33762	727-572-4910	R	2*	<.1
2068	Fairfield Manufacturing Company Inc—*Raymond Marshalek*	213 Streibeigh Ln, Montourville PA 17754	570-368-8624	R	2*	<.1
2069	Grandeur Manufacturing Inc—*Mike Phillips*	PO Box 216, Jonesville NC 28642	336-526-2468	R	2*	<.1

Note: An asterisk (*) indicates an estimated financial figure. The company type code used is as follows: R = Private, P = Public, S = Private Subsidiary, B = Public Subsidiary, D = Division, J = Joint Venture, I = Investment Fund.

COMPANY RANKINGS BY SALES WITHIN 4-DIGIT SIC

Rank	Company Name—Executive Officer	Address, City, State, Zip	Phone	Type	Fin	Empls
2070	Reynolds and Company Inc—Gerald Reynolds	1916 S 25th St, Terre Haute IN 47802	812-232-5313	R	2*	<.1
2071	Alston Machine Company Inc—Ruth Craft	2 Commerce Dr, Pittsburgh PA 15239	412-795-1000	R	2*	<.1
2072	Badger Barrels Inc—Geraldine Stallman	PO Box 417, Bristol WI 53104	262-857-6950	R	2*	<.1
2073	Dynomach Precision Inc—Michael Olano	1146 Commercial Dr, Port Allen LA 70767	225-383-3119	R	2*	<.1
2074	Hose Technology Inc—Trajan Trajanovski	PO Box 206, Williamsport IN 47993	765-762-5501	R	2*	<.1
2075	Machining Solutions LLC—Gary Norris	PO Box 1889, Wichita Falls TX 76307	940-761-3030	R	2*	<.1
2076	Pleasant Gardens Machine Inc—Michael Queen	2708 Us 70 W, Marion NC 28752	828-724-4173	R	2*	<.1
2077	Precision Tool Work Inc—Forest Peltier	PO Box 9947, New Iberia LA 70562	337-364-1738	R	2*	<.1
2078	S and S Specialty Systems Inc—Patrick Germain	PO Box 536, Iron River WI 54847	715-372-8988	R	2*	<.1
2079	Schwartz Boring Company Inc—Robert Olson	24649 Mound Rd, Warren MI 48091	586-758-0774	R	2*	<.1
2080	Model Machine Company Inc—John Wahlhaupter	1401 S Haven St, Baltimore MD 21224	410-675-7585	R	2*	<.1
2081	Young Machine Inc—Anand Jagani	12282 Colony Ave, Chino CA 91710	909-464-0405	R	2*	<.1
2082	Aegis Sales and Engineering Inc—Joyce Armstrong	5411 Industrial Rd, Fort Wayne IN 46825	260-483-4160	R	2*	<.1
2083	Arrow Grinding Inc—John Goller	525 Vickers St, Tonawanda NY 14150	716-693-3333	R	2*	<.1
2084	Boyd Machine Company Inc—Robert Boyd	PO Box 64156, Souderton PA 18964	215-723-8941	R	2*	<.1
2085	Delong Manufacturing Company Inc—David Long	967 Parker Ct, Santa Clara CA 95050	408-727-3348	R	2*	<.1
2086	Dill Brothers Inc—William Dill	3401 20th St, Zion IL 60099	847-746-8323	R	2*	<.1
2087	EB Trottnow Machine Specialties Inc—Mary Pietsch	PO Box 29, Tonawanda NY 14151	716-694-0600	R	2*	<.1
2088	Precision Die- Cutting Inc—Lee Rademacher	PO Box 3078, Wilsonville OR 97070	503-685-9130	R	2*	<.1
2089	Service Machine Company Inc—Arthur Kneller	PO Box 2183, Loves Park IL 61130	815-654-2310	R	2*	<.1
2090	Darco Products Inc—Dennis Reasner	8406 Washington Pl Ne, Albuquerque NM 87113	505-828-0498	R	2*	<.1
2091	Graphite Electrodes Ltd—Patrick Martin	1311 N Sherman St, Bay City MI 48708	989-893-3635	R	2*	<.1
2092	Loveland Screw Machine Ltd—D Olsen	PO Box 1349, Berthoud CO 80513	970-532-3628	R	2*	<.1
2093	Loughlin Manufacturing Corp—Martin Loughlin	1601 9th Ave, Bohemia NY 11716	631-585-4422	R	2*	<.1
2094	Alpha-Omega Industries Inc—Bryan Gilbert	500 Plz Dr, Harrisonville MO 64701	816-380-4434	R	2*	<.1
2095	Dynasys Corp—Raymond Gomes	PO Box 2116, Westerly RI 02891	860-599-1872	R	2*	<.1
2096	Camano Mold Inc—Theresa Gilbertson	122 N E Camano Dr, Stanwood WA 98282	360-387-0961	R	2*	<.1
2097	Babeco Inc—Steven Hubnik	1101 Crlos Parker Blvd, Taylor TX 76574	512-352-5355	R	2*	<.1
2098	Midway Machine and Instrument Company Inc—John Mai	701 Oregon St Ste B, South Houston TX 77587	713-947-1102	R	2*	<.1
2099	Padgett Machine Tool Company Inc—Morris Padgett	4212 E Us Hwy 84, Gatesville TX 76528	254-865-9771	R	2*	<.1
2100	Ams Inc—Arthur Swanson	PO Box 1064, Saint Charles IL 60174	630-584-7291	R	2*	<.1
2101	Antrim Machine Products Inc—Gerald Witowski	PO Box 379, Mancelona MI 49659	231-587-9114	R	2*	<.1
2102	Grant-Pridco-Tube-Alloy—Mike Mcshane	410 Commercial Blvd, Broussard LA 70518	337-839-6000	R	2*	<.1
2103	Universal Wearparts Inc—Ted Weill	142 Old Hwy 98 W, Tylertown MS 39667	601-876-3442	R	2*	<.1
2104	4-D Engineering Inc—Ernie Thury	1635 W 144th St, Gardena CA 90247	310-532-2384	R	2*	<.1
2105	Avers Machine and Manufacturing Inc—Jerry Tyralski	4625 N Ronald St, Chicago IL 60706	708-867-3335	R	2*	<.1
2106	Camco Machining Inc—Richard Wright	115 Ben Abi Rd, Spartanburg SC 29307	864-579-7972	R	2*	<.1
2107	Capital City Machine Shop Inc—Charlotte Brown	PO Box 47938, Atlanta GA 30362	770-447-9545	R	2*	<.1
2108	Estes Machine Co—Stephanie Collins	256 Snowhill Dr, Mount Airy NC 27030	336-786-7680	R	2*	<.1
2109	Kilby Steel Company Inc—George Kilby	PO Box 2122, Anniston AL 36202	256-831-3010	R	2*	<.1
2110	Mcallister Machine Inc—James Mcallister	95 Industrial Park Rd, Saco ME 04072	207-282-8655	R	2*	<.1
2111	Campbell Grinding and Machine Inc—Kevin Latham	582 Benjamins Way, Lewisville TX 75057	972-221-2211	R	2*	<.1
2112	Mayfield Machine and Tool Inc—Brenda Ausenbaugh	PO Box 738, Mayfield KY 42066	270-247-0501	R	2*	<.1
2113	E and S Precision Machine Inc—Jim Elzner	4631 Enterprise Way, Modesto CA 95356	209-545-6161	R	2*	<.1
2114	Envision Tech Inc—Daniel Baur	4404 S 40th St, Saint Joseph MO 64503	816-232-0305	R	2*	<.1
2115	Markham Machine Company Inc—James Markham	160 N Union St, Akron OH 44304	330-762-7676	R	2*	<.1
2116	Metalrnite Corp—Michael Gendich	194 S Elizabeth St, Rochester MI 48307	248-651-9415	R	2*	<.1
2117	Reuther Engineering—Ken Rys	126 S 14th St, Newark NJ 07107	973-485-5800	R	2*	<.1
2118	West Machine and Tool Inc—Wayne West	PO Box 3503, Longview TX 75606	903-758-5401	R	2*	<.1
2119	Clay-Groomer Machine Shop Inc—Ellis Groomer	701 S Carlton Ave, Farmington NM 87401	505-327-7751	R	2*	<.1
2120	Cmi Technology Inc—John Howard	65 Haas Dr, Englewood OH 45322	937-832-2000	R	2*	<.1
2121	Jarvis Manufacturing Inc—Tony Grewal	195 Lewis Rd Ste 36, San Jose CA 95111	408-226-2600	R	2*	<.1
2122	Kodiak Machining Company Inc—Arthur Gaudet	PO Box 595, Ipswich MA 01938	978-356-9876	R	2*	<.1
2123	Milco Wire Edm Inc—Steven Miller	15221 Connector Ln, Huntington Beach CA 92649	714-373-0098	R	2*	<.1
2124	Mill and Motion Inc—Daniel Hala	5415 E Schaaf Rd Ste 1, Cleveland OH 44131	216-524-4000	R	2*	<.1
2125	Paul Schurman Machine Inc—Matthew Houghton	PO Box 999, Ridgefield WA 98642	360-887-3193	R	2*	<.1
2126	Geiger Manufacturing Inc—Roger Haack	PO Box 1449, Stockton CA 95201	209-464-7746	R	2*	<.1
2127	Dynatec Machine Inc—Donald Bonar	23 Spiral Dr, Florence KY 41042	859-371-7888	R	2*	<.1
2128	Rogar International Inc—Ronnie Clark	PO Box 6938, Toledo OH 43612	419-476-5500	R	2*	<.1
2129	Jem Tool and Manufacturing Co—Wesley Cassidy	797 Industrial Dr, Bensenville IL 60106	630-595-1686	R	2*	<.1
2130	Engineering Design Industries Inc—Loc Tran	9649 Rush St, South El Monte CA 91733	626-443-7741	EI	2*	<.1
2131	Antrim Machine Co—Sam Gates	PO Box 187, Greencastle PA 17225	717-369-3184	R	2*	<.1
2132	Delaware Tool and Machine Company Inc—Kevin Yum	544 Industrial Park Dr, Yeadon PA 19050	610-259-1810	R	2*	<.1
2133	Johnson Manufacturing Inc—Colleen Johnson	15201 Connector Ln, Huntington Beach CA 92649	714-903-0393	R	2*	<.1
2134	Washington Iron Works Inc—Scott Totten	400 E Lamar St, Sherman TX 75090	903-892-8145	R	2*	<.1
2135	Mark Precision Inc—Thomas Egan	70 Salmon St, Providence RI 02909	401-455-0558	R	2*	<.1
2136	Overbeck Machine—Wayne Overbeck	2620 Mission St, Santa Cruz CA 95060	831-425-5912	R	2*	<.1
2137	All Tool Company Inc—John Vinciguerra	899 Rahway Ave, Union NJ 07083	908-687-3636	R	2*	<.1
2138	Kelles Inc—Michael Patrick	20 Hoiles Dr Ste C, Kenilworth NJ 07033	908-241-9300	R	2*	<.1
2139	Kortzendorf Machine and Tool Inc—Tom Kortzendorf	1450 Sunday Dr, Indianapolis IN 46217	317-783-5449	R	2*	<.1
2140	Astro Precision Machine Inc—Troy Hasty	PO Box 491, Salem NH 03079	603-893-3700	R	2*	<.1
2141	Bliss Machine Inc—William Kanner	PO Box 145, Arcade NY 14009	585-492-5128	R	2*	<.1
2142	Causey Machine Works Inc—Maria Pantoja	12131 Science Dr, Orlando FL 32826	407-277-7570	R	2*	<.1
2143	Sigma Engineering and Consulting Inc—Robert Bruno	220 Lincoln Blvd Ste A, Middlesex NJ 08846	732-356-3046	R	2*	<.1
2144	Sugaro Corp—Patrick Hart	1971 W Mcmillan St, Tucson AZ 85705	520-293-7818	R	2*	<.1
2145	Ultra-Metric Tool Co—Steven Huy	2952 N Leavitt St, Chicago IL 60618	773-281-4200	R	2*	<.1
2146	Acal Universal Grinding Co—Joseph Elsesser	20200 Cornillie Dr, Roseville MI 48066	586-296-3900	R	2*	<.1
2147	GP Manufacturing Inc—Greg Gilbert	541 W Briardale Ave, Orange CA 92865	714-974-0288	R	2*	<.1
2148	Pacific Roller Die Company Inc—Baris Degertekin	1321 W Winton Ave, Hayward CA 94545	510-782-7242	R	2*	<.1
2149	H and S Machine Company Inc—George Younker	PO Box 897, Lawrence MA 01842	978-686-2321	R	2*	<.1
2150	Tennessee Metal Works Inc—Dale Isaacs	1887 Elm Tree Dr, Nashville TN 37210	615-871-0300	R	2*	<.1
2151	Heinhold Engineering and Machine Company Inc—Kenneth Heinhold	1261 S Redwood Rd Ste, Salt Lake City UT 84104	801-972-0109	R	2*	<.1
2152	Machined Metals Manufacturing Inc—Matthias Soehn	1450 Jarvis Ave, Elk Grove Village IL 60007	847-364-6116	R	2*	<.1
2153	Pahl Tool Service—Peter Pinaha	12213 Sprecher Ave, Cleveland OH 44135	216-433-1711	R	2*	<.1
2154	Hutson Brothers Inc—Billy Purvis	PO Box 311, Breckenridge TX 76424	254-559-7557	R	2*	<.1
2155	Centrex International LLC—Alan Jamison	PO Box 73568, Houston TX 77273	281-370-0720	R	2*	<.1
2156	Southern Ohio Manufacturing Inc—Dave Rechtin	1147 Clough Pke, Batavia OH 45103	513-943-2555	R	2*	<.1
2157	American Precision Machining Inc—Nicholas Troisi	2350 W Shangri La Rd, Phoenix AZ 85029	602-870-5600	R	2*	<.1
2158	Carolina Textile Sales Of Gastonia Inc—Pam Grimsley	PO Box 637, Kings Mountain NC 28086	704-739-1646	R	2*	<.1

Rank	Company Name—*Executive Officer*	Address, City, State, Zip	Phone	Type	Fin	Empls
2159	Dilco Industries Inc—*Robert Dillon*	PO Box 859, Salem OH 44460	330-337-6732	R	2*	<.1
2160	LMI Manufacturing—*Ralph Gundrum*	PO Box 97, Allenton WI 53002	262-629-5527	R	2*	<.1
2161	Miller Machine and Tool Company Inc—*Carl Leach*	PO Box 2704, Winchester VA 22604	540-662-6512	R	2*	<.1
2162	Minnesota Fabrication and Machine Inc—*Kenneth Millslagle*	18489 Twin Lakes Rd Nw, Elk River MN 55330	763-441-2733	R	2*	<.1
2163	Precision West Engineered Products Inc—*Jan Bild*	6803 Walnut Ave, Orangevale CA 95662	916-989-2614	R	2*	<.1
2164	Spot Master Inc—*David Gardikis*	473 Pleasant St, Fall River MA 02721	508-672-0844	R	2*	<.1
2165	Wayne Burt Machine—*Wayne Burt*	510 Industrial Rd, Grove OK 74344	918-786-4415	R	2*	<.1
2166	Williams Manufacturing Corp—*Robert Fowlkes*	PO Box 387, Fort Lauderdale FL 33302	276-228-5441	R	2*	<.1
2167	Accur-Cut Machine Company Inc—*Joseph Harris*	PO Box 272, North Webster IN 46555	574-834-2877	R	2*	<.1
2168	Carolina Precision Machining Inc—*Steven Vick*	1500 N Main St, Mocksville NC 27028	336-751-7788	R	2*	<.1
2169	Olivia Machine and Tool Inc—*Terry Thomas*	PO Box 351, Olivia NC 28368	919-499-6021	R	2*	<.1
2170	Suburban Metal Products Inc—*D Kempton*	1050 Tarlton Rd, Circleville OH 43113	740-474-4237	R	2*	<.1
2171	Superior Machine and Pattern Inc—*Larry Dalton*	PO Box 6080, Talladega AL 35161	256-362-1385	R	2*	<.1
2172	United Tool Company Inc—*M Bechtol*	PO Box 242, Wabash IN 46992	260-563-3143	R	2*	<.1
2173	Wolverine Production and Engineering Inc—*Bernard Aude*	41160 Executive Dr, Harrison Township MI 48045	586-468-2890	R	2*	<.1
2174	C and G Machine Tool Company Inc—*Omer Gingras*	180 W State St, Granby MA 01033	413-467-9557	R	2*	<.1
2175	Manheim Specialty Machine Inc—*Robert Miller*	PO Box 143, Manheim PA 17545	717-665-5400	R	2*	<.1
2176	W D Lee and Co—*Dennis Lee*	PO Box 12157, Gastonia NC 28052	704-864-0346	R	2*	<.1
2177	American Deburring Inc—*Joseph Campbell*	20742 Linear Ln, Lake Forest CA 92630	949-457-9790	R	2*	<.1
2178	Daley Design Inc—*Dale Sisney*	PO Box 620, Roscoe IL 61073	815-316-8400	R	2*	<.1
2179	Farrell Brothers Holdings Inc—*Doug Farrell*	1137 N Armando St, Anaheim CA 92806	714-630-3417	R	2*	<.1
2180	Galvin Precision Machining Inc—*Jim Galvin*	404 Yolanda Ave, Santa Rosa CA 95404	707-526-5359	R	2*	<.1
2181	T and D Machine—*Brooke Smith*	5035 N 124th St, Butler WI 53007	262-781-3870	R	2*	<.1
2182	Globe Dynamics International Inc—*Herb Conway*	640 S Santa Fe St, Santa Ana CA 92705	714-973-0657	R	2*	<.1
2183	Isom Industrial Metals Inc—*Mike Isom*	PO Box 207, Caldwell ID 83606	208-459-9441	R	2*	<.1
2184	Javin Machine Corp—*Vincent Spiezio*	31 Otis St, West Babylon NY 11704	631-643-3322	R	2*	<.1
2185	Johnson Machine And Fibre Products Company Inc—*Michael Marshall*	142 Hopkins Ave, Jamestown NY 14701	716-665-2003	R	2*	<.1
2186	Monroe Tool And Manufacturing Co—*Herbert Brosnan*	3900 E 93rd St, Cleveland OH 44105	216-883-7360	R	2*	<.1
2187	Randy Martin Inc—*Randy Martin*	4457 Bethany Rd Unit C, Mason OH 45040	513-573-9487	R	2*	<.1
2188	Raymond and Lae Engineering Inc—*Donald Raymond*	104 Racquette Dr, Fort Collins CO 80524	970-484-6510	R	2*	<.1
2189	Southtowne Machining Inc—*Janusz Kwapich*	808 Corporate Centre D, O Fallon MO 63368	636-447-5521	R	2*	<.1
2190	Technical Hardfacing and Machining Inc—*Paul Egasti*	35 Ext St, Attleboro MA 02703	508-223-2900	R	2*	<.1
2191	Terry's Machine and Manufacturing Inc—*Roger Sanford*	12128 Cyrus Way Ste B, Mukilteo WA 98275	425-315-8866	R	2*	<.1
2192	Advanced Precision Machining Inc—*Nick Brackus*	PO Box 480, Meridian ID 83680	208-288-2185	R	2*	<.1
2193	ALE Hydraulic Machinery Company LLC—*Elwood Heim*	6215 Airport Rd, Levittown PA 19057	215-547-3351	R	2*	<.1
2194	Polaris Engineering Inc—*Michael Burns*	17540 15 Mile Rd, Fraser MI 48026	586-296-1603	R	2*	<.1
2195	Crystal Metal Products Company Inc—*John Cristinzio*	2700 Castor Ave, Philadelphia PA 19134	215-423-2500	R	2*	<.1
2196	Bay Precision Machining Inc—*Anne Feher*	815 Sweeney Ave Ste D, Redwood City CA 94063	650-200-3135	R	2*	<.1
2197	Devor Tool and Die Inc—*Richard Devor*	PO Box 89, Lake Mills WI 53551	920-648-2718	R	2*	<.1
2198	Industrial Precision Products Inc—*William Gallagher*	350 Mitchell St, Oswego NY 13126	315-343-4421	R	2*	<.1
2199	Palm Beach Iron Works Inc—*Jim Higgins*	7768 Belvedere Rd, West Palm Beach FL 33411	561-683-1816	R	2*	<.1
2200	Collins Corp—*James Collins*	PO Box 8439, Longview TX 75607	903-753-5411	R	2*	<.1
2201	Fosda Inc—*Nancy Foster*	14546 Hawthorne Ave, Fontana CA 92335	909-350-8040	R	2*	<.1
2202	J M T Machine Co—*Julius Kamper*	9986 Gantry Rd, Philadelphia PA 19115	215-934-7600	R	2*	<.1
2203	Lester's Machine Company Inc—*Terry Lester*	5256 Hollow Springs Rd, Bradyville TN 37026	615-765-5544	R	2*	<.1
2204	Mictron Inc—*Myron Weinstein*	6050 Porter Way, Sarasota FL 34232	941-371-6659	R	2*	<.1
2205	Talos Corp—*Gerald Popplewell*	PO Box 5765, Rodwood City CA 94063	650-364-7364	R	2*	<.1
2206	Whitman Mold Inc—*Tim Whitman*	PO Box 442, Orangeburg SC 29116	803-533-1949	R	2*	<.1
2207	Custom Machining Inc—*James Pierce*	PO Box 866, Mount Sterling KY 40353	859-498-9898	R	2*	<.1
2208	Lewis Machine And Tool Company Inc—*Ronald Lewis*	111 Midland Dr, Cuba MO 65453	573-885-4415	R	2*	<.1
2209	Journeyman Machine and Supply Company Inc—*Michael Lambeseder*	715 Sullivan Dr, Fond Du Lac WI 54935	920-923-3758	R	2*	<.1
2210	M and W Manufacturing Inc—*Neil Westervelt*	PO Box 861, Iola KS 66749	620-365-7456	R	2*	<.1
2211	Vmg Engineering Inc—*Vicente Corona*	1046 Griswold Ave, San Fernando CA 91340	818-837-6320	R	2*	<.1
2212	Brennan Machine Company Inc—*Andrew Brennan*	820 Monponsett St, Hanson MA 02341	781-293-3997	R	2*	<.1
2213	K and C Machine Company Inc—*Jeff Collins*	601 Industrial Ave, Greensboro NC 27406	336-373-0745	R	2*	<.1
2214	Marco Machine and Design Inc—*Donald Lawson*	7740 Whitepine Rd, Richmond VA 23237	804-275-5555	R	2*	<.1
2215	Mcleod Machine Works Inc—*Cal Smith*	4717 S M L King Jr Pkw, Beaumont TX 77705	409-835-0192	R	2*	<.1
2216	Api Precision Machining Inc—*Karen Lynch*	617 W Commerce St, Dallas TX 75208	214-748-4994	R	2*	<.1
2217	Biggs Tool And Die Inc—*Charles Biggs*	365 Patricia Dr, Warminster PA 18974	215-674-9911	R	2*	<.1
2218	Coffman Manufacturing Corp—*Richard Coffman*	305 Cary Point Dr, Cary IL 60013	847-639-5721	R	2*	<.1
2219	Commerce Welding and Manufacturing Company Inc—*Doug Weldon*	2200 Evanston Ave, Dallas TX 75208	214-748-8824	R	2*	<.1
2220	Damick Enterprises—*Frank Sikorski*	1801 Rochester Industr, Rochester Hills MI 48309	248-652-7500	R	2*	<.1
2221	Duyck Machine Inc—*Andy Duyck*	4200 Nw Visitation Rd, Forest Grove OR 97116	503-357-0123	R	2*	<.1
2222	Hocker Tool And Die Inc—*Ronald Hocker*	5161 Webcter St, Dayton OH 45414	937-274-3443	R	2*	<.1
2223	Littlecrest Machine Shop Inc—*Ray Kinkaid*	2708 Keeland St, Houston TX 77093	713-697-4715	R	2*	<.1
2224	Moody Corp—*Dalton Moody*	1688 Rte 288, Zelienople PA 16063	724-453-9470	R	2*	<.1
2225	Production Technology Inc—*Dennis Tiberius*	2727 W Ferguson Rd, Fort Wayne IN 46809	260-478-6767	R	2*	<.1
2226	Ram Machine Tooling Inc—*Frank Warburton*	24242 Rester Rd, Picayune MS 39466	601-799-4446	R	2*	<.1
2227	S and S Tool Inc—*Melissa Sichler*	830 Lund Blvd, Anoka MN 55303	763-427-0411	R	2*	<.1
2228	Sturdy Grinding And Machining Inc—*Ray Blake*	22814 Macomb Industria, Clinton Township MI 48036	586-463-8880	R	2*	<.1
2229	Thomas A Despres Inc—*Thomas Despres*	2830 Beech Daly Rd, Inkster MI 48141	313-562-6350	R	2*	<.1
2230	Knape Industries Inc—*Jonathan Knape*	6592 Proprietors Rd, Worthington OH 43085	614-885-3016	R	2*	<.1
2231	Paragon Automation Inc—*Donald Schreiner*	1410 Brummel Ave, Elk Grove Village IL 60007	847-593-0434	R	2*	<.1
2232	Wilmington Machine Inc—*Walter Richards*	432 W C St, Wilmington CA 90744	310-518-3213	R	2*	<.1
2233	Jessee Brothers Machine Shop Inc—*Chett Jessee*	1640 Dell Ave, Campbell CA 95008	408-866-1755	R	2*	<.1
2234	Brenco Machine And Tool Inc—*Dietrich Bronst*	6117 Factory Rd, Crystal Lake IL 60014	815-356-5100	R	2*	<.1
2235	Creative Machining Systems Inc—*Victor Scharko*	124 Youngs Rd, Trenton NJ 08619	609-586-3932	R	2*	<.1
2236	Carr Machine and Tool Inc—*Richard Carr*	1301 Jarvis Ave, Elk Grove Village IL 60007	847-593-8003	R	2*	<.1
2237	Barile Precision Grinding Inc—*Michael Barile*	12320 Plz Dr, Cleveland OH 44130	440-237-0931	R	1*	<.1
2238	Marshall Ruby and Sons Inc—*Marshall Ruby*	20501 Ruby Industrial, Frostburg MD 21532	301-689-9238	R	1*	<.1
2239	East Coast Machine and Design Inc—*Jana Lynch*	250 Douglas Rd, Whitinsville MA 01588	508-278-9854	R	1*	<.1
2240	Tecsol Manufacturing Inc—*Archie Ponder*	97 Hill Ave NW, Fort Walton Beach FL 32548	850-244-4292	R	1*	<.1
2241	Vermont Flexible Tubing Inc—*Beverly Simblest*	PO Box 46, Lyndonville VT 05851	802-626-5723	R	1*	<.1
2242	West End Machine and Welding—*John Rueger*	PO Box 9444, Richmond VA 23228	804-266-9631	R	1*	<.1
2243	Atomic City Tool Inc—*Robert Smith*	PO Box 4039, Oak Ridge TN 37831	865-482-7648	R	1*	<.1
2244	Nelson Metal Technology Inc—*Bonnie Friedly*	1311 S Main St, Payette ID 83661	208-642-4443	R	1*	<.1
2245	TAS Technical Services LLC	26007 Huntington Ln St, Valencia CA 91355	661-295-8588	R	1*	<.1

Note: An asterisk (*) indicates an estimated financial figure. The company type code used is as follows: R = Private, P = Public, S = Private Subsidiary, B = Public Subsidiary, D = Division, J = Joint Venture, I = Investment Fund.

COMPANY RANKINGS BY SALES WITHIN 4-DIGIT SIC

Rank	Company Name—Executive Officer	Address, City, State, Zip	Phone	Type	Fin	Empls
2246	Weins Machine Company Inc—Henry Weins	RR 1 Box 523, Terlton OK 74081	918-865-2187	R	1*	<.1
2247	Betech Inc—Ronald Brevard	190 Continuum Dr, Fletcher NC 28732	828-687-9917	R	1*	<.1
2248	Howell Machine Products Inc—Irene Vogt	6265 Grand River Rd St, Brighton MI 48114	517-546-0580	R	1*	<.1
2249	Longwood Manufacturing Corp—Thomas Piacentino	816 E Baltimore Pke, Kennett Square PA 19348	610-444-4200	R	1*	<.1
2250	Pending Inc—Neville Gallon	341 W Factory Rd, Addison IL 60101	630-628-1020	R	1*	<.1
2251	Pioneer Machine and Tooling Co—Yong Choe	515 Mildred Ave, Secane PA 19018	610-623-3908	R	1*	<.1
2252	Andrex Inc—William Pote	101 Bilby Rd Ste E, Hackettstown NJ 07840	908-850-5800	R	1*	<.1
2253	Automation West Inc—George Danenhauer	1605 E Saint Gertrude, Santa Ana CA 92705	714-556-7381	R	1*	<.1
2254	Ball S Machine and Manufacturing Company Inc—Joe Ball	PO Box 267, Candler NC 28715	828-667-0411	R	1*	<.1
2255	Boss Tool and Manufacturing Inc—Daniel Boss	4378a Contractors Cmn, Livermore CA 94551	925-371-8033	R	1*	<.1
2256	Budd Lake Machine And Tool Inc—Harold Nordstrom	PO Box 61, Mount Bethel PA 18343	570-897-5899	R	1*	<.1
2257	Burgess Manufacturing Inc—Allen Bassel	1911 Industrial Dr, Libertyville IL 60048	847-680-1724	R	1*	<.1
2258	Central Machine Works Inc—Max Redmond	PO Box 907, Duchesne UT 84021	435-738-2554	R	1*	<.1
2259	Cimarron Machine Service Inc—R Robb	7734 E 11th St, Tulsa OK 74112	918-835-5511	R	1*	<.1
2260	Heisler Tool Co—Timothy Mccord	38228 Western Pkwy, Willoughby OH 44094	440-951-2424	R	1*	<.1
2261	Holloway Equipment Company Inc—Paul Holloway	4856 Middle Channel Rd, Harsens Island MI 48028	810-748-9577	R	1*	<.1
2262	Horizon Machining and Manufacturing Inc—Larry Alexander	158 High Hope Rd, Six Mile SC 29682	864-868-3110	R	1*	<.1
2263	J M Fabrication Company LLC—Fernanda Belloti	415 Duncan Perry Rd, Arlington TX 76011	817-652-0526	R	1*	<.1
2264	Machine Craft Company Inc—Kim Jennison	PO Box 3665, Concord NH 03302	603-225-0958	R	1*	<.1
2265	Reliable Manufacturing Inc—Michael Murray	PO Box 1165, Round Rock TX 78680	512-255-6572	R	1*	<.1
2266	Tech Craft Inc—William Rehburg	1639 E Edinger Ave Ste, Santa Ana CA 92705	714-662-0539	R	1*	<.1
2267	Air Craftors Engineering Inc—Tim Boucher	4040 Cheyenne Ct, Chino CA 91710	909-591-3811	R	1*	<.1
2268	De Hoff Tool and Manufacturing Company Inc—Kim Dehoff	1018 S 7th St, Kansas City KS 66105	913-342-2212	R	1*	<.1
2269	Devries Instruments Inc—James Devries	7403 Domino Ln, Houston TX 77076	713-691-2509	R	1*	<.1
2270	Imagineering Machine Inc—Peter Schelitzche	6851 Oxford St, Minneapolis MN 55426	952-922-9311	R	1*	<.1
2271	Phil Matic Screw Products Inc—Larry Phillis	PO Box 1178, Willoughby OH 44096	440-942-7290	R	1*	<.1
2272	Riverside Machine Works Inc—Kerry Townsend	6301 Baldwin Ave, Riverside CA 92509	951-685-7416	R	1*	<.1
2273	Total Quality Machining Inc—Theodosa Davis	10 Shotwell Dr, Franklin OH 45005	937-746-7765	R	1*	<.1
2274	Vision Machine Works Inc—James Niemier	56540 Twin Branch Dr, Mishawaka IN 46545	574-259-6500	R	1*	<.1
2275	Cmc Corp—Mike Cusimano	PO Box 170039, Birmingham AL 35217	205-849-7421	R	1*	<.1
2276	Damar Machinery Company Inc—David Crysler	3389 3 Mile Rd Nw, Grand Rapids MI 49534	616-453-4655	R	1*	<.1
2277	SVM Group Inc—Richard Mattoni	PO Box 35667, Dallas TX 75235	214-637-1430	R	1*	<.1
2278	Cnc Machine and Design Inc—Karel Herian	368 W 600 S, Salt Lake City UT 84101	801-531-9922	R	1*	<.1
2279	Lynco Grinding Company Inc—Wayne Hogarth	PO Box 2127, Bell CA 90202	323-773-2858	R	1*	<.1
2280	Daltech Inc—David Rodeghiero	1420 Saris Souci Pkwy, Hanover Township PA 18706	570-823-9911	R	1*	<.1
2281	Jeb Florida Enterprises Inc—Jill Bauman	1710 12th St E, Palmetto FL 34221	941-722-9196	R	1*	<.1
2282	Diameters Inc—Warren Illgen	16700 W Ryerson Rd, New Berlin WI 53151	262-785-8720	R	1*	<.1
2283	Acme Grinding and Manufacturing Inc—Jennifer Zaluckyj	PO Box 509, Belvidere IL 61008	815-323-1380	R	1*	<.1
2284	Hannah Engineering Inc—Richard Barker	150 Maple St, Danvers MA 01923	978-777-5892	R	1*	<.1
2285	Kentucky Machine and Tool Co—Maurice Meisner	3107 Millers Ln, Louisville KY 40216	502-774-5733	R	1*	<.1
2286	Pick Instrument Products Company Inc—Hershel Pickens	102 Eastway St, Galena Park TX 77547	713-672-1686	R	1*	<.1
2287	Walter Lewis and Son Inc—Edward Smith	PO Box 270, Worthington WV 26591	304-287-2126	R	1*	<.1
2288	Furry Inc—Dann Furry	PO Box 453, Danville IL 61834	217-446-0084	R	1*	<.1
2289	Extrude Hone Deburring Service Inc—Robert Melendez	8800 Somerset Blvd, Paramount CA 90723	562-531-2976	R	1*	<.1
2290	Cambridge Machine and Supply Company Inc—Ralph Brock	PO Box 100, Cambridge OH 43725	740-432-2341	R	1*	<.1
2291	Collin's Precision Manufacturing Inc—Karen Sherlock	1445 N Kelly Ln, Safford AZ 85546	928-428-5226	R	1*	<.1
2292	Ja Ri Machining Company Inc—James Fredericks	226 Industrial Dr, Oak Hill WV 25901	304-469-3309	R	1*	<.1
2293	Metronic Engineering Company Inc—D Conner	32 Iron Horse Rd, Oakland NJ 07436	201-337-1266	R	1*	<.1
2294	Springfield Mold And Die Inc—Richard Smith	2420 W 4th St, Ontario OH 44906	419-747-7888	R	1*	<.1
2295	Badger Machine Inc—Patrick Heim	31 Insight Dr, Platteville WI 53818	608-348-7531	R	1*	<.1
2296	Cooper Tool and Machine Company Inc—Harry Cooper	PO Box 3295, Oxford AL 36203	256-831-4513	R	1*	<.1
2297	S and B Tool And Die Company Inc—Diane Sutton	1872 Commerce Park E, Lancaster PA 17601	717-392-8244	R	1*	<.1
2298	Ace Machining Technologies Ltd—Kenneth Maul	110 Private Rd 435, Hillsboro TX 76645	254-632-4250	R	1*	<.1
2299	Ay Machine Co—Richard Ay	PO Box 608, Ephrata PA 17522	717-733-0335	R	1*	<.1
2300	Eamco Corp—Joseph Fernandes	5275 W Coplay Rd, Whitehall PA 18052	610-262-5731	R	1*	<.1
2301	Edinburg Fixture and Machine Inc—Terri Tomazin	3101 State Rte 14, Rootstown OH 44272	330-947-1700	R	1*	<.1
2302	Hawk Quality Products Inc—Jeff Hawkes	PO Box 885, Derry NH 03038	603-432-3319	R	1*	<.1
2303	Holdren Brothers Inc—John Holdren	PO Box 459, West Liberty OH 43357	937-465-7050	R	1*	<.1
2304	Kremin Inc—Michael Kremin	2926 Universal Dr, Saginaw MI 48603	989-790-5147	R	1*	<.1
2305	Non Metallic Machining Assembly Inc—David Andersen	1525 E Lake Rd Ste C, Erie PA 16511	814-453-6787	R	1*	<.1
2306	Redding Machine Shop Inc—Paul Redding	5720 Seymour Hwy, Wichita Falls TX 76310	940-691-5218	R	1*	<.1
2307	B and J Machine Works Inc—Jon Justesen	PO Box 356, Ayden NC 28513	252-746-6022	R	1*	<.1
2308	BG Industries Inc—Gerald Cummings	6835 Monroe Blvd, Taylor MI 48180	313-292-5355	R	1*	<.1
2309	Loecy Precision Manufacturing Inc—Steve Loecy	9413 Hamilton Dr, Mentor OH 44060	440-358-0551	R	1*	<.1
2310	Bel-Pro Products Inc—Michael Belch	4752 W 60th Ave Unit B, Arvada CO 80003	303-231-0902	R	1*	<.1
2311	Production Machine Tool Co—Walter Lowe	5514 Fair Ln, Cincinnati OH 45227	513-271-0880	R	1*	<.1
2312	Saeger Machine Inc—Nancy Saeger	531 Old Skippack Rd, Harleysville PA 19438	215-256-8754	R	1*	<.1
2313	Sigma Manufacturing Industries Inc—Apostolos Siantos	1361 E Bay Ave, Bronx NY 10474	718-842-9180	R	1*	<.1
2314	Talco LLC—Richard Taylor	7835 Main St Ne, Minneapolis MN 55432	763-571-7640	R	1*	<.1
2315	American Machine Works Inc—Vic Brown	803 S 20th St, Omaha NE 68108	402-342-4783	R	1*	<.1
2316	Hetrick Manufacturing Inc—Donald Burk	210 Reimer St, New Kensington PA 15068	724-335-0455	R	1*	<.1
2317	Tower Tool and Manufacturing Company Inc—Lenard Lapchynski	2057 E Aurora Rd Ste N, Twinsburg OH 44087	330-425-1623	R	1*	<.1
2318	Tool Grinding Inc—David Scheel	5555 Boone Ave N, Minneapolis MN 55428	763-533-0202	R	1*	<.1
2319	Delta Manufacturing Inc—Ricardo Aguilar	6260 Prescott Ct, Chino CA 91710	909-590-4563	R	1*	<.1
2320	Excell Machine Company Inc—James Blair	PO Box 616, Midlothian TX 76065	817-473-6121	R	1*	<.1
2321	Aaron Tool Inc—John Gardi	2819 62nd Ave E, Bradenton FL 34203	941-758-9369	R	1*	<.1
2322	Miller Manufacturing Inc—David Miller	2320 Mason St, New Holstein WI 53061	920-898-4979	R	1*	<.1
2323	Taylor Tool and Machine Company Inc—Dennis Taylor	5311 Pineridge Dr, La Crescenta CA 91214	818-248-6134	R	1*	<.1
2324	Current River Die Sinking Inc—Laverne Beale	PO Box 27, Doniphan MO 63935	573-996-7181	R	1*	<.1
2325	Hi Electronics Inc—Steve Shin	3048 N Coolidge Ave, Los Angeles CA 90039	323-913-7982	R	1*	<.1
2326	K and W Manufacturing Company Inc—Korinna Burke	PO Box 97, Bronson MI 49028	517-369-9708	R	1*	<.1
2327	Kimble Machines Inc—Robert Kimble	124 S Jonesville St, Montpelier OH 43543	419-485-8449	R	1*	<.1
2328	Metal Mechanics Inc—Thomas Dailey	PO Box 447, Schoolcraft MI 49087	269-679-2525	R	1*	<.1
2329	APH Enterprises Inc—Axel Hillesheim	PO Box 12363, Green Bay WI 54307	920-865-7773	R	1*	<.1
2330	Custom Fabrication Inc—William Tillinghast	2611 Sharon St, Kenner LA 70062	504-469-6852	R	1*	<.1
2331	Metro Machine Works Inc—Charles Elliott	5204 S 49th W Ave, Tulsa OK 74107	918-446-2705	R	1*	<.1
2332	Bethel Machine and Manufacturing Inc—Lawrence Sakowitz	PO Box 550, Bethel Park PA 15102	412-833-5522	R	1*	<.1
2333	Bisaga Inc—Robert Bisaga	212 Ashland Ave, Somerdale NJ 08083	856-784-7966	R	1*	<.1
2334	Columbia Tool and Gage Co—Victor Herrera	250 Alice St, Wheeling IL 60090	847-520-5900	R	1*	<.1

Rank	Company Name—*Executive Officer*	Address, City, State, Zip	Phone	Type	Fin	Empls
2335	Darly Custom Technology Inc—*Yimou Yang*	PO Box 527, Windsor CT 06095	860-243-5518	R	1*	<.1
2336	Diamond Tool Inc—*Eileen Fertal*	33220 Lakeland Blvd, Eastlake OH 44095	216-481-0808	R	1*	<.1
2337	Niagara Manufacturing Co—*Edward Haynor*	2725 W 17th St, Erie PA 16505	814-838-4511	R	1*	<.1
2338	Randolph Tool Company Inc—*Patrick Franze*	750 Wales Dr, Hartville OH 44632	330-877-4923	R	1*	<.1
2339	Standish Steel Inc—*James Standish*	280 Standish Steel Dr, Bedford IN 47421	812-834-5255	R	1*	<.1
2340	Tech-Star Industries Inc—*James Stephens*	2682 Middlefield Rd St, Redwood City CA 94063	650-369-7214	R	1*	<.1
2341	Philadelphia Toboggan Coaster Inc—*Tom Rebbie*	3195 Penn St, Hatfield PA 19440	215-799-2155	R	1*	<.1
2342	Salco Machine Inc—*Raymond Saliola*	3822 Victory Ave, Louisville OH 44641	330-456-8281	R	1*	<.1
2343	Northstar Fabrication And Machine Inc—*Jack Trowbridge*	215 N Calapooia St, Sutherlin OR 97479	541-459-4845	R	1*	<.1
2344	Plus One Corp—*William Thorpe*	PO Box 673, Peabody MA 01960	978-532-3700	R	1*	<.1
2345	Phaztech Inc—*Carl Pfeufer*	PO Box 174, Saint Marys PA 15857	814-834-3262	R	1*	<.1
2346	Miniature Precision Inc—*Don Anderson*	4488 Mountain Lakes Bl, Redding CA 96003	530-244-4131	R	1*	<.1
2347	JC Milling Company Inc—*John Czaczkowski*	988 Industrial Ct, Loves Park IL 61111	815-654-1070	R	1*	<.1
2348	LE Warren Inc—*Leo Warren*	1600 S Jackson St, Jackson MI 49203	517-784-8701	R	1*	<.1
2349	Micro Tool Engineering Inc—*Fran Lacasse*	7575 Central Industria, Riviera Beach FL 33404	561-842-7381	R	1*	<.1
2350	Aram Precision Tool Die Inc—*Avi Amichai*	9758 Cozycroft Ave, Chatsworth CA 91311	818-998-1000	R	1*	<.1
2351	Batesville Tooling and Design Inc—*Gary Blair*	210 Tower Rd, Batesville MS 38606	662-563-1663	R	1*	<.1
2352	Accu Tek Inc—*Louis Victorino*	PO Box 240, Bristol RI 02809	401-253-1240	R	1*	<.1
2353	Chyna Inc—*Tom Conard*	7921 Old Branch Ave, Clinton MD 20735	301-599-6969	R	1*	<.1
2354	Gutierrez Machine Corp—*George Gutierrez*	PO Box 71, Athens PA 18810	570-888-9453	R	1*	<.1
2355	Gyro-Trac Corp—*Daniel Gaudreault*	10 Flying Cloud Dr, Summerville SC 29483	843-879-0208	R	1*	<.1
2356	Machine Rebuilders and Service Inc—*Willi Breuning*	4801 Projects Dr, Fort Wayne IN 46825	260-482-8168	R	1*	<.1
2357	Rivco Products Inc—*Richard Colano*	440 S Pine St, Burlington WI 53105	262-763-8222	R	1*	<.1
2358	Sisson Engineering Corp—*Cody Sisson*	330 Old Wendell Rd, Northfield MA 01360	413-498-2840	R	1*	<.1
2359	Systech Handling Inc—*Wendell Lantz*	120 Taylor Pkwy, Archbold OH 43502	419-445-8226	R	1*	<.1
2360	Tri R Tooling Inc—*Robert John*	220 Piper Rd, Mansfield OH 44905	419-522-8665	R	1*	<.1
2361	Accu-Turn Inc—*George Seater*	PO Box 36, Union Grove WI 53182	262-878-4432	R	1*	<.1
2362	Kenmore Development and Machine Company Inc—*Richard Roten*	1395 Kenmore Blvd, Akron OH 44314	330-753-2274	R	1*	<.1
2363	Masterbilt Inc—*Robert Michalk*	PO Box 3715, South Bend IN 46619	574-287-6567	R	1*	<.1
2364	Masterson's Manufacturing Corp—*John Nixon*	122 W Dudley Town Rd, Bloomfield CT 06002	860-243-3663	R	1*	<.1
2365	Mid-America Manufacturing Inc—*Randy Gummert*	1300 S B Ave, Nevada IA 50201	515-382-3113	R	1*	.1
2366	Steelcraft Inc—*Douglas Backman*	PO Box 111, Millbury MA 01527	508-865-4445	R	1*	<.1
2367	Mpb Industries Inc—*Jim Bowers*	505 E 31st St Ste Xx, Anderson IN 46016	765-644-9099	R	1*	<.1
2368	Tuff Automation Inc—*Monte Tuffs*	2751 Courier Dr Nw, Grand Rapids MI 49534	616-735-3939	R	1*	<.1
2369	Dynapoint Technologies Inc—*Jeffrey Beatty*	PO Box 355, Dayton OH 45401	937-859-5193	R	1*	<.1
2370	Veitch Machine Company Inc—*Wayne Veitch*	PO Box 191, Fairfield AL 35064	205-788-1683	R	1*	<.1
2371	Dobday Manufacturing Company Inc—*Desmond Dobday*	42750 Merrill Rd, Sterling Heights MI 48314	586-254-6777	R	1*	<.1
2372	H and H Machine Shop of Akron Inc—*Henry Haas*	955 Grant St, Akron OH 44311	330-773-3327	R	1*	<.1
2373	Monarch Manufacturing Inc—*Bill Baxter*	710 W Kathryn, Nixa MO 65714	417-724-2744	R	1*	<.1
2374	Taylor Manufacturing Company Inc—*Robert Taylor*	1101 W Main St, Springfield OH 45504	937-322-8622	R	1*	<.1
2375	Rbs Fab Inc—*Joann Smith*	230 Hoernerstown Rd, Hummelstown PA 17036	717-566-9513	R	1*	<.1
2376	Smithfield Manufacturing—*Ron Smithfield*	237 Kraft St, Clarksville TN 37040	931-552-4327	R	1*	<.1
2377	Solon Industrial Grinding Inc—*Richard Cermak*	1400 Miller Pkwy, Streetsboro OH 44241	330-995-9009	R	1*	<.1
2378	Atomatic Manufacturing Co—*John B Kindling*	300 Shadeland Ave, East Pittsburgh PA 15112	412-824-6400	R	1*	<.1
2379	Industrial Machine Repair Inc—*Robert Keener*	PO Box 51, Hayden IN 47245	812-346-2216	R	1*	<.1
2380	Macro Tool and Machine Company Inc—*Dan Siegel*	1397 Rte 55, LaGrangeville NY 12540	845-223-3824	R	1*	<.1
2381	Ncml-Brueggemann Inc—*Lionel Vazquez*	1207 Brooks St, Ontario CA 91762	909-986-1933	R	1*	<.1
2382	Pacific Coast Air Tool and Supply Inc—*Annette Marquardt*	3630 Placentia Ct, Chino CA 91710	909-627-0948	R	1*	<.1
2383	Precision Disc Grinding Corp—*Ron Buttner*	PO Box 350, Mineola NY 11501	516-747-5450	R	1*	<.1
2384	Stanko Products Inc—*Jeff Lloyd*	278 Donohoe Rd, Greensburg PA 15601	724-834-8080	R	1*	<.1
2385	Flextron Inc—*George Wesesku*	130 W Fay Ave, Addison IL 60101	630-543-5995	R	1*	<.1
2386	Hillcrest Precision Tool Company Inc—*Carl Rich*	75 Ellyson Ave, East Hampstead NH 03826	603-612-0039	R	1*	<.1
2387	Artic Tool and Engineering Company LLC—*Michael Gamache*	41 Ford Ln, Warwick RI 02888	401-785-2210	S	1*	<.1
2388	Kimzey Welding Works Inc—*John Kimzey*	164 Kentucky Ave, Woodland CA 95695	530-662-9331	R	1*	<.1
2389	Mercer Machine Company Inc—*Brian Robinson*	1421 S Holt Rd, Indianapolis IN 46241	317-241-9903	R	1*	<.1
2390	Willard Machine—*Jeffrey Rathmann*	73 Forest Ave, Buffalo NY 14213	716-885-1630	R	1*	<.1
2391	Alco Machine Corp—*Wayne Roache*	101a French Ave, Braintree MA 02184	781-848-5657	R	1*	<.1
2392	BTM Industries Inc—*Tim Porter*	604 Washington St, Woodstock IL 60098	815-338-6464	R	1*	<.1
2393	Green Machine and Tool Inc—*George Green*	PO Box 87785, Houston TX 77287	713-943-0402	R	1*	<.1
2394	Hammerlund Manufacturing Company Inc—*Albert Hammerlund*	607 2nd St S, Hopkins MN 55343	952-935-3454	R	1*	<.1
2395	Prodeva Inc—*Frederick Bunke*	PO Box 729, Jackson Center OH 45334	937-596-6713	R	1*	<.1
2396	Temtex Temperature Systems Inc—*Homer Wright*	700 E Houston St, Sherman TX 75090	903-813-1500	R	1*	<.1
2397	Western Magnum Corp—*James Crawley*	600 Lairport St, El Segundo CA 90245	310-640-7000	R	1*	<.1
2398	Automated Production Machining Inc—*David Shaw*	300 Taylor Ave, Gordonsville VA 22942	540-832-0835	R	1*	<.1
2399	Charles Costa Inc—*George Marino*	924 Home Ave, Akron OH 44310	330-376-3636	R	1*	<.1
2400	Pierson Products Inc *Bruce Pierson*	419 S Arch St, Janesville WI 53548	608-754-7733	R	1*	<.1
2401	B and B Manufacturing Inc—*Al Becherini*	11920 W Carmen Ave, Milwaukee WI 53225	414-358-4620	R	1*	<.1
2402	Calco Controls Inc—*Neil Sivertson*	PO Box 415, Cary IL 60013	847-639-3858	R	1*	<.1
2403	Dunham Machine Inc—*Ted Pawelec*	PO Box 391263, Cleveland OH 44139	216-398-4500	R	1*	<.1
2404	FillPro Inc—*Scott Harris*	17301 W Colfax Ave Ste, Golden CO 80401	303-278-7822	R	1*	<.1
2405	Industrial Machining And Design Services Inc—*Robert Hill*	2007 S Ave, Youngstown OH 44502	330-747-4637	R	1*	<.1
2406	Jet Grinding and Manufacturing—*Jerry Nosek*	2309 E Oakton St, Arlington Heights IL 60005	847-956-8646	R	1*	<.1
2407	Macpro Inc—*D Hughes*	1456 Fay Rd Unit B, Loveland OH 45140	513-575-3000	R	1*	<.1
2408	P and F Machine—*Wayne Rickey*	301 S Broadway, Turlock CA 95380	209-667-2515	R	1*	<.1
2409	Progressive Machine Works Inc—*Arthur Brudereck*	PO Box 209, Hamburg PA 19526	610-562-2281	R	1*	<.1
2410	RG Hanson Company Inc—*Thomas Hanson*	PO Box 1408, Bloomington IL 61702	309-661-9200	R	1*	<.1
2411	Secondary Operations Inc—*Lawrence Carrignan*	46 Manila Ave, Hamden CT 06514	203-288-8241	R	1*	<.1
2412	Tabor Machine Company Inc—*Carol Tabor*	12529 Memorial Pkwy SW, Huntsville AL 35803	256-881-4458	R	1*	<.1
2413	WP Instruments Inc—*Robert McLean*	PO Box 999, Longmont CO 80502	303-772-1325	R	1*	<.1
2414	Year-A-Round Cab Co—*C Anderson*	112 W Lind St, Mankato MN 56001	507-625-9381	R	1*	<.1
2415	Prime Machine and Tool Inc—*Emanuel Lungu*	3541 High Ridge Rd, Boynton Beach FL 33426	561-586-8419	R	1*	<.1
2416	Schmitmeyer Inc—*Jarett Schmitmeyer*	PO Box 227, Fort Loramie OH 45845	937-295-2091	R	1*	<.1
2417	Engine Clean Technologies Inc—*Bob Flynn*	5112 Heintz St, Baldwin Park CA 91706	626-814-3969	R	1*	<.1
2418	Tooling Connection—*Klee Dangler*	PO Box 238, Oakwood OH 45873	419-594-3339	R	1*	<.1
2419	Joseph Kavanagh Co—*Joseph M Kavanagh*	8100 Lynhurst Rd, Baltimore MD 21222	410-388-8070	R	1*	<.1
2420	Milco Waterjet LLC	15221 Connector Ln, Huntington Beach CA 92649	714-373-0098	R	1*	<.1
2421	Palmer Products Inc—*Len Palmer*	920 Moe Dr, Akron OH 44310	330-630-9397	R	1*	<.1
2422	Prather Engineering Inc—*Linda Prather*	3285 E 59th St, Long Beach CA 90805	562-634-5566	R	1*	<.1
2423	Blair-Fuehrer Inc—*George Blair*	PO Box 55, Dorchester IA 52140	563-497-3635	R	1*	<.1

Note: An asterisk (*) indicates an estimated financial figure. The company type code used is as follows: R = Private, P = Public, S = Private Subsidiary, B = Public Subsidiary, D = Division, J = Joint Venture, I = Investment Fund.

COMPANY RANKINGS BY SALES WITHIN 4-DIGIT SIC

Rank	Company Name—*Executive Officer*	Address, City, State, Zip	Phone	Type	Fin	Empls
2424	Trikinetics Inc—*Mark Spencer*	56 Emerson Rd, Waltham MA 02451	781-891-6110	R	1*	<.1
2425	Harley Tool and Machine Inc—*Robert Harley*	21 McDermott Pl, Bergenfield NJ 07621	201-244-8899	R	1*	<.1
2426	Heins Balancing Systems Inc—*Wallace Heins*	820 Railroad Ave, Santa Paula CA 93060	805-525-5445	R	1*	<.1
2427	Sandbagger Corp—*Tim Vandergrift*	PO Box 5798, Villa Park IL 60181	630-876-2400	R	1*	<.1
2428	EXPORTech Company Inc—*Robin R Oder*	4919 Simmons Circle, Export PA 15632	724-325-4431	R	1*	<.1
2429	V and L Tool Inc—*Gerald Schaefer*	2021 Mac Arthur Rd, Waukesha WI 53188	262-547-1226	R	1*	.1
2430	B and B Precision Inc—*Rick Bethke*	18015 S Broadway, Gardena CA 90248	562-634-9660	R	1*	<.1
2431	Borg Precision Inc—*Robert Borgstrom*	PO Box 69, Clayton WI 54004	715-948-2982	R	1*	<.1
2432	Carlson Manufacturing Inc—*Warren Carlson*	PO Box 305, Kerkhoven MN 56252	320-264-8101	R	1*	<.1
2433	Industrial Control Service Inc—*Mark Reust*	PO Box 1141, Huntington IN 46750	260-356-4698	R	1*	<.1
2434	Artisan Equipment Inc—*Stuart Brengman*	PO Box 500, Carroll OH 43112	740-756-9135	R	1*	<.1
2435	Blue Chip Industries Inc—*Larry Van Daele*	PO Box 383, Kewanee IL 61443	309-854-7100	R	1*	<.1
2436	Isco Inc—*Brian Amerine*	6360 Fiesta Dr, Columbus OH 43235	614-792-2206	R	1*	<.1
2437	J and L Turning Inc—*Helen Johnson*	5664 N River Rd, East China MI 48054	810-765-5755	R	1*	<.1
2438	Versa-Tech Inc—*Ron Schroeder*	2135 Stephenson Hwy, Troy MI 48083	248-526-1518	S	1*	<.1
2439	Boreal Controls Inc—*Gregory Smith*	3100 Channel Dr Ste 21, Juneau AK 99801	907-586-8367	R	1*	<.1
2440	Custom Honing Inc—*Stephen Keller*	24840 Us Hwy 20, South Bend IN 46628	574-233-2846	R	1*	<.1
2441	Dern Moore Machine Company Inc—*Ken Moore*	151 S Niagara St, Lockport NY 14094	716-433-6243	R	1*	<.1
2442	Etko Machine Inc—*Julius Koroshazi*	2796 Barber Rd, Norton OH 44203	330-745-4033	R	1*	<.1
2443	Flare Inc—*Allen Collins*	6210 Discount Dr, Fort Wayne IN 46818	260-490-1101	R	1*	<.1
2444	Wotkun Group Inc—*Richard Wotkun*	PO Box 68, Posen IL 60469	773-395-7969	R	1*	<.1
2445	Etna Tool and Die Corp—*Keranus Galuppo*	42 Bond St Frnt A, New York NY 10012	212-475-4350	R	1*	<.1
2446	Metal Rubber Corp—*David Kruse*	1225 S Shamrock Ave, Monrovia CA 91016	626-358-3274	R	1*	<.1
2447	Fluid Conservation Systems Corp—*Neal Summers*	502 Techne Ctr Dr B, Milford OH 45150	513-831-9335	R	1*	<.1
2448	Benny Machine Company Inc—*Jeffrey Benny*	PO Box 488, Isanti MN 55040	763-444-5508	R	1*	<.1
2449	Maplewood Machine Company Inc—*Edward Viveiros*	973 Reed Rd, Dartmouth MA 02747	508-673-6710	R	1*	<.1
2450	Billingsley Precision Machining LLC—*Debbie Kennemer*	PO Box 177097, Irving TX 75017	972-986-8998	R	1*	<.1
2451	Genuine Machine Design Inc—*Scott Vollmer*	509 E Drexel Pkwy, Rensselaer IN 47978	219-866-8060	R	1*	<.1
2452	D and R Autochuck Inc—*Ralph Kreissler*	5196 27th Ave, Rockford IL 61109	815-398-9131	R	1*	<.1
2453	Flex-Weld Inc—*Kevin Kelly* Kelco Industries Inc	1425 Lake Ave, Woodstock IL 60098	815-334-3662	S	1*	<.1
2454	Plastic Products Manufacturing Corp—*Othie Richardson*	1724 Junction Ave Ste, San Jose CA 95112	408-436-8780	R	1*	<.1
2455	Advanced Products Technology Inc—*Tim Hinds*	PO Box 247, Connersville IN 47331	765-827-1166	R	1*	<.1
2456	L and P Machine Inc—*Raymond Leap*	3440 Arden Rd, Hayward CA 94545	530-244-5849	R	1*	<.1
2457	Tectonics Inc—*Jeff Collins*	205 E Railroad Ave, Wytheville VA 24382	276-228-5565	R	1*	<.1
2458	Digital Machine—*Charles Robinson*	110 Easy St Ste B, Buellton CA 93427	805-686-1071	R	1*	<.1
2459	Melfred Borzall Inc—*Richard Melsheimer*	12115 Shoemaker Ave, Santa Fe Springs CA 90670	562-946-7524	R	1*	<.1
2460	Richard Fujikura Manufacturing Inc—*Thomas Breslin*	990 Lone Oak Rd Ste 11, Saint Paul MN 55121	651-994-6810	R	1*	<.1
2461	Theodore E Tiaga Sr—*Theodore Tiaga*	414 Borrego Ct, San Dimas CA 91773	909-592-4311	R	1*	<.1
2462	Precision Machine Company Inc—*Joe Price*	PO Box 6892, Richmond VA 23230	804-359-5758	R	1*	<.1
2463	Trebor Instrument Corp—*Zygmunt Grzesiak*	39 Balsam Dr, Dix Hills NY 11746	631-423-7026	R	1*	<.1
2464	American Durable Inc—*Jon Mathisrud*	6080 Claude Way, Inver Grove Heights MN 55076	651-455-6314	R	1*	<.1
2465	Quality Engineering And Tool Co—*Ginger Moody*	380 Wheatfield St, York PA 17403	717-854-3875	R	1*	<.1
2466	Bit Shop Inc—*Gary Clark*	1646 Watson Ct, Milpitas CA 95035	408-262-0713	R	1*	<.1
2467	Fixture Engineering Inc—*Robert Johnston*	1600 Kentucky St A5, Bellingham WA 98229	360-671-9052	R	1*	<.1
2468	Tarney Inc—*Raymond Peterson*	4520 W N Ave, Chicago IL 60639	773-235-0331	R	1*	<.1
2469	Commonwealth Machine Co—*James Watlington*	PO Box 147, Danville VA 24543	434-793-3488	R	1*	<.1
2470	Farnsworth Engineering—*Brian Farnsworth*	PO Box 105, East Liverpool OH 43920	330-385-1745	R	1*	<.1
2471	Kohl And Vick Machine Works Inc—*James Kohl*	2655 Erie St, River Grove IL 60171	708-456-0656	R	1*	<.1
2472	Edward F Bauer—*Edward Bauer*	1633 Old Bayshore Hwy, San Jose CA 95112	408-436-7670	R	1*	<.1
2473	Ab-Wey Machine and Die Company Inc—*Anthony Delacono*	PO Box 567, Hanson MA 02341	781-294-8031	R	1*	<.1
2474	Grand Harbor Yacht Sales And Service—*John Bennington*	706 Alpha Dr, Cleveland OH 44143	440-449-5815	R	1*	<.1
2475	Tait Machine Tool Inc—*Louis Schuh*	PO Box 134, Kankakee IL 60901	815-932-2011	R	1*	<.1
2476	Wagner and Sons Machine Shop Inc—*Maryjane Wagne*	420 Business Park Ln, Allentown PA 18109	610-434-6640	R	1*	<.1
2477	Nor Service Inc—*Neil Rouse*	215 S State Ave, Freeport IL 61032	815-232-8379	R	1*	<.1
2478	Grove Tools Inc—*Robert Smith*	PO Box 1306, Dubuque IA 52004	563-588-0536	R	1*	<.1
2479	Crouch Industries Inc—*Darrell Crouch*	1 Clark Rd, Shelbyville IN 46176	317-398-8600	R	1*	<.1
2480	Pomeroy Tool Inc—*Terri Malend*	19031 Triangle Rd Nw, Elk River MN 55330	763-441-3010	R	1*	<.1
2481	K Hein Machines Inc—*Walter Hein*	341 Vestal Pkwy E, Vestal NY 13850	607-748-1546	R	1*	<.1
2482	Industrial Tooling Service Of Asheville Inc—*Cliff Johnson*	PO Box 877, Leicester NC 28748	828-683-4168	R	1*	<.1
2483	R H Bolick and Company Inc—*Richard Bolick*	1210 9th Ave Ne, Hickory NC 28601	828-322-7847	R	1*	<.1
2484	Travis Machine Company Inc—*Malcolm Travis*	5875 Alma Hwy, Van Buren AR 72956	479-474-9212	R	1*	<.1
2485	Columbia Machine Works—*Henry Nichols*	934 75th Ave, Oakland CA 94621	510-568-0808	R	1*	<.1
2486	Mead Industries Inc—*Greg Mead*	PO Box 402, Wood River NE 68883	308-583-2875	R	1*	<.1
2487	Tri Tech Equipment Inc—*Calvin Bowie*	112 Us Hwy 80 E, Selma AL 36701	334-872-1650	R	1*	<.1
2488	Bill Barrett Industries Inc—*William Barrett*	216 E Mcleroy Blvd, Saginaw TX 76179	817-232-8956	R	1*	<.1
2489	Ellingson Inc—*Thomas Ellingson*	119 W Santa Fe Ave, Fullerton CA 92832	714-773-1923	R	1*	<.1
2490	Innova Pure Water Inc—*Dave Zich*	8528 Davis Blvd Ste 13, North Richland Hills TX 76182		P	1	<.1
2491	Intrasonics Inc—*Peter Rogozinski*	PO Box 186, Thomaston CT 06787	860-283-8040	R	1*	<.1
2492	Lanlyn Instrument Company Inc—*Richard Lanzetta*	28 Otis St Unit 1a, West Babylon NY 11704	631-491-8545	R	1*	<.1
2493	Hamlin Industries—*R Welden*	PO Box 1208, Pilot Mountain NC 27041	336-368-2131	R	<1*	<.1
2494	Component Machine Inc—*Thomas Crowe*	1631 Gent Ave, Indianapolis IN 46202	317-635-8929	R	<1*	<.1
2495	H and M Thread Rolling Company Inc—*Hubert Monzel*	9212 Grand Ave, Franklin Park IL 60131	847-451-1570	R	<1*	<.1
2496	Boucher Company Inc—*Joseph Boucher*	367 River Rd, North Conway NH 03860	603-356-6455	R	<1*	<.1
2497	Nixon Tool Company Inc—*Scott Nixon*	PO Box 1505, Richmond IN 47375	765-966-6608	R	<1*	<.1
2498	Ryan Machine Inc—*William Ryan*	4164 B Pl Nw, Auburn WA 98001	253-854-9000	R	<1*	<.1
2499	Concepts And Controls Inc—*Anant Venkateswar*	2530 Apple Hill Ct N, Buffalo Grove IL 60089	847-478-9296	R	<1*	<.1
2500	Dunbar Machine Co—*Robert Holsing*	75 Woodvale St, Dunbar PA 15431	724-277-8711	R	<1*	<.1
2501	Goyette Machine Associates Inc—*Paul Goyette*	23 Carrington St, Lincoln RI 02865	401-724-7772	R	<1*	<.1
2502	L and P Machine Co—*Terry Allen*	8488 State Rte 305, Garrettsville OH 44231	330-527-2108	R	<1*	<.1
2503	Permian Supply and Manufacturing—*James Martin*	PO Box 15070, Odessa TX 79768	432-366-1000	R	<1*	<.1
2504	R and B Mold And Die Inc—*David Brantley*	1560 Lake St, La Porte IN 46350	219-324-4176	R	<1*	<.1
2505	S and H Tool Inc—*Dennis Seibert*	5720 Columbia Cir, West Palm Beach FL 33407	561-845-2529	R	<1*	<.1
2506	Seme and Son Automotive Inc—*Frank Seme*	1320 E 260th St, Euclid OH 44132	216-261-0066	R	<1*	<.1
2507	Synthesis Industries Inc—*Brian Lewis*	PO Box 3535, Lewistown MT 59457	406-538-7165	R	<1*	<.1
2508	Accura Industries Inc—*Ali Karahan*	435 Trabold Rd, Rochester NY 14624	585-426-5660	R	<1*	<.1
2509	Athan Corp—*Gus Athanasiou*	50 S Linden Ave Ste 10, South San Francisco CA 94080	650-589-6111	R	<1*	<.1
2510	William A Moddrel—*William Moddrel*	888 Scholl Rd, Pottstown PA 19465	610-327-8296	R	<1*	<.1
2511	Appalachian Tool and Machine Inc—*Grace Frizsell*	1038 Old Us Hwy 70 W, Black Mountain NC 28711	828-669-0142	R	<1*	<.1
2512	Peck Precision Machine and Tool—*Gerald Peck*	PO Box 95, Friendsville PA 18818	570-553-2608	R	<1*	<.1

Rank	Company Name—*Executive Officer*	Address, City, State, Zip	Phone	Type	Fin	Empls
2513	JG Machine Inc—*James Marunich*	1984 Englewood Ave, Akron OH 44312	330-784-7700	R	<1*	<.1
2514	Hansen Research Inc—*Peter Hansen*	2759 S 300 W Ste G, Salt Lake City UT 84115	801-467-8576	R	<1*	<.1
2515	Heiting Tool And Die Inc—*Linda Heiting*	N8018 Grandy Rd, Black Creek WI 54106	920-984-3307	R	<1*	<.1
2516	Kliegel Machine Company LLC	104 Hibbard Rd, Big Flats NY 14814	607-562-3275	R	<1*	<.1
2517	RD Dane Corp—*Michael Mitchell*	45 Appleton St, Everett MA 02149	617-387-6701	R	<1*	<.1
2518	Micron Enviro Systems Inc—*Bradley Rudman*	8 Bond St Ste 121, Great Neck NY 11021	516-474-0310	P	<1	N/A
2519	Zip Tool and Die Company Inc—*David Ayres*	12200 Sprecher Ave, Cleveland OH 44135	216-267-1117	R	N/A	<.1

TOTALS: SIC 3599 Industrial Machinery Nec
Companies: 2,519 — 43,758 — 151.3

3612 Transformers Except Electronic

Rank	Company Name—*Executive Officer*	Address, City, State, Zip	Phone	Type	Fin	Empls
1	Phillips lighting—*Frans Van Houten*	10275 W Higgins Rd, Rosemont IL 60018	847-390-5000	D	1,076*	3.0
2	Howard Industries Inc—*Billy Howard*	PO Box 1588, Laurel MS 39441	601-425-3151	R	900	3.0
3	Cooper Power Systems LLC	1319 Lincoln Ave, Waukesha WI 53186	262-524-3300	S	675*	4.0
4	Central Moloney Inc—*RR (Bo) Siever*	PO Box 6608, Pine Bluff AR 71611	870-247-5320	R	252*	.7
5	Alphabet Inc—*John C Corey*	9400 E Market St, Warren OH 44484	330-856-2443	D	205*	2.8
6	Delta Star Inc—*Ivan Tepper*	PO Box 10429, Lynchburg VA 24506	434-845-0921	R	156*	.4
7	Programmable Products Div—*Frank S Hermance*	9250 Brown Deer Rd, San Diego CA 92121	858-450-0085	D	146*	.4
8	Jinpan International Ltd—*Li Zhiyuan*	390 Veterans Blvd, Carlstadt NJ 07072	201-460-8778	P	144	1.2
9	Transistor Devices Inc—*James Feely*	36 Newburgh Rd, Hackettstown NJ 07840	908-850-5088	R	142*	2.0
10	Power Partners Inc—*Steve Hollis*	200 Newton Bridge Rd, Athens GA 30607	706-548-3121	R	141*	.5
11	Maxitrol Co—*Larry Koskela*	PO Box 2230, Southfield MI 48037	248-356-1400	R	126*	.4
12	CG Power System USA Inc—*Francis Robberechts*	1 Pauwels Dr, Washington MO 63090	636-239-9300	R	108*	.3
13	Solomon Corp—*Phillip Hemmer*	PO Box 245, Solomon KS 67480	785-655-2191	R	100*	.5
14	Spellman High Voltage Electric Corp—*Loren Skeist*	475 Wireless Blvd, Hauppauge NY 11788	631-630-3000	R	78*	1.0
15	Waukesha Electric Systems Inc—*Tom Brockley*	400 S Prairie Ave, Waukesha WI 53186		R	72*	.5
16	ABB Incorporated Small Power Transformers—*Laura Kennedy*	PO Box 920, South Boston VA 24592	434-575-7971	D	69	.5
17	Fortron Source Corp—*Jackson Wang*	23181 Antonio Pkwy, Rcho Sta Marg CA 92688	949-766-9240	R	60*	<.1
18	Intermatic Inc—*David Schroeder*	7777 Winn Rd, Spring Grove IL 60081	815-675-2321	R	59*	.8
19	France/Scott Fetzer Co—*Philip Jones*	PO Box 300, Fairview TN 37062	615-799-0551	S	46	.3
20	International Rectifier HiRel Products LLC—*Alex Lidow*	1057 East St, Tewksbury MA 01876	978-534-5776	S	42*	.3
21	Electro-Mechanical Corp—*Morris Arnold*	PO Box 8200, Bristol VA 24203	276-466-8200	R	40*	.6
22	NWL Transformers Inc—*David Seitz*	312 Rising Sun Rd, Bordentown NJ 08505	609-298-7300	R	39*	.3
23	Ge Drives and Controls Inc—*Stephen Smith*	1501 Roanoke Blvd, Salem VA 24153	540-387-7000	R	39*	.9
24	Mining Controls Inc—*Randall Hurst*	PO Box 1141, Beckley WV 25802	304-252-6243	R	37*	.6
25	Niagara Transformer Corp—*Fred Darby*	PO Box 233, Buffalo NY 14225	716-896-6500	R	36*	.1
26	Deltran Corp—*Michael Prelec*	801 International Spee, Deland FL 32724	386-736-7900	R	36*	.1
27	Acme Electric Corp—*Robert Arzbaecher*	PO Box 248, Spring Grove IL 60081	815-675-6641	R	35*	.2
28	Zareba Systems Inc—*Dale A Nordquist*	13705 26th Ave N Ste 1, Minneapolis MN 55441	763-551-1125	S	32	.1
29	AFP Transformers LLC—*Tom Castle*	206 Talmadge Rd, Edison NJ 08817	732-248-0305	D	32*	.1
30	Globtek Inc—*Anna Kaplan*	186 Veterans Dr, Northvale NJ 07647	201-784-1000	R	31*	.1
31	Manutech Assemble Inc—*Lance Durban*	8181 Nw 91st Ter Ste 1, Medley FL 33166	305-888-2800	R	27*	.5
32	Kepco Inc—*Martin Kupferberg*	13130 Sanford Ave, Flushing NY 11355	718-461-7000	R	26*	.2
33	Pennsylvania Transformer Technology Inc—*Ravi Rahangdale*	30 Curry Ave Ste 2, Canonsburg PA 15317	724-873-2100	R	25*	.4
34	Meramec Electrical Products Inc—*Nichols Sanazaro*	1 Industrial Dr, Cuba MO 65453	573-885-2521	R	25*	.1
35	SNC Manufacturing Company Inc—*Kim Halverson*	101 W Waukau Ave, Oshkosh WI 54902	920-231-7370	R	24*	.4
36	Hobart Ground Power—*Ashraf Nasser*	1177 Trade Rd E, Troy OH 45373	937-332-5080	D	24*	.1
37	Standard Solar Inc—*Tony Clifford*	1355 Piccard Dr Ste 30, Rockville MD 20850	301-944-1200	R	23	.1
38	Golden Pacific Electronics Inc—*Wilson Chiu*	560 S Melrose St, Placentia CA 92870	714-993-6970	R	22*	<.1
39	Raf Tabtronics LLC—*Jim Oneill*	200 Lexington Ave, Deland FL 32724	386-736-1698	R	22*	.3
40	Universal Lighting Technologies Inc—*Pat Sullivan*	26 Century Blvd Ste 50, Nashville TN 37214	615-316-5100	R	22*	.3
41	Hitran Corp—*John Hindle*	362 State Rte 31, Flemington NJ 08822	908-782-5525	R	20*	.2
42	Quality Transformer and Electronics Inc—*Evan Mayerhoff*	963 Ames Ave, Milpitas CA 95035	408-263-8444	R	19*	.1
43	Current Controls Inc—*Sylvia Landon*	353 S Brooklyn Ave, Wellsville NY 14895	585-593-1544	R	16*	.2
44	Olsun Electrics Corp—*Cathleen Asta*	PO Box 1, Richmond IL 60071	815-678-2421	R	16*	.1
45	Industrial Power Generating Company LLC—*Mike Guyette*	2250 Dabney Rd, Richmond VA 23230	804-521-3500	R	14*	.1
46	Titan Energy Worldwide Inc—*Jeffrey W Flannery*	55800 Grand River Ste, New Hudson MI 48165	248-264-1900	P	14	.1
47	Pacific Transformer Corp—*Pat Thomas*	5399 E Hunter Ave, Anaheim CA 92807	714-779-0450	R	14*	.2
48	Neeltran Inc—*Antonio Capanna*	71 Pickett District Rd, New Milford CT 06776	860-350-5964	R	14*	.1
49	Mgm Transformer Co—*Al Gogerchian*	5701 Smithway St, Commerce CA 90040	323-726-0888	R	13*	.1
50	Powell-ESCO Manufacturing Co—*Thomas Powell*	PO Box 12818, Houston TX 77217	713-944-6900	S	13*	.1
51	Bicron Electronics Co—*Chris Skomorowski*	50 Barlow St, Canaan CT 06018	860-824-5125	R	13*	.1
52	Unique Lighting Systems Inc—*Randy Weisser*	1240 Simpson Way, Escondido CA 92029	760-489-1245	R	13*	.1
53	AMP Manufacturing And Supply Inc—*Cindi Dingmann*	PO Box 47036, Minneapolis MN 55447	763-551-1555	R	13*	.1
54	Radionic Industries Inc—*Jeffrey Winton*	6625 W Diversey Ave, Chicago IL 60707	773-804-0100	R	12*	.1
55	Datatronics Romoland Inc—*Nina Siu*	PO Box 1579, Romoland CA 92585	951-928-7700	R	12*	.1
56	V And F Transformer Corp—*Francis Foderaro*	31w222 W Bartlott Rd, Bartlett IL 60103	630-497-8070	R	12*	.1
57	Johnson Electric Coil Company Inc—*William Bockes*	821 Watson St, Antigo WI 54409	715-627-4367	R	11*	.1
58	Stangenes Industries Inc—*Magne Stangenes*	1052 E Meadow Cir, Palo Alto CA 94303	650-493-0814	R	11*	.1
59	Teal Electronics Corp—*Don Klein*	10350 Sorrento Valley, San Diego CA 92121	858-558-9000	S	11*	.1
60	ComCables—*Greg Greenwood*	2607 W 8th Ave, Denver CO 80204	303-296-1000	R	11*	<.1
61	Precision Inc (Minneapolis Minnesota)—*Dave Anderson*	1700 Freeway Blvd, Minneapolis MN 55430	763-561-6880	R	10*	.1
62	Dongan Electric Manufacturing Co—*Steve Hicks*	2987 Franklin St, Detroit MI 48207	313-567-8500	R	10*	.1
63	Energy Sciences Inc—*Tsuneo Kobayashi*	42 Industrial Way Ste, Wilmington MA 01887	978-694-9000	R	10*	.1
64	Sutton Designs Inc	215 N Cayuga St, Ithaca NY 14850	607-277-4801	R	10	.1
65	Dyco Electronics Inc—*Gregory Georgek*	7775 Industrial Park R, Hornell NY 14843	607-324-2030	R	9*	.1
66	Falcon Electric Inc—*Arthur Seredian*	5106 Azusa Canyon Rd, Irwindale CA 91706	626-962-7770	R	9*	<.1
67	Keytronics Inc—*Thomas Mills*	2200 Smithtown Ave, Ronkonkoma NY 11779	631-981-2400	R	9*	.1
68	Transformer Engineering LLC—*Justin Patrick*	2550 Brookpark Rd, Cleveland OH 44134	216-741-5282	R	9*	.1
69	Northlake Engineering Inc—*William Hardt*	PO Box 370, Bristol WI 53104	262-857-9600	R	8*	.1
70	Hindle Power Inc—*William Hindle*	1075 Saint John St, Easton PA 18042	610-330-9000	R	8*	.1
71	Duct-O-Wire Co—*James Holden*	PO Box 519, Corona CA 92878	951-735-8220	R	7*	.1
72	Wicc Ltd—*Terry Bierrie*	PO Box 252, Washington IL 61571	309-444-4125	R	7*	.1
73	Powell Electrical Manufacturing Co North Canton Div—*Bill Reffert*	8967 Pleasantwood Ave, North Canton OH 44720	330-966-1750	D	7*	.1
74	Van Tran Industries Inc—*Al Bolin*	PO Box 20128, Waco TX 76702		R	7*	.1
75	Lighting Technology Services Inc—*Russell Royal*	2801 Catherine Way, Santa Ana CA 92705	949-428-5040	R	7*	<.1
76	Custom Magnetics Inc—*Kirti Shah*	801 W Main St, North Manchester IN 46962	260-982-8508	R	7*	.1
77	Everbrite Electronics Inc—*William Fritz*	720 W Cherry St, Chanute KS 66720	620-431-7383	S	7*	.1

Note: An asterisk (*) indicates an estimated financial figure. The company type code used is as follows: R = Private, P = Public, S = Private Subsidiary, B = Public Subsidiary, D = Division, J = Joint Venture, I = Investment Fund.

COMPANY RANKINGS BY SALES WITHIN 4-DIGIT SIC

Rank	Company Name—Executive Officer	Address, City, State, Zip	Phone	Type	Fin	Empls
78	Electronic Systems Protection Inc—Kim Alfreds	517 N Industrial Dr, Zebulon NC 27597	919-269-6968	R	7*	<.1
79	Hunterdon Transformer Company Inc—Morris Bock	75 Industrial Rd, Alpha NJ 08865	908-454-2400	R	6*	.1
80	Coil Tec Of Arizona Inc—Charles Middleton	17617 N 25th Ave Ste 1, Phoenix AZ 85023	602-547-0016	R	6*	.1
81	RE Uptegraff Manufacturing Co—Susan Endersbe	PO Box 182, Scottdale PA 15683	724-887-7700	R	6*	.1
82	Lenco Electronics Inc—Lenard Duncan	1330 S Belden St, Mchenry IL 60050	815-344-2900	R	6*	<.1
83	Pacific Power Source	17692 Fitch, Irvine CA 92614	949-251-1800	R	6*	<.1
84	Sunbelt Transfomer Ltd—Kyle Queen	1922 S Mrtn Lther King, Temple TX 76504	254-771-3777	R	5*	<.1
85	M D Henry Company Inc—Patrick Henry	PO Box 40, Pelham AL 35124	205-663-6711	R	5*	<.1
86	SC Electronics Inc—Elizabeth Ibarra	200 Commerce St, Azle TX 76020	817-444-6600	R	5*	.1
87	Rising Sun Solar Electric LLC—Brad Albert	810 Kokomo Rd Ste 160, Haiku HI 96708	808-575-2202	R	5*	<.1
88	American Logistic Management International Supply—Loretta Wurm	9 Balsam Ct, Newtown PA 18940	267-249-9398	R	4*	.1
89	Betz Transformers Inc—Carrol Betz	PO Box 729, Olathe CO 81425	970-323-5177	R	4*	<.1
90	Ventex Technology Corp—Charles C Johnston	1440 W Indiantown Rd S, Jupiter FL 33458		R	4*	<.1
91	International Coil Inc—Jorge Machadinho	15 Jonathan Dr Ste 1, Brockton MA 02301	508-580-8515	R	4*	<.1
92	Warco Manufacturing Company Inc—Dale Lohmeyer	PO Box 48, Marthasville MO 63357	636-433-2212	R	4*	<.1
93	Syndevco Inc—Ronald Grobbel	PO Box 265, Southfield MI 48037	248-356-2839	R	4*	<.1
94	J B Nottingham and Company Inc—Paul Savoca	75 Hoffman Ln, Islandia NY 11749	631-234-2002	R	3*	<.1
95	Model Rectifier Corp—Frank Ritota	PO Box 6312, Edison NJ 08818	732-225-2100	R	3*	<.1
96	Magnetic Windings Company Inc—Albert Marron	2711 Freemansburg Ave, Easton PA 18045	610-253-2751	R	3*	<.1
97	Gulf South Infrasystems LLC—Susan Mims	4944 Tufts Rd, Mobile AL 36619	251-662-1390	R	3*	<.1
98	Ensign Corp—Brij Shamar	201 Ensign Rd, Bellevue IA 52031	563-872-3900	R	3*	<.1
99	B and B Transformer Inc—Dennis Betz	PO Box 96, Farmington MN 55024	651-463-2573	R	3*	<.1
100	Berkeley Magnetics Inc—Suresh Sansguiri	1836 Stone Ave, San Jose CA 95125	408-292-2023	R	3*	<.1
101	Greenville Transformer Co—Billie Pickens	PO Box 845, Greenville TX 75403	903-455-1610	R	3*	<.1
102	Mag-Tran Equipment Corp—Burt Rosenblum	3020 Red Hat Ln, City of Industry CA 90601	562-695-4200	R	3*	<.1
103	Coiltron Inc—William French	PO Box 23940, Portland OR 97281	503-620-8231	R	3*	<.1
104	Operating Technical Electronics Inc—James Dernehl	1289 Hemphill St, Fort Worth TX 76104	817-288-2600	R	3*	<.1
105	Transformer Manufacturers Inc—Alexander Gianaras	7051 W Wilson Ave, Harwood Heights IL 60706	708-457-1200	R	2*	<.1
106	Total Recoil Magnetics Inc—Dick Clarke	89 October Hill Rd Ste, Holliston MA 01746	508-429-9600	R	2*	<.1
107	Glen Magnetics Inc—John Sarro	1165 3rd Ave, Alpha NJ 08865	908-454-3717	R	2*	<.1
108	Nutech Industries Inc—Phyllis Stiles	PO Box 97276, Las Vegas NV 89193	702-597-0007	R	2*	<.1
109	Aldonex Inc—Alan Miller	PO Box 148, Bellwood IL 60104	708-547-5663	R	2*	<.1
110	Osborne Transformer Corp—James Osborne	PO Box 70, Fraser MI 48026	586-468-9410	R	2*	<.1
111	Wabash Transformer Inc—Bridge Sharma	101 Industrial Park Dr, Clarence IA 52216	563-452-3366	R	2*	<.1
112	National Air Vibrator Co—Mark Neundorfer	PO Box 40563, Houston TX 77240	713-467-3636	R	2*	<.1
113	Dow-Elco Inc—James Eldridge	PO Box 669, Montebello CA 90640	323-723-1288	R	2*	<.1
114	Heyboer Transformers Inc—Alden Arendson	17382 Hayes St, Grand Haven MI 49417	616-842-5830	R	2*	<.1
115	MagneLab Div—Phil Hemmer	600 Weaver Park Rd, Longmont CO 80501	303-772-9100	S	2*	<.1
116	Foster Transformer Co—Herman A Harrison	3820 Colerain Ave, Cincinnati OH 45223	513-681-2420	R	2*	<.1
117	Lti Power Systems—Robert Morog	10800 Middle Ave Hngr, Elyria OH 44035	440-327-5050	R	2*	<.1
118	IntelliPower Inc	1746 N St Thomas Cir, Orange CA 92865	714-921-1580	R	2*	<.1
119	Power Glass Co—Jim Holland	PO Box 581, Wauna WA 98395	253-884-4008	R	2*	<.1
120	Power Magne-Tech Corp—Leon Zelcer	653 Sayre Ave, Perth Amboy NJ 08861	732-826-4700	R	2*	<.1
121	Controlled Magnetics Inc—Michael Jagiela	126 Summit St, Brighton MI 48116	810-844-0667	R	2*	<.1
122	Lamar Enterprises Inc—Larry Stanley	PO Box 271565, Oklahoma City OK 73137	405-682-5511	R	2*	<.1
123	Frederick Cowan and Company Inc—Thomas Cowan	48 Kroemer Ave, Riverhead NY 11901	631-369-0360	R	2*	<.1
124	Yutaka Electric International Inc—Arthur Seredian	5116 Azusa Canyon Rd, Baldwin Park CA 91706	626-962-7770	R	1*	<.1
125	Virginia Transformer Corp—Prabhat Jain	220 Glade View Dr Ne, Roanoke VA 24012	540-345-9892	R	1*	.6
126	Power Control Systems Inc—James Darnell	2861 Jolly Rd Ste C, Okemos MI 48864	517-339-1442	R	1*	<.1
127	LEA International Inc—Kenneth Pitt	4726 Eisenhower Blvd, Tampa FL 33634	813-621-1324	R	1*	<.1
128	Pearson Electronics Inc	4009 Transport St, Palo Alto CA 94303	650-494-6444	R	1*	<.1
129	Soma Magnetics Corp—Harry Sidhu	585 S State College Bl, Fullerton CA 92831	714-447-0782	R	1*	<.1
130	Tortran Inc—Ulrik Poulsen	6 Waterview Dr, Shelton CT 06484	203-954-0050	R	1*	<.1
131	Energy Transformation Systems Inc—Trudy M Andresen	43353 Osgood Rd Ste B, Fremont CA 94539	510-656-2012	R	1*	<.1
132	Trans Mag Corp—Ashok Berajawala	300 Jackson St, Lowell MA 01852	978-458-1487	R	1*	<.1
133	Wirebenders Inc—Marsha Middleton	10201 N 21st Ave Ste 4, Phoenix AZ 85021	602-861-1856	R	1*	<.1
134	Nilsson Electrical Laboratory Inc—John Brown	333 W Side Ave, Jersey City NJ 07305	201-521-4860	R	1*	<.1
135	Antique Automobile Radio Inc—Daniel Schulz	700 Tampa Rd, Palm Harbor FL 34683	727-785-8733	R	<1*	<.1
136	Marina Power Company Inc—Robert Waddle	8456 Nw 61st St, Miami FL 33166	305-470-0037	R	<1*	<.1
137	L-3 Power Paragon—Jerome J Ozovek	901 E Ball Rd, Anaheim CA 92805	714-956-9200	S	<1	<.1
138	Silver Horn Mining Ltd—Daniel Bleak	3900A 31st St N, Saint Petersburg FL 33714	727-525-5552	R	<1	N/A

TOTALS: SIC 3612 Transformers Except Electronic
Companies: 138   5,771   33.2

3613 Switchgear & Switchboard Apparatus

Rank	Company Name—Executive Officer	Address, City, State, Zip	Phone	Type	Fin	Empls
1	ABB Power T and D Company Inc—Enrique Santacana	1021 Main Campus Dr, Raleigh NC 27606	919-856-2360	D	1,677	9.5
2	Littelfuse Inc—Gordon Hunter	8755 W Higgins Rd Ste, Chicago IL 60631	773-628-1000	P	665	6.0
3	Siemens Power Transmission and Distribution Inc—David Pacyna	7000 Siemens Rd, Wendell NC 27591	919-365-2200	D	648*	1.0
4	Powell-Process Systems Inc—Patrick McDonald Powell Industries Inc	8550 Mosley Dr, Houston TX 77075	713-944-6900	S	627*	1.1
5	Powell Energy Systems Inc—Patrick L McDonald Powell Industries Inc	8550 Mosley Dr, Houston TX 77075	713-944-6900	S	577*	1.0
6	Powell Industries Inc—Thomas W Powell	PO Box 12818, Houston TX 77217	713-944-6900	P	562	2.6
7	Mitsubishi Electric Power Products Inc—Jack Greaf	530 Keystone Dr, Warrendale PA 15086	724-772-2555	S	508*	.3
8	Liebert Corp—Robert Bauer	PO Box 29186, Columbus OH 43229	614-888-0246	S	440*	5.0
9	Honeywell Inc Micro Switch Div—David Cote	11 W Spring St, Freeport IL 61032	815-235-5500	D	440*	4.5
10	Takkt America Holding Inc—Thomas Loos	770 S 70th St, Milwaukee WI 53214	414-443-1700	R	415*	.8
11	Calix Inc—Carl Russo	1035 N McDowell Blvd, Petaluma CA 94954	707-766-3000	P	345	.6
12	S and C Electric Co—John Estey	6601 N Ridge Blvd, Chicago IL 60626	773-338-1000	R	289*	1.7
13	E-T-A Circuit Breakers—Tony Bright	1551 Bishop Ct, Mount Prospect IL 60056	847-827-7600	R	235*	1.2
14	Shoretel Inc—Peter Blackmore	960 Stewart Dr, Sunnyvale CA 94085	408-331-3300	P	200	.6
15	Motion Holdings Inc—Randy Bays	11380 White Rock Rd, Rancho Cordova CA 95742	916-463-9200	R	195*	.4
16	On-Line Power Corp—Abblid Gourgerchian	5701 Smithway St, Commerce CA 90040	323-721-5017	R	181*	.2
17	Cantata Technology Inc—Timothy Murray	15 Crawford St, Needham MA 02494	781-449-4100	S	159*	.4
18	Powell Electrical Manufacturing Co Powell Industries Inc	PO Box 12818, Houston TX 77217	713-944-6900	S	149*	.9
19	Russelectric Inc—Raymond Russell	99 Industrial Park Rd, Hingham MA 02043	781-749-6000	R	144*	.4
20	Cutler-Hammer De Puerto Rico Inc—Alexander Cutler	PO Box 709, Arecibo PR 00613	787-881-3640	R	143*	3.0

Rank	Company Name—*Executive Officer*	Address, City, State, Zip	Phone	Type	Fin	Empls
21	Hydra-Electric Co—*Allen Davis*	PO Box 7724, Burbank CA 91510	818-843-6211	R	71*	.2
22	Grayhill Inc—*Gene Hill*	PO Box 10373, La Grange IL 60525	708-354-1040	R	61*	.8
23	TII Network Technologies Inc—*Brian J Kelley*	141 Rodeo Dr, Edgewood NY 11717	631-789-5000	P	55	.1
24	Axesstel Inc—*Clark Hickock*	6815 Flanders Dr Ste 2, San Diego CA 92121	858-625-2100	P	54	<.1
25	Westwood Corp (Tulsa Oklahoma)—*Ernest H McKee*	12042 E 60th St, Tulsa OK 74146	918-252-0481	S	51*	.2
26	SPD Technologies Inc—*Jerry Ovovevk*	13500 Roosevelt Blvd, Philadelphia PA 19116	215-677-4900	R	50*	.4
27	Cole Hersee Co—*Robert Mayer*	20 Old Colony Ave, Boston MA 02127	617-268-2100	R	50*	.4
28	M and G Electronics Corp—*Mark Garcea*	PO Box 8187, Virginia Beach VA 23450	757-468-6000	R	46*	.7
29	Point Eight Power Inc—*Thomas Reagan*	PO Box 1850, Gretna LA 70054	504-394-6100	R	40*	.1
30	Magnetic Instrumentation Inc—*G Bradley*	8431 Castlewood Dr, Indianapolis IN 46250	317-842-7500	R	36*	.1
31	Powercon Corp—*Ralph Siegel*	PO Box 477, Severn MD 21144	410-551-6500	R	36*	.5
32	Systems Control—*Dave Brule Sr*	PO Box 788, Iron Mountain MI 49801	906-774-0440	S	34*	.2
33	Technology Research Corp—*G Gary Yetman*	5250 140th Ave N, Clearwater FL 33760	727-535-0572	S	33*	.5
34	Indicon Corp—*Paul Duhaime*	6417 Ctr Dr, Sterling Heights MI 48312	586-274-0505	R	31*	.2
35	Winona Watlow Inc—*Peter Desloge*	PO Box 5580, Winona MN 55987	507-454-5300	R	30*	.3
36	Coghlin Companies Inc—*James Coghlin*	17 Briden St, Worcester MA 01605	508-753-2354	R	30*	.3
37	Comus International Inc—*Robert Romano*	454 Allwood Rd, Clifton NJ 07012	973-777-6900	R	28*	.3
38	Professional Power Products Inc—*Carl Trent*	448 W Madison St, Darien WI 53114	262-882-9000	R	27*	.2
39	Orbit International Corp—*Dennis Sunshine*	80 Cabot Ct, Hauppauge NY 11788	631-435-8300	P	27	.1
40	E A Pedersen Co—*Frank Sommer*	3900 Dahlman Ave, Omaha NE 68107	402-734-3900	R	20*	.2
41	Superior Controls Inc—*Gerald Blankenship*	14925 Galleon Ct, Plymouth MI 48170	734-454-0500	R	20*	.1
42	Westwood Corp—*Ernie Mckee*	PO Box 35493, Tulsa OK 74153	918-250-4444	R	18*	.1
43	Kasa Companies Inc—*Mike Haug*	418 E Ave B, Salina KS 67401	785-825-7181	R	18*	.2
44	Pacs Industries Inc—*Mandel Dalis*	1211 Stewart Ave, Bethpage NY 11714	516-465-7100	R	17*	.2
45	Mitsubishi Electric Power Products—*JE Greaf*	530 Keystone Dr, Warrendale PA 15086	724-772-2555	S	17	.1
46	Trayer Engineering Corp—*John Trayer*	898 Pennsylvania Ave, San Francisco CA 94107	415-285-7770	R	15*	<.1
47	Ultrapanel Marine Inc—*Ivo Gomis*	6891 Nw 73rd Ct, Miami FL 33166	305-888-7709	R	14*	<.1
48	Piedmont Dielectrics Corp—*Michael Sexton*	PO Box 849, Woodruff SC 29388	864-476-8304	R	14*	.1
49	Kinney Electrical Manufacturing Co—*Lowell Naber*	678 Buckeye St, Elgin IL 60123	847-742-9600	R	14*	.1
50	Panel-Fab Inc—*Robert Harrison*	10520 Taconic Ter, Cincinnati OH 45215	513-771-7780	R	13*	.1
51	Control Technique Inc—*Richard Mueller*	41200 Technology Park, Sterling Heights MI 48314	586-997-3200	R	13*	.1
52	Staco Systems Inc—*Bruce Gray*	7 Morgan, Irvine CA 92618	949-297-8700	S	13*	.1
53	Myers Controlled Power LLC—*James Owens*	219 E Maple St 100-200, North Canton OH 44720	330-834-3200	R	12*	.1
54	Keystone Electrical Manufacturing Co—*Frederick Buie*	2511 Bell Ave, Des Moines IA 50321	515-283-2567	R	12*	.1
55	Pacific Air Switch Corp—*Travis Garske*	PO Box 328, Forest Grove OR 97116	503-359-3939	R	12*	.1
56	Hallmark Nameplate Inc—*Gary Stura*	1717 Lincoln Ave, Mount Dora FL 32757	352-383-8142	R	12*	.1
57	Paneltronics Inc—*Pedro Pelaez*	11960 Nw 87th Ct Ste 1, Hialeah FL 33018	305-823-9777	R	11*	.1
58	Thermal Engineering Corp—*Rachael Harper*	PO Box 868, Columbia SC 29202	803-783-0750	R	11*	.1
59	Southern Electrical Equipment Company Inc—*Barry Thomas*	PO Box 668547, Charlotte NC 28266	704-392-1396	R	11*	.1
60	Tapeswitch Corp—*Michael Steele*	100 Schmitt Blvd, Farmingdale NY 11735	631-630-0442	R	11*	.1
61	Switching Power Inc—*Melvin Kravitz*	3601 Veterans Memorial, Ronkonkoma NY 11779	631-981-7231	R	11*	.1
62	Phaostron Instrument and Electronic Co—*Paul Mc Guirk*	717 N Coney Ave, Azusa CA 91702	626-969-6801	R	11*	.1
63	KIB Enterprises Corp—*Mike Hoover*	2504 Jeanwood Dr, Elkhart IN 46514	574-262-0518	R	11*	.1
64	Romac Supply Company Inc—*David Rosenfield*	7400 Bandini Blvd, Commerce CA 90040	323-721-5810	R	10*	.1
65	Justcom Tech Inc—*Genny Wu*	2283 Paragon Dr, San Jose CA 95131	408-392-9998	R	10*	.3
66	Zultys Technologies—*Steve Rothenberg*	771 Vaqueros Ave, Sunnyvale CA 94085	408-328-0450	R	10*	<.1
67	Industrial Power Systems Inc—*William Young*	3010 Powers Ave Ste 16, Jacksonville FL 32207	904-731-8844	R	10*	<.1
68	Reliance Controls Corp—*Michael Flegel*	2001 Young Ct, Racine WI 53404	262-634-6155	R	10*	.1
69	Clary Corp—*John G Clary*	150 E Huntington Dr, Monrovia CA 91016	626-359-4486	R	9*	.1
70	Corrigent Systems Inc—*Eric Paneth*	101 Metro Dr Ste 680, San Jose CA 95110	408-392-9292	S	9*	<.1
71	Electrical Installations Inc—*Darlene Fritz*	397 Whittier Hwy, Moultonborough NH 03254	603-253-4525	R	9*	<.1
72	Berthold Gus Electric Co—*Roderick Berthold*	1900 W Carroll Ave, Chicago IL 60612	312-243-5767	R	9*	.1
73	Ran Technologies Inc—*Ann Niemer*	10710 Fallstone Rd, Houston TX 77099	281-530-3248	R	8*	<.1
74	W A Benjamin Electric Co—*D Benjamin*	1615 Staunton Ave, Los Angeles CA 90021	213-749-7731	R	8*	.1
75	States Manufacturing Corp—*Stuart Rubin*	650 Ottawa Ave N, Minneapolis MN 55422	763-588-0536	R	8*	<.1
76	Audio Authority Corp—*Jonathan Sisk*	2048 Mercer Rd, Lexington KY 40511	859-233-4599	R	8*	<.1
77	Wingfield Engineering Company Inc—*Alan Wingfield*	PO Box 68, Goodwater AL 35072	256-839-6338	R	7*	<.1
78	Htf Inc—*Eileen Leach*	415 19th St Dr SE, Hickory NC 28602	828-322-2860	R	7*	<.1
79	Carolina Power Systems Of Sumter Inc—*Robert Jones*	PO Box 1468, Sumter SC 29151	803-773-2409	R	7*	<.1
80	Deltrol Controls—*Josh Ferrer*	2740 S 20th St, Milwaukee WI 53215	414-671-6800	S	7*	.1
81	Wildwood Electronics Inc—*Rebecca Owens*	29700 Indian Springs R, Madison AL 35756	256-461-7110	R	7*	.1
82	Delta Nameplate Company Inc—*David Stahler*	1612 W N Ave, Chicago IL 60622	773-252-8900	R	7*	<.1
83	Boltswitch Inc—*James Erickson*	6208 Commercial Rd, Crystal Lake IL 60014	815-459-6900	R	7*	<.1
84	Control Design Inc—*William Harrington*	211 Ridc Park W Dr, Pittsburgh PA 15275	412-788-2280	R	7*	<.1
85	Lincoln Electric Products Company Inc—*Bruce Leff*	947 Lehigh Ave, Union NJ 07083	908-688-2900	R	7*	<.1
86	Circuit Breaker Sales Company Inc—*Finley Ledbetter*	PO Box 1098, Gainesville TX 76241	940-665-4444	R	6*	<.1
87	Penn Panel and Box Co—*George Craven*	PO Box 1458, Collingdale PA 19023	610-586-2700	R	6*	<.1
88	Chicago Switchboard Company Inc—*Richard Blomquist*	470 W Wrightwood Ave, Elmhurst IL 60126	630-833-2266	R	6*	<.1
89	Panelmatic Inc—*Richard Leach*	258 Donald Dr, Fairfield OH 45014	513-829-3666	R	6*	<.1
90	West Plains Electric Motor Service Inc—*Don Holloway*	6680 N Us Hwy 63, West Plains MO 65775	417-256-8749	R	6*	<.1
91	Satin American Corp—*Joseph Satin*	PO Box 619, Shelton CT 06484	203-929-6363	R	6*	<.1
92	Precision Digital Corp—*Jeffrey Peters*	89 October Hill Rd Ste, Holliston MA 01746	508-655-7300	R	6*	<.1
93	Acoustic Technology Inc—*M Bassiouni*	30 Jeffries St, Boston MA 02128	617-567-4969	R	6*	<.1
94	Control Works Inc—*Douglas Strief*	1179 Us 50, Milford OH 45150	513-831-9959	R	5*	<.1
95	Atlas Switch Company Inc—*Gina Paradise*	969 Stewart Ave, Garden City NY 11530	516-222-6280	R	5*	<.1
96	Innovative Controls Corp—*Louis Soltis*	1354 E Broadway St, Toledo OH 43605	419-691-6684	R	5*	<.1
97	Harold K Scholz Co—*Ross Scholz*	PO Box 27067, Omaha NE 68127	402-339-7600	R	5*	<.1
98	General Switchgear Inc—*Iraj Ahmadi*	14729 Spring Ave, Santa Fe Springs CA 90670	562-921-0605	R	5*	<.1
99	Enhancers Inc—*Frank Bruce*	W136n5239 Campbell Ct, Menomonee Falls WI 53051	262-783-5970	R	5*	<.1
100	Powertronic Systems Inc—*Gene B Stafford*	13700 Chef Menteur Hwy, New Orleans LA 70129	504-254-0383	R	5*	<.1
101	Electric Equipment and Engineering Co—*Richard Morroni*	PO Box 16383, Denver CO 80216	303-296-1476	R	5*	<.1
102	Panel Shop Inc—*Carol Crawford*	2800 Palisades Dr, Corona CA 92880	951-739-7000	R	5*	<.1
103	Nutherm International Inc—*Judy Hinson*	501 S 11th St, Mount Vernon IL 62864	618-244-6000	R	5*	<.1
104	Echolab Inc—*Nigel Spratling*	267 Boston Rd Ste 11, North Billerica MA 01862	978-715-1020	R	5*	<.1
105	Electric Controls Co—*Daniel Jerome*	2735 Mercantile Dr, Saint Louis MO 63144	314-645-2400	R	5*	<.1
106	Se-Mar Electric Company Inc—*Robert Haungs*	101 S Ave, West Seneca NY 14224	716-674-7404	R	4*	<.1
107	AC Gentrol Inc—*Angelito Capati*	PO Box 452, Chillicothe IL 61523	309-274-5486	R	4*	<.1
108	Silicon Valley World Trade Corp—*Vencent Liang*	1474 Gladding Ct, Milpitas CA 95035	408-945-6355	R	4*	<.1
109	Engineering Unlimited Inc—*Robert Werner*	1320 12th Ave N, Minneapolis MN 55411	612-522-4040	R	4*	<.1
110	Triplett Corp—*Carlo Carluccio*	850 Perimeter Rd, Manchester NH 03103	603-669-6400	S	4*	.1

Note: An asterisk (*) indicates an estimated financial figure. The company type code used is as follows: R = Private, P = Public, S = Private Subsidiary, B = Public Subsidiary, D = Division, J = Joint Venture, I = Investment Fund.

COMPANY RANKINGS BY SALES WITHIN 4-DIGIT SIC

Rank	Company Name—*Executive Officer*	Address, City, State, Zip	Phone	Type	Fin	Empls
111	Gonzales Electrical Systems LLC—*Gerald Wright*	6930 College St Ste G-, Beaumont TX 77707	409-860-3802	R	4*	.1
112	Electrol Specialties Co—*Frank Bazo*	PO Box 7, South Beloit IL 61080	815-389-2291	S	4*	.1
113	X-Bar Automation Inc—*Michael O'hagan*	961 Elmsford Dr, Troy MI 48083	248-616-9890	R	4*	<.1
114	Murray Controls Inc—*Rochelle Murray*	105 Prosperity Blvd, Piedmont SC 29673	864-845-5454	R	4*	<.1
115	Protection Controls Inc—*James Yates*	PO Box 287, Skokie IL 60076	847-674-7676	R	4*	<.1
116	Consumer Engineering Inc—*Jerrell Hollaway*	2730 Kirby Cir Ne, Palm Bay FL 32905	321-984-8550	R	4*	<.1
117	Custom Craft Controls Inc—*Kenneth Dunaway*	1620 Triplett Blvd, Akron OH 44306	330-630-9599	R	4*	<.1
118	Calo Corp—*Balan Menon*	1040 Kingsland Dr, Batavia IL 60510	630-879-2202	R	4*	<.1
119	Adgo Inc—*Robert Reynolds*	3988 Mcmann Rd, Cincinnati OH 45245	513-752-6880	R	4*	<.1
120	Control 7 Inc—*Mark Jacoby*	32 Scotland Blvd Ste 6, Bridgewater MA 02324	508-697-3197	R	4*	<.1
121	Polatis Inc—*Gerald Wesel*	1 Tech Dr Ste 210, Andover MA 01810	978-670-4910	R	4*	<.1
122	Bdisk Corp—*Seong Kang*	401 Kato Ter, Fremont CA 94539	510-492-0801	R	4*	<.1
123	Custom Control Manufacturer Of Kansas Inc—*Raymond Myers*	5601 Merriam Dr, Shawnee Mission KS 66203	913-722-0343	R	4*	<.1
124	Shallco Inc—*Jason Shallcross*	PO Box 1089, Smithfield NC 27577	919-934-3135	R	3*	<.1
125	Elite Es LLC—*Jonathan Balsfour*	900 Ninth St, Winnsboro SC 29180	803-815-8000	R	3*	<.1
126	Fic Corp—*John Linton*	12216 Parklawn Dr Ste, Rockville MD 20852	301-881-8124	S	3*	<.1
127	Controlled Power Inc—*Michael Dizard*	17909 Bothell Everett, Bothell WA 98012	425-485-1778	R	3*	<.1
128	Custom Flo Inc—*Gregory Cohron*	11275 Sebring Dr, Cincinnati OH 45240	513-742-1110	R	3*	<.1
129	Elliott Industries Inc—*Ken C Elliott Jr*	PO Box 6388, Bossier City LA 71171	318-746-3296	R	3*	<.1
130	Electric Power Equipment Co—*Ron Gutru*	5151 E 56th Ave, Commerce City CO 80022	303-288-0751	R	3*	<.1
131	American Manufacturing Company Inc (Manassas Virginia)—*Robert Mayer*	PO Box 97, Elkwood VA 22718		R	3*	<.1
132	Lovejoy Controls Corp—*Kim Lovejoy*	1301 Sentry Dr, Waukesha WI 53186	262-542-9061	R	3*	<.1
133	Tactical Power Systems Corp—*Robert Freihoff-Lewin*	PO Box 467, Rangeley ME 04970	207-864-5528	R	3*	<.1
134	Advanced Controls Inc—*Jeff Slusher*	9099 Hendricks Rd, Mentor OH 44060	440-632-0236	R	3*	<.1
135	Rexcon Inc—*Lawrence Page*	41775 Production Dr, Harrison Township MI 48045	586-468-9656	R	3*	<.1
136	Smith Control Systems Inc—*Thomas Smith*	1839 Rte 9h, Hudson NY 12534	518-828-7646	R	3*	<.1
137	Pacific Power and Engineering Inc—*Ernest Meissner*	5199 Airport Rd, Redding CA 96002	530-223-5937	R	3*	<.1
138	Controlled Automation Inc—*Dean Graham*	15421 Stony Creek Way, Noblesville IN 46060	317-776-1099	R	2*	<.1
139	Panel Monster Inc—*Donald Leetch*	222 Commerce Dr, Lagrange OH 44050	440-355-4442	R	2*	<.1
140	Applied Electronics Corp—*Bruce Austin*	114 E Main St, Saint Charles IA 50240	641-396-2716	R	2*	<.1
141	Apex Circuits Inc—*Ken Rensing*	PO Box 1190, West Chester OH 45071	513-942-4400	R	2*	<.1
142	Marwell Corp—*Larry Blackwell*	PO Box 139, Mentone CA 92359	909-794-4192	R	2*	<.1
143	Midwest Control Corp—*Ed Tunstall*	9063 S Octavia Ave, Bridgeview IL 60455	708-599-1331	R	2*	<.1
144	Precision Switching Inc—*Rodney Blair*	PO Box 100, Spring Grove IL 60081	815-675-2366	R	2*	<.1
145	Deborah Malush—*Robert Fritz*	7635 Hub Pkwy Units C, Cleveland OH 44125	216-642-1230	R	2*	<.1
146	ARC Technologies Corp—*Stanley Siegel*	PO Box 485, Yukon PA 15698	724-722-7067	R	2*	<.1
147	Auto-Tronic Control Co—*Harold Kowalka*	240 W Andrus Rd, Northwood OH 43619	419-666-5100	R	2*	<.1
148	Doranco Inc—*David Doran*	200 Gilbert St, Mansfield MA 02048	508-261-1200	R	2*	<.1
149	Ai Control Systems Inc—*Thomas Albright*	90 Water St, Reading PA 19605	610-921-9670	R	2*	<.1
150	Sti Inc—*Warner Speakman*	1861 Vanderhorn Dr, Memphis TN 38134	901-382-3632	R	2*	<.1
151	Halma Holdings Inc—*Steve Sowell*	11500 Northlake Dr Ste, Cincinnati OH 45241	513-772-5501	S	2*	<.1
152	Electrical Controls Inc—*Gregory Anderson*	8401 N University St, Peoria IL 61615	309-692-2500	R	2*	<.1
153	Coyote Electronics Inc—*Paul Boggs*	4701 Old Denton Rd, Fort Worth TX 76117	817-485-3336	R	2*	<.1
154	Coordinated Designs and Controls Inc—*John Colvin*	601 Mcfarland St Ste 1, Houston TX 77011	713-921-0220	R	2*	<.1
155	Whitmor Company Inc—*Anthony Pesce*	PO Box 249, Revere MA 02151	781-284-8000	R	2*	<.1
156	Eagle Connector Corp—*Henry Bauerle*	401 Crossen Ave, Elk Grove Village IL 60007	847-593-8737	R	2*	<.1
157	Link Control Systems Inc—*William Bowden*	16 Colt Ct, Ronkonkoma NY 11779	631-471-3950	R	2*	<.1
158	Interconnect Technology Inc—*Michael Susi*	3 Christine Dr, Hudson NH 03051	603-881-9592	R	2*	<.1
159	Robertson Controls Inc—*John Kennedy*	515 Plato Lee Rd, Shelby NC 28150	704-434-2411	R	2*	<.1
160	Kosmos Tool Inc—*John Ferguson*	PO Box 279, Spring Grove IL 60081	815-675-2200	R	2*	<.1
161	Illinois Switchboard Corp—*William Zastawny*	125 W Laura Dr, Addison IL 60101	630-543-0910	R	2*	<.1
162	Peninsula Control Panels Inc—*Sergey Krassilnikoff*	940 Commercial St Ste, San Carlos CA 94070	650-595-9900	R	2*	<.1
163	Quality Industrial Supplies Inc—*Richard Weller*	PO Box 1702, La Porte IN 46352	219-324-2654	R	1*	<.1
164	Control Services Co—*Harold Buice*	6835 E Wt Harris Blvd, Charlotte NC 28215	704-537-2806	R	1*	<.1
165	Specialty Concepts Inc—*Terry Staler*	8954 Mason Ave, Chatsworth CA 91311	818-998-5238	R	1*	<.1
166	Vanguard Instruments Company Inc—*Hai Nguyen*	1520 S Hellman Ave, Ontario CA 91761	909-923-9390	R	1*	<.1
167	Elektron Components Corp—*Charlie Fixa*	31315 Plantation Dr, Thousand Palms CA 92276	760-343-3650	R	1*	<.1
168	Schultz Controls Inc—*Rick Schultz*	809 S Lakeview Ave Ste, Placentia CA 92870	714-692-3301	R	1*	<.1
169	Morton Automatic Electric Co—*Elizabeth Crumrine*	641 W David St, Morton IL 61550	309-266-6330	R	1*	<.1
170	Cobel Technologies Inc—*Mike Warner*	822 N Grand Ave, Covina CA 91724	626-332-2100	R	1*	<.1
171	Bryant Control Inc—*Edward Henz*	2933 N Webster Ave, Indianapolis IN 46219	317-549-3355	R	1*	<.1
172	Industrial And Marine Engine Service Co—*Theresa Chandler*	PO Box 247, Fredericktown OH 43019	740-694-0791	R	1*	<.1
173	Maverick Technical Systems Inc—*D Friend*	PO Box 1588, Gladewater TX 75647	903-845-5574	R	1*	<.1
174	Panel-Oven Engineering Company Inc—*Frank Colvin*	1410 Sage St, South Plainfield NJ 07080	908-561-1545	R	1*	<.1
175	Carpenter Engineering Inc—*Richard Carpenter*	918 Mechanic St, Lebanon PA 17046	717-274-8808	R	1*	<.1
176	Circuit Breaker Logic Inc—*Larry Youngren*	1607 E Beaver Lake Dr, Sammamish WA 98075	425-392-9585	R	1*	<.1
177	Jac Manufacturing Inc—*James Christiansen*	PO Box 179, Palmyra WI 53156	262-495-2141	R	1*	<.1
178	Hayden Electrical Systems Inc—*John Hayden*	41 Ward Rd, Lancaster NY 14086	716-683-6941	R	1*	<.1
179	Control Interface Inc—*Tom Osborn*	517 Commercial Dr, Fairfield OH 45014	513-874-2062	R	1*	<.1
180	Optimal Control Systems Inc—*Owen Day*	PO Box 462, Albany OR 97321	541-967-9323	R	1*	<.1
181	Lighthouse Electric Controls Co—*Albert Clement*	1307 Lowell Ave, Erie PA 16505	814-835-2348	R	1*	<.1
182	Atlantic Control Systems Inc—*Gary Reddish*	7873 S Dupont Hwy Ste, Felton DE 19943	302-284-9700	R	1*	<.1
183	SWS Systems Inc—*James Wagner*	PO Box 940, Roebuck SC 29376	864-576-4652	R	1*	<.1
184	Dove Lighting Systems Inc—*Gary Dove*	3563 Sueldo St Ste E, San Luis Obispo CA 93401	805-541-8292	R	1*	<.1
185	Bkz Instruments Inc—*Gene Weinberger*	22 Nickman Plz, Lemont Furnace PA 15456	724-438-0332	R	<1*	<.1
186	Kilo Ampere Switch Corp—*Ann Impellitteri*	230 Woodmont Rd Ste 27, Milford CT 06460	203-877-5994	R	<1*	<.1
187	Northstar Controls Inc—*Steven Gatz*	PO Box 314, Howard Lake MN 55349	320-543-3595	R	<1*	<.1

TOTALS: SIC 3613 Switchgear & Switchboard Apparatus

	Companies: 187				10,186	52.2

3621 Motors & Generators

Rank	Company Name—*Executive Officer*	Address, City, State, Zip	Phone	Type	Fin	Empls
1	General Electric Co—*Jeffrey R Immelt*	3135 Easton Tpke, Fairfield CT 06828	203-373-2211	P	150,211	287.0
2	Emerson Electric Co—*David N Farr*	PO Box 4100, Saint Louis MO 63136	314-553-2000	P	18,588	127.7
3	SPX Corp—*Christopher J Kearney*	13515 Ballantyne Corpo, Charlotte NC 28277	704-752-4400	P	5,462	18.0
4	Asea Brown Boveri Inc—*Enrique Santacana*	PO Box 5308, Norwalk CT 06856	203-750-2200	S	4,800*	16.0
5	AMETEK Inc—*Frank S Hermance*	PO Box 1764, Berwyn PA 19312	610-647-2121	P	2,990	12.2
6	Regal-Beloit Corp—*Mark J Gliebe*	200 State St, Beloit WI 53511	608-364-8800	P	2,808	24.4
7	AO Smith Corp—*Paul W Jones*	PO Box 245008, Milwaukee WI 53224	414-359-4000	P	1,711	10.6
8	Baldor Electric Co—*Ronald Tucker*	PO Box 2400, Fort Smith AR 72902	479-646-4711	R	1,513*	7.2

Rank	Company Name—Executive Officer	Address, City, State, Zip	Phone	Type	Fin	Empls
9	Globe Motors—Steve McHenry	2275 Stanley Ave, Dayton OH 45404	937-228-3171	S	1,180*	.6
10	Franklin Electric Company Inc—R Scott Trumbull	400 E Spring St, Bluffton IN 46714	260-824-2900	P	821	3.8
11	Cummins Npower—Jim Andrews	1600 Buerkle Rd, White Bear Lake MN 55110	651-636-1000	S	780*	:4
12	Warner Electric—Stan Owens	449 Gardner St, South Beloit IL 61080	815-389-3771	R	439	.3
13	Lindgren RF Enclosures Inc—Bruce Butler	1301 Arrow Point Dr, Cedar Park TX 78613	512-531-6400	S	415*	.8
14	Cme LLC—Yoshi Takei	2945 Three Leaves Dr, Mount Pleasant MI 48858	989-773-0377	R	313*	.4
15	Marathon Electric Manufacturing Corp—James L Packard Regal-Beloit Corp	PO Box 8003, Wausau WI 54402	715-675-3311	S	308*	2.3
16	American Superconductor Corp—Daniel McGahn	64 Jackson Rd, Devens MA 01434	978-842-3000	P	287	.8
17	Toshiba International Corp—Hideya Sakaida	13131 W Little York Rd, Houston TX 77241	713-466-0277	S	263*	1.0
18	US Electrical Motors Div—Mark Gallion	PO Box 4100, Saint Louis MO 63136	314-553-2000	D	250	2.0
19	AMETEK Lamb Electric AMETEK Inc	PO Box 1599, Kent OH 44240	330-673-3451	D	188*	1.4
20	Advanced DC Motors Inc—John Jordan	6268 E Molloy Rd, East Syracuse NY 13057	315-434-9303	S	186*	.2
21	Cummins Power Generation Inc—Jack Edwards	1400 73rd Ave Ne, Minneapolis MN 55432	763-574-5000	R	147*	1.8
22	Prestolite Electric LLC—Michael Lea	46200 Port St, Plymouth MI 48170	734-582-7200	R	144*	2.5
23	YMH Torrance Inc—Steve Gallagher	1495 Hawkeye Dr, Hiawatha IA 52233	319-247-6039	R	111*	.1
24	Generac Power Systems Inc—Aaron Jagdfeld	S45w29290 Hwy 59, Waukesha WI 53189	262-544-4811	S	109*	1.4
25	Motor Products	201 S Delaney Rd, Owosso MI 48867	989-725-5151	S	103*	.2
26	EMA Corp—Frank S Hermance AMETEK Inc	PO Box 1764, Paoli PA 19301	610-647-2121	S	100*	.1
27	Solgas Power Systems LLC	PO Box 405, Hunt TX 78024	830-278-3637	R	100*	<.1
28	MCG Inc AMETEK Inc	1500 N Front St, New Ulm MN 56073	507-233-7000	S	94*	.1
29	Texas Genco Services LP—Jack Fusco	1301 Mckinney St Ste 2, Houston TX 77010	713-795-6000	R	76*	1.5
30	Moog Component Group—Bob Brady	1213 N Main St, Blacksburg VA 24060	540-552-3011	S	75*	.2
31	Kato Engineering Inc—David N Farr Emerson Electric Co	PO Box 8447, Mankato MN 56002	507-625-4011	S	71*	.5
32	Kollmorgen Industrial/Commercl—John S Stroup Kollmorgen Corp	203A W Rock Rd, Radford VA 24141	540-633-3545	D	66*	.5
33	Merkle-Korff Industries Inc—Richard Meyer	25 NW Point Blvd Ste 9, Elk Grove Village IL 60007	847-296-8800	R	65*	.4
34	Peerless-Winsmith Inc—David McCann	172 Eaton St, Springville NY 14141	716-592-9310	S	64*	.8
35	Ocean Power Technologies Inc—Charles F Dunleavy	1590 Reed Rd, Pennington NJ 08534	609-730-0400	P	54	.1
36	Skurka Aerospace Inc—Tom Sievers	PO Box 2869, Camarillo CA 93011	805-484-8884	S	52*	.1
37	Nidec America Corp—Shigenobu Nagamori	50 Braintree Hill Park, Braintree MA 02184	781-848-0970	R	52*	.1
38	Mamco Corp—William Meltzer	8630 Industrial Dr, Franksville WI 53126	262-886-9069	R	51*	.3
39	Aeroflex Laboratories Inc—Leonard Borrow	35 S Service Rd, Plainview NY 11803	516-694-6700	S	50*	.4
40	ENI Products Group—Paul M Eyerman	100 Highpower Rd, Rochester NY 14623	585-427-8300	S	49*	.4
41	ElectroCraft Arkansas—James Elsner	PO Box 260, Bald Knob AR 72010	501-724-3227	R	49*	.1
42	Johnson Electric USA—Patrick Wang	47660 Halyard Dr, Plymouth MI 48170	734-392-5308	S	42*	.3
43	Stature Electric Inc—Richard S Warzala	PO Box 6660, Watertown NY 13601	315-782-5910	S	42	.3
44	Imperial Electric Co—David Molnar	1503 Exeter Rd, Akron OH 44306	330-734-3600	R	38*	.3
45	Kb Electronics Inc—Gilbert Knauer	12095 Nw 39th St, Coral Springs FL 33065	954-346-4900	R	36*	.2
46	Swiger Coil Systems LLC—Cindy Trautman	4677 Manufacturing Ave, Cleveland OH 44135	216-362-7500	R	35*	.2
47	Groschopp Inc—Ron Didier	420 15th St Ne, Sioux Center IA 51250	712-722-4135	R	33*	.3
48	Pittman Inc—Frank S Hermance	343 Godshall Dr, Harleysville PA 19438	215-256-6601	S	30*	.2
49	Drehob Corp—James Smithers	PO Box 2023, Indianapolis IN 46206	317-231-8080	R	29*	.2
50	SL Montevideo Technology Inc—James Taylor	2002 Black Oak Ave, Montevideo MN 56265	320-269-6562	R	28	.2
51	Kirkwood Commutator Co—Tom Koechley	1239 Rockside Rd, Parma OH 44134	216-267-6200	R	28*	.2
52	Dayton-Phoenix Group Inc—Gale Kooken	1619 Kuntz Rd, Dayton OH 45404	937-496-3900	R	28*	.4
53	Kollmorgen Corp—Michael J Wall	347 King St, North Hampton MA 01060	413-586-2330	S	26*	.2
54	Southwest Windpower Inc—Dixon Thayer	1801 W Rte 66 Ste 100, Flagstaff AZ 86001	928-779-9463	R	24*	.1
55	US Hybrid—Abas Goodarzi	445 Maple Ave, Torrance CA 90503	310-212-1200	R	24*	<.1
56	Electro Sales Company Inc	100 Fellsway W, Somerville MA 02145	617-666-0500	R	24*	<.1
57	Careen Inc—Jerald Kauffman	PO Box 566, New Ulm MN 56073	507-359-2034	R	24*	.1
58	Mtu Onsite Energy Corp—Armin Groeber	PO Box 3229, Mankato MN 56002	507-625-7973	R	23*	.2
59	Reuland Electric Co—Noel Reuland	PO Box 1464, La Puente CA 91749	626-964-6411	R	23*	.2
60	Northland Motor Technologies (Watertown New York)—Timothy Galligos	2268 Fairview Blvd, Fairview TN 37062	615-799-0551	D	21*	.2
61	Buehler Motor Inc—Robert Riedford	PO Box 32849, Charlotte NC 28232	919-380-3333	R	21*	.2
62	Westerbeke Corp—John H Westerbeke Jr	150 John Hancock Rd, Taunton MA 02780	508-823-7677	R	20	.1
63	Plug Power Inc—Andrew Marsh	968 Albany Shaker Rd, Latham NY 12110	518-782-7700	P	20	.1
64	Fcx Systems Inc—Craig Walker	400 Fcx Ln, Morgantown WV 26501	304-983-0400	R	20*	.1
65	Mcmillan Electric Co—Douglas Mcmillan	400 Best Rd, Woodville WI 54028	715-698-2488	R	19*	.3
66	Victory Industrial Products LLC	4160 Half Acre Rd, Batavia OH 45103	513-575-5300	R	19*	.1
67	Hannon Co—Thomas Hannon	1605 Waynesburg Dr Se, Canton OH 44707	330-456-4728	R	18*	.1
68	Data Electronic Devices Inc—Udo Fritsch	32 Northwestern Dr, Salem NH 03079	603-893-2047	R	17*	.1
69	Ward Leonard Electric Company Inc—Jon Carter	401 Watertown Rd, Thomaston CT 06787	860-283-5801	R	16*	.1
70	Euphonix Inc—Martin Kloiber	1330 West Middlefield, Mountain View CA 94043	650-855-0400	R	16*	.1
71	Barta-Schoenewald Inc—Sandor Barta	3805 Calle Tecate, Camarillo CA 93012	805-389-1935	R	16*	.1
72	Enphase Energy Inc—Paul Nahi	201 1st St Ste 100, Petaluma CA 94952	707-763-4784	R	15*	.1
73	Coil Manufacturing Inc—Randy Rutter	940 Alton Pkwy, Birmingham AL 35210	205-838-5985	R	14*	.1
74	Engine Systems Inc—Dorman L Strahan	175 Freight Rd, Rocky Mount NC 27804	252-977-2720	S	14*	.1
75	Bay Motor Products Inc—David Space	PO Box 982, Traverse City MI 49685	231-941-0411	R	14*	<.1
76	Electric Motors And Specialties Inc—Judith Morrill	PO Box 180, Garrett IN 46738	260-357-4141	R	14*	.2
77	Fulmer Company LLC—Sharon Shearer	3004 Venture Ct, Export PA 15632	724-325-7140	R	13*	.1
78	Glentek Inc—Richard Vasak	208 Standard St, El Segundo CA 90245	310-322-3026	R	13*	.1
79	Sag Harbor Industries Inc—Mary Scheerer	1668 Sag Harbor Tpke, Sag Harbor NY 11963	631-725-0440	R	12*	.1
80	Electro-Miniatures Corp—Mark Pollack	68 W Commercial Ave, Moonachie NJ 07074	201-460-0510	R	11*	.1
81	Cole Instrument Corp—Ricardo Garcia	PO Box 25063, Santa Ana CA 92799	714-556-3100	R	10*	.1
82	Modular Devices Inc—Steven Summer	1 Roned Rd, Shirley NY 11967	631-345-3100	R	10*	.1
83	Goodman Ball Inc—George Buhrfeind	3639 Haven Ave, Menlo Park CA 94025	650-363-0113	R	10*	<.1
84	Electrocraft New Hampshire Inc—James Elsner	1 Progress Dr, Dover NH 03820	603-742-3330	R	9*	.1
85	Green Energy Industries—Robert Bado	401 N Michigan Ave Ste, Chicago IL 60611	312-836-3752	R	9*	.1
86	Schulz Electric Co—Robert Davis	30 Gando Dr, New Haven CT 06513	203-562-5811	R	9*	.1
87	Kencoil Inc—J Key	2805 Engineers Rd, Belle Chasse LA 70037	504-394-4010	R	9*	.1
88	City Machine Technologies Inc—Michael Kovach	PO Box 1466, Youngstown OH 44501	330-747-2639	R	8*	.1
89	Dumore Corp—David Mosser	1030 Veterans St, Mauston WI 53948	608-847-6420	R	8*	.1
90	Power Electronic Systems—Gregory Yurek American Superconductor Corp	8401 Murphy Dr, Middleton WI 53562	608-831-5773	D	8*	.1

Note: An asterisk (*) indicates an estimated financial figure. The company type code used is as follows: R = Private, P = Public, S = Private Subsidiary, B = Public Subsidiary, D = Division, J = Joint Venture, I = Investment Fund.

COMPANY RANKINGS BY SALES WITHIN 4-DIGIT SIC

Rank	Company Name—Executive Officer	Address, City, State, Zip	Phone	Type	Fin	Empls
91	Precise Power Corp—Ronn Barber	PO Box 9547, Bradenton FL 34206	941-723-3600	R	8*	.1
92	Motor Specialty Inc—Robert Frank	PO Box 081278, Racine WI 53408	262-632-2794	R	8*	.1
93	Electron Coil Inc—Douglas Marchant	PO Box 71, Norwich NY 13815	607-336-7414	R	7*	.1
94	Iberdrola Renewable Energies USA Ltd—Martin Mugica	201 King Of Prussia Rd, Radnor PA 19087	610-254-9800	R	7*	.1
95	TransTech of SC LP—Ian Paradis	709 Augusta Arbor Way, Piedmont SC 29673	864-299-3871	S	7*	.1
96	Bergey Windpower Company Inc—Karl Bergey	2200 Industrial Blvd, Norman OK 73069	405-364-4212	R	7*	<.1
97	Quantum Data Inc—Allen Jorgensen	2111 Big Timber Rd, Elgin IL 60123	847-888-0450	R	7*	<.1
98	Walker Power Systems Inc—Ronald Walker	1301 E Jackson St, Phoenix AZ 85034	602-257-8505	R	7*	<.1
99	Ronk Electrical Industries Inc—Larry Cearlock	PO Box 160, Nokomis IL 62075	217-563-8333	R	6*	<.1
100	Ohio Electric Motors Inc—Randy Greely	PO Box 168, Barnardsville NC 28709	828-626-2901	R	6*	.1
101	Louis Allis Co—Roberta Bailey	645 Lester Doss Rd, Warrior AL 35180		R	6*	<.1
102	ETEMCO—John Hassan	PO Box 4651, Lancaster PA 17604	717-393-9653	R	6*	<.1
103	Ion Physics Co—Helmet Milde	PO Box 165, Fremont NH 03044	603-895-5100	R	6*	<.1
104	Ecotality Inc—Jonathan R Read	4 Embarcadero Center S, San Francisco CA 94111	415-992-3000	P	6	.1
105	Tex-Am Industries Inc—Jack Heck	PO Box 986, Stafford TX 77497	281-261-7939	R	6*	<.1
106	Electric Apparatus Co—Carmen Biller	PO Box 227, Howell MI 48844	517-546-0520	R	6*	<.1
107	US Co-Tronics Corp—Paul Bullard	PO Box 168, Fairbury IL 61739	815-692-3416	R	5*	<.1
108	Stimple and Ward Co—Raymond Love	3400 Babcock Blvd, Pittsburgh PA 15237	412-364-5200	R	5*	<.1
109	Soft Switching Technologies Corp—Russel Loomis	8155 Forsythia St, Middleton WI 53562	608-662-7200	R	5*	<.1
110	Anko Products Inc—Sharon Kottke	3007 29th Ave E, Bradenton FL 34208	941-749-1960	R	5*	.1
111	Arc Systems Inc—Robert Miller	2090 Joshuas Path, Hauppauge NY 11788	631-582-8020	R	5*	<.1
112	Power Technology Southeast Inc—Gerald Hayman	PO Box 490133, Leesburg FL 34749	352-365-2777	R	4*	<.1
113	Walter C Brooks Company Inc—Walter Brooks	6758 Okridge Commerce, Austell GA 30168	770-933-0453	R	4*	<.1
114	Electronic Power Design Inc—John Janik	3609 Clinton Dr, Houston TX 77020	713-923-1191	R	4*	<.1
115	Shigamo Development Inc—Gary Hanington	2002 Idaho St, Elko NV 89801	775-777-0992	R	4*	<.1
116	Dynetic Systems Co—Jonathon Whitcomb	19128 Industrial Blvd, Elk River MN 55330	763-441-4300	R	4*	<.1
117	Small Assemblies Company Inc—Robert Cumming	4140 W Belmont Ave, Chicago IL 60641	773-202-9000	R	4*	<.1
118	Con Rel Auto Electric Inc—Kevin Relyea	3637 Carman Rd, Schenectady NY 12303	518-356-1646	R	4*	<.1
119	Mc Cully Mac M Corp—Guy Cully	12012 Hertz Ave, Moorpark CA 93021	805-529-0661	R	4*	<.1
120	Power Equipment Company Inc—Paul Toher	7 Franklin R Mckay Rd, Attleboro MA 02703	508-226-3410	R	4*	<.1
121	Cmi Integrated Technologies Inc—Anil Nanji	11250 Playa Ct, Culver City CA 90230	760-431-7003	R	4*	<.1
122	TK I Inc—Rado Starc	110 Southchase Blvd, Fountain Inn SC 29644	864-409-8784	R	4*	<.1
123	Minnesota Electric Technology Inc—J Kvamme	PO Box 3445, Mankato MN 56002	507-625-6117	R	4*	<.1
124	Kagmo Electric Motor Co—Mike Rinker	PO Box 556, Cape Girardeau MO 63702	573-335-2562	R	4*	<.1
125	Industrial Commutator Corp—Laura Lyke	1620 Robert C Jackson, Maryville TN 37801	865-983-7444	R	3*	<.1
126	Southern Automotive Wholesalers Inc—Thomas Tyson	597 N Saginaw St, Pontiac MI 48342	248-335-5555	R	3*	<.1
127	CW Silver Industrial Services Inc—Steve Rossiter	535 W 700 S, Salt Lake City UT 84101	801-531-8888	R	3*	<.1
128	Ashland Electric Products Inc—Roger Cloitre	10 Industrial Way, Rochester NH 03867	603-335-1100	R	3*	<.1
129	John G Rubino Inc—John Rubino	45 Aurelius Ave, Auburn NY 13021	315-253-7396	R	3*	<.1
130	Motor Magnetics Inc—Nancy Preis	79 E Hoffman Ave, Lindenhurst NY 11757	631-957-7850	R	3*	<.1
131	Li-Ion Motors Corp—Stacey Fling	158 Rolling Hill Rd, Mooresville NC 28117	704-662-0827	R	3*	<.1
132	Alpha Power and Technology LLC—Lou Petros	4000 Winnetka AveN Ste, Minneapolis MN 55427	763-323-4997	R	3*	<.1
133	W and W Manufacturing Company Inc—William Johnson	1944 Akron Peninsula R, Akron OH 44313	330-928-4567	R	3*	<.1
134	Electrical and Mechanical Resources Inc—William Overton	PO Box 38400, Richmond VA 23231	804-226-1600	R	3*	<.1
135	D/E Associates Inc—David Witt	PO Box 394, Shamokin PA 17872	570-648-6806	R	3*	.1
136	Electric Motor Rewind Inc—Raymond Lopez	PO Box 5335, Corpus Christi TX 78465	361-884-3185	R	3*	<.1
137	Viking Industrial Products—Aubrey Elms	PO Box 291, Marlborough MA 01752	508-481-4600	R	3*	<.1
138	Georator Corp—George Ripol	9617 Ctr St, Manassas VA 20110	703-368-2101	R	3*	<.1
139	Light Engineering Corp—Matt Johnston	5845 W 82nd St Ste 110, Indianapolis IN 46278	317-471-1800	R	2*	<.1
140	Meridian Laboratory Inc—Carlo Krause	2415 Pleasant View Rd, Middleton WI 53562	608-836-7571	R	2*	<.1
141	Ag Electrical Specialists—Andy Andrew	PO Box 36, Racine MN 55967	507-378-2101	R	2*	<.1
142	River's Edge Energy Inc—Terri Harris	1960 Mooney, Pocatello ID 83204	208-238-7697	R	2*	<.1
143	Gentec LLC—Jay Yuergens	215 S Park St, Port Washington WI 53074	262-268-7014	R	2*	<.1
144	Windamatic Systems Inc—Richard Nill	PO Box 10071, Fort Wayne IN 46850	260-637-3622	R	2*	<.1
145	Power Magnetics Inc—Carl Bannwart	377 Reservoir St, Trenton NJ 08618	609-695-1170	R	2*	<.1
146	Eylander Electric Inc—Patricia Eylander	PO Box 1479, Everett WA 98206	425-259-2161	R	2*	<.1
147	Hardin Industries Inc—Dale Hardin	400 N Commercial St, Lacon IL 61540	309-246-8456	R	2*	<.1
148	United Starters And Alternators Industries Inc—Vincent Trapani	1560 5th Ave, Bay Shore NY 11706	631-969-2222	R	2*	<.1
149	Farnor Enterprises Inc—Bud King	642 Watauga Ave, Erwin TN 37650	423-743-0167	R	1*	<.1
150	Agc Manufacturing Services Inc—Jorge Gutierrez	20701 E 81st St S Ste, Broken Arrow OK 74014	918-251-0490	R	1*	<.1
151	Cortec Enterprises LLC	1801 Jefferson St Nw, Minneapolis MN 55418	612-788-9000	R	1*	<.1
152	Electric Car Company Inc—Gary Spaniak	1903 N Barnes Ave, Springfield MO 65803	417-866-6565	P	1	<.1
153	Industrail Test Equipment Company Inc—Jay Monroe	2 Manhasset Ave, Port Washington NY 11050	516-883-1700	R	1*	<.1
154	Horlick Company Inc—William Nesbitt	91 Pacella Park Dr, Randolph MA 02368	781-963-0090	R	1*	<.1
155	Schulze Manufacturing Inc—Thomas Schulze	567 S Leonard St 1, Waterbury CT 06708	203-591-1156	R	1*	<.1
156	IEC Corp—David Peerson	3100 Longhorn Blvd, Austin TX 78758	512-836-0547	R	1*	<.1
157	Armatures Inc—Dean Cussack	28627 Grand River Ave, Farmington Hills MI 48336	248-474-2754	R	1*	<.1
158	Denyo Manufacturing Corp—Danny Hatter	1450 Minor Rd, Danville KY 40422	859-236-3405	R	1*	<.1
159	Motion Devices Technology Inc—Martin Thomas	1017 Bankton Cir, Hanahan SC 29410	843-744-5020	R	1*	<.1
160	Rees Electric Company Inc—C Basham	194 Central Ave, Beckley WV 25801	304-253-7131	R	<1*	<.1
161	Topsall Machine Tool Company Inc—Paul Huikku	14 Jacques St, Worcester MA 01603	508-755-0332	R	<1*	<.1
162	Innovative Electrical Components Limited Inc—Kurt Layland	4023 S Old Us Hwy 23, Brighton MI 48114	810-227-5254	R	<1*	<.1
163	Rotoblock Corp—Chien Chih Liu	300 B St, Santa Rosa CA 95404	707-578-5220	P	<1	<.1
164	American Security Resources Corp—Frank Neukomm	19 Briar Hollow Ln Ste, Houston TX 77027	713-465-1001	P	<1	<.1

TOTALS: SIC 3621 Motors & Generators
Companies: 164   196,416   537.2

3624 Carbon & Graphite Products

Rank	Company Name—Executive Officer	Address, City, State, Zip	Phone	Type	Fin	Empls
1	Graftech International Ltd—Craig S Shular	12900 Snow Rd, Parma OH 44130	216-676-2000	P	1,320	3.3
2	Mersen USA Bn Corp—Bernie Monsalvatge	400 Myrtle Ave, Boonton NJ 07005	973-541-4720	R	461*	1.1
3	Zoltek Companies Inc—Zsolt Rumy	3101 McKelvey Rd, Bridgeton MO 63044	314-291-5110	P	152	1.3
4	SGL Technic Inc/Polycarbon Div—Brian Green	28176 N Avenue Stanfor, Valencia CA 91355	661-257-0500	D	75*	.1
5	Morgan Advanced Materials And Technology Inc—Don Klas	441 Hall Ave, Saint Marys PA 15857	814-781-1573	R	33*	.6
6	Mwi Inc—Kevin Mahon	1269 Brighton Henriett, Rochester NY 14623	585-424-4204	R	32*	.1
7	BAE Systems Composite Structures Inc—Julie Scott	1095 Columbia St, Brea CA 92821	714-990-6300	R	23*	.1
8	Schunk Graphite Technology LLC—Heinz Volk	W146n9300 Held Dr, Menomonee Falls WI 53051	262-253-8720	R	20*	.2
9	Helwig Carbon Products Inc—Jay Koenitzer	PO Box 240160, Milwaukee WI 53224	414-354-2411	R	20*	.3
10	Asbury Louisiana Inc—Stephen Riddle	PO Box 144, Asbury NJ 08802	908-537-2155	R	19*	.3
11	Asbury Graphite Mills Inc—Stephen A Riddle Asbury Louisiana Inc	PO Box 144, Asbury NJ 08802	908-537-2155	S	18*	.2

Rank	Company Name—*Executive Officer*	Address, City, State, Zip	Phone	Type	Fin	Empls
12	C/G Electrodes LLC—*Sandra Hoffman*	800 Theresia St, Saint Marys PA 15857	814-834-2801	R	18*	.2
13	Metallized Carbon Corp—*Bruce Neri*	19 S Water St, Ossining NY 10562	914-941-3738	R	17*	.1
14	Graphite Sales Inc—*George C Hanna*	16710 W Park Circle Dr, Chagrin Falls OH 44023	440-543-8221	R	15*	.1
15	Mersen USA Greenville-Mi Corp—*Todd Taylor*	PO Box 637, Greenville MI 48838	616-754-5671	R	14*	.1
16	CompositAir	12827 E Imperial Hwy, Santa Fe Springs CA 90670	562-944-3281	D	13*	.1
17	Weaver Industries Inc—*John Weaver*	PO Box 326, Denver PA 17517	717-336-7507	R	11*	.1
18	Tris USA Inc—*Kiroshi Sasaki*	1803 Wilkinson St, Athens AL 35611	256-233-2511	R	11*	.1
19	Graphite Die Mold Inc—*Fred Wollman*	18 Airline Rd, Durham CT 06422	860-349-4444	R	10*	.1
20	Innovative Composite Engineering Inc—*Steve Maier*	PO Box 1218, White Salmon WA 98672	509-493-4484	R	6*	.1
21	Advance Carbon Products Inc—*Ronald Crader*	2036 National Ave, Hayward CA 94545	510-293-5930	R	5*	<.1
22	EDM Supplies Inc—*David Muhs*	9806 Everest St, Downey CA 90242	562-803-6563	R	5*	<.1
23	Carbon Carbon Advanced Technologies Inc—*Francis Schwind*	4704 Eden Rd, Kennedale TX 76060	817-985-2500	R	5*	<.1
24	Saturn Industries Inc—*John Lee*	PO Box 367, Hudson NY 12534	518-828-9956	R	5*	<.1
25	Nac Carbon Products Inc—*Jim Mcafoos*	PO Box 436, Punxsutawney PA 15767	814-938-7450	R	4*	<.1
26	Bay Carbon Inc—*William Clare*	PO Box 205, Bay City MI 48707	989-686-8090	R	3*	<.1
27	Cummings-Moore Graphite Co—*Michael Mares*	1646 N Green St, Detroit MI 48209	313-841-1615	R	3*	<.1
28	Kbr Inc—*David Mcmahon*	PO Box 426, Honeoye Falls NY 14472	562-436-9281	R	3*	<.1
29	Roc Industries Inc—*Pamela Carlson*	1605 Brittmoore Rd, Houston TX 77043	713-468-7744	R	3*	<.1
30	Sherbrooke Metals—*Randy Spoth*	36490 Reading Ave, Willoughby OH 44094	440-942-3520	R	2*	<.1
31	South-Land Carbon Products Inc—*Raymond Lilly*	PO Box 170799, Birmingham AL 35217	205-841-8799	R	2*	<.1
32	Micron Research Corp—*David Trinkley*	PO Box 269, Emporium PA 15834	814-486-2444	R	2*	<.1
33	Reliable Water Services LLC	7747 E 89th St, Indianapolis IN 46256	317-595-3000	S	1*	<.1

TOTALS: SIC 3624 Carbon & Graphite Products
Companies: 33   2,330   8.7

3625 Relays & Industrial Controls

Rank	Company Name—*Executive Officer*	Address, City, State, Zip	Phone	Type	Fin	Empls
1	Eaton Corp—*Alexander M Cutler*	Eaton Ctr 1111 Superio, Cleveland OH 44114	216-523-5000	P	13,715	70.0
2	TSV ELMA Inc—*Nicholas Trbovich*	PO Box 300, Elma NY 14059	716-655-5990	S	2,548	N/A
3	Duchossois Industries Inc—*Craig J Duchossois*	845 Larch Ave, Elmhurst IL 60126	630-279-3600	R	2,348*	6.0
4	Hella North America Inc—*Carl Brown*	201 Kelly Dr, Peachtree City GA 30269	770-631-7500	S	853*	.8
5	Poly-Flex Circuits Inc—*Dennis Carvalho*	28 Kenney Dr, Cranston RI 02920	401-463-3180	S	281*	.3
6	Yokogawa Industrial Automation America Inc—*Shuzo Kaihori*	12530 W Airport Blvd, Sugar Land TX 77478	281-340-3800	S	188*	.5
7	Emerson Control Techniques—*Todd Bertrand*	7078 Shady Oak Rd, Eden Prairie MN 55344	952-995-8000	S	171*	.2
8	Lutron Electronics Company Inc—*John Longenderfer*	7200 Suter Rd, Coopersburg PA 18036	610-282-3800	R	119*	1.5
9	Fife Corp—*Marcel Hage*	PO Box 26508, Oklahoma City OK 73126	405-755-1600	R	117*	.3
10	Novar Controls Corp	6060 Rockside Woods Bl, Cleveland OH 44131		S	113*	.1
11	Centrilift—*Charlie Wolley*	200 W Stuart Roosa Dr, Claremore OK 74017	918-341-9600	D	107*	1.4
12	Meter Devices Company Inc—*Jack Roessner*	PO Box 6382, Canton OH 44706	330-455-0301	R	106*	.6
13	GE Control Products—*Jeffrey R Immelt*	709 W Wall St, Morrison IL 61270	815-772-1100	S	104*	.5
14	Ram Optical Instrumentation Inc—*Mark Glowacky*	1175 North St, Rochester NY 14621	585-758-1300	R	93*	.6
15	Emerson Process Management Power and Water Solutions—*Robert Yeager*	200 Beta Dr, Pittsburgh PA 15238	412-963-4000	S	93	.6
16	Smc Corporation Of America—*Yoshiki Takada*	PO Box 1880, Noblesville IN 46061	317-899-4440	R	78*	1.1
17	Minarik Corp—*John Hegel*	905 E Thompson Ave, Glendale CA 91201	818-637-7500	R	77*	.2
18	Ametek Drexelbrook—*David A Zapico*	205 Keith Valley Rd, Horsham PA 19044	215-674-1234	D	60*	.2
19	L-3 Communications Henschel Inc—*Don Roussinos*	9 Malcolm Hoyt Dr, Newburyport MA 01950	978-462-2400	S	60*	.2
20	Phacotronics/Motortronics Inc—*Jim Mitchell*	PO Box 5988, Clearwater FL 33765	727-573-1819	R	56*	.3
21	Capsonic Automotive Inc—*Gregory Liautaud*	260 S 2nd St, Elgin IL 60123	248-754-1100	R	55	.5
22	Primus Technologies Corp—*Jerry Sullivan*	2333 Reach Rd, Williamsport PA 17701	570-326-6591	R	54*	.4
23	Balboa Water Group Inc—*David Cline*	1382 Bell Ave, Tustin CA 92780	714-384-0384	R	52*	.3
24	Unico Inc—*Thomas Beck*	PO Box 505, Franksville WI 53126	262-886-5678	R	52*	.3
25	Hansen Corp—*William Poyner*	901 S First St, Princeton IN 47670	812-385-3415	S	50	.4
26	Icm Controls Corp—*Ronald Kadah*	7313 William Barry Blv, North Syracuse NY 13212	315-233-5266	R	44*	.3
27	CII Technologies Inc—*Tom Lynch*	PO Box 4422, Santa Barbara CA 93140	805-684-4560	S	43*	.3
28	Marquardt Switches Inc—*Jochen Becker*	2711 Us Rte 20e, Cazenovia NY 13035	315-655-8050	R	43*	.3
29	Chatham Corp—*Garry Brainin*	350 Barclay Blvd, Lincolnshire IL 60069	847-634-5506	R	42	.4
30	Transdyn Controls Inc—*Gerald Marcus Thompson*	4256 Hacienda Dr Ste 1, Pleasanton CA 94588	925-225-1600	S	42*	<.1
31	Evans Enterprises Inc—*Sylynda Thrash*	PO Box 2370, Oklahoma City OK 73101	405-631-1344	R	39*	.2
32	Deltrol Corp—*Herb Schwensohn*	3001 Grant Ave, Bellwood IL 60104	708-547-0500	R	38*	.1
33	Pepperl and Fuchs Inc—*Wolfgang Mueller*	1600 Enterprise Pkwy, Twinsburg OH 44087	330-425-3555	R	38*	.3
34	Moeller Electric Corp—*Theo Kubat*	4140 World Houston Pkw, Houston TX 77032	713-933-0999	S	37*	.2
35	Banner Engineering Corp—*Robert Fayfield*	PO Box 9414, Minneapolis MN 55440	763-544-3164	R	37*	.6
36	W-Industries Inc—*Rick Lynn*	11500 Charles Rd, Jersey Village TX 77041	713-466-9463	R	35*	.5
37	Balluff Inc—*Kent Howard*	8125 Holton Dr, Florence KY 41042	859-727-2200	S	35*	.1
38	Saia-Burgess Automotive Actuators Inc—*Gary Dies*	755 Bill Jones Industr, Springfield TN 37172	615-384-8555	R	32*	.3
39	Tech/Ops Sevcon Inc—*Matthew Boyle*	155 Northboro Rd, Southborough MA 01772	508-281-5500	P	32	.1
40	Woodward Industrial Controls Branch Plant—*Tom A Gendron*	PO Box 1519, Fort Collins CO 80525	970-482-5811	S	31*	.2
41	eSilicon Corp—*Jack Harding*	501 Macara Ave, Sunnyvale CA 94085	408-616-4600	R	31	N/A
42	Valcor Engineering Corp—*Lilyan Kreitchman*	2 Lawrence Rd, Springfield NJ 07081	973-467-8400	R	30*	.2
43	Connor-Winfield Corp—*Roberta Olp*	2111 Comprehensive Dr, Aurora IL 60505	630-851-4722	R	30*	.2
44	Curtis PMC Inc—*Dave Damon*	235 E Airway Blvd, Livermore CA 94551	925-961-1088	D	27*	.1
45	Linemaster Switch Corp—*Joseph Carlone*	PO Box 238, Woodstock CT 06281	860-974-1000	R	26*	.2
46	Huntington Electric Inc—*Michael Khorshid*	PO Box 366, Huntington IN 46750	260-356-0756	R	26*	.2
47	O E M Controls Inc—*S Simons*	PO Box 894, Shelton CT 06484	203-929-8431	R	25*	.2
48	Namco Controls Corp	2100 W Broad St, Elizabethtown NC 28337	910-862-2511	S	25*	.2
49	Systems Machines Automation Components Corp—*Edward Neff*	5807 Van Allen Way, Carlsbad CA 92008	760-929-7575	R	25*	.2
50	Hamlin Electronics LP—*Antony Howell*	612 E Lake St, Lake Mills WI 53551	920-648-3000	R	25*	.2
51	Stearns—*Robert Hitt*	PO Box 100640, Cudahy WI 53110	414-272-1100	S	24*	.2
52	Inno-Flex Corp—*John Pesonen*	7101 31st Ave N, Minneapolis MN 55427	763-536-1007	R	24*	.2
53	Delphi Mechatronic Systems Inc—*Lothar Veeser*	3110 Woodcreek Dr, Downers Grove IL 60515	630-725-0600	S	23*	.2
54	Mason Industries Inc—*Norman Mason*	PO Box 410, Smithtown NY 11787	631-348-0282	R	23*	.4
55	Dolan-Jenner Industries Inc—*Mike Balas*	159 Swanson Rd, Boxborough MA 01719	978-263-1400	S	22*	.2
56	Danaher Controls—*Daniel L Comas*	1675 Delany Rd, Gurnee IL 60031	847-662-2666	S	22*	.1
57	Giddings and Lewis Control Measurement and Sensing—*Steve Patterson*	PO Box 1658, Fond du Lac WI 54936	920-921-7100	D	21*	.2
58	Kimchuk Inc—*William Kimbell*	1 Corporate Dr, Danbury CT 06810	203-790-7800	R	20*	.2
59	Enercon Engineering Inc—*Larry Tangel*	No 1 Altorfer Ln, East Peoria IL 61611	309-694-1418	R	20*	.1
60	Revere Control Systems Inc—*Bob Adams*	2240 Rocky Ridge Rd, Birmingham AL 35216	205-824-0004	R	20*	.1

Note: An asterisk (*) indicates an estimated financial figure. The company type code used is as follows: R = Private, P = Public, S = Private Subsidiary, B = Public Subsidiary, D = Division, J = Joint Venture, I = Investment Fund.

COMPANY RANKINGS BY SALES WITHIN 4-DIGIT SIC

Rank	Company Name—*Executive Officer*	Address, City, State, Zip	Phone	Type	Fin	Empls
61	Milwaukee Electronics Corp—*P Stoehr*	PO Box 90920, Milwaukee WI 53209	414-228-5000	R	20*	.1
62	Emx Controls Inc—*Richard Padovano*	35 Buxton St, Uxbridge MA 01569	508-876-9700	R	20*	<.1
63	Acromag Inc—*David Wolfe*	PO Box 437, Wixom MI 48393	248-624-1541	R	19*	.1
64	Inertia Dynamics LLC—*Todd Barnes*	31 Industrial Park Rd, New Hartford CT 06057	860-482-4444	R	19*	.1
65	Norgren Automation Solutions Inc—*Bill Gross*	1325 Woodland Dr, Saline MI 48176	734-429-4989	R	19*	.1
66	Precision Aerospace Corp—*Cindy Jones*	11661 Sorrento Valley, San Diego CA 92121	858-792-3229	R	19*	.1
67	Horner Electric Inc—*Phil Horner*	1521 E Washington St, Indianapolis IN 46201	317-639-4261	R	18*	.2
68	Control Holding Corp—*Robert Soeder*	1080 N Crooks Rd, Clawson MI 48017	248-435-0700	S	18*	<.1
69	Elecsys International Corp—*Karl Gemperli*	846 N Martway Ct, Olathe KS 66061	913-982-5672	R	17*	.1
70	Rotork Process Controls—*Mike Mahan*	5607 W Douglas Ave, Milwaukee WI 53218	414-461-9200	R	17*	.1
71	Pressure Systems Inc (Hampton Virginia)	34 Research Dr, Hampton VA 23666	757-865-1243	S	16*	.1
72	AMETEK Automation and Process Technologies—*Robert Soeder*	1080 N Crooks Rd, Clawson MI 48017	248-435-0700	D	16*	.1
73	Hydro Electronic Devices Inc—*Paul Ludwig*	2120 Constitution Ave, Hartford WI 53027	262-673-9450	R	16*	.1
74	Motor Technology Inc—*Dan Godin*	2796 Culver Ave, Dayton OH 45429	937-294-1041	S	16*	<.1
75	Rab Lighting Inc—*Richard Barna*	PO Box 970, Northvale NJ 07647	201-784-8600	R	16*	.1
76	Quality Name Plate Inc—*Craig Garneau*	PO Box 308, East Glastonbury CT 06025	860-633-9495	R	16*	.1
77	Beckwood Services Inc—*Peter Alcock*	PO Box 985, Plaistow NH 03865	603-382-3840	R	16*	.1
78	Cattron-Theimeg Inc—*John Paul*	58 W Shenango St, Sharpsville PA 16150	724-962-3571	R	15*	.1
79	Engineered Systems and Products Inc—*Faina Fradlin*	11438 Cronridge Dr Ste, Owings Mills MD 21117	410-998-9456	R	15*	.1
80	Precision Devices Inc—*Chris Sokol*	8840 N Greenview Dr, Middleton WI 53562		R	15*	<.1
81	Tympanium Corp—*Jim Liberty*	197 Commercial St, Malden MA 02148	781-324-8752	R	14*	.1
82	Harold Beck and Sons Inc—*H Beck*	11 Terry Dr, Newtown PA 18940	215-968-4600	R	14*	.1
83	Pine Instrument Co—*Theodore Hines*	101 Industrial Dr, Grove City PA 16127	724-458-6391	R	14*	.1
84	Electrical Power Products Inc—*Tim Donnell*	1800 Hull Ave, Des Moines IA 50313	515-262-8161	R	13*	.1
85	Silicon Microstructures Inc—*James Knutti*	1701 Mccarthy Blvd, Milpitas CA 95035	408-577-0100	R	13*	.1
86	Dynalco Controls	5450 NW 33rd Ave Ste 1, Fort Lauderdale FL 33309	954-739-4300	D	13*	.1
87	Hyde Park Electronics LLC—*Mike Edminston*	1875 Founders Dr, Dayton OH 45420	937-252-2121	S	12*	.1
88	I/O Controls Corp—*Jeffrey Ying*	1357 W Foothill Blvd, Azusa CA 91702	626-812-5353	R	12*	.1
89	Industrial Controls Distributors Inc—*Joe Eichelberger*	1776 Bloomsbury Ave, Wanamassa NJ 07712	732-918-9000	R	12*	<.1
90	Composite Modules Inc—*Robert Jones*	61 Union St, Attleboro MA 02703	508-226-0420	R	12*	.1
91	Barry Industries Inc—*Richard Barry*	PO Box 1326, Attleboro Falls MA 02763	508-226-3350	R	12*	.1
92	Abbott Furnace Co—*Thomas Jesberger*	PO Box 967, Saint Marys PA 15857	814-781-6355	R	12*	.1
93	Ns Controls Inc—*Noel Senogles*	5601 W Sam Houston Pkw, Houston TX 77041	713-465-7591	R	12*	<.1
94	Mercury Displacement Industries Inc—*Randy Brewers*	PO Box 710, Edwardsburg MI 49112	269-663-8574	R	11*	.1
95	Symcom Inc—*Kip Larson*	2880 N Plz Dr, Rapid City SD 57702	605-348-5580	R	11*	.1
96	Qualitrol Company LLC—*Ron Meyr*	1385 Fairport Rd Ste 2, Fairport NY 14450	585-586-1515	S	11*	.1
97	Manufacturing Resource Group Inc—*Robert Marotto*	930 Washington St, Norwood MA 02062	781-440-9700	R	11*	.1
98	Questek Manufacturing Corp—*Dale Krueger*	2570 Technology Dr, Elgin IL 60124	847-428-0300	R	11*	.1
99	MWSausse and Company Inc—*Torbjorn Helland*	28805 Industry Dr, Valencia CA 91355	661-257-3311	R	11*	.1
100	Jmr Holdings Inc—*Joel Rosenberg*	2035 Easy St, Commerce Township MI 48390	248-669-0334	R	11*	.1
101	Deltran PT	45 Hazelwood Dr, Amherst NY 14228	716-691-9100	D	10*	.1
102	Functional Devices Inc—*Kenneth Rittmann*	PO Box 368, Russiaville IN 46979	765-883-5538	R	10*	.1
103	Cybertrol Engineering LLC—*Dan Scott*	2950 Xenium Ln N Ste 1, Minneapolis MN 55441	763-559-8660	R	10*	<.1
104	Process Solutions Inc—*Todd Busby*	19115 62nd Ave Ne, Arlington WA 98223	360-403-7037	R	10*	<.1
105	Tetragenics Co—*Jeff Ruffner*	200 Technology Way, Butte MT 59701	406-533-6800	D	10*	<.1
106	United Equipment Accessories Inc—*Mark Hanawalt*	PO Box 817, Waverly IA 50677	319-352-3946	R	10*	.1
107	J and AK Inc—*Joseph Kleynjans*	5350 Campbells Run Rd, Pittsburgh PA 15205	412-787-9750	R	10*	.1
108	Milwaukee Resistor Corp—*Brian Jonas* Huntington Electric Inc	8920 W Heather Ave, Milwaukee WI 53224	414-362-8900	S	9*	.1
109	Flight Systems Industrial Products Co—*Barry Bowman*	1015 Harrisburg Pke, Carlisle PA 17013	717-254-3747	R	9*	.1
110	Rbb Systems Inc—*Bruce Hendrick*	4265 E Lincoln Way Uni, Wooster OH 44691	330-567-2906	R	9*	.1
111	Dyna-Graphics Corp—*Gregg Kline*	4080 Norex Dr, Chaska MN 55318	952-368-3344	R	9*	.1
112	Sta-Con Inc—*James Gallagher*	2525 S Orange Blossom, Apopka FL 32703	407-298-5940	R	9*	.1
113	Heatcon Composite Systems Inc—*Howard Banasky*	600 Andover Park E, Tukwila WA 98188	206-575-1333	R	9*	<.1
114	Paragon Firstronic Of NA Corp—*William Herndon*	1655 Michigan St Ne, Grand Rapids MI 49503	616-456-9220	R	9*	<.1
115	Burr Engineering and Development Company Inc—*Jack Budrow*	PO Box 460, Battle Creek MI 49016	269-965-2371	R	9*	.1
116	Filnor Inc—*Ronald Neely*	PO Box 2328, Alliance OH 44601	330-821-7667	R	9*	.1
117	Lintech—*Anthony Angelica*	1845 Enterprise Way, Monrovia CA 91016	626-358-0110	R	8*	.1
118	Technipower Systems Inc—*Gary Laskowski*	14 Commerce Dr, Danbury CT 06810	203-748-7001	P	8	.1
119	California Economizer—*Jeff Osheroff*	5622 Engineer Dr, Huntington Beach CA 92649	714-898-9963	R	8*	.1
120	O C Keckley Co—*Philip Miller*	PO Box 67, Skokie IL 60076	847-676-1613	R	8*	.1
121	Mide Technology Corp—*Marthinus van Schoor*	200 Boston Ave Ste 100, Medford MA 02155	781-306-0609	R	8*	<.1
122	Marine Exchange of Los Angeles-Long Beach Harbor Inc—*Richard B Mckenna*	PO Box 1949, San Pedro CA 90733	310-519-3134	R	8*	<.1
123	Advanced Micro Controls Inc—*William Erbs*	20 Gear Dr, Terryville CT 06786	860-585-1254	R	8*	<.1
124	Southern Electric Service Company Inc—*Gregory Smith*	PO Box 667489, Charlotte NC 28266	704-372-4832	R	8*	.1
125	Vector Systems Inc—*James Ovens*	411 Mckinney Pkwy, Mckinney TX 75071	214-544-9500	R	8*	<.1
126	Detroit Coil Co—*Robert Dugan*	2435 Hilton Rd, Ferndale MI 48220	248-658-1543	R	8*	.1
127	Keb America Inc—*Andy Delius*	5100 Valley Industrial, Shakopee MN 55379	952-224-1400	R	8*	<.1
128	Softsort Systems Inc—*Charles Keith*	1100 Northpoint Pkwy S, Acworth GA 30102	770-974-2700	R	8*	<.1
129	Remtron Inc—*Mike Pierson*	1916 Mission Rd, Escondido CA 92029	760-737-7800	R	7*	<.1
130	North Anoka Control Systems Inc—*William Doty*	13828 Lincoln St Ne, Anoka MN 55304	763-444-4747	R	7*	<.1
131	Copar Corp—*Stephen Schmidt*	5744 W 77th St, Burbank IL 60459	708-496-1859	R	7*	<.1
132	Wem Automation Inc—*Ernest Bollinger*	PO Box 510767, New Berlin WI 53151	262-782-2340	R	7*	<.1
133	Becs Technology Inc—*Brett Steinbrueck*	9487 Dielmn Rck Ind In, Saint Louis MO 63132	314-567-0088	R	7*	<.1
134	Monitor Technologies LLC (Elburn Illinois)—*Craig Russell*	PO Box 8048, Elburn IL 60119	630-365-9403	R	7*	<.1
135	Lake Shore Electric Corp—*Paul Shane*	205 Willis St, Cleveland OH 44146	440-232-0200	R	7*	.1
136	Integrated Control Corp—*Roberta Salerno*	748 Park Ave, Huntington NY 11743	631-673-5100	R	7*	<.1
137	P-Q Controls Inc—*Douglas Schumann*	95 Dolphin Rd, Bristol CT 06010	860-583-6994	R	7*	<.1
138	Lloyd Controls Inc—*Harold Lloyd*	PO Box 676, Mountlake Terrace WA 98043	425-775-1561	R	7*	<.1
139	Applied Digital—*Daniel Smith*	19315 State Hwy 413, Reeds Spring MO 65737	417-272-0761	R	7*	<.1
140	Zbe Inc—*Zac Bogart*	1035 Cindy Ln, Carpinteria CA 93013	805-576-1600	R	7*	<.1
141	Electronic Test Equipment Manufacturing Co—*John Hessen*	PO Box 4651, Lancaster PA 17604	717-393-9653	R	7*	<.1
142	Polytron Corp—*Alex Saharian*	4400 Wyland Dr, Elkhart IN 46516	574-522-0246	R	6*	.1
143	Tuffaloy Products Inc—*Michael Simmons*	1400 S Batesville Rd, Greer SC 29650	864-879-0763	R	6*	<.1
144	T and G Controls Inc—*Marta Lane*	1193 Beaver Ruin Rd St, Norcross GA 30093	770-921-6565	R	6*	<.1
145	Motion Control Systems Inc—*William Harris*	PO Box 115, New River VA 24129	540-731-0540	R	6*	.1
146	Systematix Controls Inc—*Doug Seto*	670 Industry Dr, Tukwila WA 98188	206-242-3800	R	6*	.1

Rank	Company Name—Executive Officer	Address, City, State, Zip	Phone	Type	Fin	Empls
147	Maple Systems Inc—Larry Peter	808 134th St Sw Ste 12, Everett WA 98204	425-745-3229	R	6*	<.1
148	EIC Systems Inc—Andrew N Huber	3988 E Jackson Blvd, Jackson MO 63755		R	6*	<.1
149	System Technical Support Corp—Eric Leskly	PO Box 2707, Culver City CA 90231	310-845-9400	R	6*	<.1
150	Peloton Manufacturing Corp—Jim Moll	8658 Tyler Blvd, Mentor OH 44060	440-205-1600	R	6*	<.1
151	Geier and Bluhm Inc—Jim MaGee	594 River St, Troy NY 12180	518-272-6951	R	6*	<.1
152	Strandberg Engineering Labs—John Strandberg	1302 N OHenry Blvd, Greensboro NC 27405	336-274-3775	R	6*	<.1
153	Teknic Inc—Thomas Bucella	1150 Pittsford Victor, Pittsford NY 14534	585-784-7454	R	6*	<.1
154	Appliance Controls Of Texas Corp—Edward Gray	PO Box 1068, Rowlett TX 75030	972-475-4180	R	6*	<.1
155	Various Technologies Inc—Kurt Sebben	2720 Aiello Dr Ste C, San Jose CA 95111	408-972-4460	R	6*	<.1
156	Ipc Power Resistors International Inc—Richard Field	4750 Olympic Blvd, Erlanger KY 41018	859-282-2900	R	6*	<.1
157	Accuweb Inc—Raymond Buisker	PO Box 7816, Madison WI 53707	608-223-0625	R	6*	<.1
158	Power Io LLC	537 Braemar Ave, Naperville IL 60563	630-717-7335	R	6*	.1
159	Olympic Controls Corp—Albano Andreini	1250 Crispin Dr, Elgin IL 60123	847-742-3566	R	6*	<.1
160	Divelbiss Corp—Terry Divelbiss	9778 Mount Gilead Rd, Fredericktown OH 43019	740-694-9015	R	6*	<.1
161	Snaptron Inc—Earl Tatman	960 Diamond Valley Dr, Windsor CO 80550	970-686-5682	R	6*	<.1
162	Product Resources Inc—John Erickson	148 Sohier Rd, Beverly MA 01915	978-524-8500	R	5*	<.1
163	Cable Concepts Inc—Rod Coons	468 Gradle Dr, Carmel IN 46032	317-587-1200	R	5*	<.1
164	Control Technology Corp—Gregory Woods	25 S St Ste E, Hopkinton MA 01748	508-435-9595	R	5*	<.1
165	Saminco Inc—Bonne Posma	10030 Amberwood Rd Ste, Fort Myers FL 33913	239-561-1561	R	5*	<.1
166	Contact Industries Inc—James Arnholt	PO Box 3086, Mansfield OH 44904	419-884-9788	R	5*	<.1
167	Rochester Industrial Control Inc—Eric Albert	6400 Furnace Rd, Ontario NY 14519	315-524-4555	R	5*	.1
168	Electro Inc—Frank Cuppoletti	PO Box 65912, Vancouver WA 98665	360-693-8265	R	5*	<.1
169	Hetronic USA—Max Heckl	4300 Highline Blvd Ste, Oklahoma City OK 73108	405-946-3574	R	5*	<.1
170	Custom Actuator Products Inc—Loren Noomen	2500 Niagara Ln N, Plymouth MN 55447	763-525-0844	R	5*	<.1
171	International Parallel Machines Inc—Robin Chang	50 Conduit St, New Bedford MA 02745	508-990-2977	R	5*	<.1
172	Hydro-Logic Inc—Ronald Reed	24832 Romano St, Warren MI 48091	586-757-7477	R	5*	<.1
173	Industrial Noise Control Inc—Mark Rubino	401 Airport Rd, North Aurora IL 60542	630-844-1999	R	5*	<.1
174	Bay Controls LLC—Bob Protech	6528 Weatherfield Ct, Maumee OH 43537	419-891-4390	R	5*	<.1
175	Tech Products Corp—Dan Rork	2215 Lyons Rd, Miamisburg OH 45342	937-438-1100	S	5*	<.1
176	Marlin Technologies Inc—Andy Lechtenberg	PO Box 123, Horicon WI 53032	920-485-4463	R	5*	<.1
177	Precision Machine Controls Inc—John Frano	PO Box 486, North Jackson OH 44451	330-538-2268	R	5*	<.1
178	Industrial Indexing Systems Inc—William Schnaufer	626 Fishers Run, Victor NY 14564	585-924-9181	R	5*	<.1
179	Control Stuff Inc—James Coder	PO Box 44, Cologne MN 55322	952-466-2175	R	5*	<.1
180	Omntec Manufacturing Inc—Lee Nicholson	PO Box 30, Ronkonkoma NY 11779	631-981-2001	R	5*	<.1
181	Control Resources Inc—James Kundert	11 Beaver Brook Rd, Littleton MA 01460	978-486-4160	R	5*	<.1
182	Centroid Corp—Joseph Mccullock	159 Gates Rd, Howard PA 16841	814-353-9290	R	4*	<.1
183	HI Solutions Inc—J Ivester	4040 Royal Dr Nw Ste 1, Kennesaw GA 30144	770-423-1150	R	4*	<.1
184	Afi Cybernetics Corp—Kenneth Doyle	713 Batavia St, Elmira NY 14904	607-732-3244	R	4*	<.1
185	Update Systems Inc—Joe Kittnor	10545 Baur Blvd, Saint Louis MO 63132	314-432-3282	R	4*	<.1
186	Repete Corp—Matt Peterson	W226 N6283 Village Dr, Sussex WI 53089	262-246-4541	R	4*	<.1
187	RPM Industries LLC—John Apostolides	55 Hickory St Ste 109, Washington PA 15301	724-228-5100	R	4*	<.1
188	Hurletron Inc—Garry Brainin	1820 Tempel Dr, Libertyville IL 60048	847-680-7022	S	4*	<.1
189	Circuit Interruption Technology Inc—Rick Hampton	1152 Hwy 10 No, Minneapolis MN 55432	763-535-2339	R	4*	<.1
190	Gilderfluke and Co—Douglas C Mobley	205 S Flower St, Burbank CA 91502	810-040-0184	R	4*	<.1
191	Unimar Inc—Michael Marley	3195 Vickery Rd, North Syracuse NY 13212	315-699-4400	R	4*	<.1
192	Elliott Control Company Ltd—Rick Fennell	PO Box 467, Willis TX 77378	936-228-5060	R	4*	<.1
193	Wilkes and Mclean Ltd—Roy Wilkes	17 Lakeside Ln, North Barrington IL 60010	847-381-3872	R	4*	<.1
194	Eac Electronics—John Anderberg	14090 Laurelwood Pl, Chino CA 91710	909-902-0654	R	4*	<.1
195	Southconn Technologies Inc—Thomas Shackett	PO Box 3229, West Columbia SC 29171	803-939-4700	R	4*	<.1
196	Grand Rapids Controls Company LLC—Tony Francik	PO Box 360, Rockford MI 49341	616-866-9551	R	4*	<.1
197	Elevator Systems Inc—Ignatius Alcamo	PO Box 601, Lawrence NY 11559	516-239-4044	R	4*	<.1
198	Ely Energy Inc—Richard Ely	11385 E 60th Pl, Tulsa OK 74146	918-250-6601	R	4*	<.1
199	E-Max Instruments Inc—Miguel Xavier	13 Inverness Way S, Englewood CO 80112	303-799-6640	R	4*	<.1
200	Static Controls Corp—William Yonish	30460 S Wixom Rd, Wixom MI 48393	248-926-4400	R	4*	<.1
201	Celtex Industries Inc—Tracy Acord	997 Cherokee Trce, White Oak TX 75693	903-297-8481	R	4*	<.1
202	Electrolab Inc—Karl Senghaas	2103 Mannix Dr, San Antonio TX 78217	210-824-5364	R	4*	<.1
203	SC and B Owners Inc—T Sekella	2000 Lake Rd, Elmira NY 14903	607-732-2030	R	4*	<.1
204	Infitec Inc—George Ehegartner	PO Box 2956, Syracuse NY 13220	315-433-1150	R	4*	.1
205	Powr-Ups Corp—Steven Summer	1 Roned Rd, Shirley NY 11967	631-345-5700	R	4*	<.1
206	High Country Tek Inc—Lennard Hjord	208 Gold Flat Ct, Nevada City CA 95959	530-265-3236	R	4*	<.1
207	Utility Relay Company Ltd—Patty Clayman	10100 Queens Way, Chagrin Falls OH 44023	440-708-1000	R	4*	<.1
208	Anderson Electric Controls Inc—Gary Anderson	8639 S 212th St, Kent WA 98031	253-395-3003	R	4*	<.1
209	Temperature Corporation Inc—Paul Straight	PO Box 1588, Fairmont WV 26555	304-366-4088	R	4*	<.1
210	Control Electric Co—Mike Vogt	14625 Puritas Ave, Cleveland OH 44135	216-671-8010	R	4*	<.1
211	Actus Manufacturing Inc—Timothy Nicholson	245 Roselawn Ave E Ste, Saint Paul MN 55117	651-487-8716	R	4*	<.1
212	American Teletimer Corp—Joel Rosenzweig	1167 Globe Ave, Mountainside NJ 07092	908-654-4200	R	3*	<.1
213	Hambolu LLC—Stacy Abercarbre	2940 S Jackson Dr, Independence MO 64057	816-795-0600	R	3*	<.1
214	S and N Manufacturing Inc—Nancy Paganessi	455 Stevens St, Geneva IL 60134	630-232-0275	R	3*	<.1
215	Kar-Tech Inc—Hassan Karbassi	111 Enterprise Rd, Delafield WI 53018	262-646-9444	R	3*	<.1
216	Roanoke Electronic Controls Inc—Thomas Hicks	PO Box 366, Roanoke AL 36274	334-863-7176	R	3*	<.1
217	Contrex Inc—Gary Hansen	PO Box 9000, Maple Grove MN 55311	763-424-7800	R	3*	<.1
218	F-Dyne Electronics—John Strickland	10443 Peach Ave, Mission Hills CA 91345	818-893-6068	R	3*	<.1
219	Artisan Controls Corp—John Murray	111 Canfield Ave Ste B, Randolph NJ 07869	973-598-9400	R	3*	<.1
220	Carotron Inc—Michael Jenkins	3204 Rocky River Rd, Heath Springs SC 29058	803-286-8614	R	3*	<.1
221	Lynx System Developers Inc—Douglas De Angelis	179 Ward Hill Ave, Haverhill MA 01835	978-556-9780	R	3*	<.1
222	Tel-Tron Technologies Corp—Brian Dawson	226 Fentress Blvd, Daytona Beach FL 32114	386-255-1921	R	3*	<.1
223	Bay Electronics Inc—Daniel Olsen	PO Box 397, Roseville MI 48066	586-296-0900	R	3*	<.1
224	Maxtrol Corp—Uri Ranon	1701 E Edinger Ave Ste, Santa Ana CA 92705	714-245-0506	R	3*	<.1
225	K G Moats and Sons LLC—Jack Nooney	27010 Us Hwy 24, Saint Marys KS 66536	785-437-2021	R	3*	<.1
226	Sewell Industrial Electronics Inc—Leonard Sewell	5851 Fern Valley Rd, Louisville KY 40228	502-968-3825	R	3*	<.1
227	Mehta Tech Inc—Harish Mehta	PO Box 350, Eldridge IA 52748	563-285-9151	R	3*	<.1
228	Q Com Inc—Robert Elders	30152 Esperanza, Rcho Sta Marg CA 92688	949-833-1000	R	3*	<.1
229	Entertron Industries Inc—Stephen Luft	99 Robinson Pl, Lockport NY 14094	716-438-7248	R	3*	<.1
230	Senasys Inc—Steve Dye	704 Bartlett Ave, Altoona WI 54720	715-831-6353	R	3*	<.1
231	Control Logic Inc—Tarique Islam	1724 S Nevada Way, Mesa AZ 85204	480-926-3434	R	3*	<.1
232	Electro-Pro Inc—Dan Skell	PO Box 409, Cedarburg WI 53012	262-377-6927	R	3*	<.1
233	Otek Corp—Otto Fest	4016 E Tennessee St, Tucson AZ 85714	520-748-7900	R	3*	<.1
234	Fitz-Rite Products Inc—W Fitzpatrick	1122 Naughton Dr, Troy MI 48083	248-528-8440	R	3*	<.1
235	Inductive Components Manufacturing Inc—Dirk Mooibroek	PO Box 188, Amelia OH 45102	513-752-4731	R	3*	<.1
236	Robinson Engineering Company Inc—Brad Robinson	1914 Silver St, Garland TX 75042	972-272-2001	R	3*	<.1

Note: An asterisk (*) indicates an estimated financial figure. The company type code used is as follows: R = Private, P = Public, S = Private Subsidiary, B = Public Subsidiary, D = Division, J = Joint Venture, I = Investment Fund.

COMPANY RANKINGS BY SALES WITHIN 4-DIGIT SIC

Rank	Company Name—Executive Officer	Address, City, State, Zip	Phone	Type	Fin	Empls
237	Murcal Inc—Robert Murphy	41343 12th St W, Palmdale CA 93551	661-272-4700	R	3*	<.1
238	Sterling Systems and Controls Inc—Robert Prater	PO Box 418, Sterling IL 61081	815-625-0852	R	3*	<.1
239	Automation and Control Services Inc—Roger Florkiewicz	2440 Ontario St, Schererville IN 46375	219-558-2060	R	3*	<.1
240	Tomkins Corp—John Nilsen	117 Dean Ave, Franklin MA 02038	508-528-2000	R	3*	<.1
241	Avab America Inc—Frantz Lau	434 Payran St Ste B, Petaluma CA 94952	707-778-8990	R	3*	<.1
242	Rees Inc—Daniel Breeden	PO Box 652, Fremont IN 46737	260-495-9811	R	3*	<.1
243	Textrol Inc—E White	111 W Sandy Ridge Rd, Monroe NC 28112	704-764-3400	R	3*	<.1
244	Micromod Automation Inc—Richard Keane	75 Town Centre Dr, Rochester NY 14623	585-321-9200	R	3*	<.1
245	Seatorque Control Systems LLC—Janet Stolper	2779 Se Monroe St, Stuart FL 34997	772-220-3020	R	3*	<.1
246	Avtech Inc—Thomas Manning	1430 Overlook Way, Bel Air MD 21014	410-592-7580	R	3*	<.1
247	Selectouch Corp—Raymond Stone	PO Box 38, Anna TX 75409	972-924-3289	R	2*	<.1
248	Ollila Industries Inc—Richard Ollila	17229 Lemon St Ste C, Hesperia CA 92345	909-866-8884	R	2*	<.1
249	Thomas Products Ltd—Thomas Duksa	987 W St, Southington CT 06489	860-621-9101	R	2*	<.1
250	Val-Tech Inc—Roger Beam	PO Box 9086, Newark DE 19714	302-738-0500	R	2*	<.1
251	Bwi Eagle Inc—David Festog	105 Bonnie Dr, Butler PA 16002	724-283-4681	R	2*	<.1
252	Wythe Power Equipment Company Inc—B Bradberry	PO Box 658, Wytheville VA 24382	276-228-7371	R	2*	<.1
253	Andy's Electrical Service Inc—Alva Andrew	PO Box 36, Racine MN 55967	507-378-2101	R	2*	<.1
254	MP Jackson LLC—Rich Regole	1824 River St, Jackson MI 49202	517-782-0391	R	2*	<.1
255	Brunstedt and Lambert Systems Inc—William Brunstedt	418 N Washington Ave A, Prescott AZ 86301	928-445-1770	R	2*	<.1
256	Silvatech Corp—William Rousseau	PO Box 521, Bethel VT 05032	802-234-5174	R	2*	<.1
257	Silveron Industries Inc—Steve Lee	182 S Brent Cir, Walnut CA 91789	909-598-4533	R	2*	<.1
258	Ese Inc—Mark Weber	3600 Downwind Dr, Marshfield WI 54449	715-387-4778	R	2*	<.1
259	Venus Controls Inc—Ravi Tandon	30105 8 Mile Rd, Livonia MI 48152	248-477-6520	R	2*	<.1
260	Vibration and Noise Engineering Corp—Art Cagney	3374 N Benzing Rd, Orchard Park NY 14127	716-827-4959	R	2*	<.1
261	Kanson Electronics Inc—Arthur Filson Sr	245 Forrest Ave, Hohenwald TN 38462	931-796-3050	R	2*	<.1
262	Macromatic Controls LLC—John Perdue	W134 N5345 Campbell Dr, Menomonee Falls WI 53051	262-781-3366	R	2*	<.1
263	Payne Engineering Company Inc—Henry Payne	P O Box 70, Scott Depot WV 25560	304-757-7353	R	2*	<.1
264	Autotronics Inc—Julia Womack	2700 Davis Blvd, Joplin MO 64804	417-781-1812	R	2*	<.1
265	Industrial Control Concepts Inc—John Germanos	707 N 2nd St 5th Fl, Saint Louis MO 63102	314-621-0076	R	2*	<.1
266	Microtronics Inc—Roger Jones	1219 N 10th St, Humboldt KS 66748	620-365-8264	R	2*	<.1
267	Systems Equipment Corp—Orrin Grangaard	903 3rd Ave SW, Waukon IA 52172	563-568-6387	R	2*	<.1
268	Hausermann Controls Co—Marten Hausermann	300 W Laura Dr, Addison IL 60101	630-543-6688	R	2*	<.1
269	P And B Services Inc—Jerry Powell	PO Box 800877, Houston TX 77280	713-460-8818	R	2*	<.1
270	Advantage Electronics Inc—Steven Wash	PO Box 407, Greenwood IN 46142	317-888-1946	R	2*	<.1
271	Computer Control Corp—Harvey Padden	10 Park Pl Ste 1, Butler NJ 07405	973-492-8265	R	2*	<.1
272	Control Systems West Inc—Bruce Borders	1150 Industrial Ave St, Petaluma CA 94952	707-763-1108	R	2*	<.1
273	Marine and Industrial Hydraulics Inc—John Wright	329 Ctr Ave, Mamaroneck NY 10543	914-698-2650	R	2*	<.1
274	PEC Systems Inc—Bryan Wood	PO Box 1030, Phenix City AL 36867	334-298-2821	R	2*	<.1
275	Thunderco Inc—Walter Edrington	PO Box 920795, Houston TX 77292	713-681-4686	R	2*	<.1
276	Engineering Concepts Unlimited Inc—Adam Suchko	PO Box 250, Fishers IN 46038	317-849-8470	R	2*	<.1
277	Speer Equipment Inc—Gregory Speer	PO Box 100, Hamlin NY 14464	585-964-2700	R	2*	<.1
278	Advanced Design And Control Corp—Jeff Dietterich	535 Hagey Rd, Souderton PA 18964	215-723-7200	R	2*	<.1
279	Ben Franklin Design and Manufacturing Company Inc—Edward Leyden	PO Box 502, Agawam MA 01001	413-786-4220	R	2*	<.1
280	Rogers Electro-Matics Inc—Robert Haller	PO Box 186, Syracuse IN 46567	574-457-2305	R	2*	<.1
281	Rasp Inc—Ronald Richards	22 Hudson Falls Rd Ste, South Glens Falls NY 12803	518-747-8020	R	2*	<.1
282	Indelac Controls Inc—James Robinson	6810 Power Line Dr, Florence KY 41042	859-727-7890	R	2*	<.1
283	Computer Components Inc—Gary Flor	PO Box 1378, East Granby CT 06026	860-653-9909	R	2*	<.1
284	Howman Electronics Inc—Manfred Koch	PO Box 536, Lebanon NJ 08833	908-534-2247	R	2*	<.1
285	Creative Engineering Associates Inc—Arthur Beutler	5890 Fleming Ct, Greendale WI 53129	414-421-3363	R	2*	<.1
286	Drivecon Inc—James Vandegrift	820 Lakeside Dr Ste 1, Gurnee IL 60031	847-855-9150	R	2*	<.1
287	Controllix Corp—John Kelly	21415 Alexander Rd, Cleveland OH 44146	440-232-8757	R	2*	<.1
288	Gigavac LLC	1125 Mark Ave, Carpinteria CA 93013	805-684-8401	R	2*	<.1
289	Beeco Inc—Larry Egelhoff	4175 Millersville Rd, Indianapolis IN 46205	317-547-1717	R	2*	<.1
290	Fillmore Systems Inc—James Fillmore	760 N Thornton St Ste, Post Falls ID 83854	208-773-8389	R	2*	<.1
291	Eversan Inc—Mustafa Evke	34 Main St Ste 3, Whitesboro NY 13492	315-736-3967	R	2*	<.1
292	R-K Electronics Inc—John Keller	7405 Industrial Row Dr, Mason OH 45040	513-489-4060	R	2*	<.1
293	Sieb and Meyer America Inc—Axel Schroeter	3975 Port Union Rd, Fairfield OH 45014	513-563-0860	R	2*	<.1
294	Anaheim Automation Inc—William Reimbold	910 E Orangefair Ln, Anaheim CA 92801	714-992-6990	R	2*	<.1
295	Electro-Matic Products Co—Kenneth Littwin	2235 N Knox Ave, Chicago IL 60639	773-235-4010	R	2*	<.1
296	O'neill Industrial Corp—Justin O'neill	105 Commerce Cir, Durham CT 06422	860-349-8988	R	2*	<.1
297	Reitech Corp—John Reiter	240 Shumway St S Ste 2, Shakopee MN 55379	952-895-6161	R	2*	<.1
298	Markload Systems Inc—Jan Roush	1118 N Main St Ste C, Pearland TX 77581	281-485-8600	R	2*	<.1
299	Sun State Systems Inc—Gary Armbruster	34 Industrial Loop N S, Orange Park FL 32073	904-269-2544	R	2*	<.1
300	Cieco Inc—Ronald Cejer	2401 Hookstown Grade R, Clinton PA 15026	412-262-5581	R	2*	<.1
301	Icotech Inc—Scott Pritchett	PO Box 210424, Montgomery AL 36121	334-569-2233	R	2*	<.1
302	Joliet Technologies LLC—Clay Johnson	1724 Tinsmith Ct, Crest Hill IL 60403	815-725-9696	R	2*	<.1
303	GL Engineering Company Inc—Gary Lairson	8542 Hamilton Ave, Huntington Beach CA 92646	714-374-2270	R	2*	<.1
304	American Relays Inc—Hyo Lee	10306 Norwalk Blvd, Santa Fe Springs CA 90670	562-944-0447	R	1*	<.1
305	Core Components Inc—Amy Adams	154 Easy St, Carol Stream IL 60188	630-690-0520	R	1*	<.1
306	T and M Controls Inc—Terry O'reilly	720 W Cheyenne Ave Ste, North Las Vegas NV 89030	702-240-4811	R	1*	<.1
307	Conntrol International Inc—Ronald Braaten	PO Box 645, Putnam CT 06260	860-928-0567	R	1*	<.1
308	Skjonberg Controls Inc—Knut Skjonberg	1363 Donlon St Ste 6, Ventura CA 93003	805-650-0877	R	1*	<.1
309	Booth Electrosystems Inc—E Snape	PO Box 15030, Greenville SC 29610	864-246-5811	R	1*	<.1
310	Wolff Controls Corp—Peter Wolff	PO Box 9407, Winter Haven FL 33883	863-324-0423	R	1*	<.1
311	Heritage Electrical Corp—Ronald Daugherty	7725 Whitepine Rd, Richmond VA 23237	804-743-4614	R	1*	<.1
312	Applied Control Concepts Inc—Gerald Walloch	8865 N 55th St, Milwaukee WI 53223	414-362-7880	R	1*	<.1
313	Bck Inc—Ron Cox	9520 Pulaski Hwy Ste B, Baltimore MD 21220	410-682-4400	R	1*	<.1
314	T and T Automation Inc—Ben Terkildsen	88 Pierson Ln, Windsor CT 06095	860-683-8788	R	1*	<.1
315	Valve Related Controls Inc—Fred Tasch	143 Commerce Dr, Loveland OH 45140	513-677-8724	R	1*	<.1
316	AP Seedorff and Company Inc—Kurt Simon	1338 N Knollwood Cir, Anaheim CA 92801	714-252-5330	R	1*	<.1
317	Omni Control Technology Inc—Peter Bedigian	PO Box 444, Whitinsville MA 01588	508-234-9121	R	1*	<.1
318	Pro Controls Inc—Doug Tilton	1312 Gordon Rd, Yakima WA 98901	509-457-3386	R	1*	<.1
319	Positive Safety Manufacturers Co—Jeff Sloat	34099 Melinz Pkwy Unit, Willoughby OH 44095	440-951-2130	R	1*	<.1
320	Precision Timer Company Inc—James Hunicke	PO Box 678, Westbrook CT 06498	860-399-6253	R	1*	<.1
321	Morris Products Inc—Jeff Schwartz	53 Carey Rd, Queensbury NY 12804	518-743-0523	R	1*	<.1
322	Metal-Tech Controls Corp—Glen Koedding	3441 Saint Croix Ct, Punta Gorda FL 33950	941-575-7677	R	1*	<.1
323	Systems Engineering Associates Inc—Kenneth Dixon	14989 W 69th Ave, Arvada CO 80007	303-421-0233	R	1*	<.1
324	Con-Trol-Cure Inc—Stephen Siegel	1229 W Cortland St, Chicago IL 60614	773-248-0099	R	1*	<.1
325	Mission Microsystems Inc—William Bmcdonough	5942 Edinger Ave Ste 1, Huntington Beach CA 92649	714-841-1986	R	1*	<.1

Rank	Company Name—*Executive Officer*	Address, City, State, Zip	Phone	Type	Fin	Empls
326	Relay Service Co—*John Thomas*	1300 N Pulaski Rd, Chicago IL 60651	773-252-2700	R	1*	<.1
327	Libra Systems Corp—*David Cardy*	PO Box 366, Harleysville PA 19438	215-256-1700	R	1*	<.1
328	Arrgh Manufacturing Company Inc—*Thomas Graham*	831 Vallejo Ave, Novato CA 94945	415-897-0220	R	1*	<.1
329	Aaim Controls Inc—*Arthur Marshall*	11885 Mutual Dr, Waynesboro PA 17268	717-765-9100	R	1*	<.1
330	Instrumentation and Control Systems Inc—*Marion Servos*	520 W Interstate Rd, Addison IL 60101	630-543-6200	R	1*	<.1
331	Intersol Industries Inc—*Orest Hrynewycz*	241 James St, Bensenville IL 60106	630-238-0385	R	1*	<.1
332	Motor Protection Electronics Inc—*James Gallagher*	2464 Vulcan Rd, Apopka FL 32703	407-299-3825	R	1*	<.1
333	Noise Suppression Technologies Inc—*Daniel Belcher*	4182 Fisher Rd, Columbus OH 43228	614-258-4455	R	1*	<.1
334	Control System Innovators Inc—*Darrell Whitmore*	1301 Bowes Rd Ste A, Elgin IL 60123	847-741-0007	R	1*	<.1
335	Kamp-Synergy LLC	9434 N 107th St, Milwaukee WI 53224	414-354-6700	R	1*	<.1
336	Video Control Systems Inc—*Kerry Jackson*	PO Box 939, Middlesex NC 27557	252-235-6000	R	1*	<.1
337	Cincinnati Control Dynamics Inc—*Frank Bao*	4924 Para Dr, Cincinnati OH 45237	513-242-7300	R	1*	<.1
338	Koenig-Pretempco Inc—*Robert A Koenig*	3320 Church St, Slatington PA 18080	484-263-6000	R	1*	<.1
339	Powis Corp—*Mike Powis*	2301 Nw Jefferson St, Blue Springs MO 64015	816-229-1114	R	1*	<.1
340	WSA Sales Company Inc—*Connie Garrett*	10707 E Seminole, Tulsa OK 74116	918-664-0269	R	1*	<.1
341	Kf Controls LLC	8565 Cottonwood St Nw, Minneapolis MN 55433	763-792-0205	R	1*	<.1
342	M/D Control Systems Inc—*Robert Marshall*	3306 Nw 211th Ter, Hillsboro OR 97124	503-690-7500	R	1*	<.1
343	Zahn Electronics Inc—*David Zahn*	4133 Courtney Rd Unit, Franksville WI 53126	262-835-9200	R	1*	<.1
344	Industrial Safety Sales Inc—*Brian Thomas*	PO Box 126, Kenosha WI 53141	262-652-8660	R	1*	<.1
345	JH Technology Inc—*Harry Trietley*	4233 Clark Rd Ste 9, Sarasota FL 34233	941-927-0300	R	1*	<.1
346	Industrial Control Engineering—*Robert Conway*	109 Tremont City Rd, Springfield OH 45502	937-390-9423	R	1*	<.1
347	ASI Electronics Inc—*William Jackson*	PO Box 578, Cypress TX 77410	281-373-3835	R	1*	<.1
348	Smart Relay Technology Inc—*Ron Colino*	97 Gannet Dr, Commack NY 11725	631-543-7161	R	1*	<.1
349	WH Autopilots Inc—*Will Hamm*	7995 Ne Day Rd Ste B, Bainbridge Island WA 98110	206-780-2175	R	1*	<.1
350	Lor Manufacturing Company Inc—*Lawrence Rescoe*	7131 W Drew Rd, Weidman MI 48893	989-644-2581	R	1*	<.1
351	Mission Controls Company Inc—*Frederic Heinzen*	305 Mayock Rd Ste H, Gilroy CA 95020	408-848-5250	R	1*	<.1
352	Edison Controls Fci Inc—*Jack Miller*	PO Box 2095, Fairhope AL 36533	251-928-3114	R	1*	<.1
353	Nicra Inc—*Nicholas Rao*	930 Lincoln Blvd, Middlesex NJ 08846	732-271-9400	R	1*	<.1
354	Avanti Resources LLC—*John Logsdon*	PO Box 436964, Louisville KY 40253	502-499-6561	R	1*	<.1
355	Gemtrol Inc—*Jeffrey Dombek*	1800 Broadway St Bldg, Buffalo NY 14212	716-894-0716	R	1*	<.1
356	Kinematics And Controls Corp—*John Rakucewicz*	15151 Technology Dr, Brooksville FL 34604	352-796-0300	R	1*	<.1
357	Mcm Systems Inc—*Will Green*	PO Box 205, Little Chute WI 54140	920-788-8052	R	1*	<.1
358	Signatrol Inc—*Ed Griffins*	714 Garfield Pl, Danville IL 61832	217-446-1160	R	1*	<.1
359	TD Controls Inc—*Thomas Ressler*	300 W Mountain Rd, Wind Gap PA 18091	610-759-8764	R	1*	<.1
360	Vision Controls and Automation—*Larry Stern*	3025 N Progress Dr, Appleton WI 54911	920-734-9760	R	1*	<.1
361	Applied Motor Controls Ltd—*Ian Browne*	PO Box 790786, San Antonio TX 78279	210-524-1050	R	1*	<.1
362	Control Dynamics Corp—*Harvey Shuhart*	960 Louis Dr, Warminster PA 18974	215-956-0700	R	1*	<.1
363	Futurecom Inc—*Mary Herbin*	1941 W State Rd 426, Oviedo FL 32765	407-359-9295	R	1*	<.1
364	Competition Electronics Inc—*James Bailey*	3469 Precision Dr, Rockford IL 61109	815-874-8001	R	1*	<.1
365	Wilmington Research and Development Corp—*Stephen Boyd*	50 Parker St Ste 3, Newburyport MA 01950	978-499-0100	R	1*	<.1
366	Excitron Corp—*Vern Bunch*	333 N Snowmass Cir, Superior CO 80027	303-859-9476	R	1*	<.1
367	Capstan Inc—*Graeme Henderson*	101 N Kansas Ave, Topeka KS 66603	785-232-4477	R	1*	<.1
368	Edon Controls Inc—*Norman Fender*	2891 Industrial Row Dr, Troy MI 48084	248-280-0420	R	1*	<.1
369	Advanced Control Systems Corp—*Charles Marshall*	35 Corporate Park Dr S, Pembroke MA 02359	781-829-9228	R	1*	<.1
370	Howman Associates Inc—*Howard Rood*	12 Garden St, Edison NJ 08817	732-985-7474	R	1*	<.1
371	Magnelink Inc—*Fred Hostetler*	1060 Ne 25th Ave Ste C, Hillsboro OR 97124	503-844-6620	R	1*	<.1
372	Power Efficiency Corp—*Steven Strasser*	5744 Pacific Center Bl, San Diego CA 92121	858-750-3875	P	1	<.1
373	Automation Systems and Control Inc—*Robin Rich*	303 Bill Futch Rd, Ellabell GA 31308	912-653-5440	R	1*	<.1
374	Trend Machinery Inc—*John Gordon*	7475 S Madison St Ste, Burr Ridge IL 60527	630-655-0030	R	1*	<.1
375	Corby Industries Inc—*Glenn Matz*	PO Box 4307, Bethlehem PA 18018	610-433-1412	R	1*	<.1
376	Doddridge Controls Inc—*Walter Heimbuch*	Rr 2 Box 380, Shinnston WV 26431	304-592-0634	R	1*	<.1
377	National Magnetic Sensors Inc—*Robert Bardoorian*	PO Box 64, Plantsville CT 06479	860-621-6816	R	1*	<.1
378	Universal Controls Systems—*Gordon Munn*	36324 Moravian Dr, Clinton Township MI 48035	586-790-2150	R	1*	<.1
379	Micro Decisions Corp—*Dale Agonis*	3209 Cascade Dr Ste A, Valparaiso IN 46383	219-477-2002	R	1*	<.1
380	Hms Electronics Inc—*Richard Harkey*	5935 Labath Ave Ste 1, Rohnert Park CA 94928	707-584-8760	R	1*	<.1
381	Miller Carbonic Inc—*James Rosenbaum*	530 W Root St, Chicago IL 60609	773-624-5651	R	1*	<.1
382	Crane Dorray Corp—*Ron Jaeger*	PO Box 1465, Elmhurst IL 60126	630-893-7553	R	1*	<.1
383	Bouchette Electronics Inc—*Theodore Bouchette*	N11325 County Rd Y, Clintonville WI 54929	715-823-7770	R	1*	<.1
384	Dnh Industries Inc—*David Hitt*	24100 Frampton Ave Ste, Harbor City CA 90710	310-517-1769	R	1*	<.1
385	Enetics Inc—*William Bush*	830 Canning Pkwy, Victor NY 14564	585-924-5010	R	1*	<.1
386	Interstate Industrial Technology Inc—*Merrill Dawson*	510 N Main St, Dupo IL 62239	618-286-4900	R	1*	<.1
387	Microridge Systems Inc—*John Schuldt*	PO Box 3249, Sunriver OR 97707	541-593-1656	R	1*	<.1
388	Mid-States Controls Corp—*Richard Gotthardt*	3714 S Memorial Dr, Racine WI 53403	262-554-6660	R	1*	<.1
389	Scott Electronic Services—*Dan Ghiocel*	43678 Salem Way, Fremont CA 94538	510-490-6349	R	1*	<.1
390	Automation And Mechanical Services Inc—*Joan Mcbride*	403 E Main St, Morgantown PA 19543	610-913-0410	R	1*	<.1
391	Atta Boy Automation Inc—*Bruce Walker*	384 S Main St Ste C, Ashland City TN 37015	615-792-6022	R	1*	<.1
392	Le Sueur Manufacturing Co—*Samuel Ray Le Sueur*	3220 Lorna Rd, Birmingham AL 35216	205-822-0720	R	1*	<.1
393	Radius LLC	4922 Technical Dr, Milford MI 48381	248-685-0773	R	1*	<.1
394	Sigma Switches Plus Inc—*Brian Rothbauer*	4703 Wyland Dr, Elkhart IN 46516	574-294-5776	R	1*	<.1
395	Stewart Ergonomics Inc—*Jack Stewart*	345 Park Ave, Chalfont PA 18914	215-822-8433	R	<1*	<.1
396	Domenic Stangherlin—*Domenic Stangherlin*	943 Kurtz St, Allentown PA 18102	610-434-5624	R	<1*	<.1
397	Electroneering Inc—*Stefan Vingsbo*	2400 Campbell Rd Ste C, Houston TX 77080	713-461-5206	R	<1*	<.1
398	Panish Controls Inc—*Robert Panish*	191 Bennett St Ste 203, Bridgeport CT 06605	203-333-7371	R	<1*	<.1
399	Custom Control Systems Inc—*Kevin Hagberg*	45 Sherrill Ln, New Hartford NY 13413	315-732-1990	R	<1*	<.1
400	Retzlaff Inc—*Robert Retzlaff*	50 Mitchell Blvd, San Rafael CA 94903	415-472-1177	R	<1*	<.1
401	Process Technologies Group Inc—*Jerrold Cabe*	30 W 106 Butterfield R, Warrenville IL 60555	630-393-4777	R	<1*	<.1
402	EDR Electronics Inc—*Edward Rumisek*	1504 E Algonquin Rd, Arlington Heights IL 60005	847-640-6996	R	<1*	<.1
403	3d Farms and Machine LLC	1600 E Loomis Rd, Weatherford OK 73096	580-772-5543	R	<1*	<.1
404	Brower Timing Systems—*Mark Brower*	12660 Fort St Ste 102, Draper UT 84020	801-572-5540	R	<1*	<.1
405	David T Jennings—*David Jennings*	2705a De La Vina St, Santa Barbara CA 93105	805-682-8206	R	<1*	<.1
406	Hy-Meg Corp—*Vincent Cupidro*	854 S Westgate St, Addison IL 60101	630-543-9250	R	<1*	<.1
407	Correction Controls—*Thomas Weaver*	928 Maplewood St, Willard OH 44890	419-935-1003	R	<1*	<.1
408	Acoustic Standards LLC—*Joe Bixhorn*	3890 Walnut Ave, Chino CA 91710	909-517-1133	R	<1*	<.1
409	Bird and Associates Inc—*John Bird*	PO Box 5913, Sparks NV 89432	775-358-7109	R	<1*	<.1
410	Cox Control Systems—*Boyd Cox*	4032 Shady Ln Dr Se, Smyrna GA 30080	770-433-1187	R	<1*	<.1
411	Finder Relays Inc—*Michelle Kitzrow*	4191 Capital View Dr, Suwanee GA 30024	770-271-4431	R	<1*	<.1
412	Javatec Inc—*James Van Antwerp*	300 Chaney Branch Rd, Crockett VA 24323	276-621-4572	R	<1*	<.1
413	Levex Engineering Co—*Randy Fuerst*	5211 Northrup Ave, Saint Louis MO 63110	314-772-1518	R	<1*	<.1
414	Precision Switch Design Inc—*Thorp Freeman*	PO Box 1207, Stowe VT 05672	802-253-0911	R	<1*	<.1
415	Vektron Corp—*Scott Banks*	1840 County Line Rd St, Huntingdon Valley PA 19006	215-354-0300	R	<1*	<.1

Note: An asterisk (*) indicates an estimated financial figure. The company type code used is as follows: R = Private, P = Public, S = Private Subsidiary, B = Public Subsidiary, D = Division, J = Joint Venture, I = Investment Fund.

COMPANY RANKINGS BY SALES WITHIN 4-DIGIT SIC

Rank	Company Name—Executive Officer	Address, City, State, Zip	Phone	Type	Fin	Empls
416	Bayside Controls Inc—Roger Hummel	173 Ludlow Ave, Northvale NJ 07647	201-767-1509	R	<1*	<.1
417	Boulton Machine Products Inc—Douglas Hunt	11085 E 9 Mile Rd, Warren MI 48089	586-757-6161	R	<1*	<.1
418	Fuller Enterprises Inc—Leon Fuller	11200 Se 21st Ave, Milwaukie OR 97222	503-654-0711	R	<1*	<.1
419	Vantec—Dail Villeneuve	460 Honeycutt Dr, Grants Pass OR 97526	541-471-7135	R	<1*	<.1
420	Custom Electronics Systems Inc—Robert Oppel	455 Forum Pkwy, Rural Hall NC 27045	336-969-2411	R	<1*	<.1
421	Lewus Electric Company Inc—James Lewus	1303 W Red Baron Rd, Payson AZ 85541	928-468-6320	R	<1*	<.1
422	Silent Technology LLC	1105 Travis Heights Bl, Austin TX 78704	512-912-1302	R	<1*	<.1
423	Pelton Company Inc—Robert P Peebler	1500 North Waverly, Ponca City OK 74602	580-762-6341	S	<1	<.1
424	Servos and Simulation Inc—E Bruce Baker	377 Balogh Pl, Longwood FL 32750	407-262-9042	R	<1	<.1
425	Universal Remote Control Inc—Hank Eisengrein	500 Mamaroneck Ave, Harrison NY 10528	914-835-4484	R	<1	N/A

TOTALS: SIC 3625 Relays & Industrial Controls
Companies: 425 — 24,154 — 104.3

3629 Electrical Industrial Apparatus Nec

Rank	Company Name—Executive Officer	Address, City, State, Zip	Phone	Type	Fin	Empls
1	American Power Conversion Corp—Laurent Vernerey	132 Fairgrounds Rd, West Kingston RI 02892	401-789-5735	S	1,980	7.6
2	Woodward Inc (Fort Collins Colorado)—Thomas A Gendron	PO Box 1519, Fort Collins CO 80522	970-482-5811	P	1,712	6.2
3	VICR Securities Corp—Patrizio Vinciarelli	25 Frontage Rd, Andover MA 01810	978-470-2900	S	1,025*	1.0
4	Zero Corp—Daniel Leininger	500 W 200 N, North Salt Lake UT 84054	801-298-5900	R	229*	.3
5	Cooper B-Line Inc—Kevin Kissling	509 W Monroe St, Highland IL 62249	618-654-2184	S	211*	1.2
6	Converteam Inc—Michael Archibald	610 Epsilon Dr Ste 1, Pittsburgh PA 15238	412-967-0765	R	178*	.3
7	Eaton Power Quality Group Inc—A Cutler	8609 Six Forks Rd, Raleigh NC 27615	919-872-3020	R	171*	.1
8	Gardner Bender Inc—Ed Staple	PO Box 3241, Milwaukee WI 53201	414-352-4160	S	151*	.2
9	Jerrik Inc	102 W Julie Dr, Tempe AZ 85283	480-730-5700	S	131*	.1
10	Schumacher Electric Corp—John Waldron	801 E Business Ctr Dr, Mount Prospect IL 60056	847-385-1600	R	107*	.1
11	Interpoint Corp	PO Box 97005, Redmond WA 98073	425-882-3100	S	105*	.4
12	Proton OnSite—Robert Fredland	10 Technology Dr, Wallingford CT 06492	203-678-2000	S	102*	.1
13	Powerware Corp—Mark Ascolese	PO Box 58189, Raleigh NC 27658	919-845-3569	S	100*	.6
14	IdaTech Inc—Harol Koyama	63065 NE 18th St, Bend OR 97701	541-383-3390	S	90*	.1
15	Static Control Components Inc—Edwin Swartz	PO Box 152, Sanford NC 27331	919-774-3808	R	89*	1.2
16	Acme Electric Corp (Lumberton North Carolina)—Bill Axline	4815 W 5th St, Lumberton NC 28358	910-738-1121	S	89*	.7
17	Orion Energy Services Inc—Neal R Verfuerth	2210 Woodland Dr, Manitowoc WI 54220	920-892-9340	P	86	.3
18	INSTALLS Inc—Thomas C Hunt	241 Main St 5th Fl, Buffalo NY 14203	716-854-1994	R	82*	.2
19	Active Power Inc—Jan Lindelow	2128 W Braker Ln Bldg, Austin TX 78758	512-836-6464	P	65	.2
20	Nuvera Fuel Cells Inc—Roberto Cordaro	129 Concord Rd Bldg 1, Billerica MA 01821	617-245-7500	R	60*	.1
21	Cyberex LLC	5900 Eastport Blvd Bld, Richmond VA 23231	804-236-3300	S	56*	.4
22	Werner Electric Supply Co—Lynn MacDonald	2341 Industrial Dr, Neenah WI 54956	920-729-4500	R	56*	.1
23	Ametek Rotron	627 Lake St, Kent OH 44240	330-673-3452	D	47*	.1
24	Inlet Technologies—Don Bossi	1121 Situs Ct Ste 330, Raleigh NC 27606	919-856-1080	R	45*	.1
25	American Electric Technologies Inc—Charles M Dauber	6410 Long Dr, Houston TX 77087	713-644-8182	P	39	.3
26	Ault Inc—Frederick M Green	7105 Northland Ter, Minneapolis MN 55428	763-592-1900	R	37	.7
27	Powervar Inc—George Lannert	1450 S Lakeside Dr, Waukegan IL 60085	847-596-7000	R	36*	.1
28	ADMMicro Inc—Peter Howell	2797 Frontage Rd NW St, Roanoke VA 24011	540-527-4600	S	36*	<.1
29	CopperLogic Inc—John W Hamm	4140 World Houston Par, Houston TX 77032	713-933-0999	S	35	.2
30	Delta-Unibus Corp—Tom Powell	515 RailRoad Ave, Northlake IL 60164	708-409-1200	S	34*	.1
31	Vanner Power Group Inc—Steve Funk	4282 Reynolds Dr, Hilliard OH 43026	614-771-2718	R	32*	.1
32	Quasar Power and Technologies Inc—Bruce Maroni	PO Box 810, Belmont NH 03220	603-267-8865	R	27*	<.1
33	DESCO Industries Inc—Wayne Hunter	3651 Walnut Ave, Chino CA 91710	909-627-8178	R	26*	.1
34	Avionic Instruments Inc—David Reinfeld	PO Box 498, Avenel NJ 07001	732-388-3500	S	25*	.2
35	Mcgregor-Surmount Corp—Larry Gregor	365 Carr Dr, Brookville OH 45309	937-833-6768	R	24*	.2
36	Picor Corp—Claudio Tuozzolo	PO Box 859, Slatersville RI 02876	401-235-1100	S	23*	<.1
37	Semiconductor Circuits Inc—Teddi Ritchie	14C Industrial Way, Atkinson NH 03811	603-893-2330	R	21*	<.1
38	American Radionic Company Inc—Robert Stockman	PO Box 352919, Palm Coast FL 32135	386-445-6000	R	21*	.2
39	Picosecond Pulse Labs Inc—Vance Nahman	2500 55th St, Boulder CO 80301	303-443-1249	R	20*	<.1
40	GB International Trading Company Ltd—August Garufy	408 Airport Rd, Endicott NY 13760	607-785-0938	R	20*	.2
41	Dynapower Corp—Peter Pollak	85 Meadowland Dr, South Burlington VT 05403	802-860-7200	R	19*	.2
42	Elpac Electronics Inc—Ricardo Felix	4 Westbrook Corporate, Westchester IL 60154	708-316-4407	R	18*	.2
43	Connector Castings Inc—Peter Fuerst	1600 N 22nd St, Saint Louis MO 63106	314-421-5895	R	18*	.2
44	Sure Power Industries Inc—Kirk S Hachigian	10955 SW Avery St Ste, Tualatin OR 97062	503-692-5360	S	18	.2
45	Power Dynamics Inc—James Papianni	145 Algonquin Pkwy Ste, Whippany NJ 07981	973-560-0019	R	17*	.2
46	Myers Power Products Inc—Diana Grootonk	725 E Harrison St, Corona CA 92879	951-520-1900	R	15*	.1
47	Apex Microtechnology Corp—Jason Rhode	5980 N Shannon Rd, Tucson AZ 85741	520-690-8600	S	14*	.1
48	Dei Services Corp—Jose Diaz	7213 Sandscove Ct Ste, Winter Park FL 32792	407-678-3388	R	13*	.1
49	Pauluhn Electric Manufacturing Co—Peter Guile	1616 N Main St, Pearland TX 77581	281-485-4311	S	13*	.1
50	Sparqtron Corp—Mitchell Kung	5079 Brandin Ct, Fremont CA 94538	510-657-7198	R	13*	.1
51	Acumentrics Corp—Gary Simon	20 SW Park, Westwood MA 02090	781-461-8251	R	12*	.1
52	Onda Corp—Claudio I Zanelli	592 Weddell Dr, Sunnyvale CA 94089	408-745-0383	R	12*	<.1
53	La Marche Manufacturing Co—Tom Steinke	106 Bradrock Dr, Des Plaines IL 60018	847-299-1188	R	11*	.1
54	iPhotonix—Amir Elbaz	1299 Commerce Dr, Richardson TX 75081	214-575-9300	S	11	<.1
55	Custom Power Ltd—Frank Reyna	2821 W 11th St, Houston TX 77008	713-880-0909	R	11*	<.1
56	Energy Technologies Inc—Paul Madden	219 Park Ave E, Mansfield OH 44902	419-522-4444	R	10*	.1
57	Kussmaul Electronics Company Inc—Ernest Kussmaul	170 Cherry Ave, West Sayville NY 11796	631-567-0314	R	10*	.1
58	Synergistic Technology Solutions Inc—Larry Ye	935 Lakeview Pkwy Ste, Vernon Hills IL 60061	847-968-5501	R	10*	<.1
59	Viking Technologies Ltd—David Kjeldsen	80 E Montauk Hwy, Lindenhurst NY 11757	631-957-8000	R	10*	<.1
60	Freedom Power Systems Inc—James B Russell	1620 La Jaita Dr Ste 1, Cedar Park TX 78613	512-259-0941	S	10*	<.1
61	D C Systems Inc—Douglass Campbell	1251 Industrial Pkwy N, Brunswick OH 44212	330-273-3030	R	10*	<.1
62	Elite Component Service Inc—Richard Liu	780 Montague Expy Ste, San Jose CA 95131	408-428-1088	R	10*	<.1
63	Ferro Magnetics Corp—Michael Franklin	4328 Bridgeton Industr, Bridgeton MO 63044	314-739-1414	R	9*	.1
64	Endicott Research Group Inc—John Petersen	2601 Wayne St, Endicott NY 13760	607-754-9187	R	9*	.1
65	Hydromotion Inc—Nisha Lobo	85 E Bridge St, Spring City PA 19475	610-948-4150	S	9*	<.1
66	SCI Engineered Materials Inc—Daniel Rooney	2839 Charter St, Columbus OH 43228	614-486-0261	P	9	<.1
67	Associated Equipment Corp—William Cottle	5043 Farlin Ave, Saint Louis MO 63115	314-385-5178	R	9*	<.1
68	Transbotics Corp—Claude Imbleau	3400 Latrobe Dr, Charlotte NC 28211	704-362-1115	P	8	<.1
69	Megown Test and Measurement Inc—Michael Megown	1010 Winding Creek Rd, Roseville CA 95678	916-773-5010	R	8*	<.1
70	Scott Engineering Inc—Bob Bertolli	20540 E Walnut Dr N, Walnut CA 91789	909-594-9637	R	8*	.1
71	Phoenix Electric Corp—Thomas Clark	PO Box 53, Boston MA 02137	781-821-0200	R	7*	.1
72	Digital Prototype Systems Inc—Robert Berry	4955 E Yale Ave, Fresno CA 93727	559-454-1600	R	7*	<.1
73	American Electric Equipment Inc—Perfecto Dacal	PO Box 710, Beckley WV 25802	304-255-7438	R	6*	<.1
74	Exeltech Inc—Barry Jason	7317 Jack Newell Blvd, Fort Worth TX 76118	817-595-4969	R	6*	.1
75	Ronken Industries Inc—Donald Plochocki	PO Box 161, Princeton IL 61356	815-664-5306	R	6*	<.1
76	Isc Engineering LLC—Barbara Spani	4351 Schaefer Ave, Chino CA 91710	909-596-3315	R	6*	<.1

Rank	Company Name—*Executive Officer*	Address, City, State, Zip	Phone	Type	Fin	Empls
77	Unlimited Services (Rockford)—*Shaun Merrell*	10108 Forest Hills Rd, Machesney Park IL 61115	815-399-0282	D	6*	<.1
78	Electrnic Integration Inc—*Sona Sitapara*	875 Pennsylvania Blvd, Feasterville PA 19053	215-364-3390	R	6*	<.1
79	Gulf Services Industrial LLC—*John Cradure*	PO Box 631129, Houston TX 77263	337-439-6700	R	6*	<.1
80	Diversified Supply Inc—*Dan K Anderson*	210 N Highland Park Av, Chattanooga TN 37404	423-698-1551	R	5*	<.1
81	Strata Technologies—*Jack Mazarone*	1800 Irvine Blvd Ste 2, Tustin CA 92780	714-368-9785	R	5*	<.1
82	Master Control Systems Inc—*William Stelter*	PO Box 276, Lake Bluff IL 60044	847-295-1010	R	5*	<.1
83	Empro Manufacturing Company Inc—*Gary Graf*	PO Box 26060, Indianapolis IN 46226	317-823-4478	R	4*	<.1
84	Minuteman UPS—*Rod Pullen*	1455 LeMay Dr, Carrollton TX 75007	972-446-7363	S	4*	<.1
85	Southern California Sound Image Inc—*Ross Ritto*	2415 Auto Park Way, Escondido CA 92029	760-737-3900	R	4*	<.1
86	E G Pump Controls Inc—*Samuel Jacobson*	11790 Philips Hwy, Jacksonville FL 32256	904-292-0110	R	4*	<.1
87	Engineered Abrasives Inc—*Michael Wern*	11631 S Austin Ave, Alsip IL 60803	708-389-9700	R	4*	<.1
88	Adam Electronics Inc—*Dan Kayganich*	652 Ajax Dr, Madison Heights MI 48071	248-583-2000	R	3*	<.1
89	Capax Technologies Inc—*Jagdish Patel*	24842 Ave Tibbitts, Valencia CA 91355	661-257-7666	R	3*	<.1
90	American Battery Charging Inc—*Ronald Stutzbach*	PO Box 17040, Smithfield RI 02917	401-231-5227	R	3*	<.1
91	Lightning Master Corp—*Bruce Kaiser*	PO Box 6017, Clearwater FL 33758	727-447-6800	R	3*	<.1
92	Arizona Capacitors Inc—*David Shorey*	3151 E Drexel Rd, Tucson AZ 85706	520-573-0221	R	3*	<.1
93	Quick Charge Corp—*Raymond Santilli*	1032 Sw 22nd St, Oklahoma City OK 73109	405-634-2120	R	2*	<.1
94	Ultra Electronics Precision Air Systems Inc—*Alison Todd*	5751 General Wash Dr, Alexandria VA 22312	703-914-8881	R	2*	<.1
95	Power Integrity Corp—*James Fesmire*	1834 Pembroke Rd Ste 1, Greensboro NC 27408	336-379-9773	R	2*	<.1
96	South Atlantic Controls Inc—*Craig Shupp*	PO Box 280, Williamsport MD 21795	301-223-9166	R	2*	<.1
97	Cygnus Automation Inc—*Sharon Dietrich*	1605 9th Ave, Bohemia NY 11716	631-981-0909	R	2*	<.1
98	Mrc Technology Inc—*Andrew Zaderej*	1901 S Lafayette Blvd, South Bend IN 46613	574-232-9057	R	2*	<.1
99	Innovative Peening Systems Inc—*Daniel Dickey*	2825 Simpson Cir, Norcross GA 30071	770-246-9883	R	2*	<.1
100	Lumatronix Manufacturing Inc—*Paul Shin*	1141 Ringwood Ct Ste 1, San Jose CA 95131	408-435-7820	R	2*	<.1
101	Cm Technologies Corp—*Sheldon Lefkowitz*	1026 4th Ave, Coraopolis PA 15108	412-262-0734	R	2*	<.1
102	Carsan Engineering Inc—*David Sanso*	221 Corporate Cir Ste, Golden CO 80401	303-237-9608	R	2*	<.1
103	Takk Industries Inc—*Joseph Overman*	8665 E Miami River Rd, Cincinnati OH 45247	513-353-4306	R	2*	<.1
104	Quest Microwave Inc—*Mohamad Khayat*	225 Vineyard Ct, Morgan Hill CA 95037	408-778-4949	R	2*	<.1
105	Motor Capacitors Inc—*Terry Noon*	6455 N Avondale Ave, Chicago IL 60631	773-774-6666	R	2*	<.1
106	Hi-Z Technology Inc—*Norbert Elsner*	7606 Miramar Rd Ste 74, San Diego CA 92126	858-695-6660	R	2*	<.1
107	Nytone Inc—*George Balding*	2424 S 900 W, Salt Lake City UT 84119	801-973-4090	R	2*	<.1
108	A-Systems Inc—*Floyd Artrip*	2030 Avon Ct Ste 8, Charlottesville VA 22902	434-295-7200	R	1*	<.1
109	Advanced Electronics Systems Inc—*Richard Diller*	2005 Lincoln Way E, Chambersburg PA 17201	717-263-5681	R	1*	<.1
110	Uninterruptible Power Products Inc—*Gary Jungwirth*	1567 W 11th Dr, Friendship WI 53934	608-339-2151	R	1*	<.1
111	Electronic Systems Southeast LLC	3301 N Dixie Hwy, Boca Raton FL 33431	561-955-9006	R	1*	<.1
112	Proteus Electronics Inc—*Thomas Clabaugh*	161 Spayde Rd, Bellville OH 44813	419-886-2296	R	1*	<.1
113	Meg-Alert Inc—*Laurie Zelm*	PO Box 665, Woodruff WI 54568	715-356-1499	R	1*	<.1
114	Micro-Aide Inc—*Rolf Anderson*	685 Arrow Grand Cir, Covina CA 91722	626-915-5502	R	1*	<.1
115	Strainsense Enterprises Inc—*Layne Vranka*	1080 Long Run Rd, Mckeesport PA 15132	412-751-3055	R	1*	<.1
116	Ibex Manufacturing Inc—*Richard Wharton*	218 Bennington Rd, Francestown NH 03043	603-547-6209	R	1*	<.1
117	Donald R Husband Inc—*Don Husband*	1140 E Maine Rd, Johnson City NY 13790	607-770-1990	R	1*	<.1
118	All Systems Integrated—*Michael Lindbo*	315 7th St Ne, Puyallup WA 98372	253-770-5570	R	1*	<.1
119	Larcor—*Larry Cornelius*	6614 Fm 30 S, Quinlan TX 75474	903-356-2338	R	1*	<.1
120	Thomas Instruments Inc—*Lynn Thomas*	PO Box 50, Spofford NH 03462	603-363-4500	R	1*	<.1
121	Dalec Electronics Inc—*Ted Knapczyk*	9335 Belmont Ave Ste 4, Franklin Park IL 60131	847-671-7676	R	1*	<.1
122	Gizmos-N-Gadgets—*David Clarke*	275 Gershwin Dr, Dayton OH 45458	937-272-4717	R	<1*	<.1
123	Waterloo Manufacturing Company Inc—*Thomas Ludlam*	6298 Waterloo Rd, Atwater OH 44201	330-947-2917	R	<1*	<.1
124	Brindle and Associates Inc—*Kermit Brindle*	38445 S Apache Peak Dr, Tucson AZ 85739	520-825-2426	R	<1*	<.1
125	Easton Controls Inc—*Steven Clark*	3999 Hupp Rd Bldg R 64, Kingsbury IN 46345	219-393-7218	S	<1*	<.1
126	Fill Rite Co—*Mary Olson*	43 Poplar Ave, Fox Lake IL 60020	847-587-5100	R	<1*	<.1

TOTALS: SIC 3629 Electrical Industrial Apparatus Nec
Companies: 126 — 7,922 — 27.4

3631 Household Cooking Equipment

Rank	Company Name—*Executive Officer*	Address, City, State, Zip	Phone	Type	Fin	Empls
1	Viking Range Corp—*Fred Carl Jr*	111 Front St, Greenwood MS 38930	662-455-1200	R	1,000*	1.0
2	Unaka Company Inc—*Robert Austin*	1500 Industrial Rd, Greeneville TN 37745	423-639-1171	R	89*	.8
3	WC Bradley Co—*Stephen Butler*	PO Box 140, Columbus GA 31902	706-571-6080	R	67*	.1
4	Masterbuilt Manufacturing Inc—*John Mclemore*	1 Masterbuilt Ct, Columbus GA 31907	706-327-5622	R	47*	.1
5	Weber-Stephen Products LLC—*James Stephen*	200 E Daniels Rd, Palatine IL 60067	847-934-5700	R	37*	.3
6	Keurig Inc—*Michelle Stacey*	55 Walkers Brook Dr, Reading MA 01867	781-246-3466	S	37*	.1
7	Peerless-Premier Appliance Co—*Joseph Geary*	PO Box 387, Belleville IL 62222	618-233-0475	R	32*	.3
8	Traeger Pellet Grills LLC—*David Webb*	9445 Sw Ridder Rd Ste, Wilsonville OR 97070	503-685-6219	R	20*	.1
9	United States Stove Co—*Charles Layman*	227 Industrial Park Dr, South Pittsburg TN 37380		R	17*	.1
10	Meco Corp—*Harrell Word*	1500 Industrial Rd, Greeneville TN 37745	423-639-1171	R	12*	.1
11	Fiesta Gas Grills LLC—*Mike Tidwell*	1 Fiesta Dr, Dickson TN 37055	615-446-1800	R	11*	.1
12	Challenge Tool and Manufacturing Incorporated—*Larry Redmon*	PO Box 306, New Haven IN 46774	260-749-9558	R	9*	.1
13	Strategic Products Inc—*Art Markuson*	5100 Laguna Vista Dr, Melbourne FL 32934	321-752-0441	R	8*	.1
14	Kenyon International Inc—*Phillip Williams*	PO Box 925, Clinton CT 06413	860-664-4906	R	4*	<.1
15	Oscarware Inc—*Debra Dudley*	PO Box 40, Bonnieville KY 42713	270-531-2860	R	4*	<.1
16	David B Knight and Associates Inc—*David Knight*	333 N Main St, Cape Girardeau MO 63701	573-334-6512	R	3*	<.1
17	Modern Home Products Corp—*Thomas Koziol*	150 Ram Rd, Antioch IL 60002	847-395-6556	R	3*	<.1
18	Deluxe Equipment Company Inc—*Gib Smith*	4414 28th St W, Bradenton FL 34207	941-753-4184	R	3*	<.1
19	TIMTangel Inc—*Joseph Traeger*	1385 E College St, Mount Angel OR 97362	503-845-9234	R	2*	<.1
20	Metal Fusion Incorporated—*Norman Bourgeois*	712 Saint George Ave, Jefferson LA 70121	504-736-0201	R	2*	<.1

TOTALS: SIC 3631 Household Cooking Equipment
Companies: 20 — 1,407 — 3.2

3632 Household Refrigerators & Freezers

Rank	Company Name—*Executive Officer*	Address, City, State, Zip	Phone	Type	Fin	Empls
1	Whirlpool Corp—*Jeff M Fettig*	2000 N M-63, Benton Harbor MI 49022	269-923-5000	P	18,366	71.0
2	Sub-Zero Inc—*James Bakke*	4717 Hammersley Rd, Madison WI 53711	608-271-2233	R	758*	3.0
3	Delfield Co—*Kevin Clark*	980 S Isabella Rd, Mount Pleasant MI 48858	989-773-7981	D	108*	.7
4	Cleveland Range Co—*Rick Cutler*	1333 E 179th St, Cleveland OH 44110	216-481-4900	S	39*	.2
5	Champion Industries Inc (Winston-Salem North Carolina)—*Erik Nommsen*	PO Box 4149, Winston Salem NC 27115	336-661-1556	R	28*	.1
6	Thetford Corp—*Michael Harris*	PO Box 1285, Ann Arbor MI 48106	734-769-6000	R*	26*	.4
7	U-Line Corp—*Philip Uihlein*	8900 N 55th St, Milwaukee WI 53223	414-354-0300	R	25*	.2
8	Norcold Inc—*Jack Tierney* Thetford Corp	PO Box 180, Sidney OH 45365	937-497-3080	S	23*	.4

Note: An asterisk (*) indicates an estimated financial figure. The company type code used is as follows: R = Private, P = Public, S = Private Subsidiary, B = Public Subsidiary, D = Division, J = Joint Venture, I = Investment Fund.

COMPANY RANKINGS BY SALES WITHIN 4-DIGIT SIC

Rank	Company Name—*Executive Officer*	Address, City, State, Zip	Phone	Type	Fin	Empls
9	Equipment Brokers Inc—*Jorge Defarias*	720 Northwestern Ave, Audubon IA 50025	712-563-4623	R	14*	.1
10	Larry Schlussler—*Larry Schussler*	PO Box 1101, Arcata CA 95518	707-822-9095	R	1*	<.1

TOTALS: SIC 3632 Household Refrigerators & Freezers
Companies: 10   19,388   76.2

3633 Household Laundry Equipment

Rank	Company Name—*Executive Officer*	Address, City, State, Zip	Phone	Type	Fin	Empls
1	Speed Queen Co—*Tom L'Esperance*	PO Box 990, Ripon WI 54971	920-748-1666	S	293*	1.7
2	Electrolux Home Products—*Hans Strabergs*	PO Box 212378, Augusta GA 30917	706-651-1751	D	158*	.3
3	EnviroStar Inc—*Michael S Steiner*	290 NE 68th St, Miami FL 33138	305-754-4551	P	21	<.1
4	National Home Products Inc—*Gene Reilly*	535 School House Rd, Telford PA 18969	215-723-8959	R	7*	.1
5	Staber Industries Inc—*William Staber*	4800 Homer Ohio Ln, Groveport OH 43125	614-836-5995	R	4*	<.1
6	Iron-A-Way Inc—*Reginald Smidt*	220 W Jackson St, Morton IL 61550	309-266-7232	R	3*	<.1
7	Keltner Research Inc—*Steven Keltner*	1501 W Campus Dr Ste A, Littleton CO 80120	303-795-9024	R	1*	<.1

TOTALS: SIC 3633 Household Laundry Equipment
Companies: 7   488   2.2

3634 Electric Housewares & Fans

Rank	Company Name—*Executive Officer*	Address, City, State, Zip	Phone	Type	Fin	Empls
1	Tutco Inc—*Patrick Mccaffrey*	500 Gould Dr, Cookeville TN 38506	931-432-4141	R	17,275*	.6
2	Jarden Consumer Solutions—*Andrew Hill*	2381 Executive Center, Boca Raton FL 33431	561-912-4100	S	1,870*	10.0
3	Blendtec Inc—*Tom Dickson* K-TEC Inc	1206 S 1680 W, Orem UT 84058	801-222-0888	D	744*	.3
4	Water Pik Technologies Inc	1730 E Prospect Rd, Fort Collins CO 80525		R	647*	.6
5	Applica Inc—*Harry D Schulman*	3633 Flamingo Rd, Miramar FL 33027	954-883-1000	S	556	.3
6	Hamilton Beach/Proctor-Silex Inc—*Gregory Trepp*	360 Page Rd, Washington NC 27889		S	516	.5
7	Ronco Inventions LLC—*Ron Popeil*	570 Lexington Ave 25th, New York NY 10022		R	173*	.2
8	West Bend Co—*Berhard Ziegler*	PO Box 2780, West Bend WI 53095		S	159	1.0
9	Tacony Corp—*Ken Tacony*	1760 Gilsinn Ln, Fenton MO 63026	636-349-3000	R	120*	.3
10	Oasis Corp—*Romanie Gilliland*	222 E Campus View Blvd, Columbus OH 43235	614-861-1350	S	92*	.5
11	Remington Products Company LLC—*David Jones*	PO Box 44960, Madison WI 53744	608-275-3340	S	51*	.3
12	Ecoquest Manufacturing Inc—*Michael Jackson*	55 Marley Dr, Greeneville TN 37743	423-798-6488	R	41*	.1
13	Concordia Coffee Systems—*David Isett*	1287 120th Ave NE, Bellevue WA 98005	425-453-2800	R	40*	<.1
14	K-TEC Inc—*Thomas Dickson*	1206 S 1680 W, Orem UT 84058	801-222-0888	R	24*	.1
15	Metal Ware Corp—*Wesley Drumm*	PO Box 237, Two Rivers WI 54241	920-794-3140	R	20*	.1
16	Edgecraft Corp—*Samuel Weiner*	825 Southwood Rd, Avondale PA 19311	610-268-0500	R	18*	.2
17	Vulcan Radiator Corp	260 N Elm St, Westfield MA 01085		D	15	.2
18	Mosebach Manufacturing Co—*Gordon Denny*	1417 Mclaughlin Run Rd, Pittsburgh PA 15241	412-220-0200	R	15*	.1
19	Desert Aire Corp—*Keith Coursin*	N120 W18485 Freistadt, Germantown WI 53022	262-946-7400	R	14*	.1
20	Cadet Manufacturing Co—*Hutch Johnson*	PO Box 1675, Vancouver WA 98668	360-693-2505	R	14*	.1
21	King Electrical Manufacturing Co—*Robert Wilson*	9131 10th Ave S, Seattle WA 98108	206-762-0400	R	13*	.1
22	Allied Precision Industries Inc—*Donald Reusche*	705 E N St, Elburn IL 60119	630-365-0340	R	12*	<.1
23	Hybrinetics Inc—*Richard Rosa*	PO Box 14399, Santa Rosa CA 95402	707-585-0333	R	12*	.1
24	Accu-Therm Inc—*William Lindennayer*	PO Box 249, Monroe City MO 63456	573-735-1060	R	10*	.1
25	Spruce Environmental Technologies Inc—*Alan Zucchino*	PO Box 8244, Haverhill MA 01835	978-521-0901	R	10*	.1
26	Brasch Manufacturing Company Inc—*Jerome Brasch*	11880 Dorsett Rd, Maryland Heights MO 63043	314-291-0440	R	10*	.1
27	Bkmfg Corp—*Michael Shanahan*	143 Colebrook River Rd, Winsted CT 06098	860-738-2200	R	7*	<.1
28	Glenn Electric Heater Corp—*John Finn*	PO Box 10247, Erie PA 16514	814-898-4000	R	7*	.1
29	Microtek Inc—*Anne Paradis*	36 Justin Dr, Chicopee MA 01022	413-593-1025	R	6*	.1
30	World Dryer Corp—*Tom Vic*	5700 McDermott Dr, Berkeley IL 60163	708-449-6950	R	6*	<.1
31	Aqua Massage International Inc—*David Cote*	PO Box 808, Groton CT 06340	860-536-3735	R	6*	<.1
32	Eichenauer Inc—*Donald Campbell*	292 Sunapee St, Newport NH 03773	603-863-1454	R	5*	.1
33	Edemco Dryers Inc—*Francisco Dominguez*	5675 Parachute Cir, Colorado Springs CO 80916	719-550-0500	R	3*	<.1
34	And-Dell Corp—*Jon Lobdell*	245 Sw 33rd St, Fort Lauderdale FL 33315	954-523-6478	R	3*	<.1
35	Dampp-Chaser Electronics Corp—*Gayle Mair*	PO Box 1610, Hendersonville NC 28793	828-692-8271	R	3*	<.1
36	Grayline Housewares Inc—*Fred Rosen*	PO Box 4527, Wheaton IL 60189	630-682-3330	R	2*	<.1
37	Valid Electric Corp—*Arthur Cecchini*	PO Box 577, Tarrytown NY 10591	914-631-9436	R	2*	<.1

TOTALS: SIC 3634 Electric Housewares & Fans
Companies: 37   22,519   16.4

3635 Household Vacuum Cleaners

Rank	Company Name—*Executive Officer*	Address, City, State, Zip	Phone	Type	Fin	Empls
1	Royal Appliance Manufacturing Co—*Paul R D'Alora*	7005 Cochran Rd, Glenwillow OH 44139	440-996-2000	S	425*	.6
2	Kirby Co—*Mike Nichols*	1920 W 114th St, Cleveland OH 44102	216-228-2400	S	125*	.4
3	Varian Vacuum Technologies—*Sergio Piras*	121 Hartwell Ave, Lexington MA 02421	781-861-7200	D	40*	.2
4	HMI Industries Inc—*Kirk W Foley*	13325 Darice Pkwy Unit, Strongsville OH 44149	440-846-7800	R	35*	.1
5	Metropolitan Vacuum Cleaner Company Inc—*Jules Stern*	PO Box 149, Suffern NY 10901	845-357-1600	R	11*	.1
6	Aerus LLC—*Joseph P Urso*	5420 L B Johnson 1010, Dallas TX 75240	214-378-4000	S	6*	.1
7	Better Cleaning Systems Inc—*Bill Hachtmann*	PO Box 359, Madera CA 93639	559-673-5700	R	5*	<.1
8	Buckeye Vacuum Cleaner Supply Co—*Kenard Strauss*	1820 S Cobb Industrial, Smyrna GA 30082	404-351-7300	R	5*	<.1
9	Lindsay Manufacturing Inc—*Edward Lindsay*	PO Box 1708, Ponca City OK 74602	580-762-2457	R	5*	.1
10	Ash Love-Less Company Inc—*Colleen Loveless*	1285 E 650 S, Price UT 84501	435-637-5885	R	4*	<.1
11	Lely USA Inc—*Peter Langebeeke*	PO Box 789, Wilson NC 27894	252-291-7050	R	1*	<.1
12	Rent A Mom Inc—*Linda Delaney*	4531 Hillside Rd, Seven Hills OH 44131	216-901-9599	R	1*	<.1

TOTALS: SIC 3635 Household Vacuum Cleaners
Companies: 12   663   1.7

3639 Household Appliances Nec

Rank	Company Name—*Executive Officer*	Address, City, State, Zip	Phone	Type	Fin	Empls
1	American Water Heater Co—*Kevin Wheeler*	PO Box 4056, Johnson City TN 37602	423-283-8000	R	3,984*	1.2
2	NTK Holdings Inc—*Richard L Bready*	50 Kennedy Plz, Providence RI 02903	401-751-1600	R	2,270	8.8
3	Sharp Manufacturing Co of America—*Doug Koshima*	1 Sharp Plaza Blvd, Memphis TN 38193	901-795-6510	S	1,508*	.8
4	Tadiran Ltd—*David Sopko*	2 Seaview Blvd, Port Washington NY 11050	516-632-7200	S	1,188	8.3
5	AO Smith Water Products Corp—*Ajita Rajendra*	25589 Hwy 1, Mc Bee SC 29101	843-335-8281	D	954*	.5
6	State Industries Inc	500 Tennessee Waltz Pk, Ashland City TN 37015	615-792-4371	S	538*	2.8
7	In-Sink-Erator—*Jerry Ryder*	4700 21st St, Racine WI 53406	262-554-5432	D	341*	1.0
8	AO Smith Water Products Co	500 Tennessee Waltz Pk, Ashland City TN 37015		S	317*	1.2
9	Dacor Inc—*S Michael Joseph*	600 Anton Blvd Ste 100, Costa Mesa CA 92626	626-799-1000	R	82*	.5
10	Human Touch—*Andrew Cohen*	3030 Walnut Ave, Long Beach CA 90807	562-426-8700	R	74	.1
11	Knight Inc (Lake Forest California)—*George Noa*	20531 Crescent Bay Dr, Lake Forest CA 92630	949-595-4800	S	47*	<.1
12	Nostalgia Products Group LLC—*Tom Berres*	1471 Partnership Rd, Green Bay WI 54304	920-337-9800	R	45*	.1
13	National Refrigeration Co—*James Kaufman*	563 Corbin Rd, Honea Path SC 29654	864-369-1665	R	22*	.2
14	Vaughn Manufacturing Corp—*William Newbauer*	PO Box 5431, Salisbury MA 01952	978-462-6683	R	19*	.1

Rank	Company Name—Executive Officer	Address, City, State, Zip	Phone	Type	Fin	Empls
15	Atlanta Attachment Co—Hank Little	362 Industrial Park Dr, Lawrenceville GA 30046	770-963-7369	R	18*	.1
16	Sahni Enterprises—Gary Sahni	3285 Saturn Ct, Norcross GA 30092		R	12*	<.1
17	Eemax Inc—Kevin Ruppelt	353 Christian St Ste 1, Oxford CT 06478	203-267-7890	R	11*	.1
18	Bertolotti's Ceres Disposal Inc—Bert Bertolotti	PO Box 127, Ceres CA 95307	209-537-8000	R	10*	.1
19	Cemline Corp—William Chappell	PO Box 55, Cheswick PA 15024	724-274-5430	R	6*	.1
20	Bock Water Heaters Inc—Terry Mullen	PO Box 8632, Madison WI 53708	608-257-2225	R	6*	<.1
21	Water Heater Innovations Inc—Barry Jackson	3107 Sibley Memorial H, Saint Paul MN 55121	651-688-8827	R	6*	<.1
22	AMI Inc	PO Box 1782, Stanwood WA 98292	360-629-9269	R	4*	<.1
23	Hallowell International LLC—Elizabeth Robul	110 Hildreth St, Bangor ME 04401	207-990-5600	R	4*	<.1
24	Nolting Manufacturing Inc—Daniel Terrill	1265 Hawkeye Dr, Hiawatha IA 52233	319-378-0999	R	3*	<.1
25	Old Dutch International Ltd—Ben Kan	421 N Midland Ave, Saddle Brook NJ 07663	201-794-6262	R	3*	<.1
26	Weco Industries Inc—Steve Kligis	2777 Washington Blvd, Bellwood IL 60104	708-547-6661	R	3*	<.1
27	Gammill Quilting Machine Co—Rhon Parker	1452 Gibson St, West Plains MO 65775	417-256-5919	R	3*	<.1
28	Jado Sewing Machines Inc—Onik Balian	4008 22nd St, Long Island City NY 11101	718-784-2314	R	3*	<.1
29	Hammbros Inc—Johnny Hamm	401 Rockcrest Rd, Mckinney TX 75071	972-548-0975	R	2*	<.1
30	Barrage—Tom Johnson	401 W 47th St Frnt, New York NY 10036	212-586-9390	R	1*	<.1
31	Camatron Sewing Machine Inc—Robert Ross	42 Bergenwood Rd Ste A, Fairview NJ 07022	201-941-5116	R	1*	<.1

TOTALS: SIC 3639 Household Appliances Nec

Companies: 31					11,482	26.0

3641 Electric Lamps

Rank	Company Name—Executive Officer	Address, City, State, Zip	Phone	Type	Fin	Empls
1	GE Lighting	1975 Noble Rd, Cleveland OH 44112	216-266-2121	D	4,893*	40.0
2	Philips Lighting Co—Frans van Houten	200 Franklin Sq Dr, Somerset NJ 08873		D	2,333*	10.0
3	Advanced Lighting Technologies Inc—Wayne C Hellman	32000 Aurora Rd, Solon OH 44139	440-519-0500	R	119*	1.2
4	Venture Lighting International—Wayne Hellman Advanced Lighting Technologies Inc	32000 Aurora Rd, Solon OH 44139	440-248-3510	S	99*	.3
5	Lime Energy Co—John O'Rourke	16810 Kenton Dr Ste 24, Huntersville NC 28078	704-892-4442	P	96	.4
6	TCP Inc—Ellis Yan	325 Campus Dr, Aurora OH 44202		R	78*	.2
7	Elmet Technologies Corp—Robin Cook	1560 Lisbon St, Lewiston ME 04240	207-333-6100	R	47*	.3
8	Light Process Co—Michael Hirsch	1631 Gillingham Ste 10, Sugar Land TX 77478	281-530-3600	R	40*	.1
9	HIDirect Inc Advanced Lighting Technologies Inc	32000 Aurora Rd, Solon OH 44139	440-519-0500	S	39*	.1
10	HH Fluorescent Parts Inc—Robert Hillen	PO Box 65, Cheltenham PA 19012	215-379-2750	R	31*	.2
11	Light Sources Inc—Christian Sauska	PO Box 948, Orange CT 06477	203-799-7877	R	29*	.2
12	Eye Lighting International Of North America Inc—Tsuneo Kobayashi	9150 Hendricks Rd, Mentor OH 44060	440-350-7000	R	27*	.2
13	US Lighting Tech—Richard Ham	14370 Myford Rd Ste 10, Irvine CA 92606	714-617-8800	R	26	<.1
14	Los Angeles Lighting Co—Bill Shapiro	10141 Olney St, El Monte CA 91731	626-454-8300	R	26*	.1
15	Dasol Inc—David Smith	16210 S Avalon Blvd, Gardena CA 90248	310-532-6700	R	24*	.1
16	LED Lumina USA LLC—Gerard Duffy	118 Wilbur Place, Bohemia NY 11716	631-612-9440	R	21*	.1
17	E G L Company Inc—Harold Cortese	100 Industrial Rd, Berkeley Heights NJ 07922	908-508-1111	R	13*	.1
18	Interlectric Corp—Steven Rothenberg	1401 Lexington Ave, Warren PA 16365	814-723-6061	R	12*	.1
19	Arkansas Lamp Manufacturing Company Inc—Robert Null	PO Box 452, Van Buren AR 72957	479-474-0876	R	11*	.1
20	Superior Quartz Products Inc—Dennis Losco	2701 Baglyos Cir, Bethlehem PA 18020	610-317-3450	R	10*	.1
21	Jelight Company Inc—Marinko Jelic	2 Mason, Irvine CA 92618	949-380-8774	R	9*	.1
22	Malcolite Corp—Jason Howard	1918 Raymond Dr, Northbrook IL 60062	847-562-1350	R	9*	.1
23	Environmental Lighting Concepts Inc—Donald Barry	1214 W Cass St, Tampa FL 33606	813-621-0058	R	8*	.1
24	Xenonics Holdings Inc—Jeffrey P Kennedy	3186 Lionshead Ave, Carlsbad CA 92010	760-477-8900	P	7	<.1
25	Hanovia Specialty Lighting LLC—Dario Bravar	6 Evans St, Fairfield NJ 07004	908-688-0050	R	7*	.1
26	Westron Corp—Hershel Allerhand	18 Neil Ct, Oceanside NY 11572	516-678-2300	R	7*	.1
27	Junction City Wire Harness Inc—Marilyn Sliski	PO Box 45, Junction City KS 66441	785-762-4400	R	6*	.1
28	K and H Industries Inc—Karl Baake	8656 Delamater Rd, Angola NY 14006	716-549-0135	R	6*	<.1
29	Isomet Corp	PO Box 1634, Springfield VA 22151	703-321-8301	P	4	<.1
30	American Light Bulb Manufacturing Inc—Ray Schlosser	105 American St, Mullins SC 29574	843-464-0755	R	3*	.1
31	Superior Lamp Inc—Anthony Adams	200 Century Pkwy Ste B, Mount Laurel NJ 08054	856-222-0260	R	3*	<.1
32	Preston Glass Industries Inc—Ashish Karnavat	10420 Queens Blvd Apt, Forest Hills NY 11375	718-997-8888	R	2*	<.1
33	AB Electrical Wires Inc—Wes Leiter	PO Box 1873, Muskegon MI 49443	231-737-9200	R	2*	<.1
34	Chimera Co—Gary Delfium	1812 Valtec Ln Ste 9, Boulder CO 80301	303-444-8000	R	2*	<.1
35	Louisville Lamp Co—Rick Buehner	PO Box 39126, Louisville KY 40233	502-964-4094	R	1*	<.1
36	Design Specialty Inc—David Holmes	14524 Latrobe Dr, Colorado Springs CO 80921	719-488-3036	R	<1*	<.1

TOTALS: SIC 3641 Electric Lamps

Companies: 36					8,047	54.4

3643 Current-Carrying Wiring Devices

Rank	Company Name—Executive Officer	Address, City, State, Zip	Phone	Type	Fin	Empls
1	Thomas and Betts Caribe Corp	8155 Tand B Blvd, Memphis TN 38125	901-252-8000	S	4,678	N/A
2	Hubbell Inc—Timothy H Powers	40 Waterview Dr, Shelton CT 06484	475-882-4000	P	2,872	13.5
3	Vista-Pro Automotive LLC—Steve Scharnhorst	15 Century Blvd Ste 60, Nashville TN 37214		R	1,408*	1.8
4	Panduit Corp—Tom Donovan	17301 Ridgeland Ave, Tinley Park IL 60477	708-532-1800	R	1,306*	4.0
5	Belkin International Inc—Mark Reynoso	12045 E Waterfront Dr, Playa Vista CA 90094	310-751-5100	R	796*	1.0
6	Leviton Manufacturing Company Inc—Donald Hendler	PO Box 10600, Melville NY 11747	631-812-6000	R	567*	6.0
7	Cherry Corp—Peter B Cherry	11200 88th Ave, Pleasant Prairie WI 53158	262-942-6500	S	327*	3.1
8	Electroswitch Electronic Products	2010 Yonkers Rd, Raleigh NC 27604	919-833-0707	R	194*	.2
9	Seacon Phoenix LLC—Frank Ravenelle	15 Gray Ln Ste 108, Ashaway RI 02804	401-637-4952	D	171*	.2
10	Fci Americas Holding Inc—Jean Lamy	47 E Industrial Pk Dr, Manchester NH 03109	603-647-5000	R	157*	2.9
11	Esterline Mason Controls—Robert Cremin	13955 Balboa Blvd, Sylmar CA 91342	818-361-3366	S	151*	.2
12	Molex Industrial Div—Martin Slark	4 Aviation Dr, Gilford NH 03249	603-524-5101	D	130*	.2
13	Pass and Seymour Inc—Michael Gambino	PO Box 4822, Syracuse NY 13221	315-468-6211	R	112*	1.3
14	Winchester Electronics—Michael P Driscoll	62 Barnes Industrial R, Wallingford CT 06492	203-741-5400	D	106*	.3
15	ITW Ark-Les Corp—Bruce MacNeil	1490 Central St, Stoughton MA 02072	781-297-6000	R	94*	<.1
16	Tri-Star Electronics International Inc—Terry Jarnigan	2201 Rosecrans Ave, El Segundo CA 90245	310-536-0444	S	90*	.3
17	ITW Linx—W James Farrell	425 N Gary Ave, Carol Stream IL 60188	630-315-2150	D	75*	.1
18	SEA CON/Brantner and Associates	1240 Vernon Way, El Cajon CA 92020	619-562-7071	R	69*	.4
19	Reinhausen Manufacturing Inc—Bernhard Kurth	2549 N 9th Ave, Humboldt TN 38343	731-784-7681	R	61*	.1
20	Joslyn Electronic Systems Company LLC—Alan F Joslyn	5900 Eastport Blvd, Richmond VA 23231	804-236-3300	S	52*	.2
21	Heraeus Medical Components (St Paul Minnesota)—Mark Kempf	5030 Centerville Rd, St Paul MN 55127	651-792-8500	S	49*	.2
22	Autosplice Inc—Debbie Binks	10121 Barnes Canyon Rd, San Diego CA 92121	858-535-0077	R	40*	.6
23	Fargo Assembly Co—Ron Bergan	PO Box 2340, Fargo ND 58108	701-298-3803	R	40*	.7
24	Electro Switch Corp—Howard Grey	775 Pleasant St Ste 1, Weymouth MA 02189	781-335-1195	R	38*	<.1

Note: An asterisk (*) indicates an estimated financial figure. The company type code used is as follows: R = Private, P = Public, S = Private Subsidiary, B = Public Subsidiary, D = Division, J = Joint Venture, I = Investment Fund.

COMPANY RANKINGS BY SALES WITHIN 4-DIGIT SIC

Rank	Company Name—Executive Officer	Address, City, State, Zip	Phone	Type	Fin	Empls
25	Siemon Co—Carl Siemon	PO Box 400, Watertown CT 06795	860-945-4200	R	38*	.5
26	Inncom International Inc—Duane Buckingham	277 W Main St, Niantic CT 06357	860-739-4468	R	37*	.1
27	Watt Stopper Inc—Jerome Mix	2800 De La Cruz Blvd, Santa Clara CA 95050	408-988-5331	R	36*	.1
28	Connector Manufacturing Co—William Boehm	3501 Symmes Rd, Hamilton OH 45015	513-860-4455	R	34*	.3
29	Hubbell Power Systems Inc—Bill Tolley	210 N Allen St, Centralia MO 65240	573-682-5521	D	34	.2
30	Ddh Enterprise Inc—Danny Du	2220 Oak Ridge Way, Vista CA 92081	760-599-0171	R	31*	.2
31	Minnesota Wire—Paul Wagner	1835 Energy Park Dr, Saint Paul MN 55108	651-642-1800	R	28*	.2
32	Deringer-Ney Inc—Roderick Lamm	616 Atrium Dr Ste 100, Vernon Hills IL 60061	847-932-6800	R	28*	.4
33	Souriau USA Inc—Scott Roland	25 Grumbacher Rd, York PA 17406	717-767-7963	R	27*	.2
34	Aero-Electric Connector Inc—Walter Neubauer	2280 W 208th St, Torrance CA 90501	310-618-3737	R	26*	.4
35	CMW Inc—Mark Gramelspacher	PO Box 2266, Indianapolis IN 46206	317-634-8884	R	25*	.2
36	David Cianciulli Electronics Supply Inc—David Cianciulli	PO Box 28463, San Jose CA 95159	408-947-4500	R	24*	.2
37	Penn-Union Corp—Brian Cullen	229 Waterford St, Edinboro PA 16412	814-734-1631	R	24*	.2
38	Amphenol Sine Systems Pyle Connectors Corp	PO Box 2336, Mount Clemens MI 48046	586-465-3131	D	24*	.2
39	Cooper Industries Bussmann Div—H John Riley Jr	PO Box 14460, Saint Louis MO 63178	636-527-3877	D	24*	.2
40	Thermon Industries Inc—Mark Burdick	PO Box 609, San Marcos TX 78667	512-396-5801	R	23*	.5
41	Special Mine Services Inc—Steve Simmons	PO Box 188, West Frankfort IL 62896	618-932-2151	R	21*	.1
42	King Associates Ltd—Timothy King	62 Industrial Cir, Lancaster PA 17601	717-556-5673	R	20*	.1
43	Transtector Systems Inc—Michael Thompson	10701 N Airport Rd, Hayden ID 83835	208-772-8515	R	20*	.2
44	Nsi Industries LLC—Gus Hogshead	PO Box 2725, Huntersville NC 28070	704-439-2420	R	18*	.3
45	Raymond Engineering Operations—Paul R Kuhn	217 Smith St, Middletown CT 06457	860-632-1100	R	18*	.2
46	Hi Rel Connectors Inc—Fred Baumann	760 Wharton Dr, Claremont CA 91711	909-626-1820	R	18*	.3
47	Smc Electrical Products Inc—Oliver Fearing	PO Box 880, Barboursville WV 25504	304-733-7305	R	18*	.2
48	Quick Cable Corp—John Shannon	3700 Quick Dr, Franksville WI 53126	262-824-3100	R	17*	.1
49	G and H Technology Inc—Darrell Wampler	750 W Ventura Blvd, Camarillo CA 93010	805-484-0543	S	16*	.2
50	Triton Manufacturing Company Inc—Michael Edwards	PO Box 623, Bedford Park IL 60499	708-587-4000	R	16*	.1
51	Electro Adapter Inc—Ray Fish	20640 Nordhoff St, Chatsworth CA 91311	818-998-1198	R	16*	.1
52	Mac Products Inc—Edward Gollob	PO Box 469, Kearny NJ 07032	973-344-0700	R	15*	.1
53	Ekstrom Industries Inc—Jeff Hanft	23847 Industrial Park, Farmington Hills MI 48335	248-477-0040	R	14*	.1
54	State Tool and Manufacturing Co—Manroe Raschke	1650 E Empire Ave, Benton Harbor MI 49022	269-927-3153	R	14*	.2
55	Contact Technologies Inc—John Bauer	PO Box 149, Saint Marys PA 15857	814-834-9000	R	13*	.1
56	Checon Corp—D Conaway	30 Larsen Way, Attleboro Falls MA 02763	508-809-5100	R	13*	.1
57	Ericson Manufacturing Co—John Ericson	4215 Hamann Pkwy, Willoughby OH 44094	440-951-8000	R	13*	.1
58	Gdm Electronic Assembly—Fred Koehler	2070 Ringwood Ave, San Jose CA 95131	408-945-4100	R	13*	.1
59	Raycap Inc—Kostas Samaras	806 S Clearwater Loop, Post Falls ID 83854	208-777-1166	R	13*	.1
60	Dow-Key Microwave Corp—David Wightman	4822 McGrath St, Ventura CA 93003	805-650-0260	S	12*	.1
61	Plant Enterprises Inc—Pamela Tunis	809a Calle Plano, Plano CA 93012	805-389-5335	R	12*	.1
62	Flexible Whips Of Tennessee Inc—Joyce Meadows	6341 Hwy 41a, Pleasant View TN 37146	615-746-8105	R	12*	.1
63	Zierick Manufacturing Corp—Gretchen Zierick	131 Radio Cir Dr, Mount Kisco NY 10549	914-666-2911	R	12*	.1
64	Prosource Industries LP—Steve Hyde	1700 111th St, Grand Prairie TX 75050	972-660-1400	R	12*	.1
65	Connectec Company Inc—Russell Kavezadeh	1701 Reynolds Ave, Irvine CA 92614	949-252-1077	R	12*	.1
66	Tower Manufacturing Corp—Louis Shatkin	25 Reservoir Ave, Providence RI 02907	401-467-7550	R	11*	.1
67	Sullins Electronics Corp—Soussan Sullins	PO Box 189, San Marcos CA 92079	760-744-0125	R	11*	.1
68	Tru Corp—Linda Moulton	245 Lynnfield St, Peabody MA 01960	978-532-0775	R	11*	.1
69	Woodhead LP	3411 Woodhead Dr, Northbrook IL 60062	847-353-2500	D	10*	.2
70	ITW Switches—Jerry Hill	2550 Millbrook Dr, Buffalo Grove IL 60089	847-876-9400	R	9*	.1
71	ARI Industries—Michael Cooky	381 ARi Ct, Addison IL 60101	630-953-9100	S	9*	.1
72	Remke Industries Inc—Thomas O'gara	310 Chaddick Dr, Wheeling IL 60090	847-541-3780	R	9*	.1
73	North American Electronics Components LLC—Seliga Richter	PO Box 2804, Peachtree City GA 30269	770-716-7248	R	9*	.1
74	Harger Inc—Mark Harger	301 Ziegler Dr, Grayslake IL 60030	847-548-8700	R	9*	.1
75	Mjm Industries Inc—Eric Wachob	1200 E St, Fairport Harbor OH 44077	440-350-1230	R	9*	.1
76	East Coast Lightning Equipment Inc—Mark Morgan	24 Lanson Dr, Winsted CT 06098	860-379-9072	R	8*	<.1
77	Norstan Inc (Waukegan Illinois)—James Granger	10333 82nd Ave, Pleasant Prairie WI 53158	262-947-0707	R	8*	.1
78	Easter-Owens Electric Co—David Easter	6692 Fig St, Arvada CO 80004	303-431-0111	R	8*	<.1
79	Pro Company Sound Inc—Charles Wicks	PO Box 18001, Kalamazoo MI 49019	269-388-9675	R	8*	<.1
80	Nivek Industries Inc—Kevin Pezzolla	230 E Dyer Rd Ste K, Santa Ana CA 92707	714-545-8855	R	8*	<.1
81	Garvin Industries Inc—Bart Garvin	3700 Sandra St, Franklin Park IL 60131	847-455-0188	R	8*	<.1
82	Electro-Mechanical Components Inc—Walter Trumbull	1826 Floradale Ave, South El Monte CA 91733	626-442-7180	R	7*	.1
83	Electrivert Inc—Ken Murphy	17850 E 14 Mile Rd, Fraser MI 48026	586-285-0720	R	7*	.1
84	Mercotac Inc—Timothy Leslie	6195 Corte Del Cedro S, Carlsbad CA 92011	760-431-7723	R	7*	<.1
85	Ted Manufacturing Corp—Ted Grade	PO Box 3099, Shawnee Mission KS 66203	913-631-6211	R	7*	.1
86	Thorson Manufacturing Co—Mark Thorson	PO Box 65637, West Des Moines IA 50265	515-225-6523	R	7*	<.1
87	Peak Contract Manufacturing LLC—Robert Crow	6113 Constitution Ave, Colorado Springs CO 80915	719-574-1135	R	7*	<.1
88	Ek-Ris Cable Company Inc—Gary Robinson	777 Osgood Ave, New Britain CT 06053	860-223-4327	R	7*	<.1
89	Cableconn Industries Inc—Lisa Coffman	7198 Convoy Ct, San Diego CA 92111	858-571-7111	R	6*	.1
90	Total Energy Concepts Inc—Douglas Overvold	PO Box 663, Detroit Lakes MN 56502	218-844-5848	R	6*	<.1
91	Brumall Manufacturing Corp—Rod Brumberg	7850 Division Dr, Mentor OH 44060	440-974-2622	R	6*	<.1
92	Madison Co—Steven Schickler	27 Business Park Dr, Branford CT 06405	203-488-4477	R	6*	<.1
93	Precision Technology And Manufacturing Inc—Jose Pompa	3147 Durahart St, Riverside CA 92507	951-788-0252	R	6*	<.1
94	Fin-Con Assembly Group Inc—Steve Weier	76 N Central Dr, O Fallon MO 63366	636-281-0203	R	6*	<.1
95	Joy Signal Technology LLC—Cindy Hare	1020 Marauder St Ste A, Chico CA 95973	530-891-3551	R	6*	.1
96	Electronic Connector Service Inc—Edward Stout	10541 Ashdale St, Stanton CA 90680	714-828-0570	R	5*	<.1
97	Polaris Sales Company Inc—Frank Cipolla	11625 Prosperous Dr, Odessa FL 33556	727-546-4285	R	5*	<.1
98	Senior Industries Inc—Joseph Francaviglia	610 Pond Dr, Wood Dale IL 60191	630-350-1600	R	5*	<.1
99	Alcon Inc—C Sorflaten	6522 Snider Rd, Loveland OH 45140	513-722-1037	R	5*	<.1
100	Atlee Of Delaware Inc—Gary Bergholtz	10 Bayfield Dr, North Andover MA 01845	978-681-1003	R	5*	<.1
101	Rockford Rigging Inc—John Malcotte	5401 Mainsail Dr, Roscoe IL 61073	815-877-0007	R	5*	<.1
102	Frank Condon Inc—Frank Condon	PO Box 100, Jonesville MI 49250	517-849-2505	R	5*	<.1
103	Bassin Technical Sales Co—Gilbert Bassin	1009 W Boston Post Rd, Mamaroneck NY 10543	914-698-9358	R	5*	<.1
104	Microtech Inc—Vernon Albert	1420 Conchester Hwy, Marcus Hook PA 19060	610-459-3566	R	5*	<.1
105	Pres Air Trol Corp—Arthur Bluemethal	1009 W Boston Post Rd, Mamaroneck NY 10543	914-698-2026	R	4*	<.1
106	JST Sales America Inc—Nishi Moto	37879 Interchange Dr, Farmington Hills MI 48335	248-324-1957	R	4*	<.1
107	Cable Technologies Inc—Martha O'brien	3209 Ave E E, Arlington TX 76011	817-633-9181	R	4*	<.1
108	Telegartner Inc—Ralph Souders	411 Dominic Ct, Franklin Park IL 60131	630-616-7600	R	4*	<.1
109	Thompson Lightning Protection Inc—Douglas Franklin	901 Sibley Memorial Hwy, Saint Paul MN 55118	651-455-7661	R	4*	<.1
110	Metts Brothers Inc—Marvin Metts	3307 N Washington Ave, Durant OK 74701	580-924-9303	R	4*	<.1
111	Thor Guard Inc—Peter Townsend	PO Box 451987, Fort Lauderdale FL 33345	954-835-0900	R	4*	<.1
112	Galaxy Electronics Co—Yueh Yang	201 E Arapaho Rd, Richardson TX 75081	972-234-0065	R	4*	<.1
113	Volta Corp—Alexander Norden	PO Box 1027, Laurence Harbor NJ 08879	732-583-3300	R	4*	<.1
114	Lyncole Grounding Solutions LLC—John Howard	3547 Voyager St Ste 20, Torrance CA 90503	310-214-4000	R	4*	<.1

Rank	Company Name—*Executive Officer*	Address, City, State, Zip	Phone	Type	Fin	Empls
115	Intersense Inc—*Thomas Browne*	4 Federal St, Billerica MA 01821	781-541-6330	R	3*	<.1
116	French Corp—*Thomas Kearney*	340 Washington Ave, La Grange IL 60525	708-482-3434	R	3*	<.1
117	Tip Products Inc—*Wayne Gielow*	15411 Chatfield Ave St, Cleveland OH 44111	216-252-2535	R	3*	<.1
118	Qualastat Electronics Inc—*Vernon Judy*	1270 Fairfield Rd Ste, Gettysburg PA 17325	717-253-9301	R	3*	<.1
119	Heary Brothers Lightning Protection Company Inc—*Kenneth Heary*	11291 Moore Rd, Springville NY 14141	716-941-6141	R	3*	<.1
120	International Specialty Products—*Curtiss Wright*	1720 Tate Blvd SE, Hickory NC 28602	828-326-9053	R	3*	<.1
121	Robbins Lightning Inc—*Patricia Robbins*	PO Box 440, Maryville MO 64468	660-582-3156	R	3*	<.1
122	United Universal Industries Inc—*Edward Smith*	20620 Burl Ct Ste 1, Joliet IL 60433	815-727-4445	R	3*	<.1
123	Torq Corp—*John Taylor*	32 W Monroe St, Bedford OH 44146	440-232-4100	R	3*	<.1
124	Calpico Inc—*Carey Wilson*	1387 San Mateo Ave, South San Francisco CA 94080	650-588-2241	R	3*	<.1
125	Cordmaster Engineering Company Inc—*Bernie Roche*	PO Box 1051, North Adams MA 01247	413-664-9371	R	3*	<.1
126	Lta/D-Cemco Inc—*Rick Ferguson*	550 Library St, San Fernando CA 91340	818-365-6507	R	3*	<.1
127	Gifford And Brown Inc—*Brian Gifford*	PO Box 698, Des Moines IA 50303	515-243-1257	R	3*	.1
128	Air Tite Inc—*James Darnell*	PO Box 1227, Jonesboro AR 72403	870-935-8483	R	3*	<.1
129	Dicon Connections Inc—*Jeffrey Williams*	PO Box 190, North Branford CT 06471	203-481-8080	R	2*	.1
130	Hofer Machine and Tool Company Inc—*Alan Hofer*	126 Linda Vista Ave, North Haledon NJ 07508	973-427-1195	R	2*	<.1
131	Cotton Utility Constructors Inc—*Laurence Murphy*	5101 Fm 2666 Rd, Shepherd TX 77371	936-628-3661	R	2*	<.1
132	Ava Electronics Corp—*Mario Rafalin*	PO Box 184, Drexel Hill PA 19026	610-284-2500	R	2*	<.1
133	Bussco Inc—*Robert Greenman*	2400 S Roosevelt St, Tempe AZ 85282	480-967-0624	D	2*	<.1
134	Whitman Controls Corp—*Jesse Yoder*	201 Dolphin Rd, Bristol CT 06010	860-583-1847	R	2*	<.1
135	Vantage Technology LLC	4675 S Windermere St, Englewood CO 80110	303-761-2121	R	2*	<.1
136	Harry C Johnson Co—*Kim Johnson*	PO Box 100452, Birmingham AL 35210	205-956-1456	R	2*	<.1
137	Straight River Cable Inc—*Jerry Sexton*	1872 NW 70th St, Medford MN 55049	507-455-4255	R	2*	<.1
138	Carling Technologies Inc—*Richard Sorenson*	60 Johnson Ave, Plainville CT 06062	860-793-9266	R	2*	2.6
139	Omnithruster Inc—*Kurt Widmer*	2201 Pinnacle Pkwy Ste, Twinsburg OH 44087	330-963-6310	R	2*	<.1
140	Midwest Promac Inc—*Shelby Brown*	6130 Interstate Cir, Blue Ash OH 45242	513-489-4880	R	2*	<.1
141	Jcd Manufacturing Inc—*W Justice*	140 Space Park S, Nashville TN 37211	615-833-8334	R	2*	<.1
142	Z-Axis Connector Co—*George Glatts*	PO Box 379, Jamison PA 18929	215-672-2880	R	2*	<.1
143	Rhimco Industries Inc—*Dan Massey*	4150 Britton Rd, Mansfield TX 76063	817-477-3176	R	2*	<.1
144	Altek Systems Inc—*Kirby Degnan*	PO Box 232, Lamar CO 81052	719-336-3403	R	1*	.1
145	Cord Shattuc Specialties Inc—*Russel Novak*	2340 Ernie Krueger Cir, Waukegan IL 60087	847-244-4500	R	1*	<.1
146	Total Quality Instrumentation—*Richard Grogan*	125 Security Pl, Cookeville TN 38506	931-372-0575	R	1*	<.1
147	Lightning Diversion Systems Inc—*Jack Schroeder*	16572 Burke Ln, Huntington Beach CA 92647	714-841-1080	R	1*	<.1
148	Atlanta Lightning Protection Inc—*Sue Browning*	1031 Shepherds Ln Ne, Atlanta GA 30324	404-329-8700	R	1*	<.1
149	Diversified Electrical Products Inc—*John Tiano*	PO Box 390, Bohemia NY 11716	631-567-5710	R	1*	<.1
150	Connector Products Inc—*Thomas Paladon*	PO Box 2516, Cinnaminson NJ 08077	856-829-9190	R	1*	<.1
151	American Power Connection Systems Inc—*Paul Wujek*	2460 Midland Rd, Bay City MI 48706	989-686-6302	R	1*	<.1
152	Optoelectronics Center Inc—*Alan Nieuwboer*	651 Lincoln Loop, Sauk Centre MN 56378	320-352-6556	R	1*	<.1
153	T and T Machine Products Inc—*Anthony Muscillo*	PO Box 430, Rockland MA 02370	781-878-3861	R	1*	<.1
154	Zero Surge Inc—*J Rudy Harford*	889 State Rte 12, Frenchtown NJ 08825		R	1*	<.1
155	Command Components Corp—*Jerry Sukman*	6 Cherry St, Bay Shore NY 11706	631-666-4411	R	1*	<.1
156	Hlp Systems—*Jeff Harger* Harger Inc	426 N Ave, Libertyville IL 60048	847-362-0777	S	1*	<.1
157	Wire-Rite Fabrication Inc—*John Stevens*	PO Box 637, Blacksburg SC 29702	864-839-9019	R	1*	<.1
158	Electrocom Midwest Sales Inc—*Steve Blank*	32500 Concord Dr Ste 2, Madison Heights MI 48071	248-307-1640	R	1*	<.1
159	Charlton Precision Products Inc—*Robert Charlton*	PO Box 500, Mount Marion NY 12456	845-338-2351	R	1*	<.1
160	Shore Holders—*Arthur Sinnott*	PO Box 27, Phenix VA 23959	434-542-4105	R	1*	<.1
161	Konnext Inc—*Jeffrey Barger*	7 Kane Industrial Dr, Hudson MA 01749	978-567-0800	R	1*	<.1
162	Capital Lightning Protection Company Inc—*Thomas Cottle*	PO Box 162, Raleigh NC 27602	919-832-5574	R	1*	<.1
163	Boggs Inc—*Edward Campbell*	4426 Hunt Ave, Saint Louis MO 63110	314-533-0007	R	1*	<.1
164	Southport Industries Inc—*Wayne Larsen*	PO Box 747, Winsted CT 06098	860-379-0761	R	1*	<.1
165	Surelite Products Company Inc—*Gerald Warsetsky*	1920 Nw 18th St Ste 13, Pompano Beach FL 33069	954-969-9051	R	1*	<.1
166	V E Products Inc—*Andrea Medina*	3541 Old Conejo Rd Ste, Newbury Park CA 91320	805-499-1959	R	<1*	<.1
167	Level Sensor Technology—*Bruce Smith*	3797 Sullivan Wood Trl, Isanti MN 55040	763-444-5384	R	<1*	<.1

TOTALS: SIC 3643 Current Carrying Wiring Devices
Companies: 167   14,826   50.4

3644 Noncurrent-Carrying Wiring Devices

Rank	Company Name—*Executive Officer*	Address, City, State, Zip	Phone	Type	Fin	Empls
1	NGK-Locke Inc (Baltimore Maryland)—*Koichi Nakano*	2525 Insulator Dr, Baltimore MD 21230	410-347-1700	S	941*	3.7
2	EGS Electrical Group LLC—*Peter Strong*	9377 W Higgins, Rosemont IL 60018	847-268-6000	R	653*	3.5
3	Erico Products Inc—*William Roj*	34600 Solon Rd, Cleveland OH 44139	440-248-0100	S	281*	.1
4	O-Z/GEDNEY—*David N Farr* EGS Electrical Group LLC	9377 W Higgins Rd, Rosemont IL 60018	847-268-6000	S	150	1.1
5	Arlington Industries Inc—*Thomas Stark*	Stauffer IndustrialPar, Scranton PA 18517	570-562-0270	R	89*	.3
6	Wiremold Co—*Halfey Cook*	PO Box 330639, West Hartford CT 06133	860-233-6251	R	44*	1.3
7	NGK-Locke Polymer Insulators Inc—*Shun Matsushita*	1609 Diamond Springs R, Virginia Beach VA 23455	757-460-3649	S	37*	.2
8	Electri-Flex Co—*Jason Kinander*	PO Box 72260, Roselle IL 60172	630-529-2920	R	32*	.1
9	Lindsey Manufacturing Co—*Keith E Lindsey*	PO Box 877, Azusa CA 91702	626-969-3471	R	30*	.1
10	Industrial Dielectrics Holdings Inc—*John Merrell*	PO Box 357, Noblesville IN 46061	317-773-1766	R	28*	.3
11	Minerallac Electric Co—*Jim Hlavacek*	100 Gast Rd, Hampshire IL 60140		R	28*	.1
12	Bridgeport Fittings Inc—*Paul Suzio*	PO Box 619, Bridgeport CT 06601	203-377-5944	R	27*	.2
13	Mulberry Metal Products Inc—*Richard Horn*	PO Box 443, Union NJ 07083	908-688-8850	R	24*	.1
14	Monti Inc—*Gavin Narburgh*	333 W Seymour Ave, Cincinnati OH 45216	513-761-7775	R	24*	.1
15	Durham Co—*J Russell*	PO Box 908, Lebanon MO 65536	417-532-7121	R	22*	.4
16	Austin Company Of Greensboro—*James Austin*	PO Box 2320, Yadkinville NC 27055	336-468-2851	R	16*	.1
17	Minerallac Co—*John Alton*	100 Gast Rd, Hampshire IL 60140	630-543-7080	R	15*	.1
18	Custom Materials Inc—*Greg Robinson*	16865 Park Circle Dr, Chagrin Falls OH 44023	440-543-8284	R	14*	.1
19	Creftcon Industries Inc—*Leonard Freibott*	PO Box 1269, La Puente CA 91749	626-964-6531	R	14*	.2
20	Dare Products Inc—*Robert Wilson*	PO Box 157, Battle Creek MI 49016	269-965-2307	R	12*	<.1
21	Sherman and Reilly Inc—*Glenn Brown*	PO Box 11267, Chattanooga TN 37401	423-756-5300	R	12*	.1
22	Gund Company Inc—*Paul Gund*	2121 Walton Rd, Saint Louis MO 63114	314-423-5200	R	11*	.1
23	Isovolta Inc—*Kevin Sheehy*	PO Box 848, Rutland VT 05702	802-775-5528	S	11*	.1
24	Maclean Power Systems—*Randolph Hall*	1909 Hwy 87, Alabaster AL 35007	205-663-4912	R	11*	.1
25	Red Seal Electric Co—*Samuel Stryffeler*	3835 W 150th St, Cleveland OH 44111	216-941-3900	R	10*	<.1
26	Superior Technical Ceramics Corp—*Theodore Church*	600 Industrial Park Rd, Saint Albans VT 05478	802-527-7726	R	10*	.1
27	Saf-T-Co Supply—*Patricia Mcdonald*	1300 E Normandy Pl, Santa Ana CA 92705	714-547-9975	R	8*	.1
28	Kaf-Tech Inc—*David Kruse*	2000 Tall Pines Dr, Largo FL 33771	727-539-0588	D	8*	.1
29	Queen City Plastics Inc—*Robert Chapman*	PO Box 410568, Charlotte NC 28241	803-548-0685	R	7*	.1

Note: An asterisk (*) indicates an estimated financial figure. The company type code used is as follows: R = Private, P = Public, S = Private Subsidiary, B = Public Subsidiary, D = Division, J = Joint Venture, I = Investment Fund.

COMPANY RANKINGS BY SALES WITHIN 4-DIGIT SIC

Rank	Company Name—*Executive Officer*	Address, City, State, Zip	Phone	Type	Fin	Empls
30	Connector Concepts Inc—*Tony Doctor*	1530 McCormick Blvd, Mundelein IL 60060	847-541-4020	R	6*	<.1
31	Lew Electric Fittings Co—*John Romer*	1801 Saint Charles Rd, Maywood IL 60153	708-345-2075	R	6*	<.1
32	Elec-Tron Inc—*Rose Rohleder*	2050 E Northern St, Wichita KS 67216	316-522-3401	R	5*	.1
33	Nohl Corp—*Victor Nohl*	6360 N 60th St, Milwaukee WI 53218	414-464-8480	R	5*	<.1
34	Bourbon Plastics Inc—*Richard Bennett*	PO Box 23, Bourbon IN 46504	574-342-0893	R	5*	<.1
35	Bo-Witt Products Inc—*Jon Jacobson*	500 N Walnut St, Edinburgh IN 46124	812-526-5561	R	4*	<.1
36	Armel Electronics Inc—*Walter Johnsen*	1601 75th St, North Bergen NJ 07047	201-869-4300	R	4*	<.1
37	Frase Enterprises Inc—*Robert Frase*	2230 Davis Ct, Hayward CA 94545	510-856-3600	R	4*	<.1
38	Producto Electric Corp—*Arthur Lemay*	11 Kings Hwy, Orangeburg NY 10962	845-359-4900	R	3*	<.1
39	Imperial Fabricators Co—*Robert Goehrke*	3729 W Belmont Ave, Chicago IL 60618	773-463-5522	R	3*	<.1
40	Rochling Machined Plastics—*Melinda Roberts*	161 Westec Dr, Mount Pleasant PA 15666	724-696-5200	R	3*	<.1
41	S and S Metal And Plastics Inc—*Cynthia Strickland*	3740 Morton St, Jacksonville FL 32217	904-731-4655	R	3*	<.1
42	Lutamar Electrical Assemblies Inc—*Ida Wilk*	8030 Ridgeway Ave, Skokie IL 60076	847-679-5400	R	3*	<.1
43	Steel Electric Products Company Inc—*Howard Feldsher*	6301 New Utrecht Ave, Brooklyn NY 11219	718-259-6100	R	3*	<.1
44	Precision Fiberglass Products—*Robby Ross*	3105 Kashiwa St, Torrance CA 90505	310-539-7470	R	3*	<.1
45	Park Speedway—*Royal Jones*	3590 W Picacho Ave, Las Cruces NM 88007	915-791-8749	R	2*	<.1
46	Polar-Ply Corp—*David Dittemore*	PO Box 247, San Dimas CA 91773	909-305-1450	R	2*	<.1
47	Bilken Industrial Fabricators Inc—*Kay Hochschild*	PO Box 277, Northfield MN 55057	507-645-8388	R	1*	<.1
48	Aeronautical Electric Co—*William Nordlof*	5656 N NW Hwy, Chicago IL 60646	773-774-5200	D	1*	<.1
49	Multi-Tech Industries Inc—*James Bernard*	PO Box 159, Marlboro NJ 07746	732-431-0550	R	1*	<.1
50	Nehrwess Company Inc—*Susan Nehrt*	1408 E State Rd 250, Brownstown IN 47220	812-358-3406	R	<1*	<.1
51	Boton—*Shaojie Xu*	8808 W 125th St, Shawnee Mission KS 66213	913-814-9375	R	<1*	<.1
52	No Bull Sim Racing—*Tom Linser*	5254 Spicer Rd, Toledo OH 43612	419-478-5320	R	<1*	<.1

TOTALS: SIC 3644 Noncurrent Carrying Wiring Devices
Companies: 52　　　　　　　　　　　　　　　　　　　　　　　　　　　　2,637　　13.2

3645 Residential Lighting Fixtures

Rank	Company Name—*Executive Officer*	Address, City, State, Zip	Phone	Type	Fin	Empls
1	Acuity Brands Lighting Inc—*Vernon Nagel* Acuity Brands Inc	1 Lithonia Way, Conyers GA 30012	770-922-9000	S	2,895*	6.0
2	Acuity Brands Inc—*Vernon J Nagel*	1170 Peachtree St NE S, Atlanta GA 30309	404-853-1400	P	1,796	6.0
3	Osram Sylvania Inc—*Rick Leaman*	100 Endicott St, Danvers MA 01923	978-777-1900	S	1,402*	9.5
4	Lithonia Lighting Inc—*Carol Ellis Morgan* Acuity Brands Lighting Inc	PO Box A, Conyers GA 30012		S	1,124*	4.5
5	Progress Lighting Inc—*Charlie Harris*	PO Box 6701, Greenville SC 29606	864-599-6000	S	127*	1.0
6	Lights Of America Inc—*Usman Vakil*	611 Reyes Dr, Walnut CA 91789	909-594-7883	R	88*	1.2
7	Quoizel Inc—*Rick Seidman*	6 Corporate Pky, Goose Creek SC 29445	631-273-2700	R	65*	.4
8	LD Kichler Co—*David Pamer*	PO Box 318010, Cleveland OH 44131	216-573-1000	R	43	.4
9	Blumberg Industries Ltd—*Max Blumberg*	5772 Miami Lakes Dr, Hialeah FL 33014	305-821-3850	R	40*	.6
10	Tresch Electrical Company Inc—*Manny Majano*	7400 Redwood Blvd, Novato CA 94945	415-897-4608	R	38*	.1
11	Energy Focus Inc—*Joe Kaveski*	32000 Aurora Rd, Solon OH 44139	440-715-1300	P	35	.1
12	Nulco Manufacturing Corp—*Kenneth Nulman*	123 Dyer St, Providence RI 02903	401-728-5200	R	34*	.2
13	Cooper Lighting Inc—*John Riley*	1121 Hwy 74 S, Peachtree City GA 30269	770-486-4800	S	28*	.3
14	Hubbardton Forge LLC—*Lyn Brown*	PO Box 827, Castleton VT 05735	802-468-3090	R	28*	.2
15	Robert Abbey Inc—*Jeffrey Rose*	3166 Main Ave Se, Hickory NC 28602	828-322-3480	R	27*	.3
16	Stylecraft Home Collection Inc	4325 Executive Dr Ste, Southaven MS 38672	662-429-5279	R	26*	.2
17	A Schonbek and Company Inc—*Andrew Schonbek*	61 Industrial Blvd, Plattsburgh NY 12901	518-563-7500	S	25*	.4
18	American Fluorescent Corp—*William Solomon*	2345 Ernie Krueger Cir, Waukegan IL 60087	847-249-5970	R	23*	.2
19	Duray Fluorescent Manufacturing Co—*Bernard Myers*	2050 W Balmoral Ave, Chicago IL 60625	773-271-2800	R	19*	.1
20	Architectural Area Lighting Inc—*George Preston*	16555 E Gale Ave, Hacienda Heights CA 91745	714-994-2700	S	18*	.1
21	Lightolier Inc	631 Airport Rd, Fall River MA 02720	508-679-8131	S	18*	.1
22	2nd Avenue Design—*Bob Cowen*	737 W 2nd Ave, Mesa AZ 85210		R	17*	.1
23	Jimco Lamp and Manufacturing Co—*Don Harmon*	11759 Hwy 63 N B, Bono AR 72416	870-935-6820	R	16*	.2
24	Insight Lighting Inc—*David Patterson*	4341 Fulcrum Way Ne, Rio Rancho NM 87144	505-345-0888	R	13*	.1
25	Gustafson Lighting—*Charles Gustafson*	PO Box 39, Elkhart IN 46515	574-522-0871	R	12*	.1
26	Atlas Lighting Products Inc—*Rector Hunt*	PO Box 2348, Burlington NC 27216	336-222-9258	R	12*	.1
27	Mario Industries Of Virginia Inc—*Louis Scutellaro*	PO Box 3190, Roanoke VA 24015	540-342-1111	R	11*	.1
28	Hallmark Manufacturing Company Inc—*Brad Senet*	PO Box 2313, Chatsworth CA 91313	818-885-5010	R	11*	.1
29	Prestigeline Inc—*Scott Roth*	PO Box 100, Bay Shore NY 11706	631-273-3636	R	10*	.1
30	Tempo Lighting Inc—*Lee Warder*	PO Box 133297, Hialeah FL 33013	305-835-2214	R	10*	.1
31	Irvin's Country Tinware—*Irvin Hoover*	115 Cedar Ln, Mount Pleasant Mills PA 17853	570-539-8200	R	10*	.1
32	Nessen Lighting Inc—*Robert N Haidinger Jr*	PO Box 187, Mamaroneck NY 10543	914-698-7799	R	10*	.1
33	Will-Light Inc—*C Willis*	955 Charles St, Longwood FL 32750	407-830-4305	R	10*	.1
34	Hinkley Lighting Inc—*Richard Wiedemer*	12600 Berea Rd, Cleveland OH 44111	216-671-3300	R	10*	.1
35	Visual Comfort Corporation Of America—*Andrew Singer*	2021 Bingle Rd, Houston TX 77055	713-686-5999	R	9*	.1
36	Boyd Lighting Fixture Co—*Jay Sweet*	944 Folsom St, San Francisco CA 94107	415-778-4300	R	9*	.1
37	Decora Industries Inc—*Robert Levitt*	14001 Townsend Rd, Philadelphia PA 19154	215-698-2600	R	8*	.1
38	Lava Lite LLC—*Frank Hoare*	321 W Lake St Ste G, Elmhurst IL 60126	630-315-3300	R	8*	.1
39	Metalite Corp—*Marvin Friedman*	1815 Troy St, New Albany IN 47150	812-944-6600	R	7*	.1
40	Dab Inc—*David Boose*	13415 Marquardt Ave, Santa Fe Springs CA 90670	562-623-4773	R	7*	.1
41	Command Electronics Inc—*Cary Campagna*	15670 Morris Industria, Schoolcraft MI 49087	269-679-4011	R	7*	<.1
42	Dana Creath Designs Ltd—*Dana Creath*	308 N Newport Blvd, Newport Beach CA 92663	714-662-0111	R	7*	<.1
43	Holtkoetter International Inc—*Paul Eusterbrock*	PO Box 623, South Saint Paul MN 55075	651-552-8776	R	7*	.1
44	American Plumbing Supply Co—*Max Gross*	1735 Alton Rd, Miami Beach FL 33139	305-531-3111	R	7*	<.1
45	Yawitz Inc—*John Klena*	1379 Ridgeway St, Pomona CA 91768	909-865-5599	R	6*	.1
46	James R Moder Crystal Chandelier Inc—*James Moder*	PO Box 420346, Dallas TX 75342	214-742-4488	R	6*	.1
47	Techtron Products Inc—*William Swen*	2694 W Winton Ave, Hayward CA 94545	510-293-3500	R	6*	<.1
48	FSC Inc—*Edward Yawitz*	12120 Altamar Pl, Santa Fe Springs CA 90670	562-906-2644	R	6*	<.1
49	Norwell Manufacturing Company Inc—*Alan Indursky*	PO Box 559, East Taunton MA 02718	508-822-5854	R	6*	<.1
50	Hudson Valley Lighting Inc—*David Littman*	PO Box 7459, Newburgh NY 12550	845-561-0300	R	6*	<.1
51	Atlite Inc—*Ted Pearlman*	100 Andres Rd, Hicksville NY 11801	516-470-1000	S	6	<.1
52	Natural Light Inc—*Harvey Hollingsworth*	PO Box 16449, Panama City FL 32406	850-265-0800	R	6*	.1
53	Uspar Enterprises Inc—*Khalid Parekh*	13404 Monte Vista Ave, Chino CA 91710	909-591-7506	R	6*	.1
54	Wildwood Lamps and Accents Inc—*W Kincheloe*	PO Box 672, Rocky Mount NC 27802	252-446-3266	R	6*	<.1
55	Pieri Creations LLC—*Oren Wineberg*	100 W Oxford St, Philadelphia PA 19122	215-634-4000	R	6*	.1
56	Candella Lighting Company Inc—*Eva Axelsson*	6415 Fleet St, Los Angeles CA 90040	323-278-8116	R	5*	<.1
57	H A Framburg and Co—*Malcolm Tripp*	941 Cernan Dr, Bellwood IL 60104	708-547-5757	R	5*	<.1
58	Melissa Lighting Inc—*Peter Macaluso*	4859 Olson Dr, Dallas TX 75227	214-388-7487	R	5*	<.1
59	A Boy Electric Dolan Design—*Pat Dolan*	2700 Nw Front Ave, Portland OR 97210	503-220-0799	R	5*	.1
60	SCW Corp—*Steve Weisman*	126 Chestnut St, Warwick RI 02888	401-467-8232	R	5*	<.1
61	A' Homestead Shoppe Inc—*Bruce Albert*	PO Box 254, Lapaz IN 46537	574-784-2307	R	4*	<.1

Rank	Company Name—Executive Officer	Address, City, State, Zip	Phone	Type	Fin	Empls
62	Medallion Lighting Corp—William Knuff	PO Box 51, Mentor OH 44061	440-255-8383	R	4*	<.1
63	K-B Lighting Manufacturing Co—Gary Kessel	2101 Byberry Rd, Philadelphia PA 19116	215-673-6400	R	4*	<.1
64	Prima Lighting Corp—Adam Lee	13615 Marquardt Ave, Santa Fe Springs CA 90670	562-407-3079	R	4*	<.1
65	St Nick Decorators—Jamie Limber	4902 E McDowell Rd 105, Phoenix AZ 85008	602-934-2644	R	4*	<.1
66	Light Logic Inc—Malcolm Tripp	902 Silver Ridge Rd, Hyde Park VT 05655	802-888-7984	R	4*	<.1
67	Brandon Industries Inc—Jan Hall	1601 Wilmeth Rd, Mckinney TX 75069	972-542-3000	R	4*	<.1
68	Alger Company Inc—Mishel Mikail	8690 National Blvd, Culver City CA 90232	310-229-9500	R	3*	<.1
69	J-Rie Inc—Marie Pallitto	19 E Elizabeth Ave, Linden NJ 07036	908-486-2995	R	3*	<.1
70	Rainbow Lighting Inc—Mike Stern	3545 Commercial Ave, Northbrook IL 60062	847-480-1136	R	3*	<.1
71	Daniel Lamp Co—Michael Welbel	3611 W Cermak Rd, Chicago IL 60623	773-521-1000	R	3*	<.1
72	Western Lighting Industries Inc—Lawrence Ives	511 N Virginia Ave, Azusa CA 91702	626-969-6820	R	3*	<.1
73	Patio Living Concepts—Cydney Armistad	PO Box 259, Saint Albans MO 63073	636-458-5483	R	3*	<.1
74	Murray Feiss Industries—Greg Vandia	125 Rose Feiss Blvd, Bronx NY 10454		R	3*	<.1
75	Royal Haeger Lamp Co—Nicholas Estes	PO Box 218, Macomb IL 61455	309-837-9966	R	3*	<.1
76	Inlite Corp—D Belle	939 Grayson St, Berkeley CA 94710	510-849-1067	R	3*	<.1
77	Electrodex Inc—Michael Guritz	4554 19th St Ct E, Bradenton FL 34203	941-753-5663	R	3*	<.1
78	Cedric Hartman Inc—Cedric Hartman	PO Box 3842, Omaha NE 68103	402-344-4474	R	2*	<.1
79	Remcraft Lighting Products Inc—Mitchell Robboy	PO Box 541487, Opa Locka FL 33054	305-687-9031	R	2*	<.1
80	Lt Moses Willard Inc—Christopher Nordloh	1156 Us 50, Milford OH 45150	513-248-5500	R	2*	<.1
81	Vision Lighting Inc—Kerwood Barrand	300 Vine St NW Ste 308, Washington DC 20012	202-882-5181	R	2*	<.1
82	M Lazy Inc—David Mays	69 Clark Dr, Russellville AL 35654	256-332-0026	R	2*	<.1
83	Matov Industries Inc—Alan Hochster	1011 40th Ave, Long Island City NY 11101	718-392-5060	R	2*	<.1
84	Natural Illuminating Technologies Inc—Neal Owens	19217 Orbit Dr, Gaithersburg MD 20879	301-869-5980	R	2*	<.1
85	Crystal James Corp—Jeffrey Kovacs	1300 Biddle Ave, Wyandotte MI 48192	734-285-7900	R	1*	<.1
86	Period Lighting Fixtures Inc—Christopher Burda	167 River Rd, Clarksburg MA 01247	413-664-7141	R	1*	<.1

TOTALS: SIC 3645 Residential Lighting Fixtures
Companies: 86   **8,287   34.8**

3646 Commercial Lighting Fixtures

Rank	Company Name—Executive Officer	Address, City, State, Zip	Phone	Type	Fin	Empls
1	Cooper Industries PLC—Kirk S Hachigian	PO Box 4446, Houston TX 77210	713-209-8400	P	5,066	24.8
2	LSI Greenlee Lighting—Robert J Ready / LSI Industries Inc	1417 Upfield Dr Ste 11, Carrollton TX 75006	972-466-1133	S	2,627*	1.2
3	National Service Industries Inc—Michael R Kelly	1420 Peachtree St NE, Atlanta GA 30309	404-853-1000	R	1,650*	22.0
4	Prescolite Inc—Jim Duggar	701 Millennium Blvd, Greenville SC 29607	864-678-1000	S	300*	2.2
5	LSI Industries Inc—Robert J Ready	PO Box 42728, Cincinnati OH 45242	513-793-3200	P	294	1.2
6	LSI Kentucky LLC—Robert J Ready / LSI Industries Inc	3871 Turkeyfoot Rd, Erlanger KY 41018	859-342-2273	S	272*	1.2
7	Columbia Lighting Inc—Timothy Powers	701 Millennium Blvd, Greenville SC 29607	864-678-1000	D	230*	1.4
8	Kramer Lighting—Al Ruud	1200 92nd St, Sturtevant WI 53177		R	67*	.4
9	Simkar LLC—Yoram Weiss	700 Ramona Ave, Philadelphia PA 19120	215-831-7700	R	66*	.9
10	Tempo Industries Inc—Gil Padilla	1961 McGaw Ave, Irvine CA 92614	949-442-1601	R	62*	<.1
11	Luminator Holding LP—Ben Sorrels	PO Box 278, Plano TX 75086	972-424-6511	R	36*	.2
12	LSI Midwest Lighting Inc—Robert J Ready / LSI Industries Inc	100 Funston Rd, Kansas City KS 66115	913-281-1100	D	32*	.2
13	Vari-Lite Inc	10911 Petal St, Dallas TX 75238	214-647-7880	S	32*	.2
14	Luminescent Systems Inc	4 Lucent Dr, Lebanon NH 03766	603-643-7766	S	31*	.2
15	Sun Valley Lighting Standards Inc—Joseph Straus	660 W Ave O, Palmdale CA 93551	661-233-2000	R	27*	.3
16	LSI Lightron Inc / LSI Industries Inc	500 Hudson Valley Ave, New Windsor NY 12553	845-220-3200	S	25*	.2
17	Lightolier/A Genlyte Co—William Schoettler	631 Airport Rd, Fall River MA 02720	608-679-8131	S	24*	.2
18	Prudential Lighting Corp—Jeffrey Ellis	PO Box 58736, Los Angeles CA 90058	213-746-0360	R	24*	.1
19	Winona Lighting Inc—Steve Biesanz	3760 W 4th St, Winona MN 55987	507-454-5113	R	21*	.2
20	Amerlux Inc—Charles Campagna	23 Daniel Rd, Fairfield NJ 07004	973-882-5010	R	21*	.2
21	H E Williams Inc—Mark Williams	PO Box 837, Carthage MO 64836	417-358-4065	R	20*	.3
22	Advanced Specialty Lighting Inc—Jarold Bijak	7227 W Wilson Ave, Harwood Heights IL 60706	708-867-3140	R	18*	.3
23	Forum Inc—Norman Garret	908 Old Freeport Rd, Pittsburgh PA 15238	412-781-5970	R	17*	.2
24	Linear Lighting Corp—Stanley Deutsch	3130 Hunters Point Ave, Long Island City NY 11101	718-361-7552	R	17*	.2
25	Spi Lighting Inc—Lee Doerr	PO Box 3605, Thiensville WI 53092	262-242-1420	R	17*	.2
26	Lumitex Inc—Peter Broer	8443 Dow Cir, Strongsville OH 44136	440-243-8401	R	16*	.2
27	Mercury Lighting Products Company Inc—John Fedinec	20 Audrey Pl, Fairfield NJ 07004	973-244-9444	R	16*	.1
28	Edison Price Lighting Inc—Emma Price	4150 22nd St, Long Island City NY 11101	718-685-0700	R	15*	.1
29	Light Corporation Inc—Brad Davis	14800 172nd Ave, Grand Haven MI 49417	616-842-5100	R	14*	.1
30	Hi-Lite Manufacturing Company Inc—Dorothy Ohai	13450 Monte Vista Ave, Chino CA 91710	909-465-1999	R	14*	.1
31	Focal Point LLC—Tasha Ramos	4141 S Pulaski Rd, Chicago IL 60632	773-247-9494	R	14*	.1
32	Scott Lamp Company Inc—Dennis Scott	355 Watt Dr, Suisun City CA 94534	707-864-2066	R	13*	.1
33	Harris Manufacturing Inc—Andrew Bebington	4035a Reynolds Blvd, Green Cove Springs FL 32043	904-284-1220	R	13*	<.1
34	Litelab Corp—Frederick Spaulding	251 Elm St, Buffalo NY 14203	716-856-4491	R	13*	.1
35	North Star Lighting Inc—Reginald Barrett	PO Box 6038, Maywood IL 60155	708-681-4330	R	12*	.1
36	TWR Lighting—Kenneth Meador	4300 Windfern Rd Ste 1, Houston TX 77041	713-973-6905	R	12*	.1
37	Pathway Lighting Products Inc—Fred Stark	PO Box 591, Old Saybrook CT 06475	860-388-6881	R	12*	.1
38	Focus Industries Inc—Stan Shibata	25301 Commercentre Dr, Lake Forest CA 92630	949-830-1350	R	11*	.1
39	Lighting Services Inc—Daniel Gelman	2 Holt Dr, Stony Point NY 10980	845-942-2800	R	11*	.1
40	Cooper Corelite Inc—Terry Klebey / Cooper Industries PLC	4675 Holly St, Denver CO 80216	303-393-1522	S	11	.1
41	Metaloptics Inc—Paolo Minissi	2011 W Rundberg Ln, Austin TX 78758	512-832-0025	R	11*	.1
42	Lucifer Lighting Co—Gilbert Mathews	3750 Ih 35 N, San Antonio TX 78219	210-227-7329	R	10*	.1
43	LC Doane Co—Margaret Eagan	PO Box 700, Ivoryton CT 06442	860-767-8295	R	10*	.1
44	La Mar Lighting Company Inc—Barry Kugel	PO Box 9013, Farmingdale NY 11735	631-777-7700	R	10*	.1
45	Electrix Inc—Haim Swisha	PO Box 9575, New Haven CT 06535	203-776-5577	R	9*	.1
46	RBB Corp—Raymond Bentley	PO Box 450, Ledgewood NJ 07852	973-770-1100	R	8*	.1
47	Hammerton Inc—William Shott	217 Wright Brothers Dr, Salt Lake City UT 84116	801-973-8095	R	8*	.1
48	Peerless Lighting—James S Balloun	PO Box 2556, Berkeley CA 94702	510-845-2760	D	8*	<.1
49	Environmental Lighting For Architecture Inc—Elsie Dahlin	17891 Arenth Ave, City Of Industry CA 91748	626-965-0821	R	8*	<.1
50	D and P Custom Lights and Wiring Systems Inc—Julius Smith	PO Box 90465, Nashville TN 37209	615-350-7800	R	8*	<.1
51	Lighting World Inc—Bruce Belfer	PO Box 2079, Asbury Park NJ 07712	732-493-2666	R	7*	.1
52	Lusive Decor—Terra Clark	5240 Alhambra Ave, Los Angeles CA 90032	323-227-9207	R	7	<.1
53	Swivelier Company Inc—Michael Schwartz	600 Bradley Hill Rd St, Blauvelt NY 10913	845-353-1455	R	7*	.1
54	King Luminaire Company Inc—Greg Dutton	PO Box 266, Jefferson OH 44047	440-576-9073	R	7*	<.1
55	Besa Lighting Company Inc—Bernd Hoffbauer	6695 Taylor Rd, Blacklick OH 43004	614-475-7046	R	7*	<.1

Note: An asterisk (*) indicates an estimated financial figure. The company type code used is as follows: R = Private, P = Public, S = Private Subsidiary, B = Public Subsidiary, D = Division, J = Joint Venture, I = Investment Fund.

COMPANY RANKINGS BY SALES WITHIN 4-DIGIT SIC

Rank	Company Name—Executive Officer	Address, City, State, Zip	Phone	Type	Fin	Empls
56	Thin-Lite Corp—Alan Griffin	530 Constitution Ave, Camarillo CA 93012	805-987-5021	R	7*	<.1
57	Rle Industries LLC—Scott Koenig	35 Kulick Rd, Fairfield NJ 07004	973-276-1444	R	7*	<.1
58	C W Cole and Company Inc—Stephen Cole	2560 Rosemead Blvd, South El Monte CA 91733	626-443-2473	R	6*	<.1
59	Starfire Lighting Inc—Zachary Gomes	7 Donna Dr, Wood Ridge NJ 07075	201-438-9540	R	6*	<.1
60	Teron Lighting Inc—David Bellos	33 Donald Dr Uppr, Fairfield OH 45014	513-858-6004	R	6*	<.1
61	Brownlee Lighting Inc—Curtis Brownlee	4600 Dardanelle Dr, Orlando FL 32808	407-297-3677	R	6*	<.1
62	Legion Lighting Company Inc—Sheldon Bellovin	221 Glenmore Ave, Brooklyn NY 11207	718-498-1770	R	6*	<.1
63	ZEON Corp—Michelle Thomas	321 /s /Taylor Ave Ste, Louisville CO 80027	303-666-9400	R	6*	<.1
64	New Metal Crafts Inc—James Neumann	812 N Wells St, Chicago IL 60610	312-787-6991	R	6*	.1
65	Mcfadden Lighting Company Inc—Jay Sturgeon	2601 Ohio Ave, Saint Louis MO 63118	314-773-1340	R	5*	<.1
66	Manning Lighting Inc—Andrew Manning	PO Box 1063, Sheboygan WI 53082	920-458-2184	R	5*	<.1
67	Eclipse Lighting Inc—Robert Fiermuga	PO Box 2351, Schiller Park IL 60176	847-260-0333	R	5*	<.1
68	Pacific Lighting and Standards Co—Frank Munoz	2815 Los Flores Blvd, Lynwood CA 90262	310-603-9344	R	5*	<.1
69	Michaels' Lighting Inc—Michael Conway	PO Box 192, Winona MN 55987	507-454-5560	R	5*	<.1
70	Charles Loomis Inc—Charles Loomis	11828 Ne 112th St, Kirkland WA 98033	425-823-4560	R	5*	<.1
71	Conservation Technology Ltd—John Ranshaw	2783 Shermer Rd, Northbrook IL 60062	847-559-5500	R	4*	<.1
72	St Louis Antique Lighting Company Inc—Gary Behm	801 N Skinker Blvd, Saint Louis MO 63130	314-863-1414	R	4*	<.1
73	Specialty Lighting Industries Inc—Benjamin Solomon	1306 Doris Ave, Ocean NJ 07712	732-517-0800	R	4*	<.1
74	Esco Lighting Inc—Donna Franklin	3254 N Kilbourn Ave, Chicago IL 60641	773-427-7000	R	4*	<.1
75	J and J Electronics Inc—James Rafferty	35 Hammond Ste 100, Irvine CA 92618	949-455-4460	R	4*	<.1
76	Modular International Inc—Irwin Kotovsky	3941 California Ave, Pittsburgh PA 15212	412-734-9000	R	4*	<.1
77	Creative Light Source Inc—Kenneth Walker	985 Trade Dr Ste E, North Las Vegas NV 89030	702-897-1400	R	4*	<.1
78	Crownlite Manufacturing Corp—William Siegel	1546 Ocean Ave, Bohemia NY 11716	631-589-9100	R	4*	<.1
79	Lightway Industries Inc—Jeffrey Bargman	28435 Industry Dr, Valencia CA 91355	661-257-0286	R	4*	<.1
80	Arch Lighting Group Inc—Scott Davis	30 Sherwood Dr, Taunton MA 02780	508-823-8277	R	4*	<.1
81	Ashley Lighting Inc—Blake Barber	405 Industrial Dr, Trumann AR 72472	870-483-6181	R	4*	<.1
82	Gross Chandelier Co—Nicholas Gross	9777 Reavis Park Dr, Saint Louis MO 63123	314-631-6000	R	3*	<.1
83	Morris Kurtzon Inc—Daniel Koch	1420 S Talman Ave 30, Chicago IL 60608	773-277-2121	R	3*	<.1
84	Humberto Arguelles—Humberto Arguelles	9335 Stephens St Unit, Pico Rivera CA 90660	562-908-6181	R	3*	<.1
85	Nylube Products Company LLC	2299 Star Ct, Rochester Hills MI 48309	248-852-6500	R	3*	<.1
86	Lite-Makers Inc—John Iorio	3055 Vernon Blvd, Astoria NY 11102	718-729-7700	R	3*	<.1
87	Davis Muller Lighting—Scott Davis	30 Sherwood Dr, Taunton MA 02780	508-821-4544	R	3*	<.1
88	Magni-Flood Inc—Ken Greene	7200 New Horizons Blvd, Amityville NY 11701	631-226-1000	R	3*	<.1
89	National Electric Manufacturing Corp—James Galvez	6371 Chalet Dr, Commerce CA 90040	562-928-8488	R	3*	<.1
90	Renova Lighting Systems Inc—Rick Edwards	20 Middlesex Rd, Ashaway RI 02804	401-682-1850	R	3*	<.1
91	O C White Co—Richard May	PO Box 644, Thorndike MA 01079	413-289-1751	R	3*	<.1
92	Mks Inc—Ken Brattlie	7 N Industrial Blvd, Bridgeton NJ 08302	856-451-5545	R	3*	<.1
93	Lighting and Electronic Design Inc—Janie Lynn	141 Cassia Way Ste C, Henderson NV 89014	702-568-8742	R	3*	<.1
94	Tujayar Enterprises Inc—Richard Tempkin	1346 Pioneer Way, El Cajon CA 92020	619-442-0577	R	3*	<.1
95	Peachtree Lighting Inc—Waddy Batson	7230 Industrial Blvd N, Covington GA 30014	770-787-8490	R	3*	<.1
96	O'ryan Industries Inc—Rick Grant	PO Box 1736, Vancouver WA 98668	360-892-0447	R	2*	<.1
97	Visco Inc—Chris Herring	29579 Awbrey Ln, Eugene OR 97402	541-688-7741	R	2*	<.1
98	Nu Tech Inc—Charles Trowbridge	PO Box 1425, Newtown PA 18940	215-297-8889	R	2*	<.1
99	Luxo Corp—Sam Gumins	200 Clearbrook Rd Ste, Elmsford NY 10523	914-345-0067	R	2*	<.1
100	Moffatt Products Inc—David Moffatt	222 Cessna St, Watertown SD 57201	605-886-5700	R	2*	<.1
101	S-P Products Inc—Peter Vrame	PO Box 128, Glenview IL 60025	847-593-8595	R	2*	<.1
102	Genesis Lamp Corp—Edward Zukowski	375 N Saint Clair St, Painesville OH 44077	440-354-0095	R	2*	<.1
103	Videssence Inc	10768 Lower Azusa Rd, El Monte CA 91731	626-579-0943	S	2*	<.1
104	Encapsulite International Inc—Peter Waumsley	PO Box 1086, Rosenberg TX 77471	281-239-0225	R	2*	<.1
105	Light Craft Manufacturing Inc—Jeffery Matt	220 Sullivan Rd, Fremont OH 43420	419-332-0536	R	2*	<.1
106	Toltec Co—Hugh Gregory	PO Box T, Burnsville MS 38833	662-427-9515	R	1*	<.1
107	Scientific Components Systems Inc—Juan Flores	1514 N Susan St Ste C, Santa Ana CA 92703	714-554-3960	R	1*	<.1

TOTALS: SIC 3646 Commercial Lighting Fixtures
Companies: 107 — 11,510 — 62.0

3647 Vehicular Lighting Equipment

Rank	Company Name—Executive Officer	Address, City, State, Zip	Phone	Type	Fin	Empls
1	North American Lighting Inc—Cliff Ashley	2275 S Main St, Paris IL 61944	217-465-6600	R	1,050*	2.2
2	Guide Corp—George Sloan	600 Corporation Dr, Pendleton IN 46064	765-221-7000	R	560*	3.0
3	Honeywell Grimes Aerospace—David M Cote	550 State Rte 55, Urbana OH 43078	937-484-2000	S	156	.9
4	Truck-Lite Company Inc—Brian Kupchella	PO Box 387, Jamestown NY 14702	716-665-6214	R	99*	1.3
5	Grote Industries Inc—Dominic Grote	2600 Lanier Dr, Madison IN 47250	812-273-1296	R	84*	1.2
6	Ii Stanley Company Inc—Satoshi Nakamura	1500 Hill Brady Rd, Battle Creek MI 49037	269-660-7777	R	52*	.8
7	Whelen Engineering Company Inc—John Olson	51 Winthrop Rd, Chester CT 06412	860-526-9504	R	50*	.7
8	Adronics/Elrob Manufacturing Corp—Richard Robinson	9 Sand Park Rd, Cedar Grove NJ 07009	973-239-3800	R	35*	.3
9	Lankfer Diversified Industries Inc	4311 Patterson Ave SE, Grand Rapids MI 49512	616-957-2570	S	25*	.3
10	Atc Lighting and Plastics Inc—Seymour Stein	101 Parker Dr, Andover OH 44003	440-466-7670	R	25*	.3
11	Sate-Lite Manufacturing Co—Richard Van Deventer	10 N Martingale Rd Ste, Schaumburg IL 60173	847-647-1515	S	18	.2
12	Jkl Components Corp—Joseph Velas	13343 Paxton St, Pacoima CA 91331	818-896-0019	R	17*	.1
13	Innovative Lighting Inc—Jerry Handsaker	PO Box 366, Roland IA 50236	515-388-1011	R	16*	.1
14	Transmatic Inc—Richard Solon	6145 Delfield Industri, Waterford MI 48329	248-623-2500	R	15*	.1
15	Frameworks Inc—Paul Belliveau	PO Box 312, Antrim NH 03440	603-464-5190	R	13*	.2
16	Street Glow Inc—Jack Panzarella	160 Gregg St Ste 7, Lodi NJ 07644		R	9*	<.1
17	Pwi Inc—Miklos Lorik	109 S Knight St, Wichita KS 67213	316-942-2811	R	8*	.1
18	Ramco Industries Inc—Greg Bland	420 Roske Dr, Elkhart IN 46516	574-389-0040	R	7*	.1
19	Electric Industries Corp—Frank Heffley	325 S Union St, Aurora IL 60505	630-851-1616	R	6*	<.1
20	Baader-Brown Manufacturing Co—Joseph Baader	4220 Springsfld Jmesto, Springfield OH 45502	937-323-6017	R	5*	<.1
21	Kc Hilites Inc—Michael Dehaal	PO Box 155, Williams AZ 86046	928-635-2607	R	5*	<.1
22	Heads Up Technologies Inc—Robert Harshaw	2033 Chenault Dr Ste 1, Carrollton TX 75006	972-407-1131	R	5*	<.1
23	Sierra Design Manufacturing Inc—Dennis Moore	1113 Greenville Rd, Livermore CA 94550	925-443-3140	R	3*	<.1
24	Sunbeam Trailer Products Inc—Fred Muzic	5312 Production Dr, Huntington Beach CA 92649	714-373-5000	R	2*	<.1
25	Lite-Minder Co—Atsuko Nelson	2777 Alvarado St, San Leandro CA 94577	510-352-5483	R	<1*	<.1

TOTALS: SIC 3647 Vehicular Lighting Equipment
Companies: 25 — 2,264 — 11.8

3648 Lighting Equipment Nec

Rank	Company Name—Executive Officer	Address, City, State, Zip	Phone	Type	Fin	Empls
1	AZZ Inc—David H Dingus	3100 West 7th St Ste 5, Fort Worth TX 76107	817-810-0095	P	381	1.3
2	Juno Lighting Inc—John Mabbott	PO Box 5065, Des Plaines IL 60017	847-827-9880	S	242*	1.0
3	Excelitas Technologies Holdings LLC—David Nislick	940 Winter St, Waltham MA 02451	781-663-6900	R	151*	3.0
4	Chase Corp—Peter R Chase	26 Summer St Ste 220, Bridgewater MA 02324	508-819-4200	P	123	.3
5	Dual-Lite Inc	701 Millennium Blvd, Greenville SC 29607	864-678-1000	S	77*	.4

Rank	Company Name—*Executive Officer*	Address, City, State, Zip	Phone	Type	Fin	Empls
6	Mag Instrument Inc—*Anthony Maglica*	PO Box 50600, Ontario CA 91761	909-947-1006	R	73*	.9
7	Union Metal Corp—*Darryl Dillenback*	1432 Maple Ave Ne, Canton OH 44705	330-456-7653	R	66*	.4
8	Midmark Corp—*Anne D*	PO Box 286, Versailles OH 45380	937-526-3662	R	55*	.8
9	Lamplight Farms Inc—*Joel Borgardt*	4900 N Lilly Rd, Menomonee Falls WI 53051	262-781-9590	R	50*	.3
10	J Baxter Brinkmann International Corp—*J Brinkmann*	4215 Mcewen Rd, Dallas TX 75244	972-387-4939	R	46*	.8
11	Electronic Theatre Controls Inc—*Fred Foster*	PO Box 620979, Middleton WI 53562	608-831-4116	R	45*	.6
12	Pelican Products Inc—*Lyndon Faulkner*	23215 Early Ave, Torrance CA 90505	310-326-4700	R	40*	.6
13	Acr Electronics Inc—*Joe Mentz*	5757 Ravenswood Rd, Fort Lauderdale FL 33312	954-981-3333	R	40*	.2
14	Lighting Components and Design Inc—*Gina Zamarelli*	11711 Nw 39th St, Coral Springs FL 33065	954-425-0123	S	39*	.3
15	Streamlight Inc—*Raymond Sharrah*	30 Eagleville Rd Ste 1, Eagleville PA 19403	610-631-0600	R	32*	.2
16	Re-Flek Corp—*Robert Dorsky*	PO Box 298, Fall River MA 02724	508-678-3906	R	20*	.2
17	Kw Industries Inc—*James White*	909 Industrial Blvd, Sugar Land TX 77478	281-240-0909	R	16*	.1
18	Vantage Controls Inc—*Ron Wilson*	1061 S 800 E, Orem UT 84097	801-229-2800	R	16*	.1
19	Altman Stage Lighting Company Inc—*Robert Altman*	57 Alexander St, Yonkers NY 10701	914-476-7987	R	15*	.1
20	Luminus Devices Inc—*Keith Ward*	1100 Tech Pk Dr Unit 2, Billerica MA 01821	978-528-8000	R	15*	.1
21	Koehler-Bright Star Inc—*Mark Dirsa*	380 Stewart Rd, Wilkes Barre PA 18706	570-825-1900	R	15*	.1
22	Iota Holding Co—*Stephen Shell*	PO Box 11846, Tucson AZ 85734	520-294-3292	R	15*	.1
23	Spring City Electrical Manufacturing Co—*Alan Brink*	PO Box 19, Spring City PA 19475	610-948-4000	R	14*	.1
24	W J Whatley Inc—*George Maybee*	3550 Odessa Way, Aurora CO 80011	303-287-8053	R	14*	.1
25	X-Tra Light Manufacturing Partnership Ltd—*Jerry Caroom*	8812 Frey Rd, Houston TX 77034	713-943-9927	R	13*	.1
26	Delray Lighting Inc—*Steven Feig*	7545 N Lockheed Dr, Burbank CA 91505	818-767-3793	R	13*	<.1
27	Bevolo Gas and Electric Lights Inc—*Andrew Bevolo*	521 Conti St, New Orleans LA 70130	504-522-9485	R	12*	.1
28	Control Products Corp—*H Hanks*	PO Box 531109, Grand Prairie TX 75053	972-264-0368	R	12*	.2
29	Able 2 Products Company Inc—*Jerry Watley*	PO Box 543, Cassville MO 65625	417-847-4791	R	12*	.1
30	Remote Ocean Systems Inc—*Robert Acks*	5618 Copley Dr, San Diego CA 92111	858-565-8500	R	11*	<.1
31	Nite Ize Inc—*Rick Case*	5660 Central Ave Unit, Boulder CO 80301	303-449-2576	R	11*	.1
32	Inter-Global Inc—*Larry Glazer*	6333 Etzel Ave, Saint Louis MO 63133	314-725-9800	R	10*	.1
33	Deaver Industries Inc—*Ken Deaver*	3120 Morgan Rd, Bessemer AL 35022	205-426-4309	R	9*	.1
34	Lite Touch Inc—*Don Buehner*	3400 S W Temple, Salt Lake City UT 84115	801-268-8668	R	9*	.1
35	Furnlite Inc—*Gary Alsobrook*	PO Box 159, Fallston NC 28042	704-538-3193	R	8*	.1
36	North American Signal Co—*William Neiman*	605 Wheeling Rd, Wheeling IL 60090	847-537-8888	R	8*	.1
37	Optronics Inc—*Brett Johnson*	401 S 41st St E, Muskogee OK 74403	918-286-1288	R	7*	.1
38	General Manufacturing Inc—*Paul Reiff*	1336 W Wiley Ave, Bluffton IN 46714	260-824-3440	R	7*	.1
39	Times Square Stage Lighting Company Inc—*Robert Riccadelli*	5 Holt Dr, Stony Point NY 10980	845-947-3034	R	7*	.1
40	Prime Systems Inc—*Elinor Midlik*	416 Mission St, Carol Stream IL 60188	630-681-2100	R	7*	<.1
41	Niterider Technical Lighting and Video Systems Inc—*Thomas Carroll*	8205 Ronson Rd Ste H, San Diego CA 92111	858-268-9316	R	7*	<.1
42	Lighting Innovations Inc—*Bruce Bukas*	3609 Swenson Ave, Saint Charles IL 60174	630-889-8100	R	6*	<.1
43	Carlisle And Finch Co—*Brent Finch*	4562 W Mitchell Ave, Cincinnati OH 45232	513-681-6080	R	6*	<.1
44	Benson Electric Co—*H Mahan*	1102 N 3rd St, Superior WI 54880	715-394-5547	R	6*	<.1
45	Ric-Lo Productions Ltd—*Richard Logothetis*	Kings Hwy, Sugar Loaf NY 10981	845-469-2285	R	6*	<.1
46	Gammalux Systems Inc—*Mehmet Incikaya*	248 E Arrow Hwy, San Dimas CA 91773	909-599-9669	R	6*	<.1
47	Integro LLC—*Al Lewis*	30 Peter Ct, New Britain CT 06051	860-832-8960	R	6*	<.1
48	Master Electrical Contractors Inc—*Daniel Teague*	9822 Titan Park Cir, Littleton CO 80125	303-791-4215	R	6*	<.1
49	Paul C Buff Inc—*Paul Buff*	2725 Bransford Ave, Nashville TN 37204	615-383-3982	R	5*	<.1
50	Big Beam Emergency Systems Inc—*Nick Shah*	PO Box 518, Crystal Lake IL 60039	815-459-6100	R	5*	<.1
51	CHDT Corp—*Stewart Wallach*	350 Jim Moran Blvd Ste, Deerfield Beach FL 33442	954-252-3440	P	5	<.1
52	Apollo Design Technology Inc—*Joel Nichols*	4130 Fourier Dr, Fort Wayne IN 46818	260-497-9191	R	5*	.1
53	Rulon Electric Illuminations Company Inc—*Thomas Kretzschmar*	607 Durham Dr, Houston TX 77007	713-803-1133	R	5*	<.1
54	STEU Inc—*Dan Cunado*	1625 Surveyor Ave, Simi Valley CA 93063	805-527-0987	R	5*	<.1
55	Duraguard Products Inc—*Terry Grover*	1304 Ne 154th St Ste 1, Vancouver WA 98685	360-571-9681	R	4*	<.1
56	Lehigh Electric Products Co—*Lloyd Jones*	6265 Hamilton Blvd Ste, Allentown PA 18106	610-395-3386	R	4*	<.1
57	Performance Sound and Light Inc—*Rob Carroll*	2114 Seabrook Cir, Seabrook TX 77586	281-291-8325	R	4*	<.1
58	Shimada Enterprises Inc—*Tak Shimada*	14009 Dinard Ave, Santa Fe Springs CA 90670	562-802-8811	R	4*	<.1
59	Nova Electronics Data Inc—*Stephen Hanley*	36 Dr Foote Rd, Colchester CT 06415	860-537-3471	R	4*	<.1
60	Unilux Inc—*Michael Simonis*	59 N 5th St, Saddle Brook NJ 07663	201-712-1266	R	4*	<.1
61	Urban Electric Co—*David Dawson*	2130 N Hobson Ave Ste, North Charleston SC 29405	843-576-3994	R	4*	<.1
62	Lightronics Inc—*Kevin Nelson*	509 Central Dr Ste 101, Virginia Beach VA 23454	757-486-3588	R	3*	<.1
63	Centralite Systems Inc—*James Busby*	6420 Wall St, Mobile AL 36695	251-607-9119	R	3*	<.1
64	Abl Lights Inc—*Michel Boisin*	660 Golf Club Dr, Mosinee WI 54455	715-693-1530	R	3*	<.1
65	Birchwood Lighting Inc—*Darrin Weedon*	1302 E Hunter Ave, Santa Ana CA 92705	714-550-7118	R	3*	<.1
66	Main Street Lighting Standards Inc—*Roland Burke*	1080 Industrial Pkwy, Medina OH 44256	330-723-4431	R	3*	.4
67	Julian A Mcdermott Corp—*Vernon Mcdermott*	1639 Stephen St, Ridgewood NY 11385	718-456-3606	R	3*	<.1
68	Carolina Lantern Inc—*John Henderson*	903 Poplar St, Cayce SC 29033	803-926-0001	R	3*	<.1
69	Retro Lightng and Cnsv LC	3407 Autumn Bend Dr, Sugar Land TX 77479	281-491-1195	R	3*	<.1
70	Lumenton Inc—*A Esmailzadeh*	5461 W Jefferson Blvd, Los Angeles CA 90016	323-904-0200	R	3*	<.1
71	Dabmar Lighting Inc—*Dan Davidson*	2140 Eastman Ave, Oxnard CA 93030	805-604-9090	R	3*	<.1
72	Lighting and Electronics Inc—*John Fedigan*	Market St Industrial P, Wappingers Falls NY 12590	845-297-1244	R	3*	<.1
73	Grand Stage Co—*Glenn Becker*	630 W Lake St, Chicago IL 60661	312-332-5611	R	3*	<.1
74	Lighting Accents Inc—*Tom Pontzloff*	3946 Oswald St, Pittsburgh PA 15212	412-761-5000	R	3*	<.1
75	Gti Graphic Technology Inc—*Frederic Curdy*	PO Box 3138, Newburgh NY 12550	845-562-7066	R	3*	<.1
76	Legendary Lighting LLC—*Lyle Wynn*	PO Box 321404, Flowood MS 39232	601-932-0707	R	3*	<.1
77	Plasteco Inc—*Kiyoshi Sandow*	PO Box 24158, Houston TX 77229	713-673-7710	R	3*	<.1
78	Onesolution Light And Control—*John Ortiz*	225 S Loara St, Anaheim CA 92802	714-490-5540	R	3*	<.1
79	Plastic Technologies Inc—*Arthur Schueler*	1200 Abbott Dr, Elgin IL 60123	847-488-9151	R	3*	<.1
80	Al Kramp Specialties—*Al Kramp*	PO Box 8867, Stockton CA 95208	209-464-7539	R	3*	<.1
81	Rodac USA Corp—*Daniel Primeau*	5605 Kraus Rd, Clarence NY 14031	716-741-3931	R	2*	<.1
82	Natural Lighting Co—*Paul J Bilbrey*	5636 N 53rd Dr, Glendale AZ 85301	623-463-0901	R	2*	<.1
83	Lighting Sciences Inc—*Ian Lewin*	7826 E Evans Rd, Scottsdale AZ 85260	480-991-9260	S	2*	<.1
84	Ilc Intelligent Lighting Controls Inc—*Marshal Miller*	5229 Edina IndustrialB, Minneapolis MN 55439	952-829-1900	R	2*	<.1
85	Solar Light Company Inc—*Jay Silverman*	100 E Glenside Ave, Glenside PA 19038	215-517-8700	R	2*	<.1
86	Press A Light Corp—*Paul Chabria*	300 Industrial Dr, West Chicago IL 60185	630-231-6566	R	2*	<.1
87	A Wealthy Place Arts and Theater Company Inc—*Chad Cooper*	703 Woodland Pl, Woodstock GA 30188		R	2*	<.1
88	Architectural Cathode Lighting Inc—*Eric Zimmerman*	5301 Pacific Blvd, Huntington Park CA 90255	323-581-8800	R	1*	<.1
89	Pell Artifex Co—*Michael Pell*	511 W 33rd St Fl 2, New York NY 10001	212-563-9656	R	1*	<.1
90	La'spec Industries Inc—*J Melamed*	2315 E 52nd St, Vernon CA 90058	323-588-8746	R	1*	<.1
91	Arc Light Efx Inc—*Gregory Smith*	9338 San Fernando Rd, Sun Valley CA 91352	818-394-6330	R	1*	<.1
92	Pacific Lighting Sales Inc—*Michael Everett*	23666 Birtcher Dr Ste, Lake Forest CA 92630	949-597-1633	R	1*	<.1
93	Traffic Systems and Technology LLC—*Jon Bondanella*	7853 Coppermine Dr, Manassas VA 20109	703-530-9655	R	1*	<.1

Note: An asterisk (*) indicates an estimated financial figure. The company type code used is as follows: R = Private, P = Public, S = Private Subsidiary, B = Public Subsidiary, D = Division, J = Joint Venture, I = Investment Fund.

COMPANY RANKINGS BY SALES WITHIN 4-DIGIT SIC

Rank	Company Name—*Executive Officer*	Address, City, State, Zip	Phone	Type	Fin	Empls
94	Tescor Technology Inc—*Edward Straszewski*	PO Box 606, Cedarburg WI 53012	262-377-4208	R	1*	<.1
95	Capitol Lighting Plastics—*Collin Millard*	271 Opportunity St Ste, Sacramento CA 95838	916-564-2788	R	1*	<.1
96	Roto Manufacturing Company Inc—*Roy Oto*	PO Box 1109, Fresno CA 93714	559-485-1464	R	1*	<.1
97	Cinemills Corp—*Carlos Demattos*	2021 N Lincoln St, Burbank CA 91504	818-843-4560	R	<1*	<.1

TOTALS: SIC 3648 Lighting Equipment Nec
Companies: 97 — 1,936 — 14.8

3651 Household Audio & Video Equipment

Rank	Company Name—*Executive Officer*	Address, City, State, Zip	Phone	Type	Fin	Empls
1	Sony Electronics Inc—*Phil Molyneux*	16530 Via Esprillo, San Diego CA 92127	858-942-2400	S	72,200*	180.5
2	Thomson Multimedia Inc—*Frederic Rose*	101 West 103rd street, Indianapolis IN 46290	317-587-3000	S	57,986*	32.5
3	Sony USA Inc—*Howard Stringer*	550 Madison Ave, New York NY 10022	212-833-6800	R	29,000	N/A
4	Philips Electronics North America Corp—*Scott M Weisenhoff*	3000 Minuteman Rd Ste, Andover MA 01810		D	6,690	20.9
5	Toshiba America Inc—*Masahiko Fukakushi*	1251 Ave of the Americ, New York NY 10020	212-596-0600	S	5,596*	8.0
6	Harman International Industries Inc—*Dinesh C Paliwal*	400 Atlantic St, Stamford CT 06901	203-328-3500	P	3,772	10.1
7	Vizio Inc—*William Wang*	39 Tesla, Irvine CA 92618	949-428-2525	R	2,712*	.2
8	Philips Consumer Electronics Co—*Gerard Klusterlee* Philips Electronics North America Corp	64 Perimeter Center E, Atlanta GA 30346	770-821-2629	S	2,674	8.0
9	Air Systems Components—*Terry O'Halloran*	1401 N Plano Rd, Richardson TX 75081	972-680-9126	D	2,240*	7.0
10	THOMSON Consumer Electronics Inc/RCA—*Frank E Dangeard*	10330 N Meridian St, Indianapolis IN 46290	317-587-3000	R	2,236*	3.9
11	Bose Corp—*Bob Maresca*	The Mountain, Framingham MA 01701	508-879-7330	R	2,000*	8.0
12	Mitsubishi Electric and Electronics USA—*Katsuya Takamiya*	PO Box 6007, Cypress CA 90630	714-220-2500	R	1,692*	3.0
13	MTX Audio	4545 E Baseline Rd, Phoenix AZ 85042	602-438-4545	S	1,343*	.8
14	BD Biosciences—*William Kozy*	2350 Qume Dr, San Jose CA 95131		S	1,195*	<.1
15	JBL Consumer Products—*John Carpanini* Harman Consumer Products	8400 Balboa Blvd, Northridge CA 91329	818-894-8850	S	989*	1.8
16	Sherborne Group Inc—*E Bramson*	135 E 57th St 32nd Fl, New York NY 10022	212-759-6301	R	870*	6.9
17	Zenith Electronics Corp—*Myeong-Kyu Ahn*	2000 Millbrook Dr, Lincolnshire IL 60069	847-391-7000	S	834	4.0
18	Avid Technology Worldwide Inc	1 Park W, Tewksbury MA 01876	978-640-6789	R	698*	1.6
19	Universal Electronics Inc—*Paul D Arling*	6101 Gateway Dr, Cypress CA 90630	714-820-1000	P	332	1.8
20	Rockford SalesCom Inc—*Jim Fosgate* Rockford Corp	600 S Rockford Dr, Tempe AZ 85281	480-967-3565	S	326*	.7
21	Peavey Electronics Corp—*Hartley Peavey*	5022 Hartley Peavey Dr, Meridian MS 39305	601-483-5365	R	271*	1.5
22	Hittite Microwave Corp—*Stephen G Daly*	2 Elizabeth Dr, Chelmsford MA 01824	978-250-3343	P	264	.5
23	DEI Holdings Inc—*Jim Minarik*	1 Viper Way, Vista CA 92081	760-598-6200	P	263	.6
24	Fender Musical Instruments Corp—*Matthew Janopaul*	8860 E Chaparral Rd St, Scottsdale AZ 85250	480-596-9690	R	261*	3.2
25	Sarnoff Corp—*Mark A Clifton*	PO Box 5300, Princeton NJ 08543	609-734-2553	S	230*	.5
26	Behavior Tech Computer Corp—*Daniel Yu*	4180 Business Center D, Fremont CA 94538	510-657-3956	R	223*	.5
27	QSC Audio Products Inc—*Barry Andrews*	1675 MacArthur Blvd, Costa Mesa CA 92626	714-754-6175	R	218*	.4
28	LOUD Technologies Inc—*Mark Graham*	16220 Wood-Red Rd NE, Woodinville WA 98072	425-892-6500	P	208	.5
29	Emerson Radio Corp—*Duncan Hon*	PO Box 430, Parsippany NJ 07054	973-884-5800	P	201	.1
30	Dielectric Communications—*Garrett VanAtta*	PO Box 949, Raymond ME 04071	207-655-8100	S	172*	.3
31	Toshiba America Electronic Components Inc—*Hideya Sakaida*	19900 Macarthur Blvd, Irvine CA 92612	949-623-2900	R	165*	2 3
32	Knowles Electronics Holdings Inc—*John Zei*	1151 Maplewood Dr, Itasca IL 60143	630-250-5100	S	114*	.2
33	Samson Technologies Inc—*Scott Goodman*	45 Gilpin Ave Ste 100, Hauppauge NY 11788	631-784-2200	R	110	<.1
34	Alienware Corp—*Nelson Gonzalez*	14591 SW 120 St, Miami FL 33186	305-251-9797	S	109*	.5
35	Harman Professional Signal Processing—*Rob Urry* Harman International Industries Inc	8760 Sandy Pkwy, Sandy UT 84070	801-566-8800	D	99*	.3
36	MPO Videotronics Inc—*Larry Kaiser*	5069 Maureen Ln, Moorpark CA 93021	805-499-8513	R	98*	.2
37	DTS Inc—*Jon Kirchner*	5220 Las Virgenes Rd, Calabasas CA 91302	818-436-1000	P	87	.2
38	Bosch Communications Systems—*Thomas Hanson*	12000 Portland Ave, Burnsville MN 55337	952-884-4051	R	85*	.3
39	Roku Inc—*Anthony Wood*	12980 Saratoga Ave, Saratoga CA 95070		R	60	<.1
40	ASA Corp—*Brent Barrow*	2602 Marina Dr, Elkhart IN 46514	574-264-3135	R	59*	.1
41	Marshall Optical Systems Inc—*Leonard Marshall*	1910 E Maple Ave, El Segundo CA 90245	310-333-0606	S	58*	.1
42	Rockford Corp—*William Jackson*	600 S Rockford Dr, Tempe AZ 85281	480-967-3565	P	54	.1
43	Harman Consumer Products—*Dinesh Paliwal* Harman International Industries Inc	8500 Balboa Blvd, Northridge CA 91329	818-893-8411	S	48*	.2
44	Digital Spectrum Solutions—*John Parsa*	17811 Mitchell N, Irvine CA 92614	949-252-1111	R	43*	.1
45	Koss Corp—*Michael J Koss*	4129 N Port Washington, Milwaukee WI 53212	414-964-5000	P	42	.1
46	Touchtunes Music Corp—*Charles Goldstuck*	3455 Salt Creek Lane, Arlington Heights IL 60005	847-419-3300	R	38	.1
47	Cambridge SoundWorks Inc—*Michael Mo*	120 Water St, North Andover MA 01845	978-623-4400	S	38*	.3
48	Renkus-Heinz Inc—*Harro Heinz*	19201 Cook St, Foothill Ranch CA 92610	949-588-9997	R	37*	.1
49	Metra Electronics Corp—*William Jones*	460 Walker St, Holly Hill FL 32117	386-257-1186	R	34*	.5
50	Phoenix Gold International Inc—*Jonathan Cooley*	13190 56th Court Ste 4, Clearwater FL 33760	727-572-9255	R	33*	.2
51	HT Electronics Inc—*Chuck Lokenvitz*	50 E Greg St Ste 112, Sparks NV 89431	775-331-5401	R	31*	<.1
52	SnapAV—*Jay Faison*	1800 Continental Blvd, Charlotte NC 28273		R	30	.1
53	Lexicon Inc Harman International Industries Inc	1718 W Mishawaka Rd, Elkhart IN 46517	516-594-0300	S	30*	.1
54	Antique Apparatus Co—*Glen Streeter*	2335 W 208th St, Torrance CA 90501	310-328-1306	R	29*	.1
55	Kinyo Company Inc—*Calvin Wong*	14235 Lomitas Ave, La Puente CA 91746	626-333-3711	R	29*	<.1
56	Pioneer North America Inc—*Tom Haga*	2265 E 220th St, Long Beach CA 90810	310-952-2000	S	28*	.3
57	LRAD Corp—*Thomas R Brown*	15378 Ave of Science S, San Diego CA 92128	858-676-1112	P	27	<.1
58	Lectrosonics Inc—*Larry Fisher*	PO Box 15900, Rio Rancho NM 87174	505-892-4501	R	26*	.2
59	Rih Inc—*J Johnson*	1500 Union Ave SE, Grand Rapids MI 49507	616-243-3633	R	26*	.2
60	Eminence Speaker LLC—*Chris Rose*	PO Box 360, Eminence KY 40019	502-845-5622	R	25*	.1
61	Spectra Systems Corp—*Nabil M Lawandy*	321 S Main St Ste 102, Providence RI 02903	401-274-4700	R	25*	.1
62	Immersive Media Co—*Albert Lin*	2407 SE 10th Ave, Portland OR 97214	503-231-2656	R	25*	<.1
63	Scosche Industries Inc—*Roger Alves*	1550 Pacific Ave, Oxnard CA 93033	805-486-4450	R	24*	.2
64	Meyer Sound Laboratories Inc—*John Meyer*	2832 San Pablo Ave, Berkeley CA 94702	510-486-1166	R	23*	.2
65	JTI Inc	1181 S Rogers Cir Ste, Boca Raton FL 33487	561-998-0211	R	21*	<.1
66	Sdi Technologies Inc—*Ezra Ashkenazi*	1299 Main St, Rahway NJ 07065	732-574-9000	R	20*	.1
67	VocalTec Communication Inc—*Joseph Albagli*	2 Executive Dr Ste 592, Fort Lee NJ 07024	201-228-7000	S	19*	.2
68	Communication Products Corp Loudspeaker Component Div Loudspeaker Components LLC	7596 US Hwy 61 S, Lancaster WI 53813	608-723-2127	D	19*	.1
69	Apex Digital Inc (Walnut California)—*David Ji*	301 Brea Canyon Rd, Walnut CA 91789	909-923-8686	R	18*	<.1
70	Russound/Fmp Inc—*Joe Brouillet*	5 Forbes Rd Ste 1, Newmarket NH 03857	603-659-5170	R	18*	.2
71	Goto California Inc—*Saburo Goto*	6120 Bus Ctr Ct Ste F2, San Diego CA 92154	619-691-8722	R	17*	.2
72	D2Audio Inc—*Brian Wong*	7600 B Capital of Texa, Austin TX 78731	512-343-9301	R	17*	<.1
73	Wireless Technology Inc—*Phil Fancher*	2064 Eastman Ave Ste 1, Ventura CA 93003	805-339-9696	R	15*	<.1
74	Akoo International Inc—*Elise McVeigh*	5600 N River Ave, Rosemont IL 60018	847-737-4400	R	14*	<.1

Rank	Company Name—Executive Officer	Address, City, State, Zip	Phone	Type	Fin	Empls
75	Sanyo Fisher Corp—Shin Oka	21605 Plummer St, Chatsworth CA 91311	818-998-7322	S	14*	.1
76	Genex Technologies Inc—Gino Pereira	10411 Motor City Dr St, Bethesda MD 20817	301-767-2810	R	14*	<.1
77	Thermo CIDTEC—Marc N Casper	101 Commerce Blvd, Liverpool NY 13088	315-451-9410	S	14*	<.1
78	Tv Ears Inc—George Dennis	2701 Via Orange Way St, Spring Valley CA 91978	619-797-1605	R	14*	<.1
79	Ksc Industries Inc—Jeffrey King	881 Kuhn Dr Ste 200, Chula Vista CA 91914	619-671-0110	R	13*	<.1
80	Lightspeed Technologies Inc—Jerry Ramey	11509 Sw Herman Rd, Tualatin OR 97062	503-684-5538	R	13*	.1
81	Innovative Electronic Designs—Hardison Martin	9701 Taylorsville Rd, Louisville KY 40299	502-267-7436	R	13*	.1
82	Meridian America Inc—Peter Wellikoff	8055 Troon Cir Ste C, Austell GA 30168	404-344-7111	R	13*	.1
83	Velodyne Acoustics Inc—David Hall	345 Digital Dr, Morgan Hill CA 95037	408-465-2800	R	12*	.1
84	Southern Audio Services Inc—Jon Jordan	15049 Florida Blvd, Baton Rouge LA 70819	225-272-7135	R	12*	.1
85	Gci Technologies Corp—Artie Cabasso	1 Mayfield Ave, Edison NJ 08837	732-346-0061	R	12*	.1
86	Eti Sound Systems Inc—Eli El-Kiss	3383 E Gage Ave, Huntington Park CA 90255	323-277-4100	R	12*	.1
87	Whirlwind Music Distributors Inc—Michael Laiacona	99 Ling Rd, Rochester NY 14612	585-663-8820	R	11*	.1
88	Quam-Nichols Co—William Little	234 E Marquette Rd Ste, Chicago IL 60637	773-488-5800	R	11*	.1
89	Speakercraft LLC—Jeremy Burkhardt	940 Columbia Ave, Riverside CA 92507	951-787-0543	R	11*	.1
90	Micronas USA Inc—James Mannos	560 S Winchester Blvd, San Jose CA 95128	408-625-1200	R	11*	.1
91	Cutting Edge Bridgette Inc—Michael Ehman	1825 Gillespie Way Ste, El Cajon CA 92020	619-258-7800	R	11*	<.1
92	Nady Systems Inc—John Nady	6701 Shellmound St, Emeryville CA 94608	510-652-2411	R	11*	.1
93	Mesa/Boogie Ltd—Randall Smith	1317 Ross St, Petaluma CA 94954	707-778-6565	R	11*	.1
94	Community Light and Sound Inc—Bruce Howze	333 E 5th St, Chester PA 19013	610-876-3400	R	11*	.1
95	United Gasket Corp—Mark Pahios	1633 S 55th Ave, Cicero IL 60804	708-656-3700	R	10*	.1
96	Polyline Corp—Ed Kaiser	845 N Church St, Elmhurst IL 60126	630-993-2700	R	10*	.1
97	ReQuest Inc (Ballston Spa New York)—Peter Cholnoky	100 Saratoga Village B, Ballston Spa NY 12020	518-899-1254	R	10*	.1
98	Digital Techniques Inc—Richard Mueller	13500 Watertown Plank, Elm Grove WI 53122	262-860-1000	R	10*	<.1
99	Triad Speakers Inc—Larry Pexton	15835 Ne Cameron Blvd, Portland OR 97230	503-256-2600	R	10*	.1
100	Credence Speakers Inc—Eugene Brandt	13075 Ogden Landing Rd, Kevil KY 42053	270-462-2161	R	10*	.1
101	California Instruments Corp—Brian Hull	9250 Brown Deer Rd, San Diego CA 92121	858-450-0085	D	9*	.1
102	Design Direct Sound LLC—Ivan Cole	3501 Interstate 35E S, Waxahachie TX 75165	972-923-9922	R	9*	<.1
103	Soldano Custom Amplification—Michael J Soldano Jr	4233 21st Ave W, Seattle WA 98199	206-781-4636	R	9*	<.1
104	Ten-Lab—Nidia Beltramo	27346 Oak Summit Rd, Agoura Hills CA 91301		R	9*	<.1
105	Wilson Audio Specialties Inc—David Wilson	2233 Mountain Vista Ln, Provo UT 84606	801-377-2233	R	8*	<.1
106	LR Baggs Co—Lloyd Baggs	483 N Frontage Rd, Nipomo CA 93444	805-929-3545	R	8*	<.1
107	Production Resource Group LLC—Fred Gallo	539 Temple Hill Rd, New Windsor NY 12553	845-567-5700	R	8*	.1
108	Gallien Technology Inc—Robert Gallien	2234 Industrial Dr, Stockton CA 95206	209-234-7300	R	8*	.1
109	Revolabs Inc—Martin Bodley	144 N Rd Ste 3250, Sudbury MA 01776	978-610-5400	R	8*	.1
110	Primo Microphones Inc—Osamu Wada	PO Box 1570, Mckinney TX 75070	972-548-9807	R	8*	.1
111	Dana Innovations Inc—Scott Struthers	212 Avenida Fabricante, San Clemente CA 92672	949-492-7777	R	7*	.1
112	Marantz America LLC	100 Corporate Dr, Mahwah NJ 07430	201-762-6500	S	7*	.1
113	Q Power Inc—Michael Shapiro	5610 Savoy Dr, Houston TX 77036	713-266-5295	R	6*	.1
114	GLW Inc—William B Owen	1024 Firestone Pky, La Vergne TN 37086	615-641-7200	R	6*	.1
115	Loudspeaker Components LLC—Neal Kirschbaum	7596 US Hwy 61 S, Lancaster WI 53813	608-723-2127	R	6*	.1
116	Sierra Video Systems—Adel Ghanem	PO Box 2462, Grass Valley CA 95945	530-478-1000	R	6*	.1
117	TIC Corp—Jimmy Lin	15224 E Stafford Rd, City of Industry CA 91744	626-968-0211	R	6*	<.1
118	Sherwood America Inc—Ilny Oh	14730 Beach Blvd Ste10, LaMirada CA 90638	562-741-0960	R	6*	<.1
119	Pulseworks LLC—Cleve Lawrence	5100 Highlands Pkwy Se, Smyrna GA 30082	770-916-1722	R	6*	.1
120	Misco/Minneapolis Speaker Company Inc—Dan Digre	2637 32nd Ave S, Minneapolis MN 55406	612-825-1010	R	5*	<.1
121	Electronic Engineering and Manufacturing Inc—Thomas Walker	22410 70th Ave W Ste 1, Mountlake Terrace WA 98043	425-775-8461	R	5*	<.1
122	Frazier Loudspeakers—Jay Mitchell	3030 Canton St, Dallas TX 75226	214-741-7136	R	5*	<.1
123	Harvey C Waters Inc—Harvey Waters	13780 E Rice Pl Ste 20, Aurora CO 80015	303-400-6312	R	5*	<.1
124	Musimatic Electronics Inc—Don McCampbell	6659 Tribble St, Lithonia GA 30058	770-484-8434	R	5*	<.1
125	Polaris Industries—Tom Tiller	3158 Process Dr, Norcross GA 30071	678-405-6080	R	5*	<.1
126	Dalbec Audio Lab—Richard Dalbec	58 King St, Troy NY 12180	518-272-7098	R	5*	<.1
127	Integrated Systems Corp—Douglas Underhill	7819 E Paradise Ln, Scottsdale AZ 85260	480-998-4130	R	5*	<.1
128	Cary Audio Design LLC	1020 Goodworth Dr, Apex NC 27539	919-355-0010	R	5*	<.1
129	Soundtube Entertainment Inc—David Wiener	6430 Bus Prk Loop Rd A, Park City UT 84098	435-647-9555	R	5*	<.1
130	Ultimate Sound Inc—Robert Chiu	163 University Pkwy, Pomona CA 91768	909-594-2604	R	4*	<.1
131	Astra Products Company Incorporated Of Tampa—Steve Ladoniczki	PO Box 711, Oldsmar FL 34677	813-855-3021	R	4*	<.1
132	Earthquake Sound Corp—Sabina Hohmann	2727 Mccone Ave, Hayward CA 94545	510-732-1000	R	4*	<.1
133	Sound Enhancement Products Inc—Randy Wright	325 Cary Point Dr, Cary IL 60013	847-639-4646	R	4*	<.1
134	Swanagon Inc—John Swanagon	940 Graland Pl, Highlands Ranch CO 80126	720-348-6951	R	4*	<.1
135	Quality Musical Systems Inc—Daniel Wilson	PO Box 850, Candler NC 28715	828-667-5719	R	4*	<.1
136	Magnepan Inc—James Winey	1645 9th St, Saint Paul MN 55110	651-426-1645	R	3*	<.1
137	Meisei Inc—Tsunaki Rikiishi	300 Eastgate Dr, Danville IL 61834	217-431-8551	R	3*	<.1
138	Rolls Corp—Marilyn Difrancesco	5968 S 350 W, Salt Lake City UT 84107	801-263-9053	R	3*	<.1
139	Mccauley Sound Inc—Thomas Mccauley	PO Box 731024, Puyallup WA 98373	253-848-0363	R	3*	<.1
140	Comtek Communications Technology Inc—Ralph Belgique	357 W 2700 S, Salt Lake City UT 84115	801-466-3463	R	3*	<.1
141	Jazz Inc	1355 Darius Ct, City of Industry CA 91745	626-336-2689	R	3*	<.1
142	EgglestonWorks LLC—Jim Thompson	540 Cumberland St, Memphis TN 38112	901-525-1100	R	3*	<.1
143	Jlab Audio—Josh Rosenfield	PO Box 43692, Tucson AZ 85733		R	3*	<.1
144	Legacy Audio Inc—Bill Dudleston	3023 Sangamon Ave, Springfield IL 62702	217-544-3178	S	3*	<.1
145	Record Play Tek Inc—Michael H Stoll	PO Box 790, Bristol IN 46507	574-848-5233	R	3*	<.1
146	Advanced Media Services Inc—Joseph Jangro	24 Keewaydin Dr, Salem NH 03079	603-898-7500	R	3*	<.1
147	Automated Processes Inc—Larry Droppa	8301 Patuxent Range Rd, Jessup MD 20794	301-776-7879	R	3*	<.1
148	Resonance Inc—Jassa Langford	1141 Nw 1st St, Oklahoma City OK 73106	405-239-2800	R	3*	<.1
149	Tara Labs Inc—Merrill Bergs	1020 Benson Way, Ashland OR 97520	541-488-6465	R	3*	<.1
150	Ayre Acoustics Inc—Charles Hansen	2300 Central Ave Ste B, Boulder CO 80301	303-442-7300	R	3*	<.1
151	Galaxy Audio Inc—Brock Jabara	PO Box 16285, Wichita KS 67216	316-263-2852	R	3*	<.1
152	Vtl Amplifiers Inc—Luke Manley	4774 Murietta Stste 10, Chino CA 91710	909-627-5944	R	2*	<.1
153	Edcor Electronics Corp—Phyllis Weston	7130 National Parks Hw, Carlsbad NM 88220	575-887-6790	R	2*	<.1
154	Keywest Technology Inc—Koytt Nichols	14563 W 96th Ter, Shawnee Mission KS 66215	913-492-4666	R	2*	<.1
155	Shure Electronics—Robert Godlewski	21 Zane Grey St Ste A, El Paso TX 79906	915-782-2800	R	2*	<.1
156	Mxros Inc—Mark Rose	422 Lee Rd, Mineral Wells TX 76067	940-327-8189	R	2*	<.1
157	Bretford Manufacturing Inc—David Petrick	11000 Seymour Ave, Franklin Park IL 60131	847-678-2545	R	2*	.4
158	Hawley Products Inc—Fred Yocum	1567 N 8th St, Paducah KY 42001	270-442-2344	R	2*	<.1
159	Olsen Audio Group Inc—Craig Olsen	7845 E Evans Rd Ste E, Scottsdale AZ 85260	480-998-7140	R	2*	<.1
160	Electric Picture Display Systems Inc—Robert Higgins	5131 Industry Dr Ste 1, Melbourne FL 32940	321-757-8484	R	2*	<.1
161	Abekas Inc (Menlo Park California)—Junaid Sheikh	1090 O'Brien Dr, Menlo Park CA 94025	650-470-0900	R	2*	<.1
162	Leda Corp—Joseph Tung	7080 Kearny Dr, Huntington Beach CA 92648	714-841-7821	R	2*	<.1
163	Gulick Brothers House Of Sound—Andy Gulick	21430 N 20th Ave, Phoenix AZ 85027	623-580-9338	R	2*	<.1

Note: An asterisk (*) indicates an estimated financial figure. The company type code used is as follows: R = Private, P = Public, S = Private Subsidiary, B = Public Subsidiary, D = Division, J = Joint Venture, I = Investment Fund.

COMPANY RANKINGS BY SALES WITHIN 4-DIGIT SIC

Rank	Company Name—*Executive Officer*	Address, City, State, Zip	Phone	Type	Fin	Empls
164	Vandersteen Audio Inc—*Richard Vandersteen*	116 W 4th St, Hanford CA 93230	559-582-0324	R	2*	<.1
165	Intelix LLC—*Steven Cohan*	2222 Pleasant View Rd, Middleton WI 53562	608-831-0880	R	2*	<.1
166	Audix Corporation USA—*Cliff Castle*	9400 Sw Barber St Ste, Wilsonville OR 97070	503-682-6933	R	2*	<.1
167	Electronic Auto Systems Inc—*Chang Tong*	9855 Joe Vargas Way, South El Monte CA 91733	626-575-5098	R	2*	<.1
168	Diem Digital Interiors LLC—*Megan Beasley*	2271 Sir Amant Dr, Lewisville TX 75056	972-899-1189	R	2*	<.1
169	H2o Audio Inc—*Kristian Rauhala*	11010 Roselle St, San Diego CA 92121	858-623-0339	R	2*	<.1
170	Convergent Audio Tech Inc—*Ken Stevens*	85 High Tech Dr, Rush NY 14543	585-359-2700	R	2*	<.1
171	WorxAudio Technologies Inc—*Hugh Sarvis*	620 S Elm St Ste 353, Greensboro NC 27406	336-275-7474	R	2*	<.1
172	Digital Connection—*Richard Martin*	714 Adams Ave Ste 103, Huntington Beach CA 92648	714-960-9814	R	2*	<.1
173	Viper Logic Corp—*Lance Conway*	1440 S Manzanita Ave, Palm Springs CA 92264	760-320-1414	R	2*	<.1
174	Owens Audio Video Design Inc—*Robert Owens*	7305 Gladwin Ct, Orlando FL 32836	407-363-1551	R	2*	<.1
175	CyberData Systems Inc—*Phil Goldman*	100 Glen Ave, Newton MA 02459	617-969-7700	R	2*	<.1
176	BIC America Inc	925 N Shepard St, Anaheim CA 92806		D	2*	N/A
177	Ae Techron Inc—*Larry Shank*	2507 Warren St, Elkhart IN 46516	574-295-9495	R	2*	<.1
178	Big Boys Electronics And Entertainment Ltd—*Bernard Afryman*	5070 N Kimberly Ave, Chicago IL 60630	773-304-0505	R	2*	<.1
179	Digital Sound and Lighting LLC—*Rudy Nickens*	1717 Olive St Fl 7, Saint Louis MO 63103	314-725-6415	R	2*	<.1
180	Headroom Corp—*Susan Smith*	2020 Gilkerson Dr, Bozeman MT 59715	406-587-9466	R	2*	<.1
181	Video Technology Services Inc—*Andres Sierra*	5 Aerial Way Ste 300, Syosset NY 11791	516-937-9700	R	2*	<.1
182	Bayview Entertainment LLC	107 Pink St, Hackensack NJ 07601	201-488-6110	R	2*	<.1
183	360 Systems—*Robert Easton*	3281 Grande Vista Dr, Thousand Oaks CA 91320	818-991-0360	R	2*	<.1
184	Hartley Loudspeakers Inc—*Richard Schmetterer*	5732 Oleander Dr, Wilmington NC 28403	910-392-4373	R	2*	<.1
185	Pace Scientific Inc—*Joseph Dobson*	PO Box 4418, Mooresville NC 28117	704-799-0688	R	2*	<.1
186	Cutting Edge Communications Inc—*Andre Metzger*	608 N Porter Ave, Norman OK 73071	405-360-7409	R	2*	<.1
187	Pamek Trading Corp—*Harold Ribeiro*	240 Gray Rd, Falmouth ME 04105	207-878-5550	R	2*	<.1
188	American Contract Assembly Corp—*Tenney Rensvold*	12432 Hwy 99 Bldg A78, Everett WA 98204	425-357-5650	R	1*	<.1
189	Oxmoor Corporation LLC—*Joe Bennett*	309 Cahaba Valley Pkwy, Pelham AL 35124	205-982-8200	R	1*	<.1
190	Link Electronics Inc—*Robert Henson*	2137 Rust Ave, Cape Girardeau MO 63703	573-334-4433	R	1*	<.1
191	Ksi Professional LLC	3500 Parkdale Ave, Baltimore MD 21211	410-383-2167	R	1*	<.1
192	Hudson Access Group Ii—*Thomas Mendoza*	2460 Bramfield Way, Hudson OH 44236	330-283-6214	R	1*	<.1
193	Recordex Manufacturing Inc—*Wayne Wiseman*	4080 Oak Park Dr, Suwanee GA 30024	478-237-5501	R	1*	<.1
194	Countryman Associates Inc—*Carl Countryman*	417 Stanford Ave, Redwood City CA 94063	650-364-9988	R	1*	<.1
195	Parasound Products Inc—*Richard Schram*	2250 Mckinnon Ave, San Francisco CA 94124	415-397-7100	R	1*	<.1
196	Vht Amplification Inc—*Steven Fryette*	1201 S Flower St, Burbank CA 91502	818-846-4000	R	1*	<.1
197	Pacesetter Electronics Inc—*Peter Marsac*	400 Trade Ctr Dr E, Saint Peters MO 63376	636-379-4222	R	1*	<.1
198	Dage-Mti Of Michigan City Inc—*A Moore*	701 N Roeske Ave, Michigan City IN 46360	219-872-5514	R	1*	<.1
199	Alumapro Inc—*Ken Meyer*	1 Union Special Plz, Huntley IL 60142	224-569-3650	R	1*	<.1
200	White Instruments—*Carl Van Ryswyk*	PO Box 90003, Austin TX 78709	512-389-5358	R	1*	<.1
201	Matrix Stream Technologies Inc—*Jack Chung*	1840 Gateway Dr Ste 20, San Mateo CA 94404	650-292-4982	R	1*	<.1
202	Larcan-TTC Inc—*James Wilson*	1390 Overlook Dr, Lafayette CO 80026	303-665-8000	R	1*	<.1
203	Fast Forward Video Inc—*Paul DeKeyser*	1151 Duryea Ave, Irvine CA 92614	949-852-8404	R	1*	<.1
204	Tkm Technologies Inc—*Mike Moroff*	585 Bicycle Path Ste 2, Port Jefferson Station NY 11776	631-474-4700	R	1*	<.1
205	Micro Technology Unlimited—*David Cox*	6900 Six Forks Rd Ste, Raleigh NC 27615	919-870-0344	R	1*	<.1
206	Pierre M Sprey Inc—*Pierre Sprey*	5311 Solomons Island R, Lothian MD 20711	410-867-7794	R	1*	<.1
207	Green Mountain Audio LLC—*Roy Johnson*	3333-D N El Paso St, Colorado Springs CO 80907	719-636-2500	R	1*	<.1
208	Ten Technology—*John Lin*	555 E Ocean Blvd Ste 1, Long Beach CA 90802	408-548-0018	R	1*	<.1
209	Sondpex Corporation Of America LLC—*Chuck Chen*	2031 Rte 130 Unit K, Monmouth Junction NJ 08852	732-940-4430	R	1*	<.1
210	TalkPoint Communications Inc—*Nick Balletta*	100 William St, New York NY 10038	212-909-2900	R	1	<.1
211	Monolithic Sound Inc—*Gregory Schug*	PO Box 448, Nipomo CA 93444	805-929-3251	R	1*	<.1
212	Nykon Inc—*Craig Cuvelier*	8175 Stell Rd, Sodus NY 14551	315-483-0504	R	1*	<.1
213	Mega Systems Inc—*Guillermo Cabda*	5718 Kenwick St, San Antonio TX 78238	210-684-2600	R	1*	<.1
214	Fire Fox Technologies LLC	2220 N 200 E, Provo UT 84604	801-377-1882	R	1*	<.1
215	Nova Audio Inc—*David Lee*	PO Box 40569, Houston TX 77240	713-466-1880	R	1*	<.1
216	HAS Production Inc—*Larry Hall*	3000 S Highland Dr Ste, Las Vegas NV 89109	702-434-2384	R	1*	<.1
217	Jeff Rowland Design Group Inc—*Jeff Rowland*	PO Box 7231, Colorado Springs CO 80933	719-473-1181	R	1*	<.1
218	Sonic Craft Inc—*Jeff Glowacki*	PO Box 88, Hot Springs AR 71902	501-620-4444	R	1*	<.1
219	Guy G Veralrud—*Guy Veralrud*	PO Box 1437, Cedar Ridge CA 95924	530-477-7323	R	1*	<.1
220	Atma-Sphere Music Systems—*Ralph Karsten*	1742 Selby Ave, Saint Paul MN 55104	651-690-2246	R	1*	<.1
221	Milbert Corp—*Al Milbert*	PO Box 1027, Germantown MD 20875	301-963-9355	R	1*	<.1
222	Ac Cetera Inc—*Mark Tarshis*	3120 Banksville Rd, Pittsburgh PA 15216	412-344-8609	R	1*	<.1
223	Dicon Technologies Inc—*Greg Sutherland*	2810 Louetta Rd Ste 7, Spring TX 77388	281-350-5005	R	1*	<.1
224	Navone Engineering Inc—*David Navone*	4119 Coronado Ave Ste, Stockton CA 95204	209-465-6139	R	1*	<.1
225	Jps Labs LLC	7601 Seneca St, East Aurora NY 14052	716-656-0810	R	1*	<.1
226	Opamp Labs Inc—*Bela Losmandy*	1033 N Sycamore Ave, Los Angeles CA 90038	323-934-3566	R	1*	<.1
227	Techtronics LLC	14 Fairfield Ave, Westport CT 06880	203-341-9270	R	1*	<.1
228	Digital Connection—*Frank Culmone*	4135 W Wigwam Ave, Las Vegas NV 89139	702-269-4559	R	1*	<.1
229	Eminent Technology Inc—*Bruce Thigpen*	225 E Palmer Ave, Tallahassee FL 32301	850-575-5655	R	1*	<.1
230	UHF Associates—*Gene Hill*	6068 Dolores Dr, Rohnert Park CA 94928	707-584-7844	R	1*	<.1
231	Universal Satellite Communications Inc—*Juan Renteria*	13426 Rosecrans Ave St, Norwalk CA 90650	562-483-4800	R	1*	<.1
232	Innersound LLC—*Raj Varma*	865 Kalmia Ave, Boulder CO 80304	303-939-0074	R	1*	<.1
233	Radio Oem Inc—*David Zima*	1408 Ctr Ave, Oostburg WI 53070	920-564-6620	R	<1*	<.1
234	Hilton Audio Products Inc—*Richard Henschel*	1033 Shary Cir Ste E, Concord CA 94518	925-682-8390	R	<1*	<.1
235	Sonic Inc—*Gary Hahlbeck*	3383 E Layton Ave Stop, Cudahy WI 53110	414-483-5091	R	<1*	<.1
236	Inter Electronics Corp—*Enrique Fonseca*	PO Box 1408, Solana Beach CA 92075	619-476-0577	R	<1*	<.1
237	Courterport Corp—*John Lightstone*	16938 Pidgeon Meadow R, Flushing NY 11358	718-961-4611	R	<1*	<.1
238	Video-Codes Inc—*Avi Rubinstein*	21 Firstfield Rd, Gaithersburg MD 20878	301-330-4772	R	<1*	<.1
239	Macpherson Inc—*Gordon Napes*	5520 Touhy Ave Ste 1, Skokie IL 60077	847-674-3535	R	<1*	<.1
240	Cunningham Trey—*Trey Cunningham*	7326 N Vandiver Rd, San Antonio TX 78209	210-823-6986	R	<1*	<.1
241	Rivertree Productions Inc—*John Bodkin*	PO Box 410, Bradford NH 03221	603-938-5120	R	<1*	<.1
242	Chapman Audio Systems—*Stuart Jones*	PO Box 140, Vashon WA 98070	206-463-3008	R	<1*	<.1
243	Devance Av Design Inc—*Dana Devance*	15932 Midway Rd, Addison TX 75001	214-389-4985	R	<1*	<.1
244	Roy Johnston—*Roy Johnston*	3333 N El Paso St Ste, Colorado Springs CO 80907	719-636-2500	R	<1*	<.1
245	Zed Audio Corp—*Stephen Mantz*	743 Cochran St Ste D, Simi Valley CA 93065	805-526-5315	R	<1*	<.1
246	DLW Audio Consultants Inc—*Pamela Wenger*	11 Stevens Rd, Stevens PA 17578	717-336-6675	R	<1*	<.1
247	Plus One Engineering—*Kenneth Brown*	PO Box 937, Placentia CA 92871	714-223-6600	R	<1*	<.1
248	Peter-Lisand Machine Corp—*Peter Guasti*	262 Voorhis Ave, New Milford NJ 07646	201-943-5600	R	<1*	<.1
249	Shahinian Acoustics Ltd—*Richard Shahinian*	37 Cedarhurst Ave Ste, Medford NY 11763	631-736-0033	R	<1*	<.1
250	Speaker Factory—*Ray Ihndris*	24337 Hilton Pl, Gaithersburg MD 20882	301-253-4611	R	<1*	<.1
251	Stephen Paul Audio Inc—*Stephen Paul*	10834 Burbank Blvd Ste, North Hollywood CA 91601	818-980-4772	R	<1*	<.1
252	Alarmco—*Ron Cook*	1 Bailey Dr, Guilford CT 06437	203-458-2646	R	<1*	<.1
253	Deborah Edmonson—*Deborah Edmonson*	1840 Woodmoor Dr Ste 1, Monument CO 80132	719-481-8346	R	<1*	<.1

Rank	Company Name—*Executive Officer*	Address, City, State, Zip	Phone	Type	Fin	Empls
254	First Sound Inc—*Emmanuel Go*	833 Sw Sunset Blvd L57, Renton WA 98057	425-271-7486	R	<1*	<.1
255	New Life Electronics Inc—*Robert Puff*	1350 Buffalo Rd Ste 2, Rochester NY 14624	585-436-5450	R	<1*	<.1
256	Teres Audio Inc—*Chris Brady*	80 Garden Ctr Ste 10, Broomfield CO 80020	303-466-1743	R	<1*	<.1
257	Vintage Performance LLC—*Carl Dudesh*	PO Box 200, Norfolk CT 06058	860-542-5753	R	<1*	<.1
258	Transcendent Sound Inc—*Bruce Rozenblit*	PO Box 22547, Kansas City MO 64113	816-333-7358	R	<1*	<.1
259	John Marovskis Audio System Inc—*John Marovskis*	2889 Roebling Ave, Bronx NY 10461	718-892-7419	R	<1*	<.1
260	Professional Systems Engineering Inc—*Dean Klinefelter*	7757 Aetna Ave Ne, Monticello MN 55362	763-295-1710	R	<1*	<.1
261	Threshold Audio Inc—*David Lee*	PO Box 41736, Houston TX 77241	713-466-1411	R	<1*	<.1
262	Technical Sound Development—*Kenneth Silvers*	3917 Kensington Ave, Kansas City MO 64130	816-924-5255	R	<1*	<.1
263	Sharp Electronics Corp	1 Sharp Plz, Mahwah NJ 07430	201-529-8200	S	N/A	2.5
264	New Era Production—*Benny Smith*	1912 E Dale St, Springfield MO 65803	417-869-7476	R	N/A	<.1

TOTALS: SIC 3651 Household Audio & Video Equipment
Companies: 264   200,340   322.9

3652 Prerecorded Records & Tapes

Rank	Company Name—*Executive Officer*	Address, City, State, Zip	Phone	Type	Fin	Empls
1	Sony Music Entertainment Inc—*Doug Morris*	550 Madison Ave, New York NY 10022	212-833-8000	S	1,500*	10.0
2	Technicolor Videocassette	28301 Schoolcraft Rd, Livonia MI 48150	734-853-3800	S	787*	.8
3	Universal Music Group—*Doug Morris*	1755 Broadway, New York NY 10019	212-841-8000	S	545*	1.1
4	Music City Optical Media Inc—*Tom Beld*	1045 Firestone Pkwy, La Vergne TN 37086	615-641-2271	R	500*	.3
5	WEA Manufacturing Inc—*Thomas Costabile*	Mid Valley Industria, Olyphant PA 18447	570-383-3291	S	364	2.8
6	Capitol Records Inc—*Andrew Slater*	1750 N Vine St, Hollywood CA 90028	323-462-6252	R	286*	.2
7	Muzak LLC—*Steven Richards*	3318 Lakemont Blvd, Fort Mill SC 29708	803-396-3000	S	250*	1.2
8	Sony Disc Manufacturing—*Rolf Schmidt-Holtz* Sony Music Entertainment Inc	123 International Way, Springfield OR 97477	541-988-8000	S	183*	.4
9	Integrity Media Inc—*P Michael Coleman*	PO Box 851389, Mobile AL 36685	251-633-9000	R	102*	.3
10	Hollywood Records—*Bob Cavallo*	500 S Buena Vista St, Burbank CA 91521	818-560-5670	R	97*	.1
11	Cinram Inc—*Jaime Ovadia*	1600 Rich Rd, Richmond IN 47374	765-962-9511	S	84*	.7
12	Integrity Music—*Michael Coleman*	4050 Lee Vance View, Colorado Springs CO 80918		D	67*	.1
13	Orchard The—*Brad Navin*	23 E 4th St 3rd Fl, New York NY 10003	212-201-9280	R	62	.1
14	Rykodisc Inc—*George Bruntnell*	1290 Avenue of America, New York NY 10003	212-287-6100	R	50*	.1
15	Motown Record Company LP—*Sylvia Rhone* Universal Music Group	1755 Broadway 6th Fl, New York NY 10019	212-841-8600	S	46*	.1
16	Univision Music Inc—*Gus Lopez*	5820 Canoga Ave Ste 30, Woodland Hills CA 91367	818-577-4700	S	43*	.1
17	Beachbody LLC—*Carl Daikeler*	3301 Exposition Blvd 3, Santa Monica CA 90404	323-904-5600	R	35*	<.1
18	Eastern Standard Productions Inc	37 John Glenn Dr, Buffalo NY 14228	716-691-7631	R	31*	<.1
19	Virgin Records America Inc—*Ray Cooper*	1750 Vine St, Los Angeles CA 90028	323-462-6252	R	27*	.3
20	Singing Machine Company Inc—*Gary Atkinson*	6301 NW 5th Way Ste 29, Fort Lauderdale FL 33309	954-596-1000	P	19	<.1
21	Magnetix Corp—*William Hohns*	3600 E Commerce Pl, Orlando FL 32808	407-926-2400	R	19*	.2
22	Hainbo Record Manufacturing Corp—*Steve Sheldon*	8960 Eton Ave, Canoga Park CA 91304	818-280-1100	R	18*	.2
23	Sugo Music Co—*Scott Kellner*	80 Cabrillo Hwy N Ste, Half Moon Bay CA 94019		R	17*	<.1
24	Optical Disc Solutions Inc—*Fred Austerman*	1767 Sheridan St, Richmond IN 47374	765-935-7574	R	15*	.1
25	Fantasy Inc—*Ralph Kaffel*	2600 10th St Ste 100, Berkeley CA 94710	510-549-2500	R	11*	.1
26	Axcel Photonics Inc—*Jim Hsieh*	45 Bartlett St, Marlborough MA 01752	508-481-9200	R	11*	<.1
27	Americ-Evolved Manufacturing LLC—*Donna Lock*	PO Box 669865, Charlotte NC 28266	704-395-1002	R	9*	.1
28	Ama Printing / Finishing Inc—*Marsh Shaw*	PO Box 7535, Waco TX 76714	254-776-8860	R	9*	.1
29	Abkco Music and Records Inc—*Allen Klein*	85 5th Ave Fl 11, New York NY 10003	212-399-0300	R	8*	.1
30	SOH Distributors Network Inc—*Sam Phillips*	1981 Fletcher Creek Dr, Memphis TN 38133	901-388-1579	R	7*	.1
31	Machine Head—*Stephen Dewey*	1641 20th St, Santa Monica CA 90404	310-392-8393	R	7*	<.1
32	Original Sound Records Company Inc—*Dale Berger*	7120 W Sunset Blvd, Los Angeles CA 90046	323-851-2600	R	6*	<.1
33	Talking Devices Co—*Lad Ottofy*	37 Brown St, Weaverville NC 28787	828-658-0660	R	5*	<.1
34	California Magnetics—*Don Nuzzo*	7898 Ostrow St Ste H, San Diego CA 92111	858-576-0291	R	5*	<.1
35	Covenant Communications Inc—*V Kofford*	PO Box 416, American Fork UT 84003	801-756-9966	R	4*	<.1
36	Antone's Records and Tapes—*Randolph Clendenen*	805 West Ave, Austin TX 78701	512-322-0617	R	4*	<.1
37	C and C Duplicators Inc—*Frank Carroll*	PO Box 400, Bohemia NY 11716	631-244-0800	R	4*	<.1
38	BDC Inc—*Thom Carpenter*	1185 Jansen Farm Ct, Elgin IL 60123	847-741-2233	R	4*	<.1
39	Asinni 2000 Records Inc—*J Ward*	14601 Bellaire Blvd 30, Houston TX 77083	281-564-4111	R	3*	<.1
40	Joey Records Inc—*Joe Lopez*	6703 W Commerce St, San Antonio TX 78227	210-432-7893	R	3*	<.1
41	Record Technology Inc—*Don Innis*	486 Dawson Dr Ste 4s, Camarillo CA 93012	805-484-2747	R	3*	<.1
42	United Record Pressing—*Cris Ashworth*	453 Chestnut St, Nashville TN 37203	615-259-9396	R	3*	<.1
43	Transco Products Corp—*Robert Cosulich*	609 W Elizabeth Ave, Linden NJ 07036	908-862-0030	R	3*	<.1
44	Metrolpolis Mastering LP—*Murat Aktar*	88 10th Ave 6w, New York NY 10011	212-604-9433	R	3*	<.1
45	Synchronicity Mastering Services LLC—*Shauna Baker*	5447 W 700 S Ste C, Salt Lake City UT 84104	801-533-0301	R	2*	<.1
46	Caribbean Records Manufacturing Corp—*Juan Fernandez*	3081 Nw 24th St, Miami FL 33142	305-633-4322	R	2*	<.1
47	MMO Music Group Inc—*Irving Kratka*	50 Executive Blvd Ste, Elmsford NY 10523	914-592-1188	R	2*	<.1
48	QC A Inc—*James Bosken*	2832 Spring Grove Ave, Cincinnati OH 45225	513-681-8400	R	1*	<.1
49	Clean Cuts Inc—*Jack Heyrman*	2901 Chestnut Ave, Baltimore MD 21211	410-467-4231	R	1*	<.1
50	Miami Tape Inc—*Carlos Garcia*	6200 W 21st Ct, Hialeah FL 33016	305-558-9211	R	1*	<.1
51	Red House Records Inc—*Eric Peltoniemi*	PO Box 4044, Saint Paul MN 55104	651-644-4161	R	1*	<.1
52	Advanced Audio Technology Inc—*Robert Atkins*	200 Easy St Ste E, Carol Stream IL 60188	630-665-3344	R	1*	<.1
53	Melody House Inc—*Stephen Fite*	819 Nw 92nd St, Oklahoma City OK 73114	405-840-3383	R	1*	<.1
54	Audio Productions Inc—*James Reyland*	1102 17th Ave S Ste 20, Nashville TN 37212	615-321-3612	R	1*	<.1
55	George Foreman Enterprises Inc—*Chuck Gartenhaus*	100 N Wilkes-Barre Blv, Wilkes Barre PA 18702	570-822-6277	P	<1	<.1

TOTALS: SIC 3652 Prerecorded Records & Tapes
Companies: 55   5,273   20.0

3661 Telephone & Telegraph Apparatus

Rank	Company Name—*Executive Officer*	Address, City, State, Zip	Phone	Type	Fin	Empls
1	Comverse Technology Inc—*Charles Burdick*	810 7th Ave, New York NY 10019	212-739-1000	P	1,623	5.9
2	Polycom Inc—*Andrew M Miller*	4750 Willow Rd, Pleasanton CA 94588	925-924-6000	P	1,496	3.5
3	Tellabs Inc—*Robert W Pullen*	1415 W Diehl Rd, Naperville IL 60563	630-798-8800	P	1,286	3.2
4	Hughes Network Systems Inc—*Pradman P Kaul*	11717 Exploration Ln, Germantown MD 20876	301-428-5500	B	1,043	2.3
5	Netgear Inc—*Patrick Lo*	350 E Plumeria Dr, San Jose CA 95134	408-907-8000	P	902	.7
6	US Robotics Corp—*Gerry Burns*	1300 E Woodfield Rd Rm, Schaumburg IL 60173	847-874-2000	R	899	3.3
7	Precision Communication Services Inc—*Bruce Heywood*	PO Box 11926, Tampa FL 33680	813-237-2020	R	768*	.4
8	ADTRAN Inc—*Thomas R Stanton*	PO Box 140000, Huntsville AL 35814		P	717	1.7
9	Plantronics Inc—*S Kenneth Kannappan*	345 Encinal St, Santa Cruz CA 95060	831-426-5858	P	684	3.2
10	Alcatel Lucent Submarine Network Inc—*Richard Nielson*	45195 Business Ct Ste, Sterling VA 20166	703-668-7013	D	465*	.8
11	Infinera Corp—*Tom Fallon*	140 Caspian Ct, Sunnyvale CA 94089	408-572-5200	P	454	1.1
12	ADC Broadband Access Systems Inc—*Steven Grady*	PO Box 1181, Minneapolis MN 55440	952-938-8080	S	316*	7.5
13	IPC Systems Holdings Corp—*Lance B Boxer*	1500 Plz Ten 15th Fl, Jersey City NJ 07311	201-253-2000	R	310*	.9

Note: An asterisk (*) indicates an estimated financial figure. The company type code used is as follows: R = Private, P = Public, S = Private Subsidiary, B = Public Subsidiary, D = Division, J = Joint Venture, I = Investment Fund.

COMPANY RANKINGS BY SALES WITHIN 4-DIGIT SIC

Rank	Company Name—*Executive Officer*	Address, City, State, Zip	Phone	Type	Fin	Empls
14	Xerox Omnifax—*Anne Mulcahy*	PO Box 4505, Norwalk CT 06850	203-968-3000	D	271*	.4
15	IPC Acquisition Corp—*Lance Boxer*	3 2nd St 15th Fl, Jersey City NJ 07302	201-253-2000	R	263	<.1
16	Zoom Technologies Inc—*Frank Manning*	207 South St, Boston MA 02111	617-423-1072	P	253	1.8
17	Telect Inc—*Wayne Williams*	PO Box 665, Liberty Lake WA 99019	509-926-6000	R	217*	.8
18	SymmetriCom Inc—*David Cote*	2300 Orchard Pky, San Jose CA 95131	408-433-0910	P	208	.6
19	Westell Inc Westell Technologies Inc	750 N Commons Dr, Aurora IL 60504	630-898-2500	S	207	.8
20	Fibertech Networks LLC—*John K Purcell*	300 Meridian Centre, Rochester NY 14618	585-697-5100	S	191*	.4
21	Westell Technologies Inc—*Richard S Gilbert*	750 N Commons Dr, Aurora IL 60504	630-898-2500	P	190	.4
22	Advanced Concepts Inc (Columbia Maryland)—*Arnold Crater*	9861 Broken Land Pkwy, Columbia MD 21046	410-381-3780	R	175*	.3
23	MPI Technologies Inc—*Gerard Logel*	4952 Warner Ave Ste 30, Huntington Beach CA 92649	714-840-8077	R	142*	.1
24	TTG Acquisition Corp—*Ewen R Cameron* Teltronics Inc	2150 Whitfield Industr, Sarasota FL 34243	941-753-5000	S	141*	.2
25	GN Netcom Inc—*P Michael Fairweather*	77 Northeastern Blvd, Nashua NH 03062		S	139*	.3
26	Zhone Technologies Inc—*Mory Ejabat*	7195 Oakport St, Oakland CA 94621	510-777-7000	P	129	.4
27	Communications Systems Inc—*William G Schultz*	PO Box 777, Hector MN 55342	952-996-1674	P	120	.5
28	Trillion Communications Corp—*Ralph E Brown*	3871 Pine Ln Ste 141, Bessemer AL 35022	205-481-1678	R	120*	.2
29	Aastra USA Inc—*Anthony Shen*	2811 Internet Blvd, Frisco TX 75034	469-365-3000	R	116*	.2
30	ComCore Technologies Inc—*Yong Huang*	48834 Kato Rd Ste 108, Fremont CA 94538	510-498-8858	R	110*	.2
31	Fujitsu Network Communications Inc—*Satoshi Ikeuchi*	2801 Telecom Pkwy, Richardson TX 75082	972-479-6000	R	110*	1.4
32	NEC Transmission Systems Inc	14040 Park Center Rd, Herndon VA 20171	703-834-4000	S	87*	.2
33	Xeta Technologies Inc—*Greg Forrest*	1814 W Tacoma St, Broken Arrow OK 74012	918-664-8200	S	85	.5
34	Brooktrout Inc—*Eric R Giler*	250 1st Ave Ste 300, Needham MA 02494	781-449-4100	S	80	.3
35	Compunetix Inc—*Giorgio Coraluppi*	2420 Mosside Blvd Ste, Monroeville PA 15146	412-373-8110	R	74*	.4
36	Infosonics Corp—*Joseph Ram*	4350 Executive Dr Ste, San Diego CA 92121	858-373-1600	P	73	.1
37	Tellabs (Naperville Illinois)—*Robert W Pullen* Tellabs Inc	1415 W Diehl Rd, Naperville IL 60563	630-798-8800	S	67*	.3
38	Telaid Industries Inc—*Thomas Patsiga*	PO Box 711, Niantic CT 06357	860-739-4461	R	66*	.2
39	Airvana Inc—*Randy Battat*	19 Alpha Rd, Chelmsford MA 01824	978-250-3000	R	65*	.6
40	Intecom—*Tim Whittington*	2811 Internet Blvd, Frisco TX 75034		S	65*	.5
41	American-Tel-A-Systems Inc—*Tom Curtis*	4800 Curtin Dr, MC Farland WI 53558		R	62*	.1
42	Ulticom Inc—*Bruce Swail*	1020 Briggs Rd, Mount Laurel NJ 08054	856-787-2700	S	61	.1
43	Aydin Displays Inc—*Art Mengel*	1 Riga Ln, Birdsboro PA 19508	610-404-7400	S	60*	.1
44	Bogen Corp—*Jeffery E Schwarz* Bogen Communications International Inc	50 Spring St, Ramsey NJ 07446	201-934-8500	S	59*	.1
45	Nuera Communications Inc—*Harprit Chhatwal*	27 World's Fair Dr, Somerset NJ 08873		R	59*	.1
46	Microdyne Outsourcing Inc—*John Oakes*	3100 Lomita Blvd, Torrance CA 90509		S	58	1.1
47	Osprey Technologies Inc—*George Platt*	3701 W Plano Pky Ste 3, Plano TX 75075	972-488-7200	S	56*	.1
48	Bogen Communications Inc—*Jonathan Guss* Bogen Corp	50 Spring St, Ramsey NJ 07446	201-934-8500	S	55*	.1
49	Bogen Communications LLC—*Jonathan Guss* Bogen Communications International Inc	50 Spring St, Ramsey NJ 07446	201-934-8500	S	55*	.1
50	RADvision Inc—*Vic DeBernardis*	17-17 State Hwy 208 St, Fairlawn NJ 07410	201-689-6300	S	51*	.1
51	NET Federal Inc	21660 Ridgetop Circle, Dulles VA 20166	703-948-1800	D	50*	.1
52	Sotera Engineered Solutions Inc—*John Hillen*	2200 Defense Hwy Ste 4, Crofton MD 21114	301-858-1230	R	49*	.7
53	Orbit Advanced Technologies Inc—*Israel Adan*	506 Prudential Rd, Horsham PA 19044	215-674-5100	S	49*	.1
54	Sycamore Networks Inc—*Daniel E Smith*	220 Mill Rd, Chelmsford MA 01824	978-250-2900	P	49	.3
55	SER Solutions Inc—*Joe Licata*	45925 Horseshoe Dr Ste, Dulles VA 20166	703-948-5600	S	48*	.2
56	Franklin Wireless Corp—*OC Kim*	5440 Morehouse Dr Ste, San Diego CA 92121	858-623-0000	P	47	.1
57	Bogen Communications International Inc—*Jonathan Guss*	50 Spring St, Ramsey NJ 07446	201-934-8500	P	45	.2
58	VBrick Systems Inc—*Doug Howard*	12 Beaumont Rd, Wallingford CT 06492	203-265-0044	R	44*	.1
59	dPi Teleconnect LLC—*David B Dorwart*	1330 Capitol Parkway, Carrollton TX 75006	972-488-5500	R	44*	.1
60	Solectek Corp—*Eric Lee*	6370 Nancy Ridge Dr St, San Diego CA 92121	858-450-1220	R	44*	.1
61	Teltronics Inc—*Ewen R Cameron*	2150 Whitfield Industr, Sarasota FL 34243	941-753-5000	P	43	.2
62	Katron Technologies Inc—*Robert Kae*	10415 A Westpark Dr, Houston TX 77042	713-266-3891	R	43*	.1
63	Frontrunner Network Systems Inc—*Jim Keegan*	412 Linden Ave, Rochester NY 14625		S	41*	.1
64	Pyott-Boone Electronics Inc—*Donald Fetterolf*	PO Box 809, Tazewell VA 24651	276-988-5505	R	41*	.2
65	Bay Technical Associates Inc—*Charles Ramsey*	5239 Ave A, Long Beach MS 39560	228-563-7334	R	39*	.1
66	Biscom Inc—*Don Dunning*	321 Billerica Rd, Chelmsford MA 01824	978-250-1800	R	39*	.1
67	Syntellect Inc—*Steve Dodenhoff*	2095 W Pinnacle Peak R, Phoenix AZ 85027	602-789-2800	S	38*	.3
68	Fiber Instrument Sales Inc—*Frank Giotto*	161 Clear Rd, Oriskany NY 13424	315-736-2206	R	38*	.2
69	VXI Corp—*Mike Ferguson*	271 Locust St, Dover NH 03820	603-742-2888	R	38*	.1
70	Canoga Perkins Corp—*Tim Champion*	20600 Prairie St, Chatsworth CA 91311	818-718-6300	R	37*	.1
71	Noble Systems Corp—*James K Noble*	4151 Ashford Dunwoody, Atlanta GA 30319	404-851-1331	S	37*	.1
72	Radware Inc (Mahwah New Jersey)—*Roy Zisapel*	575 Corporate Dr, Mahwah NJ 07430	201-512-9771	S	37*	<.1
73	Suttle Apparatus Corp—*Bruce Blackwood* Communications Systems Inc	1001 E Hwy 212, Hector MN 55342	320-848-6711	S	37	.2
74	Clearfield Inc—*Cheri Beranek*	5480 Nathan Ln, Plymouth MN 55442	763-476-6866	P	35	.2
75	COMARCO Wireless Technologies—*Samuel Inman*	25541 Commercentre Dr, Lake Forest CA 92630	949-599-7400	S	33*	.1
76	National Applied Computer Technologies Inc—*Arnie Goodstein*	478 S Geneva Rd, Amityville NY 11701	801-802-3000	R	33*	.1
77	MobilePro Corp—*Jay Wright*	6701 Democracy Blvd St, Bethesda MD 20817	301-571-3476	P	31	.1
78	Applied Innovation Inc—*Richard Cremona*	5800 Innovation Dr, Dublin OH 43016	614-798-2000	R	31	.1
79	Palco Telecom Service Inc—*Janice Migliore*	2914 Green Cove Rd Sw, Huntsville AL 35803	256-883-3400	R	30*	.2
80	Transition Networks Inc—*Bill Schultz* Communications Systems Inc	10900 Red Circle Dr, Minnetonka MN 55343	952-941-7600	S	29*	.1
81	Artel Video Systems Inc—*Richard Dellacanonica*	5B Lyberty Way, Westford MA 01886	978-263-5775	R	29*	.1
82	Omnitron Systems Technology Inc—*Arie Goldberg*	140 Technology Ste 500, Irvine CA 92618	949-250-6510	R	28*	.1
83	Spectra Merchandising International Inc—*Patricia Shoenberg*	4230 N Normandy Ave, Chicago IL 60634	773-202-8408	R	27*	.1
84	OnePath Networks Inc—*Jack Hotz*	Princeton Forrestal Vi, Princeton NJ 08540	609-514-1800	R	27*	<.1
85	Ringdale Inc	101 Halmar Cove, Georgetown TX 78628	512-288-9080	S	27*	<.1
86	Valcom Inc—*John Mason*	5614 Hollins Rd, Roanoke VA 24019	540-563-2000	R	27*	.2
87	dbSpectra Inc—*Chuck York*	1590 E Hwy 121 Bldg A, Lewisville TX 75056	469-322-0080	R	26*	.1
88	Cassidian Communications Inc—*Timothy Fuller*	PO Box 9007, Temecula CA 92589	951-719-2100	S	25*	.4
89	Dataradio Corp—*Robert T Rouleau*	6160 Peachtree Dunwood, Atlanta GA 30328	770-392-0002	S	25*	<.1
90	Ameritec Corp—*Bill Speight*	760 Arrow Grand Cir, Covina CA 91722	626-915-5441	R	24	.1
91	Innova Electronics Corp—*Cynthia Tsai*	17291 Mt Herrmann St, Fountain Valley CA 92708	714-241-6800	R	23*	<.1
92	Arnold A Semler Inc—*Ravi Achar*	11347 Vanowen St, North Hollywood CA 91605	818-760-1000	R	22*	<.1
93	Total Communications Inc—*Richard Lennon*	333 Burnham St, East Hartford CT 06108	860-282-9999	R	21*	.2
94	Extreme Technologies Inc—*Lisa Guidry*	PO Box 941507, Houston TX 77094	281-293-7800	R	21*	<.1
95	CT-Innovations—*Cynthia B Brussee*	2268 Welsch Industrial, Saint Louis MO 63146	636-537-4284	R	20*	<.1

Rank	Company Name—*Executive Officer*	Address, City, State, Zip	Phone	Type	Fin	Empls
96	STARTEL Corp—*Bill Lane*	16 Goodyear, Irvine CA 92618	949-863-8700	S	18*	.1
97	Monroe Systems for Business Inc—*Richard Roberts*	47 Runway DrSte G, Levittown PA 19057		R	17*	<.1
98	SEPE Inc—*Michel Remion*	245 Fischer Ave C-4, Costa Mesa CA 92626	714-241-7373	R	17*	<.1
99	AltiGen Communications Inc—*Jeremiah Fleming*	410 E Plumeria Dr, San Jose CA 95134	408-597-9000	P	17	.1
100	Quintron Systems Inc—*James Mc Glothlin*	2105 S Blosser Rd, Santa Maria CA 93458	805-928-4343	R	16*	.1
101	Best-Tronics Manufacturing Inc—*Stanley Bartosz*	18500 Graphic Ct, Tinley Park IL 60477	708-802-9677	R	16*	.2
102	Molex Premise Networks—*Dennis Curtis*	2222 Wellington Ct, Lisle IL 60532		D	16*	<.1
103	Applied Media Technologies Corp—*Clayton Burton*	4091 AMTC Ctr Dr, Clearwater FL 33764	727-531-3105	R	16*	<.1
104	Optoplex Corp—*James Sha*	3342 Gateway Blvd, Fremont CA 94538	510-490-8320	R	16*	.3
105	Dialogic Communications Corp	117 Seabord Ln Ste D-1, Franklin TN 37067	615-790-2882	S	15*	.1
106	Metal-Tech Partners—*Darcy Nunn*	PO Box 273, Bruning NE 68322	402-353-6535	R	14*	.2
107	Telco Systems Inc—*Itzik Weinstein*	15 Berkshire Rd, Mansfield MA 02048	781-551-0300	S	14*	.2
108	Ultratec Inc—*Rob Engelke*	450 Science Dr, Madison WI 53711		R	14*	.1
109	Global Technologies Group Inc	3108 Columbia Pike Ste, Arlington VA 22204	703-486-0500	R	14*	<.1
110	Walker Equipment Corp—*Carsten Thads* Plantronics Inc	4289 Bonny Oaks Dr Ste, Chattanooga TN 37406	423-622-7793	D	14*	<.1
111	Lattice Inc—*Paul Burgess*	7150 N Park Dr Ste 500, Pennsauken NJ 08109	856-910-1166	P	14	<.1
112	Veramark Technologies Inc—*Anthony C Mazzullo*	3750 Monroe Ave, Pittsford NY 14534	585-383-6806	P	13	.1
113	Autonomy etalk—*Andrew Joiner*	2200 Ross Ave Ste 3500, Dallas TX 75201	214-981-3100	R	13*	.1
114	Western Telematic Inc—*Dan Morrison*	5 Sterling, Irvine CA 92618	949-586-9950	R	13*	.1
115	Telecom Industries LLC—*Ron Lesniak*	6311 San Ignacio Ave, San Jose CA 95119	408-574-2100	R	12*	.1
116	LiveWire Mobile Inc—*Matthew Stecker*	1 Monarch Dr Ste 203, Littleton MA 01460	978-742-3100	P	12	.2
117	Patton Electronics Co—*Robert E Patton*	7622 Rickenbacker Dr, Gaithersburg MD 20879	301-975-1000	R	12*	.1
118	Fanstel Corp—*Yuan-Neng Fan*	7466 E Monte Cristo Av, Scottsdale AZ 85260	480-948-4928	R	12	.1
119	Zypcom Inc—*Karl Zorzi*	2301 Industrial Pky W, Hayward CA 94545	510-783-2501	R	12*	<.1
120	Dantel Inc—*Al Hutcheson*	2991 N Argyle Ave, Fresno CA 93727		R	11*	.1
121	Electronic Specialists Inc—*FJ Stifter*	75 Middlesex Ave, Natick MA 01760	508-655-1532	R	11*	<.1
122	Sonetronics Inc—*Gary Kuskin*	PO Box L, Belmar NJ 07719	732-681-5016	R	11*	.1
123	Phonex Broadband Corp—*John Knab*	6952 High Tech Dr, Midvale UT 84047	801-566-0100	R	10*	<.1
124	Eversun Technologies Inc—*Scott Chen*	148 S 6th Ave, City of Industry CA 91746	626-934-9868	J	10*	<.1
125	Dataprobe Inc—*David Weiss*	1B Pearl Ct, Allendale NJ 07401	201-934-9944	R	9*	<.1
126	Canary Communications Inc	6040 Hellyer Ave Ste 1, San Jose CA 95138	408-365-0609	R	9*	<.1
127	Data Communication for Business Inc—*Russ Straayer*	2949 County Rd 1000 E, Dewey IL 61840	217-897-6600	R	9*	<.1
128	ICON Resources Inc—*Alyce M Imbrie*	980 N Michigan Ave Ste, Chicago IL 60611	312-573-0142	R	9*	<.1
129	Lycatel LLC—*Sylvia Singh*	570 Broad St Ste 301, Newark NJ 07102	973-286-0771	R	9*	<.1
130	General DataComm Industries Inc—*Howard S Modlin*	6 Rubber Ave, Naugatuck CT 06770	203-729-0271	P	9	.1
131	Telefonix Inc—*Paul Burke*	2340 Ernie Krueger Cir, Waukegan IL 60087	847-244-4500	R	9*	.1
132	EXP Computer Inc—*Horace Lin*	243 Winthrop Ave Unit, Westbury NY 11590	516-333-3712	R	8*	<.1
133	Computer Peripheral Systems Inc—*Richard Fetsko*	5096 Bristol Industria, Buford GA 30518		R	8*	<.1
134	Rochelle Communications Inc—*Gilbert Amline*	8140 North Mopac Expre, Austin TX 78759	512-339-8188	R	8*	<.1
135	Voiceboard Corp (Camarillo California)—*Gregory Peacock*	473 Post St, Camarillo CA 93010	805-389-3100	R	8*	<.1
136	Notify Technology Corp—*Paul F DePond*	1054 S De Anza Blvd St, San Jose CA 95129	408-777-7930	P	7	.1
137	Electro Standards Laboratory Inc—*Raymond Sepe*	36 Western Industrial, Cranston RI 02921	401-943-1164	R	7*	.1
138	Ahead Communications Systems Inc—*Anton Kaeslin*	6 Rubber Ave, Naugatuck CT 06770	203-720-0227	R	7*	.1
139	Audio-Sears Corp—*David Hartwell*	2 S St, Stamford NY 12167	607-652-7305	R	7*	.1
140	General Photonics Corp—*Steve Yao*	5228 Edison Ave, Chino CA 91710	909-590-5473	R	6*	.1
141	Astrocom Electronics Inc—*Terry Lifgren*	115 Dk Lifgren Dr, Oneonta NY 13820	607-432-1930	R	6*	.1
142	ZyXEL Communications Inc—*Howie Chu*	1130 N Miller St, Anaheim CA 92806	714-632-0882	S	6*	.1
143	Allen Tel Products Inc—*Betty Foster*	30 TV5 Dr, Henderson NV 89014	702-451-4414	R	6*	<.1
144	Controlware Communications Systems Inc—*Eugene Wolf*	One Industrial Way W B, Eatontown NJ 07724	732-919-0400	D	6*	<.1
145	D/V Technologies Inc—*Mary P Gregg*	1935 Pauline Blvd Ste, Ann Arbor MI 48103		R	6*	<.1
146	Vytran Corp—*Eric Mies*	1400 Campus Dr, Morganville NJ 07751	732-972-2880	R	6*	<.1
147	Hose-Mccann Telephone Company Inc—*Joan Grande-Butera*	1241 W Newport Ctr Dr, Deerfield Beach FL 33442	954-429-1110	R	5*	<.1
148	CR International Inc—*Kenneth Boudris*	9105 Whiskey Bottom Rd, Laurel MD 20723	301-210-1540	R	5*	<.1
149	Advanced Communication Design Inc—*Marco Scibora*	7901 12th Ave S, Bloomington MN 55425	952-854-4000	R	5*	<.1
150	EtherCom Corp—*Nafis Ahmad*	1409 Fulton Pl, Fremont CA 94539	510-440-0242	R	5*	<.1
151	Omniphone Inc—*Les Barnett*	PO Box 8739, Mobile AL 36689	251-639-9639	R	5*	<.1
152	Greyfield Industries Inc—*George Estes*	3104 Wayne Madison Rd, Trenton OH 45067	513-860-1785	R	5*	<.1
153	BICOM Inc—*Mehmet Binal*	755 Main St Bldg 3, Monroe CT 06468	203-268-4484	R	5*	<.1
154	Page Automated Telecommunications Systems Inc	3925 Bohannon Dr, Menlo Park CA 94025	650-230-2300	R	5*	<.1
155	China Voice Holding Corp—*Bill Burbank*	327 Plz Real Ste 319, Boca Raton FL 33432	561-394-2482	P	5	<.1
156	Star Dynamic Corp—*Leonard Schwartzman*	100 Outwater Ln, Garfield NJ 07026	973-340-3883	R	5*	.1
157	Proctor International Inc—*D Proctor*	15305 Ne 95th St, Redmond WA 98052	425-881-7000	R	4*	<.1
158	Coastcom Inc—*Edward Buttner*	1141 Harbor Bay Pky St, Alameda CA 94502	510-523-6000	S	4*	<.1
159	TelVue Corp—*Jesse Lerman*	16000 Horizon Way Ste, Mount Laurel NJ 08054	856-273-8888	P	4	<.1
160	Forum Communications International—*Raj Natarajan*	1223 N Glenville Dr, Richardson TX 75081	972-680-0700	R	4*	<.1
161	Micro Seven Inc—*Dick Iwata*	PO Box 5597, Beaverton OR 97006	503-693-6982	R	4*	<.1
162	Microlog Corp—*Richard Meccariella*	401 Professional Dr St, Gaithersburg MD 20879	301-540-5500	P	4*	<.1
163	Jourdan Technologies Inc—*Ronald Wilson*	PO Box 667, Douglasville GA 30133	770-489-8608	R	4*	<.1
164	Litra Manufacturing Inc—*Georgianna Ball*	6733 Jones Mill Ct Ste, Norcross GA 30092	770-446-7050	R	3*	<.1
165	Rlh Industries Inc—*Robert Harris*	936 N Main St, Orange CA 92867	714-532-1672	R	3*	<.1
166	Voice-Tech Inc—*Tim Garofalo*	720 Commerce Dr Unit 1, Venice FL 34292	941-486-0150	R	3*	<.1
167	Digital Voice Corp—*Larry Blancett*	PO Box 1414, Grapevine TX 76099	469-635-6507	R	3*	<.1
168	Coriolis Networks Inc—*Robert Castle*	330 Codman Hill Rd, Boxboro MA 01719	978-264-1904	R	3*	.1
169	Radiodetection—*Zenya Brackett*	154 Portland Rd, Bridgton ME 04009	207-647-9495	D	3*	<.1
170	FiberPlex Inc—*Buddy Oliver*	10840-412 Guilford Rd, Annapolis Junction MD 20701	301-604-0100	R	3*	<.1
171	Reliable Cable Co—*Jay R Neidenberg*	3320 NW 53rd St Ste 20, Fort Lauderdale FL 33309	954-484-9606	R	3*	<.1
172	Cylix Corp—*James Thomas*	11381 Interchange Cir, Miramar FL 33025	954-430-6310	R	3*	<.1
173	Amtel Systems Corp	1955 Ticonderoga Blvd, Chester Springs PA 19425		R	3*	<.1
174	Freedom Technologies LLC—*Mary Gatti*	PO Box 117, East Glastonbury CT 06025	860-633-0452	R	3*	<.1
175	CallerIDcom—*Mark Sutherland*	5680 Oakbrook Pky Ste, Norcross GA 30093	770-263-7111	R	3*	<.1
176	uData Net Corp—*Lindsey Wilson*	4420 W Vickery Blvd Rm, Fort Worth TX 76107	817-420-9460	R	3*	<.1
177	Miller-Jackson Co—*Jeffrey S Brown*	PO Box 61163, Oklahoma City OK 73146	405-235-8426	R	3*	<.1
178	International Totalizing Systems Corp—*Peter Lillios*	75 Foundation Ave, Haverhill MA 01835	978-521-6700	R	3*	<.1
179	Fiberall Corp—*Isaac Zilber*	449 Sheridan Blvd, Inwood NY 11096	516-371-5200	R	3*	<.1
180	Exacom Inc—*Helmut Koch*	99 Airport Rd Ste 2, Concord NH 03301	603-228-0706	R	3*	<.1
181	North American Connection—*Larry Carter*	730 F Ave Ste 210, Plano TX 75074	972-423-4222	R	3*	<.1
182	Alston Tascom Inc—*Wayne Scaggs*	13512 Vintage Pl, Chino CA 91710	909-548-7300	R	3*	<.1
183	Hotronic Inc—*Andy Ho*	1875 Winchester Blvd S, Campbell CA 95008	408-378-3883	R	3*	<.1
184	Verifiber LLC—*Don Davis*	49 Buford Hwy, Suwanee GA 30024	678-482-4021	R	3*	<.1

Note: An asterisk (*) indicates an estimated financial figure. The company type code used is as follows: R = Private, P = Public, S = Private Subsidiary, B = Public Subsidiary, D = Division, J = Joint Venture, I = Investment Fund.

COMPANY RANKINGS BY SALES WITHIN 4-DIGIT SIC

Rank	Company Name—Executive Officer	Address, City, State, Zip	Phone	Type	Fin	Empls
185	Calmar Optcom Inc—Anthony Lin	575 N Pastoria Ave, Sunnyvale CA 94085	408-733-7800	R	2*	<.1
186	Tatic Solutions Inc—Susana Craig	915 S San Tomas Aqn Rd, Campbell CA 95008	408-288-5531	R	2*	<.1
187	Ramtel Corp—Robert Moio	115 Railroad Ave, Johnston RI 02919	401-231-3340	R	2*	<.1
188	Universal Electronics Company Inc—Joseph Turner	1940 Air Ln Dr, Nashville TN 37210	615-391-0523	R	2*	<.1
189	Uraseal Inc—John Burnham	1 Washington St Ste 20, Dover NH 03820	603-749-1004	R	2*	<.1
190	NetQuest Corp—Dan Pocek	523 Fellowship Rd Ste, Mount Laurel NJ 08054	856-866-0505	R	2*	<.1
191	Chiu Technical Corp—Eva Chiu	252 Indian Head Rd, Kings Park NY 11754	631-544-0606	R	2*	<.1
192	Phoenix Digital Corp—J O'connor	7650 E Evans Rd Ste A, Scottsdale AZ 85260	480-483-7393	R	2*	<.1
193	Database Access Systems Inc—Michael Palazzi	1 Romaine Rd, Mountain Lakes NJ 07046	973-335-0800	R	2*	<.1
194	Partners Data Systems Inc	3663 Via Mercado, La Mesa CA 91941	619-415-2000	R	2*	<.1
195	General Microsystems Inc (Chantilly Virginia)—Dan Ogelsby	43676 Trade Center Pl, Sterling VA 20166	703-661-2370	R	2*	<.1
196	Western DataCom Company Inc—Philip Ardire	959-B Bassett Rd, Westlake OH 44145	440-835-1510	R	2*	<.1
197	Hydra Systems Inc—Mark Brown	17585 El Mineral Rd, Perris CA 92570	714-772-0233	R	2*	<.1
198	Ayantra Inc—Ashok Teckchandani	47873 Fremont Blvd, Fremont CA 94538	510-623-7526	R	2*	<.1
199	Multi-Link Inc—Ron Sladon	122 Dewey Dr, Nicholasville KY 40356	859-885-6363	R	2*	<.1
200	BT S Inc—Stanley Mallory	PO Box 2002, Grand Island NE 68802	308-382-1011	R	2*	<.1
201	Eagle Telephonics Inc—Richard Riccoboni	3880 Veterans Memorial, Bohemia NY 11716	631-471-3600	R	2*	<.1
202	Us Breaker Inc—Frederick Wendt	1061 Kings Bridge Rd, Greensboro GA 30642	706-467-9575	R	2*	.1
203	Electronic Tele-Communications Inc—Dean W Danner	1915 MacArthur Rd, Waukesha WI 53188	262-542-5600	P	2	<.1
204	Adaptive Networks Inc—Michael Propp	123 Highland Ave, Needham MA 02494	781-444-4170	R	2*	<.1
205	Raven Electronics Corp—Carl Dawson	4655 Longley Ln Ste 10, Reno NV 89502	775-858-2400	R	2*	<.1
206	Brook Telephone Manufacturing and Supply Company Inc—John Crescentini	PO Box 230239, Brooklyn NY 11223	718-449-4222	R	2*	<.1
207	Telephone Equipment Supply Inc—Bob Buck	PO Box 9482, Pahrump NV 89060		R	1*	<.1
208	Wintel—Angel Ingalman	1051 Bennett Dr Ste 10, Longwood FL 32750	407-834-1188	R	1*	<.1
209	Krown Manufacturing Inc—Barabra Anders	3408 Indale Rd, Fort Worth TX 76116	817-738-2485	R	1*	<.1
210	Big Ear Inc—Glenn Hood	6660 Delmonico Dr D161, Colorado Springs CO 80919	719-531-6868	R	1*	<.1
211	Bejed Inc—Alan Brown	14325 Ne Airport Way S, Portland OR 97230	503-281-8153	R	1*	<.1
212	Conveyant Systems Inc—Timothy Kenyon	1901 Carnegie Ave Ste, Santa Ana CA 92705	949-756-7100	R	1*	<.1
213	Dac Systems Inc—Mark Nickson	4 Armstrong Rd Ste 2, Shelton CT 06484	203-924-7000	R	1*	<.1
214	American Communications—Mike Occhionero	PO Box 5115, Englewood CO 80155	303-770-4644	R	1*	<.1
215	Intelect Technologies Inc—King Hock	2200 10th St Ste 300, Plano TX 75074	469-429-7800	R	1*	<.1
216	Trimm International Inc—G Newton	407 Railroad St, Butner NC 27509	919-575-6100	R	1*	<.1
217	Radicom Research Inc—Ming Hsieh	2148 Bering Dr, San Jose CA 95131	408-383-9006	R	1*	<.1
218	Alternative Technology Corp—Tom Kadala	PO Box 357, Hastings On Hudson NY 10706	914-478-5900	R	1*	<.1
219	ReadyCom Inc—Dan King	1598 Wynkoop St, Denver CO 80202		R	1*	<.1
220	Custom Assembly Inc—Kevin Hogie	9047 Lake Blvd, Chisago City MN 55013	651-257-4028	R	1*	<.1
221	Suncoast Systems Inc—Thomas Simard	6001 S Hwy 99, Walnut Hill FL 32568	850-478-6477	R	1*	<.1
222	Dynametric Inc—Alan Morse	11636 Goldring Rd, Arcadia CA 91006	626-358-2559	R	1*	<.1
223	H and L Instruments LLC—Jeniffer Landman	PO Box 580, North Hampton NH 03862	603-964-1818	R	1*	<.1
224	Tec Inc—Art O'hare	PO Box 18356, Irvine CA 92623	949-250-9400	R	1*	<.1
225	Vasira Inc	PO Box 1197, Denville NJ 07834	973-663-2515	R	1*	<.1
226	Optical Design Manufacturing Inc—Michael Schneider	143 Lake St Ste 1e, Laconia NH 03246	603-524-8350	R	1*	<.1
227	Convex Corp—Jim Turner	1319 Shepard Dr, Sterling VA 20164	703-433-9901	R	1*	<.1
228	Annexus Data Systems—Christopher Rogers	10559 Lansford Ln, San Diego CA 92126	858-530-0019	R	1*	<.1
229	Metal-Flex Hosing Inc—Raymond Arzounian	1241 E Erie Ave Ste 1, Philadelphia PA 19124	215-535-6868	R	1*	<.1
230	Building Control Solutions LLC	PO Box 14363, Kansas City MO 64152	816-741-6282	R	1*	<.1
231	Economy Copier Service Inc—Charles Kimery	501 Memorial Pkwy Nw, Huntsville AL 35801	256-512-0067	R	1*	<.1
232	Signalcom Systems Inc—Warner Yee	1499 Bayshore Hwy Ste, Burlingame CA 94010	650-692-1056	R	1*	<.1
233	Sound Control Technologies Inc—Adolph Neaderland	28 Knight St Ste 7, Norwalk CT 06851	203-854-5701	R	1*	<.1
234	Northeast Innovations Inc—John Harrison	PO Box 120, Concord NH 03302	603-229-0500	R	1*	<.1
235	Paccomm Packet Radio Systems Inc—Gwyn Reedy	7818 Causeway Blvd Ste, Tampa FL 33619	813-874-2980	R	1*	<.1
236	Altisys Communications—Leo Liu	1289 Reamwood Ave Ste, Sunnyvale CA 94089	408-752-0800	R	1*	<.1
237	Hark Electronic Systems Inc—Shellie Hargenrader	3507 Iron Horse Rd Ste, Ladson SC 29456	843-285-7205	R	1*	<.1
238	Voice Solutions Inc—Dick Brown	3360 Annapolis Ln N St, Minneapolis MN 55447	763-595-8000	R	1*	<.1
239	Elias Spater—Elias Spater	2009 Dewberry Ct, Thousand Oaks CA 91361	805-496-8053	R	<1*	<.1
240	Craig J Phillips—Craig Phillips	800 C St, Vancouver WA 98660	360-690-4535	R	<1*	<.1
241	Skutch Electronics Inc—Mark Crawford	209 Kenroy Ln Ste 9, Roseville CA 95678	916-786-6186	R	<1*	<.1
242	Sparrevohn Engineering—Fred Sparrevohn	6911 E 11th St, Long Beach CA 90815	562-799-1577	R	<1*	<.1
243	House of Telephones—Odis Le Vrier	2677 E Valley Dr, San Angelo TX 76905	325-482-0101	R	N/A	<.1
244	Hands Free America—David Amnriquez	PO Box 232146, Encinitas CA 92023	760-942-4321	R	N/A	<.1

TOTALS: SIC 3661 Telephone & Telegraph Apparatus
Companies: 244   **17,652   59.1**

3663 Radio & T.V. Communications Equipment

Rank	Company Name—Executive Officer	Address, City, State, Zip	Phone	Type	Fin	Empls
1	Motorola Solutions Inc—Greg Brown	1303 E Algonquin Rd, Schaumburg IL 60196	847-576-5000	P	19,282	51.0
2	L-3 Communications Holdings Inc—Michael T Strianese	600 3rd Ave, New York NY 10016	212-697-1111	P	15,680	63.0
3	QUALCOMM Inc—Paul E Jacobs	PO Box 919042, San Diego CA 92121	858-587-1121	P	14,957	21.2
4	CommScope Inc—Frank Drendel	PO Box 339, Hickory NC 28602	828-324-2200	S	2,783*	11.5
5	General Dynamics Decision Systems—Chris Marzilli	8201 E McDowell Rd, Scottsdale AZ 85257	480-441-3033	S	2,759*	7.0
6	Echostar Corp—Michael T Dugan	100 Inverness Terrace, Englewood CO 80112	303-706-4000	P	2,351	2.3
7	Motorola Inc Communications Div—Greg Brown General Dynamics Decision Systems	1303 E Algonquin Rd, Schaumburg IL 60196	847-576-5000	D	2,000*	10.0
8	Orbital Sciences Corp—David W Thompson	21839 Atlantic Blvd, Dulles VA 20166	703-406-5000	P	1,346	3.5
9	Tellabs Operations Inc—Robert W Pullen	1415 W Diehl Rd, Naperville IL 60563	630-798-8800	S	1,326*	3.3
10	Radio Satellite Integrators Corp—Jonathan Michels	19144 Van Ness Ave, Torrance CA 90501	310-787-7700	R	1,280*	<.1
11	Paragon Towers Inc—Joe James	PO Box 270655, Oklahoma City OK 73137	405-948-3335	R	1,000	<.1
12	Dolby Laboratories Inc—Kevin Yeaman	100 Potrero Ave, San Francisco CA 94103	415-558-0200	P	956	1.4
13	ViaSat Inc—Mark D Dankberg	6155 El Camino Real, Carlsbad CA 92009	760-476-2200	P	802	2.2
14	Space Systems/Loral Inc—John Celli	3825 Fabian Way, Palo Alto CA 94303	650-852-4000	S	714*	1.8
15	CPI Malibu Div—O Joe Caldarelli	3760 A Calle Tecate, Camarillo CA 93012	805-383-1829	D	625*	1.5
16	Powerwave Technologies Inc—Ronald J Buschur	1801 E St Andrew Pl, Santa Ana CA 92705	714-466-1000	P	592	2.1
17	Sony Ericsson Mobile Communications (USA) Inc—Hideki Komiyama	3333 Piedmont Rd Ne St, Atlanta GA 30305	919-472-7000	R	492*	6.0
18	Aviat Networks Inc—Michael Pangia	5200 Great America Pkw, Santa Clara CA 95054	408-567-7000	P	452	1.0
19	Harmonic Inc—Patrick Harshman	4300 N 1st St, San Jose CA 95134	408-542-2500	P	423	1.1
20	SafeNet Holding Corp—Chris Fedde	4690 Millennium Dr, Belcamp MD 21017	410-931-7500	S	404*	1.6
21	CPI International Inc—O Joe Caldarelli	607 Hansen Way, Palo Alto CA 94304	650-846-2900	P	389	1.6
22	EMS Technologies Inc—Neil A MacKay	660 Engineering Dr, Norcross GA 30092	770-263-9200	R	355	1.2
23	XM Satellite Radio Inc—Mel Karmazin	1500 Eckington Pl NE, Washington DC 20002	202-380-4000	S	339*	.9

Rank	Company Name—Executive Officer	Address, City, State, Zip	Phone	Type	Fin	Empls
24	Comtech Telecommunications Corp—Fred V Kornberg	68 South Service Rd St, Melville NY 11747	631-962-7000	P	312	1.3
25	Cohu Inc—James A Donahue	12367 Crosthwaite Cir, Poway CA 92064	858-848-8100	P	309	1.2
26	Telex Communications Inc—Raymond V Malpocher	12000 Portland Ave S, Burnsville MN 55337	952-884-4051	S	308*	3.0
27	Motorola Broadband Communications Sector—Greg Brown Motorola Solutions Inc	101 Tournament Dr, Horsham PA 19044	215-323-1000	D	286*	1.0
28	Ugcom Inc—Ki Yoon	3750 Convoy St Ste 303, San Diego CA 92111	619-279-3200	R	280*	.4
29	Globecomm Systems Inc—David E Hershberg	45 Oser Ave, Hauppauge NY 11788	631-231-9800	P	274	.5
30	Ericsson Inc—Hans Vestberg	6300 Legacy Dr, Plano TX 75024	972-583-0000	S	272	2.1
31	Comtech EF Data Corp—Robert McCollum Comtech Telecommunications Corp	2114 W 7th St, Tempe AZ 85281	480-333-2200	S	236*	.6
32	SeaChange International Inc—Raghu Rau	50 Nagog Park, Acton MA 01720	978-897-0100	P	216	1.2
33	Arris Interactive LLC—Robert J Stanzione	3871 Lakefield Dr, Suwanee GA 30024	678-473-2000	S	208*	.5
34	Telecom Solutions Div—Thomas W Steipp	2300 Orchard Pkwy, San Jose CA 95131	408-433-0910	S	191*	.4
35	AM Networks Inc—C Gus Kamnitsis	1900 AM Dr, Quakertown PA 18951	215-538-8700	R	181*	.5
36	Anaren Inc—Lawrence A Sala	6635 Kirkville Rd, East Syracuse NY 13057	315-432-8909	P	179	1.0
37	Sabre Communications Corp—James Mack	PO Box 658, Sioux City IA 51102	712-224-1580	S	175*	.6
38	Trak Microwave Corp—Richard Peq	4726 Eisenhower Blvd, Tampa FL 33634	813-901-7200	S	168*	.4
39	Aries Industries Inc—Nick Kroll	550 Elizabeth St, Waukesha WI 53186	262-896-7205	R	162*	.2
40	Lifeline Systems Securities Corp	111 Lawrence St, Framingham MA 01702	508-988-1000	S	151	1.0
41	Kentrox LLC—Richard Cremona	5800 Innovation Dr, Dublin OH 43016	614-798-2000	S	146*	.4
42	Datron World Communications Inc—Art Barter	3030 Enterprise Ct, Vista CA 92081	760-597-1500	R	143*	.3
43	Draper Inc—John Pidgeon	PO Box 425, Spiceland IN 47385	765-987-7999	R	126*	.5
44	CalAmp Corp—Michael Burdiek	1401 N Rice Ave, Oxnard CA 93030	805-987-9000	P	114	.4
45	KVH Industries Inc—Martin A Kits van Heyningen	50 Enterprise Ctr, Middletown RI 02842	401-847-3327	P	112	.4
46	Cobra Electronics Corp—James Bazet	6500 W Cortland St, Chicago IL 60707	773-889-8870	P	111	.1
47	LXE Inc—James S Childress EMS Technologies Inc	125 Technology Pky, Norcross GA 30092	770-447-4224	S	102*	.4
48	Chaparral Communications Inc—Bob Taggart	950 S Bascom Ave Ste 3, San Jose CA 95128	408-294-2900	R	100*	.3
49	Codonics Inc—Yasuo Hirozawa	17991 Crosthwaite Dr, Middleburg Heights OH 44130	440-243-1198	R	99*	.2
50	EDCI Holdings Inc—Clarke Bailey	11 E 44th St Ste 1201, New York NY 10017	646-401-0084	P	97	.8
51	Microwave Transmission Systems Inc—Preston D Spurlin	541 Sterling Dr, Richardson TX 75081	972-669-0591	R	89*	.2
52	DRI Corp (Dallas Texas)—David L Turney	13760 Noel Rd Ste 830, Dallas TX 75240	214-378-8992	P	87	.3
53	Grass Valley Group—Alain Andreoli	PO Box 599000, Nevada City CA 95959	415-852-6500	S	73	.4
54	Airspan Networks Inc—Eric D Stonestrom	777 Yamato Rd Ste 310, Boca Raton FL 33431	561-893-8670	P	70	.2
55	PCTEL Inc—Martin H Singer	471 Brighton Dr, Bloomingdale IL 60108	630-372-6800	P	69	.3
56	Datron Systems Inc (Vista California)—Art Baker	3030 Enterprise Court, Vista CA 92081	760-597-1500	R	62	.3
57	Alpha Technologies Inc—Mark Schnarr	3767 Alpha Way, Bellingham WA 98226	360-647-2360	R	60*	.3
58	Versitron Co—Richard Tull	83 Albe Dr Ste C, Newark DE 19702	302-894-0699	R	60*	.1
59	Iteris Inc—Abbas Mohaddes	1700 Carnegie Ave, Santa Ana CA 92705	949-270-9400	P	59	.3
60	Mackay Communications Inc—Jeff Schlacks	3691 Trust Dr, Raleigh NC 27616	919-850-3000	R	54*	.1
61	Verrex Corp—Thomas Berry Jr	1130 Rte 22 W, Mountainside NJ 07092	908-232-7000	R	52*	.1
62	Telular Corp—Joseph A Beatty	311 S Wacker Dr Ste 43, Chicago IL 60606		P	51	.1
63	Xirrus Inc—Dirk I Gates	2101 Corporate Center, Thousand Oaks CA 91320	805-262-1600	R	50*	.1
64	Cellular Specialties Inc—Robert Wilson	670 N Commercial St St, Manchester NH 03101	603-626-6677	R	48*	.2
65	Amplifier Research Corp—Donald Shepherd	160 Schoolhouse Rd, Souderton PA 18964	215-723-8181	R	46*	.2
66	Wells-Gardner Electronics Corp—Anthony Spier	9500 W 55th St Ste A, McCook IL 60525	708-290-2100	P	46	.1
67	Thales Communications Inc—Mitchell Herbets	22605 Gateway Ctr Dr, Clarksburg MD 20871	240-864-7000	R	46*	.6
68	Eagle Comtronics Inc—William Devendorf	PO Box 2457, Syracuse NY 13220	315-622-3402	R	42*	.7
69	Ampex Corp—D Gordon Strickland	500 Broadway, Redwood City CA 94063	650-367-3365	R	42	.1
70	ClearOne Communications Inc—Zee Hakimoglu	5225 Wiley Post Way St, Salt Lake City UT 84116	801-975-7200	P	41	.1
71	Secure Communication Systems Inc—Allen Ronk	1740 E Wilshire Ave, Santa Ana CA 92705	714-547-1174	R	38*	.1
72	Fidelity Technologies Corp—Jack Gulati	2501 Kutztown Rd, Reading PA 19605	610-929-3330	R	38*	.3
73	Optelecom-NKF Inc—Dave Patterson	12920 Cloverleaf Cente, Germantown MD 20874	301-444-2200	S	36	.2
74	JLCooper Electronics	142 Arena St, El Segundo CA 90245	310-322-9990	R	35*	<.1
75	RF Monolithics Inc—Farlin Halsey	4441 Sigma Rd, Dallas TX 75244	972-233-2903	P	33	.1
76	Sunair International Sales Corp	3400 SW 60th Ave, Ocala FL 34474	352-873-4000	S	32*	.1
77	MC L Inc—Arthur Faverio	501 S Woodcreek Rd, Bolingbrook IL 60440	630-759-9500	R	31*	.5
78	Blonder Tongue Laboratories Inc—James Luksch	1 Jake Brown Rd, Old Bridge NJ 08857	732-679-4000	P	31	.2
79	Proxim Wireless Corp—Lee Gopadze	1561 Buckeye Dr, Milpitas CA 95035	408-383-7600	P	30	.2
80	Comarco Inc—Tom Lanni	25541 Commercentre Dr, Lake Forest CA 92630	949-599-7400	P	29	<.1
81	Acacia Media Technologies Corp—Dooyong Lee	500 Newport Center Dr, Newport Beach CA 92660	949-480-8300	S	28*	.1
82	Soundview Technologies Inc—Paul R Ryan	500 Newport Center Dr, Newport Beach CA 92660	949-480-8300	S	28*	.1
83	Comtech PST Corp—Larry Konopelko Comtech Telecommunications Corp	105 Baylis Rd, Melville NY 11747	631-777-8900	S	27*	.1
84	Etm--Electromatic Inc—Thomas Hayse	35451 Dumbarton Ct, Newark CA 94560	510-797-1100	R	27*	.1
85	David Clark Company Inc—Robert Vincent	PO Box 15054, Worcester MA 01615	508-751-5800	R	26*	.3
86	RL Drake Co—Ron Wysong	230 Industrial Dr, Franklin OH 45005	937-746-4556	R	26*	.1
87	Five Star Productions—Scott Woolley	6001 Park of Commerce, Boca Raton FL 33487	561-279-7827	R	26*	.1
88	Auto-Comm Engineering Corp—Ted Miller	PO Box 61280, Lafayette LA 70506	337-232-9610	R	26*	.1
89	Winegard Co—Randy Winegard	3000 Kirkwood St, Burlington IA 52601	319-754-0600	R	26*	.4
90	TCI International Inc—John W Ballard III	3541 Gateway Blvd, Fremont CA 94538	510-687-6100	S	24*	.1
91	Comsonics Inc—Gary Armentrout	1350 Port Republic Rd, Harrisonburg VA 22801	540-434-5965	R	23*	.2
92	Sensor Systems Inc—Mary E Bazar	8929 Fullbright Ave, Chatsworth CA 91311	818-341-5366	R	23*	.2
93	L-3 Telemetry-East—Rod Oren L-3 Communications Holdings Inc	PO Box 729, Bristol PA 19007	267-545-7000	D	23*	.2
94	Southwest Microwave Inc—Richard McCormick	9055 S McKemy St, Tempe AZ 85284	480-783-0201	R	23*	.1
95	Moseley Associates Inc—Jamal Hamdani	82 Coromar Dr, Santa Barbara CA 93117	805-968-9621	R	21*	.4
96	Findaway World LLC—Christopher Celeste	31999 Aurora Rd, Solon OH 44139	440-893-0808	R	20	.1
97	Cushcraft Corp—Greg Czuba	48 Perimeter Rd, Manchester NH 03103	603-627-7877	R	20*	.1
98	Tecom Industries Inc Trak Microwave Corp	4726 Eisenhower Blvd, Tampa FL 33634	813-901-7200	S	19*	.2
99	Dowslake Microsystems Corp—Dr Dan Yang	21 High St Ste 306, North Andover MA 01845	978-691-5700	R	19*	.1
100	Ditech Networks Inc—Ken Naumann	825 E Middlefield Rd, Mountain View CA 94043	650-623-1300	P	19	.1
101	Broadcast Electronics Inc—Joseph Roark	PO Box 3606, Quincy IL 62305	217-224-9600	R	18*	.2
102	ViewCastcom Inc—John Hammack	3701 W Plano Pky Ste 3, Plano TX 75075	972-488-7200	P	17	.1
103	Instrument Associates Inc—Jay Fregeau	4839 W 128th Pl, Alsip IL 60803	708-597-9880	R	17*	<.1
104	Winncom Technologies Corp—Gregory Raskin	30700 Carter St Ste A, Solon OH 44139	440-498-9510	R	16*	<.1
105	Nokia Siemens Networks Us LLC—Kristin Smith	5020 148th Ave Ne Ste, Redmond WA 98052	425-556-7401	R	16*	.3
106	Ctt Inc—David Tai	241 E Java Dr, Sunnyvale CA 94089	408-541-0596	R	16*	.1
107	Legend Wireless Group Us Inc—Ehsan Gharatappeh	2761 E Trinity Mills R, Carrollton TX 75006	972-416-1066	R	15*	<.1

Note: An asterisk (*) indicates an estimated financial figure. The company type code used is as follows: R = Private, P = Public, S = Private Subsidiary, B = Public Subsidiary, D = Division, J = Joint Venture, I = Investment Fund.

COMPANY RANKINGS BY SALES WITHIN 4-DIGIT SIC

Rank	Company Name—*Executive Officer*	Address, City, State, Zip	Phone	Type	Fin	Empls
108	L-3 ESSCO—*Apostle Cardiasmenos* L-3 Communications Holdings Inc	90 Nemco Way, Ayer MA 01432	978-568-5100	S	14*	.1
109	Reva Systems Corp—*Bruce Berger*	3 LAN Dr, Westford MA 01886	978-392-3663	R	14*	<.1
110	Applied Systems Engineering Inc—*EK Reed*	PO Box 122987, Fort Worth TX 76121	817-249-4180	R	14*	<.1
111	Express Communications LLC	PO Box 474, Eau Claire WI 54702	715-836-6455	R	14*	.4
112	Wheatstone Corp—*Gary Snow*	600 Industrial Dr, New Bern NC 28562	252-638-7000	R	13*	.1
113	Utah Scientific Inc—*Tom Harmon*	4750 Wiley Post Way St, Salt Lake City UT 84116	801-575-8801	R	13*	.1
114	FSR Inc—*Janice Sandri*	244 Bergen Blvd, Woodland Park NJ 07424	973-785-4347	R	13*	.1
115	Mfj Enterprises Inc—*Martin Jue*	PO Box 494, Mississippi State MS 39762		R	13*	.2
116	Indyme Solutions Inc—*Steve Deal*	9085 Aero Dr Ste B, San Diego CA 92123	858-268-0717	R	12*	.1
117	Nissin Precision North America Inc—*Todd Shimizu*	PO Box 399, Englewood OH 45322	937-836-1910	R	12*	.1
118	Micro-Mode Products Inc—*Michael Cuban*	1870 John Towers Ave, El Cajon CA 92020	619-449-3844	R	12*	.1
119	Technical Communications Corp—*Carl H Guild Jr*	100 Domino Dr, Concord MA 01742	978-287-5100	P	12	<.1
120	Ritron Inc—*W Rice*	PO Box 1998, Carmel IN 46082	317-846-1201	R	12*	.1
121	Pico Macom Inc—*Ian A Lerner*	6260 Sequence Dr, San Diego CA 92121	858-546-5050	S	12*	.1
122	Freewave Technologies Inc—*Stephen Wulchin*	1880 S Flatiron Ct Ste, Boulder CO 80301	303-444-3862	R	12*	.1
123	Meteorcomm LLC—*Karen Mcdonald*	1201 Sw 7th St, Renton WA 98057	253-872-2521	R	12*	.1
124	Satcom Resources LLC—*Fred Pope*	PO Box 1639, Avon CO 81620	970-748-3094	R	12*	<.1
125	Microphase Corp—*Necdet Ergul*	PO Box 960, Norwalk CT 06856	203-866-8000	R	12*	.1
126	Winntech Digital Systems Inc—*Barrett Prelogar*	7023 E 12th Ter, Kansas City MO 64126	816-241-4002	R	12*	.1
127	Commstructures Inc—*James Hobbs*	101 E Roberts Rd, Pensacola FL 32534	850-968-9293	R	11*	.1
128	Antenex Inc—*Don Cislo*	1751 Wilkening Ct, Schaumburg IL 60173	847-839-6910	R	11*	.1
129	Comtech Systems Inc—*Dick Burt* Comtech Telecommunications Corp	2900 Titan Row Ste 142, Orlando FL 32809	407-854-1950	S	11*	.1
130	Mobile Technology Inc—*Jim Pendleton*	1955 S Milestone Dr, Salt Lake City UT 84104		R	11*	.1
131	Digital Lightwave Inc—*Robert F Hussey*	1780 102nd Ave N, St Petersburg FL 33716	727-442-6677	R	11	<.1
132	Vital Systems Corp—*Hamid Zaidi*	4999 Arcenter Cir Ste, Reno NV 89502	775-828-1126	R	11*	.1
133	Radio Waves Inc—*Andy Singer*	495r Billerica Ave, North Billerica MA 01862	978-459-8800	R	11*	.1
134	Department of The Air Force—*William Scrivens*	483 N Aviation Blvd, El Segundo CA 90245	310-653-4085	R	10*	.1
135	Acrodyne Communications Inc—*Nat S Ostroff*	10706 Beaver Dam Rd, Cockeysville MD 21030	410-568-1629	S	10*	.1
136	Chelton Microwave Corp	1955 Lakeway Dr Ste 20, Lewisville TX 75057	972-221-1783	S	10*	.1
137	Corporate Computer Systems Inc—*Scott K Ginsberg*	670 N Beers St Bldg 4, Holmdel NJ 07733	732-739-5600	S	10	<.1
138	Manley Laboratories Inc—*EveAnne Manley*	13880 Magnolia Ave, Chino CA 91710	909-627-4256	R	10*	<.1
139	Centron Industries Inc—*Yong Kim*	20760 Leapwood Ave, Carson CA 90746	310-324-6443	R	10*	<.1
140	Instruments For Industry Inc—*Mark Swanson*	903 S 2nd St, Ronkonkoma NY 11779	631-467-8400	R	10*	<.1
141	Jampro Antennas Inc—*Alex Perchevitch*	6340 Sky Creek Dr, Sacramento CA 95828	916-383-1177	R	10*	.1
142	Oai Electronics Inc—*Roger Evonik*	6960 E 12th St, Tulsa OK 74112	918-836-9077	R	9*	.1
143	Telewave Inc—*Ray Collins*	660 Giguere Ct, San Jose CA 95133	408-929-4400	R	9*	<.1
144	Telonics Inc—*Mavin Swapp*	932 E Impala Ave, Mesa AZ 85204	480-892-4444	R	9*	.1
145	Wohler Technologies Inc—*Carl Dempsey*	31055 Huntwood Ave, Hayward CA 94544	510-870-0810	R	9*	.1
146	Wegener Corp—*Troy Woodbury*	11350 Technology Cir, Duluth GA 30097	770-814-4000	P	9	<.1
147	Kathrein Holding USA Inc—*Anton Kathrein*	PO Box 4580, Medford OR 97501	541-779-6500	R	9*	.1
148	Da Vinci Systems Inc—*John R Peeler*	4397 NW 124 Ave, Coral Springs FL 33065	954-688-5600	S	9*	.1
149	Broadcast Supply Worldwide Inc—*Tim Schwieger*	7012 27th St W, Tacoma WA 98466	253-565-2301	R	9*	<.1
150	Grass Valley USA LLC—*Alain Andreoli*	475 Brannan St Ste 400, San Francisco CA 94107	415-852-8500	S	9*	<.1
151	First Spin Inc—*Tony Marglia*	4401 21st St Ste 205, Long Island City NY 11101	212-504-5460	R	9*	<.1
152	Anacom Inc—*James Tom*	1996 Lundy Ave, San Jose CA 95131	408-416-0355	R	9*	.1
153	Impac Technologies Inc—*Louis Parker*	3050 Red Hill Ave, Costa Mesa CA 92626	714-427-2000	R	9*	.1
154	Superconductor Technologies Inc—*Jeffrey A Quiram*	460 Ward Dr, Santa Barbara CA 93111	805-690-4500	P	9	.1
155	PHAZAR Corp—*Garland P Asher*	101 SE 25th Ave, Mineral Wells TX 76067	940-325-3301	P	8	.1
156	Quintech Electronics and Communications Inc—*George Prush-nok*	250 Airport Rd, Indiana PA 15701	724-349-1412	R	8*	.1
157	Digital Systems Inc (Lenexa Kansas)—*David C Owen*	16801 W 116th St, Lenexa KS 66219	913-338-5550	S	8	.1
158	Magneto-Inductive Systems Ltd—*Paul Wrathall*	115 N Del Rosa Dr Ste, San Bernardino CA 92408	909-888-4662	R	8*	<.1
159	Ashly Audio Inc—*Greg Hockman*	847 Holt Rd, Webster NY 14580	585-872-0010	R	8*	<.1
160	Ils International Launch Services Inc—*Frank Mckenna*	1875 Explorer St Ste 7, Reston VA 20190	571-633-7400	R	8*	.1
161	Ar Kalmus Corp—*Donald Shepherd* Amplifier Research Corp	21222 30th Dr Se Ste 2, Bothell WA 98021	425-485-9000	S	8*	<.1
162	Harris Corp Microwave Communications Div—*Howard Lance*	1025 West NASA Blvd, Melbourne FL 32919		D	8*	<.1
163	Locus Inc—*Linn Roth*	5540 Research Park Dr, Madison WI 53711	608-270-0500	R	8*	<.1
164	Blueradios Inc—*Mark J Kramer*	7173 S Havana St Ste 6, Englewood CO 80112	303-957-1003	R	8*	<.1
165	Tini Aerospace Inc—*Michael Bokaie*	2505 Kerner Blvd, San Rafael CA 94901	415-524-2124	R	8*	.1
166	Antenna Research Associates Inc—*Pradeep Wahi*	12201 Indian Creek Ct, Beltsville MD 20705	301-937-8888	R	8*	.1
167	Renae Telecom LLC	745 Thomas St, Elizabeth NJ 07202	908-362-8112	R	8*	.1
168	Diamond Antenna and Microwave Corp—*Jeffrey Gilling*	59 Porter Rd, Littleton MA 01460	978-486-0039	R	8*	.1
169	Trivec-Avant Corp—*Allen Muesse*	17831 Jamestown Ln, Huntington Beach CA 92647	714-841-4976	R	7*	.1
170	Rpr Graphics Inc—*Richard Ruocco*	PO Box 1159, Mountainside NJ 07092	908-654-8080	R	7*	.1
171	Rotating Precision Mechanisms Inc—*Kathy Nicolai*	8750 Shirley Ave, Northridge CA 91324	818-349-8680	R	7*	<.1
172	Frc Component Products Inc—*Fawzia Elmahdawy*	1511 S Benjamin Ave, Mason City IA 50401	641-424-0370	R	7*	.2
173	Ags Technology Inc—*Kyu Cho*	4800 Alliance Gateway, Fort Worth TX 76177	205-942-4855	R	7*	.1
174	Southern Cal Microwave—*Steve Patton*	2732 Via Orange Way St, Spring Valley CA 91978	619-670-3414	S	7*	<.1
175	SkyCross Inc—*Ben Naskar*	7341 Office Park Pl St, Melbourne FL 32940	321-308-6600	R	7*	<.1
176	JW Davis and Co—*MH Earp*	PO Box 710219, Dallas TX 75371	214-651-7341	R	7*	<.1
177	West-Com Nurse Call Systems Inc—*C Peters*	2200 Cordelia Rd, Fairfield CA 94534	707-428-5900	R	7*	.1
178	New-Tronics Ltd—*Clyde Ford*	1 Newtronics Pl, Mineral Wells TX 76067	940-325-1386	R	7*	.1
179	RF Products Inc—*Robert Minke*	1500 Davis St, Camden NJ 08103	856-365-5500	R	7*	.1
180	Herotek Inc—*Cheng Lai*	155 Baytech Dr, San Jose CA 95134	408-941-8399	R	7*	<.1
181	Novak Electronics Inc—*Robert Novak*	17032 Armstrong Ave, Irvine CA 92614	949-833-8873	R	6*	<.1
182	Satellink Inc—*Robert Goodrich*	PO Box 472967, Garland TX 75047	972-487-1434	R	6*	.1
183	Shook Mobile Technology LP—*John Heaney*	7451 Fm 3009, Schertz TX 78154	210-651-5700	R	6*	.1
184	TLS Corp—*Steve Church*	1241 Superior Ave E, Cleveland OH 44114	216-241-7225	R	6*	<.1
185	Echo Mountain Realty Inc—*William Lieske*	22402 N 19th Ave, Phoenix AZ 85027	623-581-2875	R	6*	<.1
186	Antenna Products Corp PHAZAR Corp	101 SE 25th Ave, Mineral Wells TX 76067	940-325-3301	S	6*	.1
187	Rpg Diffusor Systems Inc—*Peter D'antonio*	651 Commerce Dr C, Upper Marlboro MD 20774	301-249-0044	R	6*	<.1
188	COMTEK—*Joseph Fergus*	357 W 2700 S, Salt Lake City UT 84115	801-466-3463	R	6*	<.1
189	PCT International—*Steve Youtsey*	2260 W Broadway Rd, Mesa AZ 85202	480-313-0925	R	6*	<.1
190	Anacom Systems Inc—*Henry J Wojtunik*	3434 Rt 22 W Ste 140, Branchburg NJ 08876	908-754-0646	S	6*	<.1
191	Broadcast Technology Co—*Chuck Springer*	PO Box 2581, Garden City KS 67846	620-290-2263	R	6*	<.1
192	Global Satcom Technology Inc—*Cecil Lo*	9141 Arbuckle Dr, Gaithersburg MD 20877	301-963-0088	R	6*	<.1

Rank	Company Name—*Executive Officer*	Address, City, State, Zip	Phone	Type	Fin	Empls
193	Myat Inc—*Philip Cindrich*	360 Franklin Tpke, Mahwah NJ 07430	201-684-0100	R	6*	<.1
194	Marvel Communications Company Inc—*Shelia Simmons*	6000 Old Hemphill Rd D, Fort Worth TX 76134	817-568-0177	R	6*	.1
195	Css Antenna Inc—*Dee Sobczak*	2206 Lakeside Blvd Ste, Edgewood MD 21040	410-612-0080	R	6*	<.1
196	Law Enforcement Associates Corp—*Paul Briggs*	2609 Discovery Dr Ste, Raleigh NC 27616	919-872-6210	P	6	<.1
197	Tim Hoover Enterprises—*Tim Hoover*	8532 Yarrow Ln, Riverside CA 92508	951-653-6836	R	5*	<.1
198	Kintronic Laboratories Inc—*Thomas King*	PO Box 845, Bristol TN 37621	423-878-3141	R	5*	<.1
199	Communications-Applied Technology Co—*Seth Leyman*	11250 Roger Bacon Dr S, Reston VA 20190	703-481-0068	R	5*	<.1
200	Michigan Satellite—*John Dawson*	3215 Christy Way S, Saginaw MI 48603	989-497-9544	R	5*	<.1
201	Bluewater Broadcasting Inc—*Rick Peters*	4101 Wall St Ste A, Montgomery AL 36106	334-244-1170	R	5*	<.1
202	Sti-Co Industries Inc—*Antoinette Kaiser*	11 Cobham Dr, Orchard Park NY 14127	716-662-2680	R	5*	<.1
203	Delta Electronics Inc—*John Wright*	PO Box 11268, Alexandria VA 22312	703-354-3350	R	5*	<.1
204	Joyner and Associates—*Kenner Joyner*	13760 Noel Rd Ste 750, Dallas TX 75240	972-789-1058	R	5*	.1
205	Audio Accessories Inc—*Mb Hall*	PO Box 360, Marlow NH 03456	603-446-3335	R	5*	<.1
206	Goeken Group Corp—*Jack Goeken*	1751 W Diehl Rd Ste 40, Naperville IL 60563	630-717-6700	R	5*	<.1
207	Century Metal Parts Corp—*Frank Swierzbin*	230 S Fehr Way, Bay Shore NY 11706	631-667-0800	R	5*	<.1
208	Appaient Technologies Inc—*Chris O'Donnell*	150 Lucius Gordon Dr, West Henrietta NY 14586	585-214-2460	R	5*	<.1
209	HunTel Communications Inc—*Dan Hunt*	14109 S St, Omaha NE 68137	402-493-5200	S	5*	<.1
210	Automated Assembly Corp—*Scott Lindblad*	20777 Kensington Blvd, Lakeville MN 55044	952-469-6556	R	5*	<.1
211	TSS-Radio LLC—*Taylor Mitchell*	1348 W Concord Pl 3rd, Chicago IL 60642	773-772-4340	R	5*	<.1
212	Flightcom Corp—*Brian Vanderploeg*	7340 Sw Durham Rd, Tigard OR 97224	503-684-8229	R	5*	<.1
213	Andersen Manufacturing Inc—*John Andersen*	3125 N Yellowstone Hwy, Idaho Falls ID 83401	208-523-6460	R	5*	<.1
214	Mega Industries LLC—*Peter Matthew*	28 Sanford Dr, Gorham ME 04038	207-854-1700	R	5*	<.1
215	Andrea Electronics Corp—*Douglas J Andrea*	65 Orville Dr Ste 1, Bohemia NY 11716	631-719-1800	P	5	<.1
216	GigaBeam Acquisition Corp—*Jay Lawrence*	4915 Prospectus Dr, Durham NC 27713	919-206-4426	R	5	<.1
217	Mikros Systems Corp—*Thomas J Meaney*	707 Alexander Rd Ste 2, Princeton NJ 08540	609-987-1513	P	5	<.1
218	CES Wireless Technologies Corp—*Pat Lohan*	925 S Semoran Blvd Ste, Winter Park FL 32792	407-679-9440	R	5*	<.1
219	Omni Vision Inc—*Thomas Fair*	2000 Bloomingdale Rd S, Glendale Heights IL 60139	630-893-1720	R	5*	<.1
220	Pearpoint Inc—*Paul Tistai*	39740 Garand Ln Ste B, Palm Desert CA 92211	760-343-1095	R	5*	<.1
221	E2g Partners LLC—*Eric Guerrazzi*	12160 Race Track Rd, Tampa FL 33626	813-855-2251	R	5*	<.1
222	Olson Technology Inc—*Thomas Olson*	24926 State Hwy 108, Mi Wuk Village CA 95346	209-586-1022	R	5*	<.1
223	Ten-Tec Inc—*Jack Burchfield*	1185 Dolly Parton Pkwy, Sevierville TN 37862	865-453-7172	R	4*	.1
224	TPL Communications Inc—*John Ehret*	3370 San Fernando Rd S, Los Angeles CA 90065	323-256-3000	R	4*	.1
225	Jedi Communications—*Adam Dennis*	24801 Hill Rd, Hollywood MD 20636	301-373-4815	R	4*	<.1
226	Precision Contacts Inc—*Mat Wroblewski*	990 Suncast Ln, El Dorado Hills CA 95762	916-939-4147	R	4*	<.1
227	Antennas For Communications Ocala Fl Inc—*Leslie Spivey*	350 Cypress Rd, Ocala FL 34472	352-687-4121	R	4*	<.1
228	Data Path Inc—*Adam Cohen*	20 Austin Blvd, Commack NY 11725	631-273-3527	R	4*	<.1
229	Usglobalsat Inc—*Shirley Cheng*	14740 Yorba Ct, Chino CA 91710	909-597-8525	R	4*	<.1
230	Amplitech Inc—*Fawad Maqbool*	1373 Lincoln Ave, Holbrook NY 11741	631-521-7831	R	4*	<.1
231	Pacific Radomes Inc—*John Burke*	2543 Precision Dr, Minden NV 89423	775-267-5480	R	4*	<.1
232	Clearcomm Technologies LLC	PO Box 81, Fruitland MD 21826	410-860-0500	R	4*	<.1
233	Southeastern Engineering Inc—*Harry Zeek*	PO Box 61442, Palm Bay FL 32906	321-984-2521	R	4*	<.1
234	Amplivox Sound Systems LLC—*Don Roth*	3995 Commercial Ave, Northbrook IL 60062	847-498-9000	R	4*	<.1
235	Energy-Onix Broadcast Equipment Inc—*Bernie Wise*	PO Box 801, Valatie NY 12184	518-758-1690	R	4*	<.1
236	WBWalton Enterprises Inc—*William Walton*	PO Box 1328, Riverside CA 92502	951-683-0030	R	4*	<.1
237	Fine Laboratories Inc—*Carl Hurt*	100 Ashely Pkwy, Piedmont MO 63957	573-223-2388	R	4*	.1
238	Nahuel Trading Corp—*Oscar Mouras*	17838 Ne 5th Ave, Miami FL 33162	305-932-1163	R	3*	<.1
239	Burk Technology Inc—*Peter Burk*	7 Beaver Brook Rd, Littleton MA 01460	978-486-0086	R	3*	<.1
240	Radian Audio Engineering Inc—*Richard Kontrimas*	600 N Batavia St, Orange CA 92868	714-288-8900	R	3*	<.1
241	Aci Communications Inc—*John Tai*	23307 66th Ave S, Kent WA 98032	253-854-9802	R	3*	<.1
242	Optodyne Inc—*Charles Wang*	1180 W Mahalo Pl, Compton CA 90220	310-635-7481	R	3*	<.1
243	Cobra Technologies Corp—*William Brown*	4806 Wright Dr Se Ste, Smyrna GA 30082	770-435-3309	R	3*	<.1
244	Logitek Electronic Systems Inc—*Tag Borland*	5622 Edgemoor Dr, Houston TX 77081	713-664-4470	R	3*	<.1
245	Front End Services—*George Jensen*	1100 Fountain Pkwy, Grand Prairie TX 75050	214-672-0600	R	3*	<.1
246	Comtron Inc—*Guenther Wackerman*	391 State Rte 33, Manalapan NJ 07726	732-446-7571	R	3*	<.1
247	Icon Enterprises International Inc—*Claudio Laraia*	5025 35th St, Long Island City NY 11101	718-752-9764	R	3*	<.1
248	Telemetrics Inc—*Anthony Cuomo*	6 Leighton Pl Ste 4, Mahwah NJ 07430	201-848-9818	R	3*	<.1
249	Belar Electronics Laboratory Inc—*Arno Meyer*	PO Box 76, Devon PA 19333	610-687-5550	R	3*	<.1
250	Crescend Technologies LLC—*Jim Baker*	140 E State Pkwy, Schaumburg IL 60173	847-908-5400	R	3*	<.1
251	Syn-Fab Inc—*J Kennedy*	7863 Schillinger Park, Mobile AL 36608	251-633-4942	R	3*	<.1
252	Stellar One Corp—*Lars Jonsson*	5350 Carillon Point, Kirkland WA 98033	206-467-8200	R	3*	<.1
253	Communication Devices Inc	85 Fulton St, Boonton NJ 07005	973-334-1980	R	3*	<.1
254	American Video Equipment—*Alex Twyman*	2501 Central Pkwy Ste, Houston TX 77092	281-443-2300	R	3*	<.1
255	Catv Services Inc—*Richard Richmond*	12099 Nw 98th Ave, Hialeah FL 33018	305-512-5601	R	3*	<.1
256	Swift Computers Inc—*Carl Swift*	PO Box 2288, Stafford TX 77497	832-947-1760	R	3*	<.1
257	Tft Inc—*Mike Reddy*	1953 Concourse Dr, San Jose CA 95131	408-943-9323	R	3*	<.1
258	Sierra Automated Systems and Engineering Corp—*Edward Fritz*	2821 Burton Ave, Burbank CA 91504	818-840-6749	R	3*	<.1
259	Metropole Products Inc—*Al Leaman*	PO Box 309, Stafford VA 22555	540-659-2132	R	3*	<.1
260	Acroamatics Inc—*Geoffrey Johnson*	5385 Hollister Ave Ste, Santa Barbara CA 93111	805-967-9909	R	3*	<.1
261	D W Ram Manufacturing Co—*Douglas Murdaugh*	18530 Spring Creek Dr, Tinley Park IL 60477	708-633-7900	R	3*	<.1
262	Mmcomm Inc—*Yi-Chi Shih*	2525 W 190th St, Torrance CA 90504	310-512-4225	R	3*	<.1
263	Nanlee Industries—*L Schwartzman*	1400 N Shoreline Blvd, Mountain View CA 94043	650-965-8020	R	3*	<.1
264	Smith Brodcasting Of Vermont LLC	298 Mountain View Dr, Colchester VT 05446	802-660-9333	R	3*	<.1
265	Communications Etc—*Tom Phillips*	PO Box 276255, San Antonio TX 78227	210-673-6299	R	3*	<.1
266	Commtech 2000—*Edwin Weaver*	4624 S Creyts Rd, Lansing MI 48917	517-322-2001	R	3*	<.1
267	Paso Sound Products Inc—*Paul Mastrangelo*	4750 Goer Dr Ste F, North Charleston SC 29406	843-308-9005	R	3*	<.1
268	Roselm Industries Inc—*Conrad Arguijo*	2511 Seaman Ave, South El Monte CA 91733	626-442-6840	R	3*	<.1
269	Hysen Technologies Inc—*Jay Chelo*	1725 Mendon Rd Unit 20, Cumberland RI 02864	401-312-6500	R	3*	<.1
270	Gps Networking Inc—*Steven Waite*	3915 Outlook Blvd Ste, Pueblo CO 81008	719-595-9880	R	3*	<.1
271	SOS Inc—*Fred Whiting*	7 Walnut Ave, Clark NJ 07066	732-381-0700	R	3*	<.1
272	Tech Communication Inc—*Gersald O'hearn*	5010 N Hiatus Rd, Sunrise FL 33351	954-749-1776	R	3*	<.1
273	Midian Electronics Inc—*Charles Soulliard*	2302 E 22nd St, Tucson AZ 85713	520-884-7981	R	2*	<.1
274	Radio Systems Design Inc—*Daniel Braverman*	601 Heron Dr, Swedesboro NJ 08085	856-467-8000	R	2*	<.1
275	Modular Communications Systems—*Robert Moesch*	13309 Saticoy St, North Hollywood CA 91605	818-764-1333	R	2*	<.1
276	UB Corp—*Robert Upcavage*	9829 Wilsky Blvd, Tampa FL 33615	813-884-1463	R	2*	<.1
277	Connect Systems Inc—*Jerry Wanger*	PO Box 3666, Ventura CA 93006	805-642-7184	R	2*	<.1
278	Conrad-Johnson Design Inc—*William Conrad*	2733 Merrilee Dr, Fairfax VA 22031	703-698-8581	R	2*	<.1
279	Optical Robotics LLC—*Alan Grant*	4806 Wright Dr Se Ste, Smyrna GA 30082	770-435-3309	R	2*	<.1
280	Brian Kim—*Brian Kim*	11615 La Grange Ave, Los Angeles CA 90025	310-324-6078	R	2*	<.1
281	Custom Video Design Inc—*Charlotte Kutyba*	11626 34th Pl, Beltsville MD 20705	301-595-4369	R	2*	<.1

Note: An asterisk (*) indicates an estimated financial figure. The company type code used is as follows: R = Private, P = Public, S = Private Subsidiary, B = Public Subsidiary, D = Division, J = Joint Venture, I = Investment Fund.

COMPANY RANKINGS BY SALES WITHIN 4-DIGIT SIC

Rank	Company Name—Executive Officer	Address, City, State, Zip	Phone	Type	Fin	Empls
282	Green Energy Corp—Robert Tan	5082 4th St, Baldwin Park CA 91706	626-856-6400	R	2*	<.1
283	Mobo USA Corp—Marcelo Barniquel	6000 Nw 97th Ave Unit, Doral FL 33178	305-591-0324	R	2*	<.1
284	Maranatha Industries Inc—Peggy Lee	PO Box 209, Payne OH 45880	419-263-2013	R	2*	<.1
285	Arrakis Systems Inc—Michael Palmer	6604 Powell St, Loveland CO 80538	970-461-0730	R	2*	<.1
286	Radeum Inc—Randy Bailey	266 W Ctr St, Orem UT 84057	801-467-1199	R	2*	<.1
287	Tel-Conn Manufacturing Inc—Lavone Bateman	1625 Lakes Pkwy Ste J, Lawrenceville GA 30043	770-338-4206	R	2*	<.1
288	Zephyrus Electronics Ltd—Brian Young	168 S 122nd E Ave, Tulsa OK 74128	918-437-3333	R	2*	<.1
289	Nevion USA—Eugene Keane	1600 Emerson Ave, Oxnard CA 93033	805-247-8560	R	2*	.1
290	Acousticom Corp—Mark Cochran	28180 Clay St, Elkhart IN 46517	574-293-0534	R	2*	<.1
291	Ensemble Designs Inc	PO Box 993, Grass Valley CA 95945	530-478-1830	R	2*	<.1
292	American 2 Way Radio Inc—Frank Rizzuto	2902 Harney St, Omaha NE 68131	402-345-6402	R	2*	<.1
293	JEI—Jack Mahoney	3087 Alhambra Dr, Cameron Park CA 95682	530-677-3210	R	2*	<.1
294	Microwave Dynamics—Sean Adel	14321 Chambers Rd, Tustin CA 92780	714-505-0998	R	2*	<.1
295	Dimension Technologies Inc—Arnie Lagergren	315 Mt Read Blvd, Rochester NY 14611	585-436-3530	R	2*	<.1
296	Microframe Corp—Bob Mccullough	PO Box 1700, Broken Arrow OK 74013	918-258-4839	R	2*	<.1
297	West Electronics Inc (Burlington New Jersey)—Brad Brainard	PO Box 366, Burlington NJ 08016	609-387-4300	R	2*	<.1
298	Cable Aml Inc—Francisco Bernues	2271 W 205th St Ste 10, Torrance CA 90501	310-222-5599	R	2*	<.1
299	Telescript Inc—James Stringer	445 Livingston St, Norwood NJ 07648	201-767-6733	R	2*	<.1
300	Daysequerra Corp—David Day	PO Box 1530, Voorhees NJ 08043	856-719-9900	R	2*	<.1
301	Phasetek Inc—Kurt Gorman	550 California Rd Ste, Quakertown PA 18951	215-536-6648	R	2*	<.1
302	T-Square—Nick Michaels	PO Box 279, Dyer IN 46311	219-985-4000	R	2*	<.1
303	Savr Communications Inc—John Crossno	3080 Story Rd W, Irving TX 75038	972-659-1626	R	2*	<.1
304	Loma Scientific International—J Loughboro	3115 Kashiwa St, Torrance CA 90505	310-539-8655	R	2*	<.1
305	Specialty Microwave Corp—Stephen Faber	120 Raynor Ave, Ronkonkoma NY 11779	631-737-1919	R	2*	<.1
306	Sgc World Inc—Bruce Wood	PO Box 3526, Bellevue WA 98009	425-746-6310	R	2*	<.1
307	Mu-Del Electronics Inc—Souren Hakopian	8576 Wellington Rd, Manassas VA 20109	703-709-9400	R	2*	<.1
308	Tower Works Inc—Steven Svestha	47w543 Perry Rd, Maple Park IL 60151	630-557-2221	R	2*	<.1
309	Managed Communications Services LLC	PO Box 387, Huntertown IN 46748	260-480-7885	R	2*	<.1
310	Apex Airtronics Inc—William Rosenblum	2465 Atlantic Ave, Brooklyn NY 11207	718-485-8560	R	2*	<.1
311	Earthsearch Communications Inc—Kayode Aladesuyi	120 Interstate N Pkwy, Atlanta GA 30339	770-953-4184	R	2*	<.1
312	T-Metrics Inc—Ron Kahn	4430 Stuart Andrew Blv, Charlotte NC 28217	704-525-5551	R	2*	<.1
313	Benchmark Media Systems Inc—Allen Burdick	203 E Hampton Pl Ste 2, Syracuse NY 13206	315-437-6300	R	2*	<.1
314	Haigh-Farr Inc—David Farr	43 Harvey Rd, Bedford NH 03110	603-644-6170	R	2*	<.1
315	Palmetto Shelters Inc—Cliff Hall	1125 Joe Lewis Dr, Columbia SC 29210	803-254-3766	R	2*	<.1
316	Redstone Aerospace Corp—Robert Levenduski	PO Box 1504, Longmont CO 80502	303-684-8125	R	2*	<.1
317	Mobile Satellite Connection LLC—Richard Ball	908 Lakeside Dr, Mobile AL 36693	251-666-5757	R	2*	<.1
318	Tron-Tek Inc—William Grass	6570b E 51st St, Tulsa OK 74145	918-663-4877	R	2*	<.1
319	Millennium Microwave Corp—Steven Rumney	402 S Brown St Ste C, Fruitland MD 21826	410-742-8858	R	2*	<.1
320	Protostar Ltd	50 California St Ste 2, San Francisco CA 94111	415-675-2227	R	2*	<.1
321	United Satcom Inc—Ted Park	4555 Robinson St, Flushing NY 11355	718-359-4100	R	2*	<.1
322	Dorrough Electronics Inc—Karen Dorrough	20434 Corisco St, Chatsworth CA 91311	818-998-2824	R	2*	<.1
323	Orion Tech—Jong Kim	12590 Cambridge Dr, Saratoga CA 95070	408-343-0670	R	2*	<.1
324	Wilmanco—Harold Williams	5350 Kazuko Ct, Moorpark CA 93021	805-523-2390	R	1*	<.1
325	On Call Communications Inc—James Gilbert	19631 Descartes, Foothill Ranch CA 92610	949-716-3030	R	1*	<.1
326	Wubz105 9—Michael Stapleford	315 S Atherton St, State College PA 16801	814-272-2899	R	1*	<.1
327	Heil Sound Ltd—Bob Heil	5800 N Illinois St, Fairview Heights IL 62208	618-257-3000	R	1*	<.1
328	Signa Inc—Ronald Hapanowicz	1262 Kensington Ave, Grosse Pointe Park MI 48230	313-884-1141	R	1*	<.1
329	O'donnell Manufacturing Inc—Steve O'donnell	13188 Sandoval St, Santa Fe Springs CA 90670	562-944-9671	R	1*	<.1
330	PCI Manufacturing Division Inc—Sue Edwards	2103 N Ross St, Santa Ana CA 92706	714-543-3496	R	1*	<.1
331	Z Technology Inc—James Zook	PO Box 6806, Beaverton OR 97007	503-614-9800	R	1*	<.1
332	Bel Canto Design Ltd—John Stronczer	221 N 1st St Ste 300, Minneapolis MN 55401	612-852-2501	R	1*	<.1
333	Canam Technology Inc—Michael Martinez	5318 E 2nd St Ste 700, Long Beach CA 90803	562-856-0178	R	1*	<.1
334	Metric Systems Corp—William Brown	1315 Hot Spring Way St, Vista CA 92081	760-560-0348	R	1*	<.1
335	Radiotronics Inc—John Johnston	1556 Cyprefl Dr Ste 2, Jupiter FL 33469	561-746-0935	R	1*	<.1
336	Zaxcom Inc—Glen Sanders	230 W Pky Ste 9, Pompton Plains NJ 07444	973-835-5000	R	1*	<.1
337	Core Labs LLC	3720 S Lipan St Ste A, Englewood CO 80110	303-761-0131	R	1*	<.1
338	Electronic Installations Inc—Jimmie O'daniell	PO Box 15127, Wilmington NC 28408	910-799-2901	R	1*	<.1
339	Mckee Communications Inc—Peter Mckee	6381 Rose Ln Ste A, Carpinteria CA 93013	805-684-7710	R	1*	<.1
340	Sunol Sciences Corp—G Guthrie	6780 Sierra Ct Ste R, Dublin CA 94568	925-833-9936	R	1*	<.1
341	Integrated Microwave Technologies LLC—Robert Chiarulli	200 International Dr S, Budd Lake NJ 07828	908-852-3700	R	1*	.1
342	Comtech Antenna Systems Inc—Tom Christy Comtech Telecommunications Corp	3100 Communications Rd, Saint Cloud FL 34769	407-892-6111	S	1*	<.1
343	Em Technologies Inc—O Kim	PO Box 549, Prosper TX 75078	972-347-2041	R	1*	<.1
344	Barker and Williamson Corp	603 Cidco Rd, Cocoa FL 32926	321-639-1510	R	1*	<.1
345	SEA Inc—Skip Mucaelrath	7030 220th St SW, Mountlake Terrace WA 98043	425-771-2182	S	1*	<.1
346	Emergency Beacon Corp—Joan Goodman	15 River St, New Rochelle NY 10801	914-235-9400	R	1*	<.1
347	Kelley Communications Inc—Patrick Kelley	1902 N Country Club Dr, Mesa AZ 85201	480-969-0618	R	1*	<.1
348	Sartek Industries Inc—Carl Saieva	3661 Horseblock Rd Ste, Medford NY 11763	631-924-0441	R	1*	<.1
349	Trisquare Communications Inc—Gary Staley	1420 Nw Vivion Rd Ste, Kansas City MO 64118	816-505-3575	R	1*	<.1
350	Ardax Systems Inc—Aram Gharakhanian	906 Ctr St, San Carlos CA 94070	650-591-2656	R	1*	<.1
351	Dell-Star Technologies Inc—Sunun Gibson	6334 E 13th St, Tulsa OK 74112	918-838-1973	R	1*	<.1
352	Hotlines Inc—Mike Vandevoort	427 E Kanesville Blvd, Council Bluffs IA 51503	712-388-0095	R	1*	<.1
353	Tribeam Inc—Michael Kazecki	1323 S Fernandez Ave, Arlington Heights IL 60005	847-409-9497	R	1*	<.1
354	Colby Systems Inc—Charles Colby	2991 Alexis Dr, Palo Alto CA 94304	650-941-9090	R	1*	<.1
355	Nutel Electronics Corp	95 Cliff Way, Sea Cliff NY 11579	516-676-5276	R	1*	<.1
356	AGL Services Co—Allen Leonard	PO Box 466, Canandaigua NY 14424		S	1*	<.1
357	Xintekidel Inc—John Rossi	56 W Broad St, Stamford CT 06902	203-348-9229	R	1*	<.1
358	Antenna Concepts Inc—Mark Cunningham	6626 Merchandise Way, Diamond Springs CA 95619	530-621-2015	R	1*	<.1
359	W C Laikam Co—Mike Leslie	2356 S Sarah St, Fresno CA 93706	559-266-1043	R	1*	<.1
360	Larry Mcgee Co—Mitchell Kaplan	720 Armstrong Dr, Buffalo Grove IL 60089	847-419-9960	R	1*	<.1
361	Componexx Corp—Edwin Diaz	PO Box 268293, Fort Lauderdale FL 33326	954-572-8229	R	1*	<.1
362	Kantronics Company Inc—Cheryl Seiwald	14830 W 117th St, Olathe KS 66062	913-825-0680	R	1*	<.1
363	Summary Systems Inc—Robert Montana	1100 Summit Ave Ste 10, Plano TX 75074	972-943-8882	R	1*	<.1
364	Isc Datacom Inc—Charles Whitecotton	610 E Main St Ste 410, Allen TX 75002	972-649-6100	R	1*	<.1
365	Fm Systems Inc—Frank Clatchie	3877 S Main St, Santa Ana CA 92707	714-979-3355	R	1*	<.1
366	Lpb Communications Inc—Tom Spadea	PO Box 1075, Haddonfield NJ 08033	856-365-8585	R	1*	<.1
367	Nhrc LLC—Rich Cox	415 4th Range Rd, Pembroke NH 03275	603-485-2248	R	1*	<.1
368	Vigicomm Inc—Sumeet Suri	1150 Silverado St Ste, La Jolla CA 92037	858-964-4566	R	1*	<.1
369	Antenna and Satellite Technology Inc—Patrick Hart	PO Box 146, Gig Harbor WA 98335	206-763-4940	R	1*	<.1

Rank	Company Name—*Executive Officer*	Address, City, State, Zip	Phone	Type	Fin	Empls
370	Professional Electronic Components Assembly Inc—*Ralph Douglass*	PO Box 224, Bensalem PA 19020	215-245-1550	R	1*	<.1
371	Integra Systems Corp—*Barry Nulph*	4607 S 35th St Ste 6, Phoenix AZ 85040	602-276-2880	R	1*	<.1
372	Superior Satellite Engineers Inc—*Doyle Catlett*	1743 Middle Rd, Columbia Falls MT 59912	406-257-9590	R	1*	<.1
373	Electronic Directory Systems Inc—*Clair Woertendyke*	4733 Don Dr, Dallas TX 75247	214-634-0037	R	1*	<.1
374	Wintenna Inc—*Jeff Wingard*	113a E Shockley Ferry, Anderson SC 29624	864-261-3965	R	1*	<.1
375	Blackbeard Communications Inc—*John Verbeek*	2321 Morena Blvd Ste H, San Diego CA 92110	619-276-3800	R	1*	<.1
376	Balsys Technology Group Inc—*Larry Lamoray*	930 Carter Rd Ste 228, Winter Garden FL 34787	407-656-3719	R	1*	<.1
377	Cj Component Products LLC—*David Howe*	PO Box 537, Oakdale NY 11769	631-567-3733	R	1*	<.1
378	Glenn Sound Company Inc—*Glenn Lorbiecki*	228 Dexter Ave N Ste 1, Seattle WA 98109	206-583-8112	R	1*	<.1
379	Louis Systems and Products Inc—*Gerald Barrett*	13816 N Lincoln Blvd, Edmond OK 73013	405-755-1451	R	1*	<.1
380	Morad Electronics Corp—*Ken Holland*	1125 Nw 46th St, Seattle WA 98107	206-789-2525	R	1*	<.1
381	Standard Communications LLC—*Jose Zyman*	6260 Sequence Dr, San Diego CA 92121	858-546-5300	R	1*	<.1
382	Open Terra Inc—*David Sasson*	20 Reddington Dr, Matawan NJ 07747	732-765-9600	R	1*	<.1
383	Avi Communications Inc—*Patrick Shaughnessy*	517 Huffines Blvd, Lewisville TX 75056	972-939-7135	R	1*	<.1
384	Azimuth Unlimited LLC—*Sangwon Lee*	3020 N Commerce Pkwy, Miramar FL 33025	954-436-8081	R	1*	<.1
385	Control Signal Corp—*Shepard Brodie*	5964 W Columbia Pl, Denver CO 80227	303-986-3254	R	1*	<.1
386	Hilomast LLC—*Lance Burney*	402 Chairman Ct Ste 10, Debary FL 32713	386-668-6784	R	1*	<.1
387	Max System Inc—*Thomas Bernie*	4 Gerring Rd, Gloucester MA 01930	978-281-8892	R	1*	<.1
388	Dayton Industrial Corp—*Donald Roettele*	2237 Industrial Blvd, Sarasota FL 34234	941-351-4454	R	1*	<.1
389	Rainbow Satellite Communications Inc—*Brian Wilkes*	PO Box 490395, Leesburg FL 34749	352-326-8030	R	1*	<.1
390	Crimeye Inc—*Larry Hatch*	5411 W Orange Dr Ste 1, Glendale AZ 85301	623-435-1284	R	1*	<.1
391	Digital Sound And Satellite—*Ed Lefebvre*	1757 N Nova Rd Ste 106, Holly Hill FL 32117	386-767-0097	R	1*	<.1
392	Gary J Welch—*Gary Welch*	25 Elm Park, Groveland MA 01834	978-372-3442	R	1*	<.1
393	GTX Corp (Los Angeles California)—*Patrick Bertagna*	117 W 9th St Ste 1214, Los Angeles CA 90015	213-489-3019	P	<1	<.1
394	Oak Bay Technologies Inc—*Mark Mc Kibbin*	PO Box 65494, Port Ludlow WA 98365	360-437-0718	R	<1*	<.1
395	David Kelkom Systems—*David Kellems*	418 Macarthur Ave, Redwood City CA 94063	650-366-3877	R	<1*	<.1
396	Samco Antennas Inc—*Don Sanford*	2607 W Waggoman St, Fort Worth TX 76110	817-336-4351	R	<1*	<.1
397	Glencom Inc—*Greg Halik*	5955 S Oak St, Glen Arbor MI 49636	231-334-6516	R	<1*	<.1
398	Star Warehouse Inc—*Larry Pride*	1573 N Dixie Blvd, Radcliff KY 40160	270-351-9696	R	<1*	<.1
399	Technical Material Corp—*Neil De Pasquale*	PO Box 116, Mamaroneck NY 10543	914-698-4800	R	<1*	<.1
400	Isodyne Inc—*Joe Reilly*	7706 E Osie St, Wichita KS 67207	316-682-5634	R	<1*	<.1
401	Kreco Antennas—*Glenn Kreckman*	3340 Spruce Cabin Rd, Cresco PA 18326	570-595-2212	R	<1*	<.1
402	Lakeview Company Inc—*Mike Swass*	3620 Whitehall Rd Lot, Anderson SC 29626	864-226-6990	R	<1*	<.1
403	Metz Communication Corp—*Richard Metz*	151c Elm St, Laconia NH 03246	603-528-2590	R	<1*	<.1
404	TIC General—*Carl Anderson*	1815 Robin Hood Dr, Thief River Falls MN 56701	218-681-1119	R	<1*	<.1
405	AVM Instrument Company Ltd—*Barbara Kermeen*	10072 Streeter Rd Ste, Auburn CA 95602	530-268-2369	R	<1*	<.1
406	Global Communication—*Cynthia Rains*	PO Box 406, Buckner MO 64016	816-650-6503	R	<1*	<.1
407	Telemetrix Inc—*William Becker*	6650 Gunpark Dr Ste 10, Boulder CO 80301	303-652-0103	P	<1	<.1
408	Advanced Receiver Research—*Jay Rusgrove*	PO Box 1242, Burlington CT 06013	860-485-0310	R	<1*	<.1
409	Global Networx Inc—*Gary Dickey*	50 Lost Acres Ln, Amissville VA 20106	540-937-5900	R	<1*	<.1
410	JT Communications—*James Trapani*	579 Ne 44th Ave, Ocala FL 34470	352-236-0744	R	<1*	<.1
411	Video Automation Systems Inc—*Thorsten Cook*	13 Arrow Meadow Rd, New Fairfield CT 06812	203-312-0512	R	<1*	<.1
412	Compucom Inc—*Norman Blalock*	PO Box 560833, Rockledge FL 32056	321-631-2578	R	<1*	<.1
413	Keithco Inc—*Behren Reeves*	PO Box 1806, Lake Oswego OR 97035	503-635-7604	R	<1*	<.1
414	Pas-Com Inc—*Peter Soltesz*	16608 Winterwoods Ct, Rockville MD 20853	301-774-8120	R	<1*	<.1
415	United Media—*Ray Conover*	4812 Lyndale Ave S, Minneapolis MN 55419	612-822-1611	R	<1*	<.1
416	Parkervision Inc—*Jeffrey Parker*	7915 Baymeadows Way St, Jacksonville FL 32256		P	<1	<.1
417	Cain Tree Inc—*Nelson Mcnulty*	2490 Depew St, Edgewater CO 80214	303-234-0308	R	<1*	<.1
418	Crystal Monitor Service—*Clifford Stam*	PO Box 237, Watseka IL 60970	815-432-5296	R	<1*	<.1
419	Hill Jerry Steady Cam Products—*Jerry Hill*	19160 Arminta St, Reseda CA 91335	818-772-9256	R	<1*	<.1
420	Hop-On Inc—*Peter D Michaels*	2222 Michelson Dr Ste, Irvine CA 92612	949-756-9008	P	<1	N/A
421	VertexRSI Inc—*Steve Chambers*	2600 N Longview St, Kilgore TX 75662	903-984-0555	S	N/A	.4

TOTALS: SIC 3663 Radio & T.V. Communications Equipment
Companies: 421

					79,696	234.3

3669 Communications Equipment Nec

Rank	Company Name—*Executive Officer*	Address, City, State, Zip	Phone	Type	Fin	Empls
1	Juniper Networks Inc—*Kevin Johnson*	1194 N Mathilda Ave, Sunnyvale CA 94089	408-745-2000	P	4,449	9.1
2	Ansaldo STS USA—*Sergio De Luca*	1000 Technology Dr, Pittsburgh PA 15219	412-688-2400	S	3,662*	4.2
3	CIENA Corp—*Gary B Smith*	1201 Winterson Rd, Linthicum MD 21090	410-694-5700	P	1,742	4.3
4	NES Traffic Safety LP	12225 Disk Dr, Romeoville IL 60446	815-372-2300	S	1,593*	2.5
5	Sonant Corp—*Charles Smith*	6215 Ferris Sq Ste 220, San Diego CA 92121	858-623-8180	R	1,440*	<.1
6	Sensormatic Electronics Corp—*Mike Snyder*	6600 Congress Ave, Boca Raton FL 33487	561-912-6000	S	1,097	5.7
7	ARRIS Group Inc—*Robert J Stanzione*	3871 Lakefield Dr, Suwanee GA 30024	678-473-2000	P	1,088	1.9
8	Finisar Corp—*Eitan Gertel*	1389 Moffett Park Dr, Sunnyvale CA 94089	408-548-1000	P	949	8.1
9	Corning Cable Systems LLC	PO Box 489, Hickory NC 28603	828-901-5000	S	867*	13.0
10	Checkpoint Systems Inc—*Robert van der Merwe*	One Commerce Square 20, Philadelphia PA 19103	856-848-1800	P	834	5.8
11	GE Security Inc—*Dean Seavers*	8985 Town Center Pkwy, Bradenton FL 34202	941-739-4200	S	640*	3.3
12	Silicon Laboratories Inc—*Necip Sayiner*	400 W Cesar Chavez, Austin TX 78701	512-416-8500	P	492	.9
13	Tekelec—*Ronald J de Lange*	5200 Paramount Pkwy, Morrisville NC 27560	919-460-5500	P	424	1.3
14	Titan Global Holdings Inc—*Bryan Chance*	1700 Jay Ell Dr Ste 20, Richardson TX 75081	972-470-9100	P	418	.6
15	Norment Security Group—*Greg Ergenbright*	3224 Mobile Hwy, Montgomery AL 36108	334-281-8440	S	383*	.6
16	NetLogic Microsystems Inc—*Ron Jankov*	3975 Freedom Cir, Santa Clara CA 95054	308-454-3000	P	382	.6
17	Siemens Building Technologies Fire Safety—*Daryl Dulaney*	8 Fernwood Rd, Florham Park NJ 07932	973-593-2600	S	372*	1.4
18	Telephonics Corp—*Joseph Battaglia*	815 Broad Hollow Rd, Farmingdale NY 11735	631-755-7000	S	366*	1.3
19	Sentry Products Inc—*Ken Bays*	2225 Martin Ave Ste J, Santa Clara CA 95050	408-727-1866	R	270	<.1
20	ATX Technologies Inc—*Michael Saxton*	8550 Freeport Pky, Irving TX 75063	972-753-6200	R	260*	.4
21	PictureTel Securities Corp—*Robert C Hagerty*	100 Minuteman Rd, Andover MA 01810	978-292-5000	S	245	.8
22	Comverse Inc—*Oded Golan*	200 Quannapowitt Pkwy, Wakefield MA 01880	781-224-8888	S	230*	1.5
23	Applied Signal Technology Inc—*William Van Vleet III*	400 W California Ave, Sunnyvale CA 94086	408-749-1888	P	225	.9
24	Innovation Products Inc—*Albert Johnson*	3367 Chicago Ave, Riverside CA 92507	951-682-8506	R	221*	.3
25	Checkpoint Security Group Inc—*George W Off* Checkpoint Systems Inc	2005 Market St, Philadelphia PA 19103		D	219*	.3
26	TeleNav Inc—*HP Jin*	1130 Kifer Rd, Sunnyvale CA 94086	408-245-3800	P	211	1.0
27	ICx Technologies Inc—*Colin Cumming*	2100 Crystal Dr Ste 65, Arlington VA 22202	703-678-2111	S	183	.8
28	Ge Transportation Systems Global Signaling LLC	2712 S Dillingham Rd, Grain Valley MO 64029	816-650-3112	R	175*	2.1
29	Symmetricom Puerto Rico Ltd—*Thomas Steipp*	PO Box 5219, Aguadilla PR 00605	787 658 3671	R	152*	.3
30	LoJack Corp—*Richard T Riley*	200 Lowder Brook Dr St, Westwood MA 02090	781-251-4700	P	147	.6
31	Nsoro—*Darrell Mays*	2859 Paces Ferry Rd St, Atlanta GA 30339	404-541-1300	R	135*	.2

Note: An asterisk (*) indicates an estimated financial figure. The company type code used is as follows: R = Private, P = Public, S = Private Subsidiary, B = Public Subsidiary, D = Division, J = Joint Venture, I = Investment Fund.

COMPANY RANKINGS BY SALES WITHIN 4-DIGIT SIC

Rank	Company Name—*Executive Officer*	Address, City, State, Zip	Phone	Type	Fin	Empls
32	Channell Commercial Corp—*William H Channell Jr*	PO Box 9022, Temecula CA 92592	951-719-2600	P	133	.6
33	Adaptive Optics Associates Inc (Cambridge Massachusetts)—*Jeffrey Yorsz*	10 Wilson Rd, Cambridge MA 02138	617-806-1400	S	107*	.2
34	Ansul Inc—*Steve Grisko*	One Stanton St, Marinette WI 54143	715-735-7411	S	101*	.7
35	Sypris Electronics LLC—*John J Walsh*	10901 N McKinley Dr, Tampa FL 33612	813-972-6000	S	100*	.7
36	Isonas Inc—*Charles Crenshaw*	4720 Walnut St, Boulder CO 80301	303-567-6516	R	98*	.1
37	AudioDev USA Inc—*Christer Sjostrom*	5126 Clareton Dr Ste 1, Agoura Hills CA 91301	818-540-3100	R	82*	.1
38	Jetstream of Houston LLP—*Bill Krupowicz*	5905 Thomas Rd, Houston TX 77041	832-590-1300	S	77*	.1
39	Clover Systems—*Gordon Rudd*	26241 Enterprise Ct, Lake Forest CA 92630	949-598-0700	R	74*	.1
40	technotrans america inc—*Heinz Harling*	2181 S Foster Ave, Wheeling IL 60090	847-259-3330	R	74*	.1
41	Jetstream of Houston Inc—*Bill Krupowicz*	5905 Thomas Rd, Houston TX 77041		D	74*	.1
42	Napco Security Systems Inc—*Richard L Soloway*	333 Bayview Ave, Amityville NY 11701	631-842-9400	P	71	1.0
43	Cedar Point Communications Inc—*JC Murphy*	16 Rte 111 Bldg 3, Derry NH 03038	603-898-3070	R	71*	.1
44	MaxLinear Inc—*Kishore Seendripu*	2051 Palomar Airport R, Carlsbad CA 92011	760-692-0711	P	69	.2
45	Adtec Digital Inc—*Kevin Ancelin*	408 Russell St, Nashville TN 37206	615-256-6619	R	68*	.1
46	Hitachi Communication Technologies America Inc—*Yanming Liu*	3920 Freedom Cir Ste 1, Santa Clara CA 95054	408-845-5200	S	67*	.1
47	NewTek Partners—*Jim Plant*	5131 Beckwith Blvd, San Antonio TX 78249	210-370-8000	R	67*	.1
48	Matrix Systems Inc—*James Young*	7550 Paragon Rd, Dayton OH 45459	937-438-9033	R	65*	.1
49	ThruPort Technologies—*Bruce M Waldack*	5440 Cherikee Ave, Alexandria VA 22312	703-642-6243	R	63*	.1
50	Alcatel-Lucent—*Ben Verwaayen*	600 Mountain Ave Ste 3, Murray Hill NJ 07974	908-508-8080	R	60*	.1
51	American Computer Development Inc—*William Hornbaker*	5350 Partners Ct, Frederick MD 21703		R	60*	.1
52	Asaca/Shibasoku Corp—*Takashi Shigezaki*	450 Donald J Lynch Blv, Marlborough MA 01752	508-229-0107	S	59*	.1
53	Intricon Corp—*Mark S Gorder*	1260 Red Fox Rd, Arden Hills MN 55112	651-636-9770	P	59	.5
54	Numerex Corp—*Stratton J Nicolaides*	1600 Parkwood Cir 5th, Atlanta GA 30339	770-693-5950	P	58	.1
55	Best Data Products Inc—*Bruce Zaman*	20740 Plummer St, Chatsworth CA 91311	818-773-9600	R	57*	.1
56	Sentrol—*M McCarthy* GE Security Inc	12345 SW Leveton Dr, Tualatin OR 97062	503-691-7566	S	54	.5
57	Sippican Inc—*Douglas Dapprich*	7 Barnabas Rd, Marion MA 02738	774-553-6226	S	51*	.3
58	General Dynamics Network Systems/International Telecom Group—*Lewis Von-Thaer*	PO Box 26002, Greensboro NC 27420	336-698-8000	D	49*	.1
59	Amnis—*David Basiji*	2505 Third Ave Ste 210, Seattle WA 98121	206-374-7000	R	49*	.1
60	Vicon Industries Inc—*Kenneth M Darby*	89 Arkay Dr, Hauppauge NY 11788	631-952-2288	P	47	.2
61	Infrastruct Security Inc—*James Brown*	747 N Shepherd Dr, Houston TX 77007	713-721-9732	R	47*	.1
62	Empower RF Systems—*Efraim Bainvoll*	316 W Florence Ave, Inglewood CA 90301	310-412-8100	R	46*	.1
63	Aurora Networks Inc—*Guy Sucharczuk*	5400 Betsy Ross Dr, Santa Clara CA 95054	408-235-7000	R	44*	.1
64	Beceem Communications Inc—*Babu Mandava*	3960 Freedom Cir 1st F, Santa Clara CA 95054	408-387-5000	R	44	.2
65	Microwave Data Systems Inc—*Roberto Vengoechea*	175 Science Pkwy, Rochester NY 14620	585-242-9600	D	42*	.3
66	Tango Networks Inc—*Alastair Westgarth*	5465 Legacy Dr Ste 550, Plano TX 75024	469-229-6000	R	42*	.1
67	Savi Technology Inc—*David Stephens*	351 E Evelyn Ave, Mountain View CA 94041	650-316-4700	S	40	.3
68	GAI-Tronics Corp—*Tim Powers*	PO Box 1060, Reading PA 19607	610-777-1374	S	39	.3
69	SubCom—*David Coughlan*	417 Mt Kemble Ave Ste, Morristown NJ 07960	973-656-8000	S	37*	.6
70	NSGDatacom Inc—*Richard Yalen*	3859 Centerview Dr Ste, Chantilly VA 20151	703-793-2000	R	37*	.1
71	Flint Telecom Group Inc—*Vincent Browne*	7500 College Blvd Ste, Overland Park KS 66210	913-815-1570	P	34	<.1
72	Ipitek Photonic Technology—*Michael M Salour*	2330 Faraday Ave, Carlsbad CA 92008	760-438-1010	R	34	.2
73	Arista Enterprises—*Alan Leifer*	125 Commerce Dr, Hauppauge NY 11788	631-435-0200	R	33*	.1
74	Streaming21 Inc (San Jose California)—*Joe Lin*	10670 N Tantau Ave Ste, Cupertino CA 95014	408-200-1619	R	33*	<.1
75	Tachyon Inc—*Peter A Carides*	9339 Carroll Park Dr, San Diego CA 92121	858-882-8100	R	32*	<.1
76	Monaco Enterprises Inc—*Eugene Monaco*	PO Box 14129, Spokane Valley WA 99214	509-926-6277	R	31*	.1
77	Digital Angel Corp—*Joseph J Grillo*	490 Villuame Ave, South Saint Paul MN 55075	651-552-6301	P	31	.2
78	Vocera Communications Inc—*Robert Zollars*	525 Race St Ste 150, San Jose CA 95126	408-882-5100	R	30*	.1
79	Glmnt Corp—*Don Edwards*	26776 Simpatica Cir, Lake Forest CA 92630	949-581-4464	R	29*	.2
80	Dukane Corp—*Michael W Ritschdorff*	2900 Dukane Dr, Saint Charles IL 60174	630-584-2300	R	28*	.2
81	Econolite Control Products Inc—*Michael Doyle*	PO Box 6150, Anaheim CA 92816	714-630-3700	R	28*	.2
82	TC Electronic—*Thomas Lund*	5706 Corsa Ave Ste 107, Westlake Village CA 91362	818-665-4900	R	27*	<.1
83	Mccain Inc—*Jeffrey Mc Cain*	2365 Oak Ridge Way, Vista CA 92081	760-727-8100	R	27*	.4
84	R A Miller Industries Inc—*Robert Lynas*	PO Box 858, Grand Haven MI 49417	616-842-9450	R	26*	.2
85	AutoCell Laboratories Inc—*Floyd J Backes*	125 Nagog Park, Acton MA 01720	978-264-4884	R	26*	<.1
86	RELM Wireless Corp—*David P Storey*	7100 Technology Dr, West Melbourne FL 32904	321-984-1414	P	26	.1
87	Code Blue Corp—*Kenneth Genzink*	92 E 64th St, Holland MI 49423	616-392-8296	R	25*	.2
88	Western-Cullen-Hayes Inc—*Ronald Mc Daniel*	2700 W 36th Pl, Chicago IL 60632	773-254-9600	R	25*	.1
89	Gemfire Corp—*Neil Rickardson*	2255D Martin Ave, Santa Clara CA 95050	480-380-7800	R	25*	<.1
90	VoIP Logic LLC—*Micah Singer*	529 Main St, Williamstown MA 01267	310-279-4700	R	25*	<.1
91	Maritime Communication Services Inc—*Howard Lance*	1025 W Nasa Blvd, Melbourne FL 32919	321-674-4750	S	25*	<.1
92	Star Headlight and Lantern Company Inc—*David Jacobs*	455 Rochester St, Avon NY 14414	585-226-9500	R	25*	.2
93	Deposition Sciences Inc—*Lee Bartolomei*	3300 Coffey Ln, Santa Rosa CA 95403	707-573-6700	S	25	.2
94	Omega Research and Development—*Kenneth Flick*	981 N Burnt Hickory Rd, Douglasville GA 30134	770-942-9876	R	23*	<.1
95	Potter Electric Signal Company LLC—*Randy Mcpeak*	PO Box 42037, Hazelwood MO 63042	314-595-6900	R	22*	.2
96	Linear Corp—*Grant D Rummell*	1950 Camino Vida Roble, Carlsbad CA 92008	760-438-7000	S	22*	.2
97	DTC Communications Inc—*William Panije*	486 Amherst St, Nashua NH 03062	603-546-2100	S	22*	.1
98	Daitron Inc—*Zenshiro Takamoto*	PO Box 3500, Wilsonville OR 97070	503-682-7560	R	22*	<.1
99	H M Electronics Inc—*Harrison Miyahira*	14110 Stowe Dr, Poway CA 92064	858-535-6000	R	22*	.3
100	Applied Nanotech Inc—*Zvi Yaniv* Applied Nanotech Holdings Inc	3006 Longhorn Blvd Ste, Austin TX 78758	512-339-5020	S	21*	<.1
101	AeroComm Inc—*Mike Varady*	11160 Thompson Ave, Lenexa KS 66219	913-492-2320	R	20*	<.1
102	Electronic Design Co—*Graham Henderson*	3225 E Hennepin Ave, Minneapolis MN 55413	612-355-2300	R	20*	<.1
103	American Dynamics Video Products Div—*Gene Hammond* Sensormatic Electronics Corp	6600 Congress Ave, Boca Raton FL 33431	858-642-2400	D	19*	<.1
104	Air Products and Controls Inc—*Pete Stouffer*	1749 E Highwood, Pontiac MI 48340	248-332-3900	S	19*	<.1
105	Synergx Systems Inc—*Paul Mendez*	209 Lafayette Dr, Syosset NY 11791	516-433-4700	R	19	.1
106	Rgb Networks Inc—*Adam Tom*	390 W Java Dr, Sunnyvale CA 94089	408-701-2700	R	19*	.2
107	Promix Electrotec—*Jere Harris*	539 Temple Hill Rd, New Windsor NY 12553	845-567-5700	D	18*	<.1
108	Dycam Service Company Inc	22425 Ventura Blvd, Woodland Hills CA 91364	818-826-1571	R	18*	<.1
109	JAI Pulnix	625 River Oaks Pky, San Jose CA 95134	408-383-0300	S	18	.1
110	Micrologic Inc (Westboro Massachusetts)—*Sheldon Apsell*	80-A Turnpike Rd, Westboro MA 01581	508-621-1000	S	17*	<.1
111	Getecha Inc—*Chris Koffend*	2914 Business One Dr, Kalamazoo MI 49048	269-373-8896	R	17*	<.1
112	Incipio Technologies—*Andy Fathollahi*	1842 Barranca Pky, Irvine CA 92606	949-250-4929	R	17*	<.1
113	Knogo North America Inc Sentry Technology Corp	1881 Lakeland Ave, Ronkonkoma NY 11779	631-739-2000	S	16*	.1
114	Barcoding Inc—*Jay Steinmetz*	2220 Boston St, Baltimore MD 21231	410-385-8532	R	16*	.1

Rank	Company Name—*Executive Officer*	Address, City, State, Zip	Phone	Type	Fin	Empls
115	iDirect—*Mary Cotton*	13865 Sunrise Valley D, Herndon VA 20171	703-648-8000	S	16*	.1
116	4M Systems Inc—*Stephen Grey*	4655 Old Ironsides Dr, Santa Clara CA 95054	408-970-8505	R	16*	<.1
117	Vanguard Networking Products Inc—*Ken Finley*	7412 Prince Dr, Huntington Beach CA 92647	714-842-3330	R	16*	.3
118	Microsemi-RFIS—*Jacob Inbar*	1000 Avenida Acaso, Camarillo CA 93012	805-388-1345	S	16	.1
119	System Engineering International Inc—*Martin Grolnic*	5115 Pegasus Ct Ste Q, Frederick MD 21704	301-694-9601	R	15*	<.1
120	Accusentry Inc—*Wei Siong Tan*	605 Franklin Rd SE, Marietta GA 30067	770-850-1700	R	15*	<.1
121	iDNA Inc—*James J McNamara*	415 Madison Ave 7th Fl, New York NY 10017	212-644-1400	P	15	.1
122	International Electronics Inc—*Grant Rummell Linear Corp*	1950 Camino Vida Roble, Carlsbad CA 92008	760-438-7000	S	14*	.1
123	Eventide Inc—*Jason Beck*	1 Alsan Way, Little Ferry NJ 07643	201-641-1200	R	14*	.1
124	DVC Company Inc—*Ash Prabala*	4120 Friedrich Ln Ste, Austin TX 78744	512-301-9564	R	14*	<.1
125	Home Automation Inc—*Jay McLellen*	PO Box 55967, Metairie LA 70055	504-736-9810	R	14*	<.1
126	Neuro Logic Systems Inc—*Steve Sitko*	451-C Constitution Ave, Camarillo CA 93012	805-389-5435	R	14*	<.1
127	Digital Monitoring Products Inc—*Rick Britton*	2500 N Partnership Blv, Springfield MO 65803	417-831-9362	R	14*	.1
128	Tx Rx Systems Inc—*David Hessler*	8625 Industrial Pkwy, Angola NY 14006	716-549-4700	R	14*	.1
129	Space Age Electronics Inc—*Joseph Mongeau*	58 Chocksett Rd, Sterling MA 01564	978-562-2998	R	14*	<.1
130	Tomar Electronics Inc—*Scott Sikora*	2100 W Obispo Ave, Gilbert AZ 85233	480-497-4400	R	13*	.1
131	Firecom Inc—*Paul Mendez*	39-27 59th St, Woodside NY 11377	718-899-6100	R	13*	.1
132	Solar Technology Inc—*Alice Balliet*	7620 Cetronia Rd, Allentown PA 18106	610-391-8600	R	13*	.1
133	Cubix Corp—*Al Fiegehen*	2800 Lockheed Way, Carson City NV 89706	775-888-1000	R	13*	<.1
134	Output Technology—*Steve Benner*	1314 S Grand Blvd #2-2, Spokane WA 99202	509-536-0468	R	13*	<.1
135	Patriot Scientific Corp—*Cliff Flowers*	701 Palomar Airport Rd, Carlsbad CA 92011	760-547-2700	P	12	<.1
136	Harrington Signal Inc—*Richard Eisenlauer*	PO Box 590, Moline IL 61266	309-762-0731	R	12*	.1
137	Johnston Technical Services Inc—*Jim Johnston*	5310 S Cockrell Hill R, Dallas TX 75236	972-620-1435	R	12*	<.1
138	Applied Magic—*Peter Fei*	23332 Madero Rd Ste L, Mission Viejo CA 92691	949-297-8550	R	12*	<.1
139	Digital Vision (USA) Inc—*Mikael Jacobsson*	4605 Lankershim Blvd S, North Hollywood CA 91602	818-769-8111	R	12*	<.1
140	Segue Electronics Inc—*Chris Chen*	5230 Pacific Concourse, Los Angeles CA 90045	310-643-0000	R	12*	<.1
141	Television Equipment Associates—*Bill Pegler*	PO Box 404, Brewster NY 10509	310-457-7401	R	12*	<.1
142	Wilson Electronics Inc—*James Wilson*	3301 E Deseret Dr, Saint George UT 84790	435-673-5021	R	11*	<.1
143	Pro-Bell and Snell and Wilcox—*Simon Derry*	3519 W Pacific Ave, Burbank CA 91505	818-556-2616	R	11*	<.1
144	Xtellus Inc	66 Ford Rd, Denville NJ 07834	973-326-1100	S	11*	<.1
145	Basler Inc—*Dietmar Ley*	855 Springdale Dr Ste, Exton PA 19341	610-280-0171	R	11*	<.1
146	Brown Innovations Inc—*Jeremy Brown*	1545 W Nelson Ste 1R, Chicago IL 60657	773-477-7500	R	11*	<.1
147	Enseo Inc—*Vaness Ogle*	1680 Prospect Dr, Richardson TX 75081	972-234-2513	R	11*	<.1
148	Clear-Com LLC—*Terry Skelton* H M Electronics Inc	850 Marina Village Pkw, Alameda CA 94501	510-337-6600	S	11*	.1
149	iSECUREtrac Corp—*Peter A Michel*	5078 S 111th St, Omaha NE 68137		P	11	.1
150	Tektone Sound and Signal Manufacturing Inc—*Carlos Mira*	277 Industrial Park Rd, Franklin NC 28734	828-524-9967	R	10*	.1
151	Signature Technologies Inc—*Elie Geva*	3728 Benner Rd, Miamisburg OH 45342	937-859-6323	R	10*	.1
152	Vtel Products Corp—*Richard Ford*	2324 Ridgepoint Dr Ste, Austin TX 78754	512-535-1988	R	10*	<.1
153	Conferencing Advisors Inc—*Walter Somsel*	34175 Camino Capistran, Capistrano Beach CA 92624	949-493-3614	R	10*	<.1
154	Night Optics USA Inc—*Ilya Reyngold*	15182 Triton Ln Ste 10, Huntington Beach CA 92649	714-899-4475	R	10*	<.1
155	Sentry Technology Corp—*Peter L Murdoch*	1881 Lakeland Ave, Ronkonkoma NY 11779	631-739-2000	P	10	.1
156	Cryptek Inc—*Gary Hobbs*	1501 Moran Rd, Sterling VA 20166	571-434-2000	R	10*	.1
157	Astro Gaming—*Brett Lovelady*	348 6th St, San Francisco CA 94103	415-354-6300	S	10	<.1
158	Premier Technologies Inc—*Richard Stark*	PO Box 159, Long Lake MN 55356	952-475-2317	R	9*	.1
159	Joron Electronic Systems Inc—*Jerome Chesnul*	1743 W Rosehill Dr, Chicago IL 60660	773-275-1900	R	9*	.1
160	DaTARIUS Technologies Inc—*James Steynor*	20429 Raoho Pkwy S Ste, Lake Forest CA 92630	949-452-9211	S	9*	<.1
161	George Risk Industries Inc—*Ken R Risk*	802 S Elm St, Kimball NE 69145	308-235-4645	P	9	.2
162	Brown Traffic Products Inc—*David Schiltz*	736 Federal St Ste 231, Davenport IA 52803	563-323-0009	R	9*	.1
163	Safetran Traffic Systems Inc—*Darrell Emery*	1485 Garden Of The God, Colorado Springs CO 80907	719-599-5600	R	8*	.1
164	Fire Sentry Corp—*David Castleman*	23311 La Palma Ave, Yorba Linda CA 92887	714-694-2700	R	8*	<.1
165	Applied Nanotech Holdings Inc—*Douglas P Baker*	3006 Longhorn Blvd Ste, Austin TX 78758	512-339-5020	P	8	<.1
166	Cintel Inc—*Don Edmonson*	28910 Ave Penn Ste 202, Valencia CA 91355	661-294-2310	S	8*	<.1
167	Airbourne Reconnaisance Low—*Robert Rendzio*	19844 Blue Mountain Rd, Bluemont VA 20135	334-379-9056	R	8*	.1
168	Vyyo Inc—*Wayne Davis*	6625 The Corners Pky S, Norcross GA 30092	678-282-8000	R	8	<.1
169	T-S Display Systems Inc—*John Mauro*	76 Progress Dr, Stamford CT 06902	203-964-0575	R	7*	.1
170	Lund Industries Inc—*Paul Lundberg*	303 Messner Dr, Wheeling IL 60090	847-459-1460	R	7*	<.1
171	DVS Digital Video Inc—*Peter Spoer*	300 E Magnolia Blvd St, Burbank CA 91502	818-846-3600	S	7*	<.1
172	Gearhost—*Ryan Kekos*	1517 Blake St Ste 200, Denver CO 80202	720-204-1300	R	7*	<.1
173	Ultera Systems Inc	26081 Merit Cir Ste 12, Laguna Hills CA 92653	949-367-8800	R	7*	<.1
174	International Microwave Corp—*Anthony Acri*	25 Van Zant St Ste 11A, Norwalk CT 06855	203-857-4222	S	6	<.1
175	Nearfield Systems Inc—*Greg Hindman*	19730 Magellan Dr, Torrance CA 90502	310-525-7000	R	6*	.1
176	Agiltron—*Jing Zhao*	15 Presidential Way, Woburn MA 01801	781-935-1200	R	6*	.1
177	MilesTek Corp—*Frank J Miles*	1506 Interstate Hwy 35, Denton TX 76207	940-484-9400	R	6*	<.1
178	Twinco Manufacturing Company Inc—*John Schatz*	30 Commerce Dr, Hauppauge NY 11788	631-231-0022	R	6*	<.1
179	Technisphere—*Jack Goldman*	335 W 35th St, New York NY 10001	212-777-5100	R	6*	<.1
180	Better Light Inc—*Mike Collette*	1200 Industrial Rd Uni, San Carlos CA 94070	650-631-3680	R	6*	<.1
181	PageTek—*Phil Frankenstein*	182 Wind Chime Ct Ste, Raleigh NC 27615	919-518-1828	R	6*	<.1
182	ERF Wireless Inc—*H Dean Cubley*	2911 S Shore Blvd Ste, League City TX 77573	281-538-2101	P	6	.1
183	Keltron Corp—*David Wilbourn*	101a 1st Ave A, Waltham MA 02451	781-894-8710	R	6*	<.1
184	Tabet Manufacturing Company Inc—*Jeffrey Jaycox*	1336 Ballentine Blvd, Norfolk VA 23504	757-627-1855	R	6*	<.1
185	Integrated Security Systems Inc—*Russell Cleveland*	2009 Chenault Dr Ste 1, Carrollton TX 75006	972-444-8280	P	6	<.1
186	Tc Communications Inc—*Kai Liang*	17881 Cartwright Rd, Irvine CA 92614	949-852-1972	R	6*	<.1
187	Westek Electronics Inc—*Kevin Larkin*	314 Westridge Dr, Watsonville CA 95076	831-740-6300	R	5*	<.1
188	National Sign and Signal Co—*Ronald Scherer*	301 Armstrong Rd, Battle Creek MI 49037	269-963-2817	R	5*	<.1
189	Winner International	32 W State St, Sharon PA 16146	724-981-1152	R	5*	.1
190	Videoconferencing Systems Inc—*Oliver M Cooper III*	520 Guthridge Ct Ste 2, Norcross GA 30071	678-533-1200	S	5*	<.1
191	New Bedford Panoramex Corp—*Steven Ozuna*	1480 N Claremont Blvd, Claremont CA 91711	909-982-9806	R	5*	<.1
192	Signal Communications Corp—*Robert Lapham*	PO Box 2588, Woburn MA 01888	781-933-0998	R	5*	<.1
193	Audio Technology Inc—*Edward Lindsay*	PO Box 1708, Ponca City OK 74602	214-351-2191	R	5*	<.1
194	Convergent Technologies Inc	1095 Fairchild Rd, Winston Salem NC 27105	336-722-2990	S	5*	<.1
195	Tana Wire Marker Co—*Jack Rutledge*	PO Box 370, California MO 65018	573-796-3812	R	5*	<.1
196	Transportation Control Systems Inc—*John Gillis*	1030 S 86th St, Tampa FL 33619	813-632-2800	R	5*	<.1
197	Statewide Electrical Contractors Inc—*George Fernandez*	13281 Sw 124th St Unit, Miami FL 33186	305-971-8864	R	4*	<.1
198	Intego Systems Inc—*Charles Bell*	5343 Bowden Rd, Jacksonville FL 32216	904-260-6334	R	4*	<.1
199	Electronic Marine Systems Inc—*Thomas Priola*	800 Ferndale Pl, Rahway NJ 07065	732-382-4344	R	4*	<.1
200	Expand Networks Inc—*Elie Barr*	103 Eisenhower Pky, Roseland NJ 07068	973-618-9000	R	4*	<.1
201	Orion Systems Inc—*Frank Affeldt*	3401 Masons Mill Rd St, Huntingdon Valley PA 19006	215-659-1207	R	4*	<.1
202	3SI Security Systems Inc	486 Thomas Jones Way, Exton PA 19341	610-280-2000	R	4*	<.1

Note: An asterisk (*) indicates an estimated financial figure. The company type code used is as follows: R = Private, P = Public, S = Private Subsidiary, B = Public Subsidiary, D = Division, J = Joint Venture, I = Investment Fund.

COMPANY RANKINGS BY SALES WITHIN 4-DIGIT SIC

Rank	Company Name—*Executive Officer*	Address, City, State, Zip	Phone	Type	Fin	Empls
203	Unitrol Inc	1108 Raymond Way, Anaheim CA 92801	714-871-3336	D	4*	<.1
204	Electronic Control Security Inc—*Arthur Barchenko*	790 Bloomfield Ave Bld, Clifton NJ 07012	973-574-8555	P	4	<.1
205	CourtSmart Digital Systems Inc—*Andrew Treinis*	51 Middlesex St, North Chelmsford MA 01863		R	4*	<.1
206	Andrea Systems LLC—*Mary Gigilo*	140 Finn Ct, Farmingdale NY 11735	631-390-3140	R	4*	<.1
207	Nardo Group International LLC—*Jimenez Fernando*	6868 Distribution Dr, Beltsville MD 20705	301-931-3202	R	4*	<.1
208	Deco TECHnology Group Inc—*Mike Learmouth*	749 N Main St, Orange CA 92868	714-639-3326	R	4*	<.1
209	Gordon-Cross Inc—*Robert P Bradley*	PO Box 40, West Simsbury CT 06092	860-658-1000	R	4*	<.1
210	Summation Technology LLC—*John Krainock*	1155 Kelly Johnson Blv, Colorado Springs CO 80920	719-590-6063	R	4*	<.1
211	Tapematic USA—*Luciano Perego*	6881 Kingspointe Pky S, Orlando FL 32819	407-852-1901	S	4*	<.1
212	V Maslov and Company Inc—*Fern Street*	11781 Lee Jackson Hwy, Fairfax VA 22033	703-716-4282	R	4*	<.1
213	Voice Products LLC—*Michael Kaufman*	23715 Mercantile Rd St, Cleveland OH 44122	216-360-0433	R	4*	<.1
214	Christy Industries Inc—*John Christy*	1812 Bath Ave, Brooklyn NY 11214		R	4*	<.1
215	Ironwood Communications—*Scott Little*	11226 N 23rd Ave Ste 1, Phoenix AZ 85029	602-216-2507	R	4*	<.1
216	Linc Technology Corp—*Michel Maes*	3535 Factoria Blvd Se, Bellevue WA 98006	425-882-2206	R	4*	<.1
217	Protectowire Company Inc—*Andrew Sullivan*	40 Grissom Rd Ste 200, Plymouth MA 02360	781-826-3878	R	4*	<.1
218	Visiontron Corp—*Lisa Torsiello*	720 Old Willets Path, Hauppauge NY 11788	631-582-8600	R	4*	<.1
219	Traffic Safety Solutions—*Robert Graham*	1746 S Victoria Ave St, Ventura CA 93003	805-585-2250	R	4*	<.1
220	I F Engineering Corp—*Lee Foshay*	40 Parker Rd, North Grosvenordale CT 06255	860-935-0280	R	3*	<.1
221	Nel-Tech Labs Inc—*Scott Stapleford*	4 Ash St Ext, Derry NH 03038	603-425-1096	R	3*	<.1
222	King Fisher Company Inc—*Frank Carideo*	81 Old Ferry Rd, Lowell MA 01854	978-596-0214	R	3*	<.1
223	Ocean Applied Research Corp—*Tony Bernard*	7535 Waples St, San Diego CA 92121	619-277-6790	S	3	<.1
224	Carson Manufacturing Company Inc—*Barbara Ferguson*	PO Box 20464, Indianapolis IN 46220	317-257-3191	R	3*	<.1
225	BNI Solutions LLC—*Scott R Kimbell* Numerex Corp	2820 E College Ave Ste, State College PA 16801	814-237-4073	S	3*	<.1
226	Alison Control Inc—*Gene E Benzenberg*	35 Daniel Rd, Fairfield NJ 07004	973-575-7100	R	3*	<.1
227	Global Vision Systems	9301 Oakdale Ave Ste 1, Chatsworth CA 91311	818-998-7851	R	3*	<.1
228	RACOM Products Inc—*Charles Legree*	2024 W Schaaf Rd, Cleveland OH 44109	216-351-1755	R	3*	<.1
229	Almont:MediaLAB—*Gregory Green*	5 Grapevine Way, Medway MA 02053	508-533-0333	R	3*	<.1
230	Mediatechnics Systems Inc—*Richard Wilson*	PO Box 1424, Placerville CA 95667		R	3*	<.1
231	Roving Networks Inc—*Michael Conrad*	809 University Ave, Los Gatos CA 95032	408-395-6539	R	3*	<.1
232	Disan Engineering Corp—*Billy Brown*	PO Box 632, Nowata OK 74048	918-273-1636	R	3*	<.1
233	Southwest Signal Supply Inc—*Clarence Rice*	1107 Jackson St, South Houston TX 77587	713-946-7162	R	3*	<.1
234	Fire Detection Systems LLC	1351 W 121st Ave, Westminster CO 80234	303-438-8088	R	3*	<.1
235	Traffic Operations Signal Shop—*Richard Dass*	7491 Connelley Dr, Hanover MD 21076	410-787-7676	R	3*	<.1
236	Marine Technologies Inc—*Thomas Wisniewski*	31632 N Ellis Dr Unit, Volo IL 60073	847-546-9001	R	3*	<.1
237	Rsg/Aames Security Inc—*Louis Finkle*	PO Box 849, Lakewood CA 90714	562-529-5100	R	3*	<.1
238	Uam Technologies Corp—*Naveed Mohammad*	PO Box 558196, Miami FL 33255	404-969-4568	R	3*	<.1
239	Intercall Systems Inc—*Ellis Gurman*	150 Herricks Rd, Mineola NY 11501	516-294-4510	R	2*	<.1
240	LW Bills Co—*Harold Roeder*	7 Park St, Georgetown MA 01833	978-352-6660	R	2*	<.1
241	Alarm Controls Corp—*Howard Berger*	PO Box 280, Deer Park NY 11729	631-586-4220	R	2*	<.1
242	Hochiki America Corp—*Hisham Harake*	PO Box 514689, Los Angeles CA 90051	714-522-2246	R	2*	.1
243	Preferred Technology Inc—*Lance Comstock*	9160 E Bahia Dr, Scottsdale AZ 85260	480-991-1259	R	2*	<.1
244	TX Technology Corp—*Don Black*	7 Emery Ave, Randolph NJ 07869	973-442-7500	S	2*	<.1
245	Optex America Inc—*Jim Quick*	13661 Benson Ave Bldg, Chino CA 91710	909-993-5770	R	2*	<.1
246	ISDN*tek	PO Box 3000, San Gregorio CA 94074	650-712-3000	R	2*	<.1
247	ASCI—*Eric Maccalla*	PO Box 92946, Pasadena CA 91109	626-969-8441	R	2*	<.1
248	Mater Manufacturing Inc—*Donald Makar*	149 W Irving Park Rd, Roselle IL 60172	630-529-0040	R	2*	<.1
249	Dave Jones Design—*Dave Jones*	34 Lake St, Owego NY 13827	607-687-5740	R	2*	<.1
250	Independent Audio LLC—*Frasier Jones*	43 Deerfield Rd, Portland ME 04101	207-773-2424	R	2*	<.1
251	Marubeni Disc Systems Inc—*Matt Matsubara*	17332 Von Karmen Ste 1, Irvine CA 92614	949-794-7703	S	2*	<.1
252	Cyberlink Communications—*Richi Ako*	PO Box 740022, Dallas TX 75374	214-349-9247	R	2*	<.1
253	Automation Displays Inc—*R Carroll*	3533 White Ave, Eau Claire WI 54703	715-834-9595	R	2*	<.1
254	Sigtronics Corp—*Mark Kelley*	178 E Arrow Hwy, San Dimas CA 91773	909-305-9399	R	2*	<.1
255	Evax Systems Inc—*Pete Binkley*	20 Mcdermott Rd, Branford CT 06405	203-315-5116	R	2*	<.1
256	Tech-Lite Inc—*William Maley*	120 Wampus Ln, Milford CT 06460	203-878-8567	R	2*	<.1
257	Zumro Manufacturing Inc—*Win Vanbasten*	PO Box 667227, Pompano Beach FL 33066	954-782-7779	R	2*	<.1
258	Digitize Inc—*Abraham Brecher*	158 Edison Rd, Lake Hopatcong NJ 07849	973-663-1011	R	2*	<.1
259	Engineered Electronics Inc—*Roy Caviness*	4301 Industrial Access, Douglasville GA 30134	770-949-3290	R	2*	<.1
260	Telegenix Inc—*Joseph Miller*	PO Box 577, Rancocas NJ 08073	609-265-3910	R	2*	<.1
261	Franklin County Emergency Communications—*Christy Shearin*	287 T Kemp Rd, Louisburg NC 27549	919-496-1425	R	2*	<.1
262	General Traffic Equipment Corp—*Ray Staffon*	259 Broadway, Newburgh NY 12550	845-569-9000	R	2*	<.1
263	Essential Trading Systems Corp—*Gilbert Smith*	9 Austin Dr, Marlborough CT 06447	860-295-8100	R	2*	<.1
264	Lee Electric Inc—*Andy Abramowitz*	PO Box 238, West New York NJ 07093	201-866-3656	R	2*	<.1
265	HR Kirkland Company Inc—*Bruce Kirkland*	4935 Allison St Ste 13, Arvada CO 80002	303-422-6670	R	1*	<.1
266	Modco Inc—*Robert Wehe*	806 Packer Way, Sparks NV 89431	775-331-2442	R	1*	<.1
267	ABC Control Systems Inc—*Zohra Vhora*	7425 Orangethorpe Ave, Buena Park CA 90621	714-670-0117	R	1*	<.1
268	Bers Corp—*Steve Mishory*	1280 E Walnut St, North Wales PA 19454	215-699-5766	R	1*	<.1
269	Regional Emergency Dispatch Center—*Jim Clausen*	1842 Shermer Rd, Northbrook IL 60062	847-498-5748	R	1*	<.1
270	VB Ross Corp—*Vernon Ross*	4520 Baldwin Ave Ste A, El Monte CA 91731	626-443-4187	R	1*	<.1
271	Athens Technical Specialists Inc—*Ted Gilfert*	8157 Us Hwy 50, Athens OH 45701	740-592-2874	R	1*	<.1
272	Tectron Engineering—*Michael Jackson*	13913 Duval Rd, Jacksonville FL 32218	904-394-0683	R	1*	<.1
273	Security Systems Techniques Inc—*Faye Vafaee*	7768 Arjons Dr, San Diego CA 92126	858-693-0163	R	1*	<.1
274	Prototek Corp—*Lawrence Smith*	PO Box 1700, Poulsbo WA 98370	360-779-1310	R	1*	<.1
275	Control Technologies Of Centra—*Micheal Bay*	30618 William Juergens, Tomball TX 77375	281-357-1350	R	1*	<.1
276	Housing Devices Inc—*David Jablon*	407r Mystic Ave Ste 32, Medford MA 02155	781-395-5200	R	1*	<.1
277	Intermountain Traffic Safety Inc—*Mike Knaras*	2440 S 3270 W, Salt Lake City UT 84119	801-972-6515	R	1*	<.1
278	IP Video Networks Inc—*Bob Coakley*	6650 Lusk Blvd Unit B1, San Diego CA 92121	858-366-4391	R	1*	<.1
279	Educational Technology Inc—*Mark O'Neill*	300 Bedford Ave, Bellmore NY 11710	516-221-8440	R	1*	<.1
280	Mega Rentals Inc—*Megan Decker*	PO Box 8026, Madison WI 53708	608-222-2247	R	1*	<.1
281	Safepak Corp—*Buzz Siler*	1991 NW Upshure St Ste, Portland OR 97209	503-542-0935	R	1*	<.1
282	MagicBox Inc—*Tom Searcy*	1600 SW Western Ste 13, Corvallis OR 97333	541-752-5654	R	1*	<.1
283	Audiodontics Inc—*Barry Mersky*	10401 Old Georgetown R, Bethesda MD 20814	301-530-0700	R	1*	<.1
284	Detectapro LLC	PO Box 26, Menomonee Falls WI 53052		R	1*	<.1
285	1 PC Network Inc—*Alan V Cameron*	3675 S Rainbow Blvd No, Las Vegas NV 89103		R	1*	<.1
286	AWM Mold Service US Inc—*Martin Osterode*	100 Cummings Ctr Ste 2, Beverly MA 01915	978-720-4081	R	1*	<.1
287	Griffin Chase Oliver Inc—*Jim Redfield*	25262 Monte Verde Dr, Laguna Niguel CA 92677	949-495-1144	R	1*	<.1
288	Ftc - Forward Threat Control—*Frank Zajac*	234 Jason Way, Mountain View CA 94043	650-906-7917	R	1*	<.1
289	General Fire Protection Systems Inc—*Darrell Siria*	3904 E Trent Ave, Spokane WA 99202	509-535-4255	R	1*	<.1
290	Atis Ltd—*Harvey Gobel*	1060 Windward Ridge Pk, Alpharetta GA 30005	770-664-4744	R	1*	<.1
291	Touchtable Inc—*Gerard Roccanova*	31 N Fair Oaks Ave, Pasadena CA 91103	626-639-5460	R	1*	<.1

Rank	Company Name—*Executive Officer*	Address, City, State, Zip	Phone	Type	Fin	Empls
292	SCI Tronics Inc—*Cliff Brandvold*	4630 Churchill St Ste, Saint Paul MN 55126	651-659-9247	R	1*	<.1
293	Spectrex Inc—*Eric Zinn*	218 Little Falls Rd St, Cedar Grove NJ 07009	973-239-8398	R	1*	<.1
294	Jp Telecom Inc—*Jim Posilippo*	839 La Mesa Dr, Portola Valley CA 94028	650-854-1560	R	1*	<.1
295	Nel-Logiplex Co—*William Nelson*	4855 N Lagoon Ave, Portland OR 97217	503-978-6726	R	1*	<.1
296	Dulce Systems Inc—*Carmen Palacios*	9620 Topanga Canyon Pl, Chatsworth CA 91311	818-435-6009	R	1*	<.1
297	Dynamic Traffic Systems Inc—*David Salisbury*	5050 Cohasset Rd 4, Chico CA 95973	530-343-8403	R	1*	<.1
298	Unitone Communication Systems Inc—*Lucien Bohbot*	220 E 23rd St Fl 12, New York NY 10010	212-777-9090	R	1*	<.1
299	Mastercom Inc—*Henry Gross*	1060 Ashley Dr, Valley Stream NY 11580	516-285-5755	R	1*	<.1
300	Hood River Cable Inc—*Sylvia Brown*	902 Wasco St Ste 10, Hood River OR 97031	541-387-7777	R	1*	<.1
301	Ohana Wireless Inc—*Joe Anzalone*	3500 Thomas Rd Ste A, Santa Clara CA 95054	408-656-4919	R	1*	<.1
302	Astro-Tronics Inc—*John Kodak*	9321 Calanda St, Lanham MD 20706	301-577-8431	R	1*	<.1
303	Relume Corp—*Dennis Foy*	925 N Lapeer Rd Ste B, Oxford MI 48371	248-969-3800	R	1*	<.1
304	Kentronics Inc—*Robert Davis*	PO Box 365, Sayville NY 11782	631-567-5994	R	<1*	<.1
305	Metabloc Inc—*Deborah Henry*	3230 N Susquehanna Trl, York PA 17406	717-764-4937	R	<1*	<.1
306	Unisec Inc—*Albert Hermans*	2555 Nicholson St, San Leandro CA 94577	510-352-5610	R	<1*	<.1
307	Dan Imig—*Dan Imig*	1 Bic Way Ste 3, Shelton CT 06484	203-925-1707	R	<1*	<.1
308	PositiveID Corp—*William J Caragol*	1690 S Congress Ave St, Delray Beach FL 33445	561-805-8000	P	<1	<.1
309	Theta Corp—*Paul Pinkney*	PO Box 806, Niagara Falls NY 14302	716-791-3374	R	<1*	<.1
310	Micro-Trap Corp—*David Steil*	1300 Steel Rd E Ste 2, Morrisville PA 19067	215-295-8208	R	<1*	<.1
311	Prorail Manufacturing Inc	PO Box 288, Atlantic IA 50022	712-243-5411	R	<1*	<.1
312	Empowerment Enterprises LLC—*Herman Wright*	3300 Bee Cave Rd 65022, West Lake Hills TX 78746	512-347-0529	R	<1*	<.1
313	Survey Technologies Inc—*William Peek*	PO Box 1239, Manzanita OR 97130	503-848-8500	R	<1*	<.1
314	Advanced Aero Safety Inc—*Sherman Hall*	1938 Forest Hill Rd, Stanwood WA 98282	360-387-8472	R	<1*	<.1
315	Bds Systems Inc—*Robert Balderson*	756 W Sandy Ridge Rd, Doylestown PA 18901	215-345-0436	R	<1*	<.1
316	Metaplus Inc—*Rajeeva Sharma*	1600 Saratoga Ave 238, San Jose CA 95129	408-257-5569	R	<1*	<.1
317	Traffic Signal Hardware Inc—*Deloy Tolman*	1256 W 1st St, Pomona CA 91766	909-623-4556	R	<1*	<.1
318	3DIcon Corp—*Sid Aroesty*	6804 S Canton Ave Ste, Tulsa OK 74136	918-494-0509	P	<1	<.1
319	Komtek Corp—*Sherry Spiller*	PO Box 11, Stanley NM 87056	505-832-6236	R	<1*	<.1
320	Revel Technology Inc—*Jeffrey Fink*	832 W 1st St, Birdsboro PA 19508	610-582-1730	R	<1*	<.1

TOTALS: SIC 3669 Communications Equipment Nec
Companies: 320 — 28,433 — 92.4

3671 Electron Tubes

Rank	Company Name—*Executive Officer*	Address, City, State, Zip	Phone	Type	Fin	Empls
1	Hitachi Electronic (USA) Devices Inc—*L Thomas Heiser*	1000 Hurricane Shoals, Lawrenceville GA 30043	770-409-3000	S	1,305	1.2
2	Thales Components Corp—*Stephen Shapock*	PO Box 540, Totowa NJ 07511	973-812-9000	S	181*	.1
3	Dcx-Chol Enterprises Inc—*Neal Castleman*	12831 S Figueroa St, Los Angeles CA 90061	310-965-0194	R	175*	.4
4	Maxwell Technologies Inc—*David J Schramm*	5271 Viewridge Ct Ste, San Diego CA 92123	858-503-3300	P	157	.4
5	Semicon Associates—*Jeff Waldal*	695 Laco Dr, Lexington KY 40510	859-255-3664	S	153	.1
6	Thomas Electronics of New York Inc—*David Ketchum*	330 S La Londe Ave, Addison IL 60101	630-543-6444	R	111*	.2
7	Mpd Inc—*Gary Braswell*	316 E 9th St, Owensboro KY 42303	270-685-6200	R	54*	.9
8	Imaging and Sensing Technology Corp—*Ken Neal*	100 1st Ctr, Horseheads NY 14845	607-562-4300	D	38*	.4
9	Thomas Electronics of New York Inc—*David Ketchum* Thomas Electronics of New York Inc	100 Riverview Dr, Wayne NJ 07470	973-696-5200	S	32*	.2
10	Hamamatsu Corp—*Akira Hiruma*	PO Box 6910, Bridgewater NJ 08807	908-231-0960	R	20*	.2
11	Communications and Power Industries Inc—*O Joe Caldarelli*	607 Hansen Way, Palo alto CA 94304	650-846-2900	S	19*	.1
12	CPI Econco Div Communications and Power Industries Inc	1318 Commerce Ave, Woodland CA 95776	530-662-7553	D	18*	.1
13	Tfi Telemark—*Gerald Henderson*	20936 Cabot Blvd, Hayward CA 94545	510-887-2225	R	10*	.1
14	Detector Technology Inc—*Jay Ray*	9 3rd St, Palmer MA 01069	413-284-9975	R	8*	.1
15	Lexel Imaging Systems Inc—*Ronald D Ordway*	1500 Bull Lea Rd Ste 1, Lexington KY 40511	859-243-5500	S	7	.1
16	Suntronic Inc—*John Ly*	10501 Kipp Way Ste 350, Houston TX 77099	281-879-9562	R	6*	.1
17	Remtec Inc—*Nahum Rapoport*	100 Morse St Ste 6, Norwood MA 02062	781-762-9191	R	5*	<.1
18	Spectra-Mat Inc	100 Westgate Dr, Watsonville CA 95076	831-722-4116	R	5*	.1
19	Central Baptist Breast Imaging—*Teresa Zilli*	1720 Nicholasville Rd, Lexington KY 40503	859-260-6351	R	3*	<.1
20	Troy-Onic Inc—*Michael Murphy*	PO Box 494, Kenvil NJ 07847	973-584-6830	R	3*	<.1
21	World Electronics Inc—*Murray Rinzler*	37 Hanover Pl, Glen Rock NJ 07452	201-670-1177	R	2*	<.1
22	Vacuum Tube Logic Of America Inc—*Luke Manley*	PO Box 2604, Sunnyvale CA 94087	909-627-5944	R	1*	<.1
23	Stellar Micro Devices Inc—*Mark Eaton*	2020 Centimeter Cir, Austin TX 78758	512-997-7780	R	1*	<.1
24	Filtech Inc—*G Becker*	6 Pinckney St, Boston MA 02114	617-227-1133	R	1*	<.1
25	Association of Medical Device Reprocessors—*Dan Vukelich*	1400 16th St Nw Ste 40, Washington DC 20036	202-518-6796	R	1*	<.1
26	Spiral Designs Inc—*Daniel Pringle*	5775 Arapahoe Ave, Boulder CO 80303	303-442-6553	R	1*	<.1
27	Precision Cable Inc—*Terri Walker*	3255 NW 29th Ave, Portland OR 97210	503-222-4323	R	<1	<.1
28	Hawk-Eye Picture Tube Manufacturing Inc—*Donald Avitt*	724 Scott Ave, Des Moines IA 50309	515-288-8567	R	<1*	<.1

TOTALS: SIC 3671 Electron Tubes
Companies: 28 — 2,315 — 4.6

3672 Printed Circuit Boards

Rank	Company Name—*Executive Officer*	Address, City, State, Zip	Phone	Type	Fin	Empls
1	Jabil Circuit Inc—*Timothy L Main*	10560 Dr Martin Luther, St Petersburg FL 33716	727-577-9749	P	13,409	69.0
2	Sanmina-SCI Corp—*Jure Sola*	2700 N 1st St, San Jose CA 95134	408-964-3500	P	6,602	36.8
3	Benchmark Electronics Inc—*Cary T Fu*	3000 Technology Dr, Angleton TX 77515	979-849-6550	P	2,253	10.0
4	Plexus Corp—*Dean Foate*	PO Box 156, Neenah WI 54957		P	2,231	9.0
5	TTM Technologies Inc—*Kenton K Alder*	2630 S Harbor Blvd, Santa Ana CA 92704	714-241-0303	P	1,180	17.4
6	Cookson Electronics	1 Cookson Pl, Providence RI 02903	401-228-8800	D	1,103*	5.0
7	Multi-Fineline Electronix Inc—*Reza Meshgin*	3140 E Coronado St, Anaheim CA 92806	714-238-1488	P	832	12.1
8	Methode Development Co—*Donald W Duda*	7401 W Wilson Ave, Chicago IL 60706	708-867-6777	S	700*	3.2
9	Express Manufacturing Inc	3519 W Warner Ave, Santa Ana CA 92704	714-979-2228	R	446*	.5
10	Saturn Electronics and Engineering Inc—*Wallace K Tsuha Jr*	2120 Austin Ave, Rochester Hills MI 48309	248-853-5724	P	399*	1.8
11	Raven Industries Inc—*Daniel A Rykhus*	PO Box 5107, Sioux Falls SD 57117	605-336-2750	P	315	1.1
12	DDI Corp—*Mikel H Williams*	1220 Simon Cir, Anaheim CA 92806	714-688-7200	P	263	1.6
13	Sanmina-SCI PCB—*Jure Sola* Sanmina-SCI Corp	2700 N 1st St, San Jose CA 95134	408-964-3500	D	219*	2.0
14	Pycon Inc—*Ayub Rajput*	3301 Leonard Ct, Santa Clara CA 95054	408-727-1213	R	216*	.3
15	Park Electrochemical Corp—*Brain E Shore*	48 S Service Rd Ste 30, Melville NY 11747	631-465-3600	P	212	.6
16	Reptron Manufacturing Services—*Charlie Crep*	13750 Reptron Blvd, Tampa FL 33626	813-814-5069	S	209*	1.0
17	MC Test Service Inc—*George Moore*	2755 Kirby Cir Ne, Palm Bay FL 32905	321-253-0541	R	170*	.9
18	SigmaTron International Inc—*Gary R Fairhead*	2201 Landmeier Rd, Elk Grove Village IL 60007	847-956-8000	P	152	1.8
19	Dynamic Details Inc—*Mikel Williams* DDI Corp	1220 Simon Cir, Anaheim CA 92806	714-688-7200	S	143*	1.3
20	IEC Electronics Corp—*W Barry Gilbert*	105 Norton St, Newark NY 14513	315-331-7742	P	133	.8

Note: An asterisk (*) indicates an estimated financial figure. The company type code used is as follows: R = Private, P = Public, S = Private Subsidiary, B = Public Subsidiary, D = Division, J = Joint Venture, I = Investment Fund.

COMPANY RANKINGS BY SALES WITHIN 4-DIGIT SIC

Rank	Company Name—*Executive Officer*	Address, City, State, Zip	Phone	Type	Fin	Empls
21	Micro Dynamics Corp—*Michael Davis*	6201 Bury Dr, Eden Prairie MN 55346	952-941-8071	R	131*	.5
22	Flash Electronics Inc—*Chin Fan*	4050 Starboard Dr, Fremont CA 94538	510-440-2840	R	114*	.5
23	m-Audio—*Tim Ryan*	5795 Martin Rd, Irwindale CA 91706	626-633-9050	S	107*	.1
24	Parlex Corp—*Patrick Wang*	1 Parlex Pl, Methuen MA 01844	978-685-4341	S	106	1.9
25	SMTEK International Inc—*Vinod M Khilnani*	200 Science Dr, Moorpark CA 93021	805-532-2800	S	93	.5
26	ActionTec Electronics Inc—*Dean Chang*	760 N Mary Ave, Sunnyvale CA 94085	408-752-7700	R	89*	.4
27	International Control Services Inc—*Jerry Johnson*	606 W Imboden Dr, Decatur IL 62521	217-422-6700	R	73*	.1
28	Riverside Electronics Ltd—*Stephen H Craney*	1 Riverside Dr, Lewiston MN 55952	507-523-3220	R	72*	.3
29	Resistance Technology Inc	1260 Red Fox Rd, Arden Hills MN 55112	651-636-9770	S	68*	.3
30	Rogers Corporation Advanced Circuit Materials—*Robert D Wachab*	100 S Roosevelt Ave, Chandler AZ 85226	480-961-1382	D	68*	.3
31	Advanced Circuits Inc—*John Yacoub*	21100 E 32nd Pkwy, Aurora CO 80011	303-576-6610	R	53*	.2
32	Total Electronics LLC—*Jack Chang*	1 Technology Way, Logansport IN 46947	574-739-2929	R	51*	.4
33	Tyan Computer USA—*Symon Chang*	3288 Laurelview Ct, Fremont CA 94538	510-651-8868	S	48*	.1
34	Diversified Systems Inc—*Stan Bentley*	8110 Zionsville Rd, Indianapolis IN 46268	317-405-9427	R	44*	.4
35	Philway Products Inc—*Mahendra Patel*	701 Virginia Ave, Ashland OH 44805	419-281-7777	R	44*	.2
36	Paramit Corp—*Thanh Nguyen*	18735 Madrone Pkwy, Morgan Hill CA 95037	408-782-5600	R	40*	.3
37	Mcdonald Technologies International Inc—*Pip Sivakumar*	2310 Mcdaniel Dr, Carrollton TX 75006	972-869-7101	R	38*	.2
38	Cal-Quality Electronics Inc—*Brock Koren*	2700 S Fairview St, Santa Ana CA 92704	714-545-8886	R	37*	.2
39	Pioneer Circuits Inc—*James Lee*	3000 S Shannon St, Santa Ana CA 92704	714-641-3132	R	37*	.3
40	Avg Advanced Technologies LP—*Shalabh Kumar*	343 Saint Paul Blvd, Carol Stream IL 60188	630-668-3900	R	36*	1.0
41	ABIT Computer Corp USA—*Jason Hsu*	3600 Peterson Way, Santa Clara CA 95054	408-213-2618	S	36*	<.1
42	World Electronics Sales And Service Inc—*Joseph Rado*	3000 Kutztown Rd, Reading PA 19605	610-939-9800	R	36*	.1
43	Victron Inc—*Chris Lee*	6600 Stevenson Blvd, Fremont CA 94538	510-360-2222	R	35*	.2
44	Ddi North Jackson Corp—*Mikel Williams*	PO Box 216, North Jackson OH 44451	330-538-3900	R	35*	.2
45	Sonic Manufacturing Technologies Inc—*Kenneth Raab*	48133 Warm Springs Blv, Fremont CA 94539	510-580-8500	R	35*	.3
46	Hauppauge Computer Works Inc—*Kenneth H Plotkin*	91 Cabot Ct, Hauppauge NY 11788	631-434-1600	S	35*	.1
47	Electronic Instrumentation and Technology Inc—*Joe May*	108 Carpenter Dr, Sterling VA 20164	703-478-0700	R	34*	.2
48	Elcoteq Inc	1700 International Pkwy, Richardson TX 75081	972-560-1003	S	34*	.2
49	Saturn Electronics Corp—*Nagji Sutariya*	28450 Northline Rd, Romulus MI 48174	734-941-8100	R	33*	.2
50	Synergetix	5101 Richland Ave, Kansas City KS 66106	913-342-5544	S	31*	.2
51	Symetrics Industries Inc—*Mitch Garner*	1615 W NASA Blvd, Melbourne FL 32901	321-254-1500	R	31*	.1
52	Microboard Processing Inc—*Craig Hoekenga*	4 Progress Ave, Seymour CT 06483	203-881-4300	R	30*	.2
53	Quality Systems Integrated Corp—*Kiem Le*	6720 Cobra Way, San Diego CA 92121	858-587-9797	R	30*	.3
54	Oem Worldwide LLC—*Craig Green*	PO Box 430, Watertown SD 57201	605-886-2519	R	30*	.2
55	Arc-Tronics Inc—*Conrad Goeringer*	1150 Pagni Dr, Elk Grove Village IL 60007	847-437-0211	R	28*	.2
56	Brion Technologies Inc—*Jun Ye*	4211 Burton Dr, Santa Clara CA 95054	408-653-1500	S	28*	.1
57	Printed Circuits Assembly Corp—*Sim Taing*	13221 Se 26th St Ste E, Bellevue WA 98005	425-644-7754	R	28*	.3
58	Applied Technical Services Corp—*George Hamilton*	6300 Merrill Creek Pky, Everett WA 98203	425-249-5555	R	27*	.2
59	Applied Circuit Technology Inc—*W Fillebrown*	1250 American Pkwy, Richardson TX 75081	972-664-0900	R	27*	.1
60	Siemens Manufacturing Company Inc—*John Siemens*	PO Box 61, Freeburg IL 62243	618-539-3000	R	27*	.2
61	Quality Circuits Inc—*Wayne Dirkman*	1102 Progress Dr, Fergus Falls MN 56537	218-739-9707	R	26*	.1
62	Compeq International Corp—*Webb Chang*	620 John Glenn Rd, Salt Lake City UT 84116	801-990-2000	R	26*	.4
63	Surface Mount Co—*Joe Baldassano*	230 S Siesta Ln, Tempe AZ 85281	480-967-9108	R	25*	.1
64	Sopark Corp—*Gerry Murik*	3300 S Park Ave, Buffalo NY 14218	716-822-0434	R	24*	.2
65	Unicircuit Inc—*Kerry Bode*	8122 Suthpark I n Unit, Littleton CO 80120	303-730-0505	R	24*	.2
66	Holaday Circuits Inc—*Marshall Lewis*	11126 Bren Rd W, Hopkins MN 55343	952-933-3303	R	24*	.2
67	Jaton Corp—*J Chiang*	47677 Lakeview Blvd, Fremont CA 94538	510-933-8888	R	23*	.3
68	Hunting Innova Inc—*Trey Cook*	8383 N Sam Houston Pkw, Houston TX 77064	281-653-5500	S	23*	.4
69	Ddi Denver Corp—*Mikel Williams*	10570 Bradford Rd, Littleton CO 80127	303-972-4105	R	23*	.1
70	Teknetix Inc—*Joseph Florence*	2501 Garfield Ave, Parkersburg WV 26101	304-424-9400	R	23*	.2
71	Electronic Evolution Technologies Inc—*Sonny Newman*	9455 Double R Blvd, Reno NV 89521	775-355-9191	R	23*	.2
72	First International Computer of America Inc—*Ming J Chien*	5070 Brandin Ct, Fremont CA 94538	510-252-8868	R	23*	.2
73	Electrotek Corp—*John Johnson*	7745 S 10th St, Oak Creek WI 53154	414-762-1390	R	22*	.2
74	Westak Inc—*Louise Crisham*	1225 Elko Dr, Sunnyvale CA 94089	408-734-8686	R	22*	.2
75	Electronic Solutions—*David Gallitano*	1811 W Katella Ave Ste, Anaheim CA 92804	714-469-1065	S	22	.2
76	Altron Inc—*Alan Phillips*	6700 Bunker Lake Blvd, Anoka MN 55303	763-427-7735	R	22*	.2
77	Micom Corp—*Marilyn S Walhof*	475 Old Hwy 8 NW, New Brighton MN 55112	651-636-5616	R	21*	.1
78	Amitron Inc—*Bhupen Patel*	2001 Landmeier Rd, Elk Grove Village IL 60007	847-290-9800	R	20*	.3
79	Da-Tech Corp—*Paul Litwack*	141 Railroad Dr, Warminster PA 18974	215-322-9410	R	20*	.2
80	Alternative Manufacturing Inc—*Kim Vandermeulen*	30 Summer St Ste B, Winthrop ME 04364	207-377-9377	R	20*	.3
81	Forest Silicon Electronics Inc—*Frank Nichols*	6204 E 18th St, Vancouver WA 98661	360-649-2000	R	20*	.1
82	Api Systems Inc—*Steven Pudles*	345 Pomroys Dr, Windber PA 15963	814-467-9779	R	20*	.1
83	Tri-Phase Inc—*Andy Pecota*	6190 San Ignacio Ave, San Jose CA 95119	408-637-7480	R	20*	.2
84	Cirtronics Corp—*Gerardine Ferlins*	PO Box 130, Milford NH 03055	603-249-9190	R	20*	.2
85	Precision Contract Manufacturing Inc—*Michael Hathaway*	280 Clinton St, Springfield VT 05156	802-885-6208	R	19*	.1
86	Fabricated Components Corp—*Jack Evans*	130 W Bristol Ln, Orange CA 92865	714-974-8590	R	19*	.1
87	Libra Industries Inc—*Rod Howell*	7770 Division Dr, Mentor OH 44060	440-974-7770	R	19*	.1
88	Star Circuits Inc—*James B Morgan*	405 1st Ave, Brookings SD 57006	605-697-4650	S	19*	<.1
89	Qual-Pro Corp—*Brian Shane*	18510 S Figueroa St, Gardena CA 90248	310-329-7535	R	19*	.1
90	American Board Assembly Inc—*Gene Difabritis*	5456 Endeavour Ct, Moorpark CA 93021	805-523-0274	R	19*	.1
91	Astronic—*Sang Choi*	2 Orion, Aliso Viejo CA 92656	949-900-6060	R	19*	.1
92	Progress Instruments Inc—*Stephen Patterson*	807 Nw Commerce Dr, Lees Summit MO 64086	816-524-4442	R	18*	.1
93	PNC Inc—*Peter Patel*	115 E Centre St, Nutley NJ 07110	973-284-1600	R	18*	.1
94	Teltec Corp—*Hershel Petty*	1445 Oakland Rd, San Jose CA 95112	408-294-9897	R	17*	.1
95	Conelec Of Florida LLC—*James Baynor*	421 Cornwall Rd, Sanford FL 32773	407-321-9000	R	17*	.1
96	MTI Electronics Inc—*Gregory Martinek*	W133n5139 Campbell Dr, Menomonee Falls WI 53051	262-783-6080	R	16*	.1
97	Mandaree Enterprise Corp—*Clarence O'berry*	PO Box 1030, New Town ND 58763	701-627-3042	R	16*	.1
98	All Flex Flexible Circuits LLC—*Michael Smiggen*	1705 Cannon Ln, Northfield MN 55057	507-663-7162	R	16*	.1
99	Hunter Technology Corp—*Joseph O'neil*	2921 Corvin Dr, Santa Clara CA 95051	408-245-5400	R	16*	.1
100	Texatronics Inc—*Sean Nguyen*	1501 N Plano Rd 300, Richardson TX 75081	214-379-8550	R	16*	.2
101	Mosys Inc—*Len Perham*	3301 Olcott St, Santa Clara CA 95054	408-418-7500	P	16	.2
102	SAE Circuits Colorado Inc—*Ervin Hammen*	4820 63rd St Ste 100, Boulder CO 80301	303-530-1900	R	15*	.3
103	National Technology Inc—*Roger Patel*	1101 Carnegie St, Rolling Meadows IL 60008	847-506-1300	R	15*	<.1
104	Corvalent Corp—*Ed Trevis*	1101 Arrwpint Dr Bldg, Cedar Park TX 78613	512-456-2400	R	15*	<.1
105	Apt Electronics Inc—*Tae Kim*	241 N Crescent Way, Anaheim CA 92801	714-687-6760	R	14*	.1
106	FCG Inc—*George B Stollsteimer*	222 Valley Rd, Warrington PA 18976	215-343-2300	R	14	.2
107	Circuit Express Inc—*Travis Bice* Advanced Circuits Inc	229 S Clark Rd, Tempe AZ 85281	480-966-5894	S	14*	.1
108	Nri Electronics Inc—*Roger Toikka*	PO Box 136, Aurora MN 55705	218-744-9906	R	14*	.1

Rank	Company Name—Executive Officer	Address, City, State, Zip	Phone	Type	Fin	Empls
109	Ppi/Time Zero Inc—Dana Pittman	262 Buffalo Ave, Paterson NJ 07503	973-278-6500	R	14*	.1
110	Accu-Sembly Inc—John Hykes	1835 Huntington Dr, Duarte CA 91010	626-357-3447	R	14*	.1
111	United Manufacturing Assembly Inc—Yonwen Chou	44169 Fremont Blvd, Fremont CA 94538	510-490-4680	R	13*	.1
112	Semi-Kinetics Inc—Gary Gonzalez	20191 Windrow Dr Ste A, Lake Forest CA 92630	949-830-7364	S	13*	.1
113	Irvine Electronics Inc—Jane Zerounian	1601 Alton Pkwy Ste A, Irvine CA 92606	949-250-0315	R	13*	.1
114	Enercon—Ronald Marcotte	PO Box 665, Gray ME 04039	207-657-7000	R	13*	.1
115	Tetrad Electronics Inc—Ronald Brehm	2048 Joseph Lloyd Pkwy, Willoughby OH 44094	440-946-6443	R	13*	<.1
116	General Microcircuits Inc—Stanley Cox	PO Box 748, Mooresville NC 28115	704-663-5975	R	13*	.1
117	Bay Electronic Support Tronics Inc—James Choe	2060 Ringwood Ave, San Jose CA 95131	408-432-3222	R	13*	.1
118	Aspen Electronics Manufacturing Inc—Giao Le	6262 W 91st Ave, Westminster CO 80031	303-487-5732	R	13*	.1
119	Sierra Circuits Inc—Kenneth Bahl	1108 W Evelyn Ave, Sunnyvale CA 94086	408-735-7137	R	13*	.1
120	Milford Manufacturing Services LLC—Charlie Gould	425 Fortune Blvd Ste 1, Milford MA 01757	508-478-8544	R	13*	.1
121	Saehan Electronics America Inc—John Kim	7675 Dagget St, San Diego CA 92111	858-496-1500	R	12*	.1
122	Tc Cosmotronic Inc—James Savage	16721 Noyes Ave, Irvine CA 92606	949-660-0740	R	12*	.1
123	S and Y Industries—Sandy Foust	PO Box 394, Winfield KS 67156		R	12*	.1
124	CoSystems Inc	1263 Oakmead Pky, Sunnyvale CA 94085	408-522-0500	R	12*	.1
125	Synergetics Co—David Reilly	8 Harris Ct Ste E2, Monterey CA 93940	831-648-8776	R	12*	<.1
126	Electronic Interconnect Corp—Pratish Patel	2700 Touhy Ave, Elk Grove Village IL 60007	847-364-4848	R	12*	.1
127	Custom Manufacturing Services Inc—Susan Beem	235 Main Dunstable Rd, Nashua NH 03062	603-883-1355	R	12*	<.1
128	Elreha Printed Circuits Corp—Abdul Hamadeh	2510 Terminal Dr S, Saint Petersburg FL 33712	727-327-6236	R	12*	.1
129	Pro-Tech Interconnect Solutions LLC—R Schesso	4300 Peavey Rd, Chaska MN 55318	952-442-2189	R	12*	.1
130	Milplex Circuits Inc—Bhupendra Patel	1301 Ardmore Ave, Itasca IL 60143	630-250-1580	R	12*	.1
131	Hi Tech Electronic Manufacturing Corp—Vinh Lam	9393 Waples St Ste 100, San Diego CA 92121	858-657-0908	R	12*	.1
132	Youngtron Inc—Young Kim	2873 Sterling Dr, Hatfield PA 19440	215-822-7866	R	11*	.1
133	SAE Materials Inc—Richard Maldonado	340 Martin Ave, Santa Clara CA 95050	408-492-1784	R	11*	.1
134	Epec LLC—Bob St Nge	174 Duchaine Blvd, New Bedford MA 02745	508-995-5171	R	11*	.1
135	R and D Circuits Inc—James Russell	3601 S Clinton Ave, South Plainfield NJ 07080	732-549-4554	R	11*	.1
136	Lenthor Engineering—Mark P Lencioni	1506 Gladding Ct, Milpitas CA 95035	408-945-8787	R	11*	.1
137	Cirexx International Inc—Phillip Menges	3391 Keller St, Santa Clara CA 95054	408-988-3980	R	11*	.1
138	Zentech Manufacturing Inc—Bradford J LaPray	6980 Tudsbury Rd, Baltimore MD 21244	443-348-4500	R	11*	.1
139	Pro Tech Inc—DeWayne Jensen	4300 Peavey Rd, Chaska MN 55318	952-442-2189	R	11*	.1
140	Cirtech Inc—Frank Reese	250 E Emerson Ave, Orange CA 92865	714-921-0860	R	11*	.1
141	Masterwork Electronics Inc—Robert Weed	630 Martin Ave, Rohnert Park CA 94928	707-588-9906	R	11*	.1
142	Naprotek Inc—Najat Badriyeh	2945 San Ysidro Way, Santa Clara CA 95051	408-830-5002	R	11*	.1
143	Prototron Circuits Southwest Inc—David Ryder	3760 E 43rd Pl, Tucson AZ 85713	520-745-8515	R	11*	<.1
144	Teligentems LLC—Gerald Guon	102 Technology Way, Havana FL 32333	850-539-2500	R	11*	.1
145	Precision Assembly Inc—Steve Vanbibber	1315 W 400 S, Orem UT 84058	801-229-2400	R	11*	.1
146	Ftg Circuits Inc—Brad Bourne	20750 Marilla St, Chatsworth CA 91311	818-407-4024	S	10*	.1
147	Universal Circuits Inc—Thomas Esser	W141n9240 Fountain Blv, Menomonee Falls WI 53051	262-255-0802	R	10*	.1
148	American Standard Circuits Inc—Gordhan Patel	475 Industrial Dr, West Chicago IL 60185	630-639-5440	R	10*	.1
149	TWB Inc—William Bartley	11551 Eagle St Nw Ste, Minneapolis MN 55448	763-767-4625	R	10*	.1
150	American Alpha Inc	45 Stouts Ln Ste 8, Monmouth Junction NJ 08852	732-438-0420	R	10*	<.1
151	Sibex Inc—Michael Mccarthy	1040 Harbor Lake Dr, Safety Harbor FL 34695	727-726-4343	R	10*	.1
152	Mega Circuit Inc—Hick Savani	1040 S Wootgate St, Addison IL 60101	630-629-1800	R	10*	.1
153	Eagle Electronics Inc—Mike Kalaria	1735 Mitchell Blvd, Schaumburg IL 60193	847-891-5800	R	9*	.1
154	Falconer Electronics Inc—Roger Hall	421 W Everett St, Falconer NY 14733	716-665-4176	R	9*	.1
155	Quality Contract Manufacturing LLC—Bob Bilbro	4362 Thurmon Tanner Rd, Flowery Branch GA 30542	770-965-3300	R	9*	.1
156	Quality Circuit Assembly Inc—Jeff Moss	1709 Junction Ct Ste 3, San Jose CA 95112	408-441-1001	R	9*	.1
157	Modular Components National Inc—Irka Zazulak	PO Box 453, Forest Hill MD 21050	410-879-6553	R	9*	.1
158	A and A Electronics Assembly Inc—Carole Kee	915 Kiowa Ave, Lake Havasu City AZ 86403	928-453-7717	R	9*	.1
159	South Coast Circuits Inc—Charles Benson	3506 W Lake Center Dr, Santa Ana CA 92704	714-966-2108	R	9*	.1
160	Electronic Source Co—Scott Alyn	16032 Arminta St, Van Nuys CA 91406	818-988-7696	R	9*	.1
161	Gigaram—Keller Lee	9 Spectrum Pointe Dr, Lake Forest CA 92630	949-461-9999	R	9*	<.1
162	Creative Electronics And Software Inc—Robert Kowalski	650 Sundown Rd, South Elgin IL 60177	847-695-0023	R	9*	.1
163	Morgan Newton Company LP—William Boyd	3401 Wynwood Dr, Plano TX 75074	972-212-8080	R	9*	.1
164	R-Tech Inc—Donald Ryan	108 Turnberry Ln, Rainbow City AL 35906	256-442-4116	R	9*	.1
165	Murrietta Circuits—Albert Murrietta	5000 E Landon Dr, Anaheim CA 92807	714-970-2430	R	9*	.1
166	Vermont Circuits Inc—James Lin	PO Box 1890, Brattleboro VT 05302	802-257-4571	R	9*	.1
167	Photo Fabricators Inc—Steve Brooks	7648 Burnet Ave, Van Nuys CA 91405	818-781-1010	R	9*	.1
168	Ntw Inc—Roger Patel	8701 W Bradley Rd, Milwaukee WI 53224	414-355-5300	R	8*	.1
169	Marlo Electronics Inc—Mark Goddard	4007 Ne 6th Ave, Fort Lauderdale FL 33334	954-565-4839	R	8*	.1
170	Schippers and Crew Inc—Bert Schippers	5309 Shlshl Ave Nw 100, Seattle WA 98107	206-782-2325	R	8*	.1
171	Staci Corp—Dennis Docherty	905 Lakeside Dr Ste 1, Gurnee IL 60031	847-855-9600	R	8*	.1
172	Positran Manufacturing Inc—Larry Keeney	800 E Main St, Norristown PA 19401	610-277-0500	R	8*	.1
173	Logical Products Inc—Terry Coleman	2383 N Delany Rd, Waukegan IL 60087	847-336-6160	R	8*	<.1
174	Janco Inc—Mark Janetos	PO Box 0857, Dover NH 03821	603-742-1581	R	8*	.1
175	Ridge Associates Inc—Richard Ferri	5 Astro Pl Ste A, Rockaway NJ 07866	973-586-2717	R	8*	.1
176	Assembly Plus LLC—Cindy Jeffries	1607 W Whispering Wind, Phoenix AZ 85085	623-580-8400	R	8*	<.1
177	Bustronic Corp	44350 S Grimmer Blvd, Fremont CA 94538	510-490-7388	S	8*	<.1
178	Parlex Dynaflex Corp Parlex Corp	1756 Junction Ave Ste, San Jose CA 95112	408-441-8713	S	8*	<.1
179	Valley Technologies Inc—Jerry Petrole	724 Claremont Ave, Tamaqua PA 18252	570-668-3737	R	8*	<.1
180	Innovative Circuits Arizona Inc—David Shano	130 N Pasadena St, Gilbert AZ 85233	480-497-6681	R	8*	.1
181	Electro Plate Circuitry Inc—Nicolas Garcia	1430 Century Dr, Carrollton TX 75006	972-466-0818	R	8*	.1
182	Nbs Design Inc—Craig Arcuri	300 E Canon Perdido St, Santa Barbara CA 93101	805-966-9383	R	8*	.1
183	Electronic Surface Mounted Industries—Henry Kim	6731 Cobra Way, San Diego CA 92121	858-371-7145	R	8*	.1
184	Sierra Midwest Inc—Kenneth Bahl	PO Box 578, Chanute KS 66720	620-431-0406	R	7*	.1
185	Nebraska Electronics Inc—Patrick Bystrek	12202 Cary Cir, La Vista NE 68128	402-334-8120	R	7*	.1
186	Ibs Electronics Inc—Bahman Tavi	3506 W Lake Ctr Dr D, Santa Ana CA 92704	714-751-6633	R	7*	.2
187	Ito Industries Inc—Daryl Ito	PO Box 430, Bristol WI 53104	262-857-7904	R	7*	.1
188	General Standards Corp—Paul Rainosek	8302 Whitesburg Dr Se, Huntsville AL 35802	256-880-8787	R	7*	<.1
189	SKY Computers Inc—John W Wood Jr	27 Industrial Ave, Chelmsford MA 01824	978-250-2420	R	7*	.1
190	Techtron Systems Inc—Paul Teel	760 Beta Dr Ste L, Cleveland OH 44143	440-442-6003	R	7*	.1
191	Circuit Engineering LLC—Bruce Parker	1390 Lunt Ave, Elk Grove Village IL 60007	847-806-7777	R	7*	<.1
192	Mass Design Inc—Anthony Bourassa	41 Simon St, Nashua NH 03060	603-886-6460	R	7*	.1
193	Aurora Circuits LLC—Donna Brookes	2250 White Oak Cir, Aurora IL 60502	630-978-3830	R	7*	.1
194	Electronic Design and Manufacturing Co—Robert Roberts	31 Millrace Dr, Lynchburg VA 24502	434-385-0046	R	7*	.1
195	Practical Technologies Inc—Dilip Dalvi	9600 Pulaski Park Dr S, Baltimore MD 21220	410-682-4013	R	7*	.1
196	Electromax Inc—Aaron Wong	1960 Concourse Dr, San Jose CA 95131	408-428-9474	R	7*	.1
197	Quality Production Ltd—Tom Hauge	21420 Nw Nicholas Ct G, Hillsboro OR 97124	503-617-0210	R	7*	<.1

Note: An asterisk (*) indicates an estimated financial figure. The company type code used is as follows: R = Private, P = Public, S = Private Subsidiary, B = Public Subsidiary, D = Division, J = Joint Venture, I = Investment Fund.

COMPANY RANKINGS BY SALES WITHIN 4-DIGIT SIC

Rank	Company Name—*Executive Officer*	Address, City, State, Zip	Phone	Type	Fin	Empls
198	Geometric Circuits Inc—*John Pollina*	11 Michael Ave, Farmingdale NY 11735	631-249-0230	R	7*	.1
199	Integrated Circuit Packaging Corp—*Ralph Richart*	1602 Tacoma Way, Redwood City CA 94063	650-591-8300	R	7*	.1
200	First Electronics Inc—*Chong Cho*	211 W Vaughn St, Tempe AZ 85283	480-730-1900	R	7*	.1
201	Carlton Industries Corp—*Brad Carlton*	25 Marne St, Hamden CT 06514	203-288-5605	R	7*	<.1
202	Applicad Inc—*Paul Macmillan*	5029 Industrial Rd, Wall Township NJ 07727	732-751-2555	R	7*	<.1
203	We Imagine Inc—*Barry Henley*	9371 Canoga Ave, Chatsworth CA 91311	818-709-0064	R	6*	.1
204	Colonial Circuits Inc—*Mark Osborn*	1026 Warrenton Rd, Fredericksburg VA 22406	540-752-5511	R	6*	.1
205	Dallas Electronics Inc—*Geneva Matta*	2151 Delaware Ave Ste, Santa Cruz CA 95060	831-425-8774	R	6*	.1
206	Avanti Circuits Inc—*Jim Keaton*	17650 N 25th Ave, Phoenix AZ 85023	602-866-7227	R	6*	<.1
207	Accurate Circuit Engineering Inc—*Charles Lowe*	3019 Kilson Dr, Santa Ana CA 92707	714-546-2162	R	6*	.1
208	Dca Manufacturing Corp—*Carl Proescholdt*	PO Box 476, Cumberland WI 54829	715-822-5550	R	6*	<.1
209	Rtp Corp—*Salvatore Provanzano*	PO Box 106030, Atlanta GA 30348	954-974-5500	R	6*	<.1
210	Colonial Electronic Manufacturers Inc—*Steven Holzman*	1 Chestnut St Ste 203, Nashua NH 03060	603-881-8244	R	6*	<.1
211	Ampel Inc—*Popatlal Patel*	925 Estes Ave, Elk Grove Village IL 60007	847-952-1900	R	6*	.1
212	Sabtech Industries—*Rabim Sabadia*	23231 La Palma Ave, Yorba Linda CA 92887	714-692-3800	R	6*	<.1
213	Woodward Mccoach Inc—*Thomas Woodward*	1180 Mcdermott Dr, West Chester PA 19380	610-692-9526	R	6*	<.1
214	Elbit Systems of America LLC	4700 Marine Creek Pkwy, Fort Worth TX 76179	817-234-6799	S	6	<.1
215	Communication Automation Corp—*James Bridges*	1180 McDermott Dr, West Chester PA 19380	610-692-9526	R	6*	<.1
216	Case Assembly Solutions Inc—*Gregory Cronin*	19 Norfolk Ave Ste B, South Easton MA 02375	508-238-5665	R	6*	<.1
217	Neeco-Tron Inc—*Nick Nibert*	400 Trade Ctr Dr E, Saint Peters MO 63376	636-379-1994	R	6*	<.1
218	Il Assembly Inc—*John Moffat*	3943 Quebec Ave N, Minneapolis MN 55427	763-557-6737	R	6*	<.1
219	Octagon Systems Corp—*John Kown*	7403 Church Ranch Blvd, Westminster CO 80021	303-468-1577	R	6*	.1
220	Futura Circuits Corp—*Bob Godek*	5890 89th Ave N, Pinellas Park FL 33782	727-573-3910	R	6*	.1
221	Circuit Connect Inc—*Richard Clutz*	4 State St, Nashua NH 03063	603-880-7447	R	6*	.1
222	Bay Area Circuits Inc—*Barbara Nobriga*	91 Winslow St, Redwood City CA 94063	650-367-8444	R	6*	<.1
223	Logue Industries Inc—*Michael Logue*	PO Box 1833, El Centro CA 92244	760-353-4000	R	6*	<.1
224	Printed Circuits Inc—*Kenneth Tannehill*	1200 W 96th St, Minneapolis MN 55431	952-888-7900	R	6*	<.1
225	Expert Assembly Services Inc—*Jack Quinn*	1183 Warner Ave, Tustin CA 92780	714-258-8880	R	6*	<.1
226	Electropac Company Inc—*Raymond Boissoneau*	252 Willow St, Manchester NH 03103	603-622-3711	R	5*	.1
227	A And C Electronics—*Frank Sampo*	18153 Napa St, Northridge CA 91325	818-886-8900	R	5*	<.1
228	Quantronic Corp—*Rafael Del Moral*	8300 89th Ave N, Minneapolis MN 55445	763-425-2602	R	5*	<.1
229	Onanon Inc—*Dennis Johnson*	720 S Milpitas Blvd, Milpitas CA 95035	408-262-8990	R	5*	<.1
230	Electronic Service and Design Corp—*Frank English*	5885 Grayson Rd, Harrisburg PA 17111	717-561-1995	R	5*	.1
231	A and M Electronics Inc—*Ron Simpson*	25018 Ave Kearny, Valencia CA 91355	661-257-3680	R	5*	<.1
232	Nashua Circuits Inc—*Robert Moncada*	29 Crown St, Nashua NH 03060	603-882-1773	R	5*	<.1
233	C and D Assembly Inc—*Jeffrey Cronk*	107 Corona Ave, Groton NY 13073	607-898-4275	R	5*	<.1
234	Golden West Technology—*Dan Rieth*	1180 E Valencia Dr, Fullerton CA 92831	714-738-3775	R	5*	.1
235	Axon Circuit Inc—*Chandra Patel*	424 Ware Blvd, Tampa FL 33619	813-623-5200	R	5*	.1
236	Electro Surface Technologies—*Hiroo Kirpalani*	2280 Faraday Ave, Carlsbad CA 92008	760-431-8306	R	5*	<.1
237	Absolute Turnkey Services Inc—*Jeffrey Bullis*	555 Aldo Ave, Santa Clara CA 95054	408-850-7530	R	5*	<.1
238	Agility Manufacturing Inc—*Michael McGreevy*	PO Box 1455, Dover NH 03821	603-742-8977	R	5*	<.1
239	Electro National Corp—*Spencer Nash*	PO Box 402, Canton MS 39046	601-859-5511	S	5*	<.1
240	Technical Support Inc—*Rudy Chloupek*	11253 John Galt Blvd, Omaha NE 68137	402-331-4977	R	5*	<.1
241	Yamamoto Manufacturing Inc (San Jose California)—*Atsushi Mihara*	2025 Gateway Pl Ste 37, San Jose CA 95110	408-387-5254	R	5*	<.1
242	Accusemble Electronics Inc—*Deborah Bayley*	5 Esquire Rd, North Billerica MA 01862	978-392-0211	R	5*	<.1
243	Corad Technology Inc—*K Chui*	3080 Olcott St Ste 202, Santa Clara CA 95054	408-496-5511	R	5*	<.1
244	Advanced Microelectronics Inc—*Benjamin Mikulis*	1 Chestnut St, Nashua NH 03060	603-595-0333	R	5*	<.1
245	Texas Circuitry Inc—*C Patel*	2960 Market St, Garland TX 75041	972-278-3838	R	5*	.1
246	Tech Circuits Inc—*Philip Walton*	PO Box 309, Wallingford CT 06492	203-269-3311	R	5*	<.1
247	Evenstar Inc—*David Miller*	809 Aldo Ave Ste 105, Santa Clara CA 95054	408-986-8136	R	5*	<.1
248	Brundidge Electronics Corp—*Johnny Wright*	PO Box 127, Brundidge AL 36010	334-735-3030	R	5*	<.1
249	Ormec Systems Corp—*Edward Krasnicki*	19 Linden Park, Rochester NY 14625	585-385-3520	R	5*	<.1
250	Ab Electronics Inc—*Armando Bernardo*	61 Commerce Dr, Brookfield CT 06804	203-740-2793	R	5*	<.1
251	Lifetime Memory Products Inc—*Cameron Hum*	PO Box 16669, Irvine CA 92623	949-794-9000	R	5*	<.1
252	Netvia Group LLC—*David Wetzel*	230 Irby Ln, Irving TX 75061	972-259-3699	R	5*	<.1
253	Circuit World Inc—*Vipan Patel*	751 Hilltop Dr, Itasca IL 60143	630-250-1100	R	4*	<.1
254	Eagle Circuits Inc—*Harry Savalia*	10820 Sanden Dr, Dallas TX 75238	214-349-0288	R	4*	<.1
255	Symprotek Co—*Eric Chon*	950 Yosemite Dr, Milpitas CA 95035	408-956-0700	R	4*	<.1
256	American Backplane Inc—*Thomas Zampini*	355 Bantam Lake Rd, Morris CT 06763	860-567-2360	R	4*	<.1
257	Excello Circuits Manufacturing Corp—*Anal Shah*	1924 Nancita Cir, Placentia CA 92870	714-993-0560	R	4*	<.1
258	Mer-Mar Inc—*John Merell*	7042 Santa Fe Ave E A1, Hesperia CA 92345	760-244-6149	R	4*	<.1
259	Tropical Assemblies Inc—*Randall Dietz*	4066 Ne 5th Ave, Oakland Park FL 33334	954-396-9999	R	4*	<.1
260	Circuitronix LLC—*Maria Casrejon*	201 N Gables Blvd, Wheaton IL 60187	630-668-5407	R	4*	<.1
261	New Brunswick Industries Inc—*Jim Krehbiel*	1850 Gillespie Way, El Cajon CA 92020	619-448-4900	R	4*	<.1
262	Wintronics Inc—*Ted Daigneault*	191 Pitt St, Sharon PA 16146	724-981-5770	R	4*	.1
263	Global Manufacturing Services Inc—*Arlie Keith*	140 Industrial Park Wa, West Jefferson NC 28694	336-246-5143	R	4*	<.1
264	Whitman Products Company Inc—*Elizabeth Rupp*	400 Willow St S, North Andover MA 01845	978-975-0502	R	4*	<.1
265	Contrax Technologies Inc (Hanover Maryland)—*John Credle*	7509 Connelley Dr Ste, Hanover MD 21076	410-760-6611	R	4*	<.1
266	Jre Inc—*James Tuscano*	22 Fairfield Pl, West Caldwell NJ 07006	973-808-0055	R	4*	<.1
267	Proxy Manufacturing Inc—*Shawn Foy*	55 Chase St Ste 7, Methuen MA 01844	978-687-3138	R	4*	<.1
268	Smg Circuits Corp—*Tulsi Sutaria*	120 Stationvue, Washington PA 15301	724-229-3200	R	4*	<.1
269	Rjr Circuits Inc—*Robert Rodriguez*	1830 S Bannock St, Denver CO 80223	303-778-7379	R	4*	<.1
270	California Integration Coordinators Inc—*Cherie Myers*	2929 Grandview St, Placerville CA 95667	530-626-6168	R	4*	<.1
271	Electro Circuits Corp—*Chhaganlal Aghera*	3305 Benson Ave, Baltimore MD 21227	410-525-3300	R	4*	<.1
272	JVB Electronics Inc—*Valji Mulani*	3835 Conflans Rd, Irving TX 75061	972-790-0062	R	4*	<.1
273	RRJ Company Inc—*Ronald Holford*	40 Riordan Pl, Shrewsbury NJ 07702	732-450-1390	R	4*	<.1
274	Colonial Assembly and Design LLC—*Cynthia Merritt*	3361 Shannon Airport C, Fredericksburg VA 22408	540-372-6500	R	4*	<.1
275	Circle Prime Manufacturing Inc—*James Mothersbaugh*	PO Box 112, Cuyahoga Falls OH 44222	330-923-0019	R	4*	<.1
276	American Circuit Technology Inc—*Ravi Kheni*	5330 E Hunter Ave, Anaheim CA 92807	714-777-2480	R	4*	<.1
277	Star Electronics Corp—*Subash Patel*	825 Pratt Blvd, Elk Grove Village IL 60007	847-439-0605	R	4*	<.1
278	Mountain Tech Sales and Assembly—*Dick Creer*	3424 W 2400 S, Salt Lake City UT 84119	801-975-9771	R	4*	<.1
279	Triad Circuits Inc—*Shawn Bixler*	703 Sunset Dr, Round Lake IL 60073	847-546-7722	R	4*	<.1
280	Tran Electronics Corp—*Hoa Tran*	82 2nd Ave SE, Saint Paul MN 55112	651-636-6286	R	3*	<.1
281	Foxlink World Circuit Technology Inc—*Harrison Tu*	925 W Lambert Rd Ste O, Brea CA 92821	714-256-0877	R	3*	<.1
282	Electro-Circuits Inc—*Dal Vaghasiya*	1651 Mitchell Blvd, Schaumburg IL 60193	847-352-5015	R	3*	<.1
283	Almatron Electronics Inc—*Margarito Alvarez*	644 Young St, Santa Ana CA 92705	714-557-6000	R	3*	<.1
284	Rapid Circuits Inc—*Bud Zysk*	6401 Mcpherson St, Levittown PA 19057	215-547-7710	R	3*	<.1
285	Nova Drilling Services Inc—*Mike Mckibbin*	2925 Copper Rd, Santa Clara CA 95051	408-732-6682	R	3*	<.1
286	Imi Inc—*Peter Bigelow*	140 Hilldale Ave, Haverhill MA 01832	978-373-9190	R	3*	<.1

Rank	Company Name—Executive Officer	Address, City, State, Zip	Phone	Type	Fin	Empls
287	Delta Precision Circuits Inc—Mukesh Patel	1370 Lively Blvd, Elk Grove Village IL 60007	847-758-8000	R	3*	<.1
288	Fine Line Circuits and Technology Inc—Rick Bajaria	594 Apollo St Ste A, Brea CA 92821	714-529-3958	R	3*	<.1
289	Metz Electronics Corp—Richard Metz	94 Primrose Dr, Laconia NH 03246	603-524-8806	R	3*	<.1
290	Advanced Manufacturing Service Inc—John Nucatola	124 Remington Blvd, Ronkonkoma NY 11779	631-467-8225	R	3*	<.1
291	Electro Soft Inc—James Wallace	113 Keystone Dr, Montgomeryville PA 18936	215-654-0701	R	3*	<.1
292	Concept Development Inc—James Reardon	1881 Langley Ave, Irvine CA 92614	949-623-8000	R	3*	<.1
293	Valley Circuits—Drew Janes	24940 Ave Tibbitts, Valencia CA 91355	661-294-0077	R	3*	<.1
294	Multi Lab Inc—Joseph Nasser	37 Manchester St, Lawrence MA 01841	978-682-5800	R	3*	<.1
295	Pinder Instruments Company Inc—Walter Tokarz	PO Box 4099, Hammond IN 46324	219-924-7070	R	3*	<.1
296	Excell Electronics Corp—Ushma Patel	2425 American Ln, Elk Grove Village IL 60007	847-766-7455	R	3*	<.1
297	Ipc Cal Flex Inc—Wei-Cheng Chen	1255 N Kellwood Cir, Anaheim CA 92801	714-952-0373	R	3*	<.1
298	Precise Connections Inc—Mark Ott	1114 Explorer St, Duncanville TX 75137	972-298-1040	R	3*	<.1
299	Profab Electronics Inc—Mark Levy	3860 N Powerline Rd St, Pompano Beach FL 33073	954-917-1998	R	3*	<.1
300	Lectra Circuit Inc—Dwight Fincher	2700 Winn Mountain Loo, Mountainburg AR 72946	479-369-4208	R	3*	<.1
301	Delta Circuits Inc—Mike Shawdry	730 W Hawthorne Ln, West Chicago IL 60185	630-876-3000	R	3*	<.1
302	Nationwide Circuits Inc—Alan Austin	1444 Emerson St, Rochester NY 14606	585-328-0791	R	3*	<.1
303	Adeptron Technologies USA Inc—Michael Marti	2043 Zanker Rd, San Jose CA 95131	408-436-8668	R	3*	<.1
304	Perma Plastics Inc—James Hawkins	940 Lakeside Dr, Gurnee IL 60031	847-855-6900	R	3*	<.1
305	Niche Electronics Technologies Inc—Joseph Augustine	201 Dykeman Rd, Shippensburg PA 17257	717-532-6620	R	3*	<.1
306	ALOS Micrographic Corp	118 Bracken Rd, Montgomery NY 12549	845-457-4400	S	3*	<.1
307	Electronics and Metals Industries Inc—P Reese Davis	PO Box 669, Cedar Park TX 78630	512-267-0113	R	3*	<.1
308	Integrated Microelectronics (USA) Inc—Arthur Tan	14312 Franklin Ave Ste, Tustin CA 92780	714-734-7043	S	3*	<.1
309	Test And Measurement Instrumentation Inc—Michael Colavitos	1 Chestnut St Ste 4k, Nashua NH 03060	603-465-6615	R	3*	<.1
310	Reliance Technical Services Inc—Patrick Ng	895 Kifer Rd, Sunnyvale CA 94086	408-720-8448	R	3*	<.1
311	Northern Apex Corp—Joseph Deprisco	14220 Plank St, Fort Wayne IN 46818	260-637-2739	R	3*	<.1
312	Swiss Technology Inc—Vijay Shreemal	9 Bridewell Pl, Clifton NJ 07014	973-815-1700	R	3*	<.1
313	Ardent Systems Inc—Thomas Han	52 Bonaventura Dr, San Jose CA 95134	408-526-0100	R	3*	<.1
314	Nea Manufacturing Inc—Sheik Alli	PO Box 960187, Inwood NY 11096	516-371-4200	R	3*	<.1
315	Online Electronics Inc—Aziz Ajani	1261 Jarvis Ave, Elk Grove Village IL 60007	847-290-8690	R	3*	<.1
316	Multi-Plate Circuits Inc—D Babaria	2362 Lufield Dr, Dallas TX 75229	972-243-1557	R	3*	<.1
317	Capital Electro-Circuits Inc—Arvind Sitapara	7845 Airpark Rd Ste M, Gaithersburg MD 20879	301-977-0303	R	3*	<.1
318	Copper Clad Multilayer Products Inc—Fred Ohanian	1150 N Hawk Cir, Anaheim CA 92807	714-237-1388	R	3*	<.1
319	Empire Electronics Corp—Mukess Tejani	1629 Litton Dr, Stone Mountain GA 30083	770-934-1500	R	3*	<.1
320	Streamline Electronics Manufacturing Inc—Shahab Jafri	595 Yosemite Dr, Milpitas CA 95035	408-263-3600	R	3*	<.1
321	Smith International Enterprise Ltd—Herbert Smith	20600 Chagrin Blvd Ste, Shaker Heights OH 44122	216-921-3500	R	3*	<.1
322	Network Pcb Inc—Kevin Le	1914 Otoole Way, San Jose CA 95131	408-943-8760	R	3*	<.1
323	United Printed Circuits Inc—Jimmy Caudle	1860 Sparkman Dr Nw, Huntsville AL 35816	256-830-5998	R	3*	<.1
324	Lad Technology Inc—Donna Domanovics	730 Beta Dr Ste B, Cleveland OH 44143	440-461-8002	R	3*	<.1
325	Precise Circuit Company Inc—Thomas Misencik	155 Myrtle St, Shelton CT 06484	203-924-2512	R	3*	<.1
326	Aurum Assembly Plus Inc—Karl Northwang	8829 Production Ave, San Diego CA 92121	858-578-8710	R	3*	<.1
327	Vector Electronics and Technology Inc—Rakesh Bajaria	11115 Vanowen St, North Hollywood CA 91605	818-985-8208	R	3*	<.1
328	Mentzer Electronics—Edward Mentzer	858 Stanton Rd, Burlingame CA 94010	650-697-2642	R	3*	<.1
329	Circuits West Inc—Chuck Anderson	PO Box 1528, Longmont CO 80502	303-772-9261	R	3*	<.1
330	Circuit Etching Technics Inc—Babu Patel	700 Lee St, Elk Grove Village IL 60007	847-228-1722	R	3*	<.1
331	NDE Inc—Richard Le	3301 Keller St, Santa Clara CA 95054	408-727-3955	R	3*	<.1
332	Technical Manufacturing Corp—Mary Bonito	PO Box 306, Durham CT 06422	860-349-1735	R	3*	<.1
333	CJ Rogers Eloctronics Inc—Carol Rogers	326 W Katella Ave Ste, Orange CA 92867	714-288-1144	R	3*	<.1
334	Custom Electronics Co—Richard Heflin	7851 Airpark Rd Ste 20, Gaithersburg MD 20879	301-258-0811	R	3*	<.1
335	Electronic Manufacturing Technology Inc—Jay Madhani	16464 Via Esprillo, San Diego CA 92127	858-613-1040	R	3*	<.1
336	Quality Surface Mount Inc—Steve Zielinski	965 Dillon Dr, Wood Dale IL 60191	630-350-8556	R	3*	<.1
337	Omega Circuit And Engineering Corp—James Genes	8 Terminal Rd, New Brunswick NJ 08901	732-246-1661	R	2*	<.1
338	Electronic Components and Services Inc—Greg Reagan	103 Industrial Dr, Fox Lake WI 53933	920-928-2611	R	2*	<.1
339	Advanced Electrocircuits Corp—Bharat Monpara	750 Trumbull Dr, Pittsburgh PA 15205	412-278-5200	R	2*	<.1
340	American Circuits Inc—Vithal Gondha	513 W 24th St, Charlotte NC 28206	704-376-2800	R	2*	<.1
341	M and K Industries Inc—Bimal Patel	50 Stedman St Ste 9a, Lowell MA 01851	978-458-8188	R	2*	<.1
342	Vector Fabrication Inc—Quang Luong	1629 Watson Ct, Milpitas CA 95035	408-942-9800	R	2*	<.1
343	Advanced Research and Development Corp—Willie Rosseett	2285 Industrial Blvd, Norman OK 73069	405-321-0550	R	2*	<.1
344	Accurate Engineering Inc—Rush Patel	8710 Telfair Ave, Sun Valley CA 91352	818-768-3919	R	2*	<.1
345	Dbs Inc—Dwight Fincher	2017 S 28th St, Van Buren AR 72956	479-471-8255	R	2*	<.1
346	Tritech Manufacturing Inc—Edward Uslar	2728 Commercial Rd, Fort Wayne IN 46809	260-747-9154	R	2*	<.1
347	K and F Electronic Inc—Richard Kincaid	33041 Groesbeck Hwy, Fraser MI 48026	586-294-8720	R	2*	<.1
348	Jay and Associates Inc—Roger Dhanani	3464 Howell St, Duluth GA 30096	770-622-2200	R	2*	<.1
349	Aztec Electronics Inc—Roger Loftman	PO Box 70, Saint Michael MN 55376	763-497-3200	R	2*	<.1
350	Strategy Electronics Inc—John Rathbone	4211 W Wichita St, Broken Arrow OK 74012	918-252-5550	R	2*	<.1
351	Ctc Enterprises of New York LLC—Carol Schreckengost	1000 Commerce Pkwy, Lancaster NY 14086	716-681-2097	R	2*	<.1
352	Soldermask Inc—Frank Kurisu	17905 Metzler Ln, Huntington Beach CA 92647	714-842-1987	R	2*	<.1
353	Chicago Circuits Corp—Hari Kher	2685 United Ln, Elk Grove Village IL 60007	847-238-1623	R	2*	<.1
354	Hughes Electronics Products Corp—Richard Smith	34467 Industrial Rd, Livonia MI 48150	734-427-8310	R	2*	<.1
355	Aa Circuit Tech Inc—Roberto Gutierrez	1911 N Main St, Orange CA 92865	714-685-0991	R	2*	<.1
356	King Circuit—Bhagvan Patel	1651 Mitchell Blvd, Schaumburg IL 60193	630-629-7300	R	2*	<.1
357	Circuit Connections Inc—Narendra Narayan	2310 Lundy Ave, San Jose CA 95131	408-955-9505	R	2*	<.1
358	Rb Design Inc—Ron Beales	621 S Andreasen Dr Ste, Escondido CA 92029	760-743-7459	R	2*	<.1
359	Richard M Middleton LLC	4026 E Broadway Rd Ste, Phoenix AZ 85040	602-437-2151	R	2*	<.1
360	Rigiflex Technology Inc—Dhiru Sorathia	1166 N Grove St, Anaheim CA 92806	714-688-1500	R	2*	<.1
361	United Circuit Technology Inc—Craig Johnson	18101 Mount Washington, Fountain Valley CA 92708	714-979-1561	R	2*	<.1
362	L and L Albuquerque Electronics Inc—Lisa Lidderdale	900 Lamberton Pl Ne St, Albuquerque NM 87107	505-344-1600	R	2*	<.1
363	Q Circuits Inc—Jeff Cossman	2775 Algonquin Rd, Rolling Meadows IL 60008	847-797-6678	R	2*	.1
364	Mar Tek Electronics Inc—Denise Marks	PO Box 609, Onamia MN 56359	320-532-4111	R	2*	<.1
365	Mega Circuits Inc—Brian Bundy	3015 Power Dr, Kansas City KS 66106	913-722-5020	R	2*	<.1
366	PCB Solutions Inc—Dave Woodbury	3020 N Fairfield Rd, Layton UT 84041	801-773-5509	R	2*	<.1
367	Rhr Technologies Inc—Donald Bogle	1703 Industrial Hwy St, Cinnaminson NJ 08077	856-786-0108	R	2*	<.1
368	Grt Electronics LLC—Sherry Holley	3805 Beryl Rd, Raleigh NC 27607	919-821-1996	R	2*	<.1
369	Assembly International Inc—Indra Patel	775 Touhy Ave, Elk Grove Village IL 60007	847-437-3120	R	2*	<.1
370	Jet Technologies Inc—James Holle	2120 S Calhoun Rd, New Berlin WI 53151	262-796-5050	R	2*	<.1
371	Circuit Masters Inc—Mohan Dungarani	N114 W18845 Clinton Dr, Germantown WI 53022	262-255-7117	R	2*	<.1
372	Electronic Response Inc—Robert MacDonald	6150 St Croix Ave N St, Golden Valley MN 55422	763-571-4220	R	2*	<.1
373	General Electro Corp—J Patel	1069 Bryn Mawr Ave, Bensenville IL 60106	630-595-8989	R	2*	<.1
374	Industrial Service Technology—Dick Farnsworth	3286 Kentland Ct SE, Grand Rapids MI 49548	616-247-1034	R	2*	<.1
375	IDEAMATICS Inc—David L Danner	1364 Beverly Rd Sto 10, McLean VA 22101	703-903-4972	S	2*	<.1
376	KL Electronics Inc—Michael Ton	3083 S Harbor Blvd, Santa Ana CA 92704	714-751-5611	R	2*	<.1

Note: An asterisk (*) indicates an estimated financial figure. The company type code used is as follows: R = Private, P = Public, S = Private Subsidiary, B = Public Subsidiary, D = Division, J = Joint Venture, I = Investment Fund.

COMPANY RANKINGS BY SALES WITHIN 4-DIGIT SIC

Rank	Company Name—*Executive Officer*	Address, City, State, Zip	Phone	Type	Fin	Empls
377	Delru Rigidflex Inc—*Pravina Patolia*	875 S E St, Anaheim CA 92805	714-635-2511	R	2*	<.1
378	Delta Circuits Technology Inc—*Jim Kanji*	16117 Leadwell St, Van Nuys CA 91406	818-786-8241	R	2*	<.1
379	Galaxy Circuits Inc—*Anil Patel*	383 Randy Rd, Carol Stream IL 60188	630-462-1010	R	2*	<.1
380	Multimek Inc—*Doug Mccown*	357 Reed St, Santa Clara CA 95050	408-653-1300	R	2*	<.1
381	Venture Electronics International Inc—*C Wong*	6701 Mowry Ave, Newark CA 94560	510-744-3720	R	2*	<.1
382	Transline Technology Inc—*Kishor Patel*	1106 S Technology Cir, Anaheim CA 92805	714-533-8300	R	2*	<.1
383	Assembly Technologies Inc—*Rohit Savani*	PO Box 560623, Charlotte NC 28256	704-596-3903	R	2*	<.1
384	American Circuit Systems Inc—*Ashok Sheth*	712 S Westgate St, Addison IL 60101	630-543-4450	R	2*	<.1
385	American Progressive Circuits—*Ramesh Patel*	1772 W Armitage Ct, Addison IL 60101	630-495-6900	R	2*	<.1
386	Volunteer Circuits Inc—*Bennie Mc Gee*	5956 Hwy 412 S, Bells TN 38006	731-663-2308	R	2*	<.1
387	C-Tron Inc—*Donna Albright*	22 N Main St, Franklinton NC 27525	919-494-7811	R	2*	<.1
388	Multilayer Prototypes Inc—*Steve Ferris*	2513 Teller Rd, Newbury Park CA 91320	805-498-9390	R	2*	<.1
389	Delta V Instruments Inc—*James Crossland*	1870 Firman Dr, Richardson TX 75081	972-644-6501	R	2*	<.1
390	Technical Fabrication Inc—*Bruce Beigel*	15842 Elm Dr Ste 1, New Freedom PA 17349	717-227-0909	R	2*	<.1
391	Bryit Group LLC—*Larry Boas*	1724 Church St, Holbrook NY 11741	631-563-6603	R	2*	<.1
392	RC Tronics Inc—*Donald Chiddister*	2573 Kercher Rd Ste Xx, Goshen IN 46528	574-642-3857	R	2*	<.1
393	Circuitronics Corp—*Bipin Patel*	223 Hickman Dr Ste 101, Sanford FL 32771	407-322-8300	R	2*	<.1
394	Cm Solutions Inc—*Mike Driste*	PO Box 670, Corinth MS 38835	662-287-8810	R	2*	<.1
395	Dy3 Productions Inc—*Darryl Ford*	715 Southpoint Blvd St, Petaluma CA 94954	707-766-6777	R	2*	<.1
396	Datum Dynamics USA LLC—*Chris Chapman*	39 Squantum Dr, Middletown RI 02842	401-683-5300	R	2*	<.1
397	Exceltech Inc—*Robert Wruble*	2919 Ne Rivergate St 4, Mcminnville OR 97128	503-472-8914	R	2*	<.1
398	Micron Corp—*William Theos*	89 Access Rd Ste 5, Norwood MA 02062	781-769-9951	R	2*	<.1
399	Pulsar Inc—*Yogesh Patel*	9901 Pacific Ave, Franklin Park IL 60131	847-233-0012	R	2*	<.1
400	Electronic Assembly Services Inc—*Paul Kasson*	PO Box 1382, Elk Grove Village IL 60009	847-593-5560	R	2*	<.1
401	Della Systems Inc—*John Croce*	951 S 2nd St, Ronkonkoma NY 11779	631-580-0010	R	2*	<.1
402	ABC Fabricators Inc—*William Lesmerises*	30 Cook Ct, Laconia NH 03246	603-528-6185	R	2*	<.1
403	I Technical Services LLC	6245 Shiloh Rd Ste D, Alpharetta GA 30005	770-729-0669	R	2*	<.1
404	Micro Circuit Inc—*Govind Patel*	222 W Fay Ave, Addison IL 60101	630-628-5760	R	2*	<.1
405	Electronic Concepts And Engineering Inc—*Karl Swonger*	1306 Kittle Rd, Holland OH 43528	419-861-9000	R	2*	<.1
406	Niltronix Circuits Inc—*Bharat Karsaliya*	1765a Upland Dr, Houston TX 77043	713-465-4216	R	2*	<.1
407	Alphi Technology Corp—*Alain Brunet*	1898 E Southern Ave, Tempe AZ 85282	480-838-2428	R	2*	<.1
408	E-Teknet Inc—*Shusheng Jiang*	561 E Elliot Rd Ste 18, Chandler AZ 85225	480-752-7854	R	2*	<.1
409	CA M Graphics Company Inc—*Emanuel Cardinale*	24 Central Dr, Farmingdale NY 11735	631-842-3400	R	1*	<.1
410	Roger Industry—*Shann-Mou Lee*	11552 Knott St Ste 5, Garden Grove CA 92841	714-896-0765	R	1*	<.1
411	Buildex Electronics Inc—*B Parecha*	1734 Elmhurst Rd, Elk Grove Village IL 60007	847-437-2299	R	1*	<.1
412	JDF Enterprises Inc—*John Farley*	712 Dunn Way, Placentia CA 92870	714-524-1100	R	1*	<.1
413	Madison Electronics Inc—*Tony Grida*	PO Box 2, Versailles IN 47042	812-689-4204	R	1*	<.1
414	Protoline Inc—*Paresh Jasani*	10650 Stancliff Rd, Houston TX 77099	281-561-0802	R	1*	<.1
415	WWW Electronics Inc—*Linda Wright*	PO Box 168, Earlysville VA 22936	434-973-4702	R	1*	<.1
416	Surf-Tech Manufacturing Corp—*Richard Eggert*	80 Orville Dr Ste 115, Bohemia NY 11716	631-589-1194	R	1*	<.1
417	Fineline Circuits Inc—*Sona Sitapara*	1660 Loretta Ave, Feasterville Trevose PA 19053	215-364-3311	R	1*	<.1
418	Petra Electronic Manufacturing Inc—*Jack Doornbos*	PO Box B, Moline MI 49335	616-877-1991	R	1*	<.1
419	Logi Graphics Inc—*Greg Otterbach*	17592 Metzler Ln, Huntington Beach CA 92647	714-841-3686	R	1*	<.1
420	Circuit Graphics Inc—*Ron Chamberlain*	1120 Swaner Rd, Salt Lake City UT 84104	801-974-5164	R	1*	<.1
421	Ra Company Amo Inc—*Margaret Volk*	4100 Burns Rd, Palm Beach Gardens FL 33410	561-626-7232	R	1*	<.1
422	American Technology Services—*Leonard Olivares*	1312 E 29th St, Long Beach CA 90755	562-426-0521	R	1*	<.1
423	Shivtron Inc—*Navin Patel*	447 S Vista Ave, Addison IL 60101	630-543-3453	R	1*	<.1
424	Avcom Smt Inc—*Paul Wiese*	PO Box 1516, Westerville OH 43086	614-882-8176	R	1*	<.1
425	Marja Corp—*Mary Frechette*	PO Box 431, Sanford ME 04073	207-324-2994	R	1*	<.1
426	TRC Circuits Inc—*Melanie Bera*	3300 Winpark Dr, Minneapolis MN 55427	763-546-6499	R	1*	<.1
427	Captron Corp—*Arvind Sitapara*	7429 Lindbergh Dr, Gaithersburg MD 20879	301-869-6100	R	1*	<.1
428	L and L Assemblies Inc—*Bonnie Pena*	1804 Skyway Dr Unit F, Longmont CO 80504	303-532-3376	R	1*	<.1
429	Cartessa Corp—*Darryl Kristof*	PO Box 190, Shandon OH 45063	513-738-4477	R	1*	<.1
430	Uri Tech Inc—*Sea Kim*	510 Dado St, San Jose CA 95131	408-456-0115	R	1*	<.1
431	Zyrel Inc—*H Hargrave*	15322 Lkeshore Dr Ste, Clearlake CA 95422	707-995-2551	R	1*	<.1
432	Semiconductor Hybrid Assembly Inc—*Yassin Burgol*	28065 Oakland Oaks Ct, Wixom MI 48393	248-596-9050	R	1*	<.1
433	SPS Tech Corp—*Reuben Klickstein*	PO Box 266, Carlisle MA 01741	781-376-4200	R	1*	<.1
434	Precision Circuits West Inc—*Chatur Patel*	3310 W Harvard St, Santa Ana CA 92704	714-435-9670	R	1*	<.1
435	Logic Systems Corp—*Frank Aldridge*	1567 Cypress Dr, Jupiter FL 33469	561-746-5181	R	1*	<.1
436	Assembly and Design Inc—*Douglas Bronnenberg*	425 Southlake Blvd Ste, Richmond VA 23236	804-379-5432	R	1*	<.1
437	Short Circuits Inc—*Greg Easton*	850 Commercial Ln, Palmer Lake CO 80133	719-481-9029	R	1*	<.1
438	Technical and Assembly Services Corp—*Richard Hirst*	8211 Aurora Ave N Ste, Seattle WA 98103	206-682-2967	R	1*	<.1
439	Solnix—*J Sanchez*	1307 Fulton Pl, Fremont CA 94539	510-657-3082	R	1*	<.1
440	Presscom Electronics LLC—*Lee Weathers*	1736 S Nevada Way, Mesa AZ 85204	480-892-7552	R	1*	<.1
441	New Wave Electronic Services Inc—*Kevin Burke*	59 Davis Ave Ste 9, Norwood MA 02062	781-762-7211	R	1*	<.1
442	C and S Electronics Inc—*Carl Seckel*	2565 16th Ave, Columbus NE 68601	402-563-3596	R	1*	<.1
443	Conductive Circuits Inc—*Ed Roberts*	360 State St, Garner IA 50438	641-923-2260	R	1*	<.1
444	Technical Services Labs Inc—*Andrew Corbin*	95 Ready Ave NW, Fort Walton Beach FL 32548	850-243-3722	R	1*	<.1
445	TM Systems Inc—*Walter Weiner*	203 Main St Ste 337, Flemington NJ 08822	908-788-0458	R	1*	<.1
446	J and C Co—*James Becker*	5000 N 72nd St, Lincoln NE 68507	402-467-4837	R	1*	<.1
447	Excel Electro Assembly Inc—*Hiten Bhanderi*	1595 Brummel Ave, Elk Grove Village IL 60007	847-621-2500	R	1*	<.1
448	Bitflow Inc—*Avner Butnaru*	300 Wildwood Ave Ste 2, Woburn MA 01801	781-932-2900	R	1*	<.1
449	National Research Labs Inc—*JR Shah*	650 Haines Ave NW, Albuquerque NM 87102	505-243-1757	R	1*	<.1
450	Plc-Multipoint Inc—*Norm Dittmann*	3101 111th St Sw Ste F, Everett WA 98204	425-353-7552	R	1*	<.1
451	Amtech Electrocircuits Inc—*Jay Patel*	701 Minnesota Dr, Troy MI 48083	248-583-1801	R	1*	<.1
452	Casco Circuits Inc—*Ravji Kachhadia*	10039 Canoga Ave Unit, Chatsworth CA 91311	818-882-0972	R	1*	<.1
453	ProtoQwik—*Robert Cowie*	7950 Silverton Ave Ste, San Diego CA 92126	858-578-9242	R	1*	<.1
454	Electronic Innovations Corp	3333 S Wadsworth Blvd, Lakewood CO 80227	303-987-2441	R	1*	<.1
455	Micronics Technologies Inc—*Gary Miller*	1304 Fir Ave N, Glencoe MN 55336	320-864-4648	R	1*	<.1
456	Micro-Labs Inc—*Ted Carter*	204 Lost Canyon Ct, Richardson TX 75080	972-234-5842	R	1*	<.1
457	Quik Flex Circuit Inc—*Ishwar Chauhan*	85 Nicholson Rd, Gloucester City NJ 08030	856-742-0550	R	1*	<.1
458	Arnold Electronics Inc—*Sam Bhayani*	1900 Petra Ln Ste E, Placentia CA 92870	562-694-5504	R	1*	<.1
459	Electronics Manufacturing Services—*James Wolfe*	10950 Sw 5th St Ste 18, Beaverton OR 97005	503-626-8254	R	1*	<.1
460	Electronics Aid Inc—*Joel Seavey*	32 Roxbury Rd, Marlborough NH 03455	603-876-4161	R	1*	<.1
461	Electro Circuits International Inc—*Wendell Willoughby*	5706 Green Ash Dr, Houston TX 77081	713-666-1976	R	1*	<.1
462	Excel Electrocircuit Inc—*Nipur Shah*	50 Northpointe Dr, Orion MI 48359	248-373-0700	R	1*	.1
463	Precision Products Company Inc—*Amit Kabaria*	219 Hergesell Ave, Maywood NJ 07607	201-712-5757	R	1*	<.1
464	Retcomp Inc—*Loretta Caterino*	2nd New Hampshire Tn P, New Boston NH 03070	603-487-5010	R	1*	<.1
465	Protronics Inc—*Jan Alford*	861 Old Knight Rd Ste, Knightdale NC 27545	919-217-0007	R	1*	<.1
466	Hitech Circuits Inc—*Jerambhai Patel*	1200 Woodfield Way Ste, Wilkesboro NC 28697	336-838-3420	R	1*	<.1

Rank	Company Name—*Executive Officer*	Address, City, State, Zip	Phone	Type	Fin	Empls
467	Electronic Communications Inc—*Richard Morgan*	3630 Cavalier Dr, Garland TX 75042	972-272-3581	R	1*	<.1
468	Ds Electronics Inc—*Donald Stemple*	1850 E 6th St, Tempe AZ 85281	480-967-5080	R	1*	<.1
469	Electronic Contract Assemblers Inc—*Jennifer Neverosky*	5711 Industry Ln Ste 2, Frederick MD 21704	301-631-0470	R	1*	<.1
470	Lanmark Circuits Inc—*Carol Engelking*	400 Crown Point Cir, Grass Valley CA 95945	530-272-7280	R	1*	<.1
471	Hi-Tech Applications LLC—*Sharla Dean*	614 Jerrys Ln Ste B, Buda TX 78610	512-312-1177	R	1*	<.1
472	Proto Circuits Manufacturing—*Mark Strege*	8786 Industrial Ln, Rancho Cucamonga CA 91730	909-987-7237	R	1*	<.1
473	Select Circuits—*Esther Lara*	3700 W Segerstrom Ave, Santa Ana CA 92704	714-825-1090	R	1*	<.1
474	Largo Circuit Design Inc—*Avishai Hershkovitz*	15189 Springdale St, Huntington Beach CA 92649	714-898-1588	R	1*	<.1
475	Q-Fab Inc—*Jeff Forbus*	1920 Hurd Dr, Irving TX 75038	972-573-1130	R	1*	<.1
476	Electrocard—*Lester Foraker*	7202 Hibbs Ln, Levittown PA 19057	215-943-8637	R	1*	<.1
477	Slp Limited LLC—*Bruce Stuart*	2031 E Cerritos Ave St, Anaheim CA 92806	714-517-1955	R	1*	<.1
478	Cb Ram Electronics Inc—*Fidez Bonifacio*	9665 Sw Allen Blvd Ste, Beaverton OR 97005	503-646-4344	R	1*	<.1
479	Twin Star Electronics Inc—*Myron Ostby*	8808 Monticello Ln N, Osseo MN 55369	763-424-1147	R	1*	<.1
480	Alpha Circuit Corp—*Bhagvan Vaghani*	730 N Oaklawn Ave, Elmhurst IL 60126	630-617-5555	R	<1*	.1
481	RB Manufacturing Inc—*Don Nichols*	PO Box 490, Kirkland IL 60146	815-522-3100	R	<1*	<.1
482	Manufacturing Industries Inc—*Ronald Quillen*	PO Box 612, Alderson WV 24910	304-445-2718	R	<1*	<.1
483	Electronic Plastics Co—*Ray Ottinger*	2113 Pullman Ave, Simi Valley CA 93063	805-522-4236	R	<1*	<.1
484	Journey Electronics Corp—*Michael Gorden*	902 N Garver Rd, Monroe OH 45050	513-539-9836	R	<1*	<.1
485	American Circuit Services Inc—*Nick Chaudhai*	801 Albion Ave Ste B, Schaumburg IL 60193	847-895-0500	R	<1*	<.1
486	Electro Mechanical Assembly Inc—*Sheery Hunt*	1943 Powder Branch Rd, Johnson City TN 37601	423-928-1820	R	<1*	<.1
487	Aminteron Systems Inc—*Anthony Mitsingas*	1738 Somerlane St, El Cajon CA 92021	619-449-7315	R	<1*	<.1
488	CSB Design—*Dee Cook*	2918 Louise Ave, Salt Lake City UT 84109	801-467-5080	R	<1*	<.1
489	Bencor LLC—*Blaine Nabors*	PO Box 521, Brenham TX 77834	979-830-5252	R	<1*	<.1
490	Multiplex Technologies Inc—*Vinod Patel*	9441 Baythorne Dr, Houston TX 77041	713-462-3163	R	<1*	<.1
491	Proto Quick Inc—*Mary Sweeney*	PO Box 540724, Dallas TX 75354	214-351-6642	R	<1*	<.1
492	Hildy Licht Inc—*Hildy Licht*	897 Independence Ave 3, Mountain View CA 94043	650-962-9300	R	<1*	<.1
493	Injectorall Electronics Corp—*Marilyn Friedman*	110 Keyland Ct, Bohemia NY 11716	631-563-3388	R	<1*	<.1
494	Technodrill Inc—*Cono Leon*	1479 E Warner Ave, Santa Ana CA 92705	714-556-7471	R	<1*	<.1
495	Aeromation Inc—*Lorne Hofeld*	402 Beavercreek Rd Ste, Oregon City OR 97045	503-650-3688	R	<1*	<.1
496	Ulmas—*Peter Canning*	33 Rogers Ln, Smithtown NY 11787	631-366-5179	R	<1*	<.1
497	VYTA Corp—*Paul H Metzinger*	370 17th St Ste 300, Denver CO 80202	303-592-1010	P	<1	<.1
498	Viasystems Group Inc—*David M Sindelar*	101 S Hanley Rd Ste 40, Clayton MO 63105	314-727-2087	R	N/A	25.0

TOTALS: SIC 3672 Printed Circuit Boards
Companies: 498

					35,771	234.7

3674 Semiconductors & Related Devices

Rank	Company Name—*Executive Officer*	Address, City, State, Zip	Phone	Type	Fin	Empls
1	Intel Corp—*Paul S Otellini*	PO Box 58119, Santa Clara CA 95052	408-765-8080	P	43,623	82.5
2	Siemens Corp—*Eric Spiegel*	527 Madison Ave 8th Fl, New York NY 10022	212-258-4000	S	15,981*	69.0
3	Texas Instruments Inc—*Richard (Rich) K Templeton*	PO Box 660199, Dallas TX 75266		P	13,966	28.4
4	Applied Materials Inc—*Michael R Splinter*	PO Box 58030, Santa Clara CA 95052	408-727-5555	P	9,549	14.3
5	Micron Technology Inc—*Kipp A Bedard*	PO Box 6, Boise ID 83707	208-368-4000	P	8,788	26.1
6	Broadcom Corp—*John Major*	PO Box 57013, Irvine CA 92617	949-926-5000	P	6,818	9.0
7	Kingston Technology Company Inc—*John Tu*	17600 Newhope St, Fountain Valley CA 92708	714-435-2600	R	6,500*	4.0
8	Advanced Micro Devices Inc—*Rory Read*	PO Box 3453, Sunnyvale CA 94088	408-749-4000	P	6,494	11.1
9	Siltronic AG (San Jose California)—*Wilhelm Sittenthaler*	4010 Moorpark Ave Ste, San Jose CA 95117	408-296-7887	S	5,183*	5.6
10	Freescale Semiconductor Inc—*Rich Beyer*	6501 William Cannon Dr, Austin TX 78735	512-895-2000	P	4,570	19.0
11	Marvell Technology Group Ltd—*Sehat Sutardja*	5488 Marvell Ln, Santa Clara CA 95054	408-222-2500	P	3,612	5.9
12	ON Semiconductor Corp—*Keith D Jackson*	5005 E McDowell Rd, Phoenix A7 85008	602-244-6600	P	3,442	19.4
13	Semiconductor Components Industries LLC ON Semiconductor Corp	5005 E McDowell Rd, Phoenix AZ 85008	602-244-6600	S	3,280*	7.2
14	Analog Devices Inc—*Jerald G Fishman*	3 Technology Way, Norwood MA 02062	781-329-4700	P	2,993	9.2
15	Amkor Technology Inc—*Kenneeth T Joyce*	1900 S Price Rd, Chandler AZ 85286	480-821-5000	P	2,776	18.3
16	MEMC Electronic Materials Inc—*Ahmad Chatila*	501 Pearl Dr, St Peters MO 63376	636-474-5000	P	2,716	6.4
17	Philips Semiconductors (Sunnyvale California)—*Scott McGregor*	PO Box 3409, Sunnyvale CA 94088	408-474-8142	D	2,667*	1.0
18	First Solar Inc—*Mike Ahearn*	350 W Washington St St, Tempe AZ 85281	602-414-9300	P	2,564	6.1
19	Maxim Integrated Products Inc—*Tunc Doluca*	120 San Gabriel Dr, Sunnyvale CA 94086	408-737-7600	P	2,472	9.4
20	Xilinx Inc—*Moshe Gavrielov*	2100 Logic Dr, San Jose CA 95124	408-559-7778	P	2,369	3.1
21	Sunpower Corp (San Jose California)—*Thomas H Werner* Cypress Semiconductor Corp	3939 N 1st St, San Jose CA 95134	408-240-5500	B	2,219	5.2
22	LSI Corp—*Abhi Talwalkar*	1621 Barber Ln, Milpitas CA 95035	408-443-8000	P	2,044	4.6
23	Altera Corp—*John P Daane*	101 Innovation Dr, San Jose CA 95134	408-544-7000	P	1,954	2.7
24	Sand Video Inc—*Scott A McGreggor* Broadcom Corp	200 Brickstone Sq, Andover MA 01810	978-475-8990	S	1,861*	3.7
25	Kyocera International Inc—*John Rigby*	8611 Balboa Ave, San Diego CA 92123	858-576-2600	S	1,856*	4.2
26	JDS Uniphase Corp—*Thomas Waechter*	430 N McCarthy Blvd, Milpitas CA 95035	408-546-5000	P	1,805	5.0
27	Avnet Memec—*Rick Hamada*	2211 S 47th St, Phoenix AZ 85034	480-643-2000	S	1,798*	2.4
28	Siliconix Inc—*King Owyang*	PO Box 54951, Santa Clara CA 95056	408-988-8000	S	1,699*	2.0
29	Atmel Corp—*Steve Laub*	2325 Orchard Pkwy, San Jose CA 95131	408-441-0311	P	1,664	5.2
30	Fairchild Semiconductor International Inc—*Justin Chiang*	3030 Orchard Pkwy, San Jose CA 95134	408-822-2000	P	1,589	8.8
31	Microchip Technology Inc—*Derek Carlson*	2355 W Chandler Blvd, Chandler AZ 85224	480-792-7200	P	1,487	7.0
32	International Rectifier Corp—*Oleg Khaykin*	233 Kansas St, El Segundo CA 90245	310-726-8000	P	1,177	4.9
33	Linear Technology Corp—*Lothar Maier*	1630 McCarthy Blvd, Milpitas CA 95035	408-432-1900	P	1,170	4.2
34	Spansion Inc—*John H Kispert*	915 DeGuigne Dr, Sunnyvale CA 94085	408-962-2500	P	1,070	3.4
35	OPTEK Technology Inc—*Geraint Anderson*	1645 Wallace Dr, Carrollton TX 75006	972-323-2200	S	1,028*	1.2
36	Samsung Semiconductor Inc—*Wan Hoon Hong*	3655 N 1st St, San Jose CA 95134	408-544-4000	S	1,013*	1.2
37	RF Micro Devices Inc—*Robert A Bruggeworth*	7628 Thorndike Rd, Greensboro NC 27409	336-664-1233	P	1,005	3.7
38	Cypress Semiconductor Corp—*TJ Rodgers*	198 Champion Ct, San Jose CA 95134	408-943-2600	P	995	3.4
39	Cree Inc—*Charles M Swoboda*	4600 Silicon Dr, Durham NC 27703	919-313-5300	P	988	4.8
40	OmniVision Technologies Inc—*Shaw Hong*	4275 Burton Dr, Santa Clara CA 95054	408-542-3000	P	957	1.5
41	Atheros Communications Inc—*Craig H Barratt*	1700 Technology Dr, San Jose CA 95110	408-773-5200	P	927	1.8
42	GT Advanced Technologies Inc—*Thomas Gutierrez*	243 Daniel Webster Hwy, Merrimack NH 03054	603-883-5200	P	899	.6
43	TriQuint Semiconductor Inc—*Brian Balut*	2300 NE Brookwood Pkwy, Hillsboro OR 97124	503-615-9000	P	896	2.9
44	Hemlock Semiconductor Corp—*Rick Doornbos*	12334 Geddes Rd, Hemlock MI 48626	989-301-5000	J	883*	1.0
45	Microsemi Corp—*James J Peterson*	2381 Morse Ave, Irvine CA 92614	949-221-7100	P	836	2.7
46	Kulicke and Soffa Industries Inc—*Bruno Guilmart*	1005 Virginia Dr, Fort Washington PA 19034	215-784-6000	P	830	2.9
47	Intersil Corp—*David B Bell*	1001 Murphy Ranch Rd, Milpitas CA 95035	408-432-8888	P	761	1.6
48	OSI Systems Inc—*Deepak Chopra*	12525 Chadron Ave, Hawthorne CA 90250	310-978-0516	P	656	3.7
49	PMC-Sierra Inc—*Greg Lang*	1380 Bordeaux Dr, Sunnyvale CA 94089	408-239-8000	P	654	1.6

Note: An asterisk (*) indicates an estimated financial figure. The company type code used is as follows: R = Private, P = Public, S = Private Subsidiary, B = Public Subsidiary, D = Division, J = Joint Venture, I = Investment Fund.

COMPANY RANKINGS BY SALES WITHIN 4-DIGIT SIC

Rank	Company Name—*Executive Officer*	Address, City, State, Zip	Phone	Type	Fin	Empls
50	Diodes Inc—*Keh-Shew Lu*	4949 Hedgcoxe Rd Ste 2, Plano TX 75024	972-987-3900	P	635	4.5
51	Integrated Device Technology Inc—*Theodore Tewksbury III*	6024 Silver Creek Vall, San Jose CA 95138	408-284-8200	P	626	2.1
52	Photronics Inc—*Deno Macricostas*	PO Box 5226, Brookfield CT 06804	203-775-9000	P	512	1.4
53	Kawasaki Microelectronics America—*Yukio Yamauchi*	2550 N 1st St Ste 500, San Jose CA 95131	408-570-0555	S	500*	.7
54	Allegro Microsystems Inc—*Dennis Fitzgerald*	PO Box 15036, Worcester MA 01615	508-853-5000	R	464*	2.6
55	Semtech Corp—*Alain Dantec*	200 Flynn Rd, Camarillo CA 93012	805-498-2111	P	455	1.0
56	Cabot Microelectronics Corp—*William P Noglows*	870 N Commons Dr, Aurora IL 60504	630-375-6631	P	445	1.0
57	Ultra Clean Holdings Inc—*Clarence L Granger*	26462 Corporate Ave, Hayward CA 94545	510-576-4400	P	443	1.2
58	Vishay General Semiconductor Inc—*Gerald Paul*	63 Lancaster Ave, Malvern PA 19355	402-563-6866	S	434*	5.0
59	PNY Technologies Inc—*Sam Chu*	299 Webro Rd, Parsippany NJ 07054	973-515-9700	R	428*	.5
60	Standard Microsystems Corp—*Christine King*	80 Arkay Dr, Hauppauge NY 11788	631-435-6000	P	410	1.0
61	Aruba Networks Inc—*Dominic P Orr*	1344 Crossman Ave, Sunnyvale CA 94089	408-227-4500	P	397	1.1
62	Cirrus Logic Inc—*Jason Rhode*	2901 Via Fortuna, Austin TX 78746	512-851-4000	P	370	.6
63	IXYS Corp—*Nathan Zommer*	1590 Buckeye Dr, Milpitas CA 95035	408-457-9000	P	363	1.2
64	M/A-COM Inc—*David Coughlan*	PO Box 3295, Lowell MA 01853	978-442-4700	S	339*	3.9
65	Evergreen Solar Inc—*Michael El-Hillow*	138 Bartlett St, Marlboro MA 01752	508-357-2221	P	339	1.0
66	Mattson Thermal Products Inc—*David L Dutton*	47131 Bayside Pkwy, Fremont CA 94538	510-657-5900	S	330*	.7
67	Omron Electronics LLC—*Frank Newburn*	1 Commerce Dr, Schaumburg IL 60173	847-843-7900	S	315*	.5
68	Rambus Inc—*Harold Hughes*	1050 Enterprise Way St, Sunnyvale CA 94089	408-462-8000	P	312	.3
69	Power Integrations Inc—*Balu Balakrishnan*	5245 Hellyer Ave, San Jose CA 95138	408-414-9200	P	299	.4
70	Lattice Semiconductor Corp—*Darin G Billerbeck*	5555 NE Moore Ct, Hillsboro OR 97124	503-268-8000	P	298	.7
71	Sigma Designs Inc—*Thinh Q Tran*	1778 McCarthy Blvd, Milpitas CA 95035	408-262-9003	P	287	.6
72	Integrated Silicon Solution Inc—*Scott D Howarth*	1940 Zanker Rd, San Jose CA 95112	408-969-6600	P	271	.5
73	Temic Semiconductors Atmel Corp	2325 Orchard Pky, San Jose CA 95131	408-441-0311	S	269	1.2
74	MRV Communications Inc—*Chris D King*	20415 Nordhoff St, Chatsworth CA 91311	818-773-0900	P	264	.7
75	Cavium Inc—*Syed B Ali*	2315 N 1st St, San Jose CA 95131	650-623-7000	P	259	.9
76	Mellanox Technologies Inc—*Eyal Waldman*	350 Oakmead Pky Ste 10, Sunnyvale CA 94085	408-970-3400	P	259	.8
77	Micrel Inc—*Raymond D Zinn*	2180 Fortune Dr, San Jose CA 95131	408-944-0800	P	259	.8
78	Tessera Technologies Inc—*Robert A Young PhD*	3025 Orchard Pky, San Jose CA 95134	408-321-6000	P	255	.5
79	Fujitsu Microelectronics Inc—*Shinichi Machida*	1250 E Arques Ave, Sunnyvale CA 94085	408-737-5600	S	248*	1.0
80	Applied Micro Circuits Corp—*Paramesh Gopi*	215 Moffett Park Dr, Sunnyvale CA 94089		P	248	.7
81	Conexant Systems Inc—*Sailesh Chittipeddi*	4000 MacArthur Blvd, Newport Beach CA 92660	949-483-4600	B	241	.6
82	Entropic Communications Inc—*Patrick Henry*	6290 Sequence Dr, San Diego CA 92121	858-768-3600	P	241	.2
83	SiRF Technology Holdings Inc	217 Devcon Dr, San Jose CA 95112	408-467-0410	S	233	.6
84	Monolithic Power Systems Inc—*Michael Hsing*	6409 Guadalupe Mines R, San Jose CA 95120	408-826-0600	P	219	.9
85	ANADIGICS Inc—*Ron Michels*	141 Mt Bethel Rd, Warren NJ 07059	908-668-5000	P	217	.6
86	Genesis Microchip Inc—*Claude Dardanne*	2525 Augustine Dr, Santa Clara CA 95054	408-919-8400	S	215	.6
87	Ikanos Communications Inc—*Dado Banatoao*	47669 Fremont Blvd, Fremont CA 94538	510-979-0400	P	192	.4
88	OCZ Technology Inc—*Ryan Petersen*	6373 San Ignacio Ave, San Jose CA 95119	408-733-8400	P	190	.4
89	Stmicroelectronics (North America) Holding Inc—*Laurent Bosson*	1310 Electronics Dr, Carrollton TX 75006	972-466-6000	R	177*	4.2
90	SatCon Technology Corp—*Steve Rhoades*	27 Drydock Ave, Boston MA 02210	617-897-2400	P	173	.3
91	FormFactor Inc—*Richard M Freeman*	7005 Southfront Rd, Livermore CA 94551	925-290-4000	P	169	.7
92	Wafertech LLC—*Greg Damminga*	5509 Nw Parker St, Camas WA 98607	360-817-3000	⊓	168*	.9
93	Pericom Semiconductor Corp—*Alex Chi-Ming Hui*	3545 N 1st St, San Jose CA 95134	408-435-0800	P	166	1.0
94	Volterra Semiconductor Corp—*Jeffery Staszak*	47467 Fremont Blvd, Fremont CA 94538	510-743-1200	P	156	.3
95	Mitsubishi Electric and Electronics USA Inc - Semiconductor Div—*Kenichiro Yamanishi*	5201 Great America Pkw, Santa Clara CA 95054	408-727-3111	S	155*	.3
96	ONIX Systems Inc	PO Box 9046, Waltham MA 02454	781-622-1000	S	154	.9
97	Exar Corp—*Pedro Rodriguez*	48720 Kato Rd, Fremont CA 94538	510-668-7000	P	146	.5
98	Vitesse Semiconductor Corp—*Christopher R Gardner*	741 Calle Plano, Camarillo CA 93012	805-388-3700	P	133	.4
99	Ams Acquisition Corp—*Brad Scoggins*	PO Box 80249, Austin TX 78708	512-491-7411	R	132*	.1
100	American Megatrends Inc—*Subramonian Shankar*	5555 Oakbrook Pkwy Bld, Norcross GA 30093	770-246-8600	R	125*	.4
101	Micro Power Systems Inc Exar Corp	48720 Kato Rd, Fremont CA 94538	510-668-7000	S	123*	.3
102	Kopin Corp—*John CC Fan*	200 John Hancock Rd, Taunton MA 02780	508-824-6696	P	120	.4
103	PLX Technology Inc—*Ralph Schmitt*	870 W Maude Ave, Sunnyvale CA 94085	408-774-9060	P	117	.3
104	Suniva Inc—*John W Baumstark*	5765 Peachtree Industr, Norcross GA 30092	404-477-2700	R	112*	.1
105	Arasan Chip Systems Inc—*Arasan Ganesan*	2010 N 1st St Ste 510, San Jose CA 95131	408-282-1600	R	107*	.1
106	Micro Systems Engineering Inc—*Juergen Lindner*	6024 Jean Rd Ste B, Lake Oswego OR 97035	503-635-4016	R	100*	.3
107	GSI Technology Inc—*Lee-Lean Shu*	1213 Elko Dr, Sunnyvale CA 94089	408-331-8800	P	98	.1
108	NEC Display Solutions of America Inc—*Pierre Richer*	500 Park Blvd Ste 1100, Itasca IL 60143	630-467-3000	S	96*	.1
109	American Xtal Technology Inc—*Morris Young*	4281 Technology Dr, Fremont CA 94538	510-438-4700	P	96	1.3
110	Advanced Analogic Technologies Inc—*Richard K Williams*	3230 Scott Blvd, Santa Clara CA 95054	408-330-1400	P	94	.3
111	GCT Semiconductor Inc—*Kyeongho Lee*	2121 Ringwood Ave, San Jose CA 95131	408-434-6040	R	93*	.2
112	Powerex Inc—*Craig Morrow*	173 Pavilion Ln, Youngwood PA 15697	724-925-7272	R	90*	.3
113	Kyocera America Inc—*Makoto Kawamura* Kyocera International Inc	8611 Balboa Ave, San Diego CA 92123	858-576-2600	S	88*	.8
114	Melcor Corp	1040 Spruce St, Trenton NJ 08648	609-393-4178	S	86*	.1
115	Innovation Silicon Inc—*Mark-Eric Jones*	4800 Great America Pkw, Santa Clara CA 95054	408-572-8700	R	83*	.1
116	Cypress Semiconductor Inc (Round Rock Texas)—*TJ Rodgers* Cypress Semiconductor Corp	17 Cypress Blvd, Round Rock TX 78664	512-244-7789	D	83	.4
117	MIPS Technologies Inc—*Sandeep Vij*	955 E Arques Ave, Sunnyvale CA 94085	408-530-5000	P	82	.2
118	Cybershield of Texas—*Jim Skelly*	308 Ellen Trout Dr, Lufkin TX 75904	936-633-6387	R	82*	.1
119	Mitsubishi Gas Chemical America Inc	655 3rd Ave 24th Fl, New York NY 10017	212-687-9030	R	80	.3
120	Stratos International Inc—*Phillip A Harris*	7444 W Wilson Ave, Chicago IL 60706	708-867-9600	S	80	.5
121	Entorian Technologies Inc—*Stephan Godevais*	4030 W Braker Ln Bldg, Austin TX 78759	512-334-0111	P	79	.1
122	Rubicon Technology Inc—*Raja Parvez*	9931 Franklin Ave, Franklin Park IL 60131	847-295-7000	P	77	.3
123	Ramtron International Corp—*Eric A Balzer*	1850 Ramtron Dr, Colorado Springs CO 80921	719-481-7000	P	70	.1
124	Upek Inc—*Ronald D Black*	5900 Christie Ave, Emeryville CA 94608	510-420-2600	R	70*	.1
125	Pixelworks Inc—*Bruce A Walicek*	16760 SW Upper Boones, Portland OR 97224	503-601-4545	P	70	.2
126	Global Communication Semiconductors Inc—*Jerry L Curtis*	23155 Kashiwa Ct, Torrance CA 90505		R	67*	.1
127	Kilopass Technology Inc—*Charlie Cheng*	3333 Octavius Dr Ste 1, Santa Clara CA 95054	408-980-8808	R	67*	.1
128	White Electronic Designs Corp—*Gerald R Dinkel* Microsemi Corp	3601 E University Dr, Phoenix AZ 85034	602-437-1520	S	63*	.2
129	BP Solar International LLC—*Steve Westwell*	630 Solarex Ct, Frederick MD 21703	301-698-4200	S	62*	.4
130	CNet Technology Inc—*Jiongfen Wang*	2548 Zanker Rd, San Jose CA 95131	408-934-0800	R	60*	.3
131	Memtech SSD Corp—*Manouch Moshayedi*	2107 North First St St, San Jose CA 95131	408-452-1277	R	56*	.5
132	Nextest Systems Corp—*Mike Bradley*	875 Embedded Way, San Jose CA 95138	408-960-2400	S	56*	.2

Rank	Company Name—*Executive Officer*	Address, City, State, Zip	Phone	Type	Fin	Empls
133	Catalyst Semiconductor Inc—*Gelu Voicu* ON Semiconductor Corp	2975 Stender Way, Santa Clara CA 95054	408-542-1000	S	55*	.1
134	Kayex—*Bruce Williamson*	1000 Millstead Way, Rochester NY 14624	585-235-2524	D	55*	.1
135	Minicom Advanced Systems Limited - US Office—*Eli Sasson*	414 N Wood Ave, Linden NJ 07036	905-486-2100	S	54*	.1
136	Philips Semiconductors Embedded Processor Div—*Rob Westerhof*	8375 S River Pky, Tempe AZ 85284	480-752-8574	D	53*	.2
137	PRC Corp—*Jim Rickert*	350 N Frontage Rd, Landing NJ 07850	973-347-0100	S	52*	.1
138	Tropian Inc—*Tim Unger*	20813 Stevens Creek Bl, Cupertino CA 95014	408-865-1300	R	51*	.1
139	OPTi Inc—*Bernard Marren*	3430 W Bayshore Rd Ste, Palo Alto CA 94303	650-213-8550	P	51	<.1
140	Magnum Semiconductor Inc—*Jack Guedj*	591 Yosemite Dr, Milpitas CA 95035	408-934-3700	R	50*	.2
141	PEI Genesis—*Russel Dorwart*	2180 Hornig Rd, Philadelphia PA 19116	215-673-0400	R	50	.1
142	Entrepix—*Tim Tobin*	2315 W Fairmont Dr, Tempe AZ 85282	602-426-8677	R	50*	.1
143	Optibase Inc—*Tom Wyler*	880 Maude Ave, Mountain View CA 94043	650-230-2400	S	50*	.1
144	TranSwitch Corp—*Ali Khatibzadeh*	3 Enterprise Dr, Shelton CT 06484	203-929-8810	P	50	.2
145	QPC Lasers Inc—*Jeffrey Ungar*	15632 Roxford St, Sylmar CA 91342	818-986-0000	R	49*	.1
146	Oxford Semiconductor Ltd PLX Technology Inc	870 Maude Ave, Sunnyvale CA 94085	408-774-9060	S	48*	.1
147	Microsemi Integrated Products—*James T Peterson* Microsemi Corp	11861 Western Ave, Garden Grove CA 92841	714-898-8121	D	47*	.2
148	T-Ram Semiconductor Inc—*Sam R Nakib*	620 N McCarthy Blvd, Milpitas CA 95035	408-597-3000	R	47*	.1
149	Alliance Fiber Optic Products Inc—*Peter C Chang*	275 Gibraltar Dr, Sunnyvale CA 94089	408-736-6900	P	45	1.1
150	Bernard Welding Equipment—*John Winek*	449 W Corning Rd, Beecher IL 60401	708-946-2281	S	45*	.1
151	CEVA Inc—*Gideon Wertheizer*	1943 Landings Dr, Mountain View CA 94043	650-417-7900	P	45	.2
152	AuthenTec Inc—*Larry Ciaccia*	100 Rialto Pl Ste 100, Melbourne FL 32901	321-308-1300	P	45	.2
153	INNOViON Corp—*Gary Holyoak*	2121 Zanker Rd, San Jose CA 95131	408-501-9100	R	44*	.1
154	Legend Silicon Corp—*Hong Dong*	440 Mission Ct Ste 210, Fremont CA 94539	510-656-9888	R	44*	.1
155	Luxtera Inc—*Greg Young*	2320 Camino Vida Roble, Carlsbad CA 92011	760-448-3520	R	44*	.1
156	SiTime Corp—*Rajesh Vashist*	990 Almanor Ave, Sunnyvale CA 94085	408-328-4400	R	43*	.1
157	OM Jones Inc—*Olga Jones*	PO Box 4375, Sonora CA 95370	209-532-1008	R	43*	<.1
158	Amberwave Systems Corp—*Richard J Faubert*	13 Garabedian Dr, Salem NH 03079	603-870-8700	R	42*	.1
159	Enpirion Inc—*Denis Regimbal*	685 Rte 202/206 Ste 30, Bridgewater NJ 08807		R	42*	.1
160	Solec International Inc—*Yoshinobu Takabatake*	860 Via De La Paz Ste, Pacific Palisades CA 90272	310-230-8900	R	42*	.1
161	Cast Iron Systems Inc—*Ken Comee*	375 Ravendale Dr, Mountain View CA 94043	650-230-0621	R	40*	.1
162	Astute Networks Inc—*George Pavlov*	16516 Via Esprillo Ste, San Diego CA 92127	858-673-7700	R	40*	<.1
163	SunWize Technologies Inc—*Scott L Tonn*	1155 Flatbush Rd, Kingston NY 12401	845-336-0146	S	39*	<.1
164	Apache Design Solutions Inc—*Andrew Yang*	2645 Zanker Rd, San Jose CA 95134	408-457-2000	R	39*	<.1
165	Memsic Inc—*Yang Zhao*	1 Tech Dr Ste 325, Andover MA 01810	978-738-0900	P	39	N/A
166	Global Solar Energy Inc—*Jeffrey S Britt*	8500 S Rita Rd, Tucson AZ 85747	520-546-6313	R	38*	.2
167	Maxtek Components Corp—*Tom Buzak*	2905 SW Hocken Ave, Beaverton OR 97005	503-627-4133	S	37*	.2
168	Impinj Inc—*William Colleran*	701 N 34th St Ste 300, Seattle WA 98103	206-834-1091	R	37*	.1
169	Hybrid Electronics Inc—*Mark Thomas*	PO Box 5000, Victoria MN 55386	952-443-2500	P	36	.3
170	Aeroflex Colorado Springs—*Jerry Reinsma*	4350 Centennial Blvd, Colorado Springs CO 80907	719-594-8000	S	36*	.2
171	Centaur Technology Inc—*Glenn Henry*	7600-C N Capital of Te, Austin TX 78731	512-418-5700	S	36*	.1
172	EM4 Inc—*Basil Garabet*	7 Oak Park Dr, Bedford MA 01730	781-275-7501	R	36*	<.1
173	Marvell Semiconductor Inc Marvell Technology Group Ltd	5488 Marvell Ln, Santa Clara CA 95054	408-222-2500	S	35*	.4
174	Microchip Technology Incorporated Analog and Interface Products Div—*Steve Sanghi* Microchip Technology Inc	2355 W Chandler Blvd, Chandler AZ 85224	480-792-7200	D	34*	.2
175	Dune Networks Inc Broadcom Corp	5300 California Ave, Irvine CA 92617	949-926-5000	S	34*	.1
176	Fluidigm Corp—*Gajus Worthington*	7000 Shoreline Ct Ste, South San Francisco CA 94080	650-266-6000	P	34	.2
177	ESS Technology Inc—*Robert L Blair*	48401 Fremont Blvd, Fremont CA 94538	510-492-1088	S	33*	.1
178	Polar Semiconductor Inc—*Zen Suzuki*	2800 E Old Shakopee Rd, Bloomington MN 55425	952-876-3000	R	33*	.5
179	Seakr Engineering Inc—*Raymond Anderson*	6221 S Racine Cir, Englewood CO 80111	303-790-8499	R	33*	.2
180	SANYO Semiconductor Corp—*Teruo Tabata* ON Semiconductor Corp	Park 80 W Plz2 Plaza L, Saddle Brook NJ 07663	201-825-8080	S	32*	<.1
181	Hayward Quartz Technology Inc—*Ha Ly*	1700 Corporate Way, Fremont CA 94539	510-657-9605	R	32*	.3
182	SRS Labs Inc—*Chuck Cortright*	2909 Daimler St, Santa Ana CA 92705	949-442-1070	P	31	.1
183	NVE Corp—*Daniel A Baker*	11409 Valley View Rd, Eden Prairie MN 55344	952-829-9217	P	31	.1
184	Tensilica Inc—*Jack Guedj*	3255 Scott Blvd Ste 6, Santa Clara CA 95054	408-986-8000	R	31*	.1
185	Ambric Inc—*Howard Bubb*	15655 SW Greystone Ct, Beaverton OR 97006	503-601-6500	S	31*	<.1
186	eMagin Corp—*Andrew G Sculley*	3006 Northup Way Ste 1, Bellevue WA 98004	425-284-5200	P	31	.1
187	Wintegra Inc—*Jadob Ben-Zvi*	6850 Austin Center Blv, Austin TX 78731	512-345-3808	R	30*	.2
188	Conductive Technologies Inc—*Matthew Musho*	935 Borom Rd, York PA 17404	717-764-6931	R	30*	.2
189	Comtrol Corp—*Rebecca Summers Beale*	100 5th Ave NW, Saint Paul MN 55112	763-494-4100	R	29*	.1
190	ServerWorks Corp—*Scott McGregor* Broadcom Corp	5300 California Ave Bl, Irvine CA 92617		S	29*	.1
191	Advanced Photonix Inc—*Richard Kurtz*	2925 Boardwalk, Ann Arbor MI 48104	734-864-5600	P	29	.2
192	Chip Supply Inc—*Tony Hambyy*	7725 N Orange Blossom, Orlando FL 32810	407-298-7100	R	28*	.1
193	QualCore Logic Inc—*Mahendra Jain*	1289 Anvilwood Ave, Sunnyvale CA 94089	408-541-0730	R	28*	.1
194	Nascentric Inc—*Rahm Shastry*	8303 N Mopac Expy Ste, Austin TX 78759	512-225-8800	R	27*	<.1
195	QuickLogic Corp—*Andrew Pease*	1277 Orleans Dr, Sunnyvale CA 94089	408-990-4000	P	26	.1
196	Cavendish Kinetics Inc—*Dennis Yost*	3833 N 1st St, San Jose CA 95134	408-240-7370	R	26*	<.1
197	NextIO Inc—*Kenton C Murphy*	8303 N MoPac Expy Ste, Austin TX 78759	512-439-5350	R	25*	<.1
198	Nexx Systems Inc—*Tom Walsh*	900 Middlesex Turnpike, Billerica MA 01821	718-640-4442	R	25*	<.1
199	Aware Inc—*Edmund Reiter*	40 Middlesex Tpke, Bedford MA 01730	781-276-4000	P	25	.1
200	Towa Intercon Technology Inc—*Kim Tan*	18255 Sutter Blvd, Morgan Hill CA 95037	408-778-5992	R	24*	.1
201	E2v Aerospace And Defense Inc—*Keith Atwood*	2945 Oakmead Village C, Santa Clara CA 95051	408-737-0992	R	24*	.1
202	MEMC Pasadena Inc—*Nabeel Gareeb* MEMC Electronic Materials Inc	501 Pearl Dr, Saint Peters MO 63376	636-474-7600	S	24*	<.1
203	Vlsip Technologies Inc—*Gene Wakefield*	750 Presidential Dr, Richardson TX 75081	972-437-5506	R	24*	.2
204	Promex Industries Inc—*Richard Otte*	3075 Oakmead Village D, Santa Clara CA 95051	408-496-0222	R	23*	.2
205	Futaba Corporation of America—*Joe Dorris*	711 E State Pkwy, Schaumburg IL 60173	847-884-1444	S	23*	.1
206	Telairity Semiconductor Inc—*Jim Meadlock*	3375 Scott Blvd Ste 30, Santa Clara CA 95054	408-764-0270	R	23*	<.1
207	Hytel Group Inc—*Scott Johansen*	290 Industrial Dr, Hampshire IL 60140	847-683-9800	R	22*	.1
208	Zentrix Technologies Inc—*Jordan Frazier*	22 Graf Rd, Newburyport MA 01950	978-463-6543	S	22*	<.1
209	HVVi Semiconductors Inc—*Dave Lutz*	10235 S 51st St Ste 10, Phoenix AZ 85044	480-776-3800	R	22*	<.1
210	MKS Instruments Inc Spectra Products Div—*Leo Berlinghieri*	70 Rio Robles Dr, San Jose CA 95134	408-750-0300	D	21*	.1
211	Alfalight Inc—*Mohan Warrior*	1832 Wright St, Madison WI 53704	608-240-4814	R	21*	<.1

Note: An asterisk (*) indicates an estimated financial figure. The company type code used is as follows: R = Private, P = Public, S = Private Subsidiary, B = Public Subsidiary, D = Division, J = Joint Venture, I = Investment Fund.

COMPANY RANKINGS BY SALES WITHIN 4-DIGIT SIC

Rank	Company Name—*Executive Officer*	Address, City, State, Zip	Phone	Type	Fin	Empls
212	Broadlogic Network Technologies Inc—*Danial Faizullabhoy*	1740 Technology Dr Ste, San Jose CA 95110	408-452-3300	R	21*	<.1
213	Solido Design Automation Inc—*Amit Gupta*	111 North Market St, San Jose CA 95113	408-332-5811	R	21*	<.1
214	Rsm Electron Power Inc—*Martin Saunders*	221 W Industry Ct, Deer Park NY 11729	631-586-7600	R	21*	.2
215	Ichia USA Inc—*Simon Goh*	1057 Tierra Del Rey St, Chula Vista CA 91910	619-482-2222	R	20*	.2
216	Micropac Industries Inc—*Mark King*	905 E Walnut St, Garland TX 75040	972-272-3571	P	20	.1
217	Avid Identification Systems Inc—*Hannis Stoddard*	3185 Hamner Ave, Norco CA 92860	951-371-7505	R	20*	.1
218	Darim Vision Corp—*Young Kim*	3110 Constitution Dr, Livermore CA 94551	925-251-0178	S	20*	.1
219	Berkeley Design Automation Inc—*Ravi Subramanian*	2902 Stender Way, Santa Clara CA 95054	408-496-6600	R	20*	<.1
220	Quadrant Components Inc—*Chad Yau*	4378 Enterprise St, Fremont CA 94538	510-656-9988	R	19*	.1
221	API Electronics Inc—*Brian Kahn*	2200 Smithtown Ave, Ronkonkoma NY 11779	631-981-2400	R	19*	<.1
222	Rapport Inc (Redwood City California)—*Ross Q Smith*	2603 Broadway St, Redwood City CA 94063	650-568-5910	R	19*	<.1
223	E/G Electro-Graph Inc—*Mike Reilly*	2365 Camino Vida Roble, Carlsbad CA 92011	760-438-9090	S	19*	<.1
224	Cree Lighting Co—*Chuck Swoboda* Cree Inc	340 Storke Rd, Goleta CA 93117	805-968-9460	S	18*	<.1
225	Advanced Linear Devices Inc—*Robert L Chao*	415 Tasman Dr, Sunnyvale CA 94089	408-747-1155	R	18*	<.1
226	Corwil Technology Corp—*Robert Corrao*	1635 Mccarthy Blvd, Milpitas CA 95035	408-321-6404	R	18*	.2
227	Pantronix Corp—*Stanley Wang*	2710 Lakeview Ct, Fremont CA 94538	510-656-5898	R	17*	.4
228	W G Holt Inc—*William Holt*	23351 Madero, Mission Viejo CA 92691	949-859-8800	R	17*	.1
229	CDS Engineering Inc—*Peter D Kinnear*	1803 Gears Rd, Houston TX 77067	281-591-4000	S	17*	.1
230	Interconnect Systems Inc—*William Miller*	759 Flynn Rd, Camarillo CA 93012	805-482-2870	R	17*	.1
231	Advanced Micro Devices Inc - Personal Connectivity Div—*Hector Ruiz* Advanced Micro Devices Inc	7171 Southwest Pkwy, Austin TX 78735	512-602-1000	D	17*	.1
232	Peregrine Semiconductor Corp—*James S Cable*	9380 Carroll Park Dr, San Diego CA 92121	858-731-9400	R	17*	.1
233	Mobious Microsystems Inc—*Ashok Dhawan*	111 W Evlyn Ave, Sunnyvale CA 94086	408-739-5400	R	17*	<.1
234	Real Intent Inc—*Prakash Narain*	505 N Mathilda Ave Ste, Sunnyvale CA 94085	408-830-0700	R	17*	<.1
235	Synfora Inc—*Simon Napper*	2465 Latham St Ste 100, Mountain View CA 94040	650-314-0500	R	17*	<.1
236	Sajan Inc (Whitetail Blvd, River Falls Wisconsin)—*Shannon Zimmerman*	625 Whitetail Blvd, River Falls WI 54022	715-426-9505	P	16	.1
237	I-O Corp—*Matt Brady*	1490 N 2200 W Ste 100, Salt Lake City UT 84116	801-973-6767	R	16*	.1
238	Nantero Inc—*Greg Schmergel*	25 E Olympia Ave, Woburn MA 01801	781-932-5338	R	16	.1
239	Diversified Technology Inc—*Leslie Lampton*	476 Highland Colony Pk, Ridgeland MS 39157	601-856-4121	R	16*	.1
240	Applied Ceramics Inc—*Matt Sertic*	48630 Milmont Dr, Fremont CA 94538	510-249-9700	R	16*	.1
241	Ledtronics Inc—*Pervaiz Lodhie*	23105 Kashiwa Ct, Torrance CA 90505	310-534-1505	R	15*	.1
242	Irvine Sensors Corp—*Bill Joll*	3001 Red Hill Ave Bldg, Costa Mesa CA 92626	714-549-8211	P	14	.1
243	Senior Systems Technology Inc—*Bill Johns*	600 Technology Dr, Palmdale CA 93551	661-575-8500	R	14*	.2
244	Voltage Multipliers Inc—*Dennis Kemp*	8711 W Roosevelt Ave, Visalia CA 93291	559-651-1402	R	14*	.1
245	Gage Applied Inc	900 N State St, Lockport IL 60441	815-838-0005	S	14*	.1
246	Aegis Semiconductor Inc—*Jeffrey D Farmer*	78A Olympia Ave, Woburn MA 01801	781-904-4000	R	14*	<.1
247	Ziptronix Inc—*Daniel L Donabedian*	800 Perimeter Park Dr, Morrisville NC 27560	919-459-2400	R	14*	<.1
248	iNetWorks Corp—*Mel Brashears* Irvine Sensors Corp	3001 Redhill Ave Bldg, Costa Mesa CA 92626	714-435-8900	S	14*	<.1
249	Dean Technology Inc—*Craig Dean*	PO Box 848, Farmingdale NJ 07727	732-938-4499	R	13*	.1
250	Innovative Micro Technology Inc—*Richard Balanson*	75 Robin Hill Rd, Goleta CA 93117	805-681-2800	R	13*	.1
251	Coda Octopus Group Inc—*Geoff Turner*	111 Town Square Pl Ste, Jersey City NJ 07310	201-420-9100	P	13	.1
252	Cubic Wafer—*Ed Healy*	5113 Southwest Pky Ste, Austin TX 78735	512-615-0808	R	13*	<.1
253	Foresight Technologies Inc—*Jeffrey Hull*	1301 W Geneva Dr, Tempe AZ 85282	480-967-0080	R	12*	.1
254	Virtium Technology Inc—*Phu Hoang*	30052 Tomas, Rancho Santa Margarita CA 92688	949-888-2444	R	12*	<.1
255	Iqe Inc—*Andrew Nelson*	119 Technology Dr, Bethlehem PA 18015	610-861-6930	R	12*	.1
256	Hybrid Design Associates Inc—*Fred Baldassano*	230 S Siesta Ln, Tempe AZ 85281	480-967-8989	R	12*	.1
257	Jaco Inc—*Alfred Rossini*	140 Constitution Blvd, Franklin MA 02038	508-553-1000	R	11*	.1
258	Superchips Inc—*Adam Raper*	1790 E Airport Blvd, Sanford FL 32773	407-585-7000	S	11*	.1
259	Williams Thin Film Products—*Richard Sager*	PO Box 1950 42 Mt Ebo, Brewster NY 10509	845-279-0900	S	11*	<.1
260	Silicon Light Machines—*Lars Eng*	820 Kifer Rd, Sunnyvale CA 94086	408-240-4700	S	11*	<.1
261	D F Electronics Inc—*Laughton Fine*	200 Novner Dr, Cincinnati OH 45215	513-772-7792	R	11*	.1
262	Wafer Reclaim Services LLC—*Richard Mee*	2240 Ringwood Ave, San Jose CA 95131	408-945-8112	R	11*	.1
263	Ultrasource Inc—*Michael Casper*	22 Clinton Dr, Hollis NH 03049	603-881-7799	R	11*	.1
264	National Hybrid Inc—*Steve Putles*	345 Pomroys Dr, Windber PA 15963	814-467-9060	R	10*	.1
265	LightPath Technologies Inc—*Joseph (Jim) Gaynor*	2603 Challenger Tech C, Orlando FL 32826	407-382-4003	P	10	.2
266	Clare Inc—*Nathan Zommer* IXYS Corp	78 Cherry Hill Dr, Beverly MA 01915	978-524-6700	S	10*	.1
267	Hytek Microsystems Inc—*Sudesh Arora*	400 Hot Springs Rd, Carson City NV 89706	775-883-0820	S	10*	.1
268	Telephonics Large Scale Integration—*Donald C Pastor*	780 Park Ave, Huntington NY 11743	631-470-8880	S	10*	.1
269	Xyron Semiconductor Inc—*John Peers*	PO Box 871808, Vancouver WA 98687	360-449-8800	R	10*	<.1
270	Gigoptix LLC—*Avi Katz*	130 Baytech Dr, San Jose CA 95134	408-522-3100	R	10	N/A
271	Mactronix—*John Lau*	2050 N Plano Rd Ste 30, Richardson TX 75082	972-690-0028	R	10*	.1
272	Spectrolab Inc—*David Lillington*	12500 Gladstone Ave, Sylmar CA 91342	818-365-4611	S	9	.5
273	Epson Electronics America Inc—*Koji Abe*	2580 Orchard Pkwy, San Jose CA 95131	408-922-0200	R	9*	.1
274	Condor Reliability Services Inc—*Punam Patel*	3400 De La Cruz Blvd R, Santa Clara CA 95054	408-486-9600	R	9*	.1
275	Solid State Devices Inc—*Georges Pomidou*	14701 Firestone Blvd, La Mirada CA 90638	562-404-4474	R	9*	.2
276	Veris Industries Inc—*Jean-Pascal Tricoire*	16640 SW 72nd Ave, Portland OR 97224	503-598-4564	R	9*	.1
277	Sonix Inc—*Michael Zuralow*	8700 Morrissette Dr, Springfield VA 22152	703-440-0222	R	9*	<.1
278	OSI Optoelectronics OSI Systems Inc	12525 Chadron Ave, Hawthorne CA 90250	310-978-0516	S	9*	<.1
279	Sokudo USA LLC	3303 Scott Blvd Ms1085, Santa Clara CA 95054	408-496-8064	R	9*	.1
280	Epiworks Inc—*Quesnell Hartmann*	1606 Rion Dr, Champaign IL 61822	217-373-1590	R	9*	<.1
281	Ohio Semitronics Inc—*Warren Bulman*	4242 Reynolds Dr, Hilliard OH 43026	614-777-1005	R	9*	.1
282	Winslow Automation Inc—*June Clark*	905 Montague Expy, Milpitas CA 95035	408-986-0100	R	9*	.1
283	Swissbit NA Inc—*Anthony Cerreta*	18 Willett Ave 202, Port Chester NY 10573	914-935-1400	R	8*	<.1
284	Solyndra Inc—*Brian Harrison*	47700 Kato Rd, Fremont CA 94538		R	8*	1.0
285	Aljo-Gefa Precision Manufacturing LLC—*John Addleman*	205 Sweet Hollow Rd, Old Bethpage NY 11804	516-420-3890	R	8*	<.1
286	Rocky Mountain Ram LLC—*Lisa Schaeffer*	917 Front St, Louisville CO 80027	303-413-8244	R	8*	<.1
287	Telechem International Inc—*Rene Schena*	524 E Weddell Dr, Sunnyvale CA 94089	408-744-1331	D	8*	<.1
288	Don-Ell Corp—*Donald R Sell*	8450 Central Ave, Sylvania OH 43560	419-841-1828	R	8*	<.1
289	Call Management Products Inc—*Frank Meodille*	2150 W 6th Ave Unit D, Broomfield CO 80020	303-465-0651	R	8*	<.1
290	Nitronex Corp—*Charles Shalvoy*	2305 Presidential Dr, Durham NC 27703	919-807-9100	R	8*	.1
291	DT Sale Corp—*Steven D Runkel*	5675 Hudson Industrial, Hudson OH 44236	330-655-9000	P	8	<.1
292	Prospect Products Inc—*Richard Carlson*	43 Kelsey St, Newington CT 06111	860-666-0323	R	8*	<.1
293	Relume Technologies Inc—*Michael Mcclear*	925 N Lapeer Rd Ste B, Oxford MI 48371	248-969-3800	R	7*	<.1
294	Semitronics Corp—*Henrietta Rivman*	80 Commercial St, Freeport NY 11520	516-623-9400	R	7*	<.1
295	MEC Technologies Inc—*Richard Kulkaski*	2200 Industrial Way S, Toms River NJ 08755	732-505-0308	R	7*	<.1

Rank	Company Name—*Executive Officer*	Address, City, State, Zip	Phone	Type	Fin	Empls
296	Richard Manufacturing Co—*Brent Call*	2147 Rulon White Blvd, Ogden UT 84404	801-737-4450	R	7*	<.1
297	Sgm Corp—*Shanker Patel*	12831 Royal Dr, Stafford TX 77477	281-313-6111	R	7*	<.1
298	Montco Silicon Technologies—*Richard Mee*	2240 Ringwood Ave, San Jose CA 95131	610-948-6880	R	7*	<.1
299	Applied Solar Inc—*David Field*	3560 Dunhill St, San Diego CA 92121	858-909-4080	R	7	<.1
300	Sensorphysics Inc—*Gary Forrest*	8425 S Timberline Rd, Fort Collins CO 80525	970-593-0383	R	7*	.1
301	C and D Semiconductor Services Inc—*Dong Nguyen*	2031 Concourse Dr, San Jose CA 95131	408-383-1889	R	7*	.1
302	Mcg Electronics Inc—*Michael Coyle*	12 Burt Dr, Deer Park NY 11729	631-586-5125	R	7*	.1
303	Gpd Optoelectronics Corp—*Oliver Ward*	PO Box 3065, Andover MA 01810	603-894-6865	R	7*	.1
304	Protek Devices LP—*Jeff Bankel*	2929 S Fair Ln, Tempe AZ 85282	602-431-8101	R	7*	<.1
305	Tioga Technologies Inc—*Douglas Goodyear*	1380 Redhill Blvd 106, Roseville CA 95661	916-788-1266	R	6*	.1
306	Vertical Circuits Inc—*Sunil Kaul*	10 Victor Sq Ste 100, Scotts Valley CA 95066	831-438-3887	R	6*	.1
307	Reliance Machine Products Inc—*Kelly Hill*	4265 Solar Way, Fremont CA 94538	510-438-6760	R	6*	<.1
308	Penn North Technology Inc—*Vincent Spadafora*	2294 N Penn Rd Ste A, Hatfield PA 19440	215-997-3200	R	6*	<.1
309	SV Microwave Inc—*Subi Katragadda*	2400 CentrePark W Dr, West Palm Beach FL 33409	561-840-1800	S	6*	.1
310	ChipWrights Inc—*Cary Robins*	19 Crosby Dr, Bedford MA 01730	781-271-4100	R	6*	.1
311	Polyfet Rf Devices Inc—*S Leong*	1110 Avenida Acaso, Camarillo CA 93012	805-484-4210	R	6*	<.1
312	Winnov LP—*Olivier Garbe*	683 W Maude Ave, Sunnyvale CA 94085		R	6*	<.1
313	ZMD America Inc—*Thilo von Selchow*	201 Old Country Rd, Melville NY 11747	631-549-2666	S	6*	<.1
314	Power Electronics International Inc—*Victor Habisohn*	561 Plate Dr Ste 8, East Dundee IL 60118	847-428-9494	R	6*	.1
315	Stratedge Corp—*Timothy Going*	6335 Ferris Sq Ste C, San Diego CA 92121		R	6*	<.1
316	Foxsemicon Integrated Technology Inc—*Koven Tsao*	96 Bonaventura Dr, San Jose CA 95134	408-383-9880	R	6*	<.1
317	Cooper Microelectronics Inc—*Kenneth Cooper*	1671 Reynolds Ave, Irvine CA 92614	949-553-8352	R	6*	<.1
318	Excelics Semiconductor Inc—*Tao Chow*	310 De Guigne Dr, Sunnyvale CA 94085	408-737-1711	R	6*	<.1
319	Chemwest Systems Inc—*Martin Boehm*	15865 Sw 72nd Ave Bldg, Portland OR 97224	503-639-6414	R	6*	<.1
320	Stellar Industries Corp—*Ronald Visser*	50 Howe Ave, Millbury MA 01527	508-865-1668	R	6*	<.1
321	Tellurex Corp—*Charles Cauchy*	1462 International Dr, Traverse City MI 49686	231-947-0110	R	5*	<.1
322	Verisilicon Inc—*Wayne Dai*	4699 Old Ironsides Dr, Santa Clara CA 95054	408-844-8560	R	5*	<.1
323	H-Square Corp—*Bud Barclay*	2991 Copper Rd, Santa Clara CA 95051	408-732-1240	R	5*	<.1
324	Sunrise Systems Inc—*Henry Appleton*	720 Washington St, Pembroke MA 02359	781-826-9706	R	5*	<.1
325	Bipolarics Inc—*Charles Leung*	602 Charcot Ave, San Jose CA 95131	408-456-0430	R	5*	.1
326	Apollo Display Technologies LLC—*Bernhard Staller*	87 Raynor Ave Unit 1, Ronkonkoma NY 11779	631-580-4360	R	5*	<.1
327	Piconics Inc—*Stephen Slenkert*	26 Cummings Rd, Tyngsboro MA 01879	978-649-7501	R	5*	<.1
328	Nexgen Technologies LLC—*Lee Stevens*	3389 Edward Ave, Santa Clara CA 95054	408-986-1992	R	5*	<.1
329	Sierra Technologies LLC—*Robert D Patterson*	202 Moss Wood Cir, Simpsonville SC 29681	864-458-9035	R	5*	<.1
330	ZiLOG Inc—*Nathan Zommer* IXYS Corp	1590 Buckeye Dr, Milpitas CA 95035	408-513-1500	S	5	.5
331	Micro Engineering Inc—*Larry Laforest*	1428 E Smran Blvd Ste, Apopka FL 32703	407-886-4849	R	5*	<.1
332	Robertson Precision Inc—*William Robertson*	2971 Spring St, Redwood City CA 94063	650-363-2212	R	5*	<.1
333	Tela Innovations Inc—*Scott Becker*	655 Campbell Technolog, Campbell CA 95008	408-558-6300	R	5*	<.1
334	Piezo-Metrics Inc—*Herbert Chelner*	4509 Runway St, Simi Valley CA 93063	805-522-4676	R	5*	<.1
335	Electronic Technology Corp—*William Burkland*	402 Campus Dr, Huxley IA 50124	515-597-7000	R	5*	<.1
336	Crimson Semiconductor Inc—*Robert Ross*	460 W 34th St Fl 12, New York NY 10001	212-947-8585	R	5*	<.1
337	Lsi Computer Systems Internat'l Ltd—*Alfred Muslu*	1235 Walt Whitman Rd, Melville NY 11747	631-271-0400	R	5*	<.1
338	Permlight Products Inc—*George Preston*	422 W 6th St, Tustin CA 92780	714 508-0729	R	5*	<.1
339	Semi Conductor Manufacturing Corp—*Wayne Connelly*	5 Troast Ct, Clifton NJ 07011	973-478-2880	R	4*	<.1
340	Micro Gage Inc—*Bruce Talmo*	9537 Telstar Ave Ste 1, El Monte CA 91731	626-443-1741	R	4*	<.1
341	Day Microsystems Inc—*Randall Meals*	2055 Gateway Pl Ste 65, San Jose CA 95110	408-437-0400	R	4*	.1
342	TotalView Technologies LLC—*Jim Chafel*	24 Prime Park Way, Natick MA 01760	508-652-7700	S	4*	<.1
343	Innovative Integration—*Jim Henderson*	2655 Park Ctr Dr, Simi Valley CA 93065	805-578-4200	R	4*	<.1
344	Solexel Inc—*Mehrdad Moslehi*	1530 Mccarthy Blvd, Milpitas CA 95035	408-715-9554	R	4*	<.1
345	FSI/Fork Standards Inc	668 Western Ave, Lombard IL 60148	630-932-9380	R	4*	<.1
346	Burke Products Inc—*Shiv Bakhshi*	PO Box 572, Xenia OH 45385	937-372-3516	R	4*	<.1
347	Merit Sensor Systems—*Christopher Durham*	1600 W Merit Pkwy, South Jordan UT 84095	801-208-4746	D	4*	<.1
348	OSE USA Inc—*Edmond Tseng*	2560 N 1st St Ste 100, San Jose CA 95131	408-321-7920	S	4*	<.1
349	Hybrid Sources Inc—*Richard Vogel*	2950 43rd Ave, Vero Beach FL 32960	772-563-9100	R	4*	<.1
350	Semi-Automations and Technologies Inc—*Kristin Boyce*	1510-C Dell Ave, Campbell CA 95008	408-374-9549	R	4*	<.1
351	Technical Controls Inc—*Gary Thompson*	1295 Progress Industri, Lawrenceville GA 30043	770-682-9991	R	4*	<.1
352	Accretech USA Inc—*Takeshi Kagamida*	2600 Telegraph Rd Ste, Bloomfield Hills MI 48302	248-332-0100	S	4*	<.1
353	Originalpower Inc—*Kirk Turner*	3400 Corporate Way Ste, Duluth GA 30096	770-418-1850	R	4*	<.1
354	Cascade System Technology LLC—*Mary Parker*	23176 Nw Bennett St, Hillsboro OR 97124	503-640-5733	R	4*	.1
355	Pct Systems Inc—*Henry Miranda*	44060 Old Warm Springs, Fremont CA 94538	510-657-4412	R	4*	<.1
356	Asemco Inc—*Chuck Shaw*	500 Andover Park E, Tukwila WA 98188	253-872-9053	R	4*	<.1
357	Kingbright Corp—*Wen Sung*	225 Brea Canyon Rd, City Of Industry CA 91789	909-468-0500	R	4*	<.1
358	Grinding and Dicing Services Inc—*Y Haq*	925 Berryessa Rd, San Jose CA 95133	408-451-2000	R	4*	<.1
359	Essex Electronics Inc—*Peter Kaufman*	1130 Mark Ave, Carpinteria CA 93013	805-684-7601	R	4*	<.1
360	Two In One Manufacturing Inc—*Mui Nguyen*	51 Lake St Ste 4, Nashua NH 03060	603-595-8212	R	4*	.1
361	Sussex Semiconductor Inc—*George Tibol*	12251 Towne Lake Dr, Fort Myers FL 33913	239-768-6800	R	4*	<.1
362	Chartered Semi Conductors	2070 Rte 52, Hopewell Junction NY 12533	845-892-3607	R	3*	<.1
363	Legacy Capital Equipment LLC—*Michael Mihin*	4049 E Presidio St Ste, Mesa AZ 85215	480-507-7991	R	3*	<.1
364	Perfection Products Inc—*John Vickery*	1320 Indianapolis Ave, Lebanon IN 46052	765-482-7786	R	3*	<.1
365	Semiconductor Technology Inc—*Fred Seigel*	PO Box 474, Stuart FL 34995	772-283-4500	R	3*	<.1
366	Mackenzie Laboratories Inc—*Nagy Khattar*	PO Box 1416, Glendora CA 91740	909-394-9007	R	3*	<.1
367	Omnisil—*David Clark*	5401 Everglades St, Ventura CA 93003	805-644-2514	R	3*	<.1
368	Dauber Company Inc—*William Dauber*	577 N 18tth Rd Tth, Tonica IL 61370	815-442-3569	R	3*	<.1
369	Tlc Precision Wafer Technology Inc—*Timothy Childs*	1411 W River Rd, Minneapolis MN 55411	612-341-2795	R	3*	<.1
370	MetroSpec Technology LLC—*Vic Holec*	2401 Pilot Knob Rd Ste, Mendota Heights MN 55120	651-452-4800	R	3	<.1
371	American Power Devices Inc—*Paul Flaherty*	69 Bennett St, Lynn MA 01905	781-592-6090	R	3*	<.1
372	Polishing Corporation Of America—*Stuart Becker*	442 Martin Ave, Santa Clara CA 95050	408-988-6000	R	3*	<.1
373	Filmtronics Inc—*Neal Christensen*	PO Box 1521, Butler PA 16003	724-352-3790	R	3*	<.1
374	Nanosys Inc—*Jason Hartlove*	2625 Hanover St, Palo Alto CA 94304		R	3*	<.1
375	PowerTech Inc—*Jonathan Scott*	360 E South St, Collierville TN 38017	901-850-9393	R	3*	<.1
376	Svt Associates Inc—*Peter Chow*	7620 Executive Dr, Eden Prairie MN 55344	952-934-2100	R	3*	<.1
377	Dynatex International—*Kate Henry*	5577 Skylane Blvd, Santa Rosa CA 95403	707-542-4227	R	3*	<.1
378	Reaction Technology Inc—*James Jacobson*	3400 Bassett St, Santa Clara CA 95054	408-970-9601	R	3*	<.1
379	Commtech Inc—*Arthur Alvis*	9011 E 37th St N, Wichita KS 67226	316-636-1131	R	3*	<.1
380	Aptek Industries Inc—*Bud Flesher*	414-F Umbarger Rd, San Jose CA 95111	408-363-8026	R	3*	<.1
381	HTE Research Inc—*Steve Szirom*	PO Box 2812, Bellingham WA 98227	360-676-2260	R	3*	<.1
382	Mok Industries LLC	4449 Easton Way, Columbus OH 43219	614-934-1734	R	3*	<.1
383	Crystal Deltronic Industries Inc—*Stuart Samuelson*	60 Harding Ave, Dover NJ 07801	973-361-2222	R	3*	<.1
384	Aptos Corp—*Benson Chao*	360 Kiely Blvd Ste 250, San Jose CA 95129	408-273-0390	R	3*	<.1

Note: An asterisk (*) indicates an estimated financial figure. The company type code used is as follows: R = Private, P = Public, S = Private Subsidiary, B = Public Subsidiary, D = Division, J = Joint Venture, I = Investment Fund.

COMPANY RANKINGS BY SALES WITHIN 4-DIGIT SIC

Rank	Company Name—*Executive Officer*	Address, City, State, Zip	Phone	Type	Fin	Empls
385	Hi-Rel Products Inc—*Thomas Dolan*	PO Box 116, Essex CT 06426	860-767-9031	R	3*	<.1
386	M-Pulse Microwave Inc—*Billy Long*	576 Charcot Ave, San Jose CA 95131	408-432-1480	R	3*	<.1
387	Micro-Hybrid Dimensions Inc—*Ted Meyers*	PO Box 7398, Tempe AZ 85281	480-731-3131	R	3*	<.1
388	Evans Components Inc—*Robert Evans*	7606 Sw Bridgeport Rd, Portland OR 97224	971-249-1600	R	3*	<.1
389	Control Concepts Inc—*Stanley Kintigh*	7870 Park Dr, Chanhassen MN 55317	952-474-6200	R	3*	<.1
390	Ascent Solar Technologies Inc—*Ron Eller*	12300 N Grant St, Thornton CO 80241	720-872-5000	P	3	.1
391	Time Products Inc—*John Coley*	2150 W 6th Ave Ste H, Broomfield CO 80020	303-460-7481	R	3*	<.1
392	Semiconix Corp—*Serban Porumbescu*	2968 Scott Blvd, Santa Clara CA 95054	408-986-8026	R	3*	<.1
393	Marketplace Investors Inc—*Frank Wetmore*	17 Columbia St Ste 1, Swampscott MA 01907	781-592-4600	R	3*	<.1
394	Atek Products LLC—*James Bartel*	12730 Creek View Ave, Savage MN 55378	952-746-4066	R	2*	<.1
395	Hd Pacific Inc—*Eugene Ding*	4606 107th St Sw, Mukilteo WA 98275	425-481-3031	R	2*	<.1
396	Seminex Corp—*David Bean*	100 Corporate Pl Ste 4, Peabody MA 01960	978-278-3550	R	2*	<.1
397	Dan-Mar Inc—*James Heckelman*	10319 Wikel Rd, Huron OH 44839	419-433-4479	R	2*	<.1
398	Digital Light LLC	1801 Century Park E St, Los Angeles CA 90067	310-551-9999	R	2*	<.1
399	Diablo Industries—*Malcolm Hill*	2245 Meridian Blvd Ste, Minden NV 89423	775-782-1041	R	2*	<.1
400	Hi-Tron Semiconductor Corp—*Mel Lax*	85 Engineers Rd, Hauppauge NY 11788	631-231-1500	R	2*	<.1
401	Securus Enterprises—*Paul Agronin*	596 Club Dr, San Carlos CA 94070	650-802-0170	R	2*	<.1
402	Linear Integrated Systems Inc—*John Hall*	4042 Clipper Ct, Fremont CA 94538	510-490-9160	R	2*	<.1
403	Mesta Electronics Inc—*John Mandalakas*	11020 Parker Dr, Irwin PA 15642	412-754-3000	R	2*	<.1
404	Prime Solutions Inc—*Harry Moroyan*	4261 Business Ctr Dr, Fremont CA 94538	510-490-2299	R	2*	<.1
405	Epi Tech—*Phil Gier*	740 E Campbell Rd Ste, Richardson TX 75081	972-398-5500	R	2*	<.1
406	Kinetic Ceramics Inc—*Conal O'Neill*	26240 Industrial Blvd, Hayward CA 94545	510-264-2140	R	2*	<.1
407	Evergreen Avionics Inc—*Robert Hulle*	4870 Adohr Ln, Camarillo CA 93012	805-445-6492	R	2*	<.1
408	Dynawave Corp—*Rudy Kesner*	2520 Kaneville Ct, Geneva IL 60134	630-232-4945	R	2*	<.1
409	Stedham Electronics Corp—*David Stedham*	4900 Mill St Bldg A-4, Reno NV 89502	775-826-2003	R	2*	<.1
410	Delta Technologies Ltd—*John Latza*	13960 N 47th St, Stillwater MN 55082	651-439-5741	R	2*	<.1
411	Micro Quality Semiconductor Inc Microsemi Corp	One Enterprise, Aliso Viejo CA 92656	949-380-6100	S	2*	<.1
412	WebGear Inc—*Tom Wagen*	1934 Old Gallows Rd 2n, Vienna VA 22182	703-532-1000	R	2*	<.1
413	Photosense LLC—*Alan Baron*	PO BOX 20687, Boulder CO 80308	303-449-8349	R	2*	<.1
414	Advanced Technology Marketing Inc (Orlando Florida)—*Jerry Herrington*	6005 Anno Ave, Orlando FL 32809	407-859-0127	R	2*	<.1
415	Vicor Industries Inc—*Isaac Gershoni*	225 County Rd, Tenafly NJ 07670	201-569-5001	R	2*	<.1
416	International Sensor Systems Inc—*Wayne Roblee*	PO Box 345, Aurora NE 68818	402-694-6111	R	2*	<.1
417	Semiconductor Components Inc—*Archie Brainard*	1353 E Edinger Ave, Santa Ana CA 92705	714-547-6059	R	2*	<.1
418	1366 Technologies Inc—*Frank Mierlo*	45 Hartwell Ave, Lexington MA 02421	781-861-1611	R	2*	<.1
419	Advance Data Technology Inc—*Scott Gaskell*	PO Box 791, Gloucester MA 01931	978-768-6913	R	2*	<.1
420	Accumetrics Associates Inc—*John Reschovsky*	409 Front St, Schenectady NY 12305	518-393-2200	R	2*	<.1
421	Jtm Technologies Inc—*Keisha Joyce*	204 Industrial Ct, Wylie TX 75098	972-429-6575	R	2*	<.1
422	Laurell Technologies Corp—*Kenneth Valeri*	441 Industrial Dr, North Wales PA 19454	215-699-7278	R	2*	<.1
423	Halcyon Microelectronics Inc—*Patricia Martin*	5467 2nd St, Irwindale CA 91706	626-814-4688	R	2*	<.1
424	Ion Beam Milling Of New Hampshire Inc—*Robert Quagan*	850 E Industrial Park, Manchester NH 03109	603-644-2326	R	2*	<.1
425	Siliconians Inc—*Sukgi Choi*	558 Arboleda Dr, Los Altos CA 94024	650-917-2300	R	2*	<.1
426	Gps Source Inc—*Robert Horton*	64 N Mission Dr, Pueblo West CO 81007	719-561-9520	R	2*	<.1
427	Jerry Van Dierendonck Inc—*Jerry Dierendonck*	2266 Trade Zone Blvd, San Jose CA 95131	408-263-7704	R	2*	<.1
428	Thousand Oaks Micro Systems Inc—*Lamont Hsieh*	22845 Savi Ranch Pkwy, Yorba Linda CA 92887	714-998-6688	R	2*	<.1
429	Birdsall Tool and Gage Co—*David Birdsall*	24735 Crestview Ct, Farmington Hills MI 48335	248-474-5150	R	2*	<.1
430	Vertitron Midwest Inc—*John Romnes*	19336 607th Ave, Mankato MN 56001	507-245-3399	R	2*	<.1
431	Wavelength Electronics Inc—*Mary Knighton*	PO Box 865, Bozeman MT 59771	406-587-4910	R	2*	<.1
432	Headway Research Inc—*Vern Shipman*	3713 Forest Ln, Garland TX 75042	972-272-5431	R	2*	<.1
433	Super Conductor Materials Inc—*Aftab Dar*	PO Box 701, Tallman NY 10982	845-368-0240	R	2*	<.1
434	Wafer World Inc—*Sean Quinn*	1100 Tech Pl Ste 104, West Palm Beach FL 33407	561-842-4441	R	2*	<.1
435	Sitek Process Solutions—*Jim Mullany*	233 Technology Way Ste, Rocklin CA 95765	916-797-9000	R	2*	<.1
436	Accutek Microcircuit Corp—*George Northover*	5 New Pasture Rd, Newburyport MA 01950	978-465-6200	R	2*	<.1
437	Iden Industries Inc—*Lee Iden*	45 Valley View Dr, Morristown NJ 07960	973-540-9027	R	1*	<.1
438	Applied Wireless Inc—*David Nichols*	1250 Avenida Acaso Ste, Camarillo CA 93012	805-383-9600	R	1*	<.1
439	Automated Control Logic Inc—*Preston Bruenn*	578 Commerce St, Thornwood NY 10594	914-769-8880	R	1*	<.1
440	Bold Plastics Inc—*Dennis Mortensen*	PO Box 460, West Jordan UT 84084	801-568-7300	R	1*	<.1
441	Logic Devices Inc—*William J Volz*	1375 Geneva Dr, Sunnyvale CA 94089	408-542-5400	P	1	<.1
442	Lextel Manufacturing LLC	931 Hwy 80 W Unit 112, Jackson MS 39204	601-713-8350	R	1*	<.1
443	MC Systems Inc—*Dan Bough*	2412 Richland Ave Ste, Dallas TX 75234	972-247-6785	R	1*	<.1
444	Practical Applied Computer Technology Inc—*Ronin Colman*	PO Box 535025, Grand Prairie TX 75053	972-641-0049	R	1*	<.1
445	Pixelligent Technologies LLC—*Craig Bandes*	387 Tchnology Dr Ste 3, College Park MD 20742	301-405-9284	R	1*	<.1
446	Thaler Corp—*Douglas Moore*	2015 N Forbes Blvd Ste, Tucson AZ 85745	520-882-4000	R	1*	<.1
447	Thermoptics Inc—*Lynn Phalan*	1004 Mallory Way, Carson City NV 89701	775-882-7721	R	1*	<.1
448	Micro-Precision Technologies Inc—*Etang Chen*	10 Manor Pkwy Ste C, Salem NH 03079	603-893-7600	R	1*	<.1
449	Sierra Custom Electronics Inc—*Gary Brines*	1813 Rutan Dr Ste A, Livermore CA 94551	925-449-1017	R	1*	<.1
450	Total Measurement Solutions LLC—*Ann Meche*	132 Capitol Blvd, Houma LA 70360	985-346-9000	R	1*	<.1
451	Futurefab Inc—*Derek Small*	1209 Ave N Ste 12, Plano TX 75074	972-423-6606	R	1*	<.1
452	International Radiation Detectors Inc—*Raj Korde*	2527 W 237th St Ste A, Torrance CA 90505	310-534-3661	R	1*	<.1
453	Qmagiq LLC—*Axel Reisenger*	22 Cotton Rd Ste 180, Nashua NH 03063	603-821-3092	R	1*	<.1
454	Miller Design and Equipment LLC	PO Box 5071, Bend OR 97708	541-317-1020	R	1*	<.1
455	NeoMagic Corp—*Syed Zaidi*	2372 A Qume Dr, San Jose CA 95131	408-428-9725	P	1	<.1
456	Harrison Electro Mechanical Corp—*William Piegari*	1607 Coach St, Rahway NJ 07065	732-382-6008	R	1*	<.1
457	Amest Corp—*John Iest*	30394 Esperanza, Rcho Sta Marg CA 92688	949-766-9692	R	1*	<.1
458	Foresight Processing LLC	1301 W Geneva Dr, Tempe AZ 85282	480-966-8180	R	1*	<.1
459	Future Tek Inc—*Kim Brock*	663 S Frontage Rd, Columbus MS 39701	662-328-0900	R	1*	<.1
460	Cosemi Technologies Inc—*Adrian Collins*	17110 Armstrong Ave, Irvine CA 92614	949-623-9816	R	1*	<.1
461	Douglas Electronics Inc—*Chad Pennebaker*	2777 Alvarado St, San Leandro CA 94577	510-483-8770	R	1*	<.1
462	Microtechnologies Inc—*Frank Geissler*	PO Box 7068, Plainville CT 06062	860-829-2710	R	1*	<.1
463	Vartek Corp—*Vincent Shaker*	420 S Perry Ln Ste 5, Tempe AZ 85281	480-968-6661	R	1*	<.1
464	Applied Systems Inc (Deerfield Beach Florida)—*Russell A Jones Jr*	1035 Gateway Blvd Stew, Boynton Beach FL 33426	954-233-2772	R	1*	<.1
465	Auctor Corp—*WEI-Tau Chiang*	3333 Bowers Ave Ste 24, Santa Clara CA 95054	408-980-0622	R	1*	<.1
466	Astralite—*Robert Yu*	PO Box 91, Brookfield CT 06804	203-775-0172	R	1*	<.1
467	JX Crystals Inc—*Lewis M Fraas*	1105 12th Ave NW Ste A, Issaquah WA 98027	425-392-5237	R	1*	<.1
468	Sencer Inc—*David Burt*	1 Keuka Business Park, Penn Yan NY 14527	315-536-3474	R	1*	<.1
469	Cogent Computer Systems Inc—*Ming Hsieh*	17 Industrial Dr, Smithfield RI 02917	401-349-3999	R	1*	<.1
470	Eyepvideo Systems LLC	25 Olde Rd, Danville NH 03819	603-382-2547	R	1*	<.1
471	Kadco Ceramics—*Ken Sherwood*	1175 Conroy Pl, Easton PA 18040	610-252-5424	R	1*	<.1

Rank	Company Name—*Executive Officer*	Address, City, State, Zip	Phone	Type	Fin	Empls
472	Symmetric Research—*Kip Wyss*	9101 W Sahara Ave Ste, Las Vegas NV 89117	702-341-9325	R	1*	<.1
473	Impellimax Inc—*Phil Cassista*	375 W Hollis St, Nashua NH 03060	603-886-9569	R	1*	<.1
474	Advin Systems Inc—*Wing Hui*	556 E Weddell Dr Ste 8, Sunnyvale CA 94089	408-541-9004	R	1*	<.1
475	Osemi Inc—*David Braddock*	250 Hwy 19, Red Wing MN 55066	507-285-4490	R	1*	<.1
476	Sundew Technologies LLC—*Moshe Sne*	3400 Industrial Ln Uni, Broomfield CO 80020	303-466-2341	R	1*	<.1
477	Betatron Inc—*Michael Young*	1722 Ringwood Ave, San Jose CA 95131	408-453-1880	R	1*	<.1
478	Elite Semi Conductor Products—*Robert Kravitz*	860 N Richmond Ave, Lindenhurst NY 11757	631-884-8400	R	1*	<.1
479	Intrabay Automation Inc—*Paul Whalen*	4 Harris Ct, Monterey CA 93940	408-588-4600	R	1*	<.1
480	Crosslink Technologies Inc—*Peter Chen*	20863 Stevens Creek Bl, Cupertino CA 95014	408-982-1899	R	1*	<.1
481	Brumley South Inc—*Thomas Norment*	PO Box 1237, Mooresville NC 28115	704-664-9251	R	1*	<.1
482	Florida Micro Devices Inc—*Francisco Miro*	PO Box 970260, Coconut Creek FL 33097	954-973-7200	R	1*	<.1
483	Universal Semiconductor Inc—*Vic Hejmadi*	1925 Zanker Rd, San Jose CA 95112	408-436-1906	R	1*	<.1
484	Dionics Inc—*Bernard Kravitz*	65 Rushmore St, Westbury NY 11590	516-997-7474	P	1	<.1
485	East Texas Integrated Circuits—*Ben Wagner*	275 W Campbell Rd Ste, Richardson TX 75080	972-234-5656	R	1*	<.1
486	Western Semi Solutions Inc—*Steven Javinett*	2942 N Grfield Rd Ste, Mesa AZ 85215	480-218-4645	R	1*	<.1
487	Euvis—*Neng Sheng*	685 Cochran St Ste 160, Simi Valley CA 93065	805-583-9888	R	1*	<.1
488	Maier Electronics Inc—*Siegfried Maier*	PO Box 890, Manchester Center VT 05255	802-362-1042	R	1*	<.1
489	B-Tron Corp—*Elena Skitskaia*	235 N Rte 73, West Berlin NJ 08091	856-719-8485	R	1*	<.1
490	Ht Microanalytical Inc—*Todd Christenson*	3817 Academy Pky S Ne, Albuquerque NM 87109	505-341-0466	R	1*	<.1
491	Remote Processing Corp—*Jim Rogo*	7975 E Harvard Ave Ste, Denver CO 80231	303-690-1588	R	1*	<.1
492	Solarmer Energy Inc—*Edward Chen*	3445 Fletcher Ave, El Monte CA 91731	626-456-8090	R	1*	<.1
493	Crystaltech Inc—*Charles Totty*	PO Box 56, Duncan OK 73534	580-252-8893	R	1*	<.1
494	Sonic Technology Products Inc—*Justin Reinholz*	120 Richardson St Ste, Grass Valley CA 95945	530-272-4607	R	1*	<.1
495	Bill And Amanda Hollibaugh—*Bill Hollibaugh*	PO Box 864, Petaluma CA 94953	707-763-6173	R	<1*	<.1
496	K and Us Equipment Inc—*Monty Kurek*	13350 W Park Ave Ste B, Boulder Creek CA 95006	831-338-7246	R	<1*	<.1
497	Newcastle Industries Inc—*Manoo Moheban*	2664 S La Cienega Blvd, Los Angeles CA 90034	310-845-1555	R	<1*	<.1
498	Print Tek—*Asghar Shah*	176 8 Central Ave, Farmingdale NY 11735	631-454-0014	R	<1*	<.1
499	Applied Thermal Systems Inc—*Donald Berg*	4121 Ellison St Ne Ste, Albuquerque NM 87109	505-217-0518	R	<1*	<.1
500	Sentinel Power Inc—*Kenneth Thomas*	922 Middletown Rd, New Stanton PA 15672	724-925-8181	R	<1*	<.1
501	Cintel Corp—*Dave Kyung Han*	1101 Marycrest Rd Ste, Henderson NV 89074	702-403-9577	P	<1	<.1
502	Iaq Energy Solutions Inc—*Daniel Young*	12401 Palmsprings Dr, Houston TX 77034	713-944-4801	R	<1*	<.1
503	Electro Assembly Source Inc—*Robert Seiler*	602 Sciandro Dr, Greensburg PA 15601	724-838-7023	R	<1*	<.1
504	Rochester Electronics LLC—*Dick Boissonneault*	16 Malcolm Hoyt Dr, Newburyport MA 01950	978-462-9332	R	<1*	<.1
505	AuGrid Global Holdings Corp—*Muhammad J Shaheed*	5847 San Felipe Ste 17, Houston TX 77057	713-821-1755	P	<1	<.1
506	Apogee Technology Inc—*Herbert M Stein*	129 Morgan Dr, Norwood MA 02062	781-551-9450	P	<1	<.1
507	Cascade Technologies Corp—*Daniel L Farkas*	250 N Robertson Blvd S, Beverly Hills CA 90211	310-858-1670	P	<1	<.1
508	Alliance Semiconductor Corp—*Melvin Keating*	4633 Old Ironsides Dr, Santa Clara CA 95054	408-855-4900	P	<1	<.1
509	Spatializer Audio Laboratories Inc—*Jay Gottlieb*	410 Park Ave Fl 15, New York NY 10022	212-231-8359	P	<1	<.1
510	Solarflare Communications Inc—*Russell Stern*	9501 Jeronimo Rd Ste 2, Irvine CA 92618	949-581-6830	R	N/A	<.1

TOTALS: SIC 3674 Semiconductors & Related Devices
Companies: 510

					209,257	536.1

3675 Electronic Capacitors

Rank	Company Name—*Executive Officer*	Address, City, State, Zip	Phone	Type	Fin	Empls
1	Vishay Vitramon Inc—*Gerald Paul*	One Greenwich Place, Shelton CT 06484	402-563-6866	S	4,995	27.9
2	AVX Corp—*John S Gilbertson*	1 AVX Blvd, Fountain Inn SC 29644	864-967-2150	B	1,653	11.2
3	KFMET Corp—*Per-Olof Loof*	PO Box 5928, Greenville SC 29606	864-963-6300	P	1,019	11.0
4	KEMET Electronics Corp KEMET Corp	PO Box 5928, Greenville SC 29606	864-963-6300	S	697	10.0
5	AVX Tantalum Corp—*Willie King* AVX Corp	401 Hill St, Biddeford ME 04005	207-282-5111	S	420	.1
6	Aerovox Division PPC—*Robert D Elliott*	167 John Vertente Blvd, New Bedford MA 02745	508-994-9661	S	412*	1.6
7	Philips Medical Systems Hsg—*Jorod Klesterkei*	3000 Minuteman Rd Bldg, Andover MA 01810	978-687-1501	R	144*	2.5
8	Beckwith Electric Company Inc—*Bob Beckwith*	6190 118th Ave N, Largo FL 33773	727-544-2326	R	60*	.2
9	Novacap Inc—*Joe Elias*	25136 Anza Dr, Valencia CA 91355	661-295-5920	S	51	.5
10	Cornell-Dubilier Electronics Inc—*James Kaplan*	140 Technology Pl, Liberty SC 29657	864-843-2626	R	28*	.5
11	TDK Corporation of America—*John Nelson*	1221 E Business Ctr Dr, Mount Prospect IL 60056	847-803-6100	S	24*	.2
12	Johanson Dielectrics Inc—*Norman Johanson*	PO Box 923697, Sylmar CA 91392	818-364-9800	R	24*	.2
13	Nemco Electronics Corp—*John Nolan*	675 Mariners Island Bl, San Mateo CA 94404	650-571-1234	R	15*	.2
14	Johanson Manufacturing Corp—*Nancy Johanson*	301 Rockaway Valley Rd, Boonton NJ 07005	973-334-2676	R	14*	.1
15	Presidio Components Inc—*Violet Devoe*	7169 Construction Ct, San Diego CA 92121	858-578-9390	R	14*	.1
16	Radio Frequency Intertronics Corp—*Walter F Schneider*	100 Pine Aire Dr, Bayshore NY 11706	631-231-6400	S	14*	.1
17	ASC Capacitors—*Stacey Bauer*	301 W O St, Ogallala NE 69153	308-284-3611	S	13*	.2
18	Richey Capacitor Inc—*R Richey*	PO Box 100296, Nashville TN 37224	615-254-3561	R	13*	.2
19	Steinerfilm Inc—*Else Steiner*	987 Simonds Rd, Williamstown MA 01267	413-458-9525	R	13*	.2
20	Dearborn Electronics Inc—*James Sherry*	1221 N Us Hwy 17 92, Longwood FL 32750	407-695-6562	R	12*	.1
21	Circuit Components Inc—*Robert A Greenman*	2400 S Roosevelt St, Tempe AZ 85282	480-967-0624	R	11*	.1
22	Electronic Concepts Inc—*Bill Levin*	PO Box 1278, Eatontown NJ 07724	732-542-7880	R	9*	.1
23	Zf Array Technology Inc—*Robert Zinn*	1965 Concourse Dr, San Jose CA 95131	408-433-9920	R	8*	.1
24	Custom Electronics Inc—*Michael Pentares*	87 Browne St, Oneonta NY 13820	607-432-3880	R	7*	.1
25	Voltronics Corp—*Carol Willard*	100 Ford Rd Ste 10, Denville NJ 07834	973-586-8585	R	5*	<.1
26	Electronic Film Capacitors Inc—*Jay Weiner*	41 Interstate Ln, Waterbury CT 06705	203-755-5629	R	5*	<.1
27	Oren Elliott Products Inc—*June Elliott*	PO Box 638, Edgerton OH 43517	419-298-2306	R	5*	<.1
28	Metuchen Capacitors Inc—*Stephen Ficsor*	2139 State Rte 35 Ste, Holmdel NJ 07733	732-888-9700	R	4*	<.1
29	ITW Paktron Inc—*David B Speer*	1205 McConville Rd, Lynchburg VA 24502	434-239-6941	D	4*	<.1
30	Virgil Walker Inc—*Virgil Walker*	27555 Ave Scott, Valencia CA 91355	661-257-9282	R	4*	<.1
31	Tantalum Pellet Company Inc—*Todd Knowles*	21421 N 14th Ave Ste A, Phoenix AZ 85027	623-582-5555	R	4*	<.1
32	Arco Electronics Inc—*Bing Feng*	450 Goddard, Irvine CA 92618	949-789-8888	R	3*	<.1
33	Corry Micronics Inc—*Don Pavlek*	1 Plastics Rd Ste 1a, Corry PA 16407	814-664-7728	R	3*	<.1
34	Sigma Probe Inc—*Thang Vo*	1054 Yosemite Dr, Milpitas CA 95035	408-441-8183	R	3*	<.1
35	Wright Capacitors Inc—*Casey Crandall*	2610 Oak St, Santa Ana CA 92707	714-546-2490	R	3*	<.1
36	Bishop Electronics Corp—*William Bishop*	3729 Sn Gbrl Rvr Pkwy, Pico Rivera CA 90660	562-695-0446	R	2*	<.1
37	Csi Technologies Inc—*Gary Geiser*	2540 Fortune Way, Vista CA 92081	760-682-2222	R	2*	<.1
38	Custom Capacitors Inc—*Jeffrey Fielder*	2131 Broad St, Brooksville FL 34604	352-796-3561	R	2*	<.1
39	American Capacitor Corp—*Joseph Latourelle*	5367 3rd St, Irwindale CA 91706	626-814-4444	R	2*	<.1
40	Bycap Inc—*Kenneth Yahiro*	5505 N Wolcott Ave, Chicago IL 60640	773-561-4976	R	2*	<.1
41	Tdl Inc—*Tobe Deutschmann*	550 Tpke St, Canton MA 02021	781-828-3366	R	2*	<.1
42	Tronser Inc—*Michael Tronser*	3066 John Trush Jr Blv, Cazenovia NY 13035	315-655-9528	R	1*	<.1
43	High Voltage Components Inc—*Ronald Nielsen*	PO Box 223, Cedarburg WI 53012	262-375-0172	R	1*	<.1

Note: An asterisk (*) indicates an estimated financial figure. The company type code used is as follows: R = Private, P = Public, S = Private Subsidiary, B = Public Subsidiary, D = Division, J = Joint Venture, I = Investment Fund.

COMPANY RANKINGS BY SALES WITHIN 4-DIGIT SIC

Rank	Company Name—*Executive Officer*	Address, City, State, Zip	Phone	Type	Fin	Empls
44	Hi-Rel Capacitors Inc—*Basilio Lim*	12931 Sunnyside Pl, Santa Fe Springs CA 90670	562-946-8577	R	<1*	<.1

TOTALS: SIC 3675 Electronic Capacitors
Companies: 44

					9,723	67.8

3676 Electronic Resistors

Rank	Company Name—*Executive Officer*	Address, City, State, Zip	Phone	Type	Fin	Empls
1	Dahua Electronics Corp—*Gomita Junkiji*	13412 59th Ave, Flushing NY 11355	718-886-2188	R	156*	<.1
2	Rcd Components Inc—*Louis Arcidy*	520 E Industrial Park, Manchester NH 03109	603-669-0054	R	38*	.4
3	International Resistive Company Inc—*John Nelson*	PO Box 1860, Boone NC 28607	828-264-8861	S	19*	.4
4	Caddock Electronics Inc—*Richard Caddock*	1717 Chicago Ave, Riverside CA 92507	951-788-1700	R	18*	.2
5	Prime Technology LLC—*Jim Kelly*	PO Box 185, North Branford CT 06471	203-481-5721	R	16*	.2
6	Riedon Inc—*Michael Zoeller*	300 Cypress Ave, Alhambra CA 91801	626-284-9901	R	16*	.2
7	Mini-Systems Inc—*Glen Robertson*	PO Box 69, North Attleboro MA 02761	508-695-0203	R	15*	.2
8	Stackpole Electronics Inc—*Kesao Akahane*	PO Box 58789, Raleigh NC 27658	919-850-9500	R	15*	<.1
9	State of the Art Inc—*Bob Hufnagel*	2470 Fox Hill Rd, State College PA 16803	814-355-8004	R	14*	.2
10	USSensor Corp—*Roger Dankert*	1832 W Collins Ave, Orange CA 92867	714-639-1000	R	11*	.1
11	Micropen Technologies Corp—*Edwin Petrazzolo*	93 Papermill St, Honeoye Falls NY 14472	585-624-2610	R	10*	.1
12	Powerohm Resistors Inc—*Vance Hinton*	PO Box 537, Katy TX 77492	281-391-6800	R	8*	.1
13	Polymer Products Company Inc—*Paritosh Chakrabarti*	PO Box 98, Stockertown PA 18083	610-759-3690	R	7*	.1
14	International Manufacturing Services Inc—*Thomas Moakley*	50 Schoolhouse Ln, Portsmouth RI 02871	401-683-9700	R	6*	<.1
15	Bantry Components Inc—*Bernard Perry*	160 Bouchard St, Manchester NH 03103	603-668-3210	R	5*	.1
16	Servo Instrument Corp—*Gordon R Glorch Sr*	PO Box 43, Baraboo WI 53913	608-356-6623	R	5*	.1
17	Tepro Florida Inc—*Roger C Mayo*	PO Box 18802, Clearwater FL 33757	727-796-1044	S	5*	.1
18	Ametherm Inc—*Eric Rauch*	3111 N Deer Run Rd Ste, Carson City NV 89701	775-884-2434	R	4*	<.1
19	Precision Resistive Products Inc—*Oscar Cline*	PO Box 189, Mediapolis IA 52637	319-394-9131	R	4*	.1
20	Precision Resistor Company Inc—*Fred Dusenberry*	10601 75th St, Largo FL 33777	727-541-5771	R	4*	<.1
21	K-Tronics Inc—*Robert Kidder* Stackpole Electronics Inc	PO Box 4398, Bisbee AZ 85603	520-432-5388	S	3*	.2
22	Component General Inc—*James Cook*	2445 Success Dr, Odessa FL 33556	727-376-6655	R	3*	<.1
23	Altronic Research Inc—*John Dyess*	PO Box 249, Yellville AR 72687	870-449-4093	R	3*	<.1
24	Wilbrecht Ledco Inc—*Markus Affolter*	1400 Energy Park Dr St, Saint Paul MN 55108	651-659-0919	R	2*	<.1
25	Maurey Instrument Corp—*M Maurey*	5959 W 115 St, Alsip IL 60803	708-388-9898	R	2*	<.1
26	Power Film Systems Inc—*John Dyess*	PO Box 249, Yellville AR 72687	870-449-4091	R	2*	<.1
27	Micro-Ohm Corp—*Byron Ritchey*	1088 Hamilton Rd, Duarte CA 91010	626-357-5377	R	2*	<.1
28	Gemini Controls LLC—*Gail Hoffman*	PO Box 380, Cedarburg WI 53012	262-377-8585	R	1*	<.1
29	Isotek Corp—*William Poisson*	1199 Gar Hwy, Swansea MA 02777	508-673-2900	R	1*	<.1
30	T And M Research Products Inc—*Buck Ingram*	139 Rhode Island St Ne, Albuquerque NM 87108	505-268-0316	R	1*	<.1

TOTALS: SIC 3676 Electronic Resistors
Companies: 30

					395	2.7

3677 Electronic Coils & Transformers

Rank	Company Name—*Executive Officer*	Address, City, State, Zip	Phone	Type	Fin	Empls
1	Bel Fuse Inc—*Daniel Bernstein*	206 Van Vorst St, Jersey City NJ 07302	201-432-0463	P	295	5.0
2	American Precision Industries—*Kevin Heffler*	270 Quaker Rd, East Aurora NY 14052	716-652-3600	S	195*	1.8
3	Babcock Inc	14930 E Alondra Blvd, La Mirada CA 90638	714-994-6500	S	145*	.2
4	Xfmrs Inc—*Cheri Imburgia*	7570 E Landersdale Rd, Camby IN 46113	317-834-1000	R	59*	1.1
5	USA Instruments Inc	1515 Danner Dr, Aurora OH 44202	330-562-1000	S	36*	.3
6	Hytronics Corp—*John Sollers*	PO Box 18802, Clearwater FL 33762	727-530-9555	R	35*	.4
7	Taiyo Yuden (USA) Inc	1930 N Thoreau Dr Ste, Schaumburg IL 60173	847-348-2496	S	33*	.2
8	Coils Inc—*James Plunkett*	PO Box 247, Huntley IL 60142	847-669-5115	R	23*	.5
9	South Haven Coil Inc—*Randall Webber*	05585 Blue Star Hwy, South Haven MI 49090	269-637-5201	S	20*	.2
10	Precision Inc—*David Anderson*	1800 Fwy Blvd, Minneapolis MN 55430	763-852-6700	R	18*	.1
11	Captor Corp—*Donald Cooper*	5040 S County Rd 25a, Tipp City OH 45371	937-667-8484	R	16*	.1
12	Quality Coils Inc—*Keith Gibson*	PO Box 1480, Bristol CT 06011	860-584-0927	R	16*	.2
13	Corona Magnetics Inc—*Uwe Paasch*	PO Box 1355, Corona CA 92878	951-735-7558	R	15*	.1
14	Todd Systems Inc—*SE Todd*	50 Ash St, Yonkers NY 10701	914-963-3400	R	14*	.1
15	Norlake Manufacturing Co—*James Markus*	PO Box 215, Elyria OH 44036	440-353-3200	R	12*	.1
16	Rayco Inc—*Deval Patel*	1220 W 130th St, Gardena CA 90247	310-329-2660	R	12*	.3
17	Tur-Bo Jet Products Company Inc—*Richard Bloom*	5025 Earle Ave, Rosemead CA 91770	626-285-1294	R	12*	.1
18	Qse Inc—*Anthony Imburgia*	PO Box 360, Watseka IL 60970	815-432-5281	R	12*	.2
19	Torotel Products Inc—*Herb Sizemore* Torotel Inc	620 N Lindenwood Dr, Olathe KS 66062	913-747-6111	S	12*	.1
20	Power Distribution Inc—*Rob Cannon*	4200 Oakleys Ln, Richmond VA 23223	804-737-9880	R	12*	.1
21	Bh Electronics Inc—*Richard Jackson*	12219 Wood Lake Dr Ste, Burnsville MN 55337	952-894-9590	R	12*	.1
22	Torotel Inc—*Dale H Sizemore Jr*	620 N Lindenwood Dr, Olathe KS 66062	913-747-6111	P	11	.1
23	Warsaw Coil Company Inc—*Thomas Joyner*	PO Box 1057, Warsaw IN 46581	574-267-6041	R	11*	.1
24	Mohawk Electro Techniques Inc—*Lee Broomfield*	PO Box 144, Barneveld NY 13304	315-896-2661	R	10*	.1
25	Nova Magnetics Inc—*C Davis*	1101 E Walnut St, Garland TX 75040	972-272-8287	R	10*	.1
26	Ctm Magnetics Inc—*Kenneth Mac Lennan*	820 W Fairmont Dr, Tempe AZ 85282	480-967-9447	R	10*	.1
27	Coil-Tran Corp—*Nicholas Kriadis*	160 S Illinois St, Hobart IN 46342	219-942-8511	R	9*	.1
28	Cramer Coil and Transformer Company Inc—*Terrence Wilkinson*	PO Box 80200, Saukville WI 53080	262-268-2150	R	9*	.1
29	Payne Magnetics Corp—*Jon Payne*	854 W Front St, Covina CA 91722	626-332-6207	R	8*	.1
30	Robert M Hadley Company Inc—*Jim Hadley*	4054 Transport St Ste, Ventura CA 93003	805-658-7286	R	8*	.1
31	Electronic Design and Sales Inc—*Mark Gignac*	1 Eds Way, Danville VA 24540	434-822-5561	R	8*	.1
32	Classic Coil Company Inc—*Rudolf Zeidler*	205 Century Dr, Bristol CT 06010	860-583-7600	R	7*	.1
33	Marelco Power Systems Inc—*Robert Sweaney* Power Distribution Inc	PO Box 440, Howell MI 48844	517-546-6330	S	7*	.1
34	Taycorp Inc—*John Tyrakowski*	9221 Kilpatrick Ave, Oak Lawn IL 60453	708-422-3704	R	7*	.1
35	MC Davis Company LLC—*Robert Prescott*	PO Box 2269, Arizona City AZ 85223	520-466-5151	R	7*	<.1
36	Staco Energy Products Co—*Edward Kwiatkowski*	301 Gaddis Blvd, Dayton OH 45403	937-253-1191	S	7*	.1
37	Indiana Transformer Inc—*Angela Le*	905 S Westgate St, Addison IL 60101	630-543-7756	R	7*	.1
38	Communication Coil Inc—*Elliot Goldman*	9601 Soreng Ave, Schiller Park IL 60176	847-671-1333	R	7*	.1
39	Inglot Electronics Corp—*Christopher Inglot*	4878 N Elston Ave, Chicago IL 60630	773-286-5881	R	7*	.1
40	Si Manufacturing Inc—*James Reed*	1440 S Allec St, Anaheim CA 92805	714-956-7110	R	6*	.1
41	Mag Flux Corp—*Matt Davis*	1101 E Walnut St, Garland TX 75040	972-272-8576	R	6*	.1
42	Abbott Technologies Inc—*Kay Batte*	8203 Vineland Ave, Sun Valley CA 91352	818-504-0644	R	6*	.1
43	Rayco Electronic ManufacturingInc—*Deval Patel*	1220 W 130th St, Gardena CA 90247	310-329-0162	R	5*	.1
44	Transcon Technologies Inc—*Pablo Nyarady*	PO Box 1536, Westfield MA 01086	413-562-7684	R	5*	.1
45	Jmk Inc—*James Kennedy*	15 Caldwell Dr, Amherst NH 03031	603-886-4100	R	5*	.1
46	Electro Technik Industries—*Roger Mayo*	PO Box 18802, Clearwater FL 33762	727-536-7861	R	5*	<.1
47	Badger Magnetics Inc—*Richard Noel*	7939 W Tower Ave, Milwaukee WI 53223	414-362-4441	R	5*	.1

Rank	Company Name—*Executive Officer*	Address, City, State, Zip	Phone	Type	Fin	Empls
48	Spin Magnetics—*Howard Spence*	PO Box 752, Lake Wales FL 33859	863-676-9333	R	5*	.1
49	Iml Inc—*Michael Lanes*	5238 S 31st Pl, Phoenix AZ 85040	602-243-0010	R	5*	.1
50	Electronic Transformer Corp—*Martin Gorman*	460 Totowa Ave, Paterson NJ 07522	973-942-2222	R	5*	<.1
51	Coilform Co—*Richard Mc Farlane*	2571 Kaneville Ct, Geneva IL 60134	630-232-8000	R	5*	<.1
52	Frost Magnetics Inc—*Michael Frost*	49643 Hartwell Rd, Oakhurst CA 93644	559-642-2536	R	4*	<.1
53	Pca Electronics Inc—*Morris Weinberg*	16799 Schoenborn St, North Hills CA 91343	818-892-0761	R	4*	<.1
54	Stc Inc—*Brad Cross*	1201 W Randolph St, Mc Leansboro IL 62859	618-643-2555	R	4*	<.1
55	Hisonic Inc—*Jack Cooper*	PO Box 1130, Olathe KS 66051	913-782-0012	R	4*	.1
56	Gettysburg Transformer Corp—*Charles Ritter*	PO Box 4356, Gettysburg PA 17325	717-334-2191	R	4*	.1
57	Endicott Coil Company Inc	PO Box 67, Binghamton NY 13905	607-797-1263	R	4*	.1
58	Filtronetics Inc—*Edward Haber*	6010 Parretta Dr, Kansas City MO 64120	816-231-7375	R	4*	.1
59	Synder Inc—*Edward Yeh*	4941 Allison Pkwy, Vacaville CA 95688	707-451-6060	R	4*	<.1
60	Puroflux Corp—*Henry Greenberg*	2121 Union Pl, Simi Valley CA 93065	805-579-0216	R	4*	<.1
61	Isotemp Research Inc—*Sze Cha*	1750 Broadway St, Charlottesville VA 22902	434-295-3101	R	4*	<.1
62	Laconia Magnetics Inc—*Michael Southworth*	PO Box 1457, Laconia NH 03247	603-528-2766	R	4*	<.1
63	Filter Concepts Inc—*Lester Edelberg*	2624 Rousselle St, Santa Ana CA 92707	714-545-7003	R	4*	<.1
64	Tranex Inc—*Jerry Smith*	2350 Executive Cir, Colorado Springs CO 80906	719-576-7994	R	4*	<.1
65	Gulf Enterprises—*Andres Garibay*	9167 Independence Ave, Chatsworth CA 91311	818-998-7791	R	3*	<.1
66	Able Coil And Electronics Co—*Steven Rockfeller*	PO Box 9127, Bolton CT 06043	860-646-5686	R	3*	<.1
67	Muntz Industries Inc—*David Muntz*	710 Tower Rd, Mundelein IL 60060	847-949-8280	R	3*	<.1
68	Coil Specialty Company Inc—*Keith Krick*	2730 Carolean Industri, State College PA 16801	814-234-7044	R	3*	<.1
69	Cletronics Inc—*David Sands*	2262 Port Centre Dr, Medina OH 44256	330-239-2002	R	3*	<.1
70	Atlantic Magnetics Inc	1480 SW 3rd St, Pompano Beach FL 33069	954-786-0199	R	3*	<.1
71	Sureflex Inc—*Jim Schultz*	1122 Nw Valley Ridge D, Grain Valley MO 64029	816-847-6333	R	3*	<.1
72	Crest Manufacturing Company Inc—*Gary Hood*	PO Box 368, Lincoln RI 02865	401-333-1350	R	3*	<.1
73	Cemec Inc—*James Klouda*	1516 Centre Cir, Downers Grove IL 60515	630-495-9696	R	3*	<.1
74	Wjlp Company Inc—*Weyman Lundquist*	4848 Frontier Way Ste, Stockton CA 95215	209-944-0836	R	3*	<.1
75	Allied Components International—*Neal Mcdonald*	14712 Sinclair Cir Ste, Tustin CA 92780	714-665-1140	R	3*	<.1
76	Genisco Filter Corp—*G Zittle*	5466 Complex St Ste 20, San Diego CA 92123	858-565-7405	R	3*	<.1
77	Wintron Tech LLC—*Jack Nivison*	PO BOX 285, Milesburg PA 16853	814-625-2720	D	3	<.1
78	Mitchell Electronics Corp—*Nancy Lerner*	85 W Grand St, Mount Vernon NY 10552	914-699-3800	R	3*	<.1
79	Powertran Corp—*Thomas Schalk*	1605 Bonner St, Ferndale MI 48220	248-399-4300	R	3*	<.1
80	Leightner Electronics Inc—*Paul Leightner*	1501 S Tennessee St, Mckinney TX 75069	972-542-0176	R	3*	<.1
81	Filter Research Corp—*Ahmed El-Mahdawy*	PO Box 60898, Palm Bay FL 32906	321-676-3300	R	2*	<.1
82	Caddell Burns Manufacturing Company Inc—*Vincent Burns*	258 E 2nd St, Mineola NY 11501	516-746-2310	R	2*	<.1
83	Power-Volt Inc—*Brij Sharma*	PO Box 383, Addison IL 60101	630-628-9999	R	2*	<.1
84	Sub-Tronics Inc—*Peter Voysey*	501 Apollo Dr, Circle Pines MN 55014	651-288-0446	R	2*	<.1
85	Scotts Valley Magnetics Inc—*Norma Humphries*	PO Box 66575, Scotts Valley CA 95067	831-438-3600	R	2*	<.1
86	Bone Frontier Co—*Marvin Bone*	190 W Southern St, Brighton CO 80601	303-659-4611	R	2*	<.1
87	AMI/Coast Magnetics Inc—*Satya Dosaj*	5333 W Washington Blvd, Los Angeles CA 90016	323-936-6188	R	2*	<.1
88	Cal Coil Magnetics Inc—*Scott Alvarado*	2523 Seaman Ave, El Monte CA 91733	626-455-0011	R	2*	<.1
89	JW Miller Magnetics	PO Box 2859, Gardena CA 90247	310-515-1720	S	2*	<.1
90	Acutransformers Inc—*Robert Matusiak*	1711 Rte 588, Fombell PA 16123	724-452-4130	R	2*	<.1
91	Mil-Specialties Magnetics Inc—*Shelton Gunewardena*	169 Pacific St, Pomona CA 91768	909-598-8116	R	2*	<.1
92	MoxiE Inductor Corp	7545 Irvine Center Dr, Irvine CA 92618	949-623-8328	R	2*	<.1
93	MagneComp Inc—*Tim Sullivan*	PO Box 625, Pickens SC 29671	864-878-4700	R	2*	<.1
94	Schott Magnetics—*Rob Rosi*	1401 Air Wing Rd, San Diego CA 92154	507-223-5572	S	2*	<.1
95	Rodon Products Inc—*Hobert Bertels*	15481 Flectronic Ln St, Huntington Beach CA 92649	714-898-3528	R	2*	<.1
96	Wilco Corp—*Jerry Carroll*	5352 W 79th St, Indianapolis IN 46268	317-220-9020	R	2*	<.1
97	Emi Solutions Inc—*Bob Ydens*	15 Hammond Ste 304, Irvine CA 92618	949-206-9960	R	2*	<.1
98	Frontier Electronics Corp—*Winston Gu*	667 Cochran St, Simi Valley CA 93065	805-522-9998	R	2*	<.1
99	R H Barden Inc—*Richard Barden*	4769 E Wesley Dr, Anaheim CA 92807	714-970-0900	R	2*	<.1
100	Future Manufacturing Inc—*Denis Boroski*	PO Box 23, Bristol CT 06011	860-584-0685	R	2*	<.1
101	Magnetic Coil Manufacturing Co—*Joseph Sommer*	325 Beinoris Dr Ste A, Wood Dale IL 60191	630-787-1948	R	2*	<.1
102	Magnetic Technology Inc—*Sheila Burrow*	1627 Bray Central Dr, Mckinney TX 75069	214-544-2700	R	2*	<.1
103	Power Mate Technology Inc—*Tom Niu*	4677 Old Ironsides Dr, Santa Clara CA 95054	408-262-1279	R	2*	<.1
104	Atw Electronics Inc—*Jeffrey Spinks*	24 Spice St Ste 2, Charlestown MA 02129	617-241-0292	R	1*	<.1
105	Frequency Selective Networks Inc—*Julius Tischkewitsch*	5572 61st St, Maspeth NY 11378	718-424-7500	R	1*	<.1
106	Ahn Enterprises LLC—*Leon Gay*	1240 Birchwood Dr Ste, Sunnyvale CA 94089	408-734-1878	R	1*	<.1
107	Filter Systems Inc—*Tom Wright*	PO Box 328, Mazeppa MN 55956	386-304-0411	R	1*	<.1
108	Magtech and Power Conversion Inc—*Viet Pho*	1146 E Ash Ave, Fullerton CA 92831	714-451-0106	R	1*	<.1
109	HW Jencks Inc	2435 Hilton Rd, Ferndale MI 48220	248-398-5600	S	1*	<.1
110	Jackson Engineering Co—*Ron Jackson*	9411 Winnetka Ave, Chatsworth CA 91311	818-886-9567	R	1*	<.1
111	PC Transformer Corp—*Leo Goldstein*	64 Nancy St Unit D, West Babylon NY 11704	631-491-3300	R	1*	<.1
112	Componetics Inc—*Oscar Maldanido*	2373 Teller Rd Ste 106, Newbury Park CA 91320	805-498-0939	R	1*	<.1
113	Electronic Products Design Inc—*Devera Eggimann*	PO Box 1569, Wendell NC 27591	919-365-9199	R	1*	<.1
114	Air Filtration Systems LLC—*Christopher Gabriel*	35 Mayflower Rd, Eastham MA 02642	508-240-5453	R	1*	<.1
115	Wist Enterprises Inc—*Dennis Wist*	201 Pillow St, Butler PA 16001	724-283-7230	R	1*	<.1
116	Coils Unlimited Inc—*Justo Sardinas*	315 Gus Hipp Blvd, Rockledge FL 32955	321-631-0554	R	1*	<.1
117	Unifilt Corp—*Robert Eggleston*	PO Box 1627, Wilkes Barre PA 18705	570-823-0313	R	1*	<.1
118	Aer Control Systems LLC	90 River St Ste 1, New Haven CT 06513	203-772-4700	R	1*	<.1
119	AJ Smoy Company Inc—*Ronald Smoy*	5346 N NW Hwy, Chicago IL 60630	773-775-8282	R	1*	<.1
120	Rme Filters Inc—*Roger Martin*	PO Box 838, Amherst NH 03031	603-595-4573	R	1*	<.1
121	WS Deans Co—*Robin Deans*	10875 Portal Dr, Los Alamitos CA 90720	714-828-6494	R	1*	<.1
122	Coil-Q Corp—*Larry Julie*	340 Bronxville Rd, Bronxville NY 10708	914-337-4775	R	<1*	<.1
123	D and D Marine Enterprises Inc—*David Gauss*	176 Tracey Ln, Bagdad KY 40003	502-747-8562	R	<1*	<.1
124	Creative Waste Solutions Inc—*Rexford Johnson*	10848 Sw Tltin Shrwood, Tualatin OR 97062	503-783-0762	R	<1*	<.1
125	MV Mason Electronics Inc—*Matthew Marco*	486 High Plain St, Walpole MA 02081	508-668-6200	R	<1*	<.1
126	Delnetics Inc—*Pat Morris*	PO Box 3711, Hayward CA 94540	925-778-1607	R	<1*	<.1
127	Loadstar Sensors Inc—*Div Harish*	48089 Fremont Blvd, Fremont CA 94538	510-397-9911	R	<1*	<.1
128	Azonic Products Inc—*Maurice Brown*	502 W Main St, Albion NE 68620	402-395-5081	R	<1*	<.1
129	Kens Electronics—*Ken Brakey*	445 S Lincoln St, Ponca City OK 74601	580-765-8448	R	<1*	<.1

TOTALS: SIC 3677 Electronic Coils & Transformers
Companies: 129 — Fin: 1,374 — Empls: 15.2

3678 Electronic Connectors

Rank	Company Name—*Executive Officer*	Address, City, State, Zip	Phone	Type	Fin	Empls
1	Burndy LLC USA—*Pierre Valeille*	47 E Industrial Park D, Manchester NH 03109	603-647-5000	D	3,876*	14.0
2	Molex Inc—*Martin P Slark*	2222 Wellington Ct, Lisle IL 60532	630-969-4550	P	3,587	33.0
3	Amphenol Corp—*R Adam Norwitt*	PO Box 5030, Wallingford CT 06492	203-265-8900	P	3,554	39.1
4	Thomas and Betts Corp—*Dominic J Pileggi*	8155 T & B Blvd, Memphis TN 38125	901-252-8000	P	2,298	9.4

Note: An asterisk (*) indicates an estimated financial figure. The company type code used is as follows: R = Private, P = Public, S = Private Subsidiary, B = Public Subsidiary, D = Division, J = Joint Venture, I = Investment Fund.

COMPANY RANKINGS BY SALES WITHIN 4-DIGIT SIC

Rank	Company Name—*Executive Officer*	Address, City, State, Zip	Phone	Type	Fin	Empls
5	JST Corp—*Teiji Takahashi*	1957 S Lakeside Dr, Waukegan IL 60085	847-473-1957	R	680*	.1
6	Methode Electronics Inc—*Donald W Duda*	7401 W Wilson Ave, Chicago IL 60706	708-867-6777	P	428	2.7
7	Everett Charles Technologies Inc—*Patrick T Flynn*	700 E Harrison Ave, Pomona CA 91767	909-625-5551	S	216*	.9
8	Pei/ Genesis Inc—*Steven Fisher*	2180 Hornig Rd Ste 2, Philadelphia PA 19116	215-673-0400	R	175*	.5
9	ITT Industries Inc Cannon Div—*Gerard Gendron*	666 E Dyer Rd, Santa Ana CA 92705	714-557-4700	D	161	1.1
10	Deutsch Engineered Connecting Devices Inc—*Jean-Marie Painvin*	3850 Industrial Ave, Hemet CA 92545	951-765-2250	R	147*	1.9
11	Ideal Industries Inc (Sycamore Illinois)—*Jim James*	1 W Becker Pl, Sycamore IL 60178		R	139*	1.2
12	Powell Electronics Inc—*Ernest Schilling*	200 Commodore Dr, Swedesboro NJ 08085	856-241-8000	R	99*	.2
13	Radiall America Inc—*Dominique Buttin*	6825 W Galveston St St, Chandler AZ 85226	480-682-9400	R	90*	.2
14	Switchcraft Inc—*Laurans A Mendelson*	5555 N Elston Ave, Chicago IL 60630	773-792-2700	S	75*	.5
15	Mill-Max Manufacturing Corp—*James Litke*	PO Box 300, Oyster Bay NY 11771	516-922-6000	R	55*	.2
16	Molex Inc Industrial Div—*Martin P Slark* Molex Inc	4650 62nd Ave N, Pinellas Park FL 33781	727-521-2700	D	39*	.4
17	Conxall Corp—*Rob Smith* Switchcraft Inc	601 E Wildwood Ave, Villa Park IL 60181	630-834-7504	S	34*	.2
18	Abelconn LLC—*Bobbi Becchetti*	9210 Science Ctr Dr, Minneapolis MN 55428	763-533-3533	R	28*	.2
19	Virginia Panel Corp—*Kimball Stowers*	1400 New Hope Rd, Waynesboro VA 22980	540-932-3300	R	23*	.2
20	Omnetics Connector Corp—*Gerald Simonson*	7260 Commerce Cir E, Minneapolis MN 55432	763-572-0656	R	23*	.1
21	Pennatronics Corp—*Ralph Andy*	PO Box 638, California PA 15419	724-938-1800	R	23*	.1
22	RF Industries Ltd—*Howard F Hill*	7610 Miramar Rd, San Diego CA 92126	858-549-6340	P	19	.2
23	Valdor Fiber Optics—*Michel Rondeau*	3116 Diablo Ave, Hayward CA 94545	510-293-1212	R	19*	.1
24	J - T E C H—*Walter Naubauer*	548 Amapola Ave, Torrance CA 90501	310-533-6700	R	19*	.3
25	Cristek Interconnects Inc—*Cristi Cristich*	5395 E Hunter Ave, Anaheim CA 92807	714-696-5200	R	18*	.1
26	Keystone Electronics Corp—*Richard David*	3107 20th Rd, Astoria NY 11105	718-956-8900	R	15*	.1
27	Bel Stewart Connector	11118 Susquehanna Trl, Glen Rock PA 17327	717-235-7512	S	14*	.1
28	IEH Corp—*Michael Offerman*	140 58th St Ste 8E, Brooklyn NY 11220	718-492-4448	P	14	.1
29	RF Connectors—*Howard Hill* RF Industries Ltd	7610 Miramar Rd Bldg 6, San Diego CA 92126	858-549-6340	D	12*	.1
30	EBY Holding Co—*Dennis Savine*	4300 H St, Philadelphia PA 19124	215-537-4700	R	12*	.1
31	PAVE Technology Co—*Steve Jones*	2751 Thunderhawk Ct, Dayton OH 45414	937-890-1100	R	12*	.1
32	Johnstech International Corp—*David Johnson*	1210 New Brighton Blvd, Minneapolis MN 55413	612-378-2020	R	11*	.1
33	Kemlon Products and Development Company Inc—*Russell Ring*	PO Box 2189, Pearland TX 77588	281-997-3300	R	11*	.2
34	Array Connector Corp—*William Mcpherson*	12400 Sw 134th Ct Ste, Miami FL 33186	305-234-1000	R	11*	.1
35	Component Equipment Co Inc—*Bill Rigby*	3050 Camino Del Sol, Oxnard CA 93030	805-484-0149	R	9*	.1
36	Fujipoly America Corp—*Frank Hobler*	PO Box 119, Carteret NJ 07008	732-969-0100	R	9*	<.1
37	Communication Con Connectors Inc—*Robert Farnum*	1855 Business Center D, Duarte CA 91010	626-301-4200	R	9*	.1
38	San-Tron Inc—*Wayne Sanders*	4 Newbury Port Tpke, Ipswich MA 01938	978-356-1585	R	9*	.1
39	Eagle Design Group LLC—*Walter Schroth*	45 Senn Dr, Chester Springs PA 19425	610-321-2488	R	8*	<.1
40	Circuit Assembly Corp—*Roger Lang*	18 Thomas, Irvine CA 92618	949-855-7887	R	7*	.1
41	R Kern Engineering and Manufacturing Corp—*Richard Kern*	13912 Mountain Ave, Chino CA 91710	909-664-2440	R	7*	.1
42	Seacon Advanced Products LLC—*Garry Brown*	PO Box 767, Bellville TX 77418	979-865-8846	R	6*	.1
43	Megaphase LLC—*David Lutkins*	2098 W Main St Bldg 3, Stroudsburg PA 18360	570-424-8400	R	6*	.1
44	Harting Electronik Inc—*Dietmar Harting*	1370 Bowes Rd, Elgin IL 60123	847-741-1500	S	6*	<.1
45	Major League Electronics LLC—*Douglas Coffman*	4235 Earnings Way, New Albany IN 47150	812-944-7244	R	6*	<.1
46	Incon Inc—*Robert Butler*	21 Flagstone Dr, Hudson NH 03051	603-595-0550	R	6*	<.1
47	Min-E-Con LLC—*William Charett*	17312 Eastman, Irvine CA 92614	949-250-0087	R	5*	.1
48	Resonance Technologies Inc—*George Szenczy*	109 Comac St, Ronkonkoma NY 11779	631-237-4901	R	5*	<.1
49	L and M Machining Corp—*Mike Mai*	2770 E Coronado St, Anaheim CA 92806	714-414-0923	R	5*	<.1
50	Phoenix Logistics Inc—*Ray Bellefeuille*	2507 W Geneva Dr, Tempe AZ 85282	602-231-8616	R	5*	<.1
51	Connectronics Inc—*Ronald Reese*	PO Box 246, Edinburgh IN 46124	812-526-8801	R	4*	<.1
52	Valley Precision Tool Inc—*Ronald Raudenbush*	20 Clarks Valley Rd, Tower City PA 17980	717-647-7550	R	4*	<.1
53	Kycon Cable and Connector Inc—*Chris Strangways*	1810 Little Orchard St, San Jose CA 95125	408-494-0330	R	4*	<.1
54	Continental Connector Co—*Lou Kilian*	2294 N Penn Rd, Hatfield PA 19440	215-997-3200	R	4*	<.1
55	Detoronics Corp—*Kenneth Clark*	PO Box 3805, South El Monte CA 91733	626-579-7130	R	4*	<.1
56	Unicorp Inc—*Steven Mercadante*	291 Cleveland St, Orange NJ 07050	973-674-1700	R	4*	.2
57	Appalachian Technology Inc—*Nicole Smith*	187 Elk Mountain Rd, Asheville NC 28804	828-210-8888	R	4*	<.1
58	Arq Electronics Manufacturing Services Inc—*Terry O'norrell*	13910 State Hwy 30, College Station TX 77845	979-696-5889	R	4*	<.1
59	Alpha Products Inc—*Tony Gulrajani*	351 Irving Dr, Oxnard CA 93030	805-981-8666	R	3*	<.1
60	Etg Inc—*E Gossack*	PO Box 13105, Salem OR 97309	503-364-9257	R	3*	<.1
61	Sri Connector Gage Company Inc—*James Twombly*	3950 Dow Rd, Melbourne FL 32934	321-259-9688	R	3*	<.1
62	Nea Electronics Inc—*Steven Perkins*	14370 White Sage Rd, Moorpark CA 93021	805-292-4010	R	3*	<.1
63	Tektest Inc—*Phelps Wood*	PO Box 660729, Arcadia CA 91066	626-446-6175	R	3*	<.1
64	Fada—*James Lemastus*	1224 E Oak St, Louisville KY 40204	502-583-4246	R	3*	<.1
65	Connective Design Inc—*Danya Chandler*	3010 S Tech Blvd, Miamisburg OH 45342	937-746-8252	R	3*	<.1
66	G and H Industries Inc—*Paul Haas*	419 Eleanor Dr, Centreville MI 49032	269-467-4417	R	3*	<.1
67	Elpakco Inc—*John Grant*	PO Box 72, Westford MA 01886	978-392-0400	R	2*	<.1
68	Adi Electronics Inc—*Raman Kalidas*	PO Box 710518, Dallas TX 75371	214-818-4720	R	2*	<.1
69	Supplynet Inc—*Robert Berkey*	614 Corporate Way Ste, Valley Cottage NY 10989	845-267-2655	R	2*	<.1
70	Accessories For Electronics Inc—*William Epstein*	195 Central Ave Ste Q, Farmingdale NY 11735	631-847-0158	R	2*	<.1
71	Ankim Enterprises Inc—*Stan Wright*	PO Box 569, Bellefontaine OH 43311	937-599-1121	R	2*	<.1
72	Stitch Wire Systems Corp—*Floyd Penland*	917 Lawrence Dr, Newbury Park CA 91320	805-498-6727	R	2*	<.1
73	Fastener Specialty Inc—*Beth Jones*	2435 109th St, Grand Prairie TX 75050	972-988-0064	R	1*	<.1
74	3 Sixty Manufacturing—*Susan Stenejem*	6288 San Ignacio Ave E, San Jose CA 95119	408-365-0360	R	1*	<.1
75	Filconn Inc—*Rick Taylor*	1347 E University Dr, Tempe AZ 85281	480-222-3565	R	1*	<.1
76	On-Shore Technology Inc	1917 W 3rd St, Tempe AZ 85281	480-921-3000	R	1*	<.1
77	Raycon Technology Inc—*Raymond Smith*	5252 Mcfadden Ave, Huntington Beach CA 92649	714-799-4100	R	1*	<.1
78	Rf Tec Manufacturing Inc—*Kiyoshi Endo*	1375 Redwine Rd, Fayetteville GA 30215	770-719-7579	R	1*	<.1
79	Precision Electronics Company Inc—*Ash Bhargave*	2101 Penna Ave Ste 41, York PA 17404	717-845-8704	R	1*	<.1
80	Avant-Garde Technology Inc—*Richard Tems*	PO Box 276, Jamison PA 18929	215-345-8228	R	1*	<.1
81	Wildcat Connectors Inc—*Ralph Cassone*	202 Main St, Princeton KS 66078	785-937-4385	R	1*	<.1
82	Sunflower Manufacturing Inc—*Sybill Jecker*	3620 Sacramento Dr Ste, San Luis Obispo CA 93401	805-785-0900	R	1*	<.1
83	Sytron Corp—*David Sloop*	700 Crown Industrial C, Chesterfield MO 63005	636-536-2302	R	1*	<.1
84	Usapex Corp—*David Liu*	933 La Mesa Ter Unit G, Sunnyvale CA 94086	408-730-9800	R	<1*	<.1

TOTALS: SIC 3678 Electronic Connectors
Companies: 84

					16,119	109.6

3679 Electronic Components Nec

1	Technitrol Delaware Inc—*Ralph E Faison* Pulse Electronics Corp	1210 Northbrook Dr Ste, Trevose PA 19053	215-355-2900	S	67,716*	22.8

Rank	Company Name—*Executive Officer*	Address, City, State, Zip	Phone	Type	Fin	Empls
2	ITT Federal Services Corp—*Steven Loranger*	4410 E Fountain Blvd, Colorado Springs CO 80916	719-591-3600	S	20,690*	7.0
3	Flextronics America LLC—*Mike McNamara*	2090 Fortune Dr, San Jose CA 95131	408-576-7000	S	4,699*	1.5
4	Datacard Group—*Todd G Wilkinson*	11111 Bren Rd W, Minnetonka MN 55343	952-933-1223	R	4,039*	1.4
5	Altuglas International—*Bertrand Repelin*	2000 Market St, Philadelphia PA 19103	215-419-7000	R	4,001*	1.3
6	LSI Marcole Inc—*Robert J Ready*	1108 Oakdale St, Manchester TN 37355	931-723-4442	S	3,896*	1.2
7	Panasonic Electric Works Corporation of America—*Kazushige Nishida*	629 Central Ave, New Providence NJ 07974	908-464-3550	S	3,137*	1.0
8	Sparton Electronics—*Cary Wood*	PO Box 788, De Leon Springs FL 32130	386-985-4631	S	2,732*	1.0
9	I/O Marine Systems Inc—*Robert P Peebler*	5200 Toler St, Harahan LA 70123	504-733-6061	S	2,610*	.8
10	I/O Nevada LLC—*Robert P Peebler*	2105 CityWest Blvd Ste, Houston TX 77042	281-933-3339	S	2,610*	.8
11	I/O Texas LP—*Robert P Peebler*	2105 CityWest Blvd Ste, Houston TX 77042	281-933-3339	S	2,610*	.8
12	Pacific Aerospace and Electronics Inc—*Donald A Wright*	434 Olds Station Rd, Wenatchee WA 98801	509-667-9600	R	2,466*	.8
13	I/O Marine Systems Ltd—*Robert P Peebler*	5200 Toler St, Harahan LA 70123	504-733-6061	S	2,444*	.8
14	Safran—*Marc Renick*	600 Glen Ave, Salisbury MD 21804	410-548-7800	R	2,180*	.8
15	EOS Power USA Inc—*Martin Kistner*	1540 Cornerstone Blvd, Daytona Beach FL 32117	972-273-0600	R	2,146*	.7
16	Opex Corp—*Mark Stevens*	305 Commerce Dr, Moorestown NJ 08057	856-727-1100	R	1,857*	.7
17	Signal Technology Corp—*Erin Fast*	100 First Stamford Pl, Stamford CT 06902	203-363-7300	S	1,703*	.6
18	Electronic Systems Inc—*Kurt Schmelz*	369 Edwin Dr, Virginia Beach VA 23462	757-497-8000	S	1,664*	.5
19	Stratos Optical Technologies—*Phillip A Harris*	7444 W Wilson Ave, Chicago IL 60706	708-867-9600	S	1,645*	.6
20	Powercom America Inc—*Ford Chen*	623 S State College Bl, Fullerton CA 92831	714-525-8889	S	1,567*	.5
21	I/O General LLC—*Robert P Peebler*	2105 CityWest Blvd Ste, Houston TX 77042	281-933-3339	S	1,555*	.5
22	ITT Power Solutions Inc—*Steve Loranger*	11 Interstate Dr, West Springfield MA 01089	413-263-6200	S	1,552*	.5
23	ECS Incorporated International—*Patricia S Taylor*	1105 S Ridgeview, Olathe KS 66062	913-782-7787	R	1,395*	.5
24	K and L Microwave Inc—*Dave Whiteman*	2250 Northwood Dr, Salisbury MD 21801	410-749-2424	S	1,220*	.4
25	Fox Electronics—*EL Fox Jr*	5570 Enterprise Pkwy, Fort Myers FL 33905	239-693-0099	R	1,200*	3.0
26	Trueposition Inc—*Stephen Stuut*	1000 Chesterbrook Blvd, Berwyn PA 19312	610-680-1000	S	1,174*	.4
27	Power-One Inc—*Richard J Thompson*	740 Calle Plano, Camarillo CA 93012	805-987-8741	P	1,047	3.5
28	Phonic Ear Inc—*Jens Holstebro*	2080 Lakeville Hwy, Petaluma CA 94954	707-769-1110	R	1,010*	.1
29	Materion Microelectronics and Services—*Richard Sager*	2978 Main St, Buffalo NY 14214	716-837-1000	S	879	1.1
30	Nartron Corp—*Norman Rautiola*	5000 N US-131, Reed City MI 49677	231-832-5525	R	820*	.3
31	Technical Services for Electronics Inc—*Steve Sundberg*	PO Box 616, Arlington MN 55307	507-964-2237	R	816*	.3
32	Micro-Coax Inc—*Chris Kneiyzs*	206 Jones Blvd, Pottstown PA 19464	610-495-0110	R	745*	.2
33	Aeroflex Holding Corp—*Len Borow*	PO Box 6022, Plainview NY 11803	516-694-6700	P	729	2.9
34	Natel Engineering Company Inc—*Sudesh Arora*	9340 Owensmouth Ave, Chatsworth CA 91311	818-734-6500	R	664*	.2
35	Steren Electronics International LLC—*David Shteremberg*	6260 Sequence Dr, San Diego CA 92121	858-546-5000	R	615*	.2
36	Midcon Cables Co—*Charles Wheeler*	PO Box 1786, Joplin MO 64804	417-781-4331	R	565*	.2
37	Synetics Solutions Inc	18870 NE Riverside Pkw, Portland OR 97230	503-465-6000	D	554*	.2
38	CTS Corp—*Vinod M Khilnani*	905 West Blvd N, Elkhart IN 46514	574-293-7511	P	536*	4.2
39	Advanced Energy Industries Inc—*Garry Rogerson*	1625 Sharp Point Dr, Ft Collins CO 80525	970-221-0108	P	517	1.5
40	Sumitomo Corporation of America—*Michihisa Shinagawa*	600 3rd Ave, New York NY 10016	212-207-0700	S	503*	.2
41	MtronPTI—*Greg Anderson* LGL Group Inc	100 Douglas Ave, Yankton SD 57078	605-665-9321	S	487*	.2
42	IPG Photonics Corp—*Valentin Gapontsev PhD*	50 Old Webster Rd, Oxford MA 01540	508-373-1100	P	474	2.1
43	Academy Group Materion Microelectronics and Services	5520 Midway Park Pl NE, Albuquerque NM 87109	505-346-1805	S	470*	.2
44	Pulse Electronics Corp—*Ralph E Faison*	12220 World Trade Dr, San Diego CA 92128	858-674-8100	P	433	16.1
45	Memtron Technologies Inc—*Brad Lawrence*	530 N Franklin St, Frankenmuth MI 48734	989-652-2656	S	422*	.1
46	CoorsTek Inc—*John K Coors*	16000 Table Mountain P, Golden CO 80403	303-271-7000	R	400*	2.4
47	Hoffman Enclosures Inc—*Randall Hogan*	2100 Hoffman Way, Anoka MN 55303	763-421-2240	S	351	2.5
48	HiRel Systems	11100 Wayzata Blvd Ste, Minnetonka MN 55305	952-544-1344	S	330*	.1
49	Van Meter Industrial Inc—*Mark Burgart*	850 32nd Ave SW, Cedar Rapids IA 52404	319-366-4709	R	329*	.2
50	Cobham Sensor Systems Inc—*Dave Gaggin*	3310 Carlins Park Dr, Baltimore MD 21215	410-542-1700	D	314*	.1
51	Nova Electric—*Aron Levy* Technology Dynamics Inc	100 School St, Bergenfield NJ 07621	201-385-0500	D	314*	.1
52	Controlled Power Co—*Henry Tazzia*	1955 Stephenson Hwy, Troy MI 48083	248-528-3700	R	310*	.1
53	EtherWan Systems Inc USA—*Mitch Yang*	4570 E Eisenhower Cir, Anaheim CA 92807	714-779-3800	R	300*	.1
54	Hutchinson Technology Inc—*Wayne M Fortun*	40 W Highland Park Dr, Hutchinson MN 55350	320-587-3797	P	278	2.3
55	Panamax—*Bill Pollock*	1690 Corporate Cir, Petaluma CA 94954	707-283-5900	S	277*	.1
56	Vicor Corp—*Patrizio Vinciarelli*	25 Frontage Rd, Andover MA 01810	978-470-2900	P	253	1.1
57	Americor Electronics Ltd—*Tom Pross*	675 S Lively Blvd Ste, Elk Grove Village IL 60007	847-956-6200	R	247*	.1
58	Killdeer Mountain Manufacturing Inc—*Doug Fettig*	233 Rodeo Dr, Killdeer ND 58640	701-764-5651	R	247*	.1
59	Datacolor Corporate Headquarters—*Albert Busch*	5 Princess Rd Rm 1, Lawrenceville NJ 08648	609-924-2189	R	246*	.1
60	Pioneer Speakers Inc—*Hiromi Hayashi*	2427 Hoover Ave, National City CA 91950	619-477-0850	R	245*	1.3
61	NTT Electronics Corp—*Hiroshi Yoshimura*	250 Pehle Ave Ste 706, Saddle Brook NJ 07663	201-556-1770	S	232*	.8
62	Spectrum FSY Microwave Inc Spectrum Control Inc	7100 Columbia Gateway, Columbia MD 21046	443-259-3440	S	232*	.1
63	Mercury Computer Systems Inc—*Mark Aslett*	201 Riverneck Rd, Chelmsford MA 01824	978-967-1401	P	229	.6
64	Microsource Inc—*Daniel Markowitz*	1269 Corporate Ctr Pkw, Santa Rosa CA 95407	707-527-7010	S	222*	.1
65	Silicon Image Inc—*Camillo Martino*	1060 E Arques Ave, Sunnyvale CA 94085	408-616-4000	P	221	.5
66	AAI Corp—*Frederick Strader*	PO Box 126, Hunt Valley MD 21030	410-666-1400	S	219*	1.8
67	Woodhead Industries Inc—*Philippe Lemaitre*	333 Knightsbridge Pkwy, Lincolnshire IL 60069	847-353-2500	S	215	1.5
68	Jennings Technology Company LLC—*Steve Negrini*	970 McLaughlin Ave, San Jose CA 95122	408-292-4025	S	210*	.1
69	CTS RF Integrated Modules—*Vinod M Khilnani* CTS Corp	905 West Blvd N, Elkhart IN 46514	574-293-7511	S	199	.5
70	SL Industries Inc—*William T Fejes Jr*	520 Fellowship Rd Ste, Mount Laurel NJ 08054	856-727-1500	P	190	1.6
71	Planar Systems Inc—*Gerald K Perkel*	1195 NW Compton Dr, Beaverton OR 97006	503-748-1100	P	187	.5
72	Leoni Wiring Systems Inc—*Rob Duggan*	2861 N Flowing Wells R, Tucson AZ 85705	520-741-0895	R	176*	2.1
73	Tripp Lite—*Bob Gingras*	1111 W 35th St, Chicago IL 60609	773-869-1111	R	175*	.4
74	AAMP of America—*Ron Freeman*	13160 56th Ct, Clearwater FL 33760		S	165*	.1
75	Spectrum Control Inc—*Richard A Southworth*	8031 Avonia Rd, Fairview PA 16415	814-474-2207	S	164	1.6
76	Bergquist Co—*Carl Bergquist*	18930 W 78th St, Chanhassen MN 55317	952-835-2322	R	162*	.7
77	Wallace Electronics Inc—*Steve Pilipchuk*	10551 Miller Rd Ste 10, Dallas TX 75238	214-340-0400	R	149*	.1
78	California Sales Co—*John Schultz*	1735 E Monticello Ct, Ontario CA 91761	909-930-2800	R	148*	.1
79	PolyVision Corp—*Bob Crain*	3970 Johns Creek Ct St, Suwanee GA 30024	678-542-3100	S	146*	1.1
80	Graphic Research Inc—*Pete Vaghashia*	9334 Mason Ave, Chatsworth CA 91311	818-886-7340	R	145*	.1
81	Txu Energy Services Company LLC—*Carlos Ruffino*	1601 Bryan St, Dallas TX 75201	214-812-4600	R	143*	2.0
82	Simclar Inc—*Samuel Russell*	2230 W 77th St, Hialeah FL 33016	305-556-9210	B	136	1.0
83	Behlman Electronics Inc—*Mark Tublisky*	80 Cabot Ct, Hauppauge NY 11788	631-435-0410	S	136*	.1
84	EDS Manufacturing Inc—*Luis Moreno*	PO Box 6009, Nogales AZ 85628	520-287-9711	R	134*	1.9

Note: An asterisk (*) indicates an estimated financial figure. The company type code used is as follows: R = Private, P = Public, S = Private Subsidiary, B = Public Subsidiary, D = Division, J = Joint Venture, I = Investment Fund.

COMPANY RANKINGS BY SALES WITHIN 4-DIGIT SIC

Rank	Company Name—*Executive Officer*	Address, City, State, Zip	Phone	Type	Fin	Empls
85	Cherokee International Corp—*Jeffrey Frank*	2841 Dow Ave, Tustin CA 92780	714-544-6665	R	128*	1.5
86	BARCO Projection Systems America—*Martin De Prycker*	3059 Premiere Pkwy, Duluth GA 30097		S	125*	.7
87	ELDEC Corp—*Jim Hinirn*	PO Box 97027, Lynnwood WA 98046	425-743-8321	S	122*	.8
88	Lockheed Martin Corp Tactical Defense Systems Div—*James W Dunn*	1210 Massillon Rd, Akron OH 44315	330-796-2800	S	116*	.8
89	Fusite—*Larry Flatt*	6000 Fernview Ave, Cincinnati OH 45212	513-731-2020	R	115*	.8
90	Magnetek Inc—*Peter McCormick*	N49 W13650 Campbell Dr, Menomonee Falls WI 53051	262-783-3500	P	110	.3
91	Pulizzi Engineering Inc—*Randy W Carson*	3200 S Susan St, Santa Ana CA 92704	605-334-8999	S	109*	<.1
92	Hi-Lex Corp—*Makoto Teraura*	5200 Wayne Rd, Battle Creek MI 49037	269-968-0781	R	106	.3
93	Ember Corp—*Robert LeFort*	25 Thomson Pl 2nd Fl, Boston MA 02210	617-951-0200	R	101*	<.1
94	Nortech Systems Inc—*Michael J Degen*	1120 Wayzata Blvd E St, Wayzata MN 55391	952-345-2244	P	100	.7
95	Naked Optics Corp—*Buzz Nesti*	16 Mount Bethel Rd Ste, Warren NJ 07059	908-685-0352	R	99*	<.1
96	American Technical Ceramics Corp—*Victor Insetta*	1 Norden Ln, Huntington Station NY 11746	631-622-4700	S	94	.5
97	NanoOpto Corp—*Brian A Kahn*	1600 Cottontail Ln, Somerset NJ 08873	732-627-0808	D	92*	<.1
98	Paralan Corp—*Marc Brooks*	4655 Ruffner St, San Diego CA 92111	858-560-7266	R	90*	<.1
99	Radianse Inc—*Steve Schiefen*	1600 Osgood St, North Andover MA 01845	978-681-1699	R	89*	<.1
100	Taser International Inc—*Rick Smith*	17800 N 85th St, Scottsdale AZ 85255	480-905-2000	P	87	.3
101	Ifm Efector Inc—*Vincent Zagar*	782 Springdale Dr, Exton PA 19341	610-524-2000	R	84*	.2
102	Pioneer Materials Inc—*Leon Chiu*	3357 Candlewood Rd, Torrance CA 90505	714-721-5332	R	84*	<.1
103	Inphi Corp—*Young K Sohn*	3945 Freedom Cir Ste 1, Santa Clara CA 95054	408-217-7300	P	83	.2
104	Spectral Response LLC—*Kevin Melendy*	1725 Macleod Dr Ste L, Lawrenceville GA 30043	770-476-2468	S	72*	.2
105	Innovex Inc (Maple Plain Minnesota)—*Randy Acres*	3033 Campus Dr Ste E18, Plymouth MN 55441	763-383-4000	P	71	3.3
106	Delta Design Inc—*James Donahue*	12367 Crosthwaite Cir, Poway CA 92064	858-848-8000	S	69*	.5
107	DGT Holdings Corp—*John J Quicke*	100 Pine Aire Dr, Bay Shore NY 11706	631-231-6400	P	68	.2
108	Synapse Wireless Inc—*Wade Patterson*	500 Discovery Dr, Huntsville AL 35806		R	67*	<.1
109	Tri Source Inc—*Ron Johnson*	84 Platt Rd, Shelton CT 06484	203-926-9460	R	64*	<.1
110	Infiniti Media Inc—*Saeig Esephian*	19481 Harborgate Way, Torrance CA 90501	310-618-8288	R	62*	<.1
111	Universal Display Corp—*Steven V Abramson*	375 Phillips Blvd, Ewing NJ 08618	609-671-0980	P	61	.1
112	Jolt Technology Inc—*Mitchell Morehand*	6801 NW 15th Ave, Fort Lauderdale FL 33309	954-968-8526	R	61*	<.1
113	Polyflon Co—*Will Larusso*	1 Willard Rd, Norwalk CT 06851	203-840-7555	S	61*	<.1
114	Crydom Co—*Jean-Marc Theolier*	2320 Paseo de las Amer, San Diego CA 92154		S	60*	.4
115	Master International Corp—*Charles R Dawson*	PO Box 25662, Los Angeles CA 90025	310-452-1229	R	60	.2
116	Video Display Corp—*Ronald D Ordway*	1868 Tucker Industrial, Tucker GA 30084	770-938-2080	P	59	.3
117	Black Hills Workshop and Training Center—*Jim Scull*	PO Box 2104, Rapid City SD 57709	605-343-4550	R	56*	.4
118	Nagase America Corp—*Seiji Nishimura*	546 5th Ave, New York NY 10036	212-703-1340	R	53*	<.1
119	Evogen Inc—*Sean Reineke*	8301 State Line Rd Ste, Kansas City MO 64114	816-360-3895	R	52*	<.1
120	Eclipse Marketing Group—*Chris Gastelum*	13657 NE 126th Pl, Kirkland WA 98034	425-885-6991	R	52*	<.1
121	Martek Power Inc—*Ahmad Innab*	1111 Knox St, Torrance CA 90502	310-202-8820	R	51*	.5
122	California Micro Devices Corp—*Robert V Dickinson*	490 N McCarthy Blvd St, Milpitas CA 95035	408-263-3214	S	49	.1
123	MMR Technologies Inc—*William A Little*	1400 N Shoreline Blvd, Mountain View CA 94043	650-962-9620	R	49*	<.1
124	FCI Electronics Inc—*Alain Bugat*	825 Old Trail Rd, Etters PA 17319	717-938-7200	S	48*	.2
125	Massively Parallel Technologies Inc—*Bobbi Hazard*	1221 Pearl St, Boulder CO 80302	303-926-8444	R	47*	<.1
126	Heritage Wire Harness LLC—*Jerry Waters*	152 12th St NE, Fort Payne AL 35967	256-845-1255	R	47*	<.1
127	Acer Latin America Inc—*Mario Teuffer*	1701 NW 87th Ave Ste 3, Miami FL 33172	305-392-7000	S	47*	<.1
128	LGL Group Inc—*Greg Anderson*	2525 Shader Rd, Orlando FL 32804	407-298 2000	P	47	.2
129	TMA Inc—*Greg Pflum*	3600 Osuna Rd NE, Albuquerque NM 87109	505-345-8921	R	46*	<.1
130	Jewell Instruments LLC—*Carlo Carluccio*	850 Perimeter Rd, Manchester NH 03103	603-669-6400	R	44*	.2
131	U S Airmotive Inc—*Frank Bortunk*	PO Box 522514, Miami FL 33152	305-885-4992	R	44*	<.1
132	Teledyne Cougar Inc—*Daniel Cheadle*	927 Thompson Pl, Sunnyvale CA 94085	408-522-3838	S	44*	<.1
133	Fargo Assembly Of PA Inc—*Dennis Rees*	800 W Washington St, Norristown PA 19401	610-272-6850	R	42*	.7
134	Medicore Inc—*Thomas K Langbein*	2647 W 81st St, Hialeah FL 33016	305-558-4000	R	42	.3
135	Saratoga Industries Div—*Howard Pinsley* Espey Manufacturing and Electronics Corp	233 Ballston Ave, Saratoga Springs NY 12866	518-245-4400	D	41*	.2
136	Compulink Corp—*Stephen Shevlin*	1205 Gandy Blvd N, Saint Petersburg FL 33702	727-579-1500	R	41*	.6
137	Teledyne Relays	12525 Daphne Ave, Hawthorne CA 90250		D	39*	.3
138	Components Corporation Of America—*Cary Maguire*	5950 Berkshire Ln Ste, Dallas TX 75225	214-969-0166	R	38*	.2
139	Gables Engineering Inc—*Victor Clarke*	PO Box 140880, Coral Gables FL 33114	305-774-4400	R	36*	.3
140	Micronetics Inc—*David Robbins*	26 Hampshire Dr, Hudson NH 03051	603-883-2900	P	35	.2
141	Vander-Bend Manufacturing LLC—*Mike Berg*	123 Uranium Dr, Sunnyvale CA 94086	408-245-5150	R	35*	.3
142	Synqor Inc—*Martin Schlecht*	155 Swanson Rd, Boxborough MA 01719	978-849-0600	R	35*	.3
143	Densitron Corp—*Doug Batson*	10400-4 Pioneer Blvd, Santa Fe Springs CA 90670	562-941-5000	D	33*	.2
144	Marathon Norco Aerospace Co—*Jack Stiffler*	PO Box 8233, Waco TX 76714	254-776-0650	S	33*	.2
145	Bitrage Inc—*James J Dionne*	6816 Southpoint Pkwy S, Jacksonville FL 32216	904-674-0062	R	33*	<.1
146	Amtech LLC—*Wayne Armstrong*	330a Hwy 22 W, Alexander City AL 35010	256-397-0800	R	33*	.3
147	Nelco (Green Bay Wisconsin)—*Robert R Nault*	PO Box 1157, Grand Rapids MI 49501		S	31*	.2
148	Electrocube Inc—*Clay Parrill*	3366 Pomona Blvd, Pomona CA 91768	909-595-4037	R	31*	.1
149	KR Electronics Inc—*Charles Kiall*	91 Avenel St, Avenel NJ 07001	732-636-1900	R	31*	<.1
150	Teijin Kaisei America Inc—*Naoaki Okuda*	5555 Triangle Pkwy Ste, Norcross GA 30092	770-346-8949	R	31*	<.1
151	XTEC Inc—*Albert Fernandez*	5775 Blue Lagoon Dr St, Miami FL 33126	305-265-1565	R	31*	<.1
152	Emrise Corp—*Carmine Oliva*	2530 Meridian Pky, Durham NC 27713	408-200-3040	P	31	.2
153	Kauffman Engineering Inc—*Michael Buis*	701 Ransdell Rd, Lebanon IN 46052	765-482-5640	R	30*	.3
154	Sumida America Components Inc—*Doug Malcolm*	1251 N Plum Grove Rd S, Schaumburg IL 60173	847-545-6700	R	30*	<.1
155	Southern Tool and Machine Co—*Rayrik Cmarik*	1480 SW 3rd St Bay C2, Pompano Beach FL 33069	954-943-1700	R	30*	<.1
156	Target Technology Company LLC—*Han Nee*	564 Wald, Irvine CA 92618	949-788-0909	R	30*	<.1
157	Espey Manufacturing and Electronics Corp—*Mark St Pierre*	233 Ballston Ave, Saratoga Springs NY 12866	518-245-4400	P	30	.2
158	Fair-Rite Products Corp—*Carole Parker*	PO Box 288, Wallkill NY 12589	845-895-2055	R	29*	.5
159	Merrimac Industries Inc—*Mason N Carter*	41 Fairfield Pl, West Caldwell NJ 07006	973-575-1300	S	29	.2
160	Micrometals Inc—*Jim Cox*	5615 E La Palma Ave, Anaheim CA 92807	714-970-9400	R	29*	.3
161	Federal Electronics Inc—*Romolo Evangelista*	75 Stamp Farm Rd, Cranston RI 02921	401-944-6200	R	29*	.2
162	Advanced Power Designs Inc—*Fred Sabatine*	7 Chrysler, Irvine CA 92618	949-600-6400	R	29*	<.1
163	Rhombus Industries Inc—*David Doke*	313 N Birch St, Santa Ana CA 92701	714-836-0960	R	28*	.3
164	Computer Crafts Inc—*Donald Harkins*	PO Box 264, Hawthorne NJ 07507	973-423-3500	R	28*	.3
165	Unlimited Services Inc—*William Kessenich*	170 Evergreen Rd, Oconto WI 54153	920-834-4418	R	28*	.4
166	Celltron Inc—*Michael Kim*	PO Box 98, Galena KS 66739	620-783-1333	R	26*	.3
167	Regal Research And Manufacturing Company LLC—*Gayle Glosser*	PO Box 940529, Plano TX 75094	972-494-0359	R	26*	.2
168	SL Power Electronics—*Eugene J Ruddy* SL Industries Inc	6050 King Dr, Ventura CA 93003	805-486-4565	S	26*	.7
169	DSM and T Co—*Dan Wilson*	10609 Business Dr, Fontana CA 92337	909-357-7960	R	26*	.2
170	Amphenol Borisch Technologies—*Jonathan Borisch*	4511 E Paris Ave Se, Grand Rapids MI 49512	616-554-9820	R	26*	.4

Rank	Company Name—*Executive Officer*	Address, City, State, Zip	Phone	Type	Fin	Empls
171	Stuart Manufacturing Inc—*Lionel Tobin*	1615 E Wallace St, Fort Wayne IN 46803	260-744-2261	R	26*	.2
172	Omni Connection International Inc—*Henry Cheng*	126 Via Trevizio, Corona CA 92879	951-898-6232	R	25*	.4
173	Interconnect Devices Inc—*Michael Kirkman*	5101 Richland Ave, Kansas City KS 66106	913-342-5544	R	25*	.2
174	Pulse Engineering Inc—*Kevin Foley* Pulse Electronics Corp	PO Box 12235, San Diego CA 92112	858-674-8100	S	25*	1.0
175	Dicon Fiberoptics Inc—*Ho-Shang Lee*	1689 Regatta Blvd Bldg, Richmond CA 94804	510-620-5000	R	25*	.4
176	Arnold Magnetic Technologies Corp—*Tim Wilson*	770 Linden Ave, Rochester NY 14625	585-385-8711	S	25*	.1
177	Coronado Communications Inc—*Forrest Metz*	1638 E 18th St, Tucson AZ 85719	520-628-3689	R	25*	<.1
178	Frederick Engineering Inc	832 Oregon Ave Ste M, Linthicum MD 21090	410-789-7890	R	25*	<.1
179	Kinswood Electronics Corp—*Chih Tsung Liao*	1140 Centre Dr Ste N, Walnut CA 91789	909-598-0852	R	25*	<.1
180	Micro Computer Systems Of South West Florida Inc—*Stephen Meek*	2553 Longboat Dr, Naples FL 34104	239-643-6672	R	25*	<.1
181	Millennia Technology Inc—*Michael D'ambrosio*	1105 Pittsburgh St, Cheswick PA 15024	724-274-7741	R	24*	.1
182	SAE Magnetics—*Johnson Fong*	100 S Milpitas Blvd, Milpitas CA 95035	408-956-7100	S	24*	.1
183	Crystek Crystals Corp—*Anthony Mastropole*	12730 Commonwealth Dr, Fort Myers FL 33913	239-561-3311	R	24*	.1
184	Kaiser Systems Inc—*Kenneth Kaiser*	126 Sohier Rd, Beverly MA 01915	978-922-9300	R	24*	.2
185	Elecsys Corp—*Karl B Gemperli*	846 N Mart-Way Ct, Olathe KS 66061	913-647-0158	P	24	.1
186	3 Y Power Technology Inc—*Yuan Yu*	80 Bunsen, Irvine CA 92618	949-450-0152	R	24*	<.1
187	Axsys Technologies Inc Precision Machined Products Div—*Martyn Ackerman*	6717 Alabama Hwy 157, Cullman AL 35057	256-737-5200	D	23*	.2
188	Vishay Thin Film Inc	2160 Liberty Dr, Niagara Falls NY 14304	716-283-4025	D	23*	.2
189	Byrne Electrical Specialists Inc—*Norman Byrne*	320 Byrne Industrial D, Rockford MI 49341	616-866-3461	R	23*	.2
190	Statek Corp—*Margaritha Werren*	512 N Main St, Orange CA 92868	714-639-7810	R	23*	.2
191	Delta Group Electronics Inc—*Harold Mueller*	4801 Lincoln Rd Ne, Albuquerque NM 87109	505-883-7674	R	23*	.2
192	Sendec Corp—*Kenton Fiske*	72 Perinton Pkwy, Fairport NY 14450	585-425-3390	R	22*	.2
193	Encoder Products Co—*Bill Watt*	PO Box 249, Sagle ID 83860	208-263-8541	R	22*	.1
194	WaveSplitter Technologies Inc—*Sheau Sheng Chen*	46824 Lakeview Blvd, Fremont CA 94538	510-651-7800	R	22*	.1
195	Marian Inc—*William Witchger*	1011 E Saint Clair St, Indianapolis IN 46202	317-638-6525	R	21*	.2
196	BI Technologies—*Frank Pipitone*	4200 Bonita Pl, Fullerton CA 92835	714-447-2300	S	21*	.1
197	Nexergy Inc—*Philip Glandon*	1909 Arlingate Ln, Columbus OH 43228	614-351-2191	R	21*	.3
198	Qualitel Corp—*Tuanhai Hoang*	11831 Beverly Park Rd, Everett WA 98204	425-423-8388	R	20*	.2
199	QUANTUM Fuel Systems Technologies Worldwide Inc—*Alan P Niedzwiecki*	17872 Cartwright Rd, Irvine CA 92614	949-399-4500	P	20	.1
200	Celetron USA—*Sirjang(Jugi) Lal Tandon*	2125-B Madera Rd, Simi Valley CA 93065	805-955-3600	R	20*	.1
201	Electro-Mechanisms Inc—*Susan Arnold*	515 W Allen Ave Bldg 1, San Dimas CA 91773	909-394-9953	R	20*	<.1
202	IceCode LLC—*Viktor Petrenko*	PO Box 5447, West Lebanon NH 03784	603-448-9206	R	20*	<.1
203	Midcon Cables Company Inc—*Charles Wheeler*	PO Box 1786, Joplin MO 64802	417-781-4331	R	20*	.2
204	SAE Power—*Colm Campbell*	1500 E Hamilton Ave St, Campbell CA 95008	408-369-2200	R	19*	1.2
205	Rhino Linings USA Inc—*Russell Lewis*	9151 Rehco Rd, San Diego CA 92121	858-450-0441	R	19*	.1
206	Gtran Inc—*Ray Yu*	829 Flynn Rd, Camarillo CA 93012	805-482-1088	R	19*	<.1
207	Teijin Kasei America Inc—*Mr Morino*	5555 Triangle Pkwy Ste, Norcross GA 30092	770-346-8949	R	19*	<.1
208	Tooh Dineh Industries Inc—*Alex Riggs*	Leupp School Rd Bldg 4, Leupp AZ 86035	928-686-6477	R	19*	.2
209	Woven Electronics LLC—*Terry Owings*	PO Box 189, Mauldin SC 29662	864-963-5131	R	19*	.3
210	Regal Electronics Inc—*Madeleine Lee*	PO Box 60008, Sunnyvale CA 94088	408-988-2288	R	18*	.2
211	Gavial Engineering and Manufacturing Inc—*Don Connors*	1435 W Mc Coy, Santa Maria CA 93455	805-614-0060	R	18*	.2
212	Continental-Wirt Electronics Corp—*Kalman Lifson*	130 James Way, Southampton PA 18966	215-355-7080	R	18*	.4
213	Adco Circuits—*Archie Damman*	2868 Bond St, Rochester Hills MI 48309	248-829-4675	R	18*	.1
214	Atlantic Microwave Corp—*Steve Schaeffer*	68 Main St, Bolton MA 01740	978-779-6963	D	18	.1
215	R and D Electronics Inc—*Cathy Maples*	5501 Hwy 431 S, Brownsboro AL 35741	256-534-6416	R	18*	.1
216	Merit Electronic Design Company Inc—*Guy Intoci*	190 Rodeo Dr, Edgewood NY 11717	631-667-9699	R	18*	.1
217	BEA Inc—*Bryan Gregory*	100 Enterprise Dr RIDC, Pittsburgh PA 15275	412-249-4100	S	17	3.0
218	Petron Industries Inc—*Peter Buckley*	PO Box 41166, Houston TX 77241	713-693-8700	R	17*	.2
219	Netcom Inc—*John Victor*	599 Wheeling Rd, Wheeling IL 60090	847-537-6300	R	17*	.2
220	Nexus Custom Electronics Inc—*Anna Barucco*	PO Box 250, Brandon VT 05733	802-247-6811	D	17*	.1
221	Cicon Engineering Inc—*Ali Kolahi*	6633 Odessa Ave, Van Nuys CA 91406	818-909-6060	R	17*	.2
222	Mep Acquisition Corp—*Brian Barbo*	1401 Tower Rd, Lebanon MO 65536	417-588-3128	R	16*	.3
223	Vectron International Inc—*Terry Ede*	267 Lowell Rd, Hudson NH 03051		S	16*	.2
224	GE Zenith Controls	830 W 40th St, Chicago IL 60609	773-299-6600	S	16*	.1
225	Outsource Manufacturing Inc—*Ted Fogliani*	2839 Loker Ave E, Carlsbad CA 92010	760-795-1295	R	16*	.1
226	Baier and Baier Inc—*Fred Baier*	27282 Calle Arroyo, San Juan Capistrano CA 92675	949-240-1233	R	16*	.2
227	Inservco Inc—*Dennis Sudnick*	PO Box 106, Lagrange OH 44050	440-355-5102	R	15*	.1
228	Co- Ax Technology Inc—*Hosen Varghai*	29401 Ambina Dr, Solon OH 44139	440-914-9200	R	15*	.1
229	Kevlin Corp—*John Mcnulla*	596 Lowell St, Methuen MA 01844	978-557-2400	R	15*	.1
230	Imperial Electronic Assembly Inc—*Anthony Conte*	1000 Federal Rd, Brookfield CT 06804	203-740-8425	R	15*	.1
231	Amptech Inc—*Lee Wyatt*	201 Glocheski Dr, Manistee MI 49660	231-464-5492	R	15*	.1
232	Precision Cable Assemblies LLC—*Dennis Wick*	16830 Pheasant Dr, Brookfield WI 53005	262-784-7887	R	15*	.1
233	Westcor—*Patrizio Vinciarelli* Vicor Corp	560 Oakmead Pky, Sunnyvale CA 94085	408-522-5280	D	15*	.1
234	Shafer Magnetic Components—*Dan Shafer*	4773-H Brooks St, Montclair CA 91763	909-626-2722	R	15*	<.1
235	American Products Inc—*John Eltringham*	45 Leigh Dr, York PA 17406	717-767-6510	R	15*	.1
236	Unique Electronics Inc—*George Singleton*	1320 26th St, Orlando FL 32805	407-422-3051	R	15*	.1
237	Advanced Interconnections Corp—*Michael Murphy*	5 Energy Way, West Warwick RI 02893	401-823-5200	R	15*	.1
238	Jem Electronics Inc—*John Donald*	23 National Dr, Franklin MA 02038	508-520-3105	R	15*	.1
239	Curlee Manufacturing Co—*Peters Strong*	13639 Aldine Westfield, Houston TX 77039		D	14*	.1
240	S and K Electronics Inc—*Lawrence Hall*	56301 Us Hwy 93, Ronan MT 59864	406-883-6241	R	14*	.1
241	ITT Industries Inc Conoflow Div—*Steven Loranger*	PO Box 768, Saint George SC 29477	843-563-9281	D	14*	.1
242	Burton Industries Inc—*Gary Burnett*	PO Box 250, Hazelhurst WI 54531		R	14*	.1
243	LCD Systems Corp—*Dave Forter*	1167 Oddstad Dr, Redwood City CA 94063	650-365-5222	R	14*	<.1
244	Martinez Manufacturing Inc—*Carlos Martinez*	1175 Alexander Ct, Cary IL 60013	847-516-8080	R	14*	.2
245	Maury Microwave Inc—*Marc Maury*	2900 Inland Empire Blv, Ontario CA 91764	909-987-4715	R	14*	.1
246	Tel-Instrument Electronics Corp—*Harold K Fletcher*	728 Garden St, Carlstadt NJ 07072	201-933-1600	P	14	.1
247	Hermetic Switch Inc—*Thomas Posey*	3100 S Norge Rd, Chickasha OK 73018	405-224-4046	R	13*	.3
248	Acopian Technical Co—*Gregory Acopian*	PO Box 638, Easton PA 18044	610-258-6149	R	13*	.1
249	American Precision Electronics Inc—*Michael Hall*	25 W 624 Saint Charles, Carol Stream IL 60188	630-510-8080	R	13*	.1
250	Bentek Corp—*Mitch Shock*	2350 Harris Way, San Jose CA 95131	408-954-9600	R	13*	.1
251	Triana Industries Inc—*Ralph Malone*	511 6th St, Madison AL 35756	256-772-9304	R	13*	.2
252	Rapco International Inc—*Lisa Williams*	3581 Larch Ln, Jackson MO 63755	573-243-1433	R	13*	.1
253	Adcomm Inc—*Allen Cohen*	89 Leuning St Ste 9, South Hackensack NJ 07606	201-342-6349	R	13*	.1
254	Wenzel Associates Inc—*Charles Wenzel*	PO Box 80289, Austin TX 78708	512-835-2038	R	13*	.1
255	EFI Electronics Corp—*Richard D Clasen*	1751 S 4800 W, Salt Lake City UT 84104	801-977-9009	S	13*	.1

Note: An asterisk (*) indicates an estimated financial figure. The company type code used is as follows: R = Private, P = Public, S = Private Subsidiary, B = Public Subsidiary, D = Division, J = Joint Venture, I = Investment Fund.

COMPANY RANKINGS BY SALES WITHIN 4-DIGIT SIC

Rank	Company Name—Executive Officer	Address, City, State, Zip	Phone	Type	Fin	Empls
256	SSP Solutions Inc	123 Town Sq Pl Ste 113, Jersey City NJ 07310	732-603-0010	R	13*	.1
257	BTC Electronic Components—Robert Barnett	2709 Connector Dr, Wake Forest NC 27587	919-556-8900	R	13*	.1
258	Douglas Electrical Components Inc—Edward Douglas	5 Middlebury Blvd, Randolph NJ 07869	973-627-8230	R	13*	<.1
259	Able-Age Inc—Robert Satake	3307 Edward Ave, Santa Clara CA 95054	408-727-9473	R	13*	.1
260	Xymox Technologies Inc—Salvatore Bonanno	9099 W Dean Rd, Milwaukee WI 53224	414-362-9000	R	13*	.1
261	Prime Technological Services LLC—Paulla Gaines	2925 Shawnee Industria, Suwanee GA 30024	770-232-7300	R	13*	.1
262	Sentral Assemblies and Components Inc—David Spayer	595 Bond St, Lincolnshire IL 60069	847-478-9720	R	12*	.1
263	Enercon Industries Corp—Donald Nimmer	PO Box 773, Menomonee Falls WI 53052	262-255-6070	R	12*	.1
264	Robert Warren LLC—Sandy Perkins	1 Sprucewood Ln, Westport CT 06880	203-254-7155	R	12*	.2
265	Millennium Electronics Inc—Duane Benn	300 Millennium Dr, Crystal Lake IL 60012	815-479-9755	R	12*	.1
266	Rel-Tech Electronics Inc—Rosemary Blanc	PO Box 3111, Milford CT 06460	203-877-8770	R	12*	.1
267	Surface Mount Depot Inc—Ted Davis	4001 Will Rogers Pkwy, Oklahoma City OK 73108	405-948-8763	R	12*	.1
268	Sawyer Technical Materials LLC—Paul Hervey	35400 Lakeland Blvd, Willoughby OH 44095	440-951-8770	R	12*	.1
269	Calex Manufacturing Company Inc—Stephen Cuff	2401 Stanwell Dr Frnt, Concord CA 94520	925-687-4411	R	12*	.1
270	Progressive Dynamics Inc—Ralph Mcgee	507 Industrial Rd, Marshall MI 49068	269-781-4241	R	12*	.1
271	First Electronics Corp—William Tregoning	71 Von Hillern St, Dorchester MA 02125	617-288-2430	R	12*	.1
272	Ultravolt Inc—Filippo Galluppi	1800 Ocean Ave Unit A, Ronkonkoma NY 11779	631-471-4444	R	12*	.1
273	Applied Thin-Film Products—David Adams	3620 Yale Way, Fremont CA 94538	510-661-4287	R	12*	.1
274	Lucero Cables Inc—Madeline Eliasnia	193 Stauffer Blvd, San Jose CA 95125	408-298-6001	R	12*	.1
275	Badger Technologies Inc—Phillip Mistretta	5829 County Rd 41, Farmington NY 14425	585-869-7101	R	12*	.1
276	U S Circuit Inc—Michael Fariba	2071 Wineridge Pl, Escondido CA 92029	760-489-1413	R	12*	.1
277	Pinner Wire and Cable Inc—Dick Pinner	932 N Shiloh Rd, Garland TX 75042	972-494-3333	R	11*	.1
278	Integrated Power Designs Inc—Steve Thompson	300 Stewart Rd, Hanover Township PA 18706	570-824-4666	R	11*	.1
279	Source One Technologies Inc—Craig Olsen	120 Knowles Dr, Los Gatos CA 95032	408-376-3400	R	11*	.1
280	Nortra Cables Inc—Jim Love	570 Gibraltar Dr, Milpitas CA 95035	408-942-1106	R	11*	.1
281	Rantec Power Systems Inc—Michael Bickel	1173 Los Olivos Ave, Los Osos CA 93402	805-596-6000	R	11*	.1
282	International Assemblers Inc—Richard Crocker	1161 W Plcita De La Ct, Green Valley AZ 85614	520-648-2244	R	11*	.4
283	Lowell Manufacturing Co—John Lowell	100 Integram Dr, Pacific MO 63069	636-257-3400	R	11*	.1
284	Photonic Products Group Inc—Joseph J Rutherford	181 Legrand Ave, Northvale NJ 07647	201-767-1910	P	11	.1
285	Photo Stencil LLC—Neil Mecraild	4725 Centennial Blvd, Colorado Springs CO 80919	719-599-4305	R	11*	.1
286	Electrol Wire Harness Company Inc—Nelson Head	N77w30924 Hartman Ct, Hartland WI 53029	262-966-3741	R	11*	.1
287	Diversified Traffic Products Inc—Gregory Myers	PO Box 248, Seven Valleys PA 17360	717-428-0222	R	11*	.1
288	SAME Inc—David Matheny	2100 Ne Spaulding Ave, Grants Pass OR 97526	541-476-9162	R	11*	.1
289	Deca Manufacturing Company Inc—Hansford Williams	PO Box 3269, Mansfield OH 44904	419-884-0071	R	10*	.1
290	Microwave Engineering Corp—Rudy Cheung	1551 Osgood St, North Andover MA 01845	978-685-2776	R	10*	.1
291	Precision Hermetic Technology Inc—Daniel Schachtel	1940 W Park Ave, Redlands CA 92373	909-381-6011	R	10*	.1
292	Axiom Electronics Inc—Robert Toppel	14924 Nw Greenbrier Pk, Beaverton OR 97006	503-643-6600	R	10*	.1
293	Datacon Inc—John Marshall	60 Blanchard Rd, Burlington MA 01803	781-273-5800	R	10*	.1
294	Autronics Corp	665 N Baldwin Park Blv, City of Industry CA 91746	626-851-3100	S	10*	.1
295	CE Electronics Inc—Garry Courtney	2107 Industrial Dr, Bryan OH 43506	419-636-6705	R	10*	.1
296	Nel Frequency Controls Inc—Michael Krattley	PO Box 457, Burlington WI 53105	262-763-3591	R	10*	.1
297	Hampden Engineering Corp—John Flynn	PO Box 563, East Longmeadow MA 01028	413-525-3981	R	10*	.1
298	Dyrsmith LLC—Robert Smith	246 Basher Dr Unit 2, Berthoud CO 80513		R	10*	.1
299	Vishay Americas Inc	1 Greenwich Pl, Shelton CT 06484	402-563-6866	D	10	.1
300	Bei Electronics LLC—Jon Gicchio	3817 Nicholson Rd, Franksville WI 53126	262-886-8800	R	10*	.1
301	Standard Supply Electronics Co—C Robert Stillman	3424 S Main St, Salt Lake City UT 84115	801-486-3371	R	10*	<.1
302	Symetrix Inc—Dane Butcher	6408 216th St SW Ste A, Mountlake Terrace WA 98043	425-778-7728	R	10*	<.1
303	First Computer Systems Inc—Brian Choi	6000 Dawson Blvd Ste J, Norcross GA 30093	770-729-7200	R	10	<.1
304	Meca Electronics Inc—William Davo	459 E Main St, Denville NJ 07834	973-625-0661	R	10*	<.1
305	Amsco US Inc—Mike Yazdi	15250a Texaco Ave, Paramount CA 90723	562-630-0333	R	10*	.1
306	Scott Electronics Inc—John Metzemaekers	33 Northwestern Dr, Salem NH 03079	603-893-2845	R	10*	.1
307	Accratronics Seals Corp—William Fisch	2211 Kenmere Ave, Burbank CA 91504	818-843-1500	R	10*	.1
308	Rocker Solenoid Co—Francis Goodyear	1500 240th St, Harbor City CA 90710	310-534-5660	R	10*	.1
309	Ram Electronic Industries Inc—Theodore Misbin	1704 Taylors Ln Ste 7, Cinnaminson NJ 08077	856-864-0999	R	10*	.1
310	Synergy Microwave Corp—Meta Rohde	201 Mclean Blvd, Paterson NJ 07504	973-881-8800	R	10*	.1
311	Quinstar Technology Inc—Leo Fong	24085 Garnier St, Torrance CA 90505	310-320-1111	R	10*	.1
312	Ewh Spectrum Inc—Robert Robinson	221 W Chillicothe Ave, Bellefontaine OH 43311	937-593-8010	R	9*	.1
313	Four Star Tool Inc—Helmut Hoppe	5521 Meadowbrook Ct, Rolling Meadows IL 60008	847-228-0900	R	9*	.1
314	Egide USA Inc—James Collins	4 Washington St, Cambridge MD 21613	410-901-6100	R	9*	.1
315	Guardian Electric Manufacturing Co—Kevin Kelly	1425 Lake Ave, Woodstock IL 60098	815-334-3600	R	9*	.1
316	Precision Manufacturing Company Inc—Faye Ledwick	2149 Valley Pke, Dayton OH 45404	937-236-2170	R	9*	.1
317	Northeast Electronics Corp—Armand Cantafio	455 Bic Dr, Milford CT 06461	203-878-3511	R	9*	.1
318	Itasca-Bemidji Inc—Ron Bergan	1219 Naylor Dr Se, Bemidji MN 56601	218-751-8606	R	9*	.1
319	Polytronix Inc—Guohe Huan	PO Box 833024, Richardson TX 75083	972-238-7045	R	9*	.1
320	Spinneret Inc—Gary Speaker	5151 Lafayette St, Santa Clara CA 95054	408-453-3272	R	9*	.1
321	Bourns Inc—Gordon Bourns	1200 Columbia Ave, Riverside CA 92507	909-781-5500	R	9*	.2
322	UEC Electronics LLC—Rebecca A Ufkes	5918 Howard St, Hanahan SC 29406	843-552-8682	R	9*	.1
323	Technology Dynamics Inc—Aaron Levy	100 School St, Bergenfield NJ 07621	201-385-0500	R	9*	.1
324	Dialight Corp	1501 Rte 34 S, Farmingdale NJ 07727	732-919-3119	S	9*	.1
325	I/O Interconnect Inc	1202 E Wakeham Ave, Santa Ana CA 92705	714-564-1111	R	9*	.1
326	MtronicsCom Inc—Ashok Mahbubani	325 Electronics Blvd S, Huntsville AL 35824	256-461-8883	R	9*	.1
327	Control Cable Inc—Richard Meltzer	7261 Ambassador Rd, Baltimore MD 21244	410-298-4411	R	9*	.1
328	Henry Radio Inc—James Henry	2050 S Bundy Dr, Los Angeles CA 90025	310-820-1234	R	9*	<.1
329	Hirschmann Electronics Inc—Klaus Egert	1540 OrchaRd Dr, Chambersburg PA 17201	717-263-7655	R	9*	<.1
330	Asti Corp—Henry Akiya	45 W Broad St, Bergenfield NJ 07621	201-501-8900	R	9*	<.1
331	Intercon Inc—Ted Counts	PO Box 647, Forest VA 24551	434-525-3390	R	9*	.1
332	General Reliance Corp—Sheldon Masser	88 Ford Rd Ste 20, Denville NJ 07834	973-361-1400	R	9*	<.1
333	Martek Power Laser Drive LLC—Robert Geer	5318 Ranalli Dr Ste 2, Gibsonia PA 15044	724-443-7688	R	9*	.1
334	Antenna and Radome Research Associates Corp—Florence Isaacson	PO Box 113, Old Bethpage NY 11804	631-231-8400	R	9*	.1
335	Consolidated Electronic Wire and Cable Corp—Thomas Mann	11044 King St, Franklin Park IL 60131	847-455-8830	R	9*	.1
336	Glassman High Voltage Inc—Sanford Glassman	PO Box 317, High Bridge NJ 08829	908-638-3800	R	9*	.1
337	Elec-Tec Inc—David Brown	1418 Harbin Cir Ste A, Valdosta GA 31601	229-244-1828	R	9*	.1
338	Unitec Inc—Jeffrey Ousborne	7125 Troy Hill Dr Ste, Elkridge MD 21075	443-561-1200	R	9*	.1
339	Crystal Technology LLC—Jon Fowler	1040 E Meadow Cir, Palo Alto CA 94303	650-856-7911	R	9*	.1
340	Solutions Manufacturing Inc—Patrick Mcdonough	1938 Murrell Rd, Rockledge FL 32955	321-636-2041	R	9*	.1
341	Enova Systems Inc—Mike Staran	1560 W 190th St, Torrance CA 90501	310-527-2800	P	9	.1
342	Jerome Industries Corp—John Girolamo	730 Division St, Elizabeth NJ 07201	908-353-5700	S	8*	.1
343	Massa Products Corp—Donald Massa	280 Lincoln St, Hingham MA 02043	781-749-4800	R	8*	.1
344	C R V Electronics Corp—James Vyduna	2249 Pierce Dr, Spring Grove IL 60081	815-675-6500	R	8*	.1

Rank	Company Name—*Executive Officer*	Address, City, State, Zip	Phone	Type	Fin	Empls
345	American Electronic Materials Inc—*Daniel Chang*	6610 Cobra Way, San Diego CA 92121	858-481-0210	R	8*	.1
346	Renaissance Electronics Corp—*Thampy Kurian*	12 Lancaster County Rd, Harvard MA 01451	978-772-7774	R	8*	.1
347	Circuit Manufacturing Inc—*Calvin Rasmussen*	PO Box 1038, Wilsonville OR 97070	503-682-3750	R	8*	.1
348	Electronic Technologies International Inc—*William Brink*	1100 N Main St, Fort Atkinson WI 53538	920-563-0840	R	8*	<.1
349	Logan Industries Inc—*Harold Alexander*	3808 N Sullivan Rd 5f, Spokane Valley WA 99216	509-462-7400	R	8*	.1
350	Gby Corp—*Nancy Robbins*	1001 Lloyd Ave, Latrobe PA 15650	724-539-1626	R	8*	.1
351	GM Associates Inc—*Melvyn Nutter*	9824 Kitty Ln, Oakland CA 94603	510-430-0806	R	8*	.1
352	ASCOR Inc—*Jeff Lum*	4650 Norris Canyon Rd, San Ramon CA 94583	925-328-4650	S	8	.1
353	Dynawave Inc—*Christopher Lewis*	PO Box 8224, Haverhill MA 01835	978-469-0555	R	8*	.1
354	Diversified Technical Systems Inc—*Stephen Pruitt*	909 Electric Ave Ste 2, Seal Beach CA 90740	562-493-0158	R	8*	.1
355	Integrated Microwave Corp—*Dennis Clark*	11353 Sorrento Valley, San Diego CA 92121	858-259-2600	R	7*	.1
356	BV Unitron Manufacturing Inc—*Kenneth Burks*	707 Robins St Ste 115, Conway AR 72034	501-231-4034	R	7*	.1
357	Major Custom Cable Inc—*Scott Wachter*	281 Lotus Dr, Jackson MO 63755	573-204-1008	R	7*	.1
358	Microwave Technology Inc—*Greg Zhou*	4268 Solar Way, Fremont CA 94538	510-651-6700	S	7	.1
359	BC Systems Inc—*Gus Blazek*	200 N Belle Mead Rd St, Setauket NY 11733	631-751-9370	R	7*	.1
360	De Anza Manufacturing Services Inc—*Art Takahara*	1271 Reamwood Ave, Sunnyvale CA 94089	408-734-2020	R	7*	.1
361	TREK Inc—*Toshio Uehara*	11601 Maple Ridge Rd, Medina NY 14103	585-798-3140	R	7*	.1
362	Mid-Eastern Industries Div—*Aaron Levy* Technology Dynamics Inc	100 School St, Bergenfield NJ 07621	201-385-0500	S	7*	.1
363	RLC Electronics Inc—*Charles Borck*	83 Radio Cir Dr, Mount Kisco NY 10549	914-241-1334	R	7*	.1
364	Electro-Core Inc—*Barbara Roethlisberger*	PO Box 1727, Washington MO 63090	636-239-2703	R	7*	.1
365	Airborne Power	901 E Ball Rd, Anaheim CA 92805	714-956-9280	S	7*	.1
366	Electramatic Inc—*Steve Gilbertson*	1815 Jefferson St Ne, Minneapolis MN 55418	612-781-9588	R	7*	.1
367	CTS Corp Reeves Frequency Products Div—*Vinod M Khilnani* CTS Corp	171 Covington Dr, Bloomingdale IL 60108	630-924-3500	D	7*	<.1
368	Applied Electronics—*Mike Rampmeyer*	722 Blue Crab Rd, Newport News VA 23606	757-591-9371	R	7*	<.1
369	Bomac Inc—*Kevin Knecht*	6724 Joy Rd, East Syracuse NY 13057	315-433-9181	R	7*	<.1
370	Acon Inc—*C Lin*	22 Bristol Dr, South Easton MA 02375	508-230-8022	R	7*	<.1
371	Horizon Precision Assembly Co—*David Gouge*	PO Box 602, Lyons CO 80540	303-823-5673	R	7*	.1
372	American Fibertek Inc—*Jack Fernandes*	120 Belmont Dr, Somerset NJ 08873	732-302-0660	R	7*	.1
373	Electronic Controlled Systems Inc—*Lael King*	11200 Hampshire Ave S, Minneapolis MN 55438	952-922-6889	R	7*	.1
374	Sandberg Industries Inc—*Leo Boarts*	PO Box 1385, San Juan Capistrano CA 92693	949-660-9473	R	7*	.1
375	Teejet Technologies Illinois LLC—*David Moeck*	1801 Business Park Dr, Springfield IL 62703	217-753-8451	S	7*	.1
376	Stored Energy Systems A LLC—*Terri Cogdill*	1840 Industrial Cir, Longmont CO 80501	303-678-7500	R	7*	.1
377	Bobo Engineering Inc—*Brenda Bobo*	PO Box 549, Arab AL 35016	256-586-8333	R	7*	<.1
378	Tlc Electronics Inc—*Richard Crofford*	18 Long Lake Rd, Saint Paul MN 55115	651-488-2933	R	7*	.1
379	Res-Net Microwave Inc—*Roger Mayo*	PO Box 18802, Clearwater FL 33762	727-530-9555	R	7*	.1
380	Advanced Design and Manufacturing Inc—*Ron Raby*	350 Heritage Ave Unit, Portsmouth NH 03801	603-430-7573	R	7*	.1
381	Algen Design Services Inc—*Edwin Thomas*	40 Industrial Way E, Eatontown NJ 07724	732-389-4511	R	7*	.1
382	Sinclair Manufacturing Co—*John Sinclair*	PO Box 398, Chartley MA 02712	508-222-7440	R	7*	.1
383	Ruhle Companies Inc—*Frank Ruhle*	99 Wall St, Valhalla NY 10595	914-761-2600	R	7*	.1
384	Aerospace Optics Inc—*Loren Jensen*	3201 Sandy Ln, Fort Worth TX 76112	817-451-1141	R	6*	.1
385	Assem-Tech Inc—*Michael Wilson*	1600 Kooiman Ave, Grand Haven MI 49417	616-846-3410	R	6*	.1
386	Metal Cutting Corp—*Jordan Jablons*	89 Commerce Rd, Cedar Grove NJ 07009	973-239-1100	R	6*	.1
387	Astro Labs Inc—*Steven Toma*	4 Powderhorn Dr, Warren NJ 07059	732-560-3800	R	6*	<.1
388	Southern California Braiding Company Inc—*Leo Mc Intyre*	PO Box 2068, Bell CA 90202	562-927-5531	R	6*	<.1
389	Walt A O'brien—*Walt O'brian*	901 N Hill Dr, Nashville TN 37207	865-494-0006	R	6*	.1
390	Dawn Vme Products—*Barry Burnsides*	47915 Westinghouse Dr, Fremont CA 94539	510-657-4444	P	6*	<.1
391	Silverado Cable Co—*Robert Simpson*	1840 W 1st Ave, Mesa AZ 85202	480-655-8751	R	6*	.1
392	Apc International Ltd—*Ian Henderson*	PO Box 180, Mackeyville PA 17750	570-726-6961	R	6*	.1
393	Timberline Manufacturing Inc—*Mike Johnson*	1050 Lyons Ln, Marion IA 52302	319-377-3720	R	6*	.1
394	Rem-Tronics Inc—*Abe Kadis*	192 Central Ave, Silver Creek NY 14136	716-934-2697	R	6*	.1
395	Luna Tech Inc—*Amanda M McLean*	148 Moon Dr, Owens Cross Roads AL 35763	256-725-4224	R	6*	.1
396	Paramount Industries Inc—*Mike Degrandchamp*	PO Box 1030, Boca Raton FL 33429	954-781-3755	R	6*	.1
397	S and S Research Inc—*Randy Scheffler*	89 Access Rd Ste 10, Norwood MA 02062	781-769-8086	R	6*	.1
398	Sierra Microwave Technology Inc—*John Caruso*	1 Sierra Way, Georgetown TX 78626	512-869-5007	S	6*	.1
399	United Security Products Inc—*Ted R Greene*	13250 Gregg St Ste B, Poway CA 92064	858-413-0149	R	6*	.1
400	Vas Engineering Inc—*Rohak Vora*	4750 Viewridge Ave, San Diego CA 92123	858-569-1601	R	6*	.1
401	Wilbrecht Electronics Inc Elecpac Div—*Ron Campbell*	740 Industrial Dr, Cary IL 60013		D	6*	.1
402	Amtech Microelectronics Inc—*Walter Chavez*	6541 Via Del Oro Ste D, San Jose CA 95119	408-227-8885	R	6*	<.1
403	Erie Specialty Products—*John Ciprlani*	645 W 11th St, Erie PA 16501	814-453-5611	R	6*	<.1
404	Sevcon Inc—*Matthew Boyle*	155 Northboro Rd, Southborough MA 01772	508-281-5500	S	6*	<.1
405	Thunderline-Z Inc Fusite	11 Hazel Dr, Hampstead NH 03841	603-329-4050	S	6*	<.1
406	China Products Inc—*Lee Yu*	2601 S Lemay Ave Unit, Fort Collins CO 80525	970-229-1842	R	6*	<.1
407	Stein Industries Inc—*Dan Steinhaur*	7153 Northland Dr, Brooklyn Park MN 55428	763-504-3500	R	6*	<.1
408	International Electronic Research Corp—*Donald K Schwanz* CTS Corp	413 N Moss St, Burbank CA 91502	818-842-7277	S	6*	<.1
409	Western Reserve Controls Inc—*Jim Barlow*	1485 Exeter Dr, Akron OH 44306	330-733-6662	R	6*	<.1
410	Landmark Technology Inc—*Sun Lu*	172 Component Dr Frnt, San Jose CA 95131	408-434-9302	R	6*	<.1
411	Nyden Corp—*Naoyoshi Yubazaki*	2610-B N 1st St, San Jose CA 95134	408-232-7700	S	6*	<.1
412	Intrapack Corp—*Tracy Zaffino*	10817 Sanden Dr, Dallas TX 75238	214-348-7105	R	6*	.1
413	Technipower LLC—*Melvin Becker*	PO Box 222, Danbury CT 06813	203-748-7001	R	6*	<.1
414	Ahead Magnetics Inc—*Tim Higgins*	6410 Via Del Oro, San Jose CA 95119	408-226-9991	R	6*	<.1
415	Remcon-North Corp—*Marie Remson*	PO Box 957, Meredith NH 03253	603-279-7091	R	6*	<.1
416	Magnetic Sensors Corp—*Charles Boudakian*	1365 N Mccan St, Anaheim CA 92806	714-630-8380	R	6*	<.1
417	Custom Automated Services Inc—*Harry Unger*	311 25th St Nw, Fayette AL 35555	205-932-7287	R	6*	<.1
418	Qual-Tron Inc—*Robert Kane*	9409 E 55th Pl, Tulsa OK 74145	918-622-7052	R	6*	<.1
419	Bivar Inc—*Thomas Silber*	4 Thomas, Irvine CA 92618	949-951-8808	R	6*	<.1
420	Sturges Electronics Products Company Inc—*James Koch*	PO Box 532, Dryden NY 13053	607-844-8604	R	6*	<.1
421	Masterpress Inc—*Ronald Shigeno*	10721 Midvale Ave N, Seattle WA 98133	206-524-1444	R	6*	<.1
422	Logus Manufacturing Corp—*Tom Hack*	1305 Hill Ave, West Palm Beach FL 33407	561-842-3550	R	6*	<.1
423	Micro Lambda Wireless Inc—*John Nguyen*	46515 Landing Pkwy, Fremont CA 94538	510-770-9221	R	6*	<.1
424	Miller Stuart Inc—*Arthur Hoffer*	595 Old Willets Path D, Hauppauge NY 11788	631-582-4705	R	6*	<.1
425	Ironwood Electronics Inc—*Mickiel Fedde*	11351 Rupp Dr Ste 400, Burnsville MN 55337	952-229-8200	R	6*	<.1
426	Ecliptek Inc—*Cary Rosen*	3545 Cadillac Ave Ste, Costa Mesa CA 92626	714-433-1200	R	6*	<.1
427	Heiter Electronics Inc—*Roger Heiter*	3505 N Flood Ave, Norman OK 73069	405-364-5335	R	5*	<.1
428	Bryton Technology Inc—*Rebecca Ptashnik*	PO Box 300, Toulon IL 61483	309-995-3379	R	5*	.1
429	Atc Power Systems Inc—*Joel Bedell*	45 Depot St, Merrimack NH 03054	603-429-0391	R	5*	.1
430	RS Microwave Company Inc—*Richard Snyder*	PO Box 273, Butler NJ 07405	973-492-1207	R	5*	<.1

Note: An asterisk (*) indicates an estimated financial figure. The company type code used is as follows: R = Private, P = Public, S = Private Subsidiary, B = Public Subsidiary, D = Division, J = Joint Venture, I = Investment Fund.

COMPANY RANKINGS BY SALES WITHIN 4-DIGIT SIC

Rank	Company Name—Executive Officer	Address, City, State, Zip	Phone	Type	Fin	Empls
431	American Aerospace Controls Inc—Ruth Gitlin	570 Smith St, Farmingdale NY 11735	631-694-5100	R	5*	<.1
432	Cables Unlimited Inc—Darren Clark	3 Old Dock Rd, Yaphank NY 11980	631-563-6363	R	5*	<.1
433	Kinetics Industries Inc—Ronald Secrest	140 Stokes Ave, Ewing NJ 08638	609-883-9700	R	5*	<.1
434	Naso Industries Corp—Soraya Saleh	3007 Bunsen Ave Ste S, Ventura CA 93003	805-650-1231	R	5*	<.1
435	That Corp—Leslie Tyler	45 Sumner St, Milford MA 01757	508-478-9200	R	5*	<.1
436	Tri Tek Electronics Inc—Jim Gillson	25358 Ave Stanford, Valencia CA 91355	661-295-0020	R	5*	<.1
437	Reedex Inc—Dan Reed	15526 Commerce Ln, Huntington Beach CA 92649	714-894-0311	R	5*	<.1
438	Jaxx Manufacturing Inc—Greg Liu	1912 Angus Ave, Simi Valley CA 93063	805-526-4979	R	5*	<.1
439	Thermal Electronics Inc—James Mikesell	PO Box 5000, Lake Elsinore CA 92531	951-674-7771	R	5*	<.1
440	Supreme Cable Technology Inc—Glen Tilley	12351 Grant St Unit 30, Thornton CO 80241	303-280-0907	R	5*	<.1
441	Carrio Cabling Corp—Glen Carrio	2455 Executive Cir, Colorado Springs CO 80906	719-576-4571	R	5*	<.1
442	Syvox Corp	1850 Interstate 30, Rockwall TX 75087	972-771-1653	S	5*	.1
443	Magnetico Inc	4538 Camberwell Rd, Cincinnati OH 45209	513-871-3777	S	5*	.1
444	Magnetic Circuit Elements Inc—John Conklin	1540 Moffett St, Salinas CA 93905	831-757-8752	R	5*	<.1
445	Networks International Corp—Alok Bisarya	15237 Broadmoor St, Overland Park KS 66223	913-685-3400	R	5*	<.1
446	Excel Connection Inc—Joseph Marshall	5415 S 9th St, Milwaukee WI 53221	414-769-9080	R	5*	<.1
447	Microwave Filter Company Inc—Carl F Fahrenkrug	6743 Kinne St, East Syracuse NY 13057	315-438-4700	P	5	<.1
448	SAS Manufacturing Inc—Theo Smit	405 N Smith Ave, Corona CA 92880	951-734-1808	R	5*	<.1
449	T and E Industries Inc—Edward Mcentee	215 Watchung Ave, Orange NJ 07050	973-672-5454	R	5*	<.1
450	Advanced Technical Materials—Mike Geraci	49 Rider Ave, Patchogue NY 11772	631-289-0363	R	5*	<.1
451	Phonon Corp—Tom Martin	PO Box 549, Simsbury CT 06070	860-651-0211	R	5*	<.1
452	Goddard Valve Corp—Salvatore J Vinciguerra	3181 Lear Dr, Burlington NC 27215	336-226-3244	R	5*	<.1
453	Northeimer Manufacturing Inc—Gary Northeimer	2670 Leisczs Bridge Rd, Leesport PA 19533	610-926-1136	R	5*	<.1
454	Reactel Inc—Emanuel Assurian	8031 Cessna Ave, Gaithersburg MD 20879	301-519-3660	R	5*	<.1
455	Trident Manufacturing Inc—Ron Horney	PO Box 6243, Rockford IL 61125	815-394-7405	R	5*	<.1
456	ProtoCAM—Ray Biery	3848 Cherryville Rd, Northampton PA 18067	610-261-9010	R	5*	<.1
457	Military/Aerospace Division of Pulse Pulse Engineering Inc	2 Pearl Buck Ct, Bristol PA 19007	215-781-6400	D	5*	<.1
458	QCE USA—Glenn Allen	3013 Del Prado Blvd S, Cape Coral FL 33904	561-948-4387	R	5*	<.1
459	Bigston Corp—Kimitaka Sekiguchi	1590 Touhy Ave, Elk Grove Village IL 60007	847-439-3500	R	5*	.3
460	Melstrom Manufacturing Corp—Demitrios Tsoutsas	5303 Asbury Rd, Wall Township NJ 07727	732-938-7400	R	5*	.1
461	Oxford Wire and Cable Services Inc—Yoshihiro Murakawa	10 Industrial Park Dr, Oxford MS 38655	662-234-1410	R	5*	<.1
462	Affiliated Products Inc—Stephen Schlueter	PO Box 269, Mayville WI 53050	920-387-7400	R	5*	<.1
463	Ornelas Enterprises Inc—Tino Ornelas	7395 Nw Evergreen Pkwy, Hillsboro OR 97124	503-844-9000	R	5*	<.1
464	Microvision Inc—Alexander Tokman	6222 185th Ave NE, Redmond WA 98052	425-936-6847	P	5	.1
465	Aerospace—Juanita Erwin	PO Box 8744, Kansas City MO 64114	816-333-3443	R	5*	.1
466	Lightech Fiberoptic Inc—Jimmy Ko	1987 Adams Ave, San Leandro CA 94577	510-567-8700	R	5*	<.1
467	Anatech Electronics Inc—Sam Benzacar	PO Box 2217, Garfield NJ 07026	973-772-4242	R	5*	<.1
468	Heale Manufacturing Company Inc—Elliott Erickson	PO Box 1444, Waukesha WI 53187	262-542-4496	R	5*	<.1
469	Quality Electronics Inc—Philip Lavoie	PO Box 23487, Columbia SC 29224	803-865-7065	R	5*	<.1
470	Qems Inc—Phuong Nguyen	1310 Airport Rd Ste B, Monroe NC 28110	704-996-7367	R	5*	<.1
471	Apogee Controls Inc—Trish Peters	117 Constitution Dr, Warner Robins GA 31088	478-971-7020	R	5*	<.1
472	Artech Industries Inc—Mansukh Bera	1966 Keats Dr, Riverside CA 92501	951-276-3331	R	5*	<.1
473	Dare Electronics Inc—Karen Beagle	PO Box 419, Troy OH 45373	937-335-0031	R	4*	.1
474	Ssi Electronics Inc—Daniel Anderson	8080 Graphic Dr Ne, Belmont MI 49306	616-866-8880	R	4*	<.1
475	Debron Industrial Electronics Inc—Ronald Bernot	591 Executive Dr, Troy MI 48083	248-588-7220	R	4*	<.1
476	Automated Circuit Technology Inc—William Boyer	N90w14739 Commerce Dr, Menomonee Falls WI 53051	262-255-7370	R	4*	<.1
477	Maryland Ceramics And Steatite Company Inc—Ernest Dinning	PO Box 527, Bel Air MD 21014	410-838-4114	R	4*	<.1
478	Kamtel Inc—Rati Patel	933 W Chase St, Springfield MO 65803	417-864-5004	R	4*	<.1
479	Absolute Process Instruments Inc—William Sawyer	1220 American Way, Libertyville IL 60048	847-918-3510	R	4*	<.1
480	Solar Con Inc—Donald Wells	PO Box 176, Holland OH 43528	419-865-5877	R	4*	<.1
481	Miltronics Manufacturing Services Inc—Anton Neary	95 Krif Rd, Keene NH 03431	603-352-3333	R	4*	<.1
482	Andon Electronics Corp—John Tate	4 Ct Dr, Lincoln RI 02865	401-333-0388	R	4*	<.1
483	Ember Industries Inc—Thomas Leonardis	321 Carlson Cir, San Marcos TX 78666	512-396-1911	R	4*	<.1
484	Marki Microwave Inc—Ferenc Marki	215 Vineyard Ct, Morgan Hill CA 95037	408-778-4200	R	4*	<.1
485	Advantage Medical Electronics Inc—David Kendricks	10630 Wiles Rd, Coral Springs FL 33076	954-345-9800	R	4*	<.1
486	Electronic Support Services Inc—Roger Polk	720 N Webster St, Kokomo IN 46901	765-452-9935	R	4*	<.1
487	Astro Seal Inc—Michael Hammer	827 Palmyrita Ave Ste, Riverside CA 92507	951-787-6670	R	4*	<.1
488	Staffall Inc—Ernest Crivellone	1468 Elmwood Ave, Cranston RI 02910	401-461-5554	R	4*	<.1
489	Deltronic Labs Inc—Stephen Horniak	120 Liberty Ln, Chalfont PA 18914	215-997-8616	R	4*	<.1
490	Electro-Tech Products Inc—Ramzi Bader	2001 E Gladstone St St, Glendora CA 91740	909-592-1434	R	4*	<.1
491	Essex Electro Engineers Inc—Frank Pawlowski	2015 Mitchell Blvd Ste, Schaumburg IL 60193	847-891-4444	R	4*	<.1
492	GT Microwave Inc—Antonio Baliotis	2 Emery Ave Ste 2, Randolph NJ 07869	973-361-5700	R	4*	<.1
493	Innovative Card Technologies Inc—Richard J Nathan	633 W 5th St Ste 2600, Los Angeles CA 90071	213-223-2145	P	4	<.1
494	End To End Inc—Larry C Delone	801 Water St 4th Fl, Portsmouth VA 23704	757-498-3669	R	4*	.1
495	Almega/Tru-Flex Inc—Elmo Hurst	PO Box 67, Bremen IN 46506	574-546-2113	R	4*	.1
496	Jayco Interface Technology Inc—Hemant Mistry	1351 Pico St, Corona CA 92881	951-738-2000	R	4*	<.1
497	Tate Technology Inc—Lee Tate	3102 E Trent Ave Ste 1, Spokane WA 99202	509-534-2500	R	4*	<.1
498	Hermac Inc—Kathy Aninch	PO Box 129, Auburn IN 46706	260-925-0312	R	4*	<.1
499	Caliber Electronics Inc—Randall Scheckler	208 Avenida Fabricante, San Clemente CA 92672	949-366-8700	R	4*	<.1
500	Colorado Crystal Corp—Thomas Schuyler	2303 W 8th St, Loveland CO 80537	970-667-9248	S	4*	<.1
501	Smart Power Systems Inc—Bahram Mechanic	1760 Stebbins Dr, Houston TX 77043	713-464-8000	R	4*	<.1
502	Andrew Technologies Inc—Kathleen Michals	305 Alderman Ave, Wheeling IL 60090	847-520-5770	R	4*	<.1
503	Flintec Inc—Robert Gray	18 Kane Industrial Dr, Hudson MA 01749	978-562-4548	R	4*	<.1
504	Jasper Electronics—Rob Nishimoto	1580 N Kellogg Dr, Anaheim CA 92807	714-917-0749	R	4*	<.1
505	Midland Consumer Radio Inc	5900 Parretta Dr, Kansas City MO 64120	816-241-8500	R	4*	<.1
506	Quality Quartz Engineering Inc—Scott Moseley	8484 Central Ave, Newark CA 94560	510-747-9200	R	4*	<.1
507	Strike Technology Inc—Robert Kunesh	729 W Anaheim St Ste A, Long Beach CA 90813	562-437-3428	R	4*	<.1
508	Precision Mechanisms Corp—Daniel Petrasek	50 Bond St, Westbury NY 11590	516-333-5955	R	4	<.1
509	Shelly Associates Inc—Sam Cross Jr	17171 Murphy Ave, Irvine CA 92614	949-417-8070	R	4	<.1
510	Omnitronix Corp—Allen Ernst	349 Roma Jean Pkwy, Streamwood IL 60107	630-837-1400	R	4*	<.1
511	HDR Power Systems Inc—Dan Skinner	3563 Interchange Rd, Columbus OH 43204	614-308-5500	S	4*	<.1
512	Krytar Inc—Douglas Hagan	1288 Anvilwood Ave, Sunnyvale CA 94089	408-734-5999	R	4*	<.1
513	Star Engineering Inc—Victor Neagoe	1 Vaillancourt Dr, North Attleboro MA 02763	508-316-1492	R	4*	<.1
514	Telan Corp—C Nelson	2880 Bergey Rd Ste G, Hatfield PA 19440	215-822-1234	R	4*	<.1
515	Src Cables Inc—Rudolph Hirschnitz	5590 Skylane Blvd, Santa Rosa CA 95403	707-573-1900	R	4*	<.1
516	Jfh Technologies LLC—James Harhi	300 N Dr Ste 102, Melbourne FL 32934	321-752-4580	R	4*	<.1
517	Condor Electronics Corp—Wayne Corso	PO Box 60590, Rochester NY 14606	585-235-1500	R	4*	<.1
518	LP Glassblowing Inc—Leopold Pivk	2322 Calle Del Mundo, Santa Clara CA 95054	408-988-7561	R	4*	<.1
519	Transducer Techniques Inc—Randy Baker	42480 Rio Nedo, Temecula CA 92590	951-719-3965	R	4*	<.1

Rank	Company Name—Executive Officer	Address, City, State, Zip	Phone	Type	Fin	Empls
520	Wyvern Technologies Inc—James Weber	1205 E Warner Ave, Santa Ana CA 92705	714-966-0710	R	4*	<.1
521	Circom Inc—Lisa Esczuk	505 W Main St, Bensenville IL 60106	630-595-4460	R	4*	<.1
522	Hoku Corp—Scott Paul	1288 Ala Moana Blvd St, Honolulu HI 96814	808-682-7800	P	4	.1
523	Basic Electronics Inc—Nancy Balzano	11371 Monarch St, Garden Grove CA 92841	714-530-2400	R	4*	<.1
524	Osda Contract Services Inc—David Ingraham	PO Box 3048, Milford CT 06460	203-878-2155	R	4*	<.1
525	Caron Enterprises Inc—Ronald Greer	2700 Mechanic St, Lake City PA 16423	814-774-5658	R	4*	.5
526	Amperite Company Inc—Judith Johnson	4201 Tonnelle Ave Ste, North Bergen NJ 07047	201-864-9503	R	4*	<.1
527	Kadel Engineering Corp—David Alexander	1627 E Main St, Danville IN 46122	317-745-2798	R	4*	<.1
528	Porta Phone Company Inc—John Hooper	PO Box 560, Narragansett RI 02882	401-789-8700	R	4*	<.1
529	Alan Industries Inc—William Kennedy	PO Box 1203, Columbus IN 47202	812-372-8869	R	4*	<.1
530	Advanced Technology Group Inc—Li Tao	101 Round Hill Dr, Rockaway NJ 07866	973-627-6955	R	4*	<.1
531	APM Hexseal Corp—Milton Morse	44 Honeck St, Englewood NJ 07631	201-569-5700	R	4*	<.1
532	ITS Instrument Corp—Elfrieda Collins	PO Box 69, Islip NY 11751	631-581-8020	R	4*	<.1
533	Microwave Circuit Technology Inc—Brit Andresen	44 Sarah Dr, Farmingdale NY 11735	631-845-1041	R	4*	<.1
534	Southeastern Electronic Assembly Services Inc—Dan Cox	PO Box 2249, Camden SC 29020	803-425-4258	R	4*	<.1
535	Sigma Four LP—Pramila Jain	3301 Tech Dr Ste 115, Plano TX 75074	972-423-6474	R	4*	<.1
536	Electronic Fabrication Service—Mike Bruck	PO Box 750, Dardanelle AR 72834	479-229-0013	R	4*	<.1
537	Bio-Key International Inc—Michael W DePasquale	3349 Hwy 138 Bldg D St, Wall NJ 07719	732-359-1100	P	4	<.1
538	Dynasty Electronic Corp—Mark Clark	1790 E Mcfadden Ave St, Santa Ana CA 92705	714-550-1197	R	3*	<.1
539	Quality Switch Inc—Russell Sewell	PO Box 250, Newton Falls OH 44444	330-872-5707	R	3*	<.1
540	Citala Us Inc—Ronen Lin	1277 Reamwood Ave, Sunnyvale CA 94089	408-745-8500	R	3*	<.1
541	Bluegrass Wire Harness Inc—Mike Horn	PO Box 845, Berea KY 40403	859-985-1505	R	3*	<.1
542	Ngi Electronics LLC—Carlos Navarro	PO Box 40484, Houston TX 77240	713-983-7192	R	3*	<.1
543	Omniyig Inc—William Capogeannis	3350 Scott Blvd Bldg 6, Santa Clara CA 95054	408-988-0843	R	3*	<.1
544	Total Control Solutions Inc—Jeff Forsberg	20175 County Rd 50, Hamel MN 55340	763-416-1610	R	3*	<.1
545	N and N Manufacturing Inc—John Nault	24 Graf Rd, Newburyport MA 01950	978-465-1110	R	3*	<.1
546	Casco Manufacturing Inc—Jackie James	600 Territorial Dr Ste, Bolingbrook IL 60440	630-971-9400	R	3*	<.1
547	Electronics Assemblers Inc—James Vandyke	PO Box 664, Hood River OR 97031	541-386-3227	R	3*	<.1
548	Hazlow Electronics Inc—Alma Publow	49 Saint Bridgets Dr, Rochester NY 14605	585-325-5323	R	3*	<.1
549	Mask Technology Inc—Andrew Holzmann	2601 Oak St, Santa Ana CA 92707	714-557-3383	R	3*	<.1
550	Stetron International Inc—Monique Steger	90 Broadway St Ste 1, Buffalo NY 14203	716-854-3443	R	3*	<.1
551	Compex Corp—Gerald Gordon	439 Commerce Ln Ste 1, West Berlin NJ 08091	856-335-2277	R	3*	<.1
552	Reedholm Instruments Co—Joseph Reedholm	4 Sierra Way St, Georgetown TX 78626	512-869-1935	R	3*	<.1
553	Tekquest Inc—Basil Pappademetriou	2510 Kirby Cir Ne Ste, Palm Bay FL 32905	321-768-6069	R	3*	<.1
554	Rantec Microwave Systems Corp—Richard Peterson	520 E Carmel St, San Marcos CA 92078	760-744-1544	R	3*	<.1
555	Eaglepro Industries LLC—Brian Mikels	2218 E High St Ste C, Jackson MI 49203	517-796-8800	R	3*	<.1
556	Para Systems Inc—Rod Pullen Components Corporation Of America	1455 Lemay Dr, Carrollton TX 75007	972-446-7363	S	3*	<.1
557	Spencer Industries Inc—Martin Lawrence	PO Box 128, Belleville NJ 07109	973-751-2200	R	3*	<.1
558	Caddo Connections Inc—Ronald Caddo	2833 N Goldring Rd, La Porte IN 46350	219-874-8119	R	3*	<.1
559	Channel Microwave Corp—Ken Bosswell	480 Constitution Ave, Camarillo CA 93012	805-482-7280	R	3*	.1
560	Digital Power Corp Amos Kohn	41324 Christy St, Fremont CA 94538	510-657-2635	P	3	<.1
561	Clairex Technologies Inc—Malcolm Catter	1301 E Plano Pkwy, Plano TX 75074	972-205-4900	R	3*	<.1
562	Phillips LLC	606 Baltimore Ave, Baltimore MD 21204	410-821-8123	R	3*	<.1
563	Shoals Technologies Group Inc—Dean Solon	1400 Shoals Way, Portland TN 37148	615-451-1400	R	3*	<.1
564	Csr Interconnect LLC—Ana Fernandez	2950 Saturn St Ste A, Brea CA 92821	714-572-5610	R	3*	<.1
565	Da-Green Electronics Ltd—Robert Farbotko	PO Box 267, South River NJ 08882	732-254-2735	R	3*	<.1
566	Electri-Tec Investor Group Inc—Wayne Luchenbill	509 Growth Pkwy, Angola IN 46703	260-665-1252	R	3*	<.1
567	Mmt Technology Inc—Gene Vay	1203 N 7 Hwy, Pleasant Hill MO 64080	816-540-6202	R	3*	<.1
568	Pgf Technology Group Inc—Naji Gebara	2993 Technology Dr, Rochester Hills MI 48309	248-852-2800	R	3*	<.1
569	Techtrol Cyclonetics Inc—Perry Bates	PO Box 650, Dillsburg PA 17019	717-774-2746	R	3*	<.1
570	White James C Company Inc—Tom White	PO Box 5495, Greenville SC 29606	864-288-4692	R	3*	<.1
571	Microwave Applications Group—Steve VanDyke	3030 Industrial Pkwy, Santa Maria CA 93455	805-928-5711	R	3*	<.1
572	Christian Manufacturing Inc—Joseph Christian	PO Box 220, Manchaca TX 78652	512-282-8340	R	3*	<.1
573	Delta Products Corp (Beaverton Oregon)—Bruce Cheng	15125 SW Koll Pkwy Ste, Beaverton OR 97006	503-533-8444	S	3*	<.1
574	Enon Microwave Inc Micronetics Inc	26 Hampshire Dr, Hudson NH 03051	603-883-2900	S	3*	<.1
575	Mercury United Electronics Inc	9299 9th St, Rancho Cucamonga CA 91730		R	3	<.1
576	Neutronics Enterprises Inc—Keith Finkenbiner	11421 W Bernardo Ct, San Diego CA 92127	858-674-2250	R	3*	<.1
577	Redmond Cable Corp—Jackie Fjellstad	8539 154 Ave NE, Redmond WA 98052	425-882-2009	R	3*	<.1
578	Saint Wire and Cable Company Inc—Pat St Mary	N4932 Hwy V, Fond du Lac WI 54937	920-921-2637	R	3*	<.1
579	NVIS Inc—Marc Foglia	11495 Sunset Hills Ste, Reston VA 20190	703-891-1130	R	3*	<.1
580	FCS—Daniel Vermut	PO Box 16300, Fort Lauderdale FL 33318	954-370-0000	R	3*	<.1
581	Coaxial Components Corp—David Leiman	PO Box 272486, Boca Raton FL 33427	772-287-5000	R	3*	<.1
582	Seren Industrial Power Systems Inc—Larry Hooper	1670 Gallagher Dr, Vineland NJ 08360	856-205-1131	R	3*	<.1
583	Data Drive Thru Inc—Paul Andrus	PO Box 578, Turtle Lake ND 58575	214-459-8359	R	3*	<.1
584	V-Blox Corp—David Mulvaney	13291 Vantage Way Ste, Jacksonville FL 32218	904-387-9333	R	3*	<.1
585	Alternate E-Components LLC—Tim Savoy	1136 Bridge St, Manchester NH 03108	603-670-5620	R	3*	<.1
586	Silitronics Inc—Arya Bhattacherjee	1957 Concourse Dr, San Jose CA 95131	408-954-8301	R	3*	<.1
587	Meridian Technologies Inc—Denise Shay	700 Elmont Rd, Elmont NY 11003	516-285-1000	R	3*	<.1
588	Canfield Electronics Inc—Lynn Zaun	90 Remington Blvd, Ronkonkoma NY 11779	631-585-4100	R	3*	<.1
589	International Power Dc Power Supplies Inc—Craig Johnson	360 Bernoulli Cir, Oxnard CA 93030	805-981-1188	R	3*	<.1
590	Applied Power Systems Inc—James Murphy	124 Charlotte Ave, Hicksville NY 11801	516-935-2230	R	3*	<.1
591	Cleveland Circuits Corp—Sumir Amin	15516 Industrial Pkwy, Cleveland OH 44135	216-941-2226	R	3*	<.1
592	Fabricast Inc—H Wood	PO Box 3176, South El Monte CA 91733	626-443-3247	R	3*	<.1
593	Revelation Industries Inc—Steve Nettik	101 E Oak St Ste W, Bozeman MT 59715	406-587-5978	R	3*	<.1
594	Phoenix-Lamar Corp—Kent Huffman	8868 Research Blvd Ste, Austin TX 78758	512-836-6030	R	3*	<.1
595	Rnb Enterprises Inc—Raymond Bennett	17816 N 25th Ave, Phoenix AZ 85023	602-265-7564	R	3*	<.1
596	Electrotechnics Corp—Bill Marshall	1310 Commerce St, Marshall TX 75672	903-938-1901	R	3*	<.1
597	Microwave Communications Laboratories Inc—Thiem Nguyen	7255 30th Ave N, Saint Petersburg FL 33710	727-344-6254	R	3*	<.1
598	Etron Corp—Michael Mulgrew	9639 Doctor Perry Rd 1, Ijamsville MD 21754	301-831-1394	R	3*	<.1
599	Aspen Electronics Inc—Edwardo Trelles	7288 Nw 54th St, Miami FL 33166	305-863-2151	R	3*	<.1
600	Custom Cables Inc—Marian Spahr	9125 Whiskey Bottom Rd, Laurel MD 20723	301-497-9300	R	3*	<.1
601	Manu Tec Inc—Richard Zboril	415 W Belden Ave Ste E, Addison IL 60101	630-543-3022	R	3*	<.1
602	Sos Manufacturing Inc—Steve Oakins	111 Packer Dr, Roberts WI 54023	715-749-9043	R	3*	<.1
603	Solid State Testing Inc—Alfred Patane	780 Boston Rd Ste 1, Billerica MA 01821	978-670-7300	R	3*	<.1
604	Eft Corp—Dave Repolg	28 Lanyon Dr, Cheshire CT 06410	203-439-0532	R	3*	<.1
605	Geist Plastics—Sam Featherston	5110 Nw 38th St, Lincoln NE 68524	402-470-2606	R	3*	<.1
606	Production Technologies Inc—Mark Utley	7651 Washington Ave S, Minneapolis MN 55439	952-944-1076	R	3*	<.1
607	Satpro Network Inc—Paul Colombo	7406 Spicewood Dr, Garland TX 75044	972-675-8475	R	3*	<.1

Note: An asterisk (*) indicates an estimated financial figure. The company type code used is as follows: R = Private, P = Public, S = Private Subsidiary, B = Public Subsidiary, D = Division, J = Joint Venture, I = Investment Fund.

COMPANY RANKINGS BY SALES WITHIN 4-DIGIT SIC

Rank	Company Name—Executive Officer	Address, City, State, Zip	Phone	Type	Fin	Empls
608	Wheelock Manufacturing Inc—Pat Wheelock	PO Box 680, Morocco IN 47963	219-285-8540	R	3*	<.1
609	Apogee Labs Inc—David Grebe	210 S 3rd St, North Wales PA 19454	215-699-2060	R	3*	<.1
610	International Creative Data Industries Inc—Steven Villodas	407 Brookside Rd Ste 2, Waterbury CT 06708	203-753-8551	R	3*	<.1
611	Austin American Technology Corp—Steve Stach	PO Box 1489, Burnet TX 78611	512-335-6400	R	3*	<.1
612	Integrity Technology Corp—J Young	2505 Technology Dr, Hayward CA 94545	270-812-8867	R	3*	<.1
613	Second Circuits Corp—John Atkinson	127 Aspen Rd, Egan LA 70531	337-785-9333	R	3*	<.1
614	Advanced Manufacturing Inc—Gary Kinley	12205 28th St N, Saint Petersburg FL 33716	727-573-3300	S	3*	<.1
615	Sonoma Scientific Inc—Norm Hartz	2236 Park Pl Ste A, Minden NV 89423	775-783-9100	R	3*	<.1
616	C and A Transducers Inc—Daniel Toledo	14329 Commerce Dr, Garden Grove CA 92843	714-554-9188	R	3*	<.1
617	Digital Wireless Corp—Bob Gemmell	PO Box 86486, Los Angeles CA 90086	323-276-5300	R	3*	<.1
618	Data Delay Devices Inc—Annibale Lupi	3 Mount Prospect Ave, Clifton NJ 07013	973-773-2299	R	3*	<.1
619	Edal Industries Inc—Andrew Esposito	51 Commerce St, East Haven CT 06512	203-467-2591	R	3*	<.1
620	Maro Electronics Inc—Joseph Marozzi	1246 Hayes Blvd, Bristol PA 19007	215-788-7919	R	3*	<.1
621	Electro-Connect Inc—Hassan Hamedi	N84w13562 Leon Rd, Menomonee Falls WI 53051	262-255-6665	R	3*	<.1
622	Darrah Electric Co—David Darrah	5914 Merrill Ave, Cleveland OH 44102	216-631-0912	R	3*	<.1
623	Laser Materials Corp—Paul Collins	12706 Ne 95th St Ste 1, Vancouver WA 98682	360-254-4180	R	3*	<.1
624	Dynascan Technology Inc—Alan Kaufman	7 Chrysler, Irvine CA 92618	949-421-0348	R	3*	<.1
625	Spectra Symbol Corp—David Marriott	3101 W 2100 S, Salt Lake City UT 84119	801-972-6995	R	2*	.1
626	Quality Cable and Components—Cindy Brittingham	PO Box 88, Wyoming IL 61491	309-695-3435	R	2*	<.1
627	Westoak Industries Inc—Larry Rosson	PO Box 1188, Erick OK 73645	580-526-3221	R	2*	<.1
628	Impact LLC	232 Granite St Ste 101, Corona CA 92879	951-296-9600	R	2*	<.1
629	Excel Specialty Corp—Robert Kopf	6335 N Broadway St, Chicago IL 60660	773-262-4781	R	2*	<.1
630	Mekatronics Inc—Jack Bendror	85 Channel Dr Ste 2, Port Washington NY 11050	516-883-6805	R	2*	<.1
631	American Sub-Assembly Producers—Douglas Sherblom	PO Box 417, Webster MA 01570	508-949-2320	R	2*	<.1
632	Electro Power Systems Of Utah—Roy Vincent	1600 W 200 S, Lindon UT 84042	801-796-9300	R	2*	<.1
633	Electro-Support Systems Corp—Richard Olson	27449 Colt Ct, Temecula CA 92590	951-676-2751	R	2*	<.1
634	Fastrak Manufacturing Services Inc—Phil Guzman	1095 N 7th St, San Jose CA 95112	408-298-6414	R	2*	<.1
635	Nathaniel Group Inc—Joel Melnick	101 Panton Rd Ste 1, Vergennes VT 05491	802-877-2182	R	2*	<.1
636	Per-Tech Inc—Michael Hutsell	113 Erie St S, Massillon OH 44646	330-833-8824	R	2*	<.1
637	Radiaulics Inc—Nick Komninos	7343 Rattlesnake Dr, Littleton CO 80124	303-790-2512	R	2*	<.1
638	Omega Leads Inc—Jeff Sweet	1509 Colorado Ave, Santa Monica CA 90404	310-394-6786	R	2*	<.1
639	Tecmag Inc—John Delayre	10161 Harwin Dr Ste 15, Houston TX 77036	713-667-1507	R	2*	<.1
640	D L Electronics Inc—Caroline Laschenski	6020 Palmetto St, Philadelphia PA 19111	215-742-2666	R	2*	<.1
641	Crystal Cal Lab Inc—Michele Anderson	15302 Bolsa Chica St, Huntington Beach CA 92649	714-991-1580	R	2*	<.1
642	D-Termination Wire Products Inc—Michael Gillispie	PO Box 1131, Mentor OH 44061	440-466-4908	R	2*	<.1
643	Virginia Controls Inc—Fred Landon	2513 Mechanicsville Tp, Richmond VA 23223	804-225-5530	R	2*	<.1
644	Kritech Corp—Louis Riberio	329 W 131st St, Los Angeles CA 90061	310-538-9940	R	2*	<.1
645	Wireworks Corp—Gerald Krulewicz	380 Hillside Ave, Hillside NJ 07205	908-686-7400	R	2*	<.1
646	Randolph and Baldwin Inc—Curt Baldwin	PO Box 729, Ayer MA 01432	978-772-4095	R	2*	<.1
647	Apx Technologies Inc—Yuval Ofek	264 Duffy Ave, Hicksville NY 11801	516-433-1313	R	2*	<.1
648	Corey Associates Inc—Karen Kosydar	PO Box 945, Greentown PA 18426	570-676-4800	R	2*	<.1
649	Electrosem LLC	2600 S Hardy Dr, Tempe AZ 85282	602-955-6566	R	2*	<.1
650	Industrial Control Systems Inc—Mark Romers	20 W Williamsburg Rd, Sandston VA 23150	804-737-1700	R	2*	<.1
651	Applied Resources Corp—Matthew Colello	105 W Dewey Ave Ste 31, Wharton NJ 07885	973-328-3882	R	2*	<.1
652	Electronic Systems Technology Inc—Tom L Kirchner	415 N Quay St Bldg B-1, Kennewick WA 99336	509-735-9092	P	2	<.1
653	Amber Industries Inc—Beverly Dawdy	PO Box 802822, Dallas TX 75380	972-490-9801	R	2*	<.1
654	Pal International Corp—Richard Vincent	2614 E Adams St, Phoenix AZ 85034	602-273-7151	R	2*	<.1
655	Protection Technologies Inc—James Palmer	529 Vista Blvd 3a, Sparks NV 89434	775-856-7333	R	2*	<.1
656	Aimtron Corp—Mukesh Vasani	1448 Yorkshire Dr, Streamwood IL 60107	630-372-7500	R	2*	.1
657	ICTC USA—Sareet Majumdar	16041 Flight Path Dr, Brooksville FL 34604	352-796-1716	R	2*	.1
658	JKM Manufacturing—Chad B White	PO Box 579, Eufaula AL 36072	334-687-7061	R	2*	.1
659	VIP Industries Inc—John Sonatore	90 Brighton Rd, Clifton NJ 07012	973-472-7500	R	2*	.1
660	Tri Tec Systems Inc—Gary Sheets	PO Box 965, Decatur IN 46733	260-724-8874	R	2*	<.1
661	International Crystal Manufacturing Co—Royden Freeland	PO Box 1768, Oklahoma City OK 73101	405-236-3741	R	2*	<.1
662	Action Labs Inc—John Thompson	425 Best Rd, Woodville WI 54028	715-698-2525	R	2*	<.1
663	Agi American Grippers Inc—John Barnes	171 Spring Hill Rd, Trumbull CT 06611	203-459-8345	R	2*	<.1
664	Electronic Connectors Inc—Tom Tarasewich	125 S 5th St, Reading PA 19602	610-374-3796	R	2*	<.1
665	Custom Microwave Components Inc—Gregory Mau	44249 Old Warm Springs, Fremont CA 94538	510-651-3434	R	2*	<.1
666	Electronic Prototype Development Inc—James Sullivan	978 Rte 910, Pittsburgh PA 15238	412-767-4111	R	2*	<.1
667	Werlatone Inc—Glen Werlau	PO Box 47, Brewster NY 10509	845-278-2220	R	2*	<.1
668	All Things Digital Inc—Elliott Rivera	7213 Nw 54th St, Miami FL 33166	305-887-9464	R	2*	<.1
669	Ultra-Tech Enterprises Inc—Paul Benton	4701 Taylor Rd, Punta Gorda FL 33950		R	2*	<.1
670	US Electronics Inc—Anil Arekapudi	1590 Page Industrial B, Saint Louis MO 63132	314-423-7550	R	2*	<.1
671	Ute Microwave Inc—Lennart Nilson	3500 Sunset Ave Ste D1, Ocean NJ 07712	732-922-1009	R	2*	<.1
672	Virginia Diodes Inc—Thomas Crowe	979 2nd St Se 309, Charlottesville VA 22902	434-297-3257	R	2*	<.1
673	Wilkerson Instrument Company Inc—Joe Wilkerson	PO Box 6986, Lakeland FL 33807	863-647-2000	R	2*	<.1
674	Witter Manufacturing Inc—Ione Stanley	3895 E Loop 820 S, Fort Worth TX 76119	817-475-5534	R	2*	<.1
675	Circuit Automation Inc—Thomas Meeker	5292 System Dr, Huntington Beach CA 92649	714-763-4180	R	2*	<.1
676	Mann Corp—Henry Mann	2845 Terwood Rd, Willow Grove PA 19090	215-830-1200	R	2*	<.1
677	Copesetic Inc—Eric Byer	PO Box 1119, Morrisville NY 13408	315-684-7780	R	2*	<.1
678	LBA Group Inc—Lawrence Behr	PO Box 8026, Greenville NC 27834	252-757-0279	R	2*	<.1
679	M2 Antenna Systems Inc—Myrna Staal	4402 N Selland Ave, Fresno CA 93722	559-432-8873	R	2*	<.1
680	TSi POWER Corp—Peter Nystrom	1103 W Pierce Ave, Antigo WI 54409	715-623-0636	R	2*	<.1
681	VRex Inc—Sadig Feris	6 Skyline Dr, Hawthorne NY 10532	646-539-3400	S	2*	<.1
682	Southern Microwave Inc—Joseph Olmeda	6965 Vista Pkwy N Ste, West Palm Beach FL 33411	561-687-3909	R	2*	<.1
683	Quintech Security Consultants Inc—Harold Gillens	102 Sangaree Park Ct S, Summerville SC 29483	843-695-0170	R	2*	<.1
684	Transformer Technology Inc—Bruce Gueble	PO Box 436, Durham CT 06422	860-349-1061	R	2*	<.1
685	Virtual Vision Inc	3006 Northup Way, Bellevue WA 98004	425-284-5200	S	2*	<.1
686	Dinosaur Electronics Inc—Patricia Clark	1160 Se 27th St, Lincoln City OR 97367	541-994-4344	R	2*	<.1
687	Component Express Corp	1935 W State St Ste 10, Garland TX 75042	972-805-0171	S	2*	<.1
688	Ensign Power Systems Inc—P William Harris Jr	2175 Citrine Ct, Loveland CO 80537	970-203-9255	R	2*	<.1
689	HNL Inc—John Nonaka	3250 Victor St Ste C, Santa Clara CA 95054	408-727-6091	R	2*	<.1
690	Intercon 1—Michael Degen Nortech Systems Inc	7746 Goedderz Road Ste, Baxter MN 56425	218-828-3157	D	2*	<.1
691	Pacific Electronic International Corp—Robert Lee	2530 Berryessa Rd Rm 6, San Jose CA 95132	408-236-3455	R	2*	<.1
692	Tumbler Technologies Inc—Alex Hung	3350 Scott Blvd Bldg 1, Santa Clara CA 95054	408-988-6616	R	2*	<.1
693	EMW Laser Inc—Mike Menchen	6840 114th Ave N, Largo FL 33773	727-548-0452	R	2*	<.1
694	Cmetrix Inc—Robert Mielcarski	165 Mittel Dr, Wood Dale IL 60191	630-595-9800	R	2*	<.1
695	Laurel Electronics Inc—Barret Weekes	3183 Airway Ave Ste G, Costa Mesa CA 92626	714-434-6131	R	2*	<.1
696	Workman Electronic Products Inc—Jerry Twining	11955 County Rd 10 2, Delta OH 43515	419-923-7525	R	2*	N/A

Rank	Company Name—*Executive Officer*	Address, City, State, Zip	Phone	Type	Fin	Empls
697	Graphic Display Systems Inc—*Mark Ester*	709 Keller Ave S, Amery WI 54001	715-268-6495	R	2*	<.1
698	Tristate Electronic Manufacturing Inc—*Ryan Null*	91 Western Maryland Pk, Hagerstown MD 21740	301-739-9404	R	2*	<.1
699	Lxd LLC—*Jim Morrison*	7630 First Pl Ste H, Bedford OH 44146	440-786-8700	R	2*	<.1
700	Penn Engineering Components—*Robert Washburn*	29045 Ave Penn, Valencia CA 91355	661-295-2080	R	2*	<.1
701	Fugle-Miller Laboratories Inc—*John Dobracki*	1401 Witherspoon St St, Rahway NJ 07065	732-574-3121	R	2*	<.1
702	Lexan Industries Inc—*Florence Isaacson*	15 Harold Ct, Bay Shore NY 11706	631-434-7586	R	2*	<.1
703	Parisi Associates Inc—*John Caputo*	16 Esquire Rd Unit 1, North Billerica MA 01862	978-667-8700	R	2*	<.1
704	C M R USA LLC—*John Gatto*	129 Mccarrell Ln, Zelienople PA 16063	724-452-2200	R	2*	<.1
705	Wasik Associates Inc—*Peter Wasik*	29 Diana Ln, Dracut MA 01826	978-454-9787	R	2*	<.1
706	Commodity Group LLP—*Greg Ehabe*	701 Monroe St APT 204, Rockville MD 20850	301-770-9249	R	2*	<.1
707	Esi Electronic Products Corp—*Frank Sundermeyer*	PO Box 7326, Prospect CT 06712	203-758-4401	R	2*	<.1
708	Face Electronics LC—*J Sorensen*	427 W 35th St, Norfolk VA 23508	757-624-2121	R	2*	<.1
709	Precise Cables Inc—*Billie Jane Van Ark*	1801 Iron Horse Dr Ste, Longmont CO 80501	303-678-1166	R	2*	<.1
710	Control Manufacturing Company Inc—*Sylvia Mccollum*	1825 E Plano Pkwy Ste, Plano TX 75074	972-422-2750	R	2*	<.1
711	Starled Inc—*Andres Alvarez*	1050 E Dominguez St St, Carson CA 90746	310-603-0403	R	2*	<.1
712	Special Hermetic Products Inc—*Anthony Desantis*	PO Box 269, Wilton NH 03086	603-654-2002	R	2*	<.1
713	Spinnaker Microwave Inc—*Earnest Bertram*	3281 Kifer Rd, Santa Clara CA 95051	408-732-9828	R	2*	<.1
714	La Cro Products Inc—*Daniel Kelly*	PO Box 1057, La Crosse WI 54602	608-781-1600	R	2*	<.1
715	World Technologies Ltd—*John Finlay*	9215 Pflumm Rd, Shawnee Mission KS 66215	913-438-9825	R	2*	<.1
716	M and M Technology Inc—*Majid Babaie*	PO Box 1796, Indian Trail NC 28079	704-882-9432	R	2*	<.1
717	Compac Design Electronics Manufacturing Co—*Luther Patton*	1210 W Alameda Dr Ste, Tempe AZ 85282	480-894-9511	R	2*	<.1
718	Simmons Electronics Inc—*Barbara Simmons*	PO Box 442, Pleasant Valley NY 12569	845-635-2204	R	2*	<.1
719	Thin Film Technology Corp—*Tom Lietha*	1980 Commerce Dr, North Mankato MN 56003	507-625-8445	R	2*	<.1
720	Stony Point Electronics Inc—*Wolfgang Bader*	15 Holt Dr, Stony Point NY 10980	845-786-5878	R	2*	<.1
721	Xeco Inc—*David Newmyer*	1651 N Bulldog Rd, Cedar City UT 84721	435-586-0507	R	2*	<.1
722	Ceramic To Metal Seals Inc—*Nancy Ingemi*	78 Stone Pl Ste 4, Melrose MA 02176	781-665-5002	R	2*	<.1
723	Gae Trading LLC	PO Box 2225, Goose Creek SC 29445	843-863-0880	R	2*	<.1
724	Jaguar Industries Inc—*Marvin Kigler*	PO Box 385, Haverstraw NY 10927	845-947-1800	R	2*	<.1
725	Lcl Electronics Inc—*Leann Loney*	8148 Industrial Park R, Baxter MN 56425	218-829-2990	R	2*	<.1
726	Oakdale Industrial Electronics Corp—*Abraham Mamoor*	1995 Pond Rd, Ronkonkoma NY 11779	631-737-4090	R	2*	<.1
727	Wolstenholme Machine Inc—*Robert Wolstenholme*	3075 Advance Ln, Colmar PA 18915	215-822-2525	R	2*	<.1
728	Lace Technologies Inc—*Charles Han*	3483 Swenson Ave, Saint Charles IL 60174	630-762-3865	R	2*	<.1
729	Barth Electronics Inc—*Jon Barth*	1589 Foothill Dr, Boulder City NV 89005	702-293-1576	R	2*	<.1
730	Alpha Scientific Electronics Inc—*Ron Rumrill*	1868 National Ave, Hayward CA 94545	510-782-4747	R	2*	<.1
731	Laboratory Control Systems Inc—*Stephen Davis*	2259 Scrntn Crbondale, Scranton PA 18508	570-487-2490	R	2*	<.1
732	Tellurian Technologies Inc—*William Deutschmann*	1801 Hicks Rd Ste A, Rolling Meadows IL 60008	847-934-4141	R	2*	.1
733	Electronic Connection Corp—*Ray Gorski*	125 Old Iron Ore Rd, Bloomfield CT 06002	860-243-3356	R	2*	<.1
734	Autosem Inc—*Terri Califano*	1701 S Main St, South Bend IN 46613	574-288-8866	R	2*	<.1
735	Keltron Electronics Corp—*David Levison*	2000 Artic Ave Unit A, Bohemia NY 11716	631-567-6300	R	2*	<.1
736	Concept Tool and Machine—*Aarne Reid*	380 Cooper Rd, West Berlin NJ 08091	856-767-5506	R	2*	<.1
737	Diversified Companies Inc—*Deborah Mlinar*	8260 Arthur St Ne Ste, Minneapolis MN 55432	763-784-9600	R	2*	<.1
738	Sensor Manufacturing Co—*Robert Byrum*	PO Box 955, Novi MI 48376	248-474-7300	R	2*	<.1
739	Tnp Instruments Inc—*Vu Tran*	119 Star Of India Ln, Carson CA 90746	310-532-2222	R	2*	<.1
740	Custom Cable Assemblies Inc—*Joseph Diego*	105 Whiting Way, Warner Robins GA 31088	478-953-2358	R	2*	<.1
741	EnetstarsCom—*Ed Kong*	46747 Fremont Blvd, Fremont CA 94538	510-657-3300	R	2*	<.1
742	Infinity Quick Turn Material S—*Jeff Carr*	4063 Clipper Ct, Fremont CA 94538	510-661-0555	R	2*	<.1
743	Custom Wiring Inc—*Judith Diggins*	400 Enterprise Dr, Nicholasville KY 40356	859-885-9658	R	1*	.1
744	Meehan Electronics Corp—*Bernie Larocha*	PO Box 1037, North Adams MA 01247	413-664-9371	R	1*	<.1
745	DJ Grey Company Inc—*Marla Grey*	455 Allan Ct, Healdsburg CA 95448	707-431-2779	R	1*	<.1
746	Magnetic Design Labs Inc—*Judith Kazem*	1636 E Edinger Ave Ste, Santa Ana CA 92705	714-558-3355	R	1*	<.1
747	Majr Products Corp—*Don Hester*	17540 Hwy 198, Saegertown PA 16433	814-763-3211	R	1*	<.1
748	Power Controls Inc—*Ronald Nash*	801 N Main St Ext, Wallingford CT 06492	203-284-0235	R	1*	<.1
749	La Grange Electrical Assemblies Co—*W Robin Mc Clain*	PO Box 555, Lagrange OH 44050	440-355-5388	R	1*	<.1
750	Nevron Plastics Inc—*Thomas Jarosz*	124 Ballard St, Saugus MA 01906	781-233-1310	R	1*	<.1
751	Thorndike Corp—*James Thorndike*	PO Box 533, East Bridgewater MA 02333	508-378-9797	R	1*	<.1
752	Transko Electronics Inc—*Alice Chun*	1156 N Gilbert St, Anaheim CA 92801	714-491-8089	R	1*	<.1
753	Microfab Inc—*Wayne Stauss*	180 Zachary Rd Ste 1, Manchester NH 03109	603-621-9522	R	1*	<.1
754	Commitment To Keep—*Cindy Zhang*	9272 Jeronimo Rd Ste 1, Irvine CA 92618	949-380-8585	R	1*	<.1
755	Mac Technology Inc—*Maria Egbert*	3104 Southside Byp, Klamath Falls OR 97603	541-883-3352	R	1*	<.1
756	Ebl Electronics Inc—*Joseph Zarrelli*	91 Prestige Park Cir S, East Hartford CT 06108	860-290-3737	R	1*	<.1
757	Quartztech Engineering Inc—*Joseph Herak*	9348 S 500 W, Sandy UT 84070	801-255-1600	R	1*	<.1
758	Victor Microwave Inc—*Steven Parks*	38 W Water St, Wakefield MA 01880	781-245-4472	R	1*	<.1
759	Elmech Inc—*Paul Balog*	195 San Pedro Ave Ste, Morgan Hill CA 95037	408-782-2990	R	1*	<.1
760	Crystal Bomar Co—*Robert Citron*	PO Box 10, Middlesex NJ 08846	732-356-7787	R	1*	<.1
761	Mdco Inc—*Norman Blais*	13440 Wright Cir, Tampa FL 33626	813-855-4068	R	1*	<.1
762	Labworks Inc—*Gary Butts*	2950 Airway Ave Ste A1, Costa Mesa CA 92626	714-549-1981	R	1*	<.1
763	Enertech Corp—*Pamela Hall*	PO Box 183, Hersey MI 49639	231-832-5587	R	1*	<.1
764	Spruce Pine Mica Co—*Richard Montague*	PO Box 219, Spruce Pine NC 28777	828-765-4241	R	1*	<.1
765	Columbine Technology Inc—*Jack Nelligan*	4675 S Windermere St, Englewood CO 80110	303-761-2121	R	1*	<.1
766	N Systems Inc—*Stephen Neuberth*	9050 Red Branch Rd Ste, Columbia MD 21045	410-964-8400	R	1*	<.1
767	Quality Contract Assemblies Inc—*Richard Frank*	PO Box 12868, Rochester NY 14612	585-663-9030	R	1*	<.1
768	Electronics Services Unlimited Inc—*John Lankford*	PO Box 802012, Houston TX 77280	713-683-0601	R	1*	<.1
769	Emission Control Ltd—*Ronald Burnett*	12704 W Arden Pl, Butler WI 53007	262-790-0092	R	1*	<.1
770	L and N Corp—*Nicholas Cota*	2898 Commerce Way, Ogden UT 84401	801-399-5000	R	1*	<.1
771	South Coast Technology Inc—*Brian Custodero*	5345 N Commerce Ave St, Moorpark CA 93021	805-532-1225	R	1*	<.1
772	JK Miller Corp—*Curt Bowen*	80 Wabash St, Pittsburgh PA 15220	412-922-5070	R	1*	<.1
773	Lhv Power Corp—*James Gevarges*	10221 Buena Vista Ave, Santee CA 92071	619-258-7700	R	1*	<.1
774	Florida R S Technology—*Peter Adwell*	3379-A SW 42nd Ave, Palm City FL 34990	772-221-8188	R	1*	<.1
775	Netcon Enterprises Inc—*Gary Leonard*	5085 Williams Lake Rd, Waterford MI 48329	248-673-7855	R	1*	<.1
776	Space Machine and Engineering Corp—*William Loyd*	2327 16th Ave N, Saint Petersburg FL 33713	727-323-2221	R	1*	<.1
777	Trans World Connections Ltd Unlimited Services Inc	173 Fastener Dr, Lynchburg VA 24502	434-525-0085	S	1*	<.1
778	R and R Machine Products Inc—*Donald Reiser*	760 W Mill St, San Bernardino CA 92410	909-885-7500	R	1*	<.1
779	Veetronix Inc—*James Longly*	PO Box 480, Lexington NE 68850	308-324-6661	R	1*	<.1
780	Wain Industries—*Michael Wainess*	4685 Runway St Ste C, Simi Valley CA 93063	805-581-5900	R	1*	<.1
781	General Electronic Devices Inc—*Marvin Epstein*	320 S Pacific St Ste A, San Marcos CA 92078	760-591-4170	R	1*	<.1
782	V/S Networks Inc—*Daryl Kemper*	3382 W Osborn Rd, Phoenix AZ 85017	847-414-5368	R	1*	<.1
783	Micro-Tronics—*Larry Jones*	PO Box 4375, Sonora CA 95370	209-532-1008	D	1*	<.1
784	Vestal Electronic Devices Inc—*Walter Kintner*	635 Dickson St, Endicott NY 13760	607-773-8461	R	1*	<.1
785	Accu-Glass Products Inc—*Charles Miltenberger*	700 Arroyo St, San Fernando CA 91340	818-365-4215	R	1*	<.1

Note: An asterisk (*) indicates an estimated financial figure. The company type code used is as follows: R = Private, P = Public, S = Private Subsidiary, B = Public Subsidiary, D = Division, J = Joint Venture, I = Investment Fund.

COMPANY RANKINGS BY SALES WITHIN 4-DIGIT SIC

Rank	Company Name—*Executive Officer*	Address, City, State, Zip	Phone	Type	Fin	Empls
786	American Radar Components Inc—*John Maluk*	39 Front St, Denville NJ 07834	973-627-5530	R	1*	<.1
787	Anderson Industries Inc—*Thomas Anderson*	PO Box 4348, Wichita KS 67204	316-945-4488	R	1*	<.1
788	Allied Controls Inc—*David Sudol*	150 E Aurora St, Waterbury CT 06708	203-757-4200	R	1*	<.1
789	Berkeley Telonic Inc—*Daphne Shipkey*	1080 La Mirada Ct, Vista CA 92081	760-744-8350	R	1*	<.1
790	Cardinal Industries Inc—*Jeff Franklin*	4601 W Woolworth Ave, Milwaukee WI 53218	414-358-1214	R	1*	<.1
791	Schumaker Technical Assembly—*Daniel Schumaker*	PO Box 439, Lafayette IN 47902	765-742-7176	R	1*	<.1
792	Hobbit Distributing Inc—*Larry Smith*	930 Pyott Rd Ste 110, Crystal Lake IL 60014	815-459-8532	R	1*	<.1
793	Techknow Inc—*Mark Wyman*	393 Mayfield Rd, Duncan SC 29334	864-877-1341	R	1*	<.1
794	Ditom Microwave—*Tom Weisz*	7592 N Maroa Ave Ste 1, Fresno CA 93727	559-255-7045	R	1*	<.1
795	Satellite Link Corp—*Bob Gotch*	3383 Labore Rd, Saint Paul MN 55110	651-488-7000	R	1*	<.1
796	Altaria Inc	1231 Midas Way, Sunnyvale CA 94085	408-735-6180	R	1*	<.1
797	Digital Audio Labs Inc—*Allen Pickard*	1266 Park Rd, Chanhassen MN 55317	952-401-7700	R	1*	<.1
798	McManus Microwave—*James McManus*	2419 Beans Creek Rd, Bakersville NC 28705		R	1*	<.1
799	Technological Artisans Inc—*Daniel Cohn*	5 Northview Ct Ste B, Pleasantville NY 10570	212-721-9769	R	1*	<.1
800	Etex Ltd—*Susan Fortuna*	PO Box M, Mojave CA 93502	661-824-2275	R	1*	<.1
801	Phillips Components Inc (Laguna Hills California)—*Barry Phillips*	23142 Alcalde Dr Ste A, Laguna Hills CA 92653	949-855-4263	R	1*	<.1
802	Auditec of St Louis—*William F Carver*	2515 S Big Bend Blvd, Maplewood MO 63143	314-781-8890	R	1	<.1
803	Fast Semiconductor Inc—*Roger Young*	3845 E Miraloma Ave St, Anaheim CA 92806	714-528-2550	R	1*	<.1
804	Qcm Inc—*Fred Ovchinnikoff*	PO Box 21267, Keizer OR 97307	503-371-9335	R	1*	<.1
805	LIK Inc—*Lisa Jurgens*	304 Roma Jean Pkwy, Streamwood IL 60107	630-213-1282	R	1*	<.1
806	International Telecommunications Components Inc—*Robert Smith*	94 E Jefryn Blvd Ste B, Deer Park NY 11729	631-243-1444	R	1*	<.1
807	Larkin Newco LLC—*Allen Lee*	1055 Summer St Ste 1, Stamford CT 06905	203-327-3649	R	1*	<.1
808	Remco Inc—*Clare Emery*	PO Box 4837, Florence SC 29502	843-393-8511	R	1*	<.1
809	Veritec Inc—*Van Tran*	2445 Winnetka Ave N, Golden Valley MN 55427	763-253-2670	P	1	<.1
810	Advanced Micro Systems Inc—*Roger Floyd*	171 Corbin Rd, Alstead NH 03602	603-835-6503	R	1*	<.1
811	Commercial Crystal Laboratories Inc—*Michael Urbanik*	4406 Arnold Ave, Naples FL 34104	239-643-5959	R	1*	<.1
812	Jenlor Ltd—*Joseph Ophir*	523 E Genesee St, Fayetteville NY 13066	315-637-9080	R	1*	<.1
813	Standard Crystal Corp—*James Zhang*	9940 Baldwin Pl, El Monte CA 91731	626-443-2121	R	1*	<.1
814	Arizona Microtek Inc—*Harold Muller*	1630 S Stapley Dr Ste, Mesa AZ 85204	480-962-5881	R	1*	<.1
815	Ipr Systems Inc—*Eugene Tylka*	11651 S Mayfield Ave, Alsip IL 60803	708-385-7500	R	1*	<.1
816	Metal Processing Company Inc—*Robin Perry*	75 Westech Dr, Tyngsboro MA 01879	978-649-1289	R	1*	<.1
817	Dynamic Hybirds Inc—*Don Hazelmyer*	1201 E Fayette St Ste, Syracuse NY 13210	315-426-8110	R	1*	<.1
818	Excel Technology International Corp—*Michi Chen*	4 Stryker Ln Ste 5, Hillsborough NJ 08844	908-874-4747	R	1*	<.1
819	Universal Quartz Inc—*Gerald Vetack*	2910 Norman Strasse Rd, San Marcos CA 92069	760-727-8885	R	1*	<.1
820	Edwards Scott Electronics Inc—*Scott Edwards*	PO Box 160, Sierra Vista AZ 85636	520-459-4802	R	1*	<.1
821	Thin Film Concepts Inc—*Leslie Weinman*	1 Westchester Plz Ste, Elmsford NY 10523	914-592-4700	R	1*	<.1
822	ASQ Technology Inc—*Steve Lee*	PO Box 73024, San Clemente CA 92673	949-498-4000	R	1*	<.1
823	Microwave Devices Inc—*David Mann*	PO Box 552, Franklin IN 46131	317-736-8833	R	1*	<.1
824	UQM Technologies Inc—*Eric Ridenour*	4120 Speciality Pl, Longmont CO 80504	303-682-4900	P	1	.1
825	Metavideo Inc—*Norman Noble*	718 University Ave, Los Gatos CA 95032	408-354-2525	R	1*	<.1
826	P-Rom Software Inc—*William Symmes*	PO Box 4027, Burlington VT 05406	802-862-7500	R	1*	<.1
827	Eatek—*Asghar Moghimi*	PO Box 3020, Winnetka CA 91396	818-709-7700	R	1*	<.1
828	Capital Advanced Technologies Inc—*Robert Laschinski*	309a Village Dr, Carol Stream IL 60188	630-690-1696	R	1*	<.1
829	Industrial Sensors and Instruments Inc—*Bud Dublin*	150 Texas Ave Ste 104, Round Rock TX 78664	512-255-3790	R	1*	<.1
830	OCC Technology LLC	13200 Kirkham Way Ste, Poway CA 92064	858-486-8386	R	1*	<.1
831	Electromotive Inc—*Thomas Barta*	55 Brown Ave, Springfield NJ 07081	973-564-8809	R	1*	<.1
832	Eruston Corp—*Robert Bianchi*	PO Box 4008, Orange CA 92863	714-669-9001	R	1*	<.1
833	Spectraflex Inc—*David Russell*	PO Box 1225, Defuniak Springs FL 32435	850-892-3900	R	1*	<.1
834	Conta-Clip Inc—*Rudolph Abraham*	PO Box 6510, Somerset NJ 08875	908-431-0705	R	1*	<.1
835	Piezo Systems Inc—*Robert Carter*	65 Tower Office Park, Woburn MA 01801	781-933-4850	R	1*	<.1
836	Schell Electronics Inc—*Jerry Schell*	120 N Lincoln Ave, Chanute KS 66720	620-431-2350	R	1*	<.1
837	Teknational Thermal Insulation And Hardware Inc—*Timothy Bailey*	PO Box 926, Fort Myers FL 33902	239-461-5558	R	1*	<.1
838	Wenvy Technologies Inc—*Wayne Tam*	2075 Otoole Ave, San Jose CA 95131	408-509-2119	R	1*	<.1
839	Throttle Up Corp—*Steven Dominguez*	210 Rock Point Dr, Durango CO 81301	970-259-0690	R	1*	<.1
840	Joyce Telectronics Corp—*Peter Joyce*	2049 Range Rd, Clearwater FL 33765	727-461-3525	R	1*	<.1
841	Diamond Motion Inc—*Jim Thomasson*	PO Box 1225, Port Angeles WA 98362	360-417-9791	R	1	<.1
842	Filtek Inc—*Richard Gould*	PO Box 1510, Tubac AZ 85646	520-398-2856	R	1*	<.1
843	Innocomp—*Robert Cecil*	33195 Wagon Wheel Dr, Solon OH 44139	440-248-5104	R	1*	<.1
844	Intercity Inc—*Stephen Moe*	PO Box 847, Springfield OR 97477	541-726-7613	R	1*	<.1
845	Nolatron Inc—*Mike Nolan*	1259 2nd St Ste 1, Harrisburg PA 17113	717-564-3398	R	1*	<.1
846	Pentas Controls Inc—*Kevin Doyle*	2432 W Peoria Ave Ste, Phoenix AZ 85029	602-216-0010	R	1*	<.1
847	Precision Motion Controls—*Jim Siebert*	430 S 4th St, San Jose CA 95112	408-298-0898	R	1*	<.1
848	Sound Connections International Inc—*Stuart Marcus*	203 Flagship Dr, Lutz FL 33549	813-948-2707	R	1*	<.1
849	Decade Engineering—*Michael Hardwick*	5504 Val View Dr Se, Turner OR 97392	503-743-3194	R	1*	<.1
850	Denzo Systems Inc—*Armen Martirosyan*	421 Arden Ave, Glendale CA 91203	818-230-1300	R	1*	<.1
851	Epsilon Lambda Electronics Corp—*Robert Knox*	396 Fenton Ln Ste 601, West Chicago IL 60185	630-293-7118	R	1*	<.1
852	Jo Gunn Enterprises LLC—*Paul Dill*	3138 County Rd 30, Ethelsville AL 35461	205-658-2229	R	1*	<.1
853	Mitchell Electronics Inc—*Lawrence Mitchell*	PO Box 2626, Athens OH 45701	740-594-8532	R	1*	<.1
854	Netellink Inc—*David Nguyen*	12875 Brookprinter Pl, Poway CA 92064	858-486-6705	R	1*	<.1
855	Lloyd Industries Inc—*Melvin Roche*	3081 Elm Point Industr, Saint Charles MO 63301	636-946-3300	R	1*	<.1
856	Amplitude Technical Sales—*Joseph Dagostino*	252 W Swamp Rd Ste 7, Doylestown PA 18901	215-340-0123	R	<1*	<.1
857	Photo-Tron Corp—*Roger Rowley*	2146 Avon Industrial D, Rochester Hills MI 48309	248-852-5200	R	<1*	<.1
858	Future Brite—*Tom Bobosky*	8431 S Ave, Youngstown OH 44514	330-965-9550	R	<1*	<.1
859	Joule Power Inc—*Patricia Mccarthy*	Summer Rd, Boxboro MA 01719	978-263-9712	R	<1*	<.1
860	Radiation Power Systems Inc—*Richard Huber*	2261 Fortune Dr Ste D, San Jose CA 95131	408-432-6154	R	<1*	<.1
861	Roto Form Corp—*Charles Slover*	PO Box 118, Signal Mountain TN 37377	423-266-0067	R	<1*	<.1
862	Taikan Company Inc—*Shu Wang*	PO Box 3327, Lawrence KS 66046	785-841-5538	R	<1*	<.1
863	Whan Bob and Son Electronics Inc—*Kim Whan*	11000 Metro Pkwy Ste 9, Fort Myers FL 33966	239-936-2397	R	<1*	<.1
864	Mil Electronics Inc—*Michael Gaudette*	150 Dow St Ste 401, Manchester NH 03101	603-647-9201	R	<1*	<.1
865	Auto Physics LLC	314 Townsvalley Rd, River Falls WI 54022	715-426-5457	R	<1*	<.1
866	CQ Products Inc—*Robert Normandy*	151 Willis Dr, Harkers Island NC 28531	252-728-5854	R	<1*	<.1
867	Master Signal Inc—*Byron Shaw*	PO Box 99, Lapeer MI 48446	810-664-9061	R	<1*	<.1
868	Rob Geoffroy—*Rob Geoffroy*	176 Litchfield Rd, Londonderry NH 03053	603-425-2517	R	<1*	<.1
869	Torlex Inc—*Russ Hackworth*	10539 Shale Brook Way, Strongsville OH 44149	440-268-9250	R	<1*	<.1
870	Webb Tech—*Ronald Webb*	1267 Ne Blvd Unit 2, Vineland NJ 08360	856-691-5099	R	<1*	<.1
871	Anadyne Inc—*Paul Donovan*	PO Box 1344, Santa Cruz CA 95061	831-438-4898	R	<1*	<.1
872	Andrex Systems Inc—*William Pote*	PO Box 115, Port Murray NJ 07865	908-835-1720	R	<1*	<.1

Rank	Company Name—*Executive Officer*	Address, City, State, Zip	Phone	Type	Fin	Empls
873	Entratech Systems—*Michael Richardson*	202 Fox Rd, Sandusky OH 44870	419-433-7683	R	<1*	<.1
874	Gorman-Redlich—*James Gorman*	257 W Union St, Athens OH 45701	740-593-3150	R	<1*	<.1
875	Liquid Crystal Technologies LLC—*Charles Oravec*	PO Box 31, Gates Mills OH 44040	440-232-8590	R	<1*	<.1
876	Odhner Holographics—*Jeff Odhner*	5 Lake Front St, Amherst NH 03031	603-673-8651	R	<1*	<.1
877	Precision Waveguide Components Inc—*Tom Sarver*	561 E Overdrive Cir, Hernando FL 34442	352-489-9893	R	<1*	<.1
878	Resotech—*Andre Polischuk*	13610 N Scottsdale Rd, Scottsdale AZ 85254	480-483-8400	R	<1*	<.1
879	Accelerator Systems Inc—*Douglas Moore*	3 Commerce Dr Ste 303, Atkinson NH 03811	603-898-6010	R	<1*	<.1
880	Candeltronics Corp—*Sam Candeloro*	20 Fortune Ln Apt E, Rochester NY 14626	585-720-5338	R	<1*	<.1
881	GAM Electronics Inc—*Edward Russell*	191 Varney St, Manchester NH 03102	603-627-1010	R	<1*	<.1
882	Harrison Seal Corp—*Jack Argento*	1201 Kennedy Blvd, Manville NJ 08835	908-722-3322	R	<1*	<.1
883	Micromex Inc—*Juan Garcin*	7724 E Mcgee Mountain, Tucson AZ 85750	520-748-0101	R	<1*	<.1
884	Miramar Dielectric Laboratory—*Frank Chen*	510 Coralridge Pl Ste, La Puente CA 91746	626-333-2536	R	<1*	<.1
885	Quality Quartz Of America Inc—*Carmella Petruziello*	9362 Hamilton Dr, Mentor OH 44060	440-974-9555	R	<1*	<.1
886	Rtron Management Inc—*Randy Corporron*	10900 Cash Rd, Stafford TX 77477	281-295-3200	R	<1*	<.1
887	Coast Electronic Manufacturing LLC—*Joe Camuso*	571 Haverty Ct Ste H, Rockledge FL 32955	321-205-1734	R	<1*	<.1
888	EM Design—*Ray Johnson*	22661 Hwy 62, Shady Cove OR 97539	541-878-3927	R	<1*	<.1
889	Heather Sound Amplification—*Richard Johnson*	1717 E 6th St, Mishawaka IN 46544	574-255-6100	R	<1*	<.1
890	Dalle Electronics Inc—*Dallas Gutacker*	246 W Main St, Leola PA 17540	717-661-7041	R	<1*	<.1
891	Millennium Iii Inc—*William Solomon*	290 Pratt St Ste 13, Meriden CT 06450	203-235-1806	R	<1*	<.1
892	Power Plus Controls Inc—*Richard Lussier*	200 Powers Ferry Rd Se, Marietta GA 30067	678-560-2660	R	<1*	<.1
893	Spectron Glass and Electronics Inc—*Robert Marshall*	PO Box 13368, Hauppauge NY 11788	631-582-5600	R	<1*	<.1
894	Caywood Electronics Inc—*Ralph Jannini*	8 Marblehead St, North Andover MA 01845	978-975-2711	R	<1*	<.1
895	Unit Manufacturing Co—*Robert Woods*	67 Bonaventura Dr, San Jose CA 95134	408-432-8648	R	<1*	<.1
896	Intrend International Inc—*Leo Inowlocki*	4 Ravenswood Ct, West Nyack NY 10994	845-510-9630	R	<1*	<.1
897	Trimol Group Inc—*Boris Birshtein*	1285 Ave of the Americ, New York NY 10019	212-554-4394	P	<1	N/A

TOTALS: SIC 3679 Electronic Components Nec

Companies: 897					174,416	175.3

3691 Storage Batteries

Rank	Company Name—*Executive Officer*	Address, City, State, Zip	Phone	Type	Fin	Empls
1	Spectrum Brands Holdings Inc—*David R Lumley*	PO Box 44960, Madison WI 53744	608-275-3340	P	3,187	5.9
2	Exide Technologies—*James R Bolch*	13000 Deerfield Pkwy B, Milton GA 30004	678-566-9000	P	2,888	10.0
3	EaglePicher Corp—*David L Treadwell*	2424 John Daly Rd, Inkster MI 48141		R	1,244*	4.2
4	Motorola Incorporated Energy Systems Group—*Jerry Blanton*	1700 Belle Meade Ct, Lawrenceville GA 30043	770-338-3742	D	555*	4.0
5	Ener1 Group Inc—*Charles Gassenheimer*	1751 W Cypress Creek R, Fort Lauderdale FL 33309	954-776-8489	R	423*	.8
6	Energy Conversion Devices Inc—*Jay B Knoll*	3800 Lapeer Rd, Auburn Hills MI 48326	248-293-0440	P	233	1.3
7	Crown Battery Manufacturing Co—*Hal Hawk*	PO Box 990, Fremont OH 43420	419-334-7181	R	128*	.4
8	A123 Systems Inc—*David P Vieau*	321 Arsenal St, Watertown MA 02472	617-778-5700	P	97	1.6
9	Advanced Battery Technologies Inc—*Zhiguo Fu*	15 W 39th St14th Fl, New York NY 10018	212-391-2752	P	97	<.1
10	Power Battery Company Inc—*William Rasmussen*	25 McLean Blvd, Paterson NJ 07514	973-523-8630	R	84*	.4
11	Ener1 Inc—*Alex Sorokin*	1540 Broadway Ste 25C, New York NY 10036	212-920-3500	P	77	.8
12	Arotech Corp—*Robert S Ehrlich*	1229 Oak Valley Dr, Ann Arbor MI 48108		P	74	.4
13	Innergy Power Corp—*Jerry Cooper*	9051 Siempre Viva Rd D, San Diego CA 92154	619-710-0758	R	67*	<.1
14	EnerSys Energy Products Inc—*John D Craig*	2366 Bernville Rd, Reading PA 19605	610-208-1991	S	56*	.4
15	Trojan Battery Co—*Richard Godber*	12380 Clark St, Santa Fe Springs CA 90670	562-946-8381	R	47*	.6
16	Valence Technology Inc—*Robert L Kanode*	12303 Technology Blvd, Austin TX 78727	512-527-2900	P	46	.4
17	Boston-Power Inc—*Keith Schmid*	2200 W Park Dr, Westborough MA 01581	508-366-0805	R	43*	.1
18	International Battery Inc—*Dennis Sadlowski*	6845 Snowdrift Rd, Allentown PA 18106	610-366-3925	R	30*	.1
19	Storage Battery Systems Inc—*Scott Rubenzer*	N56w16665 Ridgewood Dr, Menomonee Falls WI 53051	262-703-5800	R	23*	<.1
20	Micro Power Electronics Inc—*Mike Dubose*	13955 Sw Millikan Way, Beaverton OR 97005	503-693-7600	S	19*	.3
21	Mathews Associates Inc—*Daniel Perreault*	220 Power Ct, Sanford FL 32771	407-323-3390	R	18*	.2
22	Yardney Technical Products Inc—*Richard Scibelli*	82 Mechanic St Ste 2, Pawcatuck CT 06379	860-599-1100	R	18*	.2
23	Fedco Electronics Inc—*Steven Victor*	PO Box 1403, Fond Du Lac WI 54936	920-922-6490	R	18*	<.1
24	Superior Battery Manufacturing Company Inc—*Randolph Hart*	PO Box 1010, Russell Springs KY 42642	270-866-6056	R	18*	.2
25	R and D Batteries Inc—*Randall Noddings*	PO Box 5007, Burnsville MN 55337	952-890-0629	R	15*	<.1
26	Bulldog Battery Corp—*John Dawkins*	PO Box 766, Wabash IN 46992	260-563-0551	R	11*	.1
27	Teledyne Continental Motors Battery Products—*Robert Mehrabian*	PO Box 7950, Redlands CA 92375	909-793-3131	S	9*	.1
28	Ramcar Batteries Inc—*Clifford Crowe*	2700 Carrier Ave, Commerce CA 90040	323-726-1212	R	9*	.1
29	Dantona Industries Inc—*Sal Dantona*	3051 Burns Ave, Wantagh NY 11793	516-783-5050	R	7*	<.1
30	Ace Hobby Distributors Inc—*Jeff Fassbinder*	26021 Commercentre Dr, Lake Forest CA 92630	949-900-3300	R	7*	<.1
31	Encell Technology LLC	1037 Dean Dr Nw, Atlanta GA 30318	678-576-1982	R	7*	<.1
32	Lithium Technology Corp—*Martin Koster*	10379B Democracy Ln, Fairfax VA 22030	610-256-1567	P	6	.1
33	K2 Energy Solutions	1125 American Pacific, Henderson NV 89074	702-478-3590	R	6	<.1
34	Industrial Battery Engineering Inc—*Birger Holmquist*	9121 De Garmo Ave, Sun Valley CA 91352	818-767-7067	R	4*	<.1
35	Harding Energy Inc—*David Clow*	509 E Ellis Rd, Norton Shores MI 49441	231-798-7033	R	3*	<.1
36	Avex Electronics Corp—*Michael Hasness*	PO Box 1026, Bensalem PA 19020	215-638-3300	R	3*	<.1
37	Konarka Technologies Inc—*Howard Berke*	116 John St Ste 12, Lowell MA 01852	978-569-1400	R	3*	<.1
38	Stion Corp—*Chet Farris*	6321 San Ignacio Ave, San Jose CA 95119	408-284-7200	R	3*	<.1
39	Api Inc—*Edward Rafter*	1270 Ne Delta School R, Lees Summit MO 64064	816-795-0208	R	3*	<.1
40	Aristo-Craft Inc—*Lewis Polk*	698 S 21st St, Irvington NJ 07111	973-351-9800	R	2*	<.1
41	Bell City Battery Manufacturing Inc—*Jeanith Miller*	915 S Charles St, Belleville IL 62220	618-234-7272	R	2*	<.1
42	Span Inc—*William Baker*	4404 Guion Rd, Indianapolis IN 46254	317-347-2646	R	1*	<.1
43	New Era Technologies Co—*Carl Ranno*	23935 Madison St, Torrance CA 90505	310-373-8894	R	1*	<.1
44	Astro Flight Inc—*Robert Boucher*	13311 Beach Ave, Marina Del Rey CA 90292	310-821-0291	R	1*	<.1
45	Rolls Battery Of New England—*Joseph Mcginnis*	7 Oak St, Salem MA 01970	978-745-3333	R	1*	<.1
46	Keystone Battery—*Barry Faye*	35 Holton St, Winchester MA 01890	781-729-8333	R	1*	<.1
47	Battery Pros Inc—*Patti Novack*	PO Box 54, Horseshoe Beach FL 32648	352-498-2477	R	1*	<.1
48	Red Line Research Laboratories Inc—*Steve Leiserson*	10845 Wheatlands Ave C, Santee CA 92071	619-562-7591	R	1*	<.1
49	Magnevolt Inc—*William Davidson*	PO Box 58099, Raleigh NC 27658	919-790-9686	R	1*	<.1
50	Crim Sales And Engineering Inc—*Hollen Crim*	PO Box 360955, Birmingham AL 35236	205-988-0042	R	1*	<.1
51	Neah Power Systems Inc—*Chris D'Couto*	22118 20th Ave SE Ste, Bothell WA 98021	425-424-3324	P	<1	<.1
52	Oak Ridge Micro-Energy Inc—*Mark Meriwether*	3046 E Brighton Pl, Salt Lake City UT 84121	801-201-7635	P	<1	<.1
53	Rafael Ruiz—*Rafael Ruiz*	4122 W Fm 476, Poteet TX 78065	210-409-4646	R	<1*	<.1
54	Hedb Corp—*Adrian Zolla*	PO Box 611390, San Jose CA 95161	408-259-2823	R	N/A	<.1

TOTALS: SIC 3691 Storage Batteries

Companies: 54					9,595	32.9

3692 Primary Batteries—Dry & Wet

Rank	Company Name—*Executive Officer*	Address, City, State, Zip	Phone	Type	Fin	Empls
1	Energizer Battery Co—*Joe W McClanathan*	533 Maryville Universi, Saint Louis MO 63141	314-985-2000	S	3,807*	10.0

Note: An asterisk (*) indicates an estimated financial figure. The company type code used is as follows: R = Private, P = Public, S = Private Subsidiary, B = Public Subsidiary, D = Division, J = Joint Venture, I = Investment Fund.

COMPANY RANKINGS BY SALES WITHIN 4-DIGIT SIC

Rank	Company Name—Executive Officer	Address, City, State, Zip	Phone	Type	Fin	Empls
2	Greatbatch Inc—Thomas J Hook	10000 Wehrle Dr, Clarence NY 14031	716-759-5600	P	569	3.3
3	Ultralife Corp—Michael D Popielec	2000 Technology Pkwy, Newark NY 14513	315-332-7100	P	179	1.2
4	United Solar Ovonic LLC—Subhendu Guha	3800 Lapeer Rd, Auburn Hills MI 48326	248-293-0440	S	64*	.3
5	Powergenix—Dan Squiller	9820 Towne Centre Dr S, San Diego CA 92121	858-547-7300	R	56*	.2
6	Electrochem Commercial Power—Susan Bratton Greatbatch Inc	100 Energy Dr, Canton MA 02021	781-575-0800	S	22	.1
7	Bren-Tronics Inc—Leo Brenna	10 Brayton Ct, Commack NY 11725	631-499-5155	R	20*	.1
8	BST Systems Inc—Thomas Terjesen	78 Plainfield Pke, Plainfield CT 06374	860-564-4078	R	6*	.1
9	TAE Trans Atlantic Electronics Inc—Janet English	PO Box 817, Deer Park NY 11729	631-595-9206	R	5*	<.1
10	Plainview Batteries Inc—Bernard Erde	23 Newtown Rd, Plainview NY 11803	516-249-2873	R	3*	<.1

TOTALS: SIC 3692 Primary Batteries—Dry & Wet
Companies: 10

					4,730	15.2

3694 Engine Electrical Equipment

Rank	Company Name—Executive Officer	Address, City, State, Zip	Phone	Type	Fin	Empls
1	Marathon Redevelopment Corp—Henry W Knueppel	200 State St, Beloit WI 53511		S	8,217*	17.6
2	Remy International Inc—John Weber	600 Corporation Dr, Pendleton IN 46064	765-778-6499	S	1,101*	7.9
3	NGK Spark Plugs Inc USA—Shinichi Oda	46929 Megellan, Wixom MI 48393	248-926-6900	S	567*	.6
4	Hitachi Automotive Products Inc USA	PO Box 510, Harrodsburg KY 40330	859-734-9451	S	207*	.9
5	Prestolite Wire LLC—Paul Montrone	200 Galleria Office Ct, Southfield MI 48034	248-355-4422	R	200*	.9
6	Motorcar Parts America Inc—Selwyn Joffe	2929 California St, Torrance CA 90503	310-212-7910	P	161	.2
7	Bbb Industries LLC—Linda Bigler	5640 Commerce Blvd E, Mobile AL 36619	251-438-2737	R	156*	2.0
8	Delphi Automotive Systems Corp	12170 Rojas Dr, El Paso TX 79936	915-612-2855	R	144*	2.5
9	CTS Automotive Products Inc	1142 W Beardsley Ave, Elkhart IN 46514	574-295-3575	S	144*	.7
10	Automotive Importing Manufacturing Inc—Steve Seabourne	PO Box 100, Rancho Cordova CA 95741	916-985-8505	R	126*	.3
11	FuelCell Energy Inc—Chip Bottone	3 Great Pasture Rd, Danbury CT 06810	203-825-6000	P	123	.5
12	Diamond Electric Manufacturing Corp—Tatsu Ikenaga	110 Research Pkwy, Dundee MI 48131	734-529-5525	R	73*	.3
13	Mitsubishi Electric Automotive America Inc—Takeo Sasaki	4773 Bethany Rd, Mason OH 45040	513-398-2220	S	54*	.8
14	DRS Laurel Technologies—Mark S Newman	246 Airport Rd, Johnstown PA 15904	814-534-8900	S	48*	.3
15	Kelly Aerospace Power Systems Inc—Jeffrey Kelly	2900 Selma Hwy, Montgomery AL 36108	334-227-8306	R	31*	.3
16	R E Phelon Company Inc—Russell Phelon	2063 University Pkwy, Aiken SC 29801	803-649-1381	R	31*	.5
17	NGK Spark Plugs USA Inc—Norihiko Adachi	1 Ngk Dr, Sissonville WV 25320	304-988-0060	R	29*	.2
18	Turbine Engine Components Technologies—Robert Cohen	1211 Old Albany Rd, Thomasville GA 31792	229-228-2600	S	27	.2
19	Autotronic Controls Corp—Dan Gresham	1350 Pullman Dr, El Paso TX 79936	915-857-5200	R	25*	.4
20	Micro Craft Inc—William Brown	41129 Jo Dr, Novi MI 48375	248-476-6510	R	25*	.5
21	Xenia Manufacturing Inc—Andy Knapp	PO Box 237, Xenia IL 62899	618-678-2218	R	22*	.2
22	Edge Products Inc (Ogden Utah)—Paul Lehman	1080 S Depot Dr, Ogden UT 84404	801-476-3343	R	17*	.1
23	Electrex Inc—Peter Ochs	6 N Walnut St, Hutchinson KS 67501	620-669-9966	R	17*	.2
24	Bob Brooks Motor Co—Bob Brooks	4411 Sw 19th St, Oklahoma City OK 73108	405-681-2592	R	16*	.2
25	Interconnect Wiring Harnesses Inc—John Ashour	5024 W Vickery Blvd, Fort Worth TX 76107	817-377-9473	R	16*	.1
26	Wilcas Wire Co—Mark Patel	342 Homestead Rd, Nashville TN 37207	615-255-1665	R	13*	.1
27	Interstate Industries Of Mississippi LLC—Patricia Allen	PO Box 1285, Kosciusko MS 39090	662-289-3877	R	11*	.1
28	Wire Tech Ltd—Keith Mowry	3567 Hwy 48, Summerville GA 30747	706-857-6413	R	10*	.1
29	Suncoast Automotive Products Inc—James Ferrari	3024 Nw 25th Ave, Pompano Beach FL 33069	954-973-4822	R	10*	.1
30	USA Harness Inc—Lawrence Chambly	PO Box 793, Winnsboro TX 75494	903-342-3767	R	10*	.1
31	Taylor Cable Products Inc—Bill Beaver	301 High Grove Rd, Grandview MO 64030	816-765-5011	R	9*	.1
32	Schofield Enterprises Inc—Richard Feirn	8405 Enterprise Way, Schofield WI 54476	715-359-2497	R	9*	.2
33	Imp Holdings LLC—Henry Winters	409 Growth Pkwy, Angola IN 46703	260-665-6112	R	9*	.1
34	Maca Plastics Inc—Andrew Culbertson	3455 Cross Rd, Winchester OH 45697	937-544-8618	R	9*	.1
35	Perfect Performance Products LLC—Jim Paxton	2501 Ludelle St, Fort Worth TX 76105	817-244-6212	R	8*	.1
36	B G Service Company Inc—John Frost	PO Box 2259, West Palm Beach FL 33402	561-659-1471	R	5*	<.1
37	Noel-Smyser Engineering Corp—Jeff Noel	4005 Industrial Blvd, Indianapolis IN 46254	317-293-2215	R	5*	<.1
38	Sanders Manufacturing Company Inc—Billy Sanders	PO Box 5437, Destin FL 32540	850-837-0979	R	4*	<.1
39	Kold-Ban International Ltd—James Burke	8390 Pingree Rd, Lake In The Hills IL 60156	847-658-8561	R	3*	<.1
40	Portage Wire Systems Inc—Jerome Showalter	PO Box 567, Onekama MI 49675	231-889-4215	R	3*	<.1
41	Qualtronics LLC—Melissa Bierlein	1400 Grand Ave, Columbus IN 47201	812-375-8880	R	3*	<.1
42	Powermaster Inc—Kenneth Bennett	7501 Strwbrry Plains P, Knoxville TN 37924	865-688-5953	R	3*	<.1
43	Metal Masters Foodservice Equipment Co—Jim Hickman	1258 Titan Dr, Dallas TX 75247	214-630-9221	R	2*	<.1
44	Tucson Alternator Exchange Service Inc—Daniel Montano	1401 E 20th St, Tucson AZ 85719	520-622-7395	R	2*	<.1
45	Pluskota Electric Manufacturing Co—David Blank	PO Box 387, Palos Heights IL 60463	708-597-0200	R	2*	<.1
46	Elcor Inc—Jerry Mucha	PO Box 376, Amherst OH 44001	440-365-5941	R	2*	<.1
47	Alternators Starters Etc—Muhammed Osman	1360 White Oaks Rd Ste, Campbell CA 95008	408-559-3540	R	1*	<.1
48	Keystone Cable Corp—Thomas Scott	8200 Lynch Rd, Detroit MI 48234	313-924-9720	R	1*	<.1
49	Gauss Corp—Robert Sampson	PO Box 660, Scarborough ME 04070	207-883-4121	R	1*	<.1
50	Pacific Exchange Parts Rebuilders Inc—Amir Gorodenzik	7442 Deering Ave, Canoga Park CA 91303	818-703-0865	R	1*	<.1
51	United States Energy Corp—Pamela Higgins	1600 Missile Way, Anaheim CA 92801	714-871-8185	R	1*	<.1
52	Javelina Corp—Brian Refoy	14085 King Rd, Frisco TX 75034	972-377-9807	R	1*	<.1
53	Dynamotors Inc—William Jones	4801 Commerce Pkwy Ste, Cleveland OH 44128	216-292-7278	R	1*	<.1
54	Auto Electric and Battery Inc—James Macfarlane	1171 Se Tualatin Valle, Hillsboro OR 97123	503-648-1575	R	<1*	<.1

TOTALS: SIC 3694 Engine Electrical Equipment
Companies: 54

					11,713	39.5

3695 Magnetic & Optical Recording Media

Rank	Company Name—Executive Officer	Address, City, State, Zip	Phone	Type	Fin	Empls
1	WD Media Inc—John F Coyne	3355 Michelson Dr Ste, Irvine CA 92612	949-672-7000	S	3,016*	27.0
2	Fuji Photo Film USA Inc—Shigetaka Komori	211 Pucketts Ferry Rd, Greenwood SC 29649	864-223-8171	S	1,900*	10.0
3	Ascent Media DVD—Jose Royo	520 Broadway 5th Fl, Santa Monica CA 90401	310-434-7000	R	1,680*	4.0
4	Imation Corp—Mark E Lucas	1 Imation Way, Oakdale MN 55128	651-704-4000	P	1,290	1.1
5	Allied Vaughn Communications—Doug Olzenak	7951 Computer Ave, Minneapolis MN 55435	952-832-3100	R	837*	2.0
6	IPC Communication Services Inc—Ken Kozminski	2180 Maiden Ln, Saint Joseph MI 49085	269-983-7105	S	300*	.3
7	Quantum3D Inc—Arthur Yan	5400 Hellyer Ave, San Jose CA 95138	408-600-2500	R	166*	.1
8	Ascent Capital Group Inc—William R Fitzgerald	520 Broadway 5th Fl, Santa Monica CA 90401	310-434-7000	P	139	1.3
9	WRS Motion Picture and Video Laboratory—F Jack Naper	213 Tech Rd, Pittsburgh PA 15205	412-937-1200	R	132*	.3
10	3M Cogent Inc—Ming Hsieh	639 N Rosemead Blvd, Pasadena CA 91107	626-325-9600	S	130	.4
11	American Media International Ltd—Richard Clark	2609 Tucker St Ext, Burlington NC 27215		R	126*	.3
12	Method Studios—Bob Saloman	702 Arizona Ave, Santa Monica CA 90401	310-434-6000	S	125*	.3
13	Enovation Graphic Systems Inc (Valhalla New York) Fuji Photo Film USA Inc	200 Summit Lake Dr 2nd, Valhalla NY 10595	914-789-8100	S	111*	.3
14	OEM Inc—Gary Gordon	PO Box 7206, Charlotte NC 28241	704-504-1877	R	102*	.2
15	Panasonic Disc Services Corp—Bob Pfannkuch	20608 Madrona Ave, Torrance CA 90503	310-783-4800	S	84*	.2
16	Reel Picture LLC—David Smitjkozick	5330 Eastgate Mall, San Diego CA 92121	858-587-0301	R	84*	.2
17	DVS InteleStream—Richard Appell	2600 W Olive Ave, Burbank CA 91505	818-566-4151	R	83*	.2

Rank	Company Name—*Executive Officer*	Address, City, State, Zip	Phone	Type	Fin	Empls
18	Sypris Data Systems Inc	1527 W 13th St Ste J, Upland CA 91786	909-981-9484	S	50	.1
19	Michele Audio Corporation of America—*Ginette Gramuglia*	PO Box 566, Massena NY 13662	315-769-2448	R	44*	.2
20	Crest National—*Ryan Stain*	PO Box 68057, Anaheim CA 92807	714-666-2266	R	42*	.1
21	Digital Audio Disc Corp—*Dave Rubenstein*	1800 N Fruitridge Ave, Terre Haute IN 47804	812-462-8100	D	42*	.1
22	Magno Sound and Video—*Bob Friedman*	729 Seventh Ave 7th Fl, New York NY 10019	212-302-2505	R	42*	.1
23	Lightning Media Inc—*Stephen Buchsbaum*	27520 Ave Mentry, Valencia CA 91355	323-957-9255	R	31*	.1
24	Abkco—*Allen Kline*	1700 Broadway, New York NY 10019	212-399-0300	R	30*	.1
25	Hello World Communications—*Ron Yoshida*	118 W 22nd St, New York NY 10011	212-243-8800	R	26*	.1
26	Dering Corp—*David D Dering*	PO Box 10755, Lancaster PA 17605	717-394-4200	R	26*	.1
27	Global Publishing Inc—*Willy Chow*	4415 Technology Dr, Fremont CA 94538	510-438-0373	R	26*	.1
28	USA Studios	253 West 35th St, New York NY 10001	212-398-6400	R	25*	.1
29	Digigraphics Inc—*Bob Remakel*	2639 Minnehaha Ave S, Minneapolis MN 55406	612-721-2434	R	25*	.1
30	EchoData Group—*Stephen Roberts*	735 Fox Chase STE 101, Coatesville PA 19320	610-466-2100	R	21*	.1
31	Media Evolved LLC—*Bill Walker*	3205 Freedom Dr Ste 51, Charlotte NC 28208	704-395-1002	R	21*	.1
32	Paragon Media Inc—*George Ricci*	55 S Atlantic, Seattle WA 98134	206-808-7600	R	21*	.1
33	Chicago Recording Co—*Chris Shepard*	232 E Ohio St, Chicago IL 60611	312-822-9333	R	20*	<.1
34	Arcube Multimedia Inc—*RC Damley*	959 E Collins Blvd #12, Richardson TX 75081	972-267-1800	R	20*	<.1
35	Palace Production Center—*Wendy Lambert*	29 N Main St, South Norwalk CT 06854	203-853-1740	R	20*	<.1
36	Data Management Internationale Inc—*Carol Swezey*	55 Lukens Dr, New Castle DE 19720	302-656-1151	R	18*	<.1
37	Acoustech Mastering—*Don MacInnis*	486 Dawson Dr, Camarillo CA 93012	805-484-2747	R	17*	<.1
38	Nuvidia—*Thomas P Doyle*	9258 Bond St, Overland Park KS 66214	913-599-5200	R	17*	<.1
39	Net Source—*Joe Fannen*	8020 Shaffer PkySte 10, Littleton CO 80127	303-948-3360	R	16*	<.1
40	Contour Inc—*Marc Barrows*	3131 Western Ave Ste 4, Seattle WA 98121	206-792-5226	R	15	<.1
41	Acutrack Inc—*Raj Barman*	350 Sonic Ave, Livermore CA 94551	925-579-5000	R	15*	<.1
42	Oasis CD Manufacturing—*Micah Solomon*	5400 Carolina Pl, Springfield VA 22151	703-642-3757	R	13*	<.1
43	HD Studios—*Keith Neff*	23689 Industrial Park, Farmington Hills MI 48335	248-471-6010	D	13*	<.1
44	Victory Studios—*Conrad Denke*	2247 15th Ave W, Seattle WA 98119	206-282-1776	R	13*	<.1
45	Masterwork Recording Inc—*Pete Humphreys*	1020 N Delaware Ave, Philadelphia PA 19125	215-423-1022	R	13*	<.1
46	Devlin Video International—*Mick O'Connor*	1501 Broadway Ste 408, New York NY 10036	212-391-1313	R	12*	<.1
47	Trutone Inc—*Dina Patel*	380 Lexington Ave 17th, New York NY 10168	212-265-5636	R	12*	<.1
48	GoldenRom Inc—*Derek Signorini*	3 Vertical Dr, Canonsburg PA 15317	724-746-5807	R	11*	<.1
49	Formats Unlimited Inc—*Joyce Cosentino*	121 Carolyn Blvd, East Farmingdale NY 11735	631-249-9393	R	11*	<.1
50	Promedia Digital—*Joe Chylik*	3777 Business Park Dr, Columbus OH 43204	614-274-1600	R	11*	<.1
51	ISODISC/Software Services Group—*Alan D Kegel*	7030 N 97th Cir, Omaha NE 68122	402-453-1699	R	10*	<.1
52	NDS Media Solutions Inc—*Donald W Parker*	631 Old Hickory Blvd, Old Hickory TN 37138	615-541-0077	R	10*	<.1
53	Recordpressingcom—*Oliver Goss*	475 Haight St, San Francisco CA 94117	415-462-1992	R	10*	<.1
54	Design Video Communications—*Jad Porter*	7301 E 46th St, Indianapolis IN 46226	317-544-2150	R	9*	<.1
55	Global Information Distribution Inc—*Ernstfried Driesen*	2635 Zanker Rd, San Jose CA 95134	408-232-5500	R	9*	<.1
56	DiscFarm Corp—*Charlie Chien*	125 Klug Cir, Corona CA 92880	951-279-4034	R	8*	<.1
57	Input Center—*John Klein*	2506 N Clark St Ste 32, Chicago IL 60614	773-472-6883	R	8*	<.1
58	United Audio Video Group Inc—*Miriam Newman*	6855 Vineland Ave, North Hollywood CA 91605	818-980-6700	R	8*	.1
59	Studio Magnetics Company Inc—*George Clahane*	12 Long Island Ave, Holtsville NY 11742	631-289-3400	R	8*	<.1
60	Cd Video Manufacturing Corp—*Minh Nguyen*	12650 Westminster Ave, Santa Ana CA 92706	714-265-0770	R	7*	.1
61	Oasis Disc Manufacturing—*Micah Solomon*	33 W 19th St Ste 328, New York NY 10011	212-395-9460	R	7*	<.1
62	DataDisc Inc—*Royce White*	1289 Progress Dr, Front Royal VA 22630	540-622-5580	R	7*	<.1
63	Girard Video Inc—*Andy Hemmendinger*	1775 K St NW, Washington DC 20006	202-293-4488	R	7*	<.1
64	1st Run Computer Services—*Bob Molinari*	1261 Broadway Ste 508, New York NY 10001	212-779-0800	R	7*	<.1
65	Casscom Media—*Ollie Moyer*	6000 Industrial Dr, Greenville TX 75402	903-455-2555	R	7*	<.1
66	Loop LLC—*Thomas L Shaw*	PO Box 1266, Clearwater FL 33757	727-483-9286	R	7	.1
67	Star-Byte Inc—*Steve Derstine*	611 Jeffers Cir, Exton PA 19341		R	6*	<.1
68	Cassette Works—*Michael McKinney*	235 Bellefontaine St, Pasadena CA 91105	626-441-2024	D	6*	<.1
69	Digital Video Development Inc—*Paul C Eardley*	810 Penn Ave, Pittsburgh PA 15222	412-281-4000	R	6*	<.1
70	bitMAX LLC—*Richard Martin*	6255 Sunset Blvd Ste 1, Hollywood CA 90028	323-978-7878	R	5*	<.1
71	Video Replay Inc—*Ron Norinsky*	118 W Grand Ave, Chicago IL 60610	312-467-0425	R	5*	<.1
72	HDMG Corp—*Jamie Heuton*	6573 City W Pkwy, Eden Prairie MN 55344	952-943-1711	R	5*	<.1
73	AIX Media Group—*Mark Waldrep*	8455 Beverly Blvd Ste, West Hollywood CA 90048	323-655-4116	R	5*	<.1
74	American Recordable Media—*Alan Case*	3744 Willow Ridge Rd, Lexington KY 40514		R	5*	<.1
75	Carpel Video Inc—*Morgan Boatman*	429 E Patrick St, Frederick MD 21701	301-694-3500	R	5*	<.1
76	JG Studio HD—*Jay Gross*	10781 75th St N, Largo FL 33777	727-546-7900	R	5*	<.1
77	LION and FOX Recording—*Rob Buhrman*	9517 Baltimore Ave, College Park MD 20740	301-982-4431	R	5*	<.1
78	Star Video Duplicating—*Paul J Brown*	6910 E 5th Ave, Scottsdale AZ 85251	480-946-3699	R	5*	<.1
79	Unique Media Inc—*Champion Chen*	2991 Corvin Dr, Santa Clara CA 95051	408-733-9999	R	5*	<.1
80	Agile Network LLC	6209 Mid Rivers Mall D, Saint Peters MO 63304	636-300-0912	R	5*	.1
81	Multisupport Computer Systems—*Ramin Movahedi*	PO Box 22403, Carmel CA 93922	831-657-0122	R	4*	<.1
82	Ethority Inc—*Michael Psenka*	1583 Savannah Hwy, Charleston SC 29407	843-556-5565	R	4*	<.1
83	Test and Measurement Systems Inc—*Doreen Macdonald*	750 14th St Sw, Loveland CO 80537	970-669-6553	R	4*	<.1
84	AMG Media Group—*Joseph McCoig*	477 Oak Ridge Turnpike, Oak Ridge TN 37830		R	4*	<.1
85	CD Solutions Inc—*Jerald Worner*	PO Box 536, Pleasant Hill OH 45359	937-676-2376	R	4*	<.1
86	Digital Force Ltd—*Jerome Bunke*	149 Madison Ave 12th F, New York NY 10016	212-252-9300	R	4*	<.1
87	Gateway Mastering Studios Inc—*Bob Ludwig*	428 Cumberland Ave, Portland ME 04101	207-828-9400	R	4*	<.1
88	Gotta Have Dvd Inc—*Sondra Brunone*	400 E Royal Ln Ste 230, Irving TX 75039	972-409-9293	R	4*	<.1
89	Green Solutions Inc—*Andrew Green*	5130 E La Palma Ave, Anaheim CA 92807	714-696-5454	R	4*	<.1
90	Sound Chamber Mastering—*Eric Doscb*	2201 W Burbank Blvd, Burbank CA 91506	818-752-7581	R	4*	<.1
91	Tobin Productions Inc—*Dwight Tobin*	133 W 19th St, New York NY 10011	212-727-1500	R	4*	<.1
92	M Works Inc—*Jonathan Wyner*	1035 Cambridge St Ste, Cambridge MA 02141	617-577-0089	R	4*	<.1
93	Video Movie Magic—*Mike Jones*	26941 Cabot Rd Ste 127, Laguna Hills CA 92653	949-582-8596	R	4*	<.1
94	Chicago Producers Inc—*Bill Vala*	817 S Western Ave, Chicago IL 60612	312-226-6900	R	4*	<.1
95	Electronic Media International—*Paul Gelardi*	1 Colonel Gelardi Dr S, Kennebunk ME 04043	207-985-8800	R	4*	<.1
96	Cross Access Corp—*Michael Dering*	1 Tower Ln Ste 1700, Oakbrook Terrace IL 60181	630-928-3708	R	4*	<.1
97	Error Free Software LLC—*Alexei Gitter*	200 S Wacker Dr Ste 24, Chicago IL 60606	312-461-0300	R	3*	<.1
98	Ace Fat Inc—*Derek Bailey*	16395 E Alameda Pl, Aurora CO 80017	303-981-7601	R	3*	<.1
99	Javanni Inc—*Tim Farina*	10912 Thousand Oaks Dr, Huntersville NC 28078	704-779-1546	R	3*	<.1
100	Transfer West Duplication—*Karl Renwanz*	5850 S Polaris Ave, Las Vegas NV 89118	702-895-9900	R	3*	<.1
101	Bad Animals/Seattle—*Dave Howe*	2212 4th Ave, Seattle WA 98121	206-443-1500	R	3*	<.1
102	CD Works—*Jeffrey Starfield*	93 Park St, Beverly MA 01915	617-782-5884	R	3*	<.1
103	Santa Barbara Engineering Inc—*Edward Podwojski*	8241 E Evans Rd Ste 10, Scottsdale AZ 85260	480-948-8651	R	3*	<.1
104	Video I-D—*Sam Wagner*	105 Muller Rd, Washington IL 61571	309-444-4323	R	3*	<.1
105	Advanced Media Integration—*Adam Grostefon*	2300 Meyer Rd, Fort Wayne IN 46803	260-428-2698	R	3*	<.1
106	Analog Digital International—*Ayres D'Cunha*	20 E 49th St, New York NY 10017	212-688-5110	R	3*	<.1
107	Paradise Video Inc—*Sabra Karanian*	10148 NW 47th St, Fort Lauderdale FL 33351	954-747-1118	R	3*	<.1

Note: An asterisk (*) indicates an estimated financial figure. The company type code used is as follows: R = Private, P = Public, S = Private Subsidiary, B = Public Subsidiary, D = Division, J = Joint Venture, I = Investment Fund.

COMPANY RANKINGS BY SALES WITHIN 4-DIGIT SIC

Rank	Company Name—*Executive Officer*	Address, City, State, Zip	Phone	Type	Fin	Empls
108	Program Productions—*Robert Carzoli*	870 Oak Creek Dr, Lombard IL 60148	630-792-9700	R	3*	<.1
109	Stark Raving Solutions—*Dan Stark*	10205 Ensley Ln, Leawood KS 66206	913-383-0243	R	3*	<.1
110	Optical Disc Corp—*James Wu*	10415 Slusher Dr Ste 1, Santa Fe Springs CA 90670	562-946-3050	R	3*	<.1
111	Queues Enforth Development Inc—*David Varney*	14 Summer St Ste 2, Malden MA 02148	781-870-1100	R	3*	<.1
112	Mse Media Solutions—*Michelle Cardinale*	6013 Scott Way, Commerce CA 90040	323-721-1656	R	2*	<.1
113	E-K Media Inc—*Tim Kerry*	75A Union Ave, Sudbury MA 01776	978-440-7635	R	2*	<.1
114	Major Media Inc—*Jay Steinberg*	3326 Commercial Ave, Northbrook IL 60062	847-498-4610	R	2*	<.1
115	Aardvark Record Mastering—*Paul Brekus*	4485 Utica St, Denver CO 80212	303-455-1908	R	2*	<.1
116	ANS International—*Hasan Oguz*	220 E 23rd St 2nd Fl, New York NY 10010	212-673-3107	R	2*	<.1
117	C and C Studios—*Edward Candelora*	480 Alfred Ave, Glassboro NJ 08028	856-881-7645	R	2*	<.1
118	Champion Visions World Inc—*Kelly Dole*	1735 Westlake Ave N St, Seattle WA 98109	206-336-0535	R	2*	<.1
119	DeNoisecom LLC—*Albert Benichou*	1501 Powell St Ste A, Emeryville CA 94608	510-653-3838	R	2*	<.1
120	Megalodon CD/DVD Manufacturing—*Christine Meredith*	518 Washington St 2nd, Ashland OR 97520	541-552-1747	R	2*	<.1
121	Motion City Films—*G Michael Witt*	1424 4th St Ste 604, Santa Monica CA 90401	310-434-1272	R	2*	<.1
122	Musicol Recording—*John Hull*	780 Oakland Park Ave, Columbus OH 43224	614-267-3133	R	2*	<.1
123	Novus Media Services Inc—*Bill Schafer*	4300 Pine View Dr, Galena OH 43021	740-965-1246	R	2*	<.1
124	SAE Mastering—*Roger Seibel*	6832 N 24th Dr Ste 1, Phoenix AZ 85015	602-242-0022	R	2*	<.1
125	Syzygy Media Works Inc—*David Watts Jr*	PO Box 252, Wakefield MA 01880	781-246-9766	R	2*	<.1
126	Trackmaster Inc—*Bruce Parsons*	4701 NE 12th Ave, Oakland Park FL 33334	954-776-6603	R	2*	<.1
127	12zCD—*Ken Charnick*	10907 Snow Cloud Trl, Littleton CO 80125	303-948-7180	R	2*	<.1
128	DB Plus Digital Services—*Joel Kerr*	250 W 57th St Ste 725, New York NY 10107	212-397-4099	R	2*	<.1
129	DVDTransfercom LLC—*Jason A Spafford*	712 Ontario Ave W, Minneapolis MN 55403	612-676-1165	R	2*	<.1
130	Foothill Digital Inc—*Allan Tucker*	215 W 91st St, New York NY 10024	212-877-0973	R	2*	<.1
131	JamSync—*KK Proffitt*	PO Box 120969, Nashville TN 37212	615-320-5050	R	2*	<.1
132	Mark Custom Recording Service—*Mark J Morette*	10815 Bodine Rd, Clarence NY 14031	716-759-2600	R	2*	<.1
133	Dub-It Digital Media Services—*Brian Patterson*	1110 N Tamarind Ave, Hollywood CA 90038	323-993-9570	R	2*	<.1
134	Focused Media—*Linda Weldmen*	16655 Lakeview Ct, Lakeville MN 55044	952-435-3755	R	2*	<.1
135	Storch Products Company Inc—*Marjorie Storch*	PO Box 531356, Livonia MI 48153	734-591-2200	R	2*	<.1
136	Ed Cyber—*John Murray*	PO Box 3480, Chico CA 95927	530-230-3613	R	2*	<.1
137	Xorbix Technologies Inc—*Asif Bakar*	759 N Milwaukee St Ste, Milwaukee WI 53202	414-277-5044	R	2*	<.1
138	Nuvidia LLC—*Randy Hermance*	9258 Bond St, Shawnee Mission KS 66214	913-599-5200	R	2*	<.1
139	Imperial Technical Services—*Diane Riley*	13647 SW Hwy, Orland Park IL 60462	708-873-0071	R	2*	<.1
140	Keyin Inc—*Hank Huang*	PO Box 90533, City Of Industry CA 91715	562-690-3888	R	1*	<.1
141	Mak-System Corp—*Simon Kiskovski*	2720 S River Rd Ste 22, Des Plaines IL 60018	847-803-4863	R	1*	<.1
142	Cvc Audio and Video Supply Inc—*Frank Childs*	PO Box 3397, Fullerton CA 92834	714-871-1419	R	1*	<.1
143	3s Group Inc—*Satpal Sahni*	125 Church St Ne Ste 2, Vienna VA 22180	703-281-5015	R	1*	<.1
144	Thot Technologies Inc—*James Eckerman*	271 E Hacienda Ave, Campbell CA 95008	408-370-4600	R	1*	<.1
145	BullseyeDisc—*Curtis Kidwell*	3377 SE Division St St, Portland OR 97202	503-233-2313	R	1*	<.1
146	CDS Graphics—*Rick Goldman*	634 W Broadway, Glendale CA 91204		R	1*	<.1
147	Diskette Duplication Mirror Images Inc—*Michael Shaffer*	13300 McCutcheonville, Wayne OH 43466		R	1*	<.1
148	Dominion Post Inc—*William Parks*	6800 Fleetwood Rd Rm 1, McLean VA 22101	703-891-7400	R	1*	<.1
149	Dvideo - Digital Productions Studio—*Arie Marek*	2900 Westchester Ave S, Purchase NY 10577	914-251-9244	R	1*	<.1
150	Ardenwood Sound and DVD—*Mark Calice*	34766 Monaco Common, Fremont CA 94555	510-793-7511	R	1*	<.1
151	DVD Master—*Max Nguyen*	10500 Westminster Ave, Garden Grove CA 92843	714-658-5835	R	1*	<.1
152	ELS Productions—*Mark McLelland*	1444 Meadow Bluff Lane, Draper UT 84020	801-676-0807	R	1*	<.1
153	Immersion Media Inc—*Zachary Stewart*	1322 Oakton St, Evanston IL 60202	847-491-9112	R	1*	<.1
154	Marin Digital—*Chris Armbrust*	30 Marie St, Sausalito CA 94965	415-331-4423	R	1*	<.1
155	Mark Herlinger Productions—*Mark Herlinger*	1735 Lafayette St, Denver CO 80218	303-455-4177	R	1*	<.1
156	MasterDigital Corp—*Parker Dinkins*	2614 W 15th Ave, Covington LA 70433	504-236-6368	R	1*	<.1
157	Media Management Services—*Rick Hively*	625 22nd St, Huntington Beach CA 92648	714-536-9568	R	1*	<.1
158	mediaHYPERIUM—*Herbert Waltl*	2539 W 237th St Ste E, Torrance CA 90505	310-891-0006	R	1*	<.1
159	Tambellini Productions Inc—*Karen Timbellini*	188 E 17th St Ste 201, Costa Mesa CA 92627	949-548-7762	R	1*	<.1
160	Budget Data Services Inc—*Bill Woolen*	180 Golf Club Dr Ste 1, Pleasant Hill CA 94523	925-360-9153	R	1*	<.1
161	Digital Authoring Solutions LLC—*Joseph Aloia*	303 Louisiana Ave, Brooklyn NY 11207	212-244-8071	R	1*	<.1
162	Future Disc Systems Inc—*Steve Hall*	15851 NW Willis Rd, McMinnville OR 97128	213-361-0603	R	1*	<.1
163	Gold Street Entertainment—*Eric Michael Cap*	649 Bethany Rd, Burbank CA 91504	818-567-1911	R	1*	<.1
164	Images Productions—*Marvin Smejkal*	1001 3rd Ave SW, Cedar Rapids IA 52404	319-362-8180	R	1*	<.1
165	Mozian and Associates Inc—*Paul Mozian*	15 Presidents Pl, Kingston NY 12401	845-340-9223	R	1*	<.1
166	Study Dog—*Deme Clainos*	9720 Sw Nimbus Ave, Beaverton OR 97008	503-643-4449	R	1*	<.1
167	Spencer Grant Inc—*John Arnold*	19361 Francisca Way, Yorba Linda CA 92886	714-693-3920	R	1*	<.1
168	Cd-Rom-Works LLC—*Curtis Kidwell*	3377 Se Division St St, Portland OR 97202	503-233-2313	R	<1*	<.1
169	Recall Systems Inc—*Steve Sagussy*	1117 Perimeter Center, Atlanta GA 30338	770-551-8888	R	<1*	<.1
170	Blue City Digital—*Russ Wojtkiewicz*	5014 NW Woody Creek Dr, Kansas City MO 64151	816-343-4186	R	<1*	<.1
171	Heritage Recording Studio—*Charles Davis*	23031 Goose Creek Rd, South Bloomingville OH 43152	740-332-9155	R	<1*	<.1
172	Sunburst Sensors LLC	1226 W Broadway St, Missoula MT 59802	406-532-3246	R	<1*	<.1
173	Mammobase LLC—*J Eddlemon*	9209 Oak Ridge Hwy, Oak Ridge TN 37830	865-927-0203	R	<1*	<.1
174	Spectrotape Corp—*John Chan*	PO Box 942, Loma Linda CA 92354	909-825-6744	R	<1*	<.1
175	Data Publications—*Daniel Mohr*	6721 166th Ln Nw, Anoka MN 55303	763-753-9929	R	<1*	<.1
176	Aerco—*Jerome Chamkis*	7606 Robalo Rd, Austin TX 78757	512-451-5874	R	<1*	<.1
177	Genesis One Technologies Inc—*Richard Miller*	7470 San Clemente Pl, Boca Raton FL 33433	561-393-5813	R	<1*	<.1
178	Fancy Media Company Inc—*Christopher Pfrang*	1530 Breezeport Way St, Suffolk VA 23435	757-638-3808	R	<1*	<.1
179	Glickman Technology Inc—*Steve Glickman*	304 Nicholson Ave, Los Gatos CA 95030	408-354-4506	R	<1*	<.1
180	Nevis Group LLC—*Burt Peterson*	33834 Loland Dr, Waterford WI 53185	262-514-3001	R	<1*	<.1
181	Geo Vision Software Inc—*Michael Boender*	PO Box 2152, Fairfield IA 52556	641-472-0855	R	<1*	<.1
182	Tritone Development—*John Husser*	409 Georgia St, Blacksburg VA 24060	540-951-8043	R	<1*	<.1
183	Media Circus Inc—*Scott Brewer*	53 W Jackson Blvd Ste, Chicago IL 60604	312-588-0000	R	<1*	<.1

TOTALS: SIC 3695 Magnetic & Optical Recording Media

	Companies: 183				11,441	51.5

3699 Electrical Equipment & Supplies Nec

1	Boon Edam Inc—*Tom DeVine*	420 McKinney Pkwy, Lillington NC 27546	910-814-3800	R	7,005*	.1
2	Etec Systems Inc—*Gino Addiego*	PO Box 58039, Santa Clara CA 95052	408-727-5555	S	6,992	12.2
3	Energizer Holdings Inc—*J Patrick Mulcahy*	533 Maryville Universi, Saint Louis MO 63141	314-985-2000	P	4,248	15.5
4	Flow Systems—*James Barrett*	PO Box 1069, Saint Helena Island SC 29920	843-838-6698	R	2,681*	<.1
5	Ingenico Corp—*Christoper Justice*	6195 Shiloh Rd Ste D, Alpharetta GA 30005	678-456-1200	S	2,528*	3.0
6	Lockheed Martin Enterprise Information Systems—*Robert J Stevens*	12506 Lake Underhill Rd, Orlando FL 32825	407-306-1000	S	2,383*	4.0
7	Arco Auto and Marine Products—*Ron Miller*	3921 W Navy Blvd, Pensacola FL 32507	850-455-5476	R	2,010*	<.1
8	L-3 AMI Instruments Inc—*Michael Strianese* Link Simulation and Training	3724 W Vancouver, Broken Arrow OK 74012	918-258-0707	D	945	N/A

Rank	Company Name—*Executive Officer*	Address, City, State, Zip	Phone	Type	Fin	Empls
9	Standard Motor Products Inc—*Lawrence I Sills*	37-18 Northern Blvd, Long Island City NY 11101	718-392-0200	P	811	1.9
10	East Penn Manufacturing Company Inc—*Daniel R Langdon*	PO Box 147, Lyon Station PA 19536		R	716*	5.0
11	Rofin-Sinar Technologies Inc—*Gunther Braun*	40984 Concept Dr, Plymouth MI 48170	734-455-5400	P	598	1.8
12	United Industrial Corp	PO Box 126, Hunt Valley MD 21030	410-628-3500	S	564	2.3
13	Lamson and Sessions Co—*Michael J Merriman*	25701 Science Park Dr, Cleveland OH 44122	216-464-3400	S	561*	1.3
14	Camber Corp—*Walter Batson Jr*	635 Discovery Dr, Huntsville AL 35806	256-922-0200	R	520*	1.0
15	Link Simulation and Training—*John McNellis*	PO Box 5328, Arlington TX 76005	817-619-2000	D	443*	.8
16	C and D Technologies Inc—*Jeffrey A Graves*	PO Box 3053, Blue Bell PA 19422	215-619-2700	P	355	1.5
17	Bronner Display and Sign Advertising Inc—*Wayne Bronner*	PO Box 176, Frankenmuth MI 48734	989-652-9931	R	265*	.5
18	Electro Scientific Industries Inc—*Nicholas Konidaris*	13900 NW Science Park, Portland OR 97229	503-641-4141	P	257	.6
19	FlightSafety International Inc—*Bruce M Whitman*	PO Box 12304, Wichita KS 67277	316-220-3100	S	255*	1.8
20	Catalina Lighting Inc—*Robert Varakian*	18191 NW 68th Ave, Miami FL 33015	305-558-4777	R	210	2.2
21	FlightSafety International—*Bruce N Whitman* FlightSafety International Inc	Marine Air Terminal La, Flushing NY 11371	718-565-4100	D	200*	1.5
22	Excel Technology Inc—*Antoine Dominic*	41 Research Way, East Setauket NY 11733	631-784-6175	S	160	.7
23	Electronic Cable Specialists Inc—*Paul Smyczek*	5300 W Franklin Dr, Franklin WI 53132	414-421-5300	S	145*	.2
24	Fisher Pierce—*H Lawrence Culp Jr*	54 Commercial St, Raynham MA 02767	508-821-1597	S	117*	.2
25	Wavelight Inc	5203 S Fwy, Fort Worth TX 76134	817-293-0450	S	115*	.2
26	Woods Industries Inc—*Gary Yetman*	1530 Shields Dr, Waukegan IL 60085	847-672-2300	S	110	.8
27	NLX Corp—*Tony Syme*	22626 Sally Ride Dr, Sterling VA 20164	703-234-2100	S	104*	.7
28	Carlon Chimes Co—*Michael J Merriman Jr* Lamson and Sessions Co	25701 Science Park Dr, Cleveland OH 44122	216-464-3400	S	86*	.2
29	Rofin-Sinar Inc—*Louis Molnar* Rofin-Sinar Technologies Inc	40984 Concept Dr, Plymouth MI 48170	734-455-5400	S	85*	.3
30	Gmi Holdings Inc—*Carl Adrien*	22790 Lake Park Blvd, Alliance OH 44601	330-821-5360	S	77*	1.0
31	Broadcast Microwave Services Inc—*Graham Bunney*	12367 Crosthwaite Cir, Poway CA 92064	858-391-3050	S	69*	.1
32	Sling Media Inc—*Johnny Gilmore*	1051 E Hillsdale Blvd, Foster City CA 94404	650-293-8000	S	69*	.1
33	Synrad Inc—*Dave Clarke* Excel Technology Inc	4600 Campus Pl, Mukilteo WA 98275	425-349-3500	S	65*	.1
34	Environmental Tectonics Corp—*William F Mitchell*	125 James Way, Southampton PA 18966	215-355-9100	P	56	.3
35	Hubbell Killark—*Timothy Powers*	PO Box 5325, Saint Louis MO 63115	314-531-0460	R	54*	.4
36	Control Systemation Inc—*Greg Anderson* Excel Technology Inc	2419 Lake Orange Dr, Orlando FL 32837	407-926-0800	S	46*	.1
37	Rofin-Baasel Inc—*Lou Molnar*	68 Barnum Rd, Devens MA 01434	978-635-9100	R	45*	.1
38	Flow Robotics (Jeffersonville Indiana)—*Charles M Brown*	1635 Production Rd, Jeffersonville IN 47130	812-283-7888	S	42*	.1
39	Piller USA Inc—*Michael Barron*	45 Turner Dr, Middletown NY 10941	845-695-5300	R	39*	.1
40	Hanchett Entry Systems Inc—*Scott Baker*	22630 N 17th Ave, Phoenix AZ 85027	623-582-4626	R	39*	.1
41	Citel America Inc—*Mile Robinson*	11381 Interchange Cir, Miramar FL 33025	954-430-6310	S	35*	.2
42	Mound Laser and Photonics Center Inc—*Larry Dosser* Laser Fare Inc	PO Box 223, Miamisburg OH 45343	937-865-4070	S	34*	<.1
43	Pinpoint Systems International Inc—*William Silhan*	10 Pinehurst Dr, Bellport NY 11713	631-775-2100	R	34*	.2
44	Stanley Access Technologies	65 Scott Swamp Rd, Farmington CT 06032	860-677-2861	S	33	.3
45	Weimer Bearing and Transmission Inc—*Frank Stangl*	PO Box 667, Menomonee Falls WI 53052	262-781-1992	R	32*	.1
46	Laser Devices Inc—*Heinz Thummel*	70 Garden Ct Ste 200, Monterey CA 93940	831-373-0701	R	30*	.1
47	Dvtel Inc—*Yoav Stern*	65 Challenger Rd Ste 2, Ridgefield Park NJ 07660	201-368-9700	R	30*	.1
48	E Ink Corp—*Felix Ho*	733 Concord Ave, Cambridge MA 02138	617-499-6000	R	30*	.1
49	Hyndman Industrial Products—*Joseph E Hyndman*	3205 Carriongate Dr, Fort Wayne IN 46808	260-483-6042	R	30*	<.1
50	Aitech Defense Systems Inc—*Roger Rowe*	19756 Prairie St, Chatsworth CA 91311	818-700-2000	R	29*	.2
51	Safety Vision Inc—*Bruce H Smith*	6100 W Sam Houston Pkw, Houston TX 77041	713-896-6600	R	29*	.1
52	American Tower International Inc—*James D Taiclet Jr*	116 Huntington Ave 11t, Boston MA 02116	617-375-7500	S	28*	.1
53	Evans and Sutherland Computer Corp—*David H Bateman*	770 Komas Dr, Salt Lake City UT 84108	801-588-1000	P	27	.1
54	THK America Inc—*Akihiro Teramachi*	200 E Commerce Dr, Schaumburg IL 60173	847-310-1111	D	27*	.2
55	Laser Fare Inc—*Clifford Brockmyre* Infinite Group Inc	1 Industrial Dr S, Smithfield RI 02917	401-231-4400	S	27*	.1
56	Sonatech Inc—*John Fumo*	879 Ward Dr, Santa Barbara CA 93111	805-683-1431	R	27*	.5
57	Doorking Inc—*Thomas Richmond*	120 S Glasgow Ave, Inglewood CA 90301	310-645-0023	R	26*	.2
58	Ibis Tek LLC—*Christopher Bardakos*	912 Pittsburgh Rd, Butler PA 16002	724-586-6005	R	26*	.4
59	Adalet—*Kenneth Semelsberger*	4801 W 150th St, Cleveland OH 44135	216-267-9000	D	26*	.2
60	Pemco Corp—*Marquis Johnson*	PO Box 1319, Bluefield VA 24605	276-326-2611	R	25*	.1
61	Cubic Simulation Systems Inc—*Robert Collins*	2001 W Oak Ridge Rd, Orlando FL 32809	407-859-7410	D	25*	.1
62	MDI Security Systems	12500 Network Blvd Rm, San Antonio TX 78249	210-404-9551	S	25*	.1
63	Smart Electronics And Assembly Inc—*Shou-Lee Wang*	2000 W Corporate Way, Anaheim CA 92801	714-991-6500	R	25*	.1
64	PC Open Inc—*Richard Sheppard*	23221 E Knox Ave, Liberty Lake WA 99019	509-777-6736	R	24*	.1
65	TR Manufacturing Inc—*Dom Tran*	41938 Christy St, Fremont CA 94538	510-657-3850	R	24*	.1
66	Navitar Inc—*Julian Goldstein*	200 Commerce Dr, Rochester NY 14623	585-359-4000	R	23*	.1
67	Fusion Uv Systems Inc—*David Harbourne*	910 Clopper Rd Ste 102, Gaithersburg MD 20878	301-527-2660	R	23*	.2
68	QVS Inc—*B Cooper*	2731 Crimson Canyon Dr, Las Vegas NV 89128	702-228-3670	R	23*	<.1
69	Capco Inc—*Stephen Wood*	PO Box 1028, Grand Junction CO 81502	970-243-8750	R	23*	.2
70	Ushio America Inc—*Kenji Hamashima*	5440 Cerritos Ave, Cypress CA 90630	714-236-8600	R	23*	.2
71	Wireless Xcessories Group Inc—*Stephen Rade*	1840 County Line Rd St, Huntingdon Valley PA 19006	215-322-4600	P	23	.1
72	Electri-Cord Manufacturing Co—*Mitch Samuels*	312 E Main St, Westfield PA 16950	814-367-2265	R	22*	.2
73	Heathco LLC—*Marcia Sanders*	PO Box 90045, Bowling Green KY 42102	270-846-8400	S	22*	.2
74	Laser Shot Inc—*Paige Manard*	4214 Bluebonnet Dr, Stafford TX 77477	281-240-1122	R	22*	.1
75	Atkinson Industries Inc—*David Dingus*	PO Box 268, Pittsburg KS 66762	620-231-6900	S	22*	.1
76	Isis Surface Mounting—*Chris Hoolhorst*	2530 Zanker Rd, San Jose CA 95131	408-953-7700	R	21*	.2
77	Reveo Inc—*Sadeg Faris*	6 Skyline Dr Ste 130, Hawthorne NY 10532	646-539-3300	R	20*	<.1
78	Lambda Physik USA Inc	PO box 54980, Santa Clara CA 95056	408-764-4000	S	20*	<.1
79	Aerotech Inc—*Mark Botos*	101 Zeta Dr, Pittsburgh PA 15238	412-963-7470	R	20*	.3
80	Saginaw Control and Engineering Inc—*Frederick May*	95 Midland Rd, Saginaw MI 48638	989-799-6871	R	20*	.3
81	Thermal Circuits Inc—*Anthony Klein*	1 Technology Way, Salem MA 01970	978-745-1162	R	19*	.2
82	Synchrony Technology—*Victor Iannello*	4655 Technology Dr, Salem VA 24153	540-444-4200	R	18*	<.1
83	Xterprise Solutions Inc—*Dean Frew*	2304 Tarpley Ste 114, Carrollton TX 75006	972-690-9460	R	18*	<.1
84	kSaria Corp—*Sebastian J Sicari*	439 S Union St, Lawrence MA 01843	978-933-0000	R	18*	<.1
85	Prima North America Inc—*Terry Vanderwert*	711 E Main St, Chicopee MA 01020	413-598-5200	R	17*	.1
86	Ultra-Stereo Labs Inc—*Jack Cashin*	181 Bonetti Dr, San Luis Obispo CA 93401	805-549-0161	R	16*	<.1
87	Protective Group Inc—*Ed Careaga*	14100 Nw 58th Ct, Hialeah FL 33014	305-820-4270	R	15*	.1
88	Parker-Mccrory Manufacturing Co—*Kenneth Turner*	2000 Forest Ave, Kansas City MO 64108	816-221-2000	R	15*	.1
89	Sonics and Materials Inc—*Robert S Soloff*	53 Church Hill Rd, Newtown CT 06470	203-270-4600	R	15*	.1
90	Keri Systems Inc—*Ted Geiszler*	2305 Bering Dr, San Jose CA 95131	408-435-8400	R	15*	.1
91	Tri-Tronics Inc—*Gerald Gonda*	PO Box 17660, Tucson AZ 85731	520-290-6000	S	14*	.1

Note: An asterisk (*) indicates an estimated financial figure. The company type code used is as follows: R = Private, P = Public, S = Private Subsidiary, B = Public Subsidiary, D = Division, J = Joint Venture, I = Investment Fund.

COMPANY RANKINGS BY SALES WITHIN 4-DIGIT SIC

Rank	Company Name—Executive Officer	Address, City, State, Zip	Phone	Type	Fin	Empls
92	Microsun Technologies LLC—Alan Elshafei	1200 Internationale Pk, Woodridge IL 60517	630-968-5000	R	14*	.1
93	Pace Inc—Eric Siegel	255 Air Tool Dr, Southern Pines NC 28387	910-695-7223	R	14*	.1
94	Wand Corp—John Perrill	7593 Corporate Way, Eden Prairie MN 55344	952-361-6200	R	14*	.1
95	Inner-Tite Corp—George Davis	110 Industrial Dr, Holden MA 01520	508-829-6361	R	13*	.1
96	Operator Specialty Company Inc—Dan Stottlemyre	2547 3 Mile Rd Nw Ste, Grand Rapids MI 49534	616-453-2372	R	13*	.1
97	Altronix Corp—Alan Forman	140 58th St Ste A, Brooklyn NY 11220	718-567-8181	R	13*	.1
98	Tamarack Scientific Company Inc—Ronald Sheets	220 Klug Cir, Corona CA 92880	951-817-3700	R	13*	.1
99	Nabco Entrances Inc—Philip Stuckey	S82w18717 Gemini Dr, Muskego WI 53150	262-679-0045	R	12*	.1
100	Kidde Fire Trainers Inc—Robert Downin	17 Philips Pkwy, Montvale NJ 07645	201-300-8100	S	12*	.1
101	Optomec Inc—David Ramahi	3911 Singer Blvd NE, Albuquerque NM 87109	505-761-8250	R	12*	.1
102	High Tech Inc—Stephen Spychalski	1390 29th Ave, Gulfport MS 39501	228-868-6632	R	12*	<.1
103	Laser Mechanisms Inc—William Fredrick	25325 Regency Dr, Novi MI 48375	248-615-1251	R	12*	.1
104	Manconix Inc—Minh Leba	11011 Brooklet Dr Ste, Houston TX 77099	281-879-8849	R	11*	.1
105	Miller Edge Inc—Bearge Miller	PO Box 159, West Grove PA 19390	610-869-4422	R	11*	.1
106	Gates That Open LLC—Joseph Kelley	3121 Hartsfield Rd, Tallahassee FL 32303	850-575-0176	R	11*	.1
107	Electro-Plasma Inc—Michael Horner	4400 Moline Martin Rd, Millbury OH 43447	419-838-7365	R	11*	.1
108	Universal Laser Systems Inc—Yefim Sukhman	16008 N 81st St, Scottsdale AZ 85260	480-483-1214	R	11*	.1
109	Symetrics Industries LLC—Steve Dretzka	1615 W Nasa Blvd, Melbourne FL 32901	321-254-1500	R	11*	.1
110	Guild Technologies Ltd—Guild Group	PO Box 800205, Mesquite TX 75180	972-329-0155	R	11*	<.1
111	Kno Inc—Osman Rashid	5155 Old Ironsides Dr, Santa Clara CA 95054	408-844-8120	R	11*	.1
112	Protex International Corp—David Wachsman	180 Keyland Ct, Bohemia NY 11716	631-563-4250	R	11*	.1
113	V-Tek Inc—Dennis Siemer	PO Box 3104, Mankato MN 56002	507-387-2039	R	11*	.1
114	Aero Simulation Inc—Mike Mccarthy	4450 E Adamo Dr Ste 50, Tampa FL 33605	813-628-4447	R	10*	.1
115	Simtek Inc—Thomas Cowley	1505 Royal Pkwy, Euless TX 76040	817-283-1801	R	10*	.1
116	Cincinnati Laser Cutting LLC—Eric Rogozinski	891 Redna Ter, Cincinnati OH 45215	513-779-7200	R	10*	.1
117	Laserage Technology Corp—Steve Capp	3021 N Delany Rd, Waukegan IL 60087	847-249-5900	R	10*	.1
118	Midwest Electric Products Inc—Jeff Immelt	PO Box 910, Mankato MN 56002	507-345-2505	S	10*	.1
119	Atlantic Scientific Corp—Jim McDonald	4300 Fortune Pl Ste A, West Melbourne FL 32904	321-725-8000	S	10*	.1
120	Spinnaker Contract Manufacturing Inc—Guy Nickerson	95 Business Park Dr, Tilton NH 03276	603-286-4366	R	10*	.1
121	Rf Ideas Inc—Richard Landuyt	1435 N Plum Grove Rd A, Schaumburg IL 60173	847-870-1723	R	10*	<.1
122	Raycom Electronics Inc—Ray Fowler	PO Box 250, Dover PA 17315	717-292-3641	R	10*	.1
123	Sono-Tek Corp—Christopher L Coccio	2012 Rte 9 W, Milton NY 12547	845-795-2020	P	10	<.1
124	Fi-Shock Inc—Tom Boyd	5360 N National Dr, Knoxville TN 37914	865-524-7380	R	10*	.1
125	Electrofilm Manufacturing Company LLC—David Schmidt	PO Box 55669, Valencia CA 91385	661-257-2242	R	10*	.1
126	Infinite Group Inc—James Villa	60 Office Pky, Pittsford NY 14534	585-385-0610	P	9	.1
127	Kirby Risk Electrical Supply	PO Box 5089, Lafayette IN 47903	765-448-4567	R	9*	.1
128	Wren Associates Ltd—Andrew Wren	124 Wren Pkwy, Jefferson City MO 65109	573-893-2249	R	9*	.1
129	TNR Technical Inc—Wayne Thaw	301 Central Park Dr, Sanford FL 32771	407-321-3011	P	9	<.1
130	Maverick Industries Inc—Edward Mackin	94 Mayfield Ave, Edison NJ 08837	732-417-9666	R	9*	<.1
131	CirTran Corp—Iehab J Hawatmeh	4125 S 6000 W, Salt Lake City UT 84128	801-963-5112	P	9	<.1
132	V E Power Door Company Inc—Philip Lanzarone	PO Box 663, Commack NY 11725	631-231-4500	R	9*	.1
133	Undersea Systems International Inc—Michael Pelissier	3133 W Harvard St, Santa Ana CA 92704	714-754-7848	R	9*	.1
134	Sabine Inc—Doran Oster	13301 Us Hwy 441, Alachua FL 32615	386-418-2000	R	9*	.1
135	Biomedical Life Systems Inc—Richard Saxon	PO Box 1360, Vista CA 92085	760-727-5600	R	9*	.1
136	Electra - Cord Inc—Michael Hutsell	PO Box 875, Massillon OH 44648	330-832-8124	R	8*	.1
137	Arcos Industries LLC—Gib Gratti	394 Arcos Dr, Mount Carmel PA 17851	570-339-5200	R	8*	.1
138	Engineered Products Co—Duncan Lee	5401 Smetana Dr, Minnetonka MN 55343	952-767-8780	R	8*	.1
139	Rdm Industrial Electronics Inc—Doug Long	PO Box 969, Nebo NC 28761	828-652-8346	R	8*	.1
140	Bauer Electrotech—Fred Bauer	517 41st Ave, Winona MN 55987	507-454-5564	R	8*	<.1
141	Mr Christmas Inc	5841 East Shelby Dr, Memphis TN 38141	901-365-6040	R	8*	<.1
142	Innova Industries Inc—Richard Young	PO Box 397, Fergus Falls MN 56538	218-739-3226	R	8*	.1
143	Aes Corp—Michael Sherman	PO Box 2093, Peabody MA 01960	978-535-7310	R	8*	.1
144	Soundcraft Inc—Joel Smulson	20301 Nordhoff St, Chatsworth CA 91311	818-882-0020	R	8*	.1
145	Stapla Ultrasonics Corp—David Joy	250 Andover St Ste 2, Wilmington MA 01887	978-658-9400	R	8*	<.1
146	Sciaky Inc—Scott Phillips	4915 W 67th St, Chicago IL 60638	708-594-3800	R	7*	.1
147	Rodale Wireless Inc—John Clement	20 Oser Ave Ste 2, Hauppauge NY 11788	631-231-0044	R	7*	.1
148	Ion Corp—Wendell Maddox	7500 Equitable Dr, Eden Prairie MN 55344	952-936-9490	R	7*	.1
149	360 Services International—Kenneth A Pickl II	12623 Newburgh Rd, Livonia MI 48150	734-591-9360	R	7*	.1
150	Engine Monitor Inc—Ken Cognevich	191 James Dr W, Saint Rose LA 70087	504-620-9800	R	7*	<.1
151	Highfield Manufacturing—Joseph Mcclain	380 Mountain Grove St, Bridgeport CT 06605	203-384-2281	R	7*	.1
152	Oleco Inc—Jeff Olds	18683 Trimble Ct, Spring Lake MI 49456	616-842-6790	R	7*	.1
153	Iba Industrial Inc—Frederic Genin	151 Heartland Blvd, Edgewood NY 11717	631-254-6800	R	7*	<.1
154	Custom Ultrasonics Inc—Frank Weber	PO Box 850, Buckingham PA 18912	215-364-1477	R	7*	.1
155	Knf Clean Room Products Corp—Philip Carcara	1800 Ocean Ave, Ronkonkoma NY 11779	631-588-7000	R	7*	<.1
156	Master Appliance Corp—Scott Radwill	PO Box 68, Racine WI 53401	262-633-8840	R	7*	<.1
157	Research Electronics International LLC—Lee Jones	455 Security Pl, Cookeville TN 38506	931-537-6032	R	7*	.1
158	Huffman Corp—Roger Hayes	1050 Huffman Way, Clover SC 29710	803-222-4561	R	7*	.1
159	Digital Systems Corp—Robert Laughlin	PO Box 158, Walkersville MD 21793	301-845-4141	R	6*	<.1
160	Carey Manufacturing Company Inc—John Carey	5 Pasco Hill Rd, Cromwell CT 06416	860-828-0847	R	6*	.1
161	Morse Watchmans Inc—Manuel Pires	2 Morse Rd, Oxford CT 06478	203-264-4949	R	6*	.1
162	Vynckier Enclosure Systems Inc—James Carr	249 Mccarty St, Houston TX 77029	713-374-7850	R	6*	.1
163	Bonitron Inc—Keith Benson	521 Fairground Ct, Nashville TN 37211	615-244-2825	R	6*	.1
164	Safety Training Systems Inc—Bruce Bartovick	7373 E 38th St, Tulsa OK 74145	918-665-0125	R	6*	<.1
165	Control Micro Systems Inc—Timothy Miller	4420 Metric Dr Ste A, Winter Park FL 32792	407-679-9716	R	6*	<.1
166	Lenco Marine Inc—Sam Mullinax	4700 SE Municipal Ct, Stuart FL 34997	772-288-2662	R	6*	.1
167	Big Sky Laser International Inc—Joseph Sawyer	PO Box 8100, Bozeman MT 59719	406-586-0131	R	6*	<.1
168	Corfin Tinning Services Inc—Alan Goldberg	PO Box 18335, Huntsville AL 35804	256-650-0220	R	6*	<.1
169	Rojan Electronics Inc—Richard Empert	55 Page Park Dr, Poughkeepsie NY 12603	845-452-3411	R	6*	.1
170	Semilab Sdi LLC—Chris Moore	3650 Spectrum Blvd Ste, Tampa FL 33612	813-977-2244	R	6*	<.1
171	Ces Industries Inc—Mitchell Nesenoff	2023 New Hwy Unit C, Farmingdale NY 11735	631-293-1420	R	5*	<.1
172	Comptrol Inc—Gary Tarnowski	9505 Midwest Ave, Cleveland OH 44125	216-587-5200	R	5*	<.1
173	Control Chief Holdings Inc—Douglas S Bell	PO Box 141, Bradford PA 16701	814-362-6811	R	5	.1
174	Varflex Corp—Dorothy G Griffin	512 W Court St, Rome NY 13440	315-336-4400	R	5*	.1
175	Aerotechnic Corp—Bahram Salem	527 Jessie St, San Fernando CA 91340	818-838-1008	R	5*	.1
176	Excel Dryer Inc—Denis Gagnon	PO Box 365, East Longmeadow MA 01028	413-525-4531	R	5*	<.1
177	Laharco Inc—Harold Cope	4270 Nw Yeon Ave, Portland OR 97210	503-222-9992	R	5*	<.1
178	Quality Concepts Manufacturing Inc—Debora Wadle	1635 S Murray Blvd, Colorado Springs CO 80916	719-574-1013	R	5*	<.1
179	Yuhshin USA Ltd—Kohji Tanabe	2806 Industrial Rd, Kirksville MO 63501	660-627-1655	R	5*	<.1
180	Manor Electric Supply Corp—Kenneth Rabinowitz	2737 Ocean Ave, Brooklyn NY 11229	718-648-8003	R	5*	<.1
181	Universal Surveillance Corp—Adel Sayegh	11172 Elm Ave, Rancho Cucamonga CA 91730	909-484-7870	R	5*	<.1

Rank	Company Name—*Executive Officer*	Address, City, State, Zip	Phone	Type	Fin	Empls
182	Lasermax Inc—*Susan Walter*	PO Box 92583, Rochester NY 14692	585-272-5420	R	5*	<.1
183	Dice Corp—*Clifford Dice*	1410 S Valley Ctr Dr, Bay City MI 48706	989-891-2800	R	5*	.1
184	Emx Industries Inc—*Joseph Rozgonyi*	4564 Johnston Pkwy, Cleveland OH 44128	216-518-9888	R	5*	<.1
185	Aznet—*Roy Valley*	3450 Corporate Way Ste, Duluth GA 30096	770-623-4400	R	4*	<.1
186	Alert Stamping and Manufacturing Company Inc—*Paul Blanch*	24500 Solon Rd, Bedford Heights OH 44146	440-232-5020	R	4*	<.1
187	Door-Man Manufacturing Co—*Andrew Johnson*	2498 Commercial Dr, Auburn Hills MI 48326	248-377-9200	R	4*	<.1
188	United Manufacturing Inc—*Thomas Howell*	301 Overland Park Pl, New Century KS 66031	913-780-0056	R	4*	<.1
189	Clear Align LLC—*Angelique X Irvin*	2550 Boulevard of the, Eagleville PA 19403	484-956-0510	R	4*	.1
190	Accsys Technology Inc—*Takao Kuboniwa*	1177 Quarry Ln Ste A, Pleasanton CA 94566	925-462-6949	R	4*	<.1
191	Swantech LLC—*Tony Amato*	5440 NW 33rd Ave Ste 1, Fort Lauderdale FL 33309	954-332-6710	R	4*	<.1
192	Amtel Security Systems Inc—*Suresh Gajwani*	1691 Nw 107th Ave, Doral FL 33172	305-591-8200	R	4*	<.1
193	Fernandes Enterprises LLC—*Darryl Burk*	2801 Ontario Ave, Dayton OH 45414	937-890-6444	R	4*	<.1
194	Madgetech Inc—*Norman Carlson*	PO Box 50, Warner NH 03278	603-456-2011	R	4*	<.1
195	Amrex-Zetron—*George Bell*	641 E Walnut St, Carson CA 90746	310-527-6868	R	4*	<.1
196	Architectural Control Systems Inc—*David Senften*	2720 Clark Ave, Saint Louis MO 63103	314-652-5588	R	4*	<.1
197	Scientific Materials Corp—*Anthony Ltrunzo*	31948 Frontage Rd, Bozeman MT 59715	406-585-3772	R	4*	<.1
198	Hampton Technologies LLC	19 Industrial Blvd, Medford NY 11763	631-924-1335	R	4*	<.1
199	Fortec Medical Lithotripsy LLC	10125 Wellman Rd, Streetsboro OH 44241	330-656-4301	R	3*	.1
200	Formax Technologies Inc—*Timothy Lindsay*	305 S Soderquist Rd, Turlock CA 95380	209-668-1001	R	3*	<.1
201	Promptus Electronic Hardware Inc—*Vincent Giagni*	550 Homestead Ave, Mount Vernon NY 10550	914-699-4700	R	3*	<.1
202	Crimestopper Millenium Enterpr—*Howard Miller*	1770 Tapo St, Simi Valley CA 93063	805-526-9400	R	3*	<.1
203	Montgomery Technology Inc—*Timothy Skipper*	23 Old Stage Rd, Greenville AL 36037	334-382-7441	R	3*	<.1
204	Gil Acquisition LLC	10585 Enterprise Dr, Davisburg MI 48350	248-625-0529	R	3*	<.1
205	Hurricane Electronics Lab Inc—*Cheryl Reeve*	331 N 2260 W, Hurricane UT 84737	435-635-2003	R	3*	<.1
206	Synergy Contracting Services LLC—*James Cupp*	1125 Wayne Ave, Indiana PA 15701	724-349-4381	R	3*	<.1
207	Advanced Solder Tech Inc—*John Robinson*	571 Haverty Ct Ste R, Rockledge FL 32955	321-633-4777	R	3*	<.1
208	Paraclipse Inc—*Rodney Behlen*	PO Box 686, Columbus NE 68602	402-563-3625	R	3*	<.1
209	Projected Sound Inc—*J Hilligoss*	469 Avon Ave, Plainfield IN 46168	317-839-4111	R	3*	<.1
210	Sonicor Inc—*Michael Parker*	50 Capital Dr, Wallingford CT 06492	203-265-6048	R	3*	<.1
211	Sentinel Systems Corp—*Bonnie Reddick*	1620 Kipling St, Lakewood CO 80215	303-242-2000	R	3*	<.1
212	Parabit Systems Inc—*Robert Leiponis*	PO Box 481, Roosevelt NY 11575	516-378-4800	R	3*	<.1
213	Dactek International Corp	17150 Newhope St Ste 3, Fountain Valley CA 92708	818-787-1901	R	3*	<.1
214	JNJ Industries Inc—*Clint Bradley*	290 Beaver St, Franklin MA 02038	508-553-0529	R	3*	<.1
215	Kritzer Industries Inc—*Robert Kritzer*	PO Box 847, Scarborough ME 04070	207-883-4141	R	3*	<.1
216	Mohawk Electrical Systems Inc—*Scott Welch*	PO Box 630, Milford DE 19963	302-422-2500	R	3*	<.1
217	Laserfab Inc—*Kevin Frazer*	5406 184th St E Ste D, Puyallup WA 98375	253-846-8370	R	3*	<.1
218	GatecraftersCom—*Anthony Gaeto*	13100 State Rd 54, Odessa FL 33556	813-792-9412	R	3*	<.1
219	Mdci—*Erik Hostevedt*	PO Box 980, Doylestown PA 18901	215-712-9048	R	3*	<.1
220	Power Port Products Inc—*Douglas Murphy*	301 W Interstate Rd, Addison IL 60101	630-530-7000	R	3*	<.1
221	Raco Manufacturing Engineering Co—*Constance Brown*	1400 62nd St, Emeryville CA 94608	510-658-6713	R	3*	<.1
222	Triton Infosys Inc—*Mike Patel*	1230 Ave Of The Amrcs, New York NY 10020		R	3*	<.1
223	Select Engineered Systems Inc—*John Sheppard*	7991 W 26th Ave, Hialeah FL 33016	305-823-5410	R	3*	<.1
224	Tactical Technologies Inc—*Richard Snyder*	500 Pine St Ste 3a, Holmes PA 19043	610-522-0106	R	3*	<.1
225	Advanced Thin Films LLC—*Ramin Lalezari*	5733 Central Ave, Boulder CO 80301	720-494-4194	R	3*	<.1
226	Stracon Inc—*Son Pham*	1672 Kaiser Ave Ste 1, Irvine CA 92614	949-851-2288	R	3*	<.1
227	Laser Energetics Inc—*Robert Battis*	PO Box 7147, Princeton NJ 08543	609-587-8250	R	3*	<.1
228	Precision Cable Of Tennessee Inc—*Jim Burkhart*	PO Box 449, Portland TN 37148	615-325-5086	R	2*	<.1
229	Crawford Electric Supply Co—*Butch Cox*	200 L And A Rd, Metairie LA 70001	504-849-0675	R	2*	<.1
230	Kigre Inc—*Michael Myers*	100 Marshland Rd, Hilton Head Island SC 29926	843-681-5800	R	2*	<.1
231	Wein Products Inc—*Stan Weinberg*	115 W 25th St, Los Angeles CA 90007	213-749-6049	R	2*	<.1
232	Akr Enterprises LLC—*George Jacob*	6640 Eli Whitney Dr St, Columbia MD 21046	301-483-8930	R	2*	<.1
233	Salco Industries Inc—*Salvatore Caputo*	263 Field End St, Sarasota FL 34240	941-377-7717	R	2*	<.1
234	Security And Fire Electronics Inc—*Donald Grundy*	2590 Dobbs Rd, Saint Augustine FL 32086	904-824-8553	R	2*	<.1
235	American Industrial Equipment Corp—*Jane Weiss*	PO Box 4835, Weehawken NJ 07086	201-865-1851	R	2*	<.1
236	Tricor International Inc—*Tom Hebda*	PO Box 367, Lombard IL 60148	630-629-1213	R	2*	<.1
237	Innovative Circuits Inc—*Gary Mitchell*	311a S Pky St, Corinth MS 38834	662-287-2007	R	2*	<.1
238	Integrated Security Corp—*Morton Noveck*	46755 Magellan Dr, Novi MI 48377	248-624-0700	R	2*	<.1
239	Axion Power International Inc—*Thomas Granville*	3601 Clover Ln, New Castle PA 16105	724-654-9300	P	2	.1
240	Gamma High Voltage Research Inc—*Honora Maresco*	1096 N Us Hwy 1 Ste 10, Ormond Beach FL 32174	386-677-7070	R	2*	<.1
241	Sonobond Ultrasonics Inc—*Janet Devine*	1191 Mcdermott Dr, West Chester PA 19380	610-696-4710	R	2*	<.1
242	Bird-X Inc—*Ronald Schwarcz*	300 N Oakley Blvd, Chicago IL 60612		R	2*	<.1
243	Compu-Gard Inc—*Peter Leite*	PO Box 469, Swansea MA 02777	508-679-8845	R	2*	<.1
244	Ohmega Technologies Inc—*Alan Leve*	4031 Elenda St, Culver City CA 90232	310-559-4400	R	2*	<.1
245	Spectrum Laser and Technologies Inc—*Jeffrey Riggs*	3855 Interpark Dr, Colorado Springs CO 80907	719-264-7632	R	2*	<.1
246	Synergy Electric Inc—*Cory Ratheurn*	4701 Franklin Rd, Fairview PA 16415	814-474-4727	R	2*	<.1
247	WL Jenkins Co	1445 Whipple Ave SW, Canton OH 44710	330-477-3407	R	2*	<.1
248	Design Assistance Corp—*Glenn Woerner*	PO Box 215, Swedesboro NJ 08085	856-241-9500	R	2*	<.1
249	Malwin Electronics Corp—*Gifford Weber*	52 E 22nd St, Paterson NJ 07514	973-881-1500	R	2*	<.1
250	M/Rad Corp—*Philip Marshall*	71 Pine St, Woburn MA 01801	781-935-5940	R	2*	<.1
251	Martronic Engineering Inc—*Richard Marsh*	80 W Easy St Ste 5, Simi Valley CA 93065	805-583-0808	R	2*	<.1
252	Zenion Industries Inc—*Jim Lee*	6640 Redwood Dr Ste 10, Rohnert Park CA 94928	707-584-3663	R	2*	<.1
253	US Laser Corp—*Robert Regna*	PO Box 609, Wyckoff NJ 07481	201-848-9200	R	2*	<.1
254	Dynasound Inc—*Thomas Koenig*	6439 Atlantic Blvd, Norcross GA 30071	770-242-8176	R	2*	<.1
255	Birmingham Control Systems Inc—*Robert Snyder*	1205 8th St W, Birmingham AL 35204	205-252-2504	R	2*	<.1
256	Electronic Sensors Inc—*Gerald Rues*	2063 S Edwards St, Wichita KS 67213	316-267-2807	R	2*	<.1
257	Data Design Corp—*John Giganti*	7851 Beechcraft Ave St, Gaithersburg MD 20879	301-670-1157	R	2*	<.1
258	Pro Systems Fabricators Inc—*Edith Sugarman*	14643 Hawthorne Ave, Fontana CA 92335	909-350-9147	R	2*	<.1
259	Laserreliance Technologies—*Tim Saunders*	1075 Florida Central P, Longwood FL 32750	407-339-0737	R	2*	<.1
260	Maxmar Controls Inc—*Max Birrer*	11901 W Sample Rd, Coral Springs FL 33065	954-340-4371	R	2*	<.1
261	Castle Industries Inc—*Arthur Schloss*	120 Sylvan Ave Ste 3, Englewood Cliffs NJ 07632	201-585-8400	R	2*	<.1
262	Dakota Micro Inc—*Dave Rubey*	8659 148th Ave Se, Cayuga ND 58013	701-538-4403	R	2*	<.1
263	Intelligence Support Group Ltd—*Richard Disabatino*	PO Box 1240, Inyokern CA 93527		R	2*	<.1
264	Engineered Automation of ME Inc—*Stephen Swinburne*	14 Washington Ave, Scarborough ME 04074	207-883-4183	R	2*	<.1
265	Fastpulse Technology Inc—*Steven Goldstein*	220 Midland Ave, Saddle Brook NJ 07663	973-478-5757	R	2*	<.1
266	Kern Electronics and Lasers Inc—*Gerald Kern*	1501 Industrial Dr, Wadena MN 56482	218-631-2755	R	2*	<.1
267	Prob-Test Inc—*Sam Jannati*	364 W Tullock St, Rialto CA 92376	909-626-4232	R	2*	<.1
268	Tecnomasium Inc—*Roberto Donne*	105 Bertley Ridge Dr, Coraopolis PA 15108	412-264-7364	R	1*	<.1
269	Fuller Manufacturing Inc—*Christopher Fuller*	PO Box 999, Sutter Creek CA 95685	209-267-5071	R	1*	<.1
270	Elcom Industries Inc—*Thomas Noel*	10268 Bach Blvd, Saint Louis MO 63132	314-429-3100	R	1*	<.1
271	Presco Inc—*Philip Black*	8 Lunar Dr Ste 4, Woodbridge CT 06525	203-397-8722	R	1*	<.1

Note: An asterisk (*) indicates an estimated financial figure. The company type code used is as follows: R = Private, P = Public, S = Private Subsidiary, B = Public Subsidiary, D = Division, J = Joint Venture, I = Investment Fund.

COMPANY RANKINGS BY SALES WITHIN 4-DIGIT SIC

Rank	Company Name—Executive Officer	Address, City, State, Zip	Phone	Type	Fin	Empls
272	Integrity Security Systems—Robert Wien	7801 N Lamar Blvd Ste, Austin TX 78752	512-374-9190	R	1*	<.1
273	Magiq Technologies Inc—Bob Gelfond	11 Ward St Ste 300, Somerville MA 02143	617-661-8300	R	1*	<.1
274	Protective Technologies International Ut LC—Aaron Allred	9451 Bagley Park Rd, West Jordan UT 84081	801-280-9997	R	1*	<.1
275	CCT Laser Services Inc—Roger Underwood	25421 S Schulte Rd, Tracy CA 95377	209-833-1110	R	1*	<.1
276	Laser Automation Inc—John Herkes	16771 Hilltop Park Pl, Chagrin Falls OH 44023	440-543-9291	R	1*	<.1
277	Ritec Inc—Mark Mckenna	60 Alhambra Rd Ste 5, Warwick RI 02886	401-738-3660	R	1*	<.1
278	Total Fire Systems Inc—Mike Rohlik	PO Box 1408, Wake Forest NC 27588	919-556-9161	R	1*	<.1
279	Preferred Security Components Incorporated Of PA—David Bohannon	127 W Main St, Salunga PA 17538	717-898-0107	R	1*	<.1
280	Vinland Corp—Bertho Boman	11600 Nw 20th St, Plantation FL 33323	954-475-9093	R	1*	<.1
281	TH Grogan and Associates Inc—Tom Grogan	PO Box 2858, Acton MA 01720	978-266-9548	R	1*	<.1
282	WD Burch Inc—William Burch	26082 Getty Dr Ste B, Laguna Niguel CA 92677	949-582-3898	R	1*	<.1
283	Intellikey Corp—Singh Chhatwal	4325 Woodland Pk Dr St, Melbourne FL 32904	321-724-5595	R	1*	<.1
284	Sonotronics Inc—Marlin Gregor	PO Box 26803, Tucson AZ 85726	520-746-3322	R	1*	<.1
285	QCM Inc—Bob Jacobson	836 N St Unit 1, Tewksbury MA 01876	978-858-3550	R	1*	<.1
286	Wirewise Inc—Eric Chute	1208 Industrial Ave, Gastonia NC 28054	704-869-8884	R	1*	<.1
287	Oldaker Manufacturing Corp—Linda Ream	301 N Main St, Dunkirk OH 45836	419-759-3551	R	1*	<.1
288	American Access Systems Inc—Donald Allen	7079 S Jordan Rd Ste 6, Centennial CO 80112	303-799-9757	R	1*	<.1
289	New Line USA Inc—Ilan Bartov	20 Northwood Dr, Bloomfield CT 06002	860-242-3963	R	1*	<.1
290	Audient Inc—Jerry Rossi	20532 Crescent Bay Dr, Lake Forest CA 92630	949-830-9412	R	1*	<.1
291	Aritronix Limited Inc—Avi Sandler	16055 N Dial Blvd Ste, Scottsdale AZ 85260	480-951-1109	R	1*	<.1
292	Omnisyn Corp—Henry Bobulski	PO Box 26196, Columbus OH 43226	614-436-4595	R	1*	<.1
293	Demco Electronics Inc—Darrell Hoblack	10516 S Grevillea Ave, Inglewood CA 90304	310-677-0801	R	1*	<.1
294	Stone Technologies Corp—Arthur Stone	2311 Westrock Dr Ste 4, Austin TX 78704	512-440-1234	R	1*	<.1
295	Snyder Electronics—James Briggs	2082 Lincoln Ave, Altadena CA 91001	626-794-7139	R	<1*	<.1
296	Technocean Inc—Henry White	820 Ne 24th Ln Ste 112, Cape Coral FL 33909	239-772-9067	R	<1*	<.1
297	Nitty Gritty Record Care—Gayle Syckle	4650 Arrow Hwy Ste F4, Montclair CA 91763	909-625-5525	R	<1*	<.1
298	Plugout LLC	506 Laguardia Pl Apt 4, New York NY 10012	212-655-4428	R	<1*	<.1
299	Mixed Logic LLC	5907 E Law Rd, Valley City OH 44280	440-826-1676	R	<1*	<.1
300	Adams Electronics Inc—Robert Adams	1611 S Utica Ave Pmb 4, Tulsa OK 74104	918-622-5000	R	<1*	<.1
301	Lans Of Texas Inc—Jean Stout	1773 Westborough Dr, Katy TX 77449	281-829-2448	R	<1*	<.1
302	Laser Diode Array Inc—Alan Karpinski	100 E Genesee St, Auburn NY 13021	315-253-8292	R	<1*	<.1
303	Tetrad Inc—Terry Jenkins	3243 Register Rd, Fruitland Park FL 34731	352-728-1555	R	<1*	<.1
304	Alexy Associates Inc—Cornelius Alexy	PO Box 70, Bethel NY 12720	845-482-3000	R	<1*	<.1
305	Pulse Systems Inc—Edward Mc Lellan	166 Eastgate Dr, Los Alamos NM 87544	505-662-7599	R	<1*	<.1
306	Irdata Corp—Doug Bradford	2102 Business Ctr Dr, Irvine CA 92612	714-434-9964	R	<1*	<.1
307	Beamin' Lasers Inc—Todd Rogers	1741 W Rose Garden Ln, Phoenix AZ 85027	623-780-4668	R	<1*	<.1
308	Mosley Electronics Inc—Gerard Wardack	1325 Stylemaster Dr, Union MO 63084	636-583-8595	R	<1*	<.1
309	mPhase Technologies Inc—Ronald A Durando	150 Clove Rd, Little Falls NJ 07424	973-256-3737	P	<1	<.1

TOTALS: SIC 3699 Electrical Equipment & Supplies Nec
Companies: 309 　　　　　　　　　　　　　　　　　　　　　　　　　　　　38,316　　77.3

3711 Motor Vehicles & Car Bodies

Rank	Company Name—Executive Officer	Address, City, State, Zip	Phone	Type	Fin	Empls
1	General Motors Co—Daniel F Akerson	PO Box 33170, Detroit MI 48232	313-556-5000	P	135,592	202.0
2	Ford Motor Co—Bill Ford	PO Box 6248, Dearborn MI 48126	313-322-3000	P	128,954	164.0
3	American Honda Motor Company Inc—Satoru Kishi	1919 Torrance Blvd, Torrance CA 90501	310-783-2000	S	42,539*	25.0
4	Chrysler Group LLC—Sergio Marchionne	PO Box 21-8004, Auburn Hills MI 48321	248-576-5741	R	41,946	59.0
5	Ford VAC Corp—William J Ford Ford Motor Co	1 American Rd, Dearborn MI 48121	313-322-3000	S	15,105*	1.9
6	Saturn LLC	1420 Stephenson Hwy, Troy MI 48083		R	12,597*	10.6
7	PACCAR Inc—Mark C Pigott	PO Box 95003, Bellevue WA 98009	425-468-7400	P	10,293	17.7
8	Oshkosh Corp—Richard M Donnelly	PO Box 2566, Oshkosh WI 54903	920-235-9150	P	7,585	13.1
9	Honda of America Manufacturing Inc—Aaron Hall American Honda Motor Company Inc	24000 Honda Pkwy, Marysville OH 43040	937-642-5000	S	5,090*	13.0
10	Renco Group Inc—Ira L Rennert	1 Rockefeller Plaza 29, New York NY 10020	212-541-6000	R	5,000*	12.0
11	Freightliner LLC—Chris Patterson	4435 N Channel Ave, Portland OR 97217	503-745-8000	S	2,929*	15.0
12	WABCO Holdings Inc—Jacques Esculier	1 Centennial Ave, Piscataway NJ 08855	732-369-7450	P	2,794	10.9
13	Thor Industries Inc—Peter P Orthwein	419 W Pike St, Jackson Center OH 45334	937-596-6849	P	2,756	8.3
14	BMW Of North America LLC—Jim O'Donnell	PO Box 1227, Westwood NJ 07675	201-307-4000	S	2,690*	1.0
15	AutoAlliance International Inc—Gary Roe	1 International Dr, Flat Rock MI 48134	734-782-7600	J	2,611*	3.2
16	AM General Corp—Charles Hall Renco Group Inc	PO Box 7025, South Bend IN 46617	574-237-6222	S	2,245*	2.5
17	Nissan North America Inc	1 Nissan Way, Franklin TN 37067	615-725-1000	S	1,995*	13.0
18	Mitsubishi Motors North America Inc—Shinichi Kurihara	PO Box 6014, Cypress CA 90630	714-372-6000	S	1,198*	3.6
19	Spartan Motors Chassis Inc Spartan Motors Inc	1541 Reynolds Rd, Charlotte MI 48813	517-543-6400	S	1,030*	.8
20	Toyota Motor Manufacturing West Virginia Inc—Yoji Suzuki Toyota Motor Manufacturing North America Inc	1 Sugar Maple Ln, Buffalo WV 25033	304-937-7000	S	951*	1.0
21	Federal Signal Corp—Dennis J Martin	1415 W 22nd St Ste 110, Oak Brook IL 60523	630-954-2000	P	727	2.8
22	Toyota Motor Manufacturing Kentucky Inc—Steven Angelo	PO Box 2700, Georgetown KY 40324	502-868-2000	R	723*	6.5
23	Toyota Motor Manufacturing North America Inc—Wil James	25 Atlantic Ave, Erlanger KY 41018	859-746-4000	S	571*	7.0
24	Spartan Motors Inc—John E Sztykiel	1541 Reynolds Rd, Charlotte MI 48813	517-543-6400	P	481	1.5
25	Ford of North Miami Beach—Scott Rauber	2198 NE 163rd St, North Miami Beach FL 33162	305-493-5000	R	447*	.3
26	Detroit Chassis LLC—Michael J Guthrie	6501 Lynch Rd, Detroit MI 48234	313-571-2100	S	445*	.3
27	Jefferson Industries Corp—Hideo Hayashi	6670 State Rte, West Jefferson OH 43162	614-879-5300	R	374*	.8
28	JB Poindexter and Company Inc—John Poindexter	600 Travis St Ste 200, Houston TX 77002	713-655-9800	R	349*	2.9
29	Wheeled Coach Industries Corp—Robert Collins Collins Industries Inc	2737 Forsyth Rd, Winter Park FL 32792	407-677-7777	S	326*	.4
30	North American Bus Industries Inc—Andras Racz	106 National Dr, Anniston AL 36207	256-831-4296	R	325*	.6
31	Elgin Sweeper Co—Mark Weber Federal Signal Corp	1300 W Bartlett Rd, Elgin IL 60120	847-741-5370	S	286*	.4
32	Subaru Of Indiana Automotive Inc—Masahiro Kasai	PO Box 5689, Lafayette IN 47903	765-449-1111	S	263*	2.3
33	Vac-Con Inc—Darrell Lesage	969 Hall Park Rd, Green Cove Springs FL 32043	904-284-4200	R	204*	.3
34	Collins Industries Inc—Randall Swift	PO Box 648, Hutchinson KS 67502	620-663-5551	S	187*	.9
35	E-One Inc—Peter Guile	1601 Sw 37th Ave, Ocala FL 34474	352-237-1122	R	174*	.7
36	Am General Holdings LLC—Mark Minne	105 N Niles Ave, South Bend IN 46617	574-237-6222	R	160*	3.5
37	VSV Group—Jim Olson	25161 Leer Dr, Elkhart IN 46514	574-264-7511	P	148*	.5
38	Magna Services of America Inc—Donald Walker	600 Wilshire Dr, Troy MI 48084	248-729-2400	D	120*	.4
39	Amerigon Inc—Daniel R Coker	21680 Haggerty Rd Ste, Northville MI 48167	248-504-0500	P	112	.1
40	Sutphen Corp—Drew Sutphen	PO Box 158, Amlin OH 43002	614-889-1005	R	103*	.2

Rank	Company Name—*Executive Officer*	Address, City, State, Zip	Phone	Type	Fin	Empls
41	Executive Coach Builders Inc—*David Bakare*	4400 W Production St, Springfield MO 65803	417-935-2233	R	84*	.1
42	Smeal Fire Apparatus Co—*Delwin Smeal*	PO Box 8, Snyder NE 68664	402-568-2224	R	77*	.3
43	Saleen Special Vehicles Inc—*Rich Ranke*	1225 E Maple Rd, Troy MI 48083	248-743-4800	R	44*	.3
44	Super Products LLC—*Mike Heuvel*	PO Box 510110, New Berlin WI 53151	262-784-7100	R	44*	.1
45	Schwartz Industries Inc (Huntsville Alabama)—*Bob Faulhaber*	1055 Jordan Rd, Huntsville AL 35811	256-851-1200	R	40*	.2
46	Fwd Seagrave Holdings LP—*Jim Denis*	105 E 12th St, Clintonville WI 54929	715-823-2141	R	38*	.5
47	Fisker Automotive Inc—*Henrik Fisker*	5515 E LaPalma, Anaheim CA 92807	714-888-4255	J	35*	<.1
48	Foretravel Inc—*Lyle Reed*	1221 Nw Stallings Dr, Nacogdoches TX 75964	936-564-8367	R	35*	.5
49	Sportchassis LLC—*Tim Sinor*	2300 S 13th St, Clinton OK 73601	580-323-4100	R	33*	<.1
50	Cheetah Chassis Corp—*Frank Katz*	PO Box 388, Berwick PA 18603	570-752-2708	R	31*	.2
51	Super Vacuum Manufacturing Company Inc—*Roger Weinmeister*	PO Box 87, Loveland CO 80539	970-667-5146	R	29*	.2
52	Reinke Manufacturing Company Inc—*Chris Roth*	PO Box 566, Deshler NE 68340	402-365-7251	R	29*	.4
53	Allianz Sweeper Co—*Gabriel Charky*	2810 E Philadelphia St, Ontario CA 91761	909-613-5600	R	28*	.2
54	Braun Industries Inc—*Kim Elick*	1170 Production Dr, Van Wert OH 45891	419-232-7031	R	25*	.2
55	Ferrara Fire Apparatus Incorporated—*Christopher Ferrara*	PO Box 249, Holden LA 70744	225-567-7100	R	25*	.3
56	Agm Automotive Inc—*Robert Blinstrub*	1000 E Whitcomb Ave, Madison Heights MI 48071	248-776-0600	R	22*	.1
57	AMP Electric Vehicles Inc—*James Taylor*	4540 Alpine Ave, Cincinnati OH 45242	513-360-4704	S	21*	<.1
58	Onodi Tool and Engineering Co—*John Onodi*	19150 Meginnity St, Melvindale MI 48122	313-386-6682	R	20*	<.1
59	Accubuilt Inc—*Dan Mitchell*	4707 E Kearney St, Springfield MO 65803	417-864-4411	R	20*	.1
60	Aptera Motors Inc—*Paul B Wilbur*	2778 Loker Ave, Carlsbad CA 92010	760-431-8581	R	19*	<.1
61	Alexis Fire Equipment Co—*K Morris*	PO Box 549, Alexis IL 61412	309-482-6121	R	18*	.1
62	Farber Specialty Vehicles Inc—*Ken Farber*	7052 Americana Pkwy, Reynoldsburg OH 43068	614-863-6470	R	17*	.1
63	Braun Northwest Inc—*Jack Braun*	PO Box 1204, Chehalis WA 98532	360-748-0195	R	17*	.1
64	Spangler Racing—*Loren Spangler*	10041 1/2 Canoga Ave, Chatsworth CA 91311	818-886-3736	R	16*	<.1
65	Medical Coaches Inc—*Geoffrey Smith*	PO Box 129, Oneonta NY 13820	607-432-1333	R	15*	.1
66	Excellance Inc—*Charles Epps*	453 Lanier Rd, Madison AL 35758	256-772-9321	R	13*	.1
67	Kovatch Corp—*John Kovatch*	1 Industrial Complex, Nesquehoning PA 18240	570-669-9461	R	10*	.1
68	Custom Coach International Inc—*C Smith*	PO Box 370, Mcalester OK 74502	918-287-4445	R	9*	.1
69	Kodiak Northwest Inc—*Brek Pilling*	1350 Pomerelle Ave, Burley ID 83318	208-438-8248	R	7*	.1
70	Alpine Armoring Inc—*Fred Khoroushi*	570 Herndon Pkwy Ste 1, Herndon VA 20170	703-471-0009	R	7*	.1
71	Smart Automation Systems Inc—*Masatake Horiba*	950 S Rochester Rd, Rochester Hills MI 48307	248-651-5911	R	6*	<.1
72	Special Projects Inc—*Kenneth Yanez*	45901 Helm St, Plymouth MI 48170	734-453-3048	R	5*	<.1
73	Michels and Wilde Inc—*Andy Wilde*	2870 W 2100 S, Salt Lake City UT 84119	801-972-1601	R	5*	<.1
74	Millennium Transit Services LLC—*William Beyerle*	42 W Earl Cummings Loo, Roswell NM 88203	575-347-7500	R	3*	<.1
75	Mosler Auto Care Center Inc—*Warren Mosler*	2391 Old Dixie Hwy, Riviera Beach FL 33404	561-842-2492	R	3*	<.1
76	UB Machine Inc—*Greg Urbine*	PO Box 673, New Haven IN 46774	260-493-3381	R	2*	<.1
77	Pierce Arrow Inc—*Jeff Pierce*	549 Us Hwy 287 S, Henrietta TX 76365	940-538-5643	R	1*	<.1
78	Maxim Global Inc—*Lester Lee*	701 Hodell St Ste 101, Shelbyville IN 46176	317-398-5641	R	1*	<.1

TOTALS: SIC 3711 Motor Vehicles & Car Bodies
Companies: 78   433,275   614.5

3713 Truck & Bus Bodies

Rank	Company Name—*Executive Officer*	Address, City, State, Zip	Phone	Type	Fin	Empls
1	Navistar International Corp—*Daniel C Ustian*	4201 Winfield Rd, Warrenville IL 60555	630-753-5000	P	12,145	18.7
2	Toyota Motor Manufacturing Indiana Inc—*Seizo Okamoto*	PO Box 4000, Princeton IN 47670	812-387-2000	S	1,028*	3.9
3	Motor Coach Industries International Inc—*Tom Sorrells III*	1700 E Golf Rd Ste 300, Schaumburg IL 60173	847-285-2000	S	904*	2.0
4	Heil Co—*Michael G Jobe*	6751 Cornelison Rd Bld, Chattanooga TN 37411	423-899-9100	S	782*	.6
5	Morgan Corp—*John Poindexter*	PO Box 588, Morgantown PA 19543	610-286-5025	S	386*	1.0
6	Miller Industries Inc (Ooltewah Tennessee)—*Jeffrey I Badgley*	8503 Hilltop Dr, Ooltewah TN 37363	423-238-4171	P	307	.7
7	Thomas Built Buses Inc—*John O'Leary*	1408 Courtesy Rd, High Point NC 27260	336-889-4871	S	295*	1.6
8	Bird Blue Body Co—*Robert Shaughnessy*	PO Box 937, Fort Valley GA 31030	478-825-2021	R	251*	1.6
9	Emergency One Inc	1601 SW 37th Ave, Ocala FL 34474	352-237-1122	S	240*	.8
10	Supreme Industries Inc—*Kim Korth*	PO Box 237, Goshen IN 46527	574-642-3070	P	221	1.7
11	Peach County Holdings Inc—*Keith Ramundo*	402 Bluebird Blvd, Fort Valley GA 31030	478-825-2021	R	169*	2.2
12	Supreme Corp—*Robert Wilson*	PO Box 463, Goshen IN 46527	574-642-4888	R	152*	1.5
13	Gillig LLC—*Dennis Howard*	PO Box 3008, Hayward CA 94540	510-785-1500	R	146*	.7
14	TABC Inc—*Seiji Ikezaki*	PO Box 2140, Long Beach CA 90801		S	132*	.7
15	Kenworth Truck Co—*Ed Caudill*	10630 NE 38th Pl, Kirkland WA 98033	425-828-5000	D	103*	.3
16	Mickey Truck Bodies Inc—*Dean Sink*	PO Box 2044, High Point NC 27261	336-882-6806	R	90*	.5
17	Jerr-Dan Corp—*Jeffrey Weller*	13224 Fountainhead Plz, Hagerstown MD 21742	717-597-7111	S	78*	.3
18	Halcore Group Inc—*Michael Grimes*	3800 Mcdowell Rd, Grove City OH 43123	614-539-8181	R	73*	.1
19	Durakon Industries Inc—*Edward Gniewek*	2101 N Lapeer Rd, Lapeer MI 48446	810-664-0850	R	71*	.3
20	R and S-Godwin Truck Body Company LLC—*Pat Godwin* / Godwin Manufacturing Company Inc	PO Box 420, Allen KY 41601		S	70*	.2
21	Able Manufacturing LLC—*Jim Schwarz*	1000 S Schifferdecker, Joplin MO 64801	417-623-3060	R	59*	.3
22	Stahl—*Jim Kraschinksy*	3201 W Old Lincoln Way, Wooster OH 44691		D	56*	.5
23	Reading Body Works Inc—*Bill Darish*	PO Box 650, Shillington PA 19607	610-775-3301	R	49*	.5
24	Leer Inc	58288 Ventura Dr, Elkhart IN 46517	574-522-5337	R	49*	.3
25	ARE Inc—*Ralph Gatti*	PO Box 1100, Massillon OH 44648	330-359-5450	R	49*	.5
26	Champion Bus Inc—*John Resnik*	PO Box 158, Imlay City MI 48444	810-724-6474	S	46*	.3
27	Mclaughlin Body Co—*John Mann*	2430 River Dr, Moline IL 61265	309-762-7755	R	41*	.5
28	BorgWarner Cooling Systems	1100 Wright St, Cadillac MI 49601	231-779-7500	S	37*	.2
29	Cottrell Inc—*Leland Bull*	2125 Candler Rd, Gainesville GA 30507	770-532-7251	R	36*	.5
30	Steelweld Equipment Co—*Elaine Hunter*	PO Box 440, Saint Clair MO 63077	636-629-3704	R	35*	.2
31	Rki Inc—*Thomas Rawson*	2301 Central Pkwy, Houston TX 77092	713-688-4414	R	30*	.4
32	Omaha Standard Inc—*Thomas Moser*	3501 S 11th St Ste 1, Council Bluffs IA 51501	712-328-7444	R	30*	.4
33	Collins Bus Corp—*Kent Tyler*	PO Box 2946, Hutchinson KS 67504	620-662-9000	S	28*	.2
34	Godwin Manufacturing Company Inc—*James Godwin*	PO Box 1147, Dunn NC 28335	910-897-4995	R	26*	.2
35	Ox Bodies Inc—*Robert Fines*	PO Box 886, Fayette AL 35555	205-932-5720	R	23*	.3
36	Van Air Manufacturing Inc—*Ralph Kokot*	10896 W 300 N, Michigan City IN 46360	219-879-5100	R	20*	.1
37	Southco Industries Inc—*J Goforth*	1840 E Dixon Blvd, Shelby NC 28152	704-482-1477	R	20*	.1
38	Ati Oldco Inc—*E Dondlinger*	1420 Brewster Creek Bl, Bartlett IL 60103	630-860-5600	R	18*	.1
39	Auto Crane Co—*John Celoni*	PO Box 580697, Tulsa OK 74158	918-836-0463	R	17*	.1
40	Kolstad Company Inc—*Robert Crosson*	8501 Naples St NE, Blaine MN 55449	763-792-1033	R	15*	.1
41	Leyman Manufacturing Corp—*John Henry*	10900 Kenwood Rd, Blue Ash OH 45242	513-891-6210	R	15*	.1
42	Griffin Inc—*Greg Kay*	6562 Hwy 178, Byhalia MS 38611	662-838-2128	R	14*	.1
43	Custom Sales and Service Inc—*William Sikora*	PO Box 635, Hammonton NJ 08037	609-561-6900	R	13*	.1
44	Bridgeport Truck Manufacturing Inc—*Tony Kouri*	PO Box 217, Bridgeport TX 76426	940-683-5477	R	12*	.1
45	Kann Manufacturing Corp—*Rose Kann*	PO Box 400, Guttenberg IA 52052	563-252-2035	R	11*	.1

Note: An asterisk (*) indicates an estimated financial figure. The company type code used is as follows: R = Private, P = Public, S = Private Subsidiary, B = Public Subsidiary, D = Division, J = Joint Venture, I = Investment Fund.

COMPANY RANKINGS BY SALES WITHIN 4-DIGIT SIC

Rank	Company Name—*Executive Officer*	Address, City, State, Zip	Phone	Type	Fin	Empls
46	Courtesy Enterprises Inc—*Don Gaddis*	PO Box 8090, Cedar Rapids IA 52408	319-396-7336	R	10*	.1
47	Rogers Manufacturing Company Inc—*Stephen Blackmon*	PO Box 100187, Nashville TN 37224	615-244-9720	R	10*	.1
48	Lodal Inc—*Bernard Leger*	PO Box 2315, Iron Mountain MI 49802	906-779-1700	R	8*	.1
49	Chandler Equipment Co—*William Chandler*	PO Box 2533, Gainesville GA 30503	770-536-8891	R	8*	.1
50	Calutech Mobile Solutions Inc	3550 179th St Unit C, Hammond IN 46323	219-845-1695	R	8*	<.1
51	Hillsboro Industries Inc—*Robert Klein*	220 Industrial Rd, Hillsboro KS 67063	620-947-3127	R	7*	.1
52	Elliott Machine Works Inc—*Richard Ekin*	PO Box 955, Galion OH 44833	419-468-4709	R	7*	.1
53	Clement Industries Inc—*Grayling Hill*	PO Box 914, Minden LA 71058	318-377-2776	R	6*	.1
54	Ace Equipment Company Inc—*C Steve Eunice*	PO Box 1926, Waycross GA 31502	912-449-4355	R	6*	.1
55	James A Kiley Co—*John Kiley*	15 Linwood St, Somerville MA 02143	617-776-0344	R	6*	<.1
56	Brown Industrial Inc—*Christopher Brown*	PO Box 74, Botkins OH 45306	937-693-3838	R	6*	<.1
57	Mclellan Equipment Inc—*Dale Mclellan*	251 Shaw Rd, South San Francisco CA 94080	650-873-8100	R	5*	.1
58	Campbell International Inc—*James Campbell*	PO Box 875, Wauconda IL 60084	847-526-7300	R	5*	<.1
59	Triseal Corp—*Patricia Wales*	11920 Price Rd, Hebron IL 60034	815-648-2473	R	5*	<.1
60	Lancaster Automobile Spring Company Inc—*Louis Torres*	PO Box 4626, Lancaster PA 17604	717-394-2647	R	4*	<.1
61	MAG Trucks—*Blake Fulton*	105 S Jefferson St Ste, Kearney MO 64060		R	4	<.1
62	Triple-B Truck Body and Metal Fabricating Co—*Charles Milam*	PO Box 1756, Columbus GA 31902	706-322-2831	R	3*	<.1
63	Conrad Enterprises Inc—*Dale Martin*	PO Box 656, Cornwall PA 17016	717-274-5151	R	3*	<.1
64	Rome Truck Parts and Repair Inc—*William Dempsey*	241 Dempsey Rd Ne, Rome GA 30161	706-295-4345	R	2*	<.1
65	Hesse Inc—*Peter Roberts*	6700 Saint John Ave, Kansas City MO 64123	816-483-7808	R	<1*	<.1

TOTALS: SIC 3713 Truck & Bus Bodies
Companies: 65 — 18,504 45.8

3714 Motor Vehicle Parts & Accessories

Rank	Company Name—*Executive Officer*	Address, City, State, Zip	Phone	Type	Fin	Empls
1	Zf Lemforder LLC—*Kurt Mueller*	15811 Centennial Dr, Northville MI 48168	734-416-6200	R	25,093*	.8
2	ArvinMeritor OE LLC \n Meritor Inc	2135 W Maple Rd, Troy MI 48084	248-435-1000	S	23,491*	32.0
3	Delphi Automotive PLC—*James A Bertrand*	5725 Delphi Dr, Troy MI 48098	248-813-2000	P	16,000	146.6
4	TRW Automotive Holdings Corp—*John C Plant*	12001 Tech Center Dr, Livonia MI 48150	734-855-2600	P	14,383	61.3
5	International Automotive Components—*James Kamsickas*	28333 Telegraph Rd, Southfield MI 48034	248-455-7000	R	8,796*	12.0
6	Dana Holding Corp—*Roger J Wood*	3939 Technology Dr, Maumee OH 43537	419-887-3000	P	7,592	24.5
7	Tenneco Inc—*Gregg Sherrill*	500 N Field Dr, Lake Forest IL 60045	847-482-5000	P	7,205	24.0
8	Flex-n-Gate Corp—*Shahid Khan*	1306 E University Ave, Urbana IL 61802	217-278-2600	R	7,076*	10.0
9	Robert Bosch Corp—*Kurt W Liedtke*	2800 S 25th Ave, Broadview IL 60155	708-865-5200	S	6,782*	25.0
10	Federal-Mogul Corp—*Jose Maria Alapont*	26555 Northwestern Hwy, Southfield MI 48033	248-354-7700	P	6,219	42.7
11	BorgWarner Inc—*Timothy M Manganello*	3850 Hamlin Rd, Auburn Hills MI 48326	248-754-9200	P	5,653	17.5
12	Delphi Interior Systems—*Rodney O'Neal*	6600 E 12 Mile Rd, Warren MI 48092	810-578-3000	R	5,550	35.0
13	Meritor Inc—*Charles G (Chip) McClure*	2135 W Maple Rd, Troy MI 48084	248-435-1000	P	4,622	10.5
14	Cardone Industries Inc—*Michael Cardone*	5501 Whitaker Ave, Philadelphia PA 19124	215-912-3000	R	2,871*	4.0
15	American Axle and Manufacturing Holdings Inc—*Richard E Dauch*	1 Dauch Dr, Detroit MI 48211	313-758-2000	P	2,585	9.2
16	Cooper-Standard Automotive Inc	39550 Orchard Hill Pl, Novi MI 48375	248-596-5900	S	2,511*	21.1
17	Autoliv ASP Inc—*Lars Westerberg*	3350 Airport Rd, Ogden UT 84405	801-625-4800	S	2,432*	3.0
18	Boler Co—*Matthew J Boler*	500 Park Blvd Ste 1010, Itasca IL 60143	630-773-9111	R	2,136*	3.0
19	Sypris Technologies Marion LLC	PO Box 522, Marion OH 43302	740-223-4334	S	1,920*	2.6
20	Hayes Lemmerz International Inc—*Curtis J Clawson*	15300 Centennial Dr, Northville MI 48168	734-737-5000	R	1,904	6.4
21	HLI Operating Company Inc—*Curtis J Clawson*	15300 Centennial Dr, Northville MI 48168	734-737-5000	S	1,904	6.4
22	Affinia Group Intermediate Holdings Inc—*Terry R McCormack*	1101 Technology Dr, Ann Arbor MI 48108	734-827-5400	S	1,892	11.8
23	Rexnord Holdings Inc—*George M Sherman*	4701 W Greenfield Ave, Milwaukee WI 53214	414-643-3000	R	1,882	6.2
24	ADVICS North America Inc—*Takeshi Kawata*	45300 Polaris Ct, Plymouth MI 48170	734-414-5100	S	1,810*	.1
25	Acument Global Technologies Inc—*Patrick Paige*	840 W Long Lake Rd Ste, Troy MI 48098	248-813-6329	S	1,800*	9.0
26	Continental Automotive Corp	2400 Executive Hills B, Auburn Hills MI 48326	248-209-4000	S	1,738*	10.0
27	Genco ATC—*Todd R Peters*	100 Papercraft Park, Pittsburgh PA 15238		R	1,500	10.0
28	Modine Manufacturing Co—*Thomas A Burke*	1500 DeKoven Ave, Racine WI 53403	262-636-1200	P	1,448	6.5
29	Dura Automotive Systems Inc—*Jeffrey M Stafeil*	2791 Research Dr, Rochester Hills MI 48309	248-299-7500	S	1,395*	10.0
30	Mark IV Industries Inc—*Jim Orchard*	PO Box 810, Amherst NY 14226	716-689-4972	R	1,200*	8.0
31	CLARCOR Inc—*Norman E Johnson*	840 Crescent Centre Dr, Franklin TN 37067	615-771-3100	P	1,127	5.4
32	CLARCOR International Inc—*Norman E Johnson* \n CLARCOR Inc	840 Crescent Centre Dr, Franklin TN 37067	615-771-3100	S	1,060	5.5
33	GS Costa Mesa Inc—*Norman E Johnson* \n CLARCOR Inc	840 Crescent Centre Dr, Franklin TN 37067	615-771-3100	S	1,060	5.5
34	Gentex Corp—*Fred Bauer*	600 N Centennial St, Zeeland MI 49464	616-772-1800	P	1,024	3.5
35	Key Safety Systems Inc—*Jason Luo*	7000 19 Mile Rd, Sterling Heights MI 48314	586-726-3800	S	1,006*	8.5
36	Keihin Indiana Precision Technology Inc—*Kentaro Kato*	PO Box 668, Greenfield IN 46140	317-462-3015	S	960*	1.3
37	UCI International Inc—*Bruce Zorich*	14601 Hwy 41 N, Evansville IN 47725	812-867-4156	R	885	3.9
38	DENSO International America Inc—*Haruya Maruyama*	PO Box 5047, Southfield MI 48086	248-350-7500	S	827*	.7
39	Lund International Holdings Inc—*George Scherff*	4325 Hamilton Mill Rd, Buford GA 30518		R	823*	1.2
40	Siemens Industrial Automation Inc—*Klaus kleinfeld*	100 Technology Dr, Alpharetta GA 30005	770-751-2000	D	778*	1.1
41	Baldwin Filters—*Sam Ferrise* \n CLARCOR Inc	PO Box 6010, Kearney NE 68848	308-234-1951	S	770*	1.1
42	Accuride Corp—*Rick Dauch*	PO Box 15600, Evansville IN 47716	812-962-5000	B	764	3.0
43	Jordan Auto Aftermarket Inc—*John W Jordan*	1751 Lake Cook Rd Arbo, Deerfield IL 60015	847-945-5591	S	720*	7.2
44	Superior Industries International Inc—*Steven J Borick*	7800 Woodley Ave, Van Nuys CA 91406	818-781-4973	P	720	3.5
45	Arvin Sango Inc—*Tom Hashiguchi* \n Meritor Inc	2905 Wilson Ave, Madison IN 47250	812-265-2888	S	708*	1.0
46	Arvin International Holdings LLC—*Charles G McClurre* \n Meritor Inc	2135 W Maple Rd, Troy MI 48084	248-435-1000	S	693*	1.0
47	Eaton Truck Components Div—*Kurt Huchins*	PO Box 4013, Kalamazoo MI 49003	269-342-3000	D	687*	7.5
48	Motorola Inc AIEG Div—*Greg Brown*	4000 Commercial Ave, Northbrook IL 60062	847-480-8000	D	672	3.0
49	SRG Global Inc	23751 Amber Ave, Warren MI 48089	586-757-7800	S	670	4.0
50	JMAC Inc—*Mike Priest*	150 E Wilson Bridge Rd, Worthington OH 43085	614-436-2416	R	655*	.5
51	Stoneridge Inc—*John C Corey*	9400 E Market St, Warren OH 44484	330-856-2443	P	635	6.8
52	Sumitomo Electric Wiring Systems Inc—*Toru Kuwahara*	PO Box 90031, Bowling Green KY 42102	270-782-7397	R	635*	6.0
53	Kautex Textron North America—*Robert K Simpson*	750 Stephenson Hwy, Troy MI 48083	248-616-5100	D	625*	5.0
54	RB Management—*Richard Berman*	3400 E Walnut St, Colmar PA 18915	215-997-1800	R	617*	1.0
55	International Textile Group Inc—*Joseph L Gorga*	804 Green Valley Rd St, Greensboro NC 27408	336-379-6220	P	616	8.7
56	GenTek Inc—*William Redmond*	90 E Halsey Rd, Parsippany NJ 07054	973-515-0900	R	608	1.1
57	Hillsdale Automotive	2424 John Daly Rd, Inkster MI 48141	313-278-5956	S	598*	3.9
58	KOCH Enterprises Inc—*Robert L Koch II*	14 S Eleventh Ave, Evansville IN 47712	812-465-9800	R	577*	3.2
59	ZF Group North American Operations—*Julio Caspari*	15811 Centennial Dr, Northville MI 48168	734-416-6200	R	567*	1.6

Rank	Company Name—*Executive Officer*	Address, City, State, Zip	Phone	Type	Fin	Empls
60	Haldex Brake Products Corp—*Chuck Kleinhagen*	10930 N Pomona Ave, Kansas City MO 64153	816-891-2470	D	558*	.8
61	Cummins Filtration—*Joseph Saoud*	2931 Elm Hill Pike, Nashville TN 37214		D	503*	5.6
62	Stoneridge Electronics Inc—*John C Corey* Stoneridge Inc	11801 Miriam Dr Ste B, El Paso TX 79936	915-592-5700	S	498*	.7
63	Edelbrock Corp—*O Victor Edelbrock*	2700 California St, Torrance CA 90503	310-781-2222	R	465*	.7
64	SMI Seller Inc—*Marlon Bailey*	PO Box 102349, Atlanta GA 30368	765-825-3121	R	465*	.7
65	Sensus Precision Die Casting Inc—*Barry McReynolds*	232 Hopkinsville Rd, Russellville KY 42276	270-726-0235	S	456*	.4
66	Dorman Products Inc—*Steven L Berman*	PO Box 1800, Colmar PA 18915	215-997-1800	P	456	1.2
67	Dynamic Manufacturing Co	4211 Madison St, Hillside IL 60162	708-547-9011	R	449*	.5
68	Inergy Automotive Systems (USA) LLC—*Judy Gruner*	2710 Bellingham Dr Ste, Troy MI 48083	248-743-5700	R	449*	4.0
69	Dana Corporation Automotive Systems Group—*James E Sweetman* Dana Holding Corp	PO Box 1000, Toledo OH 43697	419-535-4635	S	441*	.6
70	Fuel Systems Solutions Inc—*Mariano Costamagna*	3030 S Susan St, Santa Ana CA 92704	714-656-1300	P	431	1.6
71	Nascote Industries—*Jim Smith*	18310 Enterprise Ave, Nashville IL 62263	618-327-4381	D	418*	.6
72	ASMO North America LLC—*Tetsuro Shimmura*	470 Crawford Rd, Statesville NC 28625	704-253-6503	S	416*	.6
73	Stoneridge Control Devices Inc—*Gerry Pisani* Stoneridge Inc	300 Dan Rd, Canton MA 02021	781-830-0340	S	355*	.5
74	Cloyes Gear Co—*Trevor Myers* Cloyes Gear and Products Inc	PO Box 528, Paris AR 72855	479-963-2105	S	348*	.5
75	Federal Mogul Corp Sealing Systems Div—*Jose Maria Alapont* Federal-Mogul Corp	26555 Northwestern Hwy, Southfield MI 48033	248-354-7700	D	348*	.3
76	Aisin Brake and Chassis Inc—*Ryoichi Koizumi* Aisin Holdings of America Inc	10550 James Adams St, Terre Haute IN 47802	812-298-1617	S	347*	.5
77	Kinedyne Corp—*James Klausmann*	151 Industrial Pkwy, Branchburg NJ 08876	908-231-1800	R	342*	.4
78	Akebono Brake Corp	310 Ring Rd, Elizabethtown KY 42701	270-234-5500	S	300*	1.2
79	American Sunroof Co—*Steve Nowicki*	6115 13 Mile Rd, Warren MI 48092	586-446-4701	S	300*	1.0
80	Morse Automotive Corp—*Peter Morse*	4130 S Morgan St, Chicago IL 60609	773-843-9000	R	299*	1.5
81	Toyota Motor Manufacturing Alabama Inc—*Stephanie Deemer*	1 Cottonvalley Dr, Huntsville AL 35810	256-716-5407	S	293*	.5
82	GKN Automotive Inc—*Phillip Cabossol*	6400 Durham Rd, Timberlake NC 27583	336-364-6200	S	280*	3.0
83	QCOnics Ventures LP—*Larry L Smith*	PO Box 329, Angola IN 46703	260-665-9493	R	277*	.4
84	Global Automotive Alliance LLC—*William F Pickard*	2627 Clark St, Detroit MI 48210	313-297-6676	R	262	.7
85	Strattec Security Corp—*Harold M Stratton II*	3333 W Good Hope Rd, Milwaukee WI 53209	414-247-3333	P	261	2.6
86	C Cowles and Co—*Lawrence C Moon Jr*	83 Water St, New Haven CT 06511	203-865-3110	R	260*	.2
87	Amak Brake LLC—*Roy Okawa*	1765 Cleveland Ave, Glasgow KY 42141	270-678-1765	S	250*	.7
88	Hi-Stat Manufacturing Company Inc—*Michael D Sloan* Stoneridge Inc	345 S Mill Rd, Lexington OH 44904	419-884-1219	D	241	.5
09	BLD Products Ltd—*Scott Bye*	534 E 48th St, Holland MI 49423	616-395-5600	S	213*	.2
90	Filtran Aftermarket Products—*Brett Wall*	PO Box 328, Des Plaines IL 60016	847-635-6670	S	203*	.3
91	Weastec Inc—*Yasusuke Sugino*	1600 N High St, Hillsboro OH 45133	937-393-6800	R	193*	.4
92	Standayne Corp—*M Jones*	92 Deerfield Rd, Windsor CT 06095	860-525-0821	R	186*	1.4
93	Total Filtration Services Inc CLARCOR Inc	2725 Commerce Pkwy, Auburn Hills MI 48326	248-377-4004	S	183*	.3
94	United States Gear Corp—*Mark Garfien*	1020 W 119th St, Chicago IL 60643		R	181*	.3
95	Vibration Control Technologies LLC—*Joseph B Anderson Jr*	2075 W Big Beaver Rd S, Troy MI 48084	248-822-8010	S	177*	.5
96	CWC Textron—*Scott G Donnelly*	1085 W Sherman Blvd, Muskegon MI 49441	231-733-1331	D	174	.3
97	Muncie Power Products Inc—*Terry Walker*	PO Box 548, Muncie IN 47308	765-284-7721	S	171*	.2
98	Neaton Auto Products Manufacturing Inc—*Haruo Furukori*	975 S Franklin St, Eaton OH 45320	937-456-7103	R	170*	.6
99	Gkn Driveline North America Inc—*Max Owen*	3300 University Dr, Auburn Hills MI 48326	248-377-1200	R	168*	1.6
100	Fiamm Technologies—*Dolcetta Alessandro*	1550 Leeson St, Cadillac MI 49601	231-775-2900	S	164*	.3
101	Sejong Alabama LLC	450 Old Fort Rd E, Fort Deposit AL 36032	334-227-0821	R	164*	.2
102	Green Tokai Company Ltd—*Fumi Hosada*	55 Robert Wright Dr, Brookville OH 45309	937-833-5444	R	162*	.8
103	Nelson Industries Inc—*Trevor Passmore*	1801 Us Hwy 51 138, Stoughton WI 53589	608-873-4200	R	161*	2.2
104	GECOM Corp—*Harusumi Sakai*	1025 Barachel Ln, Greensburg IN 47240	812-663-2270	R	157*	1.9
105	Ai-Shreveport LLC—*Mona Croff*	7699 W Bert Kouns Indu, Shreveport LA 71129	318-686-3570	R	152*	.8
106	Zf Sachs Automotive Of America Inc—*Carlos Delich*	15811 Centennial Dr, Northville MI 48168	734-416-6200	R	150*	.4
107	Mssc Inc—*Gerald Anderson*	6401 W Fort St, Detroit MI 48209	313-551-2400	R	150*	.2
108	Autoparts Holdings Ltd—*Gregory Cole*	39 Old Ridgebury Rd, Danbury CT 06810	203-830-7800	R	147*	2.4
109	Clarion Technologies Inc—*Steve Olmstead*	170 College Ave Ste 30, Holland MI 49423	616-698-7277	P	146	.8
110	Draw-Tite Inc—*Thomas Benson*	47912 Halyard Dr Ste 1, Plymouth MI 48170		R	141*	.8
111	Belmor Inc Lund International Holdings Inc	6460 W Cortland St, Chicago IL 60707		S	141*	.2
112	Nelson Global Products Inc—*Tom Gosnel*	PO Box 511, Stoughton WI 53589	608-877-3003	R	140*	.8
113	Fred Jones Enterprises LLC—*Al Dearmon*	PO Box 25068, Oklahoma City OK 73125	405-272-9261	R	140*	.1
114	Awtec USA Inc—*Takao Tohyama*	14920 Keel St, Plymouth MI 48170	734-454-1710	S	139*	.2
115	Greenville Technology Inc—*Kiyoshi Sato*	PO Box 974, Greenville OH 45331	937-548-1471	R	138*	.7
116	Newcor Inc—*David Segal*	1771 Harmon Rd Ste 200, Auburn Hills MI 48326	248-409-1070	S	136*	1.0
117	Bergstrom Inc—*David Rydell*	PO Box 6007, Rockford IL 61125	815-874-7821	R	132*	1.4
118	Autocam Corp—*John C Kennedy*	4436 Broadmoor SE, Kentwood MI 49512	616-698-0707	S	130*	1.3
119	Casco Products Corp—*Ali El Haj*	1 Waterview Dr, Shelton CT 06484	203-922-3200	S	129*	.9
120	Tongxin International Ltd—*Rudy Wilson*	199 Pierce St Ste 202, Birmingham MI 48009	248-593-8330	P	122	2.5
121	Crimson Fire Inc—*Kevin Crump*	907 7th Ave N, Brandon SD 57005	605-582-4000	S	112*	.2
122	Dometic Corp—*John Waters*	PO Box 490, Elkhart IN 46516	574-294-2511	R	110*	.6
123	Newman Technology Inc—*Noriyoshi Asami*	100 Cairns Rd, Mansfield OH 44903	419-525-1856	R	105*	1.2
124	Atwood Mobile Products—*Timothy Stephens* Dura Automotive Systems Inc	1120 N Main St, Elkhart IN 46514	574-264-2131	S	103*	.1
125	Sachs North America—*John Edwards*	909 Crocker Rd, Westlake OH 44145	440-871-4880	R	100*	.9
126	Nemak USA Inc—*Armando Tamez*	1635 Old Columbia Rd, Dickson TN 37055	615-446-8110	R	99*	1.1
127	Pierce Company Inc—*Alan Kovach*	PO Box 2000, Upland IN 46989	765-998-2712	S	93*	1.1
128	Enkei America Inc—*Makoto Miura*	2900 Inwood Dr, Columbus IN 47201	812-373-7000	R	92*	.8
129	Cadillac Products Inc—*Michael Williams*	5800 Crooks Rd Ste 100, Troy MI 48098	248-879-5000	R	89*	.9
130	Jacobs Vehicle Systems—*Scott Wine*	22 E Dudley Town Rd, Bloomfield CT 06002	860-243-1441	S	89*	.4
131	FT Precision Inc—*Mitsuo Takano*	9731 Mount Gilead Rd, Fredericktown OH 43019	740-694-1500	R	85*	.2
132	Aztec Manufacturing Corp—*Francis Lopez*	15378 Oakwood Dr, Romulus MI 48174	734-942-7433	D	84*	.1
133	US Manufacturing Corp—*Brian Simon*	28201 Van Dyke Ave, Warren MI 48093	586-467-1600	R	83*	.8
134	Cta Acoustics Inc—*Thomas Brown*	PO Box 448, Corbin KY 40702	248-544-2580	R	83*	.6
135	Douglas Autotech Corp—*Etsutaka Ogusu*	300 Albers Rd, Bronson MI 49028	517-369-2315	R	82*	.3
136	Behr Heat Transfer Systems Inc—*Hans Lange*	4500 Leeds Ave Ste 101, Charleston SC 29405	843-745-1233	R	82*	1.0
137	Schrader Bridgeport International Inc—*James Telletier*	PO Box 668, Altavista VA 24517	434-369-4741	S	80*	1.0
138	Mitsuba Bardstown Inc—*Toshifumi Kohno*	901 Withrow Ct, Bardstown KY 40004	502-348-3100	R	80*	.2

Note: An asterisk (*) indicates an estimated financial figure. The company type code used is as follows: R = Private, P = Public, S = Private Subsidiary, B = Public Subsidiary, D = Division, J = Joint Venture, I = Investment Fund.

COMPANY RANKINGS BY SALES WITHIN 4-DIGIT SIC

Rank	Company Name—*Executive Officer*	Address, City, State, Zip	Phone	Type	Fin	Empls
139	International Crankshaft Inc—*Dan Condon*	101 Carley Ct, Georgetown KY 40324	502-868-0003	R	77*	.1
140	Ghsp Inc—*Paul Doyle*	1250 S Beechtree St, Grand Haven MI 49417	616-842-5500	S	77*	.8
141	Brake Parts Inc- Chowchilla—*Ray Warner*	711 S Third St, Chowchilla CA 93610	559-665-5781	R	77*	.1
142	Distinctive Industries—*Dwight K Forrister*	PO Box 910941, Commerce CA 90091	323-888-6454	R	76*	.5
143	Romeo RIM Inc—*Chris Morin*	74000 Van Dyke Ave, Romeo MI 48065	586-752-9605	S	71*	.1
144	Aircraft Gear Corp—*James Olson*	PO Box 2066, Loves Park IL 61130	815-877-7473	R	71*	.2
145	Emhart Teknologies Inc—*Michael A Tyll*	49201 Gratiot Ave, Chesterfield MI 48051		S	70*	.5
146	Hartnack Engine Supply LLC—*Francis Baker*	1412 Phoenix Ave, Fort Smith AR 72901	479-646-4771	R	67*	.1
147	Kth Parts Industries Inc—*Toshio Inoue*	PO Box 940, Saint Paris OH 43072	937-663-5941	R	67*	.8
148	Rieter Automotive North America Inc—*David Westgate*	38555 Hills Tech Dr, Farmington Hills MI 48331	248-848-0100	S	65	.7
149	Genco ATC Logistics and Electronics—*F Antony Francis* Genco ATC	5201 Alliance Gateway, Fort Worth TX 76177	817-491-7727	S	64*	.1
150	Hutchens Industries Inc—*Jeffrey Hutchens*	PO Box 1427, Springfield MO 65801	417-862-5012	R	63*	.7
151	Luk Clutch Systems LLC—*Lesa Guthery*	PO Box 798, Wooster OH 44691	330-264-4383	R	62*	.8
152	Williams Controls Inc—*Patrick W Cavanagh*	14100 SW 72nd Ave, Portland OR 97224	503-684-8600	P	62	.3
153	Usui International Corp—*Haruyasu Ito*	1045 Reed Dr Ste A, Monroe OH 45050	513-539-4591	R	60*	.2
154	Eagle Bend Manufacturing Inc—*Michael Malivuk*	1000 J D Yarnell Indus, Clinton TN 37716	865-457-3800	S	60*	.6
155	Cloyes Gear and Products Inc—*M Trevor Myers*	6101 Phoenix Ave Ste 2, Fort Smith AR 72903	479-484-5555	R	60*	.6
156	Phillips and Temro Industries Inc—*Butch Sumpter*	9700 W 74th St, Eden Prairie MN 55344	952-941-9700	R	58*	.7
157	Lorain County Automotive Systems Inc—*Arvind Pradhan*	7470 Industrial Pkwy D, Lorain OH 44053	440-960-7470	R	58*	1.7
158	General Seating of America Inc—*Yoshinori Nakashima*	2298 W State Rd 28, Frankfort IN 46041	765-659-4781	R	58*	.3
159	Tram Inc—*Yutaka Yamauchi*	47200 Port St, Plymouth MI 48170	734-254-8500	R	58*	.7
160	Smitty Bilt Inc—*Dennis Vollmershausen*	400 W Artesia Blvd, Compton CA 90220	310-762-9944	R	58	.3
161	Hebco Products Inc—*Andrew Ason*	1232 Whetstone St, Bucyrus OH 44820	419-562-7987	R	56*	.9
162	Leon Plastics Inc	PO Box 350, Grand Rapids MI 49501	616-531-7970	R	56*	.6
163	Nissin Brake Ohio Inc—*Itsuo Miyake*	PO Box 886, Findlay OH 45839	419-425-6725	R	56*	.7
164	Quality Automotive Company Inc	PO Box 1426, Tappahannock VA 22560	804-443-5356	S	56	.3
165	F and P America Manufacturing Inc—*Hajme Fujitaki*	2101 Corporate Dr, Troy OH 45373	937-339-0212	R	55*	.7
166	Hopkins Manufacturing Corp—*Brad Kraft*	PO Box 1157, Emporia KS 66801	620-342-7320	R	55*	.7
167	Whiting Door Manufacturing Corp—*Donald Whiting*	PO Box 388, Akron NY 14001	716-542-5427	R	54*	.4
168	Ryobi Die Casting (USA) Inc—*Takashi Yokoyama*	800 W Mausoleum Rd, Shelbyville IN 46176	317-398-3398	R	54*	.6
169	SMI Crankshaft LLC—*Makoto Tsuruhara*	PO Box 1127, Fostoria OH 44830	419-435-0411	S	53*	.3
170	Hesco Parts LLC—*Larry Galchick*	PO Box 3008, Louisville KY 40201	502-589-9600	R	53*	.3
171	Machine Service Inc—*Edward Fowles*	PO Box 10265, Green Bay WI 54307	920-339-3000	R	51*	.1
172	Sellner Corp—*Norbert Dieterle*	PO Box 368, Comstock Park MI 49321	616-785-9400	R	51*	.3
173	Crane Technologies Group (Daytona Beach Florida)	1640 Mason Ave, Daytona Beach FL 32117	386-310-4875	R	50*	.3
174	Diamond Audio Technology Inc—*Rikki Farr*	PO Box 11720, Tempe AZ 85284	480-820-2075	R	49*	<.1
175	Curtis-Maruyasu America Inc—*Doug Vyverberg*	665 Metts Dr, Lebanon KY 40033	270-692-2109	R	47*	.6
176	Nsk Steering Systems America Inc—*T Komori*	4200 Goss Rd, Ann Arbor MI 48105	734-913-7500	R	47*	.5
177	Fisher and Company Inc—*Alfred Fisher*	33000 Fisher Dr, Saint Clair Shores MI 48082	586-746-2062	R	47*	.5
178	Dawn Enterprises Inc—*Robert Kovach*	9155 Sweet Valley Dr, Valley View OH 44125	216-447-1777	R	47*	.1
179	Del West Engineering Inc—*Al Sommer*	28128 Livingston Ave, Valencia CA 91355	661-295-5700	R	47*	.2
180	Indiana Pmg Corp—*John Arx*	1751 Arcadia Dr, Columbus IN 47201	812-379-4606	R	46*	.2
181	Midas International Corp—*Alan Feldman*	343 Grant St, Hartford WI 53027	262-673-2440	S	45*	.2
182	Topy America Inc—*Kenichi Nagai*	980 Chenault Rd, Frankfort KY 40601	502-695-6163	R	45*	.6
183	AMETEK Vehicular Instrumentation Systems—*Robert W Chlebek*	287 27 Rd, Grand Junction CO 81503	970-242-8863	D	44*	.3
184	Craig Manufacturing Co—*Craig Taslitt*	PO Box 1829, Montebello CA 90640	323-726-7355	R	44*	.1
185	Quality Trailer Products LP—*Jim Stubblefield*	PO Box 1349, Azle TX 76098	817-444-4518	R	44*	.5
186	Eakas Corp—*Tom Mori*	6251 State Rte 251, Peru IL 61354	815-223-8811	R	43*	.3
187	M P N Inc—*Martin Newell*	3675 Amber St, Philadelphia PA 19134	215-289-9480	R	41*	.2
188	AW Technical Center USA Inc—*Shin Sasaki*	1203 Woodridge Ave, Ann Arbor MI 48105	734-741-9900	S	41*	.1
189	Buffalo Power Electronics Ctr—*Dennis S Cascio*	PO Box 225, Buffalo NY 14240	716-651-1600	R	41*	.1
190	Carlisle Industrial Brake and Friction—*Chris Koch*	1031 E Hillside Dr, Bloomington IN 47401	812-336-3811	D	40*	.3
191	Rayloc	PO Box 908, Stephenville TX 76401		D	40*	.2
192	American Cable Co—*Carlos Gonzalez*	PO Box 46827, Philadelphia PA 19160	215-456-0700	R	40*	.3
193	Systrand Manufacturing Corp—*Sharon Cannarsa*	19050 Allen Rd, Brownstown Twp MI 48183	734-479-8100	R	40*	.2
194	Magneti Marelli Powertrain USA LLC—*Gary Walker*	PO Box 548, Sanford NC 27331	919-776-4111	R	39*	.5
195	Dacco Inc—*Alan Galtan*	PO Box 2789, Cookeville TN 38502	931-528-7581	R	39*	.5
196	Showa Aluminum Corporation Of America—*Ken Gakasuki*	10500 Oday Harrison Rd, Mount Sterling OH 43143	740-869-3333	R	39*	.5
197	Competition Cams Inc—*Ronald Coleman*	3406 Democrat Rd, Memphis TN 38118	901-795-2400	R	39*	.3
198	North American Acquisition Corp—*Ganesh Subramanian*	1875 Holmes Rd, Elgin IL 60123	847-695-8030	R	39*	.2
199	Aisin Holdings of America Inc—*Toshikazu Nagura*	1665 E 4th St, Seymour IN 47274	812-524-8144	S	38*	.1
200	Thule Inc—*Fred Clark*	42 Silvermine Rd, Seymour CT 06483	203-881-4800	R	37*	.4
201	Tie Down Inc—*Charles Mac Karvich*	255 Villanova Dr Sw, Atlanta GA 30336	404-344-0000	R	37*	.2
202	Syncro Corp—*Edwin Childress*	PO Box 890, Arab AL 35016	256-931-7800	R	37*	.2
203	Daa Draexlmaier Automotive Of America LLC—*Martin Gall*	PO Box 1345, Duncan SC 29334	864-433-8910	R	37*	.4
204	Pacific Manufacturing Ohio Inc—*Toshiteru Ando*	8955 Seward Rd, Fairfield OH 45011	513-642-0055	R	36*	.5
205	Mid-West Fabricating Co—*Jennifer Friel*	313 N Johns St, Amanda OH 43102	740-969-4411	R	36*	.2
206	Custom Fibreglass Manufacturing Co—*Hartmut Schroeder*	PO Box 121, Long Beach CA 90801	562-432-5454	R	35*	.4
207	Flowmaster Inc—*Ray Flugger*	100 Stony Point Rd Ste, Santa Rosa CA 95401	707-544-4761	R	35*	.4
208	Rockford Gkn Inc—*Marty Bowers*	1200 Windsor Rd, Loves Park IL 61111	815-633-7460	R	35*	.2
209	Injex Industries Inc—*F Petri*	30559 San Antonio St, Hayward CA 94544	510-487-4960	R	34*	.4
210	Chief Automotive Systems Inc—*Randy Gard*	PO Box 1368, Grand Island NE 68802	308-384-9747	S	34*	.2
211	Teleflex Marine Inc	155 S Limerick Rd, Limerick PA 19468	610-495-7011	D	34	.2
212	Wh Industries Inc—*Kenneth Joseph*	PO Box 155, Northvale NJ 07647	201-768-8200	R	34*	.2
213	Atsco Remanufacturing Inc—*Dale Eaton*	4525 N 43rd Ave, Phoenix AZ 85031	623-842-4047	R	33*	.2
214	Sintering Technologies Inc—*Jun Sakai*	PO Box 588, Greensburg IN 47240	812-663-5058	R	33*	.3
215	Black River Manufacturing Inc—*Jarod Hawks*	2625 20th St, Port Huron MI 48060	810-982-9812	R	32*	.2
216	Vetronix Corp—*Robert Jennings*	2030 Alameda Padre Ser, Santa Barbara CA 93103	805-966-2000	S	32*	.2
217	Aerospace Systems—*Mark Nordquist*	1120 Wayzata Blvd E St, Wayzata MN 55391	507-526-6050	D	32*	.1
218	Van Bergen and Greener Inc—*Paul Weldon*	1818 Madison St, Maywood IL 60153	708-343-4700	R	32*	<.1
219	GSW Manufacturing Inc—*Yukinobu Ukai*	PO Box 1045, Findlay OH 45839	419-423-7111	R	32*	.4
220	Somic America Inc—*Aki Hiro*	6 Baker Blvd, Brewer ME 04412	207-989-1759	R	32*	.2
221	Ilmor Engineering Inc—*Paul Ray*	43998 Plymouth Oaks Bl, Plymouth MI 48170	734-456-3600	R	32*	.1
222	Gamfg Precision LLC—*Jack Iverson*	5215 W Airways Ave, Franklin WI 53132	414-423-6400	R	32*	.4
223	Mattoon Precision Manufacturing Inc—*Robert Shamdin*	2408 S 14th St, Mattoon IL 61938	217-235-6000	R	32*	.2
224	DENSO Manufacturing Tennessee Inc—*Mack Hattori* DENSO International America Inc	1720 Robert C Jackson, Maryville TN 37801	865-982-7000	S	32	2.0
225	Jarvis Caster Co—*Sal Aliotta*	881 Lower Brownsville, Jackson TN 38301		R	31	.1

Rank	Company Name—Executive Officer	Address, City, State, Zip	Phone	Type	Fin	Empls
226	Moroso Performance Products Inc—Richard Moroso	80 Carter Dr, Guilford CT 06437	203-453-6571	R	31*	.2
227	Pioneer Automotive Technologies Inc—Steve Moerner	100 S Pioneer Blvd, Springboro OH 45066	937-746-6600	R	30*	.2
228	Hirschvogel Inc—Frank Anisits	2230 S 3rd St, Columbus OH 43207	614-445-6060	R	30*	.2
229	Ultra Wheel Co—Brian Tager	570 N Gilbert St, Fullerton CA 92833	714-449-7100	R	30*	<.1
230	Sealco Commercial Vehicle Products Inc—Jerry Holland	215 E Watkins St, Phoenix AZ 85004	602-253-1007	R	30*	.1
231	Porter Engineered Systems Inc—John Ball	19635 Us Hwy 31 N, Westfield IN 46074	317-867-0234	R	30*	.4
232	Inalfa Road System Inc—Frederick Welschen	1370 Pacific Dr, Auburn Hills MI 48326	248-371-3060	R	29*	.5
233	Transtar Industries Inc—Greg Gyllstrom	7350 Young Dr, Cleveland OH 44146	440-232-5100	R	29*	.2
234	Hi-Lex Controls Inc—Shoichi Hirai	152 Simpson Dr, Litchfield MI 49252	517-542-2955	R	29*	.2
235	Crower Cams and Equipment Co—Bruce Crower	6180 Business Center C, San Diego CA 92154	619-661-6477	R	28*	.2
236	Eagle Wings Industries Inc—Tatsunori Shigeta	400 Shellhouse Dr, Rantoul IL 61866	217-892-4322	R	28*	.4
237	Luverne Truck Equipment Inc—John Schulzetenberg	1200 Birch St, Brandon SD 57005	605-582-7200	R	28*	.2
238	Yamada North America Inc—Kiyoshi Osawa	PO Box Y, South Charleston OH 45368	937-462-7111	R	27*	.4
239	Franklin Precision Industry Inc—Kenji Kasamatsu	PO Box 369, Franklin KY 42135	270-598-4300	R	27*	.4
240	Electronic Controls Co—Jim Thompson	833 W Diamond St, Boise ID 83707		R	27*	.2
241	Westin Automotive Products Inc—David L Sharp	5200 Irwindale Ave, Irwindale CA 91706	626-960-6762	R	27	.2
242	Climate Control Inc—Richard Demirjian	2120 N 22nd St, Decatur IL 62526	217-422-0055	D	27*	.1
243	Detroit Transmission Products Co—David Peace Dacco Inc	2622 Wigwam Dr, Stockton CA 95205	931-528-7581	S	27*	<.1
244	Elsa Corp—Kiyokazu Sakamoto	1240 S State Rd 37, Elwood IN 46036	765-552-5200	R	27*	.4
245	Denso Air Systems Michigan Inc—Jerry Mcguire	300 Fritz Keiper Blvd, Battle Creek MI 49037	269-962-9676	R	27*	.3
246	State Wide Aluminum Inc—Joseph Blazek	PO Box 987, Elkhart IN 46515	574-262-2594	R	27*	.2
247	Pylon Manufacturing Corp—Chuck Fesler	1341 W Newport Ctr Dr, Deerfield Beach FL 33442	954-428-7373	R	27*	.2
248	Associated Fuel Pump Systems Corp—Wilm Uhlenbecker	PO Box 1326, Anderson SC 29622	864-224-0012	R	26*	.4
249	Jost International Corp—Lee Brace	1770 Hayes St, Grand Haven MI 49417	616-846-7700	R	26*	.2
250	Grakon LLC—Don Bartlett	PO Box 98984, Seattle WA 98198	206-824-6000	R	26*	.4
251	Ranew's Truck and Equipment Company LLC—Brian Bealand	1308 Hwy 41 N, Milner GA 30257	770-229-5090	R	26*	.1
252	Transform Automotive LLC—Tina Nowicki	7026 Sterling Ponds Ct, Sterling Heights MI 48312	586-826-8500	R	26*	.2
253	Musashi Auto Parts Michigan Inc—Ikuo Makino	195 Brydges Dr, Battle Creek MI 49037	269-965-0057	R	25*	.3
254	Johnson Welded Products Inc—Lilli Johnson	625 S Edgewood Ave, Urbana OH 43078	937-652-1242	R	25*	.2
255	Bunker Corp—Don Bunker	1131 Via Callejon, San Clemente CA 92673	949-361-3935	R	25*	.2
256	Pai Industries Inc—Habib Yavari	950 Northbrook Pkwy, Suwanee GA 30024	770-822-1000	R	24*	.1
257	Axis Products Inc—Eric Overbey	PO Box 1083, Elkhart IN 46515	574-266-8282	R	24*	.2
258	Livernois Engineering Co—Jason Berry	12163 Globe St, Livonia MI 48150	734-464-7000	D	24	.1
259	Plasticolor Molded Products Inc—Matt Bagne	PO Box 6985, Fullerton CA 92834	714-525-3880	R	24*	.3
260	Hwh Corp—Paul Hanser	2096 Moscow Rd, Moscow IA 52760	563-724-3396	R	24*	.1
261	Manley Performance Products Inc—Henry Haven Manley	1960 Swarthmore Ave, Lakewood NJ 08701	732-905-3366	R	23*	.2
262	Rich Mount Inc—Susumu Nino	PO Box 986, Skyland NC 28776	828-687-8500	R	23*	.1
263	Austin/Westran—Gene Berg	PO Box 921, Byron IL 61010	815-234-2811	R	23*	.1
264	Ridewell Corp—John Millsap	PO Box 4586, Springfield MO 65808	417-833-4565	R	23*	.2
265	Medallion Instrumentation Systems LLC—Brian Kelly	17150 Hickory St, Spring Lake MI 49456	616-850-8028	R	23*	.1
266	Ap Exhaust Products Inc—Evangelos Proimos	300 Dixie Trl, Goldsboro NC 27530	919-580-2000	R	23*	.3
267	Gkn Armstrong Wheels Inc—Doug Jazowski	PO Box 48, Armstrong IA 50514	712-864-3202	S	22*	.3
268	Engine Power Components Inc—Mark Quigg	PO Box 837, Grand Haven MI 49417	616-846-0110	R	22*	.3
269	Watson and Chalin Holding Corp—Donald Watson	725 E University Dr, Mckinney TX 75069	972-547-6020	R	22*	.2
270	Rostra Precision Controls Inc—John Strautneiks	2519 Dana Dr, Laurinburg NC 28352	910-276-4853	R	22*	.2
271	Auburn Gear Inc—Martin Palmer	400 E Auburn Dr, Auburn IN 46706	260-925-3200	R	22*	.2
272	Shrin Corp—Narendra Gupta	PO Box 9860, Anaheim CA 92812	714 860-0303	R	22*	.2
273	Brunner Corp—Peter Brunner	PO Box 111, Medina NY 14103	585-798-6000	R	22*	.2
274	Bucyrus Precision Tech Inc—Keiji Nishio	200 Crossroads Blvd, Bucyrus OH 44820	419-563-9950	R	21*	.2
275	Butler Products Corp—Frank Jakubec	7502 Mesa Rd, Houston TX 77028	713-635-6292	S	21*	<.1
276	Griffin Thermal Products Inc—Frank Darling	100 Hurricane Creek Rd, Piedmont SC 29673	864-845-5000	R	21*	.2
277	Newcor Rubber and Plastic Group—W John Weinhardt Newcor Inc	1771 Harmon Rd Ste 200, Auburn Hills MI 48326	248-409-1070	S	20*	.4
278	Consolidated Manufacturing Inc—Greg Gordon	8250 Ne Underground Dr, Kansas City MO 64161	620-663-9155	R	20*	.1
279	Millat Industries Corp—Gregory Millat	PO Box 931188, Cleveland OH 44193	937-434-6666	R	20*	.1
280	Vernon Auto Parts Inc—Mike Klapper	1559 W 134th St, Gardena CA 90249	323-249-7545	R	20*	.1
281	Hicklin Inc—Scott Giles	4060 Dixon St, Des Moines IA 50313	515-254-1654	R	20*	.1
282	Nas-Tra Automotive Industries Inc—Americo Rocchis	3 Sidney Ct, Lindenhurst NY 11757	631-225-1225	R	20*	.2
283	Virginia Fdp Inc—John Carney	PO Box 1426, Tappahannock VA 22560	804-443-5356	R	19*	.3
284	Dreison International Inc—Theodore Berger	4540 W 160th St, Cleveland OH 44135	216-265-8400	R	19*	.2
285	Bowles Fluidics Corp—Eric Koehler	PO Box 6300, Columbia MD 21045	410-381-0400	R	19*	.2
286	Monroe Engineering Products Inc—Garrett Morlack	1030 Doris Rd, Auburn Hills MI 48326	248-844-2601	R	19*	<.1
287	Johnson Power Ltd—Lisa Johnson Honig	PO Box 6399, Maywood IL 60155	708-345-4300	R	19*	<.1
288	Hanwha Machinery America Corp—Young Kim	PO Box 38, Bremen IN 46506	574-546-2261	R	19*	.3
289	NSU Corp—Yukihiro Nakagawa	9385 Sonora Rd, Sonora KY 42776	219-947-7616	R	18*	.1
290	International Space Enterprises Inc—Johan Lecoutere	12302 Kerran St, Poway CA 92064	858-413-1720	R	18*	.2
291	Morris Manufacturing And Sales Corp—Michael Morris	1015 E Mechanic St, Brazil IN 47834	812-446-6141	R	18*	.1
292	Beach Manufacturing Co—Theodore Beach	PO Box 129, Donnelsville OH 45319	937-882-6372	R	18*	.1
293	Wilwood Engineering—William Wood	4700 Calle Bolero, Camarillo CA 93012	805-388-1188	R	18*	.1
294	Henman Engineering And Machine Inc—Thomas Henman	PO Box 2633, Muncie IN 47307	765-288-8098	R	18*	.1
295	R- Squared Aluminium LLC—Naveen Bhojraj	PO Box 306, Puckett MS 39151	601-825-1171	R	17*	.1
296	Fleet Engineers Inc—Wesley Eklund	1800 E Keating Ave, Muskegon MI 49442	231-777-2537	R	17*	.1
297	Ausco Products Inc—David Mattis	PO Box 8787, Benton Harbor MI 49023	269-926-0700	R	17*	.1
298	Hercules Engine Components LLC—Jack Dienes	2770 S Erie St, Massillon OH 44646	330-830-2498	R	17*	<.1
299	Telma Retarder Inc—Mark Paolicchi	870 Lively Blvd, Wood Dale IL 60191	847-593-1098	S	17*	<.1
300	Lakeland Finishing Corp—Thomas Smith	5400 36th St Se, Grand Rapids MI 49512	616-949-8001	R	17*	.1
301	Ogura Corp—Hisashi Ukita	55025 Gratiot Ave, Chesterfield MI 48051	586-749-1900	R	16*	.1
302	Ace Controls Inc	23435 Industrial Park, Farmington Hills MI 48335	248-476-0213	S	16*	.2
303	Martin Wheel Company Inc—Jimmy Yang	PO Box 157, Tallmadge OH 44278	330-633-3278	R	16*	.1
304	Powertrain Product and Chassis LLC	20530 Hoover St, Detroit MI 48205	313-371-1740	R	15*	.1
305	Mile Marker International Inc—Alvin A Hirsch	2121 Blount Rd, Pompano Beach FL 33069	954-782-0604	P	15	.1
306	Isspro Inc—Paul Wendlick	PO Box 11177, Portland OR 97211	503-288-4488	R	15*	.1
307	Apex Precision Technologies Inc—Jerry Jackson	8824 Union Mills Dr, Camby IN 46113	317-821-1000	R	15*	.1
308	Hamlin Tool and Machine Company Inc—Patrick Pihjalic	1671 E Hamlin Rd, Rochester Hills MI 48307	248-651-6302	R	14*	.1
309	Lyle Industries Inc—G Lyle	PO Box 44, Dalton GA 30722	706-278-2500	R	14*	.1
310	Hastings Manufacturing Company LLC—Robert M Kollar	325 N Hanover St, Hastings MI 49058	269-945-2491	P	13	.2
311	Air Flow Technology Inc—Sheila Mecall	4810 70th Ave, Kenosha WI 53144	262-657-2200	R	13*	.2
312	Penntecq Inc—Nobuya Nakatani	106 Kuder Dr, Greenville PA 16125	724-646-4250	R	13*	.2
313	Alphi Manufacturing Inc—Alan Symonds	576 Beck St, Jonesville MI 49250	517-849-9945	R	13*	.1

Note: An asterisk (*) indicates an estimated financial figure. The company type code used is as follows: R = Private, P = Public, S = Private Subsidiary, B = Public Subsidiary, D = Division, J = Joint Venture, I = Investment Fund.

COMPANY RANKINGS BY SALES WITHIN 4-DIGIT SIC

Rank	Company Name—Executive Officer	Address, City, State, Zip	Phone	Type	Fin	Empls
314	Schuler Inc—Timothy Mccaughey	7145 Commerce Blvd, Canton MI 48187	734-207-7200	R	13*	.1
315	Delta Research Corp—Robert Sakuta	32971 Capitol St, Livonia MI 48150	734-261-6400	R	13*	.1
316	Emerald West Equipment Parts Inc—Jerry South	90348 Hwy 99 N, Eugene OR 97402	541-689-4321	R	13*	<.1
317	Taiho Corporation Of America—T Yoshii	194 Heritage Dr, Tiffin OH 44883	419-443-1645	R	13*	.1
318	Nagakura Engineering Works Company Inc—Shuji Nagakura	630 S Mapleton St, Columbus IN 47201	812-375-1382	R	12*	.1
319	Cycle Country Accessories Corp—Robert Davis	PO Box 257, Spencer IA 51301	712-262-4191	P	12	.1
320	Yamato Engine Specialists 1990 Ltd—Amir Dhanani	2020 E Bakerview Rd, Bellingham WA 98226	360-733-1916	R	12*	.1
321	P T M Corp—Charles Russell	6560 Bethuy Rd, Ira MI 48023	586-725-2211	R	12*	.1
322	Dna Specialty Inc—James Choi	1415 W 178th St, Gardena CA 90248	310-767-4070	R	12*	.1
323	Universal Urethane Inc—T Evans	4201 E Lone Mountain R, North Las Vegas NV 89081	702-643-3626	R	12*	.1
324	National Cycle Inc—Barry Willey	PO Box 158, Maywood IL 60153	708-343-0400	R	12*	.1
325	Kellogg Crankshaft Co—Allen Spiess	3524 Wayland Dr, Jackson MI 49202	517-788-9200	R	12*	.1
326	Ace Manufacturing And Parts Co—Kevin Ijames	300 Ramsey Dr, Sullivan MO 63080	573-468-4181	R	12*	.1
327	Supertrapp Industries Inc—Kevin Berger Dreison International Inc	4540 W 160th St, Cleveland OH 44135	216-265-8400	S	12*	.1
328	Harco Brake Systems Inc—Larry Harris	3535 Kettering Blvd, Moraine OH 45439	937-832-7000	R	11*	.1
329	Camshaft Machine Company LLC—Mike Easterday	717 Woodworth Rd, Jackson MI 49202	517-787-2040	R	11*	<.1
330	Mariah Industries Inc—Samone Delagarza	2817 Bond St, Rochester Hills MI 48309	248-237-0404	R	11*	.1
331	L and W Engineering Inc—Perry Yoder	107 Industrial Pkwy E, Middlebury IN 46540	574-825-5351	R	11*	.1
332	Spalding Automotive Inc—Javier Kuehnle	4529 Adams Cir, Bensalem PA 19020	215-638-3334	R	11*	.1
333	Electrodyn Choke Corp—Peter Petris	PO Box 906, Niagara Falls NY 14302	716-284-8747	R	10*	.1
334	Souders Industries Inc—David Souders	19 Ash St, Mont Alto PA 17237	717-749-3900	R	10*	.1
335	Ambac International Corp—Bob Stamm	PO Box 85, Columbia SC 29202	803-462-9600	R	10*	.1
336	Mueller Gas Products—Doug Murdock	1800 Clayton Ave, Middletown OH 45042	513-424-5311	R	10*	.1
337	Griner Engineering Inc—John Griner	2500 N Curry Pke, Bloomington IN 47404	812-332-2220	R	10*	.1
338	Aero Mobility Inc—Eskandar Meshkani	2345 N Grand Ave, Santa Ana CA 92705	714-973-8600	R	10	<.1
339	Leedy Manufacturing Company LLC—Thomas Brooks	210 Hall St Sw, Grand Rapids MI 49507	616-245-0517	R	10*	.1
340	J G Kern Enterprises Inc—Brian Kern	44044 Merrill Rd, Sterling Heights MI 48314	586-726-1040	R	10*	.1
341	Joseph Industries Inc—Patrick Finnegan	10039 Aurora Hudson Rd, Streetsboro OH 44241	330-528-0091	R	9*	.1
342	Automoco LLC—Brian Applegate	9142 Independence Ave, Chatsworth CA 91311	818-882-6422	R	9*	.1
343	Original California Magic Car Duster Co—Travis Ford	9525 Desoto Ave, Chatsworth CA 91311	818-998-2300	R	9*	.1
344	Dexstar Wheel Company Inc—Chi Yang	400 Collins Rd, Elkhart IN 46516	574-295-3535	R	9*	.1
345	Putco Inc—James Elwell	216 W 1st St, Story City IA 50248	515-733-5252	R	9*	.1
346	Reliable Tool and Machine Company Inc—Tom Walterhouse	PO Box 757, Kendallville IN 46755	260-347-4000	R	9*	.1
347	Moeller Products Company Inc—Donald Rochow	PO Box 1736, Greenville MS 38702	662-335-2325	S	9*	.1
348	Hypertech Inc—Mark Heffington	3215 Appling Rd, Bartlett TN 38133	901-385-1888	R	8*	.1
349	Venco Manufacturing Inc—Larry Collins	12110 Best Pl, Cincinnati OH 45241	513-772-8448	R	8*	.1
350	Haynes Corp—Laura Dixon	3581 Mercantile Ave, Naples FL 34104	239-643-3013	R	8*	.1
351	US Axle Inc—Ernie Inmon	275 Shoemaker Rd, Pottstown PA 19464	610-323-3800	R	8*	.1
352	Precision Gage Inc—John Spratt	PO Box 277, Hillsdale MI 49242	517-439-5010	R	7*	.1
353	Triplex Manufacturing Co—Art Jurges	2700 W 50th St, Chicago IL 60632	773-925-4700	R	7*	.1
354	Precision Rebuilders Inc—Thomas Bley	350 N Commercial Ave, Saint Clair MO 63077	636-629-1444	R	7*	.1
355	Wolf Manufacturing Inc—Carl Blain	1450 E Scotts Ave, Stockton CA 95205	209-334-5303	R	7*	.1
356	Profile Manufacturing Inc—James Gall	50790 Richard W Blvd, Chesterfield MI 48051	586-598-0007	R	7*	<.1
357	Zandriot Technologies Inc—Albert Wong	18 Technology Dr Ste 1, Irvine CA 92618	949-655-7500	S	7*	<.1
358	SludgeBuster International Corp—Yvonee Kapelczak	PO Box 233, Escondido CA 92033	760-747-9811	R	7*	<.1
359	Mj Manufacturing Co—Edward Arends	2441 E Bristol Rd, Burton MI 48529	810-744-3840	R	7*	.1
360	Grattan Family Enterprises LLC—Lonny Smith	1350 Jarvis St, Ferndale MI 48220	248-547-3870	R	7*	.1
361	Beasley Altoona Manufacturing Inc—Harry Benjamin	PO Box 1721, Altoona PA 16603	814-942-8538	R	6*	.1
362	Dayton Wheel Concepts Inc—Charles Schroeder	115 Compark Rd, Dayton OH 45459	937-438-0100	R	6*	.1
363	Trim Parts Inc—Carl Chadwell	2175 Deerfield Rd, Lebanon OH 45036	513-934-0815	R	6*	<.1
364	AeroGo Inc—Jun Daigo	1170 Andover Park W, Seattle WA 98188	206-575-3344	R	6*	<.1
365	Ati Performance Products Inc—James Beattie	6747 Whitestone Rd, Baltimore MD 21207	410-298-4343	R	6*	<.1
366	Robinson Fin Machines Inc—Ruth Haushalter	13670 Us Hwy 68, Kenton OH 43326	419-674-4152	R	5*	.1
367	Margus Automotive Electric Exchange Inc—Donald Lopez	165 E Jefferson Blvd, Los Angeles CA 90011	323-232-5281	R	5*	.1
368	Pittsburgh Crankshaft Service Inc—Anita Prizio	PO Box 5256, Pittsburgh PA 15206	412-361-3496	R	5*	<.1
369	Perfect Equipment Company LLC—Mike Astorino	PO Box 600, La Vergne TN 37086	615-893-0643	S	5*	.1
370	Industrial Harness Company Inc—Jeffrey Lundeen	100 Outlook Ln, Shippensburg PA 17257	717-477-0100	R	5*	.1
371	Parts Expediting And Distribution Co—Virgil Cooley	PO Box 59068, Norwalk CA 90652	562-944-3199	R	5*	<.1
372	Safco Corp—Bruce Creger	5404 W Touhy Ave, Skokie IL 60077	847-677-3204	R	5*	<.1
373	Callaway Companies Inc—E Callaway	3 High St, Old Lyme CT 06371	860-434-9002	R	5*	.1
374	Precision Manifold Systems Inc—Garold Mcpeak	700 W Frontier Ln, Olathe KS 66061	913-829-1221	R	5*	<.1
375	Bergstrom Company LP—Blane Mckelvey	640 Golden Oak Pkwy, Bedford OH 44146	440-232-2282	R	5*	<.1
376	Vehicle Monitor Corp—Mike Schoiack	6825 176th Ave Ne Ste, Redmond WA 98052	425-881-5560	R	5*	<.1
377	New Mather Metals Inc—F Kimura	326 Page Dr, Franklin KY 42134	270-598-5900	R	4*	<.1
378	Addax Inc—Mark Blose	6040 Fletcher Ave, Lincoln NE 68507	402-325-6000	R	4*	<.1
379	Pardon Inc—James Pardon	3510 State Hwy M35, Gladstone MI 49837	906-428-3494	R	4*	<.1
380	Southern Automotive Inc—Thomas M Tyson	597 N Saginaw St, Pontiac MI 48342	248-335-5555	R	4*	<.1
381	Zierden Company Inc—Peter Zierden	7355 S 1st St, Oak Creek WI 53154	414-764-6630	R	4*	<.1
382	De Feo Transit Manufacturing Supply Inc—Arturo Feo	115 Commerce Dr, Brookfield CT 06804	203-775-0254	R	4*	<.1
383	Dolphin Manufacturing Inc—Alvin Fritz	12650 Universal Dr, Taylor MI 48180	734-946-6322	R	4*	<.1
384	Custom Clutch Joint and Hydraulics Inc—David Ballantyne	3417 Saint Clair Ave N, Cleveland OH 44114	216-431-1630	R	4*	<.1
385	Steck Manufacturing Company Inc—John Brill	1115 S Broadway St, Dayton OH 45417	937-222-0062	R	4*	<.1
386	Harco Manufacturing Co—Frank Harris	1000 Industrial Pkwy, Newberg OR 97132	503-537-0600	R	3*	<.1
387	American Gorwood Corp—Darrel Brandon	PO Box 68, Fairmount IN 46928	765-948-3401	R	3*	<.1
388	JW Performance Transmission Inc—John Winters	1826 Baldwin St, Rockledge FL 32955	321-632-6205	R	3*	<.1
389	Midwest Brake Bond Co—James Taylor	26255 Groesbeck Hwy, Warren MI 48089	586-775-3000	R	3*	<.1
390	Mid-State Automotive Parts Rebuilders Inc—Becky Owens	1106 Govers Ln, Ferguson KY 42533	606-679-4339	R	3*	<.1
391	Stretch Forming Corp—Lane Kakimoto	PO Box 686, Murrieta CA 92564	951-677-3309	R	3*	<.1
392	Baldwin Precision Inc—Bruce Baldwin	1025 Clancy Ave Ne, Grand Rapids MI 49503	616-451-8333	R	3*	<.1
393	In2connect Inc—David Whittaker	2304 Industrial Dr Sw, Cullman AL 35055	256-734-2110	R	3*	<.1
394	Richland Ltd—W Dallman	PO Box 489, Spring Green WI 53588	608-588-7779	R	3*	<.1
395	Kf Fiberglass Inc—Ron Belk	8247 Phlox St, Downey CA 90241	562-869-1536	R	3*	<.1
396	Trick Flow Specialties—Brian Tooley	285 West Ave, Tallmadge OH 44278	330-630-1555	R	3*	<.1
397	International Muffler Co—Kenneth Banks	2400 Maremont Pkwy, Loudon TN 37774	865-458-4681	R	3*	<.1
398	Enceratec Inc—Joseph Bentz	1414 Franklin St, Columbus IN 47201	812-377-3188	J	3*	<.1
399	PECO Manufacturing Inc—James Conroy	1818 Hobbs Dr, Delavan WI 53115	262-740-1406	R	3*	<.1
400	Rubel Machine and Tool Inc—Robert Rubel	68 Landing Rd S, Rochester NY 14610	585-924-7780	R	3*	<.1
401	Arias Industries Inc—Nicholas Arias	13420 S Normandie Ave, Gardena CA 90249	310-532-9737	R	3*	<.1
402	Globe Turbocharger Specialties Inc—Ronnie Cannon	PO Box 30009, Reno NV 89520	775-856-7337	R	3*	<.1

Rank	Company Name—*Executive Officer*	Address, City, State, Zip	Phone	Type	Fin	Empls
403	Autocraft Manufacturing Company Inc—*Martha Leod*	PO Box 540575, Merritt Island FL 32954	321-452-1010	R	2*	<.1
404	Tko Manufacturing Services Inc—*Gary Keithley*	PO Box 2246, Dayton OH 45401	937-299-1637	R	2*	<.1
405	Precision Governors LLC—*Chad Clendening*	2322 7th Ave, Rockford IL 61104	815-229-5300	R	2*	<.1
406	Sedenquist-Fraser Enterprises Inc—*Jitu Patel*	16730 Gridley Rd, Cerritos CA 90703	562-924-5763	R	2*	<.1
407	Ohio Crankshaft Co—*Stanley Ray*	5453 SR 49 S, Greenville OH 45331	937-548-7113	S	2*	<.1
408	MagnaDrive Corp—*Alex Deriugin*	600 108th Ave NE Ste 1, Bellevue WA 98004	425-463-4700	R	2*	<.1
409	PSI Industries (Rosemead California)—*B Harris*	9103 E Garvey Ave, Rosemead CA 91770	626-288-2290	R	2*	<.1
410	Med-Kas Hydraulics Inc—*Thomas Medici*	1419 John R Rd, Troy MI 48083	248-585-3220	R	2*	<.1
411	Taap Corp—*Seymour Ivice*	300 Holbrook Dr, Wheeling IL 60090	847-215-7447	R	2*	<.1
412	Tri-Mac Manufacturing And Services Co—*William Bates*	860 Belle Ave, Hamilton OH 45015	513-896-4445	R	2*	<.1
413	Harco Industries Inc—*Larry Harris*	3535 Kettering Blvd, Moraine OH 45439	937-528-5000	R	2*	<.1
414	Gerich Fiberglass Company Inc—*Anton Gerich*	7004 Us Hwy 42, Mount Gilead OH 43338	419-362-4591	R	2*	<.1
415	A Terrycable California Corp—*Terry Davis*	17376 Eucalyptus St, Hesperia CA 92345	760-244-9351	R	2*	<.1
416	JV Products Co—*Jerrie Smith*	926 Karr Rd, Arcanum OH 45304	937-884-5523	R	1*	<.1
417	Unlimited Seams Industrial Services LLC—*Millard Dunn*	202 Long St, Pulaski TN 38478	931-363-9200	R	1*	<.1
418	US Tool and Manufacturing Co—*Raymond Foreman*	1335 W Fullerton Ave, Addison IL 60101	630-953-1000	R	1*	<.1
419	North Shore Laboratories Corp—*Robert Niconchuk*	PO Box 568, Peabody MA 01960	978-531-5954	R	1*	<.1
420	Howell Engine Developments Inc—*Mathew Howell*	6201 Industrial Way, Cottrellville MI 48039	810-765-5100	R	1*	<.1
421	Mnstar Technologies Inc—*Michael Rhodes*	PO Box 806, Grand Rapids MN 55744	218-326-5566	R	1*	.1
422	Tokico (USA) Inc	301 Mayde Rd, Berea KY 40403	859-986-2359	S	1*	<.1
423	Centech Inc—*James Stafford*	2190 Colflesh Rd, Perkiomenville PA 18074	610-754-0720	R	1*	<.1
424	Buell Manufacturing Co—*Gary Buell*	PO Box 303, Lyons IL 60534	708-447-6320	R	1*	<.1
425	Freedom Wire Inc—*Michael Hatfield*	PO Box 278, Cromwell IN 46732	260-856-3059	R	1*	<.1
426	Cragar Industries Inc—*Jeff Danbom*	2188 Hwy 86, Milford IA 51351	712-330-2340	R	1	<.1
427	Mirenco Inc—*Dwayne L Fosseen*	PO Box 343, Radcliffe IA 50230	515-899-2164	P	<1	<.1
428	Jemm Inc—*Josephine Bollwitt*	211 E 1st St, Monticello IA 52310	319-465-4691	R	<1*	<.1
429	Rebuilders Enterprises Inc—*Gerald Roberts*	9004 S Octavia Ave, Bridgeview IL 60455	708-430-0030	R	<1*	<.1
430	Shepard Thomason Co—*Thomas Ruhe*	901 Leslie St, La Habra CA 90631	714-773-5539	R	<1*	<.1
431	Sense Technologies Inc—*Bruce E Schreiner*	2535 N Carleton Ave, Grand Island NE 68803	308-381-1355	P	<1	N/A
432	Turbodyne Technologies Inc—*John R Adams*	36 E Barnett St, Ventura CA 93001	805-512-9511	P	<1	N/A
433	Regency Affiliates Inc—*Laurence S Levy*	610 Jensen Beach Blvd, Jensen Beach FL 34957	772-334-8181	P	<1	<.1
434	Trico Products Corp—*Dave Cummings*	3255 W Hamlin Rd, Rochester Hills MI 48309	248-371-1700	S	N/A	4.5
435	Pratt and Whitney PSD—*Gary Scott*	275 E Robinson Ave, Springdale AR 72764	479-750-3600	D	N/A	.2

TOTALS: SIC 3714 Motor Vehicle Parts & Accessories
Companies: 435

					217,675	801.2

3715 Truck Trailers

Rank	Company Name—*Executive Officer*	Address, City, State, Zip	Phone	Type	Fin	Empls
1	Terex Corp—*Ronald M DeFeo*	200 Nyala Farm Rd, Westport CT 06880	203-222-7170	P	6,505	22.6
2	Wabash National Corp—*Richard J Giromini*	PO Box 6129, Lafayette IN 47903	765-771-5300	P	1,187	2.6
3	Utility Trailer Manufacturing Co—*Paul Bennett*	PO Box 1299, City of Industry CA 91748	626-965-1541	R	721*	3.5
4	V F Enterprises Inc—*Lonnie Whatley*	PO Box 369, Springer OK 73458	580-653-2171	S.	353*	.2
5	Strick Corp—*Steve Burns*	301 N Polk St, Monroe IN 46772	260-692-6121	R	240*	1.3
6	Featherlite Inc—*Conrad D Clement*	PO Box 320, Cresco IA 52136	563-547-6000	S	225*	1.3
7	Pace American Enterprises Inc—*James Tennant*	11550 Harter Dr, Middlebury IN 46540	574-825-7223	R	162*	.4
8	Transcraft Corp—*Dave de Poincy* Wabash National Corp	PO Box 500, Anna IL 62906		S	157*	.2
9	Universal Trailer Holdings Corp—*Terry Carlson*	11590 Century Blvd Ste, Cincinnati OH 45246	513-671-3880	R	141*	1.9
10	Trailmobile Inc—*Edward Wanandi*	100 N Field Dr Ste 355, Lake Forest IL 60045	847-504-2000	R	141*	.6
11	Beall Corp—*James Beall*	PO Box 17095, Portland OR 97217	503-735-2110	R	120*	.5
12	Sti Holdings Inc—*Donald Wahlin*	PO Box 606, Stoughton WI 53589	608-873-2500	R	94*	.9
13	Wilson Trailer Co—*Wilson Persinger*	4400 S Lewis Blvd, Sioux City IA 51106	712-252-6500	R	70*	.7
14	Trail King Industries Inc—*Bruce Yackley*	300 E Norway, Mitchell SD 57301	605-996-6482	S	60*	.5
15	East Manufacturing Corp—*Howard Booher*	PO Box 277, Randolph OH 44265	330-325-9921	R	60*	.3
16	Hyundai Translead—*Glenn Harney*	8880 Rio San Diego Dr, San Diego CA 92108	619-574-1500	S	48*	.1
17	Road Systems Inc—*Lynn Reinbolt*	2001 S Benton St, Searcy AR 72143	501-279-0991	S	47*	.1
18	Brenner Tank Services LLC—*Harry Anderson*	PO Box 670, Fond Du Lac WI 54936	920-922-5020	R	41*	.4
19	Merritt Equipment Co—*Everett Merritt*	9339 Brighton Rd, Henderson CO 80640	303-289-2286	R	40*	.2
20	Mac Trailer Manufacturing Inc—*Michael Conny*	14599 Commerce St Ne, Alliance OH 44601	330-823-9900	R	37*	.4
21	Sooner Trailer Manufacturing Co—*Matt Rohwer*	900 E Trl Blvd, El Reno OK 73036	405-262-6471	R	36*	.2
22	Mct Industries Inc—*Ted Martinez*	7451 Pan American Fwy, Albuquerque NM 87109	505-345-8651	R	36*	.1
23	4-Star Trailers Inc—*Kenneth Waller*	PO Box 75395, Oklahoma City OK 73147	405-324-7827	R	35*	.3
24	Ledwell and Son Enterprises Inc—*Lloy Ledwell*	PO Box 1106, Texarkana TX 75504	903-838-6531	R	33*	.2
25	Wells Cargo Inc—*Jeffrey Wells*	PO Box 728, Elkhart IN 46515	574-264-9661	R	31*	.4
26	Talbert Manufacturing Inc—*Rick Odle*	1628 W State Rd 114, Rensselaer IN 47978	219-866-7141	R	30*	.2
27	Reliance Trailer Manufacturing Inc—*Brian Ling*	7911 Redwood Dr, Cotati CA 94931	707-795-0081	R	29*	.2
28	Western Trailer Co—*Jerry Whitehead*	PO Box 5598, Boise ID 83705	208-344-2539	R	29*	.2
29	R C Tway Co—*Gary Smith*	7201 Logistics Dr, Louisville KY 40258	502-637-2551	R	26*	.1
30	Rockland Products Inc—*Phillip Sykes*	4060 Iberia Ave, Rockland WI 54653	608-269-8347	R	25*	.2
31	Austin-Westran LLC—*Bob Raimer*	PO Box 921, Byron IL 61010	815-234-2811	R	23*	.3
32	XI Specialized Trailers Inc—*Scott Wall*	PO Box 400, Manchester IA 52057	563-927-4900	R	23*	.2
33	Contract Manufacturer LLC—*Melinda Henry*	200 County Rd, Madill OK 73446	580-795-5536	R	21*	.3
34	Unique Functional Products—*Bernhardt Goettker*	135 Sunshine Ln, San Marcos CA 92069	760-744-1610	R	20*	.1
35	Dakota Manufacturing Company Inc—*A Oehlerking*	PO Box 1188, Mitchell SD 57301	605-996-5571	R	18*	.1
36	Truck Equipment Service Co—*Ernest Churda*	800 Oak St, Lincoln NE 68521	402-476-3225	R	17*	.1
37	Manac Trailers USA Inc—*Charles Dutil*	8593 State Hwy 77, Oran MO 63771	573-262-2166	R	16*	.1
38	Pierce Manufacturing Inc (Bradenton Florida)—*Wilson Jones*	PO Box 2017, Appleton WI 54912	920-832-3000	R	16*	.1
39	Trinity Trailer Manufacturing Inc—*Pete Eisenman*	8200 S Eisenman Rd, Boise ID 83716	208-336-3666	R	15*	.1
40	Gooseneck Trailer Manufacturing Company Inc—*David Carrabba*	PO Box 832, Bryan TX 77806	979-778-0034	R	13*	.2
41	Warren Manufacturing Inc—*Russell Warren*	900 38th St N, Birmingham AL 35222	205-591-3002	R	13*	.1
42	Construction Trailer Specialists Inc—*Spencer Taylor*	2535 Rose Pkwy, Sikeston MO 63801	573-481-0941	R	12*	.1
43	Van Nu Technology Inc—*Fred Ufolla*	2155 Hwy 1187, Mansfield TX 76063	817-477-1734	R	12*	.1
44	Lakes Enterprises Inc—*Sarah Ralph*	1300 38th Ave W, Spencer IA 51301	712-262-2992	S	9*	.1
45	Cherokee Industries Inc—*Thomas Welchel*	11301 S I 44 Service R, Oklahoma City OK 73173	405-691-8222	R	9*	.1
46	Kiefer Built LLC—*Mike Countrymen*	PO Box 88, Kanawha IA 50447	641-762-3201	R	8*	.1
47	Summit Trailer Sales Inc—*Charles Pishock*	1 Summit Plz, Summit Station PA 17979	570-754-3511	R	7*	.1
48	Vanco USA LLC *Richard Liberatore*	1170 Florence Columbus, Bordentown NJ 08505	609-499-4141	R	7*	.1
49	Industrial Hardwood Products Inc—*Marcus Chorney*	2720 N Service Dr, Red Wing MN 55066	651-388-6150	R	7*	.1
50	Uni-Glide Manufacturing Company Inc—*Robert Dills*	155 Ctr Ct, Venice FL 34285	941-493-1993	R	6*	<.1

Note: An asterisk (*) indicates an estimated financial figure. The company type code used is as follows: R = Private, P = Public, S = Private Subsidiary, B = Public Subsidiary, D = Division, J = Joint Venture, I = Investment Fund.

COMPANY RANKINGS BY SALES WITHIN 4-DIGIT SIC

Rank	Company Name—*Executive Officer*	Address, City, State, Zip	Phone	Type	Fin	Empls
51	American Carrier Equipment Inc—*Phillip Sweet*	2285 E Date Ave, Fresno CA 93706	559-442-1500	R	5*	<.1
52	Hooper's Trailer Sales Inc—*Cecil Hooper*	2245 Bethel Church Rd, Monticello GA 31064	706-468-8414	R	5*	.1
53	Marshall Steel Inc	1555 Harbor Ave, Memphis TN 38113	901-946-1124	S	5*	<.1
54	Clark Trailer Service Inc—*Bruce Clark*	24988 Us Hwy 29, Andalusia AL 36421	334-222-7216	R	4*	<.1
55	Atoka Trailer And Manufacturing LLC—*Dana Page*	PO Box 569, Atoka OK 74525	580-889-7270	R	4*	<.1
56	Master Tow Inc—*John Tart*	783 Slocomb Rd, Fayetteville NC 28311	910-630-2000	R	4*	<.1
57	Iron Works Enterprises Inc—*Ryan Lauritson*	801 S 7th St, Modesto CA 95351	209-726-4270	R	3*	<.1
58	Circle W Trailers—*John Horton*	PO Box 205, Mc Kenzie AL 36456	334-374-2560	R	3*	<.1
59	Mate Inc—*W Paul Mc William*	PO Box 40542, Houston TX 77240	281-855-0045	R	3*	<.1
60	Advance Metalworking Co—*Richard Kull*	PO Box 465, Kewanee IL 61443	309-853-3387	R	3*	<.1
61	Magnolia Trailers Inc—*Connie Langley*	PO Box 1146, Lucedale MS 39452	601-947-7990	R	2*	<.1
62	Smithway Inc—*G Smith*	PO Box 188, Fairview NC 28730	828-628-1756	R	2*	<.1
63	Thumb Truck And Trailer Co—*Budd Elenbaum*	8305 Geiger Rd, Pigeon MI 48755	989-453-3133	R	1*	<.1

TOTALS: SIC 3715 Truck Trailers
Companies: 63   **11,069**   **43.2**

3716 Motor Homes

Rank	Company Name—*Executive Officer*	Address, City, State, Zip	Phone	Type	Fin	Empls
1	Monaco RV LLC—*Daniel C Ustian*	91320 Coburg Industria, Coburg OR 97408	541-686-8011	S	1,272*	5.3
2	Tiffin Motor Homes Inc—*Robert Tiffin*	PO Box 596, Red Bay AL 35582	256-356-8661	R	498*	.5
3	Winnebago Industries Inc—*Randy J Potts*	PO Box 152, Forest City IA 50436	641-585-3535	P	496	2.1
4	Gulf Stream Coach Inc—*Dan Shea*	PO Box 1005, Nappanee IN 46550	574-773-7761	R	109*	1.2
5	Newmar Corp—*Richard Parks*	PO Box 30, Nappanee IN 46550	574-773-7791	R	88*	1.0
6	Four Winds International Inc—*Jeff Kime*	PO Box 1486, Elkhart IN 46515	574-266-1111	S	75*	.3
7	Kan Build Inc—*Quinton Robert*	PO Box 259, Osage City KS 66523	785-528-4163	R	61*	.2
8	ElDorado National Kansas Inc	1655 Wall St, Salina KS 67401	785-827-1033	S	53*	.3
9	ElDorado National California Inc	9670 Galena St, Riverside CA 92509	909-591-9557	S	35*	.2
10	Marathon Coach Inc—*Robert Schoellhorn*	91333 Coburg Industria, Coburg OR 97408	541-343-9991	R	29*	.4
11	SMC Corp (Bend Oregon)—*Kay Toolson* Monaco RV LLC	PO Box 5639, Bend OR 97708	541-686-8011	S	25*	.2
12	Rexhall Industries Inc—*William J Rex*	46147 7th St W, Lancaster CA 93534	661-726-0565	P	18	.2
13	Fiber-Tron Corp—*William Mccaslin*	29877 Us Hwy 33, Elkhart IN 46516	574-294-8545	R	3*	<.1
14	Viking Recreational Vehicles LLC—*Gar Warlick*	PO Box 549, Centreville MI 49032	269-467-6321	S	1*	.2
15	Let's Go Aero—*Marty Williams*	3380 N El Paso St Ste, Colorado Springs CO 80907	719-630-3800	R	1*	<.1
16	Sidumpr Trailer Company Inc—*Jennifer Thompson*	PO Box 520, Plainview NE 68769	402-582-4830	R	N/A	<.1

TOTALS: SIC 3716 Motor Homes
Companies: 16   **2,764**   **12.1**

3721 Aircraft

Rank	Company Name—*Executive Officer*	Address, City, State, Zip	Phone	Type	Fin	Empls
1	Boeing Co—*W James McNerney Jr*	100 N Riverside, Chicago IL 60606	312-544-2000	P	64,306	160.5
2	Northrop Grumman Corp—*Wes Bush*	1840 Century Park E, Los Angeles CA 90067	310-553-6262	P	34,757	117.1
3	Boeing Defense Space and Security—*James Albaugh* Boeing Co	PO Box 516, Saint Louis MO 63166	314-232-0232	D	17,354*	72.0
4	Textron Inc—*Scott C Donnelly*	40 Westminster St, Providence RI 02903	401-421-2800	P	10,525	32.0
5	Cessna Aircraft Co—*Scott A Ernest* Textron Inc	PO Box 7706, Wichita KS 67277	316-517-6056	S	5,091*	10.0
6	Lockheed Martin Aeronautics Co—*Robert J Stevens*	PO Box 748, Fort Worth TX 76101	817-777-2000	S	2,740	11.0
7	Gulfstream Aerospace Corp—*Joseph T Lombardo*	PO Box 2206, Savannah GA 31402	912-965-3000	S	2,670*	8.0
8	Flight Options—*Michael J Silvestro*	26180 Curtiss Wright P, Cleveland OH 44143		S	2,477*	1.8
9	AAR Corp—*David P Storch*	1100 N Wood Dale Rd, Wood Dale IL 60191	630-227-2000	P	1,776	6.1
10	Sikorsky Aircraft Corp—*David Eherts*	6900 Main St, Stratford CT 06614	203-386-4000	S	1,600	8.0
11	Kaman Corp—*Neal J Keating*	PO Box 1, Bloomfield CT 06002	860-243-7100	P	1,498	4.6
12	Dassault Falcon Jet Corp—*John Rosanvallon*	PO Box 2000, South Hackensack NJ 07606	201-440-6700	S	812*	1.5
13	Raytheon Aircraft Co—*William Swanson*	870 Winter St, Waltham MA 02451	781-522-3000	S	632	14.6
14	McDonnell Douglas Helicopter Co—*James F Albaugh* Boeing Co	100 N Riverside Plz, Chicago IL 60606	312-544-2000	S	520*	2.8
15	Mooney Airplane Company Inc—*Dennis E Ferguson* Mooney Aerospace Group Ltd	165 Al Mooney Rd N, Kerrville TX 78028	830-896-6000	S	478*	.3
16	Kaman Aerospace Corp—*Sal Bordanelero* Kaman Corp	PO Box 2, Bloomfield CT 06002	860-242-4461	D	349*	1.4
17	Aerovironment Inc—*Timothy E Conver*	181 W Huntington Dr St, Monrovia CA 91016	626-357-9983	P	293	.8
18	Robinson Helicopter Co—*Frank Robinson*	2901 Airport Dr, Torrance CA 90505	310-539-0508	R	200*	1.2
19	Aurora Flight Sciences Corp—*John Langford*	9950 Wakeman Dr, Manassas VA 20110	703-369-3633	R	65*	.3
20	Alabama Aircraft Industries Inc—*Ronald A Aramini*	1943 50th St N, Birmingham AL 35212	205-592-0011	P	63	.6
21	Avcon Industries—*Clark D Stewart* Butler National Corp	516 Morth Oliver, Newton KS 67114	316-284-2842	S	57*	<.1
22	Butler National Corp—*Clark D Stewart*	19920 W 161st St, Olathe KS 66062	913-780-9595	P	46	.1
23	Bizjet International Sales and Support Inc—*Kai S Roepke*	3515 N Sheridan Rd, Tulsa OK 74115	918-832-7733	R	45*	.3
24	Sikorsky Military Completions Center Sikorsky Aircraft Corp	17 Aviation Dr, Horseheads NY 14845	607-378-4000	S	35*	.5
25	Philadelphia Agustawestland Corp—*Vruno Cellenne*	PO Box 16002, Philadelphia PA 19114	215-281-1400	R	33*	.4
26	Hiller Aircraft Corp—*Steven L Palm*	925 M St, Firebaugh CA 93622	559-659-5959	R	25*	<.1
27	Rail Co—*Richard N Huffman Sr*	515 E Joppa Rd, Towson MD 21286	410-583-8990	R	21*	.2
28	Corporate Fleet Services—*Tom McCune*	17039 Kenton Dr 3rd Fl, Cornelius NC 28031	704-359-0007	R	21*	<.1
29	DP Associates Inc—*Donald J Patterson Jr*	3401 Columbia Pke 4th, Arlington VA 22204	703-521-6236	S	18*	.3
30	Groen Brothers Aviation USA Inc—*David Groen* Groen Brothers Aviation Inc	2640 California Ave St, Salt Lake City UT 84104	801-973-0177	S	18*	<.1
31	Odyssey Industries Inc—*Donald Stockton*	3020 Indianwood Rd, Lake Orion MI 48362	248-814-8800	S	16*	.2
32	Thrush Aircraft Inc—*K Hughes*	PO Box 3149, Albany GA 31706	229-883-1440	R	13*	.1
33	Commander Premier Aircraft Corp—*Joel M Hartstone*	20 Stanford Dr, Farmington CT 06032	860-678-0600	R	12*	.1
34	Basler Turbo Conversions LLC—*Carrie Chappa*	PO Box 2305, Oshkosh WI 54903	920-236-7820	R	11*	.1
35	Aviat Aircraft Inc—*Stuart Horn*	PO Box 1240, Afton WY 83110	307-885-3151	R	9*	.1
36	Cargo Helicopter Program Management Office—*William Crosby*	5678 Hicks Rd, Huntsville AL 35898	256-313-4302	R	8*	.1
37	Enstrom Helicopter Corp—*Jerry Mullins*	2209 22nd St, Menominee MI 49858	906-863-1200	R	8*	.1
38	STW Composites Inc—*Burt Rutan*	1624 Flight Line, Mojave CA 93501	661-824-4541	S	7*	.1
39	Mooney Aerospace Group Ltd—*Dennis Ferguson*	165 Al Mooney Rd N, Kerrville TX 78028	830-896-6000	R	6*	.1
40	Dakota Aircraft Corp—*Allan Klapmeier*	4515 Taylor Cir, Hermantown MN 55811	218-727-2737	R	5*	.2
41	Emivest Aerospace Corp—*Ching Kuo*	1770 Skyplace Blvd, San Antonio TX 78216	210-258-3900	R	3*	<.1
42	Maule Air Inc—*David Maule*	2099 Ga Hwy 133 S, Moultrie GA 31788	229-985-2045	R	3*	<.1
43	Learjet Inc—*Jim Ziegler*	PO Box 7707, Wichita KS 67277	316-946-2000	R	2*	4.5

Rank	Company Name—*Executive Officer*	Address, City, State, Zip	Phone	Type	Fin	Empls
44	Geotronic Labs Inc—*Darwin Renner*	115 W Greenbriar Ln, Dallas TX 75208	214-946-7573	R	1*	<.1
45	Ramec Engineering—*Leonard Roberts*	1736 W 130th St, Gardena CA 90249	310-532-2573	R	1*	<.1
46	Groen Brothers Aviation Inc—*David Groen*	2640 W California, Salt Lake City UT 84104	801-973-0177	P	<1	<.1
47	Moller International—*Paul Moller*	1222 Research Park Dr, Davis CA 95616	530-756-5086	P	<1	<.1

TOTALS: SIC 3721 Aircraft
Companies: 47

					148,631	461.8

3724 Aircraft Engines & Engine Parts

Rank	Company Name—*Executive Officer*	Address, City, State, Zip	Phone	Type	Fin	Empls
1	GE Aircraft Engines—*David Joyce*	1 Neumann Way Mail Dro, Cincinnati OH 45215	513-243-2000	D	16,800	39.0
2	Pratt and Whitney—*David P Hess*	400 Main St, East Hartford CT 06108	860-565-4321	S	12,100	38.6
3	Hamilton Sundstrand Corp—*Michael Dumais*	1 Hamilton Rd, Windsor Locks CT 06096	860-654-6000	S	6,200	18.3
4	B/E Aerospace Machined Products Inc—*Amin Khoury*	2555 Birch St, Vista CA 92083	760-599-1130	S	2,385*	3.5
5	Danville Metal Stamping Company Inc—*Judd Peck*	20 Oakwood Ave, Danville IL 61832	217-446-0647	R	1,441*	.4
6	Turbomeca Engine Corp—*Russ Spray*	2709 N Forum Dr, Grand Prairie TX 75052	972-606-7600	S	1,043*	.4
7	HEICO Corp—*Laurans A Mendelson*	3000 Taft St, Hollywood FL 33021	954-987-4000	P	765	2.5
8	Utica Corp—*Ron Cable*	2 Halsey Rd, Whitesboro NY 13492	315-768-8070	R	356*	1.3
9	Jet Avion Corp—*Eric Mendelson* HEICO Aerospace Holdings Corp	3000 Taft St, Hollywood FL 33021	954-744-7602	S	255*	.4
10	West Star Aviation Inc—*Dave Krogman*	796 Heritage Way, Grand Junction CO 81506	970-243-7500	S	209*	.3
11	Strategic Industries LLC—*Robert Stift*	26 Main St Ste 200, Chatham NJ 07928	732-512-0195	R	141*	2.6
12	Unison Engine Components Inc—*Mike Sims*	401 Sweten Creek Indus, Asheville NC 28803	828-274-4540	R	140*	.4
13	Chromalloy Georgia—*Tim Ulles*	30 Dart Rd, Newnan GA 30265	770-254-6200	D	124*	.2
14	HEICO Aerospace Holdings Corp—*Eric A Mendelson* HEICO Corp	3000 Taft St, Hollywood FL 33021	954-987-4000	S	120	.7
15	Steel Improvement and Forge Co—*Michael S Lipscomb*	970 E 64th St, Cleveland OH 44103	216-881-8600	P	107	.4
16	Teledyne Continental Motors Inc—*Rhett C Ross*	PO Box 90, Mobile AL 36601	251-438-3411	S	101*	.5
17	Pemco World Air Services—*Bill Meehan*	100 Pemco Dr, Dothan AL 36303		S	83*	.6
18	GE Tri-Remanufacturing Inc—*Jim Hastings* GE Aircraft Engines	3390 E Locust St, Terre Haute IN 47803	812-234-5889	S	80*	.1
19	Edac Technologies Corp—*Dominick A Pagano*	1806 New Britain Ave, Farmington CT 06032	860-678-8140	P	73	.4
20	Senior Aerospace Jet Products Corp—*Ronald Blair*	9106 Balboa Ave, San Diego CA 92123	858-278-8400	S	72*	.3
21	Meyer Tool Inc—*Arlyn Easton*	3064 Colerain Ave, Cincinnati OH 45225	513-681-7362	R	71*	.8
22	Gkn Aerospace Chem-Tronics Inc—*Michael Beck*	PO Box 1604, El Cajon CA 92022	619-448-2320	S	57*	.7
23	Palmer Manufacturing Company LLC—*Mike White*	PO Box K, Malden MA 02148	781-321-0480	R	55*	.2
24	Fairchild Controls Corp—*Steve Orr*	540 Highland St, Frederick MD 21701	301-228-3400	S	53*	.2
25	Evangeline Airmotive Inc—*Al A Gonsoulin*	PO Box 90808, Lafayette LA 70509	337-235-2452	S	46*	.1
26	Standard Aero Alliance Inc	1524 W 14th St Ste 110, Tempe AZ 85281	480-377-3100	S	45	.2
27	Delta Industries (East Granby Connecticut)—*William Evans*	39 Bradley Park Rd, East Granby CT 06026	860-653-5041	R	42*	.2
28	Gros-Ite Industries Div—*Dominik Pagano* Edac Technologies Corp	1798 New Britain Ave, Farmington CT 06032	860-677-2603	D	38*	.2
29	Middleton Aerospace Corp—*Richard Neill*	20 Computer Dr, Haverhill MA 01832	978-774-6000	R	38*	.1
30	All Manufacturers Inc—*Jon Gerwin*	2900 Palisades Dr, Corona CA 92000	951-280-4200	R	36*	.3
31	Arrow Gear Co—*Joseph Arvin*	2301 Curtiss St, Downers Grove IL 60515	630-969-7640	R	36*	.3
32	Rolls-Royce North America Inc—*James M Guyette*	1875 Exploers St Ste 2, Reston VA 20190	703-834-1700	S	33*	.2
33	Electro-Methods Inc—*Randy Fries*	PO Box 54, South Windsor CT 06074	860-289-8661	R	30*	.2
34	Stein Seal Co—*Philip Stein*	PO Box 316, Kulpsville PA 19443	215-256-0201	R	29*	.2
35	Kreisler Manufacturing Corp—*Michael D Stern*	180 Van Riper Ave, Elmwood Park NJ 07407	201-791-0700	P	28	.2
36	Sermatech-Lehr—*Jim Mueller*	1566 Medical Dr, Pottstown PA 19464	610-819-1270	D	28*	.3
37	Cfan Co—*Benoit Cloutier*	1000 Technology Way, San Marcos TX 78666	512-353-2832	R	27*	.4
38	Barnes Aerospace/Advanced Fabrications Div—*Patrick Dempsey*	169 Kennedy Rd, Windsor CT 06095	860-298-7740	D	26*	.1
39	Therm Inc—*Robert Sprole*	PO Box 220, Ithaca NY 14851	607-272-8500	R	26*	.2
40	Beacon Group Inc—*Robert Sarkisian*	85 Granby St, Bloomfield CT 06002	860-242-3453	R	24*	.4
41	Twigg Corp—*Roy Rapp*	659 E York St, Martinsville IN 46151	765-342-7126	R	22*	.1
42	Niles Precision Co—*Jay Skalla*	PO Box 548, Niles MI 49120	269-683-0585	R	21*	.2
43	Thrun Manufacturing Inc—*Christine Thrun*	15590 Dupont Ave, Chino CA 91710	909-631-2980	R	21*	<.1
44	Budney Industries Inc—*Michael Budney*	PO Box 8316, Berlin CT 06037	860-828-1950	R	20*	.2
45	Jedco Inc—*Daniel Szymanski*	1615 Broadway Ave Nw, Grand Rapids MI 49504	616-459-5161	R	19*	.2
46	Berkshire Industries Inc—*Eckard Brause*	PO Box 828, Westfield MA 01086	413-568-8676	R	18*	.1
47	BH Aircraft Company Inc—*Daniel Kearns*	2230 Smithtown Ave, Ronkonkoma NY 11779	631-981-4200	R	17*	.1
48	Birken Manufacturing Co—*Gary Greenberg*	PO Box 65, Bloomfield CT 06002	860-242-2211	R	17*	.1
49	Aeronca Inc—*Paul Sivilotti*	2320 Wedekind Dr, Middletown OH 45042	513-422-2751	R	16*	.1
50	Columbia Manufacturing Inc—*David Bell*	165 Rte 66 E, Columbia CT 06237	860-228-2259	R	16*	.1
51	Dyna-Empire Inc—*G Patrick Mc Cart*	1075 Stewart Ave, Garden City NY 11530	516-222-2700	R	15*	.1
52	Moeller Aerospace Technology Inc—*Daniel Moellering*	8725 Moeller Dr, Harbor Springs MI 49740	231-347-9575	R	15*	.1
53	Welded Ring Products Co—*James Janosek*	2180 W 114th St, Cleveland OH 44102	216-961-3800	R	14*	.1
54	Precision Airmotive LLC—*Karen Hackett*	14800 40th Ave Ne, Marysville WA 98271	360-651-8282	R	14*	.1
55	Pointe Precision Inc—*Joseph Kinsella*	2675 Precision Dr, Plover WI 54467	715-342-5100	R	13*	.1
56	Cfm International Inc—*Paul Ebanga*	PO Box 15514, Cincinnati OH 45215	513-552-3272	S	12*	.1
57	Car-Graph Inc—*Charles Lindbloom*	1545 W Elna Rae St, Tempe AZ 85281	480-894-1356	R	11*	.1
58	Dukes Inc—*Chet Huffman*	9060 Winnetka Ave, Northridge CA 91324	818-998-9811	R	11*	.1
59	Norris Precision Manufacturing Inc—*Arthur Norris*	PO Box 1968, Pinellas Park FL 33780	727-572-6330	R	11*	.1
60	Reliable Manufacturing Company Inc—*Mark Gregoreti*	125 Highland Park Dr, Bloomfield CT 06002	860-242-5591	R	10*	.1
61	J F Fredericks Tool Company Inc—*Ash Patel*	25 Spring Ln, Farmington CT 06032	860-677-2646	R	8*	.1
62	A-1 Machining Co—*David Bovenizer*	235 John Downey Dr, New Britain CT 06051	860-223-6420	R	8*	.1
63	Phoenix Aerospace Inc—*William Sutherland*	PO Box 8744, Kansas City MO 64114	816-333-3400	R	7*	.1
64	Cam-Tech Manufacturing LP—*Bill Carlisle*	1112 N Commercial Blvd, Arlington TX 76006	817-784-8482	R	7*	.1
65	Cbs Manufacturing Co—*J Lawton*	35 Kripes Rd, East Granby CT 06026	860-653-8100	R	6*	<.1
66	Tri Aerospace LLC—*David Abrams*	1055 S Hunt St, Terre Haute IN 47803	812-872-2400	R	6*	<.1
67	Doncasters Inc New England Airfoil Products Div	36 Spring Ln, Farmington CT 06032	860-677-1376	D	5*	<.1
68	Dependable Machine Company Inc—*Robert Wagner*	1846 E 30th St, Indianapolis IN 46218	317-924-5378	R	5*	<.1
69	Boring Machine Corp—*Tom Chacon*	7922 Ranchers Rd Ne, Minneapolis MN 55432	763-786-0100	R	4*	<.1
70	Tradewind Turbines Corp—*Larry Boyd*	PO Box 31930, Amarillo TX 79120	806-335-1400	R	4*	<.1
71	General Aviation Manufacturing Inc—*William Schwemlein*	2693 Philmont Ave, Huntingdon Valley PA 19006	215-947-9349	R	2*	<.1
72	D and D Machinery And Sales Inc—*Dolores Martinez*	PO Box 591730, San Antonio TX 78259	830-438-2309	R	2*	<.1
73	Tethers Unlimited Inc—*Robert Hoyt*	11711 N Creek Pkwy S, Bothell WA 98011	425-486-0100	R	2*	<.1
74	Abdite Industries Inc—*Oliver Laszlo*	8400 Beech Daly Rd, Taylor MI 48180	313 291-1000	R	1*	<.1
75	Approved Aircraft Accessories Inc—*Gail Yancheck*	PO Box 666, Taylor MI 48180	734-946-9000	R	1*	<.1

Note: An asterisk (*) indicates an estimated financial figure. The company type code used is as follows: R = Private, P = Public, S = Private Subsidiary, B = Public Subsidiary, D = Division, J = Joint Venture, I = Investment Fund.

COMPANY RANKINGS BY SALES WITHIN 4-DIGIT SIC

Rank	Company Name—*Executive Officer*	Address, City, State, Zip	Phone	Type	Fin	Empls
76	Rolls-Royce Inc—*James Guyette*	1875 Explorer St Ste 2, Reston VA 20190	703-834-1700	S	N/A	5.7

TOTALS: SIC 3724 Aircraft Engines & Engine Parts
Companies: 76 — Fin 43,741 — Empls 124.3

3728 Aircraft Parts & Equipment Nec

Rank	Company Name—*Executive Officer*	Address, City, State, Zip	Phone	Type	Fin	Empls
1	GE Aviation—*David L Joyce*	1 Neumann Way, Cincinnati OH 45215	513-243-2000	S	8,288*	39.0
2	Spirit AeroSystems Holdings Inc—*Jeffrey L Turner*	PO Box 780008, Wichita KS 67278	316-526-9000	B	4,864	13.8
3	Rockwell Collins Inc—*Clayton M Jones*	400 Collins Rd NE, Cedar Rapids IA 52498	319-295-1000	P	4,806	20.5
4	Triumph Group Inc—*Richard C III*	899 Cassatt Rd Ste 210, Berwyn PA 19312	610-251-1000	P	2,905	12.1
5	Triumph Aerostructures - Vought Aircraft Division—*Elmer L Doty* Triumph Group Inc	9314 W Jefferson Blvd, Dallas TX 75211	972-946-2011	S	1,910*	6.0
6	Precise Machine Co—*Ronald S Saks* LMI Aerospace Inc	2201 River Hill Rd, Irving TX 75061	972-438-3995	S	1,708*	.7
7	Precise Machine Partners LLP—*Ronald S Saks* LMI Aerospace Inc	3600 Mueller Rd, Saint Charles MO 63301	636-946-6525	S	1,708*	.7
8	AAR Manufacturing Inc—*David Storch*	1100 N Wood Dale Rd 1, Wood Dale IL 60191	630-227-2000	S	1,526*	3.5
9	Spirit Aerosystems Inc—*Jeffrey Turner*	PO Box 780008, Wichita KS 67278	316-526-9000	R	1,287*	12.0
10	L-3 Display Systems—*Robert McGill*	1355 Bluegrass Lakes P, Alpharetta GA 30004	770-752-7000	S	998*	.4
11	PCC Airfoils Inc	25201 Chagrin Blvd Ste, Beachwood OH 44122	216-831-3590	D	914*	2.2
12	Mitsubishi Heavy Industries America Inc—*Hiromichi Morimoto*	630 5th Ave Ste 2650, New York NY 10111	212-969-9000	R	839	N/A
13	BAE SYSTEMS Integrated Defense Solutions	6500 Tracor Ln, Austin TX 78725	512-926-2800	D	616*	.7
14	Ducommun Technologies—*Joseph Berenato* Ducommun Inc	23301 Wilmington Ave, Carson CA 90745	310-513-7280	S	539*	.2
15	Stellex Aerospace—*Jay Fitzsimmons*	3 Werner Way, Lebanon NJ 08833	908-437-4170	R	429*	.5
16	Ducommun Inc—*Anthony J Reardon*	23301 Wilmington Ave, Carson CA 90745	310-513-7280	P	408	1.8
17	C and D Zodiac Inc—*Tom Mcfarland*	5701 Bolsa Ave, Huntington Beach CA 92647	714-934-0000	R	376*	4.0
18	Crane Aerospace Inc—*Mike Romito*	PO Box 97027, Lynnwood WA 98046	425-743-8321	S	345*	.8
19	Hydro-Aire Inc—*Gregory A Ward* Crane Aerospace Inc	PO Box 7722, Burbank CA 91510	818-526-2600	S	278*	.6
20	General Atomics Aeronautical Systems Inc—*Thomas J Cassidy Jr*	13322 Evening Creek Dr, San Diego CA 92128	858-964-6700	S	262*	2.3
21	Esterline Korry Electronics Co—*Dan McFeely*	901 Dexter Ave N, Seattle WA 98109	206-281-1300	S	242*	.6
22	LMI Aerospace Inc—*Ronald S Saks*	411 Fountain Lakes Blv, Saint Charles MO 63301	636-946-6525	P	223	1.3
23	Van's Aircraft Inc—*Richard VanGrunsven*	14401 NE Keil Rd, Aurora OR 97002	503-678-6545	R	215*	.1
24	Edwards and Associates Inc—*Greg Williams*	PO Box 3689, Bristol TN 37625	423-538-5111	S	212*	.4
25	Nordam Group Inc—*Meredith Siegfried*	PO Box 3365, Tulsa OK 74101	918-878-4000	R	205*	2.4
26	Avox Systems Inc—*James Capozzi*	225 Erie St, Lancaster NY 14086	716-683-5100	S	201*	1.0
27	General Dynamics Armament and Technical Products Inc—*Linda Hudson*	2118 Water Ridge Pky, Charlotte NC 28217	704-714-8000	S	198*	1.2
28	Astronics Corp—*Peter J Gundermann*	130 Commerce Way, East Aurora NY 14052	716-805-1599	P	196	1.0
29	Hawk Corp—*Ronald Weinberg*	200 Public Sq Ste 1500, Cleveland OH 44114	216-861-3553	S	172	1.0
30	Radiant Power Corp—*Laurans A Mendelson*	7135 16th St E Ste 101, Sarasota FL 34243	941-739-3200	S	141*	.1
31	Chromalloy Gas Turbine Corp—*Armand Lauzon*	303 Industrial Park Rd, San Antonio TX 78226	210-331-2300	S	136*	.3
32	Aerotech World Trade Corp—*Jan Endresen*	11 New King St, White Plains NY 10604	914-681-3000	R	136*	<.1
33	DeCrane Aerospace—*Roger Wolfe*	1643 S Maize Rd, Wichita KS 67209	316-448-4888	R	125*	1.0
34	Pratt and Whitney Auto-Air Inc—*Steve Foster*	5640 Enterprise Dr, Lansing MI 48911	517-393-4040	S	116*	.3
35	Johnson Technology Inc—*David M Yacavone*	2034 Latimer Dr, Muskegon MI 49442	231-777-2685	S	91	.5
36	Hawker Pacific Aerospace—*Klaus Klesfer*	11240 Sherman Way, Sun Valley CA 91352	818-765-6201	R	79*	.5
37	Gkn Westland Aerospace Inc—*Paul Cocker*	3951 Al Hwy 229 S, Tallassee AL 36078	334-283-9200	S	78*	1.0
38	Breeze-Eastern Corp—*Mike Harlan*	35 Melanie Ln, Whippany NJ 07981	973-602-1001	P	78	.2
39	Precision Machine Works Inc—*David Baublits*	PO Box 1115, Tacoma WA 98401	253-272-5119	R	54*	.2
40	Eclipse Aerospace—*Mason Holland*	2503 Clark Carr Loop S, Albuquerque NM 87106	505-245-7555	R	53*	.1
41	Parker Hannifin Corp Electronic Systems Div	300 Marcus Blvd, Hauppauge NY 11788	631-639-3737	D	51	.4
42	Triumph Fabrications Hot Springs Inc—*Tony Johnson* Triumph Group Inc	1923 Central Ave, Hot Springs AR 71901	501-321-9325	S	51*	.4
43	Jamco America Inc—*Norikazu Natsume*	1018 80th St Sw, Everett WA 98203	425-347-4735	R	50*	.4
44	Tect Aerospace Wellington Inc—*Brett Jacobson*	PO Box 70, Wellington KS 67152	620-359-5000	S	50	.4
45	BBA Aviation- Flight Support	201 S Orange Ave Ste 1, Orlando FL 32801	407-648-7230	S	48*	.1
46	Arrowhead Products Corp—*David Schramm*	4411 Katella Ave, Los Alamitos CA 90720	714-828-7770	R	47*	.6
47	CPI Aerostructures Inc—*Edward Fred*	91 Heartland Blvd, Edgewood NY 11717	631-586-5200	P	44	.1
48	Carleton Life Support Systems Inc—*Kelly Coffield*	2734 Hickory Grove Rd, Davenport IA 52804	563-383-6000	S	43*	.3
49	Triumph Structures-Long Island LLC—*Richard C III* Triumph Group Inc	717 Main St, Westbury NY 11590	516-997-5757	S	42*	.1
50	Driessen Aircraft Interior Systems Inc—*Del Hebert*	10781 Forbes Ave, Garden Grove CA 92843	714-265-2911	R	38*	.4
51	Messier Services America Inc—*Robert Granger*	45360 Severn Way, Sterling VA 20166	703-450-8200	S	38*	.2
52	Ctl-Aerospace Inc—*James Irwin*	5616 Spellmire Dr, Cincinnati OH 45246	513-874-7900	R	36*	.2
53	D-J Engineering Inc—*Rezaul Chowdhury*	PO Box 278, Augusta KS 67010	316-775-1212	R	36*	.2
54	Rogerson Aircraft Corp—*Michael Rogerson*	2201 Alton Pkwy, Irvine CA 92606	949-660-0666	R	36*	.2
55	G S Precision Inc—*Norman Schneeberger*	101 John Seitz Dr, Brattleboro VT 05301	802-257-5200	R	35*	.4
56	Applied Aerospace Structures Corp—*John Rule*	PO Box 6189, Stockton CA 95206	209-982-0160	R	34*	.2
57	JC Carter Company Inc—*Bal Melikian*	671 W 17th St, Costa Mesa CA 92627	949-764-2200	R	34*	.3
58	Woodward FST Inc	700 N Centennial St, Zeeland MI 49464	616-772-9171	S	34*	.2
59	Globe Engineering Company Inc—*Ronald Ross*	PO Box 12407, Wichita KS 67277	316-943-1266	R	34*	.2
60	Curtiss-Wright Flight Systems Inc—*Martin R Benante*	10 Waterview Blvd 2nd, Parsippany NJ 07054	973-541-3700	S	33*	.2
61	Flight Structures Inc (Tulalip Washington)—*Trevor Skelly*	6330 31st Ave NE, Marysville WA 98271	360-657-5197	S	33*	.2
62	Reinhold Industries Inc—*Clarence Hightower*	12827 E Imperial Hwy, Santa Fe Springs CA 90670	562-944-3281	S	33	.1
63	Luminator Aircraft Products—*Avi Zisman*	900 Klein Rd, Plano TX 75074	972-424-6511	D	32*	.2
64	Mountain Air Cargo Inc—*Walter Clark*	PO Box 488, Denver NC 28037	828-464-8741	S	32*	.1
65	Senior Aerospace Composites	PO Box 12950, Wichita KS 67277	316-942-3208	S	31	.2
66	Aeroflex International Inc—*Harvey Blau*	PO Box 270, Bloomingdale NJ 07403	973-838-1780	R	31*	.1
67	McCauley Propeller Systems—*Peter Wilkinson*	PO Box 7704, Wichita KS 67277	316-831-4021	R	30	.2
68	Aero Gear Inc—*Douglas Rose*	1050 Day Hill Rd, Windsor CT 06095	860-688-0888	R	30*	.1
69	Fatigue Technology Inc—*Kevin Dooley*	401 Andover Park E, Tukwila WA 98188	206-246-2010	R	29*	.2
70	Forrest Machining Inc—*Joanne Butler*	27756 Ave Mentry, Valencia CA 91355	661-257-0231	R	29*	.2
71	Luxfer Inc—*John Rhodes*	3016 Kansas Ave Bldg 1, Riverside CA 92507	951-684-5110	R	29*	.4
72	Pako Inc—*Paul Kosir*	7615 Jenther Dr, Mentor OH 44060	440-946-8030	R	29*	.2
73	B/E Aerospace Services Inc—*Amin J Khoury*	1455 Fairchild Rd, Winston-Salem NC 27105	336-767-2000	S	29	.2
74	Meggitt Inc (Londonderry New Hampshire)—*Stuart Parker*	144 Harvey Rd, Londonderry NH 03053	603-669-0940	R	28*	.2
75	Neill Aircraft Co—*Judith Carpenter*	1260 W 15th St, Long Beach CA 90813	562-432-7981	R	27*	.2

Rank	Company Name—Executive Officer	Address, City, State, Zip	Phone	Type	Fin	Empls
76	Ellanef Manufacturing Corp—N Edwards	9711 50th Ave, Corona NY 11368	718-699-4000	R	26*	.3
77	Hydroform USA Inc—Chester Jablonski	2848 E 208th St, Carson CA 90810	310-632-6353	R	25*	.1
78	Parker Hannifin Corp Airborne Div—Greg Crowe	PO Box 4032, Elyria OH 44036	440-284-6300	D	25*	.2
79	AGC Inc—Walter Layman	106 Evansville Ave, Meriden CT 06451	203-235-3361	R	25*	.2
80	Ace Clearwater Enterprises Inc—James Dodson	19815 Magellan Dr, Torrance CA 90502	310-538-5380	R	24*	.2
81	Carleton Technologies Inc—Kelly Coffield	10 Cobham Dr, Orchard Park NY 14127	716-662-0006	R	24*	.3
82	Compass Aerospace Northwest Inc—Ron Case	821 3rd Ave S, Kent WA 98032	253-852-9700	R	24*	.2
83	Stl Enterprises Inc—William Windette	15148 Bledsoe St, Sylmar CA 91342	818-362-5665	R	24*	.1
84	Exotic Metals Forming Company LLC—Mark Simon	5411 S 226th St, Kent WA 98032	253-395-3710	R	23*	.3
85	Arkwin Industries Inc—Daniel Berlin	686 Main St, Westbury NY 11590	516-333-2640	R	23*	.3
86	Avtech Corp—Jeff Smith	3400 Wallingford Ave N, Seattle WA 98103	206-695-8000	R	22*	.3
87	B and E Tool Company Inc—John Wilander	PO Box 40, Southwick MA 01077	413-569-5585	R	22*	.1
88	Hartzell Propeller Inc—James Brown	1 Propeller Pl, Piqua OH 45356	937-778-4200	R	22*	.3
89	Moritz Aerospace Inc—Claude Mercier	123 N Main St Ste 257-, Dublin PA 18917	215-996-9211	S	22*	.5
90	Frasca International Inc—Rudolf Frasca	906 Airport Rd, Urbana IL 61802	217-344-9200	R	20*	.2
91	Heizer Aerospace Inc—Charles Heizer	8750 Pevely Industrial, Pevely MO 63070	636-475-6300	R	20*	.2
92	Engineered Arresting Systems Corp—Spencer Hoos	2550 Market St, Upper Chichester PA 19014	610-494-8000	R	20*	.1
93	Hollingsead International Inc—John Martin	21652 Nanticoke Ave, Georgetown DE 19947	302-855-5888	S	20	.1
94	Acromil Corp—Gerald Niznick	18421 Railroad St, City Of Industry CA 91748	626-964-2522	R	20*	.1
95	Idd Aerospace Corp—Elizabeth Deyoung	18225 Ne 76th St, Redmond WA 98052	425-885-4353	S	19*	.2
96	Mayday Manufacturing Co—James Nelson	1500 Interstate 35 W, Denton TX 76207	940-898-8301	R	18*	.2
97	Ferco Tech Corp—Millie Blanco	291 Conover Dr, Franklin OH 45005	937-746-6696	R	18*	.1
98	Chelton Inc—Michael S Wilkerson	1955 Lakeway Dr Ste 20, Lewisville TX 75057	972-221-1783	S	18*	<.1
99	Capps Manufacturing Inc—Barney Capps	2121 S Edwards St, Wichita KS 67213	316-942-9351	R	18*	.2
100	Royell Manufacturing Inc—James Yelle	3817 Smith Ave, Everett WA 98201	425-259-9258	R	17*	.1
101	Cox and Company Inc—Stephen Landry	1664 Old Country Rd, Plainview NY 11803	212-366-0200	R	17*	.2
102	Engine Components Inc—Gary Garvens	9503 Middlex Dr, San Antonio TX 78217	210-820-8100	R	17*	.2
103	Lapeer Industries Inc—Carl Schreiber	PO Box 69, Lapeer MI 48446	810-664-1816	R	17*	.1
104	Aim Aerospace Inc—John Feutz	PO Box 9011, Renton WA 98057	425-235-2750	R	17*	.2
105	Addison Meggitt Inc—Greg Dewitt	4554 Claire Chennault, Addison TX 75001	972-407-1234	R	17*	.1
106	Western Methods Machinery Corp—Mark Heasley	2344 Pullman St, Santa Ana CA 92705	949-252-6600	R	17*	.1
107	J D Ott Company Inc—Rex Ott	2244 6th Ave S, Seattle WA 98134	206-749-0777	R	16*	.1
108	Parker Hannifin Corp Aircraft Wheel and Brake Div—Donald E Washkewicz	1160 Center Rd, Avon OH 44011	440-937-6211	D	16*	.1
109	Hoover Industries Inc—Marisa Ianante	PO Box 522337, Miami FL 33152		R	16*	.1
110	Triumph Fabrication—Richard C III Triumph Group Inc	7445 E Lancaster Ave, Fort Worth TX 76112	817-451-0620	D	16*	.1
111	Gkn Aerospace Bandy Machining Inc—Tom Fulton	PO Box 7716, Burbank CA 91510	818-846-9020	R	16*	.1
112	Gcm North American Aerospace LLC—Dean Jendro	21719 84th Ave S, Kent WA 98032	253-872-7488	R	15*	.1
113	Harper Engineering Co—O Harper	700 Sw 7th St, Renton WA 98057	425-228-4945	R	15*	<.1
114	Advanced Machine and Stretchform International Inc—John Summit	18620 S Broadway, Gardena CA 90248	310-538-3857	R	15*	.1
115	Amro Fabricating Corp—Aquilina Hutton	1430 Adelia Ave, South El Monte CA 91733	626-579-2200	R	15*	.1
116	Accra Manufacturing Inc—Joseph Rieger	17703 15th Ave Se, Bothell WA 98012	425-424-1000	R	14*	.1
117	Trailboss Enterprises Inc—Joseph Tolliver	201 E 3rd Ave, Anchorage AK 99501	907-338-8243	R	14*	.3
118	Essex Cryogenics Of Missouri Inc—Keith Guller	8007 Chivvis Dr, Saint Louis MO 63123	314-832-4500	S	14*	.1
119	Westwind Technologies Inc—J Noojln	2901 Wall Triana Hwy S, Huntsville AL 35824	256-319-0137	R	14*	.2
120	Tronair Inc—Ken Greene	1740 Eber Rd Ste E, Holland OH 43528	419-866-6301	R	14*	.1
121	Flanagan Brothers Inc—Kenneth Flanagan	911 New London Tpke, Glastonbury CT 06033	860-633-9474	R	14*	.1
122	Premier Engineering And Manufacturing Inc—Robert Derusha	2312 Sherman St, Marinette WI 54143	715-735-6440	R	14*	<.1
123	Orcon Aerospace—Hollis Bascom	1570 Atlantic St, Union City CA 94587	510-489-8100	R	13*	.2
124	Tell Tool Inc—David Smith	PO Box 1278, Westfield MA 01086	413-568-1671	R	13*	.1
125	Newbrook Machine Corp—Christopher Lanski	PO Box 231, Silver Creek NY 14136	716-934-2644	R	13*	.1
126	Quality Forming LLC—Mark Severns	22906 Frampton Ave, Torrance CA 90501	310-539-2855	R	13*	.1
127	Llamas Plastics Inc—Oswald Llamas	12970 Bradley Ave, Sylmar CA 91342	818-362-0371	R	13*	.1
128	Eagle Tool and Machine Company Inc—Charles Brougher	PO Box 179, Springfield OH 45501	937-325-1586	S	13*	.1
129	Tri-Tech Electronics Inc—Jack Zold	9480 E Colonial Dr, Orlando FL 32817	407-277-2131	R	12*	.1
130	Wayne Trail Technologies Inc—David Knapke	PO Box 257, Fort Loramie OH 45845	937-295-2120	R	12*	.1
131	Universal Technologies Inc—Jesse Rogers	PO Box 640, Estill Springs TN 37330	931-649-5171	R	12*	.1
132	Aerospace Coatings International Inc—Adelbert Marsh	PO Box 7340, Oxford AL 36203	256-241-2750	R	12*	.1
133	Brown Precision Inc—Daniel Brown	90 Shields Rd, Huntsville AL 35811	256-746-0533	R	11*	.1
134	Growth Industries Inc—Delbert Dunmire	12523 3rd St, Grandview MO 64030	816-763-7676	R	11*	.1
135	Sigma Tek Inc—Robert Castleberry	1001 Industrial Rd, Augusta KS 67010	316-775-6373	R	11*	.1
136	Operations Management Consulting Ltd—Just Mcgill	7350 E 86th St, Indianapolis IN 46256	317-570-5830	S	11*	.1
137	P and J Machining Inc—Paul Hogoboom	PO Box 310, Puyallup WA 98371	253-841-0500	R	10*	.1
138	Industrial Tube Company LLC—Richard Alderson	3091 Indian Ave, Perris CA 92571	951-657-2611	R	10*	.1
139	Triumph Accessory Services—Bob Bierk Triumph Group Inc	PO Box 10, Wellington KS 67152	620-326-2235	D	10*	.1
140	Malin Space Science Systems Inc—Michael C Malin	PO Box 910148, San Diego CA 92191	858-552-2650	R	10*	<.1
141	Meggitt Thermal Systems Inc—Rob Meyer	1915 Voyager Ave, Simi Valley CA 93063	805-584-4150	R	10*	.1
142	Allied Specialty Precision Inc—Pam Rubenstein	PO Box 543, Mishawaka IN 46546	574-255-4718	R	9*	.1
143	Ballistic Recovery Systems Inc—Larry E Williams	380 Airport Rd, S St Paul MN 55075	651-457-7491	P	9	<.1
144	Continental A L 39404400—Stan Ruth	PO Box 45446, Atlanta GA 30320	404-530-3545	R	9*	.2
145	Beranek Inc—Vilma Beranek	2340 W 205th St, Torrance CA 90501	310-328-9094	R	9*	<.1
146	Phoenix Composite Solutions LLC—Mary Morgan	5911 Mission St, Oscoda MI 48750	989-739-7108	R	9*	.2
147	Valco Manufacturing Company Inc—Roger Valdez	PO Box 2117, Oklahoma City OK 73101	580-255-4300	R	8*	.1
148	Sertco Industries Inc—Richard Crouch	100 Sertco Dr, Okemah OK 74859	918-623-0526	R	8*	<.1
149	Nassau Tool Works Inc—Vincent Carlo	34 Lamar St, West Babylon NY 11704	631-643-5000	R	8*	.1
150	DPI Labs Inc—Vic Brown	1350 Arrow Hwy, La Verne CA 91750	909-392-5777	R	7*	.1
151	Northstar Machine and Tool Company Inc—John Eagleton	4212 Enterprise Cir, Duluth MN 55810	218-720-2920	R	7*	.1
152	Notthoff Engineering L A Inc—Terry Kaller	5416 Argosy Ave, Huntington Beach CA 92649	714-894-9802	R	7*	<.1
153	Parts Tool And Die Inc—Deborah Elias	344 Shoemaker Ln, Agawam MA 01001	413-821-9718	R	7*	<.1
154	Capital Aviation Inc—Bill Boettger	5500 Philip J Rhoads A, Bethany OK 73008	405-495-1141	R	7*	<.1
155	Scott Machine Inc—Tom Dobbin	PO Box 468, Jackson MI 49204	517-787-6616	R	7*	<.1
156	United Avionics Inc—Richard Nicolari	38 Great Hill Rd, Naugatuck CT 06770	203-723-1404	R	7*	<.1
157	Truline Industries Inc—Court Durkalski	PO Box 307, Chesterland OH 44026	440-729-0140	R	7*	<.1
158	Attco Machine Products Inc—Richard Verwilst	2411 Foundation Dr, South Bend IN 46628	574-234-1063	R	7*	<.1
159	Milan Tool Corp—Mark Milan	PO Box 29336, Cleveland OH 44129	216-661-1078	R	7*	<.1
160	Yeager Manufacturing Corp—Sean Cummins	2222 E Orangethorpe Av, Anaheim CA 92806	714-879-2800	R	6*	<.1
161	Aws Industries Inc—Alvin Schaeper	2600 Henkle Dr, Lebanon OH 45036	513-932-7941	R	6*	<.1

Note: An asterisk (*) indicates an estimated financial figure. The company type code used is as follows: R = Private, P = Public, S = Private Subsidiary, B = Public Subsidiary, D = Division, J = Joint Venture, I = Investment Fund.

COMPANY RANKINGS BY SALES WITHIN 4-DIGIT SIC

Rank	Company Name—Executive Officer	Address, City, State, Zip	Phone	Type	Fin	Empls
162	MAC Aviation Services LLC—Mike Marsh	2018 W Vernon Ave, Kinston NC 28504	252-526-9677	R	6*	<.1
163	Schrillo Realty Inc—Edward Schrillo	16750 Schoenborn St, North Hills CA 91343	818-894-8241	R	6*	<.1
164	Coronado Manufacturing Inc—Allen Gowing	8991 Glenoaks Blvd, Sun Valley CA 91352	818-768-5010	R	6*	.1
165	Minutemen Precision Machining and Tool Corp—Michael Castoro	2165 5th Ave, Ronkonkoma NY 11779	631-467-4900	R	5*	<.1
166	Eck and Eck Machine Company Inc—Paul Eck	4606 W Harry St, Wichita KS 67209	316-942-5924	R	5*	<.1
167	Magnetic Seal Corp—Richard Colby	PO Box 445, Warren RI 02885	401-247-2800	R	5*	<.1
168	Min-Max Machine Ltd—Randy Neubauer	1971 Pond Rd, Ronkonkoma NY 11779	631-585-4378	R	5*	<.1
169	Paragon Precision Inc—Allan Smith	25620 Rye Canyon Rd Bl, Valencia CA 91355	661-257-1380	R	5*	<.1
170	K L Steven Company Inc—Steven Weitz	PO Box 15155, Rio Rancho NM 87174	505-892-1353	R	5*	<.1
171	Marino Enterprises Inc—Thomas Marino	10671 Civic Ctr Dr, Rancho Cucamonga CA 91730	909-476-0343	R	5*	<.1
172	Mid-Central Manufacturing Inc—Linda Jackson	1935 W Walker St, Wichita KS 67213	316-265-0603	R	5*	<.1
173	Santos Precision Inc—Francisco Santos	2220 S Anne St, Santa Ana CA 92704	714-957-0299	R	5*	<.1
174	Flame Engineering Inc—R Pivonka	W Hwy 4, La Crosse KS 67548	785-222-2873	R	5*	<.1
175	Vantage Master Machine Co—Lou Alpinieri	900 Civic Ctr Dr, National City CA 91950	619-477-6940	R	5*	<.1
176	Cub Crafters Inc—James Richmond	1918 S 16th Ave, Yakima WA 98903	509-248-9491	R	5*	<.1
177	Equipment and Supply Inc—Andrew Adams	4507 W Hwy 74, Monroe NC 28110	704-289-6565	R	5*	<.1
178	Aero Cnc Inc—Mary Layne	PO Box 35, Burleson TX 76097	817-295-0184	R	5*	<.1
179	Southwest Machine and Plastic Company Inc—W Jorgensen	620 W Foothill Blvd, Glendora CA 91741	626-963-6919	R	4*	<.1
180	Bertrand Products Inc—Paul Bonin	PO Box 3786, South Bend IN 46619	574-234-4181	R	4*	<.1
181	Boniface Tool and Die Inc—Peter Didonato	PO Box 249, Southbridge MA 01550	508-764-3248	R	4*	<.1
182	Wilson's Machine Products Inc—Paul Adams	1844 Kentucky Ave, Winter Park FL 32789	407-644-2020	R	4*	<.1
183	R and B Electronics Inc—Debra Rogers	1520 Industrial Park D, Sault Sainte Marie MI 49783	906-632-1542	R	4*	.1
184	Carden Machine Shop Inc—Lois Carden	975 N Service Rd W, Sullivan MO 63080	573-468-4194	R	4*	<.1
185	Ramar-Hall Inc—Don King	PO Box 218, Middlefield CT 06455	860-349-1081	R	4*	<.1
186	Air-Lock Inc—John Bassick	PO Box 592, Milford CT 06460	203-878-4691	S	4*	<.1
187	Jay-Em Aerospace Corp—Michael Bell	75 Marc Dr, Cuyahoga Falls OH 44223	330-923-0333	R	4*	<.1
188	US Aerospace Inc—Jim Worsham	10291 Trademark St, Rancho Cucamonga CA 91730	909-477-6504	P	4	<.1
189	Victor-Balata Belting Co—Lawrence O'neill	1118 S 25th St, Easton PA 18042	610-258-2010	R	4*	<.1
190	Flexco Inc—Erik Moller	6855 Suva St, Bell Gardens CA 90201	562-927-2525	R	4*	<.1
191	Apache Enterprises Inc—Douglas Gadberry	2985 Red Hawk Dr, Grand Prairie TX 75052	972-641-0835	R	4*	<.1
192	Asturies Manufacturing Company Inc—Manuel Perez	310 Cessna Cir, Corona CA 92880	951-270-1766	R	4*	<.1
193	Volumatic Inc—Robert Schmucker	8219 Industrial Hwy, Macon GA 31216	478-781-9300	R	3*	<.1
194	Cardona Manufacturing Corp—Louis Cardona	1869 N Victory Pl, Burbank CA 91504	818-841-8358	R	3*	<.1
195	Satellite Tool and Machine Company Inc—Jan Lukasik	185 Commerce Way, South Windsor CT 06074	860-290-8558	R	3*	<.1
196	Johnson Caldraul Inc—Douglas Johnson	220 N Delilah St Ste 1, Corona CA 92879	951-340-1067	R	3*	<.1
197	Gali Corp—Gal Lipkin	2301 Pontius Ave, Los Angeles CA 90064	310-477-1224	R	3*	<.1
198	Trans-Cal Industries Inc—John Ferrero	16141 Cohasset St, Van Nuys CA 91406	818-787-1221	R	3*	<.1
199	Spaceage Control Inc—Tom Schnell	38850 20th St E, Palmdale CA 93550	661-273-3000	R	3*	<.1
200	Carolina Metals Inc—Alan Wagner	1398 Brevard Rd, Asheville NC 28806	828-667-0876	R	3*	<.1
201	Merco Manufacturing Co—Daryl Rossman	588 Porter Way, Placentia CA 92870	714-961-9200	R	3*	<.1
202	Excelco Developments Inc—Christopher Lanski	PO Box 230, Silver Creek NY 14136	716-934-2651	R	3*	<.1
203	Dukes Titan Aviation LLC—Gary Binkley	PO Box 80727, Rochester MI 48308	419-422-9653	R	3*	<.1
204	Robert's Precision Engineering Inc—Robert Flores	1345 S Allec St, Anaheim CA 92805	714-635-4485	R	2*	<.1
205	Usher Precision Manufacturing Inc—Karl Usher	3863 24th Ave, Forest Grove OR 97/116	503-992-0015	R	2*	<.1
206	Jerames Industries Inc—Robert Hubble	9424 Abraham Way Ste A, Santee CA 92071	619-448-1220	R	2*	<.1
207	Beta Engineering Inc—Steve Austin	468 Dodson Lake Dr, Arlington TX 76012	817-265-3367	R	2*	<.1
208	Ace Air Manufacturing—Roger Brandt	1430 W 135th St, Gardena CA 90249	310-323-7246	R	2*	<.1
209	Rickman Machine Company Inc—Fred Stuart	922 N Santa Fe St, Wichita KS 67214	316-263-0841	R	2*	<.1
210	Kilgore Machine Company Inc—Bryant Kilgore	2312 S Susan St, Santa Ana CA 92704	714-540-3659	R	2*	<.1
211	K-Jack Aero Industries LLC—Mony Barkol	1560 Moonstone, Brea CA 92821	714-578-1700	R	2*	<.1
212	Pynco Inc—Jim Seib	2605 35th St, Bedford IN 47421	812-275-0900	R	2*	<.1
213	Whiteco Inc—John Calvin	106 Garden Ln, La Follette TN 37766	423-562-1111	R	2*	<.1
214	Bishop Aviation Inc—Greg Bishop	506 Jack Mountain Rd, Hot Springs AR 71913	501-525-8228	R	2*	<.1
215	Anmar Precision Components Inc—Bruno Mudy	7424 Greenbush Ave, North Hollywood CA 91605	818-764-0901	R	1*	<.1
216	Machen Inc—Steven Speer	10555 Airport Dr, Hayden Lake ID 83835	208-762-7814	R	1*	<.1
217	Winding Specialists Company Inc—David Wills	1225 Wellington Pl, Wichita KS 67203	316-265-9358	R	1*	<.1
218	Lee Air Inc—Bennie Lee	4603 S Seneca St, Wichita KS 67217	316-524-4622	R	1*	<.1
219	Bbgn Inc—Glenn Schierhold	283 Corporate Way, Upland CA 91786	909-946-5959	R	1*	<.1
220	Sea West Products Inc—Cecil Green	8801 S 228th St, Kent WA 98031	253-854-2942	R	1*	<.1
221	Atacs Products Inc—Richard Imus	PO Box 88237, Seattle WA 98138	206-433-9000	R	1*	<.1
222	National Aircraft Service Inc—Wesley Plattner	9133 Tecumseh Clinton, Tecumseh MI 49286	517-423-7589	R	1*	<.1
223	Midwest Aircraft Products Company Inc—Jerry Miller	125 S Mill St, Mansfield OH 44904	419-884-2164	R	1*	<.1
224	Val Rollers Inc—William Williams	2345 N Butler Ave, Indianapolis IN 46218	317-542-1968	R	1*	<.1
225	Ack Technologies Inc—Michael Akatiff	440 W Julian St, San Jose CA 95110	408-287-8021	R	1*	<.1
226	Aero-Tec Industries Inc—Charles Harbert	PO Box 1216, Seminole OK 74818	405-382-8501	R	1*	<.1
227	Master Swaging Inc—Daniel Gilroy	PO Box 550, Jackson Center OH 45334	937-596-6171	R	1*	<.1
228	Pifers Airmotive Inc—Richard Pifer	1660 Airport Rd, Waterford MI 48327	248-674-0909	R	<1*	<.1
229	Inertial Airline Services Inc—Laurans A Mendelson	375 Alpha Park, Highland Heights OH 44143	440-995-6555	S	<1	<.1
230	MC Gill Corp—Stephen Gill	4056 Easy St, El Monte CA 91731	626-443-4022	R	N/A	.3
231	Philadelphia Bourse Inc	120 Sallitt Dr, Stevensville MD 21666	410-604-3780	R	N/A	.1

TOTALS: SIC 3728 Aircraft Parts & Equipment Nec
Companies: 231   40,681   154.9

3731 Ship Building & Repairing

Rank	Company Name—Executive Officer	Address, City, State, Zip	Phone	Type	Fin	Empls
1	Northrop Grumman Systems Corp	PO Box 149, Pascagoula MS 39568	310-553-6262	S	5,168*	18.0
2	BAE Systems Ship Repair—Bill Clifford	PO Box 2100, Norfolk VA 23501	757-494-4000	S	2,972*	5.0
3	National Steel and Shipbuilding Co—Frederick J Harris	PO Box 85278, San Diego CA 92186	619-544-3400	S	1,091*	3.0
4	Bath Iron Works Corp—Jeffrey Geiger	700 Washington St, Bath ME 04530	207-443-3311	S	1,000	N/A
5	TDI-Halter LP—Don Covington	PO Box 2367, Orange TX 77631	409-963-2001	R	998	7.0
6	Detyens Shipyards Inc—D Loy Stewart Jr	1670 Drydock Ave Bldg, North Charleston SC 29405	843-308-8000	R	367*	.8
7	U S Marine Inc—Brett Dungan	PO Box 307, Bayou La Batre AL 36509	251-824-4151	R	313*	<.1
8	Marine Hydraulics International Inc—Gary Brandt	543 E Indian River Rd, Norfolk VA 23523	757-545-6400	R	223*	.4
9	Bollinger Shipyards Inc—Donald Bollinger	PO Box 250, Lockport LA 70374	985-532-2554	R	217*	2.9
10	Vigor Shipyards—Stephen G Welch	1801 16th Ave SW, Seattle WA 98134	206-623-1635	R	180	.8
11	Caddell Dry Dock and Repair Company Inc—Steven Kalil	PO Box 327, Staten Island NY 10310	718-442-2112	R	169*	.2
12	Bae Systems Ship Repair Inc—Bill Clifford	PO Box 2100, Norfolk VA 23501	757-494-4000	R	159*	2.6
13	Conrad Industries Inc—John P Conrad Jr	1501 Front St, Morgan City LA 79380	985-384-3060	P	139	.4
14	Metro Machine Corp—Richard Goldbach	PO Box 1860, Norfolk VA 23501	757-543-6801	R	135*	.6
15	Bae Systems Norfolk Ship Repair Inc—William Clifford	PO Box 2100, Norfolk VA 23501	757-494-4000	R	130*	1.2

Rank	Company Name—*Executive Officer*	Address, City, State, Zip	Phone	Type	Fin	Empls
16	Swiftships Shipbuilders LLC—*Calvin Leleux*	PO Box 2869, Morgan City LA 70381	985-384-1700	R	98*	.2
17	Jeffboat LLC—*Mark Holden*	1701 E Market St, Jeffersonville IN 47130	812-288-0100	S	90	.8
18	Fountain Powerboats Inc—*Reginald M Fountain Jr* Fountain Powerboat Industries Inc	1653 Whichards Beach R, Chocowinity NC 27817	252-975-2000	S	69	N/A
19	Fountain Powerboat Industries Inc—*Reginald M Fountain Jr*	1653 Whichards Beach R, Washington NC 27889	252-975-2000	R	68	.3
20	Bae Systems Southeast Shipyards Alabama LLC—*Deborah Naron*	PO Box 3202, Mobile AL 36652	251-690-7100	R	65*	.6
21	Fraser Shipyards Inc—*James Korthals*	PO Box 997, Superior WI 54880	715-394-7787	R	56*	.3
22	Gulf Marine Repair Corp—*Aaron W Hendry*	1800 Grant St, Tampa FL 33605	813-247-3153	R	51*	.2
23	North Florida Shipyards Inc—*Matt Self*	PO Box 3255, Jacksonville FL 32206	904-354-3278	R	50*	.6
24	Bay Ship and Yacht Co—*William Elliott*	2900 Main St Ste 2100, Alameda CA 94501	510-337-9122	R	44*	.3
25	North American Shipbuilding LLC—*Gary Chouest*	PO Box 580, Larose LA 70373	985-693-4072	R	35*	.5
26	Cascade General Inc—*Frank Foti*	PO Box 4367, Portland OR 97208	503-285-1111	R	33*	.3
27	Bay Shipbuilding Co—*Todd Thayse*	PO Box 830, Sturgeon Bay WI 54235	920-743-5524	D	30*	.4
28	Leevac Industries LLC—*Jeryl Bertrand*	PO Box 1190, Jennings LA 70546	337-824-2210	R	30*	.2
29	Pacific Ship Repair and Fabrication Inc—*Gary Thomas*	PO Box 13428, San Diego CA 92170	619-232-3200	R	27*	.2
30	Hydraulic and Fabrication Services Inc—*Jeremy Youngblood*	2614 Industrial Ln, Conroe TX 77301	936-494-4322	R	25*	<.1
31	Lyon Shipyard Inc—*George Lyon*	1818 Brown Ave, Norfolk VA 23504	757-622-4661	R	24*	.2
32	Derecktor Robert E Inc—*Paul Derecktor*	311 E Boston Post Rd, Mamaroneck NY 10543	914-698-5020	R	22*	.1
33	Navatek Ltd—*Steven Loui* Pacific Marine and Supply Co	PO Box 29816, Honolulu HI 96820	808-531-7001	S	22*	<.1
34	Tampa Ship LLC—*Tony Pellegrino*	1130 Mcclosky Blvd, Tampa FL 33605	813-248-9310	R	22*	.3
35	Twin Brothers Marine LLC—*John Jenkins*	PO Box 2426, Morgan City LA 70381	337-923-4981	R	19*	.1
36	J M Martinac Shipbuilding Corp—*Joseph Martinac*	401 E 15th St, Tacoma WA 98421	253-572-4005	R	19*	.1
37	Bae Systems San Francisco Ship Repair Inc—*Hugh Vanderspek* Bae Systems Ship Repair Inc	PO Box 7644, San Francisco CA 94120	415-861-7447	S	16*	.2
38	Marisco Ltd—*Alfred Anawati*	91-607 Malakole St, Kapolei HI 96707	808-682-1333	R	15*	.1
39	Main Iron Works LLC	PO Box 1918, Houma LA 70361	985-876-6302	R	15*	.1
40	Buck Kreihs Marine Repair LLC—*Mike Tonguis*	PO Box 53305, New Orleans LA 70153	504-524-7681	R	14*	.1
41	Marine Industrial Fabrication Inc—*R Burton*	PO Box 9218, New Iberia LA 70562	337-369-7004	R	13*	.1
42	Alaska Ship And Drydock Inc—*Randall Johnson*	PO Box 9470, Ketchikan AK 99901	907-225-7199	R	12*	.1
43	B and D Marine And Industrial Boilers Inc—*Toby Kearney*	PO Box 71687, Charleston SC 29415	843-414-8500	R	12*	.1
44	Christensen Shipyards Ltd—*Joe Foggia*	4400 SE Columbia Way, Vancouver WA 98661	360-695-3238	R	11*	.2
45	PacOrd Inc—*Douglas Hawks*	2427 Hoover Ave, National City CA 91950	619-336-2200	S	10	.1
46	Pacific Marine and Supply Co—*Steven Loui*	841 Bishop St Ste 1110, Honolulu HI 96813	808-531-7001	R	10*	<.1
47	Larson Al Boat Shop—*John Wall*	1046 S Seaside Ave, San Pedro CA 90731	310-514-4100	R	9*	.1
48	Hendry Corp—*Aaron Hendry*	PO Box 75036, Tampa FL 33675	813-241-9206	R	8*	.1
49	Treadwell Corp—*John Johnson*	PO Box 458, Thomaston CT 06787	860-283-8251	R	7*	<.1
50	Northrop Grumman Shipbuilding Inc—*Mike Petters*	4101 Washington Ave, Newport News VA 23607	757-380-2000	S	7	N/A
51	Navtec Inc—*Phil Castell*	351 New Whitfield St, Guilford CT 06437	203-458-3163	R	6*	.1
52	Cleveland Ship LLC—*Edward L Bartlett Jr*	6100 Oak Tree Blvd Ste, Cleveland OH 44131	216-456-4285	R	5*	<.1
53	Rigdon Marine LLC—*Bruce Streeter*	815 Walker St Ste 1001, Houston TX 77002	713-236-9100	S	4*	<.1
54	Northlake Shipyard Inc—*E Peter Kelly*	1441 N Northlake Way, Seattle WA 98103	206-632-1441	R	4*	<.1
55	Technical Marine Service Inc—*Martin Wolf*	6040 N Cutter Cir Ste, Portland OR 97217	503-285-8947	R	3*	<.1
56	Intracoastal City Drydock And Shipbuilding Inc—*Lewis Faciane*	18938 Live Oak Rd, Abbeville LA 70510	337-893-4184	R	3*	<.1
57	Tampa Bay Shipbuilding and Repair Company Inc—*David Barnett*	2415 Blanding Blvd Ste, Jacksonville FL 32210	904-334-9593	R	1*	<.1
58	TNT Custom Marine Inc—*John Tomlinson*	3030 Ne 188th St, Miami FL 33180	305-931-3157	R	1*	<.1
59	Canvas and Upholstery Center Inc—*Joseph Bowman*	404 Riberia St, Saint Augustine FL 32084	904-826-3591	R	<1*	<.1

TOTALS: SIC 3731 Ship Building & Repairing
Companies: 59   14,342   49.9

3732 Boat Building & Repairing

Rank	Company Name—*Executive Officer*	Address, City, State, Zip	Phone	Type	Fin	Empls
1	General Dynamics Corp—*Jay L Johnson*	2941 Fairview Park Dr, Falls Church VA 22042	703-876-3000	P	32,466	90.0
2	Brunswick Corp—*Dustan E McCoy*	1 N Field Ct, Lake Forest IL 60045	847-735-4700	P	3,748	15.4
3	Sea Ray Boats Corp—*Rick Stone* Brunswick Corp	2600 Sea Ray Blvd, Knoxville TN 37914	865-522-4181	S	1,017*	1.8
4	Robalo Acquisition Company LLC—*Richard A Hubbell* Marine Products Corp	PO Box 928, Nashville GA 31639	229-686-2700	S	891*	1.1
5	Taylor Made Group Inc—*Dennis Flint*	66 Kingsboro Ave, Gloversville NY 12078	518-725-0681	R	799*	1.5
6	Bombardier Motor Corporation of America (Sturtevant Wisconsin)—*Pierre Beaudoin*	10101 Science Dr, Sturtevant WI 53177	262-884-5000	S	518*	.7
7	Four Winns Inc—*Jeff Olsen*	925 Frisbie St, Cadillac MI 49601	231-775-1343	R	474*	.9
8	Brunswick Corp US Marine Div—*Stephen M Wolpert* Brunswick Corp	PO Box 9029, Everett WA 98206	360-435-5571	D	450	2.5
9	Triton Boat LLC—*Earl Bentz*	880 Butler Dr, Murfreesboro TN 37127	615-895-5190	R	346*	.5
10	Bombardier Motor Corporation of America (Waukegan Illinois)—*Laurent Beaudoin*	300 E Sea Horse Dr, Waukegan IL 60085	847-689-6000	S	185*	.3
11	Trinity Yachts LLC—*Keith Morris*	13085 Seaway Rd, Gulfport MS 39503	228-276-1000	R	150*	.6
12	Genmar Michigan LLC—*Kelly Cater*	925 Frisbie St, Cadillac MI 49601	231-775-1351	R	115*	.9
13	Sea Fox Boat Company Inc—*Fred Renken*	2550 Hwy 52, Moncks Corner SC 29461	843-761-6090	R	114*	.2
14	Marine Products Corp—*Richard Hubbell*	2801 Buford Hwy NE Ste, Atlanta GA 30329	404-321-7910	P	106	.5
15	Premier Marine Inc—*Robert Menne*	26612 Fallbrook Ave, Wyoming MN 55092	651-462-2880	R	106*	.2
16	Viking Yacht Co—*William Healey*	9 Rt No and The Bass R, New Gretna NJ 08224	609-296-6000	R	89*	.7
17	Regal Marine Industries Inc—*Duane Kuck*	2300 Jetport Dr, Orlando FL 32809	407-851-4360	R	86*	.7
18	Old Town Canoe Co	PO Box 548, Old Town ME 04468	207-827-5514	S	86*	.2
19	Fiberglass Engineering Inc—*William StClair*	1715 N 8th St, Neodesha KS 66757	620-325-2653	R	78*	.7
20	Delta Marine Industries Inc—*Ivor Jones*	1608 S 96th St, Seattle WA 98108	206-763-2383	R	70*	.3
21	Glastron Inc—*Allen Keubelbeck*	PO Box 460, Little Falls MN 56345	320-632-8395	S	67*	.8
22	Catalina Yachts Inc—*Frank Butler*	21200 Victory Blvd, Woodland Hills CA 91367	818-884-7700	R	67*	.2
23	Kcs International Inc—*Jim Viestenz*	PO Box 78, Oconto WI 54153	920-834-2211	R	66*	1.0
24	Fishing Holdings LLC—*Randy Hopper*	PO Box 179, Flippin AR 72634	870-453-2222	R	60*	.4
25	Westport Shipyard Inc—*Daryl Wakefield*	1807 Nyhus Ave, Westport WA 98595	360-268-1800	R	53*	.7
26	Pro-Line Boats Inc—*John E Walker*	PO Box 1348, Crystal River FL 34423	352-795-4111	R	53*	.1
27	Mcbc Holdings Inc—*John Dorton*	100 Cherokee Cove Dr, Vonore TN 37885	423-884-2221	R	50*	1.1
28	Bertram Yacht Inc—*Norberto Ferretti*	PO Box 520774, Miami FL 33152	305-633-8011	R	49*	.4
29	Malibu Boats LLC—*Barry Bennett*	1 Malibu Ct, Merced CA 95341	209-383-7469	R	46*	.6
30	Pfc Inc—*James Fink*	PO Box 669, Hartsville SC 29551	843-383-3660	R	43*	.2

Note: An asterisk (*) indicates an estimated financial figure. The company type code used is as follows: R = Private, P = Public, S = Private Subsidiary, B = Public Subsidiary, D = Division, J = Joint Venture, I = Investment Fund.

COMPANY RANKINGS BY SALES WITHIN 4-DIGIT SIC

Rank	Company Name—*Executive Officer*	Address, City, State, Zip	Phone	Type	Fin	Empls
31	Dakota Creek Industries Inc—*Richard Nelson*	PO Box 218, Anacortes WA 98221	360-293-9575	R	40*	.6
32	Leisure Properties LLC—*Guy Coons*	11884 Country Club Rd, West Frankfort IL 62896	618-937-6426	R	37*	.6
33	Boston Whaler Inc—*Tim Schiek* Brunswick Corp	100 Whaler Way, Edgewater FL 32141	386-428-0057	D	34*	.3
34	Rinker Boat Company LLC—*Larry Deputy*	300 W Chicago St, Syracuse IN 46567	574-457-5731	R	31*	.5
35	Hinckley Co—*Ralph Willard*	PO Box 699, Southwest Harbor ME 04679	207-244-5531	R	30*	<.1
36	Shipbuilders Of Wisconsin Inc—*James Ruffolo*	1811 Spring St, Manitowoc WI 54220	920-684-1600	R	29*	.5
37	Contender Boats Inc—*Joseph Neber*	1820 Se 38th Ave, Homestead FL 33035	305-230-1600	R	28*	.2
38	Skeeter Products Inc—*Jeff Stone*	1 Skeeter Rd, Kilgore TX 75662	903-984-0541	R	27*	.2
39	Alumacraft Boat Co—*David Benbow*	315 Saint Julien St, Saint Peter MN 56082	507-931-1050	R	27*	.2
40	Skier's Choice Inc—*Rick Tinker*	1717 Henry G Ln St, Maryville TN 37801	865-983-9924	R	26*	.2
41	Ocean Yachts Inc—*John Leek*	PO Box 312, Egg Harbor City NJ 08215	609-965-4616	R	25*	.2
42	Rybovich Spencer—*Wayne Huizenga Jr*	4200 N Flagler Dr, West Palm Beach FL 33407	561-844-1800	R	25*	.2
43	Beneteau USA Inc—*Wayne Burdick*	1313 W Hwy 76, Marion SC 29571	843-629-5300	S	25*	.2
44	Hunter Marine Corp—*Daniel Jett*	PO Box 1030, Alachua FL 32616	386-462-3077	R	23*	.4
45	Stardust Cruisers Inc—*Terrry Aff*	110 Stardust Ave, Monticello KY 42633	606-348-8466	R	23*	.2
46	Silverton Marine Corp—*John Luhrs*	301 Riverside Dr, Millville NJ 08332	856-825-4117	R	23*	.4
47	Knight and Carver Yachtcenter Inc—*Michael Oldery*	1313 Bay Marina Dr, National City CA 91950	619-336-4141	R	22*	.2
48	Parker Marine Enterprises Inc—*E Parker*	PO Box 2129, Beaufort NC 28516	252-728-5621	R	21*	.2
49	Bradford Yacht Limited Inc—*Dieter Cosman*	3051 W State Rd 84, Fort Lauderdale FL 33312	954-791-3800	R	21*	.2
50	Quality Shipyards LLC—*Joseph Badeaux*	PO Box 1817, Houma LA 70361	985-876-4846	S	20*	.2
51	Ebbtide Corp—*Thomas Trabue*	2545 Jones Creek Rd, White Bluff TN 37187	615-797-3193	R	20*	.2
52	Sumerset Acquisition LLC—*Steve Lochmueller*	200 Sumerset Blvd, Somerset KY 42501	606-679-9393	R	18*	.2
53	Teledyne Webb Research—*Thomas W Altshuler*	82 Technology Park Dr, East Falmouth MA 02536	508-548-2077	S	18*	<.1
54	Mainship Corp—*Bill Finney*	404 Riberia St, Saint Augustine FL 32084	904-829-0500	R	18*	.4
55	Moss Point Marine Inc	PO Box 1328, Pascagoula MS 39568	228-696-6888	S	17	.2
56	Destination Outdoors Inc—*John Rukavina*	111 Kayaker Way, Easley SC 29642	864-859-7518	R	17*	.5
57	Derecktor-Gunnell Inc—*Eric Derecktor*	775 Taylor Ln, Dania FL 33004	954-920-5756	R	16*	.1
58	Jupiter Marine International Holdings Inc—*Carl Herndon Sr*	1103 12th Ave E, Palmetto FL 34221	941-729-5000	P	15	N/A
59	Leisure Life Ltd—*Sandy Spielmaker*	4855 Broadmoor Ave SE, Grand Rapids MI 49512	616-698-3000	S	14*	.1
60	Avalon and Tahoe Manufacturing Inc—*Jim Wolf*	PO Box 698, Alma MI 48801	989-463-2112	R	14*	.1
61	Hewes Marine Company Inc—*Dave Hewes*	2600 N Hwy, Colville WA 99114	509-684-5235	R	14*	.1
62	Merrill-Stevens Dry Dock Co—*Fred Kirtland*	1270 Nw 11th St, Miami FL 33125	305-324-5211	R	14*	.1
63	Maverick Boat Company Inc—*Douglas Deal*	3207 Industrial 29th S, Fort Pierce FL 34946	772-465-0631	R	13*	.1
64	IJ Holdings Corp—*Roger Cloutier II*	80 S 8th St, Minneapolis MN 55402	612-339-7900	R	13*	.1
65	Fairpint Yachts Ltd—*Timothy Jackett*	1920 Fairport Nursery, Painesville OH 44077	440-354-3111	R	12*	.1
66	Willard Marine Inc—*Jojo Nery*	1250 N Grove St, Anaheim CA 92806	714-666-2150	R	12*	.1
67	Northport Corporation Of StCloud—*Dan Boettcher*	PO Box 380, Gillett WI 54124	920-855-2168	R	11*	.1
68	Robert E Derecktor Inc—*E Derecktor*	311 E Boston Post Rd, Mamaroneck NY 10543	914-698-5020	R	11*	.1
69	Gulf Craft LLC—*Kevin Tibbs*	3904 Hwy 182 W, Patterson LA 70392	985-395-5254	R	10*	.1
70	Hodgdon Yachts Inc—*Timothy Hodgdon*	PO Box 505, East Boothbay ME 04544	207-633-4194	R	10*	.1
71	Key West Boats Inc—*William Holseberg*	PO Box 399, Ridgeville SC 29472	843-873-0112	R	9*	.1
72	Novurania Of America Inc—*Robert Collada*	2105 S Us Hwy 1, Vero Beach FL 32962	772-567-9200	R	9*	.1
73	Hc Composites LLC—*Bicky Pittman*	1090 W Saint James St, Tarboro NC 27886	252-641-8000	R	9*	.1
74	Macgregor Yacht Corp—*Roger Gregor*	1631 Placentia Ave, Costa Mesa CA 92627	949-642-6830	R	9*	.1
75	North End Composites LLC—*Christopher Evans*	PO Box 548, Rockland ME 04841	207-594-8821	R	8*	.1
76	Angler Boat Corp—*Gerritt Walsh*	4450 Nw 128th St, Opa Locka FL 33054	305-691-9975	R	7*	.1
77	Kaye Sandy Enterprises Inc—*Alex Kaye*	1074 Independence Ave, Mountain View CA 94043	650-961-5334	R	4*	<.1
78	Checkmate Boats Inc—*William Combs*	3691 State Rte 4, Bucyrus OH 44820	419-562-3881	R	4*	<.1
79	Carstens Industries Inc—*James Carstens*	P O Box 185, Melrose MN 56352	320-256-3919	R	4*	<.1
80	S 2 Yachts Inc—*Robert Slikkers*	725 E 40th St, Holland MI 49423	616-392-7163	R	4*	.9
81	Adept Process Services Inc—*Jack Van Zandt*	PO Box 2130, Imperial Beach CA 91933	619-434-3194	R	4*	<.1
82	Douglas Marine Corp—*Peter Hledin*	PO Box 819, Douglas MI 49406	269-857-4308	R	3*	<.1
83	Controls Engineering Maintenance Corp—*Coleman Mcswain*	105 S 31st St, San Diego CA 92113	619-557-8373	R	3*	<.1
84	Magnum Marine Corp—*Katrin Theodoli*	2900 Ne 188th St, Miami FL 33180	305-931-4292	R	3*	<.1
85	Marquis Yachts LLC—*Paul Prestin*	PO Box 1010, Pulaski WI 54162	920-822-3214	R	1*	<.1
86	IPV Inc—*William Parker*	PO Box 232, Vivian LA 71082	318-375-3241	R	1*	.2

TOTALS: SIC 3732 Boat Building & Repairing
    Companies: 86   43,353   134.5

3743 Railroad Equipment

Rank	Company Name—*Executive Officer*	Address, City, State, Zip	Phone	Type	Fin	Empls
1	Washington Div—*Tom Zarges*	PO Box 73, Boise ID 83729	208-386-5000	D	3,398*	25.0
2	Trinity Industries Inc—*Timothy R Wallace*	PO Box 568887, Dallas TX 75356	214-631-4420	P	3,075	13.4
3	Westinghouse Air Brake Technologies Corp—*Albert J Neupaver*	1001 Air Brake Ave, Wilmerding PA 15148	412-825-1000	P	1,968	8.5
4	Progress Rail Services Corp—*William Ainsworth*	PO Box 1037, Albertville AL 35950	256-593-1260	S	1,290*	4.1
5	Greenbrier Companies Inc—*William A Furman*	1 Centerpointe Dr Ste, Lake Oswego OR 97035	503-684-7000	P	1,243	6.0
6	GE Transportation Systems—*Lorenzo Simonelli*	2901 East Lake Rd, Erie PA 16531	814-875-2234	S	747*	8.0
7	AFC Industries LLC—*James E Bowles*	101 Clark St, Saint Charles MO 63301	636-949-2399	R	579*	.5
8	Motive Power Inc (Boise Idaho)—*Mark Warner* Westinghouse Air Brake Technologies Corp	4600 Apple St, Boise ID 83716	208-947-4800	S	544*	.3
9	American Railcar Industries Inc—*James Cowan*	100 Clark St, Saint Charles MO 63301	636-940-6000	P	274	1.6
10	Loram Maintenance Of Way Inc—*Phil Homan*	PO Box 188, Hamel MN 55340	763-478-6014	R	193*	.7
11	Kawasaki Rail Car Inc—*Matichi Sakai*	29 Wells Ave Bldg 4, Yonkers NY 10701	914-376-4700	S	165*	.4
12	FreightCar America Inc—*Michael MacMahon*	2 N Riverside Pl Ste 1, Chicago IL 60606	312-928-0850	P	143	.5
13	Alstom Signaling Inc—*Patrick Kron*	1025 John St, West Henrietta NY 14586	585-783-2000	S	107*	.5
14	Portec Rail Products Inc—*Richard J Jarosinsk*	PO Box 38250, Pittsburgh PA 15238	412-782-6000	S	92	.3
15	Ellcon-National Inc—*David Rose*	PO Box 9377, Greenville SC 29604	864-277-5000	R	77*	.3
16	Trinity Rail Group—*Timothy Wallace* Trinity Industries Inc	2525 Stemmons Freeway, Dallas TX 75207	214-589-8451	S	70*	.4
17	Harsco Track Technologies—*Robert Newman*	2401 Edmund Rd, Cayce-West Columbia SC 29171	803-822-9160	D	60*	.3
18	Dynamic Corp	4750 Swisher Rd, West Lafayette IN 47906	765-742-4410	S	57*	.1
19	Miner Enterprises Inc—*David Withall*	PO Box 471, Geneva IL 60134	630-232-3000	R	42*	.3
20	Graham-White Manufacturing Co—*James Frantz*	PO Box 1099, Salem VA 24153	540-387-5600	R	29*	.3
21	Railway and Industrial Services Inc—*Richard Vetter*	2201 N Ctr St, Joliet IL 60403	815-726-4224	R	16*	.1
22	Shuttlewagon Inc—*Ed Harbour*	PO Box 777, Grandview MO 64030	816-767-0300	S	15*	.1
23	Coast Engine and Equipment Corp—*David Swanson*	PO Box 16630, Missoula MT 59808	253-922-5955	R	13*	.1
24	United Knitting Machine Company Inc—*Frank Weisbecker*	PO Box 309, Kulpsville PA 19443	215-256-4800	R	8*	<.1
25	LB Foster Co Allegheny Rail Products Div—*Stan Hasselbusch*	415 Holiday Dr Ste 1, Pittsburgh PA 15220	412-928-3500	D	8	<.1
26	Miller Felpax Corp—*Steve Blue*	PO Box 558, Winona MN 55987	507-452-2461	R	7*	.1
27	J and A Industries Inc—*James Ferree*	14 S Ewing St, Kansas City KS 66118	913-281-5722	R	3*	<.1

Rank	Company Name—Executive Officer	Address, City, State, Zip	Phone	Type	Fin	Empls
28	Dwight and Wilson Co—Julio Rubio	PO Box 5190, Lighthouse Point FL 33074	954-942-8321	R	1*	<.1
29	Robinette Inc—David Gaydos	PO Box 464, Medina OH 44258	330-725-0126	R	<1*	<.1

TOTALS: SIC 3743 Railroad Equipment
Companies: 29 — 14,224 — 71.5

3751 Motorcycles, Bicycles & Parts						
1	Harley-Davidson Motor Co—James Ziemer Harley-Davidson Inc	3700 W Juneau Ave, Milwaukee WI 53208	414-343-4056	S	11,944*	7.0
2	Harley-Davidson Inc—Keith E Wandell	PO Box 653, Milwaukee WI 53201		P	4,859	6.3
3	SRAM Corp—Stan Day Jr	1333 N Kingsbury 4th F, Chicago IL 60642	312-664-8800	R	1,090*	1.0
4	Huffy Bicycle Co—Bill Smith	6551 Centerville Busin, Centerville OH 45459	937-865-2800	S	561	3.7
5	Trek Bicycle Corp—John Burke	801 W Madison St, Waterloo WI 53594	920-478-2191	R	293*	1.1
6	Specialized Bicycle Components Inc—Mike Sinyard	15130 Concord Cir, Morgan Hill CA 95037	408-779-6229	R	292*	.3
7	RockShox Inc—Stanley R Day Jr SRAM Corp	1333 N Kingsbury, Chicago IL 60622	312-664-8800	S	74	.3
8	K and N Engineering Inc—Steven Rogers	1455 N Citrus St, Riverside CA 92507	951-826-4100	R	43*	.6
9	Pacific Cycle Inc—Alice Tillett	4902 Hammersley Rd, Madison WI 53711		S	42*	.1
10	Custom Chrome Manufacturing Inc—Megan Williams	16100 Jacqueline Ct, Morgan Hill CA 95037	408-825-5000	R	41*	.2
11	Performance Machine Inc—Perry Sands	6892 Marlin Cir, La Palma CA 90623	714-523-3000	S	25*	.2
12	Markland Industries Inc—Donald Markland	1111 E Mcfadden Ave, Santa Ana CA 92705	714-245-4923	R	24*	.2
13	Persons-Majestic Manufacturing Co	PO Box 370, Huron OH 44839	419-433-9057	S	24*	.2
14	Fmf Racing—Don Emler	18033 S Santa Fe Ave, Compton CA 90221	310-631-4363	R	19*	.2
15	Thiessen Products Inc—Jim Thiessen	555 Dawson Dr Ste A, Camarillo CA 93012	805-482-6913	R	16*	.1
16	All American Racers Inc—Daniel Gurney	PO Box 2186, Santa Ana CA 92707	714-540-1771	R	15*	.1
17	Corbin Pacific Inc—Michael Hanagan	2360 Technology Pkwy, Hollister CA 95023	831-634-1100	R	12*	.1
18	Radio Sound Inc—R Northup	1713 Cobalt Dr, Louisville KY 40299	502-267-6768	R	9*	.1
19	Klein Bicycle Corporation Of Washington—John Burke	801 W Madison St, Waterloo WI 53594	920-478-4676	R	7*	.1
20	Paladin Holdings Inc—Larry Lunan	2344 Woodridge Ave, Kingsport TN 37664	423-247-9560	P	6	.9
21	D S Manufacturing Inc—James Preisler	67 5th St Ne, Pine Island MN 55963	507-356-8322	R	6*	.1
22	Danbar Equipment Company Inc—Tom Fisher	744 W Crescent Ave, Mesa AZ 85210	480-834-2990	R	5*	.1
23	Bike Track Inc—Barry McVey	PO Box 235, Woodstock VT 05091	802-457-3275	R	5*	<.1
24	Torelli Imports—Todd Linscott	10717 Chandler Blvd, North Hollywood CA 91601	818-508-0216	R	4*	<.1
25	ZAP (Santa Rosa California)—Steven M Schneider	501 4th St, Santa Rosa CA 95401	707-525-8658	P	4	<.1
26	IMS Products Inc—Scott Wright	6240 Box Springs Blvd, Riverside CA 92507		R	3*	<.1
27	Amarillo Mop and Broom Company Inc—E Bryan	PO Box 30098, Amarillo TX 79120	806-372-8596	R	1*	<.1
28	AC International Inc—Randy Kirk	PO Box 60307, Pasadena CA 91116	805-962-2328	R	1*	<.1
29	Tri-Con Industries Ltd—Iwao Miyajima	4000 Nw 44th St, Lincoln NE 68524	402-470-3311	R	1*	<.1

TOTALS: SIC 3751 Motorcycles, Bicycles & Parts
Companies: 29 — 19,426 — 22.9

3761 Guided Missiles & Space Vehicles						
1	Lockheed Martin Missiles/Space Co—Robert J Stevens	PO Box 3504, Sunnyvale CA 94088	408-742-4321	S	2,277*	16.1
2	Lockheed Martin Astronautics—Robert J Stephens	PO Box 179, Denver CO 80201	303-977-3000	S	1,574*	8.0
3	Orbital Sciences Corporation Launch Systems Group—David W Thompson	3380 S Price Rd, Chandler AZ 85248	480-899-6000	S	807*	3.7
4	L'Garde Inc—Gayle Bilyeu	15181 Woodlawn Ave, Tustin CA 92780	714-259-0771	R	170*	<.1
5	SpaceDev Inc—Fatih Ozmen	13855 Stowe Dr, Poway CA 92064	858-375-2000	S	35	.2
6	Astrotech Corp—Thomas B Pickens	401 Congress Ave Ste 1, Austin TX 78701	512-485-9530	P	20	.1
7	Blue Origin LLC—Gail Fox	21218 76th Ave S, Kent WA 98032	253-872-0411	R	14*	.1
8	Aero Astro Inc—Paul Lithgow	20145 Ashbrook Pl, Ashburn VA 20147	703-554-6361	S	9	.1
9	Lane Industries Inc—Steven Lane	500 Mile Crossing Blvd, Rochester NY 14624	585-247-5940	R	5*	.1

TOTALS: SIC 3761 Guided Missiles & Space Vehicles
Companies: 9 — 4,911 — 28.3

3764 Space Propulsion Units & Parts						
1	GenCorp Inc—Scott J Seymour	PO Box 537012, Sacramento CA 95853	916-355-4000	P	918	3.3
2	Williams International Company LLC—Roger Cochran	PO Box 200, Walled Lake MI 48390	248-624-5200	R	250*	.8
3	Ampac-Isp Corporation LLC—Martin Weinstein	6686 Walmore Rd, Niagara Falls NY 14304	716-731-6000	D	7*	.1
4	Innovation Marine Corp—Richard Lamore	8011 15th St E, Sarasota FL 34243	941-355-7852	R	3*	<.1

TOTALS: SIC 3764 Space Propulsion Units & Parts
Companies: 4 — 1,178 — 4.1

3769 Space Vehicle Equipment Nec						
1	Ball Aerospace and Technologies Corp—David L Taylor	PO Box 1062, Boulder CO 80301	303-939-6100	S	605*	2.7
2	Aerojet—Scott Seymour	PO Box 13222, Sacramento CA 95813	916-355-4000	S	373*	2.7
3	Lockheed Martin Michoud Operations	PO Box 29304, New Orleans LA 70189	504-257-3311	S	355*	2.0
4	Aerostructures Corp—Jeffry D Frisby	1431 Vultee Blvd, Nashville TN 37217	615-361-2000	S	272*	1.2
5	BAE Systems Platform Solutions—Sean Bond	600 Main St, Johnson City NY 13790	607-770-2000	D	258*	1.4
6	Barnes Aerospace Corp—Brent Wiberg	169 Kennedy Rd, Windsor CT 06095	860-298-7740	D	230*	1.0
7	Hoke Inc (Spartanburg South Carolina)—David A Bloss Circle Seal Controls Inc	PO Box 4866, Spartanburg SC 29305	864-574-7966	S	86*	.5
8	Pratt and Whitney Rocketdyne Inc—David Hess	PO Box 49028, San Jose CA 95161	408-776-5789	D	56*	.3
9	Circle Seal Controls Inc—Carl Nasca	PO Box 3300, Corona CA 92878	951-270-6200	D	33*	.3
10	Aeroflex New Century—Michael Gorin	400 New Century Pky, New Century KS 66031	913-764-2452	S	32*	.2
11	Certified Fabricators Inc—Joseph Lauderdale	6530 Altura Blvd, Buena Park CA 90620	714-670-1491	S	29*	.2
12	Fiber Materials Inc—Spencer Tolis	5 Morin St, Biddeford ME 04005	207-282-5911	R	27*	.2
13	Gentz Industries LLC—Randy Borieo	25250 Easy St, Warren MI 48089	586-772-2500	R	27*	.2
14	Kreisler Industrial Corp—Michael Stern	180 Van Riper Ave, Elmwood Park NJ 07407	201-791-0700	S	25*	.1
15	LPI Corp—James Roubian	3000 Taft St, Hollywood FL 33021	954-989-3399	S	23*	.1
16	Astro Aerospace—Chris Yamada	6384 Via Real, Carpinteria CA 93013	805-684-6641	S	22*	.1
17	Ac Inc—George Smith	PO Box 17069, Huntsville AL 35810	256-851-9020	R	18*	.2
18	Barnes Aerospace Lansing Div—Greg Milzik Barnes Aerospace Corp	169 Kennedy Rd, Windsor CT 06095	860-298-7740	D	18	.1
19	Competitive Engineering Inc—Don Martin	3371 E Hemisphere Loop, Tucson AZ 85706	520-746-0270	R	14*	.1
20	American Automated Engineering Inc—Kenneth Christensen	5382 Argosy Ave, Huntington Beach CA 92649	714-898-9951	R	12*	.1
21	Hi-Shear Technology Corp—George W Trahan	24225 Garnier St, Torrance CA 90505	310-784-2100	S	11	.1
22	Associated Technologies Inc—Jake Johnston	2632 Saturn St, Brea CA 92821	714-996-8178	R	8*	.1
23	Honeybee Robotics Ltd—Kiel Davis	460 W 34th St, New York NY 10001	212-966-0661	R	4*	<.1

Note: An asterisk (*) indicates an estimated financial figure. The company type code used is as follows: R = Private, P = Public, S = Private Subsidiary, B = Public Subsidiary, D = Division, J = Joint Venture, I = Investment Fund.

COMPANY RANKINGS BY SALES WITHIN 4-DIGIT SIC

Rank	Company Name—Executive Officer	Address, City, State, Zip	Phone	Type	Fin	Empls
24	Lynch Brothers Manufacturing Co—Wayne Craig	4045 W Washington St, Phoenix AZ 85009	602-267-7575	R	4*	<.1
25	Micro Steel Inc—Lazar Hersko	7850 Alabama Ave, Canoga Park CA 91304	818-348-8701	R	4*	<.1
26	Cliffdale Manufacturing Inc—James Hart	20409 Prairie St, Chatsworth CA 91311	818-341-3344	R	4*	<.1
27	M-Tron Manufacturing—Robert Mcsweeney	625 Arroyo St, San Fernando CA 91340	818-361-7133	R	4*	<.1
28	Hi-Tech Machining and Engineering LLC—Celia Penn	1075 E Wieding Rd, Tucson AZ 85706	520-889-8325	R	3*	<.1
29	Energy Research and Generation Inc—Burton O Benson	900 Stanford Ave, Oakland CA 94608	510-658-9785	R	2*	<.1

TOTALS: SIC 3769 Space Vehicle Equipment Nec
Companies: 29   2,556   13.9

3792 Travel Trailers & Campers

Rank	Company Name—Executive Officer	Address, City, State, Zip	Phone	Type	Fin	Empls
1	Truck Accessories Group Inc—John Poindexter	PO Box 1128, Elkhart IN 46515	574-522-5337	R	756*	.8
2	Jayco Inc—Derald Bontrager	PO Box 460, Middlebury IN 46540	574-825-5861	R	668*	1.8
3	Airstream Inc—Bob Wheeler	PO Box 629, Jackson Center OH 45334		S	523*	.4
4	Starcraft RV Inc—Don Walter	PO Box 460, Middlebury IN 46540		R	117*	.4
5	Keystone RV Co—Ronald J Fenech	PO Box 2000, Goshen IN 46526	574-535-2100	S	101*	.4
6	Skyline Corp Nomad Div—Thomas G Deranek	PO Box 360, McMinnville OR 97128	503-472-3101	S	101*	.1
7	Northwood Manufacturing—Ron Nash	PO Box 3359, La Grande OR 97850	541-962-6274	R	68*	.4
8	Kit Home Builders West LLC—John W Hinrichs	PO Box 250, Caldwell ID 83606	208-454-5000	R	42	.4
9	Extreme RV's LLC—Don Day	PO Box 1420, Caldwell ID 83606	208-453-2500	R	35*	.1
10	Nu-Wa Industries Inc—Michael Mitchell	3701 S Johnson Rd, Chanute KS 66720	620-431-2088	R	32*	.4
11	Carriage Inc—Glenn Cushman	PO Box 246, Millersburg IN 46543	574-642-3622	R	31*	.2
12	Komfort Corp—Wade FB Thompson	12628 SE Jennifer St, Clackamas OR 97015	503-722-5199	S	31*	.2
13	Lippert Components Inc—Jason Lippert	1818 SW 9th Ave, Ocala FL 34471	352-629-5300	S	25*	.1
14	Vanguard LLC—Wanda Moyer	1047 E M 86, Colon MI 49040	269-432-3271	R	21*	.2
15	Lance Camper Manufacturing Corp—Jack Cole	43120 Venture St, Lancaster CA 93535	661-949-3322	R	21*	.3
16	Kzrv LP—Mark Campbell	985 N 900 W, Shipshewana IN 46565	260-768-4016	R	19*	.3
17	Dynamax Corp—Dewayne Creighton	PO Box 875, Elkhart IN 46515	574-262-3474	R	17*	.2
18	Chariot Eagle Inc—Robert Holliday	931 Nw 37th Ave, Ocala FL 34475	352-629-7007	R	16*	.1
19	Peterson Industries Inc—Bryan Tillett	616 E Hwy 36, Smith Center KS 66967	785-282-6825	R	14*	.2
20	Jason Industries Inc—Lon Franklin	1500 W Lusher Ave, Elkhart IN 46517	574-294-7595	R	13*	.1
21	Dodgen Industries Inc—John Dodgen	PO Box 39, Humboldt IA 50548	515-332-3755	R	13*	.1
22	Viking RV LLC—Garr Warlick	PO Box 549, Centreville MI 49032	269-467-6321	S	12*	.1
23	Astro Cap Manufacturing-West Inc—Bobby Combs	210 S Catalpa St, Garnett KS 66032	785-448-5577	R	12*	.1
24	Boston Trailer Manufacturing	1 Production Rd, Walpole MA 02081	508-668-2242	R	9	.1
25	Ranch Fiberglass Inc—Walter Stankovich	28564 Holiday Pl, Elkhart IN 46517	574-294-7550	R	8*	.1
26	Livin' Lite Recreational Vehicles—Scott Tuttle	PO Box 528, Wakarusa IN 46573	574-862-2228	R	5	.1
27	Play'mor Trailers Inc—John Willibrand	PO Box 128, Westphalia MO 65085	573-455-2387	R	5*	.1
28	Eagle Craft Inc—Charles Wicks	904 Markley Dr, Plymouth IN 46563	574-936-3196	R	2*	<.1

TOTALS: SIC 3792 Travel Trailers & Campers
Companies: 28   2,717   7.5

3795 Tanks & Tank Components

Rank	Company Name—Executive Officer	Address, City, State, Zip	Phone	Type	Fin	Empls
1	General Dynamics Land Systems Inc—Mark Roualet	PO Box 2074, Warren MI 48090	586-825-4000	S	674*	7.4
2	Palomar Medical Technologies Inc—Joseph P Caruso	15 Network Dr, Burlington MA 01803	781-993-2300	P	64	.2
3	Hardwire LLC—George C Tunis III	1947 Clarke Ave, Pocomoke MD 21851	410-957-3669	R	22*	<.1
4	Sioux Manufacturing Corp—Carl Mckay	1115 Dakotah Dr, Fort Totten ND 58335	701-766-4211	R	20*	.2
5	Tarsco Inc—Terry Warren	11905 Regentview Ave, Downey CA 90241	562-231-5400	R	18*	.1
6	Protectoseal Co—James Honan	PO Box 95588, Chicago IL 60694	630-595-0800	R	13*	.1
7	Lourdes Industries Inc—William Jakobsen	65 Hoffman Ave, Hauppauge NY 11788	631-234-6600	R	11*	.1

TOTALS: SIC 3795 Tanks & Tank Components
Companies: 7   822   8.1

3799 Transportation Equipment Nec

Rank	Company Name—Executive Officer	Address, City, State, Zip	Phone	Type	Fin	Empls
1	Polaris Industries Inc—Scott W Wine	2100 Hwy 55, Medina MN 55340	763-542-0500	P	2,657	3.9
2	San Joaquin Helicopters—James Josephson	1407 S Lexington St, Delano CA 93215	661-725-1898	R	834*	.3
3	Jacobsen Division of Textron Inc—David Withers	3800 Arco Corporation, Charlotte NC 28273	704-504-6600	D	554	.6
4	Arctic Cat Inc—Claude J Jordan	PO Box 810, Thief River Falls MN 56701	218-681-8558	P	465	1.3
5	Kawasaki Motors Manufacturing Corporation USA—Shrio Noiri	PO Box 81469, Lincoln NE 68501	402-476-6600	NE	175*	2.0
6	Sooner Trailer Manufacturing Co—Jim Garis	1515 McCurdy, Duncan OK 73533	580-255-6979	R	147*	.4
7	Exiss Aluminum Trailers Inc—Rodney Culp	900 E Trail Blvd, El Reno OK 73036	405-262-6471	S	55	.5
8	Midwest Industries Inc—Andy Brosius	122 E State Hwy 175, Ida Grove IA 51445	712-364-3365	R	54*	.3
9	Cequent Performance Products—Grant H Beard	PO Box 8, Mosinee WI 54455	715-693-1700	S	51	.3
10	EZ Loader Boat Trailers Inc—Randy Johnson	PO Box 3263, Spokane WA 99220	509-489-0181	R	51*	.4
11	Karavan Trailers Inc—Scott Boyd	PO Box 27, Fox Lake WI 53933	920-928-6200	R	29*	.2
12	Westman Freightliner Inc—Jerry Westman	2200 4th Ave, Mankato MN 56001		R	24*	.1
13	AL-KO KOBER Corp (Elkhart Indiana)	PO Box 1367, Elkhart IN 46515	574-294-6651	S	20*	.1
14	W - W Trailer Manufacturers Inc—H Watkins	PO Box 807, Madill OK 73446	580-795-5571	R	17*	.2
15	Load Rite Trailers Inc—Bill Merkel	265 Lincoln Hwy, Fairless Hills PA 19030	215-949-0500	R	16*	.1
16	Rolligon Corp—Mike Dearing	6740 Hwy 30, Anderson TX 77830	936-873-2600	R	14*	.1
17	Scaletta Moloney Armoring Corp—Suzanne Scaletta	6755 S Belt Cir Dr, Bedford Park IL 60638	708-924-0099	R	13*	.1
18	Triton Corp—Rochelle Priesgen	857 W State St, Hartford WI 53027	262-670-6514	R	12*	.1
19	Columbia Parcar Corp—Todd Sauey	PO Box 60, Reedsburg WI 53959	608-524-8888	R	12*	.1
20	Leitner-Poma Of America Inc—Rick Spear	2746 Seeber St Bldg A, Grand Junction CO 81506	970-241-4442	S	10*	.1
21	EZ Way Inc—Bill Lisle	PO Box 89, Clarinda IA 51632	712-542-5102	R	9*	.1
22	Miles Electric Vehicles—Miles Rubin	31324 Via Colinas Ste, Westlake Village CA 92362	818-879-1721	R	8*	<.1
23	CCI Manufacturing—Jane Wear	1770 E Smith St, Warsaw IN 46580	574-267-6900	D	7*	.1
24	Performance Metal Works Inc—Royce Patterson	PO Box 1338, Winnsboro TX 75494	903-967-2622	R	7*	.1
25	TJT Inc—Jerome B Light	843 N Washington Ave, Emmett ID 83617		P	6	<.1
26	Charmac Inc—Lloyd Casperson	PO Box 205, Twin Falls ID 83303	208-733-5241	R	5*	.1
27	Western Construction Components Inc—George Wilson	13465 Cmino Cnada Ste, El Cajon CA 92021	619-596-5696	R	5*	.1
28	Spreuer and Son Inc—Ron Troyer	115 E Spring St, Lagrange IN 46761	260-463-3513	R	4*	<.1
29	J-Rod Inc—Raymon Hunt	398 N Intrstate 35 Svc, Red Oak TX 75154	972-617-3770	R	3*	<.1
30	Green Valley Manufacturing Inc—Robert Johnston	100 Green Valley Dr, Mount Zion IL 62549	217-864-4125	R	3*	<.1
31	Hlt Ltd—Carl Crewson	PO Box 569, Humboldt IA 50548	515-332-1802	R	3*	.1
32	Quadra Manufacturing Inc—Eugene Lehman	PO Box 536, White Pigeon MI 49099	269-483-9633	R	2*	<.1
33	Currahee Trailers Inc—Chet Barrett	850 Tommy Irvin Rd, Mount Airy GA 30563	706-754-5396	R	2*	<.1
34	Jerald Inc—Todd Gordon	3050 Wagner Rd, Waterloo IA 50703	319-234-6195	R	2*	<.1
35	Mirage Enterprises Inc—Rob Swikert	2212 Industrial Rd, Nampa ID 83687	208-461-7776	R	1*	<.1

Rank	Company Name—*Executive Officer*	Address, City, State, Zip	Phone	Type	Fin	Empls
36	Carter Brothers Manufacturing Company Inc—*Jonathan Arn*	1871 Us Hwy 231, Brundidge AL 36010	334-735-2301	R	<1*	<.1

TOTALS: SIC 3799 Transportation Equipment Nec
Companies: 36 ... 5,277 ... 11.6

3812 Search & Navigation Equipment

Rank	Company Name—*Executive Officer*	Address, City, State, Zip	Phone	Type	Fin	Empls
1	Lockheed Martin Corp—*Robert J Stevens*	6801 Rockledge Dr, Bethesda MD 20817	301-897-6000	P	45,803	132.0
2	Honeywell International Inc—*David M Cote*	PO Box 1053, Morristown NJ 07962	973-455-2000	P	33,370	130.0
3	Raytheon Co—*William H Swanson*	870 Winter St, Waltham MA 02451	781-522-3000	P	25,183	72.0
4	Garmin Ltd—*Min Kao*	1200 E 151st St, Olathe KS 66062	913-397-8200	P	2,690	8.9
5	DRS Technologies Inc—*James M Baird*	5 Sylvan Way, Parsippany NJ 07054	973-898-1500	S	2,473	10.2
6	Honeywell International Commercial Electronic Systems Div—*Rob Gillette* Honeywell International Inc	21111 N 19th Ave, Phoenix AZ 85027	602-436-2311	S	2,280*	12.0
7	AAR Defense Systems—*David Storch*	1100 N Wood Dale Rd, Wood Dale IL 60191	630-227-2000	D	1,887*	6.0
8	FLIR Systems Inc—*Earl R Lewis*	27700A SW Parkway Ave, Wilsonville OR 97070	503-684-3731	P	1,544	3.1
9	Sierra Nevada Corp—*Fatih Ozmen*	444 Salomon Cir, Sparks NV 89434	775-331-0222	R	1,202*	2.0
10	International Launch Services Inc—*Frank McKenna* Lockheed Martin Corp	1875 Explorer St Ste 7, Reston VA 20190	571-633-7400	S	750*	.1
11	Flightline Electronics Inc—*Carlos Santiago*	7625 Omnitech Pl, Victor NY 14564	585-924-4000	R	748*	.3
12	ESCO Technologies Inc (St Louis Missouri)—*Victor Richey*	9900 Clayton Rd Ste A, Saint Louis MO 63124	314-213-7200	P	694	2.5
13	DRS C3 and Aviation Group—*Mark Newman* DRS Technologies Inc	400 Professional Dr, Gaithersburg MD 20879	301-921-8100	S	619*	2.0
14	DRS Sensors and Targeting Systems Inc—*Robert Viviano* DRS Technologies Inc	10600 Valley View St, Cypress CA 90630	714-220-3800	S	404*	1.5
15	Argon ST Inc—*Terry L Collins*	12701 Fair Lakes Cir S, Fairfax VA 22033	703-322-0881	S	366	1.1
16	Textron Defense Systems—*Frederick Strader*	201 Lowell St, Wilmington MA 01887	978-657-2100	S	312*	1.3
17	Integrated Defense Technologies Inc—*Thomas J Keenan* DRS Technologies Inc	110 Wynn Dr, Huntsville AL 35807	256-895-2000	S	304	2.1
18	Ducommun LaBarge Technologies—*Craig E LaBarge*	9900 Clayton Rd, Saint Louis MO 63124	314-997-0800	P	289	1.6
19	Woodward HRT	25200 Rye Canyon Rd, Santa Clarita CA 91355	661-294-6000	S	263*	.9
20	Raytheon Electronic Systems—*Jack Kelbe*	PO Box 902, El Segundo CA 90245	310-647-2660	R	255*	1.6
21	Astronautics Corporation Of America—*Mohammad Abdallah*	PO Box 523, Milwaukee WI 53201	414-449-4000	R	248*	1.9
22	Garmin International Inc—*Min Kao*	1200 E 151st St, Olathe KS 66062	913-397-8200	R	235*	2.5
23	Sperry Marine—*Wes Bush*	3510 Remson Ct, Charlottesville VA 22901	434-974-2000	S	225*	1.3
24	Sparton Corp—*Cary B Wood*	425 N Martingale Rd St, Schaumburg IL 60173	517-762-5800	P	203	1.0
25	Thales ATM—*Wayne Dohlman*	23501 W 84th St, Shawnee KS 66227	913-422-2600	S	203*	1.5
26	Teledyne Brown Engineering Inc—*Rex D Geveden*	PO Box 070007, Huntsville AL 35807	256-726-5555	S	187*	2.0
27	United Space Alliance Pension—*Ginger Barnes*	600 Gemini St, Houston TX 77058	281-212-6200	R	165*	5.0
28	Goodrich Sensor Systems Div—*Brian Gora*	14300 Judicial Rd, Burnsville MN 55306	952-892-4000	D	162*	1.0
29	CompuDyne Corp—*James O'Neill*	2530 Riva Rd Ste 201, Annapolis MD 21401	410-224-4415	S	147*	.7
30	Systron Donner Inertial Div—*Dean Johnson*	2700 Systron Dr, Concord CA 94518	925-979-4400	D	144*	.5
31	BAE Systems Aircraft Controls—*Mike Turner*	PO Box 442, Santa Monica CA 90406	323-298-6300	S	125	.8
32	Meggitt-USA Inc—*John Stobie*	1955 N Surveyor Ave, Simi Valley CA 93063	805-526-5700	S	120*	1.2
33	Universal Avionics Systems Corp—*Joachim Naimer*	3260 E Universal Way, Tucson AZ 85706	520-295-2300	R	82*	.6
34	Interstate Electronics Corp—*Robert Huffman*	PO Box 3117, Anaheim CA 92803	714-758-0500	S	82*	.5
35	ITT Gilfillan Inc *John Molloy*	PO Box 7713, Van Nuys CA 91409	818-988-2600	D	81*	.5
36	Northrop Grumman Norden Systems—*Ivory Tucker*	10 Norden Pl, Norwalk CT 00855	203-852-5000	S	81*	.5
37	Meggitt Safety Systems—*Grant Hintez*	1915 Voyager Ave, Simi Valley CA 93063	805-584-4100	S	69*	.5
38	Crane Aerospace and Electronics—*Mike Romito*	3000 Winona Ave, Burbank CA 91504	818-526-2600	S	69*	.4
39	DRS FPA Inc DRS Technologies Inc	5 Sylvan Way, Parsippany NJ 07054	973-898-1500	S	67*	.3
40	DRS Surveillance Support System Inc DRS Technologies Inc	5 Sylvan Way, Parsippany NJ 07054	973-898-1500	S	67*	.3
41	DRS Systems Inc DRS Technologies Inc	5 Sylvan Way, Parsippany NJ 07054	973-898-6019	S	67*	.3
42	DRS Systems Management Corp DRS Technologies Inc	5 Sylvan Way, Parsippany NJ 07054	973-898-1500	S	67*	.3
43	Sensis Corp—*Judson Gostin*	85 Collamer Crossings, East Syracuse NY 13057	315-445-0550	S	66*	.4
44	L-3 Ocean Systems—*Michael T Strianese*	15825 Roxford St, Sylmar CA 91342	818-367-0111	S	65*	.4
45	Barfield Miami—*Francois Amat*	4101 NW 29th St, Miami FL 33142	305-894-5300	S	62*	.2
46	Global Aerosystems LLC—*Mohammed Abouellnega*	10108 32nd Ave W, Everett WA 98204	425-367-4477	R	56*	.2
47	General Dynamics Information Systems—*Lewis Von Thaer*	12450 Fair Lakes Cir, Fairfax VA 22033	703-263-2800	R	48*	.3
48	Immediate Response Technologies Inc—*Harley Hughes*	7100 Holladay Tyler Rd, Glenn Dale MD 20769	301-352-8800	R	47	.2
49	Trilectron Industries Inc—*Sigmund Borax*	11001 Us Hwy 41 North, Palmetto FL 34221	941-721-1000	S	47	.3
50	Industrial Scientific Corp—*Justin McElhattan*	1001 Oakdale Rd, Oakdale PA 15071	412-788-4353	R	45*	.2
51	L-3 Telemetry-West Conic—*Michael Strianese*	9020 Balboa Ave, San Diego CA 92123	858-694-7500	D	40*	.4
52	Dayton-Granger Inc—*Gibbons Cline*	3299 Sw 9th Ave, Fort Lauderdale FL 33315	954-463-3451	R	37*	.3
53	Lowrance Electronics Inc—*Darrell J Lowrance*	12000 E Skelly Dr, Tulsa OK 74128	918-437-6881	S	37*	.3
54	HID Corp—*Denis Hebert*	15370 Barranca Pkwy, Irvine CA 92618	949-732-2000	S	36*	.2
55	Pacific Scientific HTL/Kin-Tech—*Dennis Hutton*	1800 Highland Ave, Duarte CA 91010	626-359-9317	S	34*	.2
56	L-3 Aviation Recorders	6000 Fruitville Rd, Sarasota FL 34232	941-371-0811	S	33*	.2
57	DRS Photronics Inc—*Peter Conway* DRS Technologies Inc	133 Bauer Dr, Oakland NJ 07436	201-337-3800	S	33*	.1
58	Tideland Signal Corp—*Allen Mitchener*	PO Box 52430, Houston TX 77052	713-681-6101	R	32*	.1
59	Ridge Engineering Inc—*David Tracey*	3987 Hampstead Mexico, Hampstead MD 21074	410-239-7716	R	31*	.1
60	Aerosonic Corp—*Douglas J Hillman*	1212 N Hercules Ave, Clearwater FL 33765	727-461-3000	P	30	.2
61	Parker Hannifin Corp Daedel Div—*Roger S Sherard*	1140 Sandy Hill Rd, Irwin PA 15642	724-861-8200	D	28*	.2
62	Hughes Telematics Inc—*Jeff Leddy*	41 Perimeter Center E, Atlanta GA 30346	770-391-6400	R	28*	.1
63	S Tech Corp—*Roger Smith*	1 S Tec Way, Mineral Wells TX 76067	940-325-9406	R	27*	.1
64	Commonwealth Technology Inc—*Paul Mccann*	5875 Barclay Dr, Alexandria VA 22315	703-719-6800	R	27*	.1
65	Escort Inc—*John Larsen*	5440 W Chester Rd, West Chester OH 45069	513-870-8500	S	26*	.1
66	Mistral Inc—*Eyal Banai*	7910 Woodmont Ave Ste, Bethesda MD 20814	301-913-9366	R	26*	<.1
67	Hydroscience Technologies Inc—*Fred G Woodland*	6100 Columbia Rd, Mineral Wells TX 76067	940-325-8221	S	25*	.1
68	Crossbow Technology Inc—*Mike Horton*	4145 N 1st St, San Jose CA 95134	408-965-3300	R	24*	.1
69	Chemring Energetic Devices Inc—*William Currer*	2525 Curtiss St, Downers Grove IL 60515	630-969-0620	S	23*	.1
70	Kor Electronics—*Kevin Carnino*	10855 Business Ctr Dr, Cypress CA 90630	714-898-8200	R	23*	.1
71	Garmin At Inc—*Min Kao* Garmin International Inc	2345 Turner Rd Se, Salem OR 97302	503-581-8101	R	23*	.1
72	Rogerson Kratos—*Michael Rogerson*	403 S Raymond Ave, Pasadena CA 91105	626-449-3090	S	23*	.2

Note: An asterisk (*) indicates an estimated financial figure. The company type code used is as follows: R = Private, P = Public, S = Private Subsidiary, B = Public Subsidiary, D = Division, J = Joint Venture, I = Investment Fund.

COMPANY RANKINGS BY SALES WITHIN 4-DIGIT SIC

Rank	Company Name—Executive Officer	Address, City, State, Zip	Phone	Type	Fin	Empls
73	Sensor Switch Inc—Brian Platner	900 Northrop Rd Ste A, Wallingford CT 06492	203-265-2842	R	23*	.1
74	Frontier Electronic Systems Corp—Mark Rolls	PO Box 1023, Stillwater OK 74076	405-624-1769	R	23*	.2
75	Kongsberg Underwater Technology Inc—Tom Healy	19210 33rd Ave W Ste A, Lynnwood WA 98036	425-712-1107	R	22*	<.1
76	Automatic Power Inc—Steve Trenchard	PO Box 230738, Houston TX 77223	713-228-5208	R	21*	.1
77	Peek Traffic Inc—Timothy O'Leary	2906 Corporate Way, Palmetto FL 34221	941-366-8770	S	21*	.1
78	Kelly Manufacturing Co—Justin Kelly	555 S Topeka, Wichita KS 67202	316-265-6868	R	21*	.1
79	Nextek Inc—John Roberts	201 Next Technology Dr, Madison AL 35758	256-772-0400	R	21*	.1
80	Aeroantenna Technology Inc—Joe Klein	20732 Lassen St, Chatsworth CA 91311	818-993-3842	R	20*	.1
81	Decatur Electronics Inc—Brian Brown	3433 E Wood St, Phoenix AZ 85040	217-428-4315	R	20*	.1
82	United Gear and Assembly Inc—Mike Menz	1700 Livingstone Rd, Hudson WI 54016	715-386-5867	R	19*	.2
83	Vitron Acquisition LLC—Tom Schoaf	18008 N Black Canyon H, Phoenix AZ 85053	602-548-9661	R	19*	.1
84	Cochrane Technologies Inc—Doug Cochrane	PO Box 81276, Lafayette LA 70598	337-837-3334	R	19*	.1
85	Pryer Machine and Tool Co—Scott Pryer	2230 N Sheridan Rd, Tulsa OK 74115	918-835-8885	R	19*	.2
86	Navcom Defense Electronics Inc—Clifford Christ	9129 Stellar Ct, Corona CA 92883	951-268-9205	R	19*	.1
87	Safe Flight Instrument Corp—Randau Greene	20 New King St, White Plains NY 10604	914-946-9500	R	18*	.2
88	Engineered Polymer Products Div—Marshall Larsen	6061 Goodrich Blvd, Jacksonville FL 32226	904-757-3660	D	18*	.1
89	Rantec Microwave Systems Inc—Graham Wilson	24003 Ventura Blvd, Calabasas CA 91302	818-223-5000	R	18*	.1
90	Garrett Electronics Inc—Charles Garrett	1881 W State St, Garland TX 75042	972-494-6151	R	18*	.1
91	Progressive Inc—Guinn Crousen	1030 Commercial Blvd N, Arlington TX 76001	817-467-0031	S	18*	.1
92	Inthinc Technology Solutions Inc—Todd Follmer	4225 Lake Park Blvd St, West Valley City UT 84120	801-886-2255	R	16*	.1
93	Princeton Gamma-Tech Inc—Chris Cox	303C College Rd E, Princeton NJ 08540	609-924-7310	S	15*	.1
94	L2 Consulting Services Inc—Mark Lebovitz	2100 E Hwy 290, Dripping Springs TX 78620	512-894-3414	R	15*	.1
95	Geophysical Survey Systems Inc—Christopher Hawekotte	12 Industrial Way Ste, Salem NH 03079	603-893-1109	R	14*	<.1
96	Lake Shore Cryotronics Inc—Michael Swartz	575 Mccorkle Blvd, Westerville OH 43082	614-891-2243	R	14*	.1
97	Btl Machine—Buu Vo	1168 Sherborn St, Corona CA 92879	951-808-9929	R	14*	.1
98	Williams-Pyro Inc—Della Williams	200 Greenleaf St, Fort Worth TX 76107	817-872-1500	R	13*	.1
99	Applied Energetics Inc—Joseph C Hayden	3590 E Columbia St, Tucson AZ 85714	520-628-7415	P	13	.1
100	Armatron International Inc—Charles Houseman	15 Highland Ave, Malden MA 02148	781-321-2300	R	13	.1
101	Metrotech Corp—Jeff Smith	3251 Olcott St, Santa Clara CA 95054	408-734-1400	R	13*	.1
102	Kmc Systems Inc—Patrick Mcnallen	220 Daniel Webster Hwy, Merrimack NH 03054	603-889-2500	R	13*	.1
103	Davis Instruments Corp—Robert Selig	3465 Diablo Ave, Hayward CA 94545	510-732-9229	R	12*	.1
104	M/A-COM Sigint Products	PO Box 868, Hunt Valley MD 21030	410-329-7915	S	12*	3.0
105	Fortner Aerospace Manufacturing Inc—Mark Heasley	401 N Pleasant St, Prescott AZ 86301	928-771-2434	R	12*	.1
106	Celtech Corp—Rudy Juarez	1300 Terminal Dr, Carlsbad NM 88220	505-887-2044	S	12*	<.1
107	Kongsberg Defense Corp—Ronnie Olfen	160 Jari Dr Ste 150, Johnstown PA 15904	814-266-1923	R	11*	.1
108	Aerospace and Commercial Technologies Inc—David Smith	970 Fm 2871, Fort Worth TX 76126	817-560-6600	R	11*	<.1
109	Oppenheimer Precision Products Inc—Thomas Kirk	173 Gibraltar Rd, Horsham PA 19044	215-674-9100	R	11*	.1
110	ES Ritchie and Sons Inc—Paul Sherman	PO Box 548, Pembroke MA 02359	781-826-5131	R	10*	.1
111	Ithaco Space Systems Inc—Marshall O Larsen	950 Danby Rd Ste 100, Ithaca NY 14850	607-272-7640	S	10*	.1
112	Schonstedt Instrument Company Inc—Michael Head	100 Edmond Rd, Kearneysville WV 25430	304-725-1050	R	10*	<.1
113	Brimrose Corporation Of America—Ronald Rosemeier	19 Loveton Cir, Sparks Glencoe MD 21152	410-472-7070	R	9*	.1
114	Tekscan Inc—Stephen Jacobs	307 W 1st St, Boston MA 02107	617-464-4500	R	9*	.1
115	Reno Agriculture and Electronics—Thomas Potter	4655 Aircenter Cir, Reno NV 89502	775-826-2020	R	8*	.1
116	Interface Displays and Controls Inc—William Lang	4630 N Ave, Oceanside CA 92056	760-945-0230	R	8*	.1
117	Acutronic USA Inc—Dominique Schinabeck	700 Waterfront Dr, Pittsburgh PA 15222	412-926-1200	R	8*	.1
118	Cenco Inc (New Brighton Minnesota)—Edward Carlson	639 Campus Dr, New Brighton MN 55112	651-203-6100	S	8*	.1
119	Klein Associates Inc—John Cotumaccio	11 Klein Dr, Salem NH 03079	603-893-6131	S	8*	<.1
120	Eltec Instruments Inc—Samuel Mollenkof	PO Box 9610, Daytona Beach FL 32120	386-252-0411	R	8*	.1
121	Servo Corporation of America—Steve A Barre	123 Frost St, Westbury NY 11590	516-938-9700	R	8*	.1
122	Navsys Corp—Alison Brown	14960 Woodcarver Rd, Colorado Springs CO 80921	719-481-4877	R	7*	<.1
123	Rex Systems Inc—G Rathbun	10684 43rd Ave, Chippewa Falls WI 54729	715-723-9313	R	7*	.1
124	Jsb Holdings Inc—Susan Bloom	340 N 51st Ave, Phoenix AZ 85043	602-278-7700	R	7*	<.1
125	Valentine Research Inc—Michael Valentine	10280 Alliance Rd, Blue Ash OH 45242	513-984-8900	R	6*	<.1
126	Megapulse Inc—Paul Johannessen	101 Billerica Ave Ste, North Billerica MA 01862	978-670-9960	R	6*	.1
127	Aero-Instruments Company LLC—Deborah Allen	14901 Emery Ave, Cleveland OH 44135	216-671-3133	R	6*	.1
128	Magellan Navigation Inc—Nelson Chan	960 Overland Ct, San Dimas CA 91773	909-394-5000	S	6*	.1
129	Rogers Holding Company Inc—Dal Rogers	1130 Columbia St, Brea CA 92821	714-257-4850	R	6*	<.1
130	Romer/Cimcore Inc—Hank Kraus	5145 Avenida Encinas, Carlsbad CA 92008	760-438-1725	S	6*	<.1
131	Airpath Instrument Co—Gilmore C Stone	13150 Taussig Ave, Bridgeton MO 63044	314-739-8117	R	6*	<.1
132	Penetradar Corp—Anthony J Alongi	2509 Niagara Falls Blv, Niagara Falls NY 14304	716-731-4369	R	6*	<.1
133	G and B Liquidating Corp—Glendon Whitehouse	48 Perimeter Rd, Manchester NH 03103	603-669-0600	R	6*	.1
134	Aeronautical Instrument And Radio Co—Wilfred Burke	PO Box 340, Lodi NJ 07644	973-473-0034	R	6*	<.1
135	Ability Metal Co—Steve Mucci	1355 Greenleaf Ave, Elk Grove Village IL 60007	847-437-7040	R	6*	<.1
136	Sky Probes Inc—Jack Sheriff	8711 E Pinnacle Peak R, Scottsdale AZ 85255	480-502-1434	R	6*	<.1
137	Mid Continent Controls Inc—Rick Hemphill	901 N River St, Derby KS 67037	316-789-0088	R	5*	<.1
138	Ranger Security Detectors Inc—John Turner	11900 Montana Ave, El Paso TX 79936	915-590-4441	R	5*	<.1
139	QED Inc—Randy Heartfield	2920 Halladay St, Santa Ana CA 92705	714-546-6010	R	5*	<.1
140	Antenna Associates Inc—Ronald Sandquist	21 Burke Dr, Brockton MA 02301	508-583-3241	R	5*	<.1
141	H Galow Company Inc—Michael Galow	15 Maple St, Norwood NJ 07648	201-768-0547	R	4*	<.1
142	Interocean Industries Inc—Michael Pearlman	3738 Ruffin Rd, San Diego CA 92123	858-565-8400	R	4*	<.1
143	Intertek Laboratories Inc—Denis Rybkiewicz	340 Union St, Stirling NJ 07980	908-903-1800	R	4*	<.1
144	Southern Avionics Co—Brooks Goodhue	PO Box 5345, Beaumont TX 77726	409-842-1717	R	4*	<.1
145	XCOR Aerospace—Jeff Greason	PO Box 1163, Mojave CA 93502	661-824-4714	R	4*	<.1
146	Technovation Applications Inc—James K Williams	3160-A Enterprise St, Brea CA 92821	714-996-0104	R	4*	<.1
147	Archangel Systems Inc—Michael Greene	1635 Pumphrey Ave, Auburn AL 36832	334-826-8008	R	4*	<.1
148	Agent Video Intelligence—Dieter Kondek	1660 17th St Ste 310, Denver CO 80202		R	4*	<.1
149	Data Security Inc—Brian Boles	729 Q St, Lincoln NE 68508	402-434-5959	R	4*	<.1
150	Radar Technology Inc—James Noonan	39 S Hunt Rd, Amesbury MA 01913	978-834-9700	R	4*	<.1
151	Kearflex Engineering Company Inc—Thomas Kearney	66 Cypress St, Warwick RI 02888	401-781-4900	R	3*	<.1
152	Patriot 3 Inc—Charles Fuqua	PO Box 278, Quantico VA 22134	540-891-7353	R	3*	<.1
153	Tesoro Electronics Inc—James Gifford	PO Box 10250, Prescott AZ 86304	928-771-2646	R	3*	<.1
154	Goldak Inc—Dan Mulcahey	PO Box 1988, Glendale CA 91209	818-367-0149	R	3*	<.1
155	J Diamond Inc—Joseph Harris	2020 W Harry St, Wichita KS 67213	316-264-0600	R	3*	<.1
156	Narco Avionics Inc—Barbara Barda	270 Commerce Dr Ste 20, Fort Washington PA 19034	215-643-2900	R	3*	<.1
157	Mcnab Inc—Horace Teass	383 E 29th St Ste 2, Buena Vista VA 24416	540-261-1045	R	3*	<.1
158	Sun Dial and Panel Corp—Roger Lokker	60 Passaic Ave, Fairfield NJ 07004	973-226-4334	R	3*	<.1
159	Microsensor Systems Inc—William M Lambert	121 Gamma Dr, Pittsburgh PA 15238		R	3*	<.1
160	Del Norte Technology Inc—Steven Koles	1100 Pamela Dr, Euless TX 76040	817-267-3541	R	3*	<.1
161	Ateez Corp—David Javid	3738 W Century Blvd St, Inglewood CA 90303	310-419-9068	R	3*	<.1
162	Kongsberg Maritime—Vegar Arndal	150 James Dr E Ste 160, Saint Rose LA 70087	504-712-2799	R	3*	<.1

Rank	Company Name—*Executive Officer*	Address, City, State, Zip	Phone	Type	Fin	Empls
163	Austin Digital Inc—*Thomas Mayer*	3913 Medical Pkwy Ste, Austin TX 78756	512-452-8178	R	3*	<.1
164	Dg Engineering Corp—*Aret Demiral*	13300 Ralston Ave, Sylmar CA 91342	818-364-9024	R	2*	<.1
165	Multiprens USA Inc—*Bill Tayloe*	20 Ohio Ave, Kansas City KS 66118	913-371-6999	R	2*	<.1
166	Anseri Corp—*Craig Benson*	35 Industrial Way Ste, Rochester NH 03867	603-994-2200	R	2*	<.1
167	Electronic Design and Packaging Company Inc—*Richard Bezerko*	36704 Commerce St, Livonia MI 48150	734-591-9176	R	2*	<.1
168	Critical Solutions International Inc—*Raymond Craig*	PO Box 118698, Carrollton TX 75011	972-242-8500	R	2*	<.1
169	Menches Tool and Die Inc—*John Menches*	30995 San Benito St, Hayward CA 94544	510-476-1160	R	2*	<.1
170	Sound Ocean Systems Inc—*Frank Brockett*	PO Box 2978, Redmond WA 98073	425-869-1834	R	2*	<.1
171	Remcor Technical Industries Inc—*Ron Mueller*	7025 Alamitos Ave, San Diego CA 92154	619-424-8878	R	2*	<.1
172	Whisco Component Engineering Inc—*Robert Scorza*	501 Mitchell Rd, Glendale Heights IL 60139	630-790-9785	R	2*	<.1
173	Mikelson Machine Shop Inc—*Josie Mikelson*	2546 Merced Ave, South El Monte CA 91733	626-448-3920	R	2*	<.1
174	Orbital Research Inc—*Bob Schmidt*	4415 Euclid Ave Ste 50, Cleveland OH 44103	216-649-0399	R	2*	<.1
175	TSI Prism Inc	15575 N 83rd Way Ste 4, Scottsdale AZ 85260	480-998-7700	R	2*	<.1
176	Foxtronics Inc—*Wayne Ostrander*	3448 W Mockingbird Ln, Dallas TX 75235	214-358-4425	R	2*	<.1
177	Marine Sonic Technology Ltd—*Martin Wilcox*	PO Box 730, White Marsh VA 23183	804-693-9602	R	2*	<.1
178	Facilamatic Instrument Corp—*Dennis West*	39 Clinton Ave, Valley Stream NY 11580	516-825-6300	R	2*	<.1
179	Interphase Technologies Inc—*Charles Hicks*	2880 Research Park Dr, Soquel CA 95073	831-477-4944	R	2*	<.1
180	Trilogy International Associates Inc—*William Johnson*	18711 Tiffeni Dr, Twain Harte CA 95383	209-586-5728	R	2*	<.1
181	Vti-Valtronics Inc—*Irvin Burough*	3463 Double Springs Rd, Valley Springs CA 95252	209-754-0707	R	2*	<.1
182	Comprobe Inc—*William Hawkins*	9632 Crowley Rd, Fort Worth TX 76134	817-293-7333	R	2*	<.1
183	Technofan Inc—*Rick Freeman*	7501 Hardeson Rd, Everett WA 98203	425-438-1378	R	2*	<.1
184	Infrared Components Corp—*Thomas Clynne*	2306 Bleecker St, Utica NY 13501	315-732-1544	R	1*	<.1
185	Utility Tool Company Inc—*R Plosser*	2900 Commerce Blvd, Irondale AL 35210	205-956-3710	R	1*	<.1
186	Davtron—*Kevin Torresdal*	427 Hillcrest Way, Emerald Hills CA 94062	650-369-1188	R	1*	<.1
187	Biospherical Instruments Inc—*Charles Booth*	5340 Riley St, San Diego CA 92110	619-686-1888	R	1*	<.1
188	Remcal Products Corp—*Denise Panceri*	2068 Bunnell Rd, Warrington PA 18976	215-343-5500	R	1*	<.1
189	Electro-Technic Products Inc—*Gerald Cuzelis*	4642 N Ravenswood Ave, Chicago IL 60640	773-561-2349	R	1*	<.1
190	Radio Research Instrument Company Inc—*Paul Plishner*	584 N Main St, Waterbury CT 06704	203-753-5840	R	1*	<.1
191	Rotomotion LLC	459 Jessen Ln Ste C, Charleston SC 29492	843-972-0294	R	1*	<.1
192	Sarcon Microsystems Inc—*Donald Perrine*	1001 Tuskegee Dr, Oak Ridge TN 37830	865-482-4148	R	1*	<.1
193	Select Fabricators Inc—*David Yearsley*	PO Box 119, Canandaigua NY 14424	585-393-0650	R	1*	<.1
194	Rozendal Associates Inc—*Tim Rozendal*	9530 Pathway St Ste 10, Santee CA 92071	619-562-5596	R	1*	<.1
195	Interad Limited LLC—*Deborah Christie*	18321 Pky Rd, Melfa VA 23410	757-787-7610	R	1*	<.1
196	Wema USA Inc—*Dieter Marker*	15 Ne 3rd St, Fort Lauderdale FL 33301	954-463-1075	R	1*	<.1
197	Watson Industries Inc—*William Watson*	3041 Melby St, Eau Claire WI 54703	715-839-0628	R	1*	<.1
198	Aero Products Research Inc—*Leonard Wilstein*	11201 Hindry Ave, Los Angeles CA 90045	310-641-7242	R	1*	<.1
199	New England Photoconductor Corp—*Paul Brennan*	PO Box M, Norton MA 02766	508-285-5561	R	1*	<.1
200	Aircraft Instruments Co—*Dave C Bielecki*	4039 Skyron Dr, Doylestown PA 18902	215-348-5274	R	1*	<.1
201	Alert Technologies—*Randy Barnes*	636 E 11th St, Indianapolis IN 46202	317-631-5580	R	1*	<.1
202	Aqua-Tronics Inc—*Merrill Haddon*	1795 N Yellowstone Hwy, Idaho Falls ID 83401	208-528-8875	R	1*	<.1
203	Syqwest Inc—*Robert Tarini*	222 Metro Ctr Blvd Ste, Warwick RI 02886	401-921-5170	R	1*	<.1
204	Ross Laboratories Inc—*James Ross*	3138 Fairview Ave E, Seattle WA 98102	206-324-3950	R	1*	<.1
205	Anderson Manufacturing Company Inc (St Paul Minnesota)—*Lance Anderson*	2885 Country Dr Ste 19, Saint Paul MN 55117	651-484-1316	R	1*	<.1
206	JW Fishers Manufacturing Inc—*Jack Fisher*	1953 County St, East Taunton MA 02718	508-822-7330	R	1*	<.1
207	Logan Enterprises Inc (West Liberty Ohio)—*Laurel C McCombe*	PO Box 839, West Liberty OH 43357	937-465-8170	R	1*	<.1
208	Mwt Materials Inc—*Michael Katz*	90 Dayton Ave Ste 6e, Passaic NJ 07055	973-472-5161	R	1*	<.1
209	Lapoint-Blase Industries Inc—*Guy Blase*	336 Leffingwell Ave St, Saint Louis MO 63122	314-821-1022	R	1*	<.1
210	Aeris Corp—*Toby Whitehurst*	PO Box 365, Waverly Hall GA 31831	706-323-0500	R	1*	<.1
211	Navigation Laboratories Inc—*Frank Bletzacker*	30251 Golden Lantern, Laguna Niguel CA 92677	949-766-0444	R	1*	<.1
212	Brittain Industries Inc—*Gerald Walters*	3266 N Sheridan Rd, Tulsa OK 74115	918-836-7701	R	1*	<.1
213	C-R Control Systems Inc—*Robert Seidler*	20 Airpark Rd, West Lebanon NH 03784	603-298-2113	R	1*	<.1
214	Mits LLC	19 W Las Vegas St, Colorado Springs CO 80903	719-444-0646	R	1*	<.1
215	TSE and Associates—*John Campbell*	341 Dubois Rd, Annapolis MD 21401	410-571-8551	R	<1*	<.1
216	Xtreme Alternative Defense Systems—*Pete Bitar*	2701 Enterprise Dr Ste, Anderson IN 46013	765-644-7323	R	<1*	<.1
217	RTX Systems Inc—*Richard Daly*	560 Broadhollow Rd Ste, Melville NY 11747	516-933-2130	R	<1*	<.1
218	Kolmar Technologies Inc—*Tovio Koehler*	3 Henry Graf Jr Rd Ste, Newburyport MA 01950	978-462-2905	R	<1*	<.1
219	Applied Science Products Inc—*Kenneth Wood*	924 Corridor Park Blvd, Knoxville TN 37932	865-777-3780	P	<1	<.1
220	Micromet Corp—*Carl Augustine*	3800 N 13 Rd, Mesick MI 49668	231-885-1466	R	<1*	<.1
221	Muecke's Shrimp Boiler LLP—*Johny Muecke*	6314 Sioux Dr, Pasadena TX 77503	281-487-4462	R	<1*	<.1
222	Global Ecology Corp—*Peter Ubaldi*	96 Park St, Montclair NJ 07042		P	<1	<.1
223	Daniel O Scharf—*Daniel Scharf*	65 E Palatine Rd Ste 3, Prospect Heights IL 60070	847-459-5801	R	<1*	<.1
224	Rossfelder Corp—*Richard Wilkins*	PO Box 1030, Poway CA 92074	858-679-7361	R	<1*	<.1
225	4C Controls Inc—*Jean-Robert Martin*	100 Wall St 21st Fl, New York NY 10005	908-273-4442	P	<1	N/A
226	Green Bridge Technologies International Inc—*Leonard Baxter*	15091 Poberezny Ct, Linden MI 48451	810-410-8177	P	<1	N/A
227	Ion Metrics Inc	11558 Sorrento Valley, San Diego CA 92121	858-792-1580	S	N/A	<.1

TOTALS: SIC 3812 Search & Navigation Equipment

Companies: 227					126,391	429.1

3821 Laboratory Apparatus & Furniture

Rank	Company Name—*Executive Officer*	Address, City, State, Zip	Phone	Type	Fin	Empls
1	Sartorius North America Inc—*Guenther Maaz*	131 Heartland Blvd, Brentwood NY 11717	631-254-4249	S	757*	3.6
2	Newport Corp—*Robert J Phillippy*	1791 Deere Ave, Irvine CA 92606	949-863-3144	P	480	1.7
3	Hamilton Laboratory Workstations—*Paul M Montrone*	PO Box 137, Two Rivers WI 54241	920-793-1121	S	120*	.9
4	Kewaunee Scientific Corp—*William A Shumaker*	PO Box 1842, Statesville NC 28687	704-873-7202	P	100	.6
5	CEM Corp—*Michael J Collins*	PO Box 200, Matthews NC 28106	704-821-7015	R	86*	.2
6	Restek Corp—*Don Chandless*	110 Benner Cir, Bellefonte PA 16823	814-353-1300	R	53*	.3
7	Carver Inc (Wabash Indiana)	PO Box 544, Wabash IN 46992	260-563-7577	R	49*	.1
8	Suburban Surgical Co—*Todd Pinkerman*	275 12th St Ste A, Wheeling IL 60090	847-537-9320	R	30*	.2
9	Parr Instrument Co—*Michael Steffenson*	211 53rd St, Moline IL 61265	309-762-7716	R	30*	.1
10	Nu Aire Inc—*Richard Peters*	2100 Fernbrook Ln N, Minneapolis MN 55447	763-553-1270	R	30*	.2
11	Parter Medical Products Inc—*Hormonz Foroughi*	17015 Kingsview Ave, Carson CA 90746	310-327-4417	R	25*	.2
12	ThermoGenesis Corp—*J Melville Engle*	2711 Citrus Rd, Rancho Cordova CA 95742	916-858-5100	P	23	.1
13	Henry Troemner LLC—*Jane Andrews*	201 Wolf Dr, Thorofare NJ 08086	856-686-1600	R	22*	.2
14	Buehler Ltd—*David N Farr*	PO Box 1, Lake Bluff IL 60044	847-295-6500	S	21	.2
15	Baker Company Inc—*Dennis Eagleson*	PO Box E, Sanford ME 04073	207-324-8773	R	21*	.2
16	Preston Industries Inc—*Philip Preston*	6600 W Touhy Ave, Niles IL 60714	847-647-0611	R	18*	.2
17	Schroer Manufacturing Co—*Joseph Schroer*	511 Osage Ave, Kansas City KS 66105	913-281-1500	R	18*	.1
18	Microfluidics International Corp—*Michael C Ferrara*	PO Box 9101, Newton MA 02464	617-969-5452	S	16	.1
19	QualMark Corp—*Andy Drenick*	10390 E 48th Ave, Denver CO 80238	303-254-8800	P	15	.1

Note: An asterisk (*) indicates an estimated financial figure. The company type code used is as follows: R = Private, P = Public, S = Private Subsidiary, B = Public Subsidiary, D = Division, J = Joint Venture, I = Investment Fund.

COMPANY RANKINGS BY SALES WITHIN 4-DIGIT SIC

Rank	Company Name—*Executive Officer*	Address, City, State, Zip	Phone	Type	Fin	Empls
20	Misonix Inc—*Michael McManus Jr*	1938 New Hwy, Farmingdale NY 11735	631-694-9555	P	14	.1
21	Tecan Systems—*Stephen Levers*	2450 Zanker Rd, San Jose CA 95131	408-953-3100	R	14*	.1
22	Western Slate Co—*Jeff Pope*	365 Keyes Ave, Hampshire IL 60140	847-683-4400	R	14*	.1
23	Fts Systems Inc—*Claus Kinder*	3538 Main St, Stone Ridge NY 12484	845-687-5300	R	13*	.1
24	Institutional Casework Inc—*Dale Doeve*	1865 Hwy 641 N, Paris TN 38242	731-642-4251	R	13*	.2
25	Ika-Works Inc—*Rene Stiegelmann*	2635 Northchase Pkwy S, Wilmington NC 28405	910-452-7059	R	13*	.1
26	Leonard Peterson and Company Inc—*Roger Lethander*	PO Box 2277, Auburn AL 36831	334-821-6832	R	12*	.1
27	Knf Neuberger Inc—*Martin Becker*	2 Black Forest Rd, Trenton NJ 08691	609-890-8889	R	12*	.1
28	Skc Inc—*Richard Guild*	863 Valley View Rd, Eighty Four PA 15330	724-941-9701	R	12*	.1
29	Sheldon Laboratory Systems Inc—*Eddie Adkins*	PO Box 836, Crystal Springs MS 39059	601-892-2731	S	12*	.1
30	Sartorius Tcc Co—*Scott Schuler*	6542 Fig St, Arvada CO 80004	303-431-7255	R	11*	.1
31	Genevac Inc—*Steve Graham*	815 Rte 208, Gardiner NY 12525	845-267-2211	R	11*	<.1
32	Percival Scientific Inc—*Gary Wheelock*	505 Research Dr, Perry IA 50220	515-465-9363	R	11*	.1
33	Qualigen Inc—*Wallace Ballentine*	2042 Corte Del Nogal A, Carlsbad CA 92011	760-918-9165	R	10*	<.1
34	Thoren Caging Systems Inc—*William Thomas*	PO Box 586, Hazleton PA 18201	570-455-5041	R	9*	.1
35	Janis Research Company LLC—*Thomas Pasakarnis*	2 Jewel Dr, Wilmington MA 01887	978-657-8750	R	9*	.1
36	Entech Laboratory Automation Inc—*Dan Cardin*	2207 Agate Ct, Simi Valley CA 93065	805-527-5939	R	8*	.1
37	Teclab Inc—*Darren Draves*	6450 Valley Industrial, Kalamazoo MI 49009	269-372-6000	R	8*	.1
38	Perma Pure LLC—*Richard A Curran*	PO Box 2105, Toms River NJ 08754	732-244-0010	S	7*	.1
39	Spex Certiprep Inc—*Michel Baudron*	203 Norcross Ave, Metuchen NJ 08840	732-549-7144	R	7*	<.1
40	So-Low Environmental Equipment Co—*Walter Schum*	10310 Spartan Dr, Cincinnati OH 45215	513-772-9410	R	7*	<.1
41	Microcal LLC—*Mike Kallelis*	22 Industrial Dr E, Northampton MA 01060	413-586-7720	R	6*	<.1
42	Spex Sample Prep LLC	203 Norcross Ave, Metuchen NJ 08840	732-549-7144	R	6*	.1
43	Marvac Scientific Manufacturing Inc—*George Marin*	3231 Monument Way, Concord CA 94518	925-825-4636	R	6*	<.1
44	Texas Metal Equipment Company Ltd—*Andrew Harman*	6707 Mayard Rd, Houston TX 77041	713-466-8722	R	6*	<.1
45	Kimball Physics Inc—*Charles Crawford*	311 Kimball Hill Rd, Wilton NH 03086	603-878-1616	R	5*	<.1
46	Hanson Lab Furniture Inc—*Mike Hanson*	814 Mitchell Rd, Newbury Park CA 91320	805-498-3121	R	5*	<.1
47	Laser Reference Inc—*Lee Robson*	151 Martinvale Ln, San Jose CA 95119	408-361-0220	R	5*	<.1
48	Mellen Company Inc—*Jonathan Mellen*	40 Chenell Dr, Concord NH 03301	603-228-2929	R	4*	<.1
49	Air Master Systems Corp—*Don Nelson*	6480 Norton Ctr Dr, Norton Shores MI 49441	231-798-1111	R	4*	<.1
50	MacAlaster Bicknell Company of New Jersey Inc—*Karen L Barsuglia*	PO Box 109, Millville NJ 08332	856-825-3222	R	4*	<.1
51	Eberbach Corp—*Ralph Boehnke*	PO Box 1024, Ann Arbor MI 48106	734-665-8877	R	4*	<.1
52	Vistalab Technologies Inc—*Richard Scordato*	2 Geneva Rd, Brewster NY 10509	914-244-6226	R	4*	<.1
53	Exion Technology Inc—*Gilbert Hong*	37350 Cedar Blvd Ste K, Newark CA 94560	510-494-1687	R	4*	<.1
54	Materials Research Furnaces Inc—*Peter Sanborn*	Lavoie Dr Rr 28, Suncook NH 03275	603-485-2394	R	4*	<.1
55	Bbc Biochemical Corp—*James Biesecker*	PO Box 1320, Mount Vernon WA 98273	360-542-8400	R	3*	<.1
56	SP Industries Inc (Warminster Pennsylvania)—*Charles L Grant*	935 Mearns Rd, Warminster PA 18974	215-672-7800	S	3*	.4
57	Morris And Lee Inc—*Nancy Bell*	86475 Gene Lassere Blv, Yulee FL 32097	904-225-5558	R	3*	<.1
58	Calorimetry Sciences Corp—*Dennis Hunter*	890 W 410 N Ste A, Lindon UT 84042	801-763-1500	S	3*	<.1
59	Biospherix Ltd—*Randy Yerden*	PO Box 87, Lacona NY 13083	315-387-3414	R	3*	<.1
60	Plas-Labs Inc—*David Regan*	401 E N St Ste 1, Lansing MI 48906	517-372-7177	R	3*	<.1
61	Kin-Tek Laboratories Inc—*James Kinley*	504 Laurel St, La Marque TX 77568	409-938-3627	R	2*	<.1
62	B/R Instrument Corp—*Richard Roark*	9119 Centreville Rd, Easton MD 21601	410-820-8800	R	2*	<.1
63	Alfred Technology Resources Inc—*Jon Wilder*	200 N Main St, Alfred NY 14802	607-587-9444	R	2*	<.1
64	Pinpoint Laser Systems Inc—*Albert Creighton*	56 Pulaski St Unit 5, Peabody MA 01960	978-532-8001	R	2*	<.1
65	Toroid Corp—*Anne Paelian*	PO Box 1435, Huntsville AL 35807	256-837-7510	R	2*	<.1
66	Sonford Co—*Gary Glenna*	8287 214th St W, Lakeville MN 55044	952-469-4832	R	2*	<.1
67	Hemco Corp—*Ronald Hill*	711 S Powell Rd, Independence MO 64056	816-796-2900	R	2*	<.1
68	Engineering Laboratory Design Co—*Sigurd Anderson*	PO Box 278, Lake City MN 55041	651-345-4515	R	2*	<.1
69	Sable Systems International Inc—*John Lighton*	6000 S Eastern Ave Ste, Las Vegas NV 89119	702-269-4445	R	2*	<.1
70	Security Steelcraft Corp—*Stanley Horness*	PO Box 118, Muskegon MI 49443	231-733-1110	R	1*	<.1
71	Metal Goods Manufacturing Company Inc—*Buz Mcabery*	PO Box 2096, Bartlesville OK 74005	918-336-4282	R	1*	<.1
72	Wabash Instrument Corp—*Shethar Davis*	300 Olive St, Wabash IN 46992	260-563-8406	R	1*	<.1
73	Emerson Apparatus Inc—*William Holmes*	59 Sanford Dr Unit 12, Gorham ME 04038	207-856-0055	R	1*	<.1
74	Biodesign Incorporated Of New York—*Susanne Ruddnick*	PO Box 1050, Carmel NY 10512	845-454-6610	R	1*	<.1
75	Scientific Machine and Supply Company Inc—*Edwin Phillips*	PO Box 67, Middlesex NJ 08846	732-356-1553	R	1*	<.1
76	Scientech Inc—*Tom O'Rourke*	5649 Arapahoe Ave, Boulder CO 80303	303-444-1361	R	1*	<.1
77	Research Technologies Inc—*Michael Hanchett*	115 2nd Ave N Ste 300, Edmonds WA 98020	425-670-2167	R	1*	<.1
78	Theta Industries Inc—*Gerhard Clusener*	26 Valley Rd, Port Washington NY 11050	516-883-4088	R	1*	<.1
79	Hoyt Corp (Westport Massachusetts)—*John Olinger*	251 Forge Rd, Westport MA 02790	508-636-8811	R	1*	<.1
80	S and G Enterprises Inc—*Mark J Griffith*	N115 S19000 Edison Dr, Germantown WI 53022	262-251-8300	R	1*	<.1
81	Delaware Technologies Inc—*Donald Dawson*	641 Mount Laurel Rd, Mount Laurel NJ 08054	856-235-8454	R	1*	<.1
82	Electro Mechanical Services Inc—*Richard Winder*	109 Hermosa Dr Se, Albuquerque NM 87108	505-255-9363	R	<1*	<.1

TOTALS: SIC 3821 Laboratory Apparatus & Furniture
Companies: 82   **2,254**   **11.8**

3822 Environmental Controls

1	Schneider Electric Buildings Americas Inc—*James Sandlan*	PO Box 841868, Dallas TX 75284	972-323-1111	R	3,394*	2.6
2	Watlow Electric Manufacturing Co—*Peter Desloge*	12001 Lackland Rd, Saint Louis MO 63146	314-878-4600	R	1,050*	2.0
3	Ameresco Inc—*George Sakellaris*	111 Speen St Ste 410, Framingham MA 01701	508-661-2200	P	618	.7
4	Therm-O-Disc Inc—*John Rhodes*	1320 S Main St, Mansfield OH 44907	419-525-8300	S	244*	4.0
5	NORESCO LLC—*Neil Petchers*	1 Research Dr, Westborough MA 01581	508-614-1000	S	124*	.3
6	Nailor Industries—*Mike Nailor*	4714 Winfield Rd, Houston TX 77039	281-590-1172	R	50*	.4
7	Omega Engineering Inc—*Betty Ruth Hollander*	PO Box 4047, Stamford CT 06907	203-359-1660	R	50*	.4
8	Southern Environmental Inc—*John Jernigan*	PO Box 865, Cantonment FL 32533	850-944-4475	R	36*	<.1
9	Novatech LLC—*Volker Oakey*	1720 Molasses Way, Quakertown PA 18951	484-812-6000	R	35*	.2
10	Evans Tempcon Inc—*Brenda Nestor*	701 Ann St Nw, Grand Rapids MI 49504	616-361-2681	R	34*	.4
11	Control Products Inc—*Chris Berghoff*	1724 Lake Dr W, Chanhassen MN 55317	952-448-2217	R	34*	.2
12	Nailor Industries Of Texas Inc—*Michael Nailor*	4714 Winfield Rd, Houston TX 77039	281-590-1172	R	33*	.2
13	PECO Manufacturing Company Inc—*Stephen M Scheidler*	PO Box 82189, Portland OR 97282	503-233-6401	R	31*	.3
14	Bitzer Us Inc—*Peter Schaufler*	4031 Chamblee Rd, Oakwood GA 30566	770-503-9226	R	31*	.1
15	Portage Electric Products Inc—*Brandon Wehl*	PO Box 2170, Canton OH 44720	330-499-2727	R	30*	.2
16	Thermtrol Corp—*Mark Jeffries*	PO Box 2501, Canton OH 44720	330-497-4148	R	28*	.2
17	Stulz Investment Corporation Of America—*Jurgen Stulz*	1572 Tilco Dr, Frederick MD 21704	301-620-2033	R	26*	.3
18	ADA-EX Inc—*Michael D Durham*	8100 Southpark Way Uni, Littleton CO 80120	303-734-1727	P	22	.1
19	Prentke Romich Co—*Dave Moffat*	PO Box 76079, Cleveland OH 44101	330-262-1984	R	21*	.1
20	Goldline Controls Inc—*Gilbert Conover*	61 Whitecap Dr, North Kingstown RI 02852	401-583-1100	R	20*	.1
21	NSI Tork Inc—*Sam Shankar*	1 Grove St, Mount Vernon NY 10550	914-664-3542	D	18*	.1
22	Electro Industries Inc—*Jon Smith*	PO Box 538, Monticello MN 55362	763-295-4138	R	18*	<.1

Rank	Company Name—*Executive Officer*	Address, City, State, Zip	Phone	Type	Fin	Empls
23	Hansen Technologies Corp—*Jeff Nank*	6827 High Grove Blvd, Burr Ridge IL 60527	630-325-1565	S	17*	.1
24	Channel Products Inc—*David Wozencraft*	7100 Wilson Mills Rd, Chesterland OH 44026	440-423-0113	R	17*	.1
25	Automation Components Inc—*Troy Schwenn*	2305 Pleasant View Rd, Middleton WI 53562	608-831-2585	R	17*	.1
26	Hotwatt Inc—*William Lee*	128 Maple St, Danvers MA 01923	978-777-0070	R	15*	.1
27	Precision Speed Equipment Inc—*Robert Griffioen*	PO Box 7036, Sturgis MI 49091	269-651-4303	R	15*	.1
28	Nason Company Inc—*Steve Mihaly*	PO Box 505, West Union SC 29696	864-638-9521	R	14*	.1
29	Advantage Engineering Inc—*Harold Short*	PO Box 407, Greenwood IN 46142	317-887-0729	R	14*	.1
30	In-Situ Inc—*Robert Blythe*	221 E Lincoln Ave, Fort Collins CO 80524	970-498-1500	R	13*	.1
31	Pertronix Inc—*Thomas Reh*	440 E Arrow Hwy, San Dimas CA 91773	909-599-5955	R	13*	.1
32	Integrated Development and Manufacturing Co—*Adrian Rule*	PO Box 390, Chagrin Falls OH 44022	440-247-5100	R	13*	.1
33	Dickson Co—*Michael Unger*	930 S Westwood Ave, Addison IL 60101		R	13*	.1
34	EWC Controls Inc—*Kevin Cyrana*	385 Hwy 33, Englishtown NJ 07726		R	13*	.1
35	Air Monitor Corp—*Dean Baun*	PO Box 6358, Santa Rosa CA 95406	707-544-2706	R	12*	.1
36	DR Joseph Inc—*Daniel R Joseph*	2125 S Great Southwest, Grand Prairie TX 75051	972-641-7711	R	12*	<.1
37	Optimum Controls Corp—*Michael Galiyano*	PO Box 14174, Reading PA 19612	610-375-0990	R	12*	.1
38	Degree Controls Inc—*Jagat Sisodia*	18 Meadowbrook Dr, Milford NH 03055	603-672-8900	R	11*	.1
39	Johnson Controls Building Automation Systems LLC—*Melissa Aufmuth*	50 W Watkins Mill Rd, Gaithersburg MD 20878	240-683-7600	R	11*	.1
40	Rdf Corp—*Naresh Puri*	23 Elm Ave, Hudson NH 03051	603-882-5195	R	11*	.1
41	Southeast Industries Inc—*Bill Alston*	PO Box 5267, Johnson City TN 37602	423-928-3355	R	11*	.1
42	Psg Controls Inc—*John Reilly*	1225 Tunnel Rd, Perkasie PA 18944	215-257-3621	R	10*	.1
43	Jms Southeast Inc—*Frank Johnson*	105 Temperature Ln, Statesville NC 28677	704-873-1835	R	9*	.1
44	Techniserv Inc—*Paul Heaps*	PO Box 285, Berwick PA 18603	570-759-2315	R	9*	.1
45	Rees Scientific Corp—*Rees Thomas*	1007 Whitehead Rd Ext, Ewing NJ 08638	609-530-1055	R	9*	.1
46	Heat-Timer Corp—*Michael Pitonyak*	20 New Dutch Ln, Fairfield NJ 07004	973-575-0316	R	9*	.1
47	Jordan Acquisition Group LLC—*Claudia Beerbower*	1 Technology Ln, Export PA 15632	724-733-2000	R	8*	.1
48	Laminar Flow Inc—*Anthony Diccianni*	PO Box 2427, Warminster PA 18974	215-672-0232	R	8*	.1
49	National Electrostatics Corp—*James Ferry*	PO Box 620310, Middleton WI 53562	608-831-7600	R	8*	.1
50	Electrosynthesis Company Inc—*David Genders*	72 Ward Rd, Lancaster NY 14086	716-684-0513	R	8*	<.1
51	Trolex Corp—*Richard Foster*	57 Bushes Ln, Elmwood Park NJ 07407	201-794-8004	R	6*	<.1
52	Selco Products Co (Buena Park California)—*Tim Wilkenson*	8780 Technology Way, Reno NV 89521	775-674-5100	R	6*	<.1
53	Nile Inc—*Martin Olagbegi*	9434 S Main St Ste 190, Jonesboro GA 30236	404-361-1133	R	6*	<.1
54	Hcr Inc—*Peter Smith*	PO Box 149, Lewistown MT 59457	406-538-7781	S	5*	<.1
55	Energy Options Inc—*Bradley Freeman*	256 Campus Dr, Edison NJ 08837	732-512-9100	R	5*	<.1
56	Advanced Controls Corp—*Gary Bonebright*	626 W Flores St, Tucson AZ 85705	520-620-6656	R	5*	<.1
57	Temperature Control Specialties Company Inc—*Jack Toal*	2800 Laura Ln, Middleton WI 53562	608-836-9034	R	5*	<.1
58	ATC Companies Inc—*Stephen Gajarsky*	PO Box 310, Middlesex NJ 08846	732-560-0900	R	5*	<.1
59	Betatherm Corp—*Terence Monaghan*	910 Boston Tpke Ste 7, Shrewsbury MA 01545	508-842-0516	R	5*	<.1
60	Oven Industries Inc—*Michael Carlini*	PO Box 290, Mechanicsburg PA 17055	717-766-0721	R	5*	<.1
61	Advanced Control Technologies Inc—*Gary Colip*	PO Box 502948, Indianapolis IN 46250	317-806-2750	R	5*	<.1
62	Ford Environmental Quality Office—*Andrew Hobbs*	1 Parklane Blvd Ste 14, Dearborn MI 48126	313-845-5802	R	4*	<.1
63	Wadsworth Control Systems Inc—*Gary Dean*	5541 Marshall St, Arvada CO 80002	303-424-4461	R	4*	<.1
64	Air Louver and Damper Inc—*Joseph Chalpin*	2121 44th Rd, Long Island City NY 11101	718-392-3232	R	4*	<.1
65	TE Technology Inc—*Richard Buist*	1590 Keane Dr, Traverse City MI 49686	231-929-3966	R	4*	<.1
66	Parameter Generation And Control Inc—*Clay Hile*	PO Box 129, Black Mountain NC 28711	828-669-8717	R	4*	<.1
67	Amega Scientific Corp—*Anthony Amato*	617 Stokes Rd Ste 4334, Medford NJ 08055	609-953-7295	R	4*	<.1
68	Wattmaster Controls Inc—*Gloria Brady*	8500 Nw River Pk Dr 10, Kansas City MO 64152	816-505-1100	R	4*	<.1
69	US Geological Servey—*Rob Brown*	PO Box 1230, Iowa City IA 52244	319-337-4191	R	3*	<.1
70	Geocorp Industrial Controls Inc—*George Conrad*	9010 River Rd, Huron OH 44839	419-433-1101	R	3*	<.1
71	Link Electric and Safety Control Company Inc—*James Barrett*	444 Mcnally Dr, Nashville TN 37211	615-833-4168	R	3*	<.1
72	Thermik Corp—*Fred Goeckerman*	3304 Us Hwy 70 E, New Bern NC 28560	252-636-5720	R	3*	<.1
73	Altech Controls Corp—*Richard Alsenz*	4910 Wright Rd Ste 120, Stafford TX 77477	281-207-2775	R	3*	<.1
74	Edge Mechanical Inc—*John Cherkis*	2429 Bowland Pkwy Ste, Virginia Beach VA 23454	757-228-3540	R	2*	<.1
75	Engenuity Systems Inc—*Tracy Markie*	2165 W Pecos Rd Ste 1, Chandler AZ 85224	480-782-5600	R	2*	<.1
76	Residential Control Systems Inc—*Michael Kuhlmann*	11481 Sunrise Gold Cir, Rancho Cordova CA 95742	916-635-6784	R	2*	<.1
77	Triangle Microsystems Inc—*George King*	2716 Discovery Dr, Raleigh NC 27616	919-878-1880	R	2*	<.1
78	Smart Controls LLC—*David Kniepkamp*	10000 St Clair Ave, Fairview Heights IL 62208	618-394-0300	R	2*	<.1
79	Paragon Controls Inc—*Richard Reis*	PO Box 99, Forestville CA 95436	707-579-1424	R	2*	<.1
80	Solidyne Corp—*Baha Erturk*	4215 Kirchoff Rd, Rolling Meadows IL 60008	847-394-3333	R	2*	<.1
81	Electrasem Corp—*Don Edwards*	372 Elizabeth Ln, Corona CA 92880	951-371-6140	S	2*	<.1
82	Conery Manufacturing Inc—*Scott Conery*	1380 Enterprise Pkwy, Ashland OH 44805	419-289-1444	R	2*	<.1
83	Static Solutions Inc—*Leonard Cohen*	331 Boston Post Rd E S, Marlborough MA 01752	508-480-0700	R	1*	<.1
84	Turmoil Inc—*John Parker-Hansel*	PO Box 583, West Swanzey NH 03469	603-352-0053	R	1*	<.1
85	Rbe Electronics Inc—*Roger Ernst*	16535 Jordan Ave, Jordan MN 55352	952-492-6960	R	1*	<.1
86	AESOPS Inc—*John Harrison*	PO Box 4119, Dalton GA 30719	706-226-0628	R	1*	<.1
87	Static Technologies Corp—*James Barrett*	138 Weymouth St, Rockland MA 02370	781-871-8962	R	1*	<.1
88	Earthlinked Technologies Inc—*Hal Roberts*	4151 S Pipkin Rd, Lakeland FL 33811	863-701-0096	R	1*	<.1
89	Airotech Environmental—*Thomas M Gombos*	333 Tamiami Trl S, Venice FL 34285	941-485-1204	R	1*	<.1
90	Humidity Control Systems Inc (Carson City Nevada)—*Stan Gittelman*	PO Box 21066, Carson City NV 89721	775-246-2000	R	1*	<.1
91	Repco Replacement Parts Inc—*Ronald Chandler*	1021 W Enon Ave, Fort Worth TX 76140	817-293-3639	R	1*	<.1
92	Automated Systems Engineering Inc—*Dan Mullin*	PO Box 1328, Riverside CA 92502	719-599-7477	R	1*	<.1
93	Temptek Inc—*Harry Short*	PO Box 1152, Greenwood IN 46142	317-887-6352	R	1*	<.1
94	Werecon Inc—*Joe Wantulok*	3320 N 29th Ave, Phoenix AZ 85017	602-256-0573	R	1*	<.1
95	Process Products and Service Co—*Charles Summers*	PO Box 581, Mounds OK 74047	918-827-4998	R	1*	<.1
96	Enertec Bas—*Cynthia Johnstone*	628 Plymouth St Sw, Olympia WA 98502	360-943-2952	R	<1*	<.1
97	US Energy Controls Inc—*Gerald Pindus*	7840 164th St Ste Aa, Flushing NY 11366	718-380-1004	R	<1*	<.1
98	Twinsource LLC	32333 Aurora Rd Ste 2, Solon OH 44139	440-248-6800	R	<1*	<.1
99	PGK Inc—*Michael Woodruff*	PO Box 263, Hobart WA 98025	425-432-0945	R	<1*	<.1
100	MK Hansen Co—*Mike Hansen*	PO Box 2066, Wenatchee WA 98807	509-884-1396	R	<1*	<.1
101	Healy-Ruff Company LLC—*Wendy Nortunen*	13005 16th Ave N Ste 4, Minneapolis MN 55441	651-633-7522	S	<1*	<.1
102	White-Rodgers Div—*David N Farr*	8100 W Florissant, St Louis MO 63136	314-553-3600	R	N/A	2.2

TOTALS: SIC 3822 Environmental Controls
Companies: 102 | 6,408 | 18.4

3823 Process Control Instruments

1	UOP LLC—*Carlos Guimaraes*	25 E Algonquin Rd, Des Plaines IL 60016	847-391-2000	S	4,726	4.0
2	Roper Industries Inc—*Brian D Jellison*	6901 Professional Pkwy, Sarasota FL 34240	941-556-2601	P	2,386	8.1
3	Esterline Technologies Corp—*Brad Lawrence*	500 108th Ave NE Ste 1, Bellevue WA 98004	425-453-9400	P	1,718	12.1

Note: An asterisk (*) indicates an estimated financial figure. The company type code used is as follows: R = Private, P = Public, S = Private Subsidiary, B = Public Subsidiary, D = Division, J = Joint Venture, I = Investment Fund.

COMPANY RANKINGS BY SALES WITHIN 4-DIGIT SIC

Rank	Company Name—*Executive Officer*	Address, City, State, Zip	Phone	Type	Fin	Empls
4	Custom Sensors and Technologies—*Eric Pilaud*	14401 Princeton Ave, Moorpark CA 93021	805-552-3599	S	1,180*	4.3
5	Sterling Inc—*Tom Breslin*	2900 S 160th St, New Berlin WI 53151	414-354-0970	R	929*	.8
6	MKS Instruments Inc—*Leo Berlinghieri*	2 Tech Dr Ste 201, Andover MA 01810	978-645-5500	P	823	2.4
7	Uson LP—*Mike Oldfield* Roper Industries Inc	8640 N Eldridge Pky, Houston TX 77041	281-671-2000	S	608	.1
8	Foxboro Co	33 Commercial St, Foxboro MA 02035	508-549-2424	S	520*	6.0
9	ProSoft Technology Inc—*Janice Hungerford*	5201 Truxtun Ave 3rd F, Bakersfield CA 93309	661-716-5100	R	450*	1.0
10	Dionex Corp—*Frank Witney*	PO Box 3603, Sunnyvale CA 94088	408-737-0700	S	420	1.6
11	Phoenix International—*Chuck Kaufman*	1441 44th St NW, Fargo ND 58102		S	392*	.9
12	Sypris Solutions Inc—*Jeffrey T Gill*	101 Bullitt Ln Ste 450, Louisville KY 40222	502-329-2000	P	267	1.1
13	INFICON Holding AG—*Lukas Winkler*	2 Technology Pl, East Syracuse NY 13057	315-434-1100	P	265	.8
14	Cognex International Inc—*Robert J Shillman*	1 Vision Dr, Natick MA 01760	508-650-4141	S	213*	.7
15	K-Tron International Inc—*Edward B Cloues II*	Routes 55 and 553, Pitman NJ 08071	856-589-0500	S	206*	.7
16	Rudolph Technologies Inc—*Paul F McLaughlin*	PO Box 1000, Flanders NJ 07836	973-691-1300	P	187	.6
17	Hurco Companies Inc—*Michael Doar*	1 Technology Way, Indianapolis IN 46268	317-293-5309	P	180	.5
18	Vishay Dale Electronics Inc—*Ruta Zandman*	1122 23rd St, Columbus NE 68601	402-564-3131	S	162*	.5
19	Daniel Industries Inc—*Dennis Perkins*	PO Box 19097, Houston TX 77224	713-467-6000	R	152*	2.0
20	ENGlobal Construction Resources Inc	3105 Executive Blvd, Beaumont TX 77705	409-840-2100	S	128*	.3
21	GE Fanuc Automation Corp—*Maryrose Sylvester*	2500 Austin Dr, Charlottesville VA 22911	434-978-5100	J	100*	.8
22	Dwyer Instruments Inc—*Stephen Clark*	PO Box 373, Michigan City IN 46361	219-879-8868	S	100*	.5
23	Micro Motion Inc—*Jim Mannebach*	7070 Winchester Cir, Boulder CO 80301	303-527-5200	S	90*	.7
24	KineticSystems Company LLC—*William Boston*	900 N State St, Lockport IL 60441	815-838-0005	R	78*	.1
25	Sparton Technology Inc—*Cary Wood*	2400 E Ganson St, Jackson MI 49202	517-787-8600	S	75*	.2
26	Atlas Material Testing Technology LLC—*Laurence Bond*	4114 N Ravenswood Ave, Chicago IL 60613	773-327-4520	R	70*	.3
27	EndressHauser Inc—*Todd Lucey*	2350 Endress Pl, Greenwood IN 46143	317-535-7138	R	69*	.3
28	Forney Corp—*John Conroy*	3405 Wiley Post Rd, Carrollton TX 75006	972-458-6100	S	68*	.2
29	Lee Co—*Leighton Lee*	2 Pettipaug Rd, Westbrook CT 06498	860-399-6281	R	65*	.8
30	K-Tron America Inc—*Edward Cloues* K-Tron International Inc	PO Box 888, Pitman NJ 08071	856-589-0500	S	65*	.5
31	Eurotherm International Inc—*Steve Bloomquist*	741-F Miller Dr, Leesburg VA 20175	703-443-0000	S	65*	.4
32	Lionheart Technologies Inc—*Briar Alpert*	PO Box 998 Highland Pa, Winooski VT 05404	802-655-4040	R	63*	.2
33	Vishay Measurement Group Inc	PO Box 27777, Raleigh NC 27611	919-365-3800	D	62*	.5
34	OI Analytical	PO Box 9010, College Station TX 77842	979-690-1711	S	60*	.1
35	ISCO Inc (Lincoln Nebraska)—*David Kennedy*	4700 Superior St, Lincoln NE 68504	402-464-0231	S	58*	.4
36	Malema Engineering Corp—*Dan Malani*	2225 Martin Ave Ste I, Greensboro FL 32330	561-995-0595	R	56*	<.1
37	Novatech Process Solutions LLC—*Aubrey Zey*	11500 Cronridge Dr Ste, Owings Mills MD 21117	410-753-8300	D	54*	.1
38	Emerson Process Management Inc—*Steve Sonnenberg*	PO Box 1148, Chanhassen MN 55317		S	49*	.7
39	Dynapar Corp—*Everett McElroy*	1675 N Delany Rd, Gurnee IL 60031	847-662-2666	S	49*	.1
40	Claud S Gordon Company Inc—*Peter Desloge*	PO Box 500, Richmond IL 60071	815-678-2211	R	48*	.3
41	INFICON Inc—*Lukas Winkler* INFICON Holding AG	2 Technology Pl, East Syracuse NY 13057	315-434-1100	S	48*	.2
42	Gasboy International Inc—*Greg Beason*	PO Box 22087, Greensboro NC 27420	336-547-5000	S	47*	.3
43	Hubbell Industrial Controls Inc—*Timothy Powers*	4301 Cheyenne Dr, Archdale NC 27263	336-434-2800	S	44*	.1
44	Wika Holding Corp—*Alexander Wiegand*	1000 Wiegand Blvd, Lawrenceville GA 30043	770-513-8200	R	44*	.6
45	Supreme Electronics Corp Hickok Inc	1714 Carrollton Ave, Greenwood MS 38930	662-453-6212	S	42*	.1
46	Campbell Scientific Inc—*Paul Campbell*	815 W 1800 N, Logan UT 84321	435-750-9681	R	40*	.3
47	A-Tech Corp—*Tony Tenorio*	1300 Britt St Se, Albuquerque NM 87123	505-767-1200	R	40*	.1
48	Metrix Instrument Company LP—*Rob Schulz* Roper Industries Inc	8824 Fallbrook Dr, Houston TX 77064	281-940-1802	S	39*	.1
49	Cognex Technology and Investment Corp	1 Vision Dr, Natick MA 01760	508-650-3000	S	38*	.1
50	Federal APD Inc—*Joe Wilson*	42775 Nine Mile Rd, Novi MI 48375	248-374-9600	S	36*	.2
51	FLIR Systems Boston—*Earl R Lewis*	25 Esquire Rd, North Billerica MA 01862	978-901-8000	S	35*	.3
52	Mesa Laboratories Inc—*John Sullivan*	12100 W 6th Ave, Lakewood CO 80228	303-987-8000	P	33	.2
53	Heraeus Electro-Nite Co—*Michael Midash*	1717 Langhorne Newtown, Langhorne PA 19047	215-944-9000	R	31*	.4
54	Micro Lithography Inc—*Chris Yen*	1257 Elko Dr, Sunnyvale CA 94089	408-747-1769	R	30*	.2
55	Fluid Components International—*Daniel McQueen*	1755 La Costa Meadows, San Marcos CA 92078	760-744-6950	R	30*	.2
56	Magnetrol International Inc—*Judy Stevenson*	5300 Belmont Rd, Downers Grove IL 60515	630-969-4000	R	30*	.4
57	CEC Controls Company Inc—*Robert Scheper*	14555 Barber Ave, Warren MI 48088	586-779-0222	R	25*	.1
58	Spectronics Corp—*Jonathan Cooper*	956 Brush Hollow Rd, Westbury NY 11590	516-333-4840	R	25*	.1
59	HO Trerice Co	12950 W 8 Mile Rd, Oak Park MI 48237	248-399-8000	R	25*	.1
60	International Systems and Controls Corp—*Robert S Medina*	2950 N Loop W Ste 500, Houston TX 77092	713-526-5461	R	23*	.2
61	Meriam Process Technologies—*Kenneth Semelsberger*	10920 Madison Ave, Cleveland OH 44102	216-281-1100	S	23*	.1
62	Pyromation Inc—*Peter Wilson*	5211 Industrial Rd, Fort Wayne IN 46825	260-484-2580	R	22*	.2
63	Imtech Corp—*Paul Noble*	2 Stewart Ct, Denville NJ 07834	973-366-5550	R	22*	.1
64	Fairchild Industrial Products Co—*Mark Cuthbert*	3920 Westpoint Blvd, Winston Salem NC 27103	336-659-3400	R	22*	.1
65	Spectrum Controls Inc—*Bruce Wanta*	PO Box 6489, Bellevue WA 98008	425-746-9481	R	22*	.1
66	Moog Schaeffer Magnetics Div—*Raymond Boushie*	21339 Nordhoff St, Chatsworth CA 91311	818-341-5156	D	21*	.2
67	Phoenix Controls Corp—*Bob Munro*	75 Discovery Way, Acton MA 01720	978-795-1285	S	21*	.2
68	Axelgaard Manufacturing Company Ltd—*Dan Jeffres*	520 Industrial Way, Fallbrook CA 92028	760-723-7554	R	21*	.1
69	Vacuum Instrument Corp—*Frederick Ewing*	2099 9th Ave, Ronkonkoma NY 11779	631-737-0900	R	20*	.1
70	Specialized Systems Inc—*Robert Timm*	234 33rd St Dr Se, Cedar Rapids IA 52403	319-366-4971	R	20*	<.1
71	Food Automation - Service Techniques Inc—*Bernard Koether*	PO Box 1181, Bridgeport CT 06601	203-377-4414	R	19*	.1
72	American Glass Research Inc—*Bob Cowden*	603 Evans City Rd, Butler PA 16001	724-482-2163	R	19*	.2
73	Avl Instrumentation and Test Systems Inc—*Don Manvel*	46097 Commerce Ctr Dr, Plymouth MI 48170	734-414-9600	R	18*	.1
74	Emerson Process Management Valve Actuation LLC—*John Berra*	PO Box 4100, Saint Louis MO 63136	314-553-2000	S	17	N/A
75	Sencore Inc—*Allen Bowden*	3200 Sencore Dr, Sioux Falls SD 57117	605-339-0100	R	17*	.2
76	Control Concepts And Technology Corp—*Rick Lynn*	PO Box 99, Maurice LA 70555	337-993-7425	R	17*	.1
77	Schenck Accurate Inc—*Dirk Maroske*	PO Box 208, Whitewater WI 53190	262-473-2441	R	17*	.1
78	Tayco Engineering Inc—*Charles Taylor*	PO Box 6034, Cypress CA 90630	714-952-2240	R	16*	.1
79	Beta Lasermike Inc—*Ken Wright*	8001 Technology Blvd, Dayton OH 45424	937-233-9935	R	16*	.2
80	Aerosonic Avionics Specialties Inc—*Douglas J Hillman*	PO Box 6400, Charlottesville VA 22906	434-973-3311	S	16*	.1
81	Pulse Communications Inc—*Carl Moore*	2900 Towerview Rd, Herndon VA 20171	703-417-2950	S	16*	.1
82	Dieterich Standard Inc—*John Garnett*	PO Box 9000, Boulder CO 80301	303-530-9600	S	16*	.1
83	Healy-Ruff Co—*Chris Cole*	13005 16th Ave N Ste 1, Plymouth MN 55441	763-559-0568	R	16*	<.1
84	Cincinnati Test Systems Inc—*Chris Mccoy*	5555 Dry Fork Rd, Cleves OH 45002	513-367-6699	R	16*	.1
85	Aquasol Controllers Inc—*John Falik*	1707 Townhurst Dr, Houston TX 77043	713-683-6406	R	16*	.1
86	Mamac Systems Inc—*S Gul*	8189 Century Blvd, Chanhassen MN 55441	952-556-4900	R	15*	.1
87	Cidra Corp—*Kevin Didden*	50 Barnes Park Rd N St, Wallingford CT 06492	203-265-0035	R	15*	.1

Rank	Company Name—*Executive Officer*	Address, City, State, Zip	Phone	Type	Fin	Empls
88	Sensidyne LP—*Howard Mills*	16333 Bay Vista Dr, Clearwater FL 33760	727-530-3602	R	15*	.1
89	Georg Fischer Signet LLC—*Christine Wendel*	PO Box 5770, El Monte CA 91734	626-571-2770	R	15*	.1
90	CSE Automation Engineering And Services Inc—*Johnny Canino*	PO Box 52373, Lafayette LA 70505	337-984-8054	R	15*	.1
91	Rjg Technologies Inc—*Matthew Groleau*	3111 Park Dr, Traverse City MI 49686	231-947-3111	R	15*	.1
92	Syscon International Inc—*Steve Thomas*	1108 High St, South Bend IN 46601	574-232-3900	R	15*	.1
93	Futek Advanced Sensor Technology Inc—*Javad Mokhberi*	10 Thomas, Irvine CA 92618	949-465-0900	R	15*	.1
94	Cannon Instrument Co—*Patrick Maggi*	2139 High Tech Rd, State College PA 16803	814-353-8000	R	14*	.1
95	Ati Industrial Automation Export Co—*Keith Morris*	1031 Goodworth Dr, Apex NC 27539	919-772-0115	R	14*	.1
96	AMETEK Process and Analytical Instruments—*Tom Mareice*	150 Freeport Rd, Pittsburgh PA 15238	412-828-9040	R	14*	.1
97	Amot Controls Corp—*Jake Plaia* Roper Industries Inc	8824 Fallbrook Dr, Houston TX 77064	281-940-1800	S	14*	.1
98	Venture Measurement Company LLC—*Mark Earl*	150 Venture Blvd, Spartanburg SC 29306	864-574-8960	S	14*	.1
99	TempTime—*Jean-Paul Martin*	116 American Rd, Morris Plains NJ 07950	973-984-6000	R	14*	<.1
100	Sekidenko Inc—*Doug Schatz*	2501 SE Columbia Way S, Vancouver WA 98661	360-694-7871	S	14*	<.1
101	Conax Technologies LLC—*Mike Valachoes*	2300 Walden Ave, Buffalo NY 14225	716-684-4500	R	14*	.1
102	Welker Inc—*Brian Welker*	PO Box 138, Sugar Land TX 77487	281-491-2331	R	14*	.1
103	Geophysical Research Company LLC—*Elaine Brasuell*	PO Box 581570, Tulsa OK 74158	918-834-9600	R	13*	.1
104	Weiss Instruments Inc—*John Weiss*	905 Waverly Ave, Holtsville NY 11742	631-207-1200	R	13*	.1
105	Geotech Environmental Equipment Inc—*Jerry Popiel*	2650 E 40th Ave, Denver CO 80205	303-320-4764	R	13*	.1
106	Technical Systems Inc—*Gary Conley*	2303 196th St Sw Ste B, Lynnwood WA 98036	425-775-5696	R	13*	<.1
107	Gayesco International LP—*Sean Morrison*	2859 Westside Dr, Pasadena TX 77502	713-941-8540	R	13*	.1
108	Sumitomo Cryogenics of America Inc—*David Dedman*	1833 Vultee St, Allentown PA 18103	610-791-6700	S	13*	.1
109	Asi Datamyte Inc—*Frank Voigt*	2800 Campus Dr Ste 60, Plymouth MN 55441	763-553-1040	R	13*	.1
110	Scully Signal Co—*Robert Scully*	70 Industrial Way, Wilmington MA 01887	617-692-8600	R	13*	.1
111	Paine Electronics LLC—*Dick Burkenpas*	5545 Nelpar Dr, East Wenatchee WA 98802	509-881-2100	R	13*	.1
112	Marlin Manufacturing Corp—*Al Tymkewicz*	12800 Corporate Dr, Cleveland OH 44130	216-676-1340	R	12*	.1
113	Teledyne TapTone—*Ron Marsiglio*	49 Edgerton Dr, North Falmouth MA 02556	508-563-1000	D	12*	.2
114	Santa Barbara Infrared Inc—*Steve McHugh*	30 S Calle Cesar Chave, Santa Barbara CA 93103	805-965-3669	S	12*	.1
115	Teledyne Advanced Pollution Instrumentation Inc—*Aldo Pichelli*	9480 Carroll Park Dr, San Diego CA 92121	858-657-9800	S	12*	.1
116	Sensor Electronics Corp—*Alan Petersen*	5500 Lincoln Dr Ste 17, Minneapolis MN 55436	952-938-9486	R	12*	<.1
117	Flow Technology Inc—*Alan Eschbach* Roper Industries Inc	8930 S Beck Ave Ste 10, Tempe AZ 85284	480-240-3400	D	12	.1
118	Schmitt Industries Inc—*Wayne A Case*	2765 NW Nicolai St, Portland OR 97210	503-227-7908	P	12	<.1
119	Ebtron Inc—*David Dougan*	1663 Hwy 701 S, Loris SC 29569	843-756-1828	R	11*	.1
120	Betatronix LLC—*Joseph Yanosik*	110 Nicon Ct, Hauppauge NY 11788	631-582-6740	R	11*	.1
121	Qei Inc—*Stephen Dalyai*	60 Fadem Rd, Springfield NJ 07081	973-379-7400	R	11*	.1
122	Precision Fabricating and Cleaning Company Inc—*Russell Gray*	3975 E Railroad Ave, Cocoa FL 32926	321-635-2000	R	11*	.1
123	Mensor Corp—*Paul Neilson* Wika Holding Corp	201 Barnes Dr, San Marcos TX 78666	512-396-4200	S	11*	.1
124	Gammon Technical Products Inc—*James Gammon*	PO Box 400, Manasquan NJ 08736	732-223-4600	R	11*	.1
125	Intech EDM	560 Bond St, Lincolnshire IL 60069	847-913-5300	S	11*	<.1
126	Palmer Wahl Instrumentation Group—*Stephen J Santangelo*	234 Old Weaverville Rd, Asheville NC 28804	828-658-3131	R	11*	<.1
127	Curtiss-Wright Controls Embedded Computing (Dayton Ohio)—*Matt Young*	2600 Paramount Pl Ste, Fairborn OH 45324	937-252-5601	S	11*	<.1
128	Solon Manufacturing Co—*David J Carpenter*	PO Box 207, Chardon OH 44024	440-286-7149	R	11*	<.1
129	Hoffer Flow Controls Inc—*Kenneth Hoffer*	PO Box 2145, Elizabeth City NC 27906	252-331-1997	R	11*	.1
130	Q-Lab Corp—*Douglas Grossman*	800 Canterbury Rd, Cleveland OH 44145	440-835-8700	R	11*	.1
131	World Wide Plastics Inc—*Donald Frick*	250 Andrews Rd, Langhorne PA 19053	215-357-0893	R	10*	.1
132	Aeroflex Powell	383 N Liberty St, Powell OH 43065	614-888-2700	S	10*	.1
133	Arizona Instrument LLC—*George Hays*	3375 N Delaware St, Chandler AZ 85225	602-470-1414	R	10*	.1
134	Control Instruments Corp—*Chris Schaeffer*	25 Law Dr, Fairfield NJ 07004	973-575-9114	R	10*	.1
135	Dataforth Corp—*Lee Payne*	3331 E Hemisphere Loop, Tucson AZ 85706	520-741-1404	R	10*	.1
136	Proteus Industries Inc—*Jon Heiner*	340 Pioneer Way, Mountain View CA 94041	650-964-4163	R	10*	.1
137	Quality Thermistor Inc—*Jack Ketlinski*	2108 Century Way, Boise ID 83709	208-377-3373	R	10*	<.1
138	Humble Instruments and Services Inc—*Daniel Jarvie*	143 Vision Park, Shenandoah TX 77384	281-540-6050	R	10*	<.1
139	Athena Controls Inc—*Robert Schlegel*	5145 Campus Dr Ste 1, Plymouth Meeting PA 19462	610-828-2490	R	10*	.1
140	Lux Products Corp—*Paul Balon*	6000 Commerce Pkwy Ste, Mount Laurel NJ 08054	856-234-7905	R	10*	.1
141	Pantrol Inc—*Jim Kucera*	PO Box 4387, Spokane WA 99220	509-535-9061	R	10*	<.1
142	Daq Electronics Inc—*Stanley Green*	PO Box 5028, New York NY 10087	732-981-0050	R	10*	.1
143	Koehler Instrument Company Inc—*Roy Westerhaus*	1595 Sycamore Ave, Bohemia NY 11716	631-589-3800	R	10*	.1
144	Sealant Equipment and Engineering Inc—*Nick Schultz*	PO Box 701460, Plymouth MI 48170	734-459-8600	R	9*	.1
145	Unicontrol Inc—*Dean Sung*	1111 Brookpark Rd, Cleveland OH 44109	216-398-4414	R	9*	.1
146	Dexter Research Center Inc—*Robert Toth*	7300 Huron River Dr St, Dexter MI 48130	734-426-3921	R	9*	.1
147	Hardy Instruments Inc—*Dave Ness*	9440 Carroll Park Dr S, San Diego CA 92121	858-278-2900	R	9*	.1
148	Mountz Inc—*Brad Mountz*	1080 N 11th St, San Jose CA 95112	408-292-2214	R	9*	.1
149	Lec Inc—*Harol Hogue*	PO Box 127, Brandon MS 39043	601-939-8535	R	9*	<.1
150	Agar Corporation Inc—*Joram Agar*	5150 Tacoma Dr, Houston TX 77041	832-476-5100	R	9*	.1
151	Orange Research Inc—*Paul Hoffman*	140 Cascade Blvd, Milford CT 06460	203-877-5657	R	8*	.1
152	Macrolink Inc—*David Vendor*	1500 N Kellogg Dr, Anaheim CA 92807	714-777-8800	R	8*	.1
153	Coastal Flow Measurement Inc—*Stephen Whitman*	PO Box 58965, Houston TX 77258	281-282-0622	R	8*	.1
154	Accutech (Hudson Massachusetts)—*Gene Yon*	577 Main St Ste 300, Hudson MA 01749	978-568-0500	R	8*	.1
155	King Instrument Company Inc—*Clyde King*	12700 Pala Dr, Garden Grove CA 92841	714-891-0008	R	8*	.1
156	Advanced Vacuum Company Inc—*Brian Raver*	1215 Business Pkwy N, Westminster MD 21157	410-876-8200	R	8*	<.1
157	Raytek Corp—*Carl Pickard*	1201 Shaffer Rd, Santa Cruz CA 95060	831-458-1110	S	8*	<.1
158	Kurz Instruments Inc—*Daniel Kurz*	2411 Garden Rd, Monterey CA 93940	831-646-5911	R	8*	<.1
159	David Morgan—*David Morgan*	600 Emlen Way, Telford PA 18969	215-799-0980	R	8*	.1
160	Lynn Products Co—*Daniel Cullinane*	400 Boston St Ste 1, Lynn MA 01905	781-593-2500	R	8*	.1
161	Proflow Inc—*Kurt Uihlein*	PO Box 748, North Haven CT 06473	203-248-2151	R	8*	<.1
162	Scanivalve Corp—*Addison Pemberton*	1722 N Madson St, Liberty Lake WA 99019	509-891-9970	R	8*	.1
163	Arzel Technology Inc—*Dennis Laughlin*	4801 Commerce Pkwy, Cleveland OH 44128	216-831-6068	R	8*	.1
164	Noren Products Inc—*Kimberly Dawn*	1010 O Brien Dr, Menlo Park CA 94025	650-322-9500	R	8*	.1
165	Miljoco Corp—*Howard Trerice*	200 Elizabeth St, Mount Clemens MI 48043	586-777-4280	R	8*	.1
166	Sandvik Process Systems Inc—*Walter Miller*	21 Campus Rd, Totowa NJ 07512	973-790-1600	S	7*	.1
167	Universal Flow Monitors Inc—*Lars Rosaen*	PO Box 249, Hazel Park MI 48030	248-542-9635	R	7*	<.1
168	Eagle Research Corp—*James Dutch*	4237 State Rte 34, Hurricane WV 25526	304-757-6565	R	7*	.1
169	Tel-Tru Inc—*Andrew Germanow*	408 Saint Paul St, Rochester NY 14605	585-295-0225	R	7*	<.1
170	Granville-Phillips—*Stephen S Schwartz*	6450 Dry Creek Pkwy, Longmont CO 80503	303-652-4400	D	7*	.1
171	Control Gaging Inc—*David Hayes*	5200 Venture Dr, Ann Arbor MI 48108	734-668-6750	R	7*	.1

Note: An asterisk (*) indicates an estimated financial figure. The company type code used is as follows: R = Private, P = Public, S = Private Subsidiary, B = Public Subsidiary, D = Division, J = Joint Venture, I = Investment Fund.

COMPANY RANKINGS BY SALES WITHIN 4-DIGIT SIC

Rank	Company Name—*Executive Officer*	Address, City, State, Zip	Phone	Type	Fin	Empls
172	Electro-Optical Industries Inc—*Robert Carlson*	859 Ward Dr, Santa Barbara CA 93111	805-964-6701	R	7*	.1
173	ABB Instrumentation—*Joel Blumenthal*	9716 S Virginia St Ste, Reno NV 89511	775-850-4800	R	7*	.1
174	Erdco Engineering Corp—*Bruce Nesvig*	PO Box 6318, Evanston IL 60204	847-328-0550	R	7*	.1
175	Systems Interface Inc—*Scott Demers*	22125 17th Ave Se Ste, Bothell WA 98021	425-481-1225	R	7*	<.1
176	Kds Holding LLC	41041 Black Bayou Rd, Gonzales LA 70737	225-644-5255	R	7*	<.1
177	Gammaflux LP—*Mike Brostedt*	113 Executive Dr Ste 1, Sterling VA 20166	703-471-5050	R	7*	.1
178	Palmer Instruments Inc—*Stephen Santangelo*	234 Old Weaverville Rd, Asheville NC 28804	828-658-3131	R	7*	.1
179	Onicon Inc—*Marvin Feldman*	1500 N Belcher Rd, Clearwater FL 33765	727-447-6140	R	7*	<.1
180	Mac Panel Co—*P Sedberry*	PO Box 7728, High Point NC 27264	336-861-3100	R	7*	<.1
181	Instrument Control Systems Inc—*Gary Kakach*	13005 16th Ave N Ste 1, Minneapolis MN 55441	763-559-0568	R	7*	<.1
182	Ducon Environmental Systems Inc—*Arun Govil*	19 Engineers Ln, Farmingdale NY 11735	631-420-4900	R	6*	<.1
183	Malcon Inc—*Peter Malavenda*	PO Box 463, Bedford Hills NY 10507	914-666-7146	R	6*	<.1
184	Technidyne Corp—*M Popson*	100 Quality Ave, New Albany IN 47150	812-948-2884	R	6*	<.1
185	Electro-Sensors Inc—*Bradley D Slye*	6111 Blue Circle Dr, Minnetonka MN 55343	952-930-0100	P	6	<.1
186	Noshok Inc—*James Cole*	1010 W Bagley Rd, Berea OH 44017	440-243-0888	R	6*	<.1
187	International Isotopes Inc—*Steve Laflin*	4137 Commerce Cir, Idaho Falls ID 83401	208-524-5300	P	6	<.1
188	Control Chief Corp—*Douglas S Bell*	200 Williams St, Bradford PA 16701	814-362-6811	S	6*	<.1
189	Air Logic Power Systems Inc—*David Huberfield*	3818 W Mitchell St, Milwaukee WI 53215	414-671-3332	R	6*	<.1
190	Knapp Engineering PC—*Greg Knapp*	20 Industrial Rd, Prospect CT 06712	203-758-3503	R	6*	<.1
191	New York Thermal Systems LLC	136 Old Short Hills Rd, Short Hills NJ 07078	212-731-2020	R	6*	<.1
192	Gpd Global Inc—*G Ferris*	PO Box 3836, Grand Junction CO 81502	970-245-0408	R	6*	<.1
193	Advanced Electromagnetics Inc—*Gabriel Sanchez*	PO Box 711719, Santee CA 92072	619-449-9492	R	6*	<.1
194	Midwest Timer Service Inc—*James Chapman*	PO Box 126, Benton Harbor MI 49023	269-849-2800	R	6*	<.1
195	CS Controls Inc—*Paul Srigley*	101 Dickson Rd, Houma LA 70363	985-876-6040	R	6*	<.1
196	Advanced Thermal Solutions Inc—*Kaveh Aza*	89 Access Rd Ste 27, Norwood MA 02062	781-769-2800	R	6*	<.1
197	Marsh-Mcbirney Inc—*Richard Espy*	4539 Metropolitan Ct, Frederick MD 21704	301-874-5599	R	6*	.1
198	Mija Industries Inc—*John Mc Sheffrey*	11 Commerce Rd Ste 2, Rockland MA 02370	781-871-5750	R	6*	<.1
199	Monitor Technologies LLC—*Amy Georgonsen*	PO Box 8048, Elburn IL 60119	630-365-9403	R	6*	<.1
200	Real-Time Laboratories LLC—*Sue Jason*	990 S Rogers Cir Ste 5, Boca Raton FL 33487	561-988-8826	R	6*	.1
201	NM Knight Company Inc—*Jack Narbut*	PO Box 1099, Millville NJ 08332	856-327-4855	R	5*	.1
202	Defelsko Corp—*Frank Koch*	802 Proctor Ave, Ogdensburg NY 13669	315-393-4450	R	5*	<.1
203	Nao Inc—*John Straitz*	PO Box 820503, Philadelphia PA 19182	215-743-5300	R	5*	<.1
204	Meeco Inc—*Lisa Bergson-Riddle*	250 Titus Ave, Warrington PA 18976	215-343-6600	R	5*	<.1
205	Veris Inc—*John Good*	6315 Monarch Park Pl A, Niwot CO 80503	303-652-8550	R	5*	<.1
206	Vorne Industries Inc—*Ramon Vorne*	1445 Industrial Dr, Itasca IL 60143	630-875-3600	R	5*	<.1
207	Hickok Inc—*Robert L Bauman*	10514 Dupont Ave, Cleveland OH 44108	216-541-8060	P	5	.1
208	Pyco Inc—*John Metzger*	600 E Lincoln Hwy, Langhorne PA 19047	215-757-3704	R	5*	<.1
209	Universal Analyzers Inc—*Michael Benton*	5200 Convair Dr, Carson City NV 89706	775-883-2500	S	5*	.1
210	Cimetrics Inc—*James Lee*	141 Tremont St Fl 11, Boston MA 02111	617-350-7550	R	5*	.1
211	Biomarine Inc—*Dave Stubbs*	456 Creamery Way, Exton PA 19341	610-524-8800	S	5*	.1
212	Dover Flexo Electronics Inc—*Kenneth Ekola*	217 Pickering Rd, Rochester NH 03867	603-332-6150	R	5*	.1
213	Ever Ready Thermometer Company Inc—*Duncan Ross*	2555 Kerper Blvd, Dubuque IA 52001		S	5	.1
214	PPT VISION Inc—*Joseph C Christensen*	6301 Old Shakopee Rd S, Bloomington MN 55438	952-996-9500	R	5*	<.1
215	Tigerstop LLC—*Elaine Mercer*	12909 Ne 95th St, Vancouver WA 98682	360-260-1153	R	5*	<.1
216	H-B Instrument Co—*Edward Hiergesell*	PO Box 26770, Collegeville PA 19426	610-489-5500	R	5*	<.1
217	Parvus Corp—*Less Goodman*	3222 S Washington St, Salt Lake City UT 84115	801-483-1533	R	5*	<.1
218	Furnace Parts LLC—*Scott Smith*	4755 W 150th St Ste C, Cleveland OH 44135	216-916-9601	R	5*	<.1
219	Ian-Conrad Bergan Inc—*Knut Bergan*	3119 N Davis Hwy, Pensacola FL 32503	850-434-1286	R	5*	<.1
220	Ck Technologies Inc—*Karl Zimmermann*	3629 Vista Mercado, Camarillo CA 93012	805-987-4801	R	5*	<.1
221	Energy Meter Systems Inc—*Ken Hudgeons*	1161 S Main St, Hennessey OK 73742	405-853-4976	R	5*	<.1
222	Intek Inc—*Joseph Harpster*	751 Intek Way, Westerville OH 43082	614-895-0301	R	5*	<.1
223	Jad LLC—*Daniel Raboin*	PO Box 649, South Windsor CT 06074	860-289-1551	R	5*	<.1
224	Borgwaldt Kc Inc—*Peter Nagel*	7741 Whitepine Rd, Richmond VA 23237	804-271-6471	R	5*	<.1
225	Essex Products Group Inc—*Peter Griffin*	PO Box 307, Centerbrook CT 06409	860-767-7130	R	5*	<.1
226	Pneumercator Company Inc—*Rudolph Manger*	120 Finn Ct Ste 2, Farmingdale NY 11735	631-293-8450	R	5*	<.1
227	Aggressive Systems Inc—*Gary Hine*	24269 Indoplex Cir, Farmington Hills MI 48335	248-477-5300	R	5*	<.1
228	Dusouth Industries—*William Southard*	651 Stone Rd, Benicia CA 94510	707-745-5117	R	5*	<.1
229	Alpa Precision Machine Works Inc—*Alberto Lozano*	1819 Antoine Dr, Houston TX 77055	713-680-8556	R	5*	<.1
230	Enquip Inc—*Michael Ross*	3319 N Lewis Ave, Tulsa OK 74110	918-599-8111	R	5*	<.1
231	Young Engineering and Manufacturing Inc—*Winston Young*	PO Box 3984, San Dimas CA 91773	909-394-3225	R	5*	<.1
232	Temp-Pro Inc—*Rodolfo Jacobson*	PO Box 89, Northampton MA 01061	413-584-3165	R	4*	<.1
233	Chem-Tec Equipment Co—*William Nolan*	234 Sw 12th Ave, Deerfield Beach FL 33442	954-428-8259	R	4*	<.1
234	Electronic Development Laboratories Inc—*Donald Polsky*	244 Oakland Dr, Danville VA 24540	434-799-0807	R	4*	<.1
235	Wagner Electronic Products Inc—*Ed Wagner*	326 Pine Grove Rd, Rogue River OR 97537	541-582-0541	R	4*	<.1
236	Myron L Co—*Myron L Turfitt*	2450 Impala Dr, Carlsbad CA 92008	760-438-2021	R	4*	.1
237	Alloy Engineering Company Inc—*Chris Lorch*	304 Seaview Ave, Bridgeport CT 06607	203-366-5253	R	4*	.1
238	Humidial Corp	926 S 8th St, Colton CA 92324	909-825-1793	S	4	<.1
239	Continental Controls Corp—*Ross Fisher*	8845 Rehco Rd, San Diego CA 92121	858-453-9880	R	4*	<.1
240	Gefran Isi Inc—*Ennio Franceshetti*	8 Lowell Ave, Winchester MA 01890	781-729-5249	R	4*	<.1
241	Bambeck Systems Inc—*Robert Bambeck*	1921 Carnegie Ave Ste, Santa Ana CA 92705	949-250-3100	R	4*	<.1
242	Electro Products Inc—*Richard Holscher*	PO Box 1000, Gonzalez FL 32560	850-968-4984	R	4*	<.1
243	Geomation Inc—*John Klebba*	7220 W Bonfils Ln Ste, Lakewood CO 80226	720-810-2426	S	4*	<.1
244	Greaves Company Inc—*John Greaves*	PO Box 411, La Conner WA 98257	360-466-1600	R	4*	<.1
245	WH Cooke and Company Inc—*Wayne Cooke*	PO Box 893, Hanover PA 17331	717-630-2222	R	4*	<.1
246	Xilas Medical Inc—*Don Lawson*	12665 Silicon Dr, San Antonio TX 78249	210-692-1114	R	4*	<.1
247	Howard M Trerice Corp—*Howard Trerice*	PO Box 291, Eastpointe MI 48021	586-777-4280	R	4*	<.1
248	Emcee Electronics Inc—*Max Corzilius*	520 Cypress Ave, Venice FL 34285	941-485-1515	R	4*	<.1
249	Allen Gauge and Tool Co—*Charles Allen*	PO Box 8647, Pittsburgh PA 15221	412-241-6410	R	4*	<.1
250	Custom Instrumentation Services Corp—*Leonard Richter*	7841 S Wheeling Ct, Englewood CO 80112	303-790-1000	R	4*	<.1
251	Eurotech Industries LLC	PO Box 180188, Utica MI 48318	586-493-9911	R	4*	<.1
252	Get Engineering Corp—*Greg Macneil*	9350 Bond Ave, El Cajon CA 92021	619-443-8295	R	4*	<.1
253	W A Kates Co—*John Taube*	1363 Anderson Rd Ste A, Clawson MI 48017	248-435-8225	R	4*	<.1
254	Professionalized Products And Services Inc—*William Huang*	10905 Brooklet Dr, Houston TX 77099	281-933-9427	R	4*	<.1
255	Process Sensors Corp—*Robert Winson*	113 Cedar St Ste S1, Milford MA 01757	508-473-9901	R	4*	<.1
256	Radiant Thermal Products Co—*Albert Maglio*	640 W 1st Ave, Roselle NJ 07203	908-241-7700	R	4*	<.1
257	Selective Med Components Inc—*Richard Fisher*	504 Harcourt Rd Ste 3, Mount Vernon OH 43050	740-397-7838	R	4*	<.1
258	Modutek Corp—*T Gross*	6387 San Ignacio Ave, San Jose CA 95119	408-362-2000	R	4*	<.1
259	Anchor Scientific Inc—*Margaret Potter*	PO Box 378, Long Lake MN 55356	952-473-7115	R	4*	<.1
260	Chino Works America Inc—*Koji Yanagisawa*	22301 S Western Ave St, Torrance CA 90501	310-787-8899	R	4*	<.1
261	Computer Aided Solutions LLC—*Lori Weier*	12628 Chillicothe Rd J, Chesterland OH 44026	440-729-2570	R	4*	<.1

Rank	Company Name—Executive Officer	Address, City, State, Zip	Phone	Type	Fin	Empls
262	Buck Scientific Inc—Robert Anderson	58 Fort Point St, Norwalk CT 06855	203-853-9444	R	3*	<.1
263	Vaporless Manufacturing Inc—Greg Young	8700 E Long Mesa Dr, Prescott Valley AZ 86314	928-775-5191	R	3*	<.1
264	Eldridge Products Inc—Mark Eldridge	2700 Garden Rd Ste A, Monterey CA 93940	831-648-7777	R	3*	<.1
265	Rickly Hydrological Co—Michael Rickly	1700 Joyce Ave, Columbus OH 43219	614-297-9877	R	3*	<.1
266	Compucon Corp—Robert Horeck	9307 Science Ctr Dr A, Minneapolis MN 55428	763-535-4176	R	3*	<.1
267	Winland Electronics Inc—Brian D Lawrence	1950 Excel Dr, Mankato MN 56001	507-625-7231	P	3	<.1
268	Oil Well Survey Instrument Company Inc—Charles Thrasher	PO Box 230061, Houston TX 77223	713-225-6595	R	3*	<.1
269	Caron Products And Services Inc—Steve Keiser	PO Box 715, Marietta OH 45750	740-373-6809	R	3*	<.1
270	Clinton Instrument Co—Marianne Szreders	295 E Main St, Clinton CT 06413	860-669-7548	R	3*	<.1
271	Visi-Trak Worldwide LLC—Barbara Barrick	8400 Sweet Valley Dr S, Cleveland OH 44125	216-524-2363	R	3*	<.1
272	Marathon Monitors Inc—Eric Boltz	8904 Beckett Rd, West Chester OH 45069	513-772-1000	R	3*	<.1
273	Broadley-James Corp—LS Broadley	19 Thomas, Irvine CA 92618	949-829-5555	R	3*	<.1
274	Future Controls Corp—John Williams	PO Box 130, Austinburg OH 44010	440-275-3191	R	3*	<.1
275	EMI Holding Corp Electro-Metrics Div—John A Fallone	231 Enterprise Rd, Johnstown NY 12095	518-762-2600	R	3*	<.1
276	Measurement Technology Northwest Inc—F O'neill	4211 24th Ave W, Seattle WA 98199	206-634-1308	R	3*	<.1
277	Airtrol Components Inc—Louis Atkinson	17400 W Liberty Ln, New Berlin WI 53146	262-786-1711	R	3*	<.1
278	DynaPath—Paul Bernhart Hurco Companies Inc	34155 Industrial Rd, Livonia MI 48150	248-488-0440	S	3*	<.1
279	Pdq Print Center—David Price	27 Stauffer Industrial, Taylor PA 18517	570-343-0414	R	3*	<.1
280	Mark - 10 Corp—William Fridman	11 Dixon Ave, Copiague NY 11726	631-842-9200	R	3*	<.1
281	Penn Separator Corp—Steven McNeil	PO Box 340, Brookville PA 15825	814-849-7328	R	3*	<.1
282	Electronic Controls Design Inc—Rex Breunsbach	4287 Se International, Milwaukie OR 97222	503-659-6100	R	3*	<.1
283	Automated Industrial Motion—Kurt Witham	5627 Airline Rd, Fruitport MI 49415	231-865-1800	R	3*	<.1
284	Environmental Solutions International Inc—Alexander Marcus	4200 Lafayette Ctr Dr, Chantilly VA 20151	703-263-7600	R	3*	<.1
285	Norcross Corp—Robert Norcross	255 Newtonville Ave St, Newton MA 02458	617-969-7020	R	3*	<.1
286	Automatic Firing Inc—James Pellegrino	300 Colvin Woods Pkwy, Tonawanda NY 14150	716-836-0300	R	3*	<.1
287	McIntosh Controls Corp—Harold Mattesky	215 Little Falls Rd, Fairfield NJ 07004	973-890-9400	R	3*	<.1
288	Mikron Infrared Inc / E2T—Gerry Posner	16 Thornton Rd, Oakland NJ 07436	201-405-8900	R	3*	<.1
289	EPM Inc—Chris Adams	2105 Power Ln, Fulton MO 65251	573-642-6550	R	3*	<.1
290	Ram Sensors Inc—Ron Miller	875 Canterbury Rd, Cleveland OH 44145	440-835-3540	R	3*	<.1
291	Jowa USA Inc—Per Hogdahl	59 Porter Rd, Littleton MA 01460	978-486-9800	R	3*	<.1
292	Chemtrac Systems Inc—Robert Bryant	6991 Pchtree Industry, Norcross GA 30092	770-449-6233	R	3*	<.1
293	LJ Star Inc—David Star	PO Box 1116, Twinsburg OH 44087	330-405-3040	R	3*	<.1
294	Junge Control Inc—Dave Junge	PO Box 8391, Cedar Rapids IA 52408	319-365-0686	R	3*	<.1
295	Bernard Controls Inc—Richard Upton	15740 Park Row Ste 100, Houston TX 77084	281-578-6666	R	3*	<.1
296	Impolit Environmental Control—J Andrews	800 Cummings Ctr Ste 3, Beverly MA 01915	978-927-4304	R	3*	<.1
297	Adhesive Systems Technology Corp—Steven Anderson	9000 Science Ctr Dr, Minneapolis MN 55428	763-592-2060	R	3*	<.1
298	King Nutronics Corp—J King	6421 Independence Ave, Woodland Hills CA 91367	818-887-5460	R	3*	<.1
299	Delphi Control Systems Inc—Beth Barbone	2806 Metropolitan Pl, Pomona CA 91767	909-593-8099	R	3*	<.1
300	Desert Microsystems Inc—Albert Johnson	PO Box H, Moreno Valley CA 92556	951-682-3007	R	3*	<.1
301	Coast Controls Inc—Douglas Fife	7500 Commerce Ct, Sarasota FL 34243	941-355-7555	R	3*	<.1
302	Crane Manufacturing Inc—Dreu Crane	PO Box 470945, Tulsa OK 74147	918-838-8800	R	3*	<.1
303	Algae-X International—Wout Lisseveld	5400 Division Dr Ste 1, Fort Myers FL 33905	239-690-9589	R	3*	<.1
304	Micro-Tek Laboratories Inc—Ronald Feller	154 Huron Ave, Clifton NJ 07013	973-779-5577	R	3*	<.1
305	Pavan and Kievit Enterprises Inc—Richard Pavan	473 Getty Ave, Paterson NJ 07503	973-742-8710	R	3*	<.1
306	Cambridge Viscosity Inc—Robert Kasameyer	101 Station Lndg Ste 1, Medford MA 02155	781-393-6500	R	3*	<.1
307	Analytical Instruments Corp—Bill Bonett	9845 Drysdale Ln, Houston TX 77041	713-460-5757	R	3*	<.1
308	Southeastern Process Equipment and Controls Inc—Marvin Donald	PO Box 746, Denver NC 28037	704-483-1141	R	3*	<.1
309	Weksler Glass Thermometer Corp—Kevin Marks	990 S Rogers Cir Ste 1, Boca Raton FL 33487	561-988-8003	R	3*	<.1
310	Woodlane Environmental Technology Inc—Michael Mccue	PO Box 250, Columbus NC 28722	828-894-8383	R	2*	<.1
311	Vici Metronics Inc—Stanley Stearns	26295 Twelve Trees Ln, Poulsbo WA 98370	360-394-6060	R	2*	<.1
312	Richards Arklay S Company Inc—Lincoln Richards	72 Winchester St, Newton MA 02461	617-527-4385	R	2*	<.1
313	Seventy-Three Manufacturing Company Inc—Richard Croyle	136 Stauffer Rd, Bechtelsville PA 19505	610-845-7823	R	2*	<.1
314	Universal Test Equipment Inc—David Huynh	1625 Quail Run, Charlottesville VA 22911	434-973-4545	R	2*	<.1
315	Toledo Transducers Inc—Mark Storer	PO Box 10, Holland OH 43528	419-867-4170	R	2*	<.1
316	Celamark Corp—Charles Ray	22 Commercial Blvd Ste, Novato CA 94949	415-883-3386	R	2*	<.1
317	Provar Industrial Corp—Edwin Stillman	PO Box 10728, Merrillville IN 46411	219-650-2330	R	2*	<.1
318	Rotronic Instruments Corp—Jos Horstman	PO Box 11241, Hauppauge NY 11788	631-427-3898	R	2*	<.1
319	Specialized Turning Inc—Harold Holm	7 Summit Industrial Pa, Peabody MA 01960	978-977-0444	R	2*	<.1
320	Starnet Technologies Inc—Bruce Grindeland	PO Box 374, Franksville WI 53126	262-886-0228	R	2*	<.1
321	Q-Mark Manufacturing Inc—Mark Osterstock	23332 Madero Ste D, Mission Viejo CA 92691	949-457-1913	R	2*	<.1
322	Donovan Controls LLC	PO Box 2582, Mandeville LA 70470	225-294-4133	R	2*	<.1
323	Valley Instrument Company Inc—James Magee	491 Clover Mill Rd, Exton PA 19341	610-363-2650	R	2*	<.1
324	Delta Computer Systems Inc—Peter Nachtwey	1818 SE 17th St, Battle Ground WA 98604	360-254-8688	R	2*	.1
325	Gentran Div—Jim Hawkins	42025 Osgood Rd, Fremont CA 94539	510-226-9343	R	2*	.1
326	Devar Inc—Anthony Ruscito Jr	706 Bostwick Ave, Bridgeport CT 06605	203-368-6751	R	2*	<.1
327	Perma-Cal Industries Inc—Robert Honer	1742 Orbit Way, Minden NV 89423	775-782-1026	R	2*	<.1
328	Beta Raven Inc—Don Root	40 S Corporate Hill Dr, Saint Charles MO 63301	636-255-1600	D	2*	<.1
329	Los Angeles Scientific Instruments Company Inc—Wolfgang Buerner	2451 Riverside Dr, Los Angeles CA 90039	323-662-2128	R	2*	<.1
330	Pra Inc—Robert Gubser	4821 226th Pl Ne, Arlington WA 98223	360-435-7097	R	2*	<.1
331	Electronic Design and Research Inc—Vladimir A Shvartsman	7331 Intermodal Dr, Louisville KY 40258	502-933-8660	R	2*	<.1
332	Electro-Numerics Inc—John A Wills	42213 Sarah Way, Temecula CA 92590	951-699-2437	R	2*	<.1
333	ISS Inc—P Herndon	1270 Souter Dr, Troy MI 48083	248-585-3600	R	2*	<.1
334	LT Industries Inc	811 Russell Ave, Gaithersburg MD 20879	301-990-4050	R	2*	<.1
335	Thermal Instrument Company Inc—Joseph Curran	217 Sterner Mill Rd, Langhorne PA 19053	215-355-8400	R	2*	<.1
336	Seekirk Inc—Douglas Seeley	2420 Scioto Harper Dr, Columbus OH 43204	614-278-9200	R	2*	<.1
337	Ultimate Technology Inc—Richard Clark	30 Waverly St, Taunton MA 02780	508-880-2400	R	2*	<.1
338	Marshall L H Co	270 W Ln Ave, Columbus OH 43201	614-294-6433	R	2*	<.1
339	American Sensors Corp—Francois Reizine	557 Long Rd, Pittsburgh PA 15235	412-242-5903	D	2*	<.1
340	Digitron Electronics LLC—Ron Gookin	PO Box 1250, Stevenson WA 98648	509-427-4005	R	2*	<.1
341	Southeastern Liquid Analyzers—Ronnie Roberts	308 W Liberty St, York SC 29745	803-684-4515	R	2*	<.1
342	Spectrum Company International Ltd—Douglas F Marsh	336 McKee St, Batavia IL 60510	630-879-8008	R	2*	<.1
343	Beta Control Systems Inc—Bryan Cullivan	PO Box 25507, Portland OR 97298	503-646-3399	R	2*	<.1
344	Jogler Inc—William Jackson	9715 Derrington Rd, Houston TX 77064	281-469-6969	R	2*	<.1
345	Scp Control Inc—Carl Peterson	PO Box 32022, Minneapolis MN 55432	763-572-8042	R	2*	<.1
346	Precision Coating Rods—Stephen Grandoff	600 Mount Vernon St, Oldsmar FL 34677	813-855-5054	R	2*	<.1
347	Colorado Digital Laboratories Inc—Steve Navratil	PO Box 235, Fort Garland CO 81133	719-206-2223	R	2*	<.1
348	Arga Controls Inc—Linda Halsey	128 W Chestnut Ave, Monrovia CA 91016	626-303-0301	R	2*	<.1

Note: An asterisk (*) indicates an estimated financial figure. The company type code used is as follows: R = Private, P = Public, S = Private Subsidiary, B = Public Subsidiary, D = Division, J = Joint Venture, I = Investment Fund.

COMPANY RANKINGS BY SALES WITHIN 4-DIGIT SIC

Rank	Company Name—Executive Officer	Address, City, State, Zip	Phone	Type	Fin	Empls
349	Philadelphia Instruments and Controls Inc—Eric Engelhardt	4401 N 6th St, Philadelphia PA 19140	215-329-8828	R	2*	<.1
350	Matrix Controls Company Inc—Robert Lindeman	330 Elizabeth Ave, Somerset NJ 08873	732-469-5551	R	2*	<.1
351	Systematic Controls Corp—Ami Bental	PO Box 1928, Kennesaw GA 30156	770-423-7100	R	2*	<.1
352	Photon Inc—John Fleisher	6878 Santa Teresa Blvd, San Jose CA 95119	408-226-1000	R	2*	<.1
353	Duro-Sense Corp—Jay Waterman	869 Sandhill Ave, Carson CA 90746	310-533-6877	R	2*	<.1
354	Measurementation—Kimberly Pena	1740 W 4th St Ste 105, Freeport TX 77541	979-373-9991	R	2*	<.1
355	Delta Controls Corp—Mildred Brown	585 Fortson St, Shreveport LA 71107	318-424-8471	R	2*	<.1
356	Zeltex Inc—Todd Rosenthal	130 Western Maryland P, Hagerstown MD 21740	301-791-7080	R	2*	<.1
357	R G Hansen and Associates—Robert Hansen	631 Chapala St, Santa Barbara CA 93101	805-564-3388	R	2*	<.1
358	Lewis Controls Inc—Andrew Corley	PO Box 526, Cornelius OR 97113	503-648-9119	R	2*	<.1
359	Research Applications Inc—Robert Childress	650 S 79th St, Chandler AZ 85226	480-961-4046	R	2*	<.1
360	Gem Instrument Co—Spiras Arfaras	PO Box 830, Brunswick OH 44212	330-273-6117	R	2*	<.1
361	Tsgc Inc—Richard Cook	PO Box 468, Spirit Lake IA 51360	712-336-0199	R	2*	<.1
362	Thermco Instrument Corp—Kent Richardson	PO Box 309, La Porte IN 46352	219-362-6258	R	2*	<.1
363	Agri-Tronix Corp—Terry Clarkson	2001 N Morton St, Franklin IN 46131	317-738-4474	R	2*	<.1
364	SJControls Inc—David Olszewski	2248 Obispo Ave Ste 20, Long Beach CA 90755	562-494-1400	R	2*	<.1
365	Integral Vision Inc—Charles J Drake	49113 Wixom Tech Dr, Wixom MI 48393	248-668-9230	P	2	<.1
366	Electronic System Design Inc—Harry Rueckel	418 S Vermont St, Palatine IL 60067	847-358-8212	R	2*	<.1
367	Valley Controls Inc—Verl Tyler	PO Box 1205, Reedley CA 93654	559-638-5115	R	2*	<.1
368	Infrared Associates Inc—Fred Rothe	2851 Se Monroe St, Stuart FL 34997	772-223-6670	R	2*	<.1
369	Pierry Manufacturing Inc—Russell Pierry	45 Rawhide Ridge Rd, Bozeman MT 59715	406-585-2200	R	2*	<.1
370	Promag Ltd—Jerome Medlin	11552 Merchant Dr, Baton Rouge LA 70809	225-751-7755	R	1*	<.1
371	Enerac—Bill Dascal	67 Bond St, Westbury NY 11590	516-997-2100	R	1*	<.1
372	Sensortech Systems Inc—Colin Hanson	5140 N Commerce Ave St, Moorpark CA 93021	805-378-1160	R	1*	<.1
373	Techmation Inc—David Ender	2121 S Mill Ave Ste 11, Tempe AZ 85282	480-968-9946	R	1*	<.1
374	Sensing Devices Inc—Steve Cornibert	1809 Olde Homestead Ln, Lancaster PA 17601	717-295-2311	R	1*	<.1
375	Calibron Systems Inc—Edward Francisco	7861 E Gray Rd Ste 109, Scottsdale AZ 85260	480-991-3550	R	1*	<.1
376	Avalon Vision Solutions LLC	422 Thornton Rd Ste 10, Lithia Springs GA 30122	770-944-8445	R	1*	<.1
377	Sansei Showa Company Ltd—Michihiko Kobayashi	31000 Bainbridge Rd, Cleveland OH 44139	440-248-4440	R	1*	<.1
378	Automatic Control Electronics Company Inc—Dan Faubel	5355 Dietrich Rd, San Antonio TX 78219	210-661-4111	R	1*	<.1
379	Delta Controls Company Inc—Donald Felts	12022 Knigge Cemetery, Cypress TX 77429	281-469-4891	R	1*	<.1
380	Process Thermal Dynamics Inc—Robert Beattie	801 Central Ave N, Brandon MN 56315	320-834-3370	R	1*	<.1
381	Dutile Glines and Higgins Inc—David Dutile	PO Box 5638, Manchester NH 03108	603-622-0452	R	1*	<.1
382	Hades Manufacturing Corp—Eugene Brand	135 Florida St, Farmingdale NY 11735	631-249-4244	R	1*	<.1
383	Si Industrial Instruments Inc—Frank Perch	200 Saw Mill River Rd, Hawthorne NY 10532	914-769-5700	R	1*	<.1
384	Sheridan Engineering Corp—Robert Sheridan	PO Box 312, Peabody MA 01960	978-977-3300	R	1*	<.1
385	Pmg Digital Inc—Michelle Terry	6011 43rd St, Lubbock TX 79407	806-747-7446	R	1*	<.1
386	Signal Systems International—Tom Kinney	1700 Hwy 35, Lavallette NJ 08735	732-793-4668	R	1*	<.1
387	Aec Engineering—David Audesse	172 Lower Main St, Freeport ME 04032	207-865-4190	R	1*	<.1
388	Calibrated Instruments Inc—John Shroyer	171 Brady Ave Ste 2, Hawthorne NY 10532	914-741-5700	R	1*	<.1
389	Inferno Manufacturing Corp—Allen Organick	115 Ricou St, Shreveport LA 71107	318-221-8454	R	1*	<.1
390	Kontrol Automation Inc—Edward Sharretts	PO Box 483, Primos Secane PA 19018	610-543-0215	R	1*	<.1
391	Panel-Tec Inc—A Ingram	3325 Triana Blvd Sw, Huntsville AL 35805	256-534-8132	R	1*	<.1
392	Micro-Design Inc—Helene Patel	PO Box 59449, Dallas TX 75229	972-488-8725	R	1*	<.1
393	Ameri Source Manufacturing Inc—Sam Alford	PO Box 1656, Athens TX 75751	903-677-7734	R	1*	<.1
394	Electronic Measuring Devices Inc—Frank Allia	199 Us Hwy 46, Budd Lake NJ 07828	973-691-4755	R	1*	<.1
395	Process Level Technology Ltd—Wade Donehue	PO Box 705, League City TX 77574	281-332-6241	R	1*	<.1
396	Thermometrics Corp—Jorge Hernandez	18714 Parthenia St, Northridge CA 91324	818-886-3755	R	1*	<.1
397	Check-It Electronics Corp—Richard Bettle	560 Trumbull St, Elizabeth NJ 07206	908-354-8236	R	1*	<.1
398	Gordon Engineering Corp—Steven Weighart	67 Del Mar Dr, Brookfield CT 06804	203-775-4501	R	1*	<.1
399	GRH Electronics Inc—Kenneth Hoberman	4520 S 36th St, Omaha NE 68107	402-734-4900	R	1*	<.1
400	Innovative Exhibits Ltd—Rita Viggiano	7156 W 127th St Ste 28, Palos Heights IL 60463	708-385-2787	R	1*	<.1
401	Micro-Tech Designs Inc—Mark Duvall	4312 Black Rock Rd Ste, Hampstead MD 21074	410-239-2885	R	1*	<.1
402	Air Instruments and Measurements LLC—Haecheol Baek	3579 E Foothill Blvd, Pasadena CA 91107	626-791-1912	R	1*	<.1
403	Encompass Automation and Engineering Technoligies LLC	622 Eckel Rd, Perrysburg OH 43551	419-873-0000	R	1*	<.1
404	Fjw Optical Systems Inc—Frank Warzak	322 N Woodwork Ln, Palatine IL 60067	847-358-2500	R	1*	<.1
405	SensorTec Inc (Fort Wayne Indiana)—Grant Passwater	7620 DiSalle Blvd, Fort Wayne IN 46825	260-497-8811	R	1*	<.1
406	Intra Computer Inc—Richard Eden	161-15 Rockaway Blvd S, Jamaica NY 11434	718-805-3911	R	1*	<.1
407	Senix Corp—Doug Boehm	52 Maple St Apt 3, Bristol VT 05443	802-453-5522	R	1*	<.1
408	G and W Instruments Inc—Ferdinand Weiss	277 Brooklyn St, Carbondale PA 18407	570-282-7352	R	1*	<.1
409	Scientific Engineering Instruments Inc—Robert Robercik	139 NE 1st St Ste 613, Miami FL 33132	305-851-8005	R	1*	<.1
410	TPF Inc—Charles Stiens	PO Box 15171, Cincinnati OH 45215	513-761-9968	R	1*	<.1
411	Pcf Inc—Richard Preston	1509 S 270 E Ste 4, Saint George UT 84790	435-673-7677	R	1*	<.1
412	Instec Inc—Henry Zou	5589 Arapahoe Ave Ste, Boulder CO 80303	303-444-4608	R	1*	<.1
413	Master Level Controls Co—Jim LaFortune	4255 White Bear Pkwy S, Vadnais Heights MN 55110	651-426-9085	R	1*	<.1
414	Precision Measurement Company Inc—Samuel K Clark	PO Box 7676, Ann Arbor MI 48107	734-995-0041	R	1*	<.1
415	Accurate Gas Control Systems—Michael Shepherd	640 Brooker Creek Rd S, Oldsmar FL 34677	813-818-9777	R	1*	<.1
416	Control Headquarters Inc—Barbara Miller	1491 Caton Farm Rd, Crest Hill IL 60435	815-725-8080	R	1*	<.1
417	Logical Devices Inc—David Mot	PO Box 8400, Denver CO 80201	303-861-8200	R	1*	<.1
418	Tangent Instruments Inc—Rick Williams	PO Box 932, Santa Paula CA 93061	805-642-3136	R	1*	<.1
419	Meitler Consulting Inc—Brian Meitler	11935 Kaw Dr, Kansas City KS 66111	913-422-9339	R	1*	<.1
420	Benedict Computer Co—Travis Benedict	220 Felton Dr, Menlo Park CA 94025	650-323-0148	R	1*	<.1
421	Fluidthink	2 Gold St APT 1201, New York NY 10038	917-546-2980	R	1*	<.1
422	Inventive Systems Inc—William Borland	PO Box 220, Lexington Park MD 20653	301-863-5153	R	1*	<.1
423	Louis C Eitzen Co—David Jeffers	PO Box 1210, Glenwood Springs CO 81602	970-945-7572	R	1*	<.1
424	Jr3 Inc—John Ramming	22 Harter Ave Ste 1, Woodland CA 95776	530-661-3677	R	1*	<.1
425	Oxysense Inc—Peter Gerard	13111 N Cntl Expy Ste, Dallas TX 75243	214-575-7600	R	1*	<.1
426	Slack Associates—Howard Slack	540 S Longwood St, Baltimore MD 21223	410-566-2520	R	1*	<.1
427	Lagus Applied Technology Inc—Peter Lagus	457 Corporate Dr, Escondido CA 92029	760-480-1290	R	1*	<.1
428	Thermo/Probes Inc—Troy Hopper	55 Lyerly St Ste 214, Houston TX 77022	713-699-1393	R	1*	<.1
429	Allrout Inc—Jeff Robinson	3382 Production Ct, Zeeland MI 49464	616-748-7696	R	1*	<.1
430	Komech Corp—John Mentink	PO Box 118, Schenectady NY 12301	518-382-1801	R	1*	<.1
431	A and A Engineering—Stas Andrzejewski	2521 W La Palma Ave St, Anaheim CA 92801	714-952-2114	R	1*	<.1
432	Tomantron Inc—Jiri Toman	17942 66th Ave, Tinley Park IL 60477	708-532-7430	R	1*	<.1
433	International Temperature Control—Louis Perrot	PO Box 805, Au Gres MI 48703	989-876-8075	R	1*	<.1
434	Scale Electronics Corp—Moe Hassan	1875 Angus Ave Ste D, Simi Valley CA 93063	805-306-0347	R	1*	<.1
435	Cambria Corp—Douglas Johnson	1328 N 128th St, Seattle WA 98133	206-782-8380	R	1*	<.1
436	Midwest Energy Management Inc—Lonnie Samples	10 E 22nd St Ste 111, Lombard IL 60148	630-916-8643	R	1*	<.1
437	Wincal Technology Corp—Tommy Chang	1028 S Greenwood Ave S, Montebello CA 90640	323-346-3900	R	1*	<.1
438	Micro Cooling Concepts Inc—Jack Freyer	7522 Slater Ave Ste 12, Huntington Beach CA 92647	714-847-9945	R	1*	<.1

Rank	Company Name—*Executive Officer*	Address, City, State, Zip	Phone	Type	Fin	Empls
439	Tokheim Company Inc—*Vicki Barnes*	560 31st St, Marion IA 52302	319-362-4847	R	1*	<.1
440	Applewood Controls Inc—*Ronald Ricci*	PO Box 37, Littleton MA 01460	978-486-9220	R	1*	<.1
441	Complete Controls Inc—*Mark Lewis*	3923 Option Pass, Fort Wayne IN 46818	260-489-0852	R	1*	<.1
442	Kaltec Scientific Inc—*Jon Dean*	PO Box 762, Novi MI 48376	248-349-8100	R	1*	<.1
443	Microenergy Systems Inc—*Tim Lanager*	300 Industrial Dr, Oakland MD 21550	301-334-3455	R	1*	<.1
444	Vetra Systems Corp—*Jonas Ulenas*	275 Marcus Blvd Unit J, Hauppauge NY 11788	631-434-3185	R	1*	<.1
445	Noramar Company Inc—*Norm Tomiello*	PO Box 771, Chagrin Falls OH 44022	440-338-5740	R	1*	<.1
446	Integrated Time Systems Inc—*William Tanner*	PO Box 700699, San Jose CA 95170	408-996-3822	R	1*	<.1
447	Kuhlman Instrument Co—*Mark Lacy*	PO Box 468, Norwalk OH 44857	419-668-9533	R	1*	<.1
448	LSI Controls Inc—*Walt Nuschke*	11664 Orchard Rd, Waynesboro PA 17268	717-762-2191	R	1*	<.1
449	Mars Labs LLC—*Paul Decamp*	29 C St, Laurel MD 20707	301-470-6277	R	1*	<.1
450	Smartset Automation LLC	8818 7th Ave N, Minneapolis MN 55427	763-476-5999	R	1*	<.1
451	Tru Temperature Sensors Inc—*Terry Hale*	495 Morgan Ct, Southampton PA 18966	215-396-1550	R	1*	<.1
452	Infrared Analysis Inc—*Philip Hanst*	1558 S Anaheim Blvd St, Anaheim CA 92805	714-817-9303	R	1*	<.1
453	Warner Instruments—*Gene Warner*	PO Box 604, Grand Haven MI 49417	616-842-7658	R	1*	<.1
454	Diventech Inc—*Conley Sandberg*	12495 Cornell Ct, Eden Prairie MN 55347	952-946-7934	R	1*	<.1
455	Expo Instruments—*George Rauchwerger*	1122 Aster Ave Ste E, Sunnyvale CA 94086	408-554-8822	R	1*	<.1
456	Marshall Instruments Inc—*James Lynch*	2930 E La Cresta Ave, Anaheim CA 92806	714-632-8565	R	1*	<.1
457	Deban Enterprises Inc—*Elias Aboujaoude*	2650 Indian Ripple Rd, Beavercreek OH 45440	937-426-0003	R	1*	<.1
458	Micon Systems LLC	PO Box 12848, Houston TX 77217	713-921-1899	R	1*	<.1
459	Midstates Engineering Corp—*Joel Peterson*	PO Box 1941, Fargo ND 58107	701-293-3184	R	1*	<.1
460	3d Plus USA Inc—*John Quinn*	6633 W Eldorado Pkwy, Mckinney TX 75070	214-733-8505	R	1*	<.1
461	Western Electronic Components Corp—*Mark Razegti*	521 Spectrum Cir Ste A, Oxnard CA 93030	805-988-9888	R	1*	<.1
462	Bridger Scientific Inc—*David Schlottenmier*	114 State Rd Bldg B7, Sagamore Beach MA 02562	508-888-6699	R	1*	<.1
463	A Pick Time Inc—*John Taves*	17307 Ne 13th Pl, Bellevue WA 98008	425-444-2368	R	<1*	<.1
464	Digital Technologies Inc—*Robert Francis*	2305 Ashland St, Ashland OR 97520	541-821-2800	R	<1*	<.1
465	Machine Applications Corp—*James Weit*	3410 Tiffin Ave, Sandusky OH 44870	419-621-2322	R	<1*	<.1
466	Dataman Inc—*Barry Savage*	215 Michigan Ave, Orange City FL 32763	386-774-7785	R	<1*	<.1
467	Huntington Instruments Inc—*Jeffrey Huntington*	PO Box 718, Yellow Springs OH 45387	937-767-7001	R	<1*	<.1
468	Pressure Switches Inc—*Rachel Peck*	353 California St, Grants Pass OR 97526	541-474-4444	R	<1*	<.1
469	Xco International Inc—*Bonnie Scott*	1082 Rock Rd Ln Ste A, East Dundee IL 60118	847-428-2400	R	<1*	<.1
470	Lexica Inc—*Austin Mack*	15075b Sw Koll Pkwy B, Beaverton OR 97006	503-350-0731	R	<1*	<.1
471	Microcomputer Systems Inc—*John Hilburn*	1814 Ryder Dr, Baton Rouge LA 70808	225-769-2154	R	<1*	<.1
472	American Density Materials—*Al Ashton*	3826 Spring Hill Rd, Staunton VA 24401	540-887-1217	R	<1*	<.1
473	Big Thompson Watershed Forum—*Zack Shelley*	800 S Taft Ave, Loveland CO 80537	970-613-6160	R	<1*	<.1
474	Engineered Systems and Designs Inc—*Robert Spring*	119a Sandy Dr, Newark DE 19713	302-456-0446	R	<1*	<.1
475	Common Sensing Inc—*Brian D'aoust*	PO Box 130, Clark Fork ID 83811	208-266-1541	R	<1*	<.1
476	Connecticut Industrial Gauging Inc—*John Soucy*	141 S Main St, Beacon Falls CT 06403	203-729-3400	R	<1*	<.1
477	Esc Products Corp—*Larry Douglas*	PO Box 3998, Sequim WA 98382	360-681-6904	R	<1*	<.1
478	Mount Fury Company Inc—*Daniel Pope*	PO Box 2763, Issaquah WA 98027	425-391-0747	R	<1*	<.1
479	Oregon Electro-Mec Inc—*Bradford Whiting*	PO Box 1205, Corvallis OR 97339	541-757-1100	R	<1*	<.1
480	Papec LLC	2589 W Maracay Dr, Meridian ID 83646	208-893-5493	R	<1*	<.1
481	D and M Instruments Inc—*Dudley Sheffield*	1851 Gulf Fwy S Ste 26, League City TX 77573	281-557-1002	R	<1*	<.1
482	Sensitron Associates Inc—*Michael Rutkowski*	PO Box 4184, Reading PA 19606	610-779-0939	R	<1*	<.1
483	Embroidery Studio Inc—*Lynne Redmond*	510 Audubon Dr, Greensboro NC 27410	336-292-7311	R	<1*	<.1
484	Selectronix Inc—*Jerry Numata*	16419 199th Ct Ne, Woodinville WA 98077	425-788-2979	R	<1*	<.1
485	Tettmar and Associates Inc—*Thomas Tettmar*	2141 Summitview Dr Ste, Longmont CO 80504	303-684-9598	R	<1*	<.1
486	Kahn and Company Inc—*Jeffrey Kahn*	885 Wells Rd, Wethersfield CT 06109	860-529-8643	R	<1	<.1
487	RMF Products Inc—*Richard Frieders*	PO Box 520, Batavia IL 60510	630-879-0020	R	<1	<.1
488	Optrol Inc—*George Reeves*	PO Box 37157, Raleigh NC 27627	919-779-3377	R	<1	<.1
489	Universal Detection Technology—*Jacques Tizabi*	340 N Camden Dr Ste 30, Beverly Hills CA 90210	310-248-3655	P	<1	<.1
490	Ellis John—*John Ellis*	PO Box 553, Westbrookville NY 12785	845-754-8696	R	<1*	<.1
491	Invisa Inc—*Edmund C King*	PO Box 49376, Sarasota FL 34230	941-870-3950	P	<1	N/A

TOTALS: SIC 3823 Process Control Instruments
Companies: 491

					20,163	74.2

3824 Fluid Meters & Counting Devices

Rank	Company Name—*Executive Officer*	Address, City, State, Zip	Phone	Type	Fin	Empls
1	Danaher Industrial Controls—*Larry Culp*	6095 Parkland Blvd Ste, Mayfield Heights OH 44124	803-289-1388	S	3,567*	2.4
2	Badger Meter Inc—*Richard A Meeusen*	PO Box 245036, Milwaukee WI 53224	414-355-0400	P	277	1.3
3	FMC Technologies Measurement Solutions—*Jeff Nepherland*	500 North Sam Houston, Houston TX 77067	281-260-2190	S	117	.5
4	Brooks Instrument LLC	407 W Vine St, Hatfield PA 19440	215-362-3500	D	102*	.5
5	Daniel Measurement and Control Inc—*David Hunter*	PO Box 19097, Houston TX 77224	713-467-6000	S	79*	.5
6	Designatronics Inc—*Martin Hoffman*	PO Box 5416, New Hyde Park NY 11042	516-328-3300	R	49*	1.2
7	Elster Amco Water LLC—*James Gardiner*	1100 Sw 38th Ave, Ocala FL 34474	352-732-4670	S	38*	.3
8	Master Meter Inc—*Jerry Potter*	101 Regency Pkwy, Mansfield TX 76063	817-842-8000	R	32*	.1
9	Mid-South Electronics Inc—*Harold Weaver*	2600 E Meighan Blvd, Gadsden AL 35903	256-492-8997	R	30*	.4
10	Liquid Controls Corp	105 Albrecht Dr, Lake Bluff IL 60044	847-295-1050	D	29*	.2
11	Auto Meter Products Inc—*Jeff King*	413 W Elm St, Sycamore IL 60178	815-895-8141	R	27*	.2
12	Ernst Flow Industries—*Roger Ernst*	PO Box 925, Farmingdale NJ 07727	732-938-5641	R	26*	<.1
13	Thomas G Faria Corp—*David Blackburn*	PO Box 983, Uncasville CT 06382	860-848-9271	R	24*	.2
14	Acteras US Liquid Measurement Div—*LeRoy Nosbaum*	1310 Emerald Rd, Greenwood SC 29646	864-223-1212	D	21*	.1
15	Spangler Valve Co—*Walter Jorgensen*	505 S Vermont Ave, Glendora CA 91741	626-335-4028	R	20*	<.1
16	Sonin Inc—*Chris Tufo*	15105-D John J Delaney, Charlotte NC 28277	704-540-9000	R	17*	<.1
17	Tri-Continent Scientific Inc—*Brenton Hanlon*	12555 Loma Rica Dr, Grass Valley CA 95945	530-273-8389	R	12*	.1
18	Blue-White Industries Ltd—*Frances King*	5300 Business Dr, Huntington Beach CA 92649	714-893-8529	R	12*	.1
19	Techno Inc—*George Klein* Designatronics Inc	PO Box 5416, New Hyde Park NY 11042	516-328-3970	S	11*	<.1
20	Laser Technology Inc—*Eric A Miller*	7070 S Tucson Way, Centennial CO 80112	303-649-1000	R	11	.1
21	ENM Co—*Nicholas Polydoris*	5617 N NW Hwy, Chicago IL 60646	773-775-8400	R	10*	.1
22	NT International Inc—*Chuck Gould*	5155 E River Rd, Minneapolis MN 55421		S	9*	<.1
23	Duncan Parking Technologies Inc—*Mike Nickolus*	PO Box 849, Harrison AR 72602	870-741-5481	R	9*	<.1
24	Parkeon Inc—*Yves Chambeau*	40 Twosome Dr Ste 7, Moorestown NJ 08057	856-234-8000	R	8*	.1
25	Mindrum Precision Products Inc—*Diane Mindrum*	10000 4th St, Rancho Cucamonga CA 91730	909-989-1728	R	8*	<.1
26	Maguire Products Inc—*Stephen Maguire*	PO Box 2056, Aston PA 19014	610-459-4300	R	7*	<.1
27	Silversmith Inc—*David Silvers*	PO Box 1934, Gaylord MI 49734	989-732-8988	S	7*	<.1
28	Continental Nh3 Products Company Inc—*Joyce Ward*	PO Box 225323, Dallas TX 75222	214-741-6081	R	6*	<.1
29	Monarch International Inc—*Kenneth Grabeau*	15 Columbia Dr, Amherst NH 03031	603-883-3390	R	6*	<.1
30	Advance Engineering Corp—*Thomas Brown*	440 S Mclean Blvd, Elgin IL 60123	630-628-3445	R	6*	<.1
31	Roxar Inc—*Sandy Esselmont*	14701 Saint Marys Ln S, Houston TX 77079	713-482-6400	R	6*	<.1

Note: An asterisk (*) indicates an estimated financial figure. The company type code used is as follows: R = Private, P = Public, S = Private Subsidiary, B = Public Subsidiary, D = Division, J = Joint Venture, I = Investment Fund.

COMPANY RANKINGS BY SALES WITHIN 4-DIGIT SIC

Rank	Company Name—Executive Officer	Address, City, State, Zip	Phone	Type	Fin	Empls
32	Floscan Instrument Company Inc—Charles Wurster	3016 Ne Blakeley St, Seattle WA 98105	206-524-6625	R	5*	.1
33	Pom Inc—Seth Ward	PO Box 430, Russellville AR 72811	479-968-2880	R	5*	.1
34	HF Scientific Inc	3170 Metro Pkwy, Fort Myers FL 33916	239-337-2116	S	5*	<.1
35	Bidwell Industrial Group Inc—Donald Bidwell	2055 S Main St, Middletown CT 06457	860-346-9283	R	5*	<.1
36	Melland Gear and Instrument Of Hauppauge Inc—Richard Coronato	225 Engineers Rd, Hauppauge NY 11788	631-234-0100	R	4*	<.1
37	Pmi—David Hartman	321 1st St, Aspinwall PA 15215	412-201-2420	R	4*	.1
38	Delmhorst Instrument Co—Thomas Laurenzi	51 Indian Ln E, Towaco NJ 07082	973-334-2557	R	4*	<.1
39	G H Meiser and Co—Brian Parduhn	PO Box 315, Posen IL 60469	708-388-7867	R	4*	<.1
40	US Paper Counters—Anthony Perzanowski	PO Box 837, Cairo NY 12413	518-622-2600	R	3*	<.1
41	Phoenix America Inc—Bob Loubier	4717 Clubview Dr, Fort Wayne IN 46804	260-432-9664	R	2*	<.1
42	Waukee Engineering Company Inc—Dirk Pfeil	5600 W Florist Ave, Milwaukee WI 53218	414-462-8200	R	2*	<.1
43	Max Machinery Inc—Oliver Max	33 Healdsburg Ave Ste, Healdsburg CA 95448	707-433-7281	R	2*	<.1
44	Hi-Temperature Inc—Chuck Rumbley	PO Box 478, Tuscumbia AL 35674	256-383-5066	R	1*	<.1
45	Abbott Enterprises Inc—Bobby Abbott	PO Box 9026, Pine Bluff AR 71611	870-535-4973	R	1*	<.1
46	Carlon Meter Company Inc—Raymond Pilch	1710 Eaton Dr, Grand Haven MI 49417	616-842-0420	R	1*	<.1
47	Severn Engineering Company Inc—Robert Gross	555 Old Stage Rd Ste 1, Auburn AL 36830	334-821-8995	R	1*	<.1
48	Barker Controls Inc—Harry Mansfield	2205 Old Buncombe Rd, Greenville SC 29609	864-233-2145	R	1*	<.1
49	Instruments And Control Inc—Federico Singer	540 E Main St Ste 5, Branford CT 06405	203-481-7278	R	<1*	<.1

TOTALS: SIC 3824 Fluid Meters & Counting Devices
Companies: 49

					4,629	9.3

3825 Instruments to Measure Electricity

Rank	Company Name—Executive Officer	Address, City, State, Zip	Phone	Type	Fin	Empls
1	ITT Corp—Denise L Ramos	1133 Westchester Ave, White Plains NY 10604	914-641-2000	P	10,995	40.0
2	Agilent Technologies Inc—William P (Bill) Sullivan	5301 Stevens Creek Blv, Santa Clara CA 95051	408-345-8886	P	5,444	18.5
3	Itron Inc—LeRoy Nosbaum	2111 N Molter Rd, Liberty Lake WA 99019	509-924-9900	P	2,434	9.6
4	Teradyne Inc—Michael A Bradley	600 Riverpark Dr, North Reading MA 01864	978-370-2700	P	1,429	3.2
5	Advanced Energy Voorhees Inc	1625 Sharp Point Dr, Fort Collins CO 80525	970-221-4670	S	1,351*	1.3
6	Tektronix Inc—Amir Aghdaei	PO Box 500, Beaverton OR 97075	503-627-7111	S	1,105*	4.5
7	JDS Uniphase Corp	1 Milestone Center Dr, Germantown MD 20876	301-353-1550	S	680	2.8
8	Analogic Corp—James W Green	8 Centennial Dr, Peabody MA 01960	978-326-4000	P	424	1.4
9	Ixia—Atul Bhatnagar	26601 W Agoura Rd, Calabasas CA 91302	818-871-1800	P	277	1.1
10	LTX-Credence Corp—David G Tacelli	825 University Ave, Norwood MA 02062	781-461-1000	P	250	.6
11	OYO Instruments LP—Arnold Pater	7007 Pinemont Dr, Houston TX 77040	713-986-4444	S	222*	.3
12	BAE Systems Mission Solutions—William L Ballhaus	PO Box 509009, San Diego CA 92150	858-675-2600	S	206	1.4
13	Anritsu Co—Frank Tiernan	490 Jarvis Dr, Morgan Hill CA 95037	408-778-2000	S	205*	.6
14	Spirent Communications—William Burns	1325 Borregas Ave, Sunnyvale CA 94089	408-752-7100	S	180*	.4
15	Keithley International Investment Corp—Joseph Keithley Keithley Instruments Inc	28775 Aurora Rd, Solon OH 44139	440-248-0400	S	144	N/A
16	Keithley Instruments Inc—Joseph P Keithley	28775 Aurora Rd, Solon OH 44139	440-248-0400	R	127	.5
17	Honeywell Aerospace—Robert J Gillette	PO Box 52181, Phoenix AZ 85072	602-231-1000	D	109*	.6
18	ADE Corp—Chris Koliopoulos	80 Wilson Way, Westwood MA 02090	781-467-3500	S	103	.4
19	Cascade Microtech Inc—Michael D Burger	9100 SW Gemini Dr, Beaverton OR 97008	503-601-1000	P	96	.4
20	Curtis Instruments Inc—Stuart Marwell	200 Kisco Ave, Mount Kisco NY 10549	914-666-2971	R	92*	1.0
21	Triton Services Inc—Stephen E Hincks	2014 Industrial Dr, Bowie MD 21401	443-716-0600	R	92*	.2
22	Transcat Inc—Charles Hadeed	35 Vantage Point Dr, Rochester NY 14624	585-352-9460	P	91	.3
23	Fluke Networks—Chris O'Dell	PO Box 777, Everett WA 98206	425-446-4519	S	91*	.5
24	Theragenics Corp—M Christine Jacobs	5203 Bristol Industria, Buford GA 30518	770-271-0233	P	82	.5
25	Milbank Manufacturing Co—Lavon Winkler	PO Box 419028, Kansas City MO 64141	816-483-5314	R	81*	.9
26	Allied Motion Technologies Inc—Richard S Warzala	23 Inverness Way E Ste, Englewood CO 80112	303-799-8520	P	81	.5
27	L3 Telemetry-West Telemetry and Instrumentation—Michael Strianese	9020 Balboa Ave, San Diego CA 92123	858-694-7500	D	78*	.4
28	Lansdale Semiconductor Inc—Dale Lillard	5245 S 39th St, Phoenix AZ 85040	602-438-0123	R	71*	.1
29	Aero Systems Engineering Inc—Charles Loux	358 E Fillmore Ave, Saint Paul MN 55107	651-227-7515	S	64*	.2
30	Boonton Electronics Corp Wireless Telecom Group Inc	PO Box 465, Parsippany NJ 07054	973-386-9696	S	63*	.1
31	Logitek Inc—William Forman North Atlantic Industries Inc	110 Wilbur Pl, Bohemia NY 11716	631-567-1100	S	62*	.1
32	Precision Flow Technologies Inc—Kevin Brady	PO Box 149, Saugerties NY 12477	845-247-0810	R	59*	.1
33	Megger Group Ltd	4271 Bronze Way, Dallas TX 75237		R	56*	.7
34	Rohde and Schwarz Inc	8661 Robert Fulton Dr, Columbia MD 21046	410-910-7800	S	54*	.1
35	Frequency Electronics Inc—Martin B Bloch	55 Charles Lindbergh B, Uniondale NY 11553	516-794-4500	P	53	.4
36	B and B Electronics Manufacturing Co—Don Wiencek	PO Box 1040, Ottawa IL 61350	815-433-5100	S	53*	.1
37	Bird Electronic Corp—David Hessler	30303 Aurora Rd, Solon OH 44139	440-248-1200	R	51*	.2
38	LandisGyr Inc—Richard Mora	2800 Duncan Rd, Lafayette IN 47904	765-742-1001	R	51*	.7
39	Trans-Coil Inc	7878 N 86th St, Milwaukee WI 53224	414-357-4480	R	48*	.1
40	inTEST Corp—Robert E Matthiessen	804 E Gate Dr Ste 200, Mt Laurel NJ 08054	856-505-8800	P	46	.1
41	Cues Inc—Sandy Milley	3600 Rio Vista Ave, Orlando FL 32805	407-849-0190	R	46*	.2
42	Maxima Technologies and Systems LLC	1811 Rohrerstown Rd, Lancaster PA 17601	717-581-1000	R	43*	.2
43	Plastronics Socket Company Inc—Wayne Pfaff	2601 Texas Dr, Irving TX 75062	972-258-2580	R	43*	.1
44	SPX Corporation Service Solutions—Christopher Kearney	28635 Mound Rd, Warren MI 48092	586-574-2332	D	40*	.4
45	Xyratex International Inc—Steve Barber	46831 Lakeview Blvd, Fremont CA 94538	510-687-5200	D	40*	.2
46	ManTech Test Systems Inc—George J Pedersen	14119A Sullyfield Cr 2, Chantilly VA 20151	703-814-4200	S	40*	.1
47	ORBIT/FR Inc—Per O Iversen	506 Prudential Rd, Horsham PA 19044	215-674-5100	P	36	.1
48	Dranetz—Robert Hart	PO Box 4019, Edison NJ 08818	732-287-3680	S	36*	.1
49	Environmental Systems Products Inc—Mark Fratello	7 Kripes Rd, East Granby CT 06026	860-653-0081	R	36*	.1
50	Nida Corp—Lydia Beauseigneur	300 S John Rodes Blvd, Melbourne FL 32904	321-727-2265	R	36	.1
51	Trio-Tech International—Siew W Yong	16139 Wyandotte St, Van Nuys CA 91406	818-787-7000	P	36	.5
52	Doble Engineering Co—Robert Smith	85 Walnut St, Watertown MA 02472	617-926-4900	R	36*	.2
53	Specialized Products Co—Pete Smith	1100 S Kimball Ave, Southlake TX 76092	817-329-6647	R	32*	.1
54	International Transducer Corp—R Callahan	869 Ward Dr, Santa Barbara CA 93111	805-683-2575	R	32*	.5
55	AMETEK Aerospace Inc	50 Fordham Rd, Wilmington MA 01887	978-988-4101	D	30*	8.3
56	Shokai Far East Ltd—MB Rubin	9 Elena Ct, Cortlandt Manor NY 10567	914-736-3500	R	29*	.1
57	Avtron Aerospace Inc—Jeffery Gwinnell	7900 E Pleasant Valley, Cleveland OH 44131	216-750-5152	R	28*	.1
58	Evolve Manufacturing Technologies Inc—Noreen King	960 Linda Vista Ave, Mountain View CA 94043	650-968-9292	R	28*	.1
59	Airmar Technology Corp—Stephen Boucher	35 Meadowbrook Dr, Milford NH 03055	603-673-9570	R	28*	.2
60	Hunt Technologies LLC—Jim Barutt	6436 County Rd 11, Pequot Lakes MN 56472	218-562-4877	R	28*	.2
61	Circuit Check Inc—Greg Michalko	6550 Wedgwood Rd N Ste, Maple Grove MN 55311	763-694-4100	R	27*	.1
62	Baker Instrument Co—Curt Lanham	4812 McMurry Ave, Fort Collins CO 80525	970-282-1200	D	27*	.1
63	Data I/O Corp—Frederick R Hume	6464 185th Ave NE Ste, Redmond WA 98052	425-881-6444	P	26	.1

Rank	Company Name—*Executive Officer*	Address, City, State, Zip	Phone	Type	Fin	Empls
64	AandD Technology Inc—*Eddie Koyama*	4622 Runway Blvd, Ann Arbor MI 48108	734-973-1111	S	25*	.1
65	Micro Control Co—*Harold Hamilton*	7956 Main St Ne, Minneapolis MN 55432	763-786-8750	R	25*	.2
66	Wireless Telecom Group Inc—*Paul Genova*	25 Eastmans Rd, Parsippany NJ 07054	973-386-9696	P	25	.1
67	D2D LLC	7915 Baymeadows Way St, Jacksonville FL 32256		S	24*	.1
68	Applied Precision LLC—*Ronald Suebert*	1040 12th Ave Nw, Issaquah WA 98027	425-557-1000	R	22*	.1
69	Ronan Engineering Co—*John Hewitson*	PO Box 129, Castaic CA 91310	661-702-1344	R	22*	.2
70	Giga-tronics Inc—*John R Regazzi*	4650 Norris Canyon Rd, San Ramon CA 94583	925-328-4650	P	21	.1
71	Texas Meter and Device Co—*Steve Swenke*	PO Box 154099, Waco TX 76715	254-799-0261	R	21*	<.1
72	Midtronics Inc—*Stephen Mc Shane*	7000 Monroe St, Willowbrook IL 60527	630-323-2800	R	20*	.1
73	Broudy Precision Equipment Co—*Jay Ranalli*	9 Union Hill Rd, West Conshohocken PA 19428	610-825-7200	R	19*	<.1
74	Jfw Industries Inc—*Fred Walker*	5134 Commerce Sq Dr, Indianapolis IN 46237	317-887-1340	R	19*	.1
75	Photo Research Inc—*Francis Dominic*	9731 Topanga Canyon Pl, Chatsworth CA 91311	818-725-9750	S	18*	.1
76	Altek Electronics Inc—*Richard Razza*	PO Box 1128, Torrington CT 06790	860-482-7626	R	18*	.1
77	Process Control Systems International	11993 Ravenna Rd Ste 5, Chardon OH 44024	440-286-4440	R	17*	.3
78	Phase Matrix Inc—*Pete Pragastis*	109 Bonaventura Dr, San Jose CA 95134	408-428-1000	R	17*	<.1
79	North Atlantic Industries Inc—*William Forman*	110 Wilbur Pl, Bohemia NY 11716	631-567-1100	R	16*	.1
80	Aetrium Inc—*John Pollock*	2350 Helen St, North Saint Paul MN 55109	651-770-2000	P	16	.1
81	Darmark Corp—*Darwin Zavadil*	13225 Gregg St, Poway CA 92064	858-679-3970	R	15*	.1
82	Nu-Di Products Company Inc—*Kenneth Bihn*	12730 Triskett Rd, Cleveland OH 44111	216-251-9070	R	15*	.1
83	DCI—*Karl Gemperli*	846 N Mart-Way Ct, Olathe KS 66061	913-982-5672	D	15*	.1
84	MCT Worldwide Inc—*John Moon*	121 S 8th St Ste 960, Minneapolis MN 55402	612-436-3240	R	15	.1
85	Microwave Instrumentation Technologies LLC—*Neil Cunningham*	1125 Satellit Blvd Nw, Suwanee GA 30024	678-475-8300	R	14*	.1
86	DIT-MCO International Corp—*Rick Thompson*	5612 Brighton Ter, Kansas City MO 64130	816-444-9700	S	14*	.1
87	Gold Line Connectors Inc—*Martin Miller*	PO Box 500, West Redding CT 06896	203-938-2588	R	14*	<.1
88	CXR Telcom Corp—*Eric Piaget*	894 Faulstich Ct, San Jose CA 95112	408-573-2700	D	14*	<.1
89	Aehr Test Systems—*Rhea J Posedel*	400 Kato Ter, Fremont CA 94539	510-623-9400	P	14	.1
90	Radian Research Inc—*Timothy Everidge*	3852 Fortune Dr, Lafayette IN 47905	765-449-5500	R	14*	.1
91	Xandex Inc—*Kamran Shamsavari*	1125 N Mcdowell Blvd, Petaluma CA 94954	707-763-7799	R	14*	.1
92	Reid-Ashman Manufacturing Inc—*Steven Reid*	582 N 3050 E, Saint George UT 84790	435-652-8422	R	13*	.1
93	MTI-Milliren Technologies—*Paul E Baia*	2 New Pasture Rd Ste 1, Newburyport MA 01950	978-465-6064	R	13*	.1
94	Schweitzer E O Manufacturing Company Inc—*Dan Clifford*	450 Enterprise Pkwy, Lake Zurich IL 60047	847-362-8304	R	13*	.1
95	Data Flow Systems Inc—*Thomas Smaidris*	605 N John Rodes Blvd, Melbourne FL 32934	321-259-5009	R	12*	.1
96	Sensor Systems LLC—*Nancy Preis*	PO Box 44000, Saint Petersburg FL 33743	727-347-2181	R	12*	.1
97	Dynamic Instruments Inc—*Steve Ness*	3860 Calle Fortunada, San Diego CA 92123	858-278-4900	R	12*	.1
98	Greenray Industries Inc—*Shih Chuang*	840 W Church Rd, Mechanicsburg PA 17055	717-766-0223	R	12*	<.1
99	Phase Dynamics Inc—*Bentley Scott*	1251 Columbia Dr, Richardson TX 75081	972-680-1550	R	12*	<.1
100	Loranger International Corp—*J Loranger*	817 4th Ave, Warren PA 16365	814-723-2250	R	12*	.1
101	Hanna Instruments Inc—*Martino Nardo*	584 Park E Dr, Woonsocket RI 02895	401-765-7500	R	11*	.1
102	Prime Instruments Inc—*James Moran*	9805 Walford Ave, Cleveland OH 44102	216-651-0400	R	11*	.1
103	Quadlogic Controls Corp—*Sayre Swarztrauber*	33-00 Northern Blvd, Long Island City NY 11101	212-930-9300	P	11	N/A
104	Flexstar Technology Inc—*Anthony Via*	47323 Warm Springs Blv, Fremont CA 94539	510-440-0170	S	11*	.1
105	Accurate Technologies Inc—*Robert Kasprzyk*	47199 Cartier Dr, Wixom MI 48393	248-848-9200	R	11*	.1
106	Glendinning Marine Products—*Paul Glendinning*	740 Century Cir, Conway SC 29526	843-399-6146	R	11*	.1
107	Satec Inc—*Ed Hoinowski*	10 Milltown Ct, Union NJ 07083	908-686-9510	R	11*	.1
108	QATechnology CoInc—*David Coe*	110 Towle Farm Rd, Hampton NH 03842	603-926-1193	R	10*	.1
109	Phenix Technologies Inc—*Frank Vitez*	75 Speiohor Dr, Accident MD 21520	301-746-8118	R	10*	.1
110	NH Research Inc—*Peter Swartz*	16601 Hale Ave, Irvine CA 92606	949-474-3900	R	10*	.1
111	Zumbach Electronics Corp—*Sven Naegeli*	140 Kisco Ave, Mount Kisco NY 10549	914-241-7080	S	10*	.1
112	Ems Development Corp—*Peter Crawford*	95 Horseblock Rd Unit, Yaphank NY 11980	631-345-6200	R	10*	<.1
113	Laser Design Inc—*C Martin Schuster*	9401 James Ave S Ste 1, Minneapolis MN 55431	952-884-9648	R	10*	.1
114	Spectral Dynamics Inc—*James Tucker*	2730 Orchard Pkwy, San Jose CA 95134	408-678-3500	R	10*	.1
115	Verity Instruments Inc—*Mike Whelan*	2901 Eisenhower St, Carrollton TX 75007	972-446-9990	R	10*	.1
116	ISCO International Inc—*Gordon Reichard*	1450 Arthur Ave Ste A, Elk Grove Village IL 60007	224-222-1666	R	10	<.1
117	Ideal Precision Meter Inc—*Mohamed El-Refai*	PO Box 31421, Raleigh NC 27622	919-571-2000	R	9*	.1
118	Noyes Fiber Systems Inc—*Jody Gallagher*	PO Box 398, Laconia NH 03247	603-528-7780	D	9*	.1
119	Albercorp—*Jeff Alber*	3103 N Andrews Ave, Pompano Beach FL 33064	954-623-6660	R	9*	<.1
120	Matec Instrument Companies Inc—*Ken Bishop*	56 Hudson St, Northborough MA 01532	508-393-0155	R	9*	<.1
121	Sotcher Measurement Inc—*Marc Sotcher*	175 Lewis Rd Unit 23, San Jose CA 95111	408-574-0112	R	9*	<.1
122	Sadelco Inc—*Les Kaplan*	75 W Forest Ave, Englewood NJ 07631	201-569-3323	R	9*	.1
123	Hoyt Electrical Instrument Works Inc—*Donald Hall*	23 Meter St, Concord NH 03303	603-753-6321	R	8*	.1
124	Hd Electric Co—*Mark Hoffman*	1475 S Lakeside Dr, Waukegan IL 60085	847-473-4980	R	8*	<.1
125	PDMA Corp—*Tim Owens*	5909 Hampton Oaks Pky, Tampa FL 33610	813-621-6463	R	8*	.1
126	Wilcom Inc—*Dennis McCarthy*	PO Box 508, Laconia NH 03247	603-524-2622	R	8*	.1
127	Roos Instruments Inc—*Mark Roos*	2285 Martin Ave, Santa Clara CA 95050	408-748-8589	R	8*	<.1
128	Krohn-Hite Corp—*Richard Haddad*	15 Jonathan Dr Unit 4, Brockton MA 02301	508-580-1660	R	8*	<.1
129	NETZSCH Instruments Inc—*Wolf-Dieter Emmerich*	37 N Ave, Burlington MA 01803	781-272-5353	S	8*	<.1
130	Qualitau Inc—*Gedaliahoo Krieger*	950 Benecia Ave, Sunnyvale CA 94085	408-522-9200	R	8*	.1
131	Ramsey Electronics Inc—*John Ramsey*	590 Fishers Station Dr, Victor NY 14564	585-924-4560	R	8*	.1
132	Associated Research Inc—*Michael Braverman*	13860 W Laurel Dr, Lake Forest IL 60045	847-367-4077	R	8*	<.1
133	S Himmelstein And Co—*Sydney Himmelstein*	PO Box 1134, Barrington IL 60011	847-843-3300	R	8*	<.1
134	Nutmeg Utility Products Inc—*Jeannine Lavallee*	PO Box 723, Cheshire CT 06410	203-272-2291	R	8*	<.1
135	Heateflex Corp—*Jorge Ramirez*	405 E Santa Clara St S, Arcadia CA 91006	626-599-8566	R	7*	<.1
136	Imperial Machine and Tool Co—*George Joest*	8 W Crisman Rd, Columbia NJ 07832	908-496-8100	R	7*	<.1
137	Electric Metering Corporation USA—*Steven Torsivia*	202 William Leigh Dr, Bristol PA 19007	215-949-1900	R	7*	<.1
138	Sage Instruments—*Brett M MacKinnon*	240 Airport Blvd, Freedom CA 95019	831-761-1000	R	7*	.1
139	Binsfeld Engineering Inc—*Stephen Tarsa*	4571 W MacFarlane, Maple City MI 49664	231-334-4383	R	7*	<.1
140	Advanced Probing Systems Inc—*Michelle Gesse*	PO Box 17548, Boulder CO 80308	303-939-9384	R	7*	<.1
141	Redington Counters Inc—*Frank O'neill*	PO Box 608, Windsor CT 06095	860-688-6205	R	7*	<.1
142	Scj Associates Inc—*Scott Sutherland*	60 Commerce Dr, Rochester NY 14623	585-359-0600	R	7*	<.1
143	Rika Denshi America Inc—*Larre Nelson*	112 Frank Mossberg Dr, Attleboro MA 02703	508-226-2080	R	7*	<.1
144	GGB Industries Inc—*Greg Boll*	PO Box 10958, Naples FL 34101	239-643-4400	R	7*	<.1
145	Jem America Corp—*Eddie Kazama*	3000 Laurelview Ct, Fremont CA 94538	510-683-9234	R	7*	.1
146	SR Instruments Inc—*John Siegel*	600 Young St, Tonawanda NY 14150	716-693-5977	R	6*	<.1
147	Elenco Electronics Inc—*Arthur Seymour*	150 Carpenter Ave, Wheeling IL 60090	847-541-3800	R	6*	<.1
148	Williams Wholesale Supply Of Nashville Inc—*Richard Tanner*	831a Cowan St, Nashville TN 37207	615-324-0466	R	6*	<.1
149	E F E Laboratories—*Greg Duffy*	420 Babylon Rd Ste A, Horsham PA 19044	215-672-2400	R	6*	<.1
150	San Antonio Independent School District Network Div—*Iris Amon*	1702 N Alamo St Ste 20, San Antonio TX 78215	210-299-1110	R	6*	.1
151	Summitek Instruments Inc—*Rick Hartman*	12503 E Euclid Dr Ste, Englewood CO 80111	303-768-8080	R	6*	<.1

Note: An asterisk (*) indicates an estimated financial figure. The company type code used is as follows: R = Private, P = Public, S = Private Subsidiary, B = Public Subsidiary, D = Division, J = Joint Venture, I = Investment Fund.

COMPANY RANKINGS BY SALES WITHIN 4-DIGIT SIC

Rank	Company Name—Executive Officer	Address, City, State, Zip	Phone	Type	Fin	Empls
152	GL Communications Inc—Vijay Kulkarni	818 W Diamond Ave Fl 3, Gaithersburg MD 20878	301-670-4784	R	6*	<.1
153	Load Technology Inc—David Ballweg	525 Commerce Cir, Mesquite NV 89027	702-643-8750	R	6*	<.1
154	Iet Labs Inc—Sam Sheena	534 Main St Unit 1, Westbury NY 11590	516-334-5959	R	6*	<.1
155	Royce Instruments Inc—Diane Cox	831 Latour Ct Ste C, Napa CA 94558	707-255-9078	R	6*	<.1
156	Sensorlink Corp—Karen Roth	1360 Stonegate Way, Ferndale WA 98248	360-595-1000	R	6*	<.1
157	Axiam Inc—Donald Lohin	58 Blackburn Ctr, Gloucester MA 01930	978-281-3550	R	5*	<.1
158	Precision Filters Inc—Donald Chandler	240 Cherry St, Ithaca NY 14850	607-277-3550	R	5*	<.1
159	Pile Dynamics Inc—Garland Likins	30725 Aurora Rd, Solon OH 44139	440-542-0873	R	5*	<.1
160	Martel Electronics Corp—David Devries	3 Corporate Park Dr St, Derry NH 03038	603-434-1433	R	5*	<.1
161	Ludl Electronic Products Ltd—Helmut Ludl	171 Brady Ave, Hawthorne NY 10532	914-769-6111	R	5*	<.1
162	GEOTEST - Marvin Test Systems Inc—Loofie Gutterman	1770 Kettering, Irvine CA 92614	949-263-2222	S	5*	<.1
163	Veeco Metrology Group—Lloyd Lacombe	2650 E Elvira Rd, Tucson AZ 85706	520-741-1044	S	5*	<.1
164	Metriguard Inc—James Logan	PO Box 399, Pullman WA 99163	509-332-7526	R	5*	<.1
165	Marine Electric Systems Inc—Harry Epstein	80 Wesley St, South Hackensack NJ 07606	201-531-8600	R	5*	<.1
166	Computer Service Technology Inc—Cecil Ho	2336 Lufield Dr, Dallas TX 75229	972-241-2662	R	5*	<.1
167	Etec Inc—Mark Ford	25 Worley St, West Roxbury MA 02132	617-325-6075	R	5*	<.1
168	Titan Tool Supply Inc—Stewart Pennington	PO Box 569, Buffalo NY 14217	716-873-9907	R	5*	<.1
169	Gould and Bass Company Inc—John Bass	1431 W 2nd St, Pomona CA 91766	909-623-6793	R	5*	<.1
170	Novotechnik Us Inc—Matt Pietro	155 Northboro Rd Ste 3, Southborough MA 01772	508-485-2244	R	5*	<.1
171	Test Products Inc—David Bruszewski	41255 Technology Park, Sterling Heights MI 48314	586-997-9600	R	5*	<.1
172	Programmed Test Sources Inc—Michael Lohrer	PO Box 517, Littleton MA 01460	978-486-3008	R	5*	<.1
173	Fischer Custom Communications Inc—Virginia Fischer	PO Box 5307, Torrance CA 90510	310-303-3300	R	5*	<.1
174	Huntron Inc—William Curry	15720 Main St Ste 100, Mill Creek WA 98012	425-743-3171	R	5*	<.1
175	Arbiter Systems Inc—Craig Armstrong	1324 Vendels Cir Ste 1, Paso Robles CA 93446	805-237-3831	R	5*	<.1
176	Yield Engineering Systems Inc—William Moffat	203 Lawrence Dr Ste A, Livermore CA 94551	925-373-8353	R	5*	<.1
177	MC Miller Company Inc—Melvin Miller	11640 Us Hwy 1, Sebastian FL 32958	772-794-9448	R	4*	<.1
178	Ballard Technology Inc—Richard Steegstra	11400 Airport Rd Ste 2, Everett WA 98204	425-339-0281	S	4*	<.1
179	Qxq Inc—Roger Quan	44113 S Grimmer Blvd, Fremont CA 94538	510-252-1522	R	4*	<.1
180	Chroma Systems Solutions Inc—Fred Sabatine	25612 Commercentre Dr, Lake Forest CA 92630	949-600-6400	R	4*	<.1
181	Innovative Circuits Engineering Inc—Narendra Narayan	2310 Lundy Ave, San Jose CA 95131	408-955-9505	R	4*	<.1
182	Waveline Inc—James Mc Gregor	160 Passaic Ave, Fairfield NJ 07004	973-808-9113	R	4*	<.1
183	Greening Associates Inc—Brent Greening	19465 Mount Elliott St, Detroit MI 48234	313-366-7160	R	4*	<.1
184	Eclypse International Corp—C Ferguson	265 N Joy St Ste 150, Corona CA 92879	951-371-8008	R	4*	<.1
185	Panashield Inc—Mary Girard	185r W Norwalk Rd, Norwalk CT 06850	203-866-5888	R	4*	<.1
186	Electrodata Inc—Robert J Robbins	23020 Miles Rd, Bedford Heights OH 44128	216-663-3333	R	4*	<.1
187	DigiLog Inc—Stratton Nicolaides	2360 Maryland Rd, Willow Grove PA 19090	215-830-9400	S	4*	<.1
188	Psiber Data Systems Inc—Darrell Johnson	7075-K Mission Gorge R, San Diego CA 92120	619-287-9970	R	4*	<.1
189	Process Measurement and Controls Inc—Robert Knowles	11 Old Sugar Hollow Rd, Danbury CT 06810	203-792-8686	R	4*	<.1
190	Cr Magnetics Inc—Jennifer Leslie	3500 Scarlet Oak Blvd, Saint Louis MO 63122	636-343-8518	S	4*	<.1
191	Dynamp LLC—Chuck Lockard	3735 Gantz Rd Ste D, Grove City OH 43123	614-871-6900	R	4*	<.1
192	Pulse Instruments—Sylvia Kan	1234 Francisco St, Torrance CA 90502	310-515-5330	R	4*	<.1
193	Columbia Research Laboratories Inc—Olive Alibert	1925 Macdade Blvd, Woodlyn PA 19094	610-872-3900	R	4*	.1
194	Quantem Corp—Christopher Bromberg	1457 Lower Ferry Rd St, Ewing NJ 08618	609-883-9191	R	4*	<.1
195	Dbm Optics Inc—Michael Minneman	300 S Public Rd Unit 2, Lafayette CO 80026	303-464-1919	R	4*	<.1
196	Testmetrix Inc—Christian Cojocneanu	846 Del Rey Ave, Sunnyvale CA 94085	408-730-5511	R	3*	<.1
197	Accuprobe Inc—Jeff Wake	35 Congress St Ste 2, Salem MA 01970	978-745-7878	R	3*	<.1
198	Rod L Electronics Inc—Roy Clay	PO Box 52158, Palo Alto CA 94303	650-322-0711	R	3*	<.1
199	Digalog Systems Inc—Rick Wagner	3180 S 166th St, New Berlin WI 53151	262-797-8000	R	3*	<.1
200	Kesu System and Services Inc—Sue Herrel	4210 S Industrial Dr S, Austin TX 78744	512-899-9383	R	3*	<.1
201	Cito Products Inc—Horst Wieder	PO Box 90, Watertown WI 53094	920-261-5799	R	3*	<.1
202	Nebulatronics Inc—Kenneth Rados	24542 Nobottom Rd, Olmsted Falls OH 44138	440-243-2370	R	3*	<.1
203	Test and Controls International Inc—Michael Mcmahon	11801 Diode Ct, Louisville KY 40299	502-266-7099	R	3*	<.1
204	Calogic LLC—Jonathan Kaye	237 Whitney Pl, Fremont CA 94539	510-656-2900	R	3*	<.1
205	Excel Precision Corporation USA—John Tsai	32551 Scott Blvd Ste 1, Santa Clara CA 95054	408-727-4260	R	3*	<.1
206	Morehouse Instrument Co—Harry Zumbrun	1742 6th Ave, York PA 17403	717-843-0081	R	3*	<.1
207	Lite-Check—Robert Blair	3102 E Trent Ave, Spokane WA 99202	509-535-7512	R	3*	<.1
208	Communications Manufacturing Co—John T Thompson	2234 Colby Ave, Los Angeles CA 90064	310-828-3200	R	3*	<.1
209	Dr Schenk of America LLC—Christoph Schenk	1830 Wooddale Dr Ste 5, Woodbury MN 55125	651-730-4090	R	3*	<.1
210	Orfid Corp—Winn Hong	180 N Vinedo, Pasadena CA 91107	626-641-9561	R	3*	<.1
211	RADCOM Equipment Inc—David Ripstein	6 Forest Ave, Paramus NJ 07652	201-518-0033	S	3*	<.1
212	Magnebit Holding Corp—Catherine Jacobson	9590 Chesapeake Dr Ste, San Diego CA 92123	858-573-0727	R	3*	<.1
213	Electro-Tech Systems Inc—Stan Weitz	3101 Mount Carmel Ave, Glenside PA 19038	215-887-2196	R	3*	<.1
214	Entertainment Solutions LLC	1704 Lake Rd, Altoona WI 54720	715-834-2216	R	3*	.1
215	Datacomm Management Sciences Inc—Thomas Parnon	25 Van Zant St Ste 2a, Norwalk CT 06855	203-838-7183	R	3*	<.1
216	Techtron Corp—Samuel Freedland	1400 Rail Head Blvd, Naples FL 34110	239-513-0800	R	3*	<.1
217	Electro-Fix Inc—Thomas Kade	PO Box 1775, Plainville MA 02762	508-695-0228	R	3*	<.1
218	Finley Design Services—Gerry Finley	910 Bern Ct Ste 130, San Jose CA 95112	408-437-4080	R	3*	<.1
219	Mesco Inc—Brent Ostendorff	PO Box 1949, Simpsonville SC 29681	864-228-6372	R	3*	<.1
220	Ballantine Laboratories Inc—Russell Mcadoo	312 Old Allerton Rd, Annandale NJ 08801	973-984-1900	R	3*	<.1
221	Rlc Electronic Systems Inc—Richard Kundrat	141 S 2nd St, Womelsdorf PA 19567	610-589-1988	R	3*	<.1
222	Encore Electronics Inc—Marcel Zucchino	4400 Rte 50, Saratoga Springs NY 12866	518-584-5354	R	3*	<.1
223	HJ Arnett Industries LLC—David Eales	20460 Sw Avery Ct, Tualatin OR 97062	503-692-4600	R	3*	<.1
224	Design Technology Inc—Stephen Myers	768 Burr Oak Dr, Westmont IL 60559	630-920-1300	R	2*	<.1
225	Candes Systems Inc—Daniel Signore	3131 Detwiler Rd, Harleysville PA 19438	215-256-4130	R	2*	<.1
226	Rotek Instrument Corp—Paul Lualdi	PO Box 540504, Waltham MA 02454	781-899-4611	R	2*	<.1
227	Pacific Instruments Inc—John Hueckel	4080 Pke Ln, Concord CA 94520	925-827-9010	R	2*	<.1
228	Cannon Load Banks Inc—Stanley Cannon	502 Park St, Palmetto GA 30268	770-463-0504	R	2*	<.1
229	Marena Systems Corp—Marius Enachescu	3563 Investment Blvd S, Hayward CA 94545	510-783-1907	R	2*	<.1
230	International Contact Technologies Inc—Joseph Baker	1432 Old Waterbury Rd, Southbury CT 06488	203-264-5757	R	2*	<.1
231	Quality Concepts Telecommunications Ltd—Chris Warren	19485 Harble Rd, Logan OH 43138	740-385-2003	R	2*	<.1
232	Nisene Technology Group Inc—Alan Wagner	384 Pine St, Watsonville CA 95076	831-761-7980	R	2*	<.1
233	Cactus Custom Analog Design Inc—James McDonald	60 N McClintock Dr Ste, Chandler AZ 85226	480-497-4511	R	2*	<.1
234	Loomis Industries Inc—James Loomis	1204 Church St, Saint Helena CA 94574	707-963-4111	R	2*	<.1
235	Chicago Dial Indicator Company Inc—Bruce Peterson	1372 Redeker Rd, Des Plaines IL 60016	847-827-7186	R	2*	<.1
236	AT Parker/Solar Electronics—Roy Talley	10866 Chandler Blvd, North Hollywood CA 91601	818-755-1700	R	2*	<.1
237	Sound Technology Corp—Bob Anderson	1400 Dell Ave Ste F, Campbell CA 95008	408-378-6540	R	2*	<.1
238	AH Systems Inc—Arthur Cohen	9710 Cozycroft Ave, Chatsworth CA 91311	818-998-0223	R	2*	<.1
239	Power Quality Inc—Bruce Chancellor	642 E 39th Pl Ste 5, Yuma AZ 85365	928-344-9008	R	2*	<.1
240	Xsis Electronics Inc—Jerry Dehnert	12620 Shawnee Mission, Shawnee Mission KS 66216	913-631-0448	R	2	<.1
241	Cablescan Inc—David Eubanks	3022 Inland Empire Blv, Ontario CA 91764	909-483-2436	S	2*	<.1

Rank	Company Name—*Executive Officer*	Address, City, State, Zip	Phone	Type	Fin	Empls
242	Micro Burn-In and Technology Inc—*Ken Bowers*	935 S Andreasen Dr Ste, Escondido CA 92029	760-746-2010	R	2*	<.1
243	Micro Crystal—*Tony Knezevich*	1615 Barclay Blvd, Buffalo Grove IL 60089	847-818-9825	S	2	<.1
244	Dyco Inc (Cave Creek Arizona)—*Greg Piesinger*	6225 E Saguaro Vista C, Cave Creek AZ 85331	480-585-4386	R	2*	<.1
245	Maurice Landstrass—*Maurice Landstrass*	1667 Rosita Rd, Pacifica CA 94044	650-355-5532	R	2*	<.1
246	Electronic Systems Of Wisconsin Inc—*Linda Naegeli*	5020 21st St, Racine WI 53406	262-554-1211	R	2*	<.1
247	Chiller City Corp—*Andy Wylde*	PO Box 42246, Mesa AZ 85274	480-889-1092	R	2*	<.1
248	Ball Systems Inc—*Patrick Turley*	624 S Range Line Rd St, Carmel IN 46032	317-848-0205	R	2*	<.1
249	Sts Instruments Inc—*Kevin Voelcker*	PO Box 1805, Ardmore OK 73402	580-223-4773	R	2*	<.1
250	Advanced Microtechnology Inc—*Eugene Wertz*	480 Vista Way, Milpitas CA 95035	408-945-9191	R	2*	<.1
251	Four Dimensions Inc—*James Chen*	3138 Diablo Ave 3140, Hayward CA 94545	510-782-1843	R	2*	<.1
252	Tahoe Rf Semiconductor Inc—*Irshad Rasheed*	12834 Earhart Ave, Auburn CA 95602	530-823-9786	R	2*	<.1
253	Droplet Measurement Technologies—*Darrell Baumgardner*	2545 Central Ave, Boulder CO 80301	303-440-5576	R	2*	<.1
254	Test Logic Inc—*Rod Gwillam*	17 Kenneth Dooley Dr, Middletown CT 06457	860-347-8378	R	2*	<.1
255	Sentech Inc—*Mina Patel*	2851 Limekiln Pke, Glenside PA 19038	215-887-8665	R	2*	<.1
256	Signum Systems Corp—*Jerry Lewandowski*	1211 Flynn Rd Unit 104, Camarillo CA 93012	805-383-3682	R	2*	<.1
257	Emulation Technology Inc—*Joseph Bagliere*	759 Flynn Rd, Camarillo CA 93012	408-982-0660	R	2*	<.1
258	Integrated Metering Systems Inc—*Charles Wilde*	11701 Belcher Rd S Ste, Largo FL 33773	727-539-1813	S	2*	<.1
259	Innoventions Inc—*David Feinstein*	10425 Bissonnet St, Houston TX 77099	281-879-6226	R	2*	<.1
260	Van London Company Inc—*Kurt London*	6103 Glenmont Dr, Houston TX 77081	713-772-6641	R	2*	<.1
261	Gulf Coast Power and Control Inc—*John Zimmerman*	64080 Hwy 1090, Pearl River LA 70452	985-863-2336	R	2*	<.1
262	T-Tech Inc—*John Taylor*	510 Guthridge Ct, Norcross GA 30092	770-455-0676	R	2*	<.1
263	Clarke Hess Communication Research—*Kenneth Salz*	3243 Rte 112 Ste 1, Medford NY 11763	631-698-3350	R	2*	<.1
264	Energy Control Systems Inc—*Joseph Ackerman*	2940 Cole Ct Ste A, Norcross GA 30071	770-448-0651	R	2*	<.1
265	Elm Systems Inc—*Bill Keith*	1101 Brown St, Wauconda IL 60084	847-526-5003	R	2*	<.1
266	Semprex Corp—*Karl Volk*	782 Camden Ave, Campbell CA 95008	408-379-3230	R	2*	<.1
267	Avanel Industries Inc—*Ingo Kurth*	121 Hopper St, Westbury NY 11590	516-333-0990	R	2*	<.1
268	Andeen-Hagerling Inc—*Carl Hagerling*	31200 Bainbridge Rd St, Cleveland OH 44139	440-349-0370	R	1*	<.1
269	Azimuth Electronics Inc—*Kenneth Johnson*	2605 S El Camino Real, San Clemente CA 92672	949-492-6481	R	1*	<.1
270	CPR Iii Inc—*Charles Ring*	380 S St, Rochester MI 48307	248-652-2900	R	1*	<.1
271	Durridge Company Inc—*Derek Lane-Smith*	PO Box 71, Bedford MA 01730	781-687-9556	R	1*	<.1
272	RB Watkins Inc—*Jim Rogers*	617 S Margene Dr, Oklahoma City OK 73130	405-732-9969	R	1*	<.1
273	Frequency Devices Inc—*William Franklin*	1784 Chessie Ln, Ottawa IL 61350	815-434-7800	R	1*	<.1
274	Ptek LLC	1723 Little Orchard St, San Jose CA 95125		R	1*	<.1
275	E/T Technologies Inc—*Michael Ames*	1111 W Mcnab Rd, Pompano Beach FL 33069	954-946-7100	R	1*	<.1
276	Accushim Inc—*Daniel Mottl*	PO Box 65, Lyons IL 60534	708-442-6448	R	1*	<.1
277	Linseis Inc—*Claus Linseis*	109 N Gold Dr, Trenton NJ 08691	609-799-6282	R	1*	<.1
278	Palstar Inc—*Paul Hrivnak*	PO Box 1136, Piqua OH 45356	937-773-6255	R	1*	<.1
279	Electrical Instrument Service Inc—*Michael Kane*	PO Box 272, Harrison NY 10528	914-699-9717	R	1*	<.1
280	Rfid Inc—*James Heurich*	14100 E Jewell Ave Ste, Aurora CO 80012	303-366-1234	R	1*	<.1
281	T and C Power Conversion Inc—*Tomasz Mokrzan*	110 Halstead St Ste 7, Rochester NY 14610	585-482-5551	R	1*	<.1
282	Macrodyne Inc—*Richard Murphy*	PO Box 376, Clifton Park NY 12065	518-877-3300	R	1*	<.1
283	Northeast Metrology Corp—*Basil Korbut*	2601 Genesee St, Buffalo NY 14225	716-827-3770	R	1*	<.1
284	PP M Inc—*Chas Gilmore*	30725 Aurora Rd, Solon OH 44139	216-595-3200	R	1*	<.1
285	Highrel Inc—*Gordon Cowan*	1335 N Hobson St, Gilbert AZ 85233	480-892-3233	R	1*	<.1
286	Neff Instrument Corp—*Glyn Neff*	255 E Santa Clara St, Arcadia CA 91006	626-357-2281	R	1*	<.1
287	Cpi Communications Inc—*Phil Easterling*	941 Hensley Ln, Wylie TX 75098	972-429-7160	R	1*	<.1
288	Precise Time And Frequency Inc—*David Briggs*	501 Audubon Rd, Wakefield MA 01880	781-245-9090	R	1*	<.1
289	Harris Instrument Corp—*Diane Mideleton*	155 Johnson Dr, Delaware OH 43015	740-369-3580	P	1*	<.1
290	Optimized Devices Inc—*Arthur Zuch*	220 Marble Ave, Pleasantville NY 10570	914-769-6100	R	1*	<.1
291	Eastern Time Designs Inc—*Lawrence P Stacy*	PO Box 474, Candia NH 03034	603-483-5876	R	1*	<.1
292	Centurion Non Destructive Testing Inc—*Kenneth Strass*	1400 Yorkshire Dr, Streamwood IL 60107	630-736-5500	R	1*	<.1
293	Lorlin Test Systems—*Clinton Rule* Axiam Inc	PO Box 3099, Framingham MA 01705	508-879-1827	D	1*	<.1
294	Midwest Flex Systems Inc—*Daniel Sternbergh*	415 Sb Chavez Dr, Flint MI 48503	810-424-0060	R	1*	<.1
295	Non-Linear Systems	4561-F Mission Gorge P, San Diego CA 92120		S	1*	<.1
296	Terahertz Technologies Inc—*John Gentile*	169 Clear Rd, Oriskany NY 13424	315-736-3642	R	1*	<.1
297	Hale Manufacturing Inc—*Wayne Hunter*	6235 Cupp Rd, Alanson MI 49706	231-529-6271	R	1*	<.1
298	Vuemetrix—*Jim Chu*	960 Hamlin Ct, Sunnyvale CA 94089	408-734-9974	R	1*	<.1
299	Pendulum Instruments Inc—*Harald Kruger*	5811 Racine St, Oakland CA 94609	510-428-9488	R	1*	<.1
300	Axcelerate Networks Inc—*Martin Varga*	1500 E Hamilton Ave St, Campbell CA 95008	408-626-8511	R	1*	<.1
301	Ambco Electronics—*Dennis Daniels*	15052 Red Hill Ave Ste, Tustin CA 92780	714-259-7930	R	1*	<.1
302	Mint Systems Corp—*Rudy Juang*	266 E Gish Rd, San Jose CA 95112	408-573-8885	R	1*	<.1
303	STB Electrical Test Equipment—*Patricia A Tavare*	1666 Auburn Ravine Rd, Auburn CA 95603	530-823-5111	R	1*	<.1
304	Electronic Devices Inc—*Ray Kauffman*	PO Box 15037, Chesapeake VA 23328	757-421-2968	R	1*	<.1
305	Calibrators Inc—*Michael Bruneault*	38 Morning Glory Rd, Cumberland RI 02864	401-769-0333	R	1*	<.1
306	Scientific Test Inc—*John Bailey*	1110 E Collins Blvd St, Richardson TX 75081	972-479-1300	R	1*	<.1
307	American Probe and Technologies Inc—*Kenneth Chabraya*	471 Montague Expy, Milpitas CA 95035	408-263-3356	R	1*	<.1
308	Haroutunian Aramais—*Aramais Haroutunian*	8025 Wheatland Ave Uni, Sun Valley CA 91352	818-504-2721	R	1*	<.1
309	David Gingerela—*Dave Gingerela*	7117 Arlington Ave Ste, Riverside CA 92503	951-688-3067	R	1*	<.1
310	Spectrum Instruments Inc—*Thomas Verseput*	570 E Arrow Hwy Ste D, San Dimas CA 91773	909-971-9710	R	1*	<.1
311	Crumbliss Manufacturing Company Inc—*Ronald Crumbliss*	PO Box 3201, Collegedale TN 37315	239-693-8588	R	1*	<.1
312	Deltec—*Dennis Orman*	13065 Tom White Way St, Norwalk CA 90650	562-926-2304	R	1*	<.1
313	GMH Engineering Inc—*John Gordon*	336 Mountain Way Dr, Orem UT 84058	801-225-8970	R	1*	<.1
314	Han King Inc—*Paul Robertson*	8b Middle River Dr, Stafford Springs CT 06076	860-851-9378	R	1*	<.1
315	Alpha Radio Products LLC—*Jeremy Ford*	6185 Arapahoe Rd, Boulder CO 80303	303-473-9232	R	1*	<.1
316	RKC Instrument—*Teru Hochi*	4245 Meghan Beeler Ct, South Bend IN 46628	574-273-6099	R	1*	<.1
317	Bartlett Instrument Company Inc—*Paul Bartlett*	PO Box 445, Fort Madison IA 52627	319-372-8366	R	1*	<.1
318	High Performance Test Inc—*Paramjit Singh*	48531 Warm Springs Blv, Fremont CA 94539	510-445-1182	R	1*	<.1
319	Prostat Corp—*Stephen Halperin*	1072 Tower Ln, Bensenville IL 60106	630-238-8883	R	1*	<.1
320	Alchimisti Group Inc—*Gordon Owen*	1027 Bransten Rd, San Carlos CA 94070	650-596-0130	R	1*	<.1
321	Continental Control Systems LLC—*Burl Amsbury*	3131 Indian Rd Ste A, Boulder CO 80301	303-444-7422	R	1*	<.1
322	Cortek Engineering Inc—*Katherine Homan*	1522 E Francis St Ste, Ontario CA 91761	909-930-1788	R	1*	<.1
323	PK Neuses Inc—*Gary Neuses*	PO Box 100, Arlington Heights IL 60006	847-253-6555	R	1*	<.1
324	Vertox Co—*Steven Hacker*	PO Box 2251, Garden Grove CA 92842	714-530-4541	R	1*	<.1
325	Frothingham Electronics Corp—*George Frothingham*	PO Box 629, Sanbornville NH 03872	603-522-6620	R	1*	<.1
326	California Marketing Enterprises Inc—*John Cusimano*	PO Box 53498, San Jose CA 95153	408-248-4644	R	1*	<.1
327	Data Proof—*James Marshall*	2562 Lafayette St, Santa Clara CA 95050	408-919-1799	R	1*	<.1
328	East Arizona Good Luck Enterprises Inc—*James Beck*	PO Box 579, Clarkdale AZ 86324	928-204-2597	R	1*	<.1
329	Stevens Instrument Co—*Sharon Kordt*	PO Box 193, Waukegan IL 60079	847-336-9375	R	1*	<.1
330	International Electro Magnetic Inc—*Anthony Pretto*	350 N Eric Dr Ste B, Palatine IL 60067	847-358-4622	R	1*	<.1

Note: An asterisk (*) indicates an estimated financial figure. The company type code used is as follows: R = Private, P = Public, S = Private Subsidiary, B = Public Subsidiary, D = Division, J = Joint Venture, I = Investment Fund.

COMPANY RANKINGS BY SALES WITHIN 4-DIGIT SIC

Rank	Company Name—*Executive Officer*	Address, City, State, Zip	Phone	Type	Fin	Empls
331	Omega Laboratories Inc—*Jack Moon*	245 Western Ave Ste 15, Essex MA 01929	978-948-7757	R	1*	<.1
332	Vm Solutions Inc—*Dave Brown*	PO Box 44926, Tacoma WA 98448	253-841-2939	R	1*	<.1
333	Probing Solutions Inc—*Kenneth Hollman*	9 Enterprise Way, Dayton NV 89403	775-246-0999	R	1*	<.1
334	Dgm Electronics Inc—*Dennis Makovec*	13654 Metric Rd, Roscoe IL 61073	815-389-2040	R	1*	<.1
335	Energy Tech LLC	PO Box 351, Higganum CT 06441	860-345-3993	R	1*	<.1
336	Lexseco LLC—*Thomas Clare*	4742 Allmond Ave, Louisville KY 40209	502-367-4393	R	1*	<.1
337	Autonnic Manufacturing Inc—*Edward Carmichael*	1076 Horizon Dr Ste 5, Fairfield CA 94533	707-421-0949	R	1*	<.1
338	Edaq Inc—*Michael Hagen*	1485 Tuskegee Pl Ste E, Colorado Springs CO 80915	719-576-7000	R	1*	<.1
339	Engineered Inspection Services Inc—*Dale Bletso*	PO Box 40, Brooks KY 40109	502-955-9021	R	1*	<.1
340	B and W Engineering Corp—*Garry Black*	3303 Harbor Blvd Ste E, Costa Mesa CA 92626	714-540-9975	R	1*	<.1
341	Innovative Instrumentation Inc—*Richard Josephs*	440 S Broad St Unit 26, Philadelphia PA 19146	215-659-6719	R	<1*	<.1
342	Optical Wavelength Laboratories Inc—*Daniel Welsch*	N9623 Us Hwy 12, Whitewater WI 53190	262-473-0643	R	<1*	<.1
343	Universal Synaptics Inc—*Brent Sorensen*	1801 W 21st St, Ogden UT 84401	801-731-8508	R	<1*	<.1
344	Zeta Meter Inc—*Louis Ravina*	PO Box 3008, Staunton VA 24402	540-886-3503	R	<1*	<.1
345	H6 Systems Inc—*Michael Hunter*	55 Lake St Ste 3, Nashua NH 03060	603-880-4190	R	<1*	<.1
346	Turgeon Engineering Inc—*Luke Turgeon*	1829 New Holland Rd St, Reading PA 19607	610-777-8267	R	<1*	<.1
347	Concrete Controls Corp—*Paul Mackinney*	1311 N Congress Dr, Chandler AZ 85226	480-821-5050	R	<1*	<.1
348	Holloway Shunts Inc—*Joseph Holloway*	PO Box 727, Edna TX 77957	361-782-3471	R	<1*	<.1
349	Jeff Kelley Cne—*Jeff Kelley*	2200 Morriss Ct, Flower Mound TX 75028	972-724-0085	R	<1*	<.1
350	Key Chemical and Equipment Company Inc—*James Witt*	13195 49th St N Ste A, Clearwater FL 33762	727-572-1159	R	<1*	<.1
351	Permian Electronics Inc—*Charles Wilson*	929 S L St, Midland TX 79701	432-570-6677	R	<1*	<.1
352	Practec LLC	17625 Ne 65th St Ste 1, Redmond WA 98052	425-881-8202	R	<1*	<.1
353	Omni Systems Inc—*James Mccabe*	1861 205th Ave Nw, Cedar MN 55011	763-753-3650	R	<1*	<.1
354	PC Netrix—*Mike Collins*	811 Minakwa Dr, Madison WI 53711	608-441-9400	R	<1*	<.1
355	Sigmation Inc—*James Knoth*	4549 Gateway Cir, Dayton OH 45440	937-435-2129	R	<1*	<.1
356	Television Measurement Services—*Gary Andrews*	34405 Sw Larkins Mill, Hillsboro OR 97123	503-628-3764	R	<1*	<.1
357	Test Systems Inc—*Leroy Earhart*	217 W Palmaire Ave, Phoenix AZ 85021	602-861-1010	R	<1*	<.1
358	Metara Inc—*Fred Ramberg*	1225 E Arques Ave, Sunnyvale CA 94085	408-331-5208	R	<1*	<.1
359	Macken Instruments Inc—*John Macken*	3186 Coffey Ln, Santa Rosa CA 95403	707-566-2110	R	<1	<.1
360	NCC Acquisition Corp—*Charles Dinsmore*	11358 Kumquat St Nw, Minneapolis MN 55448	763-862-8744	R	<1*	<.1
361	Test Switch—*Jere Wright*	PO Box 141252, Dallas TX 75214	214-328-4122	R	<1*	<.1
362	Reliability Inc—*Jay Gottlieb*	PO Box 218370, Houston TX 77218	281-492-0550	P	<1	N/A
363	Measurement Systems Technology—*Myron Tanner*	PO Box 167, Lodi WI 53555	608-592-5682	R	N/A	<.1

TOTALS: SIC 3825 Instruments to Measure Electricity
Companies: 363

					29,460	115.7

3826 Analytical Instruments

Rank	Company Name—*Executive Officer*	Address, City, State, Zip	Phone	Type	Fin	Empls
1	Beckman Coulter Inc—*Bob Hurley*	PO Box 8000, Brea CA 92821	714-993-5321	S	3,663	11.9
2	Life Technologies Corp—*Gregory T Lucier*	5791 Van Allen Way, Carlsbad CA 92008	760-603-7200	P	3,588	11.0
3	Bio-Rad Laboratories Inc—*Norman Schwartz*	1000 Alfred Nobel Dr, Hercules CA 94547	510-724-7000	P	2,074	7.0
4	PerkinElmer Inc—*Robert F Friel*	940 Winter St, Waltham MA 02451		P	1,921	7.2
5	Merck Millipore—*Martin Madaus*	290 Concord Rd, Billerica MA 01821	978-715-4321	D	1,654	6.1
6	Bruker Corp—*Frank H Laukien*	40 Manning Rd, Billerica MA 01821	978-663-3660	P	1,305	5.4
7	Waters Corp—*Douglas A Berthiaume*	34 Maple St, Milford MA 01757	508-482-2000	P	1,167	5.4
8	Illumina Inc—*Jay T Flatley*	9885 Towne Centre Dr, San Diego CA 92121	858-202-4566	P	1,056	2.2
9	Coherent Inc—*John R Ambroseo*	PO Box 54980, Santa Clara CA 95056	408-764-4000	P	803	3.3
10	Abbott Laboratories Diagnostic Div	1921 Hurd Dr, Irving TX 75038	972-518-6000	D	306*	2.0
11	Cepheid—*John L Bishop*	904 Caribbean Dr, Sunnyvale CA 94089	408-541-4191	P	278	.7
12	Perkin-Elmer Instruments—*Robert Friel* PerkinElmer Inc	940 Winter St, Waltham MA 02451	203-925-4600	D	154*	.9
13	Siemens Applied Automation Inc—*Riener Pallmann*	500 W Hwy 60, Bartlesville OK 74003	918-662-7000	D	136*	.3
14	Bruker Daltonics Corp Bruker Corp	40 Manning Rd, Billerica MA 01821	978-663-3660	S	121*	.7
15	World Precision Instruments Inc—*Harry Fein*	175 Sarasota Center Bl, Sarasota FL 34240	941-371-1003	R	113*	.1
16	International Remote Imaging Systems Inc—*Cesar M Garcia*	9172 Eton Ave, Chatsworth CA 91311	818-709-1244	P	108	.4
17	Clarient Inc—*Ronald A Andrews Jr*	31 Columbia, Aliso Viejo CA 92656	949-425-5700	P	92	.4
18	Ysi Inc—*Richard Omlor*	PO Box 279, Yellow Springs OH 45387	937-767-7241	R	90*	.3
19	ABB Inc Process Analytics Div—*Frank DeThomas*	PO Box 831, Lewisburg WV 24901	304-647-4358	D	84*	.2
20	Phenomenex Inc—*Farshad Mahjoor*	411 Madrid Ave, Torrance CA 90501	310-212-0555	R	75*	.4
21	REVCO Technologies Inc—*Guy Broadbent*	275 Aiken Rd, Asheville NC 28804	828-645-3981	S	73	.5
22	Foerster Instruments Inc—*Tommie Nilson*	140 Industry Dr, Pittsburgh PA 15275	412-788-8976	R	62*	.1
23	Thorlabs Inc—*Alex Cable*	PO Box 366, Newton NJ 07860	973-579-7227	R	54*	.7
24	HACH Ultra Analytics (Grants Pass Oregon)—*Simon Appleby*	PO Box 389, Loveland CO 80539		S	54*	.2
25	Roche NimbleGen Inc—*Frank Pitzer*	504 S Rosa Rd, Madison WI 53719	608-218-7600	S	51	.1
26	Physical Electronics USA Inc—*Retsu Oiwa*	18725 Lake Dr E, Chanhassen MN 55317	952-828-6100	R	49*	.1
27	Union Biometrica Inc	84 October Hill Rd, Holliston MA 01746	508-893-3115	S	48*	.1
28	ABB Automation Analytical Div—*Jurgen Dormann*	PO Box 831, Lewisburg WV 24901	304-647-4358	D	44*	.2
29	Li Cor Inc—*William Biggs*	PO Box 4425, Lincoln NE 68504	402-467-3576	R	37*	.3
30	GE Analytical Instruments—*David Calhoun*	6060 Spine Rd, Boulder CO 80301	303-444-2009	D	37*	.2
31	Owen Mumford USA Inc—*Robert Shaw*	1755 W Oak Commons Ct, Marietta GA 30062	770-977-2226	R	35*	<.1
32	Ocean Optics Inc—*Saul Arcos*	PO Box 2249, Dunedin FL 34697	727-733-2447	R	35*	.3
33	Aperio Technologies Inc—*Dirk G Soenksen*	1360 Park Ctr Dr, Vista CA 92081		R	34*	.1
34	Pacific Biosciences of California Inc—*Michael W Hunkapiller*	1380 Willow Rd, Menlo Park CA 94025	650-521-8000	P	34	.3
35	Bioanalytical Systems Inc—*Anthony S Chilton*	2701 Kent Ave, West Lafayette IN 47906	765-463-4527	P	33	.3
36	Trilithic Inc—*Bruce Malcolm*	9710 Park Davis Dr, Indianapolis IN 46235	317-895-3600	R	32*	.2
37	Bruker Medical Inc—*Frank Laukien* Bruker Daltonics Corp	15 Fortune Dr, Billerica MA 01821	978-663-3360	S	30*	.2
38	Exergen Corp—*Francesco Pompei*	400 Pleasant St, Watertown MA 02472	617-923-9900	R	30*	.1
39	Brookfield Engineering Laboratories Inc—*David Brookfield*	11 Commerce Blvd, Middleboro MA 02346	508-946-6200	R	29*	.2
40	Horiba Instruments Inc—*Mike Pohl*	17671 Armstrong Ave, Irvine CA 92614	949-250-4811	R	29*	.1
41	Rotex Global Lcc—*William Herkamp*	1230 Knowlton St, Cincinnati OH 45223	513-541-1236	R	27*	.2
42	Westover Scientific Inc—*Steve Lytle*	18421 Bothell-Everett, Mill Creek WA 98012	425-398-1298	R	22*	.1
43	Teledyne Analytical Instruments—*Tom Compas*	PO Box 1580, La Puente CA 91749		S	21*	.1
44	Transgenomic Inc—*Craig J Tuttle*	12325 Emmet St, Omaha NE 68164		P	20	.2
45	Analytical Sensors and Instruments Ltd—*Peter Cai*	12800 Park One Dr, Sugar Land TX 77478	281-565-8818	R	20	.1
46	OI Corp—*J Bruce Lancaster*	PO Box 9010, College Station TX 77842	979-690-1711	S	20	.1
47	Foss Nirsystems Inc—*Torben Ladegaard*	7703 Montpelier Rd Ste, Laurel MD 20723	301-680-9600	R	19*	.1
48	La Motte Chemical Products Company Inc—*David Motte*	PO Box 99, Swedesboro NJ 08085	410-778-3100	R	19*	.1
49	Quality Electrodynamics LLC	777 Beta Dr, Mayfield Village OH 44143	440-638-5106	R	17	.1
50	M Braun Inc—*Chris Chausse*	14 Marin Way, Stratham NH 03885	603-773-9333	R	16*	.1

Rank	Company Name—Executive Officer	Address, City, State, Zip	Phone	Type	Fin	Empls
51	Whatman Inc—Bill Emhiser	200 Park Ave Ste 210, Florham Park NJ 07932	973-245-8300	D	16*	.1
52	Esa Biosciences Inc—Walter Giusto	22 Alpha Rd, Chelmsford MA 01824	978-250-7000	R	15*	.1
53	RS Technical Services Inc—Rod Sutliff	PO Box 750579, Petaluma CA 94975	707-778-1974	R	15*	.1
54	Spectrum Systems Inc—Reginald Davis	3410 W Nine Mile Rd, Pensacola FL 32526	850-944-3392	R	15*	<.1
55	Dogwood Pharmaceuticals—Drew Fromkin	1 Gateway Ctr Ste 702, Newton MA 02458	617-527-9933	S	13	.2
56	Envirologix Inc—Bruce Ferguson	500 Riverside Industri, Portland ME 04103	207-797-0300	R	13*	.1
57	Hanson Research Corp—Roy Hanson	9810 Variel Ave, Chatsworth CA 91311	818-882-7266	R	13*	<.1
58	Bahnson Environmental Specialties LLC—Chris Berrier	4412 Tryon Rd, Raleigh NC 27606	919-829-9300	S	13*	.1
59	Wyatt Technology Corp—Philip Wyatt	6300 Hollister Ave, Goleta CA 93117	805-681-9009	R	12*	.1
60	TM Microscopes	3601 Calle Tecate Ste, Camarillo CA 93012	805-388-3326	D	12*	.1
61	Southern Flow Companies Inc—Gary Gray	PO Box 51475, Lafayette LA 70505	337-233-2066	S	11*	.2
62	Med Associates Inc—Bridget Garibay	PO Box 319, Saint Albans VT 05478	802-527-2343	R	11*	.1
63	Lincoln Laser Co—Robert Nehrbas	234 E Mohave St, Phoenix AZ 85004	602-257-0407	R	11*	.1
64	Florida Radiology Imaging At Lake Mary LLC—Richard Lewis	875 Concourse Pkwy S S, Maitland FL 32751	407-949-6439	R	11*	.1
65	Edgeone LLC—Betty Sundberg	19 Brigham St Unit 8, Marlborough MA 01752	508-263-5900	R	10*	.1
66	Lambda Research Optics Inc—Mark Youn	1695 Macarthur Blvd, Costa Mesa CA 92626	714-327-0600	R	10*	.1
67	Distek Inc—Gerald Brinker	121 N Ctr Dr, North Brunswick NJ 08902	732-422-7585	R	10*	.1
68	California Analytical Instruments Inc—R Furton	1312 W Grove Ave, Orange CA 92865	714-974-5560	R	9*	.1
69	Warner Instruments LLC—Victor Pantani	1125 Dixwell Ave, Hamden CT 06514	203-776-0664	S	9*	<.1
70	Automated Precision Inc—Kam Lau	15000 J Hpkins Dr Ste, Rockville MD 20850	240-268-0391	R	9*	.1
71	Regis Technologies Inc—Louis Glunz	8210 Austin Ave, Morton Grove IL 60053	847-967-6000	R	9*	.1
72	A2 Technologies LLC—Phyllis Bender	14 Commerce Dr, Danbury CT 06810	203-312-1000	R	8*	<.1
73	Columbus Instruments International Corp—Jan Czekajewski	950 N Hague Ave, Columbus OH 43204	614-276-0861	R	8*	<.1
74	Alliance Hni LLC—Andrew Heyek	525 S Gould St, Owosso MI 48867	989-729-2804	R	8*	.1
75	Interscan Corp—Richard Shaw	PO Box 2496, Chatsworth CA 91313	818-882-2331	R	8*	<.1
76	Dry Vac Environmental Inc—Dan Simpson	864 Saint Francis Way, Rio Vista CA 94571	707-374-7500	R	7*	.1
77	Wescor Inc—Wayne Barlow	370 W 1700 S, Logan UT 84321	435-752-6011	R	7*	.1
78	Chemetrics Inc—Gordon Rampy	4295 Catlett Rd, Calverton VA 20138	540-788-9026	R	7*	.1
79	ICX Photonics—Martin Pralle	215 First St, Cambridge MA 02142	617-441-8871	S	7*	<.1
80	J A Woollam Company Inc—John Woollam	645 M St Ste 102, Lincoln NE 68508	402-477-7501	R	7*	<.1
81	Beckart Environmental Inc—Arthur Fedrigon	6900 46th St, Kenosha WI 53144	262-656-7680	R	7*	<.1
82	Boekel Industries Inc—Leo Synnestvedt	855 Pennsylvania Blvd, Feasterville Trevose PA 19053	215-396-8200	R	7*	<.1
83	Griffin Analytical Technologies LLC—Dennis Barket	3000 Kent Ave Ste E1, West Lafayette IN 47906	765-775-1701	R	6*	<.1
84	Delta F Corp—Joseph Capua	4 Constitution Way Ste, Woburn MA 01801	781-935-4600	R	6*	<.1
85	Tescor Inc—Jacques Boudin	341 Ivyland Rd, Warminster PA 18974	215-957-9112	R	6*	<.1
86	Cargille-Sacher Laboratories Inc—John Cargille	55 Commerce Rd, Cedar Grove NJ 07009	973-239-6633	R	6*	<.1
87	Scientific Industries Inc—Helena R Santos	70 Orville Dr, Bohemia NY 11716	631-567-4700	P	6*	<.1
88	Metrolaser Inc—Cecil Hess	8 Chrysler, Irvine CA 92618	949-553-0688	R	6*	<.1
89	Cybortronics Inc—Brian Supplee	13845 Alton Pkwy Ste C, Irvine CA 92618	949-855-2814	R	6*	<.1
90	Mectron Engineering Company Inc—James Hanna	400 S Industrial Dr, Saline MI 48176	734-944-8777	R	6*	<.1
91	Ilx Lightwave—Lawrence Johnson	PO Box 6310, Bozeman MT 59771	406-586-1244	R	6*	<.1
92	Chemimage Filter Technologies LLC	7301 Penn Ave, Pittsburgh PA 15208	412-241-7335	R	5*	<.1
93	Wasson-Ece Instrumentation Inc—John Wasson	101 Rome Ct, Fort Collins CO 80524	970-221-9179	R	5*	<.1
94	Scientific Systems Inc—Andrew Charney	349 N Science Park Rd, State College PA 16803	814-234-7317	R	5*	<.1
95	GOW-MAC Instrument Co—Jeffery Lawson	PO Box 25444, Lehigh Valley PA 18002	610-954-9000	R	5*	<.1
96	E A Fischione Instruments Inc—Paul Fischione	9003 Corporate Cir, Export PA 15632	724-325-5444	R	5*	<.1
97	Analytical Spectral Devices—Dave Rzasa	2555 55th St Ste 100, Boulder CO 80301	303-444-6522	R	5*	<.1
98	Analytical Scientific Instruments Inc—Stephen Graham	425 Appian Way, El Sobrante CA 94803	510-669-2250	R	5*	<.1
99	Applied Separations Inc—Rolf Schlake	PO Box 20032, Lehigh Valley PA 18002	610-770-0900	R	5*	<.1
100	RHK Technology Inc—Adam Kollin	1050 E Maple Rd, Troy MI 48083	248-577-5426	R	4*	<.1
101	Screening Systems Inc—Susan Baker	PO Box 3931, Laguna Hills CA 92654	949-855-1751	R	4*	<.1
102	Shore Western Manufacturing Inc—Don Schroeder	225 W Duarte Rd, Monrovia CA 91016	626-357-3251	R	4*	<.1
103	Designs and Prototype—Jacob Newby	1280 Hopmeadow St Ste, Simsbury CT 06070	860-658-0458	R	4*	<.1
104	Bemco Inc—Randy Bruskrud	2255 Union Pl, Simi Valley CA 93065	805-583-4970	R	4*	<.1
105	Industrial Test Systems Inc—Ivars Jaunakais	1875 Langston St, Rock Hill SC 29730	803-329-9712	R	4*	<.1
106	CDS Analytical Inc—Charles Close	PO Box 277, Oxford PA 19363	610-932-3636	R	4*	<.1
107	CombiMatrix Corp—Judd Jessup	300 Goddard Ste 100, Irvine CA 92618	949-753-0624	P	4	<.1
108	Mcpherson Inc—Chris Schoeffel	7a Stuart Rd, Chelmsford MA 01824	978-256-4512	R	4*	<.1
109	Associated Environmental Systems—John Orourke	31 Willow Rd Ste 1, Ayer MA 01432	978-772-0022	R	3*	<.1
110	Anasazi Instruments Inc—Craig Bradley	4101 Cashard Ave Ste 1, Indianapolis IN 46203	317-783-4126	R	3*	<.1
111	Morton Grove Medical Imaging LLC—Susan Blum	9000 Waukegan Rd Ste 1, Morton Grove IL 60053	847-213-2700	R	3*	<.1
112	Arrayit Corp—Rene Schena	524 E Weddell Dr, Sunnyvale CA 94089	408-744-1331	P	3	<.1
113	Eci Technology Inc—Edward Rabinovitch	60 Gordon Dr, Totowa NJ 07512	973-773-8686	R	3*	.1
114	Porous Materials Inc—Krishna Gupta	20 Dutch Mill Rd, Ithaca NY 14850	607-257-5544	R	3*	<.1
115	Quicksilver Analytics Inc—Rodney Hudson	1309 Continental Dr St, Abingdon MD 21009	410-676-4300	R	3*	<.1
116	Infrared Laboratories Inc—Dave Dozor	1808 E 17th St, Tucson AZ 85719	520-622-7074	R	3*	<.1
117	Torion Technologies Inc—Douglas Later	796 E Utah Valley Dr S, American Fork UT 84003	801-705-6600	R	3*	<.1
118	Williamson Corp—William Barron	70 Domino Dr, Concord MA 01742	978-369-9607	R	3*	<.1
119	Brookhaven Instruments Corp—Walther Tscharnuter	750 Blue Point Rd, Holtsville NY 11742	631-758-3200	R	3*	<.1
120	Applied Image Inc—Bruno Glavich	1653 E Main St Ste 1, Rochester NY 14609	585-482-0300	R	3*	<.1
121	Sprite Industries Inc—David Farley	1791 Railroad St, Corona CA 92880	951-735-1015	R	3*	<.1
122	Stanford Research Systems Inc—William Green	1290 Reamwood Ave Ste, Sunnyvale CA 94089	408-744-9040	R	3*	<.1
123	Bioscan Inc—Seth Shulman	4590 Macarthur Blvd Nw, Washington DC 20007	202-338-0974	R	3*	<.1
124	Clark-Mxr Inc—William Clark	7300 Huron River Dr St, Dexter MI 48130	734-426-2803	R	3*	<.1
125	Conspec Controls Inc—Nancy Mccullough	6 Guttman Blvd, Charleroi PA 15022	724-489-8450	R	3*	<.1
126	Illinois Instruments Inc—Richard Smith	2401 Hiller Rdg Ste A, Johnsburg IL 60051	815-344-6212	R	2*	<.1
127	Orthometrix Inc—Reynald G Bonmati	106 Corporate Park Dr, White Plains NY 10604	914-694-2285	P	2*	<.1
128	LA M Incorporated De—Malinda Cochran	620 Wheat Ln Ste B, Wood Dale IL 60191	630-860-9700	R	2*	<.1
129	Umass M R I and Imaging Center—Kristina Mcgowan	214 Shrewsbury St, Worcester MA 01604	508-756-7300	R	2*	<.1
130	Energy Beam Sciences Inc—Michael Nesta	29 Kripes Rd Ste B, East Granby CT 06026	860-653-0411	R	2*	<.1
131	UV Aetek Systems Inc—Meredith Stines	212 S Mount Zion Rd, Lebanon IN 46052		R	2*	<.1
132	Food Technology Corp—Shirl C Lakeway Jr	45921 Marie's Rd Ste 1, Sterling VA 20166	703-444-1870	R	2*	<.1
133	Bio-Brite Inc—Kirk Renaud	4330 E W Hwy Ste 310, Bethesda MD 20814	301-961-5940	R	2*	<.1
134	Comstock Inc—William Gibson	1005 Alvin Weinberg Dr, Oak Ridge TN 37830	865-483-7690	R	2*	<.1
135	Rame-Hart Inc—Thor Stadil	8 Morris Ave, Mountain Lakes NJ 07046	973-335-0560	R	2*	<.1
136	DiaSys Corp—Frederic Neikrug	405 Lexington Ave 26th, New York NY 10174	212-541-2458	P	2	<.1
137	Yokogawa Leisure Analysis Div—David Johnson	910 Gemini St, Houston TX 77058	281-488-0409	R	2*	<.1
138	Jodon Engineering Associates Inc—Michael Gillespie	62 Enterprise Dr, Ann Arbor MI 48103	734-761-4044	R	1*	<.1
139	Chemplex Industries Inc—Monte Solazzi	2820 Sw 42nd Ave, Palm City FL 34990	772-283-2700	R	1*	<.1
140	BioForce NanoSciences Holdings Inc—Kerry Frey	609 E Lincoln Way Ste, Ames IA 50010	515-233-8333	P	1	<.1

Note: An asterisk (*) indicates an estimated financial figure. The company type code used is as follows: R = Private, P = Public, S = Private Subsidiary, B = Public Subsidiary, D = Division, J = Joint Venture, I = Investment Fund.

COMPANY RANKINGS BY SALES WITHIN 4-DIGIT SIC

Rank	Company Name—*Executive Officer*	Address, City, State, Zip	Phone	Type	Fin	Empls
141	Xitech Instruments Inc—*Dwight Patterson*	PO Box 1127, Placitas NM 87043	505-867-0008	R	1*	<.1
142	Accelr8 Technology Corp—*Thomas V Geimer*	7000 N Broadway Ste 3-, Denver CO 80221	303-863-8088	P	1	<.1
143	Network Analysis Inc—*Ron Behee*	4151 W Lindbergh Way, Chandler AZ 85226	480-756-0512	R	1*	<.1
144	Infrared Industries Inc—*Mark Russell*	25590 Seaboard Ln, Hayward CA 94545	510-782-8100	R	1*	<.1
145	GBC Scientific Equipment Corp—*Mike Lynch*	PO Box 339, Hampshire IL 60140	847-683-9870	S	1*	<.1
146	La Pine Scientific Co—*Robert J La Pine*	PO Box 780, Blue Island IL 60406	708-388-4030	R	1*	<.1
147	Micro Probe Inc—*Martin Bak*	18247 D Flower Hill Wa, Gaithersburg MD 20879	301-330-9788	R	1*	<.1
148	Biotage Inc—*David B Patteson*	1725 Discovery Dr, Charlottesville VA 22911	434-979-2319	S	1*	<.1
149	Custom Sample Systems Inc—*Michael Ponstingl*	531 Axminister Dr, Fenton MO 63026	636-305-0666	R	1*	<.1
150	Hydrolynx Systems Inc—*Kimberly Blair*	950 Riverside Pkwy Ste, West Sacramento CA 95605	916-374-1800	R	1*	<.1
151	Timberline Instruments LLC	PO Box 20356, Boulder CO 80308	303-440-8779	R	1*	<.1
152	Eldex Laboratories Inc—*Stephen Amendola*	30 Executive Ct, Napa CA 94558	707-224-8800	R	1*	<.1
153	Omnion Inc—*Frank Mcgovern*	PO Box O, Rockland MA 02370	781-878-7200	R	1*	<.1
154	Sentech Corp—*Jerry Spore*	5745 Progress Rd, Indianapolis IN 46241	317-248-1988	R	1*	<.1
155	Rad Electric Inc—*Frederick Stieff*	5716 Industry Ln Ste A, Frederick MD 21704	301-694-0011	R	1*	<.1
156	Scientific Adsorbents Inc—*Leslie Storey*	3342 International Pk, Atlanta GA 30316	770-455-1140	R	1*	<.1
157	Metricon Corp—*John Jackson*	PO Box 63, Pennington NJ 08534	609-737-1052	R	1*	<.1
158	Agricultural Electronics Corp—*Willam Gensler*	PO Box 50291, Tucson AZ 85703	520-624-7656	R	1*	<.1
159	Advanced Vehicle Technologies Inc—*Michael Riley*	1509 Manor View Rd, Davidsonville MD 21035	410-798-4038	R	1*	<.1
160	Rudolph Instruments Inc—*Kumar Utukuri*	400 Morris Ave Ste 120, Denville NJ 07834	973-983-6700	R	1*	<.1
161	Calypte Biomedical Corp—*Adel Karas*	15875 SW 72nd Ave, Portland OR 97224	503-726-2227	P	<1	<.1
162	Analytical Technologies Inc—*David Gross*	11 Holt St, Westfield NY 14787	716-326-6444	R	<1*	<.1
163	Spectronics Inc—*Wallace Masters*	11230 Nw Reeves St, Portland OR 97229	503-643-8030	R	<1*	<.1
164	St John Associates Inc—*Peter John*	4805 Prince Georges Av, Beltsville MD 20705	301-595-5605	R	<1*	<.1
165	Monitor Instruments Inc—*Van Anderson*	437 Dimmocks Mill Rd S, Hillsborough NC 27278	919-732-5400	R	<1*	<.1
166	Advanced Research Instruments Corp—*Jozef Lebiedzik*	PO Box 7427, Golden CO 80403	303-463-5500	R	<1*	<.1
167	Ken-Tech Products Corp—*Lloyd Koeppel*	S6695 County Rd Pf, North Freedom WI 53951	608-522-3381	R	<1*	<.1
168	PMS Instrument Co—*Brian Cleary*	1725 Geary St Se, Albany OR 97322	541-704-2299	R	<1*	<.1
169	Laser Atlanta LLC—*Adrian Curry*	6090 Northbelt Pkwy St, Norcross GA 30071	770-446-3866	R	<1*	<.1
170	Haber Inc—*Albert B Conti*	58 Medford St, Arlington MA 02474	781-643-2727	P	<1	<.1
171	Aethlon Medical Inc—*James A Joyce*	8910 University Center, San Diego CA 92122	858-459-7800	P	<1	<.1
172	Waters Technologies Corp Waters Corp	34 Maple St, Milford MA 01757	508-478-2000	D	N/A	5.0

TOTALS: SIC 3826 Analytical Instruments
Companies: 172

					20,371	78.8

3827 Optical Instruments & Lenses

Rank	Company Name—*Executive Officer*	Address, City, State, Zip	Phone	Type	Fin	Empls
1	KLA-Tencor Corp—*Richard P (Rick) Wallace*	1 Technology Dr, Milpitas CA 95035	408-875-3000	P	3,175	5.5
2	Bausch and Lomb Inc Eyewear Div—*Brent L Saunders*	1 Bausch And Lomb Pl, Rochester NY 14604	585-338-6000	D	1,680*	11.0
3	3M Precision Optics Inc—*George W Buckley*	3997 McMann Rd, Cincinnati OH 45245	513-752-7000	S	690*	1.3
4	II-VI Inc—*Francis Kramer*	375 Saxonburg Blvd, Saxonburg PA 16056	724-352-4455	P	503	6.2
5	Optical Coating Laboratory Inc—*Thomas Waechter*	430 N McCarthy Blvd, Milpitas CA 95035	408-546-5000	S	357*	1.5
6	AXSYS Technologies Inc—*Stephen Bershad*	175 Capital Blvd Ste 1, Rocky Hill CT 06067	860-257-0200	S	246	1.0
7	Pentax of America Inc—*Ikuzo Okamoto*	600 12th St, Golden CO 80403	303-799-8000	D	224*	.6
8	Oplink Communications Inc—*Joseph Y Liu*	46335 Landing Pky, Fremont CA 94538	510-933-7200	P	199	3.6
9	NeoPhotonics Corp—*Timothy S Jenks*	2911 Zanker Rd, San Jose CA 95134	408-232-9200	P	184	3.1
10	Sumitomo Electric Light Wave—*Hiroaki Horima*	PO Box 13445, Research Triangle Park NC 27709	919-541-8100	S	161	.5
11	DRS Optronics Inc—*Mark S Newman*	5 Sylvan Way, Parsippany NJ 07054	973-898-1500	S	141*	.5
12	Cyoptics Inc—*Ettore Coringrato*	9999 Hamilton Blvd, Breinigsville PA 18031	484-397-2000	R	108*	.6
13	Trijicon Inc—*Stephen Bindon*	PO Box 930059, Wixom MI 48393	248-960-7700	R	100*	.2
14	Suncoast Medical Clinic—*Josh Adler*	601 7th St S, Saint Petersburg FL 33701	727-894-1818	R	85*	.3
15	Semrock Inc—*Victor Mizrahi*	3625 Buffalo Rd Ste 6, Rochester NY 14624	585-594-7050	S	66*	.1
16	Perceptron Inc—*Harry T Rittenour*	47827 Halyard Dr, Plymouth MI 48170	734-414-6100	P	59	.2
17	CyberOptics Corp—*Kathleen P Iverson*	5900 Golden Hills Dr, Minneapolis MN 55416	763-542-5000	P	57	.2
18	Seiler Instrument And Manufacturing Company Inc—*Eric Seiler*	3433 Tree Crt Industri, Saint Louis MO 63122	314-968-2282	R	49*	.2
19	Leupold and Stevens Inc—*Calvin Johnston*	PO Box 688, Beaverton OR 97075	503-646-9171	R	43*	.5
20	Orange 21 Inc—*Carol Montgomery*	2070 Las Palmas Dr, Carlsbad CA 92011	760-804-8420	P	35	.1
21	Optical Gaging Products Inc—*Edward Polidor*	850 Hudson Ave, Rochester NY 14621	585-544-0450	R	34*	.2
22	Awareness Technology Inc—*Mary Freeman*	PO Box 1679, Palm City FL 34991	772-283-6540	R	31*	.1
23	Zebra Imaging Inc—*Albert E Wargo*	9801 Metric Blvd Ste 2, Austin TX 78758	512-251-5100	R	31*	.1
24	BE Meyers and Company Inc—*Brad Meyers*	14540 Ne 91st St, Redmond WA 98052	425-881-6648	R	30*	.2
25	Schott-Fostec LLC—*Doug Roberts*	62 Columbus St, Auburn NY 13021	315-255-2791	S	28*	.1
26	CVI Melles Griot Inc—*Stuart Schoenmann*	2051 Palomar Airport R, Carlsbad CA 92011	760-438-2131	S	27*	.2
27	Meade Instruments Corp—*Steven G Murdock*	27 Hubble, Irvine CA 92618	949-451-1450	P	26	.4
28	Exotic Electro-Optics Inc—*Andrew Riser* II-VI Inc	36570 Briggs Rd, Murrieta CA 92563	951-926-2994	S	26*	.2
29	New Focus Inc	3635 Peterson Way, Santa Clara CA 95054	408-919-1500	S	24*	.2
30	Moxtek Inc—*Hiroyuki Iseki*	452 W 1260 N, Orem UT 84057	801-225-0930	R	23*	.2
31	Stereographics Corp—*Michael V Lewis*	100 N Crescent Dr Ste, Beverly Hills CA 90210	310-385-4000	S	21*	<.1
32	Anorad Corp—*Keith Nosbusch*	100 Precision Dr, Shirley NY 11967	631-344-6600	D	20*	.3
33	Chroma Technology Corp—*Paul Millman*	10 Imtec Ln, Bellows Falls VT 05101	802-428-2500	R	20*	.1
34	Optimax Systems Inc—*Michael Mandina*	6367 Dean Pkwy, Ontario NY 14519	585-217-0729	R	19*	.2
35	Directed Energy Solutions—*David K Neumann*	890 Elkton Dr Ste 101, Colorado Springs CO 80907	719-593-7848	R	18*	<.1
36	Research Electro-Optics Inc—*Terry Moshier*	5505 Airport Blvd Ste, Boulder CO 80301	303-938-1960	R	18*	.1
37	Eyeonics—*Andy Corley*	26970 Aliso Viejo Pkwy, Aliso Viejo CA 92656	949-916-9352	S	17	.1
38	Wilcox Industries Corp—*James Teetzel*	25 Piscataqua Dr, Newington NH 03801	603-431-1331	R	16*	.1
39	Adaptive Optics Associates Inc—*Thomas Price*	115 Jackson Rd, Devens MA 01434	978-772-0352	R	16*	.1
40	ProPhotonix Ltd—*Mark W Blodgett*	32 Hampshire Rd, Salem NH 03079	603-893-8778	P	15	.2
41	Sunoptic Technologies LLC—*Janice Lee*	6018 Bowdendale Ave, Jacksonville FL 32216	904-737-7611	R	15*	.1
42	Polymicro Technologies LLC—*Gary Nelson*	18019 N 25th Ave, Phoenix AZ 85023	602-375-4100	S	14*	.1
43	Machine Vision Products Inc—*George Ayoub*	5940 Darwin Ct Ste A, Carlsbad CA 92008	760-438-1138	R	14*	.1
44	United Optical Co—*Michael Simmons*	933 E 3300 S, Salt Lake City UT 84106	801-486-1001	R	14*	<.1
45	Lightworks Optics Inc—*Michael Minailo*	14242 Chambers Rd, Tustin CA 92780	714-247-7100	R	14*	.1
46	Micro-Vu Corporation Of California—*Edward Amornino*	7909 Conde Ln, Windsor CA 95492	707-838-6272	R	14*	.1
47	Rochester Precision Optics LLC—*William Hurley*	850 John St, West Henrietta NY 14586	585-292-5450	R	14*	.1
48	Celestron Acquisition LLC—*Joseph Lupica*	2835 Columbia St, Torrance CA 90503	310-328-9560	R	14*	.1
49	Gurley Precision Instruments Inc—*O Brady*	514 Fulton St, Troy NY 12180	518-272-6300	R	13*	.1
50	Corning Tropel Corp	60 O'Connor Rd, Fairport NY 14450	585-388-3500	S	13*	.1
51	Scientific Microscopes Inc—*Costa Tsobanakis*	578 Division St, Campbell CA 95008	408-739-2631	R	13*	<.1
52	Plx Inc—*Jack Lipkins*	25 W Jefryn Blvd Ste A, Deer Park NY 11729	631-586-4190	R	13*	<.1

Rank	Company Name—*Executive Officer*	Address, City, State, Zip	Phone	Type	Fin	Empls
53	Omega Optical Inc—*Robert Johnson*	21 Omega Dr, Brattleboro VT 05301	802-251-7300	R	12*	.1
54	NovaSol—*David Van Buren*	1001 Bishop St, Honolulu HI 96813	808-441-3600	R	12*	.1
55	Three Rivers Optical Co—*William Seibert*	260 Bilmar Dr, Pittsburgh PA 15205	412-928-2020	R	12*	.1
56	Accutome Inc—*Brian Chandler*	3222 Phoenixville Pke, Malvern PA 19355	610-889-0200	R	12*	.1
57	Xradia Inc—*Rod Browning*	4385 Hopyard Rd Ste 10, Pleasanton CA 94588	925-701-3600	R	12*	<.1
58	Insaco Inc—*Robert Haines*	PO Box 9006, Quakertown PA 18951	215-536-3500	R	12*	.1
59	JML Optical Industries Inc—*Joseph Lobozzo*	820 Linden Ave, Rochester NY 14625	585-248-8900	R	12*	.1
60	Edmund Optical Manufacturing LLC—*Jennifer Barndt*	601 Montgomery Ave, Pennsburg PA 18073	215-679-6272	R	11*	.1
61	Deltronic Corp—*Robert Larzelere*	3900 W Segerstrom Ave, Santa Ana CA 92704	714-545-0401	R	11*	.1
62	Siskiyou Design Inc—*Robert Hodge*	110 Sw Booth St, Grants Pass OR 97526	541-479-8697	R	11*	.1
63	Gooch and Housego LLC (Melbourne Florida)—*Pat Shannon-house*	4005 Opportunity Dr, Melbourne FL 32934	321-242-7818	R	11*	.1
64	Bsa Industries Inc—*Matt Carmen*	6510 Huntley Rd, Columbus OH 43229	614-846-5515	R	10*	.1
65	Hardin Optical Co—*Larry Hardin*	PO Box 219, Bandon OR 97411	541-347-9467	R	10*	.1
66	Labsphere Inc—*Tim Kardish*	PO Box 70, North Sutton NH 03260	603-927-4266	S	10*	.1
67	Metavac Inc	4000 Point St, Holtsville NY 11742	631-447-7700	S	10*	<.1
68	Cyth Systems LLC—*Andy Long*	9939 Via Pasar, San Diego CA 92126		R	10*	<.1
69	Rigaku Innovative Technologies Inc—*John Mcgill*	1900 Taylor Rd, Auburn Hills MI 48326	248-232-6400	S	9*	.2
70	Miller-Holzwarth Inc—*David Hartman*	PO Box 270, Salem OH 44460	330-337-8736	R	9*	.1
71	American Technology Network Corp—*Marc Morgovsky*	1341 San Mateo Ave, South San Francisco CA 94080	650-875-0130	R	9*	.1
72	Adolf Meller Co—*David Lydon*	PO Box 6001, Providence RI 02940	401-331-3717	R	9*	.1
73	Sellers Optical Inc—*Rod Randolph*	869 W 17th St, Costa Mesa CA 92627	949-631-6800	R	8*	.1
74	Photon Technology International Inc—*Charles Marianik*	PO Box 272, Birmingham NJ 08011	609-894-4420	R	8*	.1
75	Ocular Instruments Inc—*Phil Erickson*	2255 116th Ave Ne, Bellevue WA 98004	425-455-5200	R	8*	.1
76	Videk Inc—*Thomas Slechta*	1387 Frport Rd Bldg 10, Fairport NY 14450	585-377-0377	R	7*	<.1
77	Brunson Instrument Company Inc—*Deighton Brunson*	8000 E 23rd St, Kansas City MO 64129	816-483-3187	R	7*	<.1
78	Halo Optical Products Inc—*Peter Leonardi*	PO Box 1369, Gloversville NY 12078	518-773-4256	R	7*	.1
79	Bond Optics LLC—*Elliot Matteson*	PO Box 422, Lebanon NH 03766	603-448-2300	R	7*	.1
80	Spitz Inc—*Jon Shaw*	PO Box 198, Chadds Ford PA 19317		S	7*	.1
81	Instrument Technology Inc—*Gregory Carignan*	PO Box 381, Westfield MA 01086	413-562-3606	R	7*	.1
82	Qioptiq Imaging Solutions—*David Marks*	78 Schuyler Baldwin Dr, Fairport NY 14450	585-223-2370	S	7*	<.1
83	Model Optics Inc—*Erhard Gersbach*	10 Dixon Ave, Woodstock NY 12498	845-219-1678	R	7*	<.1
84	General Scientific Corp—*Byung Chang*	77 Enterprise Dr, Ann Arbor MI 48103	734-996-9200	R	7*	.1
85	Laurel Industries Inc—*Carl Lambrecht*	280 Laurel Ave, Highland Park IL 60035	847-432-8204	R	7*	.1
86	Andover Corp—*Richard Bennett*	4 Commercial Dr, Salem NH 03079	603-893-6888	R	6*	<.1
87	Dibok Inc—*Robert Kathe*	1050 W Main St Ste 102, Mesa AZ 85201	480-894-8770	R	6*	.1
88	Wilson Optical Laboratory Inc—*John Wilson*	9450 Pineneedle Dr, Mentor OH 44060	440-357-7000	R	6*	.1
89	Cleveland Hoya Corp—*William Bennedict*	94 Pelret Industrial P, Berea OH 44017	440-234-5703	R	6*	.1
90	Computer Optical Products Inc—*Richard D Smith*	9355 Eton Ave, Chatsworth CA 91311	818-882-0424	S	6*	<.1
91	Opt-Sciences Corp—*Anderson L McCabe*	PO Box 221, Riverton NJ 00077	856-829-2800	P	6	<.1
92	Lattice Materials LLC—*Jessica Higgins*	516 E Tamarack St, Bozeman MT 59715	406-586-2122	R	6*	<.1
93	Precision Photonics Corp—*Chris Myatt*	3180 Sterling Cir Ste, Boulder CO 80301	303-444-9948	R	6*	<.1
94	Fraser-Volpe Corp—*John Hornberger*	1025 Thomas Dr, Warminster PA 18974	215-443-5240	R	6*	<.1
95	Cambridge Research and Instrumentation Inc—*George Abe*	35b Cabot Rd, Woburn MA 01801	781-935-9099	R	6*	<.1
96	Alpine Research Optics LLC—*Annette Sowl*	6810 Winchester Cir, Boulder CO 80301	303-444-3420	R	6*	<.1
97	Ecco Products—*Gary Steneken*	171 Oak Ridge Rd, Oak Ridge NJ 07438	973-697-3700	R	5*	<.1
98	Liebmann Optical Company Inc—*Hobert Sparrow*	1 Industrial Pkwy, Easthampton MA 01027	413-527-0079	R	5*	<.1
99	Fiber SenSys Inc—*Dwayne Thompson*	2925 NW Aloclek Dr Ste, Hillsboro OR 97124	503-692-4430	S	5*	<.1
100	Metron Optics Inc—*Charles Kempf*	PO Box 690, Solana Beach CA 92075	858-755-4477	R	5*	<.1
101	Intra Action Corp—*John Lekavich*	3719 Warren Ave, Bellwood IL 60104	708-547-6644	R	5*	<.1
102	Reynard Corp—*Forrest Reynard*	1020 Calle Sombra, San Clemente CA 92673	949-366-8866	R	5*	<.1
103	O and S Research Inc—*Anderson Cabe*	PO Box 221, Riverton NJ 08077	856-829-2800	R	4*	<.1
104	Vibgyor Optical Systems Corp—*Bharat Verma*	1140 N Phelps Ave, Arlington Heights IL 60004	847-818-0788	R	4*	<.1
105	Automatic Inspection Systems Inc—*Jerry Pollard*	7000 Dtton IndustrialP, Caledonia MI 49316	616-554-1000	R	4*	<.1
106	Harold Johnson Optical Laboratories Inc—*Harold Johnson*	1826 W 169th St, Gardena CA 90247	310-327-3051	R	4*	<.1
107	Diagnostic Instruments Inc—*Patrick Merlo*	6540 Burroughs Ave, Sterling Heights MI 48314	586-731-6000	R	4*	<.1
108	Pacific Quartz Inc—*E Dickson*	1404 E Saint Gertrude, Santa Ana CA 92705	714-546-8133	R	4*	.1
109	Ferson Optics Inc—*Louis Peters*	5801 Gulf Tech Dr, Ocean Springs MS 39564	228-875-8146	S	4*	<.1
110	French Reflection Inc—*Alice Myers*	8899 Beverly Blvd, Los Angeles CA 90048	310-659-3800	R	4*	<.1
111	Galvanic Applied Sciences USA Inc—*Gerald Hipple*	41 Wellman St, Lowell MA 01851	978-848-2701	S	4*	<.1
112	Minuteman Laboratories Inc—*DM Schoeffel*	7A Stuart Rd, Chelmsford MA 01824	978-256-4512	S	4*	<.1
113	Vision Training Products Inc—*Craig Andrews*	4016 N Home St, Mishawaka IN 46545	574-259-2070	R	4*	<.1
114	Keeler Instruments Inc—*David Keeler*	456 Parkway, Broomall PA 19008	610-353-4350	S	4*	<.1
115	Vingtech Corp—*Per Aas*	15 Morin St Ste B, Biddeford ME 04005	207-571-5850	R	4*	<.1
116	Hinds International Inc—*Paul Hinds*	7245 Nw Evergreen Pkwy, Hillsboro OR 97124	503-690-2000	R	4*	<.1
117	Mems Optical Inc—*Gregg Borek*	205 Import Cir Nw, Huntsville AL 35806	256-859-1886	R	4*	<.1
118	Diverse Optics Inc—*Deborah Demelo*	1318 Palomares St, La Verne CA 91750	909-593-9330	R	4*	<.1
119	Lenox Instrument Company Inc—*John Lang*	265 Andrews Rd, Trevose PA 19053	215-322-9990	R	4*	<.1
120	Bernell Corp—*Craig Andrews* Vision Training Products Inc	4016 N Home St, Mishawaka IN 46545	574-259-2070	D	4	<.1
121	SheerVision Inc—*Suzanne Lewsadder*	4030 Palos Verdes Dr N, Rolling Hills Estates CA 90274	310-265-8918	P	4	<.1
122	Aura Systems Inc—*Melvin Gagerman*	2330 Utah Ave, El Segundo CA 90245	310-643-5300	P	4	.1
123	Retina Systems Inc—*Floyd Moir*	146 Day St, Seymour CT 06483	203-881-1311	R	3*	<.1
124	Bern Optics Inc—*Bernd Gottschalk*	579 Southampton Rd Ste, Westfield MA 01085	413-568-6800	R	3*	<.1
125	Bay Area Eye Center—*Steven Updgarff*	160138 Ave N, Saint Petersburg FL 33704	727-551-2020	R	3*	<.1
126	Tfd Inc—*Saleem Shaikh*	1180 N Tustin Ave, Anaheim CA 92807	714-630-7127	R	3*	<.1
127	International Crystal Laboratories—*Theresa Herpst*	11 Erie St Ste 2, Garfield NJ 07026	973-478-8944	R	3*	<.1
128	Advanced Vision Science Inc—*Khalid Mentak*	5743 Thornwood Dr, Goleta CA 93117	805-683-3851	R	3*	<.1
129	Pacific Coast Optics—*Charles Gaugh*	1361 E Edinger Ave, Santa Ana CA 92705	714-835-1888	R	3	<.1
130	Opticraft Inc—*Dennis Mcallister*	17d Everberg Rd, Woburn MA 01801	781-938-0456	R	3*	<.1
131	Sela USA Inc—*Shams Tabrez*	2000 Wyatt Drive Ste #, Santa Clara CA 95050	408-235-8500	R	3*	<.1
132	Tele-Vue Optics Inc—*Albert Nagler*	32 Elkay Dr, Chester NY 10918	845-469-4551	R	3*	<.1
133	Opco Laboratory Inc—*Saverio Maldari*	704 River St, Fitchburg MA 01420	978-345-2522	R	3*	<.1
134	Karl Lambrecht Corp—*Alvin Lambrecht*	4204 N Lincoln Ave, Chicago IL 60618	773-472-5442	R	3*	<.1
135	JP Manufacturing Inc—*Gloria Kania*	13 Lovely St, Southbridge MA 01550	508-764-2538	R	3*	<.1
136	Mark Optics Inc—*Julie Houser*	1424 E Saint Gertrude, Santa Ana CA 92705	714-545-6684	R	3*	<.1
137	Redfern Integrated Optics Inc—*Radv Barsan*	3350 Scott Blvd Bldg 6, Santa Clara CA 95054	408-970-3500	R	3*	<.1
138	Gaertner Scientific Corp—*Rusty Kutko*	3650 Jarvis Ave, Skokie IL 60076	847-673-5006	R	3*	<.1
139	Lear Engineering Corp—*Dennis Swing*	1310 Research Park Dr, Beavercreek OH 45432	937-429-0534	R	2*	<.1
140	Astro-Physics Inc—*Roland Christen*	11250 Forest Hills Rd, Machesney Park IL 61115	815-282-1513	R	2*	<.1

Note: An asterisk (*) indicates an estimated financial figure. The company type code used is as follows: R = Private, P = Public, S = Private Subsidiary, B = Public Subsidiary, D = Division, J = Joint Venture, I = Investment Fund.

COMPANY RANKINGS BY SALES WITHIN 4-DIGIT SIC

Rank	Company Name—*Executive Officer*	Address, City, State, Zip	Phone	Type	Fin	Empls
141	National Aperture Inc—*George Mauro*	16 Northwestern Dr, Salem NH 03079	603-893-7393	R	2*	<.1
142	Sadler Brothers Inc—*Thomas Sadler*	PO Box 3005, Attleboro MA 02703	508-761-8352	R	2*	<.1
143	Ross Optical Industries Inc—*Ed Ross*	1410 Gail Borden Pl A3, El Paso TX 79935	915-595-5417	R	2*	<.1
144	Gradient Lens Corp—*Douglas Kindred*	207 Tremont St Ste 1, Rochester NY 14608	585-235-2620	R	2*	<.1
145	Westwood Group—*Arthur Kennedy*	24832 Ave Rockefeller, Valencia CA 91355	661-702-8603	R	2*	<.1
146	Buk Optics Inc—*Daniel Bukaty*	3600 W Moore Ave, Santa Ana CA 92704	714-540-0126	R	2*	<.1
147	Shadowfax Inc—*Nicholas Bentley*	141 S 7th St, Reading PA 19602	610-373-5177	R	2*	<.1
148	Collimated Holes Inc—*Richard Mead*	460 Division St, Campbell CA 95008	408-374-5080	R	2*	<.1
149	EMF Corp—*Paul M Schulz*	239 Cherry St, Ithaca NY 14850	607-272-3320	R	2*	<.1
150	Cascade Optical Coating Inc—*Lawrence Hundsdoerfer*	1225 E Hunter Ave, Santa Ana CA 92705	714-543-9777	R	2*	<.1
151	Computer Optics Inc—*Gordon Kane*	PO Box 240, Hudson NH 03051	603-889-2116	R	2*	<.1
152	LensCom Inc—*Bill Odem*	PO Box 366, Louisiana MO 63353	573-754-3600	R	2*	<.1
153	Optima Precision Inc—*Richard Schmitz*	775 Sw Long Farm Rd, West Linn OR 97068	503-638-2525	R	2*	<.1
154	Coating Design Group Inc—*William Roy*	165 Pepes Farm Rd, Milford CT 06460	203-878-3663	R	2*	<.1
155	Metaphase Technologies Inc—*Oliver Sveto*	3412 Progress Dr Ste C, Bensalem PA 19020	215-639-0124	R	2*	<.1
156	Genvac Aerospace Corp—*Gerald Mearini*	PO Box 12105, Birmingham AL 35202	440-646-9986	R	1*	<.1
157	Promet International Inc—*Lubomir Koudelka*	4611 Chatsworth St N, Saint Paul MN 55126	651-481-9661	R	1*	<.1
158	Spawr Industries Inc—*Walter Spawr*	2051 Spawr Cir, Lake Havasu City AZ 86403	928-453-8800	R	1*	<.1
159	Davro Optical Systems Inc—*John Daveler*	500 N Cannon Ave, Lansdale PA 19446	215-362-3870	R	1*	<.1
160	Atlas Instrument Company Inc—*Terry Olson*	144 Oyler Dr, Chambersburg PA 17201	717-267-1250	R	1*	<.1
161	Sine Patterns LLC—*David Doubledee*	236 Henderson Dr, Penfield NY 14526	585-381-2185	R	<1*	<.1

TOTALS: SIC 3827 Optical Instruments & Lenses
Companies: 161   **9,349**   **45.0**

3829 Measuring & Controlling Devices Nec

Rank	Company Name—*Executive Officer*	Address, City, State, Zip	Phone	Type	Fin	Empls
1	Thermo Fisher Scientific Inc—*Marc N Casper*	81 Wyman St, Waltham MA 02454	781-622-1000	P	10,789	37.2
2	Rockwell Automation Inc—*Keith D Nosbusch*	1201 S 2nd St, Milwaukee WI 53204	414-382-2000	P	6,000	21.0
3	Vishay Intertechnology Inc—*Gerald Paul*	63 Lancaster Ave, Malvern PA 19355	610-644-1300	P	2,594	20.9
4	Trimble Navigation Ltd—*Steven W Berglund*	935 Stewart Dr, Sunnyvale CA 94085	408-481-8000	P	1,644	5.3
5	Cubic Corp—*Walter J Zable*	PO Box 85587, San Diego CA 92186	858-277-6780	P	1,285	7.8
6	Teledyne Odom Hydrographic Inc—*Aldo Pichelli*	1450 Seaboard Ave, Baton Rouge LA 70810	225-769-3051	S	573	<.1
7	MTS Systems Corp—*William V Murray*	14000 Technology Dr, Eden Prairie MN 55344		P	467	2.0
8	Dataspan Inc—*Gerry Smith*	PO Box 678310, Dallas TX 75267	214-630-9625	R	425*	.3
9	IPOP Management Inc—*Robert P Peebler*	2105 CityWest Blvd Ste, Houston TX 77042	281-933-3339	S	403*	.8
10	Kulite Semiconductor Products Inc—*Anthony D Kurtz*	1 Willow Tree Rd, Leonia NJ 07605	201-461-0900	R	307*	.6
11	Geospace Engineering Resources International LP—*Gary Owens* OYO Geospace Corp	7007 Pinemont Dr, Houston TX 77040	713-986-4444	S	301*	.6
12	Measurement Specialties Inc—*Frank D Guidone*	1000 Lucas Way, Hampton VA 23666	757-766-1500	P	275	2.9
13	Faro Technologies Inc—*Jay W Freeland*	250 Technology Park Dr, Lake Mary FL 32746	407-333-9911	P	254	.9
14	ABB Industrial Systems Inc—*Enrique Santacana*	579 Executive Campus D, Westerville OH 43082	203-750-2200	S	250*	1.5
15	Nanometrics Inc—*Timothy J Stultz*	1550 Buckeye Dr, Milpitas CA 95035	408-545-6000	P	188	.5
16	OYO Geospace Corp—*Gary D Owens*	7007 Pinemont Dr, Houston TX 77040	713-986-4444	B	173	1.0
17	Instron Corp—*James O Garrison*	825 University Ave, Norwood MA 02062	724-458-9610	S	155*	1.2
18	Dolphin Medical Inc—*Manoocher Mansouri*	12525 Chadron Ave, Hawthorne CA 90250	310-978-0516	S	154*	.3
19	Deltec Inc (St Paul Minnesota)—*Ralph Reynolds*	1265 Grey Fox Rd, Saint Paul MN 55112	651-633-2556	S	150*	.5
20	Abaxis Inc—*Clinton H Severson*	3240 Whipple Rd, Union City CA 94587	510-675-6500	P	144	.4
21	Fairfield Industries Inc—*Walter Pharris*	14100 SW Freeway Ste 6, Sugar Land TX 77478	281-275-7500	R	140*	.4
22	TSI Inc—*James Doubles*	500 Cardigan Rd, Shoreview MN 55126	612-483-0900	R	133*	.8
23	Adesta Communications Inc—*Robert Sommerfeld*	1200 Landmark Ctr Ste, Omaha NE 68102	402-233-7700	R	130*	.3
24	Cornerstone Therapeutics Inc—*Craig A Collard*	1255 Crescent Green Dr, Cary NC 27518		P	125	.1
25	Springfield Precision Instruments—*Bill Vogt*	76 Passaic St, Wood Ridge NJ 07075	973-777-2900	R	106*	.2
26	Electronic Warfare Associates Inc (Fort Huachuca Arizona)—*Carl Guerreri*	13873 Park Ctr Rd Ste, Herndon VA 20171	703-904-5700	R	97*	.8
27	Manitex International Inc (Bridgeview Illinois)—*David Langevin*	9725 Industrial Dr, Bridgeview IL 60455	708-430-7500	P	96	.2
28	RAE Systems Inc (Sunnyvale California)—*Robert I Chen*	3775 N 1st St, San Jose CA 95134	408-952-8200	P	87	1.3
29	Oyo Corporation USA—*Earnest Hall*	7007 Pinemont Dr, Houston TX 77040	713-343-5662	S	67*	.5
30	MTI Instruments Inc—*Peng Lim* Mechanical Technology Inc	325 Washington Ave Ext, Albany NY 12205	518-218-2550	S	62*	.1
31	Fisher Research Laboratory Inc—*John Griffin* First Texas Products	1465-H Henry Brennen, El Paso TX 79936	915-225-0333	S	55*	.1
32	Digital Instruments Veeco Metrology Group—*John Peeler*	112 Robin Hill Rd, Santa Barbara CA 93117	516-677-0200	S	51*	.3
33	Sequenom Inc—*Harry Hixson*	3595 John Hopkins Ct, San Diego CA 92121	858-202-9000	P	48	.2
34	Redwood Instrument Co—*Peter Newgard*	17248 Rivendale Ln SE, Rainier WA 98576	360-446-2860	R	46*	<.1
35	Kimray Inc—*Garman Kimmell*	PO Box 18949, Oklahoma City OK 73154	405-525-6601	R	45*	.3
36	Martin Engineering Co—*Scott Hutter*	1 Martin Pl, Neponset IL 61345	309-594-2384	R	43*	.6
37	First Texas Products—*Tom Walsh*	1465 Henry Brennan Dr, El Paso TX 79936	915-633-8354	R	42*	.1
38	Eckert and Ziegler Isotope Products Inc—*Frank Yeager*	24937 Avetibbitts, Valencia CA 91355	661-309-1010	R	41*	.1
39	Southern Cross Corp—*David Crawford*	4487 S Old Peachtree R, Norcross GA 30071	770-441-0403	R	39*	.3
40	Faro Delaware Inc Faro Technologies Inc	125 Technology Pk, Lake Mary FL 32746	407-333-9911	S	38*	.1
41	Link Manufacturing Inc—*Roy Link*	43855 Plymouth Oaks Bl, Plymouth MI 48170	734-453-0800	R	36*	.2
42	Sage Laboratories Inc—*David McIntosh*	8 Executive Dr, Hudson NH 03051	603-459-1600	S	35*	.1
43	Ludlum Measurements Inc—*Donald Ludlum*	PO Box 810, Sweetwater TX 79556	325-235-5494	R	35*	.3
44	Alabama Specialty Products Inc—*Donald Johnson*	PO Box 8, Munford AL 36268	256-358-4202	R	34*	.3
45	Beta Technology Inc—*Dermott Corr*	2841 Mission St, Santa Cruz CA 95060	831-457-5709	R	32*	.2
46	Image Sensing Systems Inc—*Ken Aubrey*	500 Spruce Tree Ctr 16, Saint Paul MN 55104	651-603-7700	P	32	.1
47	MOCON Inc—*Robert L Demorest*	7500 Mendelssohn Ave N, Minneapolis MN 55428	763-493-6370	P	32	.1
48	Sensotec Inc—*Beth Wozniak*	2080 Arlingate Ln, Columbus OH 43228	614-850-5000	S	30*	.3
49	Cooper-Atkins Corp—*Carol Wallace*	PO Box 450, Middlefield CT 06455	860-349-3473	R	30*	.2
50	SJE - Rhombus—*Laurie Lawandowski*	PO Box 1708, Detroit Lakes MN 56502	218-847-1317	R	28*	.2
51	Geokon Inc—*J Sellers*	48 Spencer St, Lebanon NH 03766	603-448-1562	R	28*	.1
52	Contec Inc—*John Mcbride*	PO Box 530, Spartanburg SC 29304	864-503-8333	R	27*	.2
53	L and N Metallurgical Products Co—*David Araneicka*	3 Fountain Ave, Ellwood City PA 16117	724-758-4541	R	26*	.2
54	Rosemount Analytical Inc—*David N Farr*	2400 Barranca Pkwy, Irvine CA 92606	949-757-8500	D	26*	.2
55	Presco Polymers LP—*Josh James*	1201 E Pecan St, Sherman TX 75090	903-870-2131	R	26*	.2
56	Kuka Assembly And Test Corp—*Scott Orendach*	PO Box 1968, Saginaw MI 48605	989-777-2111	R	26*	.2
57	Bacharach Inc—*Stacy Brovitz*	621 Hunt Valley Cir, New Kensington PA 15068	724-334-5000	R	25*	.1
58	Hommel-Etamic America Corp—*Christian Sommermeyer*	1505 W Hamlin Rd, Rochester Hills MI 48309	248-853-5888	R	25*	.1
59	Azonix Corp—*Greg Balesta*	900 Middlesex Tpke Bld, Billerica MA 01821	978-670-6300	S	25*	.1

Rank	Company Name—Executive Officer	Address, City, State, Zip	Phone	Type	Fin	Empls
60	Adcole Corp—Addison Cole	PO Box 39, Marlborough MA 01752	508-485-9100	R	25*	.2
61	Honeywell Analytics	651 S Main St, Middletown CT 06457	860-344-1079	D	24*	.2
62	Testek Inc—Harish Patel	28320 Lakeview Dr, Wixom MI 48393	248-573-4980	R	24*	.1
63	Topcon Positioning Systems Inc—Raymond O'connor	7400 National Dr, Livermore CA 94550	925-245-8300	R	24*	.3
64	X-Ray Industries Inc—Scott Tharms	1961 Thunderbird St, Troy MI 48084	248-362-2242	R	23*	.2
65	JMAR/SAL NanoLithography Inc JMAR Technologies Inc	10905 Technology Pl, San Diego CA 92127	858-946-6800	S	23*	.1
66	Sutron Corp—Raul McQuivey	22400 Davis Dr, Sterling VA 20164	703-406-2800	P	23	.1
67	Advanced Industrial Tech—Andy Caffyn	1525 Fairlane Cir, Allen Park MI 48101	248-476-7875	R	21*	.1
68	GE Reuter-Stokes Inc—Jeff Immelt	8499 Darrow Rd, Twinsburg OH 44087	330-425-3755	S	21*	.2
69	Harco Laboratories Inc—Robert Wise	PO Box 10, Branford CT 06405	203-483-3700	R	21*	.1
70	Bitrode Corp—Paolo Canova	1642 Manufacturers Dr, Fenton MO 63026	636-343-6112	R	20*	.1
71	Unholtz-Dickie Corp—Michael Reen	6 Brookside Dr, Wallingford CT 06492	203-265-3929	R	20*	<.1
72	Refraction Technology Inc—Paul R Passmore	1600 10th St Ste A, Plano TX 75074	214-440-1265	R	20*	<.1
73	Tuppas Software Corp—Paul Tupciauskas	PO Box 171, Waterville OH 43566	419-897-7902	R	20*	.2
74	Randolph Co—Oliver Ring	PO Box 721230, Houston TX 77272	281-983-4040	R	20*	<.1
75	Novatron Corp—Charles Debeau	6000 Rinke Ave, Warren MI 48091	586-755-1300	R	19*	.2
76	Balance Technology Inc—Thomas Plunkett	7035 Jomar Dr, Whitmore Lake MI 48189	734-769-2100	R	19*	.1
77	VLSI Standards Inc—Brad Scheer	5 Technology Dr, Milpitas CA 95035	408-875-1000	S	18	<.1
78	Schneeberger Inc—Hans Schneeberger	11 Deangelo Dr, Bedford MA 01730	781-271-0140	R	18*	<.1
79	Interstates Control Systems Inc—Jack Woelber	PO Box 260, Sioux Center IA 51250	712-722-1663	R	17*	.4
80	Testing Machines Inc—John Sullivan	40 Mccullough Dr, New Castle DE 19720	302-613-5600	R	17*	.1
81	Ag Leader Technology Inc—Allen Myers	2202 S Riverside Dr, Ames IA 50010	515-232-5363	R	16*	.1
82	SKF Condition Monitoring Inc—Jan Brons	5271 Viewridge Ct, San Diego CA 92123	858-496-3511	S	16*	.1
83	Ideal Aerosmith Inc—John Mohn	3001 S Washington St, Grand Forks ND 58201	701-757-3400	R	16*	.1
84	Preferred Utilities Manufacturing Corp—David Bohn	31-35 S St, Danbury CT 06810	203-743-6741	R	16*	.1
85	Baron Services Inc—Robert Baron	4930 Research Dr Nw, Huntsville AL 35805	256-881-8811	R	15*	.1
86	Pressco Technology Inc—Don Cochran	29200 Aurora Rd, Cleveland OH 44139	440-498-2600	R	15*	.1
87	Magnetic Analysis Corp—William Gould	103 Fairview Park Dr, Elmsford NY 10523	914-530-2000	R	15*	.1
88	Met One Instruments Inc—Thomas Pottberg	1600 Nw Washington Blv, Grants Pass OR 97526	541-471-7111	R	15*	.1
89	Geometrics Inc—Mark Prouty Oyo Corporation USA	2190 Fortune Dr, San Jose CA 95131	408-954-0522	S	15*	.1
90	Laser Technology Inc (Norristown Pennsylvania)—John Newman	1055 W Germantown Pke, Norristown PA 19403	610 631 4846	R	15*	<.1
91	Applus AutoLogic LLC—William Nicholson	N56 W24701 N Corporate, Sussex WI 53089	262-820-9672	R	15*	<.1
92	Microanalytics Instrumentation Corp—Robert Forbesberg MOCON Inc	2011A Lamar Dr, Round Rock TX 78664	512-218-9873	S	15*	<.1
93	Field Controls LLC—Patrick Holleran	2630 Airport Rd, Kinston NC 28504	252-522-3031	R	15*	.1
94	Quantachrome Corp—F Lowell	1900 Corporate Dr, Boynton Beach FL 33426	561-731-4999	R	15*	.1
95	Valpey-Fisher Corp—Michael J Ferrantino Jr	75 South St, Hopkinton MA 01748	508-435-6831	S	15	.1
96	Sierra Monitor Corp—Gordon R Arnold	1991 Tarob Ct, Milpitas CA 95035	408-262-6611	P	14	.1
97	Capintec Inc—Jessica Bede	6 Arrow Rd Ste 208, Ramsey NJ 07446	201-825-9500	R	14*	.1
98	Projects Inc—Michael Kenyon	PO Box 190, Glastonbury CT 06033	860-633-4615	R	14*	.1
99	Horiba/Stec Inc—Kensuke Nakagawa	3265 Scott Blvd, Santa Clara CA 95054	408-730-8795	R	14*	.1
100	Lansmont Corp—Joseph Driscoll	17 Mandeville Ct, Monterey CA 93940	831-655-6600	R	14*	.1
101	Kessler-Ellis Products Co—Peter Sabat	10 Industrial Way E, Eatontown NJ 07724	732-935-1320	R	14*	<.1
102	Msp Corp—Ben Liu	5910 Rice Creek Pkwy S, Saint Paul MN 55126	651-287-8100	R	14*	<.1
103	International Electronic Machines Corp—Zack Mian	60 4th Ave, Albany NY 12202	518-268-1636	R	14*	<.1
104	Serveron Corp—Wang Peng	3305 Nw Aloclek Dr, Hillsboro OR 97124	503-924-3200	R	14*	.1
105	Astrata Group Inc—Anthony Harrison	1801 Century Pk E Ste, Los Angeles CA 90067	310-777-8889	R	13	.1
106	Alvarado Manufacturing Company Inc—James Armatas	PO Box 5135, Chino CA 91708	909-591-8431	R	13*	.1
107	Spectrum Laboratories Inc—Anthony MacDonald	18617 Broadwick St, Rancho Dominguez CA 90220	310-885-4600	R	13*	.1
108	Kistler-Morse Corp—Mark Earl	150 Venture Blvd, Spartanburg SC 29306	864-574-2763	S	13*	.1
109	Brunton Outdoor Inc—John Smithbaker	2255 Brunton Ct, Riverton WY 82501	307-856-6559	R	13*	<.1
110	Paksense—David W Light	9939 W Emerald St Bldg, Boise ID 83704		R	13*	<.1
111	IDSC Holdings LLC	2950 Water View Dr, Rochester Hills MI 48309	248-293-8200	S	13	.1
112	Optivus Proton Therapy Inc—Jon Slater	PO Box 608, Loma Linda CA 92354	909-799-8300	R	12*	.1
113	Thermoscan Inc—AJ Lafley	10421 Pacific Center C, San Diego CA 92121		S	12*	.1
114	Kistler Instrument Corp—Nick Wilks	75 John Glenn Dr, Amherst NY 14228	716-691-5100	R	12*	.1
115	R M Young Co—Thomas Young	2801 Aero Park Dr, Traverse City MI 49686	231-946-3980	R	12*	<.1
116	Dynamic Sciences International Inc—Eli Shiri	6130 Variel Ave, Woodland Hills CA 91367	818-226-6262	R	12*	<.1
117	Chauvin Arnoux Inc—Winthrop Smith	15 Faraday Dr, Dover NH 03820	603-749-6434	R	12*	.1
118	Quantum Group Inc—Mark Goldstein	7737 Kenamar Ct, San Diego CA 92121	858-566-9959	R	11*	.1
119	Maryland Meggitt Inc—Derek Carbin	20511 Seneca Meadows P, Germantown MD 20876	301-330-8811	R	11*	.1
120	Uster Technologies Inc—Hossein Ghorashi	456 Troy Cir, Knoxville TN 37919	865-588-9716	R	11*	.1
121	Kinemetrics Inc—Mel Lund Oyo Corporation USA	222 Vista Ave, Pasadena CA 91107	626-795-2220	S	11*	.1
122	Radiation Monitoring Devices Inc—Gerald Entine	44 Hunt St Ste 2, Watertown MA 02472	617-926-1167	R	11*	.1
123	Bauer Inc—Lou Auletta	175 Century Dr, Bristol CT 06010	860-583-9100	R	10*	.1
124	Hamilton Associates Inc—Douglas Hamilton	11403 Cronridge Dr Ste, Owings Mills MD 21117	410-363-9020	R	10*	.1
125	JMAR Precision Systems Inc—Chandu Vanjani	20447 Nordhoff St, Chatsworth CA 91311	818-700-8977	R	10*	.1
126	Ectron Corp—Earl Cunningham	8159 Engineer Rd, San Diego CA 92111	858-278-0600	R	10*	<.1
127	Environmental Instruments Leasing Company Inc—William Stortz	5650 Imhoff Dr Ste A, Concord CA 94520	925-686-4474	R	10*	<.1
128	ODV Inc—Scott Obrien	13386 International Pk, Jacksonville FL 32218	904-485-1836	R	10*	<.1
129	Ames Engineering Inc—John Maurer	PO Box 310, Ames IA 50010	515-292-8194	R	10*	<.1
130	Second Wind Systems Inc—Larry Letteney	366 Summer St, Somerville MA 02144	617-776-8520	R	10*	.1
131	Spectracom Corp—Elizabeth Withers	1565 Jefferson Rd Ste, Rochester NY 14623	585-321-5800	R	10*	.1
132	Ssi Technology Inc—Robert Bloom	1235 Spartan St, Madison Heights MI 48071	248-582-0600	R	10*	.1
133	Tsa Systems Ltd—Allan Frymire	14000 Mead St, Longmont CO 80504	970-535-9949	R	10*	<.1
134	Avionics Interface Technologies LLC—Bill Fleissner	3703 N 200th St, Elkhorn NE 68022	402-763-9644	R	10*	.1
135	Sonoscan Inc—Lawrence Kessler	2149 Pratt Blvd, Elk Grove Village IL 60007	847-437-6400	R	10*	.1
136	Thwing-Albert Instrument Company Inc—Joseph Raab	14 W Collings Ave, West Berlin NJ 08091	856-767-1000	R	10*	.1
137	Technology For Energy Corp—William Simpkins	10737 Lexington Dr, Knoxville TN 37932	865-966-5856	R	10*	.1
138	Tricor Systems Inc—Timothy Allen	1650 Todd Farm Dr, Elgin IL 60123	847-724-5542	R	9*	<.1
139	Chart Cryogenic Systems—Tom Carey	407 7th St NW, New Prague MN 56071	952-758-4484	D	9*	.1
140	Lafayette Instrument Company Inc—Roger Clellan	PO Box 5729, Lafayette IN 47903	765-423-1505	R	9*	.1
141	DeltaTRAK Inc—Frederick Wu	PO Box 398, Pleasanton CA 94566	925-249-2250	R	9*	.1
142	Geosonics Inc—D Froedge	PO Box 506, Warrendale PA 15086	724-934-2900	R	9*	<.1
143	Inter Basic Resources Inc—George Grundelman	PO Box 250, Grass Lake MI 49240	517-522-8453	R	9*	<.1

Note: An asterisk (*) indicates an estimated financial figure. The company type code used is as follows: R = Private, P = Public, S = Private Subsidiary, B = Public Subsidiary, D = Division, J = Joint Venture, I = Investment Fund.

COMPANY RANKINGS BY SALES WITHIN 4-DIGIT SIC

Rank	Company Name—Executive Officer	Address, City, State, Zip	Phone	Type	Fin	Empls
144	Irrometer Company Inc—Tom Penning	PO Box 2424, Riverside CA 92516	951-689-1701	R	9*	<.1
145	Intoximeters Inc—M Forrester	PO Box 798313, Saint Louis MO 63179	314-429-4000	R	9*	.1
146	Magtrol Inc—William Mulroy	70 Gardenville Pkwy W, Buffalo NY 14224	716-668-5555	R	9*	.1
147	Gamma Scientific LLC—Valeria Cotter	8581 Aero Dr, San Diego CA 92123	858-279-8034	R	9*	<.1
148	Detcon Inc—Dan Alpha	PO Box 8067, The Woodlands TX 77387	713-559-9200	R	9*	.1
149	Liquid Crystal Resources LLC—Linda Booth	1911 Pickwick Ln, Glenview IL 60026	847-998-8580	R	9*	.1
150	Humboldt Manufacturing Co—Dennis Burgess	3801 25th Ave, Schiller Park IL 60176	708-456-6300	R	9*	<.1
151	Sun Nuclear Corp—William Simon	425 Pineda Ct Ste A, Melbourne FL 32940	321-259-6862	R	8*	<.1
152	California Sensor Corp—Ralph Miller	2075 Corte Del Nogal P, Carlsbad CA 92011	760-438-0525	R	8*	<.1
153	Audio Precision Inc—David Schmoldt	PO Box 2209, Beaverton OR 97075	503-627-0832	R	8*	<.1
154	J L Shepherd And Associates—Joseph Shepherd	1010 Arroyo St, San Fernando CA 91340	818-898-2361	R	8*	<.1
155	Industrial Tool Die and Engineering Inc—Guy Theriault	4765 S Overland Dr, Tucson AZ 85714	520-745-8771	R	8*	.1
156	Shadin LP—Jason Bruggeman	6831 Oxford St, Saint Louis Park MN 55426	952-927-6500	R	8*	.1
157	Team Corp—Robert Tauscher	11591 Watertank Rd, Burlington WA 98233	360-757-8601	R	8*	.1
158	General Nuclear Corp—Rick Lang	PO BOx 400, New Stanton PA 15672	724-925-3565	R	8*	<.1
159	Kahler Automation Corp—Wayne Kahler	808 Timberlake Rd, Fairmont MN 56031	507-235-6648	R	8*	<.1
160	Windrock Inc—J Follmar	1832 Midpark Rd Ste 10, Knoxville TN 37921	865-330-1100	R	8*	<.1
161	Dyne Systems Inc—Alan Brown	PO Box 18, Jackson WI 53037	262-677-9300	R	8*	<.1
162	RENS Metal Detectors—Michael Nelson	4270 NW Yeon Av, Portland OR 97210	503-222-9992	D	8*	<.1
163	Clean-Flo Laboratories Inc—Brian Kling	540 E Union St Ste 1, West Chester PA 19382	610-431-1934	R	8*	<.1
164	Daily Thermetrics Corp—Jeffrey Daily	5700 Hartsdale Dr, Houston TX 77036	713-780-8600	R	8*	.1
165	Applied Physics Systems—William Goodman	1245 Space Park Way St, Mountain View CA 94043	650-965-0500	R	8*	.1
166	Gagemaker LP—Linda Birdwell	PO Box 87709, Houston TX 77287	713-472-7360	R	8*	.1
167	Power Test Inc—Alan Petelinsek	N60w 22700 Silver Spri, Sussex WI 53089	262-252-4301	R	8*	.1
168	Vacuum Technology Of Tennessee Inc—George Solomon	1003 Alvin Weinberg Dr, Oak Ridge TN 37830	865-481-3342	R	8*	.1
169	Standard Imaging Inc—Ed Neumueller	3120 Deming Way, Middleton WI 53562	608-831-0025	R	8*	<.1
170	Radcal Partners la California LP—Paul Sunde	426 W Duarte Rd, Monrovia CA 91016	626-359-4575	R	7*	<.1
171	Rohrback Cosasco Systems Inc—Brent Ford	11841 Smith Ave, Santa Fe Springs CA 90670	562-949-0123	R	7	.9
172	Mechanical Technology Inc—Peng K Lim	431 New Karner Rd, Albany NY 12205	518-533-2218	P	7	.1
173	Automation And Control Technology Inc—Charles Totel	PO Box 3667, Dublin OH 43016	614-495-1120	R	7*	<.1
174	Tek-Air Systems Inc—A Siemer	41 Eagle Rd Ste 2, Danbury CT 06810	203-791-1400	R	7*	.1
175	Standards Testing Laboratories Inc—Darryl Fuller	PO Box 758, Massillon OH 44648	330-833-8548	R	7*	.1
176	Hart Scientific Inc—Chris Juchau	799 E Utah Valley Dr, American Fork UT 84003	801-763-1600	S	7*	.1
177	MIDAC Corp—Jerry Auth	130 McCormick Ave Ste, Costa Mesa CA 92626	714-546-4322	R	7*	.1
178	Gilson Screen Inc—David Cody	PO Box 99, Malinta OH 43535	419-256-7711	R	7*	<.1
179	Burns Engineering Inc—Jim Burns	10201 Bren Rd E, Minnetonka MN 55343	952-935-4400	R	7*	<.1
180	Proprietary Controls Systems Corp—Masami Kosaka	3541 Challenger St, Torrance CA 90503	310-303-3600	R	7*	<.1
181	Respironics - New Jersey—Daniel Bevevino	41 Canfield Rd, Cedar Grove NJ 07009	973-857-3414	S	7*	<.1
182	L N D Inc—Peter Neyland	3230 Lawson Blvd, Oceanside NY 11572	516-678-6141	R	7*	<.1
183	Teletrol Systems Inc—Andy Mcmillan	286 Commercial St Ste, Manchester NH 03101	603-645-6061	R	7*	<.1
184	Kld Labs Inc—Steven Magnus	300 Broadway, Huntington Station NY 11746	631-549-4222	R	6*	<.1
185	Production Control Units Inc—Thomas Hoge	2280 W Dorothy Ln, Moraine OH 45439	937-299-5594	R	6*	.1
186	Systems Analysis and Integration Inc—Susan Corrales-Diaz	2200 N Glassell St, Orange CA 92865	714-998-0900	R	6*	.1
187	Cosense Inc—Naim Dam	155 Ricefield Ln, Hauppauge NY 11788	631-231-0735	R	6*	<.1
188	Thermo Electric Company Inc—Richard Rodelli	1193 McDermott Dr, West Chester PA 19380	610-692-7990	R	6*	.1
189	Information Processing Systems Of California Inc—Clarence Boice	70 Glenn Way Ste 2, San Carlos CA 94070	650-592-1742	R	6*	<.1
190	AMS Inc (American Falls Idaho)—Marc Chipps	105 Harrison St, American Falls ID 83211	208-226-2017	R	6*	<.1
191	Hypres Inc—Richard Hitt	175 Clearbrook Rd Ste, Elmsford NY 10523	914-592-1190	R	6*	<.1
192	Lawler Manufacturing Corp—Joseph Cekada	7 Kilmer Ct, Edison NJ 08817	732-777-2040	R	6*	<.1
193	Colorado Video Inc—Kirk Fowler	PO Box 928, Boulder CO 80306	303-530-9580	R	6*	<.1
194	CST Inc (Dallas Texas)—Cecil Ho	2336 Lu Field Rd, Dallas TX 75229	972-241-2662	R	6*	<.1
195	Vermont Photonics Inc—Michael Mross	22 Browne Ct, Brattleboro VT 05301	802-275-5210	R	6*	<.1
196	CTRL Systems Inc—Robert H Roche	1004 Littlestown Pike, Westminster MD 21157	410-876-5676	R	6*	<.1
197	Galiso Inc—Charles Grenci	22 Ponderosa Ct, Montrose CO 81401	970-249-0233	R	6*	<.1
198	Aja International Inc—William Hale	PO Box 246, Scituate MA 02060	781-545-7365	R	6*	<.1
199	Blatek Industries Inc—Stuart Blacker	2820 E College Ave Ste, State College PA 16801	814-231-2085	R	6*	.1
200	Accurate Measurement Controls Inc—Mike Arceneaux	PO Box 268, Broussard LA 70518	337-369-9222	R	6*	<.1
201	Chant Engineering Company Inc—L Chant	59 Industrial Dr, New Britain PA 18901	215-230-4260	R	6*	<.1
202	Tekvisions Inc—Thomas Cramer	40970 Anza Rd, Temecula CA 92592	951-506-9709	R	6*	<.1
203	Eustis Company Inc—Carrold Paulson	PO Box 1095, Mukilteo WA 98275	425-423-9996	R	6*	<.1
204	Quest Controls Inc—Edward Goggin	208 9th St Dr W, Palmetto FL 34221	941-729-4799	R	6*	<.1
205	Systems Integrated LLC	2200 N Glassell St, Orange CA 92865	714-998-0900	R	6*	<.1
206	Maxant Technologies Inc—Raynor Sturgis	7540 N Caldwell Ave, Niles IL 60714	847-588-2280	R	6*	<.1
207	Bay Cast Technologies Inc—Scott Holman	PO Box 676, Bay City MI 48707	989-892-9500	R	6*	<.1
208	Tegam Inc—Andrew Brush	10 Tegam Way, Geneva OH 44041	440-466-6100	R	5*	<.1
209	Morphix Technologies—Bart Heenan	2557 Production Rd, Virginia Beach VA 23454	757-431-2260	R	5*	<.1
210	Ultrasonic Sciences Inc—John Kennelly	333 E Key Palm Rd, Boca Raton FL 33432	561-391-4302	R	5*	<.1
211	Imaginant Inc—Todd Jackson	3800 Monroe Ave Ste 29, Pittsford NY 14534	585-264-0480	R	5*	<.1
212	Modern Machine And Tool Company Inc—Brent Meadors	11844 Jefferson Ave, Newport News VA 23606	757-873-1212	R	5*	.1
213	Becon Inc	46 Schweir Rd, South Windsor CT 06074	860-528-9641	R	5*	.1
214	Comten Industries—Betty Giebner	6405 49th St N, Pinellas Park FL 33781	727-520-1200	R	5*	.1
215	Spiricon Inc—Gray Wagner	3050 N 300 W, North Logan UT 84341	435-753-3729	R	5*	<.1
216	Alpha Sensors Inc—Fernando Marchitelli	17151 Gillette Ave, Irvine CA 92614	949-250-6578	R	5*	<.1
217	Frye Electronics Inc—George Frye	PO Box 23391, Tigard OR 97281	503-620-2722	R	5*	<.1
218	CJ Instruments Inc—C Tucker	PO Box 570430, Tarzana CA 91357	818-996-4131	R	5*	<.1
219	Ralston Instruments LLC—Douglas Ralston	PO Box 340, Novelty OH 44072	440-247-6575	R	5*	<.1
220	Vemco Drafting Products Corp—Jackson Albright	PO Box 549, San Dimas CA 91773	909-287-0687	R	5*	<.1
221	Grape Networks Inc—Peter Tsepeleff	231 Market Pl Ste 206, San Ramon CA 94583	925-389-7387	R	5*	<.1
222	SensorTran—Sandy Esslemont	4401 Freidrick Ln Ste, Austin TX 78744	512-583-3520	R	5*	<.1
223	Advanced Systems And Controls Inc—Andrew Zundel	15773 Leone Dr, Macomb MI 48042	586-992-9684	R	5*	<.1
224	Automatic Tool Control And Management Systems Inc—Hemi Sagi	4037 Guion Ln, Indianapolis IN 46268	317-328-8492	R	5*	<.1
225	U E Systems Inc—Michael Osterer	14 Hayes St, Elmsford NY 10523	914-592-1220	R	5*	<.1
226	National Patent Analytical System Inc—John Fusco	PO Box 1435, Mansfield OH 44901	419-526-6727	R	5*	<.1
227	Anter Corp—Peter Gaal	1700 Universal Rd Ste, Pittsburgh PA 15235	412-795-6410	R	5*	<.1
228	Metronics Inc—Carmel Boucher	136 Harvey Rd Ste A001, Londonderry NH 03053	603-222-5600	R	5*	<.1
229	Laser Sensor Technology Inc—Johnnie Ridgeway	14833 Ne 87th St, Redmond WA 98052	425-881-7117	R	5*	<.1
230	C W Brabender Instruments Inc—Richard Thoma	PO Box 2127, South Hackensack NJ 07606	201-343-8425	R	5*	<.1
231	Holmes Brothers Inc—Robert Muirhead	510 Junction St, Danville IL 61832	217-442-7950	R	5*	<.1

Rank	Company Name—Executive Officer	Address, City, State, Zip	Phone	Type	Fin	Empls
232	Integrated Sensing Systems Inc—Nader Najafi	391 Airport Industrial, Ypsilanti MI 48198	734-547-9896	R	5*	<.1
233	Valentine LLC—Curtis Arcement	129 Valentine Dr, Lockport LA 70374	985-532-2541	R	5*	<.1
234	Mb Dynamics Inc—Richard Mc Cormick	25865 Richmond Rd, Cleveland OH 44146	216-292-5850	R	5*	<.1
235	Shortridge Instruments Inc—B Shortridge	PO Box 13085, Scottsdale AZ 85267	480-991-6744	R	5*	<.1
236	M - R Electronics Inc—Melva Roesler	700 Industrial Blvd, Sugar Land TX 77478	281-240-9400	R	5*	<.1
237	Tucker-Davis Technologies Inc—Tim Tucker	11930 Research Cir, Alachua FL 32615	386-462-9622	R	5*	<.1
238	Strain Measurement Devices Inc—Frederick Jackson	55 Barnes Park Rd N, Wallingford CT 06492	203-294-5800	R	4*	<.1
239	Forney Holdings Inc—Jeff Gziki	1565 Broadway Rd, Hermitage PA 16148	724-346-7400	R	4*	<.1
240	United Calibration Corp—Robert Graves	5802 Engineer Dr, Huntington Beach CA 92649	714-893-1821	R	4*	.1
241	Hines Industries Inc—Dawn Hines	793 Airport Blvd, Ann Arbor MI 48108	734-769-2300	R	4*	<.1
242	Micro-G Lacoste Inc—Tim Niebauer	1401 Horizon Ave, Lafayette CO 80026	303-828-3499	R	4*	<.1
243	Clio Inc—Reva Johnson	12981 166th St, Cerritos CA 90703	562-926-3724	R	4*	<.1
244	Strainsert Co—Tim Foley	12 Union Hill Rd, West Conshohocken PA 19428	610-825-3310	R	4*	<.1
245	Sensor Scientific Inc—G Brinley	6 Kingsbridge Rd Ste 4, Fairfield NJ 07004	973-227-7790	R	4*	.2
246	International Sensor Technology Inc—Jack Chou	3 Whatney Ste 100, Irvine CA 92618	949-452-9000	R	4*	<.1
247	Climatronics Corp—John Robertson	140 Wilbur Pl, Bohemia NY 11716	631-567-7300	R	4*	<.1
248	Turner Designs Inc—Jim Crawford	845 W Maude Ave, Sunnyvale CA 94085	408-749-0994	R	4*	<.1
249	Precision Measurements Inc (Atlanta Georgia)—Bill Roberts	3715 Northcrest Rd Ste, Atlanta GA 30340	770-457-7099	R	4*	<.1
250	International Diagnostic Systems Corp—Deborah K Morris	PO Box 799, Saint Joseph MI 49085	269-428-8400	S	4*	<.1
251	Material Testing Technology Co—W Scott Thielman	1676 S Wolf Rd, Wheeling IL 60090	847-215-7448	R	4*	<.1
252	Siko Products Inc—Darrell Davey	PO Box 279, Dexter MI 48130	734-426-3478	R	4*	<.1
253	Home Safeguard Industries LLC—Margaret Feiter	107 Garlisch Dr, Elk Grove Village IL 60007	847-427-8340	R	4*	<.1
254	Clark Solutions	10 Brent Dr, Hudson MA 01749	978-568-3400	R	4*	<.1
255	Ultrasonic Power Corp—Dolores Schnoes	239 E Stephenson St, Freeport IL 61032	815-235-6020	R	4*	<.1
256	Accu-Sport International Inc—Randall Tuttle	4310 Enterprise Dr Ste, Winston Salem NC 27106	336-759-3300	R	4*	<.1
257	Thermo Sensors Corp—John Medcalf	PO Box 461947, Garland TX 75046	972-494-1566	R	4*	<.1
258	Telog Instruments Inc—Barry Ceci	830 Canning Pkwy, Victor NY 14564	585-742-3000	R	4*	<.1
259	Automated Quality Technologies Inc—Donald Martin	563 Shoreview Park Rd, Saint Paul MN 55126	651-484-6544	R	4*	<.1
260	Gfg Instrumentation Inc—H Huebner	1194 Oak Valley Dr Ste, Ann Arbor MI 48108	734-769-0573	R	4*	<.1
261	General Nucleonics Inc—Sam Dominey	2807 Metropolitan Pl, Pomona CA 91767	909-593-4985	R	4*	<.1
262	Kocour Co—Dennis Masarik	4800 S Saint Louis Ave, Chicago IL 60632	773-847-1111	R	4*	<.1
263	Perey Turnstiles Inc—M Hendrickson	308 Bishop Ave, Bridgeport CT 06610	203-333-9400	R	4*	<.1
264	Aviation Technology Inc—John Verderame	225 E Industrial Park, Manchester NH 03109	603-666-0200	R	4*	<.1
265	Electronic Electromechanical Equipment Assembly Inc—Kamal Armaly	PO Box 369, Mauldin SC 29662	864-963-3651	R	4*	<.1
266	Plasticoid Manufacturing Inc—Jonathan Shoham	32 N Rd Rear, East Windsor CT 06088	860-623-1361	R	4*	<.1
267	Soilmoisture Equipment Corp—Percy Skaling	PO Box 30025, Santa Barbara CA 93130	805-964-3525	R	4*	<.1
268	Arrow-Tech Inc—Carol James	PO Box 1240, Rolla ND 58367	701-477-6461	R	4*	<.1
269	Rainhart Co—Robert Durr	PO Box 4533, Austin TX 78765	512-452-8848	R	4*	<.1
270	Temprel Inc—John Bertsch	206 Industrial Pky Dr, Boyne City MI 49712	231-582-6585	R	3*	<.1
271	Warren Industries Inc—John Warren	2045 Bennett Rd, Philadelphia PA 19116	215-464-9300	R	3*	<.1
272	National Ultrasound Inc—Joe Wiliams	2730 N Brkly Lake Rd N, Duluth GA 30096	770-551-8797	R	3*	<.1
273	Helm Instrument Company Inc—Richard Wilhelm	361 W Dussel Dr, Maumee OH 43537	419-893-4356	R	3*	<.1
274	California Dynamics Corp—Donald Benkert	5572 Alhambra Ave, Los Angeles CA 90032	323-223-3882	R	3*	<.1
275	Dynamic Systems Inc (Poestenkill New York)—Todd Bonesteel	PO Box 1234, Poestenkill NY 12140	518-283-5350	R	3	<.1
276	Lenox Laser Corp—Joseph D'entremont	12530 Manor Rd, Glen Arm MD 21057	410-592-3106	R	3*	<.1
277	Helmel Engineering Products Inc—Erwin Helmel	6520 Lockport Rd, Niagara Falls NY 14305	716-297-8644	R	3*	<.1
278	Mechanized Science Seals Inc—Jon Hamren	5322 Mcfadden Ave, Huntington Beach CA 92649	714-898-5602	R	3*	<.1
279	Akers Biosciences Inc—Thomas Nicolette	201 Grove Rd, Thorofare NJ 08086	856-848-8698	H	3*	<.1
280	Aqua Measure Instrument Co—John Lundstrom	1712 Earhart, La Verne CA 91750	909-392-5833	R	3*	<.1
281	Gamry Instruments Inc—Gregory Martinchek	734 Louis Dr, Warminster PA 18974	215-682-9330	R	3*	<.1
282	Auto Tran Inc—Greg Sedivy	7638 Washington Ave S, Eden Prairie MN 55344	952-942-8743	R	3*	<.1
283	Rycom Instruments Inc—E Reitz	9351 E 59th St, Raytown MO 64133	816-353-2100	R	3*	<.1
284	Spectrum Sensors And Controls Inc—Richard Southworth	2236 N Clvland Msslion, Akron OH 44333	330-659-3312	R	3*	<.1
285	Optiphase Inc—Ira Bush	7652 Haskell Ave, Van Nuys CA 91406	818-782-0997	R	3*	<.1
286	Airmate Company Inc—Carol Rogers	16280 County Rd D, Bryan OH 43506	419-636-3184	R	3*	.1
287	CMI Inc—Gary Braswell	316 E 9th St, Owensboro KY 42303		S	3*	<.1
288	Kohlman Systems Research Inc—Thomas Rawlings	2500 W 31st St Ste H, Lawrence KS 66047	785-843-4099	R	3*	<.1
289	Imc Instruments Inc—Louis Frias	468 Liberty Dr, Wittenberg WI 54499	715-253-2801	R	3*	<.1
290	Calder Testers Inc—John Emmitte	8402 Scranton St, Houston TX 77061	713-333-0260	R	3*	<.1
291	Hogentogler and Company Inc—Thomas Nolan	PO Box 2219, Columbia MD 21045	410-381-2390	R	3*	<.1
292	MEECO Inc (Warrington Pennsylvania)—Lisa Bergson	250 Titus Ave, Warrington PA 18976	215-343-6600	R	3*	<.1
293	Narmac Corp—Daniel Nanigian	11 Mayhew St, Framingham MA 01702	508-872-4811	R	3*	<.1
294	Precision Samplers Inc—Israel Broome	147 11th Ave Ste 200, South Charleston WV 25303	304-744-5534	R	3*	<.1
295	Schap Specialty Machine Inc—William Schap	17309 Taft Rd Ste A, Spring Lake MI 49456	616-846-6530	R	3*	<.1
296	SE International Inc—Susan Skinner	PO Box 39, Summertown TN 38483	931-964-3561	R	3*	<.1
297	Global Gauge Corp—Tim Mccormick	PO Box 3040, Dayton OH 45401	937-254-3500	R	3*	<.1
298	AST Products Inc—Carl Cummings	9 Linnell Cir, Billerica MA 01821	978-667-4500	R	3*	<.1
299	Capacitec Inc—Robert Foster	PO Box 819, Ayer MA 01432	978-772-6033	R	3*	<.1
300	NovaLynx Corp—Joseph Andre	PO Box 240, Grass Valley CA 95945	530-823-7185	R	3*	<.1
301	MiE America Inc—Norman Vonhollen	420 Bennett Rd, Elk Grove Village IL 60007	847-981-6100	S	3*	<.1
302	Dakota Technologies Inc—Randy St Germain	2201 12th St N Ste A, Fargo ND 58102	701-237-4908	R	3*	<.1
303	Indiana Standards Laboratory—Richard Chance	2919 Shelby St, Indianapolis IN 46203	317-787-6578	R	3*	<.1
304	Keco R and D Inc—Tom Kimbell	1400 B Graham Dr, Tomball TX 77375	281-516-3950	S	3*	<.1
305	REMTECH Inc—Jean-Michel Fage	2 Red Oak Rd, Saint James NY 11780	303-772-6825	R	3*	<.1
306	Precision Speed Instruments Inc—Ann Bogert	PO Box 27430, Phoenix AZ 85061	602-973-1055	R	3*	<.1
307	Ascend Geo LLC	500 Corporate Cir Ste, Golden CO 80401	720-881-4000	R	3*	<.1
308	Highland Technology—John Larkin	18 Otis St, San Francisco CA 94103	415-551-1700	R	3*	<.1
309	PBS Control—Mike Larimer	6 Pearl Ct, Allendale NJ 07401	201-327-9500	R	3*	<.1
310	World Magnetics Co—James Lievense	810 Hastings St, Traverse City MI 49686	231-946-3800	R	3*	<.1
311	Thermalogic Corp—Louis Grein	22 Kane Industrial Dr, Hudson MA 01749	978-562-5974	R	3*	<.1
312	Science Pump Corp—Steven Schwartz	1431 Ferry Ave, Camden NJ 08104	856-963-7700	R	3*	<.1
313	Thunderbird International Corp—Walter Wunsch	PO Box 360, Emigrant MT 59027	406-333-4967	R	3*	<.1
314	Interlaken Technology Corp—Thomas Driggers	8175 Century Blvd, Chaska MN 55318	952-942-7499	R	3*	<.1
315	Magnetic Automation Corp—Dieter Schwald	3160 Murrell Rd, Rockledge FL 32955	321-635-8585	R	3*	<.1
316	Thermocouple Technology Inc—Gerald Shea	350 New St, Quakertown PA 18951	215-529-9394	R	3*	<.1
317	Miller and Weber Inc—Deanne Miller	1637 George St, Ridgewood NY 11385	718-821-7110	R	3*	<.1
318	Quality Gage Inc—David D'agostino	18346 Hearthside Ln, Clinton Township MI 48038	586-263-0093	R	3*	<.1
319	Bonal International Inc—A George Hebel III	1300 N Campbell Rd, Royal Oak MI 48067	248-582-0900	P	3	<.1
320	Emission Methods Inc—Kenneth Parker	1307 S Wanamaker Ave, Ontario CA 91761	909-605-6800	R	3*	<.1

Note: An asterisk (*) indicates an estimated financial figure. The company type code used is as follows: R = Private, P = Public, S = Private Subsidiary, B = Public Subsidiary, D = Division, J = Joint Venture, I = Investment Fund.

COMPANY RANKINGS BY SALES WITHIN 4-DIGIT SIC

Rank	Company Name—*Executive Officer*	Address, City, State, Zip	Phone	Type	Fin	Empls
321	Visualant Inc—*Ronald P Erickson*	500 Union St Ste 406, Seattle WA 98101	206-903-1351	P	3*	<.1
322	Barnette Industries Inc—*Barbara Barnette*	5860 Laird Rd, Loomis CA 95650	916-652-7050	R	3*	<.1
323	Princeton Measurements Corp—*Harry Reichard*	31 Airpark Rd Ste 2, Princeton NJ 08540	609-924-7885	R	2*	<.1
324	Michael A Yedinak—*Michael Yedinak*	15 Reef Ct, Portsmouth VA 23703	757-953-1121	R	2*	<.1
325	Migatron Corp—*Frank Wroga*	PO Box 1229, Woodstock IL 60098	815-338-5800	R	2*	<.1
326	Delraye Investments Corp—*Daniel Mchugh*	4921 Carver Ave, Langhorne PA 19053	215-322-4700	R	2*	<.1
327	Blaze Technical Services Inc—*Ralph Hickman*	1445 Commerce Dr, Stow OH 44224	330-923-0409	R	2*	<.1
328	Quality First Systems Inc—*Richard Shore*	10301 Enterprise Dr, Davisburg MI 48350	248-922-4780	R	2*	<.1
329	Beamco Inc—*James Bergman*	20487 470th Ave Nw, Oslo MN 56744	218-965-4660	R	2*	<.1
330	Resource Technology Corp—*Robert Rucinski*	PO Box 1346, Laramie WY 82073	307-742-5452	R	2*	<.1
331	Scientific Process and Research Inc—*Joe Klein*	67 Veronica Ave, Somerset NJ 08873	732-846-3477	R	2	<.1
332	Semco—*Shawn Martin*	1495 S Gage St, San Bernardino CA 92408	909-799-9666	R	2*	<.1
333	Thermacal Inc—*Jerry Nickol*	30275 Bainbridge Rd, Solon .OH 44139	440-498-1005	R	2*	<.1
334	Lpg Industries Inc—*Kenneth Gabriel*	PO Box 600, Clifton Heights PA 19018	610-338-0746	R	2*	<.1
335	Headwall Photonics Inc—*David Bannon*	601 River St, Fitchburg MA 01420	978-353-4100	R	2*	<.1
336	Rainwise Inc—*Bunny Emerson*	PO Box 443, Bar Harbor ME 04609	207-288-5169	R	2*	<.1
337	RC Electronics Inc—*Richard Renck*	6464 Hollister Ave, Santa Barbara CA 93117	805-685-7770	R	2*	<.1
338	STI Automation Sensor Div—*Randy Anderson*	1025 West 1700 North, Logan UT 84321	435-753-7300	R	2*	<.1
339	Echometer Co—*James Mccoy*	5001 Ditto Ln, Wichita Falls TX 76302	940-767-4334	R	2*	<.1
340	Quint Measuring Systems Inc—*Carol Quint*	PO Box 280, San Ramon CA 94583	925-952-9484	R	2*	<.1
341	Automation Technology Inc—*Robert Storar*	1900 Troy St, Dayton OH 45404	937-233-6084	R	2*	<.1
342	Vibrac Corp—*Tom Rogers*	PO Box 840, Amherst NH 03031	603-882-6777	R	2	<.1
343	Chen Instrument Design—*Shane Chin*	4901 NW Camas Meadows, Camas WA 98607	360-833-8835	S	2*	<.1
344	UDT Instruments—*Mark Decker* Gamma Scientific LLC	8581 Aero Dr, San Diego CA 92123	858-279-8035	S	2*	<.1
345	Arnel Inc—*Clarence Wentzel*	3145 Bordentown Ave, Parlin NJ 08859	732-721-4300	R	2*	<.1
346	Balmac Inc—*Mark Slebodnik*	8205 Estates Pkwy Ste, Plain City OH 43064	614-873-8222	R	2*	<.1
347	Kahl Scientific Instrument Corp—*Joseph Kahl*	PO Box 1166, El Cajon CA 92022	619-444-5944	R	2*	<.1
348	Dispersion Technology Inc—*Andre Doukhin*	364 Adams St, Bedford Hills NY 10507	914-241-4777	R	2*	<.1
349	Quad Group Inc—*J Maria Riegert*	1815 S Lewis St, Spokane WA 99224	509-458-4558	R	2*	<.1
350	Telatemp Corp—*Dan Stack*	351 S Raymond Ave, Fullerton CA 92831	714-879-2901	R	2*	<.1
351	Weather Metrics Inc—*Peter Levy*	PO Box 7071, Shawnee Mission KS 66207	913-438-2666	R	2*	<.1
352	Instrumented Sensor Technology Inc—*Gregory Hoshal*	PO Box 955, Okemos MI 48805	517-349-8487	R	2*	<.1
353	Biosynergy Inc—*Fred Suzuki*	1940 E Devon Ave, Elk Grove Village IL 60007	847-956-0471	R	2*	<.1
354	Adaptive Technologies Inc—*Sam Silverberg*	7845 Cessna Ave, Gaithersburg MD 20879	301-519-1174	R	2*	<.1
355	Campbell Security Equipment Co—*Tony Harris*	875 A Island Dr Ste 35, Alameda CA 94502	510-864-8010	R	2*	<.1
356	Feole Technologies Inc—*Robert A Feole*	2220 Plainfield Pike, Cranston RI 02921	401-943-3141	R	2*	<.1
357	NDT International Inc—*Victor Kelly*	711 S Creek Rd, West Chester PA 19382	610-793-1700	R	2*	<.1
358	DL Instruments LLC—*Dave Woolston*	233 Cecil A Malone Dr, Ithaca NY 14850	607-277-8498	R	2*	<.1
359	Guth Laboratories Inc—*Ted Pauley*	590 N 67th St, Harrisburg PA 17111	717-564-5470	R	2*	<.1
360	Advanced Components Inc—*James Cline*	14230 Jetport Loop W, Fort Myers FL 33913	239-561-8622	R	2*	<.1
361	Evans and Company Inc—*Robley Evans*	7930 Zeigler Blvd, Mobile AL 36608	251-633-6008	R	2*	<.1
362	Testron Inc—*Timothy Amburn*	34153 Industrial Rd, Livonia MI 48150	734-513-6820	R	2*	< 1
363	Arc Drilling Inc—*Lee Trem*	9551 Corporate Cir, Cleveland OH 44125	216-525-0920	R	2*	<.1
364	Applied Roller Technology Inc—*Don Bigham*	PO Box 26825, Charlotte NC 28221	704-598-9500	R	2*	<.1
365	Marathon Technology Corp—*Robert Howitt*	8280 Nw 56th St, Doral FL 33166	305-592-1340	R	2*	<.1
366	Far West Technology Inc—*John Rickey*	330 S Kellogg Ave Ste, Goleta CA 93117	805-964-3615	R	2*	<.1
367	Service Center LLC—*Sue Chiattetta*	2000 S 25th Ave Ste S, Broadview IL 60155	708-345-0894	R	2*	<.1
368	Bw Technologies LLC—*Jimmy Blont*	3279 W Pioneer Pkwy, Pantego TX 76013	817-274-2487	R	2*	<.1
369	Advanced Designs Corp—*Martin Riess*	PO Box 1907, Bloomington IN 47402	812-333-1922	R	2*	<.1
370	Convectronics Inc—*Philip Aberizk*	111 Neck Rd, Haverhill MA 01835	978-374-7714	R	2*	<.1
371	Eppley Laboratory Inc—*Tom Kirk*	PO Box 419, Newport RI 02840	401-847-1020	R	2*	<.1
372	Dunn's Valve Testers Inc—*Emmett Dunn*	PO Box 489, Spring TX 77383	281-350-4767	R	2*	<.1
373	NDS Products Inc—*Noel Smith*	111 Anderson St, Pasadena TX 77506	713-475-2986	R	2*	<.1
374	Golf Coast Products LLC	3661 Wild Pines Dr A30, Bonita Springs FL 34134	239-947-3481	R	2*	<.1
375	American Ndt Inc—*Donald Constantini*	671 E Walnut St, Lancaster OH 43130	740-687-1321	R	2*	<.1
376	Sensor Developments Inc—*Albert Brendel*	PO Box 290, Lake Orion MI 48361	248-391-3000	R	2*	<.1
377	Mab Enterprises Inc—*Marlene Bennett*	225 Grand St, Paterson NJ 07501	973-345-8282	R	2*	<.1
378	Quality Engineering Associates Inc—*Ming-Kai Tse*	755 Middlesex Tpke 3, Billerica MA 01821	978-528-2034	R	2*	<.1
379	Richmond Instruments And Systems Inc—*Dennis Mach*	21392 Carlo Dr, Clinton Township MI 48038	586-954-3770	R	2*	<.1
380	Texas Electronics Inc—*Jason Burson*	PO Box 7225, Dallas TX 75209	214-631-2490	R	2*	<.1
381	Browns Hill Engineering and Controls LLC—*Joan Garner*	8119 Shaffer Pkwy Unit, Littleton CO 80127	720-344-7771	R	2*	<.1
382	Controlled Access Inc—*Louis Chaki*	1515 W 130th St Ste A, Hinckley OH 44233	330-273-6185	R	2*	<.1
383	High Precision Devices Inc—*William Hollander*	1668 Valtec Ln Ste C, Boulder CO 80301	303-447-2558	R	2*	<.1
384	Modern Blending Technologies Inc—*Robert Stempel*	2061 Hartel Ave, Levittown PA 19057	267-580-1000	R	2*	<.1
385	Chemdaq Inc—*David Hilliker*	135 Industry Dr, Pittsburgh PA 15275	412-787-0202	R	2*	<.1
386	Bayou Gauging Services Inc—*Steve Cheramie*	PO Box 617, Lockport LA 70374	985-532-9300	R	1*	<.1
387	Ponam Limited Inc—*Earl Foster*	6618 San Fernando Rd, Glendale CA 91201	818-243-3135	R	1*	<.1
388	Assurance Technologies Inc—*Kenneth Losacco*	1251 Humbracht Cir Ste, Bartlett IL 60103	630-550-5000	R	1*	<.1
389	Optron Scientific Company Inc—*Robert Goldstein*	7051 Eton Ave, Canoga Park CA 91303	818-883-7043	R	1*	<.1
390	Theory Development Corp—*Thomas Phillips*	31 Industrial Ave Ste, Mahwah NJ 07430	201-934-8015	R	1*	<.1
391	King Engineering Corp—*Harvard Lefevre*	PO Box 1228, Ann Arbor MI 48106	734-662-5691	R	1*	<.1
392	Pressure BioSciences Inc—*Richard T Schumacher*	14 Norfolk Ave, South Easton MA 02375	508-230-1828	P	1	<.1
393	Integrated Controls Inc—*Jay Norris*	930 Duell Rd, Traverse City MI 49686	231-941-1030	R	1*	<.1
394	Libco Industries Inc—*Brian Belardi*	PO Box 470, Roscoe IL 61073	815-623-7677	R	1*	<.1
395	Irm Group Inc—*Michael Ramsey*	3940 Gantz Rd Ste E, Grove City OH 43123	614-277-4810	R	1*	<.1
396	John B Long Co—*Steve Campbell*	1040 Dutch Valley Dr, Knoxville TN 37918	865-522-8686	R	1*	<.1
397	Olympic Instruments Inc—*Kevin Britz*	16901 Westside Hwy Sw, Vashon WA 98070	206-463-3604	R	1*	<.1
398	Spiracle Technology LLC—*Sam Lin*	16520 Harbor Blvd Ste, Fountain Valley CA 92708	714-418-1091	R	1*	<.1
399	International Medcom Inc—*Dan Sythe*	6871 Abbott Ave Ste 7, Sebastopol CA 95472	707-823-0336	R	1*	<.1
400	Heitman Laboratories Inc—*Lynn Heitman*	PO Box 941390, Plano TX 75094	972-509-2400	R	1*	<.1
401	Suncoast Tool and Gage Industries Inc—*Michael Powers*	11625 54th St N, Clearwater FL 33760	727-572-8000	R	1*	<.1
402	Multibeam Systems Inc—*David Lan*	1900 Wyatt Dr Ste 15, Santa Clara CA 95054	408-855-8400	R	1*	<.1
403	David L Ellis Company Inc—*Richard Ellis*	310 Old High St, Acton MA 01720	978-897-1795	R	1*	<.1
404	Krumor Inc—*Robert Mikals*	7655 Hub Pkwy Ste 206, Cleveland OH 44125	216-328-9802	R	1*	<.1
405	Us Ultratek Inc—*Song Cui*	4070 Nelson Ave Ste B, Concord CA 94520	925-687-7688	R	1*	<.1
406	Parker Research Corp—*S Parker*	PO Box 1406, Dunedin FL 34697	727-796-4066	R	1*	<.1
407	Protean Instrument Corp—*Phillip Cole*	231 Sam Ray Burn Pkwy, Lenoir City TN 37771	865-717-3456	R	1*	<.1
408	Triple Five Industries LLC—*Megan Mcgurkin*	242 Rte 156 Ste A, Trenton NJ 08620	609-585-5588	R	1*	<.1
409	Maximum Inc—*Peter Kilgore*	30 Samuel Barnet Blvd, New Bedford MA 02745	508-995-2200	R	1*	<.1

Rank	Company Name—Executive Officer	Address, City, State, Zip	Phone	Type	Fin	Empls
410	Advanced Calibration Designs—Kurt Ballard	2024 W McMillan St, Tucson AZ 85705	520-290-2855	R	1*	<.1
411	Metal Detectors Inc—Harry Peltzer	PO Box 26440, Eugene OR 97402	541-345-7454	R	1*	<.1
412	Senso-Metrics Inc—Gary Johnson	4584 Runway St, Simi Valley CA 93063	805-527-3640	R	1*	<.1
413	Fenner and Associates Inc—Richard Fenner	13518 Cypress Ln, Cypress TX 77429	281-970-9977	R	1*	<.1
414	Datatest Inc—Douglas Hasbrouck	PO Box 801, Belle Mead NJ 08502	908-369-1590	R	1*	<.1
415	Rel-Tek Corp—Albert Ketler	610 Beatty Rd Ste 5, Monroeville PA 15146	412-373-6700	R	1*	<.1
416	Concept Technology Inc—Thomas Hornung	144 Wimbleton Dr, Birmingham MI 48009	248-642-7766	R	1*	<.1
417	Upa Technology Inc—Michael Justice	PO Box 8172, West Chester OH 45069	513-755-1380	R	1*	<.1
418	Gamma Products Inc—Nancy Meier	PO Box 190, Palos Park IL 60464	708-974-4100	R	1*	<.1
419	GTC Falcon Inc—Gerald Leto	118 Long Pond Rd Ste E, Plymouth MA 02360	508-746-0200	R	1*	<.1
420	King Tester Corp—Ana Borgersen	201 King Manor Dr Ste, King Of Prussia PA 19406	610-279-6010	R	1*	<.1
421	Marlin Controls Inc—Moe Chigani	PO Box 550457, Dallas TX 75355	214-553-5700	R	1*	<.1
422	Ordela Inc—Manfred Kopp	1009 Alvin Weinberg Dr, Oak Ridge TN 37830	865-483-8675	R	1*	<.1
423	Phipps and Bird Inc—Wes Skaperdas	1519 Summit Ave, Richmond VA 23230	804-254-2737	R	1*	<.1
424	Control Electronics Inc—Eugene Traband	PO Box 330, Brandamore PA 19316	610-942-3190	R	1*	<.1
425	Marks Products Inc—Franklin Marks	1243 Burnsville Rd, Williamsville VA 24487	540-396-4740	R	1*	<.1
426	Lois A Valeskie—Lois Valeskie	1300 22nd St Ste A, San Francisco CA 94107	415-641-2570	R	1*	<.1
427	Gilmore Diamond Tools Inc—Michael Mihalec	1231 County St, Attleboro MA 02703	508-226-0053	R	1*	<.1
428	Compix Inc—Richard Crall	PO Box 885, Tualatin OR 97062	503-639-8496	R	1*	<.1
429	General Pump and Equipment Co—David Lapp	PO Box 6380, Canton OH 44706	330-455-2100	R	1*	<.1
430	Herman H Sticht Company Inc—Paul Plotkin	45 Main St Ste 701, Brooklyn NY 11201	718-852-7602	R	1*	<.1
431	Scientronix Inc—Jack Wiens	484 Auzerais Ave, San Jose CA 95126	408-297-7303	R	1*	<.1
432	Colby Instruments Inc—Victor Chinn	1715 114th Ave SE Ste, Bellevue WA 98004	425-452-8889	R	1*	<.1
433	Torfino Enterprises Inc—Lise DeTorfino	11924 Forest Hill Blvd, Wellington FL 33414	561-790-0111	R	1*	<.1
434	Lasers Etc—Ray Weatherbee	117 Manchester St, Concord NH 03301	603-224-5556	R	1*	<.1
435	Integrator Services Inc—Don Smith	PO Box 582, Cleveland OK 74020	918-358-3546	R	1*	<.1
436	Regin HVAC Products Inc—Ronnie Magnusson	315 Riggs St Unit 1, Oxford CT 06478		R	1*	<.1
437	Wyoming Test Fixtures Inc—Donald F Adams	2960 E Millcreek Canyo, Salt Lake City UT 84109	801-484-5055	R	1*	<.1
438	JMAR Technologies Inc—C Neil Beer	10905 Technology Pl, San Diego CA 92127	858-946-6800	P	1	<.1
439	Chemical Automation Technologies Inc—Patrick Sweeney	10101 Molecular Dr Ste, Rockville MD 20850	301-990-8825	R	1*	<.1
440	Corporate Consulting Service Instruments Inc—Jack Warner	PO Box 382, Bath OH 44210	330-376-3600	R	1*	<.1
441	Infrared Telemetrics Inc—Glen Barna	PO Box 70, Houghton MI 49931	906-482-0012	R	1*	<.1
442	Tensitron Inc—Stanley Saxl	733 S Bowen St, Longmont CO 80501	303-702-1980	R	1*	<.1
443	ACO Pacific Inc—Noland Lewis	2604 Read Ave, Belmont CA 94002	650-595-8588	R	1*	<.1
444	AVK Industries Inc—Andrew Cherinka	2052 St Johns Bluff Rd, Jacksonville FL 32246	904-998-8400	R	1*	<.1
445	CKC Industries Inc—Charles Cheng	PO Box 151012, Tampa FL 33684	813-888-9468	R	1*	<.1
446	Hydraulic Technology Inc—Daniel Stokes	3833 Cincinnati Ave, Rocklin CA 95765	916-645-3317	R	1*	<.1
447	M Squared Electronics Inc—Frederick Robinson	1610 Manning Blvd Ste, Levittown PA 19057	215-945-6658	R	1*	<.1
448	Tool Technologies Van Dyke—Steven Vandyke	PO Box 256, Milford Center OH 43045	937-349-4900	R	1*	<.1
449	Trinity Brand Industries Inc—Ron Supeter	PO Box 560, La Grange IL 60525	708-482-4980	R	1*	<.1
450	Solvetech Inc—Douglas Lawrence	PO Box 9245, Wilmington DE 19809	302-798-5400	R	1*	<.1
451	Nitv LLC—Charles Humble	11400 Fortune Cir, West Palm Beach FL 33414	561-798-6280	R	1*	<.1
452	Industrial Protection Devices LLC—Russel Phipps	7768 W 78th St, Minneapolis MN 55439	952-941-0146	R	1*	<.1
453	Carlen Controls Inc—Eric Carlen	6560 Commonwealth Dr, Roanoke VA 24018	540-772-1736	R	1*	<.1
454	Electric Speed Indicator Co—Robert Riley	12234 Triskett Rd, Cleveland OH 44111	216-251-2540	R	1*	<.1
455	Machine Diagnostics Inc—Glen Hutto	PO Box 1003, Americus GA 31709	229-924-3030	R	1*	<.1
456	Ecklund-Harrison Technologies Inc—Leonard Darsey	11000 Metro Pkwy Ste 3, Fort Myers FL 33966	239-936-6032	R	1*	<.1
457	Unimeasure Inc—Thomas Peterson	4175 Sw Research Way, Corvallis OR 07333	541-757-3158	R	1*	<.1
458	Dakim Inc—Dan Michel	2121 Cloverfield Blvd, Santa Monica CA 90404	310-573-7161	R	1*	<.1
459	Ransom International Corp—Cheri Lewis	PO Box 3845, Prescott AZ 86302	928-778-7899	R	1*	<.1
460	Andor Design Corp—Ralph Silvera	20 Pond View Dr, Syosset NY 11791	516-364-1619	R	1*	<.1
461	Isc Instrument Service Co—Bennett Grieb	2859 Westside Dr, Pasadena TX 77502	281-745-0231	S	1*	<.1
462	Mechanical Control Systems—Al Woodman	1501 Main St Ste 30, Tewksbury MA 01876	978-640-9994	R	1*	<.1
463	Storage Control Systems Inc—Jim Schaefer	PO Box 304, Sparta MI 49345	616-887-7994	R	1*	<.1
464	Doco Inc—Collins Fitzsimmons	320 Stevens Rd, Gallitzin PA 16641	814-886-4153	R	1*	<.1
465	Palmer Electronics Inc—Victor Palmeri	156 Belmont Ave, Garfield NJ 07026	973-772-5900	R	1*	<.1
466	Eais—Mahammed Barjasteh	PO Box 5191, Englewood CO 80155	662-287-5477	R	1*	<.1
467	St Acquisitions LLC—Dan Delzer	1461 Tallevast Rd, Sarasota FL 34243	941-753-1095	R	1*	<.1
468	Cement Test Equipment Inc—Wc Jones	5704 E Admiral Blvd, Tulsa OK 74115	918-835-4454	R	1*	<.1
469	Eastern Technology Corp—Carol Freidman	42 Nelson St, East Hartford CT 06108	860-528-9821	R	1*	<.1
470	Rice Nuclear Diagnostics LP—James Caplan	1414 S Loop W Ste 120, Houston TX 77054	713-796-2752	R	1*	<.1
471	Chem-Dyne Research Corp—Victor Janule	PO Box 30430, Mesa AZ 85275	480-924-1744	R	1*	<.1
472	Industrial Measurement Systems Inc—Donald Yuhas	2760 Beverly Dr Ste 4, Aurora IL 60502	630-236-5901	R	1*	<.1
473	Instrumentors Inc—Robert Heinrich	22077 Drake Rd, Strongsville OH 44149	440-238-3430	R	1*	<.1
474	Sports Technology Inc—Robert Rankin	9839 13th Ave N, Plymouth MN 55441	763-546-0437	R	1*	<.1
475	Cld Dynamics Inc—Kenneth Metzgar	5731 Palmer Way Ste A, Carlsbad CA 92010	760-438-4949	R	1*	<.1
476	Custom Scientific Instruments Inc—Paul Sud	1125 Conroy Pl, Easton PA 18040	610-923-6500	R	1*	<.1
477	Emat Ultrasonics Inc—Ron Alers	PO Box 1889, San Luis Obispo CA 93406	805-545-0675	R	1*	<.1
478	Frazier Precision Instrument Company Inc—John Scrivener	925 Sweeney Dr, Hagerstown MD 21740	301-790-2585	R	1*	<.1
479	High Point Control Systems Inc—Jeff Hutchings	PO Box 3484, Apache Junction AZ 85117	480-633-3001	R	1*	<.1
480	PJ Electronics Inc—Peter Mlynar	575 Davidson Rd, Pittsburgh PA 15239	412-793-3912	R	1*	<.1
481	Zls Corp—James Adams	7801 N Lamar Blvd E184, Austin TX 78752	512-453-0288	R	1*	<.1
482	ASI Instruments Inc—Chris Chiodo	12900 E 10 Mile Rd, Warren MI 48089	586-756-1222	R	1*	<.1
483	Scans Group Corp—Richard Werner	2208 Hartwick Hwy, Lincoln Park MI 48146	313-382-7311	R	1*	<.1
484	Dietert Foundry Testing Equipment Inc—David Miller	9190 Roselawn St, Detroit MI 48204	313-491-4680	R	1*	<.1
485	Physical Testing Equipment Services Inc—Anthony Sepe	PO Box 19108, Johnston RI 02919	401-944-4760	R	1*	<.1
486	Kemkraft Engineering Inc—Edward Kemski	47650 Clipper St, Plymouth MI 48170	734-414-6500	R	1*	<.1
487	Pixe International Corp—J Nelson	PO Box 2744, Tallahassee FL 32316	850-574-6469	R	1*	<.1
488	Reico Technology—William Fujita	274 W Fairview Ave, San Gabriel CA 91776	626-284-0212	R	1*	<.1
489	Albion Devices Inc—Paul Sagar	538 Stevens Ave Ste O, Solana Beach CA 92075	858-792-9585	R	1*	<.1
490	Aurora Technical Services Ltd—Karen Wright	PO Box 103, East Aurora NY 14052	716-652-6041	R	1*	<.1
491	Cdex Inc—Jeffrey K Brumfield	4555 S Palo Verde Ste1, Tucson AZ 85714	520-745-5172	P	1	<.1
492	Dositec Inc—Sam Hsu	63 S St Ste 275, Hopkinton MA 01748	508-497-8998	R	1*	<.1
493	L-Ray—Joe Welmers	118 Indianwood Rd, Lake Orion MI 48362	248-814-6900	R	1*	<.1
494	Thermotech Inc—Sherman Barker	2900 N 1000 W, Ogden UT 84414	801-782-2233	R	1*	<.1
495	HSI Fire And Safety Group—Jack Ackerman	107 Garlisch Dr, Elk Grove Village IL 60007	847-427-8340	R	1*	<.1
496	Phoenix Small Tool Inc—Donald Weeks	835 W 22nd St Ste 109, Tempe AZ 85282	602-256-7011	R	1*	<.1
497	Instrument Personnel Inc—Marcia Durbin	17156 Bellflower Blvd, Bellflower CA 90706	562-804-7772	R	<1*	<.1
498	Ramer Products Inc—William Racine	PO Box 1027, Niles MI 49120	269-684-7710	R	<1*	<.1
499	Cyberdyne Inc—Harold Holsopple	205 Main St, New Eagle PA 15067	724-258-8440	R	<1*	<.1

Note: An asterisk (*) indicates an estimated financial figure. The company type code used is as follows: R = Private, P = Public, S = Private Subsidiary, B = Public Subsidiary, D = Division, J = Joint Venture, I = Investment Fund.

COMPANY RANKINGS BY SALES WITHIN 4-DIGIT SIC

Rank	Company Name—*Executive Officer*	Address, City, State, Zip	Phone	Type	Fin	Empls
500	FW and T A Corp—*Frank Wall*	27955 Cabot Rd, Laguna Niguel CA 92677	949-582-7633	R	<1*	<.1
501	GFV Associates Inc—*G Vanderschmidt*	52 Louders Ln, Boston MA 02130	617-524-0465	R	<1*	<.1
502	Heather Design Ltd—*Robert Schellig*	5740 Becker Dr, Rochester MI 48306	248-601-3909	R	<1*	<.1
503	Hmc Int'l Division Inc—*Tito Howard*	5996 S Crocker St, Littleton CO 80120	303-794-2510	R	<1*	<.1
504	Klein Optical Instruments Inc—*Luhr Jensen*	321 Sw 4th Ave Ste 200, Portland OR 97204	503-245-1012	R	<1*	<.1
505	Rotex Industries LLC—*Meighan Lassen*	PO Box 560428, Dallas TX 75356	214-630-9616	R	<1*	<.1
506	Litek Inc—*Charles Kanavle*	392 Pine Grove Rd, Rogue River OR 97537	541-582-1581	R	<1*	<.1
507	Temp-Cal Enterprises LLC—*Charlie Crisel*	2015 E 5th St Ste 6, Tempe AZ 85281	480-968-1623	R	<1*	<.1
508	Fatigue Dynamics Inc—*Milton Weber*	969 Decker Rd, Walled Lake MI 48390	248-669-6100	R	<1*	<.1
509	Innovative Test Systems Inc—*Walter Wozniak*	115 Industrial Dr, Sulphur LA 70663	337-626-8200	R	<1*	<.1
510	Paper Research Materials Inc—*Janelle Unbehend*	2828 Sw 171st St, Burien WA 98166	206-248-2050	R	<1*	<.1
511	Carolyn Adkinson—*Carolyn Atkinson*	1270 Sw Covered Bridge, Palm City FL 34990	772-286-6588	R	<1*	<.1
512	Control Measurement Inc—*Steve Kovach*	1400 Mentor Ave Ste 5, Painesville OH 44077	440-639-0020	R	<1*	<.1
513	Standard Testing Equipment Co—*Randall Lucius*	938 W Church St Ste 10, Jasper GA 30143	706-692-2828	R	<1*	<.1
514	Engineers Tool Corp—*William Bernau*	116 W Main St, Lake City IA 51449	712-464-3591	R	<1*	<.1
515	Industrial Detection Systems—*Vince Gifford*	715 White Spar Rd, Prescott AZ 86303	928-541-1522	R	<1*	<.1
516	Measurements International Inc—*Duane Brown*	812 Proctor Ave, Ogdensburg NY 13669	315-393-1323	R	<1*	<.1
517	PC Rc Products LLC—*Jim Bellistri*	2424 Northline Industr, Maryland Heights MO 63043	314-344-4421	R	<1*	<.1
518	VitaminSpice—*Edward Bukstel*	996 Old Eagle Rd Ste 1, Wayne PA 19087	484-367-7401	P	<1	<.1
519	Jeffrey Dombach—*Jeffrey Dombach*	2818 Marietta Ave, Lancaster PA 17601	717-892-1100	R	<1*	<.1
520	Earth Search Sciences Inc—*Larry Vance*	PO Box 386, Lakeside MT 59922	406-844-3300	P	<1	<.1
521	Lifeline BioTechnologies Inc—*Jim Holmes*	1325 Airmotive Way Ste, Reno NV 89502	775-324-1933	P	<1	<.1
522	Protune Corp—*Jesse Aronstein*	PO Box 1808, Poughkeepsie NY 12601	845-462-6452	R	<1*	<.1
523	Sumatron Inc—*Tom Baker*	24601 Steffy Dr, Laguna Niguel CA 92677	949-360-0386	R	<1*	<.1
524	Bison Instruments Inc—*Barrie D Rose*	7725 Vasserman Trl, Chanhassen MN 55317	952-938-1055	P	<1	N/A
525	Quartzdyne Inc—*Robert Wiggins*	4334 W Links Dr, Salt Lake City UT 84120	801-266-6958	S	N/A	.1

TOTALS: SIC 3829 Measuring & Controlling Devices Nec
Companies: 525   30,896   130.7

3841 Surgical & Medical Instruments

Rank	Company Name—*Executive Officer*	Address, City, State, Zip	Phone	Type	Fin	Empls
1	Abbott Diabetes Care	1360 S Loop Rd, Alameda CA 94502	510-749-5400	S	18,514*	60.0
2	Baxter International Inc—*Robert L Parkinson Jr*	PO Box 154, Deerfield IL 60015	847-948-2000	P	12,843	48.0
3	GE Medical Systems—*Joseph M Hogan*	3000 N Grandview Blvd, Waukesha WI 53188	262-544-3011	S	9,625*	27.5
4	Becton Dickinson and Co—*Edward J Ludwig*	1 Becton Dr, Franklin Lakes NJ 07417	201-847-6800	P	7,829	29.4
5	Boston Scientific Corp—*J Raymond Elliot*	1 Boston Scientific Pl, Natick MA 01760	508-650-8000	P	7,806	25.0
6	Stryker Corp—*Curt Hartman*	2825 Airview Blvd, Kalamazoo MI 49002	269-385-2600	P	7,320	20.0
7	CareFusion Corp—*Kieran Gallahue*	3750 Torrey View Ct, San Diego CA 92130	858-617-2000	P	3,528	14.0
8	CR Bard Inc—*Timothy M Ring*	730 Central Ave, Murray Hill NJ 07974	908-277-8000	P	2,720	11.7
9	Siemens Medical Systems Inc—*Thomas McCausland*	51 Valley Stream Pkwy, Malvern PA 19355		S	2,200	5.5
10	Cordis Endovascular Systems Inc—*Daniel Hall* Cordis Corp	14201 NW 60th Ave, Miami Lakes FL 33014	786-313-2000	S	1,974*	7.0
11	Hill-Rom Holdings Inc—*John J Greisch*	1069 State Rte 46 E, Batesville IN 47006	812-934-7777	P	1,592	6.2
12	Cadwell Laboratories Inc—*Carl Cadwell*	909 N Kellogg St, Kennewick WA 99336	509-735-6481	R	1,583*	.1
13	Wampole Laboratories LLC—*John Bridgen*	2 Research Way, Princeton NJ 08540	609-627-8000	S	1,565*	1.1
14	Teleflex Inc—*Benson F Smith*	155 S Limerick Rd, Limerick PA 19468	610-948-5100	P	1,529	11.5
15	Edwards Lifesciences Corp—*Michael A Mussallem*	1 Edwards Way, Irvine CA 92614	949-250-2500	P	1,447	7.0
16	Varian Oncology Systems—*Timothy Guertin*	3100 Hansen Way, Palo Alto CA 94304	650-493-4000	D	1,395*	4.8
17	ResMed Inc—*Peter C Farrell*	9001 Spectrum Center B, San Diego CA 92123	858-836-5000	P	1,243	3.5
18	Cook Group Inc—*William A Cook*	PO Box 489, Bloomington IN 47402	812-339-2235	R	969*	6.3
19	McKesson Medical-Surgical—*Brian Tyler*	8741 Landmark Rd, Richmond VA 23228	804-264-7500	D	934*	3.0
20	Haemonetics Corp—*Brian Concannon*	400 Wood Rd, Braintree MA 02184		P	677	2.2
21	VIASYS Healthcare Inc—*Ronald A Ahrens*	227 Washington St Ste, Conshohocken PA 19428	610-862-0800	S	610	2.4
22	BD Medical Systems—*Edward Ludwig* Becton Dickinson and Co	1 Becton Dr, Franklin Lakes NJ 07417	201-847-6800	D	577*	1.2
23	Gen-Probe Inc—*Carl W Hull*	10210 Genetic Center D, San Diego CA 92121	858-410-8000	P	576	1.4
24	Arrow International Inc—*Carl Anderson* Teleflex Inc	PO Box 12888, Reading PA 19612	610-378-0131	S	482	4.0
25	ev3 Inc	3033 Campus Dr, Plymouth MN 55441	763-398-7000	S	449	1.4
26	Medrad Inc—*Sam Liang*	100 Global View Dr, Warrendale PA 15086		R	435*	.8
27	Allyn Welch Holdings Inc—*Julie Shimer*	PO Box 220, Skaneateles Falls NY 13153	315-685-4100	R	422*	2.8
28	Kyphon Inc—*Richard W Mott*	1221 Crossman Ave, Sunnyvale CA 94089	408-548-6500	S	408	1.1
29	GSI Group Inc (Billerica Massachusetts)—*John Roush*	125 Middlesex Tpke, Bedford MA 01730	781-266-5700	P	384	1.6
30	Merit Medical Systems Inc—*Fred P Lampropoulos*	1600 W Merit Pkwy, South Jordan UT 84095	801-253-1600	P	359	2.4
31	Puritan-Bennett Corp—*Kristin Garvin*	4280 Hacienda Dr, Pleasanton CA 94588		S	337	2.7
32	Cantel Medical Corp—*Andrew A Krakauer*	150 Clove Rd 9th Fl, Little Falls NJ 07424	973-890-7220	P	322	1.2
33	Cordis Corp	430 Rte 22 East, Bridgewater NJ 08807	908-541-4100	S	315	2.0
34	ICU Medical Inc—*George A Lopez*	951 Calle Amanecer, San Clemente CA 92673	949-366-2183	P	285	2.2
35	Ventana Medical Systems Inc—*Christopher M Gleeson*	1910 Innovation Park D, Tucson AZ 85755	520-887-2155	R	237*	.8
36	Accuray Inc—*Euan S Thomson*	1310 Chesapeake Ter, Sunnyvale CA 94089	408-716-4600	P	222	1.1
37	AngioDynamics Inc—*Joe DeVivo*	14 Plaza Dr, Latham NY 12110	518-795-1400	P	216	.7
38	Roche Diagnostics Corp—*Michael Tillmann*	9115 Hague Rd, Indianapolis IN 46256	317-521-2000	S	215	2.0
39	Vital Signs Inc—*Omar S Ishrak*	20 Campus Rd, Totowa NJ 07512	973-790-1330	D	205*	1.3
40	Medtronic Xomed Inc	6743 Southpoint Dr N, Jacksonville FL 32216	904-296-9600	S	201*	.7
41	Alphatec Holdings Inc—*Dirk Kuyper*	5818 El Camino Rd, Carlsbad CA 92008	760-431-9286	P	198	.5
42	FoxHollow Technologies Inc—*John B Simpson* ev3 Inc	740 Bay Rd, Redwood City CA 94063	650-421-8400	S	193	.6
43	DePuy DePuy Acromed and Codman—*Gary Frechetti*	325 Paramount Dr, Raynham MA 02767	508-880-8100	S	174*	.4
44	Stryker Puerto Rico Ltd—*Ronald Elenbaas*	PO Box 329, Arroyo PR 00714	787-839-7688	R	160*	.9
45	Medtronic Puerto Rico Inc—*Bill Hawkins*	24 Rd 31 Hm 4, Juncos PR 00777	787-561-2200	R	153*	2.4
46	Insulet Corp—*Duane DeSisto*	9 Oak Park Dr, Bedford MA 01730	781-457-5000	P	152	.6
47	Empi Inc—*Les Cross*	599 Cardigan Rd, Saint Paul MN 55126	651-415-9000	S	150*	.8
48	Bard Access Systems Inc—*Jim Beasley* CR Bard Inc	605 N 5600 W, Salt Lake City UT 84116	801-522-5000	D	150*	.5
49	Barnstead-Thermolyne Corp	81 Wyman St, Waltham MA 02451	781-622-1000	S	144*	.5
50	Conceptus Inc—*Mark M Sieczkarek*	331 E Evelyn Ave, Mountain View CA 94041	650-962-4000	P	141	.3
51	I-Flow Corp—*Donald M Earhart*	20202 Windrow Dr, Lake Forest CA 92630	949-206-2700	S	133	.3
52	Advanced Neuromodulation Systems Inc—*Christopher G Chavez*	6901 Preston Rd, Plano TX 75024	972-309-8800	S	121	.5
53	CryoLife Inc—*Steven G Anderson*	1655 Roberts Blvd NW S, Kennesaw GA 30144	770-419-3355	P	120	.4
54	Osteometer MediTech Inc—*Deepak Chopra*	12515 Chadron Ave, Hawthorne CA 90250	310-978-3073	S	111*	.4

Rank	Company Name—*Executive Officer*	Address, City, State, Zip	Phone	Type	Fin	Empls
55	Atrion Corp—*David A Battat*	1 Allentown Pky, Allen TX 75002	972-390-9800	P	109	.4
56	Harvard Bioscience Inc—*Chane Graziano*	84 October Hill Rd, Holliston MA 01746	508-893-8999	P	108	.4
57	Research and Diagnostic Systems Inc—*Thomas E Oland*	614 McKinley Pl NE, Minneapolis MN 55413	612-379-2956	S	99*	.6
58	Micrus Endovascular Corp—*John T Kilcoyne*	821 Fox Ln, San Jose CA 95131	408-433-1400	S	91	.3
59	Vascular Solutions Inc—*Howard Root*	6464 Sycamore Ct, Minneapolis MN 55369	763-656-4300	P	90	.4
60	CooperSurgical Inc—*Nicholas J Pichotta*	95 Corporate Dr, Trumbull CT 06611	203-601-5200	S	85*	.4
61	Meridian Medical Technologies Inc—*Dennis O'Brian*	6350 Stevens Forest Rd, Columbia MD 21046	443-259-7800	S	82*	.5
62	Kloehn Company Ltd—*Michael Marshall*	10000 Banburry Cross D, Las Vegas NV 89144	702-243-7727	S	80*	.2
63	Cardiovascular Systems Inc—*David L Martin*	651 Campus Drive, St Paul MN 55112	651-259-1600	P	79	.3
64	DexCom Inc—*Terrance H Gregg*	6340 Sequence Dr, San Diego CA 92121	858-200-0200	P	76	.5
65	Diasorin Inc	1951 Northwestern Ave, Stillwater MN 55082	651-439-9710	S	76*	.2
66	Stryker Sustainability Solutions—*Ricardo M Ferreirar* Stryker Corp	10232 S 51st St, Phoenix AZ 85044	480-763-5300	D	74*	.2
67	ev3 Neurovascular ev3 Inc	9775 Toledo Way, Irvine CA 92618	949-837-3700	D	72*	.3
68	Kensey Nash Corp—*Joseph W Kaufmann*	735 Pennsylvania Dr, Exton PA 19341	484-713-2100	P	72	.3
69	Othy Inc—*John Byrd*	486 W 350 N, Warsaw IN 46582	574-267-8700	R	69*	1.0
70	Animas Corp—*Katherine D Crothall*	200 Lawrence Dr, West Chester PA 19380	610-644-8990	S	68	.3
71	Endologix Inc—*John McDermott*	11 Studebaker, Irvine CA 92618	949-595-7200	P	67	.3
72	King Systems Corp—*Don Dumoulin*	15011 Herriman Blvd, Noblesville IN 46060	317-776-6823	R	67*	.5
73	BioForm Medical Inc	1875 S Grant St Ste 20, San Mateo CA 94402	650-286-4000	S	67	.3
74	Haemonetics Enterprises Inc Haemonetics Corp	400 Wood Rd, Braintree MA 02184	781-848-7100	S	65*	.3
75	Medtronic PS Medical Inc—*Omar Ishrak*	PO Box 8090, Goleta CA 93118	805-968-1546	S	63*	.2
76	Stryker Endoscopy—*Stephen MacMillan* Stryker Corp	5900 Optical Ct, San Jose CA 95138	408-754-2000	D	62*	.4
77	AtriCure Inc—*David J Drachman*	6217 Centre Park Dr, West Chester OH 45069	513-755-4100	P	59	.2
78	Anika Therapeutics Inc—*Irina B Kulinets*	32 Wiggins Ave, Bedford MA 01730	781-457-9000	P	56	.1
79	Stereotaxis Inc—*Michael P Kaminski*	4320 Forest Park Ave S, Saint Louis MO 63108	314-678-6100	P	54	.2
80	Rochester Medical Corp—*Anthony J Conway*	1 Rochester Medical Dr, Stewartville MN 55976	507-533-9600	P	53	.3
81	Ideal Instruments Inc	944 Nandino Blvd, Lexington KY 40511	859-254-1221	S	52*	.4
82	Specialty Silicone Fabricators Inc—*William Reising*	3077 Rollie Gates Dr, Paso Robles CA 93446	805-239-4284	R	49*	.3
83	Medovations Inc—*Brant Stanford*	102 E Keefe Ave, Milwaukee WI 53212	414-265-7620	R	44*	.1
84	Micro Stamping Corp—*Frank Semcer*	140 Belmont Dr, Somerset NJ 08873	732-302-0800	R	42*	.3
85	SwissRay International Inc	1 Tower Center Blvd, E Brunswick NJ 08816	908-353-0971	R	40*	.1
86	Mennen Medical Corp—*Danny Harel*	950 Industrial Hwy, Southampton PA 18966	215-259-1020	S	40*	.1
87	Codan US Corp—*Bernd J Larsen*	3511 W Sunflower Ave, Santa Ana CA 92704	714-545-2111	R	38*	.1
88	Memry Corp—*Nicola DiBartolomeo*	3 Berkshire Blvd, Bethel CT 06801	203-739-1100	S	37*	.2
89	Enpath Medical Inc—*John Hertig*	2300 Berkshire Ln N, Minneapolis MN 55441	763-951-8181	S	37	.3
90	Salter Labs—*Peter Salter*	100 Sycamore Rd, Arvin CA 93203	661-854-3166	R	37*	.2
91	Retractable Technologies Inc—*Thomas J Shaw*	PO Box 9, Little Elm TX 75068	972-294-1010	P	36	.2
92	Endocardial Solutions NV/SA	1 St Jude Medical Dr, Saint Paul MN 55117	651-523-6900	S	36*	.2
93	Sechrist Industries Inc—*Ed Pulwer*	4225 E La Palma Ave, Anaheim CA 92807	714-579-8400	R	35*	.1
94	Harmac Medical Products Inc—*John Somers*	2201 Bailey Ave, Buffalo NY 14211	716-897-4500	R	35*	.2
95	Arthrex Inc—*Reinhold Schmieding*	1370 Creekside Blvd, Naples FL 34108	239-643-5553	R	34*	.4
96	Manufacturing and Research Inc—*Joseph Lee*	4700 S Overland Dr, Tucson AZ 85714	520-882-7794	R	33*	.1
97	BioSphere Medical Inc—*Fred P Lamproploulus* Merit Medical Systems Inc	1050 Hingham St, Rockland MA 02370	781-681-7900	S	31	.1
98	Katecho Inc—*Lorne Scharnberg*	4020 Gannett Ave, Des Moines IA 50321	515-244-1212	R	31*	.3
99	International Technidyne Corp—*Lawrence Cohen*	20 Corporate Place S, Piscataway NJ 08854	732-548-5700	S	31*	.2
100	Welch Allyn Protocol Inc—*Julie Schimer*	8500 Sw Creekside Pl, Beaverton OR 97008	503-530-7500	R	30*	.4
101	Salient Surgical Technologies Inc—*Joseph F Army*	180 International Dr, Portsmouth NH 03801	603-742-1515	R	30	.1
102	Angeion Corp—*Gregg O Lehman*	350 Oak Grove Pkwy, Saint Paul MN 55127	651-484-4874	P	29	.1
103	iCAD Inc—*Ken Ferry*	98 Spit Brook Rd Ste 1, Nashua NH 03062	603-882-5200	P	29	.1
104	Acclarent Inc—*William M Facteau*	1525B OBrien Ave, Menlo Park CA 94025	650-687-5888	D	28*	.2
105	Utah Medical Products Texas Inc—*Kevin L Cornwell*	7043 S 300 W, Midvale UT 84047	801-566-1200	R	28*	.2
106	Micro-Aire Surgical Instruments Inc—*Frank Altenhofen*	Lock Box 96565, Chicago IL 60693	434-975-8000	R	28*	.2
107	Gaymar Industries Inc—*Kent Davies*	10 Centre Dr, Orchard Park NY 14127	716-662-2551	R	27*	.4
108	United States Endoscopy Group Inc—*Marlin Younker*	5976 Heisley Rd, Mentor OH 44060	440-639-4494	R	27*	.2
109	Microline Surgical Inc—*Jean Boulnois*	800 Cummings Ctr Ste 1, Beverly MA 01915	978-922-9810	R	27*	.1
110	Nonin Medical Inc—*Gary Tschautscher*	13700 1st Ave N, Minneapolis MN 55441	763-553-9968	R	26*	.2
111	Trimline Medical Products Corp—*Richard Jacobson*	PO Box 40, Raritan NJ 08869	908-429-0590	R	26*	.2
112	TranS1 Inc—*Ken Reali*	301 Government Center, Wilmington NC 28403	910-332-1700	P	26	.1
113	Applied Imaging Corp—*Robin C Stracey*	120 Baytech Dr, San Jose CA 95134	408-719-6400	S	26*	.2
114	Utah Medical Products Inc—*Kevin Cornwell*	7043 S 300 W, Midvale UT 84047	801-566-1200	P	25	.2
115	Surgical Specialties Corp—*Pete Molinaro*	100 Dennis Dr, Reading PA 19606	610-404-1000	R	25*	.2
116	Berchtold Corp—*Matthew Weismiller*	1950 Hanahan Rd, Charleston SC 29406	843-569-6100	R	25*	.2
117	Phillips Precision Inc—*Francis Phillips*	7 Paul Kohner Pl, Elmwood Park NJ 07407	201-797-8820	R	25*	.1
118	CardioDynamics International Corp—*Michael P Perry*	6175 Nancy Ridge Dr St, San Diego CA 92121	425-951-1200	S	25	.1
119	Bovie Medical Corp—*Andrew Makrides*	734 Walt Whitman Rd, Melville NY 11747	631-421-5452	P	24	.1
120	CAS Medical Systems Inc—*Thomas M Patton*	44 E Industrial Rd, Branford CT 06405	203-488-6056	P	24	.1
121	Gyrus ACMI Inc	136 Turnpike Rd, Southborough MA 01772	508-804-2600	S	24*	.2
122	Newport Medical Instruments Inc—*Hong-lin Du*	PO Box 2600, Newport Beach CA 92658	714-427-5811	R	23*	.1
123	D-M-S Holdings Inc—*Merwyn Dan*	1931 Norman Dr, Waukegan IL 60085	847-680-6811	S	23	.2
124	Mangar Medical Inc—*Douglas Coleman*	97 Britain Dr, Doylestown PA 18901	215-230-0300	R	23*	.2
125	Magellan Medical Technology Consultants Inc—*Susan Johnson*	120 S 6th St Ste 2150, Minneapolis MN 55402	612-677-0000	R	22*	.2
126	Caire Inc—*Samuel F Thomas*	1 Infinity Corporate C, Garfield Heights OH 44125	440-753-1490	S	22*	.1
127	Sigma International General Medical Apparatus LLC—*May Nemcik*	PO Box 756, Medina NY 14103	585-798-3901	R	22*	.3
128	Cerus Corp—*William M Greenman*	2550 Stanwell Dr, Concord CA 94520	925-288-6000	P	22	.1
129	Response Genetics Inc—*Thomas Bologna*	1640 Marengo St, Los Angeles CA 90033	323-224-3900	P	21	.1
130	Micropulse Inc—*Brian Emerick*	5865 E State Rd 14, Columbia City IN 46725	260-625-3304	R	21*	.2
131	MultiMedia Communications LLC—*Mark Spitzer*	206 Hudson Rd, Stow MA 01775	978-562-7833	R	21*	.1
132	Bose Electroforce Systems Group—*Amar Bose*	10250 Valley View Rd S, Eden Prairie MN 55344	952-278-3070	D	21*	.1
133	Precision Metal Products Inc—*William O'brien*	307 Pepes Farm Rd, Milford CT 06460	203-877-4258	R	21*	.2
134	Walter Lorenz Surgical Inc—*Adam Johnson*	1520 Tradeport Dr, Jacksonville FL 32218	904-741-4400	S	20*	.1
135	Medin Corp—*Jay Schainholz*	90 Dayton Ave Ste 94, Passaic NJ 07055	973-779-2400	R	20*	.1
136	MegaDyne Medical Products Inc—*Rob Farnsworth*	PO Box 1332, Sandy UT 84091	801-576-9669	R	20*	.2
137	Mill-Rose Co—*Paul Miller*	7995 Tyler Blvd, Mentor OH 44060	440-255-9171	R	20*	.2

Note: An asterisk (*) indicates an estimated financial figure. The company type code used is as follows: R = Private, P = Public, S = Private Subsidiary, B = Public Subsidiary, D = Division, J = Joint Venture, I = Investment Fund.

COMPANY RANKINGS BY SALES WITHIN 4-DIGIT SIC

Rank	Company Name—*Executive Officer*	Address, City, State, Zip	Phone	Type	Fin	Empls
138	Bicron Business Unit of Saint-Gobain Industrial Ceramics Inc—*Tom Kinisky*	12345 Kinsman Rd, Newbury OH 44065	440-564-2251	S	19*	.2
139	Dale Medical Products Inc—*John Brezack*	PO Box 1556, Plainville MA 02762		R	19*	.1
140	Coeur Inc—*William Cude*	100 Physicians Way Ste, Lebanon TN 37090	615-547-7923	R	19*	.1
141	Micromedics Inc—*Jeff Pembroke*	1270 Eagan Industrial, Saint Paul MN 55121	651-452-1977	R	19*	.1
142	Nspire Health Inc—*Michael Sims*	1830 Lefthand Cir, Longmont CO 80501	303-666-5555	R	19*	.1
143	Oscor Inc—*Thomas Osypka*	3816 Desoto Blvd, Palm Harbor FL 34683	727-937-2511	R	19*	.1
144	Ophthalmic Imaging Systems—*Gil Allon*	221 Lathrop Way Ste I, Sacramento CA 95815	916-646-2020	S	19	.1
145	Rusch Inc—*Jeffrey Black* Teleflex Inc	4024 Stirrup Creek Ste, Durham NC 27703		D	18	.1
146	Arkray USA Inc—*Jonathan Chapman*	5198 W 76th St, Minneapolis MN 55439	952-646-3259	R	18*	.1
147	Sten Corp—*Kenneth W Brimmer*	10275 Wayzata Blvd, Minnetonka MN 55305	952-545-2776	P	18	.1
148	Precision Medical Products Inc—*Douglas Yocom*	PO Box 300, Denver PA 17517	717-335-3700	R	18*	.1
149	NMT Innovasive Systems Inc—*Richard E Davis* NMT Medical Inc	27 Wormwood St, Boston MA 02210	617-737-0930	S	18*	.1
150	Pulse Technologies Inc—*Robert S Walsh Sr*	2000 AM Dr, Quakertown PA 18951	267-733-0200	R	17*	.1
151	Aspen Medical Products—*Dan Williamson*	6481 Oak Canyon, Irvine CA 92618	949-681-0200	R	17	.1
152	Phillips and Johnston Inc—*Christopher Kowalski*	21 W 179 Hill Ave, Glen Ellyn IL 60137	630-469-8150	S	17*	<.1
153	Cirtec Medical Systems LLC—*Barry Smith*	55 Deer Park Dr, East Longmeadow MA 01028	413-525-5700	R	17*	.1
154	Advantis Medical Inc—*Michael Bettini*	2121 Southtech Dr Ste, Greenwood IN 46143	317-859-2300	R	16*	.1
155	Advanced Medical Instruments Inc—*Gary Kinley*	3061 W Albany St, Broken Arrow OK 74012	918-250-0566	R	16*	.1
156	Viper Technologies LLC	15045 Ne Mason St, Portland OR 97230	503-654-5726	R	16*	.2
157	Designs For Vision Inc—*Richard Feinbloom*	760 Koehler Ave, Ronkonkoma NY 11779	631-585-3300	R	15*	.1
158	Aurora Imaging Technology Inc—*Olivia Cheng*	39 High St, North Andover MA 01845	978-975-7530	R	15*	.1
159	Ekos Corp—*Robert Hubert*	11911 N Creek Pkwy S, Bothell WA 98011	425-415-3100	R	15*	.1
160	Std Med Inc—*Steven Tallarida*	75 Mill St, Stoughton MA 02072	781-828-4400	R	15*	.2
161	Acist Medical Systems—*Thomas Morizio*	7905 Fuller Rd, Eden Prairie MN 55344	952-941-3507	R	15*	.1
162	Grason-Stadler Inc—*Chris Ingham*	1 Westchester Dr, Milford NH 03055	603-672-0470	R	15*	.1
163	Life-Tech Inc—*Alfred Coates*	PO Box 1849, Stafford TX 77497	281-491-6600	R	14*	.1
164	Metal Craft Machine and Engineering Inc—*Trisha Mowry*	13760 Business Ctr Dr, Elk River MN 55330	763-441-1855	R	14*	.1
165	Carstens Inc—*George Block*	7310 W Wilson Ave, Chicago IL 60706	708-669-1500	R	14*	.1
166	Trinity Biotech USA—*Rory Nealon*	400 Connell Dr Ste 710, Berkeley Heights NJ 07922	908-464-2001	D	14*	.1
167	Sklar Instruments Corp—*Don Taylor*	889 S Matlack St, West Chester PA 19382	610-430-3200	R	14*	.1
168	Asthmatx Inc—*Glendon E French*	888 Ross Dr Ste 100, Sunnyvale CA 94089	408-419-0100	R	14*	<.1
169	NeuroMetrix Inc—*Shai N Gozani MD*	62 4th Ave, Waltham MA 02451	781-890-9989	P	14	.1
170	B and M Precision Inc—*Miro Mitusina*	1225 4th St Sw, Ruskin FL 33570	813-645-1188	R	14*	.1
171	Uroplasty Inc—*David B Kaysen*	5420 Feltl Rd, Minnetonka MN 55343	952-426-6140	P	14	.1
172	Biogenex Laboratories—*Kris Kalra*	49026 Milmont Dr, Fremont CA 94538	510-824-1400	R	14*	<.1
173	VirtualScopics Inc—*Jeff Markin*	500 Linden Oaks, Rochester NY 14625	585-249-6231	P	13	.1
174	Lampire Biological Labs Inc—*Gregory Krug*	PO Box 270, Pipersville PA 18947	215-795-2838	R	13*	.1
175	NMT Medical Inc—*Richard E Davis*	27 Wormwood St, Boston MA 02210	617-737-0930	P	13	.1
176	Cardica Inc—*Bernard A Hausen*	900 Saginaw Dr, Redwood City CA 94063	650-364-9975	P	13	<.1
177	Metrix Co—*Donnelle Fuerste*	4400 Chavenelle Rd, Dubuque IA 52002	563-556-8800	R	13*	.1
178	Medivance Inc—*Robert Kline*	321 S Taylor Ave, Louisville CO 80027	303-926-1917	R	13*	.1
179	Mulholland Positioning Systems Inc—*Larry Mulholland*	839 Albion St, Burley ID 83318	208-878-3840	R	13*	<.1
180	Winslow Automatics Inc—*Janusz Podlasek*	23 Saint Claire Ave, New Britain CT 06051	860-225-6321	H	13*	.1
181	Antares Pharma Inc—*Paul K Wotton PhD*	250 Phillips Blvd Ste, Ewing NJ 08618	609-359-3020	P	13	<.1
182	Connecticut Hypodermics Inc—*Stephen Tutolo*	519 Main St, Yalesville CT 06492	203-265-4881	R	13*	.1
183	Reliance Medical Products Inc—*David Edenfield*	3535 Kings Mill Rd, Mason OH 45040	513-398-3937	R	12*	.1
184	Bradshaw Medical Inc—*Keith Easter*	10325 58th Pl, Kenosha WI 53144	262-925-1374	R	12*	.1
185	Plasma Etch Inc—*Richard DeLarge*	3522 Arrowhead Dr, Carson City NV 89706	775-883-1336	R	12*	<.1
186	L and R Manufacturing Co—*Robert Lazarus*	PO Box 607, Kearny NJ 07032	201-991-5330	R	12*	.1
187	Westmed Inc—*Robert Mckinnon*	5580 S Nogales Hwy Ste, Tucson AZ 85706	520-294-7987	R	12*	.1
188	Maxi Aids Inc—*Elliot Zaretsky*	PO Box 3209, Farmingdale NY 11735	631-752-0521	R	11*	.1
189	CardioGenesis Corp—*Paul J McCormick* CryoLife Inc	1655 Roberts Blvd, Kennesaw GA 30144	770-419-3355	S	11	<.1
190	Ranfac Corp—*Robert Adler*	PO Box 635, Avon MA 02322	508-588-4400	R	11*	.1
191	Organogenesis Inc—*Geoff MacKay*	150 Dan Rd, Canton MA 02021	781-575-0775	R	11*	.2
192	Concentric Medical Inc—*Maria Sainz*	301 E Evelyn Ave, Mountain View CA 94041	650-938-2100	R	11*	.1
193	Thermotek Inc—*Robert Nickell*	1200 Lkeside Pkwy Ste, Flower Mound TX 75028	972-874-4949	R	11*	.1
194	Instrumentation Industries Inc—*Edward C Horey*	2990 Industrial Blvd, Bethel Park PA 15102	412-854-1133	R	11*	<.1
195	Clinical Innovations LLC—*Mark King*	747 W 4170 S, Murray UT 84123	801-268-8200	R	11*	.1
196	Engineered Medical Systems Inc—*Jeffrey Quinn*	2055 Executive Dr, Indianapolis IN 46241	317-246-5500	R	11*	.1
197	Neoprobe Corp—*Mark J Pykett*	425 Metro Pl N Ste 300, Dublin OH 43017	614-793-7500	P	11	<.1
198	W A Baum Company Inc—*John Baum*	PO Box 209, Copiague NY 11726	631-226-3940	R	11*	.1
199	Diagnostic Systems Laboratories Inc—*Gopal Savjani*	445 Medical Ctr Blvd, Webster TX 77598	281-332-9678	R	11*	.1
200	Opus Iii-Vii Corp—*Mark Keffeler*	8939 F St, Omaha NE 68127	402-592-2169	R	10*	.1
201	Hospital Marketing Services Company Inc—*Brian Hurley*	162 Great Hill Rd, Naugatuck CT 06770	203-723-1466	R	10*	.1
202	United Medical Enterprise Inc—*Herschel Pitts*	4049 Allen Station Rd, Augusta GA 30906	706-790-9115	R	10*	.1
203	Micro-Surgical Technology Inc—*Larry Laks*	PO Box 2679, Redmond WA 98073	425-556-0544	R	10*	.1
204	Ace Surgical Supply Company Inc—*Jay Edward Carchidi*	1034 Pearl St, Brockton MA 02301	508-588-3100	R	10*	<.1
205	Colin Medical Instruments Corp—*Mark Rison*	5850 Farinon Dr, San Antonio TX 78249	210-690-6200	R	10*	<.1
206	PLC Medical Systems Inc—*Mark R Tauscher*	459 Fortune Blvd, Milford MA 01757	508-541-8800	S	10	<.1
207	Bryan Corp—*Frank Abrano*	4 Plympton St, Woburn MA 01801	781-935-0004	R	10*	<.1
208	Oculus Innovative Sciences Inc—*Hojabr Alimi*	1129 N McDowell Blvd, Petaluma CA 94954	707-283-0550	P	10	.1
209	Polyzen Inc—*Tilak Shah*	PO Box 1299, Apex NC 27502	919-319-9599	R	10*	.1
210	Uma Inc—*Awad Da'mes*	PO Box 100, Dayton VA 22821	540-879-2040	R	10*	<.1
211	Lab Medical Manufacturing Inc—*Leon Bester*	28 Cook St, Billerica MA 01821	978-663-2475	R	9*	.1
212	Applied Cardiac Systems Inc—*Danny Marcus*	22912 El Pacifico Dr, Laguna Hills CA 92653	949-855-9366	R	9*	.1
213	Command Medical Products Inc—*David Slick*	15 Signal Ave, Ormond Beach FL 32174	386-672-8116	R	9*	.1
214	Inviro Medical—*Gareth Clarke*	1755 N Brown Rd Ste150, Lawrenceville GA 30043	678-405-4025	R	9*	<.1
215	U S Medical Instruments Inc—*Matthew Mazur*	PO Box 928439, San Diego CA 92192	619-661-5500	R	9*	<.1
216	Alto Development Corp—*Michael Wojciechowicz*	PO Box 758, Farmingdale NJ 07727	732-938-2266	R	9*	.1
217	Xodus Medical Inc—*Craig Kaforey*	702 Prominence Dr, New Kensington PA 15068	724-337-5500	R	9*	<.1
218	Zeus Scientific Inc—*Donald Tourville*	PO Box 38, Raritan NJ 08869	908-526-3744	R	8*	.1
219	Biofilm Inc—*Daniel Wray*	3225 Executive Rdg, Vista CA 92081	760-727-9030	R	8*	.1
220	Kollsut Scientific Corp—*Arkady Teplitsky*	3001 W Hlnd Beach Blvd, Hallandale FL 33009	954-922-7332	R	8*	.1
221	Gregory Manufacturing Inc—*William Gregory*	420 Dwight St, Holyoke MA 01040	413-536-5432	R	8*	.1
222	Medtek Devices Inc—*Christopher Palmerton*	595 Commerce Dr Ste 13, Buffalo NY 14228	716-835-7000	R	8*	.1
223	PolyMedica Pharmaceuticals Inc USA—*Samuel Shanaman*	11 State St, Woburn MA 01801	781-933-2020	S	8*	<.1

Rank	Company Name—*Executive Officer*	Address, City, State, Zip	Phone	Type	Fin	Empls
224	Intella Interventional Systems Inc—*Allan May*	605 W California Ave, Sunnyvale CA 94086	408-737-7121	R	8*	.1
225	Konigsberg Instruments Inc—*William Mills*	2000 E Foothill Blvd, Pasadena CA 91107	626-449-0016	R	8*	.1
226	Tnco Inc—*Karin Gilman*	61 John Vertente Blvd, New Bedford MA 02745	781-447-6661	R	8*	.1
227	Anchor Products Co—*Robert Thrun*	52 W Official Rd, Addison IL 60101	630-543-9124	R	8*	.1
228	Pryor Products—*Jeff Pryor*	1819 Peacock Blvd, Oceanside CA 92056	760-724-8244	R	8*	.1
229	Holmed Corp—*Russell Holmes*	40 Norfolk Ave Ste 2, South Easton MA 02375	508-238-3351	R	8*	.1
230	American Medical Industries Inc—*James Fiocchi*	330 E 3rd St Ste 2, Dell Rapids SD 57022	605-428-5501	R	8*	<.1
231	Marlee Manufacturing Inc—*Russell Wells*	4711 E Guasti Rd, Ontario CA 91761	909-390-3222	R	7*	.1
232	Precise Corp—*Neal York*	2038 Hwy 116, Caryville TN 37714	865-426-7406	R	7*	.1
233	Wallach Surgical Devices Inc—*Nicholas Pichotta*	75 Corporate Dr, Trumbull CT 06611	203-799-2000	R	7*	<.1
234	Bionix Development Corp—*Andrew Milligan*	PO Box 935, Toledo OH 43697	419-727-8421	R	7*	.1
235	Naimco Inc—*John Litzinger*	4120 S Creek Rd, Chattanooga TN 37406	423-648-7730	R	7*	.1
236	Promedica Inc—*Ed Padinske*	114 Douglas Rd E, Oldsmar FL 34677	813-889-9250	R	7*	<.1
237	Electro Medical Equipment Co—*Randy H Thurman* VIASYS Healthcare Inc	12015 Industriplex Blv, Baton Rouge LA 70809	225-756-0351	S	7*	<.1
238	Kinematic Automation Inc—*David Carlberg*	PO Box 69, Twain Harte CA 95383	209-532-3200	R	7*	.1
239	Nidek Medical Products Inc—*Anand Chitlangia*	3949 Valley E Industri, Birmingham AL 35217	205-856-7200	R	7*	<.1
240	Epimed International Inc—*Gabor Racz*	141 Sal Landrio Dr, Johnstown NY 12095	518-725-0209	R	7*	.1
241	Implant Sciences Corp—*Glenn D Bolduc*	600 Research Dr, Wilmington MA 01887	978-752-1700	P	7	<.1
242	Bio-Med Devices Inc—*Dean Bennett*	61 Soundview Rd, Guilford CT 06437	203-458-0202	R	7*	<.1
243	National Biological Corp—*Kenneth Oif*	23700 Mercantile Rd, Beachwood OH 44122	216-831-0600	R	6*	<.1
244	Windstone Medical Packaging Inc—*Greg Deman*	1602 4th Ave N, Billings MT 59101	406-259-6387	R	6*	<.1
245	Inovio Pharmaceuticals Inc—*J Joseph Kim*	1787 Sentry Pky W Bldg, Blue Bell PA 19422	267-440-4200	P	6	<.1
246	Bioject—*Ralph Makar* Bioject Medical Technologies Inc	20245 SW 95th Ave, Tualatin OR 97062	503-692-8001	S	6*	.1
247	Kilgore Manufacturing Company Inc—*C Kilgore*	445 S Line St, Columbia City IN 46725	260-248-2002	R	6*	<.1
248	Techno-Aide Inc—*Jean Lagotte*	7117 Centennial Blvd, Nashville TN 37209	615-350-7030	R	6*	<.1
249	Pace Tech Inc—*Ilhan M Bilgutay*	510 Garden Ave N, Clearwater FL 33755	727-442-8118	R	6*	<.1
250	BD Vacutainer Systems—*Edward J Ludwig* Becton Dickinson and Co	1 Becton Dr, Franklin Lakes NJ 07417	201-847-6800	D	6*	<.1
251	Mark of Fitness Inc—*James Austion*	621 Shrewsbury Ave, Shrewsbury NJ 07702	732-842-7200	R	6*	<.1
252	Webster Enterprises of Jackson County Inc—*Gene Robinson*	PO Box 220, Webster NC 28788	828-586-8981	R	6*	<.1
253	Sigmedics Inc—*Frank E Zeiss*	335 N Broad St, Fairborn OH 45324	937-439-9131	R	6*	<.1
254	Bico Inc (Burbank California)—*Robert De Palma*	PO Box 6339, Burbank CA 91510	818-842-7179	R	6*	<.1
255	Anderson Tool and Die Corp—*Jack Kauffman*	1430 W Blancke St, Linden NJ 07036	908-862-5550	R	6*	.1
256	Lone Star Medical Products Inc—*Jim Fowler*	11211 Cash Rd, Stafford TX 77477	281-340-6000	R	6*	<.1
257	Lifeline Products Inc—*Carol Pinto*	PO Box 230, Wallingford CT 06492	203-265-2846	R	6*	<.1
258	Surgical Instrument Manufacturers Inc—*William Bartling*	1533b Larkin Williams, Fenton MO 63026	636-349-4960	R	6*	<.1
259	Brain Power Inc—*Herbert Wertheim*	PO Box 559501, Miami FL 33255	305-264-4465	R	6*	<.1
260	Arthrocare Medical Corp—*John Raffle*	7500 Rialto Blvd Ste 1, Austin TX 78735	512-391-3900	R	6*	<.1
261	Titertek Instruments Inc—*Olga Golovleva*	330 Wynn Dr Nw, Huntsville AL 35805	256-859-8600	R	6*	<.1
262	Bioject Medical Technologies Inc—*Ralph Makar*	20245 SW 95th Ave, Tualatin OR 97062	503-692-8001	P	6	<.1
263	Andersen Sterilizers Inc—*William Andersen*	3154 Caroline Dr, Haw River NC 27258	336-376-8622	R	6*	<.1
264	Uresil LLC—*Brett Hazuka*	5418 Touhy Ave, Skokie IL 60077	847-982-0200	R	5*	<.1
265	Diagnostic Scanning—*Kurt Meehan*	1611 S Green Rd Ste 26, Cleveland OH 44121	216-382-0704	R	5*	.1
266	Scanlan International Inc—*Timothy Scanlan*	1 Scanlan Plz Ste 1, Saint Paul MN 55107	651-298-0997	R	5*	<.1
267	Dupaco Inc—*Gregory Jordan*	4144 Avonda De La Plat, Oceanside CA 92056	760-758-4550	R	5*	<.1
268	Peregrine Surgical Ltd—*John Richmond*	51 Britain Dr, Doylestown PA 18901	215-348-0456	R	5*	<.1
269	Mettler Electronics Corp—*Mark Mettler*	1333 S Claudina St, Anaheim CA 92805	714-533-2221	H	5*	<.1
270	Nexcelom Bioscience LLC—*Jean Qiu*	360 Merrimack St Bldg, Lawrence MA 01843	978-327-5340	R	5*	<.1
271	Isoray Medical Inc—*Dwight Babcock*	350 Hills St Ste 106, Richland WA 99354	509-375-1202	R	5*	<.1
272	Modern Metals Industries Inc—*Lee Sherrill*	PO Box 701, El Segundo CA 90245	310-516-0851	R	5*	<.1
273	Inovo Inc—*George Harris*	2975 Horseshoe Dr S St, Naples FL 34104	239-643-6577	R	5*	<.1
274	Hill Laboratories Co—*Howard Hill*	PO Box 2028, Malvern PA 19355	610-644-2867	R	5*	<.1
275	Nova Technology Corp—*Michael Campbell*	29 Magnolia Ave, Manchester MA 01944	978-525-3066	R	5*	<.1
276	Sandhill Scientific Inc—*Frederick Jory*	9150 Commerce Cntr Cir, Littleton CO 80129	303-470-7020	R	5*	<.1
277	Hmd Inc—*Thomas Coneys*	81 Tpke Rd, Jaffrey NH 03452	603-532-5656	R	5*	<.1
278	Unimed Surgical Products Inc—*Lee Alexander*	10401 Belcher Rd S, Largo FL 33777		R	5*	<.1
279	Pepin Manufacturing Inc—*Jeff Solberg*	1875 S Hwy 61, Lake City MN 55041	651-345-5655	R	5*	<.1
280	Avantec Vascular Corp—*Motasim Sirhan*	605 W California Ave, Sunnyvale CA 94086	408-329-5400	R	5*	<.1
281	Gertler Industries Inc—*Bernard Gertler*	914 W 17th St, Costa Mesa CA 92627	949-631-4474	R	5*	<.1
282	Preferred Medical Products Inc—*William Bartolac*	8100 S Akron St Ste 31, Centennial CO 80112	303-649-9010	R	4*	<.1
283	Afassco Inc—*Don Schumaker*	PO Box 488, Minden NV 89423	775-783-3555	R	4*	<.1
284	Vesta Medical LLC—*Arthur Bertolero*	1555 Mcgaw Ave Ste A, Irvine CA 92614	949-660-8648	R	4*	<.1
285	Boehringer Laboratories Inc—*John Boehringer*	300 Thoms Dr, Phoenixville PA 19460	610-278-0900	R	4*	<.1
286	Buxton Medical Equipment Corp—*Carl Newman*	1178 Rte 109, Lindenhurst NY 11757	631-957-4500	R	4*	<.1
287	Depuy Spine—*Gregory Casciaro*	365 Ravendale Dr, Mountain View CA 94043	650-903-4800	R	4*	<.1
288	Quality Tech Services Inc—*Doug Wilder*	10525 Hampshire Ave S, Bloomington MN 55438	952-942-8321	R	4*	<.1
289	Bbs Enterprises Inc—*David Behrens*	55980 Russell Industri, Mishawaka IN 46545	574-255-3173	R	4*	<.1
290	Applied Medical Technology Inc—*George J Picha*	8000 Katherine Blvd, Brecksville OH 44141	440-717-4000	R	4*	<.1
291	WR Medical Electronics Co—*Jack Blais*	1700 Gervais Avenue, Maplewood MN 55109	651-430-1200	R	4*	<.1
292	Advantech Manufacturing Inc—*James Lang*	2450 S Commerce Dr, New Berlin WI 53151	262-786-1600	R	4*	<.1
293	Axya Medical Inc—*Ken Fallen*	100 Cummings Ctr Ste 4, Beverly MA 01915	978-232-9997	R	4*	<.1
294	International Medical Industries Inc—*Jonathan Vitello*	2881 W Mcnab Rd, Pompano Beach FL 33069	954-917-9570	R	4*	<.1
295	Pointe Scientific Inc—*Janusz Szyszko*	PO Box 87188, Canton MI 48187	734-487-8300	R	4*	<.1
296	Wells Johnson Co—*John Wells*	8000 S Kolb Rd, Tucson AZ 85706	520-298-6069	R	4*	<.1
297	Novostent Corp—*G Ray Martin*	1400 Terra Bella Ave S, Mountain View CA 94043	650-404-0300	R	4*	<.1
298	Medical Industries America Inc—*Dan Bunting*	26378 289th Pl, Adel IA 50003	515-993-5001	R	4*	<.1
299	Medrx Inc—*Ronald Buck*	1200 Starkey Rd Ste 10, Largo FL 33771	727-584-9600	R	4*	<.1
300	Impedimed Inc—*Greg Brown*	5959 Cornerstn Ct W St, San Diego CA 92121	858-412-0200	R	4*	<.1
301	Mira Inc—*James Clasby*	414 Quaker Hwy, Uxbridge MA 01569	508-278-7877	R	4*	<.1
302	David Kopf Instruments—*J Kopf*	PO Box 636, Tujunga CA 91043	818-352-3274	R	4*	<.1
303	Quintus Inc—*Richard Cook*	PO Box 3930, Camp Verde AZ 86322	928-567-3833	R	4*	<.1
304	Man Maven Medical Manufacturing Inc—*Paul Vaughan*	PO Box 909, Indian Rocks Beach FL 33785	727-518-0555	R	4*	<.1
305	Computerized Imaging Reference Systems Inc—*Mark Devlin*	2428 Almeda Ave Ste 31, Norfolk VA 23513	757-855-2765	R	4*	<.1
306	Radiology Support Devices Inc—*Matthew Alderson*	1904 E Dominguez St, Long Beach CA 90810	310-518-0527	R	4*	<.1
307	Clinton Industries Inc—*Robert Bohn*	1140 Edison St, York PA 17403	717-848-3519	R	4*	<.1
308	Madison Medical LLC	8 Bishop Ln, Madison CT 06443	203-245-0306	R	4*	<.1
309	MGM Instruments Inc—*George Mismas*	925 Sherman Ave, Hamden CT 06514	203-248-4008	R	4*	<.1
310	Touch International Inc—*Stewart Griffith*	PO Box 1304, Hillsborough NC 27278	919-732-6968	R	4*	<.1

Note: An asterisk (*) indicates an estimated financial figure. The company type code used is as follows: R = Private, P = Public, S = Private Subsidiary, B = Public Subsidiary, D = Division, J = Joint Venture, I = Investment Fund.

COMPANY RANKINGS BY SALES WITHIN 4-DIGIT SIC

Rank	Company Name—*Executive Officer*	Address, City, State, Zip	Phone	Type	Fin	Empls
311	Atritech Inc—*Jim Bullock*	3750 Annapolis Ln N St, Minneapolis MN 55447	763-258-0250	R	4*	<.1
312	Accutech LLC—*Madison Rodgers*	2641 La Mirada Dr, Vista CA 92081	760-599-6555	R	3*	<.1
313	Biochemical Diagnostics Inc—*Allen Panetz*	180 Heartland Blvd, Edgewood NY 11717	631-595-9200	R	3*	<.1
314	Guided Therapeutics Inc—*Mark L Faupel*	5835 Peachtree Corners, Norcross GA 30092	770-242-8723	P	3	<.1
315	Odyssey Medical Inc—*Gary Tatge*	2975 Brother Blvd, Memphis TN 38133	901-383-7777	R	3*	<.1
316	Bio Compression Systems Inc—*Robert Freidenrich*	120 W Commercial Ave, Moonachie NJ 07074	201-939-0716	R	3*	<.1
317	Biomedical Research And Development Laboratories Inc—*Bruce Kroener*	8561 Atlas Dr, Gaithersburg MD 20877	301-948-6506	R	3*	<.1
318	Electronic Waveform Lab Inc—*Ryan Haney*	5702 Bolsa Ave, Huntington Beach CA 92649	714-843-0463	R	3*	<.1
319	Gauthier Biomedical Inc—*Michael Gauthier*	1235 Dakota Dr Ste G, Grafton WI 53024	262-546-0010	R	3*	<.1
320	Vasamed Inc—*Paulita M LaPlante*	7615 Golden Triangle D; Eden Prairie MN 55344	952-944-5857	P	3	<.1
321	Banyan International Corp—*James Breckenridge*	PO Box 1779, Abilene TX 79604	325-677-1874	R	3*	<.1
322	Promextecnoligies LLC—*Jen Mcneill*	3049 Hudson St, Franklin IN 46131	317-736-0128	R	3*	<.1
323	Morrison Medical—*Donald Evans*	3735 Paragon Dr, Columbus OH 43228	614-461-4400	R	3*	<.1
324	Sierra Laboratories Inc—*Joshua H Levine*	PO Box 27005, Tucson AZ 85726	520-624-0580	S	3	<.1
325	Surgistar Inc—*Jonathan Woodward*	2310 La Mirada Dr, Vista CA 92081	760-598-2480	R	3*	<.1
326	4-D Neuroimaging—*Scott Buchanan*	9727 Pacific Heights B, San Diego CA 92121	858-453-6300	R	3*	<.1
327	Modular Medical Corp—*Jeffery Offner*	1513 Olmstead Ave, Bronx NY 10462	718-829-2626	R	3*	<.1
328	CardioFocus Inc—*Stephen W Sagon*	500 Nickerson Rd Ste 5, Marlborough MA 01752	508-658-7200	R	3*	<.1
329	Sequel Special Products LLC—*Mark Debisschop*	PO Box 11050, Waterbury CT 06703	203-759-1020	R	3*	<.1
330	MRI Interventions—*Kimble L Jenkins*	1 Commerce Sq Ste 2550, Memphis TN 38103	901-522-9300	R	3*	<.1
331	Protomatic Inc—*William Wetzel*	PO Box 21, Dexter MI 48130	734-426-3655	R	3*	<.1
332	LIFE Corp—*John Kirchgeorg*	1776 N Water St, Milwaukee WI 53202	414-272-4000	R	3*	<.1
333	Thinking Systems Corp—*Xiaoyi Wang*	750 94th Ave N Ste 211, Saint Petersburg FL 33702	727-217-0909	R	3*	<.1
334	Instead Sciences—*Daniel Pike*	4275 Executive Sq Ste, La Jolla CA 92037	858-550-1901	R	3*	<.1
335	NeoSurg Technologies Inc—*Pete O Heeron* CooperSurgical Inc	17300 El Camino Real S, Houston TX 77058	281-461-6211	S	3*	<.1
336	Astra Tool and Instrument Manufacturing Corp—*Herbert Unmann*	369 Bradhurst Ave, Hawthorne NY 10532	914-747-3863	R	3*	<.1
337	Ideal Medical Products Inc—*Mike Hohn*	1287 County Rd 623, Broseley MO 63932	573-686-0003	R	3*	<.1
338	I2s Micro Implantable Systems LLC—*Jamie Beaudry*	391 Chipeta Way Ste G, Salt Lake City UT 84108	801-582-5533	R	3*	<.1
339	Nephros Inc—*Paul A Mieyal*	41 Grand Ave, River Edge NJ 07661	201-343-5202	P	3	<.1
340	Cameron-Miller Inc—*John Martin*	5410 W Roosevelt Rd St, Chicago IL 60644	773-379-2624	R	3*	<.1
341	Pioneer Surgical Orthobiologics Inc—*Mark Metzger*	1800 N Greene St, Greenville NC 27834	252-355-4405	S	3*	<.1
342	MTI Precision Products LLC—*Moshe Meller*	175 Oberlin Ave N Ste, Lakewood NJ 08701	732-905-7440	R	3*	<.1
343	Precision Systems Inc—*Charles Bell*	16 Tech Cir Ste 100, Natick MA 01760	508-655-7010	R	3*	<.1
344	Jones Medical Instrument Co—*Bill Jones*	200 Windsor Dr Ste A, Oak Brook IL 60523	630-571-1980	R	3*	<.1
345	Walkmed Infusion LLC—*Donna Mcdaniel*	96 Inverness Dr E Ste, Englewood CO 80112	303-420-9569	R	3*	<.1
346	Chrono-Log Corp—*Paula Freilich*	2 W Park Rd, Havertown PA 19083	610-853-1130	R	3*	<.1
347	Sorb Technology Inc—*Pete Decomo*	PO Box 44500, Oklahoma City OK 73144	405-682-1993	R	3*	<.1
348	Nanosphere Inc—*William Moffitt*	4088 Commercial Ave, Northbrook IL 60062	847-400-9000	P	3	.1
349	Pharmaco-Kinesis Corp—*Eli Gang*	10524 S La Cienega Blv, Inglewood CA 90304	310-734-4447	R	3*	<.1
350	Lifemed Of California—*Thomas Hamon*	13948 Mountain Ave, Chino CA 91710	714-517-6900	R	3*	<.1
351	Physicians Services—*John Gilbert*	1721 Nicholasville Rd, Lexington KY 40503	859-224-0090	R	2*	<.1
352	Pro Surg Inc—*Ashvin Desai*	2193 Trade Zone Blvd, San Jose CA 95131	408-945-4044	R	2*	<.1
353	Cardima Inc—*Robert Cheney*	47266 Benicia St, Fremont CA 94538	510-354-0300	P	2	.1
354	Medical Screening Laboratories Inc—*Michael Bagan*	5727 W Howard St, Niles IL 60714	847-647-7911	R	2*	<.1
355	Greenwald Surgical Company Inc—*Christopher Reynolds*	2688 Dekalb St, Lake Station IN 46405	219-962-1604	R	2*	<.1
356	Hobbs Medical Inc—*Joanna Warner*	8 Spring St, Stafford Springs CT 06076	860-684-5875	R	2*	<.1
357	Harvard Clinical Technology Inc—*Diane Gargano*	22 Pleasant St, Natick MA 01760	508-655-2000	R	2*	<.1
358	Varitronics Inc—*Alan Abrams*	620 Park Way Ste 4, Broomall PA 19008	610-356-3995	R	2*	<.1
359	Extreme Molding LLC—*Lynn Momrow*	25 Gibson St, Watervliet NY 12189	518-326-9319	R	2	<.1
360	BioLife Solutions Inc—*Mike Rice*	3303 Monte Villa Pkwy, Bothell WA 98021	425-402-1400	P	2	<.1
361	Carbon Medical Technologies Inc—*Dean Klein*	1290 Hammond Rd Ste 2, Saint Paul MN 55110	651-653-8512	R	2*	<.1
362	Mastel Precision Surgical Instruments Inc—*Doug Mastel*	2843 Samco Rd Ste A, Rapid City SD 57702	605-341-4595	R	2	<.1
363	Columbia Medical Inc Utah Medical Products Inc	7043 S 300 West, Midvale UT 84047	801-566-1200	S	2*	<.1
364	DE Hokanson Inc—*Kyra Gray*	12840 NE 21st Pl, Bellevue WA 98005	425-882-1689	R	2*	<.1
365	American Medical Specialties Inc—*Richard A Furlong*	PO Box 4350, Mission TX 78573	727-561-9400	R	2	<.1
366	AxioMed Spine Corp—*Patrick McBrayer*	5350 Transportation Bl, Garfield Heights OH 44125	216-587-5566	R	2*	<.1
367	IOP Inc—*Jason Malecka*	3184-B Airway Ave, Costa Mesa CA 92626	714-549-1185	R	2*	<.1
368	Everest Biomedical Instruments Company Inc—*Eldar Causevic*	1732 Gilsinn Ln, Fenton MO 63026	636-519-7770	R	2*	<.1
369	JHM Engineering—*J Maliga*	4014 8th Ave, Brooklyn NY 11232	718-871-1810	R	2*	<.1
370	Hs International Inc—*Henry Shapiro*	5040 Commercial Cir St, Concord CA 94520	925-674-1515	R	2*	<.1
371	Kapp Surgical Instrument Co—*Albert Santilli*	4919 Warrensville Ctr, Cleveland OH 44128	216-587-4400	R	2*	<.1
372	Innovative Technology International Inc—*Frederick Wang*	10747 Tucker St, Beltsville MD 20705	301-937-3688	R	2*	<.1
373	Daxor Corp—*Joseph Feldschuh*	Empire State Building, New York NY 10118	212-330-8500	P	2	<.1
374	Hemocleanse Inc—*Robert Truitt*	3601 Sagamore Pkwy N B, Lafayette IN 47904	765-742-9392	R	2*	<.1
375	Rand-Scot Inc—*Joel Lerich*	401 Linden Ctr Dr, Fort Collins CO 80524	970-484-7967	R	2*	<.1
376	River Bank Laboratories Inc—*Robert Swanson*	PO Box 110, Geneva IL 60134	630-232-2207	R	2*	<.1
377	Neuro Kinetics Inc—*Howison Schroeder*	128 Gamma Dr, Pittsburgh PA 15238	412-963-6649	R	2*	<.1
378	BioMimetic Therapeutics Inc—*Samuel E Lynch*	389 Nichol Mill Ln, Franklin TN 37067	615-844-1280	P	2	.1
379	Andermac Inc—*C Anderson*	PO Box 152, Yuba City CA 95992	530-674-8450	R	2*	<.1
380	Vision Research Corp—*James Kennemer*	PO Box 19707, Birmingham AL 35219	205-942-8011	R	2*	<.1
381	Hypertension Diagnostics Inc—*Mark N Schwartz*	2915 Waters Rd Ste 108, Eagan MN 55121	651-687-9999	P	1	<.1
382	LKC Technologies Inc—*Jim Datovech*	2 Professional Dr Ste, Gaithersburg MD 20879	301-840-1992	R	1*	<.1
383	Pemco Inc—*William Koteles*	5663 Brecksville Rd, Cleveland OH 44131	216-524-2990	R	1*	<.1
384	Diversified Diagnostic Products Inc—*Gerald Timpe*	11603 Windfern Rd, Houston TX 77064	281-955-5323	R	1*	<.1
385	Precision Therapeutics Inc—*Sean C McDonald*	2516 Jane St, Pittsburgh PA 15203	412-432-1500	R	1*	.1
386	Apricot Designs Inc—*Felix Yiu*	681 Arrow Grand Cir, Covina CA 91722	626-966-3299	R	1*	<.1
387	Troy Manufacturing Co—*David Cseplo*	PO Box 448, Burton OH 44021	440-834-8262	R	1*	<.1
388	EyeTel Imaging Inc—*John C Garbarino*	8520 Corridor Rd Ste J, Savage MD 20763	301-483-6167	R	1*	<.1
389	New Horizons Diagnostics Corp—*Lawrence Loomis*	9110 Red Branch Rd Ste, Columbia MD 21045	410-992-9357	R	1*	<.1
390	Sound Surgical Technologies LLC—*Daniel S Goldberger*	357 McCaslin Blvd Ste, Louisville CO 80027		R	1*	<.1
391	California Professional Manufacturing Inc	PO Box 4832, Modesto CA 95352	209-527-2686	R	1*	<.1
392	Quick-Med Technologies Inc—*J Ladd Greeno*	902 NW 4th St, Gainesville FL 32601		P	1	<.1
393	Queststar Medical Inc—*Arthur Kydd*	10180 Viking Dr, Eden Prairie MN 55344	952-941-7345	R	1*	<.1
394	Itg - International Technology Group LLC—*Marc Grabis*	PO Box 11451, San Rafael CA 94912	415-454-8054	R	1*	<.1
395	AcuNetx Inc—*Robert Corrigan*	2301 W 205th Ste 102, Torrance CA 90501	310-328-0477	R	1	<.1
396	Medica Inc—*Jarka Bartl*	336 Encinitas Blvd Ste, Encinitas CA 92024	760-634-5440	R	1*	<.1

Rank	Company Name—Executive Officer	Address, City, State, Zip	Phone	Type	Fin	Empls
397	Paradigm Medical Industries Inc—Stephen L Davis	4273 S 590 W, Salt Lake City UT 84123	801-977-8970	P	1	<.1
398	Biophan Technologies Inc—John F Lanzafame	15 Schoen Pl, Pittsford NY 14534	585-267-4800	R	1	<.1
399	Xitron Technologies Inc—Greg Brown	5959 Cornerstone Ct W, San Diego CA 92121	858-530-8099	R	1*	<.1
400	World Video Sales Company Inc—John Taylor	PO Box 331, Boyertown PA 19512	610-754-6800	R	1*	<.1
401	American Health Systems Inc—Don Bolt	PO Box 26688, Greenville SC 29616	864-234-0496	R	1*	<.1
402	Savex Manufacturing Company Inc—George Wimpffen	170 Easy St, Carol Stream IL 60188	630-668-7219	R	1*	<.1
403	Myco Industries Inc—John Choate	510 Highland Ave 332, Milford MI 48381	248-685-2496	R	1*	<.1
404	Phenome Technologies Inc—Michael Wellems	23220 N Indian Creek R, Lincolnshire IL 60069	847-962-1273	R	<1*	<.1
405	CytoCore Inc—Robert McCullough Jr	414 N Orleans St Ste 5, Chicago IL 60654	312-222-9550	P	<1	<.1
406	Informedix Holdings Inc—Bruce A Kehr	5880 Hubbard Dr, Rockville MD 20852	301-984-1566	P	<1	<.1
407	Clarus Medical LLC—Randal Gatzke	1000 Boone Ave N Ste 1, Minneapolis MN 55427	763-525-8400	R	<1*	<.1
408	Venoscope LLC—Hille Domingue	PO Box 52703, Lafayette LA 70505	337-234-8993	R	<1*	<.1
409	Baap Inc—Bruno Mombrinie	PO Box 1597, Forestville CA 95436	707-836-0206	R	<1*	<.1
410	Tengion Inc—John L Miclot	2900 Potshop Ln Ste 10, East Norriton PA 19403	610-292-8364	P	<1	.1
411	Delcath Systems Inc—Eamonn P Hobbs	810 7th Ave Ste 3505, New York NY 10019	212-489-2100	P	<1	<.1
412	Mela Sciences Inc—Joseph V Gulfo	50 S Buckhout St Ste 1, Irvington NY 10533	914-591-3783	P	<1	<.1
413	OptiMedica Corp—Mark J Forchette	3130 Coronado Dr, Santa Clara CA 95054	408-850-8600	R	<1	<.1
414	TherOx Inc—Kevin T Larkin	17500 Cartwright Rd St, Irvine CA 92614	949-757-1999	R	<1	<.1
415	Capstone Therapeutics Corp—Randolph C Steer	1275 W Washington St, Tempe AZ 85281	602-286-5520	P	<1	<.1
416	Forticell Bioscience Inc—Alan Schoenbart	3960 Broadway, New York NY 10032	212-740-6910	R	<1	<.1
417	American Scientific Resources Inc—Christopher F Tirotta	1112 Weston Rd Unit 27, Weston FL 33326	847-386-1384	P	<1	<.1
418	Scivanta Medical Corp—David R LaVance	215 Morris Ave, Spring Lake NJ 07762	732-282-1620	P	<1	<.1
419	Automated Medical Products Corp—Jerry M Brown	PO Box 2508, Edison NJ 08818	732-602-7717	R	N/A	<.1
420	Medi-Globe Corp—Stefan Wohnhas	110 W Orion St, Tempe AZ 85283	480-897-2772	R	N/A	<.1
421	Oncologix Tech Inc—Anthony Silverman	PO Box 8832, Grand Rapids MI 49518	616-977-9933	P	N/A	<.1

TOTALS: SIC 3841 Surgical & Medical Instruments
Companies: 421   102,002   367.5

3842 Surgical Appliances & Supplies

Rank	Company Name—Executive Officer	Address, City, State, Zip	Phone	Type	Fin	Empls
1	Baylor Health Care System—Joel T Allison	3500 Gaston Ave, Dallas TX 75246	214-820-0111	R	6,422*	18.0
2	Baxter Healthcare Corp—Robert L Parkinson	1 Baxter Pkwy, Deerfield IL 60015	847-948-2000	S	6,380	42.0
3	St Jude Medical Inc—Daniel J Starks	1 St Jude Medical Dr, Saint Paul MN 55117	651-756-2000	P	5,165	15.0
4	Zimmer Holdings Inc—David C Dvorak	PO Box 708, Warsaw IN 46581	574-267-6131	P	4,220	8.8
5	Biomet Inc—Jeffrey R Binder	PO Box 587, Warsaw IN 46581	574-267-6639	R	2,732	3.2
6	Stryker Howmedica Osteonics—Steve MacMillan	325 Corporate Dr, Mahwah NJ 07430	201-831-5000	S	2,600	N/A
7	Medline Industries Inc—Charles S Mills	1 Medline Pl, Mundelein IL 60060	847-949-5500	R	2,346*	5.0
8	Garden City Medical Invacare Corp	1 Invacare Way, Elyria OH 44035	440-329-6000	S	2,044*	5.7
9	Invacare Corp—Gerald B Blouch	PO Box 4028, Elyria OH 44035		P	1,801	6.2
10	Intuitive Surgical Inc—Gary S Guthart PhD	1266 Kifer Rd Bldg 101, Sunnyvale CA 94086	408-523-2100	P	1,413	.7
11	STERIS Corp—Walter M Rosebrough	5960 Heisley Rd, Mentor OH 44060	440-354-2600	P	1,207	5.0
12	Respironics Inc—Donald J Spence	1010 Murry Ridge Ln, Murrysville PA 15668	724-387-5200	S	1,195	4.9
13	Mine Safety Appliances Co—William M Lambert	PO Box 426, Pittsburgh PA 15230	412-967-3000	P	1,173	5.3
14	Guidant's Cardiac Rhythm Management—William Kucheman	4100 Hamline Ave N, Saint Paul MN 55112	651-582-4000	S	1,130*	5.0
15	ArjoHuntleigh—Mark Harwood	2349 W Lake St, Addison IL 60101		S	969	4.2
16	DePuy Inc—R Michael McCaffrey	PO Box 988, Warsaw IN 46581	574-371-4865	S	770	3.2
17	Sunrise Medical Inc—Thomas Rossnagel	6899 Winchester Cir St, Boulder CO 80301	303-218-4500	R	645	4.5
18	Aearo Technologies Inc—Michael A McLain	5457 W 79th St, Indianapolis IN 46268	317-692-6666	R	591*	1.7
19	American Medical Systems Holdings Inc—Anthony P Bihl III	10700 Bren Rd W, Minnetonka MN 55343	952-930-6000	P	542	1.3
20	NuVasive Inc—Alexis V Lukianov	7475 Lusk Blvd, San Diego CA 92121	858-909-1800	P	541	1.1
21	Ethicon Inc—Clifford Holland	PO Box 151, Somerville NJ 08876	908-218-0707	S	539*	5.4
22	Wright Medical Group Inc—Robert Palmisano	5677 Airline Rd, Arlington TN 38002	901-867-9971	P	513	1.3
23	Cotton Goods Manufacturing Company Inc—Edward J Lewis	259 N California Ave, Chicago IL 60612	773-265-0088	R	472*	<.1
24	Medtronic Sofamor Danek Inc—Michael Demane	1800 Pyramid Pl, Memphis TN 38132	901-396-2695	S	470*	1.5
25	DJO Inc—Les Cross	1430 Decision St, Vista CA 92081	760-727-1280	S	413	3.0
26	DJ Orthopedics LLC DJO Inc	1430 Decision St, Vista CA 92081	760-727-1280	S	400*	1.2
27	Align Technology Inc—Thomas M Prescott	2560 Orchard Pky, San Jose CA 95131	408-470-1000	P	387	2.1
28	Mentor Corp—Joshua H Levine	201 Mentor Dr, Santa Barbara CA 93111	805-879-6000	S	376*	1.2
29	Hoveround Corp—Thomas Kruse	2151 Whitfield Industr, Sarasota FL 34243	941-739-6200	R	370*	.4
30	Invacare Technologies Corp—Gerald B Blouch Invacare Corp	PO Box 4028, Elyria OH 44036	440-329-6000	S	370*	1.7
31	Medical Action Industries Inc—Paul D Meringolo	500 Expressway Dr S, Brentwood NY 11717	631-231-4600	P	363	1.3
32	Symmetry Medical Inc—Thomas Sullivan	3724 N State Rd 15, Warsaw IN 46582	574-268-2252	P	361	2.8
33	Ethicon Endo-Surgery Inc—Bob Salerno	4545 Creek Rd, Cincinnati OH 45242	513-337-7000	S	324*	2.0
34	Medtronic MiniMed Inc—Christopher J O'Connell	18000 Devonshire St, Northridge CA 91325	818-362-5958	S	287*	1.5
35	Hollister Inc—Alan Herbert	2000 Hollister Dr, Libertyville IL 60048	847-680-1000	R	222*	2.4
36	Linvatec Corp—Joe Darling	11311 Concept Blvd, Largo FL 33773		S	203*	.9
37	3M Occupational Health and Safety Products—RL George Buckley	3M Ctr, Saint Paul MN 55144	651-737-6501	D	197*	.6
38	Sage Products Inc—Vincent Foglia	3909 3 Oaks Rd, Cary IL 60013	815-455-4700	R	195*	.6
39	Exactech Inc (Gainesville Florida)—William Petty MD	2320 NW 66th Ct, Gainesville FL 32653	352-377-1140	P	191	.6
40	Getinge USA Inc—Andrew Ray	1777 E Henrietta Rd, Rochester NY 14623	585-475-1400	R	187*	.6
41	Johnson and Johnson Medical Inc—William Clarke	Us Rt 22, Somerville NJ 08876	908-218-0707	R	179*	3.1
42	RTI Biologics Inc—Brian K Hutchison	11621 Research Cir, Alachua FL 32615	386-418-8888	P	169	.7
43	Point Blank Solutions Inc—James Henderson	2102 SW 2nd St, Pompano Beach FL 33069	954-630-0900	P	165	1.3
44	Boston Scientific (Glens Falls New York)—J Raymond Elliott	1 Boston Scientific Pl, Natick MA 01760	508-650-8000	S	160*	.8
45	Atrium Medical Corp—Steve Herweck	5 Wentworth Dr, Hudson NH 03051	603-880-1433	R	145*	.6
46	DJO Surgical—Kenneth W Davidson DJO Inc	9800 Metric Blvd, Austin TX 78758	512-832-9500	D	143	1.3
47	St Jude Medical Daig—Daniel J Starks St Jude Medical Inc	14901 Minnetonka Indus, Minnetonka MN 55345	952-933-4700	S	130	.8
48	Broda Enterprises USA Inc—Bradley T Nielson	PO Box 33046, Detroit MI 48232	519-746-8080	S	129*	.4
49	Howard Leight Industries	7828 Waterville Rd, San Diego CA 92154		S	120*	.8
50	Zimmer Orthopedic Surgical Products—Paul Blair Zimmer Holdings Inc	PO Box 10, Dover OH 44622	330-343-8801	D	120*	.4
51	Smith and Nephew Inc Wound Management Div—Oliver Bohuon	11775 Starkey Rd, Largo FL 33773	727-392-1261	D	107*	.4
52	Lakeland Industries Inc—Christopher Ryan	701 Koehler Ave Ste 7, Ronkonkoma NY 11779	631-981-9700	P	101	2.0

Note: An asterisk (*) indicates an estimated financial figure. The company type code used is as follows: R = Private, P = Public, S = Private Subsidiary, B = Public Subsidiary, D = Division, J = Joint Venture, I = Investment Fund.

COMPANY RANKINGS BY SALES WITHIN 4-DIGIT SIC

Rank	Company Name—*Executive Officer*	Address, City, State, Zip	Phone	Type	Fin	Empls
53	Sorin Group	14401 W 65 Way, Arvada CO 80004		S	98*	.5
54	Otix Global Inc—*Joseph A Lugara*	4246 S Riverboat Rd St, Salt Lake City UT 84123	801-312-1700	S	96	.5
55	Surgical Appliance Industries Inc—*L Applegate*	3960 Rosslyn Dr, Cincinnati OH 45209	513-271-4594	R	95*	.5
56	Kappler Safety Group Inc—*George P Kappler*	PO Box 490, Guntersville AL 35976	256-505-4005	R	93*	1.4
57	Synovis Life Technologies Inc—*Richard W Kramp*	2575 University Ave, Saint Paul MN 55114	651-796-7300	P	82	.3
58	Ansell Healthcare Products Inc—*Douglas Tough*	200 Schulz Dr, Red Bank NJ 07701	732-345-5400	S	76*	.2
59	ATS Medical Inc—*Michael D Dale*	3905 Annapolis Ln Ste, Minneapolis MN 55447	763-553-7736	S	76	.3
60	Aetrex Worldwide Inc—*Larry Schwartz*	414 Alfred Ave, Teaneck NJ 07666	201-833-2700	R	75*	.2
61	Minntech Corp—*Roy Malkin*	14605 28th Ave N, Minneapolis MN 55447	763-553-3300	S	72*	.4
62	Mizuho OSI—*Steve Lamb*	30031 Ahern Ave, Union City CA 94587	510-429-1500	R	67*	.3
63	Zimmer Patient Care Div—*David C Dvorak* Zimmer Holdings Inc	PO Box 10, Dover OH 44622	330-343-8801	D	66*	.3
64	Mitek Worldwide—*Rodrigo Bianchi* Ethicon Inc	325 Paramount Dr, Raynham MA 02767	508-880-8100	D	65*	.4
65	Community Products LLC—*Carol Kleinsasser*	PO Box 903, Rifton NY 12471	845-658-8799	R	63*	.3
66	GN Resound North America—*Todd Murray*	8001 E Bloomington Frw, Bloomington MN 55420	952-769-8000	S	62*	.5
67	Louis M Gerson Company Inc—*Ronald Gerson*	PO Box 600, Middleboro MA 02346	508-923-3030	R	56*	.2
68	Davol Inc—*Dan LaFevre*	PO Box 8500, Cranston RI 02920	401-463-7000	S	55*	.5
69	Sunrise Medical Inc Mobility Products Div—*Thomas Rossnagel* Sunrise Medical Inc	6899 Winchester Cir St, Boulder CO 80301	303-218-4500	D	55*	.3
70	Span-America Medical Systems Inc—*James D Ferguson*	PO Box 5231, Greenville SC 29606	864-288-8877	P	53	.3
71	Microtek Medical Inc—*Dan Lee*	512 Lehmberg Rd, Columbus MS 39702	662-327-1863	S	51	.3
72	Cairns Helmets MSA—*William Lambert* Mine Safety Appliances Co	PO Box 426, Pittsburgh PA 15230	412-967-3000	S	49*	.3
73	Bard Peripheral Vascular Inc	PO Box 1740, Tempe AZ 85280	480-894-9515	S	47*	.3
74	Allied Healthcare Products Inc—*Earl R Refsland*	1720 Sublette Ave, Saint Louis MO 63110	314-771-2400	P	47	.3
75	PC Group Inc—*W Gray Hudkins*	4 Brighton Rd Ste 320, Clifton NJ 07012		P	45	.3
76	MAKO Surgical Corp—*Maurice R Ferre*	2555 Davie Rd, Fort Lauderdale FL 33317	954-927-2044	P	44	.3
77	Closure Medical Corp—*Daniel A Pelak*	5250 Greens Dairy Rd, Raleigh NC 27616	919-876-7800	S	40	.1
78	Ossur Americas Inc—*Mahesh Mansukhani*	27051 Towne Centre Dr, Foothill Ranch CA 92610	949-362-3883	R	40*	.5
79	Moldex-Metric Inc—*Mark Magidson*	10111 Jefferson Blvd, Culver City CA 90232	310-837-6500	R	39*	.5
80	O'Gara Group—*Wilfred T O'Gara*	7870 E Kemper Rd Ste 4, Cincinnati OH 45249	513-338-0660	R	38*	1.5
81	Royal Baths Manufacturing Company Ltd—*George Dawson*	14635 Chrisman Rd, Houston TX 77039	281-442-3400	R	36*	.5
82	Sperian Respiratory Protection USA LLC—*Jack Bell*	3001 S Susan St, Santa Ana CA 92704	714-545-0410	S	36*	.1
83	Vision Quest Industries Inc—*James Knape*	18011 Mitchell S, Irvine CA 92614	949-261-3000	R	36*	.3
84	Poly-Vac Inc—*Lori Gosselin*	253 Abby Rd, Manchester NH 03103	603-647-7822	R	36*	.2
85	Synovis Micro Companies Alliance Inc—*Michael K Campbell* Synovis Life Technologies Inc	439 Industrial Ln, Birmingham AL 35211	205-941-0111	S	35*	.1
86	SAS Safety Corp—*George Heuser*	3031 Gardenia Ave, Long Beach CA 90807	562-427-2775	R	35*	.1
87	Ferno-Washington Inc—*Joseph Bourgraf*	70 Weil Way, Wilmington OH 45177	937-382-1451	R	34*	.5
88	Fillauer Inc—*Dennis Williams*	PO Box 5189, Chattanooga TN 37406	423-624-0946	R	33*	.2
89	Wright and Filippis Inc—*AJ Filippis*	2845 Crooks Rd, Rochester Hills MI 48309		R	32	.3
90	Robert Busse and Company Inc—*Emanuel Cardinale*	PO Box 11067, Hauppauge NY 11788	631-435-4711	R	31*	.3
91	ED Bullard Co—*Richard Miller*	1898 Saftey Way, Cynthiana KY 41031	859-234-6611	R	31*	.3
92	Cochlear Americas—*Chris Smith*	13059 E Peakview Ave, Centennial CO 80111	303-790-9010	D	31*	.1
93	Biodex Medical Systems Inc—*James Reiss*	20 Ramsey Rd, Shirley NY 11967	631-924-9000	R	30*	.2
94	Simpson Performance Products Inc—*Chuck Davies*	RR 328 Fm 306, New Braunfels TX 78130	830-625-1774	R	29*	.3
95	Runners Diversified Inc—*Allen Rice*	PO Box 447, Vidalia GA 30475	912-537-3024	R	28*	.3
96	First Aid Only Inc—*Mark Miller*	11101 Ne 37th Cir, Vancouver WA 98682	360-254-9291	R	28*	.2
97	Blacksheep Inc—*Bob Archer*	3220 W Gentry Pkwy, Tyler TX 75702	903-592-3853	S	27*	.5
98	Spenco Medical Corp—*Steve B Smith*	PO Box 2501, Waco TX 76702	254-772-6000	R	27*	.3
99	Boss Manufacturing Co—*G Louis Graziadio III*	1221 Page St, Kewanee IL 61443		S	27*	.2
100	US Spine—*Ben Shappley*	1885 W 2100 S, Salt Lake City UT 84119	801-839-3500	R	27*	.1
101	Medsorb Dominicana SA—*Joel Wildstein*	3 State Pier Rd, New London CT 06320	860-442-4914	R	26*	.2
102	Hartmann USA Inc—*John Gilbert*	481 Lakeshore Pkwy, Rock Hill SC 29730	803-325-7600	R	26*	.2
103	Kappler USA Inc—*Mike Willis* Kappler Safety Group Inc	PO Box 490, Guntersville AL 35976	256-505-4005	S	25	.4
104	Ohio Willow Wood Co—*Robert Arbogast*	PO Box 130, Mount Sterling OH 43143	740-869-3377	R	25*	.2
105	Helix Medical LLC—*Jorg Schneewind*	1110 Mark Ave, Carpinteria CA 93013	805-684-3304	R	24*	.2
106	Avalign Technologies Inc—*Forrest Whittaker*	801 Industrial Dr, Hicksville OH 43526	419-542-7743	R	24*	.2
107	Mutual Industries North Inc—*Edmund Dunn*	707 W Grange Ave Ste 1, Philadelphia PA 19120	215-927-6000	R	24*	.3
108	Bruno Independent Living Aids Inc—*Michael Bruno*	PO Box 84, Oconomowoc WI 53066	262-567-4990	R	23*	.3
109	Broncus Technologies Inc—*Cary B Cole*	1400 N Shoreline Blvd, Mountain View CA 94043	650-428-1600	R	23*	.1
110	Elastic Therapy LLC—*J Ramsay*	PO Box 4068, Asheboro NC 27204	336-625-0529	R	23*	.2
111	Hansen Medical Inc—*Bruce Barclay*	800 E Middlefield Rd, Mountain View CA 94043	650-404-5800	P	22	.2
112	DePuy OrthoTech	325 Paramount Dr, Raynham MA 02767		S	22*	.3
113	Ortho Development Corp—*Masao Okawa*	12187 Business Park Dr, Draper UT 84020	801-553-9991	R	22*	<.1
114	Oticon Inc—*Mikael Worning*	PO Box 6724, Somerset NJ 08875	732-560-1220	R	22*	.1
115	Innovation Sports Inc—*John Turnbull*	19762 Pauling, Foothill Ranch CA 92610	949-859-4407	R	21*	.2
116	Hal-Hen Company Inc—*Eric Spar*	180 Atlantic Ave, New Hyde Park NY 11040	516-294-3200	R	21*	.1
117	Knit-Rite Inc—*Perry Bacon*	120 Osage Ave, Kansas City KS 66105	913-281-4600	R	21*	.1
118	Hosmer-Dorrance Corp—*Karl Hovland* Fillauer Inc	561 Division St, Campbell CA 95008	408-379-5151	S	20*	.2
119	Bashlin Industries Inc—*Robert Schell*	PO Box 867, Grove City PA 16127	724-458-8340	R	20*	.1
120	Scott Specialties Inc—*Wilson Scott*	PO Box 508, Belleville KS 66935	785-527-5627	R	20*	.2
121	PACA Body Armor Inc—*Larry Ellis*	179 Mine Ln, Jacksboro TN 37757	423-562-1115	R	19	.1
122	Sharps Compliance Corp—*David P Tusa*	9220 Kirby Dr Ste 500, Houston TX 77054	713-432-0300	P	19	.1
123	Professional Products Inc—*Bryan Kilbey*	PO Box 589, Defuniak Springs FL 32435	850-892-5731	R	19*	.2
124	Wheelchairs Of Kansas—*Willard Lee Frickey*	PO Box 320, Ellis KS 67637	785-726-4885	R	19*	.1
125	Coloplast Corp—*Lars Rasmussen*	200 S 6th St Ste 900, Minneapolis MN 55402		S	18*	.2
126	Pioneer Surgical Technology Inc—*Jeffery Millin*	375 River Park Cir, Marquette MI 49855	906-226-9909	R	17*	.2
127	Becker Orthopedic Appliance Co—*Rudolf Becker*	635 Executive Dr, Troy MI 48083	248-588-7480	R	17*	.2
128	FzioMed Inc—*John Krelle*	231 Bonetti Dr, San Luis Obispo CA 93401	805-546-0610	R	17*	<.1
129	PolyMedica Healthcare Inc—*Patrick T Ryan*	11 State St, Woburn MA 01801	781-933-2020	S	17*	<.1
130	Harry J Lawall and Son Inc—*Harry Lawall*	8028 Frankford Ave, Philadelphia PA 19136	215-338-6611	R	16*	.1
131	Ehob Inc—*Scott Rogers*	250 N Belmont Ave, Indianapolis IN 46222	317-972-4600	R	16*	.1
132	Siemens Hearing Inc—*Dan Anderson*	5010 Cheshire Ln N Ste, Minneapolis MN 55446	763-268-4500	R	15*	.3
133	Euromed Inc—*Thomas Gardner*	25 Corporate Dr, Orangeburg NY 10962	845-359-4039	R	15*	.1
134	Ok 1 Manufacturing Co—*Roger Teigen*	PO Box 736, Altus OK 73522	580-482-0891	R	15*	.2
135	Mcdavid Knee-Guard Inc—*Robert Mc David*	10305 Argonne Dr, Woodridge IL 60517	630-783-0600	R	15*	.1

Rank	Company Name—*Executive Officer*	Address, City, State, Zip	Phone	Type	Fin	Empls
136	International Biomedical Ltd—*A Segars*	PO Box 143449, Austin TX 78714	512-873-0033	R	15*	.1
137	Boston Brace International Inc—*Michael Petruzzo*	20 Ledin Dr Ste 1, Avon MA 02322	508-588-6060	R	15*	.1
138	Patient Safety Technologies Inc—*Brian E Stewart*	2 Venture Ste 350, Irvine CA 92618	949-387-2277	P	15	<.1
139	Hemcon Medical Technologies Inc—*Nick Hart*	10575 Sw Cascade Ave, Portland OR 97223	503-245-0459	R	15*	.1
140	Magnatone Hearing Aid Corp—*Don Campbell*	PO Box 180964, Casselberry FL 32718	407-339-2422	R	14*	.1
141	Structure Medical LLC—*Kevin Confoy*	9935 Business Cir, Naples FL 34112	239-262-5551	R	14*	.1
142	National Fabrication Inc—*Jeff Rosen*	9561 Satellite Blvd St, Orlando FL 32837	407-852-6170	S	14*	<.1
143	Avcor Health Care Products Inc—*Fred Trainor*	PO Box 40500, Fort Worth TX 76140	817-551-0595	R	13*	<.1
144	Qosina Corp—*Stuart Herskovitz*	150-Q Executive Dr, Edgewood NY 11717	631-242-3000	R	13*	.1
145	H and P Industries Inc—*David Haertle*	700 W N Shore Dr, Hartland WI 53029	262-538-2900	R	13*	.1
146	Sohn Manufacturing Inc—*Wallace Beaudry*	544 Sohn Dr, Elkhart Lake WI 53020	920-876-3361	R	12*	.1
147	Acor Orthopaedic Inc—*Greg Alaimo*	18530 S Miles Rd, Cleveland OH 44128	216-662-4500	R	12*	.1
148	CardioMEMS Inc—*Jay S Yadav*	387 Technology Cir NW, Atlanta GA 30313	678-651-2300	R	12*	<.1
149	Chad Therapeutics Inc—*Earl L Yager*	2975 Horseshoe Dr S St, Naples FL 34104	239-687-1280	R	12	<.1
150	Maico Diagnostics Inc—*Ron Perlt*	7625 Golden Triangle D, Eden Prairie MN 55344	952-941-4200	S	11*	.1
151	Certified Safety Manufacturing Inc—*Pam Gerson*	PO Box 412217, Kansas City MO 64141	816-483-9090	R	11*	.1
152	Sellstrom Manufacturing Co—*David Peters*	PO Box 355, Palatine IL 60078	847-358-2000	R	10*	.1
153	Total Resources International Inc—*George Rivera*	385 S Lemon Ave Ste E1, Walnut CA 91789	909-594-1220	R	10*	.1
154	Restorative Care Of America Inc—*C Hess*	12221 33rd St N, Saint Petersburg FL 33716	727-573-1595	R	10*	.1
155	Dynamic Systems Inc (Leicester North Carolina)—*Ellie Brown*	104 Morrow Branch, Leicester NC 28748	828-683-3523	R	10*	<.1
156	Southeastern Technology Inc—*Thomas Eisenman*	905 Industrial Dr, Murfreesboro TN 37129	615-890-1700	R	10*	.1
157	Jerome Group Inc—*Ronald Kowalski* Ossur Americas Inc	1414 Metropolitan Ave, West Deptford NJ 08066	856-234-8600	S	10*	.1
158	Orthotic and Prosthetic Lab Inc—*David Osterman*	748 Marshall Ave, Saint Louis MO 63119	314-968-8555	R	10*	.1
159	Milestone Scientific Inc—*Leonard Osser*	220 S Orange Ave, Livingston NJ 07039	973-535-2717	P	10	<.1
160	WDC Holdings Inc—*Curtis Smith*	PO Box 1270, Attleboro Falls MA 02763	508-699-4412	R	10*	.1
161	Amigo Mobility International Inc—*Beth Thieme*	6693 Dixie Hwy, Bridgeport MI 48722	989-777-0910	R	10*	.1
162	Convaid Products Inc—*Mervyn Watkins*	PO Box 4209, Pls Vrds Pnsl CA 90274	310-618-0111	R	9*	.1
163	NY Orthopedic USA Inc—*Michael Rozenberg*	63 Flushing Ave Unit 3, Brooklyn NY 11205	718-852-5330	R	9*	.1
164	Kerma Medical Products Inc—*Joe Reubel*	215 Suburban Dr, Suffolk VA 23434	757-398-8400	R	9*	.1
165	Williams Health Care Systems—*Tom Kenny*	158 N Edison Ave, Elgin IL 60123	847-741-3650	R	9*	.1
166	Encon Safety Products Inc—*James Johnson*	PO Box 3826, Houston TX 77253	713-466-1449	R	9*	.1
167	Set Liquidation Inc—*Lawrence Peek*	1489 Cedar St, Holt MI 48842	517-694-2300	R	9*	.1
168	Monaghan Medical Corp—*Mitchell Baran*	5 Latour Ave Ste 1600, Plattsburgh NY 12901	518-561-7330	R	8*	.1
169	Audina Hearing Instruments Inc—*Marc Mclarnon*	165 E Wildmere Ave, Longwood FL 32750	407-331-0077	R	8*	.1
170	C H Martin Co—*George Counts*	329 Marietta St Nw, Atlanta GA 30313	404-525-1533	R	8*	.1
171	US Armor Corp—*Stephen Armellino*	16433 Valley View Ave, Cerritos CA 90703	562-207-4240	R	8*	<.1
172	Consensus Orthopedics—*Colleen Gray*	1115 Windfield Way Ste, El Dorado Hills CA 95762	916-355-7100	R	8*	<.1
173	VitalWear Inc—*Howard Edelman*	384 Oyster Point Blvd, S San Francisco CA 94080		R	8	<.1
174	General Econopak Inc—*James Baxter*	1725 N 6th St, Philadelphia PA 19122	215-763-8200	R	8*	.1
175	Premier Brands Of America Inc—*Steven Corsun*	31 S St Ste 2s, Mount Vernon NY 10550	914-667-6200	R	8*	.1
176	Instrumedical Technologies Inc—*H Miller*	727 N Detroit St, Warsaw IN 46580	574-269-1982	R	8*	.1
177	Opportunity Inc—*Lawrence Rosser*	PO Box 1349, Deerfield IL 60015	847-831-9400	R	8*	.1
178	Wellman Holding Co—*Maynard Wellman*	13800 Luick Dr, Chelsea MI 48118	734-475-9165	R	8*	.1
179	Chase Ergonomics Inc—*David Chase*	PO Box 92497, Albuquerque NM 87199	505-345-8488	R	7*	.1
180	Coolsystems Inc—*Tom Oliver*	1201 Marina Village Pk, Alameda CA 94501	510-868-2120	R	7*	.1
181	Williams Sound LLC—*Paul Ingebrightsen*	10300 Valley View Rd, Eden Prairie MN 55344	952-943-2252	R	7*	.1
182	Baja Products Ltd—*Randall Price*	4065 N Romero Rd, Tucson AZ 85705	520-887-1154	R	7*	.1
183	Dental Prosthetics of Tucson Inc—*Wendell Herr*	4545 E Fort Lowell Rd, Tucson AZ 85712	520-722-4484	R	7*	<.1
184	Newton C R Company Ltd—*David R Newton*	1575 S Beretania St St, Honolulu HI 96826	808-949-8389	R	7*	<.1
185	Greendale Home Fashions LLC—*Becky Tucker*	420 Springfield Pke, Cincinnati OH 45215	513-342-4362	R	7*	.1
186	Higgins Supply Company Inc—*Cathy Gregg*	18-23 S St, Mc Graw NY 13101	607-836-6474	R	7*	.1
187	La Nair Company Inc—*Raymond Allen*	PO Box 20506, Houston TX 77225	713-524-2813	R	7*	<.1
188	Medi Manufacturing Inc—*Michael Weihermueller*	PO Box 3000, Whitsett NC 27377	336-449-4440	R	6*	.1
189	Sebotek Hearing Systems LLC—*Dianne Beechy*	2488 E 81st St Ste 200, Tulsa OK 74137	918-388-9000	R	6*	.1
190	Cropper Medical Inc—*Dean Cropper*	240 E Hersey St Ste 2, Ashland OR 97520	541-488-0600	R	6*	.1
191	Yanke Bionics Inc—*Mark Yanke*	303 W Exchange St, Akron OH 44302	330-762-6411	R	6*	.1
192	Anulex Technologies Inc—*Jeff Peters*	5600 Rowland Rd Ste 28, Minnetonka MN 55343	952-224-4000	R	6*	.1
193	Maitland Engineering Inc—*Patricia Clark*	2713 Foundation Dr, South Bend IN 46628	574-287-0155	R	6*	<.1
194	Rochester Orthopedic Laboratories Inc—*David Forbes*	460 White Spruce Blvd, Rochester NY 14623	585-272-1060	R	6*	<.1
195	Homecare Products Inc—*Don Everard*	700 Milwaukee Ave, Algona WA 98001	253-631-4633	R	6*	<.1
196	K W Griffen Co—*James Brown*	100 Pearl St, Norwalk CT 06850	203-846-1923	R	6*	.1
197	Central Fabrication Inc—*Ronald Snell*	PO Box 34488, Memphis TN 38184	901-725-0060	R	6*	<.1
198	Applied Composite Technology Inc—*Roland Christensen*	192 E 100 N, Fayette UT 84630	435-528-7199	R	6*	<.1
199	Occunomix International LLC—*Jim Preston*	585 Bicycle Path Ste 5, Port Jefferson Station NY 11776	631-741-1940	R	6*	<.1
200	Golden Ross Industries Inc—*Ron Guilani*	5720 S 2nd St, Vernon CA 90058	323-588-1999	R	5*	<.1
201	Frank Stubbs Company Inc—*David Pearson*	1830 Eastman Ave, Oxnard CA 93030	805-278-4300	R	5*	<.1
202	Authorized Earmold Labs—*Henry Smith*	806 Beaver St, Bristol PA 19007	215-788-0330	R	5*	<.1
203	Gema Inc—*Gene Bernardoni*	2434 W Peterson Ave, Chicago IL 60659	773-878-2445	R	5*	<.1
204	Swede-O Inc—*Patrick Quinn*	PO Box 610, North Branch MN 55056	651-674-8301	R	5*	<.1
205	Continental Metal Products Company Inc—*Paul Siegal*	PO Box 2295, Woburn MA 01888	781-935-4400	R	5*	<.1
206	Image Molding Inc—*Ewan Grantham*	4525 Kingston St, Denver CO 80239	303-371-3338	R	5*	<.1
207	Carwild Corp—*Joel Wildstein*	3 State Pier Rd, New London CT 06320	860-536-4914	R	5*	<.1
208	North American Rescue LLC—*Kimberly Salvi*	35 Tedwall Ct, Greer SC 29650	864-675-9800	R	5*	<.1
209	Biopro Inc—*Patrick Pringle*	2929 Lapeer Rd, Port Huron MI 48060	810-982-7777	R	5*	<.1
210	Armortex Inc—*Javier Trevino*	5926 Corridor Pkwy, Schertz TX 78154	210-661-8306	R	5*	<.1
211	Troutman Machine Shop Inc—*Ben Campbell*	424 Creamery Way, Exton PA 19341	610-363-5480	R	5*	<.1
212	American Surgical Sponges LLC—*Stephen Clifford*	82 Sanderson Ave Ste 2, Lynn MA 01902	781-592-7200	R	4*	<.1
213	Infab Corp—*Donald Cusick*	3651 Via Pescador, Camarillo CA 93012	805-987-5255	R	4*	<.1
214	Corflex Inc—*Paul Lorenzetti*	669 E Industrial Pk Dr, Manchester NH 03109	603-623-3344	R	4*	<.1
215	Hermell Products Inc—*Ronald Pollack*	PO Box 7345, Bloomfield CT 06002	860-242-6550	R	4*	<.1
216	Brown Medical Industries Inc—*Ivan Brown*	1300 Lundberg Dr W, Spirit Lake IA 51360	712-336-4395	R	4*	<.1
217	Envision Products Inc—*Alan Miller*	1711 S Pennsylvania Av, Morrisville PA 19067	215-428-1791	R	4*	<.1
218	Activeaid—*Mark Oja*	PO Box 359, Redwood Falls MN 56283	507-644-2951	R	4*	<.1
219	Mckeon Products Inc—*Devin Benner*	25460 Guenther, Warren MI 48091	586-427-7560	R	4*	<.1
220	Southwest Technologies Inc—*John Phillips*	1746 Levee Rd, Kansas City MO 64116	816-221-2442	R	4*	<.1
221	Hans Rudolph Inc—*Kevin Rudolph*	8325 Cole Pkwy, Shawnee KS 66227	913-422-7788	R	4*	<.1
222	Medi-Tech International Corp—*Jacqueline Fortunato*	26 Ct St Ste 1301, Brooklyn NY 11242	718-875-4535	R	4*	<.1
223	American Orthopedics Inc—*Richard Nitsch*	1151 W 5th Ave, Columbus OH 43212	614-291-6454	R	4*	<.1
224	Adaptive Switch Laboratories Inc—*Rucker Ashmore*	125 Spur 191 Ste C, Spicewood TX 78669	830-798-0005	S	4*	<.1

Note: An asterisk (*) indicates an estimated financial figure. The company type code used is as follows: R = Private, P = Public, S = Private Subsidiary, B = Public Subsidiary, D = Division, J = Joint Venture, I = Investment Fund.

COMPANY RANKINGS BY SALES WITHIN 4-DIGIT SIC

Rank	Company Name—*Executive Officer*	Address, City, State, Zip	Phone	Type	Fin	Empls
	Invacare Corp					
225	Southpaw Enterprises Inc—*Frank Howard*	PO Box 1047, Dayton OH 45401	937-252-7676	R	4*	<.1
226	Ansell Sandel Medical Solutions LLC—*Steve Leatherman*	19736 Dearborn St, Chatsworth CA 91311	818-534-2500	R	4*	<.1
227	Beaudry Co—*David Chenal*	PO Box 220, Frederic WI 54837	715-327-4274	R	4*	<.1
228	New Options Inc—*John Scott*	2545 Merrell Rd, Dallas TX 75229	214-638-6422	R	4*	<.1
229	Nu-Hope Laboratories Inc—*Bradley Galindo*	12640 Branford St, Pacoima CA 91331	818-899-7711	R	4*	<.1
230	Pro Orthopedic Devices Inc—*Gerald Detty*	2884 E Ganley Rd, Tucson AZ 85706	520-294-4401	R	4*	<.1
231	Arveda LLC—*Barbara Bielser*	PO Box 1230, Hays KS 67601	785-625-4674	R	4*	<.1
232	Pos-T-Vac Inc—*Edward Stewart*	PO Box 1436, Dodge City KS 67801	620-227-7434	R	4*	<.1
233	Calton Dental Lab—*Larry Calton*	119 Se 11th Ave, Gainesville FL 32601	352-376-3041	R	3*	<.1
234	Ever-Flex Inc—*Merel Epstein*	12505 Universal Dr, Taylor MI 48180	734-947-2060	R	3*	<.1
235	Sure Foot Corp—*Jon Larson*	1401 Dyke Ave, Grand Forks ND 58203	701-775-9560	R	3*	<.1
236	Junkin Safety Appliance Company Inc—*W Mercke*	3121 Millers Ln, Louisville KY 40216	502-775-8303	R	3*	<.1
237	Amken Orthopedics Inc—*Albert Sumell*	299 Duffy Ave Unit B, Hicksville NY 11801	516-933-9255	R	3*	<.1
238	New England Brace Company Inc—*Paul Guimond*	15 Nelson St Unit 1, Manchester NH 03103	603-668-8360	R	3*	<.1
239	Ortho Rite Inc—*Gregory Sands*	65 Plain Ave, New Rochelle NY 10801	914-235-9100	R	3*	<.1
240	Trulife—*Noel Murphy*	2010 E High St, Jackson MI 49203		R	3*	<.1
241	Citmed Corp—*John Basset*	PO Box 67, Citronelle AL 36522	251-866-5519	R	3*	<.1
242	Therafirm Compression Products—*James Wright*	120 Osage Ave, Kansas City KS 66105	913-281-4600	S	3*	.1
	Knit-Rite Inc					
243	A-T Surgical Manufacturing Company Inc—*Eugene Kirejczyk*	115 Clemente St, Holyoke MA 01040	413-532-4551	R	3*	<.1
244	Clear Tone Hearing Center Inc—*Jim Feeley*	2323 S Sheridan Rd, Tulsa OK 74129	918-838-1000	R	3*	<.1
245	Ongoing Care Solutions Inc—*Richard Nace*	6545 44th St N Ste 400, Pinellas Park FL 33781	727-526-0707	R	3*	<.1
246	Bio Med Packaging Systems Inc—*James Brown*	100 Pearl St, Norwalk CT 06850	203-846-1923	R	3*	<.1
247	Bar-Ray Products Inc—*Jeff Stein*	PO Box 36, Littlestown PA 17340	717-359-9100	R	3*	<.1
248	Eschen Orthotic and Prosthetics Company Inc—*Glenn Garrison*	510 E 73rd St Ste 201, New York NY 10021	212-606-1262	R	3*	<.1
249	Phoenix Biomedical Corp—*Charles Hokanson*	PO Box 80390, Valley Forge PA 19484	610-539-9300	R	3*	<.1
250	Jackson Brace and Limb Co—*Wesley Wilson*	1320 N State St, Jackson MS 39202	601-353-2477	R	3*	<.1
251	Seaberg Company Inc—*Sam Scheinberg*	4909 S Coast Hwy Ste 2, Newport OR 97365	541-867-4726	R	3*	<.1
252	Sunrise Machine and Tool Inc—*Keith Lecleir*	1380 Legion Rd, Detroit Lakes MN 56501	218-847-3386	R	3*	<.1
253	Mechanical Safety Equipment Corp—*Meyer Ostrobrod*	2070 Bennett Rd, Philadelphia PA 19116	215-676-7828	R	3*	<.1
254	Contour Pak Inc—*Alice Mayn*	PO Box 41, Forest Knolls CA 94933	925-631-9601	R	3*	<.1
255	Pulse Medical Inc—*Barbara Boyce*	4131 Sw 47th Ave Ste 1, Davie FL 33314	954-587-8867	R	3*	<.1
256	Super Seer Corp—*Steven Smith*	PO Box 700, Evergreen CO 80437	303-674-6663	R	3*	<.1
257	Ken Mar Machine Manufacturing Corp—*Kenneth Walder*	477 E 30th St, Paterson NJ 07504	973-278-5827	R	3*	<.1
258	All American Amputee—*Rod Friedland*	2763 W Old Us Hwy 441, Mount Dora FL 32757	352-383-0396	R	3*	<.1
259	C D Denison Orthopaedic Appliance Corp—*Harold Thompson*	32 W Rd Ste 120, Towson MD 21204	410-235-9645	R	3*	<.1
260	Tillges Certified Orthotic Prosthetic Inc—*Robert Tillges*	1570 Beam Ave Ste 100, Saint Paul MN 55109	651-772-2665	R	2*	<.1
261	Snug Seat Inc—*Kirk Mackenzie*	PO Box 1739, Matthews NC 28105	704-882-0668	R	2*	<.1
262	Brennen Medical LLC—*Tim Lawin*	1290 Hammond Rd Ste 2, Saint Paul MN 55110	651-429-7413	R	2*	<.1
263	Emtech Laboratories Inc—*Moses Nakhle*	PO Box 12900, Roanoke VA 24022	540-265-9156	R	2*	.1
264	Back-Mueller Inc—*Maryann Back*	2700 Clark Ave, Saint Louis MO 63103	314-531-6640	R	2*	<.1
265	Excel Prosthetics and Orthotics Inc—*Douglas Walters*	115 Albemarle Ave Se, Roanoke VA 24013	540-982-0205	R	2*	<.1
266	Sroufe Healthcare Products LLC—*Deb Glaze*	PO Box 347, Ligonier IN 46767	260-894-4174	R	2*	<.1
267	Custom Carbon Composite Creations Inc—*Eddie Rogers*	693 Hi Tech Pkwy, Oakdale CA 95361	209-845-2930	R	2*	<.1
268	Scott Sabolich Prosthetics and Research Center LLC	10201 Broadway Ext, Oklahoma City OK 73114	405-841-6800	R	2*	<.1
269	Specialty Brace and Limb—*Nancy Smith*	1222 Orange Ave Ste B, Winter Park FL 32789	407-740-7772	R	2*	<.1
270	Newgen Advanced Orthotics Laboratory—*Michael Cohen*	2092 Dalkeith Dr, Germantown TN 38139	901-756-0257	R	2*	<.1
271	J-K Prosthetics and Orthotics Inc—*Jack Caputo*	699 N Macquesten Pkwy, Mount Vernon NY 10552	914-699-2077	R	2*	<.1
272	Bath-Tec Inc—*William Griffin*	PO Box 1118, Ennis TX 75120	972-646-5279	R	2*	<.1
273	Actall Corp—*Robert Hampe*	3925 Monaco Pkwy Unit, Denver CO 80207	303-487-4222	R	2*	<.1
274	Texas Medical Industries Inc—*Susan Chambers*	1409 Industrial Dr, Royse City TX 75189	972-636-9898	R	2*	<.1
275	Lambert's Orthotics And Prosthetics Inc—*George Lambert*	PO Box 66376, Baton Rouge LA 70896	225-769-2591	R	2*	<.1
276	Cocco Brothers—*Carlo Cocco*	2745 W Passyunk Ave, Philadelphia PA 19145	215-334-3816	R	2*	<.1
277	Us Biomaterials Corp—*Randolph Scott*	1551 Atl Blvd Ste 105, Jacksonville FL 32207	386-418-1551	R	2*	<.1
278	Anjon Inc—*John Knapik*	4801 Dawin Rd, Jacksonville FL 32207	904-730-9373	R	2*	<.1
279	Jsb Orthotics and Medical Supply Inc—*Scott Becker*	509 Paul Morris Dr, Englewood FL 34223	941-473-0620	R	2*	<.1
280	Bio-Concepts Inc—*Frank Reichenbacher*	2424 E University Dr, Phoenix AZ 85034	602-267-7854	R	2*	<.1
281	Brownfields Incorporated Of Boise—*Barrett Jones*	122 N 5th St, Boise ID 83702	208-342-4659	R	2*	<.1
282	Cleveland Medical Devices Inc—*Hani Kayyali*	4415 Euclid Ave Ste 40, Cleveland OH 44103	216-791-6720	R	2*	<.1
283	Mayflower Splint Co—*Inge Krueger*	PO Box 381, Huntington Station NY 11746	631-549-5131	R	2*	<.1
284	Med-Techna Inc—*John Snowden*	297 High St, Dedham MA 02026	781-326-3939	R	2*	<.1
285	Hanger Medical Center Brace Company Inc—*Marc Kowatic*	33 S 19th St, Pittsburgh PA 15203	412-431-3553	R	2*	<.1
286	Southeastern Orthotics Prosthetics Inc—*John Gilbreath*	PO Box 3357, Chattanooga TN 37404	423-698-0184	R	2*	<.1
287	AcryMed Inc—*Dan Pike*	9560 SW Nimbus Ave, Beaverton OR 97008	503-624-9830	R	2*	<.1
288	Kingsley ManufacturingCo—*Jeffery Kingsley*	PO Box 5010, Costa Mesa CA 92628	949-645-4401	R	2*	<.1
289	Bell-Horn Inc (Carmel Indianapolis)—*Todd Katz*	4511 W 99th St, Carmel IN 46032	317-228-1144	R	2*	<.1
290	Summit Medical Inc—*Curt Miller*	1270 Eagan Industrial, Saint Paul MN 55121	651-452-1977	S	2*	<.1
291	E Benson Hood Laboratories Inc—*Lewis H Marten*	575 Washington St, Pembroke MA 02359	781-826-7573	R	2*	<.1
292	Fidelity Orthopedic Inc—*Hillmo Hodzic*	8514 N Main St, Dayton OH 45415	937-228-0682	R	2*	<.1
293	InterMed Holdings Inc—*Harry Davies*	18 Commerce Rd, Newtown CT 06470	203-270-0677	R	2*	<.1
294	ADCO South Medical Supplies Inc—*Burton Firtel*	346 Pike Rd Ste 1, West Palm Beach FL 33411	561-688-1264	S	2*	<.1
295	Bell Hearing Instruments Inc—*William Bell*	PO Box 1888, Oldsmar FL 34677	813-814-2355	R	2*	<.1
296	Andrade and Ashworth Inc—*Charles Andrade*	PO Box 939, Westbrook CT 06498	860-399-5577	R	2*	<.1
297	Tri W-G Inc—*Leigh Berg*	PO Box 905, Valley City ND 58072	701-845-3984	R	2*	<.1
298	Psi/Eye-Ko Inc—*Stacy Beriford*	804 Corporate Centre D, O Fallon MO 63368	636-447-1010	R	2*	<.1
299	Brannock Device Company Inc—*Salvatore Leonardi*	116 Luther Ave, Liverpool NY 13088	315-475-9862	R	2*	<.1
300	A-M Systems LLC—*Phil Brown*	PO Box 850, Carlsborg WA 98324	360-683-8300	R	2*	<.1
301	Pg Drives Technology Inc—*Phyllis Abramf*	2532 E Cerritos Ave, Anaheim CA 92806	714-712-7911	S	2*	<.1
302	Magister Corp—*David Maley*	PO Box 4323, Chattanooga TN 37405	423-265-3574	R	2*	<.1
303	Oxlife Of Nc LLC—*Dean Hardesty*	141 Twin Springs Rd, Hendersonville NC 28792	828-684-7353	R	2*	<.1
304	Stand Aid Of Iowa Inc—*Mike Kleinwolterink*	1009 2nd Ave, Sheldon IA 51201	712-324-2153	R	2*	<.1
305	Carolina Brace Manufacturers Inc—*Tim Owens*	PO Box 36953, Charlotte NC 28236	704-332-5143	R	2*	<.1
306	Myer Show Print Inc—*Hugo Maisnik*	5720 E Union Pacific A, Commerce CA 90022	323-727-1231	R	2	<.1
307	Alex Orthopedic Inc—*Ebrahim Lavi*	PO Box 201442, Arlington TX 76006	972-641-9680	R	2	<.1
308	Ultimatecare Services Inc—*Felix Nwadjei*	PO Box 1602, Gardena CA 90249	310-970-9727	R	1*	<.1
309	D Audio Ltd—*Ed Gauthier*	885 Roosevelt Trl, Windham ME 04062	207-893-2920	R	1*	<.1
310	Orthotic And Prostetic Specialties Inc—*Richard Gaudio*	20650 Lakeland Blvd, Euclid OH 44119	216-531-2773	R	1*	<.1
311	Becker Oregon Inc—*Kyle Scott*	2280 Three Lakes Rd Se, Albany OR 97322	541-967-1821	R	1*	<.1

Rank	Company Name—*Executive Officer*	Address, City, State, Zip	Phone	Type	Fin	Empls
312	Precision Intricast Inc—*Paul Rasmussen*	1323 W Red Baron Rd, Payson AZ 85541	928-474-9707	R	1*	<.1
313	A and L Shielding Inc—*L Roberts*	268 Old Lindale Rd Se, Rome GA 30161	706-235-8822	R	1*	<.1
314	Hyperbaric Oxygen Therapy Systems Inc—*WT Gurnee*	PO Box 1987, National City CA 91950	619-336-2022	S	1*	.2
315	Duralife Inc—*Daniel Day*	195 Phillips Park Dr S, Williamsport PA 17702	570-323-9743	R	1*	<.1
316	Zygo Industries Inc—*Lawrence Weiss*	PO Box 1008, Portland OR 97207	503-684-6006	R	1*	<.1
317	Minto Research and Development Inc	20270 Charlanne Dr, Redding CA 96002	530-222-2373	R	1*	<.1
318	MED-E-CELL—*Henri Maget*	10633 Roselle St, San Diego CA 92121	858-552-0781	R	1*	<.1
319	Hartwell Medical Corp—*Gary R Williams*	6352 Corte Del Abeto S, Carlsbad CA 92009	760-438-5500	R	1*	<.1
320	Pediatric Prosthetics Inc—*Linda Putback-Bean*	12926 Willowchase Dr, Houston TX 77070		R	1*	<.1
321	Pro-Kold Corp—*Becky Brink*	2607 N Moore Ave, Moore OK 73160	405-237-1688	R	1*	<.1
322	Maloney's Custom Ocular Prosthetics Inc—*Maureen Maloney-Schou*	4035 SW Mercantile Dr, Lake Oswego OR 97035	503-675-1320	R	1*	<.1
323	Albemarle Orthotics and Prosthetics Inc—*W Truesdale*	PO Box 1471, Elizabeth City NC 27906	252-338-3002	R	1*	<.1
324	B and B Lingerie Company Inc—*Stacie Neely*	PO Box 5731, Boise ID 83705	208-343-9696	R	1*	<.1
325	Fox Bay Industries Inc—*Wayne Walker*	4150 B Pl Nw Ste 101, Auburn WA 98001	253-941-9155	R	1*	.1
326	Smith and Nephew Inc—*Genevieve Berger*	7135 Goodlett Farms Pk, Cordova TN 38016	901-396-2121	R	1*	.1
327	Whitney Products Inc—*Steven Whitney*	6153 W Mulford St Ste, Niles IL 60714	847-470-9300	R	1*	<.1
328	Chenica Inc—*Chris Chen*	PO Box 308, Millington MI 48746	989-871-4529	R	1*	<.1
329	Pathfinder Cell Therapy Inc—*Richard Franklin*	200 Middlesex Essex Tp, Iselin NJ 08830	732-404-1117	R	<1	<.1
330	Urban Ag Corp—*Marshall Sterman*	68 Phillips Beach Ave, Swampscott MA 01907	781-389-9703	P	<1	<.1

TOTALS: SIC 3842 Surgical Appliances & Supplies
Companies: 330

					56,402	213.9

3843 Dental Equipment & Supplies

Rank	Company Name—*Executive Officer*	Address, City, State, Zip	Phone	Type	Fin	Empls
1	Nobel Biocare USA LLC—*Domenico Scala*	22715 Savi Ranch Pkwy, Yorba Linda CA 92887	714-282-4800	S	3,792*	2.4
2	DENTSPLY International Inc—*Bret W Wise*	PO Box 872, York PA 17405	717-845-7511	P	2,538	11.8
3	Sirona Dental Systems Inc—*Jost Fischer*	3030 47th Ave Ste 500, Long Island City NY 11101	718-482-2011	P	914	2.7
4	Sybron Dental Specialties Inc—*Dan Even*	1717 W Collins Ave, Orange CA 92867	714-516-7400	S	650	4.1
5	Ivoclar Vivadent Inc—*Robert A Ganley*	175 Pineview Dr, Amherst NY 14228	716-691-0010	R	508*	2.1
6	A-Dec Inc—*George Austin*	PO Box 111, Newberg OR 97132	503-538-9471	R	151*	1.9
7	Young Innovations Inc—*Alfred E Brennan*	13705 Shoreline Ct E, Earth City MO 63045	314-344-0010	P	103	.4
8	Heraeus Kulzer LLC—*Peter Bentley*	300 Heraeus Dr, South Bend IN 46614	574-299-5430	R	100*	.2
9	Hu Friedy Manufacturing Company LLC—*Ken Serota*	3232 N Rockwell St, Chicago IL 60618	773-975-6100	R	93*	.6
10	Fujinon Inc—*Takeshi Higuchi*	10 Highpoint Dr, Wayne NJ 07470	973-633-5600	R	85*	.1
11	Ormco Corp—*Don Tuttle* Sybron Dental Specialties Inc	1717 W Collins Ave, Orange CA 92867	714-516-7400	S	84*	1.2
12	Kerr Corp—*Floyd Pickrel* Sybron Dental Specialties Inc	1717 W Collins Ave, Orange CA 92867	714-516-7400	S	67*	.4
13	Takara Belmont USA Inc—*Hidetaka Yoshikawa*	101 Belmont Dr, Somerset NJ 08873	732-469-5000	R	34*	.2
14	Jeneric/Pentron Inc—*Gordon Cohen*	53 N Plains Industrial, Wallingford CT 06492	203-265-3886	R	32*	.3
15	Biolase Technology Inc—*Federico Pignatelli*	4 Cromwell, Irvine CA 92618	949-361-1200	P	26	.1
16	Whip-Mix Corp—*Allen Steinbock*	PO Box 17183, Louisville KY 40217	502-637-1451	R	26*	.2
17	Unicep Packaging Inc—*John Snedden*	1702 Industrial Dr, Sandpoint ID 83864	208-265-9696	R	21*	.1
18	Young Dental Manufacturing LLC Young Innovations Inc	13705 Shoreline Ct E, Earth City MO 63045	314-344-0010	D	18*	.1
19	CMP Industries Inc—*William Regan*	413 N Pearl St, Albany NY 12207	518-434-3147	R	16*	.1
20	Jensen Industries Slc Inc—*David Stine*	PO Box 514, North Haven CT 06473	203-239-2090	R	15*	.1
21	Aseptico Inc—*Douglas Kazen*	PO Box 1548, Woodinville WA 98072	425-487-3157	R	14*	.1
22	DENTSPLY Rinn—*Gary Kunkle* DENTSPLY International Inc	1212 Abbott Dr, Elgin IL 60123	847-742-1115	S	14*	.1
23	Parkell Products Inc—*Karen Mitchell*	300 Executive Dr, Edgewood NY 11717	631-249-1134	R	14*	.1
24	Biohorizons Implant Systems Inc—*Steve Boggan*	2300 Riverchase Ctr, Hoover AL 35244	205-967-7880	R	14*	.1
25	Centrix Inc—*William Dragan*	770 River Rd, Shelton CT 06484	203-929-5582	R	13*	.1
26	Bisco Inc—*Byoung Suh*	1100 W Irving Park Rd, Schaumburg IL 60193	847-534-6000	R	13*	.1
27	Selane Products Inc—*Rob Veis*	PO Box 4184, Van Nuys CA 91409	818-998-7460	R	11*	.1
28	Issaquah Dental Lab Inc—*Larry Searles*	640 Nw Gilman Blvd Ste, Issaquah WA 98027	425-392-5125	R	10*	.1
29	Novocol Inc—*Kent Chiu*	416 S Taylor Ave, Louisville CO 80027	303-665-7535	R	10*	.2
30	Imaging Sciences International Inc—*Henry Tancredi*	1910 N Penn Rd, Hatfield PA 19440	215-997-5666	R	9*	.1
31	Cmp Industries LLC—*Richard Adamson*	413 N Pearl St, Albany NY 12207	518-434-3147	R	9*	<.1
32	ClearCorrect Inc—*Jarrett Pumphrey*	15151 Sommermeyer St, Houston TX 77041	713-850-1036	R	9	.1
33	North Star Orthodontics Inc—*John Kelly*	PO Box 146, Park Rapids MN 56470	218-732-9503	R	9*	.1
34	Royal Dental Manufacturing Inc—*Harold Tai*	12414 Hwy 99 Ste 29, Everett WA 98204	425-743-0988	R	9*	.1
35	Boyd Industries Inc—*Bruce Livingston*	12900 44th St N, Clearwater FL 33762	727-561-9292	R	8*	.1
36	Lares Research—*Craig Lares*	295 Lockheed Ave, Chico CA 95973	530-345-1767	R	8*	.1
37	Dci Holdings Inc—*John Spencer*	305 N Springbrook Rd, Newberg OR 97132	503-538-8343	R	8*	.1
38	Pulpdent Corp—*Fred Berk*	PO Box 780, Watertown MA 02471	617-926-6666	R	7*	.1
39	Prodenco Group Inc—*Guy Watkins*	611 Omaha St, Sioux City IA 51103	712-252-4034	R	7*	.1
40	Columbia Dentoform Corp—*Jeffrey Perelman*	3424 Hunters Point Ave, Long Island City NY 11101	718-482-1569	R	7*	.1
41	Nu Life Restorations Of L I Inc—*Mark Marinbach*	PO Box 297, West Hempstead NY 11552	516-489-5200	R	7*	.1
42	Dux Industries Inc—*Don Porteous*	600 E Hueneme Rd, Oxnard CA 93033	805-488-1122	R	7*	.1
43	Camsight Company Inc—*Ben Yoo*	3368 N Sn Fernndo Rd 1, Los Angeles CA 90065	323-259-1900	R	6*	.1
44	Buffalo Dental Manufacturing Company Inc—*Donald Nevin*	PO Box 678, Syosset NY 11791	516-496-7200	R	6*	.1
45	Zirc Co—*Jim Campion*	3918 Hwy 55 SE, Buffalo MN 55313	763-682-6636	R	6*	.1
46	Lancer Orthodontics Inc—*Allen Barbieri* Biomerica Inc	2330 Cousteau Ct, Vista CA 92081	760-744-5585	B	6	<.1
47	Harry J Bosworth Co—*Mildred Goldstein*	7227 Hamlin Ave, Skokie IL 60076	847-679-3400	R	6*	.1
48	Dexta Corp—*Mark Rusin*	962 Kaiser Rd, Napa CA 94558	707-255-2454	R	6*	.1
49	Nordent Manufacturing Inc—*Richard Martin*	610 Bonnie Ln, Elk Grove Village IL 60007	847-437-4780	R	6*	<.1
50	Biotec Inc—*Harold Tai*	652 E Main Ave, Zeeland MI 49464	616-772-2133	R	5*	.1
51	Biomerica Inc—*Zackary S Irani*	17571 Von Karman Ave, Irvine CA 92614	949-645-2111	P	5	<.1
52	Dyna Flex Of Missouri LP—*Darren Buddemeyer*	10403 International Pl, Saint Ann MO 63074	314-426-4020	R	5*	<.1
53	CDB Corp—*Markus Hirsch*	9201 Industrial Blvd N, Leland NC 28451	910-383-6464	R	5*	.1
54	Lang Dental Manufacturing Company Inc—*David Lang*	PO Box 969, Wheeling IL 60090	847-215-6622	R	5*	<.1
55	Handler Manufacturing Company Inc—*William Lehman*	PO Box 520, Westfield NJ 07091	908-233-7796	R	5*	<.1
56	Proma Inc—*Harold Tai*	730 Kingshill Pl, Carson CA 90746	310-327-0035	R	4*	<.1
57	Laclede Inc—*Michael Pellico*	2103 E University Dr, Compton CA 90220	310-605-4280	R	4*	<.1
58	Temrex Corp—*Alda Levander*	112 Albany Ave, Freeport NY 11520	516-868-6221	R	4*	<.1
59	Orthopli Corp—*William Tippy*	10061 Sandmeyer Ln, Philadelphia PA 19116	215-671-1000	R	4*	<.1
60	Terrafina Inc—*Richard Jahns*	PO Box 248, Greenwood IN 46142	317-346-6655	R	4*	<.1

Note: An asterisk (*) indicates an estimated financial figure. The company type code used is as follows: R = Private, P = Public, S = Private Subsidiary, B = Public Subsidiary, D = Division, J = Joint Venture, I = Investment Fund.

COMPANY RANKINGS BY SALES WITHIN 4-DIGIT SIC

Rank	Company Name—*Executive Officer*	Address, City, State, Zip	Phone	Type	Fin	Empls
61	Danville Manufacturing Inc—*Mark Fernwood*	3420 Fostoria Way Ste, San Ramon CA 94583	925-973-0710	R	4*	<.1
62	Tech West Vacuum Inc—*John Napier*	2625 N Argyle Ave, Fresno CA 93727	559-291-1650	R	4*	<.1
63	Engle Dental Systems Inc—*Lewis Engle*	PO Box 725, Forest Grove OR 97116	503-359-9390	R	3*	<.1
64	Sterngold Dental LLC—*Austin Carr*	PO Box 2967, Attleboro MA 02703	508-226-5660	R	3*	<.1
65	Hand Piece Parts And Products Inc—*Stan Bowen*	707 W Angus Ave, Orange CA 92868	714-997-4331	R	3*	<.1
66	American Consolidated Manufacturing Co—*Rick Slack*	2 Union Hill Rd, Conshohocken PA 19428	610-825-2630	R	3*	<.1
67	Replacement Parts Industries Inc—*Ira Lapides*	PO Box 5019, Chatsworth CA 91313	818-882-8611	R	3*	<.1
68	G Hartzell and Son Inc—*Andy Hartzell*	PO Box 5988, Concord CA 94524	925-798-2206	R	3*	<.1
69	Orthodontic Technologies Inc—*Diane Johnson*	PO Box 4871, Houston TX 77210	713-861-0033	R	3*	<.1
70	Endodent Inc—*Jerry Sullivan*	851 Meridian St, Duarte CA 91010	626-359-5715	R	3*	<.1
71	Ortho Arch Laboratory Inc—*Jeffrey Maki*	PO Box 600, Kingsford Heights IN 46346	219-393-5591	R	3*	<.1
72	Cataki International Inc—*Michael Diesso*	PO Box 939, East Wareham MA 02538	508-295-9630	R	2*	<.1
73	Pascal Company Inc—*David Watton*	PO Box 1478, Bellevue WA 98009	425-827-4694	R	2*	<.1
74	Engler Engineering Corp—*Eva Engler*	1099 E 47th St, Hialeah FL 33013	305-688-8581	R	2*	<.1
75	Kinetic Instruments Inc—*William Becker*	17 Berkshire Blvd, Bethel CT 06801	203-743-0080	R	2*	<.1
76	Westar Medical Products Inc—*Ruth Haller*	4470 Chennault Beach Rd, Mukilteo WA 98275	425-290-3945	R	2*	<.1
77	Marque Dental Laboratory Inc—*Darrell Fey*	PO Box 10278, Fargo ND 58106	701-235-2932	R	2*	<.1
78	Pemaco Inc—*Ken Perkowski*	2030 S 3rd St, Saint Louis MO 63104	314-231-3399	R	2*	<.1
79	Myotronics Noromed Inc—*Fray Adib*	5870 S 194th St, Kent WA 98032	206-243-4214	R	2*	<.1
80	Viade Products Inc—*Keith Zinser*	354 Dawson Dr, Camarillo CA 93012	805-484-2114	R	2*	<.1
81	Superior Dental and Surgical Manufacturing Inc—*Donald Jochum*	1501 Se Village Green, Port Saint Lucie FL 34952	772-335-5200	R	1*	<.1
82	Jasinski Dental Lab Inc—*Hubert Jasinski*	1141 Smile Ln, Lansdale PA 19446	215-699-8861	R	1*	<.1
83	Wells Dental Inc—*Richard Wells*	PO Box 106, Comptche CA 95427	707-937-0521	R	1*	<.1
84	Rmo Inc—*Jody Whitson*	PO Box 17085, Denver CO 80217	303-592-8200	R	1*	.3
85	Ortho Arch Co—*Michael C Zerafa*	1185 Tower Rd, Schaumburg IL 60173	847-885-7805	R	1*	<.1
86	Orthogen Corp—*Harold Alexander*	505 Morris Ave, Springfield NJ 07081	973-467-2404	R	1*	<.1
87	Orthodontic Supply Corporation and Research Inc—*Evelyn Lindquist*	11793 Technology Ln, Fishers IN 46038	317-849-2618	R	1*	<.1
88	Wykle Research Inc—*Lorraine Weikel*	2222 College Pkwy, Carson City NV 89706	775-887-7500	R	1*	<.1
89	Alger Equipment Company Inc—*David Alger*	320 Flightline Rd, Lago Vista TX 78645	512-267-0383	R	<1*	<.1

TOTALS: SIC 3843 Dental Equipment & Supplies
Companies: 89

					9,633	32.7

3844 X-Ray Apparatus & Tubes

Rank	Company Name—*Executive Officer*	Address, City, State, Zip	Phone	Type	Fin	Empls
1	Varian Medical Systems Inc—*Timothy Guertin*	3100 Hansen Way, Palo Alto CA 94304	650-493-4000	P	2,597	5.7
2	Hologic Inc—*Robert Cascella*	35 Crosby Dr, Bedford MA 01730	781-999-7300	P	1,789	5.0
3	GE OEC Medical Systems Inc—*Ruben Beruman*	384 Wright Brothers Dr, Salt Lake City UT 84116	801-328-9300	S	298*	1.0
4	American Science and Engineering Inc—*Anthony R Fabiano*	829 Middlesex Tpke, Billerica MA 01821	978-262-8700	P	279	.4
5	Del Medical Imaging Corp	50 N Gary Ave, Roselle IL 60172	847-288-7000	S	194*	.1
6	DMS Health Group—*Paul Wilson*	2101 N University Dr, Fargo ND 58102	701-237-9073	S	140*	.4
7	Bruker AXS Inc—*Frank Burgazy*	5465 E Cheryl Pky, Madison WI 53711	608-276-3000	S	104*	.6
8	DMS Imaging Inc	11600 96th Ave N, Maple Grove MN 55369	763-315-1947	S	89*	.3
9	Dunlee Inc—*Patrick Fitzgerald*	555 N Commerce St, Aurora IL 60504	630-585-2000	D	78*	.3
10	Medx Inc	3456 N Ridge Ave Ste 1, Arlington Heights IL 60004	847-463-2020	R	58*	<.1
11	Rigaku Americas Corp—*Yasuhiro Sugiyama*	9009 New Trails Dr, The Woodlands TX 77381	281-362-2300	R	26*	.2
12	Mettler-Toledo Safeline Inc—*Viggo Nielsen*	6005 Benjamin Rd, Tampa FL 33634	813-889-9500	R	18*	.1
13	S and S X-Ray Products Inc—*Norman Shoenfeld*	10625 Telge Rd, Houston TX 77095	281-815-1300	R	15*	.1
14	Ziehm Imaging Inc—*Michael Palazzola*	6280 Hzltine National, Orlando FL 32822	407-615-8560	R	14*	.1
15	X-Ray Cassette Repair Company Inc—*Leo Reina*	6107 W Lou Ave, Crystal Lake IL 60014	815-356-8181	R	8*	<.1
16	Photo Medic Equipment Inc—*Len Corso*	239 S Fehr Way, Bay Shore NY 11706	631-242-6600	R	8*	.1
17	Carr Corp—*John Carr*	1547 11th St, Santa Monica CA 90401	310-587-1113	R	7*	.1
18	Lsi International Inc—*Mark Glass*	640 Miami Ave, Kansas City KS 66105	913-894-4493	R	7*	<.1
19	Intraop Medical Corp—*John Powers*	570 Del Rey Ave, Sunnyvale CA 94085	408-636-1020	P	7	<.1
20	Progeny Inc—*Ed McDough*	675 Heathrow Dr, Lincolnshire IL 60069	847-415-9800	R	6*	<.1
21	Aribex Inc—*D Clark Turner*	744 S 400 E, Orem UT 84097	801-226-5522	R	6	<.1
22	Dilon Technologies Inc—*Robert Moussa*	12050 Jefferson Ave St, Newport News VA 23606	757-269-4910	R	4*	<.1
23	Advanced Instrument Development Inc—*Edward Polic*	2545 Curtiss St, Downers Grove IL 60515	630-271-9729	R	4*	<.1
24	Orthoscan Inc—*Rob Marocco*	8212 E Evans Rd, Scottsdale AZ 85260	480-503-8010	R	4*	<.1
25	Star X-Ray Company Inc—*Eric Rosen*	200 Marine St Ste B, Farmingdale NY 11735	631-454-0010	R	3*	<.1
26	American Medical Sales Inc—*Daniel Giesberg*	218 Bronwood Ave, Los Angeles CA 90049	310-219-3200	R	3*	<.1
27	YXLON International Inc—*Joseph Kosanetzky*	3400 Gilchrist Rd, Mogadore OH 44260	330-798-4800	S	3*	<.1
28	Enhanced Video Devices Inc—*Tom Carson*	9830 Summers Ridge Rd, San Diego CA 92121	858-530-0100	R	3*	<.1
29	Omega Medical Imaging Inc—*Robert Lindquist*	675 Hickman Cir, Sanford FL 32771	407-323-9400	R	3*	<.1
30	Willick Engineering Company Inc—*Dan Guerrero*	12516 Lakeland Rd, Santa Fe Springs CA 90670	562-946-4242	R	2*	<.1
31	Glenbrook Technologies Inc—*Gilbert Zweig*	11 Emery Ave, Randolph NJ 07869	973-361-8866	R	2*	<.1
32	Envision Cmosxray LLC—*Ky Holland*	7800 King St, Anchorage AK 99518	907-563-1141	R	2*	<.1
33	Security Defense Systems Corp—*Donna Korkala*	160 Park Ave Ste 1, Nutley NJ 07110	973-235-0606	R	1*	<.1
34	Digiray Corp—*Richard Albert*	PO Box 1083, Danville CA 94526	925-838-1510	R	<1*	<.1
35	Alvord Systems Inc—*Thomas Alvord*	620 Saint Clair Ave, Clairton PA 15025	412-233-3910	R	<1*	<.1

TOTALS: SIC 3844 X Ray Apparatus & Tubes
Companies: 35

					5,780	14.9

3845 Electromedical Equipment

Rank	Company Name—*Executive Officer*	Address, City, State, Zip	Phone	Type	Fin	Empls
1	Medtronic Inc—*D Camero Findlay*	710 Medtronic Pkwy, Minneapolis MN 55432	763-514-4000	P	15,933	45.0
2	Fresenius Medical Care North America—*Rice Powell*	920 Winter St, Waltham MA 02451	781-402-9000	S	9,700	30.0
3	St Jude Medical Cardiac Rhythm Management Div—*Daniel J Starks*	PO Box 9221, Sylmar CA 91392	818-362-6822	D	5,165*	16.0
4	Mallinckrodt Inc—*Timothy R Wright*	675 McDonnell Blvd, Hazelwood MO 63042	314-654-2000	S	2,951*	12.0
5	Ortho Clinical Diagnostics (Raritan New Jersey)—*Clifford Holland*	PO Box 350, Raritan NJ 08869	908-218-1300	S	1,491*	2.5
6	Astra Tech Inc—*Peter Selley*	590 Lincoln St, Waltham MA 02451	781-890-6800	S	946*	2.2
7	CONMED Corp—*Joseph Corasanti*	525 French Rd, Utica NY 13502	315-797-8375	P	694	3.4
8	Boston Scientific Scimed Inc—*Joseph Fitzgerald*	1 Scimed Pl, Maple Grove MN 55311	763-494-1700	S	533*	3.4
9	ZOLL Medical Corp—*Richard A Packer*	269 Mill Rd, Chelmsford MA 01824	978-421-9655	P	524	1.9
10	Thoratec Corp—*Gerhard F Burbach*	6035 Stoneridge Dr, Pleasanton CA 94588	925-847-8600	P	423	.8
11	ArthroCare Corp—*David F Fitzgerald*	7500 Rialto Blvd Bldg, Austin TX 78735	512-391-3900	P	355	1.6
12	Volcano Corp—*Scott Huennekens*	3661 Valley Centre Dr, San Diego CA 92130	916-638-8008	P	344	1.3
13	SonoSite Inc—*Kevin M Goodwin*	21919 30th Dr SE, Bothell WA 98021	425-951-1200	P	275	.9
14	Terumo Cardiovascular Systems Corp—*Mark Sutter*	6200 Jackson Rd, Ann Arbor MI 48103	734-663-4145	R	241*	.7

Rank	Company Name—Executive Officer	Address, City, State, Zip	Phone	Type	Fin	Empls
15	Natus Medical Inc—James B Hawkins	1501 Industrial Rd, San Carlos CA 94070	650-802-0400	P	219	.8
16	NxStage Medical Inc—Jeffrey H Burbank	439 S Union St 5th Fl, Lawrence MA 01843	978-687-4700	P	217	2.5
17	Olympus Surgical and Industrial America Inc—F Mark Gumz	3500 Corporate Pkwy, Center Valley PA 18034	484-896-5000	S	195*	.3
18	Cyberonics Inc—Daniel J Moore	100 Cyberonics Blvd, Houston TX 77058	281-228-7200	P	191	.5
19	Spectra-Physics Lasers Inc—Bruce Craig	PO Box 7013, Mountain View CA 94039	650-961-2550	S	175*	1.0
20	Agfa Materials Corp—Wojciech Balcewicz	1658 Bushy Park Rd, Goose Creek SC 29445	843-574-2600	R	170*	.1
21	Med Services Inc—Steven Cortese	100 Knickerbocker Ave, Bohemia NY 11716	631-218-6450	R	155*	.1
22	Candela Corp—Gerard E Puorro	530 Boston Post Rd, Wayland MA 01778	508-358-7400	S	130	N/A
23	Laserscope Inc	3070 Orchard Dr, San Jose CA 95134	408-943-0636	S	124*	.3
24	Nipro Diagnostics Inc—Joseph Capper	2400 NW 55th Ct, Fort Lauderdale FL 33309	954-677-9201	S	124	.6
25	Candela Skin Care Centers of Boston Inc Candela Corp	530 Boston Post Rd, Wayland MA 01778	508-358-7400	S	120*	.2
26	Cardionet Inc—Joseph H Capper	227 Washington St Ste, Conshohocken PA 19428		P	119	.7
27	Spectranetics Corp—Scott Drake	9965 Federal Dr, Colorado Springs CO 80921	719-447-2000	P	118	.5
28	Solta Medical Inc—Stephen J Fanning	25881 Industrial Blvd, Hayward CA 94545	510-786-6946	P	111	.3
29	Aspect Medical Systems Inc—Nassib G Chamoun	1 Upland Rd, Norwood MA 02062	617-559-7000	S	99	.3
30	PerSeptive Biosystems Inc	500 Old Connecticut Pa, Framingham MA 01701	508-383-7700	S	97	.7
31	Dornier Medtech—Bryan Walsh	1155 Roberts Blvd, Kennesaw GA 30144	770-426-1315	R	96*	.5
32	Compex Technologies Inc—Serge Darcy	1811 Old Hwy 8, New Brighton MN 55112	651-631-0590	R	95*	.6
33	Fibercor Div—Roy Malkin	14605 28th Ave N, Plymouth MN 55447	763-553-3300	D	86*	.4
34	Palomar Medical Products Inc	15 Network Dr, Burlington MA 01803	781-993-2300	S	86*	.2
35	AngioCare Corp ArthroCare Corp	680 Vaqueros Ave, Sunnyvale CA 94085	408-736-0224	S	85*	.2
36	Carl Zeiss Meditec—Ralph Kaschke	PO Box 8111, Pleasanton CA 94588	925-557-4100	R	84*	.4
37	Cynosure Inc—Michael R Davin	5 Carlisle Rd, Westford MA 01886	978-256-4200	P	82	.3
38	EBI LP—Glen Kashuba	100 Interpace Pky, Parsippany NJ 07054	973-299-9300	S	75*	.4
39	Cholestech Corp—Warren Pinckert	3347 Investment Blvd, Hayward CA 94545	510-732-7200	S	75*	.2
40	Neostem Inc—Robin L Smith	420 Lexington Ave Ste, New York NY 10170	212-584-4180	P	70	1.0
41	Allstates Worldcargo Inc—Sam DiGiralomo	1 Pelican Dr Ste 1, Bayville NJ 08721	732-831-6868	R	60*	.1
42	Hospital Systems Inc—Jennifer Miller	750 Garcia Ave, Pittsburg CA 94565	925-427-7800	R	60*	<.1
43	i-STAT Corp—Miles D White	104 Windsor Center Dr, East Windsor NJ 08520	609-443-9300	S	60	.7
44	Rockwell Medical Technologies Inc—Robert L Chioini	30142 Wixom Rd, Wixom MI 48393	248-960-9009	P	60	.3
45	Care Fusion—Gary Fulbright	22745 Savi Ranch Pkwy, Yorba Linda CA 92887	714-283-2228	S	59*	.3
46	Charter Medical Ltd—Peter Ferris	3948-A Westpoint Blvd, Winston Salem NC 27103	336-768-6447	S	58*	.1
47	Synergetics USA Inc—David Hable	3845 Corporate Centre, O Fallon MO 63368	636-939-5100	P	56	.3
48	Invivo Corp—James B Hawkins	12501 Research Pkwy, Orlando FL 32826	407-275-3220	R	53	.3
49	Cutera Inc—Kevin P Connors	3240 Bayshore Blvd, Brisbane CA 94005	415-657-5500	P	53	.2
50	Quantum Medical Imaging LLC—Scott Matovich	2002 Orville Dr N, Ronkonkoma NY 11779	631-567-5800	S	49*	.1
51	IRIDEX Corp—Dominik Beck	1212 Terra Bella Ave, Mountain View CA 94043	650-940-4700	P	44	.1
52	Applied Medical Resources Corp—Said Hilal	22872 Avenida Empresa, Rcho Sta Marg CA 92688	949-713-8000	R	43*	.5
53	LifeWatch Corp—Yacov Geva	10255 West Higgins Rd, Rosemont IL 60018	847-720-2100	S	40*	.3
54	ZEVEX International Inc—David J McNally	4314 Zevex Park Ln, Salt Lake City UT 84123	801-264-1001	S	33*	.2
55	Dynatronics Corp—Kelvyn H Cullimore Jr	7030 Park Centre Dr, Salt Lake City UT 84121	801-568-7000	P	33	.2
56	Escalon Medical Corp—Richard DePiano	435 Devon Park Dr Bldg, Wayne PA 19087	610-688-6830	P	30	.2
57	Impact Instrumentation Inc—Leslie Sherman	PO Box 508, Caldwell NJ 07007	973-882-1212	R	30*	.2
58	Bio-Tek Instruments Inc—Briai Alpert	PO Box 998, Winooski VT 05404	802-655-4740	S	28*	.3
59	Lightlab Imaging LLC—Daniel J Starks	1 Technology Park Dr, Westford MA 01886	978-399-1000	D	28*	.1
60	Zynex Inc—Thomas Sandgaard	9990 Park Meadows Dr, Lone Tree CO 80124	303-703-4906	P	24	.2
61	Phamatech Inc—James Bergmark	10151 Barnes Canyon Rd, San Diego CA 92121	858-643-5555	R	24*	.2
62	Arrhythmia Research Technology Inc—James E Rouse	25 Sawyer Passway, Fitchburg MA 01420	978-345-0181	P	23	.1
63	Cook Vascular Inc—Louis Goode	1186 Montgomery Ln, Vandergrift PA 15690	724-845-8621	R	19*	.2
64	RF Technologies Inc—Glen F Jonas	3125 N 126th St, Brookfield WI 53005	262-790-1771	R	19*	.1
65	Electromed Inc—Robert D Hansen	500 6th Ave NW, New Prague MN 56071	952-758-9299	P	19	.1
66	Home Diagnostics Corp—George Holley	1 Trefoil Dr, Trumbull CT 06611	203-445-1170	R	18*	.2
67	Gish Biomedical Inc—Douglas E Whitaker	22942 Arroyo Vista, Rancho Santa Margarita CA 92688	949-635-2600	S	17*	.1
68	Nuclear Imaging Ltd	109 S Petro Ave, Sioux Falls SD 57107	605-330-9060	S	17*	<.1
69	Arteriocyte Medical Systems Inc—Donald Brown	7100 Euclid Ave Ste 15, Cleveland OH 44103		R	17*	<.1
70	Vasomedical Inc—Jun Ma	180 Linden Ave, Westbury NY 11590	516-997-4600	P	16	.1
71	Infimed Inc—Amy Ryan	121 Metropolitan Park, Liverpool NY 13088	315-453-4545	R	15*	.1
72	InterVascular Inc—M Christian Koller	14 Phillips Pky, Montvale NJ 07645	201-391-8100	S	15	.1
73	Bio-Detek Inc—Michael Dupelle ZOLL Medical Corp	525 Narragansett Park, Pawtucket RI 02861	401-729-1400	S	15*	.1
74	Cea Technologies Inc—Marcus Boggs	1735 Merchants Ct, Colorado Springs CO 80916	719-591-5300	R	14*	.1
75	Ad-Tech Medical Instrument Corp—David A Putz	1901 William St, Racine WI 53404	262-634-1555	R	14*	<.1
76	Transoma Medical Inc—Brian P Brockway	119 14th St NW, Saint Paul MN 55112	651-481-7444	R	13*	<.1
77	Instromedix Inc—Frederick Mindermann	10255 W Higgins Rd Ste, Rosemont IL 60018		S	13*	<.1
78	Machida Inc—Ron Hadani Vision-Sciences Inc	40 Ramland Rd S Ste 1, Orangeburg NY 10962	845-365-0600	S	13*	<.1
79	Urologix Inc—Stryker Warren Jr	14405 21st Ave N, Minneapolis MN 55447	763-475-1400	P	13	.1
80	DeJarnette Research Systems—Wayne T DeJarnette	401 Washington Ave Ste, Towson MD 21204	410-583-0680	R	12*	<.1
81	Noraxon USA Inc—Randy Raisanen	13430 N Scottsdale Rd, Scottsdale AZ 85254	480-443-3413	R	12*	<.1
82	Sonomed Inc—Benoit Larosse Escalon Medical Corp	1979 Marcus Ave Ste C1, Lake Success NY 11042	516-354-0900	S	12	<.1
83	Vision-Sciences Inc—Cynthia F Ansari	40 Ramland Rd S, Orangeburg NY 10962	845-365-0600	P	11	.1
84	Accelerated Care Plus Inc—John Beach	4850 Joule St Ste A-1, Reno NV 89502	775-685-4000	S	10*	.1
85	New Star Lasers Inc—David Hennings	9085 Foothills Blvd, Roseville CA 95747	916-677-1900	R	9*	<.1
86	Gammex RMI—Peggy Lescrenier	PO Box 620327, Middleton WI 53562	608-828-7000	R	8*	.1
87	Composiflex Inc—Alan Hannibal	8100 Hawthorne Dr, Erie PA 16509	814-866-8616	R	7*	.1
88	Tomtec Inc—Thomas Astle	1000 Sherman Ave, Hamden CT 06514	203-281-6790	R	7*	.1
89	Electro-Optics Technology Inc—David Scerbak	5835 Shugart Ln, Traverse City MI 49684	231-935-4044	R	7*	.1
90	Trimedyne Inc—Marvin P Loeb	25901 Commercentre Dr, Lake Forest CA 92630	949-951-3800	P	7	.1
91	Teratech Corp—John Bridge	77-79 Ter Hall Ave, Burlington MA 01803	781-270-4143	R	6*	.1
92	LaserSight Inc—David D Lui	931 S Semoran Blvd Ste, Winter Park FL 32792	407-678-9900	R	6	<.1
93	Sony Broadcast and Business Solutions Co—Steven Blum	1 Sony Dr, Park Ridge NJ 07656	201-930-7098	D	6	<.1
94	Conversion Devices Inc—Roland Roth	15481 Electronic Ln St, Huntington Beach CA 92649	714-898-6551	R	6*	<.1
95	Ivy Biomedical Systems Inc—James Biondi	11 Business Park Dr St, Branford CT 06405	203-481-4183	R	6*	<.1
96	Optim Inc—Thomas Root	64 Technology Park Rd, Sturbridge MA 01566	508-347-5100	R	6*	<.1
97	Transmedics Inc—Waleed Hassanein	200 Minuteman Rd Ste 3, Andover MA 01810	978-552-0900	R	6*	<.1
98	Accuscan Imaging LLC	199 Lee Ave Ste 657, Brooklyn NY 11211	718-504-1443	R	5*	<.1
99	Positron Corp—Patrick Rooney	7715 Loma Ct Ste A, Fishers IN 46038	317-576-0183	P	5	<.1

Note: An asterisk (*) indicates an estimated financial figure. The company type code used is as follows: R = Private, P = Public, S = Private Subsidiary, B = Public Subsidiary, D = Division, J = Joint Venture, I = Investment Fund.

COMPANY RANKINGS BY SALES WITHIN 4-DIGIT SIC

Rank	Company Name—*Executive Officer*	Address, City, State, Zip	Phone	Type	Fin	Empls
100	Artel Inc—*Kirby Pilcher*	25 Bradley Dr, Westbrook ME 04092	207-854-0860	R	4*	<.1
101	Aradigm Corp—*Igor Gonda*	3929 Point Eden Way, Hayward CA 94545	510-265-9000	P	4	<.1
102	Belmont Instrument Corp—*George Herzlinger*	780 Boston Rd Ste 3, Billerica MA 01821	978-663-0212	R	4*	<.1
103	Burton Medical Products Corp—*George Preston*	21100 Lassen St, Chatsworth CA 91311	818-701-8700	R	4*	<.1
104	Sofradir Ec Inc—*Frank Vallese*	373 Us Hwy 46 Bldg E, Fairfield NJ 07004	973-882-0211	R	4*	<.1
105	PLC Systems Inc—*Mark R Tauscher*	10 Forge Pk, Franklin MA 02038	508-541-8800	P	4	<.1
106	Amco Precision Tools Inc—*Aldo Zovich*	PO Box 442, Berlin CT 06037	860-828-5640	R	4*	<.1
107	Xdx Inc—*Pierre Cassigneul*	3260 Bayshore Blvd, Brisbane CA 94005	415-287-2300	R	3*	.1
108	BSD Medical Corp—*Harold R Wolcott*	2188 W 2200 S, Salt Lake City UT 84119	801-972-5555	P	3	<.1
109	Pioneer Optics Company Inc—*Ron Hille*	35 Griffin Rd S, Bloomfield CT 06002	860-286-0071	R	3*	<.1
110	Del Mar Avionics—*Bruce Del Mar*	1601Alton Pky Suite C, Irvine CA 92606	949-250-3200	R	3*	<.1
111	Beltronics Inc—*Robert Bishop*	124 Crescent Rd Ste 7, Needham MA 02494	617-244-8696	R	3*	<.1
112	David Saunders Inc—*David Saunders*	192 Gannett Dr, South Portland ME 04106	207-228-1887	R	3*	<.1
113	Thayer Medical Corp—*Steve Carpenter*	4575 S Palo Verde Rd S, Tucson AZ 85714	520-790-5393	R	3*	<.1
114	Cambridge Heart Inc—*Ali Khederian-Mood*	100 Ames Pond Dr Ste 1, Tewksbury MA 01876	978-654-7600	P	3	<.1
115	Sleepnet Corp—*Thomas Moulton*	5 Merrill Industrial D, Hampton NH 03842	603-758-6600	R	3*	<.1
116	Hyperbaric Technologies Inc—*W Gurnee*	3224 Hoover Ave, National City CA 91950	619-336-2022	R	3*	.1
117	Cardiac Center LLC—*James Fykes*	507 N University St, Murfreesboro TN 37130	615-895-1301	R	2*	<.1
118	World Heart Corp—*John Alexander Martin*	4750 Wiley Post Way St, Salt Lake City UT 84116	801-355-6255	P	2	.1
119	Precision Optics Corporation Inc—*Richard E Forkey*	22 E Broadway, Gardner MA 01440	978-630-1800	P	2	<.1
120	Elmed Inc—*Werner Hausner*	60 W Fay Ave, Addison IL 60101	630-543-2792	R	2*	<.1
121	Doty Scientific Inc—*F Doty*	700 Clemson Rd, Columbia SC 29229	803-788-6497	R	2*	<.1
122	Avotec Inc—*Paul Bullwinkel*	603 Nw Buck Hendry Way, Stuart FL 34994	772-692-0750	R	2*	<.1
123	Rich-Mar Corp—*Ken Coffey*	PO Box 879, Inola OK 74036	918-543-2222	R	2*	<.1
124	Longport Inc—*Michael C Boyd*	Brandywine 2 Bldg 5 Ch, Chadds Ford PA 19317	610-361-9100	R	2*	<.1
125	Nwa Heart and Vascular Center—*Rose Smithson*	601 W Maple Ave Ste 70, Springdale AR 72764	479-750-2203	R	2*	<.1
126	Dagan Corp—*Allan Erickson*	2855 Park Ave, Minneapolis MN 55407	612-827-5959	R	2*	<.1
127	Michigan Instruments Inc—*Bruce Barkalow*	4717 Talon Ct Se, Grand Rapids MI 49512	616-554-9696	R	2*	<.1
128	PTS Inc (Las Vegas Nevada)—*Marc Pintar*	2360 Corporate Cir, Henderson NV 89074	702-882-3999	S	1	<.1
129	Medical Energy Inc—*David Lewing*	8806 Paul Starr Dr, Pensacola FL 32514	850-476-8113	R	1*	<.1
130	Echo Therapeutics Inc—*Patrick T Mooney*	10 Forge Pkwy, Franklin MA 02038	508-553-8850	R	1*	<.1
131	General Hearing Instruments Inc—*Roger Juneau*	PO Box 23748, New Orleans LA 70183	504-733-3767	R	1*	<.1
132	HQ Inc—*William S Hicks*	210 9th St Dr W, Palmetto FL 34221	941-723-4197	R	1*	<.1
133	Optima Intl Components LLC	625 Pontiac St, Denver CO 80220	720-434-4063	R	1*	<.1
134	Hlpr Inc—*Deborah Hohenstein*	PO Box 341, Hamel MN 55340	763-478-8926	R	1*	<.1
135	AxoGen Inc—*Karen Zaderej*	13859 Progress Blvd St, Alachua FL 32615	386-462-6800	P	1	<.1
136	Percussionaire Corp—*Forrest Bird*	PO Box 817, Sandpoint ID 83864	208-263-2549	R	1*	<.1
137	Diapulse Corporation of America—*David M Ross*	475 Northern Blvd, Great Neck NY 11021	516-466-3030	P	1	<.1
138	Non-Invasive Monitoring Systems Inc—*Marvin A Sackner*	4400 Biscayne Blvd, Miami FL 33137	305-575-4200	P	1	<.1
139	Imaging Diagnostic Systems Inc—*Linda B Grable*	5307 NW 35th Ter, Fort Lauderdale FL 33309	954-581-9800	P	1	<.1
140	SpectraScience Inc—*Michael P Oliver*	11568 Sorrento Valley, San Diego CA 92121	858-847-0200	P	<1	<.1
141	Medis Technologies Ltd—*Jose Mejia*	805 3rd Ave, New York NY 10022	212-935-8484	R	<1	.1
142	EnteroMedics Inc—*Mark B Knudson*	2800 Patton Rd, Saint Paul MN 55113	651-634-3003	P	<1	<.1
143	Xcorporeal Inc—*Kelly J McCrann*	80 Empire Dr, Lake Forest CA 92630	949-600-4640	R	<1	<.1
144	Pori and Rowe Associates Inc—*John Pori*	1825 Palmetto Ave, Pacifica CA 94044	650-359-5175	R	<1*	<.1

TOTALS: SIC 3845 Electromedical Equipment
Companies: 144

					44,231	142.7

3851 Ophthalmic Goods

Rank	Company Name—*Executive Officer*	Address, City, State, Zip	Phone	Type	Fin	Empls
1	Bausch and Lomb Inc—*Brent L Saunders*	1 Bausch and Lomb Pl, Rochester NY 14604	585-338-6000	R	1,939*	11.0
2	Cooper Companies Inc—*Robert S Weiss*	6140 Stoneridge Mall R, Pleasanton CA 94588	925-460-3600	P	1,331	7.4
3	CIBA Vision Corp—*Andrea Saia*	11460 Johns Creek Pkwy, Duluth GA 30097	678-415-3937	S	1,040	N/A
4	Essilor Of America Inc—*John Carrier*	13555 N Stemmons Fwy, Dallas TX 75234	214-496-4000	S	788*	8.5
5	Oakley Inc—*Scott Olivet*	1 Icon, Foothill Ranch CA 92610	949-951-0991	S	768*	3.4
6	Marchon Eyewear Inc—*Al Berg*	35 Hub Dr, Melville NY 11747	631-755-2020	R	432*	1.5
7	FGX International Holdings Ltd—*A Alexander Taylor*	500 George Washington, Smithfield RI 02917	401-231-3800	B	259	3.0
8	Transitions Optical Inc—*Rick Elias*	PO Box 700, Pinellas Park FL 33780		R	164*	1.2
9	Sperian Protection Optical Inc—*Thomas Goeltz*	690 HP Way, Chester VA 23836	804-732-6121	S	88*	.4
10	Gentex Corp (Carbondale Pennsylvania)—*L Peter Frieder Jr*	324 Main St, Simpson PA 18407	570-282-3550	R	85*	.4
11	CooperVision Inc—*Dennis Murphy* Cooper Companies Inc	370 Woodcliff Dr Ste 2, Fairport NY 14450	949-597-8130	S	67*	.5
12	Signet Armorlite Inc—*Bruno Salvadori*	1001 Armorlite Dr, San Marcos CA 92069	760-744-4000	S	60*	.4
13	STAAR Surgical Co—*Barry Caldwell*	1911 Walker Ave, Monrovia CA 91016	626-303-7902	P	55	.3
14	Luxottica USA Inc—*Leonardo Del Vecchio*	44 Harbor Park Dr, Port Washington NY 11050	516-484-3800	S	49*	.4
15	Twin City Optical Co—*Dean Clause*	5205 Hwy 169 N, Minneapolis MN 55442	763-551-1000	R	46*	.4
16	Parmelee Industries Inc—*L Sankpill*	PO Box 15965, Shawnee Mission KS 66285	913-599-5555	R	41*	.3
17	Icare Industries Inc—*Scott Payne*	4399 35th St N, Saint Petersburg FL 33714	727-526-0501	R	36*	.2
18	Uvex Safety Manufacturing Ltd—*Herve Meillat*	10 Thurber Blvd, Smithfield RI 02917	401-232-1200	R	28*	.3
19	New Era Optical Co—*Herbert Natkin*	5575 N Lynch Ave, Chicago IL 60630	773-725-9600	R	27*	.2
20	Kollmorgen Corp Electro-Optical Div—*Michael J Wall*	347 King St, Northampton MA 01060	413-586-2330	D	25*	.3
21	Lantis Eyewear Corp—*Bill Deyo*	489 5th Ave, New York NY 10017	212-561-7500	S	23*	.3
22	Soderberg Inc—*Aloys Willenbring*	PO Box 7305, Saint Paul MN 55107	651-291-1400	S	21*	.3
23	Sun Rams Products Inc—*Chris Pederson*	12935 16th Ave N, Plymouth MN 55441		R	21*	.2
24	Signature Eyewear Inc—*Michael Prince*	498 N Oak St, Inglewood CA 90302	310-330-2700	P	21	.1
25	Nassau Lens Company Inc—*Michael Pildes*	160 LeGrand Ave, Northvale NJ 07647	201-767-8033	S	20*	.1
26	Moc Acquisition Corp—*Matt Iovaldi*	2360 59th St, Saint Louis MO 63110	314-533-2020	R	19*	.2
27	Eye Kraft Optical Inc—*Floyd Lehne*	PO Box 400, Saint Cloud MN 56302		R	18*	.1
28	Artcraft Optical Company Inc—*C Eagle*	57 Goodway Dr S, Rochester NY 14623	585-546-6640	R	17*	.1
29	Rite-Style Optical Co—*George Lee*	PO Box 3068, Omaha NE 68103	402-492-8822	R	17*	.1
30	Optovision Coating Labs Inc—*Peter Zuccarelli*	10510 Olympic Dr, Dallas TX 75220	214-357-1717	R	17*	.2
31	Winchester Optical Co—*Ben Lynch*	PO Box 1515, Elmira NY 14902	607-734-4251	R	16*	.1
32	Art Optical Contact Lens Inc—*Thomas Anastor*	PO Box 1848, Grand Rapids MI 49501	616-453-1888	R	15*	.1
33	Beitler-Mckee Optical Co—*W Driscoll* Essilor Of America Inc	160 S 22nd St, Pittsburgh PA 15203	412-481-4700	S	14*	.1
34	Fosta-Tek Optics Inc—*John Morrison*	320 Hamilton St, Leominster MA 01453	978-534-6511	R	14*	.1
35	Tri-Supreme Optical LLC—*Jennifer Boutges* Essilor Of America Inc	91 Carolyn Blvd, Farmingdale NY 11735	631-249-2020	S	13*	.1
36	Dispensers Optical Service Corp—*Charles Arensberg*	PO Box 35000, Louisville KY 40232	502-491-3440	R	12*	.1
37	Dioptics Medical Products Inc—*Henry Lane*	1327 Archer St, San Luis Obispo CA 93401	805-781-3300	R	12*	.1
38	Brothers Ophthalmic Laboratory Inc—*John Ragazzo*	870 N Eckhoff St, Orange CA 92868	714-634-9303	R	12*	.1

Rank	Company Name—*Executive Officer*	Address, City, State, Zip	Phone	Type	Fin	Empls
39	Optogenics Of Syracuse Inc—*Robert Cotran* Essilor Of America Inc	PO Box 4894, Syracuse NY 13221	315-446-7500	S	12*	.1
40	Hoya Optical Inc—*Fred Fink*	PO Box 580870, Modesto CA 95358	209-579-7739	R	12*	.1
41	Luzerne Optical Laboratories Ltd—*John Dougherty*	PO Box 998, Wilkes Barre PA 18773	570-822-3183	R	11*	.2
42	Classic Optical Laboratories Inc—*Monte Friedkin*	PO Box 1341, Youngstown OH 44501	330-759-8245	R	9*	.1
43	Zyloware Corp—*Christopher Shyer*	8 Slater St Ste 1, Port Chester NY 10573	718-392-3900	R	9*	.1
44	Rooney Optical Inc—*Kevin Dougher*	5440 W 164th St, Cleveland OH 44142	216-267-5600	R	9*	.1
45	Lensvector Inc—*Derek Proudian*	2307 Leghorn St, Mountain View CA 94043	650-618-0700	R	9*	.1
46	Homer Optical Company Inc—*Robert Dunn*	2401 Linden Ln, Silver Spring MD 20910	301-585-9060	R	9*	.1
47	Unilens Vision Inc—*Michael J Pecora*	10431 72nd St N, Largo FL 33777	727-544-2531	P	9	<.1
48	Duffins-Langley Optical Company Inc—*John Carrier*	8140 Marshall Dr, Shawnee Mission KS 66214	913-492-5379	R	9*	.1
49	Hydrogel Vision Corp—*Steven Schuster*	7575 Commerce Ct, Sarasota FL 34243	941-739-1382	S	8*	.1
50	Trecom Safety Corp—*Wesley Patterson*	1020 Randolph St, Thomasville NC 27360	336-476-9500	R	8*	<.1
51	Dfg Inc—*Bill Scott*	651 Critchlow Dr Ste 2, Ogden UT 84404	801-394-0865	R	8*	.1
52	Ophthonix Inc—*Stephen Osbaldeston*	1491 Poinsettia Ave St, Vista CA 92081	760-842-5600	R	8*	.1
53	Leisure Vision Of Nevada City	400 Sierra College Dr, Grass Valley CA 95945	530-272-7784	R	7*	.1
54	Hirsch Optical Corp—*Harold Rothstein*	83 Milbar Blvd, Farmingdale NY 11735	516-752-2211	R	7*	.1
55	Opticote Inc—*Edwin Ellefsen*	10455 Seymour Ave, Franklin Park IL 60131	847-678-8900	R	7*	.1
56	Toledo Optical Laboratory Inc—*Irland Tashima*	PO Box 2028, Toledo OH 43603	419-248-3384	R	7*	.1
57	Katz and Klein Inc—*Corrine Hood*	1909 H St, Sacramento CA 95811	916-444-2024	R	7*	<.1
58	Hoya Optical Laboratories—*Ray Knoll*	PO Box 1798, Tacoma WA 98401	253-474-0610	R	6*	.1
59	Opsales Inc—*Dean Friedman*	4217 Austin Blvd, Island Park NY 11558	516-889-5800	R	6	.1
60	Volkoptical Inc—*Peter Mastores*	7893 Enterprise Dr, Mentor OH 44060	440-942-6161	R	6*	.1
61	Barnett and Ramel Optical Company Of Nebraska—*Frank Besch*	PO Box 3488, Omaha NE 68103	402-453-4900	R	6*	<.1
62	Empire Optical Of California Inc—*Neil Grossman*	7633 Varna Ave, North Hollywood CA 91605	818-997-6474	R	6*	<.1
63	Optical One Inc—*Edward Deblasio*	1750 S Ave, Youngstown OH 44502	330-743-8518	R	5*	<.1
64	B and G Optics Inc—*William Hamburg*	1320 Unity St, Philadelphia PA 19124	215-289-2480	R	5*	.1
65	Sea Vision USA	4399 35th St N, Saint Petersburg FL 33714	727-525-6906	R	5*	.1
66	Tkc Optical Inc—*Steve Conley*	229 4th St, Sioux City IA 51101	712-252-1519	R	5*	.1
67	Precision Optical Company Inc—*Richard Welch* Essilor Of America Inc	PO Box 280023, East Hartford CT 06128	860-289-6023	S	5*	<.1
68	Carskadden Optical Company Inc—*Thomas Colopy*	1525 High Point Ct, Zanesville OH 43701	740-452-9306	R	5*	<.1
69	Sutherlin Optical Co—*Steven Sutherlin*	1941 Central St, Kansas City MO 64108	816-421-0369	R	5*	.1
70	Medennium Inc—*Jacob Feldman*	9 Parker Ste 150, Irvine CA 92618	949-789-9000	R	5*	<.1
71	Paragon Vision Sciences Inc—*Joe Sicari*	947 E Impala Ave, Mesa AZ 85204	480-892-7602	R	5*	<.1
72	C and H Contact Lens Inc—*Robert Cottie*	PO Box 29081, Dallas TX 75229	214-358-4433	R	5*	<.1
73	Randolph Engineering Inc—*Peter Waszkiewicz*	26 Thomas Patten Dr, Randolph MA 02368	781-961-6070	R	5*	<.1
74	Buchman Optical Inc—*Jacky Buchmann*	5360 NW 35th Ave, Fort Lauderdale FL 33309	954-733-2300	R	5*	<.1
75	Vision Craft Inc—*Gerald Mansuy* Essilor Of America Inc	3285 Martin Rd Ste 110, Commerce Township MI 48390	248-669-1130	S	5*	<.1
76	De Camp Medical Products Corp—*Dennis Decamp*	10201 Trademark St Ste, Rancho Cucamonga CA 91730	909-481-0011	R	4*	.1
77	Northeast Lens Corp—*John Flaherty*	PO Box 9117, Newton MA 02464	617-964-6797	R	4*	<.1
78	Central Optical Inc—*Lloyd Yazbek*	6981 Southern Blvd Ste, Youngstown OH 44512	330-783-9660	R	4*	<.1
79	Bristow Optical—*Bob Strohbehn*	3711 E Atlanta Ave, Phoenix AZ 85040	602-269-2522	R	4*	.1
80	Polymer Technology Corp—*Brent Saunders* Bausch and Lomb Inc	100 Research Dr Ste 2, Wilmington MA 01887	978-658-6111	S	4*	.1
81	Unilens Corporation USA—*Michael Pecora* Unilens Vision Inc	10431 72nd St N, Largo FL 33777	727-544-2531	S	4*	<.1
82	Precision Optical Laboratory Inc—*Ed Reynolds* Essilor Of America Inc	PO Box 68, Gallaway TN 38036	901-867-2991	S	4*	<.1
83	Quality Accessories Inc	9748 Indiana Pkwy, Munster IN 46321	219-922-8103	S	4*	<.1
84	Ozarks Optical Laboratories Inc—*John Noy*	PO Box 9700, Springfield MO 65801	417-890-5367	R	4*	<.1
85	Addition Technology Inc—*William Flynn*	950 Lee St Ste 210, Des Plaines IL 60016	847-297-8419	R	4*	<.1
86	Morgan Optical Inc—*Jesse Morgan*	PO Box 51446, Knoxville TN 37950	865-524-5448	R	4*	<.1
87	Motif Industries Inc—*Al Kay*	8 Commerce Rd, Fairfield NJ 07004	973-575-1800	R	4*	<.1
88	His Vision Inc—*Patrick Ho*	1260 Lyell Ave, Rochester NY 14606	585-254-0022	R	4*	<.1
89	Special Optics Inc—*David Manzi*	315 Richard Mine Rd St, Wharton NJ 07885	973-366-7289	R	4*	<.1
90	Richmond Optical Company Inc—*Alice Bose*	29425 Ruus Rd, Hayward CA 94544	510-783-1420	R	3*	<.1
91	Specialty Lens Corp—*Alan Combs* Essilor Of America Inc	3955 S 210 W, Salt Lake City UT 84107	801-288-8819	S	3*	<.1
92	Fused Kontacts Of Missouri Inc—*David Rusch*	3901 Ne 33rd Ter Ste E, Kansas City MO 64117	816-455-0500	R	3*	<.1
93	Ilixco—*Jeff Fergason*	4229 Northgate Blvd, Sacramento CA 95834	916-568-9424	R	3*	<.1
94	Hoya Largo—*Donald Behagg*	12345 Starkey Rd Ste E, Largo FL 33773	727-531-8964	R	3*	<.1
95	Optical Dimensions Inc—*Richard Kirsammer*	711 E 4th St, Royal Oak MI 48067	248-541-3790	S	3*	<.1
96	Accu Rx Inc—*Nicholas Masi*	100 Federal Way, Johnston RI 02919	401-454-2920	R	3*	<.1
97	Donegan Optical Company Inc—*Frank Donegan*	PO Box 14308, Shawnee Mission KS 66285	913-492-2500	R	3*	<.1
98	US Iol Inc—*Dhaval Shukla*	PO Box 13550, Lexington KY 40583	859-259-4925	R	3*	<.1
99	Enterprise Optical Inc—*Charles Flood*	PO Box 104, Royal Oak MI 48068	248-583-7740	R	3*	<.1
100	Young's Valley Contax Inc—*Stephen Young*	200 S Mill St, Springfield OR 97477	541-744-9393	R	3*	<.1
101	Co-Optics Of America Laboratory Inc—*Paul Strenn*	297 River St Service R, Oneonta NY 13820	607-432-0557	R	2*	<.1
102	Trioptics Inc—*H Muehlbach*	2921 S 5th Ct, Milwaukee WI 53207	414-481-9822	R	2*	<.1
103	Ocean Waves Inc—*Kevin Carlson*	525 3rd St N Apt 105, Jacksonville Beach FL 32250	904-247-7871	R	2*	<.1
104	Hi-Tech Optics Cooperative Inc—*James Kirchner*	PO Box 81726, Lincoln NE 68501	402-434-2700	R	2*	<.1
105	Capri Optics Inc	1421 38th St, Brooklyn NY 11218	718-633-2300	R	2*	<.1
106	I See Optical Laboratories Inc—*Michael Pak*	44 W Church St, Blackwood NJ 08012	856-227-9300	R	2*	<.1
107	Index 53 Optical Company Inc—*Lawrence Rudolph*	PO Box 1111, Saint Cloud MN 56302	320-252-9380	R	2*	<.1
108	Sheridan Optical Company Inc—*Edward Sheridan*	PO Box 8, Pitman NJ 08071	856-582-0963	R	2*	<.1
109	Abba Optical Inc—*Lee Dickerson*	2230 Centre Park Ct, Stone Mountain GA 30087	770-498-8545	R	1*	<.1
110	Rafi Systems Inc—*Kusum Rafiquzza*	750 N Diamond Bar Blvd, Diamond Bar CA 91765	909-593-8124	R	1*	.1
111	Dita Inc—*Jeff Solorio*	2214 Beverly Blvd, Los Angeles CA 90057		R	1*	<.1
112	Prestonwood Eye Care—*David Moigar*	5425 Belt Line Rd, Dallas TX 75244	972-980-1774	R	1*	<.1
113	Metro Optics Inc—*Al Blackburn*	11034 Shady Trl Ste 10, Dallas TX 75229	214-350-6863	R	1*	<.1
114	Kaban Optical Inc—*Susan Kabin*	77734 Country Club Dr, Palm Desert CA 92211	760-772-2210	R	1*	<.1
115	Prairie Products Inc—*Brian Laprairie*	PO Box 100, Dover PA 17315	717-292-0421	R	<1*	<.1
116	Viva International Group—*Frank Rescigna*	3140 Rte 22 W, Somerville NJ 08876	908-595-6200	S	<1	.5
117	Southeastern Ocularists Inc—*Robert Hendenite*	8426 Medical Plz Dr St, Charlotte NC 28262	704-510-9292	R	<1	<.1

TOTALS: SIC 3851 Ophthalmic Goods
Companies: 117

	7,995	46.2

Note: An asterisk (*) indicates an estimated financial figure. The company type code used is as follows: R = Private, P = Public, S = Private Subsidiary, B = Public Subsidiary, D = Division, J = Joint Venture, I = Investment Fund.

COMPANY RANKINGS BY SALES WITHIN 4-DIGIT SIC

Rank	Company Name—*Executive Officer*	Address, City, State, Zip	Phone	Type	Fin	Empls
	3861 Photographic Equipment & Supplies					
1	Xerox Corp—*Ursula M Burns*	PO Box 4505, Norwalk CT 06856	203-968-3000	P.	21,633	136.5
2	Eastman Kodak Co—*Antonio M Perez*	343 State St, Rochester NY 14650		P	6,022	17.1
3	Canon Virginia Inc—*Yusaku Azuma*	12000 Canon Blvd, Newport News VA 23606	757-881-6000	S	1,798*	1.9
4	Lexar Media Inc—*Eric B Stang*	47300 Bayside Pky, Fremont CA 94538	510-413-1200	S	853*	.3
5	Avid Technology Inc—*Gary Greenfield*	75 Network Dr, Burlington MA 01803	978-640-6789	P	678	1.8
6	Polaroid Consumer Electronics International LLC—*Mary Jeffries*	300 Baker Ave, Concord MA 01742	781-386-2000	S	664*	3.0
7	Polaroid Holding Co—*Stewart Cohen*	1265 Main St, Waltham MA 02451	781-386-2000	S	598*	2.7
8	Kodak Colorado Div Eastman Kodak Co	9952 Eastman Park Dr, Windsor CO 80551	970-686-7611	D	578*	1.8
9	Recon/Optical Inc—*J Johnson*	570 W NW Hwy, Barrington IL 60010	847-381-2400	R	393*	.2
10	Pinnacle Systems Inc—*Patti S Hart* Avid Technology Inc	280 N Bernardo Ave, Mountain View CA 94043	650-526-1600	D	347*	.9
11	Minolta Corporation Business Products Group—*Masatoshi Matuzaki*	100 Williams Dr, Ramsey NJ 07446	201-825-4000	D	300*	.6
12	Panavision Inc—*William C Bevins*	6219 De Soto Ave, Woodland Hills CA 91367	818-316-1000	S	233*	1.2
13	X-Rite Inc—*Thomas J Vacchiano Jr*	4300 44th St SE, Grand Rapids MI 49512	616-803-2100	P	223	.7
14	Panavision International LP—*Bill Bevins* Panavision Inc	6219 De Soto Ave, Woodland Hills CA 91367	818-316-1000	S	194*	1.2
15	PLUS Vision Corporation of America—*Shinichi Fukushima*	9610 SW Sunshine Ct St, Beaverton OR 97005	503-748-8700	S	180*	.1
16	Da-Lite Screen Company Inc—*Richard E Lundin*	PO Box 137, Warsaw IN 46581	574-267-8101	S	173*	.7
17	Kodak Professional Photography Div—*Antonio Perez*	343 State St, Rochester NY 14650		R	149	N/A
18	Graphic Enterprises Inc—*Austin Vanchieri*	3874 Highland Park NW, North Canton OH 44720		R	138*	.3
19	Ballantyne Strong Inc—*Gary L Cavey*	4350 McKinley St, Omaha NE 68112	402-453-4444	P	136	.3
20	Proxima Corp	13190 SW 68th Pkwy Ste, Portland OR 97223		S	122*	.4
21	West Point Products LLC—*Greg Lemasters*	PO Box 50, Valley Grove WV 26060	304-547-1360	R	66*	.2
22	Roper Scientific—*Gene Yazbak*	3660 Quakerbridge Rd, Trenton NJ 08619	609-587-9797	D	65*	.2
23	Eastman Gelatine Corp—*Gary Butler* Eastman Kodak Co	227 Washington St, Peabody MA 01960	978-573-3700	S	56*	.2
24	3M Visual Systems Div—*George Buckley*	6801 River Place Blvd, Austin TX 78726	512-984-1800	R	50*	.1
25	Fairchild Imaging Inc—*Charles Arduini*	1801 McCarthy Blvd, Milpitas CA 95035	408-433-2500	R	44*	.1
26	International Laser Group Inc—*Cindy Michaels*	PO Box 686, Woodland Hills CA 91365	818-888-0400	R	41*	.3
27	Eiki International Inc—*K Sekino*	30251 Esperanza, Rancho Santa Margarita CA 92688		R	40	<.1
28	Stewart Filmscreen Corp—*Grant Stewart*	1161 W Sepulveda Blvd, Torrance CA 90502	310-784-5300	R	35*	.2
29	Electronic Systems Engineering Company Inc—*Arthur Kaminshine*	1 E Eseco Rd, Cushing OK 74023	918-225-1266	R	30*	.1
30	Fujifilm Hunt Chemicals USA Inc—*Albert Aerts*	40 Boroline Rd, Allendale NJ 07401	201-995-2200	R	28*	.3
31	Mole-Richardson Co—*Michael Parker*	937 N Sycamore Ave, Hollywood CA 90038	323-851-0111	R	28*	.1
32	Chyron Corp—*Michael I Wellesley-Wesley*	5 Hub Dr, Melville NY 11747	631-845-2000	P	28	.1
33	Tamron USA Inc—*Takashi Inoue*	10 Austin Blvd, Commack NY 11725	631-858-8400	S	27*	.1
34	Precision Document Solutions Inc—*David Smith*	2452 Lacy Ln Ste 100, Carrollton TX 75006	972-242-7200	R	25*	.2
35	Elcan Optical Technologies—*Robert Clayton*	1601 N Plano Rd, Richardson TX 75081	972-344-8000	R	25*	.2
36	New Vad LLC—*Wayne Lusthoff*	9433 Science Ctr Dr, Minneapolis MN 55428	763-971-4400	R	25*	<.1
37	Vutec Corp—*Howard Sinkoff*	11711 W Sample Rd, Coral Springs FL 33065	954-545-9000	R	24*	.1
38	Brijot Imaging Systems Inc—*Mitchel J Laskey*	1064 Greenwood Blvd St, Lake Mary FL 32746	407-641-4370	R	21*	<.1
39	Alfa Color Inc—*Michael Trerotola*	535 W 135th St, Gardena CA 90248	310-532-2532	R	20*	.1
40	ImageWorks—*R Scott Jones*	250 Clearbrook Rd Ste, Elmsford NY 10523	914-592-6100	P	19	.1
41	MDI Inc—*James Collier Sparks*	12500 Network Blvd Ste, San Antonio TX 78249	210-477-5400	P	17	.1
42	Enhanced Laser Products—*Curtis Morris*	9075 Katy Frwy, Houston TX 77024	713-956-9481	R	17*	.1
43	Quantum Instruments Inc—*Ed Phair*	10 Commerce Dr, Hauppauge NY 11788	631-656-7400	R	17*	.1
44	Ikonics Corp—*William C Ulland*	4832 Grand Ave, Duluth MN 55807	218-628-2217	P	17	.1
45	Falcon Safety Products Inc—*Philip Lapin*	PO Box 1299, Somerville NJ 08876	908-707-4900	R	16*	<.1
46	Deepsea Power and Light Inc—*Mark Olsson*	4033 Ruffin Rd, San Diego CA 92123	858-576-1261	R	15*	<.1
47	Photo Systems Inc—*Alan Fischer*	7200 Huron River Dr, Dexter MI 48130	734-426-4646	R	14*	.1
48	Tiffen Acquisition LLC—*Stacy Gonzalez*	90 Oser Ave, Hauppauge NY 11788	631-273-2500	R	13*	.1
49	J and R Moviola—*Joe Paskal*	1135 N Mansfield Ave, Hollywood CA 90038	323-467-3107	R	13*	<.1
50	Black Bayou Productions Inc—*Kasi Lemmons*	9800 Yoakum Dr, Beverly Hills CA 90210	310-859-0010	R	13*	.1
51	Hollywood Film Co—*Vincent Carabello*	9265 Borden Ave, Sun Valley CA 91352	818-683-1130	R	13*	.1
52	Promark International Inc—*Ken Orlando*	1268 Humbracht Cir, Bartlett IL 60103	630-830-9200	R	12*	.1
53	Hf Group Inc—*Myung Lee*	203 W Artesia Blvd, Compton CA 90220	310-605-0755	R	12*	<.1
54	Cordin Co—*James Nebeker*	2230 S 3270 W, Salt Lake City UT 84119	801-972-5272	R	11*	<.1
55	Lavezzi Precision Inc—*Albert La Vezzi*	999 Regency Dr, Glendale Heights IL 60139	630-582-1230	R	10*	.1
56	A Qc Group Corp—*Mitch Howard*	200 Park Central Blvd, Pompano Beach FL 33064	954-970-8989	R	10*	.1
57	Doremi Cinema LLC—*Sherly Shamma*	1020 Chestnut St, Burbank CA 91506	818-562-1101	R	10*	<.1
58	H R Simon And Company Inc—*H Simon*	3515 Marmenco Ct, Baltimore MD 21230	410-636-5555	R	10*	<.1
59	Advance Reproductions Corp—*Thomas Nigrelli*	100 Flagship Dr, North Andover MA 01845	978-685-2911	R	9*	.1
60	Pic-Mount Imaging Corp—*Eugene Boylan*	2300 Arrowhead Dr, Carson City NV 89706	775-887-5700	R	9*	<.1
61	Sky-Skan Inc—*Steven Savage*	51 Lake St, Nashua NH 03060	603-880-8500	R	9*	<.1
62	Neumade Products Corp—*Ronald Jones*	30-40 Pecks Ln, Newtown CT 06470	203-270-1100	R	8*	<.1
63	Bidwell Industrial Group Inc/Blu-Ray Div	2055 S Main St, Middletown CT 06457	860-346-9283	D	8*	<.1
64	J L Fisher Inc—*James Fisher*	1000 W Isabel St, Burbank CA 91506	818-846-8366	R	8*	.1
65	Display Devices Inc—*Mervin Perkins*	5880 Sheridan Blvd, Arvada CO 80003	303-412-0399	R	8*	.1
66	Richards Corp—*Stanley Richards*	44931 Falcon Pl Ste 1, Sterling VA 20166	703-834-5550	R	7*	.1
67	American Business Technology	45929 Maries Rd, Dulles VA 20166	703-709-7140	S	7*	.1
68	Turner Bellows Inc—*Marilyn Yeager*	526 Child St, Rochester NY 14606	585-235-4456	R	7*	<.1
69	Advanced Microsensors Inc—*Timothy Stucchi*	333 S St Bldg 2, Shrewsbury MA 01545	508-770-6600	R	7*	<.1
70	Digital Check Technologies Inc—*Philip Barboni*	10231 Trademark St Ste, Rancho Cucamonga CA 91730	909-945-5106	R	7*	<.1
71	Ad Color Inc—*Dave Messner*	620 Adcolor Dr, Lexington KY 40511	859-253-1046	R	6*	.1
72	Joseph Merritt and Company Inc—*Edward W Perry*	650 Franklin Ave, Hartford CT 06114	860-296-2500	R	6*	.1
73	Pfaff Manufacturing—*Stephen Pfaff*	32010 Caminito Quieto, Bonsall CA 92003	760-331-3700	R	6*	<.1
74	Research Technology International Co—*Ray Short*	4700 W Chase Ave, Lincolnwood IL 60712	847-677-3000	R	6*	<.1
75	Reyhan Pgf—*Bryan Hansel*	930 Blue Gentian Rd St, Saint Paul MN 55121	651-256-0050	R	6*	<.1
76	Photoengraving Inc—*Joe Perry*	502 N Willow Ave, Tampa FL 33606	813-253-3427	R	6*	<.1
77	Pen And Incorporated Of Milwaukee Inc—*Penny Forrest*	9860 S Franklin Dr, Franklin WI 53132	414-421-8262	R	6*	<.1
78	Douthitt Corp—*Douglas Diehl*	245 Adair St, Detroit MI 48207	313-259-1565	R	5*	.1
79	QuickSet International Inc—*Andy Lareau*	3650 Woodhead Dr, Northbrook IL 60062	847-498-0700	R	5*	.1
80	Leica Camera Inc—*Roger Horn*	1 Pearl Ct Ste A, Allendale NJ 07401		S	5*	<.1
81	ConMed Linvatec	11311 Concept Blvd, Largo FL 33773	727-399-5106	D	5*	<.1
82	Visual Matrix Corp—*Pierre Yenokian*	3320 N San Fernando Bl, Burbank CA 91504	818-843-4831	R	5*	<.1

Rank	Company Name—*Executive Officer*	Address, City, State, Zip	Phone	Type	Fin	Empls
83	Argus Camera Company LLC—*Anthony Graffia*	1610 Colonial Pkwy, Inverness IL 60067		R	5*	<.1
84	Spectral Instruments Inc—*Gary Sims*	PO Box 85430, Tucson AZ 85754	520-884-8821	R	5*	<.1
85	Optima Technologies LLC—*Steve Jensen*	5313 Johns Rd Rm 210, Tampa FL 33634	727-842-9977	R	4*	.1
86	Hasselblad USA Inc—*Christian Poulsen*	15209 NE 95th St, Redmond WA 98052	425-861-6434	R	4*	<.1
87	LogEtronics Corp—*Ray Luca* ImageWorks	6521 Arlington Blvd St, Falls Church VA 22042	703-912-7745	S	4*	<.1
88	Zeta Products Inc—*Michael Naso*	1060 Garden State Rd, Union NJ 07083	908-688-0440	R	4*	<.1
89	Rosco Laboratories Inc—*Stanford Miller*	52 Harbor View Ave, Stamford CT 06902	203-708-8900	R	4*	<.1
90	Tameran Inc—*Mark Wise*	30340 Solon Indtrl Pkw, Cleveland OH 44139	440-349-7100	R	4*	<.1
91	Hilord Chemical Corp—*Donald Balbinder*	70 Engineers Rd, Hauppauge NY 11788	631-234-7373	R	4*	<.1
92	Mac Gregor Smith Blueprinters Inc—*Brenda Smith*	1500 S Division Ave, Orlando FL 32805	407-423-5944	R	4*	<.1
93	Applied Vision Company LLC—*Mike Kress*	2020 Vision Ln, Cuyahoga Falls OH 44223	330-724-9600	R	3*	<.1
94	Shadow Fax Inc—*Tim Meixelspierger*	4601 Helgesen Dr, Madison WI 53718	608-222-1918	R	3*	<.1
95	Ken-A-Vision Manufacturing Company Inc—*Steven Dunn*	5615 Raytown Rd, Raytown MO 64133	816-353-4787	R	3*	<.1
96	Laser Connection LLC—*Mike Assels*	100 E Midland Rd, Auburn MI 48611	989-662-4022	R	3*	<.1
97	Robotics Technologies Inc—*Allan Roberts*	20655 Burl Ct, Joliet IL 60433	815-722-7650	R	3*	<.1
98	Base-Line Ii Inc—*Howard Harper*	2001 N Delany Rd, Gurnee IL 60031	847-336-8403	R	3*	<.1
99	Laser's Resource Inc—*Thomas Senecal*	4770 50th St Se, Grand Rapids MI 49512	616-554-5555	R	3*	<.1
100	Santa Barbara Instrument Gp Inc—*Alan Holmes*	147 Castilian Dr Ste A, Santa Barbara CA 93117	805-571-7244	R	3*	<.1
101	Technical Film Systems Inc—*Manfred Michelson*	4725 Calle Quetzal Ste, Camarillo CA 93012	805-384-9470	R	3*	<.1
102	Logan—*Ben Conrad*	11 Brooks Ave Apt Unit, Venice CA 90291	310-314-0306	R	2*	<.1
103	Two Thirty Two Productins Inc—*Paul Dillon*	7108 Katella Ave Ste 4, Stanton CA 90680	714-317-5317	R	2*	<.1
104	Vitek Industrial Video Products Inc—*Greg Bier*	28492 Constellation Rd, Valencia CA 91355	661-294-8043	R	2*	<.1
105	Optical and Electronic Research Inc—*Frederick Bley*	11501 Sunset Hills Rd, Reston VA 20190	703-471-1645	R	2*	<.1
106	Filmdex Inc—*Ida Slattery*	PO Box 490, Centreville VA 20122	703-631-0600	R	2*	<.1
107	Cardamation Company Inc—*Robert Swartz*	1041 W Bridge St, Phoenixville PA 19460	610-935-9700	R	2*	<.1
108	Dunning Photo Equipment Inc—*Ernie Dunning*	605 W Needles St, Bixby OK 74008	918-366-4917	R	2*	<.1
109	Kelmar Systems Inc—*Andrew Marglin*	284 Broadway, Huntington Station NY 11746	631-421-1230	R	2*	<.1
110	Bescor Video Accessories Ltd—*Douglas Brandwin*	244 Rte 109, Farmingdale NY 11735	631-420-1717	R	2*	<.1
111	Speedotron Corp—*Jerry Schutt*	310 S Racine Ave Fl 4, Chicago IL 60607	312-421-4050	R	2*	<.1
112	Creatron Services Inc—*Isidore Epstein*	504 Cherry Ln, Floral Park NY 11001	516-437-5119	R	2*	<.1
113	Systems and Products Engineering Co—*George Higginbotham*	709 N 6th St, Kansas City KS 66101	913-321-3978	R	2*	<.1
114	Minco Manufacturing LLC—*William Griffith*	855 Aeroplaza Dr, Colorado Springs CO 80916	719-550-1223	R	2*	<.1
115	Bencher Inc—*Jere Benedict*	241 W Depot St, Antioch IL 60002	847-838-3195	R	1*	<.1
116	Meriden Machine Shop Inc—*Jim Surritt*	PO Box 367, Meriden KS 66512	785-484-2466	R	1*	<.1
117	Photikon Corp—*James Condon*	100 Photikon Dr, Fairport NY 11450	585-421-0540	R	1*	<.1
118	Alta Photographic Inc—*Richard Covert*	1421 International Dr, Bartlesville OK 74006	918-335-2582	R	1*	<.1
119	CDM Optics Inc—*Shaw Hong*	4001 Discovery Dr Ste, Boulder CO 80303	303-449-5593	S	1*	<.1
120	StarDot Technologies—*James Chan*	6820 Orangethorpe Ave, Buena Park CA 90620	714-228-9282	R	1*	<.1
121	Sunrise Imaging Inc—*Joe Paradiso*	1813 E Dyer Rd Ste 412, Santa Ana CA 92705	949-252-3003	S	1*	<.1
122	Micron Business Products Inc—*Harold Palmer*	2998 Syene Rd, Madison WI 53713	608-274-2099	R	1*	<.1
123	Art Research Institute Ltd—*Joey Fischer*	325 Kelson Dr, Atlanta GA 30327	770-933-1733	R	1*	<.1
124	Loersch Corporation Of PA—*Bob Kreger*	1530 E Race St, Allentown PA 18109	610-264-5641	R	1*	<.1
125	Packard Shutter Co—*Reno G Farinelli*	PO Box 1, Fiddletown CA 95629	209-245-5719	R	1*	<.1
126	Cpm Inc—*Stephen Crane*	PO Box 550367, Dallas TX 75355	214-349-6886	R	1*	<.1
127	Subsea Video Systems Inc—*Fred Meyer*	PO Box 159, Elizabeth City NC 27907	252-338-1001	R	1*	<.1
128	Eprad Inc—*Ham-Hi Lee*	28271 Cedar Park Blvd, Perrysburg OH 43551	419-666-8109	R	1*	<.1
129	Oxberry LLC—*Anna Ferraro*	180 Broad St, Carlstadt NJ 07072	201-935-3000	R	1*	<.1
130	Seitz Technical Products Inc—*Bill Matthews*	PO Box 338, Avondale PA 19311	610-268-2228	R	1*	<.1
131	Essannay Show It Inc—*Christopher Chambers*	851 W Grand Ave, Chicago IL 60642	312-733-5511	R	1*	<.1
132	Opelco Inc—*Hermann Esser*	105 Executive Dr Ste 1, Dulles VA 20166	703-437-5534	R	1*	<.1
133	Gray Engineering Laboratories Inc—*Scott Gray*	2118 W Collins Ave, Orange CA 92867	714-997-4151	R	1*	<.1
134	Popcorn Movies LLC	7095 Hollywood Blvd St, Los Angeles CA 90028	310-691-8083	R	<1*	<.1
135	Brooke Engineering and Photographic Equipment—*Jack Brooke*	PO Box 300, Hansville WA 98340	360-638-2591	R	<1*	<.1

TOTALS: SIC 3861 Photographic Equipment & Supplies
Companies: 135 — 36,619 — 177.6

3873 Watches, Clocks, Watchcases & Parts

Rank	Company Name—*Executive Officer*	Address, City, State, Zip	Phone	Type	Fin	Empls
1	Fossil Inc—*Kosta N Kartsotis*	901 S Central Expy, Richardson TX 75080	972-234-2525	P	2,567	13.1
2	Casio America Inc—*Kazuo Kashio*	570 Mt Pleasant Ave, Dover NJ 07801	973-361-5400	S	788*	.3
3	Movado Group Inc—*Efraim Grinberg*	650 From Rd Ste 375, Paramus NJ 07652	201-267-8000	P	382	1.0
4	Swatch Group Inc (Weehawken New Jersey)—*Nick Hayek*	1200 Harbor Blvd Ste 7, Weehawken NJ 07086	201-271-1400	S	322*	.7
5	Howard Miller Co—*Howard Miller*	860 E Main Ave, Zeeland MI 49464	616-772-9131	R	50*	.5
6	Seiko Corporation of America—*Shinji Hattori*	1111 Macarthur Blvd, Mahwah NJ 07430	201-529-5730	S	49*	.5
7	Sharp International Corp—*Herbert Spitz*	484 Sunrise Hwy, Rockville Centre NY 11570	516-536-1600	S	37	.1
8	Watchery—*Hans-Kristian Hoejsgaard*	626 Dean St Ste 2A, Brooklyn NY 11238		R	33*	<.1
9	Riddles Group Inc—*Jesse Riddle*	PO Box 5600, Rapid City SD 57709	605-343-2226	R	27*	.4
10	E Gluck Corp—*Eugen Gluck*	2910 Thomson Ave Fl 6, Long Island City NY 11101	718-784-0700	R	20*	.4
11	Accu-Time Systems Inc—*Peter DiMaria*	420 Somers Rd, Ellington CT 06029	860-870-5000	R	18*	.1
12	Takane USA Inc—*Kenji Hanaoka*	369 Van Ness Way Ste 7, Torrance CA 90501	310-212-1411	R	16*	.1
13	American Time and Signal Co—*Jeffrey Baumgartner*	PO Box 707, Dassel MN 55325	320-275-2101	R	8*	.1
14	Timeworks Inc—*John Kowalski*	2929 5th St, Berkeley CA 94710	510-883-0234	R	8*	.1
15	Electrodynamics Inc—*Don Spetter*	1200 Hicks Rd, Rolling Meadows IL 60008	847-259-0740	S	6*	.3
16	Now and Zen Inc—*Steve McIntosh*	PO Box 110, Boulder CO 80306	303-530-9028	R	5*	<.1
17	Time Systems International	142 S Van Brunt St, Englewood NJ 07631	201-871-1200	R	5	N/A
18	Chelsea Clock LLC—*Meg Trant*	PO Box 1082, West Chatham MA 02669	617-884-0250	R	5*	<.1
19	Electric Time Company Inc—*Thomas Erb*	PO Box 466, Medfield MA 02052	508-359-4396	R	4*	<.1
20	Terminal Rexall Pharmacy—*James Nordlund*	PO Box 996070, Miami FL 33299	305-876-0556	S	4*	.1
21	Mod Electronics Inc—*William Kaiser*	142 Sierra St, El Segundo CA 90245	310-322-2136	R	3*	<.1
22	Accusplit Inc—*W Sutton*	3090 Independence Dr S, Livermore CA 94551	925-226-0888	R	2*	<.1
23	Franklin Instrument Company Inc—*Jeremy Fischer*	233 Railroad Dr, Warminster PA 18974	215-355-7942	R	1*	<.1
24	Quality Time Components—*Mike Wallace*	404 Hughes Dr, Traverse City MI 49696	231-947-1071	R	1*	<.1

TOTALS: SIC 3873 Watches, Clocks, Watchcases & Parts
Companies: 24 — 4,361 — 17.8

3911 Jewelry & Precious Metal

Rank	Company Name—*Executive Officer*	Address, City, State, Zip	Phone	Type	Fin	Empls
1	Visant Corp—*Marc Reisch*	357 Main St, Armonk NY 10504	914-595-8218	S	1,187*	<.1

Note: An asterisk (*) indicates an estimated financial figure. The company type code used is as follows: R = Private, P = Public, S = Private Subsidiary, B = Public Subsidiary, D = Division, J = Joint Venture, I = Investment Fund.

COMPANY RANKINGS BY SALES WITHIN 4-DIGIT SIC

Rank	Company Name—Executive Officer	Address, City, State, Zip	Phone	Type	Fin	Empls
2	American Achievement Corp—Alyce Alston AAC Group Holding Corp	7211 Circle S Rd, Austin TX 78745	512-444-0571	S	906*	2.5
3	M and L Jewelry Manufacturing Inc—Michael Landver	2520 W 6th St, Los Angeles CA 90057		R	858*	.8
4	Maui Divers Of Hawaii Ltd—Robert Taylor	1451 S King St Ste 210, Honolulu HI 96814	808-943-8316	R	824*	.6
5	Jostens Inc—Timothy Larsen Visant Corp	3601 Minnesota Dr, Minneapolis MN 55435	952-830-3300	S	807*	6.7
6	Andin International Inc—Ofer Azrielant	609 Greenwich St, New York NY 10014	212-886-6000	R	625*	.5
7	AAC Group Holding Corp—Donald J Percenti American Achievement Group Holding Corp	7211 Circle S Rd, Austin TX 78745	512-444-0571	S	436*	2.5
8	American Achievement Group Holding Corp—Donald J Percenti	7211 Circle S Rd, Austin TX 78745	512-444-0571	R	436*	2.5
9	Harry Winston Inc—Ronald Winston	1330 6th Ave Fl 33, New York NY 10019	212-315-7900	R	413*	.2
10	OC Tanner Recognition Co—David Petersen	1930 S State St, Salt Lake City UT 84115	801-486-2430	S	300*	1.7
11	MA Brands Inc—Michael W Paolercio Michael Anthony Jewelers Inc	115 S MacQuesten Pky, Mount Vernon NY 10550	914-699-0000	S	148*	.7
12	Continental Jewelry—Glen Smith	405 N West Shore Blvd, Tampa FL 33609	813-286-8004	R	139*	.1
13	Black Hills Gold Jewelry By Coleman—Dwight Sobczak	PO Box 6400, Rapid City SD 57709	605-394-3700	R	123*	.1
14	Michael Anthony Jewelers Inc—Michael W Paolercio	115 S MacQuesten Pkwy, Mount Vernon NY 10550		S	119	.7
15	Marfo Co—Bill Giovanello	799 N Hague Ave, Columbus OH 43204	614-276-3352	R	85*	.1
16	Tessler and Weiss/Premesco Inc—Mark Tessler	2389 Vauxhall Rd, Union NJ 07083	908-686-0513	R	66*	.2
17	Yurman Design Inc—Paul Blum	501 Madison Ave, New York NY 10022	212-896-1550	R	58*	.2
18	Mtm Recognition Corp—Roger Mashore	PO Box 15659, Oklahoma City OK 73155	405-670-4545	R	43*	.7
19	Terryberry Company LLC—Alex Allion	PO Box 502, Grand Rapids MI 49501	616-458-1391	R	29*	.2
20	Prime Time Manufacturing Inc—Salvatore Eacuello	185 Jefferson Blvd, Warwick RI 02888	401-738-1227	R	27*	.3
21	Empire Diamond Corp—Gregory Herdemian	350 5th Ave Ste 4000, New York NY 10118	212-564-4777	R	25*	<.1
22	Tru-Kay Manufacturing Co—Alan Kaufman	PO Box 488, Lincoln RI 02865	401-333-2105	R	23*	.2
23	Krementz and Co—Richard Krementz	375 McCarter Hwy, Newark NJ 07114	973-621-8300	R	22*	.3
24	Ace Holdings Inc—John Arzoian	650 S Hill St Ste 510, Los Angeles CA 90014	213-626-6966	R	21*	.2
25	Brilliant Jewelers/Mjj Inc—Nicolay Yakubovich	902 Broadway Fl 18, New York NY 10010	212-353-2326	R	20*	.1
26	Relios Inc—H Pollack	6815 Academy Pky W Ne, Albuquerque NM 87109	505-345-5304	R	19*	.2
27	Samuel Aaron Inc—Robert Kempler	3100 47th Ave Ste 4c, Long Island City NY 11101	718-392-5454	R	18*	.3
28	A Jaffe Inc—Stanley Sikorski	154 W 14th St Ste 12a, New York NY 10011	212-843-7464	R	17*	.2
29	Kabana Inc—Stavros Eleftheriou	PO Box 25345, Albuquerque NM 87125	505-843-9330	R	17*	.3
30	Sunrise Jewelry Manufacturing Corp—Sol Levy	4425 Convoy St Ste 226, San Diego CA 92111	619-270-5624	R	16*	.3
31	Carla Corp—Ralph Fleming	33 Sutton Ave, East Providence RI 02914	401-438-7070	R	15*	.2
32	Danecraft Inc—Victor Primavera	1 Baker St, Providence RI 02905	401-941-7700	R	15*	.2
33	Larter and Sons—Stephen Schutz	PO Box 902, Laurence Harbor NJ 08879	732-290-1515	R	14*	.1
34	Armbrust International Ltd—Thomas Baker	735 Allens Ave, Providence RI 02905	401-781-3300	R	14*	.1
35	Marathon Co—Roy Forman	PO Box 419, Attleboro MA 02703	508-222-5544	R	13*	.1
36	Riva Jewelry Manufacturing Inc—Ted Doudak	4131 39th St, Long Island City NY 11104	718-361-3100	R	13*	.1
37	M S Co—Kurt Schweinshaut	PO Box 298, Attleboro MA 02703	508-222-1700	R	13*	.1
38	Charles And Colvard Ltd—Randy McCullough	300 Perimeter Park Dr, Morrisville NC 27560	919-468-0399	P	13	<.1
39	Nordt Company Incorporated John C—Robert Nordt	1420 Coulter Dr Nw, Roanoke VA 24012	540-362-9717	R	12*	.1
40	Wheeler Manufacturing Company Inc—Bradford Wheeler	PO Box 629, Lemmon SD 57638	605-374-3848	R	12*	.1
41	Klitzner Industries Inc—Alan Klitzner	44 Warren St, Providence RI 02907	401-751-7500	R	12*	.1
42	Gleim Jewelers—Georgie Gleim	540 University Ave, Palo Alto CA 94301	650-323-1331	R	12*	<.1
43	World Pacific Ullenberg Inc—Joseph K Lau	1010 Executive Dr Ste, Westmont IL 60559	630-887-8288	R	11*	.1
44	Abazias Inc—Oscar Rodriquez	5214 SW 91st Ter Ste A, Gainesville FL 32608	352-264-9940	B	6	<.1
45	Plainville Stock Co—William Weisman	PO Box 1628, Plainville MA 02762	508-699-4434	R	6*	.1
46	E Chabot Ltd—Ezra Shabot	10 W 33rd St Rm 712, New York NY 10001	212-575-1026	R	6*	.1
47	Rolyn Inc—Douglas Ricci	189 Macklin St, Cranston RI 02920	401-944-0844	R	5*	<.1
48	Metal Mafia—Vanessa Merit Nornberg	248 W 35th St Ste 601, New York NY 10001	212-279-4655	R	4*	<.1
49	Shaudra Company Inc—Shirley Sparagana	1801 Whitehead Rd, Baltimore MD 21207	410-265-5200	R	3*	<.1
50	Na Hoku Inc—Ed Sultan	3049 Ualena St 12th Fl, Honolulu HI 96819		R	3*	<.1
51	Ict Inc—Larry Kelley	1330 Industrial Park D, Shelby MI 49455	231-861-2165	R	1*	<.1

TOTALS: SIC 3911 Jewelry & Precious Metal
Companies: 51

					8,030	25.1

3914 Silverware & Plated Ware

Rank	Company Name—Executive Officer	Address, City, State, Zip	Phone	Type	Fin	Empls
1	Onedia Ltd—James E Joseph	PO Box 1, Oneida NY 13421	315-361-3000	R	348	.7
2	Syratech Corp—Alan Kanter	175 McClellan Hwy, East Boston MA 02128	617-561-2200	S	203	.7
3	Towle Manufacturing Co—Stuart Hemingway	175 McClellan Hwy, East Boston MA 02128	617-561-2200	R	62*	.2
4	Great American Products Inc	1661 S Seguin Ave, New Braunfels TX 78130	830-620-4400	S	57*	.1
5	Reed And Barton Corp—Tim Riddle	144 W Britannia St, Taunton MA 02780	508-824-6611	R	25*	.4
6	Bruce Fox Inc—James Greer	PO Box 89, New Albany IN 47151	812-945-3511	R	12*	.1
7	Vita Craft Corp—Gary Martin	PO Box 3129, Shawnee Mission KS 66203	913-631-6265	R	10*	.1
8	Stellar Recognition Inc—Roy Newton	5544 W Armstrong Ave, Chicago IL 60646	773-282-8060	R	10*	.1
9	Rada Manufacturing Co—Gary Nelson	PO Box 838, Waverly IA 50677	319-352-5454	R	9*	.1
10	Utica Cutlery Co—David Allen	PO Box 10527, Utica NY 13503	315-733-4663	R	8*	.1
11	Pdu Lad Corp—Loren Funk	1507 Kishwaukee St, Rockford IL 61104	815-969-7711	R	6*	.1
12	Endurart Inc—Stuart Levine	132 Nassau St Rm 1100, New York NY 10038	212-473-7000	R	3*	<.1
13	Zeit Company Inc—Jim Millburn	3265 Pky Blvd Ste A, Salt Lake City UT 84119	801-972-8210	R	2*	<.1

TOTALS: SIC 3914 Silverware & Plated Ware
Companies: 13

					754	2.7

3915 Jewelers' Materials & Lapidary Work

Rank	Company Name—Executive Officer	Address, City, State, Zip	Phone	Type	Fin	Empls
1	Excell Hallmark Sweet Co—Richard Powers	49 Pearl St, Attleboro MA 02703	508-222-9234	D	425*	.8
2	Hallmark Sweet—Dick Smith	PO Box 358, Attleboro MA 02703		S	61*	.2
3	Antwerp Diamond Distributing Inc—Phyllis Lisker	6 E 45th St, New York NY 10017	212-319-3300	R	32*	<.1
4	W R Cobb Co—Roderick Lichtenfels	800 Waterman Ave, East Providence RI 02914	401-467-7400	R	18*	.2
5	Carrera Casting Corp—Owen Schwartz	64 W 48th St Fl 2, New York NY 10036	212-869-8762	R	15*	.2
6	Karbra Co—Sing Liu	131 W 35th St Fl 8, New York NY 10001	212-736-9300	R	15*	.1
7	Findings Inc—Harvey O'conor	PO Box 462, Keene NH 03431	603-352-3717	R	11*	.1
8	Grobet File Company Of America Inc—John Canzoneri	750 Washington Ave, Carlstadt NJ 07072	201-939-6700	R	11*	.1
9	Victors Three-D Inc—Albert Hess	25 Brook Ave, Maywood NJ 07607	201-845-4433	R	10*	.1
10	Gemvision Corporation LLC—Jill Goodson	706 E River Dr, Davenport IA 52803	563-884-8180	R	8*	<.1
11	Microlap Technologies Inc—Steve Arvidson	PO Box 280, Rolla ND 58367	701-477-3193	R	5*	.1

TOTALS: SIC 3915 Jewelers' Materials & Lapidary Work
Companies: 11

					611	1.9

Rank	Company Name—*Executive Officer*	Address, City, State, Zip	Phone	Type	Fin	Empls
3931 Musical Instruments						
1	Steinway Musical Instruments Inc—*Michael T Sweeney*	800 South St Ste 305, Waltham MA 02453	781-894-9770	P	318	1.7
2	Nutone Inc—*David L Pringle*	9825 Kenwood Rd Ste 30, Cincinnati OH 45242		D	258*	1.0
3	Yamaha Corporation of America—*Yoshihiro Doi*	PO Box 6600, Buena Park CA 90622	714-522-9011	S	185*	1.0
4	D'addario and Company Inc—*Rick Drumm*	PO Box 290, Farmingdale NY 11735	631-439-3300	R	64*	1.1
5	Baldwin Piano Inc	309 Plus Park Blvd, Nashville TN 37217	615-871-4500	S	57*	1.0
6	CF Martin and Company Inc—*Chris Martin IV*	PO Box 329, Nazareth PA 18064	610-759-2837	R	52*	.8
7	Line 6 Inc—*Mike Meunch*	26580 Agoura Rd, Calabasas CA 91302	818-575-3600	R	41*	.2
8	Allen Organ Co—*Steven Markowitz*	PO Box 36, Macungie PA 18062	610-966-2202	R	39*	.3
9	PianoDisc—*Tom Lagomarsino* Burgett Inc	4111 N Freeway Blvd, Sacramento CA 95834	916-567-9999	D	37*	.2
10	Hohner Inc—*Clay Edwards*	PO Box 15035, Richmond VA 23227	804-515-1900	S	28	.1
11	Kawai America Corp—*Hirotaka Kawai*	PO Box 9045, Rancho Dominguez CA 90224	310-631-1771	R	26*	.2
12	GHS International Inc—*Russell Mc Fee*	PO Box 136, Battle Creek MI 49016	269-968-3351	R	26*	.3
13	Carvin Corp—*Carson Kiesel*	12340 World Trade Dr, San Diego CA 92128	858-487-1600	R	21*	.2
14	Avedis Zildjian Co—*Craigie Zildjian*	22 Longwater Dr Ste 20, Norwell MA 02061	781-871-2200	R	19*	.2
15	Taylor-Listug Inc—*Kurt Listug*	1980 Gillespie Way, El Cajon CA 92020	619-258-1207	R	18*	.3
16	QRS Music Technologies Inc—*Thomas A Dolan*	269 Quaker Dr, Seneca PA 16346	814-676-6683	P	18	.1
17	Burgett Inc—*Kirk Burgett*	4111 N Freeway Blvd, Sacramento CA 95834	916-567-9999	R	18*	.1
18	Shield Manufacturing Inc—*David Berghash*	425 Fillmore Ave, Tonawanda NY 14150	716-694-7100	R	17*	.1
19	Paul Reed Smith Guitars LP—*Laura Rausch*	380 Log Canoe Cir, Stevensville MD 21666	410-643-9970	R	17*	.2
20	Rodgers Instruments Corp—*Karl Garner*	1300 Ne 25th Ave, Hillsboro OR 97124	503-648-4181	R	16*	.2
21	Ernie Ball Inc—*Roland Ball*	PO Box 4117, San Luis Obispo CA 93403	805-544-7726	R	15*	.2
22	Lyon and Healy Holding Corp—*Antonio Forero*	168 N Ogden Ave, Chicago IL 60607	312-786-1881	R	14*	.1
23	I T Verdin Co—*Robert Verdin*	444 Reading Rd, Cincinnati OH 45202	513-241-4010	R	12*	.1
24	Midi Music Center Inc—*Naoki Mori*	PO Box 1270, La Grange Park IL 60526	708-352-3388	R	11*	<.1
25	Fox Products Corp—*Alan Fox*	PO Box 347, South Whitley IN 46787	260-723-4888	R	10*	.1
26	E and O Mari Inc—*Richard Cocco*	PO Box 869, Newburgh NY 12551	845-562-4400	R	10*	.1
27	US Music Corp—*Rudolph Schlacher*	444 E Courtland St, Mundelein IL 60060	847-949-0444	R	9*	.1
28	Ovation Instruments—*Paul Kuhn* Kaman Music Corp	55 Griffin Rd S, Bloomfield CT 06002	860-379-7575	D	8	.1
29	Schulmerich Carillons Inc—*Nevin Scholl*	PO Box 903, Sellersville PA 18960	215-257-2771	R	5*	.1
30	Calato J D Manufacturing Company Inc—*Joseph Calato*	4501 Hyde Park Blvd, Niagara Falls NY 14305	716-285-3546	R	5*	<.1
31	Gemeinhardt Company LLC—*Steve Lynn*	PO Box 788, Elkhart IN 46515	574-295-5280	R	5*	<.1
32	Dean Markley Strings Inc—*Dean Markley*	3350 Scott Blvd Bldg 4, Santa Clara CA 95054	408-988-2456	R	2*	<.1
33	Santa Cruz Guitar Corp—*Richard Hoover*	151 Harvey W Blvd C, Santa Cruz CA 95060	831-425-0999	R	2*	<.1
34	Tei Electronics Inc—*Danilo Alonso*	750 W 18th St, Hialeah FL 33010	305-888-3980	R	2*	<.1
35	Brian Moore Guitars Inc—*Patrick Cummings*	290 Main St Ste 3, Cold Spring NY 10516	845-809-5347	R	2*	<.1
36	Mike Balter Mallets—*Mike Balter*	15 E Palatine Rd Ste 1, Prospect Heights IL 60070	847-541-5777	R	1*	<.1
37	LA Sax Co—*James Gavigan*	325 Nolan St, San Antonio TX 78202	210-637-0414	S	1*	<.1
38	WD Music Products Inc—*Larry Davis*	17570 N Tamiami Trail, North Fort Myers FL 33903	239-543-3625	R	1*	<.1
39	Halo Custom Guitars Inc—*Belinda Lee*	21621 Stevens Creek Bl, Cupertino CA 95014	408-873-8606	R	<1*	<.1
TOTALS: SIC 3931 Musical Instruments Companies: 39					**1,390**	**10.1**
3942 Dolls & Stuffed Toys						
1	Mattel Inc—*Robert A Eckert*	333 Continental Blvd, El Segundo CA 90245	310-252-2000	P	5,856	31.0
2	JAKKS Pacific Inc—*Stephen G Berman*	2174 Baker Pky, Walnut CA 91789	909-594-7771	P	765	.8
3	Ty Inc—*H Ty Warner*	PO Box 5377, Oak Brook IL 60522	630-920-1515	R	750*	.6
4	Kid Brands Inc—*Raphael Benaroya*	1800 Valley Rd, Wayne NJ 07470	201-405-2400	P	276	.3
5	Boyds Operations Inc—*Jan Murley*	350 S St, McSherrystown PA 17344	717-633-9898	S	226*	.2
6	Gund Inc—*Jim Madonna*	PO Box 852, Edison NJ 08818	732-248-1500	R	223*	.2
7	Playmates Toys Inc—*Lou Novak*	909 N Sepulveda Blvd S, El Segundo CA 90245	310-252-8005	S	118*	.1
8	Trade Union International Inc—*Mei Lien Chang*	4651 State St, Montclair CA 91763	909-628-7500	R	110*	.1
9	Vermont Teddy Bear Company Inc—*Jonathan Gilbert*	PO Box 965, Shelburne VT 05482	802-985-3001	R	58*	.3
10	Franklin Mint LLC—*Bruce Newman*	801 Springdale Dr Ste, Exton PA 19341	610-884-4800	R	30*	.5
11	Manhattan Group LLC—*Arete Passas*	430 1st Ave N Ste 500, Minneapolis MN 55401	612-337-9600	D	25*	.1
12	Alexander Doll Company Inc—*Gale Jarvis*	615 W 131st St Fl 6, New York NY 10027	212-283-5900	R	25*	.5
13	Bestever Inc—*Kwang Joong Kim*	17727 S Susana Rd, Rancho Dominguez CA 90221	310-515-7030	R	24*	<.1
14	Tonner Doll Company Inc—*Robert Tonner*	PO Box 4410, Kingston NY 12402	845-339-9537	R	18*	<.1
15	Creations by Alan Stuart Inc—*Stuart Kalinsky*	7 W 34th St, New York NY 10001	212-719-5511	R	6*	<.1
16	Lovee Doll and Toy Company Inc—*Sam Horowitz*	286 5th Ave, New York NY 10001	212-242-1545	R	5*	<.1
17	Goldberger Company LLC—*Steven Strauss*	36 W 25th St Fl 14, New York NY 10010	212-924-1194	R	2*	<.1
18	Charisma Brands LLC—*Anthony Shutts*	23482 Peralta Dr Ste A, Laguna Hills CA 92653	949-587-9400	R	2	<.1
TOTALS: SIC 3942 Dolls & Stuffed Toys Companies: 18					**8,519**	**34.8**
3944 Games, Toys & Children's Vehicles						
1	Hasbro Inc—*Brian Goldner*	PO Box 1059, Pawtucket RI 02862	401-431-8697	P	4,002	5.8
2	Little Tikes—*Rory Leyden*	2180 Barlow Rd, Hudson OH 44236		D	675*	2.0
3	LEGO Systems Inc—*Soren Torp Laursen*	PO Box 1600, Enfield CT 06083	860-763-6731	S	585*	1.5
4	LeapFrog Enterprises Inc—*John Barbour*	6401 Hollis St Ste 100, Emeryville CA 94608	510-420-5000	B	455	.5
5	Sony Computer Entertainment America Inc—*Jack Tretton*	919 E Hillsdale Blvd, Foster City CA 94404	650-655-8000	S	315*	.8
6	Milton Bradley Co—*George Ditomassi* Hasbro Inc	443 Shaker Rd, East Longmeadow MA 01028	413-525-6411	S	237	1.6
7	Mad Catz Interactive Inc—*Darren Richardson*	7480 Mission Valley Rd, San Diego CA 92108	619-683-9830	P	184*	.3
8	Fisher-Price Inc—*Neil Friedman*	636 Girard Ave, East Aurora NY 14052	716-687-3000	S	156*	.9
9	Uniek Inc—*Thomas F Pyle*	805 Uniek Dr, Waunakee WI 53597	608-849-9999	R	141*	.4
10	Nintendo of America Inc—*Tatsumi Kimishima*	PO Box 957, Redmond WA 98073	425-882-2040	S	139*	1.0
11	Big Fish Games Inc—*Jeremy Lewis*	333 Elliott Ave W Ste, Seattle WA 98119	206-282-4923	R	132*	.4
12	Exx Inc—*David A Segal*	1350 E Flamingo Rd Ste, Las Vegas NV 89119	702-598-3223	P	118	.7
13	Summit Products Inc—*Mike Searls*	PO Box 620, Trussville AL 35173	205-661-1774	R	87*	<.1
14	United States Playing Card Co—*Phil Dolci*	300 Gap Way, Erlanger KY 41018		S	74*	.5
15	Gaming Partners International Corp—*Greg Gronau*	1700 S Industrial Rd, Las Vegas NV 89102	702-384-2425	P	60	.6
16	American Plastic Toys Inc—*John Gessert*	PO Box 100, Walled Lake MI 48390	248-624-4881	R	51*	.3
17	Poof Slinky Inc—*Raymo Dallavecchia*	PO Box 701394, Plymouth MI 48170	734-454-9552	R	34*	.1
18	Educational Insights Inc—*James B Whitney*	380 N Fairway Dr, Vernon Hills IL 60061		S	30*	.3
19	Small World Kids Inc—*Debra Fine*	1451 W Knox St, Torrance CA 90501	310-645-9680	P	28	.1
20	Ohio Art Co—*William C Killgallon*	PO Box 111, Bryan OH 43506	419-636-3141	P	25	.2

Note: An asterisk (*) indicates an estimated financial figure. The company type code used is as follows: R = Private, P = Public, S = Private Subsidiary, B = Public Subsidiary, D = Division, J = Joint Venture, I = Investment Fund.

COMPANY RANKINGS BY SALES WITHIN 4-DIGIT SIC

Rank	Company Name—Executive Officer	Address, City, State, Zip	Phone	Type	Fin	Empls
21	Buffalo Games Inc—Paul Dedrick	220 James E Casey Dr, Buffalo NY 14206	716-827-8393	R	20*	.1
22	Kids Ii Inc—Ryan Gunnigle	555 N Point Ctr E Ste, Alpharetta GA 30022	770-751-0442	R	19*	.2
23	Athearn Inc—Tim Geddes	2883 E Spring St Ste 1, Long Beach CA 90806	310-763-7140	R	18*	.2
24	Poolmaster Inc—Lee Tager	PO Box 340308, Sacramento CA 95834	916-567-9800	R	18*	.1
25	Universal Manufacturing Co (Kansas City Missouri)—Jim Lepore	5450 Deramus, Kansas City MO 64120	816-231-2771	R	15*	.3
26	Small World Toys Inc—John Nelson	1451 W Knox St, Torrance CA 90501		R	15	<.1
27	Mag-Nif Inc—William Knox	PO Box 720, Mentor OH 44061	440-255-9366	R	15*	.2
28	Edaron Inc—Louis Moretti	100 Appleton St, Holyoke MA 01040	413-533-7159	R	14*	.1
29	Radio Flyer Inc—Robert Pasin	6515 W Grand Ave, Chicago IL 60707	773-542-7100	R	13*	.1
30	Atlas Model Railroad Company Inc—Thomas Haedrich	378 Florence Ave, Hillside NJ 07205	908-687-0880	R	10*	.1
31	Norscot Group Inc—Scott Stern	PO Box 998, Thiensville WI 53092	262-241-3313	R	9*	.1
32	Decipher Inc—Warren Holland	259 Granby St Ste 100, Norfolk VA 23510	757-664-1111	R	7*	.1
33	Alexander Global Promotions Inc—Malcolm Alexander	PO Box 52885, Bellevue WA 98015	425-637-0610	R	7*	<.1
34	Family Amusement Corp—David Peck	876 N Vermont Ave, Los Angeles CA 90029	323-660-8180	R	6*	<.1
35	Action Products International Inc—Gary Polistena	419 Lafayette St, New York NY 10003		P	5	<.1
36	Gamepal Inc—Adrian Robey	3209 Gresham Lake Rd S, Raleigh NC 27615	919-757-9648	R	5*	.1
37	Parris Manufacturing Co—Craig Phillips	PO Box 338, Savannah TN 38372	731-925-3918	R	5	<.1
38	Little Kids Inc—James Engle	1015 Newman Ave, Seekonk MA 02771	401-454-7600	R	5*	<.1
39	Parma International Inc—Michael Macdowell	13927 Progress Pkwy, North Royalton OH 44133	440-237-8650	R	5*	<.1
40	Scott Resources Inc—Michael Warring	PO Box 2121, Fort Collins CO 80522	970-484-7445	D	4*	<.1
41	Chardan Corp—Daniel Johns	705 S Union St, Bryan OH 43506	419-636-6900	R	4*	<.1
42	Instant Products Inc—Heather Boone	PO Box 33068, Louisville KY 40232	502-367-2266	R	3*	<.1
43	Bingo Cactus Supply Inc—Sam Whitlock	3210 E Roeser Rd Ste 1, Phoenix AZ 85040	602-268-2848	R	2*	<.1
44	Con-Cor International Ltd—James Conway	8101 E Research Ct, Tucson AZ 85710	520-721-8939	R	2*	<.1
45	Lite Machines Corp—Paul Arlton	1291 Cumberland Ave, West Lafayette IN 47906	765-463-0959	R	1*	<.1
46	Yomega Corp—Alan Amaral	145 Globe St, Fall River MA 02724	508-672-7399	R	1*	<.1
47	Magic Makers Inc—Rob Stiff	501 Presentation St, Sioux Falls SD 57104	605-338-3900	R	1*	<.1
48	Gameco Inc—Steven Rouke	12319 Plaza Dr, Parma OH 44130	216-676-5000	R	1*	<.1

TOTALS: SIC 3944 Games, Toys & Children's Vehicles

	Companies: 48				7,757	19.6

3949 Sporting & Athletic Goods Nec

Rank	Company Name—Executive Officer	Address, City, State, Zip	Phone	Type	Fin	Empls
1	AMF Bowling Centers Inc—Frederick R Hipp	7313 Bell Creek Rd, Mechanicsville VA 23111	804-559-8600	S	5,536*	9.8
2	Amer Sports Co—Juha Vaisanen	8750 W Bryn Mawr Ave F, Chicago IL 60631	773-714-6400	R	4,351*	2.7
3	AMF Beverage Company of Oregon Inc—Fredrick R Hipp	7313 Bell Creek Rd, Mechanicsville VA 23111	804-559-8600	S	3,524*	10.0
4	AMF Bowling Centers Holdings Inc—Fredrick R Hipp	7313 Bell Creek Rd, Mechanicsville VA 23111	804-730-4000	S	3,524*	10.0
5	AMF Worldwide Bowling Centers Holdings Inc—Fredrick R Hipp	7313 Bell Creek Rd, Mechanicsville VA 23111	804-730-4301	S	3,524*	10.0
6	Acushnet Co—Walter R Uihlein	333 Bridge St, Fairhaven MA 02719	508-979-2000	S	2,206*	4.6
7	Top-Flite Golf Co	2180 Rutherford Rd, Carlsbad CA 92008	760-931-1771	S	1,504*	3.2
	Callaway Golf Co					
8	Under Armour Inc—Kevin A Plank	1020 Hull St 3rd Fl, Baltimore MD 21230	410-454-6428	P	1,473	5.4
9	North Face Inc—Mike Egeck	2013 Farallon Dr, San Leandro CA 94577	510-618-3500	S	1,200	.8
10	Arnold Palmer Golf Management—Jim Hinckley	5080 Spectrum Dr Ste 1, Addison TX 75001	972-419-1400	R	1,159*	3.0
11	Callaway Golf Co—George Fellows	2180 Rutherford Rd, Carlsbad CA 92008	760-931-1771	P	968	2.1
12	IHF Holdings Inc—Scott R Watterson	1500 S 1000 West, Logan UT 84321	435-750-5000	S	836*	5.4
	Icon Fitness Corp					
13	ICON Health and Fitness Inc	1500 S 1000 W, Logan UT 84321	435-750-5000	D	742*	3.3
	IHF Holdings Inc					
14	Huffy Corp—Michael Buenzow	6551 Centerville Busin, Centerville OH 45459		R	438*	1.1
15	Precor Inc—Paul Byrne	PO Box 7202, Woodinville WA 98072	425-486-9292	S	411*	.6
16	Johnson Outdoors Inc—Helen P Johnson-Leipold	555 Main St, Racine WI 53403	262-631-6600	P	407	1.2
17	Icon Fitness Corp—Scott R Watterson	1500 S 1000 W, Logan UT 84321	435-750-5000	R	391*	2.5
18	Golfsmith International Holdings Inc—Martin E Hanaka	11000 N IH-35, Austin TX 78753	512-837-8810	B	352	1.6
19	Aqua Glass Corp—Robert Ball	320 Industrial Park Dr, Adamsville TN 38310	731-632-0911	D	318*	.9
20	IHF Capital Inc—Scott R Watterson	1500 S 1000 W, Logan UT 84321	435-750-5000	R	310*	2.0
21	Sitca Corp	555 Theodore Fremd Ave, Rye NY 10580	914-967-9400	S	289*	1.0
22	Sport Brands International LLC—Steve Wynne	340 Madison Ave 3rd FL, New York NY 10173	212-726-5900	R	249*	.7
23	Bauer Nike Hockey Inc—Chris Zimmerman	150 Ocean Rd, Greenland NH 03840	603-430-2111	S	226*	.5
24	NordicTrack Inc—Scott Watterson	1500 S 1000 W, Logan UT 84321		S	220*	2.0
	ICON Health and Fitness Inc					
25	Karsten Manufacturing Corp—John A Solheim	PO Box 82000, Phoenix AZ 85071	602-687-5000	R	213	.4
26	Bell Sports Corp	1924 County Rd 3000 N, Rantoul IL 61866	217-893-9300	S	207	1.3
27	Life Fitness Consumer Div—Kevin Grodzki	10601 Belmont Ave, Franklin Park IL 60131	847-288-3300	D	203*	.4
28	Cobra Golf Inc—Bob Philion	1818 Aston Ave, Carlsbad CA 92008	508-979-2000	S	170*	1.0
29	Nautilus Inc—Bruce M Cazenave	16400 SE Nautilus Dr, Vancouver WA 98683	360-859-2900	P	169	.3
30	Miracle Recreation Equipment Comapny Inc—Dan Gutherie	878 Hwy 60, Monett MO 65708	417-235-6917	R	168*	.5
31	Varsity Brands Inc—Jeffrey G Webb	6745 Lenox Center Ct S, Memphis TN 38115	901-387-4300	R	156	.5
32	Zodiac Pool Systems Inc—Tony Purdhomme	2620 Commerce Way, Vista CA 92081	707-776-8200	S	150*	.1
33	Schutt Sports Inc—Kenneth Nimmons	710 Industrial Dr, Litchfield IL 62056	217-324-3978	R	148*	.4
34	Eaton Corp Golf Grip Div	16900 Aberdeen Rd, Laurinburg NC 28352	910-277-3770	D	131*	1.3
35	Lifetime Products Inc—Barry Mower	PO Box 160010, Clearfield UT 84016	801-776-1532	R	129*	1.7
36	Playcore Inc—Bob Farnsworth	401 Chestnut St Ste 31, Chattanooga TN 37402	423-265-7529	R	126*	.7
37	Wright and McGill Co—John Jilling	4245 E 46th Ave, Denver CO 80216	720-941-8700	R	126*	.3
38	CYBEX International Inc—John Aglialoro	10 Trotter Dr, Medway MA 02053	508-533-4300	P	123	.6
39	Escalade Inc—Robert J Keller	817 Maxwell Ave, Evansville IN 47711	812-467-4449	P	121	.6
40	Rawlings Sporting Goods Company Inc—Robert Parish	510 Maryville Universi, Saint Louis MO 63141	314-819-2800	S	112*	.6
41	True Temper Sports Inc—Scott C Hennessy	8275 Tournament Dr Ste, Memphis TN 38125	901-746-2000	R	111*	.7
42	True Temper Sports LLC	717 Fifth Ave, New York NY 10022	607-739-4544	R	107	.7
43	Worth Inc—James E Lillie	510 Maryville Universi, Saint Louis MO 63141	314-819-2800	S	106*	.7
44	Heartland Industries Inc—Thomas Vandermeulen	1000 Ternes Dr, Monroe MI 48162	734-242-6900	S	89*	.6
45	Ride Manufacturing Inc—Robert Marcovitch	4201 6th Ave S, Seattle WA 98108	206-805-4800	S	87*	.3
46	Adams Golf Inc—Oliver Brewer III	2801 E Plano Pky, Plano TX 75074	972-673-9000	P	86	.1
47	Shakespeare Fishing Tackle—Scott Hogsett	3801 Westmore Dr, Columbia SC 29223	803-754-7000	S	75*	.2
48	Grandoe Corp—Eric Friedman	PO Box 713, Gloversville NY 12078	518-725-8641	R	71*	.2
49	American Recreation Products Inc—George Grabner	600 Kellwood Pky, Chesterfield MO 63017	314-576-3100	D	70	.6
50	K2 Sports—Wayne Merck	19215 Vashon Hwy SW, Vashon Island WA 98070	206-463-8830	S	65	.5
51	Star Trac	14410 Myford Rd, Irvine CA 92606	714-669-1660	R	62*	.2
52	Rossignol Ski Co—Francois Goulet	PO Box 981060, Park City UT 84098		S	60	.1

Rank	Company Name—*Executive Officer*	Address, City, State, Zip	Phone	Type	Fin	Empls
53	Spirit Manufacturing Inc—*Chris Cox*	PO Box 2037, Jonesboro AR 72402	870-935-1107	R	57*	<.1
54	PlayPower LT Farmington Inc—*Tyler Brohm*	PO Box 897, Farmington MO 63640	573-756-4591	R	56*	.5
55	Aldila Inc—*Peter R Mathewson*	14145 Danielson St Ste, Poway CA 92064	858-513-1801	P	55	1.2
56	Cascade Designs—*Lee Formson*	4000 1st Ave S, Seattle WA 98134	206-505-9500	R	54*	.4
57	Ektelon Prince Sports Group Inc	1 Advantage Ct, Bordentown NJ 08505	609-291-5800	D	54*	.2
58	Penn Racquet Sports—*Dave Haggerty*	306 S 45th Ave, Phoenix AZ 85043		S	50*	.4
59	Wham-O Inc	6301 Owensmouth Ave St, Woodland Hills CA 91367	510-596-4202	R	50	N/A
60	Parker Compound Bows Inc—*Robert O Errett*	PO Box 105, Mint Spring VA 24463	540-337-5426	R	47*	.1
61	Prince Sports Group Inc—*Alistair Thorburn*	1 Advantage Ct, Bordentown NJ 08505		R	45*	.1
62	Columbia IT Solutions—*Mike Allbritton*	PO Box 13430, San Antonio TX 78213	210-343-3400	R	44*	.3
63	Rainbow Play Systems Inc—*C Foster*	500 Rainbow Pkwy, Brookings SD 57006	605-692-1500	R	42*	.7
64	Mountain Hardwear Inc—*Topher Gaylord*	1414 Harbour Way S Ste, Richmond CA 94804		S	40*	.1
65	Shane Group Inc—*DC Shaneour*	200 Industrial Dr, Hillsdale MI 49242	517-439-4316	R	37*	.2
66	Adams Golf Direct Response Ltd—*Oliver Brewer* Adams Golf Inc	2801 E Plano Pky, Plano TX 75074	972-673-9000	S	37*	.1
67	Ringside Inc—*John Brown*	14865 W 105th St, Lenexa KS 66215		R	36*	.1
68	Mizuno USA Inc—*Robert Puccini*	4925 Avalon Ridge Pkwy, Norcross GA 30071	770-441-5553	R	34*	.3
69	Storm Products Inc—*John Chrisman*	165 S 800 W, Brigham City UT 84302	435-723-0403	R	33*	.1
70	Zebco—*Jeff Pontius*	6105 E Apache, Tulsa OK 74115		S	32*	.2
71	Dreams Products Inc	2 S University Dr Ste, Plantation FL 33324	954-377-0002	S	29*	.1
72	Mckenzie Sports Products LLC—*Jody Lefler*	PO Box 480, Granite Quarry NC 28072	704-279-7985	R	28*	.5
73	Haas Outdoors Inc/Mossy Oak—*Toxey Haas*	PO Box 757, West Point MS 39773	662-494-8859	R	28*	.1
74	True Fitness Technology Inc—*Frank Trulaske*	865 Hoff Rd, O Fallon MO 63366	636-272-7100	R	28*	.2
75	Kent Sporting Goods Company Inc—*J Tipton*	433 Park Ave, New London OH 44851	419-929-7021	R	27*	.6
76	Hoyt Inc—*Randy Walk*	543 Neil Armstrong Rd, Salt Lake City UT 84116	801-363-2990	R	27*	.2
77	Odyssey Golf Inc—*George Fellows* Callaway Golf Co	2180 Rutherford Rd, Carlsbad CA 92008		S	26*	.2
78	Water Gremlin Co—*Robert Neal*	1610 Whitaker St, White Bear Lake MN 55110	651-429-7761	R	26*	.2
79	Riddell Inc—*Dan Arment* Varsity Brands Inc	669 Sugar Ln, Elyria OH 44035	440-366-8225	S	25*	.1
80	Olhausen Billiard Manufacturing Inc—*Donald Olhausen*	1124 Vaughn Pkwy, Portland TN 37148	615-323-8522	R	23*	.2
81	Sure Grip International Inc—*Iowne Ball*	5519 Rawlings St, South Gate CA 90280	562-923-0724	R	23*	.1
82	Landscape Structures Inc—*Pat Faust*	601 7th St S, Delano MN 55328	763-972-3391	R	22*	.4
83	Rusty Inc—*Rusty Preisendorfer*	8495 Commerce Ave, San Diego CA 92121	858-578-0414	R	21*	<.1
84	Imperial Pools Inc—*John Maiuccoro*	33 Wade Rd, Latham NY 12110	518-786-1200	R	20*	.4
85	Porter Athletic Equipment Co—*Greg Hege*	PO Box 1790, Champaign IL 61824	217-367-8438	R	20*	.2
86	Easton Technical Products Inc—*Greg Easton*	5040 Harold Gatty Dr, Salt Lake City UT 84116	801-539-1400	R	20*	.4
87	Kolpin Outdoors Inc—*Patrick Gantert*	PO Box 107, Fox Lake WI 53933	920-928-3118	R	19*	.1
88	DeMarini Sports Inc—*Natthan Baldwin* Amer Sports Co	6435 NW Croeni Rd, Hillsboro OR 97124	503-531-5500	D	18*	.1
89	Paramount Fitness Corp—*Steve Rhodes*	6450 E Bandini Blvd, Los Angeles CA 90040	323-721-2121	R	17*	.1
90	AMF Bowling Products Inc—*Fred Hipp*	Utica Blvd, Lowville NY 13367	315-376-6541	S	16*	.1
91	Connelly Skis Inc—*Thomas Stephens* Kent Sporting Goods Company Inc	PO Box 716, Lynnwood WA 98046	425-775-5416	S	16*	.1
92	Women's Golf Unlimited Inc—*Robert L Ross*	18 Gloria Ln, Fairfield NJ 07004	973-227-7783	R	16*	<.1
93	Playworld Systems Inc—*Dale Miller*	1000 Buffalo Rd, Lewisburg PA 17837	570-522-9800	R	16*	.3
94	Jk Products and Services Inc—*Hans-Juergen Kreitz*	1 Walter Kratz Dr, Jonesboro AR 72401	870-268-2976	R	15*	.1
95	Hoppe's	Airport Industrial Mal, Coatesville PA 19320	610-384-6000	S	14	.1
96	Southbend Sporting Goods Inc—*Jory Katlin*	1910 Techny Rd, Northbrook IL 60062	847-715-1400	R	14*	<.1
97	NHS Inc—*Richard Novak*	PO Box 2718, Santa Cruz CA 95063	831-459-7800	R	14*	.1
98	SR Smith LLC—*Bryan Dunam*	PO Box 400, Canby OR 97013	503-266-2231	R	14*	.1
99	American Underwater Products—*Robert Hollis*	2002 Davis St, San Leandro CA 94577	510-562-0500	R	13*	.1
100	Northland Industries Inc—*Patrick Ellis*	2201 12th Ave, South Milwaukee WI 53172	414-764-4068	R	13*	.1
101	Mervin Manufacturing Inc—*Mike Olson*	65 Banana Way, Sequim WA 98382	306-683-9414	S	13*	.1
102	Vectra Fitness Inc—*Doug Maclean*	7901 S 190th St, Kent WA 98032	425-291-9550	R	13*	.1
103	Classic Sport Companies Inc—*Mike Nally*	5151 Bannock St Ste D, Denver CO 80216	303-991-8010	R	13	.1
104	Mathews Inc—*Matt Mcpherson*	PO Box 247, Sparta WI 54656	608-269-2728	R	12*	.1
105	Swimline Corp—*Larry Schwimmer*	191 Rodeo Dr, Edgewood NY 11717	631-254-2155	R	12*	.1
106	Gary Yamamoto Custom Baits Inc—*Gary Yamamoto*	PO Box 1000, Page AZ 86040	928-645-3812	R	12*	.1
107	Martin Archery Inc—*Gail Martin*	3134 Heritage Rd, Walla Walla WA 99362	509-529-2554	R	12*	.1
108	Bison Inc—*Nicholas Cusick*	603 L St, Lincoln NE 68508	402-474-3353	R	12*	.1
109	Hoist Fitness Systems Inc—*Jeffrey Partrick*	9990 Empire St Ste 130, San Diego CA 92126	858-578-7676	R	11*	.1
110	Strong Industries Inc—*Wade Spicer*	PO Box 108, Northumberland PA 17857	570-275-2700	R	11*	.1
111	Zevo Golf Company Inc—*Roberto Buaron* Golfsmith International Holdings Inc	42000 Zevo Dr, Temecula CA 92590	909-296-2030	S	11	.1
112	Sun Mountain Sports Inc—*Edwin Kowachek*	301 N 1st St W, Missoula MT 59802	406-728-9224	R	11*	.1
113	Nash Manufacturing Inc—*Russell Miller*	PO Box 11526, Fort Worth TX 76110	817-926-5223	R	11*	.1
114	Title Boxing LLC—*Tina Jaworski*	14711 W 112th St, Lenexa KS 66215	913-438-4427	R	10*	.1
115	Mid Atlantic Sports LLC—*Melissa Aleman*	10078 Tyler Ct, Ijamsville MD 21754	301-607-4747	R	10*	<.1
116	Activate Inc—*Anthony Macaluso*	2533 N Carson St Ste 2, Carson City NV 89706	775-888-9709	R	10*	<.1
117	Delair Group LLC—*Gerald Herson*	8600 River Rd, Delair NJ 08110	856-663-2900	R	10*	.1
118	Park View Manufacturing Corp—*John Mansfield*	2510 S Broadway Ave, Salem IL 62881	618-548-9054	R	10*	.1
119	Fox Pool Of Lancaster Inc—*Robert Seitz*	PO Box 549, York PA 17405	717-764-8581	R	10*	.1
120	Pro-Kennex—*Kevin Gilbert*	1159 Monterey Pl, Encinitas CA 92024		R	9*	.1
121	Peak Body Systems Inc—*Julie Lobdell*	5555 Central Ave Ste 2, Boulder CO 80301	303-998-1531	R	9*	<.1
122	Ninja Jump Inc—*Rouben Gourchounian*	3221 N San Fernando Rd, Los Angeles CA 90065	323-255-5418	R	9*	.1
123	Diving Unlimited International Inc—*Richard Long*	1148 Delevan Dr, San Diego CA 92102	619-236-1203	R	9*	.1
124	Barnett International Inc—*Michael Houllis*	13447 Byrd Dr, Odessa FL 33556	813-920-4796	R	9*	.1
125	Eufaula Manufacturing Company Inc—*Francis Oelerich*	965 State Docks Rd, Eufaula AL 36027	334-687-2904	R	9*	.1
126	Riedell Shoes Inc—*Robert Riegelman*	122 Cannon River Ave N, Red Wing MN 55066	651-388-8251	R	9*	.1
127	Yellowstone Company LLC—*Dennis Potzman*	PO Box 507, Manhattan MT 59741	406-284-3193	R	9*	.1
128	Diver's Supply Company Inc—*Jean Brigham*	PO Box 88100, Indianapolis IN 46208	317-923-4523	R	9*	.1
129	Arachnid Inc—*John Martin*	PO Box 2901, Loves Park IL 61132	815-654-0212	R	8*	<.1
130	Scubapro/Uwatec—*Helen Johnson-Leipold* Johnson Outdoors Inc	1166 Fesler St, El Cajon CA 92020	619-402-1023	D	8*	.1
131	Mitsushiba International Inc—*Richard Tcheng*	2300 E Walnut Ave, Fullerton CA 92831	714-870-1900	R	8*	<.1
132	ProGolfcom Inc—*Thomas W Ifit* Pro Golf International Inc	32751 Middlebelt Rd St, Farmington Hills MI 48334	248-994-0553	S	8*	<.1
133	G and H Decoy Inc—*Richard Gazalski*	PO Box 1208, Henryetta OK 74437	918-652-3314	R	8*	.1

Note: An asterisk (*) indicates an estimated financial figure. The company type code used is as follows: R = Private, P = Public, S = Private Subsidiary, B = Public Subsidiary, D = Division, J = Joint Venture, I = Investment Fund.

COMPANY RANKINGS BY SALES WITHIN 4-DIGIT SIC

Rank	Company Name—Executive Officer	Address, City, State, Zip	Phone	Type	Fin	Empls
134	Rel Corp—Mark Lundstrum	1462 US Rte 20 Byp, Cherry Valley IL 61016	815-332-4951	R	7*	.1
135	Southern Plastics Company Inc—Terry Spence	2 Humminbird Ln, Eufaula AL 36027	334-687-5758	R	7*	.1
136	Mitchell Golf Equipment Co—Gwen Mitchell	954 Senate Dr, Centerville OH 45459	937-436-1314	R	7*	<.1
137	Ferrari Importing Co—Harry Ferrari	200 Waterfront Dr, Pittsburgh PA 15222	412-323-0335	R	6*	<.1
138	Snag Proof Manufacturing Inc—Harry Ehlers	11387 Deerfield Rd, Cincinnati OH 45242	513-589-6483	R	6*	<.1
139	Moultrie Feeders LLC—Teresa Grimen	150 Industrial Rd, Alabaster AL 35007	205-664-6700	R	6*	.1
140	Bohning Company Ltd—Larry Griffith	7361 N 7 Mile Rd, Lake City MI 49651	231-229-4247	R	6*	<.1
141	Macho Products Inc—Amir Shadab	10045 102nd Ter, Sebastian FL 32958	772-388-9892	R	5*	.1
142	Jugs Inc—Kerry Paulson	PO Box 365, Tualatin OR 97062	503-692-1635	R	5*	<.1
143	Pro Golf International Inc—Thomas W Itin	32751 Middlebelt Rd St, Farmington Hills MI 48334	248-994-0553	R	5*	<.1
144	Pro Golf of America Inc—Thomas W Itin Pro Golf International Inc	32751 Middlebelt Rd St, Farmington Hills MI 48334	248-994-0553	S	5*	<.1
145	D and J Plastics Inc—Dennis Montgomery	PO Box 741, Georgetown GA 39854	229-334-4200	R	5*	.1
146	Outdoor Connection Inc—Floyd Hightower	PO Box 7751, Waco TX 76714	254-772-5575	R	5*	<.1
147	Mann's Bait Company Inc—Francis Oelerich	1111 State Docks Rd, Eufaula AL 36027	334-687-5716	R	5*	.1
148	Dacor—Dave Haggerty	1 Sellock St, Norwalk CT 06855	203-852-1079	R	4*	<.1
149	3M Scientific Anglers—Jim Klug	4100 James Savage Rd, Midland MI 48642	989-496-3401	D	4*	<.1
150	Lamartek Inc—Lamar Hires	175 NW Washington St, Lake City FL 32055	386-752-1087	R	4*	<.1
151	GLoomis Inc—Toyo Shimano	1359 Down River Dr, Woodland WA 98674	360-225-6516	R	4*	<.1
152	Sellmark Corp—James Sellers	2421 Callender Rd Ste, Mansfield TX 76063	817-225-0310	R	4*	<.1
153	Annwil Inc—Geneva Carroll	5204 Saint Paul St, Tampa FL 33619	813-623-2277	R	4*	<.1
154	Slivnik Machining Inc—Leo Slivnik	1070 Linda Vista Dr St, San Marcos CA 92078	760-744-8692	R	3*	<.1
155	Graphite Design International Inc—Megumi Yamada	9045 Balboa Ave, San Diego CA 92123	619-671-0505	R	3*	<.1
156	Creative Urethanes Inc—Richard Heitfield	250 Independence Rd, Winchester VA 22602	540-542-6676	R	3*	<.1
157	Marine Construction and Design Company Inc—Peter Schmidt	4259 22nd Ave W, Seattle WA 98199	206-285-3200	R	3*	<.1
158	Amusement Products LLC—Jay Grant	5954 Brainerd Rd, Chattanooga TN 37421	423-892-7264	R	3*	<.1
159	Aqua Xtremes Inc—Scott Webber	1005 Terminal Way Ste, Reno NV 89502	775-324-8531	S	3*	<.1
160	Meredith Industries Inc—Thomas Meredith	406 Dixon St, Vidalia GA 30474	912-537-8242	R	3*	<.1
161	Bcs International Inc—James Wied	PO Box 8955, Green Bay WI 54308	920-430-3700	R	2*	<.1
162	Strikeforce Bowling LLC—Mike Stout	2001 Parkes Dr, Broadview IL 60155	708-863-1200	R	2*	<.1
163	Brownies Marine Group Inc—Robert Carmichael	940 NW 1st St, Fort Lauderdale FL 33311	954-462-5570	P	2	<.1
164	Sportsgraphics Inc—Larry Conlon	1791 Page Ave, Clarion IA 50525	515-532-2857	R	2*	<.1
165	Indian Industries Inc Escalade Inc	817 Maxwell Ave, Evansville IN 47711	812-467-4449	S	2*	<.1
166	Maravia Corporation Of Idaho—Douglas Tims	PO Box 404, Boise ID 83701	208-322-4949	R	2*	<.1
167	Hawg-Ly Lure Co—Larry Davidson	29 Smallwood St, Indian Orchard MA 01151	413-478-7396	R	2*	<.1
168	Fun Spot Trampolines—Andy Adams	1323 E Franklin St, Hartwell GA 30643	706-376-8989	R	2*	<.1
169	Besler Industries Inc—Herbert Besler	40855 W, Cambridge NE 69022	308-697-4698	R	2*	<.1
170	Sports Design And Development Inc—Wesley Higgins	PO Box 7959, Alexandria LA 71306	318-487-0352	R	2*	<.1
171	Bumper Bowling Inc—Greg Langston	PO Box 560121, Dallas TX 75356	214-630-0304	R	2*	<.1
172	Victoria Skimboards—Charles Haines	2955 Laguna Canyon Rd, Laguna Beach CA 92651	949-494-0059	R	1*	<.1
173	McHenry Metals Golf Inc—Mel Rodelli	4502 Marquette Ave, Jacksonville FL 32210	904-384-4334	R	1*	<.1
174	Vermont Ski Safety Equipment Inc—Carl Ettlinger	PO Box 85, Underhill Center VT 05490	802-899-4738	R	1*	<.1
175	Game Country Inc—Arletta Sanders	2403 Commerce Ln, Albany GA 31707	229-883-4706	R	1*	<.1
176	Van Staal Sales LLC—Jeff Pontius	PO Box 270, Tulsa OK 74101	918-831-6952	R	1*	<.1
177	Bowl-Tronics Enterprises Inc—Richard Gehee	1115 Sherwood Ave, Elgin IL 60120	847-741-4500	R	1*	<.1
178	Summit Gear Inc—Ann Anderson	7685 W Bridle Trl, Flagstaff AZ 86001	928-774-0724	R	<1*	<.1
179	Xertech Inc—Catherine Lamberti	1956 Palma Dr Ste J, Ventura CA 93003	805-477-0202	P	<1	N/A

TOTALS: SIC 3949 Sporting & Athletic Goods Nec
Companies: 179 — 39,494 — 113.9

3951 Pens & Mechanical Pencils

Rank	Company Name—Executive Officer	Address, City, State, Zip	Phone	Type	Fin	Empls
1	Sanford LP—Mark Ketchum	2707 Butterfield Rd, Oak Brook IL 60523	708-547-5731	S	192*	.7
2	AT Cross Co—David G Whalen	1 Albion Rd, Lincoln RI 02865	401-333-1200	P	158	1.0
3	Mark Dri Products Inc—Charles Reichmann	15 Harbor Park Dr, Port Washington NY 11050	516-484-6200	R	21*	.2
4	Rotary Pen Corp—Warren Shea	746 Colfax Ave, Kenilworth NJ 07033	908-245-2437	R	10*	.1
5	Harper Products Ltd—Robert Perlmutter	PO Box 692, Westbury NY 11590	516-997-2330	R	9*	.1
6	Streamline Plastics Company Inc—Joseph Bartner	2590 Park Ave, Bronx NY 10451	718-401-4000	R	4*	<.1
7	Pelican Products Company Inc—Kenneth Silver	1049 Lowell St, Bronx NY 10459	718-860-3220	R	4*	<.1
8	Garland Industries Inc—Louise Lanoie	1 S Main St, Coventry RI 02816	401-821-1450	R	2*	<.1

TOTALS: SIC 3951 Pens & Mechanical Pencils
Companies: 8 — 400 — 2.1

3952 Lead Pencils & Art Goods

Rank	Company Name—Executive Officer	Address, City, State, Zip	Phone	Type	Fin	Empls
1	Plaid Enterprises Inc—Michael Mccooey	PO Box 7600, Norcross GA 30091	678-291-8100	R	900*	.3
2	Dixon Ticonderoga Co—Richard Asta	195 International Pky, Heathrow FL 32746	407-829-9000	S	88*	1.4
3	Koh-I-Noor Inc	1 River Rd, Leeds MA 01053	413-584-5446	R	53*	.4
4	Conversion Technology Company Inc—Jim Newkirk	PO Box 4341, West Hills CA 91308	805-378-0033	R	27*	.1
5	Musgrave Pencil Co—Henry Hulan	PO Box 290, Shelbyville TN 37162	931-684-3611	R	16*	.1
6	Golden Artist Colors Inc—Mark Golden	188 Bell Rd, New Berlin NY 13411	607-847-6154	R	12*	.1
7	Polytex Environmental Inks Ltd—Andy Yamnraj	820 E 140th St, Bronx NY 10454	718-402-2000	R	12*	.1
8	Badger Air Brush Co—Ken Schlotfeldt	9128 Belmont Ave, Franklin Park IL 60131	847-678-3104	R	11*	.1
9	General Pencil Company Inc—James Weissenborn	67 Fleet St, Jersey City NJ 07306	201-653-5351	R	10*	.1
10	Harcourt Industries Inc—Jean Harcourt	PO Box 128, Milroy IN 46156	765-629-2625	R	10*	.1
11	Paasche Airbrush Co—John Pettersen	4311 N Normandy Ave, Chicago IL 60634	773-867-9191	R	8*	.1
12	PBS Supply Company Inc—David Strecker	7013 S 216th St, Kent WA 98032	253-395-5550	R	7*	<.1
13	Spaulding and Rogers Manufacturing Inc—Huck Spaulding	PO Box 439, Voorheesville NY 12186	518-768-2070	R	7*	.1
14	Rupert Gibbon and Spider Inc—Michael Katz	PO Box 425, Healdsburg CA 95448	707-433-9577	R	3*	<.1
15	Meadowbrook Inventions Inc—Harold Sutton	PO Box 960, Bernardsville NJ 07924	908-766-0606	R	3*	<.1
16	Leisure Time Products Inc—Robert E Boyer	2650 Davisson St, River Grove IL 60171	708-452-5400	R	2	<.1
17	Graphic Chemical and Ink Company Inc—Dean Clark	PO Box 7027, Villa Park IL 60181	630-832-6004	R	1*	<.1

TOTALS: SIC 3952 Lead Pencils & Art Goods
Companies: 17 — 1,170 — 3.0

3953 Marking Devices

Rank	Company Name—Executive Officer	Address, City, State, Zip	Phone	Type	Fin	Empls
1	Shachihata Incorporated USA—Shinkitiro Funahashi	PO Box 2017, Torrance CA 90505		S	700*	.9
2	Pamarco Technologies Inc—Terrance Ford	235 E 11th Ave, Roselle NJ 07203	908-241-1200	R	201*	1.1
3	Weber Marking Systems Inc—Dennis McGrath	711 W Algonquin Rd, Arlington Heights IL 60005	847-364-8500	R	134*	.7
4	Diagraph Corp—Robert Quarles	1 Missouri Research Pa, Saint Charles MO 63304	636-300-2000	S	84*	.5
5	Telesis Technologies Inc—Steven Sheng	PO Box 1000, Circleville OH 43113	740-477-5000	R	35*	.2

Rank	Company Name—Executive Officer	Address, City, State, Zip	Phone	Type	Fin	Empls
6	Thermopatch Corp—Tom Depuit	PO Box 8007, Syracuse NY 13217	315-446-8110	R	27*	.3
7	Crown Marking Equipment Co—John Donnelly	352 N Fail Rd Ste 6, La Porte IN 46350	219-362-9921	R	20*	.1
8	Bunting Inc—Joseph Bunting	20 River Rd, Verona PA 15147	412-820-2200	R	19*	.2
9	Schwaab Inc—Douglas Lane	PO Box 26069, Milwaukee WI 53226	414-771-4150	R	16*	.4
10	Pannier Corp—Scott Heddaeus	207 Sandusky St, Pittsburgh PA 15212	412-323-4900	R	14*	.1
11	Dab-O-Matic Corp—Gerard Magaletti	PO Box 3839, Mount Vernon NY 10553	914-699-7070	R	12*	.1
12	Millennium Marking Co—Craig Petersen	2600 Greenleaf Ave, Elk Grove Village IL 60007	847-806-1750	R	9*	.1
13	Dixie Seal and Stamp Company Inc—Curtis Schmidt	PO Box 2188, Tucker GA 30085	404-875-8883	R	7*	.1
14	Keson Industries Inc—Clyde Torp	810 N Commerce St, Aurora IL 60504	630-820-4200	R	6*	.1
15	General Graphics Corp—Charles Wilson	PO Box 2101, Jacksonville FL 32203	904-695-1600	R	6*	.1
16	Mark Maker Company Inc—Robert Pettijohn	4157 Stafford Ave Sw, Grand Rapids MI 49548	616-538-6980	R	5*	.1
17	Lebanon Valley Engraving Inc—Neil Rhine	PO Box 31, Lebanon PA 17042	717-273-7301	R	5*	<.1
18	Schwerdtle Stamp Co—Katherine Saint	PO Box 1461, Bridgeport CT 06601	203-330-2750	R	4*	<.1
19	Automated Industrial Systems Inc—Robert Lindenberger	4238 W 12th St, Erie PA 16505	814-838-2270	R	3*	<.1
20	Atomic Screen Printing and Embroidery—Laura Walden	329 W Columbia Dr, Kennewick WA 99336	509-585-2866	R	2*	<.1
21	Rite Mark Stamp Co—Donald Bailey	4141 N Atlantic Blvd, Auburn Hills MI 48326	248-391-7600	R	2*	<.1
22	Pavement Tool Manufacturing Inc—Patty Smith	PO Box 1048, Gladewater TX 75647	903-734-7531	R	1*	<.1
23	Numberall Stamp and Tool Company Inc—Herman Bayerdorffer	PO Box 187, Sangerville ME 04479	207-876-3541	R	1*	<.1
24	Mecco Partners LLC—Gerallyn Friel	PO Box 5004, Cranberry Township PA 16066	724-779-9555	R	1*	<.1
25	Ellis Graphics Inc—Harry Ellis	5350 115th Ave N, Clearwater FL 33760	727-572-8700	R	1*	<.1
26	Lectroetch Co—David Badt	5342 Evergreen Pkwy, Sheffield Village OH 44054	440-934-1249	R	1*	<.1

TOTALS: SIC 3953 Marking Devices
Companies: 26   1,317   5.0

3955 Carbon Paper & Inked Ribbons

Rank	Company Name—Executive Officer	Address, City, State, Zip	Phone	Type	Fin	Empls
1	NER Data Products Inc—Francis C Oatway	307 S Delsea Dr, Glassboro NJ 08028	856-881-5524	R	83*	.5
2	Nukote Inc—C Baiocchi	2400 Dallas Pkwy Ste 2, Plano TX 75093	972-398-7100	R	79*	1.3
3	Turbon USA Inc—Dean C Edwards	4350 Haddonfield Rd, Pennsauken NJ 08109	856-665-6650	D	50*	.2
4	International Imaging Materials Inc—Vince Dowell	310 Commerce Dr, Amherst NY 14228	716-691-6333	R	40*	.6
5	Inkcycle Inc—Rick Krska	11100 W 82nd St, Shawnee Mission KS 66214	913-894-8387	R	28*	.5
6	Coding Products—David B Speer	111 W Park Dr, Kalkaska MI 49646	231-258-5521	D	14*	.1
7	Guy Brown Management LLC—Ashoke Mukherji	9003 Overlook Blvd, Brentwood TN 37027	615-777-1500	R	12*	<.1
8	California Ribbon and Carbon Company Inc—Robert Picou	4720 S Eastern Ave, Los Angeles CA 90040	323-724-9100	R	9*	.1
9	Aspen Imaging International Inc—Robert H Kanner	3830 Kelley Ave, Cleveland OH 44114	216-881-5300	S	7	<.1
10	Golden Ribbon Corp—Lee Manuel	PO Box 3370, Seminole FL 33775	727-545-4499	R	6*	.1
11	Imaging Systems LLC—Marie Oharek	4160 Ctr Park Dr, Colorado Springs CO 80916	719-591-9660	R	4*	<.1
12	Rayzist Photomask Inc—Randy Willis	955 Park Ctr Dr, Vista CA 92081	760-727-8185	R	4*	<.1
13	Summit Imaging Products LLC—Dawn Christ	2655 S Santa Fe Dr 4h, Denver CO 80223	303-783-0336	R	4*	<.1
14	L1 Corp—Michael Yarbrough	712 4th Ave S, Nashville TN 37210	615-726-1111	R	2*	<.1
15	Copi-Mate Inc—Robert Reese	PO Box 56, Milltown NJ 08850	732-828-1045	R	2*	<.1
16	Laserquipt Inc—David Naas	4870 12th Ave E, Shakopee MN 55379	952-496-3100	R	2*	<.1
17	InkjetsincCom Of Florida Inc—Lisa Picciotti	8695 College Pkwy Ste, Fort Myers FL 33919	239-541-1234	R	1*	<.1

TOTALS: SIC 3955 Carbon Paper & Inked Ribbons
Companies: 17   346   3.5

3961 Costume Jewelry

Rank	Company Name—Executive Officer	Address, City, State, Zip	Phone	Type	Fin	Empls
1	Uncas Manufacturing Co—John M Corsini	150 Niantic Ave, Providence RI 02907	401-944-4700	R	465*	.2
2	Swarovski North America Ltd—Daniel Cohen	1 Kenney Dr, Cranston RI 02920	401-463-6400	R	68*	.9
3	Monet International Inc—William L McComb	1441 Broadway, New York NY 10018	212-354-4900	D	59	.7
4	American Ring Company Inc—Anthony Calandrelli	19 Grosvenor Ave, East Providence RI 02914	401-438-9060	R	38*	.1
5	Tsi Accessory Group Inc—Dee Marino	8350 Lehigh Ave, Morton Grove IL 60053	847-965-1700	R	32*	.6
6	Narragasett Jewelry Inc—Gary Jacobsen	100 Dupont Dr, Providence RI 02907	401-944-2200	R	23*	.2
7	Mel Bernie And Company Inc—Melvyn Bernie	PO Box 7761, Burbank CA 91510	818-841-1928	R	22*	.3
8	International Inspirations—Shaya Reiter	362 5th Ave, New York NY 10001	212-465-8500	R	21*	<.1
9	Dyna Group International Inc—Roger R Tuttle	1661 S Seguin Ave, New Braunfels TX 78130	830-620-4400	R	13	.2
10	Magic Novelty Company Inc—Alex Neuburger	308 Dyckman St, New York NY 10034	212-304-2777	R	11*	.1
11	WBPromotions—Azim Makanojiya	1303 El Camino Village, Houston TX 77058		R	7	<.1
12	Bob Siemon Designs Inc—Laura Lung	3501 W Segerstrom Ave, Santa Ana CA 92704	714-549-0678	R	6*	.1
13	Ubio Inc—John Clemente	3890 Post Rd Ste 4, Warwick RI 02886	401-541-9172	R	3*	<.1
14	Esposito Jewelry Inc—Joseph Esposito	PO Box 72777, Providence RI 02907	401-943-1900	R	1*	<.1

TOTALS: SIC 3961 Costume Jewelry
Companies: 14   768   3.4

3965 Fasteners, Buttons, Needles & Pins

Rank	Company Name—Executive Officer	Address, City, State, Zip	Phone	Type	Fin	Empls
1	YKK USA Inc—Max Mazota	7680 The Bluffs Ste 10, Austell GA 30168	678-838-6000	S	372*	3.2
2	Avibank Manufacturing Inc—David Arnold	11500 Sherman Way, North Hollywood CA 91605	818-392-2100	D	82*	.4
3	Anstro Manufacturing Inc—Robert Bosco	238 Wolcott Rd, Wolcott CT 06716	203-879-1423	S	56*	.1
4	Whitesell Corp—Neil Whitesell	PO Box 2570, Muscle Shoals AL 35662	256-248-8500	R	54*	.9
5	Scovill Fasteners Inc—Stewart Little	PO Box 44, Clarkesville GA 30523	706-754-1000	R	37*	.3
6	Ideal Fastener Corp—Ralph Gut	PO Box 548, Oxford NC 27565	919-693-3115	R	29*	.3
7	Brunner Manufacturing Company Inc—Ronald Brunner	PO Box 225, Mauston WI 53948	608-847-6667	R	27*	.3
8	Triad Fastener Corp—Richard Merrick	PO Box 130, Alda NE 68810	308-384-1780	R	24*	.3
9	Spencer Products Co—Robert Tuttle	1859 Summit Commerce P, Twinsburg OH 44087	330-487-5200	R	22*	.1
10	Termax Corp—William Smith	1155 Rose Rd Ste A, Lake Zurich IL 60047	847-519-1500	R	21*	.2
11	Rightway Fasteners Inc—Kazumasa Arima	7945 S International D, Columbus IN 47201	812-342-2700	R	20*	.2
12	Aplix Inc—Patrick Billarant	PO Box 7505, Charlotte NC 28241	704-588-1920	R	17*	.3
13	Braxton Manufacturing Company Inc—Joseph Triano	PO Box 429, Watertown CT 06795	860-274-6781	R	17*	.2
14	Mona Slide Fasteners Inc—Joel Barrocas	4510 White Plains Rd, Bronx NY 10470	718-325-7700	R	16*	.2
15	US Button Corp—Larry Jacobs	328 Kennedy Dr, Putnam CT 06260	860-928-2707	R	13*	.1
16	Prym Dritz Corp—Johan Starrenburg	PO Box 5028, Spartanburg SC 29304		S	13*	.1
17	Morton Grinding Inc—Wallace Morton	17341 Sierra Hwy, Santa Clarita CA 91351	661-298-0895	R	11*	.1
18	ITW Waterbury Buckle Co—Earl Reilly	952 S Main St, Waterbury CT 06706	203-753-1161	R	11*	.1
19	Southeastern Bolt And Screw Inc—Walter Andrews	PO Box 758, Birmingham AL 35201	205-328-4551	R	10*	.1
20	Bergamot Brass Works Inc—Daniel Baughman	820 E Wisconsin St, Delavan WI 53115	262-728-5572	R	6*	.1
21	Micron Products Inc	25 Sawyer Passway, Fitchburg MA 01420	978-345-5000	S	5*	.1
22	Ribco Manufacturing Inc—Kevin Redmond	192 Georgia Ave, Providence RI 02905	401-467-4300	R	5*	.1
23	W H Bagshaw Company Inc—Arron Bagshaw	1 Pine St Ext Ste 135, Nashua NH 03060	603-883-7758	R	3*	<.1
24	Marchel Industries Inc—Ricky Pitts	100 SW Dr, Spartanburg SC 29303	864-574-6318	R	3*	<.1

Note: An asterisk (*) indicates an estimated financial figure. The company type code used is as follows: R = Private, P = Public, S = Private Subsidiary, B = Public Subsidiary, D = Division, J = Joint Venture, I = Investment Fund.

COMPANY RANKINGS BY SALES WITHIN 4-DIGIT SIC

Rank	Company Name—Executive Officer	Address, City, State, Zip	Phone	Type	Fin	Empls
25	Eaglehead Manufacturing Company Inc—Harris Phillips	23555 Euclid Ave, Euclid OH 44117	216-692-1240	R	3*	<.1
26	Crumrine Manufacturing Jewelers—Jeanne Lashelle	20 Towhee Way, Reno NV 89508	775-786-3712	R	3*	<.1
27	Badge Parts Inc—Joseph Bruno	1520 Paramount Dr, Waukesha WI 53186	262-650-9991	R	2*	<.1
28	Threaded Products Inc—Dave Konrardy	21050 N Brady St Frnt, Davenport IA 52806	563-386-1160	R	2*	<.1
29	Beacon Safety Products Inc—Richard Suhm	226 Vinewood Dr, Avon Lake OH 44012	440-933-8678	R	<1*	<.1

TOTALS: SIC 3965 Fasteners, Buttons, Needles & Pins
Companies: 29   885   7.7

3991 Brooms & Brushes

Rank	Company Name—Executive Officer	Address, City, State, Zip	Phone	Type	Fin	Empls
1	Team Technologies Inc—Steve Henrikson	5949 Commerce Blvd, Morristown TN 37814	423-587-2199	R	117*	.5
2	Worldwide Energy and Manufacturing USA Inc—Jeff Watson	408 N Canal St Ste A a, South San Francisco CA 94080	650-794-9888	P	100	.6
3	Fuller Brush Co—Norbert Schneider	1 Fuller Way, Great Bend KS 67530		R	50*	.5
4	Evercare Co—Tom Penner	3440 Preston Ridge Rd, Alpharetta GA 30005	770-570-5000	R	48*	.7
5	Weiler Corp—Christopher Weiler	PO Box 149, Cresco PA 18326	570-595-7495	R	26*	.4
6	Libman Co—Robert Libman	220 N Sheldon St, Arcola IL 61910	217-268-4200	R	26*	.3
7	Harper Brush Works Inc—Barry Harper	400 N 2nd St, Fairfield IA 52556	641-472-5186	R	24*	.2
8	Carlisle Sanitary Maintenance Products Inc—Dave Shannon	PO Box 53006, Oklahoma City OK 73152	405-475-5600	S	17	.2
9	Old Dominion Brush Company Inc—Tim Brizzolara	5118 Glen Alden Dr, Richmond VA 23231	804-226-4433	R	12*	.1
10	Malish Corp—Jeffery Malish	4260 Hamann Pkwy, Willoughby OH 44094	440-951-5356	R	12*	.1
11	Sanderson-Macleod Inc—Eric Sanderson	PO Box 50, Palmer MA 01069	413-283-3481	R	11*	.1
12	Detroit Quality Brush Manufacturing Company Inc—Donald Weinbaum	32165 Schoolcraft Rd, Livonia MI 48150	734-525-5660	R	11*	.1
13	Pferd Milwaukee Brush Company Inc—James Henderson	W142 N 9251 Fountain B, Menomonee Falls WI 53051	262-255-3200	R	10*	.1
14	Felton Inc—Ben Boehm	7 Burton Dr, Londonderry NH 03053	603-425-0200	R	8*	.1
15	Crystal Lake Manufacturing Inc—Edward Pearson	PO Box 159, Autaugaville AL 36003	334-365-3342	R	6*	.1
16	Industrial Brush Corp—John Cottam	PO Box 2608, Pomona CA 91769	909-591-9341	R	6*	<.1
17	Smith Equipment and Supply Co—Ginger Smith	3825 Maine Ave, Lakeland FL 33801	863-665-4904	R	4*	<.1
18	Rollercoat Industries Inc—Joseph Lancaster	10135 E Us Hwy 92, Tampa FL 33610	813-621-4668	R	4*	<.1
19	Whit Holdings Inc—W Whitaker	5068 Us Hwy 64 E, Franklinville NC 27248	336-824-2321	R	3*	<.1
20	Lakim Industries Inc—Song Kim	1 World Trade Ctr Ste, Long Beach CA 90831	310-637-8900	R	3*	<.1
21	Kingsolver Inc—Keith Kingsolver	PO Box 3106, Santa Fe Springs CA 90670	562-945-7590	R	3*	<.1
22	HW Fairway International Inc—Lee Strange	716 N Mantua St, Kent OH 44240	330-678-2540	R	2*	<.1
23	Radius Corp—Kevin Foley	207 Railroad St, Kutztown PA 19530	610-683-9400	R	2*	<.1
24	Cardinal Comb and Brush Manufacturing Corp—Anthony Mazzaferro	106 Carter St Ste 3, Leominster MA 01453	978-537-6330	R	2*	<.1
25	American Brush Company Inc—Allen Benson	112 Industrial Blvd, Claremont NH 03743	603-542-9951	S	2*	<.1

TOTALS: SIC 3991 Brooms & Brushes
Companies: 25   508   4.2

3993 Signs & Advertising Displays

Rank	Company Name—Executive Officer	Address, City, State, Zip	Phone	Type	Fin	Empls
1	Daktronics Inc—James B Morgan	PO Box 5128, Brookings SD 57006	605-692-0200	P	442	2.6
2	Signmark Div—Frank Jaennert	PO Box 2131, Milwaukee WI 53201		D	351*	2.7
3	Group M Worldwide Inc—Scott Neslund	498 7th Ave Fl 4, New York NY 10018	212-297-7000	H	342*	5.0
4	Rock-Tenn Converting Co—James R Rubright	PO Box 4098, Norcross GA 30091	770-448-2193	S	187*	.7
5	Derse Inc—Adam Beckett	3800 W Canal St, Milwaukee WI 53208	414-257-2000	R	127*	.4
6	Icon Identity Solutions Inc—Greg Goulette	1418 Elmhurst Rd, Elk Grove Village IL 60007	847-364-2250	R	117*	.5
7	Pop Displays USA LLC—Hideto Yamamoto	555 Tuckahoe Rd, Yonkers NY 10710	914-771-4200	R	116*	1.2
8	Alliance Display and Packaging	5950 Grassy Creek Blvd, Winston Salem NC 27105	336-661-1700	D	81*	.4
9	Architectural Graphics Inc—Craig Rohde	PO Box 9175, Virginia Beach VA 23450	757-427-1900	R	62*	.3
10	Everbrite LLC—Tom Rubenalt	PO Box 20020, Milwaukee WI 53220	414-529-3500	R	58*	.9
11	RTC Industries Inc—Richard Nathan	2800 Golf Rd, Rolling Meadows IL 60008	847-640-2400	R	46*	.2
12	Fluoresco Lighting-Sign Maintenance Corp—Ladd Kleiman	PO Box 27042, Tucson AZ 85726	520-623-7953	R	45*	.4
13	Frank Mayer and Associates Inc—Michael Mayer	PO Box 105, Grafton WI 53024	262-377-4700	R	45*	.1
14	Blair Cos—Phillip Devorris	PO Box 2566, Altoona PA 16603	814-949-8280	R	45*	.3
15	UPSHOT Direct Inc—Brian Kristofek	350 N Orleans St 5th F, Chicago IL 60654	312-943-0900	S	33*	.2
16	New England Wooden Ware Corp—David Urquhart	205 School St Ste 201, Gardner MA 01440	978-632-3600	R	32*	.1
17	Apco Graphics Inc—Ronald Cobb	388 Grant St Se, Atlanta GA 30312	404-688-9000	R	31*	.3
18	Coast Sign Inc—Afshan Alemi	1500 W Embassy St, Anaheim CA 92802	714-999-1900	R	30*	.2
19	Noteworthy Industries Inc—Carol Constantino	PO Box 490, Amsterdam NY 12010	518-842-2660	R	30*	.3
20	Fallon Visual Products Corp—Douglas Bagin	7325 Oak Ridge Hwy Ste, Knoxville TN 37931	865-207-4707	R	30*	.2
21	Gold Bond Inc—Donald Godsey	PO Box 967, Hixson TN 37343	423-842-5844	R	29*	.3
22	Adaptive Micro Systems Inc—Richard Johnson	7840 N 86th St, Milwaukee WI 53224	414-357-2020	R	28*	.3
23	Thomas Sign and Awning Company Inc—Priscilla Thomas	4590 118th AveN, Clearwater FL 33762	727-573-7757	R	28*	.2
24	Marketing Displays International—Thomas Lacey	38271 W Twelve Mile Rd, Farmington Hills MI 48331	248-553-1900	R	28	.2
25	Encore Image Group Inc—Tom Johnson	1445 Sepulveda Blvd, Torrance CA 90501	310-534-7500	R	28*	.1
26	Allen Industries Inc—Thomas Allen	6434 Burnt Poplar Rd, Greensboro NC 27409	336-668-2791	R	28*	.2
27	EGads LLC—Julie Grant	3235 Polaris Ave, Las Vegas NV 89102	702-314-7777	R	27*	.2
28	Ovation Instore—Ben Weshler	57-13 49th St, Maspeth NY 11378	718-628-2600	R	27*	.2
29	Kentek Corp—Tom McMillan	1 Elm St, Pittsfield NH 03263	603-435-5580	R	27*	.1
30	Fellers Inc—Frank Fellers	6566 E Skelly Dr, Tulsa OK 74145	918-621-4400	R	26*	.2
31	International Patterns Inc—Shelley Beckwith	50 Inez Dr, Bay Shore NY 11706	631-952-2000	R	26	.1
32	Gallo Displays Inc—Don Lockwood	4922 E 49th St, Cleveland OH 44125	216-431-9500	R	25*	.2
33	Display Producers Inc—Joseph Laurite	1260 Zerega Ave, Bronx NY 10462	718-904-1200	R	24*	.3
34	Chandler Signs LP LLP—Rockford Gray	3201 Manor Way, Dallas TX 75235	214-902-2000	R	24*	.3
35	Work Area Protection Corp—Thomas Bednar	PO Box 4087, Saint Charles IL 60174	630-377-9100	S	24*	.1
36	Aerostar International Inc—Mark West	PO Box 5057, Sioux Falls SD 57117	605-331-3500	S	22*	.3
37	Hi-Tech Electronic Displays	13900 US Hwy 19 N, Clearwater FL 33764	727-531-4800	R	22*	.2
38	Sunshine Electronic Display Corp—Kendall Randolph	PO Box 727, Saint Joseph MO 64502	816-232-4224	R	21*	<.1
39	Affinity Displays and Expositions Inc—Timothy Murphy	1301 Glendale Milford, Cincinnati OH 45215	513-771-2339	R	20*	.3
40	Kubik Maltbie Inc—Sam Kohn	7000 Commerce Pkwy Ste, Mount Laurel NJ 08054	856-234-0052	R	20*	<.1
41	Bullet Line Inc—William Rosenfeld	PO Box 694470, Miami FL 33269	305-623-9223	R	20*	.3
42	Tube Art Displays Inc—Frank Dupar	1705 4th Ave S, Seattle WA 98134	206-223-1122	R	20*	.1
43	Interstate Highway Sign Corp—Robert Brown	7415 Lindsey Rd, Little Rock AR 72206	501-490-3812	R	19*	.1
44	White Way Sign and Maintenance Company Inc—Robert Flannery	451 Kingston Ct, Mount Prospect IL 60056	847-391-0200	R	19*	.2
45	Shorewood Display Co—John Faraci	33 Phoenix Dr, Thorofare NJ 08086	856-853-7000	D	19*	.2
46	Tradenet Publishing Inc—Tom Mertz	PO Box 158, Gardner KS 66030	913-884-7300	R	18*	.1
47	Centerpoint Marketing Inc—Joel Turnen	375 Riverfown Dr, Saint Paul MN 55125	651-578-3600	R	18*	.1
48	H B Stubbs Holdings Inc—Scott Stubbs	27027 Mound Rd, Warren MI 48092	586-574-9700	R	18*	.2
49	Felbro Inc—Norman Feldner	3666 E Olympic Blvd, Los Angeles CA 90023	323-263-8686	R	17*	.2

Rank	Company Name—*Executive Officer*	Address, City, State, Zip	Phone	Type	Fin	Empls
50	Rocal Inc—*Robert Lightle*	PO Box 640, Frankfort OH 45628	740-998-2122	R	17*	.1
51	Lamar Company LLC—*Kevin Reilly*	1986 Beaumont Dr, Baton Rouge LA 70806	225-923-3113	S	17*	.1
52	Eighth Floor Promotions LLC—*Jeff Adams*	1 Visions Pkwy, Celina OH 45822	419-586-6433	R	17*	.2
53	East Coast Sign Advertising Company Inc—*Greg Goulette*	5058 Rte 13, Bristol PA 19007	215-781-8500	R	17*	.1
54	Windsor Marketing Group Inc—*Kevin Armata*	2 Industrial Rd, Windsor Locks CT 06096	860-627-5927	R	17*	.1
55	Crown Products Co—*Bob Bickert*	3107 Halls Mill Rd, Mobile AL 36660	251-476-7777	R	16*	.2
56	Quick Point Inc—*John Goessling*	1717 Fenpark Dr, Fenton MO 63026	636-343-9400	R	16*	.2
57	Fairmont Sign Co—*David Haddad*	3750 E Outer Dr, Detroit MI 48234	313-368-4000	R	16*	.2
58	Persona Inc—*David Holien*	PO Box 210, Watertown SD 57201	605-882-2244	R	15*	.3
59	Formetco Inc—*Lawrence Garrett*	PO Box 1989, Duluth GA 30096	770-476-7000	R	15*	.1
60	Quikey Manufacturing Company Inc—*Michael Burns*	1500 Industrial Pkwy, Akron OH 44310	330-633-8106	R	15*	.3
61	Massillon-Cleveland-Akronsign Co—*Sam Mollet*	PO Box 555, Massillon OH 44648	330-833-3165	R	15*	.1
62	Metal Art Of California Inc—*Gene Sobel*	640 N Cypress St, Orange CA 92867	714-532-7100	R	15*	.1
63	California Display Co—*Irv Bush*	7142 Condor Ave, Commerce CA 90040	323-278-9720	R	15*	.1
64	Wishoo Inc—*David Bolling*	3105 E 98 St Ste 100, Indianapolis IN 46280	317-705-9640	S	15*	<.1
65	Kayco Leasing—*Ladd Kleiman*	PO Box 27042, Tucson AZ 85726	520-623-7953	R	15*	.2
66	Product Miniature Company Inc—*William Ford*	627 Capitol Dr, Pewaukee WI 53072	262-691-1700	R	14*	.1
67	Dee Sign Co—*Braden Huenefeld*	6163 Allen Rd, West Chester OH 45069	513-779-3333	R	14*	.1
68	New Dimensions Research Corp—*Timothy Mason*	260 Spagnoli Rd, Melville NY 11747	631-694-1356	R	14*	.1
69	Signcraft Inc—*Sandra Redington*	100 A J Harle Dr, Galena IL 61036	815-777-3030	R	14*	.1
70	Dublin Management Associates Of New Jersey Inc—*Michael Carrozza*	7 Campus Dr, Burlington NJ 08016	609-387-1600	R	13*	.1
71	Lamar Outdoor Advertising Co—*Kevin P Reilly Jr*	PO Box 6157, York PA 17406	717-252-1528	D	13*	.1
72	Stout Industries Inc—*Pat Conners*	6425 W Florissant Ave, Saint Louis MO 63136	314-385-4600	R	13*	.1
73	Howard Company Inc—*Michael Kopacz*	1375 N Barker Rd, Brookfield WI 53045	262-782-6000	R	12*	.1
74	Sign Faces LLC—*Bill Uline*	PO Box 320096, Birmingham AL 35232	205-591-7777	R	12*	.1
75	American Greenwood Inc—*Edward Sokolofski*	3035 W 47th St, Chicago IL 60632	773-650-1600	R	12*	.1
76	Janis Plastics Inc—*Manu Graditor*	330 N Ave, Antioch IL 60002	847-838-5500	R	12*	.1
77	Eastern Metal Of Elmira Inc—*Michael Knapp*	1430 Sullivan St, Elmira NY 14901	607-734-2295	R	12*	.1
78	Milwaukee Sign Company LLC—*Robert Aiken*	2076 1st Ave, Grafton WI 53024	262-375-5740	R	12*	.1
79	Capitol Sign Company Inc—*Piero Cappelli*	Broad St and Rte 309, Lansdale PA 19446	215-822-0166	R	11*	.1
80	Nimlok Co—*Simon Perutz*	7420 N Lehigh Ave, Niles IL 60714	847-647-1012	R	11*	.1
81	Cicogna Electric And Sign Co—*Frank Cicogna*	4330 N Bend Rd, Ashtabula OH 44004	440-998-2637	R	11*	.1
82	Sargent-Sowell Co—*George Ittner*	930 W North Carrier Pk, Grand Prairie TX 75050	972-641-4911	R	11	.1
83	Markley Enterprise Inc—*Timothy Markley*	800 Lillian Ave, Elkhart IN 46516	574-295-4195	R	11*	.1
84	Acrylic Design Associates Inc—*William Neely*	6050 Nathan Ln N, Minneapolis MN 55442	763-559-8392	R	11*	.1
85	Climax Packaging Inc—*Patt Purdy*	PO Box 579, Saint Joseph MO 64502	816-233-3181	R	10*	.1
86	Nevco Inc—*Gayla Moore*	301 E Harris Ave, Greenville IL 62246	618-664-0360	R	10*	.1
87	Downing Displays Inc—*Michael Scherer*	550 Techne Ctr Dr, Milford OH 45150	513-248-9800	R	10*	.1
88	Colite International Ltd—*Marty Brown*	5 Technology Cir, Columbia SC 29203	803-926-7926	R	10*	.1
89	Acme Sign Hanger Inc—*Darrel Schultze*	1313 Vernon St, Kansas City MO 64116	816-842-8980	R	10*	.1
90	Kinder Group Inc—*Jeff Cardwell*	1915 E N St, Kokomo IN 46901	765-457-5966	H	10*	.2
91	Architectural Signing Inc—*Bill Tolar*	3044 Adriatic Ct, Norcross GA 30071	770-448-2026	R	10*	.1
92	Southwest Sign Group Inc—*Charles Jones*	7208 S Ww White Rd, San Antonio TX 78222	210-648-3221	R	10*	.1
93	Hall Signs Inc—*Larry Hall*	4495 W Vernal Pke, Bloomington IN 47404	812-332-9355	R	10*	.1
94	Ad-Mart Attractions Inc—*Rand Krikorian*	PO Box 68, Danville KY 40423	859-236-7600	R	9*	.1
95	Trans-Lux West—*J M Allain*	1700 Delaware Ave, Des Moines IA 50317	515-265-5305	S	9	.1
96	Hamilton Exhibits LLC—*Larey Gibson*	9150 E 33rd St, Indianapolis IN 46235	317-898-9300	R	9*	.1
97	Okt/Colson Company Inc—*John Jedd*	PO Box 211, Paris IL 61944	217-465-7535	R	9*	.2
98	Adams McClure Inc—*Steve Oldani*	1245 S Inca St, Denver CO 80223	303-777-1984	S	9*	.1
99	Sign-Lite Corp—*Bill Holsman*	12655 Coit Rd, Cleveland OH 44108	216-851-1000	R	9*	.1
100	Programmed Products Corp—*Charles Voydanoff*	44311 Grand River Ave, Novi MI 48375	248-348-7755	R	9*	.1
101	Baird Display—*Neil Wickert*	W220N507 Springdale Rd, Waukesha WI 53186		R	9*	<.1
102	General Display Inc—*Arthur Mastrodicasa*	6 Industrial Park Rd, Medway MA 02053	508-533-6676	R	9*	.1
103	William P Gelberg Inc—*Neil Brami*	6511 Chillum Pl Nw, Washington DC 20012	202-882-7733	R	8*	.1
104	Esco Manufacturing Inc—*Mark Stein*	PO Box 1237, Watertown SD 57201	605-886-9668	R	8*	.1
105	Lewtan Industries Corp—*Douglas Lewtan*	PO Box 2049, Hartford CT 06145	860-278-9800	R	8*	.1
106	Barlo Signs International Inc—*Arthur Bartlett*	158 Greeley St, Hudson NH 03051	603-882-2638	R	8*	.1
107	Lakeshore Display Company Inc—*Daniel Casper*	PO Box 983, Sheboygan WI 53082	920-457-3695	R	8*	.1
108	Harper Mullholland Co—*Patrick Hanrahan*	24778 Meeting House Rd, Denton MD 21629	410-479-1300	R	7*	.1
109	Daysol Inc—*Dennis Polvere*	40 Boright Ave, Kenilworth NJ 07033	908-272-5900	R	7*	.1
110	Magna-Tel Inc—*Mary Farmer*	PO Box A, Cape Girardeau MO 63702	573-334-3096	R	7*	.1
111	Victory Sign Industries Ltd—*Richard Paryse*	2109 Lafayette Rd, Fort Oglethorpe GA 30742	706-866-7999	R	7*	.1
112	Group Delphi—*Justin Hursh*	950 W Tower Ave, Alameda CA 94501	510-749-6890	R	7*	.1
113	Kroy Sign Systems LLC—*Edward Hunter*	7575 E Redfield Rd Ste, Scottsdale AZ 85260	480-619-6070	S	7*	<.1
114	Blair Inc—*Scott Jackson*	7001 Loisdale Rd, Springfield VA 22150	703-922-0976	R	7*	.1
115	R D Niven and Associates Ltd—*Don Hubbard*	955 Kimberly Dr, Carol Stream IL 60188	630-580-6000	R	7*	.1
116	Chicago Scenic Studios Inc—*Robert F Doepel*	1315 N North Branch St, Chicago IL 60642	312-274-9900	R	6*	.1
117	Electronic Billboard Technology Inc—*Zvi Yaniv*	3006 Longhorn Blvd Ste, Austin TX 78758	512-339-5020	S	6*	<.1
118	Advance Graphic Systems Inc—*James Hall*	1806 Rochester Industr, Rochester Hills MI 48309	248-656-8000	R	6*	.1
119	Chameleon Color Cards Ltd—*Phyllis Duha*	6530 S Transit Rd, Lockport NY 14094	716-625-9452	R	6*	.1
120	Highlight Inc—*Allen Lofald*	PO Box 538, Sparta WI 54656	608-269-3191	R	6*	.1
121	Mitchell Signs Inc—*Melanie Mitchell*	3200 Hwy 45 N, Meridian MS 39301	601-482-7471	R	6*	.1
122	Data Graphics Inc—*Robert Welter*	3800 Progress Blvd, Mount Dora FL 32757	352-589-1312	R	6*	.1
123	Epnm Inc—*David Pelletier*	PO Box 6465, Albuquerque NM 87197	505-243-3771	R	6*	<.1
124	Farmington Displays Inc—*Sabastian Ditomosso*	21 Hyde Rd Ste 1, Farmington CT 06032	860-677-2497	R	6*	<.1
125	Cypress Multigraphics LLC—*Casey Kurik*	8500 185th St Ste A, Tinley Park IL 60487	708-633-1166	R	5*	<.1
126	Strong Group Inc—*David Cutter*	PO Box 1195, Gloucester MA 01931	978-281-3300	R	5*	.1
127	Jaf Converters Inc—*John Flandina*	60 Marconi Blvd, Copiague NY 11726	631-842-3131	R	5*	<.1
128	Morrow Technologies Corp—*Sharon Morrow*	12000 28th St N Fl 1, Saint Petersburg FL 33716	727-531-4000	R	5*	<.1
129	Decker Supply Company Inc—*Jane Decker*	PO Box 8008, Madison WI 53708	608-249-2405	R	5*	<.1
130	Schult Industries LLC—*Jeff Journagan*	900 Nw Hunter Dr, Blue Springs MO 64015	816-874-4600	R	5*	<.1
131	National Beverage Screen Printers Inc—*Will Roberson*	12000 Main St, Williston SC 29853	803-266-5272	R	5*	<.1
132	Damon Company Of Salem Inc—*Samuel Newsom*	PO Box 995, Salem VA 24153	540-389-8609	R	4*	<.1
133	Endagraph Inc—*Terry Lollar*	9000 Corporate Cir, Export PA 15632	724-327-9384	R	4*	<.1
134	Bass Industries Inc—*Robert Baron*	3485 Nw 65th St, Miami FL 33147	305-751-2716	R	4*	<.1
135	General Clay Co—*Adolphus Orthwein*	PO Box 999, Cape Girardeau MO 63702	573-334-5041	R	4*	<.1
136	Vgu Industries Inc—*Brian Stransky*	4747 Manufacturing Ave, Cleveland OH 44135	216-676-9093	R	4*	<.1
137	William Frick and Co—*William Frick*	2600 Commerce Dr, Libertyville IL 60048	847-918-3700	R	4*	<.1
138	Noventri—*David Linetdky*	20940 Twin springs Dr, Smithsburg MD 21783		R	4*	<.1

Note: An asterisk (*) indicates an estimated financial figure. The company type code used is as follows: R = Private, P = Public, S = Private Subsidiary, B = Public Subsidiary, D = Division, J = Joint Venture, I = Investment Fund.

COMPANY RANKINGS BY SALES WITHIN 4-DIGIT SIC

Rank	Company Name—*Executive Officer*	Address, City, State, Zip	Phone	Type	Fin	Empls
139	Bacon Signs Inc—*Bruce Bacon*	PO Box 3, Minot ND 58702	701-852-0331	R	4*	<.1
140	Always In Mind Inc—*Beryl Sullivan*	404 Green St Ste B, Thibodaux LA 70301	985-447-1818	R	4*	<.1
141	Bay State Associates Inc—*James Moore*	PO Box 392, Middleboro MA 02346	508-947-6700	R	4*	<.1
142	Brinker Industries—*Didier Blanc*	88 King St Ste 1, Dover NJ 07801	973-678-1200	R	4*	<.1
143	Advance Finishing And Display Corp—*Ross Swigert*	8460 Hopewell Rd, Cincinnati OH 45242	513-921-6161	R	3*	<.1
144	Ideaman Inc—*Ted Swoboda*	7 Cedar Ct, Union MO 63084	636-583-1145	R	3*	<.1
145	Auld Co—*Daniel Auld*	180 Outerbelt St, Columbus OH 43213	614-755-2853	R	3*	<.1
146	Ross Name Plate Co—*Harry Ross*	2 Red Plum Cir, Monterey Park CA 91755	323-725-6812	R	3*	<.1
147	Berline Group Inc—*James Berline*	70 E Long Lake, Bloomfield Hills MI 48304	248-593-4744	R	3*	<.1
148	Signs Now Corp—*Steve White*	6976 Professional Pkwy, Sarasota FL 34240	941-373-1958	R	3*	<.1
149	Grate Signs Inc—*Anton Grate*	PO Box 2788, Joliet IL 60434	815-729-9700	R	3*	<.1
150	Fossil Industries Inc—*Howard Decesare*	44 W Jefryn Blvd Ste A, Deer Park NY 11729	631-254-9200	R	3*	<.1
151	R and M Deese Inc—*Raymond Deese*	PO Box 2317, Corona CA 92878	951-734-1812	R	3*	<.1
152	On Time Promotions Inc—*Larry Weiler*	6280 Oakton St, Morton Grove IL 60053	847-470-1190	R	3*	<.1
153	Interwest Safety Supply Inc—*Bryce Sorenson*	PO Box 31, Provo UT 84603	801-375-6321	R	3*	<.1
154	Infinity Watch Corp—*Patrick Tam*	21078 Commerce Point D, Walnut CA 91789	626-289-9878	R	3*	<.1
155	Nite-Bright Sign Company Inc—*David Mathey*	16061 Pine Ridge Rd, Fort Myers FL 33908	239-466-2616	R	3*	<.1
156	American Name Plate and Metal Decorating Co—*Michael Stevens*	4501 S Kildare Ave, Chicago IL 60632	773-376-1400	R	2*	<.1
157	Adhesa-Plate Manufacturing Co—*Craig Mitchell*	PO Box 84723, Seattle WA 98124	206-682-0141	R	2*	<.1
158	Displaymaker Productions Inc—*Byron Trostle*	1000 S Weller St, Seattle WA 98104	206-623-1058	R	2*	<.1
159	George Eschbaugh Advertising Inc—*Stephen Eschbaugh*	PO Box 130, Wilson KS 67490	785-658-2105	R	2*	<.1
160	Concepts Inc—*Jay Cranford*	PO Box 33219, Decatur GA 30033	404-296-1041	R	2*	<.1
161	Signologies Inc—*Philip Carlman*	37 Plaistow Rd Unit 11, Plaistow NH 03865	603-378-9119	R	2*	<.1
162	Virginia Logos LLC—*Jason Newcomber* Interstate Logos LLC	10001 Patterson Ave St, Richmond VA 23238	804-754-0970	S	2*	<.1
163	National Readerboard Supply Company Inc—*Patrick T Case*	PO Box 430, Poncha Springs CO 81242	719-539-9626	R	2*	<.1
164	Interstate Logos LLC—*Floyd Williams*	PO Box 66338, Baton Rouge LA 70808	225-927-9408	S	2*	<.1
165	Ohio Logos Inc—*Roger Rose* Interstate Logos LLC	4384 Tuller Rd, Dublin OH 43017	614-717-0833	S	2*	<.1
166	Utah Logos Inc—*Gary Turner* Interstate Logos LLC	5278 S Pinemont Dr Ste, Murray UT 84123	801-263-2263	S	2*	<.1
167	South Carolina Logos Inc—*Lee Stewart* Interstate Logos LLC	1221 Atlas Rd, Columbia SC 29209	803-783-1288	S	2*	<.1
168	Nebraska Logos Inc—*Kurtis Griffin* Interstate Logos LLC	315 S 9th St Ste 207, Lincoln NE 68508	402-435-5646	S	2*	<.1
169	Austin Architectural Graphics Inc—*Thomas Dunn*	1406 E 5th St, Austin TX 78702	512-473-2075	R	2*	<.1
170	Custom Hot Stamp Inc—*Donald Williamson*	5055 Ne 13th Ave, Fort Lauderdale FL 33334	954-491-0141	R	2*	<.1
171	Electronic Displays Inc—*Judith Holmberg*	135 S Church St Ste A, Addison IL 60101	630-628-0658	R	2*	<.1
172	Flow-Eze Co—*Patrick Mc Carren*	3209 Auburn St, Rockford IL 61101	815-965-1062	R	2*	<.1
173	Economy Pencil Company Inc—*Joseph Pitner*	PO Box 230, Shelbyville TN 37162	931-684-5434	R	2*	<.1
174	All Sign Systems Inc—*Tina Lockwood*	PO Box 36184, Phoenix AZ 85067	602-230-0614	R	2*	<.1
175	Associated Sign Co—*Michael Shano*	3335 W Vernon Ave, Phoenix AZ 85009	602-278-8464	R	2*	<.1
176	Craft Master Sign Corp—*John Brennard*	1756 Grand Ave, Phoenix AZ 85007	602-484-9588	R	1*	<.1
177	STM Russell Manufacturing Co—*Richard Whipple*	151 Industry Rd, Georgetown KY 40324	502-863-4548	R	1*	<.1
178	AutoComm Inc—*Duane Weber*	1200 S Lynndale Dr, Appleton WI 54914	920-380-8637	R	1*	<.1
179	Georgia Logos LLC—*Bill Jones* Interstate Logos LLC	6597 Peachtree Industr, Norcross GA 30092	770-447-6399	S	1*	<.1
180	Kansas Logos Inc—*Tana Mock* Interstate Logos LLC	2231 SW Wanamaker Rd S, Topeka KS 66614	785-272-1771	S	1*	<.1
181	Minnesota Logos Inc—*David DeSutter* Interstate Logos LLC	201 West Travelers Tra, Burnsville MN 55337	952-895-8079	S	1*	<.1
182	Missouri Logos LLC—*Eric Knox* Interstate Logos LLC	3218 Emerald Ln Ste A, Jefferson City MO 65109	573-893-6662	S	1*	<.1
183	New Jersey Logos LLC—*Lee Haddaway* Interstate Logos LLC	1230 Parkway Ave Ste 1, West Trenton NJ 08628	609-406-9525	S	1*	<.1
184	Kentucky Logos LLC—*JR Jarvis* Interstate Logos LLC	2129 Commerical Dr Ste, Frankfort KY 40601	502-227-0802	S	1*	<.1
185	Mississippi Logos LLC—*Johnny Durrett* Interstate Logos LLC	113 Village Blvd Ste C, Madison MS 39110	601-853-7100	S	1*	<.1
186	Tecnolux Inc—*Michael Emoff*	103 14th St, Brooklyn NY 11215	718-369-3900	R	1*	<.1
187	Florida Logos Inc—*Andrew Hennosy* Interstate Logos LLC	3764 New Tampa Hwy, Lakeland FL 33815	863-686-5261	S	1*	<.1
188	Oklahoma Logos LLC—*Everett Stewart* Interstate Logos LLC	4334 NW Expressway, Oklahoma City OK 73116	405-840-1550	S	1*	<.1
189	Michigan Logos LLC—*Michael Kovalchick* Interstate Logos LLC	5030 Northwind Dr Ste, East Lansing MI 48823	517-337-2267	S	1*	<.1
190	American Led-Gible Inc—*Charles Morrison*	1776 Lone Eagle St, Columbus OH 43228	614-851-1100	R	1*	<.1
191	Fkn Systek Inc—*Klaus Heimann*	86 Kendall Ave, Framingham MA 01702	508-935-2282	R	1*	<.1
192	Doppler Systems—*David Cunningham*	PO Box 2780, Carefree AZ 85377	480-488-9755	R	1*	<.1
193	ACL Equipment Corp—*Martin Reinfeld*	Northfield Rd, Livingston NJ 07039	973-740-9800	R	<1*	<.1
194	Image Matters Inc—*Roger Laudy*	1808 Ramhurst Dr, Clemmons NC 27012	336-940-3000	R	<1*	<.1
195	Highway Handyman Products Inc—*Gary Wood*	4881 Biscayne Ave, Eagan MN 55123	651-423-1968	R	<1*	<.1

TOTALS: SIC 3993 Signs & Advertising Displays
Companies: 195　　　　　　　　　　　　　　　　　　　　　　　　　　　　　3,895　　31.0

3995 Burial Caskets

Rank	Company Name—*Executive Officer*	Address, City, State, Zip	Phone	Type	Fin	Empls
1	Batesville Casket Company Inc—*Joe A Raver*	1 Batesville Blvd, Batesville IN 47006	812-934-7500	S	638	3.3
2	York Group Inc—*James Doyle*	2 NorthShore Center St, Pittsburgh PA 15212	412-995-1600	S	192*	1.7
3	Aurora Casket Company Inc—*William Backman*	PO Box 29, Aurora IN 47001	812-926-1111	R	49*	.9
4	Clark Grave Vault Co—*David Beck*	PO Box 8250, Columbus OH 43201	614-294-3761	R	24*	.2
5	Casket Shells Inc—*Joseph Semon*	PO Box 172, Archbald PA 18403	570-876-2642	R	21*	<.1
6	JM Hutton and Company Inc—*Richard Jeffers*	PO Box 129, Richmond IN 47375	765-962-3591	R	20*	.1
7	Freeman Metal Products Inc—*Morris Freeman*	PO Box 785, Ahoskie NC 27910	252-332-5390	R	12*	.2
8	Astral Industries Inc—*Charles B Shaw*	PO Box 638, Lynn IN 47355	765-874-2525	R	12*	.1
9	Greenwood Inc—*Donna Darby-Walthall*	3901 N Vermilion St, Danville IL 61834	217-442-9224	R	10*	.1
10	Schuylkill Haven Casket Company Inc—*Donald Houck*	PO Box 179, Schuylkill Haven PA 17972	570-385-0296	R	10*	.1
11	Eternal Image Inc—*Clint Mytych*	28800 Orchard Lake Rd, Farmington Hills MI 48334	248-932-3333	P	<1	<.1

TOTALS: SIC 3995 Burial Caskets
Companies: 11　　　　　　　　　　　　　　　　　　　　　　　　　　　　　987　　6.6

Rank	Company Name—*Executive Officer*	Address, City, State, Zip	Phone	Type	Fin	Empls
3996 Hard Surface Floor Coverings Nec						
1	Mannington Mills Inc—*Tom Davis*	PO Box 30, Salem NJ 08079	856-935-3000	R	440*	2.2
2	Forbo Industries Inc—*Tom Kaiser*	PO Box 667, Hazleton PA 18201	570-459-0771	R	40*	.1
3	Natco Products Corp—*Michael Litner*	PO Box 190, West Warwick RI 02893	401-828-0300	R	34*	.6
4	Tuplex Corp—*Richard Deneau*	2012 Corporate Ln Ste, Naperville IL 60563	630-579-6456	S	8*	<.1
5	The Motz Group—*Joseph E Motz*	3607 Church St Ste 300, Cincinnati OH 45244	513-533-6452	S	2*	<.1

TOTALS: SIC 3996 Hard Surface Floor Coverings Nec
Companies: 5   524   2.9

Rank	Company Name—*Executive Officer*	Address, City, State, Zip	Phone	Type	Fin	Empls
3999 Manufacturing Industries Nec						
1	ConvaTec—*David I Johnson*	100 Headquarters Park, Skillman NJ 08558		R	28,561*	8.0
2	Milliken Chemical—*Joe Salley*	920 Milliken Rd, Spartanburg SC 29303	864-503-2200	R	3,317*	10.0
3	International Game Technology Inc—*Patti S Hart*	PO Box 10580, Reno NV 89510	775-448-7777	P	1,957	4.6
4	Provisur Technologies Inc—*Mel Cohen*	9150 191st St, Mokena IL 60448	708-479-3500	P	1,351*	.5
5	Brady Corp—*Frank M Jaehnert*	PO Box 571, Milwaukee WI 53201		P	1,340	6.5
6	Blyth Inc—*Robert B Goergen*	1 E Weaver St, Greenwich CT 06831	203-661-1926	P	1,221	2.3
7	Yankee Candle Company Inc—*Harlen Kent*	16 Yankee Candle Way, South Deerfield MA 01373	413-665-8306	P	885*	5.3
8	WMS Industries Inc—*Brian R Gamache*	800 S Northpoint Blvd, Waukegan IL 60085	847-785-3000	P	783	1.9
9	Royer Corp—*Roger Williams*	805 East St, Madison IN 47250	812-265-3133	R	776*	.1
10	Ceradyne Inc—*Joel P Moskowitz*	3169 Red Hill Ave, Costa Mesa CA 92626		P	572	2.1
11	Mid-South Industries Inc—*Harold R Weaver*	2620 E Meighan Blvd, Gadsden AL 35903	256-494-3265	R	563*	1.6
12	WMS Gaming Inc—*Orrin J Edidin* WMS Industries Inc	3401 N California Ave, Chicago IL 60618	773-961-1620	S	398*	.8
13	Enesco Corp—*Jeff F Cauley*	225 Windsor Dr, Itasca IL 60143	630-875-5300	S	384	1.8
14	UNICEF—*Anthony Lake*	3 United Nations Plz, New York NY 10017	212-326-7000	R	352*	1.0
15	Quanta Systems Corp QDI Div—*Philip M Blackmon*	510 Spring Street Suit, Herndon VA 20170	301-590-3300	D	249*	.1
16	Midwest Grain Products Inc—*Tim Newkirk*	PO Box 130, Atchison KS 66002		P	248	.2
17	Summer Infant Inc—*Jason P Macari*	1275 Park E Dr, Woonsocket RI 02895	401-671-6550	P	238	.2
18	Lowell Engineering Corp—*Frank Stronach*	6151 Bancroft Ave SE, Alto MI 49302	616-868-6122	D	233*	.7
19	Shuffle Master Inc—*Gavin Isaacs*	1106 Palms Airport Dr, Las Vegas NV 89119	702-897-7150	P	228	.7
20	Oil-Dri Corporation of America—*Daniel S Jaffee*	410 N Michigan Ave Ste, Chicago IL 60611	312-321-1515	P	227	.8
21	Day-Timers Inc—*Bob Dorney*	1 Willow Ln, East Texas PA 18046	610-398-1151	S	200*	1.3
22	Garelick Farms Inc—*Larry Zelkind*	1199 W Central St, Franklin MA 02038	508-528-9000	S	192*	1.6
23	OtterBox—*Curt Richardson*	209 S Meldrum St, Fort Collins CO 80521	970-493-8446	R	169	.3
24	Blackbourn Media Packaging—*Micheal B Ziebell*	200 4th Ave N, Edgerton MN 56128	507-442-3642	S	166*	.3
25	Amdec Inc—*Kathy Carmody*	2623 Manana Dr, Dallas TX 75220	214-654-0560	R	158*	.1
26	Piston Automotive LLC—*Steven Hayworth*	12723 Telegraph Rd, Redford MI 48239	313-541-8674	R	143*	.1
27	Wahl Clipper Corp—*Patrick Anello*	PO Box 578, Sterling IL 61081	815-625-6525	R	129*	2.0
28	ACMI Corp	136 Turnpike Rd, Southborough MA 01772	508-804-2600	S	105*	.3
29	American Biophysics Corp—*Raymond Iannetta*	140 Frenchtown Rd, North Kingstown RI 02852	401-884-3500	R	102*	.2
30	Bally Technologies—*Robert Luciano*	300 Sierra Manor Dr, Reno NV 89511	775-850-1500	S	101*	.1
31	Ravenswood Studio Inc—*Michael Shapiro*	6900 N Central Park Av, Lincolnwood IL 60712	847-679-2800	R	99*	<.1
32	Ferry Morse Seed Co—*Daniel Schrodt*	PO Box 1620, Fulton KY 42041	270-472-3400	R	98*	.3
33	General Foam Plastics Corp—*Ascher Chase*	3321 E Princess Anne R, Norfolk VA 23502	757-857-0153	R	96*	1.5
34	Walter Kidde Portable Equipment Inc—*Michael Leblanc*	1016 Corporate Park Dr, Mebane NC 27302	919-563-5911	R	91*	.3
35	Epolin Holding Corp—*Greg Amato*	358-364 Adams St, Newark NJ 07105	973-465-9495	S	84*	<.1
36	Polk Audio Inc—*James Minarik*	5601 Metro Dr, Baltimore MD 21215	410-358-3600	S	83*	.1
37	Caffco International—*Lamar Thompson*	PO Box 3508, Montgomery AL 36109	334-272-2140	R	71*	.5
38	Cinnabar CA—*Jonathan Katz*	4571 Electronics Pl, Los Angeles CA 90039	818-842-8190	R	68*	.2
39	Thermospas Inc—*Andy Tournas*	155 E St, Wallingford CT 06492	203-265-6133	R	60*	.4
40	Zippo Manufacturing Company Inc—*Greg Booth*	PO Box 364, Bradford PA 16701	814-368-2700	R	60*	1.0
41	Sakura Finetek USA Inc—*Anthony Marotti*	1750 W 214th St, Torrance CA 90501	310-972-7800	R	54*	.1
42	Sakata Seed America Inc—*Dave Armstrong*	PO Box 880, Morgan Hill CA 95038	408-778-7758	S	50*	.2
43	Pioneer Balloon Co—*Ted Vlamis*	5000 E 29th St N, Wichita KS 67220	316-685-2266	R	48*	.1
44	PrimeTech Inc—*John Taylor*	3131-B N Franklin Rd, Indianapolis IN 46226	317-715-1100	S	44*	.1
45	Cast-Crete Corp—*John Stanton*	PO Box 24567, Tampa FL 33623	813-621-4641	R	42	.3
46	Santa's Best—*William Protz Jr*	3750 W Deerfield Rd St, Riverwoods IL 60015	920-684-4448	R	40*	.4
47	Cross Match Technologies Inc—*David Buckley*	3950 RCA Blvd Ste 5001, Palm Beach Gardens FL 33410	561-622-1650	R	40*	.2
48	SA Technology—*Michael Cappello*	3985 S Lincoln Ave Ste, Loveland CO 80537	970-663-1431	R	40*	.1
49	Masterspas Inc—*Robert Lauter*	6927 Lincoln Pkwy, Fort Wayne IN 46804	260-436-9100	R	40*	.2
50	Ride Inc—*Robert Marcovitch*	8160 304th Ave SE, Preston WA 98050	425-222-6015	R	40	.3
51	Pacific Trade International Inc—*Mei Xu*	5515 Security Ln Ste 1, Rockville MD 20852	301-816-4200	R	33*	<.1
52	Arizona Natural Resources Inc—*George Dembow*	2525 E Beardsley Rd, Phoenix AZ 85050	602-569-6900	R	32*	.3
53	Insignia Systems Inc—*Scott Drill*	8799 Brooklyn Blvd, Minneapolis MN 55445	763-392-6200	P	30	.1
54	Pacific Columns Inc—*Robert Sellek*	505 W Lambert Rd, Brea CA 92821	714-257-9600	R	30*	.1
55	Buckeye Fire Equipment Co—*Thomas Bower*	110 Kings Rd, Kings Mountain NC 28086	704-739-7415	R	30*	.3
56	Hogan Manufacturing Inc—*Mark Hogan*	PO Box 398, Escalon CA 95320	209-838-7323	R	29*	.3
57	Trend Enterprises Inc—*Kay Fredericks*	PO Box 64073, Saint Paul MN 55164	651-631-2850	R	28*	.2
58	Hanna's Candle Co—*Burt Hanna*	PO Box 3557, Fayetteville AR 72702	479-718-7700	R	27*	.5
59	Shuttlelift Inc	49 E Yew St, Sturgeon Bay WI 54235	920-743-8650	S	27*	.2
60	American Educational Products Inc—*Michael Anderson*	PO Box 2121, Fort Collins CO 80522	970-484-7445	R	27*	.1
61	Vestil Manufacturing Corp—*Ralph Trine*	PO Box 507, Angola IN 46703	260-665-7586	R	26*	.3
62	Ira Green Inc—*Michael Allister*	177 Georgia Ave, Providence RI 02905	401-467-4770	R	26*	.2
63	Andis Co—*Matthew Andis*	PO Box 085005, Racine WI 53408	262-884-2600	R	26*	.4
64	Trans-Lux Corp—*JM Allain*	26 Pearl St, Norwalk CT 06850	203-853-4321	P	24	.2
65	Maddak Inc—*Kurt Landsberger*	6 Industrial Rd, Pequannock NJ 07440	973-628-7600	S	24*	.3
66	Al Root Co—*John A Root*	PO Box 706, Medina OH 44256	330-725-6677	R	24*	.3
67	Entertainment Gaming Asia Inc—*Clarance Chung*	40 E Chicago Ave Ste 1, Chicago IL 60611	312-867-0848	P	22	.3
68	Badger Fire Protection—*Vic Modic*	944 Glenwood Station L, Charlottesville VA 22901		S	22*	.2
69	Teledyne Benthos—*Ronald Marsiglio*	49 Edgerton Dr, North Falmouth MA 02556	508-563-1000	S	22*	.3
70	Marquis Corp—*John Schrenk*	596 Hoffman Rd, Independence OR 97351	503-838-0888	R	21*	.3
71	J Kinderman and Sons Inc—*AS Kinderman*	2900 S 20th St, Philadelphia PA 19145	215-271-7600	R	21*	.1
72	Grand Products Inc—*David Marofske*	1757 Winthrop Dr, Des Plaines IL 60018	847-795-0400	R	20*	.3
73	Orlandi Inc—*Sven Dobler*	131 Executive Blvd, Farmingdale NY 11735	631-756-0110	R	20*	.2
74	Columbian Home Products LLC—*Dick Ryan*	550 N Rand Rd, Lake Zurich IL 60047	847-307-8621	R	20*	.2
75	Film Technologies International Inc—*Don Wheeler*	2544 Terminal Dr S, St Petersburg FL 33712	727-327-2544	R	20*	.1
76	Nu-Dell Manufacturing Company Inc—*David Block*	2250 E Devon Ave Ste 3, Des Plaines IL 60018	847-803-4500	R	20*	.1
77	Inverness Corp—*William Mead*	PO Box 2973, Attleboro MA 02703	774-203-1130	R	20*	.1
78	Greneker Inc—*Erik Johnson*	3110 E 12th St, Los Angeles CA 90023	323-263-9000	R	20*	.1

Note: An asterisk (*) indicates an estimated financial figure. The company type code used is as follows: R = Private, P = Public, S = Private Subsidiary, B = Public Subsidiary, D = Division, J = Joint Venture, I = Investment Fund.

COMPANY RANKINGS BY SALES WITHIN 4-DIGIT SIC

Rank	Company Name—*Executive Officer*	Address, City, State, Zip	Phone	Type	Fin	Empls
79	Stageright Corp—*O Rogers*	495 Pioneer Pkwy, Clare MI 48617	989-386-7393	R	19*	.2
80	Ami Entertainment Network Inc—*Mike Maas*	155 Rittenhouse Cir, Bristol PA 19007	215-826-1400	R	18*	.2
81	Replogle Globes Inc—*Dan Dillon*	2801 S 25th Ave, Broadview IL 60155	708-343-0900	R	18*	.2
82	Health Pro Inc—*Bart Greenhut*	2532 Strozier Ave, South El Monte CA 91733		R	18*	.1
83	Seastone LLC—*Eric Child*	5152 N Edgewood Dr Ste, Provo UT 84604	801-762-0088	R	17*	<.1
84	Filtrona Greensboro Inc—*Roger Bird*	PO Box 49421, Greensboro NC 27419	336-605-0293	R	17*	.2
85	LC Bullfrog International—*Ash Capital*	668 W 14600 S, Riverton UT 84065	801-565-8111	R	17*	.2
86	Silvestri Studio Inc—*E Levi*	PO Box 512198, Los Angeles CA 90051	323-277-4420	R	16*	.2
87	Fortunet Inc—*Yuri Itkis*	2950 S Highland Dr, Las Vegas NV 89109	702-796-9090	R	16	.1
88	Alene Candles LLC—*Michael Fahey*	51 Scarborough Ln, Milford NH 03055	603-673-5050	R	15*	.1
89	Dadant and Sons Inc—*Tim Dadant*	51 S 2nd St Ste 2, Hamilton IL 62341	217-847-3324	R	14*	.2
90	Dain Betty Creations Inc—*Gerald Leebow*	PO Box 133010, Hialeah FL 33013	305-769-3451	R	14*	.2
91	Akon Inc—*Surya Sareen*	2135 Ringwood Ave, San Jose CA 95131	408-432-8039	R	14*	.1
92	Learning Resources Inc—*Etienne Veber*	380 N Fairway Dr, Vernon Hills IL 60061	847-573-8400	R	13*	.1
93	Diversified Service Technologies Inc—*Brenda Lewo*	34364 Goddard Rd, Romulus MI 48174	734-941-5400	R	13*	.2
94	BargainLockscom—*Steve Maxim*	7239 Wales Ave NW, North Canton OH 44720		R	13*	<.1
95	Softub Inc—*Edward Mcgarry*	13495 Gregg St, Poway CA 92064	661-702-1401	R	13*	.1
96	J Harris and Sons Co—*Jack Harris*	50 26th St, Pittsburgh PA 15222	412-391-5532	R	13*	.1
97	Peerless Umbrella Company Inc—*Gene Moscowitz*	427 Ferry St, Newark NJ 07105	973-578-4900	R	12*	.1
98	Micro Design International (USA) Inc—*Martin Hegart*	45 Skyline Dr Ste 1017, Lake Mary FL 32746	407-472-6000	R	12*	<.1
99	Stagecraft Industries Inc—*William Walter*	PO Box 4442, Portland OR 97208	503-286-1600	R	12*	.1
100	Village Candle Inc—*Paul Aldrich*	PO Box 889, Wells ME 04090	207-725-9223	R	12*	.1
101	Liberty-Pittsburgh Systems Inc—*Kevin Weir*	3498 Grand Ave, Pittsburgh PA 15225	412-771-8000	R	12*	.1
102	Maine Machine Products Co—*David Macmahon*	PO Box 260, South Paris ME 04281	207-743-6344	R	11*	.1
103	Four Paws Products Ltd—*Allen Simon*	50 Wireless Blvd, Hauppauge NY 11788	631-434-1100	S	11*	.1
104	Atlas Match LLC—*Carolyn Bernard*	PO Box 1227, Euless TX 76039	817-354-7474	R	11*	.1
105	Plantscape Inc—*Steve Falatovich*	3101 Liberty Ave, Pittsburgh PA 15201	412-281-6352	R	10*	.1
106	Assemblers Inc—*Joel Rosenbacher*	2850 W Columbus Ave, Chicago IL 60652	773-378-3000	R	10*	.3
107	Candle-Lite Co—*John Gerlach*	PO Box 42364, Cincinnati OH 45242	513-563-1113	S	10*	.1
108	Highland Labs Inc—*Peter Lewis*	42b Pope Rd, Holliston MA 01746	508-429-2918	R	10*	<.1
109	Cover-Pools Inc—*Rick Clark*	66 E 3335 S, Salt Lake City UT 84115	801-484-2724	R	10*	.1
110	ITW Shakeproof Assembly Components—*David B Speer*	2550 S 27th Ave, Broadview IL 60155	708-681-3891	S	9	.1
111	Whitney Originals Inc—*David Whitney*	5 Bridge St, Machias ME 04654	207-255-3392	R	9*	.1
112	Lumi-Lite Candle Co—*George Pappas*	PO Box 97, Norwich OH 43767	740-872-3248	R	9*	.1
113	Mold-In Graphics Systems Inc—*Ralph Roney*	PO Box 1650, Clarkdale AZ 86324	928-634-8838	R	8*	.1
114	Quality Label Inc—*Chad Johnson*	17823 Industrial Cir N, Elk River MN 55330	763-862-1285	R	8*	<.1
115	Nature's Envy Inc—*Loren Brown*	1099 Baker St Ste B, Costa Mesa CA 92626	714-241-8111	R	8*	.1
116	Koken Manufacturing Company Inc—*Masahiro Kanaya*	1631 Dr Martin L King, Saint Louis MO 63106	314-231-7383	R	7*	.1
117	Dennis Green Ltd—*Dennis Green*	12850 E 40th Ave Ste 8, Denver CO 80239		R	7*	<.1
118	Olympic Awards Inc—*Tom Rudig*	PO Box 26429, Wauwatosa WI 53226	414-773-9000	R	7*	<.1
119	Graphic Packaging Resources—*Jeffrey Willinger*	648 W Randolph St, Chicago IL 60661	312-441-1980	R	7*	<.1
120	Buztronics Inc—*Edward Lewis*	4343 W 62nd St, Indianapolis IN 46268	317-876-3413	R	7*	.1
121	Pem Systems Inc—*Paul Moskaluk*	PO Box 586, Cranford NJ 07016	908-276-0211	R	7*	<.1
122	Mostly Memories Inc—*Patricia Derges*	1020 N Hawks Perch St, Nixa MO 65714	417-581-8555	R	6*	.1
123	Promotional Development Inc—*Henry Lombardi*	909 Remsen Ave, Brooklyn NY 11236	718-485-8550	R	6*	.1
124	Omni Components Corp—*William Holka*	46 River Rd, Hudson NH 03051	603-882-4467	R	6*	.1
125	Promotions By Design Inc—*Cliff Bassmann*	1210 Northbrook Dr Ste, Trevose PA 19053	215-354-1515	R	6*	<.1
126	Fiberlok Inc—*Brown Abrams*	PO Box 1727, Fort Collins CO 80522	970-221-1200	R	6*	.1
127	PokerTek Inc—*Mark Roberson*	1150 Crews Rd Ste F, Matthews NC 28105	704-849-0860	P	6	<.1
128	Sunstar SpA Covers Inc—*Edward Mcgarry* Softub Inc	13495 Gregg St, Poway CA 92064	760-744-2172	S	6*	.1
129	Impact Fulfillment Services—*J Porterfield*	PO Box 2628, Burlington NC 27216	336-227-1130	R	6*	.1
130	Alexander Plastics Inc—*Ben Goldfarb*	12750 Perimeter Rd Ste, Dallas TX 75228	972-686-7836	R	6*	.1
131	Cardinal Laboratories Inc—*Tony Devos*	710 S Ayon Ave, Azusa CA 91702	626-969-3305	R	6*	.1
132	Thomson Grass Valley—*Nathan Armstrong*	2300 Decker Lake Blvd, Salt Lake City UT 84119	801-972-8000	R	6*	.1
133	Misty Mate Inc—*David Bandawat*	2910 S Hardy Dr Ste 10, Tempe AZ 85282		R	6*	<.1
134	RSR Electronics Inc—*Eli Rosenbaum*	365 Blair Rd Ste B, Avenel NJ 07001	732-381-8777	R	5*	<.1
135	State Line Scrap Company Inc—*David Bourque*	PO Box 3029, Attleboro MA 02703	508-399-8300	R	5*	.1
136	Dlm Inc—*Edward Maguire*	PO Box 460, Malvern AR 72104	501-332-5495	R	5*	.1
137	Munchkin Inc (North Hills California)—*Steven B Dunn*	16689 Schoenborn St, North Hills CA 91343	818-893-5000	R	5*	.1
138	Earth Sun Moon Trading Company Inc—*Nathan A Depew*	111 N Center St, Grove City PA 16127		R	5*	<.1
139	Card USA Inc—*Marc Rochman*	201 N Ocean Dr, Hollywood FL 33019	954-862-1300	R	5*	<.1
140	Astoria-Pacific Inc—*Raymond Pavitt*	PO Box 830, Clackamas OR 97015	503-657-3010	R	5*	<.1
141	MCM Environmental Technologies Inc—*Dwight Morgan*	1 University Plz, Hackensack NJ 07601	201-342-1222	S	5*	<.1
142	Usm Inc—*Joyce Johnson*	12303 Fuqua St, Houston TX 77034	281-619-0144	R	5*	.1
143	Technical Sales And Services Inc—*Scott Mckye*	2380 N Lark Dr, Fenton MO 63026	636-677-6610	R	5*	.1
144	Age Manufacturers Inc—*Yosel Avtzon*	10624 Ave D, Brooklyn NY 11236	718-927-0048	R	5*	.1
145	Attainment Company Inc—*Donald Bastian*	PO Box 930160, Verona WI 53593	608-845-7880	R	5*	<.1
146	Hydrofarm Inc—*Stuart Dvorin*	2249 S Mcdowell Blvd, Petaluma CA 94954	707-765-9990	R	4*	<.1
147	Apollo Antenna and Sales Inc—*Steve Donald*	720 N Fancher Rd, Spokane Valley WA 99212	509-534-6972	R	4*	<.1
148	Langley/Empire Candle LLC—*Linda Rucker*	2925 Fairfax Trfy, Kansas City KS 66115	913-621-4555	R	4*	.1
149	Haidar Inc—*Christiano Jorge*	2906 Springbrook Rd, Crystal Lake IL 60012	815-788-1337	R	4*	<.1
150	Biomedic Data Systems Inc—*Neil Campbell*	1 Silas Rd, Seaford DE 19973	302-628-4100	R	4*	<.1
151	Sherpa's Pet Trading Co—*Gayle Martz*	300 Roundhill Dr, Rockaway NJ 07866	973-625-5900	R	4*	<.1
152	Tempico Inc—*Scott Miller*	PO Box 1607, Hammond LA 70404	985-429-9929	R	4*	<.1
153	Advanced Cosmetic Research Labs Inc—*Kitty Juan*	20550 Prairie St, Chatsworth CA 91311	818-709-9945	R	4*	<.1
154	Americhem Systems Inc—*Joseph Garbarski*	1770 W Cortland Ct, Addison IL 60101	630-495-9300	R	4*	<.1
155	Smart Industries Corp—*Gordon Smart*	1626 Delaware Ave, Des Moines IA 50317	515-265-9900	R	4*	.1
156	Hydra Sponge Co—*Theodore Tripolitis*	800 Biltmore Dr, Trenton MO 63026	636-349-5656	R	4*	<.1
157	Schmit Laboratories Inc—*Robert Schmit*	5837 S Oakley Ave, Chicago IL 60636	773-476-0072	R	4*	<.1
158	Cal Cover Products Inc—*Rick Vanderpool*	4475 Eucalyptus Ave St, Chino CA 91710	909-393-4575	R	4*	<.1
159	Professional Security Corp—*Richard Olson*	PO Box 128, Hiawatha IA 52233	319-373-4713	R	4*	<.1
160	King Model Co—*Gifford Wells*	365 Kenmore Blvd, Akron OH 44301	330-633-0491	R	3*	<.1
161	Barrango—*William Barrango*	360 Swift Ave Ste 1, South San Francisco CA 94080	650-871-1931	R	3*	<.1
162	Magnet Works Ltd—*Sue Todd*	12927 Gravois Rd, Saint Louis MO 63127	314-333-5001	R	3*	<.1
163	Books Of Love Inc—*Peter Bond*	PO Box 3199, Davenport FL 33836	863-422-6001	R	3*	<.1
164	Microscreen LLC—*Thomas Roose*	1106 S High St, South Bend IN 46601	574-232-4358	R	3*	<.1
165	Parker Systems Inc—*John Parker*	PO Box 6380, Chesapeake VA 23323	757-485-2952	R	3*	<.1
166	GTT/FlexPoint—*Elmer Harris*	PO Box 5019, Montgomery AL 36103		R	3	<.1
167	MadeToOrder—*Barbara Brown*	1244A Quarry Ln, Pleasanton CA 94566	925-484-0600	R	3*	<.1

Rank	Company Name—*Executive Officer*	Address, City, State, Zip	Phone	Type	Fin	Empls
168	Intruder Inc—*Mark Johnson*	230 W Colman St, Rice Lake WI 54868	715-234-1202	R	3*	<.1
169	Plastic Development Co—*David Livingston*	PO Box 4007, Williamsport PA 17701	570-323-3060	R	3*	.1
170	B Barine Inc—*Barbara Marino*	145 18th St, Brooklyn NY 11215	718-499-5650	R	3*	.1
171	Bradley Industries Inc—*Jonathan Bradley*	PO Box 1227, Euless TX 76039	815-469-2314	R	3*	.1
172	Scentations Inc—*Peggy Fender*	PO Box 505, Pocahontas AR 72455	870-892-4933	R	3*	.1
173	Rm International Inc—*Charley Moody*	370 Mountain Springs R, Stevensville MT 59870	406-777-2181	R	3*	<.1
174	Tulsa Centerless Bar Processing Inc—*Judi Hudson*	PO Box 581251, Tulsa OK 74158	918-438-0000	R	3*	<.1
175	Sun Badge Co—*Rick Hamilton*	2248 S Baker Ave, Ontario CA 91761	909-930-1444	R	3*	<.1
176	Mar-Kal Products Corp—*Hans Schmid*	145 Commerce Rd, Carlstadt NJ 07072	973-783-7155	R	3*	<.1
177	Paul Ferrante Inc—*Thomas Raynor*	8464 Melrose Pl, West Hollywood CA 90069	323-653-4142	R	2*	<.1
178	Vision Gaming and Technology Inc—*Marie Pierson*	2055 Boggs Rd, Duluth GA 30096	770-923-9900	R	2*	<.1
179	Heathkit Company Inc—*Lori Marciniak*	2024 Hawthorne Ave, Saint Joseph MI 49085	269-925-6000	R	2*	<.1
180	Denoyer - Geppert Science Co—*Mark Gilbert*	7701 Austin Ave, Skokie IL 60077	847-965-9600	R	2*	<.1
181	Prima Technologies Inc—*Arturo Desantes*	24837 Sherwood, Center Line MI 48015	586-759-0250	R	2*	<.1
182	Jamaica Lamp Corp—*Irving Shernock*	21220 Jamaica Ave, Queens Village NY 11428	718-465-1405	R	2*	<.1
183	Clamp Swing Pricing Company Inc—*Ben Garfinkle*	8386 Capwell Dr, Oakland CA 94621	510-567-1600	R	2*	<.1
184	Dolphin Spas Inc—*Kareem Azizeh*	701 W Foothill Blvd, Azusa CA 91702	626-334-0099	R	2*	<.1
185	Midwest Modelmakers Inc—*Ed Watson*	5742 N Post Rd, Indianapolis IN 46216	317-257-5131	R	2*	<.1
186	Puritan Systems Inc—*Roger Arnold*	2713 York Dr, Stow OH 44224	330-686-0527	R	2*	<.1
187	Security Intelligence Technologies Inc—*Ben Y Jamil*	145 Huguenot St, New Rochelle NY 10801	914-738-0640	R	2	<.1
188	Midwest Computer Register Corp—*Rick Salvesen*	PO Box 376, Hampton IA 50441	641-456-4847	R	2*	<.1
189	Criminalistics Inc—*Robert Worsham*	7560 Nw 82nd St, Medley FL 33166	305-885-6444	R	2*	<.1
190	Gold Seal Inc—*Darryl Bufford*	PO Box 417, Heber Springs AR 72543	501-362-7096	R	2*	<.1
191	Welsh Gold Stampers Inc—*Edwin Wallace*	139 Ludlow St, New York NY 10002	212-505-9200	R	2*	<.1
192	B and R Scenery Inc—*Brian Sullivan*	486 Constitution Ave, Camarillo CA 93012	805-388-8555	R	2*	<.1
193	Dj Products Inc—*Jeff Berg*	1009 4th St Nw, Little Falls MN 56345	320-632-4100	R	2*	<.1
194	Product Dynamics Ltd—*Peter Harrsen*	2080 Hartel Ave, Levittown PA 19057	215-943-8606	R	2*	<.1
195	Promotional Arts LLC—*Blaine Callaway*	2305 E Belt Line Rd St, Carrollton TX 75006	972-820-0329	R	1*	<.1
196	Independent Industries Inc—*Donna Brignolo*	101 N Main St, Middletown OH 45042	513-342-8787	R	1*	<.1
197	US Tape Company Inc—*Peter Rosenquist*	2452 Quakertown Rd Ste, Pennsburg PA 18073	215-541-1850	R	1*	<.1
198	Tubari Inc—*Michelle Glass*	90 Dayton Ave Ste 48, Passaic NJ 07055	973-779-8600	R	1*	<.1
199	Master Model Makers Inc—*Gene Kresser*	PO Box 1539, Addison IL 60101	630-628-1979	R	1*	<.1
200	Advanced Animations—*Peggy Toth*	PO Box 34, Stockbridge VT 05772	802-746-8974	R	1*	<.1
201	Archetype 3d Images Inc—*Craig Martin*	197 S 104th St Unit B, Louisville CO 80027	303-449-0878	R	1*	<.1
202	Penn Shadecrafters Inc—*Stephen Carter*	941 Sanderson Ave, Scranton PA 18509	570-342-3193	R	1*	<.1
203	Spraymation Inc—*Eric J Cocks*	5320 NW 35th Ave, Fort Lauderdale FL 33309	954-484-9700	R	1*	<.1
204	Dorfman Museum Figures Inc—*Robert Dorfman*	6224 Holabird Ave, Baltimore MD 21224	410-284-3248	R	1*	<.1
205	Adam and Gillian's Sensual Whips and Toys—*Adam Selene*	40 Grant Ave, Copiague NY 11726	631-842-1711	R	1*	<.1
206	Ped-Stuart Corp—*Stuart Walasek*	PO Box 15550, Brooksville FL 34604	352-754-6001	R	1*	<.1
207	Hdtv Electronic Assembly Inc—*Viet Vu*	1742 W Katella Ave Ste, Orange CA 92867	714-771-5731	R	1*	<.1
208	Studio One Midwest Inc—*Michael Clark*	74 Leonard Wood Rd, Battle Creek MI 49037	269-962-2124	R	1*	<.1
209	Vista International Inc—*Johan Smith*	8310 S Valley Hwy Ste, Englewood CO 80112	720-222-3032	P	1	<.1
210	Creative Engineering Inc—*Aaron Fechter*	47 W Jefferson St, Orlando FL 32801	407-425-1001	R	<1*	<.1
211	Greenview Manufacturing Company Inc—*Terry Wendt*	PO Box 319, Rogersville MO 65742	417-753-2822	R	<1*	<.1
212	Visual Odyssey Inc—*Bruce Goldsmith*	22 Windridge Ln, Temple GA 30179	770-646-8031	R	<1*	<.1
213	Mallard Frame Inc—*Martha Arnold*	216 Main St, Whitesburg GA 30185	770-834-2094	R	<1*	<.1
214	NeuroPace Inc—*Frank M Fischer*	1375 Shorebird Way, Mountain View CA 94043	650-237-2700	R	<1	.1
215	DayStar Technologies Inc—*Peter Lacey*	1010 S Milpitas Blvd, Milpitas CA 95035	408-582-7100	P	<1	<.1
216	National Patent Development Corp—*Harvey P Eisen*	PO Box 1960, East Hanover NJ 07936	973-428-4600	P	<1	<.1
217	United Tote Co—*Jeff True*	5901 Desoto Ave, Woodland Hills CA 91367	818-668-2100	R	<1	N/A
218	Virtual Medical International Inc—*Francis G D'Ambrosio*	469 St Pierre Rd, Los Angeles CA 90077	310-470-2616	P	<1	N/A
219	Lawnview Industries Inc—*Micheal Misler*	PO Box 829, Urbana OH 43078	937-653-5217	R	N/A	.2

TOTALS: SIC 3999 Manufacturing Industries Nec
Companies: 219   48,081   74.9

4011 Railroads—Line-Haul Operating

Rank	Company Name—*Executive Officer*	Address, City, State, Zip	Phone	Type	Fin	Empls
1	Burlington Northern Santa Fe LLC—*John O Ambler*	2650 Lou Menk Dr, Fort Worth TX 76131		P	19,548	39.0
2	Union Pacific Corp—*J Michael Hemmer*	1400 Douglas St, Omaha NE 68179	402-544-5000	P	16,965	42.9
3	Burlington Northern and Santa Fe Railway Co—*Matthew K Rose* Burlington Northern Santa Fe LLC	2650 Lou Menk Dr 2nd F, Fort Worth TX 76131	817-867-6427	S	14,450*	40.0
4	Union Pacific Railroad Co—*James R Young* Union Pacific Corp	1400 Douglas St, Omaha NE 68179	402-544-5000	S	12,158*	43.5
5	CSX Corp—*Michael J Ward*	500 Water St 15th Fl, Jacksonville FL 32202	904-359-3200	P	10,636	30.0
6	Norfolk Southern Corp—*Charles W Moorman*	PO Box 3040, Norfolk VA 23514	757-629-2680	P	9,516	28.6
7	Norfolk Southern Railway Co—*Charles W Moorman* Norfolk Southern Corp	3 Commercial Pl, Norfolk VA 23510	757-629-2600	S	7,176	28.1
8	CSX Transportation Inc—*Michael J Ward* CSX Corp	500 Water St 15th Fl, Jacksonville FL 32202	904-359-3200	S	5,730*	32.0
9	Consolidated Rail Corp—*David M LeVan* Conrail Inc	PO Box 41416, Philadelphia PA 19101	215-209-4594	S	3,686	24.0
10	Kansas City Southern—*David L Starling*	PO Box 219335, Kansas City MO 64121	816-983-1303	P	2,098	6.1
11	Genesee and Wyoming Inc—*John C Hellmann*	66 Field Point Rd, Greenwich CT 06830	203-629-3722	P	630	2.5
12	CG Railway Inc—*Erik Johnsen*	11 N Water St Ste 1829, Mobile AL 36602	251-243-9120	S	622*	.6
13	Dakota Minnesota and Eastern Railroad Corp—*Ed Terbell*	140 N Phillips Ave, Sioux Falls SD 57104		S	586*	1.0
14	RailAmerica Inc—*John E Giles*	7411 Fullerton St Ste, Jacksonville FL 32256	904-538-6100	P	551	1.8
15	Kansas City Southern Railway Co—*David L Starling* Kansas City Southern	PO Box 219335, Kansas City MO 64121		S	537*	2.6
16	Canadian Pacific Railway (Minneapolis Minnesota)—*Fred J Green*	501 Marquette Ave, Minneapolis MN 55402		R	462*	3.5
17	Florida East Coast Industries Inc—*Adolfo Henriques*	2855 Le Jeune Road I 4, Coral Gables FL 33134	305-520-2300	R	458	1.1
18	SFP Pipeline Holdings Inc—*Matthew Rose* Burlington Northern and Santa Fe Railway Co	2650 Lou Menk Dr 2nd F, Fort Worth TX 76131	817-333-2000	S	183	.4
19	OmniTrax Inc—*Gary R Long*	50 S Steele St Ste 250, Denver CO 80209	303-398-4500	S	172	.3
20	Paducah and Louisville Railway Inc—*Tom Garrett*	1500 Kentucky Ave, Paducah KY 42003	270-444-4300	R	130*	.3
21	Pan Am Railways—*David Fink*	1700 Iron Horse Park, North Billerica MA 01862	978-663-1131	R	122*	1.0
22	Alaska Railroad Corp—*Christopher Aadnesen*	PO Box 107500, Anchorage AK 99510	907-265-2300	R	116*	.4
23	Illinois and Midland Inc—*John C Hellmann* Genesee and Wyoming Inc	PO Box 139, Springfield IL 62705	217-788-8601	S	73*	.1

Note: An asterisk (*) indicates an estimated financial figure. The company type code used is as follows: R = Private, P = Public, S = Private Subsidiary, B = Public Subsidiary, D = Division, J = Joint Venture, I = Investment Fund.

COMPANY RANKINGS BY SALES WITHIN 4-DIGIT SIC

Rank	Company Name—*Executive Officer*	Address, City, State, Zip	Phone	Type	Fin	Empls
24	Springfield Terminal Railway Co—*David Fink* Pan Am Railways	Iron Horse Pk, North Billerica MA 01862	978-663-1130	S	72*	.3
25	Boston and Maine Corp Pan Am Railways	1700 Iron Horse Park, North Billerica MA 01862	978-663-1191	S	55*	.3
26	Alabama and Florida Railway Company Inc—*J Michael Carr* Pioneer Railcorp	1510 E 3 Notch St, Andalusia AL 36420		S	52*	.1
27	Decatur Junction Railway Co—*J Michael Carr* Pioneer Railcorp	308 S Chestnut St, Assumption IL 62510		S	52*	.1
28	Elkhart and Western Railroad Co—*J Michael Carr* Pioneer Railcorp	PO Box 1468, Elkhart IN 46515		S	52*	.1
29	Fort Smith Railroad Co—*J Michael Carr* Pioneer Railcorp	22 N B St, Fort Smith AR 72901		S	52*	.1
30	Garden City Western Railway Co—*J Michael Carr* Pioneer Railcorp	708 N VFW Rd, Garden City KS 67846		S	52*	.1
31	Gettysburg and Northern Railroad Co—*J Michael Carr* Pioneer Railcorp	750 Mummasburg Rd, Gettysburg PA 17325		S	52*	.1
32	Indiana Southwestern Railway Co—*J Michael Carr* Pioneer Railcorp	1603 Allen Ln, Evansville IN 47710		S	52*	.1
33	Kendallville Terminal Railway Co—*J Michael Carr* Pioneer Railcorp	PO Box 239, White Pigeon MI 49099		S	52*	.1
34	Keokuk Junction Railway Co—*Michael Carr* Pioneer Railcorp	100 Mississippi Dr, Keokuk IA 52632		S	52*	.1
35	Michigan Southern Railroad Co—*Michael Carr* Pioneer Railcorp	PO Box 239, White Pigeon MI 49099		S	52*	.1
36	Mississippi Central Railroad Co—*Michael Carr* Pioneer Railcorp	542 E Van Dorn Ave, Holly Springs MS 38635		S	52*	.1
37	Pioneer Industrial Railway Co—*Michael Carr* Pioneer Railcorp	1318 S Johanson Rd, Peoria IL 61607	309-697-1400	S	52*	.1
38	Shawnee Terminal Railway Co—*Michael Carr* Pioneer Railcorp	PO Box 343, Cairo IL 62914		S	52*	.1
39	Vandalia Railroad Co—*Michael Carr* Pioneer Railcorp	609 W Main St, Vandalia IL 62471		S	52*	.1
40	West Michigan Railroad Co—*Michael Carr* Pioneer Railcorp	115 Industrial Dr, Paw Paw MI 49079		S	52*	.1
41	Cedar Rapids and Iowa City Railway Co—*Kevin Burke* Alliant Energy Transportation Inc	2330 12th St SW, Cedar Rapids IA 52404	319-786-3698	S	32*	.1
42	Iowa Interstate Railroad Ltd—*DH (Dennis) Miller*	5900 6th St SW, Cedar Rapids IA 52404	319-298-5400	R	30*	.2
43	New York Susquehanna and Western Railway Corp—*Nathan Fenno*	1 Railroad Ave, Cooperstown NY 13326	607-547-2555	R	29*	.2
44	Providence and Worcester Railroad Co—*Scott Conti*	75 Hammond St, Worcester MA 01610	508-755-4000	P	29	.1
45	Chicago Rail Link LLC—*Mike Shore* OmniTrax Inc	2728 E 104th St, Chicago IL 60617	773-721-4000	S	27*	.1
46	Alliant Energy Transportation Inc—*Paul Treangen*	2330 12th St SW, Cedar Rapids IA 52404	319-786-3663	S	24*	.1
47	Georgetown Rail Equipment—*Steven Orrell*	111 Cooperative Way St, Georgetown TX 78626	512-869-1542	R	19*	.1
48	Pioneer Railcorp—*J Michael Carr*	1318 S Johanson Rd, Peoria IL 61607	309-697-1400	P	17	.1
49	Chicago SouthShore and Freight—*Andrew Fox*	505 N Carroll Ave, Michigan City IN 46360	219-874-9000	R	15*	.1
50	Twin Cities and Western Railroad Co—*Mark Wegner*	2925 12th St E, Glencoe MN 55336	320-864-7200	R	14*	.1
51	Tarantula Corp—*Tom schlosser*	6300 Ridgley Pl Ste 12, Fort Worth TX 76116	817-763-8297	R	12*	.1
52	Modesto and Empire Traction Co—*Joseph Mackil*	PO Box 3106, Modesto CA 95353	209-524-4631	R	8*	<.1
53	Alabama Railroad Co Pioneer Railcorp	RR2 Box 209, Monroeville AL 36460	251-743-3314	S	5*	<.1
54	Rail Management Corp—*Kay Older*	2605 Thomas Dr, Panama City Beach FL 32408	850-230-8331	R	4*	<.1
55	Bauxite and Northern Railway Company Inc—*Clifton Sheridan* RailAmerica Inc	PO Box 138, Bauxite AR 72011	501-776-4619	S	3*	<.1
56	Conrail Inc—*Gregory Weber* Norfolk Southern Corp	PO Box 41419, Philadelphia PA 19101	215-209-2000	S	2*	20.0
57	Belt Line Railroad Co—*Charles Mather*	620 Chestnut St Ste 62, Philadelphia PA 19106	215-592-7775	R	2*	<.1
58	Maryland Midland Railway Inc—*Jonathan Rudman* Genesee and Wyoming Inc	PO Box 1000, Union Bridge MD 21791	410-775-7718	S	N/A	<.1

TOTALS: SIC 4011 Railroads— Line-Haul Operating
Companies: 58

					107,784	353.3

4013 Switching & Terminal Services

1	Long Island Rail Road Co—*Kenneth Bauer*	9302 Archer Ave, Jamaica NY 11435	718-558-7400	S	1,300*	6.0
2	Indiana Harbor Belt Railroad Co—*Jim Roots*	2721 161st St, Hammond IN 46323	219-989-4703	R	87*	.8
3	Belt Railway Company of Chicago—*Patrick OBrien*	6900 S Central Ave, Bedford Park IL 60638		R	64*	.5
4	Central California Traction Co—*Dave Buccolo*	2201 W Washington St S, Stockton CA 95203	209-466-6927	S	2*	<.1

TOTALS: SIC 4013 Switching & Terminal Services
Companies: 4

					1,453	7.3

4111 Local & Suburban Transit

1	Coach USA Inc—*Edward Hodgson*	160 S Rte 17 N, Paramus NJ 07652	201-225-7500	S	784*	5.0
2	MV Transportation Inc—*Carter Pate*	4620 Westamerica Dr, Fairfield CA 94534	707-863-8980	R	494*	12.0
3	Triboro Coach Corp—*Stephen Eagar*	8501 24th Ave, Flushing NY 11370	718-335-1000	R	273*	.5
4	Northern Virginia Transportation Commission—*Richard Taube*	4350 Fairfax Dr Ste 72, Arlington VA 22203	703-524-3322	R	152*	<.1
5	Connecticut Limousine LLC	80 Middletown Ave, New Haven CT 06513	203-974-4700	R	80*	.1
6	Mears Transportation Group—*Charles E Carnes*	324 W Gore St, Orlando FL 32806	407-422-4561	R	52*	2.0
7	Bell Trans Inc—*Breck Opega*	1900 Industrial Rd, Las Vegas NV 89102	702-739-7990	R	24*	.5
8	Central New York Regional Transportation Authority—*HJ Hubert*	PO Box 820, Syracuse NY 13205	315-442-3400	R	24*	.5
9	San Diego Trolley Inc—*Paul Jablonski*	1255 Imperial Ave Ste, San Diego CA 92101	619-595-4949	S	19*	.5
10	Connecticut Limousine Service Inc Connecticut Limousine LLC	230 Old Gate Ln, Milford CT 06460		S	19*	.4
11	Nationwide Trucking Inc—*Ed Sandoval*	PO Box 26338, Los Angeles CA 90026		R	10	.2
12	Continental Air Transport Co—*John McCarthy*	1200 W 35th St, Chicago IL 60609		R	9*	.2
13	Fairfield City Transit System—*Lance Atencil*	827 Missouri St Ste 6, Fairfield CA 94533	707-422-2877	S	4*	.1
14	Kahului Trucking and Storage Inc—*John Jackson*	140 Hobron Ave, Kahului HI 96732	808-877-5001	S	3*	.1
15	Trolley Tours of Cleveland Inc—*Sherrill Paul*	PO Box 91658, Cleveland OH 44101	216-771-4484	R	2*	.1
16	Veolia Transportation Inc—*Mark L Joseph*	720 E Butterfield Rd S, Lombard IL 60148	630-571-7070	S	2*	<.1
17	Alexander City Flying Service Inc—*Mike Smith*	997 TC Russell Dr, Alexander City AL 35010	256-329-9057	S	1*	<.1

Rank	Company Name—*Executive Officer*	Address, City, State, Zip	Phone	Type	Fin	Empls
18	Grayline of Seattle—*Mollie Jones*	4500 W Marginal Way SW, Seattle WA 98106		S	N/A	.2

TOTALS: SIC 4111 Local & Suburban Transit
Companies: 18   1,951   22.2

4119 Local Passenger Transportation Nec

Rank	Company Name—*Executive Officer*	Address, City, State, Zip	Phone	Type	Fin	Empls
1	Emergency Medical Services LP—*William A Sanger*	6200 S Syracuse Way St, Greenwood Village CO 80111	303-495-1200	S	2,859	17.5
2	American Medical Response—*Mark Bruning* Emergency Medical Services LP	6200 S Syracuse Way St, Greenwood Village CO 80111	303-495-1200	S	1,055*	17.8
3	Rural/Metro Corp—*Michael P DiMino*	9221 E Via de Ventura, Scottsdale AZ 85258	480-994-3886	P	531	8.2
4	TransCare Pennsylvania—*Jamye Burgman*	400 Seco Rd, Monroeville PA 15146	412-373-6300	R	417*	2.0
5	Southwest Ambulance of Casa Grande Inc—*Jeff Sargent* Rural/Metro Corp	1125 N Pinal Ave, Casa Grande AZ 85222	520-836-0284	S	184*	1.0
6	Carey International Inc—*Gary Kessler*	4530 Wisconsin Ave NW, Washington DC 20016	202-895-1200	R	165*	.8
7	Van Pool Services Inc—*R Jeffrey Hening*	1220 Rankin Dr, Troy MI 48083	248-597-3500	S	118*	.1
8	Abbott Ambulance Inc—*Mark Corley* Emergency Medical Services LP	2500 Abbott Pl, Saint Louis MO 63143	314-768-1000	S	75*	.4
9	Em-Star Ambulance Service—*David Incorvaia*	300 Domino Ln, Philadelphia PA 19128	215-969-0630	R	69*	.3
10	Rural/Metro of Indiana Inc—*John Karolzak*	3450 Developers Rd, Indianapolis IN 46227	317-955-3500	S	50*	.3
11	Tauck World Tours Inc—*Author Tauck*	10 Norden Pl, Norwalk CT 06855	203-899-6500	R	48*	.4
12	Hunter Ambulette-Ambulance Inc—*Danny Libowitz*	28 Sheridan Blvd, Inwood NY 11096	516-371-2622	R	41*	.2
13	Sunteck Transport Company Inc—*Harry Wachtel*	6413 Congress Ave Ste, Boca Raton FL 33487		S	12*	.1
14	First Leasing and Rental Corp—*Orlando Berges-Gonzalez*	1519 Ponce de Leon Ave, Santurce PR 00908	787-729-8200	S	12*	<.1
15	Custom Transportation Service—*Philip J Gilpin* Carey International Inc	66 Rocsam Park Rd, Braintree MA 02184	781-848-6803	S	6*	.2
16	Specialized Transportation for Outpatient Services Inc—*Bob Jarvis*	8855 Grissom Pkwy, Titusville FL 32780		R	6*	<.1
17	Schoolman Transportation Group—*Bill Schoolman*	1600 Locust Ave, Bohemia NY 11716	631-567-5100	R	6*	<.1
18	ABC Worldwide Chauffeured Transportation—*Jeffrey Bowles*	65 Glen Rd Ste 656, Garner NC 27529	919-934-7800	R	2*	<.1
19	Elliott's Evening Star Limousine—*Elliott Calvetti*	7077 E 5th Ave, Scottsdale AZ 85251	480-947-9934	R	2*	<.1
20	Chicagoland Transportation Solutions Inc—*Brian Whitaker*	PO Box 3278, Barrington IL 60011	847-844-2920	R	2*	<.1
21	Digest Publications Inc—*Eric Alpert*	29 Fostertown Rd, Medford NJ 08055	609-953-4900	R	2*	.1

TOTALS: SIC 4119 Local Passenger Transportation Nec
Companies: 21   5,662   49.3

4121 Taxicabs

Rank	Company Name—*Executive Officer*	Address, City, State, Zip	Phone	Type	Fin	Empls
1	Whittlesea Blue Cab Co—*Brent Bell*	PO Box 15333, Las Vegas NV 89114	702-382-7060	R	529*	.5
2	Yellow Cab Company Inc—*Jeff Feldman*	2231 South Wabash, Chicago IL 60616	312-225-7440	R	42*	.1
3	Yellow Checker Cab Company Inc—*Larry Silva*	1880 S 7th St, San Jose CA 95112	408-286-3400	R	33*	.1
4	Liberty Cab Company Inc—*Jerry Brady*	PO Box 91092, Houston TX 77291	713-695-6700	R	19*	<.1
5	Best Cab Co—*Pam Reetz*	102 W Broadway, Waukesha WI 53186	262-549-6622	R	7*	<.1
6	1 Cab LLC—*Rafat Alawneh*	525 Southgate Ave, Iowa City IA 52240		R	3*	<.1
7	Coastal Cab Company Inc—*Joe Duke*	1202 7th Ave, Kill Devil Hills NC 27948	252-449-8787	R	1*	<.1

TOTALS: SIC 4121 Taxicabs
Companies: 7   634   .7

4131 Intercity & Rural Bus Transportation

Rank	Company Name—*Executive Officer*	Address, City, State, Zip	Phone	Type	Fin	Empls
1	Greyhound Lines Inc—*David Leach*	PO Box 660362, Dallas TX 75266	214-849-8000	S	924	13.4
2	New Jersey Transit Corp—*James Weinstein*	1 Penn Plz, Newark NJ 07105		R	588*	10.5
3	San Diego Transit Corp—*Paul Jablonski*	1255 Imperial Ave Ste, San Diego CA 92101	619-238-0100	R	265*	1.2
4	Railcrew Xpress LLC—*John Bickerstaff*	15729 College Blvd, Lenexa KS 66219	913-928-5000	R	149*	4.5
5	Peter Pan Bus Lines Inc—*Peter A Picknelly*	P O Box 1776, Springfield MA 01102	413-781-2900	R	106*	1.5
6	Jefferson Partners LP—*Charles A Zelle*	2100 E 26th St, Minneapolis MN 55404	612-332-8745	R	20	.3
7	Carolina Coach Company Inc—*Elvis Latiolais* Carolina Associates Inc	1201 S Blount St, Raleigh NC 27601	919-833-3601	S	18*	.2
8	Carolina Associates Inc—*William C Steele*	1201 S Blount St, Raleigh NC 27601	919-833-3601	R	16*	.3
9	Greater Richmond Transit Co—*John M LewisJr*	301 E Belt Blvd, Richmond VA 23224	804-358-4782	R	11*	.4
10	Vermont Transit Company Inc—*Robert N Bergesen* Greyhound Lines Inc	345 Pine St, Burlington VT 05401		S	10	.1

TOTALS: SIC 4131 Intercity & Rural Bus Transportation
Companies: 10   2,106   32.3

4141 Local Bus Charter Service

Rank	Company Name—*Executive Officer*	Address, City, State, Zip	Phone	Type	Fin	Empls
1	SuperShuttle International Inc—*R Brian Wier*	14500 N Northsight Blv, Scottsdale AZ 85260	480-609-3000	S	750*	16.0
2	Martz Group—*Craig Smith*	PO Box 1007, Wilkes Barre PA 18773	570-821-3838	R	30*	.6

TOTALS: SIC 4141 Local Bus Charter Service
Companies: 2   780   16.6

4142 Bus Charter Service Except Local

Rank	Company Name—*Executive Officer*	Address, City, State, Zip	Phone	Type	Fin	Empls
1	Western Pioneer Inc—*Alton Dupree*	4601 Shilshole Ave NW, Seattle WA 98107	206-789-1930	R	58*	.2
2	MTR Western—*Darren Berg*	1501 4th Ave Ste 1900, Seattle WA 98101	206-838-8125	R	21*	.2

TOTALS: SIC 4142 Bus Charter Service Except Local
Companies: 2   79   .3

4151 School Buses

Rank	Company Name—*Executive Officer*	Address, City, State, Zip	Phone	Type	Fin	Empls
1	Durham School Services—*John Elliott*	4300 Weaver Pkwy, Warrenville IL 60555	630-435-8000	D	415*	11.0
2	First Transit Inc—*Brad Thomas*	600 Vine St Ste 1400, Cincinnati OH 45202	513-241-2200	S	365*	15.5
3	Atlantic Express Transportation Group Inc—*Domenic Gatto*	7 North St, Staten Island NY 10302	718-442-7000	R	358*	7.6
4	Student Transportation of America Inc—*Denis J Gallagher*	3349 Hwy 138 Bldg B St, Wall NJ 07719	732-280-4200	R	135*	.2
5	Nelson's Bus Service Inc—*Christopher Arnett*	W8608 Willis Ray Rd, Whitewater WI 53190	262-473-6680	R	14*	<.1
6	C J's Bus Supplies And Service Inc—*Carla Hoffman*	732 Buck Rd, Monroeville NJ 08343	856-863-0779	R	3*	.1

TOTALS: SIC 4151 School Buses
Companies: 6   1,290   34.4

4173 Bus Terminal & Service Facilities

Rank	Company Name—*Executive Officer*	Address, City, State, Zip	Phone	Type	Fin	Empls
1	Greatwide Logistics Services—*Leo Suggs*	12404 Park Central Dr, Dallas TX 75251	972-228-7300	R	727*	3.1
2	Serco Management Services Inc—*Ed Casey*	1818 Library St Ste 10, Reston VA 20190	703-939-6000	R	142*	6.0

TOTALS: SIC 4173 Bus Terminal & Service Facilities
Companies: 2   869   9.1

Note: An asterisk (*) indicates an estimated financial figure. The company type code used is as follows: R = Private, P = Public, S = Private Subsidiary, B = Public Subsidiary, D = Division, J = Joint Venture, I = Investment Fund.

COMPANY RANKINGS BY SALES WITHIN 4-DIGIT SIC

Rank	Company Name—*Executive Officer*	Address, City, State, Zip	Phone	Type	Fin	Empls
	4212 Local Trucking Without Storage					
1	Schwerman Trucking Co—*Jack Schwerman* Tankstar USA Inc	PO Box 1601, Milwaukee WI 53201	414-671-1600	S	8,625*	.7
2	GE Fleet Services—*Clarence Nunn*	3 Capital Dr, Eden Prairie MN 55344	952-828-1000	D	7,676*	2.9
3	Savage Industries Inc (Salt Lake City Utah)—*Allan B Alexander*	6340 S 3000 E Ste 600, Salt Lake City UT 84121	801-944-6600	R	6,080*	2.0
4	Slay Industries Inc—*EP Slay*	PO Box 39904, Saint Louis MO 63139	314-647-7529	R	4,604*	.8
5	JB Hunt Transport Services Inc—*John N Roberts III*	PO Box 130, Lowell AR 72745	479-820-0000	P	4,527	15.6
6	Schneider National Inc—*Christopher Lofgren*	PO Box 2545, Green Bay WI 54306	920-592-2000	R	3,367*	18.2
7	USF Glen Moore Transport Inc—*Matt Stoll*	1513 Commerce Ave, Carlisle PA 17013	717-245-0788	R	1,312*	1.0
8	MGM Transport Corp—*George Massood*	PO Box 1823, High Point NC 27261	336-887-3054	R	1,214*	.4
9	ABC Global Rigging—*Jeff Mueller*	5405 County TKR, Manitowoc WI 54220	920-652-9407	R	580*	.1
10	UPS Supply Chain Solutions Inc—*Bob Stoffel*	12380 Morris Rd, Alpharetta GA 30005	678-746-4365	S	551*	1.0
11	US Xpress Inc—*Max L Fuller*	4080 Jenkins Rd, Chattanooga TN 37421	423-510-3000	S	509*	5.6
12	R and L Carriers—*Larry Roberts*	600 Gilliam Rd, Wilmington OH 45177	773-927-1597	R	360*	2.0
13	PLS Logistics Services—*John Gallardo*	3120 Unionville Rd Bld, Cranberry Township PA 16066	724-709-9000	R	342	.2
14	Trimac Transport Inc—*Jeff McCaig*	PO Box 3000, Rapid City SD 57709	605-348-1063	S	330*	.3
15	Tankstar USA Inc—*Dan Bulinski*	611 S 28th St, Milwaukee WI 53215	414-671-3039	R	312*	.1
16	Romar Transportation Systems Inc—*Robert Marden*	3500 S Kedzie Ave, Chicago IL 60632	773-376-8800	R	264*	.2
17	Mbi Holding Inc—*Neeraj Mital*	2627 E 139th St, Burnham IL 60633	708-868-0059	R	180*	<.1
18	Anderson Services LLC—*Sara Carrington*	6016 Brookvale Ln 110b, Knoxville TN 37919	865-584-6714	R	157*	2.3
19	Experienced Mail Transport Inc—*Sidney Saunders*	1072 Leeda Dr, Jacksonville FL 32254	904-354-4855	R	150*	<.1
20	Schneider National Bulk Carriers Inc—*Christopher Lofgren* Schneider National Inc	PO Box 2545, Green Bay WI 54306	920-592-2000	S	93*	1.0
21	Distribution Technologies Inc (Newbury Ohio)—*Richard J Manfredi*	14841 Sperry Rd, Newbury OH 44065	440-338-1010	R	87*	.5
22	Seiler Tank Truck Service Inc—*Scott Hammontree*	26791 W Michigan Ave, Albion MI 49224	517-629-4810	S	67*	<.1
23	Carroll Fulmer and Company Inc—*Elliott Ogden*	PO Box 5000, Groveland FL 34736	352-429-5000	R	66*	.5
24	Con-way Freight Inc—*Gregory Lehmkuhl*	2211 Old Earhart Rd Rm, Ann Arbor MI 48105	734-769-0203	S	47*	.4
25	Admiral Merchants Motor Freight Inc—*Brian Short*	215 S 11th St, Minneapolis MN 55403	612-332-4819	R	45*	.4
26	Dart America Inc—*Lee Stoneburner*	11017 Market St, North Lima OH 44452	330-549-0994	R	37*	.2
27	Electronic Data Carriers Inc—*George Gilbert*	2228 Wirtcrest Ln Ste, Houston TX 77055		R	36*	.2
28	Terminal Trucking Co—*Paul Matthews*	PO Box 1623, Concord NC 28025	704-786-0189	R	34*	.2
29	Hodges Truck Company Inc—*Joe Hodges*	PO Box 270660, Oklahoma City OK 73137	405-947-7764	R	31*	.2
30	CPS Delivery System Inc—*Ron Kauffman*	3000 Rohr Rd, Groveport OH 43125	614-492-0000	R	31*	.1
31	KBS Inc—*Bill Paulette*	PO Box 7, Thomasville PA 17364	717-792-1800	R	31*	<.1
32	Dart Services Inc—*Ronald Klingle* Dart America Inc	11017 Market St, North Lima OH 44452	330-549-0094	S	29*	.1
33	JP Donmoyer Inc—*Frank Constanzo*	PO Box 74, Ono PA 17077	717-865-2148	R	26*	.2
34	Shaw Trucking Inc—*Kim Baker*	PO Box 7479, Delray Beach FL 33482	561-278-6295	R	23*	<.1
35	Northwest Containers Services Inc—*Gary Cardwell*	11920 N Burgard St, Portland OR 97203	503-286-4873	R	22*	.1
36	Duncan Machinery Movers Inc—*Tom Bennington*	2004 Duncan Machinery, Lexington KY 40504	859-233-7333	R	13*	.2
37	Hess Trucking Company Inc—*William G Nelson*	PO Box 4193, Harrisburg PA 17111	717-561-8344	R	13*	.2
38	Hurley Transportation Cos—*William Ewing*	22600 N 19th Ave, Phoenix AZ 85027	623-434-0590	R	13*	.1
39	NE Finch Co—*Thomas E Finch*	PO Box 5187, Peoria IL 61601	309-671-1444	R	12*	.1
40	California Transport Enterprises—*Ira Shepnick*	PO Box 471, South Gate CA 90280	323-357-1720	R	12*	<.1
41	Movers Specialty Service Inc—*Timothy Hughes*	211 Commerce Dr, Montgomeryville PA 18936	215-393-1900	R	12*	.1
42	Double M Trucking Inc—*John R Martin*	710 Dutton St, Winters CA 95694	530-795-4181	R	10*	.1
43	George D L and Sons Transportation Inc—*John George*	20 E 6th St, Waynesboro PA 17268	717-765-4700	R	9*	.1
44	Klepper Oil—*Ken Klepper*	PO Box 4119, Wichita KS 67204	316-838-9341	R	9*	.1
45	Lindeman Moving Company Inc—*Joy Henry*	2010 Greenwood St, Harrisburg PA 17104	717-236-9044	R	9*	.1
46	Movex Inc—*Stuart Suddath*	12183 W Linebaugh Ave, Tampa FL 33626	813-908-5557	R	9*	<.1
47	Harry Kuhn W Inc—*Woody Griffin*	207 Illinois Ave, Saint Charles IL 60174	630-945-3829	R	9*	.1
48	Metro Transport Inc—*Earl Lafave*	30069 Wixom Rd, Wixom MI 48393	248-624-5544	R	8*	<.1
49	Harlis R Ellington Construction Inc—*Larry Davison*	PO Box 257, Lake Butler FL 32054	386-496-2134	R	8*	.1
50	Zappi Oil and Gas Co—*Pete Zappi*	44 Bridge St, Washington PA 15301	724-222-9188	R	7*	<.1
51	M and P Transport Company Inc—*Thomas Valente*	3635 S 43rd Ave Ste 30, Phoenix AZ 85009	602-272-2637	R	7*	.1
52	Desert Equipment Company Inc—*Craig Hills*	1495 W Melody Dr, Gilbert AZ 85233	480-898-7414	R	6*	.1
53	HB Phillips Inc—*Cathy Coats*	1763 E Person Ave, Memphis TN 38114	901-775-1424	R	6*	.1
54	Truckstaff LLC	2815 E Skelly Dr Ste 8, Tulsa OK 74105	918-712-9193	R	6*	.1
55	Paradis Inc—*Roger Paradis*	PO Box 97, Brooks MN 56715	218-698-4613	R	6*	.1
56	MBE Inc—*Stuart Mathis*	6060 Cornerstone Ct W, San Diego CA 92121	858-455-8800	R	6*	<.1
57	Ranco Sand and Stone Corp—*Marilyn Horan*	151 S St, Manorville NY 11949	631-874-3939	R	6*	<.1
58	Etheredge Manufacturing Company Inc—*Charles Etheredge*	PO Box 128, Iron City TN 38463	931-845-4187	R	6*	.1
59	A-1 Delivery Company Inc—*Joe Romine*	19805 Business Pkwy, Walnut CA 91789	909-444-1220	R	6*	.1
60	Gary Transfer Company Inc—*Carlos Ruiz Jr*	912 W Ave H, East Chicago IN 46312	219-980-1165	R	5*	<.1
61	United Freight and Transport Inc—*William McCormick*	1701 E 1st Ave, Anchorage AK 99501	907-272-5700	R	5*	.1
62	Whittaker and Gooding Trucking Co—*George Ausail*	5800 Cherry Hill Rd, Ypsilanti MI 48198	734-483-4775	S	4*	.1
63	Reese Trucking Inc—*Eugene Reese*	PO Box 99, Dover OH 44622	330-343-3341	R	4*	<.1
64	Global CFS Inc—*Lou Capizzi*	860 Foster Ave, Bensenville IL 60106	630-238-1164	R	4*	<.1
65	WWR International	PO Box 336, Winfield IL 60190	630-682-4007	R	4*	<.1
66	Innovative Postal Services Inc—*Steve Riggin*	920 2nd St S, Great Falls MT 59405	406-761-8965	R	3*	<.1
67	Central States Non-Stock Coop—*Tom Ladehoff*	1745 N Airport Rd, Fremont NE 68025	402-721-2898	R	3*	<.1
68	Don Frame Trucking Company Inc—*Donald Frame*	5485 W Lake Rd, Fredonia NY 14063	716-672-4306	R	3*	<.1
69	Rausch Brothers Trucking of Ionia—*Richard Rausch*	1521 220th St, Ionia IA 50645	641-394-4384	R	3*	<.1
70	Guyer the Mover Inc—*John Guyer II*	PO Box 1096, Peru IN 46970	765-473-3802	R	3*	<.1
71	Hoover Transportation Services Inc—*Ken Hoover*	PO Box 890, Reynoldsburg OH 43068	614-868-0577	R	3*	<.1
72	Puryear Tank Lines Inc—*Donnie Puryear*	405 Raleigh St, Wilmington NC 28412	910-793-9900	R	3*	<.1
73	Franklin Express Inc—*Ron Mantlo*	PO Box 473, Franklin KY 42135	270-586-3296	R	3	<.1
74	Bullseye Trucking LC—*Natasha Mccory*	3220 Dixon St, Des Moines IA 50313	515-262-2141	R	3*	<.1
75	Hampton Roads Crane and Rigging Co—*James Speegle*	525 J Clyde Morris Blv, Newport News VA 23601	757-595-5838	R	2*	<.1
76	Two Men and A Truck International Inc—*Brig Sorber*	3400 Belle Chase Way, Lansing MI 48911	517-394-7210	R	2*	<.1
77	Smithey Environmental Services LLC	PO Box 757, Sand Springs OK 74063	918-245-1070	R	2*	<.1
78	Dennis Fink Trucking Inc—*Dennis Fink*	4871 Rte 9G, Germantown NY 12526	518-537-4739	R	2*	<.1
79	Lattavo Brothers Inc—*Phillip Lattavo*	2230 Shepler Church Av, Canton OH 44706	330-456-4571	R	2*	<.1
80	Vital Link Trucking Services	1098 Melody Ln Ste 302, Roseville CA 95678	916-773-2688	R	2*	<.1
81	Wilson Truck Service—*Norman Wilson*	18846 N State Hwy 21, Cadet MO 63630	573-438-4967	R	2	<.1
82	HJG Trucking Inc—*Sharon Fentress*	701 Denair St, Fort Worth TX 76111	817-834-7181	R	1*	<.1
83	TransCorr LLC—*Steven Harris*	PO Box 681548, Indianapolis IN 46268	317-879-3900	R	N/A	.4

TOTALS: SIC 4212 Local Trucking Without Storage
Companies: 83

					42,120	60.0

Rank	Company Name—*Executive Officer*	Address, City, State, Zip	Phone	Type	Fin	Empls
	4213 Trucking Except Local					
1	United Parcel Service Inc—*D Scott Davis*	55 Glenlake Pkwy NE, Atlanta GA 30328	404-828-6000	P	49,545	400.6
2	USF Reddaway—*TJ O'Connor*	16277 SE 130th Ave, Clackamas OR 97015		S	32,053*	2.6
	YRC Regional Transportation Inc					
3	Exel Direct Inc—*John Gilbert*	570 Polaris Pkwy, Westerville OH 43082	614-865-8500	R	23,714*	40.0
4	FedEx Express Corp—*David Bronczek*	942 South Shady Grove, Memphis TN 38120	901-818-7200	S	11,302*	95.0
5	Artic Express Inc—*Dick Durst*	PO Box 129, Hilliard OH 43026	614-876-4008	R	6,036*	.5
6	Con-Way Inc—*Douglas W Stotlar*	PO Box 130588, Ann Arbor MI 48113		P	5,290	27.8
7	Brink's Inc—*Thomas C Schievelbein*	555 Dividend, Coppell TX 75019	469-549-6000	S	4,767	39.0
8	Triple Crown Services Co—*Jim Newton*	2720 Dupont Commerce C, Fort Wayne IN 46825	260-416-3600	S	3,566*	.3
9	Swift Transportation Co—*Jerry Moyes*	PO Box 29243, Phoenix AZ 85043	602-269-9700	P	3,334	16.5
10	Averitt Express Inc—*Gary D Sasser*	PO Box 3166, Cookeville TN 38502	931-526-3306	R	3,232*	6.0
11	Yellow Transportation Inc—*Phil Gaines*	10990 Roe Ave, Overland Park KS 66211	913-344-3000	S	3,152	13.1
12	Crete Carrier Corp—*Tonn Ostergard*	PO Box 81228, Lincoln NE 68501	402-475-9521	R	3,104*	6.1
13	Dart Transit Company Inc—*Dave Oren*	PO Box 64110, Saint Paul MN 55164	651-688-2000	R	3,016	.3
14	United Van Lines Inc—*Carl Walters*	1 United Dr, Fenton MO 63026	636-343-3900	S	2,742*	1.8
	UniGroup Inc					
15	CH Robinson International Inc—*John Wiehoff*	14701 Charlson Rd, Eden Prairie MN 55347	952-937-8500	S	2,704*	5.8
16	FedEx Freight East Inc—*Larry C Miller*	PO Box 840, Harrison AR 72602	870-741-9000	S	2,689	9.8
17	Landstar System Inc—*Henry H Gerkens*	13410 Sutton Park Dr S, Jacksonville FL 32224	904-389-9400	P	2,649	1.4
18	YRC Regional Transportation Inc—*Thomas E Bergmann*	8550 West Bryn Mawr Av, Chicago IL 60631	773-824-1000	R	2,395	20.0
19	Roadway Express Inc—*Terrence Gilbert*	PO Box 471, Akron OH 44309	330-384-1717	S	2,328*	23.0
20	UniGroup Inc—*Richard McClure*	1 Premier Dr, Fenton MO 63026	636-305-5000	R	2,200*	1.1
21	Werner Enterprises Inc—*Gregory L Werner*	PO Box 45308, Omaha NE 68145	402-895-6640	P	2,003	11.4
22	Arkansas Best Corp—*Judy R McReynolds*	PO Box 10048, Fort Smith AR 72917	479-785-6000	P	1,908	10.0
23	Old Dominion Freight Line Inc—*David S Congdon*	500 Old Dominion Way, Thomasville NC 27360	336-889-5000	P	1,883	12.0
24	CR England Inc—*Wayne Cederholm*	4701 W 2100 S, Salt Lake City UT 84120	801-972-2712	R	1,777*	3.3
25	ABF Freight System Inc—*Roy Slagle*	PO Box 10048, Fort Smith AR 72917		S	1,730	11.3
	Arkansas Best Corp					
26	SIRVA Inc—*Wes Lucas*	700 Oakmont Ln, Westmont IL 60559	630-570-3047	R	1,699	2.6
27	Ryder Integrated Logistics—*Gregory T Swienton*	11690 NW 105th St, Miami FL 33178	305-500-3726	S	1,421*	8.0
28	KLLM Transport Services Inc—*James M Richards*	135 Riverview Dr, Richland MS 39218	601-939-2545	R	1,353*	2.0
29	US Xpress Enterprises Inc—*Max Fuller*	4080 Jenkins Rd, Chattanooga TN 37421	423-510-3000	R	1,352*	10.0
30	Estes Express Lines Inc—*Rob W Estes Jr*	PO Box 25612, Richmond VA 23260	804-353-1900	R	1,295*	12.4
31	Wilson Trucking Corp—*CL Wilson*	PO Box 200, Fishersville VA 22939	540-949-3200	R	1,257*	1.8
32	AEP Industries Inc—*J Brendan Barba*	125 Phillips Ave, South Hackensack NJ 07606	201-641-6600	R	1,162*	2.1
33	Kenan Transport Co—*Lee P Shaffer*	PO Box 2729, Chapel Hill NC 27515	919-967-8221	S	1,025*	1.7
	Kenan Advantage Group Inc					
34	APX Logistics—*Bradley Garberich*	9939 Norwalk Blvd, Santa Fe Springs CA 90670	562-906-6300	S	979*	1.9
35	Landair Transport Inc—*Scott Niswonger*	PO Box 938, Greeneville TN 37744	423-783-1300	R	914*	1.3
36	Saia Inc—*Richard D O'Dell*	11465 Johns Creek Pkwy, Johns Creek GA 30097		P	903	7.5
37	Saia Motor Freight Line Inc—*Richard O'Dell*	11465 Johns Creek Pkwy, Duluth GA 30097	770-232-5067	S	903	7.5
	Saia Inc					
38	Penske Logistic Inc—*Vincent W Hartnett Jr*	PO Box 563, Reading PA 19603	610-775-6291	S	866	4.0
39	FedEx Custom Critical Inc—*Virginia C Albanese*	PO Box 5000, Green OH 44232	234-310-4090	S	863*	2.0
40	Landstar Ligon Inc—*Henry H Gerkens*	13410 Sutton Park Dr S, Jacksonville FL 32224	904-308 0100	S	844*	1.0
	Landstar System Holdings Inc					
41	Groendyke Transport Inc—*John D Groendyke*	2510 Rock Island Blvd, Enid OK 73701	580-234-4663	R	752*	1.5
42	Lakeville Motor Express Inc—*Peter Martin*	PO Box 130280, Saint Paul MN 55113	651-636-8900	R	750*	.8
43	TK Stanley Inc—*Steve Farrar*	PO Box 31, Waynesboro MS 39367	601-735-2855	R	748*	1.3
44	Knight Transportation Inc—*Kevin P Knight*	5601 W Buckeye Rd, Phoenix AZ 85043	602-269-2000	P	697	4.7
45	Cardinal Logistic Managment Inc—*Tom Hostetler*	PO Box 1389, Concord NC 28026	704-786-6125	D	691*	1.5
46	Waggoners Trucking—*David Waggoner*	PO Box 31357, Billings MT 59107	406-248-1919	R	666*	1.4
47	Covenant Transport Group Inc—*David R Parker*	400 Birmingham Hwy, Chattanooga TN 37419	423-821-1212	P	650	4.7
48	USF Holland Inc—*Jeff Rogers*	750 E 40th St, Holland MI 49423	616-395-5000	S	647*	6.7
49	CRST International Inc—*David L Rusch*	PO Box 68, Cedar Rapids IA 52406	319-396-4400	R	636*	3.5
50	Quality Carriers Inc—*Gary R Enzor*	4041 Park Oaks Blvd St, Tampa FL 33610		R	622	3.1
51	Universal Truckload Services Inc—*Donald B Cochran*	12755 E Nine Mile Rd, Warren MI 48089	586-920-0100	P	606	.7
52	Marten Transport Ltd—*Randolph L Marten*	129 Marten St, Mondovi WI 54755		P	604	2.7
53	Celadon Trucking Services Inc—*Bart Middleton*	9503 E 33rd St, Indianapolis IN 46235	317-972-7000	S	586*	3.0
	Celadon Group Inc					
54	Southeastern Freight Lines—*WT Cassels III*	PO Box 1691, Columbia SC 29202	803-794-7300	R	565	2.7
55	Prime Inc—*Robert E Low*	PO Box 4208, Springfield MO 65808	417-521-6886	R	565*	3.3
56	Celadon Group Inc—*Stephen Russell*	9503 E 33 Rd St, Indianapolis IN 46235	317-972-7000	P	557	3.5
57	Central Freight Lines Inc—*Robert V Fasso*	PO Box 2638, Waco TX 76702	254-741-5305	R	533*	4.0
58	Heartland Express Inc—*Michael J Gerdin*	901 N Kansas Ave, North Liberty IA 52317	319-626-3600	P	529	2.9
59	FFE Transportation Services Inc—*S Russell Stubbs*	PO Box 655888, Dallas TX 75265		S	488*	2.5
	Frozen Food Express Industries Inc					
60	FFE Transportation and American Eagle Lines—*Stoney Stubbs*	PO Box 655888, Dallas TX 75265	214-630-8090	R	474	2.1
61	AAA Cooper Transportation—*Reid Dove*	1751 Kinsey Rd, Dothan AL 36303	334-793-2284	R	469*	5.5
62	USA Truck Inc—*Clifton Beckham*	3200 Industrial Park R, Van Buren AR 72956	479-471-2500	P	460	2.9
63	Ergon Trucking Inc—*Leslie B Lampton*	PO Box 1639, Jackson MS 39232	601-933-3000	S	452*	2.5
64	USF Logistics Services Inc	1000 Veterans Pkwy, Bolingbrook IL 60440	630-754-3000	S	446*	4.8
65	Navajo Shippers Inc—*Don Digby*	1400 W 64th Ave, Denver CO 80221	303-287-3800	R	432*	.8
66	Dependable Logistics Services—*Rob Massman*	2555 E Olympic Blvd, Los Angeles CA 90023	323-526-2222	R	426*	.6
67	Midwest Motor Express Inc—*Marlin Kling*	PO Box 1058, Bismarck ND 58502	701-223-1880	R	413*	.6
68	New Penn Motor Express Inc—*Steven Gast*	625 S 5th Ave, Lebanon PA 17042	717-274-2521	S	406*	2.0
69	Comcar Industries Inc—*R Mark Bostick*	PO Drawer 67, Auburndale FL 33823	863-967-1101	R	405*	4.5
70	New World Van Lines Inc—*David Marx*	5875 N Rogers Ave, Chicago IL 60646	773-685-3399	R	394*	.5
71	Logisticare Inc—*Herman M Schwarz*	1275 Peachtree St NE 6, Atlanta GA 30309	770-907-7596	R	388*	.7
72	John Christner Trucking Inc—*John Christner*	19007 W Hwy 33, Sapulpa OK 74066	918-227-1600	R	385*	.8
73	Landstar Ranger Inc	PO Box 19060, Jacksonville FL 32245	904-398-9400	S	380*	1.1
	Landstar System Holdings Inc					
74	Brookside Trucking Inc—*Rick Uppenkamp*	PO Box 68, Maria Stein OH 45860	419-925-4457	R	375*	.1
75	Vitran Express—*Dave Kimack*	6500 E 30th St, Indianapolis IN 46219	317-803-6400	S	375	.9
76	Atlas Van Lines Inc—*Glen Dunkerson*	1212 St George Rd, Evansville IN 47711	812-424-2222	S	370*	.8
77	Frozen Food Express Industries Inc—*S Russell Stubbs*	PO Box 655888, Dallas TX 75265	214-630-8090	P	369	2.3
78	Pacer Stacktrain	2300 Clayton Rd Ste 12, Concord CA 94520	925-887-1400	S	367*	.7
79	Kenan Advantage Group Inc—*Dennis A Nash*	4895 Dressler Rd Ste 1, Canton OH 44718	330-491-0474	S	365*	3.5

Note: An asterisk (*) indicates an estimated financial figure. The company type code used is as follows: R = Private, P = Public, S = Private Subsidiary, B = Public Subsidiary, D = Division, J = Joint Venture, I = Investment Fund.

COMPANY RANKINGS BY SALES WITHIN 4-DIGIT SIC

Rank	Company Name—Executive Officer	Address, City, State, Zip	Phone	Type	Fin	Empls
80	Dayton Freight Lines Inc—Thomas Cronin	PO Box 340, Vandalia OH 45377	937-264-4060	R	362*	2.0
81	Alan Ritchey Inc—Alan Ritchey	PO Box 249, Valley View TX 76272	940-726-3276	R	358*	.5
82	Ruan Transport Corp—Mike Kandris	666 Grand Ave, Des Moines IA 50309	515-245-2749	R	352	1.3
83	Land Span Inc—Roger Reed	1120 W Griffin Rd, Lakeland FL 33805	863-688-1102	S	352*	.5
	Watkins Associated Industries Inc					
84	Roadrunner-Dawes Transport Inc—Mark DiBlasi	PO Box 8903, Cudahy WI 53110	414-615-1500	S	348*	.7
85	National Carriers Inc—Richard Rees	PO Box 1358, Liberal KS 67905	620-624-1621	R	343*	.7
86	Shaffer Trucking Inc—Ray Dunn	PO Box 418, New Kingstown PA 17072	717-766-4708	S	343*	.6
	Crete Carrier Corp					
87	Velocity Express—Gerald Vento	11104 W Airport Blvd S, Stafford TX 77477		R	343	N/A
88	Stevens Transport Inc—Steven L Aaron	PO Box 279010, Dallas TX 75227	972-216-9000	R	341*	1.7
89	Super Service LLC—Harvey Gainey	6000 Clay Ave SW, Grand Rapids MI 49548	616-530-8558	R	340*	1.2
90	Dependable Highway Exp Inc—Ronald Massman	2555 E Olympic Blvd, Los Angeles CA 90023	323-526-2255	R	332*	.6
91	PAM Transportation Services Inc—Daniel Cushman	297 W Henri De Tonti B, Tontitown AR 72770	479-361-9111	P	332	2.7
92	deBoer Transportation Inc—Ronald DeBoer	PO Box 145, Blenker WI 54415	715-652-2911	R	330*	<.1
93	Classic Transport Inc—Bill Garvey	57784-2 CR3 South, Elkhart IN 46517	574-389-5014	R	318*	.5
94	PAM Transport Inc—Bob Weaver	PO Box 188, Tontitown AR 72770	479-361-9111	S	313*	.8
	PAM Transportation Services Inc					
95	Mercer Transportation Company Inc—James Stone	1128 W Main St, Louisville KY 40203	502-584-2301	R	312*	1.5
96	Mayflower Transit LLC—Richard McClure	PO Box 26150, Fenton MO 63026	636-305-4000	S	311*	.5
	UniGroup Inc					
97	Interstate Distributor Co—George Payne	11707 21st Avenue Ct S, Tacoma WA 98444		R	307*	2.0
98	Con-way Truckload—Herbert J Schmidt	4701 E 32nd St, Joplin MO 64804	417-623-5229	D	300*	3.0
	Con-Way Inc					
99	Continental Van Lines Inc—Greg Blaine	4501 W Marginal Way SW, Seattle WA 98106	206-937-2261	R	300*	.1
100	National Freight—Ike Brown	71 W Park Ave, Vineland NJ 08360	856-691-7492	S	299*	1.5
101	Service Transport Co—Claude Lewis	7900 Almeda Genoa Rd, Houston TX 77075	713-209-2500	R	296*	.5
102	Alabama Motor Express Inc—Scott White	PO Box 487, Ashford AL 36312	334-899-5136	R	289*	.5
103	Centra Inc—Manuel Moroun	12225 Stephen Rd, Warren MI 48089	810-939-7100	R	286	4.0
104	Tropical Shipping and Construction Company Ltd—Rick Murrell	4 E Port Rd, Riviera Beach FL 33404	561-881-3900	S	285*	.9
105	Milan Express Company Inc—John Ross	1091 Kefauver Dr, Milan TN 38358	731-686-7428	R	284*	1.5
106	Midwest Systems—Steve Williamson	5911 Hall St, Saint Louis MO 63147	314-389-6280	R	281*	.4
107	Sentinel Transportation/DuPont-ConocoPhilips—Ralph Benson	3521 Silverside Rd Ste, Wilmington DE 19810	302-477-1640	R	277*	.5
108	Kephart Trucking Co—Timothy Kephart	PO Box 386, Bigler PA 16825	814-857-7704	R	277*	.4
109	Tri-State Motor Transit Co—Glen Garrett	PO Box 113, Joplin MO 64802		S	275	N/A
	Bed Rock Inc					
110	Cardinal Freight Logistics Management—Tom Hosteller	5333 Davidson Hwy, Concord NC 28027	704-786-6125	R	262*	1.4
111	Atlantic Distribution Systems—Ted Alger	1314 Chattahoochie Ave, Atlanta GA 30318	404-351-5311	R	262*	.1
112	Transport Corporation of America Inc—Scott C Arves	1715 Yankee Doodle Rd, Eagan MN 55121	651-686-2500	S	258	1.4
113	Landstar System Holdings Inc	13410 Sutton Park Dr S, Jacksonville FL 32224	904-398-9400	S	256*	.4
	Landstar System Inc					
114	PI and I Motor Express Inc—Joseph Kerola	PO Box 685, Sharon PA 16146	330-448-4035	R	254*	.5
115	Towne Air Freight LLC—Tom Downey	24805 US Hwy 20 W, South Bend IN 46628	574-233-3183	R	248*	.5
116	Con-Way Freight-Western—Kevin Hartman	6301 Beach Blvd Ste 30, Buena Park CA 90621	714-562-0110	D	244*	3.0
117	Coleman American Moving Services—William Brakefield	PO Box 960, Midland City AL 36350	334-983-6500	R	244*	.4
118	DM Bowman Inc—James Ward	10226 Governor Lane Bl, Williamsport MD 21795	301-223-6900	R	242*	.4
119	Danny Herman Trucking Inc—Joe Herman	PO Box 55, Mountain City TN 37683	423-727-9061	R	239*	.3
120	Bancroft and Sons Transportation—Charles Bancroft	3390 High Prairie Rd, Grand Prairie TX 75050	972-790-3777	R	237*	.4
121	Dry Storage Corp—Ann Drake	1750 S Wolf Rd, Des Plaines IL 60018	847-390-6800	R	233*	2.5
122	Bridge Terminal Transport Inc—Thomas Zervos	725 Lawton Rd, Charlotte NC 28216		R	229*	1.5
123	Western Express Holdings Inc—Wayne Wise	7135 Centennial Pl, Nashville TN 37209	615-259-9920	R	226*	1.7
124	Interstate Van Lines Inc—Donald J Morrissette	5801 Rolling Rd, Springfield VA 22152	703-569-2121	R	226*	.2
125	Sharkey Transportation Inc—Jack R Sharkey	3803 Dye Rd, Quincy IL 62305	217-228-6555	R	225*	.4
126	JP Noonan Transportation—Paul Noonan	415 W St, West Bridgewater MA 02379	508-583-2880	R	222*	.4
127	Modco Inc—Brad Baumert	PO Box 33101, Louisville KY 40202	502-515-6590	R	220*	.1
128	Jack Cooper Transport Co—Greg May	2345 Grand Blvd Ste 40, Kansas City MO 64108	816-983-4000	R	219*	.8
129	Turner Brothers LLC—David Ramm	PO Box 83017, Oklahoma City OK 73148	405-680-5100	R	215*	.4
130	Stan Koch and Sons Trucking Inc—Dave Koch	4200 Dahlberg Dr, Minneapolis MN 55422	763-302-5400	R	212*	1.0
131	Cargo Transporters Inc—John Pope	PO Box 850, Claremont NC 28610	828-459-3282	R	212*	.4
132	US 1 Industries Inc—Michael E Kibler	336 W US Hwy 30 Ste 20, Valparaiso IN 46385	219-476-1300	P	211	.1
133	Watkins Associated Industries Inc—John Watkins	PO Box 1738, Atlanta GA 30301	404-872-3841	R	210*	1.8
134	McClymonds Supply and Transit Company Inc—Mark McClymonds	PO Box 296, Portersville PA 16051	724-368-8040	R	210*	.3
135	Paschall Truck Lines Inc—Randall Waller	3443 US Hwy 641 S, Murray KY 42071	270-753-1717	R	209	1.0
136	Roehl Transport Inc—Rick Roehl	PO Box 750, Marshfield WI 54449	715-591-3795	R	206*	1.6
137	Cassens Transport Co—Richard Suhre	145 N Kansas St, Edwardsville IL 62025	618-656-3006	R	204*	.9
138	Davison Transport Inc	PO Box 310, Ruston LA 71273	318-255-3850	S	196*	.4
139	Schilli Corp—John Koons	887 Bolger Ct, Fenton MO 63026	636-717-2600	R	196*	.4
140	Ace Doran Hauling and Rigging Co—Daniel Doran	1601 Blue Rock St, Cincinnati OH 45223	513-681-7900	R	195*	.3
141	Gordon Trucking Inc—Larry Gordon	151 Stewart Rd SW, Pacific WA 98047		R	194*	2.5
142	Hilldrup Transfer and Storage—Charles McDaniel	4022 Jefferson Davis H, Stafford VA 22554	703-221-7155	R	186*	.6
143	Tiger Lines LLC—Donald Altnow	PO Box 1940, Lodi CA 95241	209-334-4102	R	186*	.3
144	Highway Transport Chemical LLC—Gary Reagan	Box 50068, Knoxville TN 37950	865-584-8631	R	184*	.3
145	Globe Transport Inc—Paul Rizzo	1207 N Harrison St, Fort Wayne IN 46808		R	182	2.3
146	Motor Cargo Inc—Pete Morrow	845 W Ctr St, North Salt Lake UT 84054	801-936-1111	S	181	.9
	United Parcel Service Inc					
147	Suddath Cos—Barry S Vaughn	815 S Main St, Jacksonville FL 32207	904-638-8058	R	180*	1.2
148	Superior Solvents and Chemicals—Ray Roembke	1402 N Capitol Ave Ste, Indianapolis IN 46202	317-781-4400	R	180	N/A
149	Lone Star Transportation LLC—Kevin Jordan	1100 Northway Dr, Fort Worth TX 76131	817-306-1000	S	177*	.5
	Tex Robbins Transportation LLC					
150	Tex Robbins Transportation LLC—Kevin Jordan	1100 Northway Dr, Fort Worth TX 76131	817-306-1000	R	177*	.5
151	Jack B Kelley Inc—Mark Davis	Po Box 50539, Amarillo TX 79159	806-353-3553	R	176*	.9
152	New England Motor Freight—Michael S Bare	1-71 N Ave E, Elizabeth NJ 07201	908-965-0100	S	175	2.7
153	Hunt Transportation Inc—Richard Anderson	10770 I St, Omaha NE 68127	402-339-3003	S	175*	.3
	Crete Carrier Corp					
154	Schilli Transportation Services Inc—Tom Schilli	6358 W US Hwy 24, Remington IN 47977	219-261-2101	R	174*	1.1
155	Guardian Moving and Storage Co—Eugene Smoot	1901 Light St, Baltimore MD 21230	410-752-0500	R	170*	.1

Rank	Company Name—*Executive Officer*	Address, City, State, Zip	Phone	Type	Fin	Empls
156	Arpin Group Inc—*David Arpin*	PO Box 1302, East Greenwich RI 02818	401-828-8111	R	170*	.6
157	Greatwide Logistics Services LLC—*Leo Suggs*	12404 Park Central Dr, Dallas TX 75251	972-228-7344	R	169*	2.8
158	Urs Gores Holdings Corp—*Alex Gores*	10877 Wilshire Blvd St, Los Angeles CA 90024	310-209-3010	R	168*	2.3
159	Barr-Nunn Transportation Inc—*Bob Sturgeon*	PO Box 518, Granger IA 50109	515-999-2525	R	168*	.9
160	Fred Taylor Co—*James F Taylor*	PO Box 1156, Albany GA 31702	229-883-5200	R	167*	.5
161	Maverick USA Inc—*Steve Williams*	P O Box 16173, North Little Rock AR 72231		R	166	1.0
162	Landstar Inway Inc—*Henry Gerkens* Landstar System Holdings Inc	PO Box 7013, Rockford IL 61125	815-972-5000	S	166*	.3
163	Consolidated Delivery and Logistics—*Albert Van Ness Jr*	104 Sunfield Ave, Edison NJ 08837	732-417-1880	R	166*	<.1
164	Cassens Corp—*Richard Suhre*	145 N Kansas St, Edwardsville IL 62025	618-656-3006	R	165*	.9
165	Wheaton Van Lines Inc—*Stephen F Burns*	8010 Castleton Rd, Indianapolis IN 46250	317-849-7900	R	162*	.3
166	Superior Bulk Logistics Inc—*Richard Lewis*	711 Jorie Blvd Ste 101, Oak Brook IL 60523	630-573-2555	R	162*	.2
167	Bavarian Motor Transport Inc—*Warren Lasch*	3681 Okemos Rd Ste 500, Okemos MI 48864	517-349-3011	S	161*	.4
168	Arrow Trucking Co—*Doug Filstickler*	PO Box 3570, Tulsa OK 74101	918-446-1441	R	160	N/A
169	Boyd Brothers Transportation Inc—*Gail B Cooper*	3275 Hwy 30, Clayton AL 36016	334-775-1400	R	160*	.9
170	Watkins and Shepard Trucking Inc—*Ray Kuntz*	PO Box 5328, Missoula MT 59806	406-532-6121	R	160*	.9
171	Trucks Inc—*Helen Willis*	105 Short Rd, Jackson GA 30233	770-775-4999	R	160*	.3
172	Brown Transport Inc—*Mickey Brown*	PO Box 6, West Alexandria OH 45381	513-787-3512	R	160*	<.1
173	Willis Shaw Express—*Chris Kozak* Comcar Industries Inc	201 N Elm St, Elm Springs AR 72728	479-248-7261	S	157*	1.1
174	Keen Transport Inc—*William Keen*	PO Box 389, New Kingstown PA 17072	717-243-6622	R	155*	.2
175	CTS Advantage Logistics—*Steve Haney*	2071 Ringwood Ave, San Jose CA 95131		R	154*	.3
176	Active USA Inc / ATC Leasing—*Bruce Jackson*	10801 Corporate Dr, Pleasant Prairie WI 53158	262-564-7952	R	154	.6
177	Cheeseman LLC—*Ed Zumstein*	2200 State Rt 119, Fort Recovery OH 45846		R	153*	.3
178	Slay Transportation Company Inc—*Gary Slay*	1441 Hampton Ave, Saint Louis MO 63139	314-647-7529	R	152*	.8
179	Heyl Truck Lines Inc—*Don Heyl*	PO Box 500, Akron IA 51001	712-568-2451	R	152*	.3
180	Pegasus Transportation Inc—*Gary Hanke*	2903 S English Station, Louisville KY 40299		R	152*	.3
181	Unigroup Worldwide Inc—*Mike Kranisky*	1 Worldwide Dr, Fenton MO 63026	636-326-3100	R	151*	1.3
182	USF Bestway Inc—*Doug Wagner* YRC Regional Transportation Inc	PO Box 31001-0925, Pasadena CA 91110	480-760-1675	S	151*	1.8
183	Maverick Transportation LLC—*Chris Leurquin*	PO Box 15428, Little Rock AR 72231	501-955-1222	R	150*	1.8
184	PJAX Inc—*Donald Hammel*	PO Box 1290, Gibsonia PA 15044	724-449-9000	R	150	1.0
185	Howard Sheppard Inc—*Cliff Sheppard*	PO Box 797, Sandersville GA 31082	478-552-5127	R	148*	.3
186	Southern Freight Inc—*Robert Fauls Jr*	99 University Ave SW, Atlanta GA 30315	404-688-5300	R	148*	.3
187	Decker Truck Line Inc—*Donald Decker*	PO Box 915, Fort Dodge IA 50501	515-576-4141	R	146*	.8
188	Roadrunner Dawes Freight Systems Inc—*Mark DiBlasi*	4900 S Pennsylvania Av, Cudahy WI 53110	414-615-1500	R	143*	.2
189	Standard Forwarding Company Inc—*John Ward*	2925 Morton Dr, East Moline IL 61244	309-755-4504	R	141*	.2
190	New York Carolina Express—*Jeffrey Bump*	1314 Conklin Rd, Conklin NY 13748	607-723-7977	R	140*	.2
191	Teton Transportation Inc—*Larry Hammond*	PO Box 909, Knoxville TN 37901	865-546-3846	R	140*	.2
192	Glenn Machine Works Inc—*James Glenn*	PO Box 2205, Columbus MS 39704	662-328-4611	R	140*	.1
193	Navajo Express Inc—*Donald Digby*	1400 W 64th Ave, Denver CO 80221	303-287-3800	R	138*	.8
194	Exel Transportation Services Inc—*Chris Marchetti*	965 Ridge Lake Blvd St, Memphis TN 38120	901-767-4455	D	138*	.3
195	Gaines Motor Lines Inc—*Jeffrey Shortt*	PO Box 1549, Hickory NC 28603	828-322-2000	R	138*	.2
196	Bulkmatic Transport Co—*Albert Bingham*	2001 N Cline Ave, Griffith IN 46319	219-972-7630	R	137*	1.1
197	Dallas and Mavis Specialized Carrier Co—*Tom Mills*	625 55th St, Kenosha WI 53140		R	136*	.1
198	Sunset Pacific Transportation—*Charles King*	PO Box 805, Chino CA 91708	909-464-1677	R	135*	1.0
199	Atlantic Relocation Systems—*Ted Alger*	1314 Chattahoochee Ave, Atlanta GA 30318	404-351-5311	R	135*	.7
200	Transport Service Co—*Robert Schurer* Kenan Advantage Group Inc	2001 Spring Rd Ste 400, Oak Brook IL 60523	630-472-5900	S	135*	.7
201	Johnson Storage and Moving Company Inc—*James R Johnson*	7009 S Jordan Rd, Centennial CO 80112	303-690-2600	R	135*	.3
202	Cowan Systems LLC—*Joseph Cowan*	4555 Hollins Ferry Rd, Baltimore MD 21227	410-247-0800	R	134*	1.0
203	Keystone Freight Corp—*Raymond Wisniewski*	2820 16th St, North Bergen NJ 07047	201-330-1900	D	134*	.7
204	YRC Glen Moore—*Mike Smid*	PO Box 760, Carlisle PA 17013	717-245-0788	S	134	1.1
205	TransAm Trucking Inc—*Russ McElliotte*	15910 S Hwy 169, Olathe KS 66051	913-782-5300	R	132	N/A
206	A and R Transport Inc—*James E Bedeker*	8440 South Tabler Rd, Morris IL 60450	815-729-1308	R	131*	.7
207	Spee Dee Delivery Service—*Donald Weeres*	PO Box 1417, Saint Cloud MN 56302	320-251-6697	R	128*	1.4
208	FAF Inc—*Bruce A Campbell*	430 Airport Rd, Greeneville TN 37745	423-636-7000	R	128	.9
209	The TransVantage Group—*Shirley Sooy*	58 Chambers Brook Rd, Somerville NJ 08876	908-526-8700	R	126*	.2
210	Liedtka Trucking Inc—*Phillip Liedtka*	PO Box 8607, Trenton NJ 08650	609-586-2080	R	125*	.2
211	Carlile Transportation Systems—*Harry McDonald*	1800 E 1st Ave, Anchorage AK 99501	907-276-7797	R	123*	.2
212	Commercial Carrier Corp—*Kevin Nixon*	502 E Bridgers Ave, Auburndale FL 33823	863-967-1101	R	120	1.1
213	Lisa Motor Lines Inc FFE Transportation Services Inc	PO Box 655888, Dallas TX 75265	214-819-5625	S	120*	.3
214	Transport Investments Inc—*Douglas McAdams*	100 Industry Dr, Pittsburgh PA 15275	412-788-8878	R	120*	.2
215	Universal Am-Can Ltd Universal Truckload Services Inc	PO Box 2007, Warren MI 48090	586-920-0100	S	118	.9
216	Southern Ag Carriers Inc—*Henry H Griffin*	P O Box 50335, Albany GA 31703	229-432-9696	R	118*	.2
217	Wynne Transport Service Inc—*Donald W Wynne*	2222 N 11th St, Omaha NE 68110	402-342-4001	R	116*	.2
218	McCollister's Transportation Systems—*Daniel McCollister*	PO Box 9, Burlington NJ 08016		R	115	.4
219	Cressler Trucking Inc—*William Keen* Keen Transport Inc	PO Box 312, Shippensburg PA 17257	717-532-6315	S	114*	.2
220	Great Plains Trucking Inc—*Sherwin Fast*	PO Box 166, Salina KS 67402	785-823-3276	S	113*	1.0
221	Smith Transport Inc—*Barry Smith*	331 E Closson Rd, Roaring Spring PA 16673		R	112	.8
222	Ozark Motor Lines Inc—*Steve Higginbotham*	3934 Homewood Rd, Memphis TN 38118	901-251-9711	R	111	.7
223	Kinard Trucking Inc—*Dave Meckley*	310 N Zarfoss Dr, York PA 17404	717-792-3632	R	111*	.2
224	American Security LLC—*John Gilge*	1717 University Ave W, Saint Paul MN 55104	651-644-1155	R	111*	.2
225	Nu-Way Transportation Services—*Vernon Schrof*	25 Access Way, Bloomington IL 61704	309-820-9797	R	111*	.2
226	Colonial Freight Systems Inc—*Tom McBride*	PO Box 22168, Knoxville TN 37933	865-966-9711	R	110*	.3
227	Truckers Express Inc—*Robert Froehlich*	3501 W Broadway St, Missoula MT 59808	406-721-6002	R	109*	.6
228	J Grady Randolph Inc—*Charles Randolph*	PO Box 2128, Gaffney SC 29342	864-488-9030	R	109*	.2
229	Southwestern Motor Transport—*Chris Withers*	4600 Goldfield, San Antonio TX 78218	210-662-2390	R	109	.9
230	K-Five Construction Corp—*George Krug Jr*	13769 Main St, Lemont IL 60439	630-257-5600	R	108*	.5
231	Super Service Inc—*Roger Waddle*	PO Box 3070, West Somerset KY 42564	606-679-1141	R	107*	.8
232	Lonestar Transportation Inc—*Tex Robbins*	1100 N Way Dr, Fort Worth TX 76131		R	107*	.7
233	Builders Transportation Company LLC—*Frank Phillips*	PO Box 16369, Memphis TN 38186	901-396-1220	R	107*	.2
234	Enterprise Transportation Co—*Michael Creel*	PO Box 4324, Houston TX 77210	713-880-6500	S	106*	1.0
235	TRANS International System—*Mark Stewart*	130 E Wilson Bridge Rd, Worthington OH 43085	614-891-4942	R	106*	.2
236	WL Logan Trucking Co—*William Logan Jr*	3224 Navarre Rd SW, Canton OH 44706	330-478-1404	R	105*	.2
237	Wiley Sanders Truck Lines—*Bobby Brown*	PO Box 707, Troy AL 36081	334-566-5184	R	104	.8

Note: An asterisk (*) indicates an estimated financial figure. The company type code used is as follows: R = Private, P = Public, S = Private Subsidiary, B = Public Subsidiary, D = Division, J = Joint Venture, I = Investment Fund.

COMPANY RANKINGS BY SALES WITHIN 4-DIGIT SIC

Rank	Company Name—*Executive Officer*	Address, City, State, Zip	Phone	Type	Fin	Empls
238	Liquid Transport Corp—*Keith Lewis*	8470 Allison Pointe Bl, Indianapolis IN 46250	317-841-4200	R	104	.6
239	Jordan Carriers Inc—*Kenneth Jordan*	PO Box 1066, Natchez MS 39121	601-446-8899	R	102*	.2
240	NAPA Transportation Inc—*Ron Accomando*	PO Box 959, Mechanicsburg PA 17055	717-920-9840	R	102*	.2
241	FT Silfies Inc—*Jim Niness*	1275 Glenlivet Dr Ste, Allentown PA 18106		R	101*	.2
242	L and H Trucking Company Inc—*Glenn Longstreth*	860 Gitts Run Rd, Hanover PA 17331	717-633-1710	R	101*	.2
243	LCL Transit Co—*Robert J Schaupp*	PO Box 19009, Green Bay WI 54307	920-431-3500	R	100*	.2
244	Panella Trucking Inc—*Robert Panella*	5000 E Fremont St, Stockton CA 95215	209-943-5000	R	100*	.2
245	Home Run Inc—*Gary Harlow*	1299 Lavelle Dr, Xenia OH 45385	937-376-4316	R	100*	.2
246	Trade Winds Trucking—*Julie Wolff*	PO Box 265, Alpha IL 61413	309-761-4232	R	100	<.1
247	Florida Rock and Tank Lines Inc—*Robert Sandlin*	501 Riverside Ave Ste, Jacksonville FL 32202	904-396-5733	R	99	.5
248	Market Transport Ltd—*Gary Wilson*	110 N Marine Dr, Portland OR 97217	503-283-2405	R	98*	.5
249	Navajo Express Inc (Denver Colorado)—*Donald Digby*	1400 W 64th Ave, Denver CO 80221	303-287-3800	R	98*	.5
250	Pottle's Transportation Inc—*Barry E Pottle*	15 Page Rd W, Hermon ME 04401	207-947-2179	R	98*	.2
251	B-H Transfer Co—*Frank Young*	PO Box 151, Sandersville GA 31082	478-552-5119	R	98*	.1
252	Special Dispatch Inc—*Brian Kuntz*	5830 Fee Fee Rd, Hazelwood MO 63042	314-731-2240	R	98*	.1
253	Fleet Car Carriers—*Walter Tripp*	7563 Dahlia St, Commerce City CO 80022	303-288-4600	R	97	.5
254	Liberty Moving and Storage Co—*Michael Federico*	350 Moreland Rd, Commack NY 11725	631-234-3000	R	97*	.2
255	Elmer Buchta Trucking LLC—*Elmer Buchta*	PO Box 68, Otwell IN 47564	812-354-6300	R	97*	.2
256	TH Ryan Cartage Co—*Tim Ryan*	111 S 7th Ave, Maywood IL 60153	708-345-0900	R	97*	.2
257	National Retail Transportation—*Raymond Wisniewski*	2201 Garry Rd, Cinnaminson NJ 08077	856-786-0865	D	97	.3
258	Q Carriers Inc—*Greg Gorvin*	1415 Maras St S, Shakopee MN 55379	952-445-8718	R	95*	.2
259	Foodliner Inc—*Greg McCoy*	PO Box 1565, Dubuque IA 52003		R	94	.5
260	Epes Transport System Inc—*Bill Fobert*	PO Box 35605, Greensboro NC 27425	336-668-3358	S	94*	.7
261	Mason and Dixon Truck Lines—*Donald B Cochran* Universal Truckload Services Inc	PO Box 2122, Warren MI 48090	586-920-0100	S	94	.6
262	A Anastasio and Sons Trucking Co—*Andrew Anastasio*	80 Middletown Ave, New Haven CT 06513	203-787-5746	R	93*	.5
263	Anderson Trucking Service Inc—*William A Woolsey Jr*	725 Opportunity Dr, Saint Cloud MN 56301	320-255-7400	R	92*	.5
264	Amstan Logistics—*Michael Seboria*	101 Knightsbridge Dr, Hamilton OH 45011	513-863-4627	R	92*	.1
265	Oak Harbor Freight Lines Inc—*David Vander Pol*	PO Box 1469, Auburn WA 98071	253-288-8300	R	91*	1.2
266	Atkinson Freight Lines—*Joseph B Atkinson III*	PO Box 984, Bensalem PA 19020	215-638-1130	R	91*	.2
267	Gordon Sevig Trucking Co—*Gordon Sevig*	400 Hwy 151 E, Walford IA 52351	319-846-5500	R	91*	.2
268	Opies Transport Inc—*Danny Opie*	PO Box 89, Eldon MO 65026	573-392-6525	R	91*	.1
269	Gypsum Express Ltd—*John Wight*	PO Box 268, Baldwinsville NY 13027	315-638-2201	R	90*	.7
270	McCoy Group Inc (Shullsburg Wisconsin)—*Robert Shullsburg*	PO Box 368, Shullsburg WI 53586	608-965-4462	R	90*	.5
271	Caledonia Haulers Inc—*Dennis Gavin*	PO Box 31, Caledonia MN 55921	507-725-9000	R	89*	.2
272	GDS Express Inc—*Jack Delaney*	1270 Hilbish Ave, Akron OH 44312	330-794-8868	R	89*	.2
273	Rinchem Company Inc—*Bill Moore*	6133 Edith Blvd NE, Albuquerque NM 87107	505-345-3655	R	89*	.2
274	Ward Trucking Corp—*Bill T Ward*	PO Box 1553, Altoona PA 16603	814-944-0803	R	88*	1.1
275	AD Transport Express Inc—*Gary Percy*	5601 Belleville Rd, Canton MI 48188	734-397-7100	R	88*	.6
276	Lester Coggins Trucking Inc—*Dan Denhof*	PO Box 55, Okahumpka FL 34762	352-326-8800	R	88*	.5
277	Caldwell Freight Lines Inc—*David Brenner*	PO Box 1950, Lenoir NC 28645	828-728-9231	R	88*	.4
278	Kaplan Trucking Co—*David Ferrante*	6600 Bessemer Ave, Cleveland OH 44127	216-341-3322	R	85*	.6
279	Pitt Ohio Inc—*Charles Hammel*	15 27th St, Pittsburgh PA 15222	412-232-3015	R	84*	< 1
280	Dupre' Transport LLC—*Reggie Dupre*	201 Energy Pkwy Ste 5, Lafayette LA 70508	337-237-8471	R	84*	.5
281	South Shore Transportation Company Inc—*Cole Hanley*	4010 Columbus Ave, Sandusky OH 44870	419-625-0710	R	84*	.2
282	Davis-Express Inc—*James Davis*	PO Box 1276, Starke FL 32091	904-964-6619	R	84*	.1
283	Penn's Best Inc—*Patrick Healey*	PO Box 128, Meshoppen PA 18630	570-833-2583	R	84*	.1
284	Billy Barnes Enterprises Inc—*Terry Kilpatrick*	PO Box 745, Monroeville AL 36461	251-267-3153	R	83*	.2
285	Dedicated Transport LLC—*Frank Wagner*	6551 Grant Ave, Cleveland OH 44105	216-641-2500	R	83*	.2
286	Ralph Moyle Inc—*Ralph Moyle*	PO Box 248, Mattawan MI 49071	269-668-4531	R	83*	.2
287	James Group International Inc—*John James*	4335 W Fort St, Detroit MI 48209	313-841-0070	R	82*	.5
288	Landstar Express America Inc—*Henry H Gerkins* Landstar System Inc	PO Box 19136, Jacksonville FL 32224	904-398-9400	S	82	.4
289	Wheaton World Wide Moving—*Steve Burns*	8010 Castleton Rd, Indianapolis IN 46250	317-849-7900	R	81	.7
290	West Side Transport Inc—*Don Vogt*	4201 16th Ave SW, Cedar Rapids IA 52404	319-390-4466	R	81*	.5
291	L and B Transport LLC—*Jody Gullory*	PO Box 74870, Baton Rouge LA 70874	225-387-0894	R	81*	.2
292	Access America Transport—*James Large*	1110 Market St Ste 315, Chattanooga TN 37402	423-821-8044	R	81*	.2
293	Horizon Freight Systems Inc—*David Ferrante*	6600 Bessemer Ave, Cleveland OH 44127	216-341-7410	R	81	.6
294	Warren Transport Inc—*Robert Molinaro*	PO Box 420, Waterloo IA 50704	319-233-6113	R	80	.2
295	Lile International Cos—*Diane DeKutremont*	8060 SW Pfaffle St Ste, Portland OR 97223	503-726-4800	R	80*	.4
296	Bisson Moving and Storage—*Robert Cooper*	76 New Meadows Rd, West Bath ME 04530	207-442-7991	R	80*	.2
297	Petron Inc—*Steve Ayres*	PO Box 8718, Alexandria LA 71306	318-445-5685	R	80*	.2
298	Mission Petroleum Carriers—*David Fontenot*	8450 Mosley Rd, Houston TX 77075	713-943-8250	R	79*	.5
299	Cresco Lines Inc—*Robert Stranczek*	15220 S Halstead St, Harvey IL 60426		R	79*	.2
300	Charles G Lawson Trucking—*Charles Lawson*	7815 Mobile Hwy, Hope Hull AL 36043	334-284-3220	R	79*	.2
301	Star Transportation Inc—*Jim Brower*	PO Box 100925, Nashville TN 37224	615-256-4336	R	78	.6
302	Sunco Carriers Inc—*Joe Whitfield* Watkins Associated Industries Inc	1025 N Chestnut Rd, Lakeland FL 33805	863-688-1948	S	78*	.1
303	Northeast Express Transportation Inc—*Kevin Malone*	PO Box 549, Windsor Locks CT 06096	860-254-6398	R	78*	<.1
304	Schneider Specialized Carriers Inc—*Christopher Lofgren*	PO Box 2545, Green Bay WI 54306		S	77*	.7
305	Thom's Transport Company Inc—*Darrell Thomas*	4842 Gilman Rd, Blackshear GA 31516	912-449-3316	R	77*	.1
306	G and P Trucking Company Inc—*Clifton Parker*	126 Access Rd, Gaston SC 29053	803-791-5500	R	77	.7
307	RE Garrison Trucking—*Wyles Griffith*	PO Box 890, Cullman AL 35056		R	76*	.4
308	Tri-Union Express Inc—*Patricia Parchem*	1939 N Lafayette Ct, Griffith IN 46319	219-838-5400	R	76*	.2
309	Commonwealth Warehouse and Storage—*Ross Aiello*	123 36th St, Pittsburgh PA 15201	412-687-6600	R	76*	<.1
310	Godfrey Transport Inc—*Michael Martinez*	50 E 91st St Ste 305, Indianapolis IN 46240		R	75	1.0
311	Lanter Co—*Steve Lanter*	PO Box 68, Madison IL 62060		R	75*	.9
312	Tango Transport Inc—*Robert Gorman*	6009 Financial Plz, Shreveport LA 71129	318-683-6700	R	75	.6
313	Tonyan Brothers Inc—*Jim Tonyan*	P O Box 70, Ringwood IL 60072	815-385-0856	R	75*	.1
314	Moeller Trucking Inc—*Gary Moeller*	8100 Industrial Dr, Maria Stein OH 45860	419-925-4799	R	74*	.1
315	Kenan Advantage Group West—*Chet Friday*	4076 Seaport Blvd, West Sacramento CA 95691	916-371-8241	R	73	.7
316	Eagle Transport Corp—*A Donald Stallings*	300 S Wesleyan Blvd St, Rocky Mount NC 27804	252-937-2464	R	73*	.5
317	Freightmasters Inc—*Ronald Have*	3703 Kennebec Dr, Eagan MN 55122	651-688-6800	R	73*	.5
318	Great Coastal Express Inc Heartland Express Inc	1501 Ware Bottom Sprin, Chester VA 23836	804-768-0023	D	73	N/A
319	Scully Distribution Services—*Steven Scully*	10641 Almond Ave, Fontana CA 92337	909-356-8555	S	71*	.5
320	Barney Trucking Inc—*Brad Barney*	235 South SR 24, Salina UT 84654		R	71*	.4
321	Kane Transport Inc—*Robert Kane*	PO Box 126, Sauk Centre MN 56378	320-352-2762	R	71*	.1
322	Flexway Trucking Inc—*John McBride*	4849 Park 370 Blvd, Hazelwood MO 63042	314-429-6444	R	71*	.1
323	Gentle Giant Moving Company Inc—*Larry O'Toole*	29 Harding St, Somerville MA 02143	617-661-3333	R	70*	.4

Rank	Company Name—*Executive Officer*	Address, City, State, Zip	Phone	Type	Fin	Empls
324	Tetco Inc—*Tom Turner*	1100 NE Loop 410 Ste 9, San Antonio TX 78209	210-821-5900	R	70*	.2
325	Woody Bogler Trucking Co—*Woody Bogler*	PO Box 229, Rosebud MO 63091	573-764-3700	R	70*	.1
326	Fremont Contract Carriers Inc—*Michael Herre*	PO Box 489, Fremont NE 68026	402-721-3020	R	70*	.1
327	Hedge and Herberg Inc—*Gayle Hedge*	PO Box 98, Big Stone City SD 57216	605-862-8143	R	70*	.1
328	Palmer Moving and Storage Co—*Jeffrey Palmer*	24660 Dequindre Rd, Warren MI 48091	586-834-3400	R	70*	.1
329	Riegel Transportation Inc—*Robert Riegel*	174 Cabot St, West Babylon NY 11704	631-753-1500	R	70*	.1
330	Mckenzie Tank Lines Inc—*James Shaeffer*	PO Box 1200, Tallahassee FL 32302	850-576-1221	R	69*	.8
331	Millis Transfer Inc—*David Millis*	PO Box 550, Black River Falls WI 54615	715-284-4384	R	69*	.5
332	North Park Transportation Co—*Peter Kooi*	5150 Columbine St, Denver CO 80216	303-295-0300	R	69*	.3
333	O and S Trucking Inc—*James O'Neal*	3769 E Evergreen St, Springfield MO 65803	417-864-4780	R	69	.4
334	CTL Distribution Inc—*Thomas Hindle*	PO Box 376, Mulberry FL 33860	863-428-2373	R	68*	.6
335	H and M Bay Inc—*Walter Messick*	PO Box 280, Federalsburg MD 21632		R	68*	<.1
336	Steel Warehouse Inc—*Dave Lerman*	PO Box 1377, South Bend IN 46624		R	67*	.6
337	Jack Cooper Transport—*Greg May* Jack Cooper Transport Co	1100 Walnut Street, Kansas City MO 64106	816-983-4000	S	67*	.4
338	Lynden Transport Inc—*Alex McKallor*	3027 Rampart Dr, Anchorage AK 99501	907-276-4800	S	67*	.2
339	CaseStack Inc—*Dan Sanker*	2850 Ocean Park Blvd S, Santa Monica CA 90405		R	65	.4
340	Blue Flash Express Inc—*Rod Bentley*	23356 Old Scenic Hwy, Zachary LA 70791	225-293-0185	R	65*	.3
341	Marina Cartage Inc—*Michael Tadin*	4450 S Morgan St, Chicago IL 60609	773-254-3644	R	65*	.1
342	Schulz Transportation Service—*Allan Schulz*	4301 W Adams St, Lincoln NE 68524	402-470-0600	R	65*	.1
343	Marine Pollution Control Corp—*David Usher*	8631 W Jefferson Ave, Detroit MI 48209	313-849-2333	R	65*	.1
344	Barton Solvents Inc—*Leon Casten*	PO Box 221, Des Moines IA 50301	515-265-7998	R	65*	.1
345	Planes Moving and Storage Inc—*John Planes*	9823 Cincinnati Dayton, West Chester OH 45069	513-759-6000	R	65	.2
346	Raven Transport Company Inc—*W Randolph Lee*	6800 Broadway Ave, Jacksonville FL 32254	904-880-1515	R	64*	.4
347	Grayson Mitchell Inc—*H Grayson Mitchell Jr*	PO Box 128, Emporia VA 23847	434-634-9159	R	64*	.3
348	Safeway Transportation Co—*Greg Stewart*	PO Box 74790, Baton Rouge LA 70874	225-387-6623	R	64*	.1
349	Evans Delivery Company Inc—*Albert Evans*	100-110 W Columbia St, Schuylkill Haven PA 17972	570-385-9048	R	63	.6
350	Titus Transportation LLC—*Brent Hagenbuch*	2500 Westcourt Rd Bldg, Denton TX 76207	940-566-1962	R	63*	.4
351	Sherman Brothers Heavy Trucking—*Bart Sherman*	PO Box 706, Harrisburg OR 97446	541-995-7751	R	63*	.4
352	Interstate Carrier Xpress—*Mike Gully*	3820 Wisman Ln, Quincy IL 62305	217-224-0770	R	63*	.1
353	Tri-Modal Distribution Services—*Gregory Owen*	2011 E Carson St, Carson CA 90810	310-522-5506	R	63*	.1
354	J Bar B Foods—*Danny Janeck*	PO Box 7, Waelder TX 78959	830-788-7511	R	63*	<.1
355	ADM Trucking Inc—*Patricia A Woertz*	4666 Faries Pkwy, Decatur IL 62526	217-424-5200	R	63	.5
356	Southern Refrigerated Transport—*Tony Smith*	8055 Hwy 67 N, Texarkana AR 71854	870-898-3337	R	62*	.4
357	Acme Truck Line Inc—*Mike Coatney*	PO Box 183, Harvey LA 70059	504-368-2510	R	62*	.1
358	Carlen Transport Inc—*Leonard Peters*	81 Mecaw Rd, Hampden ME 04444	207-990-4507	R	62*	.1
359	Arrow Concrete Co—*Kurt Meby*	1601 E Houston St, Broken Arrow OK 74012	918-258-8693	R	62*	.1
360	S and M Moving Systems—*Steve Todare*	3637 E Miami Ave, Phoenix AZ 85040	602-586-3200	R	62	.1
361	Berks Transportation Inc—*John Hannon*	PO Box 9000, Wyomissing PA 19610	610-374-5131	R	62	.1
362	Trailiner Corp—*H E Whitener*	PO Box 5270, Springfield MO 65803	417-866-7258	R	61*	.4
363	Fleetwood Transportation Services—*Mark Prowell*	PO Box 430, Diboll TX 75941	936-829-4735	R	61*	.4
364	Coshocton Trucking Inc—*James Woodie*	PO Box 1210, Coshocton OH 43812	740-622-1311	R	61*	.1
365	Cape Cod Express Inc—*Stephen Hoss*	1 Express Dr, Wareham MA 02571	508-291-1600	R	61*	.1
366	First Class Services Inc—*Randy Stroup*	PO Box 478, Lewisport KY 42351	270-295-3746	R	61*	.1
367	Perdido Trucking Service Inc—*Huston Hollister*	3164 Midtown Park S, Mobile AL 36606	251-470-0355	R	61*	.1
368	Reeve Trucking Co—*Donald E Reeve*	5050 Carpenter Rd, Stockton CA 95215	209-948-4061	R	61*	.1
369	RRR Transportation Inc—*John Reeves*	PO Box 863, Calhoun GA 30703	706-625-9229	R	61*	.1
370	Safeway Moving Systems Inc—*Edward Hart*	2828 N Emerson Ave, Indianapolis IN 46218	317-545-7533	R	61*	.1
371	Superior Carriers Inc—*Len F Fletcher*	711 Jorie Blvd Ste 101, Oak Brook IL 60523	630-573-2555	R	61*	.1
372	Buske Lines Inc—*John Babington*	PO Box 929, Edwardsville IL 62025	618-931-6091	R	60	.4
373	Shipper's Transport Co—*Cheryl Hulshof*	3750 Stewarts Ln, Nashville TN 37218		R	60	.5
374	Nelson Westerberg Inc—*John R Westerburg*	1500 Arthur Ave, Elk Grove Village IL 60007	847-437-2080	R	60*	.4
375	Office Movers Inc—*John Kane*	6500 Kane Way, Elkridge MD 21075		R	60*	.2
376	Jones Motor Group Inc—*James Koegel*	654 Enterprise Dr, Limerick PA 19468	610-948-7900	R	60*	.1
377	Mid Cities Motor Freight Inc—*Robert Whetsell*	6006 Lake Ave, Saint Joseph MO 64504	816-238-8000	R	60*	.1
378	South Bend Motor Freight—*Abraham Marcus*	PO Box 1228, South Bend IN 46624	574-239-1310	R	60*	.1
379	Brown's Transport Inc—*Brian Kinsey*	6908 Chapman Rd, Lithonia GA 30058	770-482-6521	R	59*	.6
380	Cypress Truck Lines Inc—*David Penland*	1414 Lindrose St, Jacksonville FL 32206	904-356-9322	R	59*	.5
381	Land Air Express of New England—*William Spencer*	59 Ave C, Williston VT 05495	802-863-5062	R	58*	.4
382	Armellini Express Lines Inc—*Richard Armellini*	PO Box 678, Palm City FL 34991	772-287-0575	R	58*	.3
383	Sodrel Truck Lines Inc—*Noah Sodrel*	1 Sodrel Dr, Jeffersonville IN 47130	812-282-7433	S	58*	.3
384	Melton Truck Lines Inc—*Robert A Peterson*	808 N 161st E Ave, Tulsa OK 74116	918-234-8000	R	57*	.8
385	Dohrn Transfer Co—*Gary Dohrn*	625 3rd Ave, Rock Island IL 61201	309-794-0723	R	57*	.5
386	Pohl Transportation Inc—*Harold Pohl*	PO Box 334, Versailles OH 45380	937-526-5046	R	57*	.1
387	West Brothers Transportation Services—*Michael Flanagan*	PO Box 21019, Durham NC 27703	919-281-1151	R	56*	.5
388	Earl L Henderson Trucking Co—*John Kaburick*	1 Industrial Dr, Salem IL 62881	618-548-4667	R	56*	.4
389	American Transport Group LLC	1700 W Cortland St, Chicago IL 60622	773-413-6502	R	56*	.1
390	Bo-Mark Transport Inc—*John R Phillips*	4884 Old Louisville Rd, Garden City GA 31408	912-964-8620	R	56*	.1
391	Hardinger Transfer Company Inc—*William Schaal*	1314 W 18th St, Erie PA 16502	814-453-6587	R	56*	.1
392	United Petroleum Transports—*Greg Price*	4312 S Georgia Pl, Oklahoma City OK 73129	405-677-6633	R	55*	.5
393	Tony's Express Inc—*George Raluy*	10613 Jasmine St, Fontana CA 92337	909-427-8700	R	55*	.3
394	Pleasant Trucking—*Nancy A Morrow*	PO Box 778, Connellsville PA 15425	724-628-5347	R	55*	.1
395	Advanced Industrial Services—*Michael Yergo*	3250 N Susquehanna Trl, York PA 17402	717-764-9811	R	55*	.1
396	Atlantic and Pacific Freightways—*Dan Wyatt*	PO Box 17007, Portland OR 97217	360-699-2057	R	55*	.1
397	EH Hamilton Trkg and Wholesale Service—*Byron Bayne*	2612 W Morris St, Indianapolis IN 46221	317-916-2600	R	55*	.1
398	Flanary and Sons Trucking Inc—*Curtis Flanary*	900 Holliston Mills Rd, Church Hill TN 37642	423-357-8357	R	55*	.1
399	Jeffco Leasing Company Inc—*Ryan Abeln*	1700 Kosciusko St, Saint Louis MO 63104	314-385-2545	R	55*	.1
400	Reliable Transportation Specialists—*Kevin Lhotak*	139 Venturi Dr, Chesterton IN 46304	219-926-8850	R	55*	.1
401	Southern Intermodal Xpress Inc—*David Kennedy*	PO Box 929, Mobile AL 36601	251-438-2749	R	55*	.1
402	Barnhart Crane and Rigging Co—*Alan Barnhart*	PO Box 13364, Memphis TN 38113	901-775-3000	R	54	.1
403	Martin Transportation Systems—*Rich Dabney*	7300 Clyde Park Ave SW, Byron Center MI 49315	616-455-8850	R	54*	.5
404	Hornady Transportation—*BC Hornady*	PO Box 846, Monroeville AL 36461	251-575-4811	R	54*	.5
405	Combined Transport Inc—*Michael Card*	PO Box 3667, Central Point OR 97502	541-734-7418	R	54*	.3
406	Badger Express Inc—*Barry Turner*	181 Quality Ct, Fall River WI 53932	920-484-5808	R	54*	.1
407	Beam Brothers Trucking Inc—*Gerald Beam*	PO Box 183, Mount Crawford VA 22841	540-234-8545	R	54*	.1
408	Payne Inc—*Daniel Payne*	1101 International Pkw, Fredericksburg VA 22406	540-898-0045	R	54*	.1
409	Central Trucking Inc—*Mark Roberts*	11930 N Hartman Dr Ste, Edinburgh IN 46124	812-526-9737	R	54	.5
410	DS Distribution Inc—*William deRodes*	PO BOX 477, Wooster OH 44691	330-264-7400	R	53*	.1
411	Duplainville Transport Inc—*Tom Quadricci*	N63W23075 Hwy 74, Sussex WI 53089	414-566-2102	R	53*	.1
412	Hyland Enterprises Inc—*Doug Dowlin*	PO Box 2377, Rawlins WY 82301	307-328-0668	R	53*	.1

Note: An asterisk (*) indicates an estimated financial figure. The company type code used is as follows: R = Private, P = Public, S = Private Subsidiary, B = Public Subsidiary, D = Division, J = Joint Venture, I = Investment Fund.

COMPANY RANKINGS BY SALES WITHIN 4-DIGIT SIC

Rank	Company Name—*Executive Officer*	Address, City, State, Zip	Phone	Type	Fin	Empls
413	Jaro Transportation Services—*James Stiffy*	975 Post Rd NW, Warren OH 44483	330-393-5659	R	53*	.1
414	Karl's Transport Inc—*Karl Schulz*	PO Box 333, Antigo WI 54409	715-623-2033	R	53*	.1
415	Midwest Specialized Transportation—*Allen Koenig*	P O Box 6418, Rochester MN 55903	507-288-5649	R	53*	.1
416	Amhof Trucking Inc—*Randy Amhof*	PO Box 285, Eldridge IA 52748	563-285-9887	R	53*	.1
417	Cowen Truck Line Inc—*LaVone Cowen*	PO Box 480, Perrysville OH 44864	419-938-3401	R	53*	.1
418	Oakley Transport Inc—*Thomas E Oakley*	PO Box 4170, Lake Wales FL 33859	863-638-1435	R	53*	.1
419	EL Hollingsworth Group Inc—*Christopher Shepard*	3039 Airpark Dr N, Flint MI 48507	810-233-7331	R	53	.4
420	Advantage Tank Lines—*Dennis Nash* Kenan Advantage Group Inc	4895 Dressler Rd NW St, Canton OH 44718	330-491-0474	S	52	.5
421	Apex Bulk Commodities Inc—*Glen Warner*	12531 Violet Rd, Adelanto CA 92301	760-246-6077	R	52*	.4
422	Jim Palmer Trucking Inc—*Jim Palmer*	9730 Derby Dr, Missoula MT 59808	406-721-5151	R	52*	.4
423	Tri Isle Inc—*Richard N Barreras*	860 Eha St, Wailuku HI 96793	808-244-1800	R	52*	.1
424	National Logistics Management Inc—*Scott Taylor*	14320 Joy Rd, Detroit MI 48228		R	52*	.1
425	G and D Transportation Inc—*Joseph O'Neil*	50 Commerce Dr, Morton IL 61550	309-266-1177	R	51*	.4
426	Carlyle Van Lines Inc—*Roy Carlyle*	PO Box 47, Warrensburg MO 64093	660-747-8128	R	51*	.1
427	CRH Transportation Inc—*Gary Mantei*	100 Marion St, Saint Louis MO 63104	314-231-6060	R	51*	.1
428	Don Hummer Trucking Corp—*Don Hummer*	1486 Hwy 6 NW, Oxford IA 52322	319-828-2000	R	51*	.1
429	Idaho Milk Transport Inc—*Xana Brice*	P O Box 1185, Burley ID 83318	208-878-5000	R	51*	.1
430	Michigan Produce Haulers Inc—*Robert Gilliland*	1340 Locust St, Fremont MI 49412	231-924-4600	R	51*	.1
431	Norsemen Trucking Inc—*David Steffens*	106 E Main St, Lake Mills IA 50450	641-592-5060	R	51*	.1
432	Redbank Transport Inc—*John Jackson*	910 US Hwy 50, Milford OH 45150	513-831-6231	R	51*	.1
433	3PD Inc—*Karl Meyer*	1851 W Oak Pkwy Ste 10, Marietta GA 30062		R	50*	.3
434	Admiral Transport Corp—*Louis Pfrangle*	PO Box 726, Worland WY 82401	307-347-8266	R	50*	.1
435	Baggett Transportation Co—*Joseph Donald*	2 32nd St S, Birmingham AL 35233	205-322-6501	R	50*	.1
436	Freeport Transport Industries—*Don Smetanick*	Drawer A, Freeport PA 16229	724-295-2181	R	50*	.1
437	Kix Kutzler Express Inc—*Robert Kutzler*	12737 60th St, Kenosha WI 53144	262-857-7945	R	50*	.1
438	Landes Trucking Inc—*Rusty Landes*	PO Box 1152, Jacksonville IL 62651	217-245-9753	R	50*	.1
439	Martin's Bulk Milk Service—*Allan Martin*	1101 Walker St, Wilton WI 54670	608-435-6561	R	50*	.1
440	Pacific Storage Co—*Greg Tudor*	PO Box 334, Stockton CA 95201		R	50*	.1
441	Plainfield Trucking Inc—*Greg Ruffalo*	PO Box 306, Plainfield WI 54966	715-335-6375	R	50*	.1
442	Richard Carrier Trucking Inc—*Richard Carrier*	PO Box 718, Skowhegan ME 04976	207-474-6293	R	50*	.1
443	E and J Transportation Inc—*Robert Rudolph*	PO Box 69, Murray KY 42071	270-753-0686	R	50*	.1
444	MC Van Kampen Trucking Inc—*Marvin Van Kampen*	5841 Clay Ave SW, Grand Rapids MI 49548	616-531-9931	R	49*	.1
445	Marrlin Transit Inc—*Marrlynn Bearden*	PO Box 645, Van Buren AR 72957	479-474-2325	R	49*	.1
446	Garner Trucking Inc—*Jean Garner*	PO Box 1506, Findlay OH 45839	419-422-5742	R	49*	.1
447	D and W Truck Lines Inc—*Daniel Wilfong*	PO Box 366, Parsons WV 26287	304-478-2430	R	49*	.1
448	Cool Transports Inc—*Ron Nuckels*	P O Box 341, Bloomington CA 92316	562-630-6500	R	49*	.1
449	VPL Transport Inc—*Phil Loduca*	PO Box 600, Lodi CA 95241	209-368-1369	R	49*	.1
450	Gold Coast Freightways Inc—*Gary C Maxwell*	12250 NW 28th Ave, Miami FL 33167	305-687-3560	R	49*	.1
451	R and R Trucking Inc—*Jeff Herr*	PO Box 545, Duenweg MO 64841	417-623-6885	R	48	.3
452	Kreilkamp Trucking Inc—*John Kreilkemp*	PO Box 268, Allenton WI 53002	262-629-5000	R	48*	.4
453	Hallamore Corp—*Sheldon Thomason*	795 Plymouth St, Holbrook MA 02343	781-767-2000	R	48*	.3
454	Zone Transportation Co—*Robert Lehman*	PO Box 1379, Elyria OH 44036	440-324-3544	R	48*	.1
455	J Bauer Trucking Inc—*John Bauer*	N 3090 Bauer Dr, Medford WI 54451	715-748-3207	R	48*	.1
456	LCT Transportation Services—*Dan Denhof*	PO Box 55, Okahumpka FL 34762	352-326-8900	R	48	.4
457	Transystems Inc—*Scott Lind*	1901 Benefis Ct, Great Falls MT 59404	406-727-7500	R	47	.6
458	Cardinal Transport Inc—*Jack Riley*	PO Box 6, Coal City IL 60416	815-634-4443	R	47*	.4
459	Selland Auto Transport Inc—*Ann Selland*	615 S 96th St, Seattle WA 98108	206-767-5960	R	47*	.3
460	Morristown Driver's Service Inc—*Terry K Wolfe*	PO Box 2158, Morristown TN 37816	423-581-6048	R	47*	.1
461	Gibco Motor Express LLC—*Larry Meeks*	PO Box 8358, Evansville IN 47716	812-424-8782	S	47	.2
462	Mawson and Mawson Inc—*Timothy G Durbin*	PO Box 248, Langhorne PA 19047	215-750-1100	R	46*	.4
463	Robert Heath Trucking Inc—*Jimmy Shankle*	PO Box 2501, Lubbock TX 79408	806-747-1651	R	46*	.2
464	Frame's Motor Freight Inc—*Robert Temple*	PO Box 1600, West Chester PA 19380	610-696-2950	R	46*	.1
465	M and M Trucking Company Inc—*Brett McAnally*	980 Lee Rd 10, Auburn AL 36830		R	46*	.1
466	Greentree Transportation Co—*Kenneth Slafka* Transport Investments Inc	100 Industry Dr, Pittsburgh PA 15275	412-788-3680	S	46*	<.1
467	CapSource Financial Inc—*Steven A Museles*	2305 Canyon Blvd Ste 1, Boulder CO 80302	303-245-0515	P	46	<.1
468	Kee Trans Inc—*Bob Mariano*	PO Box 473, Milwaukee WI 53201	414-231-5130	R	45	.5
469	Butler Transport Inc—*George Butler*	347 N James St, Kansas City KS 66118	913-321-0047	R	45*	.4
470	Bestway Systems Inc—*Jeffrey Wenham*	876 Davis Dr SE, Conyers GA 30094	770-922-8502	R	45*	.3
471	Purdy Brothers Trucking Company Inc—*Doug Surrett*	PO Box 39, Loudon TN 37774	865-458-4642	R	44*	.3
472	Van Eerden Trucking Company Inc—*Daniel Van Eerden*	10299 S Kent Dr SW, Byron Center MI 49315	616-877-0192	R	44*	.3
473	WEL Companies Inc—*Bruce Tielens*	PO Box 5610, De Pere WI 54115	920-339-0110	R	44*	.3
474	Lee's Trucking Inc—*Jimmy Lee*	PO Box 1552, El Dorado AR 71731	870-862-5477	R	44*	.1
475	Cimarron Express Inc—*Glenn Grady*	21611 State Rte 51, Genoa OH 43430	419-855-7713	R	44*	.1
476	Andrews Transport LP—*Bill Andrew*	PO Box 163469, Fort Worth TX 76161	817-498-6000	R	43	.3
477	Carlisle Carrier Corp—*David Metzger*	PO BOX 1549, Mechanicsburg PA 17050	717-691-8600	R	43*	.2
478	M-K Express Co—*Norman Gottschalk*	PO Box 509, East Butler PA 16029		R	43*	.1
479	Great Lakes Cartage Co—*James Cleary*	PO Box 4704, Youngstown OH 44515	330-793-9331	R	43*	.1
480	Washington Trucking Inc—*Art Wright*	2810 34th St, Everett WA 98201	425-259-5115	R	43*	.1
481	Rabb Brothers Trucking Inc—*Roy Rabb*	7304 S Placer Ave, San Joaquin CA 93660	559-693-4325	R	43*	.1
482	Saturn Freight Systems Inc—*Phillip Bouchez*	PO Box 87468, Carol Stream IL 60188	630-221-0400	R	43*	.1
483	ACI Motor Freight Inc—*Robert Carriker*	PO Box 17025, Wichita KS 67217	316-522-5559	R	43*	.1
484	FV Martin Trucking Co—*Floyd Martin*	2325 Merry Ln, White City OR 97503	541-826-6014	R	43*	.1
485	Venture Express—*Jimmy Allen*	131 Industrial Blvd, La Vergne TN 37086	615-793-9500	R	42*	.5
486	Bonneville Transloaders Inc—*Claire Anderson*	642 S Federal Blvd, Riverton WY 82501	307-856-7480	R	42*	.3
487	National Distributors Leasing Inc—*Keith Vaughn*	1517 Avco Blvd, Sellersburg IN 47172	812-246-6306	R	42*	.3
488	WTI Transport Inc—*Rendy Taylor* Boyd Brothers Transportation Inc	1526 51St Ave, Tuscaloosa AL 35401	205-752-1608	S	42*	.1
489	Central American Transportation and Distribution—*David Szubart*	10320 Werch Dr, Woodridge IL 60517	630-972-0707	R	42*	.1
490	Dedicated Distribution Services—*Richard Augustine*	600 Kolter Dr, Indiana PA 15701	724-349-7816	R	42*	.1
491	DMT Trucking Inc—*Paul Petryszak*	1200 Chesapeake Ave, Baltimore MD 21226	410-355-6060	R	42*	.1
492	Royster Enterprises Inc—*Randall Royster*	PO Box 400, Ashland AL 36251	256-354-5900	R	42*	.1
493	Cartwright International Van Lines Inc—*Andy Cartwright*	11901 Cartwright Ave, Grandview MO 64030	855-210-5359	R	42*	.1
494	DL Belknap Trucking Inc—*Denver Belknap*	3526 Baird Ave SE, Paris OH 44669	330-868-7766	R	42*	.1
495	Budd Van Lines—*David Budd*	24 Schoolhouse Rd, Somerset NJ 08873	732-627-0600	R	41	.1
496	Halvor Lines Inc—*Jon Vinje*	PO Box 16087, Duluth MN 55816	715-392-8161	R	41*	.3
497	Daily Express Inc—*Robert Long*	PO Box 39, Carlisle PA 17013	717-243-5757	R	41*	.1
498	FTI/Bill Thompson Transport Inc—*Wade Thompson*	26600 Van Born Rd, Dearborn Heights MI 48125	313-295-0502	R	41*	.1

Rank	Company Name—*Executive Officer*	Address, City, State, Zip	Phone	Type	Fin	Empls
499	GG Barnett Transport Inc—*Greg Barnett*	W 7530 County I, Juneau WI 53039	920-386-2236	R	.41*	.1
500	HO Wolding Inc	9642 Western Way, Amherst WI 54406	715-824-4200	R	40*	.5
501	Rosedale Transport Inc—*Arvis Harris*	1821 Wendell St, Dalton GA 30721	706-226-1003	R	40*	.4
502	AW Coulter Trucking—*Arthur Coulter*	23311 Ave 95, Terra Bella CA 93270	559-535-4831	R	40*	.2
503	Midwest Coast Transport—*Matt Stanifzewski* Comcar Industries Inc	1600 E Benson Rd, Sioux Falls SD 57104	605-339-8400	S	40*	.2
504	Computer Van Lines USA—*James Woods*	1150 Swift Rd Ste A, Addison IL 60101	630-543-0600	R	40*	.1
505	Pallet Express Inc—*Michael Briggs*	2821 Assembly Rd, Greensboro NC 27405	336-621-2266	R	40*	.1
506	Belmont Freight Corp—*Rob Robbins*	2825 Maxx Rd, Evansville IN 47711	812-423-5425	R	40*	.1
507	Ross Neely Systems Inc—*Thomas Neely*	1500 2nd St, Birmingham AL 35214	205-798-1137	R	40*	.1
508	Wolford and Wethington Lumber Co—*Douglas Wolford*	1805 Casey Creek Rd, Liberty KY 42539	606-787-6677	R	40*	.1
509	Mid-States Express Inc—*Terry Hartman*	540 W Galena Blvd, Aurora IL 60506	630-906-0250	R	39	.6
510	Andrus Transportation Services—*James Andrus*	3185 E Deseret Dr, Saint George UT 84790	435-673-1566	R	39*	.4
511	Dolphin Cartage Inc—*Edward Barnicle*	5274 S Archer Ave, Chicago IL 60632	773-767-1234	R	39*	.4
512	KC Transportation Inc—*Kenyon S Calender*	PO Box 268, Carleton MI 48117	734-654-0010	R	39*	.3
513	Best Specialized and Logistics—*Mike Herman*	PO Box 679, South Point OH 45680	740-894-2215	R	39*	.3
514	Clark Transfer Inc—*Norma Deull*	800A Paxton St, Harrisburg PA 17104	717-238-6581	R	39*	.1
515	Robert Bearden Inc—*Robert Bearden*	PO Box 870, Cairo GA 39828	229-377-6928	R	39*	.1
516	Parks Moving and Storage Inc—*Barton Williams*	740 Commonwealth Dr, Warrendale PA 15086	724-776-3224	R	39*	.1
517	Thomas Trucking Inc—*Callis Thomas*	2350 Seymour Ave, Cincinnati OH 45212	513-731-8411	R	39*	.1
518	M and T Trucking Inc—*Mark Cole*	532 Peoria Rd, Pavilion NY 14525	585-584-3763	R	39*	.1
519	Cornhusker Motor Lines Inc—*Edward Trout*	PO Box 27249, Omaha NE 68127	402-895-7211	R	39	.2
520	Island Transportation Corp—*Peter Fioretti*	299 Edison Ave Ste A, West Babylon NY 11704	631-694-4800	R	38	.3
521	McKelvey Trucking Co—*Dale Fink*	PO Box 23155, Phoenix AZ 85063	623-936-9434	R	38	.2
522	Cliff Viessman Inc—*Wayne Viessman*	PO Box 175, Gary SD 57237	605-272-5241	R	38*	.4
523	Puget Sound Truck Lines Inc—*Cliff Bennet*	3720 Airport Way S, Seattle WA 98134	206-623-1600	R	38*	.4
524	Nebraska Transport Company Inc—*Brent Holliday*	P O Box 1646, Scottsbluff NE 69363	308-635-1214	R	38*	.3
525	Schuster Company Inc—*Steve Schuster*	2605 Lincoln Ave SW, Le Mars IA 51031	712-546-5124	R	38*	.3
526	Jim's Water Service Inc—*Jimmie Rodgers*	205 Newton Rd, Gillette WY 82716	307-682-4051	R	38	.2
527	City Dash Inc—*Troy Burt*	949 Laidlaw Ave, Cincinnati OH 45237	513-562-2000	R	38*	.2
528	Linden Bulk Transportation Co—*Paul DeFalco*	4200 Tremley Point Rd, Linden NJ 07036	908-862-3883	R	38*	.2
529	John R Lawson Rock and Oil Inc—*John Lawson*	PO Box 9899, Fresno CA 93794	559-275-2221	R	38*	.1
530	Ingram Trucking Inc—*Venita Ingram*	PO Box 249, Morgantown KY 42261	270-526-3727	R	38*	.1
531	On Time Delivery Inc—*James Jenkins*	1800 Preble Ave, Pittsburgh PA 15233	412-231-4813	R	38*	.1
532	Perfetti Trucking Inc—*John D Perfetti*	186 Perfetti Ln, Blairsville PA 15717	724-459-8451	R	38*	.1
533	Todd Transit Inc—*Richard Todd*	1355 Capital Dr, Rockford IL 61109	815-398-5115	R	38*	.1
534	Am-Can Transport Service Inc—*Swain Thompson*	PO Box 770, Anderson SC 29622	864-226-3476	R	38	.2
535	Land Air Express Inc—*Joseph Schneller*	PO Box 2250, Bowling Green KY 42102	270-781-0655	R	37	.3
536	James Helwig and Son Inc—*John Jacobson Jr* TransAm Trucking Inc	15910 S Hwy 169, Olathe KS 66051	972-771-0927	S	37	.2
537	BH Trucking Inc—*Thomas W De Silva*	PO Box 388, Burlington MA 01803	781-229-6380	R	37*	.4
538	Carter Express Inc—*John Paugh*	4020 W 73rd St, Anderson IN 46011	765-778-6960	R	37*	.4
539	HVH Transportation Inc—*Bruce Holder*	PO Box 16610, Denver CO 80216	303-292-3656	R	37*	.3
540	Reynolds Nationwide—*Dennis Reynolds*	PO Box 201720, San Antonio TX 78220	210-648-7770	R	37*	.3
541	Watsontown Trucking Company Inc—*Steven Patton*	60 Belford Blvd, Milton PA 17847	570-552-9820	R	37*	.2
542	B and G Supply Company Inc—*Jack Fricks*	PO Box 748, Albertville AL 35950	256-878-2928	R	37*	.1
543	R and R Trucking LLC—*Richard Marple*	48 Allen Marple Dr, Oakland MD 21550	301-334-3111	R	37*	<.1
544	Cooper and Cooper Moving Inc—*Jay Cooper*	5161 Wilfong Rd, Memphis TN 38134	901-382-2083	R	36*	.4
545	Transus Intermodal LLC—*Kent Troxler*	112 Krog St NE Ste 10, Atlanta GA 30307	404-627-1124	R	36	.3
546	Matheson Fast Freight Inc—*Mark Matheson*	PO Box 910, Elk Grove CA 95759	916-686-4600	R	36*	.2
547	Wrag-Time Air Freight Inc—*Leonard Emrick*	400 White Horse Pike, Haddon Heights NJ 08035		R	36*	.1
548	Midwest Continental Inc—*Deborah Weaver*	PO Box 3289, Sioux City IA 51102	712-239-1613	R	36*	.1
549	B and T Mail Service Inc—*Betty Gutenberger*	19625 W Lincoln Ave, New Berlin WI 53146	262-544-6010	R	36*	.1
550	Engles Trucking Services Inc—*Timothy Engles*	803 Atlantic Ave, Franklin PA 16323	814-437-2499	R	36*	.1
551	Crystal Motor Express Inc—*Ronald Masiello*	PO Box 501, Wakefield MA 01880	781-245-6988	R	36*	.1
552	PAM Dedicated Services Inc—*Randy Englehart* PAM Transportation Services Inc	1450 N Bailey Rd, North Jackson OH 44451	330-270-7900	S	36*	<.1
553	Haney Truck Line Inc—*Michael Richardson*	3710 Gun Club Rd, Yakima WA 98901	509-248-2996	R	35*	.3
554	Texas Star Express—*Gary Amerson*	PO Box 1779, Rockwall TX 75087	972-771-5655	R	35	.3
555	Zimmerman Truck Lines Inc—*Ronald Zimmerman*	PO Box 130, Mifflintown PA 17059	717-436-2141	R	35	.3
556	Hartt Transportation Systems Inc—*William Hartt*	PO Box 1385, Bangor ME 04402	207-947-1106	R	35*	.3
557	Churchill Transportation Inc—*Don Federnoko*	2455 24th St, Detroit MI 48216	313-896-1500	R	35*	.2
558	Grand Island Express Inc—*Thomas Pirnie*	PO Box 2122, Grand Island NE 68802	308-384-8555	R	35*	.2
559	Suffolk Cement Products Inc—*Mark Lohr*	PO Box 241, Calverton NY 11933	631-727-2317	R	35*	.1
560	Western Box Meat Distributors Inc—*Jay Leavy*	PO Box 4796, Portland OR 97208	503-284-3314	R	35*	.1
561	Hickman Transport Company Inc—*Cameron Hickman*	PO Box 5325, Valdosta GA 31603	229-247-4150	R	35*	.1
562	Quality Transport Inc—*Sam Lampo*	PO Box 74339, Baton Rouge LA 70874	225-355-6353	R	35*	.1
563	Ohio Pacific Express Inc—*Kenneth McCormack*	PO Box 617, Benton MO 63736	573-545-3100	R	35*	.1
564	Supervan Service Company Inc—*Walter M Brauer Jr*	121 Bremen Ave, Saint Louis MO 63147	314-231-8444	R	35*	.1
565	Wills Trucking Inc—*Paul W Wills II*	3185 Columbia Rd, Richfield OH 44286	330-659-9381	R	35	.2
566	Trailer Transit Inc—*James Lippert*	1130 E US Hwy 20, Porter IN 46304	219-926-2111	R	34	.3
567	Western Distributing Transportation Corp—*Vieri Gaines*	6655 N York St, Denver CO 80229	303-292-1626	R	34	.3
568	KKW Trucking Inc—*Dennis Firestone*	PO Box 2960, Pomona CA 91768	909-869-1200	R	34*	.4
569	Pritchett Trucking Inc—*John Pritchett*	PO Box 311, Lake Butler FL 32054	386-496-2630	R	34*	.4
570	Logex/Logistics Express Inc—*Gary Mooney*	333 S Anita Dr Ste 400, Orange CA 92868	714-972-0445	R	34*	.3
571	Nationwide Truck Brokers Inc—*Henry Schwarz*	1240 84th St SW, Byron Center MI 49315	616-878-5554	R	34*	.3
572	Crown Express LLC—*Paul Sihota*	3545 E Date Ave, Fresno CA 93725		R	34*	.3
573	James H Clark and Son Inc—*Greg McCandless*	4100 S 500 W, Salt Lake City UT 84123	801-266-9322	R	34*	.2
574	Bright Transportation Inc—*Charles Lawson*	3115 Denton Dr, Garland TX 75041	972-271-2000	R	34*	.2
575	Crosby Trucking Service Inc—*Jeffrey Crosby*	PO Box 28, Mount Sidney VA 24467	540-234-9268	R	34*	.2
576	Central Penn Transportation Inc—*Chic Rhoads*	425 Steel Way, Lancaster PA 17601	717-295-2442	R	34*	.2
577	Glass Trucking Company Inc—*Ike Glass*	PO Box 447, Newkirk OK 74647	580-362-6221	R	34*	.1
578	Schwend Inc—*Charles Schwend*	28945 Johnston Rd, Dade City FL 33523	352-588-2220	R	34*	<.1
579	Great American Lines Inc—*Jim McManus*	PO Box 550, Murrysville PA 15668	724-327-3993	R	33	.4
580	Frontier Transport Corp—*Richard Gaetz*	1560 W Raymond St, Indianapolis IN 46221	317-636-2242	S	33*	.3
581	S and H Express—*Stephen Shellenberger*	Po Box 20219, York PA 17402	717-848-5015	R	33*	.2
582	Evans Dedicated Systems Inc—*Cleo Evans*	6279 E Slauson Ave Ste, Los Angeles CA 90040	323-725-2928	R	33*	.2
583	OmniSource Transport LLC—*Leonard Rifkin*	7575 W Jefferson Blvd, Fort Wayne IN 46804	260-422-5541	R	33*	.2
584	S and S Transport Inc—*June Seng*	PO Box 12579, Grand Forks ND 58208	701-746-8484	R	33*	.1
585	McKinley Trucking Company Inc—*Phillip McKinley*	652 N Williams St, Carson City MI 48811	989-584-3177	R	33*	.1

Note: An asterisk (*) indicates an estimated financial figure. The company type code used is as follows: R = Private, P = Public, S = Private Subsidiary, B = Public Subsidiary, D = Division, J = Joint Venture, I = Investment Fund.

COMPANY RANKINGS BY SALES WITHIN 4-DIGIT SIC

Rank	Company Name—*Executive Officer*	Address, City, State, Zip	Phone	Type	Fin	Empls
586	Millwood Trucking Inc—*Mark Millwood*	170 Hwy 27 S, Nashville AR 71852	870-845-1796	R	33*	.1
587	Tri-State Expedited Service—*Glenna Chidester*	PO Box 307, Perrysburg OH 43552	419-837-2401	R	33*	.1
588	A and G Trucking Inc—*Greg Deline*	26789 Hwy 195, Double Springs AL 35553	205-489-0002	R	33*	.1
589	IFCO Transport Inc—*Michael J Mascari*	PO Box 68931, Indianapolis IN 46268	317-546-2425	R	33*	.1
590	J and D Burgess Inc—*Dennis Burgess*	PO Box 1002, Anniston AL 36202	256-831-1165	R	33*	.1
591	West Northwest Transportation—*Bryan Beneux*	PO Box 627, Mulberry AR 72947	479-997-1683	R	33*	.1
592	Golden Ring Trucking Inc—*Gerald Krog*	1728 N 1st Ave, Fergus Falls MN 56537	218-739-2662	R	33*	<.1
593	JET Intermodal Inc—*Jon Krohn*	445 W Oklahoma Ave, Milwaukee WI 53207	414-744-5225	R	33*	<.1
594	Transco Lines Inc—*Micheal Barr*	PO Box 1400, Russellville AR 72811		R	33	.3
595	Tennessee Commercial Warehouse Inc—*Scott George*	22 Stanley St, Nashville TN 37210	615-255-1122	R	32	.3
596	Beaver Express—*Michael Stone*	PO Box 1147, Woodward OK 73802	580-256-6460	R	32	.2
597	American Central Transport Inc—*Tom Kretsinger*	PO Box 516, Liberty MO 64069	816-781-9600	R	32*	.3
598	Waller Truck Company Inc—*Robert Waller*	400 S McCleary Rd, Excelsior Springs MO 64024	816-629-3400	R	32*	.3
599	Hiner Transport Inc—*Paul James*	1350 S Jefferson St, Huntington IN 46750	260-356-8218	R	32*	.2
600	Peninsula Truck Lines Inc—*Stanley Vander Pol*	PO Box 587, Auburn WA 98071	253-929-2000	R	32*	.2
601	Rich Thompson Trucking Inc—*Richard Thompson*	PO Box 969, Concord VA 24538	434-993-2195	R	32*	.1
602	Teal's Express Inc—*Michael Teal*	PO Box 6010, Watertown NY 13601	315-788-6437	R	32*	<.1
603	C Bean Transport Inc—*Tim Bean*	PO Box 180236, Fort Smith AR 72918	870-342-9531	R	32*	.4
604	Lemore Transportation Inc—*Mike Querio*	1420 Royal Industrial, Concord CA 94520	925-689-6441	R	31	.2
605	M and L Trucking Inc—*Robert Williams*	PO Box 4140, Rome NY 13442	315-339-2550	R	31	<.1
606	Southwest Freightlines—*Gustavo Jimenez*	PO Box 371736, El Paso TX 79937	915-860-8592	R	31*	.3
607	Fil-Mor Express Inc—*Richard Olson*	PO Box 518, Cannon Falls MN 55009	507-263-2608	R	31*	.3
608	RBX Inc—*Patrick Blasi*	PO Box 2118, Springfield MO 65801	417-862-7258	R	31*	.2
609	MHF Express Inc—*James Wylie*	613 E Butler Rd, Butler PA 16002	724-431-0365	R	31*	.2
610	Herman R Ewell Inc—*Calvin Ewell*	4635 Division Hwy, East Earl PA 17519	717-354-4556	R	31*	.2
611	Nilson Van and Storage—*Phyllis Nilson*	PO Box 3219, Columbia SC 29230	803-786-1090	R	31*	.1
612	Tryon Trucking Inc—*Barry Meklir*	PO Box 68, Fairless Hills PA 19030	215-295-6622	R	31*	.1
613	Double J Trucking Co—*Kenneth Hoover*	PO Box 890, Reynoldsburg OH 43068	440-542-4410	S	31*	.1
614	Moorman Farms Inc—*Rob Moorman*	1127 E Marksberry Rd, Utica KY 42376	270-733-4909	R	31*	.1
615	Erickson Transport Corp—*Jim Erickson*	PO Box 10068, Springfield MO 65808	417-862-6741	R	31*	.1
616	Horwith Trucks Inc—*Frank Horwith*	PO Box 7, Northampton PA 18067	610-261-2220	R	31*	.1
617	TMCI Inc—*Thomas Manville*	12448 Sprtsman Rd, Highland IL 62249	618-654-8624	R	31*	.1
618	Omni Crown Trucking Inc—*Hilda Medina*	PO Box 882135, Los Angeles CA 90009	310-672-1763	R	31*	<.1
619	Erdner Brothers Inc—*Richard Erdner*	PO Box 68, Swedesboro NJ 08085	856-467-0900	R	31*	<.1
620	Renner Trucking—*JE Renner*	116 Jasmine Dr, Newport TN 37821	423-623-2480	R	31*	<.1
621	Sanyo Transportation Co—*Hideki Yamagata*	8400 Milliken Ave, Rancho Cucamonga CA 91730	909-987-7854	S	31	<.1
622	Tombigbee Transport Corp—*Ron Curtis*	320 Industrial Rd, Adamsville TN 38310	731-632-4800	S	31	.2
623	Reliable Trucking Inc—*Jim Luke*	5141 Commercial Cir, Concord CA 94520	951-780-5658	R	30	.1
624	R and O Transportation LLC—*Richard Bauer*	PO Box 721668, Newport KY 41072		R	30	.1
625	Lanter Co Transportation Div—*Steve Lanter* Lanter Co	PO Box 68, Madison IL 62060	618-452-7100	D	30*	.4
626	Walpole Leasing Inc—*Ed Walpole*	PO Box 1177, Okeechobee FL 34973	863-763-5593	R	30*	.3
627	Thomas H Ireland Inc—*Thomas Ireland*	361 N Old Pacific Hwy, Myrtle Creek OR 97457	541-863-5241	R	30*	.2
628	MP Environmental Services Inc—*Dawn Calderwood*	3400 Manor St, Bakersfield CA 93308	661-393-1151	R	30*	.1
629	Garrett Trucking—*Charles Garrett*	PO Box 900, Tuttle OK 73089	405-381-2211	R	30*	.1
630	Lance Trucking Corp—*John Lance*	PO Box 8, Blue Ridge GA 30513	706-632-2248	R	30*	.1
631	Leon Jones Feed and Grain Inc—*Leon Jones*	4880 Leland Dr, Cumming GA 30041	770-887-6117	R	30*	.1
632	Mid Seven Transportation Co—*LW Simpson*	2323 Delaware Ave, Des Moines IA 50317	515-266-5181	R	30*	.1
633	SMF Inc—*Thomas M Dooley*	9357 General Dr Ste 12, Plymouth MI 48170	734-454-4090	R	30*	.1
634	Van's Delivery Service Inc—*Ron Van Zytveld*	PO Box 630, Comstock Park MI 49321	616-365-3200	R	30*	.1
635	Longhorn Produce Co—*Mark Cross*	890 E C Hwy, Lamar MO 64759	417-681-0200	R	30*	.1
636	Refrigerated Delivery Service—*Tom Ferguson*	PO Box 50247, Tulsa OK 74150	918-835-1195	R	30*	.1
637	Kindsvater Inc—*Dennis Kindsvater*	2301 E Trl St, Dodge City KS 67801	620-227-6191	R	30	.1
638	Ray Jones Trucking Inc—*Carol Ann Jones*	3296 State Rt 181 S, Greenville KY 42345	270-338-2417	R	30*	.1
639	Louisville Cartage Company Inc—*Jimmie Johnson*	PO Box 16219, Louisville KY 40256	502-447-4252	R	30*	<.1
640	McKlim Milk Transit Inc—*Larry McKimm*	1145 Adams St SE, Hutchinson MN 55350	320-587-3167	R	30*	<.1
641	Big Red LTL Transport Inc—*Michael Pryslak*	PO Box 88, Great Meadows NJ 07838	908-475-3220	R	30*	<.1
642	Kennesaw Transportation Inc—*Pat Patrick*	3794 Hgwy 411 NE, Rydal GA 30171	770-382-3748	R	30	.3
643	Usher Transport Inc—*Bill Usher*	3801 Shanks Ln, Louisville KY 40216	502-449-4000	R	30	.2
644	Wheels Clipper—*Walt Whitt*	9014 Heritage Pkwy Ste, Woodridge IL 60517	630-739-0700	R	30	N/A
645	Gemini Transfer Sales Inc—*Harry Winrow*	41 Distribution Blvd, Edison NJ 08817	732-287-8899	R	29	.2
646	Nussbaum Trucking Inc—*Brent Nussbaum*	2200 N Main St, Normal IL 61761	309-452-4426	R	29*	.3
647	Best Way Express Inc (Vincennes Indiana)—*Shepard Dunn*	PO Box 728, Vincennes IN 47591	812-882-6448	R	29*	.3
648	Florilli Transportation LLC—*Murry Fitzer*	PO Box 186, West Liberty IA 52776	319-627-2678	R	29*	.3
649	Harbor Express Inc—*Peter Kim*	501 Quay Ave, Wilmington CA 90744	310-513-6478	R	29*	.3
650	Williams Tank Lines—*Michael Williams*	1477 Tillie Lewis Dr, Stockton CA 95206	209-944-5613	R	29*	.3
651	Hamm and Phillips Service Co—*Harold Hamm*	PO Box 3907, Enid OK 73701	580-242-1876	R	29*	.2
652	AN Webber Inc—*Alan Webber*	PO Box 95, Chebanse IL 60922	815-939-2235	R	29*	.2
653	Pemberton Truck Lines Inc—*Bob Pemberton*	2530 Mitchell St, Knoxville TN 37917	865-524-5592	R	29	.2
654	Gra-Bell Truck Line Inc—*Tom Van Wyk*	PO Box 1019, Holland MI 49422		R	29*	.2
655	Security Van Lines Inc—*Mark Johnson*	PO Box 830, Kenner LA 70063	504-466-4449	R	29*	.1
656	Triple G Express Inc—*Randy Guillot*	PO Box 10485, New Orleans LA 70181	504-731-2841	R	29*	.1
657	Stock Transport Inc—*Bob Stock*	10037 Faust Rd, Lebanon IL 62254	618-537-8440	R	29*	.1
658	National Highway Express Inc—*WS Dutcher*	PO Box 20262, Columbus OH 43220	614-459-4900	R	29*	.1
659	Morris Trucking Corp—*Mike Morris*	3201 Erie Canal Rd, Terre Haute IN 47802	812-232-1984	R	29*	<.1
660	Quicksilver Express Courier of MN—*Mike Crary*	203 Little Canada Rd E, Little Canada MN 55117	651-484-1111	R	29	<.1
661	Louis J Kennedy Trucking Co—*Frederick Kennedy*	342 Schuyler Ave, Kearny NJ 07032	201-998-4142	R	29	.3
662	Dart Trucking Company Inc—*Tim Kephart*	PO Box 60, Columbiana OH 44408	330-856-8430	S	28	.2
663	Fraley and Schilling Inc—*Robert Schilling*	1920 S State Rd 3, Rushville IN 46173	765-932-5977	R	28*	.3
664	CLI Transport LLP—*Paul Casado*	RR 1 Box 587, Claysburg PA 16625	814-239-1490	R	28*	.3
665	Rogers Cartage Co—*Thomas Budnik*	611 S 28th St, Milwaukee WI 53215	414-671-3039	S	28*	.2
666	Four Truckers Inc—*Eric Clarke*	PO Box 1296, Morganton NC 28680	828-584-1018	R	28*	.2
667	Bulk Transportation—*Gary Cross*	PO Box 390, Walnut CA 91789	909-594-2855	R	28*	.2
668	Triad Transport Inc—*John Titsworth*	PO Box 818, McAlester OK 74502	918-426-4751	R	28*	.2
669	Bullocks Express Transportation—*Bruce Bullock*	PO Box 16441, Denver CO 80216	303-296-0302	R	28*	.2
670	Cox Transportation Services Inc—*John A Cox*	10448 Dow Gil Rd, Ashland VA 23005	804-798-1477	R	28*	.2
671	Wilson Lines Inc—*Larry Hofstad*	2131 2nd Ave, Newport MN 55055	651-459-2384	R	28*	.1
672	Hinkle Trucking Inc—*Gary Hinkle*	PO Box 65, Circleville WV 26804	304-567-2900	R	28*	.1
673	Cargocare Transportation Co—*Charles Thorne*	PO Box 4433, Rocky Mount NC 27803	252-446-8256	R	28*	.1
674	Central Delivery Service of Wash—*Lawrence Mawn*	9435 Washington Blvd S, Laurel MD 20723	301-725-8841	R	28*	.1

Rank	Company Name—*Executive Officer*	Address, City, State, Zip	Phone	Type	Fin	Empls
675	Gazelle Transportation Inc—*Ron Lallo*	4939 Gilmore Ave, Bakersfield CA 93308	661-322-8868	R	28*	.1
676	Jerry Holliday Construction Inc—*Joey Holliday*	PO Box 502, Blanding UT 84511	435-678-2028	R	28*	.1
677	JM Bozeman Enterprises Inc—*James Bozeman*	166 Seltzer Ln, Malvern AR 72104	501-844-4060	R	28*	.1
678	John N John Truck Line—*John John*	PO Box 921, Crowley LA 70527	337-783-3394	R	28*	.1
679	Lotz Trucking Inc—*Donald Muffler*	807 E Dayton Rd, Ottawa IL 61350	815-587-6090	R	28*	.1
680	Palmetto State Transportation—*Bob Dumit*	1050 Park W Blvd, Greenville SC 29611	864-848-3800	R	28*	.1
681	Premier Transportation and Warehousing—*Gregory Chandler*	851 E Watson Ctr Rd, Long Beach CA 90745	310-835-9207	R	28*	.1
682	Richers Trucking Inc—*James Richers*	1727 346th Ave, Wever IA 52658	319-372-9420	R	28*	.1
683	Tantara Transportation Corp—*Michael Riggan*	2420 Stewart Rd, Muscatine IA 52761	563-262-8621	R	28*	.1
684	Western Transport—*Craig Scheckla*	PO Box 671, Sheridan WY 82801	307-674-6305	R	28*	.1
685	Roy E Lay Trucking Inc—*Bob Hensley*	1218 E Kentucky Ave, Woodland CA 95776	530-662-1711	R	28*	<.1
686	Sinclair Cartage Inc—*Kenneth J St Clair Sr*	PO Box 3249, Oak Brook IL 60522		R	28*	<.1
687	Barnets Inc—*Gary Gregg*	1619 Barnetts Mill Rd, Camden OH 45311	937-452-1218	R	28*	<.1
688	D and V Trucking Inc—*Danny Fowler*	12803 Columbiana Canfi, Columbiana OH 44408	330-482-9440	R	28*	<.1
689	Flat-Bed Services Inc—*Floyd Fiedler*	PO Box 3377, Sioux City IA 51102	712-239-2030	R	28*	<.1
690	Gabler Trucking Inc—*Harold C Gabler Jr*	5195 Technology Ave, Chambersburg PA 17201		R	28*	<.1
691	Jack Treier Moving and Storage Inc—*Jack Treier*	140 Marble Dr, Lancaster PA 17601	717-397-2808	R	28*	<.1
692	KL Harring Transportation and Warehousing—*Keith L Harring*	PO Box 56, Bethel PA 19507	717-933-5992	R	28*	<.1
693	G3 Enterprises—*Robert Lubeck*	502 W Whitmore Ave, Modesto CA 95358	209-341-4048	R	28	<.1
694	Rochester Armored Car Co—*Joseph Shea*	3937 Leavenworth St, Omaha NE 68105	402-558-9323	R	27*	.6
695	Mike Campbell and Associates Ltd—*Kevin McHugh*	981 Corporate Center D, Pomona CA 91768	909-242-7940	R	27*	.4
696	Taylor Truck Line Inc—*Robert Taylor*	31485 Northfield Blvd, Northfield MN 55057	507-645-4531	R	27*	.4
697	Spirit Truck Lines Inc—*Raul Garza*	PO Box 87, San Juan TX 78589	956-781-7715	R	27*	.2
698	All Truck Transportation Co—*Mathew Alagna*	4924 S Austin Ave, Chicago IL 60638	708-594-2500	R	27*	.2
699	Dalton Trucking Inc—*Terrance Klenske*	PO Box 5025, Fontana CA 92335	909-823-0663	R	27*	.2
700	Equity Transportation Co—*Edwin Stoga*	3685 Dykstra Dr NW, Walker MI 49544	616-785-3800	R	27*	.2
701	Sadler Brothers Trucking and Leasing Inc—*Chester Sadler*	436 Enos Reed Dr, Nashville TN 37210		R	27*	.1
702	Pan American Express Inc—*Ricardo Guardado*	PO Box 3317, Laredo TX 78044	956-723-4848	R	27*	.1
703	Findlay Truck Line Inc—*Greg Cassidy*	420 Trenton Ave, Findlay OH 45840	419-422-1945	R	27*	.1
704	East Penn Trucking Co—*Dale Schleicher*	681 W Lizard Creek Rd, Lehighton PA 18235	610-377-3194	R	27*	.1
705	AJ Weigand Inc—*John Boynton*	PO Box 130, Dover OH 44622	330-878-5501	R	27*	.1
706	B-D-R Transport Inc—*Gregory Gay*	7994 U S Rt 5, Westminster VT 05158	802-463-0606	R	27*	.1
707	CBSL Transportation Services—*Thomas Heaney*	4750 S Merrimac Ave, Chicago IL 60638	708-496-1100	R	27*	.1
708	CWT Inc—*Curtis Tharpe*	3030 Tollhouse Rd, Drakes Branch VA 23937	434-568-4171	R	27*	.1
709	DP Curtis Trucking Inc—*Dent Curtis*	1450 S Hwy 118, Richfield UT 84701	435-896-4417	R	27*	.1
710	Draxler Transport Inc—*Martin Draxler*	10592 County Rd A, Marshfield WI 54449	715-591-2222	R	27*	.1
711	Edens Distributing Company Inc—*Charles Edens*	PO Box 994, Pulaski VA 24301	540-980-6866	R	27*	.1
712	Fallen Trucking—*Dolly Fallen*	1103 Dill Tuck Hwy, South Boston VA 24592	434-572-9188	R	27*	.1
713	Jacobson Southwest Storage and Distribution Co—*Fred Gretsch Sr*	1 N 59th Ave, Phoenix AZ 85043	602-233-3296	S	27*	.1
714	Key Trucking Inc—*Gary Castagno*	19801 78th Ave S, Kent WA 98032	206-624-3626	R	27*	.1
715	Korth Transfer Inc—*Levi Hagen*	PO Box 99, Hillpoint WI 53937	608-727-2551	R	27*	.1
716	Wyatt Transfer Inc—*David Chewning*	PO Box 24326, Richmond VA 23224	804-743-3800	R	27*	.1
717	CD Haugen Inc—*Holly Young*	3857 Cardinal Rd NW, Bemidji MN 56601	218-751-2738	R	27*	<.1
718	Dennis Truck Lines Inc—*Carol Dukes*	PO, Box 1066, Vidalia GA 30475	912-537-7939	R	27*	<.1
719	TVS Inc—*Edmond Doss*	PO Bux 5545, Birmingham AL 35207	205-326-0490	R	27*	<.1
720	Gentry Trucking LLC—*James Gentry*	PO Box 481, Greenwood LA 71033	318-938-5396	R	27*	<.1
721	Werhane Enterprises Ltd—*Robert Werhane*	509 E Main St, Lena IL 61048	815-369-4760	R	27	.1
722	RAC Transport Company Inc—*James Perea*	PO Box 17459, Denver CO 80217	303-289-5500	R	26	.2
723	CoreTrans LLC—*Mike Whitaker*	PO Box 3210, West Somerset KY 42564	606-679-0000	R	26	N/A
724	CRST Inc—*David L Rusch* CRST International Inc	PO Box 68, Cedar Rapids IA 52406	319-396-4400	S	26*	.3
725	McLeod Express LLC—*Mark McLeod*	PO Box 3520, Decatur IL 62524	217-876-0570	R	26*	.2
726	Point Dedicated Services—*Ross Hare*	1300 E Big Beaver Rd, Troy MI 48083	248-680-1996	R	26*	.2
727	McGriff Transportation Inc—*Barry McGriff*	86 Walnut St NW, Cullman AL 35055	256-739-0780	R	26	.2
728	Baylor Trucking Inc—*Robert Baylor*	9269 E State Rd 48, Milan IN 47031	812-623-2020	R	26*	.2
729	Tidewater Transit Company Inc—*Eric Emerson*	PO Box 189, Kinston NC 28502	252-523-4103	R	26*	.2
730	Timblin Transit Inc—*William Timblin*	PO Box 188, Eden WI 53019	920-477-4364	R	26*	.2
731	Brown Transfer Co—*Dwayne Brown*	PO Box 158, Kearney NE 68848	308-237-2244	R	26*	.2
732	Walpole Inc—*Edwin Walpole*	PO Box 1177, Okeechobee FL 34973	863-763-5593	R	26*	.2
733	Advanced Delivery Systems Inc—*Stuart Levine*	1071 Post Rd E, Westport CT 06880	203-291-6840	R	26*	.2
734	R and R Transportation Inc—*Roger Westlund*	PO Box 216, Audubon MN 56511	218-439-6144	R	26*	.1
735	ALTL Inc—*Ross Luurtsema*	PO Box 100, Hudsonville MI 49426	616-669-6060	R	26*	.1
736	Bross Trucking Inc—*Chester Bross*	PO Box 1438, Hannibal MO 63401	573-221-5958	R	26*	.1
737	Bud's and Son Trucking Inc—*Larry Willingham*	12570 Hwy 67 Ste 8, Lakeside CA 92040	619-938-8090	R	26*	.1
738	Eilen and Sons Trucking—*Tom Eilen*	PO Box 98, Hampton MN 55031	651-437-4001	R	26*	<.1
739	Massey Hauling Company Inc—*Brian Buckner*	PO Box 566, Oneonta AL 35121	205-625-3855	R	26*	<.1
740	Risinger Brothers Transfer Inc—*Stan Risinger*	225 W Courtland St, Morton IL 61550	309-266-9555	R	26	.2
741	Starving Students Inc—*Bear Barnes*	1850 Sawtelle Blvd Ste, Los Angeles CA 90025		R	25	.2
742	Associated Petroleum Carriers—*Larry Brock*	PO Box 2808, Spartanburg SC 29304	864-573-9301	R	25	.2
743	Williams Brothers Trucking—*Roger Williams*	PO Box 188, Hazlehurst GA 31539	912-375-7777	R	25	.2
744	Leonard's Express Inc—*Patricia Johnson*	PO Box 25130, Farmington NY 14425	585-924-8140	R	25	.1
745	Sun Coast Resources Inc—*Kathy Lehne*	6922 Cavalcade St, Houston TX 77028	713-844-9600	R	25*	.5
746	Barrett Moving and Storage Co—*Randy Koepsell*	7100 Washington Ave S, Eden Prairie MN 55344	952-944-6550	R	25*	.3
747	Sea-Logix LLC—*Chuck Raymond*	220 W Manville St, Compton CA 90220	323-983-2311	S	25*	.2
748	Cross-Country Courier Inc—*Duane Tietz*	PO Box 4030, Bismarck ND 58502	701-222-8498	R	25*	.2
749	Dick Lavy Trucking Inc—*Dick Lavy*	8848 State Rt 121, Bradford OH 45308	937-448-2104	R	25*	.2
750	Fort Worth Carrier Corp—*Robert Durden*	4501 N Beach St, Fort Worth TX 76137	817-831-5231	R	25	.2
751	AT Systems Northwest Inc—*Richard Irvin*	1401 E Yesler Way, Seattle WA 98122	206-322-8848	S	25*	.2
752	Chizek Elevator and Transport—*Mike Chizek*	PO Box 147, Cleveland WI 53015	920-726-4244	R	25*	.2
753	J and R Schugel Trucking Inc—*Rick Schugel*	PO Box 278, New Ulm MN 56073	507-359-2037	R	25*	.2
754	Raider Express Inc—*Michael P EggletonSr*	3100 Produce Row Ste 1, Houston TX 77023	713-923-4545	R	25*	.2
755	EW Wylie Corp—*Marv Skar*	1520 2nd Ave NW, Fargo ND 58103	701-282-5550	S	25*	.2
756	Bass Transportation Company Inc—*James L Mattes*	PO Box 391, Easton PA 18042	484-373-0720	R	25*	.2
757	Boyle Transportation Inc—*Marc Boyle*	15 Riverhurst Rd, Billerica MA 01821	978-670-3400	R	25*	.2
758	Lisk Trucking Inc—*Howard Lisk*	PO Box 70, Polkton NC 28135	704-272-7641	R	25*	.2
759	Paxton Van Lines Inc—*Frederick Paxton*	5300 Port Royal Rd, Springfield VA 22151	703-321-7600	R	25*	.1
760	Bob's Transport and Storage Co—*Robert Pfeffer*	PO Box 1305, Jessup MD 20794	410-799-0832	R	25*	.1
761	Craig Transportation Co—*Lance Craig*	PO Box 1010, Perrysburg OH 43552	419-872-3333	R	25*	.1
762	Lo-Vac Inc—*Jay Bolden*	PO Box 69, Lottie LA 70756	225-637-3634	R	25*	.1

Note: An asterisk (*) indicates an estimated financial figure. The company type code used is as follows: R = Private, P = Public, S = Private Subsidiary, B = Public Subsidiary, D = Division, J = Joint Venture, I = Investment Fund.

COMPANY RANKINGS BY SALES WITHIN 4-DIGIT SIC

Rank	Company Name—*Executive Officer*	Address, City, State, Zip	Phone	Type	Fin	Empls
763	Mark's Transportation Inc—*Mark Frederickson*	PO Box 75, Junction City WI 54443	715-457-2936	R	25*	.1
764	Motor West Inc—*Dennis Moss*	PO Box 1178, Caldwell ID 83606	208-454-9238	R	25*	.1
765	RAM Trucking Inc—*Dale Latimer*	PO Box 398, Brownsville OR 97327	541-466-5022	R	25*	.1
766	RF Chamberland Inc—*Mark Chamberland*	PO Box 188, Saint Agatha ME 04772	207-543-6607	R	25*	.1
767	Trans-United Inc—*Jeff Fleming*	1123 N State Rd 149, Burns Harbor IN 46304	219-762-3111	R	25*	.1
768	West Wisconsin Transport Inc—*Gary Nowak*	6300 Alter Rd, Eau Claire WI 54703	715-874-4760	R	25*	.1
769	Whitley Mobile Homes Inc—*Daryl Eberly*	702 S State St, South Whitley IN 46787	260-723-5402	R	25*	.1
770	Zar Tran Inc—*Walter Raybun*	150 Prior Station Rd, Cedartown GA 30125	770-748-2124	R	25*	.1
771	M and M Cartage Inc—*Steven Person*	PO Box 3202, Des Moines IA 50316	515-698-5551	R	25*	<.1
772	Augusta Transportation Inc—*Melton Rose*	940 Molly Pond Rd, Augusta GA 30901	706-722-5383	R	25*	<.1
773	Potter Transport Inc—*Randy Potter*	PO Box 273, Boonville MO 65233	660-882-2100	R	25*	<.1
774	Van Auken Express Inc—*John Van Auken*	PO Box 339, Greenville NY 12083	518-966-4499	R	25*	<.1
775	Union Machinery—*Glen Corlett*	PO Box 498, Union MO 63084	636-583-3689	R	25*	<.1
776	Keim TS Inc—*Stan Keim*	PO Box 226, Sabetha KS 66534	785-284-2147	R	25	.2
777	Continental Express Inc—*Russell L Gottemoeller*	10450 State Rt 47, Sidney OH 45365	937-497-2100	R	25	.1
778	West Brothers Transfer and Storage—*Tony Lovette*	PO Box 7327, Charlotte NC 28241		R	25	N/A
779	Roadlink USA—*Mike Haley*	112 Krog St NE, Atlanta GA 30307	404-624-1124	R	24*	N/A
780	Priority Dispatch Inc—*Jeff Thomas*	4665 Malsbury Rd, Cincinnati OH 45242	513-791-1300	R	24	.1
781	Miller Transporters Inc—*Lee Miller*	PO Box 1123, Jackson MS 39215	601-922-8331	R	24*	.3
782	Air Ground Xpress Inc—*Phillip Fall*	PO Box 438, Clinton PA 15026	724-695-1110	R	24*	.3
783	OST Trucking Company Inc—*Richard Amato*	1205 68th St, Baltimore MD 21237	410-866-7700	R	24*	.3
784	Bilbo Transports Inc—*Clifford Bilbo*	PO Box 560109, Dallas TX 75356	214-441-0021	R	24*	.2
785	TAX Airfreight Inc—*Mark Zeidler*	PO Box 070911, Milwaukee WI 53207	414-769-6565	R	24*	.2
786	D and D Sexton Inc—*Dean Sexton*	PO Box 156, Carthage MO 64836	417-358-8727	R	24*	.2
787	Cooke Trucking Company Inc—*David Smith*	1759 S Andy Griffith P, Mount Airy NC 27030	336-786-5181	R	24*	.1
788	Black Hills Trucking Inc—*Diemer True*	PO Box 2360, Casper WY 82602	307-237-9301	R	24*	.1
789	National Van Lines Inc—*Maureen Beal*	2800 Roosevelt Rd, Broadview IL 60155	708-450-2900	R	24*	.1
790	AMA Transportation Company Inc—*Mark Bruzzese*	28 Plank St, Billerica MA 01821	978-667-9133	R	24*	.1
791	DHT Transport—*David Hausbeck*	5150 Rosa Parks Blvd, Detroit MI 48208	313-895-1300	R	24*	.1
792	RWI Transportation LLC—*Richard Bower*	PO Box 721668, Newport KY 41072	859-572-0920	R	24*	.1
793	Shetler Moving and Storage Inc—*Thomas J Shetler Sr*	1253 E Diamond Ave, Evansville IN 47711	812-421-7750	R	24*	.1
794	Fetch Logistics Inc—*Robert Closs II*	25 Northpointe Pkwy St, Amherst NY 14228	716-689-4556	R	24*	.1
795	FWCC Inc—*Robert Durden*	PO Box 863, Muldrow OK 74948	918-427-3258	R	24*	.1
796	Hutchins Trucking Co—*Mark Hutchins*	75 Dartmouth St, South Portland ME 04106	207-767-1692	R	24*	.1
797	Triple L Transport Inc—*Kim Lund*	PO Box 730, Gunnison UT 84634	435-528-3748	R	24*	<.1
798	Paris Transport Inc—*Dean Smittkamp*	PO Box 283, Paris IL 61944	217-463-7030	R	24*	<.1
799	Double VV Inc—*Arlin Van Voorst*	25 S Water St, Kansas City KS 66118	913-621-1608	R	24*	<.1
800	Ed Thayer Inc—*Floyd Thayer*	PO Box 858, Oxford ME 04270	207-539-8241	R	24*	<.1
801	Pro Fleet Transport Corp—*Chris Wood*	601 Middleton Run Rd, Elkhart IN 46516	574-522-4415	R	24*	<.1
802	Al Forte Inc—*Robert Forte*	139 Ryerson Ave, Wayne NJ 07470	973-628-7707	R	24*	<.1
803	Fleming's Transportation Inc—*Shaun Fleming*	720 Thompsonville Rd, Suffield CT 06078	860-668-0206	R	24*	<.1
804	Jack Gray Transport Inc—*John S Gray*	4600 E 15th Ave, Gary IN 46403	219-938-7020	R	24*	<.1
805	Landstar Gemini Inc—*Henry H Gerkins* Landstar Ranger Inc	13410 Sutton Park Dr S, Jacksonville FL 32224	904-398-9400	S	24*	<.1
806	Blue Ribbon Transport Inc—*Philip Caito*	3120 N Post Rd, Indianapolis IN 46226	317-897-2009	R	24	.1
807	American Red Ball Transit Co—*Jack Griffin*	1335 Sadlier Cir E Dr, Indianapolis IN 46239	206-526-1730	R	24	.2
808	Butler Trucking Co—*DS Butler*	PO Box 88, Woodland PA 16881	814-857-7644	R	23*	.3
809	Miller Truck Lines Inc—*James Miller*	PO Box 665, Stroud OK 74079	918-447-2143	R	23*	.2
810	Whiteline Express Ltd—*William P Young*	41605 Ann Arbor Rd, Plymouth MI 48170	734-455-4700	R	23*	.2
811	Transport Distribution Co—*Larry Kloeppel*	PO Box 306, Joplin MO 64802	417-624-3814	R	23*	.2
812	V and S Midwest Carriers Corp—*Dave Venhandle*	PO Box 107, Kaukauna WI 54130	920-766-9696	R	23*	.2
813	Abilene Motor Express—*Keith Jones*	1700 Willis Rd, Richmond VA 23237	804-275-0224	R	23*	.1
814	Fort Transfer—*Brad Kahler*	PO Box 457, Morton IL 61550	309-263-2000	R	23*	.1
815	Seneca Beverage Corp—*John F Potter*	2085 Lake Rd, Elmira NY 14903	607-734-6111	R	23*	.1
816	Eastern Logistics—*Richard Linsenbach* Eastern Consolidation and Distriburion Services Inc	405 Sterling St, Camp Hill PA 17011	717-761-6720	S	23*	.1
817	Pittsburgh-Fayette Express—*Francis Prezioso*	PO Box 141, Charleroi PA 15022	724-929-2220	R	23*	<.1
818	Rocking-T Transportation—*Richard Schilling*	12150 Cactus Feeders R, Cactus TX 79013	806-966-3664	R	23*	<.1
819	Pennway Express Inc—*Barb Williams*	PO Box 1083, Du Bois PA 15801	814-375-3648	S	23*	<.1
820	Osterkamp Trucking Inc—*Hank Osterkamp*	P O Box 600, Pomona CA 91769	909-590-8200	R	23	.2
821	America's Service Line Inc—*Tom McClone*	300 Elizabeth St, Green Bay WI 54302	920-430-8427	R	23	.2
822	APL Logistics Freight Systems	2001 Eagle Rd, Normal IL 61761	309-452-2410	S	23	.1
823	Courier Systems Inc—*Henry Murad*	30 Pulaski St, Bayonne NJ 07002	201-432-0550	R	23	.1
824	Valley Trucking Company Inc—*Dwayne Tyner*	4550 Coffeeport Rd, Brownsville TX 78521	956-831-4511	R	22	.2
825	Steel Transport Inc—*Kenneth Paulan*	6701 Melton Rd, Gary IN 46403	219-939-3000	R	22	.2
826	Kelly Trucking—*Mary Kelly*	PO Box 170, Wadley AL 36276		R	22	.2
827	May Trucking Co—*C Marvin May*	PO Box 9039, Salem OR 97305		R	22*	.4
828	K and R Transportation Inc California Cartage Co	PO Box 92829, Long Beach CA 90809	310-537-1432	S	22	.2
829	Air-Land Transport Service—*John Gray*	PO Box 968, Morton IL 61550	309-673-1227	R	22*	.2
830	All Freight Systems Inc—*Robert Smith*	1134 S 12th St, Kansas City KS 66105	913-281-1203	R	22*	.2
831	DTX Inc/Dart Container Corp—*Bob Dart*	500 Hogsback Rd, Mason MI 48854	517-676-3800	R	22*	.2
832	Energy Dispatch LLC—*Eric Williams*	PO Box 105554, Atlanta GA 30348	770-431-7601	R	22*	.2
833	Food Express Inc—*Walt Keeney*	521 N 1st Ave, Arcadia CA 91006		R	22*	.2
834	Material Delivery Service—*Robert Schilli* Schilli Corp	334-C Business Cir, Pelham AL 35124	205-358-1500	S	22*	.2
835	WW Rowland Trucking Company Inc—*WW Rowland*	10000 Wallisville Rd, Houston TX 77013	713-675-1200	R	22*	.2
836	Murphy Warehouse Co—*Richard T Murphy Jr*	701 24th Ave SE, Minneapolis MN 55414	612-623-1200	R	22*	.2
837	Van Wyk Inc—*Dave Van Wyk*	PO Box 389, Sheldon IA 51201	712-324-4687	R	22*	.2
838	Mountain Valley Express Co—*Scott Blevins*	P O Box 2569, Manteca CA 95336	209-823-2168	R	22*	.2
839	Seward Motor Freight Inc—*Joanie Tanderup*	970 280th Rd, Seward NE 68434	402-643-4503	R	22*	.2
840	D and T Trucking Company Inc—*Robert Dolle*	11530 Hudson Blvd N, Lake Elmo MN 55042	651-482-1000	R	22*	.2
841	Johnsrud Transport Inc—*Jackie Johnsrud*	200 SE 34th St, Des Moines IA 50317	515-263-8265	R	22*	.2
842	System Freight Inc—*Michael Pagliuca*	PO Box 554, Jamesburg NJ 08831	609-395-8600	R	22*	.1
843	Wannemacher Enterprises Inc—*Greg Wannamecher*	400 E Hanthorn Rd, Lima OH 45804	419-225-9060	R	22*	.1
844	Certified Freight Lines Inc—*Rick Perry*	PO Box 5819, Santa Maria CA 93456	805-925-9900	R	22*	.1
845	Mesa Systems Inc—*Michele Bisbee*	681 Railroad Blvd, Grand Junction CO 81505	970-242-1565	R	22*	.1
846	Road Scholar Transport Inc—*James Barrett*	130 Monahan Ave, Dunmore PA 18512		R	22*	.1
847	Harrison-Nichols Company Ltd—*Randall Harrison*	5265 4th St, Irwindale CA 91706	626-337-5020	R	22*	.1
848	RAM Nationwide Inc—*Ronald Murphy*	240 W North Bend Rd, Cincinnati OH 45216	513-821-0010	R	22*	.1

Rank	Company Name—Executive Officer	Address, City, State, Zip	Phone	Type	Fin	Empls
849	Fred Burrows Trucking and Excavation—Frederick Burrows	437 Oriskany Blvd, Whitesboro NY 13492	315-736-1971	R	22*	.1
850	Haynes Motor Lines LLC—Sam Haynes	1100 Mansfield St, Baton Rouge LA 70802	225-383-3100	R	22*	<.1
851	Evans Seafood Transport LLC—T Armistead Perry	PO Box 534, Washington NC 27889	252-946-7173	R	22*	<.1
852	Oehme Carrier Corp—Thomas Oehme	PO Box 220, Lititz PA 17543	717-626-8260	R	22*	<.1
853	Tomar Inc—Oral Markle	PO Box 580, Keyser WV 26726	304-788-1845	R	22*	<.1
854	Whitehurst Transport Inc—Wilson Whitehurst	2800 Deepwater Termina, Richmond VA 23234	804-233-9296	R	22*	<.1
855	J-M Transports Inc—Barry Jacobson	PO Box 284, Newark IL 60541	815-695-5463	R	22*	<.1
856	Schafer's Fisheries Inc—Michael Schafer	PO Box 399, Thomson IL 61285	815-589-3368	R	22*	<.1
857	Phoenix Transportation Services—Kevin Warren	335 E Yusen Dr, Georgetown KY 40324	502-863-0108	R	22	.3
858	Bohren's Moving and Storage—Ted Froehlich	3 Applegate Dr S, Robbinsville NJ 08691	609-208-1470	R	22	.1
859	Dunham Express Corp—Mark McDonald	3633 Lexington Ave, Madison WI 53714	608-242-1000	R	22	.2
860	Dick Harris and Son Trucking Co—Jim Harris	PO Box 539, Madison Heights VA 24572	434-528-6700	R	21	.2
861	Gary W Gray Trucking Inc—Gary Gray	PO Box 48, Delaware NJ 07833	908-475-3797	R	21	.1
862	Royal Express Inc—Paul Sihota	3545 E Date Ave, Fresno CA 93725	559-272-3500	R	21	.2
863	McNay Truck Line—Richard McNay	700 N 2nd St, Quincy IL 62301	217-222-0248	R	21	.2
864	Tri Star Freight System Inc—Kathleen Nance	5407 Mesa Dr, Houston TX 77028	713-631-1095	R	21*	.2
865	AD Conner Inc—William McEnery	160 S La Grange Rd, Frankfort IL 60423	708-479-3801	R	21*	.2
866	Conley Transport II Inc—Rory Conley	2104 Eastline Rd, Searcy AR 72143	501-268-4672	R	21*	.2
867	Basin Western Inc—Lloyd Dean	PO Box 877, Roosevelt UT 84066	435-722-3378	R	21*	.2
868	KOLEASECO Inc—JP Koop	PO Box 366, Hudsonville MI 49426	616-896-5170	R	21*	.2
869	Cushing Transportation Inc—Anthony Pacella	3756 S Cicero Ave, Cicero IL 60804	708-656-5050	R	21*	.1
870	High Country Transportation—Donald Crowley	1915 Menaul Blvd NE St, Albuquerque NM 87107	970-565-6402	R	21*	.1
871	McRyan Hauling Inc—Judy Stinnett	PO Box 1669, Roanoke TX 76262	817-430-3213	R	21*	.1
872	T and T Trucking Inc—Terry Tarditi	11396 N Hwy 99, Lodi CA 95240	209-931-6000	R	21*	.1
873	Western Transport Inc—Alan Ginkel	3916 W 65 S, Idaho Falls ID 83402	208-529-9327	R	21*	<.1
874	Heim Trucking—Michael Heim	5022 Shirley Rd, Denmark WI 54208	920-863-2924	R	21*	<.1
875	Cumpton Trucking Inc—Lawrence Cumpton	13565 State Hwy 36 E, Red Bluff CA 96080	530-527-4102	R	21*	<.1
876	Harrington Trucking Inc—Craig Andersen	510 Delong St, Salt Lake City UT 84104	801-972-4974	R	21*	<.1
877	Keeney Truck Lines Inc—Dan Hubbard	3500 Fruitland Ave, Maywood CA 90270	323-589-3231	R	21*	<.1
878	Casco Services Inc—Norman Swenson	275 Pacific St, Newark NJ 07114	973-624-8601	R	21*	<.1
879	DMX Transportation Inc—Wayne Merritt	960 Berry Shoals Rd, Duncan SC 29334	864-877-7709	R	21*	<.1
880	Excalibur Transportation Group—Darren Cummings	PO Box 1230, Texarkana TX 75504	903-794-2777	R	21*	<.1
881	JR's Trucking Inc—Cleve Roberson	575 Barnett Hwy, Brewton AL 36426	251-867-7738	R	21*	<.1
882	Shoun Trucking Company Inc—Shiela Shoun	1247 Hwy 126, Bristol TN 37620	423-968-7630	R	21*	<.1
883	Southern Tier Express Inc—John Mills	558 Lane School Rd, Andover NY 14806	607-478-8503	R	21*	<.1
884	Sunbelt Auto Carriers Inc—Bruce Lawrence	PO Box 530206, Debary FL 32753	386-668-5377	R	21*	<.1
885	Holman Distribution Center of WA—Hobert Downie	22430 76th Ave S, Kent WA 98032	253-872-7140	R	21*	<.1
886	Avondale Trucking Div—Tim Stancell	43 Central Ave, Sylacauga AL 35150	256-208-2000	S	21	.1
887	Howard Transportation Inc—Michael Howard	PO Box 1588, Laurel MS 39441	601-425-3151	S	21	.2
888	Sea Lane Express Inc—Guy Mazarin	60 Cuttermill Rd Ste 2, Great Neck NY 11021	516-466-4278	R	21	.1
889	Empire Express Inc—Tim Gatlin	PO Box 13468, Memphis TN 38113	901-942-3300	R	20	.2
890	Petroleum Transport Company Inc—James York	PO Box 490, Pilot Mountain NC 27041		R	20	.2
891	Black Horse Carriers Inc—Gerald Niedert	150 Village Ct, Carol Stream IL 60188	630-690-8368	R	20	.4
892	M and C Trucking Company Inc—John Muchesko	PO Box 430, Seward PA 15954		R	20	.2
893	Blackhawk Transport Inc—Kevin McGrath	1431 Manchester Rd, Beloit WI 53511	608-364-4040	R	20*	.3
894	Ohio Transport Corp—Bill Hill	9426 N Fwy Dr, Macedonia OH 44056	330-908-0266	R	20*	.3
895	Swing Transport Inc—Dan Summitt	1405 N Salisbury Ave, Salisbury NC 28144	704-633-3567	R	20*	.3
896	Hot-Line Freight System Inc—Larry Johnson	PO Box 205, West Salem WI 54669	608-486-1600	R	20*	.2
897	C and C Trucking of Duncan Inc—Charles Tapp	PO Box 705, Duncan SC 29334	864-848-3755	R	20*	.2
898	Walt's Drive-A-Way Service Inc—Don Meisler	321 N Kerth, Evansville IN 47711	812-424-8927	R	20*	.2
899	Benny Whitehead Inc—Benny Whitehead	3265 S Eufaula Ave, Eufaula AL 36027	334-687-8055	R	20*	.2
900	Double D Express Inc—Gary Dahl	PO Box 606, Peru IL 61354	815-224-1924	R	20*	.2
901	Gresham Transfer Inc—Rick Ulmer	24001 NE Sandy Blvd, Wood Village OR 97060	503-255-7900	R	20*	.2
902	Service Trucking Inc—Daniel Baugh	PO Box 188, Eustis FL 32727	352-357-1300	R	20*	.2
903	RC Moore Inc—Shawn Moore	8 Ginn Rd, Scarborough ME 04074	207-883-5184	R	20*	.1
904	VL Watkins Transport Co—Greg Hibbitts	2169 Center Industrial, Jenison MI 49428	616-669-4302	R	20*	.1
905	Transland Inc—Mike Walker	1601 W Old Rte 66, Strafford MO 65757	417-864-5710	R	20*	.1
906	FMI Express Corp—Ernie De Saye	800 Federal Blvd, Carteret NJ 07008	732-750-9000	R	20*	.1
907	Hall Brothers Transportation Co—Frank Hall	8390 N State Rd 37, Orleans IN 47452	812-865-2443	R	20*	.1
908	Bealine Service Company Inc—Jack D Beal Jr	9717 Chemical Rd, Pasadena TX 77507	281-474-7772	R	20*	.1
909	Brothers Trucking Company Inc—Edward Brothers	40 Willow Springs Cir, York PA 17402	717-764-5800	R	20*	.1
910	EF Transit Inc—Edwin French	PO Box 438, Indianapolis IN 46206	317-247-0742	R	20*	.1
911	Pegasus Transportation Group—John McFadden	1675 American Way, Cedar Hill TX 75104	972-293-8561	R	20*	.1
912	Geo F Alger Co—Dean Styles	28650 Hildebrandt St, Romulus MI 48174	734-946-7556	R	20*	.1
913	Scriptfleet	5590 Ulmerton Rd, Clearwater FL 33760	727-539-8400	R	20*	.1
914	Galasso Trucking Inc—Frank Galasso	2 Galasso Pl, Maspeth NY 11378	718-456-1800	R	20*	<.1
915	Aim Transportation Inc—W Sosnowski	660 Hariton St, Orange CA 92868	714-997-5390	R	20*	<.1
916	Cooley Transport Inc—Jeff Cooley	3637 Peppertown Rd, Fulton MS 38843	662-862-5434	R	20*	<.1
917	Emrick's Van and Storage Inc—Paul Baker	4021 NW 3rd St, Oklahoma City OK 73107	405-946-4405	R	20*	<.1
918	J and N Trucking Company Inc—Don Eddins	PO Box 696, Greenwood MS 38935	662-453-0437	R	20*	<.1
919	Lake City Trucking—James Gobert	PO Box 16545, Lake Charles LA 70616	337-494-6900	R	20*	<.1
920	Mad River Transportation Inc—Martin Warner	PO Box 1296, Dayton OH 45401	937-228-2166	R	20*	<.1
921	Sidney Transportation Services—Steve Wooderuff	PO Box 748, Sidney OH 45365	937-498-2323	R	20*	<.1
922	Dorn's Delivery and Transfer Inc—Larry Dorn	PO Box 1471, Appleton WI 54912	920-739-4215	R	20*	<.1
923	Francis Powell Enterprises—Francis Powell	23980 Hwy 84, Grove Hill AL 36451	251-275-4171	R	20*	<.1
924	Rowe Machinery Inc—William Rowe	PO Box 818, Haleyville AL 35565	205-486-9237	R	20*	<.1
925	Berlin Transportation Inc—Tom Wengerd	7576 State Rt 241, Millersburg OH 44654	330-674-3395	R	20*	<.1
926	Ronnie Bledsoe Trucking Inc—Ronnie Bledsoe	1760 Braly Ln, Pulaski TN 38478	931-363-8749	R	20*	<.1
927	United Express System Inc—Brad Westrom	PO Box 1628, Aurora IL 60507	630-922-4200	R	20*	<.1
928	Styline Transportation Inc—Robert Menke	PO Box 200, Huntingburg IN 47542		R	20	.2
929	Robinson Transport Inc—Kim Robinson	850 W Main St, Salina UT 84654	435-529-7472	R	20	.1
930	Sharp Transport Inc—Allie Schwalb	PO Box 155, Ethridge TN 38456	931-829-2194	R	19	.2
931	Givens Transportation—Edward Reed	1720 S Military Hwy, Chesapeake VA 23320	757-233-4300	R	19	N/A
932	Hazmat Environmental Group—Ricky Wickham	60 Commerce Dr, Buffalo NY 14218	716-827-7200	R	19	.1
933	Peoples Cartage Inc—Ronald R Sibila	Po Box 20109, Canton OH 44701	330-453-3709	R	19	<.1
934	Container Freight EIT LLC—Patrick McGurk	6150 N Paramount Blvd, Long Beach CA 90805	562-220-2433	R	19*	.2
935	Cox Petroleum Transport—Daniel Mairs	7641 Edison Hwy, Bakersfield CA 93307	661-366-3236	R	19*	.2
936	Clark Freight Lines Inc—Roneil Clark	PO Box 5250, Pasadena TX 77508	281-487-3160	R	19*	.2

Note: An asterisk (*) indicates an estimated financial figure. The company type code used is as follows: R = Private, P = Public, S = Private Subsidiary, B = Public Subsidiary, D = Division, J = Joint Venture, I = Investment Fund.

COMPANY RANKINGS BY SALES WITHIN 4-DIGIT SIC

Rank	Company Name—*Executive Officer*	Address, City, State, Zip	Phone	Type	Fin	Empls
937	Bulldog Hiway Express—*Philip Byrd*	3390 Buffalo St, North Charleston SC 29418	843-744-1651	R	19*	.1
938	McIlvaine Trucking International McIlvaine Trucking Inc	7556 Cleveland Rd, Wooster OH 44691	330-345-7033	S	19*	.1
939	Barlow Truck Lines Inc—*James Lindsay*	1305 Grand DD SE, Faucett MO 64448	816-238-3373	R	19*	.1
940	AM Express Inc—*Patrick Barron*	PO Box 721, Escanaba MI 49829	906-786-0645	R	19*	.1
941	Mabe Trucking Company Inc—*Roger Mabe*	PO Box 1081, Eden NC 27289	336-635-1793	R	19*	.1
942	Riechmann Transport Inc—*Jim Riechmann*	3328 W Chain Of Rocks, Granite City IL 62040	618-797-6700	R	19*	.1
943	Dalbo Inc—*Tony George*	355 S 1000 E 8407B, Vernal UT 84078	435-789-0743	R	19*	.1
944	Arrow Freight Management Inc—*Fred Urban*	PO Box 371974, El Paso TX 79928	915-778-3999	R	19*	.1
945	ITA Inc—*Jack Gill*	PO Box 473, Milwaukee WI 53201	414-231-7301	D	19*	.1
946	Elliott Truck Line Inc	PO Box 1, Vinita OK 74301	918-256-5534	R	19*	<.1
947	Glazier Trucking Inc—*Michael Glazier*	PO Box 938, Kiefer OK 74041	918-321-9623	R	19*	<.1
948	Farmers Oil Company Inc—*Larry Graves*	PO Box 311, Anthony KS 67003	620-842-3117	R	19*	<.1
949	Brunozzi Transfer and Truck Rental—*Joan Brunozzi*	455 Tuckahoe Rd, Vineland NJ 08360	856-696-8302	R	19*	<.1
950	Dynamex Operations West Inc—*James Welch*	5429 LBJ Frwy Ste 1000, Dallas TX 75240	214-560-9000	S	19*	<.1
951	Can-Am Express Inc—*Mohammad Abu-Ghazaleh*	241 Sevilla Ave, Coral Gables FL 33134	305-520-8400	S	19	.1
952	RG Transport Inc—*Richard Deboer*	PO Box 103, Elwood IN 46036	765-552-3381	R	19	.1
953	JKC Trucking Inc—*John Kucharski*	5450 S Ctr Ave, Summit IL 60501	708-496-3901	R	18	.1
954	Central Refrigerated Service Inc—*Jon Isaacson*	5175 W 2100 S, West Valley City UT 84120		R	18	N/A
955	Roadmasters Transport Co—*Larry Moran*	1201 Hwy 175 W, Athens TX 75751	903-675-8550	S	18	.2
956	Trans-Continental Systems—*Gary Stone*	10801 Evendale Dr, Cincinnati OH 45241	513-769-4774	R	18	.2
957	Texas Transeastern Inc—*Johnny Isbell Jr*	PO Box 5339, Pasadena TX 77508	281-604-3100	R	18*	.2
958	Freymiller Inc—*David Freymiller*	8125 SW 15th St, Oklahoma City OK 73128	405-491-2800	R	18*	.2
959	Truck Transport Inc—*Robert Schilli* Miller Transporters Inc	2280 Cassens Dr, Fenton MO 63026	636-343-1877	S	18	.2
960	Wenger Truck Line Inc—*Robert Murray*	PO Box 3427, Davenport IA 52808	563-333-4500	R	18*	.2
961	Wooster Motor Ways Inc—*Paul Williams*	PO Box 19, Wooster OH 44691	330-264-7690	R	18*	.2
962	A and M Transport Inc—*Suzan Donner*	PO Box 310, Glendale OR 97442	541-832-2183	R	18*	.2
963	Lumber Transport Inc—*Buddy Hamrick*	P O Box 312, Cochran GA 31014	478-934-6251	R	18*	.2
964	M Bruenger and Company Inc—*Butch Bruenger*	6250 N Broadway St, Wichita KS 67219	316-744-0494	R	18*	.2
965	Baldwin Distribution Services Ltd—*Dudley Baldwin*	PO Box 51618, Amarillo TX 79159	806-383-7650	R	18	.1
966	Stevens Trucking Co—*Kenny Stevens*	PO Box 19608, Oklahoma City OK 73144	405-745-2363	R	18*	.1
967	Redding Lumber Transport—*Al Shufelberger*	P O Box 992257, Redding CA 96099	530-241-8193	R	18*	.1
968	Robbie D Wood Inc—*Robbie Wood*	PO Box 125, Dolomite AL 35061	205-744-8440	R	18*	.1
969	Walbon and Company Inc—*Darby Walbon*	4230 Pine Bend Trl, Rosemount MN 55068	651-437-2011	R	18*	.1
970	Britt Trucking Co—*Tomy Churchwell*	PO Box 707, Lamesa TX 79331	806-872-3353	R	18*	.1
971	Gurney Trucking Inc—*Scott Gurney*	PO Box 360, Aurora UT 84620	435-529-3831	R	18*	.1
972	Hahn Transportation Inc—*Barbara Windsor*	PO Box 8, New Market MD 21774	301-865-5467	R	18*	.1
973	Wagner Moving and Storage Inc—*Robert Wagner*	PO Box 1300, Paducah KY 42002	270-443-5361	R	18*	.1
974	Arabie Brothers Trucking Inc—*Sandy Arabie*	163 Lincoln Ln, Thibodaux LA 70301	985-448-1121	R	18*	.1
975	Jones Brothers Transport Inc—*Schley Jones*	PO Box 15039, Florence SC 29506	843-667-4585	R	18*	.1
976	Five Star Trucking Inc—*John Gramc*	4380 Glenbrook Rd, Willoughby OH 44094	440-953-9300	R	18*	<.1
977	IE Miller of Eunice Inc—*Sherry Flato*	PO Box 472, Eunice LA 70535	337-457-0922	R	18*	<.1
978	Murphy Transportation Inc—*Greg Murphy*	6720 Kilby Rd, Harrison OH 45030	513-367-2990	R	18*	<.1
979	Scott Transportation Inc—*Ron Scott*	PO Box 2640, La Pine OR 97739	541-536-3636	R	18*	<.1
980	TM Brown Trucking Inc—*Odell Burgess*	PO Box 673, Houston MS 38851	662-456-1325	R	18*	<.1
981	P and B Transportation Inc—*Patrick Riggle*	601 Marco Rd, Apollo PA 15613	724-727-3477	R	18*	<.1
982	Bailey's Express Inc—*Bernard Kowalski*	61 Industrial Park Rd, Middletown CT 06457	860-632-0388	R	18*	<.1
983	Barnett Transportation Inc—*David Rouse*	PO Box 2468, Tuscaloosa AL 35403	205-759-5113	R	18*	<.1
984	Capitol Express Inc—*Larry Yeaton*	8125 Stayton Dr, Jessup MD 20794		R	18*	<.1
985	Eagle Valley Inc—*Steve Downen*	P O Box 490, Shawneetown IL 62984	618-269-3111	R	18*	<.1
986	LSSD Inc—*Steve Dunhan*	PO Box 167, Griggsville IL 62340	217-285-2808	R	18*	<.1
987	Macera and Martini Trans Inc—*Wayne Martini*	2227 Plainfield Pke, Johnston RI 02919	401-944-4747	R	18*	<.1
988	Pray Trucking Inc—*Robert Reed*	132 Old Fall River Rd, Seekonk MA 02771	508-336-5011	R	18*	<.1
989	Stan Suarez Trucking Inc—*Stan Suarez*	32740 Camphora Rd, Soledad CA 93960	831-678-1099	R	18*	<.1
990	Temp-Distribution of Maryland Inc—*Thomas Wolfgang*	4711 Hollins Ferry Rd, Baltimore MD 21227	410-242-6550	R	18*	<.1
991	3-J Fuels Inc—*James Smith*	61 W Service Rd, Champlain NY 12919	518-298-2555	R	18*	<.1
992	M and J Transportation—*Mike Ashpaugh*	PO Box 10716, Kansas City MO 64188	816-231-6733	R	18*	<.1
993	Resource Transportation of America—*Paul Wagner*	110 Alvin St, Cameron LA 70631	337-775-8200	R	18*	<.1
994	Sea Transfer Corp—*Vincent Chester*	328 Tiffany St, Bronx NY 10474	718-328-0600	R	18*	<.1
995	Walton Hauling and Warehouse Corp—*Eugene P Walton*	609 W 46th St, New York NY 10036	212-246-8685	R	18*	<.1
996	Suburban Oil Company Inc—*Jeff Pyle*	4291 State Rte 741 S, Mason OH 45040	513-459-8100	R	18*	<.1
997	Protected Cargo Transport—*Chuck Reich*	2671 Coulee Crossing R, Woodworth LA 71485	318-448-7241	R	18*	<.1
998	Robinson Transport Inc—*Richard Robinson*	2499 McGaw Rd, Columbus OH 43207	614-492-1920	R	18	.1
999	Turner Trucking Co—*Talmadge Turner*	PO Box 1096, Boiling Springs NC 28017	704-434-5080	R	18	.1
1000	VB Hook and Company Inc—*Gary Martin*	315 Wholesale Ln, West Columbia SC 29172	803-799-0504	R	18	<.1
1001	First Choice Logistics—*Richard Jousma*	12550 S Stony Island A, Chicago IL 60633	708-210-3160	R	18	.1
1002	Mid South Transport—*Ronnie Lancaster*	2765 Profit Dr, Memphis TN 38132	901-332-8600	R	17	.1
1003	American Motor Lines Inc	36253 Michigan Ave, Wayne MI 48184	734-722-9500	R	17	.1
1004	H and M Trucking Inc—*Randy Mueller*	2522 Edward Babe Gomez, Omaha NE 68107	402-431-9410	R	17	.1
1005	American Pacific Forwarders	13951 Magnolia Ave, Chino CA 91710	909-627-6050	R	17	.1
1006	Floyd and Beasley Transfer Company Inc—*Jeff McGrady*	PO Box 8, Sycamore AL 35149	256-245-4385	R	17*	.3
1007	Southwest Int'l Freight Services—*Richard Eberhart*	8189 S Central Expy, Dallas TX 75241	214-371-1901	R	17*	.2
1008	Sunbelt Furniture Xpress Inc—*Jake Wood*	PO Box 487, Hickory NC 28603	828-464-7240	R	17*	.2
1009	Ready Trucking Inc—*Don Dougherty*	2717 Campbell Blvd, Ellenwood GA 30294	404-361-5473	R	17*	.2
1010	Trimac USA (Houston Texas)—*Tom Conrad*	15333 John F Kennedy B, Houston TX 77032	281-985-0000	R	17*	.1
1011	Hyway Trucking Co—*Roger Lenhart*	10060 State Rd 224 W, Findlay OH 45840	419-423-7145	R	17*	.1
1012	Truline Corp—*Paul Truman*	9390 Redwood St, Las Vegas NV 89139	702-362-7495	R	17*	.1
1013	Skinner Transfer Corp—*Evelyn Skinner*	PO Box 438, Reedsburg WI 53959	608-524-2326	R	17*	.1
1014	Guy Shavender Trucking Inc—*Guy Shavender*	PO Box 206, Pantego NC 27860	252-943-3379	R	17*	.1
1015	Calex Express Inc—*Nelson Fey*	58 Pittston Ave, Pittston PA 18640	570-603-0180	R	17*	.1
1016	Star Transportation Co—*Beth Franklin*	PO Box 3089, Plant City FL 33563	813-659-1002	R	17*	.1
1017	Lester R Summers Inc—*J Hearld Summers*	PO Box 239, Ephrata PA 17522	717-733-6556	R	17*	.1
1018	D and D Transportation Services Inc—*Ira Young*	P O Box 116, Gooding ID 83330	208-934-4451	R	17*	.1
1019	Chemical Transfer Company Inc—*Michael Ellis*	PO Box 6036, Stockton CA 95206	209-466-3554	R	17*	.1
1020	Jack Jones Trucking Inc—*Valerie Liese*	1090 E Belmont St, Ontario CA 91761	909-456-2500	R	17*	.1
1021	Penser Transportation Inc—*Shawn Barnett*	11001 Pritchard Rd, Jacksonville FL 32219	904-345-3956	R	17*	<.1
1022	A and A Tank Truck Co—*Marshall Brackin*	PO Box 862, Norman OK 73070	405-364-2601	R	17*	<.1
1023	D Pierce Transportation Inc—*David Pierce*	PO Box 453, Murrysville PA 15668	724-334-6880	R	17*	<.1
1024	Don Farr Moving Co—*Donald Fix*	4920 Buttermilk Hollow, West Mifflin PA 15122	412-469-9700	R	17*	<.1

Rank	Company Name—*Executive Officer*	Address, City, State, Zip	Phone	Type	Fin	Empls
1025	Brownlee Trucking Inc—*Frank Brownlee*	PO Box 51, West Middletown PA 15379	724-587-3876	R	17*	<.1
1026	Cooke's Crating Inc—*Bryan Cooke*	3124 E 11th St, Los Angeles CA 90023	323-268-5101	R	17*	<.1
1027	Goodluck Refrigeration Service—*John Goetgeluck Sr*	62910 N Ave, Ray MI 48096	586-749-5158	R	17*	<.1
1028	Ho Ho Ho Express Inc—*Eric Ho*	6333 Rothway St, Houston TX 77040	281-820-5555	R	17*	<.1
1029	LC Trucking Inc—*Larry Catron*	2775 Wards Rd, Altavista VA 24517	434-369-1801	R	17*	<.1
1030	Whalen Trucking Inc—*Richard Whalen*	PO Box 106, Waverly IL 62692	217-435-2231	R	17*	<.1
1031	Valley Spreader Inc—*Martin Gordon*	260 N 9th St, Brawley CA 92227	760-344-1526	R	17*	<.1
1032	Yowell International—*Jay Yowell*	PO Box 1502, Melbourne FL 32902	321-725-3611	R	17*	<.1
1033	Borwegen Trucking Inc—*Teresa Borwegen*	6570 State Rt 81, Greenville NY 12083	518-966-4561	R	17*	<.1
1034	JN Moser Trucking Inc—*Bill Moser*	PO Box 309, Montgomery IL 60538	630-892-8216	R	17	.1
1035	TNI USA—*Jeffrey Herr*	PO Box 545, Duenweg MO 64841	417-623-6885	R	17	.1
1036	JTM Materials Inc—*Lynn Johnson*	PO Box 2496, Denton TX 76202	940-243-8530	R	17	.1
1037	Guy M Turner Inc—*Jimmy Clark*	PO Box 7776, Greensboro NC 27417	336-294-4660	R	17	.1
1038	Consolidated Cargo Carriers—*Steve Holtschlag*	650 Rosewood Dr, Columbia SC 29202	803-771-7920	R	16	.1
1039	Michigan Metal Transporters—*Edward Battier*	36253 Michigan Ave, Wayne MI 48184	734-722-9500	R	16	<.1
1040	Davis Transport Inc—*Jim McKinny*	PO Box 8129, Missoula MT 59807	406-728-5510	R	16	.2
1041	Mike Brooks Inc—*Mike Brooks*	PO Box 443, Knoxville IA 50138	641-828-7280	R	16*	.2
1042	Dancor Transit Inc—*Dan Bearden*	PO Box 849, Van Buren AR 72957	479-474-9756	R	16*	.2
1043	Davis Transfer Company Inc—*Todd Davis*	PO Box 650, Carnesville GA 30521	706-384-2030	R	16*	.2
1044	Miller Brothers Express LC—*Kris Miller*	PO Box E, Hyrum UT 84319	435-245-6025	R	16*	.2
1045	Rist Transport Ltd	369 Bostwick Rd, Phelps NY 14532	315-789-8871	R	16*	.1
1046	Saia (Waunakee Wisconsin)	900 Uniek Dr, Waunakee WI 53597	608-849-6371	R	16*	.1
1047	Southland Transportation—*R Cummings*	PO Box 99, Boonville NC 27011	336-367-4767	R	16	.1
1048	Palmentere Brothers Cartage Services—*Loree Huttinger*	801 Forest Ave, Kansas City MO 64106	816-421-4482	R	16*	.1
1049	Express-1 Inc—*Jeff Curry*	PO Box 210, Buchanan MI 49107	269-695-2700	S	16*	.1
1050	Dandy Service Corp—*Daniel Lang*	916 Brush Creek Rd, Warrendale PA 15086	724-935-1920	R	16*	.1
1051	Pan Western Corp—*Mitchell Truman*	4910 Donovan Way Ste A, North Las Vegas NV 89081	702-632-2931	R	16*	.1
1052	Machine Transportation Co—*James Caskey*	3180 Utica St, Jackson MS 39209	601-353-9382	R	16*	.1
1053	BT Trucking Inc—*Mike Irwin*	2500 S 25th Ave, Broadview IL 60155	708-450-1295	R	16*	.1
1054	Cascade Express—*Larry Gordon*	PO Box 887, Albany OR 97321	541-928-4091	R	16*	.1
1055	Floyd Blinsky Trucking Inc—*Floyd Blinsky*	PO Box 10147, Yakima WA 98909	509-457-3484	R	16*	.1
1056	GB 'Boots' Smith Corp—*James Smith*	PO Box 1987, Laurel MS 39441	601-649-1220	R	16*	.1
1057	H and W Trucking Company Inc—*Gary Harold*	PO Box 1545, Mount Airy NC 27030	336-789-2188	R	16*	.1
1058	Holiday Express Corp—*Basil Roberts*	PO Box 452, Estherville IA 51334	712-362-5812	R	16*	.1
1059	Milton Transportation Inc—*Ray Bowersox*	5505 State Rte 405, Milton PA 17847	570-742-8774	R	16*	.1
1060	Warren Trucking Company Inc—*Richard Eanes*	PO Box 5224, Martinsville VA 24115	276-956-3181	R	16*	.1
1061	Manuel Huerta Trucking Inc—*Manuel Huerta*	PO Box 7089, Nogales AZ 85628	520-281-2058	R	16*	.1
1062	LW Miller Transportation Inc—*Larry Miller*	1050 W 200 N, Logan UT 84321	435-753-8350	R	16*	.1
1063	Harbor Freight Transport Corp—*Steve Liberti*	301 Craneway St, Newark NJ 07114	973-589-6700	R	16*	.1
1064	Owen Trucking LLC—*Lucky Owen*	PO Box 1595, Lorton VA 22199	703-541-5501	R	16*	.1
1065	Twin City Transportation Inc—*Herb Martin*	2300 W 60th St, Little Rock AR 72209	501-562-5591	R	16*	.1
1066	Copy Carriers Inc—*Tina Saxe*	16930 S Main St, Gardena CA 90248	310-324-9922	R	16*	.1
1067	Stringer's Oilfield Service—*Johnnie Stringer*	PO Box 323, Columbia MS 39429	601-736-4498	R	16*	<.1
1068	Logan Trucking Inc—*Edward Schaye*	PO Box 41, South Beloit IL 61080	815-389-2286	R	16*	<.1
1069	North East Transfer Inc—*Edward Deets*	484 S Mountain Blvd, Mountain Top PA 18707	570-474-6771	R	16*	<.1
1070	Barrett Trucking Company Inc—*John Barrett*	1G Austin Dr, Burlington VT 05401	802-863-1311	R	16*	<.1
1071	Chuck Foster Trucking Inc—*James Foster*	4004 Burkey Rd, Youngstown OH 44515	330-223-1164	R	16*	<.1
1072	Dettinburn Transport Inc—*Gary Hinkle*	Hc 78 Box 99, Riverton WV 26814	304-567-6000	R	16*	<.1
1073	Reis Trucking Inc—*Paul Reis*	10080 Valley Junction, Cleves OH 45002	513-353-1960	R	16*	<.1
1074	Gene Hansen and Sons Trucking Inc—*Ivan Hansen*	PO Box 60, Herron MI 49744	989-379-2718	R	16*	<.1
1075	DSC Integrated Logistics—*Ann M Drake*	1750 S Wolf Rd, Des Plaines IL 60018	847-390-6800	R	16*	<.1
1076	Contaminant Control Inc—*Mark Vestal*	PO Box 64399, Fayetteville NC 28306		R	16*	<.1
1077	Bucolo Cold Storage Inc—*Jerry Bucolo*	5796 Wilson Burt Rd, Burt NY 14028	716-778-7631	R	16*	<.1
1078	Online Transport Inc—*Dan Cook*	6311 Stoner Dr, Greenfield IN 46140	317-894-2159	R	16*	.1
1079	UP Special Delivery Inc—*Terry Reed*	821 E Blvd, Kingsford MI 49802	906-774-1931	R	16	.1
1080	RE West Inc—*Bob West*	14 Bluegrass Dr, Ashland City TN 37015	615-792-1526	R	16	.1
1081	Bork Transportation of Illinois—*Thomas Rowe*	PO Box 500, Summit IL 60501	708-594-5551	R	16	.1
1082	Brennen Transportation Services—*Terrance Brennan*	50 Connecticut Dr, Burlington NJ 08016	609-239-7950	R	15	.1
1083	Trimac Transportation Services USA—*Jeff McCaig*	PO Box 674421, Houston TX 77267	281-985-0000	R	15	N/A
1084	Jefferson Trucking Co—*Lee Radcliffe*	2363 S National City R, National City MI 48748	989-756-2711	R	15	.1
1085	Delta Express Inc—*Robbie Rollins*	2520 E Outer Rd N, Scott City MO 63780		R	15*	.2
1086	Blue Max Trucking Inc—*Denton Williams*	1015 E Westinghouse Bl, Charlotte NC 28273	704-588-8780	R	15*	.2
1087	Seahorse Transportation Inc—*Mark Haynes*	PO Box 3767, Brownsville TX 78523	956-831-0600	R	15*	.2
1088	Cross Creek Trading Co—*Mike DeSimone*	PO Box 3127, Central Point OR 97502	541-773-3700	R	15*	.2
1089	Ameri-Co Carriers Inc—*James Kerr*	1702 E Overland, Scottsbluff NE 69361	308-635-3157	S	15*	.1
1090	TFX Inc—*John R Arwood*	3500 Westgate Dr Ste 8, Durham NC 27707	919-493-5311	R	15*	.1
1091	BSP Trans Inc—*Jack Law*	2500 Liberty Dr, Londonderry NH 03053	603-432-1400	R	15*	.1
1092	North Canton Transfer Co—*Carl Young* Kenan Advantage Group Inc	PO Box 35519, Canton OH 44735	330-491-0474	S	15	.1
1093	Dowell Transport Inc—*Earl Dowell*	PO Box 2436, Batesville AR 72503	870-698-1888	R	15*	.1
1094	Dolphin Line Inc—*Joel Earheart*	4521 Higgins Rd, Mobile AL 36619	251-666-2057	R	15*	.1
1095	Holland Enterprises Inc—*Chris Holland*	PO Box 9768, Fargo ND 58106	701-280-2634	R	15*	.1
1096	MSJ Trucking Inc—*J Sorrells*	1118 US Hwy 84 E, Opp AL 36467	334-493-3697	R	15*	.1
1097	Baltimore Tank Lines Inc—*William Molner*	180 8th Ave NW, Glen Burnie MD 21061	410-760-5500	R	15*	.1
1098	Berg Grain and Produce Inc—*Arnold Berg*	PO Box 1500, Fargo ND 58107	701-293-3434	R	15*	.1
1099	WM Dewey and Son Inc—*Robert McDowell*	1101 Mccarty St, Houston TX 77029	713-672-7511	R	15*	.1
1100	Carolina Tank Lines Inc—*Tony Capps*	PO Box 2827, Burlington NC 27216	336-226-7039	R	15*	.1
1101	ACT Transportation—*Phil Adams*	232 W Ctr St, North Salt Lake UT 84054	801-951-1131	R	15*	.1
1102	Boarder To Boarder Trucking—*JW Thomas*	PO Box 328, Edinburg TX 78540	956-316-4444	R	15*	.1
1103	BR Williams Trucking Inc—*Dee Brown*	PO Box 3310, Oxford AL 36203	256-831-5580	R	15*	.1
1104	Cox Transfer Inc—*William Honeg*	PO Box 168, Eureka IL 61530	309-467-4614	R	15*	.1
1105	Dirksen Transportation Inc—*Ron Lanting*	P O Box 1450, Manteca CA 95336	209-824-8877	R	15*	.1
1106	Don R Fruchey Inc—*Robert Fruchey*	5608 Old Maumee Rd, Fort Wayne IN 46803	260-749-8502	R	15*	.1
1107	Foltz Trucking Inc—*Frank Foltz*	19097 Frontage Rd, Detroit Lakes MN 56501		R	15*	.1
1108	Kopf Trucking Inc—*Kenneth Kopf*	PO Box 148, Goshen IN 46527	574-825-2152	R	15*	.1
1109	MST Express Inc—*Gene P Tate*	P O Box 908, New Albany MS 38652		R	15*	.1
1110	Severance Trucking Company Inc—*Robert H Severance*	49 McGrath Rd, Dracut MA 01826	978-275-9800	R	15*	.1
1111	Sorenson Transportation Co—*Darrell Sorenson*	PO Box 311, Chehalis WA 98532	360-748-8877	R	15*	.1
1112	Steelman Transportation Inc—*Jim Towery*	2160 N Burton, Springfield MO 65803	417-831-6300	R	15*	.1
1113	Westwood Cartage Inc—*Carol Gray McCarthy*	62 Everett St, Westwood MA 02090	781-329-4400	R	15*	.1

Note: An asterisk (*) indicates an estimated financial figure. The company type code used is as follows: R = Private, P = Public, S = Private Subsidiary, B = Public Subsidiary, D = Division, J = Joint Venture, I = Investment Fund.

COMPANY RANKINGS BY SALES WITHIN 4-DIGIT SIC

Rank	Company Name—Executive Officer	Address, City, State, Zip	Phone	Type	Fin	Empls
1114	WN Morehouse Truck Line Inc—Gerald Morehouse	4010 Dahlman Ave, Omaha NE 68107	402-733-2200	R	15*	.1
1115	Southwest Freight Inc—Kyle Johnson	PO Box 23098, Houston TX 77228	713-633-8889	R	15*	.1
1116	Action Resources Inc—Dean Flint	40 County Rd 517, Hanceville AL 35077	256-352-2689	R	15*	.1
1117	Harold Dickey Transport Inc—Dave Dickey	401 E 4th St, Packwood IA 52580	319-695-3601	R	15*	.1
1118	McFarland Truck Lines—Geoff Baker	PO Box 1008, Austin MN 55912	507-437-6651	R	15*	.1
1119	TIGHE Trucking Inc—John F Tighe II	481 Wildwood Ave, Woburn MA 01801	781-939-0925	R	15*	.1
1120	Plycon Van Lines Inc—Dean Pliaconis	280 Indian Head Rd, Kings Park NY 11754	631-269-7000	R	15*	.1
1121	Trans Continental Transport Inc—Paul Blomberg	PO Box 8868, Boise ID 83707	208-343-6400	R	15*	.1
1122	Smart Refrigerated Transport	PO Box 4278, Modesto CA 95352	209-858-2212	R	15*	.1
1123	Denton Cartage Company Inc—Lowell Denton	P O Box 57, Lyons IL 60534	708-222-3300	R	15*	.1
1124	Chrisman Heavy Hauling Inc—Michael Chrisman	PO Box 505, Ozark AR 72949	479-667-3185	R	15*	.1
1125	Skippy's Trucking Inc—Ron Carol	10407 Nokesville Rd, Manassas VA 20110	703-368-9995	R	15*	.1
1126	Antonini Enterprises LLC—Joseph Antonini	PO Box 8468, Stockton CA 95208	209-466-9041	R	15*	.1
1127	Lewis and Michael Inc—David Lewis	PO Box 97, Dayton OH 45402	937-252-5686	R	15*	<.1
1128	H and L Cartage Company Inc—John Goodman	PO Box 5719, Pearl MS 39288	601-932-8513	R	15*	<.1
1129	Hebert Brothers Inc—Robert Hebert	2 Badgers Island W, Kittery ME 03904	207-703-0431	R	15*	<.1
1130	Hilltop Transportation Inc—R Robinson	805 Cleveland Ave, Columbus OH 43201	614-297-4770	R	15*	<.1
1131	King Trucking Inc—Earl King	PO Box 1100, Amelia LA 70340	985-631-0525	R	15*	<.1
1132	Peerless Trucking Co—William Hart	PO Box 54554, Los Angeles CA 90054	310-637-3603	R	15*	<.1
1133	Two Guys and A Truck—David Underwood	45726 Elmwood Ct, Sterling VA 20166	703-406-9605	R	15*	<.1
1134	Shannon Brothers Company Inc—Mike Shannon	24478 Rd 140, Tulare CA 93274	559-686-4701	R	15*	<.1
1135	Shipley Transport—Ray Shipley	255 Adam Smith St, Sykesville MD 21784	410-795-4072	R	15*	<.1
1136	WS Emrian Trucking Inc—R Emerian	2963 S Chestnut Ave, Fresno CA 93725	559-485-9520	R	15*	<.1
1137	Gillies Trucking Inc—Randall Gillies	3931 Newton Rd, Stockton CA 95205	209-948-6268	R	15*	<.1
1138	Sound Transportation Inc—Jon Graciano	PO Box 44896, Tacoma WA 98444	253-582-2822	R	15*	<.1
1139	Darrell Andrews Trucking Inc—Darrell Andrews	PO Box 654, Siler City NC 27344	919-663-2142	R	15*	<.1
1140	Quick Courier Service Inc—Harry Sweeney	5185 Campus Dr Ste 100, Plymouth Meeting PA 19462		R	15*	<.1
1141	TCSI Inc—Mike Walker	1601 W Old Rt 66, Strafford MO 65757	417-864-5710	R	15	<.1
1142	Reynolds Trucking Company Inc—Bruce Reynolds	PO Box 2848, Indian Trail NC 28079	704-821-4717	R	15*	<.1
1143	Jet Inc—Wilbur Bontrager	PO Box 460, Middlebury IN 46540	574-825-0522	S	15	.2
1144	Sunset Transportation Inc—Peggy Alexander	PO Box 185058, Fort Worth TX 76181	817-589-7063	R	15	.1
1145	Product Distribution Co—James Leveck	3925 Produce Rd, Louisville KY 40218	502-968-8711	R	15	.2
1146	Marine Transport Inc—Robert Castelo	2421 Iorio Ct, Union NJ 07083	908-686-0086	R	14	.2
1147	Buddy Moore Trucking Inc—Eugene Moore	PO Box 10047, Birmingham AL 35202	205-254-3682	R	14	.1
1148	Gless Brothers Inc—Steve Berger	PO Box 220, Blue Grass IA 52726	563-381-1051	R	14	.1
1149	Hines Trucking Inc—Billy Hines	407 Hines Blvd, Prescott AR 71857	870-887-6693	R	14	.1
1150	Zenith Freight Lines LLC—Jack Hawn	PO Box 969, Conover NC 28613	828-465-7036	R	14*	.3
1151	Danny Nicholson Inc—Danny Nicholson	339 City Lake Rd, Lexington NC 27295	336-249-7204	R	14*	.2
1152	Grammer Industries Inc—Charles Whittington	18375 E 345 S, Grammer IN 47236	812-579-5644	R	14*	.2
1153	Ard's Trucking Company Inc—Allen Ard	1702 N Governor Willia, Darlington SC 29540	843-393-5101	R	14*	.2
1154	Ormsby Trucking Inc—Reginald Ormsby	PO Box 67, Uniondale IN 46791	260-543-2233	R	14*	.1
1155	Rodgers Trucking Co—Frank Ghiglione	14327 Washington Ave, San Leandro CA 94578	510-483-7000	R	14*	.1
1156	Central Pennsylvania Transportation—Chic Rhoads	425 Steel Way, Lancaster PA 17601	717-295-2442	R	14*	.1
1157	Hoffman Transport Inc—John Hoffman	485 Mason Dixon Rd, Greencastle PA 17225	717-597-7117	R	14*	.1
1158	BFL Inc—Milton Buskill	1883 S State Rd 161, Rockport IN 47635	812-649-9183	R	14*	.1
1159	Brandt Truck Line Inc—Steven Kubsch	1619 S Morrissey Dr, Bloomington IL 61704	309-662-3341	R	14*	.1
1160	BTI Special Commodities Inc—Tom Trustey	PO Box 4805, Des Moines IA 50306	515-288-2675	R	14*	.1
1161	Burnham Trucking Company Inc—Yvonne Meurkson	4000 Cline Ave, East Chicago IN 46312	219-399-4420	R	14*	.1
1162	Hercules Transport Inc—Tom O'Neal	PO Box 536, Choudrant LA 71227	318-768-2534	R	14*	.1
1163	Motor Carrier Service Inc—Keith Tuttle	815 Lemoyne Rd, Northwood OH 43619	419-693-6207	R	14*	.1
1164	Plains Transportation Inc—Jane Gripp	PO Box 32230, Amarillo TX 79120	806-372-9290	R	14*	.1
1165	SMP Inc—Stephen Powell	402 County Rd 519, Phillipsburg NJ 08865	908-454-4272	R	14*	.1
1166	Star Line Trucking Corp—Steve Ball	PO Box 510410, New Berlin WI 53151	262-786-8280	R	14*	.1
1167	Palm Express Inc Averitt Express Inc	PO Box 3166, Cookeville TN 38502	931-526-3306	S	14*	.1
1168	Dick Irvin Inc—David Irvin	PO Box 950, Shelby MT 59474	406-434-5583	R	14*	.1
1169	3KB Transportation Inc—Keith Baker	601 Eastside Dr, Altus OK 73521	580-477-1188	R	14*	.1
1170	ABC Transportation Inc—Aubrey Baugh	PO Box 800, Eufaula AL 36072	334-688-2616	S	14*	.1
1171	Dyno Nobel Transportation—Len Smith	2650 Deckler Lake Blvd, Salt Lake City UT 84119	801-521-2447	S	14*	.1
1172	Oregon Transfer Co—Gary Eichman	5910 N Cutter Cir, Portland OR 97217	503-943-3500	R	14*	.1
1173	Godfrey Trucking Inc—Scott Godfrey	6173 West 2100 South, West Valley City UT 84128	801-972-0660	R	14*	.1
1174	Fortune Transportation Company Inc—Donavan J Olson	PO Box 399, Windom MN 56101	507-831-2335	R	14*	.1
1175	Frock Brothers Trucking Inc—Daniel Frock	PO Box 157, New Oxford PA 17350	717-624-4431	R	14*	.1
1176	HF Campbell and Son Inc—Franklin Campbell	PO Box 260, Millerstown PA 17062	717-589-3194	R	14*	.1
1177	Lessors Inc—James Shapiro	1056 Gemini Rd, Eagan MN 55121	651-454-1202	R	14*	.1
1178	Van Wyk Freight Lines Inc—Vernon Van Wyk	PO Box 70, Grinnell IA 50112	641-236-7551	R	14*	.1
1179	GT USA—Mark Gunther	7462 Railroad Ave, Hanover MD 21076	410-766-8600	R	14*	.1
1180	Bett-A-Way Beverage Distributors—John Vaccaro	110 Sylvania Pl, South Plainfield NJ 07080	908-222-2500	R	14*	.1
1181	PAT Auto Transport Inc—George Gregory Hedges	PO Box 37701, Pensacola FL 32526	850-474-8850	R	14*	.1
1182	Suddath International—Steve Crooks Suddath Cos	815 S Main St, Jacksonville FL 32207	904-585-1200	S	14	.1
1183	RiverLift Trucking—Bob Schaefer	PO Box 532, West Elizabeth PA 15088	412-384-8420	R	14*	<.1
1184	Allen Freight Services Inc—Robert W Weaver PAM Transportation Services Inc	297 N Henri de Tonti B, Tontitown AR 72770	479-361-9111	S	14*	<.1
1185	Hoffmeier Inc—Kermit D Hoffmeier	PO Box 3667, Tulsa OK 74101	918-428-5823	R	14*	<.1
1186	J and D Hauling Inc—Don Plecher	PO Box 2582, Ardmore OK 73402	580-223-1012	R	14*	<.1
1187	Concept Freight Service Inc—Jeremy Rayl J Rayl Transport Inc	PO Box 7157, Akron OH 44306	330-724-9314	S	14*	<.1
1188	HM Kelly Inc—Edmond Frock	PO Box 186, New Oxford PA 17350	717-624-4421	R	14*	<.1
1189	Leander Trucking Company Inc—John Smith	PO Box 299, Hineston LA 71438	337-238-6826	R	14*	<.1
1190	Packard Truck Lines Inc—Claiborne Perrilliat	PO Box 1536, Harvey LA 70059	504-392-9994	R	14*	<.1
1191	Badger State Western Inc—Richard Seefluth	710 S 4th, Abbotsford WI 54405	715-223-2667	R	14*	<.1
1192	Shumaker Trucking Company Inc—Dave Shumaker	PO Box 329, Dillsburg PA 17019	717-432-9617	R	14*	<.1
1193	Albert Farms Inc—Jeffrey L Albert	696 Main St, Madawaska ME 04756	207-728-4318	R	14*	<.1
1194	Haynes Trucking LLC—Alvin Haynes	PO Box 8638, Lexington KY 40533	859-254-2385	R	14*	<.1
1195	Humboldt Storage and Moving Co—Darcy Goldman	100 New Boston Dr, Canton MA 02021	781-821-8777	R	14*	<.1
1196	Puryear Trucking Inc—Randy Menefee	3041 Gum Rd, Chesapeake VA 23321	757-638-7914	R	14*	<.1
1197	St Ann Transportation Inc—William McQueen	PO Box 485, Fort Ann NY 12827	518-747-7158	R	14*	<.1
1198	Thurel Mason Trucking Inc—Thurel Mason	PO Box 250, Aurora UT 84620	435-529-3734	R	14*	<.1
1199	Timmer's Express Inc—Timothy Siercks	2599 Mississippi St, New Brighton MN 55112	651-633-1313	R	14*	<.1

Rank	Company Name—*Executive Officer*	Address, City, State, Zip	Phone	Type	Fin	Empls
1200	John Ray Enterprises—*John Ray*	221 John Ray Ln, Eastaboga AL 36260	256-831-3746	R	14*	<.1
1201	B and Q Distribution Service Inc—*Betty Taylor*	24 Hoag Dr, Phoenix NY 13135	315-695-7271	R	14*	<.1
1202	Bastian Trucking Inc—*Russell Bastian*	PO Box 417, Aurora UT 84620	435-529-7453	R	14*	<.1
1203	Clyde's Transfer Inc—*Clyde Hostutlers*	7208 Aquarius Dr, Mechanicsville VA 23111		R	14*	<.1
1204	Lutrel Trucking Inc—*Mark Lutrel*	12856 Old River Rd, Bakersfield CA 93311	661-399-0246	R	14*	<.1
1205	Don Snow Trucking Inc—*Donald H Snow*	PO Box 606, Harpursville NY 13787	607-693-8432	R	14*	<.1
1206	Mo-Vac Service Company Inc—*Glynn Andrews*	PO Box 2677, McAllen TX 78502	956-631-9121	R	14	.1
1207	Riverside Transport Inc—*Bill Grojean*	4001 Kansas Ave, Kansas City KS 66106	913-233-5500	R	14	.1
1208	Priority Express Inc—*Don Wauters*	3915 Delaware Ave, Des Moines IA 50313	515-564-1400	R	14	.1
1209	Buchheit Trucking Service—*Ron Gjerstad*	600 Daugherty St, Scott City MO 63780	573-264-1700	R	14	.1
1210	Franks and Son Trucking LLC—*Dewayne Franks*	31303 S Hwy 69, Big Cabin OK 74332	918-783-5780	R	14	<.1
1211	Diamond Transportation System—*Paul Martinson*	PO Box 1557, Racine WI 53406	262-554-5410	R	13	.1
1212	Blue Mountain Trucking Corp—*Larry Winstead*	PO Box 307, Blue Mountain MS 38610		R	13	.1
1213	Pullen Brothers Inc—*Jerry Pullen*	1788 State Hwy HH, Sikeston MO 63801	573-471-7897	R	13	.1
1214	City Transfer Company Inc—*Tottie Ogle*	39555 Schoolcraft Rd, Plymouth MI 48170	734-354-9400	R	13	<.1
1215	John Bunning Transfer Co—*Chris Bunning*	1600 Elk St, Rock Springs WY 82901	307-362-3791	R	13	.1
1216	Murrow's Transfer Inc—*Fred Murrow*	PO Box 4095, High Point NC 27263	336-475-6101	R	13*	.2
1217	Jeff Foster Trucking Inc—*Jeff Foster*	PO Box 367, Superior WI 54880	715-394-6099	R	13*	.2
1218	Reeves Brothers Trucking Inc—*Jeff Reeves*	16105 Hwy 412 E, Lexington TN 38351	731-968-6839	R	13*	.1
1219	Evans Equipment Company Inc—*Helen F Evans*	685 E Main St, Butler IN 46721	260-868-5835	R	13*	.1
1220	FAB Express Inc—*Fred Bartuch*	11225 Joliet Rd, Lemont IL 60439	630-739-3600	R	13*	.1
1221	Witte Brothers Exchange Inc—*Brent Witte*	575 Witte Industrial C, Troy MO 63379	314-219-4200	R	13*	.1
1222	Dixon Brothers Inc—*Loren Knittel*	5093 Us Hwy 16, Newcastle WY 82701	307-746-2788	R	13*	.1
1223	Pope Transport Co—*E Pope*	1092 N Breazeale Ave, Mount Olive NC 28365	919-658-6566	R	13	.1
1224	Class 1 Transport Inc—*Dave Bradden*	PO Box 175, McVeytown PA 17051	717-899-6606	R	13*	.1
1225	Dot-Line Transportation—*Walley Watson*	PO Box 8739, Fountain Valley CA 92728	323-780-9010	R	13*	.1
1226	Ezzell Trucking Inc—*Grover Ezzell*	PO Box 67, Harrells NC 28444	910-532-4101	R	13*	.1
1227	JAT of Fort Wayne Inc—*Jim Thompson*	5031 Industrial Rd, Fort Wayne IN 46825	260-482-8447	R	13*	.1
1228	Klink Trucking Inc—*Wayne Klink*	PO Box 428, Ashley IN 46705	260-587-9113	R	13*	.1
1229	Nationwide Transportation—*Paul Moore*	PO Box 27845, Omaha NE 68127	402-592-2924	R	13*	.1
1230	Team One Transport Inc—*Kris Koals*	4161 N 150 W, Columbus IN 47201	812-376-7726	R	13*	.1
1231	Trade Winds Transit Inc—*David Monin*	1000 W John Rowan Blvd, Bardstown KY 40004	502-348-3503	R	13*	.1
1232	Yourga Trucking Inc—*Beverly Churko*	PO Box 607, Wheatland PA 16161	724-981-3600	R	13*	.1
1233	Hardy Brothers Inc—*Eddie Hardy*	6406 Siloam Rd, Siloam NC 27047		R	13	.1
1234	Prochnow Transport Inc—*Dale Prochnow*	PO Box 565, Medford WI 54451	715-748-4556	R	13*	.1
1235	Davidson Brothers Inc—*Randall Davidson*	450 Runville Rd, Bellefonte PA 16823	814-355-5513	R	13*	.1
1236	Salem Trucking Co—*Richard Salem*	2100 Yolande Ave, Lincoln NE 68521	402-477-4444	R	13*	.1
1237	Clouse Trucking Inc—*Edward Clouse*	2075 Ritner Hwy, Carlisle PA 17015	717-249-2410	R	13*	.1
1238	Comstar Enterprises Inc—*Mike Ferguson*	PO Box 6698, Springdale AR 72766	479-361-2111	R	13*	.1
1239	Klapec Trucking Co—*Cindy Urban*	PO Box 1278, Oil City PA 16301	814-676-1512	R	13*	.1
1240	Midnite Express Inc—*Lee Skistad*	448 7th St NW, West Fargo ND 58078	701-281-2511	R	13*	.1
1241	TP Trucking—*Ron Tycer*	5630 Table Rock Rd, Central Point OR 97502		R	13*	.1
1242	Grane Transportation Lines Ltd—*Allan Grane*	1011 S Laramie, Chicago IL 60644	773-379-9711	R	13*	.1
1243	PCI Transportation Inc—*Charles Smith*	PO Box 4, Galena Park TX 77547	713-673-6120	R	13*	.1
1244	Grand Rapids Transport Inc—*Robert E Fedwa*	PO Box D, Grand Rapids MI 49501	616-669-8822	R	13*	.1
1245	Jerry W Bailey Trucking Inc—*Jerry Bailey*	PO Box 9277, Fort Wayne IN 46899	260-747-3511	P	13*	1
1246	Time Critical Freight Inc—*Paul Lange*	1790 Crossroads, Odenton MD 21113		R	13*	.1
1247	Chordus Inc/Office Furniture USA—*Gary Kitchen*	273 Cahaba Valley Pky, Pelham AL 35124	205-988-5919	R	13	.1
1248	Burkhart Enterprises Inc—*Ray Burkhart*	PO Box 6131, Knoxville TN 37914	865-523-6157	R	13*	<.1
1249	Tri-Star Transport Inc—*Dallas Knepp* Bavarian Motor Transport Inc	3681 Okemos Rd Ste 500, Okemos MI 48864	517-349-3011	S	13*	<.1
1250	Capitol North American—*Mitch Rittenhouse*	1780 S Mojave Rd, Las Vegas NV 89104	702-457-5353	R	13*	<.1
1251	Century Lines Inc—*Robert Rucker*	PO Box 27469, Cleveland OH 44127	216-271-0700	R	13*	<.1
1252	CFC Transportation Inc—*Thomas Comer*	PO Box 8057, Columbus MS 39705	662-329-0019	R	13*	<.1
1253	KJ Bradley Inc—*Keith Bradley*	PO Box 369, Mount Vernon IN 47620	812-838-0961	R	13*	<.1
1254	McConnell Heavy Hauling Inc—*F McConnell*	PO Box 164918, Little Rock AR 72216	501-490-1481	R	13*	<.1
1255	Olson Carriers Inc—*Thomas Olson*	15640 Clayton Ave E, Rosemount MN 55068	651-437-6311	R	13*	<.1
1256	Statewide Express Inc—*Thomas Armanini*	5231 Engle Rd, Brookpark OH 44142	216-676-4600	R	13*	<.1
1257	Vincent Fister Inc—*Dennis Tolson*	PO Box 5063, Lexington KY 40509	859-266-2153	R	13*	<.1
1258	Carney Trucking Company Inc—*Verl Carney*	PO Box 48, Melvin AL 36913	251-771-6585	R	13*	<.1
1259	Golden Transfer Co—*Todd Winter* Atlas Van Lines Inc	PO Box 907, Longmont CO 80502	303-776-3882	S	13*	<.1
1260	Randy Rowe Trucking Inc—*Randy Rowe*	PO Box 2176, Twin Falls ID 83303	208-734-3880	R	13*	<.1
1261	Contractors Cargo Co—*Gerald Wheeler*	500 S Alameda St, Compton CA 90221	310-609-1957	R	13*	<.1
1262	T and T Truck and Crane Service Inc—*Todd Holder*	1375 N Olive St, Ventura CA 93001	805-648-3348	R	13*	<.1
1263	Great American Transport Inc—*Larry Hobson*	2787 S Willow Ave, Fresno CA 93725	559-497-1200	R	13*	<.1
1264	Volunteer Trucking Inc—*Alvin Harrison*	PO Box 837, Dayton TN 37321		R	13	.1
1265	Kasper Trucking Inc—*Gary Kasper*	5441 Forest Hills Ct, Loves Park IL 61111	815-282-3331	R	13	.1
1266	Cranston Trucking Co	25 Hopkins Hill Rd, West Greenwich RI 02817	401-397-2442	S	13	.1
1267	American Delivery Service Inc—*Sally Beck*	1501 Carmen Dr, Elk Grove Village IL 60007	847-253-0084	R	13	.1
1268	Abbott SYSCO Transportation—*Larry Abbott*	2400 Harrison Rd, Columbus OH 43204	614-272-0658	R	13	.1
1269	DTS—*Scott Weiss*	1640 Monad Rd, Billings MT 59101	406-245-4695	R	13	.1
1270	Nagle Toledo Inc—*Edwin Nagle III*	4520 Moline-Martin Rd, Walbridge OH 43465	419-661-2500	R	13	<.1
1271	First Coast Intermodal Services—*Buddy Bowser*	PO Box 26767, Jacksonville FL 32226	904-757-6008	R	13	.2
1272	Bunch Transport Inc—*Richard Bundschuh*	Po Box 41400, Charleston SC 29423	843-207-5100	R	13	.1
1273	Specialized Transportation Services—*Ramsey Hassan*	1235 Fesslers Ln, Nashville TN 37210	615-742-9944	R	13	.1
1274	CAST Transportation—*Richard Eshe*	9850 Havana St, Henderson CO 80640	303-534-6376	R	12	.1
1275	M and P Transportation Inc / Skyway—*Doug Marquardt*	PO Box 1040, Yankton SD 57078	605-665-1053	R	12	.1
1276	Lydall Transport Ltd—*Bill Franks*	11023 Washington Hwy, Glen Allen VA 23059	804-550-1993	S	12	.1
1277	Paper Transport of Green Bay—*Leonard Shefchik*	2701 Executive Dr, Green Bay WI 54304	920-497-6222	R	12	.2
1278	Air Van northAmerica—*Steven Galvagno*	10510 NE Northup Way S, Kirkland WA 98033	425-629-4101	R	12*	.2
1279	Classic Carriers Inc—*Jim Subler*	PO Box 295, Versailles OH 45380	937-526-5100	R	12*	.2
1280	Daryl Thomason Trucking Inc—*Daryl Thomason*	PO Box 219, Broken Bow OK 74728	580-584-2895	R	12*	.2
1281	Forest Products Transports Inc—*Tommy Duff*	202 Industrial Rd, Columbia MS 39429	601-736-3344	R	12*	.1
1282	Bonded Carriers Inc—*Vaughn Clatterbuck*	1014 Mid Atlantic Pkwy, Martinsburg WV 25401	304-263-0884	R	12	.1
1283	MCO Transport Inc—*Daniel McComas*	PO Box 1320, Wilmington NC 28402	910-343-8372	R	12*	.1
1284	Lone Star Trucking Inc—*Hank Weeks*	PO Box 81257, Bakersfield CA 93380	661-327-3788	R	12*	.1
1285	Daggett Truck Line Inc—*Fred Daggett*	PO Box 158, Frazee MN 56544	218-334-3711	R	12*	.1
1286	Bill Davis Trucking Inc—*Bill Davis*	810 Newport Rd, Batesville AR 72501	870-251-2806	R	12*	.1
1287	Panama Transfer Inc—*Jim Kloewer*	600 La Salle Ave, Panama IA 51562	712-489-2020	R	12*	.1

Note: An asterisk (*) indicates an estimated financial figure. The company type code used is as follows: R = Private, P = Public, S = Private Subsidiary, B = Public Subsidiary, D = Division, J = Joint Venture, I = Investment Fund.

COMPANY RANKINGS BY SALES WITHIN 4-DIGIT SIC

Rank	Company Name—Executive Officer	Address, City, State, Zip	Phone	Type	Fin	Empls
1288	Rail Delivery Services Inc—Greg Stefflre	8600 Bannana Ave, Fontana CA 92335	909-355-4100	R	12*	.1
1289	Tri-State Delivery Inc—Edward McCormick	3411 Summerhill Rd, Texarkana TX 75503	903-794-1423	R	12*	.1
1290	Bigbee Transportation Inc—Beverlee Lancaster	40158 Lackey Rd, Aberdeen MS 39730	662-369-4160	R	12*	.1
1291	W and K Express Inc—Ted Baranowski	2314 River Rd, River Grove IL 60171	708-453-8889	R	12*	.1
1292	K and K Trucking Inc—Donnie Kemp	147 Transport Dr, Gordonsville TN 38563	615-735-1420	R	12*	.1
1293	Badger Federal Services Inc—William Dougherty	PO Box 3083, Oshkosh WI 54903	920-426-6400	R	12*	.1
1294	Reliable Tank Line LLC—Graham Bennett	PO Box 2736, Winston Salem NC 27102	336-722-3441	R	12*	.1
1295	Sharp Transportation Inc—Zan Sharp	PO Box 3452, Logan UT 84323	435-245-6053	R	12*	.1
1296	Nationwide-Southeast Inc—Edsel Cleveland	1000 S River Industria, Atlanta GA 30315	404-624-0011	R	12*	.1
1297	Airline Transportation Specialists—Tom J Medved	PO Box 21344, Eagan MN 55121	651-675-0277	R	12*	.1
1298	US Transport—Steve Nelligan	241 W 56th Ave, Denver CO 80216	303-297-9779	R	12*	.1
1299	Appalachian Freight Carriers—William Pence	PO Box 307, Edinburg VA 22824	540-984-8514	R	12*	.1
1300	Autumn Transport Inc—Lowell Rieks	6550 Courtly Rd, Woodbury MN 55125	651-738-6998	R	12*	.1
1301	Utley Inc—Riley Rhoades	PO Box 207, Steele MO 63877	573-695-4431	R	12*	.1
1302	Key Logistics—Donald Jenks Jr	PO Box 92334, Rochester NY 14692	585-424-3660	R	12*	.1
1303	Ann Arbor Distribution—Frank Kolakowski	1942 McGregor Rd, Ypsilanti MI 48198	734-484-0100	R	12*	.1
1304	Leavitt's Freight Service—Terry Leavitt	3855 Marcola Rd, Springfield OR 97477	541-747-4236	R	12*	.1
1305	Short Freight Lines Inc—Bob Short	PO Box 357, Bay City MI 48707	989-893-3505	R	12*	.1
1306	Zeitner and Sons Inc—Rallen Zeitner	PO BOX 7760, Omaha NE 68107	402-731-5047	R	12*	.1
1307	Bulk Express Inc—Chris Pawlikowski	610 E 131st Pl, Hammond IN 46327	219-937-3070	R	12*	.1
1308	Driveline International Inc—Raymond Huston	PO Box 720477, McAllen TX 78504	956-787-7979	R	12*	.1
1309	Unique Express Inc—Allan Hughes	PO Box 7623, Charlotte NC 28241	704-552-5636	R	12*	.1
1310	Yarbrough Transfer Co—James Yarbrough	1500 Doune St, Winston Salem NC 27127	336-725-7552	R	12*	.1
1311	B and K Transportation Inc—Terry Kultgen	2500 W Southbranch Blv, Oak Creek WI 53154	414-761-2410	R	12*	.1
1312	Colonial Cartage Corp—Fred Keith	3000 Cobb Internationa, Kennesaw GA 30152	770-424-8811	R	12*	.1
1313	Taylor Distributing Co—Rex Taylor	2875 E Sharon Rd, Cincinnati OH 45241	513-773-2100	R	12*	.1
1314	Wise Trucking Inc—Keith Wise	37630 Hwy 91, Holly Pond AL 35083	256-796-5291	R	12*	.1
1315	Great Lakes Terminal and Transport—Steven Dehmlow	85 W Algonquin Rd Ste, Arlington Heights IL 60005	847-437-0200	R	12*	.1
1316	McLane Livestock Transport Inc—JP McLane	PO Box 309, Poplar Bluff MO 63902	573-785-0177	R	12*	.1
1317	Volpe Express Inc—Dante Volpe	565 Hollow Rd, Phoenixville PA 19460	610-630-0700	R	12*	<.1
1318	J Supor Trucking and Rigging Co—Joseph Supor III	433 Bergen Ave, Kearny NJ 07032	201-299-1100	R	12*	<.1
1319	Trans American Trucking Services—Ronald McGraw	115 Saint Nicholas Ave, South Plainfield NJ 07080	908-755-9000	R	12*	<.1
1320	DT Grantham Trucking Co—Dallas Grantham	540 - B Old Grantham R, Goldsboro NC 27530	919-734-1350	R	12*	<.1
1321	Verplank Trucking Inc—Joe Burns	705 2nd St, Ferrysburg MI 49409	616-842-1448	R	12*	<.1
1322	Parker K Bailey and Sons Inc—Craig Bailey	6 State St, Brewer ME 04412	207-989-6161	R	12*	<.1
1323	Resource Recovery Corp—Mo Azose	1629 E Alexander Ave, Tacoma WA 98421	253-383-3044	S	12*	<.1
1324	Wattrans Inc—Lyndon Watt	14022 Valley Blvd, Fontana CA 92335	909-356-7740	R	12*	<.1
1325	Richard L Hodges Inc—Richard L Hodges	PO Box 141, Unity ME 04988	207-948-2828	R	12*	<.1
1326	AAA Transfer Inc—Jamey Wills	4910 Gardner Ave, Kansas City MO 64120		R	12*	<.1
1327	Chris J Alt Inc—Chris Alt	PO Box 660, Moorefield WV 26836	304-538-2071	R	12*	<.1
1328	Reber Corp—Floyd Reber	3 Steel Rd E, Morrisville PA 19067	215-736-9662	R	12*	<.1
1329	Jennings Trucking Service Inc—Robert Jennings	11 Miles S Hwy 54, Gotebo OK 73041	580-639-2239	R	12*	<.1
1330	BD Transportation Inc—John Douglas	PO Box 813, Piqua OH 45356	937-773-9280	R	12*	<.1
1331	Chemical Transportation Inc—Greg Gibbons	P O Box 397, Rillito AZ 85654	520-624-2348	R	12*	<.1
1332	Commodity Carriers Inc—Robert Dembinski	112 Stockhouse Rd, Bozrah CT 06334	860-886-5161	R	12*	<.1
1333	Frate Service Inc—Leo Reising	1365 Spring Bay Rd, East Peoria IL 61611	309-822-8181	R	12*	<.1
1334	JB Lee Transportation Inc—James Lee	1505 N Main St, Pontiac IL 61764	815-842-2888	R	12*	<.1
1335	KP Carriers Inc—Kermit Puterbaugh	290 Maple St, Kingsland AR 71652	870-348-5337	R	12*	<.1
1336	System Transport Inc—George Engler	1710 E 29th St, Signal Hill CA 90755	562-426-5918	R	12*	<.1
1337	Tacoma Transload Inc—Gary Hofmann	501 E 19th St, Tacoma WA 98421	253-272-3075	R	12*	<.1
1338	Timberland Trucking Company Inc—Roland Crawford	PO Box 416, East Millinocket ME 04430	207-746-9394	R	12*	<.1
1339	Baker Truck Services Inc—Bradley Baker	P O Box 106, Grangeville ID 83530	208-983-1360	R	12*	<.1
1340	Triple P Trucking Inc—James Carlsen	4987 E US Hwy 27, Mayo FL 32066	386-294-3172	R	12*	<.1
1341	CLS and Associates Incorporated Trucking—Sharon Carrier	PO Box 279, Seagoville TX 75159	972-287-3266	R	12*	<.1
1342	Horseless Carriage Carriers—Frank Malatesta	61 Iowa Ave, Paterson NJ 07503		R	12*	<.1
1343	Lavalley Transportation Inc—Randy Lavalle	PO Box 547, Potsdam NY 13676	315-265-5800	R	12	.1
1344	Atlantic Carriers Inc—Joe Bateman	PO Box 457, Atlantic IA 50022		R	12	<.1
1345	Truck-Rite Distribution Systems—Peter Durante	295 Lombardy St, Brooklyn NY 11222	718-599-7400	R	12	<.1
1346	Texas Moving Co—Steve M Dumais	908 N Bowser Rd, Richardson TX 75081	972-234-6371	R	12	<.1
1347	Sunbelt Express Services Inc—John Phillips	PO Box 111, Harlingen TX 78551	956-425-6767	R	12	.1
1348	James R Smith Trucking Company Inc—James Smith	86 Cupp Rd, Cullman AL 35055	256-734-0511	R	12	.1
1349	7 Hills Transport Inc—Lyons Heyman Jr	2 Dean Dr, Cartersville GA 30121	770-382-0963	R	12	.1
1350	Ewing Brothers Inc—Rex Ewing	1200 A St, Las Vegas NV 89106	702-382-9261	R	12	<.1
1351	Ozburn-Hessey Transportation LLC—Bert Irigoyeh	7101 Executive Center, Brentwood TN 37027	615-401-6400	R	12	<.1
1352	Glasscock Company Inc—James Glasscock	PO Box 6677, Sumter SC 29154	803-494-2694	R	12*	.1
1353	Raymond Corcoran Trucking Inc—Brian Corcoran	532 Klenck Ln, Billings MT 59101	406-252-7054	R	12	.1
1354	Desert Coastal Transport Inc—Timothy Wyant	10686 Banana Ave, Fontana CA 92337	909-357-3395	R	12	.1
1355	4-Star Bulk Transport Inc—Paul Hillman	PO Box 394, Fort Edward NY 12828	518-792-6571	R	12	.1
1356	South East Carriers Inc—Paul Gobble	1905 Mahr Ave, Lawrenceburg TN 38464	931-762-0570	R	12	.1
1357	RPM Transportation Inc—Shawn Duke	13225 Marquardt Ave, Santa Fe Springs CA 90670	562-777-9510	R	12	.1
1358	Carty and Carty Inc—K Schomp	849 Nandino Blvd, Lexington KY 40511	859-255-6642	R	12	.1
1359	Stone Belt Freight Lines Inc—William Benckart	PO Box 281, Bloomington IN 47402	812-824-6741	R	12	.1
1360	Best Cartage Inc—William Ward	829 Graves St, Kernersville NC 27284	336-996-1377	R	11	.1
1361	Buel Inc—Julie Comeaux	795 Rutherfordton Hwy, Chesnee SC 29323	864-461-3415	R	11	.1
1362	Young's Commercial Transfer—Larry Young	PO Box 871, Porterville CA 93257	559-784-6651	R	11	<.1
1363	Modular Transportation Co/MTC—Evan Stouten	PO Box 9465, Wyoming MI 49509	616-241-2060	R	11	.1
1364	TeeBerry Express Inc—Tom Berry	6725 Brookshire Blvd, Charlotte NC 28216	704-393-8866	R	11	.1
1365	Cherin Transportation Inc—Salvatore Ricciardi	300 Purity Dr, Lebanon IN 46052	765-483-3730	R	11	<.1
1366	Truck One Inc—Jeff Lilly	PO Box 4070, Newark OH 43058	740-349-8144	R	11*	.2
1367	Jack Hood Transportation Inc—Jack Hood	10827 W 400 N, Michigan City IN 46360	219-874-2885	R	11*	.2
1368	AT Systems East Inc—Richard Irvin	1241 White Horse Rd, Greenville SC 29605	864-422-8480	R	11*	.2
1369	Sunrise Express Inc—Raymond Vettel Jr	PO Box 1282, Grand Island NE 68802	308-381-2251	R	11*	.2
1370	Beco Inc—Burton Hoovestol	3655 County Rd 139, New Salem ND 58563	701-843-7529	R	11*	.1
1371	BJ Cecil Trucking Inc—Christopher Cecil	PO Box 2228, Claypool AZ 85532	928-425-5781	R	11*	.1
1372	Hazen Transport Inc—Richard Palmer	27050 Wick Rd, Taylor MI 48180	313-292-4061	R	11*	.1
1373	Regency Transportation Inc—Richard Giroux	101 Constitution Blvd, Franklin MA 02038	508-520-3595	R	11*	.1
1374	J and H Trucking Inc—Carl Cooper	PO Box 131, Andover KS 67002	316-733-5000	R	11*	.1
1375	JET Delivery Systems Inc—Leland Johnson	6225 NE 112th Ave, Portland OR 97220	503-256-3621	R	11*	.1
1376	Gemi Trucking Inc—Gene Adams	PO Box 3908, Eatonton GA 31024	912-748-2800	R	11*	.1
1377	Building Systems Transportation Co—Jerry Alcott	460 E High St, London OH 43140	740-852-9700	R	11*	.1

Rank	Company Name—Executive Officer	Address, City, State, Zip	Phone	Type	Fin	Empls
1378	Dahlsten Truck Line Inc—Donna Hastings	PO Box 95, Clay Center NE 68933	402-762-3511	R	11*	.1
1379	Kohel Interstate Transport Corp—Donald Kohel	PO Box 265, Marion WI 54950	715-754-4444	R	11*	.1
1380	Roy Miller Freight Lines Inc—Wiley Miller	3165 E Coronado St, Anaheim CA 92806	714-632-5511	R	11*	.1
1381	Sparhawk Trucking Inc—Tom Sparhawk	130 25th Ave S, Wisconsin Rapids WI 54495	715-423-0380	R	11*	.1
1382	Star Leasing Inc—Randal Menscer	PO Box 64428, Fayetteville NC 28306	910-425-2539	R	11*	.1
1383	Circle City Transport Inc—Johnny Baker	PO Box 5525, Dothan AL 36302	334-792-5751	R	11*	.1
1384	Skinner Transportation Inc—Steve Skinner	PO Box 26660, Austin TX 78755	512-389-3311	R	11*	.1
1385	Apgar Brothers Inc—Matthew Wright	PO Box 631, Bound Brook NJ 08805	732-356-3900	R	11	.1
1386	Hornish Brothers Inc—Joellen Hornish	2060 E 2nd St Ste 101, Defiance OH 43512	419-785-3100	R	11	.1
1387	Shippers Express Inc—Larry Kerr	1651 Kerr Dr, Jackson MS 39204	601-948-4251	R	11*	.1
1388	Stiles Truck Line Inc—Kurt Stiles	1901 Jasmine Dr, Pasadena TX 77503	713-472-0861	R	11*	.1
1389	Trexler Trucking Inc—Douglas Trexler	3350 Liberty Rd, Gold Hill NC 28071	704-633-0690	R	11*	.1
1390	American Marine Transport	9487 Regency Square Bl, Jacksonville FL 32225	904-727-2200	R	11*	.1
1391	Bob Brink Inc—James Brink	165 Steuben St, Winona MN 55987	507-452-1568	R	11*	.1
1392	Carnes Trucking Company Inc—Gary Carnes	351 Terry Blvd, Louisville KY 40229	502-957-1990	R	11*	.1
1393	Metro Xpress—Kerry Sell	3518 Ohio St, Wichita KS 67219	316-832-9300	R	11*	.1
1394	Rand's Trucking Inc—William Rands	W8527 Gokey Rd, Ladysmith WI 54848	715-532-6663	R	11*	.1
1395	East-West Inc—Louis Linn	PO Box 19026, Asheville NC 28815	828-686-5434	R	11*	.1
1396	Morey Enterprises Inc—Gregory A Morey	384 County Rt 3, Brushton NY 12916	518-358-5920	R	11*	.1
1397	Services Transport—John Bultman	PO Box 250837, Milwaukee WI 53225	414-461-8600	R	11*	.1
1398	All-Star Transportation Inc—Carol McCoy	1547 Thornton Rd, Pacific MO 63069	636-271-6100	R	11*	.1
1399	McCauley Trucking Co—Larry McCauley	379 Industrial Park Rd, Brookville PA 15825		R	11*	.1
1400	Yowell Transportation Services—Bob Yowell	1840 Cardington Rd, Dayton OH 45409	937-294-5933	R	11*	.1
1401	CLM Freight Lines Inc—Charles Mong	PO Box 19333, Indianapolis IN 46219	317-353-8344	R	11*	.1
1402	P and C Trucking Enterprises Inc—Paul Wiltjer Jr	4410 S Ross Rd, Gary IN 46408	219-972-0193	R	11*	.1
1403	Pro Transport and Leasing Inc—Arthur Bakken	5520 32nd Ave S, Grand Forks ND 58201	701-775-5346	R	11*	.1
1404	Perkins Specialized Transportation—Andy Card	14450 Getz Rd, Noblesville IN 46060	317-297-3550	R	11*	.1
1405	PS Marston Associates Inc—Paul Marston	38B S Rd, North Hampton NH 03862	603-964-6713	R	11*	.1
1406	Lee Jennings Enterprises Inc—Lee Jennings	1465 Franklin Ave, Pomona CA 91766	909-868-1040	R	11*	.1
1407	Clark and Reid Company Inc—Donald Martin	1 Dunham Rd, Billerica MA 01821	978-670-9844	R	11*	.1
1408	Ross Express Inc—Steve Brown	195 N Main St, Boscawen NH 03303	603-753-4176	R	11*	.1
1409	US Inter-Mex Transportation—Richard Martinez	PO Box 4525, McAllen TX 78502	956-781-6606	R	11*	.1
1410	Destiny Transportation—Deborah Maggs-Quinn	105 Commerce Dr, Chatsworth GA 30705	706-517-5005	R	11*	.1
1411	Kerns Trucking Inc—Clyde C Kerns	PO Box 279, Kings Mountain NC 28086	704-739-4747	R	11*	.1
1412	Twin Express Inc—Brad McAlister	21840 Industrial Ct St, Rogers MN 55374	763-428-4969	R	11*	.1
1413	USA Transport Inc—Gary Leslie	12191 Violet Rd, Adelanto CA 92301	760-246-8620	R	11*	.1
1414	Cook Moving Systems Inc—Gregory Fierle	1845 Dale Rd, Buffalo NY 14225	716-897-0700	R	11*	<.1
1415	Gentner Inc—Bill Gentner	9685 W Michigan Ave, Saline MI 48176	734-944-0362	R	11*	<.1
1416	Moyer and Sons Inc—Gordon Moyer Jr	13050 Shawnee Ln, Clarksburg MD 20871	301-869-3896	R	11*	<.1
1417	Superior Transportation Inc—Patrick Barber	PO Box 1599, Mount Pleasant SC 29465	843-740-1840	R	11*	<.1
1418	Transwood Inc—Brian Wood	PO Box 189, Omaha NE 68105	402-346-8092	R	11*	<.1
1419	Atlas Transfer and Storage Co—Thomas Oakley	PO Box 80008, San Diego CA 92138	858-513-3800	R	11*	<.1
1420	Furness Trucking Inc—Joe Furness	310 S Main, Witt IL 62094	217-825-4242	R	11*	<.1
1421	ABC Fry-Wagner Inc—Larry Fry	15850 Santa Fe Dr, Lenexa KS 66219	913-541-0020	R	11*	<.1
1422	Carmen M Pariso Inc—Carmen Pariso	273 S Roycroft Blvd, Buffalo NY 14225	716-875-6168	R	11*	<.1
1423	Medelez Inc—Bryan Medelez	1190 E Punkin Ctr Rd, Hermiston OR 97838	541-567-4098	R	11*	<.1
1424	Granger Trucking Inc—Charles E Jackson	8001 Old Granger Rd, Garfield Heights OH 44125	216-641-5015	R	11*	<.1
1425	V Dolan Trucking Inc—Tom Brandal	PO Box 1090, Penngrove CA 94951	707-664-1409	R	11*	<.1
1426	Eckert Trucking Inc—Ervin Eckert	PO Box 1682, York PA 17405	717-843-0995	R	11*	<.1
1427	Miarer Transportation Inc—Thomas Miarer	2930 County Rd 69, Gibsonburg OH 43431	419-665-2334	R	11*	<.1
1428	Gregg Express Inc—Deborah Trimble	PO Box 81149, Cleveland OH 44181	216-476-2466	R	11*	<.1
1429	Mustang Expediting Inc—Stephanie Fleetman	35 Stanley Dr, Aston PA 19014	610-497-6360	R	11*	<.1
1430	Q Trucking Inc—Kenneth Fleekop	2701 Red Line Rd, Philadelphia PA 19114	215-992-0900	R	11*	<.1
1431	Bouche Trucking Inc—Ruben Jasso	12556 Weaver Rd, El Paso TX 79928	915-852-2324	R	11*	<.1
1432	Buchan Trucking LLC—Jerold Buchan	2787 Main St, East Troy WI 53120	262-642-3116	R	11*	<.1
1433	Carl L Jonas Inc—Carl Jonas	PO Box 943, Wytheville VA 24382	276-228-6609	R	11*	<.1
1434	Craig Van Lines Inc—Frederick Craig III	1100 Phoenix Dr, Fairfax VA 22030	703-273-8852	R	11*	<.1
1435	E and J Trucking Inc—James Route	1564 Milk Plant Rd, Liberty PA 16930	570-324-6661	R	11*	<.1
1436	Eastwood Carriers Inc—Ronald Schortmann	61 Union St, Westfield MA 01085	413-562-3661	R	11*	<.1
1437	Erich Trucking—Grace Arnold	640 S Saint Marys St, Saint Marys PA 15857	814-834-4133	R	11*	<.1
1438	Hribar Trucking Inc—Steven Hribar	1521 Waukesha Rd, Caledonia WI 53108	262-835-4401	R	11*	<.1
1439	J and C Trucking of Forest Lake Inc—Cindy Haley	20030 Ingersoll Ave N, Forest Lake MN 55025	651-464-1416	R	11*	<.1
1440	LL Smith Trucking—Roger Smith	PO Box 987, Riverton WY 82501	307-856-2491	R	11*	<.1
1441	Luecke's Hauling Inc—John Luecke	PO Box 1256, Florissant MO 63031	314-837-1700	R	11*	<.1
1442	Sanders Truck Transportation—William Byrd	3969 Goshen Industrial, Augusta GA 30906	706-792-0721	R	11*	<.1
1443	Waddell Transfer Inc—Walter Waddell	PO Box 168, Atkins VA 24311	276-783-5207	R	11*	<.1
1444	Lindsey Transport Service Inc—Jimmy Huddleston	2525 Farrisview Blvd, Memphis TN 38118	901-375-0087	R	11*	<.1
1445	Hauser Trucking Corp—Mark Hauser	PO Box 10, Watervliet NY 12189	518-271-7771	R	11*	<.1
1446	P and S Enterprises Inc—Mitch Twenter	PO Box 65, Pilot Grove MO 65276	660-834-3244	R	11*	<.1
1447	Shark Lines Inc—James Stevens	194 Morris Ave Ste 46, Holtsville NY 11742	631-447-0888	R	11*	<.1
1448	Stoughton Trucking Inc—Ed Swartout	1901 Academy St, Stoughton WI 53589	608-873-2926	R	11	.2
1449	Stanley Refrigerated Express—Peggy Stanley	1738 Empire Central, Dallas TX 75235	214-631-8420	R	11	.1
1450	Frontier Transportation Inc—Ray Takeda	3577 W Philadelphia St, Chino CA 91710	909-590-8245	R	11	.1
1451	Alabama Food Service Inc—Joe McGuire	401 Paul Rd, Montgomery AL 36108	334-262-4763	R	11	.1
1452	Storey Trucking Company Inc—Paul Storey	PO Box 126, Henagar AL 35978	256-657-3283	R	11	.1
1453	Atlantic Coastal Trucking Co—Peter Dykstra	PO Box 6550, Carlstadt NJ 07072	201-438-6500	R	11	.1
1454	Cal-Western Transport Inc—Ray Fonseca	1353 J St, Tulare CA 93274	559-687-3076	R	11	.1
1455	Joe Costa Trucking Inc—Tom Burgess	5540 W End Rd, Arcata CA 95521	707-822-2901	R	11	.1
1456	JH Sims Trucking Company Inc—James Sims	PO Box 799, Ontario CA 91762	909-986-5468	R	11	<.1
1457	Sam Broussard Trucking Company Inc—Sammy Broussard	PO Box 11507, New Iberia LA 70562	337-364-7681	R	10	.1
1458	Nationwide Magazine/Book Distrib—Ben Madill	3030 E Grauwyler Rd, Irving TX 75061	972-438-2333	R	10	.2
1459	TB and P Express Inc—Richard Burns	PO Box 71, Daleville IN 47334	765-378-5536	R	10	.1
1460	Kelworth Trucking Company Inc—Scotty Jones	PO Box 220, Poteau OK 74953	918-647-8212	R	10	.1
1461	Rollout Express Inc—Bob Ingram	2255U Hwy 70 E, Jackson TN 38305		R	10	.1
1462	L and L Transportation LLC—Joe Donnell	2817 E Wisconsin Ave, Appleton WI 54911	920-731-3771	R	10	.2
1463	Remel Sims Inc—Remel Sims	PO Box 1687, Wenatchee WA 98807	509-663-8540	R	10	.1
1464	Holland Special Delivery Inc—Jim Albers	3068 Highland Dr, Hudsonville MI 49426		R	10*	.1
1465	Fanelli Brothers Trucking Co—Dominic Fanelli	1298 Keystone Blvd, Pottsville PA 17901	570-628-5738	R	10*	.1
1466	Adrian Carriers Inc—Gary Adrian	PO Box 20, Milan IL 61264	309-787-4747	R	10*	.1
1467	Trans Valley Transport Inc—Donald Triolo	PO Box 485, Gilroy CA 95021	408-842-2188	R	10*	.1

Note: An asterisk (*) indicates an estimated financial figure. The company type code used is as follows: R = Private, P = Public, S = Private Subsidiary, B = Public Subsidiary, D = Division, J = Joint Venture, I = Investment Fund.

COMPANY RANKINGS BY SALES WITHIN 4-DIGIT SIC

Rank	Company Name—*Executive Officer*	Address, City, State, Zip	Phone	Type	Fin	Empls
1468	Farruggio's Express Inc—*Samuel Farruggio*	PO Box 362, Bristol PA 19007	215-788-5596	R	10*	.1
1469	Distribution Transportation Services—*Thomas J Komadina Sr*	PO Box 7, Wentzville MO 63385		R	10*	.1
1470	Calko Transport Company Inc—*Chong Suh*	720 E Watson Center Rd, Carson CA 90745	310-638-6791	R	10*	.1
1471	Fuchs Inc—*Scott Fuchs*	PO Box 576, Sharon WI 53585	608-643-3371	R	10*	.1
1472	Handy Truck Line Inc—*Clay Handy*	PO Box 876, Paul ID 83347	208-438-5071	R	10*	.1
1473	Nick Strimbu Inc—*William Strimbu*	PO Box 268, Brookfield OH 44403	330-448-4046	R	10*	.1
1474	PB Express Inc—*Dae Yun*	20800 Ctr Ridge Rd Ste, Rocky River OH 44116	440-356-8988	R	10*	.1
1475	Western Ports Transportation—*Steven Tyner*	9369 8th Ave S, Seattle WA 98108	206-762-2600	R	10*	.1
1476	WS Thomas Transfer Inc—*Robert Thompson*	1854 Morgantown Ave, Fairmont WV 26554	304-363-8050	R	10	.1
1477	Wicker Services Inc—*John Arwood*	PO Box 1398, Burlington NC 27215	336-227-1436	R	10*	.1
1478	Martin Trucking Inc—*Ronald Martin*	1015 W City Limits St, Hugoton KS 67951	620-544-4920	R	10*	.1
1479	KS and Company Inc—*Kenneth Simmons*	8681 Spruiell St, Leeds AL 35094	205-702-4021	R	10	.1
1480	Regional Integrated Logistics—*Robert Bengal*	2321 Kenmore Ave, Buffalo NY 14207	716-876-4645	R	10*	.1
1481	West Tennessee Express Inc—*J Michael McFarland*	58 Truck Ctr Dr, Jackson TN 38305	731-424-9791	R	10*	.1
1482	Knudsen Trucking Inc—*Perry Knudsen*	N 1811 785th St, Hager City WI 54014	715-792-5202	R	10*	.1
1483	E and B Trucking Inc—*Ed Costa*	12477 12th Ave, Hanford CA 93230	559-582-9135	R	10*	.1
1484	Fry-Wagner Moving and Storage—*Larry Fry*	3700 Rider Trl S, Earth City MO 63045	314-291-4100	R	10*	.1
1485	Riverbend Express LLC—*Norman Howard*	1391 W Redledge Rd, Washington UT 84780	435-634-9800	R	10*	.1
1486	Cooper Truck Line Inc—*Brad Cooper*	PO Box 699, Holly Springs MS 38635	662-252-5505	R	10*	.1
1487	Price Truck Line Inc—*Edward Toon*	3402 W Harry St, Wichita KS 67213	316-945-6915	R	10*	.1
1488	Temple Trucking Inc—*Stephen Temple*	3920 Shannon St, Chesapeake VA 23324	757-545-2431	R	10*	.1
1489	Arthur Wells Inc—*Hilton Kahn*	7140 N Broadway, Saint Louis MO 63147	314-592-2000	S	10*	.1
1490	Glasgow Trucking Inc—*Johnny Glasgow*	PO Box 1377, Vernon AL 35592	205-695-9120	R	10*	.1
1491	Port Jersey Transportation—*Robert Russo*	4 S Middlesex Ave, Monroe Township NJ 08831	609-860-1010	R	10*	.1
1492	Styer Transportation Co—*Mel Simon*	7870 215th St W, Lakeville MN 55044	952-469-4491	R	10*	.1
1493	Don's Trucking Inc—*Don Beverly*	1801 Coxendale Rd, Chester VA 23836	804-796-3881	R	10*	.1
1494	L and N Transport Inc—*Luther Morgan*	PO Box 6664, Phoenix AZ 85005	602-484-0563	R	10*	.1
1495	Montana Brand Produce Co—*Chris Drakes*	1483 Beck St, Salt Lake City UT 84116	801-532-2573	R	10*	.1
1496	Callaway Carriers Inc—*Henry Niles*	PO Box 110, Kingdom City MO 65262	573-642-7766	R	10*	.1
1497	DCM Transport Inc—*Terri Moore*	1745 S Henderson St, Galesburg IL 61401	309-344-1131	R	10*	.1
1498	Englund Equipment Co—*Bill Englund*	PO Box 250, Cashion AZ 85329	623-936-3365	R	10*	.1
1499	Hanna Truck Line Inc—*Pete Hanna*	PO Box 558, Fairfield AL 35064	205-780-1111	R	10*	.1
1500	Indian Valley Trucking Inc—*Robert Landis*	671 Souder Rd, Souderton PA 18964	215-723-7625	R	10*	.1
1501	Richard B Rudy Inc—*Kenneth Rudy*	1 Bernard St, Frederick MD 21701	301-663-9041	R	10*	.1
1502	Alnye Trucking—*Donald Nye*	PO Box 1118, Moravia NY 13118	315-497-3329	R	10*	.1
1503	Harrison Trucking Inc—*Harold Harrison*	8801 Olive Ln, Santee CA 92071	619-449-0840	R	10*	.1
1504	Haney Trucking Inc—*Brax Haney*	PO Box 231, Lufkin TX 75902	936-639-2434	R	10*	.1
1505	Sweeney Transportation Inc—*Martin Sweeney*	2073 Westover Rd, Chicopee MA 01022	413-593-5933	R	10*	.1
1506	Budway Enterprises Inc—*Vincent McLeod*	13600 Napa St, Fontana CA 92335	909-463-0500	R	10*	.1
1507	Michael J Collins Inc—*Mike Collins*	8228 SW 3rd St, Oklahoma City OK 73128	405-787-8233	R	10*	.1
1508	Collins Industries—*Michael A Collins*	PO Box 617, Jackson GA 30233	770-775-3333	R	10*	.1
1509	Ace Transport Ltd—*Kenneth Etheridge*	PO Box 189, Kenly NC 27542	919-284-3105	R	10*	.1
1510	Aero Bulk Carrier Inc—*Harvey Gainey* Super Service LLC	6000 Clay Ave, Grand Rapids MI 49548	616-530-8551	S	10*	.1
1511	Earl L Bonsack Inc—*Earl Bonsack*	402 Sky Harbour Dr, La Crosse WI 54603	608-783-2746	R	10	.1
1512	Mayfield Transfer Company Inc—*Raymond Emerick*	3200 W Lake St, Melrose Park IL 60160	708-681-4440	R	10	.1
1513	Raider Trucking Inc—*Ginger Stolp*	17105 Darwin, Hesperia CA 92345	760-244-4567	R	10*	.1
1514	Severt Trucking Inc—*Greg Severt*	3160 W Beaver St, Jacksonville FL 32254	904-388-8516	R	10*	.1
1515	Spirit Trucking Co—*Robert Denton*	5400 W 47th St, Chicago IL 60638	708-496-8888	R	10*	.1
1516	Starrete Trucking Company Inc—*Jack Starrette*	2019 Westside Dr, Augusta GA 30907	706-860-2060	R	10*	.1
1517	TJ Potter Trucking Inc—*Todd Potter*	13000 Sherburne Ave, Becker MN 55308	763-262-5850	R	10*	.1
1518	MoKan Container Services Inc—*Wes Seyller*	400 N Atlantic, Kansas City MO 64116	913-596-9100	R	10*	.1
1519	Charles D Goodwin Inc—*Charles Goodwin*	PO Box 1006, Sanford NC 27331	919-775-2622	R	10*	.1
1520	Good Transport Services Inc—*Lester Good*	PO Box 469, Columbia PA 17512	717-684-2228	R	10*	.1
1521	JE Williams Trucking Inc—*Bob Williams*	PO Box 30371, Billings MT 59107	406-248-7397	R	10*	.1
1522	Richard Nestor Inc—*Richard Nestor*	PO Box 1724, Sterling CO 80751	970-522-0076	R	10*	.1
1523	Shelly Moving and Storage Inc—*Robert J Bruce*	4451 Lincoln Hwy, York PA 17406	717-755-4099	R	10*	.1
1524	Truck 'N I Inc—*Carlos Urrea*	1401 Hills Pl NW, Atlanta GA 30318	404-355-5151	R	10*	.1
1525	Regional Enterprises Inc—*Gary Farrar*	410 Water St, Hopewell VA 23860	804-458-0926	S	10*	<.1
1526	Southwest Industrial Rigging—*Harry Baker*	2802 W Palm Ln, Phoenix AZ 85009	602-278-6281	R	10*	<.1
1527	Terminal Consolidation Co—*David r Nickell*	PO Box 12460, Kansas City MO 64161	816-453-5101	R	10	<.1
1528	Carolina Express Delivery Inc—*Terry Phillips*	PO Box 2574, Spartanburg SC 29304	864-503-4110	R	10*	<.1
1529	Direct Service Transport Inc—*Del Weiss*	PO Box 766, South Saint Paul MN 55075	651-450-0779	R	10*	<.1
1530	Escro Transport Ltd—*Donald Esposito*	275 Mayville Ave, Buffalo NY 14217	716-874-6155	R	10*	<.1
1531	Rainbow Trucking LLC—*Eugene Stos*	PO Box 2027, Great Bend KS 67530	620-792-3927	R	10*	<.1
1532	Tantara Transportation Inc—*Alan Fisher*	46051 Michigan Ave, Canton MI 48188	734-879-4400	R	10*	<.1
1533	Laramie Enterprises Inc—*Gordon Laramie*	PO Box 27170, Detroit MI 48227	313-279-4900	R	10*	<.1
1534	Returnable Services Inc	150 Mount Vernon Ave, Augusta ME 04330	207-623-2944	D	10*	<.1
1535	Ritter Feeds Inc—*Gary Ritter*	PO Box 306, Paxtonville PA 17861	570-837-3606	R	10*	<.1
1536	WW Owens and Sons Moving and Storage—*William Clarence Owens Jr*	501 E Ward St, Elizabeth City NC 27909	252-338-8121	R	10*	<.1
1537	Air Cargo Transit Inc—*Dewey Brown*	PO Box 24280, Phoenix AZ 85074	602-252-1000	R	10*	<.1
1538	AM and S Transportation Co—*Mateus Morais*	PO Box 23822, Oakland CA 94623	510-763-7768	R	10*	<.1
1539	Big I Trucking—*Gary Hoffman*	1201 N 16th St, Chickasha OK 73018	405-224-1333	R	10*	<.1
1540	Hi-Tech Express Inc—*Brian Honrud*	1743 W County Rd C Bld, Roseville MN 55113	763-537-1690	R	10*	<.1
1541	Howmet Transport Services—*Jeff Hill*	926 E Lincolnway, La Porte IN 46350	219-325-4127	R	10*	<.1
1542	Martinovich Trucking Inc—*Robert Martinovich*	PO Box 158, Babcock WI 54413	715-884-6363	R	10*	<.1
1543	Sweet Water Trucking Company Inc—*Rentz Lewis*	PO Box 98, Sweet Water AL 36782	334-994-4103	R	10*	<.1
1544	Grand Transportation Inc—*Frank Pso*	620 W 16th St, Long Beach CA 90813	562-432-6761	R	10*	<.1
1545	Armstrong Moving and Storage Co—*Rick Anderson*	1460 N Newport Rd, Colorado Springs CO 80916	719-475-2800	R	10*	<.1
1546	Newhaven Distribution Services—*Bill Shiffer*	999 E 149th St, Bronx NY 10455	718-292-9751	R	10*	<.1
1547	Swartz Moving and Storage Co—*Dan Allen*	9611 NE Sunderland Ave, Portland OR 97211	503-288-6564	R	10*	<.1
1548	Taylor-Made Transportation—*Michael Reynolds*	PO Box 197, Maplesville AL 36750	334-366-2269	R	10	<.1
1549	Sooner Trucking and Oilfield Services—*John Leffler*	PO Box 206, Countyline OK 73425	580-444-3318	R	10	<.1
1550	Allied Holdings—*Pam Runken*	2302 Park Lake Dr Ste, Atlanta GA 30345	404-371-0379	R	10	<.1
1551	Harris Trucking Co—*Izzy Petrill*	PO Box 529, Monroe NC 28111	704-289-5447	R	10	<.1
1552	Dino's Trucking Inc—*Constoline Vainalis*	9615 Continental Indus, Saint Louis MO 63123	314-631-3001	R	10	.1
1553	Classic Moving and Storage Inc—*Larry Hendricks*	PO Box 731, Hickory NC 28603		R	10	.1
1554	Vaughan Transport Inc—*Lonnie White*	PO Box 298, New Kingstown PA 17072		R	9	.1
1555	Cook Trucking Company Inc—*James Cook*	PO Box 70, Grimsley TN 38565	931-277-5322	R	9	.1

Rank	Company Name—*Executive Officer*	Address, City, State, Zip	Phone	Type	Fin	Empls
1556	Cope-Bestway Express Inc—*Michael Cope*	PO Box 179, Cheektowaga NY 14043	716-875-6565	R	9	<.1
1557	Fleming-Babcock Inc—*Douglas Babcock*	PO Box 681481, Riverside MO 64168	816-741-8328	R	9	<.1
1558	Freight Management LLC—*Robert O'Neill*	800 Federal Blvd, Carteret NJ 07008	732-750-9000	R	9	<.1
1559	Foothills Trucking Company Inc—*Andrew DeHart*	PO Box 192, Conover NC 28613	828-322-1380	R	9	.1
1560	J Rayl Transport Inc—*Tim Rayl*	1016 TRIPLETT BLVD, Akron OH 44306	330-784-1134	R	9	.1
1561	Gulf States Intermodal—*Scott Giroir*	100 Intermodal Dr, Chalmette LA 70043	504-279-8544	R	9	.1
1562	Everhart Transportation Inc—*Cline Everhart*	624 Midway Rd, Midway TN 37809		R	9	.1
1563	DOS Transportation Inc—*Donald O'Neal*	9101 Elm St, Seaford DE 19973	302-628-1810	R	9	<.1
1564	JT Sands Corp—*Todd Sands*	3445 Adamsville Rd, Zanesville OH 43701	740-454-1982	R	9	<.1
1565	Systems Logistics—*Richard Staley*	401 S Locust St Ste 20, Denton TX 76201	940-387-4241	R	9	.2
1566	Ray Walker Trucking Company Inc—*Ray Walker*	PO Box 469, Piedmont SC 29673	864-277-5234	R	9	.1
1567	Rajor Inc—*Toby Kemp*	PO Box 1115, Spring Hill TN 37174	931-486-1092	R	9	.1
1568	LH Chaney Materials Inc—*L Chaney*	PO Box 1665, Roanoke TX 76262	817-638-2403	R	9*	.1
1569	Jerry Lipps Inc—*Jerry Lipps*	PO Drawer F, Cape Girardeau MO 63702	573-335-8204	R	9*	.1
1570	Cargo Express Inc—*Dennis Schlegel*	1356 E Beechcraft Ct, Boise ID 83716	208-386-9446	R	9*	.1
1571	Iddings Trucking Inc—*George Loeber*	741 Blue Knob Rd, Marietta OH 45750	740-568-1780	R	9*	.1
1572	Associated Couriers Inc—*Elizabeth Anderson*	2684 Metro Blvd, Maryland Heights MO 63043	314-739-0400	R	9*	.1
1573	Horizon Moving Systems Inc—*Bruce L Dusenberry*	3600 E 36th St, Tucson AZ 85713	520-747-1400	R	9*	.1
1574	California Cartage Co—*Robert Curry*	PO Box 92829, Long Beach CA 90809	310-537-1432	R	9*	.1
1575	Chambers Leasing Systems Inc—*James Chambers*	PO Box 5337, Toledo OH 43611	419-726-9747	R	9*	.1
1576	East-West Motor Freight Inc—*Robert Chambers*	PO Box 607, Selmer TN 38375	731-645-7991	R	9*	.1
1577	Altom Transport Inc—*Thomas Warren*	7439 W Archer Ave, Summit IL 60501	773-735-6900	R	9*	.1
1578	Jet Express Inc—*Kevin Burch*	4518 Webster St, Dayton OH 45414	937-274-7033	R	9*	.1
1579	Jess Diaz Trucking Inc—*Dimas Diaz*	P O Box 367, La Mirada CA 90637	714-522-4800	R	9*	.1
1580	Alton Bean Trucking Inc—*Gary Bean*	PO Box 10, Amity AR 71921	870-342-9551	R	9*	.1
1581	Foshee Trucking Inc—*Eugene Foshee*	PO Box 3547, Montgomery AL 36109	334-215-7007	R	9*	.1
1582	JF Lomma Inc—*James Lomma*	48 3rd St, South Kearny NJ 07032	973-589-2000	R	9*	.1
1583	JL Rothrock Inc—*W Bondurant*	PO Box 77257, Greensboro NC 27417	336-854-6050	R	9*	.1
1584	Keane Thummel Trucking Inc—*Keane Thummel*	PO Box 33, New Market IA 51646	712-585-3266	R	9*	.1
1585	Oberg Freight Co—*Kent O'Berg*	22153 Old Hwy 169, Fort Dodge IA 50501	515-955-6818	R	9*	.1
1586	ProLinks Services Inc—*Richard Macko*	2738 W Entry Rd, Baldwinsville NY 13027	315-638-3368	S	9*	.1
1587	Quality Transportation Inc—*Michael Griffith*	PO Box 1530, Baker MT 59313	406-778-3304	R	9*	.1
1588	Warren C Sauers Company Inc—*Lori Trattner*	2601 Rochester Rd, Cranberry Township PA 16066	724-776-1504	R	9*	.1
1589	EL Farmer and Co—*Jamie Todd*	PO Box 3512, Odessa TX 79760		R	9*	.1
1590	Excel Transport Inc—*Bill Stellmon*	1914 5th Ave N, Lewiston ID 83501	208-746-4111	R	9*	.1
1591	Falcon Transport Inc—*James Murphy*	PO Box 11388, Lancaster PA 17605		R	9*	.1
1592	Sallee Horse Vans Inc—*Nicole Pieratt*	PO Box 13338, Lexington KY 40583	859-255-9406	R	9*	.1
1593	Wiest Truck Line Inc—*Jon Wiest*	8060 36th St SE, Jamestown ND 58401	701-252-6451	R	9*	.1
1594	A and H Inc—*Robert Hoerler*	PO Box 346, Footville WI 53537	608-876-6131	R	9*	.1
1595	Elliott Transport Systems Inc—*Jim Elliott*	PO Box 366, Moorhead MN 56561	218-236-9220	R	9*	.1
1596	Horizon Tank Lines Inc—*Charles Collie*	PO Box 2857, Durham NC 27715	919-620-3231	R	9*	.1
1597	Truck Service Inc—*Stephen Bennett*	PO Box 390, Forest City NC 28043	828-245-1637	R	9*	.1
1598	Berner Trucking Inc—*Jim Knisely*	PO Box 660, Dover OH 44622	330-343-5812	R	9*	.1
1599	February Fourteen Inc—*Bridget Carey*	4525 50th St SE, Grand Rapids MI 49512	616-656-0267	R	9*	.1
1600	Grandview Enterprises Inc—*Harold Hass*	7708 NE 99th St, Vancouver WA 98662	360-254-0181	R	9*	.1
1601	Jim Ressler Trucking Inc—*Jim Ressler*	1900 Hancock Dr, Bismarck ND 58501	701-258-3550	R	9*	.1
1602	H and W Transfer and Cartage Service—*Ray Lewis*	PO Box 448, Cedartown GA 30125	770-748-6535	R	9*	.1
1603	Rees Trucking Company Inc—*Don Storm*	PO Box 759, Licking MO 65542	573-674-9000	R	9*	.1
1604	W and A Distribution Services—*Scott Housley*	PO Box 309, Fort Atkinson WI 53538	920-563-6999	R	9*	.1
1605	Southwest Trails Inc—*Tom Donaldson*	PO Box 419, Gardena CA 90248		R	9*	.1
1606	Air Land Transport Inc—*John Snead*	11100 Calaska Cir, Anchorage AK 99515	907-248-0362	R	9*	.1
1607	B and A Hyder Trucking Company Inc—*Thomas Edward II*	314 Hyder St, Hendersonville NC 28792	828-693-5208	R	9*	.1
1608	Beverage Transportation Inc—*John Keagel*	PO Box 3, Thomasville PA 17364	717-225-5751	R	9*	.1
1609	Buckler Transport Inc—*David Buckler*	PO Box 269, Roulette PA 16746	814-544-1400	R	9*	.1
1610	Chicago Suburban Express Inc—*Douglas McClement*	5504 W 47th St, Chicago IL 60638	708-496-3300	R	9*	.1
1611	Harry's Motor Service Inc—*Jerry Kowalski*	PO Box 166, Argo IL 60501	708-458-0782	R	9*	.1
1612	Inman Trucking Management—*Tommy Spivey*	125-1 Gregory Rd NE, Leland NC 28451	910-371-3313	R	9*	.1
1613	Magra Inc—*Edward Eberle*	6400 Mount Elliott St, Detroit MI 48211	313-922-0006	R	9*	.1
1614	W Smith Cartage Company Inc—*James Smith*	7013 Sands Rd, Crystal Lake IL 60014	815-455-6161	R	9*	.1
1615	F and W Transportation Inc—*Robert Willis*	4197 Mike Padgett Hwy, Augusta GA 30906	706-796-3342	R	9*	.1
1616	Freight Systems Inc—*Richard Flynn*	21818 76th Ave S, Kent WA 98032	253-872-5191	R	9*	.1
1617	Doug Bradley Trucking Inc—*Doug Bradley*	680 E Water Well Rd, Salina KS 67401	785-826-9681	R	9*	.1
1618	Assured Aggregates Company Inc—*Barbra Chapin*	520-A Crazyhorse Canyo, Salinas CA 93907	831-443-8644	R	9*	.1
1619	Bekins Hawaiian Movers Inc—*Jim Coleman*	91-120 Hanua St, Kapolei HI 96707	808-682-6055	R	9*	.1
1620	MKP Transport Inc—*David White*	PO Box 70, Tolleson AZ 85353	623-936-6258	R	9*	.1
1621	Cannonball Express Transportation Co—*Bruce Meyers*	10064 S 134th St, Omaha NE 68138	402-894-4882	R	9*	.1
1622	McIlvaine Trucking Inc—*Doug Jonsen*	7556 Cleveland Rd, Wooster OH 44691	330-804-6054	R	9*	.1
1623	Custom Transfer Inc—*David Kamphenkel*	PO Box 157, Long Prairie MN 56347	320-732-3013	R	9*	.1
1624	McTyre Trucking—*John McTyre*	PO Box 590147, Orlando FL 32859	407-859-5171	R	9*	.1
1625	Mid-Western Car Carriers Inc—*Randall Wills*	2010 Television Drive, Kansas City MO 64126	816-836-5888	R	9*	.1
1626	North Star Ranch Inc—*Don Doty*	3575 W Grand River Ave, Howell MI 48855	517-546-3900	R	9*	.2
1627	TJ Marquart and Sons Inc—*Alexandra Marquart*	5195 Rt 19, Gainesville NY 14066	585-493-2522	R	9*	.1
1628	Tom Joy and Son Inc—*Darryl Joy*	PO Box 117, Peshtigo WI 54157	715-582-0222	R	9*	.1
1629	Weather Shield Transportation—*Edward Schield*	PO Box 309, Medford WI 54451	715-748-6555	R	9*	.1
1630	Gardner Trucking Inc—*Wayne Gardner*	PO Box 268, Pittsville WI 54466	715-884-2651	R	9	<.1
1631	Jones Brothers Trucking Inc—*William Jones*	PO Box 4414, Missoula MT 59806	406-721-4629	R	9*	<.1
1632	Oester Trucking Inc—*William Oester*	10268 Mason Dixon Hwy, Salisbury PA 15558	814-662-2702	R	9*	<.1
1633	Brantley Trucking Inc—*Kent McDaniel*	PO Box 2010, Monahans TX 79756	432-943-4057	R	9*	<.1
1634	Eagle Air Freight Inc—*Michael O'Brien*	140 Eastern Ave, Chelsea MA 02150	617-884-4436	R	9*	<.1
1635	Hutchison Transportation—*George Hutchison*	940 E Main St, Manchester IA 52057	563-927-3620	R	9*	<.1
1636	Joyce Van Lines Inc—*William Joyce*	1012 E Sumner Ave, Indianapolis IN 46227		R	9*	<.1
1637	Antonini Freight Express Inc—*Joseph Antonini*	PO Box 8468, Stockton CA 95208	209-466-9041	R	9	<.1
1638	JDS Refrigerated Transportation—*Brian De Francesco*	212 Beacham St, Everett MA 02149	617-381-9970	R	9*	<.1
1639	Coastal Courier Inc—*David Upchurch*	206 Ctr Rd, Gulf Breeze FL 32561	850-932-0782	R	9*	<.1
1640	Kentucky Container Service—*Donald Farris*	PO Box 197089, Louisville KY 40259	502-810-9800	R	9*	<.1
1641	Thomas and Sons Distributing—*Aaron Thomas*	PO Box 1030, Coos Bay OR 97420	541-267-3483	R	9*	<.1
1642	Roeder Cartage Company Inc—*Al Bishop*	1979 N Dixie Hwy, Lima OH 45801	419-221-1600	R	9	<.1
1643	Ray Moving and Storage Inc—*John Deare*	4111 Romaine St, Greensboro NC 27407	336-855-5881	R	9*	<.1
1644	RW Jones Trucking Co—*Wayne Jones*	1388 E 1000 S, Vernal UT 84078	435-789-1231	R	9*	<.1
1645	Palmer Transport Corp—*Donald Palmer*	1750 Pointe Ave, Ontario CA 91761	909-591-9240	R	9*	<.1

Note: An asterisk (*) indicates an estimated financial figure. The company type code used is as follows: R = Private, P = Public, S = Private Subsidiary, B = Public Subsidiary, D = Division, J = Joint Venture, I = Investment Fund.

COMPANY RANKINGS BY SALES WITHIN 4-DIGIT SIC

Rank	Company Name—Executive Officer	Address, City, State, Zip	Phone	Type	Fin	Empls
1646	Silvers Brothers Construction—Joe Silvers	95 Highland Ctr Blvd, Asheville NC 28806	828-667-3204	R	9*	<.1
1647	Tri-State Disposal Inc—Sheryl Germany	PO Box 627, Blue Island IL 60406	708-388-9910	R	9*	<.1
1648	Holman United—Katherine Holman United Van Lines Inc	20 E Commons Blvd, New Castle DE 19720	302-545-9708	S	9*	<.1
1649	Car-Tex Transport and Vacuum Service—Henry Howard	PO Box 387, Carthage TX 75633	903-693-6271	R	9*	<.1
1650	Colt Truck Lines Inc—R Yielding	PO Box 82729, Oklahoma City OK 73148	405-350-2015	R	9*	<.1
1651	Earl R Martin Inc—Earl Martin	PO Box 67, East Earl PA 17519	717-354-4061	R	9*	<.1
1652	Link Truck Service Inc—Robert Link	718 Industrial Dr, Sparta IL 62286	618-443-4848	R	9*	<.1
1653	Broyhill Transport Inc—Tom Foy	PO Box 100, Lenoir NC 28645	828-728-4332	S	9	<.1
1654	Amzac Enterprises Inc—Gregory Blazek	16225 S Broadway, Gardena CA 90248	310-329-7323	R	9*	<.1
1655	J Brach and Sons Trucking Inc—John Brach	1265 N 3/4 Rd, Loma CO 81524	970-858-9750	R	9*	<.1
1656	Systems II Transport Inc—William Economos	1515 Louis Ave, Elk Grove Village IL 60007	847-541-7766	R	9*	<.1
1657	Tri-R Trucking Inc—Pete Whitehead	13235 Golden State Rd, Valencia CA 91355	661-294-1430	R	9*	<.1
1658	3R Inc—William Rhodes	315 Bond Place Rm A, Greer SC 29650	864-848-1312	R	9*	<.1
1659	Keller Trucking Company Inc—Larry Keller	470 Old Skokie Rd, Park City IL 60085	847-336-0156	R	9*	<.1
1660	TCX Inc—Danny Hosea	5600 Universal Dr, Memphis TN 38118	901-368-5600	R	9*	<.1
1661	Ohio Eastern Express Inc—John Waldock	300 W Perkins Ave, Sandusky OH 44870	419-625-8433	R	9*	N/A
1662	Venture Logistics Inc—Doug Williams	1101 Harding Ct, Indianapolis IN 46217	317-787-1101	R	9	.1
1663	Tramcor Corp—Duane Braegger	908 N 2000 W, Farr West UT 84404	801-731-5522	R	9	.1
1664	GOE Enterprises Ltd—Gary Bertch	PO Box 754, Waterloo IA 50704	319-296-2987	R	9	.1
1665	Merchants Delivery Moving and Storage—Jim Eastman	1215 State St, Racine WI 53404	262-631-5680	R	9	.1
1666	Luxury Delivery Service Inc—Gary Tittle	1800 Moler Rd, Columbus OH 43207	614-221-9200	R	9	.1
1667	LLL Transport Inc—Mary Littrell	PO Box 327, Brookfield MO 64628	660-258-7661	S	9*	<.1
1668	Young Transportation Inc—Mike Schildman	PO Box 946, Jacksonville IL 62651	217-243-7077	R	9	.2
1669	AL Smith Trucking Inc—Dave Fullenkamp	8984 Murphy Rd, Versailles OH 45380	937-526-3651	R	9	.1
1670	Refrigerated Transport Inc—Mr Bishop	3300 E Park Row Dr, Arlington TX 76010	817-652-4710	R	9	.1
1671	RB Humphreys Inc—Brian Humphreys	PO Box 427, Westmoreland NY 13490		R	9	<.1
1672	Freshpoint—Brian Sturgeon	740 Massman Dr, Nashville TN 37210	615-256-8143	R	9	.2
1673	Madden Ltd—Mike Madden	2110 4th St, Boone IA 50036	515-432-8742	R	9	.1
1674	Seminole Express—Brian Young	32585 US Hwy 90, Seminole AL 36574	251-946-2072	R	9	.1
1675	Ancon Transportation Services Inc—Bret Hardin	2250 E Dominguez St, Carson CA 90810	310-522-5110	R	9	<.1
1676	Dennis Floyd Trucking Company Inc—Dennis Floyd	860 Irwin Ln, Santa Rosa CA 95401	707-544-1747	R	9	<.1
1677	TruckersB2B Inc—Stephen Russell Celadon Group Inc	9503 E 33rd St, Indianapolis IN 46235		S	9	N/A
1678	Pennfield Transport Co	711 Rohrerstown Rd, Lancaster PA 17603	717-295-8721	R	8	.1
1679	1st Express Inc—Monica Southward	227 Matzinger Rd, Toledo OH 43612	419-476-6881	R	8	.1
1680	Quality Logistics Inc—Christopher Levato	PMB 182 2131 Woodruff, Greenville SC 29607	864-879-7770	R	8	.1
1681	Viking Land Transportation Systems—Jill Fitzl	PO Box 247, New Ulm MN 56073	507-354-5055	R	8	.1
1682	R and M Leasing Corp—Ron Perry	PO Box 204, Auburn MA 01501	508-987-8533	R	8	.1
1683	Accelerated Courier Inc—Barry Pearse	515 Airpark Ctr Dr, Nashville TN 37217	615-367-0949	R	8	.1
1684	Super Cartage Company Inc—John Staggs	2300 S Throop St, Chicago IL 60608	312-733-1110	R	8	<.1
1685	Houser Transport Inc—Sam Houser	PO Box 148, Vale NC 28168	704-276-3500	R	8	.1
1686	Corney Transportation Inc—Bobby Corney	PO Box 385, Saint Pauls NC 28384	910-865-4045	R	8	.1
1687	Universe Company Inc—Robert Johnson	4909 S 33rd St, Omaha NE 68107	402-408-1014	R	8	.1
1688	Bulk Carrier Services Inc—Maxine Miller	3451 Losee Rd Ste B, North Las Vegas NV 89030	702-648-9055	R	8	<.1
1689	Werdco BC Inc—Werdna Conrad	4660 Flippin St, Las Vegas NV 89115	702-645-5848	R	8	<.1
1690	James A Smith Transportation—James R Smith	PO Box 1947, Cullman AL 35056	256-734-0511	R	8	.1
1691	Ron Burge Trucking Inc—Michael Burge	1876 W Britton Rd, Burbank OH 44214	330-624-5373	R	8	<.1
1692	Speedway Transportation—Dale Sostad	2321 E 4th Ave, Holdrege NE 68949	308-995-4491	R	8	.1
1693	Applegate Drayage Co—Michael Applegate	PO Box 981300, West Sacramento CA 95798	916-830-8320	R	8	.1
1694	Short Mountain Trucking Inc—RL Waalen	151 Silica Rd, Mooresburg TN 37811	423-921-9868	R	8	.1
1695	Don Hagan and Sons Inc—Don Hagan Jr	RR 3 Box 11A, Culbertson NE 69024	308-278-2614	R	8	<.1
1696	UTS Transportation Services—Jim Uthe	PO Box 277, Grimes IA 50111	515-986-3399	R	8	<.1
1697	Butler Refrigerated Meats—David Shapira	690 Perry Hwy, Harmony PA 16037	724-452-8936	S	8*	.1
1698	Daybreak Express Inc—Scott Fields	500 Ave P, Newark NJ 07105	973-589-5931	R	8*	.1
1699	Commercial Transport Inc—Robert White	PO Box 469, Belleville IL 62222	618-233-5260	R	8*	.1
1700	Barnes Transportation Services Inc—Keith Barnes	PO Box 7073, Wilson NC 27895	252-291-8282	R	8*	.1
1701	George Hildebrandt Inc—Alfred Bartolotta	412 Stone Mill Rd, Hudson NY 12534	518-851-3861	R	8*	.1
1702	Fundis Co—Edward Meyer	2180 Kleppe Ln, Sparks NV 89431	775-331-7200	R	8*	.1
1703	Steel and Machinery Transport—John Riley	PO Box 2310, Hammond IN 46323	219-845-5848	R	8*	.1
1704	CPS Express Inc—Bill Smerber	3401 Etiwanda Blvd Blg, Mira Loma CA 91752	951-685-1041	R	8*	.1
1705	OIX Inc—David Orscheln	1632 N Jackson Ave, Kansas City MO 64120	816-373-7595	R	8*	.1
1706	Rising Sun Express Inc—Herman McBride	PO Box 610, Jackson OH 45640	937-596-6167	R	8*	.1
1707	Total Express—Patricia Pappas	830 N Cassady Ave, Columbus OH 43219	614-253-5566	R	8*	.1
1708	BCJ Trucking Inc—Jerry Newman	PO Box 1908, Mount Airy NC 27030	336-320-3611	R	8*	.1
1709	Reed's Fuel and Trucking—Jason Reed	PO Box 1793, Springfield OR 97477	541-746-6535	R	8*	.1
1710	Curry Ice and Coal-Carlinville—Jim Curry	21149 Rte 4, Carlinville IL 62626	217-854-3101	R	8*	.1
1711	Quick Delivery Service Inc—Richard Young	PO Box 7361, Mobile AL 36670	251-471-5369	R	8*	.1
1712	Bedford Motor Service Inc—Edward Borkowski	2600 Internationale Pk, Woodridge IL 60517	630-739-6760	R	8*	.1
1713	Bell Trucking Company Inc—Eugene W Bell	PO Box 238, Shoemakersville PA 19555	610-562-5700	R	8*	.1
1714	Best Way Transportation Inc—Brett Witt	PO Box 249, Palmer TX 75152	972-845-3222	R	8*	.1
1715	McClatchy Brothers Inc—Richard Minnix	PO Box 4126, Midland TX 79704	432-694-9691	R	8*	.1
1716	WC Fore Trucking Inc—Wallace C Fore	14270 Cresote Rd, Gulfport MS 39503	228-863-1314	R	8*	.1
1717	E Mac Transportation Company Inc—Edward MacDonald	342 Compass Cir Ste D4, North Kingstown RI 02852	401-667-7440	R	8*	.1
1718	Ned Bard and Son Co—Robert Bard	PO Box 6, Leola PA 17540	717-656-2931	R	8*	.1
1719	Polman Transfer Inc—Nick Polman	PO Box 470, Wadena MN 56482	218-631-1753	R	8*	.1
1720	TS Boyd Grain Inc—Thomas Boyd	1957 E 200 N, Washington IN 47501	812-254-5599	R	8*	.1
1721	DD and S Express Inc—Richard Seleski	6600 Frankford Ave, Baltimore MD 21206	410-488-9200	R	8*	.1
1722	Valley Bulk Inc—Jeff Golson	17649 Turner Rd, Victorville CA 92394	760-951-6963	R	8*	.1
1723	Bonus Transportation Inc—William Boughan	PO Box 169, Sorrento FL 32776	352-735-0035	R	8*	.1
1724	Kuhnle Brothers Inc—Kim Taylor-Kuhnle	PO Box 375, Newbury OH 44065	440-564-7168	R	8*	.1
1725	Total Warehousing Inc—Vincent Gulisano	4411 W Roosevelt St, Phoenix AZ 85043	602-682-1800	R	8*	.1
1726	Northwest Dairy Forwarding Co—Shawn Nelson	1305 159th Ave NE, Ham Lake MN 55304	763-434-6654	R	8*	.1
1727	B and J Trucking Service Inc—Jimmy Fraley	PO Box 199, Borden IN 47106		R	8*	.1
1728	Buesing Bulk Transport Inc—Bradley Vedem	1250 Crest View Dr St, Hudson WI 54016	715-386-6264	R	8*	.1
1729	C and A Transportation Inc—Aubrey Mitchusson	2360 Spires Dr, Macon GA 31216	478-784-8652	R	8*	.1
1730	Duane Livingston Trucking—Duane Livingston	169 Blankenship Rd, Texarkana TX 75501	903-832-5373	R	8*	.1
1731	F and S Distributing Inc—Reid Wicker	4444 E 26th St, Los Angeles CA 90058	323-269-0525	R	8*	.1
1732	Lengner and Sons Produce Express—Laurence Lengner	2565 Buna St Bldg 90, Oakland CA 94607	510-625-1900	R	8*	.1
1733	PE Kramme Inc—Karl Kramme	PO Box 937, Monroeville NJ 08343	856-358-8151	R	8*	.1

Rank	Company Name—Executive Officer	Address, City, State, Zip	Phone	Type	Fin	Empls
1734	Smith Trucking Inc—Rodney Smith	PO Box 600, Bowman SC 29018	803-829-2552	R	8*	.1
1735	Valley Express Inc—Merle Jegtvig	3911 37th Ave SW, Fargo ND 58104	701-281-0521	R	8*	.1
1736	Vance Trucking Company Inc—Sam Burrows	PO Box 1119, Henderson NC 27536	252-438-6151	R	8*	.1
1737	William Thomas Trucking Inc—Steve Myers	PO Box 10238, Albuquerque NM 87184	505-344-4906	R	8*	.1
1738	Lisa Express Inc—Lisa Mattern-Stokes	13 S Industrial Park R, Milton PA 17847	570-742-7668	R	8*	.1
1739	Action Express Inc—Nick Fiore	6023 S Howell Ave, Milwaukee WI 53207	414-461-3300	R	8*	.1
1740	Carman Inc—Greg Carman	PO Box 6424, Fort Smith AR 72906	479-646-8486	R	8*	.1
1741	East River Lumber and Grain—Kent Mauck	PO Box 128, Mobridge SD 57601	605-845-7257	R	8*	.1
1742	Grand Island Contract Carriers	PO Box 2078, Grand Island NE 68802		S	8*	.1
1743	Rapid Armored Corp—Mitchell Wolf	254 Scholes St, Brooklyn NY 11237	718-366-8103	R	8*	.1
1744	Reliable Liquid Transport—Cate Summers	1041 College Ave, Santa Rosa CA 95404	707-579-2890	R	8*	.1
1745	Anderson Truck Line Inc—Jake Wood	PO Box 1196, Lenoir NC 28645	828-728-9236	•	R	8*	.1
1746	Bob's Pickup and Delivery Inc—Raymond Bell	209 14th St SE, Sidney MT 59270	406-433-1733	S	8*	.1
	Old Dominion Freight Line Inc					
1747	Responsive Trucking Inc—William Moccio Jr	PO Box 472, Feeding Hills MA 01030	413-789-1263	R	8*	.1
1748	Accela—Daniel Spreng	300 W Franklin St, Hagerstown MD 21740	301-739-6107	R	8*	.1
1749	Apollo Motor Express Inc—Michael Beckwith	221 Cherry St, Shrewsbury MA 01545	508-842-5100	R	8*	.1
1750	Behnke Inc—Mark Behnke	600 Helmer Rd N, Battle Creek MI 49015	269-962-4231	R	8*	.1
1751	D and A Truck Line Inc—Florian Dittrich	PO Box 564, New Ulm MN 56073	507-354-6086	R	8*	.1
1752	Dale Meyer Trucking Co—Linda Meyer	PO Box 3548, Odessa TX 79760	432-366-3661	R	8*	.1
1753	Heding Truck Service Inc—Harry Heding	PO Box 97, Union Center WI 53962	608-462-8441	R	8*	.1
1754	JA Frate Inc—Joseph Alger	PO Box 497, Crystal Lake IL 60039	815-459-0839	R	8*	.1
1755	Jacobson Transport Inc—Wayne Viessman	PO Box 156, Wahpeton ND 58074	701-642-4770	R	8*	.1
1756	Powerline Freight Systems—James Powers	PO Box 417, Chandler IN 47610	812-925-3431	R	8*	.1
1757	Sun Belt Transportation Inc—John Cumberworth	8100 E 14th St, Brownsville TX 78521	956-831-4282	R	8*	.1
1758	William B Altman Inc—William Altman	2916 Old Rt 422 E, Fenelton PA 16034	724-282-4063	R	8*	.1
1759	Larry's Cartage Company Inc—Larry Denton	101 Burr Ridge Pkwy St, Burr Ridge IL 60527	630-920-0772	R	8	<.1
1760	Nelson Trucking Company Inc—Peter Whitehead	PO Box 80323, Seattle WA 98108	206-723-3000	R	8*	<.1
1761	Charles E Crowe and Son Inc—Charles Crowe	2388 N Market St, Flizabethtown PA 17022	717-367-8535	R	8*	<.1
1762	Jesse Baro Inc—Stephen Baro	157 Quarry Rd, Douglassville PA 19518	610 323-8783	R	8*	<.1
1763	A and B Freight Line Inc—Frederick Blume	PO Box 6026, Rockford IL 61125	815-874-4700	R	8*	<.1
1764	Garvey Transport Inc—Kathy Perkins	2 Water St, Holbrook MA 02343	781-767-1500	R	8*	<.1
1765	Howes and Howes Trucking Inc—Richard Howes	5301 N M 37, Mesick MI 49668	231-885-1630	R	8*	<.1
1766	Larry Oswalt Trucking Inc—Larry Oswalt	2200 S Campbell Creek, Sand Springs OK 74063	918-363-8072	R	8*	<.1
1767	Pradon Construction and Trucking—Donald Pradon	2100 W 83rd Rd, Odessa TX 79764	432-362-4186	R	8*	<.1
1768	Teresi Trucking Inc—John Teresi	PO Box 1270, Lodi CA 95241	209-368-2472	R	8*	<.1
1769	Tussey Trucking Inc—Gary Tussey	PO Box 69, Saint Francisville IL 62460	618-943-3249	R	8*	<.1
1770	Ausmus Corp—James Crane	PO Box 633, Williamsville NY 14231	716-876-7373	R	8*	<.1
1771	Quality Transport Inc—Al Schorno	45051 Industrial Dr, Fremont CA 94538	510-657-4267	R	8*	<.1
1772	Bestway Transport Co—Richard Myers	PO Box 195, Plymouth OH 44865	419-687-2000	R	8*	<.1
1773	Brites Cartage Ltd—Donna Fox	17001 S State St, South Holland IL 60473	708-333-8600	R	8*	<.1
1774	Goeman Trucking Ltd—Gary Goeman	PO Box 667, Slinger WI 53086	262-644-4428	R	8*	<.1
1775	Ray Bellew and Sons Inc—Raymond Bellew	7810 Almeda Genoa Rd, Houston TX 77075	713-991-0390	R	8*	<.1
1776	Silk Road Transport Inc—Jane Karlsten	8781 State Rte 36, Arkport NY 14807	607-295-7406	R	8*	<.1
1777	Frank's Vacuum Truck Service—Frank Jurek	4500 Royal Ave, Niagara Falls NY 14303	716-284-2132	R	8*	<.1
1778	Louis P Cote Inc—John Cote	42 Cote Ave, Goffstown NH 03045	603-623-1533	R	8*	<.1
1779	BHM Express Inc—Todd Vickers	4915 Second Ave S, Birmingham AL 35222	205-591-9400	R	8*	<.1
1780	Dan Barclay Inc—Daniel Barclay	12 Cork Hill Rd, Franklin NJ 07416	973-361-4000	R	8*	<.1
1781	Holman Distribution Center of OR—Leonard Clark	2300 SE Beta St, Portland OR 97222	503-652-1912	R	8*	<.1
1782	Lucia Specialized Hauling Inc—Rick Lucia	689 Mariaville Rd, Schenectady NY 12306	518-382-0353	R	8*	<.1
1783	Nolan H Brunson Inc—Hal Brunson	PO Box 2390, Hobbs NM 88241	505-393-6169	R	8*	<.1
1784	Inovative Transport System—Perry Hanson	8401 54th Ave N, New Hope MN 55428	612-521-7357	R	8*	<.1
1785	Albert Shaffer Trucking Inc—Larry Shaffer	PO Box 251, Masontown WV 26542	304-864-5244	R	8*	<.1
1786	Goolsby Trucking Company Inc—Lee Goolsby Jr	104 Gap Dr, New Albany MS 38652		R	8*	<.1
1787	Hames Trucking Inc—John James	3546 Redwine Rd, Atlanta GA 30344	404-344-3960	R	8*	<.1
1788	Richardson Trucking Inc—Ron Richardson	PO Box 1690, Mills WY 82644	307-265-9012	R	8*	<.1
1789	Swanson Trucking Inc—Richard Swanson	PO Box 68, Ohio IL 61349	815-376-2792	R	8*	<.1
1790	Tanis Trucking Co—David Tanis	2685 Port Sheldon St, Jenison MI 49428	616-669-2490	R	8*	<.1
1791	Wal-Zon Transfer Inc—Keith Ilaug	PO Box 99, Newport MN 55055	651-738-9030	R	8*	<.1
1792	CTX-Lambie—Donald Sheeler	1060 Monroe St, Hoboken NJ 07030	201-798-8555	R	8	<.1
1793	Aetna Freight Lines Inc—Jeff Kollar	PO Box 350, Warren OH 44482	330-369-5201	S	8*	<.1
	Transport Investments Inc					
1794	Astro Moving and Storage Co—Joseph Verderber Sr	30 Jefferson Ave, Saint James NY 11780	631-584-7700	R	8*	<.1
1795	Swift Air Delivery Inc—Robert Forrest	PO Box 7202, Charlottesville VA 22906	434-985-7113	R	8*	<.1
1796	Transcon Shipping Specialists—John Mullane	234 Rider Ave, Bronx NY 10451	718-585-1600	R	8*	<.1
1797	Pierce Enterprises—Edward Pierce	11130 State Rte 31, Clyde NY 14433	315-923-5830	R	8*	<.1
1798	TGS Transportation Inc—Timothy Schneider	PO Box 2668, Fresno CA 93745	559-486-1100	R	8*	<.1
1799	Admiral Moving and Storage Inc—Robert Milkie	PO Box 1134, South Windsor CT 06074	860-528-4421	R	8*	<.1
1800	A and A Transfer and Storage Inc—Eulice Shelley	113 Hollywood Blvd NW, Fort Walton Beach FL 32548	850-244-7661	R	8	<.1
1801	Foundry Service Corp—Matthew W Milam	PO Box 2119, Vineland NJ 08362	856-692-3100	R	8	.1
1802	Bagshaw Trucking Inc—Beverly Bagshaw	13110 Blue Lick Rd, Memphis IN 47143	812-294-4060	R	8	.1
1803	Pioneer Transportation Ltd—Grant Peterson	N 2130 State Hwy 17, Merrill WI 54452	715-536-9789	R	8	.1
1804	All-Pro Transport Company Inc—Richard Fisher	PO Box 3078, Ashtabula OH 44005	440-998-5565	R	8	.1
1805	Clancy Moving Systems Inc—John Clancy	PO Box 291, Patterson NY 12563	845-878-3300	R	8	<.1
1806	Central Moving Systems Inc—Brian Coriell	PO Box 6517, Bridgewater NJ 08807	732-764-0405	R	8	<.1
1807	Artex Inc—John Jacobs	8712 Jericho City Dr, Landover MD 20785	301-350-5500	R	8	.1
1808	G and H Motor Freight Lines Inc—Tom Brown	PO Box 239, Greenfield IA 50849	641-343-7980	R	8	.1
1809	Art Pape Transfer Inc—Loras Pape	1080 E 12th St, Dubuque IA 52001	563-588-1435	R	8	<.1
1810	Indian Valley Bulk Carriers Inc—Paul Yerk Jr	PO Box 200, Tylersport PA 18971	215-257-5151	R	8	.1
1811	US Central Express Inc—Steven Hoke	23232 Hwy 6, Gretna NE 68028	402-332-0991	R	8	.1
1812	Terpening Trucking Company Inc—Dick Terpening	115 Farrell Rd, Syracuse NY 13209	315-451-8661	R	8	<.1
1813	Snoozie Shavings Inc—Dwayne Reichlin	PO Box 14, Crescent City CA 95531	707-464-6186	R	8	.1
1814	Lewiston Trucking Company Inc—Richard Washuta	PO Box 209, Model City NY 14107	716-754-4111	R	8	<.1
1815	Sagara Trucking Inc—Shuny Sagara	PO Box 1345, Woodland CA 95776	530-662-9611	R	8	N/A
1816	L and B Cartage Inc—Tony Lander	966 Bridgeview S, Saginaw MI 48604	989-759-5544	R	8	.1
1817	Mount Pleasant Transfer Inc—Steve Wade	PO Box 467, Mount Pleasant TN 38474	931-379-5521	R	8	.1
1818	Kruepke Trucking Inc—Kenneth Kruepke	2881 County Rd P, Jackson WI 53037	262-677-3155	R	8	.1
1819	P Judge and Sons Inc—Patrick Wynne	201A Export St, Newark NJ 07114	973-491-0600	R	8	.1
1820	Trans Technical Logistics Inc—Joseph Nachtrab	18487 N Dixie Hwy, Bowling Green OH 43402	419-352-3500	R	8	.1
1821	Bob Hubbard Horse Transportation—Tom Hubbard	3730 S Riverside Ave, Colton CA 92324	909-369-3770	R	8	<.1

Note: An asterisk (*) indicates an estimated financial figure. The company type code used is as follows: R = Private, P = Public, S = Private Subsidiary, B = Public Subsidiary, D = Division, J = Joint Venture, I = Investment Fund.

COMPANY RANKINGS BY SALES WITHIN 4-DIGIT SIC

Rank	Company Name—Executive Officer	Address, City, State, Zip	Phone	Type	Fin	Empls
1822	Novak Trucking Service LLC—John Novak	PO Box 67, Laona WI 54541	715-674-4211	R	7	.1
1823	Smith and Waters Inc—Danny Riddle	PO Box 570, Ware Shoals SC 29692	864-456-7421	R	7	.1
1824	Louisiana Tank Inc—Steven Jordan	PO Box 1863, Lake Charles LA 70602	337-436-1000	R	7	N/A
1825	Dilts Trucking Inc—Ellen Dilts	22926 River Rd N, Crescent IA 51526	712-545-3228	R	7	.1
1826	Watkins and Son Inc—Leon Watkins	1021 E 17th St, Chattanooga TN 37408	423-265-8500	R	7	.1
1827	Dakota Carriers Inc—Bridget Fowlds	PO Box 84907, Sioux Falls SD 57118	605-338-0002	R	7	<.1
1828	A-1 Freeman—James Freeman	2242 Manana Rd, Dallas TX 75220	972-556-1777	R	7	<.1
1829	Diamond Express Inc—Tom Brown	700 39th St N, Birmingham AL 35222	205-591-0661	R	7	<.1
1830	Clinch Mountain Transport/CMT—Elmer Kincaid	PO Box 99, Thorn Hill TN 37881	865-767-3610	R	7	.1
1831	TBI Inc—Randy Thompson	2209 E 39th St N Ste 1, Sioux Falls SD 57104	605-334-4187	R	7	<.1
1832	Wright Transportation Inc—Pat Wright	2300 Ave I, Mobile AL 36615	251-432-6390	R	7	.1
1833	Brooks Courier Service Inc—Daniel Conaty	PO Box 9560, Wilmington DE 19809	302-762-4661	R	7*	.1
1834	James Gath Trucking Inc—James Gath	4880 S Huron Rd, Standish MI 48658	989-846-9224	R	7*	.1
1835	RL Leek Industries Inc—Ronald L Leek	2210 Harrison Ave, Rockford IL 61104	815-398-1060	R	7*	.1
1836	Wayne Smith Trucking Inc—Wayne Smith	PO Box 356, Morrilton AR 72110	501-354-0995	R	7*	.1
1837	Direct Lines Inc—Steve Wendling	PO Box 763, Effingham IL 62401	217-857-6444	R	7*	.1
1838	East-West Express Inc—Richard Cangemi	PO Box 755, Villa Rica GA 30180	770-459-1159	R	7*	.1
1839	M Bar D Rail Car Tech Inc	1000 Holland Ave, Crete IL 60417	708-672-2300	R	7*	.1
1840	Wayne W Sell Corp—John W Sell	236 Winfield Rd, Sarver PA 16055	724-352-9441	R	7*	.1
1841	Gotoh Distribution Service—Tim Wells	703 Foster Ave, Bensenville IL 60106	630-451-2080	R	7*	.1
1842	M and M Transport Inc—Steve Blankenship	170 St Hwy 508, Chehalis WA 98532	360-262-9383	R	7*	.1
1843	Andrews Van Lines Inc—Clayton Andrews	PO Box 1609, Norfolk NE 68702	402-371-5440	R	7*	.1
1844	Titan Freight Systems Inc—Keith Wilson	PO Box 22005, Milwaukie OR 97269	503-652-0010	R	7*	.1
1845	Burgess Trucking Company Inc—Cecilia Burgess	PO Box 96, Sedley VA 23878	757-653-9461	R	7*	.1
1846	Old South Service Inc—James Raines	PO Box 167, Pleasant View TN 37146	615-746-3683	R	7*	.1
1847	Rye Gentry Trucking Inc—Steven Gentry	6134 W Jefferson Ave, Detroit MI 48209	313-843-2588	R	7*	.1
1848	Silica Transport Inc—Jack Knight	PO Box 9, Guion AR 72540	870-346-5811	R	7*	.1
1849	Weinrich Truck Line Inc—Donna Weinrich-Lucht	PO Box 1022, Hinton IA 51024	712-947-4887	R	7*	.1
1850	Hutt Trucking Company Inc—Jim Hutt	1362 Lincoln Ave, Holland MI 49423	616-928-2307	R	7*	.1
1851	McCracken Motor Freight Inc—Curt McCracken	PO Box 10304, Portland OR 97296	503-223-7304	R	7*	.1
1852	Nick's Transport Inc—Dwight Wilmoth	PO Box 391, Mount Vernon MO 65712		R	7*	.1
1853	Hansen Trucking—Bruce Hansen	96 Curtis St, Jerseyville IL 62052	618-498-2906	R	7*	.1
1854	Direct Transport Ltd—Jeff Brand	460 7th Ave NE, West Fargo ND 58078	701-282-7066	R	7*	.1
1855	Piqua Transfer and Storage Co—John Laughman	PO Box 823, Piqua OH 45356	937-773-3743	R	7*	.1
1856	Professional Services Transportation—Denny Price	PO Box 656, Moberly MO 65270	660-277-4624	R	7*	.1
1857	Roadmaster Transportation Inc—Ed Weeks	1640 Stone Ridge Dr, Stone Mountain GA 30083	770-934-8555	R	7*	.1
1858	Seegers Truck Line Inc—Bryce Seegers	PO Box 392, Denver IA 50622	319-984-5163	R	7*	.1
1859	Interstate Intermodal Inc—Les Peters	501 New County Rd, Secaucus NJ 07094	201-866-8000	R	7*	.1
1860	Fruitt Trucking—Jim Fruitt	32341 Old Hwy 34, Tangent OR 97389	541-928-1131	R	7*	.1
1861	R and D Transport Inc—Dan Hockaday	PO Box 34238, Clermont IN 46234	317-291-2600	R	7*	.1
1862	Hatfield Enterprizes Inc—James Hatfield	16715 E Euclid Ave, Spokane Valley WA 99216	509-927-8357	R	7*	.1
1863	Terminal Transport Inc—Brent Coatney	2982 Cleviand Ave N, Saint Paul MN 55113	651-407-6200	R	7*	.1
1864	Fort Edward Express Company Inc—Paul Hillman	PO Box 304, Fort Edward NY 12828	518-792-6571	R	7*	.1
1865	G and RG Inc—Gerald Griggs	800 S Meadow, Odessa TX 79761	432-335-9575	R	7*	.1
1866	AMST Inc—Philip Mulder	1936 Transport Ln, Holland MI 49423	616-392-5929	R	7*	.1
1867	Clark Farms Trucking Inc—Stephen Clark	12940 Pittsburg Rd, Marion IL 62959	618-997-3889	R	7*	.1
1868	JME of Monticello Inc—Jay Morrell	1401 Fallon Ave, Monticello MN 55362	763-295-3122	R	7*	.1
1869	FMC Transport—David Montgomery	PO Box 218, Willow Springs MO 65793	417-469-2777	R	7*	.1
1870	Norbet Trucking Corporation Inc—Tony Campo	400 Metuchen Rd, South Plainfield NJ 07080	908-791-9103	R	7*	.1
1871	Skagit Transportation Inc—Tim Sullivan	PO Box 400, Mount Vernon WA 98273	360-424-4214	R	7*	.1
1872	JA Trucking Inc—Arthur Francia	212 Country Ln, West Newton PA 15089	724-872-0801	R	7*	.1
1873	Becker Transportation Inc—Brian Becker	1501 S Burlington Ave, Hastings NE 68901	402-461-4454	R	7*	.1
1874	Birchwood Transport Inc—Charles Vignieri / Kenosha Beef International Ltd	PO Box 639, Kenosha WI 53141	262-859-3018	S	7*	.1
1875	Birkmire Trucking Co—Tim Birkmire	PO Box 8768, Erie PA 16505	814-833-5855	R	7*	.1
1876	Dependon Inc—John Canela	2005 Kenosha Rd, Zion IL 60099	847-731-2345	R	7*	.1
1877	Gregory Logistics Inc—Larry Gregory	PO Box 308, Poplar Bluff MO 63902	573-785-1088	R	7*	.1
1878	Holland Transfer Co—Jeff Harvey	PO Box 552, Statesville NC 28687	704-873-4374	R	7*	.1
1879	K Truck Lines Inc—Fred Knox	1565 W Hunter Ferrell, Grand Prairie TX 75050	972-263-1634	R	7*	.1
1880	Lewis Transport Inc—Pam Scott	PO Box 1029, Columbia KY 42728	270-384-4132	R	7*	.1
1881	Mayer Truck Line Inc—Ron Mayer	1207 S Riverside Dr, Jamestown ND 58402	701-252-6071	R	7*	.1
1882	Montgomery Trucking Co—Phillip Fain	PO Box 21, Wellston OH 45692	740-384-2138	R	7*	.1
1883	Page ETC Inc—Debra Titus	PO Box 290, Weedsport NY 13166	315-834-6681	R	7*	.1
1884	Poteat Motor Lines Inc—Billy Poteat	PO Box 2030, Hickory NC 28603	828-322-4597	R	7*	.1
1885	Refrigerated Food Express Inc—James L Morse	57 Littlefield St, Avon MA 02322	508-587-4600	R	7*	.1
1886	Rinehart's Trucking Corp—Jack Harris	133 Bell Rd, Branson MO 65616	417-334-2044	R	7*	.1
1887	Sunbird Transport Inc—Timothy McCarthy	295 Union St, East Walpole MA 02032	508-668-0375	R	7*	.1
1888	US Art Company Inc—Mark Lank	66 Pacella Park Dr, Randolph MA 02368	781-986-6500	R	7*	.1
1889	Northern Neck Transfer Inc—William Edwards	12284 State Rd, King George VA 22485	540-775-2121	R	7*	<.1
1890	Marine Container Services Inc—Joseph Noonan	414 Ave P, Newark NJ 07105	973-624-5200	R	7*	<.1
1891	Richardson Trucking Inc—Bill Stellmon	PO Box 933, Lewiston ID 83501	208-743-6857	R	7	<.1
1892	Levinge Transportation LLC—Richard Levinge	17463 I-45 N, Willis TX 77318	936-344-2448	R	7*	<.1
1893	A and M Cartage of Tinley Park—August Badali	PO Box 727, Tinley Park IL 60477	815-469-9005	R	7*	<.1
1894	Baumgartner Trucking Inc—Dennis Baumgartner	PO Box 2285, La Crosse WI 54602	507-895-8490	R	7	<.1
1895	Byron L Lang Inc—Roger Lang	PO Box 301, Jackson MO 63755	573-243-5266	R	7*	<.1
1896	Hardebeck Trucking—Tim Hardebeck	PO Box 432, Monticello IN 47960	574-583-3030	R	7*	<.1
1897	Jimmy T Wood Inc—James Wood	382 Klinke Ave, Memphis TN 38127	901-358-9599	R	7*	<.1
1898	K and J Trucking Inc—Sharon Koch	PO Box 1859, Sioux Falls SD 57104	605-332-5531	R	7*	<.1
1899	Texas Auto Carriers Inc—Ford Wagner	5765 Bicentennial St, San Antonio TX 78219	210-666-4444	R	7*	<.1
1900	R Conley Inc—Theodore Gaczynski	6891 Seneca St, Elma NY 14059	716-652-0430	R	7*	<.1
1901	All Chemical Transport Corp—Steven Quadrel	PO Box 2083, Lakewood NJ 08701	732-730-2110	R	7*	<.1
1902	Caine Transfer Inc—Chester Caine Jr	PO Box 376, Lowell WI 53557	920-927-3838	R	7	<.1
1903	Clark Transportation Inc—Larry Clark	PO Box 30109, Columbia MO 65205	573-445-6808	R	7*	<.1
1904	Gangloff Industries Inc—Randy Ferguson	PO Box 28, Logansport IN 46947	574-722-3888	R	7*	<.1
1905	HFCS Transport Co—Hans Schaupp	2100 Riverside Dr Ste, Green Bay WI 54301	920-431-3500	R	7*	<.1
1906	HRS Transport Inc—Howard Sodano	191 Strykers Rd, Phillipsburg NJ 08865	908-387-9566	R	7*	<.1
1907	James Reynolds Transport Inc—James Reynolds	PO Box 834, Berwick PA 18603	570-752-3500	R	7*	<.1
1908	Randolph Trucking Inc—Margie Randolph	3502 E Governor John S, Knoxville TN 37914	865-523-4241	R	7*	<.1
1909	Sojourner Trucking Inc—Charlie Sojourner	26113 Hwy 27, Crystal Springs MS 39059		R	7*	<.1
1910	Steve Kent Trucking Inc—Steve Kent	PO Box 148, Lottie LA 70756	225-637-2304	R	7*	<.1

Rank	Company Name—*Executive Officer*	Address, City, State, Zip	Phone	Type	Fin	Empls
1911	TG Stegall Trucking Company Inc—*Jeff Stegall*	PO Box 98, Matthews NC 28106	704-536-1122	R	7*	<.1
1912	WC Trucking Inc—*Harry C Warner*	2480 S Clare Ave, Clare MI 48617	989-386-4350	R	7*	<.1
1913	Bobby Fryar Trucking Company Inc—*Bobby Fryar*	1017 E 38th St, Chattanooga TN 37407	423-867-9160	R	7	<.1
1914	Price Trucking Inc FT Silfies Inc	PO Box 1057, Aberdeen MD 21001	410-272-3010	S	7*	<.1
1915	Laughlin Trucking Inc—*Larry Cubes*	PO Box 399, Carlton OR 97111	503-852-7186	R	7*	<.1
1916	P and D Curtis Enterprises Inc—*Phillip Curtis*	61276 Fox Run Rd, Montrose CO 81401	970-323-0100	R	7*	<.1
1917	Adriaansen Trucking Inc—*Kevin Adriaansen*	4627 Smith Rd, Marion NY 14505		R	7*	<.1
1918	A Santini Storage Company Inc—*Charles Sands*	One Steel Ct, Roseland NJ 07068	973-228-7211	R	7*	<.1
1919	Bart Larsen Trucking Inc—*Bart Larsen*	PO Box 228, Roberts ID 83444	208-228-2228	R	7*	<.1
1920	V Van Dyke Inc—*Cliff Bates*	150 S River St, Seattle WA 98108	206-762-2222	R	7*	<.1
1921	Spartan Warehouse and Distribution—*Ed Harmon*	4140 Lockbourne Rd, Columbus OH 43207	614-497-1777	R	7*	<.1
1922	Ristow Trucking Inc—*James Ristow*	PO Box 67, Hammond WI 54015	715-247-2626	R	7*	<.1
1923	EZE Trucking Inc—*Kirk Jensen*	2584 N Locust Ave, Rialto CA 92377	909-803-5000	R	7*	<.1
1924	Terrill Transportation Inc—*Kevin Terrill*	PO Box 1285, Lodi CA 95241	209-239-2145	R	7*	<.1
1925	Trucking Unlimited—*Bob Murray*	PO Box 2309, Santa Fe Springs CA 90670	562-946-5558	R	7*	<.1
1926	Apollo Van Lines Inc—*Brad Johnson*	10384 Dow Gil Rd, Ashland VA 23005	804-798-1556	R	7*	<.1
1927	Bed Rock Inc—*Bill Hay*	PO Box 366, Point Arena CA 95468	707-882-2323	R	7*	<.1
1928	Bryan and Bryan—*Billy Bryan*	PO Box 625, Henderson TX 75653	903-657-2391	R	7*	<.1
1929	Baton Rouge Tankwash—*Roger Dies*	4425 Plank Rd, Baton Rouge LA 70805	225-357-3035	R	7*	<.1
1930	CTC Inc—*Edward J Sheehan Jr*	100 CTC Dr, Johnstown PA 15904	814-269-2840	R	7*	<.1
1931	Ronnie Sharp Trucking Inc—*Ronnie Sharp*	4 Dixie Park Rd, Rome GA 30165	706-232-9987	R	7*	<.1
1932	WD Kerr and Sons Inc—*W Dennis Kerr*	21270 Rt 19, Cranberry Township PA 16066	724-452-5300	R	7*	<.1
1933	Bill and George Gill Trucking Inc—*George Gill*	221 Druid Hills Dr, Dickson TN 37055	615-446-7109	R	7*	<.1
1934	Hazel Trucking Company Inc—*Michael Gilbert*	PO Box 7322, Macon GA 31209	478-743-2111	R	7*	<.1
1935	RW Sanders Trucking Inc—*Richard Sanders*	PO Box 345, Bellevue OH 44811	419-483-2684	R	7*	<.1
1936	Swanner Transfer and Storage Co—*Joseph Stough*	PO Box 9127, Montgomery AL 36108	334-264-2273	R	7*	<.1
1937	Caprioni Sewerage Service Inc—*Gina Caprioni*	188 Head of River Rd, Woodbine NJ 08270	609-861-2472	R	7*	<.1
1938	Globe Storage and Moving Co—*Vincent Cibrano*	36 Bleecker St, New York NY 10012	212-925-3555	R	7*	<.1
1939	Majestic Marine Inc—*W Grunow*	N 1599 Maple Ridge Rd, Lake Geneva WI 53147	262-248-6128	R	7*	<.1
1940	Pioneer Freight Systems Inc—*Richard Kitchell*	PO Box 5, Whippany NJ 07981	973-887-0543	R	7*	<.1
1941	Steel Transport Inc—*Jeffrey Fine*	8055 Highland Pointe P, Macedonia OH 44056	330-908-2780	R	7*	<.1
1942	Syracuse Relocation Services—*Sean Cleland*	6255 E Taft Rd, North Syracuse NY 13212	315-458-9080	R	7*	<.1
1943	M and W Transportation Company Inc—*Mike McFarlin*	PO Box 100225, Nashville TN 37224	615-256-5755	R	7	.1
1944	DJ Franzen Inc—*Dennis Franzen*	PO Box 218, Altoona IA 50009	515-265-7417	R	7	.1
1945	Jessup Transportation Inc—*Robin Jessup*	641 Old Gilroy St, Gilroy CA 95020	408-848-3390	R	7	.1
1946	Uni-Bulk Inc—*Dan Kemp*	4404 Euclid Ave, East Chicago IN 46312	219-392-0062	R	7	<.1
1947	Harvey and Company Inc—*Olen Harvey*	565 Ratta Rd, Chazy NY 12921	518-846-8130	R	7	.1
1948	Haddad International Transport—*Jack Haddad*	5000 Wyoming St Ste 11, Dearborn MI 48126	313-846-4560	R	7	.1
1949	NTA Ltd—*Eugene Arbuthnot*	PO Box 831, Huron SD 57350	605-352-8404	R	7	.1
1950	McGuire Transportation Inc—*Phil McGuire*	PO Box 184, Belton TX 76513	254-791-1003	R	7	.1
1951	H and S Enterprises Inc—*Robert Drayer*	199 Strykers Rd, Phillipsburg NJ 08865	908-454-9196	R	7	<.1
1952	Olsen and Fielding Moving Services—*Reid Olsen*	6350 Sky Creek Dr, Sacramento CA 95828	916-383-8800	R	7	N/A
1953	French Trucking Inc—*Vickie French*	PO Box 958, Lexington TN 38351	731-968-5391	R	7	<.1
1954	Mobile Air Transport Inc—*John J Ingemie*	PO Box 219, Latham NY 12110	518-783-5111	R	7	<.1
1955	Heavy Duty Trux Ltd—*Vicki Busch*	PO Box 560, Bloomfield MO 63825	573-568-4576	R	7	.1
1956	Milk Transport Inc—*Blaine Hovis*	PO Box 550, Grove City PA 16127	724-458-8280	R	7	.1
1957	Superior Truck Lines—*Roger Johnson*	PO Box 538, Newark NY 14513	315-597-5102	R	7	.1
1958	Sunbelt Crane Construction and Hauling—*Vic Granowicz*	PO Box 310007, Tampa FL 33680	813-623-1111	R	7	<.1
1959	Republic Waste Services—*Pete Gutwein*	2800 Erie S St, Massillon OH 44646	330-830-9050	R	7*	N/A
1960	Willies Grain Inc—*Mike Willits*	PO Box 100, Lucerne CO 80646	970-352-1243	R	6	<.1
1961	Bowlus Trucking Company Inc—*Mitchell Lance*	PO BOX 746, Fremont OH 43420	419-332-2607	R	6	<.1
1962	Hanefeld Brothers Inc—*David Hanefeld*	N 8073 State Rd 26, Burnett WI 53922	920-689-2485	R	6	.1
1963	Al Thompson Trucking Inc—*Alvin Thompson*	PO Box 1050, Chester SC 29706		R	6	.1
1964	Pehler and Sons Inc—*Francis Pehler*	1740 E Blaschko Ave, Arcadia WI 54612	608-323-3520	R	6	<.1
1965	Timmerman Starlite Trucking—*Mark Timmerman*	3955 Starlite Dr, Ceres CA 95307	209-538-1706	R	6	.1
1966	Leicht Transfer and Storage Co—*Bob Johnson*	PO Box 2447, Green Bay WI 54306	920-432-8632	R	6	<.1
1967	Thompson Trucking Company Inc—*David Hand*	PO BOx 63385, Charleston SC 29419	843-572-0088	R	6	<.1
1968	Commodore Transport LLC—*John Quinn*	6601 N Tidewater Rd, Mooresville IN 46158	317-831-6428	R	6	<.1
1969	Ed Rocha Livestock Transportation—*Henry Dirksen*	PO Box 40, Ceres CA 95307	209-554-4113	R	6	.1
1970	Best Transportation Inc—*Tom Heingartner*	263 Distribution St, Newark NJ 07114	973-465-5310	R	6	<.1
1971	Lake State Transport Inc—*Michael Neutzling*	PO Box 944, Saint Cloud MN 56302	320-253-2261	R	6	.1
1972	Keenan Transit Co—*William B Keenan Jr*	245 E Fullerton Ave, Carol Stream IL 60188	630-784-3900	R	6	.1
1973	Sterling Express Ltd—*Maro Allen*	PO Box 1067, Valparaiso IN 46384	219-464-7880	R	6	.1
1974	Daum Trucking Inc—*Robert Daum*	PO Box 1085, Plainfield IN 46168	317-839-4173	R	6	.1
1975	Paul Marshall Produce Inc—*Paul Marshall*	PO Box 366, Elba NY 14058	585-343-1286	R	6	<.1
1976	Shelba D Johnson Trucking Inc—*Joe Wade*	PO Box 7287, High Point NC 27264	336-476-2000	R	6*	.4
1977	Arizona Pacific Transport Logistics—*Donald Tieden*	3620 E Kerr St, Springfield MO 65803	417-862-1600	R	6*	.2
1978	LeFebvre and Sons Inc—*Paul LeFebvre*	10895 171st Ave NW, Elk River MN 55330	763-441-2681	R	6*	.1
1979	WC McQuaide Inc—*Stan McQuaide*	153 Macridge Ave, Johnstown PA 15904	814-269-6000	R	6*	.1
1980	Case Enterprises Inc—*Bobby Case*	PO Box 629, Athens TN 37371	423-745-0106	R	6*	.1
1981	Jimmie Tucker Trucking Inc—*James A Tucker*	PO Box 428, Broken Bow OK 74728	580-584-9143	R	6*	.1
1982	Linn Star Transfer Inc—*Dennis Munson*	9440 Wright Brothers C, Cedar Rapids IA 52404	319-363-0444	R	6*	.1
1983	Easton Transportation Inc—*Keith Warning*	P O Box 750, Channahon IL 60410	815-467-2168	R	6*	.1
1984	Day-N-Nite Transportation—*Glen Cheh*	10700 Forest St, Santa Fe Springs CA 90670	562-946-3946	R	6*	.1
1985	Drews Trucking Inc—*Troy Drews*	710 Ralph Lemorande Dr, Oconto Falls WI 54154	920-848-3477	R	6*	.1
1986	Leeser TX Inc—*Ronald Brink*	6985 County Rd 326, Palmyra MO 63461	573-769-2227	R	6*	.1
1987	Perimeter Transportation Company LLC—*Mike Russell*	5515 E Holmes Rd, Memphis TN 38118	901-794-2900	R	6*	.1
1988	Powell Transportation Company Inc—*Barry Powell*	2348 Hwy 98 E, Columbia MS 39429	601-731-2527	R	6*	.1
1989	Woerner Turf Inc—*George Woerner*	PO Box 820, Foley AL 36536	251-943-4548	R	6*	.1
1990	IDM Trucking Inc—*Dennis Houff*	73 Railside Dr, Weyers Cave VA 24486	540-234-9185	R	6*	.1
1991	R and L Smith Trucking Inc—*Steven Smith*	PO Box 301, South Dayton NY 14138	716-988-3241	R	6*	.1
1992	Truck Air of the Carolinas—*Steve Sims*	PO Box 827, Greer SC 29652		R	6*	.1
1993	Debrick Truck Line Co—*Kevin Debrick*	PO Box 421, Paola KS 66071	913-294-5020	R	6*	.1
1994	Harold Bibbs and Sons Trucking Inc—*Harold Bibbs*	PO Box 194, Hornersville MO 63855	573-737-2428	R	6*	.1
1995	Hinz Trucking Inc—*Scott Hinz*	PO Box 370, Kearney NE 68848	308-237-3116	R	6*	.1
1996	Underwood and Weld Company Inc—*Badger Underwood*	PO Box 669, Spruce Pine NC 28777	828-765-2424	R	6*	.1
1997	CXpress Trucking Inc—*Corry Scalone*	1608 Commerce Rd, Richmond VA 23224	804-233-2403	R	6*	.1
1998	LMT Trucking Company Inc—*Curlie Threlkeld*	PO Box 1288, Batesville MS 38606	662-563-8570	R	6*	.1
1999	PVT—*John R Tucker*	202 S Rochester, Ontario CA 91761	909-390-6161	R	6*	.1

Note: An asterisk (*) indicates an estimated financial figure. The company type code used is as follows: R = Private, P = Public, S = Private Subsidiary, B = Public Subsidiary, D = Division, J = Joint Venture, I = Investment Fund.

COMPANY RANKINGS BY SALES WITHIN 4-DIGIT SIC

Rank	Company Name—*Executive Officer*	Address, City, State, Zip	Phone	Type	Fin	Empls
2000	AG Trucking Inc—*Tim Boehlke*	Po Box 453, Goshen IN 46527	574-642-3351	R	6*	.1
2001	Bertis Carlson Trucking Inc—*Bertis Carlson*	1480 S Henderson St, Galesburg IL 61401	309-343-9919	R	6*	.1
2002	Boyd and Sons Inc—*Steve Boyd*	1312 E 200 N, Washington IN 47501	812-254-6858	R	6*	.1
2003	DiPietro Trucking Co—*Arthur Di Pietro*	PO Box 5849, Kent WA 98064		R	6*	.1
2004	Hogland Transfer Co—*Steve Holtgeerts*	6605 Hardeson Rd Ste 1, Everett WA 98203	425-407-1011	R	6*	.1
2005	K and P Trucking LLC—*Kent Knaus*	PO Box 179, Willard OH 44890	419-935-8646	R	6*	.1
2006	Larry Schefus Trucking Inc—*Larry Schefus*	PO Box 545, Redwood Falls MN 56283	507-644-2125	R	6*	.1
2007	Matuszko Trucking Inc—*Ted Matuszko*	137 Damin Rd Rm B, Northampton MA 01060	413-665-8011	R	6*	.1
2008	MO Nelson and Sons Inc—*Morris Nelson*	PO Box 21733, Eugene OR 97402	541-746-0303	R	6*	.1
2009	Port City Trucking Inc—*Luther B Oakes Jr*	101 Karen St, Greenville MS 38703	662-335-8010	R	6*	.1
2010	PW Trucking Inc—*Mark Grasse*	2215 Union Ave Ste 3, Sheboygan WI 53081	920-457-4433	R	6*	.1
2011	Tri-Hi Transportation Inc—*Douglas Lokemoen*	N3163 Hwy 107, Merrill WI 54452	715-536-9860	R	6*	.1
2012	Hammer Express Inc—*Patrick Barrett*	9100 Plainfield Rd, Brookfield IL 60513	708-485-0530	R	6*	<.1
2013	Jonick and Company Inc—*William Morog*	PO Box 2095, Sheffield Lake OH 44054	440-277-0592	R	6*	<.1
2014	Edwards Transportation Co—*Keith Edwards*	PO Box 70, East Prairie MO 63845	573-649-3007	R	6*	<.1
2015	Grand Traverse Trucking Inc—*Rick Nottke*	2699 Cass Rd, Traverse City MI 49684	231-933-9204	R	6*	<.1
2016	Al's Leasing Inc—*Donald Snyder*	156 Prescott Ave, Elmira Heights NY 14903	607-733-9153	R	6*	<.1
2017	Atlas Motor Express Inc—*David Pevna*	PO Box 920, Plaistow NH 03865	603-382-6265	R	6*	<.1
2018	Cool Cargo Carriers Inc—*Burt Pedowitz*	5324 Georgia Hwy 85 St, Forest Park GA 30297	770-994-0338	R	6*	<.1
2019	D and M Express Inc—*Dave Richard*	20886 Rt 19, Cranberry Township PA 16066	724-452-8631	R	6*	<.1
2020	LB Transport Inc—*Terry Klewlet*	615 1st Ave NE, Buffalo Center IA 50424	641-562-2048	R	6*	<.1
2021	Tate Transportation Inc—*Thomas Tate*	PO Box 1296, Walla Walla WA 99362	509-522-0406	R	6*	<.1
2022	Trans Technical Leasing Inc—*Keith Garrison*	461 Harrisport Ct, Middletown PA 17057	717-939-8250	R	6	<.1
2023	Mercer Trucking Company Inc—*Steven Hanning*	PO Box 11585, Spokane WA 99211	509-535-3597	R	6*	<.1
2024	Whitaker Transportation Co—*Charles Whitaker*	PO Box 5266, Spartanburg SC 29304	864-578-6232	R	6*	<.1
2025	Denny Transport Inc—*David Denny*	3435 Industrial Pkwy, Jeffersonville IN 47130	812-282-7464	R	6*	<.1
2026	Farmers Distributing—*Bart Graff*	PO Box 910399, Saint George UT 84791	435-628-0846	R	6*	<.1
2027	Farruggio's Express—*Terry Kraft*	PO Box T, Cliffwood NJ 07721	732-583-2900	R	6*	<.1
2028	Rocking C Truck Lines Inc—*Vernon Clark*	PO Box 3327, Gulfport MS 39505	228-539-5377	R	6*	<.1
2029	Specialized Rail Service Inc—*Herb Okada*	4740 E Tropical Pkwy, Las Vegas NV 89115	702-388-9277	R	6	<.1
2030	Southern Cal Transport Co—*Alvin Reser*	15570 SW Jenkins Rd, Beaverton OR 97006	503-526-5726	R	6*	<.1
2031	Heiter Truck Line Inc—*Don Heiter*	PO Box 713, Spencer IA 51301	712-262-5723	R	6*	<.1
2032	Howe Freightways Inc—*Kenneth Howe*	2716 8th St, Rockford IL 61109	815-316-1002	R	6*	<.1
2033	Jackie B Lovett Trucking Co—*Johnny Lovett*	3975 Hwy 24 S, Waynesboro GA 30830	706-554-6732	R	6*	<.1
2034	Stahly Cartage Co—*Jeffrey Wohlford*	119 S Main St, Edwardsville IL 62025	618-656-5070	R	6*	<.1
2035	Yarmouth Lumber Inc—*William Phipps*	384 Portland Rd, Gray ME 04039	207-657-2903	R	6*	<.1
2036	Asbury Trucking—*Jerry Asbury*	6255 Webster St, Dayton OH 45414	937-667-4870	R	6*	<.1
2037	Sunshine Trucking Inc—*Alan Bostick*	PO Box 676, Red Bay AL 35582	256-356-9541	R	6	<.1
2038	Glenn-Lee Trucking Company Inc—*Joe C Sikes*	PO Box 2213, Savannah GA 31402	912-964-6972	R	6*	<.1
2039	Weston Transportation Inc—*Scott Schriner*	1600 Swift Ave, N Kansas City MO 64116	816-421-7895	R	6*	<.1
2040	AC Leasing Co—*Joe Zembrodt*	3023 E Kemper Rd, Cincinnati OH 45241	513-771-3676	R	6*	<.1
2041	Classic Transportation Services—*Larry Benton*	PO Box 385, Wayland MI 49348	616-877-0003	R	6*	<.1
2042	Environmental Transport Group—*Edward Collioud*	PO Box 296, Flanders NJ 07836	973-347-8200	R	6*	<.1
2043	Mid Atlantic Xpress Inc—*Jacquoline Kurnath*	139 US Hwy 46, Hackettstown NJ 07840	908-852-9190	R	6*	<.1
2044	Dalton Brothers Trucking—*Michael Dalton*	PO Box 308, Circleville UT 84723	435-577-2861	R	6*	<.1
2045	Quality Brands of Omaha Inc—*James Gustafson*	13255 Centech Rd, Omaha NE 68138	402-896-8900	R	6*	<.1
2046	Sound Delivery Service—*Jerry Lawrence*	PO Box 2068, Sumner WA 98390	253-200-2208	R	6*	<.1
2047	AR Paquette and Company Inc—*Allen Paquette*	1400 E International S, Deland FL 32724	386-736-9421	R	6*	<.1
2048	Barole Trucking Inc—*Ray Olson*	6805 20th Ave S, Centerville MN 55038	651-209-1104	R	6*	<.1
2049	BJ Transport Inc—*Bill Turcotte*	12720 S Hudson Rd, Afton MN 55001	651-436-4300	R	6*	<.1
2050	Camp Curtin Transfer Inc	3465 N 6th St, Harrisburg PA 17110	717-234-3145	R	6*	<.1
2051	Eagle Movers Inc—*Tom Brittain*	929 W Bruce St, Milwaukee WI 53204	414-383-1776	R	6*	<.1
2052	Henry V Rabouin Inc—*Jerry Norton*	PO Box 204, Pittsfield MA 01202	413-443-4749	R	6*	<.1
2053	Kingdom Express Inc—*Larry King*	18640 Crenshaw Blvd, Torrance CA 90504	310-258-0900	R	6*	<.1
2054	Quality Transport Co—*Curt McIntyre*	PO Box 461, Freeport IL 61032	815-235-6149	R	6*	<.1
2055	Veeco Services Inc—*Michael Arciero*	6801 W Side Ave, North Bergen NJ 07047	201-865-6200	R	6*	<.1
2056	Booker Transportation Inc—*Dennis Cowley*	2300 S Pullman Rd, Amarillo TX 79118		R	6*	<.1
2057	WDS Partners LP—*Donnie Siratt*	1102 W N Carrier Pkwy, Grand Prairie TX 75050	972-623-3756	R	6*	<.1
2058	Wherley Moving and Storage Inc—*Ed Meyer*	216 Second Street NE, East Grand Forks MN 56721	218-773-1173	R	6*	<.1
2059	Pine Bluffs Gravel and Excavating—*Tyler Kimzey*	PO Box 609, Pine Bluffs WY 82082	307-245-3426	R	6*	<.1
2060	Golan's Moving and Storage Inc—*Itzahk Eliyahu*	3600 Jarvis Ave, Skokie IL 60076	847-673-8189	R	6*	<.1
2061	Goulet Trucking Inc—*Wayne Goulet*	PO Box 259, South Deerfield MA 01373	413-584-8446	R	6*	<.1
2062	Haggard Hauling and Rigging Inc—*John Haggard*	2100 Guinotte Ave, Kansas City MO 64120	816-221-7840	R	6*	<.1
2063	High Mountain Transport LLC—*Mark Menezes*	100 Canyon Way, Sparks NV 89434	775-342-0414	R	6*	<.1
2064	Jim Keeler Enterprises Inc—*Jim L Keeler*	1279 County Hwy 2A, Defuniak Springs FL 32433	850-834-2974	R	6*	<.1
2065	Wood Trucking Corp—*Robert Wood*	101 Lakeland Park Dr, Peabody MA 01960	978-535-0894	R	6*	<.1
2066	Spinnaker Inc—*Brad Beamesderfer*	PO Box 127, Bethel PA 19507	717-933-4141	R	6*	<.1
2067	Titan Armored Car and Courier Inc—*Timothy Peloso*	101 Mill St, Newburgh NY 12550	845-562-9000	R	6*	<.1
2068	Jackie Evans Trucking Inc—*Jackie Evans*	3845 Waterlevel Hwy, Cleveland TN 37323	423-472-8412	R	6	<.1
2069	Eastern Consolidation and Distriburion Services Inc—*Carl Linsenbach*	405 Sterling St, Camp Hill PA 17011	717-761-4020	R	6*	<.1
2070	Walter Flagstone Inc—*William Walter*	RR 1 Box 40, Sugar Run PA 18846	570-746-7736	R	6*	<.1
2071	Controlled Temperature Transit—*Craig Fielder*	PO Box 21036, Indianapolis IN 46221	317-632-8288	R	6*	<.1
2072	Lesaint Logistics Transportation—*Greg Issacs*	4487 Le Saint Ct, Fairfield OH 45014	513-874-3900	R	6*	<.1
2073	Longhorn Trucking Company Inc—*Edward Logan*	6605 State Hwy 5, Fort Plain NY 13339	518-993-3480	R	6*	<.1
2074	Cantrell Motor Lines Inc—*Barry Cantrell*	609 49th St SE, Charleston WV 25304	304-925-0563	R	6*	<.1
2075	Powell Relocation Group—*William Powell*	4937 Starr St SE, Grand Rapids MI 49546	616-956-0900	R	6*	<.1
2076	Specialized Machinery Transport—*Theodore Kistner*	21 Town Forest Rd, Webster MA 01570	508-671-9188	R	6*	<.1
2077	Universal Environmental Nevada—*Wayne Turnage*	PO Box 10120, Reno NV 89510	775-331-9400	R	6*	<.1
2078	Jung Brothers Trucking—*Thomas Jung*	9825 Durand Ave, Sturtevant WI 53177	262-886-6817	R	6	<.1
2079	Lowe Trucking Co—*Dick Webber*	401 S Mission Rd, Los Angeles CA 90033	323-266-2530	R	6*	<.1
2080	AAAAdvantage Auto Transport—*Vincent Smith*	7810 S Hardy Dr Ste 10, Tempe AZ 85284	480-753-9000	R	6*	<.1
2081	Fox Marine Service—*Dennis Fox*	PO Box 113, Colchester VT 05446	802-862-7707	R	6*	<.1
2082	Keystone Carriers Inc—*Warren Shaffer*	5010 Rt 104, Mount Pleasant Mills PA 17853	570-539-4877	R	6*	<.1
2083	Yule Transport Inc—*Terry Yule*	2957 NW 76th St, Medford MN 55049		R	6*	<.1
2084	Gloucester Dispatch Inc—*James Montagnino*	186 Main St, Gloucester MA 01930	978-283-1110	R	6*	<.1
2085	BAT Express Inc—*Charles Hancock*	PO Box 145, Charlestown NH 03603	603-826-4333	R	6*	<.1
2086	Dimon and Sons Transportation Corp—*Daniel F Dimon Sr*	93 Industrial Park Blv, Elmira NY 14901	607-734-2937	R	6*	<.1
2087	Hoosier Tire Mid-Atlantic—*Robert Wirts*	2931 Industrial Park D, Finksburg MD 21048	410-833-2061	R	6*	<.1
2088	Hutchcraft Van Service Inc—*Orin Hutchraft III*	PO Box 457, Urbana IL 61803	217-328-3333	R	6*	<.1

Rank	Company Name—*Executive Officer*	Address, City, State, Zip	Phone	Type	Fin	Empls
2089	Maverig Freight Inc—*John Evans*	18765 Seaway Dr, Melvindale MI 48122	313-388-3200	R	6*	<.1
2090	MC Parcel Delivery Inc—*Andrew Laycock*	1410 Martin Luther Kin, Tacoma WA 98405	253-272-1800	R	6*	<.1
2091	Pharr Brothers Inc—*Joyce Pharr*	PO Box 69, Blanchard LA 71009	318-929-2337	R	6*	<.1
2092	Pope Transport Inc—*Lynn Panek*	5533 W 109th St Ste 20, Oak Lawn IL 60453	708-499-3737	R	6*	<.1
2093	Brent G Theobald Construction—*Brent Theobald*	215 W Industrial Dr, Washington UT 84780	435-673-4284	R	6*	<.1
2094	Galasso Trucking Service Inc—*Richard L Galasso*	2840 Hedley St, Philadelphia PA 19137	215-535-4731	R	6*	<.1
2095	Tomlin Trucking and Brokerage Inc—*Gene Tomlin*	202 N Hwy J, Hayti MO 63851	573-359-0407	R	6*	<.1
2096	Anthony M Brida Inc—*Anthony Brida*	PO Box 340, Glassboro NJ 08028	856-881-1708	R	6*	<.1
2097	Marocchi Trucking Company Inc—*Louis A Marocchi Jr*	6129 State Rt 233, Rome NY 13440	315-339-6459	R	6*	<.1
2098	Bender Transportation Co—*Chris Bender*	PO Box 11430, Reno NV 89510	775-788-8800	R	6*	<.1
2099	Valhalla Corp—*Murray Tynch*	1462 Virginia Rd, Edenton NC 27932	252-482-3426	R	6*	<.1
2100	Mid-South Express Delivery—*David Walters*	3385 Airways Blvd Ste, Memphis TN 38116	901-398-1524	R	6	.1
2101	Ashley Transport Inc—*Phil Kuyvenhoven*	PO Box 10, Ashley IN 46705	260-587-9303	R	6	.1
2102	Carbon Express Inc—*Stephen Rush*	PO Box 403, Wharton NJ 07885	973-328-0050	R	6	.1
2103	Special Service Freight-Carolinas—*Steve Perriman*	PO Box 38630, Charlotte NC 28278	704-587-0001	R	6	.1
2104	TP Freight Lines Inc—*Buck Collekon*	PO Box 580, Tillamook OR 97141	503-842-2574	R	6	.1
2105	Christy Trucking Company Inc—*Steven Beaver*	2079 Us Hwy 601 N, Mocksville NC 27028	336-492-7716	R	6	<.1
2106	Mast Trucking Inc—*Willis Mast*	6471 County Rd 625, Millersburg OH 44654	330-674-8913	R	6	<.1
2107	Copeland Truc-King Inc—*Richard Copeland*	5400 NE Main St Ste 20, Fridley MN 55421	763-572-0505	R	6	<.1
2108	Smart Move Transportation LLC—*Chris Sapyta*	1212 St George Road, Evansville IN 47711		S	6	<.1
2109	Mid Continent Van Service—*Kent Costello*	148 Millwell Dr, Maryland Heights MO 63043	314-291-8998	R	6	<.1
2110	OB Hill Trucking and Rigging Co—*Bryant Hill*	197 W Central St, Natick MA 01760	508-653-2071	R	6	<.1
2111	Link Trucking Inc—*Luther Palmer*	PO Box 27715, Salt Lake City UT 84127	801-972-6220	R	6	.1
2112	Meiko America Inc—*Naoki Ishii*	19600 Magellan Dr, Torrance CA 90502	310-483-7400	R	6	<.1
2113	Double 'S' Truck Line Inc—*Valdine Schueman*	PO Box 279, Avoca IA 51521	712-343-2644	R	6	<.1
2114	Lobiondo Brothers Motor Express—*George Lobiondo*	711 Shiloh Pike, Bridgeton NJ 08302	856-451-2410	R	6	<.1
2115	Hudson Transportation Inc—*Paul Hudson*	125 Henderson Dr, Troy AL 36081	334-566-6270	R	6	<.1
2116	Certified Van Service Inc—*Joe McNamara*	195 Oval Dr, Islandia NY 11749	631-234-6700	R	6	<.1
2117	G and R Trucking Company Inc—*Rick Justice*	5516 Tell Mynatt Rd, Knoxville TN 37938	865-922-0242	R	6	<.1
2118	Douglas and Sons Inc—*Robert Douglas*	1025 N Chipley Ford Rd, Statesville NC 28625	704-876-1257	R	6	.1
2119	Rahn's Trucking Inc—*Paul Yerk*	PO Box 26410, Collegeville PA 19426	610-489-2646	R	6	.1
2120	T and B Trucking Inc—*Edward Taylor*	6246 Dr Hess Rd, Bells TN 38006	731-772-0959	R	6	<.1
2121	Plaisted Companies Inc—*Todd Plaisted*	PO Box 332, Elk River MN 55330	763-441-1100	R	6*	<.1
2122	D and L Trucking Company Inc—*Keith Campbell*	PO Box 901375, Memphis TN 38190		R	6	<.1
2123	Odeen Hibbs Trucking Co—*Odeen Hibbs*	PO Box 14332, Austin TX 78761	512-251-2100	R	6	<.1
2124	Weatherly Truck Lines Inc—*Russell Weatherly*	PO Box 450, Bearden AR 71720	870-687-3118	R	5	<.1
2125	McLeod Inc—*Barbara McLeod*	PO Box 66, Midland VA 22728	540-788-4872	R	5	<.1
2126	CTX-TL Inc—*Donald Sheeler*	1060 Monroe St, Hoboken NJ 07030	201-798-8555	R	5	<.1
2127	NEMA Inc—*Neal Baines*	2750 Breckinridge Blvd, Duluth GA 30096	770-935-7087	R	5	<.1
2128	G and L Trucking Inc	165 Locke Rd, Locke NY 13092	607-533-4072	R	5	<.1
2129	RAD Transport Inc—*Mike Davis*	53049 Paul Dr, Elkhart IN 46514	574-266-1330	R	5	.1
2130	Springhill Services Inc—*Frank Wall*	PO Box 8, Mc Intyre GA 31054	478-946-2667	R	5	.1
2131	Meteor Express Inc—*George Jones*	PO Box 248, Scottsboro AL 35768	256-218-3000	R	5	.1
2132	Bulk Transport Corp—*Barry Brown*	720 W Us Hwy 20, Michigan City IN 46360	219-872-8618	R	5	<.1
2133	Keene's Transfer Inc—*Kerry Keene*	909 Townline Rd, Tomah WI 54660	608-372-4178	R	5	<.1
2134	White Brothers Trucking Co *James White*	PO Box 82, Wasco IL 60183	630-584-3810	R	5	<.1
2135	Gray Trucking—*Robert Gray*	735 Broad St, Beverly NJ 08010	609-386-7887	H	5	<.1
2136	Chemtrans—*Reginald Lathan*	14700 S Avalon Blvd, Gardena CA 90248	310-523-2555	R	5*	<.1
2137	Hardin Delivery Inc—*Paige Hardin*	101 Magnet Dr Ste 1, Elizabethtown KY 42701	270-765-4909	R	5	.1
2138	Kings Express—*Michael King*	3813 Broadway St, Buffalo NY 14227	716-651-9383	R	5	<.1
2139	Century Services Inc—*Linwood Guthrie*	PO Box 608, Hickory NC 28603	828-397-7376	R	5	<.1
2140	Day After Day Services—*Douglas Brewer*	PO Box 202, Union City TN 38281	731-885-3008	R	5	.1
2141	Cox Motor Express of Greensboro—*Nathan Cox*	1465 Alamance Church R, Greensboro NC 27406	336-274-7937	R	5	.1
2142	Crapo Ltd—*David Crapo*	1908 E 500 N, Saint Anthony ID 83445	208-624-3293	R	5	.1
2143	Davis Trucking Company Inc—*Denton Bowmen*	PO Box 626, Jackson OH 45640	740-286-4172	S	5	<.1
2144	Movers Unlimited Inc—*Barbara Johnson*	102 Westview Rd NW, Georgetown TN 37336		R	5	<.1
2145	Kingman Dedicated Service Inc—*Roy E Kingman*	2800 Lexington Ave, Elkhart IN 46514	574-254-7510	R	5*	.1
2146	SWT Inc—*Sam Williams*	1003 Venture St, Green Forest AR 72638	870-438-6340	R	5*	.1
2147	Ferry Transportation Inc—*William Ferry*	5 Thames Ave, Laurel MS 39440	601-425-5542	R	5*	.1
2148	Harvey Trucking Inc—*Regina Harvey*	2435 W Curtis Rd, Tucson AZ 85705	520-888-6255	R	5*	.1
2149	Jack B Wooten Co—*Jack Wooten*	847 Buffalo Shoals Rd, Statesville NC 28677	704-873-2866	R	5*	.1
2150	J Trans Inc—*JD Hodge*	2025 E 38th St, Marion IN 46953	765-674-2204	R	5*	.1
2151	AC Widenhouse Inc—*Linda Fink*	PO Box 5010, Concord NC 28027	704-782-4103	R	5*	.1
2152	A and B Leasing Inc—*James Blackmon*	PO Box 292, Montevallo AL 35115	205-665-2044	R	5*	.1
2153	Barge Terminal Trucking Inc—*John Edmier*	PO Box 636, Oswego IL 60543	630-499-5565	R	5*	.1
2154	Becker's Trucking Inc—*Rolan Becker*	6350 S 143rd St, Tukwila WA 98168	206-246-9500	R	5*	.1
2155	Dave Clinard Truck Service—*Dave Clinard*	PO Box 112, Mount Sterling IL 62353	217-773-3965	R	5*	.1
2156	Elliott Brothers Truck Line Inc—*Jim Ochletree*	PO Box 310, Dysart IA 52224	319-476-3212	R	5*	.1
2157	Golding Transport Inc—*Senator Golding*	602 N Main St, Dobson NC 27017	336-386-4920	R	5*	.1
2158	Hucks Piggyback Service Inc—*Lydia HHucks*	1200 W Craighead Rd, Charlotte NC 28206	704-596-9153	R	5*	.1
2159	J and C Stringer Trucking Inc—*Jack Stringer*	1490 N Woodcock St, Macon IL 62544	217-764-3396	R	5*	.1
2160	JD Donovan Inc—*Joan Donovan*	PO Box 364, Rockville MN 56369	320-251-1213	R	5*	.1
2161	Jowin Express Inc—*Edwin Johnson Jr*	PO Box 1348, Columbia MS 39429	601-736-0938	R	5*	.1
2162	Kentuckiana Trucking Inc—*Jerome Schneider*	PO Box 2544, Clarksville IN 47131	812-282-0908	R	5*	.1
2163	Ludtke-Pacific Trucking Inc—*Lloyd Ludtke*	4059 Bakerview Valley, Bellingham WA 98226	360-733-6670	R	5*	.1
2164	Mardel Trucking Company Inc—*Frank Julian*	PO Box 280, North East MD 21901	410-287-5700	R	5*	.1
2165	Novco Inc—*Harold Novotny*	11090 173rd Ave NW, Elk River MN 55330	763-441-0047	R	5*	.1
2166	Richard I Green Inc—*Richard Green*	PO Box 506, Enosburg Falls VT 05450	802-933-6693	R	5*	.1
2167	Way Transportation Company Inc—*Scott Way*	5916 US Hwy 31 S, Charlevoix MI 49720	231-547-9660	R	5*	.1
2168	Windy Hill Foliage Inc—*Jack Short*	PO Box 839, Marshfield WI 54449	715-384-3137	R	5*	.1
2169	Fikes Truck Line Inc—*Gary Salisbury*	PO Box 662, Hope AR 71802	870-777-6540	R	5*	<.1
2170	Rawhide Trucking Inc—*Tony Gaston*	PO Box 1768, Hutchinson KS 67504	620-663-8818	R	5*	<.1
2171	Over the Road Trucking Inc—*Mike Litt*	744 23rd St, Detroit MI 48216	734-853-6400	R	5*	<.1
2172	DiJulio Enter/Harbor Freightlines—*Paul Di Julio*	PO Box 80825, Seattle WA 98108	206-762-6100	R	5*	<.1
2173	TWL Inc—*Robert Locklear*	PO Box 2229, Pembroke NC 28372	910-521-8844	R	5	<.1
2174	August Transport Inc—*Jim August*	17 Ferry St, Leetsdale PA 15056	724-251-0500	R	5*	.1
2175	Jimmy Harris Trucking Inc—*Terri Joiner*	8163 Old Atlanta Hwy, Covington GA 30014	770-786-0061	R	5*	.1
2176	Milky-Way Transport Company Inc—*Randy Bergman*	PO Box 9266, Springfield MO 65801	417-869-3397	R	5*	.1
2177	Oldland Distributing Inc—*Jim Oldland*	PO Box 3241, Central Point OR 97502	541-664-7080	R	5*	<.1
2178	Phoenix-PDQ Inc—*Leonard Young*	15723 Texaco Ave, Paramount CA 90723	562-634-0366	R	5*	<.1

Note: An asterisk (*) indicates an estimated financial figure. The company type code used is as follows: R = Private, P = Public, S = Private Subsidiary, B = Public Subsidiary, D = Division, J = Joint Venture, I = Investment Fund.

COMPANY RANKINGS BY SALES WITHIN 4-DIGIT SIC

Rank	Company Name—*Executive Officer*	Address, City, State, Zip	Phone	Type	Fin	Empls
2179	Scott Banks Trucking Inc—*Kirk Banks*	PO Box 352, Candler NC 28715	828-667-5888	R	5*	<.1
2180	Shore Trucking Company Inc—*Johnny Shore*	PO Box 5955, Maryville TN 37802	865-984-4252	R	5*	<.1
2181	Tideport Distributing Inc—*Harold Hees*	5582 Old Brownsville R, Corpus Christi TX 78417	281-452-2865	R	5*	<.1
2182	Walter J Sheets and Son Inc—*Donnie Sheets*	300 Maplewood Ave, Lewisburg WV 24901	304-645-6001	R	5	<.1
2183	Truscott Inc—*Larry Truscott*	PO Box 1832, Twin Falls ID 83303	208-734-9350	R	5*	<.1
2184	Big State Logistics Inc—*Mervin Gilbertson*	PO Box 71540, Fairbanks AK 99707	907-452-8600	R	5*	<.1
2185	Roy N Carlson Inc—*Royce Carlson*	8506 Cedarhome Dr NW, Stanwood WA 98292	360-629-4542	R	5*	<.1
2186	Cayenne Express Inc—*Robert Christ*	410 Transpoint Dr, Dupo IL 62239	618-286-9900	R	5*	<.1
2187	Graham Ship By Truck Co—*Richard Arnold*	PO Box 2936, Kansas City KS 66110	913-621-7600	R	5*	<.1
2188	Lakeside Specialized Transportation—*James Fernhoff*	PO Box 1341, Verdi NV 89439	775-345-6900	R	5*	<.1
2189	Brook Ledge Inc—*Robert Gotwals*	PO Box 56, Oley PA 19547	610-987-6284	R	5*	<.1
2190	Cleveland Express Trucking Company Inc—*John Lamb*	3091 Rockefeller Ave, Cleveland OH 44115	216-348-1007	R	5*	<.1
2191	CV Transport Inc—*John Miltiades*	PO Box 496580, Lawrenceville GA 30049	770-513-1251	R	5*	<.1
2192	Eagle Transportation LLC—*Herb Holtzman*	601 Double Springs Rd, Bowling Green KY 42101	270-843-3363	R	5*	<.1
2193	Exclusive Transportation for Industry—*Richard Sauers*	PO Box 20022, Lehigh Valley PA 18002	610-798-0300	R	5*	<.1
2194	Joel Olson Trucking Inc—*Joel Olson*	1615 NE 78th St, Vancouver WA 98665	360-694-8610	R	5*	<.1
2195	Midcoe Transportation Co—*James Briscoe*	PO Box 189, Powderly TX 75473	903-784-1995	R	5*	<.1
2196	S and H Trucking Inc—*Glenn Holland*	3500 Alton Park Blvd, Chattanooga TN 37410	423-648-5355	R	5*	<.1
2197	Smith Brothers Trucking Inc—*Rapier Smith*	PO Box 848, Bardstown KY 40004	502-348-9423	R	5*	<.1
2198	Terminal Transportation Service—*Tom Huesman*	1801 S Clinton St, Baltimore MD 21224	410-633-8110	S	5*	<.1
2199	Trans Petro of California—*Delton Crandall*	15220 Lakewood Blvd, Bellflower CA 90706	562-867-2300	R	5*	<.1
2200	United Motor Freight Inc—*Jeff Landstrom*	3800 W Marginal Way SW, Seattle WA 98106	206-933-0515	R	5*	<.1
2201	Apache Truck Lines Inc—*Stephen Germane*	150 E Martin Dr, Goodfield IL 61742	309-467-2525	R	5*	<.1
2202	Lester M Prange Inc—*Lester K Prange*	380 Maple Shade Rd, Kirkwood PA 17536	717-529-2191	R	5*	<.1
2203	Light Express Inc—*Thomas Carver*	PO Box 508, Ironton OH 45638	740-532-6139	R	5*	<.1
2204	Marvin Ward Trucking Inc—*Marvin Ward*	2929 N Industrial Ave, Tyler TX 75708	903-593-7121	R	5*	<.1
2205	Sindall Transport Inc—*Robert Sindall*	PO Box 165, New Holland PA 17557	717-354-0606	R	5	<.1
2206	Mall Delivery Service—*Francine DeSantis*	480 Duncan Ave, Jersey City NJ 07306	201-434-6338	R	5*	<.1
2207	Adams Motor Express Inc—*Herbert Adams*	PO Box 450, Carnesville GA 30521	706-384-4533	R	5*	<.1
2208	B and G Transportation Inc—*Jerry Johnson*	PO Box 9, Madison SD 57042	605-256-9105	R	5*	<.1
2209	Crozier Trucking—*Gerald Crozier*	42009 US 70 W, Portales NM 88130	505-356-8528	R	5*	<.1
2210	Emory Rothenbuhler and Sons—*Joyce Bonar*	47126 Sunfish Creek Rd, Beallsville OH 43716	740-458-1432	R	5*	<.1
2211	Lynn H Scott Inc—*Gary Scott*	PO Box 70, Blossvale NY 13308	315-339-2900	R	5*	<.1
2212	S and R Transport Inc—*Robert Espinoza*	3550 Lee Blvd, El Paso TX 79936	915-856-6481	R	5*	<.1
2213	DL Coates Transportation—*Don Coates*	3225 Creighton Ln, Bedford TX 76021	817-545-0800	R	5*	<.1
2214	Minnesota Valley Transport—*Daniel Schumacher*	301 N Water St, New Ulm MN 56073	507-354-3276	R	5*	<.1
2215	Columbus Warehouse and Cartage—*Susan Barker*	PO Box 167, Columbus IN 47202	812-372-0753	R	5*	<.1
2216	Sisson Transportation Inc—*Cathy Sisson*	137 Law Rd, Jackson TN 38305		R	5*	<.1
2217	Sub Zero Transportation Inc—*Todd Palmer*	4429 N 23rd Plz, Omaha NE 68110	402-451-9600	R	5*	<.1
2218	Time Moving and Storage Inc	628 W 45th St, New York NY 10036	718-855-1700	R	5*	<.1
2219	American Ramp Transit Inc—*Gerry Rhodes*	4904 Luckys Bridge Rd, Dearing GA 30808	706-597-1880	R	5*	<.1
2220	Anthony Augliera Inc—*Robert Augliera*	34 Hamilton St, West Haven CT 06516	203-937-9080	R	5*	<.1
2221	Atlantic Star Trucking Inc—*Joseph Magiera*	436 Doremus Ave, Newark NJ 07105	973-465-4421	R	5*	<.1
2222	Bobby Lehmann Inc—*Bobby Lehmann*	PO Box 59, Giddings TX 78942	979-542-0889	R	5*	<.1
2223	Camrett Dedicated Logistics—*Collin Peel*	2460 N 4th St, Wytheville VA 24382	276-625-8100	R	5*	<.1
2224	Dave Evans Transports—*David Evans*	1122 Cedar Ave, Superior WI 54880	715-392-2211	R	5*	<.1
2225	Midwest Express Corp—*Greg Orscheln*	102 Abbie Ave, Kansas City KS 66103	913-371-6023	R	5*	<.1
2226	Reed Trucking Co—*Blake Reed*	522 Chestnut St, Milton DE 19968	302-684-8585	R	5*	<.1
2227	W and S Trucking Inc—*John Worden*	PO Box 638, Saint Croix Falls WI 54024	715-483-1626	R	5*	<.1
2228	Aero Transporters Inc—*Todd Polonsky*	PO Box 551, Ellenville NY 12428	845-647-7500	R	5*	<.1
2229	Marine Cross Country Inc—*Eddie Harvey*	PO Box 26778, Greenville SC 29616	864-281-0041	R	5*	<.1
2230	C and A Trucking Inc—*Brad Anderson*	7901 Derby Ln, Cotati CA 94931	707-795-9231	R	5*	<.1
2231	Chipman Moving and Storage (Spokane Washington)—*Linda Burgin*	2704 N Moore Ln, Spokane WA 99216	509-535-8761	R	5*	<.1
2232	Cordova Truck Company Inc—*Arthur Cordova*	11030 Arrow Rte, Rancho Cucamonga CA 91730		R	5*	<.1
2233	Joe Dieter and Sons Inc—*Ronald Dieter*	30W010 Ferry Rd, Naperville IL 60563	630-983-7107	R	5*	<.1
2234	LAD Truck Lines Inc—*Mack Guest III*	PO Box 749, Watkinsville GA 30677	706-769-4048	R	5*	<.1
2235	Manfredi Mushroom Inc—*John Manfredi*	PO Box 368, Kennett Square PA 19348	610-444-5832	R	5*	<.1
2236	Mario's Express Service Inc—*Mario Pereira*	45 Fernwood Ave, Edison NJ 08837	732-346-6666	R	5*	<.1
2237	Roy Brothers Inc—*Arthur Roy*	764 Boston Rd, Billerica MA 01821	978-667-1921	R	5*	<.1
2238	Sun Express Inc—*Brian Bachar*	13866 Slover Ave, Fontana CA 92337	909-350-8365	R	5*	<.1
2239	Surfaces Transport Inc—*Nick Fiore*	6066 N 76th St, Milwaukee WI 53210	414-461-8600	R	5*	<.1
2240	Whitcomb Trucking Inc—*Gary Whitcomb*	4105 Montdale Park Dr, Valparaiso IN 46383	219-465-3066	R	5*	<.1
2241	James P Poshard and Son Inc—*James Poshard*	PO Box 69, Mount Vernon IN 47620	812-838-5061	R	5*	<.1
2242	Trio Trucking Inc—*Carvel Simmons*	7750 Reinhold Dr, Cincinnati OH 45237	513-679-7100	R	5*	<.1
2243	California Tank Lines Inc—*Michael Ellis*	3105 S El Dorado St, Stockton CA 95206	209-466-3554	R	5*	<.1
2244	Haas Carriage Inc—*Terry Haas*	625 W Utica St, Sellersburg IN 47172	812-246-4481	R	5*	<.1
2245	Jack Key Auto Transportation—*Jamey Key*	9779 Hawn Fwy, Dallas TX 75217	972-557-8210	R	5*	<.1
2246	WDS Enterprises Inc—*William Switzer*	PO Box 491, Shepherd MI 48883	989-828-4900	R	5*	<.1
2247	JA Carman Trucking Company Inc—*Louie Carman*	4 Anderson Dr, Albany NY 12205	518-482-4494	R	5*	<.1
2248	Garrison Hauling Company Inc—*Harold Garrison*	PO Box 237, Thorsby AL 35171	205-646-2831	R	5*	<.1
2249	Lurgan Leasing—*Martin Reiff*	12940 Cumberland Highw, Orrstown PA 17244	717-532-6753	R	5*	<.1
2250	Rio Grande Service Center—*Robert Green*	PO Box 9798, Albuquerque NM 87119	505-877-2349	R	5*	<.1
2251	Total Metal Services Trucking—*Mark Stackpoole*	29850 Ecorse Rd, Romulus MI 48174	734-729-2550	R	5*	<.1
2252	Wallace Transport Inc—*Opie Wallace*	PO Box 67, Planada CA 95365	209-382-0131	R	5*	<.1
2253	Dillard Environmental Service—*Patricia Dillard*	PO Box 579, Byron CA 94514	925-634-6850	R	5*	<.1
2254	California Minibridge Transportation—*RA Curry*	PO Box 92829, Long Beach CA 90809	310-537-1432	R	5*	<.1
2255	Duffy Brothers Inc—*Patrick Duffy*	PO Box 250, Columbus WI 53925	920-623-4160	R	5	<.1
2256	Bassett Transportation Inc—*Phillip McKinley*	652 N Williams St, Carson City MI 48811	989-584-3177	R	5*	<.1
2257	Bingham Trucking—*Lucille Bingham*	RR 3 Box 1049, Atoka OK 74525	580-889-3410	R	5*	<.1
2258	Concrete Delivery Company Inc—*Wesley Nieman*	249 Boxart St, Rochester NY 14612	585-621-0201	R	5*	<.1
2259	Dick Jones Trucking—*Mitch Jones*	PO Box 965, Powell WY 82435	307-754-4132	R	5*	<.1
2260	Hy-Way Transit Inc—*Bonnie Depies*	N 905 Sauk Trl Rd, Cedar Grove WI 53013	920-668-6403	R	5*	<.1
2261	Intermountain Concrete Co—*Tony Frazier*	425 W 1700 S, Salt Lake City UT 84115	801-486-5311	R	5*	<.1
2262	John C Hipp Inc—*John Hipp*	PO Box 437, Millersburg OH 44654	330-674-1651	R	5*	<.1
2263	John R Loomis Inc—*Robert Loomis*	1121 Vt Rt 149, West Pawlet VT 05775	802-645-0983	R	5*	<.1
2264	National Horse Transfer Inc—*William Nichols*	50 Carnation Ave Bldg, Floral Park NY 11001	516-488-8080	R	5*	<.1
2265	Pacific Bulk Transportation Co—*James Tausz*	6250 Caballero Blvd, Buena Park CA 90620		R	5*	<.1
2266	Piedmont Express Inc—*Benjamin Smith*	PO Box 4144, Lynchburg VA 24502	434-845-2546	R	5*	<.1
2267	S and S Cartage Ltd—*Gary Seaton*	PO Box 2712, Loves Park IL 61132	815-877-1090	R	5*	<.1
2268	Warmka Transport Inc—*Rolland Warmka*	PO Box 47, Easton MN 56025	507-787-2289	R	5*	<.1
2269	Zaluzny Excavating Corp—*Walter Zaluzny*	230 Fort Bridgman Rd, Vernon VT 05354	802-254-5758	R	5*	<.1

Rank	Company Name—Executive Officer	Address, City, State, Zip	Phone	Type	Fin	Empls
2270	Hurricane Express Inc—Kaedon Steinert	17663 E Hwy 412, Springdale AR 72764	479-751-3595	R	5*	<.1
2271	American Express Trucking Co—James Shotts	554 E Foothill Blvd St, San Dimas CA 91773	909-599-6026	R	5*	<.1
2272	Crow Wing Transport Inc—James Vant	7740 Central Ave NE, Fridley MN 55432	763-780-5762	R	5*	<.1
2273	JC Duggan Inc—Gerald Cereghino	320 Maspeth Ave, Brooklyn NY 11211	718-384-3260	R	5*	<.1
2274	Warners Moving and Storage Inc—Donald Werner	PO Box 269, Red Lion PA 17356	717-244-4537	R	5*	<.1
2275	Preferred Transportation Corp—Vincent Gorta	91 N Industry Ct, Deer Park NY 11729	631-243-2612	R	5*	<.1
2276	Crown Relocations—Lezlie St Germain	600 Kahelu Ave, Mililani HI 96789	808-625-4520	R	5	N/A
2277	RE Adams—Jimmy Adams	795 Georgia Ave, Gainesville GA 30501	770-534-3608	R	5	N/A
2278	Dworkin Inc—Lew Battaglia	5400 Harvard Ave, Cleveland OH 44105	216-883-9100	R	5	.1
2279	Brankle Brothers Express Ltd—Dennis Brankle	PO Box 568, Marion IN 46952	765-664-9583	R	5	<.1
2280	James E Owen Trucking Inc—James Owen	1091 Blackwater Rd, Forest VA 24551	434-525-2175	R	5	<.1
2281	Kaiser Transport Inc—Todd Kaiser	PO Box 468, Janesville WI 53547	608-752-7271	R	5	<.1
2282	Greylawn Foods Inc—Sidney Goldman	2032 Plainfield Pike, Cranston RI 02921	401-223-4400	R	5	<.1
2283	Rapid Service Inc—Rollie Knoke	PO Box 356, Greer SC 29652	864-848-4171	R	5	.1
2284	Burningham Enterprises Inc—Gary Burningham	PO Box 974, American Fork UT 84003	801-756-8138	R	5	.1
2285	Transit Services Inc—Judith Smith	4014 S Maybelle, Tulsa OK 74107	918-446-6362	R	5	<.1
2286	Doudell Trucking Co—Armand Kunde	555 E Capitol Ave, Milpitas CA 95035	408-263-7300	R	5	<.1
2287	Hab Nab Transportation Inc—Michael Hubbard	PO Box 420, Seaford DE 19973	302-629-5090	R	5	<.1
2288	Mid-Atlantic Transportation Services LL—Tom Harrington	PO Box 1098, Roseboro NC 28382		R	5	<.1
2289	StoneGate Transport—Chuck Deinum	1803 Sheffield Blvd, Houston TX 77015	713-453-6464	R	5	<.1
2290	Pierceton Trucking Company Inc—David Nickol	895 E 200 N, Warsaw IN 46582	574-267-2286	R	5	.1
2291	Beatrice Freight Line Inc—Doug Roseland	PO Box 29136, Lincoln NE 68529		R	5	<.1
2292	Fleetwood Forwarding—Richard Brienza	100 Central Ave, Kearny NJ 07032	973-817-8970	R	5	<.1
2293	Jetco Delivery Inc—Brian Fielcow	5521 Harvey Wilson Dr, Houston TX 77020	713-676-1111	R	5	<.1
2294	Truck Lease Services Inc—Wanda R Butner	4350 Idlewild Industri, Winston Salem NC 27105	336-661-1355	R	5	<.1
2295	Charles Bailey Trucking Inc—Charles Bailey	PO Box 2998, Cookeville TN 38502	931-738-5065	R	5	<.1
2296	Aurora Logistics Inc—John Gillenwater	10944 Marsh Rd, Aurora IN 47001	812-926-1111	R	5	<.1
2297	KAS Trucking Inc—Kenneth Krupp	PO Box 326, Bellevue OH 44811		R	5	<.1
2298	Nealon Transportation Inc—Jerry Derrick	PO Box 459, Binghamton NY 13902	607-773-1581	R	5	<.1
2299	Logix Transportation Inc—Bill Dircks	3730 Macalaster Dr NE, Minneapolis MN 55421		R	5	<.1
2300	Thompson Inc—Ronald Brink	4400 N 24th St, Quincy IL 62305	217-224-9737	R	5	<.1
2301	D and R Trucking—Daniel Gamblin	201 Simpson St, Pratt KS 67124	620-672-7713	R	5	<.1
2302	Storewide Delivery Company Inc—Carmine Zeccardi	194 County Ave, Secaucus NJ 07094	201-330-1997	R	5	<.1
2303	Stuart's Household Furn Moving and Storage—Anthony Stuart	PO Box 44028, Indianapolis IN 46244	317-924-0505	R	5	<.1
2304	Liquid Cargo Inc—Mark Jackson	PO Box 482, Kearny NJ 07032	201-991-7375	R	5	<.1
2305	Relocation Systems LLP—John Licata	22884 Cedar Green Rd, Sterling VA 20166	703-925-9556	R	5	N/A
2306	Jim Bender Inc—Jim Bender	7840 F St, Omaha NE 68127	402-331-6423	R	5	<.1
2307	Turnbo Motor Express Inc—Larry Turnbo	PO Box 1148, Savannah TN 38372	731-925-6446	R	5	<.1
2308	Three Rivers Trucking Inc—Rod Pinkett	PO Box 2728, Farmington NM 87499	505-632-5300	R	5	<.1
2309	Triple R Trucking Inc—Rick Willett	1303 Woodside Ave, Essexville MI 48732	989-892-1569	R	5	<.1
2310	D and I Trucking Inc—Jerry Thigpen	PO Box 878, Maxton NC 28364	910-844-3021	R	5	<.1
2311	American Storage and Transport—Christopher Shea	1860 Walt Whitman Rd, Melville NY 11747	631-293-1700	R	5	<.1
2312	Trailer Convoys Inc—Jeff Bishop	Po Box 14, Jeffersonville IN 47131	812-283-5088	R	5	<.1
2313	Cox Refrigerated Express Inc—Billy Cox	PO Box 541235, Dallas TX 75354		R	5	<.1
2314	Thomas and Thomas Inc—Harold Thomas	218 Jim Veatch Rd, Morganfield KY 42437	270-389-4281	R	5*	<.1
2315	McClellan Truck Lines—Nick McClellan	PO Box 1327, Tifton GA 31793	229-386-5944	R	5	<.1
2316	Sercombe Trucking Company Inc—Jim Sercombe	3001 Shirley Dr, Jackson MI 49201	517-784-9137	R	5	<.1
2317	Joy Truck Lines Inc—Mack Baker	119 Maresca Dr NE, Dalton GA 30721	706-259-6303	R	5	<.1
2318	Pozas Brothers Trucking Co—Jeff Maillo	8130 Enterprise Dr, Newark CA 94560	510-742-9939	R	5	<.1
2319	Don Gray Trucking Inc—Don Gray	PO Box 5362, Kingsport TN 37663		R	5	<.1
2320	Cummings Transportation—Pam Cummings	19609 Broken Ct, Shafter CA 93263	661-746-1786	R	5	<.1
2321	Barry Trucking Inc—John Rohatsch	3073 S Chase Ave Bldg, Milwaukee WI 53207	414-274-6158	R	5*	<.1
2322	Sprinter Services Inc—James Zevalkink	2900 Dixie Ave SW, Grandville MI 49418	616-514-6001	R	5	<.1
2323	Westbury Logistics—Matthew Casamassima	21 Vandeventer Ave, Port Washington NY 11050	516-883-8400	R	5	<.1
2324	JTW Air Express Inc—Vernon Walls	30690 Cypress Rd, Romulus MI 48174	734-727-5899	R	5	<.1
2325	Guess Freighways Inc—Charles Guess	PO Box 644, Hobart IN 46342	219-947-4679	R	5	<.1
2326	J and D Trucking Inc—James Duffey	PO Box 228, Granite Falls NC 28630	828-396-5227	R	5	<.1
2327	BPI Transportation Inc—Lori Parrish	PO Box 368, Decatur AL 35602	256-355-1926	R	5	<.1
2328	Taylor Services Inc—Darryl Taylor	200 Neal Dr, Blairsville PA 15717	724-459-8901	R	4	.1
2329	Tindall Haul and Erect Inc—William Lowndes	PO Box 1778, Spartanburg SC 29304	864-576-3230	R	4	<.1
2330	WAY Delivery Services—John Wayne	1301 Harrisburg Pike, Lancaster PA 17603	717-299-0992	R	4	<.1
2331	Norgaard Trucking Inc—Shiela Norgaard	181 S Bloomingdale Rd, Bloomingdale IL 60108	630-671-1750	R	4	<.1
2332	Three Way Transfer of Arkansas—Marshall Yantis	1022 S "Y" St, Fort Smith AR 72901	479-782-8960	R	4	<.1
2333	Blue Velvet Transport Inc—Phyllis Bulso	PO Box 9477, Canton OH 44711	330-478-1426	R	4	<.1
2334	Mercury Transportation Inc—Eric Moerbe	8502 Miller Rd 3, Houston TX 77049	281-458-4340	R	4	<.1
2335	Valley Pallet Trucking Inc—Mike Hackett	PO Box 2088, Salinas CA 93902	831-422-3875	R	4	<.1
2336	White Transportation Services—Gin Durham	PO Box 3772, Lubbock TX 79452	806-745-7811	R	4	<.1
2337	Global Enterprises Inc—Stanley Golenia	699 Washington St, South Attleboro MA 02703	508-399-8270	R	4*	<.1
2338	Megatrux Transportation Inc—Karen Pelle	18725 San Jose Ave, City of Industry CA 91748		R	4	.1
2339	National Transportation Corp—Scott Lunt	1281 Jarvis Ave, Elk Grove Village IL 60007		R	4	<.1
2340	True North Trucking—Mike Conway	3710 Leharps Dr, Youngstown OH 44515	330-793-0569	R	4	<.1
2341	Bossong's Commercial Delivery—Edward Bossong	6713 Pickard Dr E, Syracuse NY 13211	315-455-7431	R	4	<.1
2342	Halls of Cross Inc—Richmond Halls	PO Box 249, Cross SC 29436	843-753-2040	R	4	<.1
2343	Merchants Forwarding Co—Thomas S Brennan	18765 Seaway Dr, Melvindale MI 48122		R	4	<.1
2344	F Smith Cartage Co—William Pavin	41 Walter Ct, Lake in the Hills IL 60156	847-854-1555	R	4	<.1
2345	Triangle Transportation and Distribution Service—Jack Moser	201 Aero Ct, Greensboro NC 27409	336-668-0156	R	4	<.1
2346	Container Transfer Corp—Scott Ford	PO Box 26053, Salt Lake City UT 84126	801-973-8207	R	4	<.1
2347	JE Phillips and Sons Inc—Billy Phillips	1500 Hernando Rd, Memphis TN 38106	901-774-7680	R	4	<.1
2348	CRW Inc—Charles Wood	3716 S Elyria Rd, Shreve OH 44676	330-264-3785	R	4	<.1
2349	Central Transport Co—Tom Abler	PO Box 249, Norfolk NE 68702	402-371-9517	R	4	<.1
2350	Target Trucking Inc—Dan McKee	2960 N 500 E, Vernal UT 84078	435-789-5758	R	4	<.1
2351	Rapco Distributing Co—Roy Van Derlinden	3984 S 500 W, Salt Lake City UT 84123	801-262-2041	R	4	<.1
2352	Leoni Motor Express Inc—Michael Leoni	501-23 Ashland Ave, Chicago Heights IL 60411	708-756-3232	R	4	<.1
2353	SACS Trucking Inc—Dan Poling	9000 Cartage Rd, Missoula MT 59808	406-541-7227	R	4	<.1
2354	Flynn Transport Inc—Sue Flynn	RR 6 Box 6027, Towanda PA 18848	570-265-3456	R	4	<.1
2355	Piepho Moving and Storage Inc—Larry Piepho	1300 Oak Forest Dr, Onalaska WI 54650	608-783-3400	R	4	<.1
2356	A and A Trucking Inc—Julie Hazen	PO Box 75608, Oklahoma City OK 73147	405-949-0515	R	4	<.1
2357	Jensen Transport Inc—Roxie Mell-Brandts	55318 State Hwy 68, Mankato MN 56001	507-387-4403	R	4	.1
2358	John R Trucking Company Inc—Thomas Mueller	205 Smalley Rd, Cincinnati OH 45215	513-733-0077	R	4	<.1
2359	Republic Express Inc—James Kelley	PO Box 628, Hudson WI 54016	715-381-1550	R	4	<.1

Note: An asterisk (*) indicates an estimated financial figure. The company type code used is as follows: R = Private, P = Public, S = Private Subsidiary, B = Public Subsidiary, D = Division, J = Joint Venture, I = Investment Fund.

COMPANY RANKINGS BY SALES WITHIN 4-DIGIT SIC

Rank	Company Name—Executive Officer	Address, City, State, Zip	Phone	Type	Fin	Empls
2360	Goodman Tank Lines Inc—Craig Goodman	463 Old Reading Pke, Pottstown PA 19464	610-970-9250	R	4*	.1
2361	Sterling Transport Company Inc—Hugh Hinton	PO Box 456, Lakeview NC 28350	910-245-6502	R	4*	.1
2362	Max Express (Carson California)—Jack Hao	22440 S Alameda St, Carson CA 90810	310-834-0888	R	4*	.1
2363	McCallum Transfer Inc—Daniel McCallum	3501 Marshall St NE, Minneapolis MN 55418	651-633-1612	R	4*	.1
2364	Spokane Transfer and Storage Co—Dale Ross	PO Box 3181, Spokane WA 99220	509-535-7636	R	4*	.1
2365	Brazil Trucking Inc—Keith Roberts	PO Box 202, Brazil IN 47834	812-442-7221	R	4*	.1
2366	JT Wein Inc—Morris Weinstein	PO Box 1120, Opelousas LA 70571	337-948-3939	R	4*	.1
2367	Wright Motor Lines Inc—Gladys Knox	PO Box 79, Armagh PA 15920	814-446-5611	R	4*	.1
2368	Cannonball Trucking Inc—Ronald Eubanks	PO Box 262523, Houston TX 77207	713-644-7300	R	4*	.1
2369	Baarts Trucking Inc—Larry Baarts	333 S 4th Ave E, Truman MN 56088	507-776-8161	R	4*	.1
2370	Charlie Baucom Inc—Charlie Baucom	PO Box 160, Belle Mina AL 35615	256-233-4870	R	4*	.1
2371	Checker Logistics Inc—Bob Johnson	1725 Dixie Rd, Neenah WI 54957	920-727-5701	R	4*	.1
2372	Elgin Milk Service Inc—Forrest Walters	PO Box 365, Elgin MN 55932	507-876-2831	R	4*	.1
2373	Enterprise Truck Lines Inc—Michael Kibler	9148 Louisiana St Unit, Merrillville IN 46410	219-736-9200	R	4*	.1
2374	Overseas Freight Inc—Robert Wang	1525 Seabright Ave, Long Beach CA 90813	562-980-1811	R	4*	.1
2375	TCT Trucking Inc—David Dossett	PO Box 470, La Follette TN 37766	423-562-9864	R	4*	.1
2376	Tree Line Transportion Inc—Jim Olson	PO Box 8, Turner OR 97392	503-743-2181	R	4*	.1
2377	TTSI HoldingsInc—Paul Temple	PO Box 421078, Indianapolis IN 46242		R	4*	.1
2378	Valley Express LLC—Ronald Jankowski	PO Box 472, Neenah WI 54957	920-231-1677	R	4*	.1
2379	Daniel Company of Springfield—Larry Daniel	3725 W Division St, Springfield MO 65803	417-869-7511	R	4*	<.1
2380	Logistics One—William McNeary IV	33 Cady Hill Blvd, Saratoga Springs NY 12866	518-587-3700	R	4*	<.1
2381	Mack Transport Inc—Jim Clement	PO Box 335, Valley City OH 44280	330-483-3111	R	4*	<.1
2382	Kallmeyer Brothers Enterprises—Larry Kallmeyer	PO Box 223, Hermann MO 65041	573-486-5714	R	4*	<.1
2383	Bigge Crane and Rigging Co—Weston J Settlemier	10700 Bigge St, San Leandro CA 94577	510-638-8100	R	4*	<.1
2384	Stack Container Service Inc—Stan Jurcevic	PO Box 19068, Cleveland OH 44119	216-531-7555	R	4*	<.1
2385	Stellar Express Inc—Frederick Schaupp	2100 Riverside Dr Ste, Green Bay WI 54301	920-431-3500	R	4*	<.1
2386	Allstate Delivery Service Co—Dale Robison	55 W 78th St, Bloomington MN 55420	952-884-0765	R	4*	<.1
2387	By-Line Transit Inc—Deborah Bywater	17075 White Stone Rd, Marysville OH 43040	937-642-2500	R	4*	<.1
2388	Freight All Kinds Inc—Sam Marcove	PO Box 5187, Denver CO 80217	303-289-5433	R	4*	<.1
2389	Nebraska Coast Inc—Fred Gach	PO Box 1865, Council Bluffs IA 51502	712-366-2551	R	4*	<.1
2390	RTI Transport Inc—Dave Devries	5635 Clay Ave SW, Grand Rapids MI 49548	616-531-1850	R	4*	<.1
2391	Runge Trucking Inc—Mark Runge	1401 7th Ave S, Saint James MN 56081	507-375-3283	R	4*	<.1
2392	Sea Truck Inc—Henry Schatz	2800 NW 105th Ave, Miami FL 33172	305-526-3144	R	4*	<.1
2393	Tipton Trucking Company Inc—Frank Tipton	397 Waterway Rd, Oxford PA 19363	610-932-5120	R	4*	<.1
2394	WJ Dillner Transfer Co—William Dillner	4160 Washington Rd Ste, McMurray PA 15317	724-942-0230	R	4*	<.1
2395	Wooten Transports Inc—Mike Lathum	153 Gaston Ave, Memphis TN 38106	901-948-9031	R	4*	<.1
2396	DeWitt Brothers Inc—Roy Mintzmyer	843 S Hwy 89, Chino Valley AZ 86323	928-636-0303	R	4*	<.1
2397	JSG Trucking Company Inc—J Giammona	19400 N Hwy 99, Acampo CA 95220	209-368-8815	R	4*	<.1
2398	TJ's Trucking Inc—Terry Jenema	6961 S 45 Rd, Cadillac MI 49601	231-775-3213	R	4	<.1
2399	Cavanaugh Trucking Inc—Reid Cavanaugh	318 Everson Valley Rd, Connellsville PA 15425	724-628-1018	R	4*	<.1
2400	Hall Transfer and Storage Inc—John Hall	67 Mall Dr, Commack NY 11725		R	4*	<.1
2401	Lee and Eastes Tank Lines Inc—Jill Eastes-Newcomb	2418 Airport Way S, Seattle WA 98134		R	4*	<.1
2402	Waccamaw Transport Inc—Roger Clark	PO Box 368, Selma NC 27576	919-965-6311	R	4*	<.1
2403	Freightmaster Inc—Keith Stokes	PO Box 865, Taylorsville NC 28681	828-632-8511	R	4*	<.1
2404	Advance Transport Inc—James Watts	PO Box 550, Advance MO 63730	573-722-3464	R	4*	<.1
2405	ASAP Express Inc—John Cummings	PO Box 1693, Taylor MI 48180	734-946-2052	R	4*	<.1
2406	Brittain Trucking Inc—Britt Brittain	PO Box 1420, Tuscaloosa AL 35403	205-345-0115	R	4*	<.1
2407	CAT Inc—Artis Williams	PO Box 6228, Pearl MS 39288	601-939-4992	R	4*	<.1
2408	KBT Inc—Tim May	PO Box 768, Sidney OH 45365	937-498-1388	R	4*	<.1
2409	Swifty Transportation Inc—Don Myers	PO Box 1002, Seymour IN 47274	812-522-1640	R	4*	<.1
2410	Wallace Transportation Inc—Joel Wallace	532 Peterbelt Ln, Woodland PA 16881		R	4*	<.1
2411	AC Wright Trucking Inc—Stanley Wright	1916 N 2nd St, Booneville MS 38829	662-728-7744	R	4*	<.1
2412	Alton Delivery Service Co—Marco Putre	PO Box 756, Mattoon IL 61938	217-235-2223	R	4*	<.1
2413	DST Inc—Steve Freckman	805 S 72nd St, Milwaukee WI 53214	414-453-5335	R	4*	<.1
2414	Elliott Bay Service Transfer—Michael Edens	305 Upland Dr, Tukwila WA 98188	206-575-9187	R	4*	<.1
2415	Force Transportation Inc—Randy Forse	PO Box 6212, Pasadena TX 77506	713-473-8378	R	4*	<.1
2416	Helser Brothers Transfer Co—James Helser	PO Box 83183, Portland OR 97283	503-978-1090	R	4*	<.1
2417	Houston Transportation Inc—Robert Houston	PO Box 121, Spruce Pine NC 28777	828-765-1733	R	4*	<.1
2418	Lewis Truck Lines Inc—LeRoy LeMaster	2025 Hwy 378, Conway SC 29527	843-248-5984	R	4*	<.1
2419	McCammon Trucking Inc—Darrell McCammon	3365 E 400 N, Hartford City IN 47348	765-348-0493	R	4*	<.1
2420	Ocoee River Transport Inc—Wanda Winters	PO Box 3663, Cleveland TN 37320	423-339-0376	R	4*	<.1
2421	Parker's Express Inc—Lin Parker	625 Dawson Dr, Newark DE 19713	302-737-7537	R	4*	<.1
2422	Piedmont Transportation of Vale NC—Gay Miller	2361 Ben Yount Ln, Vale NC 28168	704-276-1033	R	4*	<.1
2423	Tech Transportation—Marc Pierce	566 Walcott St, Pawtucket RI 02861		R	4*	<.1
2424	Watkins Transportation Inc—Larry Watkins	PO Box 1976, Sherman TX 75091	903-868-1623	R	4*	<.1
2425	BSV Transportation—Diane Roberts	PO Box 407, Plymouth WI 53073	920-892-3000	R	4	<.1
2426	Great Northern Transportation Co—David Niec	5205 E Vienna Rd, Clio MI 48420		R	4*	<.1
2427	Li-Way Transfer and Storage Inc—Wayne Pugh	55 Chamisa Rd, Covington GA 30016	770-787-8113	R	4	<.1
2428	Sugarcreek Cartage Company Inc—Doug Miller	PO Box 494, Sugarcreek OH 44681	330-852-2213	R	4*	<.1
2429	TCI Trucking and Warehousing Services—Jack Jensen Jr	3900 France Road Pkwy, New Orleans LA 70126	504-734-0561	R	4*	<.1
2430	DAE Trucking Inc—Carl Bates	PO Box 1209, Canton TX 75103	903-567-1072	R	4*	<.1
2431	Figgins Transport Ltd—Marvin Figgins	PO Box 938, Grand Rapids MN 55744	218-326-9477	R	4*	<.1
2432	Jesse Ford Trucking—Gary Ford	PO Box 16754, Louisville KY 40256	502-447-4828	R	4*	<.1
2433	Sonny Peterson Trucking Inc—Carl Peterson	PO Box 276, Swanville MN 56382	320-547-2489	R	4*	<.1
2434	Richies Delivery Inc—Richard Deslongchamps	1 Bert Dr Ste 8, West Bridgewater MA 02379	508-586-7674	R	4*	<.1
2435	TMSI Transport—Larry Krasowski	PO Box 615, Buffalo NY 14240	716-895-8674	R	4*	<.1
2436	Wes-Flo Company Inc—James Perry	5707 N 54th St, Tampa FL 33610	813-626-2171	R	4*	<.1
2437	Bones Transportation Inc—Paul Bones	PO Box 80, Ottawa KS 66067	785-242-3660	R	4*	<.1
2438	Brewton Express Inc—Harold Anderson	5794 Hwy 167 N, Winnfield LA 71483	318-628-3156	R	4	<.1
2439	DaRan Inc—Randy Hanson	PO Box 134, Zimmerman MN 55398	763-856-4000	R	4*	<.1
2440	DR Smith Trucking Inc—Devon Smith	10491 S 750 W, Akron IN 46910	260-352-2115	R	4*	<.1
2441	Drees Transportation—Thomas Drees	PO Box 154, Peshtigo WI 54157	715-582-4575	R	4*	<.1
2442	G and F Trucking Leasing Inc—Raymond Gerling	PO Box 4032, Hammond IN 46324	219-944-8695	R	4*	<.1
2443	Gem State Transportation Inc—Steve Walters	PO Box 265, Kimberly ID 83341	208-734-9062	R	4*	<.1
2444	General Delivery Inc—James Thompson	1822 Morgantown Ave, Fairmont WV 26554	304-363-4400	R	4	<.1
2445	Green Transfer and Storage Co—Norbert Trudeau	10099 N Portland Rd, Portland OR 97203	503-286-0673	R	4*	<.1
2446	Judy Jones Trucking Inc—Judy Jones	PO Box 98, Naples NC 28760	828-684-5698	R	4*	<.1
2447	Kerry Transport Inc—John F Doyle	3460 E Washington Rd, Saginaw MI 48601	989-754-6871	R	4*	<.1
2448	MC Tank Transport Inc—Timothy Anderson	10134 Mosteller Ln, West Chester OH 45069	513-771-8667	R	4*	<.1
2449	Norton Brothers Inc—Ralph Norton	40 Kellogg Rd, Essex Junction VT 05452	802-878-7112	R	4*	<.1

Rank	Company Name—Executive Officer	Address, City, State, Zip	Phone	Type	Fin	Empls
2450	Prime Time Transportation—Gerald Bachelor	9003 Tara Blvd, Jonesboro GA 30236	770-477-1755	R	4*	<.1
2451	Ren Potterfield Trucking Inc—Ren Potterfield	404 US Hwy 24/36 E, Monroe City MO 63456	573-735-4528	R	4*	<.1
2452	Rohrer Trucking Inc—Robert Rohrer	3180 Rte 6, Waterford PA 16441	814-796-6747	R	4*	<.1
2453	Senske and Son Transfer Co—James Senske	PO Box 13022, Grand Forks ND 58208	701-746-6472	R	4*	<.1
2454	Smith Truck Service Inc—Dino Rotellini	PO Box 1329, Steubenville OH 43952	740-535-0551	R	4*	<.1
2455	Triangle Trucking Inc—Patricia Counts	2250 Hein Ave, Salina KS 67401	785-827-5500	R	4*	<.1
2456	West Bend Transit and Service—Ben Schloemer	PO Box 477, West Bend WI 53095	262-334-2386	R	4*	<.1
2457	Western Refrigerated Freight System—Jeff Boley	PO Box 40, Tolleson AZ 85353	602-254-9922	R	4*	<.1
2458	Whimsy Inc—Matthew O'Mara	1901 Busse Rd, Mount Prospect IL 60056	847-690-1246	R	4*	<.1
2459	Your Town Transport Inc—Mark Heding	PO Box 56, Elroy WI 53929	608-462-5543	R	4*	<.1
2460	Fast Way Freight Systems Inc—Jeff Bosma	PO Box 40142, Spokane WA 99220	509-534-9351	R	4*	<.1
2461	Hobbs Enterprises Inc—Eric Hobbs	PO Box 413, Woodside DE 19980	302-697-2090	R	4*	<.1
2462	Maiers Transport and Warehousing—John Maiers	PO Box 218, Saint Cloud MN 56302	320-251-6882	R	4*	<.1
2463	Triple S Hauling Inc—David Poe	2602 N Stadium Blvd, Columbia MO 65202		R	4*	<.1
2464	AH Newman Inc—Richard Newman	PO Box 28, Clifford ND 58016	701-488-2778	R	4	<.1
2465	Bear Cartage and Intermodal—Nicholas Urso	8600 W Joliet Rd, McCook IL 60525	708-924-9093	R	4*	<.1
2466	Caribbean Shipping Services Inc—Paul Robins	1505 Dennis St, Jacksonville FL 32204	904-358-0027	R	4*	<.1
2467	Eidson and Ussery Inc—Charles Eidson	2451 S Odell Ave, Marshall MO 65340	660-886-6922	R	4*	<.1
2468	HH Omps Inc—John Omps	1800 Martinsburg Pke, Winchester VA 22603	540-667-4919	R	4*	<.1
2469	Regional Associates Inc—Willie Russell	2350 S Midwest Blvd St, Midwest City OK 73110	405-869-7166	R	4*	<.1
2470	Vancouver Warehouse and Distribution—Charles Bower	PO Box 61486, Vancouver WA 98666	360-693-1487	R	4*	<.1
2471	Hill Grain Inc—Richard Hill	PO Box 246, Commerce TX 75429	903-886-3133	R	4*	<.1
2472	Justa Truck Trucking Inc—Michael Burr	43581 Hwy 30, Lexington NE 68850	308-324-6366	R	4*	<.1
2473	Ralph Martinez Trucking Inc—Ralph Martinez	7255 Ivanhoe St, Commerce City CO 80022	303-288-8788	R	4*	<.1
2474	Barry Bashore Inc—Barry Bashore	PO Box 318, Bethel PA 19507	717-933-8686	R	4*	<.1
2475	Battelini Transportation Systems—Albert Battelini	PO Box 298, Landisville NJ 08326	856-697-9595	R	4*	<.1
2476	Bay Motor Transport Inc—Jeff LeClaire	PO Box 28377, Green Bay WI 54324	920-983-3400	R	4	<.1
2477	Bernard D Harner and Son Inc—Bernard Harner	PO Box 126, Washington IN 47501	812-254-2247	R	4*	<.1
2478	Graham Trucking Company Inc—Robert Graham	722 S Chicago St, Seattle WA 98108	206-762-6099	R	4*	<.1
2479	Huebner and Son Trucking Inc—Roger Huebner	PO Box 486, Boonville IN 47601	812-897-1454	R	4*	<.1
2480	Jenkins Farms Inc—Keith Jenkins	8637 State Rt 36 N, Arkport NY 14807	607-295-7726	R	4*	<.1
2481	Mhart Express Inc—Randy Gearhart	PO Box 192, Hope IN 47246	812-546-5010	R	4*	<.1
2482	Olmsted Transportation Co—Bart Smith	22529 Knapp Rd, Mount Vernon WA 98273	360-424-7528	R	4*	<.1
2483	Paul Watts Trucking Inc—Rich Johnson	3668 Summit Rd, Norton OH 44203	330-745-9278	R	4*	<.1
2484	Pouliot and Corriveau Inc—Raymond Pouliot	185 Ferno Rd, Williamstown VT 05679	802-476-3462	R	4*	<.1
2485	S and S X-Press LLC—June Seng	PO Box 12579, Grand Forks ND 58208	701-746-8484	R	4*	<.1
2486	Sandra K Easley Trucking/DET Co—Sandra Easley	PO Box 40, Ben Wheeler TX 75754	903-833-5603	R	4*	<.1
2487	TC Transportation Inc—Ron Nunes	PO Box 709, Crystal Lake IL 60039	815-459-5724	R	4*	<.1
2488	Tonawanda Tank Transport Service—Thomas Napier	PO Box H, Buffalo NY 14217	716-874-0400	R	4*	<.1
2489	Urban Express—Mike Fiorito	229 W 36th St, New York NY 10018	212-855-5555	R	4*	<.1
2490	GR Daniels Trucking Inc—Gary R Daniels	19258 Turner Ave, Hutchinson MN 55350	320-587-4002	R	4*	<.1
2491	A-1 Pioneer Moving and Storage—Douglas Bagley	2001 Warm Springs Rd, Salt Lake City UT 84116	801-328-4796	R	4*	<.1
2492	Advanced Waste Carriers Inc—Larry Lyons	1126 S 70th St, West Allis WI 53214	414-475-3100	R	4*	<.1
2493	CC Caldwell Trucking Inc—Adelle Caldwell	2204 Jackson Pike, Bidwell OH 45614	740-446-1922	R	4*	<.1
2494	Nu-Way Trucking Inc—Randall Walker	PO Box 39, Alexander City AL 35011	256-329-0022	R	4	<.1
2495	Santa Clara Transfer Service—Russ Johnson	11080 Commercial Pkwy, Castroville CA 95012	831-633-5941	R	4*	<.1
2496	Hi-Ball Trucking Inc—Trent Smith	PO Box 80325, Billings MT 59108	406-656-6700	R	4*	<.1
2497	AC Trucking Inc—Chris Athanasiadis	2 Commerce Dr, O'Fallon MO 63366	636-278-5666	R	4*	<.1
2498	Anderson Transportation Co—Keith Anderson	PO Box 352, Forreston IL 61030	815-938-2493	R	4*	<.1
2499	Charles E Groff and Sons Inc—Wilbur Groff	1284 Cloverleaf Rd, Mount Joy PA 17552	717-653-1357	R	4*	<.1
2500	CKR Transport Ltd—Helen Clark	770 N Church Rd Ste F, Elmhurst IL 60126	630-279-0412	R	4*	<.1
2501	Cornerstone Transportation Inc—Ken Kimsey	PO Box 1087, Forest Park GA 30298	404-366-4738	R	4*	<.1
2502	Don Stockley Trucking LLC—Mary Stockley	3995 S 300 W, Salt Lake City UT 84107	801-265-2220	R	4*	<.1
2503	F and T Trucking Company Inc—Antonio Ayala	6900 Nolan Ave, North Bergen NJ 07047	201-864-1889	R	4*	<.1
2504	John DeGrand and Son Inc—Tom DeGrand	PO Box 16609, West Haven CT 06516	203-933-7726	R	4*	<.1
2505	RBR Trucking Inc—Richard McArdle	PO Box 337, Rockton IL 61072	815-389-2989	R	4*	<.1
2506	RCD Trucking Inc—Ray Kramer	PO Box 0097, Kankakee IL 60901	815-939-0122	R	4*	<.1
2507	Fiamingo Moving and Storage Inc—Anthony Fiamingo	18610 Rte 6, Mansfield PA 16933	570-662-3171	R	4	<.1
2508	Cobra Transportation Services Inc	301 Eaton St, Saint Paul MN 55107	651-552-1151	R	4*	<.1
2509	Semper Truck Lines Inc—Martin Semper	8355 McMullin Grade, Fresno CA 93706	559-268-9408	R	4*	<.1
2510	TM Morley Inc—James Soave	24471 N River Rd, Mount Clemens MI 48043	586-465-6500	R	4*	<.1
2511	Gilco Trucking—Lee Gill	PO Box 112, La Fargeville NY 13656	315-658-9916	R	4*	<.1
2512	Quality Transportation Services	5220 S Cameron St, Las Vegas NV 89118	702-220-7000	S	4*	<.1
2513	Roberts Trucking Inc—Sandra Roberts	N9250 State Rd 26, Eldorado WI 54932	920-872-2281	R	4*	<.1
2514	Binghamton-Ithaca Express Inc—John Cole	PO Box 1133, Binghamton NY 13902	607-723-9433	R	4*	<.1
2515	Central Air Freight Services—Robert Conahan	PO Box 99, Hazleton PA 18201		R	4	<.1
2516	Daniel L Ribbe Trucking Inc—Daniel Ribbe	510 W 5th St, Tilton IL 61833	217-446-0207	R	4*	<.1
2517	Dump Trucks Inc—Michael Smith	PO Box 326, Clinton IN 47842	765-832-5102	R	4*	<.1
2518	Johncox Trucking Inc—Alan Stuart	5575 Wolcott Dr, Avon NY 14414	585-226-6610	R	4*	<.1
2519	Naglee Moving and Storage Inc—Philip Schweiger	PO Box 2039, Elmira NY 14903	607-733-4671	R	4*	<.1
2520	Nova Cor Ltd—Kenneth Szwaida	PO Box 2584, Buffalo NY 14240	716-823-9562	R	4*	<.1
2521	Oil Recovery Corp—Jonathan Gagnon	PO Box 1065, West Springfield MA 01090	413-737-2949	R	4*	<.1
2522	Owen's CFS Inc—Steve Sun	1595 W Walnut Pky, Compton CA 90220	310-764-1111	R	4*	<.1
2523	American International Moving—G Shelley	PO Box 2317, Fort Walton Beach FL 32549	850-243-7324	R	4*	<.1
2524	Scott Transportation Inc—Wayne Scott	232 Main St Ste 10, Fort Fairfield ME 04742	207-473-0063	R	4*	<.1
2525	Carolina Public Warehouse Inc—Larry Hicks	PO Box 4508, Winston Salem NC 27115	336-767-2891	R	4*	<.1
2526	Celli Trucking Co—E Celli	10328 Belle Plaine Ave, Schiller Park IL 60176	847-447-5530	R	4*	<.1
2527	L and S Trucking Inc—Scott Gross	3490 S 1500 E, Vernal UT 84078	435-789-7838	R	4*	<.1
2528	Transform Trucking Co—Al Jennings	1800 NE Broadway Ave, Des Moines IA 50313	515-266-1141	R	4*	<.1
2529	Lambert Moving and Storage Inc—Brian Lambert	3215 Roberson Rd, Florence AL 35630	256-764-0681	R	4*	<.1
2530	Sloane Moving and Storage Company Inc—Patrick Stanton	855 Township Line Rd, Elkins Park PA 19027	215-576-8459	R	4*	<.1
2531	Bester Brothers Transfer and Storage—Douglas Bester	260 Hardman Ave S, South Saint Paul MN 55075	651-451-1018	R	4*	<.1
2532	Elton M Harvey Trucking Inc—Peter Marsicano	1408 Perrineville Rd, Monroe Township NJ 08831	609-371-7600	R	4*	<.1
2533	Henderson Specialties Inc—Paul Henderson	2008 E 2nd St, Russellville AR 72801	479-967-3235	R	4*	<.1
2534	Leonard Transportation Corp—Leonard Gannet	475 Division St Bldg 3, Elizabeth NJ 07201	908-289-5500	R	4*	<.1
2535	Stateline Ag Service Inc—J Isch	RR 1 Box 901, Dawson NE 68337	402-855-2355	R	4*	<.1
2536	Donald L Brown Trucking—Donald Brown	PO Box 335, Warren IL 61087	815-745-3469	R	4	<.1
2537	Stempihar Brothers Distributing—John Stempihar	PO Box 21, Bessemer MI 49911	906-667-0852	R	4*	<.1
2538	Quality Cartage Inc—Jerry Reynolds	7580 State Rd, Burbank IL 60459	708-496-2500	R	4*	<.1
2539	Leeway Transportation Inc—Tish Farrell	PO Box 2145, Houston TX 77252	281-449-8777	R	4	.1

Note: An asterisk (*) indicates an estimated financial figure. The company type code used is as follows: R = Private, P = Public, S = Private Subsidiary, B = Public Subsidiary, D = Division, J = Joint Venture, I = Investment Fund.

COMPANY RANKINGS BY SALES WITHIN 4-DIGIT SIC

Rank	Company Name—*Executive Officer*	Address, City, State, Zip	Phone	Type	Fin	Empls
2540	JMW Trucking Services Inc—*John Slutz*	512 45th St SW, Canton OH 44706	330-484-2428	R	4	<.1
2541	Covered Wagon Train Inc—*Mary Ann Parmley*	1 Park Dr, Hornell NY 14843	607-324-2306	R	4	<.1
2542	Don Sumpter Trucking Inc—*Donald Sumpter*	6791 W US Hwy 50, Medora IN 47260	812-966-2919	R	4	<.1
2543	PC Transport Inc—*Violet Christopherson*	PO Box 880, Casper WY 82602	307-235-3367	R	4	<.1
2544	Midwest Cargo Systems Inc—*Robert Cunningham*	1050 W Pershing Rd 2nd, Chicago IL 60609	773-847-7800	R	4	<.1
2545	Studdard Moving and Storage—*Charles Campbell*	201 Commercial St, Leavenworth KS 66048		R	4	<.1
2546	Lakehead Trucking Inc—*Gregory Kaneski*	6035 Lavaque Rd, Duluth MN 55803	218-721-3521	R	4	<.1
2547	P and H Transportation Inc—*George Pratt*	PO Box 458, Bradford VT 05033	603-787-2085	R	4	<.1
2548	Feldspar Trucking Company Inc—*William Norris*	PO Box 705, Spruce Pine NC 28777	828-765-7491	R	4	<.1
2549	Nelson Inc—*Scott Nelson*	PO Box 38, Deerwood MN 56444	218-534-3521	R	4	<.1
2550	Hartz Truck Line Inc—*Keith Higginbotham*	PO Box 618, Thief River Falls MN 56701	218-681-3295	R	4	<.1
2551	Van Hof Trucking Inc—*Duane Van Veldhuizen*	710 E 1st St, Sanborn IA 51248	712-729-3010	R	4	<.1
2552	Winter Truck Line Inc—*Bill Winter*	1485 230th St, Mahnomen MN 56557	218-935-2236	R	4	<.1
2553	Time Auto Transportation Inc—*James Ferns*	575 E Elmwood Ave, Troy MI 48083	248-588-5200	R	4	<.1
2554	Carl McCarty Trucking LLC—*Carl McCarty*	PO Box 55, Texline TX 79087	806-362-4807	R	4	<.1
2555	Graves Trucking Inc—*John Walda*	PO Box 9121, Fort Wayne IN 46899	260-747-1842	R	4	<.1
2556	WH Fay Co—*Benjamin Gregg*	3020 Quigley Rd, Cleveland OH 44113	216-861-4232	R	4	<.1
2557	Tri-B Inc—*Michael Brummett*	PO Box 949, Burnside KY 42519	606-561-6498	R	4	<.1
2558	Paisley Trucking Inc—*Gene Paisley*	19917 Hwy 52 N, Durango IA 52039	563-552-2617	R	4	<.1
2559	Montgomery Air Freight—*Todd Vickers*	PO Box 250223, Montgomery AL 36125	334-281-9157	R	4	<.1
2560	N and N Transport Inc—*Mike Newman*	7170 Hwy 96, Belk AL 35545	205-932-4574	R	4	N/A
2561	George W Burnett Inc—*Eric Bauer*	145 Ganson St, Buffalo NY 14203	716-856-8300	R	4	<.1
2562	Moore Brothers Inc—*Terry Moore*	PO Box 1381, Norfolk NE 68702	402-371-8100	R	4	<.1
2563	Yeatts Transfer Co—*P Debernard*	PO Box 687, Altavista VA 24517	434-369-5695	R	4	<.1
2564	Duran Freight Corp—*Eric Duran*	PO Box 1037, Tecate CA 91980	619-478-5166	R	4	<.1
2565	Pacific Enterprises Ltd—*Joe Morris*	PO Box 427, Spencer IA 51301	712-262-3422	R	4	<.1
2566	Thornburg Brothers Inc—*Warren Thornburg*	6860 S 900 W, Modoc IN 47358	765-853-5687	R	4	<.1
2567	Southwest Express Inc—*Doug Martin*	1015 W City Limits, Hugoton KS 67951	620-544-7500	R	4	<.1
2568	Cliff Reed Inc—*Clifton Reed*	656 Willow Creek Rd, Corvallis MT 59828	406-961-4671	R	4	<.1
2569	Brown Produce Inc—*Carl Brown*	PO Box 309, Nixon TX 78140	830-582-1750	R	4	<.1
2570	Cason Inc—*Fred Cason*	PO Box 428, Duanesburg NY 12056	518-895-5815	R	4	<.1
2571	BA Miller and Sons Trucking Co—*Terry Miller*	PO Box 7, Liberty Center OH 43532	419-533-2871	R	4	<.1
2572	Tejas Warehouse Transportation—*Gaylan Beavers*	PO Box 1339, Waco TX 76703	254-752-9241	R	4	<.1
2573	Central Van Lines Inc—*Bonnie Brunelle*	PO Box 4501, Queensbury NY 12804	518-793-8036	R	4	<.1
2574	Sorensen Transportation Company Inc—*William Sorensen*	6 Old Amity Rd, Bethany CT 06524	203-393-0660	R	4	<.1
2575	Rock River Cartage Inc—*Doug House*	PO Box 430, Rock Falls IL 61071	815-625-1699	R	4	<.1
2576	Ameri-Line Inc—*Joseph Michgtti*	PO Box 965, Columbia Station OH 44028	440-236-3233	R	4	<.1
2577	B and C Trucking Inc—*Robert Blalock*	PO Box 271, Bolivar TN 38008	731-658-2868	R	4	<.1
2578	Owl Wire Logistics Inc—*Phil Kemper*	PO Box 187 Rte 5, Canastota NY 13032	315-697-2011	R	4	<.1
2579	TWL Corp—*Joseph Benacci*	5650 Wattsburg Rd, Erie PA 16509	814-825-1881	R	4	<.1
2580	Tucker Enterprises—*C Tucker*	PO Box 3843, Lubbock TX 79452		R	4	<.1
2581	Roadside Auto and Truck Transport—*Jim Best*	2725 Belvidere Rd, Waukegan IL 60085	847-244-4466	R	4	<.1
2582	Universe Moving Company Inc—*William Richardson*	1255 Willoughby Ave, Brooklyn NY 11237	718 628-4477	R	4	<.1
2583	Mahoney Express Inc—*William Mahoney*	1130 Elgin Ave, Forest Park IL 60130	708-689-0008	R	4*	<.1
2584	KEHM Transportation Inc—*Ron Evenson*	5634 Wildwood Dr, Rapid City SD 57702	605-341-7700	R	4	N/A
2585	Rock Transport Inc—*David Filipek*	725 Julie Ann Way, Oakland CA 94621	510-633-1528	R	4	N/A
2586	Pirollo Transport Company Inc—*Adelin Pirollo*	12th St Bldg 240, New Kensington PA 15068	724-335-4513	R	3	<.1
2587	Marshall's Express Inc—*Mark Melfi*	80 Southfield Ave, Stamford CT 06902	203-327-9807	R	3	<.1
2588	Carpenter's Motor Transport Inc—*Don Carpenter*	PO Box 754, Williston VT 05495	802-862-9669	R	3	<.1
2589	SETS LLC—*Winnie Taylor*	435 Howell Rd, Martin TN 38237	731-587-1923	R	3	<.1
2590	Scott Melvin Transportation Inc—*Scott Melvin*	200 N Main St, Rock Port MO 64482		R	3	<.1
2591	Sebring Transport Inc—*John Taufer*	2100 Carden St, San Leandro CA 94577	510-562-0872	R	3	<.1
2592	Hoerler Milk Transport Inc—*Jonathan Flint*	619 S Wright Rd, Janesville WI 53546		R	3	<.1
2593	FJD Trucking Company Inc—*Fred Drewes*	300 Michael Dr, Syosset NY 11791	516-677-0350	R	3	<.1
2594	Stranco Inc—*William Strain*	70459 Hwy 59, Abita Springs LA 70420	985-893-5308	R	3	<.1
2595	Boehmer Transportation Corp—*Laurice Boehmer*	PO Box 308, Machias NY 14101	716-353-8522	R	3	<.1
2596	Sullens Transport LLC—*Troy Sullens*	100 Hennessee Ave, Morrison TN 37357		R	3	<.1
2597	Shepherd-Will Inc—*Gene Bailey*	PO Box 400, Richburg SC 29729	803-789-3936	R	3	<.1
2598	Seacoast Asphalt Services Inc—*Jennifer Nicolai*	PO Box 98, Hatfield MA 01038	413-773-9247	R	3	<.1
2599	Wolf's Run Transport—*William Parry*	1412 Rte 438, Irving NY 14081	716-532-1737	R	3	<.1
2600	Northside Transportation LLC—*Grover McMurray*	PO Box 8050, Gallatin TN 37066	615-451-4317	R	3	<.1
2601	Hill and Williams Brothers Inc—*Delbert Williams*	625 44th St, Marion IA 52302	319-377-4801	R	3	<.1
2602	Erie Enterprises Inc—*Robert Bretz*	PO Box 233, West Middlesex PA 16159	724-528-1200	R	3	<.1
2603	Zellmer Truck Lines Inc—*Kurt Zellmer*	PO Box 606, Granville IL 61326	815-446-5131	R	3	<.1
2604	Loudoun Milk Transportation—*Tom Rust*	1591 North Valley Pike, Harrisonburg VA 22802	540-434-8766	R	3	<.1
2605	JMJ Projects Inc—*Jeff Robertson*	PO Box 5306, Kansas City KS 66119	913-621-3331	R	3	<.1
2606	Desert Empire Transfer and Storage—*Jim Prusa*	258 Commercial Rd, San Bernardino CA 92408	909-370-3077	R	3	<.1
2607	Merritt and Son Equipment Inc—*Freddy Merritt*	1280 Canal Rd, Brunswick GA 31525	912-264-1253	R	3	<.1
2608	Classic Express Inc—*Eddie Smith*	2150 Westland Dr SW, Cleveland TN 37311	423-339-2504	R	3	<.1
2609	Metro Express Inc—*Dan Holcomb*	PO Box 4207, Ontario CA 91761	909-758-9133	R	3	<.1
2610	Evergreen Express Lines Inc—*Gregory E Burns*	601 Memory LnSte D, York PA 17402	717-505-7170	S	3	<.1
2611	Genie Trucking Line Inc—*Mark Bishop*	221 Mill St, Mount Holly Springs PA 17065	717-486-5700	R	3	<.1
2612	Michigan Transport Inc—*Richard Kokila*	560 S Fordson St, Detroit MI 48217	313-842-2575	R	3	<.1
2613	McEwen Trucking Inc—*Randy A McEwen*	7860 E M 21, Corunna MI 48817	989-743-3898	R	3	<.1
2614	Downey Trucking Inc—*Joy Downey*	PO Box 39, Portland TN 37148	615-325-4031	R	3	<.1
2615	Green Motor Lines Inc—*Larry Green*	2401 Commerce Rd, Richmond VA 23234	804-233-4341	R	3	<.1
2616	Tuzze Trucking Inc—*Joseph Tuzze*	78 Cottage St, Carbondale PA 18407	570-282-1093	R	3	<.1
2617	S and S Transportation Inc—*Steven Stanley*	PO Box 336, Lincoln ME 04457	207-794-6050	R	3	<.1
2618	First Class Service Trucking Co—*Jim Alves*	2370 E Grant Line Rd, Tracy CA 95304	209-832-4669	R	3	<.1
2619	Sensenig Trucking—*John R Sensenig*	10705 State Rte 44, Watsontown PA 17777	570-649-6383	R	3	<.1
2620	Lewis and Robey Inc—*Jim Robey*	106 S Bishop St, Butler MO 64730	660-679-4179	R	3	<.1
2621	Patriot Courier Service Inc	PO Box 1265, Patchogue NY 11772	631-286-6677	R	3	<.1
2622	BJJ Company Inc—*James Blincoe*	PO Box 30010, Stockton CA 95213	209-941-8361	R	3*	.1
2623	D and E Livestock Transportation—*Rockne L Bosco*	PO Box 1267, Canon City CO 81215	719-275-2639	R	3*	.1
2624	GH Miller and Sons Inc—*Richard Miller*	421 25th Ave N, Wisconsin Rapids WI 54495	715-424-4000	R	3*	.1
2625	Commodore Express Inc—*Jerry Keen*	P O Box 507, LaVergne TN 37086	615-287-5140	R	3*	.1
2626	Coomes Inc—*Rick Coomes*	1697 E 250 Ln, Phillipsburg KS 67661	785-543-2759	R	3*	.1
2627	Pasquale Trucking Company Inc—*Thomas Pasquale*	960 W County Rd 250 S, Logansport IN 46947	574-722-4055	R	3*	.1
2628	Action Couriers Inc—*Michael McGrath*	PO Box 190981, Boise ID 83719	208-378-7500	R	3*	<.1
2629	All Star Moving and Storage Inc—*Richard Barrale*	88 Sandford St, Brooklyn NY 11205	212-254-2638	R	3*	<.1

Rank	Company Name—*Executive Officer*	Address, City, State, Zip	Phone	Type	Fin	Empls
2630	Sioux's Transportation Inc/STI—*Sue Colvin*	1849 W Henri De Tonti, Springdale AR 72762	479-361-2094	R	3*	<.1
2631	Adrian Trucking Inc—*Howard Adrian*	705 Hwy 78 E, Richland IA 52585	319-456-8111	R	3	<.1
2632	AV Transportation Inc—*Kenneth Liddle*	2103 9th Ave, Camanche IA 52730	563-259-1924	R	3*	<.1
2633	Hammonds Trkg Flatbed Div—*Steve Hammonds*	PO Box 38, Ider AL 35981	256-657-5171	R	3*	<.1
2634	Murray's Transfer and Storage Inc—*Robert Powell*	1011 Floral Ln, Davenport IA 52802	563-333-4570	R	3*	<.1
2635	Wangerin Trucking Company Inc—*Gerald Wangerin*	N7923 Cemetery Rd, Stephenson MI 49887	906-753-2235	R	3*	<.1
2636	Roadshow Services Inc—*David Kiely*	5501 3rd St, San Francisco CA 94124	415-822-3000	R	3*	<.1
2637	Savannah Transport Inc—*Hoyt Moore*	4425 NW Hwy 24, Topeka KS 66618	785-233-2190	R	3*	<.1
2638	H and H Transportation Inc—*Jeff Harbin*	645 Gerdau Ameristell, Jackson TN 38305	731-824-1400	R	3*	<.1
2639	Brenny Specialized Inc—*Todd Brenny*	PO Box 7155, Saint Cloud MN 56302	320-363-6999	R	3*	<.1
2640	GTL Transport Company Inc—*Danny Glover*	PO Box 1944, Virginia Beach VA 23479	757-934-2366	R	3*	<.1
2641	Burrows Trucking Inc—*Alfred Burrows*	8363 N 4040 Rd, Wann OK 74083	918-531-2268	R	3*	<.1
2642	Chadderton Trucking Inc—*Jerry Nighswander*	PO Box 687, Sharon PA 16146	724-981-5050	R	3*	<.1
2643	Debarr Trucking Company Inc—*David De Barr*	872 Staunton Tpke, Parkersburg WV 26104	304-485-4497	R	3*	<.1
2644	Billig Trucking Inc—*David Billig*	5316 Oakview Dr, Allentown PA 18104	610-395-9122	R	3*	<.1
2645	Boring Transport Inc—*Troy Boring*	3442 W Main St, Belleville PA 17004	717-935-2427	R	3*	<.1
2646	Honor Truck and Transfer Inc—*Ali Nikkhoo*	1100 Deforest Ave, Long Beach CA 90813	562-435-8555	R	3*	<.1
2647	Wright Trucking Inc—*Mark Wright*	517 W Railroad St, Clay KY 42404	270-664-2092	R	3	<.1
2648	Amsco Transportation Inc—*Rick Smith*	6100 Almeda Genoa Rd, Houston TX 77048	713-991-5560	R	3*	<.1
2649	Blue Mt Express Inc—*William Cooney*	291 Bucheimer Rd, Frederick MD 21701	301-663-1270	R	3*	<.1
2650	Buanno Transportation Company Inc—*Carl Buanno*	218 Riverside Dr, Fultonville NY 12072		R	3*	<.1
2651	Dixie Drayage Service Inc—*Carol Stanley*	PO Box 2274, Mobile AL 36652	251-679-1660	R	3*	<.1
2652	Interstate Wood Products Inc—*Dale Lemmons*	2308 Talley Way, Kelso WA 98626	360-425-8390	R	3*	<.1
2653	James Young Green Inc—*James Young*	PO Box 892, Weatherford TX 76086	817-594-2777	R	3*	<.1
2654	Pipco Transportation Inc—*Salvatore Pipitone*	PO Box 17, Rosenhayn NJ 08352	856-451-3212	R	3*	<.1
2655	RH Boelk Truck Lines Inc—*Mabel Boelk*	RR 2 Box 437, Mendota IL 61342	815-539-6778	R	3*	<.1
2656	Underwood Machinery Transport Inc—*Clay Smith*	PO Box 977, Indianapolis IN 46206	317-783-9235	R	3*	<.1
2657	Watkins Trucking Company Inc—*Jay Watkins*	4712 Richard Arrington, Birmingham AL 35212	205-592-3422	R	3*	<.1
2658	California Gas Transport Inc—*Ernesto Flores*	5959 Gateway Blvd W St, El Paso TX 79925	915-771-7595	R	3*	<.1
2659	H Fred Barefoot Trucking Inc—*Ricky Barefoot*	PO Box 25, Alum Bank PA 15521	814-839-2193	R	3*	<.1
2660	Land Trucking Co—*Thomas Duke*	PO Box 2620, Jacksonville FL 32203	904-353-4841	R	3*	<.1
2661	Carey Transport Inc—*Alan Carey*	3939 Reno Hwy, Fallon NV 89406	775-867-2813	R	3*	<.1
2662	Carlton Transport Inc—*Edward Robbins*	PO Box 838, Cambridge MD 21613	410-228-8700	R	3*	<.1
2663	DL George and Sons Transportation—*David George*	13321 Midvale Rd, Waynesboro PA 17268	717-765-4700	R	3*	<.1
2664	Flatout Trucking Ltd—*Anthony St Bernard*	1878 Frenchtown Center, Monroe MI 48162	734-241-2856	R	3*	<.1
2665	Frank R Ring Transfer Inc—*Albert Ring*	3220 Nebraska Ave, Council Bluffs IA 51501	712-328-8563	R	3*	<.1
2666	Robin Hood Container Express—*Robin Hood II*	PO Box 70, Benson NC 27504	910-892-5803	R	3*	<.1
2667	Same Day Inc—*Kent Okey*	3140 E State Rd 124, Bluffton IN 46714	260-824-9999	R	3*	<.1
2668	Southeastern Transfer and Storage Co—*Walter Wallace*	2561 Plant Atkinson Rd, Smyrna GA 30080		R	3*	<.1
2669	PNI Transportation Inc—*Pettis Norman*	4563 S Westmoreland Rd, Dallas TX 75237	214-331-8800	R	3*	<.1
2670	Cargo Transport Inc—*Peter Coumounduros*	44190 Mercure Cir Ste, Dulles VA 20166	703-661-6223	R	3*	<.1
2671	CLS Transportation Co—*Brian Pello*	21982 State Rt 22, Hoosick Falls NY 12090	518-686-5411	R	3*	<.1
2672	Fepco Container Inc—*Wayne Smith*	PO Box 348, Conley GA 30288	404-362-0005	R	3*	<.1
2673	General Transport Inc—*Joseph M Ostrowske*	1100 N Jenkins Blvd, Akron OH 44306	330-786-3400	R	3*	<.1
2674	Gray Rock Farms Inc—*John Douglas*	822 Mocksville Hwy, Statesville NC 28625	704-873-6901	R	3*	<.1
2675	Ideal Transportation Company Inc—*Nadeine DiGiulio*	17 Oak St, Peabody MA 01960	978-531-3161	R	3*	<.1
2676	J and M Leasing Co—*Martin Anderson*	295 Grand Ave, Clarion PA 16214	814-226-4153	R	3*	<.1
2677	Manchester Motor Freight Inc—*James McKenna*	183 Hayward St, Manchester NH 03103	603-644-2100	R	3*	<.1
2678	Moco Transportation Company Inc—*Jack Mitchell*	PO Box 65, Sylacauga AL 35150	256-245-0707	R	3*	<.1
2679	Morgan Trucking Inc—*Robert McClane*	Box 6196, Federal Way WA 98063	360-426-6255	R	3*	<.1
2680	Rodney Rohrbaugh Trucking Inc—*Rodney Rohrbaugh*	PO Box 202, Caldwell OH 43724	740-732-7382	R	3*	<.1
2681	Sully Transport Inc—*Arland Vander Leest*	PO Box 350, Sully IA 50251	641-594-3435	R	3*	<.1
2682	TD Express Inc—*Dennis Frank*	1425 N 7th Ave, Greeley CO 80631	970-356-8947	R	3*	<.1
2683	Terry Palecek Inc—*Terry Palecek*	709 3rd Ave N, Park Falls WI 54552	715-769-3306	R	3*	<.1
2684	Wheelwright Trucking Company Inc—*Johnnie Barker*	3820 S Eufaula Ave, Eufaula AL 36027	334-687-0390	R	3*	<.1
2685	Seagate Transportation Services—*Brad James*	555 F St, Perrysburg OH 43551	419-666-9919	R	3*	<.1
2686	Vesco Specialized Carriers LLC—*William Honey*	PO Box 1057, Conyers GA 30012	770-922-1097	R	3*	<.1
2687	B and H Freight Lines Inc—*Paul Billings*	468 S 26th St, Kansas City KS 66105	913-621-1840	R	3*	<.1
2688	Consolidated Transfer and Warehouse Co—*Robert Winsky*	1251 Taney St, North Kansas City MO 64116	816-221-3411	R	3	<.1
2689	LJ Rogers Jr Trucking Inc—*L Rogers*	7723 Oakwood St Ext, Mebane NC 27302	919-304-8782	R	3*	<.1
2690	Shadow Trucking Inc—*Linda Thoele*	2800 Falund St, Rockford IL 61109	815-399-0923	R	3*	<.1
2691	Terrier Transportation Inc—*David C Diaz*	4708 Fidelity St, Houston TX 77029	713-671-0204	R	3*	<.1
2692	Transpro Contract Carriers Inc—*Karl Mueller*	PO Box 79, Kaukauna WI 54130	920-766-6603	R	3*	<.1
2693	Bernard Pavelka Trucking Inc—*Thomas Pavelka*	1215 E J St, Hastings NE 68901	402-462-4650	R	3*	<.1
2694	John and Sandra Inc—*Sandra Pouland*	611 N Temple Dr, Diboll TX 75941	936-829-4040	R	3*	<.1
2695	K and K Trucking—*David Bertelsen*	5100 49th St SW, Great Falls MT 59404	406-453-2290	R	3*	<.1
2696	R and S Lines Inc—*Robert Liechty*	PO Box 410, Stryker OH 43557	419-682-7807	R	3*	<.1
2697	Sheppard Trucking Ltd—*Steven Sheppard*	1615 Maryland St Rd, Phelps NY 14532	315-548-9271	R	3*	<.1
2698	American Container Transport—*John Wright*	PO Box Ad, Moses Lake WA 98837	509-962-5006	R	3*	<.1
2699	Propane Resources Transportation—*Marty Lerum*	PO Box 2308, Mission KS 66202	913-262-8345	R	3*	<.1
2700	Aarco Equipment Inc—*James Doyle*	PO Box 408, Wisconsin Dells WI 53965	608-254-6974	R	3	<.1
2701	Accord Services Inc—*Mr Weidlan*	PO Box 2346, Kansas City KS 66110	913-281-1879	R	3*	<.1
2702	Associated Carriers LP—*Doug Lloyd*	PO Box 6178, Arlington TX 76005	817-649-6004	R	3*	<.1
2703	CA Perry and Son Transit Inc—*Sidney Perry*	4033 Virginia Rd, Hobbsville NC 27946	252-221-4463	R	3*	<.1
2704	Cedarpoint Trucking Inc—*Craig Leatham*	PO Box 429, Rexburg ID 83440	208-356-8095	R	3*	<.1
2705	City Haul Inc—*Karen Kimmey*	4101 S Morgan St, Chicago IL 60609	773-847-3710	R	3*	<.1
2706	Collins Crane and Rigging Service—*Phil Collins*	PO Box 624, East Bridgewater MA 02333	508-378-3434	R	3*	<.1
2707	Conner Trucking Inc—*Larry Calcatera*	1951 Keller Hicks Rd, Fort Worth TX 76177	817-439-4704	R	3*	<.1
2708	FEC Highway Services Inc—*John Giles*	6140 Phillips Hwy, Jacksonville FL 32256	904-737-7876	S	3*	<.1
2709	Hicks Trucking Company Inc—*Lyle Hicks*	102 N Gorman Ave, Litchfield MN 55355	320-693-3292	R	3*	<.1
2710	Kid Glove Service Inc—*Mark Anness*	PO Box 19772, Indianapolis IN 46219	317-547-6550	R	3*	<.1
2711	M and B Carriers Inc—*Rick Eidson*	16183 E Whittier Blvd, Whittier CA 90603	562-902-0161	R	3*	<.1
2712	Murphy Rigging and Erecting Inc—*Richard Murphy*	701 24th Ave SE, Minneapolis MN 55414	612-623-1270	R	3*	<.1
2713	Nestor and Sons LLC—*Michael Nestor*	122 Charter Pl, La Vergne TN 37086	615-793-6067	R	3*	<.1
2714	Ohio Valley Reload Inc—*Randy Carter*	89 Wells Cemetery Rd, Millwood KY 42762	270-879-3161	R	3*	<.1
2715	Paul Garnsey and Son Inc—*Paul Garnsey*	952 Rt 4, Schuylerville NY 12871	518-695-3346	R	3*	<.1
2716	Pier Transportation Inc—*Augie Mimica*	2901 W 31st St, Chicago IL 60623	773-847-6601	R	3*	<.1
2717	Prairie Lines Inc—*Monty Wilson*	PO Box 72, Harwood ND 58042	701-235-9926	R	3*	<.1
2718	Ralph Walker Inc—*Ralph Walker*	625 Old Hwy 49 S, Jackson MS 39218	601-939-3104	R	3*	<.1
2719	Rapid Transport Ltd—*Joe Chance*	PO Box L, Kermit TX 79745	432-586-2569	R	3*	<.1

Note: An asterisk (*) indicates an estimated financial figure. The company type code used is as follows: R = Private, P = Public, S = Private Subsidiary, B = Public Subsidiary, D = Division, J = Joint Venture, I = Investment Fund.

COMPANY RANKINGS BY SALES WITHIN 4-DIGIT SIC

Rank	Company Name—*Executive Officer*	Address, City, State, Zip	Phone	Type	Fin	Empls
2720	S and S Trucking Inc—*Carl Stewart*	1135 Old Salem Rd, Murfreesboro TN 37129	615-867-0212	R	3*	<.1
2721	SRS Trucking and Excavating Inc—*Lester Howerton*	21529 Double Arch Rd, Staunton IL 62088	618-635-8565	R	3*	<.1
2722	Titletown Express Inc—*Paul Holschuh*	PO Box 10507, Green Bay WI 54307	920-490-9930	R	3*	<.1
2723	Trevis Berry Transportation Inc—*Trevis Berry*	PO Box 1802, Gilroy CA 95021	408-842-8238	R	3*	<.1
2724	Wehrle Trucking Inc—*Marvin Wehrle*	14832 S 128th Ave E, Lynnville IA 50153	641-594-4341	R	3*	<.1
2725	A and K Transport Company Inc—*Anthony Sebastiano*	2785 Reiter Rd, New Lenox IL 60451	815-462-1900	R	3*	<.1
2726	Alto's Express Inc—*James Stuffo*	2301 Garry Rd, Cinnaminson NJ 08077	856-829-6900	R	3	<.1
2727	Burgess Transportation LLC—*Jack Burgess*	20825 Currier Rd, Walnut CA 91789	909-594-0019	R	3*	<.1
2728	Contractual Carriers Inc—*Karl Schneider*	104 Alan Dr, Newark DE 19711	302-731-7440	R	3*	<.1
2729	Dimon and Bacorn Company of Binghamton—*Daniel Dimon Sr*	93 Industrial Park Blv, Elmira NY 14901	607-734-2937	R	3*	<.1
2730	TGC Transportation Inc—*Gary Gregson*	8530 Nike Rd, Red Bud IL 62278	618-473-9397	R	3*	<.1
2731	D and M Water Service Inc—*Dale Leivestad*	PO Box 848, Baker MT 59313	406-778-3107	R	3*	<.1
2732	Happy Trucking Company Inc—*Harold Hix*	3815 Clay County Hwy, Moss TN 38575	931-258-3554	R	3	<.1
2733	R and S Transportation Inc—*David Roat*	PO Box 1641, Great Bend KS 67530	620-792-8121	R	3*	<.1
2734	Circle V Specialized Inc—*Bill Vollmer*	11301 W 57th Pl S, Sand Springs OK 74063		R	3*	<.1
2735	JK Williams LLC—*James Williams*	2331 Alabama St, Lawrence KS 66046	785-690-7390	R	3*	<.1
2736	Viner's Inc—*William Viner*	801 Morton Ave, Emerson IA 51533	712-824-7370	R	3*	<.1
2737	BCW Transportation Inc—*Bowmen Williams*	6000 Denton Dr, Dallas TX 75235	214-350-3320	R	3*	<.1
2738	Conus Transportation Inc—*Clifford Phillips*	155 Glendale Ave, Sparks NV 89431	775-358-8003	R	3*	<.1
2739	Cord Moving and Storage Inc—*Steve Ryan*	57 Marsh Dr, Belleville IL 62220	618-235-5561	R	3*	<.1
2740	Fox Trucking Inc—*Gary Fox*	29920 Dover Rd, Easton MD 21601	410-822-2966	R	3*	<.1
2741	KS and D Rentals Inc	PO Box 1419, Woodward OK 73802	580-254-5975	R	3*	<.1
2742	Roth Trucking—*David Roth*	3730 Elk Vale Rd, Rapid City SD 57703	605-341-0800	R	3*	<.1
2743	Silkey Trucking Inc—*Jimmie Silkey*	PO Box 2250, Nixa MO 65714	417-443-3111	R	3*	<.1
2744	Zachrich Trucking Inc—*Robert Zachrich*	I088 County Rd 18, Holgate OH 43527	419-762-5701	R	3*	<.1
2745	Overland Services Inc—*Elsa Merola*	2811 N 62nd St, Tampa FL 33619	813-248-6524	R	3*	<.1
2746	Packer Transportation Company Inc—*Guy Packer*	280 E Parr Blvd, Reno NV 89512	775-329-1872	R	3	<.1
2747	Industrial Engineers Inc—*Robert H Chabot*	PO Box 505, Uncasville CT 06382	860-848-8558	R	3*	<.1
2748	Davidson Transfer and Storage—*Richard Davidson*	6600 Frankford Ave, Baltimore MD 21206	410-488-9200	R	3*	<.1
2749	Day Trucking Inc—*Michael Day*	1970 NW Paula Ave, Albany OR 97321	541-928-4176	R	3*	<.1
2750	Starck Van Lines Inc—*Jerry Hurt*	12 Starck Dr, Burgettstown PA 15021	724-729-3600	R	3*	<.1
2751	Action Delivery Inc—*John Malinee*	PO Box 2346, Kansas City KS 66110	816-241-3300	R	3*	<.1
2752	Anker Trucking Inc—*William Anker*	19790 Burnham Ave, Lynwood IL 60411	708-895-0338	R	3*	<.1
2753	Eagle Panel Systems Inc—*Ken Disch*	PO Box 247, Mulberry Grove IL 62262	618-326-7132	R	3*	<.1
2754	Liberty Express Inc—*Gene Hinson*	3194 15th Ave Blvd SE, Conover NC 28613	828-465-5905	R	3*	<.1
2755	Scarr Moving and Storage Inc—*Mark Scarr*	PO Box 8, Salinas CA 93902	831-424-2784	R	3*	<.1
2756	Ziron Environmental Services—*Brian Ziron*	PO Box 68, Park Forest IL 60466	708-757-9601	R	3*	<.1
2757	Agricultural Transportation Association—*Ray Schertz*	PO Box 51, Springfield IL 62705	217-522-2500	R	3*	<.1
2758	Citizens Transportation Company Inc—*Ron Goodin*	1670 E Holt Blvd, Ontario CA 91761	909-988-7531	R	3*	<.1
2759	Edwards Moving and Rigging Inc—*Mark Edwards*	200 Everett Hall Rd, Shelbyville KY 40065	502-722-5530	R	3	<.1
2760	Galto Trucking Inc—*Andy Zurawik*	PO Box 72546, Roselle IL 60172	630-523-5555	R	3*	<.1
2761	Hydro Technology Inc—*Morris Partridge*	3143 Post Rd, Newport MI 48166	734-586-3931	R	3*	<.1
2762	Melrose Transport Systems—*Albert Ariola*	7545 S Madison St, Burr Ridge IL 60527	630-655-2233	R	3*	<.1
2763	Von Sydow's Moving and Storage—*Brad Von Sydow*	PO Box 699, Palatine IL 60078	847-934-7100	R	3*	<.1
2764	Lee Traynham Trucking Inc—*Lee Traynham*	7082 Tule Rd, Arbuckle CA 95912	530-476-2236	R	3*	<.1
2765	Roy's Transfer Inc—*Patricia Burch*	PO Box 317, Rochelle IL 61068	815-562-2160	R	3*	<.1
2766	DC Express Inc—*Gene Altenburg*	69 King St, Dover NJ 07801	973-989-5000	R	3*	<.1
2767	Nappi Trucking Corp—*Ralph Nappi*	541 Morristown Rd, Matawan NJ 07747	732-566-3000	R	3*	<.1
2768	Choice Graphics Inc—*Jeff Dalrymple*	1215 Latta St, Chattanooga TN 37406	423-622-5000	R	3*	<.1
2769	Exhibit Express Air Freight—*Armando Petruzziello*	21A 6th St, Woburn MA 01801	781-932-7330	R	3	<.1
2770	Indiana-Kentucky Trucking Inc—*Robert Parker*	PO Box 371, Carrollton KY 41008	502-732-4493	R	3	<.1
2771	Tennessee Traders and Technicians—*Gary Hooper*	385 N Pine St, Whitwell TN 37397	423-658-6517	R	3	<.1
2772	Horizon Air Services Inc—*George Mercuri*	480 William F McClella, Boston MA 02128	617-567-2660	R	3	<.1
2773	Western Trucking—*Clyde Burns*	PO Box 980, Baker MT 59313	406-778-3366	R	3	<.1
2774	Davidson Trucking Inc—*Daniel Davidson*	PO Box 162, Bradner OH 43406	419-288-3088	R	3	<.1
2775	Triple R Trucking—*Bob Reed*	PO Box 102, Laurens IA 50554	712-845-4570	R	3	<.1
2776	Try-Us Trucking Inc—*Suki Sanghera*	PO Box 1631, Empire CA 95319	209-537-4817	R	3	<.1
2777	Central Dispatch Inc—*Joni Gravolet*	PO Box 2070, Gretna LA 70054	504-362-3282	R	3	<.1
2778	Columbus Air Delivery—*Ron Chapman*	1033 Brentnell Ave Spa, Columbus OH 43219	614-252-5143	R	3	<.1
2779	SG Wilson Truck and Equipment Co—*Steve Wilson*	PO Box 2744, White City OR 97503	541-830-3966	R	3	<.1
2780	Ronwal Transportation Inc—*Ronald Carter*	PO Box 6351, Hammond IN 46325	219-932-7510	R	3	N/A
2781	Kenosha Beef International Ltd—*Dennis Vignieri*	PO Box 639, Kenosha WI 53141	262-859-2272	R	3*	.8
2782	Sea Best Express Inc—*Robert Brandano*	44 Newmarket Square, Boston MA 02118	617-428-6926	R	3	<.1
2783	Larry Jones Trucking—*Larry Jones*	131 SE Golden Ave, Topeka KS 66607		R	3	<.1
2784	CE and W Enterprises Inc—*Vernon Williams*	PO Box 87, Staley NC 27355	919-742-3409	R	3	<.1
2785	Construction Specialty—*Jeffrey Hansen*	PO Box 181, Lee Vining CA 93541	760-647-6346	R	3	<.1
2786	Mindemann Trucking Inc—*Richard Mindemann*	N8067 Maple St, Ixonia WI 53036	920-206-6583	R	3	<.1
2787	DC Sales and Trucking Inc—*Dick Caldwell*	60 Indy Ln, Inman SC 29349		R	3	<.1
2788	Galil Moving and Storage Inc—*Lisa Sadaoui*	111 Linnett St, Bayonne NJ 07002	201-823-4222	R	3	<.1
2789	G and T Air Expediting Service Inc—*Francis Troccia*	1510 Grand Central Ave, Elmira NY 14901	607-734-8153	R	3	<.1
2790	Archilla Transportation Inc—*Glenn Perry*	1 Nixon Ln, Edison NJ 08837		R	3	<.1
2791	Arlington Truck Co—*Larry Crockett*	524 Oregon Rd, Northwood OH 43619	419-666-5265	R	3	<.1
2792	T and M Trucking Inc—*Tom Ruppel*	PO Box 114, Vincennes IN 47591	812-882-1240	R	3	<.1
2793	J-West Oilfield Services Transportation—*Weston Serrano*	PO Box 523, Vernal UT 84078	435-789-2225	R	3	<.1
2794	S and L Services Inc—*Lawrence Mattern*	13 S Industrial Park R, Milton PA 17847	570-742-7984	R	3	<.1
2795	Gum Log Movers Inc—*Homer Mccarter*	1989 Mccarter Hl, Blairsville GA 30512	706-745-3107	R	3*	<.1
2796	Semi-Express Inc—*Edmond Ritter*	8271 Brock Bridge Rd, Laurel MD 20724	410-880-4333	R	3	<.1
2797	City Cartage Co—*Norman Lansdale*	PO Box 236, Mount Sterling KY 40353	859-498-4490	R	3	<.1
2798	S and W Industries Inc—*Brad Wolkoff*	PO Box 1002, Masontown WV 26542	304-864-5261	R	3	<.1
2799	International Moving Service—*George Harrington*	4412 - 4414 Wheeler Av, Alexandria VA 22304	703-751-6400	R	3	<.1
2800	WEJ Trucking Company Inc—*Jim Northington*	PO Box 51, Gattman MS 38844		R	3	<.1
2801	Recover Inc—*William McLellan*	191 Clear Springs Ct, Greenville SC 29615	864-213-2141	R	3	<.1
2802	Billy Joe Burrow Inc—*Bill Burrow*	PO Box 329, Mountain City TN 37683	423-727-6000	R	2	<.1
2803	Donald Holland Trucking Inc—*Sue Seabold*	PO Box 637, Keokuk IA 52632	319-524-1353	R	2	<.1
2804	TL Trucking Inc—*Terry Law*	3665 County Rd 14, Piedmont AL 36272	256-927-6231	R	2	<.1
2805	Herin Brothers Inc—*Terry Herin*	8121 E M 20, Hesperia MI 49421	231-854-6525	R	2	<.1
2806	William E Smith Trucking Inc—*William Smith*	2973 Riverside Dr, Mount Airy NC 27030	336-786-5815	R	2	<.1
2807	Two Men and A Truck of Charlotte—*Brig Sorber*	3400 Belle Chase Way, Lansing MI 48911	517-394-7210	R	2	<.1
2808	Emery Trucking Inc—*Wayne Emery*	PO Box 736, Martinsburg WV 25402	304-274-2501	R	2	<.1
2809	Bayou City Express Inc—*James Walker*	PO Box 431424, Houston TX 77243	713-956-6300	R	2	<.1

Rank	Company Name—Executive Officer	Address, City, State, Zip	Phone	Type	Fin	Empls
2810	NOFFS/Atlantic Relocation Systems—Ted Alger	1735 E Davis St, Arlington Heights IL 60005	847-870-3200	R	2	N/A
2811	Tradewind Enterprises Inc—Sid Smith	PO Box 1017, Hillsboro OR 97123	503-648-2823	R	2	<.1
2812	ABCD Transportation Company Inc—Danny Homan	PO Box 21, Marquand MO 63655	573-783-8558	R	2	<.1
2813	D and B Trucking—Bernie Bockhold	1905 Lincoln Ave, Tacoma WA 98421	253-383-3860	R	2	<.1
2814	Gathright Services Inc—John Gathright	899 Enterprise Way, Benton Harbor MI 49022	269-923-6677	R	2	<.1
2815	JMA Trucking Inc—James Alligood	15 Lakewood Dr Unit 13, Oakdale CT 06370	860-437-8892	R	2	<.1
2816	Tiger Trucking Inc—James Swindle	4570 Getwell Rd, Memphis TN 38118		R	2	<.1
2817	Baker Transfer and Storage Co—Richard Hunt	706 Daniels St, Billings MT 59101	406-245-3147	R	2	<.1
2818	Grangers Cooperative Association—Ronald Linsey	PO Box 54, Lebo KS 66856	620-256-6323	R	2	<.1
2819	Gale Delivery Inc—William Joel	45 Sweeneydale Ave, Bay Shore NY 11706	631-231-4444	R	2	<.1
2820	Wes Olson Trucking Inc—James Olson	1640 Baldy Mountain Rd, Sandpoint ID 83864	208-263-2578	R	2	<.1
2821	Sunward Trucking Inc—Danton Wirth	6800 E Hampden Ave, Denver CO 80224	303-759-3200	R	2	<.1
2822	George H Ratchford Inc—George Ratchford	PO Box 640, Wadley GA 30477	478-252-5524	R	2	<.1
2823	Universal Distribution Inc—Aaron Dean	PO Box 40, Simpsonville KY 40067	502-774-2597	R	2	<.1
2824	O'Neal Melton and Sons Inc—James Melton	PO Box 607, Camden TN 38320	731-584-2764	R	2	<.1
2825	K and S Tank Lines Inc—Kenneth Stuart	PO Box 1168, Copperhill TN 37317	423-496-4939	R	2	<.1
2826	J and R Express Inc—John Barnwell	PO Box 645, Fletcher NC 28732	828-891-9281	R	2	<.1
2827	George W Banks Trucking—George Banks	5032 US Rt 11, Homer NY 13077	607-749-7000	R	2	<.1
2828	Ray's Transportation Inc—Nancy Stackhouse	42 Argenio Dr, New Windsor NY 12553	845-565-7210	R	2	<.1
2829	Hydra Trucking Inc—Frank Dodd	8825 Elder Creek Rd, Sacramento CA 95828	916-383-9620	R	2	<.1
2830	Franklin Trucking Inc—Michael Santillo	212 Ohio St, Buffalo NY 14204	716-852-0480	R	2	<.1
2831	Keller Transport Inc—Barbara Hulett	1311 Taylor Pl, Billings MT 59101	406-259-2202	R	2	<.1
2832	Naco Express—David A Cohen	850 Allen St, Jamestown NY 14701	716-664-3896	R	2	<.1
2833	Prince Transport—Dennis Wessel	8351 County Rd H, Marshfield WI 54449	715-384-3105	R	2	<.1
2834	Inland Sea Inc—George Koenigsmann	9601 Carnegie Ave, El Paso TX 79925	915-592-1517	R	2	<.1
2835	Still Transfer Company Inc—Eugene Still	632 Boone St, Kingsport TN 37660	423-245-4000	R	2	<.1
2836	Stanley Brothers LLC—Stephen Stanley	PO Box 522, Lincoln ME 04457	207-794-6050	R	2	<.1
2837	Clifton Trucking Inc—Ronald Scott	PO Box 2640, La Pine OR 97739	541-536-8502	R	2	<.1
2838	D and D Trucking and Services Inc—Donald Miller	5025 N Kill Rd, Delphos OH 45833	419-692-3205	R	2*	.1
2839	Stephens Carriers Inc—Terry Stephens	PO Box 220, Hendersonville TN 37077	615-824-1617	R	2*	<.1
2840	Best Courier and Delivery Service—Carol Hinch	PO Box 6327, Libertyville IL 60048	847-816-6229	R	2*	<.1
2841	CP Transporters Inc—Raymond Kunde	2966-A E Victoria St, Compton CA 90221	310-639-9800	R	2*	<.1
2842	Hoge Motor Co—Lawrence Hoge	4269 Hwy 431 N, Springfield TN 37172	615-384-8416	R	2*	<.1
2843	Sam Freitas Trucking Inc—Sam Freitas	2420 E Eight Mile Rd, Stockton CA 95210	209-474-0924	R	2*	<.1
2844	All Ways Moving and Storage—Timothy M Moore	338 W Maiden St, Washington PA 15301	724-225-7360	R	2*	<.1
2845	Earnest Investments LLC—L Earnest	3820 W 70th St, Shreveport LA 71108	318-631-6477	R	2*	<.1
2846	Lanman Transportation Inc—Mike Lanman	PO Box 108, Charleston IL 61920	217-348-8434	R	2*	<.1
2847	Shiflett Transport Services Inc—Steven Shiflett	PO Box 570, Fletcher OK 73541	580-549-6147	R	2*	<.1
2848	John H Kooy Trucking Inc—John Kooy	19324 67th Ave NE, Arlington WA 98223	360-474-8000	R	2*	<.1
2849	Mara Transport Inc—Ray Willits	1249 Hart Ave, Union IA 50258	641-486-2223	R	2*	<.1
2850	J and B Fast Freight—Joseph Lydon	220 Flat Creek Ln, Blountville TN 37617	423-323-1224	R	2	<.1
2851	Tan Kline's—Marjorie Kline	RR 2 Box 629, Altoona PA 16601	814-944-7561	H	2	<.1
2852	Beskau Trucking Inc—Gary Beskau	19500 Goodwin Ave, Hastings MN 55033	651-437-9737	R	2*	<.1
2853	Crown Moving and Storage Inc—Gary Reynolds	8040 Castleton Rd, Indianapolis IN 46250	317-842-8111	R	2*	<.1
2854	Gary Foglio Trucking Inc—Gary Foglio	84811 Hwy 101, Florence OR 97439	541-997-3478	R	2*	<.1
2855	L and A Trucking Company Inc—J Lamb	31624 Hwy 69, Jasper AL 35504	205-384-3451	R	2*	<.1
2856	Show Me Trucking and Freight—Darrin Swaggert	PO Box 404, Harrisonville MO 64701	816-380-3933	R	2*	<.1
2857	Thompson Moving and Storage Inc—Richard Thomas	416 Tiny Town Rd, Clarksville TN 37042	931-431-6659	R	2*	<.1
2858	Transporter Inc—Russell Cook	5410 Oates Rd, Houston TX 77013	713-675-0131	R	2*	<.1
2859	Freight Expeditors Inc—Pat Roberts	PO Box 84041, Seattle WA 98124	206-767-5052	R	2*	<.1
2860	Gamble Parts Dart Inc—Dennis Gamble	PO Box 280, Mount Olive AL 35117	205-631-4705	R	2*	<.1
2861	Guntren Trucking—Tom Guntren	PO Box 2548, Sioux City IA 51106	712-255-1184	R	2	<.1
2862	BS Xpress Inc—Bart Brant	4703 SE Us Hwy 169, Saint Joseph MO 64507	816-364-2336	R	2*	<.1
2863	Pulliam Trucking Company Inc—Edwin Pulliam	2524 Hwy 25 S, Greenwood SC 29646	864-227-1022	R	2*	<.1
2864	Royce Campbell and Sons—Royce Campbell	871 Ky 80, Windsor KY 42565	270-866-3765	R	2*	<.1
2865	Vickers Distribution and Transfer—Jo Vickers	1248 Warford St, Memphis TN 38108	901-454-5577	R	2*	<.1
2866	Cooperative Transport—Larry Ray	PO Box 160, Stetsonville WI 54480	715-678-2917	R	2*	<.1
2867	Gwillim Trucking Service—Scott Gwillim	1525 Sumner St, Carlinville IL 62626	217-415-3904	R	2*	<.1
2868	AD Weaver Service Inc—A Weaver	3552 Rte 66, Export PA 15632	724-325-3997	R	2*	<.1
2869	Arlin Curtiss Trucking Inc—Arlin Curtiss	PO Box 26, Montevideo MN 56265	320-269-5581	R	2*	<.1
2870	Atlas Specialized Transport Inc—Jeannie Schubert	8425 213th St W, Lakeville MN 55044	952-985-5400	R	2*	<.1
2871	Baker's Transportation Service of Lakeland—Robert Baker Dedicated Transport LLC	2720 Crystal Lake Acre, Lakeland FL 33801	863-668-9757	S	2*	<.1
2872	Buttercup Farms Inc—Richard Decker	1619 Hanford St, Levittown PA 19057	215-945-1943	R	2*	<.1
2873	Commercial Warehouse and Cartage—Greg Parrish	3402 Meyer Rd, Fort Wayne IN 46803	260-426-7825	R	2*	<.1
2874	Cummings Moving Systems LLC	PO Box 3130, Albany OR 97321	541-928-3385	S	2*	<.1
2875	Edwin Hardy Trucking Inc—David Hardy	116 Hardy Ln, Wampum PA 16157	724-535-7376	R	2*	<.1
2876	Ellis Trucking—Glenn R Ellis	PO Box 71888, Chattanooga TN 37407	423-629-4333	R	2*	<.1
2877	ITS Global Relocation Services—James Doeneka	PO Box 11266, Portland OR 97211	503-287-2700	R	2*	<.1
2878	J-Mar Enterprises Inc—Janel Helfrich	PO Box 4143, Bismarck ND 58502	701-222-4518	R	2*	<.1
2879	Mallett and Sons Trucking Company Inc—Verlan Mallett	PO Box 241, Blythe CA 92226	760-922-2297	R	2*	<.1
2880	O and I Transport Inc—Harold Ford	14201 Prospect St Ste, Dearborn MI 48126	313-945-1530	R	2*	<.1
2881	O'Connor's Express Inc—Richard Durgin	506 Underwood Ave, Elmira NY 14905	607-732-1441	R	2*	<.1
2882	Pipe Transportation Company Inc—Aldo Bussio	PO Box 791, Orem UT 84059	801-225-2416	R	2*	<.1
2883	Ralston Trucking Co—Nan Ralston	651 Axe Ave, Valparaiso IN 46383	219-477-3770	R	2*	<.1
2884	Ramrod Trucking Inc—Tina Funderburk	3009 Hohl St, Houston TX 77093	713-699-5757	R	2*	<.1
2885	RO Wetz Transportation Co—Ernest Wetz	PO Box 729, Marietta OH 45750	740-373-2472	R	2*	<.1
2886	Smalley Trucking Company Inc—Granvel Smalley	PO Box 486, Sutherlin OR 97479	541-459-4838	R	2*	<.1
2887	TJ Stidham Inc—Melissa Stidham	2701 Airport Rd, Plant City FL 33563	813-752-4675	R	2*	<.1
2888	Wilson Hauling Inc—James Guenther	PO Box 28, Ross OH 45061	513-738-4437	R	2*	<.1
2889	Grafton Transit Inc—Mark Kurziak	PO Box 254, Grafton WI 53024	262-306-9191	R	2*	<.1
2890	Hemphill and Son Inc—Roger Hemphill	PO Box 160, Toccoa GA 30577	706-886-0002	R	2*	<.1
2891	Huff and Puff Trucking Inc—Bruce Daniel	750 Joe Daniel Rd, Bradyville TN 37026	615-765-5033	R	2*	<.1
2892	John Ferris Trucking Inc—Arthur Ferris	PO Box 591, Bath NY 14810	607-776-1010	R	2*	<.1
2893	LG Almony and Sons Inc—Linden Almony	2108 Jerrys Rd, Street MD 21154	410-692-5521	R	2*	<.1
2894	M and D Transport Inc—Mary Carman	PO Box 481, Providence RI 02901	401-946-4676	R	2*	<.1
2895	Marlow Trucking Company Inc—David Marlow	120 John Dodd Rd, Spartanburg SC 29303	864-578-9576	R	2*	<.1
2896	Fullone Trucking Inc—Chuck Fullone	10862 Mileblock Rd, North Collins NY 14111	716-337-2645	R	2*	<.1
2897	J and L Motor X-Press Inc—Jan Larkin	2015 Lake St, Kalamazoo MI 49001	269-381-9322	R	2*	<.1
2898	DL Heritage Transport Inc—Douglas L Heritage	9098 Nichols Rd, Windham OH 44288	330-527-2759	R	2*	<.1

Note: An asterisk (*) indicates an estimated financial figure. The company type code used is as follows: R = Private, P = Public, S = Private Subsidiary, B = Public Subsidiary, D = Division, J = Joint Venture, I = Investment Fund.

COMPANY RANKINGS BY SALES WITHIN 4-DIGIT SIC

Rank	Company Name—Executive Officer	Address, City, State, Zip	Phone	Type	Fin	Empls
2899	Zentner Transportation Inc—Mark Zentner	PO Box 342, Cedar Rapids NE 68627	308-358-0291	R	2*	<.1
2900	AJJ Trucking Company Inc—Arnold Lawson	808 Patterson Rd, Harrogate TN 37752	423-869-2642	R	2*	<.1
2901	Altendorf Express Inc—Martin Altendorf	PO Box 250, Minto ND 58261	701-248-3003	R	2*	<.1
2902	Bieri Trucking Inc—James Bieri	16571 Us Hwy 61, Letts IA 52754	319-729-2133	R	2*	<.1
2903	Blaschke Trucking Co—Larry Gutowsky	PO Box 40527, Houston TX 77240	713-466-1875	R	2*	<.1
2904	Butler Transport System—Marty Butler	PO Box 6, Jasper NY 14855	607-792-3882	R	2*	<.1
2905	Coast to Coast Express Inc—Kevin Fagan	PO Box 3321, Windsor Locks CT 06096	860-623-3277	R	2*	<.1
2906	EC Services Inc—Juan J Moreno	8340 Tejas Loop, Laredo TX 78045	956-722-8018	R	2*	<.1
2907	Eisenman Transportation Services—John Eisenman	1612 1st Ave, Greeley CO 80631	970-352-2990	R	2*	<.1
2908	Frerichs Freight Lines Inc—William Frerichs	209 Clara St, Belleville IL 62226	618-277-9080	R	2*	<.1
2909	George Husack Inc—George Husack	4234 Locust Dr, Schnecksville PA 18078	610-799-3623	R	2*	<.1
2910	Gray Rider Truck Lines Inc—John Lee	32555 US Hwy 90 W, Seminole AL 36574	251-946-3030	R	2*	<.1
2911	H David Pitzer Trucking Inc—Ronald Thomas	PO Box 276, Biglerville PA 17307	717-677-8147	R	2*	<.1
2912	National Freightways Inc—Gerard Spittler	PO Box 19124, Omaha NE 68119	712-347-6300	R	2*	<.1
2913	Ohio Auto Delivery Inc—David Stynchula	PO Box 268, Grove City OH 43123	614-277-1445	R	2*	<.1
2914	PDS Agent Inc—Matthew Taylor	7801 Bussing Dr, Evansville IN 47725	812-422-8700	R	2*	<.1
2915	Quandt Transport Service Inc—Eugene Quandt	2606 N 11th St, Omaha NE 68110	402-344-2304	R	2*	<.1
2916	Riggers Inc—Clayton Mays	901 Holly Springs Ave, Richmond VA 23224	804-232-1281	R	2*	<.1
2917	Sonneborn Brothers Inc—William Sonneborn	PO Box 71, Hettick IL 62649	618-778-5252	R	2*	<.1
2918	Stegall Milling Company Inc—Thomas Stegall	PO Box 607, Marshville NC 28103	704-624-2181	R	2*	<.1
2919	Trantham Services Inc—David Trantham	1260 State Farm Rd, Alexandria AL 36250	256-820-1988	R	2*	<.1
2920	Gallagher International—Robert Maloney	2401 Elysian Fields Av, New Orleans LA 70117	504-943-0200	R	2*	<.1
2921	GFC Cartage LLC—Jeffrey Daniels	4141 Murfreesboro Pke, Antioch TN 37013	615-501-9400	R	2*	<.1
2922	Lane's Equipment Rental Inc—Richmond Lane	619 Hudson Rd, Chattanooga TN 37405	423-266-7402	R	2*	<.1
2923	Will-Tech Inc—Billy Williams	5044 S Royal Atlanta D, Tucker GA 30084	770-723-1200	R	2*	<.1
2924	WL Davis Trucking—Daniel Michaels	6405 Stone Creek Canyo, Fort Worth TX 76137		R	2*	<.1
2925	Davidson Trucking Inc—Karna Gross	PO Box 67, Creston IL 60113	815-384-3123	R	2*	<.1
2926	Dayton Containerized Freight—Linda Dresback	2005 W Stanfield Rd, Troy OH 45373	937-339-1960	R	2*	<.1
2927	Abke Trucking Inc—Gerald Abke	PO Box 334, Pemberville OH 43450	419-287-3251	R	2*	<.1
2928	Arnold L Barris Trucking Inc—Virginia Barris	PO Box 254, West Middlesex PA 16159	724-528-3398	R	2*	<.1
2929	Big John's Moving Inc—John Healey	1602 1st Ave, New York NY 10028	212-734-3300	R	2*	<.1
2930	C and G Feed and Supply Co—Bob Gilmore	131 County Rd 540, Jackson MO 63755		R	2*	<.1
2931	Capitol Warehousing Corp—Paul Tessmer	PO Box 228, Windsor WI 53598	608-846-9310	R	2*	<.1
2932	Independent Operator Inc—Gerald Kissinger	2863 Country Rd N, Cottage Grove WI 53527	608-873-7267	R	2*	<.1
2933	Joseph Barton Inc—Joseph Botknecht	225 Central Ave, Farmingdale NY 11735	631-293-2113	R	2*	<.1
2934	JV Rigging Inc—Joseph Vaglia	PO Box 4097, New Kensington PA 15068	724-339-8900	R	2*	<.1
2935	L and S Trucking—Larry Frick	PO Box 1781, Wausau WI 54402	715-848-2523	R	2*	<.1
2936	McCoy Transport Inc—William Mullane	PO Box 291, Katonah NY 10536	914-242-2001	R	2*	<.1
2937	MD Miller Trucking Inc—Marlene Miller	600 W Lockport Rd, Plainfield IL 60544	815-254-4966	R	2*	<.1
2938	Priority Services Inc—William Norton	1000 N Villa Ave, Villa Park IL 60181	630-993-6000	R	2*	<.1
2939	Quality Warehouse and Distrib Co—Harold Cannata	180 Mill Rd, Edison NJ 08817	732-287-9393	R	2	<.1
2940	Stageline Express Inc—Tom Freeland	140 N 64th St, Coopersville MI 49404	616-837-8829	R	2*	<.1
2941	Dun Transportation and Stringing—Gene Johnson	304 Reynolds Ln, Sherman TX 75092	903-891-9660	R	2*	<.1
2942	Falcon Drilling and Blasting Inc—Lynda Miller	PO Box 148, Eureka WI 54934	920-685-5299	R	2*	<.1
2943	Paul C Emery Co—Craig Emery	2377 Kimberton Rd, Phoenixville PA 19460	610-933-3365	R	2*	<.1
2944	Peet Frate Line Inc—Richard Ahrens	PO Box 1129, Woodstock IL 60098	815-338-5500	R	2*	<.1
2945	Ross Caves and Son Inc—Larry Caves	N 5796 State Rd 22, Wild Rose WI 54984	920-622-3484	R	2*	<.1
2946	3R of Charleston Inc—Walton Rhodes	PO Box 1443, Goose Creek SC 29445	843-824-0711	R	2*	<.1
2947	Action Moving and Storage Inc—Carl Laroe	359 Jasper Mine Rd, Colchester VT 05446	802-893-1234	R	2*	<.1
2948	Anderson Brothers Storage and Moving—Brian Miller	3141 N Sheffield Ave, Chicago IL 60657	773-935-0013	R	2*	<.1
2949	August Pensa Modern Movers Corp—Louis Pensa	1110 Kennedy Blvd, Union City NJ 07087	201-863-3560	R	2*	<.1
2950	B and B Trucking Inc—John Bruneau	676 Bruneau Rd, Orleans VT 05860	802-754-6968	R	2*	<.1
2951	Best Delivery Systems Inc—Roger Best	13225 Bay Park Rd, Pasadena TX 77507	713-749-5900	R	2*	<.1
2952	Brent Higgins Trucking Company Inc—Brent Higgins	PO Box 827, Mulberry AR 72947	479-997-2366	R	2*	<.1
2953	Brouwer Relocation Inc—Timothy Brouwer	4800 N Velocity Ave, Sioux Falls SD 57104		R	2*	<.1
2954	Caribbean Intl Transportation and Consoli—Foster Shepherd	5440 W 5th St, Jacksonville FL 32254	904-786-0811	R	2*	<.1
2955	Chicagoland Quad Cities Express—Dottie Vavrik	7715 S 78th Ave, Bridgeview IL 60455	708-594-6767	R	2*	<.1
2956	Colma Drayage Inc—Barry Carnesecca	PO Box S, Daly City CA 94017	650-756-1905	R	2*	<.1
2957	J and D Trucking Inc—James Threet	2201 Livingston Hwy, Jamestown TN 38556	931-879-8542	R	2*	<.1
2958	Jeff's Movers Inc—Michael Fenstermaker	8900 Louisiana St, Merrillville IN 46410	219-756-9999	R	2*	<.1
2959	Lindsay Transportation Inc—Rick Parod	PO Box 156, Lindsay NE 68644	402-428-2131	S	2*	<.1
2960	Nunley Trucking Company Inc—Herman Nunley	212 County Rd 195, Iuka MS 38852	662-424-0080	R	2*	<.1
2961	Seward Sand and Gravel Inc—David Beisler	532 County Hwy 58, Oneonta NY 13820	607-432-1653	R	2*	<.1
2962	Sudbury Transportation Inc—Robert Sudbury	6100 E 21st St N Ste 2, Wichita KS 67208	316-682-1628	R	2*	<.1
2963	Triple D Supply LLC—Don Doke	350 Crawford Blvd, Las Cruces NM 88007	505-525-2477	R	2*	<.1
2964	Welpak Corp—Thomas Ryan	58-60 Grand Ave, Maspeth NY 11378	718-391-0155	R	2*	<.1
2965	Kirk Trucking Service Inc—Charles Guest	6629 Rt 22, Delmont PA 15626	724-468-8100	R	2*	<.1
2966	Paulk's Moving and Storage Inc—Ron Danzey	724 Kraft Ave, Panama City FL 32401	850-785-4333	R	2	<.1
2967	Stearly's Motor Freight Inc—Walter Stearly	PO Box 26450, Collegeville PA 19426	610-489-4141	R	2	<.1
2968	Beachler Trucking Inc—William Beachler	2334 County Rd 775, Loudonville OH 44842	419-938-7503	R	2*	<.1
2969	Dan M Ogden and Sons Inc—Norman Ogden	6230 S 1280 E, Salt Lake City UT 84121	801-262-3010	R	2	<.1
2970	Demers Brothers Trucking Inc—Gary Demers	453 S Main St, Attleboro MA 02703	508-222-2181	R	2*	<.1
2971	DLD Grain and Feed Inc—Esther Rochlitz	PO Box 180, Big Springs NE 69122	308-889-3390	R	2*	<.1
2972	JB Moving Services Inc—Joseph Barone	222 Selleck St, Stamford CT 06902	203-602-7979	R	2*	<.1
2973	Vaughan Contractors Inc—Jo Vaughan	685 Bridge City Ave, Westwego LA 70094	504-361-1347	R	2	<.1
2974	Curtis Specialized Moving and Storage—Curtis Wilson	460 W Mockingbird Lane, Dallas TX 75247	214-634-0304	R	2*	<.1
2975	Ideal Way Movers Inc—Baker McColley	1865 Swarthmore Ave, Lakewood NJ 08701	732-364-7575	R	2*	<.1
2976	MDR Equipment Transportation—Michael Nisen	PO Box 397, French Camp CA 95231	209-983-1310	R	2	<.1
2977	Shelly Ward Enterprises Inc—D Shelly Ward	7255 Radford Ave, North Hollywood CA 91605	818-255-5850	R	2*	<.1
2978	Voncannon Trucking Inc—Johnny Voncannon	2025 Carl Dr, Asheboro NC 27203	336-672-0036	R	2*	<.1
2979	Bark River Transit Inc—Donald Van Enkevort	PO Box 67, Bark River MI 49807	906-466-9905	R	2*	<.1
2980	Bushnell's Warehousing and Trucking—Dick Bushnell	2720 NW 35th Ave, Portland OR 97210	503-227-3514	R	2*	<.1
2981	DH Campbell Inc—Larry Campbell	PO Box 176, Pine Knot KY 42635	606-354-2400	R	2*	<.1
2982	East Side Van and Storage Co—Vern Tufford	PO Box 86216, Portland OR 97286	503-777-4181	R	2*	<.1
2983	Helders Motor Service Co—Robert Albrecht	3201 S Kostner Ave, Chicago IL 60623	773-523-8501	R	2*	<.1
2984	Bill Ross and Son Trucking Inc—Bill Ross	93459 M 152, Dowagiac MI 49047	269-424-5820	R	2*	<.1
2985	Coy Trucking LLC—Patricia Coy	PO Box 385, Red Oak OK 74563	918-754-2853	R	2*	<.1
2986	Livengood Trucking Inc—Rose Huppert	1108 300th St, Hiawatha KS 66434	785-742-7377	R	2*	<.1
2987	Montana Transfer Co—Thomas Northey	209 Commerce St, Missoula MT 59808	406-728-8080	R	2*	<.1
2988	MW Leahy Company Inc—Michael Leahy	PO Box 187, Ayer MA 01432	978-772-3113	R	2*	<.1

Rank	Company Name—*Executive Officer*	Address, City, State, Zip	Phone	Type	Fin	Empls
2989	North Star Delivery Inc—*Ted Sommerfeld*	8307 Brooklyn Blvd, Brooklyn Park MN 55445	763-391-8097	R	2*	<.1
2990	Pride Enterprises—*Perry Ferguson*	3900 S Coffing Brother, Kingman IN 47952	765-492-3712	R	2*	<.1
2991	Baucom Truck Service Inc—*James Baucom*	2602 Hwy 24, Camp Point IL 62320	217-593-7748	R	2*	<.1
2992	Lady Bugs Transportation Inc—*Randy Barton*	PO Box 789, Magnolia AR 71754	870-234-6500	R	2*	<.1
2993	A and R Transport—*Aaron Atwood*	3345 W 2600 N, Brigham City UT 84302	435-744-2201	R	2*	<.1
2994	Cargo Trac Inc—*Neale Jenkins*	PO Box 41, Springfield NJ 07081	908-654-3460	R	2*	<.1
2995	Fleetwood Trucking Company Inc—*Walter Sellers*	11251 Big Hurricane Rd, Brookwood AL 35444	205-556-8882	R	2*	<.1
2996	Four Seasons Messenger Service—*John Atai*	22A Commerce Dr, Hauppauge NY 11788		R	2*	<.1
2997	Lafond Express Inc—*Richard A Lafond*	PO Box 74187, Romulus MI 48174	734-941-9000	R	2*	<.1
2998	National Truck and Trailer Service LLC—*Nelson McCall*	150 Williams St, Elkton MD 21921	410-398-9350	R	2*	<.1
2999	McHone Trucking Inc—*Sonjia McHone*	1685 Robertson Rd, Salisbury NC 28146	704-633-2436	R	2*	<.1
3000	Alamo Transportation Services Co—*Chris Galvan*	1879 Hormel Dr, San Antonio TX 78219	210-229-9311	R	2	.1
3001	Frick Transfer Inc—*Paul Robison*	415 S 24th St, Easton PA 18042	610-252-2161	R	2	<.1
3002	Midwest Viking Inc—*Jack Myer*	1101 SE Lorenz Dr, Ankeny IA 50021	515-964-1933	R	2	<.1
3003	Brooks Trucking Company Inc—*Caroll Brooks*	4540 Delp St, Memphis TN 38118		R	2	<.1
3004	Haz-Mat Transportation and Disposal—*Jack Holder*	PO Box 37392, Charlotte NC 28237	704-332-5600	R	2	<.1
3005	Laz-Trans Inc—*William Lazzerini*	PO Box 10655, Bakersfield CA 93389	661-833-3787	R	2	<.1
3006	Barnet's Express Inc—*Michael DiPiazza*	28 Garfield Pl, South Hackensack NJ 07606	973-777-7307	R	2	<.1
3007	English Trucking Inc—*Lonnie English*	2525 E Malaga Ave, Fresno CA 93725	559-486-7440	R	2	<.1
3008	Enterprise Van Lines Inc—*Benito DeVivo*	360 Rt 59, Monsey NY 10952	845-357-4334	R	2	<.1
3009	Custom Industries Inc—*Lamar Powell*	PO Box 506, West Jordan UT 84084	801-280-3502	R	2	<.1
3010	Weil-Thoman Moving and Storage Co—*Joseph Thoman*	1617-29 Queen City Ave, Cincinnati OH 45214	513-251-5000	R	2	<.1
3011	Schaben and Westling Inc—*Walter Westling*	PO Box BB, Elma WA 98541	360-482-6500	R	2	<.1
3012	Father and Son Moving and Storage—*Frank Russo*	194 Frelinghuysen Ave, Newark NJ 07114	973-824-1313	R	2	<.1
3013	McMillan Transport Inc—*Daniel McMillan*	48 Abby Rd, Manchester NH 03103	603-627-9293	R	2	<.1
3014	Chariot Cartage Inc—*Margaret Kenah*	4359 S Wood St, Chicago IL 60609	773-254-3208	R	2*	<.1
3015	Brauns International Inc—*Wolfgang Makurat*	44466 Chilum Pl, Ashburn VA 20147	703-729-6200	R	2	<.1
3016	Hug-Condon Moving and Storage Co—*Michael Condon*	632 Time Saver Ave, Harahan LA 70123		R	2	N/A
3017	MM Smith Storage Warehouse Inc—*Matthew Smith*	PO Box 413, Fayetteville NC 28302		R	2	<.1
3018	Patterson Storage Warehouse Co *Tom Kiser*	472 Robeson St, Fayetteville NC 28301	910-485-3156	R	2	<.1
3019	Kolnik Trucking Inc—*Joe Kolnik*	505 W Madison St, Darien WI 53114	262-882-3282	R	2	<.1
3020	Southwest Truck Service Inc—*Robert Spear*	PO Box 1810, Watsonville CA 95077	831-724-8514	R	2	<.1
3021	Gregory Palmer and Sons—*Dennis Gregory*	5544 Ashburn Rd, Springfield TN 37172	615-384-4725	R	2	<.1
3022	Dwain Johnson and Sons Trucking—*Dwain Johnson*	1711 S 19th St, Clinton IA 52732	563-242-6046	R	2	<.1
3023	Coral Springs Moving and Storage—*Danny Margolis*	12090 NW 40th St, Coral Springs FL 33065	954-752-7366	R	2	<.1
3024	Rock Island Express—*Joe Scott*	PO Box 125, Rock Island TN 38581	931-686-2977	R	2	<.1
3025	Aspen Transportation Service—*Mike Manca*	795 W Broadway, Gardner MA 01440	978-632-0194	R	2	<.1
3026	OK Moving and Storage Company Inc—*Edward Saner*	PO Box 12848, Norfolk VA 23541	757-461-0007	R	2	<.1
3027	Dagen Trucking Inc—*Jeffrey Dagen*	566 Broadway, Albany NY 12204	518-427-9624	R	2	<.1
3028	M Lange Inc—*Glen Tucker*	900 Industrial Dr, Bensenville IL 60106	630-766-8787	R	2	<.1
3029	J and J Delivery Inc—*Jason Ayers*	PO Box 65996, West Des Moines IA 50265	515-284-5756	R	2	<.1
3030	Dooley Oil Transport Inc—*Kevin Dooley*	PO Box 370, Laramie WY 82073	307-742-5667	R	2	<.1
3031	Beck Transportation Inc—*Lynn Beck*	PO Box 324, Archbold OH 43502	419-445-3371	R	2	<.1
3032	Fallen Oak Packing LLC—*Ron Harney*	PO Box 2357, Salinas CA 93902	831-755-0955	R	2*	<.1
3033	Quick-Way Inc—*William Dunn*	1004 Conrad Industrial, Ludington MI 49431	231-845-6520	R	2	<.1
3034	Taylor Trucking Inc—*William Taylor*	PO Box 267, Camden TN 38320	731-584-7362	R	2	<.1
3035	Beamon and Lassiter Inc—*Rebecca Beamon*	1391 Air Rail Ave Ste, Virginia Beach VA 23455		R	2	<.1
3036	C Summers Inc—*Steven Summers*	112 Spruce St, Elizabethville PA 17023	717-362-8117	R	2	<.1
3037	Barkley Truck Line Inc—*Francis Kick*	PO Box 970, Watertown SD 57201	605-886-6925	R	2	<.1
3038	Dispatch Transportation Inc—*Sam Bono*	PO Box 911167, Los Angeles CA 90091	323-890-0195	R	2	<.1
3039	Mills Distributing—*Renee Miller*	PO Box 575, Brandon SD 57005	605-582-6704	R	2	<.1
3040	D and S Mobile Home Service—*Sherry Triplett*	20166 Hwy 53, Gulfport MS 39503	228-832-5681	R	2	<.1
3041	Yasutomi Warehousing and Distribution/YWD—*Yasuo Yasutomi*	1140 Sandhill Ave, Carson CA 90746	310-761-1066	R	2	N/A
3042	McKissick Trucking of Ohio Inc—*Bill McKissick*	PO Box 150, Girard OH 44420	330-539-6164	R	2	<.1
3043	Calexico Freight Lines—*Luis Rioseco*	PO Box 5675, Calexico CA 92232	760-357-2265	R	2	<.1
3044	DeLullo Trucking Corp—*Robert DeLullo*	PO Box 497, Saint Marys PA 15857	814-834-1464	R	2	<.1
3045	RPTS Express Inc—*Dante Plange*	PO Box 852, Brunswick OH 44212	330-273-7303	R	2	<.1
3046	Callahan Brothers Inc—*John Callahan*	133 E Putnam Ave, Cos Cob CT 06807	203-869-2239	R	2	<.1
3047	Moving Right Along Service Inc—*James Rueda*	8920 Cooper Ave, Glendale NY 11385	718-997-6868	R	2	<.1
3048	Nor-Cal Distribution Services	1498 Seareel Ln, San Jose CA 95131	408-416-0526	R	2	<.1
3049	Metro Air Services Inc—*Manuel Gonzalez*	109 Air Freight Blvd, Nashville TN 37217	615-361-6135	R	2	<.1
3050	TCC Dalton Inc—*Paul Hastings*	990 Spiral Blvd, Hastings MN 55033	651-480-3786	R	2	<.1
3051	Banchi Trucking LLC—*Eric Winner*	8008 N Star Fort Loram, Yorkshire OH 45388	419-582-2219	R	1	<.1
3052	Carry All Trucking Inc—*David Morrow*	PO Box 93, Winfield TN 37892	423-569-3910	R	1	<.1
3053	Morgan Trucking Co—*Donald Morgan*	PO Box 1714, Muscatine IA 52761	563-263-4140	R	1	<.1
3054	RZ Trucking—*Richard Speaker*	19413 Le Claire Ln, Redding CA 96003	530-275-4295	R	1	<.1
3055	Dawn Trucking Inc—*William Myers*	PO Box 1044, Iron Mountain MI 49801	906-779-1135	R	1	<.1
3056	Pasco Products Inc—*Johnny Davis*	PO Box 5479, Cleveland TN 37320	423-472-2159	R	1	<.1
3057	Cathie's Cartage Inc—*Catherine Morris*	PO Box 916, Griffith IN 46319	219-922-6880	R	1	<.1
3058	Floyd's of South Carolina Inc—*Floyd Edick*	PO Box 610, Chesterfield SC 29709		R	1	<.1
3059	K-C Refrigeration Transport Co—*Stephen Kowalczyk*	PO Box 545, Troy NY 12181	518-273-7505	R	1	<.1
3060	Samson Moving and Storage Company Inc—*Moshe Deutsch*	264 E Broadway Rm C 15, New York NY 10002	212-752-5040	R	1	<.1
3061	Canxpress Inc—*Wes Cannon*	PO Box 34995, Memphis TN 38184	901-372-2565	R	1	<.1
3062	Universal Delivery Systems Inc—*Rosanne Koncelik*	11402 15th Ave, College Point NY 11356	718-539-4480	R	1	<.1
3063	Henry L Taylor Trucking LLC—*Henry Taylor*	1280 Nawakwa Rd, Biglerville PA 17307	717-677-6138	R	1	<.1
3064	Palm Freight Systems Inc—*William Fields*	1717 JP Hennessy Dr, La Vergne TN 37086	615-641-1200	R	1	<.1
3065	Hurricane Trucking Inc—*Miguel Pradou*	1901 Magnolia Dr, Pasadena TX 77503		R	1	<.1
3066	W Peter Ronson Jr and Sons Inc—*Dave Ronson*	2823 Carmen Rd, Middleport NY 14105	716-735-7814	R	1	<.1
3067	Harvest Express Inc—*Craig Beam*	PO Box 611, Bardstown KY 40004	502-585-9184	R	1	<.1
3068	Morrison Freight Company Inc—*Timothy Gallagher*	2961 King Rd, Morrison TN 37357		R	1	<.1
3069	DiPinto Brothers Transportation—*Robert DiPinto*	PO Box 1375, Edison NJ 08818	732-248-8811	R	1	<.1
3070	Ryan Trucking Company Inc—*Barry Cannon*	PO Box 160, Caneyville KY 42721	270-879-3241	R	1	<.1
3071	Anderson Transfer Inc—*Gene Papa*	595 Meadowlands, Washington PA 15301		R	1	<.1
3072	Carestia Trucking Co—*Dominic Bellino*	1241 County Rd Ste 13A, Florence CO 81226	719-784-3878	R	1	<.1
3073	ER Lewis Transportation Inc—*Eric Lewis*	PO Box 870236, Woods Cross UT 84087	801-292-3491	R	1	<.1
3074	SWI Transportation Inc—*Carol Becklund*	3820 Cajon Blvd, San Bernardino CA 92407	909-880-3399	R	1	<.1
3075	Kealy Trucking Co—*Kevin Kealy*	PO Box 27469, Cleveland OH 44127	216-271-0400	R	1	<.1
3076	JJ's and Associates Inc—*John Reynolds*	736 W Elm St, Wayland MI 49348	269-792-9909	R	1	<.1
3077	Leonard Transport Inc—*John Leonard*	6358 N River Rd, Waterville OH 43566	419-872-6565	R	1	<.1
3078	Virginia Storage Services—*Adrian Pullen*	1955 Valley Ave, Winchester VA 22601	540-667-4273	R	1	<.1

Note: An asterisk (*) indicates an estimated financial figure. The company type code used is as follows: R = Private, P = Public, S = Private Subsidiary, B = Public Subsidiary, D = Division, J = Joint Venture, I = Investment Fund.

COMPANY RANKINGS BY SALES WITHIN 4-DIGIT SIC

Rank	Company Name—*Executive Officer*	Address, City, State, Zip	Phone	Type	Fin	Empls
3079	Macy Movers Inc—*Jack Macy*	200 Victory Ct, Oakland CA 94607	510-444-0100	R	1	N/A
3080	Clifford R Lathrop Inc—*Bettie Lathrop*	35w090 Lathrop Ln, Dundee IL 60118		R	1	<.1
3081	Cormier Movers Inc—*Ken Cormier*	136 Lafayette Rd, North Hampton NH 03862	603-964-4100	R	1	<.1
3082	Vito's Express Inc—*Anthony Ambrosino*	50 Maria Ave, Johnston RI 02919	401-273-9440	R	1	<.1
3083	Central Moving and Storage—*Steven Donenfeld*	374 Kosciusko St, Brooklyn NY 11221	718-726-6222	R	1	<.1
3084	Green's Moving and Storage Inc—*Brady Christofferson*	1115 E New York St, Rapid City SD 57701	605-342-7060	R	1	<.1
3085	RG Hawkes Trucking Inc—*Randy Hawkes*	PO Box 176, Litchfield MI 49252	517-767-4151	R	1	<.1
3086	Nyconn Horse Transportation Corp—*Anthony Baxendale*	183 Silver Spring Rd, Wilton CT 06897	203-762-0611	R	1	<.1
3087	Fleming-Shaw Transfer and Storage—*Michael Simpson*	PO Box 18047, Greensboro NC 27419	336-665-9411	R	1	<.1
3088	Flatbush Moving Van Co—*John Liantonio Jr*	195 Bay 19th St, Brooklyn NY 11214	718-236-8900	R	1	<.1
3089	Chas Wood and Son Moving Inc—*Alan Greenberg*	30 Hub Dr, Melville NY 11747	631-293-5550	R	1	N/A
3090	Hart Transportation Inc—*William Hart*	944 Lane Ave N, Jacksonville FL 32254	904-786-0805	R	1*	<.1
3091	Atlantic Good Services Inc—*Guillermo Sanchez*	3005-3007 NW 24th St, Miami FL 33142	305-634-9991	R	1*	<.1
3092	Continental Machinery Movers—*Terry Clyne*	1234 Fesslers Ln, Nashville TN 37210	615-256-1780	R	1*	<.1
3093	Horwith Freightliner—*Regina Horwith Grim*	PO Box 7 Rte 329, Northampton PA 18067	610-261-2220	R	1*	<.1
3094	Petersen Trucking Inc—*Richard Petersen*	PO Box 304, Dysart IA 52224	319-476-2335	R	1*	<.1
3095	Ralph H Burns and Son Inc—*William Burns*	PO Box 38, Hillsboro WV 24946	304-653-4213	R	1*	<.1
3096	J and J Drive-Away Inc	16244 Foster St, Stilwell KS 66085	913-851-4011	R	1*	<.1
3097	Richard Bellerud Trucking—*Richard Bellerud*	4520 19th Ave SW, Fargo ND 58103	701-277-8321	R	1*	<.1
3098	Trans Gulf Transportation—*William Keys*	501 Independence Pkwy, La Porte TX 77571	281-470-0500	R	1*	<.1
3099	ATL Courier Inc—*Jeff Stewart*	PO Box 569, Norcross GA 30091	770-449-5880	R	1*	<.1
3100	Piedmont Transportation Inc—*Ben Davenport*	PO Box 879, Chatham VA 24531	434-432-4491	R	1*	<.1
3101	Norwood Transportation Inc—*Steven Peterson*	2232 S 7200 W, Magna UT 84044	801-250-2030	R	1*	<.1
3102	Dynamic Transportation Co—*Lyle Braun*	955 Hamilton Ave, University Park IL 60466	708-534-9000	R	1*	<.1
3103	Gerold Moving and Warehousing Co—*Albert Crawford*	435 Hecker St, Belleville IL 62221	618-277-8636	R	1*	<.1
3104	GL Wasko and Sons LLC—*Gerald Wasko*	PO Box 806, Bridgman MI 49106	269-465-5913	R	1*	<.1
3105	Inland Transporters LLC—*Daniel Irwin*	PO Box 2050, Fontana CA 92334	909-355-8787	R	1*	<.1
3106	Judge Manning Horse Transportation—*Judge Manning*	18 Mechanic St, Amenia NY 12501	845-373-8700	R	1*	<.1
3107	Run-R-Way Express Company Inc—*Russell Hendrich*	PO Box 205, Portis KS 67474	785-346-2900	R	1*	<.1
3108	Stettner Inc—*Larry Stettner*	2206 E 14 Rd, Hampton NE 68843	402-725-3176	R	1*	<.1
3109	DRP Trucking Co—*Robert Pefley*	PO Box 188, Wabash IN 46992	260-782-2222	R	1*	<.1
3110	Rudolph Transfer and Storage Co—*Robert Tieken*	520 S Spring St, Clarksville TN 37040	931-647-3542	R	1*	<.1
3111	Dalor Transit Inc—*Dave Hughes*	6005 W Ryan Rd, Franklin WI 53132	414-421-8900	R	1*	<.1
3112	Gardner Trucking—*Michael Gardner*	PO Box 747, Chino CA 91708	909-563-5606	R	1	<.1
3113	JL Shandy Transportation—*Lynn Crotty*	PO Box 130, Saint John IN 46373	219-365-2000	R	1*	<.1
3114	PAB Moving and Storage Co—*Seth Millington*	121 S Santa Fe Ave, Norman OK 73069	405-329-1933	R	1*	<.1
3115	Reichs Ford Trailer Rentals LLC—*James Stull*	PO Box 3247, Frederick MD 21705	301-898-7150	R	1*	<.1
3116	Carter Truck Lines Inc—*Sharon Carter*	2462 S W St, Indianapolis IN 46225	317-783-3311	R	1*	<.1
3117	Titan Trucks Inc—*Shannon Himango*	PO Box 1353, Levelland TX 79336	806-894-4852	R	1*	<.1
3118	Oliver Trucking Company Inc—*David Oliver*	PO Box 53, Winchester KY 40392	859-744-7320	R	1*	<.1
3119	Clinton Moving and Packaging Inc—*Carter Jackson*	232 Utica Rd Ste 12B, Clinton NY 13323	315-853-5239	R	1*	<.1
3120	Whitney Trucking Inc—*Dan Whitney*	576 Pine Meadow Rd, Northfield MA 01360	413-498-5591	R	1*	<.1
3121	MLK Delivery Service Inc—*Marion Kats*	PO Box 87, Worth IL 60482	708-389-9050	R	1*	<.1
3122	Silva's Fxpress Inc—*John Bettencourt*	75 Phoenix Ave, Lowell MA 01852	978-459-3080	R	1*	<.1
3123	Salem '66' Auto Sales—*Richard Wunderlich*	PO Box 73, Pelham NH 03076	603-635-3222	R	1*	<.1
3124	Spinning Wheels Express—*Jason Colaccio*	152 Lynnway Ste 2D, Lynn MA 01902		R	1*	<.1
3125	Supreme Cores Transport Inc—*Warren Grossmann*	5737 W Mill Rd, Milwaukee WI 53218	414-353-7100	R	1*	<.1
3126	IWX Motor Freight—*Richard Coulter*	2750 N Barnes Ave, Springfield MO 65803	417-873-1136	R	<1	.5
3127	Osborn Transportation Inc—*Paul Skelton*	P O Box 1830, Gadsden AL 35902	256-442-2514	R	<1	.3
3128	WLA Inc—*Bill Anderson*	PO Box 1967, Mount Airy NC 27030	336-789-0545	R	<1	.2
3129	USA Cartage Inc—*Ralph Richmond*	PO Box 630, Williamsport MD 21795	301-223-7112	R	<1	.1
3130	Vernon Milling Company Inc—*Elmer Thomas*	PO Box 1617, Vernon AL 35592	205-695-7161	R	<1	.1
3131	Sugar House Van Lines—*David Greensides*	PO Box 65796, Salt Lake City UT 84165	801-487-3636	R	<1	<.1
3132	Don Jerry X-Plo Inc—*Rhonda Barber*	1080 Military Tpke Ste, Plattsburgh NY 12901	518-561-7810	R	<1	<.1
3133	Dakotaland Transportation Inc—*Jerry Fowlds*	PO Box 84424, Sioux Falls SD 57118	605-543-6640	R	<1	<.1
3134	Dana Transport Inc—*Ronald Dana*	210 Essex Ave E, Avenel NJ 07001	732-750-9100	R	N/A	.2
3135	Freight Lime and Sand Hauling—*Patrick McConnell*	PO Box 574, Green Lake WI 54941	920-294-0430	R	N/A	.1
3136	Hot Shot Express Inc—*James Keogel* Jones Motor Group Inc	PO Box 600, Spring City PA 19475	610-948-7900	S	N/A	.1
3137	Joule Yacht Transport Inc—*Larry Jensen*	12290 Automobile Blvd, Clearwater FL 33762	727-573-2627	R	N/A	.1
3138	WW Transport Inc—*Keith Whitehead*	PO Box 97, Advance MO 63730	573-722-3206	R	N/A	<.1
3139	JC Hauling Co—*Peggy Todd*	PO Box 12, Millstadt IL 62260	618-476-1900	R	N/A	<.1
3140	Colonial Van and Storage Inc—*Douglas Welton*	5901 88th St Rm 700, Sacramento CA 95828	916-546-3600	R	N/A	<.1
3141	Sava Transportation Inc—*Sredko Kondic*	1200 Greenwood Ave, Maywood IL 60153	708-731-2400	R	N/A	<.1
3142	Knight Trucking Inc—*Leroy Knight*	3475 Obannon Rd SE, Elizabeth IN 47117	812-945-3072	R	N/A	<.1
3143	Outlaw Trucking and Logistics Inc—*Patrick Heard*	1638 4th St SW, Cullman AL 35055	256-734-7762	R	N/A	<.1

TOTALS: SIC 4213 Trucking Except Local
Companies: 3,143 — 290,988 — 1,261.7

4214 Local Trucking With Storage

Rank	Company Name—*Executive Officer*	Address, City, State, Zip	Phone	Type	Fin	Empls
1	ACME Distribution Centers Inc—*Jeff Goldfogel*	18101 E Colfax Ave, Aurora CO 80011	303-340-2100	R	1,081*	.3
2	Keller Transfer Lines Inc—*Doug Devries*	5635 Clay Ave SW, Grand Rapids MI 49548	616-531-1850	R	894*	.2
3	Murray Transfer and Storage Company Inc—*David Sneeden*	1400 S 5th St, Wilmington NC 28401	910-762-6684	R	593*	.2
4	Exel Logistics Inc—*John Gilbert*	570 Polaris Pkwy, Westerville OH 43082	614-865-8500	S	225*	6.0
5	Bekins Van Lines LLC—*Greg Hoover* Bekins Co	330 S Mannheim Rd, Hillside IL 60162	708-547-2000	S	207*	.4
6	La Rosa del Monte Express Inc—*Hiran Rodriquez*	1133-35 Tiffany St, Bronx NY 10459	718-991-3300	R	198*	.1
7	Bekins Co—*Michael Petersen*	330 S Mannheim Rd, Hillside IL 60162	708-547-2000	R	167*	1.2
8	EE Ward Moving and Storage Co—*Brian Brooks*	1975 Galaxie St, Columbus OH 43207	614-321-9932	R	138*	<.1
9	Arnold Transportation Service Inc—*Michael Walters*	9523 Florida Mining Bl, Jacksonville FL 32257	904-262-4285	R	121*	1.7
10	Paul Arpin Van Lines—*David Arpin*	PO Box 1302, East Greenwich RI 02818	401-828-8111	R	116*	.5
11	Central Transportation Systems Inc—*James Alexander*	4105 Rio Bravo Ste 100, El Paso TX 79902		R	94*	<.1
12	Cord Moving and Storage Co—*Steve Ryan*	4101 Rider Trl N, Earth City MO 63045	314-291-7440	R	70*	.3
13	Intermodal Cartage Company Inc—*John Henry*	PO Box 751747, Memphis TN 38175	901-312-3011	R	60*	.2
14	HC Gabler Inc—*Harold C Gabler Jr*	PO Box 220, Chambersburg PA 17201	717-264-3609	R	45*	.1
15	George W Weaver and Son Inc	165 Lamont St, New Cumberland PA 17070	717-774-7838	S	28*	.1
16	Clausen Supply Co—*Peter Clausen*	PO Box 1386, Clinton IA 52733	563-242-4994	R	26*	.1
17	Terminal Corp—*Scott Menzies*	1801 S Clinton St Ste, Baltimore MD 21224		R	26*	.1
18	Lawrence Transportation Systems Inc—*Weldon S Lawrence*	872 Lee Hwy, Roanoke VA 24019		R	19*	.3
19	Wald Relocation Services Ltd—*Tim Martin*	8708 W Little York Rd, Houston TX 77040	713-512-4800	S	19*	.1

Rank	Company Name—*Executive Officer*	Address, City, State, Zip	Phone	Type	Fin	Empls
20	Castine Moving and Storage—*Don Castine*	1235 Chestnut St, Athol MA 01331	978-249-9105	R	15*	.1
21	Werner-Donaldson Moving Services Inc—*Kenneth J Seibert*	2901 E 10th Ave, Tampa FL 33605	813-886-8110	R	15*	<.1
22	Cruz Modular Inc—*Linda Galleran*	249 W Baywood Ave Ste, Orange CA 92865	714-283-2890	R	11*	.1
23	Accelerated Moving and Storage Inc—*Todd Wilson*	4600 Homer Ohio Ln, Groveport OH 43125	614-836-1007	R	11*	<.1
24	Meyer Equipment Company Inc—*Robert Meyer*	117 N 1st St, King City CA 93930	831-385-0601	R	9	<.1
25	Triple S Trucking Company Inc—*Jerry Sandel*	PO Box 100, Aztec NM 87410	505-334-6193	R	8*	.1
26	Intracoastal Liquid Mud Inc—*Michael Calkins*	PO Box 51784, Lafayette LA 70505	337-232-4550	R	7*	<.1
27	Frederick Industries Inc—*Henry Frederick*	8309 Sherwick Ct, Jessup MD 20794	410-792-8066	R	6*	.1
28	Falcon Express Inc—*Victor Marano*	PO Box 4897, Philadelphia PA 19124	215-992-3140	R	6	.1
29	Kid Glove Inc—*Dave Fulwider*	8430 E Evans Rd, Scottsdale AZ 85260	480-948-2442	R	5*	<.1
30	MHF Logistical Solutions Inc—*Thomas Piatak*	800 Cranberry Woods Dr, Cranberry Township PA 16066	724-772-9800	R	4*	.1
31	Store and Haul Inc—*Curt Rager*	1165 Grill Rd, Van Wert OH 45891	419-238-4284	R	4*	<.1
32	TH Helig Inc—*Ted Heiling*	541 Scull St, Lebanon PA 17046	717-272-0361	R	4*	<.1
33	Commercial Transfer Inc—*Tim Fortier*	PO Box 12004, Fresno CA 93776	559-275-0444	R	2*	<.1
34	Sugar Services Corp—*Charles Bunn*	PO Box 1402, Memphis TN 38101	901-523-0045	R	1*	<.1
35	Neoc Inc—*Dean Prescott*	36 Finnell Dr Ste 6, Weymouth MA 02188	781-331-5997	R	1*	<.1

TOTALS: SIC 4214 Local Trucking With Storage
Companies: 35

					4,237	12.5

4215 Courier Services Except by Air

1	Dynamex Inc—*Maynard Skarka*	5429 LBJ Fwy Ste 1000, Dallas TX 75240	214-560-9000	B	406	1.5
2	AutoInfo Inc—*Harry M Wachtel*	PO Box 4383, Stamford CT 06907	561-988-9456	P	280	.1
3	Fedex Ground Package System Inc—*Frederick Smith*	1000 Fed Ex Dr, Coraopolis PA 15108	412-269-1000	S	240*	1.5
4	Patriot Transportation Holding Inc—*John D Baker II*	501 N Riverside Ave St, Jacksonville FL 32202		P	111	.8
5	Aeronet Worldwide—*Tony L Medeiros*	PO Box 17239, Irvine CA 92623	949-474-3000	R	74*	.2
6	Mid-Georgia Courier Inc—*Larry Friday*	1564 Norman Dr, College Park GA 30349	770-991-1084	R	66*	.1
7	Priority Express Courier Inc—*Rob Johnstone*	5 Chelsea Pky, Boothwyn PA 19061	610-364-3300	R	48*	.1
8	Eastern Connection Operating Inc—*James E Berluti*	60 Olympia Ave, Woburn MA 01801		R	27*	.3
9	Rush Transportation and Logistics—*Jan Parker*	PO Box 2810, Dayton OH 45401	937-297-6182	R	25*	.2
10	Careful Courier Service—*Christopher Snell*	PO Box 51118, Palo Alto CA 94303	650-903-9393	R	18*	.1
11	Sunset Transportation—*Jim Williams*	11406 Gravois Rd, Saint Louis MO 63126		R	16*	<.1
12	Veterans Distribution of Chicago—*William Factor*	2220 Arthur Ave, Elk Grove Village IL 60007	312-666-3400	R	13	N/A
13	Delivery Solutions Inc—*Dave Thompson*	595 Tamarack Ave Ste D, Brea CA 92821		R	13*	.1
14	WPX Delivery Solutions LLC—*Dennis Bishop*	3320 West Valley Hwy N, Auburn WA 98001	253-876-2760	R	12*	<.1
15	Georgia Messenger Service Inc—*Dave Croom*	PO Box 48392, Atlanta GA 30362	404-681-3278	R	7*	<.1
16	Unity Courier Service—*Ron Boehm*	1132 Beecher St, San Leandro CA 94577	510-568-8890	R	4*	.1
17	Choice Parcel Service Inc—*Deborah Dudderar*	9532 Deereco Rd, Timonium MD 21093	410-560-0607	R	4*	<.1
18	United States Cargo Service Corp—*Ralph Richter*	2036 Williams Rd, Columbus OH 43207	614-449-2854	R	3*	.2
19	A-1 Express Delivery Service Inc—*Mark McCurry*	PO Box 467307, Atlanta GA 31146	404-888-9999	R	3*	<.1
20	Taylor Courier Service—*Robert Taylor*	1801 Hulman St, Terre Haute IN 47803	812-235-6899	R	1	<.1
21	Eagle One Logistics Inc—*Greg Hasley*	4001 Planters Rd, Fort Smith AR 72908	479-785-3524	R	1*	<.1

TOTALS: SIC 4215 Courier Services Except by Air
Companies: 21

					1,373	5.2

4221 Farm Product Warehousing & Storage

1	Farmers Cooperative Compress—*Ron Harkey*	PO Box 2877, Lubbock TX 79408	806-763-9431	R	181*	.1
2	Federal Compress and Warehouse Company Inc—*Larry Lively*	6060 Primacy Pkwy Ste, Memphis TN 38119	901-524-4000	R	174*	.1
3	Ray-Carroll County Grain Growers Inc—*Mike Norwald*	PO Box 158, Richmond MO 64085	816-776-2291	R	148*	.1
4	Minn-Kota Ag Products Inc—*George M Schuler III*	PO Box 175, Breckenridge MN 56520	218-643-8464	R	104*	<.1
5	Attebury Grain Inc—*Sam L Attebury*	PO Box 2707, Amarillo TX 79105	806-335-1639	R	91*	.1
6	Prairie Central Cooperative Company Inc—*Mark Heil*	33559 Hazel St, Chenoa IL 61726	815-945-7866	R	85*	<.1
7	Farmers Cooperative Association (Alva Oklahoma)—*Randy Schwerdtfeger*	PO Box 603, Alva OK 73717	580-327-3854	R	49*	.1
8	Wallace County Cooperative Equity Exchange—*Jay Minton*	PO Box 280, Sharon Springs KS 67758	785-852-4241	R	32*	<.1
9	Tillman and Deal Farm Services Inc—*Billy Tillman*	PO Box 158, Statesboro GA 30459	912-764-9657	R	2*	<.1
10	Wehah Farm Inc—*Grant Lundberg*	PO Box 369, Richvale CA 95974	530-882-4551	R	1*	.2

TOTALS: SIC 4221 Farm Product Warehousing & Storage
Companies: 10

					867	.8

4222 Refrigerated Warehousing & Storage

1	Americold Logistics LLC—*Jozef Opdeweegh*	10 Glennlake Pkwy Ste, Atlanta GA 30328	678-441-1400	R	734*	6.5
2	Burris Logistics—*Donnan R Burris*	501 SE 5th St, Milford DE 19963	302-839-5157	R	186*	1.0
3	Hall's Warehouse Corp—*William Jayne III*	PO Box 378, South Plainfield NJ 07080	908-756-6242	R	93*	.2
4	United States Cold Storage Inc—*David Harlan*	201 Laurel Rd Ste 400, Voorhees NJ 08043	856-354-8181	S	57*	.3
5	Nordic Refrigerated Services—*Don Schoenl*	4300 Pleasantdale Rd, Atlanta GA 30340	770-448-7400	R	33*	.2
6	Bellingham Cold Storage Co—*Doug Thomas*	PO Box 895, Bellingham WA 98227	360-733-1640	R	29*	.2
7	Merchants Terminal Corp—*Harry D Halpert*	501 N Kresson St, Baltimore MD 21224	410-342-9300	R	19*	.1
8	California Refrigerated Services Inc—*Peter Divona*	625 W Anaheim St, Long Beach CA 90813	562-599-5831	R	19*	<.1
9	Tex-Mex Cold Storage Inc—*Emilio Sanchez*	PO Box 4960, Brownsville TX 78523	956-831-4531	R	17*	.2
10	Main Street Produce Inc—*Paul Allen*	2165 W Main St, Santa Maria CA 93458	805-349-7170	R	17*	<.1
11	Konoike-Pacific California Inc—*Robert Smola*	1420 Coil Ave, Wilmington CA 90744	310-518-1000	R	13*	.1
12	Rainier Cold Storage Inc—*Greg Moore*	3625 First Ave South, Seattle WA 98134	206-682-5646	R	12*	<.1
13	Los Angeles Cold Storage Co—*Thom Thomas* Standard Southern Corp	400 S Central Ave, Los Angeles CA 90013	213-624-1831	S	9*	.1
14	E Street Cold Logistics LLC—*G Larson*	901 E E St, Wilmington CA 90744	310-233-7300	R	6*	.1
15	Winchester Cold Storage Company Inc—*John Scully*	PO Box 45, Winchester VA 22604	540-662-4151	R	6*	<.1
16	Barber's Poultry Inc—*David R Barber*	4950 N Washington St, Denver CO 80216	303-466-7338	R	6*	<.1
17	Berkshire Refrigerated Warehouse LLC	PO Box 09284, Chicago IL 60609	773-254-2424	R	5*	<.1
18	Atlantic Custom Processors LLC—*Cheryle Levesque*	PO Box 509, Fort Fairfield ME 04742	207-472-1000	R	5*	<.1
19	Standard Southern Corp—*Mark Rauch*	PO Box 270415, Houston TX 77277	713-627-1700	R	5*	<.1
20	New Orleans Cold Storage and Warehouse Company Ltd—*Mark Blanchard*	PO Box 26308, New Orleans LA 70186	504-944-4400	R	3*	.1
21	Ice Cold Products—*Robert Worten*	100 Frontier Way, Bensenville IL 60106	630-860-0375	R	3*	<.1

TOTALS: SIC 4222 Refrigerated Warehousing & Storage
Companies: 21

					1,277	9.1

4225 General Warehousing & Storage

1	Tecma Group LP—*Alan Russell*	2000 E Wyoming Ave, El Paso TX 79903	915-534-4252	R	1,814*	4.0

Note: An asterisk (*) indicates an estimated financial figure. The company type code used is as follows: R = Private, P = Public, S = Private Subsidiary, B = Public Subsidiary, D = Division, J = Joint Venture, I = Investment Fund.

COMPANY RANKINGS BY SALES WITHIN 4-DIGIT SIC

Rank	Company Name—*Executive Officer*	Address, City, State, Zip	Phone	Type	Fin	Empls
2	APL Logistics Ltd—*Brian Lutt*	1111 Broadway, Oakland CA 94607	510-272-8000	S	975*	4.0
3	Distribution and Marking Services Inc—*Nick Santella*	PO Box 7112, Charlotte NC 28241	704-587-3674	R	701*	.5
4	Federal Warehouse Co—*William T Cirone*	101 National Rd, East Peoria IL 61611	309-694-4500	R	698*	.6
5	Kenco Group Inc—*Andy Smith*	PO Box 1607, Chattanooga TN 37401	423-622-1113	R	408*	2.5
6	Delta Terminal Services LLC—*Richard D Kinder*	3540 River Rd, Harvey LA 70058	504-340-4911	S	185*	.2
7	Ohl LLC—*Randall Curran*	7101 Executive Ctr Dr, Brentwood TN 37027	615-401-6400	R	165*	2.5
8	Jhci Acquisition Inc—*Brian Lutt*	PO Box 224, Des Moines IA 50306	515-265-6171	R	146*	3.5
9	Kenco Logistic Services Inc—*Gary Mayfield*	PO Box 1607, Chattanooga TN 37401	423-756-5552	R	140*	2.5
10	All Metals Service and Warehousing Inc—*Harry Simon*	100 All Metals Dr Sw, Cartersville GA 30120	770-427-7379	R	128*	.1
11	Saddle Creek Corp—*Cliff Otto*	3010 Saddle Creek Rd, Lakeland FL 33801	863-665-0966	R	98*	1.2
12	Kane is Able Inc—*Richard Kane*	PO Box 931, Scranton PA 18501	570-344-9801	R	94*	.9
13	Hermann Services—*Richard Hermann*	83 Stults Rd, Dayton NJ 08810		R	93	.1
14	Mahomed Sales and Warehousing LLC—*Yousuf Mahomed*	8258 Zionsville Rd, Indianapolis IN 46268	317-472-5800	R	86*	.1
15	Jacobson Warehouse Company Inc—*Steve Bourne*	PO Box 224, Des Moines IA 50301	515-265-6171	S	81*	.8
16	Derby Industries LLC—*Diana Herold*	4451 Robards Ln, Louisville KY 40218	502-451-7373	R	78*	.4
17	Garnet Logistics Inc—*Fredrick Yohe*	3681 Leeds Ave, Charleston SC 29405	843-554-6622	R	63*	.1
18	Distribution Services of America—*David Petri*	208 North St, Foxboro MA 02035	508-543-9700	S	58*	.4
19	DD Jones Transfer and Warehouse Company Inc—*Don Goldberg*	2115 Portlock Rd, Chesapeake VA 23324	757-494-0252	R	52*	.3
20	Webgistix Corp—*Joseph DiSorbo*	2251 Constitution Ave, Olean NY 14760	716-372-5211	R	44*	.1
21	Patterson Warehouses Inc—*Samuel Bell*	5388 Airways Blvd, Memphis TN 38116	901-344-2600	R	36*	.2
22	Columbian Logistics Network—*John Zevalkink*	900 Hall St SW, Grand Rapids MI 49503	616-514-6000	R	30*	.2
23	APC Warehouse Co—*Richard Kerns*	PO Box C, Madison IL 62060	618-451-4322	R	28*	.1
24	Eltrex Industries Inc—*Matthew Augustine*	PO Box 30630, Rochester NY 14603	585-454-6100	R	26*	.3
25	Aero Fulfillment Services Corp—*Jon Gimpel*	3900 Aero Dr, Mason OH 45040	513-459-3970	R	25*	.1
26	Belt's Corp—*John Redding*	949 Fell St, Baltimore MD 21231	410-342-1111	R	24*	.2
27	Door To Door Storage Inc—*Timothy J Riley*	6718 S 216th St, Kent WA 98032	253-872-5800	R	23*	.3
28	Metro Park Warehouses Inc—*Robert Banach*	PO Box 2346, Kansas City KS 66110	816-231-0777	R	17*	.3
29	Quality Logistics Systems Inc—*Jeffery Ballard*	PO Box 5637, Meridian MS 39302	601-483-0265	R	17*	.1
30	Brokers Logistics Genpar LLC—*Elizabeth Escalada*	1000 Hawkins Blvd, El Paso TX 79915	915-778-7751	R	16*	.3
31	Ccw Group Pacesetter Inc—*Richard Kern*	PO Box 383, Circleville OH 43113	740-474-0122	R	13*	.2
32	Rite Stuff Foods Inc—*Tom Madden*	PO Box 447, Jerome ID 83338	208-324-8410	R	6*	.1
33	Airboss Polymer Products Corp—*Robert Hagerman*	200 Veterans Blvd, South Haven MI 49090	269-637-2181	R	6*	<.1
34	Hopkins Distribution Co—*Robert Hopkins*	PO Box 19040, Reno NV 89511	775-829-4440	R	4*	<.1
35	D and S Warehousing Inc—*Joachim Schneider*	104 Alan Dr, Newark DE 19711	302-731-7440	R	4*	<.1
36	Merry Maid Inc—*Marilyn Rettaliata*	PO Box 228, Bangor PA 18013	610-588-0927	R	2*	<.1

TOTALS: SIC 4225 General Warehousing & Storage
Companies: 36

					6,383	26.8

4226 Special Warehousing & Storage Nec

Rank	Company Name—*Executive Officer*	Address, City, State, Zip	Phone	Type	Fin	Empls
1	Iron Mountain Inc—*Richard Reese*	745 Atlantic Ave, Boston MA 02111	617-535-4766	P	2,774	8.8
2	Auto Warehousing Co—*Steve Seher*	2810 Marshall Ave Ste, Tacoma WA 98421	253-922-0540	R	335*	1.0
3	Vopak North America Inc—*Dick Richelle*	2000 W Loop S Ste 2200, Houston TX 77027	713-561-7200	S	192	N/A
4	GATX Terminals Holding Corp—*Brian A Kenney*	500 W Monroe St, Chicago IL 60661	312-621-6200	S	76*	.3
5	Amalie Oil Co—*Rick Barkett*	1601 McCloskey Blvd, Tampa FL 33605	813-248-1988	R	75*	.1
6	Ohio Distribution Warehouse Corp—*John R Ness*	1580 Williams Rd, Columbus OH 43207	614-497-1660	R	51*	.5
7	Oiltanking Houston LP—*Adrian De Monchy* Oiltanking Holding USA Inc	PO Box 96290, Houston TX 77213	281-457-7900	S	47*	.1
8	Iron Mountain Confidential Destruction LLC—*Bob Brennan* Iron Mountain Inc	2605 N Berkley Leg Rd, Duluth GA 30096	770-622-0886	S	28*	<.1
9	Oiltanking Holding USA Inc—*Lou Tittle*	15631 Jacintoport Blvd, Houston TX 77015	281-457-7900	S	25*	.1
10	PABTEX GP LLC—*Allen Alexander*	209 Taft Ave Ext, Port Arthur TX 77642	409-962-8343	S	19*	<.1
11	Richards and Richards—*Stephen Richards*	1741 Elm Hill, Nashville TN 37210	615-242-9600	R	12*	<.1
12	S N S South Inc—*Daniel Lione*	PO Box 8189, Seneca SC 29678	864-882-1672	R	10*	.2
13	Midwest Service Warehouse Inc—*Clyde Perfect*	4000 Schenley Pl, Greendale IN 47025	812-537-2331	R	9*	.1
14	Molding Box—*Jordan Guernsey*	12278 S Lone Peak Pky, Draper UT 84020	801-307-2224	R	5*	<.1
15	Elston-Richards Inc—*John Holmes*	3701 Patterson Ave SE, Grand Rapids MI 49512	616-698-2698	R	3*	.1
16	Excel Courier Inc—*Christian Marchetti*	PO Box 401, Herndon VA 20172	703-478-0140	R	3*	<.1
17	Dri-View Manufacturing Company Inc—*W Andriot*	3214 E Blue Lick Rd, Shepherdsville KY 40165	502-957-2700	R	3*	.1

TOTALS: SIC 4226 Special Warehousing & Storage Nec
Companies: 17

					3,667	11.3

4231 Trucking Terminal Facilities

Rank	Company Name—*Executive Officer*	Address, City, State, Zip	Phone	Type	Fin	Empls
1	Brake Systems Inc—*Harry Dozier*	2221 NE Hoyt St, Portland OR 97232	503-236-2116	R	13*	<.1
2	Baldwin Transfer Company Inc—*Richard Edwards*	PO Box 2925, Mobile AL 36652	251-433-3391	R	12	.2
3	Pacific Terminals Ltd—*Steve Frasier*	3480 W Marginal Way SW, Seattle WA 98106	206-923-2155	R	5*	<.1
4	American Industrial Werks Inc—*Craig Knickerbocker*	904 S Roselle Rd Ste 2, Schaumburg IL 60193	847-477-2648	R	5*	<.1

TOTALS: SIC 4231 Trucking Terminal Facilities
Companies: 4

					35	.2

4412 Deep Sea Foreign Transportation of Freight

Rank	Company Name—*Executive Officer*	Address, City, State, Zip	Phone	Type	Fin	Empls
1	Maersk Inc—*Eivind Kolding*	88 Black Falcon Ave St, Boston MA 02210	617-261-8700	D	7,956*	4.5
2	APL Ltd—*Ronald D Widdows*	16220 N Scottsdale Rd, Scottsdale AZ 85254	510-272-8000	S	4,700*	4.0
3	Stolt-Nielsen Transportation Group Ltd	800 Connecticut Ave Fl, Norwalk CT 06854	203-838-7100	S	2,740*	4.7
4	SEACOR Holdings Inc—*Oivind Lorentzen*	PO Box 13038, Fort Lauderdale FL 33316	954-523-2200	P	2,142	6.0
5	Enterprise Ship Company Inc—*Eric L Johnsen* Central Gulf Lines Inc	11 N Water St Ste 1829, Mobile AL 36602	251-243-9120	S	1,880*	.1
6	SEACOR Marine LLC—*Charles Fabrikant* SEACOR Holdings Inc	7910 Main St 2nd Fl, Houma LA 70360		S	1,705*	3.1
7	Sulphur Carriers Inc—*Eric F Johnsen* Waterman Steamship Corp	11 N Water St Ste 1829, Mobile AL 36602	251-243-9120	S	1,677*	.1
8	Overseas Shipholding Group Inc—*Morten Arntzen*	666 3rd Ave, New York NY 10017	212-953-4100	P	1,050	3.6
9	Seabulk International Inc—*Charles Fabrikant* SEACOR Holdings Inc	PO Box 13038, Fort Lauderdale FL 33316	954-523-2200	S	1,041	5.0
10	Orient Overseas Container Line USA Inc—*Erxin Yao*	PO Box 5100, San Ramon CA 94583	925-358-6625	S	793*	3.4
11	Canal Barge Company Inc—*Merritt Lane*	835 Union St Ste 300, New Orleans LA 70112	504-581-2424	R	543*	.5
12	Hamburg Sud North America Inc—*Klaus Meves*	465 South St, Morristown NJ 07960	973-775-5300	R	476*	.3
13	Genco Shipping and Trading Ltd—*Robert Gerald Buchanan*	299 Park Ave 20th Fl, New York NY 10171	646-443-8550	P	392	1.4
14	General Maritime Corp—*John P Tavlarios*	299 Park Ave, New York NY 10171	212-763-5600	P	387	1.1

Rank	Company Name—*Executive Officer*	Address, City, State, Zip	Phone	Type	Fin	Empls
15	International Shipholding Corp—*Niels M Johnsen*	11 N Water St Ste 1829, Mobile AL 36602	251-243-9100	P	290	.5
16	Eagle Bulk Shipping Inc—*Sophocles N Zoullas*	477 Madison Ste 1405, New York NY 10022	212-785-2500	B	265	.8
17	Atlantic Container Line Inc—*Andrew Abbott*	50 Cardinal Dr, Westfield NJ 07090	908-518-5300	S	190*	.4
18	Crowley Petroleum Services Inc—*Rockwell Smith*	9487 Regency Sq Blvd, Jacksonville FL 32225	904-727-2507	R	161*	2.2
19	Waterman Steamship Corp International Shipholding Corp	1 Whitehall St, New York NY 10004	212-747-8550	S	120*	.1
20	Trailer Bridge Inc—*Mark A Tanner*	10405 New Berlin Rd E, Jacksonville FL 32226	904-751-7100	P	118	.1
21	Westwood Shipping Lines—*Guy Stephenson*	PO Box 9777, Federal Way WA 98063	253-924-4399	S	118*	.1
22	Alcoa Steamship Company Inc—*Klaus Kleinfeld*	201 Isabella St, Pittsburgh PA 15212	412-553-4545	S	86*	.1
23	Chevron Shipping Co—*Michael Carthew*	6001 Bollinger Canyon, San Ramon CA 94583	925-842-1000	S	82*	.2
24	Central Gulf Lines Inc—*Erik F Johnsen* International Shipholding Corp	PO Box 53366, New Orleans LA 70153	504-529-5461	S	59*	.1
25	Liberty Maritime Corp—*Philip J Shapiro*	1979 Marcus Ave Ste 20, Lake Success NY 11042	516-488-8800	R	50*	<.1
26	Scorpio Tankers Inc—*Emanuele A Lauro*	150 E 58th St, New York NY 10155	212-542-1616	P	39	<.1
27	SeaRiver Maritime Inc—*Paul Revere*	5959 Las Colinas Blvd, Irving TX 75039	972-444-1000	S	38*	.3
28	Cosco Agencies Los Angeles Inc—*Guogiang Jin*	588 Harbor Scenic Way, Long Beach CA 90802	213-689-6777	S	34*	.1
29	Worldlink Logistics Inc—*Ann Wilkinson*	PO Box 895, Voorhees NJ 08043	856-566-1000	R	6*	<.1
30	Red River Shipping Corp—*John Morris III*	6110 Executive Blvd St, Rockville MD 20852	301-230-0854	R	2*	<.1
31	Stolt Parcel Tankers Inc—*Niel Stolt Nielsen* Stolt-Nielsen Transportation Group Ltd	800 Connecticut Ave 4t, Norwalk CT 06854	203-838-7100	S	<1	4.7

TOTALS: SIC 4412 Deep Sea Foreign Transportation of Freight
Companies: 31					29,140	47.6

4424 Deep Sea Domestic Transportation of Freight
1	Alexander and Baldwin Inc—*Stanley M Kuriyama*	822 Bishop St, Honolulu HI 96813	808-525-6611	P	1,646	2.3
2	ATC Leasing Co—*Michael Testman*	10801 Corporate Dr, Pleasant Prairie WI 53158	262-564-7954	R	1,258*	.9
3	Horizon Lines Inc—*Stephen H Fraser*	4064 Colony Rd Ste 200, Charlotte NC 28211	704-973-7000	P	1,163	1.9
4	Crowley American Transport Inc—*Thomas Crowley Jr*	9487 Regency Square Bl, Jacksonville FL 32225	904-727-2200	S	1,111*	3.5
5	Matson Navigation Company Inc—*Matthew J Cox* Alexander and Baldwin Inc	555 12th St Ste 700, Oakland CA 94607	510-628-4000	S	888*	.7
6	OSG America LP	2 Harbour Pl 302 Knigh, Tampa FL 33602	813-209-0600	S	286	N/A
7	American Eagle Tankers Incorporated Ltd—*Hor Weng Yew*	1900 West Loop S Ste 9, Houston TX 77027	832-615-2000	S	272*	<.1
8	Kellaway Terminal Inc—*Kendall P Kellaway Jr*	PO Box 750, Randolph MA 02368	781-961-8200	R	142*	.3
9	Totem Ocean Trailer Express Inc—*John Parrott* Saltchuk Resources Inc	PO Box 4129, Federal Way WA 98063	206-628-4343	S	102*	.2
10	Express Marine Inc	PO Box 329, Pennsauken NJ 08110	856-541-4600	R	45*	.1
11	Coastal Transportation Inc—*Peter Strong*	4025 13th Ave W, Seattle WA 98119	206-282-9979	R	32*	.1
12	Saltchuk Resources Inc—*Timothy B Engle*	1111 Fairview Ave N, Seattle WA 98109	206-652-1111	R	29*	<.1
13	IEI Barge Services Inc	18525 Hwy 20 W, East Dubuque IL 61025	815-747-3161	S	10*	<.1

TOTALS: SIC 4424 Deep Sea Domestic Transportation of Freight
Companies: 13					6,984	9.9

4432 Freight Transportation on the Great Lakes
1	American Steamship Co—*Jerome Welsch*	500 Essjay Rd, Williamsville NY 14221	716-635-0222	S	123*	.5
2	KCBX Terminals Co *Miko Gibson*	3259 E 100th St, Chicago IL 60617	773-375-3700	S	9*	<.1

TOTALS: SIC 4432 Freight Transportation on the Great Lakes
Companies: 2					132	.5

4449 Water Transportation of Freight Nec
1	Carnival Corp—*Micky Arison*	PO BOX 526170, Miami FL 33152	305-599-2600	P	14,469	89.2
2	Ingram Content Group Inc—*David Prichard*	1 Ingram Blvd, La Vergne TN 37086	615-793-5000	S	2,160	5.4
3	Kirby Corp—*Joesph H Pyne*	PO Box 1537, Houston TX 77251	713-435-1000	P	1,850	4.2
4	Ingram Barge Co—*Craig Philip* Ingram Content Group Inc	4400 Harding Rd, Nashville TN 37205	615-298-8200	S	1,669*	2.3
5	American River Transportation Co—*Patricia A Woertz*	4666 E Faries Pkwy, Decatur IL 62526	217-424-5200	S	1,400*	1.0
6	Commercial Barge Line Co—*Mark K Knoy*	1701 E Market St, Jeffersonville IN 47130	812-288-0100	B	731	2.4
7	Hornbeck Offshore Services Inc—*Todd M Hornbeck*	103 Northpark Blvd Ste, Covington LA 70433	985-727-2000	P	382	1.0
8	K-Sea Transportation Partners LP—*Timothy J Casey* Kirby Corp	One Tower Center Blvd, East Brunswick NJ 08816	732-339-6100	S	264	.9
9	US Shipping Corp—*Joseph Gehegan*	399 Thornall St, Edison NJ 08837	732-635-1500	R	177	.5
10	American Commercial Lines Inc—*Paul Bridwell*	PO Box 610, Jeffersonville IN 47131	812-288-0100	R	170*	2.6
11	AmherstMadison	2 Port Amherst Dr, Charleston WV 25306	304-926-1100	R	158*	.4
12	American Commercial Lines LLC—*Karl Kintzele*	1701 Utica Pke, Jeffersonville IN 47130	812-288-0100	R	149*	2.5
13	Rand Logistics Inc—*Laurence S Levy*	500 5th Ave 50th Fl, New York NY 10110	212-644-3450	P	118	.4
14	Marine Terminals of Arkansas Inc	3852 N County Rd 955, Blytheville AR 72315	870-763-5923	S	102*	.2
15	Western Rivers Boat Management Inc—*Charles Strait*	2308 S 4th St, Paducah KY 42003	270-444-4772	R	69*	.3
16	American Overseas Marine Corp—*Thomas W Merrell*	100 Newport Ave Ext, Quincy MA 02171	617-786-8300	S	68*	.5
17	Crounse Corp—*Stephen D Little*	400 Marine Way, Paducah KY 42003	270-444-9611	R	65*	.4
18	AEP River Operations LLC—*Mark Knoy*	16150 Main Circle Dr S, Chesterfield MO 63017	636-530-2100	S	63*	.1
19	Alter Barge Line Inc—*Jeff Goldstien*	2117 State St, Bettendorf IA 52722	563-344-5100	R	61*	.1
20	Baltic Trading Ltd—*John Wobensmith*	299 Park Ave 20th Fl, New York NY 10171	646-443-8550	B	44	.2
21	Parker Towing Co—*Charles A Haun*	PO Box 20908, Tuscaloosa AL 35402	205-349-1677	R	40*	.2
22	Warrior and Gulf Navigation LLC—*Richard Miller*	PO Box 11397, Chickasaw AL 36671		S	36*	.3
23	M/G Transport Services LLC	4101 Founders Blvd Ste, Batavia OH 45103	513-943-7300	R	6*	<.1

TOTALS: SIC 4449 Water Transportation of Freight Nec
Companies: 23					24,250	114.8

4481 Deep Sea Passenger Transportation Except Ferry
1	Royal Caribbean Cruises Ltd—*Richard D Fain*	PO Box 026053, Miami FL 33102		P	6,753	58.1
2	NCL Corporation Ltd—*Kevin Sheehan*	7665 Corporate Center, Miami FL 33126	305-436-4000	S	4,295*	1.2
3	Seabourn Cruise Line—*Pamela C Conover*	6100 Blue Lagoon Dr St, Miami FL 33126	305-463-3000	S	3,788*	3.5
4	Orient Lines—*Wayne Heller* NCL Corporation Ltd	7665 Corporate Center, Miami FL 33126	954-527-6657	S	290*	.1
5	Blount Small Ship Adventures—*Nancy Blount*	PO Box 368, Warren RI 02885	401-247-0955	R	244*	.1
6	Cunard Line—*Peter Shanks*	24303 Town Center Dr S, Valencia CA 91355		S	143*	1.3
7	Holland America Line Westours Inc—*Stein Kruse*	300 Elliott Ave W, Seattle WA 98119	206-281-3535	S	139*	1.4
8	Windstar Cruises Lines—*Kruse Stein*	2101 4th Ave Ste 210, Seattle WA 98121	206-292-9606	S	139*	.1
9	Costa Cruise Lines Inc	200 S Park Rd Ste 200, Hollywood FL 33021		S	19*	.2

Note: An asterisk (*) indicates an estimated financial figure. The company type code used is as follows: R = Private, P = Public, S = Private Subsidiary, B = Public Subsidiary, D = Division, J = Joint Venture, I = Investment Fund.

COMPANY RANKINGS BY SALES WITHIN 4-DIGIT SIC

Rank	Company Name—*Executive Officer*	Address, City, State, Zip	Phone	Type	Fin	Empls
10	Star Clippers Ltd—*Michael Krafft*	7200 NW 19th St Ste 20, Miami FL 33126	305-442-0550	R	8*	<.1
11	Travel Dynamics International—*George Papagapitos*	132 E 70th St, New York NY 10021		R	8*	<.1
12	Unique World Travel Inc—*Misha Radulovic*	154 Village Rd, Manhasset NY 11030	516-627-2636	R	5*	<.1

TOTALS: SIC 4481 Deep Sea Passenger Transportation Except Ferry
Companies: 12 — 15,831 — 65.9

4482 Ferries

Rank	Company Name—*Executive Officer*	Address, City, State, Zip	Phone	Type	Fin	Empls
1	Arcorp Properties—*Arthur Imperatore Jr*	4800 Avenue at Port Im, Weehawken NJ 07086	201-902-8711	R	1,257*	.5
2	Cross Sound Ferry Services Inc—*John Wronowski*	PO Box 33, New London CT 06320	860-443-5281	R	48*	.1
3	Black Ball Transport Inc—*Rian Anderson*	101 E Railroad Ave, Port Angeles WA 98362	360-457-4491	R	48*	<.1
4	Catalina Channel Express Inc—*Greg Bombard*	95 Berth, San Pedro CA 90731	310-519-7971	R	12*	.2

TOTALS: SIC 4482 Ferries
Companies: 4 — 1,365 — .8

4489 Water Passenger Transportation Nec

Rank	Company Name—*Executive Officer*	Address, City, State, Zip	Phone	Type	Fin	Empls
1	Hornblower Cruises and Events—*Terry MacRae*	Pier 3 on the Embarcad, San Francisco CA 94111	415-438-8300	D	1,595*	.3
2	Trico Marine Services Inc—*Richard Bachmann*	1001 Woodloch Forest D, The Woodlands TX 77380	713-780-9926	P	642	1.8
3	World Yacht Inc—*August J Ceradini Jr*	W 41st St Pier 81, New York NY 10036	212-630-8100	R	609*	.2
4	Blue and Gold Fleet	Pier 41 Marine Termina, San Francisco CA 94133	415-705-8200	S	99*	.4
5	Clipper Navigation Inc—*Meredith Tall*	2701 Alaskan Way Pier, Seattle WA 98121	206-443-2560	R	29*	.1
6	Barry Graham Oil Service LLC	PO Box 982, Bayou La Batre AL 36509	251-824-2774	R	10*	.1

TOTALS: SIC 4489 Water Passenger Transportation Nec
Companies: 6 — 2,984 — 2.8

4491 Marine Cargo Handling

Rank	Company Name—*Executive Officer*	Address, City, State, Zip	Phone	Type	Fin	Empls
1	SSA Marine Inc—*Jon F Hemingway*	1131 SW Klickitat Way, Seattle WA 98134	206-623-0304	S	1,580	13.0
2	Peeples Industries Inc—*Frank Peeples*	21 E Broad St, Savannah GA 31401	912-236-1865	R	308*	.3
3	Jackson Kearney Group—*Dan Houser*	1555 Poydras St Ste 16, New Orleans LA 70112	504-587-1100	R	252*	.2
4	Summit Logistics International Inc—*Robert O'Neill*	800 Federal Blvd, Carteret NJ 07008	732-750-9000	S	211	.8
5	Kirby Inland Marine LP—*Greg Binion*	11211 Industriplex Blv, Baton Rouge LA 70809	225-201-3000	S	181*	.2
6	Direct Container Line Inc	1477 Hamilton Pky, Itasca IL 60143	630-250-1655	R	143*	.5
7	Penn Warehousing and Distribution—*John Brown*	2147 S Columbus Ave, Philadelphia PA 19148		R	115*	.1
8	General Steamship Corporation Ltd—*Scott M Jones*	575 Redwood Hwy Ste 20, Mill Valley CA 94941	415-389-5200	R	97*	.1
9	New Haven Terminal Inc—*Joseph D Crowley*	100 Waterfront St, New Haven CT 06512	203-468-0805	R	39*	.2
10	Levin Enterprises Inc—*Gary M Levin*	402 Wright Ave, Richmond CA 94804	510-232-4422	R	36*	<.1
11	Mcginnis Inc—*Bruce Mcginnis*	PO Box 534, South Point OH 45680	740-377-4391	R	23*	.2
12	Great Western Recycling Industries Inc—*Michael Silverman*	521 Barge Channel Rd, Saint Paul MN 55107	651-224-4877	R	20*	.1
13	Marietta Industrial Enterprises Inc—*W Elliott*	17943 State Rte 7, Marietta OH 45750	740-373-2252	R	19*	.2
14	Dix Shipping Company Inc—*Bob Ostos*	5500 R L Ostos Rd, Brownsville TX 78521	956-831-4228	R	17*	.1
15	Lambert's Point Docks Inc—*Landon Hilliard*	PO Box 89, Norfolk VA 23509	757-446-1200	S	13*	<.1
16	Universal Maritime—*Griff Lynch*	1800 Seaboard Ave, Portsmouth VA 23707	757-393-4071	S	9*	<.1
17	SSA-Cooper LLC—*John Coakley* SSA Marine Inc	PO Box 1767, Savannah GA 31402	912-966-1111	S	5*	.1
18	Advent Inc—*Carl D'emilio*	890 Mountain Ave Ste 5, New Providence NJ 07974	908-795-3200	R	2*	<.1

TOTALS: SIC 4491 Marine Cargo Handling
Companies: 18 — 3,070 — 16.0

4492 Towing & Tugboat Services

Rank	Company Name—*Executive Officer*	Address, City, State, Zip	Phone	Type	Fin	Empls
1	Crowley Maritime Corp—*Thomas B Crowley Jr*	9487 Regency Sq Blvd, Jacksonville FL 32225	904-727-2200	R	1,467*	4.1
2	Foss Maritime Co—*Paul Stevens*	1151 Fairview Ave N, Seattle WA 98109	206-281-3800	S	1,173*	1.2
3	Moran Towing and Transportation Company Inc—*Edward Tregurtha* Moran Towing Corp	50 Locust Ave, New Canaan CT 06840	203-442-2800	S	102*	.1
4	Allied Marine Industries Inc—*John Stroud*	PO Box 717, Norfolk VA 23501	757-545-7301	R	98*	.3
5	Moran Towing Corp—*Paul R Tregurtha*	50 Locust Ave, New Canaan CT 06840	203-442-2800	R	89*	.9
6	Le Beouf Brothers Towing LLC—*Richard Gonsoulin*	PO Box 9036, Houma LA 70361	985-594-6691	R	66*	.4
7	Bay Houston Towing Co—*Mark E Kuebler*	PO Box 3006, Houston TX 77253	713-529-3755	R	38*	.4
8	Jantran Inc—*Joseph W Janoush*	PO Box 397, Rosedale MS 38769	662-759-6841	R	35*	.2
9	McAllister Towing and Transportation Company Inc—*Brian A McAllister*	17 Battery Pl Ste 1200, New York NY 10004	212-269-3200	R	17*	.1
10	Shaver Transportation Co—*Harry L Shaver*	PO Box 10324, Portland OR 97296	503-228-8850	R	11*	.1

TOTALS: SIC 4492 Towing & Tugboat Services
Companies: 10 — 3,096 — 7.7

4493 Marinas

Rank	Company Name—*Executive Officer*	Address, City, State, Zip	Phone	Type	Fin	Empls
1	Seven Resorts Inc—*David A Ohanesian*	PO Box 16247, Irvine CA 92623		R	26*	.7
2	Jones Boat Yard Inc—*Cleveland Jones*	3399 Nw S River Dr, Miami FL 33142	305-635-0891	R	7*	.1
3	Westrec Marina Management Inc—*William W Anderson*	16633 Ventura Blvd 6th, Encino CA 91436	818-907-0400	R	2*	.1
4	Crowley's Yacht Yard Lakeside LLC—*Grant Crowley*	3434 E 95th St, Chicago IL 60617	773-221-9990	R	2*	<.1

TOTALS: SIC 4493 Marinas
Companies: 4 — 37 — .9

4499 Water Transportation Services Nec

Rank	Company Name—*Executive Officer*	Address, City, State, Zip	Phone	Type	Fin	Empls
1	Tidewater Inc—*Dean E Taylor*	601 Poydras St Ste 190, New Orleans LA 70130	504-568-1010	P	1,051	7.5
2	Edison Chouest Offshore Inc—*Laney Chouest*	16201 E Main St, Cut Off LA 70345	985-601-4444	R	392*	2.0
3	Abdon Callais Offshore LLC—*Mike Callais*	PO Box 727, Golden Meadow LA 70357		R	367*	.3
4	Sonsub Inc—*Brian Fine*	15950 Park Row, Houston TX 77084	281-552-5600	R	239*	.2
5	Biehl International Corp—*Steen Pedersen*	5200 Hollister St Ste, Houston TX 77040	713-690-7200	R	29*	.2
6	Bisso Marine Company Inc—*William Bisso*	PO Box 4113, New Orleans LA 70178	281-897-1500	R	23*	.4
7	Main Industries Inc—*Raymond Challoner*	107 E St, Hampton VA 23661	757-380-0180	R	19*	.2
8	Zidell Marine Corp—*Jay Zidell*	3121 Sw Moody Ave, Portland OR 97239	503-228-8691	R	11*	.1
9	Gulf Fleet Holdings Inc—*Michael Hillman*	2623 Se Evangeline Trw, Lafayette LA 70508	337-210-2600	R	4*	.1

TOTALS: SIC 4499 Water Transportation Services Nec
Companies: 9 — 2,134 — 10.9

4512 Air Transportation—Scheduled

Rank	Company Name—*Executive Officer*	Address, City, State, Zip	Phone	Type	Fin	Empls
1	United Air Lines Inc—*Jeffrey A Smisek*	77 W Wacker Dr, Chicago IL 60601	312-997-8000	B	37,110	87.0
2	Continental Airlines Inc—*Robert Edwards*	PO Box 4607, Houston TX 77210	713-324-2950	S	37,110	40.0

Rank	Company Name—*Executive Officer*	Address, City, State, Zip	Phone	Type	Fin	Empls
3	Delta Air Lines Inc—*Richard H Anderson*	PO Box 20706, Atlanta GA 30320	404-715-2600	P	31,755	80.0
4	AMR Corp—*Thomas W Horton*	PO Box 619616 DFW Airp, Dallas TX 75261	817-963-1234	P	22,170	78.3
5	American Airlines Inc—*Gerard J Arpey* AMR Corp	PO Box 619616 MD 2400, Dallas TX 75261	817-963-1234	S	22,100	65.5
6	US Airways Group Inc—*W Douglas Parker*	111 W Rio Salado Pkwy, Tempe AZ 85281	408-693-0800	P	11,908	30.9
7	US Airways Inc—*Doug Parker* US Airways Group Inc	111 W Rio Salado Pkwy, Tempe AZ 85281	480-693-0800	S	6,328*	34.0
8	Astral Airlines Inc—*Timothy E Hoeksema*	6744 S Howell Ave, Oak Creek WI 53154	414-570-4000	S	5,935*	.7
9	Horizon Air Industries Inc—*Jeffrey D Pinneo* Alaska Air Group Inc	19521 International Bl, Seatac WA 98188	206-241-6757	S	4,565*	3.8
10	JetBlue Airways Corp—*David Barger*	118-29 Queens Blvd, Forest Hills NY 11375	718-286-7900	P	4,504	14.0
11	Alaska Air Group Inc—*William S Ayer*	PO Box 68900, Seattle WA 98168	206-433-3200	P	4,318	12.8
12	Evergreen International Aviation Inc—*Delford M Smith*	3850 Three Mile Ln, McMinnville OR 97128	503-472-9361	R	3,883*	2.5
13	Alaska Airlines Inc—*William S Ayer* Alaska Air Group Inc	PO Box 68900, Seattle WA 98168		S	3,819*	9.6
14	Skywest Inc—*Jerry C Atkin*	444 S River Rd, Saint George UT 84790	435-634-3000	P	3,655	18.4
15	Republic Airways Holdings Inc—*Bryan K Bedford*	8909 Purdue Rd Ste 300, Indianapolis IN 46268	317-484-6000	P	2,654	9.9
16	AirTran Holdings Inc—*Robert L Fornaro*	9955 AirTran Blvd, Orlando FL 32827		P	2,619	8.3
17	Capital Cargo International Airlines Inc—*Chris Chorley*	7100 TPC Dr Ste 200, Orlando FL 32822	407-855-2004	R	2,235*	.3
18	Nippon Express USA Inc—*Kenryo Senda*	590 Madison Ave Ste 24, New York NY 10022	212-758-6100	S	2,035*	2.0
19	Atlas Air Inc—*William J Flynn*	2000 Westchester Ave, Purchase NY 10577	914-701-8000	S	1,867*	1.2
20	Hawaiian Holdings Inc—*Mark B Dunkerley*	PO Box 30008, Honolulu HI 96820	808-835-3700	P	1,651	4.3
21	Skywest Airlines Inc—*Jerry Atkin* Skywest Inc	444 S River Rd, Saint George UT 84790	435-634-3000	S	1,332*	10.0
22	Mesa Air Group Inc—*Jonathan Ornstein*	Appling410 N 44th St S, Phoenix AZ 85008	602-685-4000	R	1,326	4.1
23	Frontier Airlines Holdings Inc—*David Siegel* Republic Airways Holdings Inc	7001 Tower Rd, Denver CO 80249	720-374-4200	S	1,171	4.3
24	ExpressJet Airlines Inc—*Patrick Kelly* ExpressJet Holdings Inc	700 N Sam Houston Pkwy, Houston TX 77067	832-353-1000	S	1,086*	7.0
25	Spirit Airlines Inc—*B Ben Baldanza*	2800 Executive Way, Miramar FL 33025	954-447-7965	P	1,071*	2.5
26	Pinnacle Airlines Corp—*Sean E Menke*	1689 Nonconnah Blvd St, Memphis TN 38132	901-348-4100	P	1,021	7.6
27	Air Transport International LLC—*James Hobson*	2800 Cantrell Rd, Little Rock AR 72202	501-615-3500	S	809*	.1
28	ExpressJet Holdings Inc—*Thomas M Hanley* Skywest Inc	700 N Sam Houston Pky, Houston TX 77067	823-353-1000	S	688	5.6
29	Midwest Air Group Inc—*Bryan Bedford* Republic Airways Holdings Inc	6744 S Howell Ave, Oak Creek WI 53154	414-570-4000	S	665	3.4
30	Allegiant Travel Co—*Maurice J Gallagher Jr*	8360 S Durango Dr, Las Vegas NV 89113	702-851-7300	P	664	1.6
31	Atlantic Southeast Airlines Inc—*Brad Holt* Skywest Inc	990 Toffie Ter, Atlanta GA 30354	404-856-1000	S	615*	4.0
32	Comair Holdings Inc—*John Bendoraitis* Delta Air Lines Inc	PO Box 75021, Cincinnati OH 45275	859-767-2550	S	470*	2.7
33	Polar Air Cargo Inc—*William J Flynn*	2000 Westchester Ave, Purchase NY 10577	914-701-8000	S	443*	.4
34	Commutair Inc—*John Sullivan*	240 Valley Rd, South Burlington VT 05403	802-951-2500	R	413*	.3
35	Mesaba Aviation Inc—*John Spanjers* Delta Air Lines Inc	1000 Blue Gentian Rd S, Eagan MN 55121	651-367-5000	S	391*	3.6
36	Blue Star Jets Inc—*Richard Sitomer*	885 Second Avenue 16th, New York NY 10017	212-446-9037	R	330*	.2
37	PSA Airlines Inc—*Keith D Houk* US Airways Group Inc	3400 Terminal Dr, Vandalia OH 45377	937-454-1116	S	310*	2.0
38	Trans States Airlines Inc—*Richard Leach*	11495 Navaid Rd Ste 34, Bridgeton MO 63044	314-222-4300	R	263*	2.0
39	Air Wisconsin Airline Corp—*James P Rankin*	W6390 Challenger Dr St, Appleton WI 54914	920-739-5123	S	249*	2.3
40	Clay Lacy Aviation—*Clay Lacy*	7435 Valjean Ave, Van Nuys CA 91406	818-989-2900	S	242*	.1
41	Comair Inc—*John Selvaggio* Comair Holdings Inc	PO Box 75021, Cincinnati OH 45275	859-767-2550	S	231*	2.2
42	American Eagle Airlines Inc—*Peter Bowler* AMR Corp	PO Box 619616, Dallas TX 75261	817-963-1234	S	175	1.4
43	Express One International Inc—*Lawrence Brinker*	1682 Hangar Rd, Sanford FL 32773	407-599-2040	R	143*	.6
44	CSA Air Inc—*Walter Clark*	260 Riverhills Rd, Kingsford MI 49802	906-774-3101	S	129*	.2
45	Great Lakes Aviation Ltd—*Charles R Howell IV*	1022 Airport Pkwy, Cheyenne WY 82001	307-432-7000	P	125	1.1
46	Arrow Air Inc—*Luis J Soto*	PO Box 523726, Miami FL 33152	305-871-3116	R	86*	.5
47	Ameriflight LLC—*Gary Richards*	4700 W Empire Ave, Burbank CA 91505	818-980-5005	R	83*	.7
48	Gulfstream International Airlines Inc—*David F Hackett*	1100 Lee Wagener Blvd, Ft Lauderdale FL 33315		R	78*	.6
49	AirTran Airways Inc—*Bob Fornaro* AirTran Holdings Inc	9955 AirTran Blvd, Orlando FL 32827	407-318-5600	S	68	.4
50	Alpine Aviation Inc	13310 Nevada City Ave, Grass Valley CA 95945	530-477-7701	S	63*	.1
51	Era Aviation Inc	6160 Carl Brady Dr, Anchorage AK 99502	907-248-4422	S	58*	.4
52	Peninsula Airways Inc—*Scott Bloomquist*	6100 Boeing Ave, Anchorage AK 99502	907-771-2500	R	56*	.4
53	USA Jet Airlines Inc	2068 E St Willow Run A, Belleville MI 48111		R	46*	.3
54	XOJET Inc—*Blair LaCorte*	2000 Sierra Point Pkwy, Brisbane CA 94005	650-676-4700	R	36*	.1
55	Island Air—*Robert Mauracher* Aloha Airgroup Inc	99 Kapalulu Pl, Honolulu HI 96819	808-840-2444	R	33*	.3
56	Scott Richard Aviation Services Inc—*Scott Inhoffer*	600 Hayden Cir, Allentown PA 18109	570-386-1265	R	25*	<.1
57	Wells Aircraft Inc—*Don Rogers*	800 Airport Rd, Hutchinson KS 67501	620-663-1546	R	22*	<.1
58	Priester Aviation Inc—*Andrew Priester*	1061 S Wolf Rd, Wheeling IL 60090	847-537-1133	R	15*	<.1
59	Ross Aviation Inc—*Douglas Hawley*	11705 Airport Way, Broomfield CO 80021	303-830-7780	R	10*	.1
60	Venture Travel LLC—*Brien Salazar*	PO Box 8495, Ketchikan AK 99901	907-225-8800	R	7*	<.1
61	Aloha Airgroup Inc—*David A Banmiller*	PO Box 30028, Honolulu HI 96820	808-836-4210	R	3*	3.0
62	Air Vegas Airlines—*James Petty*	1400 Executive Airport, Henderson NV 89012	702-501-8470	R	1*	<.1

TOTALS: SIC 4512 Air Transportation—Scheduled
Companies: 62   227,272   579.5

4513 Air Courier Services

Rank	Company Name—*Executive Officer*	Address, City, State, Zip	Phone	Type	Fin	Empls
1	United States Postal Service—*Patrick R Donahoe*	475 W L'enfant Plz SW, Washington DC 20260	202-268-2500	R	65,711	557.3
2	FedEx Corp—*Frederick W Smith*	942 S Shady Grove Rd, Memphis TN 38120	901-818-7500	P	39,304	143.0
3	Air Transport Services Group Inc—*Joseph Hete*	145 Hunter Dr, Wilmington OH 45177	937-382-5591	P	667	2.1
4	Xpress Air Inc—*Max Fuller*	4080 Jenkins Rd, Chattanooga TN 37421	423-510-3000	S	607	N/A
5	Amerijet International Inc—*David G Bassett*	2800 S Andrews Ave, Fort Lauderdale FL 33316	954-320-5300	R	385*	.6
6	Velocity Express Corp—*Mike Heiberger*	11104 W Airport Blvd S, Stafford TX 77477		S	341	1.8
7	Astar Air Cargo Inc—*John H Dasburg*	1200 Brickell Ave 16th, Miami FL 33131	305-982-0500	R	323*	1.0
8	AirNet Systems Inc—*George Gonzalez*	7250 Star Check Dr, Columbus OH 43217	614-409-4900	S	156*	.6

Note: An asterisk (*) indicates an estimated financial figure. The company type code used is as follows: R = Private, P = Public, S = Private Subsidiary, B = Public Subsidiary, D = Division, J = Joint Venture, I = Investment Fund.

COMPANY RANKINGS BY SALES WITHIN 4-DIGIT SIC

Rank	Company Name—*Executive Officer*	Address, City, State, Zip	Phone	Type	Fin	Empls
9	Flight Express Inc—*John Kirschoefer*	3614 E Amelia StSte C, Orlando FL 32803	407-895-0453	S	94*	.1
10	Air T Inc—*Walter Clark*	PO Box 488, Denver NC 28037	828-464-8741	P	83	.4
11	Bellair Expediting Service Inc—*Ed Becht*	3745 25th Ave, Schiller Park IL 60176	847-928-1500	R	22*	<.1
12	Midnite Express—*Scott Cannon*	300 N Oak St, Inglewood CA 90302	310-330-2328	R	20*	.1
13	Adcom Express Inc—*Robert F Friedman*	PO Box 3627, Bellevue WA 98009	425-462-1094	S	18*	<.1
14	Empire Airlines Inc—*Tim Komberec*	11559 N Atlas Rd, Hayden ID 83835	208-292-3850	R	10*	.1

TOTALS: SIC 4513 Air Courier Services
Companies: 14   107,742   707.1

4522 Air Transportation—Nonscheduled

Rank	Company Name—*Executive Officer*	Address, City, State, Zip	Phone	Type	Fin	Empls
1	Lynden Air Freight Inc—*Dennis Patrick*	18000 International Bl, Seattle WA 98188	206-241-8778	S	2,603*	.3
2	Jet Aviation Holdings Inc—*Peter G Edwards*	112 Charles A Lindberg, Teterboro NJ 07608	201-288-8400	R	1,730*	5.6
3	ATA Holdings Corp—*Doug Yokola*	7337 W Washington St, Indianapolis IN 46231	317-247-4000	R	1,533	6.9
4	Bristow Group Inc—*William E Chiles*	2000 W Sam Houston Pky, Houston TX 77042	713-267-7600	P	1,233	3.3
5	Gama Aviation Inc—*Greg Thomas*	480 Lordship Blvd, Stratford CT 06615	203-337-4600	R	894*	.5
6	World Airways Holding Inc—*Rob Binns*	101 World Dr HLH Bldg, Peachtree City GA 30269	770-632-8000	S	864*	2.2
7	Grasso Production Management	9821 Katy Frwy Ste 400, Houston TX 77024	713-984-1000	S	839*	.5
8	Air Methods Corp—*Aaron D Todd*	7211 S Peoria St, Englewood CO 80112	303-792-7400	P	562	3.0
9	Petroleum Helicopters Inc—*Al A Gonsoulin*	PO Box 90808, Lafayette LA 70509	337-235-2452	P	517	2.2
10	JetCorp—*John Gillespie*	657 N Bell Ave, Chesterfield MO 63005	636-530-7000	R	411*	.4
11	Pilot Freight Services—*Lou Cortese*	314 N Middletown Rd, Lima PA 19037	610-891-8100	R	373	N/A
12	Evergreen International Airlines Inc—*Delford Smith*	3850 Three Mile Ln, McMinnville OR 97128	503-472-9361	S	260*	.5
13	Active Aero Charter LLC—*Rumben Rienstra*	2068 E St, Belleville MI 48111	734-547-7200	R	140*	.1
14	Phoenix Air Group Inc—*Mark Thompson*	100 Phoenix Air Dr SW, Cartersville GA 30120	770-387-2000	R	88*	.2
15	Air Evac Services Inc—*Al A Gonsoulin* Petroleum Helicopters Inc	2800 N 44th St Ste 800, Phoenix AZ 85008	602-244-9327	S	88*	<.1
16	Arctic Slope World Services Inc—*William Sample*	6303 Ivy Ln, Greenbelt MD 20770	301-837-5500	S	80*	.8
17	ARCH Air Medical Service Inc—*Robert Stupf* Mercy Air Service Inc	2207 Scott Ave, Saint Louis MO 63103	314-655-4050	S	79*	.1
18	Mercy Air Service Inc—*David Dolstein* Air Methods Corp	PO Box 2532, Fontana CA 92334	909-357-9006	S	66*	.3
19	Aviation Capital Group Corp—*R Stephen Hannahs*	610 Newport Ctr Dr 14t, Newport Beach CA 92660	949-219-4600	S	63*	.1
20	Petroleum Helicopters International Inc—*Dale Johnson* Petroleum Helicopters Inc	PO Box 90808, Lafayette LA 70509	337-235-2452	S	54*	<.1
21	Emery Air Inc—*Steve Thomas*	PO Box 6067, Rockford IL 61125	815-968-8287	R	52*	.2
22	Grand Aire Inc—*Katrina Cheema*	11777 W Airport Servic, Swanton OH 43558	419-861-6700	R	50*	.1
23	Aviation Leasing Group	8080 Ward Pkwy Ste 407, Kansas City MO 64114	816-931-7300	R	46*	.2
24	Linear Air—*William Herp*	1724 Robins St Hangar, Hanscom AFB MA 01731	781-860-9696	R	43*	<.1
25	Richmor Aviation Inc—*Mahlon W Richards*	PO Box 423, Hudson NY 12534	518-828-9461	R	33*	.2
26	Epps Aviation Inc—*E Patrick Epps*	1 Aviation Way DeKalb, Atlanta GA 30341	770-458-9851	R	32*	.2
27	Atlantic Aero Inc—*Jim Spinder*	PO Box 35408, Greensboro NC 27425	336-668-0411	R	25*	.2
28	Flight International Inc—*George Mayer*	1 Lear Dr, Newport News VA 23602		S	22*	.2
29	Executive Jet Management—*Robert S Garrymore*	4556 Airport Rd, Cincinnati OH 45226		S	21*	.1
30	Alpine Air Express Inc—*Eugene Mallette*	1177 Alpine Air Way, Provo UT 84601	801-373-1508	P	20	.1
31	Scenic Airlines Inc—*Chad Dixon*	3900 Paradise Rd Ste 1, Las Vegas NV 89169	702-638-3300	R	15*	.3
32	Air Orlando Aviation Inc—*John Painter*	319 Crystal Lake Dr, Orlando FL 32803	407-896-0721	R	7*	<.1
33	Balloon Aviation—*Nielsen Rogers*	PO Box 2290, Yountville CA 94599	707-944-4400	R	7*	<.1
34	Coastal Helicopters Inc—*Jim Wilson*	8995 Yandukin Dr, Juneau AK 99801	907-789-5600	R	6*	<.1
35	Tavaero Jet Charter—*Renato Venturini*	PO Box 750069, Houston TX 77275	713-643-5387	R	4*	<.1
36	Jet Resource Inc—*Sandra E Laney*	455 Wilmer Ave, Cincinnati OH 45226	513-762-6909	S	3*	<.1
37	Adventures Aloft—*Nielsen Rogers*	6525 Washington St, Yountville CA 94599	707-944-4408	R	3*	<.1
38	Napa Valley Aloft Inc—*Nielsen Rogers*	PO Box 2290, Yountville CA 94599	707-944-8638	R	2*	<.1
39	Air America Jet Charter—*William B McCarter*	2323 S Voss Rd Ste 525, Houston TX 77057	713-640-2900	R	2*	<.1
40	St Louis Helicopter LLC—*Jim Robinson*	18004 Edison Ave, Chesterfield MO 63005	636-532-1177	R	1*	<.1
41	Helicopter Services Inc—*Robin Simpson*	19931 Stuebner Airline, Spring TX 77379	281-370-4354	R	1*	<.1

TOTALS: SIC 4522 Air Transportation—Nonscheduled
Companies: 41   12,871   28.5

4581 Airports, Flying Fields & Services

Rank	Company Name—*Executive Officer*	Address, City, State, Zip	Phone	Type	Fin	Empls
1	Piedmont Airlines Inc—*Stephen R Farrow*	5443 Airport Terminal, Salisbury MD 21804	410-742-2996	S	952*	4.0
2	AOG Inc—*James T Pradetto*	2742 Burbank St, Dallas TX 75235	214-350-5334	R	896*	1.2
3	Lear Siegler Services Inc—*Martin M Koffel*	20501 Seneca Meadows P, Germantown MD 20876	301-944-3100	D	873*	10.0
4	Kay and Associates Inc—*Greg Kay*	165 N Arlington Height, Buffalo Grove IL 60089	847-255-8444	R	592*	.9
5	Lockheed Martin Space Operations—*Joanne M Maguire*	6801 Rockledge Dr, Bethesda MD 20817	301-897-6000	S	500*	5.3
6	Aircraft Service International Group—*Keith Ryan*	201 S Orange Ave Ste 1, Orlando FL 32801	407-648-7373	S	330*	7.5
7	Signature Flight Support Corp—*Michael Scheeringa*	201 S Orange Ave Ste 1, Orlando FL 32801	407-648-7200	S	325*	5.2
8	TIMCO Aviation Services Inc—*Kevin Carter*	623 Radar Rd, Greensboro NC 27410	336-668-4410	R	316	3.4
9	Aviall Product Repair Services Inc—*Paul Fulchino*	PO Box 619048, Dallas TX 75261	972-586-1000	S	313*	.6
10	Duncan Aviation Inc—*Aaron Hilkemann*	3410 W Mathis St, Lincoln NE 68524	402-475-2611	R	217*	1.9
11	St Mobile Aerospace Engineering Inc—*Joseph Ng*	2100 9th St, Mobile AL 36615	251-438-8788	R	184*	1.0
12	Lockheed Martin Logistic Services Inc—*Edward Bergin*	244 Terminal Rd, Greenville SC 29605	864-236-3552	R	171*	3.0
13	Matlinpatterson Ata Holdings LLC	520 Madison Ave Fl 35, New York NY 10022	212-651-9500	R	163*	3.0
14	Tas Holding Inc—*John Cawthron*	623 Radar Rd, Greensboro NC 27410	336-668-4410	R	152*	3.4
15	AAR Airframe and Accessories Group Inc—*David Storch*	6611 S Meridian Ave, Oklahoma City OK 73159	405-681-3000	D	77*	3.0
16	Hawthorne Corp—*Steven P Levesque*	3955 Faber Place Dr St, North,Charleston SC 29405	843-553-2203	R	76*	.5
17	Limco-Piedmont Inc—*Robert Koch*	5304 S Lawton Ave, Tulsa OK 74107	918-445-4300	S	72	.3
18	Wisconsin Aviation Inc—*Jeff Baum*	1741 River Dr, Watertown WI 53094	920-261-4567	R	62*	.1
19	Northern Air Inc—*Charles R Cox*	PO Box 888380, Grand Rapids MI 49588	616-336-4711	R	58*	.1
20	EADS Barfield Inc—*Christophe Bernadini*	PO Box 25367, Miami FL 33102	305-894-5300	R	52*	.3
21	Stevens Aviation Inc—*Robert Stevens*	600 Delaware St, Greenville SC 29605	864-678-6000	R	49*	.3
22	Multi Corp—*Philip Maffei*	PO Box 361, Westminster MD 21158	410-876-5000	R	33*	.5
23	Galvin Flying Service Inc—*Peter G Anderson*	7149 Perimeter Rd, Seattle WA 98108	206-763-0350	R	30*	.2
24	Professional Aircraft Accessories Inc—*Robert Bial*	7035 Center Ln, Titusville FL 32780	321-267-1040	S	27*	<.1
25	Curtiss-Wright Accessory Services	10 Waterview Blvd Fl 2, Parsippany NJ 07054	973-541-3700	D	25*	.2
26	Global Aircraft Solutions Inc—*David T Querio*	PO Box 23009, Tucson AZ 85734	520-294-3481	P	25	.1
27	Banyan Air Service Inc—*Donald Campion*	5360 NW 20th Ter, Fort Lauderdale FL 33309	954-491-3170	R	24*	.2
28	Western Aircraft Inc—*Allen Hoyt*	4300 S Kennedy St, Boise ID 83704	208-338-1800	S	24*	.1
29	M7 Aerospace LLC—*Kevin Brown*	10823 Ne Entrance Rd, San Antonio TX 78216	210-824-9421	R	24*	.4
30	Aero Precision Repair and Overhaul Company Inc—*Alex Tearle*	580 S Military Trail, Deerfield Beach FL 33442	954-428-9500	R	19*	.1

Rank	Company Name—*Executive Officer*	Address, City, State, Zip	Phone	Type	Fin	Empls
31	Concert Group Logistics LLC—*Gerry Post*	1430 Branding Ave Ste, Downers Grove IL 60515	630-795-1300	S	18*	<.1
32	DAC International Inc (Austin Texas)—*Michael Crouch*	6702 McNeil Dr, Austin TX 78729	512-331-5323	S	16*	<.1
33	Muncie Aviation Co—*Martin Ingram*	PO Box 1169, Muncie IN 47308	765-289-7141	R	15*	.1
34	Lektro Inc—*Eric Paulson*	1190 Se Flightline Dr, Warrenton OR 97146	503-861-2288	R	14*	.1
35	Saker Aviation Services Inc—*Ronald J Ricciardi*	101 Hangar Rd, Avoca PA 18641	570-457-3400	P	12	.1
36	Denver jetCenter Inc—*Charles Haas* Jet Centers Inc	7625 S Peoria St, Englewood CO 80112	303-790-4321	S	12*	.1
37	Wood Group Turbopower LLC—*Allan Barthalomew*	14820 Nw 60th Ave, Hialeah FL 33014	305-820-3225	R	11*	.1
38	Turbine Controls Inc—*Glen Greenberg*	5 Old Windsor Rd, Bloomfield CT 06002	860-242-0448	R	11*	.1
39	Aeroparts Manufacturing and Repair Inc—*Dean Leavengood*	431 Rio Rancho Dr Ne, Rio Rancho NM 87124	505-891-6600	R	10*	.1
40	Volant Aerospace LLC—*Carlos Herrera*	11817 Westar Ln, Burlington WA 98233	360-757-2376	R	10*	.1
41	Winner Aviation Corp—*Charles Hale*	1453 Youngstwn Kingsvl, Vienna OH 44473	330-882-6852	R	8*	.1
42	Jet Centers Inc—*Randy Duncan*	7800 E Orchard, Englewood CO 80110	720-346-1123	R	8*	.1
43	JMA Solutions LLC—*Jan Adams*	Capital Gallery West 6, Washington DC 20024	202-863-2680	R	7	<.1
44	Texas Aerospace Services Limited LLP—*Cavin Hill*	3550 Maple St, Abilene TX 79602	325-695-2406	R	5*	<.1
45	AirFlite Inc—*Joe Williamson*	3250 Airflite Way, Long Beach CA 90807	562-490-6200	S	4*	.1
46	Stc Aviation Inc—*William Mavencamp*	PO Box 1599, Saint Cloud MN 56302	320-253-1500	R	4*	<.1
47	Burlington Aviation—*Allan Ostroff*	3510 Alamance Rd, Burlington NC 27215	336-227-1278	R	3*	<.1
48	Sky Helicopters Inc—*Ken Pyatt*	Garland / DFW Heliport, Garland TX 75041	214-349-7000	R	1*	<.1
49	B-Fast Corp—*Bob Atkins*	660 Newtown-Yardley Rd, Newtown PA 18940	215-860-5600	S	1*	<.1
50	Texas Skyways Inc—*Jack Johnson*	308 Boerne Stage Airfi, Boerne TX 78006	830-755-8989	R	N/A	<.1

TOTALS: SIC 4581 Airports, Flying Fields & Services
Companies: 50 — 6,829 — 57.6

4612 Crude Petroleum Pipelines

Rank	Company Name—*Executive Officer*	Address, City, State, Zip	Phone	Type	Fin	Empls
1	Koch Industries Inc—*Charles G Koch*	PO Box 2256, Wichita KS 67201	316-828-5500	R	100,000	67.0
2	Plains All American Pipeline LP—*Greg L Armstrong*	PO Box 4648, Houston TX 77210	713-646-4100	P	34,275	3.8
3	TransMontaigne Inc—*Chalres Dunlap*	PO Box 5660, Denver CO 80217	303-626-8200	S	8,584	.7
4	Enbridge Energy Management LLC—*Stephen JJ Letwin*	1100 Louisiana Ste 330, Houston TX 77002	713-821-2000	P	7,736	N/A
5	NuStar Energy LP—*Curt Anastasio*	PO Box 781609, San Antonio TX 78278	210-918-2000	P	6,575	1.5
6	CITGO Pipeline Co—*Oswaldo Contreras*	6100 S Yale Ave, Tulsa OK 74136	918-495-4000	S	1,996*	1.3
7	Williams Pipe Line Co—*Steven J Malcolm*	1 Williams Ctr, Tulsa OK 74172	918-573-2000	S	210	.7
8	Marathon Pipe Line LLC—*Don Bozell*	539 S Main St, Findlay OH 45840	419-422-2121	S	157	.5
9	BP Oil Pipeline Co—*Ross Pilladi*	28301 Ferry Rd, Warrenville IL 60555	630-420-5111	R	154*	3.0
10	Blueknight Energy Partners LP—*James C Dyer IV*	6120 S Yale Ave Ste 50, Tulsa OK 74136	918-237-4000	P	153	.5
11	TransMontaigne Partners LP—*Charles Dunlap* TransMontaigne Inc	PO Box 5660, Denver CO 80217	303-626-8200	B	151	.6
12	Unocal Pipeline Co—*David O'Reilly*	6001 Bollinger Canyon, San Ramon CA 94583	925-845-1000	S	150	.2
13	Minnesota Pipeline Co—*Katie Stavinoha* Koch Industries Inc	46729 179th Ave, Clearbrook MN 56634	218-776-3313	S	77*	<.1
14	Jayhawk Pipeline Corp—*Rick Peterson*	PO Box 1404, McPherson KS 67460	620-241-9270	J	70	.1
15	ConocoPhillips Pipeline Co—*Greg Garland*	PO Box 2197, Houston TX 77252		S	44	.6
16	KLT Gas Inc	PO Box 418679, Kansas City MO 64141	816-556-2200	S	8*	<.1

TOTALS: SIC 4612 Crude Petroleum Pipelines
Companies: 16 — 160,339 — 80.4

4613 Refined Petroleum Pipelines

Rank	Company Name—*Executive Officer*	Address, City, State, Zip	Phone	Type	Fin	Empls
1	Kinder Morgan Energy Partners LP—*Richard D Kinder*	500 Dallas St Ste 1000, Houston TX 77002	713-369-9000	P	21,861	8.1
2	Buckeye Partners LP—*Forrest E Wylie*	9999 Hamilton Blvd, Breinigsville PA 18031	610-904-4000	P	4,760	1.0
3	Atlas Pipeline Partners LP—*Eugene Dubay*	1550 Coraopolis Height, Moon Township PA 15108	412-262-2830	B	1,931	N/A
4	Magellan Midstream Partners LP—*Michael N Mears*	PO Box 22186, Tulsa OK 74121	918-574-7000	P	1,749	1.3
5	Magellan NGL LLC—*Michael N Mears* Magellan Midstream Partners LP	PO Box 22186, Tulsa OK 74121	918-574-7000	S	695*	1.0
6	WEG GP LLC—*Michael N Mears* Magellan Midstream Partners LP	PO Box 22186, Tulsa OK 74121	918-574-7000	S	695*	1.0
7	Kaneb Pipe Line Company LLC	2330 N Loop 1604 W, San Antonio TX 78248	210-918-2000	S	640*	1.1
8	Colonial Pipeline Co—*Tim Felt*	PO Box 1624, Alpharetta GA 30009	678-762-2200	R	544*	.7
9	Holly Energy Partners LP—*Matthew P Clifton*	2828 N Harwood Ste 130, Dallas TX 75201	214-871-3555	B	214	N/A
10	Buckeye Pipe Line Co—*Forrest E Wylie* Buckeye Partners LP	4741 Wilder Rd, Bay City MI 48706	989-684-5820	S	161*	.5
11	Plantation Pipe Line Co—*Thomas A Bannigan*	1435 Windward Concours, Alpharetta GA 30005	770-751-4000	R	130*	.3
12	Olympic Pipe Line Co—*Chris Maudin*	2201 Lind Ave SW, Renton WA 98057	425-235-7736	J	122*	.1
13	Black Marlin Pipeline Co—*Steven Malcolm*	PO Box 1396, Houston TX 77251	713-215-3029	S	30*	<.1
14	Pii North America Inc—*Robert Vilyus*	7105 Business Park Dr, Houston TX 77041	713-849-6300	R	4*	<.1

TOTALS: SIC 4613 Refined Petroleum Pipelines
Companies: 14 — 33,535 — 15.1

4619 Pipelines Nec

Rank	Company Name—*Executive Officer*	Address, City, State, Zip	Phone	Type	Fin	Empls
1	Sunoco Logistics Partners LP—*Lynn L Elsenhans*	525 Fritztown Rd, Sinking Spring PA 19608	610-670-3860	B	10,918	1.5
2	Texas Brine Company LLC—*Theodore Grabowski*	4800 San Felipe St, Houston TX 77056	713-877-2700	R	397*	.3
3	Cazayoux Commercial Investments LLC—*H Ansley*	26618 Prairie St, Spring TX 77373	281-350-2100	R	3*	<.1

TOTALS: SIC 4619 Pipelines Nec
Companies: 3 — 11,318 — 1.8

4724 Travel Agencies

Rank	Company Name—*Executive Officer*	Address, City, State, Zip	Phone	Type	Fin	Empls
1	Carlson Wagonlit Travel Inc—*Douglas Anderson*	701 Carlson Pky, Minneapolis MN 55459	713-212-2197	J	20,000	N/A
2	Atlantic Express Coachways	7 North St, Staten Island NY 10302	718-442-7000	S	14,478*	8.2
3	Maritz Travel Co	1375 N Hwy Dr, Fenton MO 63099	636-827-4000	D	4,830*	1.9
4	Liberty Travel Inc—*Billy McDonald*	69 Spring St, Ramsey NJ 07446	201-934-3500	R	3,583*	2.5
5	Expedia Inc—*Dara Khosrowshahi*	333 108th Ave NE, Bellevue WA 98004	425-679-7200	P	3,348	8.9
6	Travelport—*Gordon Wilson*	400 Interpace Pkwy Bld, Parsippany NJ 07054	973-939-1610	S	1,591*	3.5
7	Abacus Travel Inc—*Marla Huntley*	10 Centenial Dr, Peabody MA 01960	978-326-3100	R	1,188*	.8
8	Travel and Transport Inc—*William Tech*	2120 S 72nd St, Omaha NE 68124	402-399-4500	R	1,015*	.8
9	Frontier Enterprises Inc—*David Lippincott*	58 Hobart St, Hackensack NJ 07601	201-488-4224	R	763*	.3
10	TripAdvisor Inc—*Stephen Kaufer*	141 Needham St, Newton MA 02464	617-670-6300	S	736*	.5
11	Travizon Inc—*Joel Smith*	275 Mishawum Rd 3rd Fl, Woburn MA 01801	781-994-1200	R	588*	.4
12	San Diego Travel Group—*Tim Smith*	9710 Scranton Rd Ste 3, San Diego CA 92121	858-450-4060	R	535*	.1
13	Click Trips Inc—*David Liu*	462 Broadway 6th Fl, New York NY 10013	212-219-8555	S	477*	.4

Note: An asterisk (*) indicates an estimated financial figure. The company type code used is as follows: R = Private, P = Public, S = Private Subsidiary, B = Public Subsidiary, D = Division, J = Joint Venture, I = Investment Fund.

COMPANY RANKINGS BY SALES WITHIN 4-DIGIT SIC

Rank	Company Name—*Executive Officer*	Address, City, State, Zip	Phone	Type	Fin	Empls
14	Travel Authority—*Tom Lumluy*	702 N Shore Dr Ste 300, Jeffersonville IN 47130	812-206-5100	R	435*	.3
15	Bon Voyage Travel	1640 E River Rd Ste 11, Tucson AZ 85718	520-797-1110	R	382*	.2
16	AAA Travel (Cincinnati Ohio)—*Chip Pease*	15 W Central Pky, Cincinnati OH 45202	513-762-3100	D	378*	.5
17	Japan Travel Bureau USA Inc—*Tsuneo Irita*	156 W 56th St, New York NY 10019	212-698-4900	S	366*	.1
18	CI Travel—*Reed Atkins*	870 N Military Hwy Ste, Norfolk VA 23502	757-461-0022	R	360*	.3
19	TravelStore (Sacramento California)—*Wido Schaefer*	855 Howe Ave Ste 5, Sacramento CA 95825	916-929-5555	R	355*	.3
20	Morris Murdock Travel—*Brian Hollien*	515 S 700 E Ste 1B, Salt Lake City UT 84102	801-483-6441	R	324*	.2
21	Rail Europe Holding—*Fabrice Morel*	44 S Broadway Fl 11, White Plains NY 10601	914-682-2999	S	310*	.3
22	Garber Travel Service Inc—*Rosyln Garber*	27 Boylston St, Chestnut Hill MA 02467	617-965-2100	R	200*	.4
23	Boeing Travel Management Co—*Curt Nohavec*	325 McDonnell Blvd Mai, Hazelwood MO 63042		S	194*	.2
24	MTS Travel Inc—*James Buffendorf*	124 E Main St 4th Fl, Ephrata PA 17522	717-733-4131	R	189*	.1
25	Travel Destinations Management Group Inc—*Ira Weiner*	110 Painters Mill Rd S, Owings Mills MD 21117	410-363-3111	R	178*	.1
26	Adelman Travel Group—*Craig Adelman*	6980 N Port Washington, Milwaukee WI 53217	414-352-7600	R	175*	.3
27	Mann Travel and Cruises—*Gary Silverstein*	4400 Park Rd, Charlotte NC 28209	704-556-8311	R	169*	.2
28	Burkhalter Travel Agency Inc—*Ed Mani*	6501 Mineral Point Rd, Madison WI 53705	608-833-5200	R	154*	.1
29	Rail Europe Group Ltd—*Bernard Frelat* Rail Europe Holding	44 S Broadway 11 Fl, White Plains NY 10601	914-682-2999	S	150*	.2
30	Avantair Inc—*Steven F Santo*	4311 General Howard Dr, Clearwater FL 33762	727-538-7900	P	149	.5
31	Casto Travel Inc—*Maryles Casto*	2560 N 1st St Ste 150, San Jose CA 95131	408-984-7000	R	144*	.1
32	Cruises Only LLC	1011 E Colonial Dr, Orlando FL 32803	407-898-5353	R	143*	.4
33	Montrose Travel—*Joe McClure*	2349 Honolulu Ave, Montrose CA 91020	818-553-3200	R	142*	.2
34	Group Voyagers Inc—*Sergio Mantegazza*	5301 S Federal Cir, Littleton CO 80123		R	132*	.3
35	Europ Assistance USA—*Thierry Depois*	4330 East-West Hwy Ste, Bethesda MD 20814	240-330-1000	S	128*	.1
36	Ovation Travel Group (Harrison New York) Ovation Travel	71 5th Ave, New York NY 10003	914-698-8282	S	125*	.1
37	Balboa Travel Inc—*Jose G da Rosa*	5414 Oberlin Dr Ste 30, San Diego CA 92121	858-678-3300	R	121*	.1
38	Wright Travel Inc—*Pamela J Wright*	2505 21st Ave S, Nashville TN 37212	615-783-1111	R	117	.2
39	Alamo Travel Group Inc—*Patricia Pliego Stout*	8930 Wurzbach Rd, San Antonio TX 78240	210-593-0084	R	111*	.1
40	Stevens Travel Management Inc—*Harold Stevens*	119 W 40th St 14th Fl, New York NY 10018	212-696-4300	R	108*	.1
41	Ambassadair Travel Club Inc—*Michael E Gruninger*	PO Box 51609, Indianapolis IN 46251	317-465-1122	R	107*	.1
42	Brownell Travel Inc—*Troy Haas*	813 Shades Creek Pkwy, Birmingham AL 35209	205-802-6222	R	101*	.1
43	Nippon Express Travel USA Inc—*Shimizu Michiya*	8 California St 8th Fl, San Francisco CA 94111	415-421-1822	S	98*	.1
44	The Travel Team Inc—*Jean Covelli*	2495 Main St Ste 340, Buffalo NY 14214	716-862-7600	R	92*	.1
45	Century Travel Inc—*Gene Lashley*	5565 Glenridge Connect, Atlanta GA 30342	404-478-8888	R	89*	<.1
46	Omega World Travel Inc—*Gloria Bohan*	3102 Omega Office Park, Fairfax VA 22031	703-359-0200	R	88*	1.1
47	Frosch International Travel Inc—*Bryan Leibman*	1 Greenway Plaza Ste 8, Houston TX 77046	713-850-1566	R	88*	.1
48	Travelmore/Carlson Wagonlit Travel—*Robert Hamilton*	212 W Colfax Ave, South Bend IN 46601	574-232-3061	R	79*	.1
49	Central Holidays—*Fred Berardo*	250 Moonachie Rd, Moonachie NJ 07074	201-228-5200	R	73*	.1
50	InteleTravel 2000	PO Box 6310, Delray Beach FL 33482	561-272-7476	R	72*	.1
51	Kintetsu International Express—*Frank Lee*	1290 Ave of the Americ, New York NY 10104	212-259-9600	R	71*	.1
52	Carlson Wagonlit Travel (Tacoma Washington)—*Alex Trettin*	1142 Broadway Plz Ste, Tacoma WA 98402	253-383-8000	R	69*	<.1
53	Ovation Travel—*Paul Metselaar*	71 5th Ave 10th Fl, New York NY 10003	212-679-1600	R	67*	.1
54	Travel Holdings Inc—*Uri Argov*	220 E Central Pkwy Ste, Altamonte Springs FL 32701	407-667-8700	R	62*	.1
55	Boehm Travel Cos—*Dan Boehm*	1400 Indian Trail Lilb, Norcross GA 30093	770-931-5500	R	62*	<.1
56	Williamsburg Travel Management Cos—*Roland Williamson*	1830 Water Place Ste10, Atlanta GA 30339	770-933-2000	R	60*	.1
57	Gwin's Travel Planners—*Graydon Owen*	212 N Kirkwood Rd, Kirkwood MO 63122	314-822-1958	R	57*	.1
58	REI Adventures—*Sally Jewell*	PO Box 1938, Sumner WA 98390	253-437-1100	S	52*	<.1
59	International Travel Specialists Inc (Irvine California)—*Linda McIntosh*	2151 Michelson Dr Ste, Irvine CA 92612	949-450-8550	R	51*	.1
60	Breton Village Travel Services Inc—*John Lovell*	1910 Breton Rd SE, Grand Rapids MI 49506	616-942-0300	R	51*	<.1
61	Kayakcom—*Steve Hafner*	55 N Water St Ste 1, Norwalk CT 06854	203-899-3100	R	50*	.1
62	Travel Duet Inc Frosch International Travel Inc	520 Lake Cook Rd Ste 6, Deerfield IL 60015	847-948-5300	S	49*	.1
63	Trivision Executive Travel Inc—*Joel Smith*	10 State St, Woburn MA 01801	781-994-1300	R	48*	.2
64	Hewins/Carlson Wagonlit Travel—*Steve Hewins*	PO Box 7140, Portland ME 04112	207-772-7257	R	48*	.1
65	Miller Travel Services Inc—*Homer Miller*	4380 W 12th St, Erie PA 16505	814-833-8888	R	48*	.1
66	Apollo Travel Agency—*Azzam Hajyousis*	307 N Michigan Ave Ste, Chicago IL 60601	312-236-3939	R	46*	<.1
67	Diamond Resorts LLC	3745 Las Vegas Blvd S, Las Vegas NV 89109	702-261-1010	R	46*	.7
68	Griffin America—*Robert Westendarp*	3646 Greenbriar Dr, Houston TX 77098		S	44*	.1
69	Image Travel and Tours Inc—*Monique Kasmauskis*	2828 Kraft Ave SE, Grand Rapids MI 49512	616-957-1000	R	43*	<.1
70	Metro Travel and Tours Inc—*Bennet E Cyrus*	9298 Central Ave NE St, Minneapolis MN 55434	763-784-0560	R	43*	<.1
71	Euro Lloyd Travel Inc—*Franz J Herzig*	1640 Hempstead Turnpik, East Meadow NY 11554		R	42*	.1
72	Giselle's Travel—*Cynthia Michalski*	1300 E Ethan Way Ste 1, Sacramento CA 95825	916-922-5500	S	41*	.2
73	Azumano Travel Service Inc—*Sho G Dozono*	320 SW Stark St Ste 60, Portland OR 97204	503-223-6245	R	40*	.2
74	Teplis Travel Service—*Monica Teplis*	244 Perimeter Center P, Atlanta GA 30346	404-843-7460	R	40*	<.1
75	Andavo Travel	5680 Greenwood Plz Blv, Greenwood Village CO 80111	303-694-3322	S	39*	<.1
76	YTB International Inc—*Robert M Van Patten*	1901 E Edwardsville Rd, Wood River IL 62095	618-655-9477	P	36	.1
77	Tzell Travel Group of PA	520 E Main St, Carnegie PA 15106	412-278-2300	R	36*	<.1
78	USA Hosts—*Jennifer Patino*	3068 E Sunset Rd Ste 9, Las Vegas NV 89120	702-798-0000	R	36*	<.1
79	Cruises Inc	1415 NW 62nd St Ste 20, Fort Lauderdale FL 33309	954-958-3700	R	35*	<.1
80	Meridian World Travel—*Dan Freeman*	830 Menlo Ave Ste 110, Menlo Park CA 94025	650-328-2030	R	35*	<.1
81	World of Travel—*Ron Hersh*	5001 Horizons Dr, Columbus OH 43220	614-451-4882	R	34*	<.1
82	Agencias Condado Travel Inc—*Jose D Targa*	255 Ponce de Leon Ave, Hato Rey PR 00919	787-754-7000	R	30	.1
83	Action Travel and Tours—*Marian Hankins*	1600 Airport Dr, Jackson MS 39209	601-948-2096	R	29*	<.1
84	George Kun Travel Cruise Quarters—*George Kun*	6000 Venture Dr, Dublin OH 43017	614-459-1303	R	28*	<.1
85	Travel Beyond—*Jim Bendt*	214 S Minnetonka Ave, Wayzata MN 55391	952-475-2565	R	28*	<.1
86	Paragon Travel Agency Inc	21 Father DeValles Blv, Fall River MA 02723		R	27*	<.1
87	Meetings and Incentives in Latin America	100 S Greenleaf Ave, Gurnee IL 60031	847-249-2111	D	26*	<.1
88	Travel-On Ltd—*Karen Dunlap*	9000 Virginia Manor Rd, Beltsville MD 20705	240-387-4000	R	25*	<.1
89	Business Travel Consultants—*Mark Squillante*	2440 Sandy Plaines, Marietta GA 30066	770-952-8181	R	25*	<.1
90	Passageways Travelcom—*Tom McIntyre*	3032 Lake Lansing Rd, East Lansing MI 48823	517-351-1080	R	24*	.1
91	Smarter Travel Media LLC—*Daniel Saul*	500 Rutherford Ave 2nd, Boston MA 02129	617-886-5555	R	23*	<.1
92	Tramex Travel Inc—*Juan Portillo*	4505 Spicewood Springs, Austin TX 78759	512-343-2201	R	22*	<.1
93	Around The World Travel Inc—*Keith St Clair*	2151 LeJeune Rd Ste 30, Miami FL 33134	305-445-2999	R	22*	<.1
94	Travel Leaders/Bentley Hedges Travel Inc—*Angela Hendricks*	10011 S Pennsylvania, Oklahoma City OK 73159	405-237-3333	R	22*	<.1
95	Vacation Outlet	100 Sylvan Rd Ste 600, Woburn MA 01801		R	20	<.1
96	Rainbow Holding Company Inc—*Jay Musgrove*	PO Box 60128, Oklahoma City OK 73146	405-528-5741	R	19*	<.1
97	Aer Travel—*Gil Saidy*	5465 Morehouse Dr Ste, San Diego CA 92121	858-455-5773	R	18*	<.1
98	Tenenbaum's Vacation Stores Inc—*Barry Tenenbaum*	300 Market St, Kingston PA 18704	570-288-8747	R	18*	<.1
99	Rodgers Travel Inc—*Norma Pratt*	512 W Lancaster Ave, Wayne PA 19087	610-964-1775	R	17*	<.1

Rank	Company Name—*Executive Officer*	Address, City, State, Zip	Phone	Type	Fin	Empls
100	Regency Travel and International Market—*Terry Beaty*	416 Perkins Extended, Memphis TN 38117	901-682-9065	R	17*	<.1
101	TheTravel Society Inc—*Andrea Nicholson*	600 S Cherry St Ste 10, Denver CO 80246	303-321-0900	R	17*	<.1
102	Aladdin Travel and Meeting Planners—*Richard E ShoreJr*	485 Sheppard St, Winston Salem NC 27103	336-768-1680	R	16*	.1
103	International Travel and Resorts Inc—*Steve Hicks*	1875 Palmer Ave, Larchmont NY 10538	212-476-9450	R	15*	.1
104	All Travel Inc Wright Travel Inc	5180 Park Ave Ste 125, Memphis TN 38119	901-767-2080	S	15*	<.1
105	All World Travel Inc—*Charles Moore*	314 Gilmer St, Sulphur Springs TX 75482	903-885-0896	R	15*	<.1
106	Everest Travel Inc—*Ashish Dharamrup*	3300 Buckeye Rd Ste 33, Atlanta GA 30341	770-220-1866	R	14*	<.1
107	Flannery Enterprise Inc—*Tammy McSwain*	5700 W Plano Pky Ste 1, Plano TX 75093	972-422-4000	R	13*	<.1
108	Folsom Travel—*Kate Kurz*	620 E Bidwell St, Folsom CA 95630	916-983-7900	R	13*	<.1
109	Charlie Brown's Goodtime Travel—*Charlie Brown*	1465 N Union Blvd, Colorado Springs CO 80909	719-635-8992	R	12*	<.1
110	ATC Travel Inc—*Caroline Amenta*	239 N Broadway, Sleepy Hollow NY 10591	914-631-8301	R	12*	<.1
111	Jim's Travel Link Inc—*Jim Gray*	1250 W Mockingbird Ln, Dallas TX 75247	214-720-1000	R	12*	<.1
112	St Tours—*Rick Hysell*	8466 Lockwood Ridge Rd, Sarasota FL 34243	941-360-9851	R	12*	<.1
113	Pronto Travel Service	PO Box 862, Soledad CA 93960	831-678-0192	R	11*	<.1
114	Malmberg Travel Cos—*Robert Malmberg*	359 Boylston St 3rd Fl, Boston MA 02116	617-267-4200	R	11*	<.1
115	Tower Travel Management Corp—*John LS Smith*	53 Ogden Ave, Clarendon Hills IL 60514	630-928-7000	R	10*	<.1
116	Alvarez and Bremer Travel—*Jose Alvarez*	9336 Transit Rd, East Amherst NY 14051	716-688-4567	R	10*	<.1
117	AMTA—*Zbigniew Wegiel*	505 8th Ave Ste 801, New York NY 10018	212-586-5230	R	10*	<.1
118	Superior Travel—*Ingrid Schmitt Ream*	2467 E Hill Rd, Grand Blanc MI 48439	810-695-6170	R	10*	<.1
119	Traveltime Services Inc—*Debbie Corbett*	2838 Old 280 Ct, Birmingham AL 35243	205-969-4900	R	10*	<.1
120	Travelong Inc—*Linda Walczyk*	213 W 35th St Ste 1302, New York NY 10001	212-736-2166	R	10*	<.1
121	Menno Travel Service—*Geof Landis*	210 S Main St, Goshen IN 46526	574-534-1521	R	9*	<.1
122	Davisville Travel—*Jack Saxe*	420 2nd St, Davis CA 95616	530-758-4510	R	8*	<.1
123	Go The Travel Co—*Robert Hazucha*	330 Castro St, San Francisco CA 94114	415-255-2800	R	8*	<.1
124	Hadar Travel and Tours—*Udi Gordon*	20380 Town Center Ln R, Cupertino CA 95014	408-517-9906	R	8	<.1
125	Big Sky Travel Source Inc—*Judy Renauer*	2601 NW Expressway Ste, Oklahoma City OK 73112	405-840-8220	R	8*	<.1
126	Dillard Travel Inc—*Bill Dillard*	1600 Cantrell Rd, Little Rock AR 72201		S	7*	<.1
127	Enterprise Travel Inc—*Terry Johnson*	3508 W Galbraith Rd, Cincinnati OH 45239	513-741-9898	R	7*	<.1
128	Virginia Escape Ltd—*Jacqueline Chutter*	215 McLaws Cir Ste 1, Williamsburg VA 23185	757-229-1161	R	7*	<.1
129	Pier 'n Port Travel Inc	15 W Central Pkwy, Cincinnati OH 45202	513-763-3080	R	6*	<.1
130	Bler Travel Inc—*Sam Erenfeld*	419 Harvard St, Brookline MA 02446	617-738-0500	R	6*	<.1
131	Ray Sorrell Travel Co—*Ray Sorrell*	948 Canton St, Roswell GA 30075	770-587-0010	R	6*	<.1
132	Travelore Travel Service—*David Hawes*	204 E Main St, Batavia NY 14020	585-343-9380	R	6*	<.1
133	Travel Company Inc—*Sheila Batty*	1303 Delaware Ave Ste, Wilmington DE 19806	302-652-6263	R	6*	<.1
134	Midwest Auto Clubs LLC—*Kevin Paulasec*	5050 S 13th St Ste B, Milwaukee WI 53221	414-325-1643	R	6*	<.1
135	Rainbow Travel Service Inc—*Jay Musgrove* Rainbow Holding Company Inc	5831 NE 1st Ave, Fort Lauderdale FL 33334	954-491-9747	S	5*	<.1
136	Two Brothers Travel Inc—*Rob Schlesinger*	2750 Bellflower Blvd S, Long Beach CA 90815	562-938-7502	R	5*	<.1
137	Strong Travel Services—*Nancy Strong*	8214 Westchester Dr St, Dallas TX 75225	214-361-0027	R	4*	<.1
138	Sundance Travel Service—*Nancy Wolfe*	215 N 40th St, Phoenix AZ 85034	602-275-2400	R	4*	<.1
139	Club Europa—*Andy Benz*	802 W Oregon St, Urbana IL 61801	217-344-5863	R	4*	<.1
140	Berkshire Travel Agency Inc—*John Stevenson*	2 Woodland Rd, Wyomissing PA 19610		R	4*	<.1
141	Rainbow Travel Corp—*John Lovell*	2777 E Paris Ave, Grand Rapids MI 49546	616-957-5055	R	4*	<.1
142	Travel House Corp (Mobile Alabama)—*Josiane Landman*	1301 Azalea Rd, Mobile AL 36693	251-344-6336	R	4*	<.1
143	University Travel Service Inc—*John Bohna*	1421 Washington Ave S, Minneapolis MN 55454	612-339-9278	R	4*	<.1
144	Millbrook Travel Consultants Inc—*Susan Fay*	1508 Treemont St, Duxbury MA 02332	781-934-0906	R	4*	<.1
145	Reve Medical Tourism LLC	5715 Will Clayton Pkwy, Humble TX 77338	281-857-6112	R	4*	<.1
146	Cataract Travel Planners Inc—*Donald Masocco*	1727 Military Rd, Niagara Falls NY 14304	716-298-5490	R	4*	<.1
147	SaveOnResortscom LLC—*Kevin Schneider*	6727 Flanders Dr Ste 2, San Diego CA 92121	858-625-0630	R	4	<.1
148	Geneva Travel Inc—*Lucille Richmond Stein*	171 N Eagle St, Geneva OH 44041	440-466-5900	R	3*	<.1
149	Orient Travel Inc—*Jim McCrimmon*	1521 Azalea Garden Rd, Norfolk VA 23502	757-857-7777	R	3*	<.1
150	Ijet International Inc—*Stephen Hoffman*	910 Bestgate Rd Ste F, Annapolis MD 21401	410-573-3860	S	3*	.1
151	Just Cruisin Plus—*Sherrie S Funk*	750 Old Hickory Blvd S, Brentwood TN 37027	615-833-0922	R	2*	<.1
152	Craig Corey Travel Service—*Craig Corey*	1271 Mulberry Ln, East Lansing MI 48823	517-336-8829	R	2*	<.1
153	World Links Development Inc—*Will Knox*	8665 Wilshire Blvd Ste, Beverly Hills CA 90211	310-652-7786	R	1*	<.1
154	Kutrubes Travel Inc—*Mary Kutrubes*	328 Tremont St, Boston MA 02116	617-426-5668	R	1*	<.1

TOTALS: SIC 4724 Travel Agencies
Companies: 154   **62,093**   **39.1**

4725 Tour Operators

Rank	Company Name—*Executive Officer*	Address, City, State, Zip	Phone	Type	Fin	Empls
1	Mark Travel Corp—*William E La Macchia*	8907 N Port Washington, Milwaukee WI 53217	414-228-7472	R	2,602*	1.4
2	Certified Vacations Group Inc—*Nicholas Davison*	PO Box 1525, Fort Lauderdale FL 33301	954-522-1440	R	1,280*	.8
3	E Noa Tours—*Maki Kuroda*	3015 Koapaka St Ste G, Honolulu HI 96819	808-591-2561	R	968*	.2
4	Pleasant Holidays LLC—*Tim Irwin*	2404 Townsgate Rd, Westlake Village CA 91361	818-991-3390	R	710*	.7
5	Worldstrides—*James Hall*	218 West Water St 400, Charlottesville VA 22902	434-982-8600	S	665*	.4
6	Tourmobile Sightseeing Inc—*Tom Mack*	1000 Ohio Dr SW, Washington DC 20024	202-554-5100	R	504*	.3
7	Atlantis Adventures LLC—*Ronald Williams*	1600 Kapiolani Blvd St, Honolulu HI 96814	808-973-9800	R	367*	.2
8	Brendan Vacations—*Nico Zenner*	21625 Prairie St, Chatsworth CA 91311	818-428-6000	R	293*	.2
9	Travel Impressions Ltd—*Steven J Gorga*	465 Smith St, Farmingdale NY 11735	631-845-8000	S	225	.5
10	Argosy Cruises—*Kevin Clark*	1101 Alaskan Way Pier, Seattle WA 98101	206-623-1445	R	216*	.1
11	Mayflower Tours Inc—*John Stachnik*	PO Box 490, Downers Grove IL 60515		R	172*	.1
12	Isram World of Travel—*Ady Gelber*	233 Park Ave S, New York NY 10003		R	158*	.1
13	Atkinson Mullen and Rosso—*John J Mullen*	7 Campus Blvd, Newtown Square PA 19073	610-359-5980	R	144*	.4
14	Outdoor Adventure River Specialists Inc—*George Wendt*	PO Box 67, Angels Camp CA 95222	209-736-4677	R	140*	.1
15	Polynesian Adventure Tours Inc—*Bob George*	1049 Kikowaena Pl, Honolulu HI 96819	808-833-3000	R	117*	.3
16	Europe Through the Back Door Inc—*Rick Steves*	PO Box 2009, Edmonds WA 98020	425-771-8303	R	112*	.1
17	TOURCO Inc—*Gerald DiPietro*	PO Box 167, Nobleboro ME 04555	207-563-2288	R	111*	.1
18	Frontier Travel and Tours Inc—*David Lippincott*	PO Box 22300, Carson City NV 89701	775-882-2100	S	87*	<.1
19	Trek America Tours—*Tony Church*	PO Box 189, Rockaway NJ 07866		R	86*	.2
20	Mountain Travel-Sobek	1266 66th St Ste 4, Emeryville CA 94608	510-594-6000	R	86*	.1
21	Hamilton Miller Hudson and Fayne—*Bruce Migdal*	29566 Northwestern Hwy, Southfield MI 48034	248-827-4065	R	83*	.1
22	Bergh International Holdings Inc—*Robert Stewart*	5428 Lyndale Ave S, Minneapolis MN 55419	612-827-3666	R	81*	<.1
23	Paragon Tours Inc—*Amy Gottesdiener*	21 Father DeValles Blv, Fall River MA 02723		R	79*	.1
24	Wildland Adventures Inc—*Kurt Kutay*	3516 NE 155th St, Seattle WA 98155	206-365-0686	R	60*	<.1
25	Hawaii Forest and Trail Ltd—*Rob Pacheco*	74-5035B Queen Kaahuma, Kailua Kona HI 96740	808-331-8505	R	56*	<.1
26	Americantours International LLC—*Noel Hentschel*	6053 W Century Blvd St, Los Angeles CA 90045	310-641-9953	R	54*	.1
27	Maupintour LLC—*Bill Kirby*	2690 Weston Rd Ste 200, Weston FL 33331	954-653-3820	R	51*	.1
28	Fair Wind Inc—*Tuhi Dahanc*	78-7130 Kaleiopapa St, Kailua Kona HI 96740	808-322-2644	R	42*	<.1

Note: An asterisk (*) indicates an estimated financial figure. The company type code used is as follows: R = Private, P = Public, S = Private Subsidiary, B = Public Subsidiary, D = Division, J = Joint Venture, I = Investment Fund.

COMPANY RANKINGS BY SALES WITHIN 4-DIGIT SIC

Rank	Company Name—*Executive Officer*	Address, City, State, Zip	Phone	Type	Fin	Empls
29	Natural Habitat Adventures—*Ben Bressler*	PO Box 3065, Boulder CO 80307	303-449-3711	R	40*	.1
30	Sky Trekking Alaska Fiskehauk—*Dan Michaels*	PO Box 871370, Wasilla AK 99687	907-373-4966	R	39*	<.1
31	AHI International—*Joseph W Small*	6400 Shafer Ct, Rosemont IL 60018		R	34*	.1
32	Geographic Expeditions—*James D Sano*	PO Box 29902, San Francisco CA 94129	415-922-0448	R	33*	<.1
33	Vacation Express Inc—*Renee Yongmans*	3495 Piedmont Rd NE Bl, Atlanta GA 30305	404-315-4848	R	32*	.1
34	AdventureLink Inc—*Jeff Dossett*	2400 N Lincoln Ave, Altadena CA 91001	310-658-5180	R	30*	<.1
35	World Outdoors—*Bill Marriner*	2840 Wilderness Place, Boulder CO 80301	303-413-0938	R	25*	<.1
36	iExplore Inc—*George Deeb*	93 N Park Place Blvd, Clearwater FL 33759	312-492-9443	R	24*	<.1
37	Lindblad Expeditions—*Sven-Olof Lindblad*	96 Morton St 9th Fl, New York NY 10014	212-765-7740	R	22*	.1
38	Gadabout Vacations	1801 E Tahquitz Canyon, Palm Springs CA 92262	760-325-5556	R	21*	.1
39	Avanti Destinations Inc—*Harry Dalgaard*	1629 SW Salmon St, Portland OR 97205	503-295-2723	R	21*	.1
40	Red Sail Sports Inc—*John Pritzker*	Pier 5 The Embarcadero, San Francisco CA 94111	305-454-2538	S	20*	.3
41	Insight Vacations Inc—*Marc Kazlauskas*	801 E Katella Ave, Anaheim CA 92805	714-935-0808	R	20*	<.1
42	Ya'lla Tours USA—*Ronen Paldi*	4711 SW Huber St Bldg, Portland OR 97219	503-977-3758	R	20*	<.1
43	Picasso Travel—*Rainer Klee*	999 N Sepulveda Blvd, El Segundo CA 90245	310-645-4400	R	15*	.1
44	Sun Islands Hawaii—*Gregory A Brossier*	2299 Kuhio Ave, Honolulu HI 96815	808-926-3888	R	15*	<.1
45	Foreign Independent Tours—*Jean Paul Belmondo*	2125 Center Ave Ste 20, Fort Lee NJ 07024	201-585-1549	R	15*	<.1
46	Burke International Tours Inc—*Udean Burke*	PO Box 890, Newton NC 28658	828-465-3900	R	14*	.1
47	Beamers Hells Canyon Tours and Excursions—*Jim Koch*	PO Box 1243, Lewiston ID 83501	509-758-4800	R	14*	<.1
48	Dan Dipert Tours Inc—*Dan Dipert*	PO Box 580, Arlington TX 76004	817-543-3700	R	13*	<.1
49	African Travel Inc—*Anne Bellamy*	1100 E Broadway, Glendale CA 91205	818-507-7893	R	13*	<.1
50	Nordique Tours—*Huseyin Ozyurtcu*	11099 S La Cienega Blv, Los Angeles CA 90045	310-645-7527	R	12*	<.1
51	Ker and Downey Inc—*Dave Marek*	6703 Hwy Blvd, Katy TX 77494	281-371-2500	R	11*	<.1
52	Intergolf Vacations—*Gordon Dalgleish*	PO Box 1273, Wrightsville Beach NC 28480		R	9*	<.1
53	Horse FarmTours Inc—*Margaret Woods*	PO Box 22593, Lexington KY 40522	859-268-2906	R	9*	<.1
54	Visits Plus Inc—*Donald Yu*	3 Landmark Sq Ste 110, Stamford CT 06901	203-358-9999	R	9*	<.1
55	Perillo Tours—*Lucio Massari*	577 Chestnut Ridge Rd, Woodcliff Lake NJ 07677	201-307-1234	R	8*	<.1
56	Destination Ireland and Great Britain Inc—*Declan O'Brien*	314 W 56th St Ste 2E, New York NY 10019	212-757-5797	R	7*	<.1
57	Lewis Brothers Stages—*Richard Bizzaro*	PO Box 510247, Salt Lake City UT 84151	801-359-8677	R	6*	.2
58	Anderson House Tours—*John Hall*	1127 N Lakeshore Dr, Lake City MN 55041	651-345-1212	R	6*	<.1
59	International Bicycle Tours Inc—*Frank Behrendt*	PO Box 754, Essex CT 06426	860-767-7005	R	6*	<.1
60	Cal Events	5050 Laguna BlvdPMB 62, Elk Grove CA 95758	916-924-8661	R	5*	<.1
61	Classic Custom Vacations Inc—*Greg Bernd*	5893 Rue Ferrari, San Jose CA 95138	408-287-4550	S	4*	<.1
62	Caribbean Concepts—*Molly Sumption*	PO Box 639, Ocean Shores WA 98569	206-575-0907	R	4*	<.1
63	Molokai Mule Ride Inc—*Bruddah Roy Horner*	PO Box 200, Kualapuu HI 96757	808-567-6088	R	3*	<.1
64	Far North Tours—*Robert Greaves*	PO Box 92758, Anchorage AK 99509	907-272-7480	R	3*	<.1
65	Cartan Tours Inc	3033 Ogden Ave Ste 303, Lisle IL 60532	630-778-0300	R	2*	<.1
66	Capricorn Leisure Corp—*Jeremy Pask*	2 Haven Ave Ste 210, Port Washington NY 11050	516-944-8383	R	2*	<.1
67	Talbot Tours Inc—*Serge Talbot*	1952 Camden Ave, San Jose CA 95124	408-879-0101	R	2*	<.1
68	Blackbeard's Charters Inc—*Bruce Purdy*	3700 Hacienda Blvd Ste, Davie FL 33314	954-734-7111	R	2*	<.1
69	Holiday Cruise Center—*Donna Esposito*	1032 Tralee Dr, Toms River NJ 08753	732-270-8826	R	2*	<.1
70	PlanItMichigan—*D Stafford Nelson*	PO Box 15009, Detroit MI 48215	313-399-6160	R	1*	<.1
71	Tumlare Travel Organization Inc—*Egil Fosse*	2128 Bellmore Ave, Bellmore NY 11710	516-781-0322	S	1*	<.1

TOTALS: SIC 4725 Tour Operators
Companies: 71   **10,143**   **8.3**

4729 Passenger Transportation Arrangement Nec

Rank	Company Name—*Executive Officer*	Address, City, State, Zip	Phone	Type	Fin	Empls
1	Cumulus Telecommunications Inc—*Lewis W Dickey Jr*	3280 Peachtree Road NW, Atlanta GA 30305	404-949-0700	S	2,710*	2.8
2	GATX Corp—*Brian A Kenney*	222 W Adams St, Chicago IL 60606	312-621-6200	P	1,309	2.0
3	Orbitz Worldwide Inc—*Barney Harford*	500 W Madison St Ste 1, Chicago IL 60661	312-894-5000	B	767	1.3
4	TransCor America Inc—*Steve Kennedy*	646 Melrose Ave, Nashville TN 37211	615-251-7008	S	233*	.2
5	Erickson Air-Crane Inc—*Udo Rieder*	5550 SW Macadam Ave St, Portland OR 97239	503-505-5800	R	150*	.7
6	Lowestfarecom	800 Connecticut Ave, Norwalk CT 06854	203-299-8000	S	112*	.2
7	BostonCoach Inc—*Larry Moulter*	69 Norman St, Everett MA 02149	617-563-8600	S	90*	1.2
8	Colorado Mountain Express Inc—*Robert Tsaupp*	PO Box 580, Vail CO 81658	970-926-9800	S	17*	.1
9	Alliance Creative Group Inc—*Paul Sorkin*	214 W Ohio St 3rd Fl, Chicago IL 60654	312-324-0433	P	11	N/A

TOTALS: SIC 4729 Passenger Transportation Arrangement Nec
Companies: 9   **5,399**   **8.5**

4731 Freight Transportation Arrangement

Rank	Company Name—*Executive Officer*	Address, City, State, Zip	Phone	Type	Fin	Empls
1	CSX Intermodal Inc—*Michael Ward*	500 Water St, Jacksonville FL 32202	904-359-3200	S	95,985*	34.0
2	Landstar Logistics Inc—*Henry H Gerkens*	13410 Sutton Park Dr S, Jacksonville FL 32224	904-398-9400	S	32,558*	1.0
3	CH Robinson Worldwide Inc—*John P Wiehoff*	14701 Charlson Rd, Eden Prairie MN 55347	952-937-8500	P	9,274	7.6
4	Expeditors International of Washington Inc—*Peter J Rose*	1015 3rd Ave 12th Fl, Seattle WA 98104	206-674-3400	P	5,968	12.9
5	YRC Worldwide Inc—*Tom Gerke*	10990 Roe Ave, Overland Park KS 66211	913-696-6100	P	4,869	32.0
6	UTi Worldwide Inc—*Eric W Kirchner*	100 Oceangate Ste 1500, Long Beach CA 90802	562-552-9400	P	4,550	20.6
7	NYK Logistics Inc—*Yasumi Kudo*	300 Lighting Way, Secaucus NJ 07094	310-518-0098	S	4,000	20.9
8	Brink's Co—*Thomas C Schievelbein*	PO Box 18100, Richmond VA 23226	804-289-9600	P	3,886	71.0
9	Total Quality Logistics Inc—*Kenneth Oaks*	PO Box 799, Cincinnati OH 45206	513-831-2600	R	3,220*	1.2
10	Hub Group Inc—*David P Yeager*	3050 Highland Pkwy Ste, Downers Grove IL 60515	630-271-3600	P	2,752	1.6
11	Transplace Texas LP—*Thomas Sanderson*	3010 Gaylord Pkwy Ste, Frisco TX 75034	972-731-4500	R	1,565*	.5
12	Pacer International Inc—*Daniel W Avramovich*	2300 Clayton Rd Ste 12, Concord CA 94520	887-917-2237	P	1,479	1.0
13	Nissin International Transport Inc—*Tadakuni Shiomoto*	1540 W 190th St, Torrance CA 90501	310-222-5810	S	1,462*	.6
14	Alexander International—*Neely Mallory Jr*	4294 Swinnea Rd, Memphis TN 38118	901-367-9400	R	1,239*	.5
15	Tricor America—*Chee Louie*	12441 Eucalyptus Ave, Hawthorne CA 90250	310-676-0800	S	1,209*	.5
16	Associated Global Systems—*Norman Freeman*	3333 New Hyde Park Rd, New Hyde Park NY 11042	516-627-8910	R	1,067*	.4
17	Pilot Air Freight Corp—*Richard G Phillips*	PO Box 97, Lima PA 19037	610-891-8100	R	947*	.4
18	Walker International Transportation LLC—*Emmett Walker*	70 E Sunrise Hwy Ste 6, Valley Stream NY 11581	516-568-2080	R	887*	.4
19	Odyssey Logistics and Technology Corp—*Douglas L Clark*	39 Old Ridgebury Rd St, Danbury CT 06810	203-448-3900	R	753*	.3
20	RailWorks Corp—*Jeffrey M Levy*	5 Penn Plz 17th Fl, New York NY 10001	212-502-7900	R	636*	4.0
21	Alliance Shippers Inc—*Ronald Lefcourt*	15515 S 70th Ct, Orland Park IL 60462	708-802-7000	R	562*	.6
22	Forward Air Corp—*Bruce A Campbell*	PO Box 1058, Greeneville TN 37744	423-636-3380	P	536	2.0
23	Tricor America—*Chee B Louie*	PO Box 8100, San Francisco CA 94128	650-877-3650	R	456*	.9
24	Roadrunner Transportation Services Holdings Inc—*Mark A Di-Blasi*	4900 S Pennsylvania Av, Cudahy WI 53110	414-615-1500	R	450*	.9
25	Seaboard Marine Ltd—*Edward Gonzalez*	8001 NW 79th Ave, Miami FL 33166	305-863-4444	S	444*	.2
26	AIT Worldwide Logistics—*Vaughn Moore*	PO Box 66730, Chicago IL 60666	630-766-8300	R	355*	.7
27	Norvanco International Inc—*Robert J Juranich*	3514 142nd Ave E Ste 4, Sumner WA 98390	253-987-4000	R	353*	.2
28	James J Flanagan Shipping Corp—*Thomas M Flanagan*	490 Park St, Beaumont TX 77701	409-833-5053	R	288*	.1

Rank	Company Name—*Executive Officer*	Address, City, State, Zip	Phone	Type	Fin	Empls
29	AmeriQuest Transportation and Logistics Resources—*Douglas Clark*	457 Haddonfield Rd Ste, Cherry Hill NJ 08002	856-773-0600	R	287*	.1
30	John S Connor Inc—*Lee Connor*	799 Cromwell Park Dr, Glen Burnie MD 21061	410-863-0211	R	254*	.1
31	Golden Gate Logistics LLC—*John H Willliford*	101 University Ave Ste, Palo Alto CA 94301	650-838-1111	R	240*	.1
32	Matson Integrated Logistics—*Ronald J Forest*	1855 Gateway Blvd Ste, Concord CA 94520	925-887-6200	S	211*	.1
33	Pittsburgh Logistics Systems Inc—*John Gallardo* Quadrivius Inc	294 Massachusetts Ave, Rochester PA 15074	724-709-9000	S	208*	.2
34	Daniel F Young Inc—*A Wesley Wyatt*	1235 Westlakes Dr, Berwyn PA 19312	610-725-4000	R	201*	.1
35	Quadrivius Inc—*Gregg A Troian*	1 Century Pl, Rochester PA 15074	724-709-9000	R	190*	.2
36	XPO Logistics Inc—*Michael L Welch*	PO Box 210, Buchanan MI 49107	269-695-2700	P	177	.1
37	SeaCube Container Leasing Ltd—*Joseph Kwok*	1 Maynard Dr, Park Ridge NJ 07656	201-391-0800	P	170	.1
38	AN Deringer Inc—*Jake Holzscheiter*	PO Box 1309, Saint Albans VT 05478	802-524-8110	R	150	.5
39	Protrans International Inc—*Craig Roeder*	PO Box 42069, Indianapolis IN 46242	317-240-4100	R	150*	.1
40	Allen Lund Company Inc—*Allen Lund*	4529 Angeles Crest Hwy, La Canada CA 91011		R	144*	.3
41	Nationwide Transport LLC	PO Box 42726, Blue Ash OH 45242	813-600-6963	R	142*	<.1
42	Custom Companies Inc—*Perry Mandera*	317 W Lake St, Northlake IL 60164	708-338-8888	R	141*	.4
43	Nations Express Inc—*Bill Frazier*	1300 Altura Rd Ste 230, Fort Mill SC 29708	704-423-9911	R	127*	.1
44	Clipper Exxpress Co—*Walt Whitt*	9014 Heritage Pkwy St, Woodridge IL 60517	630-739-0700	S	115*	.2
45	ABX Logistics (USA) Inc—*Laurent Levaux*	8010 Roswell Rd Ste 30, Atlanta GA 30350	770-353-4200	R	83*	.3
46	Service By Air Inc—*Joseph Poliseno*	222 Crossways Park Dr, Woodbury NY 11797	516-576-0500	R	75*	.2
47	Mike's Loading Service Inc—*Mike Castillo*	1802 S Expy 281, Edinburg TX 78542	956-292-2700	R	57*	.1
48	Network Shipping Ltd	PO Box 149222, Coral Gables FL 33114	305-520-8400	S	55*	<.1
49	Rock-it Cargo USA Inc—*David Bernstein*	5438 W 104th, Los Angeles CA 90045	310-410-0935	R	54*	.1
50	Air-Sea Forwarders Inc—*Todd Hinkley*	PO Box 90637, Los Angeles CA 90009	310-216-1616	R	49*	.2
51	James J Boyle and Co—*Edward Inouye*	1097 Sneath Lane, San Bruno CA 94066	650-871-6334	R	45*	.1
52	SDV Inc (Houston Texas)—*Philippe Naudin*	15490 Vickery Dr, Houston TX 77032	281-443-3318	R	43*	.2
53	GlobalTranz Inc—*Andrew Leto*	5415 E High St Ste 460, Phoenix AZ 85054		R	37*	.1
54	Langham—*Catherine A Langham*	5335 W 74th St, Indianapolis IN 46268	317-290-0227	R	35*	<.1
55	Sino Global Shipping America Ltd—*Lei Cao*	136-56 39th Ave Ste 30, Flushing NY 11354	718-888-1814	P	33	.1
56	BDP International Inc—*Richard J Bolte Jr*	510 Walnut St 14th Fl, Philadelphia PA 19106	215-629-8900	R	30*	.6
57	Industrial Transport Inc—*Brian E Hall*	2330 E 79th St, Cleveland OH 44104	216-881-5052	R	28*	.2
58	Global Transportation Services Inc—*Brian Lutt*	1930 6th Ave S, Seattle WA 98134	206-624-4354	R	25*	.1
59	Distribution Transportation Services Inc—*Tom Komadina*	PO Box 74, Wentzville MO 63385	636-639-1540	R	23*	.2
60	Global Supply Solutions LLC—*Emily Whittaker*	5348 Vegas Dr, Las Vegas NV 89108	757-227-6757	R	20*	<.1
61	Access Technology Solutions—*Chris Boyle*	5252 N Edgewood Dr Ste, Provo UT 84604		R	15*	<.1
62	American Business Services Corp—*Oscar Cedeno*	4444 NW 74 Ave, Miami FL 33166	305-592-7640	R	14*	<.1
63	Alba-Wheels Up International Inc—*Salvadore J Stile II*	150-30 132nd Ave, Jamaica NY 11434	718-276-3000	R	13*	.1
64	Minority Auto Handling Specialists Inc—*Theodore Vance*	22401 Sauk Pointe Dr, Chicago Heights IL 60411	708-757-8758	R	12*	.2
65	Corrigan Dispatch Co—*FC Averill Jr*	PO Box 1240, Laredo TX 78042	956-723-4343	R	12*	.1
66	OIA Global Logistics—*Charlie Hornecker*	17230 NE Sacramento St, Portland OR 97230	503-736-5900	R	12*	.1
67	Extra Mile Transportation LLC—*Anthony Baynes*	4295 Harris Hill Rd, Buffalo NY 14221	716-276-2045	R	12*	<.1
68	Three Dog Logistics—*John Kennedy*	3012 Dunglow Rd Ste 30, Baltimore MD 21222	410-284-5494	R	12	<.1
69	Hub Group Kansas City LLC—*David Yager* Hub Group Inc	9250 Glenwood St, Overland Park KS 66212	913-381-2070	S	10*	<.1
70	Pak Mail Crating and Freight Service Inc—*P Evan Lasky* Pak Mail Centers of America Inc	7173 S Havana St Ste 6, Centennial CO 80112	303-957-1000	S	8*	<.1
71	Concentrek Inc—*John R Patterson* UTi Worldwide Inc	PO Box 888500, Grand Rapids MI 49588	616-988-5900	S	6*	.1
72	Pak Mail Centers of America Inc—*P Evan Lasky*	7173 S Havana St Ste 6, Englewood CO 80112	303-957-1000	R	6*	<.1
73	National Shipping Company of Saudi Arabia (America) Inc—*Fahad Al-Meqren*	400 E Pratt St Ste 400, Baltimore MD 21202	410-625-7000	R	6*	<.1
74	uShip Inc—*Matt Chasen*	205 Brazos St, Austin TX 78701		R	5*	.1
75	Intelligent Logistics LLC—*Tim Miller*	598 Greenhill Dr Ste C, Round Rock TX 78665	512-238-6874	R	5*	<.1
76	CASAS International Brokerage Inc—*Sylvia Casas-Jolliffe*	9355 Airway Rd Ste 4, San Diego CA 92154	619-661-6162	R	5*	<.1
77	Radix Organizations—*Pierre Schoenheimer*	551 5th Ave Ste 2405, New York NY 10176	212-697-9141	R	5*	<.1
78	Trans Harbor Services LLC	222 E G St, Wilmington CA 90744	310-241-7990	R	5*	<.1
79	Dynalink Systems Inc—*Jack Chen*	11222 La Cienega Blvd, Inglewood CA 90304	310-216-6881	R	4*	<.1
80	LimitLess International Inc—*Cheryl Stockstad*	1075 Gills Dr Ste 310, Orlando FL 32824	407-852-9225	R	4	<.1
81	M E Dey and Company Inc—*Robert Gardenier*	700 W Virginia St Ste, Milwaukee WI 53204	414-747-7000	R	4*	<.1
82	Hm Product Solutions Ltd—*Heather Maynor*	581 S Industrial Dr, Hartland WI 53029	262-754-0424	R	3*	<.1
83	Payne Lynch and Associates Inc—*Pat Lynch*	205 14th Ave E, Sartell MN 56377	320-251-7030	R	3*	<.1
84	SNS Logistics Inc—*Cary Simon*	2586 N Lane Ave, Jacksonville FL 32254	904-378-2544	R	3*	<.1
85	Universal Cargo Management Inc—*Devin Burke*	10825 Washington Blvd, Culver City CA 90232	310-216-4024	R	3*	<.1
86	Traffic Management Inc—*Dawn Montez*	1710 Douglas Dr N Ste, Minneapolis MN 55422	763-544-3455	R	3*	<.1
87	Red Sea Shipping Co—*Mohamed Anwar*	22895 Savi Ranch Pkwy, Yorba Linda CA 92887	714-998-0150	R	3	<.1
88	Matrix Mailing LLC—*Ken White*	PO Box 6509, Bend OR 97708	541-749-9095	R	3*	<.1
89	Decisions and Advanced Technology Associates Inc—*Gary Gustafson*	555 Sparkman Dr NW, Huntsville AL 35816	256-726-0277	R	2*	<.1
90	Princeton Profit Associates Inc—*Charlene Tsu*	812 State Rd Ste 223, Princeton NJ 08540	602-677-7109	R	2*	<.1

TOTALS: SIC 4731 Freight Transportation Arrangement

Companies: 90					185,545	222.8

4741 Rental of Railroad Cars

Rank	Company Name—*Executive Officer*	Address, City, State, Zip	Phone	Type	Fin	Empls
1	General Electric Railcar Services Corp—*Joe Lattanzio*	161 N Clark Ste 700, Chicago IL 60601	312-853-5000	S	1,809*	1.0
2	GATX Financial Corp	222 W Adams St, Chicago IL 60606	312-621-6200	S	974*	1.7
3	TTX Co—*Thomas F Wells*	101 N Wacker Dr, Chicago IL 60606	312-853-3223	R	293*	.3
4	Pioneer Railroad Equipment Company Ltd—*Michael Carr*	1318 S Johanson Rd, Peoria IL 61607	309-697-1400	S	79*	.1
5	Chicago Freight Car Leasing Co—*Fred R Sasser*	6250 N River Rd Ste 70, Rosemont IL 60018	847-318-8000	R	14*	<.1

TOTALS: SIC 4741 Rental of Railroad Cars

Companies: 5					3,169	3.0

4783 Packing & Crating

Rank	Company Name—*Executive Officer*	Address, City, State, Zip	Phone	Type	Fin	Empls
1	Howard Ternes Packaging Co—*Charles Ross*	12285 Dixie, Redford MI 48239	313-531-5867	R	257*	.5
2	Peacock Engineering Co—*Michael A Bilder*	1800 Averill Rd, Geneva IL 60134	630-845-9400	S	160*	.8
3	Newstar Fresh Food LLC—*David Eldredge*	PO Box 5999, Salinas CA 93915	831-758-7800	R	63*	.2
4	Flint Packaging Inc—*Stephen Landaal*	PO Box 326, Flint MI 48501	810-742-2730	R	18*	.2
5	Pierce Packaging Co—*Kevin Hogan*	PO Box 15600, Loves Park IL 61132	815-636-5650	R	16*	.3
6	Bentley World-Packaging Ltd—*Thomas Bentley*	4080 N Port Washington, Milwaukee WI 53212	414-967-8000	R	15*	.3
7	Pak-Rite Industries Inc—*Charles Lefler*	4270 High St, Detroit MI 48229	313-388-6400	R	15*	.2

Note: An asterisk (*) indicates an estimated financial figure. The company type code used is as follows: R = Private, P = Public, S = Private Subsidiary, B = Public Subsidiary, D = Division, J = Joint Venture, I = Investment Fund.

COMPANY RANKINGS BY SALES WITHIN 4-DIGIT SIC

Rank	Company Name—*Executive Officer*	Address, City, State, Zip	Phone	Type	Fin	Empls
8	Fapco Inc—*Larry Gardiner*	216 Post Rd, Buchanan MI 49107	269-695-6889	R	14*	.2
9	Prescotech Industries Inc—*Matt Schoen*	1001 W Oak St, Louisville KY 40210	502-585-5866	R	11*	.1
10	Tech Packaging Inc—*Robert Janes*	13241 Bartram Park Blv, Jacksonville FL 32258	904-288-6403	R	10*	.1
11	Bps Inc—*Alan Bartlo*	28 Phillips Rd 324, Helena AR 72342	870-572-7771	R	9*	.1
12	Sunopta Aseptic Inc—*Mark Tagatz*	3915 Minnesota St, Alexandria MN 56308	320-763-9822	R	8*	.1
13	Sisk Fulfillment Service Inc—*Michael Phillips*	PO Box 463, Federalsburg MD 21632	410-754-8141	R	7*	.1
14	Orchard Village—*Joset Wright*	7670 Marmora Ave, Skokie IL 60077	847-967-1800	R	7*	.1
15	Pinnacle Stanrick Inc—*Stanley Miller*	PO Box 589, Milan IL 61264	309-787-4100	R	7*	.1
16	Packaging and Shipping Center Inc—*Phillip Wivietsky*	721 Broadway Ave Ste 2, Holbrook NY 11741	631-567-5330	R	7*	.1
17	Bates Metal Products Inc—*James Bates*	PO Box 68, Port Washington OH 43837	740-498-8371	R	6*	.1
18	Dixie Box and Crating Inc—*Don Perry*	9 S 12th St Ste 100, Richmond VA 23219	757-625-7520	R	6*	<.1
19	Triumph Packaging Georgia LLC—*Ronnie Rogers*	600 Poplar Dr, Thomaston GA 30286	706-647-6671	R	6*	.1
20	Product Packaging West Inc—*Joe Arceo*	11921 Vose St, North Hollywood CA 91605	818-765-8037	R	5*	<.1
21	Action-Pak Inc—*Ira Smith*	PO Box 557, Bristol PA 19007	215-785-4548	R	5*	.1
22	Bartlo Packaging Inc—*Allen Bartlo*	61 Willet St, Passaic NJ 07055	973-778-6900	R	5*	<.1
23	Landmark Industries Inc—*Howard Harrington*	1111 Elmwood Ave, Rochester NY 14620	585-241-1578	R	4*	.1
24	Case Mason Filling Inc—*Alfred Mason*	PO Box 230, Joppa MD 21085	410-687-0007	R	4*	<.1
25	Park City Packaging Inc—*Richard Polzello*	480 Sniffens Ln, Stratford CT 06615	203-378-7384	R	4*	<.1
26	Bison Laboratories Inc—*Robert Morber*	100 Leslie St, Buffalo NY 14211	716-895-2707	R	3*	<.1
27	Nor Pak Services Inc—*Wayne Norton*	347 Shellybrook Dr, Pilot Mountain NC 27041	336-368-3494	R	3*	<.1
28	Liquipak Corp—*Brian Rockafellow*	PO Box 484, Alma MI 48801	989-463-5510	R	2*	<.1
29	Pak-It Inc—*Rebekah Brown*	PO Box 303, Tipp City OH 45371	937-667-6099	R	2*	<.1
30	Adampac Inc—*Ann Bass*	PO Box 1971, Colleyville TX 76034	817-571-8813	R	1*	<.1

TOTALS: SIC 4783 Packing & Crating
Companies: 30 — 677 — 4.0

4785 Inspection & Fixed Facilities

Rank	Company Name—*Executive Officer*	Address, City, State, Zip	Phone	Type	Fin	Empls
1	Itr Concession Company Holdings LLC—*Segundo De-Los-Heros*	233 N Michigan Ave Ste, Chicago IL 60601	312-552-7100	R	153*	.5
2	Detroit and Windsor Tunnel LLC—*Neal Belitsky*	100 E Jefferson Ave, Detroit MI 48226	313-567-4422	R	34*	.1
3	H3 Freeway Tunnel Control—*Lester Lau*	727 Kakoi St, Honolulu HI 96819	808-485-6200	R	3*	<.1
4	Ashley W George—*Ashley George*	773 Mccarty St, Houston TX 77029	713-672-9491	R	1*	<.1

TOTALS: SIC 4785 Inspection & Fixed Facilities
Companies: 4 — 190 — .6

4789 Transportation Services Nec

Rank	Company Name—*Executive Officer*	Address, City, State, Zip	Phone	Type	Fin	Empls
1	Menlo Worldwide Logistics Inc—*Douglas W Stotlar*	2855 Campus Dr Ste 300, San Mateo CA 94403	650-378-5200	S	8,680*	4.8
2	Hertz Global Holdings Inc—*Mark P Frissora*	225 Brae Blvd, Park Ridge NJ 07656	201-307-2000	P	7,563	22.9
3	Patriot Rail Corp—*Gary O Marino*	2255 Glades Rd Ste 342, Boca Raton FL 33431	561-443-5300	R	2,300*	2.8
4	Aircastle Ltd—*Ron Wainshal*	300 First Stamford Pl, Stamford CT 06902	203-504-1020	P	605	.1
5	Schneider Logistics Inc	PO Box 2666, Green Bay WI 54306		S	481*	.7
6	Franklin Covey Travel Inc	2200 W Parkway Blvd, Salt Lake City UT 84119	801-817-1776	S	179*	.2
7	Panther Expedited Services Inc—*Andrew Clarke*	4940 Panther Pkwy, Seville OH 44273	330-769-5830	R	174*	.3
8	Rescar Inc—*Joseph F Schieszler*	1101 31st St Ste 250, Downers Grove IL 60515	630-963-1114	R	133*	.7
9	A/G Technologies Inc—*Rory V Sanchez*	1254 Okeechobee Rd, West Palm Beach FL 33401	561-835-8351	R	119*	<.1
10	FleetNet America LLC—*Oren Summer*	PO Box 970, Cherryville NC 28021	704-435-3897	S	70*	.2
11	Lasko Products Inc—*Oscar Lasko*	820 Lincoln Ave, West Chester PA 19380	610-692-7400	R	60*	1.0
12	Ambassadors International Inc—*Eugene I Davis*	2101 4th Ave Ste 210, Seattle WA 98121	206-292-9606	P	59	.1
13	Footprint Retail Services—*William J McKenna*	2200 Western Ct Ste 15, Lisle IL 60532	630-324-3400	S	46*	.1
14	Crusader Staffing Associates LLC—*David Bandy*	1815 Union Ave Ste 202, Chattanooga TN 37404	423-243-3060	R	38*	.3
15	Holland Transportation—*Jeff Harvey*	PO Box 529, Statesville NC 28687	704-872-4269	R	22*	<.1
16	Ronson Aviation Inc—*Louis Aronson*	152 Mercer County Ap S, Trenton NJ 08628	609-771-9500	S	19*	<.1
17	Kinder Morgan Bulk Terminals Inc—*Richard Kinder*	7116 Hwy 22, Sorrento LA 70778	225-675-5387	S	19*	<.1
18	A Arnold and Sons Transfer and Storage Company Inc—*Richard Russell*	5200 Interchange Way, Louisville KY 40229	502-426-7050	R	16*	.2
19	Albert W Sisk and Son Inc	PO Box 70, Preston MD 21655	410-673-7111	R	15*	<.1
20	Lydall Distribution Services Inc—*Dale Barhart*	1 Colonial Rd, Manchester CT 06042	860-646-1233	S	13*	<.1
21	SANYO Customs Brokerage Inc—*Takeshi Nushii*	9850 Siempre Viva Rd S, San Diego CA 92173	619-661-6995	S	12*	<.1
22	SANYO Logistics Corp—*Seiichiro Sano*	8400 Milliken Ave, Rancho Cucamonga CA 91730	909-987-7854	S	11*	<.1
23	Southern California Car Transfer Inc—*Mike Magnett*	11139 Roxboro Rd, San Diego CA 92131	858-586-0006	R	8*	.1
24	Eastbiz Corp—*John Vanhara*	2972 Columbia St, Torrance CA 90503	310-211-7143	R	8	.1
25	Frit Car Inc—*Larry Lanham*	PO Box 1340, Brewton AL 36427	251-867-7752	S	6*	.1
26	CMR Railroad Salvage Co—*Charley Richardson*	PO Box 117, Ranger TX 76470	254-647-5421	R	3*	.1
27	Spectrum Transportation—*Brian Sweeney*	200C Bucknell Ct Ste C, Atlanta GA 30336	678-904-5660	R	3*	<.1
28	Go Mini's—*Bill Norris*	6982 Highway Ave, Jacksonville FL 32254	904-693-6464	R	1*	<.1
29	Crystal Creek Logistics LLC—*Cathy Hayward*	1373 Admiral Pl Ste 10, Ferndale WA 98248	360-325-8123	R	1	<.1
30	Cargo Connection Logistics Holding Inc—*Scott Goodman*	600 Bayview Ave, Inwood NY 11096	516-239-7000	P	<1	N/A

TOTALS: SIC 4789 Transportation Services Nec
Companies: 30 — 20,664 — 34.9

4812 Radiotelephone Communications

Rank	Company Name—*Executive Officer*	Address, City, State, Zip	Phone	Type	Fin	Empls
1	Verizon Wireless—*Daniel S Mead*	1 Verizon Way, Basking Ridge NJ 07920	908-559-7000	J	63,400	83.0
2	Sprint Nextel Corp—*Dan Hesse*	6391 Sprint Pkwy, Overland Park KS 66251		P	32,563	40.0
3	T-Mobile USA Inc—*Philipp Humm*	PO Box 37380, Albuquerque NM 87176	425-378-4000	S	21,347	42.0
4	Asurion—*Bret Cornolli*	648 Grassmere Park, Nashville TN 37211	615-837-3000	R	6,278*	5.0
5	NII Holdings Inc—*Steven P Dussek*	1875 Explorer St Ste 1, Reston VA 20190	703-390-5100	P	5,601	13.5
6	United States Cellular Corp—*Mary N Dillon*	8410 W Bryn Mawr Ave S, Chicago IL 60631	773-399-8900	B	4,375	8.7
7	SkyTel Communications Inc—*James Myers*	PO Box 2469, Jackson MS 39225	601-944-1300	S	3,412*	3.6
8	Leap Wireless International Inc—*S Douglass (Doug) Hutcheson*	5887 Copley Dr, San Diego CA 92111	858-882-6000	P	3,071	3.9
9	Teligent Inc	210 Brookwood Rd, Atmore AL 36502	251-368-8600	R	2,778*	2.9
10	Virgin Mobile USA Inc	10 Independence Blvd, Warren NJ 07059	908-607-4000	S	1,324	.4
	Sprint Nextel Corp					
11	Loral Space and Communications Inc—*Michael B Targoff*	600 3rd Ave, New York NY 10016	212-697-1105	P	1,159	2.7
12	iPCS Inc (Schaumburg Illinois)—*Timothy Yager*	1901 N Roselle Rd Ste, Schaumburg IL 60195	847-885-2833	S	526*	.5
	Sprint Nextel Corp					
13	ABC Phones of North Carolina Inc—*Rich Balot*	3280 Charles Blvd, Greenville NC 27858	252-317-0388	R	497*	.6
14	Knology Inc—*Rodger L Johnson*	1241 OG Skinner Dr, West Point GA 31833	706-645-8553	P	460	1.8
15	USA Mobility Inc—*Vincent D Kelly*	6850 Versar Center Ste, Springfield VA 22151	703-269-6850	P	243	.7

Rank	Company Name—*Executive Officer*	Address, City, State, Zip	Phone	Type	Fin	Empls
16	Mobile 365—*Neville Street*	4511 Singer Ct, Chantilly VA 20152	703-961-8300	R	179*	.2
17	MAP Mobile Communications Inc—*Bronwyn Humphrey*	840 Greenbrier Cir Ste, Chesapeake VA 23320	757-424-1191	R	178*	.3
18	Satellink Communications Inc—*Dawn Anderson*	1100 Northmeadow Pky S, Roswell GA 30076	770-625-2599	R	170*	.2
19	Working Assets Funding Service—*Laura Scher*	101 Market St Ste 700, San Francisco CA 94105	415-369-2000	R	166*	.1
20	Pcs Telecorp Inc—*Gerald Vento*	1010 N Glebe Rd Ste 80, Arlington VA 22201	703-236-1100	R	148*	3.6
21	LCC International Inc—*Kenneth Young*	4800 Westfields Blvd S, Chantilly VA 20151	703-873-2000	R	146	1.3
22	Grande Communications Holdings Inc—*Matthew Murphy*	900 Bugg Ln Ste 118, San Marcos TX 78666	512-878-4000	R	141*	.8
23	GTE Airfone Inc—*Kathy Harless*	2809 Butterfield Rd, Oak Brook IL 60522	630-572-1800	R	115*	.3
24	Purple Communications Inc—*Daniel R Luis*	595 Menlo Dr, Rocklin CA 95765	415-408-2300	R	109	.4
25	Otelco Inc—*Michael D Weaver*	505 3rd Ave E, Oneonta AL 35121	205-625-3574	P	104	.3
26	SiGe Semiconductor Inc (Andover Massachusetts)—*Sohail Khan*	200 Brickstone Sq Ste, Andover MA 01810	978-327-6850	S	103*	.1
27	Knology of Huntsville Inc—*Rodger L Johnson* Knology Inc	2401 10th St SW, Huntsville AL 35805	256-533-5353	S	100*	.1
28	EF Johnson Technologies Inc—*Andrew L Adams*	1440 Corporate Dr, Irving TX 75038	972-819-0700	R	92	.3
29	Lifesize Communications Inc—*Craig Malloy*	901 S Mopac Expy Bldg, Austin TX 78746	512-347-9300	R	81*	.1
30	Cellxion LLC—*James Mack*	5031 Hazel Jones Rd, Bossier City LA 71111	318-213-2900	S	80*	.9
31	FiberTower Corp—*Kurt Van Wagenen*	185 Berry St Ste 4800, San Francisco CA 94107	415-659-3500	P	76	.2
32	Smith Bagley Inc—*Smith Bagley*	1500 S White Mountain, Show Low AZ 85901	928-537-0690	R	74*	.2
33	Globalstar LLC—*Peter Dalton*	461 S Milpitas Blvd Bl, Milpitas CA 95035	408-933-4000	R	72*	.4
34	Alltel Cellular—*Lowell McAdam*	1 Allared Dr Bldg 4 3r, Little Rock AR 72204		D	57*	.2
35	Knology of Augusta Inc Knology Inc	3714 Wheeler Rd, Augusta GA 30909	706-364-1000	S	48*	.1
36	Knology of Columbus Inc Knology Inc	6050 Knology Way, Columbus GA 31909	706-221-1000	S	48*	.1
37	Knology of Knoxville Inc Knology Inc	10115 Sherrill Blvd, Knoxville TN 37932	865-357-1000	S	48*	.1
38	Knology of Montgomery Inc Knology Inc	1637 Eastern Blvd, Montgomery AL 36117	334-356-1000	S	48*	.1
39	Knology of Panama City Inc Knology Inc	13200 Panama City Beac, Panama City Beach FL 32407	850-215-1000	S	48*	.1
40	Teletouch Communications Inc—*Robert McMurrey*	5718 Airport Fwy, Fort Worth TX 76117	817-654-6100	P	40	.1
41	Nextwave Wireless Inc—*Frank Cassou*	12264 El Camino Real S, San Diego CA 92130	619-573-1570	P	40	<.1
42	CMT Partners—*Mark Bradner*	7277 164th Ave Ne Rtc1, Redmond WA 98052	425-580-6000	R	38*	1.3
43	Integrated Data Corp—*Abe Carmel*	1000 N West St Ste 120, Wilmington DE 19801	302-295-5057	P	32	N/A
44	Cellcomm Inc—*Ed Veres*	3285 Solomons Island R, Edgewater MD 21037	301-261-7100	R	28*	.1
45	Microspace Communications Corp—*Joe Amor*	3100 Highwoods Blvd St, Raleigh NC 27604	919-850-4500	S	27*	<.1
46	DukeNet Communications Inc—*William B Davis*	400 S Tryon St Ste 290, Charlotte NC 28202	704-382-7111	S	26*	<.1
47	Pro Cellular Wireless Communication Inc—*Kent Johansen*	2556 Broadway Ave, Slayton MN 56172	507-836-1012	R	25*	.2
48	Unbeatable Cellular and Beeper Accessories Inc—*Jacob Gold*	54 Freeman St, Newark NJ 07105	973-344-0344	R	23*	.1
49	Metromedia International Group Inc—*Mark S Hauf*	5960 Fairview Rd Ste 4, Charlotte NC 28210	704-496-2750	R	23	.7
50	Ultra Electronics Criticom—*Brian Garcia*	4211 Forbes Blvd, Lanham MD 20706	301-306-0600	R	20*	<.1
51	Southern Light LLC—*Andy Newton*	156 Saint Anthony St, Mobile AL 36603	251-662-1170	R	19*	<.1
52	Bravo Tech Inc—*Q He*	6185 Phyllis Dr Unit D, Cypress CA 90630	714-230-8333	R	19*	.1
53	ConferenceCallcom Inc—*Hobert Wise*	1445 MacArthur Dr Ste, Carrollton TX 75007	972-446-1216	S	18*	.1
54	NTT Multimedia Communications Laboratories Inc—*Kenji Takahashi*	101 S Ellsworth Ave, San Mateo CA 94401	650-579-0800	D	18*	<.1
55	Aquis Communications Group Inc—*Brian M Bobeck*	100 N Constitution Dr, Yorktown VA 23692	757-890-2801	R	16*	.1
56	Ellipso Inc—*David Castiel*	4410 Massachusetts Ave, Washington DC 20016	202-466-4488	R	16*	<.1
57	Pacific Wireless Communications LLC—*Mary Sensui*	710 Kakoi St, Honolulu HI 96819	808-833-3778	R	15*	.1
58	Gila River Telecommunications Inc—*Bruce M Holdridge*	7065 W Allison Dr, Chandler AZ 85226	520-796-3333	R	15*	<.1
59	InfoRad Inc—*Paul Fitzgerald*	635 E 185th St, Cleveland OH 44119	216-531-1313	R	15*	<.1
60	Massive Telecom Inc	269 S Beverly Dr Ste 6, Beverly Hills CA 90212	213-550-4492	R	15*	<.1
61	NextG Networks Inc—*Steven J Moskowitz*	890 Tasman Dr, Milpitas CA 95035		R	12*	.1
62	Acn-International Corp—*Charles Blake*	3291 Morcom Ave, Oakland CA 94619	510-437-9234	R	12*	<.1
63	Snet Springwich Inc—*Fred Bennetto*	500 Enterprise Dr Ste, Rocky Hill CT 06067	860-513-7600	R	12*	.2
64	Cleveland Unlimited Inc—*William Jarvis*	7165 E Pleasant Valley, Cleveland OH 44131	216-525-1100	R	12*	.4
65	Maxstream Inc—*Brad Walters*	PO Box 1508, Orem UT 84059	801-765-9885	S	10	<.1
66	Choice Wireless LC—*Alan Rohmer*	PO Box 8426, Wichita Falls TX 76307	940-692-1289	R	10*	<.1
67	ATI (Trabuco Canyon California)—*David Singer*	30575 Trabuco Canyon R, Trabuco Canyon CA 92679	949-265-2000	R	10*	.1
68	Socket Holding Corp—*George Pfenenger*	PO Box 7085, Columbia MO 65205	573-817-0000	R	9*	.1
69	Mountain Wireless Construction Inc—*Randy Hanson*	927 Salida Way, Aurora CO 80011	303-343-6544	R	9*	<.1
70	World Communications Inc (Seattle Washington)—*Michael Terpening*	1945 Yale Pl E, Seattle WA 98102	206-652-4470	R	9*	<.1
71	Sprint Missouri Inc—*Dan Hesse* Sprint Nextel Corp	3702 W Truman Blvd, Jefferson City MO 65109	573-632-7727	S	9*	<.1
72	Sierra Wireless America Inc—*Donna Bevington*	2200 Faraday Ave Ste 1, Carlsbad CA 92008	760-476-8700	R	9*	.1
73	Dennis Belton—*Dennis Belton*	14706 James River Ln, Houston TX 77084	281-855-7891	R	8*	.1
74	KeyOn Communications Holdings Inc—*Jonathan Snyder*	11742 Stonegate Cir, Omaha NE 68164		P	8	.1
75	Let's TalkCom Inc—*Delly Tamer*	201 Mission St Ste 300, San Francisco CA 94105	415-357-7600	R	7*	.1
76	Wholesale Carrier Services Inc—*Chris S Barton*	5471 N University Dr, Coral Springs FL 33067	561-852-3400	R	7*	<.1
77	Mailtrust—*Lanham Wapier*	755 University City Bl, Blacksburg VA 24060	540-552-3603	R	6*	.1
78	Yoder Enterprises Inc—*Alan Yoder*	PO Box 3097, Mcallen TX 78502	956-631-7243	R	6*	.1
79	Streamline Wireless Inc—*Scott Bodish*	12937 Wicker Ave A, Cedar Lake IN 46303	219-374-7509	R	6*	.1
80	Indiana Paging Network Inc—*William Eisele*	6745 W Johnson Rd, La Porte IN 46350	219-874-5000	R	6*	.1
81	Gtp Acquisition Partners Ii LLC—*Marc Ganzi*	750 Park Of Commerce B, Boca Raton FL 33487	561-886-3909	R	5*	.1
82	EvO2 Inc	159 S B St, San Mateo CA 94401	650-375-2388	R	5*	<.1
83	Wireless Ventures LLC—*Eddy Harvey*	4996 Indiana Ave, Winston Salem NC 27106	336-761-1911	R	5*	.1
84	Las Vegas Dissemination Inc—*John Gaughan*	PO Box 400550, Las Vegas NV 89140	702-739-8781	R	5*	<.1
85	Rf Communications—*Todd Moore*	6724 Alexander Bell Dr, Columbia MD 21046	301-317-9474	R	5*	.1
86	Telpage Inc—*Charles Grigg*	636 S Main St, Emporia VA 23847	434-634-5100	R	4*	<.1
87	Alphapage LLC—*Graeme Bean*	4201 E Yale Ave Ste 14, Denver CO 80222	303-698-1111	R	4*	.1
88	Health Discovery Corp—*Stephen D Barnhill MD*	2 E Bryan St Ste 601, Savannah GA 31401		P	4	<.1
89	Port City Communication Inc—*James Beckett*	942 Military St, Port Huron MI 48060	810-984-5141	R	4*	<.1
90	Kvr Communication—*Vincent Phillips*	1313 Pa Ave Se, Washington DC 20003	202-547-3560	R	4*	.1
91	ICTC Group Inc—*David S Ahl*	65 Highland Rd, Rye NY 10580	914-336-1718	P	4	N/A
92	Ztar Mobile Inc—*Kevin Haddad*	16 Village Ln Ste 250, Colleyville TX 76034	817-427-8888	R	4*	.1
93	All Star Wireless—*Sam Falk*	10001 Telegraph Rd, Redford MI 48239	313-794-1400	R	4*	<.1
94	Voice Stream Wireless—*Paul Cole*	4401 Freidrich Ln Ste, Austin TX 78744	512-437-6500	R	3*	<.1
95	Cook Telecom Inc—*Tom Cook*	2960 Kerner Blvd, San Rafael CA 94901	415-460-4900	R	3*	<.1

Note: An asterisk (*) indicates an estimated financial figure. The company type code used is as follows: R = Private, P = Public, S = Private Subsidiary, B = Public Subsidiary, D = Division, J = Joint Venture, I = Investment Fund.

COMPANY RANKINGS BY SALES WITHIN 4-DIGIT SIC

Rank	Company Name—Executive Officer	Address, City, State, Zip	Phone	Type	Fin	Empls
96	Ascendent Telecommunications Inc—Deborah Miller	2000 Bridge Pkwy Ste 1, Redwood City CA 94065		R	3*	<.1
97	Carolina Cellular Inc—John Rooney	405 Broad St, Fuquay Varina NC 27526	919-567-3282	R	3*	<.1
98	Allsafe Security Systems Inc—Paul Sargenti	9600 Sunbeam Ctr Dr, Jacksonville FL 32257	904-268-1111	R	3*	<.1
99	Wireless Connection Corp—Jeff Ussery	410 N 1st St Ste D, Hamilton MT 59840	406-363-2330	R	3*	<.1
100	Northwest Missouri Cellular LP—Roger Bundridge	PO Box 551, Maryville MO 64468	660-582-3334	R	3*	<.1
101	Super Fair Cellular Inc—Jason Najor	930 E Lewiston Ave, Ferndale MI 48220	248-547-4100	R	3*	<.1
102	True Wireless Inc—Robert Chamberlin	12657 Alcosta Blvd Ste, San Ramon CA 94583	925-362-9600	R	3*	<.1
103	Cellular Sales Of Kentucky—Joe Burns	1985 Edsel Ln Nw, Corydon IN 47112	812-738-7508	R	2*	<.1
104	Wireless Works—Mark Prunsell	94 E Geneva Sq, Lake Geneva WI 53147	262-248-9400	R	2*	<.1
105	Antietam Answering Service Inc—William Bosch	239 N Potomac St, Hagerstown MD 21740	301-739-0187	R	2*	<.1
106	Rcc Inc—Harvey Jacquin	3057 Hwy A, Washington MO 63090	636-239-7192	R	2*	<.1
107	Pathwayz Communications Inc—Paul Chapman	PO Box 19417, Amarillo TX 79114	806-355-0551	R	2*	<.1
108	Xnet Information System Inc—Arthur Zards	3080 Ogden Ave Ste 303, Lisle IL 60532	630-983-6064	R	2*	<.1
109	Kscoam 1080 Red Hot News Talk Radio—Michael Zwering	2300 Portola Dr, Santa Cruz CA 95062	831-475-1080	R	2*	<.1
110	Midland Communications Inc—Diane Hodgkins	721 School House Rd Ne, Calhoun GA 30701	706-624-9273	R	2*	<.1
111	Advanced Wireless Solutions Inc—Federico Samuel	12390 W 75th Ave, Arvada CO 80005	303-277-0388	R	2*	<.1
112	Johnson Communications Inc—John Johnson	29 Stumpfield Rd Ste B, Pensacola FL 32503	850-477-9134	R	2*	<.1
113	Western Paging And Voice Mail Systems I LP—Gene Clark	701 N Post Oak Rd Ste, Houston TX 77024	713-681-7243	R	2*	<.1
114	Baby Beepers	50 S Maple St, Akron OH 44303	330-374-6154	R	2*	<.1
115	Bridgeport Wireless LLC—Thomas Emyherhltze	4173 Main St, Bridgeport CT 06606	203-374-3600	R	2*	<.1
116	Electronics Service Company Of Hamlet LLC	PO Box 1104, Hamlet NC 28345	910-582-5411	R	2*	<.1
117	Spectracom Inc—Michael Carvin	5090 Central Hwy Ste 6, Pennsauken NJ 08109	856-910-9880	R	2*	<.1
118	Slo Cellular Inc—Harinder Kumara	PO Box 4331, San Luis Obispo CA 93403	805-543-0100	R	1*	<.1
119	International Wireless Corp—Essa Ebodi	11814 Western Ave, Stanton CA 90680	714-892-7252	R	1*	<.1
120	Northland Communications (Utica New York)—Jeremiah O Mc-Carthy	317 Court St, Utica NY 13502	315-624-2000	R	1*	.2
121	Nationwide Paging Inc—Peter Brown	382 Watertown St, Newton MA 02458	617-630-9000	R	1*	<.1
122	Kalama Telephone Co—Charlie Peterson	PO Box 1068, Kalama WA 98625	360-673-2755	S.	1	<.1
123	Incom Communications Corp—Gene Clothier	1571 Pky Loop Ste G, Tustin CA 92780	714-259-0450	R	1*	<.1
124	Farmers Cellular Telephone Co—Dennis McKeever	404 4th St, Batavia IA 52533	641-662-2373	R	1*	<.1
125	K and W and Fathers Inc—Michael Wieser	12 W 37th St Rm 500, New York NY 10018	212-867-9655	R	1*	<.1
126	Wireless Communications Unlimited—Ronald Batiste	2775 Butters Dr, Oakland CA 94602	510-530-2480	R	1*	<.1
127	LA Wireless Inc—Ramin Goel	15125 Ventura Blvd Ste, Sherman Oaks CA 91403	818-906-7222	R	1*	<.1
128	Miracon Wireless LLC	1049 Queen St Ste 4, Southington CT 06489	860-793-1700	R	1*	<.1
129	Geos Communications Inc—Andy L Berman	430 N Carroll Ave Ste, Southlake TX 76092	817-240-0200	P	<1	<.1
130	Robert Guzzo—Robert Guzzo	12 Avis Dr Rear Ste, Latham NY 12110	518-782-1300	R	<1*	<.1
131	Marconi Society Inc—Robert Lucky	500 W 120th St, New York NY 10027	212-854-7676	R	<1*	<.1
132	Seed Wireless and Accessories Co—Miguel Dada	8886 W Flagler St Apt, Miami FL 33174	305-270-3098	R	<1*	<.1
133	Accessory Store Inc—John Shawareb	6722 Nw Expy, Oklahoma City OK 73132	405-810-0077	R	<1*	<.1
134	Wireless Outreach LLC	9710 Sheet Ct, Cheltenham MD 20623	301-372-3535	R	N/A	<.1

TOTALS: SIC 4812 Radiotelephone Communications
Companies: 134

					150,248	225.4

4813 Telephone Communications Except Radiotelephone

Rank	Company Name—Executive Officer	Address, City, State, Zip	Phone	Type	Fin	Empls
1	AT and T Inc—Randall L Stephenson	208 S Akard St, Dallas TX 75202	210-821-4105	P	124,280	265.4
2	Verizon Communications Inc—Lowell McAdam	140 West St, New York NY 10007	212-395-1000	P	106,565	194.4
3	Verizon Business Verizon Communications Inc	295 N Maple Ave, Basking Ridge NJ 07920	908-559-4000	D	21,100	32.0
4	180 Connect Inc	6501 E Belleview Ave S, Englewood CO 80111	303-395-6001	S	17,246	4.0
5	Schlumberger Omnes	5599 San Felipe St, Houston TX 77056	713-513-2000	S	10,450*	1.0
6	ALLTEL Corp Verizon Communications Inc	1 Allied Dr, Little Rock AR 72202	501-905-8000	S	8,803	14.9
7	TDS METROCOM LLC—Dave Wittwer Telephone and Data Systems Inc	525 Junction Rd Ste 60, Madison WI 53717	608-663-3330	S	8,562*	10.0
8	CenturyLink—Glen F Post III	PO Box 11600, Monroe LA 71211	318-388-9000	P	7,042	20.3
9	PacifiCorp Group Holdings Co—Michael Dunn	825 NE Multnomah St, Portland OR 97232	503-813-5000	S	5,343*	6.3
10	Telephone and Data Systems Inc—LeRoy T Carlson Jr	30 N LaSalle St Ste 40, Chicago IL 60602	312-630-1900	P	5,181	12.3
11	Frontier Communications Corp—Susana D'Emic	3 High Ridge Pk, Stamford CT 06905		P	3,798	14.8
12	Windstream Corp—Jeff Gardner	4001 Rodney Parham Rd, Little Rock AR 72212	501-748-7000	P	3,712	10.1
13	Southern New England Telecommunications Corp—Rex Adams AT and T Inc	227 Church St, New Haven CT 06510	203-771-5200	S	3,000	14.5
14	Frontier Corp—Mary Wilderotter Frontier Communications Corp	180 S Clinton Ave, Rochester NY 14646	585-777-1000	S	2,594	8.2
15	IDT Corp—Howard S Jonas	520 Broad St, Newark NJ 07102	973-438-1000	P	1,556	1.3
16	XO Holdings Inc—Laura Thomas	13865 Sunrise Valley D, Herndon VA 20171	703-547-2000	R	1,521	4.0
17	Cincinnati Bell Inc—John F Cassidy	PO Box 2301, Cincinnati OH 45201	513-397-9900	P	1,462	3.1
18	Time Warner Telecom Inc—Larissa Herda	10475 Park Meadows Dr, Littleton CO 80124	303-566-1000	R	1,430*	2.9
19	iBasis Inc—Jon van Vianen	20 2nd Ave, Burlington MA 01803	781-505-7500	S	1,324	.4
20	Equinix Inc—Stephen M Smith	301 Velocity Way 5th F, Foster City CA 94404	650-513-7000	P	1,220	1.9
21	Cameron Telephone Company Inc—George Mack	PO Box 110, Sulphur LA 70664	337-583-2111	S	1,102*	.1
22	FairPoint Communications Inc—Paul H Sunu	521 E Morehead St Ste, Charlotte NC 28202	704-344-8150	P	1,071	4.0
23	ALLTEL Missouri Inc—Frank O'Mara ALLTEL Corp	920 S Springfield Ave, Bolivar MO 65613	417-326-1001	S	1,068*	.1
24	Pccw Global Inc—Marc Halbfinger	450 Springpark Pl Ste, Herndon VA 20170	703-621-1600	R	953*	16.2
25	Vonage Holdings Corp—Mark P Lefar	23 Main St, Holmdel NJ 07733	732-528-2600	P	870	1.0
26	Cincinnati Bell Telephone Co—John F Cassidy Cincinnati Bell Inc	PO Box 2301, Cincinnati OH 45202	513-397-9900	S	832*	6.0
27	Verizon Washington Verizon Communications Inc	1710 H St NW, Washington DC 20006	202-392-9900	S	814*	2.0
28	Primus Telecommunications Group Inc—Peter D Aquino	7901 Jones Branch Dr S, McLean VA 22102	703-902-2800	P	765	1.7
29	General Communication Inc—Ronald A Duncan	PO Box 99016, Anchorage AK 99509	907-265-5400	P	651	1.7
30	RCN Corp—Jim Holanda	196 Van Buren St Ste 3, Herndon VA 20170	703-434-8200	S	636	2.2
31	CenturyTel of Washington Inc CenturyLink	PO Box 9901, Vancouver WA 98668	360-905-5800	S	620*	2.1
32	Atlantic Tele-Network Inc—Michael T Prior	600 Cummings Ctr, Beverly MA 01915	978-619-1300	P	619	1.8
33	NTELOS Holdings Corp—James A Hyde	PO Box 1990, Waynesboro VA 22980	540-946-3500	P	546	1.6
34	TDS Telecom Inc—James Barr III TDS Telecommunications Corp	525 Junction Rd, Madison WI 53717	608-664-4000	S	545	2.0
35	NTELOS Inc—James A Hyde	PO Box 1990, Waynesboro VA 22980		R	530	1.3
36	Linkedin Corp—Jeffrey Weiner	2029 Stierlin Ct, Mountain View CA 94043	650-687-3600	P	522*	1.0

Rank	Company Name—Executive Officer	Address, City, State, Zip	Phone	Type	Fin	Empls
37	Simply Wireless Inc—Steven Qureshi	2730 Prosperity Ave St, Fairfax VA 22031	703-343-2700	R	498*	.5
38	Hawaiian Telcom Communications Inc—Eric K Yeaman	1177 Bishop St, Honolulu HI 96813	808-546-3442	R	484	N/A
39	Horry Telephone Cooperative Inc—Micheal Hagg	PO Box 1820, Conway SC 29528	843-365-2154	S	467*	.6
40	One Communications Corp—Howard Janzen	5 Wall St, Burlington MA 01803	781-362-5700	R	458*	2.0
41	Cbeyond Inc—James F Geiger	320 Interstate North P, Atlanta GA 30339	678-424-2400	P	452	1.9
42	Broadview Networks Inc—Michael K Robinson	800 Westchester Ave, Rye Brook NY 10573	914-922-7000	S	408*	1.0
43	TDS Telecommunications Corp—Leroy T Carlson Jr Telephone and Data Systems Inc	PO Box 628010, Middleton WI 53562	608-664-8300	S	403*	2.0
44	Innovative Communication Corp—Jeffrey J Prosser	PO Box 1730, Christiansted VI 00821	340-777-7700	R	401*	.4
45	Frontier Communications of the South Inc Frontier Communications Corp	3 High Ridge Park, Stamford CT 06905	203-614-5600	S	393*	<.1
46	Consolidated Communications Holdings Inc—Robert J Currey	121 S 17th St, Mattoon IL 61938	217-235-3311	P	383	1.0
47	ACC Corp—John Baker AT and T Inc	400 West Ave, Rochester NY 14611		S	373*	.9
48	GCI Communication Corp—Ronald A Duncan General Communication Inc	PO Box 99016, Anchorage AK 99509	907-265-5600	S	369*	1.3
49	Granite Telecommunications LLC—Robert Hale Jr	100 Newport Ave Ext, Quincy MA 02171	617-933-5500	R	361*	.6
50	Alaska Communications Systems Group Inc—Anand Vadapalli	600 Telephone Ave, Anchorage AK 99503	907-297-3000	P	342	.8
51	Lynch Telephone Corporation III—Mario J Gabelli	401 Theodore Fremd Ave, Rye NY 10580	914-921-8821	S	339*	.4
52	ATX Communications Inc—Michael Robinson Broadview Networks Inc	800 Westchester Ave, Rye Brook NY 10573	914-922-7000	S	294*	1.3
53	Terremark Worldwide Inc—Nelson Fonseca Verizon Communications Inc	2 S Biscayne Blvd Ste, Miami FL 33131	305-856-3200	S	292	.7
54	Smart City Holdings LLC—Martin Rubin	5795 W Badura Ave Ste, Las Vegas NV 89118	702-943-6000	R	274*	.3
55	Multiband Corp—James L Mandel	9449 Science Center Dr, New Hope MN 55428	763-504-3000	P	266	.1
56	Cypress Communications Holding Company Inc—Michael F Elliott	4 Piedmont Center, Atlanta GA 30305	404-869-2500	R	257*	.3
57	Verizon Avenue Corp—Ivan Seidenberg	150 N Field Dr Ste 300, Lake Forest IL 60045	847-582-8800	S	248*	.6
58	9278 Communications Inc—Sajid Kapadia	1942 Williamsbridge Rd, Bronx NY 10461	718-475-9489	R	247	.2
59	SureWest Communications—Steve C Oldham	8150 Industrial Ave Bl, Roseville CA 95678	916-786-1407	P	244	.8
60	Integra Telecom Inc—Dudley R Slater	1201 NE Lloyd Blvd Ste, Portland OR 97232	503-453-8000	R	235*	.6
61	Road Runner Holdco LLC—Jeffrey M King	13224 Woodland Park Rd, Herndon VA 20171	703-345-2400	D	214*	.4
62	Neutral Tandem Inc—G Edward Evans	550 W Adams St Ste900, Chicago IL 60661	312-384-8000	P	200	.2
63	Farmers Telephone Coop (Kingstree South Carolina)—Brad Erwin	1101 E Main St, Kingstree SC 29556	843-382-2333	R	195*	.4
64	Shenandoah Telecommunications Co—Christopher E French	PO Box 459, Edinburg VA 22824	540-984-4141	P	195	.6
65	Madison River Communications Corp—J Stephen Vander-woude	PO Box 9, Mebane NC 27302	919-563-1500	R	191	.6
66	Federal Communications Group Inc—C Byron Snyder	2328 W Huntington Dr, Tempe AZ 85282	480-379-6200	S	190*	.2
67	Nemont Telephone Cooperative Inc—Ben Boreson	PO Box 600, Scobey MT 59263	406-783-5654	R	179*	.2
68	Telegroup Business Unit (Fairfield Iowa)—Clifford Rees Primus Telecommunications Group Inc	2094 185th St, Fairfield IA 52556	641-469-4690	D	177*	.4
69	Rico Puerto Telephone Company Inc—Enrique Ortiz	1515 Roosevelt Ave, San Juan PR 00920	787-782-8282	S	171*	4.8
70	Golden West Telecommunications Cooperative Inc—Denny Law	PO Box 411, Wall SD 57790	605-279-2161	R	168*	.2
71	FSH Communications LLC—Donald V Goens	100 W Monroe St Ste 21, Chicago IL 60603	312-269-9937	R	166*	.2
72	Global Service Solutions Inc—David Sparks	3420 Oakcliff Rd Ste 1, Atlanta GA 30340	770-457-3048	R	166*	<.1
73	Hickory Tech Corp—John W Finke	PO Box 3248, Mankato MN 56002	507-387-1151	P	162	.5
74	Ontonagon County Telephone Co—Dorothy Sharkey Hiawatha Communication	618 River St, Ontonagon MI 49953	906-884-9911	S	159*	<.1
75	CTC Communications Corp—Howard Janzen	220 Bear Hill Rd, Waltham MA 02451	781-466-8080	S	153*	.6
76	ALLTEL Florida Inc—Richard H Brashear ALLTEL Corp	PO Box 409, Live Oak FL 32060	386-364-2400	S	151*	.1
77	Global Crossing North American Holdings Inc—John Legere	200 Park Ave Ste 300, Florham Park NJ 07932	973-937-0100	R	147*	3.2
78	Iowa Network Services Inc—Richard Vohs	4201 Corporate Dr, West Des Moines IA 50266	515-830-0110	R	146*	.2
79	Gruber Industries Inc—Peter Gruber	21439 N 2nd Ave, Phoenix AZ 85027	602-863-2655	R	145*	.2
80	Rio Holdings Inc—Michael Wilfley	600 Congress Ave Ste 2, Austin TX 78701	512-917-1742	R	144*	.8
81	Minnesota Southern Wireless Inc Hickory Tech Corp	PO Box 3248, Mankato MN 56002	507-387-1151	S	144*	.2
82	Electric Lightwave Inc—Mike Daniel Integra Telecom Inc	PO Box 8905, Vancouver WA 98668	360-816-3000	S	143*	.5
83	Harrisonville Telephone Co—HR Gentsch	PO Box 149, Waterloo IL 62298	618-939-6112	R	137*	.1
84	Elandia International Inc—Harley M Rollins	8200 NW 52nd Terrace S, Miami FL 33166	305-415-8830	P	136	.8
85	Global Crossing Telecommunications Inc—John Legere	225 Kenneth Dr, Rochester NY 14623	703-464-3322	D	133*	.4
86	USA Datanet Corp—David Montanaro	318 S Clinton St Ste 5, Syracuse NY 13202	315-579-7000	R	132*	.2
87	Birch Communications Inc—Vincent M Oddo	4885 Riverside Dr Ste, Macon GA 31210	478-475-9800	R	124*	.4
88	Spirit Telecom LLC—R Vernon Williams	1500 Hampton St Ste 10, Columbia SC 29201	803-771-7476	R	122*	.2
89	Logix Communications Enterprises Inc—Craig Sheetz	100 Park Ave Ste 800, Oklahoma City OK 73102		R	120*	.2
90	NewMarket Technology Inc—Bruce Noller	14860 Montfort Dr Ste, Dallas TX 75254	972-386-3372	P	118	.5
91	Consolidated Communications Inc—Robert Curry	121 S 17th St, Mattoon IL 61938	217-235-3311	R	117*	.6
92	PNG Telecommunications Inc—Bernie Stevens	100 Commercial Dr, Fairfield OH 45014	513-942-7900	R	117*	.3
93	Horizon Telcom Inc—Thomas McKell	PO Box 480, Chillicothe OH 45601	740-772-8200	R	114*	.2
94	Telrad Connegy—Zvika Bar	10 Executive Blvd, Farmingdale NY 11735	631-420-8800	S	108*	.1
95	Global Crossing Development Co—John J Legere	110 E 59th St 18th Fl, New York NY 10022	212-290-8201	S	105*	.1
96	ILD Telecommunications Inc—Michael Lewis	5000 Sawgrass Village, Ponte Vedra Beach FL 32082	904-273-2440	R	104*	.4
97	Consolidated Telephone Co—Paul Nieman Jr	PO Box 972, Brainerd MN 56401	218-454-1234	R	104*	.1
98	Canby Telephone Association—Rich Ares	190 SE 2nd Ave, Canby OR 97013	503-266-8111	R	101*	.1
99	Craw-Kan Telephone Cooperative Inc—Barry Bedene	300 N Ozark St, Girard KS 66743	620-724-8235	R	100*	.1
100	Waat Media Wireless Entertainment—Ian Aaron	14242 Ventura Blvd 3rd, Sherman Oaks CA 91423	818-301-6200	R	100*	.1
101	Panhandle Telephone Cooperative Inc—Ronald Strecker	PO Box 1188, Guymon OK 73942	580-338-2556	R	97*	.2
102	Hector Communications Corp—Curtis A Sampson	PO Box 697, New Ulm MN 56073	507-354-2500	R	97*	.1
103	France Telecom North America Inc—Marc Dandelot	1270 Ave of the Americ, New York NY 10020	212-332-2100	S	95*	.1
104	Ace Communications Group—David Schroeder	PO Box 363, Houston MN 55943	507-896-4695	R	92*	.1
105	SDS International Inc—George Gennin	1320 Central Park Blvd, Fredericksburg VA 22401	703-553-7535	R	90*	.1
106	New Horizons Telecom Inc—John S Lee	901 Cope Industrial Wa, Palmer AK 99645	907-761-6000	R	89*	.1
107	Fidelity Communications Co (Sullivan Missouri)—John T Davis	64 N Clark St, Sullivan MO 63080	573-468-8081	R	88*	.2
108	Westel Inc—Tommy K Garner	9606 N Mopac Expy Ste, Austin TX 78759	512-480-5500	R	88*	.2
109	Pine Tree Telephone and Telegraph Co—Robert Souza	92 Oak St, Portland ME 04101	207-699-2300	S	88*	.1
110	Locus Telecommunications Inc—Jason Chon	111 Sylvan Ave, Englewood Cliffs NJ 07632	201-585-3600	R	83*	.2
111	inContact Inc—Paul Jarman	7730 S Union Park Ave, Midvale UT 84047	801-320-3200	P	82	.3

Note: An asterisk (*) indicates an estimated financial figure. The company type code used is as follows: R = Private, P = Public, S = Private Subsidiary, B = Public Subsidiary, D = Division, J = Joint Venture, I = Investment Fund.

COMPANY RANKINGS BY SALES WITHIN 4-DIGIT SIC

Rank	Company Name—*Executive Officer*	Address, City, State, Zip	Phone	Type	Fin	Empls
112	Premiere Communications Inc	3280 Peachtree Rd NE S, Atlanta GA 30305	404-262-8400	S	81*	.1
113	Global Telecom and Technology Inc—*Richard D Calder Jr*	8484 Westpark Dr Ste 7, McLean VA 22102	703-442-5500	P	81	.1
114	Sunrise Telecom Inc—*Bahaa Moukadam*	302 Enzo Dr, San Jose CA 95138	408-363-8000	P	81	.4
115	AT and T Alascom—*Mike Felix* AT and T Inc	505 E Bluff Dr, Anchorage AK 99501	907-264-7000	S	80*	.6
116	CapRock Communications Corp—*Peter Shaper*	4400 S Sam Houston Pky, Houston TX 77048	832-668-2300	S	80*	.3
117	Indepedent Telecommunications Systems Inc—*Robert Sweezie*	4079 Park E Ct, Grand Rapids MI 49546	616-242-5300	R	80*	.1
118	Net2phone Inc—*Liore Alroy* IDT Corp	520 Broad St, Newark NJ 07102	973-438-3111	S	79*	.3
119	Mid-Rivers Telephone Cooperative Inc—*Robert B. Reukauf*	PO Box 280, Circle MT 59215	406-485-3301	R	75*	.2
120	Empire Telephone Corp—*Robert H Wagner*	PO Box 349, Prattsburgh NY 14873		R	75*	.1
121	Northland Telephone Systems Ltd—*Jeremiah O McCarthy*	317 Court St, Utica NY 13502	315-624-2000	R	73*	.2
122	West River Telecommunications Coop—*Mick Grosz*	PO Box 467, Hazen ND 58545	701-748-2211	R	71*	.1
123	8x8 Inc—*Bryan R Martin*	810 W Maude Ave, Sunnyvale CA 94085	408-727-1885	P	70	.2
124	Pioneer Telephone Cooperative Inc—*Richard Ruhl*	PO Box 539, Kingfisher OK 73750	405-375-4111	R	69*	.6
125	InfoHighway Communications Corp—*Michael K Robinson* Broadview Networks Inc	39 Broadway 19th Fl, New York NY 10006		S	67*	.2
126	ACT Teleconferencing Services Inc—*Peter Salas*	1526 Cole Blvd, Golden CO 80401	303-233-3500	R	66*	.4
127	American Broadband Nebraska Inc (Blair Nebraska)	1605 Washington St, Blair NV 68008	402-426-6200	S	65	.6
128	Iglou Internet Services Inc—*Dannie Gregory*	PO Box 33187, Louisville KY 40232		R	64*	.1
129	DSLi—*Mario Bustamante*	PO BOX 558350, Miami FL 33255	305-779-7777	R	62*	.1
130	Brandenburg Telephone Co—*JD Tobin Jr*	200 Telco Dr, Brandenburg KY 40108	270-422-2121	R	60*	.2
131	Lexington Telephone Long Distance Co—*Richard Reese*	PO Box 808, Lexington NC 27293	336-249-9901	R	60*	.1
132	Covista Communications Inc—*Warren Feldman*	225 E 8th St Ste 400, Chattanooga TN 37402		R	60	.2
133	Coalfield Telephone Company Inc—*Paul Gearheart*	PO Box 14109, Lexington KY 40512	606-478-9401	R	59*	.1
134	Telephone Service Co—*Lonnie D Pederson*	2 Willipie St, Wapakoneta OH 45895	419-739-2200	R	51*	.1
135	Rural Telephone Service Company Inc—*FC Brungardt*	PO Box 158, Lenora KS 67645	785-567-4281	R	49*	.2
136	DSLnet Inc—*D Craig Young*	50 Barnes Park N Ste 1, Wallingford CT 06492	203-284-6100	S	49	.1
137	Choice Communications LLC—*Tony Shepherd* Atlantic Tele-Network Inc	Al Cohen's Mall - Have, St Thomas VI 00802	340-778-8864	S	49*	.1
138	Netwolves Resicom Corp—*Scott Foote*	4710 Eisenhower Blvd S, Tampa FL 33634	813-579-3200	S	48*	.1
139	Vycera Communications Inc—*Derek M Gietzen*	12750 High Bluff Dr St, San Diego CA 92130	858-792-2400	R	47*	.3
140	Premiere Conferencing Networks Inc—*Ted Schraftt*	3399 Peachtree Rd NW S, Atlanta GA 30326	404-262-8400	S	46*	.7
141	Highland Telephone Cooperative Inc—*Fred Terry*	PO Box 119, Sunbright TN 37872	423-628-2121	R	46*	.1
142	Smart Funding Corp—*Madhu Baid*	1809 E Dyer Rd Ste 301, Santa Ana CA 92705	949-838-1810	R	43*	.1
143	Alternative Telecommunications Corp—*John W Winnen*	41 Nieske Rd, Monson MA 01057	413-267-3700	R	43*	<.1
144	Upper Peninsula Telephone Co—*Robert F Dolan*	PO Box 86, Carney MI 49812	906-639-2111	S	42*	<.1
145	SRT Communications Inc—*Steve D Lysne*	3615 N Broadway, Minot ND 58703	701-858-1200	S	40*	.3
146	Pioneer Telephone Coop (Philomath Oregon)—*Jerry Schlachter*	PO Box 640, Philomath OR 97370	541-563-3135	R	40*	.1
147	Capsule Communications Inc—*David B Hurwitz* Covista Communications Inc	2 Greenwood Sq 3331 St, Bensalem PA 19020	215-633-9400	S	37	.1
148	HOSTINGCOM Inc—*Art Zeile*	501 S 4th St, Louisville KY 40202	781-478-1950	R	37*	<.1
149	Innovative Technologies Inc—*Mario Martinez*	4115 Pleasant Valley R, Chantilly VA 20151	703-322-9400	R	35*	.1
150	Pioneer Telephone Association Inc—*Richard Veach*	PO Box 707, Ulyoooa KS 67000	620-356-3211	R	34*	.2
151	Creative Communications Inc (Salt Lake City Utah)—*Chris Nottoli*	155 N 400 W Ste 100, Salt Lake City UT 84103	801-994-4100	R	34*	<.1
152	Chasecom LP—*Tony Chase*	3311 W Alabama St, Houston TX 77098	713-874-3000	R	34	.7
153	Atlanta Datacom Inc—*Dennis Fryzel*	2915 Courtyards Dr Ste, Norcross GA 30071	770-263-9756	R	33*	.1
154	Futurewei Technologies Inc—*Tianfeng Hong*	5700 Tennyson Pkwy Ste, Plano TX 75024	214-919-6000	R	33*	.8
155	Telephone Electronics Corp—*Joseph D Fail*	700 S West St, Jackson MS 39201	601-353-9118	R	32*	.1
156	New Ulm Telecom Inc—*Bill Otis*	27 N Minnesota St, New Ulm MN 56073	507-354-4111	P	32	.1
157	HiWAAY Internet Services—*MD Smith IV*	2227 Drake Ave Ste 28, Huntsville AL 35805	256-650-4900	R	31*	<.1
158	Arrival Communications Inc—*Tony Distefano*	1800 19th St, Bakersfield CA 93301	661-716-2100	R	31*	.1
159	Chillicothe Telephone Co Horizon Telcom Inc	PO Box 480, Chillicothe OH 45601		S	30	.3
160	Ponderosa Telephone Co—*Elizabeth Silkwood*	PO Box 21, O Neals CA 93645	559-868-6000	R	30*	.1
161	Nobel Limited Co—*Thomas C Knobel*	5857 Owens Ave, Carlsbad CA 92008	760-405-0105	R	29*	.2
162	Mcgraw Communications Inc—*Francis Ahearn*	521 5th Ave Fl 14, New York NY 10175	212-849-2301	R	29*	<.1
163	Lavaca Telephone Company Inc—*Keith Gibson*	PO Box 230, Lavaca AR 72941	479-674-2211	R	29*	<.1
164	Vector Internet Services Inc—*Mike Sowada* DSLnet Inc	10290 W 70th St, Eden Prairie MN 55344	612-395-9000	S	28*	<.1
165	Glowpoint Inc—*Joseph Laezza*	430 Mountain Ave Ste 3, Murray Hill NJ 07974	805-384-4255	P	28	.1
166	Syringa Networks LLC—*Greg Lowe*	3795 S Development Ave, Boise ID 83705	208-229-6100	R	27*	.1
167	Capital Telecommunications Inc—*George V Kingsbury*	200 W Market St, York PA 17401	717-848-8800	R	27*	.1
168	South Central Rural Telephone Cooperative Corporation Inc—*Max Phipps*	PO Box 159, Glasgow KY 42142	270-678-2111	R	26*	.1
169	Arise Virtual Solutions Inc—*John Meyer*	3450 Lakeside Dr Ste 6, Miramar FL 33027	954-392-2600	R	25*	.2
170	Guadalupe Valley Telephone Coop—*Ritchie T Sorrells*	36101 FM 3159, New Braunfels TX 78132	830-885-4411	R	25*	.1
171	Graphnet Inc—*Yaakov Elkon*	40 Fulton St, New York NY 10038	212-994-1100	R	25	.1
172	Inter-Community Telephone Co—*Keith Andersen*	PO Box 8, Nome ND 58062	701-924-8815	S	25*	.1
173	Molalla Communications Co—*Steve Loutzenhiser*	PO Box 360, Molalla OR 97038	503-829-1100	R	25*	<.1
174	North State Communications—*Roster Tucker*	111 Hayden Pl, High Point NC 27260	336-886-3670	R	24*	.4
175	Warwick Valley Telephone Co—*Duane W Albro*	PO Box 592, Warwick NY 10990	845-986-8080	P	24	.1
176	Telscape International Inc—*Philip Siegel*	PO Box 30, Pasadena CA 91109	626-415-1000	R	24*	.2
177	Trans National Communications International Inc—*Brian Twomey*	2 Charlesgate W, Boston MA 02215	617-369-1000	S	24*	.1
178	Whidbey Telecom—*Marion F Henny*	PO Box 329, Langley WA 98260	360-321-1122	R	24*	.1
179	Network Operator Services Inc—*Tim Martin*	PO Box 3529, Longview TX 75606	903-323-4500	R	24*	.2
180	Orbis 1 LLC	2901 Johnston St Ste 2, Lafayette LA 70503	337-761-8024	R	24*	<.1
181	JBN Telephone Company Inc—*Gene Morris* Haviland Telephone Co	418 W 5th St Ste A, Holton KS 66436	785-362-3323	S	23*	<.1
182	Manhattan Telecommunications Corp—*Marshall Aronow*	55 Water St Fl 31, New York NY 10041	212-607-2000	R	23*	.2
183	Yadtel Telecom—*Jim Crabtree*	PO Box 368, Yadkinville NC 27055	336-463-5022	R	22*	.2
184	Qpay Inc—*Ami Shashoua*	16853 Ne 2nd Ave Ste 3, North Miami Beach FL 33162	305-650-9930	R	22*	.2
185	Eastex Telephone Cooperative Inc—*Kenneth Gladden*	PO Box 150, Henderson TX 75653	903-854-1000	R	22*	.1
186	Pioneer Directories—*Douglas Timmerman*	205 W Alona Ln, Lancaster WI 53813	608-723-4140	R	22*	<.1
187	Consolidated Communications Of Fort Bend Co—*Herbert Zureich*	121 S 17th St, Mattoon IL 61938	217-235-4402	R	21*	.1
188	Gioia P Ambrette Inc—*Gioia P Ambrette*	1140 Broadway Ste 201, New York NY 10001	212-780-9680	R	21*	.1
189	Mir3 Inc—*Amir Moussavian*	3398 Carmel Mountain R, San Diego CA 92121	858-724-1200	R	21*	.1

Rank	Company Name—Executive Officer	Address, City, State, Zip	Phone	Type	Fin	Empls
190	HTI Voice Solutions Inc—Peter B Keenan	2 Mt Royal Ave, Marlborough MA 01752	508-485-8400	R	21*	.1
191	Global Telecom Inc—Ayyad Yassin	PO Box 805, Morristown NJ 07963	973-285-9099	R	21*	<.1
192	Vision Net Inc—Rob Farris	PO Box 3068, Great Falls MT 59403	406-727-5994	R	21*	.1
193	Channel Intelligence Inc—Robert Wight	1180 Celebration Blvd, Kissimmee FL 34747	321-559-2300	R	21*	.2
194	Ambient Corp—John J Joyce	7 Wells Ave Ste 11, Newton MA 02459	617-332-0004	P	20	.1
195	Clay County Rural Telephone Cooperative Inc—Ralph Cunha	PO Box 237, Cloverdale IN 46120	765-795-4261	R	20*	<.1
196	Comporium Communications—Bill Beaty	PO Box 470, Rock Hill SC 29731	803-326-6011	R	20*	.3
197	Garden Valley Telephone Co—Ronald Engelstad	PO Box 259, Erskine MN 56535	218-687-5251	R	20*	.2
198	Triangle Telephone Cooperative Association—Rick Stevens	PO Box 1140, Havre MT 59501	406-394-7807	R	20*	.1
199	Pond Branch Telephone Company Inc—Luther Kneece	1660 Juniper Springs R, Gilbert SC 29054	803-894-3121	R	20*	.1
200	Pingtone Communications Inc—Bill Smedberg	13921 Park Center Rd, Herndon VA 20171		R	20*	<.1
201	Global Velocity Inc—Greg Sullivan	222 S Central Ave Ste, Saint Louis MO 63105	314-588-8555	R	20*	<.1
202	Arvig Communications Systems—Allen Arvig	150 2nd St SW, Perham MN 56573	218-346-4227	R	19*	.1
203	Twin Lakes Telephone Cooperative Corp—David Parsons	201 W Gore Ave, Gainesboro TN 38562	931-268-2151	R	19*	.1
204	JMSD Telecommunications Inc—John Martin	67 W Easy St Ste 105, Simi Valley CA 93065	805-522-0259	R	19*	<.1
205	Hiawatha Communication—Craig Immonen	618 River St, Ontonagon MI 49953	906-884-9911	R	19*	<.1
206	LightBound—Jack Carr	PO Box 20870, Indianapolis IN 46220	317-259-5050	R	19*	<.1
207	Beacon Enterprise Solutions Group Inc—Bruce Widener	9300 Shelbyville R Ste, Louisville KY 40222	502-657-3500	P	19	.1
208	Samsung Networks America Inc—Yihwan Jang	85 W Tasman Dr, San Jose CA 95134	408-544-5155	R	18*	<.1
209	Lafourche Telephone Company Inc	PO Box 188, Larose LA 70373	985-693-4567	S	18*	.2
210	Aries Network Inc—Kuliat Khalaf	2101 Empire Ave 2nd Fl, Burbank CA 91504	818-441-0246	R	18*	<.1
211	TouchPoint Networks—Chuck Whiteley	1150 Knutson Ave Ste 1, Medford OR 97504	541-842-1000	R	18*	<.1
212	Portables Unlimited Inc—Raja Amar	136 1st St, Nanuet NY 10954	845-507-8200	R	18*	.2
213	Blueprint Technologies Inc—Michael W Nole	15500 Roosevelt Blvd S, Clearwater FL 33760	727-535-2151	P	18	.1
214	Arctic Slope Telephone Association Cooperative Inc—Steve Merrian	4300 B St Ste 501, Anchorage AK 99503	907-563-3989	R	17*	.1
215	Business Only Broadband—Alan Rosenberg	777 Oakmont Ln Ste 200, Westmont IL 60559	630-590-6000	R	17*	<.1
216	Global Conference Partners—Chad Clawson	PO Box 289, Glendale CA 91209	323-469-3380	S	17*	<.1
217	Planet Com Internet Services Inc—Terry Chance	315 Capitol St Ste 205, Houston TX 77002		R	17*	.4
218	Answer Quick Telecommunications—Jerry Long	7415 Town S Ave, Baton Rouge I A 70808	225-766-1111	R	16*	.1
219	Spot Mobile International Ltd—Charles J Zwebner	PO BOX 414629, Miami Beach FL 33141		P	16	<.1
220	Farmers Telecommunications Coop—Randy Wright	PO Box 217, Rainsville AL 35986	256-638-2144	R	16*	.1
221	E Ritter and Co—Dan Hatzenbuehler	106 Frisco St Ste 100, Marked Tree AR 72365	870-358-4400	R	16*	.1
222	Above Telecommunications Inc—Bill Borger	655 Montgomery St Ste, San Francisco CA 94111	415-762-5123	R	16*	<.1
223	CaliforniaCom Inc—Larry Loebig	1624 Franklin St Ste 3, Oakland CA 94612	510-287-8450	R	16*	<.1
224	Cruzio Internet—Peggy Dolgenos	877 Cedar St Ste 150, Santa Cruz CA 95060	831-459-6301	R	16*	<.1
225	Great Basin Internet Services Inc—Bruce Robertson	PO Box 3115, Reno NV 89505	775-348-7299	R	16*	<.1
226	Last Mile Inc—Darol Lain	120 S 16th St, Lebanon PA 17042	717-270-1979	R	16*	<.1
227	netINS Inc—Dick Vohs	4201 Corporate Dr, West Des Moines IA 50266	515-830-0110	R	16*	<.1
228	PrismNet Ltd—Greg Stringfellow	11500 Metric Blvd Ste, Austin TX 78758	512-821-2991	R	16*	<.1
229	Profitec Business Services Inc—Richard Minervino	1s Barnes Rd, Wallingford CT 06492	203-679-7000	R	15*	.1
230	Northwestern Indiana Telephone Company Inc—Rhys Mussman	PO Box 67, Hebron IN 46341	219-996-2981	R	15*	.1
231	Ballard Rural Telephone Cooperative Corporation Inc—Harlon Parker	159 W 2nd St, La Center KY 42056	270-665-5186	R	15*	<.1
232	InfoWest Global Internet Services Inc—Kelly Nyberg	148 E Tabernacle, Saint George UT 84770	435-674-0165	R	15*	<.1
233	Digerati Technologies Inc—Arthur L Smith	3201 Cherry Ridge Dr S, San Antonio TX 78230	210-614-7240	P	15	<.1
234	Bullhorn Inc—Arthur Papas	33 Farnsworth St, Boston MA 02210	617-478-9100	R	15*	.1
235	Nushagak Electric and Telephone Cooperative Inc—Henry Strub	PO Box 350, Dillingham AK 99576	907-842-5295	R	15*	<.1
236	Peoples Rural Telephone Cooperative Corporation Inc—Donald Hughes	PO Box 159, Mc Kee KY 40447	606-593-5000	R	14*	.1
237	StreetdeliveryCom Inc—Andrew Logan	44 Merrimac St, Newburyport MA 01950	978-388-7707	R	14*	.1
238	Mvd Communications LLC—Nicole Berberich	11690 Grooms Rd, Blue Ash OH 45242	513-683-4711	R	14*	.1
239	Sunflower Telephone Co FairPoint Communications Inc	PO Box M, Leoti KS 67861	620-375-4300	S	14*	.1
240	Skyriver Communications Inc—Saeed Khorami	9370 Chesapeake Dr Ste, San Diego CA 92123	858-812-5280	R	14*	<.1
241	Noel Communications Inc—Jon F Burns	PO Box 2965, Yakima WA 98907	509-575-4780	S	14*	<.1
242	Us Telmanagement LLC	21 Sperry Ave, Stratford CT 06615	203-386-9155	R	14*	<.1
243	eOn Communications Corp—James W Hopper	1703 Sawyer Rd, Corinth MS 38834		P	14	.1
244	Mashell Telecom Inc—Brian Haynes	PO Box 639, Eatonville WA 98328	360-832-6161	R	14*	.1
245	Ecommerce Inc—Fathi Said	1774 Dividend Dr, Columbus OH 43228		R	13*	.1
246	Corr Wireless Communications LLC	PO Box 1500, Oneonta AL 35121	205-237-3581	R	13*	.1
247	3 Rivers Telephone Cooperative Inc—Steven R Krogue	PO Box 429, Fairfield MT 59436	406-467-2535	R	13*	.1
248	Woodbury Telephone Co—Donald Porter AT and T Inc	299 Main St S, Woodbury CT 06798		S	13*	.1
249	IMAP Partners LLC—James A Hickstein	795 Main St, Half Moon Bay CA 94019	612-656-1737	R	13*	<.1
250	Add2net Inc—Ronald Riddle	1360 N Hancock St, Anaheim CA 92807	714-521-8150	R	13*	.1
251	IntermediaNet Inc—Phil Koen	PO Box 03006818, Sioux Falls SD 57186	212-375-6375	R	13*	.1
252	Sage Telecom Inc—Brian Kushner	3300 E Renner Rd 350, Richardson TX 75082	214-495-4700	R	12*	.3
253	MedcenterdirectCom Inc—Robert White	3343 Peachtree Rd Ne S, Atlanta GA 30326	404-233-2563	R	12*	.1
254	Combest Inc—Richard Pusbach	1856 Corporate Dr Ste, Norcross GA 30093	770-729-0202	R	12*	.1
255	Vertseek Inc—Michael Wines	20866 Collins St, Woodland Hills CA 91367		R	12*	.5
256	Secureworks Inc—Michael R Cote	1 Concourse Pky Ste 50, Atlanta GA 30328	404-327-6339	S	12*	.1
257	Olm LLC—Chris Silkman	4 Trefoil Dr, Trumbull CT 06611	203-445-7700	R	12*	.1
258	Mountain Rural Telephone Cooperative Inc—Jimmie Jones	PO Box 399, West Liberty KY 41472	606-743-3121	R	12*	.1
259	Amerimex Communications Corp—Don Aldridge	1007 Mansell Rd Ste A, Roswell GA 30076	678-290-1500	R	12*	<.1
260	American Telephone and Data Inc—Victor Rode	PO Box 649, Wheaton IL 60187	630-752-1800	R	12*	<.1
261	Fionda LLC—Rick Stambaugh	2029 Village Ln Ste 10, Santa Barbara CA 93101	805-884-0884	R	12*	<.1
262	Direct Communications Rockland Inc—Leonard May	PO Box 269, Rockland ID 83271	208-548-2345	R	12*	<.1
263	Netwurx—David Kiernan	35 E Summer St, Hartford WI 53027		R	12*	<.1
264	Evergreen Telecom Services LLC—Alexander Rothman	1117 Desert Ln Ste 120, Las Vegas NV 89102		R	12*	.1
265	Blinkx Inc—Suranga Chandratillake	1 Market St Ste 1810, San Francisco CA 94105	415-655-1450	R	12*	.1
266	Drumbeat Digital LLC—Michelle Edwards	460 Park Ave S Fl 10, New York NY 10016	212-941-9041	R	12*	.1
267	Albion Telephone Co—O'deen Redman	PO Box 98, Albion ID 83311	208-673-5335	R	12*	<.1
268	Satcom Global Inc—Adam Thompson	1347 N Alma School Rd, Chandler AZ 85224	480-857-6656	R	12*	<.1
269	Routematch Software Inc—Bahman Irvani	1180 W Peachtree St Nw, Atlanta GA 30309	404-876-5160	R	12*	.1
270	Hotwire Communications LLC—Kristin Johnson	300 E Lancaster Ave, Wynnewood PA 19096	610-642-8570	R	11*	.3
271	Xtel Communications Inc—Don Flynn	401 Rte 73 N Ste 106, Marlton NJ 08053	856-596-4000	R	11*	<.1
272	Eastern Oregon Telecom LLC—Leroy Pilant	1475 N 1st St, Hermiston OR 97838	541-289-7000	R	11*	<.1

Note: An asterisk (*) indicates an estimated financial figure. The company type code used is as follows: R = Private, P = Public, S = Private Subsidiary, B = Public Subsidiary, D = Division, J = Joint Venture, I = Investment Fund.

COMPANY RANKINGS BY SALES WITHIN 4-DIGIT SIC

Rank	Company Name—*Executive Officer*	Address, City, State, Zip	Phone	Type	Fin	Empls
273	Extend America Inc—*Gregory L Rohde*	1915 N Kavaney Dr, Bismarck ND 58501	701-255-9500	R	11*	<.1
274	Hemisphere Communication Inc—*Julius Baldassari*	5655 S Park Ave, Hamburg NY 14075	716-646-1773	R	11*	<.1
275	4medica Inc—*Oleg Bess*	100 Crprate Pnte Ste, Culver City CA 90230	310-695-3300	R	11*	.1
276	Start Wireless Group Inc—*Abdul Andrede*	1615 Timber Wolf Dr, Holland OH 43528	419-382-8603	R	11*	.1
277	Wamego Telephone Company Inc—*Steven Sackrider*	PO Box 25, Wamego KS 66547	785-456-2237	R	11*	<.1
278	Multisoft Inc—*Tammy Lucas*	900 Cir 75 Pkwy Ste 45, Atlanta GA 30339	770-612-8411	R	11*	.1
279	Trillion Digital Communication Inc—*Terry Johnson*	2124 Christina Cv, Birmingham AL 35244	205-733-3710	R	11*	.1
280	Tularosa Basin Telephone Company Inc—*Matthew Boos*	PO Box 550, Tularosa NM 88352	575-585-0125	R	11*	<.1
281	X Tend Communications Inc—*William Shwartz*	171 Madison Ave Fl 8, New York NY 10016	212-725-2000	R	10*	.1
282	Novarra Inc—*Jayanthi Ranjarajah*	1 Pierce Pl Ste 500e, Itasca IL 60143	630-773-0000	R	10*	.1
283	Vernon Telephone Co-Operatives Inc—*Rod Olson*	PO Box 20, Westby WI 54667	608-634-3136	R	10*	<.1
284	Molalla Telephone Co—*Steve Loutzenhiser*	211 Robbins St, Molalla OR 97038	503-829-1100	R	10*	<.1
285	Rmg Direct Inc—*Randy Greenberg*	300 Tri State Internat, Lincolnshire IL 60069	847-948-7400	R	10*	.3
286	Baran Telecom Inc—*Alon Yegnes*	2355 Industrial Park B, Cumming GA 30041	678-455-1181	S	10*	.1
287	Volcano Communications Group—*Sharon J Lundgren*	PO Box 1070, Pine Grove CA 95665	209-296-7502	R	10*	.1
288	Brantley Telephone Company Inc—*A Strickland*	PO Box 255, Nahunta GA 31553	912-462-5111	R	10*	.1
289	Western New Mexico Telephone Co—*Jack Keen*	PO Box 150, Cliff NM 88028	505-535-2291	R	10*	<.1
290	CA Affinity Corp—*Brian Sledz*	1842 Centre Point Cir, Naperville IL 60563		R	10*	<.1
291	Yp Inc—*Michael Mattos*	26895 Aliso Creek Rd, Aliso Viejo CA 92656	949-230-3456	R	10*	<.1
292	Netnames USA Inc—*Geoff Wicks*	55 Broad St Rm 11c, New York NY 10004	212-627-4599	R	10*	.1
293	Interlink Global Corp—*Anastasios N Kyriakides*	6205 Blue Lagoon Dr St, Miami FL 33126	305-261-2007	P	10	<.1
294	AtlanticNet Broadband Inc—*Manoj Puranik*	440 W Kennedy Blvd Ste, Orlando FL 32810	352-375-2912	R	10*	.1
295	Barry County Telephone Co—*William Smith*	PO Box 128, Delton MI 49046	269-623-2311	R	10*	.1
296	Division Of Purchasing	Empire Stat Pz Crng Fl, Albany NY 12242	518-474-3695	R	9*	.1
297	Breda Telephone Corp—*Charles Deisbeck*	PO Box 190, Breda IA 51436	712-673-2311	R	9*	<.1
298	CP Telecom Hickory Tech Corp	209 W 1st St, Duluth MN 55802	218-722-4245	S	9*	.1
299	Reservation Telephone Coop—*Royce Aslakson*	PO BOX 68, Parshall ND 58770	701-862-3115	R	9*	.1
300	Full Service Computing Corp—*David Schwencke*	600 Grant St Ste 3075, Pittsburgh PA 15219	412-745-9000	R	9*	.1
301	Reliance Connects—*Brenda Crosby*	PO Box 189, Estacada OR 97023		R	9*	.1
302	Sandhill Telephone Coop—*Norman P Caldwell*	PO Box 519, Jefferson SC 29718	843-658-3434	R	9*	<.1
303	Academy Communications Inc—*Blair Mooney*	1446 SOM Center Rd, Mayfield Heights OH 44124		R	9*	<.1
304	Tenino Telephone Co—*Charles Peterson*	PO Box 4005, Tenino WA 98589	360-264-2915	R	9*	<.1
305	Sirius Telecommunications Inc—*Chris Edgecomb*	1933 Cliff Dr Ste 28, Santa Barbara CA 93109	805-690-2808	R	9*	.1
306	Switchroom Design LLC—*Bill Smith*	910 15th St Ste 1050, Denver CO 80202	303-571-1773	R	9*	.1
307	Ernest Communications Inc—*Joseph Ernest*	5275 Triangle Pkwy Ste, Norcross GA 30092	770-242-9069	R	9*	.1
308	HostdimeCom Inc—*Emanuel Vivar*	189 S Orange Ave 1500s, Orlando FL 32801	407-756-1126	R	9*	<.1
309	Terra Networks Operations Inc—*Fernando Rodriguez*	95 Merrick Way Ste 706, Coral Gables FL 33134	786-552-1400	R	9*	.1
310	New Hope Telephone Coop—*Tom Wing*	PO Box 452, New Hope AL 35760	256-723-4211	R	9*	<.1
311	Adchemy Inc—*Murthy Nukala*	1001 E Hillsdal Blvd F, Foster City CA 94404	650-594-4600	R	9*	.1
312	Message Technologies Inc—*Mark Abramson*	1995 N Park Pl Se, Atlanta GA 30339	770-240-8000	R	9*	.1
313	Globexplorer LLC—*Rob Shanks*	2121 N Calif Blvd Ste, Walnut Creek CA 94596	925-934-5415	R	8*	.1
314	Grid 4 Communications Inc—*Charles Hopkins*	2107 Crooks Rd, Troy MI 48084	248-244-8100	R	8*	.1
315	Cornerstone Telephone Company LLC—*Hank Decker*	PO Box 509, Troy NY 12181	518-272-1018	R	8*	.1
316	River City Communications Corp	643 W Stadium Ln, Sacramento CA 95834	916-576-8310	R	8*	.1
317	QAI Inc—*John Burke*	17942 Sky Park Cir Ste, Irvine CA 92614	949-553-0370	R	8*	.1
318	Affinity Network Inc—*F Coppy*	250 Pilot Rd Ste 300, Las Vegas NV 89119		R	8*	<.1
319	Trade Network Inc—*Robert Bonavito*	2600 Kitty Hawk Rd Ste, Livermore CA 94551	925-447-9950	R	8*	<.1
320	Rye Telephone Co—*Michelle Anderson*	PO Box 19048, Colorado City CO 81019	719-676-3131	R	8*	<.1
321	DSL Extreme Inc—*Jim Murphy*	21540 Plummer St Ste A, Chatsworth CA 91311		R	8*	<.1
322	Access Technology Inc—*Ken Sikora*	403 Twinridge Ln, Richmond VA 23235	804-320-8399	R	8*	<.1
323	Caprica Internet Services—*Kenneth Taira*	2168 S Atlantic Blvd S, Monterey Park CA 91754		R	8*	<.1
324	PortBridge Internet Services LLC—*Eric Hobbs*	PO Box 4409, Cary NC 27519	919-459-0130	R	8*	<.1
325	AeroSurf Wireless Internet Inc—*Jason Diskin*	27570 Commerce Center, Temecula CA 92590	951-304-9986	R	8*	<.1
326	Cass Telephone Company Inc—*Gerald Gill*	PO Box 230, Virginia IL 62691	217-452-3022	R	8*	.1
327	Phone Power—*Ari Ramezani*	20847 Sherman Way, Winnetka CA 91306	818-264-4400	R	8	.1
328	Red River Rural Telephone Association—*David Hendrickson*	PO Box 136, Abercrombie ND 58001	701-553-8309	R	8*	<.1
329	West Central Telephone Association Inc—*Anthony Mayer*	PO Box 304, Sebeka MN 56477	218-837-5151	R	8*	<.1
330	Silver Star Telephone Company Inc—*Allen Hoopes*	PO Box 226, Freedom WY 83120	307-883-2411	R	8*	.1
331	Stayton Cooperative Telephone Company Inc—*Don Lawrence*	PO Box 477, Stayton OR 97383	503-769-2121	R	8*	.1
332	Sts Telecom LLC—*Keith Kramer*	PO Box 822270, Pembroke Pines FL 33082	954-434-7075	R	8*	.1
333	Education Networks Of America Inc—*David Pierce*	1101 Mcgavock St Ste 3, Nashville TN 37203	615-312-6000	R	8*	.1
334	Mir3Com Inc—*Amir Moussavian*	3398 Carmel Mountain R, San Diego CA 92121	858-724-1200	R	7*	.1
335	Ardmore Telephone Company Inc—*Warren Nunn*	PO Box 549, Ardmore TN 38449	256-423-2131	R	7*	.1
336	Davinci Virtual Office Solutions—*Bill Grodnik*	2150 S 1300 E Ste 200, Salt Lake City UT 84106	801-990-9200	R	7*	.1
337	Polar Communications Mutual Aid Corp—*David L Dunning*	PO Box 270, Park River ND 58270	701-284-7221	R	7*	<.1
338	Worlddoc Inc—*Rahul Singal*	7730 W Sahara Ave Ste, Las Vegas NV 89117	702-821-0818	R	7*	<.1
339	FULLnet Inc (Jasper Indiana)—*John Fullington*	335 Southgate Center, Jasper IN 47546	812-482-3642	R	7*	.1
340	Redline Services LLC—*Jepp Walter*	4929 Atlantic Blvd, Jacksonville FL 32207		R	7*	<.1
341	Innova Communications LLC—*Richard Ellison*	528-FvBy Pass 123, Seneca SC 29678		R	7*	<.1
342	ICN Corp—*Eric Cherry*	1801 S Federal Hwy Ste, Delray Beach FL 33483	561-272-5667	R	7*	.1
343	Citizens Telephone Company Inc—*Tommy Smith*	PO Box 187, Leslie GA 31764	229-874-4145	R	7*	.1
344	Talkpoint Holdings LLC—*Nicholas Balletta*	100 William St Fl 8, New York NY 10038	212-909-2900	R	7*	.1
345	Coast International Inc—*Bijan Moaveni*	14303 W 95th St, Shawnee Mission KS 66215	913-859-9000	R	6*	.1
346	Xchange Telecom Corp—*Alfred West*	3611 14th Ave, Brooklyn NY 11218	718-972-3030	R	6*	.1
347	Webs Inc—*Haroon Mokhtarzada*	1100 Wayne Ave Ste 801, Silver Spring MD 20910	301-960-9000	R	6*	.1
348	Bevcomm—*Bill Eckles*	123 West 7th St, Blue Earth MN 56013	507-526-2822	R	6*	.1
349	Park Region Mutual Telephone Co—*Dave Bickett*	230 W Lincoln Ave, Fergus Falls MN 56537	218-998-2000	R	6*	.1
350	Merchantwired LLC—*Robert Mcbay*	731 W Henry St Ste 200, Indianapolis IN 46225	317-829-0600	R	6*	.1
351	Realitybuy Inc—*Dan Legerskar*	21 Morgan Ste 200, Irvine CA 92618	949-460-2000	R	6*	.1
352	Sandwich Isles Communications Inc—*Albert Hee*	1003 Bishop St Ste 270, Honolulu HI 96813	808-524-8400	R	6*	.1
353	National Law Enforcement Telecommunications System Inc—*Gerry Coleman*	2930 E Camelback Rd St, Phoenix AZ 85016	623-308-3500	R	6*	<.1
354	Northwest Nevada Telco Inc—*John Lawless*	2910 Mill St, Reno NV 89502	775-333-3600	R	6*	<.1
355	Vista Satellite Communications Inc—*Roy Liemer*	73-104 SW 12th Ave, Dania Beach FL 33004	954-838-0900	R	6*	<.1
356	Mid-South Telecommunications Co—*Harry E Bovay Jr*	3355 W Alabama Ste1140, Houston TX 77098	713-626-2051	R	6*	.1
357	American Telecommunications Systems Inc—*Bill Stathakaros*	4450 Belden Village St, Canton OH 44718		R	6*	<.1
358	ShoploopCom Inc—*Eyal Yechezkell*	350 7th Ave Fl 2, New York NY 10001	212-588-1180	R	6*	.1
359	Connective Communications Inc—*Michael Lessin*	43720 Trade Ctr Pl Ste, Dulles VA 20166	202-513-1000	R	6*	.1
360	Vdl Inc—*Dror Mei-Tal*	PO Box 568, Owings Mills MD 21117	410-581-4833	R	6*	<.1

Rank	Company Name—*Executive Officer*	Address, City, State, Zip	Phone	Type	Fin	Empls
361	Pdns LLC—*John Schmoldt*	PO Box 750, Harold KY 41635	606-478-9100	R	6*	.1
362	Clear Creek Mutual Telephone Co—*Mitchell Moore*	18238 S Fischers Mill, Oregon City OR 97045	503-631-2101	R	6*	<.1
363	Nefcom Inc—*Leon Conner*	130 N 4th St, Macclenny FL 32063	904-259-2261	R	6*	.1
364	Xanadoo LLC—*Raymond Harris*	225 E City Ave Ste 100, Bala Cynwyd PA 19004	610-934-7000	R	6*	.1
365	Outernet Inc—*Mike Erwin*	6200 Bridge Point Pkwy, Austin TX 78730	512-215-3500	R	5*	.1
366	Northeast Telecom LLC—*Brent Mcmilleon*	PO Box 219, Collinston LA 71229	318-325-9999	R	5*	<.1
367	Allied Telecom Group LLC—*Nak Phungephorn*	1120 20th St Nw Ste 50, Washington DC 20036	202-541-9000	R	5*	<.1
368	Volcano Telephone Company Inc—*Sharon J Lundgren* Volcano Communications Group	PO Box 1070, Pine Grove CA 95665	209-296-7502	D	5*	.1
369	Golden Belt Telephone Association Inc—*Gerald Washburn*	610 S Cosmos, Elkhart KS 67950	785-372-4236	R	5*	<.1
370	Epic Touch Company Inc—*Trent Boaldin*	610 S Cosmos, Elkhart KS 67950	620-697-2233	R	5*	<.1
371	Regional Communications Inc—*Anthony Sabino Jr*	64 E Midland Ave, Paramus NJ 07652	201-261-6600	R	5*	<.1
372	Cyworld Inc—*In Park*	575 Market St Ste 800, San Francisco CA 94105	415-543-4242	R	5*	<.1
373	North Penn Telephone Company Inc—*Robert Wagner*	PO Box 349, Prattsburgh NY 14873	607-522-3712	R	5*	<.1
374	Fasttone Inc—*Simon Wong*	1230 Stockton St, San Francisco CA 94133	415-989-3299	R	5*	<.1
375	Net World America Inc—*Allan Rees*	901 Bernardo Ct, Pinole CA 94564	510-704-7100	R	5*	<.1
376	Netease Inc—*Bill Perdue*	PO Box 11211, Santa Rosa CA 95406		R	5*	<.1
377	ServicechannelCom—*Steven Gottfried*	9 Albertson Ave Ste 1, Albertson NY 11507	516-240-6800	R	5*	.1
378	Atlantech Online Inc—*Edward Fineran*	1010 Wayne Ave Ste 630, Silver Spring MD 20910	301-589-3060	R	5*	<.1
379	Broadvox LLC—*Isaac Parampottil*	1228 Euclid Ave Ste 39, Cleveland OH 44115	216-373-4600	R	5*	<.1
380	West Side Telephone Co—*James Lauffer*	1449 Fairmont Rd, Morgantown WV 26501	304-983-2211	R	5*	<.1
381	Qbos Inc—*James Lord*	14275 Midway Rd Ste 22, Addison TX 75001	972-233-5066	R	5*	<.1
382	Singapore Telecom USA Inc—*Allen Lew*	100 Marine Pkwy Ste 45, Redwood City CA 94065	650-508-6800	R	5*	<.1
383	Giganews Inc—*Jonah Yokubaitis*	1044 Liberty Park Dr, Austin TX 78746	512-684-9750	R	5*	<.1
384	Internet Junction Corp—*Eric Feinstein*	PO Box 2218, Dunedin FL 34697	813-855-7793	R	5*	<.1
385	Microserv Computer Technologies Inc—*Travis Johnson*	1808 E 17th St, Idaho Falls ID 83404	208-528-6161	R	5*	<.1
386	Inetcity Solutions Inc—*Mark Bray*	PO Box 1148, Sterling Heights MI 48311	586-978-7222	R	5*	<.1
387	Mon-Cre Telephone Cooperative Inc—*Carl Massey*	PO Box 125, Ramer AL 36069	334-562-3242	R	5*	<.1
388	All Communications Inc—*Richard Dean*	PO Box 20368, Saint Petersburg FL 33742	727-573-2620	R	5*	<.1
389	HostrocketCom Inc—*Brendan Brader*	21 Corporate Dr Ste 20, Clifton Park NY 12065	518-371-3421	R	5*	<.1
390	Wave 3 Inc—*Robert Haefner*	15 N Main St, Sapulpa OK 74066	918-877-9200	R	5*	<.1
391	X Brand Networks Inc—*John Prather*	2511 W Shaw Ave Ste 10, Fresno CA 93711	559-420-3900	R	5*	<.1
392	Construction BiddingCom LLC—*R Fortney*	31269 Bradley Rd, North Olmsted OH 44070	440-716-4087	R	4*	.1
393	Allegiant Networks LLC—*Kara Filley*	14643 W 95th St, Shawnee Mission KS 66215	913-599-6900	R	4*	.1
394	West Wisconsin Telcom Cooperative Inc—*Randy Siler*	PO Box 115, Downsville WI 54735	715-664-8311	R	4*	<.1
395	Residential Computing	2510 Channing Way Ste, Berkeley CA 94704	510-643-8463	R	4*	.1
396	Perfectserve Inc—*Terrell Edwards*	1225 E Weisgarber Rd S, Knoxville TN 37909	865-212-5000	R	4*	<.1
397	VndirectNet LLC—*Phong Lai*	15030 Old Hearth Dr, Houston TX 77084	281-221-0055	R	4*	.1
398	Evga Corp—*Andrew Han*	2900 Saturn St Ste B, Brea CA 92821	714-528-4500	R	4*	<.1
399	Coast To Coast Wireless Inc—*Mike Winklepleck*	2633 Harbor Blvd, Costa Mesa CA 92626	714-429-9800	R	4*	<.1
400	CT Wireless—*Michael Conrad*	731 Scioto St, Urbana OH 43078	937-653-2208	R	4*	.1
401	Stormwise Concepts Inc—*Diaz Camilo*	4743 Nw 72nd Ave, Miami FL 33166	305-597-7797	R	4*	.1
402	True Ld LLC—*Mitchelle Valdivia*	2470 W Majestic Park W, Tucson AZ 85705	520-629-4333	R	4*	.1
403	Daxko LLC—*Anthony Crumley*	600 University Park Pl, Birmingham AL 35209	205-437-1400	R	4*	<.1
404	Devine Conulting Inc—*Jeffrey Devine*	39350 Civic Ctr Dr Ste, Fremont CA 94538	510-713-8800	R	4*	.1
405	SLIC Dotcom—*Mark Cornett*	PO Box 5077, Potsdam NY 13676	315-265-3400	R	4*	.1
406	Siskiyou Telephone Co—*Jim Lowers*	PO Box 157, Etna CA 96027	530-467-6000	R	4*	<.1
407	Adams Telephone Coop—*Vern Lubker*	PO Box 217, Golden IL 62339	217-696-4611	R	4*	<.1
408	Community Isp Inc—*Jeffrey Klingshirn*	3035 Moffat Rd, Toledo OH 43615	419-724-5336	R	4*	<.1
409	Hubx Inc—*Michael Murray*	39 Chapel St, Newton MA 02458	617-244-0444	R	4*	<.1
410	Cal-Ore Telephone Co	PO Box 847, Dorris CA 96023	530-397-2211	S	4*	<.1
411	Wiggins Telephone Association—*Terry Hendrickson*	PO Box 690, Wiggins CO 80654	970-483-7343	R	4*	<.1
412	Federated Telephone Co—*Kevin Beyer*	PO Box 156, Chokio MN 56221	320-324-7111	R	4*	<.1
413	Boost Mobile LLC—*Andre Smith*	8845 Irvine Center Dr, Irvine CA 92618		D	4*	<.1
414	CNG Internet Inc—*Gunter Beck*	21 Nottingham Rd, Manalapan NJ 07726	732-842-2144	R	4*	<.1
415	Creative Data Concepts Limited Inc—*Jim Nitterauer*	3 W Garden St Ste 326, Pensacola FL 32502	850-434-7645	R	4*	<.1
416	Fire 2 Wire—*Duane Severson*	PO Box 100, Hughson CA 95326	209-543-1800	R	4*	<.1
417	Internet At Cyber Mesa—*Jane Hill*	4200 Rodeo Rd, Santa Fe NM 87507	505-795-7100	R	4*	.1
418	ItworldCom—*William Reinstein*	118 Tpke Rd, Southborough MA 01772	508-303-9700	R	4*	.1
419	Tactara LLC—*Crosby Haffner*	550 S Hope St Ste 2825, Los Angeles CA 90071	213-221-3200	R	4*	<.1
420	Belcaro Group Inc—*Marc Braunstein*	7100 E Belleview Ave, Greenwood Village CO 80111	303-843-0302	R	4*	<.1
421	Internet Express Inc—*Kris Harris*	524 15th St, Moline IL 61265	309-736-8000	R	4*	<.1
422	I24x7Com—*Todd Tanner*	2818 S Redwood Rd, Salt Lake City UT 84119	801-428-4500	R	4*	<.1
423	Dc Communication LLC	11 Bragg St, East Hartford CT 06108	860-289-8550	R	4*	<.1
424	East Wind Inc—*Yoshiyuki Ito*	4446 173rd Ave Se, Bellevue WA 98006	425-643-7265	R	4*	<.1
425	Cleverbridge Inc—*Craig Vodnik*	360 N Michigan Ave Ste, Chicago IL 60601	312-922-8693	R	4*	<.1
426	Datumcom Corp—*Isaias Sudit*	6926 Royal Orchid Cir, Delray Beach FL 33446	561-210-7414	R	4*	<.1
427	Ghn-Online Inc—*Azadeh Farahmand*	12655 N Central Expy, Dallas TX 75243	214-696-5717	R	4*	<.1
428	Long Distance Partnership LLP—*Bob Cleary*	PO Box 1049, Burlington VT 05402	802-860-0378	R	4*	<.1
429	Executone/Rhode Island Inc—*Douglas Anderson*	993a Waterman Ave, East Providence RI 02914	401-434-4425	R	4*	<.1
430	Orcs Web Inc—*Brad Kingsley*	PO Box 51090, Myrtle Beach SC 29579		R	4*	<.1
431	Localtel Communications—*Dimitri Mandelis*	343 Grant Rd, East Wenatchee WA 98802	509-884-6291	R	4*	<.1
432	Wireless Innovations LLC	205 Rte 46 Ste 2, Totowa NJ 07512	973-441-3955	R	4*	<.1
433	Poplar Bluff Internet Inc—*Brian Becker*	PO Box 190, Poplar Bluff MO 63902	573-686-9114	R	4*	<.1
434	Netherland Typewriter Inc—*Dan Murray*	51 N St, Presque Isle ME 04769	207-769-2691	R	4*	<.1
435	Advanced Phone Solutions Inc—*Kurt Amos*	6700 Broken Sound Pkwy, Boca Raton FL 33487	561-208-0100	R	4*	<.1
436	Saturn Network Services—*Dennis Gallagher*	141 Lattintown Rd, Newburgh NY 12550	212-332-9898	R	4*	<.1
437	Unite Private Networks LLC	PO Box 25526, Kansas City MO 64119	816-903-9400	R	3*	<.1
438	Quick Communications Inc—*Bruce Yuille*	5850 Dixie Hwy, Clarkston MI 48346	248-623-9500	R	3*	<.1
439	Paymentone Corp—*Joe Lynam*	5883 Rue Ferrari, San Jose CA 95138	408-362-4100	R	3*	<.1
440	Washington County Rural Telephone Cooperative Inc—*Roland King*	PO Box 9, Pekin IN 47165	812-967-3171	R	3*	<.1
441	Johnson Communications—*Chad Johnson*	PO Box 366, Burleson TX 76097	817-705-1113	R	3*	<.1
442	Splitrock Properties Inc—*Don Snyders*	PO Box 349, Garretson SD 57030	605-594-3411	R	3*	.1
443	REL Communication Inc—*Robert Murray*	12 Parmenter Rd Unit D, Londonderry NH 03053	603-421-0270	R	3*	<.1
444	Aep Networks Inc—*Pat Donnellan*	347 Elizabeth Ave Ste, Somerset NJ 08873	732-652-5200	R	3*	<.1
445	Apollo Hosting Inc—*Martin Field*	3267 Bee Cave Rd, Austin TX 78746	512-261-1203	R	3*	<.1
446	Global-Pc Networks Inc—*Eduardo Camamar*	6423 Mcpherson Rd Ste, Laredo TX 78041	956-791-9999	R	3*	<.1
447	Global Access Communications Inc—*Marcus Mullings*	131 Dorchester Rd, Hackensack NJ 07601	201-343-5922	R	3*	<.1
448	Cellere LLC—*Papillon Erreca*	4110 Copper Ridge Dr S, Traverse City MI 49684	231-929-4555	R	3*	<.1

Note: An asterisk (*) indicates an estimated financial figure. The company type code used is as follows: R = Private, P = Public, S = Private Subsidiary, B = Public Subsidiary, D = Division, J = Joint Venture, I = Investment Fund.

COMPANY RANKINGS BY SALES WITHIN 4-DIGIT SIC

Rank	Company Name—Executive Officer	Address, City, State, Zip	Phone	Type	Fin	Empls
449	IC Interconnect LLC—Curt Erickson	1025 Elkton Dr, Colorado Springs CO 80907	719-533-1030	R	3*	<.1
450	Cheyenne River Sioux Tribe Telephone Authority—G Williams	PO Box 810, Eagle Butte SD 57625	605-964-2600	R	3*	<.1
451	Mid Missouri Telephone Co—Gary Romig	215 Roe St, Pilot Grove MO 65276	660-834-3311	R	3*	<.1
452	KD Marketing Inc—Michael Spinn	3500 Comanche Rd Ne A3, Albuquerque NM 87107	505-338-2300	R	3*	<.1
453	Heller Information Services Inc—Paul Heller	30 W Gude Dr Ste 220, Rockville MD 20850	301-255-0500	R	3*	.1
454	Cross Telephone Co—V David Miller II	PO Box 9, Warner OK 74469	918-463-2921	R	3*	<.1
455	Northstar Access—Mary Michaels	210 Main St S, Cambridge MN 55008	763-691-0885	R	3*	<.1
456	Farmers Mutual Telephone Co—Dale Koehler	608 E Congress St, Nora Springs IA 50458	641-749-2531	R	3*	<.1
457	Hinton Telephone Co—Kenneth Doughty	PO Box 1040, Hinton OK 73047	405-542-3262	R	3*	<.1
458	Knology—Chris Dupree	2660 Montgomery Hwy, Dothan AL 36303	334-899-3333	S	3	<.1
459	Seacoast Telecommunication Service Bureau Inc—Ken Mcdavitt	PO Box 216, Dover NH 03821	603-742-1959	R	3*	<.1
460	Telnet Worldwide Inc—Patrick Leary	1175 W Long Lake Rd St, Troy MI 48098	248-485-1000	R	3*	<.1
461	Aircanopy Internet Services Inc—Phil Walsh	3261 Fm 663 Ste D, Midlothian TX 76065	972-617-8889	R	3*	<.1
462	Ethan Interactive Inc—Jared Hunnell	2 Miranova Pl Ste 320, Columbus OH 43215	614-298-8100	R	3*	<.1
463	Haviland Telephone Co—Gene Morris	PO Box 308, Haviland KS 67059	620-862-5211	S	3*	<.1
464	Maynard Group Inc—Dean Maynard	PO Box 166, Soquel CA 95073	831-462-0777	R	3*	<.1
465	Northwind Financial Inc—Arthur Erickson	6704 Foxcroft Rd, Prospect KY 40059	502-244-1234	R	3*	<.1
466	Creative Online Computer Services Inc—Dianne Widmeyer	PO Box 2158, Granite Bay CA 95746	916-569-2900	R	3*	<.1
467	Custom Computer Designs Corp—Jonathan Smith	5700 Logan St, Denver CO 80216	303-460-0900	R	3*	<.1
468	Elegant Office Inc—Melinda Farrell	5200 Nw 43rd St Ste 10, Gainesville FL 32606	352-332-3613	R	3*	<.1
469	Blinkmind Inc—Joe Baird	2027 Briarchester Dr, Katy TX 77450	408-648-4800	R	3*	<.1
470	Idiom Communications LLC—David Sharnoff	2625 Alcatraz Ave Ste, Berkeley CA 94705	510-595-4321	R	3*	<.1
471	Network America—Steven Poole	1029 13th St, Bedford IN 47421	812-277-1499	R	3*	<.1
472	UxPro Consulting Services Inc—Don Caprio	PO Box 1487, Discovery Bay CA 94505	925-240-8649	R	3*	<.1
473	CTTS Information Services—James Lee	2658 Griffith Park Blv, Los Angeles CA 90039	323-660-7722	R	3*	<.1
474	Frontera Telecommunications Inc—Curtis Hunt	2123 Sidney Baker St, Kerrville TX 78028	830-257-9882	R	3*	<.1
475	Zangle Inc—Paul Charlton	10080 N Wolfe Rd, Cupertino CA 95014	408-350-8200	R	3*	<.1
476	Acp Interactive LLC—Camille Wehner	150 Spear St Ste 700, San Francisco CA 94105	415-357-5100	R	3*	<.1
477	Netro City Design and Information Systems Inc—James Andrus	33 S Commercial St, Manchester NH 03101	603-222-9004	R	3*	<.1
478	Protel Communications Inc—John Wittman	13851 Danielson St, Poway CA 92064	858-218-2000	R	3*	<.1
479	Road 9 Inc—Jim King	PO Box 3528, Englewood CO 80155	303-468-1829	R	3*	<.1
480	Optical and Telecommunication Solutions Inc—Sam Orendain	PO Box 2327, Addison TX 75001	972-931-0360	R	3*	<.1
481	Imagination Inc—Beth Montes	PO Box 834, Sedalia MO 65302	660-829-4638	R	3*	<.1
482	Project Austin Inc—Reza Mosin	8000 Marina Blvd Fl 8, Brisbane CA 94005	650-952-1100	R	3*	<.1
483	Jungle Lasers LLC—Amy Doidge	201 Main St Ste 2, Allenhurst NJ 07711	732-502-3100	R	3*	<.1
484	Rendition Networks—Raghav Kher	10735 Willows Rd Ne St, Redmond WA 98052	425-636-2148	R	3*	<.1
485	River Valley Telecommunications Coop—David Jacobson	PO Box 250, Graettinger IA 51342	712-859-3300	R	3*	<.1
486	Serverplus LLC—Brad Gardner	PO Box 970842, Orem UT 84097	801-426-8283	R	3*	<.1
487	Accurate Communications Corp—Ron Kirkpatrick	PO Box 772197, Memphis TN 38177	901-797-8900	R	3*	<.1
488	Radix Ii Inc—Holly Wallace	6178 Oxon Hill Rd Ste, Oxon Hill MD 20745	301-567-5200	R	3*	<.1
489	Teledata Communications LLC—Cindy Deane	10620 Widmer Rd, Lenexa KS 66215	913-663-2010	R	3*	<.1
490	F4w Inc—Patrick Callahan	39 Skyline Dr Ste 1001, Lake Mary FL 32746	407-804-1020	R	3*	<.1
491	Connectlink Inc—Phil Henson	PO Box 128, Chesapeake OH 45619	740-867-5095	R	3*	<.1
492	Ipremise Inc—Rob Bosch	8200 S Quebec St Ste A, Centennial CO 80112		R	3*	<.1
493	Italk Global Communications Inc—Jack Zhao	1101 S Cpitl Of Texas, West Lake Hills TX 78746	512-637-1450	R	3*	<.1
494	Revering Group Inc—George Revering	222 S Clayborn Ave, Parkers Prairie MN 56361	218-338-4000	R	3*	<.1
495	Mystateusa—Claudia Bitner	PO Box 809, Star ID 83669	208-377-1960	R	3*	<.1
496	U-Tec Construction Inc—Larry Wilson	926 Ridgedale Dr, Lawrenceville GA 30043	770-237-0805	R	3*	.1
497	PC Fling—Ryan Varner	1217 Walnut St, Highland IL 62249	618-654-7841	R	3*	<.1
498	Community Network Services Inc—Faye Manghir	101 Park Ave Rm 2501, New York NY 10178		R	3*	<.1
499	Southern Datacom Inc—Gina Pounds	3508 Montopolis Dr, Austin TX 78744	512-448-7800	R	3*	<.1
500	Novatel Ltd—Paul Golibart	11550 Ih 10 W Ste 110, San Antonio TX 78230	210-698-8005	R	3*	<.1
501	Nirvanix Inc—Scott Genereux	4445 Estgate Mall Ste, San Diego CA 92121	619-764-5650	R	3*	<.1
502	Eastern Telephone and Telecommunications Inc—Fusun Bubernack	2360 Ave A, Bethlehem PA 18017	610-867-7800	R	3*	<.1
503	Plexus M/2 Holdings LLC—Kyle Martell	PO Box 310820, Miami FL 33231	305-653-5352	R	3*	<.1
504	Wahkiakum West Telephone Inc—Carlton Appelo	PO Box 99, Rosburg WA 98643	360-465-2211	R	3*	<.1
505	Allnet Services Inc—Russell Wilkins	2251 Orpheus Ct, Bakersfield CA 93308	661-322-6900	R	3*	<.1
506	Internet Development Company LLC—Jan Daiker	111 N Canal St Ste 941, Chicago IL 60606	312-669-7547	R	3*	<.1
507	Isupportisp LLC—Stephan West	PO Box 328923, Columbus OH 43232	614-586-4040	R	3*	<.1
508	Venture Communications Inc—Harry Thomas	PO Box 157, Highmore SD 57345	605-852-2224	R	2*	.1
509	Econotek LLC—Lisa Scordamaglia	352 7th Ave Fl 11, New York NY 10001	212-631-7556	R	2*	<.1
510	Integrated Comtel Inc—Louis Darnell	2412 Rose St Ste 202, Honolulu HI 96819	808-356-0010	R	2*	<.1
511	International Access Inc—William Wade	725 Lakefield Rd Ste G, Westlake Village CA 91361	805-374-2460	R	2*	<.1
512	Metronet-Telecom Inc—Joseph Choma	2182 Cedar St, Holt MI 48842	517-694-1101	R	2*	<.1
513	New York Internet Company Inc—Erik Koblence	PO Box 1702, New York NY 10268	212-269-1999	R	2*	<.1
514	Teamwork Telecom Inc	8150 Garvey Ave Ste 11, Rosemead CA 91770	626-288-0772	R	2*	<.1
515	Vbnet Inc—Jack Calloway	250 N Orange Ave Ste 3, Orlando FL 32801	407-996-8000	R	2*	<.1
516	Benefitnation Inc—Mike Donohue	21355 Ridgetop Cir Ste, Dulles VA 20166	703-433-1277	R	2*	<.1
517	Home Link Of Nevada Inc—Mat Matson	6221 Industrial Rd, Las Vegas NV 89118	702-260-1588	R	2*	<.1
518	Pen Publishing Interactive Inc—Steve Pendergraft	PO Box 782302, Wichita KS 67278	316-651-0551	R	2*	<.1
519	Serverbeach Ltd—Ruben Dominguez	8500 Vicar Ste 500, San Antonio TX 78218	210-798-4400	R	2*	<.1
520	Imbris Inc—Hilary Anderson	610 W Hubbard St Ste 1, Coeur D Alene ID 83814	208-292-5000	R	2*	<.1
521	Supernova Systems Inc—Terry Miller	360 N Main St Ste G, Bluffton IN 46714	260-824-9612	R	2*	<.1
522	Golden Bridge Technology Inc—Kourosh Parsa	25 James Way, Eatontown NJ 07724	732-870-8088	R	2*	<.1
523	Servint Corp—Reed Caldwell	6861 Elm St Ste 2b, Mc Lean VA 22101	703-847-1381	R	2*	<.1
524	West Michigan Internet Services Inc—Robert Servis	2007 Eastcastle Dr Se, Grand Rapids MI 49508	616-588-9647	R	2*	<.1
525	Johnson Telephone Co—Conrad Johnson	PO Box 39, Remer MN 56672	218-566-2302	R	2*	<.1
526	Iformata LLC—Valerie Barker	130 W 2nd St Ste 1111, Dayton OH 45402	937-832-6900	R	2*	<.1
527	Zebra Network LLC	3919 Turnberry Ln, Okemos MI 48864	517-712-9199	R	2*	<.1
528	Web Fire Communications Inc—Dennis Mcaden	3406 Mcniel Ave, Wichita Falls TX 76308	940-691-7578	R	2*	<.1
529	Falcon Communications Solutions Inc—Creston Owen	PO Box 590, Manassas VA 20108	703-335-5000	R	2*	<.1
530	AgentlifeCom LLC	5350 W Kennedy Blvd, Tampa FL 33609	813-282-7400	R	2*	<.1
531	Lakefield Telephone Co—Glenn Sonnenburg	PO Box 102, Newton WI 53063	920-758-2211	R	2*	<.1
532	Mailcentro Inc—David Saykally	715 Sutter St Ste B, Folsom CA 95630	916-985-4445	R	2*	<.1
533	Speed Link—Jack Evans	1447 Keats Ave, Naperville IL 60564	630-904-5254	R	2*	<.1
534	Dynamic Solutions Worldwide Inc—Shellie Verbiest	246 Pocono Mountain La, Bushkill PA 18324	570-588-1152	R	2*	<.1
535	Fredericksburg Regional Telework Center—Jennifer Alcott	4956 Southpoint Pkwy, Fredericksburg VA 22407	540-710-5001	R	2*	<.1

Rank	Company Name—*Executive Officer*	Address, City, State, Zip	Phone	Type	Fin	Empls
536	Prescient Worldwide—*Cynthi Nappi*	1 Barnes Park S, Wallingford CT 06492	203-679-7000	R	2*	<.1
537	Link Aka Communications Corp—*Joseph Marino*	305 W Broadway, New York NY 10013	718-496-2541	R	2*	<.1
538	Talent Networks Inc—*Richard Troost*	7448 Champagne Pl, Boca Raton FL 33433	561-338-2950	R	2*	<.1
539	Texas Communications Inc—*William Bergman*	4309 Maple St, Abilene TX 79602	325-695-6962	R	2*	<.1
540	Traknet—*Alan Kurwoski*	6891 E Genesee St, Fayetteville NY 13066	315-446-2898	R	2*	<.1
541	World Online Inc—*Chand Akkineni*	4470 Chamblee Dunwoody, Atlanta GA 30338	770-458-2727	R	2*	<.1
542	Wilmur Communications Inc—*Daniel Murphy*	224 N 76th St Stop 1, Milwaukee WI 53213	414-231-0034	R	2*	<.1
543	Biltmore Communications Inc—*Jeff Levy*	817 W Peachtree St Nw, Atlanta GA 30308	404-961-7010	R	2*	<.1
544	Falcon Broadband Inc—*Randy Deyoung*	707 Hanaway Dr, Colorado Springs CO 80915	719-573-5343	R	2*	<.1
545	NewNet Inc—*Dan Sheehy*	2101 Rosecrans Ave Ste, El Segundo CA 90245	310-646-6000	R	2*	<.1
546	Sierra Communications Inc—*Anelle Briesh*	PO Box 67, Des Moines NM 88418	575-445-5364	R	2*	<.1
547	American Telesis Inc—*Monica Bauer*	PO Box 6659, Hilton Head Island SC 29938	843-842-6099	R	2*	<.1
548	Network South Inc—*Jerry Norris*	PO Box 20424, Raleigh NC 27619	919-872-4771	R	2*	<.1
549	Illinois Payphone Systems Inc—*Mark Shmikler*	7720 W 99th St, Oak Lawn IL 60457	708-598-7200	R	2*	<.1
550	Popular Front Studio Inc—*Michael Keefe*	555 1st Ave Ne, Minneapolis MN 55413	612-362-0900	R	2*	<.1
551	Secure Family Records—*Stephen Petty*	5802 Bob Bullock Loop, Laredo TX 78041	210-568-9854	R	2*	<.1
552	Clear-Tone Communications Incorporated LLC—*Anthony Laino*	166 Industrial Loop, Staten Island NY 10309	718-605-2000	R	2	<.1
553	IdeiaCom—*Bob Wollheim*	23 Renwick St, New York NY 10013	212-966-2236	R	2*	<.1
554	Virtual Clinic Inc—*Liindsey Broughs*	2047 152nd Ave Ne, Redmond WA 98052	425-562-3271	R	2*	<.1
555	Integrated Wireless Communications—*Dawit Hailab*	1421 Shadwell Cir, Lake Mary FL 32746	407-538-0001	R	2*	<.1
556	Dct Technologies Inc—*David Troup*	PO Box 33013, Green Bay WI 54303	920-436-0888	R	2*	<.1
557	Turbowave Inc—*Jacques Jonassaint*	299 S Main St Fl 17, Salt Lake City UT 84111	801-534-4430	R	2*	<.1
558	Tagmar Inc—*Timothy Gordon*	410 W Fallbrook Ave St, Fresno CA 93711	559-490-2800	R	2*	<.1
559	Trustedid Inc—*Scott Mitic*	303 Twin Dolphin Dr St, Redwood City CA 94065	650-631-8100	R	2*	<.1
560	World Net Services Inc—*Brian Adam*	9543 S 700 E Ste 200, Sandy UT 84070	801-571-0016	R	2*	<.1
561	Colonial Telephone Co—*John Pearce*	PO Box 727, Bay Springs MS 39422	601-764-3173	R	2*	<.1
562	Rawls and Winstead Inc—*Benjamin Winstead*	PO Box 7009, Rocky Mount NC 27804	252-937-4118	R	2*	<.1
563	Telescan Corp—*Roger Young*	10679 Midwest Industri, Saint Louis MO 63132	314-426-7662	R	2*	<.1
564	Vant Systems Inc—*Dirk Van Tamelen*	5210 Lewis Rd Bldg 8, Agoura Hills CA 91301	818-706-1733	R	2*	<.1
565	Ads Up LLC—*Garry Scott*	3921 14th Ave, Brooklyn NY 11218		R	2*	<.1
566	Sti Management LLC	PO Box 1317, Coshocton OH 43812	740-623-2662	R	2*	<.1
567	Tristate Bellcom Corp—*Abe Lerber*	1656 53rd St, Brooklyn NY 11204	718-435-2402	R	2*	<.1
568	Piedmont Telephone Membership Corp—*Barbara Wood*	PO Box 2066, Lexington NC 27293	336-787-5433	R	2*	<.1
569	My Therapy Net Inc—*Kathleen Derrig-Palumbo*	6455 Corbin Ave, Woodland Hills CA 91367	818-401-0302	R	2*	<.1
570	Onestop Wireless Inc—*Daniel Laue*	PO Box 370, Etiwanda CA 91739	909-355-0800	R	2*	<.1
571	Frontier Communications of Viroqua Inc—*Maggie Boulderado* Frontier Communications Corp	PO Box 191, Viroqua WI 54665	608-637-2111	S	2	<.1
572	TelephoneBiz Inc—*Hensley West*	4440 N Industrial Dr, Cumming GA 30041	678-648-5095	R	2*	<.1
573	Trans Global Communication Enterprises Inc—*Ricardo Cruz*	4995 Nw 72nd Ave Ste 3, Miami FL 33166	305-477-8686	R	2*	<.1
574	Geetingsville Telephone Company Inc	9155 N County Rd 200 E, Frankfort IN 46041	765-258-3111	R	2*	<.1
575	Diamond Lane—*Mary Nicolaus*	2415 Radley Ct Ste 1, Hayward CA 94545	510-782-6825	R	2*	<.1
576	Dobbs Inventory Services Inc—*Charles Dobbs*	PO Box 1626, Suisun City CA 94585		R	2*	<.1
577	2INTERACTIVE LLC—*Brock Eastman*	3008 Cohasset Rd, Chico CA 95973	530-343-6777	R	2*	<.1
578	Leadswell Inc—*Matthew Payne*	PO Box 170432, San Francisco CA 94117	415-518-6701	R	2*	<.1
579	TerreNAP Data Centers Inc—*Manuel D Medina* Terremark Worldwide Inc	50 NE 9th St, Miami FL 33132	305-328-8000	S	2*	<.1
580	Southwest Cyberport Inc—*Mark Costlow*	5021 Indian School Rd, Albuquerque NM 87110	505-232-7992	R	2*	<.1
581	Ec/Edi Inc—*Steve Montgomery*	2241 Pinnacle Pkwy, Twinsburg OH 44087	330-425-0580	R	2*	<.1
582	Gte Service Office—*Tommy Miller*	207 Church St, Laurens SC 29360	864-984-7311	R	2*	<.1
583	Mountain View Telephone Co—*Calvin Czeschin*	PO Box 70, Mountain View AR 72560	870-269-3232	R	2*	<.1
584	Advanced Global Communications Inc—*Chris Keller*	PO Box 177, Prospect KY 40059	502-583-6000	R	2*	<.1
585	Benton Cooperative Telephone Co—*Raymond Thompson*	2220 125th St Nw, Rice MN 56367	320-393-2115	R	2*	<.1
586	All Service Telecommunications—*Jo Bilancini*	PO Box 839, Elyria OH 44036	440-324-6644	R	2*	<.1
587	Dialup USA Inc—*Brandon Mullenberg*	4720 200th St Sw Ste 1, Lynnwood WA 98036		R	2*	<.1
588	Smsonline Net LLC—*Sharon Schroebel*	18909 Shepherdstown Pk, Keedysville MD 21756	301-432-5088	R	2*	<.1
589	Maclee Virtual Sysytems LLC—*Leon Cohen*	429 Lenox Ave, Miami Beach FL 33139		R	2*	<.1
590	Reptel Inc—*John Abram*	23623 N Scottsdale Rd, Scottsdale AZ 85255	623-935-3999	R	2*	<.1
591	Cdt Resources LLC	PO Box 143, Allendale NJ 07401	201-785-1090	R	2*	<.1
592	Herakles LLC—*Laurence Stancil*	1100 N Market Blvd, Sacramento CA 95834	916-679-2100	R	2*	<.1
593	Netstream Communications LLC—*Marisa Flores*	200 Sandy Springs Pl N, Atlanta GA 30328	404-531-0080	R	2*	<.1
594	Weatherflow Inc—*Daniel Lyons*	108 Whispering Pines D, Scotts Valley CA 95066	831-438-9740	R	2*	<.1
595	Hypernet Communications Inc—*Douglas Bowyer*	205 E Henderson St, Cleburne TX 76031	817-517-6000	R	2*	<.1
596	Bossier Parish Communications District 1 Inc—*Tracy Hilburn*	PO Box 847, Benton LA 71006	318-965-2911	R	2*	<.1
597	Lacityweb Inc—*William Watchulonis*	PO Box 8418, Van Nuys CA 91409	818-943-2197	R	2*	<.1
598	Host Depot Inc—*Mark Erskine*	12524 W Atlantic Blvd, Coral Springs FL 33071	954-340-3527	R	2*	<.1
599	Intrahome Technologies Inc—*Steven D'Addone*	74 Coit St, Irvington NJ 07111		R	2*	<.1
600	Xtelesis Corp—*Scott Strochak*	1640 Gilbreth Rd, Burlingame CA 94010	650-239-1400	R	2*	<.1
601	Freight Bay LLC—*Tom Obyrne*	5855 N 94th St Ste 3, Milwaukee WI 53225	414-463-2415	R	2*	<.1
602	Perspective Network—*Victoria Rutt*	116 E 37th St Apt 2b, New York NY 10016	212-993-1000	R	2*	<.1
603	Austin's Bestline Inc—*Grant Riemer*	500 N Capital Of Texas, Austin TX 78746	512-328-9095	R	2*	<.1
604	Pumpkin Networks Inc—*Andrew Sohn*	1245 Oakmead Pkwy Ste, Sunnyvale CA 94085	408-736-0062	R	2*	<.1
605	Mktc Telenet USA Inc—*Philip Gorbulsky*	7639 169th St, Fresh Meadows NY 11366	718-820-0551	R	2*	<.1
606	Under-Communication Inc—*David Hermansader*	198 Mullet Run, Milford DE 19963	302-424-1554	R	2*	<.1
607	Equivoice LLC—*Sheri Thomas*	200 N Harrison St Ste, Algonquin IL 60102	847-429-1700	R	2*	<.1
608	Pilosoft Inc—*Alex Pilosov*	55 Broad St Frnt 3, New York NY 10004		R	2*	<.1
609	Velocenet Inc—*Daniel Williford*	1121 Radio Rd, Statesville NC 28677	704-397-2258	R	2*	<.1
610	David C Rowe—*David Rowe*	629 Easy St, Bridgeport WV 26330	304-842-5555	R	2*	<.1
611	Triple J Communications LLC	2760 N Eastown Rd, Elida OH 45807	419-234-6432	R	2*	<.1
612	Cbi Communications—*Eric Larson*	6515 Highland Rd Ste 1, Waterford MI 48327	248-666-8880	R	2*	<.1
613	Clifford Thackson Inc—*Westley Clifford*	1040 King Stables Cir, Birmingham AL 35242	205-991-2635	R	2*	<.1
614	Commercial Wireless Solutions LP—*Richard Burchfield*	PO Box 841691, Houston TX 77284	713-472-9700	R	2*	<.1
615	Hivelocity Ventures Corp—*William Linton*	4465 W Gandy Blvd Ste, Tampa FL 33611		R	2*	<.1
616	Irides LLC—*Matthew Dennin*	1000 Wilson Blvd Ste 2, Arlington VA 22209	703-236-7900	R	2*	<.1
617	One Touch Inc—*James Scarborough*	1108a Russell Pkwy, Warner Robins GA 31088	478-922-6565	R	2*	<.1
618	Commnet Communications Network Inc—*Lonnie Danchik*	PO Box 551447, Dallas TX 75355	214-349-8521	R	2*	<.1
619	Inverselogic LLC	3439 Ocean View Blvd, Glendale CA 91208	818-542-3103	R	2*	<.1
620	Mud Lake Tele Co-Op Association Inc—*Dale Cope*	PO Box 235, Dubois ID 83423	208-374-5401	R	2*	<.1
621	Forona Technologies Inc—*Jason Rudolph*	2033 6th Ave Ste 830, Seattle WA 98121	206-973-2130	R	2*	<.1
622	Hayes And Associates Inc—*James Hayes*	PO Box 1389, Rural Hall NC 27045	336-969-1871	R	2*	<.1
623	Global Gateway Communications Inc—*Michael Nelson*	2500 Quantum Lakes Dr, Boynton Beach FL 33426	561-853-2213	R	2*	<.1

Note: An asterisk (*) indicates an estimated financial figure. The company type code used is as follows: R = Private, P = Public, S = Private Subsidiary, B = Public Subsidiary, D = Division, J = Joint Venture, I = Investment Fund.

COMPANY RANKINGS BY SALES WITHIN 4-DIGIT SIC

Rank	Company Name—*Executive Officer*	Address, City, State, Zip	Phone	Type	Fin	Empls
624	Wholesale East Coast Phone Card Express—*Tan Pham*	4947 Oriskany Dr, Annandale VA 22003	703-354-7288	R	2*	<.1
625	World Telecommunications—*Donny Fan*	453 Stanford Dr, Arcadia CA 91007	626-487-9917	R	2*	<.1
626	Microglobe Networkz Inc—*Gregory Brown*	PO Box 441261, Kennesaw GA 30160	404-526-6232	R	2*	<.1
627	Central Louisiana Communication—*Tracy Belt*	309 E Mark St, Marksville LA 71351	318-253-9912	R	1*	<.1
628	NCTC Internet—*Duncan Mcgregor*	PO Box 700, Gibbon NE 68840	308-468-6341	R	1*	<.1
629	Tri-Com LLC—*Judisch Denys*	PO Box 330, Geneseo IL 61254	309-944-2103	R	1*	<.1
630	Coin Phones Inc—*Jeffrey Bittner*	777 E Eads Pkwy Ste B, Greendale IN 47025	812-537-3301	R	1*	<.1
631	Venture Group Enterprises Inc—*Doug Turpin*	2520 Whitehall Park Dr, Charlotte NC 28273	704-676-0160	R	1*	<.1
632	Workable Programs and Systems Inc—*Bruce Jones*	3100 Arlington St, Ada OK 74820	580-332-6601	R	1*	<.1
633	Pervasip Corp—*Paul Riss*	75 S Broadway Ste 400, White Plains NY 10601	212-404-7633	P	1	<.1
634	Turtle Mountain Communications—*Ken Carlson*	501 11th St W Ste 2, Bottineau ND 58318	701-228-1101	R	1*	<.1
635	Wmg Pso LLC	12100 W Olympic Blvd, Los Angeles CA 90064	310-407-0204	R	1*	<.1
636	Indiana Data Center LLC—*Viktoria Bergman*	620 W Coliseum Blvd St, Fort Wayne IN 46808	260-407-7474	R	1*	<.1
637	Infomedia Service Corp—*Ricardo Acosta*	8300 Nw 53rd St Ste 35, Miami FL 33166	305-418-4550	R	1*	<.1
638	Telecentre Of Indiana Inc—*Craig Lyon*	45 Hickory Ridge Cir, Cicero IN 46034	317-877-4545	R	1*	<.1
639	Axletree Media Inc—*Bill Nix*	2600 E S Blvd, Montgomery AL 36116	334-613-8189	R	1*	<.1
640	Cxp Solutions LLC	900 S Shackleford Rd S, Little Rock AR 72211	501-907-6686	R	1*	<.1
641	Commercial Telephone Installations—*Bryan Henderson*	712 S Saint Marys St, San Antonio TX 78205	210-824-5035	R	1*	<.1
642	Pathway Computing Inc—*Horace Demmink*	1515 Madison Ave Se, Grand Rapids MI 49507	616-225-5224	R	1*	<.1
643	Abselcom Inc—*Dennis Lyons*	PO Box 429, Englishtown NJ 07726	212-269-1800	R	1*	<.1
644	Americall Communications Company Inc—*Eugene Dinardo*	447 N Walnut St, Springfield IL 62702	217-522-2255	R	1*	<.1
645	Adeia Technologies Inc—*Martina Miller*	18666 W 157th Ter Ste, Olathe KS 66062	913-323-6869	R	1*	<.1
646	Zezan Global Inc—*Sami Siddiqi*	5039 Prairie Sage Rd, Naperville IL 60564	630-202-4541	R	1*	<.1
647	Xiosoft Inc—*Richard Raddatz*	PO Box 2433, Parker CO 80134	303-468-2110	R	1*	<.1
648	Citizen Telephone Corp—*Gordon Laymon*	426 N Wayne St, Warren IN 46792	260-375-2111	R	1*	<.1
649	Netriver Inc—*Adam Vierra*	4200 194th St Sw Ste 1, Lynnwood WA 98036	425-741-7014	R	1*	<.1
650	Rad Video Inc—*Douglas Richardson*	1947 Fern St Ste 5, San Diego CA 92102	619-230-0363	R	1*	<.1
651	Education World Inc—*Peter Sibley*	5471 Kearny Villa Rd S, San Diego CA 92123	858-712-9341	R	1*	<.1
652	Intercage Inc—*Emil Kacperski*	200 Paul Ave, San Francisco CA 94124	415-508-2880	R	1*	<.1
653	Affiliated Sports Management Company Inc—*W Kitchen*	13747 Montfort Dr Ste, Dallas TX 75240	972-503-5501	R	1*	<.1
654	Affilisys LLC—*Mario Dorizas*	1220 N Market St, Wilmington DE 19801	302-861-1448	R	1*	<.1
655	Smart City—*Patrick Flanagan*	800 W Katella Ave, Anaheim CA 92802	714-765-8600	R	1*	<.1
656	Power Shift Computer Services Inc—*Joseph Allen*	PO Box 127, Stowe VT 05672	802-253-6287	R	1*	<.1
657	Fitness Venture Group Inc—*Richard Novelli*	8889 E Bell Rd Ste 102, Scottsdale AZ 85260	602-867-1324	R	1*	<.1
658	North Country Internet Access Inc—*Jeff Schall*	38 Glen Ave Ste 3, Berlin NH 03570	603-752-1250	R	1*	<.1
659	Arkansas Inet LLC—*Fred Wood*	10500 W Markham St Ste, Little Rock AR 72205	501-954-9090	R	1*	<.1
660	Audiology Online Inc—*Jane Weeden*	19202 Huebner Rd Ste 1, San Antonio TX 78258	210-615-6831	R	1*	<.1
661	Clickiq Inc—*Andrew Atkins*	2001 Killebrew Dr Ste, Minneapolis MN 55425	612-915-7060	R	1*	<.1
662	Mainstreet Communications LLC—*Tony Gebhardt*	831 Main St S, Sauk Centre MN 56378	320-352-1460	R	1*	<.1
663	Access Highway Inc—*Pat Prague*	96 Carleton Ave, Central Islip NY 11722	631-232-9119	R	1*	<.1
664	Dreamscape Online LLC—*Jeremiah O McCarthy*	17 Technology Pl, East Syracuse NY 13057	315-671-6200	S	1*	<.1
665	Globalscope Communications Corp—*Isabel Gonzaba*	7400 Blanco Rd Ste 200, San Antonio TX 78216	210-321-3700	R	1*	<.1
666	Web 1 Capital Inc—*Bob Sereico*	1242 Timberlane Rd, Tallahassee FL 32312	850-893-4031	R	1*	<.1
667	Syracuse Online LLC—*Michele Sardina*	5706 Widwaters Pkwy 3, Syracuse NY 13214	315-251-1810	R	1*	<.1
668	Seed Corn Advertising Inc—*Andrew Stern*	3150 Laurel Canyon Blv, Studio City CA 91604	323-822-3551	R	1*	<.1
669	Transecur Inc—*Noel Koch*	51 Monroe St Ste 110, Rockville MD 20850	301-315-2223	R	1*	<.1
670	Advantage Telecommunications Corp—*Sonya A Bly*	3001 Aloma Ave Ste 304, Winter Park FL 32792		R	1*	<.1
671	California Internet Inc—*Jim Persky*	105 W Clay St, Ukiah CA 95482	707-468-1005	R	1*	<.1
672	CorpisCom Inc—*Robert Krueger*	620 W Coliseum Blvd, Fort Wayne IN 46808	260-407-7474	R	1*	<.1
673	Hawaii Information Consortium—*Russell Castagnaro*	201 Merchant St Ste 18, Honolulu HI 96813	808-587-4220	R	1*	<.1
674	Idaho Information Consortium—*Jeff Walker*	999 Main St Ste 910, Boise ID 83702	208-332-0102	R	1*	<.1
675	Igd Solutions Corp—*Steve Hyer*	6825 Dixie Hwy Ste E, Clarkston MI 48346	248-625-0817	R	1*	<.1
676	Ignite Sales Inc—*Mitchell Orlowsky*	14785 Preston Rd Ste 5, Dallas TX 75254	972-789-5520	R	1*	<.1
677	Information 2 Extreme Inc—*Arnie Boyarsky*	5777 W Century Blvd St, Los Angeles CA 90045	310-641-6551	R	1*	<.1
678	Integrity Communications Ltd—*Jana Chapa*	PO Box 260154, Corpus Christi TX 78426	361-242-1000	R	1*	<.1
679	Network Tallahassee Inc—*Darrel Harvey*	PO Box 12035, Tallahassee FL 32317	850-671-4007	R	1*	<.1
680	Pro Tech Technologies Inc—*Richard Hennessey*	217 Westport Rd, Wilton CT 06897	203-210-7230	R	1*	<.1
681	Warren Communications Inc—*Jonathon Warren*	874 Orleans Rd Unit 8, Charleston SC 29407	843-852-2360	R	1*	<.1
682	Xert Communications—*Dave Battaglini*	215 S Union St Ste 1, Alexandria VA 22314	703-838-9847	R	1*	<.1
683	A-Web Internet Marketing Services Corp—*Ben Lee*	11615 15th Ave, College Point NY 11356	718-888-7760	R	1*	<.1
684	PC Pros Inc—*Diana Thompson*	622 W Redwood St, Coweta OK 74429	918-279-0972	R	1*	<.1
685	Information Access Technologies Inc—*Arthur Britto*	1500 Oliver Rd Ste K #, Fairfield CA 94534	510-704-0160	R	1*	<.1
686	Professional Technical Systems Inc—*Robert Perrins*	1752 Junction Ave Ste, San Jose CA 95112	408-436-4944	R	1*	<.1
687	Frontier Communications of Mondovi Inc—*Maggie Wilderrotter*	217 S Eau Claire St, Mondovi WI 54755	715-926-4141	S	1*	<.1
688	Talisman Networks—*Travis Almuti*	1450 Koll Cir Ste 109, San Jose CA 95112	408-980-7110	R	1*	<.1
689	Shop Ideas Network LLC	2125 Biscayne Blvd Ste, Miami FL 33137	305-572-0660	R	1*	<.1
690	Aadast Co—*Jerry Gullick*	4511 Windy Gorge Dr, Humble TX 77345	281-360-6661	R	1*	<.1
691	Marketing Response Solutions—*Danny Cantrell*	3939 Belt Line Rd Ste, Addison TX 75001	972-484-1600	R	1*	<.1
692	Iserve Technologies Inc—*Douglas Kaleugher*	1627 Penn Ave Fl 5, Pittsburgh PA 15222	412-281-9930	R	1*	<.1
693	A5com LLC—*David Lalande*	331 Fulton St Ste 200, Peoria IL 61602	309-820-7498	R	1*	<.1
694	Inteliport Inc—*Stephen Lane*	103 N Church St, Hertford NC 27944	252-426-4600	R	1*	<.1
695	Ascedia Inc—*Daniel Early*	161 S 1st St Ste 300, Milwaukee WI 53204	414-225-9770	R	1*	<.1
696	Solar Communications International Inc—*Robert Renfro*	8885 Rio San Diego Dr, San Diego CA 92108	619-243-2750	R	1*	<.1
697	EZ Nettools—*Alan Eckman*	238 E 3000 N, Rexburg ID 83440	208-356-8361	R	1*	<.1
698	Netegories—*Bradford Weller*	1412 N 350 W, Clearfield UT 84015	801-525-8940	R	1*	<.1
699	InphonexCom LLC	3044 Nw 72nd Ave, Miami FL 33122	305-728-6203	R	1*	<.1
700	Telecom Decision Makers Inc—*Melinda Shields*	7608 W Hwy 146 Ste 300, Pewee Valley KY 40056	502-244-1668	R	1*	<.1
701	Trademark Telecom Inc—*Miguel Gutierrez*	10690 Shadow Wood Dr S, Houston TX 77043	713-533-0751	R	1*	<.1
702	Atlantic Internet Technologies Inc—*Robert Zachok*	628 Shrewsbury Ave Ste, Tinton Falls NJ 07701	732-758-0505	R	1*	<.1
703	Internet Doctors Dba DockNet—*William Harrel*	3533 Old Conejo Rd Ste, Newbury Park CA 91320	805-383-1863	R	1*	<.1
704	Compoint Inc—*Pascale Schlegel*	5900 NW 99th Ave Unit, Doral FL 33178	305-599-3873	R	1	<.1
705	American Millennium Corporation Inc—*Bruce R Bacon*	17301 W Colfax Ave Ste, Golden CO 80401	303-279-2002	R	1	<.1
706	Netcentra Inc—*William Bradley*	556 Riverdale Dr Ste A, Glendale CA 91204	818-552-6800	R	1*	<.1
707	Oliby Inc—*Rebecca Maestas*	PO Box 35071, Albuquerque NM 87176	505-884-0444	R	1*	<.1
708	Dbisp LLC—*John Miller*	1300 N Pennsylvania St, Indianapolis IN 46202	317-222-1671	R	1*	<.1
709	Ecom Partners Inc—*Steve Kohler*	880 Riverhaven Dr, Suwanee GA 30024	678-947-6580	R	1*	<.1
710	Electronics Sonic—*Rob Lohit*	160 W 28th St, New York NY 10001	212-414-1798	R	1*	<.1
711	Elist Express LLC—*James Galvin*	607 Trixsam Rd, Sykesville MD 21784	410-549-4619	R	1*	<.1
712	Manufacturing Trade Inc—*Brian Chen*	20544 Champion St, Plainfield IL 60544	815-609-7115	R	1*	<.1
713	Msmb2b Inc—*Mark Cave*	16133 Ventura Blvd Ste, Encino CA 91436	323-525-3900	R	1*	<.1

Rank	Company Name—*Executive Officer*	Address, City, State, Zip	Phone	Type	Fin	Empls
714	Ultimate Systems Inc—*Tom Prince*	4000 Rouse Rd, Orlando FL 32817	407-977-0123	R	1*	<.1
715	Denlin Partners LLC	1614 S Broadway St Ste, Carrollton TX 75006	972-245-8343	R	1*	<.1
716	Cactus International Inc—*Monica Ray*	211 S Main St, Moscow ID 83843	208-883-5500	R	1*	<.1
717	Defentect Group Inc—*James C Ackerly*	535 Connecticut Ave 2n, Norwalk CT 06854	203-354-9164	P	1	N/A
718	Defi Global Inc—*Jeffrey P Rice*	7373 E Double Tree Ran, Scottsdale AZ 85258	310-823-8300	P	1	<.1
719	Gone Wired Cafe—*Kevin Marsh*	2021 E Michigan Ave, Lansing MI 48912	517-853-0550	R	1*	<.1
720	Power Brands—*Darin Ezra*	16501 Sherman Way Ste, Van Nuys CA 91406	818-989-5800	R	1*	<.1
721	Huntel Systems Inc—*Dan Hunt*	PO Box 400, Blair NE 68008	402-533-1000	R	1*	<.1
722	Securewebs Inc—*Scott Hirsch*	PO Box 377, Kettle Falls WA 99141	509-684-2511	R	1*	<.1
723	Xyte Inc—*Linda Mcisaac*	979 Jonathon Dr Ste B, Madison WI 53713	608-327-1000	R	1*	<.1
724	401k Datawarehouse LLC—*Thomas Laessig*	203 Bedford Ln, Lansdale PA 19446	215-368-2791	R	1*	<.1
725	VR Metro LLC	37655 Ford Rd, Westland MI 48185	734-729-7082	R	1*	<.1
726	Authority Domains Inc—*Owen Andrew*	17914 Vista Ct, Canyon Country CA 91387	714-350-9575	R	1*	<.1
727	South Florida Goline Inc—*Rita Rivero*	5245 Nw 36th St Ste 21, Miami Springs FL 33166	305-889-0027	R	1*	<.1
728	Michael Flicker—*Michael Flicker*	31 Cir Ave, Ridgewood NJ 07450	201-300-2900	R	1*	<.1
729	Cylogy Inc—*Brice Dunwoodie*	300 Broadway Ste 39, San Francisco CA 94133	415-677-9089	R	1*	<.1
730	Christy Communications Company Inc—*Paul Christy*	1260 Rankin Dr Ste L, Troy MI 48083	248-585-6030	R	1*	<.1
731	Redstick Internet Services LLC—*David Gary*	9121 Interline Ave Ste, Baton Rouge LA 70809	225-928-8888	R	1*	<.1
732	California Catalog and Technology Inc—*Steve Fetzer*	1106 E Turner Rd, Lodi CA 95240	209-365-9500	R	1*	<.1
733	Hut Man Inc—*Darrell Anderson*	1710 Douglas Dr N Ste, Golden Valley MN 55422	612-843-1400	R	1*	<.1
734	Cydian Technology—*Chris Ulrich*	445 Broadhollow Rd Ll4, Melville NY 11747	516-420-5000	R	<1*	<.1
735	Hub Of The Earth Inc—*Johnny Sparks*	1602 Gunter Ave, Guntersville AL 35976	256-571-9992	R	<1*	<.1
736	Rc Microsystems Inc—*George Chigundeni*	5610 Crawfordsville Rd, Indianapolis IN 46224	317-244-0322	R	<1*	<.1
737	SpecterwebCom LLC—*S Hall*	PO Box 687, Loxley AL 36551	251-943-3315	R	<1*	<.1
738	Tanza Technologies Inc—*Jafaar Nyang'oro*	PO Box 683038, Franklin TN 37068	615-538-1240	R	<1*	<.1
739	Threshold Communications Inc—*Jeff Matson*	16541 Redmond Way 245c, Redmond WA 98052	206-686-7800	R	<1*	<.1
740	Bayhill Capital Corp—*Bob Bench*	10757 S River Front Pk, South Jordan UT 84095	801-816-2529	P	<1	<.1
741	Iblast Inc—*Michael Lambert*	100 N Crescent Dr Fl 2, Beverly Hills CA 90210	310-385-4200	R	<1*	<.1
742	Webcanyon Inc—*Scott Hamilton*	PO Box 374, Huntsville AL 35804	256-430-1954	R	<1*	<.1
743	World Surveillance Group Inc—*Glenn Estrella*	State Rd 405 Bldg M6-3, Kennedy Space Center FL 32815	321-452-3545	P	<1	<.1
744	Portal Blocks—*Antonio Rodriguez*	9600 Great Hills Trl 1, Austin TX 78759	512-342-2090	R	<1*	<.1
745	Alenet Inc—*Sebastian Alegrett*	701 Sw 27th Ave Ste 70, Miami FL 33135	305-646-1135	R	<1*	<.1
746	Dyniverse Wireless Inc—*Terence Smith*	263 Fox Run, Exton PA 19341	610-620-4491	R	<1*	<.1
747	Cti Products Inc—*Allen Gerth*	1211 W Sharon Rd, Cincinnati OH 45240	513-595-5900	R	<1*	<.1
748	Dot Genesis LLC	1224 E Green St Ste 10, Pasadena CA 91106	626-792-8177	R	<1*	<.1
749	Switchnet Technologies—*Jerry Wentz*	2027 Cavanaugh Ct, Hartford WI 53027	262-673-3900	R	<1*	<.1
750	Ethicalhax Inc—*Keith Ramsey*	818 Florence Ave, Pittsburgh PA 15202	412-761-6546	R	<1*	<.1
751	Fibernet Inc—*Douglas Denoff*	PO Box 4050, Santa Monica CA 90411	310-314-4141	R	<1*	<.1
752	Rinestock Studios LLC—*Rich Rinehart*	15917 Lake Ave, Cleveland OH 44107	216-221-3421	R	<1*	<.1
753	NAP of the Americas Inc—*Manuel D Medena* Terremark Worldwide Inc	50 NE 9th St, Miami FL 33132	305-328-8000	S	<1	.2
754	Millington Telephone Company Inc—*Holly Starnes*	PO Box 429, Millington TN 38083	901-872-3311	R	<1*	.1
755	Pendrell Corp—*Benjamin G Wolff*	2300 Carillon Point, Kirkland WA 98033	425-278-7100	P	<1	<.1
756	Charlene Palmer—*Charlene Palmer*	402 N Pleasant St, Jackson MI 49202	517-789-5689	R	<1*	<.1
757	Redwood County Telephone Co—*Lauren Beran*	PO Box 130, Wabasso MN 56293	507-342-8000	R	<1*	<.1
758	Roberts Webforge Inc—*James Roberts*	865 Troxel Rd, Lansdale PA 19446	215-393-4757	R	<1*	<.1
759	Kim Celano—*Kim Celano*	6864 Carr St, Arvada CO 80004	303-456-9924	R	N/A	<.1

TOTALS: SIC 4813 Telephone Communications Except Radiotelephone

Companies: 759					369,811	738.1

4822 Telegraph & Other Communications

Rank	Company Name—*Executive Officer*	Address, City, State, Zip	Phone	Type	Fin	Empls
1	Petters Group Worldwide—*James Wehmhoff*	4400 Baker Rd, Minnetonka MN 55343	952-934-5000	R	2,200*	3.2
2	Ascom Wireless Solutions Inc—*Chad West*	598 Airport Blvd Ste 3, Morrisville NC 27560	919-234-2500	R	813*	1.2
3	Network Telephone Services Inc—*Joseph D Preston*	21135 Erwin St, Woodland Hills CA 91367	818-992-4300	R	350*	.5
4	j2 Global Communications Inc—*Hemi Zucker*	6922 Hollywood Blvd, Hollywood CA 90028	323-860-9200	P	330	.6
5	Adlink	11150 Santa Monica Blv, Los Angeles CA 90025	310-477-3994	R	144*	.1
6	USANET Inc—*Tim Harvey*	1155 Kelly Johnson Blv, Colorado Springs CO 80920	719-265-2930	S	41*	.1
7	E-Sync Networks Inc	35 Nutmeg Dr, Trumbull CT 06611	203-601-3000	R	40*	<.1
8	Nellymoser Inc—*John Puterbaugh*	11 Water St, Arlington MA 02476	781-646-1515	R	38*	.1
9	CallWave Inc—*Jeff Cavins*	PO Box 609, Santa Barbara CA 93102	805-690-4000	P	20	<.1
10	Intermex Wire Transfers Inc—*John Rincon*	9480 S Dixie Hwy, Miami FL 33156	305-671-8000	R	16*	.2
11	Swn Communications Inc—*Tony Schmitz*	224 W 30th St Ste 500, New York NY 10001	212-379-4900	R	10*	.1
12	Hometown Telecom—*David Schofield*	9864 Wilshire Blvd, Beverly Hills CA 90210	916-844-3330	R	8*	<.1
13	Integrated Communications Inc—*James Marineau*	PO Box 341886, Memphis TN 38184	901-366-4412	R	7*	<.1
14	iCue Corp—*Gary S Rosner*	1111 Street Rd Ste 101, Southampton PA 18966		R	6*	<.1
15	Adval Communications Inc—*Anthony Croce*	200 Galleria Office Ct, Southfield MI 48034		R	4*	<.1
16	Commtouch Inc—*Gideon Mantel*	292 Gibralter Dr Ste 1, Sunnyvale CA 94089	650-864-2000	S	4	N/A
17	ABS Fax Technologies Inc—*Kevin Chodrow*	2401 Fountain View Dr, Houston TX 77057	713-735-5100	R	3*	<.1
18	Reflect Scientific Inc—*Kim Boyce*	1270 S 1380 W, Orem UT 84058	801-226-4100	P	2	<.1
19	BoomerangCom Inc—*David Kearney*	2100 Geng Rd Ste 102, Palo Alto CA 94303	650-614-9090	R	2*	<.1
20	Answer Excellence Inc—*Tam Barendreat*	1938 N Hercules Ave St, Clearwater FL 33763	727-469-8300	R	2*	<.1
21	FaxBack Inc—*Art King*	7409 SW Tech Ctr Dr St, Portland OR 97223		R	2*	<.1
22	Sejersen Dps Inc—*Sejer Sejersen*	4930 Naples St, San Diego CA 92110	619-275-6931	R	2*	<.1
23	Quick Link Information Service LLC—*George Heudorfer*	131 Commercial Pkwy 3a, Branford CT 06405	203-483-2922	R	1*	<.1
24	Denny's Copy Stop—*Denny Louquet*	1509 S Russell St, Missoula MT 59801	406-728-3363	R	1*	<.1
25	Quality Interconnect Cabling LLC—*Lydia Groen*	PO Box 582, Barrington NH 03825	603-664-7117	R	<1*	<.1
26	Dallas Prompter and Captions Inc—*Clinton Stephenson*	PO Box 571233, Dallas TX 75357	214-275-9000	R	<1*	<.1
27	R and C Electronics—*Willie Richard*	2532 Washington Ave, Baton Rouge LA 70802	225-388-9496	R	<1*	<.1

TOTALS: SIC 4822 Telegraph & Other Communications

Companies: 27					4,046	6.2

4832 Radio Broadcasting Stations

Rank	Company Name—*Executive Officer*	Address, City, State, Zip	Phone	Type	Fin	Empls
1	CC Media Holdings Inc—*Mark P Mays*	200 E Basse Rd, San Antonio TX 78209	210-832-3700	P	5,866	20.3
2	Sirius XM Radio Inc—*Mel Karmazin*	1221 Ave of the Americ, New York NY 10020	212-584-5100	P	3,015	1.5
3	Buckley Broadcasting Corp—*Joseph M Bilotta*	166 W Putnam Ave, Greenwich CT 06830	203-661-4307	R	834*	.3
4	Cox Radio Inc—*Robert F Neil*	6205 Peachtree Dunwood, Atlanta GA 30328	678-645-0000	S	410	2.1
5	Entercom Kansas City Licensee LLC Entercom Communications Corp	7000 Squibb Rd Ste 200, Mission KS 66202	913-677-8998	S	391*	.4
6	Entercom Communications Corp—*David J Field*	401 City Ave Ste 809, Bala Cynwyd PA 19004	610-660-5610	P	383	2.0

Note: An asterisk (*) indicates an estimated financial figure. The company type code used is as follows: R = Private, P = Public, S = Private Subsidiary, B = Public Subsidiary, D = Division, J = Joint Venture, I = Investment Fund.

COMPANY RANKINGS BY SALES WITHIN 4-DIGIT SIC

Rank	Company Name—Executive Officer	Address, City, State, Zip	Phone	Type	Fin	Empls
7	Barden Companies Inc—Don H Barden	400 Renaissance Ctr St, Detroit MI 48243	313-496-2900	R	349*	4.0
8	Radio One Inc—Alfred C Liggins III	5900 Princess Garden P, Lanham MD 20706	301-306-1111	P	280	1.3
9	Cumulus Media Inc—Lewis W Dickey Jr	3280 Peachtree Road NW, Atlanta GA 30305	404-949-0700	P	263	2.3
10	Univision Radio—Jose Valle	3102 Oak Lawn Ave Ste, Dallas TX 75219	214-525-7700	D	257	1.1
11	Emmis Communications Corp—Jeffrey H Smulyan	1 Emmis Plz 40 Monumen, Indianapolis IN 46204	317-266-0100	P	251	1.2
12	Nassau Broadcasting Partners LP (Princeton New Jersey)—Louis F Mercatanti Jr	619 Alexander Rd3rd Fl, Princeton NJ 08540	609-452-9696	R	235*	.3
13	Midcontinent Media Inc—Mark S Niblick	3600 Minnesota Dr Ste, Edina MN 55435	952-844-2600	R	212*	1.5
14	Salem Communications Corp—Edward G Atsinger III	4880 Santa Rosa Rd Ste, Camarillo CA 93012	805-987-0400	P	207	1.5
15	WAMC—Alan Chartock	PO Box 66600, Albany NY 12206	518-465-5233	R	180*	.1
16	Bonneville International Corp—Bruce T Reese	PO Box 1160, Salt Lake City UT 84110	801-575-7500	R	174*	1.2
17	Fisher Broadcasting Co	140 4th Ave N Ste 500, Seattle WA 98109	206-404-7000	S	170*	.7
18	Journal Broadcast Group—Doug Kiel	333 W State St, Milwaukee WI 53203	414-332-9611	S	156*	1.0
19	Saga Communications Of Illinois LLC—Edward Christian	73 Kercheval Ave Ste 2, Grosse Pointe MI 48236	313-886-7070	R	141*	.1
20	Spanish Broadcasting System Inc—Raul Alarcon Jr	2601 S Bayshore Dr PH2, Coconut Grove FL 33133	305-441-6901	P	136	.5
21	Saga Communications Inc—Edward K Christian	73 Kercheval Ave Ste 2, Grosse Pointe Farms MI 48236	313-886-7070	P	128	1.2
22	Beasley Broadcast Group Inc—George G Beasley	3033 Riviera Dr Ste 20, Naples FL 34103	239-263-5000	P	98	.6
23	Liberman Broadcasting Corp—Jose Liberman	1845 W Empire Ave, Burbank CA 91504	818-563-5722	R	89*	.4
24	Marathon Media—Chris Devine	980 N Michigan Ave Ste, Chicago IL 60611	312-204-9900	R	88*	<.1
25	Townsquare Media LLC—Steven Price	240 Greenwich Ave, Greenwich CT 06830	208-861-0900	P	84	.8
26	Triton Media Group LLC—Neal Schore	15303 Ventura Blvd Ste, Sherman Oaks CA 91403	818-528-8860	R	81*	.4
27	Jones International Networks Ltd—Jeffrey C Wayne	9697 E Mineral Ave, Centennial CO 80112	303-792-3111	R	75*	.4
28	Big Horn Radio Network—Roger Gelder	PO Box 1210, Cody WY 82414	307-578-5000	R	72*	<.1
29	Premiere Radio Networks Inc—Charlie Rahilly	15260 Ventura Blvd 4th, Sherman Oaks CA 91403	818-377-5300	S	71*	.3
30	Krcs Hot 931 Fm—D Knight	660 Flormann St, Rapid City SD 57701	605-343-1355	R	68*	.8
31	KURM Radio—Kermit Womack	113 E New Hope Rd, Rogers AR 72758	479-636-0790	R	64*	<.1
32	Regent Broadcasting of Grand Rapids Inc—Steven Price	50 Monroe Ave NW Ste 5, Grand Rapids MI 49503	616-451-4800	S	63*	.1
33	Topeka Television Corp—Jean Turnbough Emmis Communications Corp	PO Box 2700, Topeka KS 66601	785-582-4000	S	54*	.1
34	Radio One of Charlotte LLC—Debbie Kwei Cook Radio One Inc	8809 Lenox Pointe Dr S, Charlotte NC 28273	704-548-7800	S	49*	.1
35	Cumulus Broadcasting Inc—Lewis Dickey Cumulus Media Inc	3280 Peachtree Rd NW S, Atlanta GA 30305	404-949-0700	S	47*	.1
36	Wnyc Radio—Laura Walker	160 Varick St Fl 7, New York NY 10013	646-829-4400	R	47*	.1
37	Trans World Radio—Thomas Lowell	PO Box 8700, Cary NC 27512	919-460-3700	R	40*	.5
38	Charlotte Broadcasting LLC—Barry Mayo Radio One Inc	8809 Lenox Pointe Dr S, Charlotte NC 28273	704-548-7800	S	34*	<.1
39	Radio One of North Carolina LLC—Barry Mayo Radio One Inc	8809 Lenox Pointe Dr S, Charlotte NC 28273	704-548-7800	S	34*	<.1
40	Learfield Communications Inc—Clyde G Lear	505 Hobbs Rd, Jefferson City MO 65109	573-893-7200	R	33*	.2
41	Radio One of Boston Inc—Alfred C Liggins III Radio One Inc	5900 Princess Garden P, Lanham MD 20706	301-306-1111	S	29*	<.1
42	Radio One of Boston Licenses LLC—Alfred C Liggins III Radio One of Boston Inc	500 Victory Rd, Quincy MA 02171	617-931 1090	S	29*	<.1
43	ICBC Broadcast Holdings Inc—Pierre Sutton	3 Park Ave 41st Fl, New York NY 10016	212-447-1000	R	27*	.1
44	Sandusky Newspapers Inc—David Rau	PO Box 5071, Sandusky OH 44871	419-625-5500	R	27*	.5
45	Connecticut Radio Network—Barry Berman	1 Circular Ave, Hamden CT 06514	203-288-2002	R	20*	.1
46	Maverick Media Holdings LLC—Gary Rosynedk	136 Main St Ste 202, Westport CT 06880	203-227-2800	R	20*	<.1
47	Thru The Bible Radio Network—Leo Karlyn	PO Box 7100, Pasadena CA 91109	626-795-4145	R	20*	<.1
48	Family Stations Inc—Harold Camping	290 Hegenberger Rd, Oakland CA 94621	510-568-6200	R	20*	.3
49	Bellevue Radio Inc—Mark Kaye	3650 131st Ave SE Ste, Bellevue WA 98006	425-653-9462	R	19*	.1
50	Dial Global—David Landau Triton Media Group LLC	220 W 42nd St, New York NY 10036	212-967-2888	S	17*	.1
51	Boston Celtics Communications LP—Rich Pond	226 Causeway St 4th fl, Boston MA 02114	617-854-8000	S	15*	.1
52	Buck Owens Production Company Inc—Mel Owens	3223 Sillect Ave, Bakersfield CA 93308	661-326-1011	R	14*	.1
53	Clear Channel Metroplex Inc—L Mays	200 E Basse Rd, San Antonio TX 78209	210-822-2828	R	14*	.1
54	WJPZ Radio Inc—Dave Peterson	316 Waverly Watsn Comp, Syracuse NY 13210	315-443-4689	R	13*	.2
55	GHB Radio Group—George H Buck Jr	1776 Briarcliff Rd NE, Atlanta GA 30306	404-875-1110	R	13*	.1
56	Insight For Living—Cynthia Swindoll	PO Box 251007, Plano TX 75025	972-473-5000	R	12*	.1
57	Meridian Broadcasting Inc—Joseph Schwartzel	2824 Palm Beach Blvd, Fort Myers FL 33916	239-337-2346	R	11*	.1
58	Family Life Communications Inc—Randy Carlson	7355 N Oracle Rd Ste 2, Tucson AZ 85704	520-544-5950	R	11*	<.1
59	FM 107 W F M P Real Life Conversation—Stanley Hubbard	3415 University Ave W, Saint Paul MN 55114	651-642-4107	R	10*	.1
60	Perry Broadcasting Company Inc—Russell Perry	1528 Ne 23rd St Ste A, Oklahoma City OK 73111	405-427-5877	R	10*	.1
61	Public Broadcasting Of Colorado Inc—Max Wycisk	7409 S Alton Ct, Centennial CO 80112	303-871-9191	R	10*	.1
62	Fisher Radio Seattle—Bill Kripphaene	140 4th Ave N Ste 340, Seattle WA 98109	206-421-1000	R	10*	.1
63	Keymarket Communications LLC	1370 Wash Pke Ste 406, Bridgeville PA 15017	412-279-5400	R	10*	.1
64	Raritan Valley Broadcasting Company Inc—Frank Ambrose	PO Box 100, New Brunswick NJ 08903	732-249-2600	R	9*	.1
65	Greater Philadelphia Radio Group—John Bordes	1 Bala Plz Ste 339, Bala Cynwyd PA 19004	610-667-8500	R	9*	.1
66	Benchmark Communications Inc—Bruce R Anguish	2480 Sand Hill Rd Ste, Menlo Park CA 94025	650-854-8180	R	8*	<.1
67	Wwj 950 Am—Gregory Ross	26495 American Dr, Southfield MI 48034	248-455-7200	R	8*	.1
68	Entercom Norfolk LLC—Eric Mastel	236 Clearfield Ave Ste, Virginia Beach VA 23462	757-497-2000	R	8*	.1
69	Lotus Broadcasting Corp—Howard Kalmasen	8755 W Flamingo Rd, Las Vegas NV 89147	702-876-1460	R	7*	.1
70	Wtcc Radio Station Request Line—Ernie Johnson	1 Armory Sq Ste 1, Springfield MA 01105	413-746-9822	R	7*	.1
71	Good News Broadcasting Association Inc—Woodrow M Kroll	PO Box 82808, Lincoln NE 68501		R	7*	.1
72	Charles River Broadcasting Inc—Bill Campbell	750 South St, Waltham MA 02453	781-893-7080	R	7*	<.1
73	Cincinnati Public Radio Inc—Richard Eiswerth	1223 Central Pkwy, Cincinnati OH 45214	513-241-8282	R	7*	<.1
74	Heartland Communications Inc—Thomas Bookey	PO Box 309, Eagle River WI 54521	920-882-4750	R	6*	.1
75	Beasley Broadcasting of Eastern North Carolina Inc—George Beasley	PO Box 2563, Fayetteville NC 28302	910-483-9565	R	6*	.1
76	Wchc Fm Radio Station—Gary Brooks	Holy Cross College, Worcester MA 01610	508-793-2475	R	6*	.1
77	Gold Coast Broadcasting LLC	2284 S Victoria Ave 2g, Ventura CA 93003	805-289-1400	R	6*	.1
78	WSJM Inc—Gayle Olson	580 E Napier Ave, Benton Harbor MI 49022	269-925-1111	R	5*	.1
79	Black Crow Media LLC	126 W International Sp, Daytona Beach FL 32114	386-255-9300	R	5*	.1
80	Mix 102 5—Brian Delaney	39 Kellogg Rd, New Hartford NY 13413	315-721-0102	R	5*	.1
81	Regent Broadcasting Of Utica/Rome Inc—Mary Beach	9418 State Rte 49, Marcy NY 13403	315-736-5225	R	5*	.1
82	Access One Inc—Cary Camp	PO Box 7197, Shreveport LA 71137	318-222-3122	R	5*	.1
83	WDAY-TV-AM—Kevin Weaver	PO Box 2466, Fargo ND 58108	701-237-6500	S	5*	.2
84	Gilliam Communications Inc—H Gilliam	363 S 2nd St, Memphis TN 38103	901-527-9565	R	5*	.1
85	Clear Channel Broadcasting—Ivy Elam	2743 Perimetr Pkwy Ste, Augusta GA 30909	706-396-6000	R	5*	.1
86	Forever Of PA Inc—Jim Shields	900 Waters St Downtown, Meadville PA 16335	814-827-3651	R	5*	.1

Rank	Company Name—*Executive Officer*	Address, City, State, Zip	Phone	Type	Fin	Empls
87	Withers Broadcasting Company Of West Virginia—*W Withers*	PO Box 480, Bridgeport WV 26330	304-848-5000	R	5*	.1
88	Eyewitness News At 5—*Don Mcgouiok*	1314 Gray Hwy, Macon GA 31211	478-752-1309	R	5*	.1
89	Weaz Fm—*Gerald Lee*	225 E City Ave Ste 200, Bala Cynwyd PA 19004	610-667-8400	R	5*	<.1
90	Wbhj and Wbhk Radio—*David Dubose*	950 22nd St N Ste 1000, Birmingham AL 35203	205-326-2535	R	4*	.1
91	Rodgers Broadcasting Corp—*David Rodgers*	2301 W Main St, Richmond IN 47374	765-962-6533	R	4*	.1
92	DWS Inc—*Mike Haile*	2301 S Neil St, Champaign IL 61820	217-351-5300	R	4*	<.1
93	Backyard Broadcasting Inc—*Berry Drake*	800 E 29th St, Muncie IN 47302	765-288-4403	R	4*	.1
94	Midwestern Broadcasting Co—*Ross Biederman*	314 E Front St, Traverse City MI 49684	231-947-7675	R	4*	<.1
95	Big League Broadcasting LLC—*Devra Blakley*	3350 Peachtree Rd Ne S, Atlanta GA 30326	404-237-0079	R	4*	.1
96	Kelsho Communications LP—*Ken Roberts*	3099 Mandeville Canyon, Los Angeles CA 90049	310-476-6441	R	4*	<.1
97	Sconnix Broadcasting LLC	PO Box 917, McLean VA 22101	703-356-6000	R	4*	<.1
98	WQXR FM—*Thomas Bartunek*	122 5th Ave 3rd Fl, New York NY 10011	212-633-7600	S	4*	<.1
99	KMHL Broadcasting Corp—*John Linder*	PO Box 61, Marshall MN 56258	507-532-2282	R	4*	<.1
100	Reach Media Inc—*Tom Joyner*	PO Box 801565, Dallas TX 75380	972-789-1058	R	4*	<.1
101	WAM U/Rehm Show—*Neil Kerwin*	4000 Brandywine St Nw, Washington DC 20016	202-885-1230	R	4*	.1
102	Intercom of Norfolk Inc—*Jeff Brown*	236 Clearfield Ave Ste, Virginia Beach VA 23462	757-497-1067	R	4*	<.1
103	East Kentucky Broadcasting Corp—*Walter May*	1240 Radio Dr, Pikeville KY 41501	606-437-4051	R	4*	<.1
104	Caracol Broadcasting Inc—*Sonia Dula*	2100 Coral Way Ste 126, Coral Gables FL 33145	305-285-1260	R	4*	.1
105	Radio Group—*Carrey Camp*	208 N Thomas Dr, Shreveport LA 71107	318-222-3122	R	4*	.1
106	WBBQ Radio—*Barry Kaye*	500 Carolina Spgs 300, North Augusta SC 29841	803-279-5555	R	4*	.1
107	WHMETV and Radio—*Craig Wallin*	61300 Ironwood Rd, South Bend IN 46614	574-291-8614	R	4*	.1
108	Triad Broadcasting—*David Benjiman*	PO Box 9919, Fargo ND 58106	701-237-4500	R	4*	.1
109	Kbtt—*Cary Camp*	PO Box 7197, Shreveport LA 71137	318-222-3122	R	4*	.1
110	Swick Broadcasting Co—*Steve Swick*	PO Box 999, Angola IN 46703	260-665-9554	R	4*	<.1
111	Media-Com Inc—*Richard Klaus*	PO Box 2170, Akron OH 44309	330-673-2323	R	4*	<.1
112	Centennial Broadcasting Ii LLC	6201 Towncenter Dr Ste, Clemmons NC 27012	336-766-2828	R	4*	.1
113	Kinop Sports Complex—*Kate O'rielly*	2500 E Ajo Way, Tucson AZ 85713	520-434-1334	R	4*	.1
114	Leighton Broadcasting—*Jerry Englund*	1185 9th St Ne, Thompson ND 58278	701-746-4516	R	4*	.1
115	Wvpn 88 5—*Rita Ray*	600 Capitol St, Charleston WV 25301	304-558-3000	R	3*	.1
116	Southern Communication Corp—*Shane Southern*	306 S Kanawha St, Beckley WV 25801	304-252-6452	R	3*	.1
117	Ktlr Gospel 890 Inc—*Tony Tyler*	5101 S Shields Blvd, Oklahoma City OK 73129	405-616-5500	R	3*	.1
118	American Media Investments Inc—*Gene Bicknell*	1162 E Hwy 126, Pittsburg KS 66762	620-231-7200	R	3*	<.1
119	Nassau Broadcasting Maine—*Dave Dean*	250 Ctr St Unit 2, Auburn ME 04210	207-784-4300	R	3*	.1
120	Region Broadcasting Of El Paso—*Alex Berkett*	4180 N Mesa St, El Paso TX 79902	915-544-9300	R	3*	.1
121	Wbml Radio Station—*Carlos Jenkins*	708 S Mathews Ave, Urbana IL 61801	217-333-2613	R	3*	.1
122	WNTR-1079 FM—*Tonia Lotz*	9245 N Meridian St Ste, Indianapolis IN 46260	317-816-4000	R	3*	.1
123	Lenk Broadcasting Company Inc—*Bayard Walters*	1824 Murfreesboro Pke, Nashville TN 37217	615-361-7560	R	3*	<.1
124	Sunbury Broadcasting Corp—*Roger Haddon*	1227 County Line Rd, Selinsgrove PA 17870	570-286-5838	R	3*	<.1
125	1079 Mix—*Brian Michael*	2835 E 3300 S, Salt Lake City UT 84109	801-570-1079	R	3*	.1
126	LM Communications Inc—*Lynn Martin*	401 W Main St Ste 301, Lexington KY 40507	859-252-4137	R	3*	<.1
127	WDEV—*Kenley Squier*	9 Stowe St, Waterbury VT 05676	802-244-7321	R	3*	<.1
128	WSM Inc—*Chris Kulick*	2804 Opryland Dr, Nashville TN 37214	615-889-6595	S	3*	<.1
129	Mckenzie River Broadcasting Inc—*John Tilson*	925 Country Club Rd St, Eugene OR 97401	541-484-9400	R	3*	<.1
130	Woodward Broadcasting Inc—*Charles Woodward*	PO Box 491, Fairmont MN 56031	507-235-5595	R	3*	<.1
131	Rhode Island Public Radio—*Toby Ayers*	1 Union Sta Ste 6, Providence RI 02903	401-351-2800	R	3*	<.1
132	Southern Sports Network Inc—*Glenn Herrin*	2001 Molton Ct APT 3, Birmingham AL 35216	205-643-0068	R	3*	.1
133	East Texas Broadcasting Company Inc—*John Mitchell*	PO Box 990, Mount Pleasant TX 75456	903-572-8726	R	3*	<.1
134	Zimmer Radio Group—*Amber Lee*	3125 W 6th St, Lawrence KS 66049	785-843-1320	R	3*	<.1
135	Ingleside Investments Inc—*Roger Vaughan*	503 S Front St Ste 101, Columbus OH 43215	614-224-4664	R	3*	.1
136	Midwest Family Broadcasting Inc—*Gail Olson*	PO Box 107, Saint Joseph MI 49085	269-925-9756	R	3*	.1
137	B100 Kbea - Studio—*Mat Williams*	1229 Brady St, Davenport IA 52803	563-326-2100	R	3*	.1
138	Kool 107 9 Inc—*Kevin Wodlinger*	315 Kennedy Ave, Grand Junction CO 81501	970-242-7788	R	3*	.1
139	KVSF Talk—*Fred Sena*	2502 Camino Entrada St, Santa Fe NM 87507	505-438-8255	R	3*	.1
140	Krad Inc—*Jack Hanson*	PO Box 13638, Grand Forks ND 58208	701-772-2204	R	3*	<.1
141	Black Crow Media Of Valdosta LLC—*Ralph Rosenberg*	1711 Ellis Dr, Valdosta GA 31601	229-247-9993	R	3*	.1
142	KVFX 945—*Kent Francis*	810 W 200 N, Logan UT 84321	435-752-5141	R	3*	.1
143	WOKQ 975 FM Stereo Inc—*Farid Fuelman*	PO Box 576, Dover NH 03821	603-463-9750	R	3*	<.1
144	Union Broadcasting Inc—*Chad Boeger*	6721 W 121st St, Shawnee Mission KS 66209	913-344-1500	R	3*	<.1
145	Wmbd 1470 Am—*Mike Wild*	PO Box 9050, Peoria IL 61612	309-637-3700	R	3*	<.1
146	Robinson Corp—*David Robinson*	E7601a County Rd Ss, Viroqua WI 54665	608-637-7200	R	3*	<.1
147	Southwestern Minnesota Radio Inc—*Jerry Papenfuss*	752 Bluffview Cir, Winona MN 55987	507-452-4000	R	3*	<.1
148	Pillar Of Fire Corp—*Robert Dallenbach*	3455 W 83rd Ave, Westminster CO 80031	303-428-0910	R	3*	<.1
149	WCUZ 1023 FM 102—*Kristine Foate*	2000 Lower Huntington, Fort Wayne IN 46819	260-747-1511	R	3*	<.1
150	Rfe Ri Inc—*Thomas Dine*	1201 Connecticut Ave N, Washington DC 20036	202-457-6900	R	2*	.1
151	Krcb Radio—*Nancy Dobbs*	5850 La Bath Ave, Cotati CA 94928	707-585-8522	R	2*	<.1
152	Student Broadcasting Inc—*Wes High*	379 Iowa Memorial Un, Iowa City IA 52242	319-335-9525	R	2*	<.1
153	Mcentee Broadcasting Of Florida Inc—*William Mcentee*	2090 Plm Beach Lk Blvd, West Palm Beach FL 33409	561-227-0660	R	2*	<.1
154	Forever Communications—*Christine Hillard*	1919 Scottsville Rd, Bowling Green KY 42104	270-782-0180	R	2*	<.1
155	Sky Blue Broadcasting Inc—*Kim Benefield*	327 S Marion Ave, Sandpoint ID 83864	208-263-2179	R	2*	<.1
156	Jarb Broadcasting Co—*Gary Scott*	PO Box 1180, Jacksonville IL 62651	217-245-7171	R	2*	<.1
157	Elgin Broadcasting Co—*Kenneth Jakle*	14b Douglas Ave, Elgin IL 60120	847-741-7700	R	2*	<.1
158	Wtop—*Don Pollnow*	5315 Sw 7th St, Topeka KS 66606	785-297-1490	R	2*	<.1
159	Joy Fm—*Andy Haynes*	408 W University Ave S, Gainesville FL 32601	352-351-8810	R	2*	<.1
160	Redwood Empire Stereocasters—*Gordon Zlot*	3392 Mendocino Ave Fl, Santa Rosa CA 95403	707-528-4434	R	2*	<.1
161	Odyssey Communications Inc—*Kamila Dworska*	1551 Rte 202, Pomona NY 10970	845-354-2000	R	2*	<.1
162	Kkaj 957 Fm—*David Smith*	1205 Northglen St, Ardmore OK 73401	580-226-0421	R	2*	<.1
163	WTAG 580 AM Stereo—*Sean Davey*	58 Stereo Ln, Paxton MA 01612	508-795-0580	R	2*	<.1
164	Sparta-Tomah Broadcasting Company Inc—*Zel Rice*	113 W Oak St, Sparta WI 54656	608-269-3307	R	2*	<.1
165	Wxrl 1300 Am—*Louis Schriver*	PO Box 170, Lancaster NY 14086	716-681-1313	R	2*	<.1
166	Fisher Broadcasting - SE Idaho Tv LLC—*Leslee Hammer*	1255 E 17th St, Idaho Falls ID 83404	208-522-5100	R	2*	.1
167	Good Radio Tv LLC	PO Box 619, Moberly MO 65270	660-263-6999	R	2*	.1
168	Double Z Broadcasting Inc—*Curt Teigen*	PO Box 190, Devils Lake ND 58301	701-662-7563	R	2*	<.1
169	WTBF-AM—*Joseph Gilchrist*	67 W Ct Sq, Troy AL 36081	334-566-0300	R	2*	<.1
170	WNSW AM 1430—*Aurther Liu*	449 Broadway Fl 2, New York NY 10013	212-966-8700	R	2*	<.1
171	Jack Fm—*Mike Falere*	180 N Stetson Ave Ste, Chicago IL 60601	312-870-6400	R	2*	<.1
172	Wrek Radio Station—*Aaksh Jariwala*	165 8th St Nw, Atlanta GA 30332	404-894-2468	R	2*	<.1
173	Kfia Radio—*Dale Hendry*	1425 River Park Dr Ste, Sacramento CA 95815	916-924-0710	R	2*	<.1
174	Marshalltown Broadcasting Inc—*David Nelson*	PO Box 698, Marshalltown IA 50158	641-753-3361	R	2*	<.1
175	Wolfhouse Radio Group Inc—*Nell Ahl*	PO Box 1939, Salinas CA 93902	831-757-1910	R	2*	<.1
176	Kqmx—*Harold Wright*	10040 Hwy 54, Weatherford OK 73096	580-772-5939	R	2*	<.1

Note: An asterisk ( ) indicates an estimated financial figure. The company type code used is as follows: R = Private, P = Public, S = Private Subsidiary, B = Public Subsidiary, D = Division, J = Joint Venture, I = Investment Fund.*

COMPANY RANKINGS BY SALES WITHIN 4-DIGIT SIC

Rank	Company Name—Executive Officer	Address, City, State, Zip	Phone	Type	Fin	Empls
177	Kiix Sports Radio 1410 Am—Stu Askell	1612 La Porte Ave, Fort Collins CO 80521	970-482-5991	R	2*	<.1
178	KMMX Mix 1003—Jerry Richardson	33 Briercroft Office P, Lubbock TX 79412	806-762-3000	R	2*	<.1
179	Am Kwlc—Jennifer Cantine	700 College Dr, Decorah IA 52101	563-387-1571	R	2*	<.1
180	Marshfield Broadcasting Company Inc—Edward Perry	130 Enterprise Dr, Marshfield MA 02050	781-837-1166	R	2*	<.1
181	Prettyman Broadcasting Corp—William Prettyman	1606 W King St, Martinsburg WV 25401	304-263-8868	R	2*	<.1
182	Valkyrie Broadcasting Inc—Jim Collum	12615 Jones Rd Ste 108, Houston TX 77070	281-955-8424	R	2*	<.1
183	Options University LLC—Brett Fogle	925 S Federal Hwy Ste, Boca Raton FL 33432		R	2*	<.1
184	Ksrv Inc—Dave Capps	2003 Nw 56th St, Pendleton OR 97801	541-278-2500	R	2*	<.1
185	Magic 16 Weup—Hundley Batts	PO Box 11398, Huntsville AL 35814	256-837-9387	R	2*	<.1
186	Pearl River Communications Inc—John R Pigott	PO Box 5409, Picayune MS 39466	601-798-4835	R	2*	<.1
187	Kxbz B 104 7 Fm—Seaton Stations	2414 Casement Rd, Manhattan KS 66502	785-539-1047	R	2*	<.1
188	WUHU 107 1 FM—Christine Hillart	1919 Scottsville Rd, Bowling Green KY 42104	270-843-0107	R	2*	<.1
189	Forts Radio Group LLC	400 Ardmore Blvd, Pittsburgh PA 15221	412-244-4556	R	2*	<.1
190	Kpgr Radio Station—Van Bulkley	700 E 200 S, Pleasant Grove UT 84062	801-785-5747	R	2*	<.1
191	Orca Radio Inc—Rick Taylor Sandusky Newspapers Inc	3650 131st Ave Se Ste, Bellevue WA 98006	425-373-5536	S	2*	<.1
192	KRPL Inc—Rob Prasil	PO Box 8849, Moscow ID 83843	208-882-2551	R	2*	<.1
193	Kwoz Arkansas 103—Preston Grace	PO Box 2077, Batesville AR 72503	870-269-4306	R	2*	<.1
194	Elnorah Inc—Frank Jlorle	45 County Rd 519, Phillipsburg NJ 08865	908-995-1999	R	2*	<.1
195	Kbew Inc—Jerry Papenfuss	PO Box 278, Blue Earth MN 56013	507-526-2181	R	2*	<.1
196	Maxmedia Of Pennsylvania LLC—Tom Morgan	PO Box 90, Selinsgrove PA 17870	570-374-8819	R	2*	<.1
197	S-R Broadcasting Co—Andy Skotdal	7115 Larimer Rd, Everett WA 98208	425-743-1380	R	2*	<.1
198	Kiti 1420 Am—Rod Etherton	1133 Kresky Ave Unit M, Centralia WA 98531	360-736-1355	R	2*	<.1
199	Dick Broadcasting Company Incorporated Of North Carolina—James Dick	192 E Lewis St, Greensboro NC 27406	336-274-8042	R	2*	<.1
200	WNDV U93 FM—Bob Ford	3371 Cleveland Rd Ext, South Bend IN 46628	574-273-9300	R	2*	<.1
201	MCC Broadcasting Company Inc—Stephen Mindich	25 Exchange St, Lynn MA 01901	781-595-6200	R	2*	<.1
202	Burlington Broadcasting Inc—Jay Williams	PO Box 4489, Burlington VT 05406	802-860-1818	R	2*	<.1
203	Citicasters Co—John Dimeo	1635 S Gold St, Centralia WA 98531	360-736-3321	R	2*	<.1
204	Rocket City Broadcasting LLC—Bill Thomas	1555 The Boardwalk Ste, Huntsville AL 35816	256-536-1568	R	2*	<.1
205	Kjel Radio—Dean Goodman	PO Box 1112, Lebanon MO 65536	417-588-2234	R	2*	<.1
206	Quorum Radio Partners Of Virginia Inc—Todd Fowler	PO Box 710, Covington VA 24426	540-962-1133	R	2*	<.1
207	Wgl Talk Studio Line—Dave Riethmiller	2000 Lower Huntington, Fort Wayne IN 46819	260-747-5100	R	2*	<.1
208	WDUQ—James Byrne	600 Forbes Ave, Pittsburgh PA 15219	412-396-6030	R	2*	<.1
209	Gillen Broadcasting Corp—Doug Gillen	7120 Sw 24th Ave, Gainesville FL 32607	352-331-2200	R	2*	<.1
210	Mountain Lake Broadcasting Corp—Charlie Earls	620 Hwy 5 N, Mountain Home AR 72653	870-425-3101	R	2*	<.1
211	Clancy Mance Communications Inc—Dave Mance	199 Wealtha Ave, Watertown NY 13601	315-782-1240	R	2*	<.1
212	Mountain Dog Media Inc—Randy Hopper	254 Winnebago Dr, Fond Du Lac WI 54935	920-921-1071	R	2*	<.1
213	Kfyr Radio	5584 Collection Ctr Dr, Chicago IL 60601	312-258-5555	R	2*	<.1
214	Seven Bridges Radio LLC—Steve Griffin	9090 Hogan Rd, Jacksonville FL 32216	904-641-1011	R	2*	<.1
215	Scantland Broadcasting Ltd—Tony Condo	1608 Casey Key Rd, Nokomis FL 34275	941-966-2599	R	2*	<.1
216	Haugo Broadcasting Inc—Christian Haugo	3601 Canyon Lake Dr St, Rapid City SD 57702	605-343-0888	R	2*	<.1
217	Elliott Mcgraw Broadcast—Dick Mcgraw	228 Randolph Ave, Elkins WV 26241	304-472-1400	R	2*	<.1
218	Zone Corp—Steven King	PO Box 1929, Bangor ME 04402	207-990-2000	R	2*	<.1
219	Aurora Communications—Robert Dyson	2 Pendell Rd, Poughkeepsie NY 12601	845-471-1500	R	2*	<.1
220	Wyav Wave 1041—Barry Brown	1016 Ocala St, Myrtle Beach SC 29577	843-448-1041	R	2*	<.1
221	M Belmont Verstandig Inc—John Verstandig	10960 John Wayne Dr, Greencastle PA 17225	717-597-9200	R	2*	<.1
222	Polish American Radio Program—Lisa Edwards	308 Walnut St, Philadelphia PA 19106	215-923-2888	R	2*	<.1
223	KQV Newsradio—Robert Dickey	650 Smithfield St Ste, Pittsburgh PA 15222	412-562-5900	R	2*	<.1
224	Mapleton Communications—Andrew Adams	1020 W Main St, Merced CA 95340	209-723-2191	R	1*	<.1
225	Q Hot Line—Ed Atsinger	7150 Campus Dr Ste 150, Colorado Springs CO 80920	719-388-0300	R	1*	<.1
226	WGRX Thunder 1045—Carl Haulderbus	4414 Lafayette Blvd St, Fredericksburg VA 22408	540-710-1045	R	1*	<.1
227	Wrni Radio—Joe O'connor	40 W Exchange St, Providence RI 02903	401-351-2800	R	1*	<.1
228	Forever Broadcasting—Jim Shields	Downtown Mall, Meadville PA 16335	814-724-1111	R	1*	<.1
229	Kjjr Am 880 Newstalk—Rob Dewbre	PO Box 5409, Kalispell MT 59903	406-756-5557	R	1*	<.1
230	Salem Media Of Colorado—Jules Dygert	3131 S Vaughn Way Ste, Aurora CO 80014	303-750-5687	R	1*	<.1
231	Wottfm—Jim Leven	199 Wealtha Ave, Watertown NY 13601	315-786-9552	R	1*	<.1
232	Reynolds Communications Inc—William Reynolds	PO Box 908, Monticello NY 12701	845-794-0242	R	1*	<.1
233	Wafl Wyus Broadcasting Inc—Melody Booker	1666 Blairs Pond Rd, Milford DE 19963	302-422-7575	R	1*	<.1
234	Omnicom Tower Ltd—J Williams	101 Ctr St Ste R, Woodward OK 73801	580-254-2034	R	1*	<.1
235	Opus Broadcasting Systems Inc—Henry Flock	511 Rossanley Dr, Medford OR 97501	541-772-0322	R	1*	<.1
236	Taylor Communications Inc—Kyle Bauer	1815 Meadowlark Rd, Clay Center KS 67432	785-632-5661	R	1*	<.1
237	Pat and Wes Productions—Weston Sale	2314 Duncan Dr Apt 6, Fairborn OH 45324	937-422-9512	R	1*	<.1
238	Brookings Radio—Linda Werkmeister	227 22nd Ave S, Brookings SD 57006	605-692-9102	R	1*	<.1
239	Wbhg Studio—Jack Beaton	Country Club Rd, Laconia NH 03246	603-528-7699	R	1*	<.1
240	WMVO 1300 Am—Michael Hays	17421 Coshocton Rd, Mount Vernon OH 43050	740-397-1000	R	1*	<.1
241	Wrnj Radio Inc—Norman Worth	PO Box 1000, Hackettstown NJ 07840	908-850-1000	R	1*	<.1
242	Wvrt Inc—Jim Dabney	1559 W 4th St, Williamsport PA 17701	570-601-9770	R	1*	<.1
243	Radio Central Coast—Tom Hughes	795 Buckley Rd Ste 2, San Luis Obispo CA 93401	805-786-2570	R	1*	<.1
244	Wspy 1071 Fm—Lawrence Nelson	1 Broadcast Ctr, Plano IL 60545	630-552-1000	R	1*	<.1
245	WCRX Radio Station 881—Jim Mitchem	33 E Congress Pkwy, Chicago IL 60605	312-663-3512	R	1*	<.1
246	Ashling Broadcasting—Jonathan Hoffman	738 Blowing Rock Rd, Boone NC 28607	828-264-2411	R	1*	<.1
247	Azteca Communications Inc—Javier Macias	1800 Lake Park Dr SE S, Smyrna GA 30080	770-437-8911	R	1*	<.1
248	Key Broadcasting Inc—Terry Forche	PO Box 1988, London KY 40743	606-864-2148	R	1*	<.1
249	Kma Broadcasting LP—Mark Eno	PO Box 960, Shenandoah IA 51601	712-246-5270	R	1*	<.1
250	Radio Hendersonville Inc—Arthur Cooley	PO Box 2470, Hendersonville NC 28793	828-693-9061	R	1*	<.1
251	KVSO Request Line—Kenneth Taishoff	1205 Northglen St, Ardmore OK 73401	580-226-1240	R	1*	<.1
252	WUBU 1063 FM—Esby Klien	237 W Edison Rd Ste 20, Mishawaka IN 46545	574-258-9333	R	1*	<.1
253	Wnst 1570 Am—Steve Hennessey	1550 Hart Rd, Baltimore MD 21286	410-821-9678	R	1*	<.1
254	Gradick Communications Inc—Steve Gradick	102 Parkwood Cir, Carrollton GA 30117	770-832-9685	R	1*	<.1
255	Am Wdef Fm Radio—Gary Downs	PO Box 1449, Chattanooga TN 37401	423-321-6200	R	1*	<.1
256	Kaspar Broadcasting Company Of Missouri Inc—Vernon Kaspar	PO Box 220, Warrenton MO 63383	636-456-3311	R	1*	<.1
257	KOBC Radio Station—Robert Kind	1111 N Main St, Joplin MO 64801	417-781-6401	R	1*	<.1
258	Sturgis Falls Broadcasting—James Coloff	PO Box 248, Cedar Falls IA 50613	319-277-1918	R	1*	<.1
259	Kuvo/Denver Educational Broadcasting Inc—Jene Craven	PO Box 2040, Denver CO 80201	303-480-9272	R	1*	<.1
260	Dakota News Network—Mark Swenson	PO Box 1197, Pierre SD 57501	605-224-9911	R	1*	<.1
261	Cram Communications LLC	401 W Kirkpatrick St, Syracuse NY 13204	315-472-0222	R	1*	<.1
262	KOR N/ K Q R N Radio—Clint Greenway	PO Box 921, Mitchell SD 57301	605-996-1073	R	1*	<.1
263	Kpua 670 Am—Ann Chew	1145 Kilauea Ave, Hilo HI 96720	808-935-5461	R	1*	<.1

Rank	Company Name—*Executive Officer*	Address, City, State, Zip	Phone	Type	Fin	Empls
264	Markham Broadcasting Inc—*Patrick Markham*	1445 W Harvard Ave, Roseburg OR 97471	541-672-6641	R	1*	<.1
265	Alpine Broadcasting Corp—*Norman Alpert*	11800 Tamiami Trl E, Naples FL 34113	239-793-1011	R	1*	<.1
266	Carroll Broadcasting Co—*Mary Collison*	PO Box 886, Carroll IA 51401	712-792-4321	R	1*	<.1
267	Far East Broadcasting Co—*James Cummer*	PO Box 1, La Mirada CA 90637	562-947-4651	R	1*	.1
268	WGCHAM 1490—*Michael Matter*	71 Lewis St, Greenwich CT 06830	203-869-1490	R	1*	<.1
269	K Triple L—*Scott Harris*	33 Briercroft Office P, Lubbock TX 79412	806-770-5555	R	1*	<.1
270	Hometown Broadcasting—*P Leslie*	PO Box 1228, Portsmouth OH 45662	740-353-1161	R	1*	<.1
271	Miami Valley Christian Broadcasting Association Inc—*Claud Shildler*	7333 Manning Rd, Miamisburg OH 45342	937-866-2471	R	1*	<.1
272	Power Country Inc—*Louis Bolton*	9206 W Us Hwy 90, Lake City FL 32055	386-752-0960	R	1*	<.1
273	Music Express Broadcasting Corp—*Warren Jones*	95 W Main St, Geneva OH 44041	440-466-1049	R	1*	<.1
274	South Sound Broadcasting LLC	1803 State Ave Ne, Olympia WA 98506	360-704-3143	R	1*	<.1
275	World Evangelistic Enterprise Corp—*Ryan Freed*	2265 Troy Rd, Springfield OH 45504	937-399-7837	R	1*	<.1
276	Wyep 913 Fm—*Alexa Belajac*	67 Bedford Sq, Pittsburgh PA 15203	412-381-9131	R	1*	<.1
277	WTPA FM 93 5—*Ron Giovanniello*	2300 Vartan Way Ste 10, Harrisburg PA 17110	717-238-6397	R	1*	<.1
278	Basin Broadcasting Co—*James Gober*	1515 W Main St, Farmington NM 87401	505-325-1996	R	1*	<.1
279	WDBM 89 FM—*Gary Reid*	G4 E Holden, East Lansing MI 48825	517-353-4414	R	1*	<.1
280	Advance Media—*Mike Rea*	2006 W Altorfer Dr Ste, Peoria IL 61615	309-693-2345	R	1*	<.1
281	News Radio Corp—*Tim Brown*	PO Box 7205, Avon CO 81620	970-949-0140	R	1*	<.1
282	Potomac News Service—*Nick Chiaia*	1133 19th St Ste 867, Washington DC 20005	202-783-6464	R	1*	<.1
283	Ultra Radio LLC	242 College St, New Haven CT 06510	203-772-3922	R	1*	<.1
284	Creative Rock Concepts Inc—*Dwayne Matekel*	20358 Laguna Canyon Rd, Laguna Beach CA 92651	949-349-0875	R	1*	<.1
285	WMVG Inc—*Randy Beasley*	1250 W Charlton St, Milledgeville GA 31061	478-452-0586	R	1*	<.1
286	WKPW—*Mike York*	10892 N State Rd 140, Knightstown IN 46148	765-345-9070	R	<1*	<.1
287	Flagship Broadcasting LLC	1605 1st St S Ste B16, Willmar MN 56201	320-235-1194	R	<1*	<.1
288	Patrick Henry Broadcasting Corp—*Bill Wyatt*	PO Box 3551, Martinsville VA 24115	276-632-9811	R	<1*	<.1
289	Chadrad Communications Inc—*Dennis Brown*	226 Bordeaux St, Chadron NE 69337	308-432-5545	R	<1*	<.1
290	Lac Qui Parle Broadcasting Company Inc—*Maynard Meyer*	PO Box 70, Madison MN 56256	320-598-7301	R	<1*	<.1
291	WDMLFM—*David Lister*	PO Box 1591, Mount Vernon IL 62864	618-242-3333	R	<1*	<.1
292	WPKN Inc—*Henry Minot*	244 University Ave, Bridgeport CT 06604	203-331-9756	R	<1*	<.1
293	KAZI Austin Community Radio—*David Burrell*	8906 Wall St Ste 203, Austin TX 78754	512-836-9544	R	<1*	.1
294	Whmx Fm 1057—*Pencil Boone*	PO Box 5000, Bangor ME 04402	207-947-2751	R	<1*	<.1
295	Audio Journal Inc—*Vincent Lombardi*	799 W Boylston St Ste, Worcester MA 01606	508-797-1117	R	<1*	<.1
296	Virginia Beach Educational Broadcast Foundation Inc—*Bill Verebely*	3500 Virginia Beach Bl, Virginia Beach VA 23452	757-498-9632	R	<1*	<.1
297	International Sports Broadcasting LLC—*John Lawler*	175 S W Temple Ste 650, Salt Lake City UT 84101	801-466-8080	R	<1*	<.1

TOTALS: SIC 4832 Radio Broadcasting Stations
Companies: 297   16,181   59.8

4833 Television Broadcasting Stations

Rank	Company Name—*Executive Officer*	Address, City, State, Zip	Phone	Type	Fin	Empls
1	Media General Communications Inc—*Marshall N Morton*	333 E Franklin St, Richmond VA 23219	804-649-6000	S	54,009*	7.2
2	Media General Broadcasting of South Carolina Holdings Inc—*Marhsall N Morton*	PO Box 1717, Spartanburg SC 29304	864-576-7777	S	53,987*	7.2
3	NBC Universal Inc—*Richard Cotton*	30 Rockefeller Plz, New York NY 10112	212-664-4444	S	15,416	N/A
4	CBS Corp—*Leslie Moonves*	51 W 52 St, New York NY 10019	212-975-4321	P	14,060	25.4
5	CBS Television Network - Div—*Leslie Moonves*	51 W 52nd St, New York NY 10019	212-975-4321	D	7,240	28.0
6	American Broadcasting Companies Inc—*Paul Lee*	77 W 66th St, New York NY 10023	212-456-7777	S	6,379*	20.2
7	Belo Holdings Inc Belo Corp	PO Box 655237, Dallas TX 75265	214-977-6606	S	2,652*	2.5
8	Ion Media Networks - Knoxville—*R Brandon Burgess* ION Media Networks Inc	9000 Executive Park Dr, Knoxville TN 37923	865-693-4343	S	2,503*	.5
9	ION Television—*R Brandon Burgess* ION Media Networks Inc	2600 W Olive Ste 900, Burbank CA 91505	818-524-1891	S	2,503*	.5
10	Ion Television Denver ION Media Networks Inc	3001 S Jamaica Ct Ste, Aurora CO 80014	303-751-5959	S	2,503*	.5
11	KPXO TV- Honolulu—*Brandon Burgess* ION Media Networks Inc	875 Waimanu St, Honolulu HI 96813	808-591-1275	S	2,503*	.5
12	Allbritton Communications Co—*Robert L Allbritton*	1000 Wilson Blvd Ste 2, Arlington VA 22209	703-647-8700	R	2,389*	.9
13	IAC/InterActiveCorp—*Greg Blatt*	555 W 18th St, New York NY 10011	212-314-7300	P	2,059	3.2
14	Univision Communications Inc—*Randy Falco*	605 3rd Ave 12th Fl, New York NY 10158	212-455-5200	R	1,921*	4.0
15	Tribune Broadcasting Co—*Ed Wilson*	435 N Michigan Ave Ste, Chicago IL 60611	312-222-9100	S	1,718*	5.0
16	Roberts Tower Co—*Michael Roberts Sr*	901 Locust St, Saint Louis MO 63101	314-367-4600	R	1,611*	.5
17	New England Television Corp—*Joe Amorosino* Sunbeam Television Corp	7 Bulfinch Pl, Boston MA 02114	617-725-0777	S	1,587*	.3
18	Ion Media Network - Houston—*Brandon Burgess* ION Media Networks Inc	256 N Sam Houston Pkwy, Houston TX 77060	936-756-2055	S	1,442*	.5
19	Home Shopping Club Inc—*Mindy Grossman*	11831 30th Ct N, Saint Petersburg FL 33716	727-872-1000	S	1,249*	4.5
20	NEP Broadcasting LLC—*Debbie Honkus*	2 Beta Dr, Pittsburgh PA 15238	412-826-1414	S	1,237*	.4
21	WSYX Licensee Inc—*David D Smith*	1261 Dublin Rd, Columbus OH 43215	614-481-6666	S	1,085*	.2
22	R/GA Digital Studios Inc—*Bob Greenberg*	350 W 39th St, New York NY 10018	212-946-4000	S	1,047*	.3
23	CW Network LLC—*Dawn Ostroff*	4000 Warner Blvd, Burbank CA 91522	818-977-2500	J	956*	.3
24	PRN Corp—*Richard Fisher*	600 Harrison St 4th Fl, San Francisco CA 94107	415-808-3500	S	829*	.2
25	Buzztime Entertainment Inc—*Michael J Bush* NTN Buzztime Inc	5966 La Place Ct Ste 1, Carlsbad CA 92008	760-438-7400	S	820*	.2
26	Sinclair Broadcast Group Inc—*David D Smith*	10706 Beaver Dam Rd, Hunt Valley MD 21030	410-568-1500	P	767	2.4
27	Hearst Television Inc—*David J Barrett*	300 W 57th St, New York NY 10019	212-887-6800	S	721	3.3
28	Belo Corp—*Dunia A Shive*	PO Box 655237, Dallas TX 75265	214-977-6606	P	687	2.6
29	KOCB Inc—*Scott Campbell*	1228 E Wilshire Blvd, Oklahoma City OK 73111	405-843-2525	S	627*	.1
30	WGGB Inc—*John Gormally*	1300 Liberty St, Springfield MA 01104	413-733-4040	S	627*	.1
31	WPGH Licensee LLC—*Allan Frank* Sinclair Media I Inc	750 Ivory Ave, Pittsburgh PA 15214	412-931-5300	S	627*	.1
32	AandE Television Networks—*Abbe Raven*	235 E 45th St, New York NY 10017	212-210-1400	J	625*	.6
33	KOCB Licensee LLC KOCB Inc	1228 E Wilshire Blvd, Oklahoma City OK 73111	405-478-3434	S	621*	.1
34	WKEF Licensee LP—*Dane Dittmer*	45 Broadcast Plz, Dayton OH 45408	937-263-4500	S	621*	.1
35	KABB Licensee LLC—*John Seabers*	4335 NW Loop 410, San Antonio TX 78229	210-366-1129	S	620*	.1
36	Wear Licensee LLC—*David Smith*	PO Box 12278, Pensacola FL 32591	850-456-3333	S	620*	.1
37	WGME Licensee LLC	1335 Washington Ave, Portland ME 04103	207-797-1313	S	620*	.1
38	Hubbard Broadcasting Inc—*Stanley Hubbard*	3415 University Ave, Saint Paul MN 55114	651-646-5555	R	600*	1.5

Note: An asterisk (*) indicates an estimated financial figure. The company type code used is as follows: R = Private, P = Public, S = Private Subsidiary, B = Public Subsidiary, D = Division, J = Joint Venture, I = Investment Fund.

COMPANY RANKINGS BY SALES WITHIN 4-DIGIT SIC

Rank	Company Name—*Executive Officer*	Address, City, State, Zip	Phone	Type	Fin	Empls
39	Sinclair Media I Inc—*David D Smith*	7622 Bald Cypress Pl, Tampa FL 33614	813-886-9882	S	564*	.1
40	Telefutura Houston LLC—*Joe Uva* Univision Communications Inc	9440 Kirby Dr, Houston TX 77054	713-662-4545	S	564*	.1
41	WTTO Inc—*JC Lowe*	651 Beacon Pky W Ste 1, Birmingham AL 35209	205-943-2168	S	564*	.1
42	WTWC Licensee LLC WTWC Inc	8440 Deerlake S, Tallahassee FL 32312	850-893-4140	S	559*	.1
43	WICS Licensee LLC—*Tim Mathes*	2680 E Cook St, Springfield IL 62703	217-753-5620	S	558*	.1
44	LeSEA Inc—*Peter Sumrall*	PO Box 12, South Bend IN 46624	574-291-8200	R	551*	.2
45	Sinclair Media III Inc—*David D Smith*	PO Box 11138, Charleston WV 25339	304-346-5358	S	502*	.1
46	WCHS Licensee LLC—*Harold Cooper* Sinclair Media III Inc	PO Box 11138, Charleston WV 25339	304-346-5358	S	502*	.1
47	WLFL Inc—*David D Smith*	3012 Highwoods Blvd St, Raleigh NC 27604	919-790-9535	S	502*	.1
48	WTVZ Inc—*Scott Campbell*	900 Granby St, Norfolk VA 23510	757-622-3333	S	502*	.1
49	WYZZ Inc—*Coby Cooper*	3131 N University, Peoria IL 61604	309-688-3131	S	501*	.1
50	WTTO Licensee LLC—*JC Lowe* WTTO Inc	651 Beacon Pkwy W Ste, Birmingham AL 35209	205-943-2168	S	496*	.1
51	WCGV Licensee LLC—*David Ford*	4041 N 35th St, Milwaukee WI 53216	414-442-7050	S	477*	.1
52	KGAN Licensee LLC	PO Box 3131, Cedar Rapids IA 52406	319-395-9060	S	465*	.1
53	Williams Vyvx Services—*Laura Kenny*	111 E 1st St, Tulsa OK 74103	918-573-5760	R	450*	1.5
54	KY-3 Inc—*Brian McDonough*	999 W Sunshine, Springfield MO 65807	417-268-3000	S	429*	.2
55	LIN TV Corp—*Vincent L Sadusky*	1 W Exchange St Ste 5A, Providence RI 02903	401-454-2880	P	420	1.8
56	WSYT Licensee LP	1000 James St, Syracuse NY 13203	315-472-6800	S	414*	.1
57	KFPX TV-Des Moines—*Brandon Burgess* ION Media Networks Inc	1801 Grand Ave, Des Moines IA 50309	515-242-3500	S	411*	.1
58	MobiTV—*Charlie Nooney*	6425 Christie Ave 5th, Emeryville CA 94608	510-450-5000	R	385*	.1
59	WTWC Inc	8440 Deerlake Rd S, Tallahassee FL 32312	850-893-4140	S	376*	.1
60	Raycom Media Inc—*Paul McTear*	201 Monroe St20th Fl, Montgomery AL 36104	334-206-1400	R	352*	3.0
61	WICD Licensee LLC—*Tim Mathis*	250 S Country Fair Dr, Champaign IL 61821	217-351-8500	S	335*	.1
62	Nexstar Broadcasting Group Inc—*Perry A Sook*	5215 N O'Conner Blvd S, Irving TX 75039	972-373-8800	P	313	2.1
63	Sinclair Television of Charleston Inc	4301 Arco Ln, Charleston SC 29418	843-744-2424	S	310*	.1
64	WMMP Licensee LP—*Mary M Johnson*	4301 Arco Ln, Charleston SC 29418	843-744-2424	S	310*	.1
65	WSMH Licensee LLC WSMH Inc	G-3463 W Pierson Rd, Flint MI 48504	810-785-8866	S	310*	.1
66	Gray Television Inc—*Hilton H Howell*	4370 Peachtree Rd NE, Atlanta GA 30319	404-504-9828	P	307	2.2
67	WRDW-TV Inc—*John Ray* Gray Television Inc	PO Box 1212, Augusta GA 30903		S	303*	.1
68	Fox Broadcasting Co—*Ed Wilson*	10201 West Pico Blvd, Los Angeles CA 90035	212-852-7017	S	293*	.4
69	WSMH Inc—*Scott Campbell*	G-3463 W Pierson Rd, Flint MI 48504	810-785-8866	S	282*	<.1
70	WildBlue Communications Inc—*David J Leonard*	5970 Greenwood Plz Blv, Greenwood Village CO 80111	720-554-7400	S	266*	.1
71	rVueInc—*Jason M Kates*	100 NE 3rd Ave Ste 200, Fort Lauderdale FL 33301	954-525-6464	R	263*	.1
72	WITN-TV Inc—*Hilton Howell* Gray Television Inc	PO Box 468, Washington NC 27889	252-946-3131	S	242*	.1
73	ION Media Networks Inc—*Brandon Burgess*	601 Clearwater Park Rd, West Palm Beach FL 33401	561-659-4122	R	229*	.5
74	KBSI Licensee LP—*David D Smith*	806 Enterprise, Cape Girardeau MO 63703	573-334-1223	S	207*	<.1
75	KUPN Licensee LLC	3830 S Jones Blvd, Las Vegas NV 89103	702-382-2121	S	207*	<.1
76	WDKY Inc—*Scott Campbell*	836 Euclid Ave Ste 201, Lexington KY 40502	859-269-5656	S	207*	<.1
77	WDKY Licensee LLC—*Micheal Brickey* WDKY Inc	836 Euclid Ave, Lexington KY 40502	859-269-5656	S	205*	<.1
78	Sunbeam Television Corp—*Edmund Ansin*	1401 79th St Cswy, Miami FL 33141	305-795-2633	R	202*	.4
79	Entravision Communications Corp—*Walter F Ulloa*	2425 Olympic Blvd Ste, Santa Monica CA 90404	310-447-3870	P	201	.9
80	Telemundo Group Inc—*Donald Browne*	2290 W 8th Ave, Hialeah FL 33010	305-884-8200	S	198	1.2
81	Entravision Holdings LLC Entravision Communications Corp	2425 Olympic Blvd Ste, Santa Monica CA 90404	310-447-3870	S	193*	<.1
82	Fisher Communications Inc—*Colleen B Brown*	100 4th Ave N Ste 510, Seattle WA 98109	206-404-7000	P	176	.8
83	Fox Inc—*K Murdoch*	PO Box 900, Beverly Hills CA 90213	310-369-1000	R	160*	3.2
84	Thirteen—*Neil Shapiro*	825 8th Ave Fl 14, New York NY 10019	212-560-2000	R	155*	.4
85	Young Broadcasting of Sioux Falls Inc—*Jay Huizenga*	501 S Phillips Ave, Sioux Falls SD 57104	605-336-1100	S	153*	.1
86	Ellis Communications Kdoc LLC—*John Manzi*	625 N Grand Ave Fl 1, Santa Ana CA 92701	949-442-9800	R	150*	<.1
87	WNAB-TV Channel 58—*Mary Wilson*	631 Mainstream Dr, Nashville TN 37228	615-650-5858	S	142*	<.1
88	Communications Corporation of Baton Rouge Inc—*Steve Pruett*	700 St John St Ste 300, Lafayette LA 70501	337-237-1142	R	136*	.1
89	Young Broadcasting of Davenport Inc—*Jim Graham*	805 Brady St, Davenport IA 52803	563-383-7000	S	126*	.1
90	Capitol Broadcasting Company Inc—*James Goodmon*	PO Box 12800, Raleigh NC 27605	919-890-6000	R	120*	.6
91	Fortel DTV Inc—*Makary Awadalla*	3305 Breckinridge Blvd, Duluth GA 30096	770-806-0234	R	117*	.1
92	Young Broadcasting of Lansing Inc—*Deb McDermott*	2820 E Saginaw St, Lansing MI 48912	517-372-8282	S	115*	.1
93	WRLH Licensee LLC Sinclair Television of Charleston Inc	1925 Westmoreland St, Richmond VA 23230	804-359-3510	S	111*	<.1
94	NBC 10—*Lisa Churchville* NBC Universal Inc	23 Kenney Dr, Cranston RI 02920	401-455-9100	S	106*	.3
95	KING Broadcasting Co	PO Box 24525, Seattle WA 98124	206-448-5555	S	94*	.4
96	Tribune Entertainment Co—*Richard Inouye* Tribune Broadcasting Co	5800 W Sunset Blvd, Los Angeles CA 90028	323-460-5800	S	91*	.1
97	Outdoor Channel Holdings Inc—*Roger L Werner Jr*	43445 Business Park Dr, Temecula CA 92590	951-699-4749	P	83	.2
98	KPXM TV-Minneapolis—*R Brandon Burgess* ION Media Networks Inc	22601 176th St NW, Big Lake MN 55309	763-236-8666	S	82*	<.1
99	Citadel Comunications Ltd—*Philip Lombardo*	44 Pondfield Rd, Bronxville NY 10708	914-793-3400	R	76*	.1
100	Trinity Broadcasting Network Inc	PO Box A, Santa Ana CA 92711	714-832-2950	R	68*	.4
101	WTBC 1230—*Ronnie Quarles*	PO Box 2000, Tuscaloosa AL 35403	205-752-9822	S	63*	<.1
102	Granite Broadcasting Corp—*Don Cornwell*	767 3rd Ave 34th Fl, New York NY 10017	212-826-2530	R	57*	.5
103	Kqed Inc—*John Boland*	PO Box 410865, San Francisco CA 94141	415-864-2000	R	57*	.3
104	Telefutura Tampa LLC—*Joe Uva* Univision Communications Inc	15001 Boyette Rd, Tampa FL 33602	813-684-5550	S	50*	<.1
105	WBNA TV-Louisville—*Bob Rodgers* ION Media Networks Inc	3701 Fern Valley Rd, Louisville KY 40219	502-964-2121	S	49*	<.1
106	WBPX TV-Boston—*Brandon Burgess* ION Media Networks Inc	1120 Soldiers Field Rd, Boston MA 02134	617-787-6868	S	49*	<.1
107	WCPX TV-Chicago—*Brandon Burgess* ION Media Networks Inc	333 S Desplaines St, Chicago IL 60661	312-376-8520	S	49*	<.1
108	WNPX TV-Nashville—*R Brandon Burgess* ION Media Networks Inc	1281 N Mt Juliet Rd, Mount Juliet TN 37122	615-773-6100	S	49*	<.1

Rank	Company Name—*Executive Officer*	Address, City, State, Zip	Phone	Type	Fin	Empls
109	WPXX TV-Memphis—*R Brandon Burgess* ION Media Networks Inc	5050 Poplar Ave STE 90, Memphis TN 38157	901-821-8593	S	49*	<.1
110	KLAS-TV Inc	PO Box 15047, Las Vegas NV 89114	702-792-8888	S	42*	.2
111	WPXJ TV-Buffalo—*Brandon Burgess* ION Media Networks Inc	726 Exchange St, Buffalo NY 14210	716-852-1818	S	39*	<.1
112	Roberts Broadcasting Co—*Michael V Roberts* Roberts Tower Co	901 Locust St, Saint Louis MO 63101	314-367-4600	S	38*	.1
113	Diversified Communications Inc—*Dustin Fain*	2000 M St NW Ste 340, Washington DC 20036	202-775-4300	R	36*	<.1
114	WLPX TV-Charleston—*Brandon Burgess* ION Media Networks Inc	600 Prestige Park Dr, Hurricane WV 25526	304-760-1029	S	33*	<.1
115	WPXA TV-Atlanta—*Brandon Burgess* ION Media Networks Inc	200 N Cobb Pkwy, Marietta GA 30062	770-919-0575	S	33*	<.1
116	WUPX TV-Lexington—*R Brandon Burgess* ION Media Networks Inc	2166 Mccausey Ridge Rd, Frenchburg KY 40322	216-344-7465	S	33*	<.1
117	Twin Cities Public Television Inc—*James Pagliarini*	172 4th St E, Saint Paul MN 55101	651-222-1717	R	33*	.2
118	Window to the World Communications Inc—*Dan Schmidt*	5400 N St Louis Ave, Chicago IL 60625	773-583-5000	R	31*	.3
119	NBC Internet Inc—*Chris Kitze* NBC Universal Inc	225 Bush St, San Francisco CA 94104	415-375-5000	S	28*	.5
120	Kob-Tv LLC—*Robert Hubbard*	PO Box 1351, Albuquerque NM 87103	505-243-4411	R	27*	.2
121	Jones Education Co—*Glenn R Jones*	9697 E Mineral Ave, Centennial CO 80112	303-792-3111	S	27*	.1
122	Shadow Broadcast Services Inc	201 State Rte 17 N 9th, Rutherford NJ 07070	201-939-1888	R	27*	<.1
123	NTN Buzztime Inc—*Michael Bush*	2231 Rutherford Rd Ste, Carlsbad CA 92008	760-438-7400	P	25	.1
124	Yuma Broadcasting Co—*James Rogers*	1385 S Pacific Ave, Yuma AZ 85365	928-782-1111	R	/25*	.7
125	WJAC Inc—*Jim Edgar*	49 Old Hickory Ln, Johnstown PA 15905	814-255-7600	R	25*	.1
126	WFMY Television Corp—*Larry Audus*	1615 Phillips Ave, Greensboro NC 27405	336-379-9369	S	24*	.1
127	WGPX TV- Greensboro—*Brandon Burgess* ION Media Networks Inc	1114 N O'Henry Blvd, Greensboro NC 27405	336-272-9227	S	23*	<.1
128	WYPX TV-Albany—*Brandon Burgess* ION Media Networks Inc	1 Charles Blvd Ste 1, Guilderland NY 12084	518-464-9842	S	23*	<.1
129	LeSEA Broadcasting Corp—*Peter Sumrall* LeSEA Inc	61300 S Ironwood Rd, South Bend IN 46614	574-291-8200	S	22*	.2
130	Newschannel 11s New Media Sales—*Thomas Hoffman*	338 E Main St, Johnson City TN 37601	423-434-4543	R	22*	.1
131	Max Media LLC—*Gene Loving*	900 Laskin Rd, Virginia Beach VA 23451	757-437-9800	R	21	<.1
132	KULR Corp—*Bruce Cummings*	PO Box 80810, Billings MT 59108	406-656-8000	R	20	.1
133	New Jersey Public Broadcasting Authority—*Elizabeth Christo-pherson*	PO Box 777, Trenton NJ 08625	609-777-5000	R	20*	.2
134	Kcts Television—*William Mohler*	401 Mercer St, Seattle WA 98109	206-728-6463	R	20*	.1
135	Price Communications Corp—*Robert Price*	45 Rockefeller Plz, New York NY 10020	212-757-6600	R	19	<.1
136	Griffin Communications LLC—*David F Griffin*	7401 N Kelley Ave, Oklahoma City OK 73111	405-843-6641	R	19*	.2
137	VHR Broadcasting of Springfield Inc—*Mark Gordon* Nexstar Broadcasting Group Inc	2650 E Division St, Springfield MO 65803	417-862-1010	S	19*	.1
138	Sinclair Radio of St Louis Inc—*David D Smith*	10706 Beaver Dam Rd, Hunt Valley MD 21030	410-568-1500	S	19*	<.1
139	Blue Sky Productions—*John McElroy*	39201 Schoolcraft Rd S, Livonia MI 48150	734-542-7000	R	18*	<.1
140	Bay City Television Inc—*Robert Taylor*	8253 Ronson Rd, San Diego CA 92111	858-279-6666	R	17*	.1
141	Wqed Multimedia—*George Miles*	4802 5th Ave Ste 1, Pittsburgh PA 15213	412-622-1300	R	17*	.1
142	Connecticut Public Broadcasting Inc—*Jerry Franklin*	1049 Asylum Ave, Hartford CT 06105	860-278-5310	R	17*	.1
143	Meyer Broadcasting Co—*Judith Johnson*	PO Box 1738, Bismarck ND 58502	701-255-5757	R	17*	.3
144	Authority For Educational Television Kentucky—*Mac Wall*	600 Cooper Dr, Lexington KY 40502	859-258-7104	R	16*	.2
145	KPXR TV-Cedar Rapids—*Brandon Burgess* ION Media Networks Inc	1957 Blairs Ferry Rd N, Cedar Rapids IA 52402	319-378-1260	S	16*	<.1
146	Wboc Inc—*Thomas Draper*	1729 N Salisbury Blvd, Salisbury MD 21801	410-749-1111	R	15*	.1
147	Draper Communications Inc—*Thomas H Draper*	PO Box 2057, Salisbury MD 21802	410-749-1111	R	15*	.2
148	ACME Communications Inc—*Doug Gealy*	2101 E 4th St Ste 202, Santa Ana CA 92705	714-245-9499	P	15	.1
149	Hampton Roads Educational Telecommunications Association Inc—*Bert Schmidt*	5200 Hampton Blvd, Norfolk VA 23508	757-889-9400	R	14*	.1
150	Panhandle Telecasting LP—*Wilson Leftwich*	PO Box 10, Amarillo TX 79105	806-383-1010	R	14*	.1
151	Long Island Educational TV Council Inc—*Terrell Cass*	PO Box 21, Plainview NY 11803	516-367-2100	R	14*	.1
152	Heritage Broadcasting Group—*Mario Iacobelli* Sinclair Broadcast Group Inc	PO Box 627, Cadillac MI 49601	231-775-3478	S	13*	.1
153	Next Star Broadcasting Group LLC—*Perry Sook*	8455 Peach St, Erie PA 16509	814-864-2400	R	13*	.1
154	Care Tv—*John Remes*	8811 Olson Memorial Hw, Minneapolis MN 55427	763-546-1111	R	13*	.2
155	Virginia West Educational Broadcasting—*Dennis Adkins*	600 Capitol St, Charleston WV 25301	304-556-4900	R	12*	.1
156	New Orleans Hearst-Argyle Television Inc—*David Barrett*	846 Howard Ave, New Orleans LA 70113	504-679-0600	R	12*	.1
157	WLBT Inc—*Dan Modisett* Raycom Media Inc	715 S Jefferson St, Jackson MS 39201	601-948-3333	S	12*	<.1
158	Wsjv Television Inc—*Thomas Oakley*	PO Box 28, South Bend IN 46624	574-679-9758	R	11*	.1
159	Fox 17 Studio Productions—*David Birdsong*	631 Mainstream Dr, Nashville TN 37228	615-244-1717	R	11*	.2
160	WJLA Inc—*Fred Ryan* Allbritton Communications Co	1100 Wilson Blvd, Arlington VA 22209	703-236-9552	D	11*	.2
161	Gray Kentucky Television Inc—*Wayne M Martin* Gray Television Inc	2851 Winchester Rd, Lexington KY 40509	859-299-0411	D	11*	.1
162	Ottumwa Media Holding LLC—*Tom Henson*	820 W 2nd St, Ottumwa IA 52501	641-684-5415	R	11*	.1
163	Northland Television Inc—*Joseph Fuchs*	3217 County G, Rhinelander WI 54501	715-365-8812	R	11*	<.1
164	Virginia Broadcasting Corp—*Harold Wright*	PO Box 769, Charlottesville VA 22902	434-220-2900	R	10*	.1
165	Azadi Television Inc—*Harvard Palmer*	21045 Superior St, Chatsworth CA 91311	818-700-0666	R	10*	<.1
166	Florida West Coast Public Broadcasting Inc—*Dick Lobo*	1300 N Blvd, Tampa FL 33607	813-254-9338	R	9*	.1
167	Wipb Tv Channel 49—*Thomas Thise*	Ball State UniversityB, Muncie IN 47306	765-285-1249	R	9*	.1
168	Bet Television Station—*Debra Lee*	1235 W St Ne, Washington DC 20018	202-608-2100	R	8*	.4
169	Nvt Savannah LLC	10001 Abercorn St, Savannah GA 31406	912-925-0022	R	8*	.1
170	Pappas Telecasting Of Centralnebraska LP—*Dennis Davis*	PO Box 220, Kearney NE 68848	308-743-2494	R	8*	.1
171	KTSM-TV—*Gary Sotir*	801 N Oregon St, El Paso TX 79902	915-532-5421	R	8*	.1
172	OBN Holdings Inc—*Roger Neal Smith*	8275 S Eastern Ave Ste, Las Vegas NV 89123	702-938-0467	P	8	<.1
173	Kfox-Tv Inc—*Armando Maldonado*	6004 N Mesa St, El Paso TX 79912	915-833-8585	R	8*	.1
174	Unavision—*Steve Stuck*	1150 9th St Ste 1505, Modesto CA 95354	209-578-1900	R	8*	.1
175	Kwbb—*Larry Boyer*	PO Box 7128, Beaumont TX 77726	409-924-9099	R	7*	.1
176	Channel Three Productions—*Andy Combs*	615 N Front St, Wilmington NC 28401	910-762-8581	R	7*	.1
177	WFPX TV-Fayetteville—*Brandon Burgess* ION Media Networks Inc	19234 NC Hwy 71 N, Lumber Bridge NC 28357	910-827-4801	S	7*	<.1
178	Nyc Media Group—*Arick Wierson*	1 Centre St Rm 2000n, New York NY 10007	212-669-7400	R	7*	.1
179	Smith Television Of Ny Inc—*David Streeter*	PO Box 2, Utica NY 13503	315-733-0404	R	7*	.1

Note: An asterisk (*) indicates an estimated financial figure. The company type code used is as follows: R = Private, P = Public, S = Private Subsidiary, B = Public Subsidiary, D = Division, J = Joint Venture, I = Investment Fund.

COMPANY RANKINGS BY SALES WITHIN 4-DIGIT SIC

Rank	Company Name—Executive Officer	Address, City, State, Zip	Phone	Type	Fin	Empls
180	Midessa Television LP—Lawton Cablevision	PO Box 60150, Midland TX 79711	432-567-9999	R	6*	.1
181	Kgns Laredo Inc—Juan Cue	120 W Del Mar Blvd, Laredo TX 78041	956-727-8888	R	6*	.1
182	Pollacks-Belz Broadcasting CoLlc—William Pollack	5650 S Broadway St, Eureka CA 95503	707-443-3123	R	6*	<.1
183	Nashville Broadcasting LP—J Hannan	631 Mainstream Dr, Nashville TN 37228	615-650-5858	R	6*	<.1
184	Centex Television LP—Jerry Pursley	PO Box 2522, Waco TX 76702	254-754-2525	R	5*	.1
185	Herring Broadcasting Company Inc—Robert Herring	4757 Morena Blvd, San Diego CA 92117	858-270-6900	R	5*	.1
186	Greater Nebraska Television Inc—Cynda Walker	PO Box 749, North Platte NE 69103	308-532-2222	R	5*	.1
187	Atlanta Wupa Cw—John Bryner	2700 Ne Expy Ne Bldg A, Atlanta GA 30345	404-325-6969	R	5*	.1
188	Mexicanal LLC	1532 Dnwody Village Pk, Atlanta GA 30338	770-396-7850	R	5*	<.1
189	Weny Inc—Kevin Lilly	474 Old Ithaca Rd, Horseheads NY 14845	607-739-0344	R	5*	<.1
190	KTRETV Station	Hwy 69 N, Pollok TX 75969	936-569-0998	R	5*	.1
191	Cinedigm Digital Media Services Division—A Dale Mayo	20640 Bahama St, Chatsworth CA 91311	818-678-2000	S	5	<.1
192	Lehigh Valley Public Telecommunications Corp—Patricia Simon	123 Sesame St, Bethlehem PA 18015	610-867-4677	R	5*	.1
193	Colorado Public Television Inc—Willard Rowland	PO Box 1740, Denver CO 80201	303-296-1212	R	5*	<.1
194	Kcen Operating Company LLC—Gayle Kiger	111 W Central Ave, Temple TX 76501	254-773-1633	R	5*	.1
195	Ktlm Tv—Sam Vale	3900 N 10th St Fl 7, Mcallen TX 78501	956-686-0040	R	5*	<.1
196	Sunbelt Multimedia Co—Sam Vale	PO Box 156, Rio Grande City TX 78582	956-686-0040	R	4*	<.1
197	Retirement Living Tv LLC—Erin Knapp	991 Corporate Blvd, Linthicum MD 21090	410-402-9618	R	4*	<.1
198	Woods Communication Corp—David Woods	1 Wcov Ave, Montgomery AL 36111	334-288-7020	R	4*	<.1
199	WOHL Tv Fox 25 And Metro Video Inc—Greg Phipps	PO Box 1689, Lima OH 45802	419-224-8867	R	4*	<.1
200	KRQE—Bill Anderson	13 Broadcast Plz SW, Albuquerque NM 87104		D	4*	<.1
201	Sutro Tower Inc	1 La Avanzada St, San Francisco CA 94131	415-681-8850	R	4*	<.1
202	Coronet Communications Inc—Heather Voudrie	231 18th St, Rock Island IL 61201	309-786-5441	R	4*	.1
203	Wzup—Phil Waterman	10000 Perkins Rd, Baton Rouge LA 70810	225-214-1313	R	4*	.1
204	Telefutura 49 Kstr—Becky Diaz	2323 Bryan St Ste 1900, Dallas TX 75201	214-953-7100	R	4*	.1
205	Acme Television Of Tennessee LLC—Anna Robins	10427 Cogdill Rd Ste 1, Knoxville TN 37932	865-777-9220	R	4*	<.1
206	M Network Television Inc—Jonathan Murray	6007 Sepulveda Blvd, Van Nuys CA 91411	818-756-5150	R	4*	.1
207	World News Saturday/Sunday—Vinnie Malhotra	47 W 66th St Fl 2, New York NY 10023	212-456-4083	R	4*	.1
208	Fox 46—William Pharis	PO Box 573, Fort Smith AR 72902	479-785-4600	R	4*	<.1
209	Kqtv—Perry Soot	PO Box 8369, Saint Joseph MO 64508	816-233-1606	R	4*	.1
210	Krxi—David West	4920 Brookside Ct, Reno NV 89502	775-856-1100	R	4*	.1
211	Seekonk Local Cable Studio—Russ Hart	301 Taunton Ave Ste 7, Seekonk MA 02771	508-336-6770	R	4*	<.1
212	Shenandoah Valley Educational Television Corp—Steve Shenk	298 Port Republic Rd, Harrisonburg VA 22801	540-434-5391	R	4*	<.1
213	Red Lion Television Inc—John Norris	PO Box 88, Red Lion PA 17356	717-246-1681	R	4*	<.1
214	Asia Star Broadcasting Inc—Hasmukh Shah	76 National Rd, Edison NJ 08817	732-650-1100	R	3*	<.1
215	Wollmann Video Production Ltd—Richard Wollmann	19 Bontecou View Dr, New Paltz NY 12561	845-255-5348	R	3*	<.1
216	Mph Entertainment Inc—James Milio	1033 N Hollywood Way C, Burbank CA 91505	818-441-5040	R	3*	<.1
217	WHDFT V-15—Louann Thomson	200 Andrew Jackson Way, Huntsville AL 35801	256-536-1550	R	3*	<.1
218	Mountain Broadcasting Corp—Sun Joo	99 Clinton Rd, Caldwell NJ 07006	973-852-0300	R	3*	<.1
219	WBNS Tv—Fred Barnes	121 Old Cline Rd, Ghent WV 25843	304-787-5959	R	3*	<.1
220	Public Broadcasting of Northwest Pennsylvania—Dwight Miller	8425 Peach St, Erie PA 16509	814-864-3081	R	3*	<.1
221	Bluebonnet Communications Inc—Lester Langley	129 W Prien Lake Rd, Lake Charles LA 70601	337-474-1316	R	3*	<.1
222	Asia Network Enterprise Inc—Jaeh Chung	6430 W Sunset Blvd Ste, Los Angeles CA 90028	323-465-1100	R	3*	<.1
223	Kansas Public Telecommunications Service Inc—Michele Cook	320 W 21st St N, Wichita KS 67203	316-838-3090	R	3*	<.1
224	Tulsa Communications LLC—Derek Criss	233 S Detroit Ave Ste, Tulsa OK 74120	918-270-1919	R	3*	<.1
225	Wyomedia Corp—Jerry Friedman	1856 Skyview Dr, Casper WY 82601	307-577-5923	R	3*	<.1
226	Duluth Superior Area Educational Tv Corp—Allen Harmon	632 Niagara Ct, Duluth MN 55811	218-724-8567	R	3*	<.1
227	Nextar Broadcasting—Nadia Bashir	PO Box 8655, Fort Wayne IN 46898	260-471-5555	R	3*	<.1
228	Jovon Broadcasting Inc—Joe Stroud	18600 Oak Park Ave, Tinley Park IL 60477	708-633-0001	R	3*	<.1
229	VTN Victory Television Network—Happy Caldwell	700 S Church St, Jonesboro AR 72401	870-935-4848	R	2*	<.1
230	Global Sports Marketing Corp—Wayne Butler	PO Box 556, Bryn Athyn PA 19009	610-688-1765	R	2*	<.1
231	WTSN Channel 63—Dan Robbin	44 Main St, Evansville IN 47708	812-464-4444	R	2*	<.1
232	Kktu Television—Sonya Humphery	1896 Skyview Dr, Casper WY 82601	307-237-3711	R	2*	<.1
233	WB Cable 6—Peter Padilla	940 Matley Ln Ste 15, Reno NV 89502	775-786-6666	R	2*	<.1
234	Go Inc—Scott Thomas	1050 Gemini St, Houston TX 77058	281-212-1022	R	2*	<.1
235	WFXG TV—Barry Bart	3933 Washington Rd, Augusta GA 30907	706-650-5400	R	2*	<.1
236	Viet Hai Ngoai-Television Corp—Bruce Tran	16055 Brookhurst St, Fountain Valley CA 92708	714-531-8884	R	2*	<.1
237	Faith For Today Inc—Stewart Harty	PO Box 1000, Thousand Oaks CA 91359	805-955-7700	R	2*	<.1
238	Wowk Tv—Bray Cary	1900 Kanawha Blvd E St, Charleston WV 25305	304-343-1313	R	2*	<.1
239	Good Life Broadcasting Inc—Ken Mikesel	31 Skyline Dr, Lake Mary FL 32746	407-423-5200	R	2*	<.1
240	Sainte Partners—Chester Smith	142 N 9th St Ste 8, Modesto CA 95350	209-466-3400	R	2*	<.1
241	WGBC-TV LLC—Carol Lisenbe	1151 Crestview Cir, Meridian MS 39301	601-485-3030	R	2*	<.1
242	Tv Station—Laura Wolf	1550 W Interstate 20, Odessa TX 79763	432-580-0113	R	2*	<.1
243	Vtv Varsity Television Inc—Kelly Hoffman	6500 River Pl Blvd 2, Austin TX 78730	512-527-2500	R	2*	<.1
244	Telewizja Polska USA Inc—Bob Spanski	1350 Remington Rd Ste, Schaumburg IL 60173	847-882-2000	R	2*	<.1
245	Motor Week—John Davis	11767 Owings Mills Blv, Owings Mills MD 21117	410-581-4212	R	2*	<.1
246	Max Media Of Kentucky—Jeff Cash	325 Emmett Ave Ste N, Bowling Green KY 42101	270-781-2140	R	2*	<.1
247	Tri-State Family Broadcasting Inc—Marcus Lamb	PO Box 2320, Ashland KY 41105	606-329-2700	R	2*	<.1
248	Redwood Empire Public Television Inc—Ronald Schoenherr	PO Box 13, Eureka CA 95502	707-445-0813	R	1*	<.1
249	Kcft 20 Christian Family Tv Inc—Tom Speigleman	6401 E Nrthn Lghts Fl, Anchorage AK 99504	907-337-2020	R	1*	<.1
250	Trinity Broadcasting Of Arizona—Paul Crouch	3551 E Mcdowell Rd, Phoenix AZ 85008	602-273-1477	R	1*	<.1
251	Elearning Media Inc—Steven Russak	2808 Blazing Star Dr, Thousand Oaks CA 91362	805-493-4402	R	1*	<.1
252	Channel 8 Wpsj Tv—Paul Wilson	339 State Rte 73 N, Winslow NJ 08095	856-767-8884	R	1*	<.1
253	Spartan Communications Inc—Kimberly Carter	PO Box 1717, Spartanburg SC 29304	864-599-0054	R	1*	<.1
254	Quinn Broadcasting Inc—James F Quinn	415 N High St, Millville NJ 08332	856-327-8800	R	1*	<.1
255	Channel 38 Christian Television—Andrew Pascell	6400 Escondido Dr, El Paso TX 79912	915-585-8838	R	1*	<.1
256	Herald Of Truth Ministries Inc—John Hall	PO Box 2439, Abilene TX 79604	325-698-4370	R	1*	<.1
257	Michigan Government Television Inc—Bill Trevarthen	111 S Capitol Ave Fl 4, Lansing MI 48933	517-373-4250	R	1*	<.1
258	Regional Educational Technology Network—Scott Campitelli	PO Box 2386, South Burlington VT 05407	802-654-7980	R	1*	<.1
259	Signet International Holdings Inc—Ernest W Letiziano	205 Worth Ave Ste 316, Palm Beach FL 33480	561-832-2000	P	<1	<.1
260	Thirteen / WNET—Neal Shapiro	825 8th Ave, New York NY 10019	212-560-1313	R	N/A	5.0
261	WLOX Inc—Paul McTear Raycom Media Inc	PO Box 4596, Biloxi MS 39535	228-896-0761	S	N/A	.2
262	Paxson Communications of Birmingham-44 Inc—Brandon Burgess ION Media Networks Inc	2085 Golden Crest Dr, Birmingham AL 35209	205-870-4404	S	N/A	<.1
263	WPXD TV-Detroit—Brandon Burgess ION Media Networks Inc	3975 Varsity Dr, Ann Arbor MI 48108	734-973-7900	S	N/A	<.1

TOTALS: SIC 4833 Television Broadcasting Stations
Companies: 263   212,235   164.5

Rank	Company Name—*Executive Officer*	Address, City, State, Zip	Phone	Type	Fin	Empls
	4841 Cable & Other Pay Television Services					
1	Comcast Corp—*Brian L Roberts*	1 Comcast Ctr, Philadelphia PA 19103		P	37,937	102.0
2	Time Warner Cable Inc—*Glenn A Britt*	60 Columbus Cir 17th F, New York NY 10023	212-364-8200	P	18,868	47.5
3	Viacom Inc—*Philippe P Dauman*	1515 Broadway, New York NY 10036	212-258-6000	P	14,914	10.6
4	Dish Network Corp—*Joseph P Clayton*	PO Box 6660, Englewood CO 80155	303-723-1000	P	12,641	22.0
5	Liberty Global Inc—*Michael T Fries*	12300 Liberty Blvd, Englewood CO 80112	303-220-6600	P	9,017	20.0
6	Cablevision Systems Corp—*James L Dolan*	1111 Stewart Ave, Bethpage NY 11714	516-803-2300	P	7,231	18.1
7	Charter Communications Inc—*Thomas M Rutledge*	12405 Powerscourt Dr, Saint Louis MO 63131	314-965-0555	P	7,059	16.6
8	Liberty Associated Inc	12300 Liberty Blvd, Englewood CO 80112	720-875-5400	S	5,354*	13.7
9	Discovery Communications Inc—*David M Zaslav*	1 Discovery Pl, Silver Spring MD 20910	240-662-2000	P	3,773	4.2
10	Turner Broadcasting System Inc—*Philip Kent*	1 CNN Ctr, Atlanta GA 30303	404-827-1700	S	3,226*	10.0
11	Home Box Office—*Bill Nelson*	1100 Ave of the Americ, New York NY 10036	212-512-1000	D	2,386*	3.0
12	Cable News Network Inc—*Kenneth Estenson* Turner Broadcasting System Inc	1 Cnn Ctr, Atlanta GA 30303	404-827-1700	S	2,107*	4.0
13	Scripps Networks Interactive Inc—*Kenneth W Lowe*	PO Box 51850, Knoxville TN 37950	865-694-2700	P	2,067	2.0
14	Viacom International Inc—*Phillippe Dauman* Viacom Inc	1515 Broadway, New York NY 10036	212-258-6000	S	1,900*	5.0
15	Insight Communications Company Inc—*Michael S Willner*	810 7th Ave, New York NY 10019	917-286-2300	R	1,053	2.9
16	Mediacom Communications Corp—*Rocco Commisso*	100 Crystal Run Rd, Middletown NY 10941	845-695-2600	R	968*	3.0
17	Television Food Network—*Kenneth W Lowe*	75 9th Ave 2nd Fl, New York NY 10011	212-398-8836	S	946*	1.0
18	Lifetime Entertainment Services—*Abbe Raven*	309 W 49th St, New York NY 10019	212-424-7000	S	900*	.4
19	Insight Midwest LP—*Michael Willner* Insight Communications Company Inc	810 7th Ave, New York NY 10019	917-286-2300	S	702	3.0
20	DIRECTV Inc—*Michael White* DIRECTV Holdings LLC	2230 E Imperial Hwy, El Segundo CA 90245	310-535-5000	S	588*	1.5
21	Midcontinent Communications—*Pat McAdaragh*	529 S 7th St, Bismarck ND 58504		S	524*	.8
22	AMC Networks Inc—*Joshua W Sapan*	11 Penn Plaza, New York NY 10001	212-324-8500	P	499*	2.0
23	Oceanic Cablevision Inc—*Nate Smith*	200 Akimainui St, Mililani HI 96789	808-625-2100	R	478*	.9
24	E! Entertainment Television Inc—*Ted Halbert* Comcast Corp	5750 Wilshire Blvd, Los Angeles CA 90036	323-954-2400	S	461*	.7
25	Charter Communications VII LP—*Neil Smit* Charter Communications Inc	12405 Powerscourt Dr, St Louis MO 63131	314-965-0555	S	457	N/A
26	Tvmax Holdings Inc—*Ronald Dorchester*	10300 Wstffice Dr Ste, Houston TX 77042	713-784-0171	R	438*	.7
27	Block Communications Inc—*Gary Blair*	405 Madison Ave Ste 21, Toledo OH 43604	419-724-6212	R	434*	3.0
28	Starz Entertainment Group LLC—*Chris Albrecht* Starz LLC	8900 Liberty Cir, Englewood CO 80112	720-852-7700	S	372*	.8
29	US Cable Corp—*James D Pearson*	28 W Grand Ave, Montvale NJ 07645	201-930-9000	R	336*	.5
30	Crown Media Holdings Inc—*William Abbott*	12700 Ventrua Blvd Ste, Studio City CA 91604	818-755-2400	B	323	.2
31	ABC Cable and International Broadcast Group—*Anne M Sweeney*	77 W 66th St 13th Fl, New York NY 10023	212-456-7777	S	317*	.6
32	Midcontinent Communications Inc—*Mark S Niblick*	3901 N Louise Ave, Sioux Falls SD 57107		S	305*	1.0
33	Comedy Partners LP—*Larry Divney*	1775 Broadway 10th Fl, New York NY 10019	212-767-8600	J	296	N/A
34	Bresnan Communications Inc—*James Dolan* Cablevision Systems Corp	1111 Stewart Ave, Bethpage NY 11714	516-803-2300	S	263*	1.4
35	Black Entertainment Television LLC—*Debra L Lee* BET Holdings Inc	1235 W St NE, Washington DC 20018	202-608-2000	S	238*	.4
36	Golf Channel—*Page Thompson*	7580 Commerce Center D, Orlando FL 32819	407-355-4653	S	230*	.4
37	TiVo Inc—*Jeff Klugman*	PO Box 2160, Alviso CA 95002	408-519-9100	P	220	.6
38	Knology (Sioux Falls South Dakota)	5100 S Broadband Ln, Sioux Falls SD 57108		S	186*	.4
39	CoxCom Inc—*Patrick Esser*	5159 Federal Blvd, San Diego CA 92105	619-263-9251	S	180*	1.1
40	Resort Television Cable Company Inc	410 Airport Rd Ste H, Hot Springs AR 71913	501-624-5781	R	153	N/A
41	BET Holdings Inc—*Debra L Lee* Viacom Inc	1235 W St NE, Washington DC 20018	202-608-2000	S	147*	.5
42	Corporate Technologies LLC—*Jim Griffith*	6210 Bury Dr, Eden Prairie MN 55346	952-715-3500	S	127*	.2
43	TVN Entertainment Corp—*Ramu Potarazu*	15301 Ventura Blvd Bld, Sherman Oaks CA 91403	818-526-5000	R	125*	.2
44	Millennium Digital Media Holdings LLC—*Kelvin R Westbrook*	16305 Swingley Ridge R, Saint Louis MO 63107	636-534-7400	R	124*	.4
45	Inspirational Network Inc—*C David Cerullo*	PO Box 7750, Charlotte NC 28241	803-578-1000	R	122*	.2
46	MSNBC Cable LLC—*Charles Tillinghast*	1 Microsoft Way, Redmond WA 98052	212-664-6605	J	122*	.2
47	Comcast Cablevision of Maryland Inc—*Brian Roberts* Comcast Corp	20 W Gude Dr, Rockville MD 20850	301-294-7600	S	121*	.5
48	Starz LLC—*Robert B Clasen*	8900 Liberty Cir, Englewood CO 80112	720-852-7700	S	114*	.3
49	Etan Industries Inc—*Nathan A Levine*	PO Box 802068, Dallas TX 75380	972-385-9101	R	106	.3
50	Spacenet Corp—*Andreas M Georghiou*	1750 Old Meadow Rd, McLean VA 22102	703-848-1000	S	105*	.2
51	ChicagoLand Television News Inc—*Steve Barber*	2501 W Bradley Pl, Chicago IL 60618	630-368-4000	S	95*	.1
52	Jones Interactive Systems Inc—*Timothy J Burke*	9697 E Mineral Ave, Centennial CO 80112	303-792-3111	S	84*	.1
53	Newwave Communications—*Jim Gleason*	1 Montgomery Plz 4th F, Sikeston MO 63801	573-472-9500	R	80*	.1
54	Tennis Channel Inc	2850 Ocean Park Blvd S, Santa Monica CA 90405	310-314-9400	R	80	.1
55	Hawkeye Communications Of Clinton—*Dan Summers*	2205 Ingersoll Ave, Des Moines IA 50312	515-246-1890	R	79*	.2
56	Tele-Media Corporation of Delaware—*Robert E Tudek*	804 Jacksonville Rd, Bellefonte PA 16823	814-353-2025	R	75*	.4
57	MetroCast Cablevision of New Hampshire LLC—*James J Bruder*	9 Apple Rd, Belmont NH 03220	603-524-4425	R	68*	.1
58	Move Networks Inc—*Rosanne Austin*	796 E Utah Valley Dr, American Fork UT 84003	801-756-5805	R	67*	.1
59	Current Media LLC—*Mark Rosenthall*	118 King St, San Francisco CA 94107	415-995-8200	R	64*	.4
60	Bravo Networks—*Lauren Zalaznick*	3000 W Alameda Ave, Burbank CA 91523	310-828-7005	D	63*	.3
61	Comcast Cablevision of Detroit Inc Comcast Corp	12775 Lyndon St, Detroit MI 48227	313-934-2600	S	60	.3
62	Outdoor Channel Inc	43445 Business Park Dr, Temecula CA 92590		S	60*	.1
63	Souris River Television Coop—*Steve D Lysne*	PO Box 2027, Minot ND 58702	701-858-1200	R	58*	.2
64	Cass Communications Management Inc—*Gerald S Gill*	PO Box 200, Virginia IL 62691	217-452-7725	R	58*	.1
65	Bend Cable Communications LLC—*Amy Tykeson*	63090 Sherman Rd, Bend OR 97701	541-382-5551	R	55*	.1
66	American Telecasting Inc—*Robert D Hostetler*	5575 Tech Center Dr St, Colorado Springs CO 80919	719-260-5533	S	48	.3
67	James Cable LLC—*Kate Adams*	38710 Woodward Ave Ste, Bloomfield Hills MI 48304	248-647-1080	R	44*	.2
68	Jones International Ltd—*Glenn R Jones*	9697 E Mineral Ave, Centennial CO 80112	303-792-3111	R	40*	.3
69	Massillon Cable TV Inc—*Bob Gessner*	PO Box 1000, Massillon OH 44648	330-833-4134	R	40*	.1
70	Knology Holdings Inc—*Rodger Johnson*	1241 Og Skinner Dr, West Point GA 31833	706-645-3000	R	31*	1.2
71	World Cinema Inc—*Chester E Dickson*	9801 Westheimer Rd Ste, Houston TX 77042	713-266-2686	R	30*	<.1
72	Chambers Communications Corp	PO Box 7009, Eugene OR 97401	541-485-5611	R	26*	.3
73	New England Cable News	160 Wells Ave, Newton MA 02459	617-630-5000	R	26*	.2
74	Selectronics Corp—*Gregg Haskin*	PO Box 9, Waitsfield VT 05673	802-496-3391	R	26*	.1

Note: An asterisk (*) indicates an estimated financial figure. The company type code used is as follows: R = Private, P = Public, S = Private Subsidiary, B = Public Subsidiary, D = Division, J = Joint Venture, I = Investment Fund.

COMPANY RANKINGS BY SALES WITHIN 4-DIGIT SIC

Rank	Company Name—Executive Officer	Address, City, State, Zip	Phone	Type	Fin	Empls
75	Stt Video Partners LP—Rick White	1633 Broadway Fl 40, New York NY 10019	212-767-4600	R	25*	.1
76	Fox Sports Pittsburgh—Rupert Murdock	2 Alligheny Ctr Ste 10, Pittsburgh PA 15212	412-322-9500	R	23*	.1
77	Classic Telephone Inc	3733 Eastern Ave SE, Grand Rapids MI 49508	616-245-5500	R	23*	.1
78	Louisiana Baptist Convention—David Hankins	PO Box 311, Alexandria LA 71309	318-448-3402	R	22*	.1
79	WorldGate Communications Inc—Christopher Vitale	3800 Horizon Blvd Ste, Trevose PA 19053	215-354-5100	P	22	.1
80	In Demand LLC—Robert Benya	345 Hudson St, New York NY 10014	646-486-1010	R	21*	.1
81	Americable International Inc—Joan Hermanowski	10735 SW 216th St Ste, Miami FL 33170	305-256-6844	R	21*	<.1
82	Bulk TV and Internet—Robert Vogelsang	8537 Six Forks Rd Ste, Raleigh NC 27615	919-792-3500	R	21*	<.1
83	DIRECTV Holdings LLC—Micheal D White	2230 E Imperial Hwy, El Segundo CA 90245	310-964-5000	S	19*	16.3
84	Product Information Network—Mark Russo	2600 Michelson Dr, Irvine CA 92612	949-263-9900	R	19*	<.1
85	MGM Networks Latin America LLC—Gladys Sans	800 S Douglas Rd Fl 10, Coral Gables FL 33134	305-445-4350	R	17*	<.1
86	Jack Kent Cooke Inc—Lawrence Kutner	44325 Woodridge Pkwy, Lansdowne VA 20176	703-723-8000	R	16*	<.1
87	Japan Network Group Inc—Susumu Tanimura	100 Broadway Fl 15, New York NY 10005	212-262-3377	R	15*	<.1
88	Service Electric Cable Television Inc—John E Walson	2260 Ave A, Bethlehem PA 18017	610-865-9100	R	13*	<.1
89	WaveDivision Holdings LLC	4120 Citrus Ave, Rocklin CA 95677		R	12*	.1
90	Oasis Communications LLC	PO Box 55386, Houston TX 77255	281-955-0007	R	11*	.1
91	Advocate Communications Inc—Mary Schurz	PO Box 149, Danville KY 40423	859-236-2551	R	11*	.1
92	Ohio Valley Cable Services—Douglas Tompkins	1030 Fwy Dr N Bldg 6, Columbus OH 43229	614-890-1782	R	10*	.3
93	Fidelity Cablevision Inc—Bill Drewry	64 N Clark St, Sullivan MO 63080		S	8*	<.1
94	Armstrong Utilities Inc—Jeffrey A Ross	1 Armstrong Pl, Butler PA 16001	724-283-0925	S	7*	<.1
95	Ropir Industries Inc—Billie Pirnie	PO Box 240967, Montgomery AL 36124	334-279-8201	R	7*	<.1
96	Stratos Offshore Services Co—Nick Pugh	1710 W Willow St, Scott LA 70583	337-761-2000	R	6*	.1
97	Satellite Dish Communications—Robert Greenwood	11144 Ellenton St, Barnwell SC 29812	803-541-3333	R	6*	.1
98	Catalyst Learning Co—M Lynn Fischer	310 W Liberty St Ste 4, Louisville KY 40202	502-584-7337	R	6*	<.1
99	SCT Cable Corp—Richard Straight	2050 V I P Way, Fairmont WV 26554	304-366-0845	R	6*	.1
100	Cable Corps Inc—James Balkovic	2509 Gettysburg Rd, Camp Hill PA 17011	717-975-7800	R	5*	.1
101	A and L Cable Service Inc—Arnold Jones	525 Dunn Rd, Fayetteville NC 28312	910-486-6064	R	5*	<.1
102	United Cable Systems Inc—Robert Thacker	PO Box 1410, Hindman KY 41822	606-633-0778	R	5*	<.1
103	Telecom Assemblies Plus Inc—Rick Rodgers	11535 183rd Pl Ste 119, Orland Park IL 60467	708-479-7999	R	5*	<.1
104	Boxco Incorporated Of Maryland—Christopher Kalisz	PO Box 10768, Gaithersburg MD 20898	301-258-7600	R	5*	.1
105	Manhattan Community Access Corp—Dan Coughlin	537 W 59th St, New York NY 10019	212-757-2670	R	5*	<.1
106	RoomLinX Inc—Michael S Wasik	2150 W 6th Ave Ste H, Broomfield CO 80020	303-544-1111	P	5	<.1
107	Clearwater Cable Vision Inc—Kendall Mikesell	PO Box 800, Clearwater KS 67026	620-584-2077	R	4*	.1
108	Home2us Communications Inc—Emrah Ozkan	2325 Dulles Corner Blv, Herndon VA 20171	703-766-3810	R	4*	<.1
109	NEPSK—Peter Kozloski	12 Brewer Rd, Presque Isle ME 04769	207-764-4461	R	4*	<.1
110	Pencor Services Inc—Fred Reinhard	PO Box 215, Palmerton PA 18071	610-826-9311	R	4*	<.1
111	Ngtv—John Burns	9944 Santa Monica Blvd, Beverly Hills CA 90212	310-556-8600	R	4*	.1
112	Straight Cable And Tower Service Corp—Richard Straight	523 Benoni Ave, Fairmont WV 26554	304-366-3221	R	4*	<.1
113	Contract Technologies International Inc—Long Tran	1228 Albany St, Schenectady NY 12304	518-382-5723	R	4*	<.1
114	COI Telecom Inc—Ken Toll	118 E Turbo Dr, San Antonio TX 78216	210-829-8900	R	3*	.1
115	Tv Options—Betty Willcutt	65 Curry Hwy, Jasper AL 35503	205-384-1980	R	3*	.1
116	Tsc Television Inc—Terrance Schwieterman	PO Box 408, Wapakoneta OH 45895	419-739-2200	R	3*	.1
117	Blue Ridge Communication Tv 13—Kimberley Bell	936 Elm St, Lehighton PA 18235	610-767-8060	R	3*	<.1
118	MSTI Holdings Inc—Frank T Matarazzo	259-263 Goffle Rd, Hawthorne NJ 07506	973-304-6080	P	3	<.1
119	T Js Catv Inc—Jay Mills	60 E Main St, Bloomfield NY 14469	585-657-5465	R	3*	<.1
120	Ruffin Enterprises Inc—Penny Wade	PO Box 8450, Biloxi MS 39535	205-349-0000	R	3*	<.1
121	Boston Community Access and Programing Foundation Inc—Curtis Henderson	3025 Washington St, Roxbury MA 02119	617-708-3200	R	3*	<.1
122	Total Vision Of The Gulf States LLC—Sussan Cossoan	8465 State Hwy 59, Foley AL 36535	251-967-1783	R	3*	<.1
123	Cable Installers and Designers Inc—Muhammad Akhter	PO Box 42583, Houston TX 77242	713-785-9044	R	3*	<.1
124	Computer Facilities Service Corp—William Bick	12969 Manchester Rd, Saint Louis MO 63131	314-993-8053	R	3*	<.1
125	Michael Termondt—Michael Termondt	25 Creek Ln Ste A, Oak View CA 93022	805-649-1384	R	3*	<.1
126	Choice Media Satellite Systems Inc—Will Watkins	6311 Fairview Ave, Westmont IL 60559	312-735-2870	R	2*	<.1
127	4 Peaks Satellite And Sound Inc—Robert Arend	5861 S Kyrene Rd Ste 1, Tempe AZ 85283	480-726-3344	R	2*	<.1
128	Ocean Cable Group Inc—Robert Mills	112 Woodland Ave Ste 2, Somers Point NJ 08244	609-653-0844	R	2*	<.1
129	Kings Bay Communications Inc—Donald Trednick	PO Box 1267, Kingsland GA 31548	912-729-3883	R	2*	<.1
130	Willamette Broadband LLC	PO Box 568, Woodburn OR 97071	503-982-4085	R	2*	<.1
131	Avenue Tv Cable Service Inc—Stephen George	PO Box 1458, Ventura CA 93002	805-648-5253	R	2*	<.1
132	Community Antenna Service Inc—Arthur Cooper	1525 Dupont Rd, Parkersburg WV 26101	304-420-2470	R	2*	<.1
133	Small Cities Cable Television—John Rigas	PO Box 190, Shelburne VT 05482	802-985-3308	R	2*	<.1
134	Vertical Television Inc—Bill Shiverick	PO Box 672137, Marietta GA 30006	404-352-2488	R	2*	<.1
135	Cablesystem—Patrick Deville	409 E Market St, Sandusky OH 44870	419-627-0800	R	2*	<.1
136	Loosbrock Digging Service Inc—Bruce Loosbrock	221 W 4th St, Lismore MN 56155	507-472-8448	R	2*	<.1
137	Sweetwater Television Co—Albert Carollo	602 Broadway St, Rock Springs WY 82901	307-362-3773	R	2*	<.1
138	TV Allen's Cable Service Inc—Gregory Price	PO Box 2643, Morgan City LA 70381	985-384-8335	R	2*	<.1
139	Cn2—Ron Schwallie	135 S Elizabeth Ln, Rock Hill SC 29730	803-326-2777	R	2*	<.1
140	Fox Network Center—Rupert Murdoch	10201 W Pico Blvd 101, Los Angeles CA 90064	310-369-9369	R	2*	<.1
141	3 Rivers D B S Inc—Steve Krogue	PO Box 159, Fairfield MT 59436	406-467-3650	R	2*	<.1
142	Waycross Cable Company Inc—John Harrison	PO Box 37, Waycross GA 31502	912-283-2332	R	2*	<.1
143	Rhn Splicing Inc—Ronald Notter	645 Miriam Ln, Lusby MD 20657	410-326-9698	R	2*	<.1
144	Triple J Community Broadcasting—Joseph Gans	1059 E 10th St, Hazleton PA 18201	570-455-4251	R	2*	<.1
145	Range Television Cable Company Inc—Frank Befera	PO Box 13201, Miami FL 33101	218-262-1071	R	2*	<.1
146	Current Media LLC—James Dubern	118 King St, San Francisco CA 94107	415-995-8200	R	2*	<.1
147	Peak Uplink Inc—Bruce Fauser	458 Silverhorn Dr, New Castle CO 81647	970-984-9765	R	2*	<.1
148	Fox Sports Networks—David Hill	10201 W Pico, Los Angeles CA 90035	310-369-1000	S	2	N/A
149	Signature Cable Manufacturing Technology Inc—Mohamad Sasa	140 Comstock Pkwy Unit, Cranston RI 02921	401-383-1008	R	1*	<.1
150	Mediaone International Holding Inc—Gary Ames	188 Inverness Dr W, Englewood CO 80112	303-858-5800	R	1*	<.1
151	Korean Channel Inc—Sang Han	1838 131st St, College Point NY 11356	718-353-8970	R	1*	<.1
152	Lowry Telephone Company LLC	PO Box 336, Hoffman MN 56339	320-283-5101	R	1*	<.1
153	Interstate Cablevision Co—Ed Buchanan	PO Box 229, Truro IA 50257	641-765-4203	R	1*	<.1
154	Great Western Satellite Communications—Dewey Peterson	840 Garden Breeze Way, Las Vegas NV 89123	702-361-8384	R	1*	<.1
155	Belhaven Cable T V Inc—Guinn Leverett	235 Pamlico St, Belhaven NC 27810	252-943-3736	R	1*	<.1
156	Sound and Signal Inc—Ronald Morgan	277 Rickenbacker Cir, Livermore CA 94551	925-455-1778	R	1*	<.1
157	Cabling Systems Inc—John Narron	10386 Southard Dr, Beltsville MD 20705	301-595-1933	R	1*	<.1
158	Urban Communications Transport Corp—Stuart Reid	369 E 149th St Fl 6, Bronx NY 10455	718-401-5913	R	1*	<.1
159	MTV Networks Inc—Judy McGrath Viacom International Inc	1515 Broadway Lbby, New York NY 10036	212-258-8000	S	1	2.0
160	Nc Iv Inc—Robert Price	1788 Barber Rd, Sarasota FL 34240	941-378-9133	R	1*	<.1
161	Horizon Cable TV Inc—Kevin Daniel	PO Box 1240, Point Reyes Station CA 94956	415-663-9610	R	1*	<.1

Rank	Company Name—*Executive Officer*	Address, City, State, Zip	Phone	Type	Fin	Empls
162	Omega Communications Inc—*Robert E Schloss*	PO Box 1766, Indianapolis IN 46206	317-264-4010	R	1*	<.1
163	Tucson Community Cable Corp—*Sam Behrend*	124 E Broadway Blvd, Tucson AZ 85701	520-624-9833	R	1*	<.1
164	Chatmoss Cablevision—*John Shoemaker*	PO Box 5064, Martinsville VA 24115	434-685-1521	R	1*	<.1
165	Bass' Electronics Inc—*Haywood Bass*	2080 Aubin Ln, Baton Rouge LA 70816	225-272-1394	R	1*	<.1
166	Tampa Educational Cable Consortium—*Glenda Inda*	703 N Willow Ave, Tampa FL 33606	813-254-2253	R	1*	<.1
167	Medical Media Television Inc—*Philip N Cohen*	5625 W Waters Ave Ste, Tampa FL 33634		R	<1	<.1
168	Cablesuite 541—*Jim Suplee*	224 State St, Conneaut OH 44030	440-599-2000	R	<1*	<.1
169	Altec Datacom LLC—*Abraham Mendez*	3601 Commerce Blvd Ste, Kissimmee FL 34741	407-846-4142	R	<1*	<.1
170	Dr Dish Selective Systems Inc—*Chris Schaler*	4230 Madison Ave, Indianapolis IN 46227	317-783-0077	R	<1*	<.1
171	Cable Line Installation Services Inc—*Kevin Diehl*	PO Box 95, Perkasie PA 18944	215-258-1380	R	<1*	<.1
172	Ron's Tv—*Dawn Phillips*	141 Country Manor Rd, Piedmont SC 29673	864-845-5124	R	<1*	<.1
173	Cable Technologies Corp—*Dave Burgett*	30951 Walden Dr, Westlake OH 44145	440-785-2631	R	<1*	<.1
174	Home Satellite Services Inc—*Paul Gearheart*	PO Box 383, Craynor KY 41635	606-478-4388	R	<1*	<.1
175	Home and Garden Television—*Jim Samples*	PO Box 50970, Knoxville TN 37950	865-694-2700	S	N/A	6.0
176	Laurel Cable LP—*Dale Maust*	936 Stoystown Rd, Somerset PA 15501	814-443-6250	R	N/A	<.1

TOTALS: SIC 4841 Cable & Other Pay Television Services
Companies: 176 | | | | | 143,440 | 341.7

4899 Communications Services Nec

Rank	Company Name—*Executive Officer*	Address, City, State, Zip	Phone	Type	Fin	Empls
1	DIRECTV Group Inc—*Michael White*	2230 E Imperial Hwy, El Segundo CA 90245	310-964-5000	P	24,102	25.1
2	L-3 Satellite Networks—*Michael T Strianese*	600 3rd Ave, New York NY 10016	212-697-1111	S	9,000	N/A
3	MetroPCS Communications Inc—*Roger D Linquist*	PO Box 601119, Dallas TX 75360	214-570-5800	P	4,847	3.7
4	American Tower Corp—*James D Taiclet*	116 Huntington Ave 11t, Boston MA 02116	617-375-7500	P	1,985	1.7
5	Crown Castle International Corp—*W Benjamin Moreland*	1220 Augusta Dr Ste 50, Houston TX 77057	713-570-3000	P	1,879	1.2
6	PAETEC Holding Corp—*Arunas A Chesonis*	600 WillowBrook Office, Fairport NY 14450		P	1,624	4.5
7	Suddenlink Communications—*Jerry Kent*	12444 Powerscourt Dr, St Louis MO 63131	314-965-2020	R	1,491*	5.0
8	TW Telecom Inc—*Larissa L Herda*	PO Box 172567, Denver CO 80217	303-566-1000	P	1,367	3.1
9	Yipes Enterprise Services Inc—*John Scanlon*	114 Sansome St 11th Fl, San Francisco CA 94104	415-901-2000	S	1,261*	.4
10	Clearwire Corp—*Erik Prusch*	4400 Carillon Point, Kirkland WA 98033	425-216-7600	P	1,254	.9
11	XM Satellite Radio Holdings Inc—*Mel Karmazin*	1500 Eckington Pl NE, Washington DC 20002	202-380-4000	S	1,242	N/A
12	Arinc Inc—*John Belcher*	2551 Riva Rd, Annapolis MD 21401	410-266-4000	R	1,083*	3.0
13	WOW! Internet Cable and Phone—*Colleen Abdoulah*	7887 E Belleview Ave, Englewood CO 80111		R	923*	1.0
14	Paetec Communications Inc	600 WillowBrook Office, Fairport NY 14450	585-340-2500	S	851*	1.1
15	Intelsat Global Service Corp—*Thierry Guillemin*	3400 International Dr, Washington DC 20008	202-944-6800	R	823*	.8
16	American Tower Management Inc—*James D Taiclet Jr* American Tower Corp	116 Huntington Ave 11t, Boston MA 02116	617-375-7500	S	565*	.7
17	DataPath Inc—*Andy Mullins*	2205 Northmont Pky, Duluth GA 30096	678-597-0300	S	551*	.6
18	Arkadin Inc—*Thomas Boudier*	1 Penn Plz Ste 2200, New York NY 10119	646-495-7600	R	522*	.5
19	Syniverse Holdings Inc—*Jeff Gordon*	8125 Highwoods Palm Wa, Tampa FL 33647	813-637-5000	B	483	1.3
20	TracFone Wireless Inc—*Frederick J Pollak*	9700 NW 112th Ave, Miami FL 33178	305-640-2000	S	469*	.5
21	GlobalFluency—*Donovan Neale-May*	4151 Middlefield Rd, Palo Alto CA 94303	650-328-5555	R	465*	.5
22	LodgeNet Interactive Corp—*Scott C Petersen*	3900 W Innovation St, Sioux Falls SD 57107	605-988-1000	P	452	1.0
23	Premiere Global Services Inc—*Boland T Jones*	3280 Peachtree Rd NE S, Atlanta GA 30305		P	442	1.7
24	Cable One Inc—*Thomas Might*	1314 N 3rd St, Phoenix AZ 85004	602-364-6000	S	410*	1.7
25	PBS Enterprises Inc—*Paula Kerger*	2100 Crystal Dr, Arlington VA 22202	703-739-5400	R	352*	.5
26	GeoEye Inc—*Matthew M O'Connell*	2325 Dulles Corner Blv, Herndon VA 20171	703-480-7500	P	330	.7
27	Atlantic Broadband Inc—*David J Keefe*	1 Batterymarch Pk Ste, Quincy MA 02169	617-786-8800	R	289*	.7
28	ISPcom—*George Napso*	265 E 100 S Ste 240, Salt Lake City UT 84111		S	288*	.3
29	RMS Communications Group Inc—*James Mosieur*	4551 NW 44 Ave, Ocala FL 34482	352-369-3888	R	274*	.1
30	Boxnet Inc—*Aaron Levie*	220 Portage, Palo Alto CA 94306	650-329-1210	R	264*	.2
31	MultiLing Corp—*Michael Sneddon*	PO Box 1998, Provo UT 84603	801-377-2000	R	233*	.4
32	GreatCall Inc—*David Inns*	12680 High Bluff Dr, San Diego CA 92130	858-720-7500	R	204*	.2
33	Telenity Inc—*Ilhan Bagoren*	755 Main St Bldg 7, Monroe CT 06468	203-445-2000	R	192*	.2
34	Genesys Conferencing Inc—*Francois Legros*	1861 Wiehle Ave, Reston VA 20190	703-736-7100	S	180	N/A
35	Linderlake Corp—*Victoria A Juskie*	9981 W 190th St, Mokena IL 60448	708-478-7012	R	167*	.2
36	Telekenex—*Brandon Chaney*	3221 20th St, San Francisco CA 94110	415-869-9000	R	162*	.2
37	ThruPoint Inc—*Rami Musallam*	1040 Ave of the Americ, New York NY 10018	646-562-6000	R	160*	.4
38	Masergy—*Chris MacFarland*	2740 N Dallas Pkwy Ste, Plano TX 75093	214-442-5663	R	157*	.1
39	Hipcricket—*Paul R Arena*	4400 Carillon Point, Kirkland WA 98033	425-452-1111	R	156*	.1
40	RaySat Inc—*Ilan Kaplan*	8460-D Tyco Rd, Vienna VA 22182	703-584-3770	R	139*	.2
41	Mediawhiz Holdings LLC—*Jonathan Sharpiro*	75 Broad St 23rd Fl, New York NY 10004	646-442-0074	R	130*	.1
42	Aicent Inc—*Lynn Liu*	2540 N 1st St 2nd Fl, San Jose CA 95131	408-324-1830	R	129*	.1
43	TowerCo—*Richard Byrne*	5000 Valleystone Dr, Cary NC 27519	919-469-5559	R	125	.1
44	EA Technologies—*Edward Willner*	150 Motor Pkwy Ste LL3, Hauppauge NY 11788	631-434-9600	R	122*	.1
45	Vero Systems Inc—*Brian Cafferty*	4585 US Hwy 9 N, Howell NJ 07731	732-730-1330	R	121*	.1
46	Tropos Networks Inc—*Tom Ayers*	555 Del Ray Ave, Sunnyvale CA 94085	408-331-6800	R	109*	.1
47	Alpheus Communications LP—*Paul W Hobby*	1301 Fannin St 20th Fl, Houston TX 77002		R	108*	.1
48	TeleBright Corp—*Chet Thaker*	1700 Research Blvd Ste, Rockville MD 20850	301-296-3800	R	106*	.1
49	Communication Technologies Inc (Chantilly Virginia)—*Joseph E Fergus*	3684 Centerview Dr Ste, Chantilly VA 20151	703-961-9080	R	99*	1.2
50	WPCS International Inc—*Andrew Hidalgo*	1 E Uwchlan Ave Ste 30, Exton PA 19341	610-903-0400	P	97	.5
51	Imagine Communications Inc—*Sebastiano Tevarotto*	12235 El Camino Real S, San Diego CA 92130	858-480-0110	R	93*	.1
52	RigNet Inc—*Mark Slaughter*	1880 S Dairy Ashford S, Houston TX 77077	281-674-0100	P	93	.2
53	Continental Broadband Inc—*Charlie Watkins*	100 W Plume St Ste 2E, Norfolk VA 23510	757-222-5300	S	81*	.1
54	CFN Services Inc—*Mark Casey*	13454 Sunrise Valley D, Herndon VA 20171	703-788-6633	R	80*	.1
55	kgb USA—*Robert A Pines*	3864 Courtney St Ste 4, Bethlehem PA 18017	610-997-1000	R	78*	2.5
56	US Satellite Corp—*Don Blanchard*	935 W Bullion St, Murray UT 84123	801-263-0519	S	78*	<.1
57	MeziMedia—*James R Zarley*	222 E Huntington Dr St, Monrovia CA 91016	626-408-9100	S	76*	.1
58	Clairmail Inc—*Pete Daffern*	781 Lincoln Ave Ste 20, San Rafael CA 94901	415-526-7000	R	73*	.1
59	SDV Telecommunications Inc (Grass Valley California)—*Timothy J Voors*	124 Clydesdale Ct Ste, Grass Valley CA 95945	530-271-0382	R	73*	.1
60	Globalstar Inc—*James Monroe III*	300 Holiday Square Blv, Covington LA 70433	408-933-4000	P	68	.3
61	IntrexNet—*David Peachey*	3601 Bastion Ln Ste B, Raleigh NC 27604	919-573-5488	R	67*	.1
62	Xfone Inc—*Guy Nissenson*	5307 W Loop 289, Lubbock TX 79414	806-771-5212	P	59	.3
63	Fiberlink Communications Corp—*James Sheward*	1787 Sentry Pky W Bldg, Blue Bell PA 19422	215-664-1600	R	58*	.2
64	Carl Group Inc—*Timothy S Carl*	282 Dry Creek Rd, Aptos CA 95003	831-708-2609	R	57*	.1
65	Davel Communications Inc—*Tammy L Martin*	200 Public Sq BP Tower, Cleveland OH 44114	216-241-2555	R	56	.2
66	Henry Brothers Electronics Inc—*James E Henry*	17-01 Pollitt Dr, Fair Lawn NJ 07410	201-794-6500	S	55	.2
67	ATX Group Inc—*Michael Saxton*	8550 Freeport Pkwy, Irving TX 75063	972-753-6200	R	54*	.4

Note: An asterisk (*) indicates an estimated financial figure. The company type code used is as follows: R = Private, P = Public, S = Private Subsidiary, B = Public Subsidiary, D = Division, J = Joint Venture, I = Investment Fund.

COMPANY RANKINGS BY SALES WITHIN 4-DIGIT SIC

Rank	Company Name—*Executive Officer*	Address, City, State, Zip	Phone	Type	Fin	Empls
68	ACT Teleconferencing Inc—*Peter E Salas*	1526 Cole Blvd Ste 300, Golden CO 80401	303-233-3500	R	54	.3
69	Citel Technologies—*Jose David*	221 Commerce Dr, Amherst NY 14228	206-957-6270	R	53*	.1
70	uReach Technologies Inc—*Krishnamurty Kambhampati*	2137 State Hwy 35 and, Holmdel NJ 07733	732-335-5400	R	51*	<.1
71	Virtela Communications Inc—*BV Jaqadeesh*	5680 Greenwood Plz Blv, Greenwood Village CO 80111	720-475-4000	R	50*	.1
72	OuterLink Corp—*Andrew Joseph*	175 Cabot St Ste 311, Lowell MA 01854	978-856-0007	R	49*	<.1
73	Airband Communications Inc—*Michael Ruley*	14800 Landmark Blvd St, Dallas TX 75254	469-791-0000	R	47*	.1
74	HBE Acquisition Corp—*James Henry* Henry Brothers Electronics Inc	17-01 Pollitt Dr, Fair Lawn NJ 07410	201-794-6500	S	47*	.1
75	New World Network USA Inc—*Paul W Scott*	15950 W Dixie Hwy, North Miami Beach FL 33162	786-274-7400	R	47*	.1
76	Smaato Inc—*Ragnar Kruse*	3 Lagoon Dr Ste 170, Redwood City CA 94065	650-286-1198	R	46*	<.1
77	New Global Telecom Inc—*Don Petampel*	600 12th St Ste 200, Golden CO 80401	303-278-0700	R	45*	.1
78	South Valley Internet Inc—*Bob Brentnall*	PO Box 1246, San Martin CA 95046	408-683-4533	R	45*	.1
79	Community Communications Inc—*Jose A Fajardo*	11510 E Colonial Dr, Orlando FL 32817	407-273-2300	R	44*	.1
80	WebMessenger Inc—*Val Babajov*	6708 Foothill Blvd Ste, Tujunga CA 91042	818-352-7800	S	44*	.1
81	AnswersMedia Inc—*Jeff Bohnson*	400 W Erie St, Chicago IL 60654	312-421-0113	R	43*	<.1
82	Kodiak Networks Inc—*John Vice*	1501 10th St Ste 130, Plano TX 75074	972-665-0200	R	42*	<.1
83	Atrinsic Inc—*Stuart Goldfarb*	469 7th Ave, New York NY 10018	212-716-1977	P	40	<.1
84	Rave Wireless Inc—*Tom Axbey*	50 Speen St, Framingham MA 01701		R	40*	<.1
85	Trafficcom Inc—*Robert N Verratti*	851 Duportail Rd Ste 2, Wayne PA 19087	610-725-9700	S	39*	.6
86	Santur Corp—*Paul Meissner*	40931 Encyclopedia Cir, Fremont CA 94538	510-933-4100	S	38*	<.1
87	O1 Communications Inc—*Brad Jenkins*	5190 Golden Foothill P, ElDorado CA 95162	916-554-2100	R	37*	.1
88	SyChip Inc—*George Barber*	2805 N Dallas Pkwy Ste, Plano TX 75093	972-202-8900	S	37*	<.1
89	ORBCOMM Corp—*Marc J Eisenberg*	2115 Linwood Ave Ste 1, Fort Lee NJ 07024	703-433-6300	P	37	.1
90	Mercom Corp—*Stella Mercado Colwell*	235 Commerce Dr Ste 30, Pawleys Island SC 29585	843-979-9957	R	36*	<.1
91	Wireless Matrix Corp (Reston Virginia)—*J Richard Carlson*	13645 Dulles Technolog, Herndon VA 20171	703-262-0500	P	35	.1
92	Satellite Communication Systems Inc—*Ernie S Hux*	5741 Cleveland St Ste, Virginia Beach VA 23462	757-723-0835	R	32*	<.1
93	Stelera Wireless LLC—*Edward Evans*	4700 Gaillardia Pky St, Oklahoma City OK 73142	405-751-3525	R	32*	<.1
94	Acquirgy Inc—*Paul Soltoff*	877 Executive Center D, Saint Petersburg FL 33702	727-576-6630	R	31	.1
95	Internet Nebraska Inc—*Eric R Erlandson*	PO Box 5301, Lincoln NE 68505	402-434-8680	R	30*	<.1
96	Tacher Co—*Mick Tacher*	7150 SW Hampton Ste 20, Tigard OR 97223	425-885-3758	R	30*	<.1
97	Phonoscope Ltd—*Charles Miracle*	6105 Westline Dr, Houston TX 77036	713-272-4600	R	29*	.1
98	Weintraub Telecomm LLC—*Bruce Weintraub*	1002 W 9th Ave, King of Prussia PA 19406	610-337-1333	R	28*	<.1
99	MDU Communication International Inc—*Sheldon B Nelson*	60-D Commerce Way, Totowa NJ 07512	973-237-9499	P	28	.1
100	Bytemobile Inc—*Hugh Barton*	2860 De La Cruz Blvd S, Santa Clara CA 95050	408-327-7700	R	27*	.3
101	Hillcrest Labs Inc—*Daniel S Simpkins*	15245 Shady Grove Rd S, Rockville MD 20850	240-386-0600	R	27*	<.1
102	SDN Global—*Timothy R McKee*	PO Box 7668, Charlotte NC 28241	704-588-2233	S	27*	<.1
103	StarNet Inc—*Russ Intravartolo*	579 N First Bank Dr St, Palatine IL 60067	847-963-0116	R	27*	<.1
104	InterWorld Communications Inc (Torrance California)—*Ralph E Whitmore III*	2531 W 237th St Ste 10, Torrance CA 90505	310-856-0550	R	27*	<.1
105	Matrix Visual Solutions—*Paul Motal*	2915 Daimler St, Santa Ana CA 92705	949-756-5500	S	25*	.1
106	Shaffer Communication Services Inc—*Joe Shaffer*	1239-B W 19th St, Houston TX 77008	713-463-0022	R	25*	<.1
107	Madison Group Inc—*Mary Bowen*	2785 Summer Oaks Dr Rm, Bartlett TN 38134	901-381-2624	R	25*	<.1
108	yousendit Inc—*Ivan Koon*	1919 S Bascom Ave 3rd, Campbell CA 95008	408-879-9118	R	24*	.1
109	MetaSwitch—*Kevin DeNuccio*	1001 Marina Village Pk, Alameda CA 94501	510-748-8230	D	24*	<.1
110	Airimba Wireless Inc—*Robert H Turner*	75 5th St NW Ste 460, Atlanta GA 30308	214-413-3221	R	24*	<.1
111	Mtone Wireless Corp—*Victor Wang*	3080 Olcott St Ste 100, Santa Clara CA 95054	408-986-8988	R	22*	.3
112	TriNET Systems Inc—*Jim Tinnell*	780 Dedham St, Canton MA 02021		R	22*	.1
113	Nexus Group—*Steve Brugman*	1661 Murfreesboro Pke, Nashville TN 37217	615-221-4200	R	22*	<.1
114	Telesphere Networks Inc—*Clark Peterson*	9237 E Via De Ventura, Scottsdale AZ 85258	480-385-7000	R	22	.1
115	Gazelle—*Israel Ganot*	25 Thomsson Pl 3rd Fl, Boston MA 02210	617-440-7582	R	21	.1
116	MDI Electrical Construction Inc—*Robert Heiderscheidt*	5627 W 120th St, Alsip IL 60803	708-597-0111	R	21*	<.1
117	Network Management Corp—*Richard Moreno*	111 Derek Pl, Roseville CA 95678	916-332-5841	R	21*	<.1
118	A-Tech Consulting Inc—*JD Wigginton*	3901 W Osborne Ave, Tampa FL 33614	813-887-1178	R	21*	<.1
119	Ensequence Inc—*Peter Low*	111 SE 5th Ave Ste 140, Portland OR 97204	503-416-3800	R	21*	<.1
120	Linguistic Systems Inc—*Martin Roberts*	201 Broadway, Cambridge MA 02139	617-864-3900	R	20*	<.1
121	Mobile Telesystems Inc—*Doug Thomas*	205 Perry Pkwy Ste 14, Gaithersburg MD 20877	301-963-5970	R	20*	<.1
122	Where Inc—*Walter A Doyle Jr*	60 Canal St 2nd Fl, Boston MA 02114	617-502-3100	R	19*	<.1
123	CCT Telecommunications Inc—*Steve Fetzer*	1106 E Turner Rd, Lodi CA 95240	209-365-9500	R	18*	<.1
124	Skyhook Wireless Inc—*Ted Morgan*	34 Farnsworth St 4th F, Boston MA 02210	617-314-9802	R	17*	<.1
125	Adaptix Inc—*Michael Pisterzi*	4100 Midway Road Ste 2, Carrollton TX 75007	206-326-1000	R	15*	<.1
126	LocalNet Corp—*Marc P Silvestri*	170 Lawrence Bell Dr, Williamsville NY 14221		R	15	.1
127	Biddeford Internet Corp—*Fletcher Kittredge*	8 Pomerleau St, Biddeford ME 04005	207-286-8686	R	14*	<.1
128	Freeport Technologies—*John Mc Greevy*	470 Springpark Pl Ste, Herndon VA 20170	571-262-0400	R	14*	<.1
129	Relay House Inc—*Randy Johnson*	9277 Meridian Ave S, Montrose MN 55363	763-972-8008	R	14*	<.1
130	Thinkom Solutions Inc—*Michael Burke*	20000 Mariner Ave Ste, Torrance CA 90503	310-371-5486	R	13*	<.1
131	SONNET Networking LLC—*Roberta Curnow*	PO Box 5093, Sonora CA 95370	209-532-2750	R	13*	<.1
132	Full Web Inc	201 Robert S Kerr Ave, Oklahoma City OK 73102	405-236-8200	S	13*	<.1
133	Inter-Community Telephone Company LLC—*Keith Anderson*	PO Box 8, Nome ND 58062	701-924-8815	S	13*	<.1
134	Single Touch Interactive Inc—*Anthony Macaluso*	2235 Encinitas Blvd St, Encinitas CA 92024	760-438-0100	R	13*	<.1
135	Access US—*Victor Madison*	712 N 2nd St Ste 300, Saint Louis MO 63102	314-655-7700	R	13*	<.1
136	SingleHop Inc—*Zachary Boca*	621 W Randoph St 3rd F, Chicago IL 60661	312-447-2580	R	13	<.1
137	Great Works Internet—*Fletcher Kittredge*	8 Pomerleau St, Biddeford ME 04005	207-286-8686	R	12*	.1
138	Telkonet Inc—*Jason L Tienor*	10200 Innovation Rd St, Milwaukee WI 53226	414-223-0473	P	11	.1
139	InterMetro Communications Inc—*Charles Rice*	2685 Park Center Dr Bl, Simi Valley CA 93065	805-433-8000	R	11*	<.1
140	Global IP Solutions Inc—*Emerick Woods*	642 Harrison St 2nd Fl, San Francisco CA 94107	415-397-2555	R	10*	.1
141	Bandwidthcom Inc—*David Morken*	4001 Weston Pkwy Ste 1, Cary NC 27513	919-297-1100	R	10*	.1
142	Powercom Electrical Services Inc	37 Plain Ave, New Rochelle NY 10801	914-632-2600	R	10*	<.1
143	BandCon—*Ari Benowitz*	151 Kalmus Dr Ste M-2, Costa Mesa CA 92626	714-727-2800	R	10*	<.1
144	SkyMira LLC—*Robert Landsfield*	167 Cherry St Ste 430, Milford CT 06460	203-987-3336	R	10*	<.1
145	Sprint Healthcare Systems Inc—*Gary D Forsee*	2001 Edmund Halley Dr, Reston VA 20191	703-433-4000	S	10	N/A
146	IP5280 Communications Inc—*Jeffrey Pearl*	391 Inverness Pky, Englewood CO 80112	303-800-0000	R	9*	<.1
147	New England Satellite Systems Inc—*John Foley Jr*	786 Hartford Tpk, Shrewsbury MA 01545	508-842-4328	R	9*	<.1
148	Inter-Community Telephone Company II LLC—*Keith Andersen*	PO Box 8, Nome ND 58062	701-924-8815	S	9*	<.1
149	International Contact Inc—*Carla Itzkowich*	351 15th St, Oakland CA 94612	510-836-1180	R	9*	<.1
150	Leadcom Integrated Solutions USA Inc—*Uri Dotan*	2645 Executive Park Dr, Weston FL 33331	954-385-1620	R	9*	<.1
151	Omni Telecommunications Inc (Greenville South Carolina)—*Nick Arkon*	PO Box 25873, Greenville SC 29616		R	9*	<.1
152	Telisimo International—*Linda G Hobbs*	2468-150 Historic Deca, San Diego CA 92106		R	9*	<.1
153	United Systems Access Inc—*Stephen J Gilbert*	5 Bragdon Ln Ste 200, Kennebunk ME 04043	207-467-8000	R	9*	<.1
154	Zoomy Communications Inc—*Diane Kruse*	402 7th St Ste 111, Glenwood Springs CO 81601	970-928-7722	R	9*	<.1

Rank	Company Name—Executive Officer	Address, City, State, Zip	Phone	Type	Fin	Empls
155	Loral Skynet—Robert A Hedinger	500 Hills Dr, Bedminster NJ 07921	908-698-4900	R	9*	<.1
156	Whec-Tv LLC—Arnold Klinsky	191 E Ave, Rochester NY 14604	585-546-5670	R	9*	.1
157	Lenco Mobile Inc—Michael Levinsohn	345 Chapala St, Santa Barbara CA 93101	805-308-9198	P	8	.1
158	River View Solutions Corp—Lisa Reisfield	12 Grace Ct W, Great Neck NY 11021	917-620-5463	R	8*	.1
159	Beacon Technologies Inc (Nashville Tennessee)—Terry Sutton	1441 Donelson Pke, Nashville TN 37217	615-301-5020	R	7*	.1
160	AtlanticNet Internet Services Inc—Manoj Puranik	440 W Kennedy Blvd Ste, Orlando FL 32810		R	7*	.1
161	Logical Net Corp—Richard Frederick	1462 Erie Blvd, Schenectady NY 12305		R	7*	.1
162	World Tower Company Inc—Doug Walker	PO Box 508, Mayfield KY 42066	270-247-3642	R	6*	<.1
163	Single Digits Inc—Robert Goldstein	749 E Industrial Park, Manchester NH 03109	603-580-1539	R	6*	.1
164	Comtech Mobile Datacom Corp—Daniel S Wood	20430 Century Blvd, Germantown MD 20875	240-686-3300	S	6*	.1
165	Giant Communications Inc—Mario J Gabelli	418 W 5th St Ste C, Holton KS 66436	785-362-9331	S	6*	.1
166	Sirus Inc—Lincoln Bauer	675 E 16th St Ste 200, Holland MI 49423	616-394-0558	R	6*	<.1
167	Sunset Net LLC—Barry Sherwood	PO Box 1104, Chico CA 95927	530-879-5660	R	6*	<.1
168	Paladyne Corp—Sameer Shalaby	420 Lexington Ave Ste, New York NY 10170	646-214-3700	R	6	<.1
169	P Value Communications LLC—Patrick Defeo	400 Interpace Pkwy Ste, Parsippany NJ 07054	973-984-6129	R	5*	.1
170	Stake Center Locating Inc	2920 W Directors Row, Salt Lake City UT 84104	801-381-4825	R	5*	.1
171	Rizzo Consulting Inc—Joseph Rizzo	5420 Newport Dr, Rolling Meadows IL 60008	847-788-9300	R	5*	<.1
172	Grovesite Inc—Thomas I Selling	3104 E Camelback Rd St, Phoenix AZ 85016	602-952-9880	R	5*	<.1
173	MaineStreet Communications Inc—Jason Chambers	208 Portland Rd, Gray ME 04039	207-657-5078	R	5*	<.1
174	Marion Computer Technologies LLC—Gale Atkins	201 E Main St Centre S, Marion VA 24354	276-783-6986	R	5*	<.1
175	NileNet Ltd—Andy Sandoval	PO Box 13558, Denver CO 80201	303-825-1950	R	5*	<.1
176	SkyPoint Communications Inc—Greg Kemnitz	PO Box 567, Plymouth MN 55447	763-548-2600	R	5*	<.1
177	Digital Map Products Inc—James Skurzynski	18831 Von Karman Ave, Irvine CA 92612	714-727-1234	R	5*	<.1
178	Smart Cabling Solutions Inc—Ron Wagner	1250 N Winchester St K, Olathe KS 66061	913-390-9501	R	5*	<.1
179	NextWeb Inc	515 S Flower St 47th F, Los Angeles CA 90071		S	4*	<.1
180	Affinity Internet Inc—James Collins	3250 W Commercial Blvd, Fort Lauderdale FL 33309	954-334-8000	R	4*	.2
181	One Call Now—Leib Lurie	726 Grant St, Troy OH 45373	937-335-3336	R	4*	<.1
182	Videocom Satellite Associates Inc—Daniel V Swartz	502 Sprague St, Dedham MA 02026	781-329-4080	R	4*	<.1
183	Qc Tv Corp—Wanda Palmer	PO Box 691165, Houston TX 77269	281-583-1000	R	4*	<.1
184	Sorvive Technologies Inc—Larry Galaviz	2090 Buford Hwy Ste 1b, Buford GA 30518	770-614-3122	R	4*	<.1
185	Atlantic Metro Communications—Stephen M Klenert	4 Century Dr Ste 102, Parsippany NJ 07054		R	4	<.1
186	ARC Wireless Solutions Inc—Jason T Young	6330 N Washington St S, Denver CO 80216	303-421-4063	P	4	<.1
187	National Datacast Inc—Jacqueline Weiss PBS Enterprises Inc	2100 Crystal Dr Ste 75, Arlington VA 22202	703-739-2786	S	4*	<.1
188	Music A La Carte—Rene Barge	2574 SW 27th Ln, Miami FL 33133	305-854-1810	R	4*	<.1
189	Lightriver Technologies Inc—Glenn Johansen	2150 John Glenn Dr Ste, Concord CA 94520	925-363-9000	R	4*	.1
190	Moftware LLC—Kumaran Baskaran	648 S Pickett St, Alexandria VA 22304		R	4*	.1
191	Cross Connection Communications Inc—Donald Cross	11137 Dayton Pke, Soddy Daisy TN 37379	423-332-6006	R	3*	.1
192	Nighthawk Total Control Inc—Charles Kitowski	6116 N Central Expy St, Dallas TX 75206	214-234-7571	R	3	.1
193	Elontec—Ginger Clayton	5402 W Roosevelt St St, Phoenix AZ 85043	623-445-0055	R	3*	<.1
194	American Teleconnect Inc—David Jannetti	PO Box 2939, Southampton NY 11969	631-204-1891	R	3*	<.1
195	IDT Spectrum Inc—Ira Greenstein	520 Broad St, Newark NJ 07102	973-438-1000	S	3*	<.1
196	LookNet LLC—Peter Weyland	PO Box 308, Lorton VA 22199	703-550-7565	R	3*	<.1
197	Midtown Computer Services—Don Kuhwarth	PO Box 191246, Sacramento CA 95819	916-448-1290	R	3*	<.1
198	Widearea Systems—Nate Wallace	201A Broadway St, Frederick MD 21701	301-418-6180	S	3*	<.1
199	Yankee Microwave Inc—Bill Bockus	PO Box 305, Harrison ME 04040	207-583-4670	R	3*	<.1
200	C-Tech Associates Inc—Bill Brady	PO Box 463, Sparta NJ 07871	973-726-9000	R	3*	<.1
201	West Virginia Pcs Alliance LC—Keith Collins	500 Summers St 300, Charleston WV 25301	304-353-8900	R	3*	.1
202	Educational Technology Consultants International—Mary Markowsky	24 W Railroad Ave Ste, Tenafly NJ 07670	201-567-9183	R	3*	<.1
203	Cascade Communication Services Inc—Michael Macaluso	1616a Dowell Rd, Grants Pass OR 97527	541-474-4696	R	2*	<.1
204	FullTel Inc Full Web Inc	201 Robert S Kerr Ave, Oklahoma City OK 73102	405-236-8200	S	2*	<.1
205	MHO Networks—Vinh Phan	1190 S Colorado Blvd, Denver CO 80246	303-692-9409	R	2*	<.1
206	Computer Network Solutions Inc—Jeff Penland	819 Francis St, Saint Joseph MO 64501	816-232-9919	R	2*	<.1
207	Datfax Services Corp—Ramiro Rotas	6175 Nw 167th St Ste G, Hialeah FL 33015	305-653-1633	R	2*	<.1
208	Chesapeake Network Installations Inc—Paddy Sullivan	371 Lake Shore Dr, Pasadena MD 21122	410-271-1233	R	2*	<.1
209	Mrsw Management LLC—Djuana White	PO Box 6941, Austin TX 78762	512-322-2347	R	2*	<.1
210	New Skies Networks Inc—Dan Goldberg	8000 Gainsford Ct, Bristow VA 20136	703-330-3305	R	2*	<.1
211	Prime Home Entertainment Inc—Walt Obrien	901 N Hill Dr, Nashville TN 37207	615-262-9100	R	2*	<.1
212	Global Digital Datacomm Services Inc—Angela Depascale	400 W Main St Ste 330, Babylon NY 11702	631-661-5700	R	2*	<.1
213	Summit Corporate Car Inc—John Acierno	1440 39th St, Brooklyn NY 11218	718-972-7770	R	2*	<.1
214	Norris Satellite Communications Inc—John Norris	Windsor Rd, Red Lion PA 17356	717-244-3145	R	1*	<.1
215	Ace Answering Service Inc—Andy Krishak	270 Walker Dr Ste 104, State College PA 16801	814-231-8223	R	1*	<.1
216	Htn Communications LLC	11 Penn Plz Ste 2205, New York NY 10001	212-239-3710	R	1*	<.1
217	Commercial Communications LLC—Heather Young	5211 Hwy 42, Hattiesburg MS 39401	601-584-9026	R	1*	<.1
218	HS3 Technologies Inc—Robert A Morrison	1800 Boulder St Ste 60, Denver CO 80211	303-455-2550	P	1	<.1
219	Transaria Inc—Todd Graetz	7330 Shedhorn Dr, Bozeman MT 59718	406-556-1700	R	1*	<.1
220	Peace City International Inc—Guustaaf Damave	1802 N Carson St Ste 2, Carson City NV 89701	310-860-7565	R	1*	<.1
221	Wisecarver Communications Inc—Robert Read	222 S Loudoun St, Winchester VA 22601	540-662-6311	R	1*	<.1
222	Nu-Tel Communications Of New Jersey Inc—Ralph Meyers	12 Daniel Rd Ste 305, Fairfield NJ 07004	973-227-9664	R	1*	<.1
223	Vision Accomplished Inc—Craig Landis	PO BOX 700362, Kapolei HI 96709	808-478-9580	R	1	<.1
224	Antenna Sites Inc—Richard Bonifasi	7725 E Red Bird Rd Ste, Scottsdale AZ 85266	480-998-7222	R	1*	<.1
225	AgriStar Global Networks Ltd—Kip E Pendleton	70 W Madison Ave, Chicago IL 60602	312-595-1200	R	1*	<.1
226	WeatherVision—Edward I St Pe'	PO Box 786, Jackson MS 39205	601-352-6691	R	1*	<.1
227	Megatel Industries Corp—Karen Huang	6 Crimson Dr, Norristown PA 19401	610-239-8812	R	1*	<.1
228	a2i Communications—Rahul Dhesi	1211 Park Ave Ste 215, San Jose CA 95126	408-293-9706	R	1*	<.1
229	Unison Partners LLC—Patrice Samara	1010 Wisconsin Ave Nw, Washington DC 20007	202-337-7887	R	1*	<.1
230	Nikolas Management Group Inc—Larry Kavulich	PO Box 1062, Zanesville OH 43702	740-454-7515	R	1*	<.1
231	Biomedical Communications—Larry Moore	301 Kimberly Dr, Auburn AL 36832	334-844-4095	R	1*	<.1
232	Mediajoe Inc—Joe Melton	PO Box 18972, Spokane WA 99228	509-489-8980	R	1*	<.1
233	Sail Inc—Joan Okeefe	602 Dock St Ste 105, Ketchikan AK 99901	907-225-4753	R	1*	<.1
234	Blue Sky Network LLC—Brian Mycroft	1298 Prospect St Ste 1, La Jolla CA 92037	858-551-3898	R	<1*	<.1
235	Basin 2 Way Radio Inc—Tommy Hildebran	1808 Scurry St, Big Spring TX 79720	432-264-7034	R	<1*	<.1
236	TerreStar Corp—Jeffrey Epstein	12010 Sunset Hills Rd, Reston VA 20190	703-483-7806	P	<1	.1
237	Republic Data Products Inc—Stanley Bailin	PO Box 273, Maplewood NJ 07040	973-761-5151	R	<1*	<.1
238	GetFugu Inc—Michael J Solomon	415 Madison Ave 14th F, New York NY 10017		P	<1	<.1
239	Natural Blue Resources Inc—Phil Braeuning	36 Commerce Way 2nd Fl, Woburn MA 01801	781-933-4333	P	<1	<.1
240	Champion Communication Services Inc—Albert F Richmond	2739 Wisteria Walk, Spring TX 77388	281-216-6808	P	<1	N/A
241	Interlink Us Network Ltd—A Frederick Greenberg	10390 Wilshire Blvd Pe, Los Angeles CA 90024	310-777-0012	P	<1	N/A

Note: An asterisk (*) indicates an estimated financial figure. The company type code used is as follows: R = Private, P = Public, S = Private Subsidiary, B = Public Subsidiary, D = Division, J = Joint Venture, I = Investment Fund.

COMPANY RANKINGS BY SALES WITHIN 4-DIGIT SIC

Rank	Company Name—*Executive Officer*	Address, City, State, Zip	Phone	Type	Fin	Empls
242	Lithium Corp—*Tom Lewis*	200 S Virginia St 8th, Reno NV 89501	714-475-3512	P	<1	N/A
243	Skypilot Networks—*Paul Gordon*	2055 Laurelwood Rd, Santa Clara CA 95054		R	N/A	<.1

TOTALS: SIC 4899 Communications Services Nec
Companies: 243 — Fin: 66,444 — Empls: 79.4

4911 Electric Services

Rank	Company Name—*Executive Officer*	Address, City, State, Zip	Phone	Type	Fin	Empls
1	Empire District Electric Co—*Bradley Beecher*	PO Box 127, Joplin MO 64802	417-625-5100	P	576,870	.7
2	Duke Energy Corp—*James E Rogers*	526 S Church St, Charlotte NC 28202	704-594-6200	P	59,090	18.4
3	Southern Co—*Thomas A Fanning*	30 Ivan Allen Jr Blvd, Atlanta GA 30308	404-506-5000	P	55,032	25.9
4	NextEra Energy Inc—*Lewis Hay III*	700 Universe Blvd, Juno Beach FL 33408	561-694-4000	P	52,994	10.0
5	American Electric Power Company Inc—*Michael G Morris*	1 Riverside Plz, Columbus OH 43215	614-716-1000	P	50,455	18.7
6	Tennessee Valley Authority—*Tom D Kilgore*	400 W Summit Hill Dr, Knoxville TN 37902	865-632-2101	P	46,393	12.9
7	Edison International—*Theodore F Craver Jr*	PO Box 976, Rosemead CA 91770	626-302-2222	P	45,530	20.1
8	Energy Future Holdings Corp—*John F Young*	1601 Bryan St Energy P, Dallas TX 75201	214-812-4600	R	44,077	9.3
9	Dominion Resources Inc—*Thomas F Farrell II*	PO Box 26532, Richmond VA 23261	804-819-2000	P	42,817	15.8
10	AES Corp—*Philip Odeen*	4300 Wilson Blvd 11th, Arlington VA 22203	703-522-1315	P	40,511	29.0
11	Entergy Corp—*J Wayne Leonard*	639 Loyola Ave, New Orleans LA 70113	504-576-4000	P	38,685	15.0
12	FirstEnergy Corp—*Anthony J Alexander*	76 S Main St, Akron OH 44308		P	34,805	13.3
13	Progress Energy Inc—*William (Bill) D Johnson*	410 S Wilmington St, Raleigh NC 27601	919-546-6111	P	33,054	11.0
14	PPL Corp—*James H Miller*	2 N 9th St, Allentown PA 18101	610-774-5151	P	32,837	14.0
15	Southern California Edison Co—*Ronald L Litzinger* Edison International	PO Box 800, Rosemead CA 91770	626-302-1212	S	28,179*	15.5
16	Vermont Electric Cooperative Inc—*David Hallquist*	42 Wescom Rd, Johnson VT 05656	802-635-2331	R	27,687*	.1
17	NRG Energy Inc—*David Crane*	211 Carnegie Ctr, Princeton NJ 08540	609-524-4500	P	26,896	5.0
18	DTE Energy Co—*Gerard M Anderson*	1 Energy Plz, Detroit MI 48226	313-235-4000	P	24,896	9.8
19	MidAmerican Energy Co—*William Fehrman* MidAmerican Energy Holdings Co	PO Box 657, Des Moines IA 50303	515-242-4300	S	24,154*	9.7
20	First Wind Holdings Inc—*Paul Gaynor*	179 Lincoln St Ste 500, Boston MA 02111	617-960-2888	R	23,817	.1
21	Virginia Electric and Power Co—*Paul D Koonce* Dominion Resources Inc	PO Box 26543, Richmond VA 23261	804-819-2000	B	23,544	6.8
22	Florida Power and Light Co—*Lewis Hay III* NextEra Energy Inc	PO Box 025576, Miami FL 33102	561-694-4000	S	22,810*	10.4
23	Duke Capital Corp—*James E Rogers*	PO Box 1005, Charlotte NC 28201	704-382-3853	S	20,600	N/A
24	CenterPoint Energy Inc—*David M McClanahan*	PO Box 4567, Houston TX 77210	713-207-1111	P	20,111	8.8
25	Constellation Energy Group Inc—*Mayo A Shattuck III*	PO Box 1475, Baltimore MD 21203	410-470-2800	P	20,019	7.6
26	MidAmerican Energy Holdings Co—*William J Fehrman*	666 Grand Ave Ste 500, Des Moines IA 50309	515-281-2458	S	18,646*	16.8
27	Calpine Corp—*Jack A Fusco*	717 Texas Ave Ste 1000, Houston TX 77002	713-830-2000	P	17,256	2.1
28	PPL Energy Supply LLC—*James H Miller* PPL Corp	2 N 9th St, Allentown PA 18101	610-774-5151	S	16,796	7.1
29	PacifiCorp—*Gregory E Abel* PacifiCorp Holdings Inc	825 NE Multnomah St, Portland OR 97232	503-813-5000	S	14,907	6.5
30	Northeast Utilities—*Charles W Shivery*	PO Box 270, Hartford CT 06141		P	14,522	6.2
31	Pepco Holdings Inc—*Joseph M Rigby*	701 9th St NW, Washington DC 20001	202-872-2000	P	14,480	5.1
32	Pinnacle West Capital Corp—*Donald E Brandt*	PO Box 53999 Mail Sta, Phoenix AZ 85072	602-250-1000	P	12,363	6.7
33	GenOn Energy—*Edward Meuller*	PO Box 3795, Houston TX 77253	832-357-3000	P	12,269	3.1
34	Puget Sound Energy Inc—*Kimberly J Harris* Puget Energy Inc	PO Box 97034, Bellevue WA 98009	425-454-6363	S	11,929	2.8
35	Puget Energy Inc—*Kimberly Harris*	PO Box 97034, Bellevue WA 98009	425-454-6363	R	11,900	N/A
36	Detroit Edison Co—*Steven Kurmas* DTE Energy Co	1 Energy Plz, Detroit MI 48226	313-235-4000	S	10,373*	8.0
37	PacifiCorp Holdings Inc—*Greg Abel*	825 NE Multnomah Ste 2, Portland OR 97232	503-813-5000	S	9,715*	6.4
38	Alliant Energy Corp—*William D Harvey*	PO Box 77007, Madison WI 53707		P	9,688	4.3
39	Hawaiian Electric Industries Inc—*Constance H Lau*	PO Box 730, Honolulu HI 96808	808-543-5662	P	9,593	3.7
40	Nashville Electric Service Co—*Decosta Jenkins*	1214 Church St, Nashville TN 37246	615-736-6900	R	9,437*	1.0
41	Great Plains Energy Inc—*Michael J Chesser*	PO Box 418679, Kansas City MO 64141	816-556-2200	P	9,118	3.1
42	TXU Energy Retail Company LLC—*Jim Burke* Energy Future Holdings Corp	1601 Bryan St, Dallas TX 75201	214-812-4600	S	8,951*	7.3
43	Commonwealth Edison Co—*Frank M Clark*	PO Box 805398, Chicago IL 60680	312-483-3220	S	8,204*	6.0
44	Nstar—*Tom May*	1 NSTAR Way, Westwood MA 02090		P	7,934	3.0
45	San Diego Gas and Electric Co—*Jessie J Knight Jr*	PO Box 25111, Santa Ana CA 92799	619-696-2000	S	7,890*	5.0
46	TECO Energy Inc—*Sherrill Hudson*	702 N Franklin St, Tampa FL 33602	813-228-4111	P	7,322	4.0
47	Ameren Missouri—*Warner Baxter*	PO Box 66301, Saint Louis MO 63166	314-342-1111	S	7,116*	4.2
48	Arizona Public Service Co—*Jack Davis* Pinnacle West Capital Corp	PO Box 53933 Sta 3200, Phoenix AZ 85072	602-371-7171	S	6,944*	6.6
49	Energy Northwest—*Mark Reddemann*	PO Box 968, Richland WA 99352	509-372-5000	R	6,618	1.1
50	Portland General Electric Co—*Jim Piro*	PO Box 4404, Portland OR 97208	503-464-8000	P	5,733	2.6
51	PPL Electric Utilities Corp—*David G DeCampli* PPL Corp	827 Hausman Rd, Allentown PA 18104	610-774-4745	B	5,705	2.3
52	Oglethorpe Power Corp—*Thomas A Smith*	PO Box 1349, Tucker GA 30085	770-270-7600	R	5,508*	.2
53	Entergy Texas—*Joe Domino* Entergy Corp	350 Pine St, Beaumont TX 77701	409-838-6631	S	5,349*	1.3
54	Potomac Electric Power Co Pepco Holdings Inc	701 9th St NW, Washington DC 20068	202-872-2000	S	5,286	3.6
55	Connecticut Light and Power Co—*Jeffery Butler* Northeast Utilities	PO Box 270, Hartford CT 06141	860-947-2000	S	5,227*	2.2
56	US Power Generating Co—*Mark R Sudbey*	505 5th Ave 21st Fl, New York NY 10017	212-792-0800	R	5,004*	.4
57	IDACorp Inc—*J LaMont Keen*	PO Box 70, Boise ID 83707	208-388-2200	P	4,961	2.1
58	ITC Holdings Corp—*Joseph L Welch*	27175 Energy Way, Novi MI 48377	248-946-3000	P	4,823	.5
59	Sacramento Municipal Utility District—*John DiStasio*	PO Box 15830, Sacramento CA 95852	916-452-3211	R	4,741*	2.2
60	Nebraska Public Power District—*Ron Asche*	PO Box 499, Columbus NE 68602	402-564-8561	R	4,361*	2.0
61	Tampa Electric Co—*Charles R Black* TECO Energy Inc	PO Box 111, Tampa FL 33601	813-228-1111	S	4,182*	2.5
62	Black Hills Corp—*David R Emery*	PO Box 1400, Rapid City SD 57709	605-721-1700	P	4,127	2.0
63	Central Louisiana Electric Company Inc—*Bruce Williamson*	PO Box 5000, Pineville LA 71361	318-484-7400	P	4,050	1.2
64	UniSource Energy Corp—*Paul J Bonavia*	1 S Church Ave Ste 100, Tucson AZ 85701	520-571-4000	P	3,985	2.0
65	Indiana Michigan Power Co—*Paul Chodak* American Electric Power Company Inc	PO Box 60, Fort Wayne IN 46801		S	3,886*	2.8
66	LG and E Energy Systems Inc—*Victor Staffieri* E-ON US LLC	PO Box 32010, Louisville KY 40232	502-627-2000	S	3,707	5.4
67	Baltimore Gas and Electric Co—*Kenneth W DeFontes Jr* Constellation Energy Group Inc	PO Box 1475, Baltimore MD 21203	410-685-0123	S	3,704*	6.0

Rank	Company Name—*Executive Officer*	Address, City, State, Zip	Phone	Type	Fin	Empls
68	Tri-State Generation and Transmission Association Inc—*Ken Ansderson*	PO Box 33695, Denver CO 80233	303-452-6111	R	3,689	1.2
69	Mississippi Power—*Ed Day* Southern Co	2992 W Beach Blvd, Gulfport MS 39501	228-864-1211	B	3,672	1.3
70	Public Service Company of Oklahoma—*Michael G Morris* American Electric Power Company Inc	PO Box 201, Tulsa OK 74102	918-599-2000	B	3,284	1.2
71	Jersey Central Power and Light Co—*Wes Taylor* FirstEnergy Corp	76 S Main St, Akron OH 44308	973-455-8200	S	3,255*	1.4
72	Goodhue County Cooperative Electric Association—*Doug Fingerson*	1410 Northstar Dr, Zumbrota MN 55992	507-732-5117	R	3,037*	<.1
73	Nana Development Corp—*Helvi Sandvik*	1001 E Benson Blvd, Anchorage AK 99508	907-265-4100	S	2,964*	1.3
74	Tenaska Inc—*Howard L Hawks*	1044 N 115th St Ste 40, Omaha NE 68154	402-691-9500	R	2,950*	.7
75	PSEG Power LLC	PO Box 570, Newark NJ 07101	973-430-7000	S	2,893*	3.1
76	Gulf Power Co—*Susan Story* Southern Co	One Energy Pl, Pensacola FL 32520	850-444-6111	S	2,879	1.3
77	Pennsylvania Electric Co—*Michael J Chesser* FirstEnergy Corp	2800 Pottsville Pike, Reading PA 19605	610-929-3601	S	2,785*	3.0
78	Toledo Edison Co FirstEnergy Corp	76 S Main St, Akron OH 44308	419-249-5380	S	2,667	1.0
79	Cleco Power LLC—*Bruce Williamson* Central Louisiana Electric Company Inc	PO Box 5000, Pineville LA 71361	318-484-7400	S	2,664*	1.2
80	Salt River Project—*John M Williams Jr*	1521 N Project Dr, Tempe AZ 85281	602-236-8888	R	2,656*	4.4
81	Public Service Company of New Hampshire—*Gary Long* Northeast Utilities	PO Box 330, Manchester NH 03105	603-669-4000	S	2,544*	1.2
82	National Grid USA—*Steven Holliday*	25 Research Dr, Westborough MA 01582	508-389-2000	S	2,483*	1.5
83	El Paso Electric Co—*David W Stevens*	PO Box 982, El Paso TX 79999	915-543-5711	P	2,365	1.0
84	FPL Energy LLC—*Jim Robo* NextEra Energy Inc	PO Box 14000, Juno Beach FL 33408	561-691-7171	S	2,360*	1.8
85	Iberdrola Renewables—*Ralph Currey*	1125 NW Couch St Ste 7, Portland OR 97209	503-796-7000	S	2,254*	.9
86	Metropolitan Edison Co—*Donald Brennen* FirstEnergy Corp	2800 Centre Ave, Reading PA 19605	610-929-3601	S	2,248*	1.0
87	Pedernales Electric Cooperative Inc—*RB Sloan*	PO Box 1, Johnson City TX 78636	830-868-7155	R	2,193*	.8
88	Southwestern Public Service Co—*Richard Kelly*	PO Box 1261, Amarillo TX 79105	806-378-2121	S	2,182	1.3
89	Tucson Electric Power Co—*Paul Bonavia* UniSource Energy Corp	PO Box 711, Tucson AZ 85702	520-623-7711	S	2,052*	1.2
90	Ormat Technologies Inc—*Yehudit Bronicki*	6252 Neil Rd, Reno NV 89511	775-356-9029	P	2,043	1.1
91	Hawaiian Electric Company Inc—*Constance Lau* Hawaiian Electric Industries Inc	PO Box 730, Honolulu HI 96808	808-543-7771	S	1,948*	1.2
92	E-ON US LLC—*Victor A Staffieri*	PO Box 32010, Louisville KY 40232	502-627-2000	S	1,753*	3.5
93	IPALCO Enterprises Inc—*Ann D Murtlow* AES Corp	PO Box 1595, Indianapolis IN 46206	317-261-8261	S	1,655*	1.5
94	Old Dominion Electric Coop—*Jackson E Reasor*	4201 Dominion Blvd, Glen Allen VA 23060	804-747-0592	R	1,640*	.1
95	Jacksonville Electric Authority—*Jim Dickenson*	21 W Church St, Jacksonville FL 32202	904-665-6000	R	1,573*	2.0
96	Kansas City Power and Light Co—*William Downey* Great Plains Energy Inc	PO Box 418679, Kansas City MO 64141	816-556-2200	S	1,517*	3.2
97	GenOn Mid-Atlantic LLC—*Edward Muller*	1000 Main St, Houston TX 77002	832-357-3000	R	1,426*	.7
98	Indianapolis Power and Light Co—*Ann Murtlow* IPALCO Enterprises Inc	PO Box 1595, Indianapolis IN 46206	317-261-8261	S	1,304*	1.5
99	Noble Environmental Power Inc—*Kay Mann*	8 Railroad Ave, Essex CT 06426	860-581-5010	R	1,291*	.2
100	Foster Wheeler Power Systems Inc—*Gary Nedelka*	PO Box 4000, Clinton NJ 08809	908-730-4000	S	1,256*	.7
101	Indiana-Kentucky Electric Corp Ohio Valley Electric Corp	3932 US Route 23, Piketon OH 45661		S	1,148*	.7
102	Entergy Arkansas Inc—*Hugh McDonald* Entergy Corp	PO Box 551, Little Rock AR 72203	501-377-4000	B	1,127	1.4
103	Otter Tail Corp—*Edward J McIntyre*	PO Box 496, Fergus Falls MN 56538		P	1,106	3.9
104	Seminole Electric Cooperative Inc—*Timothy S Woodbury*	PO Box 272000, Tampa FL 33688	813-963-0994	R	1,106*	.5
105	Pennsylvania Power Co—*Anthony Alexander* FirstEnergy Corp	PO Box 3687, Akron OH 44309		S	1,034	2.0
106	North Carolina Electric Membership Corp—*Richard Thomas*	PO Box 27306, Raleigh NC 27611	919-872-0800	R	999*	.2
107	Central Maine Power Co—*Sara Burns*	83 Edison Dr, Augusta ME 04336	207-623-3521	S	993*	1.4
108	Idaho Power Co—*J LaMont Keen* IDACorp Inc	PO Box 70, Boise ID 83707	208-388-2200	S	979*	2.0
109	Western Massachusetts Electric Co—*Peter J Clarke* Northeast Utilities	PO Box 2010, West Springfield MA 01090	413-785-5871	S	967*	.4
110	Nevada Power Co	PO Box 30086, Las Vegas NV 89173	702-367-5000	S	949*	1.8
111	Hoosier Energy Rural Electric Cooperative Inc—*J Steven Smith*	PO Box 908, Bloomington IN 47402	812-876-2021	R	932*	.5
112	Arkansas Valley Electric Co-operative Corp—*Bill Peters*	PO Box 47, Ozark AR 72949	479-667-2176	R	910*	.2
113	UGI Utilities Inc Electric Div—*Dave Trego*	PO Box 3200, Wilkes Barre PA 18704	570-819-1212	D	849*	2.0
114	Black Hills Power Inc—*Lee DeLange* Black Hills Corp	1060 Main St, Sturgis SD 57785	605-720-2440	S	835*	.4
115	System Energy Resources Inc—*J Wayne Leonard* Entergy Corp	PO Box 31995, Jackson MS 39286	601-368-5000	S	816*	.5
116	Entergy Louisiana LLC—*Bill Mohl* Entergy Corp	446 North Blvd, Baton Rouge LA 70802	504-840-2734	B	815	.9
117	Lee County Electric Cooperative Inc—*Dennis Hamilton*	PO Box 3455, North Fort Myers FL 33918	239-995-2121	R	809*	.4
118	East Kentucky Power Cooperative Inc—*Bob Marshall*	PO Box 707, Winchester KY 40392	859-744-4864	R	803*	.7
119	Maui Electric Company Ltd—*Ed Rhinehardt* Hawaiian Electric Company Inc	210 W Kamehameha Ave, Kahului HI 96732	808-871-8461	S	774*	.3
120	Southwest Louisiana Electric Membership Corp—*JU Gajan*	PO Box 90866, Lafayette LA 70509	337-896-5384	R	744*	.3
121	Alabama Power Co—*Charles D McCrary* Southern Co	600 N 18th St, Birmingham AL 35291	205-257-1000	B	716	6.7
122	Central Vermont Public Service Corp—*Lawrence Reilly*	77 Grove St, Rutland VT 05701	802-773-2711	P	711	.5
123	Great River Energy—*David Saggau*	PO Box 800, Elk River MN 55330	763-445-5000	R	698*	.9
124	Indeck Energy Services Inc—*Lawrence Lagowski*	600 N Buffalo Grove Rd, Buffalo Grove IL 60089	847-520-3212	R	690*	.3
125	Associated Electric Cooperative Inc—*James J Jura*	PO Box 754, Springfield MO 65801	417-881-1204	R	686*	.7
126	United Illuminating Co—*James Torgerson*	PO Box 1564, New Haven CT 06506	203-499-2000	S	680	1.2
127	Cardinal Power Plant—*Doug Shearn*	306 Country Rd 7E, Brilliant OH 43913	740-598-4164	S	677*	.5
128	Kentucky Power Co—*Greg Pauley* American Electric Power Company Inc	PO Box 5190, Frankfort KY 40602	502-696-7000	S	654*	.4

Note: An asterisk (*) indicates an estimated financial figure. The company type code used is as follows: R = Private, P = Public, S = Private Subsidiary, B = Public Subsidiary, D = Division, J = Joint Venture, I = Investment Fund.

COMPANY RANKINGS BY SALES WITHIN 4-DIGIT SIC

Rank	Company Name—Executive Officer	Address, City, State, Zip	Phone	Type	Fin	Empls
129	Guadalupe Valley Electric Cooperative Inc—Darren Schauer	PO Box 118, Gonzales TX 78629	830-857-1200	R	634*	.3
130	CMS Generation Co	1 Energy Plz Dr, Jackson MI 49201	517-788-0550	S	602*	.3
131	Anchorage Municipal Light and Power—James M Posey	1200 E 1st Ave, Anchorage AK 99501	907-279-7671	R	600*	.2
132	Western Farmers Electric Coop—Gary R Roulet	PO Box 429, Anadarko OK 73005	405-247-3351	R	594*	.4
133	Middle Tennessee Electric Membership Corp—Frank Jennings	555 New Salem Rd, Murfreesboro TN 37129	615-890-9762	R	587*	.4
134	Ohio Valley Electric Corp	PO Box 468, Piketon OH 45661	740-289-7200	R	574*	.8
135	GreyStone Power Corp—Gary A Miller	PO Box 897, Douglasville GA 30133	770-942-6576	R	570*	.3
136	Dakota Electric Association—Greg Miller	4300 220th St W, Farmington MN 55024	651-463-7134	R	532*	.2
137	Chugach Electric Association Inc—Brad Evans	PO Box 196300, Anchorage AK 99519	907-563-7494	R	517*	.4
138	Hawaii Electric Light Company Inc—John Perreira Hawaiian Electric Company Inc	PO Box 730, Honolulu HI 96808	808-543-5662	S	502*	.4
139	Northern Virginia Electric Coop—Stan C Feuerberg	PO Box 2710, Manassas VA 20108	703-335-0500	R	492*	.3
140	Rappahannock Electric Coop—Kent Farmer	PO Box 7388, Fredericksburg VA 22404	540-898-8500	R	467*	.3
141	Dairyland Power Coop—William L Berg	PO Box 817, La Crosse WI 54602	608-788-4000	R	437*	.6
142	Cogentrix Energy LLC—Larry Kellerman	9405 Arrowpoint Blvd, Charlotte NC 28273	704-525-3800	R	425*	.2
143	Flathead Electric Cooperative Inc—Jim Sutherland	2510 Hwy 2 E, Kalispell MT 59901	406-751-4483	R	424*	.2
144	Ambit Energy Holdings LLC—Jere Thompson Jr	PO Box 864589, Plano TX 75086		R	418	.2
145	First Electric Cooperative Corp—Neil Frizzell	1000 S JP Wright Loop, Jacksonville AR 72076	501-982-4545	R	407	.2
146	Arizona Electric Power Cooperative Inc—Donald Kimball	PO Box 670, Benson AZ 85602	520-586-3631	R	396*	.3
147	Arkansas Electric Cooperative Corp—Gary C Voigt	PO Box 194208, Little Rock AR 72219	501-570-2200	R	395*	.2
148	Entergy Mississippi Inc—Haley Fisackerly Entergy Corp	308 E Pearl St, Jackson MS 39201	601-368-5000	B	393	.7
149	Powder River Energy Corp—Michael Easley	PO Box 930, Sundance WY 82729	307-283-3531	R	387*	.3
150	Direct Energy Marketing Ltd—Chris Weston	1001 Liberty Ave 12th, Pittsburgh PA 15222		S	377	6.0
151	Carroll Electric Cooperative Corp—Rob Boaz	PO Box 4000, Berryville AR 72616	870-423-2161	R	362*	.3
152	Duck River Electric Membership Corp—Jim Allison	PO Box 89, Shelbyville TN 37162	931-684-4621	R	351*	.2
153	Colquitt Electric Membership—Danny Nichols	PO Box 3608, Moultrie GA 31776	229-985-3620	R	348*	.2
154	Trico Electric Cooperative Inc—Vincent Nitido	PO Box 930, Marana AZ 85653	520-744-2944	R	348*	.1
155	Cumberland Electric Membership Corp—Joe H Whitaker	PO Box 3300, Clarksville TN 37043	931-645-2481	R	335	.2
156	Golden Valley Electric Association—Brian Newton	PO Box 71249, Fairbanks AK 99707	907-452-1151	R	333*	.3
157	New Hampshire Electric Cooperative Inc—Fred Anderson	PO Box 9612, Manchester NH 03108	603-536-1800	R	329*	.2
158	South Mississippi Electric Power Association—James Compton	PO Box 15849, Hattiesburg MS 39404	601-268-2083	R	310*	.2
159	Horry Electric Cooperative Inc—James P Howle	PO Box 119, Conway SC 29528	843-369-2211	R	301*	.1
160	Cobb Electric Membership Corp—Dwight T Brown	PO Box 369, Marietta GA 30061	770-429-2100	R	298*	.6
161	Energy Cooperative of Ohio—John Zornes	790 Windmiller Dr Ste, Pickerington OH 43147	614-856-3599	R	287*	.2
162	Corn Belt Power Coop—Ken Kuyper	PO Box 508, Humboldt IA 50548	515-332-2571	R	280*	.1
163	South Central Power Co—Ralph E Luffler	PO Box 250, Lancaster OH 43130	740-653-4422	R	275*	.2
164	Linn County Rural Electric Coop—Gary Schropp	PO Box 69, Marion IA 52302	319-377-1587	R	274*	.1
165	Manitowoc Public Utilities—Nilaksh Kothari	PO Box 1090, Manitowoc WI 54221	920-683-4600	R	274*	.1
166	Brunswick Electric Membership Corp—Robert Leavitt Jr	PO Box 826, Shallotte NC 28459	910-754-4391	R	265*	.1
167	Edison Mission Marketing and Trading Inc—Theodore Craver	160 Federal St 4th Fl, Boston MA 02110	617-912-6000	S	263*	.1
168	Northeast Oklahoma Electric Coop—Sheila Allgood	PO Box 948, Vinita OK 74301	918-256-6405	R	262*	.2
169	Matanuska Electric Association Inc—Joe Griffith	PO Box 2929, Palmer AK 99645	907-745-3231	R	262*	.1
170	Holy Cross Energy Inc—Del Woorley	PO Box 2150, Glenwood Springs CO 81602	970-945-5491	R	260*	.2
171	East River Electric Power Coop—Jeff Nelson	PO Box 227, Madison SD 57042	605-256-4536	R	256*	.1
172	Black River Electric Coop (Fredericktown Missouri)—Tom Steska	PO Box 31, Fredericktown MO 63645	573-783-3381	R	256*	.1
173	Habersham Electric Membership Corp—Todd A Pealock	PO Box 25, Clarkesville GA 30523	706-754-2114	R	249*	.1
174	Central Georgia Electric Membership Co-op—George Weaver	923 S Mulberry St, Jackson GA 30233	770-775-7857	R	247*	.2
175	West Florida Electric Cooperative Association—Bill Rimes	PO Box 127, Graceville FL 32440	850-547-9325	R	247*	.1
176	Cleco Generation Services LLC—Bruce Williamson Central Louisiana Electric Company Inc	2030 Donahue Ferry Rd, Pineville LA 71360	318-484-7400	S	242*	.1
177	Acadia Power Partners LLC—Bruce Williamson Central Louisiana Electric Company Inc	2030 Donahue Ferry Rd, Pineville LA 71360	318-484-7400	S	231*	.1
178	Cleco Evangeline LLC—Bruce Williamson Central Louisiana Electric Company Inc	2030 Donahue Ferry Rd, Pineville LA 71360	318-484-7400	S	231*	.1
179	Cleco Marketing and Trading LLC—Bruce Williamson Cleco Midstream LLC	2030 Donahue Ferry Rd, Pineville LA 71360	318-484-7400	S	231*	.1
180	Cleco Midstream Resources LLC—Bruce Williamson Central Louisiana Electric Company Inc	2030 Donahue Ferry Rd, Pineville LA 71360	318-484-7400	S	231*	.1
181	Cleco Support Group LLC—Bruce Williamson Central Louisiana Electric Company Inc	PO Box 5000, Pineville LA 71361	318-484-7400	S	231*	.1
182	Intermountain Rural Electric Association—Tim L White	PO Drawer A, Sedalia CO 80135	303-688-3100	R	225*	.2
183	Mid-South Synergy—Kerry Kelton	PO Box 970, Navasota TX 77868	936-825-5100	R	221*	.1
184	PJM Interconnection LLC—Craig Glazer	955 Jefferson Ave, Norristown PA 19403	610-666-8980	R	215*	.6
185	Dominion Clearinghouse—Thomas Farrell Virginia Electric and Power Co	120 Tredegar St, Richmond VA 23219	804-819-2000	S	215*	.2
186	Ozarks Electric Cooperative Corp—Mitchell Johnson	PO Box 848, Fayetteville AR 72702	479-521-2900	R	215*	.2
187	Duke Energy Group Inc—John F Norris	400 S Tryon St Ste 180, Charlotte NC 28285	704-382-9800	R	214*	.2
188	Sho-Me Power Electric Coop—Chris Hamon	PO Box D, Marshfield MO 65706	417-468-2615	R	213*	.1
189	Texas-New Mexico Power Co—Pat Vincent-Collawn	577 N Garden Ridge Blv, Lewisville TX 75067		S	213	.4
190	Kenergy Corp—Sanford Novick	PO Box 18, Henderson KY 42419		S	210*	.2
191	Dixie Electric Membership Corp—Jeff Kilpatrick	PO Box 15659, Baton Rouge LA 70895	225-261-1221	R	202*	.2
192	Green Mountain Power Corp—Mary G Powell	163 Acorn Ln, Colchester VT 05446	802-864-5731	S	201*	.1
193	Mountain Electric Cooperative Inc—Joseph Thacker	PO Box 180, Mountain City TN 37683	423-727-1800	R	196*	.1
194	Mid-Carolina Electric Coop—Jack F Wolfe	PO Box 669, Lexington SC 29071	803-749-6400	R	194*	.1
195	Union Power Coop—BL Starnes	PO Box 5014, Monroe NC 28111	704-289-3145	R	192*	.1
196	Woodruff Electric Coop—Billy C Martin III	PO Box 1619, Forrest City AR 72336	870-633-2262	R	182*	.1
197	Southwest Electric Coop—James Ashworth	1023 S Springfield, Bolivar MO 65613	417-326-5244	R	181*	.1
198	Southern Illinois Power Cooperative Inc—Larry Lovel	11543 Lake of Egypt Rd, Marion IL 62959	618-964-1448	R	180*	.1
199	Concho Valley Electric Cooperative Inc—Sid Long	PO Box 3388, San Angelo TX 76902	325-655-6957	R	180*	.1
200	Sunflower Electric Power Corp—L Earl Watkins	PO Box 1020, Hays KS 67601	785-628-2845	R	179*	.4
201	Washington-St Tammany Electric Coop—Francis Cefalu	PO Box N, Franklinton LA 70438	985-839-3562	R	178*	.1
202	Illinois Municipal Electric Agency—Ronald Earl	3400 Conifer Dr, Springfield IL 62711	217-789-4632	R	177*	<.1
203	Platte River Power Authority—M Dave	2000 E Horsetooth Rd, Fort Collins CO 80525	970-226-4000	R	177*	.2
204	Central Electric Cooperative Inc—Dave Markham	PO Box 846, Redmond OR 97756	541-548-2144	R	176*	.1
205	Lake County Power—Charles Mistek	2810 Elida Dr, Grand Rapids MN 55744		R	175	.1
206	Magic Valley Electric Coop—John W Herrera	PO Drawer 267, Mercedes TX 78570		R	174*	.2
207	Connexus Energy—Richard Newland	PO Box 1808, Ramsey MN 55303	763-323-2600	R	174*	.2

Rank	Company Name—*Executive Officer*	Address, City, State, Zip	Phone	Type	Fin	Empls
208	Black Hills/Colorado Electric Utility Company LP—*Jason Ketchum*	105 S Victoria Ave, Pueblo CO 81003	719-546-6589	R	174*	.2
209	Constellation Energy Nuclear Group LLC—*Henry Barron*	100 Constellation Way, Baltimore MD 21202	410-470-2800	R	173*	2.3
210	Sumter Electric Cooperative Inc—*James P Duncan*	PO Box 301, Sumterville FL 33585	352-793-3801	R	173*	.4
211	Southern Electric Generating Co Alabama Power Co	PO Box 2641, Birmingham AL 35291	205-257-1000	S	173	N/A
212	Great Lakes Energy Coop—*Steve Boeckman*	1323 Boynce Ave, Boyne City MI 49712	231-652-1651	R	171*	.2
213	Washington Electric Membership Corp—*Frank Askew Jr*	PO Box 598, Sandersville GA 31082	478-552-2577	R	170*	.1
214	BlueStar Energy Services Inc—*Guy H Morgan*	363 W Erie St Ste 700, Chicago IL 60654	312-327-0090	R	169*	.1
215	Northeast Texas Electric Cooperative Inc—*John Dugen*	1127 Judson Rd Ste 249, Longview TX 75601	903-757-3282	R	167*	<.1
216	San Bernard Electric Cooperative Inc—*James W Marricle*	PO Box 1208, Bellville TX 77418	979-865-3171	R	166*	.1
217	Suwannee Valley Electric Cooperative Inc—*John Martz*	PO Box 160, Live Oak FL 32060	386-362-2226	R	166*	.1
218	Flint Energies—*Bob Ray*	PO Box 308, Reynolds GA 31076	478-847-3415	R	165*	.2
219	Volunteer Energy Coop—*Rody Blevins*	PO Box 1183, Decatur TN 37322	423-334-7001	R	165*	.1
220	Marshall-DeKalb Electric Coop—*James W Stewart*	PO Box 724, Boaz AL 35957	256-593-4262	R	165*	.1
221	Shenandoah Valley Electric Cooperative Inc—*C Wine*	PO Box 236, Mount Crawford VA 22841	540-434-2200	R	164*	.1
222	Amicalola Electric Membership—*Robert Payne*	544 Hwy 515 S, Jasper GA 30143	706-253-5200	R	163*	.1
223	Navopache Electric Coop—*David Plumb*	PO Box 308, Lakeside AZ 85929	928-368-5118	R	163*	.1
224	Pacific Northwest Generating Coop—*Joseph Nadal*	711 Ne Halsey St, Portland OR 97232	503-288-1234	R	163*	<.1
225	Wiregrass Electric Cooperative Inc—*MIchael S McWaters*	PO Box 158, Hartford AL 36344	334-588-2223	R	162*	.1
226	Entergy Nuclear Generation Co—*John Herron*	1340 Echelon Pkwy Ste, Jackson MS 39213	601-368-5000	R	161*	2.2
227	KAMO Electric Cooperative Inc—*J Chris Cariker*	PO Box 577, Vinita OK 74301	918-256-5551	R	160*	.1
228	Piedmont Electric Membership Corp—*R G Brecheisen*	PO Drawer 1179, Hillsborough NC 27278	919-732-2123	R	158*	.1
229	West Penn Power Co—*Joseph Richardson*	800 Cabin Hill Dr, Greensburg PA 15601	724-837-3000	R	154*	1.5
230	Natchez Trace Electric Power Association—*Norma F Kilgore*	PO Box 609, Houston MS 38851	662-456-3037	R	154*	.1
231	Buckeye Rural Electric Cooperative Inc—*C Tonda Meadows*	PO Box 200, Rio Grande OH 45674	740-379-2025	R	152*	.1
232	Energy Plus Holdings LLC—*Brigitte Addimando*	3711 Market St Ste 910, Philadelphia PA 19104		R	151*	.1
233	NW Electric Power Coop—*Don McQuitty*	PO Box 565, Cameron MO 64429	816-632-2121	R	150*	.1
234	Great Lakes Energy—*Steve Boeckman*	1323 Boyne Ave, Boyne City MI 49712	231-582-6521	R	150*	.2
235	People's Electric Coop—*R Ethridge*	PO Box 429, Ada OK 74821	580-332-3031	R	148*	.1
236	Oklahoma Municipal Power Authority—*David Osburn*	PO Box 1960, Edmond OK 73083	405-340-5047	R	148*	.1
237	Columbia Power and Water System—*John Collier*	PO Box 379, Columbia TN 38402	931-388-4833	R	147*	.1
238	Polk-Burnett Electric Coop—*Bill Schmidt*	1001 State Rd 35, Centuria WI 54824	715-646-2191	R	147*	.1
239	APX Inc (Santa Clara California)—*Brian M Storms*	224 Airport Pkwy Ste 6, San Jose CA 95110	408-517-2100	R	146*	.1
240	Municipal Energy Agency Of Nebraska—*J Stauffer*	PO Box 95124, Lincoln NE 68509	402-474-4759	R	145*	.1
241	Tri-County Electric Coop (St Matthews South Carolina)—*B Robert Pauling*	PO Box 217, Saint Matthews SC 29135	803-874-1215	R	144*	.1
242	East River Electric Power Cooperative Inc—*Jeffrey Nelson*	PO Box 227, Madison SD 57042	605-256-4536	R	142*	.1
243	La Plata Electric Association Inc—*Greg Munro*	PO Box 2750, Durango CO 81302	970-247-5786	R	140*	.1
244	Safe Harbor Water Power Corp—*Juan Kimble*	1 Powerhouse Rd, Conestoga PA 17516	717-872-5441	J	140*	.1
245	Clark Energy Cooperative Corp—*Paul Embs*	PO Box 748, Winchester KY 40392	859-744-4251	R	137*	.1
246	Pioneer Electric Cooperative Inc (Greenville Alabama)—*Stephen A Harmon*	PO Box 40, Sardis AL 36775	334-875-2223	R	137*	.1
247	Caney Valley Cooperative Association Inc—*Kenny Bates*	PO Box 308, Cedar Vale KS 67024	620-758-2262	R	137*	.1
248	Homer Electric Association Inc—*Brad Janorschke*	3977 Lake St, Homer AK 99603	907-235-8551	R	136*	.1
249	Orcas Power and Light Coop—*Randy Conelius*	183 Mt Baker Rd, Eastsound WA 98245	360-376-3500	R	136*	.1
250	Fall River Rural Electric Coop—*Bryan Case*	1150 N 3400 E, Ashton ID 83420	208-652-7431	R	133*	.1
251	Wayne-White Counties Electric Coop—*Daryl Donjon*	PO Box E, Fairfield IL 62837	618-842-2196	R	132*	.1
252	Diverse Power Inc—*Wayne Livingston*	PO Box 160, LaGrange GA 30241	706-845-2000	R	130*	.1
253	York Electric Cooperative Inc—*E Paul Basha Jr*	PO Box 150, York SC 29745	803-684-4247	R	130*	.1
254	Salem Electric—*Jeff Anderson*	PO Box 5588, Salem OR 97304	503-362-3601	R	128*	.1
255	International Transmissionn Co—*Joseph L Welch* ITC Holdings Corp	27175 Energy Way, Novi MI 48377		S	126*	.1
256	Mitchell Electric Membership Corp—*Tony F Tucker*	PO Box 409, Camilla GA 31730	229-336-5221	R	126*	.1
257	Graham County Electric Cooperative Inc—*Steve Lines*	PO Drawer B, Pima AZ 85543	928-485-2451	R	125*	.1
258	Jones-Onslow Electric Membership Corp—*J Ronald McEl-heney*	259 Western Blvd, Jacksonville NC 28546	910-353-1940	R	124*	.2
259	Randolph Electric Membership Corp—*Dale F Lambert*	PO Box 40, Asheboro NC 27204	336-625-5177	R	124*	.1
260	Maine and Maritimes Corp—*Brent Boyles*	PO Box 789, Presque Isle ME 04769	207-760-2499	P	123	.1
261	Palmetto Electric Cooperative Inc—*G Thomas Upshaw*	PO Box 820, Ridgeland SC 29936		R	123*	.1
262	Commerce Energy Group Inc—*Rohn Crabtree*	1 Centerpointe Dr Ste, La Palma CA 90623		B	122	.2
263	Harrison County Rural Electric Coop (Corydon Indiana)—*David Lett*	PO Box 517, Corydon IN 47112		R	121*	.1
264	Citizens Electric Corp—*Van Robinson*	PO Box 311, Sainte Genevieve MO 63670	573-883-3511	R	118*	.1
265	Minnkota Power Cooperative Inc—*David Loer*	PO Box 13200, Grand Forks ND 58208	701-795-4000	S	117*	.4
266	East Central Oklahoma Electric Cooperative Inc—*Jimmy Eller*	PO Drawer 1178, Okmulgee OK 74447	918-756-0833	R	116*	.1
267	Lea County Electric Cooperative Inc	PO Box 1447, Lovington NM 88260	575-396-3631	R	115*	.1
268	Lyntegar Electric Cooperative Inc—*Greg L Henley*	PO Box 970, Tahoka TX 79373	806-561-4588	R	115*	.1
269	Northeastern Rural Electric Membership Coop—*Gregg Kiess*	4901 E Park 30 Dr, Columbia City IN 46725	260-244-6111	R	115*	.1
270	Oklahoma Electric Co-Operative Inc—*Bob Usry*	PO Box 1208, Norman OK 73070	405-321-2024	R	114*	.1
271	Southern Rivers Energy—*Raleigh Henry*	PO Box 40, Barnesville GA 30204	770-358-1383	R	113*	.1
272	Coos-Curry Electric Coop—*Roger Meader*	PO Box 1268, Port Orford OR 97465	541-332-3931	R	113*	.1
273	Twin County Electric Power Association—*John W Mosley*	PO Box 158, Hollandale MS 38748	662-827-2262	R	111*	.1
274	Pickwick Electric Coop—*Karl W Dudley*	PO Box 49, Selmer TN 38375	731-645-3411	R	110*	.1
275	Riverland Energy Coop—*Dave Oelkers*	PO Box 277, Arcadia WI 54612	608-323-3381	R	110*	<.1
276	Big Rivers Electric Corp—*Michael H Core*	PO Box 24, Henderson KY 42419	270-827-2561	R	108*	.1
277	Elkhorn Rural Public Power—*Thomas Rudloff*	PO Box 310, Battle Creek NE 68715	402-675-2185	R	107*	<.1
278	Central Iowa Power Coop—*Dennis Murdock*	PO Box 2517, Cedar Rapids IA 52406	319-366-8011	R	106*	.2
279	Wheatland Electric Cooperative Inc—*Neil K Norman*	101 Main St, Scott City KS 67871	620-872-5885	R	106*	.1
280	Mohave Electric Cooperative Inc—*Robert Broz*	PO Box 1045, Bullhead City AZ 86430	928-763-4115	R	106*	.1
281	Wells Rural Electric Co—*Clay R Fitch*	PO Box 365, Wells NV 89835	775-752-3328	R	106*	<.1
282	Kiamichi Electric Coop—*Stephen Bryan*	PO Box 340, Wilburton OK 74578	918-465-2338	R	106*	<.1
283	Umatilla Electric Cooperative Association—*Steve Eldridge*	PO Box 1148, Hermiston OR 97838	541-567-6414	R	105*	.1
284	Tri-State Electric Membership Corp—*Grady Anderson*	PO Box 68, McCaysville GA 30555	706-492-3251	R	105*	<.1
285	Kentucky Utilities Co—*Vic Staffieri* E-ON US LLC	1 Quality St, Lexington KY 40507		S	104*	1.7
286	United Electric Cooperative Inc—*Brenda Swartzlander*	PO Box 688, Du Bois PA 15801	814 371-8570	R	104*	.1
287	Pioneer Rural Electric Cooperative Inc—*Ronald Salyer*	PO Box 604, Piqua OH 45356	937-773-2523	R	104*	.1
288	Tri-County Electric Cooperative Inc (Madison Florida)—*Julius Hackett*	PO Box 208, Madison FL 32341	850-973-2285	R	103*	<.1

Note: An asterisk (*) indicates an estimated financial figure. The company type code used is as follows: R = Private, P = Public, S = Private Subsidiary, B = Public Subsidiary, D = Division, J = Joint Venture, I = Investment Fund.

COMPANY RANKINGS BY SALES WITHIN 4-DIGIT SIC

Rank	Company Name—Executive Officer	Address, City, State, Zip	Phone	Type	Fin	Empls
289	Poudre Valley Rural Electric Association Inc—Brad Gaskill	PO Box 272550, Fort Collins CO 80527	970-226-1234	R	102*	.1
290	Butler County Rural Electric Coop	PO Box 98, Allison IA 50602	319-267-2726	R	102*	<.1
291	Butler Rural Electric Cooperative Association Inc—Olin Claassen	PO Box 1242, El Dorado KS 67042	316-321-9600	R	102*	<.1
292	Warren Rural Electric Cooperative Corp—Gary K Dillard	951 Fairview Ave Ste 2, Bowling Green KY 42101	270-842-6541	R	100*	.2
293	Choptank Electric Cooperative Inc—Frederick L Hubbard	PO Box 430, Denton MD 21629	410-479-0380	R	98	.2
294	Black River Electric Coop (Sumter South Carolina)—C H Leaird	PO Box 130, Sumter SC 29151	803-469-8060	R	98*	.1
295	Santee Electric Cooperative Inc—Floyd L Keels	PO Box 548, Kingstree SC 29556	843-355-6187	R	96*	.2
296	Cotton Electric Cooperative Inc—Warren Langford	226 N Broadway St, Walters OK 73572	580-875-3351	R	96*	.1
297	Truckee Donner Public Utility District—Michael D Holley	PO Box 309, Truckee CA 96160	530-587-3896	R	96*	.1
298	Scenic Rivers Energy Coop—Richard E Kolb	231 N Sheridan, Lancaster WI 53813	608-723-2121	R	93*	<.1
299	Southwest Tennessee Electric Membership Corp—Kevin Murphy	PO Box 959, Brownsville TN 38012	731-772-1322	R	92*	.1
300	Callaway Electric Coop—Charles Schmid	PO Box 250, Fulton MO 65251	573-642-3326	R	92*	<.1
301	Slash Pine Electric Membership	PO Box 356, Homerville GA 31634	912-487-5201	R	90*	<.1
302	Continental Divide Electric Coop—Richard A Shirley	PO Box 1087, Grants NM 87020	505-285-6656	R	87*	.1
303	Southern Pine Electric Cooperative Inc—Vince Johnson	PO Box 528, Brewton AL 36427	251-867-5415	R	87*	.1
304	Appalachian Electric Coop	PO Box 400, New Market TN 37820	865-475-2032	R	86*	.1
305	Adams Columbia Electric Coop—Martin Hillert	401 E Lake St, Friendship WI 53934	608-339-3346	R	85*	.1
306	West Central Electric Coop—Charles Oller	PO Box 17, Murdo SD 57559	605-669-2472	R	85*	<.1
307	Rockland Electric Co—Victor Blanchet	82 E Allendale Rd Ste, Saddle River NJ 07458	845-352-0600	R	84*	.1
308	Coast Electric Power Association—Robert Occhi	PO Box 2430, Bay Saint Louis MS 39521	228-467-6535	R	83*	.3
309	Central Texas Electric Cooperative Inc—Robert Loth	PO Box 553, Fredericksburg TX 78624	830-997-2126	R	83*	.1
310	Canadian Valley Electric Coop—George Hand	PO Box 751, Seminole OK 74818	405-382-3680	R	83*	.1
311	Osage Valley Electric Coop—Daryl Veatch	PO Box 151, Butler MO 64730	660-679-3131	R	82*	.1
312	Yazoo Valley Electric Power Association—CH Shelton	PO Box 8, Yazoo City MS 39194	662-746-4251	R	82*	.1
313	Rayle Electric Membership Corp—Philip J Brown	PO Box 1090, Washington GA 30673	706-678-2116	R	81*	.1
314	Cumberland Valley Rural Electric Cooperative Corp	6219 US Hwy 25E, Gray KY 40734		R	81*	.1
315	Pea River Electric Coop—Randy Brannon	PO Box 969, Ozark AL 36361	334-774-2545	R	80*	.1
316	Oconee Electric Membership Corp—Marty Smith	PO Box 37, Dudley GA 31022	478-676-3191	R	79*	.1
317	Shelby Electric Cooperative Inc	PO Box 560, Shelbyville IL 62565	217-774-3986	R	79*	.1
318	Little Ocmulgee Electric Membership Corp—Grant Rowe	PO Box 150, Alamo GA 30411	912-568-7171	R	78*	<.1
319	Tellico Electric Co—Chris Stokes	1200 W Broadway St, Lenoir City TN 37771	865-986-9330	R	77*	<.1
320	Southeastern Electric Cooperative Inc—Brad Schardin	PO Box 388, Marion SD 57043	605-648-3619	R	76*	.1
321	Hancock-Wood Electric Cooperative Inc—George B Walton	PO Box 190, North Baltimore OH 45872	419-257-3241	R	76*	<.1
322	Kaw Valley Electric Coop—Dan O'Brien	PO Box 750640, Topeka KS 66675	785-478-3444	R	76*	<.1
323	Beacon Power Corp—F William Capp	65 Middlesex Rd, Tyngsboro MA 01879	978-694-9121	P	76	.1
324	Blue Ridge Electric Membership Corp—Doug Johnson	PO Box 112, Lenoir NC 28645	828-758-2383	R	75*	.2
325	People Electric Coop—Randy J Ethridge	PO Box 429, Ada OK 74821	580-332-3031	R	75*	.1
326	Doswell LP—Lou Hay FPL Energy LLC	10098 Old Ridge Rd, Ashland VA 23005	804-227-3330	S	74*	<.1
327	Irwin Electric Membership Corp—Randy Crenshaw	PO Box 125, Ocilla GA 31774	229-468-7415	R	73*	.1
328	Northern Plains Electric Coop—Tracy Boe	1515 W Main Ave, Carrington ND 50421	701-968-3314	R	73*	.1
329	Red River Valley Rural Electric Association—Brent Hartin	PO Box 220, Marietta OK 73448	580-276-3364	R	73*	<.1
330	McDonough Power Coop—Steve Epperson	PO Box 352, Macomb IL 61455	309-833-2101	R	73*	<.1
331	CoServ—Mike Drewspring	7701 S Stemmons, Corinth TX 76210	940-321-7800	R	72*	.3
332	Cass County Electric Coop—Scott W Handy	4100 32nd Ave SW, Fargo ND 58104	701-356-4400	R	72*	.1
333	Altamaha Electric Membership Corp—Robert E Youmans	PO Box 346, Lyons GA 30436	912-526-8181	R	72*	.1
334	West Central Electric Cooperative Inc—Clark Bredehoeft	7867 S Hwy 13 PO Box 4, Higginsville MO 64037	660-584-2131	R	72*	<.1
335	Nobles Cooperative Electric—Henry A Hanson	PO Box 788, Worthington MN 56187	507-372-7331	R	72*	<.1
336	Lumbee River Electric Membership Corp—Randall Jones	PO Box 830, Red Springs NC 28377	910-843-4131	R	71*	.1
337	Adams Electric Cooperative Inc—Steve Rasnussen	PO Box 1055, Gettysburg PA 17325	717-334-9211	R	71*	.1
338	Northern Lights Inc—Annie Terracciano	PO Box 269, Sagle ID 83860	208-263-5141	R	71*	.1
339	Berkeley Electric Cooperative Inc—EE Strickland	PO Box 1234, Moncks Corner SC 29461	843-761-8200	R	70*	.2
340	North Central Electric Coop—Wayne Martian	538 11th St W, Bottineau ND 58318	701-228-2202	R	70*	<.1
341	KLT Inc—Michael Chesser Great Plains Energy Inc	PO Box 418679, Kansas City MO 64141	816-556-2200	S	70*	<.1
342	Northeast Missouri Electric Power Coop—Emery Geisendorfer	PO Box 191, Palmyra MO 63461	573-769-2107	R	69*	.1
343	SEMO Electric Coop—Reuben L Jeane	PO Box 520, Sikeston MO 63801	573-471-5821	R	68*	<.1
344	Heartland Power Coop—John Leerar	216 Jackson St, Thompson IA 50478	641-584-2251	R	68*	<.1
345	Mor-Gran-Sou Electric Cooperative Inc—Donald A Franklund	PO Box 297, Flasher ND 58535	701-597-3301	R	68*	<.1
346	Cullman Electric Coop—Grady Smith	PO Box 1168, Cullman AL 35056	256-737-3200	R	67*	.1
347	Upper Peninsula Power Corp—Gary Erickson	PO Box 19076, Green Bay MI 54307	906-487-5000	S	66*	.1
348	Somerset Rural Electric Cooperative Inc—Wayne E Sechler	PO Box 270, Somerset PA 15501	814-445-4106	R	66*	<.1
349	Wolverine Power Systems Inc—Glenn Emmert	3229 80th Ave, Zeeland MI 49464	616-879-0040	S	66*	<.1
350	Delaware Electric Coop—William Andrews	PO Box 600, Greenwood DE 19950	302-349-9090	R	65*	.1
351	North Arkansas Electric Cooperative Inc—Mel Coleman	PO Box 1000, Salem AR 72576	870-895-3221	R	65*	.1
352	Platte-Clay Electric Coop—Mike Torres	PO Box 100, Kearney MO 64060	816-628-3121	R	65*	.1
353	Cloverland Electric Coop—Dan Dasho	2916 W M-28, Dafter MI 49724	906-635-6800	R	65*	<.1
354	Lamb County Electric Cooperative Inc	2415 S Phelps Ave, Littlefield TX 79339	806-385-5191	R	65	<.1
355	Moon Lake Electric Association Inc—Grant J Earl	PO Box 278, Roosevelt UT 84066		R	64*	.1
356	Beltrami Electric Cooperative Inc—Lyle Robinson	PO Box 488, Bemidji MN 56619	218-444-2540	R	64*	.1
357	Jeff Davis Electric Cooperative Inc—Michael Heinen	PO Box 1229, Jennings LA 70546	337-824-4330	R	64	<.1
358	Central Power Electric Coop—Tom Meland	525 20th Ave SW, Minot ND 58701	701-852-4407	R	64*	<.1
359	Upper Cumberland Electric Membership Corp—Jimmy Gregory	PO Box 159, Carthage TN 37030	615-735-2940	R	63*	.1
360	Kit Carson Electric Coop—Luis A Reyes	PO Box 587, Taos NM 87571	575-758-2258	R	63*	.1
361	Runestone Electric Association—Bill O'Brien	PO Box 9, Alexandria MN 56308	320-762-1121	R	63*	<.1
362	Tombigbee Electric Power Association—William W Long	PO Box 1789, Tupelo MS 38802	662-842-7635	R	62*	.1
363	Win Energy REMC—David A Jones	PO Box 270, Sullivan IN 47882	812-882-5140	R	62*	.1
364	A and N Electric Coop—Vernon N Brinkley	PO Box 290, Tasley VA 23441	757-787-9750	R	60*	<.1
365	Sequachee Valley Electric Coop—Bob Matheny	PO Box 31, South Pittsburg TN 37380	423-837-8605	R	59*	.1
366	Kootenai Electric Cooperative Inc—Doug Elliot	PO Box 278, Hayden ID 83835	208-765-1200	R	58*	.1
367	Butler Rural Electric Cooperative Inc—Michael L Sims	3888 Stillwell Beckett, Oxford OH 45056	513-867-4400	R	58*	<.1
368	Itasca-Mantrap Co-op Electrical Association—Michael Munsrod	PO Box 192, Park Rapids MN 56470	218-732-3377	R	58*	<.1
369	Kankakee Valley Rural Electric Co—Dennis Weiss	PO Box 157, Wanatah IN 46390	219-733-2511	R	57*	<.1
370	Capital Electric Coop—Lars Nygren	PO Box 730, Bismarck ND 58502	701-223-1513	R	57*	<.1
371	Dakota Valley Electric Cooperative Inc—Jay Jacobson	14051 Hwy 13, Milnor ND 58060	701-427-5242	R	57*	<.1
372	High Plains Power Inc—Jeff Hohn	PO Box 713, Riverton WY 82501	307-856-9426	R	56*	.1
373	Barc Electric Coop—Micheal Keyser	PO Box 264, Millboro VA 24460		R	56*	<.1

Rank	Company Name—*Executive Officer*	Address, City, State, Zip	Phone	Type	Fin	Empls
374	Oconto Electric Coop—*Byron Nolde*	PO Box 168, Oconto Falls WI 54154	920-846-2816	R	56*	<.1
375	Southwest Texas Electrical Cooperative Company Inc—*William Whitten*	PO Box 677, Eldorado TX 76936	325-853-2544	R	55*	.1
376	Wyrulec Co—*Julie Kilty*	PO Box 359, Lingle WY 82223	307-837-2225	R	55*	<.1
377	Tri County Electric Coop (Lancaster Missouri)—*David Ramsey*	PO Box 159, Lancaster MO 63548	660-457-3733	R	54*	<.1
378	Pearl River Valley Electric Power Association—*Randy Wallace*	PO Box 1217, Columbia MS 39429	601-736-2666	R	53*	.1
379	Jemez Mountain Electric Coop—*Johnny Jaramilto*	PO Box 128, Espanola NM 87532	505-753-2105	R	53	.1
380	South Louisiana Electric Cooperative Association—*Joe Ticheli*	PO Box 4037, Houma LA 70361	985-876-6880	R	53*	.1
381	Eastern Illini Electric Coop—*David Champion*	PO Box 96, Paxton IL 60957	217-379-2131	R	53*	.1
382	Garkane Energy Cooperative Inc—*Carl Albrecht*	120 W 300 S, Loa UT 84747	435-836-2795	R	53*	.1
383	Northwest Iowa Power Coop—*Kent D Pauling*	PO Box 240, Le Mars IA 51031	712-546-4141	R	52*	<.1
384	Alfalfa Electric Cooperative Inc—*Kent McMahan*	PO Box 39, Cherokee OK 73728	580-596-3333	R	51*	<.1
385	Deep East Texas Electric Coop—*SW Carter*	PO Box 736, San Augustine TX 75972	936-275-2314	R	50*	.2
386	Cuivre River Electric Cooperative Inc—*Dan L Brown*	1112 E Cherry St, Troy MO 63379		R	50*	.1
387	PKM Electric Cooperative Inc—*Chuck Riesen*	PO Box 108, Warren MN 56762	218-745-4711	R	50*	<.1
388	Rayburn Country Electric Cooperative Inc—*John W Kirkland*	PO Box 37, Rockwall TX 75087	972-771-1336	R	50*	<.1
389	Rutherford Electric Membership Corp—*Joseph N Quinn*	186 Hudlow Rd, Forest City NC 28043	828-245-1621	R	49*	.2
390	Loup Power District—*Neal Suess*	PO Box 988, Columbus NE 68602	402-564-3171	R	49*	.1
391	Gibson Electric Membership Corp—*Dan Rodamaker*	PO Box 47, Trenton TN 38382	731-855-4740	R	49*	.1
392	Kodiak Electric Association Inc—*Darron Scott*	PO Box 787, Kodiak AK 99615	907-486-7700	R	49*	.1
393	South Central Arkansas Electric Cooperative Inc—*Kevin Brownlee*	PO Box 476, Arkadelphia AR 71923	870-246-6701	R	49*	<.1
394	Central Electric Coop—*Larry S Adams*	PO Box 329, Parker PA 16049	724-399-2931	R	48*	.1
395	Grayson-Collin Electric Coop—*David McGinnis*	PO Box 548, Van Alstyne TX 75495	903-482-7100	R	48*	.1
396	Lakeview Light and Power—*Thomas F McDonald*	PO Box 98979, Lakewood WA 98498	253-584-6060	R	48*	<.1
397	East Mississippi Electric Power Association—*Gloria Welch*	PO Box 5517, Meridian MS 39302	601-483-7361	R	47*	.1
398	Southeast Colorado Power Association—*Richard Wilson*	PO Box 52, La Junta CO 81050	719-384-2551	R	47*	.1
399	Union Rural Electric Coop—*Roger G Yoder*	15461 State Rt 36, Marysville OH 43040	937-642-1826	R	47*	<.1
400	Prince George Electric Coop—*M Dale Bradshaw*	PO Box 168, Waverly VA 23890	804-834-2424	R	46*	<.1
401	Newberry Electric Cooperative Inc—*Daniel P Murphy*	PO Box 477, Newberry SC 29108	803-276-1121	R	45*	<.1
402	Jackson Purchase Energy Corp—*G Kelly Nuckols*	PO Box 4030, Paducah KY 42002	270-442-7321	R	44*	.1
403	South Alabama Electric Cooperative Inc—*Max Davis*	PO Box 449, Troy AL 36081	334-566-2060	R	44*	.1
404	Wheatbelt Public Power District—*Doug Smith*	2104 Illinois St, Sidney NE 69162	308-254-5871	R	44*	<.1
405	Miami Cass County Rural Electric Membership Corp—*Jim Yates*	P O Box 310, Covington IN 47932	765-473-6668	R	44*	<.1
406	Mecklenburg Electric Coop—*John Lee*	PO Box 2451, Chase City VA 23924	434-372-6100	R	43*	.2
407	Hill County Electric Coop—*William L Allen*	PO Box 127, Itasca TX 76055	254-687-2331	R	43*	.1
408	Frontier Power Co—*Robert Wise*	770 S 2nd St, Coshocton OH 43812	740-622-6755	R	43*	<.1
409	Columbus Electric Cooperative Inc—*Michael D Fletcher*	PO Box 631, Deming NM 88031	575-546-8838	R	43*	<.1
410	Henry County Rural Electric Membership Corp—*Don Cross*	PO Box D, New Castle IN 47362	765-529-1212	R	43*	<.1
411	Ralls County Electric Coop—*Dan Strode*	PO Box 157, New London MO 63459	573-985-8711	R	43*	<.1
412	Jasper County Rural Electric Membership Corp—*Kenneth Deyoung*	PO Box 129, Rensselaer IN 47978	219-866-4601	R	43*	<.1
413	Dixie Electric Power Association—*Mack Mauldin*	PO Box 88, Laurel MS 39441	601-425-2535	R	42*	.1
414	Consolidated Electric Coop—*Michael Fuller*	PO Box 540, Mexico MO 65265	573-581-3630	R	42*	.1
415	Karnes Electric Cooperative Inc—*Leroy T Skloss*	PO Box 7, Karnes City TX 78118	830-780-3952	R	42*	.1
416	Nrg El Segundo Operations Inc—*John Ragan*	301 Vista Del Mar, El Segundo CA 90245	310-615-6344	H	42*	.1
417	Distributed Energy Systems Corp—*Bernard Cherry*	10 Technology Dr, Wallingford CT 06492	203-678-2000	P	42	.2
418	North Central Mississippi Electric Power Association—*Curtis Thompson*	PO Box 405, Byhalia MS 38611	662-838-2151	R	41*	.1
419	Mountain Parks Electric Inc—*Joe Pandy*	PO Box 170, Granby CO 80446	303-377-2525	R	41*	.1
420	Community Electric Coop—*James M Reynolds*	PO Box 267, Windsor VA 23487	757-242-6181	R	41*	<.1
421	Pemiscot Dunklin Electric Coop—*Thomas Fisher*	PO Box 657, Bragg City MO 63827	573-757-6641	R	41*	<.1
422	Kiwash Electric Cooperative Inc—*Dennis Krueger*	PO Box 100, Cordell OK 73632	580-832-3361	R	41*	<.1
423	Meade County Rural Electric—*Burns Mercer*	PO Box 489, Brandenburg KY 40108	270-422-2162	R	40*	.1
424	Ouachita Electric Cooperative Corp—*Marc Cayce*	PO Box 877, Camden AR 71711	870-836-5791	R	40*	<.1
425	Roughrider Electric Cooperative Inc—*William Retterath*	PO Box 1038, Dickinson ND 58602	701-483-5111	R	40*	<.1
426	Benton Rural Electric Association—*Charles Dawsey*	PO Box 1150, Prosser WA 99350	509-786-2913	R	39*	.1
427	Verendrye Electric Cooperative Inc—*Everett Dobrinski*	615 Hwy 52 W, Velva ND 58790	701-338-2855	R	39*	.1
428	Southern Iowa Electric Cooperative Inc—*Mark Aeilts*	PO Box 70, Bloomfield IA 52537	641-664-2277	R	39*	<.1
429	Central Alabama Electric Coop—*Thomas M Stackhouse*	PO Box 681570, Prattville AL 36068	334-365-6762	R	38*	.1
430	Catamount Resources Corp—*James Moore* Central Vermont Public Service Corp	71 Allen St Ste 101, Rutland VT 05701	802-773-6684	S	38*	<.1
431	Buzzard Power Corp—*Kam Tejwani*	1 Cate St 4th Fl, Portsmouth NH 03801	603-431-1780	S	38*	<.1
432	Catamount Energy Corp Catamount Resources Corp	71 Allen St Ste 101, Rutland VT 05701	802-773-6684	S	37*	<.1
433	Cordova Electric Cooperative Inc—*Clay Koplin*	PO Box 20, Cordova AK 99574	907-424-5555	R	37*	<.1
434	Western Illinois Electrical Coop—*Paul Dion*	PO Box 338, Carthage IL 62321		R	37*	<.1
435	Bowie-Cass Electric Coop—*Steve Delaughter*	PO Box 47, Douglasville TX 75560	903-846-2311	R	36*	.1
436	Navasota Valley Electric Cooperative Inc—*Billie Sue Corry*	PO Box 848, Franklin TX 77856	979-828-3232	R	36*	.1
437	Dartmouth Power Associates Ltd—*James Gordon*	1 Energy Rd, North Dartmouth MA 02747	508-995-0269	S	36*	<.1
438	Missouri Rural Electric Coop—*David Wright*	PO Box 111, Palmyra MO 63461	573-769-2104	R	36*	<.1
439	Farmers Electric Cooperative Corp—*Gene Sweat*	PO Box 708, Newport AR 72112	870-523-3691	R	35*	<.1
440	Lewis County Electric Rural Cooperative Association—*John Bloom*	PO Box 68, Lewistown MO 63452	573-215-4000	R	35*	<.1
441	Slope Electric Cooperative Inc—*Clayton Hoffman*	PO Box 338, New England ND 58647	701-579-4191	R	35*	<.1
442	City Of Tallahassee Electric Utilities—*Kevin Wailes*	2602 Jackson Bluff Rd, Tallahassee FL 32304	850-891-5023	R	35*	.3
443	Caney Fork Electric Cooperative Inc—*Hubert King*	PO Box 272, Mc Minnville TN 37111	931-473-3116	R	34*	.1
444	Boone County Rural Electric Membership Corp—*Dale Geiselman*	PO Box 563, Lebanon IN 46052	765-482-2390	R	34*	<.1
445	Crow Wing Cooperative Power and Light Co—*Bruce Kraemer*	PO Box 507, Brainerd MN 56401	218-829-2827	R	33*	.1
446	Broad River Electric Cooperative Inc—*Norris R Fowler*	PO Box 2269, Gaffney SC 29342	864-489-5737	R	33*	<.1
447	Kaydon Group LLC—*James O'Leary*	125 John Hancock Rd, Taunton MA 02780	508-884-5050	R	32	.2
448	Bangor Hydro-Electric Co—*Peter Dawes*	PO Box 932, Bangor ME 04402	207-945-5621	S	32*	.6
449	Tallahatchie Valley Electric Power Association—*Brad Robison*	PO Box 513, Batesville MS 38606	662-563-4742	R	32*	.1
450	Meriwether Lewis Electric Coop—*Hal Womble*	PO Box 240, Centerville TN 37033	931-729-3558	R	32*	.1
451	White County Rural Electric Membership Coop—*Randy W Price*	PO Box 599, Monticello IN 47960	574-583-7161	R	32*	<1
452	Fergus Electric Cooperative Inc—*Bob Evans*	84423 US Hwy 87, Lewistown MT 59457	406-538-3465	R	32*	<.1

Note: An asterisk (*) indicates an estimated financial figure. The company type code used is as follows: R = Private, P = Public, S = Private Subsidiary, B = Public Subsidiary, D = Division, J = Joint Venture, I = Investment Fund.

COMPANY RANKINGS BY SALES WITHIN 4-DIGIT SIC

Rank	Company Name—*Executive Officer*	Address, City, State, Zip	Phone	Type	Fin	Empls
453	Chippewa Valley Electric Coop—*Todd Howard*	PO Box 575, Cornell WI 54732	715-239-6800	R	32*	<.1
454	Covington Electric Cooperative Inc—*WB Smith Jr*	18836 US Hwy 84, Andalusia AL 36421	334-222-4121	R	31*	.1
455	Southeastern Indiana Rural Electric Membership Corp—*Robert H Mackey*	PO Box 196, Osgood IN 47037	812-689-4111	R	31*	.1
456	Valley Rural Electric Cooperative Inc—*Wayne F Miller*	PO Box 477, Huntingdon PA 16652	814-643-2650	R	31*	.1
457	Maquoketa Valley Rural Electric Coop—*Jim M Lauzon*	109 N Huber St, Anamosa IA 52205	319-462-3542	R	31*	.1
458	North West Rural Electric Coop—*Lyle Korver*	1505 Albany Pl SE, Orange City IA 51041	712-707-4935	R	31*	<.1
459	Access Energy Coop—*Robert Swindell*	PO Box 440, Mount Pleasant IA 52641	319-385-1577	R	31*	<.1
460	Sheridan Electric Cooperative Inc—*Richard Sampsen*	PO Box 227, Medicine Lake MT 59247	406-789-2231	R	31*	<.1
461	Inter County Energy Cooperative Inc—*Jim Jacobus*	PO Box 87, Danville KY 40423	859-236-4561	R	30*	.1
462	REA Energy Cooperative Inc—*Gary R Grindle*	PO Box 70, Indiana PA 15701	724-349-4800	R	30*	<.1
463	Navarro County Electric Cooperative Inc—*Billy P Jones*	PO Box 616, Corsicana TX 75151	903-874-7411	R	30*	<.1
464	Decatur County Rural Electric Membership Coop—*Tim Gauck*	PO Box 46, Greensburg IN 47240	812-663-3391	R	30*	<.1
465	Clinton County Electric Cooperative Inc—*Ralph Kuhl*	PO Box 40, Breese IL 62230	618-526-7282	R	30*	<.1
466	Verdigris Valley Electric Cooperative Inc—*Alice Houston*	PO Box 219, Collinsville OK 74021	918-371-2584	R	29	.1
467	Tennessee Valley Electric Coop—*Gerald Taylor Jr*	PO Box 400, Savannah TN 38372	731-925-4916	R	29*	.1
468	Roanoke Electric Membership Corp—*Allen Speller*	PO Box 440, Rich Square NC 27869	252-539-2236	R	29*	.1
469	Citizens Electric Co—*Eric Winslow*	PO Box 551, Lewisburg PA 17837	570-524-2231	R	29*	<.1
470	Foster Wheeler Martinez Inc—*Gary Nedelka* Foster Wheeler Power Systems Inc	550 Solano Way, Martinez CA 94553	925-313-0800	S	29*	<.1
471	Lower Valley Energy—*James R Webb*	PO Box 188, Afton WY 83110	307-885-3175	R	28*	.1
472	Alcorn County Electric Power Association—*Bruce Dillingham Jr*	PO Box 1590, Corinth MS 38835	662-287-4402	R	28*	.1
473	Swisher Electric Cooperative Inc—*Charles Castleberry*	PO Box 67, Tulia TX 79088	806-995-3567	R	28*	<.1
474	Logan County Cooperative Power Light Association Inc—*Doug Miller*	1587 County Rd 32 N, Bellefontaine OH 43311	937-592-4781	R	28*	<.1
475	Jackson County Rural Electric Membership Corp—*John Trinkle*	274 E Base Rd, Brownstown IN 47220	812-358-4458	R	27*	.1
476	Clearwater Power Company Inc—*Robert Foss*	PO Box 997, Lewiston ID 83501	208-743-1501	R	27*	<.1
477	Paulding-Putnam Electric Cooperative Inc—*George Carter*	910 N Williams St, Paulding OH 45879	419-399-5015	R	26*	<.1
478	Albemarle Electric Membership Corp—*Jeff Edwards*	PO Box 69, Hertford NC 27944	252-426-5735	R	26*	<.1
479	ABB Energy Ventures	202 Carnegie Ctr Ste 1, Princeton NJ 08540	609-243-7575	S	25	N/A
480	Wild Rice Electric Cooperative Inc—*Mark Habedank*	PO Box 438, Mahnomen MN 56557	218-935-2517	R	25*	<.1
481	Edgecombe-Martin County Electric Membership Corp—*Bob McDuffie*	PO Box 188, Tarboro NC 27886	252-823-2171	R	25*	<.1
482	Duncan Valley Electric Coop—*Johnnie Frie*	PO Box 440, Duncan AZ 85534	928-359-2503	R	25*	<.1
483	Fulton County Rural Electric Corp—*Eldon Umbarger*	PO Box 230, Rochester IN 46975	574-223-3156	R	25*	<.1
484	HomeWorks Tri-County Electric Cooperative Inc—*Mark Kappler*	PO Box 379, Portland MI 48875	517-647-7554	R	24*	.1
485	Southwest Rural Electric Association Inc—*Mike R Hagy*	PO Box 310, Tipton OK 73570	580-667-5281	R	24*	<.1
486	Haywood Electric Membership Corp—*Norman Sloan*	376 Grindstone Rd, Waynesville NC 28785	828-452-2281	R	23*	.1
487	Clark Electric Coop—*Tim Stewart*	124 N Main St, Greenwood WI 54437	715-267-6188	R	23*	<.1
488	Southern Indiana REC Inc—*Michael E Hammack*	PO Box 219, Tell City IN 47586	812-547-2316	R	23*	<.1
489	Columbia Basin Electric Cooperative Inc—*Lori Anderson*	PO Box 398, Heppner OR 97836	541-676-9146	R	22*	<.1
490	Edd Helms Group Inc—*W Edd Helms Jr*	17850 NE 5th Ave, Miami FL 33162	305-653-2520	I	22	.1
491	Claverack Rural Electric Cooperative Inc—*Bobbi Kilmer*	32750 Route 6, Wysox PA 18854	570-265-2167	R	21*	.1
492	Bailey County Electric Coop—*David Marricle*	PO Drawer 1013, Muleshoe TX 79347	806-272-4504	R	21*	.1
493	Highline Electric Association Inc—*Mark Farnsworth*	PO Box 57, Holyoke CO 80734	970-854-2236	R	21*	.1
494	Kosciusko County Rural Electric Membership Corp—*Steve Rhodes*	PO Box 588, Warsaw IN 46581	574-267-6331	R	21*	<.1
495	Choctawhatchee Electric Cooperative Inc—*JE Smith*	PO Box 512, Defuniak Springs FL 32435	850-892-2111	R	20*	.1
496	Alaska Power and Telephone Co—*Robert S Grimm*	PO Box 3222, Port Townsend WA 98368	360-385-1733	R	20*	.1
497	Cherryland Electric Co-op—*Tony Anderson*	PO Box 298, Grawn MI 49637	231-486-9200	R	20*	<.1
498	Noble Rural Electric Membership Coop—*Monte Egolf*	PO Box 137, Albion IN 46701	260-636-2113	R	20*	<.1
499	United Rural Electric Membership Corp—*Rob Pearson*	PO Box 605, Markle IN 46770	260-758-3155	R	20*	<.1
500	Upson Electric Membership Corp—*Neal Trice*	PO Box 31, Thomaston GA 30286	706-647-5475	R	20*	<.1
501	Lane Electric Cooperative Inc—*Rick Crinklaw*	PO Box 21410, Eugene OR 97402	541-484-1151	R	20	<.1
502	Baldwin County Electric Membership Corp—*Bucky Jakins*	PO Box 220, Summerdale AL 36580	251-989-6247	R	19*	.2
503	Western Cooperative Electric Association Inc—*David L Schneider*	PO Box 278, Wakeeney KS 67672	785-743-5561	R	19*	.1
504	Tipmont Rural Electric Membership Corp—*Tim McCarthy*	PO Box 20, Linden IN 47955	765-339-7211	R	19*	.1
505	McCook Public Power District—*Jim Phinney*	PO Box 1147, McCook NE 69001	308-345-2500	R	19*	<.1
506	Jump River Electric Coop—*John Kmosena*	PO Box 99, Ladysmith WI 54848	715-532-5524	R	19*	<.1
507	Lyon-Lincoln Electric Cooperative Inc—*Tom O'Leary*	PO Box 639, Tyler MN 56178	507-247-5505	R	19*	<.1
508	Springer Electric Cooperative Inc—*David Spradlin*	PO Box 698, Springer NM 87747	575-483-2421	R	19*	<.1
509	Wise Electric Cooperative Inc—*Glenn Hughes*	PO Box 269, Decatur TX 76234	940-627-2167	R	18*	.1
510	Empire Electric Association Inc—*Neal Stephens*	PO Box K, Cortez CO 81321	970-565-4444	R	18*	.1
511	Tombigbee Electric Cooperative Inc—*Steve Foshee*	PO Box 610, Guin AL 35563	205-468-3325	R	18*	<.1
512	TIP Rural Electric Coop—*Darrel Heetland*	PO Box 534, Brooklyn IA 52211	641-522-9223	R	18*	<.1
513	Bayfield Electric Cooperative Inc—*Earl Anderson*	PO Box 68, Iron River WI 54847	715-372-4287	R	18*	<.1
514	Central Missouri Electric Cooperative Inc—*Don Thiel*	PO Box 939, Sedalia MO 65302	660-826-2900	R	17*	.1
515	Cimarron Electric Cooperative Inc—*Mark Snowden*	PO Box 299, Kingfisher OK 73750	405-375-4121	R	17*	.1
516	Northern Neck Electric Coop—*Greg White*	PO Box 288, Warsaw VA 22572	804-333-3621	R	17*	.1
517	Consolidated Electric Cooperative Inc—*Jerry Lauer*	PO Box 111, Mount Gilead OH 43338	419-947-3055	R	17*	<.1
518	Agralite Electric Coop—*Kory Johnson*	PO Box 228, Benson MN 56215	320-843-4150	R	17*	<.1
519	Farmers Rural Electric Cooperative Corp—*William T Prather*	504 S Broadway St, Glasgow KY 42141	270-651-2191	R	16	.1
520	North Star Electric Cooperative Inc—*Steve Arnesen*	PO Box 719, Baudette MN 56623	218-634-2202	R	16*	<.1
521	Bedford Rural Electric Cooperative Inc—*Owen Miller*	PO Box 335, Bedford PA 15522	814-623-5101	R	16*	<.1
522	Coosa Valley Electric Cooperative Inc—*Leland Fuller*	PO Box 837, Talladega AL 35161	256-362-4180	R	15*	.1
523	Rita Blanca Electric Cooperative Inc—*Aubrey L Neff*	PO Box 1947, Dalhart TX 79022	806-249-4506	R	15*	<.1
524	Northeast Utilities Inc—*Charles W Shivery*	56 Prospect St, Hartford CT 06103	860-665-3355	R	15	N/A
525	Farmers Electric Cooperative Inc (Chillicothe Missouri)—*Mike Sanders*	PO Box 680, Chillicothe MO 64601	660-646-4281	R	14*	.1
526	Northern Plains Electric Coop (Carrington North Dakota)—*Tracy Boe*	PO Box 180, Carrington ND 58421	701-652-3156	R	14*	.1
527	Big Country Electric Cooperative Inc—*Carl Williams*	PO Box 518, Roby TX 79543	325-776-2244	R	14*	.1
528	Bartholomew County Rural Electric Membership Coop—*Jim Turner*	PO Box 467, Columbus IN 47202	981-418-9882	R	14*	<.1
529	Barton County Electric Coop—*Virginia Erwin*	PO Box 459, Lamar MO 64759	417-682-5636	R	13*	<.1
530	Southern Illinois Electric Coop—*Larry Lovell*	PO Box 100, Dongola IL 62926	618-827-3555	R	13*	<.1
531	Rosebud Electric Cooperative Inc—*Bart Birkeland*	PO Box 439, Gregory SD 57533	605-835-9624	R	13*	<.1
532	Washington Electric Cooperative Inc—*Ken Schilling*	PO Box 800, Marietta OH 45750	740-373-2141	R	13*	<.1
533	Deister Electronics USA Inc—*William Nuffer*	9303 Grant Ave, Manassas VA 20110	703-368-2739	R	13*	<.1

Rank	Company Name—*Executive Officer*	Address, City, State, Zip	Phone	Type	Fin	Empls
534	O'connell Electric—*Dorithy Roberts*	301 Staoutenger E, Syracuse NY 13201	315-437-0829	R	13*	.1
535	Grady Electric Membership Corp—*Thomas A Rosser*	PO Box 270, Cairo GA 39828	229-377-4182	R	12*	.1
536	Barry Electric Coop—*David Cupps*	PO Box 307, Cassville MO 65625	417-847-2131	R	12*	<.1
537	Steele Waseca Cooperative Electric—*Donald Kolb*	PO Box 485, Owatonna MN 55060	507-451-7340	R	12*	<.1
538	White Water Valley Rural Electric Membership Corp—*Boyd Huff*	101 Brownsville Ave, Liberty IN 47353	765-458-5171	R	12*	<.1
539	Warren Electric Cooperative Inc—*Gary Franklin*	PO Box 208, Youngsville PA 16371	814-563-7548	R	12*	<.1
540	Concordia Electric Co—*Billy Harris*	PO Box 98, Jonesville LA 71343	318-339-7969	R	11*	.1
541	Gascosage Electric Coop—*John Greenlee*	PO Drawer G, Dixon MO 65459	573-759-7146	R	11*	<.1
542	Grand Valley Rural Power Lines Inc—*Dennis Haberkorn*	PO Box 190, Grand Junction CO 81502	970-242-0040	R	11*	<.1
543	North Plains Electric Cooperative Inc—*Randy Mahannah*	PO Box 1008, Perryton TX 79070	806-435-5482	R	11*	<.1
544	Lane-Scott Electric Cooperative Inc—*Earl Steffens*	PO Box 758, Dighton KS 67839	620-397-2321	R	11*	<.1
545	Sedgwick County Electrical Cooperative Association Inc—*John Hillman*	PO Box 220, Cheney KS 67025	316-542-3131	R	11*	<.1
546	J-A-C Electric Cooperative Inc—*Kim Hooper*	PO Box 278, Bluegrove TX 76352	940-895-3311	R	11*	<.1
547	Thumb Electric Cooperative Inc—*Louis Wenzlaff*	2231 Main St, Ubly MI 48475	989-658-8571	R	10*	<.1
548	Timber Energy Resources Inc	PO Box 199, Telogia FL 32360	850-379-8341	S	10*	<.1
549	KC Electric Association Coop—*John Huppert*	P O Box 8, Hugo CO 80821	719-743-2431	R	10*	<.1
550	Pitt and Greene Electric Membership Corp—*Mark Suggs*	PO Box 249, Farmville NC 27828	252-753-3128	R	10*	<.1
551	Spoon River Electric Cooperative Inc—*Jack L Clark*	PO Box 340, Canton IL 61520	309-647-2700	R	10*	<.1
552	Jay County Rural Electric Membership—*John G Nill*	PO Box 904, Portland IN 47371	260-726-7121	R	10*	<.1
553	Allamakee-Clayton Electric Cooperative Inc—*Roger Arthur*	PO Box 715, Postville IA 52162	563-864-7611	R	9*	.1
554	Rural Electric Coop (Lindsay Oklahoma)—*Gary Jones*	PO Box 609, Lindsay OK 73052	405-756-3104	R	9*	<.1
555	Northern Electric Cooperative Inc—*Jim Moore*	PO Box 457, Bath SD 57427	605-225-0310	R	9*	<.1
556	Midwest Electric Inc—*Rick D Gerdeman*	PO Box 10, Saint Marys OH 45885	419-394-4110	R	9*	<.1
557	City Public Service Energy—*Milton B Lee*	PO Box 1771, San Antonio TX 78205	210-353-2222	R	9	3.6
558	Adams Electric Coop—*Jim Thompson*	PO Box 247, Camp Point IL 62320	217-593-7701	R	8*	<.1
559	South Central Power Co Belmont Div—*Rick Lemonds* South Central Power Co	PO Box 270, Barnesville OH 43713	740-425-4018	D	8*	<.1
560	Glacier Electric Cooperative Inc—*Jasen Bronec*	PO Box 2090, Cut Bank MT 59427	406-873-5566	R	8*	<.1
561	North Central Missouri Electric Cooperative Inc—*Melvin Scott*	PO Box 220, Milan MO 63556	660-265-4404	R	8*	<.1
562	Todd-Wadena Electric Coop—*Robin Doege*	PO Box 431, Wadena MN 56482	218-631-3120	R	8*	<.1
563	Jackson Electric Coop—*Gary Woods*	PO Box 546, Black River Falls WI 54615	715-284-5385	R	8*	<.1
564	Darke Rural Electric Cooperative Inc—*Jack Kitchel*	PO Box 278, Greenville OH 45331	937-548-4114	R	8*	<.1
565	Coahoma Electric Power Association—*WH Hardin*	PO Box 188, Lyon MS 38645	662-624-8321	R	7*	<.1
566	Northeast Nebraska Public Power District—*Don Larsen*	PO Box 350, Wayne NE 68787	402-375-1360	R	7*	<.1
567	Dunn County Electric Coop—*James Hathaway*	PO Box 220, Menomonie WI 54751	715-232-6240	R	7*	<.1
568	Federated Rural Electric Association—*Richard Burud*	PO Box 69, Jackson MN 56143	507-847-3520	R	7*	<.1
569	Vigilante Electric Cooperative Inc—*Dave Alberi*	PO Box 1049, Dillon MT 59725	406-683-2327	R	7*	<.1
570	Hickman-Fulton Counties RECC—*Greg Grissom*	PO Box 190, Hickman KY 42050	270-236-2521	R	7*	<.1
571	Intercontinental Energy Group LLC—*Stephen Roy*	350 Lincoln St Ste 111, Hingham MA 02043	781-749-9800	R	7*	<.1
572	Enerstar Power Corp—*Peter E Kollinger*	11597 Illinois Hwy 1, Paris IL 61944	217-463-4145	R	6*	<.1
573	Big Horn Rural Electric Co—*Don Russel*	208 S 5th, Basin WY 82410	307-568-2419	R	6*	<.1
574	Jasper-Newton Electric Cooperative Inc—*Mark Tamplin*	812 S Margaret Ave, Kirbyville TX 75956	409-423-2241	R	6*	<.1
575	Red River Valley Cooperative Power Association—*Lauren Brorby*	PO Box 358, Halstad MN 56548	218-456-2139	R	6*	<.1
576	Basin Electric Power Coop—*Ronald Harper*	1717 E Interstate Ave, Dismarck ND 58503	701-223-0441	R	5	4.0
577	Georgia Power Co—*Michael Garrett* Southern Co	241 Ralph McGill Blvd, Atlanta GA 30308	404-506-6526	S	5*	8.9
578	Harrison County Rural Electric Coop—*Joe Farley*	PO Box 2, Woodbine IA 51579	712-647-2727	R	5*	<.1
579	Wheatland Rural Electric Association—*Robert Brockman*	PO Box 1209, Wheatland WY 82201	307-322-2125	R	5*	<.1
580	South Central Electric Association—*Albert Haler*	PO Box 150, Saint James MN 56081	507-375-3164	R	5*	<.1
581	Tricounty Rural Electric Cooperative Inc—*Larry Maassel*	PO Box 100, Malinta OH 43535	419-256-7900	R	5*	<.1
582	Raser Technologies Inc—*Nicholas Goodman*	5152 N Edgewood Dr, Provo UT 84604	801-765-1200	P	4	<.1
583	Rgm Industries Inc—*Ronald Goigel*	3300 Lillian Blvd, Titusville FL 32780	321-269-4720	R	4*	<.1
584	Big Sandy Rural Electric Coop—*David A Estepp*	504 11th St, Paintsville KY 41240	606-789-4095	R	4*	<.1
585	Dahlberg Light and Power Co—*Dave Dahlberg*	PO Box 300, Solon Springs WI 54873	715-378-2205	R	4	<.1
586	Cuming County Public Power—*Elwood Moore*	PO Box 256, West Point NE 68788	402-372-2463	R	4*	<.1
587	The New World Power Corp—*Brad Dotson*	32234 Paseo Adelanto S, San Juan Capistrano CA 92675	949-248-8185	R	4	<.1
588	Force Electronics—*Bob Clap*	6701 Katella Ave Ste 2, Cypress CA 90630	714-220-3965	R	4*	<.1
589	Santaniello Electric LLC	1401 Witherspoon St, Rahway NJ 07065	732-815-1005	R	3*	<.1
590	Synergics Energy Development Inc—*Wayne Rogers*	191 Main St, Annapolis MD 21401	410-268-8820	R	3*	<.1
591	Twin Valleys Public Power District—*James P Dietz*	PO Box 160, Cambridge NE 69022	308-697-3315	R	3*	<.1
592	PSEG Nuclear LLC	80 Park Plz, Newark NJ 07102	973-430-7000	S	3	N/A
593	Ennis Power Company LLC—*Linda Rasco*	4001 W Ennis Ave, Ennis TX 75119	972-875-2993	R	2*	<.1
594	Natural Power Inc—*S Rowland*	2730 Rowland Rd, Raleigh NC 27615	919-876-6722	R	2*	<.1
595	Zbb Energy Corp—*Eric Apfelbach*	N93 W14475 Whittaker W, Menomonee Falls WI 53051	262-253-9800	P	2	.1
596	Kesio Inc—*Hsin Zengchen*	4117 Covecrest Ct, Pomona CA 91766	949-725-0382	R	2*	<.1
597	Vinson Electric Supply Inc—*Joe Vinson*	PO Box 1103, Russellville AR 72811	479-968-1296	R	2*	<.1
598	K Mac Inc—*Paul Vogel*	1174 Renton Rd, Pittsburgh PA 15239	412-795-3660	R	<1*	<.1
599	PowerVerde Inc—*George Konrad*	23429 N 35th Dr, Glendale AZ 85310	623-780-3321	P	<1	<.1
600	Menard Electric Coop—*Gary L Martin*	PO Box 200, Petersburg IL 62675	217-632-7746	R	N/A	<.1
601	Kandiyohi Cooperative Electric Power Association—*David George*	PO Box 40, Spicer MN 56288	320-796-1155	R	N/A	<.1

TOTALS: SIC 4911 Electric Services
Companies: 601   1,913,332   598.8

4922 Natural Gas Transmission

Rank	Company Name—*Executive Officer*	Address, City, State, Zip	Phone	Type	Fin	Empls
1	El Paso Corp—*Douglas L Foshee*	PO Box 2511, Houston TX 77252	713-420-2600	P	25,270	4.9
2	Williams Companies Inc—*Alan Armstrong*	1 Williams Ctr, Tulsa OK 74172	918-573-2000	P	24,972	5.0
3	Williams Alaska Petroleum Inc—*Alan Armstrong*	1 Williams Ctr, Tulsa OK 74172	918-573-2000	S	23,993	3.7
4	Energy Transfer Partners LP—*Kelcy L Warren*	3738 Oak Lawn Ave, Dallas TX 75219	214-981-0700	B	15,519	1.9
5	OneOk Partners LP—*John W Gibson*	100 W 5th St, Tulsa OK 74103	918-588-7000	P	7,920	N/A
6	Boardwalk Pipeline Partners LP—*Stanley Horton*	9 Greenway Plz Ste 280, Houston TX 77046		P	6,771	1.2
7	Duncan Energy Partners LP—*W Randall Fowler*	PO Box 4324, Houston TX 77210	713-381-6500	P	5,572	N/A
8	Trans Texas Gas Corp—*Arnold Brackenridge*	1300 N Sam Houston Pkw, Houston TX 77032	281-987-8600	R	4,830*	2.0
9	Algonquin Gas Transmission Co—*Rick Priory*	890 Winter St Ste 300, Waltham MA 02451	617-254-4050	S	4,760*	2.0
10	El Paso Natural Gas Co El Paso Corp	PO Box 1087, Colorado Springs CO 80944	713-420-1200	S	3,724	.7

Note: An asterisk (*) indicates an estimated financial figure. The company type code used is as follows: R = Private, P = Public, S = Private Subsidiary, B = Public Subsidiary, D = Division, J = Joint Venture, I = Investment Fund.

COMPANY RANKINGS BY SALES WITHIN 4-DIGIT SIC

Rank	Company Name—*Executive Officer*	Address, City, State, Zip	Phone	Type	Fin	Empls
11	Targa Resources Partners LP—*Rene R Joyce*	1000 Louisiana St Ste, Houston TX 77002	713-584-1000	P	3,658	1.1
12	Atlas Energy LP—*Edward Cohen*	1550 Coraopolis Height, Moon Township PA 15108	412-262-2830	P	2,684	.7
13	Spectra Energy Partners LP—*Julie Dill*	5400 Westheimer Ct, Houston TX 77056	713-627-4963	P	2,457	N/A
14	Western Gas Partners LP—*Donald Sinclair*	1201 Lake Robbins Dr, The Woodlands TX 77380	832-636-6000	P	2,452	N/A
15	TC PipeLines LP—*Steven D Becker*	13710 FNB Pkwy, Omaha NE 68154		P	2,082	N/A
16	Copano Energy LLC—*R Bruce Northcutt*	2727 Allen Pkwy Ste 12, Houston TX 77019	713-621-9547	P	1,907	.4
17	DCP Midstream Partners LP—*Mark A Borer*	370 17th St Ste 2775, Denver CO 80202	303-633-2911	P	1,904	<.1
18	Texas Gas Service Co—*Greg Phillips*	1301 S MoPac Expresswa, Austin TX 78746		D	1,803*	.7
19	Cheniere Energy Partners LP—*Charif Souki*	700 Milam St Ste 800, Houston TX 77002	713-375-5000	B	1,737	N/A
20	Mississippi River Transmission Corp—*David McClanahan*	1111 Louisiana Fl 11, Houston TX 77002	713-207-5184	S	1,525*	.6
21	ANR Pipeline—*Lee Hobbs*	PO Box 2446, Houston TX 77252	832-320-5000	S	1,131*	.4
22	Crestwood Midstream Partners LP—*Robert G Phillips*	717 Texas St, Houston TX 77002	832-519-2200	P	1,027	N/A
23	Columbia Gas Transmission Company—*Tommy Kilpatrick*	1700 NacCorkle Ave SE, Charleston WV 25314		S	1,020*	3.0
24	Exterran Partners LP—*Ernie Danner*	16666 Northchase Dr, Houston TX 77060	281-836-7000	P	991	N/A
25	Great Lakes Gas Transmission LP—*Lee G Hobbs* El Paso Corp	717 Texas St, Houston TX 77002	832-320-5000	S	915*	.3
26	Northern Natural Gas Co—*Mark A Hewett*	PO Box 3330, Omaha NE 68103	402-398-7200	R	900*	.3
27	Columbia Gulf Transmission Co—*Christopher Helms*	5151 San Felipe Ste 25, Houston TX 77056	713-267-4100	S	804*	1.3
28	Texas Gas Transmission LLC—*Rolf Gafvert* Boardwalk Pipeline Partners LP	3800 Frederica St, Owensboro KY 42301	270-926-8686	S	686*	.7
29	Trunkline Gas Company LLC	5444 Westheimer, Houston TX 77056	713-989-7000	S	470*	.3
30	Florida Gas Transmission Co—*Rockford G Meyer*	PO Box 4967, Houston TX 77210	713-989-7000	S	467	.5
31	Williams Pipelines Partners LP—*Steven J Malcolm*	1 Williams Ctr, Tulsa OK 74172	918-573-2000	B	434	N/A
32	Questar Exploration and Production Co	1050 17th St Ste 500, Denver CO 80265	303-672-6900	S	427*	.2
33	Iroquois Gas Transmission Company LP—*EJ Holm*	1 Corporate Dr Ste 600, Shelton CT 06484	203-925-7200	S	372*	.2
34	Dominion Cove Point LNG LP	2100 Cove Point Rd, Lusby MD 20657	410-286-5100	S	319*	.1
35	Gas Transmission Northwest Corp—*Harold Kvisle*	1400 SW 5th Ave Ste 90, Portland OR 97201	503-833-4000	S	297*	.1
36	Cook Inlet Energy Supply	333 Clay St Ste 4550, Houston TX 77002	713-275-6100	S	180*	.1
37	Williston Basin Interstate Pipeline Co—*Steven L Bietz*	1250 W Century Ave, Bismarck ND 58503	701-530-1600	S	148*	.3
38	Oasis Pipe Line Company Texas LP—*Jim Labauve*	12012 Wickchester Ln, Houston TX 77079	281-391-3289	R	110*	<.1
39	Mountaineer Gas Co—*Paul Jefferson*	2401 Sissonville Dr, Charleston WV 25312		R	74*	.3
40	Wolverine Gas and Oil Corp—*Sid Jansma Jr*	1 Riverfront Pl 55 Cam, Grand Rapids MI 49503	616-458-1150	S	69*	<.1
41	EQUITRANS LP—*Murry Gerber*	225 North Shore Dr, Pittsburgh PA 15212	412-553-5700	S	28*	<.1
42	Basin Pipeline Corp—*Mike Warren*	605 Richard Arrington, Birmingham AL 35203	205-326-2700	S	15*	<.1
43	Gateway Energy Corp—*Fredrick M Pevow Jr*	1415 Louisiana St Ste, Houston TX 77002	713-336-0844	P	14	<.1
44	Bluefield Gas Co—*John Williamson III*	PO Box 589, Bluefield WV 24701	304-327-7161	S	10*	<.1
45	Targa Resources Corp—*Rene R Joyce* Targa Resources Partners LP	1000 Louisiana Ste 430, Houston TX 77002	713-584-1000	B	7	1.1
46	Tennessee Gas Pipeline Co—*Norman Holmes* El Paso Corp	PO Box 2511, Houston TX 77252		S	5*	1.3
47	Blue Dolphin Pipe Line Co—*Ivar Siem*	801 Travis St Ste 2100, Houston TX 77002	713-568-4725	S	2*	<.1

TOTALS: SIC 4922 Natural Gas Transmission
Companies: 47 — 156,462 / 35.4

4923 Gas Transmission & Distribution

Rank	Company Name—*Executive Officer*	Address, City, State, Zip	Phone	Type	Fin	Empls
1	Enron Creditors Recovery Corp—*John Ray*	PO Box 1188, Houston TX 77251	713-853-6161	R	47,300	9.0
2	Kinder Morgan Kansas Inc—*Richard D Kinder*	500 Dallas St Ste 1000, Houston TX 77002	713-369-9000	P	21,861	8.1
3	ONEOK Inc—*John W Gibson*	PO Box 87, Tulsa OK 74102	918-588-7000	P	12,499	4.8
4	Equitable Resources Inc—*David L Porges*	625 Liberty Ave Ste 17, Pittsburgh PA 15222	412-553-5700	P	7,098	1.8
5	Southwestern Energy Co—*Steven L Mueller*	2350 N Sam Houston Pkw, Houston TX 77032	281-618-4700	P	6,018	2.1
6	PNM Resources Inc—*Pat Vincent-Collawn*	Alvarado Sq, Albuquerque NM 87158	505-241-2700	P	5,205	2.0
7	Philadelphia Gas Works Co—*Thomas Knudsen*	800 W Montgomery Ave, Philadelphia PA 19122	215-236-0500	R	4,444*	1.8
8	Southern California Gas Co—*Michael W Allman*	PO Box 3150, San Dimas CA 91773		S	4,400*	7.1
9	Shell Energy Trading North America—*Glenn Wright*	909 Fannin St Ste 700, Houston TX 77010	713-767-5400	S	2,600*	1.2
10	Tenaska Gas Co—*Jerry K Crouse*	1044 N 115th St Ste 40, Omaha NE 68154	402-691-9500	S	2,308*	.7
11	Peoples Gas Light and Coke Co—*Richard E Terry*	130 E Randolph Dr 24th, Chicago IL 60601	312-240-4000	S	1,558	2.6
12	SEMCO Energy Gas Co—*David McCowen*	PO Box 5004, Port Huron MI 48061		S	1,338*	1.6
13	Equitable Gas Co—*Murray Gerber* Equitable Resources Inc	625 Liberty Ave Rm 170, Pittsburgh PA 15222	412-553-5700	S	1,312*	1.5
14	Enbridge Midcoast Energy Inc—*Patrick D Daniel*	1100 Louisiana St Ste, Houston TX 77002	713-650-8900	S	1,037*	.4
15	Colorado Interstate Gas Co—*James J Cleary*	PO Box 1087, Colorado Springs CO 80901	719-473-2300	S	828*	1.1
16	NiSource Energy Partners LP	801 E 86th Ave, Merrillville IN 46410		S	734*	.3
17	Chesapeake Utilities Corp—*Michael P McMasters*	909 Silver Lake Blvd, Dover DE 19904	302-734-6799	P	671	.7
18	Northwest Pipeline Corp—*Steven Malcolm*	PO Box 58900, Salt Lake City UT 84158	801-584-6000	S	573*	.3
19	US Energy Development Corp—*Joseph M Jayson*	2350 N Forest Rd Ste17, Getzville NY 14068		R	395*	.1
20	Delta Natural Gas Company Inc—*Glenn R Jennings*	3617 Lexington Rd, Winchester KY 40391	859-744-6171	P	175	.2
21	US Gas and Electric Inc—*Douglas Marcille*	333 Mamaroneck Ave Ste, White Plains NY 10605		R	152	.1
22	Kentucky West Virginia Gas Co—*Murry S Gerber* Equitable Resources Inc	630 N Lake Dr, Prestonsburg KY 41653	606-886-2311	S	151*	.2
23	RGC Resources Inc—*John B Williamson III*	PO Box 13007, Roanoke VA 24030	540-777-4427	P	126	.1
24	Nashville Gas Co—*Thomas Skains*	PO Box 533500, Atlanta GA 30353		D	115	.5
25	Flo-Gas Corp	PO Box 3395, West Palm Beach FL 33402	561-832-0872	S	103*	.4
26	TW Phillips Gas and Oil Co—*Rex Tillerson*	PO Box 1231, Butler PA 16003	724-287-2751	S	93*	.2
27	Virginia Gas Co—*Hank Linginfelter*	1096 Ole Berry Dr, Abingdon VA 24210	404-558-2307	S	65	.1
28	ProLiance Energy LLC—*John Talley*	111 Monument Cir Ste 2, Indianapolis IN 46204	317-231-6400	S	50*	.1
29	Vermont Gas Systems Inc—*Don Gilbert*	PO Box 467, Burlington VT 05402	802-863-4511	S	48*	.1
30	Corning Natural Gas Corp—*Michael I German*	PO Box 58, Corning NY 14830	607-936-3755	P	45	.1
31	Fidelity Natural Gas Inc—*John Davis*	64 N Clark St, Sullivan MO 63080	573-468-8081	S	8*	<.1
32	UGI Utilities Inc—*David W Trego*	100 Kachel Blvd Ste 40, Reading PA 19607	610-796-3400	S	2*	<.1

TOTALS: SIC 4923 Gas Transmission & Distribution
Companies: 32 — 123,311 / 49.1

4924 Natural Gas Distribution

Rank	Company Name—*Executive Officer*	Address, City, State, Zip	Phone	Type	Fin	Empls
1	AGL Resources Inc—*John W Somerhalder II*	PO Box 4569, Atlanta GA 30302	404-584-4000	P	13,913	6.4
2	Southern Union Co—*George L Lindemann*	5051 Westheimer Rd, Houston TX 77056	713-989-2000	P	8,271	2.4
3	SemGroup LP—*Norman Szydlowski*	6120 S Yale Ave Ste 70, Tulsa OK 74136	918-524-8100	R	5,663*	2.2
4	NICOR Inc—*Russ M Strobel*	PO Box 3014, Naperville IL 60566	630-305-9500	P	4,497	3.8
5	Columbia Gas Of Ohio Inc—*Jack Cartridge*	PO Box 117, Columbus OH 43216	614-460-6000	S	4,373*	1.2
6	Atmos Energy Corp—*Kim R Cocklin*	PO Box 650205, Dallas TX 75265	972-934-9227	P	4,348	4.8
7	Southwest Gas Corp—*Jeffrey W Shaw*	PO Box 98890, Las Vegas NV 89193	702 876 7011	P	4,276	2.3

Rank	Company Name—*Executive Officer*	Address, City, State, Zip	Phone	Type	Fin	Empls
8	Peoples Energy Corp—*Paul Babcock*	130 E Randolph Dr, Chicago IL 60601	312-240-4000	S	3,822	2.2
9	WGL Holdings Inc—*Terry D McCallister*	101 Constitution Ave N, Washington DC 20080	703-750-2000	P	3,809	1.4
10	Piedmont Natural Gas Company Inc—*Thomas E Skains*	PO Box 33068, Charlotte NC 28233	704-364-3120	P	3,054	1.8
11	New Jersey Resources Corp—*Laurence M Downes*	1415 Wyckoff Rd, Wall NJ 07719	732-938-1000	P	3,009	.9
12	Cheniere Energy Inc—*Charif Souki*	700 Milam St Ste 800, Houston TX 77002	713-375-5000	P	2,915	.2
13	Otter Tail Energy Services Company Inc—*Chuck MacFarlane*	215 S Cascade St, Fergus Falls MN 56538	218-739-8200	S	2,907*	.8
14	Northwest Natural Gas Co—*Gregg S Kantor*	PO Box 6017, Portland OR 97228	503-226-4211	P	2,747	.6
15	Washington Gas Light Co—*James Lafond* WGL Holdings Inc	101 Constitution Ave N, Washington DC 20080	703-750-1400	S	2,505*	1.9
16	South Jersey Industries Inc—*Edward J Graham*	1 S Jersey Plz, Folsom NJ 08037	609-561-9000	P	2,077	.7
17	National Fuel Gas Co—*David F Smith*	6363 Main St, Williamsville NY 14221	716-857-7000	P	1,779	1.8
18	Arkansas Western Gas Co—*Alan N Stewart*	655 E Milsap Dr, Fayetteville AR 72703	479-521-5400	S	1,758*	.5
19	Constellation NewEnergy - Gas Div—*Kevin Watson*	9960 Corporate Campus, Louisville KY 40223	502-426-4500	D	1,683*	.5
20	Laclede Group Inc—*Douglas H Yaeger*	720 Olive St Rm 1517, Saint Louis MO 63101	314-342-0873	P	1,603	1.6
21	Martin Resource Management Corp—*Ruben S Martin*	4200 Stone Rd, Kilgore TX 75662	903-983-6287	R	1,540*	1.8
22	Energen Corp—*James T McManus II*	605 Richard Arrington, Birmingham AL 35203	205-326-2700	P	1,484	1.5
23	Atlanta Gas Light Co—*John W Somerhalder* AGL Resources Inc	PO Box 4569, Atlanta GA 30302	404-584-4000	S	1,072*	2.9
24	Alabama Gas Corp—*Dudley Reynolds* Energen Corp	605 Richard Arrington, Birmingham AL 35203	205-326-2700	S	963*	1.2
25	SEMCO Energy Inc—*George A Schreiber Jr*	PO Box 5004, Port Huron MI 48061		R	907*	.5
26	Wisconsin Gas Co—*Gale Kloppa*	PO Box 2046, Milwaukee WI 53201	414-221-2345	S	863	1.1
27	National Fuel Gas Supply Corp (Williamsville New York)—*John R Pustulka* National Fuel Gas Co	6363 Main St, Williamsville NY 14221	716-857-7000	S	858	2.2
28	South Jersey Gas Co—*Edward T Graham* South Jersey Industries Inc	1 S Jersey Plz, Hammonton NJ 08037	609-561-9000	S	813*	.7
29	Bill Barrett Corp—*Fredrick J Barrett*	1099 18th St Ste 2300, Denver CO 80202	303-293-9100	P	771	.3
30	Oklahoma Natural Gas Co—*Roger Mitchell*	PO Box 401, Oklahoma City OK 73101	405-551-6500	D	751*	1.2
31	Columbia Gas of Pennsylvania Inc—*Carol Fox*	501 Technology Dr, Canonsburg PA 15317	724-416-6300	S	666*	.9
32	Connecticut Natural Gas Corp—*Robert Allessio*	PO Box 2411, Hartford CT 06146	860-727-3000	S	542*	.6
33	Tatum Development Corp—*Robert Tatum*	11 Parkway Blvd, Hattiesburg MS 39401	601-544-6043	R	514*	.6
34	UGI Utilities Inc Gas Utility Div—*David W Trego*	PO Box 12677, Reading PA 19612		D	510*	1.1
35	Yankee Energy System Inc	107 Selden Dr, Berlin CT 06037		S	410*	.6
36	Laclede Gas Co—*Douglas H Yaeger* Laclede Group Inc	720 Olive St, Saint Louis MO 63101	314-342-0800	S	368*	1.5
37	Columbia Gas of Massachusetts—*Stephen H Bryant*	PO Box 2025, Springfield MA 01102	508-836-7000	S	362*	1.0
38	Yankee Gas Services Co—*Leon Olivier* Yankee Energy System Inc	107 Selden St, Berlin CT 06037		S	356*	.6
39	Intermountain Industries Inc—*Bill Glynn*	PO Box 7608, Boise ID 83707	208-377-6000	R	319*	.4
40	TOPP Portable Air—*Dan Topp*	12 Crozerville Rd, Aston PA 19014	610-459-5515	R	303*	<.1
41	Public Service Company of North Carolina Inc—*Jerry Richardson*	PO Box 1398, Gastonia NC 28053	704-864-6731	S	299*	.9
42	The Gas Co—*Jeffrey M Kissel*	PO Box 3000, Honolulu HI 96802	808-535-5933	S	257*	.3
43	Columbia Gas of Virginia Inc—*Peggy Landini*	1809 Coyote Dr, Chester VA 23836	804-323-5300	S	232*	.3
44	North Shore Gas Co—*Steven Nance* Peoples Energy Corp	130 E Randolph Dr, Chicago IL 60601	312-240-4000	S	231*	.3
45	PPL Gas Utilities Corp—*James Miller*	PO Box 508, Lock Haven PA 17745		S	223*	.5
46	Southern Connecticut Gas Co—*Robert Allessio*	77 Hartland St 4th FL, East Hartford CT 06108		S	217*	.3
47	V-1 Oil Co	PO Box 2436, Idaho Falls ID 83403	208-522-1210	S	209*	.3
48	ENSTAR Natural Gas Co SEMCO Energy Inc	PO Box 190288, Anchorage AK 99519	907-277-5551	D	192*	.2
49	Clearwater Enterprises LLC—*Angela Allan*	5637 N Classen Blvd, Oklahoma City OK 73118	405-842-9200	R	157*	<.1
50	Energy West Development Inc—*Kevin J Degenstein* Gas Natural Inc	PO Box 2229, Great Falls MT 59403	406-791-7500	S	138*	<.1
51	Gas Natural Inc—*Richard M Osborne*	PO Box 2229, Great Falls MT 59403	406-791-7500	P	137	.2
52	Energy West Resources Inc—*Kevin Degenstein* Gas Natural Inc	PO Box 2229, Great Falls MT 59403	406-791-7500	S	137*	<.1
53	Dominion Hope Inc	PO Box 26532, Richmond VA 23261	304-623-8600	S	120	.4
54	Commercial Energy LLC—*Ron Perry*	PO Box 548, Cut Bank MT 59427	406-873-3300	R	100*	<.1
55	Valley Energy—*Robert Tumes*	PO Box 340, Sayre PA 18840	570-888-9664	S	85*	<.1
56	Berkshire Gas Co—*Robert M Allessio*	115 Cheshire Rd, Pittsfield MA 01201	413-442-1511	S	79*	.1
57	Kokomo Gas and Fuel Co—*Mark Maassel*	PO Box 13007, Merrillville IN 46411	765-459-4101	S	74*	.1
58	Roanoke Gas Co	PO Box 13007, Roanoke VA 24030	540-777-4427	S	57*	.2
59	Elkton Gas—*Paula Rosput Reynolds* AGL Resources Inc	PO Box 4569, Elkton MD 21921	410-398-4626	S	57*	<.1
60	Columbia Gas of Maryland Inc—*Carol Fox*	121 Champion Way, Canonsburg PA 15317	724-416-6300	S	52*	.1
61	Natural Gas Processing Corp—*David L Hamilton*	PO Box 541, Worland WY 82401	307-347-9281	R	41*	.1
62	St Lawrence Gas Company Inc—*Richard Campbell*	PO Box 270, Massena NY 13662	315-769-3511	S	40*	<.1
63	Middle Tennessee Natural Gas Utility District—*Leslie B Enoch II*	PO Box 670, Smithville TN 37166	615-597-4300	R	39*	.1
64	National Fuel Resources Inc—*Donna DeCarolis* National Fuel Gas Co	PO Box 9072, Williamsville NY 14231	716-630-6778	S	35*	<.1
65	North Atlantic Utilities Inc—*Stefan Geiringer*	54 Factory Pond Rd, Glen Cove NY 11542	516-759-5400	R	30*	<.1
66	Ohio Valley Gas Corp—*Ron Loyd*	PO Box 469, Winchester IN 47394	765-584-6842	S	27*	.1
67	Wyoming Gas Co—*David L Hamilton* Natural Gas Processing Corp	PO Box 541, Worland WY 82401	307-347-2416	D	26*	<.1
68	Cost Management Services Inc—*Douglas Betzold*	2737 78th Ave SE Ste 1, Mercer Island WA 98040	206-236-8808	R	25*	<.1
69	Midwest Natural Gas Corp—*Michael V Crouch*	PO Box 707, Scottsburg IN 47170	812-752-2230	R	21*	<.1
70	Walden Energy LLC—*Tamara J Walden*	8908 S Yale Ste 402, Tulsa OK 74137	918-645-7409	R	17*	<.1
71	Service One—*Chuck Hoag*	PO Box 159, Lawrence KS 66044		R	14*	<.1
72	Energy West Wyoming—*Richard Osborne* Gas Natural Inc	PO Box 970, Cody WY 82414	307-587-4281	D	4	<.1
73	M T Deason Company Inc—*Michael Deason*	PO Box 101807, Birmingham AL 35210	205-956-2266	R	4*	<.1
74	Mountain Fuel Supply Co—*Ronald W Jibson*	PO Box 45433, Salt Lake City UT 84145	801-324-5000	S	2*	2.3

TOTALS: SIC 4924 Natural Gas Distribution
Companies: 74

					96,758	65.9

4925 Gas Production & Distribution Nec

1	AmeriGas Propane LP—*Eugene VN Bissell*	PO Box 965, Valley Forge PA 19482	610-337-7000	S	13,931*	6.0

Note: An asterisk (*) indicates an estimated financial figure. The company type code used is as follows: R = Private, P = Public, S = Private Subsidiary, B = Public Subsidiary, D = Division, J = Joint Venture, I = Investment Fund.

COMPANY RANKINGS BY SALES WITHIN 4-DIGIT SIC

Rank	Company Name—*Executive Officer*	Address, City, State, Zip	Phone	Type	Fin	Empls
2	AmeriGas Inc	460 N Gulph Rd Ste 100, King of Prussia PA 19406	610-337-7000	S	1,456*	6.0
3	Dowdle Gas and Appliance Center—*Jim McSweeney*	PO Box 9129, Columbus MS 39705	662-328-2080	R	1,003*	.5
4	AmeriGas Eagle Propane LP—*Eugene VN Bissell* AmeriGas Propane LP	PO Box 965, Valley Forge PA 19482	610-337-7000	S	711*	.4
5	Freeman Gas and Electric Company Inc—*Jim Cannon*	1186 Asheville Hwy PO, Spartanburg SC 29303	864-582-5475	R	578	.2
6	Texas Energy Holdings Inc—*Phillip Willis*	3320 Oak Grove Ave, Dallas TX 75204	214-231-4000	R	339*	.1
7	Luminant Generation Company LLC—*David Campbell*	500 N Akard St, Dallas TX 75201	214-812-4600	R	144*	2.0
8	Flint Energy Services Inc—*Bryce Satter*	PO Box 3044, Tulsa OK 74101	918-294-3030	S	100*	1.0

TOTALS: SIC 4925 Gas Production & Distribution Nec
Companies: 8 — 18,262 — 16.2

4931 Electric & Other Services Combined

Rank	Company Name—*Executive Officer*	Address, City, State, Zip	Phone	Type	Fin	Empls
1	Exelon Corp—*John W Rowe*	PO Box 805398, Chicago IL 60680	312-394-7398	P	52,240	19.2
2	Consolidated Edison Inc—*Kevin Burke*	PO Box 1528, New York NY 10009	212-460-4600	P	36,146	15.2
3	Public Service Enterprise Group Inc—*Ralph Izzo*	PO Box 570, Newark NJ 07101	973-430-7000	P	29,909	10.0
4	Xcel Energy Inc—*Benjamin GS Fowke*	PO Box 9477, Minneapolis MN 55484	612-330-5500	P	27,388	11.4
5	Ameren Corp—*Thomas R Voss*	PO Box 66149, Saint Louis MO 63166	314-621-3222	P	23,515	9.5
6	Northern States Power Co Xcel Energy Inc	414 Nicollet Mall Fl 4, Minneapolis MN 55401	612-330-5500	S	21,760*	9.0
7	Wisconsin Energy Corp—*Gale E Klappa*	PO Box 1331, Milwaukee WI 53201	414-221-2345	P	13,060	4.6
8	SCANA Corp—*Kevin B Marsh*	220 Operation Way, Cayce SC 29033	803-217-9000	P	12,968	5.9
9	National Grid Holdings Inc—*William Edwards*	300 Erie Blvd W, Syracuse NY 13202	315-474-1511	S	12,642	7.6
10	Niagara Mohawk Power Corp—*William F Edwards*	300 Erie Blvd W, Syracuse NY 13202	315-474-1511	S	12,642	7.6
11	PG and E Corp—*C Lee Cox*	1 Market Spear Twr Ste, San Francisco CA 94105	415-267-7000	P	12,096	19.4
12	Long Island Power Authority—*Kevin S Law*	333 Earle Ovington Blv, Uniondale NY 11553	516-222-7700	R	11,931*	5.2
13	NV Energy Inc—*Michael W Yackira*	PO Box 10100, Reno NV 89520	702-402-5000	P	11,635	2.8
14	Integrys Energy Group Inc—*Charles Schrock*	130 E Randolph Dr, Chicago IL 60601	312-228-5400	P	9,817	4.6
15	Public Service Company of Colorado—*Tim E Taylor* Xcel Energy Inc	1225 17th St, Denver CO 80202	303-571-7511	S	9,795*	2.8
16	South Carolina Electric and Gas Co—*Kevin B Marsh* SCANA Corp	1426 Main St, Columbia SC 29201	803-217-9000	S	9,052	3.1
17	OGE Energy Corp—*Peter B Delaney*	PO Box 321, Oklahoma City OK 73101	405-553-3000	P	8,906	3.5
18	Westar Energy Inc—*William B Moore*	PO Box 889, Topeka KS 66675	785-575-6300	P	8,683	2.4
19	Public Service Electric and Gas Co Public Service Enterprise Group Inc	PO Box 570, Newark NJ 07101	973-430-7000	S	8,500*	6.0
20	Oklahoma Gas and Electric Co—*Peter Delany* OGE Energy Corp	PO Box 321, Oklahoma City OK 73101	405-553-3000	S	8,283*	3.1
21	Louisville Gas and Electric Co—*Victor Staffieri*	220 W Main St, Louisville KY 40202	502-589-1444	S	6,942*	2.6
22	Pacific Gas and Electric Co—*Christopher P Johns* PG and E Corp	PO Box 0001, San Francisco CA 94101	415-973-7000	S	4,813*	19.3
23	Avista Corp—*Scott Morris*	PO Box 3727, Spokane WA 99220	509-489-0500	P	4,215	1.6
24	Interstate Power and Light Co—*William D Harvey*	Alliant Energy Tower 2, Cedar Rapids IA 52401	319-786-4411	S	4,211*	1.5
25	Rochester Gas and Electric Corp—*James P Laurato* RGS Energy Group Inc	PO Box 5300, Ithaca NY 14852	585-546-2700	S	3,816*	2.0
26	DPL Inc—*Paul M Barbas*	1065 Woodman Dr, Dayton OH 45432	937-224-6000	P	3,813	1.3
27	Public Service Company of New Mexico—*Pat Vincent-Collawn*	Alvarado Sq MS 1110, Albuquerque NM 87158	505-241-2700	S	3,761*	3.3
28	Delmarva Power and Light Co—*David Velazquez*	PO Box 17000, Wilmington DE 19850	302-454-0300	S	3,745	4.8
29	NorthWestern Corp (Sioux Falls South Dakota)—*Robert C Rowe*	3010 W 69th St, Sioux Falls SD 57108	605-978-2900	P	3,038	1.4
30	ALLETE Inc—*Alan Hodnik*	30 W Superior St, Duluth MN 55802	218-279-5000	P	2,876	1.4
31	PECO Energy Co—*Corbin A McNeill Jr* Exelon Corp	PO Box 8699, Philadelphia PA 19101	215-841-4000	S	2,795*	2.5
32	RGS Energy Group Inc—*James Laurito*	PO Box 5300, Ithaca NY 14852	585-771-4444	S	2,472*	2.0
33	AmerenIP—*Scott A Cisel* Ameren Corp	500 S 27th St, Decatur IL 62521		S	1,886*	1.2
34	CH Energy Group Inc—*Steven V Lant*	284 South Ave, Poughkeepsie NY 12601	845-452-2000	P	1,730	.8
35	NV Energy NV Energy Inc	PO Box 10100, Reno NV 89520	775-834-3600	S	1,555*	1.7
36	Madison Gas and Electric Co—*Gary Wolter*	PO Box 1231, Madison WI 53701	608-252-4744	S	1,541*	.5
37	Wisconsin Public Service Corp—*Larry Weyers* Integrys Energy Group Inc	PO Box 19001, Green Bay WI 54307	920-433-4901	S	1,268	2.4
38	Orange and Rockland Utilities Inc—*William G Longhi* Consolidated Edison Inc	1 Blue Hill Plz, Pearl River NY 10965	845-352-6000	S	957*	1.1
39	Stream Energy—*Rob Snyder*	1950 Stemmons Fwy Ste, Flower Mound TX 75027		R	848*	.3
40	Northern States Power Co—*Michael L Swenson*	1414 W Hamilton Ave, Eau Claire WI 54701	715-839-2582	R	825	.9
41	Unitil Corp—*Laurence M Brock*	6 Liberty Ln W, Hampton NH 03842	603-772-0775	P	800	.5
42	Midland Cogeneration Venture LP—*Rodney E Boulanger*	100 Progress Pl, Midland MI 48640	989-839-6000	J	667*	.1
43	Dayton Power and Light Co—*Allen M Hill* DPL Inc	PO Box 1247, Dayton OH 45401	937-331-3900	S	514*	.9
44	Colorado Springs Utilities—*Jerry Forte*	111 S Cascade, Colorado Springs CO 80903	719-448-4800	R	415*	2.0
45	Alaska Electric Light and Power—*Tim McLeod*	5601 Tonsgard Ct, Juneau AK 99801	907-780-2222	R	237*	.1
46	Edison Mission Group Inc—*Ronald Litzinger*	2244 Walnut Grove Ave, Rosemead CA 91770	626-302-2222	R	174*	2.7
47	Public Utilities Board—*John Bruciak*	PO Box 3270, Brownsville TX 78523	956-983-6100	R	155*	.5
48	US Energy Service—*Bill Bathe*	605 N Hwy 169 Ste 1200, Plymouth MN 55441	763-543-4600	R	148*	.1
49	Diamond Energy Inc	333 S Grand Ave Ste 15, Los Angeles CA 90071	213-473-0080	S	115*	<.1
50	Midwest Energy Inc—*Earnie Lehman*	PO Box 898, Hays KS 67601	785-625-3437	P	107*	.3
51	Superior Water Light and Power Co—*Eugene G McGillis* ALLETE Inc	PO Box 519, Superior WI 54880	715-394-2200	S	83*	.1
52	Energy Services Providers Inc—*Franklin C Lewis*	877 South St, Pittsfield MA 01201		R	79*	<.1
53	Presque Isle Electric and Gas Coop—*Brian Burns*	PO Box 308, Onaway MI 49765	989-733-8515	R	63*	.1
54	Franklin Heating Station—*Toni-Rae Musel*	119 Third St SW, Rochester MN 55902	507-289-3534	R	58*	<.1
55	StarTex Power—*Robert Zlotnik*	PO Box 4802, Houston TX 77210	713-357-2800	R	17*	<.1
56	Rosenberry Consulting Ltd—*Steven Rosenberry*	1404 Durwood Dr, Reading PA 19609	610-670-9090	R	8*	<.1
57	Vycon Inc—*Vatche Artinian*	23695 Via Del Rio, Yorba Linda CA 92887	714-386-3800	R	3*	.1
58	Modern Electric Water Company Inc—*John Conners*	PO Box 14008, Spokane WA 99214	509-928-4540	R	3*	<.1
59	Powerbridge Inc—*James Clements*	3710 Rawlins Ste 1060, Dallas TX 75219	214-520-8177	S	2*	<.1

TOTALS: SIC 4931 Electric & Other Services Combined
Companies: 59 — 401,722 — 212.7

Rank	Company Name—*Executive Officer*	Address, City, State, Zip	Phone	Type	Fin	Empls

4932 Gas & Other Services Combined

Rank	Company Name—*Executive Officer*	Address, City, State, Zip	Phone	Type	Fin	Empls
1	NiSource Inc—*Robert C Skaggs Jr*	801 E 86th Ave, Merrillville IN 46410	219-853-5200	P	19,939	7.6
2	Sempra Energy—*Debra L Reed*	101 Ash St, San Diego CA 92101	619-696-2000	P	14,345	13.5
3	Vectren Utility Holdings Inc—*Carl Chapman* Vectren Corp	20 NW 4th St, Evansville IN 47708	812-491-4000	S	9,645*	1.7
4	UGI Corp—*Lon R Greenberg*	PO Box 858, Valley Forge PA 19482	610-337-1000	P	6,091	5.8
5	Vectren Corp—*Carl L Chapman*	PO Box 209, Evansville IN 47702	812-491-4000	P	4,879	4.5
6	MDU Resources Group Inc—*Terry D Hildestad*	PO Box 5650, Bismarck ND 58506	701-530-1000	P	4,051	8.0
7	Clean Energy Fuels Corp—*Andrew J Littlefair*	3020 Old Ranch Pky Ste, Seal Beach CA 90740	562-493-2804	P	212	.7
8	Promet Energy Partners LLC—*Gregory R White*	1 E Delaware, Chicago IL 60611	312-202-9303	R	29*	<.1
9	Northern Indiana Fuel and Light Company Inc—*Eileen Odom* NiSource Inc	PO Box 13007, Merrillville IN 46411	260-925-2700	S	23*	.1
10	Whitmer Fuels Inc—*Kevin Whitmer*	PO Box 469, Sunbury PA 17801	570-286-6744	R	2*	<.1
11	Texzon Utilities Ltd—*Steve Wilson*	204 N I-35 Ste A, Red Oak TX 75154	972-938-0533	R	2*	<.1
12	TXU Energy Trading Co—*Jim Burke*	PO Box 650700, Dallas TX 75265	972-791-2828	S	N/A	.3

TOTALS: SIC 4932 Gas & Other Services Combined
Companies: 12   59,217   42.2

4939 Combination Utility Nec

Rank	Company Name—*Executive Officer*	Address, City, State, Zip	Phone	Type	Fin	Empls
1	Edison Mission Energy—*Theodore Craver*	18101 Von Karman Ave, Irvine CA 92612	949-752-5588	D	17,879*	1.8
2	AEI Services LLC—*Ron Haddock*	700 Milam St Ste 600, Houston TX 77002	713-345-5200	R	5,384*	8.3
3	Northern Indiana Public Service Co—*Robert C Skaggs Jr*	801 E 86th Ave, Merrillville IN 46410	219-853-5200	S	3,703*	5.9
4	Covanta Energy Corp—*Anthony J Orlando*	40 Ln Rd, Fairfield NJ 07004	973-882-9000	S	1,871	1.8
5	MGE Energy Inc—*Gary J Wolter*	PO Box 1231, Madison WI 53701	608-252-7000	P	1,459	.7
6	Atlas Energy Inc—*Edward E Cohen*	Westpointe Corporate C, Moon Township PA 15108	412-262-2830	P	936	.3
7	Ignite Ltd	1950 Stemmons Fwy Ste, Dallas TX 75207	214-800-4500	S	900*	.1
8	AmerenCIPS—*Gary L Rainwater*	607 E Adams St, Springfield IL 62701	217-523-3600	S	497*	.7
9	Dalton Utilities—*Don Cope*	PO Box 869, Dalton GA 30722	706-278-1313	R	258*	.3
10	Florida Public Utilities Co—*John R Schimkaitis*	PO Box 3395, West Palm Beach FL 33402	561-832-0872	S	209	.3
11	East Texas Electric Cooperative Inc—*Debra Robinson*	PO Box 631623, Nacogdoches TX 75963	936-560-9532	R	172*	<.1
12	PSEG Global LLC—*Robert Dougherty*	35 Waterview Blvd, Parsippany NJ 07054	973-541-6000	S	61*	<.1
13	Alteris Renewables Inc—*Steve Kaufman*	523 Danbury Rd, Wilton CT 06897	203-210-7710	R	56*	.1
14	Consumers Energy Co—*John G Russell*	1 Energy Plz, Jackson MI 49201	517-788-0550	S	15	N/A
15	Greenspring Energy LLC—*Paul Whittmann*	30 W Aylesbury Rd, Timonium MD 21093	443-322-7000	R	11	<.1
16	Trigen-St Louis Energy Corp—*Cyrille du Peloux*	1 Ashley St, Saint Louis MO 63102	314-621-3550	S	10*	<.1
17	Hunt Global Resources Inc—*Geroge Sharp*	24 Waterway Ave Ste 20, The Woodlands TX 77380	281-825-5000	P	6	N/A
18	Pfister Energy—*Dieter Pfisterer*	80 E 5th St, Paterson NJ 07524	973-653-9880	R	5	<.1

TOTALS: SIC 4939 Combination Utility Nec
Companies: 18   33,431   20.4

4941 Water Supply

Rank	Company Name—*Executive Officer*	Address, City, State, Zip	Phone	Type	Fin	Empls
1	American Water Works Company Inc—*Jeffry Sterba*	1025 Laurel Oak Rd, Voorhees NJ 08043	856-346-8200	B	47,080	7.6
2	Aqua America Inc—*Nicholas DeBenedictis*	762 W Lancaster Ave, Bryn Mawr PA 19010	610-525-1400	P	3,469	1.6
3	Aqua Illinois Inc—*Nicholas DeBenedictis* Aqua America Inc	762 W Lancaster Ave, Bryn Mawr PA 19010	610-525-1400	S	2,878*	1.5
4	California Water Service Group—*Peter C Nelson*	1720 N 1st St, San Jose CA 95112	408-367 8200	P	1,855	1.1
5	American States Water Co—*Robert Sprowls*	630 E Foothill Blvd, San Dimas CA 91773	909-394-3600	P	1,192	.7
6	SJW Corp—*W Richard Roth*	110 W Taylor St, San Jose CA 95110		P	935	.4
7	IWC Resources Corp—*James T Morris*	PO Box 1220, Indianapolis IN 46206	317-639-1501	R	868*	.5
8	Philadelphia Suburban Water Co—*Nicholas DeBenedictis* Aqua America Inc	762 W Lancaster Ave, Bryn Mawr PA 19010	610-525-1402	S	832*	.8
9	Las Vegas Valley Water District—*Patricia Mulroy*	1001 S Valley View Blv, Las Vegas NV 89107	702-870-2011	R	556*	1.1
10	New Jersey-American Water Co—*John Bigelow* American Water Works Company Inc	PO Box 5079, Cherry Hill NJ 08034	856-310-2200	S	549*	.4
11	Golden State Water Co American States Water Co	630 E Foothill Blvd, San Dimas CA 91773	909-394-3600	S	500*	.5
12	Middlesex Water Co—*Dennis W Doll*	PO Box 1500, Iselin NJ 08830	732-634-1500	P	489	.3
13	Connecticut Water Service Inc—*Eric W Thornburg*	93 W Main St, Clinton CT 06413	860-669-8630	P	425	.2
14	Southwest Water Co—*Floyd E Wicks*	624 S Grand Ave Ste 29, Los Angeles CA 90017	213-929-1800	R	400	1.2
15	Artesian Resources Corp—*Dian C Taylor*	PO Box 15004, Wilmington DE 19850	302-453-6900	P	372	.2
16	San Gabriel Valley Water Co—*Michael Whitehead*	PO Box 6010, El Monte CA 91734	626-448-6183	R	282*	.2
17	York Water Co—*Jeffrey R Hines*	PO Box 15089, York PA 17405	717-845-3601	P	260	.1
18	Connecticut Water Co—*Eric W Thornburg* Connecticut Water Service Inc	93 W Main St, Clinton CT 06413	860-669-8636	S	251*	.2
19	Aquarion Water Company of Connecticut—*Charles V Firlotte* Aquarion Water Co	200 Monroe Tpke, Monroe CT 06468	203-445-7310	S	238*	.3
20	California-American Water Co—*Jeremy Pelczer* American Water Works Company Inc	4701 Beloit Dr, Sacramento CA 95838		S	212*	.2
21	Pennichuck Corp—*Duane C Montopoli*	PO Box 1947, Merrimack NH 03054	603-882-5191	P	182	.1
22	Aqua North Carolina Inc Aqua America Inc	706 N Regional Rd, Greensboro NC 27409		S	176*	.2
23	Missouri-American Water Co—*Harry Roels* American Water Works Company Inc	727 Craig Rd, Saint Louis MO 63141		S	170*	.2
24	Connecticut Water Emergency Services Inc Connecticut Water Service Inc	93 W Main St, Clinton CT 06413	860-669-8636	D	170*	.2
25	Suburban Water Systems Southwest Water Co	1325 N Grand Ave Ste 1, Covina CA 91724	626-543-2500	S	161*	.1
26	Laurel Holdings Inc—*Kim Kunkle*	PO Box 1287, Johnstown PA 15907	814-533-5777	R	159*	.3
27	Tampa Bay Water A Regional Water Supply Authority—*Ann Hildebrand*	2575 Enterprise Rd, Clearwater FL 33763	727-796-2355	R	155*	.1
28	Long Island Water Corp—*William Varley* American Water Works Company Inc	733 Sunrise Hwy, Lynbrook NY 11563	516-596-4800	S	153*	.2
29	Board Of Water Supply—*Wayne Hoshiro*	630 S Beretania St, Honolulu HI 96843	808-748-5100	R	152*	.6
30	West Virginia-American Water Co—*Wayne Morgan* American Water Works Company Inc	PO Box 1906, Charleston WV 25327	304-353-6300	S	144*	.2
31	Pittsburgh Water and Sewer Authority—*Gregory Tutsock*	1200 Penn Ave Ste 100, Pittsburgh PA 15222	412-255-8935	R	140*	.3
32	New Mexico-American Water Co—*Kathy Wright* American Water Works Company Inc	PO Box 430, Clovis NM 88101	505-763-5538	S	125*	.2
33	Aqua New Jersey—*Nicholas DeBenedictis* Aqua America Inc	10 Black Forest Rd, Hamilton NJ 08691	609-587-8222	S	107*	.1

Note: An asterisk (*) indicates an estimated financial figure. The company type code used is as follows: R = Private, P = Public, S = Private Subsidiary, B = Public Subsidiary, D = Division, J = Joint Venture, I = Investment Fund.

COMPANY RANKINGS BY SALES WITHIN 4-DIGIT SIC

Rank	Company Name—*Executive Officer*	Address, City, State, Zip	Phone	Type	Fin	Empls
34	Mesa Consolidated Water District—*Paul E Shoenberger*	PO Box 5008, Costa Mesa CA 92628	949-631-1200	R	107*	.1
35	Iowa-American Water Co—*Brock Earnhardt* American Water Works Company Inc	5201 Grand Ave, Davenport IA 52807	563-324-3264	S	106*	.1
36	Aqua Ohio Inc—*Nicholas DeBenedictis* Aqua America Inc	7955 Market St, Youngstown OH 44512	330-726-8151	S	104*	.2
37	Aquarion Water Co—*Charles V Firlotte*	200 Monroe Tpke, Monroe CT 06468	203-445-7310	S	95*	.3
38	United Water Idaho Inc—*Greg Wyatt*	8248 W Victory Rd, Boise ID 83709	208-362-7304	S	91*	.1
39	Louisville Water Co—*Greg Heitzman*	550 S 3rd St, Louisville KY 40202	502-569-3600	R	80*	.4
40	Arizona-American Water Co—*Don Correll* American Water Works Company Inc	19820 N 7th St Ste 201, Phoenix AZ 85024	612-445-2400	S	59*	.1
41	Park Water Co	9750 Washburn Rd, Downey CA 90241	562-923-0711	R	58*	.1
42	Pennichuck Water Works Inc Pennichuck Corp	PO Box 1947, Merrimack NH 03054	603-882-5191	S	56*	.1
43	Ohio-American Water Co—*David Little* American Water Works Company Inc	365 E Center St, Marion OH 43302	740-383-0935	S	51*	.1
44	Goleta Water District—*De Witt*	4699 Hollister Ave, Goleta CA 93110	805-964-6761	R	51*	.1
45	Valencia Water Co—*Robert DiPrimio*	24631 Avenue Rockefell, Valencia CA 91355	661-294-0828	S	49*	.1
46	Cadiz Inc—*Keith Brackpool*	550 S Hope St Ste 2850, Los Angeles CA 90071	213-271-1600	P	49	<.1
47	East Valley Water District—*George E Wilson*	3654 E Highland Ave St, Highland CA 92346	909-889-9501	R	47*	.1
48	United Water New York Inc—*Bertrand Camus*	360 W Nyack Rd, West Nyack NY 10994	845-620-3320	S	46*	.1
49	Pennsylvania-American Water Co—*Dan Warnock* American Water Works Company Inc	800 W Hersheypark Dr, Hershey PA 17033	717-533-5000	S	44*	1.1
50	Aqua Maine—*Nicholas DeBenedictis* Aqua America Inc	855 Rockland St, Rockport ME 04856	207-236-8428	S	43*	<.1
51	Consolidated Mutual Water Co—*Thomas J Murray*	12700 W 27th Ave, Lakewood CO 80215	303-238-0451	R	39*	.1
52	Mojave Water Agency—*George Wilson*	22450 Headquarters Ave, Apple Valley CA 92307	760-946-7000	R	36*	<.1
53	Biddeford and Saco Water Co—*CS Mansfield Jr*	PO Box 304, Biddeford ME 04005	207-282-1543	R	36*	<.1
54	Baton Rouge Water Works Co—*Gene Owen*	PO Box 96016, Baton Rouge LA 70896	225-925-2011	R	31*	.2
55	Jenks Public Works Authority—*V Ewing*	PO Box 2007, Jenks OK 74037	918-299-5883	R	26*	.1
56	Birmingham Utilities Inc—*Mac Underwood*	3600 1st Ave N, Birmingham AL 35222	205-244-4000	R	24*	<.1
57	American States Utility Services Inc—*Robert Sprowls* American States Water Co	535 Anton Blvd Ste 350, Costa Mesa CA 92626	714-689-1188	R	23*	<.1
58	Sun Belt Water Inc—*Jack B Lindsey*	PO Box 92229, Santa Barbara CA 93190	617-948-9678	R	18*	<.1
59	Chaparral City Water Co	12021 N Panorama Dr, Fountain Hills AZ 85268	480-837-9522	S	12*	<.1
60	New Mexico Water Service Co—*Robert W Fox* California Water Service Group	401 Horner St, Belen NM 87002	505-864-2218	S	9*	<.1
61	Virginia American Water Co American Water Works Company Inc	PO Box 25405, Alexandria VA 22313	703-549-7080	D	7*	.1
62	Hartselle Utilities—*Mark Gunter*	PO Box 488, Hartselle AL 35640	256-773-3340	R	6*	.1
63	Beckley Water Co—*Jack R Vickers*	PO Drawer U, Beckley WV 25802	304-255-5121	R	4*	.1
64	Monroeville Municipal Authority—*John A Capor*	219 Speelman Ln, Monroeville PA 15146	412-372-2677	R	4*	<.1
65	R E Erickson Company Inc—*David Labonte*	595 Providence Hwy, Walpole MA 02081	508-668-9330	R	2*	<.1
66	Washington Water Service Co—*Michael P Ireland* California Water Service Group	PO Box 336, Gig Harbor WA 98332	253-851-4060	S	1*	<.1
67	Rio Rico Utilities Inc—*Don Baker*	PO Box 4165, Rio Rico AZ 85648	520-281-7000	S	<1	<.1
68	Halox Technologies Inc—*Dennis Williams*	304 Bishop Ave, Bridgeport CT 06610	203-334-6278	E	N/A	<1

TOTALS: SIC 4941 Water Supply
Companies: 68 — 67,051 — 25.4

4952 Sewerage Systems

Rank	Company Name—*Executive Officer*	Address, City, State, Zip	Phone	Type	Fin	Empls
1	Carylon Corp—*Julius Hemmelstein*	2500 W Arthington St, Chicago IL 60612	312-666-7700	R	482*	1.0
2	Louisville and Jefferson County Metropolitan Sewer District—*Herbert Scharttein*	PO Box 740011, Louisville KY 40201	502-540-6000	R	172*	.6
3	Hampton Roads Sanitation District—*Ted Henifin*	PO Box 5915, Virginia Beach VA 23471	757-460-2261	R	172*	.7
4	Sacramento Regional Waste Water Treatment Plant—*Maria Cablao*	8521 Laguna Station Rd, Elk Grove CA 95758	916-875-9000	R	18*	.4
5	Cascade Earth Sciences Ltd—*Steel Maloney*	3511 Pacific Blvd SW, Albany OR 97321	541-926-7737	S	15*	<.1
6	Florida Community Services Corporation of Walton Count—*Dewey Wilson*	70 Logan Ln, Santa Rosa Beach FL 32459	850-231-5114	R	15*	.1
7	Atlantic City Sewerage Co—*Louis Walters*	1200 Atlantic Ave Ste, Atlantic City NJ 08401	609-345-0131	R	8*	<.1
8	Thermo Energy Corp—*Cary G Bullock*	10 New Bond St, Worcester MA 01606	508-854-1628	R	8*	<.1
9	Global Water Group Inc—*Alan Weiss*	8601 Sovereign Row, Dallas TX 75247	214-678-9866	R	3*	<.1
10	ThermoEnergy Corp—*Cary G Bullock*	124 W Capitol Ave Ste, Little Rock AR 72201	501-376-6477	P	<1	<.1

TOTALS: SIC 4952 Sewerage Systems
Companies: 10 — 891 — 2.9

4953 Refuse Systems

Rank	Company Name—*Executive Officer*	Address, City, State, Zip	Phone	Type	Fin	Empls
1	Republic Services Inc—*Donald W Slager*	18500 N Allied Way, Phoenix AZ 85054	480-627-2700	P	19,462	30.0
2	Philip Industrial Services Group Inc—*Bruce Roberson*	5151 San Felipe Ste 16, Houston TX 77056	713-623-8777	S	11,125*	8.0
3	Browning-Ferris Industries Inc—*J Gregory Muldoon* Republic Services Inc	16800 Greenspoint Park, Houston TX 77060	281-673-2030	S	5,000*	26.0
4	Rumpke Container Services Inc—*Bill Rumpke Sr* Rumpke Consolidated Companies Inc	10795 Hughes Rd, Cincinnati OH 45251		S	3,472*	2.5
5	Waste Connections Inc—*Ronald J Mittelstaedt*	2295 Iron Point Rd Ste, Folsom CA 95630	916-608-8200	P	3,328	5.9
6	ICF Kaiser Advanced Technology New Mexico—*Sudhakar Kesavan*	9300 Lee Hwy, Fairfax VA 22031	703-934-3603	R	2,524*	3.5
7	Clean Harbors of Braintree Inc—*Alan S McKim* Clean Harbors Inc	PO Box 9149, Norwell MA 02061	781-792-5000	S	2,484*	4.4
8	Allied Waste Industries of Northwest Indiana Inc—*James E O'Connor* Republic Services Inc	865 Wheeler St, Crown Point IN 46307	219-662-8600	S	2,236*	3.1
9	Allied Waste of California Inc—*Thomas E O'Connor* Republic Services Inc	441 N Buchanan Cir, Pacheco CA 94553	925-685-4716	S	2,236*	3.1
10	Rumpke Consolidated Companies Inc—*Bill Rumpke Sr*	10795 Hughes Rd, Cincinnati OH 45251		R	2,225*	3.0
11	Clean Harbors Inc—*Alan S McKim*	PO Box 9149, Norwell MA 02061	781-792-5000	P	2,086	8.3
12	Allied Waste Industries of Illinois Inc—*John J Zillmer* Republic Services Inc	12976 St Charles Rock, Bridgeton MO 63044	314-739-7517	S	1,617*	3.0
13	Shaw Environmental and Infrastructure Inc—*Ronald W Oakley*	245 Bufer Ave, Lancaster PA 17601	717-390-9892	D	1,323	7.5
14	Recology—*Michael Sangiacomo*	50 California St Fl 24, San Francisco CA 94111	415-875-1000	R	1,315*	1.8
15	Wheelabrator Technologies Inc—*Mark Weldman*	4 Liberty Ln W, Hampton NH 03842	603-929-3000	S	1,152*	4.4

Rank	Company Name—*Executive Officer*	Address, City, State, Zip	Phone	Type	Fin	Empls
16	IESI Corp—*Keith Carrigan*	2301 Eagle PkwySte 200, Fort Worth TX 76177	817-314-5800	S	1,053*	1.4
17	Safety-Kleen Services Inc—*Frederick J Florjancic Jr* Safety-Kleen Holdco Inc	5360 Legacy Dr Ste 100, Plano TX 75024	972-265-2000	S	925	4.5
18	Deffenbaugh Industries Inc—*Mark Rosenau*	PO Box 3220, Shawnee KS 66203	913-631-3300	S	837*	1.5
19	National Recovery Systems Inc—*Bruce Roth*	5222 Indianapolis Blvd, East Chicago IN 46312	219-397-0200	R	826*	16.0
20	Safety-Kleen Holdco Inc—*Frederick J Florjancic Jr*	5360 Legacy Dr Bldg 2, Plano TX 75024	972-265-2000	R	705*	4.3
21	Casella Waste Systems Inc—*John W Casella*	25 Greens Hill Ln, Rutland VT 05701	802-775-0325	P	691	1.8
22	Synagro Technologies Inc—*Robert C Boucher Jr*	1800 Bering Dr Ste 100, Houston TX 77057	713-369-1700	S	570*	1.0
23	Baylor Hudson Corp—*Scott Tenney*	PO Box 947, Newburgh NY 12551	845-561-0160	R	536*	.4
24	Rumpke Consolidated Inc—*Bill Rumpke Sr* Rumpke Consolidated Companies Inc	10795 Hughes Rd, Cincinnati OH 45251	513-851-0122	S	500*	.5
25	WCA Waste Corp—*Tom J Fatjo Jr*	1 Riverway Ste 1400, Houston TX 77056	713-292-2400	P	440	1.1
26	Waste Industries USA Inc—*Ven Poole*	3301 Benson Dr Ste 601, Raleigh NC 27609	919-325-3000	R	409*	1.6
27	TRC Alton Geoscience Inc	4393 Viewridge Ave, San Diego CA 92123	858-505-8881	S	401	2.5
28	Residual Technologies LP—*Robert Boucher* Synagro Technologies Inc	1800 Bering Dr Ste 100, Houston TX 77057	203-754-9337	S	320	1.0
29	Waste Management Northwest Region—*Duane Woods*	7227 NE 55th Ave, Portland OR 97218	503-331-2221	D	305*	.4
30	Texas Disposal Systems Landfill—*Bob Gregory*	12200 Carl Rd, Creedmoor TX 78610	512-421-1300	R	294*	.2
31	US Ecology Idaho Inc—*Jim Baumgardner* US Ecology Inc	PO Box 400, Grand View ID 83624	208-834-2275	S	273*	.4
32	Emerald Services—*J Stephan Banchero*	7343 E Marginal Way S, Seattle WA 98108	206-832-3000	R	262*	.4
33	Metcalf and Eddy Inc—*Stephen Guttenplan*	701 Edgewater Dr, Wakefield MA 01880	781-246-5200	S	217*	1.4
34	US Ecology Inc—*James Baumgardner*	300 E Mallard Dr Ste 3, Boise ID 83706	208-331-8400	P	203	.4
35	EQ-The Environmental Quality Co—*David Lusk*	36255 Michigan Ave, Wayne MI 48184	734-329-8000	R	198*	.4
36	Carmel Marina Corp—*David Steiner*	11240 Commercial Pkwy, Castroville CA 95012	813-384-5000	S	190	.1
37	Re Community Holdings Ii Inc—*Shean Duffy*	809 W Hill St, Charlotte NC 28208	704-697-2015	R	180*	.6
38	Bfi Waste Systems Of North America Inc—*Thomas Weelden*	15880 N Grnway Hyden L, Scottsdale AZ 85260	480-627-2700	R	159*	3.0
39	CWM Chemical Services LLC	PO Box 200, Model City NY 14107	716-286-1550	S	151*	.1
40	Heritage Environmental Services Inc—*Ken Price*	7901 W Morris St, Indianapolis IN 46231	317-243-0811	R	150*	.9
41	Cyn Environmental Services Inc—*Steven Tucci*	PO Box 119, Stoughton MA 02072	781-341-1777	R	148*	.2
42	Allied Waste Services of Phoenix—*Mark Creswell* Republic Services Inc	PO Box 6644, Phoenix AZ 85005	602-237-2078	S	141*	.3
43	GZA GeoEnvironmental Inc—*William R Beloff*	1 Edgewater Dr, Norwood MA 02062	781-278-3700	S	133*	.5
44	Perma-Fix Environmental Services Inc—*Louis F Centofanti*	8302 Dunwoody Pl Ste 2, Atlanta GA 30350	770-587-9898	P	125	.7
45	Envirite Corp—*S Thomas Yablonski*	2050 Central Ave SE, Canton OH 44707	330-456-6238	R	123*	.2
46	Environmental Specialists Inc—*Alan Wolfe*	3001 E 83rd St, Kansas City MO 64132	816-523-5081	S	111*	.1
47	Sunset Waste Services—*Trent Williams*	PO Box 109, Jenison MI 49429	616-669-7888	R	111*	.1
48	Newpark Environmental Services LLC—*Paul L Howes*	207 Town Center Pky 2n, Lafayette LA 70506	337-988-4516	S	109*	.2
49	RecycleBank LLC—*Jonathan Hsu*	1800 JFK Blvd Ste 502, Philadelphia PA 19103	215-564-2224	R	107*	.2
50	EXP Pharmaceutical Services Corp—*Gus Changaris*	48021 Warm Springs Blv, Fremont CA 94539	510-476-0909	R	102*	.1
51	Perma-Fix of Florida Inc—*Raymond Whittle* Perma-Fix Environmental Services Inc	1940 NW 67th Pl, Gainesville FL 32653	352-373-6066	S	100*	.7
52	Basin Disposal Inc—*John Dietrich*	PO Box 3850, Pasco WA 99302	509-547-2476	R	96*	.1
53	EG and G Defense Materials Inc—*Martin M Koffel*	11600 Stark Rd, Tooele UT 84074	435-882-8450	S	95*	.6
54	Fibrek Recycling US Inc—*Pierre Gabriel*	702 Afr Dr, Fairmont WV 26554	304-368-0900	R	93*	.1
55	Rhode Island Resource Recovery Corp—*Michael O'Connell*	65 Shun Pike, Johnston RI 02919	401-942-1430	R	92*	.1
56	Heritage-Crystal Clean Inc—*Joseph Chalhoub*	2175 Point Blvd Ste 37, Elgin IL 60123	847-836-5670	P	90	.6
57	Sevenson Environmental Services Inc—*Michael A Elia*	2749 Lockport Rd, Niagara Falls NY 14305	716-284-0431	R	83*	.2
58	Coulter Companies Inc—*Royal J Coulter*	PO Box 9071, Peoria IL 61612	309-686-8033	R	79*	.5
59	American Ash Recycling Corp—*George Albright*	1072 Roosevelt Ave, York PA 17404	717-846-0846	S	76*	.1
60	Comanco Environmental Corp	4301 Storling Commerce, Tampa FL 33637	813-988-8829	R	68*	.1
61	Texas Molecular LP—*Casey Borowski*	PO Box 1914, Deer Park TX 77536	281-930-2540	R	66*	.2
62	Antea Group—*Gary Wisniewski*	5910 Rice Creek Pky St, Saint Paul MN 55126	651-639-9449	S	63*	.7
63	Inland Waters Pollution Control Inc—*Robert Williams*	2021 S Schaefer Hwy, Detroit MI 48217	313-659-0100	R	60*	.3
64	Operations Management International Inc—*Elisa M Speranza*	9191 SJamaica St Ste 4, Englewood CO 80112	303-740-0019	S	59*	1.6
65	Entact Inc—*Dean Piasani*	1010 Executive Ct, Westmont IL 60559	630-986-2900	R	59*	.4
66	Vertex Energy Inc—*Benjamin P Cowart*	1331 Gemini St Ste 250, Houston TX 77058		P	58	<.1
67	Perma-Fix of South Georgia Inc—*Lou Centofanti* Perma-Fix Environmental Services Inc	1612 James P Rodgers C, Valdosta GA 31601	229-244-0474	S	58*	.1
68	Sigma Environmental Services Inc—*Dave Scherzer*	1300 W Canal St, Milwaukee WI 53233	414-643-4200	R	57*	.1
69	Disposal Services	100 Vassar, Reno NV 89520	775-329-8822	S	54*	.3
70	VFL Technology Corp—*Dick Patton*	16 Hagerty Blvd, West Chester PA 19382	610-918-1000	R	49*	.3
71	Avalon Holdings Corp—*Steven M Berry*	1 American Way, Warren OH 44484	330-856-8800	P	47	.3
72	Waste Management of Kentucky LLC—*Lawrence O'Donnell III*	7501 Grade Ln, Louisville KY 40218	502-969-2355	S	47*	.3
73	Tetra Technologies Inc Specialty Chemicals Recycling Div—*Geoffrey M Hertel*	24955 I-45 N, The Woodlands TX 77380	281-367-1983	D	47*	.3
74	RHO-Chem Div	PO Box 6021, Inglewood CA 90301	323-776-6233	R	46*	.1
75	Materials and Energy Corp—*Lou Centofanti* Perma-Fix Environmental Services Inc	2010 Hwy 58 Bldg K-100, Oak Ridge TN 37830	865-574-0149	S	45*	.1
76	Browning-Ferris Industries of Colorado (Commerce City Colorado)—*Scott Eden* Browning-Ferris Industries Inc	5075 E 74th Ave, Commerce City CO 80022	303-287-8043	S	44*	.3
77	Diversified Scientific Services Inc—*Joe Crider* Perma-Fix Environmental Services Inc	657 Gallaher Rd, Kingston TN 37763	865-376-0084	S	43*	.1
78	Reuter Recycling of Florida Inc—*David Steiner*	PO Box 297110, Pembroke Pines FL 33029	954-436-9500	S	43*	.1
79	Spring Grove Resource Recovery Inc—*Alan S McKim* Clean Harbors Inc	4879 Spring Grove Ave, Cincinnati OH 45232	513-681-6242	S	42*	.1
80	DuraTherm Inc—*Kevin M Trant*	PO Box 58466, Houston TX 77258	281-339-1352	R	41*	.1
81	Cadence Environmental Energy Inc—*Ted Reese*	PO Box 770, Michigan City IN 46360	219-879-0371	R	41*	<.1
82	Lefco Environmental Technology—*John Sandling*	330 Rayfo Rd Ste 352, Spring TX 77386	281-465-0930	R	41*	<.1
83	CleanScapes Inc—*Chris Martin*	117 S Main Ste 300, Seattle WA 98104	206-859-6700	R	39*	.3
84	de maximis Inc—*Bennie Underwood*	450 Montbrook Ln, Knoxville TN 37919	865-691-5052	R	37*	.1
85	Systech Environmental Corp—*Carl Evers*	3085 Woodman Dr Ste 30, Dayton OH 45420	937-643-1240	S	34*	.1
86	Green Team of San Jose—*Paul Nelson*	1333 Oakland Rd, San Jose CA 95112	408-282-4400	R	34*	.1
87	American Landfill Inc—*Frank Clark*	7916 Chapel St SE, Waynesburg OH 44688	330-866-3265	S	34*	<.1
88	EL Harvey and Sons Inc—*James Harvey*	68 Hopkinton Rd, Westborough MA 01581	508-836-3000	R	34*	.2
89	Harold Lemay Enterprises Inc—*Nancy Lemay*	4111 192nd St E, Tacoma WA 98446	253-537-8687	R	32*	.2
90	Sims Recycling Solutions Holdings Inc—*Steve Skurnac*	1600 Harvester Rd, West Chicago IL 60185	630-231-6060	R	31*	1.0
91	Peoria Disposal Co Coulter Companies Inc	PO Box 9071, Peoria IL 61612	309-686-8033	S	29*	.5

Note: An asterisk (*) indicates an estimated financial figure. The company type code used is as follows: R = Private, P = Public, S = Private Subsidiary, B = Public Subsidiary, D = Division, J = Joint Venture, I = Investment Fund.

COMPANY RANKINGS BY SALES WITHIN 4-DIGIT SIC

Rank	Company Name—*Executive Officer*	Address, City, State, Zip	Phone	Type	Fin	Empls
92	JC Duncan Company Inc—*Nick Stefkovich* Republic Services Inc	1212 Harrison, Arlington TX 76011	817-317-2000	D	28*	.3
93	UXB International Inc—*Richmond Dugger III*	2020 Kraft Dr Rm 2100, Blacksburg VA 24060	540-443-3700	R	27*	.5
94	Healthcare Waste Solutions Inc—*Joseph Mayernik*	4357 Ferguson Dr Ste 1, Cincinnati OH 45245		R	24*	.2
95	International Polymers Corp—*Blair Manning*	PO Box 593, Allentown PA 18105	610-437-5463	R	23*	.1
96	Cycle Systems Inc—*Bruce Brenner*	PO Box 611, Roanoke VA 24004	540-981-1211	R	23*	.2
97	Waste Management of Oklahoma Inc—*David P Steiner*	5600 NW 4th St, Oklahoma City OK 73127	405-949-2121	S	23*	.2
98	Waste Management of Iowa Inc—*Curtis Hill*	201 SE 18th St, Des Moines IA 50317	515-265-5267	S	23*	.1
99	All Chemical Disposal Inc—*Fred Murabito*	21 Great Oaks Blvd, San Jose CA 95119	408-363-1660	R	22*	<.1
100	American Commodities Inc—*Mark Lieberman*	2945 Davison Rd, Flint MI 48506	810-767-3800	R	21*	.1
101	Mercury Waste Solutions LLC—*Brad J Buscher*	21211 Durand Ave, Union Grove WI 53182	262-878-2599	S	21*	<.1
102	American Waste Management Services Inc—*Ken McMahon* Avalon Holdings Corp	1 American Way, Warren OH 44484	330-856-8800	S	21*	<.1
103	Southeastern Chemical and Solvent Co—*Gary Pechota*	PO Box 1755, Sumter SC 29151	803-773-1400	R	19*	.1
104	Perma-Fix of Fort Lauderdale Inc—*Lou Centofanti*	3701 SW 47th Ave Ste 1, Davie FL 33314	954-583-3795	S	19*	<.1
105	Clean Harbors of Connecticut Inc—*Alan S McKim* Clean Harbors Inc	51 Broderick Rd, Bristol CT 06010	860-583-8917	S	18*	<.1
106	Newpark Environmental Management Company LLC—*Paul L Howes*	207 Town Center Pky 2n, Lafayette LA 70506	337-984-4445	S	16*	<.1
107	Harbor Management Consultants Inc—*Alan S McKim* Clean Harbors Inc	30 Joseph St, Kingston MA 02364	781-585-5112	S	16*	<.1
108	Louisiana Plastic Converting Corp—*John Wilhite*	503 Downing Pines Rd, West Monroe LA 71292	318-387-5490	R	15*	.1
109	Dynecol Inc—*James B Nicholson*	6520 Georgia St, Detroit MI 48211	313-571-7140	S	14*	<.1
110	Elk Environmental Services—*Harry O'Neill*	1420 Clarion St, Reading PA 19601	610-372-4760	R	14*	.1
111	Fpt Cleveland LLC—*Andrew Luntz*	8550 Aetna Rd, Cleveland OH 44105	216-441-3800	S	13*	.1
112	Wrr Environmental Services Company Inc—*James Hager*	5200 Ryder Rd, Eau Claire WI 54701	715-834-9624	R	12*	.1
113	Mission Trail Waste Systems Inc—*Louie Pellegrini*	1060 Richard Ave, Santa Clara CA 95050	408-727-5365	R	12*	.1
114	Omni Environmental LLC—*James F Cosgrove*	321 Wall St, Princeton NJ 08540	609-924-8821	S	12*	.1
115	Beaver Oil Company Inc—*Roger Vintika*	6037 Lenzi Ave, Hodgkins IL 60525	708-354-4040	R	11*	.1
116	Environmental Enterprises Inc—*Daniel McCabe*	10163 Cincinnati Dayto, Cincinnati OH 45241	513-772-2818	R	11*	.1
117	Anderson Solid Waste Inc—*Greg Johnson* Republic Services Inc	18703 Cambridge Rd, Anderson CA 96007	530-347-5236	S	11*	<.1
118	Cycle-Tex Inc—*H Neff*	702 S Thornton Ave Ste, Dalton GA 30720	706-226-1116	R	11*	.1
119	Realco Recycling Company Inc—*Andrew Senesac*	8707 Somers Rd S, Jacksonville FL 32226	904-757-7311	R	11*	<.1
120	New England Organics Inc—*James Ecker* Casella Waste Systems Inc	135 Presumpscot St, Portland ME 04103		S	10*	<.1
121	Radiation Technical Services Co—*Andrew Goss*	2600 Moss Ln, Harvey LA 70058	504-368-2448	R	10*	<.1
122	American Processing Co—*Tim Richardson*	9747 Olson Dr, San Diego CA 92121	619-622-0548	R	10*	<.1
123	M and M Chemical and Equipment Company Inc—*Lester Studebaker*	1229 Valley Dr, Attalla AL 35954	256-538-3800	R	9*	.1
124	United Plastic Recycling Inc—*John Sullivan*	4290 Alatex Rd, Montgomery AL 36108	334-288-5002	R	9*	.1
125	Cougle's Recycling Inc—*Robert Cougle*	1000 S 4th St, Hamburg PA 19526	610-562-8336	R	9*	.1
126	Pleasanton Garbage Service Inc—*Robert J Molinaro*	PO Box 399, Pleasanton CA 94566	925-846-2042	R	9*	.1
127	Land Air Water Environmental Services Inc—*Christine Lamprecht*	PO Box 372, Center Moriches NY 11934	631-874-2112	R	9*	<.1
128	Grason Inc—*Marian Eilenfeld*	440 S Illinois Ave, Mansfield OH 44907	419-526-4440	R	8*	.1
129	3Cl Complete Compliance Corp—*Otley L Smith III*	1517 W North Carrier P, Grand Prairie TX 75050		S	8*	.1
130	Maine Recycling Corp—*Charlie Kanning*	61 Capital Ave, Lisbon Falls ME 04252	207-353-7142	R	8*	.1
131	Plastic Recycling Inc—*Alan Shaw*	2015 S Pennsylvania St, Indianapolis IN 46225	317-780-6100	R	8*	.1
132	Spectraserv Inc—*Steven A Townsend*	75 Jacobus Ave, South Kearny NJ 07032	973-589-0277	R	7*	.1
133	Eagle Environmental Technologies Ltd—*Brian Wilmot*	50 W Liberty St Ste 88, Reno NV 89501	209-736-4530	R	7*	<.1
134	Mahoning Landfill Inc—*David Steiner*	3510 Garfield Rd, New Springfield OH 44443	330-549-5357	S	7*	<.1
135	Ted's Trash Service Inc—*Ted Ferrell*	PO Box 520230, Independence MO 64052	816-252-1594	R	6*	<.1
136	Asbestos Removal Technologies Inc—*George Riegel Jr*	21421 Hilltop St Ste 1, Southfield MI 48034	248-358-3311	R	6*	<.1
137	Greene Company Works Wastewater Treatment—*Larry Cole*	420 Factory Rd, Dayton OH 45434	937-426-4540	R	6*	.1
138	Medina Recycling Inc—*Ken Rupp*	370 Lake Rd, Medina OH 44256	330-723-4334	R	6*	.1
139	Colt Inc—*Bill Vincent*	PO Box 1408, Scott LA 70583	337-235-0353	R	6*	.1
140	A-1 Perfection Of Northwest Illinois Inc—*David Heitman*	1745 S Ihm Blvd, Freeport IL 61032	815-232-0908	R	5*	.1
141	Industrial Recovery and Recycling Inc—*John Marler*	3100 Green Rd, Greer SC 29651	864-879-1186	R	5*	<.1
142	Denton Plastics Inc—*Dennis Denton*	18811 Ne San Rafael St, Portland OR 97230	503-257-9945	R	5*	<.1
143	Waste Microbes Inc—*Joseph Jennings*	4901 Milwee Ste 109, Houston TX 77092	713-956-4001	R	5*	<.1
144	Rainier Plastics Inc—*William Shields*	PO Box 9125, Yakima WA 98909	509-248-1473	R	5*	<.1
145	Tri-State Iron and Metal Co—*Howard Glick*	PO Box 775, Texarkana TX 75504	870-773-8409	R	5*	<.1
146	Brandywine Enterprises Inc—*Donald Wolf*	5800 Sheriff Rd, Capitol Heights MD 20743	301-925-8100	R	4*	<.1
147	Strong Environmental Inc—*Richard Verch*	6264 Crooked Creek Rd, Norcross GA 30092	770-409-1500	R	4*	.1
148	Rpg Inc—*William Hutira*	400 Westlake Dr, Ashland OH 44805	419-289-1998	R	4*	.1
149	Galamba Metals Group/Kaw River Shredding Inc—*Richard Galamba*	PO Box 3010, Kansas City KS 66103	913-621-2711	S	4*	<.1
150	Kelly Run Sanitation Inc—*David Steiner*	PO Box 298, Elizabeth PA 15037	412-384-7569	S	4*	<.1
151	Commodore Advanced Sciences Inc—*Walt Foutz*	9769 W 119th Dr Ste 31, Broomfield CO 80021	303-421-1511	S	4*	<.1
152	Midwest Recycling Co—*Tom George*	2324 Mound Rd, Rockdale IL 60436	815-744-4922	R	4*	<.1
153	Colorado Iron and Metal Inc—*Kent Garvin*	903 Buckingham St, Fort Collins CO 80524	970-482-7707	R	4*	<.1
154	Nelson Paper Recycling Inc—*Denver Nelson*	30880 Smith Rd, Romulus MI 48174	734-721-0197	R	3*	<.1
155	Ridge Recyclers Inc—*Jeff Kindale*	PO Box 568, Johnston SC 29832	803-275-5111	R	3*	<.1
156	Lamp Recyclers Of Louisiana Inc—*Lynn Macdonald*	11441 Fontana Ln, Independence LA 70443	985-878-3333	R	3*	<.1
157	Wasatch Metal Recycling—*Dave Holtman*	205 W 3300 S, Salt Lake City UT 84115	801-484-3511	R	3*	<.1
158	Design Ready Controls Inc—*Dave Peterson*	2100 Summer St NE Ste, Minneapolis MN 55413	763-565-3000	R	3*	<.1
159	Vectre Corp	21 Griffin Rd N, Windsor CT 06095	860-298-9692	S	3*	<.1
160	Pittsburgh Recycling Services LLC	50 Vespucius St, Pittsburgh PA 15207	412-420-6000	R	3*	<.1
161	Modern Densifying Inc—*Joe Morgan*	PO Box 2312, Shelby NC 28151	704-434-8335	R	3*	<.1
162	Waste Conversion Technologies Inc—*Richard Wills*	PO Box 17250, Stamford CT 06907	203-882-5840	R	3*	<.1
163	River City Steel and Recycling Inc—*Justin Triesch*	PO Box 14507, San Antonio TX 78214	210-924-1254	R	3*	<.1
164	Interstate General Company LP—*Mark Augenblick*	PO Box 1280, Middleburg VA 20118	540-687-3177	R	3	<.1
165	Metalife Resources Inc—*Gabe Hudock*	16 S Washington St, Donora PA 15033	724-379-9535	R	2*	<.1
166	Hog Brothers Recycling LLC	9607 Dearborn St, Detroit MI 48209	313-841-8658	R	2*	<.1
167	Tacoma Metals Inc—*Robert Pollock*	1754 Thorne Rd, Tacoma WA 98421	253-627-1440	R	2*	<.1
168	CHHJ Franchising LLC—*Nick Friedman*	4836 W Gandy Blvd, Tampa FL 33689		R	2*	<.1
169	Sand Trap Service Company Inc—*Gary Beavers*	PO Box 1823, Fort Worth TX 76101	817-877-5800	R	2*	<.1
170	Source Technologies LLC—*Daniel Sandoval*	320 Gold Ave SW Ste 50, Albuquerque NM 87102	505-877-4499	R	2*	<.1
171	Civic Recycling—*Brett Allen*	3300 Brown Station Rd, Columbia MO 65202	573-474-9526	R	2*	<.1

Rank	Company Name—*Executive Officer*	Address, City, State, Zip	Phone	Type	Fin	Empls
172	Ontario Recycling Inc—*James Kubrich*	12 Cairn St, Rochester NY 14611	585-328-4253	R	<1*	<.1
173	GS EnviroServices Inc—*Kevin Kreisler*	14B Jan Sebastian Dr, Sandwich MA 02563	212-994-5374	P	<1	<.1
174	Kaiser Group Holdings Inc—*Douglas W McMinn*	9300 Lee Hwy, Fairfax VA 22031	703-934-3665	P	<1	<.1
175	Washington Closure Hanford LLC—*Carol Johnson*	2620 Fermi Ave, Richland WA 99354	509-375-4640	S	N/A	.8

TOTALS: SIC 4953 Refuse Systems
Companies: 175   **76,632**   **179.0**

4959 Sanitary Services Nec

Rank	Company Name—*Executive Officer*	Address, City, State, Zip	Phone	Type	Fin	Empls
1	Stericycle Inc—*Mark C Miller*	28161 N Keith Dr, Lake Forest IL 60045	847-367-5910	P	3,177	11.1
2	Oakleaf Waste Management LLC—*Steve Preston*	415 Day Hill Rd, WIndsor CT 06095	860-290-1250	R	433*	.7
3	Advanced Cleanup Technologies Inc—*Ruben Garcia*	18414 S Santa Fe Ave, Compton CA 90221	310-763-1423	R	357*	.3
4	TRC Companies Inc—*Christopher P Vincze*	650 Suffolk St Wannala, Lowell MA 01854	978-970-5600	P	333	2.3
5	Murphy's Waste Oil Service Inc—*Alan Mckim*	252 Salem St, Woburn MA 01801	781-935-9066	S	208*	.1
6	Northeast Ohio Regional Sewer District—*Darnell Brown*	3900 Euclid Ave, Cleveland OH 44115	216-881-6600	R	167*	.6
7	Weston Solutions Inc—*Patrick McCann*	PO Box 2653, West Chester PA 19380	610-701-3000	S	147*	1.8
8	Clean Venture Inc—*Michael Persico*	201 S First St, Elizabeth NJ 07206	908-354-0210	R	144*	.1
9	Lewis Environmental Services Inc—*Richard D Lewis*	PO Box 639, Royersford PA 19468	610-495-3000	R	138*	.1
10	Shaw Environmental and Infrastructure Inc (Trenton New Jersey)—*J M Bernhard Jr*	200 Horizon Center Blv, Trenton NJ 08691	609-584-8900	S	66*	<.1
11	Tabasco Drilling Corp—*Joseph Tabasco*	PO Box 1676, Mount Laurel NJ 08054	856-722-5593	R	49*	<.1
12	Maxymillian Technologies Inc—*Neil Maxymillian*	800 Winter St Ste 225, Waltham MA 02451	781-890-8670	R	33*	.2
13	PDG Environmental Inc—*John C Regan*	1386 Beulah Rd Bldg 80, Pittsburgh PA 15235	412-243-3200	P	26	.1
14	OP-TECH Environmental Services Inc—*Charles B Morgan*	One Adler Dr, East Syracuse NY 13057	315-437-2065	P	17	.1
15	Greenshift Corp—*Kevin Kreisler*	5950 Shiloh Rd E Ste N, Alpharetta GA 30005	212-994-5374	P	15	<.1
16	Reynolds Transport Co—*Jeff Reynolds*	4520 N State Rd 37, Orleans IN 47452	812-865-3232	R	13*	.2
17	Panther Technologies Inc—*Peter J Palko*	220 Rte 70 E Ste B, Medford NJ 08055	609-714-2420	R	11*	.1
18	National Response Corp—*Steven Candito*	3500 Sunrise Hwy Ste T, Great River NY 11739	631-224-9141	S	9*	.1
19	Aquagenix Inc—*Andrew P Chesler*	1460 SW 3rd St Ste B, Pompano Beach FL 33069	954-943-5118	D	9*	<.1
20	ECO2 Plastics Inc—*Rod Rougelot*	PO Box 760, Riverbank CA 95367	209-863-6200	R	7	<.1
21	Contra Costa Mosquito And Vector Control District—*Craig Downs*	155 Mason Cir, Concord CA 94520	925-685-9301	R	6*	<.1
22	T and T Marine Salvage Inc—*Hudy Teichman*	9723 Teichman Rd, Galveston TX 77554		R	4*	<.1
23	Micah Group LLC—*Aaron Jamison*	746 Westland Dr Ste 11, Lexington KY 40504	859-260-7760	R	3*	<.1
24	Industrial Cleanup Inc—*Rustin Johnson*	5240 Gateway Dr, Geismar LA 70734	225-673-6847	R	2*	<.1
25	RMA Road Yard 2—*Henry Hash*	14001 Ave 256, Visalia CA 93292	559-685-2625	R	2*	<.1
26	Mosquito Abatement District—*Gary Hatch*	85 N 600 W, Kaysville UT 84037	801-544-3736	R	1*	<.1
27	Caprius Inc—*Dwight Morgan*	1 University Plz Ste 4, Hackensack NJ 07601	201-342-0900	S	1	<.1
28	Biomedical Technology Solutions Holdings Inc—*Jonathan Bricken*	9800 Mount Pyramid Ct, Englewood CO 80112	303-653-0100	P	1	<.1
29	Commodore Applied Technologies Inc—*Tom Colatosti*	PO Box 3, Lexington MA 02420		P	1	<.1

TOTALS: SIC 4959 Sanitary Services Nec
Companies: 29   **5,379**   **18.1**

4961 Steam & Air-Conditioning Supply

Rank	Company Name—*Executive Officer*	Address, City, State, Zip	Phone	Type	Fin	Empls
1	Trigen Energy Corp—*Richard E Kessel*	1 Water St, White Plains NY 10601	914-286-6600	S	728	.8
2	Trigen-Boston Energy Corp—*Alan Murphy*	99 Summer St, Boston MA 02110	617-482-8080	S	86*	.1
3	Trigen-Nassau Energy Corp—*Stewart A Wood* Trigen Energy Corp	185 Charles Lindbergh, Garden City NY 11530	516-222-2884	S	27*	<.1
4	Trigen-Baltimore Energy Corp—*Stewart Wood* Trigen Energy Corp	1400 Ridgley St, Baltimore MD 21230		S	24*	.1
5	Trigen-Oklahoma Energy Corp—*Cyrille du Peloux* Trigen Energy Corp	320 S Boston Ave, Tulsa OK 74103	918-582-2212	S	16*	.1
6	Miami Air Mechanical Inc—*Michael Joffe*	7805 Nw 55th St, Doral FL 33166	305-592-5780	R	7*	.1

TOTALS: SIC 4961 Steam & Air-Conditioning Supply
Companies: 6   **888**   **1.2**

4971 Irrigation Systems

Rank	Company Name—*Executive Officer*	Address, City, State, Zip	Phone	Type	Fin	Empls
1	United Water Inc—*Bertrand Camus*	200 Old Hook Rd, Harrington Park NJ 07640	201-767-9300	S	71,728*	62.0
2	New Mexico Utilities Inc—*Richard G Newman*	PO Box 1293, Albuquerque NM 87103	505-768-3655	S	24*	<.1

TOTALS: SIC 4971 Irrigation Systems
Companies: 2   **71,752**   **62.0**

5012 Automobiles & Other Motor Vehicles

Rank	Company Name—*Executive Officer*	Address, City, State, Zip	Phone	Type	Fin	Empls
1	Fiat USA Inc	375 Park Ave Ste 2703, New York NY 10152	212-355-2600	S	92,248*	7.0
2	Manheim—*Sandy Schwartz*	4900 Buffington Rd, Atlanta GA 30349		R	76,614*	35.0
3	Mitsubishi Motor Sales of America Inc—*Pierre Gagnon*	PO Box 6011, Cypress CA 90630	714-372-6000	R	25,939	1.1
4	Southeast Toyota Distributors LLC—*Ed Sheehy* JM Family Enterprises Inc	100 Jim Moran Blvd, Deerfield Beach FL 33442	954-429-2000	S	14,027*	2.5
5	Volkswagen of America Inc—*Stefan Jacoby*	3800 Hamlin Rd, Auburn Hills MI 48326	248-340-5000	S	9,300*	2.1
6	JM Family Enterprises Inc—*Colin Brown*	100 Jim Moran Blvd, Deerfield Beach FL 33442	954-429-2000	R	9,169*	3.8
7	Hyundai Motor America—*John Krafcik*	PO Box 20850, Fountain Valley CA 92728		S	8,546	.9
8	Friedkin Companies Inc—*Toby Hynes*	7701 Wilshire Pl Dr, Houston TX 77040	713-580-3300	R	6,529*	3.1
9	Gulf States Toyota Inc—*Thomas N (Toby) Hynes* Friedkin Companies Inc	PO Box 40306, Houston TX 77240	713-580-3300	S	4,100	1.2
10	Subaru of America Inc—*Yoshio Hasanuma*	PO Box 6000, Cherry Hill NJ 08034	856-488-8500	S	4,100*	.6
11	Central Atlantic Toyota Distributors Inc—*Marshal Johnson* Toyota Motor Sales USA Inc	6710 Baymeadow Dr, Glen Burnie MD 21060	410-760-1500	D	3,730*	.3
12	Crown Automotive Co—*Michael Kearney*	3633C W Wendover Ave, Greensboro NC 27407	336-851-3400	S	2,875*	1.5
13	Akron Auto Auction Inc—*Jeff Bailey*	2471 Ley Dr, Akron OH 44319	330-773-8245	R	2,497*	.2
14	Lexus—*Dennis E Clements* Toyota Motor Sales USA Inc	PO Box 2991 - Mail Dro, Torrance CA 90509	310-328-2075	D	2,380*	1.5
15	Kar Auction Services Inc—*Brian T Clingen*	13085 Hamilton Crossin, Carmel IN 46032		P	1,886	12.2
16	Volvo Cars of North America Inc—*Doug Speck*	1 Volvo Dr, Rockleigh NJ 07647		S	1,684*	.6
17	Woodpecker Truck and Equipment Inc—*Woody Clark*	PO Box 1306, Pendleton OR 97801	541-276-5515	R	1,244*	.1
18	Wolfington Body Company Inc—*Richard Wolfington*	PO Box 218, Exton PA 19341	610-458-8501	R	1,243*	.1
19	Amparts International Inc—*Rodrolfo Duemicatm*	9117 San Mateo Dr Ste, Laredo TX 78045	956-727-3933	R	1,182*	.1
20	ADESA Inc—*Tom Caruso* Kar Auction Services Inc	13085 Hamilton Crossin, Carmel IN 46032	317-815-1100	S	1,104*	11.9

Note: An asterisk (*) indicates an estimated financial figure. The company type code used is as follows: R = Private, P = Public, S = Private Subsidiary, B = Public Subsidiary, D = Division, J = Joint Venture, I = Investment Fund.

COMPANY RANKINGS BY SALES WITHIN 4-DIGIT SIC

Rank	Company Name—Executive Officer	Address, City, State, Zip	Phone	Type	Fin	Empls
21	Yamaha Motor Corporation USA—Akira Sano	6555 Katella Ave, Cypress CA 90630	714-761-7300	R	999	.6
22	Kawasaki Motors Corporation USA—Takeshi Teranishi	PO Box 25252, Santa Ana CA 92799	949-770-0400	S	839*	.4
23	Thomason Auto Group—Poncho Redfern	2575 Automall Pkwy, Fairfield CA 94533	707-402-5700	S	713*	.3
24	Force Protection Inc—Michael Moody	1520 Old Trolley Rd, Summerville SC 29485	843-574-7000	P	656	1.3
25	WD Larson Companies Limited Inc—William D Larson	10700 Lyndale Ave S, Bloomington MN 55420	952-888-4934	R	646*	.5
26	Kenworth Sales Company Inc—R Kyle Treadway	PO Box 65829, Salt Lake City UT 84165	801-487-4161	R	542*	.2
27	Porsche Cars North America Inc—Detlev von Platen	980 Hammond Dr NE Ste, Atlanta GA 30328	770-290-3500	S	455*	.2
28	Gray Daniels Auto Group—Bobby Gray	6060 I 55 N, Jackson MS 39211	601-956-6060	S	428*	.2
29	Kia Motors America Inc—Byung Mo	111 Peters Canyon Rd, Irvine CA 92606	949-468-4800	S	360*	.3
30	Southwest International Trucks Inc—Russ Trimble	PO Box 520, Arlington TX 76004	817-461-2931	R	314*	.3
31	MHC Kenworth—Tim Murphy	1524 N Corrington, Kansas City MO 64120	816-483-7035	R	297*	.2
32	Waters Truck and Tractor Company Inc	PO Box 831 Hwy 82 W, Columbus MS 39703	662-328-1575	R	277*	.1
33	Mission Valley Ford Trucks Sales Inc—Ernie Speno	PO Box 611150, San Jose CA 95161	408-933-2300	R	277*	.1
34	Zipcar Inc—Scott Griffith	25 1st St 4th Fl, Cambridge MA 02141	617-995-4231	P	242	.5
35	Right Honda—Jay Francis	7875 E Frank Lloyd Wri, Scottsdale AZ 85260	480-778-2510	R	241*	.1
36	Around The Clock Freightliner Group LLC	PO Box 272428, Oklahoma City OK 73137	405-942-8827	R	235*	.5
37	Great Lakes Peterbilt Inc—Steve Buha	5900 Southport Rd, Portage IN 46368	219-763-7227	R	235*	.1
38	Audi of America Inc—Johan de Nysschen Volkswagen of America Inc	3800 Hamlin Rd, Auburn Hills MI 48326	248-754-5000	S	220	<.1
39	Tesla Motors Inc—Elon Musk	3500 Deer Creek, Palo Alto CA 94304	650-681-5000	P	204	1.4
40	Fyda Freightliner Columbus Inc—Timothy Fyda	1250 Walcutt Rd, Columbus OH 43228	614-851-0002	R	183*	.1
41	American Suzuki Motor Corp—Kinji Saito	PO Box 1100, Brea CA 92822	714-996-7040	S	179*	.5
42	RDO Truck Center Co—Ronald D Offutt	PO Box 9030, Fargo ND 58106	701-282-5400	S	154*	.1
43	Manning Equipment Inc—Michael Stich	PO Box 23229, Louisville KY 40223	502-426-5210	R	153*	.1
44	Auto Body Panels Inc—Lawana Tzeiranakis	11950 Mosteller Rd, Cincinnati OH 45241	513-771-2886	R	149*	.2
45	Jaguar Land Rover North America LLC—Charles R Hughes	555 MacArthur Blvd, Mahwah NJ 07430		S	141*	.2
46	Matheny Motor Truck Co—Mike Matheny	PO Box 1304, Parkersburg WV 26102	304-485-4418	R	124*	.1
47	Triumph Motorcycles America Ltd—Mark Kennedy	385 Walt Sanders Memor, Newnan GA 30265	678-854-2010	R	123*	.1
48	Premier Truck Centers Inc—TJ Willings	PO Box 820, Fultondale AL 35068	205-841-4450	R	112*	.1
49	McLean County Truck Company Inc—Dan Ryan	607 Truckers Ln, Bloomington IL 61701	309-828-1331	R	98*	.1
50	Rush Truck Center Whittier—Authur Fraser	2450 Kella Ave, Whittier CA 90601	562-692-7267	R	94*	.1
51	Schetky Northwest Sales Inc—Randy Schetky	8430 NE Killingsworth, Portland OR 97220	503-287-4141	R	93*	<.1
52	Buffalo Truck Center Inc	271 Dingens St, Buffalo NY 14206	716-821-9911	R	92*	<.1
53	Peterbilt of Las Vegas Inc—Stuart R Engs Jr	PO Box 335070, North Las Vegas NV 89033	702-657-1500	S	85*	.3
54	Kenworth of Tennessee Inc—Lester Turner Jr	550 Spence Ln, Nashville TN 37210	615-366-5454	R	83*	.3
55	Badger Truck Center Inc—Paul Schlagenhauf	2326 W St Paul Ave, Milwaukee WI 53201	414-344-9500	R	82*	.2
56	Ferrari North America Inc	250 Sylvan Ave, Englewood Cliffs NJ 07632	201-816-2600	S	76*	<.1
57	Crain M-M Sales Inc	770 Pickens Dr Ext, Marietta GA 30062	770-428-4421	R	72*	<.1
58	Holcomb Freightliner Inc—Dave Larsen	PO Box 1747, Sioux Falls SD 57101	605-336-2995	R	71*	.1
59	CrankyApecom—Jay Davis	6352 320th St, Cannon Falls MN 55009	507-263-9234	R	68*	.1
60	Southeast Toyota Port Processing—Ed Sheehy JM Family Enterprises Inc	1751 Talleyrand Ave, Jacksonville FL 32206	904-358-4400	S	63*	.3
61	Duckett Truck Center Inc—Robby Philips	3792 US Hwy 67 N, Poplar Bluff MO 63901	573-785-0193	R	61*	.1
62	OS Hill and Company Inc—Jack Hill	PO Box 2170, East Liverpool OH 43920	330-386-6440	R	56*	.2
63	Sadisco of Florence—Darlene Strickland	2419 W Sumter St, Florence SC 29502	843-669-1941	R	54*	.1
64	Peterbilt Of Utah Inc—Eric Jackson	PO Box 65616, Salt Lake City UT 84165	801-486-8781	R	50*	.1
65	Mike Shaw Texas Motors Inc—Mike Shaw	8015 S Ih 35, San Antonio TX 78224	210-928-1500	R	50*	.1
66	Charlotte Truck Center Inc—Frank Ellett	PO Box 26548, Charlotte NC 28221	704-597-1110	R	49*	.1
67	Montana Peterbilt (BillingsMT)—Kevin Gustaines	PO Drawer 2511, Billings MT 59103	406-252-5867	R	48*	.1
68	Truck Equipment Inc—Steve Kwaterski	PO Box 11296, Green Bay WI 54307	920-494-7451	R	47*	.1
69	Pacific Materials Handling Solutions Inc—Ralph Logan	30361 Whipple Rd, Union City CA 94587	510-429-0303	R	46*	.1
70	Bloomington Subaru—Rudy Luther	7801 Lyndale Ave S, Bloomington MN 55420	952-881-6200	S	45*	<.1
71	Irv Seaver Motorcycles—Evan Bell	607 W Katella Ave, Orange CA 92867	714-532-3700	R	43*	<.1
72	National Car Mart Inc—Stuart Evans	9255 Brookpark Rd, Cleveland OH 44129	216-398-4125	R	42*	<.1
73	Lotus Cars USA Inc—Robert Braner	2236 Northmont Pky, Duluth GA 30096	770-476-6540	R	41*	<.1
74	Parts Central Inc—Milton Butler	3243 Whitfield St, Macon GA 31204	478-745-0878	R	40*	.2
75	Jilco Equipment Leasing Company Inc—Gilbert Pavone	PO Box 455, Cranbury NJ 08512	609-655-5001	R	38*	<.1
76	Pete Store—Carter Baker	5218 Rutledge Pike, Knoxville TN 37924	865-546-9553	R	37*	.1
77	Phoenix Motorcars Inc—Daniel J Elliott	401 S Doubleday Ave, Ontario CA 91761	909-987-0815	R	35*	<.1
78	Nelson Leasing Inc—Dale Nelson	PO Box 993, Willmar MN 56201	320-235-2770	R	34*	.1
79	Trucks and Parts Of Tampa Inc—Lex Goldenberg	1015 S 50th St, Tampa FL 33619	813-247-6636	R	33*	.1
80	Fleet Equipment Corp—Richard Pearson	567 Commerce St, Franklin Lakes NJ 07417	201-337-7332	R	31*	<.1
81	Harbor Truck Sales And Service Inc—Edward Dentz	2723 Annapolis Rd, Baltimore MD 21230	410-685-4474	R	30*	.1
82	Dow Chevrolet Oldsmobile Inc—Ed Dow	1313 S Pacific St, Mineola TX 75773	903-569-2621	R	27*	<.1
83	Haaker Equipment Co—Edward Blackman	2070 N White Ave, La Verne CA 91750	909-542-0800	R	26*	.1
84	Toyota Motor Sales USA Inc—Yukitoshi Funo	19001 S Western Ave, Torrance CA 90501	310-468-4000	S	26*	6.2
85	Western Bus Sales Inc—Marlan Rohlena	30355 Se Hwy 212, Boring OR 97009	503-905-0002	R	26*	.1
86	Don's Truck Sales Inc—Jean Carpenter	PO Box 346, Fairbank IA 50629	319-635-2751	R	23*	<.1
87	Landmark International Trucks Inc—Jim Jablonski	PO Box 6539, Knoxville TN 37914	865-637-4881	R	22*	.1
88	Brasher's Cascade Auto Auction Inc—John Brasher	PO Box 55850, Portland OR 97238	503-492-9200	R	19*	.2
89	Minuteman Trucks Inc—Richard Witcher	2181 Providence Hwy, Walpole MA 02081	508-668-3112	R	19*	.1
90	Bond Equipment Company Inc—Andy Bond	2946 Irving Blvd, Dallas TX 75247	214-637-0760	R	19*	<.1
91	Kenworth Of Cincinnati Inc—John Nichols	PO Box 62477, Cincinnati OH 45262	513-771-5831	R	18*	.1
92	Eck's Garage Inc—Robert Fish	PO Box 269, Muncy PA 17756	570-433-3177	R	18*	<.1
93	Viper Motorcycle Co—John Silseth	2458 W Tech Ln, Auburn AL 36832	334-887-4445	R	18*	<.1
94	C-B Kenworth Inc—Arthur Hicks	42 Wallace Ave, South Portland ME 04106	207-775-6328	R	18*	.1
95	Schoolcraft Auto Auction Inc—Donald Devries	PO Box 697, Schoolcraft MI 49087	269-679-5021	R	17*	.2
96	Brasher's Northwest Auto Auction Inc—Larry Brasher	90485 Auction Way, Eugene OR 97402	541-689-3901	R	16*	.1
97	Globe Trailer Manufacturing Inc—Jeffrey Walters	3101 59th Ave Dr E, Bradenton FL 34203	941-753-2199	R	15*	<.1
98	Trans West Truck Inc—Richard Textor	PO Box 1220, Fontana CA 92334	909-829-8801	R	15*	.1
99	Suncall America Inc—Uji Isono	505 Industrial Pkwy, Richmond IN 47374	765-966-9656	R	15*	.1
100	Abc Minneapolis LLC—Chuck Eck	PO Box 360, Osseo MN 55369	763-428-8777	R	15*	.1
101	Elliott/Wilson Trucks LLC—George H Wilson Jr	327 N Aurora St, Easton MD 21601	410-822-0066	R	14*	<.1
102	Superior Auto Sales Inc—Richard J Izzo	5201 Camp Rd, Hamburg NY 14075	716-649-6695	R	14*	<.1
103	Glover's Transmission And Rear End Inc—James Glover	PO Box 16084, Little Rock AR 72231	501-945-2000	R	13*	.1
104	Fyda Freightliner Youngstown Inc—Walter Fyda	5260 76 Dr, Youngstown OH 44515	330-797-0224	R	13*	.1
105	Motor Power Equipment Co—Bruce Sunwall	PO Box 80030, Billings MT 59108	406-252-5651	R	13*	.1
106	Mid-America Auto Auction Inc—Brad Phillips	4716 S Santa Fe St Ste, Wichita KS 67216	316-522-8195	R	12*	.1
107	First Choice Auto Auction Inc—John Nichols	825 Rankin Rd, Houston TX 77073	281-821-2300	R	12*	.1
108	Jack Doheny Supplies Inc—Jack Doheny	PO Box 609, Northville MI 48167	248-349-0904	R	12*	.1

Rank	Company Name—*Executive Officer*	Address, City, State, Zip	Phone	Type	Fin	Empls
109	Greater Rockford Auto Auction Inc—*Dwight Clark*	5937 Sandy Hollow Rd, Rockford IL 61109	815-874-7800	R	11*	.1
110	Albany Auto Auction Inc—*Wilburn Ivy*	1421 Liberty Expy Se, Albany GA 31705	229-435-7708	R	11*	.1
111	Graa LP—*Mark Capel*	2380 Port Sheldon Ct, Jenison MI 49428		R	10*	.1
112	Orlando Auto Auction Inc—*Daniel Berry*	4636 W Colonial Dr, Orlando FL 32808	407-290-2813	R	10*	.1
113	Pittsburgh Mack Sales and Service Inc—*James Feucht*	1501 Beaver Ave, Pittsburgh PA 15233	412-237-6000	R	10*	.1
114	H A Dehart and Son—*Dennis Noon*	311 Crown Point Rd, Thorofare NJ 08086	856-845-2800	R	10*	<.1
115	Jacksonville Auto Auction Inc—*Ben Lange*	11982 New Kings Rd, Jacksonville FL 32219	904-764-7653	R	10*	.1
116	North American Autonet Inc—*Blake Morris*	2400 Lkeview Pkwy Ste, Alpharetta GA 30009	770-740-1330	R	10*	<.1
117	Deluxe International Trucks Inc—*Eugene Sidor*	600 S River St, Hackensack NJ 07601	201-641-2000	R	10*	<.1
118	West Houston Volkswagen LLC—*Carol Durden*	17113 Katy Fwy, Houston TX 77094	281-675-8600	R	10*	.1
119	Diesel Truck Sales Inc—*Jeff Warren*	PO Box 1428, Saginaw MI 48605	989-753-4481	R	10*	.1
120	Adesa St Louis—*Jim Hallett*	7858 Us Hwy 61/67, Barnhart MO 63012	636-475-9311	R	9*	.1
121	Ducati North America Inc—*Michael Lock*	10443 Bandley Dr, Cupertino CA 95014	408-253-0499	R	9*	<.1
122	New York Bus Sales LLC—*Don Bielby*	7765 Lakeport Rd, Chittenango NY 13037	315-687-3969	R	9*	.1
123	Central Mass Auto Auction Inc—*Michael Saad*	PO Box 346, Oxford MA 01540	508-987-6803	R	9*	.1
124	Martin Apparatus Inc—*Leon Martin*	14233 Interdrive W, Houston TX 77032	281-442-6806	R	8*	<.1
125	Pinnacle Truck and Trailer Sales LLC	176 Charter Pl, La Vergne TN 37086	615-793-9890	R	8*	.1
126	Rochester Syracuse Auto Auction LP—*Scott Prankie*	PO Box 129, Waterloo NY 13165	315-539-5006	R	8*	.1
127	FSR Inc—*Nick Pund*	PO Box 247, Fall Branch TN 37656	423-348-8419	R	8*	.1
128	Gainesville Truck Center Inc—*Michael Allison*	PO Box J, Gainesville GA 30503	770-532-8463	R	8*	<.1
129	B and G Equipment Inc—*Robert Mathews*	3960 W Fort St, Detroit MI 48216	313-554-4400	R	8*	<.1
130	Kassbohrer All Terrain Vehicles Inc—*John Gilbert*	750a S Rock Blvd, Reno NV 89502	775-857-5000	R	7*	<.1
131	Charles Watkins Automobiles Inc—*Terry Watkins*	PO Box 919, Forest City NC 28043	828-245-0128	R	7*	<.1
132	Cedar Rapids Truck Center Inc—*George Grask*	PO Box 67, Cedar Rapids IA 52406	319-848-4131	R	7*	<.1
133	Sioux Falls Kenworth Inc—*William Rush*	4500 N Cliff Ave, Sioux Falls SD 57104	605-332-7112	R	7*	.1
134	Gilbert Motor Company Inc—*Curtis Gilbert*	PO Box 337, Chesnee SC 29323	864-461-7015	R	7*	.1
135	Fleet Lease Disposal Inc—*Ronald Sanders*	272 Se 5th Ave, Delray Beach FL 33483	561-266-8704	R	7*	<.1
136	De Luxe Sales And Service Inc—*Arthur Stein*	600 S River St, Hackensack NJ 07601	201-641-2000	R	7*	.1
137	Trailer Equipment Inc—*Ross Wellman*	1701 Steele Ave Sw, Grand Rapids MI 49507	616-248-0600	R	7*	<.1
138	Bryant Motors Inc—*William Bryant*	1300 Bronson Way N, Renton WA 98057	425-255-3478	R	7*	<.1
139	Milea Hudson Valley Truck Center Corp—*John Degnan*	1708 Rte 9, Wappingers Falls NY 12590	845-297-3988	R	7*	<.1
140	Mc Cormick Motors Inc—*Bernie Beer*	1255 W Market St, Nappanee IN 46550	574-773-3134	R	6*	<.1
141	Elder Equipment Leasing Of Wyoming—*Bruce Grath*	663 Cir Dr, Casper WY 82601	307-265-0450	R	6*	<.1
142	Mc Equipment Inc—*John Mcgill*	1171 S Williams Dr, Columbia City IN 46725	260-244-7661	R	6*	<.1
143	Muster Associates Inc—*John Muster*	PO Box 160, Calhoun KY 42327	270-273-3619	R	6*	<.1
144	Obs Inc—*Robert Ferne*	PO Box 6210, Canton OH 44706	330-453-3725	R	6*	<.1
145	West Colonial Hyundai Inc—*Carl Atkinson*	4110 W Colonial Dr, Orlando FL 32808	407-578-5337	R	6*	<.1
146	Dickirson Group Ltd—*David Dickirson*	PO Box 750, Ripley WV 25271	304-372-9111	R	6*	<.1
147	National Bus Sales And Leasing Inc—*John Smith*	PO Box 6549, Marietta GA 30065	770-422-8920	R	6*	<.1
148	Wills Brothers Muncie Auto Auction—*Chet Wills*	PO Box 2022, Muncie IN 47307	765-288-1861	R	6*	<.1
149	WMI Auto Auction LLC—*David Lubinski*	PO Box 38, Holmen WI 54636	608-526-9316	R	6*	<.1
150	Kasp Inc—*Frances Williams*	5921 Athens Boonesboro, Lexington KY 40509	859-263-2129	R	6*	<.1
151	Lynnway Auto Auction Inc—*Jim Lamb*	732r Lynnway, Lynn MA 01905	781-596-8500	R	6*	<.1
152	H and H Mack Sales Inc—*William Horne*	PO Box 693, Rockaway NJ 07866	973-625-3330	R	5*	<.1
153	Sharron Group Inc—*Thomas Ewers*	7605 Commerce Pl, Plain City OH 43064	614-873-5856	R	5*	<.1
154	Baker Truck Equipment Co—*David Beltzeo*	PO Box 482, Hurricane WV 25526	304-722-3814	R	5*	<.1
155	D and K Truck Co—*Ed Bennett*	319 E N St, Lansing MI 48906	517-484-1905	R	5*	<.1
156	Ljl Truck Center Inc—*Timothy Lockooky*	PO Box 27510, Macon GA 31221	478-784-3100	R	5*	.1
157	Bay City Motors Inc—*Van Fortier*	PO Box 338, Abbeville LA 70511	337-893-3126	R	5*	<.1
158	Mack Mid-Hudson Inc—*Albert Perratore*	135 Neelytown Rd, Montgomery NY 12549	845-457-7000	R	5*	<.1
159	ICA Auctions—*Stanley Torgerson*	1265 S Gilbert Rd, Gilbert AZ 85296		R	5*	<.1
160	Autometrics—*John Hafez*	10200 San Pablo Ave, El Cerrito CA 94530	510-524-0225	R	5*	<.1
161	United Auto Sales Of Utica Inc—*Joseph Steet*	PO Box 28, New York Mills NY 13417	315-736-3362	R	5*	<.1
162	Dave Gill Trucks Inc—*David Gill*	3901 N Main St, East Peoria IL 61611	309-698-7162	R	5*	<.1
163	Reliable Trailer Systems Inc—*Tom Beale*	PO Box 42210, Indianapolis IN 46242	317-241-7180	R	5*	<.1
164	Peter Garafano and Son Inc—*Peter Garafano*	500 Marshall St, Paterson NJ 07503	973-345-9200	R	5*	<.1
165	Mack L Victoria LC—*Tomi Rayburn*	PO Box 2551, Victoria TX 77902	361-575-0675	R	5*	<.1
166	Liddell Trailers LLC—*Betty Bagley*	PO Box 20010, Tuscaloosa AL 35402	205-467-3990	R	4*	<.1
167	Meshkani Company Inc—*David Aynehchi*	2345 N Grand Ave, Santa Ana CA 92705	714-973-8600	R	4*	<.1
168	Taylor Transfer Inc—*Kevin Taylor*	PO Box 668, Boardman OR 97818	541-481-2736	R	4*	<.1
169	Rushent Sales Inc—*Anthony Rushent*	PO Box 2274, Woodinville WA 98072	425-481-6541	R	4*	<.1
170	J and D Equipment Inc—*Douglas Keith*	3250 Harvester Rd, Kansas City KS 66115	913-342-1450	R	4*	<.1
171	Us Connection—*Peter Marosi*	PO Box 1383, Hermosa Beach CA 90254	310-669-3090	R	4*	<.1
172	Segebarth General Contracting Inc—*Bradley Segebarth*	PO Box 72, Lebanon MO 65536	417-532-9808	R	4*	<.1
173	Zeiger Enterprises Inc—*Shelly Zeiger*	1701 New Willow St, Trenton NJ 08638	609-394-1000	R	4*	<.1
174	Bugbasher Inc—*Mark Leresche*	2910 W Apache Trl, Apache Junction AZ 85120	480-346-0600	R	4*	<.1
175	Peach Chevrolet—*Chard Peach*	2227 Douglas Ave, Brewton AL 36426	251-867-0506	R	4*	<.1
176	T-W Truck Equippers Of Central New York Inc—*Patrick Hodgson*	PO Box 414, Depew NY 14043	716-683-2250	R	4*	<.1
177	B and G Auto Sales Inc—*Shirley Chadwick*	PO Box 590, Colton CA 92324	909-825-1173	R	4*	<.1
178	A-B International Truck Inc—*S Alexander*	2131 Hanover Ave, Allentown PA 18109	610-433-5167	R	4*	<.1
179	General Gmc Truck Sales and Service Inc—*Madeline Santi*	360 S Military Trl, West Palm Beach FL 33415	561-686-8906	R	4*	<.1
180	Desert Trailer Systems Inc—*Jack Kaslly*	2733 W Buckeye Rd, Phoenix AZ 85009	602-272-8910	R	4*	<.1
181	Dealers Auto Auction Of Idaho LLC—*Todd Carlson*	3323 Port St, Nampa ID 83687	208-463-8250	R	3*	<.1
182	Carolina Auto Auction Inc—*Henry Stanley*	PO Box 5677, Anderson SC 29623	864-231-7000	R	3*	<.1
183	Car Zone Auto Sales Inc—*Mark Ramahi*	5350 Austell Rd, Austell GA 30106	770-739-5817	R	3*	<.1
184	NE Penna Salvage Company Inc—*Jean Conlon*	PO Box 596, Pittston PA 18640	570-654-1709	R	3*	<.1
185	Jenkins Hyundia Of Leesburg—*Jason Kirkland*	PO Box 895190, Leesburg FL 34789	352-326-3585	R	3*	<.1
186	Jerry's Transmission Service Inc—*Walter Pawelk*	18448 County Rd 9, Lester Prairie MN 55354	320-395-2529	R	3*	<.1
187	Mel's Auto Specialists Inc—*Shawn Samuels*	4203 Glenwood Rd, Brooklyn NY 11210	718-421-0525	R	3*	<.1
188	Boyd Chevrolet Of South Hill Va Inc—*Charles Boyd*	200 W Danville St, South Hill VA 23970	434-447-3111	R	3*	<.1
189	Capital Bus Sales and Service Of Texas Inc—*Don Paull*	PO Box 1758, Leander TX 78646	512-528-0001	R	3*	<.1
190	Delaware Public Auto Auction—*Doug Powell*	2323 N Dupont Pkwy, New Castle DE 19720	302-656-0500	R	3*	<.1
191	Robert Mcdorman—*Robert Mcdorman*	1305 N Main St, Vidor TX 77662	409-783-9020	R	3*	<.1
192	United Taxi Cab Company Inc—*Loretta Chapman*	1600 Shirley Ave, Joppa MD 21085	410-676-2200	R	3*	<.1
193	Manheim Indianapolis Auto Auction	3110 S Post Rd, Indianapolis IN 46239	317-862-8622	R	3*	<.1
194	Deerfield Auto Tag Agency Inc—*Paul Espinel*	2265 W Hillsboro Blvd, Deerfield Beach FL 33442	954-596-2134	R	3*	<.1
195	Alpha Trx Inc—*Zayda Villarreal*	6402 Mcpherson Rd Apt, Laredo TX 78041	210-858-6575	H	2*	<.1
196	Central Motors—*Kelly Eikenborg*	5660 392nd St, North Branch MN 55056	651-674-7017	R	2*	<.1
197	Center Point Ambulance Services—*Michael Techau*	PO Box 202, Center Point IA 52213	319-849-3865	R	2*	<.1

Note: An asterisk (*) indicates an estimated financial figure. The company type code used is as follows: R = Private, P = Public, S = Private Subsidiary, B = Public Subsidiary, D = Division, J = Joint Venture, I = Investment Fund.

COMPANY RANKINGS BY SALES WITHIN 4-DIGIT SIC

Rank	Company Name—*Executive Officer*	Address, City, State, Zip	Phone	Type	Fin	Empls
198	Wabash Trailer Sales LLC—*Susan Rudewicz*	3217 Alton Park Blvd, Chattanooga TN 37410	423-266-9100	R	2*	<.1
199	Central Arkansas Auto Auction Inc—*Kelton Keathley*	205 Foster Dr, Beebe AR 72012	501-882-6447	R	2*	<.1
200	Blue Ridge Enterprizes Inc—*Michael Jacobs*	4139 Blue Mountain Rd, Oxford NC 27565	919-661-9711	R	2*	<.1
201	Ben Shives Truck Super Center Inc—*Ben Shives*	2000 9th St W, Bradenton FL 34205	941-714-0300	R	2*	<.1
202	Jim Taylor Chevrolet Olds Pontiac Gmc Truck Inc—*Jim Taylor*	2410 St Charles St, Fort Benton MT 59442	406-622-3321	R	2*	<.1
203	Moped Mafia—*Adria Lesher*	43451 Shasta Pl, Indio CA 92201	760-397-7456	R	1*	<.1
204	Point Pleasant Plumsteadville Ems—*Lynn Fillman*	PO Box 391, Plumsteadville PA 18949	215-766-7285	R	1*	<.1
205	Haddam Volunteer Ambulance Service Inc—*Scott Stoppa*	PO Box 48, Higganum CT 06441	860-345-2500	R	<1*	<.1
206	Kansas City Auto Auction Inc Manheim	3901 N Skiles Ave, Kansas City MO 64161	816-452-4084	S	N/A	.4
207	Premier Truck Sales and Rental Inc—*Joseph Lojek*	5800 W Canal Rd, Cleveland OH 44125	216-642-5000	R	N/A	<.1

TOTALS: SIC 5012 Automobiles & Other Motor Vehicles
Companies: 207

					282,782	109.1

5013 Motor Vehicle Supplies & New Parts

Rank	Company Name—*Executive Officer*	Address, City, State, Zip	Phone	Type	Fin	Empls
1	Ford Motor Service Co—*William Ford Jr*	1 American Rd, Dearborn MI 48121	313-322-3000	S	26,239*	1.9
2	Genuine Parts Co—*Thomas C Gallagher*	2999 Circle 75 Pkwy, Atlanta GA 30339	770-953-1700	P	11,208	29.5
3	Visteon Corp—*Donald J Stebbins*	1 Village Center Dr, Van Buren Township MI 48111	734-710-5000	P	8,047	26.0
4	GM Service Parts Operation—*JF Smith*	PO Box 6020, Grand Blanc MI 48480	810-606-2000	R	5,070*	12.0
5	GM Service Parts Operations—*Frederick A Henderson*	6060 Bristol Rd, Flint MI 48554	810-635-5000	D	5,000	15.0
6	Delphi Saginaw Steering Systems	5725 Delphi Dr, Troy MI 48098	248-813-2000	D'	4,214*	10.1
7	FleetPride Inc—*Todd Dunn*	8708 Technology Forest, The Woodlands TX 77381		R	3,241*	2.5
8	LDI Ltd—*David N Shane*	54 Monument Cir Ste 80, Indianapolis IN 46204	317-237-5400	R	3,225*	2.0
9	General Parts Inc—*O Temple Sloan Jr*	PO Box 26006, Raleigh NC 27611	919-573-3000	S	3,118*	18.0
10	MCI Service Parts Inc—*Tom Sorrells*	1700 E Golf Rd, Schaumburg IL 60173	847-285-2000	S	1,863*	2.0
11	Great Dane Trailers Inc—*Scott Ashley*	PO Box 67, Savannah GA 31402	912-232-4471	R	1,828*	4.3
12	CARQUEST Corp—*Robert Blair*	PO Box 26929, Raleigh NC 27611	919-573-3000	R	1,800*	18.0
13	Qualitor Inc—*Richard Snell*	24800 Denso Dr Ste 255, Southfield MI 48033	248-204-8600	R	1,576*	.8
14	Universal Cooperative Inc—*Terry Bohman*	1300 Corporate Center, Eagan MN 55121	651-239-1000	R	1,357*	.8
15	US Farathane Corp—*Bill Kemner*	38000 Mound Rd, Sterling Heights MI 48310	586-978-2800	R	1,240*	.9
16	Creation Group Inc	1120 N Main St, Elkhart IN 46514		S	1,143*	1.0
17	RB Matheson Trucking Inc—*Robert B Matheson*	9785 Goethe Rd, Sacramento CA 95827	916-685-2330	R	1,084*	1.0
18	Tucker Rocky Distributor Inc—*Steve Johnson* LDI Ltd	4900 Alliance Gateway, Fort Worth TX 76177	817-258-9000	S	909*	.6
19	Lacy Diversified Industries—*David Shane*	54 Monument Cir Ste 80, Indianapolis IN 46204	317-237-5400	R	855*	<.1
20	Keystone Automotive Industries Inc—*Richard L Keister*	700 E Bonita Ave, Pomona CA 91767	909-624-8041	S	714	3.8
21	AAP St Marys Corp—*Randy Wendel*	1100 McKinley Rd, Saint Marys OH 45885	419-394-7840	S	690*	.4
22	Auto Wares Inc—*Fred Bunting*	440 Kirtland St SW, Grand Rapids MI 49507	616-243-2125	R	661*	1.6
23	S and S Automotive Inc—*R Kushner*	740 N Larch Ave, Elmhurst IL 60126	630-279-1600	R	658*	.4
24	Interstate Battery System of Dallas Inc—*Carlos Sepulveda*	12770 Merit Dr Ste 400, Dallas TX 75251		R	590*	.5
25	Insurance Auto Auctions Inc—*Thomas C O'Brien*	2 Westbrook Corp Ctr S, Westchester IL 60154	708-492-7000	S	441*	1.2
26	Henniges Automotive North America Inc—*Rob Depierre*	36600 Corporate Dr, Farmington Hills MI 48331	248-553-5300	R	426*	.2
27	O'Reilly Ozark Automotive—*Greg Henslee*	PO Box 15178, Little Rock AR 72231	501-945-8383	R	414*	.3
28	Mighty Distributing System of America Inc—*Ken VoelkerBarry*	650 Engineering Dr, Norcross GA 30092	770-448-3900	R	410*	.3
29	Airtex Products LP—*Bruce Zorich*	407 W Main St, Fairfield IL 62837	618-842-2111	R	299*	.8
30	Factory Motor Parts Co—*Elliot Badzin*	1380 Corporate Center, Eagan MN 55121	651-405-3600	R	296*	.2
31	Johnson Industries—*Bret Robyck* Genuine Parts Co	5944 Peachtree Corners, Norcross GA 30071	770-441-1128	S	295*	.2
32	Automotive Supply Associates Inc—*George Segal*	129 Manchester St, Concord NH 03301	603-225-4000	R	213*	.1
33	B/T Western Corp—*Steve Rosenbluth*	4 Upper Newport Plz Ste 120, Newport Beach CA 92660	949-476-8424	R	211*	<.1
34	PACCAR Inc Parts Div—*Bill Jackson*	750 Houser Way N, Renton WA 98055	425-254-4400	D	210*	.3
35	Middle Atlantic Warehouse Distributor Inc—*Jacques Landreville*	601 Vickers St, Tonawanda NY 14150	716-694-0200	R	204*	1.6
36	Midas Inc—*Alan D Feldman*	1300 Arlington Heights, Itasca IL 60143	630-438-3000	P	192	.9
37	Henderson Wheel and Warehouse Supply—*Michael S Henderson*	1825 S 300 West, Salt Lake City UT 84115	801-486-2073	R	162*	.1
38	Austin Hardware and Supply Inc—*Donald Austin*	PO Box 887, Lees Summit MO 64063	816-246-2800	R	161*	.1
39	Medart Inc (Fenton Missouri)—*Michael Medart*	124 Manufacturers Dr, Arnold MO 63010	636-282-2300	R	161*	.1
40	Automotive Supply Co—*Casey Wewerka*	PO Box 145, Appleton WI 54912	920-734-2651	R	148*	.1
41	Motorcycle Stuff Inc—*Frank Espanito*	18225 Serene Dr Ste 15, Morgan Hill CA 95037	408-778-0500	R	148*	.1
42	Zf Technologies LLC—*Greg White*	15811 Centennial Dr, Northville MI 48168	734-416-6200	R	146*	.4
43	Dorman Products Div—*Richard Berman*	25 Dorman Dr, Warsaw KY 41095	859-567-7000	D	123*	.3
44	LeMans Corp—*Fred Fox*	PO Box 5222, Janesville WI 53547	608-758-1111	R	122*	.5
45	Hahn Automotive Warehouse Inc—*Eli N Futerman*	415 W Main St, Rochester NY 14608	585-235-1595	R	110*	1.0
46	Coast Distribution System Inc—*James I Musbach*	350 Woodview Ave, Morgan Hill CA 95037	408-782-6686	P	109	.3
47	Marvin Land Systems—*Jerry Friedman*	261 W Beach Ave, Inglewood CA 90302	310-674-5030	R	105*	.3
48	Southwest Brake and Parts Inc—*Anthony Holaski*	951 S Dix St, Detroit MI 48217	313-842-8000	R	96*	.1
49	Interamerican Motor Corp—*Bart Noyes*	PO Box 3939, Canoga Park CA 91304		R	84*	.2
50	Yazaki North America Inc—*George Perry*	6801 N Haggerty Rd, Canton MI 48187	734-983-1000	R	82*	1.5
51	Southern Pump and Tank Co—*Charley Tew*	PO Box 31516, Charlotte NC 28231	704-596-4373	R	73*	.2
52	Lg Chem Michigan Inc—*Prabhakar Patil*	10717 Adams St, Holland MI 49423	248-307-1800	R	73*	.2
53	Zitco Inc—*Lowell Zitzloff*	5251 W 74th St, Minneapolis MN 55439	952-392-6060	R	69*	.2
54	Aamco Transmissions Inc—*Marc Graham*	201 Gibraltar Rd, Horsham PA 19044	215-643-5885	R	67*	.2
55	Aisin World Corporation of America—*Yasuhito Yamaucki*	46501 Commerce Center, Plymouth MI 48170	734-453-5551	S	63*	.2
56	Cummins Southern Plains LLC—*David Gillikin*	600 N Watson Rd, Arlington TX 76011	817-640-6801	S	63*	.2
57	Frank Edwards Co—*Robert Edwards Jr*	3626 W Parkway Blvd, Salt Lake City UT 84120	801-736-8000	R	63*	.2
58	Regional International Corp—*James Carello*	1007 Lehigh Station Rd, Henrietta NY 14467	585-359-2011	R	62*	.2
59	Western States Equipment—*Tommy Harris*	PO Box 38, Boise ID 83707	208-888-2287	R	62*	.6
60	Stag/Parkway Inc—*Stanley I Sunshine*	PO Box 43463, Atlanta GA 30336	404-349-1918	R	61*	.3
61	Pacific Supply Co—*Sanford Wayne*	6545 Caballero Blvd, Buena Park CA 90620	714-670-3100	R	60*	.4
62	Ack Controls Inc—*Ryuichi Kinase*	PO Box 1297, Glasgow KY 42142	270-678-6200	R	59*	.7
63	LoJack of New Jersey Corp—*Richard Riley*	12 N Rte 17, Paramus NJ 07652	201-368-8716	S	58*	<.1
64	Asher Management Group Ltd—*Ronald Levene*	PO Box 688, Buckingham PA 18912	607-723-8600	R	58*	.2
65	Lionel Harris Oil Company Inc—*Lionel Harris*	PO Box 112, Cushing OK 74023	918-225-2759	R	58*	<.1
66	Arnold Motor Supply Co—*Grant Schenk*	PO Box 320, Spencer IA 51301	712-262-1141	R	55*	.2
67	KOI Siferd-Hossellman Co—*Carl Stephens*	PO Box 450, Lima OH 45801	419-228-1221	R	55*	<.1
68	Falls Auto Parts and Supplies Inc—*James Nelessen*	N89w16688 Grant Ave, Menomonee Falls WI 53051	262-251-0400	R	54*	<.1
69	Fallsway Equipment Company Inc—*Harry F Fairhurst*	PO Box 4537, Akron OH 44310	330-633-6000	R	52*	.1
70	PBE Jobbers Warehouse Inc—*Paul Monroe*	2921 Syene Rd, Madison WI 53713	608-274-8797	R	52*	.1
71	Carnegie Body Co—*Rick Sippola*	9500 Brookpark Rd, Cleveland OH 44129	216-749-5000	R	48*	.1
72	Exedy Globalparts Corp—*Tetsuya Yoshinaga*	8601 Haggerty Rd, Belleville MI 48111	734-397-3333	R	46*	<.1

Rank	Company Name—*Executive Officer*	Address, City, State, Zip	Phone	Type	Fin	Empls
73	Integrated Supply Network LLC—*D Weber*	PO Box 90009, Lakeland FL 33804	863-603-0777	R	44*	.3
74	Drive Train Industries Inc—*James Burke Sr*	5555 Joliet St, Denver CO 80239	303-292-1100	R	44*	.2
75	Distributors Warehouse Inc (Paducah Kentucky)—*Steve Korte*	PO Box 7239, Paducah KY 42002	270-442-8201	R	44*	<.1
76	Tmd Friction Inc—*Le Gentil Xavier R*	1035 Crooks Rd, Troy MI 48084	248-280-4050	R	42*	.3
77	RBI Corp—*William T Miller*	10201 Cedar Ridge Dr, Ashland VA 23005	804-550-2210	R	42*	.1
78	Six Robblees Inc—*Andy Robblee*	11010 Tukwila Intl Blv, Tukwila WA 98168	206-767-7970	R	40*	.2
79	Vesuvius Inc—*Robert Berkstresser*	2516 N Lee Hwy, Lexington VA 24450	540-463-3478	R	40*	.1
80	Aluminum Line Products Co—*Ed Murray*	24460 Sperry Cir, Westlake OH 44145	440-835-8880	R	39*	<.1
81	Gold Eagle Co—*Marc Blackman*	4400 S Kildare Ave, Chicago IL 60632	773-376-4400	R	39*	.2
82	Interstate Diesel Service Inc—*Alfred Buescher*	4901 Lakeside Ave E, Cleveland OH 44114	216-881-0015	R	38*	.3
83	Fleet Specialties Co—*Richard Van Dyke*	31700 Bainbrook Ct, Westlake Village CA 91361	818-889-1716	R	37*	<.1
84	Lindbergh Liquidating Inc—*Brian Bauchamp*	11109 Lindbergh Busine, Saint Louis MO 63123	314-894-9868	R	37*	.1
85	Rim and Wheel Service Inc—*Dick Brockston*	1014 Gest St, Cincinnati OH 45203	513-721-6940	R	35*	.1
86	Roppel Industries Inc—*Thomas V Roppel*	829 Logan St, Louisville KY 40204	502-581-1004	R	34*	.1
87	Penda Corp—*Ulf Buergel*	PO Box 449, Portage WI 53901	608-742-5301	R	32*	.8
88	Valley Truck Parts Inc—*Jack Goodale*	1900 Chicago Dr Sw, Grand Rapids MI 49519	616-241-5431	R	31*	.2
89	Cyton Industries Inc—*John Graham*	5558 Bill Cody Rd, Hidden Hills CA 91302	818-999-3398	R	31*	.1
90	Nc Auto Parts LLC—*Steven Crystal*	1150 Matley Ln, Reno NV 89502	775-329-0707	R	31*	.1
91	Jead Auto Supply Inc—*David Barbag*	1810 E Tremont Ave, Bronx NY 10460	718-792-7113	R	30*	.1
92	NTW—*Ross Scullion*	20 Fairfield Pl, West Caldwell NJ 07006	973-808-4639	S	30*	.1
93	Xl Parts Partnership Ltd—*Ali Attayi*	15701 NW Fwy, Jersey Village TX 77040	713-983-1100	R	30*	.2
94	Shop Auto Parts Inc—*Paul Machenry*	201 Executive Dr, Moorestown NJ 08057	856-273-9252	R	29*	.1
95	Northern Factory Sales Inc—*Roger Gauquie*	PO Box 660, Willmar MN 56201	320-235-2288	R	29*	.1
96	D and W Diesel Inc—*Douglas Wayne*	1503 Clark St Rd, Auburn NY 13021	315-253-2324	R	28*	.2
97	Automotive Parts Headquarters Inc—*John Bartlett*	PO Box 1338, Saint Cloud MN 56302	320-252-5411	R	28*	.7
98	Kunkel Services Co—*John Kunkel*	PO Box 676, Abingdon MD 21009	410-679-1200	D	28*	.3
99	Ring and Pinion Service Inc—*Randy Lyman*	10411 Airport Rd SE, Everett WA 98204	425-347-1199	R	28*	.1
100	Performance Warehouse Co—*Lyle Moore*	9440 N Whitaker Rd, Portland OR 97217	503-286-7130	R	27*	.2
101	Shinn Fu Company Of America Inc—*Steven Huang*	10939 N Pomona Ave, Kansas City MO 64153	816-891-6390	R	27*	.1
102	Rowerdink Inc—*John Rowerdink*	211 Fuller Ave Ne, Grand Rapids MI 49503	616-459-3274	R	27*	.1
103	Atlantic Pacific Automotive LP—*Judy Brown*	PO Box 381900, Germantown TN 38183	901-755-5555	R	26*	.2
104	Wal Inc—*William Walaska*	PO Box 5910, Providence RI 02903	401-751-5866	R	25*	.1
105	Monroe Truck Equipment Inc—*David Quade*	1051 W 7th St, Monroe WI 53566	608-328-8127	R	25*	.7
106	Reviva Inc—*Josh Stahls*	5130 Main St Ne, Minneapolis MN 55421	763-535-8900	R	25*	.2
107	Peugeot Citroen Engines—*Richard A Darienzo*	150 Clove Rd, Little Falls NJ 07424	973-812-7600	D	25*	<.1
108	Kyb America LLC—*Michael Casper*	140 N Mitchell Ct Ste, Addison IL 60101	630-620-5555	R	24*	.1
109	Buyers Products Co—*James Kleinman*	9049 Tyler Blvd, Mentor OH 44060	440-974-8888	R	24*	.2
110	Service Champ Ii LP—*Fred Berman*	180 New Britain Blvd, Chalfont PA 18914	215-822-8500	R	23*	.2
111	Sosmetal Products Inc—*Milton Soskin*	PO Box 4763, Philadelphia PA 19134	215-739-6200	R	22*	.2
112	Jack Young Company Inc—*Irwin Young*	354 Cambridge St, Boston MA 02134	617-782-1250	R	22*	.1
113	Levins Auto Supply LLC—*Kim Thayer*	8141 Elder Creek Rd, Sacramento CA 95824	916-381-8555	R	22*	.1
114	Wheeler Brothers Inc—*David Wheeler*	PO Box 737, Somerset PA 15501	814-443-7000	R	22*	.2
115	R F Berkheimer And Sons Inc—*Dean Berkheimer*	2770 Lewisberry Rd, York PA 17404	717-767-6544	R	21*	.1
116	Brock Supply Co—*Jerry Brock*	PO Box 1000, Tempe AZ 85280	480-968-2222	R	20*	<.1
117	Mckay Auto Parts Inc—*James Kay*	PO Box 70, Litchfield IL 62056	217-324-3971	R	20*	.2
118	Europacific Parts International Inc—*James Piper*	PO Box 28989, Santa Ana CA 92799	949-553-3900	R	20*	.2
119	Florig Equipment Company Inc—*Marrissa Florig*	906 W Ridge Pke, Conshohocken PA 19428	610-825-0900	R	19*	.1
120	Fleet Acquisitions LLC	6510 Golden Groves Ln, Tampa FL 33610	813-621-1734	R	19*	.1
121	Kay Automotive Distributors Inc—*Jona Karadish*	14650 Calvert St, Van Nuys CA 91411	818-781-6850	R	19*	.1
122	Radiator Express Warehouse—*Joe Rippey*	4401 Park Rd, Benicia CA 94510	707-747-7400	R	19*	.1
123	Crown Automotive Sales Company Inc—*Herbert Gerber*	PO Box 607, Marshfield MA 02050	781-319-3100	R	19*	.1
124	Motive Parts Company Of St Louis—*Dave Jackson*	11109 Lindbergh Bus Ct, Saint Louis MO 63123	314-894-9868	R	18*	.1
125	Precision International Automotive Products Inc—*Dennis Marshall*	PO Box 540, Yaphank NY 11980	631-567-2000	R	18*	.1
126	Ideal Automotive and Truck Accessories Corp—*Daniel Cramer*	6560 Powerline Rd, Fort Lauderdale FL 33309	954-493-9800	R	18*	.1
127	Southeastern Automotive Warehouse Inc—*W Ward*	460 Decatur St Se, Atlanta GA 30312	404-523-5591	R	18*	.1
128	Sb Midwest Holding Corp—*James Scales*	PO Box 336, Boonville IN 47601	812-897-0900	R	18*	.1
129	Toyota Motor Distributors Inc—*Chris Cento*	440 Forbes Blvd, Mansfield MA 02048	508-339-5701	S	18*	.1
130	Hilite International Inc—*Joseph W Carreras*	127 Public Square, Cleveland OH 44114	216-771-6700	R	17*	<.1
131	Twinco Romax LLC—*Marc Hasko*	PO Box 12, Hamel MN 55340	763-478-2360	R	17*	.1
132	Cook Brothers Automotive Inc—*Richard Cook*	12600 Naves Cross Rd N, Cumberland MD 21502	301-722-2525	R	17*	<.1
133	Parts Plus Of New Mexico Inc—*Adam Honegger*	5900 Office Blvd Ne, Albuquerque NM 87109	505-341-7000	R	16*	.1
134	Wetherill Associates Inc—*Jeffery Sween*	411 Eagleview Blvd Ste, Exton PA 19341	484-875-6600	R	16*	.4
135	Coast To Coast International—*Mitch Nunes*	8820 Maislin Dr, Tampa FL 33637	813-980-6166	R	16*	.1
136	Clf Warehouse Inc—*Dan Straszewski*	PO Box 3267, Santa Fe Springs CA 90670	562-946-0066	R	16*	.1
137	Concho Supply Inc—*Jack Hinson*	PO Box 3487, San Angelo TX 76902	325-949-4649	R	16*	.1
138	Weldon Parts Inc—*David Settles*	711 W California Ave, Oklahoma City OK 73102	405-272-0417	R	15*	.1
139	All Products Automotive Inc—*Greg Wintroub*	4701 W Cortland Ave, Chicago IL 60639	773-889-4500	R	15*	.1
140	General Truck Parts and Equipment Co—*Gregg Chudacoff*	3835 W 42nd St, Chicago IL 60632	773-247-6900	R	15*	<.1
141	Hoffman Brothers Auto Electric Inc—*James Walsh*	PO Box 6008, South Bend IN 46660	574-239-1030	R	15*	.1
142	Herbert E Orr Company Inc—*Greg Johnson*	PO Box 209, Paulding OH 45879	419-399-4866	R	14*	.1
143	Crow's Truck Service Inc—*William Crow*	5278 Us Hwy 78, Memphis TN 38118	901-366-6611	R	14*	.1
144	Wtd Supply Inc—*Neil Staub*	16 Rewe St, Brooklyn NY 11211	718-782-2300	R	14*	.1
145	S and A Distributing Corp—*Kenneth Marks*	175 Wfm Hwy 5, Boston MA 02128	617-884-8875	R	14*	.1
146	Gary Nelson Inc—*Gary Nelson*	PO Box 4220, Renton WA 98057	206-575-8252	R	14*	.1
147	Rex Auto Parts	1233 Gordon Park Rd, Augusta GA 30901	706-722-7526	R	14*	.1
148	Parts Warehouse Distributors Inc—*Larry Chew*	449 Littlefield Ave, South San Francisco CA 94080	650-616-4988	R	14*	.1
149	Empire Auto Parts Supply Inc—*Leon Young*	141 Lanza Ave Bldg 1a, Garfield NJ 07026	973-772-4206	R	14*	.1
150	White Brothers Auto Supply Inc—*Richard White*	356 Walnut St, Macon GA 31201	478-745-1162	R	14*	.1
151	Illinois Auto Truck Company Inc—*Leonard Stein*	1669 Marshall Dr, Des Plaines IL 60018	847-299-1100	R	14*	.1
152	Autobody Products Inc—*Dom Palermo*	133 S Monroe St, Butler PA 16001	724-287-7726	R	14*	.1
153	Distributors Warehouse Inc—*Stephen Korte*	PO Box 7239, Paducah KY 42002	270-442-8201	R	14*	.1
154	Mcbee Supply Corp—*Ann Buescher*	4901 Lakeside Ave E, Cleveland OH 44114	216-881-0015	R	13*	.1
155	Abm Equipment and Supply LLC	333 2nd St Ne, Hopkins MN 55343	952-938-5451	R	13*	<.1
156	Ion Alloy Wheels—*Mark Plumer*	12905 S Spring St, Los Angeles CA 90061	310-329-2695	R	13*	<.1
157	Monroe Enterprises Inc—*Edwin Monroe*	13500 US Hwy 19 N, Clearwater FL 33764	727-531-3551	R	13*	<.1
158	Kaspar Ranch Hand Equipment LP—*Lois Bernshausen*	PO Box 667, Shiner TX 77984	361-594-4608	R	13*	.1
159	Charles W Carter Co-Hawaii Inc—*Thomas Work*	1299 Kaumualii St, Honolulu HI 96817	808-832-6292	R	13*	.1
160	Klines Auto Inc—*Allen Gribben*	630 N 13th St, Allentown PA 18102	610-434-7470	R	13*	.1

Note: An asterisk (*) indicates an estimated financial figure. The company type code used is as follows: R = Private, P = Public, S = Private Subsidiary, B = Public Subsidiary, D = Division, J = Joint Venture, I = Investment Fund.

COMPANY RANKINGS BY SALES WITHIN 4-DIGIT SIC

Rank	Company Name—Executive Officer	Address, City, State, Zip	Phone	Type	Fin	Empls
161	United Transmission Exchange Inc—Adam Curtis	21 Ramah Cir N, Agawam MA 01001	413-789-4340	R	12*	.1
162	Standard Parts Corporation Inc—Richard Davis	168 140th St S, Tacoma WA 98444	253-531-5763	R	12*	.1
163	Plaza Fleet Parts—Louis J Boggeman	1520 S Broadway, Saint Louis MO 63104	314-231-5047	R	12*	.1
164	Brake and Wheel Parts Industries—Edward Goldberg	2415 W 21st St, Chicago IL 60608	773-847-7000	R	12*	<.1
165	Pro-Cut International Limited LLC—Gina Hutchins	10 Technology Dr Ste 4, West Lebanon NH 03784	603-298-5200	R	12*	<.1
166	Dreyco Inc	263 Veterans Blvd, Carlstadt NJ 07072	201-896-9000	R	12*	.1
167	Aci Parts Warehousing Inc—Shirley Koevering	330 32nd St Se, Grand Rapids MI 49548	616-247-7771	R	12*	.1
168	Hamilton Automotive Warehouse Inc—Mark Wessendorf	630 Maple Ave, Hamilton OH 45011	513-896-4100	R	12*	.1
169	Svi International Inc—Doug Climenhaga	155 Harvestore Dr, Dekalb IL 60115	815-754-5075	R	12*	<.1
170	Carlex Glass Co—Central Amercia	77 Excellence Way, Vonore TN 37885	423-884-1105	R	12*	.4
171	Ogburn Truck Parts LP—Kathy Hunter	PO Box 4510, Fort Worth TX 76164	817-332-1511	R	12*	.1
172	Continental Auto Parts LLC	768 Frelinghuysen Ave, Newark NJ 07114	973-621-0006	R	12*	.1
173	B and B Auto Parts Inc—William Bastardi	1255 E 180th St, Bronx NY 10460	718-597-4000	R	11*	.1
174	Fred Beans Parts Inc—Fred Beans	131 Doyle St, Doylestown PA 18901	215-348-0202	R	11*	.1
175	Remington Industries Inc—Robert Lockaby	PO Box 119, Ooltewah TN 37363	423-238-3455	R	11*	<.1
176	Dr Schneider Automotive Systems Inc—Juergen Schnappauf	5775 Brighton Pines Ct, Howell MI 48843	517-545-8275	R	11*	.1
177	Eastern Industries Inc—David Wall	PO Box 59925, Panama City FL 32412	850-769-1200	R	11*	.1
178	LAX Wheel Refinishing Inc—Jesus Sanchez	1520 Spence St, Los Angeles CA 90023	323-269-1484	R	11*	.1
179	Gipe Automotive East Inc—Thomas Gipe	PO Box 987, Owensboro KY 42302	270-685-2901	R	11*	.1
180	Automotive Manufacturing and Supply Company Inc—Melvin Minoff	90 Plant Ave Ste 1, Hauppauge NY 11788	631-435-1400	R	10*	.1
181	Alpena Supply Co—William Kelly	410 S Eleventh St, Alpena MI 49707	989-354-2181	R	10*	<.1
182	Advanced Composites Technology LLC—Kevin Heronimus	1862 Sparkman Dr, Huntsville AL 35816	256-721-1331	R	10*	<.1
183	Southeast Worldwide Manufacturers—Bernardo Davila	7575 NW 74th Ave, Miami FL 33166	305-885-8689	R	10*	<.1
184	JK Auto Parts Inc—George Henard	3439 Carlin Springs Rd, Baileys Crossroads VA 22041	703-845-7000	R	10*	.1
185	DG Nicholas Co—James Nicholas	PO Box 270, Scranton PA 18501	570-342-7683	R	10*	.1
186	One Stop Brake Supply Santa Ana Inc—Selwyn Illman	1201 E Normandy Pl, Santa Ana CA 92705	714-432-7252	R	10*	.1
187	Lee Transport Equipment Inc—John Wilson	PO Box 26, Columbia SC 29202	803-799-7860	R	9*	.1
188	Terrace Supply Co—Gary Lichtenheld	710 N Addison Rd, Villa Park IL 60181	630-530-1000	R	9*	.1
189	Cee-Kay Tires and Service—Robert Butts	4949 Birney Ave, Moosic PA 18507	570-457-7464	R	9*	.1
190	Iap West Inc—Louis Berg	20036 S Via Baron, Compton CA 90220	310-667-9720	R	9*	.1
191	Marco Supply Inc—Bill Martindale	402 E Chambers St, Cleburne TX 76031	817-645-7222	R	9*	.1
192	Ned R Healy And Company Inc—Dennis Jolliffe	PO Box 2120, Huntington Beach CA 92647	714-848-2251	R	9*	<.1
193	Hawkeye Truck Equipment Co—Thomas Steinkamp	PO Box 3283, Des Moines IA 50316	515-289-1755	R	9*	.1
194	Decker Auto Supply Inc—Ron Decker	2545 N Blackstone Ave, Fresno CA 93703	559-244-0214	R	9*	.1
195	Al Jeff Corp—Scott Peterson	6990 S State St, Midvale UT 84047	801-561-2251	R	9*	.1
196	Leach Enterprises Inc—Richard Leach	4304 State Rte 176, Crystal Lake IL 60014	815-459-6917	R	9*	.1
197	Truck and Trailer Equipment Company Inc—Fred Naegele	PO Box 557, Lake Charles LA 70602	337-433-0629	R	9*	<.1
198	Mack and Rosa Inc—Randy Walker	1611 Martin Luther Kin, Monroe LA 71202	318-323-6676	R	8*	<.1
199	Nelson Truck Equipment Company Inc—Roy Nelson	20063 84th Ave S, Kent WA 98032	253-395-3825	R	8*	.1
200	Glynn Trolz And Associates Inc—Gary Trolz	PO Box 249, Jackson MI 49204	517-764-0700	R	8*	.1
201	Mohawk Manufacturing and Supply Co—John Brown	7200 N Oak Park Ave, Niles IL 60714	847-647-9350	R	8*	<.1
202	Total Automotive Warehouse Inc—William Goldkranz	222 Lake Ave Ste 1, Yonkers NY 10701	914-965-8180	R	8*	<.1
203	Jasper Engines And Transmissions Exchange Inc—Mark Harrah	PO Box 8051, Greensboro NC 27419	336-299-4017	R	8*	<.1
204	Heavy Parts International—Edward Kin	6515 N 50th str, Tampa FL 33610	813-991-7001	H	8*	<.1
205	Everdrive LLC—Steve Sindelar	PO Box 29968, Midlothian VA 23114	804-608-3050	R	8*	.1
206	Automotive Parts Sales Inc—David Olson	510 Deere Dr, New Richmond WI 54017	715-246-4517	R	8*	.1
207	Weaver Distributors Inc—James Weaver	4015 Danielsville Rd, Athens GA 30601	706-543-7394	R	8*	.1
208	Drum Corp—Steven Stich	4904 W 12th St, Sioux Falls SD 57107	605-336-0405	R	8*	.1
209	North Hollywood Carburetor and Ignition Inc—Robert Miller	5535 Lankershim Blvd, North Hollywood CA 91601	818-769-0040	R	8*	<.1
210	Wsj Worldwide Inc—Wong Wan	16775 E Johnson Dr, City Of Industry CA 91745	626-968-8228	R	8*	.1
211	Api International Inc—M Behbahany	12505 Sw Herman Rd, Tualatin OR 97062	503-692-3800	R	8*	.1
212	Meyer's Western Import Parts Inc—Jose Meyer	3540 Boulder Hwy, Las Vegas NV 89121	702-431-8000	R	8*	.1
213	Pacific Jobbers Warehouse Inc—Tetsuji Ideta	2809 Kaihikapu St, Honolulu HI 96819	808-834-7757	R	8*	<.1
214	Northstar Automotive Glass Inc—Gary Dunnegan	1340 N Mosley St, Wichita KS 67214	316-263-0415	R	7*	.1
215	Johnson Equipment Sales and Service Inc—Kyle Johnson	PO Box 25159, Farmington NY 14425	585-924-8900	R	7*	<.1
216	Power Train Components Inc—Jack Nihart	PO Box 805, Bryan OH 43506	419-636-4430	R	7*	.1
217	Automart International Inc—Eric Liou	1200 N Greenbriar Dr C, Addison IL 60101	630-812-2888	R	7*	<.1
218	Tire Service Equipment Mfg Co Inc—Warren Green	3451 S 40th St, Phoenix AZ 85040	602-437-5020	S	7*	<.1
219	Upstate Auto Body Warehouse Inc—Peter Sarratori	100 Anderson Ave, Rochester NY 14607	585-244-0510	R	7*	<.1
220	Earl Owen Co—Earl Owen	334 N Hall St, Dallas TX 75226	214-747-7549	R	7*	.1
221	CH Morris Company Inc—Hershel Swedlove	8539 Nuevo Ave, Fontana CA 92335	909-822-4481	R	7*	<.1
222	Aiken Chemical Company Inc—Dennis Schwab	PO Box 27147, Greenville SC 29616	864-968-1250	R	7*	<.1
223	Wickford Inc—Mark Dudenhoeffer	1001 Rockland St, Reading PA 19604	610-921-3558	R	7*	.1
224	234 Culpepper Inc—David Chertoff	1635 Elmwood Ave, Buffalo NY 14207	716-877-2458	R	7*	<.1
225	New Image Auto Glass LLC—John Bombinski	8270 S Kyrene Rd Ste 1, Tempe AZ 85284	480-753-3680	R	7*	<.1
226	Gwartney Automotive Group Inc—Steve Gwartney	7008 Nw 129th St, Oklahoma City OK 73142	405-722-4834	R	7*	.1
227	WNY Bus Parts Inc—William Gorman	691 Bullis Rd, Elma NY 14059	716-675-3859	R	7*	<.1
228	Weaver Automotive Inc—Roger Weaver	PO Box 480, Carnesville GA 30521	706-384-4422	R	6*	<.1
229	Universal Imports Parts Inc—Eugene Velasco	380 W 78th Rd, Hialeah FL 33014	305-266-9687	R	6*	<.1
230	Best Battery Company Inc—Roland Best	4015 Fleet St, Baltimore MD 21224	410-342-8060	R	6*	<.1
231	Ford Boyer Trucks Inc—Mark Olson	1202 Susquehanna Ave, Superior WI 54880	715-394-2460	R	6*	.1
232	JT Automotive Warehouse Inc—James Turner	1393 Springfield Ave, Irvington NJ 07111	973-375-8575	R	6*	.1
233	C and T Equipment Company Inc—Elwood Twiford	7954 Cessna Ave, Gaithersburg MD 20879	301-417-7777	R	6*	<.1
234	SB International Inc—Brian Bender	PO Box 100180, Nashville TN 37224	615-248-6281	R	6*	.1
235	Consolidated Transmission Parts Inc—Hargis Chadwick	2850 W Airport Blvd, Sanford FL 32771	407-321-2055	R	6*	.1
236	Sno-Way International Inc—Gary Wendorff	120 N Grand Ave, Hartford WI 53027	262-673-7200	R	6*	.1
237	Bookcliff Auto Parts Inc—Mike Akens	PO Box 4858, Grand Junction CO 81502	970-242-2077	R	6*	.1
238	Lake County Parts Warehouse Inc—Joseph Vidmar	3382 N Ridge Rd, Perry OH 44081	440-259-5049	R	6*	.1
239	J and R Automotive Inc—John Carlborg	889 N Larch Ave Ste 10, Elmhurst IL 60126	630-941-1950	R	6*	<.1
240	Transport Diesel Service Inc—Garth Thornley	PO Box 512, Logan UT 84323	435-753-4944	R	6*	.1
241	Advantage Truck Accessories Inc—Terry Dickie	PO Box 1747, Elkhart IN 46515	574-522-2853	R	6*	.1
242	Sabry Lee Inc—Johnson Tsai	21301 Ferrero, Walnut CA 91789	909-839-0202	R	6*	.1
243	Alds Inc—Daniel Glen	7373 Mohawk St, La Mesa CA 91942	619-589-7171	R	6*	<.1
244	Marysville Auto Parts Inc—David Lanza	960 Gray Ave, Yuba City CA 95991	530-822-2730	R	6*	<.1
245	Phoenix Wheel Company Inc—Chris Luhnow	2611 Commerce Way Ste, Vista CA 92081	760-598-1960	R	6*	<.1
246	Wheel Repair By Adam Inc—Ned Edwards	PO Box 541508, Dallas TX 75354	214-357-5762	R	6*	<.1
247	Egge Machine Co—Robert Egge	11707 Slauson Ave, Santa Fe Springs CA 90670	562-945-3419	R	6*	<.1
248	Kentucky Motor Service South Inc—David Wesselman	PO Box 14240, Cincinnati OH 45250	513-357-2415	R	6*	.1

Rank	Company Name—*Executive Officer*	Address, City, State, Zip	Phone	Type	Fin	Empls
249	All Used Transmission Parts Inc—*Jack Eaton*	1333 N 21st Ave, Phoenix AZ 85009	602-233-3835	R	6*	<.1
250	Central Motor Parts Corp—*George Hyman*	PO Box 1623, Trenton NJ 08607	609-396-7544	R	6*	<.1
251	Regional Automotive Warehouse Corp—*Joseph Principe*	401 Frelinghuysen Ave, Newark NJ 07114	973-824-9476	R	6*	<.1
252	Fort Myers Automotive And Industrial Supply Inc—*Doyle Alexander*	PO Box 7106, Fort Myers FL 33911	239-936-3917	R	6*	<.1
253	US Trailer Parts Inc—*Adam Cyze*	4334 S Tripp Ave, Chicago IL 60632	773-927-0600	R	6*	<.1
254	Chicago Parts and Sound LLC—*Jackie Lederer*	1150 Lively Blvd, Elk Grove Village IL 60007	630-350-1500	R	6*	<.1
255	Niles Inc—*Rick Iancey*	240 Wyandot St, Denver CO 80223	303-722-5900	R	6*	<.1
256	Performance Automotive Inc—*Timothy Stone*	3300 E Michigan Ave, Jackson MI 49202	517-783-2627	R	6*	<.1
257	Tri-City Automotive Warehouse Corp—*Eugene Poinsatte*	PO Box 8578, Fort Wayne IN 46898	260-471-1649	R	5*	<.1
258	Northwest Mack Parts And Service Co—*Eugene Celli*	2090 N Mannheim Rd, Melrose Park IL 60160	847-447-5500	R	5*	<.1
259	Performance Industries Manufacturing Inc—*Matt Griffin*	1900 Gunn Hwy, Odessa FL 33556	813-386-1012	R	5*	<.1
260	Enovapremier Of Michigan LLC—*Brian Springfield*	403 Parkland Dr, Charlotte MI 48813	517-541-3200	R	5*	.1
261	Fuji Component Parts USA Inc—*Makoto Maehara*	4115 W 54th St, Indianapolis IN 46254	317-347-4115	R	5*	<.1
262	Youngstown-Kenworth Inc—*Tomiel Mikes*	7255 Hubbard Masury Rd, Hubbard OH 44425	330-534-9761	R	5*	<.1
263	Bokan Brothers Inc—*Anthony Bokan*	4101 Franklin Blvd, Sacramento CA 95820	916-451-6541	R	5*	<.1
264	Brentwood Auto Parts Inc—*Richard Wilson*	7881 Brentwood Blvd, Brentwood CA 94513	925-634-3952	R	5*	<.1
265	Custom Autosound Manufacturing Inc—*Carlton Sprague*	1030 Williamson Ave, Fullerton CA 92833	714-773-1423	R	5*	<.1
266	AW Imported Auto Parts Inc—*Arnold Wenzel*	52 State Rte 35 S, Eatontown NJ 07724	732-542-5600	R	5*	<.1
267	Motor Parts Distributors Inc—*Jerry Bubeck*	710 10th St, Modesto CA 95354	209-529-8276	R	5*	<.1
268	Auto Appearance Specialists—*Matt Hagge*	3315 S 66th Ave Cir, Omaha NE 68106	402-399-9292	R	5*	<.1
269	Ni Autowindow Systems Inc—*Al Noll*	1312 Russell Cave Rd, Lexington KY 40505	859-977-2844	R	5*	<.1
270	B and L Auto Parts Inc—*Gerald Doane*	1292 Hammond St, Bangor ME 04401	207-989-6515	R	5*	<.1
271	Automotive Systems Warehouse Inc—*Robert Van Kirk*	PO Box 269, Wildwood PA 15091	412-487-4800	R	5*	<.1
272	CA Mccourt and Associates Inc—*Charles Mccourt*	1314 Centerview Cir, Copley OH 44321	330-666-0149	R	5*	<.1
273	Sherman and Associates Inc—*James Sherman*	61166 Van Dyke Rd, Washington MI 48094	586-677-6800	R	5*	<.1
274	Stellar Srkg Acquisition LLC—*Nora Howsare*	4935 Panther Pkwy, Seville OH 44273	330-769-8484	R	5*	<.1
275	Ohio Automotive Supply Company Inc—*Thomas Winklejohn*	PO Box 209, Findlay OH 45839	419-422-1655	R	5*	<.1
276	Waukegan Color Supply Inc—*David Pareti*	307 S Green Bay Rd, Waukegan IL 60085	847-336-1785	R	5*	<.1
277	RNS International Inc—*Hans Nocher*	PO Box 19867, Charlotte NC 28219	704-329-0444	R	5*	<.1
278	Painters Supply Company Inc—*Francis Heckendorf*	3701 S Santa Fe Dr Ste, Englewood CO 80110	303-762-1789	R	5*	<.1
279	Morris Roco Auto Parts Inc—*Lawrence Rose*	2129 E Michigan Ave, Kalamazoo MI 49048	269-345-0123	R	5*	<.1
280	Dixie Distributing Co—*Helen Coil*	200 W High St, Springfield OH 45506	937-322-3014	R	5*	<.1
281	Tasco LLC—*Cal Wilkins*	40 S Main St Ste 1500, Memphis TN 38103	901-365-6451	R	5*	<.1
282	A-Rod LP—*Garrick Hatfield*	500 Gulf Fwy S, League City TX 77573	281-554-9100	R	5*	<.1
283	Salem Ventilating International Inc—*Timothy Kelly*	PO Box 885, Salem VA 24153	540-387-0217	R	5*	<.1
284	Dnw Automotive And Detail Supply Inc—*Dennis Noell*	1711 E Parker Rd, Jonesboro AR 72404	870-972-5827	R	5*	<.1
285	Truck Specialties LLC—*Paul Bedke*	345 W Karcher Rd, Nampa ID 83687	208-887-7788	R	5*	<.1
286	Japan Engine Inc—*Jimmy Lin*	4401 Oakport St, Oakland CA 94601	510-532-7878	R	5*	<.1
287	B and A Friction Materials Inc—*George Botelho*	1164 Old Bayshore Hwy, San Jose CA 95112	408-286-9200	R	4*	<.1
288	Atlas Bus Sales Inc—*Steven Hoelter*	2828 S 16th St, Milwaukee WI 53215	414-672-8500	R	4*	.1
289	Ace Drive Products and Servics Inc—*David Giladi*	520 York St, Elizabeth NJ 07201	908-820-4343	R	4*	<.1
290	Cobalt Truck Equipment LLC	4620 E Trent Ave, Spokane WA 99212	509-534-0446	R	4*	<.1
291	Whatcom Electric Company Inc—*Daniel Bell*	2021 Toledo St, Bellingham WA 98229	360-734-7723	R	4*	<.1
292	Sf Alternator Starter Exchange Inc—*Vincent Hui*	2200 Jerrold Ave Ste K, San Francisco CA 94124	415-282-4077	R	4*	<.1
293	Wichita Falls Freightliner LP—*Vic Corley*	PO Box 5128, Wichita Falls TX 76307	940-767-9201	R	4*	<.1
294	A-C Brake Co—*Mary Czerwonka*	PO Box 1989, Louisville KY 40201	502-584-6226	P	4*	<.1
295	B and L Sales Inc—*James Lekas*	1112 E 30th St, Baltimore MD 21218	410-243-6100	R	4*	<.1
296	Best Bumper Supply Inc—*Glenn Coterill*	415 N Interstate 45 Sv, Hutchins TX 75141	972-225-1852	R	4*	.1
297	Colortec Inc—*Greg Laube*	854 Bridgeview S, Saginaw MI 48604	989-793-2200	R	4*	<.1
298	Barrco Automotive Warehouse Distributors Inc—*Robert Barr*	87 Albany St, Springfield MA 01105	413-781-0135	R	4*	<.1
299	Western Trailer Equipment and Manufacturing Company Of Abilene—*Tommy King*	PO Box 994, Abilene TX 79604	325-673-8311	R	4*	<.1
300	Razorback Bumper Service Inc—*Franklin Jewell*	PO Box 191008, Little Rock AR 72219	501-568-4088	R	4*	<.1
301	Brakes Express Inc—*Chad Abraham*	3650 Nw 15th St, Lauderhill FL 33311	954-583-6610	R	4*	<.1
302	Cano Auto Electric Inc—*Miguel Cano*	2723 N Pulaski Rd, Chicago IL 60639	773-486-4543	R	4*	<.1
303	Sport Truck USA Inc—*Lonnie Avra*	100 S Michigan Ave, Coldwater MI 49036	517-278-7144	R	4*	<.1
304	Botts Welding and Truck Service Inc—*Gordon Botts*	PO Box 430, Woodstock IL 60098	815-338-0594	R	4*	<.1
305	Valley Truck Parts and Service Inc—*Steven Corcoran*	1717 Central Ave Nw, East Grand Forks MN 56721	218-773-3486	R	4*	<.1
306	Equalizer Industries Inc—*Ray Asberry*	2611 Oakmont Dr, Round Rock TX 78665	512-388-7715	R	4*	<.1
307	Spal-Usa Inc—*Tom Phillipes*	1731 Se Oralabor Rd, Ankeny IA 50021	515-289-7000	R	4*	<.1
308	Lyons Parts Distributors Inc—*Randy Pieroni*	2345 S Pulaski Rd, Chicago IL 60623	773-521-4600	R	4*	<.1
309	Cedar Valley Supply Inc—*Bill Bass*	911 Commercial St, Waterloo IA 50702	319-235-1455	R	4*	<.1
310	DACCO/Detroit of Pennsylvania Inc—*Robert Douglass*	PO Box 2789, Cookeville TN 38502	913-528-7581	S	4*	<.1
311	Northwest Friction Distributors—*Jerry Weis*	201 N Columbia Blvd, Portland OR 97217	503-283-3106	R	4*	<.1
312	Acme Auto Electric Inc—*Ed Evans*	508 Baxter Ave, Louisville KY 40204	502-584-6208	R	4*	<.1
313	Truck And Auto Supply Inc—*Janna Vicario*	1340 S Claudina St, Anaheim CA 92805	714-999-7777	R	4*	<.1
314	P and G Auto Inc—*Gregory Bandini*	80 Leuning St, South Hackensack NJ 07606	201-343-8001	R	4*	<.1
315	Drive Line Service Of Portland Inc—*Roger Vrilakas*	9041 Ne Vancouver Way, Portland OR 97211	503-289-2264	R	4*	<.1
316	Ogburns Truck Parts Inc—*Tom Ogburn*	3215 Irving Blvd, Dallas TX 75247	214-637-0516	R	4*	<.1
317	Fuel Injection Sales And Service Inc—*James Blewitt*	5332 W Tilghman St, Allentown PA 18104	610-395-3718	R	4*	<.1
318	Best Bilt Parts Company Inc—*Mark Hagan*	2527 E Kearney St, Springfield MO 65803	417-869-0703	R	4*	<.1
319	Meadow Creek Truck Supply Inc—*Todd Baur*	756 S Jason St Unit 8, Denver CO 80223	303-698-9800	R	4*	<.1
320	Parts Fit Industry Co—*Roger Lo*	1005 W Republic Dr Ste, Addison IL 60101	630-458-1060	R	4*	<.1
321	Quick Auto Parts Distributors Inc—*Lloyd Shochat*	2 Bloomingdale Rd, Hicksville NY 11801	516-938-4900	R	4*	<.1
322	A and B Auto Body Supply Inc—*Art Eade*	PO Box 1295, La Salle IL 61301	815-224-2080	R	4*	<.1
323	Gsl Inc—*George Lowe*	PO Box 635, Conley GA 30288	404-361-9777	R	4*	<.1
324	Gerard Thomas Company Inc—*Thomas Bolz*	3000 Town Ctr Ste 407, Southfield MI 48075	248-358-1030	R	4*	<.1
325	American International Auto Parts Inc—*Danny Beyda*	4619 2nd Ave, Brooklyn NY 11232	718-748-1300	R	4*	<.1
326	Ksi Trading Corp—*Albert Jan*	7270 Park Cir Dr Ste E, Hanover MD 21076	410-712-9580	R	4*	<.1
327	Chassis Engineering Inc—*William Edwards*	1500 Ave R Ste 200, Riviera Beach FL 33404	561-863-2188	R	4*	<.1
328	P and M Exhaust Systems Warehouse Inc—*Ranga Gorrepati*	11843 Kemper Springs D, Cincinnati OH 45240	513-825-2660	R	4*	<.1
329	Mike and Jerry's Paint and Supply—*Michael Bohte*	828 Central Ave, Jefferson LA 70121	504-736-9004	R	4*	<.1
330	A1 Radiator Repair Inc—*Kenneth Zeal*	875 E 2nd St, Reno NV 89502	775-322-0191	R	4*	<.1
331	Rex Sales Company Inc—*Scott Crawford*	53205 Grand River Ave, New Hudson MI 48165	248-486-6600	R	4*	<.1
332	Fazzino Auto Parts Inc—*Wayne Fazzino*	120 N Colony Rd, Wallingford CT 06492	203-269-8779	R	3*	<.1
333	Herkomi Inc—*Juan Gutierrez*	12975 Sw 132nd St, Miami FL 33186	305-971-4997	R	3*	<.1
334	Bert's Truck Equipment Inc—*Wayne Gregorie*	2506 Business Hwy 2, East Grand Forks MN 56721	218-773-1194	R	3*	<.1
335	Auto Shop Equipment Company Inc—*Stephen Rogers*	6675 Doolittle Ave, Riverside CA 92503	951-359-6100	R	3*	<.1
336	Herrero and Sons Corp—*Miriam Herrero*	7575 Nw 82nd St, Medley FL 33166	305-885-7922	R	3*	<.1

Note: An asterisk (*) indicates an estimated financial figure. The company type code used is as follows: R = Private, P = Public, S = Private Subsidiary, B = Public Subsidiary, D = Division, J = Joint Venture, I = Investment Fund.

COMPANY RANKINGS BY SALES WITHIN 4-DIGIT SIC

Rank	Company Name—Executive Officer	Address, City, State, Zip	Phone	Type	Fin	Empls
337	Mayne-Mc Kenney Inc—Edward Mayne	100 W Long Lake Rd Ste, Bloomfield Hills MI 48304	248-258-0300	R	3*	<.1
338	Intercontinental Auto Parts Inc—Dan Steinfeld	133 Williams Dr, Ramsey NJ 07446	201-825-4235	R	3*	<.1
339	Precision Brake and Wheel—Patricia Witt	PO Box 1111, Porterville CA 93258	559-784-5138	R	3*	<.1
340	Carefree Distributing Inc—Richard Hawkes	3945 E Main St, Mesa AZ 85205	480-830-3220	R	3*	<.1
341	Pacific National Auto Parts Inc—Jerry Foreman	PO Box 8010, Tacoma WA 98419	253-475-7860	R	3*	<.1
342	Summit Motor Works Inc—Sanford Landa	PO Box 7478, North Brunswick NJ 08902	732-249-3484	R	3*	<.1
343	Car Parts Distributors Ltd—Bruce Goldstein	1616 W Hunting Park Av, Philadelphia PA 19140	215-329-1132	R	3*	<.1
344	Motor Parts and Equipment Inc—James Schneider	PO Box 48, Winona MN 55987	507-454-5930	R	3*	<.1
345	Tucker Automotive Corp—Jerry Tucker	714 Patton Dr, Buffalo Grove IL 60089	847-991-9560	R	3*	<.1
346	Aapco Automotive Co—Lawrence Haupert	2997 E La Palma Ave, Anaheim CA 92806	714-630-5600	R	3*	<.1
347	LoJack of California Corp—Richard T Riley	9911 W Pico Blvd Ste 1, Los Angeles CA 90035	310-286-2610	S	3*	<.1
348	Southern Sales Inc—Billy Hawkins	PO Box 1106, Travelers Rest SC 29690	864-836-8143	R	3*	<.1
349	Mofoco Enterprises Inc—Randall Henning	102 W Capitol Dr Stop, Milwaukee WI 53212	414-963-1020	R	3*	<.1
350	Quality Bumper Service Of Dallas/Fort Worth Inc—Joe Landtroop	1155 S Haskell Ave, Dallas TX 75223	214-824-7300	R	3*	<.1
351	A and Jay Automotive Warehouse Inc—Thomas Vancleave	11980 Dixie, Redford MI 48239	313-255-1122	R	3*	<.1
352	Midwest Trading Co—Janet Moody	3641 E Kiest Blvd, Dallas TX 75203	214-942-8741	R	3*	<.1
353	Commercial Motors—Arthur Tedeschi	2101 Auiki St, Honolulu HI 96819	808-842-6082	R	3*	<.1
354	International Precision Parts Corp—Dennis Connell	1476 Ben Sawyer Blvd S, Mount Pleasant SC 29464	843-881-8457	R	3*	<.1
355	Auto Craft Radiators—Norman Horton	17105 E Colonial Dr, Orlando FL 32820	321-952-0220	R	3*	<.1
356	Double E Auto Parts Corp—Ira Perlman	7224 61st St, Glendale NY 11385	718-417-9600	R	3*	<.1
357	Grtw Corp—Pyung Kim	14220 S Western Ave, Gardena CA 90249	310-327-2411	R	3*	<.1
358	Landmark Trailers Parts and Services Inc—James Jablonski	4801 Rutledge Pke, Knoxville TN 37914	865-546-9781	R	3*	<.1
359	Effingham Automotive Warehouse Inc—Chad Dust	PO Box 581, Effingham IL 62401	217-342-6868	R	3*	<.1
360	Berrodin South Inc—John Berrodin	20 Mccullough Dr, New Castle DE 19720	302-575-0500	R	3*	<.1
361	Louisville Auto Spring and Brake Company Inc—David Washbish	530 S 13th St, Louisville KY 40203	502-584-2181	R	3*	<.1
362	Richmond Bumper Service Inc—Norman Seay	8820 Park Central Dr, Richmond VA 23227	804-266-4982	R	3*	<.1
363	Royal Sales Inc—Craig Johnstone	429 Wilson St Ne, Minneapolis MN 55413	612-379-8302	R	3*	<.1
364	Advantech International Inc—Jeffrey Lang	PO Box 6739, Somerset NJ 08875	732-805-1900	R	3*	<.1
365	Mt Top Auto Supply—Harry Wolford	Hc 63 Box 3590, Romney WV 26757	304-822-5675	R	3*	<.1
366	Central Nebraska Auto Supply—Mike Taggart	PO Box 880, Grand Island NE 68802	308-384-5120	R	3*	<.1
367	Mendenhall Motor Co—Thomas Mcclure	600 S Theresa Ave, Saint Louis MO 63103	314-652-1315	R	3*	<.1
368	Spokes Inc—David Greer	4972 Virginia Beach Bl, Virginia Beach VA 23462	757-499-4146	R	3*	<.1
369	Ben's Auto Parts Corp—Roger Schnier	3687 White Plains Rd, Bronx NY 10467	718-515-9100	R	3*	<.1
370	Winchester Pacific Batteries USA Inc—Said Senan	1 Industrial St, San Francisco CA 94124	415-647-5575	R	3*	<.1
371	B and B Equipment Sales Inc—Boyd Woodard	6995 Nw 32nd Ave, Miami FL 33147	305-696-3621	R	3*	<.1
372	Tunnessen's Inc—Robert Tunnessen	PO Box 38, Hazleton PA 18201	570-455-7761	R	3*	<.1
373	Auto Master—Brian Laning	PO Box 639, Tontitown AR 72770	479-756-9300	R	3*	<.1
374	Brass Alignment Inc—Wayne Dangle	111 Rose St, Williamsport PA 17701	570-326-4194	R	3*	<.1
375	Pioneer Auto Parts and Service Company Inc—Delight Breidegam	480 Commerce Dr, Lansdowne PA 19050	610-622-6650	R	3*	<.1
376	Brd Supply Inc—Ron Dempster	503 Bloomingdale Dr, Bristol IN 46507	574-848-4256	R	3*	<.1
377	Snow Brothers Inc—Lynn Snow	1940 Janice Ave, Melrose Park IL 60160	708-681-3800	R	3*	<.1
378	A and B Auto Electric Inc—R Spencer	9225 Manchester St, Houston TX 77012	713-928-3286	R	3*	<.1
379	Unique Industry Corp—Chuck Iannacone	4506 L B Mcleod Rd Ste, Orlando FL 32811	407-835-1000	R	3*	<.1
380	Ultimate Linings Ltd—Desmond Chan	6630 Roxburgh Dr Ste 1, Houston TX 77041	713-466-0302	R	3*	<.1
381	Partsmax Inc—Manny Roman	3355 Nw 73rd St, Miami FL 33147	305-691-1313	R	3*	<.1
382	Star Envirotech Inc—Jim Saffie	17852 Gothard St, Huntington Beach CA 92647	714-427-1244	R	3*	<.1
383	Tower Distributing Inc—Ronald Ouimet	PO Box 1478, Lanesboro MA 01237	413-458-0373	R	3*	<.1
384	Adept International Inc—John Chen	308 W Mockingbird Ln, Dallas TX 75247	214-689-4607	R	3*	<.1
385	D and M Enterprises Inc—Steve Zabawa	2506 Phyllis Ln, Billings MT 59102	406-656-3947	R	3*	<.1
386	Fiber-Tech Auto Parts Inc—Richard Hopper	PO Box 713168, Santee CA 92072	619-448-0221	R	3*	<.1
387	Hite Parts Exchange Inc—Thomas Blake	2235 Mckinley Ave, Columbus OH 43204	614-272-5115	R	2*	<.1
388	Clyde Jones Distributing Company Inc—Clyde Jones	PO Box 1853, Boone NC 28607	828-264-9064	R	2*	<.1
389	International Car Parts Of New Hampshire LLC	176 Lake Ave, Manchester NH 03103	603-669-5500	R	2*	<.1
390	Valley Auto Parts Co—Louis Castagnero	329 Airbrake Ave, Wilmerding PA 15148	412-823-3200	R	2*	<.1
391	Gri Engineering and Development LLC—Craig Gordon	6700 Wildlife Way, Long Grove IL 60047	847-383-8478	S	2*	<.1
392	After Market Technologies Corp—David Helm	554 N Columbia Blvd, Portland OR 97217	503-240-2840	R	2*	<.1
393	Dorcas and Kalam Company Ltd—Arnold Lai	810 S Broadway, Hicksville NY 11801	516-349-1500	R	2*	<.1
394	Bamjak Inc—Barbara Riedel	PO Box 204, Prospect Heights IL 60070	847-394-1020	R	2*	<.1
395	Custom Truck Accessories Inc—Jim Langer	13408 Hwy 65 Ne, Anoka MN 55304	763-757-5326	R	2*	<.1
396	CV Source Inc—Ernest Roberts	3027 Summer Oak Pl, Buford GA 30518	678-889-4118	R	2*	<.1
397	Cmn Inc—Nick Kuzdak	14015 24 Mile Rd, Shelby Township MI 48315	586-677-7954	R	2*	<.1
398	Skeeter Enterprises LLC	PO Box 1629, Pharr TX 78577	956-504-2627	R	2*	<.1
399	Dealer Service Network Inc—E Mccoy	3283 Luyung Dr, Rancho Cordova CA 95742	916-852-8555	R	2*	<.1
400	Refinishing Material Specialties Inc—Terry Midkiff	2108 Pennsylvania Ave, Charleston WV 25302	304-346-9661	R	2*	<.1
401	J and D Auto Electric—James Ferrie	1800 Greensburg Rd, Campbellsville KY 42718	270-789-2889	R	2*	<.1
402	Greensboro Auto Parts Company Inc—Thomas Bigham	3720 Burlington Rd, Greensboro NC 27405	336-375-5809	R	2*	<.1
403	Highland Auto Parts Inc—Thomas Legere	625 Mcgrath Hwy, Somerville MA 02145	617-666-1733	R	2*	<.1
404	Colton Truck Supply—Brian Heller	PO Box 159, Montrose CO 81402	970-240-4484	R	2*	<.1
405	Raybestos Powertrain LLC	PO Box 227, Sullivan IN 47882	812-268-1211	R	2*	<.1
406	S and L Warshawsky Inc—Leon Warshawsky	431 S Main St, Rockford IL 61101	815-968-9800	R	2*	<.1
407	Adam's Used Auto Parts—Frank Adam	3986321 N Brushman St, Endicott KY 41653	606-886-8762	R	2*	<.1
408	Dave Schmidt Truck Service Inc—David Schmidt	1 Amann Ct, Belleville IL 62220	618-233-1470	R	2*	<.1
409	Springfield Parts Warehouse LLC—Linda Climer	2829 S Scenic Ave, Springfield MO 65807	417-887-4422	R	2*	<.1
410	Js Alternator and Starter Supply Inc—Bret Fuller	PO Box 41177, Eugene OR 97404	541-461-0081	R	2*	<.1
411	Robert Lundquist—Robert Lundquist	255 N 121st St, Milwaukee WI 53226	414-282-5660	R	2*	<.1
412	Kenwood Service Inc—David Vandewater	577 Englewood Ave, Buffalo NY 14223	716-835-0667	R	2*	<.1
413	Pawtucket Auto Supply Inc—Robert Brennan	35 Smith Hill Rd, Harrisville RI 02830	401-568-6643	R	2*	<.1
414	Martinrea Metal Industries Inc—Nick Orlando	2800 Livernois Rd Ste, Troy MI 48083	248-823-5700	S	2*	.1
415	Howard's Automotive Supply Inc—Haskell Parks	3301 Gulfway Dr, Port Arthur TX 77642	409-982-9478	R	2*	<.1
416	Atlas Lock and Tool Inc—Diane Moya	1644 Ne 148th St, Miami FL 33181	305-949-9424	R	2*	<.1
417	Ram Electric Inc—Pollyanna Mosley	100 Industrial Dr, Clarksville TN 37040	931-552-2202	R	1*	.1
418	WL Leonhardt Company Inc—William L Leonhardt	2218 W 2nd St, Santa Ana CA 92703	714-543-4858	R	1*	<.1
419	Pro-Motor Engines Inc—Peter Guild	102 S Iredell Industri, Mooresville NC 28115	704-664-6800	R	1*	<.1
420	Bowes Seal Fast LLC—Barbara Azbell-Colby	7159 E 46th St, Indianapolis IN 46226	317-549-1723	R	1*	<.1
421	Wheel Creations Plus Inc—George Oliver	414 P St, Fresno CA 93721	559-233-3654	R	1*	<.1
422	Pasha Group Co—George W Pasha IV	5725 Paradise Dr Ste 1, Corte Madera CA 94925	415-927-6400	R	N/A	.3

TOTALS: SIC 5013 Motor Vehicle Supplies & New Parts
Companies: 422

	96,377	189.5

Rank	Company Name—*Executive Officer*	Address, City, State, Zip	Phone	Type	Fin	Empls

5014 Tires & Tubes

Rank	Company Name—*Executive Officer*	Address, City, State, Zip	Phone	Type	Fin	Empls
1.	American Tire Distributors Holdings Inc—*William Berry*	PO Box 3145, Huntersville NC 28070	704-992-2000	R	1,525	2.5
2	TBC Corporation Inc—*Lawrence C Day*	4300 TBC Way, Palm Beach Gardens FL 33410	561-383-3100	S	1,480*	7.5
3	Hercules Tire and Rubber Co—*Larry Seawell*	16380 East US Rte 224, Findlay OH 45840	419-425-6400	R	300*	.4
4	WheelWorks—*Stu Waterson*	120 El Camino Real, Belmont CA 94002	650-592-3200	R	233*	.4
5	Redburn Tire—*JD Chastain*	3801 W Clarendon Ave, Phoenix AZ 85019	602-272-7601	R	181*	.3
6	Merchant's Inc—*J Riggan*	9073 Euclid Ave, Manassas VA 20110	703-368-3171	R	178*	1.5
7	Capital Tire Inc—*Thomas B Geiger Jr*	1001 Cherry St, Toledo OH 43608	419-241-5111	R	149*	.1
8	Bauer Built Inc—*Jerry M Bauer*	PO Box 248, Durand WI 54736	715-672-4295	R	137*	.5
9	Kumho Tires USA Inc—*JongHo Kim*	10299 6th St, Rancho Cucamonga CA 91730	909-428-3999	S	92*	.1
10	Player Wire Wheels Ltd	116 S Meridian Rd, Youngstown OH 44509	330-799-0128	R	75*	.1
11	Friend Tire Co—*Donald L Isbell*	11 Industrial Dr, Monett MO 65708	417-235-7836	S	73*	.2
12	Et Wholesale Ltd—*Majed Saleh*	12001 Corporate Dr, Dallas TX 75228	972-613-3020	R	61*	.1
13	Bridgestone/Firestone Tire Sales Co—*Mark E Emkes*	535 Marriott Dr, Nashville TN 37214	615-937-1000	S	57*	.6
14	Tech Supply Inc—*Jack Clifford*	PO Box 14310, Shawnee Mission KS 66285	913-492-6440	R	54*	<.1
15	Burggraf Tire Supply Inc—*Joe Karnes*	PO Box 738, Quapaw OK 74363	918-674-2281	R	50*	.1
16	Toyo Tire Corp (Cypress California)	6261 Katella Ave Ste 2, Cypress CA 90630	714-236-2080	S	43*	.1
17	Donald B Rice Tire Company Inc—*Ken Rice*	909 N East St, Frederick MD 21701	301-662-0166	R	43*	.1
18	Gateway Tire Company Inc—*William A Patton*	4 W Crescentville Rd, Cincinnati OH 45246	513-874-2500	R	37*	<.1
19	Millersburg Tire Service Inc—*Brad Schmucker*	7375 State Rte 39 E, Millersburg OH 44654	330-674-1085	R	35*	<.1
20	Lucy's Tire Inc—*Jose Rios*	12950 Nw S River Dr, Medley FL 33178	305-593-2028	R	34*	<.1
21	Harold's Tire and Auto—*Robbie Medlin*	709 Liberty Dr, Easley SC 29640	864-859-3741	R	30*	<.1
22	Statewide Tire Distributors Inc—*Roger Cornelius*	PO Box 359, Vandalia IL 62471	618-283-1102	R	26*	<.1
23	Samaritan Wholesale Tire Company Inc—*Jay Halvorson*	5100 W 35th St, Minneapolis MN 55416	612-729-8000	R	23*	<.1
24	Maxxis Corp—*James Tzen*	215 Walt Sanders Memor, Newnan GA 30265	770-502-9992	R	21*	.1
25	Phelps Tire Company Inc—*Norval Phelps*	PO Box 24968, Seattle WA 98124	206-622-8977	R	20*	.1
26	Barron's Wholesale Tire LLC—*David Barron*	1302 Eastport Rd, Jacksonville FL 32218	904-751-2449	R	19*	.1
27	Rott-Keller Supply Co—*Herb F Rott Jr*	PO Box 390, Fargo ND 58107	701-235-0563	R	19*	<.1
28	Countrywide Tire And Rubber Inc—*Robert Stone*	17200 Medina Rd Ste 10, Minneapolis MN 55447	763-546-1636	R	19*	<.1
29	ITD California Inc—*John Farkas*	6737 E Washington Blvd, Commerce CA 90040	323-722-8542	R	18*	<.1
30	Dealer Tire LLC—*Nancy Fletcher*	3711 Chester Ave, Cleveland OH 44114	216-432-0088	R	17*	.1
31	Bruneel Tire Factory Inc—*Craig Bruneel*	1519 Main St, Lewiston ID 83501	208-746-9873	R	16*	.1
32	Falken Tire Corp—*Richard Smallwood*	13649 Valley Blvd, Fontana CA 92335		S	15*	<.1
33	Steve Shannon Tire Company Inc—*Steven Shannon*	PO Box 803, Bloomsburg PA 17815	570-387-6387	R	14*	.1
34	D and J Wholesale Tire LLC	PO Box 1719, Tioga LA 71477	318-640-5489	R	14*	.1
35	Butler Tire Distributors Inc—*David Mckivigan*	8 Pittsburgh Rd, Butler PA 16001	724-287-7088	R	13*	<.1
36	Performance Plus Tire and Auto	3910 Cherry Ave, Long Beach CA 90807	562-988-0211	R	12*	<.1
37	Southern Tire Sales Of Jackson LLC—*Deanie Aswalt*	555 Hwy 80 E, Pearl MS 39208	601-932-0706	R	12*	.1
38	T M Tire Company Inc—*Thomas Accomando*	4201 Midlothian Tpke, Crestwood IL 60445	708-597-3078	R	12*	.1
39	Hoosier Racing Tire Corp—*Joyce Newton*	PO Box 538, Lakeville IN 46536	574-784-3152	R	11*	.1
40	Robison Tire Company Inc—*Joe Robison*	PO Box 545, Laurel MS 39441	601-649-8104	R	11*	<.1
41	Bobby Henard Inc—*Robert Henard*	PO Box 608, Brinkley AR 72021	870-734-1044	R	11*	<.1
42	R H Scales Company Inc—*David Scales*	240 University Ave Ste, Westwood MA 02090	781-320-0005	R	10*	<.1
43	Cherokee Industrial Tires Inc—*Katherine Koon*	PO Box 437, Lexington SC 29071	803-359-3599	R	10*	<.1
44	Ball And Prier Tire Inc—*Michael Ball*	PO Box 136, Golden MO 65658	417-271-3299	R	9*	<.1
45	Jca Ventures Inc—*Patrick Assali*	PO Box 228293, Miami FL 33222	305-887-9015	R	9*	<.1
46	BC Tire Service Inc—*Joel Caplan*	1266 Stelton Rd, Piscataway NJ 08854	732-985-6100	R	9*	<.1
47	Expedited Fleet Systems Inc—*Rupert Williams*	484 Old Hwy 17, Crescent City FL 32112	386-698-1266	R	9*	.1
48	Hanson Tire Service Inc—*Randy Eastvold*	510 Hwy 56 W, Le Roy MN 55951	507-324-5638	R	8*	<.1
49	Chicago Tire Inc—*John Wagner*	16001 Van Drunen Rd St, South Holland IL 60473	708-331-8980	R	7*	<.1
50	Inland Industrial Tire North Inc—*Linda Griffin*	30900 San Antonio St, Hayward CA 94544	510-429-2999	R	7*	<.1
51	Speck Sales Inc—*Esther Speck*	17746 N Dixie Hwy, Bowling Green OH 43402	419-353-8312	R	7*	<.1
52	Fred Harz and Son Inc—*Frederick Harz*	PO Box 1030, Elmer NJ 08318	856-358-8128	R	7*	<.1
53	Walters Tire Service Inc—*James Walters*	733 Smoky Ridge Rd, Schellsburg PA 15559	814-445-4124	R	6*	<.1
54	Philadelphia Tire Service Inc—*John Morrone*	3375 Richmond St, Philadelphia PA 19134	215-425-9980	R	6*	<.1
55	Lionshead Specialty Tire and Wheel LLC—*Melissa Mcnally*	PO Box 731, Goshen IN 46527	574-533-6169	R	6*	<.1
56	Toby Sexton Tire Company Inc—*Tolbert Sexton*	PO Box 1768, Loganville GA 30052	770-466-1060	R	6*	<.1
57	Kings Tire Service Inc—*Ed King*	Rr 52 Box Bluewell, Bluefield WV 24701	304-589-3756	R	6*	<.1
58	S and S Wholesale Tire Of Knoxville Inc—*Jerry Browning*	208 Humes St, Knoxville TN 37917	865-525-0356	R	6*	<.1
59	Northwest Tire Factory LLC—*Jan Warren*	6102 N Marine Dr, Portland OR 97203	503-283-6494	R	6*	<.1
60	Commercial Tire Co—*Jesse Albright*	5790 Washington Blvd, Elkridge MD 21075	410-796-4330	R	6*	<.1
61	Kent's Tire Service Inc—*Kent Teague*	1026 E Fort Worth St, Wichita Falls TX 76301	940-761-1349	R	5*	<.1
62	Diprima Marketing Services Inc—*Romeo Diprima*	56 Direct Connection D, Rossville GA 30741	706-891-5000	R	5*	<.1
63	Van Kleeck's Tire Inc—*Clayton Vankleeck*	1987 Rte 9w, Lake Katrine NY 12449	845-382-1292	R	5*	<.1
64	Hudson Tire Exchange—*Fred Novak*	PO Box 4009, South Hackensack NJ 07606	201-487-2112	R	4*	<.1
65	Western States Manufacturing Company Inc—*James Levich*	PO Box 3655, Sioux City IA 51102	712-252-4248	R	4*	<.1
66	Tire Sales and Service Inc—*Eugene Julian*	600 First State Blvd, Wilmington DE 19804	302-658-8955	R	4*	<.1
67	Quality Truck Tires Inc—*Stanley Dickerson*	PO Box 60366, Midland TX 79711	432-563-5301	R	4*	<.1
68	Djr Holding Corp—*Dewey Veenstra*	PO Box 407, Pella IA 50219	641-628-3153	R	4*	<.1
69	Rmg International LLC	2750 N Hayden Island D, Portland OR 97217	503-247-7115	R	4*	<.1
70	Tire Town Inc—*Duane Becker*	PO Box 87, Leavenworth KS 66048	913-682-3201	R	3*	<.1
71	Southern Tire Mart—*Jim Duff*	10941 W Fairmont Pkwy, La Porte TX 77571	281-842-8800	R	2*	<.1

TOTALS: SIC 5014 Tires & Tubes

Companies: 71					5,371	16.7

5015 Motor Vehicle Parts—Used

Rank	Company Name—*Executive Officer*	Address, City, State, Zip	Phone	Type	Fin	Empls
1	LKQ Corp—*Robert L Wagman*	120 N LaSalle St Ste 3, Chicago IL 60602	312-621-1950	P	3,270	17.9
2	National Parts LLC—*Lonnie Margol*	11554 Davis Creek Ct, Jacksonville FL 32256	904-886-9991	R	38*	.1
3	Midwest Wrecking Co—*Benjamin Kates*	PO Box 14668, Oklahoma City OK 73113	405-478-8833	R	29*	.1
4	Whatever It Takes Transmissions and Parts Inc—*Kenneth Hester*	PO Box 547, Hillview KY 40129	502-955-6035	R	25*	.2
5	Universal Manufacturing Co—*Donald D Heupel*	PO Box 190, Algona IA 50511	515-295-3557	P	15	.2
6	Alken-Ziegler Inc—*Gilbert Ziegler*	25575 Brest, Taylor MI 48180	734-946-4444	R	14*	.1
7	Midway Auto Parts Inc—*Danielle Wilcox*	4210 Gardner Ave, Kansas City MO 64120	816-241-0500	R	9*	.1
8	Nordstrom Automotive Inc—*Art Nordstrom*	25513 480th Ave, Garretson SD 57030	605-594-3910	R	8*	.1
9	Jantz's Yard 4 Automotive Inc—*Alfred Jantz*	2500 Washington Rd, Kenosha WI 53140	262-658-1392	R	5*	<.1
10	Powertrain Recycling Inc—*Barry Blank*	PO Box 5862, Harrisburg PA 17110	717-231-3793	R	4*	<.1
11	Liberty Auto Salvage—*Mark Maurer*	1064 E Morgan Ave, Evansville IN 47711	812-422-9373	R	4*	<.1

Note: An asterisk (*) indicates an estimated financial figure. The company type code used is as follows: R = Private, P = Public, S = Private Subsidiary, B = Public Subsidiary, D = Division, J = Joint Venture, I = Investment Fund.

COMPANY RANKINGS BY SALES WITHIN 4-DIGIT SIC

Rank	Company Name—*Executive Officer*	Address, City, State, Zip	Phone	Type	Fin	Empls
12	Harbor Auto Liquidators—*Lewis Canfield*	17800 S Vermont Ave, Gardena CA 90248	714-934-8310	R	4*	<.1
13	Cylinder Heads International—*Glen Nied*	3900 E Jefferson St, Grand Prairie TX 75051	972-264-3449	R	4*	<.1
14	Elgin Super Auto Parts Inc—*Sheldon Hoffman*	225 Willard Ave, Elgin IL 60120	847-695-4000	R	4*	<.1
15	Silverthorne Motors—*Wayne Kieffer*	171 W 7th St, Silverthorne CO 80498	970-262-9488	R	4*	.1
16	Jordan Auto Parts Inc—*David Jordan*	217 Moffit Rd, Dilliner PA 15327	724-943-3522	R	4*	<.1
17	Vans Carburetor And Electric Inc—*Richard Valleymen*	PO Box 51797, Indianapolis IN 46251	317-240-5900	R	3*	<.1
18	Illiana Truck Parts Inc—*Andrew Nickel*	909 N 25th St, Terre Haute IN 47803	812-232-6453	R	3*	<.1
19	Crosstown Used Auto Parts—*Russ Payne*	218 Pascal St N, Saint Paul MN 55104	612-861-3020	R	3*	<.1
20	Brown Recycling and Manufacturing Inc—*Cecil Brown*	1274 Gravel Ridge Rd, Somerville AL 35670	256-778-8756	R	3*	<.1
21	Abe's Auto Recyclers Inc—*Theresa Kauhane*	96-1268 Waihona St, Pearl City HI 96782	808-455-4200	R	3*	<.1
22	Motor Works Inc—*Michael Ulrick*	1026 N Haven St, Spokane WA 99202	509-535-9240	R	3*	<.1
23	Meridian Auto Wrecking—*Austin Davis*	20011 Meridian Ave E, Graham WA 98338	253-847-1922	R	3*	<.1
24	AB and B Auto Parts Inc—*Barnett Thompson*	540111 Us Hwy 1, Callahan FL 32011	904-879-3045	R	3*	<.1
25	Kennedy Diversified Inc—*John Kennedy*	3844 William Flynn Hwy, Slippery Rock PA 16057	724-794-6913	R	3*	<.1
26	Gregory T Blair Inc—*Gregory Blair*	11801 W Montgomery Rd, Houston TX 77086	281-447-3801	R	3*	<.1
27	Cote E T and Son Auto Exchange Inc—*Robert Cote*	37 9th St, Leominster MA 01453	978-537-2420	R	3*	<.1
28	Hi Way Auto Inc—*James Cooley*	PO Box 1946, Brownwood TX 76804	325-646-8254	R	2*	<.1
29	Bill's Used Auto Parts Inc—*Ken Harvey*	1415 Radford Rd, Christiansburg VA 24073	540-382-3972	R	2*	<.1
30	Garcia And Sons Auto and Used Parts—*Obie Garcia*	E State Hwy 107, Edinburg TX 78540	956-380-6653	R	2*	<.1
31	Jean's Used Auto Parts—*Donald Whaley*	7144 S 45 Rd, Cadillac MI 49601	231-775-2645	R	2*	<.1
32	Condon's Auto Parts Inc—*Ralph Condon*	1218 Martin Dr, Westminster MD 21157	410-848-4140	R	2*	<.1
33	N and S Used Foreign Car Parts—*Mohammad Rahimi*	361 Herron Dr, Nashville TN 37210	615-256-1293	R	2*	<.1
34	Auto Recyclers Inc—*Todd Peacock*	8209 Old Stage Rd, Moss Point MS 39562	228-475-9100	R	2*	<.1
35	Discovery Auto Parts Inc—*Stall Hiegan*	5503 Blue Star Hwy, Holland MI 49423	616-393-7998	R	2*	<.1
36	Richard J Cassidy Inc—*David French*	PO Box 245, Tioga Center NY 13845	607-687-4100	R	1*	<.1
37	Stoneman Avenue Corp—*Dennis Wang*	5029 Calmview Ave, Baldwin Park CA 91706	626-338-8998	R	1*	<.1

TOTALS: SIC 5015 Motor Vehicle Parts—Used
Companies: 37

					3,491	19.4

5021 Furniture

Rank	Company Name—*Executive Officer*	Address, City, State, Zip	Phone	Type	Fin	Empls
1	Wasserstrom Co—*Rodney Wasserstrom*	477 S Front St, Columbus OH 43215	614-228-6525	R	298*	1.1
2	Business Resource Group—*Traci Doane*	1732 N 1st St, San Jose CA 95112	408-325-3225	R	285*	.4
3	Waldner Business Environment—*John Gallivan*	215 Lexington Ave, New York NY 10016	212-696-7500	R	280*	.2
4	Southern Sales and Marketing Group Inc—*Joseph Frazier*	4400 Commerce Cir Sw, Atlanta GA 30336	404-505-5900	R	224*	.1
5	Business Furniture Corp—*David G Bratton*	6102 Victory Way, Indianapolis IN 46278	317-216-1600	R	212*	.1
6	Target Commercial Interiors—*Joseph Perdew*	81S 9th St Ste 350, Minneapolis MN 55402	612-343-0868	S	192	.2
7	Finger Office Furniture—*Robert S Finger*	4001 Gulf Fwy, Houston TX 77003	713-221-4441	R	180*	.5
8	Coppel Corp—*Ruben Coppel*	503 Scaroni Ave, Calexico CA 92231	760-357-3707	R	152*	.1
9	Office Depot Inc Business Services Div—*Dave Trudnowski*	3366 E Willow St, Signal Hill CA 90755	562-490-1100	D	149*	.9
10	Continental Office Enviroments Inc—*Ira Sharfin*	2601 Silver Dr, Columbus OH 43211	614-262-5010	R	135*	.4
11	Furniture Consultants Inc—*Chris Stevenson*	641 Ave of the America, New York NY 10011	212-229-4500	R	124*	.2
12	OfficeScapes Business Furniture—*Bob Deibel*	9900 E 51st Ave, Denver CO 80238	303-574-1115	R	115*	.2
13	Office Furniture USA—*Brad Armacost*	273 Cahaba Valley Pky, Pelham AL 35124	205-988-5919	R	113*	.1
14	Bank and Office Interiors—*Tim Jones*	5601 6th Ave S, Seattle WA 98108	206-768-8000	R	103*	.1
15	Pivot Interiors—*Ken Baugh*	2740 Zanker Rd Ste 100, San Jose CA 95134	408 432 5600	R	101*	.2
16	Sam Flax Inc—*Mark Honigsfeld*	1401 E Colonial Dr, Orlando FL 32803	407-898-9785	R	99*	<.1
17	National Business Furniture Inc—*Rick Wachowiak*	PO Box 514052, Milwaukee WI 53203		R	95	.2
18	Wilson Group Ltd—*B Don Hill*	1444 Oak Lawn Ave Rm 5, Dallas TX 75207	972-488-4100	R	92*	.1
19	New WPI LLC	30800 Telegraph Rd Ste, Bingham Farms MI 48025		R	90*	.3
20	Rucker Fuller Co—*Dave Ferrari*	333 Pine St, San Francisco CA 94104	415-445-3000	R	85*	.2
21	Intereum Inc—*Brett Abbott*	845 Berkshire Ln N, Plymouth MN 55441	763-417-3300	R	85*	.1
22	Imports by Four Hands LP—*Brett Hatton*	2090 Woodward St, Austin TX 78744	512-371-7575	R	84*	.1
23	Brunschwig and Fils Inc—*Olivier Peardon*	245 Central Ave S, Bethpage NY 11714		R	82*	.3
24	Missco Corporation of Jackson—*Vick Smith*	PO Box 5349, Jackson MS 39296	601-987-8600	R	75*	.2
25	Carithers-Wallace-Courtenay Inc—*Paul Conley*	4343 Northeast Expy, Atlanta GA 30340	770-493-8200	R	75*	.2
26	Workspace Development LLC—*Claudia Church*	PO Box 45897, San Francisco CA 94145	206-768-8000	R	75*	.1
27	Business Interiors Northwest Inc—*Rich Lacher*	10848 E Marginal Way S, Seattle WA 98168	206-762-8818	R	70*	.2
28	International Contract Furnishings Inc—*James Kasschau*	19 Ohio Ave, Norwich CT 06360		R	63*	.1
29	Miles Treaster and Associates—*Miles Treaster*	3480 Industrial Blvd, West Sacramento CA 95691	916-373-1800	R	60*	.1
30	Kinfine USA Inc—*Xiaoqiao Zhang*	1693 Yeager Ave, La Verne CA 91750	909-596-2863	R	60*	<.1
31	Lincoln Office Supply Company Inc—*Bill Pape*	205 Eastgate Dr, Washington IL 61571	309-663-1835	R	57*	.2
32	Fraenkel Wholesale Furniture Company Inc—*Brian Akchin*	PO Box 15385, Baton Rouge LA 70113	225-275-4242	R	56*	.3
33	Coaster Company of America—*Harvey N Dondero*	12928 Sandoval St, Santa Fe Springs CA 90670	562-944-7899	R	53*	.3
34	Numark Office Interiors—*Joel Johanneson*	3600 136th Pl SE Bldg, Bellevue WA 98006	425-274-7500	R	52*	.1
35	Dancker Sellew and Douglas Inc—*Scott Douglas*	291 Evans Way, Somerville NJ 08876	908-231-1600	R	51*	.1
36	Pride Family Brands Inc—*Jamie Lowsky*	PO Box 100936, Fort Lauderdale FL 33310	954-735-9800	R	50*	<.1
37	Douron Inc—*Ronald Hux*	30 New Plant Ct, Owings Mills MD 21117	410-363-2600	R	46	.2
38	Thomas Interior Systems Inc—*Thomas Klobucher*	476 Brighton Dr, Bloomingdale IL 60108	630-980-4200	R	46*	<.1
39	One Workplace L Ferrari—*David Ferrari*	1057 Montague Expwy, Milpitas CA 95035	408-263-1001	R	43*	.3
40	Price Modern LLC—*Robert S Carpenter*	2604 Sisson St, Baltimore MD 21211	410-366-5500	R	43*	.2
41	Alpha Office Supplies Inc—*James Brown*	2066 W Hunting Park Av, Philadelphia PA 19140	215-226-2690	R	42*	.1
42	AD Wynne Company Inc—*Arthur Wynne*	710 Baronne St 1st Fl, New Orleans LA 70113	504-522-9558	R	40*	.1
43	Parron-Hall Corp—*James Herr*	7700 Ronson Rd Ste 100, San Diego CA 92111	858-268-1212	R	39*	<.1
44	Barclay Dean—*Scott Harrison*	11100 NE 8th St Ste 90, Bellevue WA 98004	425-451-8940	R	37*	.1
45	Hilton Supply Management—*Christopher J Nassetta*	9350 Civic Center Dr, Beverly Hills CA 90210	703-883-1000	S	36*	<.1
46	American Office Equipment Company Inc—*David Kuntz*	309 N Calvert St, Baltimore MD 21202	410-539-7529	R	36*	.2
47	Loth Mbi Inc—*Mike Geoppinger*	3574 E Kemper Rd, Cincinnati OH 45241	513-554-4900	R	34*	.1
48	Omnia Italian Design Inc—*Sal Zolferino*	4950 Edison Ave, Chino CA 91710	909-393-4400	R	32*	.1
49	Thomas W Ruff and Company of Florida Inc—*Jack Gorman* LOTH	3201 Commerce Pky, Miramar FL 33025	954-435-7300	S	31	.1
50	Pacific Design Center LLC—*Charles Cohen*	8687 Melrose Ave, West Hollywood CA 90069	310-657-0800	R	31*	<.1
51	Castleberry Office Furnishings	3614 Chamble Dunwoody, Atlanta GA 30341	770-452-6600	R	30*	<.1
52	Carringer Company Inc—*Raymond Carringer*	3658 Hawkshead Dr, Clermont FL 34711	352-243-8834	R	30*	<.1
53	Business Furniture Inc—*Dan Morley*	133 Rahway Ave, Elizabeth NJ 07202	908-355-3400	R	28*	<.1
54	United Corporate Furnishings Inc—*Mark Hoag*	1780 N Market Blvd, Sacramento CA 95834	916-553-5900	R	27*	.1
55	Solidus Inc—*Mark Charette*	40 Cold Spring Rd, Rocky Hill CT 06067	860-257-4900	R	26*	<.1
56	LOTH—*John Johnson* Loth Mbi Inc	3574 E Kemper Rd, Cincinnati OH 45241	513-554-4900	S	26*	.1
57	Forrer Business Interiors Inc—*Randy S Howard*	555 W Estabrook Blvd, Milwaukee WI 53212	414-906-3200	R	26*	.1
58	Desks Inc (Chicago Illinois)—*Jim Ford*	225 W Ohio St Rm 500, Chicago IL 60654	312-334-3375	R	26*	.1

Rank	Company Name—*Executive Officer*	Address, City, State, Zip	Phone	Type	Fin	Empls
59	Walker Edison Furniture Company LLC	4350 W 2100 S Ste A, Salt Lake City UT 84120	801-433-3008	R	25*	.1
60	Desks Inc—*Jay Stark*	445 Bryant St Unit 8, Denver CO 80204	303-777-7778	R	25*	<.1
61	Wells and Kimich Inc—*Mikle Wells*	PO Box 19216, Houston TX 77224	713-856-9900	R	24*	<.1
62	Artlite Office Supply and Furniture Co—*Steve Light*	1851 Piedmont Rd, Atlanta GA 30324	404-875-7271	R	24*	.1
63	Business Office Systems Inc—*Harold Weibel*	365 E N Ave, Carol Stream IL 60188	630-761-0545	R	23*	.1
64	Pigott Inc—*John Stenberg*	3815 Ingersoll Ave, Des Moines IA 50312	515-279-8879	R	22*	.1
65	Commercial Furniture Services Inc—*Bill Higgins*	PO Box 24220, Houston TX 77229	713-673-2100	R	22*	.1
66	Burkett's Office Furnishings and Supplies—*Randy Mael*	8520 Younger Creek Dr, Sacramento CA 95828	916-387-8900	R	22*	<.1
67	US Business Interiors Inc—*William Rice*	8800 Lottsford Rd, Upper Marlboro MD 20774	301-350-8700	R	21*	.1
68	Atlantic Corporate Interiors Inc—*Doug Bruns*	4600 Powder Mill Rd St, Beltsville MD 20705	301-931-3600	R	21*	<.1
69	WB Wood Co—*Michael Kopelman*	100 5th Ave 12th Fl, New York NY 10011	212-206-9500	R	21*	.1
70	Braxton Culler Inc—*Braxton Culler*	PO Box 248, High Point NC 27261	336-861-5800	R	20*	.2
71	King Business Interiors Inc—*Darla King*	6155 Huntley Rd Ste D, Columbus OH 43229	614-430-0020	R	20*	<.1
72	Omnifics Inc—*Ann Whitcomb*	5845 Richmond Hwy Ste, Alexandria VA 22303	703-548-4040	R	20*	.1
73	Offices Limited Inc—*Bruce Blueweiss*	76 9th Ave Rm 313, New York NY 10011	212-704-9848	R	19*	.1
74	Commercial Office Interiors Inc—*Doug Salkville*	2601 4th Ave Ste 700, Seattle WA 98121	206-448-7333	R	19*	.1
75	Acme Furniture Industry Inc—*Chi-Chu Chen*	18895 Arenth Ave, City Of Industry CA 91748	626-964-3456	R	19*	.1
76	Innvision Hospitality Supply Inc—*Walter Jones*	504 Carver Rd, Griffin GA 30224	678-967-2020	R	18*	<.1
77	Carroll's Discount Office Furniture Co—*Frank Carroll*	5615 S Rice Ave, Houston TX 77081	713-667-6668	R	18*	<.1
78	Central Business Equipment Co—*Stephen Jones*	10839 Indeco Dr, Blue Ash OH 45241	513-891-4430	R	18*	.1
79	Tom Sexton and Associates Inc—*Thomas Sexton*	65 Cummings Dr, Walton KY 41094	859-485-7065	R	17*	<.1
80	A Pomerantz and Co—*Gary Maddox*	123 S Broad St, Philadelphia PA 19109	215-408-2100	R	16*	.1
81	Inside Source—*Dave Denny*	985 Industrial Rd Ste, San Carlos CA 94070	650-508-9101	R	16*	<.1
82	Peabody Office Furniture Corp—*Christopher Peabody*	234 Congress St, Boston MA 02110	617-542-1902	R	15*	.1
83	SIS-USA Inc—*Alan Morse*	55 Wentworth Ave, Londonderry NH 03053	603-432-4495	S	15*	.1
84	OFIS by Powell—*Bob Crawmer*	7110 Old Katy Rd Ste 2, Houston TX 77024	713-629-5599	R	14	<.1
85	Jofran Sales Inc—*Robert Roy*	1 Jofran Way, Norfolk MA 02056	508-384-6019	R	14*	.1
86	Zocalo—*Jeremy Sommer*	1551 Bancroft Ave 1508, San Francisco CA 94124	415-293-1600	R	13*	.1
87	Minton-Jones Co—*Travis Jones Jr*	PO Box 277465, Atlanta GA 30384	770-449-4787	R	13*	<.1
88	Contemporary Galleries of West Virginia Inc—*Mary Russell*	PO Box 2829, Charleston WV 25330	304-344-1231	R	13*	.1
89	GuildMaster Inc—*Steve Crowder*	1938 E Phelps, Springfield MO 65802	417-879-3326	P	13	.6
90	Southwestern Interior Contracting Company Inc—*Robert Allee*	PO Box 18697, Oklahoma City OK 73154	405-525-9411	R	13*	.1
91	WWM S Inc—*W O'neal*	1516 E Reelfoot Ave, Union City TN 38261	731-885-6471	R	13*	<.1
92	Interform Commercial Interiors Inc—*Richard Watts*	3000 Executive Pkwy St, San Ramon CA 94583	925-867-1001	R	13*	<.1
93	Carroll Seating Company Inc—*Patrick J Carroll*	2105 Lunt, Elk Grove Village IL 60007	847-434-0909	R	12*	<.1
94	Mccartney's Inc—*John Baker*	PO Box 1714, Altoona PA 16603	814-944-8139	R	11*	.1
95	L Walker Marvin and Associates Inc—*Marvin Walker*	PO Box 5600, Norcross GA 30091	770-446-0030	R	11*	<.1
96	Privilege International Inc—*Eddy Sarraf*	2419 Firestone Blvd, South Gate CA 90280	323-585-0777	R	11*	.1
97	Office Planning Group Inc—*John Rotty*	11330 Sunrise Park Dr, Rancho Cordova CA 95742	916-638-2999	R	10*	<.1
98	Interspace Office Furniture Inc—*Steve Laughman*	1025 International Pl, Kennesaw GA 30152	770-988-0091	R	10*	<.1
99	Pelican Reef Inc—*Angel Calzadilla*	4900 Nw 167th St, Hialeah FL 33014	305-558-2100	R	10*	.1
100	Ols Trading Inc—*Scott Cornblantt*	6 Triple Crown Ct, North Potomac MD 20878	301-296-3100	R	10*	<.1
101	National Furniture Liquidators I LLC—*Vince Gallo*	2870 Plant Atkinson Rd, Smyrna GA 30080	404-872-7280	R	10*	.1
102	Milton Terry Associates Inc—*Glenn Marthens*	95 Chamberlain Rd, Oak Ridge NJ 07438	973-697-7227	R	10*	<.1
103	Walter H Hopkins Company Inc—*Walter Hopkins*	2125 Corp Dr Se Ste 10, Marietta GA 30067	770-955-5025	R	10*	<.1
104	Ladco Inc—*Phillip Ladin*	PO Box 701039, Houston TX 77270	713-868-2828	R	9*	<.1
105	Syracuse Office Equipment Corp—*Walter Sweeney*	375 Erie Blvd W, Syracuse NY 13202	315-476-9091	R	9*	<.1
106	Springfield Business Equipment Co—*J Lindeman*	100 W N St, Springfield OH 45504	937-322-3828	R	8*	<.1
107	M L Bath Company Ltd—*F Todaro*	PO Box 20048, Shreveport LA 71120	318-221-7141	R	8*	.1
108	Legato A Vanguard California Corp—*Darlene Patch*	2121 Williams St, San Leandro CA 94577	510-351-3333	R	8*	.1
109	Jules Seltzer and Associates—*Grant Seltzer*	8833 Beverly Blvd, Los Angeles CA 90048	310-274-7243	R	8*	<.1
110	Commercial Furniture Interiors Inc—*Ray Blau*	1135 Spruce Dr Ste 2, Mountainside NJ 07092	908-518-1670	R	7*	<.1
111	Victory Land Group Inc—*Jeff Yao*	1350 Munger Rd, Bartlett IL 60103	630-540-7000	R	7*	<.1
112	Target Marketing Systems Inc—*Richard Koh*	146 Alexandra Way, Carol Stream IL 60188	630-784-1188	R	7*	<.1
113	Globe Office Equipment And Supplies Inc—*Scott Robertson*	6454 Centre Park Dr, West Chester OH 45069	513-771-5550	R	7*	<.1
114	Williams Import Company Inc—*David Chang*	2788 S Maple Ave, Fresno CA 93725	559-233-8899	R	7*	<.1
115	Rje Interiors Inc—*Dennis Sponfel*	621 E Ohio St, Indianapolis IN 46202	317-293-4051	R	6*	<.1
116	MngnExcel Business Supplies Inc—*Mike Standley*	PO Box 65250, West Des Moines IA 50265	515-225-2025	R	6*	<.1
117	Km Group LLC	14231 Willard Rd Ste 5, Chantilly VA 20151	703-817-0220	R	6*	<.1
118	Evansville Corporate Design Inc—*J Small*	PO Box 97, Evansville IN 47701	812-422-3000	R	6*	<.1
119	Cedar Recycling Inc—*Jerald Eck*	411 W Valley Hwy S, Pacific WA 98047	253-804-0404	R	6*	<.1
120	Stow's Office Furniture Inc—*Jerry Stow*	PO Box 1074, Oklahoma City OK 73101	405-235-3131	R	6*	<.1
121	Spacesaver Northwest LLC—*Lawrence Roybal*	9877 40th Ave S, Seattle WA 98118	206-764-8864	R	6*	<.1
122	Jamesville Office Furnishing—*Yum Armstrong*	11309-B Folsom Blvd, Rancho Cordova CA 95742	916-638-4050	R	6*	<.1
123	OnTimeSuppliescom—*Andre Scott*	PO Box 888016, Atlanta GA 30356		R	6*	<.1
124	Ruby and Quiri Leasing Corp—*Richard Ruby*	307 N Comrie Ave, Johnstown NY 12095	518-762-7829	R	6*	<.1
125	Grooms Office Systems Inc—*Henry Grooms*	1285 E Montclair St, Springfield MO 65804	417-883-4646	R	6*	<.1
126	O'brien Installation Inc—*Carol O'brien*	1 Liberty St, Sandwich MA 02563	508-888-8228	R	6*	<.1
127	Ergocraft Contract Solutions—*Daisy Liang*	10730 Bell Ct, Rancho Cucamonga CA 91730	909-373-2808	R	6*	<.1
128	Cj and Associates Inc—*Curtis Rudy*	16915 W Victor Rd, New Berlin WI 53151	262-786-1772	R	6*	<.1
129	Premier Office Solutions Inc—*Paul Barr*	374 S Warminster Rd, Hatboro PA 19040	215-734-2300	R	6*	<.1
130	Frank Cooney Company Inc—*Kevin Cooney*	1226 N Michael Dr Ste, Wood Dale IL 60191	630-694-8800	R	6*	<.1
131	Designed Business Interiors Of Topeka Inc—*Kevin Sutcliffe*	107 Sw 6th Ave Ste A, Topeka KS 66603	785-233-2078	R	6*	<.1
132	Matresspro—*Keith Gullo*	9333 Research Blvd Bld, Austin TX 78759	512-231-0888	R	5*	.1
133	Worksquared of Northern Michigan—*David Langvelde*	1101 Hammond Rd W, Traverse City MI 49686	231-922-9508	R	5*	<.1
134	Beechwood Mountain LLC—*Alex Gross*	500 Broadway Ste A, Brooklyn NY 11211	718-418-3205	R	5*	<.1
135	On The Web Marketing Group Inc—*Alex Salmon*	2651 Crimson Canyon Dr, Las Vegas NV 89128	702-304-0909	R	5*	<.1
136	Oak Furniture West LLC	PO Box 431498, San Ysidro CA 92143	619-661-5522	R	5*	<.1
137	Dof Holdings LLC	130 Broadhollow Rd Ste, Farmingdale NY 11735	631-753-3601	R	5*	<.1
138	O'Rourke Brothers Incorporated of Atlanta—*Jeff O'Rourke*	6085 Lagrange Blvd SW, Atlanta GA 30336	404-346-9863	R	5*	<.1
139	Fulton Packaging Inc—*Juf Crippen*	PO Box 7205, Tupelo MS 38802	662-862-5633	R	5*	<.1
140	Mariner Trading Company Inc—*Scott Mcmurray*	3165 Diablo Ave, Hayward CA 94545	510-732-7888	R	5*	<.1
141	Bellia Office Furniture Inc—*Anthony Bellia*	1047 N Broad St, Woodbury NJ 08096	856-845-2234	R	5*	<.1
142	Exhibits South Corp—*Marlene Kelly*	1000 Satellit Blvd Nw, Suwanee GA 30024	678-225-5200	R	5*	<.1
143	Malachi Mattress America Inc—*Tanya Bettencourt*	10500 Ulmerton Rd Ste, Largo FL 33771	727-584-1123	R	4*	<.1
144	Action Business Furniture Inc—*Byron Richmond*	3802 S Cedar St, Tacoma WA 98409	253-627-8633	R	4*	<.1
145	Mark David A Divison Of Baker Knapp and Tubbs—*Brenda Collins*	PO Box 7924, High Point NC 27264	336-821-2250	R	4*	<.1
146	Allegheny Fabricating and Supplies Inc—*Faye Ritter*	PO Box 91040, Pittsburgh PA 15221	412-828-3320	R	4*	<.1
147	Red Dragon Imports Inc—*Sean Scott*	2101 Garcia St Ne, Albuquerque NM 87112	505-681-4711	R	4*	<.1

Note: An asterisk (*) indicates an estimated financial figure. The company type code used is as follows: R = Private, P = Public, S = Private Subsidiary, B = Public Subsidiary, D = Division, J = Joint Venture, I = Investment Fund.

COMPANY RANKINGS BY SALES WITHIN 4-DIGIT SIC

Rank	Company Name—*Executive Officer*	Address, City, State, Zip	Phone	Type	Fin	Empls
148	Ruland's Used Office Furnishings—*Stephen Ruland*	215 N 16th St, Sacramento CA 95811	916-441-0706	R	4*	<.1
149	Techline Studio Furniture That Fits Inc—*Leslie Bisharat*	11225 Trade Center Dr, Rancho Cordova CA 95742	916-638-1991	R	4*	<.1
150	Joseph Khabbaz and Co—*Pierre Khabbaz*	1418 Potrero Ave, El Monte CA 91733	626-350-4335	R	4*	<.1
151	Huntington Wholesale Furniture Co—*Charles Hanshaw*	PO Box 1300, Huntington WV 25714	304-523-9415	R	4*	<.1
152	Second Systems Inc—*Fred Sanders*	1040 W Thorndale Ave, Itasca IL 60143	630-250-7555	R	4*	<.1
153	Chase Office Supplies Ltd—*David Vallone*	63 Flushing Ave Unit 2, Brooklyn NY 11205	718-852-9400	R	4*	<.1
154	Astoria Imports Inc—*Bob Gross*	1601 N Powerline Rd, Pompano Beach FL 33069	954-623-6600	R	4*	<.1
155	Premier Home Improvements Inc—*Littleton Dryden*	PO Box 7078, Newark DE 19714	302-455-1902	R	4*	<.1
156	Dynateck America Inc—*Peter Tsai*	19706 Normandie Ave St, Torrance CA 90502	310-515-0315	R	3*	<.1
157	Quattro Investments Inc—*Dennis Ammons*	1612 Heathcliff Rd, High Point NC 27262	336-889-7306	R	3*	<.1
158	Metro Office Solutions Inc—*Minh Duc Thi Sherida*	4692 Millennium Dr Ste, Belcamp MD 21017	410-297-6666	R	3*	<.1
159	Goldstar U S A Inc—*Vern Padgett*	2705 Pacific Ave, Tacoma WA 98402	253-627-4000	R	3*	<.1
160	Knock On Wood—*Karen Hunter*	3725 E Fort Lowell Rd, Tucson AZ 85716	520-881-4249	R	3*	<.1
161	M and W Sales Inc—*James Dowell*	PO Box 758, Belmont MS 38827	662-454-9419	R	3*	<.1
162	Jones-Campbell Co—*Craig Campbell*	PO Box 277788, Sacramento CA 95827	916-362-0123	R	3*	<.1
163	Winchendon Furniture Inc—*Richard Ladeau*	13 Railroad St, Winchendon MA 01475	978-297-0131	R	3*	<.1
164	Saladino Furniture Inc—*John Saladino*	200 Lexington Ave Rm 1, New York NY 10016	212-684-3720	R	3*	<.1
165	Just PC Inc—*Mary Wong*	605 S Milliken Ave Ste, Ontario CA 91761	909-390-7676	R	3*	<.1
166	BriMar Wood Innovations Inc—*Brian Roe*	2108 Eisenhower Dr N, Goshen IN 46526	574-535-0024	R	3	<.1
167	Rents and Sales—*Jim Atwood*	601 Kasold Dr Ste B105, Lawrence KS 66049	785-841-7111	R	3*	<.1
168	BDB Service and Supply Company Inc—*Albert Brauner*	6215 14th Ave, Brooklyn NY 11219	718-241-6716	R	3*	<.1
169	Fred Martin and Associates—*Fred Martin*	PO Box 968, Martinsville VA 24114	276-638-2840	R	2*	<.1
170	Frankel Furniture Industries Inc—*Annie Kwok*	15 Vela Way, Edgewater NJ 07020	201-248-6383	R	2*	<.1
171	Precision Seating LLC—*Lesa Mc Culley*	6621 Wilbanks Rd, Knoxville TN 37912	865-219-7304	R	2*	<.1
172	Educational Furnishings Of Arizona LLC—*Deb Toler*	7885 N Glen Harbor Blv, Glendale AZ 85307	602-484-7331	R	2*	<.1
173	Online Commerce Group LLC—*Scott McGlon*	3180 Wetumpka Hwy, Montgomery AL 36110	334-558-0863	R	2*	<.1
174	Daniel Minzer Co—*Daniel Minzner*	2100 Liberty St, Easton PA 18042	610-258-5449	R	2*	<.1
175	G L Mattress Inc—*Luis Aviles*	603 Central Florida Pk, Orlando FL 32824	407-373-0668	R	2*	<.1
176	Mike McMahan Desk Inc—*Martin Schlom*	20492 Crescent Bay Dr, Lake Forest CA 92630	949-597-0123	R	2*	<.1
177	Cinema Tech Seating Inc—*Michael Murphy*	4319 Lindbergh Dr, Addison TX 75001	972-381-1071	R	2*	<.1
178	Abilene Printing and Stationery Company Inc—*Patsy Lacy*	PO Box 1560, Abilene TX 79604	325-677-2673	R	1*	<.1
179	Chair Place—*Allan Kent*	531 Bryant St, San Francisco CA 94107	415-278-9640	R	1*	N/A
180	Mary Spencer Company Inc—*Mary Spencer*	2121 N Akard St Ste 10, Dallas TX 75201	214-720-0345	R	<1*	<.1

TOTALS: SIC 5021 Furniture
Companies: 180

					6,008	14.4

5023 Homefurnishings

Rank	Company Name—*Executive Officer*	Address, City, State, Zip	Phone	Type	Fin	Empls
1	CCA Global Partners—*Howard Brodsky*	4301 Earth City Expy, Earth City MO 63045		R	9,255*	.1
2	Gexpro—*Jeff Schaper*	PO Box 861, Shelton CT 06484	203-944-3100	R	1,100*	2.2
3	American Hotel Register Co—*Larry Morse*	100 S Milwaukee Ave, Vernon Hills IL 60061		R	597*	.9
4	Lasalle Bristol LP—*Ray Cole*	PO Box 98, Elkhart IN 46515	574-295-4400	R	491*	.6
5	Stark Carpet Corp—*John S Stark*	979 3rd Ave, New York NY 10022	212-752-9000	R	397*	.5
6	Tandus Group—*Glen A Hussmann*	PO Box 1447, Dalton GA 30722	706-259-9711	R	325	N/A
7	Andrea by Sadek—*Jim Sadek*	PO Box 717, New Rochelle NY 10802	914-633-8090	R	312*	.2
8	Capel Inc—*John Magee*	PO Box 828, Troy NC 27371	910-572-7000	R	293*	.4
9	WS Badcock Corp—*Donald C Marks*	PO Box 497, Mulberry FL 33860	863-425-4921	R	286*	1.2
10	Bishop Distributing Co—*Bill Morrissey*	5200 36th St SE, Grand Rapids MI 49512	616-942-9734	R	268*	.3
11	Waterford-Wedgwood USA—*Don Henderson*	1330 Campus Pky, Wall NJ 07719	732-938-5800	R	232*	.6
12	Marietta Drapery and Window Coverings Company Inc—*F Bentley*	PO Box 569, Marietta GA 30061	770-428-3335	R	224*	.2
13	Ontel Products Corp—*Charles Khubani*	21 Law Dr Ste 1, Fairfield NJ 07004	973-439-9000	R	187*	<.1
14	Idea Nuova Inc—*Nathan Accad*	302 5th Ave Fl 5, New York NY 10001	212-643-0680	R	171*	.2
15	Sure Fit Inc—*Hugh Rovit*	8000 Quarry Rd Ste C, Alburtis PA 18011	610-264-7300	R	143*	.1
16	Acme Mills Co—*James Colman*	550 Hulet Dr Ste 103, Bloomfield Hills MI 48302	248-203-2000	R	133*	.2
17	Divatex Home Fashion Inc—*Avi Gross*	295 5th Ave Ste 515, New York NY 10016	212-252-0802	R	130*	.1
18	Koval Marketing Inc—*Roy Koval*	11208 47th Ave W, Mukilteo WA 98275	425-347-4249	R	114*	<.1
19	Powell Co	PO Box 1408, Culver City CA 90232	310-204-2224	R	110*	.1
20	Ellery Homestyles LLC—*Michael Zhang*	295 5th Ave Ste 1212, New York NY 10016	212-684-5364	R	105*	.1
21	Bytheway's Manufacturing Inc—*Mervin Bytheway*	2080 Enterprise Blvd, West Sacramento CA 95691	916-453-1212	R	91*	.3
22	Regal Home Collections Inc—*Elyahu Cohen*	271 5th Ave Frnt A, New York NY 10016	212-213-3323	R	90*	.1
23	Momeni Inc—*Aliakbar Momeni*	60 Broad St, Carlstadt NJ 07072	201-549-7220	R	77*	.1
24	Charles Sadek Import Company Inc—*Jim Sadek*	PO Box 717, New Rochelle NY 10802	914-633-8090	R	67*	.1
25	Bradshaw International Inc—*Michael Rodrigue*	9409 Buffalo Ave, Rancho Cucamonga CA 91730	909-476-3884	S	65*	.1
26	Derr Flooring Co—*Chester Derr Jr*	PO Box 912, Willow Grove PA 19090	215-657-6300	R	57*	.2
27	Phoenix Textile Corp—*Palmer A Reynolds*	13652 Lakefront Dr, Earth City MO 63045	314-291-2151	R	54*	.1
28	Elements International Group LLC—*Jack Wurster*	2020 Industrial Blvd, Rockwall TX 75087	972-722-3888	R	54*	.1
29	Adleta Corp—*John Sher*	1645 Diplomat Dr, Carrollton TX 75006	972-620-5600	R	53*	.1
30	Zak Designs Inc—*Irv Zakheim*	PO Box 19188, Spokane WA 99219	509-244-0555	R	52*	.2
31	Heritage Lace Inc—*Mark De Cook*	PO Box 328, Pella IA 50219	641-628-4949	R	52*	.1
32	Wanke Cascade—*Jim Johnson*	6330 N Cutter Cir, Portland OR 97217	503-289-8609	R	50*	.1
33	Dealers Supply Co—*Russell Barringer Jr*	PO Box 2628, Durham NC 27715	919-383-7451	R	46*	.1
34	Allure Home Creation Company Inc—*Stanley Ho*	85 Fulton St, Boonton NJ 07005	973-402-8888	R	42*	.1
35	All Tile Inc—*Robert Weiss*	1201 Chase Ave, Elk Grove Village IL 60007	847-979-2500	R	42*	.1
36	Harold Import Company Inc—*Robert Laub*	747 Vassar Ave, Lakewood NJ 08701	732-367-2800	R	38*	.1
37	B and F System Inc—*John Meyer*	3920 S Walton Walker B, Dallas TX 75236	214-333-2111	R	37*	.1
38	William M Bird and Company Inc—*Maybank Hagood*	PO Box 20040, Charleston SC 29413	843-554-3040	R	37*	.1
39	Focus Products Group LLC—*Theresa Lareo*	300 Knightsbridge Pkwy, Lincolnshire IL 60069	224-513-2007	R	35*	.3
40	New Orleans Flooring Supply Inc—*Robert Chehardy*	PO Box 19165, New Orleans LA 70179	504-821-8111	R	33*	<.1
41	Kraus/Sound—*Scott Radcliffe*	300 SW 27th St Ste 100, Renton WA 98057		R	30*	.1
42	Eastside Wholesale Supply Co—*Don Lovely*	6450 E 8 Mile Rd, Detroit MI 48234	313-891-2902	R	25*	.1
43	Larson Distributing Company Inc—*John L Larson Jr*	5925 N Broadway, Denver CO 80216	303-296-7253	R	25*	.1
44	Mariak Industries Inc—*Leonard Elinson*	575 W Manville St, Rancho Dominguez CA 90220	310-661-4400	R	24*	.2
45	Gulf Coast American Blind Corp—*Carlos Diaz*	3705 Westview Dr, Naples FL 34104	239-643-2460	R	23*	.2
46	Yves Delorme Inc—*Dominique Fremaux*	1725 Broadway St, Charlottesville VA 22902	434-979-3911	R	23*	.2
47	Thompson Olde Inc—*Jeff Shumway*	3250 Camino Del Sol, Oxnard CA 93030	805-983-0388	R	21*	.2
48	Sewing Source Inc—*Janet Sload*	PO Box 639, Spring Hope NC 27882	252-478-3900	R	21*	.2
49	Interstate Supply Co—*Gary K Morrow*	9245 Dielman Industria, Saint Louis MO 63132	314-995-9900	R	21*	.1
50	Revere Mills Inc—*John Vandenberg*	3000 S River Rd, Des Plaines IL 60018	847-759-6800	R	20*	<.1
51	Brownstone Gallery Ltd	295 5th Ave Ste 412, New York NY 10016	212-696-4663	R	19*	.1
52	Cash Moulding Sales Of Alabama Inc—*Jim West*	436 Industrial Ln, Birmingham AL 35211	205-942-2909	R	19*	<.1

Rank	Company Name—*Executive Officer*	Address, City, State, Zip	Phone	Type	Fin	Empls
53	Erickson's Flooring and Supply Company Inc—*Richard Walters*	1013 Orchard St, Ferndale MI 48220	248-543-9663	R	18*	.1
54	Johnson Wholesale Floors Inc—*Melinda Mcchesney*	PO Box 250479, Atlanta GA 30325	404-352-2700	R	18*	.1
55	Picture Galleries Inc—*Lance Saunders*	PO Box 1000, Meridian ID 83680	208-321-9500	R	16*	.2
56	Jackson Pottery Inc—*Robert Jackson*	2146 Empire Central, Dallas TX 75235	214-357-9819	R	16*	.1
57	Engelsen Frame and Moulding Company Inc—*Norval Engelsen*	48260 Frank St, Wixom MI 48393	248-960-9500	R	16*	.1
58	Harbor Linen LLC—*Earl Waxman*	2 Foster Ave, Gibbsboro NJ 08026	856-435-2000	R	16*	.1
59	Boston Warehouse Trading Corp—*Peter Jenkins*	59 Davis Ave, Norwood MA 02062	781-769-8550	R	15*	.1
60	Three Hands Corp—*Shant Anan*	13259 Ralston Ave, Sylmar CA 91342	818-833-1200	R	15*	.1
61	Discover Marble and Granite Inc—*Victor Deoliveira*	4 Latti Farm Rd, Millbury MA 01527	508-438-6900	R	14*	.1
62	Hank's Specialties Inc—*Randy Grachek*	PO Box 120150, New Brighton MN 55112	651-633-5020	R	14*	.1
63	Next Day Blinds Corp—*Steve Freishtat*	8251 Preston Ct Ste B, Jessup MD 20794	240-568-8800	R	13*	.4
64	Unique Wholesale Distributors Inc—*Sam Pampenella*	6811 Nw 15th Ave, Fort Lauderdale FL 33309	954-975-0227	R	13*	.1
65	Pampered Chef Ltd—*Marla Gottschalk*	1 Pampered Chef Ln, Addison IL 60101	630-261-8900	S	13*	.8
66	Jacobs Trading Co—*Irwin Jacobs*	8090 Excelsior BLVD, Hopkins MN 55343	763-843-2000	R	13*	<.1
67	Westfloor Inc—*Jeff Henick*	202 Wythe Ave, Brooklyn NY 11249	718-782-0333	R	13*	.1
68	Midwest Floor Coverings Inc—*John Parrish*	PO Box 65768, Salt Lake City UT 84165	801-972-1125	R	13*	.1
69	Ajr Flooring LLC	PO Box 1894, Bensalem PA 19020	215-639-6300	R	12*	<.1
70	Over and Back Inc—*Bernard Levitan*	90 Adams Ave Ste B, Hauppauge NY 11788	631-357-8140	R	12*	<.1
71	Butler Group Inc (Atlanta Georgia)—*Ed Butler*	230 Spring St Ste 1212, Atlanta GA 30303	404-577-6941	R	12*	<.1
72	Kincaid and Decker Inc—*Richard Decker*	15800 Straden St, Van Nuys CA 91406	818-785-1528	R	12*	.1
73	Robinson Home Products Inc—*Robert Skerker*	PO Box 550, Cheektowaga NY 14225	716-206-1100	R	12*	.1
74	Town and Country Linen Corp—*Marc Breslof*	475 Oberlin Ave S Ste, Lakewood NJ 08701	732-364-2000	R	11*	.1
75	Valley Wholesale Supply Corp—*David Labowitz*	10708 Vanowen St, North Hollywood CA 91605	818-769-5656	R	11*	.1
76	Mastercraft Flooring Distributors Inc—*Thomas Barbaglia*	13001a Nw 38th Ave, Opa Locka FL 33054	305-688-7771	R	11*	<.1
77	Sterling Cut Glass Company Inc—*Michael Dyas*	3233 Mineola Pke, Erlanger KY 41018	859-283-2333	R	11*	.1
78	L Bornstein and Company Inc—*Leslie Bornstein-Stacks*	321 Washington St, Somerville MA 02143	617-776-3555	R	11*	<.1
79	Rainbow Linens Inc—*Bruce Tucker*	107 Trumbull St Bldg 4, Elizabeth NJ 07206	908-965-0905	R	11*	<.1
80	Bp Industries Inc—*Don Kim*	5300 Concours, Ontario CA 91764	909-481-0227	R	11*	.1
81	Don-Mar Creations Inc—*Donald Marino*	862 Waterman Ave, East Providence RI 02914	401-633-1410	R	11*	.1
82	Design Material Inc—*Marty Wessinger*	241 S 55th St, Kansas City KS 66106	913-342-9796	R	11*	<.1
83	Redi-Floors Inc—*Peter Brookner*	1791 Williams Dr, Marietta GA 30066	770-590-7334	R	10*	.1
84	Dhi Corp—*Todd Witte*	5205 W Donges Bay Rd, Mequon WI 53092	262-242-5205	R	10*	.1
85	Fssco Inc—*Lawrence Stephens*	905 Mclaughlin Ave, San Jose CA 95122	408-280-0222	R	10*	.1
86	Lvc Window Blinds Inc—*Lance Calcar*	176 Kansas St, Hackensack NJ 07601	201-525-0222	R	10*	<.1
87	Crossroads Distributors Inc—*Jeff Fuehrer*	120 Commerce Dr, Danville IN 46122		R	10*	<.1
88	Tabb Textiles Company Inc—*Alan Fenster*	PO Box 2707, Opelika AL 36803	334-745-6762	R	9*	.1
89	Kjb Supply Company Inc—*Stephen Kleinhans*	2802 W Virginia Ave, Phoenix AZ 85009	602-442-2200	R	9*	.1
90	Hom-Excel Inc—*Gene Provenzano*	21945 Us Hwy 19 N, Clearwater FL 33765	727-723-8700	R	9*	.1
91	Pfpc Enterprises Inc—*James Coffaro*	5750 Hillside Ave, Cincinnati OH 45233	513-941-6200	P	8*	.3
92	Tile and Stone Accents Ino *Rod Britain*	145 W Chilton Dr, Chandler AZ 85225	480-898-8135	R	8*	.1
93	Sferra Brothers Ltd—*Paul Hooker*	PO Box 6690, Edison NJ 08818	732-225-6290	R	8*	<.1
94	Blackton Inc—*Michael Blackton*	1714 Alden Rd, Orlando FL 32803	407-898-2661	R	8*	<.1
95	Abrahams Oriental Rugs—*Samuel Abraham*	5120 Woodway Dr Ste 18, Houston TX 77056	713-622-4444	R	8*	<.1
96	Aurora Hardwoods Inc—*Bill Backman*	PO Box 457, Piney Flats TN 37686	423-764-6127	R	8*	<.1
97	Kreative Kamaaina Enterprises LLC—*Cindy Yoshimito*	1804 Hart St, Honolulu HI 96819	808-841-8731	R	7*	<.1
98	Nl and A Collections Inc—*Daniel Edelist*	6323 Maywood Ave, Huntington Park CA 90255	323-277-6266	R	7*	<.1
99	Huff Floorcovering Inc—*C Huff*	1878 Petersburg Rd, Hebron KY 41048	859-680 7053	R	7*	<.1
100	Camden Flooring Co *Robert Sweigart*	1300 Rte 38, Cherry Hill NJ 08002	856-662-4830	R	7*	<.1
101	Pictures And More Inc—*Daniel Eagan*	512 Pecan Dr, Clinton KY 42031	270-653-2645	R	7*	.1
102	Art Floor Inc—*William Bartoshesky*	9 Jefferson Ave, Wilmington DE 19805	302-636-9201	R	7*	<.1
103	Art Chinese Gallery Inc—*Siu Kam*	1020 E Levee St, Dallas TX 75207	214-745-1341	R	7*	<.1
104	Tti Holding International Inc—*Linda Galbraitch*	1000 Nolen Dr Ste 100, Grapevine TX 76051	817-424-5300	R	7*	<.1
105	Kinder-Harris Inc—*Kristina Lindsey*	PO Box 1390, Stuttgart AR 72160	870-673-1518	R	6*	<.1
106	Flooring Design Associates Inc—*Kenneth Bauer*	3770 Paris St, Denver CO 80239	303-371-2929	R	6*	<.1
107	Portu-Sunberg and Associates Inc—*Larry Barnett*	50 S 10th St Ste 550, Minneapolis MN 55403	612-455-2130	R	6*	<.1
108	Progressive Specialty Glass Company Inc—*Dean Rosow*	123 Whiting St Ste R, Plainville CT 06062	860-410-9980	R	6*	<.1
109	Fierst Distributing Co—*Steven Feinstein*	746 Trumbull Dr, Pittsburgh PA 15205	412-429-9300	R	6*	<.1
110	CPI Manufacturing Company Inc—*Steve Benbasat*	5945 Ravenswood Rd Ste, Fort Lauderdale FL 33312	954-961-9100	R	6*	<.1
111	MAFInc—*Phillip Maffei*	PO Box 2855, Fairfield CA 94533	707-427-5120	R	6*	<.1
112	Arakelian Inc—*Eddie Arakelian*	324 N Minnewawa Ave, Clovis CA 93612	559-297-8802	R	6*	<.1
113	Nanshing America Inc—*Xing Li*	5822 E 61st St, Commerce CA 90040	323-887-3888	R	6*	<.1
114	Aluminum Frame Company Of America—*Stephen Kress*	PO Box 12727, Philadelphia PA 19134	215-288-8040	R	5*	<.1
115	Krohns Inc—*Michael Quadhamer*	702 Clark Pl, Colorado Springs CO 80915	719-471-4851	R	5*	<.1
116	Stanley Stephens Company Inc—*Stephen Seidman*	PO Box 2205, Bristol PA 19007	215-788-1515	R	5*	<.1
117	Genis Inc—*Salo Grosfeld*	19401 W Dixie Hwy, Miami FL 33180	305-933-7100	R	5*	<.1
118	Cartwright Distributing Inc—*Bill Cartwright*	4851 Kingston St, Denver CO 80239	303-371-7950	R	5*	<.1
119	Marquis Industries Inc—*Tim Bailey*	PO Box 1308, Chatsworth GA 30705	706-695-1060	R	5*	<.1
120	Pacific Mat and Commercial Flooring LLC—*Lance Kohler*	18414 80th Ct S, Kent WA 98032		R	5*	<.1
121	R and S Carpet Service Inc—*Roy Paswaters*	1142 E Acacia Ct Ste A, Ontario CA 91761	909-923-2511	R	5*	<.1
122	Charter Distributing Co—*Dennis Nehro*	4054 Dolan Dr, Flint MI 48504	810-789-5071	R	5*	<.1
123	Ebisons Harounian Imports—*Michael Harounian*	44 E 32nd St, New York NY 10016	212-686-4262	R	5*	<.1
124	Dave's Design Center Iii—*David Lindquist*	5300 S Watt Ave, Sacramento CA 95826	916-383-1555	R	5*	<.1
125	Venture Technology Groups—*Mike Fitzpatrick*	3754 Hordyk St Ne, Grand Rapids MI 49525	616-361-3690	R	5*	.1
126	Bs Trading Co—*Troy Ratterree*	3605 S Cooper St, Arlington TX 76015	817-417-7847	R	5*	<.1
127	Old Dominion Floor Company Inc—*Derek Dunlap*	3350 Speeks Dr, Midlothian VA 23112	804-674-0315	R	5*	<.1
128	Heyder Florida Inc—*Arno Heyder*	3450 Vineland Rd Ste C, Orlando FL 32811	407-423-7011	R	5*	<.1
129	Bashian Brothers Inc—*George Bashian*	100 Park Plz Dr 104n, Secaucus NJ 07094	201-330-1001	R	5*	<.1
130	SCI Floor Covering Inc—*James Robinson*	21440 Melrose Ave, Southfield MI 48075	248-359-3500	R	5*	<.1
131	Crystal Blanc Company Inc—*Barry Dyas*	225 Gap Way, Erlanger KY 41018	859-283-0039	R	5*	<.1
132	Tru-Bamboo LLC—*Rafiq Hassan*	1115 Gateway Blvd, Boynton Beach FL 33426	561-832-0628	R	5*	<.1
133	LA Destination Inc—*Iqbal Dada*	3815 S Grand Ave, Los Angeles CA 90037	213-741-1300	R	4*	<.1
134	Dixie Building Products Inc—*Alfred Silverstein*	PO Box 6023, Roanoke VA 24017	540-342-6787	R	4*	<.1
135	Monterrey Tile Co—*Ed York*	225 W Baseline Rd, Gilbert AZ 85233	480-507-7966	R	4*	<.1
136	California Closet Company Of Orange County/Long Beach Inc—*Scott Seigel*	5921 Skylab Rd, Huntington Beach CA 92647	714-899-4905	R	4*	<.1
137	Ski and Sea International Inc—*Jennifer Miner*	1445 W Tufts Ave, Englewood CO 80110	303-761-5800	R	4*	<.1
138	Blaze Fireplace Of Northern California—*Bruce Weitzman*	101 Cargo Way, San Francisco CA 94124	415-495-2002	R	4*	<.1
139	B and P Lamp Supply Company Inc—*Paul Barnes*	843 Old Morrison Hwy, Mcminnville TN 37110	931-473-3016	R	4*	<.1
140	Gerflor North America—*Dean Morgan*	206 W Campus Dr, Arlington Heights IL 60004	847-394-3944	R	4*	<.1
141	World Image Corp—*Alex Herzog*	8210 Cleary Blvd Apt 2, Plantation FL 33324	954-472-9884	R	4*	.1

Note: An asterisk (*) indicates an estimated financial figure. The company type code used is as follows: R = Private, P = Public, S = Private Subsidiary, B = Public Subsidiary, D = Division, J = Joint Venture, I = Investment Fund.

COMPANY RANKINGS BY SALES WITHIN 4-DIGIT SIC

Rank	Company Name—*Executive Officer*	Address, City, State, Zip	Phone	Type	Fin	Empls
142	Builders Fireplace and Supply Inc—*Ronnie Boles*	5323 Surrett Dr, High Point NC 27263	336-861-5440	R	4*	<.1
143	Mehdi Dilmaghani and Company Inc—*Dennis Dilmaghani*	540 Central Park Ave, Scarsdale NY 10583	914-472-1700	R	4*	<.1
144	Salvatore Polizzi—*Salvator Polizzi*	340 S La Brea, Los Angeles CA 90036	323-731-6390	R	4*	<.1
145	M and M Tile Co—*Bill Mussino*	PO Box 46, Tontitown AR 72770	479-361-2551	R	4*	<.1
146	Microtex Inc—*Steve Barak*	5301 Nw 161st St, Hialeah FL 33014	305-622-7135	R	4*	<.1
147	DJH Inc—*Marvin Tuchklaper*	PO Box 4811, Miami Lakes FL 33014	305-620-1990	R	4*	<.1
148	Floor Resources Inc—*John Gill*	PO Box 774, Pleasantville NJ 08232	609-646-3171	R	4*	.1
149	Builders Service Company Of Fort Worth—*Lori Yeager*	2008 Exchange Dr, Arlington TX 76011	817-640-3885	R	4*	<.1
150	SE Arnold And Company Inc—*Steven Arnold*	7619 Cantrell Rd Ste A, Little Rock AR 72227	501-225-3840	R	4*	<.1
151	Aram Michael Inc—*Michael Aram*	2102 83rd St, North Bergen NJ 07047	201-758-2551	R	4*	<.1
152	Mister Ralph's Inc—*Doug Morris*	1000 Dragon St, Dallas TX 75207	214-744-5111	R	4*	<.1
153	Surbuban Floor Covering Inc—*Steve Abeles*	2120 Beaver Rd, Landover MD 20785	301-773-4111	R	4*	<.1
154	Creative Flooring Designs Inc—*David Harvey*	PO Box 3905, Sedona AZ 86340	928-204-5542	R	4*	<.1
155	Commercial Window Coverings Inc—*Doris Williams*	12027 E 51st St Ste 46, Tulsa OK 74146	918-250-0025	R	4*	<.1
156	Robina Inc—*Robby Loh*	825 Great Sw Pkwy Sw, Atlanta GA 30336	678-819-1489	R	3*	<.1
157	Dudson Group USA Inc—*Russel Plum*	5604 Departure Dr, Raleigh NC 27616	919-877-0200	R	3*	<.1
158	Extreme Carpets LLC—*Tony Terrosi*	612 Berriman St, Brooklyn NY 11208	718-257-9666	R	3*	<.1
159	Olson Floor Covering Inc—*Galen Olson*	PO Box 607, Wausau WI 54402	715-359-9221	R	3*	<.1
160	Putnam Stainless Tubes Inc—*James Schlenker*	1163 Us Hwy 22, Mountainside NJ 07092	908-232-9200	R	3*	<.1
161	Duroc USA—*Albert Tor*	PO Box 351208, Los Angeles CA 90035	323-278-1111	R	3*	<.1
162	Prosource Management Inc—*David Krieling*	4301 Earth City Expy, Earth City MO 63045	314-291-0000	R	3*	<.1
163	Evald Moulding Company Inc—*Jon Hauser*	PO Box 139, Watertown WI 53094	920-261-8857	R	3*	<.1
164	Lelia Industries Inc—*Kenny Shaevel*	711 Pico Blvd, Santa Monica CA 90405	310-450-6080	R	3*	<.1
165	Apollo Propane Inc—*Walter Fritzsche*	2680 Viking Ln, Moraine OH 45439	937-298-0300	R	3*	<.1
166	Imperial Flooring Company Inc—*Robert Galeano*	PO Box 208, Bohemia NY 11716	631-567-4707	R	3*	<.1
167	Northeastern Import Export Inc—*Ronald Tuscano*	80 Crossway E, Bohemia NY 11716	631-563-3188	R	3*	<.1
168	H T Barnes Co—*Donald Watler*	PO Box 1327, Foley AL 36536	251-943-8303	R	3*	<.1
169	C and L International Co—*Michael Lee*	1351 Distribution Way, Vista CA 92081	760-599-5803	R	3*	<.1
170	Tech-Styles Window Covering Products Inc—*Rory Mcneil*	300 Graves Ave Ste A, Oxnard CA 93030	805-751-2751	R	3*	<.1
171	United Wholesale Flooring Inc—*Pedram Foroohar*	1250 Rancho Conejo Blv, Newbury Park CA 91320	805-214-0992	R	3*	<.1
172	David W Taylor and Associates—*David Taylor*	4331 S Main St, Salt Lake City UT 84107	801-262-2997	R	3*	<.1
173	Curtis D Turner Company Inc—*Steven Turner*	8220 Commonwealth Dr, Eden Prairie MN 55344	952-944-9220	R	3*	<.1
174	All American Hardwood Inc—*Angela Ma*	1735 E Grevillea Ct, Ontario CA 91761	909-947-3232	R	3*	<.1
175	Williams Flooring Sales Inc—*James Leslie*	201 W N St, Akron OH 44303	330-535-9189	R	3*	<.1
176	Rajpootana Holdings Ltd—*Rahul Bhargava*	46 Constitution Way, Jersey City NJ 07305	201-779-6063	R	3*	<.1
177	Star Kitchen and Bath—*Don Kriemin*	19414 Londelius St, Northridge CA 91324	818-654-9090	R	3*	<.1
178	Chickies Club South Inc—*Norris Jimoresi*	2388 N University Dr, Coral Springs FL 33065	954-341-9990	R	3*	<.1
179	Van Wyck Window Fashions Inc—*Harold Lamm*	2127 Borden Ave, Long Island City NY 11101	718-482-6666	R	3*	<.1
180	Zelco Industries Inc—*Adele Zeller*	65 Haven Ave, Mount Vernon NY 10553	914-699-6230	R	3*	<.1
181	MZ Carpet Inc—*Mehrbanoo Ziai*	PO Box 341705, Pacoima CA 91334	818-994-1555	R	3*	<.1
182	Triple "j" Custom Interiors Inc—*Charles Johnson*	PO Box 8003, Fort Mohave AZ 86427	928-768-7666	R	3*	<.1
183	AH Furnico Inc—*Ben Liu*	6425 English Ave Ste 1, Indianapolis IN 46219	317-802-9363	R	3*	<.1
184	Framesource Manufacturing Corp—*Howard Perl*	58 Grant Ave, Carteret NJ 07008	732-541-2603	R	3*	<.1
185	Clayton Miller Hospitality Carpet—*Clayton Miller*	2304 Dalton Industrial, Dalton GA 30721	706-281-4501	R	3*	<.1
186	Elegant Linens and Table Skirting—*Vic Martin*	5712 Granger St, Corona NY 11368	718-760-9401	R	2*	<.1
187	Garden Ridge—*Bill Howard*	1996 Pavillon Way, Lexington KY 40509	859-543-8039	R	2*	<.1
188	South Mountain Moulding Inc—*Mike Bull*	1120 W Alameda Dr Ste, Tempe AZ 85282	480-731-9715	R	2*	<.1
189	Rosle U S A Corp—*Eric Jones*	802 Centerpoint Blvd, New Castle DE 19720	302-326-4801	R	2*	<.1
190	Edward P Boutross Inc—*Edward Boutross*	PO Box 441, Windsor NJ 08561	609-897-1000	R	2*	<.1
191	Denny Lamp Company Inc—*E Denman*	PO Box 455, Smithville TN 37166	615-597-7671	R	2*	<.1
192	H J Weber Carpet Co—*Henry Weber*	3140 W 25th St, Cleveland OH 44109	216-351-1200	R	2*	<.1
193	Canopy Designs Ltd—*Merrie Shinder*	4261 24th St Fl 1, Long Island City NY 11101	718-361-3040	R	2*	<.1
194	Kronoswiss Of America LLC—*Derick Dudley*	7811 N Shepherd Dr Ste, Houston TX 77088	281-445-7680	R	2*	<.1
195	Thai Trade Development Corp—*Niwat Kitirattragarn*	231 Main St, Little Falls NJ 07424	973-237-1210	R	2*	<.1
196	Sunteca Systems Inc—*Gustavo Etably*	Ave A Bldg 2, Leetsdale PA 15056	412-749-5200	R	2*	<.1
197	Frame It And Company Inc—*Jerry Greenberg*	767 3rd Ave, Brooklyn NY 11232	718-768-7375	R	2*	<.1
198	Carpet Company Op—*Jeff Jaggers*	2690 Oxford Ave, Turlock CA 95382	209-669-9027	R	2*	<.1
199	Hsi Accessories Inc—*Terry Frisk*	1323 11th Ave N, Nampa ID 83687	208-468-0297	R	2*	<.1
200	Imported Interiors Inc—*Sudhir Chand*	18571 Oak Park Dr, Riverside CA 92504	951-776-4645	R	2*	<.1
201	Karsen Co—*Jeffry Karsen*	PO Box 653, Elk Grove Village IL 60009	847-364-6760	R	2*	<.1
202	Robina Wood Inc—*Jason Loh*	825 Great Sw Pkwy Sw, Atlanta GA 30336	678-626-0510	R	2*	<.1
203	Southwest Glassware Co—*W Stellbrink*	7521 N I10 Eb Frontage, Tucson AZ 85743	520-292-0556	R	2*	<.1
204	James M Depaul—*James Depaul*	PO Box 735, Lake Forest CA 92609	714-751-9190	R	2*	<.1
205	Casafina Enterprises Ltd—*Donna Smith*	301 Fields Ln Ste 13, Brewster NY 10509	845-277-5700	R	2*	<.1
206	Summerour Lamps—*Paul Summerour*	2220 Thrift Rd, Charlotte NC 28208	704-332-1897	R	1*	<.1
207	CC Works Inc—*Greg Harkison*	12118 Duncan Rd Ste 10, Houston TX 77066	281-440-0123	R	1*	<.1
208	Eldridge Acrylics Inc—*Karen Eldridge*	475 Oak St, Mansfield OH 44907	419-526-2678	R	1*	<.1
209	Pieceworks Inc—*Cathy Roberts*	PO Box 133, Liberty ME 04949	207-589-4123	R	1*	<.1

TOTALS: SIC 5023 Homefurnishings

	Companies: 209					
					17,166	18.4

5031 Lumber, Plywood & Millwork

Rank	Company Name—*Executive Officer*	Address, City, State, Zip	Phone	Type	Fin	Empls
1	Stock Building Supply Inc—*Jeff Rea*	8020 Arco Corporate Dr, Raleigh NC 27617	919-431-1000	J	3,953*	10.9
2	Boise Cascade Holdings LLC—*Thomas Carlile*	PO Box 50, Boise ID 83728	208-384-6161	R	2,248	4.2
3	Pope and Talbot Lumber Sales Inc—*Harold N Stanton*	1500 SW 1st Ave Ste 20, Portland OR 97201	503-228-9161	S	2,100*	2.5
4	Pope and Talbot Pulp Sales USA Inc—*Harold N Stanton*	1500 SW 1st Ave Ste 20, Portland OR 97201	503-228-9161	S	2,100*	2.5
5	Bradco Supply Corp—*Larry Stoddard*	13 Production Way, Avenel NJ 07001	732-382-3400	R	1,982*	3.2
6	BlueLinx Holdings Inc—*George R Judd*	4300 Wildwood Pkwy, Atlanta GA 30339	770-953-7000	P	1,755	1.9
7	LP Building Products	414 Union St Ste 2000, Nashville TN 37219	615-986-5600	S	1,705	5.1
8	Dyke Industries Inc—*Fred Edick*	309 Ctr St, Little Rock AR 72201	501-376-2921	R	1,089*	.5
9	Crane Composites—*Jeff Craney*	23525 W Eames, Channahon IL 60410	815-467-8600	S	988*	1.0
10	North Pacific Group Inc—*Jay Ross*	PO Box 3915, Portland OR 97208	503-231-1166	R	977*	.6
11	Plum Creek MDF Inc—*Rick R Holley*	999 3rd Ave Ste 4300, Seattle WA 98104	206-467-3600	S	906*	1.2
12	Pacific Coast Building Products Inc—*David Lucchetti*	PO Box 419074, Rancho Cordova CA 95741	916-631-6500	R	899*	3.2
13	Plum Creek Northwest Plywood Inc—*Rick R Holley*	999 3rd Ave Ste 4300, Seattle WA 98104	206-467-3600	S	876*	1.2
14	Builders FirstSource Inc—*Floyd F Sherman*	2001 Bryan St Ste 1600, Dallas TX 75201	214-880-3500	B	779	2.5
15	Bison Building Materials LLC—*Pat Bierschwale*	PO Box 19849, Houston TX 77224	713-467-6700	R	449*	.7
16	Empire Company Inc—*Thomas Highly*	PO Box 17, Zeeland MI 49464	616-772-7272	R	396*	.4
17	TWP Enterprises Inc—*Michael Cassidy*	8101 Snouffer School R, Gaithersburg MD 20879	301-840-9600	R	395*	.4
18	Forest City Trading Group LLC—*Craig Johnston*	PO Box 4209, Portland OR 97208	503-246-8500	R	381*	.4

Rank	Company Name—*Executive Officer*	Address, City, State, Zip	Phone	Type	Fin	Empls
19	Brockway-Smith Co (Andover Massachusetts)—*Charles Smith*	146 Dascomb Rd, Andover MA 01810	978-475-7100	R	373*	.4
20	Radford Co—*Michael Walsh*	PO Box 2688, Oshkosh WI 54903	920-426-2600	R	356*	.2
21	Reico Distributors Inc—*Richard Maresco*	7619 Little River Turn, Annandale VA 22003	703-256-6400	R	320*	.4
22	Seven D Wholesale—*Donald A DeGol Sr*	PO Box 67, Gallitzin PA 16641		D	300*	.4
23	International Industries Inc	PO Box 18370, South Charleston WV 25303	304-746-6021	R	299*	.3
24	Mid-AM Building Supply Inc—*Alan Knaebel*	PO Box 645, Moberly MO 65270	660-263-2140	R	262*	.4
25	Roberts and Dybdahl Inc—*Ted Roberts*	PO Box 1908, Des Moines IA 50306		R	243*	.4
26	Building Products Inc—*Lee Schull*	PO Box 1390, Watertown SD 57201	605-886-3495	R	208*	.2
27	VerHalen Inc—*John Calawerts*	PO Box 11968, Green Bay WI 54307	920-435-3791	R	201*	.3
28	Diamond Hill Plywood Company Inc—*JohnC Ramsey*	PO Box 529, Darlington SC 29540	843-393-2803	S	200	.3
29	Hundman Lumber Do-it Center Inc—*Mike Hundman*	1707 Hamilton Rd, Bloomington IL 61704	309-662-0339	R	196*	.3
30	Building Material Distributors Inc—*Jeff Gore*	PO Box 606, Galt CA 95632	209-745-3001	R	191*	.2
31	WM Tinder Inc—*W Michael Tinder*	PO Box 2188, Manassas VA 20108	703-368-9544	R	187*	.2
32	Snavely Forest Products Inc—*Stephen V Snavely*	600 Delwar Rd, Pittsburgh PA 15236	412-885-4005	R	165*	.3
33	Tumac Lumber Company Inc—*Brad McMurchie*	805 SW Broadway Ste 17, Portland OR 97205	503-226-6661	R	160*	.2
34	EE Newcomer Enterprises Inc—*Rex Newcomer*	PO Box 12517, Kansas City MO 64116	816-221-0543	R	156*	1.0
35	Patrick Lumber Company Inc—*Jim Rodway*	812 SW 10th Ave Ste 20, Portland OR 97205	503-222-9671	R	155*	.1
36	Shamrock Building Materials Inc—*Michael Gambee*	PO Box 23208, Eugene OR 97402	541-688-5444	R	154*	.1
37	Millman Lumber Co—*Richard Millman*	9264 Manchester Rd, Saint Louis MO 63144	314-968-1700	R	152*	.1
38	Cooley Industries Inc—*Dean L Cooley*	PO Box 20188, Phoenix AZ 85036	602-276-2402	R	146*	.2
39	Shelter Products Inc—*George Beechler*	PO Box 42100, Portland OR 97242	503-872-3600	R	144*	.1
40	Pacific Mutual Door Co—*Jon Lambert*	1525 W 31st St, Kansas City MO 64108	816-531-0161	R	131*	.2
41	Wheeler's Corp—*James T Manis*	550 Riverside Pkwy NE, Rome GA 30161	706-232-2400	R	131*	.2
42	JE Higgins Lumber Co—*Jonathan R Long*	6999 Southfront Rd, Livermore CA 94551	925-245-4300	R	122*	.5
43	Lawrence R Mccoy and Company Inc—*Richard Dale*	120 Front St Ste 800, Worcester MA 01608	508-368-7700	R	121*	<.1
44	Mill Creek Lumber and Supply Co—*Jeff Dunn*	6201 S 129th E Ave, Tulsa OK 74145	918-461-9090	R	115*	.5
45	Lumbermen's Inc—*Roger A Vanderheide*	4433 Stafford Ave SW, Grand Rapids MI 49548	616-261-3200	R	112*	.2
46	Amerhart Ltd—*Mark Kasper*	PO Box 10097, Green Bay WI 54307	920-494-4744	R	109*	.2
47	Lake States Lumber Inc—*Keith Logan*	PO Box 310, Aitkin MN 56431	218-927-2125	R	108*	.1
48	HW Culp Lumber Co—*Henry W Culp Jr*	PO Box 235, New London NC 28127	704-463-7311	R	104*	.1
49	United Plywood and Lumber Inc—*John Mims*	1640 Mims Ave SW, Birmingham AL 35211	205-925-7601	R	101*	.1
50	Allied Building Stores Inc—*David Stiles*	PO Box 8030, Monroe LA 71211	318-699-9100	R	85*	.1
51	Griffin Wood Company Inc—*Corin Harrison Jr*	PO Box 669, Marion AL 36756	334-683-9073	R	84*	.1
52	Matheus Lumber Company Inc—*Gary Powell*	PO Box 2260, Woodinville WA 98072	425-489-3000	R	82*	.1
53	Miller and Company Inc—*Bobby Buchanon*	PO Box 770, Selma AL 36702	334-874-8271	R	81*	.3
54	Stanford Home Centers	1173 State Rte 356, Leechburg PA 15656	724-845-8104	R	81*	.1
55	Fessenden Hall Inc—*Ed Birdsall*	1050 Sherman Ave, Pennsauken NJ 08110	856-665-2210	R	80*	.1
56	Niehaus Home Center—*Bernard F Niehaus*	PO Box 667, Vincennes IN 47591	812-882-2710	R	79*	.1
57	TBM Hardwoods—*Baird McIlvain*	100 Filbert St, Hanover PA 17331		R	73*	.1
58	Virginia Hardwood Co—*Gary Henzie*	1000 W Foothill Blvd, Azusa CA 91702	626-815-0540	R	73*	.1
59	Redwood Empire Inc—*Rodger Burch*	PO Box 1300, Morgan Hill CA 95038	408-779-7354	R	71*	<.1
60	Rew Material Inc	15720 W 108th St, Lenexa KS 66219	913-438-4142	R	71*	<.1
61	National Industrial Lumber Co—*Michael Hoag*	1 Chicago Ave, Elizabeth PA 15037	412-384-3900	R	68*	.1
62	Idaho Pacific Lumber Company Inc—*Chip Estey*	7255 W Franklin Rd, Boise ID 83709	208-375-8052	R	65*	<.1
63	Pfr Acquistons LLC	1325 Airport Rd, Fall River MA 02720	508-676-6820	R	65*	.1
64	Dealers Supply and Lumber Inc—*Knox Wherry*	PO Box 5025, Greenville SC 29606	864-242-6571	R	64*	<.1
65	Prince Corp—*Jay Emling*	8351 County Rd H, Marshfield WI 54449	715-384 3105	R	61*	.1
66	Winco Distributors Inc	2253 Cordova Ave, Le Center MN 56057	507-357-6831	R	60*	.2
67	Reliable Wholesale Lumber Inc—*Jerome Higman*	PO Box 191, Huntington Beach CA 92648	714-848-8222	R	52*	.3
68	Builders General Supply Co—*Timothy J Shaheen*	PO Box 95, Little Silver NJ 07739	732-747-0808	R	52*	.1
69	Pine Cone Lumber Company Inc—*Brian Cilker*	PO Box 61207, Sunnyvale CA 94088	408-736-5491	R	52*	.1
70	William M Young Co—*Harold West*	PO Box 10487, Wilmington DE 19850	302-654-4448	R	52*	.1
71	Western Woods Inc—*Gerald Richter*	PO Box 4402, Chico CA 95927	530-343-5821	R	52*	.1
72	WindowPRO—*John Radie Zahnow Jr*	16900 Bagley Rd, Middleburg Heights OH 44130		R	50*	.1
73	Morgan-Wightman Supply Company Inc—*Stuart P Wells*	739 Goddard Ave, Chesterfield MO 63005	636-536-9729	R	48*	.2
74	Sprenger Midwest Inc—*Steven Sprenger*	PO Box 2436, Sioux Falls SD 57101	605-334-7705	R	47*	<.1
75	Stringfellow Lumber Co—*Bill Fisher*	901 2nd Ct W, Birmingham AL 35204		S	46*	<.1
76	Central Woodwork Of Nashville Inc—*William Schaefer*	870 Keough Rd, Collierville TN 38017	901-363-4141	R	46*	.2
77	Holmes Lumber and Building Center Inc—*Paul Miller*	6139 SR 39, Millersburg OH 44654	330-674-9060	R	46*	.2
78	Thomas and Proetz Lumber Co—*Charles E Thomas*	3400 Hall St, Saint Louis MO 63147	314-231-9343	S	45*	.1
79	Grand Rapids Sash and Door Co—*Doug Lachniet*	PO Box E, Grand Rapids MI 49501	616-245-1222	R	43*	.1
80	Standard Supplies Inc—*Deborah Murphy*	4 Meem Ave, Gaithersburg MD 20877	301-948-2690	R	42*	.1
81	Schutte Lumber Company Inc—*Dan Fuhrman*	3001 Southwest Blvd, Kansas City MO 64108	816-753-6262	R	41*	<.1
82	Maner Builders Supply Company LLC—*James Broome*	PO Box 204598, Augusta GA 30917	706-863-6191	R	41*	.2
83	Cascade Lumber Co—*Ray Noonan*	PO Box 220, Cascade IA 52033	563-852-3232	R	39*	.2
84	Riddio Construction Company Inc—*James Riddiough*	5870 88th St, Sacramento CA 95828	916-387-8642	R	38*	.3
85	Pdc Glass And Metal Services Inc—*Richard Clinton*	100 Business Ctr Dr, Cheswick PA 15024	724-274-9050	R	37*	.3
86	Louis J Grasmick Lumber Company Inc—*Louis J Grasmick*	6715 Quad Ave, Baltimore MD 21237	410-325-9663	R	37*	.1
87	Edward Hines Lumber Co—*Edward Hines*	1000 Corporate Grove D, Buffalo Grove IL 60089	847-353-7700	R	36*	.8
88	Newman Lumber Co—*Roy Newman*	PO Box 2580, Gulfport MS 39505	228-832-1899	R	36*	<.1
89	Doka USA Ltd—*Daniel Winters*	214 Gates Rd, Little Ferry NJ 07643	201-641-6500	S	35*	.2
90	Rhodes Supply Company Inc—*Gene Rhodes*	9793 State Rte 303, Mayfield KY 42066	270-382-2185	R	34*	.1
91	Darant Distributing Corp	1832 E 68th Ave, Denver CO 80229	303-385-1364	R	34*	.1
92	Penrod Co—*Edward Heidt Jr*	2809 S Lynnhaven Rd St, Virginia Beach VA 23452	757-498-0186	R	33*	.1
93	Magnolia Forest Products Inc—*Dennis Berry*	PO Box 99, Terry MS 39170	601-878-2581	R	33*	.1
94	Empire Enterprises Inc—*Peter Carroll*	PO Box 1248, Bath OH 44210	330-665-7800	R	30*	<.1
95	Shuster's Builders Supplies Inc—*Anthony Shuster*	2920 Clay Pke, Irwin PA 15642	412-351-0979	R	30*	.2
96	Mentor Lumber and Supply Company Inc—*Robert Sanderson*	7180 Center St, Mentor OH 44060	440-255-8814	R	30*	.1
97	Plywood Supply Inc—*Ralph Swanson*	PO Box 82300, Kenmore WA 98028	425-485-8585	R	29*	.1
98	California Panel and Veneer Co—*John Fahs*	PO Box 3250, Cerritos CA 90703	562-926-5834	R	29*	<.1
99	Case Engineered Lumber Inc—*Kevin Case*	4650 Thurmon Tanner Pk, Flowery Branch GA 30542	678-866-8600	R	29*	<.1
100	Colorado Doorways Inc—*Jerry Ladd*	3333 E 52nd Ave, Denver CO 80216	303-291-0900	R	28*	.1
101	Holt And Bugbee Co—*Phillip Pierce*	PO Box 37, Tewksbury MA 01876	978-851-7201	R	28*	.2
102	Lee Roy Jordan Redwood Lumber Co—*Lee Jordan*	2425 Burbank St, Dallas TX 75235	214-357-7317	R	27*	.1
103	Eldredge Lumber and Hardware Inc—*Scott Eldredge*	PO Box 69, Cape Neddick ME 03902	207-363-2004	R	27*	.1
104	Allen Millwork Inc—*Burrows Wheless*	PO Box 6480, Shreveport LA 71136	318-868-6541	R	26*	.1
105	Potter Roemer LLC—*Maggie Mejia*	PO Box 3527, City Of Industry CA 91744	626-855-4890	R	26*	.1
106	Genesee Reserve Supply Inc—*Richard Buck*	PO Box 20619, Rochester NY 14602	585-292-7040	R	26*	<.1
107	Berlin Building Supply—*Albert Fleischman*	W3053 County Rd F, Berlin WI 54923	920-361-2833	R	26*	<.1
108	Nova USA Wood Products LLC—*Jonathan Vanaffe*	1022 NW Marshall St Un, Portland OR 97209	503-419-6407	R	26*	<.1

Note: An asterisk (*) indicates an estimated financial figure. The company type code used is as follows: R = Private, P = Public, S = Private Subsidiary, B = Public Subsidiary, D = Division, J = Joint Venture, I = Investment Fund.

COMPANY RANKINGS BY SALES WITHIN 4-DIGIT SIC

Rank	Company Name—*Executive Officer*	Address, City, State, Zip	Phone	Type	Fin	Empls
109	Emco Enterprises Inc—*Joe Pauly*	PO Box 853, Des Moines IA 50306	515-265-6101	R	26*	.7
110	Tru-Fit Frame and Door Corp—*Lawrence Ciletti*	PO Box 198, Pennsauken NJ 08110	856-488-8843	R	25*	.1
111	Hardwoods of Morganton Inc—*Charles F Hopkins*	PO Box 1099, Morganton NC 28680	828-437-0761	R	25*	<.1
112	Service Construction Supply Inc—*Gil Roberts*	PO Box 13405, Birmingham AL 35202	205-252-3158	R	25*	.1
113	R and K Building Supplies Inc—*Chad Coons*	PO Box 4740, Mesa AZ 85211	480-892-0025	R	24*	.2
114	Horner Millwork Corp—*Peter Humphrey*	1255 Grand Army Hwy, Somerset MA 02726	508-679-6479	R	24*	.2
115	Clem Lumber Distributing Company Inc—*Jerry Davis*	PO Box 2238, Alliance OH 44601	330-821-2130	R	24*	.1
116	Soult Wholesale Co—*Lancelot Soult Jr*	PO Box 1112, Clearfield PA 16830	814-765-5591	R	24*	.1
117	Scholl Forest Inc—*Ward Scholl*	PO Box 41558, Houston TX 77241	713-329-5300	R	24*	<.1
118	Keystone Building Products Inc—*Bruce Witkop*	PO Box 423, Selinsgrove PA 17870	570-374-7565	R	24*	<.1
119	Manufacturers Reserve Supply Inc—*Brian Boyd*	40 Woolsey St, Irvington NJ 07111	973-373-1881	R	24*	<.1
120	Great Lakes Veneer Inc—*Peter Rogers*	222 S Parkview Ave, Marion WI 54950	715-754-2501	S	24*	.3
121	National Wood Products Inc—*Donald Meyer*	PO Box 65599, Salt Lake City UT 84165	801-977-1171	R	24*	.2
122	Swaner Hardwood Company Inc—*Gary Swaner*	P O Box 4200, Burbank CA 91503	818-953-5350	R	23*	.2
123	Refrigeration Supply Inc	9700 Manchester Rd, Saint Louis MO 63119	314-961-2000	R	23*	.1
124	Lansing Building Products Inc—*J Lansing*	PO Box 9489, Richmond VA 23228	804-266-8893	R	23*	.6
125	Omaha Hardwood Lumber Co—*Sbill Sauter*	8109 F St, Omaha NE 68127	402-342-4489	R	23*	<.1
126	Allen and Allen Company Inc—*Bobby Joe Miller*	PO Box 5140, San Antonio TX 78201	210-733-9191	R	22*	.1
127	Rafferty Aluminum and Steel Company Inc—*Sean Lorden*	1 Spratt Technology Dr, Sterling MA 01564	978-422-8130	R	22*	<.1
128	Arthur Lumber Trading Co—*Robert Borghorst*	5550 SW Macadam Ave St, Portland OR 97239	503-228-8160	R	22*	<.1
129	Forest Plywood Sales—*Joseph Bolton*	14711 Artesia Blvd, La Mirada CA 90638	714-523-1721	R	22*	.1
130	W L Hall Co—*W Hall*	530 15th Ave S, Hopkins MN 55343	952-937-8400	R	21*	<.1
131	Architectural Sales Inc—*John Der Werf*	PO Box 5836, Phoenix AZ 85010	602-437-1900	R	21*	.2
132	Fort Worth Lumber Co—*Emily Fiesler*	PO Box 969, Fort Worth TX 76101	817-293-5211	R	21*	.1
133	TW Hager Lumber Company Inc—*Gary Vitale*	PO Box 912, Grand Rapids MI 49509	616-452-5151	R	21*	.1
134	KC Company Inc—*Kevin Cassidy*	12100 Baltimore Ave St, Beltsville MD 20705	301-957-7000	R	20*	.2
135	Hawkeye Building Supply Co—*William H Engelen*	PO Box 1343, Sioux City IA 51102	712-277-4001	R	20*	<.1
136	GV Moore Lumber Company Inc—*Calvin Moore*	22 W Main St, Ayer MA 01432	978-772-0900	R	20*	<.1
137	Window Classics Corp—*Jose Garcia*	PO Box 4198, Hollywood FL 33083	954-966-1148	R	20*	<.1
138	Building and Industrial Wholesale Co—*Revis Stevenson*	PO Box 3365, Parkersburg WV 26103	304-485-6500	S	20*	<.1
139	Capitol Plywood Inc—*Mike Bozich*	160 Commerce Cir, Sacramento CA 95815	916-922-8861	R	20*	<.1
140	Texas Plywood And Lumber Company Inc—*Geoffrey Yates*	PO Box 535429, Grand Prairie TX 75053	972-262-1331	R	19*	.1
141	Mariotti Building Products Inc—*Eugene Mariotti*	1 Louis Industrial Dr, Old Forge PA 18518	570-457-6774	R	18*	.1
142	William S Trimble Company Inc—*William Scott Trimble Jr*	2200 Atchley St, Knoxville TN 37920	865-573-1911	R	18*	.1
143	MKS Industries Inc—*Mark R Martino*	PO Box 4948, Syracuse NY 13221	315-437-1511	R	18*	.1
144	Dougherty Lumber Co—*Marcus Hanna*	6000 Harvard Ave, Cleveland OH 44105	216-271-2400	R	18*	<.1
145	Boehm-Madisen Lumber Company Inc	N16W22100 Jericho Dr, Waukesha WI 53186	262-544-4660	R	18*	<.1
146	Dodson Wholesale Lumber Company Inc—*Bob Dodson*	PO Box 1851, Roswell NM 88202	575-622-3278	R	18*	<.1
147	Eastex Lumber and Supply Ltd—*Bobbie Schiel*	5429 Hartwick Rd, Houston TX 77093	281-442-2591	R	18*	.1
148	Precision Countertops Inc—*Marcus Neff*	PO Box 387, Wilsonville OR 97070	503-692-6660	R	18*	.1
149	Gold and Reiss Corp—*Shimon Eidlisz*	254 Bay Ridge Ave, Brooklyn NY 11220	718-680-2600	R	18*	<.1
150	Randall Brothers Inc—*Luther Randall*	PO Box 1678, Atlanta GA 30371	404-892-6666	R	18*	.1
151	Intermountain Wood Products Inc—*Ben Banks*	PO Box 65970, Salt Lake City UT 84165	801-486-5414	R	17*	.1
152	S and P Architectural Products Inc—*Curtis Sunday*	1721 Blount Rd Ste A, Pompano Beach FL 33069	954-968-3701	R	17*	.1
153	J Gibson McIlvain Co—*John McIlvain III*	PO Box 222, White Marsh MD 21162	410-335-9600	R	17*	.1
154	Chopp and Company Inc—*Michael Cannon*	11850 Pika Dr, Waldorf MD 20602	301-843-2167	R	17*	.1
155	Quality Wood Products Ltd—*Jacob Haleva*	3001 N Nellis Blvd, Las Vegas NV 89115	702-369-3008	R	16*	.1
156	Jay-Kay Independent Lumber Corp—*Dean Kelly*	PO Box 378, New Hartford NY 13413	315-735-4475	R	16*	.1
157	Western Pacific Building Materials Inc—*Robert Harrison*	2805 Nw 31st Ave, Portland OR 97210	503-224-9142	R	16*	.1
158	Fargo Tank And Steel Co—*Ole Rommesmo*	PO Box 2044, Fargo ND 58107	701-282-2345	R	16*	.1
159	South Atlantic Forest Products Inc—*O Raymond Gaster Jr*	15010 Abercorn St, Savannah GA 31419	912-927-1112	R	16*	.1
160	Kaplan Lumber Company Inc—*Leonard Kaplan*	PO Box 340, Saint Peters MO 63376	636-745-7371	R	16*	.1
161	Cook County Lumber Co—*Monty Falb*	200 E 130th St, Chicago IL 60628	773-928-2100	R	16*	<.1
162	Interior Supply Inc—*Robert Pickard*	481 E 11th Ave, Columbus OH 43211	614-424-6611	R	16*	<.1
163	Allegheny Plywood Company Inc—*Donald Huber*	3433 Smallman St, Pittsburgh PA 15201	412-621-6804	R	16*	<.1
164	Muhler Company Inc—*Henry Hay*	PO Box 60970, North Charleston SC 29419	843-572-9727	R	15*	.1
165	American Forest Products LLC—*Daniel Rosenthal*	1620 Webster Ave, Bronx NY 10457	718-901-1700	R	15*	.1
166	Kilroy Metal Products Inc—*Charles Krobot*	283 Greene Ave, Brooklyn NY 11238	718-638-2503	R	15*	.1
167	Baltimore Door And Frame Inc—*Richard Schmitt*	PO Box 7370, Baltimore MD 21227	410-737-2000	R	15*	.1
168	Millwork Sales Georgia LLC	335 Riverside Pkwy, Austell GA 30168	770-799-0355	R	15*	<.1
169	Wood Flooring International Inc—*John Himes*	207 Carter Dr, West Chester PA 19382	856-764-2501	R	15*	<.1
170	Cleveland Plywood Co—*Chris Schlabach*	5900 Harvard Ave, Cleveland OH 44105	216-641-6600	S	15*	<.1
171	Wilson John S Company Of Baltimore County—*William O'donnell*	PO Box 280, West Friendship MD 21794	410-442-2400	R	15*	<.1
172	Taylor Brothers Architectural Products Inc—*Claire Taylor*	2934 Riverside Dr, Los Angeles CA 90039	323-805-0200	R	15*	<.1
173	KSJ Associates LLC	1 Muller Ave Bldg 19, Norwalk CT 06851	203-846-8974	R	15*	<.1
174	Vytex Corp—*Andy Weinrub*	9425 Washington Blvd N, Laurel MD 20723	301-362-1000	R	15*	.1
175	Delmarva Millwork Corp—*James Bounds*	PO Box 4068, Lancaster PA 17604	717-299-2364	R	15*	.1
176	Central Supply Company Inc—*James Stone*	PO Box 986, Bainbridge GA 39818	229-246-2929	R	15*	.2
177	Ruffin and Payne Inc—*George Haw*	PO Box 27286, Richmond VA 23261	804-329-2691	R	15*	.1
178	Joffe Lumber and Supply Company Inc—*Sol Joffe*	PO Box 2309, Vineland NJ 08362	856-825-9550	R	15*	.1
179	Deer Park Lumber Inc—*Ron Andrews*	3042 Sr 6, Tunkhannock PA 18657	570-836-1133	R	14*	.1
180	Dakota Craft Inc—*Shannon Thornburg*	PO Box 2650, Rapid City SD 57709	605-341-6100	R	14*	.1
181	Brand-Vaughan Lumber Company Inc—*Cranston Vaughan*	PO Box 1439, Tucker GA 30085	770-414-9876	R	14*	.1
182	Cleary Millwork Company Inc—*Kenneth Bussmann*	235 Dividend Rd, Rocky Hill CT 06067	860-721-0520	R	14*	.1
183	Warren Trask Co—*Vincent Micale*	PO Box 589, Stoughton MA 02072		R	14*	<.1
184	Millwork Distributors Inc—*Thomas Hoxie*	PO Box 2465, Oshkosh WI 54903	920-235-8110	R	14*	.1
185	Super Pallet Recycling Corp—*Gyan Kalwani*	PO Box 1832, Elk Grove CA 95759	916-686-1700	R	14*	.1
186	Nashville Sash and Door Company Inc—*Hill Mcalister*	PO Box 40780, Nashville TN 37204	615-254-1371	R	14*	.1
187	Robert Weed Plywood Corp—*David Weed*	PO Box 487, Bristol IN 46507	574-848-4408	R	14*	.4
188	Sphero Trading Corp—*Charles Taylor*	PO Box 365469, North Las Vegas NV 89036	702-643-8268	R	13*	.1
189	Jarvis Steel and Lumber Company Inc—*Victor Frenkil*	1030 E Patapsco Ave, Baltimore MD 21225	410-355-3000	R	13*	.1
190	Hughes Hardwood International Inc—*William Hughes*	PO Box 38, Collinwood TN 38450	931-724-6258	R	13*	.1
191	M-G-M Co—*Todd Floyd*	3296 S Zuni St, Englewood CO 80110	303-761-7033	R	13*	.1
192	Consolidated Supply Company Inc—*Sam Marchese*	10325 J St, Omaha NE 68127	402-331-0500	R	13*	.1
193	Holland Southwest International Inc—*JoAnn Gillebaard*	PO Box 330249, Houston TX 77233	713-644-1966	R	13*	<.1
194	Wilson Plywood and Door Inc—*James Preddy*	PO Box 461546, Garland TX 75046	972-494-3545	R	13*	.1
195	Apple Valley Woodworks LLC—*Patricia Larvvie*	74 Spring St, Southington CT 06489	860-620-9330	R	13*	.1
196	Falmouth Lumber Inc—*Scott Augusta*	670 Teaticket Hwy, Teaticket MA 02536	508-548-6868	R	13*	.1
197	Ar-Jay Building Products Inc—*Ralph Palmer*	PO Box 10017, Cedar Rapids IA 52410	319-393-5885	R	13*	.1

Rank	Company Name—*Executive Officer*	Address, City, State, Zip	Phone	Type	Fin	Empls
198	Ciraulo Brothers Building Co—*Vincenzo Ciraulo*	7670 19 Mile Rd, Sterling Heights MI 48314	586-731-3670	R	13*	.1
199	Gerretsen Building Supply Co—*G Gerretsen*	1900 Ne Airport Rd, Roseburg OR 97470	541-672-2636	R	13*	.1
200	Comfort View Products LLC—*Maureen Gabner*	PO Box 368, Newnan GA 30264	770-251-4050	R	13*	.1
201	Younger Brothers Door and Trim LLC—*Bob Eldridge*	3910 E Wier Ave, Phoenix AZ 85040	602-304-1000	R	12*	.1
202	Alexander Lumber Co—*Walter Alexander*	PO Box 831, Aurora IL 60507	630-844-5123	R	12*	.4
203	Hull Supply Company Inc—*Rick Hull*	5117 E Cesar Chavez St, Austin TX 78702	512-385-1262	R	12*	.1
204	US Window Factory Inc—*Angelo Alfieri*	13011 Atlantic Ave, Jamaica NY 11418		R	12*	.2
205	Pioneer Industries LLC—*Brad Baker*	PO Box 537, Owensville MO 65066	573-437-4104	R	12*	.1
206	Dale and Maxey Inc—*Albert Dale*	915 6th Ave S, Nashville TN 37203	615-254-3454	R	12*	.1
207	FS Van Hoose and Company Inc—*Joe H Van Hoose*	PO Box 1618, Paintsville KY 41240	606-789-4075	R	12*	<.1
208	Hatch And Bailey Co—*Brian Mellick*	1 Meadow St Ext, Norwalk CT 06854	203-866-5515	R	12*	<.1
209	Lumbermen's of Indiana	4433 Stafford Ave SW, Grand Rapids MI 49548	616-261-3200	R	12*	<.1
210	CJ Link Lumber Co—*Chris Mergel*	PO Box 1085, Warren MI 48090	586-773-1200	R	12*	<.1
211	Colonial Building Supply LLC—*Angie Jones*	PO Box 459, Centerville UT 84014	801-295-9471	R	12*	.1
212	Penn Wood Products Inc—*Brian Markle*	PO Box 766, East Berlin PA 17316	717-259-9551	R	12*	.1
213	Accent Surfaces LLC—*Jen Kruletz*	4103 S 500 W, Salt Lake City UT 84123	801-269-0701	R	12*	.1
214	Architectural Division 8 Inc—*Kerry Kirby*	2425 Brockton St Ste 1, San Antonio TX 78217	210-826-6616	R	12*	.1
215	Gunton Corp—*Mark Mead*	26150 Richmond Rd, Cleveland OH 44146	216-831-2420	R	12*	.4
216	Chick Lumber Inc—*Douglas Fagone*	PO Box 3060, North Conway NH 03860	603-356-6371	R	12*	.1
217	Greenfield Lumber Co—*James Peterson*	28575 Grand River Ave, Farmington MI 48336	248-474-6610	R	11*	<.1
218	Maglebys Custom Cabinets—*Paul Magleby*	PO Box 990, Pleasant Grove UT 84062	801-785-9998	R	11*	.1
219	Architectural Doors Inc—*Robert Crane*	11700 Monarch St, Garden Grove CA 92841	714-898-3667	R	11*	.1
220	S and M Lumber Co—*Scott Sharp*	424 W Main, Flushing MI 48433	785-437-2268	R	11*	<.1
221	Pallet Central Enterprises Inc—*Su So-Longman*	2B Lenox Pointe, Atlanta GA 30342	404-814-1048	R	11*	.1
222	Heppner Hardwoods Inc—*Lorraine Heppner*	555 W Danlee St, Azusa CA 91702	626-969-7983	R	11*	.1
223	Southwest Window And Door Inc—*Richard Schreiber*	PO Box 302, Fort Myers FL 33902	239-454-5959	R	11*	.1
224	Home Lumber Of New Haven Inc—*Alan Korte*	PO Box 386, New Haven IN 46774	260-493-4436	R	11*	.1
225	Hagle Lumber Company Inc—*Ralph Hagle*	PO Box 120, Somis CA 93066	805-987-3887	R	11*	<.1
226	M-D Building Material Company Of Illinois Inc—*Ralph Menn*	953 Seton Ct, Wheeling IL 60090	847-541-0002	R	11*	.1
227	Cabinet Distributors Of Georgia Inc—*Ryan Kempf*	5158 Kennedy Rd Ste B, Forest Park GA 30297	404-361-5200	R	11*	<.1
228	Roadside Lumber and Hardware Inc—*Michael Tuchman*	PO Box 339, Agoura Hills CA 91376	818-991-1880	R	10*	.1
229	American Lumber Company LP—*Andy Lander*	PO Box 6, Hamburg NY 14075	814-438-7888	R	10*	.1
230	John E Quarles Co—*Nancy Stuck*	1801 Park Pl Ave, Fort Worth TX 76110	817-926-1761	R	10*	<.1
231	Tampa Bay Hardwoods and Lumber Supply Inc—*Richard Lee*	8408 Temple Ter Hwy, Tampa FL 33637	813-987-9663	R	10*	.1
232	Nt Window Inc—*Danny Ferguson*	PO Box 40547, Fort Worth TX 76140	817-572-4994	R	10*	.1
233	Banner Supply Co—*Barney Landers*	7195 Nw 30th St, Miami FL 33122	305-593-2946	R	10*	<.1
234	North American Plywood Corp—*Clifford Lowy*	12343 Hawkins St, Santa Fe Springs CA 90670	562-941-7575	R	10*	<.1
235	EN Beard Hardwood Lumber Inc—*Tom Beard*	PO Box 13608, Greensboro NC 27415	336-378-1265	R	10*	.1
236	Pluswood—*Joe Nowak*	PO Box 2248, Oshkosh WI 54903	920-235-0440	D	10*	<.1
237	Chapman Lumber Company Inc—*William Chapman*	19585 Fullers Mill Rd, Boykins VA 23827	757-654-9330	R	10*	.1
238	Jantek Industries LLC—*Walt Litke*	230 Rte 70, Medford NJ 08055	609-654-1030	R	10*	.1
239	Johnson Richard A Cedar Products Inc—*Fred Nix*	5640 S Durango St Ste, Tacoma WA 98409	253-383-4603	R	10*	.1
240	Lexington Building and Supply Company Inc—*John Booher*	PO Box 55254, Lexington KY 40555	859-254-8834	R	10*	.1
241	Western Reflections LLC—*David Killoran*	261 Commerce Way Galla, Gallatin TN 37066	615-451-9700	S	10*	.4
242	American Lumber Company Inc—*Barry Kaye*	PO Box 111, Walden NY 12586	845-778-1111	R	10*	<.1
243	Homan Lumber Mart Inc—*Robert Homan*	PO Box 818, Elkhart IN 46515	574-293-6595	R	10*	.1
244	Midwest Walnut Company Iowa—*James Plowman*	1914 Tostevin St, Council Bluffs IA 51503	712-325-9191	R	10*	.1
245	Gaiennie Lumber Company LLC—*John Olivier*	PO Box 1240, Opelousas LA 70571	337-948-3066	R	10*	.1
246	Thompson Mahogany Co—*Donald Thompson*	7400 Edmund St, Philadelphia PA 19136	215-624-1866	R	10*	<.1
247	Gancedo Lumber Company Inc—*Martin Perez*	9300 Nw 36th Ave, Miami FL 33147	305-836-7030	R	9*	.1
248	Mann And Parker Lumber Co—*Stephen Bushman*	335 N Constitution Ave, New Freedom PA 17349	717-235-4834	R	9*	.1
249	E and E Aquisitions LLC—*Tracey Edgemon*	2605 Rodney Ln, Dallas TX 75229	972-241-3571	R	9*	<.1
250	Calibamboo LLC—*Jeff Goldberg*	9365 Waples St Ste D, San Diego CA 92121	858-200-9540	R	9	<.1
251	Browne Lumber Inc—*Robert Browne*	PO Box 577, Friday Harbor WA 98250	360-378-2168	R	9*	.1
252	Lumber Products Inc—*Rosalie Wood*	PO Box 9510, Metairie LA 70055	504-834-8444	R	9*	<.1
253	Cedar Supply Inc—*C Carrington*	PO Box 110229, Carrollton TX 75011	972-242-6567	R	9*	<.1
254	Atlantic Builders Supply Inc—*Robert Kirchoff*	1350 S Dixie Hwy E, Pompano Beach FL 33060	954-946-4421	R	9*	<.1
255	West Haven Lumber Co—*James Shanbrom*	PO Box 398, West Haven CT 06516	203-933-1641	R	9*	<.1
256	Thomas Supply Inc—*Roy Thomas*	PO Box 1256, Livingston TX 77351	936-327-3851	R	9*	<.1
257	Ray Anderson Company Inc—*Ron Willis*	2322 Sw 6th Ave, Topeka KS 66606	785-233-7454	R	9*	<.1
258	Hansen Marketing Services Inc—*James Frensley*	PO Box 640, Walled Lake MI 48390	248-669-2323	R	9*	<.1
259	Hammerhead Distribution Inc—*Paul Haefcke*	925 Fell St Fl 2, Baltimore MD 21231	443-573-8080	R	8*	.1
260	Beck and Son Incorporated Clayborne C—*Ronald Beck*	11410 N Club Dr, Fredericksburg VA 22408	540-898-0401	R	8*	.1
261	Savage Wholesale Building Materials Inc—*Andrew Mcdonald*	PO Box 8100, Tacoma WA 98419	253-383-1727	R	8*	<.1
262	Reese Kitchens Inc—*David Reese*	1057 E 54th St, Indianapolis IN 46220	317-253-1569	R	8*	<.1
263	Olathe Millwork Co—*Keith North*	16002 W 110th St, Lenexa KS 66219	913-894-5010	R	8*	<.1
264	Rigidply Rafters Inc—*Steve Shirk*	701 E Linden St, Richland PA 17087	717-866-6581	R	8*	.2
265	Roswell Lumber Co—*Bruce Ellis*	PO Box 1673, Roswell NM 88202	575-622-1630	R	8*	.1
266	Cabinet And Bath Supply Inc—*David Paris*	882 W Tracker Rd, Nixa MO 65714	417-725-2525	R	8*	.1
267	Collins and Co—*Richard Collins*	PO Box 1009, Bristol IN 46507	574-848-7778	R	8*	<.1
268	Bristol Doors Corp—*George Cain*	PO Box 205, Bristol PA 19007	215-788-9279	R	8*	.1
269	Hartzell Hardwoods Inc—*John Owsiany*	PO Box 919, Piqua OH 45356	937-773-6295	R	8*	.1
270	Ketcham Lumber Company Inc—*Gerald D Iverson*	2811 E Madison St, Seattle WA 98112	206-329-2700	R	8*	<.1
271	Cole Hardwood Inc—*William Cole*	1611 W Market St, Logansport IN 46947	574-753-3151	R	8*	.1
272	Commercial Door Company Of Houston Inc—*John Malone*	11533 S Main St, Houston TX 77025	713-667-1757	R	8*	.1
273	American Building Services LLC	953 Seton Ct, Wheeling IL 60090	847-541-0002	R	8*	.1
274	Builders Support and Supply Inc—*Bruce Leveto*	PO Box 668, Saegertown PA 16433	814-763-9663	R	8*	<.1
275	Hankins Lumber Company Inc—*Albert Hankins*	PO Box 1397, Grenada MS 38902	662-226-2961	R	8*	.2
276	I T Dealers Supply Inc—*Wayne Quinn*	122 Rte 32, North Franklin CT 06254	860-887-2531	R	8*	<.1
277	Sanford-Lussier Inc—*William Pechstedt*	2200 Nadeau St, Huntington Park CA 90255	323-585-2811	R	7*	<.1
278	Whitlock Brothers Inc—*E Whitlock*	5588 Raby Rd, Norfolk VA 23502	757-461-3127	R	7*	<.1
279	Jlr Enterprises Inc—*Jeff Rueb*	1966 E Deer Valley Rd, Phoenix AZ 85024	602-867-9316	R	7*	<.1
280	Humboldt Redwood Company LLC—*Pierce Baymiller*	PO Box 37, Scotia CA 95565	707-764-4472	R	7*	.3
281	H and H Overhead Door Company Inc—*Rick Huegele*	PO Box 3542, Victoria TX 77903	361-578-3664	R	7*	<.1
282	Canby Builders Supply Co—*Richard Morse*	102 S Pine St, Canby OR 97013	503-266-2244	R	7*	<.1
283	Reisen Lumber and Millwork Co—*Daniel Reisen*	PO Box 340, Kenilworth NJ 07033	908-276-6200	R	7*	<.1
284	Albeni Falls Building Supply Inc—*David Melbourn*	520 E Hwy 2, Oldtown ID 83822	208-437-3153	R	7*	<.1
285	Knudson Lumber Co—*Robert Knudson*	1791 Vantage Hwy, Ellensburg WA 98926	509-962-9811	R	7*	.1
286	McDonald Lumber Company Inc	126 Cedar Creek Rd, Fayetteville NC 28302	910-483-0381	R	7*	.1
287	Southeastern Dock and Door Inc—*James Foster*	667 Perimeter Rd, Greenville SC 29605	864-277-8877	R	7*	<.1

Note: An asterisk (*) indicates an estimated financial figure. The company type code used is as follows: R = Private, P = Public, S = Private Subsidiary, B = Public Subsidiary, D = Division, J = Joint Venture, I = Investment Fund.

COMPANY RANKINGS BY SALES WITHIN 4-DIGIT SIC

Rank	Company Name—*Executive Officer*	Address, City, State, Zip	Phone	Type	Fin	Empls
288	Irmscher Suppliers Inc—*Max Irmscher*	PO Box 10324, Fort Wayne IN 46851	260-456-4581	R	7*	<.1
289	Washington Hardwoods Company LLC—*Mitch Lober*	3257 17th Ave W, Seattle WA 98119	206-283-7574	R	7*	<.1
290	Christian Building Materials Inc—*Roger Johnson*	1841 N Batavia St, Orange CA 92865	714-998-5919	R	7*	<.1
291	Premier Sash and Door Ltd—*Brian Redpath*	12901 Nicholson Rd Ste, Dallas TX 75234	972-484-3020	R	7*	<.1
292	McGinnis Lumber Company Inc—*JE McGinnis III*	PO Box 2049, Meridian MS 39302	601-483-3991	R	7*	<.1
293	Tds Investments Inc—*Lael Peterson*	4435 S 134th Pl, Tukwila WA 98168	206-241-8242	R	7*	<.1
294	Goldon Windows and Mirrors Inc—*Gregory Jacobs*	6990 Murthum Ave, Warren MI 48092	586-446-8900	R	7*	<.1
295	Granite Hardwoods Inc—*William Buchanan*	PO Box 226, Granite Falls NC 28630	828-396-3395	R	7*	<.1
296	Ams Of Indiana Inc—*Rex Simpson*	3933 E Jackson Blvd, Elkhart IN 46516	574-293-5526	R	7*	<.1
297	Joyner Lumber and Supply Co—*Robert Joyner*	301 S Central Ave, Lakeland FL 33815	863-682-8101	R	7*	<.1
298	Overhead Door Company Of Beaumont Inc—*Gary Coe*	1547 Main Ln, Beaumont TX 77713	409-866-2535	R	7*	<.1
299	Park-Olson Lumber Co—*Mark Olson*	PO Box 156, La Mesa CA 91944	619-466-0511	R	7*	<.1
300	Fitzgerald Lumber Co—*Calvert Fitzgerald*	PO Box 188, Buena Vista VA 24416	540-261-3430	R	7*	.1
301	Bondurant Lumber Wholesale And Export Division Inc—*John Bondurant*	PO Box 1097, Flomaton AL 36441	251-296-5600	R	7*	.1
302	Lauderbach Builders Supply Company Inc—*Dennis Lauderbach*	PO Box 5563, Tucson AZ 85703	520-623-8443	R	7*	.1
303	Precision Metals And Hardware Inc—*Don Shrader*	5265 N 124th St, Milwaukee WI 53225	262-781-3240	R	7*	<.1
304	Georgia Hardwoods Inc—*Robert Dyson*	PO Box 504, Buford GA 30515	770-932-0640	R	7*	<.1
305	Overhead Door Company Of Madison Inc—*Ronald Ryan*	917 Watson Ave, Madison WI 53713	608-271-4288	R	7*	<.1
306	Pine Tree Building Materials—*James Karabian*	5317 E Home Ave, Fresno CA 93727	559-252-7314	R	7*	<.1
307	Die-Boards Inc—*Norman Roberts*	45 N Industry Ct Ste C, Deer Park NY 11729	631-586-7700	R	6*	<.1
308	Ybl LLC—*Evan Bowers*	8525 N 75th Ave, Peoria AZ 85345	602-230-0367	R	6*	<.1
309	Hi-Standard Equipment and Supply Company Inc—*Bruce Fowler*	320 E Broadway Ave, Fort Worth TX 76104	817-332-2373	R	6*	<.1
310	Builders Supply Company Of Cookeville—*W Ray*	50 Scott Ave, Cookeville TN 38501	931-526-9704	R	6*	<.1
311	Block Iron and Supply Company Inc—*Chuck Williams*	PO Box 557, Oshkosh WI 54903	920-231-8645	R	6*	.1
312	Forest Products Northwest Inc—*Thomas Read*	PO Box 64817, Tacoma WA 98464	253-272-6062	R	6*	<.1
313	Trumark Industries Inc—*Jack Brace*	PO Box 11956, Spokane Valley WA 99211	509-534-0644	R	6*	<.1
314	Dean Lawther Inc—*David Lawther*	PO Box 1099, League City TX 77574	281-332-9351	R	6*	<.1
315	Architectural Millwork Manufacturing Co—*Jerry Mosophski*	PO Box 2809, Eugene OR 97402	541-689-1331	R	6*	<.1
316	Dwight G Lewis Lumber Co—*Dwight G Lewis*	PO Box A, Hillsgrove PA 18619	570-924-3507	R	6*	<.1
317	Bryant Church Hardwoods Inc—*Tim Church*	PO Box 995, Wilkesboro NC 28697	336-973-3380	R	6*	<.1
318	Building Supply Trading Corp—*Andy Berardinelli*	75 Union Ave, Rutherford NJ 07070	201-939-1200	R	6*	<.1
319	Allied Structural Lumber Products Inc—*Stuart Allmon*	PO Box 12318, Albuquerque NM 87195	505-856-5244	R	6*	<.1
320	Potocnie Enterprises Inc—*James Potocnie*	4498 Commerce Dr, Whitehall PA 18052	610-262-3530	R	6*	<.1
321	G S and D Inc—*Mark Iannuzzi*	315 N Ave, Mount Clemens MI 48043	586-463-8667	R	6*	<.1
322	Builders Hardware And Hollow Metal Inc—*Janice Jacque*	W165n5690 Continental, Menomonee Falls WI 53051	262-781-5525	R	6*	<.1
323	Pella Window and Door LLC—*Elaine Sagers*	PO Box 2268, Irmo SC 29063	803-407-1112	R	6*	<.1
324	Metropolitan Rolling Door Inc—*Robert Bell*	9620 Gerwig Ln, Columbia MD 21046	410-995-6336	R	5*	<.1
325	Northwest Millwork Co—*Richard Hybiak*	455 Jarvis Ave, Des Plaines IL 60018	847-699-2040	R	5*	<.1
326	Quality Lumber Building Wholesalers Inc—*Timothy Pierson*	PO Box 488, Richmond MI 48062	586-727-7001	R	5*	<.1
327	Reserve Warehouse Corp—*James Dunbar*	PO Box 67, Chattanooga TN 37401	423-265-1677	R	5*	<.1
328	American Lumber Corp—*Howard Farbman*	520 S Caton Ave, Baltimore MD 21229	410-566-7800	R	5*	<.1
329	Cudahy Lumber Co—*Michael Cudahy*	PO Box 25200, Portland OR 97298	503-648-0831	R	5*	<.1
330	PA Hicks and Sons Inc—*Olive Hicks*	120 Main St, Colebrook NH 03576	603-237-5531	R	5*	<.1
331	Western Building Specialties Of Sacramento—*Byron Younger*	6050 S Watt Ave, Sacramento CA 95829	916-383-1070	R	5*	<.1
332	Glen Rock Building Supply Inc—*Stephen Leone*	RR 2545, Fair Lawn NJ 07410	201-796-4500	R	5*	<.1
333	Dixie Plywood Company Of Dallas Inc—*Daniel Bradley*	3060 W Miller Rd, Garland TX 75041	972-271-4607	R	5*	<.1
334	JW Werntz and Son Inc—*Patrick Werntz*	1002 Kerr St, South Bend IN 46601	574-232-4881	R	5*	<.1
335	Peter Meier Incorporated LLC—*Troy Walkup*	1255 S Park Dr, Kernersville NC 27284	336-996-7774	R	5*	<.1
336	Wildwood Cabinets Inc—*Ken Allender*	1103 Clendenen Rd, Maryville TN 37801	865-983-1466	R	5*	<.1
337	Lumberman's Wholesale Distributors Inc—*John Moore*	PO Box 91060, Nashville TN 37209	615-321-3038	R	5*	<.1
338	AP Hubbard Wholesale Lumber Corp—*Marion Hubbard*	PO Box 14100, Greensboro NC 27415	336-275-1343	R	5*	<.1
339	Plastics Advanced Research Technology Inc—*Dennis Denton*	1427 Old N Main St, Clover SC 29710	803-222-7771	R	5*	<.1
340	Millwork Sales of Valdosta LLC—*Teresa Carter*	1693 Clay Rd, Valdosta GA 31601	229-219-0889	R	5*	<.1
341	Western Wood Preserving Co—*Mike Reimer*	PO Box 1250, Sumner WA 98390	253-863-8191	R	5*	<.1
342	Maly Companies LLC—*Tim Mulcahy*	2050 E Ctr Cir Ste 200, Minneapolis MN 55441	612-788-9688	R	5*	<.1
343	Atlantic Coast Cabinet Distributors—*William Konkle*	PO Box 1257, Youngsville NC 27596	919-554-8165	R	5*	<.1
344	Spooner's Building Products—*Chris Spooner*	13200 Kirkham Way Ste, Poway CA 92064	858-748-9687	R	5*	<.1
345	Front Range Lumber Co—*John Gunzner*	1741 S Wadsworth Blvd, Lakewood CO 80232	303-988-5980	R	5*	<.1
346	Wyoming Building Supply Inc—*Robert Ingram*	2104 Fairgrounds Rd, Casper WY 82604	307-265-7935	R	5*	<.1
347	Northwest Door And Supply Inc—*Thomas Holmes*	PO Box 68, Tualatin OR 97062	503-692-9494	R	5*	<.1
348	Wixom Technologies LLC—*Debbie Cawthon*	4921 Product Dr, Wixom MI 48393	248-685-0691	S	5*	<.1
349	Commercial Door Company Of Dallas Inc—*John Malone*	2617 Andjon Dr, Dallas TX 75220	214-350-4621	R	5*	<.1
350	H and B Holdings Inc—*Harvey Robbins*	4630 Hickory Ln, Tuscumbia AL 35674	256-332-8974	R	5*	<.1
351	Diamond Tool Co—*Jon Gray*	8051 Penn Randall Pl, Upper Marlboro MD 20772	301-967-2844	R	5*	<.1
352	Charles F Shiels and Company Inc—*Marc Shiels*	PO Box 14387, Cincinnati OH 45250	513-241-0239	R	5*	<.1
353	Williamsburg Plumbing Inc—*Moishe Katz*	485 Flushing Ave, Brooklyn NY 11205	718-596-1500	R	5*	<.1
354	Rickenbaugh Building Supply Inc—*Timothy Rickenbaugh*	PO Box 67, Mc Alisterville PA 17049	717-463-3721	R	4*	<.1
355	Minton Door Co—*Allen Minton*	1150 Elko Dr, Sunnyvale CA 94089	408-743-9220	R	4*	<.1
356	Winco Window Company Inc—*Gantt Miller*	6200 Maple Ave, Saint Louis MO 63130	314-725-8088	R	4*	<.1
357	Nashville Plywood Inc—*Wynton Overstreet*	PO Box 90134, Nashville TN 37209	615-320-7877	R	4*	<.1
358	Hy Mark Wood Products Inc—*Dale Bartsch*	2625 E Spangle Waverly, Spangle WA 99031	509-245-3285	R	4*	<.1
359	Horstmeier Lumber Company Inc—*Joseph Galvin*	PO Box 27019, Baltimore MD 21230	410-752-0532	R	4*	<.1
360	Spring Overhead Door Inc—*Walter Lindley*	33206 Buckshot Ln, Magnolia TX 77354	281-355-6600	R	4*	<.1
361	Performance Films Distributing Inc—*George Lewis*	6365 Shier Rings Rd St, Dublin OH 43016	614-766-4602	R	4*	<.1
362	Entrada Iron And Wood Doors LLC—*Jeremy Dell*	3231 Commander Dr, Carrollton TX 75006	469-621-3667	R	4*	<.1
363	Diamond Builders Wholesale Inc—*Doug Mccullough*	PO Box 11580, Chandler AZ 85248	480-895-1132	R	4*	<.1
364	Idaho Western Inc—*Richard Chaffin*	6200 E Hunt Ave, Nampa ID 83687	208-465-7800	R	4*	<.1
365	Overhead Door Company Of Jacksonville—*Rick Ward*	6884 Phillips Pkwy Dr, Jacksonville FL 32256	904-268-1627	R	4*	<.1
366	GR Wood Inc—*Gunther Rodatz*	260 S Park Dr, Mooresville IN 46158	317-831-8060	R	4*	<.1
367	Contractor Express Inc—*Robert Lucas*	389 Atlantic Ave, Oceanside NY 11572	516-764-0388	R	4*	<.1
368	Armstrong Landon Company Inc—*Christopher Riesen*	PO Box 988, Kokomo IN 46903	765-457-5333	R	4*	<.1
369	Noroestana De Exportaciones Cxa—*Virgilio Cabrera*	9805 Nw 52nd St Apt 10, Doral FL 33178	305-639-6772	R	4*	<.1
370	Kansas City Hardwood Corp—*Dan Schneider*	1675 Argentine Blvd, Kansas City KS 66105	913-621-1975	R	4*	<.1
371	Diversified Forest Products Inc—*Michael Caviness*	2221 W Deer Valley Rd, Phoenix AZ 85027	623-869-8073	R	4*	<.1
372	Westwood Millwork Inc—*Tracy Edgemon*	225 Gibson Ln, Valley View TX 76272	940-726-5016	R	4*	<.1
373	Crawford Sales Inc—*Matt Booker*	PO Box 4878, Evansville IN 47724	812-423-6417	R	4*	<.1
374	Grandview Window and Door Inc—*Dudley Schaefer*	3400 Brother Blvd 3813, Bartlett TN 38133	901-383-1600	R	4*	<.1

Rank	Company Name—*Executive Officer*	Address, City, State, Zip	Phone	Type	Fin	Empls
375	Lampasas Builder's Mart Inc—*Britt Brown*	PO Box 588, Lampasas TX 76550	512-556-6291	R	4*	<.1
376	Brooklyn Installations Inc—*Peter Lutrario*	2200 Mcdonald Ave, Brooklyn NY 11223	718-449-1382	R	4*	<.1
377	Gutchess International Inc—*David Gutchess*	PO Box 5435, Cortland NY 13045	607-753-8201	R	4*	<.1
378	Colonial Forest Products Inc—*Thomas Palmer*	PO Box 168, Crewe VA 23930	434-538-0306	R	4*	<.1
379	Neuens Fredonia Lumber Company Inc—*John Janik*	PO Box 277, Fredonia WI 53021	262-692-2456	R	4*	<.1
380	Berkeley Lumber Co—*William Epstein*	9330 Natural Bridge Rd, Saint Louis MO 63134	314-428-7000	R	4*	<.1
381	Sweetwater Lumber and Land Inc—*Clay Anderson*	PO Box 66, Austell GA 30168	770-941-4932	R	4*	<.1
382	Erick's Lumber Company Inc—*Moises Gonzalez*	5714 Cerrito Prieto Ct, Laredo TX 78041	956-726-3309	R	4*	<.1
383	Hogan and Sons Lumber Company Inc—*James Hogan*	1700 Hlness Campground, Cleveland GA 30528	706-865-2570	R	4*	<.1
384	Performance Woodworking Inc—*David Watkins*	6125 E 56th Ave, Commerce City CO 80022	303-227-9441	R	4*	<.1
385	Midwest Cabinet and Counter Inc—*Timothy Labadie*	PO Box 14815, Detroit MI 48214	313-822-0142	R	4*	<.1
386	Weathershield Supply Inc—*Henry Glime*	228 Orchard Lake Rd, Pontiac MI 48341	248-335-1111	R	3*	<.1
387	Noble Wholesale Inc—*John Bowman*	1395 Jarvis St, Ferndale MI 48220	248-545-6800	R	3*	<.1
388	Abode Building Materials Co—*Marilyn Ewert*	8308 Shaver Rd, Portage MI 49024	269-329-1800	R	3*	<.1
389	Palatine Builders Supply Inc—*Robert Schuttler*	2251 Nicholas Blvd, Elk Grove Village IL 60007	847-952-1400	R	3*	<.1
390	Gibson Access Controls Inc—*Gail Gibson*	2741 Losee Rd Ste B, North Las Vegas NV 89030	702-399-7744	R	3*	<.1
391	JW Custom Cabinets and Countertops—*Jim Willis*	PO Box 163, Fairdealing MO 63939	573-857-2144	R	3*	<.1
392	Premier Forest Products Inc—*Jim Carlson*	5159 Us Hwy 101, Humptulips WA 98552	360-288-2693	R	3*	<.1
393	Goad Lumber Company Inc—*Paul Goad*	2090 Fancy Gap Hwy, Hillsville VA 24343	276-728-7282	R	3*	<.1
394	Tru Kut Door Corp—*Michael Kitta*	PO Box 23, Elkton VA 22827	540-298-8996	R	3*	<.1
395	Architectural Door And Millwork Inc—*Michael Wujczyk*	30150 S Hill Rd, New Hudson MI 48165	248-437-3900	R	3*	<.1
396	Stafford Building Products Inc—*Russell Stafford*	1235 Waterville Monclo, Waterville OH 43566	419-878-3070	R	3*	<.1
397	Northeast Wholesale Lumber Inc—*Richard Davies*	PO Box 841, East Longmeadow MA 01028	413-525-3323	R	3*	<.1
398	Premiere Builders Supply Inc—*Robert Arnold*	630 S Orchard Ln, Beavercreek OH 45434	937-426-1010	R	3*	<.1
399	Suburban Materials Co—*Jim Costello*	211 W Oak Ln, Glenolden PA 19036	610-583-4478	R	3*	<.1
400	Quality Lumber Company LLC—*Bradlee Clapp*	PO Box 51428, Knoxville TN 37950	865-588-7431	R	3*	<.1
401	Heavy Construction Lumber Inc—*Henry Giorgi*	380 Morgan Ave, Brooklyn NY 11211	718-387-7257	R	3*	<.1
402	Gold Arc Inc—*Greg Stromberg*	PO Box 308, Carlsbad CA 92018	909-394-7311	R	3*	<.1
403	Righter Group Inc—*Donald Miller*	11 Upton Dr, Wilmington MA 01887		R	3*	<.1
404	Chaney Lumber Company Inc—*Edwin Jones*	PO Box 909, London KY 40743	606-864-7375	R	3*	<.1
405	Scavolini USA Inc—*Francesco Farina*	1775 Broadway Ste 417, New York NY 10019	212-265-8787	R	3*	<.1
406	George Squires—*George Squires*	2059 Camden Ave Ste 32, San Jose CA 95124	408-971-9663	R	3*	<.1
407	Muth Lumber Company Inc—*Richard Muth*	1301 Adams Ln, Ironton OH 45638	740-533-0800	R	3*	<.1
408	Acme Brick And Supply Co—*Michael Gray*	1405 Belvidere Rd, Waukegan IL 60085	847-662-8245	R	3*	<.1
409	Calvert Lumber Company Inc—*James Hill*	7160 Poorhouse Farm Dr, Port Tobacco MD 20677	301-934-7158	R	3*	<.1
410	Johnson International Inc—*Lisa Johnson*	20205 59th Pl S, Kent WA 98032	253-479-9900	R	3*	<.1
411	Sterling Cabinets Inc—*Leonard Caldararo*	380a Rabro Dr, Hauppauge NY 11788	631-582-5454	R	3*	<.1
412	Nephew Lewis Company LLC	PO Box 1007, Monument CO 80132	719-488-2236	R	3*	<.1
413	US Lumber Co—*Irving Schwartz*	PO Box 314, Pine Plains NY 12567	518-398-5333	R	3*	<.1
414	S and L Materials Inc—*James Davis*	210 S Hoagland Blvd, Kissimmee FL 34741	407-870-0066	R	3*	<.1
415	Longs Distributing Inc—*John Long*	8888 E 34 Rd, Cadillac MI 49601	231-876-3667	R	3*	<.1
416	Opening Solutions Group LLC	400 Industry St, Pittsburgh PA 15210	724-740-1777	R	3*	<.1
417	J and W Counter Tops Inc—*Walter Justison*	600 N St, Springfield IL 62704	217-544-0876	R	3*	<.1
418	Elko Inc—*Randall Kanter*	940 N Boeke Rd, Evansville IN 47711	812-473-8430	R	3*	<.1
419	Brock Cabinets and Appliances Inc—*Ikie Howard*	35 Weathers Ct, Youngsville NC 27596	919-266-3345	R	3*	<.1
420	Kitchen Creations Inc—*Joseph Ross*	110 S Laurel St, Bridgeton NJ 08302	856-451-4500	R	3*	<.1
421	Aayco Pallet Systems LLC	PO Box 462453, Escondido CA 92046	760-737-0300	R	3*	<.1
422	Lumberjack's Lll Inc—*Jack Allen*	723 E Tallmadge Ave St, Akron OH 44310	330-762-2401	R	2*	<.1
423	Madana Manufacturing—*Chaim Neuberg*	6001 Santa Monica Blvd, Los Angeles CA 90038	323-469-0856	R	2*	<.1
424	Overhead Door Company Of Roswell Inc—*Bruce Ellis*	PO Box 1673, Roswell NM 88202	575-622-0149	R	2*	<.1
425	Panel Center Inc—*Charles Nagel*	850 Kaderly Dr, Columbus OH 43228	614-274-6000	R	2*	<.1
426	Tri-City Wood Works Inc—*John Fowlds*	202 Old Dixie Hwy, West Palm Beach FL 33403	561-842-4666	R	2*	<.1
427	Pigeon Creek Hardwoods Inc—*Terry Koxlien*	N37895 Us Hwy 53 121, Whitehall WI 54773	715-538-4285	R	2*	<.1
428	Architectural Specialty Products Inc—*Rena Jahn*	6312 W 74th St, Chicago IL 60638	708-563-8510	R	2*	<.1
429	Pallets-R-Us Ii—*Ed Kolaczkowski*	854 Sherman Ave, Springfield OH 45503	937-323-5210	R	2*	<.1
430	Peninsula Building Materials Company Inc—*Joseph Morey*	PO Box 5807, Redwood City CA 94063	650-365-8500	R	2*	<.1
431	Lumbermen's Merchandising Corp—*Anthony J DeCarlo*	PO Box 6790, Wayne PA 19087	610-293-7000	R	2*	.2
432	Building Specialties Company Inc—*W Caddell*	PO Box 788, Birmingham AL 35201	205-956-1600	R	2*	.1
433	Edwards Lumber Company Inc—*James Edwards*	PO Box 289, Orangeburg SC 29116	803-536-2684	R	2*	<.1
434	Oriental Lumber Land Inc—*Joan Chao*	1154 Flushing Ave, Brooklyn NY 11237	718-386-8200	R	2*	<.1
435	Southern Supply Inc—*Richard Skaff*	PO Box 3216, Mooresville NC 28117	704-663-1563	R	2*	<.1
436	Collins Cashway Lumber Inc—*Floyd Wernimont*	PO Box 7449, Loveland CO 80537	970-669-6043	R	2*	<.1
437	Holmquist Lumber Inc—*Calvin Anderson*	200 N Logan Ave, Oakland NE 68045	402-685-5641	R	2*	<.1
438	Willett Lumber Co—*Robert Willett*	1419 E Washington St, Louisville KY 40206	502-581-1207	R	2*	<.1
439	JR Metal Frames Manufacturing Inc—*Robert Pepin*	PO Box 503, Belgrade ME 04917	207-465-9066	R	2*	<.1
440	L and M Drywall LLC—*Steve Lawrence*	3 Industrial Way, Tyngsboro MA 01879	978-649-8750	R	2*	<.1
441	Universal Used Pallets Inc—*Jose Lesteiro*	6350 Nw 72nd Ave, Miami FL 33166	305-594-2776	R	2*	<.1
442	National Wood Products Of Maine—*Joseph Woodbury*	822 Main St, Oxford ME 04270	207-539-4462	R	2*	<.1
443	Wappoo Wood Products Inc—*Thomas Baker*	12877 Kirkwood Rd, Sidney OH 45365	937-492-1166	R	2*	<.1
444	American Specialty Window and Door Inc—*Walter Stroud*	1402 River St, Wilkesboro NC 28697	336-838-4458	R	2*	<.1
445	Willis Lumber Co—*Bruce Willis*	PO Box 84, Wshngtn Ct Hs OH 43160	740-335-2601	R	1*	<.1
446	Crosby Export Specialties—*John Crosby*	PO Box 1178, Bay Minette AL 36507	251-580-0705	R	1*	<.1
447	Louisiana Millwork LLC—*Jennifer Palomino*	1949 Merganser St, Lake Charles LA 70615	337-721-7676	R	1*	<.1
448	Ike International Corp—*Ted Fischer*	500 E Maple St, Stanley WI 54768	715-644-5777	R	1*	<.1
449	Cascade Forest Group LLC—*Jeff Morris*	PO Box 1766, Lake Oswego OR 97035	503-636-8633	R	1*	<.1
450	Kessel Lumber Supply Inc—*Lawrence Kessel*	PO Box 84, Keyser WV 26726	304-788-3371	R	<1*	<.1
451	Davis Brothers Produce Boxes Inc—*Bedford Davis*	PO Box 69, Evergreen NC 28438	910-654-4913	R	<1*	<.1
452	Emmet Vaughn Lumber Co—*Jerry V Vaughn*	3932 Martin Mill Pke, Knoxville TN 37920	865-577-7577	R	N/A	<.1

TOTALS: SIC 5031 Lumber, Plywood & Millwork
Companies: 452   35,631   75.8

5032 Brick, Stone & Related Materials

Rank	Company Name—*Executive Officer*	Address, City, State, Zip	Phone	Type	Fin	Empls
1	Louisville Tile Distributors Inc—*Randy Parker*	4520 Bishop Ln, Louisville KY 40218	502-452-2037	R	406*	.2
2	American Tile Supply Inc—*Dennis Knautz*	2244 Luna Rd Ste 160, Carrollton TX 75006	972-243-2378	R	201*	.3
3	Interceramic Inc—*Victor Almeida Garcia*	2333 S Jupiter Rd, Garland TX 75041	214-503-5500	S	194	.6
4	Granite Rock Co—*Bruce W Woolpert*	350 Technology Dr, Watsonville CA 95076	831-768-2000	R	166*	.6
5	Delaney Group Inc—*Timothy Delaney*	PO Box 219, Mayfield NY 12117	518-661-5304	R	145*	.3
6	Walker and Zanger Inc—*Leon Zanger*	13190 Telfair Ave, Sylmar CA 91342	818-252-4005	R	105*	.4
7	Alpha Tile Distributors Inc—*Scott Bennett*	2443 East Meadow Blvd, Tampa FL 33619	813-620-9000	S	103*	<.1

Note: An asterisk (*) indicates an estimated financial figure. The company type code used is as follows: R = Private, P = Public, S = Private Subsidiary, B = Public Subsidiary, D = Division, J = Joint Venture, I = Investment Fund.

COMPANY RANKINGS BY SALES WITHIN 4-DIGIT SIC

Rank	Company Name—Executive Officer	Address, City, State, Zip	Phone	Type	Fin	Empls
8	Alley-Cassetty Companies Inc—Fred Cassetty	2 Oldham St, Nashville TN 37213	615-244-7077	R	82*	.2
9	Dixie Cut Stone And Marble Inc—Kim Kueffner	5917 Dixie Hwy, Saginaw MI 48601	989-777-0420	R	81*	.1
10	Cen-Cal Wallboard Supply Co	1300 S River Rd, West Sacramento CA 95691	916-372-2320	S	80*	<.1
11	Ralph Clayton and Sons LLC—Joe Forestieri	PO Box 3015, Lakewood NJ 08701	732-751-7600	R	76*	.3
12	Corriveau-Routhier Inc—David Corriveau	266 Clay St, Manchester NH 03103	603-627-3805	R	74*	.1
13	Haskell Lemon Construction Co—Kent Wert	PO Box 75608, Oklahoma City OK 73147	405-947-6069	R	60*	.2
14	Modern Builders Supply Inc—Larry Leggett	PO Box 9393, Youngstown OH 44513	330-726-7000	R	39*	.8
15	Cemex Construction Materials Inc—Gilberto Perez	PO Box 4120, Ontario CA 91761	909-974-5400	R	38*	.3
16	Schildberg Construction Company Inc—Mark Schildberg	PO Box 358, Greenfield IA 50849	641-743-2131	R	37*	.3
17	Clay Ingels Company Inc—Bill Chapman Jr	PO Box 2120, Lexington KY 40588	859-252-0836	R	35*	.1
18	George L Wilson and Company Ltd—Edward Krokosky	220 East General Robin, Pittsburgh PA 15212	412-231-3217	R	30*	<.1
19	Bierschbach Equipment and Supply Company Inc—Michael Thuringer	PO Box 1444, Sioux Falls SD 57101	605-332-4466	R	29*	.1
20	Virginia Contractors' Supply Inc—Zulmira Morais	9106 Owens Dr, Manassas Park VA 20111	703-368-2950	R	28*	<.1
21	Tri-State Brick and Stone Of New York Inc—Robert Turzilli	333 7th Ave Fl 5, New York NY 10001	212-366-3939	R	28*	.1
22	Corliss Resources Inc—Harry Corliss	PO Box 487, Sumner WA 98390	253-924-0104	R	28*	.2
23	Barton Leasing Inc—Donnie Barton	14800 E Moncrieff Pl, Aurora CO 80011	303-576-2200	R	27*	.2
24	Amboy Aggregates—Richard Rosamilia	PO Box 3220, South Amboy NJ 08879	732-525-0620	R	25*	<.1
25	Rio Grande Co—Bruce Peterson	PO Box 17227, Denver CO 80217	303-825-2211	R	25*	.2
26	Texas Architectural Aggregate Inc—Joe Williams	PO Box 608, San Saba TX 76877	325-372-5105	R	23*	.1
27	Ontario Stone Corp—Carl Baracelli	34301 Chardon Rd, Willoughby Hills OH 44094	440-943-9556	R	20*	.1
28	Patuxent Materials Inc—Francis Gardiner	2124 Priest Bridge Dr, Crofton MD 21114	443-332-4700	R	19*	.2
29	Dura Sales Inc—Rodger Costello	2481 Bull Creek Rd, Tarentum PA 15084	724-224-7700	R	19*	<.1
30	Keystone Aggregate Products Co—Michael Raub	PO Box A, Bath PA 18014	610-837-2211	R	19*	.3
31	Masonry Center Inc—Scott Chandler	PO Box 7825, Boise ID 83707	208-375-1362	R	18*	.1
32	Nu Steel Supply Inc—Verne Kooten	2901 S Santa Fe Dr, Englewood CO 80110	303-789-7554	R	18*	.1
33	A B Property Services Inc—Shlomo Bonan	180 Nw 183rd St Ste 10, Miami FL 33169	305-932-5582	R	18*	<.1
34	Augusta Ready Mix Inc—Charles Davis	PO Box 204018, Augusta GA 30917	706-733-9781	R	17*	.1
35	Elegant Surfaces—John Polimeno	551 Carnegie St, Manteca CA 95337	209-823-9388	R	15*	.1
36	Hudson Cos—Tom Hudson	89 Ship St, Providence RI 02903	401-274-2200	R	15*	<.1
37	Winroc Corp (Minneapolis Minnesota)—Paul Vanderberg	5262 Glenbrook Ave N, Saint Paul MN 55128	651-777-8222	R	14*	.1
38	Feltes Sand and Gravel Co—Timothy Feltes	1s194 Hwy 47, Elburn IL 60119	630-365-3600	R	14*	<.1
39	Dale Tile Co—Alan Dale	8400 89th Ave N Ste 44, Minneapolis MN 55445	763-488-1880	R	13*	<.1
40	Carder Inc—Ron Peterson	PO Box 732, Lamar CO 81052	719-336-3479	R	13*	.1
41	Concrete Express Inc—Donald Mullin	46 Skyline Dr, Salem CT 06420	860-859-2312	R	13*	.1
42	EPC America LLC—Amparo Castro	3356 NW 78th Ave, Miami FL 33122	305-629-2020	R	12*	<.1
43	Nexgen Enterprises Inc—Richard Wolgemuth	PO Box 1036, West Chester OH 45071	513-618-0300	R	12*	.3
44	French Quarry Inc—David Rose	2425 E Rose Garden Ln, Phoenix AZ 85050	480-998-7745	R	11*	.1
45	Oldcastle Apg Texas Inc—Steve Bond	2624 Joe Field Rd, Dallas TX 75229	972-488-8131	S	11*	.3
46	Tile Market Of Delaware Inc—John Watson	37 Germay Dr, Wilmington DE 19804	302-777-4663	R	11*	.1
47	L and W Stone Corp—Scott Laine	PO Box 1224, Orland CA 95963	530-865-5085	R	11*	.1
48	Dimock Gould and Co—Gordon R Ainsworth	190 22nd St, Moline IL 61265	309-797-0650	R	11*	<.1
49	Robert F Henry Tile Company Inc—Robert Henry	PO Box 211209, Montgomery AL 36121	334-269-2518	R	11*	.1
50	Richards Brick Co—John Motley	234 Springer Ave, Edwardsville IL 62025	618-656-0230	R	10*	.1
51	Supply House Inc—Fornando Figueira	7204 Nw 79th Ter, Medley FL 33166	305-883-2131	R	10*	<.1
52	Greenville Ready Mix Concrete Inc—Derek Dunn	PO Box 1639, Wintorville NC 28590	252-756-0119	R	10*	.1
53	Concrete Tie Industries Inc—Paul Schoendienst	PO Box 5406, Compton CA 90224	310-886-1000	R	10*	.1
54	Concrete Formwork and Accessories Inc—Edward Douglass	10414 Perrin Beitel Rd, San Antonio TX 78217	210-653-1980	R	10*	.1
55	Encinitas Natural Stone—Mike Schzotka	597 Westlake St, Encinitas CA 92024	760-633-4242	R	10*	<.1
56	Key-James Brick and Supply Inc—James Large	4130 Jersey Pke, Chattanooga TN 37421	423-821-3547	R	10*	.1
57	Valley Caliche Products Inc—R Thompson	PO Box 1086, Mission TX 78573	956-581-2751	R	10*	.1
58	Hedberg Aggregates Inc—Stephen Hedberg	1205 Nathan Ln N, Minneapolis MN 55441	763-545-4400	R	9*	.1
59	Ohm International Inc—Pinakin Pathak	195 Prospect Plains Rd, Monroe NJ 08831	609-655-7787	R	9*	.1
60	US Technical Ceramics Inc—Walt Carbonell	15400 Concord Cir, Morgan Hill CA 95037	408-779-0303	R	9*	<.1
61	Hutcherson Tile Co—Raymond Hutcherson	130 Mitchell Rd, Houston TX 77037	281-447-6354	R	9*	<.1
62	DC Materials Inc—Robert Catterton	3334 Kenilworth Ave St, Hyattsville MD 20781	301-403-0200	R	9*	.1
63	E H Perkins Construction Inc—Edward Perkins	PO Box 752, Hudson MA 01749	978-562-3436	R	9*	.1
64	Capital Quarries—Eric Strope	PO Box 105050, Jefferson City MO 65110	573-635-8578	R	9*	.1
65	Asplin Excavating Inc—David Asplin	3100 41st St Sw, Fargo ND 58104	701-277-0048	R	9*	.1
66	Boomer Co—George Gill	1940 E Forest Ave, Detroit MI 48207	313-832-5050	R	8*	<.1
67	FTG Construction Materials Inc—Anthony Alegre	PO Box 1508, Lodi CA 95241	209-334-4038	R	7*	<.1
68	Ferazzoli Imports Inc—Antonio Ferazzoli	2110 N Andrews Ave Ext, Pompano Beach FL 33069	954-975-7775	R	7*	<.1
69	Nu-Way Concrete Forms Southeast LLC—Paul Donovan	4788 Old Cape Rd E, Jackson MO 63755	573-204-0100	R	7*	<.1
70	Marble Granite Tiles Inc—Neklan Mittenwald	1022 N Sabina St, Anaheim CA 92801	714-502-5700	R	7*	.1
71	Big Johnsons Concrete Pumping—Walter Bryun	4066 Evans Ave Ste 11, Fort Myers FL 33901	239-275-0096	R	7*	.1
72	Image Asphalt Maintenance Inc—Kevin Miller	8225 Bltmore Annplis B, Pasadena MD 21122	410-439-9200	R	7*	.1
73	Littleton And Sons Sand And Supply Inc—Joe Littleton	7610 Lake Rd Ste B, Indianapolis IN 46217	317-882-0878	R	7*	.1
74	Specialty Tile Products Inc—Josette Callol	1275 Oakbrook Dr Ste D, Norcross GA 30093	770-246-9224	R	6*	.1
75	Corriher Trucking Inc—Harold Corriher	225 Corriher Gravel Rd, China Grove NC 28023	704-857-0166	R	6*	<.1
76	Crawford Material Co—Stuart Wind	3949 W Palmer St, Chicago IL 60647	773-252-1188	R	6*	.1
77	Worcester Sand And Gravel Company Inc—Michael Trotto	182 Holden St, Shrewsbury MA 01545	508-852-1683	R	6*	.1
78	Paramount Stone Company Inc—Steve Riviere	338 Courtland Ave, Stamford CT 06906	203-353-9119	R	6*	<.1
79	Mgq Inc—Tim Bell	PO Box 130, Old Fort OH 44861	419-992-4236	R	6*	<.1
80	Brauntex Materials Inc—Dean Fischer	1504 Wald Rd, New Braunfels TX 78132	830-625-6276	R	6*	<.1
81	Dernis International Marketing Company Inc—Neil Mulligan	2600 Reliance Dr, Virginia Beach VA 23452	757-427-1142	R	6*	<.1
82	Plourde Sand and Gravel Company Inc—Oscar Plourde	PO Box 220, Suncook NH 03275	603-485-3061	R	6*	.1
83	Kb Concrete Inc—Kevin Bloxham	PO Box 43, Rigby ID 83442	208-745-8980	R	5*	<.1
84	Suburban Marble and Granite Inc—John Menarde	1010 Pulinski Rd, Warminster PA 18974	215-956-9711	R	5*	<.1
85	21st Century Tile Inc—Mark Terrill	12600 W Silver Spring, Butler WI 53007	262-790-8453	R	5*	<.1
86	Richmond Ceramic Tile Distributors Inc—Anthony Vanario	31 N Bridge St, Staten Island NY 10309	718-317-8500	R	5*	<.1
87	Akdo Intertrade Inc—Hakki Akbulak	1435 State St, Bridgeport CT 06605	203-336-5199	R	5*	<.1
88	Zamaroni Quarry Inc—Louie Zamaroni	3500 Petaluma Hill Rd, Santa Rosa CA 95404	707-543-8400	R	5*	<.1
89	Maxxon Corporation—Clyde Jorgenson	PO Box 253, Hamel MN 55340	763-478-6000	R	5*	<.1
90	A Marinelli And Sons Inc—Francis Marinelli	405 N Walnut St Fl 1, West Chester PA 19380	610-344-0793	R	5*	<.1
91	Jointa Galusha LLC—John Sharron	269 Ballard Rd, Gansevoort NY 12831	518-792-5029	R	5*	<.1
92	Sunshine Rock Inc—Rafael Caballero	129th Ave 202nd St, Miami FL 33018	305-829-8807	R	5*	<.1
93	Carolina Sand Inc—John Taylor	PO Box 850, Johnsonville SC 29555	843-386-2021	R	5*	<.1
94	Kimball Sand Company Inc—Robert Kimball	PO Box 29, Mendon MA 01756	508-883-1798	R	5*	<.1
95	Leamar Industries Inc—Marcello Mallegni	171 Locke Dr Ste 114, Marlborough MA 01752	508-786-5964	R	4*	<.1
96	Legacy Stone Products Inc—Dave Wurtsbaugh	2531 W 62nd Ct, Denver CO 80221	303-456-4672	R	4*	<.1

Rank	Company Name—Executive Officer	Address, City, State, Zip	Phone	Type	Fin	Empls
97	Stonewall Products Inc—Donald Atkinson	6935 Aliante Pkwy Ste, North Las Vegas NV 89084	702-644-9497	R	4*	<.1
98	Pesch Redi Mix Inc—Leonard Pesch	PO Box 210798, Milwaukee WI 53221	414-281-8542	R	4*	.1
99	Colonial Construction Materials Inc—Timothy Branin	PO Box 333, Oilville VA 23129	804-264-0128	R	4*	<.1
100	Cornerstone Materials Corp—Steven Lohnes	PO Box 5990, Lancaster CA 93539	661-285-5595	R	4*	<.1
101	San Francisco Gravel Company Inc—Michael Nicolai	552 Berry St, San Francisco CA 94107	415-431-1273	R	4*	<.1
102	Paragon Supply Inc—David Kellish	PO Box 1079, Syracuse NY 13201	315-475-5115	R	4*	<.1
103	Siena Marble and Granite Inc—Anthony Dinorcia	3963 Domestic Ave, Naples FL 34104	239-435-7875	R	4*	<.1
104	Kobrin Builders Supply Of Sarasota Inc—Harvey Kobrin	1688 Global Ct, Sarasota FL 34240	941-926-4494	R	4*	<.1
105	Davis Block Company Inc—Scott Davis	225 Birch Pl, Soldotna AK 99669	907-262-5106	R	4*	<.1
106	Frontier Pavement Specialists Inc—William Ferichs	105 Tower Dr, San Antonio TX 78232	210-496-2070	R	4*	<.1
107	Atlas Construction Specialties Company Inc—David Connors	4044 22nd Ave W, Seattle WA 98199	206-283-2000	R	4*	<.1
108	Marble Emporium Inc—Louiza Kourkouvis	2200 Carlson Dr, Northbrook IL 60062	847-205-4000	R	4*	.1
109	F and H Supply Inc—David Hannagan	PO Box 470410, Tulsa OK 74147	918-663-3807	R	4*	<.1
110	Quad-City Brick and Stone Inc—Bill Pender	PO Box 315, Bettendorf IA 52722	563-355-0276	R	4*	<.1
111	B and B Marble Inc—Jackie Li	341 Beach Rd, Burlingame CA 94010	650-548-1628	R	4*	<.1
112	Art Design Concrete—Aaron Mills	1015 37th Ave Ct Ste 1, Greeley CO 80634	970-346-8327	R	4*	<.1
113	Dutchess Quarry and Supply Company Inc—Joseph Arborio	PO Box 651, Pleasant Valley NY 12569	845-635-8151	R	4*	<.1
114	Henniker Sand And Gravel Company Inc—Rodney Patenaude	PO Box 2040, Henniker NH 03242	603-428-7756	R	4*	<.1
115	Lone Star Materials Inc—Bruce Bonnet	PO Box 140405, Austin TX 78714	512-834-8611	R	4*	<.1
116	Diniz Design Inc—Paulo Diniz	11962 Lakeland Park Bl, Baton Rouge LA 70809	225-755-0114	R	4*	<.1
117	Engineering Aggregates Corp—Joseph Jones	PO Box 538, Logansport IN 46947	574-722-3040	R	4*	<.1
118	Belmarmi Inc—Jerrold Dixon	436 Atlantic Blvd, Neptune Beach FL 32266	904-241-3407	R	4*	<.1
119	Brisky Supply Company Inc—Robert Brisky	10269 Old Rte 31, Clyde NY 14433	315-923-7775	R	4*	<.1
120	Access Drywall Supply Company Inc—Robert Porter	PO Box 550, Westerville OH 43086	614-890-2111	R	4*	<.1
121	Greenville Gravel Co—Stan Ingram	PO Box 220, Greenville MS 38702	662-332-8039	R	4*	<.1
122	Tennessee Building Stone Inc—David Rose	1313 Chestnut Hill Rd, Crossville TN 38555	931-484-9121	R	4*	<.1
123	Adelman Sand and Gravel Inc—Linda Adelman	34 Bozrah St, Bozrah CT 06334	860-889-3394	R	4*	<.1
124	Mobile Concrete Inc—Arthur Boatright	PO Box 1119, Casper WY 82602	307-237-9333	R	4*	<.1
125	Artistic Granite and Marble Inc—Stan Rosenquist	2444 Maggio Cir, Lodi CA 95240	209-369-6449	R	4*	<.1
126	Buffkin Ceramic Tile Supply Inc—Robert Buffkin	3350 N Courtenay Pkwy, Merritt Island FL 32953	321-452-2282	R	3*	<.1
127	Antoniello and Company Inc—Antonio Antoniello	8735 Bradley Ave, Sun Valley CA 91352	818-768-7866	R	3*	<.1
128	Ceramic Technics Ltd—Gerry King	1298 Old Alpharetta Rd, Alpharetta GA 30005	770-740-0050	R	3*	<.1
129	Dente Trading Company Inc—Gerard Dente	30 Canfield Rd, Cedar Grove NJ 07009	973-857-4050	R	3*	<.1
130	Mountain Materials Inc—Daniel Shea	PO Box 2154, Lakeside CA 92040	619-390-9932	R	3*	<.1
131	E and A Materials Inc—John Pitts	6007 Seymour Hwy, Wichita Falls TX 76310	940-692-3290	R	3*	<.1
132	Decatur Mill Service Co—Edward Levy	4301 Iverson Blvd Ste, Trinity AL 35673	256-306-9477	S	3*	<.1
133	Architectural Tile and Stone Ltd—Katie Albrecht	9315 Neils Thompson Dr, Austin TX 78758	512-420-9989	R	3*	<.1
134	Imperial Design Group Inc—Shane Khazai	PO Box 25879, Los Angeles CA 90025	310-837-7797	R	3*	<.1
135	Jrb Company Inc—James Bird	5603 Anderson Rd, Tampa FL 33614	813-886-7761	R	3*	<.1
136	Serra Stone Corp—Joe Serra	2324 Stewart Ave, Silver Spring MD 20910	301-587-8100	R	3*	<.1
137	Stone Coffman Company LLC	6015 Taylor Rd, Gahanna OH 43230	614-861-4668	R	3*	<.1
138	Medina Robert and Sons Concrete And Sand Inc—Robert Medina	PO Box 766, Taos NM 87571	575-758-3217	R	3*	<.1
139	Stone Center Of Indiana Inc—Dave Sawyer	5272 E 65th St, Indianapolis IN 46220	317-849-9100	R	3*	<.1
140	Waterford Sand and Gravel Co—Joan Wurst	15871 Sturgis Rd, Union City PA 16438	814-796-6250	R	3*	<.1
141	Alan Good Shop—Alan Good	265 Rupp Rd, Toledo WA 98591	360-864-2975	R	3*	<.1
142	Us Granite-Nevada Inc—Mike Simonelli	5350 Capital Ct Ste 10, Reno NV 89502	775-857-4700	R	3*	<.1
143	JW Brett Inc—John Brett	9660 71st St Ne, Albertville MN 55301	763-497-7351	R	3*	<.1
144	Cangelosi Co—Donae Cangelosi	PO Box 608, Missouri City TX 77459	281-499-0561	R	3*	<.1
145	Porter-Trustin-Carlson Co—Gerald Kuehn	PO Box 11158, Omaha NE 68111	402-453-2000	R	3*	<.1
146	Tennessee Stone Products LLC—Robert Brokus	626 Old Hickory Blvd C, Nashville TN 37209	615-356-5800	R	3*	<.1
147	Bill Ledbetter's Dry Wall Sales Inc—Pam Sexton	3115 Railroad Ave, Ceres CA 95307	209-537-9164	R	3*	<.1
148	Hinesburg Sand and Gravel Company Inc—Paul Casey	14818 Rte 116, Hinesburg VT 05461	802-482-2342	R	3*	<.1
149	Dade Concrete Pumping Inc—Ricardo Gonzalez	5900 Sw 122nd Ave, Miami FL 33166	305-823-1722	R	3*	<.1
150	Damar Natural Stone Imports Inc—David Gambaccini	750 Anthony Trl, Northbrook IL 60062	847-272-6666	R	3*	<.1
151	Buendia and Partners Inc—Carlos Cardin	9030 Aero St, San Antonio TX 78217	210-828-0011	R	3*	<.1
152	Pyne Sand and Stone Company Inc—James Pyne	1 Lackey Dam Rd, East Douglas MA 01516	508-234-6400	R	3*	<.1
153	Sierra Mining and Crushing Company LLC	PO Box 22110, Tucson AZ 85734	520-807-0558	R	3*	<.1
154	Appalachian Stone Company Inc—Kevin Washburn	PO Box 1598, Marion NC 28752	828-756-4287	R	3*	<.1
155	Ccs Stone Inc—Donald Mitnick	9 Caesar Pl Ste 11, Moonachie NJ 07074	201-933-1515	R	3*	<.1
156	Milpitas Materials Co—Jon Minnis	PO Box 360003, Milpitas CA 95036	408-262-0656	R	3*	<.1
157	Tile and Design Concepts Inc—Kathy Reed	310 W Wilshire Blvd, Oklahoma City OK 73116	405-842-8551	R	3*	<.1
158	Imperial Stone Corp—Ioan Bartos	739 Nw 2nd St, Hallandale Beach FL 33009	954-964-5996	R	3*	<.1
159	Abram Cleason Company Inc—James Cleason	5486 Tellier Rd, Newark NY 14513	315-597-5241	R	3*	<.1
160	Ceramica Italiana Center Inc—Jack Cohen	290 Ne 183rd St, Miami FL 33179	305-652-3353	R	3*	<.1
161	Maxim Douglas—Doug Grigg	1726 N Ventura Ave Ste, Ventura CA 93001	805-648-7761	R	3*	<.1
162	Olathe Aggregate Inc—Thomas Fry	23200 W 159th St, Olathe KS 66061	913-829-1122	R	3*	<.1
163	Quality Building Stone Inc—Velina Miller	993 W 14730 S, Riverton UT 84065	801-255-2911	R	3*	<.1
164	Specialized Building Products LLC—Brad Baker	145 W Meats Ave, Orange CA 92865	714-279-1042	R	3*	<.1
165	M and M Interiors Inc—Michael Phillips	8148 Vine St, Cincinnati OH 45216	513-821-1441	R	3*	<.1
166	Speer Concrete Inc—Clayton Speer	PO Box 280, Carthage NC 28327	910-947-3144	R	3*	<.1
167	Arcadia Limestone Co—Annabell Lenz	PO Box 106, Arcadia IL 51430	712-689-2299	R	3*	<.1
168	Bauch Quarry Products—David Bauch	PO Box 425, Roscoe IL 61073	815-239-1211	R	3*	<.1
169	Cambrian Granite and Stone Inc—Joseph Griffith	5814 Westminster Dr St, Cedar Falls IA 50613	319-266-7160	R	3*	<.1
170	Modern Masonry Products Inc—Pete Schneider	PO Box 400, Slidell LA 70459	985-863-6161	R	3*	<.1
171	Standard Gravel Company Inc—Andrew Alexander	PO Box 810, Bearden AR 71720	870-687-3131	R	3*	<.1
172	Wellington Tile and Marble—Francisco Tropeano	2091 Indian Rd, West Palm Beach FL 33409	561-686-5800	R	3*	<.1
173	Southampton Tile and Stone LLC	303 Winding Rd Ste 2, Old Bethpage NY 11804	516-777-2000	R	2*	<.1
174	Commercial Sand Company Inc—Rick Martini	1306 E Anderson Rd, Houston TX 77047	713-433-2421	R	2*	<.1
175	Solberg Aggregate Co—Robert Solberg	3615 145th St E, Rosemount MN 55068	651-437-6672	R	2*	<.1
176	Spiers Concrete Sysmtem And Excavation LLC—Shelly Leikvold	655 E Shortline St, Kuna ID 83634	208-922-3723	R	2*	<.1
177	Tri-County Aggregate Inc—Joseph White	PO Box 419, Medford MN 55049	507-446-0825	R	2*	<.1
178	Red Rock Gravel LLC—Clyde Townsend	PO Box 212, Louise TX 77455	979-648-2589	R	2*	<.1
179	Dover Sand And Gravel Inc—Richard Proulx	Mast Rd, Dover NH 03820	603-740-0013	R	2*	<.1
180	S and S Rock Inc—Dennis Stafford	316 Stafford Rd, Oldfort TN 37362	423-338-2599	R	2*	<.1
181	Santee Redi-Mix Corp—Scott Askin	815 Oldfield Cir, Florence SC 29501	843-761-8811	R	2*	<.1
182	Greenwald Supply Inc—James Greenwald	8090 Alban Rd, Springfield VA 22150	703-912-5900	R	2*	<.1
183	Material Sand and Stone Corp—Robert Pezza	618 Greenville Rd, North Smithfield RI 02896	401-767-3420	R	2*	<.1
184	Tilework Reinhardt Brothers—Laszlo Reindhardt	1450 W 228th St Ste 17, Torrance CA 90501	310-325-0174	R	2*	<.1

Note: An asterisk (*) indicates an estimated financial figure. The company type code used is as follows: R = Private, P = Public, S = Private Subsidiary, B = Public Subsidiary, D = Division, J = Joint Venture, I = Investment Fund.

COMPANY RANKINGS BY SALES WITHIN 4-DIGIT SIC

Rank	Company Name—*Executive Officer*	Address, City, State, Zip	Phone	Type	Fin	Empls
185	Concrete Structural Imaging Inc—*Pevhten Rainwater*	7800 Cucamonga Ave, Sacramento CA 95826	916-454-4220	R	2*	<.1
186	Tbr Marble and Granite Inc—*Ron Bresse*	9 Spring Brook Rd, Foxboro MA 02035	508-543-9487	R	2*	<.1
187	Union Concrete Construction Corp—*Anthony Folino*	PO Box 853, Marlborough MA 01752	508-485-8078	R	2*	<.1
188	Akropois Marble And Granite LLC—*Jackie Lignos*	88 Tyler Pl, South Plainfield NJ 07080	908-561-3700	R	2*	<.1
189	Naumann Equipment Company Inc—*H Naumann*	8800 Ramirez Ln, Austin TX 78742	512-385-0690	R	2*	<.1
190	Shenandoah Sand Inc—*Vicki Newlin*	PO Box 2528, Winchester VA 22604	540-667-1660	R	2*	<.1
191	St Charles Sand Company Inc—*Richard Viehmann*	14580 Mmouri Bottom Rd, Bridgeton MO 63044	314-739-0111	R	2*	<.1
192	Cushing Stone Company Inc—*John Tesiero*	725 State Hwy 5s, Amsterdam NY 12010	518-887-2521	R	2*	<.1
193	Virginia Beach Marble Co—*Mose Mast*	506 Viking Dr, Virginia Beach VA 23452	757-340-3686	R	2*	<.1
194	Central Transit Inc—*Charles Egbert*	W1282 S St, Green Lake WI 54941	920-294-0189	R	2*	<.1
195	Banfill Supply Inc—*Doug Hammond*	PO Box 840, Lewisburg OH 45338	937-962-9424	R	1*	<.1
196	Horizon International—*Joe Kotoch*	PO Box 7405, Fitchburg MA 01420	978-375-1339	R	1*	<.1
197	Lake Cumberland Stone Inc—*Henry Hinkle*	PO Box 740, Burnside KY 42519	606-561-4115	R	1*	<.1
198	Ldw Inc—*Fred Koermer*	N3211 Hwy H, Lake Geneva WI 53147	262-248-2000	R	1*	<.1
199	Riva Marble and Granite—*Mark Gebolske*	149 Grove St, Watsonville CA 95076	831-722-2241	R	1*	<.1
200	Sun Marble At Fresno Inc—*Wen Shu*	447 W Fallbrook Ave, Fresno CA 93711	559-448-8988	R	1*	<.1
201	Hastings Tile and Bath Inc—*Michael Homola*	30 Commercial St, Freeport NY 11520	516-379-3500	R	1*	<.1

TOTALS: SIC 5032 Brick, Stone & Related Materials
Companies: 201

					3,138	11.9

5033 Roofing, Siding & Insulation

Rank	Company Name—*Executive Officer*	Address, City, State, Zip	Phone	Type	Fin	Empls
1	American Builders and Contractors Supply Company Inc—*David Luck*	PO Box 838, Beloit WI 53512	608-362-7777	R	5,143*	9.0
2	Harvey Industries Inc—*Thomas Bigony*	1400 Main St Fl 3, Waltham MA 02451	781-899-3500	R	3,338*	1.6
3	Beacon Roofing Supply Inc—*Paul M Isabella*	1 Lakeland Park Dr, Peabody MA 01960		P	1,817	2.3
4	Irex Corp—*W Kirk Liddell*	PO Box 1268, Lancaster PA 17602	717-397-3633	R	1,525*	2.5
5	Specialty Products and Insulation Co—*Robert M Rayner*	1097 Commercial Ave, East Petersburg PA 17520	717-569-3900	R	449*	.7
6	Sunniland Corp—*Thomas Moore*	PO Box 8001, Sanford FL 32772	407-322-2425	R	284*	.2
7	Roofing Wholesale Company Inc—*Harley Lisherness*	1918 W Grant St, Phoenix AZ 85009	602-258-3794	R	203*	.3
8	Houston Rsgrp Ltd—*Janet Braney*	PO Box 671627, Houston TX 77267	281-447-7759	R	160*	.1
9	Shook and Fletcher Insulation Co—*Wayne W Killion Jr*	PO Box 380501, Birmingham AL 35238	205-991-7606	R	152*	.2
10	Eikenhout and Sons Inc—*Richard Sonneveldt*	PO Box 2806, Grand Rapids MI 49501	616-459-4523	R	147*	.2
11	Missouri Petroleum Products Company LLC	1620 Woodson Rd, Saint Louis MO 63114	314-991-2180	R	146*	.3
12	Badger Corrugating Co—*Michael J Sexauer*	PO Box 1837, La Crosse WI 54602	608-788-0100	R	94*	.2
13	Dallas Wholesale Builders Supply Inc—*Byron Potter*	PO Box 1660, DeSoto TX 75123	214-381-2200	R	92*	.1
14	Gulf Eagle Supply Inc—*James Resch*	501 N Reo St, Tampa FL 33609	813-636-9808	R	83*	.3
15	Standard Roofings Inc—*John Askin*	PO Box 1410, Eatontown NJ 07724	732-542-3300	S	79*	.1
16	Burton Building Products Inc—*Jessi Hudson*	5424 S 103rd E Ave, Tulsa OK 74146	918-665-6223	R	68*	.1
17	Western Products Inc (Fargo North Dakota)	474 45th St S, Fargo ND 58103	701-293-5310	R	64*	.1
18	Cooperative Reserve Supply Inc—*Jack Moynihan*	115 Fawcett St, Cambridge MA 02138	617-864-1444	R	50*	<.1
19	Wimsatt Brothers Inc—*John Heitel* Shelter Distribution Inc	405 N English Station, Louisville KY 40213	502-245-8891	S	35*	.1
20	J and S Supply Corp—*Michael Diamond*	5302 37th St, Long Island City NY 11101	718-786-3044	R	35*	<.1
21	SG Wholesale Roofing Supply Inc—*Roger Glazer*	PO Box 1464, Santa Ana CA 92701	714-568-1906	R	34*	.1
22	Mid-South Building Supply of Maryland Inc—*John Driggs*	5640 Sunnyside Ave Ste, Beltsville MD 20705	301-513-9000	R	32*	.1
23	Britton Lumber Company Inc—*Douglas Britton*	PO Box 389, Fairlee VT 05045	802-333-4388	R	29*	.1
24	Remedy Roofing Inc—*Greg Arnim*	21925 Franz Rd Ste 402, Katy TX 77449	281-391-8555	R	27	<.1
25	Wood Feathers Inc—*Lee Gotcher*	PO Box 17566, Portland OR 97217	503-289-8813	R	25*	.1
26	Sellmore Industries Inc—*James Yoviene*	PO Box 885, Buffalo NY 14240	716-854-1600	R	25*	.1
27	Alpha Systems Inc—*David Smith*	5120 Beck Dr, Elkhart IN 46516	574-295-5206	R	25*	.2
28	Lumberyard Suppliers Inc—*Troy Reed*	3405 N Main St, East Peoria IL 61611	309-694-4356	R	25*	.1
29	Wilson Enterprises of Illinois Inc—*William Wilson*	405 Barrington Rd, Wauconda IL 60084	630-637-0750	R	19*	<.1
30	Philadelphia Reserve Supply Co—*Frank Dalinsky*	200 Mack Dr, Croydon PA 19021		R	19*	<.1
31	Buckley Industries Inc—*David Mcarthur*	PO Box 574, Wichita KS 67201	316-744-7587	R	16*	.1
32	Hydra-Matic Packing Company Inc—*Mark Kenna*	PO Box 96, Huntingdon Valley PA 19006	215-676-2992	R	16*	.1
33	Rsgrp Dallas-Fort Worth Inc—*Vin Perella*	PO Box 540817, Dallas TX 75354	214-358-2600	R	15*	.1
34	Harrington and Co—*Stephen Booth*	PO Box 25723, Salt Lake City UT 84125	801-972-3131	R	15*	.1
35	Dakota Roofing Supply Inc—*Mark Jackson*	PO Box 12878, Grand Forks ND 58208	701-775-5369	R	14*	.1
36	Fligg Holding Co—*Robert Fligg*	PO Box 489, Ankeny IA 50021	515-963-9170	R	11*	.1
37	Tri-Valley Supply Inc—*James Peterson*	707 Aldridge Rd Ste A, Vacaville CA 95688	707-469-7470	R	11*	.1
38	Pacor Inc—*Paul Fraatz*	2603 River Rd Ste 1, Cinnaminson NJ 08077	856-303-8802	R	11*	.1
39	Tri-State Roofing and Siding Wholesale Inc—*Carl Maturo*	9630 S 76th Ave, Hickory Hills IL 60457	708-599-9770	R	10*	.1
40	Crimson Insulations Company Inc—*Nancy Woolbright*	PO Box 70786, Tuscaloosa AL 35407	205-752-6777	R	10*	.1
41	Pacific Insulation Co—*Robert Fults*	2741 Yates Ave, Commerce CA 90040	323-278-8350	S	10*	.1
42	Roofline Inc—*Ronald Ross*	PO Box 24038, Eugene OR 97402	541-345-1253	R	8*	.1
43	Contractors Roofing and Supply Company Inc—*Jerry Schulte*	1760 W Terra Ln, O Fallon MO 63366	636-474-2710	R	8*	.1
44	Welty Custom Exteriors Inc—*Bruce Welty*	300 N Bunnell St, Frankfort IN 46041	765-654-7231	R	8*	.1
45	B and S Insulation Inc—*Timothy Brant*	208 N Goldenrod Rd, Orlando FL 32807	407-658-1925	R	7*	<.1
46	E O Wood Company Inc—*Merry Kaastad*	PO Box 7614, Fort Worth TX 76111	817-834-8811	R	7*	<.1
47	Heritage Wholesalers Inc—*Steven Field*	PO Box 362, Malden MA 02148	781-324-8100	R	7*	<.1
48	Statewide Wholesale Inc—*Randy Rehbein*	PO Box 36216, Denver CO 80236	303-744-7111	R	7*	<.1
49	G and F Roof Supply Inc—*Ron Farrell*	PO Box 3169, Santa Fe Springs CA 90670	562-929-7100	R	6*	<.1
50	Bill Wahl Supply Inc—*William Wahl*	106 Sicklerville Rd, Blackwood NJ 08012	856-228-8220	R	6*	<.1
51	Wholesale Roofing Supply Inc—*Rick Mcclaughlin*	104 E Trinity Blvd, Grand Prairie TX 75050	972-263-8190	R	6*	<.1
52	Gulf Coast Building Products Inc—*Raymond Mayer*	3350 Mclemore Dr, Pensacola FL 32514	850-477-6050	R	5*	<.1
53	Weather Port LLC	1860 1600 Rd, Delta CO 81416	970-874-6373	R	5*	.3
54	Gibson Enterprises Inc—*Hsin Tang*	4982 4th St, Irwindale CA 91706	626-960-2038	R	5*	<.1
55	United Subcontractors Inc—*Tim Portland*	49 Venture Way, Sykesville MD 21784	410-795-0600	R	5*	<.1
56	Mc Donald Metal and Roofing Supply Corp—*Richard Rosenthal*	1 Ave M, Brooklyn NY 11230	718-339-0555	R	4*	<.1
57	Wesco Cedar Inc	PO Box 40847, Eugene OR 97404	541-688-5020	R	4*	<.1
58	Custom Molded Products Of Georgia LLC—*Jeeny Roy*	140 Celtic Blvd, Tyrone GA 30290	770-632-7112	R	4*	<.1
59	Indital US Management LLC—*Keith Sorosiak*	7947 Mesa Dr, Houston TX 77028	713-694-6065	R	4*	<.1
60	Vande Hey Roof Tile Installation Inc—*Kenneth Hendricks*	1565 Bohm Dr, Little Chute WI 54140	920-766-0156	R	3*	<.1
61	Midwest Siding Distributors—*Kelly Opy*	1601 S Taft Ave, Mason City IA 50401	641-424-4717	R	3*	<.1
62	A All Pro Roofing Inc—*Jeffery Tackett*	4630 Ne 35th St, Ocala FL 34479	352-236-2719	R	2*	<.1
63	Reserve Supply of Central New York Inc—*Tom Handley*	200 Midler Park Dr, Syracuse NY 13206	315-463-4557	R	2*	<.1
64	Shelter Distribution Inc—*Paul G Haefcke* Beacon Roofing Supply Inc	1602 Lavon Dr, McKinney TX 75069	972-369-8000	S	2	.4

Rank	Company Name—*Executive Officer*	Address, City, State, Zip	Phone	Type	Fin	Empls
65	Thomas Roofing Supply Co—*Daniel Thomas*	PO Box 374, Seaford DE 19973	302-629-4521	R	2*	<.1

TOTALS: SIC 5033 Roofing, Siding & Insulation
Companies: 65 — 14,479 — 21.6

5039 Construction Materials Nec

Rank	Company Name—*Executive Officer*	Address, City, State, Zip	Phone	Type	Fin	Empls
1	Acoustical Material Services—*Ruben Mendoza* Allied Building Products Corp	PO Box 2071, Montebello CA 90640	323-721-9011	S	1,054*	.7
2	Allied Building Products Corp—*Bob Feury Jr*	15 E Union Ave, East Rutherford NJ 07073	973-267-1576	S	794*	3.1
3	Parksite Group—*George Pattee*	1563 Hubbard Ave, Batavia IL 60510		R	325*	.4
4	ACI Distribution—*Charles Witherington*	12139 Los Nietos, Santa Fe Springs CA 90670	562-345-1248	D	303*	.3
5	Butler-Johnson Corp—*Rolston Johnson*	PO Box 612110, San Jose CA 95161	408-259-1800	R	265*	.2
6	Plastival Inc—*Jim Quinn*	907 Wesemann Dr, West Dundee IL 60118	847-931-4771	S	231*	.2
7	WA Wilson Glass Inc—*Robert Hartong II*	6 Industrial Park Dr, Wheeling WV 26003		R	158*	.1
8	Central Wholesale Supply Corp	1532 Ingleside Rd, Norfolk VA 23502	757-855-3131	R	106*	.1
9	King Supply Company LLC—*Stewart King*	PO Box 271169, Dallas TX 75227	214-388-9834	R	100*	.3
10	Fontaine International Inc—*Henry Bell*	7574 Commerce Cir, Trussville AL 35173	205-661-4900	S	76*	.3
11	Spohn Associates Inc—*Jack Spohn*	7150 Winton Dr Ste 100, Indianapolis IN 46268	317-921-0021	R	68*	<.1
12	Riggs Supply Corp—*A Riggs III*	320 Cedar St, Kennett MO 63857	573-888-9501	R	65*	.3
13	Kobrin Builders Supply Inc—*Harvey Kobrin*	1924 W Princeton St, Orlando FL 32804	407-843-1000	R	65*	.2
14	Hallmark Building Supplies Inc—*O Joe Balthazar*	2120 Pewaukee Rd Rm 10, Waukesha WI 53188		R	55*	.1
15	Nu-Way Concrete Forms Inc—*Gerald Rhomberg*	4190 Hofmeister Ave, Saint Louis MO 63125	314-544-1214	R	50*	.1
16	JO Galloup Co	130 Helmer Rd N, Battle Creek MI 49037	269-965-4005	R	46*	.2
17	Fargo Glass and Paint Co—*Dan Martinson*	1801 7th Ave N, Fargo ND 58102	701-235-4441	R	42*	.1
18	Kesseli Morse Company Inc—*George P Kustigian Jr*	242 Canterbury St, Worcester MA 01603	508-752-1901	R	34*	.2
19	Dairyman's Supply Co—*George Cook Jr*	PO Box 528, Mayfield KY 42066	270-247-5641	R	31*	.1
20	Brin Glass Co—*Douglas Nelson*	2300 N 2nd St, Minneapolis MN 55411	612-529-9671	R	24*	.2
21	Carter-Waters Corp—*Mike Lang*	PO Box 412676, Kansas City MO 64141	816-471-2570	S	23*	.1
22	Architectural Interior Products Inc—*Thomas Mccarty*	2268 Williams Hwy, Williamstown WV 26187	304-375-6395	R	20*	.1
23	Edward George Co	4251 W 129th St, Alsip IL 60803	708-371-0660	R	18*	.1
24	Waldo Brothers Co—*Brenda Colgan*	202 Southampton St, Boston MA 02118	617-445-3000	R	17*	.1
25	Cookson Door Sales Of Arizona Inc—*Joseph Engel*	705 W 22nd St, Tempe AZ 85282	480-377-8777	R	14*	.1
26	Velux-America Inc—*Tim Miller*	PO Dox 5001, Greenwood SC 29648	864-941-4700	R	14*	.4
27	Eastern Wholesale Fence Company Inc—*Peter Williams*	274 Middle Island Rd, Medford NY 11763	631-698-0975	R	14*	.3
28	Champion Fabricating And Supply Co—*Floyd Pease*	PO Box 247, Midvale UT 84047	801-566-1211	R	12*	<.1
29	Sunshine Supply Company Inc—*James Pyle*	4946 Naples St, San Diego CA 92110	619-276-7442	R	12*	<.1
30	Rollac Shutter Of Texas Inc—*Walter Konrad*	5331 W Orange St, Pearland TX 77581	281-485-1911	R	11*	.1
31	Diamond West Lumber Company LLC—*Megan Granhomn*	PO Box 610, Cottage Grove OR 97424	541-929-2902	R	11*	.1
32	Custom Glass Distributors Inc—*Kevin Depaoli*	1095 E 2nd St, Reno NV 89502	775-329-4265	R	10*	.1
33	Go-Glass Corp—*Thomas Huff*	PO Box 390, Salisbury MD 21803	410-742-1151	R	8*	.1
34	Metal Building Supply Inc—*Jim Britton*	19601 N Mount Olive Rd, Gravette AR 72736	479-787-6264	R	7*	<.1
35	Pacific Southwest Sales Company Inc—*Don Beisswanger*	PO Box 58919, Vernon CA 90058	323-582-6852	R	7*	<.1
36	Joseph G Pollard Company Inc—*Brian Dougan*	200 Atlantic Ave, New Hyde Park NY 11040	516-746-0842	R	7*	<.1
37	Hawkins Glass Wholesalers LLC	35 Venture Dr, Stafford VA 22554	540-288-9111	R	6*	<.1
38	W H Basnight And Company Inc—*Michael Basnight*	PO Box 1365, Ahoskie NC 27910	252-332-3131	R	6*	<.1
39	Holmes Drywall Supply Inc—*Jeanne Mcgrath*	1701 W 25th St, Kansas City MO 64108	816-471-7595	R	5*	<.1
40	Basic Components Inc—*Russ Chappell*	1201 S 2nd Ave, Mansfield TX 76063	817-473-7224	R	5*	<.1
41	Greystar E I G LP—*Scott Zimmerman*	12112 Almeda Rd Bldg F, Houston TX 77045	713-433-2700	R	5*	.1
42	Appertain Inc—*Paul Dugan*	520 Township Line Rd, Blue Bell PA 19422	610-812-1030	R	5*	.1
43	L M Barnes Co—*Larry Barnes*	PO Box 25755, Eugene OR 97402	541-686-5647	R	5*	<.1
44	Keusch Glass Inc—*Timothy Keusch*	PO Box 487, Jasper IN 47547	812-482-2566	R	4*	<.1
45	Maryland Glass and Mirror Co—*David Dalbke*	710 W Ostend St, Baltimore MD 21230	410-727-1050	R	4*	<.1
46	Building Concepts Of America Inc—*Anthony Ferrara*	101 Peoples Dr, Newark DE 19702	302-292-0200	R	4*	<.1
47	Townsend Holdings Inc—*Fred Linthicum*	62971 Plateau Dr Ste 2, Bend OR 97701	541-382-2974	R	4*	<.1
48	South Camden Iron Works Inc—*Mitchell Kowal*	PO Box 238, Mickleton NJ 08056	856-423-1107	R	4*	<.1
49	Palm Springs Mirror And Glass Inc—*Virginia Clark*	PO Box 759, Cathedral City CA 92235	760-328-0888	R	3*	<.1
50	Gray Supply Corporation 70—*Pete Hermes*	120 Parker Ave, Forked River NJ 08731	609-971-3302	R	3*	<.1
51	Wolf Glass and Paint Company Inc—*Winnie Bodner*	308 E Market St, New Albany IN 47150	812-944-2264	R	3*	<.1
52	Ibex Futurebilt JV—*Ray Adams*	1023 Laskin Rd Ste 109, Virginia Beach VA 23451	757-422-6800	R	3*	<.1
53	Kennys Home Plaza—*Kenneth Hyatt*	116 Hwy 17, Little River SC 29566	843-841-0207	R	3*	<.1
54	Paragon Pipe and Steel Inc—*Michael Penny*	18919 Aldine Westfield, Houston TX 77073	281-410-2037	R	3*	<.1
55	Addison Truss And Building Supply Inc—*Cecil Pigg*	PO Box 389, Addison AL 35540	256-747-1561	R	3*	<.1
56	Niepraschk Enterprises Inc—*Michael Mcdonald*	544 Central Dr Ste 110, Virginia Beach VA 23454	757-463-1446	R	3*	<.1
57	Mobile Home Stuff Store Inc—*Anthony Widowsky*	N7428 Osborn Way, Fond Du Lac WI 54937	920-923-0098	R	3*	<.1
58	Kassis Superior Sign Company—*Joseph Kassis*	6699 Old Thompson Rd, Syracuse NY 13211	315-463-7446	R	3*	<.1
59	Continental Divide Fence Inc—*Ken Grenemyer*	5610 Pecos St, Denver CO 80221	303-455-1101	R	3*	<.1
60	Heartland Manufacturing Group Inc—*Larry Shipp*	PO Box 588, Peculiar MO 64078	816-779-6441	R	3*	<.1
61	Rainier Stained Glass Inc—*Sun Lee*	8720 S Tacoma Way, Lakewood WA 98499	253-531-2300	R	3*	<.1
62	All Secure Technologies Inc—*Bill Mills*	1316 29th St, Orlando FL 32805	407-423-4962	R	3*	<.1
63	Barfield Fence and Wall Inc—*Lindsay Whittaker*	2266 Clark St, Apopka FL 32703	321-396-0001	R	2*	<.1
64	Olathe Glass Company Inc—*Trey Schroeder*	510 E Santa Fe St, Olathe KS 66061	913-782-7444	R	2*	<.1
65	Harvard Steel Inc—*Shawn Stoddard*	3512 B St Sw, Auburn WA 98001	253-804-8884	R	2*	<.1
66	Robodock and Door—*Ron Stelly*	251 Excell Dr, Jackson MS 39208	601-664-0270	R	2*	<.1
67	Code Precast Products Inc—*Richard Morales*	PO Box 879, Shafter CA 93263	661-746-0466	R	2*	<.1
68	Gator Glass Co—*Norma Gosnell*	1931 S Whiting Cir, Palmer AK 99645	907-745-1600	R	1*	<.1

TOTALS: SIC 5039 Construction Materials Nec
Companies: 68 — 4,203 — 9.2

5043 Photographic Equipment & Supplies

Rank	Company Name—*Executive Officer*	Address, City, State, Zip	Phone	Type	Fin	Empls
1	Konica Minolta Photo Imaging USA Inc—*Tomohisa Saito*	725 Darlington Ave, Mahwah NJ 07430	201-574-4000	S	5,374*	.3
2	Arri Inc—*Volker Bahnemann*	617 Rte 303, Blauvelt NY 10913	845-353-1400	S	667*	.6
3	Pitman Co—*Stefan Vanhooran*	721 Union Blvd, Totowa NJ 07512		S	546*	.5
4	Nikon Inc—*Yasuyuki Okamoto*	1300 Walt Whitman Rd, Melville NY 11747	631-547-4200	S	355*	.6
5	Recognition Systems Inc—*John E McCusker*	30 Harbor Park Dr, Port Washington NY 11050	516-625-5000	R	193*	.1
6	Heartland Imaging Companies Inc—*Ty Roth*	1211 Cambridge Cir Dr, Kansas City KS 66103	913-621-1211	R	141*	.4
7	Anderson and Vreeland Inc—*Darin Lyon*	PO Box 527, Bryan OH 43506		R	130*	.1
8	Witt Co—*Bill Witt*	1150 Commerce St, Tacoma WA 98402		R	119*	.1
9	Comprehensive Video Group—*Scott Schaefer*	55 Ruta Ct, South Hackensack NJ 07606		R	52*	.1
10	Supercircuits Inc—*Brian Wood*	11000 N Mopac Expwy St, Austin TX 78759	512-260-0333	R	50*	.1
11	Bron Imaging Group	17 Progress St, Edison NJ 08820	908-754-5800	R	24*	<.1

Note: An asterisk (*) indicates an estimated financial figure. The company type code used is as follows: R = Private, P = Public, S = Private Subsidiary, B = Public Subsidiary, D = Division, J = Joint Venture, I = Investment Fund.

COMPANY RANKINGS BY SALES WITHIN 4-DIGIT SIC

Rank	Company Name—Executive Officer	Address, City, State, Zip	Phone	Type	Fin	Empls
12	Christie Digital Systems USA Inc—Kenji Hamashima	10550 Camden Dr, Cypress CA 90630	714-236-8610	R	24*	.2
13	Dot Line Corp—Stanley Offman	9414 Eton Ave, Chatsworth CA 91311	818-700-9997	R	23*	<.1
14	Sigma Corporation of America—Michihiro Yamaki	15 Fleetwood Ct, Ronkonkoma NY 11779	631-585-1144	S	22*	<.1
15	Boxlight Corp—Herb Myers	PO Box 2609, Belfair WA 98528	360-464-2119	R	20*	<.1
16	Hitachi Kokusai Electric America Ltd—Yuchi Otsuka	PO Box 512408, Philadelphia PA 19175	516-921-7200	R	20*	<.1
17	Comp-View Inc—Scott Birdsall	PO Box 518, Beaverton OR 97075	503-641-8439	R	19*	.1
18	Inserts East Inc—Gino Maiale	7045 Central Hwy, Pennsauken NJ 08109	856-663-8181	R	19*	.1
19	Eye Communication Systems Inc—John Bessent	PO Box 620, Hartland WI 53029	262-367-1360	R	17*	<.1
20	Murphy Co (Columbus Ohio)	455 W Broad St, Columbus OH 43215	614-221-7731	R	17*	<.1
21	Foto Fantasy Inc—Dale Valvo	8a Industrial Way, Salem MA 03079	603-324-3240	R	15*	.1
22	MAC Group—Jan Lederman	8 Westchester Plz, Elmsford NY 10523	914-347-3300	R	13	<.1
23	Savage Universal Corp—Richard Pressman	550 E Elliot Rd, Chandler AZ 85225		R	12*	.1
24	Noritsu America Corp—Akihiko Kuwabara	PO Box 5039, Buena Park CA 90622	714-521-9040	R	12*	.3
25	Image Labs International—Brian Smithgall	PO Box 1545, Belgrade MT 59714	406-585-7225	S	11*	<.1
26	Edgewise Media Services Inc—David Cohen	602 N Cypress St, Orange CA 92867	714-919-2020	R	10*	.1
27	UV Process Supply Inc—Stephen Siegel	1229 W Cortland St, Chicago IL 60614	773-248-0099	R	9*	<.1
28	Hakuba USA Inc—Richard Darrow	10621 Bloomfield St St, Los Alamitos CA 90720	973-428-9800	D	9	<.1
29	Rovinter Inc—Oscar Rovito	675 Nw 97th St, Miami FL 33150	305-757-5577	R	8*	<.1
30	Diversified Photo Supply Corp—Darrell Benton	333 W Alondra Blvd Ste, Gardena CA 90248	310-328-8577	R	6*	<.1
31	JOS Projection Systems Inc—Alice Schellin	180 S Prospect Ave, Tustin CA 92780	858-535-1111	R	6	<.1
32	Drops and Props Inc—Jay Gupta	3540 Seagate Way, Oceanside CA 92056	760-547-2900	R	5*	<.1
33	Cmsp Corp—Amauri Augusto	44 Plauderville Ave, Garfield NJ 07026	973-546-0055	R	4*	<.1
34	Camera Tester Service Inc—Mark Treadwell	250 N 54th St, Chandler AZ 85226	480-940-1103	R	4*	<.1
35	Audio Visual Aids Co—Robert Tumlinson	2903 N Flores St, San Antonio TX 78212	210-732-1234	R	4*	<.1
36	Internet Alliance Inc—Jeffrey Sheffer	3901 Commerce Park Dr, Raleigh NC 27610		R	3*	<.1
37	Technotape USA Inc—Daniel Thomas	959 Columbia St, Crete IL 60417	708-709-9000	R	3*	<.1
38	Buffalo Printers Supply Inc—Thomas Nelson	PO Box 36, Tonawanda NY 14151	716-693-7000	R	3*	<.1
39	Lawrence Photo and Video	2550 S Campbell St, Springfield MO 65807	417-883-8300	R	3*	<.1
40	Logistics Concepts Inc—Robert Lyons	5420 Summerwood Ln, Yorba Linda CA 92886	714-996-0268	R	3*	<.1
41	D/A Mid South Inc—Jim Bartley	9000 Jameel Rd, Houston TX 77040	713-895-0090	R	2*	<.1
42	21st Century Film Company LLC	9760 Sw 99th St, Miami FL 33176	305-573-7339	R	2*	<.1
43	Kinetronics Corp—Mike Murdock	1459 Tallevast Rd, Sarasota FL 34243	941-951-2432	R	1*	<.1
44	Central Audio Visual Equipment Inc—Michael Bashir	375 Roma Jean Pkwy, Streamwood IL 60107	630-372-8100	R	1*	<.1
45	Elden Enterprises—Ted Elden	PO Box 3201, Charleston WV 25332	304-344-2335	R	1*	<.1
46	Optigraph Systems Inc—Vasile Muresan	215 E 12 Mile Rd, Madison Heights MI 48071	248-398-2424	R	1*	<.1
47	Continental Photo—Sam Mitchelson	1670 61st St, Brooklyn NY 11204	718-232-3910	R	<1*	<.1

TOTALS: SIC 5043 Photographic Equipment & Supplies
Companies: 47

					7,983	4.3

5044 Office Equipment

Rank	Company Name—Executive Officer	Address, City, State, Zip	Phone	Type	Fin	Empls
1	Canon Business Solutions West—Bill Joseph	110 W Walnut St, Gardena CA 90248	310-217-3000	S	3,265*	.6
2	Lanier Worldwide Inc—Nori Goto	2300 Parklake Dr NE, Atlanta GA 30345	770-496-9500	S	1,223*	4.5
3	Savin Corp—Kevin Togashi	5 Dedrick Pl, West Caldwell NJ 07006	973-882-2000	S	1,058*	1.9
4	Brother International Corporation USA—Toshikazu Koike	100 Somerset Corporate, Bridgewater NJ 08807	908-704-1700	S	704*	1.2
5	Casio Inc—Toshio Kashio	570 Mt Pleasant Ave, Dover NJ 07801	973-361-5400	S	630*	.3
6	Imagistics International Inc—Joseph Skzypczak	100 Oakview Dr, Trumbull CT 06611	203-365-7000	S	609*	3.6
7	Quill Corp—Michael Patriarca	PO Box 94080, Palatine IL 60094	847-634-6559	D	378*	1.4
8	Electronic Systems of Richmond Inc—Dan Cooper	10406 Lakeridge Pky St, Ashland VA 23005	804-550-0660	S	301*	.5
9	Coast to Coast Business Equipment Inc—Paul M Faus	8 Vanderbilt, Irvine CA 92618	949-457-7300	R	254*	<.1
10	Toshiba America Business Solutions Inc—Mark Mathews	2 Musick, Irvine CA 92618	949-462-6000	S	191*	3.3
11	Ohio Calculating Inc—Carl Eichler	20160 Center Ridge Rd, Rocky River OH 44116	440-333-7310	R	142*	<.1
12	Carr Business Systems Inc—Mitchell Cohen	130 Spagnoli Rd, Melville NY 11747	631-249-9880	S	120*	.2
13	Offtech Inc—Stephen Albano	800 Research Dr Ste 1, Wilmington MA 01887	978-988-0700	R	94*	.4
14	Capitol Office Solutions Inc—Steve Rolla	9065 Guilford Rd, Columbia MD 21046	301-210-4360	S	94*	.2
15	Lewan and Associates Inc—Fred F Cannataro	1400 S Colorado Blvd, Denver CO 80222	303-759-5440	S	75*	.1
16	Carolina Office Systems—Clark King	730 Salisbury Rd, Statesville NC 28677	704-873-5281	S	62*	.1
17	Georgia Duplicating Products—Leon Strickland	5675 Oakbrook Pkwy Ste, Norcross GA 30093	770-248-1020	R	59*	.1
18	Stargel Office Solutions—Jack Stargel	4700 Blalock Rd, Houston TX 77041	713-461-5382	R	58*	.1
19	Lake Business Products Inc—Jack Slattery	37200 Research Dr, Eastlake OH 44095	440-953-1199	R	55*	.2
20	American Photocopy Equipment Company of Pittsburgh—Anthony Massari	PO Box 4, Imperial PA 15126	724-695-7391	S	51*	.1
21	AXSA Document Solutions Inc—Ed McLaughlin	4673 Oak Fair Blvd, Tampa FL 33610	813-740-2224	R	46*	.1
22	Metro - Sales Inc—Jerry Mathwig	1640 E 78th St, Minneapolis MN 55423	612-861-4000	R	45*	.3
23	WJS Enterprises Inc—Cy Hosch	PO Box 6620, Metairie LA 70009	504-837-5666	R	42*	.1
24	Econ-O-Copy Inc—Johnny Buiton	4437 Trenton St Ste A, Metairie LA 70006	504-457-0032	R	37*	<.1
25	Select Office Solutions—Frank Mendicina	6229 Santos Diaz St, Irwindale CA 91702	626-334-0383	R	32*	.2
26	Conway Office Products Inc—Paul Mosley	PO Box 6060, Nashua NH 03063	603-889-1665	S	32*	.1
27	Advance Business Systems—Alan I Elkin	PO Box 627, Cockeysville MD 21030	410-252-4800	R	31*	.2
28	PDME Inc—PD Morrison	1120 Toro Grande Blvd, Cedar Park TX 78613	512-335-7173	R	27*	<.1
29	Global Imaging Finance Co	PO Box 273478, Tampa FL 33688	813-960-5508	S	26*	.1
30	Eastern Copy Products Inc—William Gage Conway Office Products Inc	1224 W Genesee St, Syracuse NY 13204	315-474-7000	S	26*	<.1
31	Laser Life Inc—Murray Martin	1625 Williams Dr, Marietta GA 30066	770-425-5928	S	25*	<.1
32	Business Equipment Unlimited—Tom Kane Conway Office Products Inc	275 Read St, Portland ME 04103	207-878-8500	S	24*	<.1
33	Copiers Northwest Inc—Mark Petrie	601 Dexter Ave N, Seattle WA 98109	206-282-1200	R	22*	.1
34	Cash Register Sales Inc—David Sanders	4851 White Bear Pkwy, Saint Paul MN 55110	651-294-2700	R	22*	.1
35	International Merchant Services—Neil Johnson	1441 Airport Fwy Ste 1, Euless TX 76040	817-868-1810	R	21*	<.1
36	Copy Systems Inc—Mike Rebick	721 W 9th St, Little Rock AR 72201	501-376-2679	R	20*	.1
37	ATM Express Inc—Marty Ambuehl	PO Box 20439, Billings MT 59102		R	20*	<.1
38	Illinois Wholesale Cash Register Inc—Al Moorhouse	2790 Pinnacle Dr, Elgin IL 60124	847-310-4200	R	20*	.1
39	Marimon Business Systems Inc—Yolanda Marimon	7300 N Gessner Rd, Houston TX 77040	713-856-2000	R	19*	.1
40	NovaCopy Inc—Darren Metz	15 Lindsley Ave, Nashville TN 37210	615-577-7677	R	18*	.1
41	Standard Duplicating Machine Corp—L Guy Reny	10 Connector Rd, Andover MA 01810	978-470-1920	R	18	.1
42	Advantage Sign Supply Inc—Russ Herman	PO Box 888684, Grand Rapids MI 49588	616-554-3300	R	17*	.1
43	Posera USA Inc—James Gillis	11057 8th Ave Ne, Seattle WA 98125	206-364-8686	R	16*	.1
44	Ban-Koe Systems Inc—William Bangtson	9100 W Bloomington Fwy, Minneapolis MN 55431	952-888-6688	R	16*	.1
45	RICOH Business Systems Inc	10 Bloomfield Ave, Pine Brook NJ 07058	973-227-4264	S	16*	.1
46	Business Imaging Systems Inc—Dan Rotelli	13900 N Harvey Ave, Edmond OK 73013	405-507-7000	R	16*	.1
47	Northern Stationers Inc—Denise Bouschor	502 W Washington St St, Marquette MI 49855	906-228-7702	R	15*	.1

Rank	Company Name—*Executive Officer*	Address, City, State, Zip	Phone	Type	Fin	Empls
48	Royal Consumer Information Products Inc—*Solomon Suwalsky*	379 Campus Dr 2nd Fl, Somerset NJ 08873	732-627-9977	S	15*	.1
49	USI Inc (Madison Connecticut)	PO Box 92, Brattleboro VT 05302		R	14*	.1
50	Northeast Copier Systems Inc—*John Uttero*	23 Birch St, Milford MA 01757	508-478-3530	S	14*	<.1
51	Subon Data Co—*Carol Bonnet*	PO Box 1234, Maple Glen PA 19002	215-628-8720	R	14*	<.1
52	Burtronics Business Systems Inc—*Tom Thompson*	PO Box 1170, San Bernardino CA 92402	909-885-7576	R	14*	.1
53	Southwest Office Systems Inc—*Victor Puente*	PO Box 612248, Dallas TX 75261	817-730-8000	R	14*	.1
54	Duplicating Products Inc—*Matt Nix*	PO Box 1548, Gainesville GA 30503	770-532-9932	R	14*	<.1
55	Image Iv Systems Inc—*Ronald Warren*	512 S Varney St, Burbank CA 91502	818-841-0756	R	13*	.1
56	Business World Inc (Little Rock Arkansas)—*Jerry Carlisle*	PO Box 34165, Little Rock AR 72203	501-374-7000	R	13*	.1
57	David Martin Inc—*David Martin*	4113 Service Rd, Jonesboro AR 72401	870-972-0180	R	13*	<.1
58	Manhattan Information Systems Inc—*Anthony Candido*	228 E 45th St Fl 6, New York NY 10017	212-557-0123	R	13*	.1
59	Imaging Alliance Group LLC—*Corey Tansom*	2601 Minnehaha Ave, Minneapolis MN 55406	612-588-9944	R	13*	.1
60	Cash Register Services Inc—*Curtis Fuller*	5808 4th St, Lubbock TX 79416	806-792-2885	R	12*	.1
61	Electronic Office Systems—*Andrew W Ritshel*	330 Fairfield Rd, Fairfield NJ 07004	973-808-0100	R	12*	<.1
62	Liberty Business Systems Inc—*Ron Fuhrman*	PO Box 9887, Fargo ND 58106	701-241-8504	R	12*	<.1
63	F M Office Express Inc—*Fabricio Morales*	1 Woodbury Blvd, Rochester NY 14604	585-238-2880	R	12*	.1
64	Postec Inc—*David Shaw*	1125 Northmeadow Pkwy, Roswell GA 30076	678-424-4011	R	11*	.1
65	Document Solutions Inc—*Kenneth Holes*	500 Garden City Plz, Monroeville PA 15146	412-373-6500	R	11*	<.1
66	Dumac Business Systems Inc—*David Carthy*	19 Corporate Cir Ste 1, East Syracuse NY 13057	315-463-1010	R	11*	.1
67	Imaging Supplies Depot Inc—*Eyal Alcoby*	PO Box 2736, Riverside CA 92516	714-978-7291	R	10*	.1
68	Buyonlinenowcom—*Robert Herman*	4865 19th St NW Ste 11, Rochester MN 55901		R	10*	<.1
69	Oklahoma Office Systems Inc—*L Wortham*	PO Box 270538, Oklahoma City OK 73137	405-942-6674	R	10*	.1
70	Elite Technology NY Inc—*Han Lu*	1001 6th Ave 24th FL, New York NY 10018	212-967-5009	R	9*	<.1
71	James Imaging Systems Inc—*Lola Tegeder*	PO Box 330, Brookfield WI 53008	262-781-7700	R	9*	<.1
72	Automated Business Resources Inc—*Lynn Hortman*	15 Chatham Ctr S, Savannah GA 31405	912-527-7777	R	9*	<.1
73	Copyfax Inc—*Larry Foor*	6631 Executive Park Ct, Jacksonville FL 32216	904-296-1600	R	8*	.1
74	Word Systems Inc—*Richard J Baretto*	9225 Harrison Park Ct, Indianapolis IN 46216	317-544-0499	R	8*	<.1
75	Connex Systems Inc—*Greg Walter*	2033 Chenault Dr Ste 1, Carrollton TX 75006	972-387-8885	R	8*	<.1
76	Midwest Copier Exchange LLC—*Chris Lento*	3300 Washington St, Waukegan IL 60085	847-599-9001	R	8*	<.1
77	Fisher's Document Systems Inc—*Christopher Taylor*	575 E 42nd St, Garden City ID 83714	208-375-4410	R	8*	<.1
78	Bruce Office Supply Inc—*Scott Bruce*	2625 2nd Ave N, Birmingham AL 35203	205-328-4081	R	8*	<.1
79	Lorain County Stationery and Office Equipment Company Inc—*William Shepard*	1953 Coper Foster Pk R, Amherst OH 44001	440-960-7070	R	7*	<.1
80	Latoff Wainer and Co—*Thomas Latoff*	1 Barleycone Ln, Bryn Mawr PA 19010	610-525-6440	R	7*	.1
81	Cr Acquisition Corp—*Cuyler Tremayne*	5732 Buckingham Pkwy, Culver City CA 90230	310-417-3544	R	7*	<.1
82	Ami Imaging Systems Inc—*Susan Olson*	7815 Telegraph Rd, Bloomington MN 55438	952-828-0080	R	7*	<.1
83	Illinois Blueprint Corp—*Lyn Smith*	800 SW Jefferson Ave, Peoria IL 61605	309-676-1300	R	7*	<.1
84	Transition Products Inc—*Jeff Trotier*	777 Goodale Blvd Ste 2, Columbus OH 43212	614-227-7000	R	7*	<.1
85	Wilmac Business Equipment Company Inc—*William Donnell*	PO Box 14387, Rochester NY 14614	585-454-1160	R	7*	.1
86	Copy Vend Inc—*Keith Webb*	6666 E Stapleton Dr S, Denver CO 80216	303-393-0027	R	7*	<.1
87	Heritage Business Systems Inc—*Thomas Lizzio*	PO Box 684, Pennsauken NJ 08110	856-722-7001	R	7*	<.1
88	Center For Business Innovation Inc—*Gary Rainsberger*	801 S Waverly Rd Ste 2, Lansing MI 48917	517-484-3939	R	7*	<.1
89	Davis Typewriter Company Inc—*Larry Davis*	PO Box 416, Worthington MN 56187	507-343-2001	R	7*	<.1
90	RTR Business Products Inc—*Richard Mccormick*	PO Box 67, Murrysville PA 15668	724-733-7373	R	6*	<.1
91	Osam Document Solutions Inc—*Ronald Thompson*	3520 N 16th St, Phoenix AZ 85016	602-263-9432	R	6*	<.1
92	Damasco Inc—*Mark Grimes*	8727 Irvington Rd, Omaha NE 68122	402-571-5577	R	6*	<.1
93	USA Datafax Inc—*Elizabeth Ezelle*	821 Jupiter Rd Sto 407, Plano TX 75074	469-467-7900	R	6*	<.1
94	Merchants Solutions—*Gary Hornstra*	4422 Roosevelt Rd, Hillside IL 60162	708-449-6650	R	6*	<.1
95	JJ Bender LLC—*Jeffrey J Bender*	457 Castle Ave, Fairfield CT 06825	203-336-4034	R	6*	<.1
96	Ultra Imaging Soltuions—*Bob Christie*	4018 W Chandler, Santa Ana CA 92704	949-553-9030	R	6*	<.1
97	Best Image Systems Inc—*Pete Rivera*	PO Box 702985, Dallas TX 75370	972-386-1860	R	6*	<.1
98	Premier Business Products Inc—*Craig Zimmerman*	1744 Maplelawn Dr, Troy MI 48084	248-822-3535	R	6*	<.1
99	Professional Business Systems Inc—*Matthew Mawby*	PO Box 2730, Bentonville AR 72712	479-636-0001	R	6*	<.1
100	Fuchs Business Solutions Inc—*James Fuchs*	12200 W Adler Ln, Milwaukee WI 53214	414-778-0210	R	6*	<.1
101	Sel-Mor Distributing Co—*A Lieberman*	6520 W Lake St, Minneapolis MN 55426	952-929-0888	R	5*	<.1
102	Xerographic Solutions Inc—*Mark Perlo*	1387 Frport Rd Ste 100, Fairport NY 14450	585-388-5550	R	5*	<.1
103	Cvk Group Inc—*Christopher Horne*	1400 L St Nw Ste C0101, Washington DC 20005	202-546-5468	R	5*	<.1
104	e/Doc Systems—*Tom Pease*	7891 Stage Hills Blvd, Memphis TN 38133	901-367-9500	R	5*	<.1
105	MICROS-Fidelio Southeast Inc—*Gary Kaufman*	7031 Columbia Gateway, Columbia MD 21046	443-285-6000	S	5*	<.1
106	Multi-Media Solutions Inc—*Mike White*	PO Box 113, Alcoa TN 37701	865-681-2575	R	5*	<.1
107	Whitaker Brothers Business Machines Inc—*Joseph Mitchell*	3 Taft Ct, Rockville MD 20850	301-354-3000	R	5*	<.1
108	Office Connection Inc—*Ezekiel Guerra*	3747 Robertson Blvd, Culver City CA 90232	310-838-5818	R	5*	<.1
109	Copy Free Technology Inc—*Shi Wei*	601 S San Gabriel Blvd, San Gabriel CA 91776	626-285-0911	R	5*	<.1
110	Copy Images Inc—*Joel Lund*	10200 Valley View Rd S, Eden Prairie MN 55344	952-833-3623	R	5*	<.1
111	Copy and Camera Inc—*Mark Landgrave*	PO Box 2067, Lafayette LA 70502	337-232-7120	R	4*	<.1
112	Precision Marketing—*Mike Dickson*	1430 Village Way Ste K, Santa Ana CA 92705	323-721-3677	R	4*	.1
113	Copy Link Inc—*Kevin Marshall*	3441 Main St, Chula Vista CA 91911	619-424-8000	R	4*	<.1
114	DocuSource LLC—*Les Walker*	10450 Pioneer Blvd Ste, Santa Fe Springs CA 90670	562-447-2600	R	4*	<.1
115	North Shore Office Machine Company Inc—*Nicholis Kirtz*	9114 58th Pl Ste 100, Kenosha WI 53144	262-657-3355	R	4*	<.1
116	ITE Distributing—*Doug Nelson*	PO Box 7017, Villa Park IL 60181	312-733-1200	R	4*	<.1
117	Imagex Inc—*Nancy Gretzinger*	1985 Isaac Newton Sq, Reston VA 20190	703-883-2500	R	4*	<.1
118	Advanced Video Inc—*Ed Beamen*	PO Box 24409, Columbia SC 29224	803-714-6536	R	4*	<.1
119	Blue Ribbon Business Products Co—*Scott Kessler*	930 SE Sherman St, Portland OR 97214	503-233-7288	R	4*	<.1
120	Filing Source Inc—*Candice Bobeck*	7529 Salisbury Rd, Jacksonville FL 32256	904-398-3600	R	4*	<.1
121	Sioux City Stationery Company Inc—*Charles Wolfe*	PO Box 9000, Sioux City IA 51102	712-277-7000	R	4*	<.1
122	Borden Office Equipment Co—*Jerry Simpson*	PO Box 249, Steubenville OH 43952	740-283-3321	R	4*	<.1
123	Skyway Technology Group Inc—*Byron Norrie*	5014 Tampa W Blvd, Tampa FL 33634	813-249-0101	R	4*	<.1
124	South Arkansas Business Solutions Inc—*Bruce Mitchell*	PO Box 1066, Pine Bluff AR 71613	870-879-6400	R	4*	<.1
125	Copiersnow Inc—*Paul Archer*	5275 E Mineral Cir, Centennial CO 80122	303-221-0733	R	4*	<.1
126	Konica Copiers—*Brian Goetz*	717 Perry St, Sioux City IA 51103	712-255-8892	R	4*	<.1
127	Robinett Business Systems Inc—*Mark Robinett*	PO Box 2501, Springfield MO 65801	417-886-0400	R	4*	<.1
128	Document Solutions Of Dayton—*Anthony Hill*	3033 Kettering Blvd St, Moraine OH 45439	937-461-0246	R	3*	<.1
129	Mountainland Business Systems Inc—*Scott Diamond*	180 W 2950 S, Salt Lake City UT 84115	801-487-8508	R	3*	<.1
130	Cook County Photocopy Co—*John King*	1600 Jarvis Ave, Elk Grove Village IL 60007	847-690-1920	R	3*	<.1
131	Atlanta Computer Group Inc—*H Alderman*	PO Box 550, Alpharetta GA 30009	770-442-9800	R	3*	<.1
132	Toner Sales Inc—*Natalie Weiss*	8858 W Schlinger Ave, Milwaukee WI 53214	414-475-0522	R	3*	<.1
133	D and R Products Inc—*Robert Mantle*	1409 Duff Dr, Fort Collins CO 80524	970-493-6223	R	3*	<.1
134	Copier Fax Business Technologies Inc	465 Ellicott St, Buffalo NY 14203	716-853-5000	R	3*	<.1
135	Coastal Business Supplies Inc—*J Pickering*	2444 Northline Industr, Maryland Heights MO 63043	314-447-2100	R	3*	<.1
136	IDEAL Scanners and Systems Inc—*Jay Magenheim*	11810 Parklawn Dr, Rockville MD 20852	301-468-0123	R	3*	<.1

Note: An asterisk (*) indicates an estimated financial figure. The company type code used is as follows: R = Private, P = Public, S = Private Subsidiary, B = Public Subsidiary, D = Division, J = Joint Venture, I = Investment Fund.

COMPANY RANKINGS BY SALES WITHIN 4-DIGIT SIC

Rank	Company Name—Executive Officer	Address, City, State, Zip	Phone	Type	Fin	Empls
137	Hane Security Safe Inc—Kay Gopp	1753 Addison Way, Hayward CA 94544	510-732-8710	R	3*	<.1
138	Point of Sale System Services Inc—Jeff Swann	2 Shaker Rd Ste F100, Shirley MA 01464	978-425-3003	R	3*	<.1
139	Brooks Duplicator Co—Allan Brooks	10402 Rockley Rd, Houston TX 77099	281-568-9787	R	3*	<.1
140	Shipman-Ward Inc—Dominic Vespia	320 W Commercial Ave S, Moonachie NJ 07074	201-933-4900	R	3*	<.1
141	Business Equipment Center Inc—Paul Rayburn	PO Box 224, Spokane WA 99210	509-624-0116	R	3*	<.1
142	Logan Business Machines Inc—Hal Logan	417b Ne Us Hwy 24, Topeka KS 66608	785-233-1102	R	3*	<.1
143	Universal Toner Plus—David Klein	540 President St, Brooklyn NY 11215		R	3*	<.1
144	Laser Solutions International LLC—Mark Abrahams	PO Box 230932, Encinitas CA 92023	760-597-5900	R	3*	<.1
145	Alternative Business Suppliers Inc—Daniel Cullen	7101 S Adams St Ste 4, Willowbrook IL 60527	630-789-0333	R	3*	<.1
146	Imagetek Partners LLC—Beverly Oakes	320 Westway Pl Ste 500, Arlington TX 76018	817-465-2450	R	3*	<.1
147	Coyle Business Products Inc—Gregory Coyle	5507 Export Blvd, Savannah GA 31408	912-964-9154	R	2*	<.1
148	Vericomm—Doug Gamacino	PO Box 61687, Honolulu HI 96839	808-285-7873	R	2*	<.1
149	International Safe Manufacturing Inc—Eric Mueller	510 Washington Blvd, Montebello CA 90640	323-724-5885	R	2*	<.1
150	Benchmark Business Solutions—Rick Thollman	720 S Tyler St Ste 112, Amarillo TX 79101	806-376-7576	R	2*	<.1
151	Kinney Office Systems—Crawford Kinney	83 Farm Rd, Bangor ME 04401	207-947-3321	R	2*	<.1
152	MaxMpact—Max Daniel	PO Box 7148, Charlotte NC 28241	704-588-8882	R	2*	<.1
153	Hermann Associates Inc—James Nuss	1405 Indiana St, San Francisco CA 94107	415-285-8486	R	2*	<.1
154	Advanced Office Automation Inc—Paul Evans	7915 L St Ste 100, Omaha NE 68127	402-339-2991	R	2*	<.1
155	Key Print Shop Inc—Paul Kornechuk	PO Box 966, Dodge City KS 67801	620-227-2101	R	2*	<.1
156	Desktop Solutions Inc—Art Ordonez	2366 N Glassell St Ste, Orange CA 92865	714-637-8200	R	1*	<.1
157	Eastern Business Systems Inc—Edward Williams	125 Wilbur Pl Ste 210, Bohemia NY 11716	631-567-8111	R	1*	<.1
158	Smarketing Business Systems Inc—Le Jones	2525 W Bellfort St Ste, Houston TX 77054	713-529-5898	R	1*	<.1
159	Kilpatrick Equipment Co—Steve Kilpatrick	PO Box 35786, Dallas TX 75235	214-358-4346	R	1*	<.1
160	Mark Feldstein and Associates Inc—Mark Feldstein	6500 Weatherfield Ct, Maumee OH 43537	419-867-9500	R	1*	<.1
161	Audio Equipment Co—Foy Rose	PO Box 14937, Oklahoma City OK 73113	405-842-9659	R	1*	<.1
162	Automated Data Systems Inc—Gene Miller	PO Box 1076, Hickory NC 28603	828-328-9365	R	1*	<.1

TOTALS: SIC 5044 Office Equipment
Companies: 162   10,779   24.8

5045 Computers, Peripherals & Software

Rank	Company Name—Executive Officer	Address, City, State, Zip	Phone	Type	Fin	Empls
1	Ingram Micro Inc—Dale Laurance	PO Box 25125, Santa Ana CA 92799	714-566-1000	P	34,589	15.7
2	Tech Data Corp—Robert M Dutkowsky	5350 Tech Data Dr, Clearwater FL 33760	727-539-7429	P	24,376	8.7
3	Arrow Electronics Incorporated Commercial Systems Group—Michael Long	50 Marcus Dr, Melville NY 11747	631-847-2000	R	13,752*	11.3
4	IKON Office Solutions Inc	70 Valley Stream Pky, Malvern PA 19355	610-296-8000	S	4,168*	25.0
5	Whitlock Group—Doug Hall	12820 W Creek Pwy, Richmond VA 23238	804-273-9100	R	4,145*	.1
6	World Wide Technology Inc—James P Kavanaugh	PO Box 957653, Saint Louis MO 63195	314-569-7000	S	3,400*	1.7
7	Expert Server Group—Doug Weisberg	318 S River Rd, Bedford NH 03110	603-668-9800	R	2,899*	.1
8	Infogate Online Ltd—Yoram Friedman	900 Corporate Dr, Mahwah NJ 07430	201-828-9040	R	2,843*	3.0
9	ScanSource Inc—Michael L Baur	6 Logue Ct, Greenville SC 29615	864-288-2432	P	2,667	1.4
10	Axiom Technology Inc (Chino California)—Yu Te Yang	18138 Rowland St, City of Industry CA 91748	626-581-3232	R	2,501*	.1
11	Ingram Book Group Inc—David Prichard	1 Ingram Blvd, La Vergne TN 37086	615-793-5000	S	2,389*	2.5
12	CompuCom Systems Inc—James W Dixon	7171 Forest Ln, Dallas TX 75230	972-856-3600	S	2,367*	12.4
13	American Systems Corp—William C Hoover	14151 Park Meadows Dr, Chantilly VA 20151	703-968-6300	R	1,906*	1.5
14	Bell and Howell LLC—Leslie F Stern	3791 S Alston Ave, Durham NC 27713	919-767-4401	R	1,794*	1.3
15	Atrenta Inc—Ajoy Bose	2077 Gateway Pl Ste 30, San Jose CA 95110	408-453-3333	R	1,533*	.1
16	ASI Corp—Dennis Adams	48289 Fremont Blvd, Fremont CA 94538	510-226-8000	R	1,300*	.9
17	ASI Computer Technologies Inc	48289 Fremont Boulevar, Fremont CA 94538	510-226-8000	R	1,200	.8
18	Bull Hn Information Systems Inc—David Bradbury	285 Billerica Rd Ste 2, Chelmsford MA 01824	978-294-6000	R	1,094*	.5
19	Intcomex Inc—Anthony Shalom	3505 NW 107th Ave, Miami FL 33178	305-477-6230	R	1,072	1.5
20	Prosys Information Systems Inc—Michelle Clery	PO Box 536761, Atlanta GA 30353	678-268-1300	R	1,041*	.4
21	Publitek Inc—Rick Wintersberger	21155 Watertown Rd, Waukesha WI 53186	262-717-0600	R	1,035*	<.1
22	Autotote Lottery Corp—A Lorne Weil	750 Lexington Ave 25th, New York NY 10022	212-754-2233	S	926*	1.0
23	ePlus Inc—Phillip G Norton	13595 Dulles Technolog, Herndon VA 20171	703-984-8400	P	863	.7
24	Harvey Whitney Books Co—Harvey Whitney	PO Box 42696, Cincinnati OH 45242	513-793-3555	R	828*	<.1
25	Media Supply Inc—Jonathan Bradlee	611 Jeffers Cir, Exton PA 19341		R	822*	<.1
26	Connecting Point Computer Centers—Jeff Thomas	545 Stevens St, Medford OR 97504	541-773-9861	R	821*	<.1
27	First Advantage Corp—Anand Nallathambi	12395 1st American Way, Poway CA 92064	619-938-7500	S	780	4.0
28	Sejin America Inc—Sang-Young Lee	2144 Zanker Rd, San Jose CA 95131	408-487-9000	S	779*	.6
29	En Pointe Technologies Sales Inc / En Pointe Technologies Inc	18701 S Figueroa St, Gardena CA 90248	310-337-5200	S	722*	.5
30	En Pointe Technologies Ventures Inc / En Pointe Technologies Inc	18701 S Figueroa St, Gardena CA 90248	310-337-5200	S	722*	.5
31	Southern Electronics Distributors Inc—Jonathan Elster / SED International Holdings Inc	4916 N Royal Atlanta D, Tucker GA 30084	770-491-8962	S	701*	.3
32	Government Technology Services Inc—Sterling E Phillips	2553 Dulles View Dr St, Herndon VA 20171	703-502-2000	P	667	.4
33	Network Hardware Resale LLC—Mike Sheldon	26 Castilian Dr Ste A, Santa Barbara CA 93117	805-964-9975	R	664*	.2
34	SED International Holdings Inc—Jonathan Elster	4916 N Royal Atlanta D, Tucker GA 30084	770-491-8962	P	607	.4
35	Log-Net Inc—John Motley	230 Half Mile Rd 3rd F, Red Bank NJ 07701	732-758-6800	R	575*	<.1
36	Pomeroy IT Solutions Inc—Christopher C Froman	1020 Petersburg Rd, Hebron KY 41048	859-586-0600	R	566*	2.0
37	Virtutech—John Lambert	2001 Gateway Pl Ste 20, San Jose CA 95110	408-392-9150	R	522*	.6
38	Navarre Corp—Richard S Willis	7400 49th Ave N, Minneapolis MN 55428	763-535-8333	P	491	.4
39	Dataflex Corp—Richard C Rose	3920 Park Ave, Edison NJ 08820	908-791-2200	R	472	.8
40	Wacom Technology Corp—Masahiko Yamada	1311 SE Cardinal Ct, Vancouver WA 98683	360-896-9833	S	464*	.4
41	Reflexis Systems Inc—Prashanth Palakurthi	3 Allied Dr, Dedham MA 02026	781-493-3400	R	450*	.4
42	Massive Inc—JJ Richards	627 Broadway 7th Fl, New York NY 10012	212-778-3500	S	447*	<.1
43	International Purchase Systems Inc—Micheal Brooks	534 Furnas Dock Rd, Cortlandt Manor NY 10567	914-788-5400	R	411*	<.1
44	Pactolus Communications Software Corp—Paul Blondin	200 Nickerson Rd Ste 4, Marlborough MA 01752	508-616-0900	S	399*	.3
45	Digital River Inc—Joel A Ronning	10380 Bren Rd W, Minnetonka MN 55343	952-253-1234	P	398	1.4
46	Atempo Inc—Neal Ater	2465 E Bayshore Rd Ste, Palo Alto CA 94303	650-494-2600	S	379*	.3
47	Eagle Investment Systems Corp—John Lehner	65 LaSalle Rd Ste 305, West Hartford CT 06107	860-561-4602	S	370*	.3
48	Verari Systems Inc—David B Wright	9449 Carroll Park Dr, San Diego CA 92121	858-874-3800	R	360*	.3
49	Axis Communications Inc	100 Apollo Dr, Chelmsford MA 01824	978-614-2000	S	359*	.3
50	En Pointe Technologies Inc—Bob Din	18701 S Figueroa St, Gardena CA 90248	310-337-5955	R	352*	1.2
51	Diskovery Educational Systems Corp—Dan Wechsler	1860 Old Okeechobee Rd, West Palm Beach FL 33409	561-683-8410	R	332*	<.1
52	INX Inc—Mark T Hilz	11757 Katy Fwy Ste 500, Houston TX 77079	713-795-2000	P	312	.5
53	Freehand Systems Inc—Kim Lorz	95 1st St Ste 200, Los Altos CA 94022	650-941-0742	R	304*	.3
54	Aetea Information Technology Inc—Jeffery Sardis	1445 Research Blvd Ste, Rockville MD 20850	301-721-4200	R	284*	.3
55	PCS Wireless Inc—Mitch Black	11 Vreeland Rd, Florham Park NJ 07932	973-805-7400	R	274*	.2

Rank	Company Name—*Executive Officer*	Address, City, State, Zip	Phone	Type	Fin	Empls
56	Ohc Group Inc—*Mark Metz*	6625 The Corners Pkwy, Norcross GA 30092	770-447-1951	R	265*	.1
57	Loglogic Inc—*Guy Churchward*	110 Rose Orchard Way S, San Jose CA 95134	408-215-5900	R	263*	.2
58	Atlantix Global Systems—*Neil Hobbs*	1 Sun Ct, Norcross GA 30092		S	257*	.2
59	Vantage Learning—*Peter Murphy*	110 Terry Dr Ste 100, Newtown PA 18940	215-579-8390	R	254*	.2
60	Control4—*Will West*	11734 S Election Rd, Draper UT 84020	801-523-3100	R	253*	.2
61	Fujitsu Computer Products of America Inc—*Etsuro Sato*	1250 E Arques Ave, Sunnyvale CA 94085	408-746-6000	S	251*	.2
62	Wayside Technology Group Inc—*Simon F Nynens*	1157 Shrewsbury Ave, Shrewsbury NJ 07702	732-389-0932	P	250	.1
63	Approva Corp—*John Becker*	1950 Roland Clarke Pl, Reston VA 20191	703-956-8300	R	248*	.2
64	Vocalocity Inc—*Boris Jerkunica*	1375 Peachtree St NE R, Atlanta GA 30309	678-528-9000	R	245*	.2
65	Openspirit Corp—*Mark Godfrey*	4800 Sugar Grove Blvd, Stafford TX 77477	281-295-1400	R	238*	.3
66	Horizon Software International LLC—*Randy Eckels*	2915 Premier Park Way, Duluth GA 30097	770-554-6353	R	230*	.2
67	Escalate Inc—*Stewart Bloom*	9890 Towne Centre Dr S, San Diego CA 92121	650-769-3000	S	223*	.2
68	Lansa USA Inc—*Steve Gapp*	3010 Highland Pky Ste, Downers Grove IL 60515	630-874-7000	R	220*	.2
69	Archos Technology—*Henri Crohas*	7951 E Maplewood Ave S, Greenwood Village CO 80111	303-962-3350	R	220*	.2
70	Imprivata Inc—*Omar Hussain*	10 Maguire Rd, Lexington MA 02421	781-674-2700	R	217*	.2
71	Raritan Computer Inc—*Ching-I Hsu*	400 Cottontail Ln, Somerset NJ 08873	732-764-8886	R	212*	.1
72	PRODUCT4 Inc—*Daniel Moskowitz*	12400 Olive Blvd Ste 1, Saint Louis MO 63141	314-434-1999	S	206*	<.1
73	Innopath Software—*John Fazio*	1195 W Fremont Ave, Sunnyvale CA 94087	408-962-9200	R	201*	.2
74	Airespace Inc—*Brett Galloway*	110 Nortech Pkwy, San Jose CA 95134	408-526-4000	S	200*	.2
75	Zomax International Inc—*Anthony Angelini*	5353 Nathan Ln, Plymouth MN 55442	763-553-9320	R	199*	1.3
76	Dell and ASAP Software	PO Box 95414, Chicago IL 60694	847-465-3700	S	196*	.4
77	Fios Inc—*John Hesse*	921 SW Washington St S, Portland OR 97205	503-265-0700	R	191*	.2
78	Netezza Corp—*David Flaxman*	26 Forest St, Marlborough MA 01752	508-382-8200	B	191	.4
79	Benchmarc360 Inc—*Ann Godi*	3220 Pointe Pkwy Ste 5, Norcross GA 30092	678-291-0011	R	190*	.2
80	Smart DB Corp—*Sam Elias*	3340 Peachtree Rd NE S, Atlanta GA 30326	404-760-1560	S	190*	.2
81	ExaGrid Systems Inc—*Bill Andrews*	2000 W Park Dr Ste 110, Westborough MA 01581	508-898-2872	R	189*	.2
82	MontaVista Software Inc—*Vincent Rerole*	2929 Patrick Henry Dr, Santa Clara CA 95054	408-572-8000	R	188*	.2
83	NWP Services Corp—*Micheal Radice*	PO Box 19661, Irvine CA 92614	949-253-2500	R	188*	.2
84	Classic Components Corp—*Jeff Klein*	23605 Telo Ave, Torrance CA 90505	310-539-5500	R	187*	.3
85	Troux Technologies—*David Hood*	8601 FM 2222 Bldg 3 St, Austin TX 78730	512-536-6270	R	187*	.1
86	Digium Inc—*Danny J Windham*	445 Jan Davis Dr NW, Huntsville AL 35806	256-428-6000	R	184*	.2
87	Ruckus Wireless Inc—*Selina Lo*	880 W Maude Ave Ste101, Sunnyvale CA 94085	650-265-4200	R	177*	.1
88	Column Technologies Inc—*Timothy Yario*	1400 Opus PlSte 110, Downers Grove IL 60515	630-515-6660	R	176*	.1
89	Phihong USA Corp—*Fei Lin*	47800 Fremont Blvd, Fremont CA 94538	510-445-0100	R	170*	.1
90	Almo Corp—*Gene Chaiken*	2709 Commerce Way, Philadelphia PA 19154	215-698-4000	R	169*	.3
91	Arbitech LLC—*Torin Pavia*	15330 Barranca Pkwy, Irvine CA 92618	949-376-6650	R	166*	.1
92	STM Networks Inc—*Emil Youssefzadeh*	2 Faraday, Irvine CA 92618	949-273-6800	R	165*	.1
93	Formosa USA Inc—*David Toung*	21540 Prairie St Unit, Chatsworth CA 91311	818-407-4965	S	164*	.2
94	XOS Digital—*Randy Eccker*	101 Billerica Ave Bld, North Billerica MA 01862	978-294-0200	R	163*	.1
95	Optimi Corp—*Juan Melero*	75 14th St NE Ste 2200, Atlanta GA 30309	404-249-9559	R	162*	.2
96	Saleslogic LLC—*Bob Howard*	15455 N Dallas Pkwy St, Dallas TX 75248	214-498-9649	R	161*	.2
97	CRF Inc—*Rachel King*	4000 Chemical Rd Ste 4, Plymouth Meeting PA 19462	267-498-2300	R	159*	.1
98	Arbor Networks Inc—*Colin Doherty*	6 Omni Way, Chelmsford MA 01824	978-703-6600	S	158*	.1
99	AQS Inc—*David Kerford*	1325 Walnut Ridge Dr, Hartland WI 53029	262-369-7500	R	151*	.2
100	Micro Star Software Inc—*Stephen Benedict*	2245 Camino Vida Roble, Carlsbad CA 92011		R	151*	.1
101	Teliris Ltd—*Neil Hobbs*	55 Broadway 14th FL, New York NY 10006	212-490-1065	R	150*	.2
102	Westcon—*Dean Douglas*	520 White Plains Rd, Tarrytown NY 10591	914-829-7170	D	148*	.3
103	Star Computer Group Inc—*Henry Waissmann*	2175 Nw 115th Ave, Miami FL 33172	305-471-6101	R	148*	.1
104	Mtc Direct Inc—*Roy Ilan*	17837 Rowland St, City Of Industry CA 91748	626-839-6800	R	143*	.1
105	Fox Technologies Inc—*Subhash Tantry*	883 N Shoreline Blvd B, Mountain View CA 94043	650-687-6300	R	138*	.1
106	ASI Computer Systems Inc—*David Wirth*	PO Box 338, Cedar Falls IA 50613	319-266-7688	R	137*	.1
107	Airdefense Inc	1125 Sanctuary Rd, Alpharetta GA 30009		S	128*	.1
108	CCS Presentation Systems Inc—*David Riberi*	3331 Jack Northrop Ave, Hawthorne CA 90250	424-675-2600	R	128*	.1
109	Kurzweil Educational Systems Inc—*Michael Sokol*	100 Crosby Dr, Bedford MA 01730	781-276-0600	S	127*	.1
110	Park Place International—*Ed Kenty*	7227 Chagrin Rd, Chagrin Falls OH 44023		R	127*	.1
111	ObjectVideo—*Raul Fernandez*	11600 Sunrise Valley D, Reston VA 20191	703-654-9300	R	126*	.1
112	Colubris Networks Inc	304290 Hanover St, Palo Alto CA 94304	650-857-1501	S	125*	.1
113	MedSeek Inc—*Peter Kuhn*	3000 Riverchase Galler, Birmingham AL 35244	805-694-3100	R	125*	.1
114	Isilon Systems Inc—*Sujal Patel*	3101 Western Ave, Seattle WA 98121	206-315-7500	D	124	.4
115	3e Technologies International Inc—*Benga Erinle*	9715 Key West Ave Ste, Rockville MD 20850	301-670-6779	S	123*	.1
116	DriveCam Inc—*Brandon Nixon*	8911 Balboa Ave, San Diego CA 92123	858-430-4000	R	123*	.1
117	Prime Systems—*Vicky Chang*	10402 Harwin Dr, Houston TX 77036	713-933-0934	R	120*	.1
118	New Age Electronics Inc—*Adam Carroll*	21950 Arnold Center Rd, Carson CA 90810	310-549-0000	S	119*	.1
119	Advantech Corp—*Ke-Cheng Liu*	380 Fairview Way, Milpitas CA 95035	408-519-3800	R	117*	.2
120	Revonet Inc—*Scott Howard*	125 Elm St, New Canaan CT 06840	203-972-9488	R	115*	.1
121	Champion Computer Corp—*Chris Pyle*	791 Park of Commerce B, Boca Raton FL 33487	561-997-2900	R	113*	.1
122	Norris Systems LLC—*Gerald Brunton*	2659 Nova Dr, Dallas TX 75229	972-385-2600	R	111*	<.1
123	Tadiran Telecom Inc—*Zeev Aviv*	265 Executive Dr Ste 2, Plainview NY 11803		S	106*	.1
124	SafeHarbor Technology Corp—*Annette Jacobs*	150 Technology Way Bld, Elma WA 98541	360-482-1500	R	104*	.1
125	mBlox Ltd—*Steve Love*	430 N Mary Ave Ste 100, Sunnyvale CA 94085	408-617-3700	R	103*	.1
126	Cyberpower Inc—*Stanley Ho*	5175 Commerce Dr, Baldwin Park CA 91706	626-813-7730	R	101*	.1
127	Nexiant—*Michael J Hammons*	2 S Pointe Dr Ste 220, Lake Forest CA 92630	949-766-9933	R	101*	.1
128	Unitech America Inc—*Vincent Shu*	6182 Katella Ave, Cypress CA 90630	714-891-6400	R	100*	.1
129	Logic Product Development—*Michael Davis*	411 Washington Ave N S, Minneapolis MN 55401	612-672-9495	R	100*	.1
130	Sayers Group LLC—*Gale Sayers*	1150 Feehanville Dr, Mount Prospect IL 60056	847-391-4040	R	100	.1
131	Ften Inc—*Ted Myerson*	885 3rd Ave 29th Fl, New York NY 10022	212-808-8440	S	98*	.1
132	Cubix Latin America LLC—*Fernado Diaz*	2841 Nw 107th Ave, Doral FL 33172	305-599-2742	R	97*	<.1
133	Parts Now! Inc—*Bruce Hagan*	3150 Pleasant View Rd, Middleton WI 53562	608-203-1500	R	96	.2
134	Arsenal Digital Solutions Worldwide Inc—*Frank Brick*	8000 Regency Pky Ste 1, Cary NC 27511	919-466-6700	R	95*	.1
135	Results Technology—*John French*	7939 Flint St, Lenexa KS 66214	913-928-8300	R	95*	.1
136	Wasp Technologies Inc—*Tom O'Shea*	1400 10th St, Plano TX 75074		R	95*	.1
137	Ubicom Inc—*Gangesh Ganesan*	195 Baypointe Pkwy, San Jose CA 95134	408-433-3330	R	94*	.1
138	Quaero Corp—*Naras Eechambadi*	1930 Camden Rd Ste 206, Charlotte NC 28203	704-414-0200	S	92*	.1
139	Amcat—*Jim Texter*	300 Johnny Bench Dr, Oklahoma City OK 73104	405-216-8080	S	91*	.1
140	Meru Networks Inc—*Ihab Abu-Hakima*	894 Ross Dr, Sunnyvale CA 94089	408-215-5300	P	91	.3
141	Faronics Corp—*Vik Khanna*	2411 Old Crow Canyon R, San Ramon CA 94583	604-637-3333	R	90*	.1
142	Neon Enterprise Software Inc—*Lacy Edwards*	14100 SW Fwy Ste 400, Sugar Land TX 77478	281-491-6366	R	90*	.1
143	Magnetic Products and Services Inc—*Michelle Morey*	7500 Boone Ave N, Brooklyn Park MN 55428	763-424-2700	R	90*	.1
144	Websourced Inc—*Lewis Finch*	300 Perimeter Park Dr, Morrisville NC 27560	919-433-3030	S	90*	.1
145	Q1 Labs Inc—*Shaun McConnon*	890 Winter St Ste 230, Waltham MA 02451	781-250-5800	R	88*	.1

Note: An asterisk (*) indicates an estimated financial figure. The company type code used is as follows: R = Private, P = Public, S = Private Subsidiary, B = Public Subsidiary, D = Division, J = Joint Venture, I = Investment Fund.

COMPANY RANKINGS BY SALES WITHIN 4-DIGIT SIC

Rank	Company Name—*Executive Officer*	Address, City, State, Zip	Phone	Type	Fin	Empls
146	Quest International Inc (Irvine California)—*Shawn Arshadi*	65 Parker, Irvine CA 92618	949-581-9900	R	88*	.1
147	Parts Now LLC—*Mike Cox*	PO Box 88632, Milwaukee WI 53288	608-203-1500	R	85*	.2
148	Guardian Mortgage Documents Inc—*Mike O'Leary*	225 Union Blvd Ste 200, Lakewood CO 80228	303-232-7770	S	85*	.1
149	Vertica Systems Inc—*Christopher Lynch*	8 Federal St 1st Fl, Billerica MA 01821	978-600-1000	R	84*	.1
150	PointRoll Inc—*James Tafler*	951 E Hector St, Conshohocken PA 19428	267-558-1300	S	84*	.1
151	Gbs Corp—*Eugene Calabria*	PO Box 2340, Canton OH 44720	330-494-5330	R	83*	.3
152	Sirius Enterprise Systems Group LLC—*Harvey Najim*	7670 S Chester St Ste, Englewood CO 80112	303-706-1700	S	82*	.1
153	Signiant Inc—*Dennis Albano*	10 2nd Ave, Burlington MA 01803	781-221-4000	R	81*	.1
154	Echopass Corp—*Vincent Deschamps*	6601 Koll Center Pky S, Pleasanton CA 94566	801-258-7000	R	81*	.1
155	Hi-Touch Imaging Technologies Inc—*Wen Lee*	727 Brea Canyon Rd Ste, Walnut CA 91789	909-974-0099	R	80*	<.1
156	Precision Computer Services Inc (Shelton Connecticut)—*Irene FitzSimons*	175 Constitution Blvd, Shelton CT 06484	203-929-0000	R	78*	.1
157	Hatteras Networks Inc—*Kevin Sheehan*	PO Box 110025, Research Triangle Park NC 27709	919-991-5440	R	77*	.1
158	Packet Design LLC—*Jack Bradley*	2455 Augustine Dr, Santa Clara CA 95054	408-490-1000	R	77*	.1
159	Greenpages Inc—*Ron Dupler*	PO Box 9001, Kittery ME 03904	207-439-7310	R	76*	.1
160	MessageLabs Inc—*Adrian Chamberlain*	512 7th Ave, New York NY 10018	646-519-8100	R	76*	.1
161	Spinnaker Networks Inc—*Ron Bianchini*	8001 Irvine Ctr Dr Ste, Irvine CA 92618	949-268-1500	S	76*	.1
162	Nallatech Inc—*Craig Anderson*	759 Flynn Rd, Camarillo CA 93012	805-383-8997	S	76*	.1
163	Second Foundation Consulting—*Dave Popoiwch*	3250 W Lake Rd Ste 4, Erie PA 16505	814-454-5215	R	76*	.1
164	Orc Software Inc—*Thomas Bill*	420 Lexington Ave Rm 2, New York NY 10170	212-507-0000	R	75*	<.1
165	Woot Inc	4121 International Pky, Carrollton TX 75007	214-445-2891	R	74*	.1
166	Clearspeed Technology Ltd—*Russell David*	800 W El Camino Real S, Mountain View CA 94040	650-943-2329	R	72*	.1
167	Shareholdercom—*Douglas Ventola*	12 Clock Tower Pl, Maynard MA 01754	978-461-3111	R	72*	.1
168	Compurex Systems Corp—*Christopher E Pernock*	580 Myles Standish Blv, Taunton MA 02780	508-230-3700	R	72*	.1
169	Lssi Data	1 Sentry Pky Ste 6000, Blue Bell PA 19422	610-276-4300	S	72*	.1
170	JBoss Inc	3340 Peachtree Rd Ste, Atlanta GA 30326	404-467-8555	S	71*	.1
171	Azimuth Systems Inc—*Jim Iuliano*	35 Nagog Park, Acton MA 01720	978-263-6610	R	71*	.1
172	Glimmerglass Networks Inc—*Robert Lundy*	26142 Eden Landing Rd, Hayward CA 94545	510-723-1900	R	71*	.1
173	Vha Yu Technologies Corp—*Jeffrey Hudson*	100 Cooper Ct, Los Gatos CA 95032	408-354-9810	R	70*	.1
174	Liquid Machines Inc—*Michael A Ruffolo*	486 Totten Pond Rd, Waltham MA 02451	781-693-3600	R	69*	.1
175	Intermountain Technology Group—*Harry Kasparian*	4795 Emerald Ste L, Boise ID 83706	208-319-2701	S	69*	.1
176	Primeon Inc—*Leon Stevens*	18 Commerce Way Fl 3, Woburn MA 01801	917-699-8165	R	68*	.1
177	Lightedge Solutions Inc—*Jim Masterson*	215 10th St Ste 1220, Des Moines IA 50309	515-471-1000	R	66*	.1
178	Verdasys Inc—*Jim Ricotta*	404 Wyman St Ste 320, Waltham MA 02451	781-788-8180	R	65*	.1
179	Corestreet Ltd—*Chris Broderick*	1 Alewife Ctr Ste 200, Cambridge MA 02140	617-661-3554	R	64*	.1
180	ASA Computers Inc—*Arvind Bhargava*	645 National Ave, Mountain View CA 94043	650-230-8000	R	64*	.1
181	Bocada Inc—*Nancy Hurley*	720 Fourth Ave Ste 100, Kirkland WA 98033	425-818-4400	R	64*	.1
182	Invoke Solutions Inc—*Ben Cesare*	375 Totten Pond Rd Ste, Waltham MA 02451	781-810-2700	R	64*	.1
183	Masterworks International Inc—*Robert Munn*	PO Box 40726, Houston TX 77240	713-896-0101	R	64*	.1
184	Oclaro (Acton Massachusetts)—*Terry F Unter*	35 Nagog Park, Acton MA 01720	978-635-1380	D	64*	.1
185	ORODAY Inc—*Joel Oropesa*	2393 Teller Rd Ste 104, Newbury Park CA 91320	805-498-9344	R	64*	.1
186	Automated Resources Group Inc—*Ray Butkus*	135 Chestnut Ridge Rd, Montvale NJ 07645	201-391-1500	R	63*	.1
187	Universal Business Matrix LLC—*Sunir Kapooor*	11808 Northup Way Ste, Bellevue WA 98005	425-285-0200	R	63*	.1
188	Arcis Co The—*Dave Boone*	7950 NW 53rd St, Miami FL 33166	786-871-0085	R	62*	.1
189	Kubotek USA Inc—*Naotako Kakishita*	2 Mount Royal, Marlborough MA 01752		S	62*	<.1
190	QSR Automations Inc—*Lee Leet*	2301 Stanley Gault Pkw, Louisvillo KY 40223	502-297-0221	R	62*	<.1
191	Astoria Software Inc—*Michael Rosinski*	300 Broadway St Ste 8, San Francisco CA 94133	650-357-7477	R	61*	.1
192	Devicescape Software Inc—*Dave Fraser*	1001 Bayhill Dr Ste 18, San Bruno CA 94066	650-249-6565	R	60*	.1
193	Lyme Computer Systems Inc—*Judy Vinson*	PO Box 290, Lyme NH 03768	603-795-4000	R	59*	<.1
194	World Data Products Inc—*Neil Vill*	121 Cheshire Ln Ste 10, Minnetonka MN 55305		R	58*	.1
195	MemoryTen Inc—*Kennneth Olsen*	2800 Bowers Ave, Santa Clara CA 95051	408-588-0077	R	58*	<.1
196	Ld Products Inc—*Aaron Leon*	2500 Grand Ave, Long Beach CA 90815	562-986-6940	R	57*	.1
197	Sanrad North America—*Oded Ilan*	900 Corporate Dr, Mahwah NJ 07430		S	57*	.1
198	Arrow ECS—*Andrew S Bryant*	11545 Wills Rd Ste 200, Alpharetta GA 30009	770-625-7500	D	56*	.1
199	Cadre—*Sandra E Laney*	255 E 5th St Ste 1200, Cincinnati OH 45202	513-762-7350	R	56*	<.1
200	American Consulting and Distribution Corp—*Mohammed Hussein*	1201 Cornwall Rd, Sanford FL 32773	407-324-2700	R	55*	<.1
201	Monoprice Inc—*Sean Lee*	11701 6th St, Rancho Cucamonga CA 91730	909-989-6887	R	54*	.2
202	Prostor Systems Inc—*Frank Harbist*	5555 Central Ave Ste 1, Boulder CO 80301	303-545-2535	R	54*	<.1
203	Automating Peripherals Inc—*JP Fingado*	1550 Innovation Way, Hartford WI 53027	262-673-6815	R	54*	<.1
204	Computer Sales International Inc—*Kenneth B Steinback*	9990 Old Olive St Rd S, Saint Louis MO 63141	314-997-7010	R	53*	.4
205	Xifin Inc—*Lale White*	3394 Carmel Mountain R, San Diego CA 92121	858-793-5700	R	53*	.1
206	Clear-Vu Products—*Michael Lax*	29 New York Ave, Westbury NY 11590		S	52*	.1
207	Otter Computer Inc—*Yuan Tsai*	3350 Scott Blvd Bldg 4, Santa Clara CA 95054	408-735-7358	R	52*	<.1
208	Agrizzi Enterprises Corp—*Saulo Sousa*	10505 Nw 37th Ter, Doral FL 33178	305-468-1890	R	52*	.1
209	Merkle Inc—*David Williams*	7001 Columbia Gateway, Columbia MD 21046	443-542-4000	S	51*	.1
210	OpVista Inc—*Karl May*	870 N McCarthy Blvd, Milpitas CA 95035	408-719-6100	R	51*	.1
211	Server Technology Inc—*Brandon Ewing*	1040 Sandhill Dr, Reno NV 89521	775-284-2000	R	51*	.1
212	Digital Storage Inc—*Simon N Garneau*	7611 Green Meadows Dr, Lewis Center OH 43035	740-548-7179	R	50*	<.1
213	Intransa Inc—*Bud Broomhead*	10710 N Tantay Ave, Cupertino CA 95014	408-678-8600	R	50*	<.1
214	XS International Inc—*Todd A Bone*	1005 Alderman Dr Ste 2, Alpharetta GA 30005	770-740-0040	R	50*	<.1
215	EIZO Nanao Technologies Inc—*Yoshitaka Jitsumori*	5710 Warland Dr, Cypress CA 90630	562-431-5011	S	50	<.1
216	Action International Marketing Inc—*Robert Beckett*	1571 Gehman Rd, Harleysville PA 19438	267-421-5328	R	50*	<.1
217	Tomba Communications and Electronics Inc—*Tom Tomba*	718 Barataria Blvd, Marrero LA 70072	504-340-2448	R	49*	.1
218	Dspcon Inc—*Alfred N Brower*	380 Foothill Rd, Bridgewater NJ 08807	908-722-5656	S	49*	<.1
219	High Point Solutions Inc—*Michael T Mendiburu*	5 Gail Ct, Sparta NJ 07871	973-940-0040	R	48*	.1
220	OrCAD Inc—*Lip Bu Tan*	13221 SW 68th Pkwy Ste, Portland OR 97223	503-968-4874	S	47	.3
221	Shotspotter Inc—*Ralph A Clark*	1060 Terra Bella Ave, Mountain View CA 94043	650-960-9200	R	47*	.1
222	Insite One Inc—*James Champagne*	135 N Plains Industria, Wallingford CT 06492	203-265-6111	R	47*	<.1
223	Chicago Soft Ltd—*Peter Mclaughlin*	4757 N Hermitage Ave, Chicago IL 60640	773-506-1900	R	47*	<.1
224	NOW Micro Inc—*Patrick Finn*	1645 Energy Park Dr St, Saint Paul MN 55108	651-393-2100	R	46*	<.1
225	Logical Choice Technologies Inc—*Cynthia B Kaye*	1045 Progress Cir, Lawrenceville GA 30043	770-564-1044	R	45*	.2
226	Edge Access Inc—*Rob Veschi*	5440 Beaumont Center B, Tampa FL 33634	813-249-1177	R	45*	.1
227	StoredIQ Inc (Austin Texas)—*James Schellhase*	4401 West Gate Blvd St, Austin TX 78745	512-334-3100	R	45*	.1
228	Clearswift Ltd—*Jon Lee*	1715 114th Ave SE Ste, Bellevue WA 98004	425-460-6000	R	45*	<.1
229	Promark Technology—*Dale Foster*	10900 Pump House Rd St, Annapolis Junction MD 20701	240-280-8030	R	45*	<.1
230	Wandering WiFi LLC—*John Marshall*	1425 Ellsworth Industr, Atlanta GA 30318	404-478-7400	R	45*	<.1
231	eDial Inc—*Scott Petrack*	266 2nd Ave, Waltham MA 02451	781-895-3600	S	45*	<.1
232	mValent Inc	230 Third Ave, Waltham MA 02451		S	44*	<.1
233	Datel Systems Inc—*William Blue*	5636 Ruffin Rd, San Diego CA 92123	858-571-3100	R	43*	<.1

Rank	Company Name—*Executive Officer*	Address, City, State, Zip	Phone	Type	Fin	Empls
234	Certeon Inc—*Peter Dougherty*	4 Van de Graaf Dr, Burlington MA 01803	781-425-5200	R	43*	<.1
235	SalePoint Inc—*Larry Haworth*	9909 Huennekens St Ste, San Diego CA 92121	858-546-9400	R	42*	.1
236	Aberdeen LLC—*Moshe Ovadya*	9130 Norwalk Blvd, Santa Fe Springs CA 90670	562-699-6998	R	42*	<.1
237	Augmentix Inc—*Stephan Godevais*	4030 W Braker Ln Ste 2, Austin TX 78759	512-334-0111	S	39*	<.1
238	Government Acquisitions Inc—*Dennis Obial*	231 W 4th St, Cincinnati OH 45202	513-721-8700	R	39*	<.1
239	Worldcom Exchange Inc—*Belisario A Rosas*	6 Delaware Dr, Salem NH 03079	603-893-0900	R	39*	<.1
240	Breece Hill LLC—*Robert J Schaefer*	10955 Westmoor Dr Ste, Westminster CO 80021	303-664-8200	R	39*	<.1
241	Redsky Technologies Inc—*Anthony Maier*	925 W Chicago Ave Ste, Chicago IL 60622	312-432-4300	R	39*	<.1
242	Perot Systems Healthcare Solutions Inc—*Salvatore Lanuto*	120 Royall St, Canton MA 02021	781-575-1100	R	38*	.2
243	Orcom Solutions LLC—*Paul Sweeny*	1001 Sw Disk Dr Ste 10, Bend OR 97702	214-576-1223	R	38*	.4
244	Interlink Communication Systems Inc—*Joe Serra*	4400 140th Ave N Ste 2, Clearwater FL 33762	727-524-8663	R	38*	<.1
245	Precision Data Products Inc—*Gail A Huff*	PO Box 8367, Grand Rapids MI 49518	616-698-2242	R	38*	<.1
246	TekVizion PVS Inc—*Sach Vengurlekar*	2301 N Greenville Ave, Richardson TX 75082	214-242-5900	R	38*	<.1
247	Inland Associates Inc—*Peggy Meader*	PO Box 940, Olathe KS 66051	913-764-7977	R	37*	<.1
248	WebGen Systems Inc—*Bob Potter*	41 Linskey Way, Cambridge MA 02142	617-349-0724	R	37*	<.1
249	Asante Networks Inc—*John Hwang*	47436 Fremont Blvd, Fremont CA 94538	408-435-8388	R	37*	<.1
250	Network Outfitters Inc—*Kurt Rawlings*	375 S 640 West, Pleasant Grove UT 84062		R	37*	<.1
251	US-Analytics Solutions Group LLC—*Scott Preszler*	600 E Las Colinas Blvd, Irving TX 75039	214-630-0081	R	37*	<.1
252	Acuo Technologies LLC—*Jeff Timbrook*	7200 Hudson Blvd Ste 2, Saint Paul MN 55128	952-905-3440	R	36*	<.1
253	Sensitron Inc—*Rajiv Jaluria*	830 Stewart Drive Ste, Sunnyvale CA 94085	408-744-6911	R	36*	<.1
254	Agama Systems Inc (Houston Texas)—*David Chang*	9912 Brooklet Dr, Houston TX 77099	713-772-1788	R	36*	<.1
255	Copan Systems Inc—*Mark B Ward*	1900 Pike Rd, Longmont CO 80501	303-532-0200	R	35*	<.1
256	InterBase Corp—*Tejas Modi*	1240 N Lakeview Ave St, Anaheim CA 92807	714-701-3600	R	35*	<.1
257	M Farris and Associates—*Mark Farris*	4032 Del Rey Ave, Marina Del Rey CA 90292	310-306-9740	R	35*	<.1
258	Roland Digital Group America—*Bob Curtis*	15363 Barranca Pky, Irvine CA 92618	949-727-2100	S	34*	.1
259	Ecutel Systems Inc—*Thomas P Matthews*	590 Herndon Pky Ste 35, Herndon VA 20170	703-787-3568	R	33*	<.1
260	eLynx Ltd—*Sharon Matthews*	7870 E Kemper Rd Ste 2, Cincinnati OH 45249	513-612-5969	R	33*	<.1
261	Scientific Systems and Software International Corp—*A Nayab Siddiqui*	5950 Symphony Woods Rd, Columbia MD 21044	410-715-5700	R	33*	<.1
262	Silver Bullet Technology Inc—*Bryan Clark*	25 West Cedar St Ste 4, Pensacola FL 32502	850-437-5880	R	33*	<.1
263	Midwest Collaborative for Library Services—*Randy DykLuis*	1407 Rensen St Ste 1, Lansing MI 48910	517-394-2420	R	33*	<.1
264	BASON Company Inc—*R J Yeh*	555 E Easy St Ste B, Simi Valley CA 93065	805-426-1000	R	32*	<.1
265	C Hoelzle Associates Inc—*Chris Hoelzle*	40 Tesla Bldg A, Irvine CA 92618	949-251-9000	R	32*	<.1
266	Colfax International—*Gautam Shah*	750 Palomar, Sunnyvale CA 94085	408-730-2275	R	32*	<.1
267	CPAcinccom—*JoAnn Moffit*	22700 Savi Ranch Pky S, Yorba Linda CA 92887	714-692-5044	R	32*	<.1
268	RK Software and Hardware Inc—*Anil Parekh*	11428 E Artesia Blvd S, Artesia CA 90701	562-865-5340	R	32*	<.1
269	Strictly Business Computer Systems Inc—*Michael G Owens*	PO Box 2076, Huntington WV 25720	304-529-0401	R	32*	<.1
270	Allied Network Solutions Inc—*Roger Schnorenberg*	1358 Blue Oaks Blvd St, Roseville CA 95678	916-774-2670	R	32*	<.1
271	Cranel Inc—*James Wallace*	8999 Gemini Pkwy, Columbus OH 43240	614-431-8000	R	31*	.2
272	Novariant Inc—*Herb Satterlee*	45700 Northport Loop E, Fremont CA 94538	510-933-4800	R	31*	.1
273	Infinite Solutions Group Inc—*Garrett Diduck*	3678 N Peachtree Rd St, Chamblee GA 30341	770-986-8180	R	31*	.1
274	Hall Research Technologies—*Ali Hagijoo*	1163 Warner Ave, Tustin CA 92780	714-641-6607	R	31*	<.1
275	Intalio Inc—*Ismael Ghalimi*	644 Emerson St, Palo Alto CA 94301	650-596-1800	R	31*	<.1
276	Lord's Computer Group Partners Inc—*Kevin Brown*	4045 Nine McFarland, Alpharetta GA 30004	770-475-8000	R	31*	<.1
277	Mate Co—*Marie Dunn*	42148 Sarah Way, Temecula CA 92590	415-454-5425	R	31*	<.1
278	Systems House Inc—*Seymour Fertig*	1033 Rte 46 E, Clifton NJ 07013	973-777-8050	R	31*	<.1
279	Cantaloupe Systems Inc—*Mandeep Arora*	612 Howard St Ste 600, San Francisco CA 94105	415-525-8100	R	31*	<.1
280	B Peters Associates Inc—*Boris Peters*	901 Curtain Ave, Baltimore MD 21218	410-662-6380	R	30*	<.1
281	mGen Inc—*Scot Peterson*	100 Foxborough Blvd St, Foxborough MA 02035	508-549-0970	R	30*	<.1
282	Satori Group Inc—*David Libesman*	1010 Spring Mill Ave S, Conshohocken PA 19428	610-862-6300	R	30*	<.1
283	Junction Solutions Inc—*Jeff Grell*	9785 S Maroon Cir Ste, Englewood CO 80112	303-327-8800	R	30*	<.1
284	Comsource Inc—*Kevin Hanlon*	8104 Cazenovia Rd Ste, Manlius NY 13104	315-682-4115	R	30*	<.1
285	WAV Inc—*Norm Dumbroff*	2380 A Prospect Dr, Aurora IL 60502	630-818-1000	R	29*	<.1
286	Microlink Enterprises Inc—*Renn Don Liang*	20955 Pathfinder Rd St, Diamond Bar CA 91765	562-205-1888	R	29*	<.1
287	Terra Technology—*Robert F Byrne*	20 Glover Ave, Norwalk CT 06850	203-847-4007	R	29*	<.1
288	AccuCode Inc—*Kevin Price*	6886 South Yosemite St, Centennial CO 80112	303-639-6111	R	28*	<.1
289	SynTel LLC—*Steve Smith*	3401 One Pl, Jonesboro AR 72404	870-802-3191	R	28*	<.1
290	Edgewater Networks Inc—*David G Norman*	2895 Northwestern Pkwy, Santa Clara CA 95051	408-351-7200	R	28*	<.1
291	Dot Hill Systems Inc (Longmont Colorado)	1351 S Sunset St, Longmont CO 80501	303-845-3200	S	28*	<.1
292	Nordix Computer Corp—*Atef Ibrahim*	3350 Scott Blvd Ste 49, Santa Clara CA 95054	408-492-1800	R	28*	<.1
293	OLSolutions—*Arsenio Vatoy*	7777 Center Ave Ste 43, Huntington Beach CA 92647	714-465-2665	R	27	<.1
294	Xelerated Inc—*Eva Lindqvist*	2700 Augustine Dr Ste, Santa Clara CA 95054	408-844-9259	R	27*	<.1
295	M and A Technology Inc—*Magdy Elwany*	2045 Chenault Dr, Carrollton TX 75006	972-490-5803	R	26*	.1
296	DataSynapse Inc—*Peter Lee*	632 Broadway 5th Fl, New York NY 10012	212-842-8842	R	26	.1
297	General Datatech LP—*John Roberts*	999 Metro Media Pl, Dallas TX 75247	214-857-6100	R	26*	<.1
298	JDR Microdevices Inc—*Jeffrey D Rose*	1723 Rogers Ave Ste O, San Jose CA 95112		R	26*	<.1
299	McCormick Computer Resale—*Jeff McCormick*	14925 Energy Way, Apple Valley MN 55124	952-891-2322	R	26*	<.1
300	Passport Systems Inc—*Robert Ledoux*	70 Treble Cove Rd 1st, Billerica MA 01862	978-263-9900	R	26*	<.1
301	Liberty Parts Team Inc—*David Reinke*	3517 W Beltline Hwy, Madison WI 53713	608-268-7600	R	25*	.1
302	Baxter Planning Systems Inc—*Greg Baxter*	7801 N Capital of Texa, Austin TX 78731	512-323-5959	R	25*	<.1
303	Bluespec Inc—*Charlie Hauck*	14-16 Spring St Ste 3, Waltham MA 02451	781-250-2200	R	25*	<.1
304	Disk-o-Tape Inc—*Phil Peretz*	23775 Mercantile Rd, Cleveland OH 44122	216-765-8273	R	25*	<.1
305	Novo Innovations Inc—*Robert Connely*	3600 Mansell Rd Ste 22, Alpharetta GA 30022		R	25*	<.1
306	ROC Software LP—*Janet Slack*	3305 Northland Dr Ste, Austin TX 78731	512-336-4200	R	25*	<.1
307	Unistar-Sparco Computers Inc—*Soo-Tsong Lim*	7089 Ryburn Dr, Millington TN 38053	901-872-2272	R	25*	<.1
308	E-Glue USA Inc—*Omer Geva*	79 Hudson St Ste Llc, Hoboken NJ 07030	201-217-0022	R	24*	<.1
309	Software Information Systems LLC—*Steve Sigg*	455 Park Pl Ste 301, Lexington KY 40511	859-977-4747	R	24	<.1
310	Bellamax Inc—*Richard Marotta*	182 Howard St Ste 138, San Francisco CA 94105	415-344-7800	R	24*	<.1
311	Business Media Inc—*Bruce Christensen*	300 Oak Creek Dr, Lincoln NE 68528	402-476-6222	R	24*	<.1
312	Dollar Computer Corp—*Harry Clinton*	15551 RedHill Ave Ste, Tustin CA 92780	714-247-2200	R	24*	<.1
313	Ensim Corp—*David J Wippich*	2900 Lakeside Dr Ste 2, Santa Clara CA 95054	408-496-3700	R	24*	<.1
314	MRK Technologies Ltd—*Michael Kennedy*	1200 Mildred Ave, Westlake OH 44145	216-535-4100	R	24*	<.1
315	NetMap Analytics—*Richard McLean*	480 Olde Worthington R, Westerville OH 43082	614-865-6000	D	24*	<.1
316	Quest Solutions Inc—*Edward Mueller*	PO Box 22736, Eugene OR 97402	541-607-1161	R	24*	<.1
317	Verdiem Corp—*John Scumniotales*	1601 2nd Ave Ste 701, Seattle WA 98101	206-838-2800	R	24*	<.1
318	R and D Industries Inc—*Don Van Oort*	812 10th St, Milford IA 51351	712-338-2999	R	24*	<.1
319	One Source Printer Service and Supply	2154 Paragon Dr, San Jose CA 95131	408-392-9900	R	24*	<.1
320	Technical and Scientific Application Inc—*Bill Smith*	2050 W Sam Houston Pkw, Houston TX 77043	713-935-1500	R	24*	<.1
321	X1—*John Nardone*	470 Park Ave S, New York NY 10016	212-741-4222	R	24*	<.1
322	Patriot Memory LLC—*Steve Gaeta*	47027 Benicia St, Fremont CA 94538	510-979-1021	R	24*	.2

Note: An asterisk (*) indicates an estimated financial figure. The company type code used is as follows: R = Private, P = Public, S = Private Subsidiary, B = Public Subsidiary, D = Division, J = Joint Venture, I = Investment Fund.

COMPANY RANKINGS BY SALES WITHIN 4-DIGIT SIC

Rank	Company Name—*Executive Officer*	Address, City, State, Zip	Phone	Type	Fin	Empls
323	Spectrum Communications Cabling Services Inc—*Robert Rivera*	226 N Lincoln Ave, Corona CA 92882	951-371-0549	R	23*	.1
324	Eastern Data Inc—*Robert Reich*	2798 Dean Dr Ste B, Virginia Beach VA 23452	757-498-1600	R	23*	<.1
325	Samsung Electro-Mechanics America Inc—*Mike Noos*	3345 Michelson Dr Ste, Irvine CA 92612	949-797-8000	R	23*	.2
326	Real Time Consultants Inc—*John Iaccarino*	777 Corporate Dr, Mahwah NJ 07430	201-512-1777	R	22*	<.1
327	Communications Resource Inc—*Victoria Johnson*	8280 Greensboro Dr Ste, Mc Lean VA 22102	703-245-4120	R	22*	.1
328	Source Office Products—*John Givens*	13350 W 43rd Dr, Golden CO 80403	303-964-8100	R	22*	<.1
329	Applied Systems Technology and Resources—*David Reiss*	2640 Rte 9 W, Cornwall NY 12518	845-534-7100	R	22*	<.1
330	Workspeed Inc—*Derrick Chen*	317 Madison Ave Ste 16, New York NY 10017	917-369-9025	R	22*	<.1
331	Finite Technologies Inc—*Scott A Henderson*	3763 Image Dr, Anchorage AK 99504	907-339-8085	R	22*	<.1
332	Asus Computer International Inc—*Ivan Hoe*	800 Corporate Way, Fremont CA 94539	510-739-3777	R	21*	.1
333	RS Knapp Company Inc—*Gary Wilbur*	PO Box 234, Lyndhurst NJ 07071	201-438-1500	R	21*	.1
334	Talyst—*Carla Corkern*	11100 NE 8th St 6th Fl, Bellevue WA 98004	425-289-5400	R	21*	.1
335	Midwest Media Group Inc—*John Connolly*	135 E Algonquin Rd, Arlington Heights IL 60005	847-228-5588	R	21*	<.1
336	DTC Computer Supply—*Mike Kinsley*	9033 9th St, Rancho Cucamonga CA 91730	909-466-7680	R	21*	<.1
337	Cadient Group—*Stephen Way*	2520 Renaissance Blvd, King of Prussia PA 19406	484-351-2800	R	21*	<.1
338	Hickey and Associates—*Robert B Hickey*	3 Clarendon Ave, Brockton MA 02301	508-559-5130	R	21*	.1
339	TransNet Corp—*Steven J Wilk*	45 Columbia Rd, Somerville NJ 08876	908-253-0500	P	21	.1
340	Supplies Distributors Inc—*Mark Layton*	PO Box 910089, Dallas TX 75391	972-881-2900	R	21*	.2
341	MySQL AB—*Marten Mickos*	20450 Stevens Creek Bl, Cupertino CA 95014	208-338-8100	R	20*	.2
342	Servigistics Inc—*Eric Hinkle*	2300 Windy Ridge Pkwy, Atlanta GA 30339	770-565-2340	R	20*	.2
343	RPL Supplies Inc—*Larry Milazzo*	141 Lanza Ave Bldg 3A, Garfield NJ 07026	973-767-0880	R	20*	<.1
344	Open Systems of Cleveland Inc	22999 Forbes Rd Ste A, Cleveland OH 44146	440-439-2332	R	20*	<.1
345	Gemalto Inc—*Paul Beverly*	9442 N Cap Of Texas Hw, Austin TX 78759	512-257-3900	R	19*	.5
346	Insight Inc—*Jefferey Karrenbauer*	7960 Donegan Dr Ste 23, Manassas VA 20109	703-366-3061	R	19*	<.1
347	Intellitrack Inc—*James Budniakiewicz*	5 Shawan Rd Ste200, Hunt Valley MD 21030	410-771-3060	R	19*	<.1
348	Moyer Group—*Chris Moyer*	3580 Pierce Drm Rm 160, Chamblee GA 30341	404-229-1127	R	19*	<.1
349	PointB Communications Inc—*Rob Grusin*	750 North Orleans Ste, Chicago IL 60610	312-867-7750	R	19*	<.1
350	DSS Networks Inc—*Jerry Marcinko*	23 Spectrum Pointe Ste, Lake Forest CA 92630	949-716-9051	R	19*	<.1
351	GeoVantage Inc—*William 'Bill' Pevear*	3 Centennial Dr Ste 35, Peabody MA 01960	978-538-6400	R	19*	<.1
352	VerityThree Inc—*Jonathan R Smith*	733 Ridgeview Dr, McHenry IL 60050	815-385-4474	R	19*	<.1
353	Gwj Sourcenet Distribution Inc—*Gayle Barnes*	PO Box 5685, Round Rock TX 78683	512-248-8848	R	18*	<.1
354	Vox Technologies Corp—*John Oshodi*	1180 Commerce Dr, Richardson TX 75081	972-234-4343	S	18*	<.1
355	Anjin Computing—*Andy Baker*	PO Box 203715, Austin TX 78720	512-450-1197	R	18*	<.1
356	Compass Computer Group Inc (Twinsburg Ohio)—*Doyle Stutzman*	9408 Ravenna Rd, Twinsburg OH 44087	330-963-0800	R	18*	<.1
357	Computer Enhancement Systems—*Rich Robertson*	8038d Liberty Rd, Frederick MD 21701	301-620-1580	R	18*	<.1
358	Source Code Corp—*Hassan Yazdi*	159 Overland Rd, Waltham MA 02451	781-255-2022	R	17*	.1
359	SciVantage Inc—*Adnance Charchour*	10 Exchange Pl 13th Fl, Jersey City NJ 07302	646-452-0050	R	17*	.1
360	Computer Lab International Inc—*Thomas Fei*	580 S Melrose St, Placentia CA 92870	714-572-8000	R	17*	.1
361	Select Sales—*Chris Conroy*	7750 W 78th St, Bloomington MN 55439	952-941-9388	R	17*	<.1
362	William K Bradford Publishing Co	31 Main St, Maynard MA 01754		R	17*	<.1
363	Cutting Edge (El Cajon California)—*Michael Ehman*	435 West Bradley Ave S, El Cajon CA 92020	619-258-7800	R	17*	.1
364	SanSpot—*Vanil Walia*	50 Alexander Ct, Ronkonkoma NY 11779	631-737-0206	R	17*	<.1
365	Essex Technology Group Inc—*Robert Echols*	2728 Eugenia Ave Ste 1, Nashville TN 37211	615-846-3938	R	17*	.1
366	Seagull Software Systems Inc—*Donald P Addington*	3340 Peachtree Rd NE S, Atlanta GA 30326	404-760-1560	R	16*	.3
367	Abraham Technical Services Inc—*Steve Schmidt*	12560 Fletcher Ln Ste, Rogers MN 55374	763-428-3170	R	16*	.1
368	Data Source Media Inc—*Mark H Tallman*	PO Box 4397, Lincoln NE 68504	402-466-3342	R	16*	<.1
369	Tech101 - Arcus Inc—*Grace Chiu*	11520 Warner Ave, Fountain Valley CA 92708	714-435-0505	R	16*	<.1
370	Engineering Design Systems Inc—*Kevin Meredith*	3780 Peters Creek Rd E, Roanoke VA 24018	540-345-1410	R	16*	<.1
371	Marsden Company Inc—*William Marsden*	2055 Washington St, Hanover MA 02339	781-871-9992	R	16*	<.1
372	Delta Computer Services Inc—*John Kamen*	4 Dubon Ct, Farmingdale NY 11735	631-845-0400	R	16*	.1
373	D and K Properties Inc—*Mike Trabilcock*	21555 Drake Rd, Strongsville OH 44149	440-238-0102	R	16*	.2
374	Diskriter Inc—*Willard Hull*	3257 W Liberty Ave, Pittsburgh PA 15216	412-344-9700	R	16*	.1
375	I2c Inc—*Amir Wain*	1300 Island Dr Ste 105, Redwood City CA 94065	650-593-5400	R	15*	.4
376	IQ Systems Inc (Reno Nevada)—*Steve Cerocke*	4655 Longley Ln Ste 10, Reno NV 89502	775-352-2301	R	15*	<.1
377	AVerMedia Technologies Inc—*Arthur S Pait*	423 Dixon Landing Rd, Milpitas CA 95035	408-263-3828	R	15*	<.1
378	Cal Micro Inc—*Khaled Hamade*	712 Charcot Ave, San Jose CA 95131	408-321-9777	R	15*	<.1
379	Automated Power Technologies—*Jerry Zechmeister*	24 Rancho Pkwy, Lake Forest CA 92630	949-768-5965	R	15*	<.1
380	Monosphere Inc—*Ralph S Hubregsen*	5 Polaris Way, Aliso Viejo CA 92656	949-754-8000	S	15*	<.1
381	Sendio Inc—*Jonathan Niednagel*	4911 Birch St Ste 150, Newport Beach CA 92660	949-274-4375	R	15*	<.1
382	Visual Apex Inc—*Paul Gilmore*	7950 NE Day Rd Ste B, Bainbridge Island WA 98110	206-780-8192	R	15*	<.1
383	Ceven Corp—*Janet Garcia*	11380 Nw 36th Ter, Doral FL 33178	305-477-5558	R	15*	<.1
384	Professional Graphics Systems And Services Inc—*Guy Livoti*	3 W Main St Ste 1, Elmsford NY 10523	914-345-3033	R	15*	.1
385	General Microsystems Inc (Bellevue Washington)—*Earl W Overstreet II*	3220 118th Ave SE Ste, Bellevue WA 98005	425-644-2233	R	14*	<.1
386	Syslink Computer Corp	1648 Range Crt, Diamond Bar CA 91765	909-563-2678	R	14*	<.1
387	Technology Transfer—*Richard Mandel*	5323 Pennsylvania Ave, Boulder CO 80303	303-499-1525	R	14*	<.1
388	POSitive Software Co—*John Hickey*	2290 Robertson Dr, Richland WA 99354	509-371-0600	R	14*	.1
389	Imagestat Corp—*Robert Milne*	2951 28th St Ste 2005, Santa Monica CA 90405	310-392-1100	R	14*	.1
390	Sherwood Iss LLC—*Prem Menon*	200 Business Park Dr, Armonk NY 10504	914-273-1717	R	13*	.1
391	Impromed LLC—*Ronald Detjen*	304 Ohio St, Oshkosh WI 54902	920-236-7070	R	13*	.1
392	Source Technologies Inc—*Bill Bouverie*	2910 Whitehall Park Dr, Charlotte NC 28273	704-969-7500	R	13*	<.1
393	Blackhawk Inc—*Brad Hurley*	PO Box 21600, Saint Paul MN 55121	651-846-0225	R	13*	<.1
394	ASCII Group Inc—*Alan Weinberger*	7101 Wisconsin Ave Ste, Bethesda MD 20814	301-718-2600	R	13*	<.1
395	American Business Network Inc—*Carol L Walters*	2544 S 156th Cir, Omaha NE 68130	402-691-8248	R	13*	<.1
396	Microgear—*Neil Popli*	225 Bush St Ste 370, San Francisco CA 94104	415-547-7800	R	13*	<.1
397	Ocean Interface Company Inc—*Mei Chen*	20545 Paseo Del Prado, Walnut CA 91789	909-595-1212	R	13*	<.1
398	Spartan Corp—*Jovius Marginus*	190 Rockland St, Hanover MA 02339	781-829-8660	R	13*	<.1
399	Vendely Communications Inc—*Elizabeth Vendely*	4609 Ventura Canyon Av, Sherman Oaks CA 91423	818-783-3707	R	13*	<.1
400	Data Robotics Inc—*Tom Buiocchi*	1705 Wyatt Dr, Santa Clara CA 95054	408-567-3100	R	13*	.1
401	Suntel Services LLC—*Bob Babadi*	1095 Crooks Rd Ste 100, Troy MI 48084	248-654-3600	R	13*	.1
402	Gar Enterprises—*Nathan Sugimoto*	418 E Live Oak Ave, Arcadia CA 91006	626-574-1175	R	13*	.1
403	Interactive Business Information Systems Inc—*Andy Vabulas*	30 Technology Pkwy S S, Norcross GA 30092	770-368-4000	R	13*	.1
404	Vss LLC—*Butch Bates*	303 Brame Rd, Ridgeland MS 39157	601-853-8550	R	12*	.1
405	Divihn Integration Inc—*Herald Manjooran*	2500 W Higgins Rd Ste, Hoffman Estates IL 60169	847-882-0585	R	12*	.1
406	Bomgar Inc—*Joel Bomgaars*	578 Highland Colony Pk, Ridgeland MS 39157	601-519-0123	R	12	.1
407	Acom Solutions Inc—*Patrick McMahon*	2850 E 29th St, Long Beach CA 90806	562-424-7899	R	12*	.1
408	Cadec Global Inc—*Tom Bassett*	645 Harvey Rd Ste 2, Manchester NH 03103	603-668-1010	R	12*	.1
409	Development Through Self-Reliance Inc—*Dan Hogan*	921 Mercantile Dr Ste, Hanover MD 21076	410-579-4508	R	12*	<.1

Rank	Company Name—*Executive Officer*	Address, City, State, Zip	Phone	Type	Fin	Empls
410	Quickshot Technology Inc—*Phil Li*	PO Box 6279, El Monte CA 91734	626-810-3890	S	12*	<.1
411	Audio Intervisual Design Inc—*Larry Deeds*	1155 N La Brea Ave, West Hollywood CA 90038	323-845-1155	R	12*	<.1
412	O'hare Systems Corp—*Wallace Shun*	PO Box 1492, Melrose Park IL 60161	708-547-9375	R	12*	<.1
413	U and S Services Inc—*Russell Stuber*	233 Fillmore Ave Ste 1, Tonawanda NY 14150	716-693-4490	R	12*	<.1
414	Winners Circle Systems—*Andy Jong*	2930 Shattuck Ste 304, Berkeley CA 94705	510-845-2400	R	12*	<.1
415	Apex Data Systems Inc—*Dwight Babcock*	6464 E Grant Rd, Tucson AZ 85715	520-298-1991	R	12*	<.1
416	Burlington A/V Recording Media Inc—*Ruth Schwartz*	106 Mott St, Oceanside NY 11572	516-678-4414	R	12*	<.1
417	Entersect Corp—*Geoffrey Lee*	2700 N Main St Ste 535, Santa Ana CA 92705	714-564-9077	S	12*	<.1
418	MicroSearch Inc—*Kan Yeung*	3903 Stoney Brook, Houston TX 77063	713-988-2818	R	12*	<.1
419	Nickel Technologies Inc—*Daniel Nickel*	7 Burroughs, Irvine CA 92618	949-586-5051	R	12*	<.1
420	Red Bend Software Inc—*Yoram Salinger*	400-1 Totten Pond Rd S, Waltham MA 02451	781-890-2090	R	12*	<.1
421	Solstice Technologies—*Ian Robertson*	10302 S Federal Hwy St, Port Saint Lucie FL 34952	240-235-0602	R	12*	<.1
422	Worldwide Circuit Technologies—*Cheng Chang*	5724 W Las Positas Blv, Pleasanton CA 94588	510-623-9000	R	12*	<.1
423	Rayco International—*David Tayyanipour*	27371 Via Fineza, Mission Viejo CA 92691	949-586-2400	R	12*	<.1
424	Microland Electronics Corp—*Abraham Chen*	1883 Ringwood Ave, San Jose CA 95131	408-441-1688	R	12*	.1
425	Bronto Software Inc—*Joe Colopy*	324 Blackwell St Ste 4, Durham NC 27701	919-226-9363	R	11*	.1
426	Golden Road Industries Inc—*Frank Sadler*	624 W Hastings Rd Ste, Spokane WA 99218	509-468-1580	R	11*	.1
427	Trisco Resources Inc—*Michael Noori*	21418 Osborne St, Canoga Park CA 91304	818-717-9980	R	11*	.1
428	Onix Networking Corp—*Tim Needles*	18519 Detroit Ave, Lakewood OH 44107	216-529-3000	R	11*	<.1
429	Coridian Technologies Inc—*Mike Cleary*	1725 Lake Dr W, Chanhassen MN 55317	952-361-9980	R	11*	<.1
430	Currie Peak and Frazier Inc—*Beau Currie*	PO Box 593747, Orlando FL 32859	407-855-0843	R	11*	<.1
431	WebVMC LLC—*Scott Sheppard*	917 Commercial St, Conyers GA 30012	770-602-3189	R	11*	<.1
432	InfoNow Corp—*Mark Geene*	1875 Lawrence St Ste 1, Denver CO 80202	303-293-0212	P	11	.1
433	Technology Resource Center Inc—*John Edwardson*	749 S 8th St Rte 31, West Dundee IL 60118	847-426-9898	R	11	<.1
434	Citadel Security Software Inc—*Steven B Solomon*	5420 Lyndon B Johnson, Dallas TX 75240		S	10	.1
435	Software Services Group Inc—*Alex Ellingsen*	6395 Technology Ave St, Kalamazoo MI 49009	269-375-8996	R	10*	.1
436	Sdn Technologies LLC	2900 W 10th St, Sioux Falls SD 57104	605-334-7185	R	10*	.1
437	Peter J Phethean—*Peter Phethean*	363 Cliffwood Park St, Brea CA 92821	562-694-5924	R	10*	<.1
438	Sword AgencyPort	51 Sleeper St, Boston MA 02210	617-646-4550	D	10*	.1
439	Gold Type Business Machines Inc—*Richard Picolli*	PO Box 305, East Rutherford NJ 07073	201-935-5090	R	10*	<.1
440	Axis Business Solutions Ltd—*Peter Estes*	53b Green St, Portsmouth NH 03801	603-294-4256	R	10*	<.1
441	Hallogram Publishing—*Gaylen Hall*	16633 W Archer Ave, Golden CO 80401	303-340-3404	R	10*	<.1
442	Peripheral Resources Inc—*Paul Landazuri*	2721 La Cienega Blvd, Los Angeles CA 90034	310-837-5888	R	10*	<.1
443	Office Automation—*Ken Showalter*	216 W Jackson Blvd Ste, Chicago IL 60606	312-739-9800	R	10*	<.1
444	Shinko Technologies Inc	100 Randolph Rd, Somerset NJ 08873	732-271-7304	R	10*	<.1
445	Tele-Vue Service Company Inc—*Randy Prade*	947 Federal Blvd, Denver CO 80204	303-623-3330	R	10*	<.1
446	Aptron Corp—*Thomas Makosky*	25 Hanover Rd, Florham Park NJ 07932	973-822-0700	R	10*	<.1
447	Golden Surplus	3397 E 19th St, Signal Hill CA 90755	562-481-3281	R	10*	<.1
448	Mini Computer Exchange Inc—*John Maydonovitch*	150 Charcot Ave Ste A, San Jose CA 95131	408-733-4400	R	10*	<.1
449	Multi-Link Communications Products—*Eric Tanaka*	2420 W Carson St Ste 1, Torrance CA 90501	310-320-1451	R	10*	<.1
450	Source One Computer Products Inc—*Sandra Jaeger*	8343 N Steven Rd, Milwaukee WI 53223	414-355-9448	R	10*	<.1
451	Tritech Graphics Inc—*Roy A Filinson*	PO Box 222, Highwood IL 60040	847-656-3435	R	10*	<.1
452	Ocean Trading Inc—*Patricia Cardenas*	3240 Quartz Ln, Fullerton CA 92831	714-865-5376	R	10*	<.1
453	Leadertech Systems Of Chicago Inc—*Leechin Su*	210 Mittel Dr, Wood Dale IL 60191	630-238-9988	R	10*	.1
454	Comstor Corp—*Thomas Dolan*	14850 Confrnce Ctr Dr, Chantilly VA 20151	703-345-5100	R	10*	.1
455	American Future Technology Corp—*Alex Hou*	11581 Federal Dr, El Monte CA 91731		R	10*	.1
456	USA Notebook Inc—*Eva Kluger*	1408 Sw 13th Ct, Pompano Beach FL 33069	954-941-1417	R	10*	<.1
457	Rts Realtime Systems Inc—*Steffen Gemuenden*	311 S Wacker Dr Ste 98, Chicago IL 60606	312-630-9006	R	10*	.1
458	Legacy Inc—*Edward Mckinley*	56 Chancellor Dr, Roselle IL 60172	630-622-2001	R	10*	.1
459	Unical Enterprises Inc—*Frank Liu*	16960 Gale Ave, City Of Industry CA 91745	626-965-5588	R	10*	.1
460	Midland Computer Inc—*Wayne Clure*	11011 Q St Ste 103c, Omaha NE 68137	402-691-8900	R	9*	.1
461	Cyveillance Inc—*Panos Anastassiadis*	2677 Prosperity Ave St, Fairfax VA 22031	703-351-1000	R	9*	.1
462	Retro-Fit Technologies Inc—*Timothy Lawlor*	455 Fortune Blvd Ste 2, Milford MA 01757	508-478-2222	R	9*	.1
463	Solver Inc—*Per Solli*	10780 Santa Monica Blv, Los Angeles CA 90025	310-691-5300	R	9*	<.1
464	Brainstorm USA LLC—*Maral Cappotto*	8800 Roswell Rd Ste 20, Atlanta GA 30350	770-587-5880	R	9*	<.1
465	Chassis Plans—*Marc Dematteo*	10123 Carroll Canyon R, San Diego CA 92131	858-571-4330	R	9*	<.1
466	Computerware Inc—*Charles Evans*	8480 Tyco Rd Ste 1i, Vienna VA 22182	703-821-8200	R	9*	<.1
467	Direct Data Corp—*Robert A Rao*	2300 Computer Ave Ste, Willow Grove PA 19090	267-913-1000	R	9*	<.1
468	Sunnytech Inc—*Oscar Wang*	30 Ruta Ct, South Hackensack NJ 07606	201-883-1130	R	9*	<.1
469	Ashwood Computer Company Inc—*Rod Owens*	10671 Techwoods Cir St, Cincinnati OH 45242	513-563-2800	R	9*	<.1
470	Data Memory Systems Inc—*Norman Macinnis*	24 Keewaydin Dr Ste 5, Salem NH 03079	603-898-7750	R	9*	<.1
471	Appropriate Solutions Inc—*Raymond Cote*	PO Box 458, Peterborough NH 03458	603-924-6079	R	9*	<.1
472	ePM LLC—*Gerry Sepe*	9600 Great Hills Trail, Austin TX 78759		R	9*	<.1
473	Whitney Worldwide Inc—*Les Layton*	553 Hayward Ave N, St Paul MN 55128	651-748-5000	R	9*	<.1
474	Mini-Mcro Supply Inc (New York New York)—*John Kim*	2735 Jackson Ave Fl 1, Long Island City NY 11101	718-482-8600	R	9*	<.1
475	A1 Datacom Supply Co—*Marianne Padros*	931 Albion Ave, Schaumburg IL 60193	847-584-1000	R	9*	<.1
476	B and C Data Systems	PO Box 1369, Shady Cove OR 97539	541-601-8282	R	9*	<.1
477	NWS Corp	101 Castleton St Ste 2, Pleasantville NY 10570	914-773-7000	R	9*	<.1
478	Physimetrics Inc—*Rubin Uribe*	5020 Old Ellis Pt Ste, Roswell GA 30076	770-642-6858	R	9*	<.1
479	Tangent Communications Inc—*Gary Sapp*	200 E Howard Ste 238, Des Plaines IL 60018	847-954-4284	R	9*	<.1
480	Wright Williams and Kelly—*David Jimenez*	6200 Stoneridge Mall R, Pleasanton CA 94588	925-399-6246	R	9*	<.1
481	Phoenix Group—*Scoot Rutladge*	6705 Keaton Corp Pkwy, O Fallon MO 63368	636-300-8094	R	9*	.1
482	Caylx Software Limited Inc—*Howard Bing*	16428 12th Ave Sw, Burien WA 98166	206-241-9877	R	9*	<.1
483	Digitek Computer Products Inc—*Paul Martorana*	44258 Mercure Cir, Dulles VA 20166	703-421-0300	R	9*	<.1
484	Chipco Computer Distributors Inc—*Fred Babaee*	PO Box 23097, Columbia SC 29224	803-786-8646	R	9*	<.1
485	Comparts Inc—*Ken Menendez*	7876 Stage Hills Blvd, Memphis TN 38133	901-382-9933	R	9*	<.1
486	Cooperatives Computer Center Inc—*Scott Woodward*	5159 Woodlane Cir, Tallahassee FL 32303	850-562-0121	R	8*	.1
487	Computer Service Professionals Inc—*Bradford Epple*	805 W Stadium Blvd, Jefferson City MO 65109	573-635-1281	R	8*	.1
488	Technology Upgrade Corp—*Luis Baquero*	2456 NW 94th Ave, Doral FL 33172	305-436-1421	R	8*	<.1
489	Yada Systems Inc—*Robert Yauk*	2717 Lincoln Dr, Saint Paul MN 55113	651-631-3237	R	8*	.1
490	Ex-Cel Solutions Inc—*Dave Bandars*	14618 Grover St, Omaha NE 68144	402-333-6541	R	8*	.1
491	Minnesota Computers Corp—*Richard Quigley*	5733 International Pkw, Minneapolis MN 55428	763-577-0803	R	8*	<.1
492	Office World Inc—*Chuck Greeley*	3820 S Dixie Hwy, Lima OH 45806	419-991-4694	R	8*	.1
493	Uniplex Software Inc—*Gerald Troy*	716 Figueroa St, Folsom CA 95630	916-985-4445	S	8*	.1
494	ADVANCED BusinessLink Corp—*Chris Lategan*	5808 Lake Washington B, Kirkland WA 98033	425-602-4777	R	8*	.1
495	Asentinel LLC—*David Perdue*	6410 Poplar Ave Ste 20, Memphis TN 38119	901-752-6200	R	8*	<.1
496	Metronome Inc—*Erick Lee*	2154 Michelson Dr, Irvine CA 92612	714-429-0031	R	8*	<.1
497	Rosetta Technologies Corp—*Robert W Hullar*	5912 Breckenridge Pky, Tampa FL 33610	813-623-6205	R	8*	<.1
498	E-Media Plus Inc—*James Jarman*	71 Schrieffer St, South Hackensack NJ 07606	201-525-0100	R	8*	<.1
499	Nexus Consortium Inc—*George Riesco*	1933 Hwy 35 Ste 356, Wall Township NJ 07719	732-643-1700	R	8*	<.1

Note: An asterisk (*) indicates an estimated financial figure. The company type code used is as follows: R = Private, P = Public, S = Private Subsidiary, B = Public Subsidiary, D = Division, J = Joint Venture, I = Investment Fund.

OMPANY RANKINGS BY SALES WITHIN 4-DIGIT SIC

Rank	Company Name—Executive Officer	Address, City, State, Zip	Phone	Type	Fin	Empls
500	Trek Equipment Corp—Michael Creazzi	4000 Bridgeway Blvd St, Sausalito CA 94965	415-332-1555	R	8*	<.1
501	United Microsystems Inc—Futien Chen	1180 Miraloma Way Ste, Sunnyvale CA 94085	408-737-8267	R	8*	<.1
502	Twin Data Corp—Russell Todaro	1025 Commerce Ave, Union NJ 07083	908-688-8100	R	8*	<.1
503	Versatile Mobile Systems Inc—John Hardy	19105 36th Ave W Ste 2, Lynnwood WA 98036	425-778-8577	R	8*	.1
504	Hula Networks Inc—Joe Commendatore	340 E Middlefield Rd, Mountain View CA 94043	650-625-4100	R	8*	<.1
505	CA T S Co—Jacques Haddad	2100 W Big Beaver Rd S, Troy MI 48084	248-816-2287	R	8*	.1
506	CS Business Systems Inc—Michael Choo	1236 Main St, Buffalo NY 14209	716-886-6521	R	8*	<.1
507	Dirxion LLC—Brian Eby	1859 Bowles Ave Ste 10, Fenton MO 63026	636-717-2300	R	7*	.1
508	Fds Infotech Inc—Mukund Altekar	245 Park Ave Fl 39, New York NY 10167	212-792-4288	R	7*	.1
509	Atlantic Computer Products Inc—Shian-Te Chu	10772 Noel St, Los Alamitos CA 90720	714-952-2274	R	7*	<.1
510	Network Suppliers—Mitch Propster	4270 Aloma Ave 124-28c, Winter Park FL 32792		R	7*	<.1
511	Warkentine Inc—Roger Warkentine	PO Box 890185, Oklahoma City OK 73189	405-799-5282	R	7*	<.1
512	Sds Financial Technologies Inc—George Maragos	111 Broadway Rm 601, New York NY 10006	212-349-3300	R	7*	<.1
513	Dakcoll Inc—George Westphal	2000 Schafer St Frnt, Bismarck ND 58501	701-255-2409	R	7*	.1
514	Vartech Systems Inc—C Wayne Prater	11529 Sun Belt Ct, Baton Rouge LA 70809	225-298-0300	R	7*	<.1
515	USA Microcraft Inc—Adelino Sousa	8220 Belvedere Ave Ste, Sacramento CA 95826	916-273-1600	R	7*	<.1
516	Four J's Development Tools Inc—Jean-Georges Schwartz	251 Oconnor Rdg Ste 12, Irving TX 75038	972-893-7300	R	7*	<.1
517	Oliver Worldclass Labs Inc—Randy Oliver	PO Box 1686, Benicia CA 94510	707-747-1537	R	7*	<.1
518	Advanced Imaging Concepts Inc—Tim L Krongard	301 N Harrison St Bldg, Princeton NJ 08540	609-921-3629	R	7*	<.1
519	Attorney's Briefcase—Garrett C Dailey	2914 McClure St, Oakland CA 94609	510-836-2743	R	7*	<.1
520	Aurora Information Systems—Jerry Cully	1873 Rte 70 E Ste 220, Cherry Hill NJ 08003	856-596-4180	R	7*	<.1
521	ZI Technologies Inc—Kon Leong	2000 Concourse Dr, San Jose CA 95131	408-240-8989	R	7*	.1
522	Hi-Class Business Systems Of America Inc—Max Higgs	PO Box 832030, Richardson TX 75083	972-234-4444	R	7*	.1
523	Data Physics Corp—Sri Welaratna	1741 Tech Dr Ste 260, San Jose CA 95110	408-437-0100	R	7*	<.1
524	Microtech Computers Inc—Mike Zheng	4921 Legends Dr, Lawrence KS 66049	785-841-9513	R	7*	<.1
525	Coeco Office Systems Greenville Inc—Ca Robbins	PO Box 2088, Rocky Mount NC 27802	252-321-2400	R	7*	<.1
526	Mesa Systems Inc—John Lange	PO Box 10607, Pleasanton CA 94588	925-443-9491	R	7*	<.1
527	SOS Computers LLC—Dennis Ray	508 N Kentucky St Ste, Kingston TN 37763	865-717-4912	R	6*	<.1
528	Uptime Solutions Associates Inc—James Davidson	PO Box 24488, Dayton OH 45424	937-237-3400	R	6*	<.1
529	Xnet Systems Inc—Laurie Tate	PO Box 682786, Houston TX 77268	281-645-6701	R	6*	<.1
530	BI Trading LLC—Laurie Kimball	145 Webster St Ste 1, Hanover MA 02339	781-982-9664	R	6*	<.1
531	Aserdiv Inc—Philip Lanctot	940 W Sproul Rd, Springfield PA 19064		R	6*	<.1
532	Nextance Inc—Scott Buoy	6011 W Courtyard Dr, Austin TX 78730	512-377-9700	R	6*	.1
533	Advanced Technology Distributors Inc—James Lawson	1571 E Whitmore Ave, Ceres CA 95307	209-541-1111	R	6*	<.1
534	Wiscomp Systems Inc—Deb Ansay	417 W Michigan St, Port Washington WI 53074	414-727-1900	S	6*	<.1
535	Computer Design and Integration LLC—Rich Falcone	696 Us Hwy 46, Teterboro NJ 07608	201-931-1420	R	6*	<.1
536	Bracken Technology Services Inc—Ryan Bracken	4518 128th Ave, Holland MI 49424	312-226-4062	R	6*	<.1
537	DP Equipment Marketing Inc—Sherry Gilbert	3801 E Roeser Rd Ste 1, Phoenix AZ 85040	602-431-9779	R	6*	<.1
538	Midland Information Systems Inc—Michael Illies	2130 Platinum Rd, Apopka FL 32703	407-571-3100	R	6*	<.1
539	Computer Wholesale Distributors—Jim Wishnia	12385 Sw Allen Blvd St, Beaverton OR 97005	503-641-5856	R	6*	<.1
540	CD-ROM Access—Cheryl Jensen	6870 Comstock Rd, College Grove TN 37046	615-595-0950	R	6*	<.1
541	Marketex Computer Corp—Russell Schneider	1601 Civic Center Dr S, Santa Clara CA 95050	408-241-3677	R	6	<.1
542	Covigna Inc—Atif Rafig	1300 Crittenden Ln Ste, Mountain View CA 94043	650-641-7950	R	6*	<.1
543	Duane Whitlow and Company Inc—Duane Whitlow	4950 Keller Springs Rd, Addison TX 75001	972-931-3001	R	6*	<.1
544	IBEX Systems—Mary Balır	150 Greenfield Dr, Bloomingdale IL 60108	630-307-3634	R	6*	<.1
545	Insync Corp (Woods Cross Utah)—Wayne Pillard	1780 S 40 W, Salt Lake City UT 84115	801-466-9149	R	6*	<.1
546	JCL Company Ltd	7510 Jurupa Ave Ste 10, Riverside CA 92504	951-359-8898	R	6*	<.1
547	Millennial Net Inc—Dieter Schill	285 Billerica Rd, Chelmsford MA 01824	978-569-1921	R	6*	<.1
548	Quinn Data Corp—Sharren Harkins	PO Box 26293, Wilmington DE 19899	302-429-7450	R	6*	<.1
549	Scsistuff LLC—Keith Dugas	800 Industrial Blvd St, Grapevine TX 76051	817-481-5904	R	6	<.1
550	Magic Moments Inc—Bill Rodriguez	5699 Kanan Rd 374, Agoura Hills CA 91301	818-706-0473	R	6*	<.1
551	Emergitech Inc—Mark Collins	2545 Farmers Dr Ste 25, Columbus OH 43235	614-866-6712	R	6*	<.1
552	Omni Data Systems Limited LLP—Gary Fsuttles	PO Box 691828, Houston TX 77269	281-469-4365	R	6*	<.1
553	Mcenroe Voice and Data Corp—Kathleen Del Monte	10955 Golden W Dr A, Hunt Valley MD 21031	410-785-1600	R	6*	.1
554	Cartridge Care Inc—Charles Pydych	2256 Terminal Rd, Saint Paul MN 55113	612-331-7757	R	6*	<.1
555	Edgerton Corp—Robert Walters	22560 Lunn Rd, Strongsville OH 44149	440-268-0000	R	6*	<.1
556	Micro Solutions Plus Inc—John Elton	120 Bethlehem Pke Ste, Colmar PA 18915	215-996-9000	R	6*	<.1
557	Dalton Instrument Corp—Mei Lein	PO Box 701271, Dallas TX 75370	469-522-1200	R	6*	<.1
558	International Computer Marketing Corp—James Simpson	3370 Sugarloaf Pkwy G2, Lawrenceville GA 30044	770-381-2947	R	6*	<.1
559	Telrepco Inc—John Krawski	PO Box 780, Wallingford CT 06492	203-284-0566	R	6*	<.1
560	Ultimate Image Marketing Inc—Daniel Rees	3324 N San Marcos Pl S, Chandler AZ 85225	480-966-8973	R	6*	<.1
561	Advanced Digital Logic Inc—Peter Engels	4411 Morena Blvd Ste 1, San Diego CA 92117	858-490-0597	R	6*	<.1
562	National Parts Depot Inc—Kenneth Bram	31 Elkay Dr, Chester NY 10918	845-469-4800	R	5*	<.1
563	Combined Systems Technology Inc—Scot Lewton	2165 Nw 108th St Ste D, Des Moines IA 50325	515-270-5300	R	5*	<.1
564	Easy Technology Inc—Julio Garcia	10316 Norris Ave Ste B, Pacoima CA 91331	818-686-8265	R	5*	<.1
565	Itox LLC—Ben Buono	8 Elkins Rd, East Brunswick NJ 08816	732-390-2815	R	5*	<.1
566	Alepo USA—Jonathan Garini	3415 Greystone Dr Ste, Austin TX 78731	512-879-1030	R	5*	.2
567	Lite-On Trading USA Inc—Sonny Chao	720 S Hillview Dr, Milpitas CA 95035	408-946-4873	R	5*	<.1
568	Equipment Supply Company Inc—Grace Caldwell	350 Clubhouse Rd, Hunt Valley MD 21031	410-584-9573	R	5*	<.1
569	Jet Software—Azi Elbachri	204 Cobblestone Dr, San Rafael CA 94903	415-492-8999	R	5*	<.1
570	Real Estate Data X-Change Inc—Mark Leck	2335 S State St Ste 10, Provo UT 84606	801-437-0106	R	5*	<.1
571	Mccormick Computer Resale Inc—Jeff Mccormick	5995 149th St W Ste 10, Saint Paul MN 55124	952-891-2322	R	5*	<.1
572	Ascendix Technologies Inc—Wesley Snow	13140 Coit Rd Ste 310, Dallas TX 75240	972-889-8090	R	5*	<.1
573	Topower Computer USA Inc—Kent Chou	18529 Gale Ave, City Of Industry CA 91748	626-935-1688	R	5*	<.1
574	MPS Multimedia Inc—Steve Chen	1222 S Amphlett Blvd, San Mateo CA 94402	650-872-7100	R	5*	<.1
575	A Dan America Inc—Lan Lin	243 Winthrop Ave, Westbury NY 11590	516-333-2019	R	5*	<.1
576	Bti Computers Inc—Joseph Rotenberg	1626 Nw 82nd Ave, Doral FL 33126	305-477-0000	R	5*	<.1
577	Eis Data Systems Inc—Sherry Johnson	PO Box 3066, Wilmington NC 28406	910-791-6461	R	5*	<.1
578	Construction Link Inc—Lance R Ward	3394 Sutton Rd, Geneva NY 14456	315-789-4333	R	5*	<.1
579	Yohay Associates—Norman Yohay	80 Cutter Mill Rd, Great Neck NY 11021	516-487-9640	R	5*	<.1
580	TechQuest Inc—Marlene Chidiac	9012 Venice Blvd, Culver City CA 90232	310-287-2444	R	5*	<.1
581	Crown International—James Cox	103 Christian Louis Ct, Bloomington IL 61701	309-828-5195	R	5*	<.1
582	Excess Trade LLC—Sourabh Pathak	60 Tanbark Dr, Parlin NJ 08859	732-234-3871	R	5*	<.1
583	GalaxyHardware Publishers Inc—Ricki Shipway	5075 Nectar Way, Eugene OR 97405	541-345-1817	R	5*	<.1
584	Software Power Inc—Andy Kwang	507 S Myrtle Ave, Monrovia CA 91016	626-303-2006	R	5*	<.1
585	Top-Tier Technologies Inc—Kashef Mahmud	1040 N Quincy St Apt 6, Arlington VA 22201	703-798-9754	R	5*	<.1
586	Pearl Technology Corp—Gary Pearl	1200 E Glen Ave, Peoria IL 61616	309-679-0320	R	5*	<.1
587	Restaurant Data Concepts Inc—William Fuller	491 Kilvert St Ste 100, Warwick RI 02886	401-732-5700	R	5*	<.1
588	Bnl Technologies Inc—Behzad Eshghieh	20525 Manhattan Pl, Torrance CA 90501	310-320-7272	R	5*	<.1
589	Csgi LLC—John Shoaker	5440 Cherokee Ave Fl 1, Alexandria VA 22312	703-642-2933	R	5*	.1

Rank	Company Name—*Executive Officer*	Address, City, State, Zip	Phone	Type	Fin	Empls
590	Dynamic Network Factory Inc—*Mo Tahmasebi*	21353 Cabot Blvd, Hayward CA 94545	510-265-1122	R	5*	<.1
591	Professional Network Services Inc—*Robert Lunsford*	6711 Peters Creek Rd S, Roanoke VA 24019	540-265-1200	R	5*	<.1
592	Advanced Computer Connections Inc—*Michael Cowan*	166 Milan Ave, Norwalk OH 44857	419-668-4880	R	5*	<.1
593	Instruments and Equipment Co—*Joseph Trobert*	2 Wilson Dr Ste 1, Sparta NJ 07871	973-579-0009	R	5*	<.1
594	Vecmar Corp—*Greg Pluscusky*	7595 Jenther Dr, Mentor OH 44060	440-953-1119	R	5*	<.1
595	Pos America Inc—*Stephen Passas*	110 Kresson Gibbsboro, Voorhees NJ 08043	856-741-0395	R	5*	<.1
596	M and M Computers Inc—*Stewart Finck*	1539 Union St, Brooklyn NY 11213	718-576-1045	R	5*	<.1
597	Softdocs Inc—*Mike Murphy*	920 Hemlock Dr, Columbia SC 29201	803-695-6044	R	4*	<.1
598	American Eagle Systems Inc—*William Herrschaft*	160 Wilbur Pl Ste 600, Bohemia NY 11716	631-207-4400	R	4*	<.1
599	Micrologic Business Systems Inc—*Richard Hollander*	2745 W Clay St Ste C, Saint Charles MO 63301	636-946-6681	R	4*	<.1
600	Centurian Surplus Inc—*Jorge Lovato*	375 Tennant Ave, Morgan Hill CA 95037	408-778-2001	R	4*	<.1
601	BTB Inc—*William Pardini*	3586 N Hazel Ave, Fresno CA 93722	559-222-4100	R	4*	<.1
602	Technical Reality Inc—*Joseph Faris*	15005 Concord Cir Ste, Morgan Hill CA 95037	408-776-8299	R	4*	<.1
603	Selektro Power Inc—*Luis Ventura*	3620 Nw 115th Ave, Doral FL 33178	305-599-6096	R	4*	<.1
604	Avolution Ltd—*David Epperly*	5009 Ravensworth Rd, Annandale VA 22003	703-941-0001	R	4*	.1
605	Omnipro Systems Inc—*Ranjan Costa*	50 Mendell St Ste 2, San Francisco CA 94124	415-648-1121	R	4*	<.1
606	Flair Data Systems—*Bob Burgess*	10499 Bradford Rd Ste, Littleton CO 80127	303-904-2700	R	4*	.1
607	Composite Software Inc—*Jim Green*	2655 Campus Dr Ste 200, San Mateo CA 94403	650-227-8200	S	4*	<.1
608	Teseda Corp—*Armagan Akar*	6915 SW Macadam Ave St, Portland OR 97219	503-223-3315	R	4*	<.1
609	Progressive Computer Services Inc—*Martin Becker*	4250 Wissahickon Ave, Philadelphia PA 19129	215-226-2220	R	4*	<.1
610	Lake Companies Inc—*Greg Lake*	2980 Walker Dr, Green Bay WI 54311	920-406-3030	R	4*	<.1
611	Area Electronics Systems Inc—*William Huang*	1247 N Lakeview Ave St, Anaheim CA 92807	714-993-0300	R	4*	<.1
612	Bandspeed Inc—*Bill Eversole*	4301 Westbank Dr Bldg, Austin TX 78746	512-358-9000	R	4*	<.1
613	Pmi Computer Supplies Inc—*John Bussmann*	10407 Baur Blvd, Saint Louis MO 63132	314-994-3050	R	4*	<.1
614	Numeridex Inc—*Alberto Hoyos*	632 Wheeling Rd, Wheeling IL 60090	847-541-8840	R	4*	<.1
615	Alternative Computer Technology Inc—*Tom Farrell*	7908 Cincinnati Dayton, West Chester OH 45069	513-755-1957	R	4*	<.1
616	Options Technologies Inc—*Eddie Marquez*	7022 Nw 50th St, Miami FL 33166	305-591-2300	R	4*	<.1
617	Eritech International—*Andy Issagholian*	1515 W Glenoaks Blvd, Glendale CA 91201	818-244-6242	R	4*	<.1
618	Anysystem Group Holdings LLC—*Melanie Mayer*	239 Braen Ave, Wyckoff NJ 07481	201-445-3122	R	4*	<.1
619	Computer and Networking Services Inc—*Matthew Vandenbergh*	14813 Morningside Dr, Poway CA 92064	858-486-4707	R	4*	<.1
620	Future Computer Technologies Inc—*Wendy Ward*	605 Spice Island Dr St, Sparks NV 89431	775-329-0909	R	4*	<.1
621	Associates in Software International	1413 Tonne Rd, Elk Grove Village IL 60007	847-593-2626	R	4*	<.1
622	Computer Systems Inc—*Greg Jacobs*	14510 F St Ste 102, Omaha NE 68144	402-330-3600	R	4*	<.1
623	Aero Direct Inc—*Karen Wong*	1995 Kerns Ave, San Marino CA 91108	626-309-0800	R	4*	<.1
624	C and C Logistic Device Corporation Inc—*Chris Lillie*	18261 Enterprise Ln St, Huntington Beach CA 92648	714-848-3599	R	4*	<.1
625	Mega Tech Express Inc—*Jim Joachimczyk*	2550 Knights Station R, Lakeland FL 33810	863-853-5904	R	4*	<.1
626	Techfarm Inc—*Gordon Campbell*	2275 E Bayshore Rd Rm, Palo Alto CA 94303	650-934-0900	R	4*	<.1
627	Coastal International Inc—*Lew F Boyd*	29 Water St Ste 204, Newburyport MA 01950	978-462-2436	R	4*	<.1
628	Dopar Support Systems Inc—*Douglas M Doggett*	2727 2nd Ave Ste 136, Detroit MI 48201	313-871-0900	R	4*	<.1
629	Mirror Image Media Solutions Inc—*Tory Wiese*	2094 Beckett Dr, El Dorado Hills CA 95762	916-939-9927	R	4*	<.1
630	Amigo Business Computers—*William Teller*	412 Larkfield Rd, East Northport NY 11731	631-486-4521	R	4*	<.1
631	Analytic Associates—*Robert W Feakins*	4817 Browndeer Ln, Rolling Hills Estates CA 90275	310-541-0418	R	4*	<.1
632	Bullard's Computer Solutions Inc—*Drew Bullard*	3405 College Ave, Snyder TX 79549	325-573-4801	R	4*	<.1
633	Digiconcepts—*Lori Potter*	6006 Seaview Ave NW St, Seattle WA 98107	206-829-8242	R	4*	<.1
634	Dynamic Computer Products Inc—*Joe Mastrocola*	PO Box 410, Southbury CT 06488		R	4*	<.1
635	National Toner and Ink—*Neil Marzacano*	PO Box 1773, Oakhurst CA 93644	559-683-4862	R	4*	<.1
636	Silicon Heights Computers Inc—*Judith Muldawer*	PO Box 14428, Albuquerque NM 87191	505-293-4077	R	4*	<.1
637	Software Video Co—*Stacy Gajus*	PO Box 10444, Newport Beach CA 92658	951-230-1842	R	4*	<.1
638	Dca Inc—*Doug Carson*	1515 E Pine St, Cushing OK 74023	918-225-0346	R	4*	<.1
639	Techcess Solutions Inc—*Hugh Sazegar*	3100 Timmons Ln Ste 35, Houston TX 77027	832-741-9485	R	4*	<.1
640	Digital Dimensions Inc—*Patrick Lindsay*	3934 Murphy Canyon Rd, San Diego CA 92123	858-279-2557	R	4*	<.1
641	Amos Data Systems Inc—*Gary Amos*	1653 Merriman Rd Ste 2, Akron OH 44313	330-836-3132	R	4*	<.1
642	Maxxess Systems Inc—*Kevin Daly*	1040 N Tustin Ave, Anaheim CA 92807	714-772-1000	R	4*	<.1
643	May Ventures LLC	455 Elizabeth Ave Apt, Newark NJ 07112	973-679-4490	R	4*	<.1
644	Onyx Soft Inc—*Nelson Roach*	10470 Nw 26th St Ste B, Doral FL 33172	305-513-0035	R	4*	<.1
645	Global Computeronics Inc—*Kay Kuba*	655 County Rd E W, Saint Paul MN 55126	651-604-5700	R	4*	<.1
646	Mk Management Inc—*Mohammed Kiani*	15 Hammond Ste 309, Irvine CA 92618	949-581-3036	R	4*	<.1
647	Systech Synergy Inc—*Naveen Chanana*	2461 W 205th St Ste B1, Torrance CA 90501	310-218-0933	R	4*	<.1
648	Vcc Of Lima Inc—*William Graves*	3720 Converse Roselm R, Fort Jennings OH 45844	419-331-9050	R	4*	<.1
649	E-Brain Solutions LLC—*Peter Warren*	1200 Mountain Creek Rd, Chattanooga TN 37405	423-308-4900	R	4*	<.1
650	Add-On Computer Peripherals LLC	34 Mauchly Ste A, Irvine CA 92618	949-861-2800	R	4*	<.1
651	Pattco Priority Printer Solutions Inc—*Kenneth Harford*	2140 New Market Pkwy S, Marietta GA 30067	770-874-4680	R	4*	<.1
652	Trg Products Inc—*Mark Kubovich*	2859 104th St, Des Moines IA 50322	515-252-7522	R	4*	<.1
653	Technology Specialists Inc—*Lee White*	4861 Telsa Dr Ste B, Bowie MD 20715	301-352-4400	R	4*	<.1
654	Tlic Worldwide Inc—*Steven Palange*	400 S County Trl A208, Exeter RI 02822	401-295-2244	R	4*	<.1
655	Anton Systems Inc—*Michael Antonelli*	13798 Nw 4th St Ste 30, Sunrise FL 33325	954-315-9000	R	4*	<.1
656	Control House International Inc—*Chad Knutson*	1450 Park Ct Ste 1, Chanhassen MN 55317	952-474-1200	R	4*	<.1
657	Superclone Inc—*Kooi Lim*	7204 Nw 31st St, Miami FL 33122	305-592-4040	R	4*	<.1
658	Bennett Office Technologies Inc—*Russell Bennett*	312 24th Ave Sw, Willmar MN 56201	320-235-6425	R	4*	<.1
659	Data Guard Systems Inc—*Timothy Maliyil*	10 Magazine St Apt 707, Cambridge MA 02139	617-702-1100	R	4*	<.1
660	Apex Computers Inc—*Mark Keane*	105 Ferry St A, Malden MA 02148	781-321-8888	R	4*	<.1
661	Forcom Corp—*Chester Yang*	3930 E Miraloma Ave St, Anaheim CA 92806	714-632-3268	R	4*	<.1
662	Zoomland Inc—*Mark Yang*	3080 Ashbourne Cir, San Ramon CA 94583	925-838-7988	R	4*	<.1
663	American Technology Solutions Inc—*Laurie Jenzer*	1457 Park Rd, Chanhassen MN 55317	952-401-4780	R	4*	<.1
664	Judy Jeong—*Judy Jeong*	75 S Milpitas Blvd, Milpitas CA 95035	408-898-6001	R	4*	<.1
665	PC Export House Corp—*Javier Pedrazzoli*	3100 Nw 72nd Ave Ste 1, Miami FL 33122	305-406-2767	R	4*	<.1
666	American Infoserv Inc—*Fernando Silva*	50 Cragwood Rd Ste 307, South Plainfield NJ 07080	908-791-9300	R	3*	<.1
667	AC Systems Inc—*Joe Zuffoletto*	3990 S Lipan St, Englewood CO 80110	303-771-5000	R	3*	<.1
668	Apparel Business Systems LLC—*Karen Eichelberger*	2 W Lafayette St Ste 3, Norristown PA 19401	610-592-0880	R	3*	<.1
669	Case Technologies Inc—*Touf Hassoun*	208 Pine St, Carnegie PA 15106	412-276-0500	R	3*	<.1
670	Achieveit New York Inc—*Timothy Singleton*	640 Belle Terre Rd Ste, Port Jefferson NY 11777	631-543-3200	R	3*	<.1
671	Consumer Safety Technology Inc—*Kevin Doyle*	10520 Hickman Rd Ste F, Des Moines IA 50325	515-331-7643	R	3*	<.1
672	Aleratec Inc—*Perry Solomon*	9851 Owensmouth Ave, Chatsworth CA 91311	818-678-6900	R	3*	<.1
673	Prestige International Inc—*Marc Bruh*	333 W Merrick Rd Ste 1, Valley Stream NY 11580	516-678-4141	R	3*	<.1
674	Tcs International Inc—*Nadene Parzych*	55 Union Ave, Sudbury MA 01776	978-443-2527	R	3*	<.1
675	Hi-Link Computer Corp—*Jerry Lin*	76 Progress Dr Ste 1, Stamford CT 06902	203-975-9335	R	3*	<.1
676	Idilus LLC—*Michael Colucci*	2100 Manchester Rd Ste, Wheaton IL 60187	630-544-3299	R	3*	<.1
677	Nonagon Technology Corp—*Chandra Mutha*	PO Box 1486, El Cerrito CA 94530	510-215-3400	R	3*	<.1
678	Abi International Group Corp—*Ariel Sojete*	1315 Nw 98th Ct Unit 3, Doral FL 33172	786-228-8122	R	3*	<.1

Note: An asterisk (*) indicates an estimated financial figure. The company type code used is as follows: R = Private, P = Public, S = Private Subsidiary, B = Public Subsidiary, D = Division, J = Joint Venture, I = Investment Fund.

COMPANY RANKINGS BY SALES WITHIN 4-DIGIT SIC

Rank	Company Name—*Executive Officer*	Address, City, State, Zip	Phone	Type	Fin	Empls
679	A2b Tracking Solutions Inc—*David Collins*	207 Highpoint Ave Ste, Portsmouth RI 02871	401-683-5215	R	3*	<.1
680	Srs Computers Inc—*Rafia Versi*	416 Commerce Way Ste 1, Longwood FL 32750	407-478-2626	R	3*	<.1
681	Bond International Software Inc—*David Read*	8720 Stony Point Pkwy, Richmond VA 23235	804-266-3300	R	3*	<.1
682	Platform Solutions Inc—*John Hawes*	201 S St Ste 615, Boston MA 02111	617-217-2819	R	3*	<.1
683	Isg Solutions—*Charles Oakley*	2400 Res Blvd Ste 350, Rockville MD 20850	301-519-3776	R	3*	<.1
684	Gp Solutions Inc—*James Brenza*	201 N Charles St Ste 2, Baltimore MD 21201	410-244-8548	R	3*	<.1
685	Hush-Hush Entertainment Inc—*Andrew Stoddard*	22287 Mulholland Hwy S, Calabasas CA 91302	818-376-1595	R	3*	<.1
686	Device Tech Inc—*Bruce Flesher*	215 Industrial Dr Ste, Hampshire IL 60140	847-683-7235	R	3*	<.1
687	Aveva Engineering IT	10350 Richmond Ave Ste, Houston TX 77042	713-977-1225	S	3*	<.1
688	Bestco Group Inc—*Benjamin Wang*	1485 Andrew Dr Ste K, Claremont CA 91711	909-626-8886	R	3*	<.1
689	Horizon Datacom Solutions Inc—*Vicky Nosbisch*	400 Lazelle Rd Ste 7, Columbus OH 43240	614-847-0400	R	3*	<.1
690	In-Synch Systems LLC—*Kirk Farra*	129 Mccarrell Ln Ste 3, Zelienople PA 16063	724-452-8611	R	3*	<.1
691	Micro Development Services Inc—*William Schroeder*	PO Box 72945, Phoenix AZ 85050	602-493-3570	R	3*	<.1
692	Laser Saver Inc—*Paul Hawker*	8451 Miralani Dr Ste R, San Diego CA 92126	858-693-8838	R	3*	<.1
693	Nri Data And Business Products Inc—*James Bates*	PO Box 623, Langhorne PA 19047	215-736-1134	R	3*	<.1
694	A 2 Z Computers Inc—*Doug Sender*	325 Harris Dr Ste A, Aurora OH 44202	330-995-3355	R	2*	<.1
695	SANBlaze Technology Inc—*Steven Munroe*	5 Clock Tower Pl Ste 1, Maynard MA 01754	978-897-1888	R	3*	<.1
696	Skkn Inc—*David Ghadoushi*	16027 Ventura Blvd Ste, Encino CA 91436	818-449-2022	R	3*	<.1
697	Tech Superpowers Inc—*Michael Oh*	252 Newbury St, Boston MA 02116	617-267-9716	R	3*	<.1
698	Xinya (USA) Electronics Inc—*Francis Yuen*	23785 Cabot Blvd Ste 3, Hayward CA 94545	510-887-8999	R	3*	<.1
699	Read Technologies Inc—*Carolyn Woodberry*	8001 Irvine Ctr Dr Ste, Irvine CA 92618	949-743-9800	R	3*	<.1
700	Computer On Queue Inc—*Richard Quarantiello*	18 Graf Rd Unit 20, Newburyport MA 01950	978-499-0049	R	3*	<.1
701	Inventory Conversion Inc	64 Lafayette Rd Unit 1, North Hampton NH 03862	603-926-0300	R	3*	<.1
702	Paxcell Group Inc	360 S Abbott Ave, Milpitas CA 95035	408-945-8054	R	3*	<.1
703	Ammadis LLC	5302 Delong St, Cypress CA 90630		R	3*	<.1
704	Kennihan and Company Inc—*Tom Kennihan*	505 Cole St Apt 1, Raleigh NC 27605	919-848-0932	R	3*	<.1
705	Telassist Inc—*Martha Sullivan*	534 Maywood Rd, York PA 17402	717-840-7900	R	3*	<.1
706	PowerData Corp—*Marck Robinson*	15193 SE 54th Pl, Bellevue WA 98006	425-957-7988	R	3*	<.1
707	RMA Electronics Inc—*Ronald A Massa Sr*	35 Pond Park Rd Unit 1, Hingham MA 02043	781-749-9700	R	3*	<.1
708	Salmen Tech Company Inc—*Kenneth Salmen*	533 N St, Bethel Park PA 15102	412-854-1822	R	3*	<.1
709	Applications Plus Software Services Inc—*Jay Williams*	21602 Figueroa St Ste, Carson CA 90745	310-328-0155	R	3*	<.1
710	ArborWay Inc—*Paul Zellweger*	82 Fresh Pond, Cambridge MA 02138	617-864-1040	R	3*	<.1
711	Coast to Coast Computer Products—*Rick Roussin*	4277 Valley Fair St, Simi Valley CA 93063		R	3*	<.1
712	Decision Graphics—*Jim Pruitt*	1104-A Gleneagles Dr, Huntsville AL 35801	256-417-6640	R	3*	<.1
713	Impediment Inc—*Alexander Sunguroff*	333 Franklin St, Duxbury MA 02332	781-834-3800	R	3*	<.1
714	MacGurus—*Rick Stephens*	207 Mill Creek Ln, Grangeville ID 83530	208-983-9999	R	3*	<.1
715	MacServices—*Dave Provine*	8378 Veterans Hwy, Millersville MD 21108	410-544-2750	R	3*	<.1
716	MCA Computer Corp—*Christine Kashkarian*	17921 Sky Park Cir Bld, Irvine CA 92614	949-260-3909	R	3*	<.1
717	Memory Man Inc—*Jay Oreman*	757 SE 17th St Ste 139, Fort Lauderdale FL 33316	954-522-3000	R	3*	<.1
718	Computer Networks Inc—*Steve Jones*	1 Embarcadero Ctr Ste, San Francisco CA 94111	415-690-6582	R	3*	<.1
719	Ncds Medical—*David Polo*	7550 Lucerne Dr Ste 40, Cleveland OH 44130	440-234-8833	R	3*	<.1
720	Adcomp Systems Inc—*Mansur Plumber*	160 Broadway Lbby E, New York NY 10038	212-267-3245	R	3*	<.1
721	Petroleum Data Specialists Inc—*John Dyer*	3240 N Colorado St Ste, Chandler AZ 85225	480-892-2828	R	3*	<.1
722	Serverware Corp—*Sandra Kegelmeyer*	1250 Pttsfd Victr 100, Pittsford NY 14534	585-785-6100	R	3*	<.1
723	Knowledge Computers Inc *Dave Potter*	2360 Daniels St, Long Lake MN 55356	952-249-9940	R	3*	<.1
724	Shiloh Technologies LLC—*Edward Moore*	2003 S Horsebarn Rd St, Rogers AR 72758	479-464-4598	R	3*	<.1
725	Avantstar Inc—*Patrick Bray*	18872 Lake Dr E, Chanhassen MN 55317	952-351-8500	R	3*	<.1
726	Advanced Processing and Imaging Inc—*Melvin Rothberg*	1350 E Newport Ctr Dr, Deerfield Beach FL 33442	954-425-0018	R	3*	<.1
727	Granite Business Solutions Inc—*Paul Dhanota*	233 Technology Way Ste, Rocklin CA 95765	916-577-2180	R	3*	<.1
728	United Solutions Inc—*Gregory Kirshe*	28 Lord Rd Ste 285, Marlborough MA 01752	508-460-0045	R	3*	<.1
729	Cornerstone Solutions of Illinois Inc—*Dom Pernai*	120 W 22nd St Ste 350, Oak Brook IL 60523	630-571-4500	R	3*	<.1
730	Comp Limited LLC—*Aaron Yadidi*	463 N Oak St, Inglewood CA 90302	310-671-4444	R	3*	<.1
731	Mcp Computer Products Inc—*Rikki Ghai*	1565 Creek St Ste 103, San Marcos CA 92078	760-471-5383	R	3*	<.1
732	Multinational Technologies Inc—*Yigal Ziv*	3170 Martin Rd, Commerce Township MI 48390	248-960-5989	R	3*	<.1
733	Legacy Holdings LLC	8500 W 95th St, Overland Park KS 66212	913-385-7800	R	3*	<.1
734	Ngen LLC—*Thecla Alem*	1101 Merc Ln Ste 100, Largo MD 20774	301-531-9700	R	3*	<.1
735	Bramasol Inc—*Louise Putron*	601 Gateway Blvd Ste 1, South San Francisco CA 94080	650-636-8811	R	3*	<.1
736	Americom Imaging Systems Inc—*Dave Dillenberger*	100 Green Park Industr, Saint Louis MO 63123	314-894-1154	R	3*	<.1
737	Rjd Computers Inc—*Stephen Chien*	15870 El Prado Rd Ste, Chino CA 91708	909-393-3555	R	3*	<.1
738	Computer Solutions 2000—*Hafiz Rahaman*	1651 W Foothill Blvd D, Upland CA 91786	909-920-1233	R	3*	<.1
739	DFM Associates—*Thomas Diebolt*	10 Chrysler Ste B, Irvine CA 92618	949-859-8700	R	3*	<.1
740	Dyna Communication Corp—*Ronny Ma*	230 Paseo Sonrisa, Walnut CA 91789	909-594-6282	R	3*	<.1
741	Insideview Technologies Inc—*Umberto Milletti*	444 De Haro St Ste 210, San Francisco CA 94107	415-728-9300	R	3*	<.1
742	Office Machine Mart—*C Lee*	111 W 31st St, Kansas City MO 64108	816-756-2400	R	3*	<.1
743	Paradigm System Solutions Inc—*Jeff White*	3200 Corp Center Dr St, Burnsville MN 55306	952-882-9888	R	3*	<.1
744	Intertech Trading Corp—*Edgardo Insignares*	8933 Nw 23rd St, Doral FL 33172	305-592-8090	R	3*	<.1
745	Ne Computing Corp—*Frank Richardson*	2 Centennial Dr Ste 4b, Peabody MA 01960	978-531-9915	R	3*	<.1
746	R Associates Inc—*Herbert Riley*	6610 Gant Rd, Houston TX 77066	713-973-1500	R	3*	<.1
747	Jcomp Technologies Inc—*Robert Carns*	630 Pate St, Baraboo WI 53913	608-356-1700	R	3*	<.1
748	Point To Point Technology (USA) Inc—*Brett Haysom*	503 Interchange Blvd, Newark DE 19711	302-359-5343	R	3*	<.1
749	Floyd Thomas LLC	1300 Bluff St, Austin TX 78704	512-345-7996	R	3*	<.1
750	Mmk Trading Inc—*Mariya Kliss*	1192 Gravesend Neck Rd, Brooklyn NY 11229	718-490-1913	R	3*	<.1
751	Heatwave Interactive Inc—*Donn Clendenon*	13805 Research Blvd, Austin TX 78750	512-501-3600	R	2*	<.1
752	Azentek LLC—*Krista Hulett*	6070 S Saginaw Rd, Grand Blanc MI 48439	810-694-4500	R	2*	<.1
753	Computer Circulation Center Inc—*Elias Zeitoune*	4040 Avenida De La Pla, Oceanside CA 92056	760-724-2404	R	2*	<.1
754	Bennett/Porter and Associates Inc—*Sue Bennett*	12559 Sw 69th Ave, Tigard OR 97223	503-620-3484	R	2*	<.1
755	Computer Aided Products Inc—*Dana Seero*	2 Centennial Dr Ste 6b, Peabody MA 01960	978-977-9889	R	2*	<.1
756	Financial Modeling Specialists Inc—*Luke Chung*	8150 Lsburg Pke Ste 11, Vienna VA 22182	703-356-4700	R	2*	<.1
757	Human Scale Inc—*Bob King*	3728 S Willow Ave, Fresno CA 93725	559-459-0374	R	2*	<.1
758	S and L Computer Services Inc—*Leo Worner*	704 28th St Sw, Fargo ND 58103	701-298-3725	R	2*	<.1
759	Cistera Networks Inc—*Gregory Royal*	6509 Windcrest Dr Ste, Plano TX 75024	972-381-4699	P	2	<.1
760	EtechnologycorpCom—*Peter Kaufman*	15 Research Dr 3, Woodbridge CT 06525	203-397-5806	R	2*	<.1
761	Northland Systems Inc—*Robert Bernu*	17300 Medina Rd Ste 60, Minneapolis MN 55447	952-525-0700	R	2*	<.1
762	Elmo Data Supply Inc—*Eleanor Estes*	PO Box 691479, West Hollywood CA 90069	310-657-0140	R	2*	<.1
763	Laser Action Plus Inc—*Carmel Connor*	1228 Sw 15th Ave, Ocala FL 34471	352-622-1786	R	2*	<.1
764	Integrated Pos Inc—*Matthew Bamberg*	PO Box 127, Winnebago IL 61088	815-335-1429	R	2*	<.1
765	Data Base Architects Inc—*William Braasch*	1195 Park Ave Ste 206, Emeryville CA 94608	510-658-9900	R	2*	<.1
766	Hospitality Management Systems Inc—*Mark Carroll*	8064 Reeder St, Shawnee Mission KS 66214	913-438-5040	R	2*	<.1
767	Pssc Labs—*Janice Lesser*	20432 N Sea Cir, Lake Forest CA 92630	949-380-7288	R	2*	<.1
768	System Support Inc—*Kirby Eddie*	PO Box 71008, Clive IA 50325	515-225-7337	R	2*	<.1

Rank	Company Name—*Executive Officer*	Address, City, State, Zip	Phone	Type	Fin	Empls
769	Ecosea Adventure Inc—*Gerardo Rio*	3000 Lakewood Ln, Hollywood FL 33021	954-983-6609	R	2*	<.1
770	Infortrend Corp—*Stone Lo*	2200 Zanker Rd Ste 130, San Jose CA 95131	408-988-5088	R	2*	<.1
771	Computer Brokers USA Inc—*Ken Biggs*	1212 Taney St, North Kansas City MO 64116	816-920-5558	R	2*	<.1
772	High Tech Systems Inc—*Raymond Fouladian*	8726 S Sepulveda Blvd, Los Angeles CA 90045	310-670-8117	R	2*	<.1
773	Houston Dataflow Inc—*Randall Bell*	245 Commerce Green Blv, Sugar Land TX 77478	281-340-4700	R	2*	<.1
774	Techmart Computer Products Inc—*Eugene Cleary*	1424 Odenton Rd Ste A, Odenton MD 21113	410-674-8202	R	2*	<.1
775	ACC Inc—*Calvin Phan*	1500 Buckeye Dr, Milpitas CA 95035	408-432-8811	R	2*	<.1
776	KI Fenix Corp—*Kim Young*	19401 S Main St Ste 10, Gardena CA 90248	310-851-5888	R	2*	<.1
777	Pan-International Electronics Inc—*Sf Liu*	48010 Fremont Blvd, Fremont CA 94538	510-623-3898	R	2*	<.1
778	Cypress Technology Inc—*James Baer*	8565a Somerset Dr Ste, Largo FL 33773	727-557-0911	R	2*	<.1
779	Pfenyan Kappa International Inc—*Pao Kuo*	386 Beech Ave Ste 3, Torrance CA 90501	310-618-0433	R	2*	<.1
780	Ipt Northwest LLC	2705 E Burnside St Ste, Portland OR 97214	503-235-0664	R	2*	<.1
781	William H Buckpitt—*William Buckpitt*	PO Box 977, Taylor AZ 85939	928-536-7134	R	2*	<.1
782	Klassen Business Computer—*Joel Classen*	4955 Jeffreys St Unit, Las Vegas NV 89119	702-798-3543	R	2*	<.1
783	New England Computer Resources Inc—*Vin O'grady*	215 Brow St, Providence RI 02906	401-453-1234	R	2*	<.1
784	CQI Solutions Inc—*Roger Kelly*	555 Ih 35 Ste 310, New Braunfels TX 78130	830-620-5462	R	2*	<.1
785	Fugro-Jason Inc—*Joe Kasparek*	6100 Hillcroft St Ste, Houston TX 77081	713-369-6900	R	2*	<.1
786	Mega Computer Corp—*Peng Lim*	PO Box 270820, San Diego CA 92198	858-618-5880	R	2*	<.1
787	J Magnum Products Inc—*Warren Estlack*	575 N Rte 73 Ste A3, West Berlin NJ 08091	856-768-2500	R	2*	<.1
788	Leslie Foumberg—*Leslie Foumberg*	5115 Douglas Fir Rd St, Calabasas CA 91302	818-222-0555	R	2*	<.1
789	Handshake Software Inc—*Douglas Horton*	2222 Old St Augustine, Tallahassee FL 32301	850-877-3992	R	2*	<.1
790	Computer Aided Business Solutions Inc—*Chris Khacherian*	1750 Montgomery St Fl, San Francisco CA 94111	415-874-3048	R	2*	<.1
791	Data Information Services Systems—*Tom Swidarski*	3001 Douglas Blvd Ste, Roseville CA 95661	916-716-6400	R	2*	<.1
792	Microsystems Technology Inc—*Charles Jackson*	401 E Jackson St Ste 1, Tampa FL 33602	813-222-0414	R	2*	<.1
793	Resource Data Services Inc—*Robert Arnold*	12614 S Kroll Dr, Alsip IL 60803	708-371-6526	R	2*	<.1
794	Iskra Computers USA Inc—*Russell Mollica*	340 Franklin St, Bloomfield NJ 07003	973-566-6270	R	2*	<.1
795	Wulff Enterprise—*Scott Wulff*	8000 Frank Ave Nw, Canton OH 44720	330-478-4778	R	2*	<.1
796	American Digital Cartography Inc—*Michael F Bauer*	338 W College Ave Ste, Appleton WI 54911	920-733-6678	R	2*	<.1
797	Modern Banking Systems Inc—*Russel Smith*	3430 Lorna Ln, Birmingham AL 35216	205-823-4820	R	2*	<.1
798	Tnt Technologies Inc—*Shirley Sandell*	2530 Berryessa Rd 435, San Jose CA 95132	408-213-2080	R	2*	<.1
799	Compusource Tech Inc—*Ahmed Nawar*	1600 Integrity Dr E, Columbus OH 43209	614-444-4438	R	2*	<.1
800	Caring Health Associate—*J Mcmillan*	1863 Craig Park Ct, Saint Louis MO 63146	314-576-5187	R	2*	<.1
801	Discount Micro Sales—*Faisal Ismail*	1504 W Commwl Ave Ste, Fullerton CA 92833	714-821-3354	R	2*	<.1
802	Kopy Kat Copier—*Christine Olson*	1550 N Farnsworth Ave, Aurora IL 60505	630-851-9822	R	2*	<.1
803	American Netronic Inc—*Steven Mauss*	5212 Katella Ave Ste 1, Lakewood CA 90715	562-795-0147	S	2*	<.1
804	Advance Solutions—*Rick Oprisu*	9711 Sycamore Rd, Carmel IN 46032	317-872-9606	R	2*	<.1
805	C3 Sales Inc—*Eddie Jones*	4309 Palladio Dr, Austin TX 78731	512-418-1107	R	2*	<.1
806	Nexon Technology Distribution LLC	2005 Tree Fork Ln Ste, Longwood FL 32750	407-951-8937	R	2*	<.1
807	Alfonso Vastola—*Alfonso Vastola*	1441 E Long Pl, Centennial CO 80122	303-797-1532	R	2*	<.1
808	Apogee Data Systems—*Steven Keane*	35 Hazel Dr, Hampstead NH 03841	603-329-5676	R	2*	<.1
809	Central House Technologies—*Joseph G Rohde*	PO Box 1030, Plymouth CA 95669	209-245-5900	R	2*	<.1
810	CWC Group Inc—*Ken C Chao*	1290 E Acacia St, Ontario CA 91761	909-773-0688	R	2*	<.1
811	Hitron Systems Inc—*Yeong Choi*	1800 Wyatts Dr Ste 6, Santa Clara CA 95054	408-980-8588	R	2*	<.1
812	Input Automation Inc—*Jay O'Donnell*	2501 W 237th St Ste C, Torrance CA 90505	310-539-3598	R	2*	<.1
813	Larsen Associates Inc—*Pete Auxier*	N96 W17695 Riversbend, Germantown WI 53022	262-293-9402	R	2*	<.1
814	Dallastone System Solutions Inc—*Barry Dacks*	9422 Silhouette Ln, Jacksonville FL 32257	904-739-5844	R	2*	<.1
815	Guaranteed Solutions Inc—*James Reed*	6501 Scarlet Oak Ln, Charlotte NC 28226	704-362-5015	R	2*	<.1
816	Positive Source Inc—*Natta Haung*	1427 Mauna Kea Ln, San Jose CA 95132	408-941-9899	R	2*	<.1
817	Select Electronics Corp—*Mark Petronaci*	PO Box 3127, Winter Park FL 32790	321-638-8948	R	2*	<.1
818	Atlantis Software Inc—*Rick Gordon*	34740 Blackstone Way, Fremont CA 94555	510-796-2180	R	2*	<.1
819	Mti Tech Products Inc—*Mark Hirshberg*	7000 E Shea Blvd Ste 2, Scottsdale AZ 85254	480-850-4390	R	2*	<.1
820	PC MAX—*Lee Shornick*	PO Box 942119, Atlanta GA 31141	770-729-1418	R	2*	<.1
821	Tecmark—*Steve Schaffran*	6822 Del Monte Ave, Richmond CA 94805	510-237-5597	R	2*	<.1
822	Tt-Dav LLC	2805 Broce Dr, Norman OK 73072	405-447-5025	R	2*	<.1
823	Southwest Modern Data Systems—*David Glles*	7508 NW 40th St, Bethany OK 73008	405-789-5541	R	2*	<.1
824	Summit Design Inc (Burlington Massachusetts)—*Charles Hale*	35 Corporate Dr 4th Fl, Burlington MA 01803	781-685-4954	R	2*	<.1
825	Xpto International Inc—*Peter Yaw Lee*	120 E Oakland Park Blv, Oakland Park FL 33334	954-563-8665	R	2*	.1
826	Ambry International Ltd—*Brad Fraley*	4404 Sunbelt Dr, Addison TX 75001	214-357-5710	R	2*	<.1
827	Hospitality Control Solutions Of West Tennessee LLC—*Jane Frey*	PO Box 40308, Nashville TN 37204	615-385-4275	R	2*	<.1
828	Lionzden Inc—*Dallas Delhousaye*	PO Box 452, Laurel MT 59044	406-628-5957	R	2*	<.1
829	F and M Micro Products Inc—*Farhad Vatandoust*	6917 Woodley Ave, Van Nuys CA 91406	818-908-2080	R	2*	<.1
830	Telios Tech LLC—*Giannis Gaitanis*	26081 Merit Cir Ste 12, Laguna Hills CA 92653	949-831-8471	R	2*	<.1
831	Trans International LLC—*Mike Kahn*	2120 E Howell Ave Ste, Anaheim CA 92806	714-634-1583	R	2*	<.1
832	Digital Society Computer Center Inc—*Michael Rowe*	60 E 10th St Frnt 1, New York NY 10003	212-777-3093	R	2*	<.1
833	Abacad Inc—*Graham Wood*	222a Nicholsen Rd, Ethel WA 98542	360-864-4022	R	2*	<.1
834	Etribeca LLC	134 W 26th St Fl 8, New York NY 10001	212-219-1521	R	2*	<.1
835	Suburban Software Systems Inc—*Frank Hughes*	2800 Dartmouth Ave, Bessemer AL 35020	205-481-4440	R	2*	<.1
836	Bangert Computer Systems Inc—*Kurt Bangert*	706 Jefferson St, Burlington IA 52601	319-752-5484	R	2*	<.1
837	Kelly Computer Supply Company LLC—*Ray Blau*	3584 Hoffman Rd E, Saint Paul MN 55110	651-773-1109	R	2*	<.1
838	Computer Solutions Group Inc—*David Rodrigues*	2740 Wyming Blvd Ne St, Albuquerque NM 87111	505-345-8000	R	2*	<.1
839	Greendata Inc—*Passam Yusef*	8501 Nw 17th St, Doral FL 33166	305-592-9225	R	2*	<.1
840	Siso International USA Corp—*Peter Chen*	260 W Arrow Hwy Ste F, San Dimas CA 91773	909-394-3055	R	2*	<.1
841	EDP Computer Systems—*Karl Nelson*	410 Main St W, Cannon Falls MN 55009	507-263-5849	R	2*	<.1
842	Casing Inc—*Henry Lai*	5 Chris Ct Ste G, Dayton NJ 08810	732-438-6150	R	2*	<.1
843	Praxis Engineering Products LLC—*Kelly Hall*	135 National Business, Annapolis Junction MD 20701	301-490-4299	R	2*	<.1
844	People Signs—*Charles Kelly*	1857 W Walnut St, Allentown PA 18104	610-434-3613	R	2*	<.1
845	Fmaudit LLC	PO Box 6760, Jefferson City MO 65102	573-632-2461	R	2*	<.1
846	Us Positioning Group—*Edward Rose*	5810 S Sossaman Rd Ste, Mesa AZ 85212	480-988-1000	R	2*	<.1
847	GMS International Inc—*David Rockower*	7 Reuten Dr Ste F, Closter NJ 07624	201-568-8600	R	2*	<.1
848	American Computer Resources Inc—*Hubert Bowen*	10 Montagne Dr, Shelton CT 06484	203-402-0420	R	2*	<.1
849	Computer Quick Corp—*Josh Daniels*	500 Tamal Plz Ste 504, Corte Madera CA 94925	415-945-1770	R	2*	<.1
850	A Prompt Corp—*Risa Stolly*	PO Box 20463, Lehigh Valley PA 18002	610-770-9204	R	2*	<.1
851	Jpmc Inc—*Jimmy Chau*	1016 Lawson St Ste B, City Of Industry CA 91748	626-839-5633	R	2*	<.1
852	Bluesky Capital Partners LLC	65 Water St Ste 2, Worcester MA 01604	508-449-3864	R	2*	<.1
853	Pps Plus Software—*John Shinn*	PO Box 8906, Biloxi MS 39535	228-594-9660	R	2*	<.1
854	Active Endpoints—*Mark Taber*	3 Enterprise Dr Ste 41, Shelton CT 06484	203-929-9400	R	2*	<.1
855	R and N Leasing Inc—*Nathan Kraiem*	472 E 101st St, Brooklyn NY 11236	718-257-0800	R	2*	<.1
856	Young Computer Technologies—*Michael Young*	15043 Gaffney Cir, Gainesville VA 20155	202-486-3228	R	2*	<.1
857	Softel USA—*Sam Pemberton*	800 Connecticut Ave 1e, Norwalk CT 06854	203-354-4602	R	2*	<.1

Note: An asterisk (*) indicates an estimated financial figure. The company type code used is as follows: R = Private, P = Public, S = Private Subsidiary, B = Public Subsidiary, D = Division, J = Joint Venture, I = Investment Fund.

COMPANY RANKINGS BY SALES WITHIN 4-DIGIT SIC

Rank	Company Name—*Executive Officer*	Address, City, State, Zip	Phone	Type	Fin	Empls
858	Ac Marketing Inc—*Yu-Chu Cheng*	4601 Telephone Rd Ste, Ventura CA 93003	805-650-6728	R	2*	<.1
859	Epac Software Technologies Inc—*Paul Oberg*	42 Ladd St Ste 316, East Greenwich RI 02818	401-884-5512	R	2*	<.1
860	Leoleo International Inc—*Lawrence Tu*	1411 E Campbell Rd Ste, Richardson TX 75081	972-680-3373	R	2*	<.1
861	Professional Computer Solutions Inc—*Brad Timberlake*	434 W 2nd St, Ottumwa IA 52501	641-682-4691	R	2*	<.1
862	Sunnytech—*Kevin Yuan*	2 Gill St J, Woburn MA 01801	978-658-8500	R	2*	<.1
863	Techlan Inc—*Leland Lee*	4794 Mercer University, Macon GA 31210	478-477-1541	R	2*	<.1
864	Miracle Tv Corp—*Miguel Kramis*	810 Hwy 6 S Ste 145, Houston TX 77079	281-646-1650	R	2*	<.1
865	Custom Computer Solutions Inc—*Gerard Nappi*	51 Monroe Ave, Toms River NJ 08755	732-473-0066	R	2*	<.1
866	Global Midrange Technologies Inc—*Michael Henderson*	6882 Edgewatr Commerce, Orlando FL 32810	407-521-5468	R	2*	<.1
867	Westech Recyclers Inc—*Earl Knudsen*	1008 W Madison St, Phoenix AZ 85007	602-256-7626	R	2*	<.1
868	Computer Management Corp—*Rita Wen*	56 Ethel Rd.W Ste 10, Piscataway NJ 08854	732-985-0100	R	2*	<.1
869	Prodecom International Corp—*Carlos Silva*	9990 Nw 14th St Ste 10, Miami FL 33172	305-715-7272	R	2*	<.1
870	A and P Enterprises Inc—*Richard Fan*	28281 Somerset, Mission Viejo CA 92692	949-581-2892	R	2*	<.1
871	Compufox USA Corp—*Rachid Elkhamlichi*	7601 E Treasure Dr Ste, North Bay Village FL 33141	305-865-8517	R	2*	<.1
872	Balco Enterprises Inc—*Lawrence Schneider*	3526 White Ct, Torrance CA 90503	310-370-4142	R	2*	<.1
873	Pci Micro Corp—*Wing Li*	2919 Westbourne Pl, Rowland Heights CA 91748	626-839-6043	R	2*	<.1
874	Nextwarehouse Inc—*Yi Juan*	14712 Franklin Ave Ste, Tustin CA 92780		R	2*	<.1
875	Quimbik Inc—*Joe Bella*	340 Brannan St Ste 300, San Francisco CA 94107	415-227-0773	R	2*	<.1
876	Scicom Inc—*Deanne Mcevoy*	123 S St Ste 103, Oyster Bay NY 11771	516-922-7154	R	2*	<.1
877	Touchstone Technologies Inc—*Mark Stacey*	1500 Industry Rd Ste H, Hatfield PA 19440	267-222-8687	R	2*	<.1
878	Accelerated Data Systems Inc—*Travis Justus*	5295 Dtc Pkwy, Greenwood Village CO 80111	303-706-1101	R	2*	<.1
879	Aerionx Inc—*Mark Jones*	1375 Greg St Ste 108, Sparks NV 89431	775-359-1500	R	2*	<.1
880	Howell and Howell Inc—*Howard Hsieh*	39 Haddonfield Rd, Cherry Hill NJ 08002	856-488-1245	R	2*	<.1
881	Mini Computer Services Inc—*Samir Zebian*	91 Bartlett St Ste 1, Marlborough MA 01752	508-624-5500	R	2*	<.1
882	Advanced Technologies Research Group Inc—*Eugene Laykthman*	307 7th Ave Rm 707, New York NY 10001	212-620-4170	R	2*	<.1
883	Computer Lab Inc—*Ronald Gibson*	345 Broad St, New London CT 06320	860-447-1079	R	2*	<.1
884	Blue Star Computer Corp—*Kenneth Smith*	7 October Hill Rd Ste, Holliston MA 01746	508-429-3001	R	2*	<.1
885	Bridge Associates Inc—*Richard Kontrimas*	600 N Batavia St, Orange CA 92868	714-744-8400	R	2*	<.1
886	Computer Supplies Inc—*Taylor Quarles*	3069 Mccall Dr Ste 14, Atlanta GA 30340	770-986-0135	R	2*	<.1
887	Netkomp—*Madan Dhamija*	16113 Copperhead Ct, Fontana CA 92336	909-350-4655	R	2*	<.1
888	System One International Inc—*Carlos Roman*	7509 Yardley Way, Tampa FL 33647	813-972-5539	R	2*	<.1
889	RH Enterprises—*Richard Hamilton*	650 Partridge Dr, West Chicago IL 60185	630-876-1376	R	2*	<.1
890	Sure Scan Inc—*John Ryan*	9631 W 153rd St Ste 32, Orland Park IL 60462	708-226-0002	R	2*	<.1
891	Energy Technology Solutions LLC	8 Falling Water Ct, Reisterstown MD 21136	410-453-0080	R	1*	<.1
892	Cluster Systems LLC—*Laxmi Ram*	68 Spruce Ln Ste 203, Haledon NJ 07508	973-423-2265	R	1*	<.1
893	Intellimagic Inc—*Gilbert Houtekamer*	558 Silicon Dr Ste 101, Southlake TX 76092	214-432-7920	R	1*	<.1
894	Computer Choices Inc—*Michael Mooney*	8302 Old Courthouse Rd, Vienna VA 22182	703-790-3600	R	1*	<.1
895	CAD/CAM Systems Inc—*James Epperson*	5291 28th Ave, Rockford IL 61109	815-399-4433	R	1*	<.1
896	Etech Micro Supply Inc—*En Chen*	1019 Prouty Way, San Jose CA 95129	408-255-2525	R	1*	<.1
897	Hte Inc—*Daniel Reed*	1100 N Opdyke Rd Ste 3, Auburn Hills MI 48326	248-371-1918	R	1*	<.1
898	On-Line Computing Inc—*Ted Murphy*	5210 Maryland Way Ste, Brentwood TN 37027	615-377-1000	R	1*	<.1
899	Acu-Tek Solutions Inc—*Carter Smith*	1560 Superior Ave Ste, Costa Mesa CA 92627	949-554-1560	R	1*	<.1
900	Complete Inspection Systems Inc—*Lana Blakeney*	334 4th Ave, Indialantic FL 32903	321-952-2490	R	1*	<.1
901	Mars International Inc—*Kumar Setty*	465 Boston Tpke Ste D-, Shrewsbury MA 01545	508-842-3932	R	1*	<.1
902	Wintel Corp—*Sergio Morantes*	2741 Nw 82nd Ave, Doral FL 33122	305 599-1191	R	1*	<.1
903	Macdaddy Computers—*Tim Hackman*	1321 Mchenry Ave Ste A, Modesto CA 95350	209-527-6227	R	1*	<.1
904	Westwood Computers LLC	15500 Erwin St Ste 400, Van Nuys CA 91411	818-988-0161	R	1*	<.1
905	Notebook Computers Inc—*Zack Alawi*	3213 Duke St, Alexandria VA 22314	703-823-8325	R	1*	<.1
906	Quantum Systems International Corp—*Eli Willner*	95 Rockwell Pl, Brooklyn NY 11217	718-834-4545	R	1*	<.1
907	Esp Computers And Software Inc—*Brian Rummel*	26 W Villard St, Dickinson ND 58601	701-225-6884	R	1*	<.1
908	Clark Management Services Inc—*Paul Sahni*	53-59 Westfield Ave, Clark NJ 07066	732-396-9500	R	1*	<.1
909	Compupack Inc—*Phuoc-Long Huynh*	7101 Rainbow Dr Apt 5, San Jose CA 95129	408-446-1868	R	1*	<.1
910	Data Tech Computer Services Inc—*Cynthia Dayton*	5910 Gateway Dr Ste C, Alpharetta GA 30004	770-772-0200	R	1*	<.1
911	Mediawave Inc—*David Hwang*	46755 Fremont Blvd, Fremont CA 94538	510-490-6768	R	1*	<.1
912	Ami Corp—*Tony Marcon*	3910 S Decatur St, Englewood CO 80110	303-761-3999	R	1*	<.1
913	Lynxtron Connections—*Mark Hanna*	972 Rincon Cir, San Jose CA 95131	408-577-0328	R	1*	<.1
914	Innovative Inc—*Jason Rappaport*	222 E Oak Ridge Dr Ste, Hagerstown MD 21740	301-739-7414	R	1*	<.1
915	Taylor Technology Inc—*Joseph Taylor*	PO Box 302, Chalfont PA 18914	215-357-9370	R	1*	<.1
916	Cebtt Inc—*Takahiro Shintani*	PO Box 3615, Seattle WA 98124	206-679-1855	R	1*	<.1
917	Comp America Inc—*Hari Maddur*	13800 Coppermine Rd, Herndon VA 20171	571-203-1400	R	1*	<.1
918	Innovative Technology Ltd—*R Sorelle*	PO Box 726, Elk City OK 73648	580-243-1559	R	1*	<.1
919	Greatmark—*Michael Klein*	110 Bell Canyon Rd, Bell Canyon CA 91307	310-753-9327	R	1*	<.1
920	Rg Technology—*Cheryl Coffey*	607 California Ave, Pittsburgh PA 15202	412-761-3699	R	1*	<.1
921	360 Vantage LLC—*Nino Davi*	3165 S Price Rd, Chandler AZ 85248	480-335-8230	R	1*	<.1
922	Unotron Inc—*Joseph Carabello*	2515 Willowbrook Rd St, Dallas TX 75220	972-438-8900	R	1*	<.1
923	Buy Direct Corp—*Kevin Lye*	1829 S Broadway, Los Angeles CA 90015	213-749-3019	R	1*	<.1
924	Decurtis Corp—*David Decurtis*	2314 Longmoore Ct, Orlando FL 32835	407-522-8722	R	1*	<.1
925	Olympic Software—*Bill Mcnaughton*	PO Box 4008, Auburn WA 98063	253-946-2690	R	1*	<.1
926	Wisdom Way LLC—*Rose Connell*	6624 Gulton Ct Ne, Albuquerque NM 87109	505-314-2500	R	1*	<.1
927	Computer Intelligence Association Inc—*Ray Rashidian*	10425 Dalebrooke Ln, Potomac MD 20854	301-762-1051	R	1*	<.1
928	Critical Power Services Inc—*Britt Harris*	4732 Lebanon Rd Ste C, Mint Hill NC 28227	704-545-8658	R	1*	<.1
929	Guestclick Inc—*Aaron Shepherd*	3301 Bonita Beach Rd S, Bonita Springs FL 34134	239-498-3558	R	1*	<.1
930	Offis Corp—*Richard Harvey*	61 N Plains Industrial, Wallingford CT 06492	203-265-6700	R	1*	<.1
931	Redsis Corp—*Mario Habib*	12233 Sw 55th St Ste 8, Cooper City FL 33330	954-252-5043	R	1*	<.1
932	Hi-Tech Distribution Inc—*Craig Cox*	19968 W 162nd St, Olathe KS 66062	913-338-4808	R	1*	<.1
933	Symerix Business Essentials Inc—*Eric Goodman*	237 W 35th St, New York NY 10001	212-736-5868	R	1*	<.1
934	Integration Computers Inc—*Mike Sung*	3909 Saint Timothy Ln, Saint Ann MO 63074	314-426-5987	R	1*	<.1
935	Polymath Inc—*David Guckenberger*	830 Armour Rd Ste 1b, Oconomowoc WI 53066	262-569-1200	R	1*	<.1
936	Lpc Technology Inc—*Timothy Lin*	243 Paseo Sonrisa, Walnut CA 91789	909-598-1266	R	1*	<.1
937	Comertec LLC—*Carmen Bernier*	2371 Sw 195th Ave, Miramar FL 33029	954-442-0500	R	1*	<.1
938	Computing Solutions Inc—*Kenneth Stokes*	PO Box 9, Indian Trail NC 28079	704-289-4499	R	1*	<.1
939	Opinionmeter Inc—*Robert Strickland*	4720 La Vlla Mrina Uni, Marina Del Rey CA 90292	310-821-4126	R	1*	<.1
940	Commercial Micro-Systems Inc—*Robert Hestenes*	3547 Old Conejo Rd Ste, Newbury Park CA 91320	805-499-7561	R	1*	<.1
941	New England Computer Remarketing Inc—*Steve Lombari*	238 Rockingham Rd Ste, Derry NH 03038	603-437-7400	R	1*	<.1
942	Triaxis Inc—*Tom Mumford*	642 Hilliard St Ste 11, Manchester CT 06042		R	1*	<.1
943	Desktop Services Inc—*David Wheelock*	18889 Santa Catherine, Fountain Valley CA 92708	714-444-1444	R	1*	<.1
944	ABC Enterprise Systems Inc—*Simon A Kniveton*	2033 Gateway Pl Ste 50, San Jose CA 95110	408-961-8708	S	1	.1
945	Ameri-Cad Inc—*Jimmy Moore*	202 E Bethany Dr, Allen TX 75002	972-747-7880	R	1*	<.1
946	Cypress Inland Corp—*James Harris*	6262 Red Canyon Dr Rm, Littleton CO 80130	303-317-8195	R	1	<.1

Rank	Company Name—*Executive Officer*	Address, City, State, Zip	Phone	Type	Fin	Empls
947	Diverse Technology Solutions Inc—*MC Hart IV*	2949 Sunrise Hwy, Islip Terrace NY 11752	631-224-1200	R	1*	<.1
948	Sun Moon Star	17800 Castleton St Ste, City of Industry CA 91748	626-854-5157	R	1*	<.1
949	Dateapp Inc—*Cataldi John-Michael*	5885 Cumming Hwy Ste 1, Sugar Hill GA 30518	678-318-3696	R	1*	<.1
950	Gene-IT USA—*Richard Resnick*	1700 West Park Dr Ste, Westborough MA 01581	508-616-0100	R	1*	<.1
951	H and H Computers—*Roger Hoss*	4616 Roseville Rd Ste, North Highlands CA 95660	916-362-4884	R	1*	<.1
952	Liconix Industries Inc	78-35 Springfield Blvd, Oakland Gardens NY 11364	718-217-7900	R	1*	<.1
953	Audioscribe Corp—*Adria Johnson*	PO Box 321, Breaux Bridge LA 70517	337-332-0680	R	1*	<.1
954	Forsythe and Associates Inc—*Mike Forsythe*	5931 Nieman Rd Ste 200, Shawnee KS 66203	913-631-1221	R	1*	<.1
955	Multipath Corp—*Ronald Young*	PO Box 8210, Incline Village NV 89450	775-831-4400	R	1*	<.1
956	Peak Computer Solutions—*Vince Chiechi*	25031 Ave Stanford Ste, Valencia CA 91355	818-240-0036	R	1*	<.1
957	A and S Electronics Inc—*Alan Lin*	372 Turquoise St, Milpitas CA 95035	408-582-5000	R	1*	<.1
958	Delta Marketing Group Inc—*Michael Hankerson*	16410 N 91st St Ste 10, Scottsdale AZ 85260	480-367-6698	R	1*	<.1
959	Network Access Corp (Pittsburgh Pennsylvania)—*Jim Barnes*	4580 McKnight Rd, Pittsburgh PA 15237	412-931-1111	R	1*	<.1
960	Aeromatrix Inc—*Ming Xu*	10500 Nw 29th Ter, Doral FL 33172	305-477-6333	R	1*	<.1
961	Barrington Enterprises Inc—*Fereydoun Shoraka*	17975 Sky Park Cir Ste, Irvine CA 92614	949-261-9771	R	1*	<.1
962	Bridgeway Systems Inc—*Frederick Schuchardt*	4040 Civic Ctr Dr Ste, San Rafael CA 94903	415-492-1484	R	1*	<.1
963	Alpha Base Systems Inc—*Barry Weingart*	1898 N Stanley Ave, Los Angeles CA 90046	323-850-6575	R	1*	<.1
964	Crucial Computers Inc—*Brian Galasso*	200 Washington St, Madison VA 22727	540-948-6424	R	1*	<.1
965	DMD Systems Recovery Inc—*Morris Scott*	1315 E Gibson Ln Bldg, Phoenix AZ 85034	602-307-0180	R	1*	<.1
966	Portable One Inc—*Ivan Gospich*	5627 Stoneridge Dr Ste, Pleasanton CA 94588	925-924-0558	R	1*	<.1
967	Rohr Systems Inc—*Bruce Hyman*	5033 Industrial Rd Ste, Wall Township NJ 07727	732-751-2700	R	1*	<.1
968	Sharevis Inc—*Nail Sudin*	701 Palomar Airport Rd, Carlsbad CA 92011	760-230-2771	R	1*	<.1
969	Vivek Systems Inc—*Bose Vivek*	2163 Avon Industrial D, Rochester Hills MI 48309	248-293-1070	R	1*	<.1
970	Creative Technology Services Group LLC	4809 Ewell Rd Ste 100, Fredericksburg VA 22408	540-891-0700	R	1*	<.1
971	Expert Technology Group Inc—*Lizbell Rincon*	5987 Nw 102nd Ave, Doral FL 33178	305-500-9374	R	1*	<.1
972	Internet 123 Inc—*Dan Irvin*	24275 Northwestern Hwy, Southfield MI 48075	586-716-1700	R	1*	<.1
973	Ckot Inc—*Rick Corcoran*	33 Main St Ste 302, Nashua NH 03064	603-889-0800	R	1*	<.1
974	Emerald Datacom Products Inc—*Donald Tittle*	PO Box 5534, River Forest IL 60305	708-366-7800	R	1*	<.1
975	Form First Inc—*Christopher Whan*	13309 Bridgeview Way, Mount Vernon WA 98273	360-336-1593	R	1*	<.1
976	Impression Technology Inc—*Adrian J Van Meir*	250 East Dr Ste E, Melbourne FL 32904	321-254-8700	R	1*	<.1
977	Independent Technologies LLC—*Greg Myhre*	60 N Dr, East Brunswick NJ 08816	732-735-6520	R	1*	<.1
978	Keyways Inc—*R Miller*	204 S 3rd St, Miamisburg OH 45342	937-847-2300	R	1*	<.1
979	Parts Port Inc—*Cathy Sebastian*	10605-C Patterson Ave, Richmond VA 23238	804-750-1444	R	1*	<.1
980	BCSR Inc—*Dan Hiatt*	2020 124th Ave NE Ste, Bellevue WA 98005	425-823-1188	R	1*	<.1
981	Echo Imaging Inc—*Barbara Milloy*	2645 Wooster Rd, Rocky River OH 44116	440-356-4720	R	1*	<.1
982	Cyperceptions Inc—*Steve Jones*	7 Jones Ave, Flourtown PA 19031	215-886-4718	R	1*	<.1
983	Network Spectrum Inc—*Josefine Lecuyer*	111 Lepes Rd, Portsmouth RI 02871		R	1*	<.1
984	Larry Moxon—*Larry Moxon*	338 Indigo St, Mystic CT 06355	860-536-8200	R	1*	<.1
985	Autochart Inc—*Harding Orin*	703 Pleasant Dr, Greensboro NC 27410	336-601-8410	R	1*	<.1
986	Premiere Computer Systems Inc—*Serge Remillard*	125 Commerce Cir, Fayetteville GA 30214	770-461-6500	R	1*	<.1
987	Abc Technical Solutions Inc—*Rick Walker*	1054 31st St Nw Ste 41, Washington DC 20007	202-393-5999	R	1*	<.1
988	Jd Research Inc—*Amy Wang*	1247 N Glassell St Ste, Orange CA 92867	714-282-3995	R	1*	<.1
989	Linktek Corp—*David Greenbaum*	1005 Drew St, Clearwater FL 33765	727-442-1822	R	1*	<.1
990	Yas Corp—*Yasmin Majd*	79 Newbury St Ste 200, Boston MA 02116	617-585-9999	R	1*	<.1
991	Acl Computers Inc—*Ana Lomas*	1711 W 38th Pl Ste 110, Hialeah FL 33012	305-826-5000	R	1*	<.1
992	Jjc Group Inc—*Margaret Gadbois*	1335 Lakeside Dr Unit, Romeoville IL 60446	630-226-5800	R	1*	<.1
993	World Computer Inc—*Deborah Hunter*	2438 N Pantano Rd, Tucson AZ 85715	520-327-2881	R	1*	<.1
994	Main Street Technologies—*Michele Wion*	PO Box 4000, Angels Camp CA 95221	209-736-2712	R	1*	<.1
995	Wound Management Technologies Inc—*Scott A Haire*	777 Main St Ste 3100, Fort Worth TX 76102	817-820-7080	P	1	<.1
996	Skyvantage Corp—*Cory Robin*	5526 W 13400 S Ste 207, Herriman UT 84096	801-649-2925	R	1*	<.1
997	Techsoft Inc—*Navin Gupta*	900 Briggs Rd Ste 410, Mount Laurel NJ 08054	856-642-7500	R	1*	<.1
998	HZS Inc—*Henry Schwarz*	64 Parsons Ave, Columbus OH 43215	614-228-3636	R	1*	<.1
999	Bto Servers Inc—*George Lai*	322 Paseo Sonrisa, Walnut CA 91789	909-839-0363	R	1*	<.1
1000	Dj Power International LLC—*Saied Motaei*	360 Childe Dr, Colorado Springs CO 80906	719-527-6937	R	1*	<.1
1001	Comp-U-Tech Of America Inc—*Eddie Berez*	157 Kings Hwy, Brooklyn NY 11223	718-236-9222	R	1*	<.1
1002	Laserland Inc—*Steven Michlin*	2655 Orchard Lake Rd S, Sylvan Lake MI 48320	248-738-5800	R	1*	<.1
1003	Multimedia Express Inc—*Ivy Chi*	1714 Ringwood Ave, San Jose CA 95131	408-573-1011	R	1*	<.1
1004	Princeton Display Technologies Inc—*Suprasad Baidyaroy*	812 State Rd Ste 206, Princeton NJ 08540	609-430-0690	R	1*	<.1
1005	Security Lab Inc—*Mark Pursley*	PO Box 326, Colleyville TX 76034	972-243-2000	R	1*	<.1
1006	TAC Computer Inc—*Tom Craven*	7603 First Pl Ste 10, Bedford OH 44146	440-232-2555	R	1*	<.1
1007	Hasco/Graphix Inc—*Robert Lee*	23040 Miles Rd, Cleveland OH 44128	216-662-7474	R	1*	<.1
1008	Imogen Corp—*Tammy Montgomery*	9580 Oak Ave Pkwy Ste, Folsom CA 95630	916-988-2950	R	1*	<.1
1009	ITS Barcode Solutions—*Juan Merchant*	259 Northland Blvd 315, Cincinnati OH 45246	513-772-5252	R	1*	<.1
1010	First Capital International Inc—*Alex Genin*	5120 Woodway Dr Ste 90, Houston TX 77056	713-629-4866	P	1	<.1
1011	Ndev Technology—*Dennis Scholler*	9201 N 25th Ave Ste 26, Phoenix AZ 85021	602-749-9933	R	1*	<.1
1012	Act Iii Office Supplies LLC	484 W 43rd St Apt 36m, New York NY 10036	212-868-1813	R	1*	<.1
1013	Application Consultants Inc—*Dianne Grundy*	PO Box 915770, Longwood FL 32791	407-788-0877	R	1*	<.1
1014	Applied Chemometrics Inc—*Richard Kramer*	PO Box 100, Sharon MA 02067	781-784-7700	R	1*	<.1
1015	Archon Distribution Inc—*Richard Patel*	361 Franklin Ave, Nutley NJ 07110	973-667-3001	R	1*	<.1
1016	Future Information Design—*Bill Williams*	1517 N Wilmot Rd 233, Tucson AZ 85712	520-327-1415	R	1*	<.1
1017	Image Computer Products—*Michael Clayton*	16 Hughes Ste 104, Irvine CA 92618	949-837-7794	R	1*	<.1
1018	Simon Systems Inc—*Don Christensen*	323 Lake Hazeltine Dr, Chaska MN 55318	952-448-9922	R	1*	<.1
1019	Blue Wire Networks Inc—*Surinder Singh*	PO Box 295, Concord CA 94522	925-680-9700	R	1*	<.1
1020	Calcomp Graphics LLC	26741 Portola Pkwy Ste, Foothill Ranch CA 92610	949-589-0053	R	1*	<.1
1021	Columbia Data Systems Inc—*Stephen Baker*	PO Box 864, Columbia TN 38402	931-381-4616	R	1*	<.1
1022	Geologic Computer Systems Inc—*Charles Julian*	2505 Williams Dr, Waterford MI 48328	248-335-8863	R	1*	<.1
1023	Micro Parts and Supplies Inc—*Eugene Brown*	9606 Fox Shores Dr, Algonquin IL 60102	847-516-0191	R	1*	<.1
1024	Thomas Tran—*Thomas Tran*	3513 Main St Ste 104, Chula Vista CA 91911	619-407-6710	R	1*	<.1
1025	Technical Education Solutions LLC	64 Benz St, Ansonia CT 06401	203-732-3600	R	1*	<.1
1026	Texas Media Systems Ltd—*Ronald Nixon*	4311 Medical Pkwy, Austin TX 78756	512-440-1400	R	1*	<.1
1027	Kypipe LLC	3229 Brighton Pl Dr, Lexington KY 40509	859-263-2234	R	1*	<.1
1028	Mdg Studio Inc—*Jorge Mateo*	3900 Shamrock St W, Tallahassee FL 32309	850-576-2239	R	1*	<.1
1029	21st Century Computer Inc—*Brian Harper*	3148 Staunton Tpke, Parkersburg WV 26104	304-485-6823	R	1*	<.1
1030	Circo Technology Corp—*Eric Lin*	20454 Carrey Rd, Walnut CA 91789	909-468-3790	R	1*	<.1
1031	Memosun Inc—*Diana Kong*	17665 Newhope St Ste A, Fountain Valley CA 92708	714-424-3900	R	1*	<.1
1032	Vita-Charge—*Bill Digirolamo*	2510 Ligonier St, Latrobe PA 15650	724-537-2375	R	1*	<.1
1033	Wrk Technologies Inc—*Bill Kaltwasser*	PO Box 1084, Du Bois PA 15801	814-375-9130	R	1*	<.1
1034	Ampem Electronics and Services Inc—*Amar Agarwal*	PO Box 721200, Houston TX 77272	281-568-5100	R	1*	<.1
1035	Industrial Data Entry Automation Systems Inc—*John Hattersley*	27 Fennell St, Skaneateles NY 13152	315-685-8311	R	1*	<.1
1036	i Brands Corp—*Paul R Smith*	PO Box 5085, Canton GA 30114		P	1	<.1

Note: An asterisk (*) indicates an estimated financial figure. The company type code used is as follows: R = Private, P = Public, S = Private Subsidiary, B = Public Subsidiary, D = Division, J = Joint Venture, I = Investment Fund.

COMPANY RANKINGS BY SALES WITHIN 4-DIGIT SIC

Rank	Company Name—*Executive Officer*	Address, City, State, Zip	Phone	Type	Fin	Empls
1037	Linkspace LLC	PO Box 455, Mc Lean VA 22101	703-848-9841	R	1*	<.1
1038	Mossor Computers—*Craig Mossor*	6299 Dressler Rd Nw St, Canton OH 44720	330-966-3825	R	1*	<.1
1039	Ariel Design Inc—*Glenn Brodie*	9 W End Way, Norwell MA 02061	781-982-8800	R	1*	<.1
1040	Channel Group Inc—*Charles Satuloff*	12 Seneca Trl, Harrison NY 10528	914-835-1400	R	1*	<.1
1041	Risenheart Consulting—*James Walters*	1414 Williams Blvd, Richland WA 99354	509-943-8685	R	1*	<.1
1042	Webicing Inc—*Robert Braun*	9815 Sam Furr Rd J304, Huntersville NC 28078	704-992-6171	R	1*	<.1
1043	Eastex Laser Corp—*Annette Baldwin*	PO Box 218481, Houston TX 77218	281-579-2500	R	1*	<.1
1044	Miamibras Inc—*Celso Lopes*	10431 Nw 28th St Ste E, Doral FL 33172	305-594-0227	R	1*	<.1
1045	Cpi Technologies Inc—*Robert Rose*	2625 Walnut St, Harrisburg PA 17103	717-214-5274	R	1*	<.1
1046	PC Distributors LLC	3611 Sycamore Dairy Rd, Fayetteville NC 28303	910-867-4171	R	1*	<.1
1047	Target Micro Inc—*Bernardo De La Espriella*	9990 Nw 14th St Ste 11, Miami FL 33172	305-597-9798	R	1*	<.1
1048	Chenex Inc—*Michael Chen*	1840 W Whittier Blvd 3, La Habra CA 90631	562-697-8231	R	1*	<.1
1049	Circa Inc—*John Taylor*	7608 N Hudson Ave, Oklahoma City OK 73116	405-751-8806	R	1*	<.1
1050	Ferotech Solution Services Inc—*Ahsan Khan*	6816 N Frostwd Pkwy St, Peoria IL 61615	309-589-0342	R	<1*	<.1
1051	Techone Trading Company Inc—*Greg Harper*	4951 Airport Pkwy Ste, Addison TX 75001	972-490-6666	R	<1*	<.1
1052	Bek Tronic Technology Inc—*Triple Chiang*	15 Kent Pl Ste 1, Pompton Plains NJ 07444	973-628-7778	R	<1*	<.1
1053	E - Micro Inc—*Mee Kim*	2455 Waterbury Ln, Buffalo Grove IL 60089	847-478-1714	R	<1*	<.1
1054	Miami Micro Export Inc—*Salvadore Boria*	2648 Nw 112th Ave, Doral FL 33172	305-599-0056	R	<1*	<.1
1055	Alante Corp—*Bruno Van Den Bosch*	1156 York Ln, Saint Helena CA 94574	707-967-4100	R	<1*	<.1
1056	CR Electronics Inc—*Christopher Rahilly*	PO Box 1210, Seabrook NH 03874	603-474-5600	R	<1*	<.1
1057	East West Trading Corp—*Paul Kavalchuk*	PO Box 559, Rye NH 03870	603-427-6545	R	<1*	<.1
1058	International Purchasing and Supply Inc—*Nicholas Mouttet*	4709 Nw 72nd Ave, Miami FL 33166	305-629-8449	R	<1*	<.1
1059	Cardio Logic Inc—*David Kuo*	1200 Industrial Rd Ste, San Carlos CA 94070	650-622-9078	R	<1*	<.1
1060	Distraction Media LLC—*Matthew Lindenburg*	3235 Nw 66th St, Seattle WA 98117	206-297-6030	R	<1*	<.1
1061	Jem Systems Inc—*Joe Schmidt*	10078 Flanders Ct Ne S, Minneapolis MN 55449	763-788-2100	R	<1*	<.1
1062	Multi Metrics Inc—*William Tandler*	865 Lemon St, Menlo Park CA 94025	650-328-0200	R	<1*	<.1
1063	Softel Systems Inc—*Tahir Mahmood*	8824 217th St, Queens Village NY 11427	718-740-4689	R	<1*	<.1
1064	Icomputerland LLC	60 Newtown Rd Ste 4, Danbury CT 06810	203-778-1100	R	<1*	<.1
1065	Laser Resource—*Rama Khanna*	1340 Fulton Pl, Fremont CA 94539	415-989-2404	R	<1*	<.1
1066	World Insulation and Chemicals Inc—*Henry Wroblewski*	1120 Mitchell Rd, Schenectady NY 12303	518-377-3377	R	<1*	<.1
1067	Lion's Den Software—*Raymond Kerney*	335 Candlewood Lake Rd, Brookfield CT 06804	203-775-1315	R	<1*	<.1
1068	Salima Technologies—*Nadia Boumaza*	1103 Huntridge Cir, Austin TX 78758	512-834-0542	R	<1*	<.1
1069	SinglesourceitCom Inc—*Josh Davda*	100 E Campus View Blvd, Columbus OH 43235	614-930-2300	R	<1*	<.1
1070	Matrix Integration—*Brenda Stallings*	417 Main St, Jasper IN 47546	812-634-1550	R	<1	.3
1071	Siscom Inc—*Bruce Cornet*	130 W Second St Ste 11, Dayton OH 45402	937-222-8150	R	<1	<.1
1072	Non Literal Inc—*Chuck Lawson*	3303 Lemmontree Ln, Plano TX 75074	214-764-3836	R	<1*	<.1
1073	Object Nirvana Inc—*Michael Mcray*	510 Old Bonhomme Rd, Saint Louis MO 63130	314-863-6770	R	<1*	<.1
1074	Ontario Corp—*Tony Reisz*	1150 W Kilgore Ave, Muncie IN 47305	765-751-7000	R	<1	N/A
1075	MindTouch Inc—*Aaron Fulkerson*	401 W A St Ste 250, San Diego CA 92101	619-795-8459	R	N/A	<.1

TOTALS: SIC 5045 Computers, Peripherals & Software
Companies: 1,075   156,585   147.9

5046 Commercial Equipment Nec

Rank	Company Name—*Executive Officer*	Address, City, State, Zip	Phone	Type	Fin	Empls
1	Strategic Equipment and Supply Corp—*Jeff Hull*	5010 Riverside Dr Ste, Irving TX 75039	972-401-5300	R	1,222*	.5
2	HB Communications—*Mackey Barron*	60 Dodge Ave, North Haven CT 06473	203-234-9246	R	829*	.4
3	Enprotech Corp—*Pedro Garcia*	4259 E 49th St, Cleveland OH 44125	216-206-0081	S	518*	.1
4	Maines Paper and Food Service Inc Equipment and Supply Div—*Christopher Mellon*	101 Broome Corporate P, Conklin NY 13748	607-779-1200	D	486*	1.7
5	For-A-Corporation of America—*Keizo Kiyohara*	11155 Knott Ave Ste H, Cypress CA 90630	714-894-3311	R	441*	.2
6	Kanawha Scales and Systems—*Jim Bradbury*	PO Box 125, Saint Marys PA 15857	814-781-3048	R	421*	.2
7	Haldeman-Homme Inc—*Mike Propp*	430 Industrial Blvd, Minneapolis MN 55413	612-331-4880	R	366*	.2
8	Le Creuset of America Inc—*Paul Van Zuydam*	PO Box 67, Early Branch SC 29916	803-943-4308	S	167*	.1
9	PFG Lester Company Inc—*Mac Pearce*	PO Box 340, Lebanon TN 37088	615-444-2010	S	142*	.5
10	Lee Hartman and Son Inc—*Lee Hartman Jr*	PO Box 13365, Roanoke VA 24033	540-366-3493	R	122*	.1
11	Hockenberg Equipment Co—*Tom Schreck*	4267 109th St, Urbandale IA 50322	515-282-0033	R	117*	.1
12	Storage Solutions Inc—*Craig McElheny*	910 E 169th St, Westfield IN 46074	317-867-2001	R	110*	<.1
13	Bargreen-Ellingson Inc—*Paul Ellingson*	6626 Tacoma Mall Blvd, Tacoma WA 98409	253-475-9201	R	101*	.3
14	HD Sheldon and Company Inc—*Robert Metros*	143 W 29th St, New York NY 10001	212-924-6920	R	78*	<.1
15	Russell T Bundy Associates Inc—*Russell Bundy*	PO Box 150, Urbana OH 43078	937-652-2151	R	69*	.2
16	Sundance Digital Inc—*Robert C Johnson*	545 E John Carpenter F, Irving TX 75062	972-444-8442	S	69*	<.1
17	Direct Source Inc—*John Hillen*	8176 Mallory Ct, Chanhassen MN 55317	952-934-8000	R	67*	.1
18	DirectNET Inc—*Alan Mamane*	11800 Ridge Pkwy Ste 1, Broomfield CO 80021		R	66*	<.1
19	Server Racks Online LLC—*Alan Mamane* DirectNET Inc	12202 Airport Way Ste, Broomfield CO 80021	720-284-6206	D	66*	<.1
20	THOMSON Multimedia—*Frederic Rose*	16935 W Bernardo Dr St, San Diego CA 92127		S	61*	<.1
21	Premier Technology Inc—*Douglas Sayer*	1858 W Bridge Rd, Blackfoot ID 83221	208-785-2274	R	58*	.4
22	Boelter Companies Inc—*Bill Boelter*	N22W23685 Ridgeview Pk, Waukesha WI 53188	262-523-6200	R	58*	.2
23	Alpine Solutions Inc—*Ed Misokanis*	3222 Corte Malpaso Ste, Camarillo CA 93012	805-388-1699	R	57*	<.1
24	Hubert Co—*Bart Kohler*	9555 Dry Fork Rd, Harrison OH 45030	513-367-8600	R	56*	.4
25	Houston's Inc—*Bill Paolo*	9799 SW Freeman Dr, Wilsonville OR 97070	503-582-1121	R	56*	.2
26	NetBank Payment Systems Inc—*Douglas K Freeman*	200 Briarwood W Dr, Jackson MS 39206	601-956-1222	R	55*	.1
27	Singer Equipment Company Inc—*Fred Singer*	150 S Twin Valley Rd, Elverson PA 19520	610-387-6400	R	50*	.2
28	Tri Mark United East—*Robert Halpern*	505 Collins St, South Attleboro MA 02703	508-399-2400	R	50*	.2
29	Interstate Electric Company Inc—*Ed Urlick*	2240 Yates Ave, Commerce CA 90040	323-803-2000	R	39*	.1
30	Addvantage Technologies Group Inc—*Kenneth A Chymiak*	1221 E Houston, Broken Arrow OK 74012	918-251-9121	P	38	.1
31	Federal Telecommunications Inc—*Paul A Bouck*	26074 Ave Hall Ste 7, Valencia CA 91355	661-295-0212	R	38*	<.1
32	Electrified Discounters Inc—*John E Bougoin*	110 Webb St, Hamden CT 06517	203-787-4246	R	36*	<.1
33	Buffalo Hotel Supply Company Inc—*James Bedard III*	375 Commerce Dr, Amherst NY 14228	716-691-8080	R	33*	.1
34	Atlanta Fixture and Sales Company Inc—*Paul Klein*	3185 Northeast Expwy, Atlanta GA 30341	770-455-8844	R	32*	.2
35	Nitel Inc—*Rick Stern*	1101 W Lake St 6th Fl, Chicago IL 60607		R	32	.1
36	Sam Tell And Son Inc—*Mark Tell*	300 Smith St, Farmingdale NY 11735	631-501-9700	R	31*	.2
37	National Bankcard Systems Inc—*Penny Baker*	5316 US 290 Ste 130, Austin TX 78735	512-494-9200	R	31*	.3
38	Mark-Costello Co—*Hugh Gilland*	1145 E Dominguez St St, Carson CA 90746	310-637-1851	R	30*	<.1
39	Toshiba TEC America Inc—*William Hosken*	4401-A Bankers Cir, Atlanta GA 30360	770-449-3040	S	29*	.1
40	Nelson Wholesale Corp—*John D Harkey*	PO Box 370, Brownwood TX 76804	325-643-3636	R	29*	<.1
41	M Tucker Company Inc—*Stephen Tucker*	1200 Madison Ave, Paterson NJ 07503	973-484-1200	R	28*	.1
42	Nexxtworks Inc—*Richard A Cartagena*	30798 US Hwy 19 N, Palm Harbor FL 34684	727-725-0400	R	26*	<.1
43	Mobile Fixture And Equipment Company Inc—*Walne Donald*	1155 Montlimar Dr, Mobile AL 36609	251-342-0455	R	25*	.1
44	Mg Concepts Inc—*Jay Austrien*	355 S Technology Dr, Central Islip NY 11722	631-348-1772	R	24*	.3

Rank	Company Name—*Executive Officer*	Address, City, State, Zip	Phone	Type	Fin	Empls
45	Hockenbergs Equipment And Supply Company Inc—*Tom Schrack*	7002 F St, Omaha NE 68117	402-339-8900	R	24*	.1
46	Zesco Products Inc—*Mark Zoll*	PO Box 6157, Indianapolis IN 46206	317-269-9300	R	20*	.1
47	Dascoa Inc—*Joe Schmitt*	PO Box 307, Marion IA 52302	319-447-1670	R	20*	<.1
48	A-1 Scale Service—*Bubba Buchhorn*	4807 NW Industrial Dr, San Antonio TX 78238	210-521-7848	R	20*	<.1
49	United Radio Inc—*Steve Cuntz*	PO Box 75030, Cincinnati OH 45275	859-371-4423	R	20*	.1
50	Admiral Craft Equipment Corp—*Matthew Lobman*	940 S Oyster Bay Rd, Hicksville NY 11801		R	19*	.1
51	Bintz Restaurant Supply Co—*Roger Brown*	PO Box 1350, Salt Lake City UT 84110	801-463-1515	R	19*	<.1
52	Tri-State Video Services—*James T Wachtel*	1379 Pittsburgh Rd, Valencia PA 16059	724-898-1630	R	18*	<.1
53	Dometek Inc—*Klaus Bierwagen*	75 Sawyer Passway, Fitchburg MA 01420	978-345-8001	R	18*	<.1
54	Entech Signs—*Steve Teas*	1905 W Arbor Rose, Grand Prairie TX 75050	972-641-0390	R	18*	<.1
55	Struve Distributing Company Inc—*Trevor Larsen*	276 W 100 S, Salt Lake City UT 84101	801-328-1636	R	18*	<.1
56	S S Kemp and Co—*Mark Fishman*	4567 Willow Pkwy, Cleveland OH 44125	216-271-7700	R	18*	.1
57	Amano Mcgann Inc—*Terrence Mcgann*	651 Taft St Ne, Minneapolis MN 55413	612-331-2020	R	17*	.1
58	Tundra Specialties Inc—*Michael Lewis*	PO Box 20670, Boulder CO 80308	303-440-4142	R	17*	.1
59	Keating Of Chicago Inc—*Eliza Moravec*	8901 W 50th St, Mc Cook IL 60525	708-544-6500	R	16*	.1
60	Aireps Inc—*Sheri Chaffin*	1529 N Harmony Cir, Anaheim CA 92807	714-777-9850	R	16*	.1
61	Plexus Co—*Kevin Bouma*	PO Box 2925, Fargo ND 58108	701-232-4428	R	16*	.1
62	Rave Computer Association Inc—*Rick Darter*	7171 Sterling Ponds Ct, Sterling Heights MI 48312	586-939-8230	R	16*	<.1
63	Display Specialties Inc—*Douglas Bray*	9 Beacon Dr, Wilder KY 41076	859-781-7711	R	16*	.1
64	Specialty Store Services Inc—*Malcolm Finke*	454 Jarvis Ave, Des Plaines IL 60018	847-470-7000	R	15*	.1
65	Z and S Electronics Inc—*Samuel Pinchassi*	967 E 11th St, Los Angeles CA 90021	213-623-8001	R	15*	<.1
66	Schultz Supply Co—*James Schultz*	3215 S 59th Ave, Cicero IL 60804	708-652-2020	R	15*	<.1
67	Pioneer Equipment Rental LLC	1402 W Cherry Ave, Ponca City OK 74601	580-762-5717	R	15*	.1
68	Econoco Corp—*Barry Rosenberg*	PO Box 29, Hicksville NY 11802	516-935-7700	R	15*	.1
69	Sherlock Systems—*Dave Saloander*	1584 Barclay Blvd, Buffalo Grove IL 60089	847-520-7711	R	14*	<.1
70	Filter Fresh of Northern Virginia Inc	378 University Ave, Westwood MA 02090	781-461-8734	D	13*	<.1
71	Henderson Auctions Inc—*Jeffrey Henderson*	PO Box 336, Livingston LA 70754	225-686-2252	R	13*	<.1
72	Grand Rapids Scale Co—*Richard Spruit*	4215 Stafford Ave Sw, Grand Rapids MI 49548	616-538-7080	R	13*	.1
73	Atlantic Scale Company Inc—*Fred Algieri*	136 Washington Ave, Nutley NJ 07110	973-661-7090	R	13*	<.1
74	Exclusively Expo Inc—*James Buehner*	1225 Naperville Dr, Romeoville IL 60446	630-378-1600	P	13*	.1
75	Optec Displays Inc—*Shu Wu*	716 Nogales St, City Of Industry CA 91748	626-369-7188	R	12*	.1
76	Resnick Supermarket Equipment Corp—*Daniel Resnick*	PO Box Q, Mountain Dale NY 12763	845-434-8200	R	12*	.1
77	AVM Enterprises Inc—*A Daniel*	PO Box 22283, Chattanooga TN 37422	423-847-4700	R	12*	.1
78	Antibus Scales and Systems Inc—*Agnes Antibus*	4809 Illinois Rd, Fort Wayne IN 46804	260-432-3591	R	12*	<.1
79	Saeco USA Inc—*Courtney Mahan*	7905 Cochran Rd Ste 10, Solon OH 44139	440-528-2000	R	12*	<.1
80	Store Supply Warehouse LLC—*John Mcmann*	9801 Page Ave, Saint Louis MO 63132	314-427-8887	R	11*	.1
81	Dick Gerharz Syrup Distributors—*Richard Gerharz*	6146 E Molloy Rd, East Syracuse NY 13057	315-463-0639	R	11*	<.1
82	MFried Store Fixtures Inc—*Michael Fried*	176 Flushing Ave, Brooklyn NY 11205	718-624-2999	R	10*	.1
83	Reb Steel Equipment Corp—*Thomas Lesko*	4556 W Grand Ave, Chicago IL 60639	773-252-0400	R	10*	.1
84	Trendco Supply Inc—*Brad Oblinger*	673 Ethel St Nw, Atlanta GA 30318	404-876-5002	R	10*	.1
85	W L Streich Equipment Company Inc—*Steven Streich*	833 S 3rd Ave, Wausau WI 54401	715-842-0531	R	10*	.1
86	Run-PCcom—*Brenda Gomez*	812 S Date Ave Ste F, Alhambra CA 91803	626-308-0100	R	10*	<.1
87	Taylor Utlimate Services Co—*Raul Piedra*	1780 N Commerce Pkwy, Weston FL 33326	954-217-9100	R	10*	<.1
88	Lippert Inc—*David Wax*	600 W 172nd St, South Holland IL 60473	708-333-6900	R	10*	<.1
89	Supreme Custom Fabricators Inc—*John Hampel*	PO Box 193655, Little Rock AR 72219	501-455-2552	R	9*	<.1
90	Quality Supply Co—*Leland Manders*	4020 Rev Dr, Cincinnati OH 45232	513 542 7000	R	9*	.1
91	Brenmar Company Inc—*Marlene Hytrok*	11701 Centennial Rd, La Vista NE 68128	402-592-3303	R	9*	.1
92	George R Ruhl and Son Inc—*George R Ruhl*	PO Box 250, Hanover MD 21076	410-796-0203	R	9*	.1
93	Robert H Ham Associates Ltd—*Nancy Ham*	PO Box 77398, Greensboro NC 27417	336-299-3422	R	9*	<.1
94	G T Michelli Company Inc—*Gasper Michelli*	130 Brookhollow Esplan, Harahan LA 70123	504-733-9822	R	9*	.1
95	Matrix Automation Inc—*William Kaman*	340 Main St, Huron OH 44839	419-433-4013	R	8*	.1
96	State Restaurant Equipment Inc—*Edmon Haddad*	3163 S Highland Dr, Las Vegas NV 89109	702-733-1515	R	8*	<.1
97	Kavanaugh's Restaurant Supplies Inc—*Kevin Kavanaugh*	2920 Bryant Rd, Madison WI 53713	608-271-8514	R	8*	<.1
98	Quality International Packaging Ltd—*Moses Gancfried*	20 Sand Park Rd, Cedar Grove NJ 07009	201-909-8100	R	8*	.1
99	Dixie Store Fixtures and Sales Company Inc	2425 1st Ave N, Birmingham AL 35203	205-322-2442	R	8*	<.1
100	Carlson JPM Store Fixtures Co—*Ken Keller*	7147 Northland Dr N, Brooklyn Park MN 55428	763-504-3547	D	8*	<.1
101	American Weigh Scales Inc—*Lee Vantine*	3285 Saturn Ct, Norcross GA 30092	770-542-0230	R	7*	<.1
102	Chan and Fung's Hardware Inc—*Peter Chang*	183 Bowery, New York NY 10002	212-254-9720	R	7*	<.1
103	Advance Fixture Mart Inc—*David Axon*	3702 Hawthorn Ct, Waukegan IL 60087	847-249-6000	R	7*	<.1
104	Bolton and Hay Inc—*Lew Bolton*	PO Box 3247, Des Moines IA 50316	515-265-2554	R	7*	<.1
105	Earl F Anderson Associates Inc—*Warren Anderson*	9701 Penn Ave S Ste 10, Bloomington MN 55431	952-884-7300	R	7*	<.1
106	Willco Sales and Services Inc—*Scott Tague*	PO Box 320003, Fairfield CT 06825		R	7*	<.1
107	Florida Seating Inc—*Maria Nikolova*	PO Box 17660, Clearwater FL 33762	727-536-2074	R	7*	<.1
108	Hot Supply Inc—*Kurt Ambami*	731 W Racquet Club Dr, Addison IL 60101	630-543-5244	R	7*	<.1
109	B and C Computer Vision and Atari Sales and Service—*Bruce Carso*	5917 Stopeway, El Dorado CA 95623	530-295-9270	R	7*	<.1
110	DK Display Corp—*David Terveen*	147 W 25th St Fl 4, New York NY 10001	212-807-0499	R	7*	<.1
111	Zelcor Media Duplication and Supplies—*Diane Hebel*	1324 Clarkson Clayton, Ellisville MO 63011	636-256-0044	R	7*	<.1
112	Tassone Equipment Corp—*Donald Tassone*	130 Eileen Way, Syosset NY 11791	516-921-6400	R	7*	<.1
113	Alfa International Corp—*Roger Madigan*	4 Kaysal Ct, Armonk NY 10504	914-273-2222	R	7*	<.1
114	Elmer Schultz Services Inc—*W Mallon*	540 N 3rd St, Philadelphia PA 19123	215-627-5400	R	6*	<.1
115	Institutional Equipment Inc—*Franklin Fiene*	704 Veterans Pkwy Ste, Bolingbrook IL 60440	630-771-0990	R	6*	<.1
116	Jake's Equipment and Repair Inc—*James Rollings*	6060 Romona Blvd, Houston TX 77086	281-999-5142	R	6*	<.1
117	Tung Hsin Trading Corp—*Kent Tseng*	20420 Business Pkwy, Walnut CA 91789	909-348-0288	R	6*	<.1
118	B and J Food Service Equipment Of Missouri Inc—*Bill Mosburg*	1616 Dielman Rd, Saint Louis MO 63132	314-428-1247	R	6*	<.1
119	Penguin Point Franchise Systems Inc—*Wallace Stouder*	PO Box 975, Warsaw IN 46581	574-267-3107	R	6*	<.1
120	Surfas Inc—*Les Surfas*	8777 W Washington Blvd, Culver City CA 90232	310-559-4770	R	6*	<.1
121	Megasource Hospitality Resources Inc—*Rudy Dostal*	3104 E Camelbck Rd Ste, Phoenix AZ 85016	602-508-8400	R	6*	<.1
122	Advance Scale Company Inc—*Jim Santarpio*	2400 Egg Harbor Rd, Lindenwold NJ 08021	856-627-0700	R	6*	<.1
123	Rocky Duron and Associates Inc—*Marciano Duron*	PO Box 560264, Dallas TX 75356	214-358-3455	R	6*	<.1
124	Ballentine Equipment Company Inc—*Russell Ballentine*	PO Box 476, Greenville SC 29602	864-232-4691	R	6*	<.1
125	California Butcher Supply Inc—*E Ekren*	PO Box 360801, Milpitas CA 95036	408-946-2820	R	5*	<.1
126	B and B Equipment and Supply Inc—*Patricia Bible*	PO Box 55, Russellville TN 37860	423-586-5877	R	5*	<.1
127	Foley and Wallace Associates Inc—*Joseph Wallace*	13 Robbie Rd, Avon MA 02322	508-583-9600	R	5*	<.1
128	Northwest Scale Systems Inc—*Madelane Radke*	PO Box 1191, Tualatin OR 97062	503-691-2420	R	5*	<.1
129	Scardina Refrigeration Company Inc—*Lin Mercil*	11848 Coursey Blvd, Baton Rouge LA 70816	225-214-6948	R	5*	<.1
130	Perkins Scale Corp—*Larry Perkins*	4184 Reservoir Ave, Louisville KY 40213	502-459-4333	R	5*	<.1
131	Kittredge Equipment Company Inc—*Wendy Webber*	100 Bowles Rd, Agawam MA 01001	413-304-4100	R	5*	<.1

Note: An asterisk (*) indicates an estimated financial figure. The company type code used is as follows: R = Private, P = Public, S = Private Subsidiary, B = Public Subsidiary, D = Division, J = Joint Venture, I = Investment Fund.

COMPANY RANKINGS BY SALES WITHIN 4-DIGIT SIC

Rank	Company Name—*Executive Officer*	Address, City, State, Zip	Phone	Type	Fin	Empls
132	Britcan Inc—*Jim Hollen*	3809 Ocean Ranch Blvd, Oceanside CA 92056	760-722-2300	R	5*	<.1
133	Dispenser Services Inc—*Steven Harth*	1327 Ashley River Rd S, Charleston SC 29407	843-554-6854	R	5*	<.1
134	Industrial Scales and Systems Inc—*Randall Black*	4295 Cromwell Rd Ste 6, Chattanooga TN 37421	423-499-2210	R	5*	<.1
135	Signs Plus New Ideas-New Technology Inc—*Robert Klinger*	4242 Mcintosh Ln, Sarasota FL 34232	941-378-4262	R	5*	<.1
136	John A Belanger Associates Inc—*Peter Belanger*	PO Box 80767, Saint Clair Shores MI 48080	586-447-0010	R	5*	<.1
137	ABS Imaging Systems Inc—*Robert J Atkinson Jr*	PO Box 447, Silverdale PA 18962	215-258-1229	R	5*	<.1
138	Excalibur Films—*Vicente Sanchez*	578 Explorer St, Brea CA 92821		R	5*	<.1
139	Southwestern Scale Company Inc—*Dean Dumont*	PO Box 8760, Phoenix AZ 85066	602-243-3951	R	5*	<.1
140	Nordon Inc—*James Gaerthofner*	3300 E Winslow Ave, Appleton WI 54911	920-739-6202	R	5*	<.1
141	National Equipment Company Inc—*Edward Redhair*	3401 E Truman Rd, Kansas City MO 64127	816-920-6800	R	5*	<.1
142	Vbs Inc—*Don Berg*	770 7th St Nw, Sioux Center IA 51250	712-722-1181	R	5*	<.1
143	Dervey Distributing Co—*Donald Davis*	2580 S Tejon St, Englewood CO 80110	303-825-0171	R	5*	<.1
144	Hospitality Depot LLC—*George Dent*	PO Box 7578, Panama City FL 32413	850-235-8063	R	5*	<.1
145	Ternion Inc—*Wendy Ressing-Seitz*	8600 Sweet Valley Dr, Cleveland OH 44125	216-642-6180	R	4*	<.1
146	Displays Depot Inc—*Roberto Dauber*	1890 Nw 7th Ave, Miami FL 33136	305-325-8200	R	4*	<.1
147	Eastern Food Equipment Inc—*Thomas Hamberis*	1930 Healy Dr, Winston Salem NC 27103	336-760-2686	R	4*	<.1
148	Pucci International Ltd—*Ralph Pucci*	44 W 18th St Fl 12, New York NY 10011	212-633-0452	R	4*	<.1
149	Ventana Distributing Company Inc—*Donald Metzger*	2825 E Chambers St, Phoenix AZ 85040	602-268-3386	R	4*	<.1
150	Ion Exhibits LLC—*Andrea Miller*	700 District Dr, Itasca IL 60143	630-285-9500	R	4*	<.1
151	Northern Nevada Equipment LLC	1343 W Idaho St, Elko NV 89801	775-777-3092	R	4*	<.1
152	Bezac Equipment Co—*Bill Custer*	3721 Mahoning Ave Ste, Youngstown OH 44515	330-797-1550	R	4*	<.1
153	Always Equipment Inc—*Richard Press*	200 Raritan Ctr Pkwy, Edison NJ 08837	732-346-4480	R	4*	<.1
154	Essex Equipment—*Jason Morse*	26 Kellogg Rd, Essex Junction VT 05452	802-879-0767	R	4*	<.1
155	Bargreen Ellingson Of Hawaii Inc—*Paul Ellingson*	98-107 Kamehameha Hwy, Aiea HI 96701	808-848-0234	R	4*	<.1
156	Insight Distributing Inc—*Kenneth Pearlstein*	PO Box 307, Sandpoint ID 83864	509-534-5901	R	4*	<.1
157	American Fixture and Display Corp—*Samuel Pure*	1504 130th St, College Point NY 11356	718-463-2176	R	4*	<.1
158	Dms/Sign Connection Inc—*James Schwartz*	102 Lookout Ave, Mount Airy MD 21771	301-831-7530	R	4*	<.1
159	Texas Hotel and Restaurant Equipment Inc—*Curtis Cargo*	2616 White Settlement, Fort Worth TX 76107	817-921-6146	R	4*	<.1
160	Abco Corp—*Ralph Freeman*	5751 Gen Washngtn Dr E, Alexandria VA 22312	703-941-9200	R	4*	<.1
161	Yamato Corp—*Shozo Kawanishi*	PO Box 15070, Colorado Springs CO 80935	719-591-1500	R	4*	<.1
162	Wahltek Inc—*Bruce Fagerstrom*	2711 Grand Ave, Des Moines IA 50312	515-309-3935	R	4*	<.1
163	Advanced World Products—*David Broderick*	44106 Old Warm Springs, Fremont CA 94538	510-226-9062	R	4*	<.1
164	Equipment Preference Inc—*William Cassidy*	1800 E State Hwy 114, Southlake TX 76092	817-552-5500	R	4*	<.1
165	International Supplies And Construction LLC	5514 Belridge Ct, Saint Louis MO 63136	910-545-9584	R	4*	<.1
166	Buccaneer Brokerage Inc—*Murray Shelton*	2210 Defoor Hills Rd N, Atlanta GA 30318	404-351-0107	R	4*	<.1
167	Dunbar Systems Inc—*George Dunbar*	1186 Walter St, Lemont IL 60439	630-257-2900	R	4*	<.1
168	Losurdo Inc—*Mark Losurdo*	220 E Lake St Ste 220, Addison IL 60101	630-833-4650	R	4*	<.1
169	Safety Light Corp—*C White*	4150a Old Berwick Rd, Bloomsburg PA 17815	570-784-4344	R	4*	<.1
170	All American Scales Inc—*Patrick Moody*	PO Box 30125, East Canton OH 44730	330-862-8100	R	4*	<.1
171	Weight and Test Solutions Inc—*Robert Voreis*	PO Box 4296, Brownsville TX 78523	956-350-4588	R	4*	<.1
172	Restaurant Equipment Paradise Inc—*Kenneth Swerdlick*	465 Park Ave, East Hartford CT 06108	860-282-8733	R	4*	<.1
173	Session Fixture Company Inc—*Charles Session*	6044 Lemay Ferry Rd, Saint Louis MO 63129	314-487-2670	R	4*	<.1
174	JB Prince Company Inc—*Judith Prince*	36 E 31st St Fl 11, New York NY 10016	212-683-3553	R	3B*	<.1
175	Division 10 Inc—*Christine Saunders*	7730 Trinity Rd Ste 10, Cordova TN 38018	901-755-2623	R	3*	<.1
176	Inland Showcase and Fixture Company Inc—*James Boone*	1473 N Thesta St, Fresno CA 93703	559-237-4158	R	3*	<.1
177	Admor Restaurant And Equipment Supplies—*Ari Theoharakis*	204 Bowery, New York NY 10012	212-226-3878	R	3*	<.1
178	Brandway Inc—*Rocco Brandonisio*	4285 Wagon Trl Ave, Las Vegas NV 89118	702-597-9999	R	3*	<.1
179	Wingfield Scale Company Inc—*Charles Wingfield*	2205 S Holtzclaw Ave, Chattanooga TN 37404	423-698-3346	R	3*	<.1
180	Seidman Brothers Inc—*Allen Seidman*	25 6th St, Chelsea MA 02150	617-884-8110	R	3*	<.1
181	E and S Cabinets and Fixtures—*Randy Stockwell*	PO Box 5427, Pasadena TX 77508	281-476-4722	R	3*	<.1
182	Brucken's Inc—*Roger Griffin*	PO Box 3406, Evansville IN 47733	812-423-4414	R	3*	<.1
183	Loubat Equipment Company Inc—*Christine Briede*	4141 Bienville St Ste, New Orleans LA 70119	504-482-2554	R	3*	<.1
184	Globe Equipment Company Inc—*Jay Ringelheim*	300 Dewey St, Bridgeport CT 06605	203-367-6611	R	3*	<.1
185	Stockton Graham and Co—*Jeffrey Vojta*	4320 Delta Lake Dr Ste, Raleigh NC 27612	919-881-8271	R	3*	<.1
186	American Fun Food Company Inc—*Laurie Jones*	6010 N Broadway St, Park City KS 67219	316-838-9329	R	3*	<.1
187	Garber Scale Co—*Jay Garber*	520 E Oregon Rd Ste 10, Lititz PA 17543	717-393-1708	R	3*	<.1
188	Central City Scale Inc—*Thomas Hawthorne*	PO Box 197, Central City NE 68826	308-946-3591	R	3*	<.1
189	FD Stella Products Co—*Frank D Stella*	7000 Fenkell Ave, Detroit MI 48238	313-341-6400	R	3*	<.1
190	Hardwick's Bar And Restaurant Supplies Inc—*Carson Hardwick*	PO Box 74, North Myrtle Beach SC 29597	843-399-4434	R	3*	<.1
191	Jimson Inc—*James Loucks*	5001 Ambassador Row, Corpus Christi TX 78416	361-851-1002	R	3*	<.1
192	Space Design and Display Inc—*Brian Nelson*	1832 Railroad St, Corona CA 92880	951-734-2990	R	3*	<.1
193	Ambex Inc—*Terry Davis*	1947 Drew St, Clearwater FL 33765	727-442-2727	R	3*	<.1
194	Retail Design Services LLC	2246 90th St E, Northfield MN 55057	612-963-0245	R	3*	<.1
195	North Dallas Warehouse Equipment Inc—*Gene Bolton*	2203 Joe Field Rd, Dallas TX 75229	972-241-9177	R	3*	<.1
196	Ccs Stateline Scale Company LLC	4096 Interstate Blvd, Loves Park IL 61111	815-885-4448	R	3*	<.1
197	Hol-N-One Donut Company Of Ark Inc—*Jerry Rogers*	PO Box 669, Fordyce AR 71742	870-352-3189	R	3*	<.1
198	Consolidated Vending—*John Maiale*	71 Kean St, Babylon NY 11704	631-643-5557	R	3*	<.1
199	Custom Cabinet and Rack Inc—*Heinrich Gerdes*	PO Box 19047, Topeka KS 66619	785-862-2211	R	3*	<.1
200	Enhance America Inc—*Jackson Ling*	3463 Grapevine St, Mira Loma CA 91752	951-361-3000	R	3*	<.1
201	Fepsco Inc—*Alfred Cadinha*	PO Box 17789, Honolulu HI 96817	808-847-4871	R	3*	<.1
202	Continental Display Inc—*Leta Nichols*	2324 Auburn Blvd, Sacramento CA 95821	916-482-3545	R	3*	<.1
203	Ace Fixture Company Inc—*Dennis Berger*	7101 Lincoln Ave, Buena Park CA 90620	714-226-9800	R	3*	<.1
204	Horizon Signal Technologies Inc—*Albert Voehringer*	202 Conestoga Rd, Wayne PA 19087	610-687-8975	R	3*	<.1
205	Krueger Inc—*Fred Krueger*	PO Box 18715, Oklahoma City OK 73154	405-528-8883	R	3*	<.1
206	Elevations Inc—*William Mchenry*	426 Littlefield Ave, South San Francisco CA 94080	650-588-9115	R	3*	<.1
207	Greco Sales Inc—*Alfonso Greco*	PO Box 4226, Springfield IL 62708	217-528-2548	R	3*	<.1
208	Quad City Equipment—*John Locassuy*	1625 34th St, Rock Island IL 61201	309-786-2232	R	3*	<.1
209	Dai Hing Fat Inc—*Zi Huang*	8296 Patuxent Range Rd, Jessup MD 20794	410-880-8513	R	3*	<.1
210	CAS Corp—*Chung Kwon*	99 Murray Hill Pkwy St, East Rutherford NJ 07073	201-933-9002	R	3*	<.1
211	Dean Distributing LLC	4990 W Chinden Blvd, Boise ID 83714	208-322-7773	R	3*	<.1
212	Topos Mondial Warehouse Corp—*Michael Morabido*	Queen S and Adams St, Pottstown PA 19464	610-970-2270	R	3*	<.1
213	Pos Plus Inc—*Steven Shipley*	8185 Upland Cir, Chanhassen MN 55317	952-448-9797	R	3*	<.1
214	Rosito And Bisani Imports Inc—*Rosanna Rosito*	940 S La Brea Ave, Los Angeles CA 90036	323-937-1888	R	3*	<.1
215	Hotel Supplies-Online LLC—*Cynthia Cicchini*	PO Box 37287, Philadelphia PA 19148	334-271-6900	R	3*	<.1
216	Dci Food Equipment Inc—*Remo Antoniolli*	9890 Gibbs Rd, Clarkston MI 48348	248-922-1523	R	3*	<.1
217	Rhino Equipment Corp—*James Rhodes*	8240 S Kyrene Rd Ste 1, Tempe AZ 85284	480-940-1826	R	3*	<.1
218	Worcester Scale Company Inc—*Steven Hoogasian*	228 Brooks St, Worcester MA 01606	508-853-2886	R	3*	<.1
219	Sarraff and Son Inc—*Osvaldo Sarraff*	1655 Nw 36th St, Miami FL 33142	305-638-3115	R	3*	<.1
220	C and H Store Equipment Company Inc—*Cheonil Kim*	2530 S Broadway, Los Angeles CA 90007	213-748-7165	R	3*	<.1
221	Galy USA Inc—*Cheng Lin*	969 Newark Tpke Ste 1, Kearny NJ 07032	201-991-9394	R	3*	<.1

Rank	Company Name—*Executive Officer*	Address, City, State, Zip	Phone	Type	Fin	Empls
222	Advantage Fixtures Inc—*Holly Hubbard*	4540 S Pinemont Dr Ste, Houston TX 77041	972-501-0804	R	3*	<.1
223	Bay Coin Distributors Inc—*Mitchell Kaufman*	13210 Jamaica Ave, Richmond Hill NY 11418	718-291-5757	R	3*	<.1
224	Central Vending Service Inc—*Tracy Seaver*	N3476 County Rd H, Lake Geneva WI 53147	262-248-6300	R	3*	<.1
225	Hobart Sales and Service—*George Eakett*	PO Box 1228, Arden NC 28704	828-654-9005	R	3*	<.1
226	Dixie Neon Supply Co—*Susan Fowler*	PO Box 7281, Charlotte NC 28241	704-588-2565	R	3*	<.1
227	Monterey Bay Restaurant Equipment Inc—*Bill Locklar*	325 Elder Ave Ste A, Seaside CA 93955	831-899-1422	R	3*	<.1
228	Pro Design and Vending Technologies Inc—*Michael Garceau*	68 Rte 125, Kingston NH 03848	603-642-9290	R	3*	<.1
229	Main Store Display and Fixtures—*Susie Chang*	1810 S Main St, Los Angeles CA 90015	213-747-4600	R	3*	<.1
230	Fixture Resource Group Inc—*William Birmingham*	4000 Webster Ave, Norwood OH 45212	513-531-8185	R	3*	<.1
231	J and R World Trading Group Inc—*Joseph Rousseau*	4967 Sw 75th Ave, Miami FL 33155	305-662-2274	R	3*	<.1
232	Restaurant Equipment Marketing Co—*Frank Kurtz*	5104 Gatehouse Way, Ellicott City MD 21043	410-313-9911	R	3*	<.1
233	Fixture Plus Install Action Inc—*Joanne Bently*	663 Park Meadow Rd Ste, Westerville OH 43081	614-818-9447	R	2*	<.1
234	Sortiumusa—*Richard Sherwood*	400 Bayou Vis, Southlake TX 76092	817-313-1100	R	2*	<.1
235	Primalyn Enterprises Inc—*Richard Wallenhorst*	447 Adirondack St, Rochester NY 14606	585-254-5050	R	2*	<.1
236	BSI Scales Inc—*John Kennedy*	16155 W Lincoln Ave, New Berlin WI 53151	262-789-5650	R	2*	<.1
237	Wenzl and Co—*Richard Wenzl*	3018 N Laramie Ave, Chicago IL 60641	773-777-3737	R	2*	<.1
238	Schmidt Equipment and Supply Inc—*Dale Schmidt*	411 Eichelberger St, Saint Louis MO 63111	314-771-4565	R	2*	<.1
239	Webco Distribution Inc—*Richard Thomas*	2301 Ingleside Rd, Norfolk VA 23513	757-248-5331	R	2*	<.1
240	Britz Store Equipment Inc—*John Britz*	PO Box 657, Buckman MN 56317	320-468-6294	R	2*	<.1
241	Red Star Restaurant Equipment Inc—*Sammy Hou*	40 Camptown Rd, Irvington NJ 07111	973-375-3388	R	2*	<.1
242	Horizon Food Service and Supply Ltd—*Judith Jones*	28595 Interstate 10 W, Boerne TX 78006	830-981-5812	R	2*	<.1
243	Midwest Electrical Appliance Service Center Inc—*Ben Buttitto*	PO Box 885, Elmhurst IL 60126	630-279-8000	R	2*	<.1
244	Nuova Distribution USA LLC—*Sandra Southwick*	6940 Salashan Pkwy Bld, Ferndale WA 98248	360-366-2226	R	2*	<.1
245	Premium Seating Products Inc—*Todd Knopp*	489 E 300 S, Burley ID 83318	208-677-2100	R	2*	<.1
246	Vendors Equipment Inc—*Roger Malagutti*	PO Box 4832, Waterbury CT 06704	203-574-5983	R	2*	<.1
247	Detroit Store Fixture Company Inc—*Lawrence Rosenthal*	7545 W 8 Mile Rd, Detroit MI 48221	313-341-3255	R	2*	<.1
248	Palmetto Scale Services—*Dan Wallace*	1467 Old Dunbar Rd, West Columbia SC 29172	803-755-6630	R	2*	<.1
249	Equinox Systems and Services Corp—*Heather Lindsey*	PO Box 31213, Jackson MS 39286	601-982-5588	R	2*	<.1
250	Mill Hardware and Food Service Inc—*Jeffrey Davis*	4855 E 345th St, Willoughby OH 44094	440-946-9444	R	2*	<.1
251	American Scale Corp—*Daniel Coyle*	3540 Bashford Ave, Louisville KY 40218	502-451-5040	R	2*	<.1
252	Corbo Hotel Restaurant and Bar Supply Inc—*Lester Reiff*	PO Box 1351, Asbury Park NJ 07712	732-774-1341	R	2*	<.1
253	Market Northwest Inc—*Terry Thompson*	25329 74th Ave S Ste A, Kent WA 98032	253-373-0015	R	2*	<.1
254	Rembert Company Inc—*Blake Edmunds*	PO Box 5641, Columbia SC 29250	803-799-3950	R	2*	<.1
255	Bakery Equipment Service—*Kenneth Lind*	118 Nevin Ave, Richmond CA 94801	510-233-8265	R	2*	<.1
256	Shelving Depot Inc—*Richard Kurland*	419 W Elizabeth Ave, Linden NJ 07036	908-474-8000	R	2*	<.1
257	Tennessee Scale Works Inc—*Steven Hunt*	7103 Juniper Rd, Fairview TN 37062	615-352-4400	R	2*	<.1
258	Tri City H P—*Wilburn Rees*	527 W 4th St, Davenport IA 52801	563-322-5382	R	2*	<.1
259	A-1 Scale Service Inc—*Bubba Buchhorn*	4807 NW Industrial Dr, San Antonio TX 78238	210-521-7848	R	2*	<.1
260	Desco U S A—*John Cora*	9630 Joliet Rd, Countryside IL 60525	708-588-1099	R	2*	<.1
261	Holmes Equipment and Supply LLC—*Dave Harrington*	714 W 20th St, Cheyenne WY 82001	307-634-6542	R	2*	<.1
262	United Distributors Inc (Wichita Kansas)—*Mark Blum*	420 S Seneca St, Wichita KS 67213	316-263-6181	R	2*	<.1
263	Fountain American Soda Exchange Inc—*Ray Schy*	455 N Oakley Blvd, Chicago IL 60612	312-733-5000	R	2*	<.1
264	D and S Sign and Supply Inc—*Dave Willis*	PO Box 7960, Beaumont TX 77726	409-842-1546	R	2*	<.1
265	Epicurean Industries Inc—*Carol Deibler*	30 Canidae St, Burlington NJ 08016	609-386-9997	R	2*	<.1
266	Midwest Food Service Equipment Inc—*William Jewell*	220 S Starr Ln, Peoria IL 61604	309-633-0400	R	2*	<.1
267	American Material Handling Company Inc—*Jackie Lackie*	9013 Hwy 165, North Little Rock AR 72117	501-375-6611	R	2*	<.1
268	Division Ten Building Specialties Inc—*Jim Tombyll*	PO Box 218, Spotswood NJ 08884	732-390-6100	R	2*	<.1
269	Bard Business Systems Inc—*Timothy Bard*	PO Box 643, Bryn Mawr PA 19010	610-924-9300	R	2*	<.1
270	Creative Store Design Inc—*Douglas Hammetter*	3728 N Fratney St, Milwaukee WI 53212	414-963-1900	R	2*	<.1
271	Thompson Equipment Supply Inc—*Steve Mckay*	3249 E Kemper Rd Ste 2, Cincinnati OH 45241	513-761-7784	R	2*	<.1
272	AC Lister and Company Inc—*Albert Lister*	8992 Cotter St, Lewis Center OH 43035	740-548-8112	R	2*	<.1
273	Seika Machinery Inc—*Kevin McClay*	3528 Torrance Blvd Ste, Torrance CA 90503	310-540-7310	S	2*	<.1
274	Southeastern Microwave Inc—*Frank Gannon*	34d Freedom Ct, Greer SC 29650	864-848-3378	R	2*	<.1
275	Total Equipment Suppliers Inc—*Tracey Umansky*	17535 Nw 66th Ct, Hialeah FL 33015	305-718-9550	R	2*	<.1
276	DVDR4Less—*Bijan Chad*	14008 Ventura Blvd, Sherman Oaks CA 91423	818-990-2222	R	2*	<.1
277	Quipcon Inc—*John Schaumberg*	20 Hi-Line Dr, Union MO 63084	636-583-8200	R	2*	<.1
278	Image Management Systems Inc—*Jack Berry*	239 W 15th St, New York NY 10011	212-741-8765	R	2*	<.1
279	We R Signs International Inc—*Mark Langman*	1830 Bath Ave Apt 101, Brooklyn NY 11214	718-837-8480	R	2*	<.1
280	SWI Trading Inc—*Shannon Illingworth*	2320 Whiteoak Ln, Corona CA 92882	714-368-0623	R	2*	<.1
281	Deskin Scale Company Inc—*Charles Harrison*	PO Box 3272, Springfield MO 65808	417-883-0055	R	2*	<.1
282	M and J Frank Inc—*Andrew Becker*	29 Eagle Rock Ave, East Hanover NJ 07936	973-887-1040	R	2*	<.1
283	Southern Exhibits Inc—*William Dorff*	4360 36th St, Orlando FL 32811	407-423-2860	R	2*	<.1
284	Triple C Technologies Inc—*Allan Kastanik*	344 Taft St Ne, Minneapolis MN 55413	612-331-5724	R	2*	<.1
285	W B Porter and Co—*Mark Porter*	1721 Lake Wheeler Rd, Raleigh NC 27603	919-828-1750	R	2*	<.1
286	Minot Restaurant Supply Company Inc—*David Forthun*	PO Box 94, Minot ND 58702	701-852-1244	R	2*	<.1
287	Royal Manufacturing Company Inc—*Mansour Feramazipour*	1900 E 25th St, Vernon CA 90058	323-231-9999	R	2*	<.1
288	Az Department Transportation Equipment Services—*Carl Eyrich*	5701 E Railhead Ave, Flagstaff AZ 86004	928-526-0915	R	2*	<.1
289	Sunbelt Import—*Salvatore Albelice*	10525 Kinghurst St Ste, Houston TX 77099	281-879-4300	R	2*	<.1
290	Pacwest Scale—*David Eccles*	21326 E Arrow Hwy, Covina CA 91724	909-394-3555	R	2*	<.1
291	Wichita Restaurant Supply Company Inc—*Sandy Hay*	PO Box 2069, Wichita Falls TX 76307	940-766-4389	R	2*	<.1
292	Frank M Waters Inc—*Peggy Waters*	3046 Sykesville Rd, Westminster MD 21157	410-876-7066	R	2*	<.1
293	Big Valley Equipment LLC—*Vickie Gardner*	40 Country Club Ln, Waterloo IL 62298	618-939-8568	R	2*	<.1
294	Braswell Scale and Equipment Company Inc—*John Farlow*	PO Box 5422, Asheville NC 28813	828-274-3771	R	2*	<.1
295	Fabian Enterprises Inc—*Virgilio Fabian*	4208 W Dr Martin Luthe, Tampa FL 33614	813-876-8787	R	2*	<.1
296	A and M Truck Equipment And Fabrication—*Bob Applegate*	3601 W 48th St, Tulsa OK 74107	918-445-2600	R	2*	<.1
297	All-Line Equipment Inc—*Steve Disselhorst*	PO Box 5257, Quincy IL 62305	217-224-9725	R	2*	<.1
298	Integrated Display Company LLC—*Dannie Warren*	601 W 26th St Ste 401, New York NY 10001	212-924-6400	R	2*	<.1
299	Tennessee Marketing Association Inc—*Terry Mcgovern*	2916 Sidco Dr, Nashville TN 37204	615-726-0351	R	2*	<.1
300	Display Options Inc—*Scott Thomas*	9517 Monroe Rd Ste A, Charlotte NC 28270	704-525-5300	R	2*	<.1
301	Fairborn Equipment Company Mid-Atlantic LLC—*Kim Oconnor*	1411 Ford Rd, Bensalem PA 19020	215-547-9557	R	2*	<.1
302	Joe Kirwan Company Inc—*Bob Nalesnik*	PO Box 1002, Old Bridge NJ 08857	732-679-1900	R	2*	<.1
303	Leroy's Food Service Equipment Inc—*Leroy Willingham*	PO Box 36817, Birmingham AL 35236	205-985-2021	R	2*	<.1
304	Refrigeration Specialties Inc—*Bill Olmstead*	3223 N Market St, Spokane WA 99207	509-624-4972	R	2*	<.1
305	Retail Service Company Inc—*Donald Tomkinson*	2108 Broadway Unit A, South Portland ME 04106	207-772-8888	R	2*	<.1
306	Total Systems Control Inc—*Robert Stosic*	1002 Oak St, Clairton PA 15025	412-384-3311	R	2*	<.1
307	Abc Restaurant Supplies and Equipment Inc—*Robert Sorota*	1345 N Miami Ave, Miami FL 33136	305-325-1200	R	2*	<.1
308	Eagle Marketing Group Inc—*Paul Fellencer*	PO Box 869, Spring TX 77383	281-355-0271	R	2*	<.1
309	America's Classic Foods LLC	1298 Warren Rd, Cambria CA 93428	805-927-0745	R	2*	<.1
310	Affordable Warehouse Equipment Inc—*Paul Wildenhaus*	PO Box 38458, Olmsted Falls OH 44138	216-961-1688	R	2*	<.1

Note: An asterisk (*) indicates an estimated financial figure. The company type code used is as follows: R = Private, P = Public, S = Private Subsidiary, B = Public Subsidiary, D = Division, J = Joint Venture, I = Investment Fund.

COMPANY RANKINGS BY SALES WITHIN 4-DIGIT SIC

Rank	Company Name—Executive Officer	Address, City, State, Zip	Phone	Type	Fin	Empls
311	Monarch Toilet Partition Inc—John Prend	PO Box 108, Freeport NY 11520	516-379-2700	R	2*	<.1
312	Daniels Display Company Inc—Daniel Benjamin	1267 Mission St, San Francisco CA 94103	415-861-4400	R	2*	<.1
313	Industrial Scale Service Inc—Dennis Byrne	S81w19077 Apollo Dr, Muskego WI 53150	262-679-9900	R	2*	<.1
314	Kendall Sign Company Inc—Thomas Kendall	8947 Fullbright Ave, Chatsworth CA 91311	818-908-0388	R	2*	<.1
315	Triboro Bar and Restaurant Supply Company Inc—John Ferrando	1803 Bronxdale Ave, Bronx NY 10462	718-863-8721	R	1*	<.1
316	Edmar Inc—Glenn Feiner	35 E Broad St, Burlington NJ 08016	609-387-3888	R	1*	<.1
317	Repssouth Inc—Michael Whitten	278 Franklin Rd Ste 29, Brentwood TN 37027	615-370-1311	R	1*	<.1
318	Cohen Technology Inc—Charles Cohen	PO Box 30, Pearl River NY 10965	845-735-7907	R	1*	<.1
319	Midwest Distributing Corp—Ken Leiderbrand	3104 Cuming St, Omaha NE 68131	402-341-5600	R	1*	<.1
320	Si Stainless International Inc—Ted Lambertson	2650 Mercantile Dr Ste, Rancho Cordova CA 95742	916-638-7370	R	1*	<.1
321	RK Sales Inc—Kelsey Deguchi	94-1175 Ka Uka Blvd St, Waipahu HI 96797	808-677-9373	R	1*	<.1
322	AAA Restaurant Equipment and Supplies—Buriel Renford	2908 Ne 21st Way, Gainesville FL 32609	352-373-0501	R	1*	<.1
323	Allied Technologies Food Equipment Inc—Philip Powell	PO Box 501, Greenwood IN 46142	317-887-2020	R	1*	<.1
324	Budget Restaurant Equipment Co—Ronald Woodsby	1246 Central Florida P, Orlando FL 32837	407-859-7951	R	1*	<.1
325	Indon International LLC—Joe Goodson	PO Box 1039, West Point MS 39773	662-494-8928	R	1*	<.1
326	Mei Equipment Inc—Gery Marcombe	PO Box 177, Broussard LA 70518	337-359-9012	R	1*	<.1
327	Stump Equipment Co—Patrick Stump	2224 W Willow St, Lansing MI 48917	517-482-4395	R	1*	<.1
328	BL Sizemore And Associates Inc—Sean Sizemore	PO Box 512, Kernersville NC 27285	336-996-2727	R	1*	<.1
329	Dillon/Quality Plus Inc—George Dillon	3501 N Kimball Dr, Kansas City MO 64161	816-453-7600	R	1*	<.1
330	Equipex Ltd—Gary Licht	765 Westminster St, Providence RI 02903	401-273-3300	R	1*	<.1
331	Holly Sales and Service Inc—Robert Fann	PO Box 702127, Tulsa OK 74170	918-834-6855	R	1*	<.1
332	Performance Food Equipment Group Inc—Ken Kurzweil	495 Blvd Ste 2, Elmwood Park NJ 07407	201-797-2266	R	1*	<.1
333	Lace Foodservice Corp—Luis Fernandez	PO Box 652953, Miami FL 33265	305-513-5223	R	1*	<.1
334	Commonwealth Trading Corp—Harvison Hunt	1060 Kapp Dr, Clearwater FL 33765	727-631-0096	R	1*	<.1
335	Flamex Sales Co—Michael Malamud	18331 Pines Blvd 112, Pembroke Pines FL 33029	954-322-5850	R	1*	<.1
336	SRE Specialty Restaurant Equipment Inc—Domenic Seminara	941 Ave G, Arlington TX 76011	817-640-3131	R	1*	<.1
337	Modern Store Fixtures Manufacturing Company Inc—Sidney Knopf	2505 N Stemmons Fwy, Dallas TX 75207	214-634-2505	R	1*	<.1
338	Cms Services Inc—Jeffrey Howitson	3095 Richmond Pkwy Ste, San Pablo CA 94806	510-758-8001	R	1*	<.1
339	Par 4 Inc—Anthony Tomasello	223 Pratt St, Hammonton NJ 08037	609-704-9086	R	1*	<.1
340	Northwest Equipment Inc—Mark Snoddy	PO Box 6421, Bend OR 97708		R	1*	<.1
341	Pontchartrain Fresh Foods LLC—Cheryl Quartararo	5604 Crawford St Ste A, Harahan LA 70123	504-733-9881	R	1*	<.1
342	Educor International Inc—John Dunker	7721 Cheri Ct, Tampa FL 33634	813-889-0800	R	1*	<.1
343	Genuine Sales Inc—Yita Weiss	PO Box 724, Harriman NY 10926	845-774-1245	R	1*	<.1
344	Giovonni Foods Inc—Paul Boscarino	50 Camden St, Paterson NJ 07503	973-247-2322	R	1*	<.1
345	Humdinger Enterprises Inc—Chad Phares	PO Box 64865, Lubbock TX 79464		R	1*	<.1
346	E H Thompson Co—Jeffrey Simon	4655 Lenox Ave, Jacksonville FL 32205	904-358-1555	R	1*	<.1
347	Shari Neff—Shari Neff	1505 Main St, Hastings PA 16646	814-247-8887	R	1*	<.1
348	Bowerman Associates Inc—Ron Bowerman	PO Box 616, Liverpool NY 13088	315-453-5288	R	1*	<.1
349	Great Western Inc—David Kao	1929 S Campus Ave, Ontario CA 91761	909-923-9258	R	1*	<.1
350	Mountain Scales Inc—Thomas Susa	12445 E 39th Ave Unit, Denver CO 80239	303-371-3966	R	1*	<.1
351	Superior Scale Inc—Steven Daniels	PO Box 766, Fort Mill SC 29716	803-548-3320	R	1*	<.1
352	Tor Rey USA Inc—Juan Rodriguez	3737 Yale St, Houston TX 77018	281-564-3150	R	1*	<.1
353	Ziggy International Inc—Andrew Steele	4024 Dr Mrtn Luther Ki, Fort Myers FL 33916	239-334-8750	R	1*	<.1
354	Vieux Carre Creation Inc—Mark Singerman	4704 N Turnbull Dr, Metairie LA 70002	504-832-3114	R	1*	<.1
355	International Restaurant Equipment Company Inc	PO Box 35497, Los Angeles CA 90035	323-933-1896	R	1*	<.1
356	Starship Industries—John Ritchey	605 Utterback Store Rd, Great Falls VA 22066	703-450-5780	R	1*	<.1
357	Paul Taylor—Paul Taylor	1152 Skyview Dr, Wylie TX 75098	972-429-9498	R	1*	<.1
358	Bridge Kitchenwares Corp—Steven Bridge	563 Eagle Rock Ave Ste, Roseland NJ 07068	973-287-6163	R	1*	<.1
359	Economy Bar and Restaurant Supply Inc—Bruce Simon	712 N Stone Ave, Tucson AZ 85705	520-624-0301	R	1*	<.1
360	Chou And Associates Inc—Heinz Rimann	130 Doolittle Dr Ste 2, San Leandro CA 94577	707-561-7080	R	1*	<.1
361	Kent Sign Company Inc—William Craven	2 E Bradys Ln, Dover DE 19901	302-697-2181	R	1*	<.1
362	Southern Sweets—Nancy Cole	186 Rio Cir Ste A, Decatur GA 30030	404-373-8752	R	1*	<.1
363	International Restaurant Equipment and Supplies—George Balatinos	6501 Market St, Upper Darby PA 19082	610-352-6500	R	1*	<.1
364	Sanstrom Scale Company Inc—Jeff Sanstrom	4010 N 2615 E, Twin Falls ID 83301	208-324-7500	R	1*	<.1
365	Tank Equipment Inc—Jerry Popelka	3752 Imperial St Unit, Frederick CO 80516	303-457-0513	R	1*	<.1
366	B Andrews Inc—Dale Destree	200 Applebee St Ste 20, Barrington IL 60010	847-381-7444	R	1*	<.1
367	Multi Distributing LLC	23600 College Blvd Ste, Olathe KS 66061	913-393-1417	R	1*	<.1
368	H and A Clarke Inc—Harold Clarke	103 S Main St Ste 8, Newtown CT 06470	203-270-6904	R	1*	<.1
369	Phoenix Scale Company Inc—Bruce Bettis	6802 N 47th Ave Ste 9, Glendale AZ 85301	623-435-9511	R	1*	<.1
370	Christian E Lewis—Christian Lewis	26 Florescent Dr, Slate Hill NY 10973	845-355-2651	R	1*	<.1
371	Mile High Food Equipment Inc—Terry Brown	18150 E 32nd Pl Ste E, Aurora CO 80011	303-371-9292	R	1*	<.1
372	Bridge Industries Inc—Jerry Deporter	309 S Cloverdale St D1, Seattle WA 98108	206-652-5075	R	<1*	<.1
373	Johnson's Restaurant And Hotel Supply Company Inc—James Johnson	427 Nw Broadway, Portland OR 97209	503-223-8495	R	<1*	<.1
374	Neon and Beyond Inc—David Rajotte	67 W St, Bristol CT 06010	860-585-5191	R	<1*	<.1
375	Overman Mark and Richard Bean—Richard Bean	1090 John Stark Hwy, Newport NH 03773	603-542-6649	R	<1*	<.1
376	Kaspar Scale Inc—James Kaspar	30311 Clemens Rd Ste 1, Westlake OH 44145	440-871-3500	R	<1*	<.1
377	DPL Surveillance Equipment—Monty Henry	PO Box 370516, Reseda CA 91337	818-344-3742	R	<1*	<.1
378	Stage-Kolstad Associates—Frederick Kolstad	9135 Alabama Ave Ste C, Chatsworth CA 91311	818-349-5787	R	<1*	<.1
379	SGT Enterprises—Sven Tveter	PO Box 466, Placerville CA 95667	408-727-4800	R	<1*	<.1
380	Omagine Inc—Frank Drohan	350 Fifth Ave Ste 1103, New York NY 10118	212-563-4141	P	<1	<.1
381	Metro Lifts and Equipment LLC—Terra Lowe	5319 Hwy 90 W Ste 102, Mobile AL 36619	251-661-5454	R	<1*	<.1
382	Northwest Mannequin—Joseph Miller	6318 E Green Lake Way, Seattle WA 98103	206-522-7292	R	<1*	<.1
383	Jetrion LLC—Kenneth Stack	1260 James L Hart Pky, Ypsilanti MI 48197	734-641-3062	S	<1	.1
384	Sumter Textile Machinery—Jung Choi	555 W Redondo Beach Bl, Gardena CA 90248	310-323-8883	R	<1*	<.1
385	Action/Reaction Techniques—John Wallace	124 W Main St, Oyster Bay NY 11771	516-922-1922	R	<1*	<.1
386	Lehigh Equipment Company Inc—James Troutt	5545 Regal Ridge Dr, Burlington KY 41005	859-586-9124	R	<1*	<.1
387	M F S E Inc—Richard Forsblad	218 E Superior St, Duluth MN 55802	218-722-0035	R	<1*	<.1

TOTALS: SIC 5046 Commercial Equipment Nec
Companies: 387 7,977   14.6

5047 Medical & Hospital Equipment

Rank	Company Name—Executive Officer	Address, City, State, Zip	Phone	Type	Fin	Empls
1	Owens and Minor Inc—Craig R Smith	PO Box 27626, Richmond VA 23261	804-723-7000	P	8,628	4.8
2	Henry Schein Inc—Stanley M Bergman	135 Duryea Rd, Melville NY 11747	631-843-5500	P	7,527	13.5
3	VWR International LLC—John M Ballbach; VWR Funding Inc	PO Box 6660, Radnor PA 19087	610-386-1700	S	4,716*	7.0
4	VWR Funding Inc—John M Ballbach	1310 Goshen Pkwy, West Chester PA 19380	610-431-1700	S	3,593*	6.5

Rank	Company Name—*Executive Officer*	Address, City, State, Zip	Phone	Type	Fin	Empls
5	Patterson Companies Inc—*Paul A Guggenheim*	1031 Mendota Heights R, St Paul MN 55120	651-686-1600	P	3,416	7.1
6	PSS World Medical Inc—*Delores M Kesler*	PO Box 550560, Jacksonville FL 32255	904-332-3000	P	2,035	3.9
7	Henry Schein Inc Dental Div Henry Schein Inc	135 Duryea Rd, Melville NY 11747	631-843-5500	D	1,672*	5.0
8	MWI Veterinary Supply Inc—*James F Cleary Jr*	3041 W Pasadena Dr, Boise ID 83705		P	1,565	1.2
9	GF Health Products Inc—*Beatrice Scherer*	2935 Northeast Pkwy, Atlanta GA 30360		R	1,457*	2.2
10	Omron Healthcare Inc—*Isao Ogino*	1200 Lakeside Dr, Bannockburn IL 60015	847-680-6200	R	1,299*	.2
11	Bellco Health Corp—*Neil Goldstein*	5500 New Horizons Blvd, North Amityville NY 11701	631-789-6300	R	1,185*	.2
12	Grifols USA—*Victor Grifols*	2410 Lillyvale Ave, Los Angeles CA 90032		J	394*	.6
13	Twin Med LLC—*Shlomo Rechnitz*	11333 Greenstone Ave, Santa Fe Springs CA 90670	323-582-9900	R	327*	.5
14	InnoMed Technologies Inc—*R Patrick Karem*	6601 Lyons Rd Ste B1 -, Pompano Beach FL 33073	561-208-3770	R	244*	.4
15	Midwest Veterinary Supply Inc—*Guy Flickinger*	11965 Larc Industrial, Burnsville MN 55337	952-894-4350	R	216*	.3
16	Basic American Medical Products Inc GF Health Products Inc	PO Box 907, Fond Du Lac WI 54937	920-929-8200	S	186*	.3
17	Nipro Medical Corp—*Luis Candelario*	3150 Nw 107th Ave, Doral FL 33172	305-599-7174	R	171*	<.1
18	Broadlane Group Inc—*Patrick Ryan*	13727 Noel Rd Ste 1400, Dallas TX 75240	972-813-7500	R	168*	.7
19	MMS A Medical Supply Co—*Gary Reeve*	13400 Lakefront Dr, Earth City MO 63045	314-291-2900	R	163*	.5
20	Aprima Medical Software Inc—*Michael Nissenbaum*	3330 Keller Springs St, Carrollton TX 75006	214-466-8000	R	159*	.3
21	Distribution Operations Center LLC—*Keith Howells*	1801 Lind Ave Sw, Renton WA 98057	425-525-3073	R	152*	<.1
22	Carefusion Solutions LLC—*Bob Dietsch*	3750 Torrey View Ct, San Diego CA 92130	858-617-2100	R	144*	3.6
23	Hitachi Medical Systems America Inc—*Don Broomfield*	1959 Summit Commerce P, Twinsburg OH 44087	330-425-1313	S	142*	.2
24	Moore Medical LLC—*John Hammergren*	1690 New Britain Ave, Farmington CT 06032	860-826-3600	S	141*	.3
25	Siemens Healthcare Diagnostics Inc—*Donal Quinn*	5210 Pacific Concourse, Los Angeles CA 90045	310-645-8200	R	141*	2.4
26	Chindex International Inc—*Roberta Lipson*	4340 E West Hwy Ste 11, Bethesda MD 20814	301-215-7777	P	137	1.1
27	Patterson Dental Supply Inc—*Scott Anderson* Patterson Companies Inc	1031 Mendota Heights R, Saint Paul MN 55120	651-686-1600	S	134*	.3
28	Nds Surgical Imaging LLC—*Fred B Parks*	5750 Hellyer Ave, San Jose CA 95138	408-776-0085	R	130*	.1
29	Cassling Diagnostic Imaging Inc—*Michael Cassling*	13808 F St, Omaha NE 68137	402-334-5000	R	125*	.1
30	Archbold Health Services Inc—*Ken E Beverly*	PO Box 1018, Thomasville GA 31799	912-227-6809	R	122*	.3
31	Gulf South Medical Supply Inc PSS World Medical Inc	4345 Southpoint Blvd, Jacksonville FL 32216	904-332-3000	S	120	.3
32	Permobil Inc—*Larry Jackson*	300 Duke Dr, Lebanon TN 37090	615-547-1889	R	109*	.1
33	Nationshealth Inc—*Glenn M Parker*	13621 NW 12th St Ste 1, Sunrise FL 33323	954-903-5000	S	100	.6
34	Mycone Dental Supply Company Inc—*Cary Robinson*	616 Hollywood Ave, Cherry Hill NJ 08002	856-663-4700	R	100*	.3
35	Medical Specialties Distributors Inc—*Jim Beck*	800 Technology Center, Stoughton MA 02072	781-344-6000	R	80*	.2
36	Grogan's Healthcare Supply Inc—*Alan Grogan*	1016 S Broadway, Lexington KY 40504	859-254-6661	R	80*	.1
37	La Salle International Inc—*Albert Kirakosian*	9667 Owensmouth Ave, Chatsworth CA 91311	818-233-8000	R	80*	.1
38	Jordan Reses Supply Company LLC—*Drema Tomnsend*	PO Box 496, Ann Arbor MI 48106	734-213-5528	R	64*	<.1
39	Mp Biomedicals LLC—*Yasin Alsayyad*	3 Hutton Cntre Dr Ste, Santa Ana CA 92707	949-833-2500	R	63*	.4
40	Lambert Vet Supply LLC	714 5th St, Fairbury NE 68352	402-729-3044	R	61*	.1
41	Mabis DMI Healthcare Inc—*Mike Mazza*	1931 Norman Dr S, Waukegan IL 60085		R	57*	.1
42	Community Surgical Supply Of Toms River Inc—*Michael Fried*	PO Box 4686, Toms River NJ 08754	732-349-2990	R	55*	.3
43	Burkhart Dental Supply—*Lori Burkhart Isbell*	2502 S 78th St, Tacoma WA 98409	253-474-7761	R	54*	.4
44	Health Management Services Inc—*John Goodman*	9100 Southwest Fwy Ste, Houston TX 77074	713-541-2727	R	53*	.1
45	Esaote North America—*Claudio Bertolini*	8000 Castleway Dr, Indianapolis IN 46250		S	52*	.1
46	Med-Lab Supply Company Inc—*Gonzalo A Sr Diaz*	923 NW 27th Ave, Miami FL 33125	305-642-5144	R	51*	.1
47	Laboratory Supply Company Inc—*Charles E Davis*	250 Ottawa Ave, Louisville KY 40209	502-363-1891	R	46*	.2
48	Clinical Specialties Inc—*Edward Rivalsky*	6955 Treeline Dr, Brecksville OH 44141	440-717-1700	R	46*	.1
49	eCardio Inc—*Larry Lawson*	1717 N Sam Houston Pky, Houston TX 77038		R	45*	.3
50	Mohawk Hospital Equipment Inc—*Thomas Spellman*	PO Box 27, Utica NY 13503	315-797-0570	R	44*	.1
51	CHF Solutions Inc—*Dave Springer*	7601 Northland Dr Ste, Brooklyn Park MN 55428	763-463-4600	R	44*	.1
52	Associated Medical—*Phyllis Forman*	2901 Southampton Rd, Philadelphia PA 19154	215-677-0589	R	42*	.1
53	Shared Service Systems Inc—*David Koraleski*	1725 S 20th St, Omaha NE 68108	402-536-5300	S	41*	.2
54	Mammoth Medical Inc—*Larry Shirley*	10620 Scottsville Rd, Glasgow KY 42141	270-646-3024	R	39*	<.1
55	Phadia Us Inc—*David Esposito*	4169 Commercial Ave, Portage MI 49002	269-492-1976	S	38*	.3
56	H Enterprises International Inc—*John E Byrne*	120 S 6th St Ste 2300, Minneapolis MN 55402	612-340-8849	R	38*	.1
57	Midland Medical Supply Co—*Al Borchhardt*	4850 Old Cheney Rd, Lincoln NE 68516	402-423-8877	R	38*	.1
58	Accumed Technologies Inc—*Thomas Blaszczykiewicz*	160 Bud Mil Dr, Buffalo NY 14206	716-853-1800	R	34*	.2
59	Sarstedt Inc—*Walter Sarstedt*	PO Box 468, Newton NC 28658	828-465-4000	R	32*	.2
60	Polar Electro Inc—*Jeff Padovan*	1111 Marcus Ave Ste M1, Lake Success NY 11042	516-364-0400	R	32*	.1
61	Mercedes Medical Inc—*Alexandra Miller*	7590 Commerce Ct, Sarasota FL 34243		R	32*	<.1
62	Timm Medical Technologies Inc—*Jerry Timm*	P O Box 5679, Hopkins MN 55343	952-947-9410	S	31*	.1
63	Respitek Inc—*Gary Anzulewicz*	8257 Causeway Blvd, Tampa FL 33619	813-626-3333	R	29*	.1
64	J and B Medical Supply Company Inc—*Mary Shaya*	50496 Pontiac Trl Ste, Wixom MI 48393	248-896-6201	R	29*	.2
65	Practicewares Dental Supply Inc—*John Boresi*	11291 Sunrise Park Dr, Rancho Cordova CA 95742	916-638-8020	R	28*	.1
66	Pro-Dex Inc—*Mark Murphy*	2361 McGaw Ave, Irvine CA 92614	949-769-3200	P	27	.1
67	Vallen Corp—*David Gabriel*	521 N Sam Houston Pkwy, Houston TX 77060	281-500-4500	S	27*	.1
68	Associated Healthcare Systems Inc—*Peter Storey*	85 Woodridge Dr, Amherst NY 14228	716-564-4500	R	27*	<.1
69	Jorgensen Laboratories Inc—*Irvin Jorgensen*	1450 Van Buren Ave, Loveland CO 80538	970-669-2500	R	27*	<.1
70	Armstrong Medical Industries Inc—*Warren G Armstrong*	PO Box 700, Lincolnshire IL 60069	847-913-0101	R	26*	.1
71	Ortho-Tex Inc—*J Randolph Harig*	1211 Arion Pky, San Antonio TX 78216	210-366-2990	R	26*	<.1
72	Hardy Media—*Jay Hardy*	1430 W Mccoy Ln, Santa Maria CA 93455	805-346-2766	R	25*	.2
73	Richard Wolf Medical Instruments Corp—*Alfons Notheis*	353 Corporate Woods Pk, Vernon Hills IL 60061	847-913-1113	R	25*	.2
74	Alcohol Monitoring Systems Inc—*Michael Iiams*	1241 W Mineral Ave Ste, Littleton CO 80120	303-989-8900	R	22*	<.1
75	Specialty Surgical Instrumentation Inc—*Lou Wallace*	200 River Hills Dr, Nashville TN 37210	615-883-9090	R	22*	.1
76	Fujifilm Medical Systems USA Inc—*Takuski Nasu*	419 W Ave, Stamford CT 06902	203-324-2000	R	22*	.4
77	American Hearing Systems Inc—*Carsten Buhl*	8001 E Bloomington Fwy, Bloomington MN 55420	763-404-1122	R	21*	.1
78	Dc Dental Supplies LLC—*Harvey Friedman*	1133 Greenwood Rd Ste, Baltimore MD 21208	410-653-7500	R	21*	.1
79	Mada Medical Products Inc—*Jeffrey Adam*	625 Washington Ave, Carlstadt NJ 07072	201-460-0454	R	20*	.1
80	Ampronix Inc—*Nausser Fathollahi*	15 Whatney, Irvine CA 92618	949-273-8000	R	20*	.1
81	McBain Systems—*Michael Crump*	2665 Park Center Dr Bl, Simi Valley CA 93065	805-581-6800	R	20*	.1
82	Nelson Laboratories LP—*Roberta Bruget*	4001 N Lewis, Sioux Falls SD 57104	605-336-2451	R	20*	.1
83	Sysmex America Inc—*John Kershaw*	1 Nelson C White Pkwy, Mundelein IL 60060	847-996-4500	R	20*	.5
84	Aggio Medical Inc—*Vince Coleht*	3222 Wellington Ct Ste, Raleigh NC 27615	919-878-6666	R	20*	.1
85	Medikmark Inc—*David Sanders*	3600 Bur Wood Dr, Waukegan IL 60085	847-887-8400	R	19*	.1
86	A Plus International Inc—*Wayne Lin*	5138 Eucalyptus Ave, Chino CA 91710	909-591-5168	R	18*	.1
87	A Plus Medical and Mobility	1225 Walton Way, Augusta GA 30901	706-722-0276	R	18*	<.1
88	Dedicated Distribution Inc—*Steven Cole*	640 Miami Ave, Kansas City KS 66105	913-371-2200	R	18*	<.1
89	Kpi Ultrasound Inc—*William Ipsen*	887 Marlborough Ave, Riverside CA 92507	951-367-0872	R	18*	<.1
90	Biotech Medical LLC—*Samuel Parker*	7800 Whipple Ave Nw, Canton OH 44767	330-494-5504	R	16*	.8

Note: An asterisk (*) indicates an estimated financial figure. The company type code used is as follows: R = Private, P = Public, S = Private Subsidiary, B = Public Subsidiary, D = Division, J = Joint Venture, I = Investment Fund.

COMPANY RANKINGS BY SALES WITHIN 4-DIGIT SIC

Rank	Company Name—*Executive Officer*	Address, City, State, Zip	Phone	Type	Fin	Empls
91	Wrymark Inc—*L Matthews*	11833 Westline Industr, Saint Louis MO 63146	314-991-3891	R	16*	<.1
92	Tactile Systems Technology Inc—*Irene Waldridge*	1331 Tyler St NE Ste 2, Minneapolis MN 55413		R	16*	.1
93	Total Pharmacy Supply Inc—*Cindy Moses*	3400 Ave E East, Arlington TX 76011	817-861-4416	R	16*	<.1
94	Grand X-Ray Supplies Co—*Richard Riley*	PO Box 2442, Grand Rapids MI 49501	616-459-0145	R	16*	<.1
95	Integrated Medical Systems Inc—*Patrick Orio*	12600 S Holiday Dr, Alsip IL 60803	708-597-7105	R	15*	.1
96	Brasseler Holdings Peter LP—*Bill Miller*	1 Brasseler Blvd, Savannah GA 31419	912-925-8525	R	15*	.4
97	Nihon Kohden America Inc—*Michael Ohsawa*	90 Icon St, Foothill Ranch CA 92610	949-580-1555	S	15*	<.1
98	Swiss Gotham—*Neal Rossner*	26 Broadway Ste 400, New York NY 10004	212-529-8859	R	15*	<.1
99	Tri-State Surgical Supply and Equipment Ltd—*George Hoffman*	409 Hoyt St, Brooklyn NY 11231	718-624-1000	R	14*	.1
100	Kentec Medical Inc—*Steve Becsi*	17871 Fitch, Irvine CA 92614	949-863-0810	R	14*	<.1
101	Cornell Surgical Co—*Howard Shiffman*	30 New Bridge Rd, Bergenfield NJ 07621	201-384-9000	R	14*	.1
102	Cameron Health Inc—*Kevin Hykes*	905 Calle Amanecer Ste, San Clemente CA 92673	949-498-5630	R	14*	.1
103	Gatti Medical Supply Inc—*William Gatti*	574 Philadelphia St St, Indiana PA 15701	724-349-4400	R	14*	.1
104	Richie's Pharmacy And Medical Supply Inc—*Richie Ray*	12820 Hwy 105 W, Conroe TX 77304		R	14*	<.1
105	School Health Corp—*Susan Rogers*	865 Muirfield Dr, Hanover Park IL 60133	630-582-0024	R	13*	.1
106	Oncology Services International Inc—*Philip Podmore*	400 Rella Blvd Ste 123, Montebello NY 10901	845-357-6560	R	13*	<.1
107	HITEC Group International Inc—*Madelaine W Uzuanis*	1743 Quincy Ave Ste 15, Naperville IL 60540	630-654-9200	R	13*	.1
108	Medela Inc—*Carolin Archibald*	PO Box 660, Mchenry IL 60051	815-363-1166	R	12*	.3
109	Mosso's Medical Supply Company Inc—*Mike Stubbs*	RR 6 Box 15 Center Dr, Latrobe PA 15650	724-537-9377	S	12*	.1
110	MediQuip International—*Ralph Armstrong*	P O Box 941227, Plano TX 75094		R	12*	<.1
111	Phase 2 Medical Manufacturing Inc—*Adam Prime*	88 Airport Dr Ste 100, Rochester NH 03867	603-332-8900	R	12*	.1
112	Jentree Inc—*Jeff Hammontree*	1140 Deerfoot Industri, Rainbow City AL 35906	256-413-0633	R	12*	.1
113	Inland Imaging Business Associates LLC—*Melissa Gage*	801 S Stevens St, Spokane WA 99204	509-456-5600	R	11*	.1
114	Freedom Medical Inc—*Frank Gwynn*	219 Welsh Pool Rd, Exton PA 19341	610-903-0200	R	11*	.1
115	Still River Systems Inc—*Joseph Jachinowski*	300 Foster St Ste 3, Littleton MA 01460	978-540-1500	R	11*	.1
116	Pharmalucence Inc—*Glenn Alto*	10 Deangelo Dr, Bedford MA 01730	781-275-7120	R	11*	.1
117	Quality Assured Services Inc—*Michael R Visnich*	70 S Keller Rd, Orlando FL 32810	407-563-2860	R	11*	.1
118	Comfort Medical Supply LLC—*Craig Daley*	615 S Yonge St, Ormond Beach FL 32174	386-673-6902	R	11*	.1
119	Midwest Scientific Inc—*Larry Degenhart*	280 Vance Rd, Valley Park MO 63088	636-225-9997	R	11*	<.1
120	Ardus Medical Inc—*Troy J Powell*	11297 Grooms Rd, Cincinnati OH 45242	513-469-7867	R	11*	<.1
121	Graham-Field Bandage Inc—*Kenneth Spett* GF Health Products Inc	2935 Northeast Parkway, Atlanta GA 30360	770-368-4700	S	11*	.1
122	Euclid Spiral Paper Tube Corp—*Leonard Buckner*	PO Box 458, Apple Creek OH 44606	330-698-4711	R	10*	.1
123	Med Share Inc—*Prakash Gandhi*	26222 Telg Rd Ste 100, Southfield MI 48033	248-827-7200	R	10*	.1
124	California Radiographics Inc—*Ken Henton*	3335 Soquel Dr, Soquel CA 95073	831-462-8399	R	10*	<.1
125	Treatment Systems Inc—*Paul Schubert*	6300 Westgate Rd Ste A, Raleigh NC 27617	919-782-9050	R	10*	.1
126	National Medical Supply Company Inc—*Edward Jarosz*	495 Woodcreek Dr, Bolingbrook IL 60440	630-378-0700	R	10*	.1
127	MarketLab Inc—*Mike Bieker*	PO Box 77000, Detroit MI 48277	616-656-2484	R	10*	.1
128	Burgoon Co—*Nancy Evans*	PO Box 1168, Galveston TX 77553	409-766-1900	R	10*	<.1
129	Adenna Inc—*Maxwell Lee*	11932 Baker Pl, Santa Fe Springs CA 90670	562-777-8026	R	10*	<.1
130	Nextron Medical Technologies—*Dr Eruzzi*	45 Kulick Rd, Fairfield NJ 07004		R	10*	.1
131	Sentech Medical Systems Inc—*Abbey Daniels*	4200 Nw 120th Ave, Coral Springs FL 33065	954-340-0500	R	10*	.1
132	Binding Site Inc—*Richard Rowland*	5889 Oberlin Dr Ste 10, San Diego CA 92121	858-453-9177	R	10*	.1
133	Valeda Company LLC—*Rose Ferreira*	PO Box 403529, Atlanta GA 30384	954-986-6665	R	10*	.1
134	Atlantic Coast Orthopaedic Medical Supplies Inc—*Stuart Ross*	PO Box 26785, Charlotte NC 28221	704-921-0116	R	10*	<.1
135	Origio Inc—*Deborah Bryant*	2400 Hunters Way, Charlottesville VA 22911	434-979-4000	R	9*	.1
136	Southern Anesthesia and Surgical Inc—*Mike Stamps*	1 Southern Ct, West Columbia SC 29169	803-739-1452	R	9*	.1
137	Global Medical Imaging LLC—*Kate Hoffmann*	222 Rampart St, Charlotte NC 28203	704-940-7755	R	9*	.1
138	Rps Inc—*David Price*	1815 Washington St, Michigan City IN 46360	219-874-8424	R	9*	.1
139	ADCO Surgical Supply Inc—*Karen Wright*	PO Box 1328, Bangor ME 04402	207-942-5273	R	9*	<.1
140	Secure Care Products Inc—*Forrest Mckerley*	39 Chenell Dr, Concord NH 03301	603-223-0745	R	9*	.1
141	Image Stream Medical Inc—*Eddie Mitchell*	1 Monarch Dr Ste 102, Littleton MA 01460	978-486-8494	R	9*	.1
142	Sklar Corp—*Donald Taylor*	889 S Matlack St, West Chester PA 19382	610-430-3200	R	9*	.1
143	Grove Medical Inc—*Larry Lollis*	1089 Park W Blvd, Greenville SC 29611	864-269-0283	R	9*	.1
144	Regional Medical Rental and Sales—*Harvey Mitchell*	11712 Florida Blvd, Baton Rouge LA 70815	225-272-5919	R	9*	.1
145	Ems Innovations Inc—*Joseph Ferko*	PO Box 239, Pasadena MD 21123	410-255-3314	R	8*	<.1
146	Advacare Home Services Inc—*Tammy Zelenko*	200 Villani Dr Ste 300, Bridgeville PA 15017	412-249-9000	R	8*	.1
147	Care Rehab and Orthopaedic Products Inc—*Christian Hunt*	PO Box 916, Mc Lean VA 22101	703-448-9644	R	8*	.1
148	Miller Veterinary Supply Company Inc—*Wilma Smith*	PO Box 470, Fort Worth TX 76101	817-335-5487	R	8*	<.1
149	Prime Medical Supply Corp—*NJ Davis*	5723 New Utrecht Ave, Brooklyn NY 11219	718-437-0066	R	8*	<.1
150	Omnica Corp—*Rex Bare*	15560 Rockfield Blvd C, Irvine CA 92618	949-472-0275	R	8*	<.1
151	Medgyn Products Inc—*Lakshman Agadi*	PO Box 3126, Oak Brook IL 60522	630-627-4105	R	8*	.1
152	Dixie Dental Inc—*Alma Whittington*	PO Box 13913, Jackson MS 39236	601-354-5411	R	8*	<.1
153	American Dental Coop—*James Stover*	402 B N A Dr Ste 500, Nashville TN 37217	615-366-3230	R	7*	.1
154	Sterling Medical Products Inc—*Carrie Woodburn*	8 Holland, Irvine CA 92618	949-586-0411	R	7*	.1
155	Excalibur Lab Specialists Inc—*Robert Skach*	2232 Meridian Blvd Ste, Minden NV 89423	775-783-1701	R	7*	<.1
156	Cone Instruments Inc—*Patrick Beck*	5201 Naiman Pkwy, Solon OH 44139	440-248-1035	R	7*	<.1
157	Universal Marine Medical Supply Co—*Julius R Nasso*	PO Box 199035, Brooklyn NY 11219	718-438-4804	R	7*	<.1
158	Direct Dental Supply Co—*Kathy Warren* Patterson Companies Inc	1267 Spice Island Dr, Sparks NV 89431	775-331-4300	S	7*	<.1
159	Fischer Medical Technologies Inc—*Ronald B Shores*	325 Interlocken Pky Bl, Broomfield CO 80021	303-280-2311	R	7*	<.1
160	Kaneka Pharma America LLC—*Kunihiko Fujii*	546 5th Ave Fl 21, New York NY 10036	212-705-4340	R	7*	<.1
161	Hospital Associates—*Cindy Juhas*	2886 E Blue Star St, Anaheim CA 92806		R	7*	.1
162	Fisher and Paykel Healthcare Inc—*Justin Callahan*	15365 Barranca Pkwy, Irvine CA 92618	949-453-4000	R	7*	.1
163	Biosensors International USA—*Mike Kleine*	PO Box 60069, Irvine CA 92602	949-553-8300	R	7*	.1
164	Zimmer Thomson Associates Inc—*Frederick Thomson*	W165n5815 Ridgewood Dr, Menomonee Falls WI 53051	262-252-4500	R	7*	.1
165	PromedixCom Inc—*Skip Klintworth*	1136 S 3600 W Ste 600, Salt Lake City UT 84104		R	7*	.1
166	Capital X-Ray Inc—*Terry Stiff*	PO Box 780337, Tallassee AL 36078	334-283-8410	R	7*	.1
167	Island Dental Supply Co—*Kurt Larsen*	300 Jericho Quadrangle, Jericho NY 11753	516-688-6480	R	7*	<.1
168	Fortec Medical Inc—*Drew Forham*	9238 Shortridge Ave, Saint Louis MO 63144	314-918-7360	R	6*	.1
169	Marine Medical Inc—*Gregory Porter*	PO Box 1145, Dickinson TX 77539	281-309-9919	R	6*	.1
170	Personal Support Medical Suppliers Inc—*David Hatooka*	270 Geiger Rd Bldg F, Philadelphia PA 19115	215-464-7304	R	6*	<.1
171	Pruett Medical Ltd—*Thomas Pruett*	1609 W 92nd St, Kansas City MO 64114	816-363-5331	R	6*	.1
172	Griffin Medical Products Inc—*Bruno Basile*	PO Box 457, Bridgeton NJ 08302	856-455-6870	R	6*	.1
173	Pemco Dental Corp—*Richard Balfour*	PO Box 249, Springfield NJ 07081	973-564-9622	R	6*	.1
174	Life-Assist Inc—*Ramona Davis*	11277 Sunrise Park Dr, Rancho Cordova CA 95742	916-635-3822	R	6*	<.1
175	Toray Marketing and Sales Inc (New York New York)—*Sad-ayuki Sakakibura*	461 5th Ave Fl 9, New York NY 10017	212-697-8150	S	6*	<.1
176	Premier Medical Supplies Inc—*Allen McCann*	18234 S Miles Rd, Cleveland OH 44128	216-823-2777	R	6*	.1
177	Sentry Medical Products Inc—*Edwin Novak*	795 Coronis Way, Green Bay WI 54304	920-337-0201	R	6*	.1

Rank	Company Name—*Executive Officer*	Address, City, State, Zip	Phone	Type	Fin	Empls
178	Amfit Inc—*Tony Tadin*	5408 Ne 88th St Ste D4, Vancouver WA 98665	360-573-9100	R	6*	<.1
179	Kimmey Plumbing Co—*J Kimmey*	496 W Sharon Rd, Cincinnati OH 45246	513-825-4023	R	6*	.1
180	Berkeley Medevices—*Dieter Kubny*	1330 S 51st St, Richmond CA 94804	510-231-2474	R	6*	<.1
181	Medical Supply Corp—*Thomas Sternfels*	1421 E 8 Mile Rd, Ferndale MI 48220	248-547-8100	R	6*	<.1
182	Sourcetech Medical LLC—*Frank Lyman*	295 E Lies Rd, Carol Stream IL 60188	630-933-7610	R	5*	<.1
183	Savoy Medical Supply Company Inc—*Guy Savia*	745 Calebs Path, Hauppauge NY 11788	631-234-7003	R	5*	<.1
184	Miat Inc—*Joseph Wosner*	5700 49th St, Maspeth NY 11378	718-381-5555	R	5*	<.1
185	Uromed Inc—*Jim Weatherford*	7340 Mcginnis Ferry Rd, Suwanee GA 30024	770-232-5821	R	5*	<.1
186	Deaf Link Inc—*Kay Chiodo*	PO Box 701826, San Antonio TX 78270	210-590-7446	R	5*	.1
187	Extrakare LLC—*Scott Lloyd*	PO Box 922575, Norcross GA 30010	770-449-6898	R	5*	<.1
188	Radebaugh-Fetzer Co—*Donald Boggs*	22400 Ascoa Ct, Strongsville OH 44149	440-878-4700	R	5*	<.1
189	HomeReach Inc—*Francis L Baby*	404 E Wilson Bridge Rd, Worthington OH 43085	614-566-0888	R	5*	<.1
190	Universal Pharmaceutical Medical Supply Company Inc—*Julius Nasso*	5824 12th Ave, Brooklyn NY 11219	718-438-4804	R	5*	<.1
191	Medico-Mart Inc—*Gerald Walsh*	2323 Corporate Dr, Waukesha WI 53189	262-446-2323	R	5*	<.1
192	Research Products International Corp—*Robert Chudy*	410 N Business Ctr Dr, Mount Prospect IL 60056	847-635-7330	R	5*	<.1
193	Midstate Medical Supply and Equipment Rental Inc—*Todd Ross*	PO Box 2138, Conway AR 72033	501-932-0033	R	5*	<.1
194	Vssi Inc—*Craig Hart*	PO Box 431, Carthage MO 64836	417-358-0141	R	5*	<.1
195	Mark Debiase Inc—*Mark Debiase*	1525 A The Greensway, Ponte Vedra Beach FL 32082	904-280-6973	R	5*	<.1
196	Advanced Medical Center Inc—*Pejman Bady-Moghaddam*	PO Box 6380, Pahrump NV 89041	775-727-5509	R	5*	<.1
197	Kol Bio-Medical Instruments Inc—*Timothy Mcinerney*	PO Box 220630, Chantilly VA 20153	703-378-8600	R	5*	<.1
198	Metrohm-Peak LLC—*Bobbie Cooley*	12521 Gulf Fwy, Houston TX 77034	281-484-5000	R	5*	<.1
199	Clinical Technology Inc—*Dennis Forchione*	1 Corporation Ctr, Cleveland OH 44147	440-526-0160	R	4*	<.1
200	Diamond Springs 2 Inc—*Mitchell Waldman*	4150 Carr Ln Ct, Saint Louis MO 63119	314-351-2730	R	4*	<.1
201	Advanced Rehabilitation Technologies—*Richard Harris*	PO Box 915, Cardiff By The Sea CA 92007	858-621-5959	R	4*	<.1
202	Cedaron Medical Inc—*Karen Bond*	PO Box 2100, Davis CA 95617	530-758-7007	R	4*	<.1
203	Soma Medical Inc—*Peter Leonidas*	166 Highland Park Dr, Bloomfield CT 06002	860-218-2575	R	4*	<.1
204	Amber Diagnostics Inc—*Robert Serros*	2180 Premier Row, Orlando FL 32809	407-438-7847	R	4*	<.1
205	Federal Medical Supplies Inc—*J Bowen*	3316 Perkins Rd, Augusta GA 30906	706-793-6786	R	4*	<.1
206	Home Care Delivered Inc—*Gordon Fox*	4144 Innslake Dr Ste A, Glen Allen VA 23060	804-354-1578	R	4*	<.1
207	AMS Group Inc—*James Stevens*	PO Box 36882, Birmingham AL 35236	205-685-9090	R	4*	<.1
208	Med1Online Inc—*Scott Carson*	4403 Table Mountain Dr, Golden CO 80403	720-888-1591	R	4*	<.1
209	Endolite North America Ltd—*Chris Nolan*	1031 Byers Rd, Miamisburg OH 45342	937-291-3636	R	4*	<.1
210	Alpin Surgical Specialties Inc—*Gary Mckindree*	105 Lincoln Ave, Butler PA 16001	724-285-6324	R	4*	<.1
211	Alpha Imaging Inc—*Albert Perrico*	4455 Glenbrook Rd, Willoughby OH 44094	440-953-3800	R	4*	<.1
212	Professional Health Sales Inc—*William Bevan*	532 W Market St, Perkasie PA 18944	215-453-5214	R	4*	<.1
213	South Jersey Medical Equipment Ltd—*David Gold*	7 Holden Rd, Cherry Hill NJ 08034	856-482-5225	R	4*	<.1
214	Advanced Medical Concepts Inc—*Tina Nowakowski*	9 Gwynns Mill Ct Ste H, Owings Mills MD 21117	410-902-7900	R	4*	<.1
215	Kadence Healthcare Inc—*Greg Kahn*	10840 Walker St, Cypress CA 90630	714-220-0071	R	4*	<.1
216	Lourdes At Home—*Sally Hoffman*	4102 Vestal Rd, Vestal NY 13850	607-772-1598	R	4*	.1
217	Haemotronic Ltd—*Silvio Eruzzi*	45 Kulick Rd, Fairfield NJ 07004	973-575-0614	R	4*	<.1
218	Radiation Services Of Indiana Inc—*James Comer*	422 Park 800 Dr, Greenwood IN 46143	317-881-7269	R	4*	<.1
219	Kalamazoo X-Ray Sales Inc—*Jim White*	9136 Portage Industria, Portage MI 49024	269-327-6296	R	4*	<.1
220	Health Care Suppliers Inc—*Cliff Herd*	8831 S 117th St, La Vista NE 68128	402-597-3088	R	4*	<.1
221	Size Wise Rentals—*Trever Frickey*	200 Walnut St, Kansas City MO 64106	816-841-0101	R	3*	<.1
222	Cresscare Medical Inc—*Todd Cressler*	133 S 5th St Ste 100, Newport PA 17074	717-567-9114	R	3*	<.1
223	Marina Medical Instruments Inc—*Alexander Barron*	955 Shotgun Rd, Sunrise FL 33326	954-924-4418	R	3*	<.1
224	Katena Products Inc—*Michael Vedral*	4 Stewart Ct, Denville NJ 07834	973-989-1600	R	3*	<.1
225	Medical Imaging Systems Inc—*Marc Shaefer*	2900 6th Ave S, Birmingham AL 35233	205-324-9729	R	3*	<.1
226	American Medical Supplies And Equipment Inc—*Victor Amat*	8361 Nw 36th St, Doral FL 33166	305-592-3422	R	3*	<.1
227	Sound Surgical Technologies LL—*Donald Wingerter*	13952 Denver W Pkwy St, Lakewood CO 80401	303-384-9133	R	3*	.1
228	Columbine Oxygen Service Inc—*Vince Cissell*	2453 W Church Ave, Littleton CO 80120	303-794-9111	R	3*	<.1
229	ABS Med Inc—*Andrew Bala*	116 Shore Dr, Burr Ridge IL 60527	630-286-8411	R	3*	<.1
230	Bsi Corp—*Jeremy Linder*	52 E Centre St Ste 2, Nutley NJ 07110	973-667-8400	R	3*	<.1
231	Zest Anchors Inc—*Paul Zuest*	2061 Wineridge Pl Ste, Escondido CA 92029	760-743-7744	R	3*	<.1
232	Biomed Resource Inc—*Jim Liu*	6466 Doolittle Ave, Riverside CA 92503	951-616-1988	R	3*	<.1
233	Globe Scientific Inc—*Milton Diamond*	PO Box 1625, Paramus NJ 07653	201-599-1400	R	3*	<.1
234	Orange County Dental Supply Corp—*Shiang-Fa Yu*	1131 Olympic Dr, Corona CA 92881	951-898-8888	R	3*	<.1
235	Team Orthopaedics—*Jim Meyer*	13040 W Lisbon Rd Ste, Brookfield WI 53005	262-754-6100	R	3*	<.1
236	Medical Marketing Associates Inc—*Ronald Gorman*	PO Box 170442, Milwaukee WI 53217	414-962-2405	R	3*	<.1
237	Hometown Oxygen Inc—*Jay Costner*	1005 S Kings Dr, Charlotte NC 28207	704-347-2233	R	3*	<.1
238	Bisco Dental Products Co—*Byoung Suh*	1100 W Irving Park Rd, Schaumburg IL 60193	847-534-6000	R	3*	<.1
239	DRG International Inc	1167 US Hwy 22 E, Mountainside NJ 07092	908-233-2079	R	3*	<.1
240	Phoenix Instruments Inc (Naperville Illinois)—*Arshad Javed*	2368 Corporate Ln, Naperville IL 60563	630-221-1820	R	3	<.1
241	Anderson Home Health Supply—*Christine Stapleton*	4063 Henderson Blvd, Tampa FL 33629	813-289-3811	R	3*	<.1
242	Complete Medical Products Inc—*James K McNeely*	2562 N Decatur Rd, Decatur GA 30033	404-373-6572	R	3*	<.1
243	Innovative Kitchens and Baths LLC	17313 Bell N Dr, Schertz TX 78154	210-651-0076	R	3*	<.1
244	Carefirst Of Fort Wayne Inc—*Chad Bachert*	PO Box 8866, Fort Wayne IN 46898	260-373-1600	R	3*	<.1
245	Associated X-Ray Corp—*Gary Johnson*	PO Box 120559, East Haven CT 06512	203-466-2446	R	3*	<.1
246	Jms Berkshire Resources Inc—*James Skesavage*	3535 Rte 66 Ste 4, Neptune NJ 07753	732-918-8115	R	3*	<.1
247	Classic X-Ray Ltd—*Jodell Basile*	1945 Wright Blvd, Schaumburg IL 60193	847-895-1817	R	3*	<.1
248	Vascular Care International Inc—*Cassandre Miller*	12966 County Rd 153, East Liberty OH 43319	937-642-4100	R	3*	<.1
249	CNY Medical Products Inc—*John Kumoda*	5 Lombard St Ste 1, Schenectady NY 12304	518-344-7024	R	3*	<.1
250	Scientific Device Laboratory Inc—*Stewart Lipton*	PO Box 1006, Des Plaines IL 60017	847-803-9495	R	3*	<.1
251	Colonial Surgical Supply Inc—*Mike Saleh*	1812 1/2 N Vermont Ave, Los Angeles CA 90027	323-666-4044	R	3*	<.1
252	Permatype Company Inc—*Mark Tulin*	83 NW Dr, Plainville CT 06062	860-747-9999	R	3*	<.1
253	Shofu Dental Corp—*Robert Noble*	1225 Stone Dr, San Marcos CA 92078	760-736-3277	R	3*	<.1
254	Carlin Employment Services Inc—*Robert Pherson*	15819 Schoolcraft St, Detroit MI 48227	313-493-4900	R	3*	<.1
255	Cardiocommand Inc—*Maynard Ramsey*	4920 W Cypress St Ste, Tampa FL 33607	813-289-5555	R	3*	<.1
256	Xpdent Corp—*Ellen Kuch*	12145 Sw 131st Ave, Miami FL 33186	305-233-3312	R	2*	<.1
257	Lifetec Inc—*Michael Christoi*	1710 S Wolf Rd, Wheeling IL 60090	847-459-7500	R	2*	<.1
258	Med Supply Cabinet Inc—*Thomas Doran*	777 Schwab Rd Ste U, Hatfield PA 19440	215-393-8672	R	2*	<.1
259	Newhouse Dental Supply—*Carl Alford*	2619 Oak St, Santa Ana CA 92707	714-557-9044	R	2*	<.1
260	Medsupply Corporation Inc—*Muhammed Quazi*	33333 Dequindre Rd Ste, Troy MI 48083	248-597-9004	R	2*	<.1
261	Acra-Cut Inc—*John Baker*	989 Main St, Acton MA 01720	978-263-2210	R	2*	<.1
262	Dreyer Materials Management—*John Potter*	501 W Fabyan Pkwy, Batavia IL 60510	630-482-9100	R	2*	<.1
263	Universal Medical Supply Corp—*Jerry Cook*	726 W Walnut St, Rogers AR 72756	479-936-8404	R	2*	<.1
264	Pari Innovative Manufacturers Inc—*Werner Gutmann*	2943 Oak Lake Blvd, Midlothian VA 23112	804-639-7235	R	2*	<.1
265	Summitek Inc—*Soon Kim*	13133 31st Ave, Flushing NY 11354	718-747-6363	R	2*	<.1

Note: An asterisk (*) indicates an estimated financial figure. The company type code used is as follows: R = Private, P = Public, S = Private Subsidiary, B = Public Subsidiary, D = Division, J = Joint Venture, I = Investment Fund.

COMPANY RANKINGS BY SALES WITHIN 4-DIGIT SIC

Rank	Company Name—*Executive Officer*	Address, City, State, Zip	Phone	Type	Fin	Empls
266	Stat Medical Supply Co—*Russ Hansen*	4894 South 300 West St, Murray UT 84107	801-261-4363	R	2*	<.1
267	ULTIMED Inc—*Tom Erickson*	287 E 6th St, Saint Paul MN 55101	651-291-7909	R	2*	<.1
268	Reavis Respiratory and Medical Equipment—*Jack Justice*	110 Burr Ave, Pauls Valley OK 73075	580-332-7773	R	2*	<.1
269	Armstrong Industries Inc—*Ralph Armstong*	PO Box 6589, Mckinney TX 75071	972-547-1400	R	2*	<.1
270	Emergency Resources International Inc—*Jennifer Rudolph*	1992 Player Cir S, Melbourne FL 32935	321-254-4320	R	2*	<.1
271	Home Medical Care Inc—*Joseph Draden*	PO Box 440, Waverly TN 37185	931-296-5000	R	2*	<.1
272	Omnis Health LLC	535 Enterprise Ave, Conway AR 72032	501-450-9063	R	2*	<.1
273	Schaerer Mayfield USA Inc—*Michal Palazzola*	4900 Charlemar Dr Bldg, Cincinnati OH 45227	513-561-2241	R	2*	<.1
274	Metron Home Care—*Mark Piersma*	5601 W Main St Ste 4, Kalamazoo MI 49009	269-382-4337	R	2*	<.1
275	Starliteworld Trading Co—*Ike Umenta*	25309 147th Rd, Rosedale NY 11422	718-723-3095	R	2*	<.1
276	Lamb and Assoc—*Allen Lamb*	115 Lees Cut 1, Wrightsville Beach NC 28480	910-256-2407	R	2*	<.1
277	Premiere Medical—*Barbara Maestas*	4201 Yale Blvd Ne Ste, Albuquerque NM 87107	505-343-8761	R	2*	<.1
278	Continental Medical Labs Inc—*Gary Swanson*	813 Ela Ave, Waterford WI 53185	262-534-2787	R	2*	<.1
279	Pro Med Center—*Cornelia Krieger*	174 Grand St, White Plains NY 10601	914-328-8077	R	1*	<.1
280	Louisiana Mobility Of Central La Inc—*Francis Harrison*	5508 Monroe Hwy, Ball LA 71405	318-640-0988	R	1*	<.1
281	International Respiratory Systems Inc—*Daniel Sheehan*	95 Ann St, Newburgh NY 12550	845-562-5546	R	1*	<.1
282	Hi Delta Tech Inc—*Glade James*	3762 S 150 E, Salt Lake City UT 84115	801-263-0975	R	1*	<.1
283	Titronics Research and Development Co—*Roger Titone*	PO Box 470, Tiffin IA 52340	319-545-7377	R	1*	<.1
284	Permark Inc—*Joseph M Cooperstein*	450 Raritan Center Pkw, Edison NJ 08837	732-225-3700	R	1*	<.1
285	American Liberty Corp—*Tony Adams*	1031 Providence Blvd, Providence Village TX 76227	214-335-3456	R	1*	<.1
286	Toshiba America Medical Systems Inc—*Hiromitsu Igarashi*	PO Box 2068, Tustin CA 92781	714-730-5000	R	1*	.9
287	Medical Store Of Palm Beach County Inc—*David Fielding*	300 Nrthpint Pkwy Ste, West Palm Beach FL 33407	561-840-7800	R	1*	<.1
288	TechniScan Inc—*David C Robinson*	3216 S Highland Dr Ste, Salt Lake City UT 84106	801-521-0444	P	<1	<.1
289	Salvadorini Consulting LLC	111 Linden Ln, Lexington NC 27292	336-238-6141	R	<1*	<.1

TOTALS: SIC 5047 Medical & Hospital Equipment
Companies: 289 .... 44,124 80.9

5048 Ophthalmic Goods

1	Charmant USA	400 American Rd, Morris Plains NJ 07950	973-538-1511	S	800*	3.5
2	Walman Optical Co—*Martin Bassett*	801 12th Ave N Ste 2, Minneapolis MN 55411	612-520-6000	R	182*	.8
3	Safilo USA—*Claudio Gottardi*	801 Jefferson Rd, Parsippany NJ 07054	973-952-2800	S	139*	.3
4	Pech Optical Corp—*Robert Pech*	PO Box 9100, Sioux City IA 51102	712-277-3937	S	72*	.3
5	City Optical Company Inc—*Lawrence Tavel*	2839 Lafayette Rd, Indianapolis IN 46222	317-924-1300	R	37*	.3
6	Charmant Inc—*Haruhiko Aida*	400 American Rd, Morris Plains NJ 07950	973-538-1511	R	32*	.1
7	Barbara Creations Inc—*Yisroel Gluck*	8230 Austin Ave, Morton Grove IL 60053	847-679-1012	R	25*	<.1
8	Oliver Peoples Inc—*David Schulte*	8570 W Sunset Blvd Ste, Los Angeles CA 90069	310-734-5000	S	23*	.1
9	Atlantic Optical Company Inc—*Sheldon Lehrer*	PO Box 3519, Chatsworth CA 91313	818-407-1890	R	14*	.1
10	New Hampshire Optical Company Inc—*Dennis Bresslin*	40 Terrill Park Dr Unit, Concord NH 03301	603-225-7121	R	13*	.1
11	Optovision Technologies Inc—*Peter Zuccarelli*	10495 Olympic Dr, Dallas TX 75220	214-351-1155	R	13*	.1
12	X Wiley Inc—*Myles Freeman*	7800 Patterson Pass Rd, Livermore CA 94550	925-243-9810	R	13*	.1
13	Mj Optical Inc—*Mary Hagge*	PO Box 3169, Omaha NE 68103	402-339-4029	R	12*	.1
14	Marco Ophthalmic Inc—*David Marco*	PO Box 16938, Jacksonville FL 32245	904-642-9330	R	11*	.1
15	Visionweb Holdings LLC—*Abraham Gracia*	8601 Ranch Rd 2222 3-4, Austin TX 78730	512-241-8500	R	10*	.1
16	Barry Optical Laboratories Inc—*Jeffrey Baraban*	200 Dixon Ave Ste B, Amityville NY 11701	631-532-6269	R	9*	<.1
17	McGee Group Inc—*A McGee*	510 Commerce Park Dr S, Marietta GA 30060	770-422-0010	R	9*	<.1
18	Nidek Inc—*Motoki Ozawa*	47651 Westinghouse Dr, Fremont CA 94539	510-226-5700	R	8*	.1
19	Robertson Optical Labratories Inc—*Calvin Robertson*	2309 Hwy 81, Loganville GA 30052	770-554-3000	R	7*	.1
20	Eyekon Medical Inc—*Mark Robinson*	2451 Enterprise Rd, Clearwater FL 33763	727-793-0170	R	7*	<.1
21	Sun Optics—*Laura Raile*	1785 S 4490 W, Salt Lake City UT 84104	801-924-0440	R	7*	<.1
22	Lens Masters Inc—*Bernard Singer*	6611 Nw 15th Way, Fort Lauderdale FL 33309	954-975-8600	R	7*	<.1
23	Associated Development Corp—*Lee Hodges*	PO Box 1170, Pinellas Park FL 33780	727-525-2153	R	6*	<.1
24	Moria Inc—*Patrick Dougherty*	1050 Crosskeys Dr, Doylestown PA 18902	215-230-7662	R	5*	<.1
25	Allentown Optical Corp—*Michael Gassler*	PO Box 25003, Lehigh Valley PA 18002	610-433-5269	R	4*	<.1
26	Mancine Optical Company Inc—*Joseph Mancine*	2910 Rte 130 Ste 1, Delran NJ 08075	856-764-0200	R	4*	<.1
27	Hoya Lens Of Chicago Inc—*Paul Ingraffia*	3531 Martens St, Franklin Park IL 60131	847-678-4700	R	4*	<.1
28	Gulf States Optical Laboratories Inc—*Pierre Bezou*	313 Coolidge St, Jefferson LA 70121	504-834-1646	R	4*	<.1
29	Professional Ophthalmic Laboratories Inc—*Diane Strickler*	PO Box 8865, Roanoke VA 24014	540-345-7303	R	3*	<.1
30	Sunburst Optics Inc—*Jeremy Gnade*	PO Box 11577, Syracuse NY 13218	315-471-5161	R	3*	<.1
31	Skaggs And Gruber Ltd—*Jeff Skaggs*	2970 Sutro St, Reno NV 89512	775-359-6667	S	3*	<.1
32	Optics Inc—*Dale Springer*	2936 Westway Dr, Brunswick OH 44212	330-273-5111	R	3*	<.1
33	Pelican Optical Labs Inc—*Dennis Camp*	6850 Whitfield Industr, Sarasota FL 34243	941-751-4437	R	3*	<.1
34	Exclusively Ours Inc—*Edward Chernoff*	2 Neil Ct, Oceanside NY 11572	516-255-0179	R	3*	<.1
35	Aco Optical Lab—*Maurice Choi*	2101 S Atlantic Blvd, Commerce CA 90040	323-266-3030	R	3*	<.1
36	Sans Pareil Inc—*Steven Lipawsky*	4151 Nw 124th Ave, Coral Springs FL 33065	954-656-1822	R	2*	<.1
37	Gateway Optical Company Inc—*Chris Federonko*	PO Box 7268, Saint Louis MO 63177	314-968-1905	R	2*	<.1
38	Ambler Surgical Corp—*Martin Anthony*	404 Gordon Dr, Exton PA 19341	610-280-7361	R	2*	<.1
39	Coyote Vision USA—*Steven Carhart*	PO Box 277, Pittsford NY 14534	585-385-7580	R	2*	<.1
40	John S Milam Optical Co—*John Milam*	109 16th Ave S, Nashville TN 37203	615-242-3372	R	2*	<.1
41	Hi Tech Optical Inc—*Tom Ryan*	PO Box 1443, Saginaw MI 48605	989-799-9390	R	1*	<.1
42	Eagle Optical Inc—*James Novak*	2755 Indiana Ave, Lansing IL 60438	708-474-3500	R	1*	<.1
43	LensCrafters Inc—*Dave Browne*	4000 Luxottica Pl, Mason OH 45040	513-765-6000	S	N/A	14.0

TOTALS: SIC 5048 Ophthalmic Goods
Companies: 43 .... 1,511 20.7

5049 Professional Equipment Nec

1	Carl Zeiss Inc—*Jim Sharp*	1 Zeiss Dr, Thornwood NY 10594	914-747-1800	S	4,829*	.5
2	KGP Telecommunications Inc—*Kathleen G Putrah*	3305 Hwy 60 W, Faribault MN 55021	507-334-2268	R	1,762*	1.2
3	Global Imaging Systems Inc—*Michael Shea*	PO Box 273478, Tampa FL 33688	813-960-5508	S	1,031	4.2
4	Sony Precision Technology America Inc—*Ryoji Chubachi*	20381 Hermana Cir, Lake Forest CA 92630	949-770-8400	S	750	N/A
5	Supelco Inc—*Rakesh Sahdev*	595 N Harrison Rd, Bellefonte PA 16823	814-359-3441	S	276*	.3
6	MTI Corporation (Paramus New Jersey)—*Patrick Sandell*	11515 Vanstory Dr, Huntersville NC 28078	704-875-8332	S	170*	.3
7	Strategic Distribution Inc—*Donald C Woodring*	1414 Radcliffe St Ste, Bristol PA 19007	215-633-1900	R	137	.4
8	ALMART Enterprises Inc—*Alan Smith*	1383 Frey Rd, Pittsburgh PA 15235	412-380-1335	R	126*	<.1
9	Construction Specialties Inc—*Ronald F Dadd*	3 Werner Wy, Lebanon NJ 08833	908-236-0800	R	112*	.7
10	Cameca Instruments Inc—*Georges Antier*	5500 Nobel Dr, Madison WI 53711	608-274-6880	S	110*	.3
11	PrimeSource Food Service Equipment Inc—*Fritzi Woods*	1409 S Lamar St Ste 10, Dallas TX 75215	214-273-4900	R	106*	.1
12	Jeol USA Inc—*Peter Genovese*	PO Box 6043, Peabody MA 01961	978-535-5900	R	106*	.3
13	Shimadzu Scientific Instruments Inc—*Takeshi Kaumi*	7102 Riverwood Dr, Columbia MD 21046	410-381-1227	R	102*	.2
14	Government Scientific Source Inc—*Wayne Bardsley*	12351 Sunrise Valley D, Reston VA 20191	703-734-1805	R	99*	.1
15	Safeware Inc (Landover Maryland)—*Charles Simons*	3200 Hubbard Rd, Landover MD 20785		R	63*	.1

Rank	Company Name—Executive Officer	Address, City, State, Zip	Phone	Type	Fin	Empls
16	Satisloh North America Inc—Lawrence Clarke	PO Box 664, Germantown WI 53022	262-255-6001	R	57*	.1
17	Gesswein—Dwight Gesswein	PO Box 3998, Bridgeport CT 06605	203-366-5400	R	54*	.1
18	Eastern Tools and Equipment Inc—David Fan	1040 S Rockefeller Ave, Ontario CA 91761	909-390-8989	R	51*	<.1
19	Skaggs Companies Inc—Don Skaggs	3828 S Main St, Salt Lake City UT 84115	801-261-4400	R	39*	.1
20	Kurt J Lesker Co—Kurt Lesker	PO Box 10, Clairton PA 15025	412-387-9200	R	39*	.2
21	Thomas Scientific—Richard Drew	PO Box 99, Swedesboro NJ 08085	856-467-2000	R	39*	.2
22	ReCellular Inc—Steve Manning	2555 Bishop Cir W, Dexter MI 48130	734-205-2200	R	38*	.2
23	North Coast Medical Inc—Mark E Biehl	8100 Camino Arroyo, Gilroy CA 95020	408-776-5000	R	37*	.1
24	Alvin and Company Inc—Scott Shoham	PO Box 188, Windsor CT 06095	860-243-8991	R	35*	.1
25	Connexion Technologies Inc—Glen Lang	111 Corning Rd, Cary NC 27518	919-674-0036	R	30	.6
26	Universal Photonics Inc—Neil Johnson	495 W John St, Hicksville NY 11801	516-935-4000	R	27*	.1
27	Intellidot Corp—Thomas G Klopack	13520 Evening Creek Dr, San Diego CA 92128	858-746-3100	R	25*	<.1
28	Fiber Optic Center Inc—Neal H Weiss	23 Centre St, New Bedford MA 02740	508-992-6464	R	21*	<.1
29	Siemens Audio Inc—George Nolen	153 E 53rd St 56th Fl, New York NY 10022	212-258-4000	S	20*	<.1
30	Ocenture LLC—Cheryl Lynch	4899 Belfort Rd Ste 40, Jacksonville FL 32256	940-766-1600	R	18*	<.1
31	Wilkens-Anderson Co—Bruce Wilkens	4525 W Division St, Chicago IL 60651	773-384-4433	R	16*	<.1
32	Broadcasters General Store Inc—David Kerstin	2480 SE 52nd St, Ocala FL 34480	352-622-7700	R	16*	.1
33	Duhadaway Tool And Die Shop Inc—Robert Du Hadaway	801 Dawson Dr, Newark DE 19713	302-366-0113	R	16*	<.1
34	Chiral Technologies Inc—Thomas B Lewis	800 N Five Points Rd, West Chester PA 19380	610-594-2100	R	15*	<.1
35	Tierney Brothers Inc—James Tierney	3300 University Ave Se, Minneapolis MN 55414	612-331-5500	R	14*	.1
36	Key Blue Prints Inc—David Key	195 E Livingston Ave, Columbus OH 43215	614-228-3285	R	14*	.1
37	Continental Laboratory Products Inc—Paul Nowak	6190 Cornerstone Ct E, San Diego CA 92121	858-279-5000	R	13*	.1
38	Abc School Equipment Inc—Gary Stell	1451 E 6th St, Corona CA 92879	951-817-2200	R	13*	.1
39	TW Medical Veterinary Supply—Mark Ziller	3610 Lohman Ford Rd, Lago Vista TX 78645		S	13	<.1
40	Sargent-Welch Scientific Co—Jim Rogers	PO Box 4130, Buffalo NY 14217		D	13*	.1
41	National Laboratory Specialists Inc—Gene Cornstubble	103 Roundabout Ln, Huntsville TX 77320	936-295-6220	R	13*	.1
42	MacAlaster Bicknell Company Inc (New Haven Connecticut)—Larry Bee	PO Box 3257, New Haven CT 06515	203-624-4191	R	12*	<.1
43	Sovereign Scientific Inc—Daniel Garibotto	2020 Ne 153rd St Ste 1, North Miami Beach FL 33162	305-757-8000	R	11*	<.1
44	Foss North America Inc—Christian Svensgaard	8091 Wallace Rd, Eden Prairie MN 55344	952-974-9892	R	11*	.1
45	Ace Educational Supplies Inc—Richard Ludwig	5595 S University Dr, Davie FL 33328	954-434-2773	R	11*	.1
46	Numax Inc—David B Speer	1073 Rte 94 Ste 11, New Windsor NY 12553	545-674-9060	S	11*	<.1
47	Palm Optical Company Inc—Stan Besner	PO Box 600189, Miami FL 33160	305-651-1373	R	11*	<.1
48	Practical Systems Inc—Glen Hernandez	11617 Prospect Rd, Odessa FL 33556	727-376-7900	R	11*	<.1
49	Polatis Photonics Inc—Gerald Wesel	1 Tech Dr Ste 210, Andover MA 01810	978-670-4910	R	11*	.1
50	Thoma Inc—Brian Thoma	201 Commerce Dr Ste 1, Moorestown NJ 08057	856-608-6887	R	11*	<.1
51	Control Analytics Inc—C Banchiere	6017 Enterprise Dr, Export PA 15632	724-837-3418	R	10*	<.1
52	GT Distributors Inc—William Orr	PO Box 16080, Austin TX 78761	512-451-8298	R	10*	.1
53	Hettich Instruments LP—Horst Eberle	100 Cummings Ctr Ste 1, Beverly MA 01915	978-232-3957	R	10*	<.1
54	HL Technologies LP—Brian Hardy	10711 Cash Rd, Stafford TX 77477	281-275-6600	R	9*	.1
55	Norcostco Inc—Erik Schindler	825 Rhode Island Ave S, Minneapolis MN 55426	763-544-0601	R	9*	.1
56	California Surveying and Drafting Supply Inc	4733 Auburn Blvd, Sacramento CA 95841	916-344-0232	R	9*	.1
57	GPS Insight LLC—Robert Donat	21803 N Scottsdale Rd, Scottsdale AZ 85255	480-663-9454	R	9*	<.1
58	St Jude Shop Inc—Norma Cocco	21 Brookline Blvd, Havertown PA 19083	610-789-1300	R	8*	.1
59	Alpha Resources Inc—Philip Lunsford	PO Box 199, Stevensville MI 49127	269-465-5559	R	8*	<.1
60	F-D-C Corp—Ronald Hawley	PO Box 1047, Elk Grove Village IL 60009	630-629-6900	R	8*	<.1
61	Omicron Nanotechnology USA LLC—Eric Peterson	14850 Scenic Heights R, Eden Prairie MN 55344	952 345 5240	R	8*	<.1
62	Graphaids Inc—Frank Festa	3030 La Cienega Blvd, Culver City CA 90232	310-204-1212	R	7*	<.1
63	Krackeler Scientific Inc—Robert Krackeler	PO Box 1849, Albany NY 12201	518-462-4281	R	6*	<.1
64	Atm Systems Corp—Lee Lovett	19650 Club House Rd St, Montgomery Village MD 20886	301-987-0100	R	6*	<.1
65	Technical Instrument San Francisco—Francis Lundy	1826 Rollins Rd Ste 10, Burlingame CA 94010	650-651-3000	R	6*	<.1
66	Tonini Church Supply Co—Elmore Tonini	966 Breckenridge Ln, Louisville KY 40207	502-897-7100	R	6*	<.1
67	Horizon Technology Inc—Robert Johnson	45 Northwestern Dr, Salem NH 03079	603-893-3663	R	5*	<.1
68	Morrell Instrument Company Inc—Peter Morrell	502 Walt Whitman Rd, Melville NY 11747	631-423-4800	R	5*	<.1
69	Mueller Optical Co—Eric Mueller	PO Box 888, Columbia IL 62236	618-281-3344	R	5*	<.1
70	ISS (USA) Inc—Beniamino Barbieri	PO Box 6930, Champaign IL 61826	217-359-8681	R	5*	<.1
71	Modern School Supplies Inc—M Shoham	PO Box 958, Hartford CT 06143	860-243-9565	R	5*	<.1
72	Jeff Dudley LLC—Jeff Dudley	8121 E Holmes Rd, Memphis TN 38125	901-755-0934	R	5*	<.1
73	Creative Street Media Group Inc—Mike Wylie	345 Massachusetts Ave, Indianapolis IN 46204	317-822-3715	R	5*	<.1
74	De Toro Optical Inc—Lorenzo Toro	5434 Sw 8th St, Coral Gables FL 33134	305-444-8676	R	5*	<.1
75	Commercial Blueprint Inc—Douglas Schmidt	416 N Cedar St, Lansing MI 48912	517-372-8360	R	5*	<.1
76	System Component Sales Co—Lee Wolfson	5301 N Las Casitas Pl, Phoenix AZ 85016	602-264-6006	R	5*	<.1
77	Suzanne L Kilmer—Suzanne Kilmer	3835 J St, Sacramento CA 95816	916-456-0400	R	4*	<.1
78	Yorktowne Optical Co—Christine Knepp	PO Box 276, Emigsville PA 17318	717-767-6406	R	4*	<.1
79	Protein Technologies Inc—Mahendra Menakuru	4675 S Coach Dr, Tucson AZ 85714	520-629-9626	R	4*	<.1
80	San Jose Scientific Company Inc—Dave Clemson	1043 Di Giulio Ave, Santa Clara CA 95050	408-727-7301	R	4*	<.1
81	Engineering Design Manufacturing Service Inc—Frank Cole	661 Millers Bluff Rd, Surgoinsville TN 37873	423-345-5086	R	4*	<.1
82	Lgc Scientific Supply Inc—Maria Amorim-Ciambare	3705 Nw 115th Ave Unit, Doral FL 33178	305-592-3171	R	4*	<.1
83	Pence Company J H—William Pence	1334 8th St Sw, Roanoke VA 24015	540-343-2434	R	4*	<.1
84	Apple Scientific Inc—Peggy Lucas	PO Box 778, Chesterland OH 44026	440-729-3056	R	4*	<.1
85	Kansas Blue Print Company Inc—Jerry Sims	PO Box 793, Wichita KS 67201	316-264-9344	R	4*	<.1
86	Backgrounds Unlimited Inc—Scott Cline	PO Box 327, Mount Sidney VA 24467	540-248-0355	R	4*	<.1
87	Hamilton Safe Products Company Inc—Brad Hunter	4770 NW Pkwy, Hilliard OH 43026	614-268-5530	R	4*	<.1
88	Gibson Associates Inc—Robert Gibson	325 Boston Post Rd Ste, Sudbury MA 01776	978-443-8160	R	4*	<.1
89	Buhler Sortex Inc—Bruno Kilshaw	2385 Arch Airport Rd S, Stockton CA 95206	209-983-8400	R	4*	<.1
90	Ncl Of Wisconsin Inc—Emily Tobisch	PO Box 8, Birnamwood WI 54414	715-449-2673	R	3*	<.1
91	Appropriate Technical Resources Inc—Stephen Mitchell	9157 Whiskey Bottom Rd, Laurel MD 20723	410-792-2907	R	3*	<.1
92	Genesee Scientific Corp—Kenneth Fry	8430 Juniper Creek Ln, San Diego CA 92126	858-453-9966	R	3*	<.1
93	Philip E Sikora and Sons Inc—Arthur Brown	147 Market St, Passaic NJ 07055	973-473-5246	R	3*	<.1
94	Champion Optical Network Engineering LLC—Lish Engel	23645 Mercantile Rd St, Beachwood OH 44122		R	3*	<.1
95	Medax International Inc—John Timpson	4026 S W Temple, Salt Lake City UT 84107	801-265-3413	R	3*	<.1
96	Cascade Scientific Inc—Steve Rodgers	132 247th Ave Se, Sammamish WA 98074	425-313-9944	R	3*	<.1
97	Major Theatre Equipment Corp—Arthur Porter	190 Dorchester Ave, Boston MA 02127	617-464-0444	R	3*	<.1
98	Rocky Mountain Transit and Laser Inc—Jeff Burton	612 Confluence Ave, Murray UT 84123	801-262-0066	R	3*	<.1
99	CSC Scientific Company Inc—Arthur Gatenby	PO Box 2468, Merrifield VA 22116	703-564-4306	R	3*	<.1
100	Blake Brothers West Inc—William Blake	451 E 58th Ave Ste 433, Denver CO 80216	303-297-2800	R	3*	<.1
101	Harvey Instruments Inc—Karen Harvey	18 Mcconkey Dr, Buffalo NY 14223	716-874-6694	R	3*	<.1
102	Icon Scientific Inc—Terri Cohen	12613 High Meadow Rd, North Potomac MD 20878	301-840-1484	R	3*	<.1
103	Hma Lab Supply Inc—John Muhlke	3435 W Leigh St, Richmond VA 23230	804-353-9499	R	3*	<.1
104	Bioautomation Corp—Jeff Scheumack	8408 Kenning Ct, Plano TX 75024	972-335-2525	R	3*	<.1

Note: An asterisk (*) indicates an estimated financial figure. The company type code used is as follows: R = Private, P = Public, S = Private Subsidiary, B = Public Subsidiary, D = Division, J = Joint Venture, I = Investment Fund.

COMPANY RANKINGS BY SALES WITHIN 4-DIGIT SIC

Rank	Company Name—Executive Officer	Address, City, State, Zip	Phone	Type	Fin	Empls
105	Vectors Inc—Matthew Nawrocki	8811 E Hampden Ave Ste, Denver CO 80231	303-283-0343	R	3*	<.1
106	Western Analytical Products Inc—Cheryl Kessler	PO Box 1576, Wildomar CA 92595	951-471-2005	R	3*	<.1
107	Edap Technomed Inc—Antoine Tetard	100 Pinnacle Way Ste 1, Norcross GA 30071	770-446-9950	R	3*	<.1
108	Vhg Labs Inc—Susan Evens-Norris	276 Abby Rd, Manchester NH 03103	603-622-7660	R	3*	<.1
109	T H Stemper Company Inc—Daniel Stemper	1125 E Potter Ave, Milwaukee WI 53207	414-744-3610	R	3*	<.1
110	SL Discount Distributor Corp—Fhu-San Lee	5912 37th Ave, Woodside NY 11377	718-779-6889	R	3*	<.1
111	Lpkf Distribution Inc—Stephan Schmidt	12555 Sw Leveton Dr, Tualatin OR 97062	503-454-4240	R	3*	<.1
112	Xia LLC—Mark Daly	31057 Genstar Rd, Hayward CA 94544	510-401-5760	R	3*	<.1
113	Industrial Arts Supply Co—Michael Raymond	5724 W 36th St, Minneapolis MN 55416	952-920-7393	R	3*	<.1
114	Microscope Store LLC—Michelle Crookenden	1222 Mcdowell Ave Ne, Roanoke VA 24012	540-904-0880	R	3*	<.1
115	Consolidated Lab Service Inc—Lawrence Fox	PO Box 1148, Bay Shore NY 11706	631-667-7800	R	3*	<.1
116	Hawaii Engineering Services Inc—Michael Elhoff	240 Puuhale Rd Ste 202, Honolulu HI 96819	808-841-0033	R	3*	<.1
117	Gulf States Distributors Inc—Charles Dees	PO Box 241387, Montgomery AL 36124	334-271-2011	R	2*	<.1
118	A California Labchoice Inc—Mike Forouzesh	3045 Kashiwa St, Torrance CA 90505	310-530-2000	R	2*	<.1
119	Ken Martin School Supply Inc—Greg Martin	PO Box 263, Midway AR 72651	870-481-6020	R	2*	<.1
120	Trek Digital Products Inc—Ed Armistead	3700 Easton Dr Ste 1, Bakersfield CA 93309	661-282-8735	R	2*	<.1
121	General Laboratory Supply Of Houston Inc—Steven Sneed	PO Box 7120, Pasadena TX 77508	281-487-0633	R	2*	<.1
122	Visionspring Inc—Jordan Kassalow	322 8th Ave Ste 12a-02, New York NY 10001	212-375-2599	R	2*	<.1
123	IR Industries Inc—M Mcdaniel	512 18th St Ste 1, Orlando FL 32805	407-423-7882	R	2*	<.1
124	Lab Depot Inc—Don Westall	PO Box 1300, Dawsonville GA 30534	706-265-2320	R	2*	<.1
125	Basics Plus Inc—Melvin Brown	PO Box 1093, Mustang OK 73064	405-577-7718	R	2*	<.1
126	Vibgyor Optics Inc—Bharat Verma	1140 N Phelps Ave, Arlington Heights IL 60004	847-818-0788	R	2*	<.1
127	Central Optical Laboratories Inc—William Scheuerman	412 Diagonal St, Clarkston WA 99403	509-758-1791	R	2*	<.1
128	Kaufer's Religious Supplies Inc—David Kaufers	1455 Custer Ave, San Francisco CA 94124	415-593-4650	R	2*	<.1
129	Pion Inc—Alex Avdeef	5 Constitution Way, Woburn MA 01801	781-935-8939	R	2*	<.1
130	Caron East Inc—Mike Clites	PO Box 1378, Cumberland MD 21501	301-724-4490	R	2*	<.1
131	Continental Equipment Company Inc—James Bell	PO Box 488, Tonganoxie KS 66086	913-845-2148	R	2*	<.1
132	Neuralynx Inc—Keith Stengel	105 Commercial Dr Ste, Bozeman MT 59715	406-585-4542	R	2*	<.1
133	Rocky Mountain Lasers and Instruments Inc—Brad Neeley	5385 Quebec St, Commerce City CO 80022	303-853-0311	R	2*	<.1
134	Western Engineering Supply Company Inc—Jim Castellanos	343 Stealth Ct 6743, Livermore CA 94551		R	2*	<.1
135	Kjolhede Inc—Kurt Kolhede	2506 Technology Dr, Hayward CA 94545	510-887-4040	R	2*	<.1
136	Anderson Machinery Co—Stuart C Anderson	PO Box 245, Stratford CT 06615	203-375-4481	R	2*	<.1
137	Iota Consulting Services Inc—Joseph Robinson	15868 Nw W Union Rd St, Portland OR 97229	503-705-6351	R	2*	<.1
138	Buckeye Exports—Khursheed Ahmad	20600 Chagrin Blvd Ste, Shaker Heights OH 44122	216-295-0202	R	2*	<.1
139	Diversified Business Products and Sales LLC	460 Firelite Ln Ste 30, Suwanee GA 30024	770-888-6883	R	2*	<.1
140	JF Morrow and Sons Inc—Kenneth Morrow	6015 N Milwaukee Ave, Chicago IL 60646	773-631-8844	R	2*	<.1
141	Cruisers Inc—Keith Wallaker	988 Rickett Rd, Brighton MI 48116	810-229-0122	R	2*	<.1
142	Draftech Blueprinting Inc—Mike Coero	1544 Ter Way, Santa Rosa CA 95404	707-578-9442	R	2*	<.1
143	Yoas Services Inc—Robert Yoas	509 W 4th St, Williamsport PA 17701	570-326-2041	R	2*	<.1
144	Stepper Equipment Inc—Robert Sharpe	4151 Citrus Ave, Rocklin CA 95677	916-632-1031	R	2*	<.1
145	Capra Optical Inc—Steven Kannel	13 Mercer Rd, Natick MA 01760	508-650-9700	R	2*	<.1
146	Integrated Surveying Solutions Inc—Mel Zohrob	24037 Acacia, Redford MI 48239	313-535-5252	R	2*	<.1
147	Bankers Supply Inc—Richard Parker	PO Box 2463, Macon GA 31203	478-743-1543	R	2*	<.1
148	General Transworld Corp—Johnny Tsai	24412 Main St Ste 106, Carson CA 90745	310-241-7988	R	2*	<.1
149	Virginia Lab Supply Corp—Jean Shano	PO Box 9870, Richmond VA 23228	804-261-3700	R	2*	<.1
150	Enforcement Technology Group Inc—Dave Schwonek	400 N Broadway Ste 400, Milwaukee WI 53202	414-276 4471	R	2*	<.1
151	Post Apple Scientific Inc—Gordon Post	PO Box 86, North East PA 16428	814-725-3330	R	2*	<.1
152	Sexton and Sexton School Supply Inc—Billy Sexton	PO Box 346, Apache OK 73006	580-588-3686	R	2*	<.1
153	Abbott Gage Inc—R Abbott	PO Box 327, Childersburg AL 35044	256-378-3286	R	2*	<.1
154	Amico Scientific Corp—Larry Ripley	7231 Garden Grove Blvd, Garden Grove CA 92841	714-894-6633	R	2*	<.1
155	Argos Technologies Inc—Geralyn Kneisel	1551 Scottsdale Ct Ste, Elgin IL 60123	847-622-0456	R	2*	<.1
156	E-R Productions LLC	PO Box 593647, Orlando FL 32859	407-264-4400	R	2*	<.1
157	Analytical Services Co—Craig Amerigian	2075 Corte Del Nogal T, Carlsbad CA 92011	760-431-2655	R	2*	<.1
158	Glass Expansion Inc—Gerald Dulude	4 Barlows Landing Rd, Pocasset MA 02559	508-563-1800	R	2*	<.1
159	Carol School Supply Company Inc—Carol Pick	17928 Union Tpke, Flushing NY 11366	718-380-4203	R	2*	<.1
160	Topcon Lasers By Branco—Brad Conover	1205 N Mcqueen Rd, Gilbert AZ 85233	480-892-5657	R	2*	<.1
161	Sper Scientific Ltd—Devin Sper	7720 E Redfield Rd Ste, Scottsdale AZ 85260	480-948-4448	R	2*	<.1
162	Warzyn Sales Inc—Thomas Warzyn	755 Larry Ct, Waukesha WI 53186	262-798-4243	R	2*	<.1
163	Pegasus Scientific Inc—Scott Berhman	9710 Traville Gateway, Rockville MD 20850	301-668-9464	R	2*	<.1
164	Gel Electrophoresis Company Inc—Greg Richardson	665 3rd St Ste 240, San Francisco CA 94107	415-247-8760	R	2*	<.1
165	Sheppard International Inc—Mary Sheppard	880 Dogwood Ln, Hermitage PA 16148	724-981-8764	R	2*	<.1
166	Advanced Process—Jon Kolaja	PO Box 894, Missouri City TX 77459	281-208-5200	R	2*	<.1
167	March Analytical—Gary Glenna	8287 214th St W, Lakeville MN 55044	952-469-2474	R	1*	<.1
168	Prestige Lens Lab Inc—Carol Mori-Prange	PO Box 967, South San Francisco CA 94083	650-266-8584	R	1*	<.1
169	Fotodyne Inc—Richard Vitek	950 Walnut Ridge Dr St, Hartland WI 53029	262-369-7000	R	1*	<.1
170	Bay Sales LLC	113 Fillmore St, Bristol PA 19007	215-331-6466	R	1*	<.1
171	Crawford International Theatrical Corp—Gary Crawford	1420 80th St Sw Ste D, Everett WA 98203	425-776-4950	R	1*	<.1
172	Royce International Eyeware—William Royce	PO Box 850, Morris NY 13808	607-263-2353	R	1*	<.1
173	Design Products Company Inc—Charles Wollensak	17025 W Rogers Dr, New Berlin WI 53151	262-786-3440	R	1*	<.1
174	Rmc Group Inc—T Hughes	1970 Swarthmore Ave St, Lakewood NJ 08701	732-363-8401	R	1*	<.1
175	Enviro-Tech Services Company Inc—Frederick Ousey	4851 Sunrise Dr Ste 10, Martinez CA 94553	925-370-1541	R	1*	<.1
176	Harold W Griffith Inc—Harold Griffith	363 Ragland Rd, Beckley WV 25801	304-256-1600	R	1*	<.1
177	Jailcraft Inc—Ronald Mullar	PO Box 340, Stevensville MD 21666	410-643-1771	R	1*	<.1
178	Clarkson Laboratory and Supply Inc—Sheley Shannon	350 Trousdale Dr, Chula Vista CA 91910	619-425-1932	R	1*	<.1
179	Industrial Lab Equipment Co—William Floyd	PO Box 220245, Charlotte NC 28222	704-357-3930	R	1*	<.1
180	Man-Tech Associates Inc—Edward Godman	600 Main St, Tonawanda NY 14150	716-743-1320	R	1*	<.1
181	Hub-City Blueprint and Supply Company Inc—Clint Murchinson	PO Box 514, Jackson TN 38302	901-386-2083	R	1*	<.1
182	Next Events Meeting Productions Inc—Kristopher Plourde	13695 Alton Pkwy, Irvine CA 92618	949-829-8029	R	1*	<.1
183	Seqgen Inc—Si-Lin Yang	1725 Del Amo Blvd, Torrance CA 90501	310-895-0038	R	1*	<.1
184	SciencelabCom Inc—Robert Tyler	14025 Smith Rd, Humble TX 77396	281-441-4400	R	1*	<.1
185	Pp System International Inc—Michael Doyle	110 Haverhill Rd Ste 3, Amesbury MA 01913	978-834-0505	R	1*	<.1
186	United Products and Instruments Inc—Albert Chang	182 Ridge Rd Ste E, Dayton NJ 08810	732-274-1155	R	1*	<.1
187	Meegan Tool Sales Co—Gerald Cavanna	160 Oak St Ste 306, Glastonbury CT 06033	860-633-2400	R	1*	<.1
188	Drysdale Enterprises Inc—Leslie Drysdale	758 N Batavia St Ste C, Orange CA 92868	714-744-3974	R	1*	<.1
189	Klinger Educational Products Corp—Irwin Malleck	11219 14th Rd, College Point NY 11356	718-461-1822	R	1*	<.1
190	Pittsburgh Embossing Services Inc—John Milhoan	185 Linnwood Rd, Eighty Four PA 15330	724-222-5240	R	1*	<.1
191	Jewel Swiss Co—Philip Steel	325 Chestnut St Ste 50, Philadelphia PA 19106	215-925-2867	R	1*	<.1
192	Lukas Microscope Service Inc—Mark Lukas	PO Box 306, Skokie IL 60076	847-673-2600	R	1*	<.1
193	Selsi Company Inc—Walter Silbernagel	PO Box 10, Midland Park NJ 07432	201-612-9200	R	1*	<.1
194	Dresco Reproduction Inc—Trudy Guy	12000 E Slauson Ave Un, Santa Fe Springs CA 90670	562-696-5848	R	1*	<.1

Rank	Company Name—*Executive Officer*	Address, City, State, Zip	Phone	Type	Fin	Empls
195	Csm Instruments Inc—*Jacques Francoise*	197 1st Ave Ste 120, Needham MA 02494	781-444-2250	R	1*	<.1
196	Saaya Inc—*Fumiaki Sato*	2111 Greenway Village, Katy TX 77494	281-395-3049	S	1*	<.1
197	Teacher Access Inc—*Craig Thuneman*	332 Byron Ave, Bloomingdale IL 60108	630-539-7693	R	1*	<.1
198	Universe Kogaku America Inc—*Mike Ohtsuki*	116 Audrey Ave, Oyster Bay NY 11771	516-624-2444	R	1*	<.1
199	Applied Instruments Corp—*Kathy Kelly*	27126 Paseo Espada B70, San Juan Capistrano CA 92675	949-661-9900	R	1*	<.1
200	Kintek Corp—*Kenneth Johnson*	7604 Sandia Loop Ste C, Austin TX 78735	512-471-0434	R	1*	<.1
201	Tescan USA Inc—*John Van Noy*	508 Thomson Park Dr, Cranberry Township PA 16066	724-772-7433	R	1*	<.1
202	B and B International Inc—*Pedro Bernal*	451 Tram Pl, Chula Vista CA 91910	619-420-5646	R	1*	<.1
203	Altec Equipment Inc—*Pedro Bocchini*	5030 Champion Blvd G6-, Boca Raton FL 33496	561-278-9118	R	1*	<.1
204	Zimmerman School Equipment Inc—*Nancy Zimmerman*	PO Box 209, Blacklick OH 43004	614-861-6383	R	1*	<.1
205	Scope Shoppe Inc—*Patrick Schlinder*	PO Box 8058, Elburn IL 60119	630-365-9499	R	1*	<.1
206	Ajax School and Office Source LLC	PO Box 2804, Jackson MS 39207	601-957-8520	R	1*	<.1
207	Checkwriter Associates International Inc—*Dan Rike*	320 Brookes Dr Ste 108, Hazelwood MO 63042	314-731-3335	R	1*	<.1
208	Mississippi Police Supply Co—*James Jenkins*	PO Box 36, Ruleville MS 38771	662-756-2011	R	1*	<.1
209	Alpha Liberty Co—*Bernd Rau*	PO Box 276, West Chester OH 45071	513-777-1525	R	1*	<.1
210	Lmi Safety Inc—*Claris Dozier*	5805 Krueger Dr, Jonesboro AR 72401	870-910-6607	R	1*	<.1
211	Physicians Eyecare Network LLC—*William Fogle*	48 Courtenay Dr, Charleston SC 29403	843-577-5830	R	1*	<.1
212	Pulcir Inc—*J Eddlemon*	9209 Oak Ridge Hwy, Oak Ridge TN 37830	865-927-6358	R	1*	<.1
213	Surveyors Materials Inc—*Donna Owen*	PO Box 5808, Saint Louis MO 63134	314-521-9041	R	1*	<.1
214	Bolton Smith Inc—*Stephen Smith*	30262 Crown Valley Pkw, Laguna Niguel CA 92677	949-369-7974	R	1*	<.1
215	Sage Action Inc—*Donald Ordway*	PO Box 416, Ithaca NY 14851	607-844-8448	R	1*	<.1
216	Metastable Instruments Inc—*George Dube*	PO Box 3858, Chesterfield MO 63006	636-447-9555	R	1*	<.1
217	Opti-Vue Inc—*Yordan Vulich*	224 James St, Bensenville IL 60106	630-274-6121	R	1*	<.1
218	Action Blueprint And Supplies LLC	284 Broad St, Manchester CT 06040	860-647-1223	R	1*	<.1
219	Company Seven Astro-Optics Div—*Martin Cohen*	14300 Cherry Ln Ct Ste, Laurel MD 20707	301-953-2000	R	<1*	<.1
220	Geonor Inc—*Ed Brylawski*	109 Greenwood Cir, Milford PA 18337	570-296-4884	R	<1*	<.1
221	Meteorological Products Inc—*James Welinski*	1346 W Arrowhead Rd 31, Duluth MN 55811	218-624-5677	R	<1*	<.1
222	Detector Electronics Corp—*Sondra Bernzweig*	23 Tpke Rd, Southborough MA 01772	508-626-0244	S	<1*	<.1
223	Richland Industrial Inc—*Jackie Stout*	PO Box 1486, Richland WA 99352	509-946-2367	R	<1*	<.1
224	Spectra Hardware Inc—*Keith Pealstrom*	PO Box 368, Westmoreland City PA 15692	724-863-7527	R	<1*	<.1
225	Sales Unlimited Inc—*Orlando Segarra*	1810 Nw 94th Ave, Doral FL 33172	305-592-3845	R	<1*	<.1
226	Southgate Process Equipment Inc—*Terry Morin*	4412 Derwent Dr Ne, Roswell GA 30075	770-594-9970	R	<1*	<.1
227	Hawks Nest—*Kathy Williams*	29995 W 12 Mile Rd, Farmington Hills MI 48334	248-489-3487	R	<1*	<.1
228	Nidatech Inc—*John Lorentzen*	6409 Brass Bucket Ct, Gaithersburg MD 20882	301-208-0998	R	<1*	<.1
229	Valdada Enterprises LLC	PO Box 270095, Littleton CO 80127	303-979-4578	R	<1*	<.1

TOTALS: SIC 5049 Professional Equipment Nec
Companies: 229

					11,022	14.2

5051 Metals Service Centers & Offices

Rank	Company Name—*Executive Officer*	Address, City, State, Zip	Phone	Type	Fin	Empls
1	Easton Steel Service Inc—*Chris Marvel*	1011 Frank Adams Indus, Federalsburg MD 21632	410-822-1393	R	9,167*	.1
2	Reliance Steel and Aluminum Co—*David H Hannah*	350 S Grand Ave Ste 51, Los Angeles CA 90071	213-687-7700	P	8,135	10.7
3	Commercial Metals Co—*Anthony Massaro*	PO Box 1046, Dallas TX 75221	214-689-4300	P	7,918	11.4
4	Marubeni America Corp—*Fumiya Kokubu*	375 Lexington Ave, New York NY 10017	212-450-0100	S	6,552*	.2
5	Combined Metals of Chicago LLC—*Dan Joewright*	2401 W Grant Ave, Bellwood IL 60104	708-547-8800	S	5,668	.3
6	Bushwick Metals Inc—*Rick Perlen*	560 N Washington Ave, Bridgeport CT 06604	203-576-1800	R	5,520*	.2
7	Ryerson Holding Corp—*Michael Arnold*	2621 W 15th Pl, Chicago IL 60608	773-762-2121	S	4,839*	4.2
8	Misa Metals Inc—*Hiro Fujisawa*	PO Box 8712, West Chester OH 45071	513-896-2700	R	4,035*	.4
9	Earle M Jorgensen Co—*R Neil McCaffery* Reliance Steel and Aluminum Co	10650 Alameda St, Lynwood CA 90262	323-567-1122	S	3,844*	1.7
10	Macsteel Service Centers USA—*Michael Hoffman*	888 San Clemente Dr St, Newport Beach CA 92660	949-219-9000	S	3,700*	1.6
11	O'Neal Steel Inc—*Holman Head*	PO Box 2623, Birmingham AL 35202	205-599-8000	R	2,930*	4.4
12	Copper and Brass Sales Inc—*William Sabol*	22355 W 11 Mile Rd, Southfield MI 48034	248-233-5600	D	2,403*	2.0
13	Columbia Ventures Corp—*Kenneth D Peterson Jr*	12503 SE Mill Plain Bl, Vancouver WA 98684	360-816-1840	R	2,401*	1.1
14	California Steel Services Inc—*Parviz Razavian*	1212 S Mountain View A, San Bernardino CA 92408	909-796-2222	R	1,861*	<.1
15	Metals USA Holdings Corp—*C Laurenco Goncalves*	2400 E Commercial Blvd, Ft Lauderdale FL 33308	954-202-4000	P	1,292	1.8
16	Olympic Steel Inc—*Michael D Siegal*	5096 Richmond Rd, Bedford Heights OH 44146	216-292-3800	P	1,262	1.7
17	R and S Steel Co—*Mike Rolnick* Triple-S Steel Holdings Inc	3811 Joliet St, Denver CO 80239	303-321-9660	D	1,113*	.5
18	AM Castle and Co—*Michael H Goldberg*	1420 Kensington Rd Ste, Oak Brook IL 60523	847-455-7111	P	944	1.6
19	Stahl Specialty Co—*Jim Splding*	PO Box 6, Kingsville MO 64061	816-597-3322	R	936*	1.1
20	Kanematsu USA Inc—*Hiroshi Iwakuma*	75 Rockefeller Plz 22n, New York NY 10019	212-704-9400	S	867*	1.0
21	Steel and Pipe Supply Company Inc	555 Poyntz Ave, Manhattan KS 66505	785-587-5100	R	863*	.4
22	Firestone Metal Products LLC—*Jim Baxter*	1001 Land Blvd, Anoka MN 55303	763-576-9595	R	757*	.3
23	Metal Traders Inc—*Fred White*	3480 Grand Ave, Pittsburgh PA 15225	412-331-7772	R	641*	.1
24	Mitsui and Co USA Inc—*Mitsuhiko Kawai*	200 Park Ave 36th Fl, New York NY 10166	212-878-4000	S	610*	.3
25	New Process Steel LP—*Richard Fant*	PO Box 55205, Houston TX 77255	713-686-9631	R	575*	.5
26	Worthington Steel Co—*Mark A Russell*	200 Old Wilson Bridge, Columbus OH 43085	614-438-3205	D	426*	.5
27	Robert-James Sales Inc—*James Bokor Jr*	PO Box 7999, Buffalo NY 14225	716-651-6000	R	422*	.2
28	Central Steel and Wire Co—*Michael Cronin*	PO Box 5100, Chicago IL 60680	773-471-3800	R	400*	1.1
29	ALRO Steel Corp—*Mark Alyea*	PO Box 927, Jackson MI 49204	517-787-5500	R	393*	.2
30	Everett J Prescott Inc—*PE Prescott*	PO Box 600, Gardiner ME 04345	207-582-1851	R	380*	.2
31	Metals USA Specialty Flat Rolled-Northbrk Metals USA Holdings Corp	3000 Shermer Rd, Northbrook IL 60062	847-291-2400	D	362*	.2
32	Burns Brothers Contractors—*DS Burns*	400 Leavenworth Ave, Syracuse NY 13204	315-422-0261	R	350*	.3
33	Hysco America Co—*Yong Shin*	200 Team Member Ln, Greenville AL 36037	334-382-9100	R	342*	.2
34	North Shore Supply Company Inc—*William K Nemzin*	PO Box 9940, Houston TX 77213	713-453-3533	R	324*	.2
35	Liebovich Brothers Inc—*Michael J Tulley* Reliance Steel and Aluminum Co	2116 Preston St, Rockford IL 61102	815-987-3200	S	315*	.3
36	Denman and Davis—*David N Deinzer*	1 Broad St, Clifton NJ 07013	973-684-3900	R	303*	.1
37	Intsel Steel West—*Gary Stein*	1887 S 700 W, Salt Lake City UT 84104	801-973-0911	R	295*	.1
38	Lyon Conklin and Company Inc—*Daved Brown*	7030 Troy Hill Dr Ste, Elkridge MD 21075	410-540-4880	R	285*	.2
39	Phoenix Metals Co—*Steve Almond* Reliance Steel and Aluminum Co	4685 Buford Hwy, Norcross GA 30071	770-447-4211	S	276*	.1
40	Kelly Pipe Company LLC—*Leonard Gross*	PO Box 2827, Santa Fe Springs CA 90670	562-868-0456	R	252*	.2
41	Energy Alloys—*Dave Warren*	350 Glenborough Dr Ste, Houston TX 77067	832-601-5800	R	251*	.4
42	Blue Tee Corp—*William Kelly*	250 Park Ave S, New York NY 10003	212-598-0880	R	243*	.9
43	Future Metals Inc—*Luis Benitez*	10401 State St, Tamarac FL 33321	954-724-1400	R	243*	.1
44	Bohler Uddeholm America Inc—*Erik Svendsen*	2505 Millenium Dr, Elgin Il 60124		R	234*	.2
45	Pacesetter Steel Service Inc—*Steven Leebow*	PO Box 100007, Kennesaw GA 30156	770-919-8000	R	217*	.3

Note: An asterisk (*) indicates an estimated financial figure. The company type code used is as follows: R = Private, P = Public, S = Private Subsidiary, B = Public Subsidiary, D = Division, J = Joint Venture, I = Investment Fund.

COMPANY RANKINGS BY SALES WITHIN 4-DIGIT SIC

Rank	Company Name—*Executive Officer*	Address, City, State, Zip	Phone	Type	Fin	Empls
46	Triple-S Steel Holdings Inc—*Gary Stein*	PO Box 21119, Houston TX 77226	713-697-7105	R	216*	.4
47	Benedict-Miller LLC—*John Benedict*	123 N 8th St, Kenilworth NJ 07033	908-497-1477	R	216*	.1
48	Gibbs Wire and Steel Company Inc—*William Torres*	PO Box 520, Southington CT 06489	860-621-0121	R	213*	.2
49	J Rubin and Co—*Phillip E Rubin*	PO Box 1657, Rockford IL 61110	815-964-9471	R	186*	.3
50	Liberty Steel Products Inc—*Andrew Weller*	PO Box 175, North Jackson OH 44451	330-538-2236	R	185*	.2
51	Contractors Steel Co—*Donald Simon*	PO Box 3364, Livonia MI 48151	734-464-4000	R	184*	.3
52	Mi-Tech Steel Inc—*Bradford T Ray*	210 Mi-Tech Dr, Murfreesboro TN 37130	615-896-7401	J	184*	.1
53	Commonwealth Metal Corp Commercial Metals Co	2050 Center Ave Ste 25, Fort Lee NJ 07024	201-569-2000	D	178*	.1
54	Jemison-Demsey LLC—*Peter Heinke*	3800 Colonnade Pkwy St, Birmingham AL 35243	205-986-6600	R	173*	.1
55	Hd Supply Waterworks Group Inc—*Joseph Deangelo*	501 W Church St Ste 10, Orlando FL 32805	407-841-4755	R	171*	3.0
56	New Jernberg Sales Inc—*George Phanopoulos*	39475 W 13 Mile Rd Ste, Novi MI 48377	248-479-2699	S	170*	<.1
57	Ryerson Procurement Corp—*James Delaney*	PO Box 8000, Chicago IL 60680	773-762-2121	R	165*	2.7
58	Tubular Steel Inc—*Dan Hauck*	1031 Executive Pkwy Dr, Saint Louis MO 63141	314-851-9200	R	164*	.4
59	Cristal Us Inc—*Jamal Nahas*	20 Wight Ave Ste 100, Hunt Valley MD 21030	410-229-4441	R	163*	4.0
60	TrueNorth Steel—*Bob Sieve*	3272 Lien St, Rapid City SD 57702	605-394-7200	R	162*	.1
61	Harris Supply Solutions Inc—*Mark Hennings*	1700 7th Ave Ste 2100, Seattle WA 98101	425-208-6000	R	155*	<.1
62	Kataman Metals Inc—*Joseph P Reinmann*	7733 Forsyth Blvd Ste, Saint Louis MO 63105	314-863-6699	R	154*	<.1
63	Century Steel LLC—*Joel Lewis*	PO Box 38, Chicago Heights IL 60412	708-758-0900	R	153*	.2
64	Titan Industrial Corp—*Michael S Levin*	555 Madison Ave, New York NY 10022	212-421-6700	R	150*	.1
65	Chatham Steel Corp—*David Hannah* Reliance Steel and Aluminum Co	PO Box 2567, Savannah GA 31402	912-233-5751	D	148*	.3
66	Metals USA Plates And Shapes Southcentral Inc—*David Martens*	PO Box 3528, Enid OK 73702	580-233-0411	R	143*	.1
67	Shinsho American Corp—*Shutoku Ota*	26200 Town Ctr Dr Ste, Novi MI 48375	248-675-0058	R	142*	.1
68	Traxys North America LLC—*Tim Monson*	825 3rd Ave Fl 9, New York NY 10022	212-918-8000	R	140*	.3
69	Leeco Steel Products Inc—*Robert Pepoff*	1011 Warrenville Rd St, Lisle IL 60532	630-427-2100	R	140*	.1
70	Brauer Supply Co—*James L Truesdell*	1218 S Vandeventer Ave, Saint Louis MO 63110	314-534-7150	R	139*	.1
71	Mcnichols Co—*Scott Mcnichols*	PO Box 30300, Tampa FL 33630	813-282-3828	R	136*	.3
72	Maas-Hansen Steel Corp—*Mark Tinyo*	PO Box 58364, Vernon CA 90058	323-583-6321	R	136*	.1
73	Xora Inc—*Anne Bonaparte*	501 Ellis St, Mountain View CA 94043	650-314-6460	R	136*	.2
74	Dixie Pipe Sales Inc—*Charles Mcguire*	PO Box 300650, Houston TX 77230	713-796-2021	R	130*	.1
75	Duferco Steel Inc—*Joe Deverter*	100 Matawan Rd Ste 400, Matawan NJ 07747	732-566-3130	S	130*	.1
76	Vulcanium Metals Inc—*Richard Leopold*	3045 Commercial Ave, Northbrook IL 60062	847-498-3111	R	124*	.1
77	Precision Strip Inc—*Joe Wollf* Reliance Steel and Aluminum Co	PO Box 104, Minster OH 45865	419-628-2343	S	122*	.3
78	Custom Alloy Sales Inc—*Kenneth Cox*	13329 Ector St, City Of Industry CA 91746	626-369-3641	R	119*	.1
79	Fedco Steel Corp—*Charles Cumella*	785 Harrison Ave, Harrison NJ 07029	973-481-1424	R	116*	.1
80	Fisher Brothers Steel Corp—*Rick Perlen* Bushwick Metals Inc	25 Rockwood Pl 3rd Fl, Englewood NJ 07631	201-567-2400	S	115*	.1
81	Metals USA Plates and Shapes-Philadelphia—*Tom Dilullo* Metals USA Holdings Corp	11200 Roosevelt Blvd, Philadelphia PA 19116	215-673-9300	D	113*	.1
82	Metals USA Specialty Flat Rolled - Kansas City—*K Krausse* Metals USA Holdings Corp	2840 E Heartland Dr, Liberty MO 64068	816-415-0004	S	112*	.1
83	Columbia Pipe and Supply—*William D Arenberg*	1120 W Pershing Rd, Chicago IL 60609	773-927-6600	R	111*	.3
84	PDM Steel Service Centers Inc—*Tim Kline* Reliance Steel and Aluminum Co	PO Box 310, Stockton CA 95201	209 043 0555	S	108*	.3
85	Coast Aluminum And Architectural Inc—*Thomas Clark*	PO Box 2144, Santa Fe Springs CA 90670	562-946-6061	R	107*	.3
86	Brown Metals Co—*Carolyn Brown*	8635 White Oak Ave, Rancho Cucamonga CA 91730	909-484-3124	R	107*	.1
87	A and K Railroad Materials Inc—*Rhonda Nicoloff*	PO Box 30076, Salt Lake City UT 84130		R	100*	.5
88	Alpert and Alpert Iron and Metal Inc—*Alan Alpert*	1815 S Soto St, Los Angeles CA 90023	323-265-4040	R	100*	.1
89	Samuel Specialty Metal—*Tom Toth*	2303 Century Centre Bl, Irving TX 75062	972-438-3949	R	98*	<.1
90	Kenwal Steel Corp—*Kenneth Eisenberg*	PO Box 4359, Dearborn MI 48126	313-739-1000	R	96*	.2
91	Aerodyne Alloys LLC—*Greg Chase* O'Neal Steel Inc	350 Pleasant Valley Rd, South Windsor CT 06074	860-289-6011	S	94*	<.1
92	Texas Pipe and Supply Company Inc—*Jerry R Rubenstein*	2330 Holmes Rd, Houston TX 77051	713-799-9235	R	93	.1
93	Sun Steel Company LLC—*Sheffield Wolk*	2500 Euclid Ave, Chicago Heights IL 60411	708-756-0400	R	89*	.1
94	Jabo Supply Corp—*Kevin Roach*	PO Box 238, Huntington WV 25707	304-736-8333	R	87*	.1
95	Atlas Steel Products Co—*John Adams*	7990 Bavaria Rd, Twinsburg OH 44087	330-425-1600	R	82*	.1
96	West Coast Wire Rope and Rigging Inc—*Karen Newton*	PO Box 5999, Portland OR 97228	503-228-9353	R	75*	.1
97	Bobco Metal Co—*Hamid Shooshani*	2000 S Alameda St, Los Angeles CA 90058	213-748-5171	R	75*	.1
98	Howco Metals Management LP—*David Birch*	PO Box 841329, Houston TX 77284	281-649-8800	R	70*	.2
99	Lane Steel Company Inc—*Paul Gedeon*	4 River Rd Ste 2, Mc Kees Rocks PA 15136	412-777-1700	R	69*	.1
100	National Specialty Alloys LLC—*Mark Russ*	18250 Kieth Harrow Blv, Houston TX 77084	281-345-2115	R	68*	.1
101	Mapes and Sprowl Steel Ltd—*Gary Hamity*	1100 E Devon Ave, Elk Grove Village IL 60007	847-364-0055	R	66*	.1
102	Metro Group Inc (Salt Lake City Utah)—*Jim Bond*	401 W 900 S, Salt Lake City UT 84101	801-328-2051	R	64*	.1
103	Steel Engineers Inc—*Mike Zech*	716 W Mesquite Ave, Las Vegas NV 89106	702-386-0023	R	60*	.4
104	Pacific Machinery and Tool Steel Co—*Dave Chatkin*	3445 NW Luzon St, Portland OR 97210	503-226-7656	R	59*	.1
105	Allied Metals Inc—*Harry Caldwell*	2220 Canada Dry St, Houston TX 77223	713-923-9491	R	58*	<.1
106	E Jordan Brookes Company Inc—*Robert J Brookes Jr*	10634 Shoemaker Ave, Santa Fe Springs CA 90670	562-968-2100	R	52*	.1
107	Tell Steel Inc—*Greg More*	2345 W 17th St, Long Beach CA 90813	562-435-4826	R	51*	.1
108	Berlin Metals LLC—*Roy Berlin*	3200 Sheffield Ave, Hammond IN 46327	219-933-0111	R	50*	.1
109	All Metals Industries Inc—*Paul Koza*	PO Box 807, Belmont NH 03220	603-267-7023	R	49*	.1
110	Corridor Recycling—*Gilbert Dobson*	22500 S Alameda St, Long Beach CA 90810	310-835-9109	R	49*	<.1
111	Block Steel Corp—*Larry Wolfson*	6101 W Oakton St, Skokie IL 60077	847-966-3000	R	48*	.1
112	Bushwick-Koons Steel—*Frank Koons III*	PO Box 476, Parker Ford PA 19457	610-495-9100	R	48*	<.1
113	Reliance Steel Co—*John Becknell* Reliance Steel and Aluminum Co	2537 E 27th St, Los Angeles CA 90058	323-583-6111	D	48*	<.1
114	Mid-West Materials Inc—*Brian Robbins*	PO Box 345, Perry OH 44081	440-259-5200	R	47*	<.1
115	Pro Met Steel Inc—*Nick Laphen*	900 E 103rd St Ste C, Chicago IL 60628	773-995-0317	R	45*	.1
116	President Titanium Company Inc—*Joseph Mac Leod*	PO Box 36, Hanson MA 02341	781-294-0000	R	45*	<.1
117	Dennen Steel Company—*Andrew Dennen*	PO Box 3200, Grand Rapids MI 49501	616-784-2000	R	44*	.1
118	Pierce Aluminum Company Inc—*Jeff Pierce*	PO Box F, Franklin MA 02038	508-541-7007	R	44*	.1
119	American Stainless and Supply LLC—*Cambron Beck*	815 State Rd, Cheraw SC 29520	843-537-5231	R	43*	.1
120	Delta Metals Company Inc—*Darren Aghabeg*	PO Box 70286, Memphis TN 38107	901-525-5000	R	43*	.1
121	Independent Steel Company LLC—*Mark Schwertner*	PO Box 472, Valley City OH 44280	330-558-5777	R	43*	.1
122	Albco Sales Inc—*Gary Staffeld*	230 Maple St, Lisbon OH 44432	330-424-9446	R	43*	.1
123	Castle Metals AM Castle and Co	3400 Wolf Rd, Franklin Park IL 60131	847-455-7111	D	43	.1
124	Rolled Steel Products Corp—*Steven Alperson*	2187 S Garfield Ave, Los Angeles CA 90040	323-723-8836	R	42*	.1

Rank	Company Name—*Executive Officer*	Address, City, State, Zip	Phone	Type	Fin	Empls
125	Oliver Steel Plate Co—*Jim Stevenson* AM Castle and Co	7851 Bavaria Rd, Twinsburg OH 44087	330-425-7000	S	42*	.1
126	Olympic Steel Inc (Schaumburg Illinois)—*Michael D Siegal* Olympic Steel Inc	1901 Mitchell Blvd, Schaumburg IL 60193	847-584-4000	D	42*	.1
127	Tw Metals Inc—*Jack Elrod*	PO Box 644, Exton PA 19341	610-458-1300	R	42*	.7
128	Sabel Industries Inc—*Keith Sabel*	PO Box 4747, Montgomery AL 36103	334-265-6771	S	40	.2
129	Kivort Steel Inc—*Stanley Kivort*	380 Hudson River Rd, Waterford NY 12188	518-590-7233	R	40	<.1
130	City Pipe And Supply Corp—*Brett Lossin*	PO Box 2112, Odessa TX 79760	432-332-1541	R	40*	.1
131	Central Illinois Steel Co—*Dan Millard*	PO Box 78, Carlinville IL 62626	217-854-3251	R	39*	.1
132	RKR Corp—*Greg Danglias*	4600 Grape St, Denver CO 80216	303-321-7610	R	39*	<.1
133	Steel Services Inc—*Garland Harwood*	9800 Mayland Dr, Richmond VA 23233	804-673-3810	R	39*	.1
134	Thompson Steel Company Inc—*Mary Ryan*	120 Royall St Ste 2, Canton MA 02021	781-828-8800	R	39*	.3
135	United Steel Service LLC—*Steven Friedman*	PO Box 149, Brookfield OH 44403	330-448-4057	R	38*	.1
136	Pipe Distributors Inc—*Stan T Rawley*	PO Box 23237, Houston TX 77228	713-635-4200	R	37*	.1
137	Gerber Metal Supply Co—*Charles Calabrese*	2 Boundary Rd, Somerville NJ 08876	908-823-9150	R	37*	<.1
138	Burgon Tool Steel Company Inc—*Eric Burgon*	20 Durham St, Portsmouth NH 03801	603-430-9200	R	37*	<.1
139	Hascall Steel Company Inc—*Dag Hascall*	4165 Spartan Industria, Grandville MI 49418	616-531-8600	R	36*	.1
140	Farwest Steel Corp—*Jack Clark*	PO Box 889, Eugene OR 97440	541-686-2000	R	35*	.7
141	Quality Metals Inc—*Benjamin Silverberg*	2575 Doswell Ave, Saint Paul MN 55108	651-645-5875	R	35*	.1
142	Pusan Pipe America Inc—*Howard Lee*	9615 Norwalk Blvd Ste, Santa Fe Springs CA 90670	562-692-0600	R	35*	<.1
143	Sioux City Foundry Co—*Andrew Galinsky*	PO Box 3067, Sioux City IA 51102	712-252-4181	R	35*	.2
144	Majestic Steel USA Inc—*Dennis Leebow*	31099 Chagrin Blvd Ste, Cleveland OH 44124	440-786-2666	R	35*	.2
145	Service Steel Inc—*Edward Westerdahl*	5555 N Channel Ave Bld, Portland OR 97217	503-224-9500	R	34*	.1
146	Murphy And Nolan Inc—*John Murphy*	PO Box 6689, Syracuse NY 13217	315-474-8203	R	34*	.1
147	Lusk Metals and Plastic—*Eric Schneider* Reliance Steel and Aluminum Co	26587 Corporate Ave, Hayward CA 94545	510-785-6400	S	34*	<.1
148	Harrison Piping Supply Co—*Jeffery Harrison*	38777 Schoolcraft Rd, Livonia MI 48150		R	33*	.1
149	Dave Steel Company Inc—*Jeffrey Dave*	PO Box 2630, Asheville NC 28802	828-252-2771	R	33*	.1
150	Colonial Metal Products Inc—*Williams Thomas*	PO Box 415, Wheatland PA 16161	724-346-5550	R	33*	<.1
151	William Reisner Corp—*William M Reisner*	33 Elm St, Clinton MA 01510	978-365-4585	R	31*	<.1
152	Klein Steel Service Inc—*Joseph Klein*	105 Vanguard Pkwy, Rochester NY 14606	585-328-4000	R	31*	.2
153	Rolled Alloys Inc—*Russ Hoogendooren*	PO Box 310, Temperance MI 48182	734-847-0561	R	31*	.2
154	Caprock Pipe and Supply Inc—*David Murray*	PO Box 1535, Lovington NM 88260	575-396-5881	R	30*	<.1
155	Aluminum and Stainless Inc—*Joseph Wolf* Reliance Steel and Aluminum Co	PO Box 3484, Lafayette LA 70502	337-837-4381	S	30*	<.1
156	Metals USA Plates and Shapes-Shreveport Div—*Chalres La-borde*	PO Box 8745, Shreveport LA 71148	318-686-1300	S	30*	<.1
157	Steel Cities Steels Inc—*Marianne Vangel*	395 Melton Rd, Burns Harbor IN 46304	219-787-9500	R	30*	<.1
158	Morse Industries Inc—*Terry Morse*	PO Box 1779, Kent WA 98035	253-852-1399	R	30*	<.1
159	Tex Isle Supply Inc—*Curtis Kayem*	10000 Memorial Dr Ste, Houston TX 77024	713-461-1012	R	30*	<.1
160	Tomson Steel Co—*Stephen Lutz*	PO Box 940, Middletown OH 45044	513-420-8600	R	30*	<.1
161	US Metals and Supply Inc—*Richard Killebrew*	PO Box 27, Saint Louis MO 63166	314-658-0200	R	30*	<.1
162	Delaco Steel Corp—*Gerald Diez*	8111 Tireman Ave Ste 1, Dearborn MI 48126	313-491-1200	R	30*	<.1
163	Jack Rubin and Sons Inc—*Bruce Rubin*	PO Box 3005, Compton CA 90223	310-635-5407	R	30*	.1
164	National Nail Corp—*Scott Baker*	2964 Clydon Ave Sw, Wyoming MI 49519	616-538-8000	R	29*	.2
165	Ulbrich of California Inc—*Chris Ulbrich*	5455 E Home Ave, Fresno CA 93727	559-456-2310	S	29*	<.1
166	Bmg Metals Inc—*Kingsbery Gay*	PO Box 7536, Richmond VA 23231	804-226-1024	R	29*	.2
167	Steel Fabricators LLC—*Sid Blaauw*	721 Ne 44th St, Oakland Park FL 33334	954-772-0440	R	28*	.2
168	Sampson Steel Corp—*Jay Eisen*	PO Box 2392, Beaumont TX 77704	409-838-1611	R	28*	<.1
169	National Tube Supply Co—*Gary Chess*	925 Central Ave, University Park IL 60484	708-534-2700	R	27*	.1
170	Jim's Supply Company Inc—*Doreen Boylan*	PO Box 668, Bakersfield CA 93302	661-324-6514	R	27*	.1
171	B and B Surplus Inc—*Mike Georgino*	7020 Rosedale Hwy, Bakersfield CA 93308	661-589-0381	R	27*	.1
172	Curtis Steel Company Inc—*Arthur Curtis*	4565 Wynn Rd, Las Vegas NV 89103	702-952-3000	R	27*	<.1
173	Nashville Steel Corp—*Okey Johnson III*	PO Box 90267, Nashville TN 37209	615-350-7933	R	27*	<.1
174	Bakersfield Pipe And Supply Inc—*Dan Byrum*	PO Box 639, Bakersfield CA 93302	661-589-9141	R	27*	.2
175	Aladdin Steel Inc—*Eugene Eschbacher*	PO Box 89, Gillespie IL 62033	217-839-2121	R	26*	.1
176	Mst Steel Corp—*Richard Thompson*	24417 Groesbeck Hwy, Warren MI 48089	586-773-5460	R	26*	.1
177	Lynch Metals Inc—*Clinton Lynch*	1075 Lousons Rd, Union NJ 07083	908-686-8401	R	25*	<.1
178	Consumers Pipe And Supply Co—*Michael Abeling*	10927 Jasmine St, Fontana CA 92337	909-728-4828	R	25*	<.1
179	C and B Piping Inc—*Curtis Estes*	PO Box 942, Leeds AL 35094	205-699-0455	R	25*	.1
180	Lexington Steel Corp—*Robert Douglass*	5443 W 70th Pl, Bedford Park IL 60638	708-594-9200	R	25*	.1
181	Mill Steel Co—*David Samrick*	PO Box 8827, Grand Rapids MI 49518	616-949-6700	R	25*	.1
182	R L Perlow Corp—*Mark Perlow*	2900 S 25th Ave, Broadview IL 60155	708-865-1200	R	25*	<.1
183	Dayton Steel Service Inc—*Mary Ryan* Thompson Steel Company Inc	3911 Dayton Park Dr, Dayton OH 45414	937-236-6940	S	24*	.1
184	Peerless Steel Co—*Randy Remdenok*	2450 Austin Dr, Troy MI 48083	248-528-3200	R	24*	.2
185	Specialty Steel Service CoInc—*Malcolm Weiss*	3300 Douglas Blvd Ste, Roseville CA 95661	916-771-4737	R	24*	.2
186	Kasle Steel Corp—*Michael Limauro*	4343 Wyoming St, Dearborn MI 48126	313-943-2500	S	24*	.1
187	Lake Steel Ltd—*C Sehorn*	PO Box 31748, Amarillo TX 79120	806-383-7141	R	24*	.1
188	H and D Steel Service Inc—*Joe Bubba*	9960 York Alpha Dr, North Royalton OH 44133	440-237-3390	R	24*	.1
189	Admiral Metals Servicenter Company Inc—*James Burstein*	11 Forbes Rd, Woburn MA 01801	781-933-8300	R	24*	.1
190	Steel Etc Holding Co—*Robert Mcintyre*	1408 52nd St N, Great Falls MT 59405	406-771-0012	R	24*	<.1
191	Taco Metals Inc—*Jon Kushner*	50 Ne 179th St, Miami FL 33162	305-652-8566	R	24*	.2
192	Lapham-Hickey Steel Corp—*William Hickey*	PO Box 71114, Chicago IL 60694	708-496-6111	R	23*	.5
193	Western Titanium Inc—*Dan Schroeder*	8015 Silverton Ave, San Diego CA 92126	858-271-7727	R	23*	<.1
194	American Douglas Metals Inc—*Edward Raimonde*	783 Thorpe Rd, Orlando FL 32824	407-855-6590	R	23*	<.1
195	Monico Alloys Inc—*Barbara Zenk*	3039 E Ana St, Compton CA 90221	310-928-0168	R	23*	.1
196	Russellville Steel Company Inc—*Trish Henry*	PO Box 1538, Russellville AR 72811	479-968-2211	R	23*	.1
197	SSCI Inc—*Buzz James*	PO Box 3625, Seattle WA 98124	206-343-0700	R	23*	.1
198	Durrett Sheppard Steel Company Inc—*Timothy Schauman* Reliance Steel and Aluminum Co	6800 E Baltimore St, Baltimore MD 21224	410-633-6800	S	23*	.1
199	General Steel Inc—*Henry Oliner*	PO Box 20008, Macon GA 31205	478-746-2794	R	23*	.1
200	Synergy Steel Inc—*Andy Moir*	1450 Rochester Rd, Troy MI 48083	248-583-9740	R	23*	<.1
201	Doral Steel Inc—*Cam Smith*	1500 Coining Dr, Toledo OH 43612	419-470-7070	R	23*	.1
202	Grammer Dempsey and Hudson Inc—*James Hudson*	PO Box 1059, Newark NJ 07101	973-589-8000	R	23*	.2
203	Sr Metals Inc—*Matthew Mc Hugh*	PO Box 931, Havertown PA 19083	610-449-6100	R	23*	<.1
204	Precision Steel Services Inc—*David Kelley*	31 E Sylvania Ave, Toledo OH 43612	419-476-5702	R	23*	.1
205	Raco Steel Company Inc—*Dennis Erickson*	2100 W 163rd Pl, Markham IL 60428	708-596-0000	R	22*	.1
206	Chapin and Bangs Co—*Richard Hoyt*	PO Box 1117, Bridgeport CT 06601	203-333-4183	R	22*	.1
207	Brugg Wire Rope LLC—*Kevin Heling*	1801 Parrish Dr Se, Rome GA 30161	706-235-6315	R	21*	<.1

Note: An asterisk (*) indicates an estimated financial figure. The company type code used is as follows: R = Private, P = Public, S = Private Subsidiary, B = Public Subsidiary, D = Division, J = Joint Venture, I = Investment Fund.

COMPANY RANKINGS BY SALES WITHIN 4-DIGIT SIC

Rank	Company Name—*Executive Officer*	Address, City, State, Zip	Phone	Type	Fin	Empls
208	Alaskan Copper Companies Inc—*Kermit Rosen*	PO Box 3546, Seattle WA 98124	206-623-5800	R	21*	.5
209	AMI Metals Inc—*Scott Smith* Reliance Steel and Aluminum Co	1738 General George Pa, Brentwood TN 37027	615-377-0400	S	21*	.2
210	MetalMart International Inc—*Bill Lippman* Metals USA Holdings Corp	5828 Smithway St, Commerce CA 90040	562-692-9081	D	21*	<.1
211	RTI Pierce-Spafford—*John Spafford*	7550 Chapman Ave, Garden Grove CA 92841	714-895-7756	S	21*	<.1
212	Metalmark Inc—*Michael Breen*	14077 Cedar Rd, Cleveland OH 44118	216-371-1333	R	21*	<.1
213	Richardson Trident Co—*Thomas Bentley*	PO Box 853900, Richardson TX 75085	972-231-5176	R	21*	.5
214	Amsco Steel Co—*Stephen Sikes*	PO Box 11037, Fort Worth TX 76110	817-926-3355	R	21*	.1
215	Cincinnati Tool Steel Co—*Brian Cincinnati*	PO Box 5664, Rockford IL 61125	815-226-8800	R	21*	.1
216	All Steel Products Inc—*Michael Favre*	PO Box 270, Staunton IL 62088	618-635-7777	R	21*	<.1
217	Harris Steel Co—*Thomas Eliasek*	1223 S 55th Ct, Cicero IL 60804	708-656-5500	R	20*	.1
218	Miami Valley Steel Service Inc—*Louis Moran*	PO Box 1191, Piqua OH 45356	937-773-7127	R	20*	.1
219	Harbor Pipe And Steel Inc—*Joseph Beattie*	1495 Columbia Ave Bldg, Riverside CA 92507	951-369-3990	R	20*	.1
220	Miller Metals Service Corp—*Wayne Miller*	2400 Bond St, University Park IL 60484	708-534-7200	R	20*	<.1
221	Crystal Steel Corp—*John Diamont*	PO Box 980, Middleton MA 01949	978-774-9988	R	20*	<.1
222	Three D Metals Inc—*David Dickens*	5462 Innovation Dr, Valley City OH 44280	330-220-0451	R	20*	.1
223	Inter-Wire Products Inc—*Deborah Cardile*	355 Main St Ste 2, Armonk NY 10504	914-273-6633	R	20*	.1
224	Westfield Steel Inc—*Charles Prine*	530 State Rd 32 W, Westfield IN 46074	317-896-5587	R	19*	.1
225	Tinplate Purchasing Corp—*Alan Kaufman*	PO Box 2410, Newark NJ 07114	973-242-9300	R	19*	.1
226	Voestalpine Rotec Inc—*Andrew Ball*	3709 Us Hwy 52 S, Lafayette IN 47905	765-471-2808	R	19*	.1
227	Harbor Steel And Supply Corp—*David Folkert*	PO Box 4250, Muskegon MI 49444	231-739-7152	R	19*	.1
228	101 Pipe and Casing Inc—*Fidel Nabor*	30101 Agoura Ct Ste 20, Agoura Hills CA 91301	818-707-9101	R	19*	.1
229	Special Metals Inc—*Mike Potts*	PO Box 94670, Oklahoma City OK 73143	405-677-7700	R	19*	.1
230	United Sales—*Tom Andrews*	425 Shrewsbury St, Worcester MA 01604	508-752-7073	R	18*	.1
231	Everglades Steel Corp—*Orlando Gomez*	PO Box 667510, Miami FL 33166	305-591-9460	R	18*	<.1
232	Whitney Blake Co—*Sheldon Scott*	PO Box 579, Bellows Falls VT 05101	802-463-9558	R	18*	.1
233	Delta Centrifugal Corp—*Robert Rose*	PO Box 1043, Temple TX 76503	254-773-9055	R	18*	.1
234	Ford Steel Co—*Anthony Morrison*	PO Box 54, St Louis MO 63043	314-567-4680	R	18*	<.1
235	Ecp American Steel LLC—*Frederick Bickel*	3122 Engle Rd, Fort Wayne IN 46809	260-478-4700	R	17*	.1
236	Den-Col Supply Co—*Dewayne Deck*	4630 Washington St, Denver CO 80216	303-295-1683	R	17*	.1
237	Albany Steel Inc—*Peter Hess*	PO Box 4006, Albany NY 12204	518-436-4851	R	17*	.1
238	Bell Processing Inc—*Duwaybe Bell*	PO Box 2604, Wichita Falls TX 76307	940-322-8621	R	17*	.1
239	Gutterman's Supply Corporation Of America—*Kenneth Cripps*	1620 Ne Argyle Dr, Portland OR 97211	503-285-2500	R	17*	<.1
240	Affiliated Metals—*Shawn Wardle* Reliance Steel and Aluminum Co	PO Box 22990, Salt Lake City UT 84122	801-363-1711	D	17*	<.1
241	Service Steel Aerospace Corp—*Terry Wilson* Reliance Steel and Aluminum Co	939 E F St, Tacoma WA 98421	253-627-2910	S	17*	<.1
242	Howard Precision Metals Inc—*Donald Howard*	PO Box 240127, Milwaukee WI 53224	414-355-9611	R	17*	.1
243	State Steel Supply Co—*Jack Bernstein*	PO Box 3224, Sioux City IA 51102	712-277-4000	R	17*	.1
244	S and S Steel Services Inc—*Barry Sharp*	PO Box 129, Chesterfield IN 46017	765-622-4545	R	17*	.1
245	Remelt Sources Inc—*David Drage*	27151 Tungsten Rd, Cleveland OH 44132	216-289-4555	R	17*	.1
246	Victory Tube Company Inc—*Victor Cassesa*	4521 Willow Pkwy, Cleveland OH 44125	216-641-9339	R	17*	.1
247	Paco Steel and Engineering Corp—*Nelson Paik*	19818 S Alameda St, Compton CA 90221	310-537-6375	R	17*	.1
248	Ici Aluminum/North Inc—*Jeff Dordalampe*	2353 Davis Ave, Hayward CA 94545	510-786-3750	R	16*	.1
249	Alliance Steel Inc—*Keith Butler*	PO Box 2441, Birmingham MI 48012	248-443-4990	D	16*	<.1
250	All Foils Inc—*Robert Papp*	16100 Imperial Pkwy, Cleveland OH 44149	440-572-3645	R	16*	.1
251	Totten Tubes Inc—*Dave Totten*	500 Danlee, Azusa CA 91702	626-812-0220	R	16*	.1
252	Columbus Pipe and Equipment Co—*Bruce Silberstein*	PO Box 7843, Columbus OH 43207	614-444-7871	R	16*	<.1
253	Parker Steel Co—*Paul Goldner*	PO Box 2883, Toledo OH 43606	419-473-2481	R	16*	<.1
254	Okaya USA Inc—*Osamu Sugimoto*	52 Marks Rd Ste 1, Valparaiso IN 46383	219-477-4488	S	16*	<.1
255	Pioneer Steel Corp—*Donald Sazama*	7447 Intervale St, Detroit MI 48238	313-933-9400	R	16*	.1
256	Blackhawk Steel Corp—*Mark Herman*	1700 W 74th Pl, Chicago IL 60636	773-778-4100	R	16*	.1
257	Arbon Steel and Service Company Inc—*Daniel O'connor*	2355 Bond St, University Park IL 60484	708-534-6800	R	16*	.1
258	Fay Industries Inc—*Richard Schnaterbeck*	PO Box 360947, Cleveland OH 44136	440-572-5030	R	16*	.1
259	Industrial Steel and Wire Company Of Illinois LLC—*Joan Smith*	1901 N Narragansett Av, Chicago IL 60639	773-804-0404	R	16*	.1
260	St Lawrence Steel Corp—*Henry Beechler*	PO Box 2490, Streetsboro OH 44241	330-562-9000	R	15*	.1
261	Macuch Steel Products Inc—*William Macuch*	PO Box 3285, Augusta GA 30914	706-823-2420	R	15	.1
262	Southern Tool Steel Inc—*Arnold Erwin*	PO Box 699, Hixson TN 37343	423-807-7888	R	15*	.1
263	Cyclone Steel Services Inc—*Steve Lesikar*	PO Box 682017, Houston TX 77268	713-635-5555	R	15*	<.1
264	Hudd Steel Corp—*William Lynch*	PO Box 10, South Plainfield NJ 07080	908-753-2200	R	15*	<.1
265	Piping Supply Company Inc—*Jeff Howell*	PO Box 5099, Chattanooga TN 37406	423-698-8996	R	15*	<.1
266	Dix Metals Inc—*Robert Dix*	14801 Able Ln Ste 101, Huntington Beach CA 92647	714-677-0777	R	15*	.1
267	Tampa Bay Steel Corp—*Cleveland Mc Innis*	6901 E 6th Ave, Tampa FL 33619	813-621-4738	R	15*	.1
268	Borrmann Metal Center—*Robert Wedeen*	110 W Olive Ave, Burbank CA 91502	818-846-7171	R	15*	.1
269	American Consolidated Industries Inc—*Josh Kaufman*	4650 Johnston Pkwy, Cleveland OH 44128	216-587-8000	R	15*	.1
270	Champion Steel Of Central Florida Corp—*Ellison Marsil*	1856 Patterson Ave, Deland FL 32724	386-734-5009	R	14*	.1
271	Steel Supply Co—*Donald Hjortland*	5105 Newport Dr, Rolling Meadows IL 60008	847-255-2460	R	14*	<.1
272	Soudan Metals Company Inc—*Thomas Soudan*	PO Box 09044, Chicago IL 60609	773-548-7600	R	14*	.1
273	Industrial Stainless Supply Inc—*Mike Tschida*	5265 Hanson Ct N, Minneapolis MN 55429	763-535-5866	R	14*	.1
274	Arlington Metals Corp—*Ted Orlowski*	11355 Franklin Ave, Franklin Park IL 60131	847-451-9100	R	14*	.1
275	Northwest Aluminum Specialties Inc—*William Reid*	2929 W 2nd St, The Dalles OR 97058	541-298-0867	R	14*	.1
276	Winchester Metals Inc—*Donald Phelps*	195 Ebert Rd, Winchester VA 22603	540-667-9000	R	14*	.1
277	Northstar Steel and Aluminum Inc—*James Macvane*	PO Box 4886, Manchester NH 03108	603-668-3600	R	14*	.1
278	Duhig and Company Inc—*Tom Card*	5071 Telegraph Rd, Los Angeles CA 90022	323-263-7161	R	14*	<.1
279	Mead Metals Inc—*John Allyn*	555 Cardigan Rd, Saint Paul MN 55126	651-484-1400	R	14*	<.1
280	Trotter Nathan and Company Inc—*Russell Etherington*	PO Box 1066, Exton PA 19341	610-524-1440	R	14*	<.1
281	Northwest Steel and Pipe Inc—*Michael Wax*	PO Box 11247, Tacoma WA 98411	253-473-8888	R	14*	.1
282	Remington Steel Inc—*Roy Kohl*	PO Box 1491, Springfield OH 45501	937-322-2414	R	14*	.1
283	Metrolina Steel Inc—*Thomas Hurt*	2601 Westinghouse Blvd, Charlotte NC 28273	704-598-7007	R	14*	.1
284	Wisconsin Steel and Tube Corp—*Michael Poehlmann*	PO Box 26365, Milwaukee WI 53226	414-453-4441	R	14*	.1
285	Diversified Metals Inc—*Kenneth Hamel*	PO Box 65, Monson MA 01057	413-267-5101	R	14*	<.1
286	Steel Warehouse Quad City LLC—*Glenn Beal*	4305 81st Ave W, Rock Island IL 61201	309-756-0495	R	14*	.1
287	Scheu Steel Supply Co—*Allyn Scheu*	PO Box 250, Upland CA 91785	909-982-8933	R	14*	.1
288	Mid-America Steel Corp—*Morton Kaufman*	20900 Saint Clair Ave, Cleveland OH 44117	216-692-3800	R	13*	.1
289	Coosa Steel Corp—*E Saville*	PO Box 187, Rome GA 30162	706-235-7011	R	13*	.1
290	Champagne Metals LLC—*Robert Ailshie*	PO Box 849, Glenpool OK 74033	918-322-1131	R	13*	.1
291	Stainless Sales Corp—*Marilyn Kutzen*	3301 S Justine St, Chicago IL 60608	773-247-9060	R	13*	<.1
292	Pohang Steel America Corp—*Ku-Taek Lee*	2 Executive Dr Ste 805, Fort Lee NJ 07024	201-585-3060	S	13*	<.1
293	Wholesale Sheet Metal Inc—*Pat Chilen*	PO Box 3153, Kansas City KS 66103	913-432-7100	R	13*	.1

Rank	Company Name—*Executive Officer*	Address, City, State, Zip	Phone	Type	Fin	Empls
294	Livingston Pipe and Tube Inc—*Ronald Mueller*	PO Box 300, Staunton IL 62088	618-635-8700	R	13*	.1
295	Energy Steel and Supply Co—*Lisa Rice*	3123 John Conley Dr, Lapeer MI 48446	810-538-4990	R	13*	.1
296	Supra Alloys Inc—*Lawrence Buhl*	351 Cortez Cir, Camarillo CA 93012	805-388-2138	R	13*	<.1
297	Dubose National Energy Services Inc—*Carl Rogers*	PO Box 499, Clinton NC 28329	910-590-2151	R	13*	.1
298	Round Ground Inc—*Andrew Strzalkowski*	4825 Turnberry Dr, Hanover Park IL 60133	630-539-5300	R	13*	.1
299	Connector Specialists Inc—*Joann Sutton*	175 James Dr E, Saint Rose LA 70087	504-469-1659	R	13*	.1
300	Bbc Steel Corp—*Diana Boyer*	2001 S Township Rd, Canby OR 97013	503-263-6343	R	13*	.1
301	Haskins Steel Company Inc—*Sterling Haskins*	PO Box 4219, Spokane WA 99220	509-535-0657	R	12*	.1
302	ABC Metals Inc—*John Barnes*	500 W Clinton St Ste 1, Logansport IN 46947	574-753-0471	R	12*	.1
303	E J Enterprises Inc—*Eric Johnson*	7280 Bltmore Annplis B, Glen Burnie MD 21061	410-625-8200	R	12*	<.1
304	White Star Steel Inc—*Stephanie Carter*	PO Box 15518, Houston TX 77220	713-675-6501	R	12*	.1
305	Light Enterprises Inc—*Timothy Light*	13318 Maugansville Rd, Hagerstown MD 21740	301-791-7179	R	12*	.1
306	Bobco Metals LLC	2000 S Alameda St, Vernon CA 90058	213-748-5171	R	12*	<.1
307	Sedalia Steel Supply Inc—*Wayne Lamb*	1900 Rissler Rd, Sedalia MO 65301	660-826-7600	R	12*	<.1
308	Arika Metals Inc—*R Mckeever*	1922 N Main St, Orange CA 92865	714-363-0151	R	12*	<.1
309	Camalloy Inc—*William Campbell*	PO Box 248, Washington PA 15301	724-228-1880	R	12*	<.1
310	Cincinnati Steel Products Co—*James Todd*	4540 Steel Pl, Cincinnati OH 45209	513-871-4444	R	12*	.1
311	Jadco Manufacturing Inc—*James Davison*	PO Box 465, Zelienople PA 16063	724-452-5252	R	12*	.1
312	Northern Illinois Steel Supply Co—*Michael Ruth*	PO Box 2146, Joliet IL 60434	815-467-9000	R	12*	<.1
313	Midland Steel Warehouse Corp—*Robert Allen*	1120 Leggett Ave, Bronx NY 10474	718-328-4600	R	12*	<.1
314	Rancocas Metals Corp—*John Eden*	PO Box 157, Rancocas NJ 08073	609-267-4120	R	12*	<.1
315	Hulick Metals Inc—*Scott Hulick*	4738 American Rd, Rockford IL 61109	815-874-8040	R	11*	.1
316	Specialty Metals Corp—*James Stice*	8300 S 206th St, Kent WA 98032	253-872-8000	R	11*	<.1
317	Admiral Steel LLC—*Mark Tolliver*	4152 W 123rd St, Alsip IL 60803	708-388-9600	R	11*	<.1
318	Medley Steel And Supply Inc—*Orlando Gomez*	9925 Nw 116th Way, Medley FL 33178	305-863-7480	R	11*	<.1
319	Great Central Steel Co—*Eugene Wagner*	85 Ames St, Marlborough MA 01752	617-625-3232	R	11*	<.1
320	Royal Metal Industries Inc—*Michael Jacobs*	1036 W Ironwood St, Olathe KS 66061	913-829-3000	R	11*	<.1
321	Sunbelt Metal Service Inc—*Larry Norred*	PO Box 7961, Shreveport LA 71137	318-222-9462	R	11*	<.1
322	Siegal Steel Co—*Leonard Siegal*	4747 S Kedzie Ave, Chicago IL 60632	773-927-7600	R	11*	<.1
323	Hubbard Iron Doors Inc—*Ron Hubbard*	7407 Telegraph Rd, Montebello CA 90640	323-724-6500	R	11*	<.1
324	West Troy Tool and Machine Inc—*Warren Davidson*	155 Marybill Dr S, Troy OH 45373	937-339-2192	R	11*	<.1
325	Stulz-Sickles Steel Company Inc—*Philip Stasio*	PO Box 273, Elizabeth NJ 07207	908-351-1776	R	11*	<.1
326	Northern Steel Castings Inc—*Tom Nowak*	80 Oliver St, Wisconsin Rapids WI 54494	715-423-8040	R	10*	<.1
327	Rimex Metals (USA) Inc—*John Horbal*	2850 Woodbridge Ave, Edison NJ 08837	732-549-3800	R	10*	<.1
328	Crawford Steel Company Inc—*Michael Isaacs*	3141 W 36th Pl, Chicago IL 60632	773-376-6969	R	10*	<.1
329	A and C Metals-Sawing Inc—*David Girk*	9170 Davenport St Ne, Minneapolis MN 55449	763-786-1048	R	10*	<.1
330	Tri-State Aluminium Inc—*Marc Schupan*	1663 Tracy St, Toledo OH 43605	419-666-0100	R	10*	<.1
331	Delta Sales Corp—*David Speier*	PO Box 681, Selbyville DE 19975	302-436-6063	R	10*	.1
332	Merfish Pipe and Supply LP—*Mark Facer*	PO Box 15879, Houston TX 77220	713-869-5731	R	10*	<.1
333	Fedmet International Corp—*Edward Siegle*	30403 Bruce Industrial, Solon OH 44139	440-248-9500	R	10*	<.1
334	Roberts and Sons Aluminum Inc—*Robert F Hinely Jr*	PO Box 71669, Newnan GA 30271	770-252-2323	R	10*	<.1
335	CRU Price Risk Management—*James Southwood*	2000 Corporate Dr Ste, Wexford PA 15090	724-940-7100	R	10*	<.1
336	Consolidated Steel Inc—*Brenda Justus*	PO Box 110, Pounding Mill VA 24637	276-964-4461	R	10*	<.1
337	Great Plains Stainless—*Joseph Gibbons*	1004 N 129th E Ave, Tulsa OK 74116	918-437-5400	R	10*	<.1
338	Great South Metals Co—*John Kingery*	2670 Hickory Grove Rd, Acworth GA 30101	770-917-9000	R	10*	<.1
339	Nightingale Metals Inc—*David Slaven*	3 Crownmark Dr, Lincoln RI 02865	401-333-2100	R	10*	<.1
340	Two Rivers Enterprises Inc—*Robert Warzecha*	PO Box 70, Holdingford MN 56340	320 746 3156	P	10*	<.1
341	Calko Steel Inc—*Young Kwon*	6921 Avalon Blvd, Los Angeles CA 90003	323-789-5730	R	10*	<.1
342	Valley Machine Company Inc—*Gary Sledd*	7500 Shadwell Dr Ste A, Roanoke VA 24019	540-345-4247	R	9*	<.1
343	Stress Con Inc—*Joe Ramey*	PO Box 471070, Tulsa OK 74147	918-836-0021	R	9*	<.1
344	Stark Metal Sales Inc—*Arthur Reiber*	432 Keystone St, Alliance OH 44601	330-823-7383	R	9*	<.1
345	Galvmet Inc—*Ernest Ketcham*	8600 Ne Underground Dr, Kansas City MO 64161	816-453-8500	R	9*	<.1
346	Jacklin Steel Supply Co—*Fred Cerasoli*	2410 Aero Park Dr, Traverse City MI 49686	231-946-8434	R	9*	<.1
347	Arrow Thompson Metals Inc—*Henry Williams* Thompson Steel Company Inc	6880 Troost Ave, North Hollywood CA 91605	818-765-0522	S	9*	<.1
348	Vita Needle Co—*Frederick Hartman*	PO Box 920236, Needham MA 02492	781-444-1780	R	9*	<.1
349	Western Branch Metals LC—*Thomas Boze*	1006 Obici IndustrialB, Suffolk VA 23434	757-215-1500	R	9*	<.1
350	Van Bebber Brothers—*Rick Bebber*	PO Box 760, Petaluma CA 94953	707-762-4528	R	9*	<.1
351	Christy Metals Inc—*Creighton Helms*	PO Box 8206, Northfield IL 60093	847-729-5744	R	9*	<.1
352	Design Manufacturing Inc—*Gary Hull*	500 James Rollo Dr, Grain Valley MO 64029	816-847-7270	R	9*	<.1
353	Scion Inc—*Carlos Hurches*	21555 Mullin Ave, Warren MI 48089	586-755-4000	R	9*	<.1
354	JRD Trading Inc—*Jose Ramirez*	12925 S Alameda St, Compton CA 90222	310-631-7499	R	9*	<.1
355	Macsteel International USA Corp—*Salvatore Purpura*	333 Westchester Ave S1, White Plains NY 10604	914-872-2700	R	9*	<.1
356	Select Steel Inc—*Jeffrey Gotthardt*	1825 Hunter Ave, Niles OH 44446	330-652-1756	R	8*	<.1
357	Dalco Metals Inc—*Richard Ring*	PO Box 1905, Walworth WI 53184	262-275-6175	R	8*	<.1
358	O'rourke and Sons Inc—*Michael O'rourke*	992 S Bolmar St, West Chester PA 19382	610-436-0932	R	8*	<.1
359	Lehman's Pipe and Steel Inc—*R Lehman*	803 Robertson Loop, Pollok TX 75969	936-853-2211	R	8*	<.1
360	Benco Steel Inc—*Judy White*	PO Box 2053, Hickory NC 28603	828-328-1714	R	8*	<.1
361	Contractors Material Company Inc—*John Caldwell*	PO Box 6137, Pearl MS 39288	601-932-2106	R	8*	<.1
362	Sunbelt-Turret Steel Inc—*Wayne Gould*	527 Atando Ave, Charlotte NC 28206	704-342-4321	R	8*	<.1
363	Schwartz Steel Service Inc—*William Schwartz*	PO Box 1055, Gastonia NC 28053	704-865-9576	R	8*	<.1
364	Tarco Steel Inc—*Eugene Taren*	13 Spud Ln, Binghamton NY 13904	607-775-1500	R	8*	<.1
365	Turner Steel Company Inc—*Carl Turner*	PO Box 399, West Bridgewater MA 02379	508-583-7800	R	8*	.1
366	Steel Works LLC—*Larry Dunn*	PO Box 366, Granite City IL 62040	618-452-2833	R	8*	<.1
367	Ts Steel Inc—*Terry Shanks*	5230 Wilson St Ste C, Riverside CA 92509	951-682-2031	R	8*	<.1
368	M/K Huron Steel—*Frank Lester*	181 W Madison St 26th, Chicago IL 60602	312-372-9500	S	8*	<.1
369	Gassett Metals Ltd—*Glen Gassett*	8815 Mississippi St, Houston TX 77029	713-675-9291	R	8*	<.1
370	Allied Crawford Inc (Lakeland Florida)—*Gary Stern*	1500 Fish Hatchery Rd, Lakeland FL 33801	863-667-4966	R	8*	<.1
371	A Tube Bending Corp—*Fred Weinstein*	4825 W Grand Ave, Chicago IL 60639	773-745-0116	R	8*	.1
372	Midwest Metals Inc—*Eugene Pierce*	PO Box 4050, Davenport IA 52808	563-324-5244	R	8*	<.1
373	Delaco-Kasle LLC—*Desiree Opperman*	PO Box 673256, Detroit MI 48267	734-692-8000	R	8*	<.1
374	M C Steel Inc—*Thomas Mcclanahan*	43160 N Crawford Rd, Antioch IL 60002	847-350-9618	R	8*	<.1
375	Norca Corp—*Russell Stern*	PO Box 220427, Great Neck NY 11022	516-466-9500	R	8*	<.1
376	Cox Die Casting Inc—*Robert Cox*	1528 W 178th St, Gardena CA 90248	310-532-7544	R	8*	<.1
377	Nowell Steel and Supply Company Inc—*Reginald Lawrence*	10746 Springdale Ave, Santa Fe Springs CA 90670	562-944-0371	R	8*	<.1
378	Decker Steel and Supply Inc—*John Decker*	4500 Train Ave, Cleveland OH 44102	216-281-7900	R	8*	<.1
379	Advantage Metal Services Inc—*Bernard Hribar*	9835 Kale St, South El Monte CA 91733	626-579-1099	R	8*	<.1
380	Quality Steels Corp—*Larry Cartwright*	2221 Arbor Blvd, Moraine OH 45439	937-294-4133	R	7*	<.1
381	Vitco Steel Supply Corp—*Dominic Vitucci*	144th St and Robey Ave, Posen IL 60469	708-388-8300	R	7*	<.1
382	Mattsco Supply Co—*Carlyn Mattox*	PO Box 2925, Tulsa OK 74101	918-836-0451	R	7*	<.1

Note: An asterisk (*) indicates an estimated financial figure. The company type code used is as follows: R = Private, P = Public, S = Private Subsidiary, B = Public Subsidiary, D = Division, J = Joint Venture, I = Investment Fund.

COMPANY RANKINGS BY SALES WITHIN 4-DIGIT SIC

Rank	Company Name—*Executive Officer*	Address, City, State, Zip	Phone	Type	Fin	Empls
383	Sugar Steel Corp—*Robert Sugar*	2521 State St Ste 1, Chicago Heights IL 60411	708-757-9500	R	7*	<.1
384	Components Company Inc—*Joseph Wittig*	3320 Intertech Dr, Brookfield WI 53045	262-790-6868	R	7*	<.1
385	Solman Inc—*Joe Halter*	2716 Shepler Church Av, Canton OH 44706	330-580-5188	R	7*	.1
386	Shear-Rite Steel Corp—*Peter Cavaleri*	80 Newtown Rd, Plainview NY 11803	516-752-4250	R	7*	<.1
387	Wire Sales Inc—*Patricia Moore*	PO Box 911568, Sherman TX 75091	903-786-7733	R	7*	<.1
388	Craco Metal Supply Inc—*Randy Adams*	PO Box 1105, York SC 29745	803-684-5544	R	7*	<.1
389	Specialty Pipe and Tube Inc—*Steven Baroff*	PO Box 516, Mineral Ridge OH 44440	330-505-8262	R	7*	<.1
390	H and H Metal Source International Inc—*Brian Harris*	1909 Turner Ave Nw, Grand Rapids MI 49504	616-364-0113	R	7*	<.1
391	M Gervich and Sons Inc—*Douglas Gervich*	PO Box 67, Marshalltown IA 50158	641-753-3359	R	7*	<.1
392	Ed Fagan Inc—*Edward Fagan*	PO Box 328, Wyckoff NJ 07481	201-891-4003	R	7*	<.1
393	Oak Steel Supply Co—*Kenneth Linderborg*	6601 99th Pl, Chicago Ridge IL 60415	708-499-5200	R	7*	<.1
394	Hunterspoint Steel LLC—*Doug Baum*	2903 Hunters Point Ave, Long Island City NY 11101	718-786-3760	R	7*	<.1
395	Universal Pipe and Steel Supply Inc—*Steven Lehman*	2200 Flint Dr, Fort Myers FL 33916	239-332-2525	R	7*	<.1
396	Dynamic Metals Inc—*Michael Wright*	1713 S 2nd St, Piscataway NJ 08854	908-769-5111	R	7*	<.1
397	International Global Metals Inc—*Bernard Leibov*	1701 Nw 31st Ave, Fort Lauderdale FL 33311	954-486-2010	R	7*	<.1
398	Northeast Air Solutions Inc—*Robert Couture*	3 Lopez Rd, Wilmington MA 01887	978-988-2000	R	7*	<.1
399	Subconn Inc—*Galynn Dexter*	840 G St, Burwell NE 68823	308-346-4874	R	6*	.1
400	Abc Sign Products Inc—*Brian Brooks*	2028 Se Frontage Rd, Fort Collins CO 80525	970-482-5225	R	6*	<.1
401	Titan Formworks Systems LLC—*Michael Heisley*	2900 Ne Brooktree Ln S, Kansas City MO 64119	816-459-7000	R	6*	<.1
402	General Supply And Metals Inc—*John Patys*	47 Nauset St, New Bedford MA 02746	508-993-9212	R	6*	<.1
403	P and K Steel Service Inc—*Fred Pylman*	PO Box 739, Grandville MI 49468	616-243-2358	R	6*	<.1
404	Pipe and Steel Industrial Fabricators Inc—*Kylie Sparks*	PO Box 1486, Denham Springs LA 70727	225-665-0407	R	6*	<.1
405	Mace Metal Sales Inc—*Anita Huseth*	5555 E Slauson Ave, Commerce CA 90040	323-726-6783	R	6*	<.1
406	P Kay Metal Inc—*Larry Kay*	2448 E 25th St, Los Angeles CA 90058	323-585-5058	R	6*	<.1
407	Chappell Steel Company Inc—*Warren Chappel*	3545 Scotten St, Detroit MI 48210	313-897-6670	R	6*	<.1
408	Viking Industrial Corp—*Spencer Brog*	620 Clark Ave, Pittsburg CA 94565	925-427-2518	R	6*	<.1
409	Rohr Steel Inc—*Christopher Rohr*	1281 E 3rd St, Pomona CA 91766	909-469-1634	R	6*	<.1
410	Production Supply Company Of Florida Inc—*John Westeyn*	14400 S Figueroa St, Gardena CA 90248	323-321-1700	R	6*	<.1
411	Savannah Recycling LLC—*Nico Berlin*	PO Box 1585, Savannah GA 31402	912-232-8882	R	6*	<.1
412	Jdr Cable Systems Inc—*Roger Herbert*	7906 N S Hou Park W 20, Houston TX 77064	713-466-6671	R	6*	<.1
413	Crown Steel Sales Inc—*Lynne Mccutcheon*	3355 W 31st St, Chicago IL 60623	773-376-1700	R	6*	<.1
414	Steel Yard Inc—*Leland Waltuck*	PO Box 4828, Portland OR 97208	503-282-9273	R	6*	<.1
415	Thermal Conductive Bonding Inc—*Wayne Simpson*	1430 Tully Rd Ste 401, San Jose CA 95122	408-920-0255	R	6*	<.1
416	Area Iron and Steel Works Inc—*Karen Edmonston*	PO Box 13265, El Paso TX 79913	915-833-9494	R	6*	<.1
417	Peterson Steel Corp—*Douglas Peterson*	PO Box 60328, Worcester MA 01606	508-853-3630	R	6*	<.1
418	Birmingham Hot Metal Coatings Inc—*Ed Lambert*	1513 Industrial Blvd, Birmingham AL 35221	205-925-0429	R	6*	<.1
419	Besco Steel Supply Of Georgia Inc—*Tim Simpson*	PO Box 2065, Lawrenceville GA 30046	678-963-9812	R	6*	<.1
420	All Metal Sales Inc—*Tom Klocker*	29260 Clemens Rd Ste 3, Westlake OH 44145	440-617-1234	R	6*	<.1
421	Palmetco Inc—*Henrik Palme*	10830 Iota Dr, San Antonio TX 78217	210-655-4444	R	6*	<.1
422	Integrity Steel Co—*Bayrd Berger*	6300 Sterling Dr N, Sterling Heights MI 48312	586-826-3700	R	6*	<.1
423	Eramet North America Inc—*Stephen Wilkinson*	333 Rouser Rd Ste 600, Coraopolis PA 15108	412-604-0308	S	6*	<.1
424	Cardinal Steel Supply Inc—*Chris Cauttrell*	6335 Mckissock Ave, Saint Louis MO 63147	314-385-4270	R	6*	<.1
425	Benner Metals Corp—*Francis Benner*	1220 S State College B, Fullerton CA 92831	714-879-6477	R	6*	<.1
426	Unisteel LLC—*Melissa Loder*	6155 Sims Dr, Sterling Heights MI 48313	586-826-8040	R	6*	<.1
427	Cdw Service Center D and B Ltd—*Laura Perigni*	5221 W 164th St, Cleveland OH 44142	216-267-5500	R	6*	<.1
428	Falcon Steel Inc—*Terry Heinz*	PO Box 4351, Springfield MO 65808	417-866-6000	R	6*	<.1
429	Griffon Steel Corp—*John Koppinger*	1561 Highwood E, Pontiac MI 48340	248-339-5300	R	6*	<.1
430	Southern Tubular Products Inc—*Dan Smith*	PO Box 1628, Bessemer AL 35021	205-426-9764	R	6*	<.1
431	Petroleum Pipe and Supply Company Inc—*Paul Maisch*	PO Box 545, Carnegie PA 15106	412-279-7710	R	5*	<.1
432	Harris Metals Inc—*Clarence Harris*	3694 County Rd 216, Hanceville AL 35077	256-734-5035	R	5*	<.1
433	HMS Holding Company Inc—*Terry Heinz*	2610 N Eastgate Ave, Springfield MO 65803	417-866-6000	R	5*	<.1
434	Colonial Steel Corp—*Arnold Cohen*	PO Box 701, Bronx NY 10452	718-993-5500	R	5*	<.1
435	Mountain Alloys Corp—*Ronald Crume*	PO Box 1836, Grants Pass OR 97528	541-479-9755	R	5*	<.1
436	Century Tubes Inc—*Christine Young*	7910 Dunbrook Rd, San Diego CA 92126	858-586-0550	R	5*	<.1
437	Peninsula Concrete And Steel Inc—*Chrystal Colvin*	3105 Millers Landing R, Gloucester VA 23061	804-694-4906	R	5*	<.1
438	Diehl Steel Co—*Michael Sheehan*	PO Box 17010, Cincinnati OH 45217	513-242-8900	R	5*	<.1
439	South St Paul Steel Supply Company Inc—*David Berg*	200 Hardman Ave N, South Saint Paul MN 55075	651-451-6666	R	5*	<.1
440	Allegheny Metal Corp—*John Wagner*	PO Box 80, Delmont PA 15626	724-468-4300	S	5*	<.1
441	Heaton Steel and Supply Inc—*Marc Hodder*	428 S Spring St, Klamath Falls OR 97601	541-882-3426	R	5*	<.1
442	Cragin Metals LLC—*Joel Weber*	2900 N Kearsarge Ave, Chicago IL 60641	773-283-2201	R	5*	<.1
443	Gottlieb Inc—*Robert Gottlieb*	5603 Grand Ave, Pittsburgh PA 15225	412-269-0708	R	5*	<.1
444	Summerlot Engineered Products Inc—*Raymond Summerlot*	PO Box 5216, Terre Haute IN 47805	812-466-7266	R	5*	<.1
445	Star Metals Inc—*Chris Nance*	1715 S Bon View Ave, Ontario CA 91761	909-930-1588	R	5*	<.1
446	Associated Steel Company Inc—*Gilda Cohen*	PO Box 28335, Cleveland OH 44128	216-475-8000	R	5*	<.1
447	Klure and Harris Inc—*Robert Harris*	2727 Main St, Riverside CA 92501	951-683-3787	R	5*	<.1
448	Ford Tool Steels Inc—*Gary Heien*	5051 Pattison Ave, Saint Louis MO 63110	314-772-3322	R	5*	<.1
449	Western Reserve Metals Inc—*Tod Theodore*	PO Box 126, Masury OH 44438	330-448-4092	R	5*	<.1
450	Acorn Metal Service Inc—*Kenneth Linderborg*	6601 99th Pl, Chicago Ridge IL 60415	708-499-5300	R	5*	<.1
451	C and R Pipe And Steel Inc—*Dennis Wilfer*	PO Box 70743, Fairbanks AK 99707	907-456-8386	R	5*	<.1
452	Metalmart Co—*Roger Palmer*	PO Box 440, Lehi UT 84043	801-768-3332	R	5*	<.1
453	Cohen Steel Supply Inc—*Peter Webster*	10 Basin St, Concord NH 03301	603-225-2047	R	5*	<.1
454	Los Alamitos Ornamental Castings Inc—*Kathryn Lloyd*	10742 Walker St, Cypress CA 90630	714-828-6382	R	5*	<.1
455	Paramount Wire Company Inc—*Charles Coats*	2-8 Central Ave, East Orange NJ 07018	973-672-0500	R	5*	<.1
456	Tigrett Steel and Supply Company Inc—*Hugh Tigrett*	PO Box 107, Tupelo MS 38802	662-844-2551	R	5*	<.1
457	Ciralsky and Associates Inc—*William Ciralsky*	1604 Prosperity Rd, Toledo OH 43612	419-470-8406	R	5*	<.1
458	Aci Industries Ltd—*Scott Fischer*	970 Pittsburgh Dr, Delaware OH 43015	740-368-4160	R	4*	<.1
459	BM Kramer and Company Inc—*Duane Swager*	69 S 20th St, Pittsburgh PA 15203	412-481-3000	R	4*	<.1
460	Bangor Steel Service Inc—*Richard Nickerson*	PO Box 1900, Bangor ME 04402	207-947-2773	R	4*	<.1
461	B C Industrial Supply Inc—*Robert Heavican*	2720 E Regal Park Dr, Anaheim CA 92806	714-666-8000	R	4*	.1
462	Aluminum Supply Company Inc—*Nancy Marshall*	14359 Meyers Rd, Detroit MI 48227	313-491-5040	R	4*	<.1
463	Gator Metal Products Inc—*Jim Jacobs*	1139 Eldridge St, Clearwater FL 33755	727-441-2492	R	4*	<.1
464	Jas Steel Co—*Donald Nelson*	5645 Imlay City Rd, Attica MI 48412	810-724-8165	R	4*	<.1
465	Reliance Sheet and Strip Co Inc—*Roger Abendroth*	2301 W 10th St, Antioch CA 94509	925-706-1061	R	4*	<.1
466	Intermet Metals Services Inc—*Timothy Jaster*	1375 E Wdfield Rd Ste, Schaumburg IL 60173	847-605-1300	R	4*	<.1
467	Metropolitan Alloys Corp—*Murray Spilman*	17385 Ryan Rd, Detroit MI 48212	313-366-4443	R	4*	<.1
468	Premium Metals Inc—*Robert Pelles*	PO Box 602690, Cleveland OH 44102	216-961-1780	R	4*	<.1
469	Bar Tie Reinforcing Inc—*Mary Kincaid*	14748 Red Hog Pke, Rising Sun IN 47040	812-534-3707	R	4*	<.1
470	Wilmington Sales LLC	PO Box 572, Unionville PA 19375	215-465-5120	R	4*	<.1
471	Coil Slitting International LLC—*Dave Bickler*	624 Hamilton Rd, Weirton WV 26062	304-748-8520	R	3*	<.1
472	Becker Iron And Metal Inc—*Jason Becker*	703 Fairview St, Marshall MN 56258	507-537-0571	R	3*	<.1

Rank	Company Name—*Executive Officer*	Address, City, State, Zip	Phone	Type	Fin	Empls
473	Aero Specialties Material Corp—*Elizabeth Smith*	20 Burt Dr, Deer Park NY 11729	631-242-7200	R	3*	<.1
474	Rbs Family Corp—*Gerald Sorensen*	224 N Justine St, Chicago IL 60607	312-421-3450	R	3*	<.1
475	Converse All Steel Services Inc—*Rose Converse*	450 W Main St, Canfield OH 44406	330-533-2377	R	3*	<.1
476	Durant Iron and Metal Inc—*James Clark*	PO Box 563, Durant OK 74702	580-924-0595	R	3*	<.1
477	Timberline Pvf Inc—*Charles Folsom*	6195 Clermont St, Commerce City CO 80022	303-289-2557	R	3*	<.1
478	United Supply Inc—*Gary Usher*	PO Box 819, Dalhart TX 79022	806-249-5654	R	3*	<.1
479	Macomb Steel Inc—*James Baxendale*	7830 Ackley St, Detroit MI 48211	313-925-2550	R	3*	<.1
480	Cunha International Inc—*Jose Estivez*	19828 30th Ave, Flushing NY 11358	718-352-8564	R	3*	<.1
481	Specialty Steel Company Inc—*Theodore Cohen*	PO Box 28152, Cleveland OH 44128	216-475-8200	R	3*	<.1
482	Royal Metal Building Component LLP—*Patt Pace*	39312 I 10 W, Boerne TX 78006	830-249-3331	R	3*	<.1
483	Ameron International Water Transmission Group—*Packron George*	5101 Williams St SE, Albuquerque NM 87105	505-877-8773	R	3*	<.1
484	Holston Steel Services Inc—*Kennith Smith*	PO Box 789, Bristol TN 37621	276-466-6000	R	3*	<.1
485	Harry E Orkin Inc—*Robert Orkin*	PO Box 175, Slatington PA 18080	610-767-3845	R	3*	<.1
486	Amsco Steel Products Co—*Gene Fulmer*	1101 S Main St, Altus OK 73521	580-482-4476	R	3*	<.1
487	North American Steel Co—*Theodore Cohen*	PO Box 28126, Cleveland OH 44128	216-475-7300	R	2*	<.1
488	Plant Two G A—*John Ball*	701 E Savidge St, Spring Lake MI 49456	616-850-8528	R	2*	<.1
489	Bissett Steel Co—*Barbara Bissett*	9005 Bank St, Cleveland OH 44125	216-447-4000	R	2*	<.1
490	Cwc Industries Inc—*Peter Chan*	185 Foundry St Ste 2, Newark NJ 07105	973-344-1434	R	2*	<.1
491	Ace Drill Corp—*Alfred Brown*	PO Box 160, Adrian MI 49221	517-265-5184	R	2*	<.1
492	Western Steel Cutting Inc—*Donald Pearlman*	6210 Garfield Ave, Commerce CA 90040	562-776-1810	R	2*	<.1
493	DT Sari Company Inc—*Katheryn Sari*	PO Box 1862, Upland CA 91785	909-463-3299	R	2*	<.1
494	Oblivion Events—*Joseph O'dell*	2945 E Beltline Ave Ne, Grand Rapids MI 49525	616-361-1995	R	2*	<.1
495	Isis Supply and Service Co—*Vanessa Braddock*	337 E Church Ln, Philadelphia PA 19144	215-849-1336	R	2*	<.1
496	Leico Industries Inc—*Leon Eisenmann*	250 W 57th St Ste 1601, New York NY 10107	212-765-5290	R	2*	<.1
497	Cabletech Sling and Supply Co—*Greg Ganyard*	4965 Moline St, Denver CO 80239	303-371-7648	R	2*	<.1
498	Promet Processing Corp—*Charles Barnes*	951 Frontenac Rd, Naperville IL 60563	630-983-9777	R	2*	<.1
499	Ewrc Inc—*Mark Quinlivan*	1709 S Eastern Ave, Oklahoma City OK 73129	405-672-0531	R	2*	<.1
500	Innovative Supply Inc—*Timothy Green*	4417 State Rte 30 B, Latrobe PA 15650	724-537-0300	R	2*	<.1
501	Keith Const Custom Metal—*Bill Keith*	540 W Dutton Rd Unit 5, Eagle Point OR 97524	541-830-4877	R	2*	<.1
502	Industrial Steel Products LLC—*Lisa Eckstein*	8517 Herrington Ct, Pevely MO 63070	636-475-4441	R	2*	<.1
503	Pennsylvania Steel Corp—*Kurt Zecman*	12380 Beech Daly Rd, Redford MI 48239	313-937-3970	R	2*	<.1
504	G and J Import and Export Inc—*Joe Carrero*	10800 Biscayne Blvd St, Miami FL 33161	305-466-4464	R	2*	<.1
505	Toma Metals Inc—*Daniel T Yunetz* Reliance Steel and Aluminum Co	740 Cooper Ave, Johnstown PA 15906	814-536-3596	S	1*	.1
506	Rogers Iron and Metal Corp—*Jason Ryle*	PO Box 1806, Rogers AR 72757	479-636-2666	R	1*	<.1
507	Moses Lake Steel Supply Inc—*R Wayne Rimple*	PO Box 1122, Moses Lake WA 98837	509-765-1741	R	1*	<.1
508	Harry H Reich Company Inc—*Harry Reich*	PO Box 218, Trussville AL 35173	205-655-2121	R	1*	<.1
509	TCT Stainless Steel Inc—*Kurt Friedmann*	6300 19 Mile Rd, Sterling Heights MI 48314	586-254-5333	R	1*	<.1
510	Alloy Tool Steel Inc—*Hano Chen*	13525 Fwy Dr, Santa Fe Springs CA 90670	562-921-8605	R	1*	<.1
511	West Coast Tube and Pipe—*Erik Moore*	28445 Driver Ave, Agoura Hills CA 91301	818-991-6000	R	<1*	<.1
512	CCC Steel Inc—*Bernd Hildebrandt* Reliance Steel and Aluminum Co	2576 E Victoria St, Rancho Dominguez CA 90220	310-637-0111	S	<1	.1
513	Uranium Resources Inc—*Donald C Ewigleben*	405 State Hwy 121 Bypa, Lewisville TX 75067	972-219-3330	P	<1	<.1
514	Mckinsey Steel and Supply Of Florida Inc—*Warren Thomas*	817 Nw 5th Ave, Fort Lauderdale FL 33311	954-524-7055	R	<1*	<.1
515	Nippon Steel USA Inc—*Akio Mimura*	780 3rd Ave 34th Fl, New York NY 10017	212-486-7150	S	N/A	<.1

TOTALS: SIC 5051 Metals Service Centers & Offices
Companies: 515   98,945   93.4

5052 Coal, Other Minerals & Ores

1	Progress Fuels Corp—*Paula Sims*	PO Box 15208, Saint Petersburg FL 33733	727-820-5151	S	1,500	4.5
2	Hickman Williams and Co—*William Snyder*	250 E 5th St Ste 300, Cincinnati OH 45202	513-621-1946	R	793*	.2
3	Robindale Energy Services Inc—*Neil Hedrick*	PO Box 228, Armagh PA 15920	814-446-6700	R	164*	.1
4	Manhattan Brass and Copper Company Inc—*Mark Bernstein*	PO Box 780145, Maspeth NY 11378	718-381-5390	R	120*	<.1
5	HM Royal Inc—*Joe Royal*	689 Pennington Ave, Trenton NJ 08618	609-396-9176	R	60*	.1
6	Summers Fuel Inc—*William N Clements III*	28 Allegheny Ave, Baltimore MD 21204	410-825-8555	R	43*	<.1
7	Rockford Metals—*Rodney Robito*	13 Delta Dr Unit 8, Londonderry NH 03053	603-965-4367	R	40*	<.1
8	Emerald International Corp—*Jack Wells*	6895 Burlington Pike, Florence KY 41042	859-525-2522	R	26*	.1
9	Graphel Corp—*Cliff Kersker*	PO Box 369, West Chester OH 45071	513-779-6166	R	13*	.1
10	Five Star Mining Inc—*Donnie Blankenburger*	6594 W State Rd 56, Petersburg IN 47567	812-354-2401	R	10*	.1
11	Global Minerals Corp—*Michael Xu*	6701 Democracy Blvd St, Bethesda MD 20817	301-571-2449	R	9*	.1
12	Minmetals Inc—*Shuxin Yu*	1200 Harbor Blvd Fl 8, Weehawken NJ 07086	201-809-1898	R	6*	<.1
13	Barakat Associates Ltd—*John Rich*	10 Gilberton Rd, Gilberton PA 17934	570-874-1602	R	5*	.1
14	Angstrom Sciences Inc—*Mark Bernick*	40 S Linden St, Duquesne PA 15110	412-469-8466	R	5*	<.1
15	Lakeshore Coal Handling Corp—*Ted Beemsterboer*	16807 S Park Ave, South Holland IL 60473	708-331-6182	R	4*	<.1
16	Connecticut Coal Inc—*Robert Osborne*	122 Broad St, Milford CT 06460	203-878-5071	R	4*	<.1
17	Southeast Fuels Inc—*Ralph K Shelton*	PO Box 4061, Greensboro NC 27404	336-854-1106	R	2*	<.1

TOTALS: SIC 5052 Coal, Other Minerals & Ores
Companies: 17   2,804   5.4

5063 Electrical Apparatus & Equipment

1	Anixter International Inc—*Robert J Eck*	2301 Patriot Blvd, Glenview IL 60026	224-521-8000	P	6,147	8.2
2	WESCO International Inc—*John J Engel*	225 W Station Square D, Pittsburgh PA 15219	412-454-2200	P	6,126	7.1
3	Brightstar Corp—*R Marcelo Claure*	9725 NW 117th Ave Ste, Miami FL 33178	305-421-6000	R	4,400*	3.5
4	Consolidated Electrical Distributors Inc—*H Dean Bursh*	31356 Via Colinas Ste, Westlake Village CA 91362	818-597-3050	R	2,766*	5.0
5	Anixter Inc—*Robert Eck* Anixter International Inc	2301 Patriot Blvd, Glenview IL 60026	224-521-8000	S	2,298*	7.5
6	Communications Supply Corp—*David Bemoras* WESCO International Inc	200 E Lies Rd, Carol Stream IL 60188	630-221-6400	S	2,254*	1.0
7	EnerSys Inc—*John D Craig*	2366 Bernville Rd, Reading PA 19605	610-208-1991	P	1,965	8.4
8	State Electric Supply Co—*Clarence Martin*	PO Box 5397, Huntington WV 25703	304-523-7491	R	1,653*	.7
9	Interstate Battery System of America Inc—*Carlos Sepulveda*	12770 Merit Dr Ste 100, Dallas TX 75251	520-573-9210	R	1,500*	1.4
10	Radio Holland USA—*Jack Haynie*	8943 Gulf Frwy, Houston TX 77017	713-378-2100	S	840*	1.0
11	United Electric Supply Inc—*George Vorwick*	10 Bellecor Dr, New Castle DE 19720		R	710*	.3
12	AFA Protective Systems Inc—*Richard Kleinman*	155 Michael Dr, Syosset NY 11791	516-496-2322	R	670*	.3
13	Crescent Electric Supply Co—*Martin Burbridge*	PO Box 500, East Dubuque IL 61025	815-747-3145	R	630*	1.7
14	Border States Electric Supply—*Tammy Miller*	PO Box 2767, Fargo ND 58108	701-293-5834	R	605*	1.4
15	Standard Electric Co—*Vern Weber*	PO Box 5289, Saginaw MI 48603	989-497-2100	R	593*	.3

Note: An asterisk (*) indicates an estimated financial figure. The company type code used is as follows: R = Private, P = Public, S = Private Subsidiary, B = Public Subsidiary, D = Division, J = Joint Venture, I = Investment Fund.

COMPANY RANKINGS BY SALES WITHIN 4-DIGIT SIC

Rank	Company Name—*Executive Officer*	Address, City, State, Zip	Phone	Type	Fin	Empls
16	Springfield Electric Supply Company Inc (Springfield Ilinois)—*William Schnirring Jr*	PO Box 4106, Springfield IL 62708	217-788-2100	R	584*	.3
17	Stanion Wholesale Electric Company Inc—*Bill Keller*	PO Drawer F, Pratt KS 67124	620-672-5678	R	514*	.2
18	Western Extralite Co—*Thomas E Isenberg*	1470 Liberty St, Kansas City MO 64102	816-421-8404	R	493*	.2
19	Washington Energy Services Co—*Craig Olson*	2800 Thorndyke Ave W, Seattle WA 98199	206-282-4700	R	489*	.2
20	Oclaro Inc—*Alain Couder*	2560 Junction Ave, San Jose CA 95134	408-383-1400	P	467	3.1
21	Turtle and Hughes Inc—*Suzanne Turtle Millard*	1900 Lower Rd, Linden NJ 07036	732-574-3600	R	392*	.5
22	Anixter Holdings Inc—*Robert J Eck* Anixter Inc	2301 Patriot Blvd, Glenview IL 60026	224-521-8000	S	385	N/A
23	Arthur Weisburg Enterprises Inc—*Arthur Weisberg*	PO Box 5397, Huntington WV 25703	304-523-7491	R	384*	.6
24	Revere Electric Supply Co—*Paul McCool*	2501 W Washington Blvd, Chicago IL 60612	312-738-3636	R	375*	.2
25	Summit Electric Supply Inc—*Victor R Jury Jr*	PO Box 6409, Albuquerque NM 87197	505-884-4400	R	336*	.5
26	Houston Wire and Cable Co—*Charles A Sorrentino*	10201 N Loop E, Houston TX 77029	713-609-2100	P	309	.4
27	Loeb Electric Co—*Charles A Loeb*	915 Williams Ave, Columbus OH 43212	614-294-6351	R	307*	.1
28	Sager Electronics Inc—*Raymond Norton*	19 Leona Dr, Middleborough MA 02346	508-947-8888	R	300*	.6
29	Cooper Electric Supply Co—*Mike Dudas*	70 Apple St, Tinton Falls NJ 07724	732-747-2233	R	270*	.4
30	Interstate Companies Inc—*Travis Penrod*	2601 American Blvd E, Bloomington MN 55425	952-854-2044	R	270*	<.1
31	Stuart C Irby Co—*Mike Wigton*	PO Box 1819, Jackson MS 39215	601-969-1811	R	263*	.6
32	McNaughton-McKay Electric Company Inc—*John R McNaughton III*	1357 E Lincoln Ave, Madison Heights MI 48071	248-399-7500	R	259*	.9
33	Mayer Electric Supply Co—*Nancy Goedecke*	PO Box 1328, Birmingham AL 35201	205-583-3500	R	250*	.6
34	Horizon Wind Energy—*Gabriel Alonso*	808 Travis St Ste 700, Houston TX 77002	713-265-0350	S	244*	.3
35	Eastern Industrial Automation—*Richard Gorsey*	158 Lexington St, Waltham MA 02452	781-899-3952	R	240*	.1
36	Braid Electric Company Inc—*Ben Gambill*	PO Box 23710, Nashville TN 37202	615-242-6511	S	236*	.1
37	Platt Electric Supply Inc—*Harvey Platt*	4650 SW Pacific Ave, Beaverton OR 97005	503-643-4671	R	210*	.8
38	Rumsey Electric Inc—*Gerald Lihota*	PO Box 61, New Castle DE 19720	610-832-9000	R	197*	.3
39	Steiner Electric Co—*Harold M Kerman*	1250 W Touhy Ave, Elk Grove Village IL 60007	847-228-0400	R	190*	.5
40	Eck Enterprises Inc—*Edgar Eck*	PO Box 85618, Richmond VA 23285	804-359-5781	R	179*	.4
41	John Deere Landscapes Inc—*Dave Werning*	1060 Windward Ridge Pk, Alpharetta GA 30005	770-410-9544	R	175*	3.0
42	Dakota Supply Group Inc—*Todd Kumm*	PO Box 2886, Fargo ND 58108	701-237-9440	R	162*	.4
43	Mirion Technologies Inc—*Thomas Logan*	3000 Executive Pky Ste, San Ramon CA 94583	925-543-0800	S	157*	.7
44	JH Larson Co—*Greg Pahl*	10200 51st Ave N, Plymouth MN 55442	763-545-1717	R	155*	.3
45	Gresco Utility Supply Inc—*Jere Thorne*	1135 Rumble Rd, Forsyth GA 31029	478-315-0850	R	150*	.1
46	Kendall Electric Inc—*Axel Johnson*	131 Grand Trunk Ave, Battle Creek MI 49015	269-965-6897	R	150	.6
47	Murray Feiss Import LLC—*Joe Belcovich*	125 Rose Feiss Blvd, Bronx NY 10454	718-292-2024	R	145*	.2
48	Wille Electric Supply Co—*Larry Robinson III*	PO Box 3246, Modesto CA 95353	209-527-6800	R	143*	.1
49	Electrical Engineering And Equipment Co—*Jeff Stroud*	953 73rd St, Des Moines IA 50324	515-273-0100	R	137*	.2
50	Hannan Supply Co—*Bruce Brockenborough*	PO Box 270, Paducah KY 42002	270-442-5456	R	129*	.1
51	Tampa Armature Works Inc—*James Turner*	6312 S 78th St, Riverview FL 33578	813-621-5661	R	128*	.7
52	Granite City Electric Supply Co—*Phyllis Papani Godwin*	19 Quincy Ave, Quincy MA 02169	617-472-6500	R	128*	.2
53	Insulectro Corp—*Tim Redfern*	20362 Windrow Dr, Lake Forest CA 92630	949-587-3200	R	123*	.2
54	Mersen USA Newburyport-Ma LLC	374 Merrimac St, Newburyport MA 01950	978-462-6662	R	120*	.8
55	Paige Electric Company LP—*Henry Coffey*	PO Box 368, Union NJ 07083	908-687-7810	R	115*	.1
56	Wholesale Electric Supply Company of Houston Inc—*Marge Rutland*	PO Box 230197, Houston TX 77223	713-748-6100	R	110	.3
57	Universal Power Group Inc—*Ian Edmonds* Zunicom Inc	1720 Hayden Dr, Carrollton TX 75006	469-892-1122	B	107	.1
58	Capitol Light and Supply Co—*David Mullane*	270 Locust St, Hartford CT 06141	860-549-1230	R	93*	.3
59	Richards Manufacturing Company Sales Inc—*Bruce Bier*	517 Lyons Ave, Irvington NJ 07111	973-371-1771	R	92*	<.1
60	Energy International Corp—*Ned M Fawaz*	6850 N Haggerty Rd, Canton MI 48187	734-354-2000	R	88*	.3
61	Schaedler Yesco Distribution Inc—*James D Schaedler*	PO Box 4990, Harrisburg PA 17111	717-233-1621	R	85*	.2
62	Comer Inc—*Arlin Perry*	PO Box 410305, Charlotte NC 28241	704-588-8400	R	84*	<.1
63	Frost Electric Supply Co—*John Frost*	PO Box 66522, Saint Louis MO 63166	314-567-4004	R	82*	.1
64	XP Power Ltd—*Larry Tracey*	990 Benecia Ave, Sunnyvale CA 94085	408-732-7777	R	80*	.1
65	Walker and Associates Inc—*Virginia Walker*	PO Box 1029, Welcome NC 27374	336-731-6391	R	78*	.1
66	Mabuchi Motor America Corp—*Kaoru Kato*	3001 W Big Beaver Rd S, Troy MI 48084	248-816-3100	R	78*	<.1
67	Motive Energy Inc—*Bob Istwan*	125 E Commercial St St, Anaheim CA 92801	714-888-2525	R	77*	.1
68	Stusser Electric Co—*Joe Anderson* Consolidated Electrical Distributors Inc	660 S Andover St, Seattle WA 98108	206-623-1501	S	76*	.3
69	Western United Electric Supply Corp—*Michael Prom*	100 Bromley Business P, Brighton CO 80603	303-659-2356	R	76*	<.1
70	Stoneway Electric Supply Co—*Clifton Kelly*	PO Box 4037, Spokane WA 99220	509-535-2933	R	71*	.2
71	Eoff Electric Company Inc—*Les Williamson*	3241 NW Industrial St, Portland OR 97210	503-363-9251	R	71*	.2
72	Electrical Insulation Suppliers Inc—*Robert W Thomas*	2018 Power Ferry Rd St, Atlanta GA 30339	678-255-3600	S	70*	.2
73	B and K Electric Wholesale—*Kathleen Ellison*	PO Box 3080, City of Industry CA 91744	626-965-5040	R	70*	.1
74	Sunray Electric Supply Co—*Phil Latterman*	PO Box 489, McKeesport PA 15132	412-678-8826	R	70*	<.1
75	Cain Electrical Supply Corp—*Tom R Ross*	PO Box 2158, Big Spring TX 79721	432-263-8421	R	67*	.3
76	Electrical Distributors Co—*Chet Lehmann*	1135 Auzerais St, San Jose CA 95126	408-293-5818	R	67	.1
77	Georgia Lighting—*Robert Nardelli*	530 14th St NW, Atlanta GA 30318	770-384-5853	S	66*	.2
78	JA Becker Co—*Dave Adkinson*	1341 E 4th St, Dayton OH 45402	937-226-1341	R	66*	.1
79	Utilicor Corp—*Rick Morrison*	367 N Prk War Ste B3, Jackson TN 38305	731-423-0071	R	65*	<.1
80	Calvert Wire and Cable Corp—*Brian Coughlan* Communications Supply Corp	5091 W 164th St, Brook Park OH 44142	216-433-7600	S	64*	.1
81	Power/mation Inc—*Jim Landes*	1310 Energy Ln, St Paul MN 55108	651-605-3300	R	63*	.2
82	Stokes Electric Co—*Dave Frazier*	1701 McCalla Ave, Knoxville TN 37915	865-525-0351	R	62*	.1
83	Ace Wire and Cable Company Inc—*Jerry Firestone*	7201 51st Ave, Woodside NY 11377	718-458-9200	R	62*	.1
84	Dominion Electric Supply Co Inc—*Richard A Williams*	5053 Lee Hwy, Arlington VA 22207	703-536-4400	R	61*	.2
85	Topaz Lighting Corp—*Timothy Gomes*	925 Waverly Ave, Holtsville NY 11742	631-758-5507	R	60*	.1
86	Codale Electric Supply Inc—*Dale Holt*	PO Box 702070, Salt Lake City UT 84170	801-975-7300	R	60*	.2
87	Benfield Electric Supply Inc—*Daniel J McLaughlin*	25 Lafayette Ave, White Plains NY 10603	914-948-6660	R	60*	.2
88	Swift Electrical Supply Co—*August Sodora*	100 Hollister Rd, Teterboro NJ 07608	201-462-0900	R	58*	.1
89	Eck Supply Co—*Edgar Eck Jr*	PO Box 85618, Richmond VA 23285	804-359-5781	R	57*	.1
90	California Lighting Sales Inc—*Roger David*	4900 Rivergrade Rd C11, Baldwin Park CA 91706	626-775-6000	R	55*	.1
91	Oriental Motor U S A Corp—*Jake Kitayama*	1001 Knox St, Torrance CA 90502	310-325-0040	R	55*	.1
92	Bulbman Inc	630 Sunshine Ln, Reno NV 89502	775-788-5661	R	54*	.1
93	Electro-Matic Products Inc—*James Baker*	23409 Industrial Park, Farmington Hills MI 48335	248-478-1182	R	54*	.1
94	FD Lawrence Electric Co	3450 Beekman St, Cincinnati OH 45223	513-542-1100	R	53*	.1
95	Hite Co—*R Lee Hite*	PO Box 1754, Altoona PA 16603	814-944-6121	R	52*	.2
96	Fletcher-Reinhardt Co—*James Reinhardt*	3105 Corporate Exchang, Bridgeton MO 63044	314-506-0700	R	52*	.1
97	Allied Wire and Cable Inc—*Daniel Flynn*	PO Box 26157, Collegeville PA 19426	484-928-6700	R	51*	.1
98	Ralph Pill Electric Supply Co	560 Oak St, Brockton MA 02301	617-532-2010	S	50*	.2

Rank	Company Name—*Executive Officer*	Address, City, State, Zip	Phone	Type	Fin	Empls
99	H Hoffman Co—*Al Hoffman*	7330 W Montrose Ave, Norridge IL 60706	708-456-9600	R	50*	.1
100	Gross Electric Inc—*Laurie Gross*	PO Box 352377, Toledo OH 43635	419-537-1818	R	50*	.1
101	Peninsular Electric Distributors Inc—*John Larmoyeux*	1301 Okeechobee Rd, West Palm Beach FL 33401	561-832-1626	R	50*	.1
102	Vanguard Holdings Inc—*Sylvester C Formey*	107 NE Lathrop Ave, Savannah GA 31415	912-236-1766	R	49*	<.1
103	H Leff Electric Co—*Bruce Leff*	4700 Spring Rd, Cleveland OH 44131	216-432-3000	R	48*	.1
104	Electro-Wire Inc—*Mickey Hamano*	933 E Remington Dr, Schaumburg IL 60173	847-944-1500	R	48*	.1
105	Hunzicker Brothers Inc—*Mike Lockard*	PO Box 25248, Oklahoma City OK 73125	405-239-7771	R	47*	.2
106	Aee Solar Inc—*David Katz*	PO Box 339, Redway CA 95560	707-923-2277	R	47*	.1
107	Reliable Fire Equipment Co—*Ernest E Horvath*	12845 S Cicero Ave, Alsip IL 60803	708-597-4600	R	47*	.1
108	Claymore Sieck Co—*W Claymore Sieck*	311 E Chase St, Baltimore MD 21202	410-685-4660	R	47*	.1
109	McGowan Electric Supply Inc—*Michael J McGowan*	PO Box 765, Jackson MI 49204	517-782-9301	R	47*	<.1
110	Wichita Falls Nunn Electrical Supply—*Coyal Francis Jr*	1300 Indiana Ave, Wichita Falls TX 76301	940-766-4203	R	45*	<.1
111	Shealy Electrical Wholesalers Inc—*William E De Loache*	422 Fairforest Way, Greenville SC 29607	864-242-6880	R	44*	.1
112	Cvs Systems Inc—*Jerry Collins*	PO Box 1990, Marion IN 46952	765-662-0037	R	44*	.1
113	Idlewood Electric Supply Inc—*John Stonehouse*	317 W Northwest Hwy, Barrington IL 60010	847-304-8000	R	44*	<.1
114	Virginia West Electric Supply Co—*Herbert Colker*	PO Box 6668, Huntington WV 25773	304-525-0361	R	43*	.1
115	Ligon Electric Supply Co State Electric Supply Co	PO Box 5098, Winston Salem NC 27113	336-723-9656	D	43*	.1
116	Paratek Microwave Inc—*Ralph Pini*	22 Technology Way Mill, Nashua NH 03060	603-598-8880	R	43*	<.1
117	Mid-Island Electrical Sales Corp—*Flora Greenberg*	PO Box 9027, Commack NY 11725	631-864-4242	R	42*	.1
118	Villa Lighting Supply Company Inc	2929 Chouteau Ave, St Louis MO 63103	314-531-2600	R	42*	.1
119	Billows Electric Supply Co—*Jeff Billows*	9100 State Rd, Philadelphia PA 19136	215-332-9700	R	41*	.2
120	Dolan Northwest LLC—*Steven Fitzpatrick*	1919 Nw 19th Ave, Portland OR 97209	503-225-9009	R	40*	.3
121	Minka Lighting Inc—*Marian Tang*	1151 Bradford Cir, Corona CA 92882	951-735-9220	R	38*	.3
122	Crest Operations LLC—*Kenneth Robison*	4725 Hwy 28 E, Pineville LA 71360	318-448-8287	R	38*	.3
123	Communications Products and Services Inc	1740 W Warren Ave, Englewood CO 80110	303-922-4519	S	38*	<.1
124	Western Automation Inc	23011 Moulton Pky Unit, Laguna Hills CA 92653	949-859-6988	R	38*	<.1
125	Advantor Systems Corp—*Todd Flemming*	12612 Challenger Pkwy, Orlando FL 32826	407-859-3350	R	37*	.2
126	Roden Electrical Supply Co—*Sam McCamy III*	170 Mabry Hood Rd, Knoxville TN 37922	865-546-8755	R	37*	.1
127	POS World Inc—*Joseph Bushey*	2100 Powers Ferry Rd S, Atlanta GA 30339	770-984-0241	R	37*	<.1
128	Standard Electric Supply Co—*Larry Stern*	222 N Emmber Ln, Milwaukee WI 53233	414-272-8100	R	36*	.1
129	Monarch Electric Company Inc—*Carl Brand*	1527 Livingston Ave, North Brunswick NJ 08902	732-249-1616	R	35*	.1
130	Decision Distribution LLC—*Daniel Goldman*	33 S Delavue Rd Ste 10, Yardley PA 19067	215-493-4400	R	35	<.1
131	Gaffney-Kroese Supply Corp—*John Kroese*	60 Kingsbridge Rd, Piscataway NJ 08854	732-885-9000	R	34*	.1
132	Industrial Electronic Supply Inc—*David Doyal*	2321 Texas Ave, Shreveport LA 71103	318-222-9459	R	34*	.1
133	Granite City Electric Supply Co—*William Raney*	10 Lowell Junction Rd, Andover MA 01810	978-470-1300	R	34*	.3
134	Mansfield Electric Supply Inc Furbay Electric Supply Co	2255 Stumbo Rd, Mansfield OH 44906		S	33*	.1
135	Treadway Electric Company Inc—*Terry Rogers*	3300 W 65th St, Little Rock AR 72209	501-562-2111	R	33*	.2
136	Electric Supply and Equipment Co—*Brad McCormick*	1812 E Wendover Ave, Greensboro NC 27405	336-272-4123	R	32*	.1
137	Sandusky Electric Inc—*Jerry Stevens*	1513 Sycamore Line, Sandusky OH 44870	419-625-4915	R	32*	.1
138	Clifford of Vermont Inc—*Maynard Nelson*	PO Box 51 Rt 107, Bethel VT 05032	802-234-9921	R	32*	<.1
139	MW McWong International Inc—*Margaret Wong*	2544 Industrial Blvd, West Sacramento CA 95691	916-371-8080	R	32*	<.1
140	Crum Electrical Supply Inc—*David Crum*	1165 English Ave, Casper WY 82601	307-266-1278	R	31*	.1
141	Multicom Inc (Phoenix Arizona)—*Dan Gibbons*	2930 N 24th St, Phoenix AZ 85016	602-244-1100	R	31*	<.1
142	Pioneer Electric Inc—*Dan Peterson*	228 Mohonua Pl, Honolulu HI 96819	808-841-0107	R	31*	<.1
143	Townsend Supply Co—*Gordon Ruggles*	120 Johnson St, Jackson TN 38301	901-424-4300	R	30	.1
144	Erie Bearings Co—*Michael Ketchel*	PO Box 10307, Erie PA 16514	814-453-6871	R	30*	.1
145	Republic Electric Co—*Mark Kilmer*	737 Charlotte St, Davenport IA 52803	563-322-6204	R	30*	.1
146	Hartford Electric Supply Co—*B Patrick De Pasq*	30 Inwood Rd Ste 1, Rocky Hill CT 06067	860-236-6363	R	30*	<.1
147	Varta Batteries Inc—*Thomas Brodrick*	1311 Mamaroneck Ave, White Plains NY 10605	914-592-2500	R	29*	<.1
148	Tai Ham Heon—*Tai Ham*	901 W Walnut St, Compton CA 90220	310-638-1881	R	29*	<.1
149	Dauphin Electrical Supply Co—*Bob Twomey*	PO Box 2206, Harrisburg PA 17105	717-986-9300	R	28*	.1
150	Advance Electrical Supply Co—*Steven Anixter*	263 N Oakley Blvd, Chicago IL 60612	312-421-2300	R	28*	.1
151	Electric Motor Sales And Supply Company Inc—*Bill Stone*	1724 Central Ave, Chattanooga TN 37408	423-493-8900	R	28*	.1
152	Mercedes Electric Supply Inc—*Mercedes C LaPorta*	8550 NW South River Dr, Miami FL 33166	305-887-5550	R	28*	<.1
153	Baldor of Texas LP	3040 Quebec, Dallas TX 75247	214-634-7271	S	28*	.1
154	Tri-State Armature and Electrical Works Inc—*Lonnie Loeffel*	PO Box 466, Memphis TN 38101	901-527-8412	R	28*	.1
155	Energy Federation Inc—*Bradley Steele*	40 Washington St Ste 2, Westborough MA 01581	508-870-2277	R	28*	.1
156	Denney Electric Supply Of Ambler Inc—*Benjamin Denney*	PO Box 519, Ambler PA 19002	215-628-8880	R	27*	.1
157	Shepherd Electric Supply Company Inc—*Bobby Jordan* State Electric Supply Co	PO Box 58787, Raleigh NC 27658	919-821-5320	S	27*	.1
158	CELL-CON Inc—*Michael Mumma*	305 Commerce Dr Ste 30, Exton PA 19341	610-280-7630	R	27*	<.1
159	Davis Electrical Supply Company Inc—*Richard A Di Vita*	24 Anderson Rd, Buffalo NY 14225	716-896-0100	R	27*	<.1
160	Gabron and Gabron Inc—*Kenneth Gabron*	PO Box 8229, Lancaster PA 17604	717-397-9710	R	27*	<.1
161	St Louis Electric Supply Inc—*William Frisella*	6801 Hoffman Ave, Saint Louis MO 63139	314-645-5656	R	27*	.2
162	Electrical Wholesale Supply Company Inc—*Kreg Davis*	1355 Fremont Ave, Idaho Falls ID 83402	208-523-2901	R	26*	.1
163	Melhinch Inc—*Charles Melhinch*	2905 Industrial Dr, Raleigh NC 27609	919-829-3511	R	26*	<.1
164	Go Electronics Inc—*Joseph Oxborough*	360 Hickman Dr, Sanford FL 32771	407-328-8011	R	26*	<.1
165	Warner Enterprises Inc—*Steven Latorra*	6575 Hinson St, Las Vegas NV 89118	702-649-7160	R	25*	<.1
166	Rockingham Electrical Supply Company Inc—*James Pender*	437 Shattuck Way, Newington NH 03801	603-436-2310	R	25*	.1
167	Revere Electric Supply Co (Rockford Illinois)—*Tom Eiseman* Revere Electric Supply Co	2501 W Washington Blvd, Chicago IL 60612		D	25*	.1
168	Pacific Radio Electronics Inc—*Joseph Phillips*	969 N La Brea Ave, Hollywood CA 90038	323-969-2035	R	25*	<.1
169	Superior Electric Supply Co (Elyria Ohio)—*Timothy King*	9445 W Ridge Rd, Elyria OH 44035	440-323-5451	R	25*	<.1
170	Wedco Inc—*Brian Elmore*	450 Toano St, Reno NV 89512	775-329-1131	R	25*	<.1
171	Sherburn Electronics Inc—*James Burke*	175 K Commerce Dr, Hauppauge NY 11788	631-231-4300	R	25*	<.1
172	ICX Global Inc—*Dennis Carson*	8206 E Park Meadows Dr, Lone Tree CO 80124	720-873-8400	S	25*	<.1
173	Wolberg Lighting Design and Electrical Supply	35 Industrial Park Rd, Albany NY 12206	518-489-8451	R	23*	.1
174	Dreisilker Electric Motors Inc—*Leo Dreisilker*	352 Roosevelt Rd, Glen Ellyn IL 60137	630-469-7510	R	23*	.2
175	K and N Electric Motors Inc—*Janet Schmidlkofer*	PO Box 303, Spokane WA 99210	509-838-8000	R	22*	.1
176	KJ Electric Inc—*Ken Jacobs*	5894 E Molloy Rd, Syracuse NY 13211	315-454-5535	R	22*	.1
177	Brance-Krachy Company Inc—*Tim Schulte*	4411 Navigation Blvd, Houston TX 77011	713-225-6661	R	22*	.1
178	Maltby Electric Supply Company Inc—*John Maltby*	336 7th St, San Francisco CA 94103	415-863-5000	R	22*	.1
179	Marco Supply Company Inc—*Marshall Jones*	812 Pocahantas Ave, Roanoke VA 24012	540-344-6211	R	22*	.1
180	Allied Trade Group Inc—*Gary Rubens*	11410 NE 122nd Way Ste, Kirkland WA 98034	425-814-2515	R	22*	<.1
181	South Dade Lighting Inc—*Don Elliott*	PO Box 560965, Miami FL 33256	305-233-8020	R	21*	<.1
182	MIControls Inc—*Steve Roe*	6516 5th Pl S, Seattle WA 98108	206-767-0140	R	21*	<.1
183	G and G Electric Supply Company Inc—*Joseph Fusco*	137 W 24th St, New York NY 10011	212-243-0051	R	21*	<.1
184	Scurlock Electric LLC—*Nancy Foret*	1903 Grand Caillou Rd, Houma LA 70363	985-868-2253	R	21*	<.1

Note: An asterisk (*) indicates an estimated financial figure. The company type code used is as follows: R = Private, P = Public, S = Private Subsidiary, B = Public Subsidiary, D = Division, J = Joint Venture, I = Investment Fund.

COMPANY RANKINGS BY SALES WITHIN 4-DIGIT SIC

Rank	Company Name—Executive Officer	Address, City, State, Zip	Phone	Type	Fin	Empls
185	Texas Light Bulb Supply Co—Steve Byrne	4201 S Congress Ave, Austin TX 78745	512-444-6761	R	21*	<.1
186	Mathes Of Alabama Electric Supply Company Inc—Kimberley Cheney	PO Box 1208, Foley AL 36536	251-943-8551	R	20*	<.1
187	Igus Bearings Inc—Frank Blase	PO Box 14349, East Providence RI 02914	401-438-2200	R	20*	.2
188	Cardello Electric Supply Co—Nick Cardello	401 N Point Dr, Pittsburgh PA 15233	412-322-8031	R	20*	.1
189	Wholesale Electric Supply Company Inc (Texarkana Texas)—Buddy McCulloch	PO Box 1258, Texarkana TX 75504	903-794-3404	R	20*	.1
190	Path Master Inc—Randall Scoy	1960 Midway Dr, Twinsburg OH 44087	330-425-4994	R	20*	<.1
191	Baldwin Supply Co—Dave LaRue	601 11th Ave S, Minneapolis MN 55415	612-338-6911	R	20*	<.1
192	Wirenetics Co—Michael Weiss	27737 Ave Hopkins, Valencia CA 91355	661-257-2400	R	19*	.1
193	Gopher Electronics Co—Whit Carnes	222 Little Canada Rd, Saint Paul MN 55117	651-490-4900	R	19*	.1
194	Kiesub Corp—George Zwerdling	3185 S Highland Dr Ste, Las Vegas NV 89109	702-733-0024	R	19*	<.1
195	Sy Kessler Sales Inc—Sy Kessler	10455 Olympic Dr, Dallas TX 75220	214-351-0380	R	19*	<.1
196	Russell Belden Electric Co—Scott Belden	1027 S Virginia Ave, Joplin MO 64801	417-624-5650	R	19*	<.1
197	No-Go International—Michael Knapp	8839 Exposition Blvd, Culver City CA 90232	310-815-8422	R	19*	<.1
198	Kistler-O'brien Fire Protection—Fred Eberting	2210 City Line Rd, Bethlehem PA 18017	610-266-7100	R	18*	.1
199	Multilink Inc—Steven Kaplan	PO Box 955, Elyria OH 44036	440-366-6966	R	18*	.1
200	Satco Products Inc—Herbert Gildin	110 Heartland Blvd, Edgewood NY 11717	631-243-2022	R	18*	.1
201	Meletio Electrical Supply—Sharon Paschall	PO Box 540816, Dallas TX 75354	214-352-3900	R	18*	.1
202	South Central Company Inc	3055 State St, Columbus IN 47201	812-376-3343	S	18*	.1
203	Valley Electric Supply Corp—Dick Cannon	PO Box 724, Vincennes IN 47591	812-882-7860	R	18*	<.1
204	Tennessee Electric Motor Co—Edwin Grant	PO Box 22839, Nashville TN 37202	615-255-7331	R	18*	<.1
205	Valley Power Inc—Steven Carr	850 Davisville Rd, Willow Grove PA 19090	215-784-9150	R	18*	<.1
206	Boettcher Supply Inc—Jarold Boettcher	PO Box 486, Beloit KS 67420	785-738-5781	R	18*	<.1
207	Sommer Electric Corp—Robert W Krause	818 3rd St NE, Canton OH 44704	330-455-9454	R	18*	<.1
208	Jademar Corp—Joseph DeMartino	2010 NW 84th Ave 2nd F, Miami FL 33122	305-640-0465	R	18*	<.1
209	Wazee Companies LLC—Al Taylor	2020 W Barberry Pl, Denver CO 80204	303-623-8658	R	18*	.1
210	Evergreen Supply Co—Colleen Kramer	9901 S Torrence Ave, Chicago IL 60617	773-375-4750	R	18*	<.1
211	Stroudsburg Electric Supply Company Inc—Robert Friedman	20 N 5th St 26, Stroudsburg PA 18360	570-424-5402	R	18*	.1
212	Electric Pump and Tool Service Inc—Richard Miller	4280 E 14th St, Des Moines IA 50313	515-265-2222	R	17*	.1
213	Westinghouse Lighting Corp—Raymond Angelo	12401 Mcnulty Rd Ofc, Philadelphia PA 19154	215-671-2000	R	17*	.5
214	Werner Electric Ventures LLC—Greg Miller	7450 95th St S, Cottage Grove MN 55016	651-769-6841	R	17*	.2
215	Wago Corp—Thomas Artman	PO Box 1015, Germantown WI 53022	262-255-6222	R	17*	.2
216	Electric Fixture and Supply Co—Barry Tegels	PO Box 898, Omaha NE 68101	402-342-3050	R	17*	.1
217	Southwest Electronic Energy Corp—Claude Benckenstein	PO Box 848, Stafford TX 77497	281-240-4000	R	17	.1
218	Omnicor	1170 Foster City Blvd, Foster City CA 94404	650-572-0122	R	17*	<.1
219	Litetronics International Inc—Robert Sorensen	4101 W 123rd St, Alsip IL 60803	708-389-8000	R	17*	<.1
220	BrickHouse Security—Todd Morris	980 Avenue of the Amer, New York NY 10018	212-643-7449	R	17	<.1
221	Ems Industrial Inc—William Hinnendael	4901 Prairie Dock Dr, Madison WI 53718	608-241-8866	R	17*	.1
222	Active Electrical Supply Co—Raymond Fox	4240 W Lawrence Ave, Chicago IL 60630	773-282-6300	R	16*	.1
223	Hughes-Peters Inc—Mike Okel	8000 Technology Blvd, Huber Heights OH 45424	937-235-7100	R	16*	.1
224	Wieland Electric Inc—Nicholas Fleming	49 International Rd, Burgaw NC 28425	910-259-5050	R	16*	.1
225	Yale Electric Supply Company Inc—Warren Sheinkopf	55 Shawmut Rd, Canton MA 02021	781-737-2500	R	16*	.1
226	Mustang Electric Supply LLC	2525 E State Hwy Ste 3, Lewisville TX 75056	972-436-8326	R	16*	<.1
227	Micro Mo Electronics Inc—Fritz Faulhaber	14881 Evergreen Ave, Clearwater FL 33762	727-572-0131	R	16*	.1
228	Innerwireless Inc—Ed Cantwell	1155 Kas Dr Ste 200, Richardson TX 75081	972-479-9898	R	16*	.1
229	Robinson Electric Supply Company Inc—Deborah Bridgmon	PO Box 5358, Meridian MS 39302	601-693-3131	R	16*	.1
230	Heyward-Charlotte Inc—Douglas Wilson	2101 Cmbrdg Bltwy Dr A, Charlotte NC 28273	704-583-2305	R	16*	<.1
231	Wls Inc—Dean Pritchard	PO Box 100519, Fort Worth TX 76185	817-731-0020	R	16*	.1
232	Mnm Group Inc—Gregory Carson	2421 Wyandotte Rd Ste, Willow Grove PA 19090	215-672-9600	R	15*	.1
233	Advanced Protection Technologies Inc—R Chapman	14550 58th St N, Clearwater FL 33760	727-535-6339	R	15*	.1
234	Womack Electric and Supply Company Inc—Burke Herring	PO Box 521, Danville VA 24543	434-793-5134	R	15*	.1
235	Berkshire Systems Group Inc—Robert Yerger	50 S Museum Rd, Reading PA 19607	610-374-1300	R	15*	.1
236	Interpower Corp—Michael Boyle	PO Box 115, Oskaloosa IA 52577	641-673-5000	R	15*	.1
237	Action Electric Sales Co—Philip Garoon	3900 N Rockwell St, Chicago IL 60618	773-539-1800	R	15*	.1
238	Cayce Mill Supply Co—Breck Cayce	PO Box 689, Hopkinsville KY 42241	270-886-3335	R	15*	.1
239	Flolo Corp—Arne Flolo	PO Box 586, Bensenville IL 60106	630-595-1010	R	15*	.1
240	Nelson Electric Supply Company Inc—Thomas Leuenberger	PO Box 1528, Racine WI 53404	262-635-5050	R	15*	.1
241	Norvell Electronics Inc—Chris Tvrdik	2251 Chennault Dr, Carrollton TX 75006	972-858-3713	R	15*	.1
242	Micro Alarm Systems Inc—Ramin Youabian	4825 S Soto St, Vernon CA 90058	323-589-9999	R	15*	<.1
243	AA Electric SE Inc—Warren Rybak	2011 S Combee Rd, Lakeland FL 33801	863-665-6941	R	15*	<.1
244	B and S Electric Supply Company Inc—Clarence Robie	PO Box 44769, Atlanta GA 30336	404-696-8284	R	15*	.1
245	Richard Greene Co—Richard Greene	PO Box 8397, Saint Louis MO 63132	314-423-8989	R	15*	<.1
246	Wabash Power Equipment Co—Richard Caitung	PO Box 427, Wheeling IL 60090	847-541-5600	R	15*	<.1
247	Coastal Electric Construction Corp—Kevin Mckosky	185 Waverly Ave, Patchogue NY 11772	631-289-3233	R	15*	.2
248	Phoenix Contact Services Inc—Jack Nehlig	PO Box 4100, Harrisburg PA 17111	717-944-1300	R	15*	.4
249	Kcm Marketing Inc—Mark Wels	1631 S Sinclair St, Anaheim CA 92806	714-937-1033	R	15*	.1
250	Beyond Components Of Massachusetts Inc—Louis Dinkel	5 Carl Thompson Rd, Westford MA 01886	978-392-9191	R	15*	.1
251	Independent Electric Supply Corp—William Gray	41 Innerbelt Rd, Somerville MA 02143	617-625-5155	R	15*	.1
252	Tulsat Corp—Deidre Howard	1221 E Houston St, Broken Arrow OK 74012	918-251-2887	R	14*	.1
253	Star Struck Ltd—Kenneth Karlan	PO Box 295, Bethel CT 06801	203-778-4925	R	14*	.1
254	Johnson Electric Supply Co—Douglas N Johnson	1841 Eastern Ave, Cincinnati OH 45202	513-421-3700	R	14*	.1
255	Murdock Companies Inc—Brenda Blazer	PO Box 2775, Wichita KS 67201	316-263-8106	R	14*	.1
256	Service Electric Supply Inc—Eric Braidwood	15424 Oakwood Dr, Romulus MI 48174	734-229-9100	R	14*	<.1
257	Reulet Electric Supplies Inc—Lynn Reulet	PO Box 15276, Baton Rouge LA 70895	225-293-5432	R	14*	<.1
258	Red Peacock International Inc—Ruby G Mansukhani	1945 Gardena Ave, Glendale CA 91204	818-407-8822	R	14*	<.1
259	Bulbtronics Inc—Bruce Thaw	45 Banfi Plz N, Farmingdale NY 11735	631-249-2272	R	14*	.1
260	Hughes Corp—David Hughes	16900 Foltz Pkwy, Strongsville OH 44149	440-238-2550	R	14*	.1
261	Leader Instruments Corp—Masahiro Sawa	6484 Commerce Dr, Cypress CA 90630	714-527-9300	R	14*	<.1
262	Southland Electrical Supply Inc—James Griggs	PO Box 1329, Burlington NC 27216	336-227-1486	R	14*	.1
263	Mid-Coast Electric Supply Inc—Steve Barker	PO Box 2505, Victoria TX 77902	361-575-6311	R	14*	.1
264	Brownstown Electric Supply Company Inc—Gregg Deck	PO Box L, Brownstown IN 47220	812-358-4555	R	14*	.1
265	Allsale Electric Inc—Ed Ratzlaff	7950 Deering Ave, Canoga Park CA 91304	818-715-0181	R	13*	.1
266	Black Electrical Supply Inc—Robert Hamilton	PO Box 134, Greenville SC 29602	864-233-4142	R	13*	.1
267	National Distribution Warehouse Inc—Edit Winik	2721 E 63rd St, Brooklyn NY 11234	718-251-0096	R	13*	<.1
268	Mercer-Zimmerman Inc—Shon Yust	9123 Barton St, Overland Park KS 66214	913-438-4546	R	13*	<.1
269	Smk Electronics Corporation USA—Paul Evans	1055 Tierra Del Rey, Chula Vista CA 91910	619-216-6400	R	13*	.1
270	Power Home Technologies—Ben Brookhart	4905 Green Rd Ste 107A, Raleigh NC 27616		R	13*	.2
271	Williams Supply Inc—Tom Moody	PO Box 2766, Roanoke VA 24001	540-343-9333	R	13*	.1
272	Fay Electric Wire Corp—Donald Novak	752 N Larch Ave, Elmhurst IL 60126	630-530-7500	R	13*	<.1

Rank	Company Name—Executive Officer	Address, City, State, Zip	Phone	Type	Fin	Empls
273	C N Robinson Lighting Supply Co—Robert Mills	4318 Washington Blvd, Baltimore MD 21227	410-242-4172	R	13*	<.1
274	Angstrom Lighting—Frans Klinkenberg	837 N Cahuenga Blvd, Hollywood CA 90038	323-462-4246	R	13*	<.1
275	Teal Electric Company Inc—Victor L Kochajda	1200 Naughton Dr, Troy MI 48083	248-689-3000	R	13*	<.1
276	Lightwedge LLC—Jamey Bennett	320 Nevada St 5th Fl, Newton MA 02460	617-969-2700	R	13*	<.1
277	Sealcon LLC—Jerry Anderson	14853 E Hinsdale Ave D, Centennial CO 80112	303-699-1135	R	13*	<.1
278	Sjh Inc—Tony Wu	415 W Golf Rd Ste 51, Arlington Heights IL 60005	847-956-1188	R	13*	<.1
279	Magnetika Inc—Francis Ishida	2041 W 139th St, Gardena CA 90249	310-527-8100	R	12*	.1
280	Technical Building Services Inc—Gerald Jannicelli	12 Commerce Dr, Ballston Spa NY 12020	518-885-4444	R	12*	.1
281	Targetti Poulsen USA Inc—Kent Pedersen	3260 Meridian Pkwy, Weston FL 33331	954-349-2525	R	12*	.1
282	Angelus Corp—James Griffin	PO Box 330, Sussex WI 53089	262-246-0500	R	12*	<.1
283	Rig-A-Lite Ltd—Cheryl Leonard	PO Box 12943, Houston TX 77217	713-943-0340	R	12*	.1
284	Commercial Lighting Industries Inc—Frank Halcovich	81161 Indio Blvd, Indio CA 92201	760-343-2704	R	12*	.1
285	Wangs Alliance Corp—Tony Wang	615 S St, Garden City NY 11530	516-515-5000	R	12*	.1
286	Teche Electric Supply Inc—Bruin R Hays	410 Eraste Landry Rd, Lafayette LA 70506	337-234-7420	R	12*	.1
287	Nesco Electrical Distributors Inc—Bob Gatlin	2344 S Green St, Tupelo MS 38801	662-840-4750	R	12*	<.1
288	Dover Electric Supply Company Inc—Bernard Tudor	1631 S DuPont Hwy, Dover DE 19901	302-674-0115	R	12*	<.1
289	Jesco Lighting Group LLC—Richard Kurtz	6625 Traffic Ave Ste 1, Glendale NY 11385	718-366-3211	R	12*	<.1
290	Root Neal and Company Inc—Joseph F Neal Sr	PO Box 101, Buffalo NY 14240	716-824-6400	R	12*	<.1
291	Rueff Lighting Co—William P Rueff	523 E Broadway, Louisville KY 40202	502-583-1617	R	12*	<.1
292	Triphase Automation Inc—Matthew Miller	604 Northshore Dr, Hartland WI 53029	262-367-6900	R	12*	<.1
293	Beacon Electrical Distributors Inc—Richard Marco	461 Riverside Ave, Medford MA 02155	781-395-3888	R	12*	<.1
294	Harbor Wholesale Electric Supply Inc—Bruce Mahboobian	3203 S Harbor Blvd, Santa Ana CA 92704	714-434-2800	R	12*	<.1
295	Kenclaire Electrical Agencies Inc—AR Stuchbury	714 Old Country Rd, Westbury NY 11590	516-333-7373	R	12*	<.1
296	Tech Electric Company Inc—Ron Wick	PO Box 308, Butler WI 53007	262-783-2222	R	12*	<.1
297	McCaskey Co—Ken Rieck	PO Box 11484, Cedar Rapids IA 52410	319-743-3730	R	12*	<.1
298	Atlantic Telecom Inc—Jack Cowlishaw	50 Williams Pkwy, East Hanover NJ 07936		R	12	N/A
299	Heco Industrial Service Groups Inc—Mark Hatfield	3509 S Burdick St, Kalamazoo MI 49001	269-381-7200	R	12*	.1
300	Mid-West Wholesale Lighting Corp—Alan Frandzel	PO Box 27339, Los Angeles CA 90027	323-469-1641	R	12*	.1
301	Diversified Lighting Associates Inc—Richard Spugnardi	825 Mearns Rd, Warminster PA 18974	215-442-0700	R	11*	.1
302	LB Electric Supply Company Inc—Carol Lifton	5202 New Utrecht Ave, Brooklyn NY 11219	718-438-4700	R	11*	.1
303	E D Supply Company Inc—Robert Brown	PO Box 2458, Salisbury MD 21802	410-546-2201	R	11*	.1
304	Queen City Electrical Supply Company Inc—Jerry Gelfman	PO Box 1288, Allentown PA 18105	610-439-0525	R	11*	<.1
305	Hacienda Lighting Inc—David Pritchett	N Greenway Hayden Loop, Scottsdale AZ 85260	480-991-6767	R	11*	.1
306	Vincent Lighting Systems Co—Paul Vincent	6161 Cochran Rd Ste D, Solon OH 44139	216-475-7600	R	11*	.1
307	Furbay Electric Supply Co—Timothy A Furbay	208 Schroyer Ave, Canton OH 44706	330-454-3033	R	11*	.1
308	Holzmueller Corp—Richard P Gentschel	1000 25th St, San Francisco CA 94107	415-826-8383	R	11*	<.1
309	OK Electric Supply Co—Bernard J Erickson Jr	224 Washington St, Perth Amboy NJ 08861	732-826-6100	R	11*	<.1
310	Arktel Inc—Scott Seay	PO Box 9496, Fayetteville AR 72703	479-935-9113	R	11	<.1
311	Alpan Lighting Products Inc—Daniel Sooferan	451 Constitution Ave E, Camarillo CA 93012	805-383-8880	R	11*	.4
312	Autonomy Technology Inc—Greg Knowles	PO Box 263, Bend OR 97709	541-617-9311	R	11*	<.1
313	Henry L Wolfers Inc—Louis Barber	103 N Beacon St, Boston MA 02134	617-254-0700	R	11*	.1
314	Sumitomo Machinery Corporation Of America—Ronald Smith	4200 Holland Blvd, Chesapeake VA 23323	757-485-3355	R	10*	.3
315	Richards Electric Motor Co—Bill Bietrich	426 State St, Quincy IL 62301	217-222-7154	R	10*	.1
316	Anthony California Inc—James Chang	4980 Eucalyptus Ave, Chino CA 91710	909-627-0351	R	10*	.1
317	Alamo Transformer Supply Co—Thomas Zimmerman	PO Box 39908, San Antonio TX 78218	210-661-8411	R	10*	.1
318	Emergency Systems Service Co—Robert Hafich	401 Oneill Rd, Quakertown PA 18951	215-536-4973	R	10*	<.1
319	Chugai USA LLC—Art Castenada	3780 Hawthorn Ct, Waukegan IL 60087	047-244-0025	R	10*	<.1
320	Barbizon Capitol Inc—Jonathan Resnick	6437g General Green Wa, Alexandria VA 22312	703-750-3900	R	10*	<.1
321	Beeco Motors and Controls Inc—Gary Muslin	5630 Guhn Rd Ste 110, Houston TX 77040	713-690-0311	R	10*	<.1
322	North Electric Supply Inc—Frank Nutt	1290 N Opdyke Rd, Auburn Hills MI 48326	248-373-1070	R	10*	<.1
323	Telecommunication Resources Inc—Najib Yamini	25 Edwards Ct Ste 105, Burlingame CA 94010	650-342-8314	R	10*	<.1
324	Nerk Enterprises LLP—Nick Baker	2113 Franklin Dr, Fort Worth TX 76106	817-626-0044	R	10*	<.1
325	Alpha Novatech Inc—Tetsuji Kataoka	473 Sapena Ct Ste 12, Santa Clara CA 95054	408-567-8082	R	10*	<.1
326	Electrical Distribution Services Inc—Kate Nugent	1077 River Rd Apt 803, Edgewater NJ 07020	201-886-9346	R	10*	<.1
327	Roy E Wilson Co—R Chastain	4020 Tradeport Blvd, Atlanta GA 30354	404-767-6677	R	10*	<.1
328	Kraus and Naimer Inc—Joachim Naimer	760 New Brunswick Rd, Somerset NJ 08873	732-560-1240	R	10*	.1
329	Systems Sales Corp—John Ventrella	1345 Campus Pkwy, Wall Township NJ 07753	732-751-0600	R	10*	.1
330	Craig Snair Security Inc—Craig Snair	75180 Mediterranean, Palm Desert CA 92211	760-341-3593	R	10*	.1
331	Rome Electric Motor Works Inc—Robert Bowling	36 Westside Industrial, Rome GA 30165	706-232-4483	R	10*	.1
332	Warren Electric Supply Inc—Gerard Nudi	22 Wade Rd, Latham NY 12110	518-785-6677	R	10*	.1
333	M and M Lighting LP—Allan Margolin	PO Box 1027, Bellaire TX 77402	713-667-5611	R	10*	<.1
334	Satellite 2000 Systems International Corp—Fred Joubert	PO Box 4453, Thousand Oaks CA 91359	818-991-9794	R	10*	<.1
335	I Am Smart Technologies LLC—Michael Haynes	6140-K6 Gnclub Rd Ste, Aurora CO 80016	303-726-1211	R	10*	<.1
336	Brithinee Electric—Wallace Brithinee	620 S Rancho Ave, Colton CA 92324	909-825-7971	R	9*	.1
337	Continental Sales and Marketing Inc—Steven Scheiner	2360 Alvarado St, San Leandro CA 94577	510-895-1881	R	9*	.1
338	Helsel-Jepperson Electrical Inc—Delores Helsel	PO Box 310, Chicago Heights IL 60412	708-756-5600	R	9*	.1
339	Connecticut Electric Equipment Company Inc—Elsa Bradford	170 Pond View Dr, Meriden CT 06450	203-237-8944	R	9*	<.1
340	Rock Springs Winlectric Co—Tony Medina	PO Box 2520, Rock Springs WY 82902	307-382-9150	R	9*	.1
341	Drogens Electric Supply—Arnold Drogen	PO Box 867, Oneonta NY 13820	607-432-9010	R	9*	.1
342	Barber-Nichols Inc—Kenneth Nichols	6325 W 55th Ave, Arvada CO 80002	303-421-8111	R	9*	.1
343	K And N Electric Inc—Jerry Schmidlkofer	PO Box 303, Spokane WA 99210	509-535-8751	R	9*	.1
344	Electric Switches Premier—Jeff Goldrun	9601 Owensmouth Ave St, Chatsworth CA 91311		R	9*	.1
345	Kennewick Industrial and Electrical Supply Inc—Augustan Kittson	113 E Columbia Dr, Kennewick WA 99336	509-582-5156	R	9*	.1
346	Global Mine Service Inc—James Watson	PO Box 188, Fayette City PA 15438	724-929-8700	R	9*	<.1
347	Business Phones Direct—Joel Ellis III	6107 Obispo Ave, Long Beach CA 90805	562-424-0072	R	9*	<.1
348	Cannon Security Inc—John Cannon	400 Hobbs Rd Ste 207, League City TX 77573	281-481-2233	R	9*	<.1
349	Houston Communications Inc—Duane Johnson	1105 Industrial Blvd, Sugar Land TX 77478	281-491-1616	R	9*	<.1
350	Rayvern Lighting Supply Company Inc—Helen Andersen	7617 Somerset Blvd Ste, Paramount CA 90723	562-634-7020	R	9*	<.1
351	R Stahl Inc—Matthias Kuch	9001 Knight Rd, Houston TX 77054	713-792-9300	R	9*	.1
352	Kilowatts Electric Supply Corp—Roger Chaguaceda	401 Sw 71st Ave, Miami FL 33144	305-261-3600	R	9*	<.1
353	Liberty Electrical Supply Company Inc—Harvey Dall	10203 Ave D, Brooklyn NY 11236	718-688-3110	R	9*	<.1
354	T Stats Supply Inc—James Strippy	3931 Penn Belt Pl, Forestville MD 20747	301-420-7300	R	9*	<.1
355	American Encoder Repair Servic—Karen Lagrou	7115 W Lynwood Dr, Michigan City IN 46360	219-872-2822	R	9*	<.1
356	Quermback Electric Inc—Peter Quermback	215 Genesee St 217, Buffalo NY 14203	716-856-6644	R	9*	<.1
357	Crn Solutions Inc—Crystal Navock	36595 Kevin Rd Ste 139, Wildomar CA 92595	951-824-1571	R	9*	<.1
358	Seikoh Giken USA Inc—Hiroshi Tanguchi	4405 International Blv, Norcross GA 30093	770-279-6602	R	9*	<.1
359	Colotex Electric Supply Co—Douglas Hample	PO Box 2409, Loveland CO 80539	970-663-4951	R	8*	.1
360	Mathes Electric Supply Company Inc—Jerry Mathes	PO Box 9699, Pensacola FL 32513	850-432-4161	R	8*	<.1
361	Southern California Illumination—Thomas Thompson	1881 Mcgaw Ave, Irvine CA 92614	949-622-3000	R	8*	.1

Note: An asterisk (*) indicates an estimated financial figure. The company type code used is as follows: R = Private, P = Public, S = Private Subsidiary, B = Public Subsidiary, D = Division, J = Joint Venture, I = Investment Fund.

COMPANY RANKINGS BY SALES WITHIN 4-DIGIT SIC

Rank	Company Name—Executive Officer	Address, City, State, Zip	Phone	Type	Fin	Empls
362	Satellite Receivers Ltd—David Charles	1740 Cofrin Dr Ste 2, Green Bay WI 54302	920-432-5777	R	8*	<.1
363	Norton and Norton Electric Company Ltd—Walter Norton	PO Box 86048, Los Angeles CA 90086	323-222-7181	R	8*	<.1
364	Lubbock Electric Co—Steve Moffett	1108 34th St, Lubbock TX 79411	806-744-2336	R	8*	.1
365	EMSCO Electric Supply Company Inc—Larry Allen	1101 W Sheridan Ave, Oklahoma City OK 73106	405-235-6331	R	8*	.1
366	Gulf Electroquip Management LLC—Michael Roush	PO Box 745, Houston TX 77001	713-675-2525	R	8*	.1
367	Pro Brand International Inc—Cecilia Shou	1900 W Oak Cir, Marietta GA 30062	770-423-7072	R	8*	<.1
368	Tepper Electric Supply Inc—Fay Tepper	608 S Neil St, Champaign IL 61820	217-356-3755	R	8*	<.1
369	Custom Communications Inc—Dave Cruse	PO Box 44458, Tacoma WA 98448	253-536-9183	R	8*	<.1
370	Rexel Norcal Valley—Alan Rosenfeld	PO Box 492417, Redding CA 96049	530-221-7200	S	8*	<.1
371	Electrical Power Products Of SC Inc—Larry Sloan	2 Rugosa Way, Greer SC 29650	864-801-0464	R	8*	<.1
372	Bell Electric Company of Penna Inc—Robert Friedman	PO Box 564, Scranton PA 18501	570-343-2461	R	8*	<.1
373	Astro Technical Services Inc—Chris Comire	1801 Hurd Dr, Irving TX 75038	972-253-7783	R	8*	<.1
374	Flann Microwave Inc—Colleen Fleming	12 Alfred St Ste 300, Woburn MA 01801	617-621-7034	R	8*	.1
375	Advance Controls Inc—Don Panuce	4505 18th St E, Bradenton FL 34203	941-746-3221	R	8*	<.1
376	Valley Lighting LLC—Rick Intyre	601 N Hammnds Fry Rd U, Linthicum Heights MD 21090	410-636-6010	R	8*	<.1
377	Atlantic Electric Supply Corp—Morton Lessans	3726 10th St Ne, Washington DC 20017	202-526-1300	R	8*	<.1
378	Nkk Switches Of America Inc—Kiyoko Toyama	PO Box 13570, Scottsdale AZ 85267	480-991-0942	R	8*	.1
379	West 1 Catv Supplies Inc—Kelley West	202 Lea Plant Rd, Waynesville NC 28786	828-452-2255	R	8*	<.1
380	Kanouse-Harper And Associates—William Kanouse	2327 E Sahuaro Dr, Phoenix AZ 85028	602-971-9786	R	8*	<.1
381	Lighting Depot Inc—Edward Fischer	321 Norristown Rd Ste, Ambler PA 19002	215-591-2800	R	8*	<.1
382	Thomas Door Controls Inc—Scott Thomas	4196 Indianola Ave, Columbus OH 43214	614-267-6391	R	8*	<.1
383	Lane and Lane Inc—Michael Lane	240 Peachtree St Nw Bs, Atlanta GA 30303	404-688-0909	R	8*	<.1
384	Pacific Lamp and Supply Co—John Kelly	5935 4th Ave S, Seattle WA 98108	206-767-5334	R	7*	<.1
385	Coastal Traffic Systems Inc—Steven Beiber	1261 Logan Ave, Costa Mesa CA 92626	714-641-3744	R	7*	.1
386	Healey Fire Protection Inc—Robert Burkland	134 Northpointe Dr, Orion MI 48359	248-373-7800	R	7*	<.1
387	Bass-United Fire and Security Systems Inc—Brad Higdon	1480 Sw 3rd St Ste 9, Pompano Beach FL 33069	954-785-7800	R	7*	<.1
388	Lester Sales Company Inc—Brian Chase	4312 W Minnesota St, Indianapolis IN 46241	317-244-7811	R	7*	<.1
389	T-R Associates Inc—Thomas Speicher	PO Box 116, Archbald PA 18403	570-876-4067	R	7*	<.1
390	Southwestern Electric Supply Company Inc—Pat Jeffreys	PO Box 64300, Lubbock TX 79464	806-745-6243	R	7*	<.1
391	Caniff Electric Supply Company Inc—Douglas Bemis	PO Box 12490, Detroit MI 48212	313-365-8144	R	7*	<.1
392	Total Fire and Safety Inc—Robert Damesworth	7909 Carr St, Dallas TX 75227	214-381-6116	R	7*	<.1
393	Ohlin Sales Inc—Paul Ohlin	6024 Culligan Way, Minnetonka MN 55345	952-294-0222	R	7*	<.1
394	Cornerstone Telecommunications Inc—Jim Highstreet	46560 Fremont Blvd Ste, Fremont CA 94538	510-661-9299	R	7*	<.1
395	Security Telecommunications of Porterville Inc—Ron Irish	768 N Prospect, Porterville CA 93257	559-781-3310	R	7*	<.1
396	Control Sales Inc—Gene Bond	306 Main St, Beech Grove IN 46107	317-786-2272	R	7*	<.1
397	Total Electric Distributors Inc—Lenore Schwartz	388 South Ave, Staten Island NY 10303	718-273-9300	R	7*	<.1
398	Lynn Elliott Company Kc Inc—Marion Boggs	5400 W 61st Pl Ste 260, Shawnee Mission KS 66205	913-722-6500	R	7*	<.1
399	Branscombe Cable Co—Penelope Johnson	5742 S Park Ave, Hinsdale IL 60521	630-789-0037	R	7*	<.1
400	John Patsey Sales Inc—John Patsey	PO Box 385, Somerset KY 42502	606-679-1092	R	7*	<.1
401	Light Brite Distributing Inc—Timothy Klein	PO Box 156, Trenton IL 62293	618-224-7314	R	7*	<.1
402	Carolina Time Equipment Company Inc—Henry Allen	PO Box 18158, Charlotte NC 28218	704-536-2700	R	7*	<.1
403	Jewel Electric Supply Co—Herbert Goldman	455 3rd St, Jersey City NJ 07302	201-653-1613	R	7*	<.1
404	Bill Casey Electric Sales Inc—William Casey	1001 Industrial Dr, Bensenville IL 60106	630-860-3600	R	7*	<.1
405	Multicom Inc—Sherman Miller	1076 Florida Central P, Longwood FL 32750	407-331-7779	R	7*	<.1
406	Conway Communications Company LLC	065 Stillwater Rd Ste, West Sacramento CA 95605	916-374-9007	R	7*	<.1
407	Lightspec Inc—David Seconi	107 Norris Dr Ste C, Rochester NY 14610	585-242-8888	R	7*	<.1
408	Astrosystems Inc—Paul Kwan	4210 Production Ct, Las Vegas NV 89115	702-643-1600	R	7*	.1
409	Nancy Brownstein—Nancy Brownstein	PO Box 11642, Philadelphia PA 19116	215-671-1540	R	7*	.1
410	Lamptronix Company Ltd—Tammy Goberstein	3362 Commercial Ave, Northbrook IL 60062	847-509-0550	R	7*	<.1
411	Classic Lighting Corp—Joseph Duran	6100 Philips Hwy Ste 3, Jacksonville FL 32216	904-645-5000	R	7*	<.1
412	Aldan Electric Supply Inc—Lee Williams	734 Brookhaven Dr, Orlando FL 32803	407-896-7761	R	7*	<.1
413	Commercial Lighting Sales—James Wheeler	6797 Dorsey Rd Ste 3, Elkridge MD 21075	410-796-1033	R	7*	<.1
414	Diebold Fire Services Virginia Inc—James Newell	7800 Whitepine Rd, Richmond VA 23237	804-271-8338	R	6*	<.1
415	R B Allen Company Inc—R Allen	PO Box 770, North Hampton NH 03862	603-964-8140	R	6*	<.1
416	Firetrace USA LLC—Laurel Eckholm	15690 N 83rd Way Ste B, Scottsdale AZ 85260	480-607-1218	R	6*	<.1
417	Curtis Engine and Equipment Company Inc—Thomas Koch	3920 Vero Rd Ste I and, Baltimore MD 21227	410-536-1203	R	6*	<.1
418	Alliance Specialty Motors Inc—Bruce Bailey	645 Lester Doss Rd, Warrior AL 35180	205-590-2986	R	6*	<.1
419	Amperage Electrical Supply Inc—Vito Pelagio	359 W Irving Park Rd A, Roselle IL 60172	630-894-8100	R	6*	<.1
420	Customized Support Services Inc—Patrick Mcgettigan	319 Yard Dr, Verona WI 53593	608-827-1105	R	6*	<.1
421	Quail Electronics Inc—Greg Ruppert	2171 Research Dr, Livermore CA 94550	925-373-6700	R	6*	<.1
422	Tennessee Wire Technologies LLC—Freda Whitaker	1350 Hwy 149 W, Cumberland City TN 37050	931-827-4000	R	6*	<.1
423	Irvin's Inc—Irvin Hoover	102 Cedar Ln, Mount Pleasant Mills PA 17853	570-539-8717	R	6*	.1
424	Supreme Securities Services—Steven Mallen	PO Box 60558, Staten Island NY 10306	718-987-2338	R	6*	.1
425	Omni Cable Corp—Jeff Siegfried	2 Hagerty Blvd, West Chester PA 19382	610-701-0100	R	6*	<.1
426	Billow Electric Supply Company Fe Inc—Jeffrey Billow	1810 Baltic Ave, Atlantic City NJ 08401	609-345-6154	R	6*	<.1
427	Delta Electric Inc—Tom Bannister	PO Box 1497, Logan WV 25601	304-752-4625	R	6*	<.1
428	Incon Industries Inc—Mark Hudson	PO Box 2083, Sanford FL 32772	407-323-5630	R	6*	<.1
429	Tri-State Lighting and Supply Company Inc—Wayne Jeffers	1159 E Diamond Ave, Evansville IN 47711	812-423-4257	R	6*	<.1
430	Semix Inc—Norio Sugano	3350 Scott Blvd Bldg 2, Santa Clara CA 95054	510-578-2808	R	6*	<.1
431	Triangle Electric Supply Co—Tom Kincaid Consolidated Electrical Distributors Inc	3815 Durazno Ave, El Paso TX 79905	915-533-5981	S	6*	<.1
432	Western Carolina Electrical Supply Co—Lyle Jensen	908 Morganton Blvd SW, Lenoir NC 28645	828-754-5811	R	6*	<.1
433	Telecom Electric Supply Co—Fred Moses	PO Box 860307, Plano TX 75086	972-422-0012	R	6*	<.1
434	Cbmc Inc—Russell Miller	5855 Kopetsky Dr Ste G, Indianapolis IN 46217	317-780-8350	R	6*	<.1
435	AMP King Battery Company Inc—Brad Streelman	10 Loomis St, San Francisco CA 94124	415-648-7650	R	6*	<.1
436	Hatley and Associates Inc—Mark Hatley	5002 Forest Oaks Dr, Greensboro NC 27406	336-674-7131	R	6*	<.1
437	Peter F Sheridan Inc—Peter Sheridan	PO Box 1506, Englewood Cliffs NJ 07632	201-567-0353	R	6*	<.1
438	Milliken Investments Inc—William Milliken	PO Box 2267, Shallotte NC 28459	910-754-6000	R	6*	<.1
439	Carrier and Gable Inc—Daniel Carrier	24110 Research Dr, Farmington Hills MI 48335	248-477-8700	R	6*	<.1
440	Purkey's Fleet Electric Inc—Veronica Purkey	221 N 14th St, Rogers AR 72756	479-621-8282	R	6*	<.1
441	Electrorep Inc—Ronald Haedt	2015 Bridgeway Ste 201, Sausalito CA 94965	415-332-4100	R	6*	<.1
442	Automatic Entrances Of Wisconsin Inc—William Holcomb	1712 Paramount Ct, Waukesha WI 53186	262-549-8600	R	6*	<.1
443	State Systems Inc—Robert Mcbride	PO Box 18439, Memphis TN 38181	901-542-0612	R	6*	.1
444	A Loss Prevention System By Sonitrol—Bill Price	815 Woodridge Ctr Dr, Charlotte NC 28217	704-423-1111	R	6*	<.1
445	Matlock Electric Company Inc—Thomas Geoppinger	2780 Highland Ave, Cincinnati OH 45212	513-731-9600	R	6*	<.1
446	Bay State Wire and Cable Company Inc—Donald Ranagan	PO Box 1093, Lowell MA 01853	978-454-2444	R	6*	<.1
447	Communication Company Of South Bend Inc—Dan Schmidtendorff	5320 S Main St, South Bend IN 46614	574-299-0020	R	6*	<.1
448	United Electric Supply Co—Douglas Gronna	15497 Dupont Ave, Chino CA 91710	909-393-4700	R	6*	<.1
449	Carol Lighting and Supply Inc—A Price	3527 E Fort Lowell Rd, Tucson AZ 85716	520-571-8818	R	6*	<.1

Rank	Company Name—*Executive Officer*	Address, City, State, Zip	Phone	Type	Fin	Empls
450	American Fitting Corp—*Henry Fischbein*	17-10 Willow St, Fair Lawn NJ 07410	201-666-2753	R	6*	<.1
451	Richards Lighting Distributors Inc—*Bradley Lapidus*	1811 University Dr Nw, Huntsville AL 35801	256-533-1460	R	6*	<.1
452	16500 Sixteen Five Hundred—*Paul Mcdowell*	2001 Broadway Fl 4th, Oakland CA 94612	510-208-5005	R	5*	<.1
453	Bulbrite Industries Inc—*Andrew Choi*	PO Box 4108, South Hackensack NJ 07606	201-531-5900	R	5*	<.1
454	Channel Way Industries Inc—*W West*	1209 W 17th St, Houston TX 77008	713-864-2478	R	5*	<.1
455	Grant Industrial Controls Inc—*William Harrington*	1 Zesta Dr, Pittsburgh PA 15205	412-787-9770	R	5*	<.1
456	HM Cross and Sons Inc—*Paul Harrison*	PO Box 20700, Rochester NY 14602	585-424-5500	R	5*	<.1
457	Energetics Industrial Distributors Inc—*William Westphal*	4901 Prairie Dock Dr, Madison WI 53718	608-241-8866	R	5*	<.1
458	Imperial Electric and Lighting Supply Inc—*John Morris*	1125 Sw 101st Rd, Davie FL 33324	954-370-3000	R	5*	<.1
459	A and A Fire and Security Inc—*Thomas Binish*	PO Box 11354, Green Bay WI 54307	920-434-9082	R	5*	<.1
460	State Electric Co—*Gerard Baum*	PO Box 28589, Saint Louis MO 63146	314-569-2140	R	5*	<.1
461	Sterris Energy Systems Inc—*Dan Sterling*	PO Box 151, Spring TX 77383	281-355-7400	R	5*	<.1
462	Cls Facilities Management Services Inc—*Robert Waldrip*	8061 Tyler Blvd, Mentor OH 44060	440-602-4600	R	5*	<.1
463	Weinstock Lamp Company Inc—*Morris Weinstock*	3430 Steinway St, Long Island City NY 11101	718-729-4848	R	5*	<.1
464	Goldfarb Electric Supply Company Inc—*Jack Goldfarb*	PO Box 3319, Charleston WV 25333	304-342-2153	R	5*	<.1
465	Douglas T Ewing and Associates—*Diane Ewing*	2210 Piney Creek Rd St, Chester MD 21619	410-827-5300	R	5*	<.1
466	Bender Systems—*Ronald Bender*	8 Commercial Blvd Ste, Novato CA 94949	415-472-7033	R	5*	<.1
467	ECP Tech Services Inc—*Phil Collins*	PO Box 729, Houston TX 77001	713-222-9195	R	5*	.1
468	Valwest Technologies Inc—*Lorenzo Valenzuela*	6033 W Sherman St, Phoenix AZ 85043	623-435-9778	R	5*	<.1
469	Lakeland Engineer Equipment Co—*William C Fox*	5735 Lindsay St, Minneapolis MN 55422	763-544-0321	R	5*	<.1
470	Amelex Inc—*Gary Newkirk*	445 S Ingram Mill Rd, Springfield MO 65802	417-864-8987	R	5*	<.1
471	Besco Electic Supply Company of Florida Inc—*Douglas W Braun*	PO Box 491366, Leesburg FL 34749	352-787-4542	R	5*	<.1
472	Anderson-Bolds Inc—*Steve Sords*	24050 Commerce Park St, Cleveland OH 44122	216-360-9800	R	5*	<.1
473	C E Beckman Co—*Charles Beckman*	PO Box 971, New Bedford MA 02741	508-994-9674	R	5*	<.1
474	Clp Corp—*Lester Hohl*	4307 Papin St, Saint Louis MO 63110	314-534-1090	R	5*	<.1
475	Service Electrical Supply Company Inc—*Albert Panza*	5200 Penn Ave, Pittsburgh PA 15224	412-363-1800	R	5*	<.1
476	M-Tron Components Inc—*Mark H Kealey*	1891 Lakeland Ave, Ronkonkoma NY 11779	631-467-5100	R	5*	<.1
477	Alpha Source Inc—*Norine Carlson-Weber*	6619 W Calumet Rd, Milwaukee WI 53223	414-760-2222	R	5*	<.1
478	Eastern Electric Supply Co—*Perry Watson III*	716 Ricks St, Rocky Mount NC 27804	252-442-5156	R	5*	<.1
479	Staab Battery Manufacturing Company Inc—*Peter J Staab*	931 S 11th St, Springfield IL 62703	217-528-0421	R	5*	<.1
480	Big Ocean Corp—*Mike Chuang*	PO Box 1637, Chino CA 91708	909-590-5950	R	5*	<.1
481	Port Electric Supply Corp—*Hank Barnes*	248 3rd St, Elizabeth NJ 07206	908-355-1900	R	5*	<.1
482	Nassor Electrical Supply Company Inc—*George Nassor*	200 Moonachie Ave, Moonachie NJ 07074	201-438-4900	R	5*	<.1
483	New Wave Systems Inc—*Andy Felton*	2800 Highwoods Blvd, Raleigh NC 27604	919-878-8747	R	5*	<.1
484	Lessman Electric Supply Company Inc—*Harlan Lessman*	PO Box 3558, Sioux City IA 51102	712-277-8040	R	5*	<.1
485	Villarreal Electric Company Inc	PO Box 760, Laredo TX 78042	956-722-2771	R	5*	<.1
486	Heat Tracing Specialties West Inc—*William Washington*	8152 Southpark Ln, Littleton CO 80120	303-979-5000	R	5*	<.1
487	Philips and Co—*Gary Bradley* Consolidated Electrical Distributors Inc	1915 Pennsylvania Dr, Columbia MO 65202	573-474-2800	D	5*	<.1
488	Digital Connections Inc (Omaha Nebraska)—*Robert Heist*	4701 Innovation Dr CB, Lincoln NE 68521	402-323-0707	R	5*	<.1
489	Esco Electric Supply Co—*Robert Hafter*	820 N 2nd St, Philadelphia PA 19123	215-923-6050	R	5*	<.1
490	Premier Electric Supply Inc—*Samuel Obie*	1024 White St Sw, Atlanta GA 30310	404-753-8900	R	5*	<.1
491	E and B Electric Supply Co Consolidated Electrical Distributors Inc	615 Strong Hwy, El Dorado AR 71730	870-862-8101	S	5*	<.1
492	Q-Mark—*Bobbie Gentile*	5963 Kentshire Dr, Dayton OH 45440	937-438-8923	R	5*	<.1
493	First Coast Lighting Inc—*Daniel Clements*	1825 University Blvd W, Jacksonville FL 32217	904-730-0222	R	6*	<.1
494	Genlyte-Lightolier—*Tom Kendrick*	201 Flagship Dr Ste 10, Lutz FL 33549	813-932-7277	R	5*	<.1
495	Esu Inc—*Edward Friedlein*	7666 Formula Pl Ste C, San Diego CA 92121	858-695-2850	R	5*	<.1
496	Mid West Co—*Jeff Roberts*	307 Merlin Dr, Weldon Spring MO 63304	636-477-9466	R	5*	<.1
497	Batteries Direct Inc—*W Lynn Fuller*	408 37th St, Parkersburg WV 26101	304-428-2296	R	5*	<.1
498	Certified Alarm Technician—*Ewell Miller*	1401 Neptune Dr, Boynton Beach FL 33426	561-752-5555	R	5*	.1
499	Midway Winnelson Co—*Danas Johnson*	4329 N Us Hwy 31, Seymour IN 47274	812-522-5199	R	5*	<.1
500	Hdw Electronics Inc—*Henning Oetjen*	89 S Commerce Way Ste, Bethlehem PA 18017	610-861-8862	R	5*	<.1
501	American Light Co—*John Stubbs*	PO Box 2280, Zanesville OH 43702	740-452-3676	R	5*	<.1
502	AA Macpherson Company Inc—*Thomas Sabin*	1 Pequot Way, Canton MA 02021	781-828-9400	R	5*	<.1
503	Kelly Generator and Equipment Inc—*John Kelly*	1955 Dale Ln, Owings MD 20736	410-257-5225	R	5*	<.1
504	Wired Investment Group Inc—*Glen Rodolico*	3411 S 44th St, Phoenix AZ 85040	602-437-0760	R	5*	<.1
505	Advanced Safety Systems Inc—*William Kay*	141 Summit St Ste 2, Peabody MA 01960	978-532-5730	R	5*	<.1
506	B and K Precision Corp—*Victor Tolan*	22820 Savi Ranch Pkwy, Yorba Linda CA 92887	714-921-9095	R	5*	<.1
507	Globe Electric Supply Company Inc—*Julius Rosenzweig*	PO Box 6258, Long Island City NY 11106	718-932-1820	R	5*	<.1
508	Terry-Durin Co—*George Durin*	PO Box 39, Cedar Rapids IA 52406	319-364-4106	R	5*	<.1
509	Ellison Electric Supply Inc—*Joel Wendt*	PO Box 1235, Fond Du Lac WI 54936	920-921-8910	R	5*	<.1
510	M and M Sales Inc—*Marco Castellon*	3336 Greencastle Rd, Burtonsville MD 20866	301-937-1650	R	5*	<.1
511	Conserve Electrical Supply—*Lawrence Sullivan*	3905 Crescent St, Long Island City NY 11101	718-937-6671	R	5*	<.1
512	Neon Engineering Inc—*James Greenebaum*	1425 Spring Lawn Ave, Cincinnati OH 45223	513-681-3300	R	5*	<.1
513	Lou Bo Inc—*Stephen Schanne*	459 Mantua Ave, Woodbury NJ 08096	856-845-5177	R	5*	<.1
514	Electrorep-Energy Products Inc—*Fred Herdlick*	PO Box 460200, Saint Louis MO 63146	314-991-2600	R	5*	<.1
515	IDC Corp—*Lewis Alspaugh*	PO Box 418, Dimondale MI 48821	517-646-0358	R	5*	.1
516	JCH Enterprises Inc—*James Hinshaw*	4527 Losee Rd, North Las Vegas NV 89081	702-639-4000	R	5*	.1
517	New England Electric Motor Service Corp—*Robert Tilton*	25 Griffin Way, Chelsea MA 02150	617-884-9200	R	5*	<.1
518	Stealth Systems Inc—*Howard Radde*	1323 N Ironwood Dr, South Bend IN 46615	574-968-0784	R	4*	<.1
519	Global Fire and Safety—*Jerry Chatel*	10975 E 47th Ave, Denver CO 80239	303-367-1959	R	4*	<.1
520	Madison Lighting Ltd—*Tom Woodward*	6701 Watts Rd, Madison WI 53719	608-271-6911	R	4*	<.1
521	H Schacht Electrical Supply Inc—*Ronald Schacht*	PO Box 380781, Brooklyn NY 11238	718-857-1000	R	4*	<.1
522	Electrical-Mechanical Drives Inc—*Heard Cunningham*	PO Box 5968, Jacksonville FL 32247	904-731-9977	R	4*	<.1
523	JH Service Company Inc	PO Box 237, Bellaire OH 43906	812-983-2525	R	4*	<.1
524	Gulf Electrical Wholesale Inc—*Wade Foster*	PO Box 2180, Alice TX 78333	361-668-1735	R	4*	<.1
525	Techflex Inc—*William Dermody*	PO Box 119, Sparta NJ 07871	973-300-9242	R	4*	<.1
526	Des Inc—*Mark Pantalone*	132 Silvermine Rd Ste, Seymour CT 06483	203-888-7500	R	4*	<.1
527	Mulcrone and Associates Inc—*Michael Mulcrone*	725 N Edgewood Ave, Wood Dale IL 60191	630-860-2250	R	4*	<.1
528	Structured Cable Products Inc—*David Spiller*	5607 Hiatus Rd Ste 500, Tamarac FL 33321	954-691-4240	R	4*	<.1
529	Control Source Inc—*Sam Jenkins*	PO Box 551177, Gastonia NC 28055	704-824-5335	R	4*	<.1
530	Signal Service Inc—*Joseph Ferguson*	1020 Andrew Dr, West Chester PA 19380	610-429-8073	R	4*	<.1
531	D and F Liquidators Inc—*Gregory Womble*	PO Box 4717, Hayward CA 94540	510-785-9600	R	4*	<.1
532	T Gray Electric Company Inc—*Troy Gray*	3404 Jane Ln, Dallas TX 75247	214-631-1188	R	4*	<.1
533	Accent Lighting Inc—*Pat Graf*	2020 N Woodlawn St Ste, Wichita KS 67208	316-636-1278	R	4*	<.1
534	Power Line Hardware LLC	6841 Phillips Pkwy Dr, Jacksonville FL 32256	904-695-9080	R	4*	<.1
535	Silvine Inc—*Norman Silver*	PO Box 1, Abington PA 19001	215-657-2345	R	4*	<.1
536	Konnerth Sales Associates LLC—*Jason Solis*	1200 Central Ave Ste B, Bartlett IL 60133	630-307-6955	R	4*	<.1

Note: An asterisk (*) indicates an estimated financial figure. The company type code used is as follows: R = Private, P = Public, S = Private Subsidiary, B = Public Subsidiary, D = Division, J = Joint Venture, I = Investment Fund.

COMPANY RANKINGS BY SALES WITHIN 4-DIGIT SIC

Rank	Company Name—Executive Officer	Address, City, State, Zip	Phone	Type	Fin	Empls
537	Putterman Scharck and Associates Inc—Michael Scharck	10855 Tanner Rd, Houston TX 77041	713-664-7111	R	4*	<.1
538	Guy Gray Supply Co—Jerry Mcelya	PO Box 2287, Paducah KY 42002	270-554-4206	R	4*	<.1
539	United Lighting Company Inc—Roger Steel	PO Box 210565, Montgomery AL 36121	334-279-9050	R	4*	<.1
540	MP Productions Co—Mike Pope	6700 Allied Way, Little Rock AR 72209	501-562-7425	R	4*	<.1
541	WN de Sherbinin Products Inc—Lawrence Greenhaus	PO Box 3471, Danbury CT 06813	203-791-0494	R	4*	<.1
542	Earnhardt Electric Service Inc—Tommy Earnhardt	PO Box 1019, Roebuck SC 29376	864-576-5922	R	4*	<.1
543	Flannigan Electric Co—Steve Flannigan	PO Box 8657, Jackson MS 39284	601-354-2756	R	4*	<.1
544	Lighthouse Electrical Suppliers Inc—David Fullmer	204 North St, La Porte IN 46350	219-362-8595	R	4*	<.1
545	Keystone Electrical Supply Company Inc—Robert Stern	PO Box 188, Butler PA 16003	724-285-4217	R	4*	<.1
546	Sitler Electric Supply Inc—Lana Weeks	PO Box 542, Washington IA 52353	319-653-2128	R	4*	<.1
547	Wsa Systems-Boca Inc—Brad Golub	442 Nw 35th St, Boca Raton FL 33431	561-393-2933	R	4*	<.1
548	Coast Air Inc—Fred Sutherland	11134 Sepulveda Blvd, Mission Hills CA 91345	818-898-2288	R	4*	<.1
549	Lee Electric Supply Company Inc—John Lee	240 Hickory St, Scranton PA 18505	570-348-6741	R	4*	<.1
550	Nichols Electric Supply Inc—John Nichols	PO Box 5516, Evansville IN 47716	812-492-1600	R	4*	<.1
551	One Wish LLC	34565 Seminole Way, Cleveland OH 44139		R	4*	<.1
552	Sunon Inc	1075 W Lambert Rd Ste, Brea CA 92821	714-255-0208	S	4*	<.1
553	Wolf Industries LP—David Louis	5910 Hamblen Dr, Humble TX 77396	281-441-9321	R	4*	<.1
554	HMC Electronics—Stanley Goldberg	PO Box 526, Canton MA 02021	781-821-1870	R	4*	<.1
555	Target Electronics Inc—Mike Weseloh	16120 Caputo Dr, Morgan Hill CA 95037	408-778-0408	R	4*	<.1
556	Wholesale Electric Supply Company Inc (Bowling Green Kentucky)—Marge Rutland	PO Box 2500, Bowling Green KY 42102	270-842-0156	R	4*	<.1
557	Kahant Electrical Supply Co—James L Crummy	437 Rte 10 E, Randolph NJ 07869	973-366-2966	R	4*	<.1
558	Automated Power Co—Mac Marsh	4364 Mangum Dr, Flowood MS 39232	601-936-4900	R	4*	<.1
559	Electric Supply Connection Inc—Kevin Naydavood	12220 W Pico Blvd, Los Angeles CA 90064	310-442-2002	R	4*	<.1
560	Meier Transmission Inc	1845 E 40th St, Cleveland OH 44103	216-881-0444	S	4*	<.1
561	Security Engineering Company Inc—O Swanson	PO Box 746, Clemmons NC 27012	336-766-9902	R	4*	<.1
562	Cotner Wholesale Lighting and Electric Supply Inc—Habibollah Rashidi	2228 Cotner Ave, Los Angeles CA 90064	310-473-0555	R	4*	<.1
563	Cablelan Products Inc—Jan Pirrong	PO Box 196, Norfolk MA 02056	508-384-7811	R	4*	<.1
564	Joseph T Fewkes and Co—RE Gillin	6 Eves Dr, Marlton NJ 08053	856-762-0149	R	4*	<.1
565	Stewart Electric Supply Inc—Don Noble	PO Box 1905, Bakersfield CA 93303	661-325-5061	R	4*	<.1
566	Adventure Lighting Supply Ltd—Jack Huff	90 Washington Ave, Des Moines IA 50314	515-288-0444	R	4*	<.1
567	All-Phase Electric Supply Co—Dean Bursch Consolidated Electrical Distributors Inc	3905 S M 139, Saint Joseph MI 49085	269-429-1700	D	4*	<.1
568	De Landsheer Sales Incorporated—Robert Delandsheer	1011a W 46th Ave, Denver CO 80211	303-202-2990	R	4*	<.1
569	Lazer Telecommunications Inc—Keith D Horton	1048 Serpentine Ln Ste, Pleasanton CA 94566	925-462-0505	R	4*	<.1
570	Sensortags Inc—Mark Fouts	2 Plaza North Shopping, Terre Haute IN 47804	812-877-9930	R	4*	<.1
571	Ambient LLC—Ed Edelman	6845 west FryeRoad, Chandler AZ 85226	480-346-3388	R	4*	<.1
572	C R J Enterprises Inc—Gary Jones	854 Texas Ave, Shreveport LA 71101	318-222-7474	R	4*	<.1
573	Queen Enterprises Inc—Paul Jeko	2930 Tpke Dr, Hatboro PA 19040	215-957-9403	R	4*	<.1
574	C and I Electrical Supply Corp—Frank Walden	PO Box 2010, Jonesboro AR 72402	870-972-1392	R	4*	<.1
575	Ddc Electric Supply Inc—David Chee	307 S Dogwood Rd, El Centro CA 92243	760-312-9988	R	4*	<.1
576	Fairfield Lighting And Design Center Inc—Frank Zemola	356 Black Rock Tpke, Fairfield CT 06825	203-384-2209	R	4*	<.1
577	Industrial Electrical Sales Of Tulsa Inc—Bill Drotar	4237 S 74th E Ave, Tulsa OK 74145	918-665-6888	R	4*	<.1
578	Allied Electric Supply Co—Philip Ross	23020 Telegraph Rd, Southfield MI 48033	248-358-2800	R	4*	<.1
579	David Whitnack Distributing Inc—David Whitnack	PO Box 43144, Philadelphia PA 19129	215-849-5755	R	4*	<.1
580	Alabama Electric Motor Services LLC—Tracy Somers	1714 Wall St, Sheffield AL 35660	256-383-1490	R	4*	<.1
581	Telco Intercontinental Corp—Frank Liang	9812 Whithorn Dr, Houston TX 77095	281-855-2218	R	4*	<.1
582	General Engineering and Equipment Co—Thomas Pugh	7920 Powell Rd, Hopkins MN 55343	952-936-0003	R	4*	<.1
583	Electric Motor Service Inc—Richard Spiczka	PO Box 1224, Saint Cloud MN 56302	320-251-8691	R	4*	<.1
584	Conley Equipment LLC—Mathew Roberts	PO Box 5528, Denver CO 80217	303-371-6777	R	4*	<.1
585	Lighting Sales and Service—Dennis Nance	PO Box 926, Fairview TN 37062	615-804-2337	R	4*	<.1
586	Feller LLC—Meredith Linkous	9100 Industrial Blvd N, Leland NC 28451	910-383-6920	R	4*	<.1
587	Atash Fire and Safety Equipment Company Inc—John Puttrich	2925 S Wabash Ave Ste, Chicago IL 60616	312-842-8480	R	4*	<.1
588	Colonial Tin Works Inc—Tom Rose	PO Box 49909, Greensboro NC 27419	336-668-4126	R	4*	<.1
589	Emerson Electric Supply Co—Philip Picciotto	1105 Broadway Ave, Farrell PA 16121	724-981-3040	R	4*	<.1
590	Johnson Electric Supply Inc—Robert Johnson	PO Box 1508, Sagamore Beach MA 02562	508-833-8836	R	4*	<.1
591	Duplex Electrical Supply Corp—Herbert Slater	95 Seaview Blvd Ste 10, Port Washington NY 11050	516-625-8181	R	4*	<.1
592	High Rise Security Systems LLC—Jackie Bayne	762 Burr Oak Dr, Westmont IL 60559	630-920-0100	R	4*	<.1
593	Advanced Electro Mechanical Sales Inc—Donald Gerard	8581 154th Ave Ne, Redmond WA 98052	425-881-2618	R	4*	<.1
594	Cabco Inc—Carl Toth	1538 Arona Rd, Irwin PA 15642	724-864-3400	R	4*	<.1
595	Bcb Group Inc—James Bessey	105 W Laura Dr, Addison IL 60101	630-628-9588	R	4*	<.1
596	Kurz Electric Solutions Inc—Richard Nowak	1325 McMahon Dr, Neenah WI 54956	920-886-8200	R	4	<.1
597	Lloyd And Bouvier Inc—Carter Lloyd	56 Sterling St Ste 103, Clinton MA 01510	978-365-5700	R	4*	<.1
598	Jth Lighting Alliance Inc—John Hartley	6885 146th St W, Saint Paul MN 55124	651-456-0806	R	4*	<.1
599	A and S Electric Supply Inc—Thomas Smith	3140 Crescent Ave Unit, Erlanger KY 41018	859-727-1111	R	4*	<.1
600	Connect-Air International Inc—Michael Jones	4240 B St Nw, Auburn WA 98001	253-813-5599	R	4*	<.1
601	Rts Transformers Inc—Diana Roberts	2234 Apopka Blvd, Apopka FL 32703	407-880-2524	R	4*	<.1
602	Winar 1 Sales Inc—Bill Winar	PO Box 270, Richfield OH 44286	330-659-4200	R	4*	<.1
603	Queens Industrial Electric Corp—David Mollet	9412 150th St, Jamaica NY 11435	718-526-7198	R	4*	<.1
604	Advance Gift Enterprises Inc—James Chen	2646 River Ave Ste A, Rosemead CA 91770	626-307-9895	R	4*	<.1
605	Industrial Battery Warehouse Inc—Brian Grill	2969 Chicago Dr Sw, Grandville MI 49418	616-530-8918	R	4*	<.1
606	Jnt Lighting Inc—Charles French	128 E Dyer Rd Ste C, Santa Ana CA 92707	714-754-7668	R	4*	<.1
607	Skinner Electrical Sales Inc—Ronald Skinner	3611 Whetstone Pl N, Wilson NC 27896	252-291-4321	R	4*	<.1
608	Nes Of Commerce—Charles Mathis	4150 Maysville Rd, Commerce GA 30529	706-654-0896	R	3*	<.1
609	Skarshaug Testing Laboratory Inc—John Miller	505 S Bell Ave, Ames IA 50010	515-292-1422	R	3*	<.1
610	Gordon J Gow Technologies—Joseph Perfito	6448 Pinecastle Blvd S, Orlando FL 32809	407-855-0497	R	3*	<.1
611	Manufacturing Systems and Equipment Inc—Charles Earhart	2812 Chamber Dr, Monroe NC 28110	704-283-2086	R	3*	<.1
612	Sai Inc—Robert Shannon	2595 24th Ave N, Saint Petersburg FL 33713	727-323-4300	R	3*	<.1
613	Atlantic Controls Corp—Anthony Brown	107a 11th St, Saint Augustine FL 32080	904-460-9112	R	3*	<.1
614	Aes Electric Supply Inc—Nancy Trunnell	3350 Trailer St, Fairbanks AK 99709	907-474-2075	R	3*	<.1
615	Integrated Power Sources Of Virginia Inc—Steven Schenkelberger	2260 Dabney Rd, Richmond VA 23230	804-359-9471	R	3*	<.1
616	Distributor Sales Southwest Inc—Richard Near	8221 Chancellor Row, Dallas TX 75247	214-630-0200	R	3*	<.1
617	Porter's Electric Motor Service Inc—Heyward Porter	PO Box 429, Gaffney SC 29342	864-487-7551	R	3*	<.1
618	Powerfields—Jim Williams	3520 Arthur St, Caldwell ID 83605		R	3*	<.1
619	Seco-Larm USA Inc—S Hwang	16842 Millikan Ave, Irvine CA 92606	949-261-2999	R	3*	<.1
620	Electri-Products Group Inc—Phillip Hedrick	PO Box 18009, Greensboro NC 27419	336-294-6230	R	3*	<.1
621	Fischer Panda Generators Inc—Anthony Rushton	4345 Ne 12th Ter, Oakland Park FL 33334	954-462-2800	R	3*	<.1
622	Sec Electrical Inc—Robert Davis	100 Messina Dr Ste H, Braintree MA 02184	781-848-2111	R	3*	<.1

Rank	Company Name—Executive Officer	Address, City, State, Zip	Phone	Type	Fin	Empls
623	Firepower Inc—Bartley Onoday	10220 N Nevada St Ste, Spokane WA 99218	509-468-3204	R	3*	<.1
624	Kay Electric Supply Company Inc—Linda Deneberg	317 Ridge Pke, Conshohocken PA 19428	610-825-0100	R	3*	<.1
625	Service Trade Corp—John Novales	10250 Nw 89th Ave Ste, Medley FL 33178	305-882-1766	R	3*	<.1
626	Keystone Wire And Cable—Michael Schmittinger	2704 Lawing Ln Ste 300, Rowlett TX 75088	972-412-7239	R	3*	<.1
627	Brenaman Electrical Service Inc—Lester Brenaman	PO Box 5, Mount Joy PA 17552	717-653-1910	R	3*	<.1
628	Electric Battery Company LLC	17815 Eveleth Rd, Jamaica NY 11434	718-978-1900	R	3*	<.1
629	Discount Plumbing and Electrical Supply—Susie Brake	101 Century Ct, Franklin TN 37064	615-794-1068	R	3*	<.1
630	All Electric and Specialty Systems Inc—Rachel All	1712 Frost Dr, Savannah GA 31404	912-238-9005	R	3*	<.1
631	Ssi Cable Corp—Kent Gilchrist	820 E Hiawatha Blvd, Shelton WA 98584	360-426-5719	R	3*	<.1
632	Tri Power Mpt Inc—Richard Wiley	1447 S Main St, Akron OH 44301	330-773-3307	R	3*	<.1
633	Heights Armature Works Inc—Barbara Segal	12250 Taylor Rd, Houston TX 77041	713-869-3356	R	3*	<.1
634	Utica Valley Electric Supply Company Inc—Lawrence Thibault	PO Box 230, Yorkville NY 13495	315-732-5197	R	3*	<.1
635	P and S Electric Supply Company Inc—Ernest Pugh	505 Smyrna Rd Sw, Conyers GA 30012	770-922-6101	R	3*	<.1
636	Manning Electric Inc—Daniel Manning	154 27th St, Brooklyn NY 11232	718-832-2488	R	3*	<.1
637	Eagle Engineering and Supply Co—Curtis Eagle	101 N Industrial Hwy, Alpena MI 49707	989-356-4526	R	3*	<.1
638	Fire Control Electrical Systems Inc—Vincent Bianco	320 Essex St Ste 3, Stirling NJ 07980	908-756-3700	R	3*	<.1
639	Jo El Electric Supply Co—Ted Barry	615 Strong Hwy, El Dorado AR 71730	870-863-5555	R	3*	<.1
640	Florida Bulb and Ballast Inc—Brenna Hoffman	1617 Cooling St, Melbourne FL 32935	321-259-7882	R	3*	<.1
641	Advanced Lighting Inc—Bruno Kossin	3099 S 1030 W, Salt Lake City UT 84119	801-972-9530	R	3*	<.1
642	Houston Motor and Control Inc—Philip Land	5210 N Sam Houston Pkw, Houston TX 77032	713-464-3910	R	3*	<.1
643	Pomona Wholesale Electric Inc—Eric Stevens	2120 S Reservoir St, Pomona CA 91766	909-591-8100	R	3*	<.1
644	Fiber Optic Supply Inc—Nichole Cortonmage	740 Clipper Hill Rd, Danville CA 94526	925-362-8378	R	3*	<.1
645	Basin-River Electrical Supply LLC—Kenny Gilbert	PO Box 306, Plaquemine LA 70765	225-687-6391	R	3*	<.1
646	City Lights and Supply Company Inc—Prentice Tuck	5037 Cleveland St, Virginia Beach VA 23462	757-499-4252	R	3*	<.1
647	Beiner Inc—Lance Beiner	PO Box 2214, Camarillo CA 93011	805-650-3008	R	3*	<.1
648	Alton Winlectric Co—Michael Webb	2615 E Broadway, Alton IL 62002	618-462-3112	R	3*	<.1
649	Blc International Inc—Thomas Ciurczak	11266 Monarch St Ste B, Garden Grove CA 92841	714-889-4116	R	3*	<.1
650	Design/Systems Group Inc—Ovid Morphew	402 S Ctr St, Grand Prairie TX 75051	972-262-3332	R	3*	<.1
651	Total Lighting Concepts Inc—Phillip Willhite	733 E San Bernardino R, Covina CA 91723	626-966-1611	R	3*	<.1
652	Lightning Group Northwest—William Howard	PO Box 80585, Seattle WA 98108	206-763-2573	R	3*	<.1
653	Power Equipment Co (Rochester New York)—Mark Kolko	PO Box 20531, Rochester NY 11602	585 235 1662	R	3*	<.1
654	Sterling Electric Corp—Dale Beaumont	8616 Xylon Ave N Ste H, Minneapolis MN 55445	763-493-4900	R	3*	<.1
655	SS Industrial Cable Corp—Claire Sullivan	PO Box 146, Port Washington NY 53074	262-284-8989	R	3*	<.1
656	Lance Wire and Cable Inc—Chris Hulen	2413 Lance Ct, Loganville GA 30052	770-554-3206	R	3*	<.1
657	BL Robinson Electric Supply Co—Garth Workman	2515 Mount Pleasant St, Burlington IA 52601	319-752-4557	R	3*	<.1
658	Blankenship And Associates Inc—David Blankenship	PO Box 13103, Spokane Valley WA 99213	509-535-6006	R	3*	<.1
659	FR Industries Inc—Francois Reizine	557 Long Rd, Pittsburgh PA 15235	412-242-5903	R	3*	<.1
660	Transmission Equipment International Inc—Jim Gambardella	134 S Turnpike Rd, Wallingford CT 06492	203-269-8751	R	3*	<.1
661	Electric Supply Co (Raleigh North Carolina)—KD Kennedy Jr	PO Box 6427, Raleigh NC 27608	919-834-7364	R	3*	<.1
662	Murray Lighting Inc—Mark Thompson	520 N Loop 288, Denton TX 76209	940-387-9571	R	3*	<.1
663	Grand Electrical Equipment and Supply Corp—Pong Leung	71 Allen St 73, New York NY 10002	212-966-8833	R	3*	<.1
664	Valley Lightsource Inc—Mark Havens	1429 N Maple Ave, Fresno CA 93703	559-453-9231	R	3*	<.1
665	Smd Enterprises Inc—Manuel Gomez	2621 S 21st St, Phoenix AZ 85034	602-275-0524	R	3*	<.1
666	Atlantic Telephone and Data Solutions Inc—Dawn Elliott	93 Clark St, Harrington DE 19952	302-398-8505	R	3*	<.1
667	Criterion Cellular—Mike Passantino	PO Box 2460, San Rafael CA 94912	510-223-0233	R	3*	<.1
668	Electrical Systems International LLC	11767 S Dixie Hwy, Miami FL 33156	305-591-5900	R	3*	<.1
669	Marvol Aero International Inc Scott Marvol	20381 Lake Forest Dr B, Lake Forest CA 92630	949-029-0204	R	3*	<.1
670	Applied Quality Test Inc—Karen Ajlouni	1906 Crestmont Dr, San Jose CA 95124	408-531-5300	R	3	<.1
671	Shaztec (USA) Inc—Nadeem Syed	1128 Tabor Ln, Philadelphia PA 19111	215-695-0801	R	3*	<.1
672	Landreth Inc—Tom Landreth	1009 Maitlnd Ctr Cmns, Maitland FL 32751	407-682-6255	R	3*	<.1
673	Elektran Inc—Richard Adams	PO Box 1027, Rockingham NC 28380	910-997-5061	R	3*	<.1
674	Beaudry Electric Motors and Equipment Company Inc—Robert Beaudry	N7317 State Hwy 42, Sheboygan WI 53083	920-565-3993	R	3*	<.1
675	Classic Lighting LP—Bryant Dussetschleger	PO Box 2052, Stafford TX 77497	281-494-0300	R	3*	<.1
676	Putnam Rf Components Inc—David Kane	720 Union St, Manchester NH 03104	603-623-0700	R	3*	<.1
677	Capital Electric Wire And Cable—Michael Harpster	W231n2840 Roundy Cir E, Pewaukee WI 53072	262-650-1400	R	3*	<.1
678	Chicago Lighting Inc—Larry Bisaillon	9854 Farragut St, Rosemont IL 60018	847-671-6200	R	3*	<.1
679	East Coast Electrical Equipment Company Inc—David Pearce	245 Bert Winston Rd, Youngsville NC 27596	919-562-8122	R	3*	<.1
680	Lewis Motor Repair Inc—John Carlson	3015 4th St S, Waite Park MN 56387	320-252-0352	R	3*	<.1
681	Industrial Automation Controls Inc—David Henry	PO Box 161296, Memphis TN 38186	901-345-7000	R	3*	<.1
682	Total Machine Solutions Inc—Marvin Goldman	PO Box 799, Plainview NY 11803	516-942-5125	R	3*	<.1
683	Merchants Paper Co—Anthony Nicola	4625 Se 24th Ave, Portland OR 97202	503-235-2171	R	3*	<.1
684	Jimmy D Hill Inc—Jimmy Hill	226 Calle Pintoresco, San Clemente CA 92672	949-369-8000	R	3*	<.1
685	Seth's Lighting and Accessories Inc—Jeffie Billings	8250 Us Hwy 64, Memphis TN 38133	901-377-5222	R	3*	<.1
686	UL Wholesale Lighting Fixtures Corp—Kyriacos Papastylianou	405 26th Ave Ste 5, Astoria NY 11102	718-726-7500	R	3*	<.1
687	Adcon Engineering Company Inc—Joseph Raftry	20102 Progress Dr Ste, Strongsville OH 44149	440-238-3915	R	3*	<.1
688	Light Bulbs Etc Inc—Colleen Black	14821 W 99th St, Shawnee Mission KS 66215	913-894-9030	R	3*	<.1
689	Warshaw Inc—Howard Elman	893 Shepherd Ave, Brooklyn NY 11208	718-257-2111	R	3*	<.1
690	Continental Lighting Systems Inc—Carmen Sherbert	129 W 29th St Fl 9, New York NY 10001	212-564-6162	R	3*	<.1
691	Lamp Technology Inc—Edith Reuter	1645 Sycamore Ave Ste, Bohemia NY 11716	631-567-1800	R	3*	<.1
692	Powers Generator Service LLC—Sheena Royce	PO Box 10005, Swanzey NH 03446	603-352-9334	R	3*	<.1
693	Viking Representatives Inc—Howard Beresford	192 Clifford St, Newark NJ 07105	973-466-3411	R	3*	<.1
694	Nord's Electric Supply Company Inc—Bert Loucks	PO Box 9550, Spokane WA 99209	509-328-3900	R	3*	<.1
695	Architectural Sales and Illumination Inc—Bruce Myers	1815 University Blvd N, Jacksonville FL 32211	904-744-7000	R	3*	<.1
696	Lumen Power Sources West Inc—Ron Rowe	3198 Soaring Eagle Ln, Castle Rock CO 80109	303-789-3400	R	3*	<.1
697	Kymco USA Inc—Eric Bondy	5 Stan Perkins Rd, Spartanburg SC 29307	864-327-4744	R	3*	<.1
698	National Breaker Services LLC—Bob Fox	298 Hawkins St, Derby CT 06418	203-734-7898	R	3*	<.1
699	PL and E Sales Inc—Michael Folk	200 E Woodlawn Rd Ste, Charlotte NC 28217	704-561-9650	R	3*	<.1
700	Blond Lighting Fixture Supply Company Inc—Gary Loeffel	PO Box 12766, San Antonio TX 78212	210-732-9936	R	3*	<.1
701	Lincoln Winlectric Company Inc—Gary Reese	PO Box 1127, Dayton OH 45401	402-423-3100	R	3*	<.1
702	Murphy's Electric Supply Co—Matt Berry	671 Rudolph Way, Greendale IN 47025	812-537-0222	R	3*	<.1
703	Jenkins and Associates Inc—Dennis Jenkins	1122 Foster Ave Ste 20, Nashville TN 37210	615-256-7606	R	3*	<.1
704	Pittsburgh Wire And Cable Inc—James Carlowski	PO Box 3666, Pittsburgh PA 15230	412-920-7190	R	3*	<.1
705	Electrical Supplies Unlimited Inc—Donald Thomas	PO Box 1179, Buford GA 30515	678-541-0280	R	3*	<.1
706	Westburgh Electric Inc—Daniel Blixt	16 Scott St, Jamestown NY 14701	716-488-1172	R	3*	<.1
707	Lands Plus Centennial Inc—Jim Finkle	6340 S Sandhill Rd Ste, Las Vegas NV 89120	702-436-3560	R	3*	<.1
708	Pyro-Matic Inc—Lawrence Elliott	11901 W Dearbourn Ave, Milwaukee WI 53226	414-453-1171	R	3*	<.1
709	Rack-Rite Inc—Richard Steggeman	3629 N Teutonia Ave, Milwaukee WI 53206	414-871-5700	R	3*	<.1
710	Hico America—Henry Heungkean	125 Theobold Ave, Greensburg PA 15601	724-834-1202	R	3*	<.1
711	Bill's Electronics Inc—Bill Browning	PO Box 1559, Logan WV 25601	304-752-8667	R	3*	<.1

Note: An asterisk (*) indicates an estimated financial figure. The company type code used is as follows: R = Private, P = Public, S = Private Subsidiary, B = Public Subsidiary, D = Division, J = Joint Venture, I = Investment Fund.

COMPANY RANKINGS BY SALES WITHIN 4-DIGIT SIC

Rank	Company Name—*Executive Officer*	Address, City, State, Zip	Phone	Type	Fin	Empls
712	Arrow Battert Edco—*Randy Banker*	PO Box 3212, Dayton OH 45401	937-223-4149	R	3*	<.1
713	Colacino Industries Inc—*Jim Colacino*	126 Harrison St Ste A, Newark NY 14513	315-331-1330	R	3*	<.1
714	Great Valley Systems Corp—*Dominic Macchione*	PO Box 368, Uwchland PA 19480	610-458-8202	R	3*	<.1
715	Light Source—*Daniel Shea*	355 E 2100 S, Salt Lake City UT 84115	801-487-2020	R	3*	<.1
716	Aim Electronics Distributors Inc—*James Dunn*	160 Bordentown Rd, Bristol PA 19007	215-946-3900	R	3*	<.1
717	Roy's Electric Motor Service Inc—*Winston Dowell*	3201 Norfolk St, Richmond VA 23230	804-355-5713	R	3*	<.1
718	Electro-Sense Of Pennsylvania Inc—*Peter Smith*	2216 Pottstown Pke, Pottstown PA 19465	610-469-0850	R	3*	<.1
719	Klode Co—*Fritz Klode*	9313 Glacier Rdg, Richmond IL 60071	815-678-6700	R	3*	<.1
720	Partex Marking Systems Inc—*Janet Szigeti*	770 N Church Rd Ste A, Elmhurst IL 60126	630-516-0400	R	3*	<.1
721	Verifier Inc—*Addi Aloya*	7280 W Palmetto Park R, Boca Raton FL 33433	561-910-3980	R	3*	<.1
722	Alarm Security—*Richard Lail*	441 Church St, Peak SC 29122	803-345-5052	R	2*	<.1
723	Colorado Fastners Inc—*Graeme Doyle*	PO Box 279, Edwards CO 81632	970-926-3301	R	2*	<.1
724	Tapco Circuit Supply Inc—*Todd Palmer*	13200 10th Ave N Ste E, Plymouth MN 55441	763-513-7300	R	2*	<.1
725	AcmelitesCom Inc—*Daniel Rhoades*	12150 W 44th Ave Unit, Wheat Ridge CO 80033	303-456-9700	R	2*	<.1
726	Rj Technologies Group LLC—*Jeff Cobb*	123 Se Pky Ct Ste 100, Franklin TN 37064	615-366-3411	R	2*	<.1
727	A and E International Inc—*Lim Hwang*	432 Park Ave S Ste 130, New York NY 10016	212-490-6794	R	2*	<.1
728	American Auto Wire Systems Inc—*Michael Manning*	150 Heller Pl 17w, Bellmawr NJ 08031	856-933-9301	R	2*	<.1
729	Consolidated Electrical Distributors Inc—*H Bursch*	2904 N Hibiscus St, Pharr TX 78577	956-702-3530	R	2*	<.1
730	Georgia Electric Supply Inc—*Wendell Fetzer*	19 Westgate Blvd, Savannah GA 31405	912-236-1840	R	2*	<.1
731	Industrial Automation Supply Inc—*Christopher Lebel*	75 Industrial Way, Portland ME 04103	207-797-2345	R	2*	<.1
732	Professional Lighting and Supply Inc—*Rebecca Phillips*	412 Gallimore Dairy Rd, Greensboro NC 27409	336-605-5888	R	2*	<.1
733	Calkins Electric Supply Company Inc—*Wendi Levitt*	PO Box 3498, Shawnee Mission KS 66203	913-631-6363	R	2*	<.1
734	Wagner Electric Of Fort Wayne Inc—*Peter Bell*	3610 N Clinton St, Fort Wayne IN 46805	260-484-5532	R	2*	<.1
735	Tradinter Development Company Inc—*Mario Obeso*	8035 Nw 60th St, Miami FL 33166	305-477-4414	R	2*	<.1
736	WECS Electric Supply Inc—*Bruce Hammett*	PO Box 580276, North Palm Springs CA 92258	760-251-0040	R	2*	<.1
737	United Central Station—*Edward Minicozzi*	111 S St Ste 10, Oyster Bay NY 11771	516-333-9797	R	2*	<.1
738	CGF Design—*Ted Mathews*	PO Box 911, Morton Grove IL 60053	847-470-1411	R	2*	<.1
739	Ceam Corp—*Corey Eisenberg*	490 Jericho Tpke, Mineola NY 11501	516-747-0651	R	2*	<.1
740	Beals Lighting Gallery Inc—*Clyde Beals*	6200 Veterans Pkwy, Columbus GA 31909	706-571-3333	R	2*	<.1
741	Spectrum Lighting Inc—*Rick Vollhardt*	1001 Kinnear Rd, Columbus OH 43212	614-486-5354	R	2*	<.1
742	Supertech Inc—*Steven Hamelin*	79 Rossotto Dr, Hamden CT 06514	203-288-3900	R	2*	<.1
743	Kenneth R Brand—*Kenneth Brand*	PO Box 2292, South Hamilton MA 01982	978-468-4877	R	2*	<.1
744	Spectrum Lighting Ltd—*Bret Reichert*	N8w22520 Johnson Dr St, Waukesha WI 53186	262-970-0300	R	2*	<.1
745	Hcs Electrical Supply LLC—*Stephenie Trescott*	4640 S Decatur Blvd, Las Vegas NV 89103	702-733-1191	R	2*	<.1
746	Source One Distributors Inc—*Randy Cates*	PO Box 701, Winfield KS 67156	620-221-8919	R	2*	<.1
747	Evelec Corp—*D'Kieswetter*	590 E Gutierrez St Ste, Santa Barbara CA 93103	805-963-6519	R	2*	<.1
748	Freelite Inc—*Chester Marvin*	331 W Mcdowell Rd, Phoenix AZ 85003	602-233-1981	R	2*	<.1
749	Gemco Sales Inc—*Jack Lype*	3150 Smallman St, Pittsburgh PA 15201	412-562-9300	R	2*	<.1
750	Hi-Tech Controls and Automation Inc—*Kelly Gains*	3470 S Dixie Hwy, Dalton GA 30720	706-278-1311	R	2*	<.1
751	Suhaimi Inc—*Sunthurs Suhaimi*	417 Agostino Rd, San Gabriel CA 91776	626-287-0700	R	2*	<.1
752	Fagan Associates Inc—*Richard Fagan*	118 Green Bay Rd Ste 6, Thiensville WI 53092	262-242-9120	R	2*	<.1
753	Ecg Industrial Co—*Emilio Cervera*	5823 Northgate Ln Ste, Laredo TX 78041	956-727-3186	R	2*	<.1
754	Nitech Inc—*Paul Alex*	84 Business Park Dr St, Armonk NY 10504	914-273-8727	R	2*	<.1
755	American Electric Supply Inc—*James Hunt*	PO Box 1930, Jonesboro AR 72403	870-932-4591	R	2*	<.1
756	Ltl Supply Inc—*Frank Suring*	2161 Speaker Ct, Green Bay WI 54313	920-434-4999	R	2*	<.1
757	Thomas J Madden and Associates Inc—*Thomas Madden*	935 Hwy 124 Ste 400, Braselton GA 30517	678-963-2060	R	2*	<.1
758	Auto Page Inc—*Michael Northup*	960 Knox St Bldg B, Torrance CA 90502	310-323-1800	R	2*	<.1
759	Gemini Circuits Inc—*Avinash Ayachit*	11510 S Petropark Dr, Houston TX 77041	713-849-5000	R	2*	<.1
760	County Electrical Distributors Inc—*Jim Martin*	100 Londonderry Ct Ste, Woodstock GA 30188	770-517-1970	R	2*	<.1
761	FW Kauphusman Inc—*Richard Kauphusman*	10943 W Executive Dr, Boise ID 83713	208-377-1600	R	2*	<.1
762	George E Anderson Company Inc—*Howard Butcher*	1700 S Ervay St, Dallas TX 75215	214-428-3731	R	2*	<.1
763	Penncat Corp—*Jerry Kane*	432 N Spring Garden St, Ambler PA 19002	610-272-0505	R	2*	<.1
764	Sail Electric Inc—*Shawn Barton*	911 Slater Rd, Bellingham WA 98226	360-383-0911	R	2*	<.1
765	Flowstar Corp—*Debbie Currier*	6800 Silacci Way, Gilroy CA 95020	408-842-2400	R	2*	<.1
766	Tasco Industries Inc—*Thomas Miller*	13885 Ramona Ave, Chino CA 91710	909-396-6139	R	2*	<.1
767	IBS Of Central Mass Inc—*Ken Machonis*	PO Box 169, Millbury MA 01527	508-791-7904	R	2*	<.1
768	Pinmax Corp—*Zev Herman*	3530 Nw 53rd St, Fort Lauderdale FL 33309	954-733-4511	R	2*	<.1
769	LW French Inc—*Larry French*	4470 Cox Rd Ste 100, Glen Allen VA 23060	804-270-3205	R	2*	<.1
770	OT Hall And Sons Inc—*Dale Hall*	8370 Veterans Hwy Ste, Millersville MD 21108	410-987-5990	R	2*	<.1
771	Spectrum Lighting Group Inc—*Robert Pierce*	807 Pressley Rd Ste 41, Charlotte NC 28217	704-522-8066	R	2*	<.1
772	Cascade Western Representatives Inc—*Richard Betts*	PO Box 42370, Portland OR 97242	503-238-8800	R	2*	<.1
773	Gary Edmunds Inc—*Gary Edmunds*	1271 N Wishon Ave, Fresno CA 93728	559-266-0433	R	2*	<.1
774	Intraline Inc—*Pete Varma*	379 Beach Rd, Burlingame CA 94010	650-340-9133	R	2*	<.1
775	Jdc Power Systems Inc—*James Roselle*	84 Busineny Pk Dr Ste, Armonk NY 10504	914-773-1234	R	2*	<.1
776	Magna Electric Supply Company Inc—*John Sebek*	15644 Cicero Ave, Oak Forest IL 60452	708-560-7700	R	2*	<.1
777	Fast Action Alarms—*Robert Spetta*	56 Enter Ln, Islandia NY 11749	631-582-5641	R	2*	<.1
778	Ag Crystal Lighting Inc—*Enayat Elkadi*	PO Box 658, Englishtown NJ 07726	732-251-2727	R	2*	<.1
779	United Electrical Sales Ltd—*Robin Clement*	4496 36th St, Orlando FL 32811	407-246-1992	R	2*	<.1
780	Minnick Supply Company Inc—*Gary Minnick*	PO Box 470, Chillicothe MO 64601	660-646-5390	R	2*	<.1
781	Power Now LLC	PO Box 1535, Cypress TX 77410	832-448-0478	R	2*	<.1
782	Precision Lighting Company Inc—*Richard Kahn*	8407 Pinehurst Dr, Tampa FL 33615	813-889-0578	R	2*	<.1
783	Wild West Lighting Inc—*Sam Kramer*	15550 N 84th St Ste 20, Scottsdale AZ 85260	480-368-9909	R	2*	<.1
784	Electric Motor Rewind Of Rupert Idaho Inc—*Kevin Thurston*	214 S Hwy 24, Rupert ID 83350	208-436-4658	R	2*	<.1
785	JV Int'l Trading Corp—*Javier Vila*	13935 Sw 252nd St, Princeton FL 33032	305-257-1497	R	2*	<.1
786	OMJC Signal Inc—*Arlen Yost*	403 Chestnut St, Waterloo IA 50703	319-236-0200	R	2*	<.1
787	Salinger Electric Co—*LN Cotsonika*	1755 E Maple Rd, Troy MI 48083	248-585-8330	R	2*	<.1
788	Battery Specialties Inc—*Gerald Kanen*	3530 Cadillac Ave, Costa Mesa CA 92626	714-755-0888	R	2*	<.1
789	Coley Electric and Plumbing Supply Of Jesup Inc—*Henry Coley*	1285 W Pine St, Jesup GA 31545	912-427-4985	R	2*	<.1
790	Ems Weeks Inc—*Mike Genechten*	1057 Cottage Grove St, Grand Rapids MI 49507	616-243-8866	R	2*	<.1
791	Franklite Corp—*Abraham Gaies*	PO Box 297, Troy NY 12181	518-274-6931	R	2*	<.1
792	Rouzer Sales Company Inc—*Tony Blinkhorn*	2738 Winnetka Ave N St, Minneapolis MN 55427	763-544-3145	R	2*	<.1
793	A-Max Wire and Cable Inc—*Stuart Fiedelman*	990 Richard Ave Ste 11, Santa Clara CA 95050	408-727-3234	R	2*	<.1
794	Automation Control Company Inc—*James Gerald*	11914 Cloverland Ct, Baton Rouge LA 70809	225-752-0337	R	2*	<.1
795	Griesser Sales Company Inc—*John Smith*	2163 Saint Clair Ave N, Cleveland OH 44114	216-771-6120	R	2*	<.1
796	Innovative Energy Systems—*Doug Keller*	PO Box 5047, Baltimore MD 21220	410-344-1800	R	2*	<.1
797	Intelligent Products Company Inc—*Dale Perry*	1178 Industry Rd, Lexington KY 40505	859-259-0692	R	2*	<.1
798	Lensco Inc—*Duane Willoughby*	PO Box 660549, Birmingham AL 35266	205-328-0064	R	2*	<.1
799	Service Electric Supply Company Inc—*Larry Stickell*	PO Box 5022, Alexandria LA 71307	318-445-7176	R	2*	<.1
800	Star and Son Electric Supply Company Inc—*Ronald Star*	719 Hempstead Tpke, Franklin Square NY 11010	516-538-1432	R	2*	<.1

Rank	Company Name—*Executive Officer*	Address, City, State, Zip	Phone	Type	Fin	Empls
801	Colorado Wire and Cable Company Inc—*Les Anderson*	485 Osage St, Denver CO 80204	303-534-0114	R	2*	<.1
802	Ideal Lighting Inc—*Anthony Rose*	812 Little Farms Ave, Metairie LA 70003	504-737-7176	R	2*	<.1
803	Precision Lighting Systems Inc—*Jay Blumer*	114 Lacey St, Hot Springs AR 71913	501-624-5566	R	2*	<.1
804	White Electric Supply Co (Lincoln Nebraska)—*Logan Ireland*	PO Box 83007, Lincoln NE 68501	402-476-7687	S	2*	<.1
805	Specialty Control Systems Inc—*L Jay Armstrong*	629 Hwy 3 S, League City TX 77573	281-332-0999	R	2*	<.1
806	Peninsula Battery Inc—*Nick Plist*	1139 Airport Blvd, South San Francisco CA 94080	650-583-6735	R	2*	<.1
807	Cd Pro-Power Cords Inc—*Clayton Diekman*	6842 Washington Ave S, Eden Prairie MN 55344	952-944-1044	R	2*	<.1
808	Springfield Electric Supply Company Inc—*Benjamin Brown*	888 Supaex Blvd Ste 1, Broomall PA 19008	610-544-4180	R	2*	<.1
809	State Electrical Supply Inc—*Ellen Ramberg*	509 W Milwaukee St, Janesville WI 53548	608-752-9451	R	2*	<.1
810	Instrument Engineers—*Jimm Hoffmann*	12335 World Trade Dr S, San Diego CA 92128	858-673-3644	R	2*	<.1
811	Lee Butter and Associates Inc—*Lee Butter*	20 Lively Blvd Ste 200, Elk Grove Village IL 60007	847-437-7600	R	2*	<.1
812	Rpm Industrial Sales LLC	PO Box 180074, Delafield WI 53018	262-524-0746	R	2*	<.1
813	Safety House of Southwest Louisiana LLC—*Kay Boyette*	801 E Prien Lake Rd, Lake Charles LA 70601	337-477-7878	R	2*	<.1
814	Bestec Inc—*Jerry Mangum*	PO Box 40005, Raleigh NC 27629	919-790-8988	R	2*	<.1
815	Donald Masi—*Don Masi*	1 Sunnie Ter, West Caldwell NJ 07006	973-618-6288	R	2*	<.1
816	Dynamic Bar Code Systems Inc—*Bill Gregory Jr*	2106 Florence Ave, Cincinnati OH 45206	513-272-1010	R	2*	<.1
817	Kohyo Telecommunications Inc—*Gary Maeda*	2281 W 205th St Ste 10, Torrance CA 90501	310-787-0632	R	2*	<.1
818	Sentex Corp—*Jacques Franque*	5869 S Kyrene Rd Ste1, Tempe AZ 85283	480-705-4022	R	2*	<.1
819	Utility Sales And Engineering Services LLC	7508 New Lgrange Rd St, Louisville KY 40222	502-412-2838	R	2*	<.1
820	Metro Fire Detection LLC—*Tim Gilmore*	1267 S Lipan St, Denver CO 80223	303-457-8088	R	2*	<.1
821	Teco Electric Motors Inc—*William Overton*	4640 International Tra, Richmond VA 23231	804-226-1600	R	2*	<.1
822	Atlantic Montana Corp—*Marcello Occhionero*	1027 Sw 30th Ave, Deerfield Beach FL 33442	305-613-5876	R	2*	<.1
823	DM Mattson Inc—*Kim Mattson*	2241 N 200 E Rd, Mc Lean IL 61754	309-874-2700	R	2*	<.1
824	Olympia Lighting Center Inc—*Joseph Heerensperger*	2633 Martin Way E, Olympia WA 98506	360-956-1953	R	2*	<.1
825	Electric Control and Supply Inc—*Herbert Hobgood*	300 Buckner Rd, Columbia SC 29203	803-691-9600	R	2*	<.1
826	Fire Alarm Control Systems Inc—*Duane Hannasch*	12961 Park Central Ste, San Antonio TX 78216	210-344-2901	R	2*	<.1
827	New Hippodrome Hardware Inc—*Aaron Landsman*	PO Box 1022, New York NY 10002	212-840-2791	R	2*	<.1
828	Yuma Winlectric Co—*Robert Goin*	PO Box 489, Yuma AZ 85366	928-782-9258	R	2*	<.1
829	A Special Electric Service And Supply Co—*Robert Lehman*	230 W Irving Park Rd, Wood Dale IL 60191	630-595-7670	R	2*	<.1
830	Bloomfield Electrical Supply Company Inc—*William Kent*	PO Box 686, Bloomfield NJ 07003	973-743-3441	R	2*	<.1
831	Cmd Powersystems Inc—*William Perry*	42 Daves Way, Hermon ME 04401	207-848-7702	R	2*	<.1
832	Hoover Instrument Service Inc—*Lowell Weeks*	401 Home Rd N, Ontario OH 44906	419-529-3226	R	2*	<.1
833	Central Communications Systems Inc—*Vincent Maiuri*	420 Boston Tpke Ste 20, Shrewsbury MA 01545	774-670-0500	R	2*	<.1
834	Electrol Systems Inc—*Art Meiners*	433 Recoleta Rd, San Antonio TX 78216	210-599-6485	R	2*	<.1
835	Joe Fox Wholesale Electric and Lighting Inc—*Joseph La-lezarian*	5074 Santa Monica Blvd, Los Angeles CA 90029	323-665-8000	R	2*	<.1
836	Light Lines Inc—*Bradt Kirsti*	3337 Rauch St, Houston TX 77029	713-673-7502	R	2*	<.1
837	Remote Connections Inc—*Joyce Randolph*	PO Box 52066, Tulsa OK 74152	918-743-3355	R	2*	<.1
838	Rocky Mountain Power Generation Inc—*David Coxson*	6301 Broadway, Denver CO 80216	303-428-3611	R	2*	<.1
839	Ward and Jacobs Inc—*Stephen Ward*	130 W Monroe Ave, Saint Louis MO 63122	314-821-7800	R	2*	<.1
840	S and B Electric Supply Corp—*Glen Bessner*	255 Kings Hwy, Brooklyn NY 11223	718-266-0432	R	2*	<.1
841	Uusco Of Illinois Inc—*Laura Pold*	395 Industrial Dr Ste, West Chicago IL 60185	630-231-1680	R	2*	<.1
842	Energy Efficient Motors and Controls Inc—*Dennis Conner*	7755 Pinemont Dr, Houston TX 77040	713-460-3600	R	2*	<.1
843	Eastern Industries Group Inc—*Fred Martin*	3411 Bernese Ct, Carson City NV 89705	775-267-4425	R	2*	<.1
844	Vehicle Lighting Solutions Inc—*David Gant*	12577 S 265 W Ste 1a, Draper UT 84020	801-676-4983	R	2*	<.1
845	Big City Sales Inc—*Carol Fortner*	6 Dyke Rd, Setauket NY 11733	631-751-3502	R	2*	<.1
846	Allied Battery Systems—*Cory Thettoll*	2580 N Orange Blossom, Kissimmee FL 34744	407-846-6070	R	2*	<.1
847	Baker Outlet—*Dennis Robins*	1088 N Robertson Rd, Casper WY 82604	307-234-5772	R	2*	<.1
848	Dawn Communications Inc—*John Joslin*	3340 S Lapeer Rd, Orion MI 48359	248-391-9200	R	2*	<.1
849	Greenlite Lighting Corporation USA—*Tarana Gupta*	10 Corporate Park Ste, Irvine CA 92606	949-261-5300	R	2*	<.1
850	Laser Electric Supply Inc—*Marlene Liberman*	PO Box 337, Walworth WI 53184	262-275-5775	R	2*	<.1
851	Related Components Inc—*Henry Kornatoski*	3186 Plainfield Rd, Dayton OH 45432	937-253-6116	R	2*	<.1
852	SFRT Inc—*Lou Becker*	PO Box 587, Toledo OH 43697	419-321-6787	R	2*	<.1
853	All Pro Sales Inc—*David Johansen*	9033 Premier Row, Dallas TX 75247	214-905-0052	R	2*	<.1
854	All Star Lighting Supplies Inc—*George Pscherhofer*	33 Randolph Ave, Avenel NJ 07001	732-882-1500	R	2*	<.1
855	Lakeville Winlectric Co—*Josh Garrahe*	21653 Cedar Ave Ste 1, Lakeville MN 55044	952-985-7072	R	2*	<.1
856	Marion Industrial Electric Supply Inc—*Michael Lugg*	202 N State St, Marion OH 43302	740-387-0009	R	2*	<.1
857	Standard Magneto Sales Company Inc—*Lottie Malinowski*	4119 W Grand Ave 25, Chicago IL 60651	773-235-2010	R	2*	<.1
858	Angel Vincent Inc—*Kark Vincent*	2910 Torrence Dr, Greensboro NC 27406	336-273-3628	R	2*	<.1
859	CSS Alarms and Services Inc—*John Tipps*	6949 Charlotte Pke Ste, Nashville TN 37209	615-356-2101	R	2*	<.1
860	M and L Enterprises Inc—*Linda Guillot*	5936 Las Positas Rd, Livermore CA 94551	925-456-9890	R	2*	<.1
861	PC Electrocraft Inc—*Frank Colaruotolo*	725 W Battery St Ste D, San Pedro CA 90731	310-832-2064	R	2*	<.1
862	Sat Pak Communications Inc—*Bill Park*	1492 N 6th St, Redmond OR 97756	541-923-0467	R	2*	<.1
863	Specialty Optical Systems Inc—*Sandra Petty*	PO Box 740813, Dallas TX 75374	214-340-8574	R	2*	<.1
864	Ventura Protection Inc—*Douglas Sullivan*	31139 Via Colinas Ste, Westlake Village CA 91362	805-379-1200	R	2*	<.1
865	Kelburn Engineering Co—*Don Fries*	851 N Industrial Dr, Elmhurst IL 60126	630-930-5700	R	2*	<.1
866	Magnetics Test Lab—*Thuy Tran*	1816 Railroad St, Corona CA 92880	951-270-0215	R	2*	<.1
867	Energy Saving Technology Inc—*Howard Hanson*	PO Box 85, Sauk City WI 53583	608-643-5000	R	2*	<.1
868	Associated Battery Co—*Dwight Hobbs*	PO Box 1590, Indian Trail NC 28079	704-821-8311	R	2*	<.1
869	Hardware Electric and Plumbing Supply Company Inc—*Hugh Corry*	PO Box 950, Lebanon MO 65536	417-532-9183	R	2*	<.1
870	Safety Systems Specialist Inc—*Juan Rodriguez*	PO Box 830383, Miami FL 33283	305-262-6163	R	2*	<.1
871	American Battery Corp—*Dennis Loso*	525 W Washington Ave, Escondido CA 92025	760-746-8010	R	2*	<.1
872	Dcpande Inc—*Wilson Clifton*	PO Box 613, Dickson TN 37056	615-446-2895	R	2*	<.1
873	Everglades Electric Supply Inc—*Ronnie Martin*	841 Ne 44th St, Oakland Park FL 33334	954-772-4526	R	2*	<.1
874	Mccomb Electric Supply Company Inc—*Stephanie Moore*	PO Box 707, Mccomb MS 39649	601-684-1160	R	2*	<.1
875	Ramapo Lighting and Electric Supplies Inc—*Abe Shwartz*	32 S Central Ave, Spring Valley NY 10977	845-425-7750	R	2*	<.1
876	Lighting Virginia LLC—*Carter Adams*	400 Southlake Blvd Ste, Richmond VA 23236	804-379-7777	R	2*	<.1
877	Parker Power Systems Inc—*Charles Parker*	1540 Valwood Pkwy, Carrollton TX 75006	972-484-9044	R	2*	<.1
878	Wholesale Lighting Inc—*Cliff Vest*	PO Box 16039, Memphis TN 38186	901-345-9550	R	2*	<.1
879	Tri-County Electrical Supply Inc—*Joanna Bisler*	175 Jacksonville Rd, Warminster PA 18974	215-443-8300	R	2*	<.1
880	American Connectors Inc—*Robert Findley*	2006 Martin Luther Kin, Fort Worth TX 76104	817-535-6268	R	2*	<.1
881	A J's Power Source Inc—*James Vaupel*	PO Box 1459, Land O Lakes FL 34639	813-996-2583	R	2*	<.1
882	Ansaldo Energy Inc—*Giuseppe Zampini*	188 State Rte 1 Ste 32, East Hanover NJ 07936	973-781-1500	R	2*	<.1
883	Applied Machine and Motion Control Inc—*David Locke*	617 N Wayne Ave Fl 2n, Cincinnati OH 45215	513-769-1111	R	2*	<.1
884	Automatic Control Systems Inc—*Edith Alexander*	PO Box 1516, Port Washington NY 11050	516-944-9498	R	2*	<.1
885	Databahn Inc—*Edward Lindsley*	14812 Venture Dr, Dallas TX 75234	972-620-1430	R	2*	<.1
886	Davis Flourescent—*Dan Davis*	8530 Venice Blvd, Los Angeles CA 90034	310-836-4860	R	2*	<.1
887	GN Inc—*Sharlotte Nolen*	115 E Chestnut St, Gadsden AL 35903	256-547-0542	R	2*	<.1
888	Jayborl Inc—*John Brown*	4704 L B Mcleod Rd, Orlando FL 32811	407-839-6261	R	2*	<.1

Note: An asterisk (*) indicates an estimated financial figure. The company type code used is as follows: R = Private, P = Public, S = Private Subsidiary, B = Public Subsidiary, D = Division, J = Joint Venture, I = Investment Fund.

COMPANY RANKINGS BY SALES WITHIN 4-DIGIT SIC

Rank	Company Name—Executive Officer	Address, City, State, Zip	Phone	Type	Fin	Empls
889	Lincoln Service LLC—Mike Jozwyak	11862 Brookfield St, Livonia MI 48150	810-230-0808	R	2*	<.1
890	Menage Automation Inc—Jeff Fisher	10600 S De Anza Blvd, Cupertino CA 95014	408-257-4406	R	2*	<.1
891	Breaker And Control Company Inc—Thad Davis	8151 Almeda Genoa Rd, Houston TX 77075	713-991-0444	R	2*	<.1
892	Everything Electric Inc—Robert Dow	3874 State Rte 11, Malone NY 12953	518-483-9740	R	2*	<.1
893	Liberty Electric Sales Inc—Ed McMahon	6602 Joy Rd, East Syracuse NY 13057	315-437-8100	R	2*	<.1
894	Lighting Dynamics Inc—Kevin Wood	211 Springside Dr, Akron OH 44333	330-665-9090	R	2*	<.1
895	Security Consulting Services Inc—Jeffrey Siproin	PO Box 2723, Farmington Hills MI 48333	248-788-0898	R	2*	<.1
896	Stuart Electric Supply Inc—Harry Irvine	3003 S 300 W, Salt Lake City UT 84115	801-466-8603	R	2*	<.1
897	ECS International Inc—Jeff Edwards	5500 E Loop 820 S Ste, Fort Worth TX 76119	817-483-8497	R	2*	<.1
898	Alarm Digital Telecommunications Corp—Nancy Ascanio	2522 Sw 113th Ct, Miami FL 33165	305-207-9974	R	2*	<.1
899	Power Quality Equipment Inc—Randy Rumley	13501 100th Ave Ne 517, Kirkland WA 98034	425-820-8660	R	2*	<.1
900	Powerhouse Battery Inc—Michael Clark	5725 Polk St, Houston TX 77023	713-923-2246	R	2*	<.1
901	Gene Oswald Co—David Vest	519 N Hydraulic St, Wichita KS 67214	316-263-7191	R	2*	<.1
902	JH Castro Designs Corp—Angelica Rodriguez	9705 Klingerman St, South El Monte CA 91733	626-448-5956	R	2*	<.1
903	Don Dennis And Associates Inc—Dennis Don	125 Baker St E Ste 175, Costa Mesa CA 92626	714-957-0844	R	2*	<.1
904	C and D Factory Direct Inc—Jeff Fisher	6601 E Adamo Dr, Tampa FL 33619	813-621-3338	R	2*	<.1
905	G and M Electric Sales Company Inc—George Pappas	PO Box 19063, New Orleans LA 70179	504-586-8100	R	2*	<.1
906	Golden Fortune Semiconductor Inc—James Wang	3350 Scott Blvd Bldg 4, Santa Clara CA 95054	408-988-0822	R	2*	<.1
907	Lighting Gallery LLC—Gordon Smith	4113 S Access Rd, Chattanooga TN 37406	423-629-1427	R	2*	<.1
908	Roanoke Electric Zupply Inc—Robert Zimmerman	PO Box 1031, Roanoke VA 24005	540-982-8564	R	2*	<.1
909	Protection Systems Technologies Inc—Bryan Futch	PO Box 411821, Charlotte NC 28241	704-525-8905	R	2*	<.1
910	Superior Electrical and Electronic Distributors Co—Millie Tonarely	2121 Nw 79th Ave, Doral FL 33122	305-591-9606	R	2*	<.1
911	A L Pickens Company Inc—Mike Klein	2500 Data Dr, Louisville KY 40299	502-491-4215	R	2*	<.1
912	Bulbworks Inc—Dennis Barker	PO Box 586, Succasunna NJ 07876	973-584-7171	R	2*	<.1
913	K and L Wholesale Inc—Keith Wiggins	PO Box 310, Baxley GA 31515	912-367-3664	R	2*	<.1
914	Canoga Electric Supply Company Inc—David Khakshoy	21410 Sherman Way, Canoga Park CA 91303	818-710-8242	R	2*	<.1
915	Midland Electric Supply Inc—Donald Brown	5818 Massachusetts Ave, Indianapolis IN 46218	317-542-1096	R	2*	<.1
916	Mid-West Electrical Supply Inc—Randy Cubbage	925 N Mosley St, Wichita KS 67214	316-265-0562	R	2*	<.1
917	Sancor Lighting Inc—John Pecora	PO Box 314, Millwood NY 10546	914-941-5511	R	2*	<.1
918	Horsepower Sales—Terry Smith	7222 Pine St, Cincinnati OH 45216	513-821-0444	R	2*	<.1
919	Memeco Sales and Service Corp—Donald Jenkinson	6600 N Lincoln Ave Ste, Lincolnwood IL 60712	847-329-9393	R	2*	<.1
920	Penn Yan Plumbing And Heating Inc—Donald D'amico	100 Horizon Park Dr, Penn Yan NY 14527	315-536-2541	R	2*	<.1
921	Eja International—William O'hara	PO Box 1506, Englewood Cliffs NJ 07632	201-568-2930	R	2*	<.1
922	Medina Electric—Rey Medina	13823 Perthshire Rd, Houston TX 77079	281-496-4803	R	2*	<.1
923	Smp Services—Mike Morrison	2645 Aero Dr, Grand Prairie TX 75052	972-206-2133	R	1*	<.1
924	Lee Baxter Enterprises Inc—Richard Smith	219 Anderson St Ste 1, Portland ME 04101	207-774-2336	R	1*	<.1
925	AR Neubauer Inc—Andrew Neubauer	333 Mendocino Way, Discovery Bay CA 94505	925-449-1932	R	1*	<.1
926	Kirker Kubala Inc—Paul Kubala	4004 Commercial Blvd S, Cincinnati OH 45245	513-753-5400	R	1*	<.1
927	Viking Industrial Electric Inc—Mark Wolfe	10851 Capital St, Oak Park MI 48237	248-547-7730	R	1*	<.1
928	Appalachian Electrical Supply Inc—Shannon Wells	PO Box 276, Rush KY 41168	606-436-8544	R	1*	<.1
929	Lighting and Design Inc—Bob Sprague	Whipple Ave Nw Ste 660, Canton OH 44720	330-966-1314	R	1*	<.1
930	Stat-Comp Inc—Jim Gilloth	1977 Safari Trl, Saint Paul MN 55122	612-616-6699	R	1*	<.1
931	Tri Star Industrial Lighting Inc—Henry Giurini	9500 Ogden Ave Ste F, Brookfield IL 60513	708-485-6300	R	1*	<.1
932	Capital Wholesale Lighting and Electric Supply Inc—Abraham Pouldian	5812 Washington Blvd, Culver City CA 90232	323-937-4444	R	1*	<.1
933	Lighting Solutions Of Illinois Inc—Stephen Davis	703 Childs St, Wheaton IL 60187	630-462-0230	R	1*	<.1
934	Poklar Power And Motion Inc—Thomas Daddario	PO Box 497, Wickliffe OH 44092	440-585-2121	R	1*	<.1
935	Bosco Inc—Scott Boswell	180 Paradise Blvd, Athens GA 30607	706-613-8163	R	1*	<.1
936	Dixie Electrical Supply Company Inc—Steve Rogers	2795 Goodwin Ave, Crestview FL 32539	850-682-1230	R	1*	<.1
937	Kehoe Electronic and Electrical Products Co—Thomas Kehoe	803 Gateway Pkwy, Marble Falls TX 78654	830-693-5599	R	1*	<.1
938	Row Electrical Equipment Inc—J Row	PO Box 2812, Toledo OH 43606	419-248-4479	R	1*	<.1
939	Steel City Lighting Co—Kurt Allerman	9001 Dutton Dr, Twinsburg OH 44087	330-963-4484	R	1*	<.1
940	Tamini Transformers USA—Frank Damico	2803 Bttrfeld Rd Ste 3, Oak Brook IL 60523	630-368-9907	R	1*	<.1
941	Frabil Industries Inc—William Hollingworth	PO Box 970, Hartwell GA 30643	770-887-4006	R	1*	<.1
942	Cnn Electronics Inc—Fred Whiting	5 Orchard Ter, Clark NJ 07066	732-388-0848	R	1*	<.1
943	Starlight—Annon Barnea	327 Washington Ave, Hackensack NJ 07601	201-968-0300	R	1*	<.1
944	Ajk Electric Company Inc—Joseph Raccuia	224 Washington St, Perth Amboy NJ 08861	732-826-6501	R	1*	<.1
945	Baco Controls Inc—Thomas Rogers	PO Box 570, Cazenovia NY 13035	315-655-8372	R	1*	<.1
946	M and M Lighting Sales Inc—Tim Gebel	8191 Birchwood Ct Unit, Johnston IA 50131	515-727-0676	R	1*	<.1
947	Parasense Inc—Peter Radford	PO Box 1444, Madison VA 22727	540-948-9919	R	1*	<.1
948	Quinn Andersen Inc—Joseph Quinn	701 Decatur Ave N Ste, Minneapolis MN 55427	763-544-5451	R	1*	<.1
949	Raztech Lighting LLC	980 990 Richard Rd, Dyer IN 46311	219-322-8800	R	1*	<.1
950	Automatic Door Service Of Grand Rapids Inc—Nathan Nymeyer	2464 Fuller Ave Ne, Grand Rapids MI 49505	616-363-6554	R	1*	<.1
951	Integra Sales Inc—Richard Bassney	445 W Commercial St St, East Rochester NY 14445	585-328-2110	R	1*	<.1
952	Loyd Armature Works Inc—Gary Hamilton	4754 Ctr Park Blvd, San Antonio TX 78218	210-599-4515	R	1*	<.1
953	Unilight Corp—Frank Lalezarian	1824 Lincoln Blvd, Santa Monica CA 90404	310-264-7171	R	1*	<.1
954	Young Power Equipment Company Nm—Randy Sutton	7505 E Greenway Rd, Scottsdale AZ 85260	480-991-9191	R	1*	<.1
955	Energy Efficient Products Company Inc—Steven Riley	659 S Hickory St, Fond Du Lac WI 54935	920-922-7711	R	1*	<.1
956	Field Instruments And Controls Inc—James Sullivan	9629 N Colfax Rd, Spokane WA 99218	509-466-8226	R	1*	<.1
957	Fluorescent Company Of America Inc—Ken Rubenstein	58 Hackensack Ave, Weehawken NJ 07086	201-330-1770	R	1*	<.1
958	Maynard Supply Company Inc—Joseph Calabro	145 Powder Mill Rd, Maynard MA 01754	978-897-9901	R	1*	<.1
959	Optex Technologies Inc—Robert Blair	3882 Del Amo Blvd Ste, Torrance CA 90503	310-214-8644	R	1*	<.1
960	Smoke Detectors Inc—Ronald Feinstein	15002 Delano St, Van Nuys CA 91411	818-989-7377	R	1*	<.1
961	Allcable Inc—Darrel Schultz	PO Box 5405, Oxnard CA 93031	805-981-2553	R	1*	<.1
962	American Electronic Systems Inc—Moses Casielles	2027 Bergenline Ave, Union City NJ 07087	201-348-3663	R	1*	<.1
963	Generator Power Systems—Ivan Tims	292 E Mallory Ave, Memphis TN 38109	901-775-1204	R	1*	<.1
964	Mc Kenney Supply Inc—Frank Mc Kenney	106 E Pleasure Ave, Searcy AR 72143	501-268-8422	R	1*	<.1
965	Motors And Drives LLC—Karin Pinto	262a Quarry Rd, Milford CT 06460	203-877-5828	R	1*	<.1
966	Inelec Corp—Alben Moreno	PO Box 621315, Oviedo FL 32762	407-977-1713	R	1*	<.1
967	Electric Parts and Service Co—Eleanor Huprich	5075 Taylor Dr Ste B, Cleveland OH 44128	216-475-8800	R	1*	<.1
968	Lithgow Agency—Jeff Lithgow	117 W Fulton St, Waupaca WI 54981	715-256-0313	R	1*	<.1
969	Hialeah Meter Co—Eugene Bixby	450 W 28th St Ste 4, Hialeah FL 33010	305-887-8931	R	1*	<.1
970	H and H Transformer Inc—Robert Hodapp	PO Box 273, Commerce City CO 80037	303-289-2802	R	1*	<.1
971	Kolga U S A—Nick Nohara	2480 N 1st St Ste 100, San Jose CA 95131	408-570-0900	R	1*	<.1
972	Florida Coast Lighting Inc—William Pino	7035 Sw 47th St Ste A, Miami FL 33155	305-666-4210	R	1*	<.1
973	KD Johnson Inc—Kenneth Johnson	PO Box 1208, Leonard TX 75452		R	1*	<.1
974	Power House Electrical Supply—Garry Capps	PO Box 224107, Dallas TX 75222	214-631-7770	R	1*	<.1
975	Power Tech Electrical Sales Inc—Mark Johnston	2005 Mcdaniel Dr Ste 1, Carrollton TX 75006	972-421-0871	R	1*	<.1

Rank	Company Name—*Executive Officer*	Address, City, State, Zip	Phone	Type	Fin	Empls
976	Electrical Representatives West—*Pete Pachl*	505 3rd Ave W 101, Seattle WA 98119	206-767-7722	R	1*	<.1
977	Lachut Electrical Sales Inc—*Ronald Lachut*	318 S Main St, North Syracuse NY 13212	315-458-6486	R	1*	<.1
978	Sacramento Computer Power Inc—*Tod Wagner*	829 W Stadium Ln, Sacramento CA 95834	916-923-2772	R	1*	<.1
979	Victory America Inc—*Richard Ruan*	330 Zachary St Unit 10, Moorpark CA 93021	805-530-1100	R	1*	<.1
980	B and B Lighting Inc—*Jack Blackshear*	PO Box 461388, Garland TX 75046	972-276-5151	R	1*	<.1
981	Binaca Products Inc—*Paul Gupta*	32218 Corte Tomatlan, Temecula CA 92592	951-296-3397	R	1*	<.1
982	Earl's Electrical Service Inc—*Richard Smith*	1448 Campbell Ridge Rd, Royston GA 30662	706-245-6925	R	1*	<.1
983	Hillcrest Enterprises Inc—*William Farmer*	PO Box 6008, Ashland VA 23005	804-798-8390	R	1*	<.1
984	Knight Protect Inc—*Thomas Mcenaney*	PO Box 685, Katonah NY 10536	914-232-0003	R	1*	<.1
985	Power And Control Distributors Inc—*Glenn Woodbury*	1772 Ross Ln, Medford OR 97501	541-779-8062	R	1*	<.1
986	First Light Of New Orleans Inc—*Scott Moine*	1020 Distributors Row, New Orleans LA 70123	504-733-4004	R	1*	<.1
987	Lighting Showroom Inc—*M Seitzman*	137 Bowery, New York NY 10002	212-431-3880	R	1*	<.1
988	Whitaker Security Inc—*Frank Begovich*	4501 Lantern Pl Ste 11, Alexandria VA 22306	703-768-5025	R	1*	<.1
989	Cummings Lighthouse Inc—*Rebecca Goranson*	7462 N Us Hwy 31, Seymour IN 47274	812-523-1034	R	1*	<.1
990	Birdman Distribution Corp—*Didier De Nier*	4268 E Los Angeles Ave, Simi Valley CA 93063	805-527-2288	R	1*	<.1
991	Bob Jones and Associates Inc—*Robert Jones*	3837 E Anne St, Phoenix AZ 85040	602-437-1111	R	1*	<.1
992	Moberg Electric Inc—*Kathy Vanhelden*	1763 20th Ave, Rice Lake WI 54868	715-234-7961	R	1*	<.1
993	Ocean State Signal Co—*Susan Namara*	27 Thurber Blvd, Smithfield RI 02917	401-231-6780	R	1*	<.1
994	Schaeffer Marketing Group Inc—*Michael Schaeffer*	PO Box 510290, Saint Louis MO 63151	314-894-1100	R	1*	<.1
995	Accurate Temperature Control Corp—*Stephen Hahnert*	3500 Pky Center Ct, Orlando FL 32808	407-292-6800	R	1*	<.1
996	JD Hudson Company Inc—*Jim Hudson*	2209 Dickens Rd Ste 20, Richmond VA 23230	804-282-1864	R	1*	<.1
997	Kearney Winlectric Inc—*Steve Anderson*	1924 Central Ave, Kearney NE 68847	308-236-9060	R	1*	<.1
998	S and J Lighting/Lense Supply Inc—*Steve Parsley*	2316 Watterson Trl, Louisville KY 40299	502-499-5516	R	1*	<.1
999	Select Equipment Company Inc—*Douglas Bray*	101 W N St, Kokomo IN 46901	765-459-5191	R	1*	<.1
1000	Sentec Automation Components—*Bill Bolyard*	1531 Highwood E, Pontiac MI 48340	248-334-4024	R	1*	<.1
1001	Arkansas Electrical Outlet Inc—*Billy Paulman*	PO Box 247, Forrest City AR 72336	870-633-4997	R	1*	<.1
1002	Delmo Inc—*William Moseby*	112 Lincoln Ave, Fisk MO 63940	573-967-3483	R	1*	<.1
1003	National Fuse Products Inc—*Marian Graham*	PO Box 771269, Lakewood OH 44107	440-356-8181	R	1*	<.1
1004	Rec Protective Systems Inc—*Dwayne Shipley*	PO Box 6620, Moore OK 73153	405-794-2388	R	1*	<.1
1005	Allied General Fire and Security Inc—*Ken Webster*	PO Box 140329, Garden City ID 83714	208-367-9100	R	1*	<.1
1006	El Cerrito Lighting Inc—*Fiorlea Canepa*	10330 San Pablo Ave, El Cerrito CA 94530	510-525-3266	R	1*	<.1
1007	Dynamic Telecommunications Inc—*Krista Kaminski*	205 Technology Park Ln, Fuquay Varina NC 27526	919-577-2700	R	1*	<.1
1008	Lamar Wholesale Supply Inc—*Edwin McGary*	6318 Burnet Rd, Austin TX 78757	512-453-2852	R	1*	<.1
1009	Mustang Industries Inc—*Dale Merrill*	PO Box 2201, Laguna Hills CA 92654	949-582-2711	R	1*	<.1
1010	Smarter Security Systems Ltd—*Jeff Brown*	1515 S Capital of Texa, Austin TX 78746	512-328-7277	R	1*	<.1
1011	Za Control Services—*Zenon Aguilar*	1183 Brittmoore Rd Ste, Houston TX 77043	713-461-3411	R	1*	<.1
1012	Bunell and Associates Inc—*Mike Doland*	250 Regency Ct Ste 200, Brookfield WI 53045	262-784-0994	R	1*	<.1
1013	Don Griffin—*Don Griffin*	1102 W Laurel Ste 5, San Antonio TX 78201	210-340-1400	R	1*	<.1
1014	Lighting Trends Inc—*Bobby Davis*	1520 Liberty St, Knoxville TN 37921	865-523-8745	R	1*	<.1
1015	Northwest Electric Motor Co—*Samson Jindoyan*	3917 25th Ave, Schiller Park IL 60176	847-671-4400	R	1*	<.1
1016	Golden Isles Supply Company Inc—*Carroll Williams*	9722 Golden Isle W, Baxley GA 31513	912-367-5850	R	1*	<.1
1017	Rains Electrical Sales Inc—*James Rains*	11721 W 62nd Ter, Shawnee Mission KS 66203	913-962-0801	R	1*	<.1
1018	Ses America Inc—*Lionnel Couche*	90 Douglas Pke, Smithfield RI 02917	401-232-3370	R	1*	<.1
1019	Consolidated Electronics Inc—*Steven Coy*	PO Box 20070, Dayton OH 45420	937-252-5662	R	1*	<.1
1020	Electric Motor Sales Inc—*William Ball*	5637 King Hwy, Kalamazoo MI 49048	269-388-2020	R	1*	<.1
1021	Home Lighting Ltd—*Frank Southall*	1575a Standing Ridge D, Powhatan VA 23139	804-378-3640	R	1*	<.1
1022	Joseph and Sammel Inc—*Ray Joseph*	407 Baylor St, Austin TX 78703	512-320-0000	R	1*	<.1
1023	National Power Equipment Inc—*Ken Prince*	5400 W 161st St, Cleveland OH 44142	216-898-2680	R	1*	<.1
1024	Sentry Security Systems Inc—*Deborah Chultz*	PO Box 270105, Kansas City MO 64127	816-474-5565	R	1*	<.1
1025	Battery Products Inc—*Michael Meyers*	PO Box 589, Hartland WI 53029	262-367-2411	R	1*	<.1
1026	Pontiac Electric Motor Works Inc—*Peter Polk*	224 W Sheffield Ave, Pontiac MI 48340	248-332-4622	R	1*	<.1
1027	Vitus Electric Supply Co	PO Box 2789, Eugene OR 97402	541-484-6333	R	1*	<.1
1028	Jackson and Dial Inc—*Dewey Jackson*	PO Box 550, Lorena TX 76655	254-857-4111	R	1*	<.1
1029	Lwr Time Ltd—*Jeffery Roth*	15 S Franklin St Ste 2, Wilkes Barre PA 18701	570-408-1640	R	1*	<.1
1030	Philtek Power Corp—*Philip Pong*	PO Box 1, Blaine WA 98231	360-332-7252	R	1*	<.1
1031	Advanced Marketing Telecommunications Inc—*Mark Brown*	5933 Sea Lion Pl Ste 1, Carlsbad CA 92008	760-918-8755	R	1*	<.1
1032	Del Mar Lighting LLC—*Peter Caldwell*	829 Pipers Ln, Brentwood TN 37027	615-376-4566	R	1*	<.1
1033	Fanchiou Satellite Tv Corp—*Alex Yu*	12338 Valley Blvd Ste, El Monte CA 91732	626-442-3688	R	1*	<.1
1034	Electronic Security Protection LLC—*Lee Mullineaux*	5 Ridgeside Ct Ste 203, Mount Airy MD 21771	301-829-8240	R	1*	<.1
1035	ATR Systems Inc—*Thomas Hoover*	2049 Stout Dr Ste A1, Warminster PA 18974	215-443-8720	R	1*	<.1
1036	Beacon Advanced Components—*Michael Farrell*	2526 Mount Vernon Rd B, Atlanta GA 30338	770-662-8190	R	1*	<.1
1037	Ensales Inc—*Benjamin Nauss*	1392 Massey Rd, Newton Grove NC 28366	910-594-1539	R	1*	<.1
1038	Aero K A P Inc—*Robert Stabler*	PO Box 661240, Arcadia CA 91066	626-574-1704	R	1*	<.1
1039	GP Batteries Marketing (Latin America) Inc—*Steve Vega*	8370 Nw 66th St, Miami FL 33166	305-471-7717	R	1*	<.1
1040	Thermocoax Inc—*Claude Capron*	6825 Shiloh Rd E Ste B, Alpharetta GA 30005	678-947-5510	R	1*	<.1
1041	Allied Trading Inc—*Yaqoob Ashai*	10555 Guilford Rd Ste, Jessup MD 20794	301-604-6777	R	1*	<.1
1042	Lou Marks and Sons Inc—*Rodney Marks*	4018 Bishop Ln, Louisville KY 40218	502-969-5116	R	1*	<.1
1043	Power Drive Enterprises Inc—*Richard Rogalski*	PO Box 347147, Cleveland OH 44134	216-459-1703	R	1*	<.1
1044	Rosenblatt And Associates Inc—*John Rosenblatt*	PO Box 240772, Charlotte NC 28224	704-525-1852	R	1*	<.1
1045	Circuit Breakers Inc—*Christine Hardman*	4068 Mount Royal Blvd, Allison Park PA 15101	412-487-9090	R	1*	<.1
1046	Zunicom Inc—*William Tan*	4315 W Lovers Ln, Dallas TX 75209	214-352-8674	P	1	<.1
1047	Bays Company Inc—*Mark Perot*	961 Ford Rd, Homer LA 71040	318-927-2457	R	1*	<.1
1048	Richard Enterprises Inc—*Richard Stpierre*	1 Great Oak Ln, Unionville CT 06085	860-673-1566	R	1*	<.1
1049	A Ray Lite Inc—*Terry Thomason*	PO Box 6115, Lubbock TX 79493	806-762-1880	R	1*	<.1
1050	Alarm Components Distributing Corp—*Gordon White*	31 Hanford St, Rochester NY 14607	585-461-4440	R	1*	<.1
1051	Bowling Green Winlectric Co—*James Bennett*	1001 Shive Ln Ste A, Bowling Green KY 42103	270-842-6153	R	1*	<.1
1052	Lucas Industrial—*Michael Lucas*	PO Box 293, Cedar Hill TX 75106	972-291-6400	R	1*	<.1
1053	Techrep Components Inc—*Tom Felts*	25332 Narbonne Ave Ste, Lomita CA 90717	310-539-9070	R	1*	<.1
1054	TPR Enterprises Ltd—*Thomas Fay*	644 Fayette Ave, Mamaroneck NY 10543	914-698-1141	R	1*	<.1
1055	Big Frog Mountain Corp—*Thomas Tripp*	PO Box 159, Oldfort TN 37362	423-265-0307	R	1*	<.1
1056	Ergytech Inc—*Julio Rivas*	2400 Augusta Dr Ste 31, Houston TX 77057	713-953-0300	R	1*	<.1
1057	Norm and Doe Electrical Supply Inc—*Annette Dettmer*	295 Suthbound Gratiot, Mount Clemens MI 48043	586-468-2000	R	1*	<.1
1058	Phoenix Wire And Cable LLC	1255 Buford Hwy Ste 20, Suwanee GA 30024	770-904-4135	R	1*	<.1
1059	Utility Products Of Arizona Inc—*Bruce Sears*	PO Box 15665, Phoenix AZ 85060	602-840-3455	R	1*	<.1
1060	Wrico International LLC	PO Box 41555, Eugene OR 97404	541-744-4333	R	1*	<.1
1061	Dade Bulb Inc—*Ashley Hennings*	12451 S Dixie Hwy, Miami FL 33156	305-235-2852	R	1*	<.1
1062	Artisan Power LLC—*Davis Gan*	577 Main St Ste 430, Hudson MA 01749	978-562-4300	R	1*	<.1
1063	Alfa Transformer Co—*Becky Mallard*	PO Box 6316, Fort Smith AR 72906	479-646-1668	R	1*	<.1
1064	Chatham Components Inc—*Richard Perst*	33 River Rd Ste C, Chatham NJ 07928	973-635-8075	R	1*	<.1
1065	Ferrari Technical Sales LLC	8660 Calle Quebrada, Rancho Cucamonga CA 91730	951-684-8034	R	1*	<.1

Note: An asterisk (*) indicates an estimated financial figure. The company type code used is as follows: R = Private, P = Public, S = Private Subsidiary, B = Public Subsidiary, D = Division, J = Joint Venture, I = Investment Fund.

COMPANY RANKINGS BY SALES WITHIN 4-DIGIT SIC

Rank	Company Name—*Executive Officer*	Address, City, State, Zip	Phone	Type	Fin	Empls
1066	Kalb Corp—*Mike Kalb*	521 Matthews Ct, Oneida IL 61467	309-483-3600	R	1*	<.1
1067	Hawaii Electrical Export Co—*David Conway*	328 Uluniu St Ste 202, Kailua HI 96734	808-261-1524	R	1*	<.1
1068	Am Trade Systems Inc—*Joe Glaser*	13720 Wayne Rd, Livonia MI 48150	734-522-9500	R	1*	<.1
1069	Unigearusa Inc—*Stephen Hounsome*	29 Water St, Newburyport MA 01950	978-463-4444	R	1*	<.1
1070	Web Warrior Inc—*Tracy Markham*	67 S Dillard St, Winter Garden FL 34787	407-877-8177	R	1*	<.1
1071	Hutton Contracting Company Inc—*Burton Hutton*	1600 Clifty Hwy, Hindsville AR 72738	479-789-2550	R	1*	<.1
1072	Lite Line Illuminations Inc—*Tal Mashhadian*	51 University Ave Ste, Los Gatos CA 95030	408-399-9000	R	1*	<.1
1073	New Trend—*Jim Case*	3833 Duck Creek Dr Ste, Stockton CA 95215	209-463-5095	R	1*	<.1
1074	Bergen Protective Systems Inc—*Joseph Cioffi*	30 Sylvan Ave, Englewood Cliffs NJ 07632	201-947-3114	R	1*	<.1
1075	Az Security and Equipment Inc—*Fabio Morales*	7324 Nw 56th St, Miami FL 33166	305-882-8940	R	1*	<.1
1076	B and D Sales Inc—*Michael Roemig*	1133 Minnie Dr, Raleigh NC 27603	919-803-5015	R	1*	<.1
1077	Transportation Technical Services Inc—*William Mcelroy*	104 Peckham Ln, Coventry RI 02816	401-392-1017	R	1*	<.1
1078	Moore Protection—*Don Moore*	1650 S Pacific Coast H, Redondo Beach CA 90277	310-540-7229	R	1*	<.1
1079	Tecnomatic Corp—*Julio Minela*	130 Lenox Ave Ste 6, Stamford CT 06906	203-359-9036	R	1*	<.1
1080	Alabama Lighting Associates Inc—*David Rexrode*	7624 Commerce Ln, Trussville AL 35173	205-655-6350	R	<1*	<.1
1081	Dorsey Alexander Inc—*John Calder*	6580 Corporate Dr, Blue Ash OH 45242	513-530-0400	R	<1*	<.1
1082	Blink Electric Motors Inc—*Kathy Buschbom*	116 N 1st Ave Rear, Marshalltown IA 50158	641-752-3036	R	<1*	<.1
1083	Neomark Inc—*Robert Bagwell*	255 Plz Dr Ste A, Oviedo FL 32765	407-366-7505	R	<1*	<.1
1084	Research Service and Engineering—*Bill Archer*	4411 E La Palma Ave, Anaheim CA 92807	714-529-9889	R	<1*	<.1
1085	Rj Controls Inc—*Randy Lindsey*	33427 Pacific Hwy S St, Federal Way WA 98003	253-661-1931	R	<1*	<.1
1086	Brown and Ross Of New Jersey Inc—*Peter Ross*	60 Kingsbridge Rd, Piscataway NJ 08854	201-659-3211	R	<1*	<.1
1087	Harry Horn Inc—*Michael Kurland*	120 Arch St, Philadelphia PA 19106	215-925-4660	R	<1*	<.1
1088	RMS Purchases Inc—*Mike Epstein*	1802 Nance St, Houston TX 77020	713-236-0924	R	<1*	<.1
1089	H and W Products—*Louis Williams*	5415 Saturn Dr Unit 33, Dallas TX 75237	214-339-3030	R	<1*	<.1
1090	Amer Electric Motion Inc—*Federica Battistella*	15 Cliff Rd W, Burnsville MN 55337	952-890-5454	R	<1*	<.1
1091	Approved Lightning Protection Company Inc—*Thomas Kelly*	65 Mahan St, West Babylon NY 11704	631-643-6327	R	<1*	<.1
1092	Automation Systems and Services—*George Shahbazian*	PO Box 90174, Los Angeles CA 90009	323-776-2424	R	<1*	<.1
1093	Equipment Source Company Inc—*Tom Flagg*	1777 Yucca Rd, Oceanside CA 92054	760-439-1200	R	<1*	<.1
1094	Microtech Electronics Inc—*William Johnson*	4177 Sucia Dr, Ferndale WA 98248	360-380-3800	R	<1*	<.1
1095	Powertronics Inc—*Mark Dahlin*	2055 105th Ave Ne, Minneapolis MN 55449	763-571-2325	R	<1*	<.1
1096	Tarnov Co—*Charlotte Hayes*	605 Park Ave, Arcata CA 95521	707-822-5658	R	<1*	<.1
1097	City Alarm Co—*Joe Lamaccia*	1940 Mitchell Pl, Saint Louis MO 63139	314-645-5500	R	<1*	<.1
1098	Gulfaccess Inc—*Brad Sprowls*	5365 Jaeger Rd, Naples FL 34109	239-514-2252	R	<1*	<.1
1099	Mccoy Associates Inc—*Jane Cherney*	2009 14th St N Ste 604, Arlington VA 22201	703-243-0200	R	<1*	<.1
1100	Ostrander Implement and Farm Center Inc—*Michael Kelley*	9265 Marysville Rd, Ostrander OH 43061	740-666-2300	R	<1*	<.1
1101	Suburban Electric Supply Inc—*William Mcgroarty*	PO Box 67, Chester PA 19016	610-872-4048	R	<1*	<.1
1102	Vu1 Corp—*Scott Blackstone*	469 7th Ave 3rd Fl, New York NY 10018	212-359-9503	P	<1	<.1
1103	Unlimited Security Systems—*Larry Golden*	45 Warwick St, Bethlehem PA 18018	610-866-4115	R	<1*	<.1
1104	Nixon Power Services Co—*Bryant Phillips*	5038 Thoroughbred Lane, Brentwood TN 37027	615-309-5823	D	N/A	.1
1105	Waytek Inc—*David Wellstrom*	PO Box 690, Chanhassen MN 55317	952-949-0765	R	N/A	<.1

TOTALS: SIC 5063 Electrical Apparatus & Equipment
Companies: 1,105   53,757   100.7

5064 Electrical Appliances—Television & Radio

Rank	Company Name—*Executive Officer*	Address, City, State, Zip	Phone	Type	Fin	Empls
1	D and H Distributing Co—*Israel Schwab*	PO Box 5967, Harrisburg PA 17110	717-236-8001	R	2,111*	1.0
2	Funai Corporation Inc—*Yoshikazu Uemura*	201 Rte 17 Ste 903, Rutherford NJ 07070	201-727-4560	R	1,404*	.1
3	Samsung Electronics America Inc—*CS Choi*	105 Challenger Rd, Ridgefield Park NJ 07660	201-229-4000	S	793*	1.7
4	Helen of Troy Ltd—*Gerald J Rubin*	1 Helen of Troy Plz, El Paso TX 79912	915-225-8000	P	777	1.3
5	Roth Distributing Co—*John Thielen*	17801 E 40th Ave, Aurora CO 80011	303-373-9090	S	637*	.4
6	Projector People—*Jennifer Blomberg*	6301 Benjamin Rd Ste 1, Tampa FL 33634	813-261-7184	R	580*	.5
7	Clarion Corporation Of America—*Matt Matsuda*	6200 Gateway Dr, Cypress CA 90630	310-327-9100	R	468*	.2
8	H Betti Industries Inc—*Peter Betti*	303 Paterson Plank Rd, Carlstadt NJ 07072	201-438-1300	R	367*	.3
9	Uniden America Corp—*Brendan Morris*	4700 Amon Carter Blvd, Fort Worth TX 76155	817-858-3300	S	361*	.3
10	Tatung Company of America Inc—*Andrew Sun*	2850 El Presidio St, Long Beach CA 90810	310-637-2105	S	355*	.3
11	Digital Products International (St Louis Missouri)—*William Fetter*	900 N 23rd St, Saint Louis MO 63106	314-621-3314	S	333*	.5
12	Hadco Inc—*John Drillot*	325 Horizon Dr, Suwanee GA 30024	770-932-7282	R	300*	.1
13	Climatic Corp—*John H Bailey*	PO Box 25189, Columbia SC 29224	803-765-2595	R	263*	.2
14	Gotham Sales Co—*Daniel Schwartzstein*	302 Main St, Millburn NJ 07041	973-912-8412	R	244*	.1
15	Kenwood USA Corp—*Joe Classett*	PO Box 22745, Long Beach CA 90801	310-639-9000	R	233*	.2
16	Gaggenau USA Corp—*Franz Bosshard*	780 Dedham St, Canton MA 02021		S	215*	.1
17	Helen of Troy Texas Corp—*Gerald J Rubin* Helen of Troy Ltd	1 Helen of Troy Plz, El Paso TX 79912	915-225-8000	S	167*	.3
18	Falcon Fine Wire and Wire Products Inc—*William D LeCount*	2401 Discovery Blvd, Rockwall TX 75032	214-771-3441	R	110*	.1
19	City Animation Co—*Eric D Schultz*	2595 Bellingham, Troy MI 48083		R	109*	.1
20	Electrolux International—*Hans Straberg*	3 Pkwy Ctr, Pittsburgh PA 15220	412-928-0252	S	104	N/A
21	Toshiba America Consumer Products Inc—*Atsushi Murasawa*	82 Totowa Rd, Wayne NJ 07470	973-628-8000	S	94*	.2
22	Roth Corp—*John Thielen*	17801 E 40th Ave, Aurora CO 80011	303-373-9090	R	84*	.1
23	Madison Electric Co—*Joseph Schneider*	31855 Van Dyke Ave, Warren MI 48093	586-825-0200	R	82*	.2
24	Sues Young and Brown Inc	5151 Commerce Dr, Baldwin Park CA 91706	626-338-3800	R	82*	<.1
25	Elna USA	10 Industrial Ave Ste, Mahwah NJ 07430		S	73*	<.1
26	Electrical Distributing Inc—*AM Cronin III*	PO Box 2720, Portland OR 97208	503-226-4044	R	72*	.1
27	Sanyo Sales and Supply Corp (Wood Dale Illinois)—*Masami Murata*	1300 Michael Dr Ste A, Wood Dale IL 60191	630-694-8216	S	69*	.1
28	Auto Chlor System Inc—*George Griesbeck*	746 Poplar Ave, Memphis TN 38105	901-579-2300	R	68*	.1
29	Rowenta Inc—*Mark Nebar*	2199 Eden Rd, Millville NJ 08332	781-396-0600	S	68*	<.1
30	Durkopp Adler America Inc—*Patrick Weissgerber*	5875 Peachtree Industr, Norcross GA 30092	770-446-8162	R	64*	.1
31	DeLonghi America Inc—*James McCusker*	250 Pehle Ave Ste 405, Saddle Brook NJ 07663	201-909-4000	R	63*	.1
32	Westye Group - South Central LP—*Todd Shane*	2615 E Belt Line Rd, Carrollton TX 75006	972-416-6677	R	60*	.1
33	Bernina of America Inc—*Martin Favre*	3702 Prairie Lake Ct, Aurora IL 60504	630-978-2500	S	54*	.1
34	Four Seasons Sales and Service Inc—*Ed Jerger*	PO Box 1308, Paris TN 38242	731-642-0234	R	53*	.1
35	Priceless Resource Inc—*Isaac Meisels*	63 Flushing Ave Ste 11, Brooklyn NY 11205	718-643-8951	R	53*	<.1
36	C and L Supply Co—*Fred Kidd*	335 S Wilson St, Vinita OK 74301		R	50*	.1
37	Paragon Communications Inc—*Michael Prefontaine*	101 Union St,2nd Fl, Ashland MA 01721		R	47*	<.1
38	White Sewing Machine Co	31000 Viking Pkwy, Westlake OH 44145		D	46*	.1
39	Orion America Inc—*Makoto Katsuki*	PO Box 1129, Princeton IN 47670	812-386-3000	R	44*	.1
40	Persinger Supply Co	PO Box 188, Prichard WV 25555	304-486-5401	R	43*	.1
41	Wave Electronics Inc—*Gary Wermuth*	8648 Glenmont Dr Ste 1, Houston TX 77036	713-849-2710	R	40*	<.1
42	Sound Com Corp—*Paul Fussner*	227 Depot St, Berea OH 44017	440-234-2604	R	33*	.1
43	Target Distributing Co	19560 Amaranth Dr, Germantown MD 20874	301-296-9400	R	30*	<.1

Rank	Company Name—*Executive Officer*	Address, City, State, Zip	Phone	Type	Fin	Empls
44	Dey Distributing Inc—*Denny Dey*	PO Box 10698, Saint Paul MN 55110	651-490-9191	R	27*	.1
45	Potter Distributing Inc—*Douglas Potter*	4037 Roger B Chaffee B, Grand Rapids MI 49548	616-531-6860	R	25*	<.1
46	Jarrell Distributors Inc—*James Jarrell Jr*	2651 Fondren Dr, Dallas TX 75206	214-363-7211	R	25*	<.1
47	SOS Associates Inc—*Hamid Razipour*	1500 S Central Ave Ste, Los Angeles CA 90021	213-749-2211	R	25*	<.1
48	Woodson and Bozeman Inc—*Edwin D Bozeman IV*	PO Box 18450, Memphis TN 38181	901-362-1500	R	24*	<.1
49	Seen On Tv Inc—*Daniel Fasano*	80 Oconnor Rd Ste 1, Fairport NY 14450	585-295-8601	R	23*	<.1
50	Key Boston Inc—*Steve Moran*	PO Box 247, Franklin MA 02038	508-528-4500	R	22*	<.1
51	Fretz Corp—*Tom Dolan*	2001 Woodhaven Rd, Philadelphia PA 19116		R	22*	<.1
52	Electro Brand Inc	1127 S Mannheim Rd Ste, Westchester IL 60154	708-338-4400	R	22*	<.1
53	Stone Appliances Inc—*James Cozby*	9901 Broadway St Ste 1, San Antonio TX 78217	210-826-9652	R	21*	.2
54	Factory Direct Appliance Inc—*Dennis Birkestrand*	14105 Marshall Dr, Shawnee Mission KS 66215	913-888-8028	R	19*	.1
55	Litex Industries Ltd—*John Mares*	3401 Trinity Blvd, Grand Prairie TX 75050	972-871-4350	R	18*	.1
56	Lite Source Inc—*David Lu*	30690 Hill St, Thousand Palms CA 92276	760-343-4700	R	18*	<.1
57	Brooke Distributors Inc—*David Rutter*	16250 NW 52nd Ave, Hialeah FL 33014	305-624-9752	R	18*	<.1
58	Collins Appliance Parts Inc—*R D Collins*	1533 Metropolitan St, Pittsburgh PA 15233		R	18*	<.1
59	R and B Wholesale Distributors Inc—*Robert Burggraf*	2350 S Milliken Ave, Ontario CA 91761	909-230-5400	R	17*	.1
60	First Coast Supply Inc—*Stanley Kantor*	6860 Phillips Industri, Jacksonville FL 32256	904-388-1217	R	16*	<.1
61	Crystal Promotions Inc—*Arsalan Dokhanian*	3030 E Vernon Ave, Vernon CA 90058	213-746-4740	R	16*	.1
62	Audio-Video Corp—*Theodore M Klarsfeld*	213 Broadway, Albany NY 12204	518-449-7213	R	15*	.1
63	Appliance Solutions By Brock's Appliance Inc—*Frank Brock*	215 Industrial Blvd, Ballwin MO 63011	314-731-6282	R	15*	<.1
64	Eagle Distributors Holding Company LLC—*Mickey Ural*	2439 Albany St, Kenner LA 70062	504-464-5991	R	14*	.1
65	Marta Cooperative of America—*Robert Thompson*	515 E Carefree Hwy Ste, Phoenix AZ 85085	480-443-0211	R	14*	<.1
66	Metropark Communications Inc—*Glen Conley*	10405 Baur Blvd Ste A, St Louis MO 63132	314-439-1900	R	14*	<.1
67	Monroe Communications Inc—*Doug Denmon*	1909 Auburn Ave, Monroe LA 71201	318-323-6441	R	14*	<.1
68	Gene Schick Co—*Gene Schick*	30826 Santana St, Hayward CA 94544	510-429-8200	R	13*	<.1
69	Schawbel Corp—*William Schawbel*	26 Crosby Dr, Bedford MA 01730	781-541-6900	R	13*	.1
70	Yeomans Distributing Co	1503 W Altorfer Dr, Peoria IL 61615	309-691-3282	R	12*	<.1
71	Quality Mobile Communications LLC—*Nick Ruark*	12200 NE 60th Way Ste, Vancouver WA 98682	360-254-9505	R	12*	<.1
72	Midwest Sales and Service Inc—*Trell Wechter*	917 S Chapin St, South Bend IN 46601	574-287-3365	R	11*	<.1
73	Riverwood Home Appliances Inc—*Deborah Williams*	1313 Harding St, Jackson MS 39202	601-932-6900	R	10*	<.1
74	Williams Corp—*Todd Williams*	1217 Harrison Ave, Panama City FL 32401	850-769-7043	R	10*	<.1
75	Cascadia Corp—*Doug Loughran*	PO Box 58544, Tukwila WA 98138	206-575-6774	R	10*	<.1
76	Rogers Stereo Inc—*Frank Rogers*	525 Woodruff Rd, Greenville SC 29607	864-585-6035	R	9*	.1
77	Westye Group - Southeast Inc—*Jim Donlin*	9777 Satellite Blvd St, Orlando FL 32837	407-857-3777	R	9*	.1
78	Eton Corp—*Esmail Hozour*	PO Box 2307, Menlo Park CA 94026	650-903-3866	R	9*	<.1
79	A and L Distributing Co—*W James Cox*	7933 Southwest Cirrus, Beaverton OR 97008	503-684-9384	R	9*	<.1
80	Setzers and Company Inc—*Allen Setzer*	PO Box B, Jacksonville FL 32203	904-731-4100	R	9*	.1
81	Car Phone Factory Inc—*Ron Nathan*	1107 S Robertson Blvd, Los Angeles CA 90035	310-724-8181	R	8*	<.1
82	Mountain West Distributors Inc—*Frederick Reynolds*	PO Box 651236, Salt Lake City UT 84165	801-487-5694	R	8*	<.1
83	McPhail Fuel Co—*Bruce MacPhail*	PO Box 960, Cotati CA 94931	707-285-3525	R	8*	<.1
84	Proton Corp—*Walter Schroeder*	15364 E Valley Blvd, City of Industry CA 91746	626-855-2128	R	8*	<.1
85	Star Electronic Sales Inc—*Adrian Aymerich*	6926 NW 46th St, Miami FL 33166	305-592-9506	R	8*	<.1
86	T and W Sales Inc—*Jason Taylor*	13592 Stemmons Hwy, Dallas TX 75234	972-243-3265	R	8*	<.1
87	Onkyo USA Corp—*Kenji Miyagi*	18 Pky, Upper Saddle River NJ 07458	201-785-2600	R	8*	<.1
88	Bay Air Conditioning Inc—*David Hutchins*	8021 W Gulf To Lake Hw, Crystal River FL 34429	352-795-2665	R	8*	.1
89	Vcp International Inc—*D Russell*	PO Box 550999, Dallas TX 75355	972-271-7474	R	7*	<.1
90	Kar-Gor Inc—*Gordon Dale*	PO Box 5948, Salem OR 97304	503-315-9899	R	7*	<.1
91	Lewis Furniture Company Inc—*Daryl Gamerman*	6316 Reisterstown Rd, Baltimore MD 21215	410-358-4433	R	7*	<.1
92	Prudential Builders Center—*Steve Brandon*	PO Box 3088, Spokane WA 99220	509-535-2701	R	7*	<.1
93	Reil and Associates Inc—*Dennis Reil*	5454 Washington St Ste, Denver CO 80216	303-294-0600	R	7*	<.1
94	Diplomat Trading Inc—*David Bradman*	8890 Nw 24th Ter, Doral FL 33172	305-594-0437	R	7*	<.1
95	Lawrence Street Industry LLC—*Bill Fields*	4700 Lawrence St, Hyattsville MD 20781	301-985-4090	R	7*	<.1
96	Texan Waste Equipment Inc—*Larry Davis*	5900 Wheeler St, Houston TX 77023	713-923-7600	R	6*	<.1
97	Rieman and Arszman Custom Distributors Inc—*Ken Rieman*	9190 Seward Rd, Fairfield OH 45014	513-874-5444	R	6*	<.1
98	Clark Wholesale Inc—*Robin Clark*	2575 Bridger Rd, Salt Lake City UT 84104	801-973-4343	R	6*	<.1
99	All Major Appliances Inc—*Sol Drimmer*	1608 Coney Island Ave, Brooklyn NY 11230	718-338-3500	R	6*	<.1
100	Oregon Scientific Inc—*Paul Zimmerman*	19861 Sw 95th Ave, Tualatin OR 97062	503-783-5100	R	6*	<.1
101	Marrone and Company Inc—*Micheal Marrone*	14020 Interdrive W, Houston TX 77032	713-462-2500	R	5*	<.1
102	Michael and Morris Enterprises Inc—*Mansoor Malekan*	1801 E 41st Pl Ste A, Los Angeles CA 90058	323-234-6801	R	5*	<.1
103	Electronic Parts Unlimited Inc—*Elliot Satinoff*	2629 Us Hwy 19, Holiday FL 34691	727-934-1800	R	5*	<.1
104	General Appliance and Electronic Distributors Inc—*Ernesto Rodriguez*	2650 Nw 74th Ave, Miami FL 33122	305-477-6206	R	5*	<.1
105	Awad Brothers LLC—*Rebeca Olmos*	11035 Harry Hines Blvd, Dallas TX 75229	214-351-0977	R	5*	<.1
106	Gametech Marketing Inc—*Farzad Saghian*	15210 Keswick St, Van Nuys CA 91405	818-908-9904	R	5*	<.1
107	Goli Enterprises Inc—*David Goldban*	10535 Wilshire Blvd St, Los Angeles CA 90024	323-589-2000	R	5*	<.1
108	Detroit Recycling Center Inc—*Barry Schwartz*	20300 Mount Elliott St, Detroit MI 48234	313-368-3500	R	5*	<.1
109	Express Industries—*Gary Cullen*	22755 Savi Ranch Pkwy, Yorba Linda CA 92887	714-453-2326	R	5*	<.1
110	Sunbelt Electronic Representative Associates Inc—*Jim Durnal*	3361 Boyington Dr Ste, Carrollton TX 75006	972-490-3240	R	5*	<.1
111	Brookmeade Hardware and Supply Co—*Roswell Nourse*	PO Box 50700, Nashville TN 37205	615-882-0755	R	5*	<.1
112	Nda Distributors LLC	1281 Puerta Del Sol, San Clemente CA 92673	949-492-4399	R	5*	<.1
113	Boeckeler Instruments Inc—*Warren Brey*	4650 S Butterfield Dr, Tucson AZ 85714	520-745-0001	R	5*	<.1
114	Lucky Star Industries Inc—*Lee Tim*	888 Vintage Ave, Ontario CA 91764	909-980-1028	R	4*	<.1
115	Custom Light And Sound Inc—*Lee Phelps*	2506 Guess Rd, Durham NC 27705	919-286-0011	R	4*	<.1
116	A and B Audio Video Sales Corp—*Joe Safaradi*	261 N Robertson Blvd, Beverly Hills CA 90211	310-858-7750	R	4*	<.1
117	Creative Marketing Concepts Corp—*Carol Abramo*	96 Audubon Rd, Wakefield MA 01880	978-532-7517	R	4*	<.1
118	American International Exports Inc—*Robert Dhyani*	8834 Monard Dr, Silver Spring MD 20910	301-585-7448	R	4*	<.1
119	HB Electronics Inc—*Helida Bordier*	6000 Gateway Blvd E, El Paso TX 79905	915-775-2552	R	4*	<.1
120	Crown Magnetics Inc—*Charles Musser*	1223 Bittner Blvd, Lebanon PA 17046	717-274-2812	R	4*	<.1
121	Lake Electronic Service Inc—*Andrew Mirabile*	1650 Central Ave, Albany NY 12205	518-869-8424	R	4*	<.1
122	Riccar America Inc	1800 E Walnut Ave, Fullerton CA 92831	714-525-4400	D	4*	<.1
123	Total Recall Corp—*Jordan P Heilweil*	17 Washington Ave, Suffern NY 10901	845-368-3700	R	4*	<.1
124	Larriva's Corp—*Leonilo Larriva IV*	2021 N Grand Ave, Nogales AZ 85621	520-287-5815	R	4*	<.1
125	Liberty Distributors Inc—*Dennis Baranowski*	520 S Commerce St, Wichita KS 67202	316-264-7393	R	4*	<.1
126	W N L Inc—*Greg Lundbom*	PO Box 427, Clackamas OR 97015	503-655-2563	R	4*	<.1
127	Kei Trading Company Inc—*Kwang Chung*	933 E 11th St, Los Angeles CA 90021	213-689-9494	R	4*	<.1
128	Bush Refrigeration Inc—*Jeffery Bush*	1700 Admiral Wilson Bl, Pennsauken NJ 08109	856-963-1800	R	4*	<.1
129	Loran International Sales Inc—*Don Lafferty*	PO Box 60359, Houston TX 77205	281-219-1114	R	4*	<.1
130	Samson Electronics Inc—*Parviz Parvizi*	3400 Slauson Ave, Maywood CA 90270	323-585-6393	R	3*	<.1
131	Japer Electronics Inc—*Luis Marsano*	12255 Kirkham Rd Ste 3, Poway CA 92064	858-486-7266	R	3*	<.1
132	Farmour Security Service—*Michael Jenkins*	PO Box 37, Kodak TN 37764	865-429-3643	R	3*	<.1

Note: An asterisk (*) indicates an estimated financial figure. The company type code used is as follows: R = Private, P = Public, S = Private Subsidiary, B = Public Subsidiary, D = Division, J = Joint Venture, I = Investment Fund.

COMPANY RANKINGS BY SALES WITHIN 4-DIGIT SIC

Rank	Company Name—*Executive Officer*	Address, City, State, Zip	Phone	Type	Fin	Empls
133	Advanced Marketing and Distribution Inc—*Thomas Gaspar*	16691 Noyes Ave, Irvine CA 92606	949-251-1851	R	3*	<.1
134	Benny Lee Enterprises Inc—*Benny Lee*	PO Box 7768, Shawnee Mission KS 66207	816-584-9700	R	3*	<.1
135	Lehigh Acres Concrete Supply Company Inc—*P Page*	2330 Bruner Ln, Fort Myers FL 33912	239-482-8300	R	3*	<.1
136	Precision Interface Electronics Inc—*Bill Summers*	9601 Mason Ave Ste A, Chatsworth CA 91311	818-678-3690	R	3*	<.1
137	Home Entertainment Systems Of Nj Inc—*Scott Bellone*	98 Vanderburg Rd, Marlboro NJ 07746	732-303-0088	R	3*	<.1
138	Denmark Inc—*Mark Thompson*	520 N Loop 288, Denton TX 76209	972-434-2607	R	3*	<.1
139	A-Ok Wholesale Appliances and Electronics Inc—*James Young*	600 Kenrick Dr Ste C34, Houston TX 77060	281-999-3200	R	3*	<.1
140	Lobright Manufacturing Company Inc—*Angini Locascio*	PO Box 280457, Queens Village NY 11428	718-464-2721	R	3*	<.1
141	Pdq Supply Inc—*Philip Ernst*	PO Box 4543, Carol Stream IL 60197	630-406-1016	R	3*	<.1
142	Texas Sales And Marketing Inc—*Charles Beck*	4747 Langfield Rd, Houston TX 77040	713-460-2400	R	3*	<.1
143	Sonnet Industries Inc—*Brent Solomon*	30 E Adams St Ste 810, Chicago IL 60603	312-922-9890	R	3*	<.1
144	Best Housekeeping Industries Inc—*Fredrick Stern*	17 Ave A, New York NY 10009	212-677-8808	R	3*	<.1
145	Ameriwaste Inc—*Janell Marin*	PO Box 1351, Alvin TX 77512	281-331-8400	R	3*	<.1
146	Chenal Heating and Air Inc—*Elton Gray*	28624 Bandy Rd, Little Rock AR 72223	501-821-6948	R	3*	<.1
147	M and V Wholesale Distributors Inc—*Manoj Narang*	27 Canal St, New York NY 10002	212-260-6017	R	3*	<.1
148	Alaska R and C Communications Inc—*Scott Romine*	2241 Cinnabar Loop, Anchorage AK 99507	907-333-1044	R	3*	<.1
149	Kamcor Ltd—*Daniel Kammin*	17 Madison Ave, Paterson NJ 07524	973-684-8666	R	3*	<.1
150	Bradlee Distributors USA Inc—*Gerald Isbister*	1400 Elliott Ave W, Seattle WA 98119	206-284-8400	R	3*	<.1
151	Competition Tv and Appliance—*Mike Widmer*	411 S 3rd St, Mccall ID 83638	208-634-3676	R	3*	<.1
152	Pyramid Audio and Video Ltd—*Jeffrey Schneider*	2440 Seward Hwy Ste C, Anchorage AK 99503	907-272-9111	R	3*	<.1
153	M and M Representatives Inc—*Martin Mcgee*	4849 Scott St Ste 110, Schiller Park IL 60176	847-671-0444	R	2*	<.1
154	Adaptive Controls Inc—*Brian Smith*	6333 212th St Sw, Lynnwood WA 98036	425-672-0464	R	2*	<.1
155	Howard Payne Co—*Howard Payne*	3583 Chamblee Tucker R, Atlanta GA 30341	770-451-0136	R	2*	<.1
156	Electrolux Vacuum Cleaners and Polishers—*Frank Karimi*	16401 Northern Blvd, Flushing NY 11358	718-359-0116	R	2*	<.1
157	Intertrade International Inc—*Janeen Mahajan*	PO Box 88, Martinsville NJ 08836	732-271-7733	R	2*	<.1
158	Karaoke Now Inc—*M Charlesworth*	7828 N 19th Ave Ste 14, Phoenix AZ 85021	602-864-1995	R	2*	<.1
159	Schoettler Research And Engineering Corp—*Harold Schoettler*	5582 Research Dr, Huntington Beach CA 92649	714-891-9901	R	2*	<.1
160	Phong Le Co—*Phong Le*	14037 Westheimer Rd, Houston TX 77077	281-988-7988	R	2*	<.1
161	Power Plus Sound and Lighting Inc—*Lane Rickard*	2460 Grand Ave, Vista CA 92081	760-727-1717	R	2*	<.1
162	Shifting Sands Stereo Distributors Inc—*Michael Sajelki*	10850 Nw 27th St, Doral FL 33172	305-594-4947	R	2*	<.1
163	Midwest Appliance Parts Co—*Louis Cole*	2601 W Diversey Ave, Chicago IL 60647	773-278-1300	R	2*	<.1
164	Rangel Distributing Co—*Josephine C Rangel*	1327 St Louis Ave, Kansas City MO 64101	816-842-7933	R	2*	<.1
165	Unisol International Corp—*Mauricio Jessurun*	8024 Nw 90th St, Medley FL 33166	305-885-2656	R	2*	<.1
166	Lello Appliances Corp—*Galileo Buzzi-Ferraris*	355 Murray Hill Pky St, East Rutherford NJ 07073	201-939-2555	R	2*	<.1
167	Grecian Imports—*Eugene Afentoulis*	PO Box 30626, Las Vegas NV 89173	702-876-4211	R	2*	<.1
168	Gaka Trading Inc—*Gustavo Abaunza*	PO Box 652801, Miami FL 33265	305-412-3039	R	2*	<.1
169	Solutions For Everything Inc—*Irfan Batada*	837 W Robindale St, West Covina CA 91790	626-338-1083	R	2*	<.1
170	A and E Electrical Services And Parts Inc—*Roger Estopinal*	PO Box 3243, Bay Saint Louis MS 39521	228-466-9857	R	2*	<.1
171	Microtherm Inc—*David Seitz*	223 W Airtex Blvd, Houston TX 77090	281-876-3300	R	2*	<.1
172	Unirex Corp—*Youness Neman*	2288 E 27th St, Vernon CA 90058	323-589-4000	R	2*	<.1
173	Frontier Radio Inc—*Roger Combs*	270 E Pamalyn Ave Ste, Las Vegas NV 89119	702-739-2940	R	2*	<.1
174	House Of Fans Inc—*Thomas Oconnor*	894 Post St, San Francisco CA 94109	415-885-1947	R	2*	<.1
175	Appliance City Inc—*Donald Rodrigue*	68 Holland St, Lewiston ME 04240	207-786-0723	R	2*	<.1
176	OWI Inc—*Ned Morioka*	17141 Kingsview Ave, Carson CA 90746	310-515-1900	R	2*	<.1
177	Video Accessory Corp—*Amy Frey*	1243 Sherman Dr Ste 8, Longmont CO 80501	303-443-1319	H	2*	<.1
178	Dey Appliance Parts Of Wisconsin Inc—*Denny Dey*	PO Box 10698, Saint Paul MN 55110	651-490-9191	R	2*	<.1
179	NRS Appliance Brokers Ltd—*Allyn Ehrlich*	502 Park Ave Apt 15g, New York NY 10022	212-759-6181	R	2*	<.1
180	DB Sales Inc—*Mark Mourton*	4100 Embassy Pkwy, Akron OH 44333	330-665-1660	R	2*	<.1
181	Plaza Imports International Inc—*Mozafar Nourmand*	1521 S Hill St, Los Angeles CA 90015	213-747-1234	R	2*	<.1
182	Green's Communications Inc—*Robert Green*	210 W Market St, Pottsville PA 17901	570-628-5556	R	2*	<.1
183	Carizan Hospitality Inc—*Errol Boothe*	9999 Summerbreeze Dr S, Fort Lauderdale FL 33322	954-748-7898	R	2*	<.1
184	Global Micro-Parts Depot Inc—*Harlan Leeds*	11151 Denton Dr, Dallas TX 75229	972-241-9470	R	2*	<.1
185	Mercury BE LLC—*Sima Ebrahimi*	3255 Saco St, Vernon CA 90058	323-588-4700	R	2*	<.1
186	Meridian Services Inc—*Robert Lantz*	1018 El Dorado Dr, Fullerton CA 92835	714-871-9625	R	2*	<.1
187	Appliance Specialty Of Florida Inc—*Doug Floyd*	6705 E 113th Ave, Temple Terrace FL 33617	813-626-6655	R	2*	<.1
188	Asia General Corp—*Valice Lim*	1013 Woodcrest Ave, Brea CA 92821	714-671-7872	R	2*	<.1
189	Atlantic Reps—*Howard Love*	811 Lingo Dr, Warminster PA 18974	215-364-2272	R	2*	<.1
190	Builder's Sales and Service Co—*Rupert Pridemore*	PO Box 8784, Fort Worth TX 76124	817-457-7900	R	1*	<.1
191	Innovative Marketing Services Inc—*Scott Edwards*	9693 Gerwig Ln Ste L, Columbia MD 21046	410-312-9070	R	1*	<.1
192	Arthur E Selnick Associates Inc—*Arthur Selnick*	6605 Selnick Dr, Elkridge MD 21075	410-796-1414	R	1*	<.1
193	Allcomm Technologies Inc—*David Cook*	5105 State Rte 33, Wall Township NJ 07727	732-919-1144	R	1*	<.1
194	Excel Electronics Company Inc—*Elie Marciano*	3700 S Santa Fe Ave, Vernon CA 90058	323-826-1955	R	1*	<.1
195	Maybrook Corp—*Nathan Feterman*	7161 Nw 52nd St, Miami FL 33166	305-715-9555	R	1*	<.1
196	Vacuflo Of Kentucky Inc—*Phillip Deddens*	2175 Watterson Trl, Louisville KY 40299	502-267-7045	R	1*	<.1
197	Logicom Sales Inc—*Prakash Thanky*	10706 Spicewood Pkwy, Austin TX 78750	512-346-5054	R	1*	<.1
198	Rochester Visual Horizons Inc—*Stanley Feingold*	180 Metro Park, Rochester NY 14623	585-424-5300	R	1*	<.1
199	Hitron International Inc—*K Chung*	941 Berryessa Rd Ste C, San Jose CA 95133	408-437-0244	R	1*	<.1
200	Sangean America Inc—*Kevin Wang*	2651 Troy Ave, South El Monte CA 91733	626-579-1600	R	1*	<.1
201	Health Labs Plus Inc—*Igor Sobolev*	1602 Alton Rd 505, Miami FL 33139	305-439-1722	R	1*	<.1
202	GCI Mobile—*Robert Goldberg*	PO Box 71480, Richmond VA 23255	804-228-5718	R	1*	<.1
203	Cunningham Corp—*Marvin Cunningham*	904 W 10th St, Pueblo CO 81003	719-543-2612	R	1*	<.1
204	SP Systems LLC—*Ferro Pagliai*	PO Box 7098, Santa Monica CA 90406	310-449-1492	R	1*	<.1
205	Fast Track Communications Inc—*Gwen Mitchell-Beard*	1510 Huber St, Atlanta GA 30318	404-875-9316	S	1*	<.1
206	Mbi Communications Inc	15271 SW 114 Terr, Miami FL 33196	305-385-0655	R	1*	<.1
207	Tana Sales And Marketing Inc—*Craig Andrews*	13815 S Lakeview Cir, Olathe KS 66061	913-522-9744	R	1*	<.1
208	Roy Brake and Associates LLC	8800 W 58th Ave Ste 10, Arvada CO 80002	303-431-5791	R	1*	<.1
209	Hollywood Sound International Corp—*Christopher Ueng*	135 E Chestnut Ave Ste, Monrovia CA 91016	626-301-7828	R	1*	<.1
210	Aga LLC—*Abraham Ali*	26300 W 8 Mile Rd, Southfield MI 48033	248-827-1020	R	1*	<.1
211	Liberty Appliances Trading Corp—*Om Sharma*	41 Greenpoint Ave, Sunnyside NY 11104	718-433-1263	R	1*	<.1
212	SAC - Sulamerica Corp—*Enesto Queiroz*	6030 Nw 99th Ave Unit, Doral FL 33178	305-477-1300	R	1*	<.1
213	Bush Refrigeration—*Jeff Bush*	1001 Line St, Camden NJ 08103	856-342-8398	R	<1*	<.1
214	Earlex Inc—*Julian Baseley*	8261 Hwy 73 Ste F, Stanley NC 28164	704-827-7889	R	<1*	<.1
215	Hennigh's Warehouse Outlet—*Ronald Hennigh*	35033 Lake Rd Ste 101, Centerville PA 16404	814-694-2606	R	<1*	<.1
216	B Frank Inc—*Bernard Frank*	300 71st St Ste 435, Miami Beach FL 33141	305-861-8227	R	<1*	<.1
217	D and K USA Inc—*Deepak Khemlani*	10475 Nw 37th Ter, Doral FL 33178	305-599-1040	R	<1*	<.1
218	Miracle Exclusives Inc—*George Drake*	PO Box 2508, Danbury CT 06813	203-796-5493	R	N/A	<.1
219	AVES Audio Visual Systems Inc—*Sandra Ramos*	PO Box 500, Sugar Land TX 77487	281-295-1300	R	N/A	<.1

TOTALS: SIC 5064 Electrical Appliances— Television & Radio
Companies: 219   12,334   13.1

Rank	Company Name—*Executive Officer*	Address, City, State, Zip	Phone	Type	Fin	Empls
	5065 Electronic Parts & Equipment Nec					
1	ADT Security Services Inc—*Theodore Vail*	1 Town Ctr Rd, Boca Raton FL 33431	561-988-3600	S	31,617*	15.0
2	Avnet Inc—*Rick Hamada*	2211 S 47th St, Phoenix AZ 85034	480-643-2000	P	26,534	17.6
3	Arrow Electronics Inc—*Michael J Long*	7459 S Lima St, Englewood CO 80112	303-824-4000	P	18,745	12.7
4	TE Connectivity Ltd—*Tom Lynch*	1050 Westlakes Dr, Berwyn PA 19312	610-893-9800	P	14,312	95.0
5	Brightpoint Inc—*Robert J Laikin*	7635 Interactive Way S, Indianapolis IN 46278		P	5,244	4.0
6	Graybar Electric Company Inc—*Robert A Reynolds Jr*	P O BOX 7231, Saint Louis MO 63177	314-573-9200	R	4,616	7.0
7	United Chemi-Con Inc—*N Kakizaki*	9801 W Higgins Rd Ste, Rosemont IL 60018	847-696-2000	R	4,590*	.4
8	Black Box Network Services (Minnetonka Minnesota)—*Terry Blakemore*	5101 Shady Oak Rd, Minnetonka MN 55343	952-352-4300	S	4,455*	1.5
9	International Electric Supply Corp	6606 LBJ Fwy Ste 184, Dallas TX 75240	972-387-3600	S	3,500	4.7
10	Vtech Communications Inc—*Nicholas Delany*	9590 Sw Gemini Dr Ste, Beaverton OR 97008	503-643-8981	R	2,808*	.1
11	Hitachi America Ltd (Brisbane California)—*Chiaki Fujiwara*	2000 Sierra Point Pkwy, Brisbane CA 94005	650-589-8300	S	2,127*	4.4
12	Rexel Inc (Dallas Texas)—*Dick Waterman*	PO Box 9085, Addison TX 75001	972-387-3600	S	1,958*	4.7
13	Astrokam—*Dick Rose*	9800 Rockside Rd, Cleveland OH 44125	216-447-0404	R	1,400*	<.1
14	Compass Technology of Burlington Massachusetts—*Kirk Rheault*	84 Sherman St 3rd Fl, Cambridge MA 02140	617-497-1700	R	1,119*	<.1
15	Panasonic Consumer Electronics Co—*Don Iwatani*	1 Panasonic Way, Secaucus NJ 07094	201-348-7000	D	857*	2.0
16	Hawk Electronics—*TA Hyde Jr*	5718 Airport Fwy, Fort Worth TX 76117		D	746*	.3
17	Reptron Electronics Inc—*Paul J Plante*	13700 Reptron Blvd, Tampa FL 33626	813-854-2000	S	710	3.5
18	Agilysys Inc—*James H Denedy*	28925 Fountain Pky, Solon OH 44139	440-519-8700	P	676	1.2
19	Nu Horizons Electronics Corp—*Martin Kent* Arrow Electronics Inc	70 Maxess Rd, Melville NY 11747	631-396-5000	S	671	.8
20	Mouser Electronics Inc—*Glen Smith*	1000 N Main St, Mansfield TX 76063	817-804-3888	S	610*	.4
21	Tessco Technologies Inc—*Robert B Barnhill Jr*	11126 McCormick Rd, Hunt Valley MD 21031	410-229-1000	P	605	.9
22	JVC Professional Products Co—*Kunihiko Sato*	1700 Valley Rd, Wayne NJ 07470	973-317-5000	S	570*	.2
23	VOXX International—*Patrick Lavelle*	180 Marcus Blvd, Hauppauge NY 11788	631-436-6499	P	562	1.0
24	Smith and Associates International Inc—*Robert G Ackerley*	5306 Hollister Rd, Houston TX 77040	713-430-3000	R	509	N/A
25	Power and Telephone Supply Company Inc—*Jim Pentecost*	2673 Yale Ave, Memphis TN 38112	901-866-3300	R	504*	.4
26	Brix Group Inc—*David Shapiro*	541 Division St, Campbell CA 95008	408-374-7900	R	503*	.2
27	Digi-Key Corp—*Mark Larson*	701 Brooks Ave S, Thief River Falls MN 56701	218-681-6674	R	500*	2.0
28	America II Electronics—*Michael Galinski*	2600 118th Ave N, Saint Petersburg FL 33716	727-573-0900	R	486*	.2
29	Rawson and Company Inc—*Tom Comstock*	PO Box 924288, Houston TX 77292	713-684-1400	R	474*	.3
30	NF Smith and Associates LP—*Robert G Ackerley*	5306 Hollister St, Houston TX 77040	713-430-3000	R	472*	.3
31	JBL Professional Inc—*John Carpanini*	8400 Balboa Blvd, Northridge CA 91329	818-894-8850	S	443*	1.8
32	Solid State Inc—*Andrew Licari*	46 Farrand St, Bloomfield NJ 07003	973-429-8700	R	343*	.1
33	PEAK Technologies Inc—*Ross M Young*	10330 Old Columbia Rd, Columbia MD 21046		S	312*	.5
34	Suntron Corp—*Ed Wheeler*	2401 W Grandview Rd, Phoenix AZ 85023	602-789-6600	R	285*	1.1
35	OKI Semiconductor—*Takaburni Asahi*	1173 Borregas Ave, Sunnyvale CA 94089	408-720-1900	S	283*	.1
36	Bearcom Operating LLC—*David Kennedy*	PO Box 559001, Dallas TX 75355	214-340-8876	R	282*	.5
37	Golden Companies Inc—*Ruby G Bowden*	PO Box 2120, Greensboro NC 27402	336-274-6700	R	267*	.1
38	DCE Corp—*Michael D Drobot*	27 Danbury Rd 3rd Fl, Wilton CT 06897	203-761-0782	R	257*	.1
39	DATAVOX Inc—*Ross Ferguson*	2000 W Sam Houston Pkw, Houston TX 77042	713-881-5300	R	238*	.1
40	SKC Communication Products Inc—*Tray Vedock*	8320 Hedge Ln Ter, Shawnee Mission KS 66227	913-422-4222	R	215*	.2
41	Jaco Electronics Inc—*Joel Girsky*	145 Oser Ave, Hauppauge NY 11788		P	194	.2
42	Versa Co—*Brock Philip*	3943 Quebec Ave N, New Hope MN 55427	763-557-6737	R	183*	.2
43	All American Semiconductor Inc—*Bruce M Goldberg*	16115 NW 52nd Ave, Miami FL 33014	305-621-8282	P	165*	.1
44	KOA Speer Electronics Inc—*Scott Rice*	PO Box 547, Bradford PA 16701	814-362-5536	R	160*	.2
45	Richardson Electronics Ltd—*Edward J Richardson*	PO Box 393, Lafox IL 60147	630-208-2200	P	159	.3
46	Edge Entertainment Distribution—*Harry Singer*	11012 Aurora Hudson Rd, Streetsboro OH 44241		R	153*	.1
47	California Eastern Laboratories Inc—*Paul Minton*	4590 Patrick Henry Dr, Santa Clara CA 95054		R	153*	.1
48	Motorola Sales And Services Inc—*Edward Fitzpatrick*	1303 E Algonquin Rd, Schaumburg IL 60196	847-576-1000	R	153*	2.5
49	Carlton-Bates Co—*Bill Carlton*	3600 W 69th St, Little Rock AR 72209	501-562-9100	S	149*	.5
50	Bluff City Electronics—*Alfred Cowles*	3339 Fontaine Rd, Memphis TN 38116	901-345-9500	R	145*	.1
51	Premier Technical Sales Inc—*Steve Dowdell*	825 San Antonio Rd Ste, Palo Alto CA 94303	650-847-1856	S	144*	.1
52	Intertrade Ltd—*Clayton M Jones*	4700 N River Blvd NE, Cedar Rapids IA 52411	319-378-3500	S	144*	.1
53	Northern Catv Sales Inc—*Andrew Tresness*	185 Ainsley Dr, Syracuse NY 13210	315-422-1230	R	133*	.5
54	Summit Electric Supply—*Victor R Jury Jr*	8718 W Little York Rd, Houston TX 77040	713-230-6300	S	133*	.3
55	NTE Electronics Inc—*Andrew Licari*	44 Farrand St, Bloomfield NJ 07003	973-748-5089	R	105*	.1
56	BridgeLux Inc—*William D Watkins*	101 Portola Ave, Livermore CA 94551	925-583-8400	R	102*	.1
57	Bell Industries Inc—*Clinton Coleman*	8888 Keystone Crossing, Indianapolis IN 46240	317-704-6000	R	101	.6
58	Force Electronics Inc—*Bob Clapp* Heilind Electronics Inc	1440 S Priest Dr Ste 1, Tempe AZ 85281	480-968-3900	S	100*	.5
59	Progressive Concepts Inc—*Robert McMurrey*	5718 Airport Fwy, Fort Worth TX 76117		S	100*	.3
60	Farmstead Telephone Group Inc (Windsor Connecticut)—*George J Taylor Jr*	725 marshall Phelps Rd, Windsor CT 06095	860-610-6000	R	100*	.1
61	Bisco Industries Inc—*Glen Seiley*	1500 N Lakeview Ave, Anaheim CA 92807	714-876-2400	S	96*	.3
62	Call One Inc—*Berchet O'daniel*	PO Box 9002, Cape Canaveral FL 32920	321-783-2400	R	93*	.1
63	Jae Electronics Inc—*Shinsuke Takahashi*	142 Technology Dr Ste, Irvine CA 92618	949-753-2600	R	92*	.2
64	Heartland Label Printers Inc—*Peter Helander*	PO Box 347, Little Chute WI 54140	920-788-7720	R	92*	.1
65	Peerless Electronics Inc—*Alvin Shankman*	PO Box 9052, Bethpage NY 11714	516-594-3500	R	86*	.1
66	Midland Radio Corp—*Daniel Devling*	5900 Parretta Dr, Kansas City MO 64120	816-241-8500	R	86*	.1
67	Associated Industries—*Ravi Achar*	11347 Vanowen St, North Hollywood CA 91605	818-760-1000	D	84*	<.1
68	Strata Inc—*Denise Lorenz*	PO Box 2988, Seattle WA 98116	425-259-6016	R	84*	<.1
69	Lemo USA Inc—*Peter Mueller*	PO Box 2408, Rohnert Park CA 94927	707-578-8811	R	82*	.1
70	Intellisys Group—*Don Esters*	140 E Dana St, Mountain View CA 94041	650-969-5212	R	80	.5
71	GC/Waldom Electronics Inc—*C Michael Jacobi*	1801 Morgan St, Rockford IL 61102	815-968-9661	S	76*	.1
72	KTS Network Solutions Inc	11132 Winners Cir Ste1, Los Alamitos CA 90720		R	75*	<.1
73	Bursma Electronic Distributing Inc—*David Van Randwyk*	2851 Buchanan SW, Grand Rapids MI 49548	616-831-0080	R	73*	.1
74	Blue Violet Networks—*Ed Lynch*	215 Baker St E Ste 150, Costa Mesa CA 92626	714-754-4000	R	72*	<.1
75	Csr Electronics Inc—*John Covey*	303 Williams Ave Sw St, Huntsville AL 35801	256-533-2444	R	70*	<.1
76	Ronco Communications and Electronics Inc—*Patricia Wasp*	595 Sheridan Dr, Tonawanda NY 14150	716-873-0760	R	67*	.3
77	Sencommunications Inc—*Frances Senory*	1611 Allison Woods Ln, Tampa FL 33619	813-626-4404	R	66	<.1
78	Relay Specialties Inc—*Barry Sauer*	17 Raritan Rd, Oakland NJ 07436	201-337-1000	R	65*	<.1
79	Elma Electronic Inc—*Fred Ruegg*	44350 S Grimmer Blvd, Fremont CA 94538	510-656-3400	R	64*	.3
80	Hammond Electronics Inc—*John Hammond*	1230 W Central Blvd, Orlando FL 32805	407-849-6060	R	61*	.2
81	MTS Telecommunications Management Inc—*Donald L Simons*	249 N Brand Blvd Ste 5, Glendale CA 91203	425-401-1000	S	61*	<.1
82	RS Electronics Inc—*Winston Stalcup*	34443 Schoolcraft Rd, Livonia MI 48150	734-525-1155	R	59*	.1
83	Air Electro Inc—*Michael McGuire*	PO Box 2231, Chatsworth CA 91311	818-407-5400	R	59*	<.1

Note: An asterisk (*) indicates an estimated financial figure. The company type code used is as follows: R = Private, P = Public, S = Private Subsidiary, B = Public Subsidiary, D = Division, J = Joint Venture, I = Investment Fund.

COMPANY RANKINGS BY SALES WITHIN 4-DIGIT SIC

Rank	Company Name—Executive Officer	Address, City, State, Zip	Phone	Type	Fin	Empls
84	Trustin Technology LLC—Jim Holden	9231 Irvine Blvd, Irvine CA 92618	949-916-7030	R	59*	<.1
85	Dow Electronics Inc—John J Yodzis	PO Box 5155, Tampa FL 33675	813-626-5195	R	56*	.2
86	B and S International Inc—Jassy Singh	9 Quail Dr, Old Bridge NJ 08857	732-360-1290	R	56*	<.1
87	Semikron Inc—Thomas O'reilley	PO Box 66, Hudson NH 03051	603-883-8102	R	55*	<.1
88	Hirose Electric (USA) Inc—Mitsugu Sugino	2688 Westhills Ct, Simi Valley CA 93065	805-522-7958	R	55*	.1
89	Trinkle Sales Inc—Tom Amaral	102 F Centre Blvd, Marlton NJ 08053	856-988-9900	R	48*	<.1
90	Iloka Inc—Sam V Kumar	5600 Greenwood Plaza B, Greenwood Village CO 80111	303-373-4444	R	46*	<.1
91	Digicorp Inc—Milton Kuyers	2322 W Clybourn St, Milwaukee WI 53233	414-343-1080	R	46*	<.1
92	Century Fasteners Corp—Jack Schlegel	5020 Ireland St, Elmhurst NY 11373	718-446-5000	R	45*	.2
93	Dataq Internet Equipment Corp—Andy Silverman	530 S Henderson Rd A-C, King Of Prussia PA 19406	610-354-9070	R	45*	<.1
94	Carswell Distributing Company Inc—William Parsley	PO Box 4193, Winston Salem NC 27115	336-767-7700	R	45*	.1
95	TriNet Communications Inc—Jon Fernandez	6567 Brisa St, Livermore CA 94550	925-294-1720	R	43*	<.1
96	Aspect Systems Inc—Dennis Key	375 E Elliot Rd Ste 6, Chandler AZ 85225	480-892-7020	R	40*	<.1
97	Integrated Electronics Corp—Craig J Walker Walker Component Group	1795 E 66th Ave, Denver CO 80229	303-292-9594	D	40*	.2
98	NJR Corp—Tony Murata	125 Nicholson Ln, San Jose CA 95134	408-321-0200	R	39*	<.1
99	Digital Connections Inc—Lee Williams	152 Molly Walton Dr, Hendersonville TN 37075	615-826-5000	R	39*	.3
100	Pics Telecom International Corp—Timothy Williams	1920 Lyell Ave, Rochester NY 14606	585-295-2000	R	39*	.1
101	Marsh Electronics Inc	1563 S 101st St, Milwaukee WI 53214	414-475-6000	R	39*	.1
102	Stellar Microelectronics Inc—Gregory Horton	28454 Livingston Ave, Valencia CA 91355	661-775-3500	R	39*	.2
103	Franklin Electric Co (Philadelphia Pennsylvania)—William Walker	1511-37 N 26th St, Philadelphia PA 19121	215-765-3965	R	38*	.1
104	Bomar Interconnect Products Inc—Bob Behrent	1850 Us Hwy 46 Ste 1, Ledgewood NJ 07852	973-347-4040	R	38*	<.1
105	PI Manufacturing Corp—Bill Chang	20732 Currier Rd, Walnut CA 91789	909-598-3718	R	37*	<.1
106	JI Audio Inc—Lucio Proni	10369 N Commerce Pkwy, Miramar FL 33025	954-443-1100	R	36*	.3
107	Asset Management Services	3900 Willow Lake Blvd, Memphis TN 38118	901-362-8600	S	36*	.3
108	Hutton Communications Inc—John Walker	2520 Marsh Ln, Carrollton TX 75006	972-417-0100	R	36	.1
109	Janesway Electronic Corp—Michael Cola	404 N Ter Ave, Mount Vernon NY 10552	914-699-6710	R	36*	<.1
110	Audiobahn Inc—Nasser Abdo	114 S Berry St, Brea CA 92821	714-988-0400	R	35*	.1
111	Bertech-Kelex Inc—Mike Moon	640 Maple Ave, Torrance CA 90503	310-787-0337	R	35*	<.1
112	Southwest Telephone and Computer Inc—Rich Fitzgeorge	3625 W MacArthur Blvd, Santa Ana CA 92704	714-556-5552	R	35*	<.1
113	Aesco Electronics Inc—William Feth	2230 Picton Pkwy, Akron OH 44312	330-245-2630	R	35*	.2
114	Durel Div—Robert Wachob	2225 W Chandler Blvd, Chandler AZ 85224	480-917-6000	D	33*	.2
115	Camtek USA Inc—Roy Porat	2000 Wyatt Dr Rm 4, Santa Clara CA 95054		S	33*	.1
116	Niles Audio Corp—Grant Rummell	PO Box 160818, Miami FL 33116	305-238-4378	R	33*	.1
117	Communications Distributors Inc—Richard Rohn	4501 Magnolia Cove Dr, Kingwood TX 77345	281-359-1115	R	32*	<.1
118	Snader And Associates Inc—John Beritzhoff	PO Box 8444, San Rafael CA 94912	415-257-8480	R	32*	.1
119	Heilind Electronics Inc—Robert Clapp	PO Box 1320, Wilmington MA 01887	978-657-4870	R	31*	.6
120	Califone International Inc—Ross Anthony	1145 Arroyo St Ste A, San Fernando CA 91340	818-407-2400	R	31*	<.1
121	Pdi Communications Inc—Barbara Edelman	6353 W Rogers Cir Ste, Boca Raton FL 33487	561-998-0600	R	31*	.1
122	Harting Incorporated Of North America—Rolf Meyer	1370 Bowes Rd, Elgin IL 60123	847-741-1500	R	30*	.1
123	Snd Electronics LLC—Michael Benedetto	14 High Bridge Rd, Sandy Hook CT 06482	203-304-4300	R	30*	<.1
124	Unique Communications Inc—Patricia Parker	3650 Coral Ridge Dr St, Coral Springs FL 33065	954-735-4002	R	30*	<.1
125	Tredent Data Systems Inc—Charles Beck	3241 Grande Vista Dr, Newbury Park CA 91320	805-375-4911	R	30*	<.1
126	Phoenix Capital Management Inc—Gary Erber	1125 Orca St, Anchorage AK 99501	907-274-8525	R	30*	<.1
127	Acg Systems Inc—Robert Dick	133 Defense Hwy Ste 20, Annapolis MD 21401	410-224-0224	R	29*	<.1
128	Barbey Electronics Corp—Jim Tabegna	PO Box 2, Reading PA 19603	610-916-7955	R	29*	<.1
129	Encore Broadcast Equipment Sales Inc—Susan Burgireno	2104 W Kennedy Blvd, Tampa FL 33606	813-253-2774	R	29*	<.1
130	Sensible Micro Corp—Ferdinand Torrioni	2339 Destiny Way, Odessa FL 33556		R	29*	<.1
131	Telecommunications Concepts Inc—Daniel Testa	5554 Port Royal Rd, Springfield VA 22151	703-321-3030	S	29*	<.1
132	Phase Technology Corp—Ken Hecht	6400 Youngerman Cir, Jacksonville FL 32244	904-777-0700	R	29*	<.1
133	Guess Technology Company Inc—Dave Guess	561 Holcombe Ave, Mobile AL 36601	251-478-0455	R	29*	<.1
134	Justin Electronics Corp—Peter Monticelli	400 Oser Ave Ste800, Hauppauge NY 11788	631-951-4900	R	27*	.1
135	Shop By Design Inc—Chris Wade-West	9710 Research Dr, Irvine CA 92618	949-333-5022	R	27*	<.1
136	Teleco Inc—William Rogers	430 Woodruff Rd Ste 30, Greenville SC 29607	864-297-4400	R	26*	.1
137	Ase (US) Inc—Pien Wu	1255 E Arques Ave, Sunnyvale CA 94085	408-636-9500	R	25*	.1
138	Prime Controls LP—Jason Eggl	815 Office Park Cir, Lewisville TX 75057	972-221-4849	R	25*	.1
139	NetVersant Solutions - Chesapeake	777 Post Oak Blvd Ste, Houston TX 77056	713-403-3800	D	25*	.1
140	Trax Distributors—Ernie Taylor	16851 Victory Blvd Ste, Lake Balboa CA 91406	818-902-0618	R	25*	<.1
141	Bliley Technologies Inc—John Cline	PO Box 3428, Erie PA 16508	814-838-3571	R	25*	.2
142	Shindengen America Inc—Peter Gajewski	2333 Waukegan Rd Ste 1, Bannockburn IL 60015	847-444-1363	R	25*	<.1
143	Compass Components Inc—Jack Maxwell	48502 Kato Rd, Fremont CA 94538	510-656-4700	R	24*	.2
144	Corstar Holdings Inc—Jeffrey Michael	10901 Red Cir Dr Ste 3, Hopkins MN 55343	952-931-0078	R	23*	.3
145	Technical Telephone Systems Inc	14 Worlds Fair Dr Ste, Somerset NJ 08873	732-563-6600	R	23*	.1
146	Tygh Silicon Inc—Steven Tygh	34145 Pacific Coast Hw, Dana Point CA 92629	925-371-1223	R	23*	<.1
147	Happ Controls Inc—Tom Happ	1743 S Linneman Rd, Mount Prospect IL 60056	847-593-6130	R	22*	.2
148	Shields Environmental Inc—Toni Gibbs	4150 Church St Ste 101, Sanford FL 32771	407-708-1875	R	22*	<.1
149	We Sell Cellular Inc—Brian Tepfer	762 Summa Ave, Westbury NY 11590	516-334-6400	R	22*	<.1
150	Lg Electronics Mobilecomm USA Inc—Kyung Hwang	10101 Old Grove Rd, San Diego CA 92131	858-635-5300	R	22*	.2
151	P D Circuits Inc—David Wolff	10 Starwood Dr, Hampstead NH 03841	603-329-4551	R	22*	.1
152	Zack Electronics Inc—Dennis Awad	1070 Hamilton Rd, Duarte CA 91010	626-303-0655	R	21*	<.1
153	Newall Electronics Inc	1778 Dividend Dr, Columbus OH 43228	614-771-0213	R	21*	<.1
154	Falcon Technologies Inc—John Baragiola	2631 Metro Blvd, Maryland Heights MO 63043	314-994-9066	R	21*	<.1
155	Cornet Technology Inc—Natarajan Kumar	6800 Versar Ctr Ste 21, Springfield VA 22151	703-658-3400	R	20*	.1
156	Lex Products Corp—Robert Luther	15 Progress Dr, Shelton CT 06484	203-363-3738	R	20*	.2
157	Airway Technologies Inc—Michael Grubbs	2205 Global Way, Hebron KY 41048	859-689-0223	R	20*	.1
158	VI Electronics Inc—Tony Tsoi	125 N Sunset Ave, City Of Industry CA 91744	626-968-4120	R	20*	<.1
159	Computer Add-Ons Inc—Asad Ali	14316 45th Ave, Flushing NY 11355	718-939-7976	R	20*	<.1
160	Cutting Edge Audio Group LLC—Jeff Briss	290 Division St Ste 10, San Francisco CA 94103	415-487-2323	R	20*	<.1
161	Leading Edge Distribution Ltd—Tracy Jones	7850 Northfield Rd, Cleveland OH 44146	440-786-2444	R	20*	<.1
162	Dailey And Wells Communications Inc—Richard Wells	3440 E Houston St, San Antonio TX 78219	210-893-6500	R	19*	.1
163	Richardson Technology Systems Inc—Joseph Ciotti	PO Box 908973, Gainesville GA 30501	678-376-8884	R	18*	.1
164	Music People Inc—Jim Hennesey	154 Woodlawn Rd Ste C, Berlin CT 06037	860-829-9229	R	18*	.1
165	Ranger Communications Inc—Joe Banos	401 W 35th St, National City CA 91950	619-426-3199	R	18*	<.1
166	Engenius Technologies Inc—Tommy Tsai	1580 Scenic Ave, Costa Mesa CA 92626	714-432-8668	R	18*	<.1
167	Telquest International Corp—Alfred Adel	26 Commerce Rd Ste B, Fairfield NJ 07004	973-808-4588	R	18*	.2
168	Macronix America Inc—Alan Portnoy	680 N Mccarthy Blvd St, Milpitas CA 95035	408-262-8887	R	17*	.1
169	Domital Corp—Juan Coccarello	7255 Nw 19th St Ste A, Miami FL 33126	305-594-0873	R	17*	.2
170	Arizona Components Company Inc—Roger Lamoure	2901 W Mcdowell Rd, Phoenix AZ 85009	602-269-5655	R	17*	.1
171	Datex Corp	10320 49th St, Clearwater FL 33762	727-571-4159	R	17*	<.1

Rank	Company Name—*Executive Officer*	Address, City, State, Zip	Phone	Type	Fin	Empls
172	Don Blackburn and Co—*Ron Clark*	13335 Farmington Rd, Livonia MI 48150	734-261-9100	R	17*	<.1
173	Intellimar Inc—*Mark O Oakes*	7560 Main St, Sykesville MD 21784	410-552-9940	R	17*	<.1
174	Midstate Electronics Co—*Mark Fortier*	71 S Tpke Rd Ste 1, Wallingford CT 06492	203-265-9900	R	17*	<.1
175	Protel Inc—*Regis Mellon*	4150 Kidron Rd, Lakeland FL 33811	863-644-5558	R	17*	.1
176	Erc Parts Inc—*Charles Rollins*	4001 Cobb Internationa, Kennesaw GA 30152	770-984-0276	R	16*	.1
177	Semtronic Associates Inc—*Ronald Camillone*	195 W Pine Ave, Longwood FL 32750	407-831-8233	R	16*	<.1
178	Bay Communications Inc—*Steve Elias*	2040 Radisson St, Green Bay WI 54302	920-468-5426	R	16*	<.1
179	Radicom Inc—*Phillip Bartmann*	2604 N Chapel Hill Rd, Mchenry IL 60051	815-385-4224	R	16*	<.1
180	GP Johnston Inc—*Philip Johnston*	PO Box 390, Kearny NJ 07032	201-991-7400	R	16*	.1
181	BGE and C Inc—*Bill Gonzalez*	1610 N Interstate 35 H, Carrollton TX 75006	972-492-7877	R	16*	<.1
182	Ectaco Inc—*David Lubinitsky*	3121 31st St, Long Island City NY 11106	718-728-6110	R	16*	.2
183	Knox Associates Inc—*Don Trempala*	1601 W Deer Valley Rd, Phoenix AZ 85027	623-687-2300	R	16*	.1
184	Masterlink Corp—*Bruce Magnuson*	PO Box 485, Butler WI 53007	262-783-8780	R	15*	.1
185	Tritronics Inc—*Kimberly Wagner*	1306 Continental Dr, Abingdon MD 21009	410-676-7300	R	15*	.1
186	Global Link Networking Solutio—*Angela Suddarth*	242 W Main St Ste 190, Hendersonville TN 37075	615-447-1430	R	15*	<.1
187	Digitel Corp—*Jerry Bailey*	2600 School Dr, Atlanta GA 30360	770-451-1111	R	15*	.1
188	L Merrill Michael and Associates Inc—*Michael Merrill*	PO Box 279, Brea CA 92822	714-256-2206	R	15*	<.1
189	Sea View Technologies Inc—*Roland Brewer*	22 Industrial Dr, Exeter NH 03833	603-436-3733	R	15*	<.1
190	Laube Technology Inc	550 Via Alondra, Camarillo CA 93012	805-388-1050	R	15*	<.1
191	Noble USA Inc—*Y Honda*	5450 Meadowbrook Indus, Rolling Meadows IL 60008	847-364-6038	R	15*	<.1
192	Electro-Line Inc—*Bruce A Jump*	PO Box 1688, Dayton OH 45401	937-461-5683	R	15*	<.1
193	Intermetra Corp—*Michael Maiden*	10100 NW 116 Way Ste 1, Medley FL 33178	305-889-1194	R	15*	<.1
194	Meunier Electronics Supply Inc—*James Meunier*	3409 E Washington St, Indianapolis IN 46201	317-635-3511	R	15*	<.1
195	Modafferi and Maether—*Scott Caliel*	6101 E Molloy Rd Ste 5, East Syracuse NY 13057	315-431-1001	R	15*	<.1
196	MBR Industries Inc—*Bernard Pomeranc*	3201 Nw 116th St, Miami FL 33167	305-769-1000	R	15*	.1
197	Electronics Supply Company Inc—*Joanne Labelle*	4100 Main St, Kansas City MO 64111	816-931-0250	R	15*	<.1
198	Waldom Electronics Corp—*Pasel Nizam*	1801 Morgan St, Rockford IL 61102	815-968-9661	R	15*	.1
199	1 Nation Investment Corp—*David Key*	4027 Tampa Rd Ste 3000, Oldsmar FL 34677	813-349-6852	R	15*	.1
200	Mobile Line Communications Corp—*Dennis Curtis*	1402 Morgan Cir, Tustin CA 92780	714-247-2500	R	15*	.1
201	Atrion Networking Corporation Inc—*Charles Nault*	30 Service Ave, Warwick RI 02886	401-736-6400	R	15*	.1
202	Optelec US Inc—*Michiel Shaik*	3030 Enterprise Ct Ste, Vista CA 92081	760-536-0077	R	15*	<.1
203	Carlin Systems Inc—*John Giovan*	31 Floyds Run, Bohemia NY 11716	631-471-2000	R	15*	<.1
204	Tecore Inc—*Jay Salkini*	7061 Columbia Gateway, Columbia MD 21046	410-872-6000	R	14*	.1
205	Ralphs Of Lafayette Inc—*David Jordan*	PO Box R, Lafayette LA 70502	337-233-0105	R	14*	.1
206	Si-Tex Marine Electronics Inc—*Ted Bodtmann*	25 Enterprise Zone Dr, Riverhead NY 11901	631-996-2690	S	14*	.1
207	Morley-Murphy Co—*Stephen Stiles*	200 S Washington St, Green Bay WI 54303	920-499-3171	R	14*	<.1
208	Milano Brothers International Corp—*Piero Guidugli*	1456 W Newport Ctr Dr, Deerfield Beach FL 33442	954-420-5000	R	14*	.1
209	3rd Wave Solutions Inc—*Bruce Anderson*	444 N 44th St Ste 222, Phoenix AZ 85008	602-797-1000	R	14*	<.1
210	Gerber Radio Supply Co—*Ben Speigel*	128 Carnegie Row, Norwood MA 02062	781-769-6000	R	14*	<.1
211	Aerospace Materials Corp—*Jerry Deland*	1940 Petra Ln Ste D, Placentia CA 92870	714-528-3002	R	14*	<.1
212	Phone Labs Technology Company Inc	955 Connecticut Ave St, Bridgeport CT 06607		R	14*	<.1
213	Hyundai Electronics Pacific Inc—*Sung Ahn*	4800 Great America Pkw, Santa Clara CA 95054	408-844-8066	R	14*	<.1
214	Sound Inc—*Todd Channell*	1550 Shore Rd, Naperville IL 60563	630-369-2900	R	14*	.1
215	Amtec Communications Inc—*Russ Goeckner*	1894 Commercenter W St, San Bernardino CA 92408	909-884-9497	R	14*	.1
216	Meritek Electronics Corp—*Pa-Shih Su*	11824 Hamden Pl, Santa Fe Springs CA 90670	562-948-2236	R	14*	.1
217	Crest Electronics Inc—*Corey Tisthammer*	PO Box 727, Dassel MN 55325	320-275-3382	R	13*	.1
218	Fowler Productions Inc—*Ron English*	PO Box 721378, Norman OK 73070	405-321-8122	R	13*	.1
219	Trade Wings Inc—*Todd Adelman*	130 International Dr, Portsmouth NH 03801	603-766-7000	R	13*	<.1
220	Universal Security Instruments Inc—*Harvey Grossblatt*	11407 Cronhill Dr Ste, Owings Mills MD 21117	410-363-3000	P	13	<.1
221	Ria Connect Inc—*Albert Metz*	200 Tornillo Way Ste 1, Tinton Falls NJ 07712	732-389-1300	R	13*	<.1
222	Iverify Inc—*Mike May*	150 Iverify Dr, Charlotte NC 28217	704-525-2701	R	13*	.2
223	Audio-Technica US Inc—*Phil Cajka*	1221 Commerce Dr, Stow OH 44224	330-686-2600	R	13*	.1
224	Walker Component Group	1795 E 66th Ave, Denver CO 80229	303-292-9594	D	13*	.1
225	Simcona Electronics Corp—*Angelo Casciani*	PO Box 60967, Rochester NY 14606	585-328-3230	R	13*	.1
226	Martco Inc—*Spencer Martin*	PO Box 7429, Louisville KY 40257	502-635-1600	R	13*	.1
227	Executone Telecommunications LLC—*Pat Reinfeldt*	1017 Naughton Dr, Troy MI 48083	248-457-9430	R	13*	.1
228	Ksm Electronics Inc—*Stephen Benjamin*	5607 Hiatus Rd Ste 600, Tamarac FL 33321	954-971-5900	R	13*	.3
229	Neteam Systems LLC—*Patrick Aulizia*	4125 Highlander Pkwy S, Richfield OH 44286	330-523-5100	R	12*	<.1
230	Dean Enterprises and Associates Inc—*Jim Dean*	PO Box 926, Divide CO 80814		R	12*	<.1
231	Odu-Usa Inc—*Joseph Cisi*	4010 Adolfo Rd, Camarillo CA 93012	805-484-0540	R	12*	.1
232	Linak US Inc—*Soren Stig-Nielsen*	2200 Stanley Gault Pkw, Louisville KY 40223	502-253-5595	R	12*	.1
233	Foreign Trade Corp—*Ramin Rostami*	130 W Cochran St, Simi Valley CA 93065	805-823-8400	R	12*	.1
234	LKG Industries Inc—*Kittikarn Mejudhon*	PO Box 6386, Rockford IL 61125	815-874-2301	R	12*	.1
235	Altex Engineered Electronic Solutions—*Ben Weidberg*	17201 Westfield Park R, Westfield IN 46074	317-867-4000	R	12*	<.1
236	Dove Electronic Components Inc—*Matthew Waite*	39 Research Way, East Setauket NY 11733	631-689-7733	R	12*	<.1
237	Summit Electronics Corp—*Richard Rosenstein*	751 Park of Commerce D, Boca Raton FL 33487	561-226-8500	R	12*	<.1
238	Ceiba Technologies Inc—*John Vargas*	410 N Roosevelt Ave, Chandler AZ 85226	480-705-4541	R	12*	<.1
239	Visual Solutions Distributing Inc—*Tony Wiggins*	135 Short St Ste B, Lawrenceburg IN 47025	812-539-1866	R	12*	.1
240	Hype Technology—*Hung Chen*	16289 Gale Ave, City Of Industry CA 91745	909-632-6385	R	12*	.1
241	Southwest Tel-Supply LLC—*Jeanie Prather*	PO Box 60366, San Angelo TX 76906	325-658-1228	R	12*	<.1
242	Magtrol Inc (Tucson Arizona)—*Jack Wissen*	1555 E Apache Park Plz, Tucson AZ 85714	520-622-7802	R	12*	.1
243	Comproducts Inc—*Thomas Harb*	1330 Stimmel Rd Ste B, Columbus OH 43223	614-276-5552	R	12*	.2
244	Anderson Electronics Inc—*William Anderson*	PO Box 89, Hollidaysburg PA 16648	814-695-4428	R	12*	.1
245	Robert Mckeown Company Inc—*Dawson Mckeown*	111 Chambers Brook Rd, Branchburg NJ 08876	908-218-9000	R	12*	<.1
246	Zettacom Inc—*Daryn Lau*	2901 Coronado Dr, Santa Clara CA 95054	408-869-7000	R	12*	.1
247	Peruno USA—*James Atterdige*	4400 Nw Pacific Rim Bl, Camas WA 98607	360-833-5012	R	11*	.1
248	Zte (USA) Inc—*Lixin Cheng*	2425 N Central Expy St, Richardson TX 75080	972-671-8885	R	11*	.1
249	Belmont Trading Company Inc—*Igor Boguslavsky*	3160 Macarthur Blvd, Northbrook IL 60062	847-412-9690	R	11*	.1
250	Interactive Solutions Inc (Memphis Tennessee)—*Jay B Myers*	3860 Forest Hill Irene, Memphis TN 38125	901-866-1474	R	11*	<.1
251	Wise Components Inc—*Scott Blaustein*	79 Harborview Ave, Stamford CT 06902		R	11*	.1
252	Surge Components Inc—*Ira Levy*	95 E Jefryn Blvd, Deer Park NY 11729	631-595-1818	R	11	<.1
253	Great Lakes Automation Supply	702 N 20th St, Battle Creek MI 49037	269-963-6282	D	11*	<.1
254	Aegis Electronic Group Inc—*Elizabeth Carnes*	1465 N Fiesta Blvd Ste, Gilbert AZ 85233	480-635-8400	R	11*	<.1
255	National Communication Service—*Ben Hayes*	14110 Ne 21st St, Bellevue WA 98007	425-378-8080	R	11*	.1
256	Elna Ferrite Laboratories Inc—*Joseph Ferraro*	203 Malden Tpke, Saugerties NY 12477	845-247-2000	R	11*	.1
257	Toko America Inc—*J Onodera*	1250 Feehanville Dr, Mount Prospect IL 60056	847-297-0070	R	11*	.1
258	Minco Technology Labs LLC—*Connie Allen*	1805 Rutherford Ln, Austin TX 78754	512-834-2022	R	11*	.1
259	Awi Inc—*Sarabjit Lamba*	206 Terminal Dr, Plainview NY 11803	516-813-9500	R	10*	.1
260	Filco Discount Center Inc—*David J Saca*	1415 Fulton Ave, Sacramento CA 95825	916-483-4526	R	10*	.2
261	Rogers Electric Supplies Co—*Jim Pfeister*	PO Box 1767, Sioux City IA 51102	712-252-3251	R	10*	<.1

Note: An asterisk (*) indicates an estimated financial figure. The company type code used is as follows: R = Private, P = Public, S = Private Subsidiary, B = Public Subsidiary, D = Division, J = Joint Venture, I = Investment Fund.

COMPANY RANKINGS BY SALES WITHIN 4-DIGIT SIC

Rank	Company Name—*Executive Officer*	Address, City, State, Zip	Phone	Type	Fin	Empls
262	Rose Electronic Components Inc—*Joseph Galinski*	4615 Gulf Blvd Ste 217, Saint Pete Beach FL 33706	727-363-6658	R	10*	<.1
263	Global Advance Inc—*W Kim*	30423 Canwood St Ste 1, Agoura Hills CA 91301	818-889-7054	R	10*	<.1
264	Lindberg Enterprises Inc—*Lina Lin*	700 Milik St, Carteret NJ 07008	732-969-1880	R	10*	<.1
265	Advanced Data Marketing Inc—*Reed Ahlquist*	PO Box 806, Parker CO 80134	303-841-4903	R	10*	<.1
266	Record A Phone Corp—*Benjamin Goldstein*	1 Rewe St, Brooklyn NY 11211	212-674-5436	R	10*	<.1
267	Dynamic Systems Integration Inc—*James Butt*	2649 Production Rd, Virginia Beach VA 23454	757-431-5000	R	10*	.1
268	Cumberland Electronics Inc—*Donald Smeltz*	PO Box 8003, Harrisburg PA 17105		R	10*	.1
269	Millennium Technology Partners LLC—*Ryan Jakic*	N1886 Hwy 120, Lake Geneva WI 53147	262-249-8705	R	10*	<.1
270	C and D Electronics Inc—*Mark Cutting*	28 Appleton St, Holyoke MA 01040	413-493-1200	R	10*	<.1
271	Mibar Marketing Corp—*Barry Goldstein*	125 Wireless Blvd Ste, Hauppauge NY 11788	631-261-6900	R	9*	<.1
272	Union Electronics Inc—*David Cecich*	311 E Corning Rd, Beecher IL 60401	708-946-9500	R	9*	.1
273	Mid-State Communications and Electronics Inc—*Sandra Corney*	185 Clear Rd, Oriskany NY 13424	315-736-3061	R	9*	.1
274	Koambra Inc—*Young Yu*	2392 E Artesia Blvd, Long Beach CA 90805	562-422-3636	R	9*	<.1
275	El Paso Communication Systems Inc—*Jorge Saad*	1630 E Paisano Dr Ste, El Paso TX 79901	915-533-5119	R	9*	<.1
276	Shawntech Communications Inc—*Lance Fancher*	1700 Lyons Rd Unit C, Dayton OH 45458	937-898-4900	R	9*	.1
277	Silicon Turnkey Solutions Inc—*Zef Malik*	801 Buckeye Ct, Milpitas CA 95035	408-432-1790	R	9*	.1
278	AdvanTel Inc—*Roger McGibbon*	2222 Trade Zone Blvd, San Jose CA 95131	408-954-5100	R	9*	.1
279	Standard Electronics Corp—*Mark Kennedy*	1001 W Washington St F, Norristown PA 19401	610-272-6300	R	9*	<.1
280	Electronic Components and Equipment—*Jamil Nizam*	3100 NW 36th St, Miami FL 33142	305-638-2000	R	9*	<.1
281	SW Marketing Associates Inc—*JR Ramsey*	10557 Metric Dr, Dallas TX 75243	214-340-0265	R	9*	<.1
282	Dv8 Enterprises Ltd—*Craig Clark*	21 Inverness Way E, Englewood CO 80112	303-884-3282	R	9*	<.1
283	Interep Associates Inc—*Perry Hughey*	401 Holmes Ave Ne Ste, Huntsville AL 35801	256-881-1096	R	9*	<.1
284	Audissey—*Gerald Luke*	841 Pohukaina St Ste B, Honolulu HI 96814	808-591-2791	R	9*	<.1
285	Tocos America Inc—*Don Schimizu*	1177 E Twr Rd, Schaumburg IL 60173	847-884-6664	S	9*	<.1
286	Industrial Representatives Inc—*Mark Mitchell*	5215 Old Orchard Rd St, Skokie IL 60077	847-967-8430	R	9*	.1
287	GC Fabrication Inc—*Joseph Abbatiello*	119 Rockland Ave Ste G, Northvale NJ 07647	201-767-6100	R	9*	.1
288	Pair Gain Communications Inc—*Paul Henson*	6260 S Bay Rd, Cicero NY 13039	315-698-4411	R	9*	.1
289	Questar Inc—*Albert Nader*	PO Box 11345, Chicago IL 60611	312-266-9400	R	9*	<.1
290	Above Board Electronics Inc—*James Wahl*	2151 Otoole Ave Ste I, San Jose CA 95131	408-325-7000	R	9*	<.1
291	Allstar Magnetics LLC—*Brad Smith*	6205 Ne 63rd St, Vancouver WA 98661	360-693-0213	R	9*	<.1
292	Components Specialties Inc—*Louis Keller*	PO Box 726, Amityville NY 11701	631-957-8700	R	9*	<.1
293	Innovative Communication Concepts Inc—*William Wenzel*	519 8th Ave Frnt 4, New York NY 10018	212-629-3366	R	8*	.1
294	Betatron Electronics Inc—*Richard Gallegos*	1381 Flightway Ave Se, Albuquerque NM 87106	505-821-1122	R	8*	<.1
295	East Coast Microwave Sales and Distribution Inc—*Bruce Cooper*	70 Tower Office Park, Woburn MA 01801	781-279-0900	R	8*	<.1
296	Btx Technologies Inc—*Greg Schwartz*	5 Skyline Dr Ste 115, Hawthorne NY 10532	914-592-1800	R	8*	<.1
297	Cal-Chip Electronics Inc—*Jerry Giuliano*	59 Steam Whistle Dr, Warminster PA 18974	215-942-8900	R	8*	.1
298	Hycon Corp—*David Heyer*	414 Plz Dr Ste 308, Westmont IL 60559	630-655-7070	R	8*	<.1
299	Cutter Communications Inc—*David Mcginnis*	PO Box 2119, Van Alstyne TX 75495	903-482-7000	R	8*	<.1
300	Systems Plus Telecom Inc—*Mark Stewart*	645 E Elliott Ave, Saint Louis MO 63122	314-835-0282	R	8*	<.1
301	Communications Televideo Ltd—*Han Jan*	9301 Georgia Ave, Silver Spring MD 20910	301-585-6311	R	8*	<.1
302	Professional Telecommunication Services Inc—*Joey Hazenfield*	2119 Beechmont Ave, Cincinnati OH 45230	513-232-7700	R	8*	<.1
303	Business Telecommunication Systems Inc—*Teresa Vorgna*	549 Bateman Cir, Corona CA 92880	951-272-3100	R	8*	<.1
304	Global Circuit Solutions—*Raul Barragan*	4130 Flat Rock Dr Unit, Riverside CA 92505	951-353-2780	R	8*	<.1
305	Phillips Communication and Equipment Co—*Harold Phillips*	PO Box 6160, Charlottesville VA 22906	434-985-3600	R	8*	<.1
306	Qualiton Imports Ltd—*Anita Quittner*	2402 40th Ave, Long Island City NY 11101	718-937-8515	R	8*	<.1
307	Interconsal Associates Inc—*Kathy Leipelt*	12425 Ranchero Way, Grass Valley CA 95949	530-268-1078	R	8*	<.1
308	Baldan Inc—*Julio Gonzalves*	245 Se 1st St Ste 438, Miami FL 33131	305-374-5695	R	8*	<.1
309	Biomimetic Solutions Plus Inc—*Bud Garrett*	1904 Canyon Creek Ct, Pearland TX 77581	281-997-9318	R	8*	<.1
310	Four S Group Inc—*Simone Kfoury*	4621 Ponce De Leon Blv, Coral Gables FL 33146	305-666-7474	R	8*	<.1
311	Westwood Associates Inc—*Kenneth Downey*	PO Box 2007, North Haven CT 06473	203-974-1333	R	8*	<.1
312	Executone Systems Company Of Louisiana Inc—*Frank Labiche*	PO Box 68, Metairie LA 70004	504-838-9600	R	8*	<.1
313	Baltimore Sound Engineering Inc—*David Soul*	6308 Blair Hill Ln, Baltimore MD 21209	410-583-8900	R	7*	<.1
314	Global Semisolutions Inc—*Robert Ramirez*	24671 Us Hwy 19 N Ste, Clearwater FL 33763	727-781-6090	R	7*	<.1
315	Taitron Components Inc—*Stewart Wang*	28040 W Harrison Pky, Valencia CA 91355	661-257-6060	P	7	<.1
316	Olympia TradingCom Inc—*Wilder Cordero*	171 Ne 1st St, Miami FL 33132	305-371-9490	R	7*	<.1
317	Spacecraft Components Corp—*Ed Wiseman*	3040 N Clayton St, North Las Vegas NV 89032	702-851-7600	R	7*	.1
318	American Connector LLC—*Neal Bonavia*	PO Box 5397, Hialeah FL 33014	305-591-7530	R	7*	.1
319	Pletronics Inc—*K Lee*	PO Box 2607, Lynnwood WA 98036	425-776-1880	R	7*	<.1
320	Nexus Office Systems Inc—*Bill Rockwood*	898 Featherstone Rd, Rockford IL 61107	815-227-0170	R	7*	<.1
321	RoData Inc—*John Rodella*	1207 Muriel St, Pittsburgh PA 15203	412-316-6000	R	7*	<.1
322	CAL-TEK Company Inc—*Dan Wiswell*	20 Republic Rd, North Billerica MA 01862	978-667-8541	R	7*	<.1
323	Etchomatic Inc—*Peter Loven*	179 Olde Canal Dr, Lowell MA 01851	978-656-0011	R	7*	<.1
324	Exley Mixon Inc—*Exley Mixon*	270 E Caribbean Dr, Sunnyvale CA 94089	408-752-1560	R	7*	<.1
325	Electronic Hardware Ltd—*Richard Degn*	PO Box 15039, North Hollywood CA 91615	818-982-6100	R	7*	<.1
326	Lintech Components Company Inc—*Ken Linden*	710 Union Pkwy Ste 8, Ronkonkoma NY 11779	631-580-9500	R	7*	<.1
327	Mark Electronics Inc—*Thomas Koebert*	PO Box 635, Glenside PA 19038	215-887-2317	R	7*	<.1
328	Central Station Inc—*Don Minyard*	PO Box 610220, Birmingham AL 35261	205-838-4145	R	7*	<.1
329	Time Mark Inc—*Stan Allina*	11440 E Pine St, Tulsa OK 74116	918-438-1220	R	7*	<.1
330	Nano Electronics Inc—*Nir Fraind*	10205 67th Dr Ste B, Flushing NY 11375	718-275-7775	R	7*	<.1
331	First Security and Communications Sales Inc—*William Smith*	1811 High Grove Ln Ste, Naperville IL 60540	630-961-5900	R	7*	.1
332	Famlee Electronics Inc—*George Streiter*	20150 Sunburst St, Chatsworth CA 91311	818-703-8892	R	7*	<.1
333	IK Systems Inc—*Melkon Babigian*	7625 Main St Fishers, Victor NY 14564	585-924-9000	R	7*	<.1
334	Realm Communications Group Inc—*John Russell*	PO Box 612380, San Jose CA 95161	408-945-6626	R	7*	<.1
335	Test Equipment Remarketers Inc—*Laura Wilson*	120 Brisbayne Cir, La Grange NC 28551	252-492-5401	R	7*	<.1
336	Advance Technical Sales Inc—*Richard Larsen*	111 W Spring Valley Rd, Richardson TX 75081	915-849-0606	R	7*	<.1
337	Arva-Hudson Inc—*Mark Zamalloa*	19119 N Creek Pkwy Ste, Bothell WA 98011	425-489-5700	R	7*	<.1
338	Capacitors Plus Inc—*Katherine Sawyer*	PO Box 820, Cordova TN 38088	901-937-0777	R	6*	<.1
339	Personal Communications Center Inc—*Patricia Sinha*	3940 30th St, Long Island City NY 11101	718-764-8300	R	6*	<.1
340	Koehlke Components Inc—*Tom Koehlke*	1201 Commerce Ctr Dr, Franklin OH 45005	937-435-5435	R	6*	<.1
341	Mavco Inc—*John Timinsky*	555 Nw 95th St, Miami FL 33150	305-757-5000	R	6*	<.1
342	Pharos Science and Applications Inc—*James Oyang*	411 Amapola Ave, Torrance CA 90501	310-212-7088	R	6*	<.1
343	Brevan Electronics Inc—*Bob Purcell*	6 Continental Blvd, Merrimack NH 03054	603-429-1900	R	6*	<.1
344	888 Digital Inc—*Al Palacci*	1416 E Linden Ave, Linden NJ 07036	908-583-9300	R	6*	<.1
345	Structured Communication Systems Inc—*Ronald Fowler*	12901 Se 97th Ave Ste, Clackamas OR 97015	503-513-9979	R	6*	<.1
346	Pedigree Technologies LLC—*David Batcheller*	1810 Ndsu Research Cir, Fargo ND 58102	701-231-5263	R	6*	<.1
347	Toa Electronics Inc—*Kazuo Musa*	601 Gateway Blvd Ste 3, South San Francisco CA 94080	650-452-1200	R	6*	<.1
348	International Protection Group LLC—*Jerry Heying*	481 8th Ave 1570, New York NY 10001	212-947-1681	R	6*	.4

Rank	Company Name—*Executive Officer*	Address, City, State, Zip	Phone	Type	Fin	Empls
349	Union Technology Corp—*David Chu*	718 Monterey Pass Rd, Monterey Park CA 91754	323-266-6603	R	6*	.1
350	Abacus Industries Inc—*David Macdougal*	3894 Mannix Dr Ste 208, Naples FL 34114	239-304-1110	R	6*	<.1
351	Nave Communications Co—*Doug Nave*	PO Box 615, Jessup MD 20794	301-725-6283	R	6*	<.1
352	Rapport Inc—*Shirley Lehman*	13180 W 43rd Dr, Golden CO 80403	303-202-9599	R	6*	<.1
353	MMC Metrology Lab Inc—*William Marcum*	4989 Cleveland St, Virginia Beach VA 23462	757-456-2220	R	6*	<.1
354	Ametrade Inc—*Karina Doracio*	3057 Nw 107th Ave, Doral FL 33172	305-594-7971	R	6*	<.1
355	NSI Communications Inc—*Yuri Sushkin*	1941 Lake Whatcom Blvd, Bellingham WA 98229		R	6*	<.1
356	American Sound and Electronics Inc—*Richard Toerner*	1800 Russell St, Covington KY 41014	859-261-9024	R	6*	<.1
357	American Microsemiconductor Inc—*William Foley*	PO Box 104, Madison NJ 07940	973-377-9566	R	6*	<.1
358	Norcomp Inc—*Scott Carpenter*	1267 Oakmead Pkwy, Sunnyvale CA 94085	408-733-7707	R	6*	<.1
359	Lubbock Audio Visual Inc—*Stan Wagnon*	PO Box 1935, Lubbock TX 79408	806-744-2559	R	6*	<.1
360	TDK Electronics Corp—*Hajime Sawabe*	PO Box 9302, Garden City NY 11530	516-535-2600	S	6	.1
361	Capitol Cable and Technology Inc—*Sten Tegner*	7905 Airpark Rd, Gaithersburg MD 20879	301-840-5700	R	6*	<.1
362	Cecol Inc—*Osamu Yamada*	951 N Plum Grove Rd St, Schaumburg IL 60173	847-619-6700	R	6*	<.1
363	Bluzona	1601 McCarthy Blvd, Milpitas CA 95035	408-546-0660	R	6*	.1
364	Equiptex Industrial Products Corp—*Robert Ramsey*	14 N Bleeker St, Mount Vernon NY 10550	914-668-4841	R	6*	<.1
365	General Telcom Inc—*Nate Gordon*	2930 Scott Blvd, Santa Clara CA 95054	408-988-7744	R	6*	<.1
366	Atlantic Components Inc—*Eugene Megna*	PO Box 847073, Boston MA 02284	781-933-9966	R	6*	<.1
367	Comtel Systems Corp—*Michael Butler*	2602 E 7th Ave Ste 200, Tampa FL 33605	813-623-3974	R	5*	<.1
368	Atlantic Business Communications Of Orlando Inc—*Joel Botbol*	4319 35th St Ste E, Orlando FL 32811	407-872-1170	R	5*	<.1
369	Ct Group LLC—*Charles Schindo*	10814 Nw 33rd St Ste 1, Doral FL 33172	305-715-7171	R	5*	<.1
370	Innovasic Inc—*Keith Prettyjohns*	3737 Princeton Dr Ne S, Albuquerque NM 87107	505-883-5263	R	5*	<.1
371	CTW Electrical Company Inc—*Edward Fiorenza*	601 Sayre Ct, Greenwood IN 46143	317-881-3785	R	5*	<.1
372	R and J Components Corp—*Tyrell Schneck*	360 Rabro Dr, Hauppauge NY 11788	631-234-3330	R	5*	<.1
373	Mosier Automation Inc—*James Mcmillan*	9851 Park Davis Dr, Indianapolis IN 46235	317-895-6200	R	5*	<.1
374	Professional Video Supply Inc—*Brad Bartholomew*	9201 Cody St, Shawnee Mission KS 66214	913-492-1787	R	5*	<.1
375	Telephone Associates Inc—*William Torrey*	PO Box 1436, Superior WI 54880	715-392-8101	R	5*	<.1
376	Motor City Services Inc—*Karen Grace*	16576 Harrison St, Livonia MI 48154	734-466-9728	R	5*	<.1
377	Inter-Commercial Business Systems Inc—*Nancy Lutringer*	601 Century Pkwy Ste 1, Allen TX 75013	972-649-4949	R	5*	<.1
378	Orion Engineering and Service Inc—*Eonsu Chanj*	PO Box 2768, Calexico CA 92232	760-352-2547	R	5*	<.1
379	Derf Electronics Corp—*Randolph Derf*	253 N Grand Ave, Poughkeepsie NY 12603	845-790-9900	R	5*	<.1
380	Promotek Inc—*Raymond Lee*	901 S Fremont Ave Ste, Alhambra CA 91803	626-308-0992	R	5*	.3
381	P4c Global Inc—*Steven Hopwood*	9327 Deering Ave, Chatsworth CA 91311	818-341-8301	R	5*	.1
382	Beyond Security Inc—*Aviram Jenik*	1616 Anderson Rd, Mc Lean VA 22102	703-286-7725	R	5*	<.1
383	Electrical and Electronics Controls Inc—*Bruce Beutler*	3881 Danbury Rd Ste 2, Brewster NY 10509	914-769-5000	R	5*	<.1
384	Illinois Capacitor Inc—*Basil Jacobson*	3757 W Touhy Ave, Lincolnwood IL 60712	847-675-1760	R	5*	<.1
385	West Side Communications Inc—*James Lauffer*	1449 Fairmont Rd, Morgantown WV 26501	304-983-8642	R	5*	<.1
386	Control Switches International Inc—*Donald Armstrong*	2425 Mira Mar Ave, Long Beach CA 90815	562-498-7331	R	5*	<.1
387	Multimedia Integrated Technology Inc—*Joe Russo*	1863 N Case St, Orange CA 92866	714-937-1484	R	5*	<.1
388	BG Electronics Inc BGE and C Inc	1610 Interstate 35 N B, Carrollton TX 75006	972-492-7877	D	5	<.1
389	Ram Meter Inc—*Richard Troyanek*	1903 Barrett Dr, Troy MI 48084	248-362-0990	R	5*	<.1
390	Independent Telephone Network Inc—*Pam Branner*	8741 Shirley Ave, Northridge CA 91324	818-882-0000	R	5*	<.1
391	Saddle Brook Controls—*Gary Laurita*	280 N Midland Ave, Saddle Brook NJ 07663	201-794-9588	R	5*	<.1
392	Global Communications—*Isaac Pinter*	3611 14th Ave Ste 501, Brooklyn NY 11218	718-369-2400	R	5*	<.1
393	Right Connection Electronics Inc—*Kuelee Lin*	22745 Old Canal Rd, Yorba Linda CA 92887	714-685-6800	R	5*	<.1
394	Nova Marketing Ltd—*Tod Danhoucor*	508 Twilight Trl Ste 2, Richardson TX 75080	214-570-0400	R	5*	<.1
395	Cameron Computers Inc—*Joseph Cameron*	27 Tobey wods, Pittsford NY 14534	585-381-3090	R	5	<.1
396	Prime Image Inc—*Frank Alioto*	458 S Hillview Dr, Milpitas CA 95035	408-867-6519	R	5*	<.1
397	Tsc Electronics Ltd—*Shi Tsai*	1610 Lockness Pl, Torrance CA 90501	310-534-2738	R	5*	<.1
398	Telnet USA Inc—*Jose Miguel*	111 Trellingwood Dr, Morrisville NC 27560	919-523-8333	R	5*	<.1
399	Oilfield Motor and Control Inc—*Watts Cutter*	10035 Tanner Rd, Houston TX 77041	713-690-3600	R	5*	<.1
400	Applied Specialties Of California Inc—*Ursula Weiss*	280 E Hamilton Ave Ste, Campbell CA 95008	408-370-2644	R	5*	<.1
401	Techtel Marketing Inc—*Richard Miano*	6860 S Yosemite Ct Ste, Centennial CO 80112	303-721-9626	R	5*	<.1
402	Digital Telecom Inc	6176 126th Ave, Largo FL 33773	727-571-3300	R	5*	<.1
403	Joel Wasserman Associates Inc—*Joel Wasserman*	829 Moseley Rd, Highland Park IL 60035	847-266-1566	R	5*	<.1
404	Industrial Automation Supply Co—*A McCulloch Jr*	1665 Gwin Rd, McKinleyville CA 95519	707-839-9682	D	5*	<.1
405	JEPICO America Inc—*Kin-ichi Ohno*	5 Charlotte Pl, Old Tappan NJ 07675	201-666-1813	S	5*	<.1
406	Best Buy—*Cara Epps*	3480 Buskirk Ave Ste 2, Concord CA 94523	925-935-9494	R	5*	.1
407	Dfw Business Telephones Inc—*Kenneth Newell*	1260 Shiloh Rd, Plano TX 75074	972-424-4242	R	5*	<.1
408	Tape Specialty Inc—*Steven Feldman*	24831 Ave Tibbitts, Valencia CA 91355	661-702-9030	R	5*	<.1
409	Preferred Sales Agency Ltd—*Todd Malone*	PO Box 1410, Carthage TX 75633	903-693-4466	R	5*	<.1
410	Cellworks International Inc—*Jose Collado*	975 Florida Central Pk, Oviedo FL 32766	407-937-9090	R	5*	<.1
411	Samwha USA Inc—*David Yoo*	2555 Melksee, San Diego CA 92154	619-671-0870	R	5*	<.1
412	Kjb Security Products Inc—*Jill Johnston*	841 Fesslers Pkwy Ste, Nashville TN 37210	615-620-1370	R	5*	<.1
413	Gamut Communications—*Tom Johnson*	8 Twin Tree Ct, Cedar Crest NM 87008	505-286-9555	R	5*	<.1
414	Transocean International Trading Inc—*Laerte Falavigna*	4155 Ne 30th St, Homestead FL 33033	305-247-3156	R	5*	<.1
415	S/G Industries Inc—*Gerald Symeon*	9113 Macon Rd, Cordova TN 38016	901-624-7030	R	5*	<.1
416	Inland Empire Components Inc—*Ron Jiron*	598 Crane St, Lake Elsinore CA 92530	951-245-6555	R	5*	<.1
417	Tonar Industries Inc—*Perry Fox*	419 Franklin Ave Ste 4, Rockaway NJ 07866	973-586-9000	R	5*	<.1
418	State Electronics Parts Corp—*Thomas Sutcliffe*	36 State Rte 10 Ste 6, East Hanover NJ 07936	973-887-2550	R	5*	<.1
419	Great Lakes Mp—*Dominic Torres*	540 N Lapeer Rd 378, Lake Orion MI 48362	586-530-5208	R	5*	<.1
420	NeedacellCom Inc—*Avi Reif*	PO Box 849147, Hollywood FL 33084	954-430-5553	R	5*	<.1
421	Delconn Wireless LLC	2400 E Cerritos Ave, Anaheim CA 92806	714-978-9330	R	5*	<.1
422	Peter Parts Electronics Inc—*Peter Parts*	6285 Dean Pkwy, Ontario NY	585-265-2000	R	5*	<.1
423	Access Control Consultants Inc—*Larry Blumenfeld*	3518 Associate Dr, Greensboro NC 27405	336-358-0060	R	5*	<.1
424	Sharp Communication Services Inc—*Lennie Sharp*	7184 Troy Hill Dr Ste, Elkridge MD 21075	410-309-7320	R	4*	<.1
425	Violet Blue Networks—*Patrick Meaders*	215 Baker St E Ste 150, Costa Mesa CA 92626	714-754-4000	R	4*	<.1
426	Chris Electronics Distributors Inc—*Colleen Christianson*	2023 County Rd C2 W, Saint Paul MN 55113	651-631-2647	R	4*	<.1
427	Marlac Electronics Inc—*Joanne Lacanfora*	311 New Albany Rd, Moorestown NJ 08057	856-234-4200	R	4*	<.1
428	Fuji Novel Batteries Inc—*Vic Chandok*	PO Box 478, Mahwah NJ 07430	201-512-0033	R	4*	<.1
429	Quick Connect Communications Inc—*Elmer Barnes*	11400 Cronridge Dr Ste, Owings Mills MD 21117	410-524-2345	R	4*	<.1
430	Wbe Network Systems Inc—*Leslie Murphy*	90 Hill Rd, Novato CA 94945	415-898-1400	R	4*	<.1
431	Heartland Video Systems Inc—*Dennis Klas*	1311 Pilgrim Rd, Plymouth WI 53073	920-893-4204	R	4*	<.1
432	Moviola Inc—*Joe Paskal*	545 W 45th St, New York NY 10036	212-247-0972	R	4*	<.1
433	Trionics LLC—*Kenneth D'ancicco*	16910 Texas Ave Ste A8, Webster TX 77598	281-338-2688	R	4*	<.1
434	Motion Engineering Company Inc—*Ronald Jones*	PO Box 501223, Indianapolis IN 46250	317-849-3638	R	4*	<.1
435	Component Enterprises Company Inc—*Michael Hoffman*	PO Box 189, Norristown PA 19404	610-272-7900	R	4*	<.1
436	Syncom Electronics Corp—*Christopher Gray*	309 Campbell Ave Sw, Roanoke VA 24016	540-343-2220	R	4*	<.1
437	Ideacom Integrated Technologies Inc—*Bradford Little*	PO Box 449, Stratham NH 03885	603-778-1763	R	4*	<.1

Note: An asterisk (*) indicates an estimated financial figure. The company type code used is as follows: R = Private, P = Public, S = Private Subsidiary, B = Public Subsidiary, D = Division, J = Joint Venture, I = Investment Fund.

COMPANY RANKINGS BY SALES WITHIN 4-DIGIT SIC

Rank	Company Name—*Executive Officer*	Address, City, State, Zip	Phone	Type	Fin	Empls
438	Shelton Technologies Inc—*Gail Shelton*	1420 Stamy Rd, Hiawatha IA 52233	319-398-9898	R	4*	<.1
439	Acs Inc—*Mike Scholl*	647 Blackhawk Dr, Westmont IL 60559	630-325-2700	R	4*	<.1
440	Electrical Power and Controls Inc—*Jack Armstrong* Control Switches International Inc	2425 Mira Mar Ave, Long Beach CA 90815	562-498-6699	S	4*	<.1
441	Vision Electronics Inc—*Mike Farrell*	1175 Spring Ctr S, Altamonte Springs FL 32714	407-774-8282	R	4*	<.1
442	C and H Technology Inc—*Thomas Heelan*	6121 Baker Rd Ste 108, Minnetonka MN 55345	952-933-6190	R	4*	<.1
443	Don Baker Inc—*Don Baker*	27142 Burbank, Foothill Ranch CA 92610	949-472-9050	R	4*	<.1
444	Operations Technology Inc—*Richard Amon*	PO Box 408, Blairstown NJ 07825	908-362-6200	R	4*	<.1
445	Bendek Cellulars And Accessories International Corp—*Arturo Bendek*	1890 Nw 95th Ave, Doral FL 33172	305-436-1310	R	4*	<.1
446	Test Equipment Solution Today—*Diane Gelb*	1755 E Byshore Rd Ste, Redwood City CA 94063	650-365-8877	R	4*	<.1
447	HB Distributors—*Pam Branner* Independent Telephone Network Inc	21612 Marilla St, Northridge CA 91324	818-882-0000	D	4*	<.1
448	C and S Products Inc—*Ken Sluder*	1411 N Batavia St Ste, Orange CA 92867	714-288-2660	R	4*	<.1
449	Dawn Satellite Inc	3340 S Lapeer Rd, Orion MI 48359	248-391-9200	R	4*	<.1
450	American Electronic Supply Company Inc—*Ted Self*	13 W Park Cir, Birmingham AL 35221†	205-942-4656	R	4*	<.1
451	Barno Electronics Corp—*Mary M Barno-Frost*	PO Box 93, McKeesport PA 15135	412-751-5966	R	4*	<.1
452	AC Atel Electronics Corp—*Gerald Lang*	PO Box 3500, Great River NY 11739	631-756-2835	R	4*	<.1
453	American Accurate Components Inc—*Alan Sun*	188 Technology Dr Ste, Irvine CA 92618	714-255-9123	R	4*	<.1
454	Islero Inc—*Thomas Moody*	535 Suncourt Ter, Glendale CA 91206	818-956-2177	R	4*	<.1
455	Florida Electronic Business Resource Company Inc—*Evy Finch*	PO Box 15051, Panama City FL 32406	850-763-5290	R	4*	<.1
456	Hollmann Manufacturing Technologies—*Jerry Hollmann*	3 N Pond Rd, Cheshire CT 06410	203-271-3911	R	4*	<.1
457	Ultimate Entertainment Marketing Inc—*Russell Graham*	50 Dalor Ct, Woodbury NY 11797	516-364-8831	R	4*	<.1
458	Nsb Electronics Inc—*Julius White*	3755 Washington Blvd S, Fremont CA 94538	510-657-3102	R	4*	<.1
459	Electec Norcal LLC—*Julie Aitken*	4701 Patrick Henry Dr, Santa Clara CA 95054	408-496-0706	R	4*	<.1
460	Telecom Management Inc—*Richard Rasmussen*	1315 Louis Ave, Elk Grove Village IL 60007	847-806-8100	R	4*	<.1
461	Electronic Expeditors Inc—*Robert Conley*	N15w22180 Watertown Rd, Waukesha WI 53186	262-574-4400	R	4*	<.1
462	Peerless Electronic Equipment Company Inc—*Lawrence Baines*	PO Box 3286, Louisville KY 40201	502-637-7674	R	4*	<.1
463	Bravo Electro Components Inc—*Laura Kramar*	1990 Russell Ave Ste 1, Santa Clara CA 95054	408-733-9090	R	4*	<.1
464	Accurate Corrosion Control Inc—*Paul Sedlet*	10487 N 91st Ave Ste 6, Peoria AZ 85345	623-486-7800	R	4*	<.1
465	Jevco International Inc—*Joe Valosay*	915 26th Ave Nw Ste A1, Gig Harbor WA 98335	253-858-2605	R	4*	<.1
466	Ultra Power Battery Inc—*Sal Dantona*	PO Box 3300, Wantagh NY 11793	516-783-5050	R	4*	<.1
467	Dmc Security Services Inc—*Chester Donati*	4455 147th St, Midlothian IL 60445	708-388-6500	R	4*	<.1
468	Tekena USA LLC	1701 Elmhurst Rd, Elk Grove Village IL 60007	847-290-8250	R	4*	<.1
469	Iinchip Inc—*Yunbong Lee*	1824 Oak Creek Dr Apt, Palo Alto CA 94304	650-327-9784	R	4*	<.1
470	Major Electronix Corp—*William Rowell*	33801 Curtis Blvd Ste, Eastlake OH 44095	440-942-0054	R	4*	<.1
471	Phones Plus Inc—*Robert Sodemann*	2745 S Calhoun Rd, New Berlin WI 53151	262-784-2311	R	4*	<.1
472	First Line Communications Inc—*Tim Maio*	3240 118th Ave Se Ste, Bellevue WA 98005	425-688-1634	R	4*	<.1
473	Fuller Engineering Company LLC—*Karen Keen*	4135 W 99th St, Carmel IN 46032	317-228-5800	R	4*	<.1
474	Dm Technology and Energy Inc—*Victor Deng*	4615 State St, Montclair CA 91763	909-627-1600	R	4*	<.1
475	Practical Components Inc—*Kevin Laphen*	10762 Noel St, Los Alamitos CA 90720	714-252-0010	R	4*	<.1
476	Marvol USA Corp—*Mario Volfzon*	245 Se 1st St Ste 329, Miami FL 33131	305-358-4305	R	4*	<.1
477	Tradelynx International—*Mark Barkhordar*	23852 Pacific Coast Hw, Malibu CA 90265	818-225-0245	R	4*	<.1
478	Van Hauser LLC	230 5th Ave Ste 800, New York NY 10001	212-689-9094	R	4*	<.1
479	Colorado Telecommunications Center Inc—*Joseph Williams*	1230 S Parker Rd, Denver CO 80231	303-755-6500	R	4	<.1
480	Benq Latin America Corp—*Peter Tan*	8200 Nw 33rd St Ste 20, Doral FL 33122	305-421-1200	R	4*	<.1
481	Ken Smith Inc—*Kenneth Smith*	8661 Monroe Rd Ste C, Charlotte NC 28212	704-536-1300	R	4*	<.1
482	Stan Clothier Co—*Ron Schultz*	10025 Valley View Rd S, Eden Prairie MN 55344	952-944-3456	R	4*	<.1
483	Alliance Wireless Technologies Inc—*Darrick Reed*	9940 W Sam Houston Pkw, Houston TX 77099	713-690-4100	R	4*	<.1
484	Seibold Security Inc—*John Seibold*	37 Richmond St, Rochester NY 14607	585-546-4990	R	4*	<.1
485	Ricom Inc—*Richard Stasior*	188 Technology Dr Ste, Irvine CA 92618	949-788-9939	R	4*	<.1
486	Virtual Supply Inc—*Chuck Taylor*	9700 Sw Harvest Ct Ste, Beaverton OR 97005	503-670-1170	R	4*	<.1
487	North American Technology Exchange Inc—*Wade Luther*	PO Box 7510, Broomfield CO 80021	303-443-1984	R	4*	<.1
488	SMI Export Industries Ltd—*Victor Nelson*	999 Grand Blvd, Deer Park NY 11729	631-242-2300	R	4*	.1
489	Vertu Americas Inc—*Nigel Litchfield*	595 Madison Ave Fl 37, New York NY 10022	212-705-5402	R	4*	<.1
490	Jhc Inc—*James Hann*	901 S Fremont Ave Ste, Alhambra CA 91803	626-308-0180	R	4*	<.1
491	Financial Equipment Company Inc—*Dennis Wick*	PO Box 245, Germantown WI 53022	262-255-6350	R	4*	<.1
492	Datalink Networks Inc—*Donald Wisdom*	28110 Ave Stanford A, Valencia CA 91355	661-294-8822	R	4*	<.1
493	Oxygen Electronics LLC—*Chris Debalko*	56 Lafayette Ave, White Plains NY 10603	914-289-0202	R	4*	<.1
494	Equipment Technologies Inc—*Jon Pelletier*	19 Park Ave, Hudson NH 03051	603-881-5253	R	4*	<.1
495	Chris Supply Company Inc—*Rick Brown*	114 E Blvd N, Rapid City SD 57701	605-342-5900	R	4*	<.1
496	Urs Electronics Inc—*Mark Twietmeyer*	PO Box 14040, Portland OR 97293	503-233-7151	R	4*	<.1
497	Inter-Pacific Inc—*Richard Kuk*	250 Chaddick Dr, Wheeling IL 60090	847-808-2100	R	4*	<.1
498	Us Tel Inc—*John Becz*	203 Paterson Ave Ste 2, Wallington NJ 07057	973-473-4411	R	4*	<.1
499	Equipment Technologies West LLC—*Debi Blood*	756 California Way, Longview WA 98632	360-423-8466	R	4*	<.1
500	SEI Capacitors Inc—*Terri Noone*	6455 N Avondale Ave, Chicago IL 60631	773-774-6666	R	3*	<.1
501	Jade Associates Inc—*Larry Feinstein*	275 Andrews Rd Ste 1, Langhorne PA 19053	215-322-7040	R	3*	<.1
502	Tidewater Communications and Electronics Inc—*Claude Hinkle*	216 N Witchduck Rd, Virginia Beach VA 23462	757-497-4321	R	3*	<.1
503	Phase 1 Technology Corp—*Rusty Ponce De Leon*	46 W Jefryn Blvd Ste B, Deer Park NY 11729	631-254-2600	R	3*	<.1
504	Menard Electronics Inc—*William Menard*	6451 Choctaw Dr, Baton Rouge LA 70805	225-355-0323	R	3*	<.1
505	Servo Systems Co—*Anthony Villano*	PO Box 97, Montville NJ 07045	973-335-1007	R	3*	<.1
506	Forbes Distributing Inc—*William Forbes*	PO Box 1478, Birmingham AL 35201	205-251-4104	R	3*	<.1
507	Chroma Digital Corp—*Sergio Toledo*	6994 Nw 42nd St, Miami FL 33166	305-471-8145	R	3*	<.1
508	Answer Network Paging Inc—*Sue Larosa*	PO Box 10440, Santa Ana CA 92711	949-472-4444	R	3*	<.1
509	Mwm Acoustics LLC—*Gary Roberson*	6602 E 75th St Ste 520, Indianapolis IN 46250	317-849-8177	R	3*	<.1
510	Pulsar Microwave Corp—*Charlie Bobroski*	48 Industrial St W, Clifton NJ 07012	973-779-6262	R	3*	<.1
511	North Atlantic Inc—*Kevin Austin*	301 Brogdon Rd Ste A, Suwanee GA 30024	678-992-2023	R	3*	<.1
512	Marsilli North America Inc—*Kumar Rajasekhara*	11445 Cronridge Dr Ste, Owings Mills MD 21117	410-654-2425	R	3*	<.1
513	Responsive Information Management Systems and Service Inc—*Tom Jarrett*	2710 Treble Creek, San Antonio TX 78258	210-493-3394	R	3*	<.1
514	Allstar Communications Inc—*Kevin Caldwell*	3810 Superior Ridge Dr, Fort Wayne IN 46808	260-482-2282	R	3*	<.1
515	Microbiz Security Co—*Dave Chritton*	444 Jessie St, San Francisco CA 94103	415-777-1151	R	3*	<.1
516	New Horizons Communications Inc—*William Langman*	929 W Liberty Dr, Wheaton IL 60187	630-510-1660	R	3*	<.1
517	North American Video And Sound Company Inc—*Danny Bramlett*	PO Box 7266, Huntsville AL 35807	256-461-6000	R	3*	<.1
518	Asian Pacific Ltd—*Jennifer Chou*	3100 Airway Ave Ste 11, Costa Mesa CA 92626	714-662-0688	R	3*	<.1
519	Mall Telecommunications—*Donn Mall*	1475 Powell St Ste 205, Emeryville CA 94608	510-297-2100	R	3*	<.1
520	Dan-Mar Components Inc—*Daniel Martin*	150 W Industry Ct, Deer Park NY 11729	631-242-8877	R	3*	<.1

Rank	Company Name—*Executive Officer*	Address, City, State, Zip	Phone	Type	Fin	Empls
521	Carolina Communications and Fire Equipment Inc—*Hoyte Fowler*	2205 Commerce Dr, Monroe NC 28110	704-283-1127	R	3*	<.1
522	Connectors Unlimited Inc—*Juan Figueroa*	PO Box 611654, San Jose CA 95161	408-287-6041	R	3*	<.1
523	Intercon Industries Inc—*Jesse Galindo*	PO Box 90429, Houston TX 77290	281-590-6434	R	3*	<.1
524	Q Source Inc—*Stephen Quail*	227 Knickerbocker Ave, Bohemia NY 11716	631-563-0600	R	3*	<.1
525	Network Access Corp—*James Barnes*	PO Box 15155, Pittsburgh PA 15237	412-931-1111	R	3*	<.1
526	Star Satellite Products Inc—*Steven Penner*	4555 Nw 103rd Ave Ste, Sunrise FL 33351	954-742-8000	R	3*	<.1
527	QSI Systems Inc—*Alfred Smilgis*	PO Box 718, Salem NH 03079	603-893-7707	R	3*	<.1
528	Technical Services Group Inc—*Arthur Hoover*	12015 Cloverland Ct, Baton Rouge LA 70809	225-751-9800	R	3*	<.1
529	Computel Communication Systems Inc—*Stephen De Bello*	170 Chngbrdge Rd Bldg, Montville NJ 07045	973-575-6600	R	3*	<.1
530	Dx Electric Co—*Beckey Fuller*	PO Box 140005, Irving TX 75014	972-438-4947	R	3*	<.1
531	BR Simpson Telephone Sales and Service Inc—*Richard Mcconnell*	1222 S Brady St, Du Bois PA 15801	814-371-4634	R	3*	<.1
532	Cbm Industries Inc—*Eric Dingley*	470 Constitution Dr, Taunton MA 02780	508-821-4555	R	3*	<.1
533	Northwest Electronics Distributing Co—*Roger Zumwalt*	5410 Se International, Milwaukie OR 97222	503-496-0343	R	3*	<.1
534	Ho Chien Electronic Group Inc—*C Lin*	1687 Curtiss Ct, La Verne CA 91750	909-596-6298	R	3*	<.1
535	FEC Technology Corp—*Mati Oren*	1 Dupont St Ste 100, Plainview NY 11803	516-576-7070	R	3*	<.1
536	Genesis Telecom Inc—*Debra Boultinghouse*	1225 N Loop W Ste 100, Houston TX 77008	713-868-5415	R	3*	<.1
537	Halted Specialties Co—*Manfred Zielinsky*	3500 Ryder St, Santa Clara CA 95051	408-732-1573	R	3*	<.1
538	American Manufacturing Services Inc—*David Beck*	202 S 7th St, Okemah OK 74859	918-623-2880	R	3*	<.1
539	Orevox USA Corp—*Main-Liang Wu*	248 Puente Ave, City Of Industry CA 91746	626-333-6803	R	3*	<.1
540	Great Valley Industries Inc—*Eric Lorgus*	PO Box 675, Downingtown PA 19335	484-691-1100	R	3*	<.1
541	Hedtke Inc—*Dennis Hedtke*	PO Box 255, Hamel MN 55340	763-478-2120	R	3*	<.1
542	Data Media Products Inc—*Caryl Galassini*	1946 Lehigh Ave Ste B, Glenview IL 60026	847-729-2020	R	3*	<.1
543	Riva Networks Inc—*Robin Gamble*	555 Riva Ave, East Brunswick NJ 08816	732-940-5555	R	3*	<.1
544	Apacer Memory America Inc—*Lawrence Lo*	386 Fairview Way Ste 1, Milpitas CA 95035	408-518-8699	R	3*	<.1
545	Communication Specialists Inc—*William Hoovler*	35 Commerce Pkwy, Fredericksburg VA 22406	540-373-0778	R	3*	<.1
546	Intelliphone Inc—*Chuck Garabedian*	191 Chandler Rd, Andover MA 01810	978-291-1000	R	3*	<.1
547	Garrett Electronics Corp—*Donna Garrett*	1320 W Mc Coy, Santa Maria CA 93455	805-922-0594	R	3*	<.1
548	Forgy Process Instruments Inc—*Randal Forgy*	1879 Craig Rd, Saint Louis MO 63146	314-439-9149	R	3*	<.1
549	Diotec Electronics Corp—*Joo Lin*	18020 S Hobart Blvd St, Gardena CA 90248	310-767-1052	R	3*	<.1
550	Raymar Information Technology	7325 Roseville Rd, Sacramento CA 95842	916-783-1951	R	3	<.1
551	O'gara Satellite Systems Inc—*Adam Thompson*	1347 N Alma S Ste 150, Chandler AZ 85224	631-586-5100	R	3*	<.1
552	Colucci Sales Inc—*Ken Colucci*	57 Mahan St, West Babylon NY 11704	631-491-7880	R	3*	<.1
553	Da-Sh Components Inc—*David Friedman*	41 Brigham St Unit 9, Marlborough MA 01752	508-624-7484	R	3*	<.1
554	Sara Sales Co—*Sherman Fishman*	295 Stevenson Dr, Pleasant Hill CA 94523	925-934-1331	R	3*	<.1
555	Northwest Marketing Team LLC	1334 Stonehaven Dr, West Linn OR 97068	503-635-5869	R	3*	<.1
556	Velle and Associates Inc—*Faye Velle*	20280 N 59th Ave Ste 1, Glendale AZ 85308	623-445-0391	R	3*	<.1
557	Daval Technologies LLC—*Daniel Leitman*	PO Box 27, Chappaqua NY 10514	914-251-9220	R	3*	<.1
558	Epstein and Siebel Associates Inc—*Paul Epstein*	1000d Lake St Ste 2, Ramsey NJ 07446	201-236-1002	R	3*	<.1
559	Jimenez Manuel Dba Telemetrics—*Manuel Jimenez*	255 Warren St, Jersey City NJ 07302	201-420-1055	R	3*	<.1
560	Audio Sounds Electronics Inc—*Karen Camacho*	10858 Nw 27th St, Doral FL 33172	305-594-0559	R	3*	<.1
561	Mid-America Telephone Systems Inc—*Linda Sanders*	740 Goddard Ave, Chesterfield MO 63005	636-728-1333	R	3*	<.1
562	New York Components Inc—*Avi Shushan*	102 05 B 67th Dr, Forest Hills NY 11375	718-275-7775	R	3*	<.1
563	Ue Systems International Corp—*Michael Osterer*	14 Hayes St, Elmsford NY 10523	914-592-1220	R	3*	<.1
564	Calrad Electronics Inc—*Robert Shupper*	819 N Highland Ave, Los Angeles CA 90038	323-465-2131	R	3*	<.1
565	Endless Wireless Group Inc—*George Kunz*	10 21st St, Brooklyn NY 11232	718-369-0070	R	3*	<.1
566	Lucas And Greer Inc—*James Greer*	3643 Willbnd Bldg 610, Houston TX 77054	713-799-1815	R	3*	<.1
567	Quad City Satellite—*Kathy Rashid*	901 E Kimberly Rd Ste, Davenport IA 52807	563-359-3474	R	3*	<.1
568	Rankin Communication Systems Inc—*Robert Rankin*	5444 Nw 96th St Ste C, Johnston IA 50131	515-986-5654	R	3*	<.1
569	Route Electronics 22 Inc—*Kathleen Mccarthy*	PO Box 1339, Mountainside NJ 07092	908-654-8283	R	3*	<.1
570	On-Line Electronics Inc—*Colton Rickert*	1000 Brioso Dr, Costa Mesa CA 92627	949-645-9900	R	3*	<.1
571	Dco Distribution Inc—*Diana O'sullivan*	5965 Peachtree Cors E, Norcross GA 30071	678-990-7963	R	3*	<.1
572	Argus Technologies Inc—*Grace Borsari*	3765 Alpha Way, Bellingham WA 98226	360-671-7054	R	3*	<.1
573	Dan Lee Communications Inc—*Lawrence Goldberg*	155 Adams Ave, Hauppauge NY 11788	631-231-1414	R	3*	<.1
574	Rcm and Associates—*Roger Merriman*	1829 E Oakton St, Des Plaines IL 60018	847-298-8100	R	3*	<.1
575	Semicore Equipment Inc—*Matthew Hughes*	5027 Preston Ave, Livermore CA 94551	925-373-8201	R	3*	<.1
576	Saturn Enterprises Inc—*Behnam Carmili*	263 Jericho Tpke, Mineola NY 11501	516-616-1111	R	3*	<.1
577	Source Research Inc—*Erik Petersen*	PO Box 7537, Clearwater FL 33758	727-443-7001	R	3*	<.1
578	Bell Component Sales Inc—*Samuel Bell*	2317 Roosevelt Dr Ste, Arlington TX 76016	817-461-5303	R	3*	<.1
579	Ordnance Unlimited Inc—*Michael Epstein*	21500 Gledhill St, Chatsworth CA 91311	818-407-5371	R	3*	<.1
580	Professional Component Sales Inc—*Robert Cook*	1501 Main St Ste 31, Tewksbury MA 01876	978-858-0100	R	3*	<.1
581	F and K Delvotec Inc—*Farhad Farassat*	27182 Burbank, Foothill Ranch CA 92610	949-595-2200	R	3*	<.1
582	Integrated Components Source—*Thomas Justus*	1740 Emerson Ave, Oxnard CA 93033	805-822-5100	R	3*	<.1
583	Miltimore Sales Inc—*Colin Miltimore*	22765 Heslip Dr Ste 10, Novi MI 48375	248-349-0260	R	3*	<.1
584	Security Integrators And Consulting Inc—*Richard Peinado*	11875 W Little St Ste 704, Houston TX 77041	281-895-7233	R	3*	<.1
585	State Industrial Supply Inc—*Bruce Hansen*	6801 Northpark Blvd St, Charlotte NC 28216	704-597-0536	R	3*	<.1
586	Bell's Paging Inc—*Robert Gold*	9920 Westpark Dr Ste B, Houston TX 77063	713-266-7243	R	3*	<.1
587	Aerotron-Repco Sales Inc—*Anthony Kostantinidis*	4602 Pkwy Commerce Blv, Orlando FL 32808	407-856-1953	R	3*	<.1
588	Electronic Game Solutions Inc—*John Smolic*	149 Weldon Pkwy Ste 10, Maryland Heights MO 63043	314-692-2600	R	3*	<.1
589	Loras Industries Inc—*Steven Loras*	2640 Freewood Dr, Dallas TX 75220	214-351-1234	R	3*	<.1
590	Aethra Inc—*Giorgio Viezzoli*	1221 Brickell Ave, Miami FL 33131	305-375-0010	R	3*	<.1
591	Septronics International Inc—*Christopher Sepe*	5835 Trouble Creek Rd, New Port Richey FL 34652	727-842-9100	R	3*	<.1
592	ICE Components Inc—*Danny Snow*	1165 Allgood Rd Ste 20, Marietta GA 30062	678-560-9172	R	3*	<.1
593	Stevens Sales Co—*Clark Lowder*	PO Box 65596, Salt Lake City UT 84165	801-487-8971	R	3*	<.1
594	Adema Technologies Inc—*George Fiegl*	5201 Great America Pkw, Santa Clara CA 95054	650-961-6100	R	3*	<.1
595	Feed Control Corp—*Robert Aslan*	1644 Cambridge Dr, Elgin IL 60123	847-488-9200	R	3*	<.1
596	International Security Inc—*Ferdinand Hauslein*	383 Las Colinas Blvd E, Irving TX 75039	972-444-9456	R	3*	<.1
597	Communications World of Dallas Inc—*Kevin Granham*	2636 Walnut Hill Ln St, Dallas TX 75229	214-350-3494	R	3*	<.1
598	Advanced Tech Sales Inc—*Steven Neri*	352 Park Pl W Ste 102, North Reading MA 01864	978-664-0888	R	3*	<.1
599	Tiltrac—*Peter Kiddy*	16115 Dooley Rd, Addison TX 75001	972-980-6991	R	3*	<.1
600	Varitech International Inc—*Ken Linxwiler*	1850 N Greenville Ave, Richardson TX 75081	972-644-7020	R	3*	<.1
601	Delta Technical Systems Inc—*Thomas Estilow*	122 N York Rd Ste 9, Hatboro PA 19040	215-957-0600	R	3*	<.1
602	Spec-Tech Industrial Electric Inc—*Terry Mocker*	203 Vest Ave, Valley Park MO 63088	636-537-0202	R	3*	<.1
603	Sws Electronics Inc—*Fred Kasper*	3731 E Speedway Blvd, Tucson AZ 85716	520-628-1613	R	3*	<.1
604	JP Electronics Import and Export Inc—*Onelia Pujol*	1740 Nw 93rd Ave, Doral FL 33172	305-592-3700	R	3*	<.1
605	Superior Wireless Communication Inc—*Jeffrey Ziemann*	409 W Touhy Ave, Des Plaines IL 60018	847-299-5075	R	3*	<.1
606	Kurol International Corp—*Sumio Yonemoto*	497 Pini Rd, Royal Oaks CA 95076	831-761-8977	R	3*	<.1
607	Ems LLC	2447 Executive Plz Rd, Pensacola FL 32504	850-266-7355	R	2*	<.1
608	M and P Quality Goods Inc—*Philip Green*	1506 Ave J, Brooklyn NY 11230	718-258-5160	R	2*	<.1

Note: An asterisk (*) indicates an estimated financial figure. The company type code used is as follows: R = Private, P = Public, S = Private Subsidiary, B = Public Subsidiary, D = Division, J = Joint Venture, I = Investment Fund.

COMPANY RANKINGS BY SALES WITHIN 4-DIGIT SIC

Rank	Company Name—Executive Officer	Address, City, State, Zip	Phone	Type	Fin	Empls
609	Arcadia Components LLC	455 White Pine Dr, Salt Lake City UT 84123	801-261-5300	R	2*	<.1
610	Integrated Communication Services Inc—George Raffoul	916 Pleasant St Ste 21, Norwood MA 02062	781-769-2927	R	2*	<.1
611	Sumer Inc—Craig Anderson	1675 Hicks Rd, Rolling Meadows IL 60008	847-991-8500	R	2*	<.1
612	Irving Langbaum Associates Inc—Irving Langbaum	950 Rte 45, Pomona NY 10970	845-362-1141	R	2*	<.1
613	EMC Schaffner Inc—F Mellen	52 Mayfield Ave, Edison NJ 08837	732-225-9533	R	2*	<.1
614	Acamard Technologies Inc—Brenda Waters	2385 Hammond Dr Ste 9, Schaumburg IL 60173	847-303-9670	R	2*	<.1
615	Delta V Electronics Inc—John Truong	17330 Newhope St Ste E, Fountain Valley CA 92708	714-545-8880	R	2*	<.1
616	Leon Hand-Crafted Speakers Inc—Jeff Gordon	715 W Ellsworth Rd, Ann Arbor MI 48108	734-213-2151	R	2*	<.1
617	Mayday Communications Inc—Jean Casazone	19 Gazza Blvd, Farmingdale NY 11735	631-752-0250	R	2*	<.1
618	Neosong USA Inc—Mei-Yu Yang	718 W Longview Ln, Palatine IL 60067	847-934-4975	R	2*	<.1
619	Construction Audio—Jon Peterson	13421 Sagewood Dr, Poway CA 92064	858-673-3997	R	2*	<.1
620	Tec South Sales Inc—William Roberts	404 Hall Cove Rd, Warne NC 28909	828-389-8850	R	2*	<.1
621	Westco Systems Inc—Jeff Caryl	4655 Juneau Ln N, Minneapolis MN 55446	763-559-7046	R	2*	<.1
622	Kx-TdCom Inc—John White	13506 Summerport Villa, Windermere FL 34786	407-581-7200	R	2*	<.1
623	Worldviz LLC—Phil Schlageter	27 W Anapamu St 101-12, Santa Barbara CA 93101	805-966-0786	R	2*	<.1
624	Chesapeake Communications Inc—Daniel Trimmer	11351 Business Ctr Dr, Richmond VA 23236	804-379-8800	R	2*	<.1
625	Caito and Klein Associates Inc—Gary Caito	8333 Clairemont Mesa B, San Diego CA 92111	858-279-0420	R	2*	<.1
626	Cooper-General Corp—Michael Fresco	1785 Nw 79th Ave, Doral FL 33126	305-223-6399	R	2*	<.1
627	Mtm Wireless Inc—Albert Baajour	5410 Nw 72nd Ave, Miami FL 33166	305-944-7243	R	2*	<.1
628	SSE Inc—Ann Braun	203 Mcmillan St, Nashville TN 37203	615-340-9033	R	2*	<.1
629	Next Electronic Systems Inc—Dan McLaughlin	3698 FM 620 S Ste 106, Austin TX 78738	512-263-9700	R	2*	<.1
630	ICT International Cellular Telephone Inc—Fred Posada	PO Box 521333, Miami FL 33152	305-640-2424	R	2*	<.1
631	M Gottlieb Associates Inc—Marvin Gottlieb	6009 N Milwaukee Ave, Chicago IL 60646	773-775-1151	R	2*	<.1
632	Rco Sales Inc—Mark Camp	815 W Liberty St Ste 4, Medina OH 44256	330-725-3705	R	2*	<.1
633	Emiex Corp—Eduardo Ramos	5959 Nw 102nd Ave, Doral FL 33178	305-436-0411	R	2*	<.1
634	Brook Marketing Inc—Patrick Cooksey	1112 Huntleigh Dr, Naperville IL 60540	630-968-4700	R	2*	<.1
635	Manix Manufacturing Inc—Daniel Martin	1650 Loretta Ave, Feasterville Trevose PA 19053	215-953-9797	R	2*	<.1
636	American Scitec Inc—Lawrence Chen	3505 Cadillac Ave Ste, Costa Mesa CA 92626	714-549-8680	R	2*	<.1
637	Olcr Inc—Tracy Bogans	20 E 5th St, Chester PA 19013		R	2*	<.1
638	Vitec Electronics Corp—Dick Lee	6213 El Camino Real, Carlsbad CA 92009	760-918-8831	R	2*	<.1
639	Hexatech Inc—Zlatko Sitar	991 Aviation Pkwy Ste, Morrisville NC 27560	919-481-4412	R	2*	<.1
640	Orange County Components Inc—Richard Hintermeyer	2925 College Ave Ste A, Costa Mesa CA 92626	714-979-3597	R	2*	<.1
641	Surface Mountable Electronic Components Inc—Marie Chaudhari	3317 El Salido Pkwy, Cedar Park TX 78613	512-249-0017	R	2*	<.1
642	A and A Telecom Group Inc—Phillip Neely	PO Box 81891, Austin TX 78708	512-327-3277	R	2*	<.1
643	Corner Electronics Inc—Danny Kalra	295 Oser Ave Ste 1, Hauppauge NY 11788	631-434-9700	R	2*	<.1
644	No Time Delay Electronics Inc—Nick Jesson	7491 Talbert Ave, Huntington Beach CA 92648	714-842-3720	R	2*	<.1
645	Time Sight Systems—Charles Foley	16000 Horizon Way Ste, Mount Laurel NJ 08054	856-206-9739	R	2*	<.1
646	Tyler Griffin Company Inc—John Griffin	46 Darby Rd, Paoli PA 19301	610-647-1550	R	2*	<.1
647	Empire Page Inc—Yong Hwang	5735 N 5th St, Philadelphia PA 19120	215-548-3656	R	2*	<.1
648	Wafer Works Corp—Pat Chiao	47338 Fremont Blvd, Fremont CA 94538	510-933-7688	R	2*	<.1
649	Davilyn Corp—David Kasper	1300 Pacific Ave, Oxnard CA 93033	805-483-7830	R	2*	<.1
650	Peak Communication Systems Inc—Steven Rubin	6180 Lake Shore Ct, Colorado Springs CO 80915	719-590-7325	R	2*	<.1
651	Carrera Investment Corp—Kyle Schroeder	1039 Inca St, Denver CO 80204	303-628-7722	R	2*	<.1
652	Langie Audio Visual Systems Company Inc—Ed Ali	PO Box 147, East Rochester NY 14445	585-385-4880	R	2*	<.1
653	Norcon Electronics Inc—Norman Schlaff	510 Burnside Ave, Inwood NY 11096	516-239-0300	R	2*	<.1
654	Unlimited Manufacturing Services Inc—Joseph Leone	234 Orinoco Dr, Brightwaters NY 11718	631-665-5800	R	2*	<.1
655	Electronic Service Products Corp—William Hrubiec	1070 N Farms Rd Ste 1, Wallingford CT 06492	203-265-4167	R	2*	<.1
656	Gila Electronics Of Yuma Inc—Harold Hendricks	2481 E Palo Verde St, Yuma AZ 85365	928-726-0896	R	2*	<.1
657	Products Plus Inc—Bruce Warneck	6550 Brem Ln Ste A, Gilroy CA 95020	408-847-7111	R	2*	<.1
658	Cable World Technologies Inc—George Fernandez	7315 Nw 56th St, Miami FL 33166	305-468-1589	R	2*	<.1
659	Full Power Enterprises Inc—Oscar Fonseca	10470 Nw 26th St Ste A, Doral FL 33172	305-238-1302	R	2*	.1
660	Southeast Assemblies Inc—Patricia Arasi	PO Box 996, Eustis FL 32727	352-357-3311	R	2*	<.1
661	Central California Electronics Inc	139 E Belmont Ave, Fresno CA 93701	559-485-1254	R	2*	<.1
662	Horizon Telephone Systems Inc—Troy Salinas	12918 Flagship Dr, San Antonio TX 78247	210-495-5520	R	2*	<.1
663	Lloyd F McKinney Associates Inc—Betty Harmoney	25350 Cypress Ave, Hayward CA 94544	510-783-8043	R	2*	<.1
664	PhoneAmerica Corp—Charlie Reimel	8 N Bacton Hill Rd, Frazer PA 19355	610-296-2850	R	2*	<.1
665	Tescom Inc—Fran Collmann	15527 Ranch Rd 620 N, Austin TX 78717	512-244-6689	R	2*	<.1
666	Moyer Electronics Supply Co—William Moyer	PO Box 1164, Pottsville PA 17901	570-622-7866	R	2*	<.1
667	C and G Electronics Co—L Ross Norberg	PO Box 1304, Tacoma WA 98401	253-272-3181	R	2*	<.1
668	Solar Technologies Inc—George Lim	26180 Enterprise Way, Lake Forest CA 92630	949-458-1080	R	2*	<.1
669	Ebert Jacques Associates Inc—Jacques Ebert	PO Box 211, Locust Valley NY 11560	516-671-6123	R	2*	<.1
670	Ewing Electronics Inc—Phillip Hawley	8 Prestige Cir Ste 120, Allen TX 75002	469-519-2900	R	2*	<.1
671	Fisher Systems Inc—Richard Mcmillen	2117 12th Ave, Lewiston ID 83501	208-746-1071	R	2*	<.1
672	Hartcom Inc—Mark Hartley	1411 W Saint James St, Tarboro NC 27886	252-641-6950	R	2*	<.1
673	Ital Sales Inc—Paul Bruneio	2483 E Orangethorpe Av, Fullerton CA 92831	714-632-2500	R	2*	<.1
674	PicturePhone Direct—Jeremy Goldstein	200 Commerce Dr, Rochester NY 14623	585-334-9040	D	2*	<.1
675	RC Merchant and Company Inc—John Merchant	23735 Research Dr Ste, Farmington Hills MI 48335	248-476-4600	R	2*	<.1
676	Wired Accessories Inc—Alex Chazan	9601 Owensmouth Ave St, Chatsworth CA 91311	818-280-0251	R	2*	<.1
677	Bluewire Communications Inc—Deta Itaya	1955 Raymond Dr Ste 10, Northbrook IL 60062	847-205-0088	R	2*	<.1
678	Acumen Technologies Inc—Rick Schuchart	500 W Calumet St, Appleton WI 54915	920-832-8000	R	2*	<.1
679	Advanced Fire and Security Systems Inc—Jeffery Lavery	12540 S Holiday Dr Ste, Alsip IL 60803	708-385-2149	R	2*	<.1
680	Blue Star Distributors Corp—Fredo Lowenhaar	8884 Nw 24th Ter, Doral FL 33172	305-406-1636	R	2*	<.1
681	Electronic Resources Inc—Ray Aubrey	534 Ohohia St Ste A, Honolulu HI 96819	808-526-2422	R	2*	<.1
682	GUS Distributing Corp—Abdul Shatara	200 S Main St, Belle Glade FL 33430	561-996-9863	R	2*	<.1
683	Scandic Electronics Inc—Kenneth Pettersson	1978 S Garrison St Ste, Lakewood CO 80227	303-984-0522	R	2*	<.1
684	Tucker Electronics Co—James Tucker	PO Box 551419, Dallas TX 75355	214-348-8800	R	2*	<.1
685	Blue Star Radios Inc—Jeff Mcmurphy	7113 W 135th St Ste 31, Overland Park KS 66223	913-890-2054	R	2*	<.1
686	Alaska Instrument Company Inc—Steve Barnett	PO Box 230087, Anchorage AK 99523	907-561-7511	S		<.1
687	Digitalks Inc—Amiel Dabush	14 Marshall Ln, Weston CT 06883	203-221-8181	R	2*	<.1
688	Scantek Inc—Richard Peppin	6430 Dobbin Rd Ste C, Columbia MD 21045	410-290-7726	R	2*	<.1
689	Service Group Inc—Walter Blackwood	PO Box 700, Lilburn GA 30048	770-638-1000	R	2*	<.1
690	Outdoor Outfitters of Wisconsin Inc—Theresa Otto	824 N Hartwell Ave, Waukesha WI 53186		R	2*	<.1
691	Life Enterprise USA Inc—Joshua Suh	6 Wright Pl, Princeton Junction NJ 08550	201-707-8111	B	2*	<.1
692	Z-Band Inc—Earl Hennenhoefer	848 N Hanover St Ste B, Carlisle PA 17013	717-249-2606	R	2*	<.1
693	Connors Co—Don Luckinbille	3245 S Kendall St, Denver CO 80227	303-466-9628	R	2*	<.1
694	Kenix Global Technologies LLC	15207 N 75th St Ste 10, Scottsdale AZ 85260	480-556-9671	R	2*	<.1
695	Process Physics Inc—Peter Dusza	320 Martin Ave Ste C, Santa Clara CA 95050	408-727-9244	R	2*	<.1
696	Smith Myers U S A Inc—Peter Myers	1418 Norman St Ne Ste, Palm Bay FL 32907	321-726-8815	R	2*	<.1
697	Admiral Sales Co—Arthur Petty	402 Fairview Dr, Richardson TX 75081	972-437-1828	R	2*	<.1

Rank	Company Name—*Executive Officer*	Address, City, State, Zip	Phone	Type	Fin	Empls
698	Bestel Corp—*John Duque*	1387 Nw 165th Ave, Pembroke Pines FL 33028	954-401-3090	R	2*	<.1
699	Chronix International Inc—*Bob Blaskvitch*	605 Louis Dr Ste 508b, Warminster PA 18974	215-443-8995	R	2*	<.1
700	ES Source Inc—*Dale Pedersen*	707 7th Ave, Marion IA 52302	319-364-1989	R	2*	<.1
701	Windhover Industries—*Myung-Goo Choi*	1068 Woodlyn Farm Way, Lancaster PA 17601	717-892-2787	R	2*	<.1
702	Schafer International—*Paul Schafer*	220 Surrey Dr, Bonita CA 91902	619-267-9000	R	2*	<.1
703	Pivotel LLC—*David Walker*	PO Box 609, Norwich NY 13815	607-337-7400	R	2*	<.1
704	Cablecon Inc—*Robert Moir*	6400 Chillum Pl Nw, Washington DC 20012	202-726-7082	R	2*	<.1
705	Altior Inc—*Charles Spackman*	444 State Rte 35 S, Eatontown NJ 07724	732-440-1280	R	2*	<.1
706	Seidio Inc—*David Chang*	10415 Westpark Dr B, Houston TX 77042	832-204-1118	R	2*	<.1
707	Moore Sales Company Inc—*Gary Moore*	11 Gilbert Rd, Burkburnett TX 76354	940-569-1463	R	2*	<.1
708	Dgm 4 Parts Inc—*Mort Hanan*	622 State Rte 10 Ste 6, Whippany NJ 07981	973-560-1111	R	2*	<.1
709	Straube Associates Inc—*Gene Straube*	2551 Casey Ave, Mountain View CA 94043	650-969-6060	R	2*	<.1
710	21st Century Communications Of Midamerican Inc—*Lane Zehnder*	150 W 88th St Ste 10, Minneapolis MN 55420	952-890-0442	R	2*	<.1
711	Southern Telephone Corp—*Carol Fox*	3939 4th St N, Saint Petersburg FL 33703	727-823-3333	R	2*	<.1
712	Key Life Network Inc—*Stephen Brown*	PO Box 945000, Maitland FL 32794	407-539-0001	R	2*	<.1
713	Component Sources International Inc—*Stephen Doody*	121 Flanders Rd, Westborough MA 01581	508-986-2300	R	2*	<.1
714	Applied Products No 1 Inc—*Michael Castanon*	9111 Jollyville Rd, Austin TX 78759	512-832-9804	R	2*	<.1
715	Caravan International Corp—*Ursula Cernuschi*	641 Lexington Ave Fl 1, New York NY 10022	212-223-7190	R	2*	<.1
716	D-Mac International Inc—*Daniel Coomb*	10575 Us Hwy 98, Sebring FL 33876	863-655-6221	R	2*	<.1
717	Bcd Electro Inc—*Robert Harris*	2525 W Commerce St, Dallas TX 75212	214-630-4298	R	2*	<.1
718	Spacecom—*A Loyd*	905 Town And Country D, Southaven MS 38671	662-280-4151	R	2*	<.1
719	Heat Barrier Systems Inc—*Bob Lloyd*	PO Box 840, Caddo Mills TX 75135		R	2*	<.1
720	Los Gatos Telephone Answering Service—*Thomas Bellew*	649 University Ave, Los Gatos CA 95032	408-399-2100	R	2*	<.1
721	Standard Data Resources Inc—*Alireza Fatemi*	951 Calle Negocio Ste, San Clemente CA 92673	949-455-0355	R	2*	<.1
722	Buffa Company Inc—*John Buffa*	22735 La Palma Ave, Yorba Linda CA 92887	714-692-8880	R	2*	<.1
723	Dii Computers Inc—*Thomas Drummond*	PO Box 420, Horsham PA 19044	215-657-5055	R	2*	<.1
724	Electronic Tracking Systems LLC—*Rick Battelle*	2545 Tarpley Rd, Carrollton TX 75006	469-574-4000	R	2*	<.1
725	L and M Merchandising Corp—*Robert Thompson*	PO Box 4023, Covina CA 91723	626-332-5210	R	2*	<.1
726	Recovery Direct Inc—*Joe Wood*	PO Box 2000, Georgetown TX 78627	512-863-2005	R	2*	<.1
727	TFC Communications Inc—*Timothy Murnano*	PO Box 16124, Cleveland OH 44116	440-333-5903	R	2*	<.1
728	Centramark America Inc—*Patrick Hannan*	PO Box 450877, Garland TX 75045	972-414-8188	R	2*	<.1
729	Ept Inc—*Bernhard Gugler*	805 Liberty Way, Chester VA 23836		R	2*	<.1
730	Linrose Electronics Inc—*Linda Landau*	29 Cain Dr, Plainview NY 11803	516-293-2520	R	2*	<.1
731	Legend Engraving Company Inc—*Todd Conforti*	553 W Carboy Rd, Mount Prospect IL 60056	847-952-0090	R	2*	<.1
732	International Wafer Service Inc—*Susan Hausler*	850 Coyote Hill Rd, Colfax CA 95713	530-637-5266	R	2*	<.1
733	Phoenix Rep Sales Inc—*Robert Derby*	515 W Harris Ave Ste 2, San Angelo TX 76903	325-658-7784	R	2*	<.1
734	Leisure Associates Inc—*R Leizure*	10090 Dudley Dr, Ijamsville MD 21754	301-607-6240	R	2*	<.1
735	RT Engineering Service Corp—*Chadwick Blair*	4 Walpole Park S Ste 8, Walpole MA 02081	508-668-2060	R	2*	<.1
736	Best Paging Inc—*Carl Whaley*	322 S Market St, Inglewood CA 90301	310-680-1616	R	2*	<.1
737	United Digital Technologies LLC	1775 Hwy 34 Ste D11, Wall Township NJ 07727	732-449-3434	R	2*	<.1
738	Video Service Of America Inc—*Dawn Norrod*	8445 Glazebrook Ave, Richmond VA 23228	804-798-4290	R	2*	<.1
739	Acclaim Electronics LLC—*Kay Cowan*	5967 Harrison Dr Ste 1, Las Vegas NV 89120	702-869-4900	R	2*	<.1
740	Serenity Electronics Inc—*Gary Thorne*	60 Firemens Way Ste 4, Poughkeepsie NY 12603	845-486-5195	R	2*	<.1
741	Asset Recovery Center LLC—*John Lynch*	107 Research Dr, Milford CT 06460	203-874-1400	R	2*	<.1
742	Communitech Services Inc—*Neal Shact*	2340 S Arlgtn Heights, Arlington Heights IL 60005	847-981-1200	R	2*	<.1
743	North Atlantic Telecom Inc—*Leonard Jones*	715 Chaney Cv Ste 1, Collierville TN 38017	901-371-9071	R	2*	<.1
744	Global Distributors International LLC—*Frank Coburn*	9550 Warner Ave 250-06, Fountain Valley CA 92708	714-593-1149	R	2*	<.1
745	Juliana Co—*Mike Juliana*	4304 Boca Raton Dr, Lewisville TX 75056	972-625-1075	R	2*	<.1
746	Paul Davis Automation Inc—*Paul Davis*	12250 Nantucket Dr, Chardon OH 44024	440-285-9597	R	2*	<.1
747	K and M Distributing LLC	2804 Jeanwood Dr Ste 1, Elkhart IN 46514	574-295-8710	R	2*	<.1
748	Milo Stallcop—*Milo Stallcop*	16417 7th Pl W, Lynnwood WA 98037	425-743-9516	R	2*	<.1
749	Micro Sales Inc—*Cal Evans*	1001 W Hawthorn Dr, Itasca IL 60143	630-285-1000	R	2*	<.1
750	American Telecom Solutions LLC—*Gary Dumbrowsky*	645 Baltimore Annapoli, Severna Park MD 21146	410-544-7300	R	2*	<.1
751	Emerge Technologies—*Eric Meyn*	44 W Jefryn Blvd Ste K, Deer Park NY 11729	631-253-3444	R	2*	<.1
752	Sun Tech Circuits Inc—*Tudor Melville*	5355 W Chandler Blvd S, Chandler AZ 85226	480-753-0771	R	2*	<.1
753	Total Electronics Corp—*Lee Norwood*	PO Box 82006, San Diego CA 92138	619-224-3291	R	2*	<.1
754	GAIN Communications Inc—*Gary Katen*	407 Sette Dr Ste S4, Paramus NJ 07652	201-261-0700	R	2*	<.1
755	Electronic Components Inc—*Richard Nadeau*	296 Irving St, Framingham MA 01702	508-881-8399	R	2*	<.1
756	Presentation Media Inc—*Carol Emmens*	214 Little Falls Rd St, Fairfield NJ 07004	973-785-1500	R	2*	<.1
757	Kelly Communications Systems Inc—*Matt Kaveney*	1135 Spruce Dr Ste 1, Mountainside NJ 07092	908-232-1860	R	2*	<.1
758	Digital Speech Systems Inc—*Lev Frenkel*	1241 N Glenville Dr, Richardson TX 75081	972-235-2999	R	2*	<.1
759	Comdie Inc—*Liz Coker*	1889 Yokley Rd, Lynnville TN 38472	931-527-0021	R	2*	<.1
760	Nippon America Inc—*Delia Martinez*	1195 Nw 97th Ave, Doral FL 33172	305-592-2616	R	2*	<.1
761	Abyx Business Systems Inc—*Efraim Palacios*	609 E Dewey Pl, San Antonio TX 78212	210-223-2299	R	2*	<.1
762	Amick Sound Inc—*Michael Amick*	PO Box 2399, Rapid City SD 57709	605-348-3633	R	2*	<.1
763	Francis Bearsch—*Francis Bearsch*	2520 W 3rd St, Bloomington IN 47404	812-339-5208	R	2*	<.1
764	Jms Electronics Inc—*Martin Klopert*	13125 Saticoy St, North Hollywood CA 91605	818-764-3303	R	2*	<.1
765	Mclean and Mclean Security and Intercom Inc—*Ingerd Mclean*	39 W 32nd St Rm 703, New York NY 10001	212-465-2088	R	2*	<.1
766	Thorson Company Southwest—*Joe Bonick*	4445 Alpha Rd Ste 109, Dallas TX 75244	972-233-5744	R	2*	<.1
767	YS Tech USA Inc—*Arik Vrobel*	12691 Monarch St, Garden Grove CA 92841	714-230-6122	R	2*	<.1
768	Planet Dj Inc—*Chris Whybrew*	1315 Greg St Ste 101, Sparks NV 89431	775-323-1540	R	2*	<.1
769	Falcon Sales And Technology Inc—*Bret Gann*	2598 Fortune Way Ste J, Vista CA 92081	760-598-7418	R	2*	<.1
770	Fiber Solutions Inc—*Carol Spoolstra*	17740 Hoffman Way, Homewood IL 60430	708-206-1565	R	2*	<.1
771	A and M Electronics Supply Inc—*C Chan*	4254 Bluebonnet Dr, Stafford TX 77477	281-240-8999	R	2*	<.1
772	Electrospec Sales Inc—*Robert Vielock*	3504 Enfield Rd, Austin TX 78703	512-671-3774	R	2*	<.1
773	American Little Swan Inc—*Jim Soux*	13336 41st Rd Apt 10b, Flushing NY 11355	718-539-2802	R	2*	<.1
774	Hurley Communications Inc—*James Hurley*	1113 Washington St, Norwood MA 02062	781-762-3313	R	2*	<.1
775	KmpartsCom Inc—*Gerald Shallow*	925 Stoner Rd, Englewood FL 34223	941-473-0073	R	2*	<.1
776	Mil-Com Distributors Inc—*Jim Ingold*	8989 122nd Ave, Largo FL 33773	727-559-7600	R	2*	<.1
777	Southern Advantage Company Inc—*Herbert Sturt*	11935 Ramah Church Rd, Huntersville NC 28078	704-992-6251	R	2*	<.1
778	Tel-Phone Resources Co—*Allan Walker*	3305 W Bismark Ave, Spokane WA 99205	509-324-0400	R	2*	<.1
779	Mercantile International NA Inc—*Rajesh Matta*	140 Ethel Rd W Ste M, Piscataway NJ 08854	732-650-9400	R	2*	<.1
780	Midori America Corp—*Terumi Tsugawa*	2501 E Chapman Ave Ste, Fullerton CA 92831	714-446-8668	R	2*	<.1
781	Sunbird Industries Inc—*Claudia Edam*	475 Scrub Oak Cir, Monument CO 80132	719-481-2900	R	2*	<.1
782	Telesodt Technologies Inc—*Robert Downham*	4340 Georgetown Sq Ste, Atlanta GA 30338	770-454-6001	R	2*	<.1
783	World Link Electronics LLC—*Hamze Samar*	1180 Springs Ctr S Blv, Altamonte Springs FL 32714	407-681-5050	R	2*	<.1
784	Cammar Enterprises Inc—*Henry Camilleri*	222 Martling Ave Apt 2, Tarrytown NY 10591	914-332-4132	R	2*	<.1
785	Gilland Electronics—*John Stover*	305 Vineyard Town Ctr, Morgan Hill CA 95037	408-778-9049	R	2*	<.1
786	Data Image Corporation Of North America Inc—*Han Liu*	2500 Meadowbrook Pkwy, Duluth GA 30096	770-623-9811	R	2*	<.1

Note: An asterisk (*) indicates an estimated financial figure. The company type code used is as follows: R = Private, P = Public, S = Private Subsidiary, B = Public Subsidiary, D = Division, J = Joint Venture, I = Investment Fund.

COMPANY RANKINGS BY SALES WITHIN 4-DIGIT SIC

Rank	Company Name—*Executive Officer*	Address, City, State, Zip	Phone	Type	Fin	Empls
787	JV Hii/Ske—*Carlos Ramos*	5205 Leesburg Pke Ste, Falls Church VA 22041	703-243-0412	R	1*	<.1
788	Mr Window Tinting—*Joel Leitson*	1776 Polk St Apt 67, Hollywood FL 33020	954-274-7963	R	1*	<.1
789	Southwestern Telecom Inc—*Raymond Stone*	401 Old Trenton Rd, Clarksville TN 37040	931-387-2682	R	1*	<.1
790	Tritech Electronics Inc—*Steven Hauste*	349 W Commercial St St, East Rochester NY 14445	585-385-6500	R	1*	<.1
791	Grip Gear Inc—*Billy Mourad*	8827 Shirley Ave, Northridge CA 91324	818-700-8076	R	1*	<.1
792	Lectro Communications Inc—*Philip Parton*	15555 Stony Creek Way, Noblesville IN 46060	317-774-1867	R	1*	<.1
793	K 2 W Group Inc—*Kenneth Buss*	1612 Nw Boca Raton Blv, Boca Raton FL 33432	561-391-5553	R	1*	<.1
794	Vz Solutions Inc—*Zenny Mera*	3317 Nw 97th Ave, Doral FL 33172	305-477-4470	R	1*	<.1
795	Aero-Tech Communications Inc—*Billie Bowmer*	PO Box 337, Imlay City MI 48444	810-724-7200	R	1*	<.1
796	Capacitor Supply Inc—*Pauline Wright*	16551 Burke Ln, Huntington Beach CA 92647	714-596-5600	R	1*	<.1
797	D1 International Inc—*Bron Kutny*	95 E Main St Ste 2, Huntington NY 11743	631-673-6866	R	1*	<.1
798	Dakota Alert Inc—*Andrew Quam*	PO Box 130, Elk Point SD 57025	605-356-2772	R	1*	<.1
799	Japan Electronic Manufacturers—*Peter Oyama*	1000 Skokie Blvd Ste 1, Wilmette IL 60091	847-251-3738	R	1*	<.1
800	Metropolitan Audio Visual Company LLC—*Karen Roundtree*	111 Carpenter Dr Ste A, Sterling VA 20164	703-834-0004	R	1*	<.1
801	Ryder Communications Inc—*Thomas Ryder*	10 Peary Dr, Sussex NJ 07461	973-702-9656	R	1*	<.1
802	Titan Photonics Inc—*Eric Liu*	48501 Warm Springs Blv, Fremont CA 94539	510-687-0098	R	1*	<.1
803	Electronic Parts Specialists Inc—*David Turner*	711 Kelso St, Flint MI 48506	810-238-7311	R	1*	<.1
804	Ohio Valley 2-Way Radio Inc—*Larry Brown*	2035 E Parrish Ave, Owensboro KY 42303	270-683-4963	R	1*	<.1
805	Weber Sensors LLC—*Gunthner Weber*	4462 Bretton Ct Nw Ste, Acworth GA 30101	770-592-6630	R	1*	<.1
806	Ancom Communications Inc—*David Anderson*	1800 Cliff Rd E Ste 17, Burnsville MN 55337	952-808-0033	R	1*	<.1
807	Beam Radio Inc—*Manuel Alvarez*	2200 Nw 102nd Ave Ste, Doral FL 33172	305-477-2326	R	1*	<.1
808	Lookout Security Systems Inc—*Luke Tripp*	200 Dexter Ave Ste 1, Watertown MA 02472	617-923-2576	R	1*	<.1
809	Ph Cellular Inc—*Luis Rojas*	3034 Nw 82nd Ave, Doral FL 33122	305-718-3535	R	1*	<.1
810	Schmitt Industrial Marketing Corp—*Richard Vairo*	738 Smithtown Byp Ste, Smithtown NY 11787	631-979-1313	R	1*	<.1
811	Bert's Electric Supply Company Inc—*Eileen Klapman*	PO Box 156, North Quincy MA 02171	617-770-1111	R	1*	<.1
812	Industrial Electronics and Controls Inc—*Michael Zielinski*	1455 W 12th Pl, Tempe AZ 85281	480-894-2375	R	1*	<.1
813	Sol Telecommunication Services Inc—*Hector Solis*	PO Box 12765, Newport Beach CA 92658	562-907-4367	R	1*	<.1
814	Canal Merchandise—*Minh Guyen*	331 Canal St, New York NY 10013	212-334-0378	R	1*	<.1
815	Preferred Manufacturing Associates LLC—*Rick Smith*	7479 Dalt Rd, Jackson MI 49201	517-764-7073	R	1*	<.1
816	Demco Group NA Inc—*Stephen Demoff*	3857 Birch St Ste 560, Newport Beach CA 92660	949-440-5800	R	1*	<.1
817	Fossman Corp—*Chris Foss*	1610 Potomac Ave Ste 1, Pittsburgh PA 15216	412-344-9000	R	1*	<.1
818	World Eyecam Inc—*Frank Le*	24551 Raymond Way Ste, Lake Forest CA 92630	949-305-6550	R	1*	<.1
819	Bohenstiehel Electric Co—*Tom Bohnenstiehl*	810 Jefferson Hwy, Jefferson LA 70121	504-834-0351	R	1*	<.1
820	Cedes Corporation Of America—*Steven Freedman*	7107 Ohms Ln, Edina MN 55439	612-424-8400	R	1*	<.1
821	Electronic Marketing Associates Inc—*Robert Denny*	185 Wind Chime Ct Ste, Raleigh NC 27615	919-847-8800	R	1*	<.1
822	Kcomm Inc—*Craig Kennedy*	10815 Gulfdale St, San Antonio TX 78216	210-344-3311	R	1*	<.1
823	King Communications USA Inc—*Robert Geaghan*	1583 E Silver Star Rd, Ocoee FL 34761	407-654-3786	R	1*	<.1
824	Opti-Com Manufacturing Network Inc—*Linda Cousin*	PO Box 23802, New Orleans LA 70183	504-736-0331	R	1*	<.1
825	Quorum Technical Sales—*Joe Obot*	4701 Patrick Henry Dr, Santa Clara CA 95054	408-980-0812	R	1*	<.1
826	Agt Technologies Inc—*David Arghavani*	22900 Ventura Blvd Ste, Woodland Hills CA 91364	818-591-8777	R	1*	<.1
827	Bank Vault Service and Equipment—*Mike Coffas*	535 S Broadway Ste 212, Hicksville NY 11801	516-433-8884	R	1*	<.1
828	Bext Inc—*Dennis Pieri*	1045 10th Ave, San Diego CA 92101	619-239-8462	R	1*	<.1
829	Raith USA Inc—*George Lanzarotta*	2805 Veterans Hwy Ste, Ronkonkoma NY 11779	631-738-9500	R	1*	<.1
830	Communication Service Inc—*Steven Johnson*	12403 Maccorkle Ave, Charleston WV 25315	304-949-4160	R	1*	<.1
831	Comtronics Inc—*James Gray*	1213 Main St, Grandview MO 64030	816-765-1800	R	1*	<.1
832	Gw Electronics Ltd—*George Wagner*	PO Box 107, Oconomowoc WI 53066	262-567-9445	R	1*	<.1
833	Hughes Xerographic Equipment Agency Inc—*Nancy Hughes-Karvelli*	3114 Belmont St, Bellaire OH 43906	740-676-8000	R	1*	<.1
834	Madell Technology Corp—*Shaolin Bi*	1957 E Cedar St, Ontario CA 91761	909-418-6951	R	1*	<.1
835	Asset Exchange Ltd—*Mariana Cardos*	3502 E Broadway Rd, Phoenix AZ 85040	602-437-9481	R	1*	<.1
836	Business Telecom Products Inc—*Marilyn Torrison*	PO Box 997, Carnation WA 98014	425-649-9262	R	1*	<.1
837	Colemans Mining And Electrical Equipment Inc—*Harold Coleman*	40 Bowers Way, Salt Lake City UT 84115	801-484-5238	R	1*	<.1
838	Listen Inc—*Michael Carrane*	661 W Lake St Ste 1n, Chicago IL 60661	312-207-0100	R	1*	<.1
839	Technical Service Corp—*David Bow*	2618 S 4th St, Louisville KY 40208	502-636-1496	R	1*	<.1
840	Tom Tech Systems Inc—*Laura Tomasino*	46 W Jefryn Blvd Ste B, Deer Park NY 11729	631-586-9676	R	1*	<.1
841	Samas Telecom—*Seokuk MA*	3425 Pomona Blvd Ste F, Pomona CA 91768	909-598-0250	R	1*	<.1
842	Seimac Inc—*Charlie Stuff*	8486 Kao Cir, Manassas VA 20110	703-393-0110	R	1*	<.1
843	Civils Associates Inc—*Charles Civils*	714 N Allyson Dr, Baton Rouge LA 70815	225-928-0651	R	1*	<.1
844	Fiberoptic Supply Inc—*Bryan Hogan*	2171 S Trenton Way Ste, Denver CO 80231	303-743-0916	R	1*	<.1
845	Palmborg Associates—*Rod Palmborg*	PO Box 200, Mercer Island WA 98040	206-232-3444	R	1*	<.1
846	Gator Security Inc—*Virginia Lewis*	106 Se 5th St, Okeechobee FL 34974	561-214-4628	R	1*	<.1
847	Communication Controls Inc—*Donald Isakson*	PO Box 967, Avon CT 06001	860-793-9621	R	1*	<.1
848	Advanced Engineering Corp—*Gilbert Yuen*	PO Box 4277, San Leandro CA 94579	510-352-7860	R	1*	<.1
849	Video Masters Inc—*Kenneth Cleveland*	PO Box 681100, Kansas City MO 64168	816-587-0000	R	1*	<.1
850	Commeg Systems Inc—*Mark Golonka*	141 W Home Ave, Villa Park IL 60181	630-833-3305	R	1*	<.1
851	Paramount Technologies Inc—*Eric Mcgrew*	PO Box 243, Follansbee WV 26037	304-527-4700	R	1*	<.1
852	River City Communications Inc—*Jerry Bernhard*	820 S Pennsylvania Ave, Mason City IA 50401	641-424-0164	R	1*	<.1
853	Voyager Components Inc—*Allen Orloff*	1208 Eska Way, Silverton OR 97381	503-873-4499	R	1*	<.1
854	Nexlink Communications LLC—*Mike Clink*	3355 Bald Mountain Rd, Auburn Hills MI 48326	248-409-2511	R	1*	<.1
855	Qos Telesys—*Kevin Cliff*	7035 Orangethorpe Ave, Buena Park CA 90621	714-224-4700	R	1*	<.1
856	Randolph and Hale Inc—*James Hale*	PO Box 1011, Hopkinsville KY 42241	270-885-5357	R	1*	<.1
857	Vertex Trading Corp—*Carlos Hoffman*	9805 Nw 52nd St Apt 21, Doral FL 33178	305-471-7773	R	1*	<.1
858	Mag-Trol Associates Inc—*Anthony Mennillo*	708 Celis St, San Fernando CA 91340	818-361-5015	R	1*	<.1
859	Atometron—*Chris Wolf*	1085 N Main St Ste M, Orange CA 92867	714-204-0285	R	1*	<.1
860	Joseph P Mazzeo Associates Inc—*Joseph Mazzeo*	354 Curlew St, Rochester NY 14613	585-458-7851	R	1*	<.1
861	Imron Corp—*Imron Hussain*	15375 Barranca Pkwy B1, Irvine CA 92618	949-341-0947	R	1*	<.1
862	North Coast Technical Sales Inc—*Dave Sexton*	8251 Mayfield Rd Ste 1, Chesterland OH 44026	440-729-7540	R	1*	<.1
863	Br Technology LLC—*Julissa Ortiv*	1501 Zephyr Ave, Hayward CA 94544	510-475-5502	R	1*	<.1
864	Imtronics Industries Inc—*Steven Cohen*	11930 31st Ct N, Saint Petersburg FL 33716	727-572-9010	R	1*	<.1
865	RF Kimball Company Inc—*Richard Kimball*	1200 Executive Dr E St, Richardson TX 75081	972-231-3447	R	1*	<.1
866	1st Call Electronics Inc—*Jerry Robinson*	22837 Islamare Ln, Lake Forest CA 92630	949-348-3100	R	1*	<.1
867	Apple Corporate Technologies Inc—*Jack Zubli*	312 Jericho Tpke, Floral Park NY 11001	516-352-7151	R	1*	<.1
868	Baypoint Components Inc—*Sam Chambers*	PO Box 443, Shirley NY 11967	631-399-5500	R	1*	<.1
869	Comp Tech Sales—*Russ Muniz*	232 Blvd Ste 11, Hasbrouck Heights NJ 07604	201-288-7400	R	1*	<.1
870	Delay Line Distributors Inc—*Stanley Wacow*	13455 Ventura Blvd Ste, Sherman Oaks CA 91423	818-986-9455	R	1*	<.1
871	Purcelltel Inc—*Patrick Purcell*	1334 Shepard Dr Ste E, Sterling VA 20164	703-406-4300	R	1*	<.1
872	Aatfab Corp—*David Carpenter*	PO Box 518, Butler WI 53007	262-783-7770	R	1*	<.1
873	Alliedus Corp—*Charles Lim*	780 Montague Expy Ste, San Jose CA 95131	408-432-8805	R	1*	<.1
874	Barron Communications Inc—*Rita Barron*	253 Chesterfield Indus, Chesterfield MO 63005	636-519-0303	R	1*	<.1

Rank	Company Name—*Executive Officer*	Address, City, State, Zip	Phone	Type	Fin	Empls
875	Cardinal Sound and Communcations Corp—*Scott Reidinger*	2219 Kansas Ave, Silver Spring MD 20910	301-589-3700	R	1*	<.1
876	Clermont Communications Corp—*Paul Levine*	245 8th Ave Ste 114, New York NY 10011	212-255-7155	R	1*	<.1
877	Comlink Wireless Technologies Inc—*Larry Dewitt*	1724 Lacy Dr Ste 106, Fort Worth TX 76177	817-546-8410	R	1*	<.1
878	Lafayette Electronic Supply Inc—*Ronald Hurst*	405 N Earl Ave Ste B, Lafayette IN 47904	765-447-9660	R	1*	<.1
879	Security Data and Cable Hq Ltd—*Billy Rinn*	5400 Mitchelldale St B, Houston TX 77092	713-686-7111	R	1*	<.1
880	Profactive Corp—*Matthew Burns*	7949 Sw Cirrus Dr Ste, Beaverton OR 97008	503-644-3222	R	1*	<.1
881	Newark InOne—*Paul Tallentine*	4801 N Ravenswood Ave, Chicago IL 60640	773-784-5100	S	1*	1.5
882	KCG Communications Inc—*Charles Beram*	5701 E Evans Ave, Denver CO 80222	303-773-1200	R	1	<.1
883	Herbach and Rademan Co—*Frank Lobascio*	353 Crider Ave, Moorestown NJ 08057	856-802-0422	R	1*	<.1
884	Innovative Control Systems Inc—*Larry Cinpinski*	10125 S 52nd St, Franklin WI 53132	414-423-1088	R	1*	<.1
885	Twisted Pair/BT Services Inc—*Frank Hanna*	6850 Regional St Ste 1, Dublin CA 94568		R	1*	<.1
886	Futronics Inc—*Mike Gruss*	550 State Rte 19 S, Fremont OH 43420	419-332-5681	R	1*	<.1
887	Bud Electronic Supply Co—*Al Pontecore*	22 N Jackson St, Danville IL 61832	217-446-0925	R	1	<.1
888	Uptime Studios—*Derek Wielend*	251 W 30th St Ste 8fw, New York NY 10001	212-695-5088	R	1*	<.1
889	Agency Mechanical Services Inc—*Ernest Schuck*	900 Creek Rd Ste A, Bellmawr NJ 08031	856-933-0393	R	1*	<.1
890	Alhambra Productions Inc—*Nabila Hanson*	231 Market Pl, San Ramon CA 94583	510-690-0098	R	1*	<.1
891	Fintel Inc—*Robert Brunton*	48790 Plomosa Rd, Fremont CA 94539	510-657-8645	R	1*	<.1
892	Westmoreland Telephone Co—*John Durbin*	572 Woodward Dr, Greensburg PA 15601	724-838-7723	R	1*	<.1
893	All 4-Pcb North America Inc—*Torsten Reckert*	4218 San Fernando Rd, Glendale CA 91204	818-230-2346	R	1*	<.1
894	Foneco Business Systems Inc—*H Sanders*	1331 E Hwy 80 Ste 18, Mesquite TX 75150	972-288-7070	R	1*	<.1
895	Hathaway Electronics Inc—*Steven Stanford*	PO Box 8, Lexington MA 02420	781-861-7010	R	1*	<.1
896	HC Johnson Agencies Inc—*William Reeves*	2488 Browncroft Blvd, Rochester NY 14625	585-586-0777	R	1*	<.1
897	Network Electronic Marketing Inc—*Dixie Lovejoy*	5719 E Indian School R, Phoenix AZ 85018	480-994-8242	R	1*	<.1
898	Priority Components LLC	PO Box 810, Carnation WA 98014	425-333-4304	R	1*	<.1
899	Ring Communications Inc—*Peter Lean*	57 Trade Zone Dr, Ronkonkoma NY 11779	631-585-7464	R	1*	<.1
900	Sunny Components Inc—*Sunil Merchant*	1370 E Cypress St Ste, Covina CA 91724	626-966-6259	R	1*	<.1
901	Visics Corp—*T Hopkins*	70 Hastings St Ste 3, Wellesley MA 02481	781-235-8926	R	1*	<.1
902	Communication Source Data Inc—*Andrew Kayworth*	200 Waler Way Unit 1, Saint Augustine FL 32086	904-829-8922	R	1*	<.1
903	Edwards Major Electronics Supply Corp—*David Leven*	23 Summer St, Pawtucket RI 02860	401-725-7400	R	1*	<.1
904	Infinity Information Inc—*Richard Ramras*	PO Box 67, Seaside CA 93955	831-655-7676	R	1*	<.1
905	Paez-Fletcher Co—*Marcelo Paez*	1638 Nw 108th Ave, Miami FL 33172	305-593-0227	R	1*	<.1
906	Price Telecommunications Inc—*Gary Price*	3237 S Cherokee Ln Ste, Woodstock GA 30188	770-977-9999	R	1*	<.1
907	Qcsystems Inc—*Pauline Yong*	4009 Clipper Ct, Fremont CA 94538	510-979-1626	R	1*	<.1
908	Ridex Integral Inc—*Yoichi Sakaguchi*	25600 Rye Canyon Rd St, Valencia CA 91355	661-775-0419	R	1*	<.1
909	Taw Electronics Inc—*Laura Salci*	4215 W Burbank Blvd, Burbank CA 91505	818-846-3911	R	1*	<.1
910	Thousand Value Limited Corp—*Robert Jones*	1625 Ramona Dr, Camarillo CA 93010	805-987-1279	R	1*	<.1
911	All Phase Video-Security Inc—*John Destefano*	70 Cain Dr, Brentwood NY 11717	631-435-4788	R	1*	<.1
912	B and R Electronics Inc—*Richard Cameron*	17 Raritan Rd, Oakland NJ 07436	201-670-7200	R	1*	<.1
913	Micro Ray Electronics Inc—*Raymond Vito*	212 Midstreams Pl, Brick NJ 08724	732-892-8799	R	1*	<.1
914	Elkays Electronics—*Leslie Kacev*	7558 Trade St, San Diego CA 92121	858-268-4400	R	1*	<.1
915	Fones West Digital Systems—*Mark Felsen*	PO Box 6741, Denver CO 80206	303-205-4500	R	1*	<.1
916	Arbon Inc—*Rick Jarosz*	3911 Wesley Ter, Schiller Park IL 60176	708-456-7956	R	1*	<.1
917	Capacitor Sales and Engineering Inc—*Gerald Voyles*	6321 Porter Rd Ste 3, Sarasota FL 34240	941-342-1677	R	1*	<.1
918	Mjl Sales and Marketing Inc—*Mitch Levine*	66 Scudders Rd, Sparta NJ 07871	732-766-1870	R	1*	<.1
919	Shieldtech Systems LLC—*Stephen Ward*	823 Hollywood Blvd, Crownsville MD 21032	410-923-8622	R	1*	<.1
920	Westel Communications Inc—*Dick Sullivan*	PO Box 681215, Houston TX 77268	281-537-8363	R	1*	<.1
921	Rnj Electronics Inc—*Jeffrey Mutterperl*	PO Box 667, Amityville NY 11701	631 226 2700	P	1*	<.1
922	North Star Communications Inc—*Thomas Klasnick*	802 Millers Run Rd Ste, Cecil PA 15321	412-221-5155	R	1*	<.1
923	Phyco/Jm Inc—*John Mc Gee*	1740 Junction Ave Ste, San Jose CA 95112	408-441-1275	R	1*	<.1
924	Resource Electronics LLC	24008 Bough Ave Bldg B, Mission Viejo CA 92691	949-457-1244	R	1*	<.1
925	Bettridge and Ryan Sales Inc—*Jack Ryan*	16414 N 91st St, Scottsdale AZ 85260	480-348-0555	R	1*	<.1
926	HR Distributors Inc—*Scott Raymond*	PO Box 8682, Portland ME 04104	207-773-2552	R	1*	<.1
927	Marketing Associates Inc—*Dick Rose*	6300 Rockside Rd Ste 2, Cleveland OH 44131	216-447-0404	R	1*	<.1
928	Nr Electronics LLC—*Liza Ordonez*	1450 Harbour Dr, Longwood FL 32750	407-331-5149	R	1*	<.1
929	Power Sources Unlimited Inc—*Ray Newby*	200 Stonewall Blvd Ste, Wrentham MA 02093	508-384-1419	R	1*	<.1
930	Digital Broadcast Equipment Inc—*Hildegard Castaneda*	14127 Jnes Maltsberger, San Antonio TX 78247	210-805-0606	R	1*	<.1
931	SR Components Inc—*Scott Russell*	3590 Oceanside Rd Ste, Oceanside NY 11572	516-536-2250	R	1*	<.1
932	Teletechnologies Inc—*Sal Suppa*	166 Ridgedale Ave Ste, Morristown NJ 07960	973-539-9995	R	1*	<.1
933	Cds Telco Inc—*Casey Smith*	5241 Secor Rd Ste S, Toledo OH 43623	419-475-1166	R	1*	<.1
934	Powerhouse Systems LLC	3139 Macarthur Blvd, Northbrook IL 60062	847-205-1112	R	1*	<.1
935	RGS Communications Inc—*Robert Simpkiss*	21 Wibraham St Ste 102, Palmer MA 01069	413-283-2882	R	1*	<.1
936	Bill H Battles—*Bill Battles*	PO Box 898, Carmichael CA 95609	916-966-8284	R	1*	<.1
937	Government Network Solutions—*Kathleen Williams*	5527 Preston Fall City, Fall City WA 98024	425-222-6082	R	1*	<.1
938	AR Communication—*Angel Rodriguez*	91 Main St, Eatontown NJ 07724	732-542-8695	R	1*	<.1
939	Telesavers—*Leslie Skeans*	PO Box 726, Chesterfield VA 23832	804-275-7000	R	1*	<.1
940	Components Electronic Systems—*Doug Evans*	1528 W San Pedro St St, Gilbert AZ 85233	480-361-9500	R	1*	<.1
941	Compostar Inc—*Hua Components*	18019 Sky Park Cir Ste, Irvine CA 92614	949-260-9678	R	1*	<.1
942	Levco Communication—*Frank Gildersleeve*	PO Box 1123, Erie PA 16512	814-452-3487	R	1*	<.1
943	Cascade Laser Corp—*Douglas Geier*	101 N Elliott Rd, Newberg OR 97132	503-554-1926	R	1*	<.1
944	Mbm Engineering Inc—*Jim Giubilato*	2320 Walsh Ave Ste A, Santa Clara CA 95051	408-360-1300	R	1*	<.1
945	Tecdia Inc—*Etsuo Koyama*	2700 Augustine Dr Ste, Santa Clara CA 95054	408-748-0100	R	1*	<.1
946	Viacell International Inc—*James Schliestett*	6917 Woodley Ave Ste B, Van Nuys CA 91406	818-901-9100	R	1*	<.1
947	E and R Marine Electronics Inc—*Joseph Esfeller*	PO Box 607, Bayou La Batre AL 36509	251-824-7051	R	1*	<.1
948	Foxtronix Inc—*Christopher Sweeney*	2240 E Central Ave Ste, Miamisburg OH 45342	937-866-2112	R	1*	<.1
949	Simi Components Inc—*Katherine Hillman*	1736 Erringer Rd Ste 2, Simi Valley CA 93065	805-581-1621	R	1*	<.1
950	Suma Distributors LLC	2051 Nw 112th Ave Ste, Miami FL 33172	305-470-9429	R	1*	<.1
951	Elecom Supply Co—*Alfredo Giovanelli*	3646 Midway Dr, San Diego CA 92110	619-223-4294	R	1*	<.1
952	Tony Abiecunas—*Tony Abiecunas*	22800 Lakeland Blvd, Cleveland OH 44132	216-289-9190	R	1*	<.1
953	K and K Sound Systems Inc—*Dieter Kaudel*	PO Box 626, Coos Bay OR 97420	541-888-3517	R	1*	<.1
954	Aspen Solutions Inc—*Paul Sandles*	PO Box 1554, Aspen CO 81612	480-778-1300	R	1*	<.1
955	Access Office Electronics Inc—*James Becker*	1192 W Main St, Stroudsburg PA 18360	570-421-0648	R	1*	<.1
956	Custom Thermoelectric Inc—*Andrew Masters*	11941 Industrial Park, Bishopville MD 21813	410-352-3442	R	1*	<.1
957	Kemp Instruments Inc—*Bryon Hale*	1201 Richardson Dr Ste, Richardson TX 75080	972-437-9100	R	1*	<.1
958	Broomfield and Associates Inc—*John Broomfield*	PO Box 3749, Lilburn GA 30048	770-992-8820	R	1*	<.1
959	Micro Electronics Corp—*Ronnie Zau*	3375 Scott Blvd Ste 22, Santa Clara CA 95054	408-988-1101	R	1*	<.1
960	Secure Tech Peripherals Inc—*Stephen Stone*	336 N Gaffey St Fl 2, San Pedro CA 90731	310-547-8501	R	1*	<.1
961	Soffa Industries Inc—*Adele Soffa*	5901 Corvette St, Commerce CA 90040	323-728-0230	R	1*	<.1
962	Ivey Sound Lighting and Multimedia—*Chris Ivey*	PO Box 82468, Conyers GA 30013	770-785-9977	R	1*	<.1
963	Logistics Supply Corp—*Claudio Bittner*	7813 Valleyfield Dr, Springfield VA 22153	703-569-8151	R	1*	<.1
964	Fleet Electronics Inc—*Robert Farakos*	227 Bridgeport Ave, Milford CT 06460	203-877-2577	R	1*	<.1

Note: An asterisk (*) indicates an estimated financial figure. The company type code used is as follows: R = Private, P = Public, S = Private Subsidiary, B = Public Subsidiary, D = Division, J = Joint Venture, I = Investment Fund.

COMPANY RANKINGS BY SALES WITHIN 4-DIGIT SIC

Rank	Company Name—Executive Officer	Address, City, State, Zip	Phone	Type	Fin	Empls
965	G and G Technologies Inc—Robert Greenberg	280 N Midland Ave Ste, Saddle Brook NJ 07663	201-791-1400	R	1*	<.1
966	Choice Communications—Jan O'dell	59 Calle De Paz, Alamogordo NM 88310	575-437-5983	R	1*	<.1
967	Cd Technologies LLC	9170 E Bahia Dr Ste 11, Scottsdale AZ 85260	480-419-8265	R	1*	<.1
968	LMS Marketing—John Mandabach	6501 Tussing Rd, Reynoldsburg OH 43068	614-575-2000	R	1*	<.1
969	Custom Drilling Technologies Inc—Timothy Clougherty	31 Conrad Rd, Melrose MA 02176	781-665-1127	R	1*	<.1
970	Inntechnology Inc—Randy Stryker	206 S Brand Blvd, Glendale CA 91204	818-552-2345	R	1*	<.1
971	Ultimate Group Corp—Paulo Ramirez	6914 NW 51st St, Miami FL 33166	305-513-0627	R	1*	<.1
972	Us Alert LLC—Robert Osullivan	164 W Royal Palm, Boca Raton FL 33432	561-394-9969	R	1*	<.1
973	Benton Electronics Supply Inc—Michael Morse	1465 E Main St, Benton Harbor MI 49022	269-925-0069	R	1*	<.1
974	Champ Inc—Mike Peters	PO Box 61297, Raleigh NC 27661	919-855-0122	R	1*	<.1
975	Surf Electronics Inc—Boris Vishnevkine	1100 Coney Island Ave, Brooklyn NY 11230	718-859-5222	R	1*	<.1
976	L Rivas Enterprises Inc—Lupe Rivas	7733 Densmore Ave Ste, Van Nuys CA 91406	818-997-3838	R	1*	<.1
977	Lee Haimowitz—Lee Haimowitz	5439 S Porter Rd, Onaway MI 49765	989-733-7622	R	1*	<.1
978	Hull Speed Data Products Inc—James Deloatche	7612 Emerald Dr, Melbourne FL 32904	321-768-0063	R	1*	<.1
979	Arnold Technical Sales Inc—Steve Arnold	1250 Oakmead Pkwy Ste, Sunnyvale CA 94085	408-245-0400	R	1*	<.1
980	Daily Electronics Inc—James Grimes	19311 Ne 91st St, Vancouver WA 98682	360-896-8856	R	1*	<.1
981	Ebg LLC—Elain Tressler	PO Box 519, Middletown PA 17057	717-737-9877	R	1*	<.1
982	IS Motorsport Inc—Neo Casserly	286 Gasoline Aly Ste A, Indianapolis IN 46222	317-244-6643	R	1*	<.1
983	Far International Corporation Of America—Roberto Fazio	7014 Nw 50th St, Miami FL 33166	305-592-7747	R	1*	<.1
984	Holzberg Communications Inc—Andrew Holzberg	PO Box 322, Totowa NJ 07511	973-389-9600	R	1*	<.1
985	Intelk Inc—Abe Fraindlich	637 Michelle Pl, Valley Stream NY 11581	516-792-0379	R	1*	<.1
986	Wizard Technologies Inc—Jeffery Jacobs	910 Boston Post Rd E S, Marlborough MA 01752	508-624-8888	R	1*	<.1
987	CF Systems Inc—Gayle Durham	16 Cliff Dr, Englewood NJ 07631	201-871-7100	R	<1*	<.1
988	Edge Electronics Inc—Adrian Giannone	10 Tower Office Park S, Woburn MA 01801	781-376-1551	R	<1*	<.1
989	Invecom Inc—Frank Wilke	N288 W8056 Park Dr N 2, Hartland WI 53029	262-538-1397	R	<1*	<.1
990	Jarrdd Inc—David Farber	141 Shreve Ave, Barrington NJ 08007	856-310-0100	R	<1*	<.1
991	JM Electronics—Jerry Mabie	970 Sunshine Ln Ste E, Altamonte Springs FL 32714	407-862-3363	R	<1*	<.1
992	Master Key Industrial Inc—Neil Elbirlik	5536 Renaissance Ave 3, San Diego CA 92122	858-587-8886	R	<1*	<.1
993	Hobbs-Crump Inc—Jack Hobbs	PO Box 59385, Birmingham AL 35259	205-252-7341	R	<1*	<.1
994	Jbr Engineering—Dick Braun	2330 Graffenburg Rd, Sauquoit NY 13456	315-737-9432	R	<1*	<.1
995	Jon B Jolly Inc—Jon Jolly	5416 California Ave Sw, Seattle WA 98136	206-938-4166	R	<1*	<.1
996	Ideacom Healthcare Communications Of Florida Inc—Donald Musselman	PO Box 7637, Tampa FL 33673	813-229-9331	R	<1*	<.1
997	Newmik International Corp—Takayoshi Miki	PO Box 41310, San Jose CA 95160	408-264-4391	R	<1*	<.1
998	Vision Pro Inc—John Davison	7207 Chagrin Rd Ste 6, Chagrin Falls OH 44023	440-893-9330	R	<1*	<.1
999	D and L Technical Sales Inc—Nicholas Vecchio	6139 S Rural Rd Ste 10, Tempe AZ 85283	480-730-9553	R	<1*	<.1
1000	Axcess Technology Source LLC	2430 Lacy Ln Ste 116, Carrollton TX 75006	972-247-1177	R	<1*	<.1
1001	Mescon Technologies Inc—Moshe Weissberg	9502 Gulfstream Rd A, Frankfort IL 60423	815-464-5004	R	<1*	<.1
1002	Semiconductor Test Inc—Larry Johnson	18645 Sw Farmington Rd, Beaverton OR 97007	503-439-1500	R	<1*	<.1
1003	Sonic Studios—Leonard Lombardo	1311 Sunny Ct, Sutherlin OR 97479	541-459-8839	R	<1*	<.1
1004	Commwise Inc—William Wisely	2820 Audubon Village D, Norristown PA 19403	610-635-3400	R	<1*	<.1
1005	American Telecommunications Corp—Robert Henze	PO Box 59441, Schaumburg IL 60159	847-310-1700	R	<1*	<.1
1006	Kaytek—Teddy Kumada	2554 Lincoln Blvd Ste, Venice CA 90291	310-306-6727	R	<1*	<.1
1007	BUSE Industries Inc	177 Northwest Industri, Bridgeton MO 63044	314-344-1166	S	<1*	<.1
1008	Mystery Electronics—John Ryan	0430 Morton Rd, Greenbrier TN 37073	615-643-8460	R	<1*	<.1
1009	Robert P Powell—Robert Powell	611 Hall St Nw, Warren OH 44483	330-392-6800	R	<1*	<.1
1010	ARC Technical Resources Inc—Jerry Ramie	2006 Lockwood Dr, San Jose CA 95132	408-263-6486	R	<1*	<.1
1011	Econo' Scope—Dennis Amiot	17405 Kincaid Rd, San Jose CA 95140	408-954-0855	R	<1*	<.1
1012	Shanks and Wright Inc—Richard Shanks	7370 Opportunity Rd St, San Diego CA 92111	858-715-0176	R	<1*	<.1
1013	Healthcomm Interactive Inc—Phil Sutton	260 E 11th Ave, Eugene OR 97401	541-342-7227	R	<1*	.1
1014	H and R Enterprises Inc—George Streiter	20150 Sunburst St, Chatsworth CA 91311	818-703-8892	R	<1	<.1
1015	Martele—Marlene Satkiewicz	116 Stonetree Cir, Rochester Hills MI 48309	248-370-0381	R	<1*	<.1
1016	Hosales Inc—Jose Fuerte	2345 E Riviera Dr, Tempe AZ 85282	480-831-2129	R	<1*	<.1
1017	Pico Systems—John Elson	543 Lindeman Rd, Saint Louis MO 63122	314-965-5523	R	<1*	<.1

TOTALS: SIC 5065 Electronic Parts & Equipment Nec
Companies: 1,017   146,065   220.9

5072 Hardware

Rank	Company Name—Executive Officer	Address, City, State, Zip	Phone	Type	Fin	Empls
1	Ace Hardware Corp—Ray A Griffith	2200 Kensington Ct, Oak Brook IL 60523	630-990-6600	R	3,709	4.5
2	True Value Co—Lyle Heidemann	8600 W Bryn Mawr Ave, Chicago IL 60631	773-695-5000	R	1,865	3.0
3	Makita USA Inc—Gary Morikawa	14930 Northam St, La Mirada CA 90638	714-522-8088	R	1,048*	.7
4	Orgill Inc—Ron Beal	3742 Tyndale Dr, Memphis TN 38125	901-754-8850	R	1,040*	1.7
5	Western Supply Corp—Kevin Kiker	PO Box 13430, Salem OR 97309	503-371-1411	R	675*	.2
6	White Cap Industries Inc—Ted Nark	PO Box 1770, Costa Mesa CA 92628	714-850-0900	R	410*	1.4
7	Long Lewis Hardware Co—Michael Brady	430 N 9TH St, Birmingham AL 35202	205-322-2561	R	377*	.2
8	California Hardware Co—Joe Wildman	3601 E Jurupa St, Ontario CA 91761	909-390-6100	R	267*	.2
9	House-Hasson Hardware Inc—Don Hasson	3125 Water Plant Rd, Knoxville TN 37914	865-525-0471	R	200	.2
10	EB Bradley Co—Don Lorey	5080 S Alameda St, Los Angeles CA 90058		R	189*	.2
11	Dolmar Gmbh—Tray Brown	1005 Alderman Dr Ste 1, Alpharetta GA 30005	770-569-4945	R	165*	<.1
12	Howard Berger Company Inc—Howard Berger	324 A Half Acre Rd, Cranbury NJ 08512	609-860-9990	R	163*	.2
13	US Lock Corp	77 Rodeo Dr, Brentwood NY 11717		S	134*	.1
14	Builders Hardware and Supply Company Inc—Greg Lunde	PO Box C-79005, Seattle WA 98119	206-281-3700	R	129*	.1
15	Emery Waterhouse Co—Stephen M Frawley	PO Box 659, Portland ME 04104	207-775-2371	R	126*	.3
16	Five Star Products Inc—David Babcock	750 Commerce Dr, Fairfield CT 06825	203-336-7900	R	117*	.2
17	Wallace Hardware Co—Doyle Wallace	5050 S Davy Crockett P, Morristown TN 37813	423-586-5650	R	111*	.2
18	Shepler's Equipment Company Inc—Murray R McClean	9103 E Almeda Rd, Houston TX 77054	713-799-1150	D	109*	.3
19	White Outdoor Products Co—Andy Outcalt	PO Box 368023, Cleveland OH 44136	330-225-8883	D	94*	.4
20	Blish-Mize Co—Johnathan Mize	PO Box 249, Atchison KS 66002	913-367-1250	R	89*	.3
21	Cascade Wholesale Hardware—Michael Parr	5650 NW Wagon Way, Hillsboro OR 97124	503-614-2600	R	86*	.1
22	Airgas Rutland Tool and Supply Company Inc—Brad Frost	PO Box 997, Whittier CA 90608	562-566-5000	S	84*	.4
23	Hardware Distribution Warehouses Inc—Kenny Beauvais	PO Box 3945, Shreveport LA 71133	318-686-8527	R	84*	.3
24	Colonial Commercial Corp—William Pagano	275 Wagaraw Rd, Hawthorne NJ 07506	973-427-8224	P	80	.2
25	Bostwick-Braun Co—Bill Bollin	7439 Crossleigh Ct, Toledo OH 43617	419-259-3600	R	78*	.3
26	CH Briggs Hardware Co—Julia Klein	PO Box 15188, Reading PA 19612		R	75*	.2
27	Monroe Hardware Co—Carl Belk	101 N Sutherland Ave, Monroe NC 28110	704-291-3121	R	71*	.3
28	Red Streak Corp—Bryan Folk	1627 Main St Ste 901, Kansas City MO 64108	816-471-6979	R	71*	.2
29	Fasteners Inc—Bill Jones	5220 E Broadway Ave, Spokane WA 99212	509-535-9022	R	64*	<.1
30	Holloway-Houston Inc—Charles Chapman	5833 Armour Dr, Houston TX 77020	713-674-5631	R	60*	.2
31	Ace Tool Co—Michael Huling	7337 Bryan Dairy Rd, Largo FL 33777	727-544-6114	S	58*	.2
32	United Hardware Distributing Co—Steve Draeger	5005 Nathan Ln N, Plymouth MN 55442	763-559-1800	R	58*	.1

Rank	Company Name—*Executive Officer*	Address, City, State, Zip	Phone	Type	Fin	Empls
33	Heads and Threads International LLC—*Bill Marthens*	200 Kennedy Dr, Sayreville NJ 08872	732-727-5800	D	54	.2
34	Brighton-Best Socket Screw Manufacturing Inc—*Perry Rosenstein*	1665 Heraeus Blvd, Buford GA 30518	678-288-1000	R	50*	.2
35	Star Stainless Screw Co—*Wayne Golden*	30 W End Rd, Totowa NJ 07512	973-256-2300	R	50*	.2
36	General Tool and Supply Co—*William C Derville*	2705 NW Nicolai St, Portland OR 97210	503-226-3411	S	50*	.1
37	Jensen Distribution Services—*Mike Jensen*	PO Box 3708, Spokane WA 99220		R	48*	.1
38	Kentec Inc—*George W Morgan*	3250 Centerville Hwy S, Snellville GA 30039	770-985-1907	R	48*	.1
39	JZ Allied International Holdings Inc—*John R Lowden*	13207 Bradley Ave, Sylmar CA 91342	818-364-2333	R	43*	.1
40	Thruway Fasteners Inc	4669 Crossroads Dr, Liverpool NY 13088	315-451-7910	R	40*	.1
41	Techni-Tool Inc—*Paul Weiss*	PO Box 1117, Worcester PA 19490	610-941-2400	R	40*	.1
42	Relli Technology Inc—*Reuven Ginton*	1200 S Rogers Cir Ste, Boca Raton FL 33487	561-886-0200	R	39*	.1
43	Amarillo Hardware Co—*Joe Wildman*	PO Box 1891, Amarillo TX 79172	806-376-4722	R	35*	.1
44	Ram Tool and Supply Co—*Mariam Head*	PO Box 320979, Birmingham AL 35232	205-714-3300	R	32*	.1
45	Merit Fasteners Corp—*Don Rogers*	2510 Ronald Reagan Blv, Longwood FL 32750	407-331-4815	R	32*	.1
46	Great Neck Saw Manufacturers Inc—*Sydney Jacoff*	PO Box 3, Mineola NY 11501	516-746-5352	R	30*	.7
47	Quality Bolt and Screw Corp—*James Power*	5290 Gateway Dr, Geismar LA 70734	225-744-1100	R	29*	.1
48	Tulnoy Lumber Inc—*Herbert Tulchin*	1620 Webster Ave, Bronx NY 10457	718-901-1700	R	28*	.1
49	Hahn Systems—*Scott Brown*	5762 W 74th St, Indianapolis IN 46278	317-243-3796	R	27*	.1
50	Charles McMurray Co—*Louis McMurray*	2520 N Argyle Ave, Fresno CA 93727	559-292-5751	R	27*	.1
51	Watters and Martin Inc—*Brooks Gornto*	3800 Village Ave, Norfolk VA 23502	757-857-0851	R	25*	.1
52	Horizon Distribution Inc—*Ken Marble*	PO Box 1021, Yakima WA 98907	509-453-3181	R	24	.1
53	Outwater Plastics Inc—*Peter Kessler*	PO Box 500, Bogota NJ 07603	201-498-8750	R	23*	.2
54	Hardware Specialty Company Inc—*Edward Kaufman*	48-75 36th St, Long Island City NY 11101	718-361-9393	R	22*	.1
55	Leight Sales Company Inc—*Alan Moskowitz*	1051 E Artesia Blvd, Carson CA 90746	310-223-1000	R	22*	.1
56	Sommer and Maca Industries Inc—*Allan Maca*	5501 W Ogden Ave, Cicero IL 60804	773-242-2871	R	22*	.2
57	Central Indiana Hardware Co—*Norm Bristley*	PO Box 501850, Indianapolis IN 46250	317-558-5700	R	21*	.1
58	Bommer Industries Inc—*Charles Martin*	PO Box 187, Landrum SC 29356	864-457-3301	R	21*	.2
59	Chown Inc—*David Chown*	PO Box 2888, Portland OR 97208	503-243-6500	R	21*	.1
60	Earnest Machine Products Co—*John Zehnder*	12502 Plaza Dr, Cleveland OH 44130	216-362-1100	R	20*	.1
61	Fasteners Inc—*John Szlenkier*	PO Box 8397, Grand Rapids MI 49518	616-241-3448	R	20*	.1
62	Mullins Buildings Products Inc—*Charles Mullins*	5631 Clifford Cir, Birmingham AL 35210	205-836-0011	R	20*	<.1
63	American Fasteners Inc—*James Delp*	9129 E Us Hwy 36, Avon IN 46123	317-271-6100	R	19*	.1
64	Darling Bolt Co—*Tim Heacock*	PO Box 2035, Warren MI 48090	586-757-4100	R	18*	.1
65	Beacon Metals Inc—*Kenneth Riches*	PO Box 65462, Salt Lake City UT 84165	801-486-4884	R	17*	.1
66	Wilco Supply	PO Box 3047, Oakland CA 94609		R	17*	<.1
67	Midwest Tool Distributors—*Chris Anthony*	8811 S 77th Ave, Bridgeview IL 60455	708-293-8888	R	17*	.1
68	Arena Distributors Inc—*James Arena*	PO Box 1410, Buffalo NY 14240	716-825-7377	R	16*	.1
69	L A Benson Company Inc—*Lee Benson*	PO Box 2137, Baltimore MD 21203	410-342-9225	R	16*	<.1
70	Weinstein and Holtzman Inc—*Ira Hymowitz*	29 Park Row Frnt 1, New York NY 10038	212-233-4651	R	16*	.1
71	ACF Components and Fasteners Inc—*Gary P Rees*	31012 Huntwood Ave, Hayward CA 94544	510-487-2100	R	15*	.1
72	Interstate Distributors Of Dunn Inc—*William Lasater*	PO Box 1145, Dunn NC 28335	910-892-4143	R	15*	<.1
73	Freud America Inc—*Sebastian Ruggiero*	PO Box 7187, High Point NC 27264	336-434-3171	R	15*	.1
74	Drivekore Inc—*Dan Emanuel*	PO Box 2004, Mechanicsburg PA 17055	717-766-7636	R	15*	.1
75	La Force Inc—*Kenneth Metzler*	PO Box 10068, Green Bay WI 54307	920-497-7100	R	14*	.4
76	Anderson Lock Company Ltd—*Eugene Anderson*	PO Box 2294, Des Plaines IL 60017	847-296-1157	R	14*	.1
77	Bamal Corp—*Chris Brown*	2580 Ross St, Sidney OH 45365	937-492-9484	R	14*	.1
78	Mcgard LLC—*David Roy*	3875 California Rd, Orchard Park NY 14127	716-662-0900	R	14*	.4
79	Christian Wholesale Distributors Inc—*James Christian*	11048 Grissom Ln, Dallas TX 75229	972-241-0633	R	13*	.1
80	Norwood Hardware and Supply Company Inc—*Gloria Chabot*	2906 Glendale Milford, Cincinnati OH 45241	513-733-1175	R	13*	.1
81	Custom-Bilt Cabinet And Supply Inc—*William Lea*	PO Box 8969, Shreveport LA 71148	318-865-1412	R	13*	.1
82	Budd Charles Corp—*Richard Steier*	PO Box 280127, East Hartford CT 06128	860-289-6861	R	13*	<.1
83	Circle Bolt and Nut Company Inc—*Joseph Milazzo*	158 Pringle St, Kingston PA 18704	570-718-6001	R	13*	.1
84	Fabory USA Ltd—*Jerry Krick*	8715 Byron Cmn Ste A, Byron Center MI 49315	616-583-1456	R	12*	.1
85	WBH Industries—*Richard Page*	PO Box 98, Arlington TX 76004	817-701-3418	R	12*	<.1
86	Arrow Tools Fasteners and Saw Inc—*Jeffrey Silverman*	7635 Burnet Ave, Van Nuys CA 91405	818-780-1464	R	11*	.1
87	US Industrial Products Corp—*Peter Kubicek*	9612 43rd Ave, Corona NY 11368	718-335-3300	R	11*	.1
88	Mid-State Bolt and Nut Company Inc—*Dave Broehm*	1575 Alum Creek Dr, Columbus OH 43209	614-253-8631	R	11*	.1
89	Becknell Wholesale Co—*Eugene Becknell*	PO Box 2008, Lubbock TX 79408	806-747-3201	R	11*	.1
90	Southern Hardware Company Inc—*Thomas G Miller Jr*	PO Box 2508, West Helena AR 72390	870-572-6761	R	11*	<.1
91	JLM Wholesale Inc—*Raymond Baldwin*	3095 Mullins Ct, Oxford MI 48371	248-628-6440	R	11*	<.1
92	JBL Hawaii Ltd—*Mark Ballantyne*	905 Kokea St, Honolulu HI 96817	808-847-4021	R	11*	.1
93	Neu's Building Center Inc—*Harvey Neu*	PO Box 665, Menomonee Falls WI 53052	262-251-6550	R	10*	.1
94	S W Anderson Co—*Richard Worcester*	PO Box 460, Downers Grove IL 60515	630-964-2600	R	10*	.1
95	Caprice Electronics Inc—*Regina Laufer*	63 Flushing Ave Unit 1, Brooklyn NY 11205	718-222-0436	R	10*	<.1
96	Fabtex Inc—*Robert Snyder*	111 Woodbine Ln, Danville PA 17821	570-275-7500	R	10*	.3
97	Dave Grattan and Sons Inc—*Jack Grattan*	PO Box 2264, Irwindale CA 91706	626-969-1703	R	10*	<.1
98	Kendell Doors and Hardware Inc—*Jack Cornwell*	222 E 2nd St, Winona MN 55987	507-454-1723	R	9*	.1
99	Leonard's Hardware Inc—*Shirley Leonard*	PO Box 637, Russellville AR 72811	479-968-2142	R	9*	.1
100	American Bolt Corp—*Kevin Gogin*	PO Box 510440, New Berlin WI 53151	262-786-6530	R	9*	.1
101	Cordova Bolt Inc—*Moses Cordova*	5601 Dolly Ave, Buena Park CA 90621	714-739-7500	R	9*	<.1
102	Okura Hardware and Lumber Inc—*Luis Martinez*	2245 Nw 72nd Ave, Miami FL 33122	305-593-9228	R	9*	.1
103	Motor City Fastener Inc—*Robert Puskas*	PO Box 219, Hazel Park MI 48030	248-399-2830	R	9*	<.1
104	Daytona Bolt And Nut Co—*Norman James*	PO Box 1391, Daytona Beach FL 32115	386-255-0248	R	9*	<.1
105	J G Edelen Company Inc—*John Healy*	8901 Kelso Dr, Baltimore MD 21221	410-918-1200	R	9*	<.1
106	Metabo Corp—*Martin Cross*	PO Box 2287, West Chester PA 19380	610-436-5900	R	9*	.1
107	Great Lakes Custom Tool Manufacturing Inc—*Russell Martin*	PO Box 152, Peshtigo WI 54157	715-582-3884	R	8*	.1
108	Pacfas—*Howard Beaman*	PO Box 897, South Houston TX 77587	713-946-4962	R	8*	.1
109	Interstate Screw Corp—*Ronald Seiden*	475 W 18th St, Hialeah FL 33010	305-888-8700	R	8*	<.1
110	Bluegrass Tool Warehouse Inc—*Kevin Moss*	PO Box 55378, Lexington KY 40555	859-281-6146	R	8*	<.1
111	Milspec Industries Inc—*Galen Ho'o*	5825 Greenwood Ave, Commerce CA 90040	213-680-9690	S	8*	.1
112	Ameriwest Industries Inc—*Qian Zhang*	1455 E Francis St, Ontario CA 91761	909-930-1898	R	8*	.1
113	National Tool Supply Inc—*Lawrence Weiner*	5725 W Hllandale Beach, West Park FL 33023	954-963-7222	R	8*	<.1
114	Duo-Fast Northeast—*Richard Steier*	22 Tolland St, East Hartford CT 06108	860-289-6861	D	8*	<.1
115	Strauss Acquisition Corp—*Dan Swift*	PO Box 42367, Des Moines IA 50323	515-276-7030	R	8*	<.1
116	Brown-Rogers-Dixson Co—*Ronny Dixson*	111 Cloverleaf Dr Ste, Winston Salem NC 27103	336-722-1112	R	8*	<.1
117	Access Hardware Supply Inc—*Steven Harris*	14359 Catalina St, San Leandro CA 94577	510-483-5000	R	8*	<.1
118	Woodbury Cement Products Company Inc—*Ray Tresch*	630 S Evergreen Ave, Woodbury NJ 08097	856-845-2652	R	8*	<.1
119	Ott Inc—*Jeffrey Ott*	PO Box 23138, Columbus OH 43223	614-875-8613	R	8*	<.1
120	Clyde Hardware Company Inc—*Margaret Walden*	4808 N 15th St, Phoenix AZ 85014	602-264-2106	R	8*	<.1
121	Illinois Industrial Tool Inc—*Lance Ericson*	8811 S 77th Ave, Bridgeview IL 60455	708-597-6000	R	8*	<.1

Note: An asterisk (*) indicates an estimated financial figure. The company type code used is as follows: R = Private, P = Public, S = Private Subsidiary, B = Public Subsidiary, D = Division, J = Joint Venture, I = Investment Fund.

COMPANY RANKINGS BY SALES WITHIN 4-DIGIT SIC

Rank	Company Name—Executive Officer	Address, City, State, Zip	Phone	Type	Fin	Empls
122	Camstar International Inc—Bingqing LI	1525 W 13th St Ste A, Upland CA 91786	909-931-2540	R	8*	.1
123	Omaha Wholesale Hardware Co—Bill Stock	PO Box 3628, Omaha NE 68103	402-444-1673	R	7*	.1
124	Barker-Jennings Corp—Don Smith	PO Box 11289, Lynchburg VA 24506	434-846-8471	R	7*	<.1
125	Harris Hardware Sales Corp—Kirk Henin	4 Harbor Park Dr, Port Washington NY 11050	516-484-4440	R	7*	<.1
126	Amash Imports Inc—Attallah Amash	3707 R B Chaffee Mmrl, Grand Rapids MI 49548	616-243-2443	R	7*	<.1
127	Swanson Hardware Supply Inc—Wayne Swanson	533 N E Ave, Vineland NJ 08360	856-691-7900	R	7*	<.1
128	Roseburrough Tool Inc—Jack Roseburrough	PO Box 1307, Orange CA 92856	714-538-6015	R	7*	<.1
129	Brabner And Hollon Inc—James Hollon	PO Box 7551, Mobile AL 36670	251-479-5408	R	7*	.1
130	Sy's Supplies Inc—Daniel Applebaum	235 N Jog Rd, West Palm Beach FL 33413	561-689-7711	R	7*	<.1
131	Mercer Tool Corp—Michael Wallick	300 Suburban Ave, Deer Park NY 11729	631-243-3900	R	7*	<.1
132	Berg Wholesale Inc—Arthur Berg	PO Box 3050, Tualatin OR 97062	503-454-5454	R	7*	<.1
133	Cal-Royal Products Inc—Sina Yashar	6605 Flotilla St, Commerce CA 90040	323-888-6601	R	7*	<.1
134	Beacon Fasteners And Components Inc—Robert Wegner	198 Carpenter Ave, Wheeling IL 60090	847-541-0404	R	6*	<.1
135	National Builders Hardware Co—Myla Fiesterman	PO Box 14609, Portland OR 97293	503-233-5381	R	6*	<.1
136	Boston Lumber and Builders Corp—Raleigh Felton	PO Box 1338, South Boston VA 24592	434-572-6991	R	6*	<.1
137	Roberts Tool and Supply Company Inc—Robert Sherman	16 Midland Ave, Elmwood Park NJ 07407	201-791-8787	R	6*	<.1
138	J and L Fasteners And General Maintenance Supplies Inc—James Belford	6944 Parrish Ave, Hammond IN 46323	219-845-8500	R	6*	<.1
139	Washington Chain and Supply Inc—Gabriel Benavidez	PO Box 3645, Seattle WA 98124	206-623-8500	R	6*	<.1
140	Morrison's Home Center Inc—K Morrison	PO Box 845, Nashville GA 31639	229-686-2014	R	6*	<.1
141	Locks Co—Milton Dorn	1175 Nw 159th Dr, Miami Gardens FL 33169	305-949-0700	R	6*	<.1
142	Industrial Rivet and Fastener Co—William Goodman	200 Paris Ave, Northvale NJ 07647	201-750-1040	R	6*	<.1
143	Slh Manufacturing Inc—Granville Smith	15403 Andrews Rd, Kansas City MO 64147	816-331-4131	R	6*	<.1
144	Bell's Hardware Of Klamath Falls Inc—John Bell	528 Main St, Klamath Falls OR 97601	541-882-7246	R	6*	<.1
145	SH Trading Inc—Hyuk Sul	1025 N Armando St, Anaheim CA 92806	714-575-0010	R	5*	<.1
146	Builders Supply Inc—William Cochran	3271 Us Hwy 84, Blackshear GA 31516	912-449-4726	R	5*	<.1
147	Hollywood Builders Hardware Inc—Kenneth Yowell	PO Box 7949, Houston TX 77270	713-644-8301	R	5*	<.1
148	R-B Industries Inc—Ronald Baade	6366 W Gross Point Rd, Niles IL 60714	847-647-5900	R	5*	<.1
149	Contractors Supply Company Inc—John Hessel	PO Box 1376, Oklahoma City OK 73101	405-525-7431	R	5*	<.1
150	Allerdice Building Supply Inc—Wallace Allerdice	41 Walworth St, Saratoga Springs NY 12866	518-587-6633	R	5*	.1
151	Raywen Enterprises Inc—Greagory Locke	351 Ratcliff St, Shreveport LA 71104	318-208-1132	R	5*	.1
152	SCI Corp—Patrick Gibbons	PO Box 490, Streator IL 61364	815-672-2957	R	5*	<.1
153	Kaylim Supplies Inc—Len Gamss	630 E 133rd St, Bronx NY 10454	718-585-2882	R	5*	<.1
154	US Futaba Inc—Karl Fournell	PO Box 26829, Santa Ana CA 92799	714-751-1593	R	5*	<.1
155	Alabama Bolt and Supply Inc—Charles Ferguson	PO Box 9429, Montgomery AL 36108	334-269-9560	R	5*	<.1
156	Allen Industrial Supply LP—John Sariaf	1309 Businetx Pk Dr St, Mission TX 78572	956-584-2000	R	5*	<.1
157	KR Tools Inc—Randy Nulman	PO Box 9185, Oxnard CA 93031	805-988-0513	R	5*	<.1
158	Riggsbee Hardware Company Inc—Edith O'brien	PO Box 230398, Houston TX 77223	713-224-6734	R	5*	<.1
159	Burgess Sales and Supply Inc—Frank Burgess	2121 W Morehead St, Charlotte NC 28208	704-333-8933	R	4*	<.1
160	J Milano Company Inc—Gary Milano	PO Box 688, Stockton CA 95201	209-944-0902	R	4*	<.1
161	Long Cabinet Co—Leon Jackson	139 Roosevelt Ave, National City CA 91950	619-477-2776	R	4*	<.1
162	MS Berkoff Company Inc—Arnold Fischman	2114 Coyle St, Brooklyn NY 11229	718-891-9000	R	4*	<.1
163	Summit Northstar Inc—Betsy Sather	PO Box 1888, Silverthorne CO 80498	970-513-1575	R	4*	<.1
164	Contract Builders Hardware Inc—Ben Yellin	1203 S NW Hwy, Barrington IL 60010	847-381-7060	R	4*	<.1
165	Del Pro Corp—Richard Stefani	343 Somerset St, Stirling NJ 07980	908-047-0500	R	4*	<.1
166	Central Lock and Hardware Supply Company Inc—David Glixman	PO Box 640938, Miami FL 33164	305-947-4853	R	4*	<.1
167	Bredemus Hardware Company Inc—E Bredemus	1285 Sylvan St, Saint Paul MN 55117	651-489-6250	R	4*	<.1
168	Wallace Supply Company Inc—Patricia Moffit	1434 Rte 9, Fort Edward NY 12828	518-793-5131	R	4*	<.1
169	Schuppann Corp—James Lind	230 E Ridgeway Ave, Waterloo IA 50702	319-235-0457	R	4*	<.1
170	Bridgecraft USA Inc—Yosuf Abedi	14680 Alondra Blvd, La Mirada CA 90638	714-523-2222	R	4*	<.1
171	John F Mahaney Co—Stephen Mahaney	PO Box 15745, Sacramento CA 95852	916-922-8306	R	4*	<.1
172	D and E Builders Supply Inc—Leonard Elliott	PO Box 7731, Waco TX 76714	254-772-5655	R	4*	<.1
173	Screw Products Inc—William Marthens	1212 Dolton Dr Ste 302, Dallas TX 75207	214-630-9393	R	4*	<.1
174	Friedlander M and R Supply Company Inc—Alfred Friedlander	PO Box 928, Bronx NY 10455	718-665-3300	R	4*	<.1
175	Link and Associates Inc—Theodore Link	PO Box 4705, Mcallen TX 78502	956-631-5465	R	4*	<.1
176	Siya Inc—Sudhir Mundhra	10233 Palm Dr, Santa Fe Springs CA 90670	562-633-3002	R	4*	<.1
177	Hank Thorn Co—Mayford Thorn	29164 Wall St, Wixom MI 48393	248-348-7800	R	4*	<.1
178	Marshall's Industrial Hardware Inc—John Marshall	8423 Production Ave, San Diego CA 92121	858-271-5555	R	4*	<.1
179	Concept Electronics Inc—Glenn Mccullough	6243 Renoir Ave, Baton Rouge LA 70806	225-927-8614	R	3*	<.1
180	Fastening Systems International Inc—Roger Nikkel	PO Box 1372, Sonoma CA 95476	707-935-1170	R	3*	<.1
181	Sparcon Import Corp—George Liebner	PO Box 9882, Englewood NJ 07631	201-569-1600	R	3*	<.1
182	Alliance Hardware and Supply—Dan Anderson	PO Box 1555, Sunset Beach CA 90742	562-236-1900	R	3*	<.1
183	Servtronics Inc—Dale Spears	7200 Sandscove Ct, Winter Park FL 32792	407-677-8191	R	3*	<.1
184	Gamalski Building Specialties Inc—John Gamalski	3851 Auburn Rd, Auburn Hills MI 48326	248-852-7050	R	3*	<.1
185	G-U Hardware Inc—Julius Resch	PO Box 14250, Newport News VA 23608	757-877-9020	R	3*	<.1
186	Robert Skeels and Co—Ken Jordan	PO Box 512183, Los Angeles CA 90051	310-639-7240	R	3*	<.1
187	Saffron Supply Co—Morris H Saffron	325 Commercial St NE, Salem OR 97301	503-581-7501	R	3*	<.1
188	Finishing Technologies Inc—Todd Elmer	PO Box 5128, Portland OR 97208	503-222-9741	R	3*	<.1
189	Home Hardware—Charles Wollmershauser	10545 S Memorial Dr, Tulsa OK 74133	918-369-7800	R	3*	<.1
190	Knoxville Bolt and Screw Inc—W Clark	PO Box 9149, Knoxville TN 37940	865-573-1991	R	3*	<.1
191	Top Notch Distributors Of Missouri Inc—Charles Jurgensen	3906 Ventures Way, Earth City MO 63045	314-291-4499	R	3*	<.1
192	May Star Corp—William Ouyang	238 Longley Way, Arcadia CA 91007	626-445-0784	R	2*	<.1
193	Handyman's Inc—Douglas Severson	604 E Saint Germain St, Saint Cloud MN 56304	320-251-3292	R	2*	<.1
194	Fasteners and Fire Equipment Inc—Michael Bateman	123 E International Ai, Anchorage AK 99518	907-562-2777	R	2*	<.1
195	Morrison Supply Company Inc—Thomas Morrison	PO Box 81103, Atlanta GA 30366	770-455-8244	R	2*	<.1
196	Ace Bolt and Screw Company Of San Antonio Inc—Eric Heydenreich	200 Brooklyn Ave, San Antonio TX 78215	210-226-0244	R	2*	<.1
197	Avanti Engineering Inc—Rocco Bratta	200 W Lake Dr, Glendale Heights IL 60139	630-260-1333	R	2*	<.1
198	Do It Best 3761—Bruce Ellis	200 S Main St, Roswell NM 88203	575-622-7841	R	2*	<.1
199	Pier 19 Inc—Rodney Williams	506 E Happy Valley St, Cave City KY 42127	270-773-2025	R	2*	<.1
200	Markwell Manufacturing Company Inc—Samuel Opland	692 Pleasant St, Norwood MA 02062	781-769-6610	R	2*	<.1
201	Greg Foemmel Inc—Greg Foemmel	1802 Sublette Rd, Sublette IL 61367	815-849-5107	R	1*	<.1
202	Corrections Products Company Ltd—Christian Hunter	5802 Rocky Pt, San Antonio TX 78249	210-829-7951	R	1*	<.1
203	John A Eberly Inc—John Lee	PO Box 8047, Syracuse NY 13217	315-449-3034	R	1*	<.1
204	Eagle Vision International—John Diblasi	2145 Grassy Basin Ct S, Jacksonville FL 32224	904-866-4562	R	1*	<.1
205	Jackson's Hardware Inc—Matthew Olson	PO Box 10247, San Rafael CA 94912	415-454-3740	R	1*	.1
206	Tamco Manufacturing Co—Tony Asoera	PO Box 1794, Elkhart IN 46515	574-294-1909	R	<1*	<.1
207	Save The World Air Inc—Cecil Bond Kyte	735 State St Ste 500, Santa Barbara CA 93101	805-845-3581	P	<1	<.1

Rank	Company Name—*Executive Officer*	Address, City, State, Zip	Phone	Type	Fin	Empls
208	Atlas Copco Tools and Assembly Systems LLC—*Anders Hoberg*	2998 Dutton Rd, Auburn Hills MI 48326	248-373-3000	S	N/A	.1

TOTALS: SIC 5072 Hardware

	Companies: 208				13,871	27.1

5074 Plumbing & Hydronic Heating Supplies

Rank	Company Name—*Executive Officer*	Address, City, State, Zip	Phone	Type	Fin	Empls
1	Ferguson Enterprises Inc—*John Stegeman*	PO Box 2778, Newport News VA 23609	757-874-7795	S	9,650*	22.0
2	Ferguson Enterprises Inc (Newport News Virginia)—*John Stegeman*	655 Ethicon Cir, Cornelia GA 30531	706-776-5675	S	2,667*	8.0
3	HD Supply Inc—*Joe DeAngelo*	3100 Cumberland Blvd S, Atlanta GA 30339		R	1,933*	14.5
4	Noland Co—*Lloyd U Noland III*	3110 Kettering Blvd, Dayton OH 45439	937-294-5331	S	516*	1.3
5	FW Webb Co—*Don Rondeau*	160 Middlesex Tpke, Bedford MA 01730	781-273-9322	R	511*	1.1
6	Hajoca Corp—*Rick Klau*	127 Coulter Ave, Ardmore PA 19003	610-649-1430	R	459*	1.3
7	Consolidated Pipe and Supply Company Inc—*Howard Kerr*	PO Box 2472, Birmingham AL 35201	205-323-7261	R	419*	.5
8	Slakey Brothers Inc—*Frank Nisonger*	2215 Kausen Dr Ste 1, Elk Grove CA 95758	916-478-2000	R	334*	.5
9	Western Nevada Supply Co—*Jack T Reviglio*	950 S Rock Blvd, Sparks NV 89431	775-359-5800	R	304*	.4
10	Thos Somerville Co—*Patrick J Mcgowan*	16155 Trade Zone Ave, Upper Marlboro MD 20774	301-390-9575	R	299*	.4
11	Barnett Inc—*Jeff Bartruff*	3333 Lenox Ave, Jacksonville FL 32254	904-384-6530	D	278*	.9
12	United Pipe and Supply Company Inc—*Wayne Miller*	7600 SE Johnson Creek, Portland OR 97206	503-788-8813	R	261*	.4
13	Granite Group Wholesalers LLC—*William Hilfinger*	6 Storss St, Concord NH 03301	603-224-1901	R	259*	.4
14	LCR-M Corp—*Karl Triche*	PO Box 951, Baton Rouge LA 70821	225-292-9915	R	207*	.6
15	RE Michel Company Inc—*JWH Michel*	1 RE Michel Dr, Glen Burnie MD 21060	410-760-4000	R	186*	1.0
16	Pittsburgh Plumbing and Heating Supply Corp—*Jay Blaushild*	434 Melwood Ave, Pittsburgh PA 15213	412-622-8100	R	165*	.3
17	Keller Supply Co—*Nick Keller*	PO Box 79014, Seattle WA 98119	206-285-3300	R	142*	.6
18	Wolverine Brass Inc—*Lloyd Coppedge*	2951 E Hwy 501, Conway SC 29526	843-347-3121	R	111*	.2
19	Security Supply Corp—*Keith W Bennett*	196 Maple Ave, Selkirk NY 12158	518-767-2226	R	106*	.1
20	Redlon and Johnson Inc—*Tom Mullen*	172-174 St John St, Portland ME 04102	207-773-4755	R	104	.3
21	Waxman Industries Inc—*Melvin Waxman*	24460 Aurora Rd, Bedford Heights OH 44146	440-439-1830	R	92*	.6
22	Suburban Plumbing Supply Co—*William Weber*	6363 Hwy 7, Saint Louis Park MN 55416	952-929-1377	R	87*	.3
23	Premier Power Renewable Energy Inc—*Miguel Anquin*	4961 Windplay Dr Ste 1, El Dorado Hills CA 95762	916-939-0400	R	87*	.1
24	Gateway Supply Company Inc—*SP Williams Jr*	PO Box 56, Columbia SC 29202	803-771-7160	R	86*	.1
25	Engineering and Equipment Co—*Collins Knight III*	PO Box 588, Albany GA 31702	229-435-5601	R	85*	.1
26	Plumb Supply Co Templeton Coal Company Inc	1622 NE 51st Ave, Des Moines IA 50313	515-262-9511	S	79*	.3
27	Plumber's Supply Co—*Bruce Madison*	1000 E Main St, Louisville KY 40206	502-582-2261	R	78*	.3
28	Nu-Way Supply Company Inc—*Larry Merritt*	5227 Auburn Rd, Utica MI 48317	586-731-4000	R	76*	.1
29	SG Supply Co—*Norman E Weiss*	12900 S Throop St, Calumet Park IL 60827	708-371-8800	R	74*	.1
30	Visionary Baths and More	908 Niagara Falls Blvd, N Tonawanda NY 14120	716-692-3200	R	73*	.3
31	Wolff Brothers Supply Inc—*Howard Wolff*	6078 Wolff Rd, Medina OH 44256	330-725-3451	R	65*	.3
32	Fresno Distributing Co—*Ryan Cloud*	PO Box 6078, Fresno CA 93703	559-442-8800	R	63*	.1
33	Briggs Incorporated of Omaha	14549 Grover St, Omaha NE 68144	402-330-3400	R	63*	.1
34	Robertson Heating Supply Co—*Scott Robertson*	PO Box 2448, Alliance OH 44601	330-821-9180	R	62*	.2
35	Herman Goldner Company Inc—*Herman Goldner*	7777 Brewster Ave, Philadelphia PA 19153	215-365-5400	R	62*	.2
36	Trumbull Industries Inc—*Murray Miller*	PO Box 30, Warren OH 44482	330-393-6624	R	61*	.2
37	Lee Supply Corp	PO Box 681430, Indianapolis IN 46268	317-290-2500	R	61*	.2
38	Teeco Products Inc—*D Goodwin*	16881 Armstrong Ave, Irvine CA 92606	949-261-6295	R	60*	.1
39	Cast Products Corp—*Tom Nagy*	PO Box 1368, Elkhart IN 46515	574-294-2684	R	56*	.1
40	Crescent Supply Of Penna Inc—*Stephen Baker*	PO Box 40110, Pittsburgh PA 15201	412-782-3300	R	56*	<.1
41	Aaron And Company Inc—*Barry Portnoy*	PO Box 8310, Piscataway NJ 08855	732-752-8200	R	55*	N/A
42	JGB Enterprises Inc (Liverpool New York)—*Jay G Bernhardt*	115 Metropolitan Dr, Liverpool NY 13088	315-451-2770	R	54*	.2
43	Minnesota Air Inc—*Mike Metzger*	6901 W Old Shakopee Rd, Minneapolis MN 55438	952-918-8000	R	51*	.1
44	AY McDonald Supply Company Inc—*Michael B McDonald*	PO Box 508, Dubuque IA 52004	563-583-7311	S	51*	.3
45	Wholesale Supply Group Inc—*Lloyd D Rogers*	885 Keith St NW, Cleveland TN 37311	423-478-1191	R	50*	.3
46	Tba LLC—*Thomas Brooks*	6700 Enterprise Dr, Louisville KY 40214	502-367-0222	R	48*	.1
47	Parnell-Martin Co—*Craig McGomery*	PO Box 30067, Charlotte NC 28230	704-375-8651	R	48*	.2
48	Nutley Heating and Cooling Supply Company Inc—*Richard Cancelosi*	50 Page Rd, Clifton NJ 07012	973-470-8844	R	45*	<.1
49	Watts Radiant Inc—*Mike Chiles*	4500 E Progress Pl, Springfield MO 65803	417-864-6108	S	43*	.1
50	Goodin Co—*Greg Skagerberg*	2700 N 2nd St, Minneapolis MN 55411	612-588-7811	R	42*	.2
51	Mountainland Supply Co—*Robert Rasmussen*	1505 W 130 S, Orem UT 84058	801-224-6050	R	40*	.1
52	Kelly's Pipe and Supply Co—*Bradley Shoen*	PO Box 14750, Las Vegas NV 89114	702-382-4957	R	40*	.1
53	American Copper and Brass Inc—*William Smith*	PO Box 652, Hillsdale MI 49242	517-439-9368	R	40*	.1
54	Perry Supply Company Inc—*David Perry*	PO Box 6486, Albuquerque NM 87197	505-884-6972	R	40*	.1
55	John M Hartel and Company Inc—*Frederick Hartel*	PO Box 280, Montvale NJ 07645	201-391-5000	R	36*	<.1
56	Wisconsin Supply Corp—*Joe Poehling*	PO Box 8124, Madison WI 53708	608-222-7799	R	32*	.1
57	Mountain States Pipe and Supply Co—*Paul Carroll*	PO Box 698, Colorado Springs CO 80903	719-634-5555	R	31*	.1
58	APR Supply Co—*Scott Weaver*	749 Guilford St, Lebanon PA 17046	717-274-5999	R	30*	.1
59	Davidson Pipe Supply Company Inc—*Peter Davidson* Ferguson Enterprises Inc	5002 2nd Ave, Brooklyn NY 11232	718-439-6300	D	30*	.1
60	World Marketing Of America Incorporated A Close Corp—*Delmont Sunderland*	PO Box 192, Mill Creek PA 17060	814-643-6500	R	30*	<.1
61	Templeton Coal Company Inc—*Thomas Templeton*	701 Wabash Ave Ste 501, Terre Haute IN 47807	812-232-7037	R	29*	.8
62	Torrington Supply Company Inc—*Joel S Becker*	PO Box 2838, Waterbury CT 06723	203-756-3641	R	28*	.1
63	N Merfish Plumbing Supply Co—*Robert Setzekorn*	PO Box 15870, Houston TX 77220	713-869-5731	R	27*	.1
64	United Plumbing and Heating Supply Co—*Chip Roska*	PO Box 250850, Milwaukee WI 53225	414-464-5100	R	27*	<.1
65	Vamac Inc—*Christopher Perry*	4201 Jacque St, Richmond VA 23230	804-353-7996	R	26*	.1
66	Watts Spacemaker Inc—*Patrick S O'Keefe*	1918 W Chestnut St, Santa Ana CA 92703	714-542-4649	S	26*	.1
67	Action Plumbing Supply Co—*Stuart Berke*	5411 Nw 15th St, Margate FL 33063	954-971-7782	R	26*	<.1
68	V and W Supply Company Inc—*James Herritt*	PO Box 1628, Birmingham AL 35201	205-324-9521	R	25*	.1
69	Dana Kepner Co—*Wayne E Johnson*	700 Alcott St, Denver CO 80204	303-623-6161	R	25*	.1
70	Deacon Industrial Supply Company Inc—*William S Vail*	PO Box 62485, King of Prussia PA 19406	610-265-5322	R	24*	.1
71	G and C Supply Company Inc—*James Halford*	PO Box 459, Atwood TN 38220	731-662-7193	R	24*	.1
72	Utility Pipe Sales Company Inc—*Edward Zausch*	11802 N Green River Rd, Evansville IN 47725	812-867-7471	R	24*	<.1
73	Baxter-Rutherford Inc—*Robert Norwood*	PO Box 24324, Seattle WA 98124	206-762-4888	R	24*	<.1
74	Puget Sound Pipe And Supply Co—*Gary Stratiner*	7816 S 202nd St, Kent WA 98032	253-796-9350	R	24*	.1
75	Gensco Inc—*Charles Walters*	4402 20th St E, Fife WA 98424	253-922-3003	R	23*	.5
76	Rundle-Spence Manufacturing Co—*David Spence*	2075 S Moorland Rd, New Berlin WI 53151	262-782-3000	R	23*	.1
77	Keidel Supply Co—*Barry Keidel*	2026 Delaware Ave, Norwood OH 45212	513-351-1600	R	21*	.1
78	Porter Pipe and Supply Co—*James Porter*	303 S Rohlwing Rd, Addison IL 60101	630-543-8145	R	21*	.1

Note: An asterisk (*) indicates an estimated financial figure. The company type code used is as follows: R = Private, P = Public, S = Private Subsidiary, B = Public Subsidiary, D = Division, J = Joint Venture, I = Investment Fund.

COMPANY RANKINGS BY SALES WITHIN 4-DIGIT SIC

Rank	Company Name—Executive Officer	Address, City, State, Zip	Phone	Type	Fin	Empls
79	CB and K Supply Inc—Rodney Katz	PO Box 1037, Janesville WI 53547	608-755-5100	R	21*	<.1
80	General Plumbing Supply CoInc—Richard Amaro	PO Box 4666, Walnut Creek CA 94596	925-939-4622	R	20*	.1
81	ID Booth Inc—John S Booth Jr	PO Box 579, Elmira NY 14902	607-733-9121	R	20*	.1
82	Hydronic and Steam Equipment Company Inc—Dennis Kring	PO Box 50430, Indianapolis IN 46250	317-577-8326	R	19*	<.1
83	Pinewood Plumbing Supply Inc—Barry Menscher	9590 Nw 7th Ave, Miami FL 33150	305-693-1931	R	19*	<.1
84	Creative Bath Products Inc—Mathias Meinzinger	250 Creative Dr, Central Islip NY 11722	631-582-8000	R	19*	.5
85	Wayne Pipe and Supply Inc—James Wilson	6040 Innovation Blvd, Fort Wayne IN 46818	260-423-9577	R	19*	.1
86	Ral Supply Group Inc—Charlie Milich	PO Box 429, Middletown NY 10940	845-343-1456	S	19*	<.1
87	Carbon Block Technology Inc—H Rice	7251 Cathedral Rock Dr, Las Vegas NV 89128	702-304-7960	R	19*	.2
88	Ez-Flo International Inc—Saleem Lahlouh	2750 E Mission Blvd, Ontario CA 91761	909-947-5256	R	18*	.1
89	York Corrugating Co—Kim Raub	PO Box 1192, York PA 17405	717-845-3511	R	18*	.1
90	A and A Mechanical Inc—William T Allen	1111 Ulrich Ave, Louisville KY 40219	502-968-0164	R	18*	.1
91	Milwaukee Stove and Furnace Supply Company Inc—Tom Engler	5070 W State St, Milwaukee WI 53208	414-258-0300	R	18*	.1
92	DC Sales Company Inc—John Dovolis	2700 Minnehaha Ave, Minneapolis MN 55406	612-728-8700	R	18*	<.1
93	Riback Supply Company Inc—Marty Riback	2412 Business Loop 70, Columbia MO 65201	573-875-3131	R	17*	.1
94	Greensboro Plumbing Supply Co—Robert Skirboll	501 E Washington St, Greensboro NC 27401	336-274-7615	R	17*	<.1
95	United Pipe And Steel Corp—David Cohen	83 Tpke Rd, Ipswich MA 01938	978-356-9300	R	17*	.1
96	Westar Contract Kitchen and Bath Corp—Elyse Sioles	9025 S Kyrene Rd Ste 1, Tempe AZ 85284	602-271-0100	R	16*	.1
97	Viega LLC—Alberto Fonseca	301 N Main St Ste 900, Wichita KS 67202	316-425-7400	R	16*	.5
98	Smith Plumbing Company Inc—Donald Smith	208 S Country Club Dr, Mesa AZ 85210	480-834-5817	R	16*	.1
99	ATR Supply Co—Scott Weaver	749 Guilford St, Lebanon PA 17046	717-274-5999	R	15*	.2
100	Banner Plumbing Supply Company Inc—Lee Greenspon	7255 S Cottage Grove A, Chicago IL 60619	773-483-4900	R	14*	.1
101	Purcell-Murray Company Inc—Timothy Murray	185 Park Ln, Brisbane CA 94005	415-468-6620	R	14*	.1
102	Robertson Supply Inc—Thomas W Malson Sr	PO Box 1366, Nampa ID 83653	208-466-8907	R	14*	.1
103	Illco Inc—John Glass	PO Box 1330, Aurora IL 60507	630-892-7904	R	14*	.1
104	Bruce Supply Corp—Bruce Wecksler	8805 18th Ave, Brooklyn NY 11214	718-259-4900	R	14*	.1
105	Shelton Winnelson Co—Prisco Panza	PO Box 761, Shelton CT 06484	203-929-6344	R	13*	<.1
106	Reeves-Wiedeman Co—Ted Wiedeman	14861 W 100th St, Lenexa KS 66215	913-492-7100	R	13*	.1
107	Kelly Supply Company of Iowa—Kasey Kelly	PO Box 1328, Grand Island NE 68802	308-382-5670	R	13*	.1
108	Wallace Supply Co	PO Box 829, Vineland NJ 08362	856-692-4800	R	13*	.1
109	Best Plumbing Supply Inc—Melvin Weiner	3333 Crompond Rd Ste 1, Yorktown Heights NY 10598	914-736-2468	R	12*	.1
110	Woodhill Supply Inc—Arnold Kaufman	4665 Beidler Rd, Willoughby OH 44094	440-269-1100	R	12*	.1
111	Mercury Partners 90 Bi Inc—David Sobut	1200 Greenleaf Ave, Elk Grove Village IL 60007	847-437-9690	R	12*	<.1
112	Schmidt's Wholesale Inc—Gary Schmidt	PO Box 5100, Monticello NY 12701	845-794-5900	R	12*	.1
113	Seelye Plastics Inc—Richard Mc Namara	9700 Newton Ave S Ste, Minneapolis MN 55431	952-881-2658	R	12*	.1
114	Shoemaker Inc—Dave Shoemaker	PO Box 1108, Holland MI 49422	616-392-7135	R	12*	.1
115	Burt Process Equipment Inc—Stephen Burt	PO Box 185100, Hamden CT 06518	203-287-1985	R	12*	.1
116	Chandler Systems Inc—Bill Chandler	220 Ohio St, Ashland OH 44805	419-281-5767	R	12*	.1
117	Rex Pipe and Supply Co—Joseph Cleary	10311 Berea Rd, Cleveland OH 44102	216-651-1900	R	11*	.1
118	Sonny's Home Center Inc—Elmer Smaller	PO Box 920, Canon City CO 81215	719-275-1544	R	11*	.1
119	Bradley S Shoen Inc—Shoen Bradley	PO Box 14750, Las Vegas NV 89114	702-382-4957	R	11*	.1
120	Kessler Industries Inc (Paterson New Jersey)—Neil Kessler	500 Green Street, Woodbridge NJ 07095	973-684-2130	R	11*	<.1
121	Ridgewood Corp—Jules Weinstein	2 Bailey Farm Rd, Harriman NY 10926	845-782-4261	R	11*	<.1
122	Leonard S Stern Plumbing—Eugene Stern	3666 Coral Way, Miami FL 33145	305-445-1345	R	11*	<.1
123	Peacock Sales Company Inc—Richard Peacock	3683 N Peachtree Rd, Atlanta GA 30341	770-451-7905	R	11*	<.1
124	Ultraviolet Devices Inc—Peter Veloz	26145 Technology Dr, Valencia CA 91355	661-295-8140	R	11*	.1
125	Forrer Supply Company Inc—Stephen Forrer	PO Box 220, Germantown WI 53022	262-255-3030	R	10*	<.1
126	State Supply Co—Patrick Lambardo	597 E 7th St, Saint Paul MN 55101	651-774-5985	R	10*	<.1
127	Rexford - Albany Municipal Supply Company Inc—George Beaudoin	14 Arch St Ste 1, Watervliet NY 12189	518-273-6300	R	10*	<.1
128	Montour Industrial Supply Inc—William Ondrasik	1400 2nd Ave, Coraopolis PA 15108	412-262-7460	R	10*	<.1
129	Salem Plumbing Supply Company Inc—Ralph Sevinor	PO Box 510, Beverly MA 01915	978-921-1200	R	10*	<.1
130	Auburn Supply Co—Myrtle Smith	3850 W 167th St, Markham IL 60428	708-596-9800	R	9*	<.1
131	Quinsig Ave Overflow Treatment—Matt Labovites	70 Quinsigamond Ave, Worcester MA 01610	508-754-6970	R	9*	<.1
132	Mechanical Supply Co—Scott Reid	PO Box 709, Matthews NC 28106	704-847-9641	R	9*	<.1
133	Norman Supply Co—Mike Knight	825 SW 5th St, Oklahoma City OK 73109	405-235-9511	R	9*	<.1
134	Southland Plumbing Supply Inc—Alan Vinturella	2321 N Arnoult Rd, Metairie LA 70001	504-835-8411	R	9*	<.1
135	Henry Quentzel Plumbing Supply Company Inc—Ann Quentzel	379 Throop Ave, Brooklyn NY 11221	718-455-6600	R	8*	<.1
136	Dellon Sales and Marketing Ltd—Scott Dellon	5 Albertson Ave, Albertson NY 11507	516-625-2626	R	8*	<.1
137	Wisco Supply Inc—Lawrence Berry	PO Box 214, El Paso TX 79942	915-544-8294	R	8*	<.1
138	Bangor Pipe and Supply Inc—Thomas Smith	PO Box 1569, Bangor ME 04402	207-942-1200	R	8*	<.1
139	Newman Associates Inc—Henry Newman	80 Hudson Rd Ste 200, Canton MA 02021	781-329-4000	R	8*	<.1
140	Joyce Agency Inc—Gary Joyce	8442 Alban Rd, Springfield VA 22150	703-866-3111	R	8*	<.1
141	East End Plumbing Supply Inc—Robert Anderson	PO Box 991243, Louisville KY 40269	502-491-4070	R	8*	<.1
142	Jack Farrelly Co—J Farrelly	97 Old Poquonock Rd, Bloomfield CT 06002	860-243-9714	R	8*	<.1
143	A and S Supply Company Inc—Cheryl Gifford	PO Box 736, Flint MI 48501	810-232-0136	R	7*	<.1
144	Harry Martz Supply Co—Scott Younggreen	5330 Pecos St, Denver CO 80221	303-421-6665	R	7*	<.1
145	Horizon SpA and Pool Parts Inc—Ralph Raub	3120 E Medina Rd, Tucson AZ 85756	520-295-9750	R	7*	<.1
146	Mid-American Water and Plumbing Inc—Bruce Ewing	5009 Murray Rd, Manhattan KS 66503	785-537-1072	R	7*	<.1
147	Amarillo Winnelson Co—Gerald Brandt	1400 W 6th St, Amarillo TX 79101	806-372-2259	R	7*	<.1
148	Portland Valve and Fitting Company Inc—Jim Trolinger	815 Se Sherman St, Portland OR 97214	503-288-6901	R	7*	<.1
149	Honold and La Page Inc—William Honold	PO Box 491, Sheboygan WI 53082	920-457-7755	R	7*	<.1
150	Hose and Fittings Etc—Denise Brock	1811 Enterprise Blvd, West Sacramento CA 95691	916-372-3888	R	7*	<.1
151	Golden West Pipe and Supply Company Inc—Shirley Lutgen	PO Box 39129, Downey CA 90239	562-803-4321	R	7*	<.1
152	Advanced Heating and Cooling Inc—Charles Huff	1211 Ivy Rd, Bremerton WA 98310	360-415-9335	R	7*	<.1
153	Empire Plumbing Supply Inc—Sam Beakey	5124 S Peoria Ave, Tulsa OK 74105	918-587-4431	R	7*	<.1
154	Alpine Water Systems LLC—Steffany Tipton	PO Box 94436, Las Vegas NV 89193	702-798-7220	R	6*	<.1
155	Lakes Pipe and Supply Corp—John Hurley	PO Box 429, Niagara Falls NY 14302	716-285-6631	R	6*	<.1
156	Centime Industries Inc—Anne Smith	5405 Centime Dr Ste 10, Wichita Falls TX 76305	940-692-2121	R	6*	<.1
157	Adel Wholesalers Inc—Ralph Gibson	1101 State St, Bettendorf IA 52722	563-355-4734	R	6*	.1
158	Morris Merchants Inc—Joseph McCarthy	77 Green St, Foxboro MA 02035	508-203-2010	R	6*	<.1
159	Howard C Fletcher Company Inc—Joseph Hudelson	16912 Von Karman Ave, Irvine CA 92606	949-660-0200	R	6*	<.1
160	Masda Corp—Daniel Darche	22 Troy Rd, Whippany NJ 07981	973-386-1100	R	6*	<.1
161	Herbeau Creation Of America Inc—Holger Baron	3600 Westview Dr, Naples FL 34104	239-417-5368	R	6*	<.1
162	Colonial Plumbing And Heating Supply Inc—Louis Marozzi	130 Railroad Ave, Albany NY 12205	518-459-6000	R	6*	<.1
163	Milford Supply Co—Timothy Milford	PO Box 6970, Saint Louis MO 63123	314-894-1991	R	6*	<.1
164	Maumee Plumbing and Heating Supply Inc—Douglas Williams	PO Box 309, Perrysburg OH 43552	419-874-7991	R	6*	<.1
165	Arizona Boiler Company Inc—Terry Melot	8282 N 75th Ave, Peoria AZ 85345	623-979-3301	R	6*	<.1
166	H and H Machine Company Inc—Kenneth Hunt	20 W Water St, Taunton MA 02780	508-823-1745	R	6*	<.1

Rank	Company Name—*Executive Officer*	Address, City, State, Zip	Phone	Type	Fin	Empls
167	Crest/Good Manufacturing Company Inc—*Philip Goerler*	PO Box 468, Syosset NY 11791	516-921-7260	R	6*	<.1
168	Hulbert Holding Corp—*Dale Miner*	PO Box 806, Plattsburg NY 12901	518-561-5400	R	5*	<.1
169	Crown Hardware and Plumbing Supply Inc—*Marvin Edelstein*	PO Box 12144, Milwaukee WI 53212	414-374-5100	R	5*	<.1
170	L and B Pipe And Supply Co—*Bob Grosher*	22515 S Western Ave, Torrance CA 90501	310-328-2060	R	5*	<.1
171	Mid Continent Marketing Services—*Gary Hull*	1275 Lakeside Dr, Romeoville IL 60446	630-953-1211	R	5*	<.1
172	John Hoadley And Sons Inc—*John Hoadley*	672 Union St, Rockland MA 02370	781-878-8098	R	5*	<.1
173	Coastal Plumbing Supply Company Inc—*Alexander Federico*	480 Bay St, Staten Island NY 10304	718-447-2692	R	5*	<.1
174	Decker's Plumbing Supply Inc—*Gregory Decker*	2794 S 1900 W, Ogden UT 84401	801-394-4600	R	5*	<.1
175	Rio Grande Plumbing Supply Inc—*Rex Widle*	PO Box 3330, Mcallen TX 78502	956-686-9557	R	5*	<.1
176	Culligan Water Conditioning Inc	6901 E 38th St, Indianapolis IN 46226	317-925-6484	S	5*	.1
177	Tipton Co—*Ty Tipton*	3301 Commerce St, Houston TX 77003	713-225-1086	R	5*	<.1
178	Teter's Faucet Parts Corp—*Jack Teter*	PO Box 141075, Dallas TX 75214	214-823-2153	R	5*	<.1
179	UP Electric/Wittock Supply Co—*Vern Weber*	701 Balsam St, Kingsford MI 49802	906-774-4455	R	5*	<.1
180	National Water Purifiers Inc—*Judith Prado*	1065 E 14th St, Hialeah FL 33010	305-887-7065	R	5*	<.1
181	Argen Inc—*Arthur Blankenship*	996 E Fwy Dr Se, Conyers GA 30094	770-760-1500	R	5*	<.1
182	B-K Plumbing Supply Inc—*Susan Terry*	PO Box 826, Keller TX 76244	817-379-1117	R	5*	<.1
183	Norland International Inc—*Don Liu*	PO Box 67189, Lincoln NE 68506	402-441-3737	R	5*	<.1
184	Wisconsin Tubing Inc—*Gary Derber*	PO Box 414, Omro WI 54963	920-685-2711	R	4*	<.1
185	Davies Supply Co—*George Fuka*	6601 W Grand Ave, Chicago IL 60707	773-637-7800	R	4*	<.1
186	H and S Supply Inc—*John Summers*	310 Lincoln Way E, New Oxford PA 17350	717-624-2171	R	4*	<.1
187	Stearns Plumbing Inc—*Keith Stearns*	PO Box 88, North Vernon IN 47265	812-346-4413	R	4*	<.1
188	Altherm Inc—*Donald Schink*	255 Humphrey St, Englewood NJ 07631	201-871-0500	R	4*	<.1
189	Summit Sales Inc—*Mitch Giles*	PO Box 189, Gustine CA 95322	209-854-2421	R	4*	<.1
190	Caylor Industrial Sales Inc—*Raymond Caylor*	PO Box 4659, Dalton GA 30719	706-226-3198	R	4*	<.1
191	HA Campbell Supply Co—*Dennis Campbell*	2671 Division Ave S, Grand Rapids MI 49507	616-243-0144	R	4*	<.1
192	Webstone Company Inc—*Michael E Reck*	PO Box 59, Worcester MA 01613		R	4*	<.1
193	BJ Terroni Company Inc—*John Terroni*	3190 Tucker Rd, Bensalem PA 19020	215-639-3600	R	4*	<.1
194	Caroplast Inc—*Louis Raymond*	PO Box 668405, Charlotte NC 28266	704-394-4191	R	4*	<.1
195	Lee Dopkin—*Rick Garber* Hajoca Corp	2100 W Cold Spring Ln, Baltimore MD 21209	410-466-3500	S	4*	<.1
196	PC McKenzie Co—*Mark Good*	PO Box 112638, Pittsburgh PA 15241	412-257-8866	R	4*	<.1
197	C Herzog Supply Inc—*Dennis Herzog*	PO Box 707, East Worcester NY 12064	607-397-8292	R	4*	<.1
198	Allied Systems Inc—*James Dermott*	2200 E Douglas Ave, Des Moines IA 50313	515-223-6642	R	4*	<.1
199	Edos Manufacturer's Representatives Inc—*Robert Os*	PO Box 27, Granby MA 01033	413-467-9161	R	4*	<.1
200	Avco Supply Inc—*Gary Verofsky*	PO Box 700, Levittown PA 19058	215-949-1550	R	4*	<.1
201	Peach Street Properties Inc—*Frederick Veith*	4818 Peach St, Erie PA 16509	814-864-4896	R	4*	<.1
202	Trinity Wholesale Distributors Inc—*Kevin Walsh*	PO Box 186, New Haven IN 46774	260-493-2574	R	4*	<.1
203	Alhern-Martin Industrial Furnace Co—*James Van Etten*	2155 Austin Dr, Troy MI 48083	248-689-6363	R	4*	<.1
204	Superlon Plastics Company Inc—*Reidar Ilvedson*	2116 Taylor Way, Tacoma WA 98421	253-383-5877	R	4*	<.1
205	Marketing Affiliates Inc—*Steve Vanstraten*	107 Cypress St Sw, Reynoldsburg OH 43068	740-927-6880	R	3*	<.1
206	Western Pottery LLC—*Shawn Bacon*	14405 Best Ave, Norwalk CA 90650	562-229-0910	R	3*	<.1
207	Probst Supply Company Inc—*Richard Probst*	PO Box 352, Marion OH 43301	740-383-6071	R	3*	<.1
208	Eddington Industries LLC	575 St Rd, Bensalem PA 19020	215-639-0675	R	3*	<.1
209	Crisp Distribution Inc—*Winston Mixon*	501 S Harris St, Cordele GA 31015	229-273-6681	R	3*	<.1
210	Warwick Hanger Company Inc—*Michael Ellery*	34 Canal St, Westerly RI 02891	401-596-8062	R	3*	<.1
211	Bristol Hose and Fitting Inc—*Carol Tuminaro*	1 W Lake St, Northlake IL 60164	708-343-1046	R	3*	<.1
212	O'connor Sales Inc—*Michael Dunn*	16107 Piuma Ave, Cerritos CA 90703	562-403-3848	R	3*	<.1
213	Dupage Water Conditioning Company Inc—*Robert Lenz*	27w250 N Ave, West Chicago IL 60185	630-293-7500	R	3*	<.1
214	Keenan Supply—*Eric Augustin* Hajoca Corp	5801 San Leandro St, Oakland CA 94621	510-261-8261	D	3*	<.1
215	Electron Solar Energy—*Christopher Quinn*	2801 NW 6th, Miami FL 33127	305-756-6789	P	3	N/A
216	Cogenra Solar Inc—*Gilad Almogy*	365 E Middlefield Rd, Mountain View CA 94043	650-230-3400	R	3*	<.1
217	Prime Supply Co—*Samuel Tredilcock*	PO Box 520, Iron Mountain MI 49801	906-779-5522	R	3*	<.1
218	Clearly H2o Inc—*Henry Mcguire*	28243 Beck Rd Ste B13, Wixom MI 48393	248-374-8951	R	3*	<.1
219	Energy Products and Design Inc—*Sandra Buchan*	497 37th St Ne, Rochester MN 55906	507-289-7496	R	2*	<.1
220	Kewanee Burner Supply and Sales—*Vincent Calluchi*	2884 Nostrand Ave, Brooklyn NY 11229	718-258-9803	R	2*	<.1
221	Out Today—*Gary Jeffen*	13300 Se 30th St, Bellevue WA 98005	425-688-8632	R	2*	<.1
222	Stern Brothers Plumbing Inc—*Eugene Stern*	3666 Coral Way, Miami FL 33145	305-445-1345	R	2*	<.1
223	Aquionics Inc—*William Decker*	21 Kenton Lands Rd Ste, Erlanger KY 41018	859-341-0710	R	2*	<.1
224	Michigan Pipe Supply LLC—*Brad Faahr*	PO Box 442, Mount Pleasant MI 48804	989-772-2225	R	2*	<.1
225	Food Process and Control Inc—*Humberto Suarez*	7786 Beech St Ne Ste 2, Minneapolis MN 55432	763-571-6200	R	2*	<.1
226	Premiere Sales—*Anthony Special*	3771 Kelton Dr, Oceanside CA 92056	760-433-7238	R	2*	<.1
227	Special Plastic Systems Inc—*Dan Conklin*	385 W Valley St, San Bernardino CA 92401	909-888-2531	R	1*	<.1
228	Superior Aqua Enterprises Inc—*James Muha*	4556 Mcashton St, Sarasota FL 34233	941-923-2221	R	1*	<.1
229	ProVision Technologies Inc—*Marco Mangelsdorf*	69 Railroad Ave Ste A-, Hilo HI 96720	808-969-3281	S	1*	<.1

TOTALS: SIC 5074 Plumbing & Hydronic Heating Supplies

Companies: 229					22,847	69.9

5075 Warm Air Heating & Air-Conditioning

Rank	Company Name—*Executive Officer*	Address, City, State, Zip	Phone	Type	Fin	Empls
1	WW Grainger Inc—*James T Ryan*	100 Grainger Pkwy, Lake Forest IL 60045	847-535-1000	P	7,182	18.5
2	Watsco Inc—*Albert H Nahmad*	2665 S Bayshore Dr Ste, Coconut Grove FL 33133	305-714-4100	P	2,978	4.3
3	Famous Supply Co—*Jay Blaufeild*	PO Box 1889, Akron OH 44309	330-434-5194	R	252*	.7
4	ACR Group Inc—*Tony Maresca* Watsco Inc	3200 Wilcrest Dr Ste 4, Houston TX 77042	713-780-8532	S	240	.5
5	Total Supply Inc—*Ronnie Floyd* ACR Group Inc	5158 Kennedy Rd Ste F, Forest Park GA 30297	404-608-0059	S	204	N/A
6	Lee Technologies Group Inc—*John C Lee IV*	12150 Monument Dr Ste, Fairfax VA 22033	703-968-0300	R	168*	.2
7	Lexington Corporate Enterprises Inc—*Raymond Mungo*	17725 Volbrecht Rd, Lansing IL 60438	708-418-0700	R	164*	.2
8	American International Management Corp—*E Schroeter*	PO Box 5070, Lighthouse Point FL 33074	954-943-3025	R	152*	<.1
9	Johnson Supply and Equipment Corp—*Carl Johnson*	10151 Stella Link, Houston TX 77025	713-661-6666	R	141*	.3
10	Mingledorffs Inc—*LB Mingledorff*	6675 Jones Mill Ct, Norcross GA 30092	770-446-6311	R	114*	.2
11	Behler-Young Co—*Douglas R Young*	PO Box 946, Grand Rapids MI 49509	616-531-3400	R	111*	.2
12	Century Air Conditioning Supply Inc—*Dennis Bearden*	10510 W Sam Houston Pk, Houston TX 77099	281-530-2859	R	99*	.3
13	Robertshaw Uni-Line North America—*Ulf Henriksson*	515 S Promenade, Corona CA 92879	951-734-2600	D	95*	.2
14	Temperature Equipment Corp—*Skip Mungo*	17725 Volbrecht Rd Ste, Lansing IL 60438	708-418-3062	R	93*	.2
15	Gunder and Associates LLC—*Marshall Gunder*	1920 Hutton Ct Ste 200, Dallas TX 75234	972-620-2801	R	85*	<.1
16	Mccall's Incorporated Of Johnsonville SC—*Dairen Jacobs*	PO Box 39, Johnsonville SC 29555	843-386-3323	R	80*	.2
17	Bryant-I labegger Co—*John Dorr*	4995 Winton Rd, Cincinnati OH 45232	513-681-5600	R	77*	.2
18	KSW Inc—*Floyd Warkol*	37-16 23rd St, Long Island City NY 11101	718-361-6500	P	76	<.1

Note: An asterisk (*) indicates an estimated financial figure. The company type code used is as follows: R = Private, P = Public, S = Private Subsidiary, B = Public Subsidiary, D = Division, J = Joint Venture, I = Investment Fund.

COMPANY RANKINGS BY SALES WITHIN 4-DIGIT SIC

Rank	Company Name—Executive Officer	Address, City, State, Zip	Phone	Type	Fin	Empls
19	Refrigeration Sales Corp—Warren W Farr Jr	9450 Allen Dr Ste A, Valley View OH 44125	216-525-8100	R	64*	.1
20	Three States Supply Co—Ronald Wigginton Watsco Inc	PO Box 646, Memphis TN 38101	901-565-0636	S	63*	.2
21	Coastline Distribution Inc—Albert Nahmad Watsco Inc	PO Box 2954, Jacksonville FL 32203	904-407-4500	S	60*	.2
22	Williams Distributing Co—Michael Koster	PO Box 2585, Grand Rapids MI 49501	616-456-1613	R	54*	.3
23	Geary Pacific Corp—Pat Geary	1908 N Enterprise St, Orange CA 92865	714-279-2950	R	52*	.1
24	Acme Refrigeration of Baton Rouge Inc—Sheila Long	11844 S Choctaw Dr, Baton Rouge LA 70815	225-273-1740	R	50*	.1
25	Temperature Systems Inc—Terry Riker	PO Box 8030, Madison WI 53708	608-271-7500	R	48*	.1
26	Equipment Sales Corp—Herbert Hughes Sr	703 Western Dr, Mobile AL 36607	251-476-2220	R	45*	.1
27	Kele Inc—Tim Vargo	PO Box 34817, Memphis TN 38184	901-382-4300	R	41*	.2
28	Hvac Distributors Inc—David Mcilwaine	PO Box 160, Mount Joy PA 17552	717-653-6674	R	39*	.1
29	Carr Supply Inc—Roger Essig	1415 Old Leonard Ave, Columbus OH 43219	614-252-7883	R	35*	.1
30	Burke Engineering Company Inc—Kelly Trolia	9700 Factorial Way, El Monte CA 91733	626-579-0037	R	34*	.1
31	Comfort Supply Inc	2151 W Hillsboror Blvd, Deerfield Beach FL 33442	954-246-2665	S	32*	.1
32	Delcard Associates Inc—Roger Wells	31 Blevins Dr Ste A Ai, New Castle DE 19720	302-221-4822	R	29*	.1
33	Ince Distributing Inc—Raymond Ince	2233 Nw Loop 410, San Antonio TX 78230	210-341-7161	R	28*	.2
34	Evans Electric Co—Dan Evans	1130 High St, Portsmouth VA 23704	757-399-3044	R	25*	.1
35	Weathertech Distributing Company Inc—Spencer Atkins	PO Box 100609, Birmingham AL 35210	205-956-5400	R	25*	.1
36	Standard Air and Lite Corp—Robert W Wilson	PO Box 44445, Pittsburgh PA 15201	412-920-6505	R	24*	.1
37	Royal Sovereign Corp—TK Lim	2 Volvo Dr, Rockleigh NJ 07647	201-750-1020	R	24*	<.1
38	Winger Contracting Co—Tom Keck	PO Box 637, Ottumwa IA 52501	641-682-3407	R	23*	.2
39	California Hydronics Corp—David Attard	PO Box 5049, Hayward CA 94540	510-293-1993	R	22*	.1
40	John R Seiberlich Inc—John Seiberlich	66 Southgate Blvd, New Castle DE 19720	302-395-0200	R	22*	.1
41	Tom Barrow Co—Thomas Barrow	2800 Plant Atkinson Rd, Smyrna GA 30080	404-351-1010	R	21*	.2
42	Meier Supply Company Inc—Frank Meier	123 Brown St, Johnson City NY 13790	607-797-7700	R	20*	.1
43	G-A-P Supply Corp—Gregory Popma	PO Box 1668, Tualatin OR 97062	503-597-7200	R	20*	.1
44	Mckenzie Compressed Air Solutions Inc—Mary Mckenzie	9260 Bryant St, Houston TX 77075	713-946-1413	R	20*	.1
45	Air Products Equipment Co—Michael Wyatt	1555 Louis Ave, Elk Grove Village IL 60007	847-437-5952	R	20*	<.1
46	Rose Corp—Brian Higgins	PO Box 15208, Reading PA 19612	610-376-5004	R	20*	.1
47	Corken Steel Products Co—Jeffrey Corken	7920 Kentucky Dr, Florence KY 41042	859-291-4664	R	19*	.1
48	Heating and Cooling Supply Inc—Marc Greer Watsco Inc	1669 Brandywine Ave St, Chula Vista CA 91911	619-591-4615	S	18*	.1
49	Anguil Environmental Systems Inc—Gene Anguil	8855 N 55th St, Milwaukee WI 53223	414-365-6400	R	17*	<.1
50	S G Torrice Company Inc—Stephen Torrice	80 Industrial Way Ste, Wilmington MA 01887	978-657-7779	R	16*	.1
51	Mid-Way Supply Inc—Kenneth Sisson	2502 Deborah Ave, Zion IL 60099	847-872-5481	R	16*	<.1
52	Contractors Heating and Supply Co ACR Group Inc	70 Santa Fe Dr, Denver CO 80223	303-893-6915	S	16*	.1
53	Refri-Parts Inc—Pedro Dedesma	590 W 84th St, Hialeah FL 33014	305-362-2666	R	16*	<.1
54	Sabol and Rice Inc—George Sabol Sr	PO Box 25957, Salt Lake City UT 84125	801-973-2300	R	15*	<.1
55	Dmg Corp—Ronald Sweet	2603 Pacific Park Dr, Whittier CA 90601	562-692-1277	R	14*	.1
56	Benoist Brothers Supply Co—Jack Benoist	107 N 16th St, Mount Vernon IL 62864	618-242-0344	R	13*	.1
57	Aces A/C Supply Inc—Bill Davenport	PO Box 330130, Houston TX 77233	713-738-3800	R	13*	.1
58	Lohmiller and Co—Roger Lee	4800 Osage St Ste 100, Denver CO 80221	303-825-4328	R	12*	.1
59	Mills Heating and Air Conditioning Inc—Larry Batchelor	237 Bulldog Rd, Freeport FL 32430	850-862-4796	R	12*	.1
60	Barron Fan Technology Inc—Willard Brown	PO Box 1883, Alabaster AL 35007	205-621-4321	R	12*	.1
61	HVAC Sales and Supply Company Inc—William D Bomar	2015 Thomas Rd, Memphis TN 38134	901-373-2395	R	11*	<.1
62	Luce Schwab and Kase Inc—James Luce	9 Gloria Ln, Fairfield NJ 07004	973-227-4840	R	11*	.1
63	Haldeman—Tom Haldeman	2937 Tanager Ave, Commerce CA 90040	323-726-7011	R	10*	.1
64	Smith Services Inc—Chip Woody	1306 29th St, Vero Beach FL 32960	772-589-7666	R	10*	.1
65	Bill Voorhees Company Inc—Terri Borders	1133 Polk Ave, Nashville TN 37210	615-242-4481	R	9*	<.1
66	Continental Fan Manufacturing Inc—Victor Afanasiev	203 Eggert Rd, Buffalo NY 14215	716-842-0670	R	9*	<.1
67	West Coast Copper and Supply Inc—Brian Mesa	12155 Magnolia Ave Ste, Riverside CA 92503	951-637-0720	R	8*	<.1
68	Knipp Equipment Inc—John Knipp	PO Box 595, Wichita KS 67201	316-265-9655	R	8*	<.1
69	GF Morin Co—Kevin Morin	8667 Cherry Ln, Laurel MD 20707	301-953-7770	R	8*	<.1
70	Tfc Automation Inc—William Wolford	806 Race Rd, Baltimore MD 21221	410-686-8600	R	8*	<.1
71	Jorban-Riscoe Associates Inc—Mark Riscoe	9808 Alden St, Lenexa KS 66215	913-438-1244	R	8*	<.1
72	Ed's Supply Company Inc—Larry Sigler	2611 W 7th St, Little Rock AR 72205	501-375-9851	R	8*	<.1
73	Tidewater Air Filter Fabrication Company Inc—James Grubbs	228 Pennsylvania Ave, Virginia Beach VA 23462	757-497-2311	R	7*	<.1
74	Monitor Products Inc—Fumio Miyamoto	PO Box 3408, Princeton NJ 08543	609-584-0505	R	7*	<.1
75	Vorys Brothers Inc—Roger Wallace	834 W 3rd Ave, Columbus OH 43216	614-294-4701	R	7*	<.1
76	Alfieri-Proctor Associates Trust—Alex Alfieri	PO Box 682, Randolph MA 02368	781-986-5900	R	6*	<.1
77	Air Conditioning Installations By Rusher Inc—George Rusher	19626 Normandie Ave, Torrance CA 90502	310-323-7201	R	6*	.1
78	Brothers Supply Corp—John Esposito	3448 31st St, Long Island City NY 11106	718-392-1200	R	6*	<.1
79	Thermo-Trol Systems Inc—Floyd Evans	PO Box 2775, Virginia Beach VA 23450	757-428-4646	R	6*	<.1
80	MidSouth Geothermal LLC—Scott Triplett	8275 Tournament Dr Ste, Memphis TN 38125	901-748-9095	R	6*	<.1
81	Hubbell Mechanical Supply Co—Jack Hubbell	PO Box 3813, Springfield MO 65808	417-865-5531	R	6*	<.1
82	Manufacturer's Products Inc—John Walsh	342 N 400 E, Valparaiso IN 46383	219-462-6951	R	6*	<.1
83	Tri State Parts Co—Joe Callahan	8 Union Hill Rd, Conshohocken PA 19428	610-941-9550	R	6*	<.1
84	Del-Ren Associates Inc—Sam Fiorelli	100 W Narbaeth Ter, Collingswood NJ 08108	856-541-1776	R	6*	<.1
85	Air Engineers LLC—Patti Baker	PO Box 380157, Birmingham AL 35238	205-991-6850	R	6*	<.1
86	Air Duct Aseptics Inc—Petrina Tebor	1059 Nw 31st Ave, Pompano Beach FL 33069		R	6*	<.1
87	Besco Supply Co—Steven Bender	12214 E 55th St, Tulsa OK 74146	918-252-4585	R	6*	<.1
88	George Holden and Associates Inc—Walter Schwarz	6675 Jones Mill Ct, Norcross GA 30092	770-458-4000	R	6*	<.1
89	Air Filter Engineers Inc—John Dibunno	385 Kimberly Dr, Carol Stream IL 60188	630-384-0400	R	5*	<.1
90	Air Cleaning Systems Inc—George Bunting	1966 W Holt Ave, Pomona CA 91768	909-620-7114	R	5*	<.1
91	Ambrose Air Inc—Patrick Ambrose	448 W Landstreet Rd, Orlando FL 32824	407-857-0889	R	5*	<.1
92	E H Arbuckle Distributing Inc—Boyd Fullmer	PO Box 65499, Salt Lake City UT 84165	801-486-4401	R	5*	<.1
93	H And B Products Inc—Sean Welsh	4200 Forbes Blvd Ste 1, Lanham MD 20706	301-918-0245	R	5*	<.1
94	Innovair Corp—Julio Gomez	11490 Nw 39th St Ste 1, Doral FL 33178	305-463-9998	R	5*	<.1
95	Filter And Coating Technology Inc—Steve Billmeier	5706 W River Dr Ne, Belmont MI 49306	616-784-3228	R	5*	<.1
96	Allegheny Engineering Co—Robert Densmore	PO Box 12567, Pittsburgh PA 15241	724-941-8500	R	5*	<.1
97	Wadsworth and Associates Inc—Britt Wadsworth	1500 Michael Owens Way, Perrysburg OH 43551	419-861-8181	R	5*	<.1
98	Upstate Systems Inc—Jody Swanson	3277 Brighton Henriett, Rochester NY 14623	585-272-9400	R	4*	<.1
99	Airdusco Inc—Adam Lancaster	4739 S Mendenhall Rd, Memphis TN 38141	901-362-6610	R	4*	<.1
100	Budget Heating and Cooling LLC—Michelle Davis	PO Box 586, Clarksville TN 37041	931-905-2356	R	4*	<.1
101	Wilspec Technologies Inc—Larry Wilhelm	6000 Nw 2nd St Ste 500, Oklahoma City OK 73127	405-495-8989	R	4*	<.1
102	Sherwood-Turner Corp—Jerry Brasher	5065 American Way, Memphis TN 38115	901-332-1414	R	4*	<.1
103	Earth Energy Technology and Supply Inc—Charles Young	PO Box 219, Marietta OK 73448	580-276-9455	S	4*	<.1
104	ETS Inc—John McKenna	1401 Municipal Rd NW, Roanoke VA 24012	540-265-0004	R	4*	<.1

Rank	Company Name—*Executive Officer*	Address, City, State, Zip	Phone	Type	Fin	Empls
105	Sandifer Engineering and Control—*Robert Sandifer*	PO Box 410, Goddard KS 67052	316-794-8880	R	4*	<.1
106	Vesco Inc—*Richard Foster*	840 N Addison Ave, Elmhurst IL 60126	630-834-8600	R	4*	<.1
107	Bush Wholesalers Inc—*Edward Light*	637 Sackett St, Brooklyn NY 11217	718-624-5900	R	4*	<.1
108	Commercial Specialists Inc—*Randy Grimme*	1925 Westwood Ave, Cincinnati OH 45214	513-921-2724	R	4*	<.1
109	Bud Griffin Customer Support—*Bill Walton*	PO Box 1710, Bellaire TX 77402	713-666-2828	R	3*	<.1
110	Edward C Smyers Co—*B Smyers*	223 Fort Pitt Blvd, Pittsburgh PA 15222	412-471-3222	R	3*	<.1
111	Famous Supply Co—*Jay Blaushield*	2300 Market St, Wheeling WV 26003	304-232-3310	R	3*	<.1
112	Perfect-Climate Heating And Air Conditioning Inc—*Bobby Beavers*	11232 St Jhns Industry, Jacksonville FL 32246	904-646-1020	R	3*	<.1
113	Cincinnati Air Filter Sales and Service Inc—*Edward Flick*	4815 Para Dr, Cincinnati OH 45237	513-242-3400	R	3*	<.1
114	Grillo's Filter Sales—*Deanna Debrunner*	6331 Industrial Ave, Riverside CA 92504	951-688-8687	R	3*	<.1
115	Parsons Sales Company Inc—*Anthony Bartoletti*	310 George Ave, Wilkes Barre PA 18705	570-655-3587	R	3*	<.1
116	Passaic Metal Building Supply—*Bob Becker*	1957 Rutgers Universit, Lakewood NJ 08701	732-886-9410	R	3*	<.1
117	Manufactured Duct and Supply—*Sherry Holland*	2805 Premiere Pkwy Ste, Duluth GA 30097	678-474-0052	R	2*	<.1
118	Chief Bauer Heating and Air Conditioning—*Rick Houchens*	520 N Hickory St, Champaign IL 61820	217-429-1738	R	2*	<.1
119	Compressor Sales Inc—*Leonard Jolley*	3021 Joe Rawlings Rd, Cookeville TN 38506	931-432-1415	R	2*	<.1
120	Oem Parts Outlet—*Julie O'donnell*	1815 W Sylvania Ave, Toledo OH 43613	419-472-2237	R	2*	<.1
121	Envitec Inc—*Walter Kleinberg*	46 Elmar Cir, Royersford PA 19468	610-792-1275	R	2*	<.1
122	Air Systems Distributors Inc—*Albert Nahmad* Watsco Inc	2151 W Hillsboro Blvd, Deerfield Beach FL 33442	954-246-2665	S	1*	<.1

TOTALS: SIC 5075 Warm Air Heating & Air-Conditioning
Companies: 122   13,812   32.1

5078 Refrigeration Equipment & Supplies

Rank	Company Name—*Executive Officer*	Address, City, State, Zip	Phone	Type	Fin	Empls
1	Next Day Gormet and Superior Cataloge Outlet—*Willie Voss*	PO Box 64177, St Paul MN 55164	651-636-1110	R	161*	.3
2	Baker Distributing Co—*Carol Poindexter*	PO Box 2954, Jacksonville FL 32203	904-407-4500	S	160	.4
3	Wittichen Supply Co—*David Henderson*	1600 3rd Ave S, Birmingham AL 35233	205-251-8500	R	159*	.2
4	Refrigeration Supplies Distributor—*Brian Martin*	26021 Atlantic Ocean D, Lake Forest CA 92630	949-380-7878	R	111*	.4
5	Young Supply Co—*John Grillo*	52000 Sierra Dr, Chesterfield MI 48047	586-421-2400	R	78*	.2
6	ABCO Refrigeration Supply Corp	49-70 31st St, Long Island City NY 11101	718-937-9000	R	67*	.2
7	Southern Refrigeration Corp—*Jack Lang*	PO Box 12646, Roanoke VA 24027	540-342-3493	R	40*	.1
8	WA Roosevelt Co—*Todd Eber*	PO Box 1208, La Crosse WI 54602	608-781-2000	R	39*	.1
9	Hudson Technologies Inc—*Kevin Zugibe*	1 Blue Hill Plz, Pearl River NY 10965	845-735-6000	P	37	.1
10	Thermal Supply Inc—*Mike Fry*	717 S Lander St, Seattle WA 98134	206-624-4590	R	37*	.1
11	Transport Refrigeration Sales and Service Inc—*K Macdonald*	500 Daniel Payne Dr, Birmingham AL 35214	205-328-7278	R	27*	.1
12	GoldStar Products Company Ltd—*Jeff Applebaum*	21680 Coolidge Hwy, Oak Park MI 48237	248-548-9840	R	20*	<.1
13	Refrigeration and Electric Supply Co—*Carl H Miller Jr*	1222 S Spring St, Little Rock AR 72202	501-374-6373	R	18*	.1
14	Chernoff Sales Inc—*Joe Andisman*	3308 Park Central Blvd, Pompano Beach FL 33064	954-972-1414	R	18*	.1
15	Boatright Company Inc—*Randy King*	653b Black Creek Rd, Birmingham AL 35217	205-841-4406	R	17*	.1
16	Thermo King Christensen Inc—*Oscar Christensen*	7508 F St, Omaha NE 68127	402-331-6116	R	16*	.1
17	S W H Supply Co—*Robert Anderson*	242 E Main St, Louisville KY 40202	502-589-9287	R	14*	.1
18	Allied Supply Company Inc—*Thomas Homan*	1100 E Monument Ave, Dayton OH 45402	937-224-9833	R	14*	.1
19	Yeti Coolers—*Roy Seiders*	PO Box 163686, Austin TX 78716	512-394-9384	R	13	.1
20	Thermo King Of Houston LP—*Ken George*	772 Mccarty St, Houston TX 77029	713-671-2700	R	12*	<.1
21	Lane Equipment Co—*Robert Lane*	PO Box 540909, Houston TX 77254	713-529-5761	R	12*	.1
22	Brock-McVey Co—*Reggie Hickman*	PO Box 55487, Lexington KY 40555	859-255-1412	S	10*	.1
23	Hoffman Supply Company Inc—*Karl Bunselmeyer*	PO Box 1477, Springfield MO 65001	417-862-6771	R	6*	<.1
24	Norms' Refrigeration And Ice Equipment Inc—*Tim Mcgillicuddy*	1175 N Knollwood Cir, Anaheim CA 92801	714-236-3600	R	6*	<.1
25	Fenco Supply Company Inc—*William Fennell*	PO Box 3906, Knoxville TN 37927	865-637-1821	R	5*	<.1
26	Chaparral Distributing LLC—*Rebacca Palacils*	3800 Drossett Dr Ste A, Austin TX 78744	713-952-3951	R	5*	<.1
27	Carlon Inc—*Lee Spencer*	241 Sw 21st Ter, Fort Lauderdale FL 33312	954-584-7330	R	5*	<.1
28	Rite-Temperature Associates Inc—*David Botscheller*	101 S Lackawanna Trl, Dalton PA 18414	570-563-2923	R	5*	<.1
29	Thermo King East Inc—*Don Ebenstein*	650 Dell Rd, Carlstadt NJ 07072	201-939-4822	R	4*	<.1
30	Minnesota Petroleum Service Inc—*Terri Swan*	682 39th Ave Ne, Minneapolis MN 55421	763-780-5191	R	4*	<.1
31	Hudson Technologies Company Inc—*Kevin J Zigibe* Hudson Technologies Inc	1 Blue Hill Plz, Pearl River NY 10965	845-512-6000	S	4*	<.1
32	Frank's Quality Services Inc—*Frank Troglauer*	1784 Two Notch Rd, Lexington SC 29073	803-957-4946	R	4*	<.1
33	San Antonio Thermo King Inc—*Ron Pruett*	5807 Dietrich Rd, San Antonio TX 78219	210-661-4611	R	4*	<.1
34	Src Inc—*Craig Richert*	6615 19 Mile Rd, Sterling Heights MI 48314		R	3*	<.1
35	Washita Refrigeration and Equipment Company Inc—*David Cribbs*	PO Box 577, Tishomingo OK 73460	580-371-3112	R	3*	<.1
36	Automatic Ice Machine Company Inc—*A Lewallen*	501 E 2nd St, Odessa TX 79761	432-337-1681	R	3*	<.1
37	Alamo Service Company Inc—*John Stafford*	1450 N Flores St, San Antonio TX 78212	210-227-7571	R	3*	<.1
38	Carrier Transcold Of Maine—*Jeffery Manning*	432 Warren Ave, Portland ME 04103	207-797-9225	R	3*	<.1
39	North Star Refrigeration Heating and Cooling—*Anthony Chabot*	3120 Pond Rd, Leonard MI 48367	248-969-8000	R	3*	<.1
40	Celsius Joint Venture A California LP—*Clair Moline*	877 Monterey Pass Rd, Monterey Park CA 91754	323-729-6000	R	2*	.1
41	HMC Shipping—*Harold Mcclarty*	13138 S Bethel Ave, Kingsburg CA 93631	559-897-4149	R	2*	<.1
42	Koldkiss LLC—*Daniel Hemerlein*	PO Box 1435, Baltimore MD 21203	410-675-6675	R	2*	<.1
43	Unified Enterprises Corp—*Rodney Shimoko*	3031A Puhala Rise, Honolulu HI 96822	808-235-5923	R	2*	<.1
44	LSK Enterprises Inc—*Mark Shimandle*	PO Box 62885, Virginia Beach VA 23466	757-366-0166	R	1*	<.1

TOTALS: SIC 5078 Refrigeration Equipment & Supplies
Companies: 44   1,159   3.4

5082 Construction & Mining Machinery

Rank	Company Name—*Executive Officer*	Address, City, State, Zip	Phone	Type	Fin	Empls
1	American Equipment Company Inc—*Gary Bernardez*	PO Box 688, Greenville SC 29602	864-295-7800	S	2,791*	2.5
2	Applied Industrial Technologies Inc—*John F Meier*	1 Applied Plz, Cleveland OH 44115	216-426-4000	P	2,213	4.6
3	Empire Southwest LLC—*Jeffrey S Whiteman*	PO Box 2985, Phoenix AZ 85062	480-633-4000	R	1,537*	1.4
4	Whayne Supply Co—*Monty Boyd*	PO Box 35900, Louisville KY 40232	502-774-4441	R	756*	1.3
5	Fabick Cat—*Harry Fabick*	1 Fabick Dr, Fenton MO 63026	636-343-5900	R	733*	.6
6	Holt Cat—*Peter Holt*	PO Box 207916, San Antonio TX 78220	210-648-1111	R	648*	1.8
7	MacAllister Machinery Company Inc—*Chris MacAllister*	7515 E 30th St PO Box, Indianapolis IN 46206	317-545-2151	R	508*	.5
8	FABCO Equipment Inc—*Jere Fabick*	11200 W Silver Spring, Milwaukee WI 53225	414-461-9100	R	475*	.5
9	Komatsu Equipment Co—*John Pfisterer*	2350 W 1500 S, Salt Lake City UT 84104	801-972-3660	R	457*	.2
10	Rish Equipment Co—*Daniel Pochick*	PO Box 330, Bluefield WV 24701	304-327-5124	R	382*	.3
11	Beckwith Machinery Company Inc—*G Beckwith*	4565 William Penn Hwy, Murrysville PA 15668	724-327-1300	R	368*	.7
12	Carolina Tractor and Equipment Company Inc—*Edward Weisiger*	PO Box 1095, Charlotte NC 28201	704-596-6700	R	282*	.7
13	Gregory Poole Equipment Co—*Gregory Poole III*	PO Box 469, Raleigh NC 27602	919-828-0641	R	269*	.7
14	Western Tool Supply Inc—*Kevin Kiker*	PO Box 13430, Salem OR 97309	503-588-8222	R	254*	.1

Note: An asterisk (*) indicates an estimated financial figure. The company type code used is as follows: R = Private, P = Public, S = Private Subsidiary, B = Public Subsidiary, D = Division, J = Joint Venture, I = Investment Fund.

COMPANY RANKINGS BY SALES WITHIN 4-DIGIT SIC

Rank	Company Name—*Executive Officer*	Address, City, State, Zip	Phone	Type	Fin	Empls
15	Peterson Tractor Co—*Jerry Lopus*	PO Box 5258, San Leandro CA 94577	510-357-6200	R	250*	.4
16	Stowers Machinery Corp—*Dave Waddilove*	6301 Old Rutledge Pke, Knoxville TN 37924	865-546-1414	R	249*	.4
17	Patten Industries Inc—*Garrett Patten*	635 W Lake St, Elmhurst IL 60126	630-279-4400	R	223*	.6
18	HO Penn Machinery Company Inc—*CE Thomas Cleveland*	122 Noxon Rd, Poughkeepsie NY 12603	845-452-1200	R	222*	.4
19	Mustang Tractor and Equipment Co—*F Louis Tucker Jr*	PO Box 1373, Houston TX 77251	713-460-2000	R	213*	.8
20	Chadwick-BaRoss Inc—*Micheal Sullivan*	160 Warren Ave, Westbrook ME 04092	207-854-8411	R	203*	.2
21	MA Deatley Construction Inc—*Mark Deatley*	PO Box 490, Clarkston WA 99403	509-751-1580	R	196*	.1
22	Puckett Machinery Co—*Richard Puckett*	PO Box 3170, Jackson MS 39207	601-969-6000	R	174*	.4
23	Road Machinery Co—*Dennise Romanson*	PO Box 4425, Phoenix AZ 85030	602-252-7121	R	168*	.3
24	JA Riggs Tractor Co—*John Riggs*	PO Box 1399, Little Rock AR 72203	501-570-3100	R	158*	.5
25	Wolverine Tractor and Equipment Co—*Ric Simon*	PO Box 19336, Detroit MI 48219	248-356-5280	R	158*	.1
26	Arnold Machinery Co (Salt Lake City Utah)—*Russ Fleming*	PO Box 30020, Salt Lake City UT 84130	801-972-4000	R	150*	.5
27	Peterson CAT—*Jeff Goggin*	4421 NE Columbia Blvd, Portland OR 97218	503-288-6411	S	149*	.4
28	Liebherr-America Inc—*Ronald Jacobson*	PO Box O, Newport News VA 23605	757-245-5251	S	140*	.4
29	Rudd Equipment Co—*Mark Burris*	PO Box 32427, Louisville KY 40232	502-456-4050	R	138*	.3
30	Tyler Equipment Corp—*M Brooke Tyler III*	PO Box 544, East Longmeadow MA 01028	413-525-6351	R	135*	.1
31	Anderson Equipment Co—*Bob Stein Jr*	PO Box 339, Bridgeville PA 15017	412-343-2300	R	130*	.4
32	Cleveland Brothers Equipment Company Inc—*Jay W Cleveland Jr*	5300 Paxton St, Harrisburg PA 17111	717-564-2121	R	126*	.5
33	ITOCHU International Inc—*Yoshihisa Suzuki*	335 Madison Ave, New York NY 10017	212-818-8000	S	124*	.3
34	Nebraska Machinery Co—*Rich Swanson*	11002 Sapp Bros Dr, Omaha NE 68138	402-891-8600	R	120*	.6
35	Vermeer Equipment Of Texas Inc—*Whit Perryman*	3025 State Hwy 161, Irving TX 75062	972-255-3500	S	120*	.1
36	Victor L Phillips Co—*Butch Teppe* VLP Holding Co	PO Box 4915, Kansas City MO 64120	816-241-9290	S	119*	.1
37	Dean Ag Services—*Lori Dean*	14069 LIV 261, Chillicothe MO 64601	660-240-0900	R	110*	.3
38	Warren Equipment Co—*Richard Folger*	PO Box 60758, Midland TX 79711	432-563-1170	R	110*	.2
39	Berry Companies Inc—*Dan Scheer*	PO Box 829, Wichita KS 67201	316-832-0171	R	109*	.4
40	Tom Growney Equipment Inc—*Tom D Growney*	2301 Candelaria Rd NE, Albuquerque NM 87107	505-884-2900	R	109*	.1
41	Scott Machinery Co—*David M Scott*	4055 S 500 W, Salt Lake City UT 84123	801-262-7441	R	99*	.1
42	GW Van Keppel Co—*William S Walker*	PO Box 2923, Kansas City KS 66110	913-281-4800	R	96*	.3
43	Roland Machinery Co—*Raymond E Roland*	816 N Dirksen Pky, Springfield IL 62702	217-789-7711	R	96*	.2
44	Briggs Equipment Inc—*Dave Bratton*	10540 N Stemmons Freew, Dallas TX 75220	214-630-0808	S	92*	.3
45	Yukon Equipment Inc—*Maurice Hollowell*	2020 E 3rd Ave, Anchorage AK 99501	907-277-1541	S	90*	<.1
46	Stribling Equipment LLC—*Gary Broadwater*	PO Box 6038, Jackson MS 39288	601-939-1000	R	85*	.2
47	Lyons Equipment Company Inc—*John Lyons*	PO Box 107, Little Valley NY 14755	716-938-9175	R	81*	.1
48	Halton Co—*Duane Doyle* Peterson CAT	PO Box 3377, Portland OR 97208	503-288-6411	S	77*	.3
49	White Star Machinery and Supply Company Inc—*Glenn Engels* Berry Companies Inc	3223 N Hydraulic St, Wichita KS 67219	316-838-3321	S	77*	.1
50	Foley Equipment Co—*Ann Konecny*	1600 E Wyatt Earp Blvd, Dodge City KS 67801	620-225-4121	R	74*	.2
51	Southeastern Equipment Company Inc (Cambridge Ohio)—*William L Baker*	10874 E Pike Rd, Cambridge OH 43725	740-432-6303	R	74*	.2
52	Sellers Equipment Inc—*David Sellers*	400 N Chicago St, Salina KS 67401	785-823-6378	R	73*	.1
53	Triad Machinery Inc—*Kristine Gittins*	4530 NE 148th Ave, Portland OR 97230	503-254-5100	R	66*	.1
54	McCann Industries Inc—*Dennis Kruepke*	543 S Rohlwing Rd, Addison IL 60101	630-627-0000	R	60*	.2
55	Tri-State Truck and Equipment Inc—*Dewit Boyd*	5250 Midland Rd, Billings MT 59101	406-245-3188	R	59*	.1
56	New Holland Construction—*Bob Bernardi*	700 State St, Racine WI 53403		S	58*	.1
57	Power Motive Corp—*Bill Blount*	5000 Vasquez Blvd, Denver CO 80216	303-355-5900	R	55*	.1
58	Lynn Ladder And Scaffolding Company Inc—*Alan Kline*	PO Box 8096, Lynn MA 01904	781-598-6010	R	52*	.2
59	American Certified Equipment Inc—*Rick Roberts*	1650 Swan Lake Rd, Bossier City LA 71111	318-425-0266	R	50*	.1
60	VLP Holding Co—*Butch Teppe*	PO Box 4915, Kansas City MO 64120	816-241-9290	R	50*	.1
61	Doyle Equipment Co—*David M Smail*	20400 Rte 19 N, Cranberry Township PA 16066	724-776-3636	R	49*	<.1
62	TreeCon Resources Inc—*John Langford*	6004 US Hwy 59 S, Lufkin TX 75901	936-634-3365	P	47	.1
63	Monroe Tractor and Implement Company Inc—*Janet E Felosky*	1001 Lehigh Station Rd, Henrietta NY 14467	585-334-3867	R	47*	.1
64	J H Fletcher and Co—*Doug Hardman*	PO Box 2187, Huntington WV 25722	304-525-7811	R	47*	.2
65	Dom-Ex LLC	109 Grant St, Hibbing MN 55746	218-262-6116	R	45*	<.1
66	Power Equipment Co (Knoxville Tennessee)—*Chris Gaylor*	PO Box 2311, Knoxville TN 37901		S	41*	.2
67	Multiquip Inc—*Tom Yasuda*	PO Box 6254, Carson CA 90749	310-537-3700	R	41*	.7
68	Mine and Mill Supply Company Inc—*Wayne Hart*	2500 S Combee Rd, Lakeland FL 33801	863-665-5601	R	40*	<.1
69	Bandit Industries Inc—*Jerry Morey*	6750 W Millbrook Rd, Remus MI 49340	989-561-2270	R	37*	.2
70	Universal Fremont Packaging—*William Niggemyer*	325 E Stahl Rd, Fremont OH 43420	419-334-8741	R	36*	<.1
71	Mcclung-Logan Equipment Company Inc—*Thomas Logan*	4601 Washington Blvd A, Baltimore MD 21227	410-242-6500	R	33*	.1
72	Extech Building Materials Inc—*Timothy Feury*	87 Bowne St, Brooklyn NY 11231	718-852-7090	R	31*	.2
73	Hub Construction Specialties Inc—*Robert Gogo*	PO Box 1269, San Bernardino CA 92402	909-889-0161	R	30*	.1
74	Eagle Power And Equipment Corp—*Gerald Mcdonald*	PO Box 425, Montgomeryville PA 18936	215-699-5871	R	29*	.1
75	Linder Industrial Machinery Co—*Jeffrey Cox*	PO Box 4589, Plant City FL 33563	813-754-2727	R	29*	.5
76	CL Boyd Company Inc—*Robert H Crews*	PO Box 26427, Oklahoma City OK 73126	405-942-8000	R	28*	.1
77	Sokkia Corp	16900 W 118th Ter, Olathe KS 66061	913-492-4900	S	27*	.1
78	Bobcat of Atlanta—*Jess Huneven*	6972 Best Friend Rd, Atlanta GA 30340	770-242-6500	S	27*	<.1
79	Wall-Ties and Forms Inc—*Ross Worley*	4000 Bonner Industrial, Shawnee KS 66226	913-441-0073	R	26*	.2
80	Stephenson Equipment Inc—*Dennis Heller*	7201 Paxton St, Harrisburg PA 17111	717-564-3434	R	26*	.1
81	Formula Equipment Inc—*Steven Palundo*	PO Box 36, Rock Tavern NY 12575	845-567-1314	R	26*	<.1
82	Eastern Equipment Inc—*William Mcgee*	PO Box 220, Northford CT 06472	860-828-6371	R	24*	.1
83	North American Trade Corp—*Jorge Guiloff*	13901 HWY 105 W, Conroe TX 77304	936-588-1010	R	24*	<.1
84	Balzer Pacific Equipment Co—*Michael B Allen*	2136 SE 8th Ave, Portland OR 97214	503-232-5141	R	23*	.1
85	Npk Construction Equipment Inc—*Dan Tyrell*	7550 Independence Dr, Bedford OH 44146	440-232-7900	R	22*	.1
86	OCT Equipment Inc—*Dale Vaughn*	7100 SW 3rd Ave, Oklahoma City OK 73128	405-789-6812	R	22*	.1
87	Southwestern Suppliers Inc—*Martin Koch*	6815 E 14th Ave, Tampa FL 33619		R	22*	.1
88	Twin City Tractor and Equipment Inc	7200 Landers Rd, North Little Rock AR 72117	501-834-9999	R	22*	.1
89	RDO Equipment Co Minnesota Construction Equipment Div—*Matt Dull*	12500 Dupont Ave S, Burnsville MN 55337	952-890-8880	D	22*	<.1
90	Aring Equipment Company Inc—*James Hock*	PO Box 912, Butler WI 53007	262-781-3770	R	20*	.1
91	West Side Tractor Sales Inc—*Steven Benck*	1400 W Ogden Ave, Naperville IL 60563	630-355-7150	R	20*	.1
92	Pacific American Commercial Co—*Brian Waller*	PO Box 3742, Seattle WA 98124	206-762-3550	R	20*	.1
93	Russell Knickerbocker Company Inc—*Russell Keith*	4759 Campbells Run Rd, Pittsburgh PA 15205	412-494-9233	R	20*	<.1
94	Air Cooled Engines—*Kenneth Stanglin*	2324 Evanston Ave, Dallas TX 75208	214-748-0050	R	20*	<.1
95	Form Services Inc—*Joseph Papparotto*	PO Box 60, Linthicum Heights MD 21090	410-247-9500	R	20*	.1
96	Jack's Truck And Equipment—*Gary Chafee*	PO Box 1628, Gillette WY 82717	307-686-0608	R	19*	.1
97	McAllister Equipment Co—*Jack L Moser*	12500 S Cicero Ave, Alsip IL 60803	708-389-7700	R	19*	.1
98	Hoffman International Inc—*Tim Watters*	300 S Randolphville Rd, Piscataway NJ 08855	732-752-3600	R	19*	.1

Rank	Company Name—*Executive Officer*	Address, City, State, Zip	Phone	Type	Fin	Empls
99	Powerscreen Mid-Atlantic Inc—*Andrew Coney*	PO Box 2505, Kernersville NC 27285	336-992-9755	R	19*	<.1
100	Birch Equipment Company Inc—*Sarah Rothenbuhler*	PO Box 30918, Bellingham WA 98228	360-734-5744	R	19*	.1
101	Coast Crane Company Of Washington Inc—*Dan Goodell*	8250 5th Ave S, Seattle WA 98108	206-622-1151	R	19*	.1
102	W I Clark Co—*Gordon Clark*	PO Box 300, Wallingford CT 06492	203-265-6781	R	18*	.1
103	Texas Contractors Supply Co—*Jim Bilderback*	PO Box 2455, Fort Worth TX 76113	817-332-4117	R	18*	.1
104	James W Bell Company Inc—*John Bell*	PO Box 727, Cedar Rapids IA 52406	319-362-1151	R	18*	.1
105	Export Oil Field Supply Company Inc—*Edward Carney*	3350 Bingle Rd, Houston TX 77055	713-939-1200	R	18*	<.1
106	Steves Equipment Service Inc—*Steve Martines*	1400 Powis Rd, West Chicago IL 60185	630-231-4840	R	17*	.1
107	Diesel Machinery Inc—*Dan Healy*	PO Box 85825, Sioux Falls SD 57118	605-336-0411	R	17*	.1
108	RB Everett and Co—*J Farrel Henderson*	PO Box 7300, Pasadena TX 77508	281-991-8161	R	17*	<.1
109	Scott Van Keppel LLC—*Joe Spreitzer*	PO Box 1288, Cedar Rapids IA 52404	319-365-9155	R	17*	.1
110	Mississippi Valley Equipment Co—*Harry Fry*	1198 Pershall Rd, Saint Louis MO 63137	314-388-2254	R	17*	.1
111	Wrench Limited Co—*Gary Gleckler*	4805 Scooby Ln, Carroll OH 43112	740-654-5304	R	17*	.1
112	Leppo Eqjipment Inc—*Glenn Leppo*	176 West Ave, Tallmadge OH 44278	330-633-3999	R	15*	.1
113	Jasper Engineering and Equipment Company Inc—*Tom Jamar*	3800 5th Ave W Ste 1, Hibbing MN 55746	218-262-3421	R	15*	<.1
114	Ben Meadows Company Inc	PO Box 5277, Janesville WI 53547		S	15*	<.1
115	Joe Money Machinery Co—*Charles S Money*	PO Box 997, Birmingham AL 35201	205-841-7000	R	15*	<.1
116	Malvese Equipment Company Inc—*Albert Cooley*	1 Henrietta St, Hicksville NY 11801	516-681-7600	R	15*	.1
117	Crawler Supply Company Inc—*Danny Cloy*	PO Box 52729, Baton Rouge LA 70892	225-357-7515	R	15*	.1
118	Psi Sales Inc—*Van Woodham*	PO Box 488, Theodore AL 36590	251-957-2114	R	15*	.1
119	Miller Sales and Engineering Inc—*Bruce Greene*	3801 N Hwy Dr, Tucson AZ 85705	520-888-4101	R	14*	.1
120	MRL Equipment Company Inc—*John Gonitzke*	PO Box 31154, Billings MT 59107	406-869-9900	R	14*	.1
121	National Capital Industries Inc—*Andrew Kramer*	PO Box 287, Bladensburg MD 20710	301-864-4150	R	14*	<.1
122	Cavotec USA Inc—*Stefan Widegren*	124 Hatfield Rd, Statesville NC 28625	704-873-3009	R	14*	<.1
123	Richmond Machinery And Equipment Company Inc—*Michael Colley*	PO Box 6588, Richmond VA 23230	804-359-4048	R	14*	<.1
124	Cogar Manufacturing Inc—*Lowell Cogar*	PO Box 532, Beckley WV 25802	304-252-4435	R	13*	.1
125	Croushorn Equipment Company Inc	101 Sunshine Pk, Harlan KY 40831	606-573-2454	R	13*	<.1
126	John Sakash Company Inc—*John Sakash*	PO Box 210, Elmhurst IL 60126	630-833-3940	R	12*	.1
127	Herman Grant Company Inc—*Paula Shuford*	PO Box 15006, Chattanooga TN 37415	423-266-6138	R	12*	.1
128	US Municipal Supply Inc—*Paul Statler*	PO Box 574, Huntingdon PA 16652	814-627-4671	R	11*	.1
129	H and R Construction Parts and Equipment Inc—*Stephen Hansen*	20 Milburn St, Buffalo NY 14212	716-891-4311	R	11*	.1
130	Anderson Machinery Company Inc—*Hudson Anderson*	PO Box 4806, Corpus Christi TX 78469	361-289-6043	R	11*	<.1
131	Sequoia Equipment Company Inc—*Dennis Monahan*	PO Box 2747, Fresno CA 93745	559-441-1122	R	11*	<.1
132	Brandeis Machinery and Supply Corp—*Charles Leis*	1801 Watterson Trail, Louisville KY 40299	502-491-4000	S	11*	.1
133	D A F Inc—*Daniel Falatok*	121 John Dodd Rd, Spartanburg SC 29303	864-578-9335	R	11*	.1
134	Snead Agricultural Supply and Services Inc—*Steve Clowdus*	PO Box 548, Snead AL 35952	205-466-7163	R	11*	<.1
135	JC Smith Inc—*Josephine Smith*	345 Peat St, Syracuse NY 13210	315-428-9903	R	11*	.1
136	Milan Supply Co—*John Gall*	PO Box 309, Mount Pleasant MI 48804	989-773-9938	R	10*	.1
137	Oliver Stores Inc—*Alan MacLean*	21 Freedom Park, Hermon ME 04401	207-848-7840	R	10*	<.1
138	Triangle Equipment Company Inc—*Barbara Mangum*	PO Box 91327, Raleigh NC 27675	919-781-7910	R	10*	<.1
139	Liebherr Construction Equipment Co—*Duane Wilder* Liebherr-America Inc	4100 Chestnut Ave, Newport News VA 23605	757-245-5251	S	10*	<.1
140	MD Moody and Sons Inc—*Maxey Moody*	PO Box 5350, Jacksonville FL 32247	904-737-4401	R	10*	<.1
141	Roofmaster Inc—*James Yundt*	PO Box 63309, Los Angeles CA 90063	323-261-5122	R	9*	<.1
142	Mccoy Investments Inc—*Brian Mccoy*	2717 Tobey Dr, Indianapolis IN 46219	317-545-0665	R	9*	<.1
143	Wireline Technologies Inc—*Alan Carmichael*	PO Box 1535, Spring TX 77383	281-209-9111	R	9*	<.1
144	Scott Equipment Inc—*Richard Scott*	14635 Valley Blvd, Fontana CA 92335	909-822-2200	R	9*	<.1
145	MJ Allen Inc—*Jay Allen*	819 S 5th St, Paragould AR 72450	870-239-6066	R	9*	.1
146	Solar Thin Films Inc—*Robert Rubin*	116 John St Ste 1120, New York NY 10038	609-288-7586	P	9	<.1
147	Advanced Specialty Products—*Kenneth Kujawa*	PO Box 210, Bowling Green OH 43402	419-354-2844	R	8*	<.1
148	For-Shor Co—*James Snarr*	4446 W 1730 S, Salt Lake City UT 84104	801-487-1656	R	8*	<.1
149	Reckart Equipment Co—*Darrell Reckart*	PO Box 216, Beverly WV 26253	304-338-4300	R	8*	<.1
150	GAR International Corp—*George McKinney*	15712 SW 41st St Ste 8, Davie FL 33331	954-306-4800	R	8*	<.1
151	Dean Machinery International Inc—*Walter Dean*	6855 Shiloh Rd E, Alpharetta GA 30005	678-947-8550	R	8*	<.1
152	Advance Equipment Co—*Terry Haug*	1400 Jackson St, Saint Paul MN 55117	651-489-8881	R	8*	<.1
153	Erb Equipment Company Of Illinois Inc—*Stanley Erb*	PO Box 8124, Mitchell IL 62040	618-931-1034	R	8*	<.1
154	Ballantine Inc—*Joe Newfield*	840 Mckinley St, Anoka MN 55303	763-427-3959	R	8*	<.1
155	California Service Tool Inc—*Bob Larue*	26250 Corporate Ave St, Hayward CA 94545	510-782-1000	R	8*	<.1
156	Tro-Cal Inc—*Bill Calhoun*	PO Box 70, Tomahawk KY 41262	606-298-7707	R	8*	<.1
157	Tuffi Products Inc—*Edward Shidler*	526 E 64th St, Holland MI 49423	616-392-7207	R	7*	.1
158	Guyan Machinery Company Inc—*Todd Meloy*	PO Box 1270, Chapmanville WV 25508	304-855-8021	R	7*	<.1
159	Aluminum Plus—*Sahi Melamed*	16200 Ventura Blvd, Encino CA 91436	818-783-3155	R	7*	<.1
160	Endeavor Homes Inc—*Del Fleener*	PO Box 1947, Oroville CA 95965	530-534-0300	R	7*	<.1
161	Holden Machine and Fabrication Inc—*Aaron Rice*	PO Box 678, Holden WV 25625	304-239-6302	R	7*	<.1
162	Lincoln Manufacturing Inc—*Jason Piatt*	198 Meadowlands Blvd, Washington PA 15301	724-222-2700	R	7*	<.1
163	Hollerbach Equipment Company Inc—*Thomas Hollerbach*	8414 Washington Blvd, Jessup MD 20794	410-792-0683	R	7*	<.1
164	Pyramid Tubular Products LP—*Ted Bigelow*	2 Northpoint Dr Ste 61, Houston TX 77060	281-405-8090	R	6*	<.1
165	Loader Services and Equipment Inc—*John Howland*	319 Bearden Rd, Pelham AL 35124	205-320-1000	R	6*	<.1
166	American Contractors Equipment Co—*Jim Bolger*	PO Box 838, Indianola PA 15051	412-828-6960	R	6*	<.1
167	Masonry Equipment and Supply Co—*Del Lewis*	295 S Redwood Rd, North Salt Lake UT 84054	801-936-3890	R	5*	<.1
168	Skyjack Corp—*Wolfgang Haessler*	3451 Swenson Ave, Saint Charles IL 60174	630-262-0005	R	5*	<.1
169	Hunting Oilfield Services—*Frank Jarvaux*	113 Capitol Blvd, Houma LA 70360	985-876-4368	R	5*	<.1
170	R W Thompson Company Inc—*Jonathan Williams*	3311 Berlin Tpke, Newington CT 06111	860-666-3654	R	5*	<.1
171	Fontanesi And Kann Co—*Joseph Fontanesi*	13380 Capital St, Oak Park MI 48237	248-543-0095	R	5*	<.1
172	Cessco Inc—*Eric Schamp*	4222 Ne Columbia Blvd, Portland OR 97218	503-288-1242	R	5*	<.1
173	Ditch Witch Of Maryland Inc—*Lind Roter*	12975 Livestock Rd, Sykesville MD 21784	410-442-1510	R	5*	<.1
174	Cambria Tractor and Equipment Co—*Fred Fadden*	PO Box 149, Ebensburg PA 15931	814-472-7300	R	5*	<.1
175	Gibson Machinery LLC—*Ester Schechter*	181 Oak Leaf Oval, Cleveland OH 44146	440-439-4000	R	5*	<.1
176	Spokane Machinery Co—*James Peplinski*	PO Box 4306, Spokane WA 99220	509-535-1576	R	5*	<.1
177	Philipps Brothers Supply Inc—*Ferdinand Philipps*	2525 Kensington Ave, Buffalo NY 14226	716-839-4800	R	5*	<.1
178	Lanford Equipment Company Inc—*R Lanford*	900 Ed Bluestein Blvd, Austin TX 78721	512-385-2800	R	5*	<.1
179	Terry L Marion—*Terry Marion*	PO Box 717, Dunseith ND 58329	701-244-5351	R	5*	<.1
180	Moxy Trucks Of America LLC	2905 Shawnee Industria, Suwanee GA 30024	770-831-2200	R	4*	<.1
181	Lake Beaver Transport Inc—*Bob May*	2496 W Hudson Rd, Rogers AR 72756	479-636-1348	R	4*	<.1
182	Dozier Crane and Machinery Inc—*Dozier Cook*	PO Box 1137, Pooler GA 31322	912-748-2684	R	4*	<.1
183	So Cal Tractor Sales Company Inc—*James Utz*	8655 Tamarack Ave, Sun Valley CA 91352	818-252-1900	R	4*	<.1
184	Ransome Engine Inc—*Wayne Brownly*	720 Pulaski Hwy, Bear DE 19701	302-328-8261	R	4*	<.1
185	B and B Sooner Inc—*Tracy Rogers*	PO Box 2410, Farmington NM 87499	505-324-0222	R	4*	<.1

Note: An asterisk (*) indicates an estimated financial figure. The company type code used is as follows: R = Private, P = Public, S = Private Subsidiary, B = Public Subsidiary, D = Division, J = Joint Venture, I = Investment Fund.

COMPANY RANKINGS BY SALES WITHIN 4-DIGIT SIC

Rank	Company Name—*Executive Officer*	Address, City, State, Zip	Phone	Type	Fin	Empls
186	Tri Steel Inc—*Ronald Hall*	8209 Cardinal Ln, Fort Worth TX 76182	817-577-3588	R	4*	<.1
187	Tsk Holdings LLC—*Niel Anderson*	765 York St, Elizabeth NJ 07201	908-527-1211	R	4*	<.1
188	River Falls Machinery Sales Inc—*Joel Pate*	PO Box 225, River Falls AL 36476	334-427-3039	R	4*	<.1
189	Diamond Discs International LLC—*Gary Damaste*	8530 W National Ave, Milwaukee WI 53227	414-543-4545	R	4*	<.1
190	Emeco USA—*Bruce Kah*	4885 Olde Towne Pkwy S, Marietta GA 30068	770-321-2601	R	4*	<.1
191	Baker and Sons Equipment Company Inc—*James Baker*	45381 State Rte 145, Lewisville OH 43754	740-567-3317	R	4*	<.1
192	Ditch Witch Iowa Inc—*Jeffery Chlupach*	1000 W Sixth Ave, Slater IA 50244	515-685-3521	R	4*	<.1
193	Stevenson Tractor Inc—*William Stevenson*	1792 S Military Hwy, Chesapeake VA 23320	757-420-4220	R	4*	<.1
194	Kern County Tractor Parts Inc—*Randy Roelofsen*	29527 Pond Rd, Mc Farland CA 93250	661-792-2188	R	4*	<.1
195	Tramac Corp—*Denis Bataille*	26 Eastmans Rd, Parsippany NJ 07054	973-887-7700	R	4*	<.1
196	B and W Equipment Company Inc—*Paul Gick*	5810 Moeller Rd, Fort Wayne IN 46806	260-422-0945	R	4*	<.1
197	Tri State Machinery Co—*Don Shilling*	13400 Bryant Ave S, Burnsville MN 55337	952-224-1500	R	3*	<.1
198	Wood Masonry Supply Inc—*Buddy Wood*	633 E King St, Boone NC 28607	828-264-2109	R	3*	<.1
199	Badger Ladder Inc—*Brian Michaud*	2040 S Ashland Ave, Green Bay WI 54304	920-429-0308	R	3*	<.1
200	Construction and Marine Equipment Company Inc—*John Dengel*	330 S Front St, Elizabeth NJ 07202	908-820-9500	R	3*	<.1
201	Gulf Coast International LLC—*Jennifer Angelle*	7608 Hwy 90 W, New Iberia LA 70560	337-365-0459	R	3*	<.1
202	Napo Associates Inc—*Mike Nasti*	180 Townline Rd, Kings Park NY 11754	631-368-4788	R	3*	<.1
203	Holt Equipment Company Inc—*Ben Holt*	3279 Lexington Rd, Richmond KY 40475	859-623-2030	R	3*	<.1
204	Pelican Equipment Company Inc—*Edward Parker*	1055 Ponce De Leon Blv, Clearwater FL 33756	727-581-1156	R	3*	<.1
205	Sharpco Inc—*James Sharplin*	8770 Frontage Rd, Monroe LA 71202	318-343-4328	R	3*	<.1
206	NC Mach C0 E Wenatchee—*John Harnish*	5535 Baker Flats Rd, East Wenatchee WA 98802	509-886-5561	R	3*	<.1
207	Virgil Geary—*Virgil Geary*	2431 Fm 1781, Rockport TX 78382	361-463-6137	R	2*	<.1
208	Pitts Engine And Transmission Inc—*Mike Pitts*	PO Box 668407, Miami FL 33166	305-592-6540	R	2*	<.1
209	Northwest Manufacturing and Distribution Inc—*Timothy King*	2050 Main St, Billings MT 59105	406-259-9525	R	2*	<.1
210	ALAC Contracting Corp—*Anthony Carpiniello*	421 Broadway, West Babylon NY 11704	631-422-3870	R	2*	<.1
211	Byles Welding And Tractor Company Inc—*Clauriste Byles*	PO Box 970, Many LA 71449	318-256-9238	R	1*	<.1
212	Garlock-East Equipment Co—*Mark Hefty*	2601 Niagara Ln N, Minneapolis MN 55447	763-553-1935	R	1*	<.1
213	WB Thompson Company Inc—*Doug Thompson*	137 N Hooper St, Kingsford MI 49802	906-774-6543	R	1*	<.1
214	Pfw Industries Corp—*Bradford Wyatt*	18 Grafton St Fl 4, Worcester MA 01604	508-798-8546	R	<1*	<.1
215	Vermeer Mid Atlantic Inc—*David Hahn*	10900 Carpet St, Charlotte NC 28273	704-588-3238	R	N/A	.1

TOTALS: SIC 5082 Construction & Mining Machinery
Companies: 215

					19,303	35.9

5083 Farm & Garden Machinery

Rank	Company Name—*Executive Officer*	Address, City, State, Zip	Phone	Type	Fin	Empls
1	Gea Westfalia Separator Inc—*Michael Vick*	PO Box 178, Northvale NJ 07647	201-767-3900	R	3,819*	.5
2	Gea Farm Technologies Inc—*Dirk Hejnal* Gea Westfalia Separator Inc	1880 Country Farm Dr, Naperville IL 60563	630-369-8100	S	2,335*	.3
3	RDO Agriculture Equipment Co—*Ronald D Offutt* RDO Equipment Co	PO Box 2445, Pasco WA 99301	509-547-0541	S	1,422*	•1.6
4	Titan Machinery—*David Meyer*	644 E Beaton Dr, West Fargo ND 58078	701-356-0130	P	1,095	1.9
5	RDO Equipment Co—*Ronald D Offutt*	PO Box 7160, Fargo ND 58103	701-239-8735	R	723*	1.6
6	Scott Truck and Tractor Company Inc—*Scott Cumming*	PO Box 4948, Monroe LA 71211		R	450*	1.0
7	Pantropic Power Products Inc	8205 NW 58th St, Miami FL 33166	305-592-4944	R	367*	.2
8	Husqvarna Professional Products Inc—*Rashad Abdulllah*	9335 Harris Corners Pk, Charlotte NC 28269	704-597-5000	H	330*	.1
9	Sloan Implement Company Inc—*Tom Sloan*	120 N Business 51, Assumption IL 62510	217-226-4411	R	187*	.3
10	Rotary Corp—*Edward Nelson*	801 W Barnard St, Glennville GA 30427	912-654-3433	R	156*	.4
11	Liechty Farm Equipment Inc—*Gene Roth*	PO Box 67, Archbold OH 43502	419-445-1565	R	135*	.1
12	Hector Turf—*Jim Mantey*	1301 NW 3rd St, Deerfield Beach FL 33442	954-429-3200	R	116*	.1
13	Northfield Tractor and Equipment Inc—*Gregory Langer*	32980 Northfield Blvd, Northfield MN 55057	507-645-4886	R	110*	.1
14	Mclean Implement Inc—*Robert Mason*	Rr Ste 4 Box 100, Albion IL 62806	618-445-3676	R	98*	<.1
15	Bucklin Tractor and Implement—*Letty Bachelor*	PO Box 127, Bucklin KS 67834	620-826-3271	R	80*	.1
16	Kubota Tractor Corp—*Satoshi Iida*	3401 Del Amo Blvd, Torrance CA 90503	310-370-3370	S	79*	.4
17	Barbee-Neuhaus Implement Co—*Earl Neuhaus*	PO Box 386, Weslaco TX 78596	956-968-7502	R	72*	.1
18	Wilbanks International Inc—*John Coors*	555 Ne 53rd Ave, Hillsboro OR 97124	503-615-0926	R	72*	1.4
19	Grossenburg Implement Inc—*Barry Grossenburg*	31341 US Hwy 18, Winner SD 57580	605-842-2040	R	71*	.1
20	Garton Tractor Inc—*Bill Garton*	PO Box 1849, Turlock CA 95381	209-632-3931	R	67*	.2
21	Straub International Inc—*Larry Straub*	PO Box 1606, Great Bend KS 67530	620-792-5256	R	65*	.1
22	Grassland Equipment And Irrigation Corp—*Kirk Pogge*	892 Troy Schenectady Rd, Latham NY 12110	518-785-5841	R	65*	.1
23	Baker Implement Co—*Paul T Combs*	915 Homecrest St, Kennett MO 63857	573-888-4646	R	63*	.1
24	Glade and Grove Supply Inc—*George Cooper*	PO Drawer 760, Belle Glade FL 33430	561-996-3095	R	59*	.1
25	Berchtold Equipment Company Inc—*Mark Berchtold*	PO Box 3098, Bakersfield CA 93385	661-323-7817	R	59*	.1
26	Hamilton Equipment Inc—*Robert Hamilton*	PO Box 478, Ephrata PA 17522	717-733-7951	R	55*	.1
27	Jamestown Implement Inc—*Roger Nelson*	PO Box 1958, Jamestown ND 58401	701-252-0580	R	53*	.1
28	Sunshine Equipment Inc—*Kenneth Rodrigue*	PO Box 429, Donaldsonville LA 70346	225-473-9609	R	50*	.1
29	Arizona Machinery Group Inc—*Ferenc Rosztoczy*	11111 W Mcdowell Rd, Avondale AZ 85392	623-936-7131	R	49*	.3
30	Finch Services Inc—*Rey Finch*	1127 Littlestown Pke, Westminster MD 21157	410-876-2211	R	49*	.2
31	Tru-Part Manufacturing Corp—*Fred Korndorf*	7800 3rd St N Ste 1000, Oakdale MN 55128	651-455-6681	R	45*	.1
32	Phelps Implement Corp—*Larry Phelps*	1502 G Ave, Grundy Center IA 50638	319-824-5247	R	39*	.1
33	Weaks Martin Implement Co—*John Morris*	PO Box 910, Mission TX 78573	956-585-1618	R	39*	.1
34	Dixie Sales Company Inc—*Harold Reiter*	5920 Summit Ave, Browns Summit NC 27214	336-375-7500	R	38*	.2
35	Implement Sales LLC—*Mitch Elkins*	1574 Stone Ridge Dr, Stone Mountain GA 30083	770-908-9439	S	36*	<.1
36	Williams Tractor Inc—*Doug Williams*	PO Box 1346, Fayetteville AR 72702	479-442-8284	R	36*	.1
37	Spartan Distributors Inc—*Dawn Johnson*	487 W Division St, Sparta MI 49345	616-887-7301	R	35*	.1
38	Stull Enterprises Inc—*Rodman W Smith*	201 Windsor Rd, Pottstown PA 19464	610-495-7441	R	32*	.1
39	Hopf Equipment Inc—*Charles Hopf*	506 E 19th St, Huntingburg IN 47542	812-683-2763	R	32*	<.1
40	Gardner Inc	3641 Interchange Rd, Columbus OH 43204	614-456-4000	R	31*	.1
41	Brakke Implements Inc—*Jeff Brakke*	17551 Killdeer Ave, Mason City IA 50401	641-423-2412	R	30*	<.1
42	M M Weaver And Sons Inc—*Ervin Weaver*	169 N Groffdale Rd, Leola PA 17540	717-656-2321	R	30*	<.1
43	Kenney Machinery Corp—*Mike Kenney*	8420 Zionsville Rd, Indianapolis IN 46268		R	29*	<.1
44	Advanced Systems Technology—*Jim Stubbs*	PO Box 1607, Huntsville AL 35807	256-721-9090	R	29*	<.1
45	Jacobi Sales Inc—*Brian Jacobi*	PO Box 67, Palmyra IN 47164	812-364-6141	R	28*	.1
46	Hayward Distributing Co—*Ronald Monroe*	4061 Perimeter Dr, Columbus OH 43228	614-272-5953	R	27*	<.1
47	Mountain View Equipment Company Inc—*Tom Nicholson*	PO Box 690, Meridian ID 83680	208-888-1593	R	27*	.1
48	Kayton International Inc—*Roger Turnus*	2630 State Hwy 14, Albion NE 68620	402-395-2181	R	27*	.1
49	John Day Co—*John D Fonda*	POBox 3541, Omaha NE 68103	402-455-8000	R	26*	.1
50	Nelson-Jameson Inc—*John Nelson*	PO Box 647, Marshfield WI 54449	715-387-1151	R	26*	.1
51	Abilene Machine Inc—*Randy Roelofsen*	PO Box 129, Abilene KS 67410	785-655-9455	R	25*	.1
52	Arends Brothers Inc—*Kent Arends*	Highway 54 N, Melvin IL 60952	217-388-7717	R	25*	.1
53	Schmidt Machine Co—*Randy Schmidt*	7013 State Hwy 199, Upper Sandusky OH 43351	419-294-3814	R	25*	<.1

Rank	Company Name—*Executive Officer*	Address, City, State, Zip	Phone	Type	Fin	Empls
54	Sioux Automation Center Inc—*Ron Hulshof*	877 1st Ave Nw, Sioux Center IA 51250	712-722-1488	R	24*	.1
55	Washington County Tractor Inc—*Carol Jensen*	PO Box 1619, Brenham TX 77834	979-836-4591	R	22*	.1
56	Longhorn Inc—*Loyd Evans*	PO Box 59929, Dallas TX 75229	972-406-0222	R	22*	.1
57	Rain Cal-West Inc—*Jim Martin*	PO Box 306, Kerman CA 93630	559-846-5326	R	20*	.1
58	Vucovich Inc—*Steve Vucovich*	PO Box 2513, Fresno CA 93745	559-486-8020	R	19*	.1
59	Hood Equipment Company Inc—*Ken Hood*	PO Box 1596, Batesville MS 38606	662-563-4546	R	18*	<.1
60	Harold Implement Company Inc—*Paul Moore*	701 N Missouri, Corning AR 72422	870-857-3931	R	17*	<.1
61	N and S Tractor Co—*Arthur Nutcher*	PO Box 910, Merced CA 95341	209-383-5888	R	17*	.1
62	Plains Equipment Group—*Perry Case*	977 280th, Seward NE 68434	402-643-3616	R	17*	<.1
63	Pals Inc—*Richard Huisinga*	PO Box 753, Willmar MN 56201	320-235-8860	R	16*	.1
64	Valley Implement and Motor Company Inc—*Sid Titensor*	PO Box 195, Preston ID 83263	208-852-0430	R	16*	.1
65	Alma Tractor and Equipment Inc—*Jim Barker*	PO Box 2169, Alma AR 72921	479-632-6300	R	16*	<.1
66	Carl F Statz and Sons Inc—*Ron Statz*	6101 Hogan Rd, Waunakee WI 53597	608-849-4101	R	16*	<.1
67	Wade Inc—*W Litton*	PO Box 5487, Greenville MS 38704	662-332-8108	R	16*	<.1
68	Lake Norman Tractor Co—*Bob Cockerham*	18309 Stateville Rd, Cornelius NC 28031	704-892-6750	R	16*	<.1
69	Smiths South-Central Sales Co—*W Smith*	PO Box 578, Springhill LA 71075	318-539-2594	R	16*	<.1
70	American Implement Inc—*Duane Koster*	PO Box 855, Garden City KS 67846	620-275-4114	R	15*	.1
71	CPS Distributors Inc—*Larry Shandy*	1105 W 122nd Ave, Westminster CO 80234	303-394-6040	S	15*	.1
72	Fields Equipment Company Inc—*Charles E Fields Jr*	PO Box 113, Winter Haven FL 33882	863-967-0602	R	15*	.1
73	Rosenau Equipment Company Inc—*Gaylen Rosenau*	PO Box 300, Carrington ND 58421	701-652-3144	R	15*	<.1
74	Tesco South Inc—*James Mantey*	1301 Nw 3rd St, Deerfield Beach FL 33442	954-429-3200	R	15*	.1
75	U S Dairy Systems Inc—*Jerry Higley*	PO Box 170, Jerome ID 83338	208-324-3213	R	15*	.1
76	Southard Implement Co—*Larry Southard*	3006 S Ctr St, Marshalltown IA 50158	641-752-1527	R	14*	.1
77	Farmer Boy Ag Systems Inc—*Dale Martin*	PO Box 435, Myerstown PA 17067	717-866-7565	R	14*	.1
78	Lampson Tractor and Equipment Company Inc—*Allan Kelly*	27000 Asti Rd, Cloverdale CA 95425	707-857-3443	R	14*	<.1
79	Matejcek Implement Co—*Paul Matejcek*	3040 Hwy 60 W, Faribault MN 55021	507-334-2233	R	14*	.1
80	Tractor Place Inc—*Brian Mize*	PO Box 689, Knightdale NC 27545	919-266-5846	R	14*	.1
81	Greenline Service Corp—*Frank Hopkins*	PO Box 7208, Fredericksburg VA 22404	540-373-7520	R	14*	.1
82	Burks Tractor Company Inc—*Douglas Burks*	3140 Kimberly Rd, Twin Falls ID 83301	208-733-5543	R	14*	.1
83	Turf Equipment And Supply Company Inc—*William Hughes*	8015 Dorsey Run Rd Ste, Jessup MD 20794	410-799-5575	R	14*	.1
84	Troxel Equipment Company LLC—*Linda Reinhard*	5068 E 100 N, Bluffton IN 46714	260-565-3659	R	13*	.1
85	Kaye Corp—*Marlin Lloyd*	1910 Lookout Dr, North Mankato MN 56003	507-625-5293	R	13*	<.1
86	Schenkelberg Implement Co—*Gary Schenkelberg*	PO Box 306, Carroll IA 51401	712-792-1400	R	13*	.1
87	Marion Ford Tractor Inc—*Gary Lashley*	6953 Covington Hwy, Lithonia GA 30058	770-808-5500	R	13*	<.1
88	Holdrege Irrigation Inc—*Lamar Schmidt*	2011 4th Ave, Holdrege NE 68949	308-995-4000	R	12*	.1
89	Ernie Williams Ltd—*Ed Wilcox*	PO Box 737, Algona IA 50511	515-295-3561	R	12*	<.1
90	Mccormick International USA Inc—*Rodney Miller*	2590 Breckenridge Blvd, Duluth GA 30096	678-924-9885	R	11*	.1
91	W P Law Inc—*Thomas Plumblee*	303 Riverchase Way, Lexington SC 29072	803-461-0599	R	11*	.1
92	Puck Implement Co—*Warren Puck*	402 6th St, Manning IA 51455	712-653-2594	R	11*	<.1
93	Dodge City Implement Inc—*Dan Cammack*	PO Box 139, Dodge City KS 67801	620-227-2165	R	11*	<.1
94	Fry Equipment Company Inc—*Robert Fry*	PO Box 367, Piggott AR 72454	870-598-3848	R	11*	<.1
95	Con-Wal Inc—*Julie Hines*	PO Box 1257, Rogers AR 72757	479-636-6943	R	11*	.1
96	Castongia's Inc—*Jon P Castongia*	PO Box 157, Rensselaer IN 47978	219-866-5117	R	11	<.1
97	Cook Tractor Company Inc—*Ronald Cook*	PO Box 38, Clinton MO 64735	660-885-2287	R	10*	<.1
98	A and B Packing Equipment Inc—*Robert Williamson*	67602 62nd St, Hartford MI 49057	269-621-3837	R	10*	.1
99	Gruett's Inc—*Steve Gruett*	PO Box 52, Potter WI 54160	920-853-3516	R	10*	<.1
100	Mies Equipment Inc—*Steve Mies*	PO Box 436, Watkins MN 55389	320-764-5310	R	10*	.1
101	Melrose Supply and Sales Corp—*Dominic Pagano*	271 E Oakland Park Blv, Oakland Park FL 33334	954-563-1303	R	10*	<.1
102	Hillsboro Equipment Inc—*Donald Slama*	PO Box 583, Hillsboro WI 54634	608-489-2275	R	10*	<.1
103	Fred Haar Company Inc—*Robert Haar*	PO Box 796, Yankton SD 57078	605-665-3762	R	10*	<.1
104	D and D Equipment Company Inc—*Stephen Dvorak*	PO Box 31, Chilton WI 53014	920-849-9304	R	10*	<.1
105	Srw Products Inc—*David Orton*	PO Box 70, Princeton MN 55371	763-389-2722	R	10*	<.1
106	Steven Willand Inc—*Scott Willand*	PO Box 9, Augusta NJ 07822	973-579-5656	R	10*	<.1
107	Interstate Service Of Fergus Fls—*Leland Rogness*	I 94 County Rd 1, Fergus Falls MN 56537	218-739-3284	R	10*	<.1
108	J J Nichting Company Inc—*Sylvan Nichting*	PO Box 14, Pilot Grove IA 52648	319-469-4461	R	9*	<.1
109	Lakeside Systems Inc—*Tim Honigschmidt*	PO Box 516, Menasha WI 54952	920-898-5702	R	9*	<.1
110	Planters Equipment Company Inc—*J Gibbs*	PO Box 309, Cleveland MS 38732	662-843-2741	R	9*	<.1
111	Agri-Lines Irrigation Inc—*Harry Bingham*	PO Box 660, Parma ID 83660	208-722-5121	R	9*	<.1
112	Billiou's—*John Billiou*	1343 S Main St, Porterville CA 93257	559-784-4102	R	9*	<.1
113	Air Bozeman Rental LLP—*Lowell Anderson*	115 Mt Hwy 221, Choteau MT 59422	406-466-5741	R	9*	.1
114	Fortier and Fortier Inc—*Paul Fortier*	PO Box 592, Reedley CA 93654	559-638-3583	R	9*	<.1
115	W B Young Company Inc—*Karl Caldwell*	PO Box 400, Marshall MO 65340	660-886-7427	R	8*	.1
116	Plains Power and Equip Inc—*Perry Case*	3221 N Lincoln Ave, York NE 68467	402-362-6607	R	8*	.1
117	Empire Stone Co—*Kevin Spencer*	63265 Jamison St, Bend OR 97701	541-617-9711	R	8*	.1
118	WN Cooper And Son Inc—*William Cooper*	621 Morgnec Rd, Chestertown MD 21620	410-778-3464	R	8*	<.1
119	Ken Griffin Landscaping Contractors Inc—*Ken Griffin*	3004 Westfield Rd, Gulf Breeze FL 32563	850-932-9304	R	8*	<.1
120	Stettler Supply Co—*William Martinak*	1810 Lana Ave Ne, Salem OR 97301	503-585-5550	R	8*	<.1
121	John Schmidt and Sons Inc—*Leroy Schmidt*	12903 E Silver Lake Rd, Mount Hope KS 67108	316-445-2103	R	8*	<.1
122	Chula Farmers Coop—*Zane Jones*	PO Box 10, Chula MO 64635	660-639-3125	R	8*	<.1
123	Kes Science and Technology—*John Hayman*	3625 Kennesaw N Indust, Kennesaw GA 30144	770-427-6500	R	8*	<.1
124	Horvick Inc—*Tim Pederson*	4350 48th Ave N, Fargo ND 58102	701-280-2862	R	8*	<.1
125	Automatic Irrigation Supply Company Indiana Inc—*Steven Christie*	116 Shadowlawn Dr, Fishers IN 46038	317-842-3123	R	7*	<.1
126	Oliver M Dean Inc—*Richard Eldon*	125 Brooks St, Worcester MA 01606	508-856-9100	R	7*	<.1
127	Tru-Power Inc—*Chester Pinto*	22520 Temescal Canyon, Corona CA 92883	951-277-3180	R	7*	<.1
128	R-J Intn'l Inc—*J Joseph*	PO Box 894, Greenville MS 38702	662-335-5822	R	7*	<.1
129	A and M Farm Center Inc—*Lou Abbett*	300 S State Rd 49, Valparaiso IN 46383	219-464-8640	R	7*	<.1
130	Red River Implement Company Inc—*Ronald Offutt*	905 Buffalo Ave, Breckenridge MN 56520	218-643-2601	R	7*	<.1
131	Diversified Imports Division Co—*Henry Stern*	556 Industrial Way W S, Eatontown NJ 07724	732-363-2333	R	7*	<.1
132	Magic City Implement Inc—*Leann Zablotney*	PO Box 105, Minot ND 58702	701-838-8884	R	7*	<.1
133	Nelson Tractor And Equipment Of Sikeston Inc—*Mike Nelson*	101 County Line Rd, Sikeston MO 63801	573-471-2531	R	7*	<.1
134	Triebold Implement Inc—*Mark Triebold*	PO Box 266, Whitewater WI 53190	262-473-2090	R	7*	<.1
135	Hance Distributing Inc—*Thomas Hance*	1 Loring Rd, Hopkins MN 55305	952-935-6429	R	7*	.1
136	M and S Equipment Inc—*Thomas Scott*	PO Box 2119, Coolidge AZ 85128	520-723-4181	R	7*	<.1
137	Porter Henderson Implement Co—*Joe Henderson*	3993 Tractor Trl, San Angelo TX 76905	325-653-4541	R	7*	<.1
138	Greenway Equipment Inc—*Marshall Stewart*	PO Box 710, Kensett AR 72082	870-256-4121	R	6*	<.1
139	Braun Electric Inc—*Richard Braun*	PO Box 177, Saint Nazianz WI 54232	920-773-2143	R	6*	<.1
140	Stan Bonham Company Inc—*Brent Bonham*	PO Box 57246, Salt Lake City UT 84157	801-262-2574	R	6*	<.1
141	Taylor Forbes Equipment Company Inc—*Earl Carter*	PO Box 243, Farmville VA 23901	434-392-4139	R	6*	<.1
142	Ranchers Tractor Company Inc—*Jerry Dingeldein*	PO Box 660, Merced CA 95341	209-722-8031	R	6*	<.1

Note: An asterisk (*) indicates an estimated financial figure. The company type code used is as follows: R = Private, P = Public, S = Private Subsidiary, B = Public Subsidiary, D = Division, J = Joint Venture, I = Investment Fund.

COMPANY RANKINGS BY SALES WITHIN 4-DIGIT SIC

Rank	Company Name—*Executive Officer*	Address, City, State, Zip	Phone	Type	Fin	Empls
143	Mid-State Group Inc—*Curtis Hanson*	N8690 High Rd, Watertown WI 53094	920-261-8118	R	6*	<.1
144	Caprock Tractors Inc—*Brent Snodgrass*	2101 Lubbock Hwy, Lamesa TX 79331	806-872-5474	R	6*	<.1
145	Belarus Tractor International Inc—*Richard Schuelke*	7842 N Faulkner Rd, Milwaukee WI 53224	414-355-2000	R	6*	<.1
146	Arends Brothers LLC	PO Box 250, Ashmore IL 61912	217-349-8338	R	6*	<.1
147	Green Power Inc—*R Chambers*	725 Burlington Ave, Logansport IN 46947	574-753-7535	R	6*	<.1
148	R L Ryerson Company Inc—*John Eimerman*	N58w14500 Shawn Cir, Menomonee Falls WI 53051	262-252-2000	R	6*	<.1
149	Smarter Sprinklers Inc—*Wade Martinez*	9312 Louetta Rd, Spring TX 77379	281-894-5296	R	5*	<.1
150	Acme Systems Inc—*Thomas Laur*	6101 N Flint Rd, Milwaukee WI 53209	414-351-8866	R	5*	<.1
151	Tool Systems Inc—*Charles Post*	2220 Centre Park Ct, Stone Mountain GA 30087	770-879-3500	R	5*	<.1
152	Unkefer Homer Farm Equipment Company Inc—*Homer Unkefer*	PO Box 87, Minerva OH 44657	330-868-6419	R	5*	<.1
153	Jackson Truck Center Inc—*R Deviney*	1023 Deviney Dr, Raymond MS 39154	601-373-9531	R	5*	<.1
154	Twin Falls Tractor And Implement Co—*Gene Glenn*	1935 Kimberly Rd, Twin Falls ID 83301	208-733-8687	R	5*	<.1
155	Irrigators Inc—*Mel Updegrave*	PO Box 449, Moses Lake WA 98837	509-765-8861	R	5*	<.1
156	Aquatech Inc—*Dan Holliday*	210 Arden Dr, Belgrade MT 59714	406-388-3315	R	5*	<.1
157	Cahall Brothers Inc—*Calvin Cahall*	50 Cahall Brothers Ln, Georgetown OH 45121	937-378-6439	R	5*	<.1
158	Linco Equipment Inc—*James Pfab*	PO Box 37, El Paso IL 61738	309-527-6455	R	5*	<.1
159	Homestead Lawn and Tractor Co—*Neil Groothuis*	3529 Apd 40, Cleveland TN 37311	423-559-1958	R	5*	<.1
160	Umbergers Of Fontana Inc—*Donald Umberger*	1067 Horseshoe Pke, Lebanon PA 17042	717-867-5161	R	5*	<.1
161	Highlands Tractor Motorsports Inc—*Keith Coble*	227 N Main St, Highlands TX 77562	281-426-4216	R	5*	<.1
162	Winnsboro Specialty Parts International Inc—*Xerlene Alexander*	PO Box 28, Winnsboro TX 75494	903-342-3551	R	5*	<.1
163	London Farm Service Inc—*Troy Ingram*	PO Box 614, London KY 40743	606-864-2214	R	5*	<.1
164	San Joaquin Valley Dairy Equipment—*Steve Whitten*	14125 Costajo Rd, Bakersfield CA 93313	661-827-8494	R	5*	<.1
165	Normangee Tractor and Implement Company Inc—*Marion Stawnicz*	190 Hwy 39 S, Normangee TX 77871	936-396-3101	R	5*	<.1
166	Christiansen Implement Of Burley Inc—*H Christiansen*	119 N Overland Ave, Burley ID 83318	208-678-5585	R	5*	<.1
167	Joe's Refrigeration Inc—*Steve Frankewicz*	W5496 County Rd X, Withee WI 54498	715-229-2321	R	5*	<.1
168	Portland Implement Inc—*Brian Wang*	20 State Hwy 33, Cashton WI 54619	608-654-5575	R	5*	<.1
169	Midwest Farm Service Co—*William Pierce*	PO Box 485, Gering NE 69341	308-632-6137	R	5*	<.1
170	Burrows Tractor Inc—*William Kabrich*	1308 E Mead Ave, Union Gap WA 98903	509-457-8105	R	5*	<.1
171	Olsen Distributing Co—*Robert Olsen*	969 Pepper Rd, Barrington IL 60010	847-381-9333	R	4*	<.1
172	Bohn Implement Co—*Bill Bohn*	8508 Rogers Rd, Castalia OH 44824	419-684-7301	R	4*	<.1
173	Mast-Lepley Silo Inc—*Claire Nussbaum*	7787 E Lincoln Way, Apple Creek OH 44606	330-264-9292	R	4*	<.1
174	S and S Seeds Inc—*Victor Schaff*	PO Box 1275, Carpinteria CA 93014	805-684-0436	R	4*	<.1
175	Big Sky Irrigation Inc—*Thelma Hamby*	523 Roxy Ln, Billings MT 59105	406-252-8175	R	4*	<.1
176	Michigan Valley Irrigation Co—*Neal Krieger*	4802 Caro Rd, Vassar MI 48768	989-673-6741	R	4*	<.1
177	Darocha's Outdoor Power Equipment—*Frank Melone*	227 Plain St, Rehoboth MA 02769	508-252-3429	R	4*	<.1
178	Central Nebraska Implement Inc—*Dennis Bauer*	PO Box 149, Albion NE 68620	402-395-2173	R	4*	<.1
179	Erb and Roberts Inc—*Thomas Erb*	PO Box 140297, Gainesville FL 32614	352-376-4888	R	4*	<.1
180	Rickreall Farms Supply Inc—*John Hochstetler*	PO Box 67, Rickreall OR 97371	503-623-2365	R	4*	<.1
181	Horizon Equipment Inc—*Dean Habrock*	3607 S Belt Hwy, Saint Joseph MO 64503	816-364-1990	R	4*	<.1
182	Richmond Farm and Lawn Inc—*Gregg Steele*	PO Box 287, Richmond MO 64085	816-776-2261	R	4*	<.1
183	Countryside Nursery—*Joe Kupiloas*	23800 Ne Airport Rd, Aurora OR 97002	503-678-3248	R	4*	<.1
184	Lawson Cattle and Equipment Inc—*Marcus Lawson*	700 Dyer Blvd, Kissimmee FL 34741	407-348-4576	R	4*	<.1
185	Tulare Dairy Center Inc—*Tony Leal*	1873 S K St, Tulare CA 93274	559-688-3622	R	4*	<.1
186	Mainjoy Unlimited Inc—*J Melhorn*	608 W Main St, Mount Joy PA 17552	717-492-0123	R	4*	<.1
187	Fergus International Inc—*Darrell Gillespie*	2096 College Way, Fergus Falls MN 56537	218-736-5496	R	4*	<.1
188	Dittamore Implement Co—*Michael Dittamore*	PO Box 280, Teutopolis IL 62467	217-857-3193	R	4*	<.1
189	Tri-County Implement Inc—*Darrell Kuhn*	PO Box 1090, Lakin KS 67860	785-672-3272	R	4*	<.1
190	Rosy Brothers Inc—*Steven Roszczewski*	5727 Dryden Rd, Dryden MI 48428	810-796-3770	R	4*	<.1
191	South Florida New Holland Equipment Corp—*Jose Cardenal*	1995 Ne 8th St, Homestead FL 33033	305-247-1321	R	4*	<.1
192	Marion County Implement Company Inc—*Carolyn Andresen*	PO Box 507, Palmyra MO 63461	573-769-2112	R	3*	<.1
193	Steenhoek Implement Co—*Kendall Steenhoek*	1442 N Shore Dr, Knoxville IA 50138	641-842-4003	R	3*	<.1
194	Medlin Equipment Company Of Mississippi County Inc—*Don Medlin*	PO Box 506, Charleston MO 63834	573-683-2601	R	3*	<.1
195	Delongs Gizzard Supply Inc—*Pat Delong*	152 Garrison Rd, Macon GA 31211	478-743-9134	R	3*	<.1
196	Carlson Industries Inc—*Ed Carlson*	PO Box 290, San Bernardino CA 92402	909-799-5571	R	3*	<.1
197	Triple D Equipment Inc—*C Delong*	2820 Firehouse Rd, Deland FL 32720	386-734-2119	R	3*	<.1
198	Lyman Parts Depot Inc—*Les Lynan*	1261 Depot Ln, Walnut Grove CA 95690	916-776-0087	R	3*	<.1
199	Schoffman's Inc—*Patrick Schoffman*	PO Box 379, Redwood Falls MN 56283	507-637-2978	R	3*	<.1
200	Mid-Co Implement Inc—*Don Hommertzheim*	PO Box 865, Pratt KS 67124	620-672-5606	R	3*	<.1
201	Pivot Power Inc—*Donald Nix*	47063 104th St, Sioux Falls SD 57108	605-368-5301	R	3*	<.1
202	Thorstad Construction Company Inc—*Larry Bosch*	PO Box 275, Maynard MN 56260	320-367-2159	R	3*	<.1
203	Beidler's Implement Inc—*Margaret Beidler*	PO Box 1180, Maquoketa IA 52060	563-652-4936	R	3*	<.1
204	Nasby Agri Systems Co—*Chris Nasby*	PO Box 48, Fairmont MN 56031	507-235-9506	R	3*	<.1
205	Ray Lee Equipment—*Aaron Lee*	PO Box 608, Dimmitt TX 79027	806-647-3324	R	3*	<.1
206	United Farmers Supply—*Hr Barron*	2501 S Hwy 87, Lamesa TX 79331	806-497-6757	R	2*	<.1
207	D And D Supply—*George Dunham*	1341 42nd St Nw, Winter Haven FL 33881	863-965-2881	R	2*	<.1
208	Denny Kincer Inc—*Denny Kincer*	3509 Globe Ave, Lubbock TX 79404	806-762-1069	R	2*	<.1
209	Farm Equipment Center—*Kenth Day*	2700 Virgil Gray Dr, Brownwood TX 76801	325-752-7022	R	2*	<.1
210	Tri-Ag Corp—*Loyal Andersen*	555 N 1000 W, Logan UT 84321	435-753-1950	R	2*	<.1
211	Marquette Grain Systems Inc—*Lawrence Marquette*	1305 Frontage Rd Nw, Byron MN 55920	507-775-6234	R	2*	<.1
212	Spencer Farm Equip—*Charles Spencer*	10338 Ne Spencer Rd, Elgin OK 73538	580-492-4841	R	2*	<.1
213	Continental Agra Grain Equipment Inc—*Dan Hirschler*	1400 S Spencer Rd, Newton KS 67114	316-283-9602	R	2*	<.1
214	Washington North Implement Co—*Jim Hale*	830 Evergreen St, Lynden WA 98264	360-354-2186	R	1*	<.1
215	Hollins Organic Products Inc—*Doug Hollins*	6247 Falls Rd Ste 12, Baltimore MD 21209	410-828-0210	R	1*	<.1
216	Murphy Equipment Co—*David Murphy*	6400 Sw Hunter Rd, Augusta KS 67010	316-775-2137	R	1*	<.1
217	Mosby and Moore Inc—*Paul Mosby*	603 Harrison St, Sumner WA 98390	253-405-6322	R	<1*	<.1

TOTALS: SIC 5083 Farm & Garden Machinery

Companies: 217					14,366	18.4

5084 Industrial Machinery & Equipment

1	Toshiba Machine Company America—*Hiroshi Iva*	755 Greenleaf Ave, Elk Grove Village IL 60007	847-593-1616	R	8,783*	.1
2	MSC Industrial Direct Company Inc—*David Sandler*	75 Maxess Rd, Melville NY 11747	516-812-2000	P	2,022	4.5
3	Ring Power Corp—*Charles Hathaway*	500 World Commerce Pkw, St Augustine FL 32092	904-737-7730	R	1,968*	2.0
4	Nortrax Inc—*James A Earnshaw*	2020 52nd Ave, Moline IL 61265	309-765-1644	R	1,544*	1.1
5	Aviall Inc—*Paul Fulchino*	PO Box 619048, Dallas TX 75261		S	1,300*	1.2
6	Global Power Equipment Group Inc—*David L Keller*	5119 N Mingo Rd, Tulsa OK 74117	918-488-0828	R	1,229*	1.8
7	Furmanite Worldwide Inc—*Jeff Chick*	2435 N Central Expwy S, Richardson TX 75080	972-301-4000	S	1,184*	1.2

Rank	Company Name—*Executive Officer*	Address, City, State, Zip	Phone	Type	Fin	Empls
8	Hobart Corp—*David Spears*	701 S Ridge Ave, Troy OH 45374	937-332-3000	S	1,018*	1.2
9	Tractor and Equipment Co—*John J Harnish*	1835 Harnish Blvd, Billings MT 59101	406-656-0202	R	834*	.9
10	Valerus Compression Services—*Pete Lane*	919 Milam St Ste 1000, Houston TX 77002	713-744-6100	R	747*	.8
11	DXP Enterprises Inc—*David R Little*	7272 Pinemont, Houston TX 77040	713-996-4700	P	656	1.1
12	Atlas Lift Truck Rentals—*Gary Klein*	9500 River St, Schiller Park IL 60176	847-678-3450	R	486*	.2
13	Nomura America Corp—*Minoru Nomura*	2 World Financial Ctr, New York NY 10281	212-667-9300	S	422*	<.1
14	Barloworld USA—*Brandon Diamond*	PO Box 410050, Charlotte NC 28241	704-587-1003	S	394*	1.8
15	Hawthorne Machinery Inc—*Tee K Ness*	16945 Camino San Berna, San Diego CA 92127	858-674-7000	R	392*	.2
16	Womack Machine Supply—*Mike Rowlett*	13835 Senlac Dr, Farmers Branch TX 75234		R	369*	.4
17	Pacific Power Products—*Jerry Tyrrell*	600 S 56th Pl, Ridgefield WA 98642	360-887-7400	R	350*	.4
18	Dillon Supply Co—*Dean Wagoner*	PO Box 14535, Raleigh NC 27620	919-838-4200	S	329*	.4
19	NC Machinery Co (Seattle Washington)—*John Harnish*	PO Box 3562, Seattle WA 98124	425-251-5800	R	309*	1.0
20	Stiles Machinery Inc—*Peter Kleinschmidt*	3965 44th St SE, Grand Rapids MI 49512	616-698-7500	R	292*	.4
21	Halliburton WellDynamics—*David J Lesar*	445 Woodline Dr, Spring TX 77386	281-297-1208	R	281*	.2
22	Morrison Industries Inc—*Roger Troost*	PO Box P, Grand Rapids MI 49501	616-447-3800	R	276*	.3
23	Wisconsin Lift Truck Corp—*Jerry Weidmann*	3125 Intertech Dr, Brookfield WI 53045	262-781-8010	R	266*	.3
24	Associated Material Handling Industries Inc—*Mike Romano*	133 N Swift Rd, Addison IL 60101	630-588-8800	R	258*	.3
25	Watson Truck and Supply Inc	PO Box 10, Hobbs NM 88240	505-397-2471	R	252*	.3
26	Valley Welders Supply Inc—*Ron Adkins*	320 N 11th St, Billings MT 59103	406-256-3830	R	227*	.1
27	Riekes Equipment Co—*Duncan Murphy*	6703 L St, Omaha NE 68117	402-593-1181	R	225*	.1
28	Unarco Material Handling Inc—*Gary Slater*	PO Box 547, Springfield TN 37172	615-384-3531	R	220*	.8
29	Crane Engineering Sales Inc—*Lance Crane*	PO Box 38, Kimberly WI 54136	920-733-4425	R	219*	.1
30	Rockford Industrial Welding Supply Inc—*Gary R Bertrand*	4646 Linden Rd, Rockford IL 61109	815-226-1900	R	217*	.1
31	Clausing Industrial Inc—*Donald Haselton*	1819 N Pitcher St, Kalamazoo MI 49007	269-345-7155	R	217*	.1
32	Cummins Great Plains Inc—*Tim Solso*	10088 S 136th St, Omaha NE 68138	402-551-7678	S	216*	.3
33	Durand Forms Inc—*Brian Ward*	9026 E Lansing Rd, Durand MI 48429	989-288-2626	R	208*	.1
34	Mahar Tool Supply Company Inc—*Mike Kovaleski*	PO Box 1747, Saginaw MI 48605	989-799-5530	R	207*	.1
35	Rite-Hite Company LLC—*Tony Stokman*	8900 N Arbon Dr, Milwaukee WI 53223	414-355-2600	R	201*	.3
36	Convenience Food Systems Inc—*Paul Conover*	PO Box 2459, Frisco TX 75034	214-618-1100	S	199*	.2
37	Drago Supply Company Inc—*Sam Drago*	PO Box 647, Port Arthur TX 77641	409-983-4911	S	192*	.2
38	Darr Equipment Company Inc	350 Bank St, Southlake TX 76092	817-410-4800	R	191*	.2
39	Pac-Van Inc—*Ted Mourouzis*	2995 S Harding St, Indianapolis IN 46225	317-791-2030	R	186*	.2
40	Kelly Tractor Co—*L Patrick Kelly*	8255 NW 58th St, Miami FL 33166	305-592-0556	R	180*	.6
41	Mountain Valley Spring Company Inc—*Taylor Cranor*	PO Box 1610, Hot Springs AR 71902	501-623-6671	R	176*	2.6
42	Wartsila North America Inc—*Frank Donnelly*	16330 Air Center Blvd, Houston TX 77032	281-233-6200	S	175*	.4
43	Atec Inc (Stafford Texas)—*Howard Lederer*	12600 Executive Dr, Stafford TX 77477	281-276-2700	P	172*	.1
44	Triumph Instruments and Avionics—*Richard C III*	2840 N Ontario St, Burbank CA 91504	818-246-8431	R	170*	.1
45	ANCA Inc (Wixom Michigan)—*Pat Boland*	31129 Century Dr, Wixom MI 48393	248-926-4466	R	163*	.3
46	United Engines LLC—*Pat Arnold*	PO Box 960110, Oklahoma City OK 73196	405-947-3321	S	160*	.2
47	Hull Lift Truck Inc—*Brian Hull*	28747 Old US 33 W, Elkhart IN 46516		R	158*	.1
48	Hagemeyer Pps Ltd—*David Gabriel*	1460 Tobias Gadson Blv, Charleston SC 29407	843-745-2400	S	157*	3.2
49	Hillman Group Inc—*Max W Hillman*	PO Box 31012, Cincinnati OH 45231	513-851-4900	S	153*	.7
50	Hydradyne Hydraulics LLC—*Fred Hohenschultz*	PO Box 760, Harvey LA 70059	504-227-0254	R	153*	.4
51	Draeger Safety Inc—*Ralf Drews*	101 Technology Dr, Pittsburgh PA 15275	412-787-8383	R	150*	.4
52	Tencarva Machinery Co—*Rodney Lee*	PO Box 35705, Greensboro NC 27425	336-665-1435	R	146*	.3
53	Wyoming Machinery Co—*Rich Wheeler*	PO Box 2335, Casper WY 82602	307-472-1000	R	144*	.5
54	Windmoeller and Hoelscher Corp—*Hans Deamer*	23 New England Way, Lincoln RI 02865	401-333-2770	R	144*	.1
55	Voss Equipment Inc—*Darrell Davis*	15241 S Commercial Ave, Harvey IL 60426	708-596-7000	R	138*	.1
56	KMT Waterjet Systems—*Dwayne Johnson*	PO Box 231, Baxter Springs KS 66713	620-856-2151	S	135*	.2
57	Forklift of Minnesota Inc—*Clayton Schubert*	2201 W 94th St, Bloomington MN 55431	952-887-5400	R	132*	.2
58	Illinois Auto Electric Co—*H Bruce Sirotek*	700 Enterprise St, Aurora IL 60505	630-862-3300	R	130*	.2
59	Bingham Equipment Co—*Bob Hoffman*	1655 S Country Club Dr, Mesa AZ 85210	480-969-5516	R	126*	.2
60	Airgas West Inc—*Sam Thompson*	4007 Paramount Blvd St, Lakewood CA 90712	562-497-1991	S	119*	1.0
61	Robert Reiser and Company Inc—*Peter Mellon*	725 Dedham St, Canton MA 02021	781-821-1290	R	119*	.1
62	Michael Business Machines—*Ned Ginsburg*	PO Box 40249, Charleston SC 29423	843-552-2700	R	115*	<.1
63	Atlantic Detroit Diesel Allison LLC—*Thomas Hogan*	PO Box 950, Lodi NJ 07644	201-678-2584	R	113*	.4
64	FCx Performance Inc—*Charlie Simon*	3000 E 14th Ave, Columbus OH 43219	614-324-6050	S	110*	.2
65	C and H Distributors Inc—*Phil Areddia*	PO Box 14770, Milwaukee WI 53214	414-443-1700	R	109*	.4
66	3D Instruments LLC—*Gary L Cooper*	2900 E White Star, Anaheim CA 92806	714-399-9200	R	107*	.1
67	Associated Packaging Inc	435 Calvert Dr, Gallatin TN 37066	615-452-2131	R	106*	.1
68	Smith Power Products Inc—*Michael Smith*	PO Box 27527, Salt Lake City UT 84127	801-415-5000	R	105*	.3
69	Komori America Corp—*Yoshiharu Komori*	5520 Meadowbrook Indus, Rolling Meadows IL 60008	847-806-9000	R	102*	.1
70	Cascade Machinery and Electric Inc—*John Spring*	PO Box 3575, Seattle WA 98124	206-762-0500	R	100*	.1
71	Rex Supply Co	2488 W Cardinal Dr, Beaumont TX 77705	409-842-5176	R	96*	.4
72	Green Bull Ladder—*William T Allen*	11225 Bluegrass Pky, Louisville KY 40299	502-267-5577	R	96*	.1
73	Hayden-Murphy Equipment Co—*Len Kirk*	9301 E Bloomington Fwy, Minneapolis MN 55420	952-884-2301	R	96*	<.1
74	Eastern Lift Truck Co—*Mike Pruitt*	549 E Linwood Ave, Maple Shade NJ 08052	856-779-8880	R	92*	.5
75	Cummins Bridgeway LLC—*Greg Boll*	54250 Grand River Ave, New Hudson MI 48165	248-573-1600	D	92*	.1
76	Haggard and Stocking Associates Inc—*Herb Haggard*	5318 Victory Dr, Indianapolis IN 46203	317-788-4661	R	92*	.1
77	Mitutoyo America Corp—*Mikio Yamashita*	965 Corporate Blvd, Aurora IL 60502	630-820-9666	R	91*	.3
78	Gosiger Inc—*George Trissler*	108 McDonough St, Dayton OH 45402	937-228-5174	R	90*	.1
79	Sydnor Hydrodynamics Inc—*Steve Marusco*	PO Box 27186, Richmond VA 23261	804-643-2725	R	89*	.1
80	John Henry Foster Co (St Louis Missouri)—*Bob Gau*	4700 Le Bourget Dr, Saint Louis MO 63134	314-427-0600	R	87*	.1
81	Delta Materials Handling Inc—*Greg Costa*	4676 Clarke Rd, Memphis TN 38141	901-795-7230	R	84*	.1
82	Abatix Corp—*Terry W Shaver*	2400 Skyline Dr Ste 40, Mesquite TX 75149	214-381-0322	P	83	.1
83	AGL Welding Supply Company Inc—*Patrick M Fenelon*	600 Rt 46, Clifton NJ 07013	973-478-5000	R	83*	.1
84	Coast Counties Truck and Equipment Co—*Robert Archer*	PO Box 757, San Jose CA 95106	408-453-5510	R	82*	.1
85	United States Strong Tool Co—*Cedric Beckett*	1251 E 286th St, Cleveland OH 44132	216-289-2450	S	81*	.1
86	Suhner Manufacturing Inc—*Paul Luthi*	PO Box 1367, Rome GA 30162	706-235-8046	R	80*	.2
87	Western Branch Diesel Inc—*Herbert Haneman*	PO Box 7788, Portsmouth VA 23707	757-673-7000	R	80*	.3
88	Scott Industrial Systems Inc—*Mark Bryan*	PO Box 1387, Dayton OH 45401	937-233-8146	R	79*	.1
89	Poclain Hydraulics Inc—*Laurent Bataille*	PO Box 801, Sturtevant WI 53177	262-321-0676	R	78*	.2
90	WW Williams Co—*William S Williams*	835 W Goodale Blvd, Columbus OH 43212	614-228-5000	R	78*	.9
91	Doosan Infracore America Corp—*JY Lee*	2905 Shawnee Industria, Suwanee GA 30024	770-831-2200	S	78*	.1
92	Murata Machinery USA Inc—*Masahiko Hattori*	PO Box 667609, Charlotte NC 28266	704-394-8331	S	78*	.2
93	Nachi America Inc—*Toshio Sugiura*	17500 23 Mile Rd, Macomb MI 48044	586-226-5151	S	76*	.1
94	Morrison Industrial Equipment Co—*Roger Troost* Morrison Industries Inc	1825 Monroe Ave NW, Grand Rapids MI 49505	616-447-3800	S	75*	.4
95	Airline Hydraulics Corp—*Joseph Loughran*	PO Box 8505, Bensalem PA 19020	215-638-4700	R	75*	.2
96	Kraft Power Corp—*Owen Duffy*	PO Box 2189, Woburn MA 01888	781-938-9100	R	74*	.2

Note: An asterisk (*) indicates an estimated financial figure. The company type code used is as follows: R = Private, P = Public, S = Private Subsidiary, B = Public Subsidiary, D = Division, J = Joint Venture, I = Investment Fund.

COMPANY RANKINGS BY SALES WITHIN 4-DIGIT SIC

Rank	Company Name—*Executive Officer*	Address, City, State, Zip	Phone	Type	Fin	Empls
97	Century Equipment Inc—*Marty O'Brien*	5959 Angola Rd, Toledo OH 43615	419-865-7400	R	74*	.1
98	Roberts Motor Co—*Vittz J Ramsdell*	550 NE Columbia Blvd, Portland OR 97211	503-240-6282	R	72*	.1
99	Ilapak Inc—*Andrew Axberg*	105 Pheasant Run, Newtown PA 18940	215-579-2900	R	72*	<.1
100	S and K Acquisition Corp—*Don Portugal*	PO Box 1279, Mattoon IL 61938	217-258-8500	R	71*	.1
101	OKI Systems Ltd	10685 Medallion Dr, Cincinnati OH 45241	513-874-2600	S	70*	.3
102	Tubular Textile Machinery Inc—*Will Lotzhar*	113 Woodside Dr, Lexington NC 27292	336-956-6444	R	69*	.2
103	Diesel Injection Service Inc—*Robert Breunig*	PO Box 7485, Madison WI 53707	608-842-5100	R	68*	.1
104	Empire Power Systems—*Jeffrey S Whiteman*	840 N 44th Ave, Phoenix AZ 85009	602-333-5600	D	67*	.1
105	Mahr Federal Inc—*Tony Picone*	1144 Eddy St, Providence RI 02905	401-784-3100	R	67*	.3
106	Abel-Womack Integrated Handling Solutions—*John Croce*	1 International Way, Lawrence MA 01843	978-989-9400	R	65*	.2
107	St Cloud Industrial Products Inc—*Don Schiffler*	2629 Clearwater Rd, Saint Cloud MN 56301	320-251-7252	R	65*	.1
108	Campbell Sorensen Company Inc—*Harry Sorensen*	111 Premier Dr, Lake Orion MI 48359	248-340-8600	R	64*	.3
109	Eam-Mosca Corp—*Ralph Morini*	675 Jaycee Dr, Hazle Township PA 18202	570-459-3426	R	64*	.1
110	Machinery Systems Inc—*Joseph J Romanowski*	614 E State Pkwy, Schaumburg IL 60173	847-882-8085	R	64*	.1
111	Mississippi Welders Supply Company Inc—*Bradley Peterson*	PO Box 1036, Winona MN 55987	507-454-5231	R	63*	.1
112	White's Tractor and Truck Inc—*D Steve White*	PO Box 3817, Wilson NC 27895	252-291-0131	R	62*	.2
113	Mutual Wheel Co—*David Engstrom*	2345 4th Ave, Moline IL 61265	309-757-1200	R	62*	.1
114	Ohio Transmission and Pump Co—*Bob Korb*	1900 Jetway Blvd, Columbus OH 43219	614-342-6123	R	60*	.3
115	Sigma Supply Inc—*Daniel Hamby*	PO Box 20980, Hot Springs AR 71903	501-760-1511	R	60*	.1
116	Htp Inc—*David Davis*	PO Box 429, East Freetown MA 02717	508-763-8071	R	59*	.2
117	Allied Industrial Equipment Corp—*Steve Mattis*	9388 Dielman Industria, Saint Louis MO 63132	314-569-2100	R	58*	.1
118	Pearce Industries Inc—*Louis Pearce III*	PO Box 35068, Houston TX 77235	713-723-1050	R	57*	.6
119	Jefferds Corp—*K Richard Sinclair*	PO Box 757, Saint Albans WV 25177	304-755-8111	R	57*	.3
120	MG Newell Company Inc—*John Sherrill Jr*	PO Box 18765, Greensboro NC 27419	336-393-0100	R	57*	.1
121	Harris Industrial Gases Inc—*Kevin Maloney*	10481 Gold Flat Rd, Nevada City CA 95959	530-478-0226	R	57*	<.1
122	Cummins Rocky Mountain LLC—*Bill Wolpert*	651 N 101st Ave, Avondale AZ 85323	623-474-2600	S	55*	.2
123	Reading Crane and Engineering Co—*Jim Friedman*	11 Vanguard Dr, Reading PA 19606	610-582-7203	R	55*	.1
124	Woodworker's Supply Inc—*John Wirth Jr*	1108 N Glenn Rd, Casper WY 82601		R	54*	.2
125	Rjms Corp—*Richard Andres*	31010 San Antonio St, Hayward CA 94544	510-675-0500	R	52*	.2
126	Kba North America Inc—*Ralf Sammeck*	PO Box 619006, Dallas TX 75261		R	52*	.1
127	Star CNC Machine Tool Corp—*Noriaki Okamoto*	PO Box 9, Roslyn Heights NY 11577	516-484-0500	D	52*	.1
128	Bobst Group North America Inc—*Robert Pordon*	146 Harrison Ave, Roseland NJ 07068	973-226-8000	R	52*	.3
129	Drillers Service Inc—*Richard Redden*	PO Box 1407, Hickory NC 28603	828-322-1100	R	51*	.2
130	Terex Utilities Inc—*Thomas J Riordan*	PO Box 23009, Portland OR 97281	503-620-0611	S	50*	.2
131	Interstate Lift Trucks Inc—*Philip Graffy*	5667 E Schaaf Rd, Cleveland OH 44131	216-328-0970	R	50*	.1
132	Kawasaki Motors Corp USA Engine Div	PO Box 703, Wood Dale IL 60191		D	50*	.1
133	Mbo Binder and Company Of America—*Manfred Minich*	400 Highland Dr, Westampton NJ 08060	609-267-2900	R	50*	.1
134	Afp Industries Inc—*Richard Kish*	PO Box 490, Chesterfield VA 23832	804-275-1436	R	49*	.1
135	Orion South Inc—*Thomas Reagan*	PO Box 1850, Gretna LA 70054	504-368-9760	R	49*	.3
136	Toyotalift Inc—*Garland Pierce*	PO Box 710280, Santee CA 92072	619-562-5438	R	49*	.1
137	Bailey Company Inc—*Gordon Morrow*	501 Cowan St, Nashville TN 37207	615-242-0351	R	49*	.3
138	Texas Process Equipment Co—*Don Grogg*	5880 Bingle Rd, Houston TX 77092	713-460-5555	R	49*	.1
139	Force America Inc—*Steve Loeffler*	501 Cliff Rd E Ste 100, Burnsville MN 55337	952-707-1300	R	48*	.2
140	Stopol Inc—*Neil Kruschke*	31005 Bainbridge Rd, Solon OH 44139	440-498-4000	R	48*	.1
141	Weldstar Co	1750 Mitchell Rd, Aurora IL 60505	630-859-3100	R	48*	.1
142	George W Warden Company Inc—*Ranse Holcomb*	PO Box 17727, Seattle WA 98127	206-633-0382	R	47*	<.1
143	Preferred Pump and Equipment LP—*Eddie Broussard*	2201 Scott Ave Ste 100, Fort Worth TX 76103	817-536-9800	R	46*	.2
144	Ulvac Technologies Inc—*Wayne Anderson*	401 Griffin Brook Dr, Methuen MA 01844	978-686-7550	R	46*	.1
145	Hydromat Inc—*Bruno Schmitter*	11600 Adie Rd, Maryland Heights MO 63043	314-432-4644	R	46*	.2
146	Cse Corp—*S Shearer*	600 Seco Rd, Monroeville PA 15146	412-856-9200	R	46*	.1
147	Picanol of America Inc—*Luc Tack*	1801 Rutherford Rd, Greenville SC 29609	864-288-5475	R	45*	.2
148	Heavy Machines Inc	3926 E Raines Rd, Memphis TN 38118		R	44*	.2
149	Rutledge Company Inc—*Scott Rutledge*	6705 Keaton Corp Pkwy, O Fallon MO 63368	636-625-8094	R	44*	.1
150	Toolmex Corp—*Arkadiusz Kielb*	1075 Worcester Rd Ste, Natick MA 01760	508-653-8897	R	44*	.1
151	Bell-Mark Sales Company Inc—*John Marozzi*	PO Box 2007, Pine Brook NJ 07058	973-882-0202	R	43*	.1
152	Talladega Machinery and Supply Company Inc—*James Heacock*	301 N Johnson Ave, Talladega AL 35160	256-362-4124	R	42*	.3
153	Hirsch International Corp—*Paul Gallagher*	PO Box 18004, Hauppauge NY 11788	631-436-7100	R	42*	.1
154	Pride Equipment Corp—*Charles Noto*	150 Nassau Ave, Islip NY 11751	631-224-5000	R	42*	.1
155	Imta Manufacturing Technology and Automation Company Inc—*Tino Oldani*	707 Fulton Ave, Rockford IL 61103	815-968-4682	R	42*	<.1
156	Bottcher America Corp—*Larry Lowe*	4600 Mercedes Dr, Belcamp MD 21017	410-273-7000	R	41*	.2
157	Material Handling Supply Inc—*Robert Levin*	15 Old Salem Rd, Brooklawn NJ 08030	856-541-1290	R	41*	.1
158	Werres Corp—*Dan Senecal*	807 E South St, Frederick MD 21701	301-620-4000	R	41*	.1
159	R S Stover Co—*Don Turbiville*	PO Box 398, Marshalltown IA 50158	641-753-5557	R	40*	<.1
160	Adobe Equipment Holdings—*Bob Young*	7801 Broadway Ste 100, San Antonio TX 78209	713-300-1700	D	40*	.2
161	Cummins-Wagner Company Inc—*Doug Ardinger*	10901 Pump House Rd, Annapolis Junction MD 20701	410-792-4230	R	40*	.2
162	REM Sales Inc—*Brad Morris*	910 Day Hill Rd, Windsor CT 06095	860-687-3400	R	40*	.1
163	Alimak Hek Inc—*William Ayles*	8400 Villa Dr, Houston TX 77061	713-640-8500	R	39*	.2
164	Motor Services Hugo Stamp Inc—*Are Friesecke*	3190 Sw 4th Ave, Fort Lauderdale FL 33315	954-763-3660	R	39*	.1
165	Western Integrated Technologies Inc—*William Hill*	13406 Se 32nd St, Bellevue WA 98005	425-747-0927	R	38*	.1
166	Cummins West Inc—*Paul V Bleeker*	14775 Wicks Blvd, San Leandro CA 94577	510-351-6101	S	38*	.1
167	Continental Engines Inc—*Jeff Cooper*	60 Pelham Davis Cir, Greenville SC 29615	864-242-5567	R	38*	<.1
168	Man Turbo Incorporated USA—*Peter Roth*	2901 Wilcrest Dr Ste 3, Houston TX 77042	713-780-4200	R	37*	.2
169	Brock White Co—*Richard Garland*	2575 Kasota Ave, Saint Paul MN 55108	651-647-0950	R	37*	.1
170	Sooner Pipe LLC—*John B Shoaff*	1331 Lamar St Ste 970, Houston TX 77010	713-759-1200	S	37*	<.1
171	Park Hyde Partners—*Clifton Vann*	PO Box 7207, Charlotte NC 28241	704-588-3670	R	37*	.2
172	Hatfield and Company Inc—*George R Hatfield*	206 S Town East Blvd, Mesquite TX 75149	972-285-0115	R	36*	.1
173	Nestor Sales Company LLC—*Robert Nestor*	7337 Bryan Dairy Rd, Largo FL 33777	727-544-6114	R	35	.2
174	Logan Corp—*CM England III*	PO Box 58, Huntington WV 25706	304-526-4700	R	35*	.1
175	Johnson and Towers Inc—*Walter F Johnson*	2021 Briggs Rd, New Lisbon NJ 08064	856-234-6990	R	35*	.1
176	Rihm Kenworth—*John W Rihm*	2108 University Ave W, Saint Paul MN 55114	651-646-7833	R	35*	.1
177	Domino Holdings Inc—*Garry Havens*	1290 Lakeside Dr, Gurnee IL 60031	847-244-2501	R	34*	.2
178	Nitco Materials Handling Solutions—*Steve O'Leary*	6 Jonspin Rd, Wilmington MA 01887	978-658-5900	R	34*	.2
179	Bohl Equipment Co—*Douglas Bohl*	534 W Laskey Rd, Toledo OH 43612	419-476-7525	R	34*	<.1
180	Phillips Corp Federal Div—*Ronald Schulze*	7390 Coca Cola Dr, Hanover MD 21076	301-953-7200	D	34*	<.1
181	HIA Inc—*Alan C Bergold*	4275 Forest St, Denver CO 80216	303-394-6040	R	34	.1
182	AJ Jersey Inc—*David Rizzo*	PO Box 587, South Plainfield NJ 07080	908-754-7333	R	33*	.1
183	Cross Co—*William S Cross III*	PO Box 18508, Greensboro NC 27419	336-856-6000	R	33*	.2
184	Hydraulic Controls Inc—*Richard A Cotter*	4700 San Pablo Ave, Emeryville CA 94608	510-658-8300	R	33*	<.1

Rank	Company Name—*Executive Officer*	Address, City, State, Zip	Phone	Type	Fin	Empls
185	Shively Brothers Inc—*Scott Shively*	PO Box 1520, Flint MI 48501	810-232-7401	R	33*	.2
186	Heidenhain Corp—*Rick Korte*	333 E State Pkwy, Schaumburg IL 60173	847-490-1191	R	32*	.1
187	Towlift Inc—*David H Cannon*	1395 Valley Belt Rd, Cleveland OH 44131	216-749-6800	R	32*	.3
188	Hubbard Supply Co—*Robert Fuller*	901 W 2nd St, Flint MI 48503	810-234-8681	R	32*	<.1
189	Tomita USA Inc—*Kaoru Tomita*	7801 Corp Blvd Unit G, Plain City OH 43064	614-873-6509	R	32*	<.1
190	Gcic LLC	PO Box 926109, Houston TX 77292	832-467-4600	R	32*	.2
191	Lehman Pipe And Plumbing Supply Inc—*Dennis Lehman*	PO Box 370417, Miami FL 33137	305-576-3054	R	31*	<.1
192	Staubli Corp—*Yves Staubli*	PO Box 189, Duncan SC 29334	864-433-1980	R	30*	.1
193	Oscar Wilson Engines and Parts Inc—*Daniel Wright*	826 Lone Star Dr, O Fallon MO 63366	636-978-1313	R	30*	.1
194	Machinery Sales Co—*Guy Stolzenburg*	9802 N Vancouver Way, Portland OR 97217	503-285-6691	R	30*	<.1
195	Coordinated Equipment Co—*Philip Gibson*	1707 E Anaheim St, Wilmington CA 90744	310-834-8535	R	30*	<.1
196	Red Ball Oxygen Company Inc—*Gary Kennedy*	PO Box 7316, Shreveport LA 71137	318-425-3211	R	30*	.2
197	Yanmar America Corp—*Naka Oka*	101 International Pkwy, Adairsville GA 30103	770-877-9894	R	29*	.1
198	Gallus Inc—*Jonathan C Guy*	2800 Black Lake Pl, Philadelphia PA 19154	215-677-9600	R	29*	<.1
199	Seitz Corp—*Michael Sullivan*	PO Box 1398, Torrington CT 06790	860-489-0476	R	29*	.2
200	Lampton Welding Supply Company Inc—*Marvin Lampton*	PO Box 765, Wichita KS 67201	316-263-3293	R	28*	.1
201	Gerotech Inc—*Jay Haas*	29220 Commerce Dr, Flat Rock MI 48134	734-379-7788	R	28*	.1
202	E and M Electric And Machinery Inc—*Steven Deas*	126 Mill St, Healdsburg CA 95448	707-473-3100	R	28*	.1
203	Mill-Log Equipment Company Inc—*Dennis Hoff*	PO Box 8099, Coburg OR 97408	541-485-2203	S	28*	<.1
204	Peerless Supply Inc—*Bruce Iler*	PO Box 3307, Des Moines IA 50316	515-265-9905	R	28*	<.1
205	Best Label Company Inc—*Ernest Wong*	13260 Moore St, Cerritos CA 90703	562-926-1432	R	27*	.2
206	Mee Enterprises Inc—*Pamela Bourque*	11721 W Carmen Ave, Milwaukee WI 53225	414-353-3300	R	27*	.1
207	Adco Manufacturing—*Kate King*	2170 Academy Ave, Sanger CA 93657	559-875-5563	R	27*	.1
208	Renishaw Inc—*David McMarty*	5277 Trillium Blvd, Hoffman Estates IL 60192	847-286-9953	S	27*	.1
209	Lister-Petter Americas Inc	815 E Hwy 56, Olathe KS 66061	913-764-3512	S	27*	<.1
210	Mitsui Seiki (USA) Inc—*Scott Walker*	563 Commerce St, Franklin Lakes NJ 07417	201-337-1300	R	27*	.1
211	Marposs Corp—*Edward Vella*	3300 Cross Creek Pkwy, Auburn Hills MI 48326	248-370-0404	R	27*	.1
212	J-Line Pump Co—*Ron Cheek*	185 Progress Rd, Collierville TN 38017	901-860-2300	R	26*	.1
213	Glatt Air Techniques Inc—*Reinhard Nowak*	20 Spear Rd, Ramsey NJ 07446	201-825-8700	R	26*	.2
214	Liftech Handling Inc—*Joe Verzino*	6847 Ellicott Dr, East Syracuse NY 13057	315-463-7333	R	26*	.2
215	Kbc Tools Inc—*Sheila Bass*	PO Box 8006, Sterling Heights MI 48311	586-264-6600	R	26*	.2
216	Heartland Pump Rental And Sales Inc—*Mae Payne*	1800 Supply Rd A, Carterville IL 62918	618-985-5110	R	26*	.1
217	Scotsco Inc—*Steve Byerly*	16750 SE Kens Ct, Milwaukie OR 97267	503-653-7791	R	26*	<.1
218	Symtech Inc—*Hans J Balmer*	PO Box 2627, Spartanburg SC 29304	864-578-7101	R	26*	<.1
219	Midvale Industries Inc—*Webb Kane*	6310 Knox Industrial D, Saint Louis MO 63139	314-647-5604	R	26*	<.1
220	World Market Supply Inc—*Mark Myers*	10842 Galt IndustrialB, Saint Louis MO 63132	314-426-0026	R	26*	<.1
221	Kentmaster Manufacturing Company Inc—*Ralph Karubian*	1801 S Mountain Ave, Monrovia CA 91016	626-359-8888	R	26*	.1
222	Statco Engineering and Fabricators Inc—*James Statham*	7595 Reynolds Cir, Huntington Beach CA 92647	714-375-6300	R	26*	.1
223	Permadur Industries Inc—*William Schneider*	PO Box 1032, Somerville NJ 08876	908-359-9767	R	25*	<.1
224	Benoit Machine Inc—*Maurice Benoit*	PO Box 1419, Houma LA 70361	985-879-2487	R	25*	.1
225	Osg Tap And Die Inc—*Gohei Osawa*	676 E Fullerton Ave, Glendale Heights IL 60139	630-790-1400	R	24*	.1
226	Martin Calibration—*Rick Braun*	11965 12th Ave S, Burnsville MN 55337	952-882-1528	R	24*	<.1
227	NetMotion Inc—*Norio Sugano*	4160 Technology Dr, Fremont CA 94538	510-578-2808	R	24*	<.1
228	Brauer Material Handling Systems Inc—*Jeff Brauer*	226 Molly Walton Dr, Hendersonville TN 37075	615-859-2930	R	24*	.1
229	Carotek Inc—*Deryl Bell*	PO Box 1395, Matthews NC 28106	704-844-1100	R	23*	.1
230	Catching Fluidpower Inc—*Richard Guminski*	881 Remington Blvd, Bolingbrook IL 60440	630-771-3800	S	23*	.1
231	M and L Industries Inc—*Marvin Marmande*	1210 St Charles St, Houma LA 70360	985-876-2280	R	23*	.1
232	Minnesota Supply Co—*John Stromsness*	6470 Flying Cloud Dr, Eden Prairie MN 55344	952-828-7300	R	23*	.1
233	Perry Videx LLC—*Gregg P Epstein*	25 Mt Laurel Rd, Hainesport NJ 08036	609-267-1600	R	23*	.1
234	JD Rush Company Inc—*Jim Varner*	5900 E Lerdo Hwy, Shafter CA 93263	661-392-1900	R	23*	.1
235	Fuchs Machinery Inc—*Tom Berger*	5401 F St, Omaha NE 68117	402-734-1991	R	23*	.1
236	Chaparral Technologies Inc—*Ashwin Kalia*	2600 Gravel Dr Bldg 7, Fort Worth TX 76118	972-988-0067	R	23	N/A
237	Maxon Lift Corp—*Casey Lugash*	11921 Slauson Ave, Santa Fe Springs CA 90670	562-464-0099	R	23*	.1
238	Okk USA Corp—*Yoshihide Morimoto*	100 Regency Dr, Glendale Heights IL 60139	630-924-9000	R	23*	<.1
239	EBM-Papst Inc—*Robert Sobolewski*	PO Box 4009, Farmington CT 06034	860-674-1515	R	22*	.5
240	Hub Supply Inc—*Dave Byerley*	2546 S Leonine Rd, Wichita KS 67217	316-265-9608	S	22*	<.1
241	Buckeye Supply Co—*Stephen R Straker*	999 Zane St, Zanesville OH 43701	740-452-3641	R	22*	.1
242	Smith Auto Parts Inc—*Jon Cochran*	216 S Bridge St, Visalia CA 93291	559-734-1526	R	22*	.1
243	AGV Products Inc—*Terry Dunn*	8012 Tower Point Dr, Charlotte NC 28227	704-845-1110	R	22*	.1
244	Hodge Co—*Tim Hodge*	7465 Chavenelle Rd, Dubuque IA 52002	563-583-9781	R	22*	.1
245	JV Equipment Co—*Valerie Mehis*	PO Box 509, Edinburg TX 78540	956-383-0777	R	22*	.1
246	Toyotalift Of Arizona Inc—*Garland Pierce*	1445 N 26th Ave, Phoenix AZ 85009	602-278-2371	R	22*	.1
247	Palm Peterbilt-Gmc Trucks Inc—*David Weiger*	2441 S State Rd 7, Davie FL 33317	954-584-3200	R	21*	.1
248	Fred V Fowler Company Inc—*Fred Fowler*	PO Box 66299, Auburndale MA 02466	617-332-7004	R	21*	<.1
249	Austin Pump and Supply Co—*Charles Sterzing*	PO Box 17037, Austin TX 78760	512-442-2348	R	21*	<.1
250	Brodie Inc—*Ronald C McCluskey*	10 Ballard Rd, Lawrence MA 01843	978-682-6300	R	21*	.1
251	Aaron Equipment Company Inc—*Jerrold Cohen*	PO Box 80, Bensenville IL 60106	630-350-2200	R	21*	.1
252	Handling and Storage Concepts Inc—*Thomas Nolan*	PO Box 4671, Chesterfield MO 63006	314-776-8146	R	21*	<.1
253	Yale Industrial Trucks Pittsburgh Inc—*Christopher Burns*	1050 Rico Rd, Monroeville PA 15146	412-856-9253	R	21*	.1
254	Fab-Con Machinery Development Corp—*Frank Catallo*	PO Box 591, Port Washington NY 11050	516-883-3999	R	20*	.1
255	Fres-Co Systems USA Inc—*Tullio Vigano*	3005 State Rd, Telford PA 18969	215-721-4600	R	20*	.4
256	Michigan Fluid Power Inc—*Roger Betten*	4556 Spartan Industria, Grandville MI 49418	616-538-5700	R	20*	<.1
257	Ilmo Products Co—*Linda Standley*	PO Box 790, Jacksonville IL 62651	217-245-2183	R	20*	.1
258	Hy-Tek Material Handling Inc—*Sam Grooms*	2222 Rickenbacker Pkwy, Columbus OH 43217	614-497-2500	R	20*	.1
259	Northwest Pump and Equipment Co—*Greg Miller*	2275 Manya St, San Diego CA 92154	619-239-2282	R	20*	.1
260	Squibb-Taylor Inc—*Milford Therrell*	10480 Shady Trl Ste 10, Dallas TX 75220	214-357-4591	R	20*	<.1
261	Neuenhauser Inc—*Bernd Keen*	PO Box 3491, Fort Mill SC 29708	864-879-3650	R	20*	<.1
262	Moritani America Inc—*Hiroshi Kato*	300 Park Blvd Ste 320, Itasca IL 60143	630-250-9898	R	20*	<.1
263	Forklifts Of St Louis Inc—*Heather Hinds*	4720 Laguardia Dr, Saint Louis MO 63134	314-426-4040	R	20*	.1
264	Oil Equipment Company Inc—*Gerald Tigges*	4701 Lien Rd, Madison WI 53704	608-249-2881	R	20*	<.1
265	Custom Bilt Holdings LLC—*Norma Fernandez*	13940 Magnolia Ave, Chino CA 91710	909-664-1500	R	20*	.1
266	Traffic Control Products Company Inc—*Wendy Garner*	PO Box 820, Brandon MS 39043	601-939-2415	R	20*	<.1
267	Glen H Womack—*Glen Womack*	2701 I 20 W, Odessa TX 79766	432-366-7829	R	19*	.1
268	Davis Inotek Instruments LLC—*Lee Rudow*	4701 Mount Hope Dr, Baltimore MD 21215	410-358-3900	R	19	.1
269	Michael Weinig Inc—*Jeffrey Davidson*	PO Box 3158, Mooresville NC 28117	704-799-0100	R	19*	.1
270	Kardex Remstar LLC—*Richard Steer*	41 Eisenhower Dr, Westbrook ME 04092	207-854-1861	R	19*	.1
271	Deleet Merchandising Corp—*Barry Kronman*	26 Blanchard St, Newark NJ 07105	973-589-7800	R	19*	.1
272	Claude Laval Corp—*Melinda Laval*	PO Box 6119, Fresno CA 93703	559-255-1601	R	19*	.1
273	Cee Kay Supply Co—*Thomas Dunn*	5835 Manchester Ave, Saint Louis MO 63110	314-644-3500	R	19*	.1
274	Wilson Co (Addison Texas)—*Richard Bills*	16301 Addison Rd, Addison TX 75001	972-931-8666	R	19*	.1

Note: An asterisk (*) indicates an estimated financial figure. The company type code used is as follows: R = Private, P = Public, S = Private Subsidiary, B = Public Subsidiary, D = Division, J = Joint Venture, I = Investment Fund.

COMPANY RANKINGS BY SALES WITHIN 4-DIGIT SIC

Rank	Company Name—*Executive Officer*	Address, City, State, Zip	Phone	Type	Fin	Empls
275	Detroit Pump and Manufacturing Co—*Paul Horvath*	450 Fair St Bld D, Ferndale MI 48220	248-544-4242	R	19*	<.1
276	Northeast Engineering Inc—*Paul S Tierney*	PO Box 97, Cataumet MA 02534	508-564-7854	R	19*	<.1
277	Eurotherm Inc—*John Searle*	44621 Guilford Dr Ste, Ashburn VA 20147	703-724-7300	S	19*	<.1
278	Arbor Material Handling Inc—*David Bennett*	2465 Maryland Rd Ste 1, Willow Grove PA 19090	215-657-2700	R	19*	.1
279	Gray Lift Inc—*John Waugh*	PO Box 2808, Fresno CA 93745	559-268-6621	R	18*	.1
280	Freeman Manufacturing and Supply Co—*Lou Turco*	1101 Moore Rd, Avon OH 44011	440-934-1902	R	18*	.1
281	Interlatin Inc—*Alejandro Carillo*	300 S Alto Mesa Dr A a, El Paso TX 79912	915-298-5450	R	18*	.2
282	Zemarc Corp—*Zeke Zahid*	6431 Flotilla St, Commerce CA 90040	323-721-5598	R	18*	.1
283	Hougen Manufacturing Inc—*Randall Hougen*	PO Box 2005, Flint MI 48501	810-635-7111	R	18*	.1
284	Satake (USA) Inc—*Junjiro Naoki*	10905 Cash Rd, Stafford TX 77477	281-276-3600	R	18*	.1
285	M and M Supply Co (Duncan Oklahoma)—*HE Foreman*	PO Box 548, Duncan OK 73534	580-252-7879	R	18*	.1
286	General Air Service and Supply Company Inc—*Gary Armstrong*	1105 Zuni St, Denver CO 80204	303-892-7003	R	18*	.1
287	Agi Industries Inc—*David George*	PO Box 3604, Lafayette LA 70502	337-233-0626	R	18*	.1
288	Crouch Supply Company Inc—*Brad Barns*	PO Box 163829, Fort Worth TX 76161	817-332-2118	R	18*	<.1
289	Industrial Tool Products Inc	919 N Central Ave, Wood Dale IL 60191	630-766-4040	R	18*	<.1
290	Oil Equipment Supply Corp—*Dan Esposito*	PO Box 21188, Indianapolis IN 46221	317-243-3120	R	18*	<.1
291	RedMax Komatsu Zenoah America Inc—*Kunio Watanabe*	9335 Harris Corners Pk, Charlotte NC 28269		R	18*	<.1
292	Aronson-Campbell Industrial Supply Inc—*John Buckberger*	10925 E Montgomery Dr, Spokane WA 99206	509-891-4047	R	18*	<.1
293	Harbor Diesel And Equipment Inc—*Mike Zupanovich*	PO Box 21399, Long Beach CA 90801	562-591-5665	R	18*	.1
294	Daifuku America Corp—*M Inoue*	6700 Tussing Rd, Reynoldsburg OH 43068	614-863-1888	R	18*	.3
295	Construction Machinery Industrial LLC—*Erik Frazier*	5400 Homer Dr, Anchorage AK 99518	907-563-3822	R	18*	.1
296	Mack Boring And Parts Co—*Steven Mcgovern*	PO Box 3116, Union NJ 07083	908-964-0700	R	18*	.1
297	AA Anderson and Company Inc—*Greg Domino*	PO Box 523, Brookfield WI 53008	262-784-3340	R	18*	<.1
298	Fna Ip Holdings Inc—*Gus Alexander*	1825 Greenleaf Ave, Elk Grove Village IL 60007	847-348-1500	R	17*	.1
299	Ekato Corp—*Helmut Gaenser*	48 Spruce St, Oakland NJ 07436	201-825-4684	R	17*	<.1
300	Morrell Inc—*Steven Tallman*	3333 Bald Mountain Rd, Auburn Hills MI 48326	248-373-1600	R	17*	.3
301	Abrasive-Tool Corp—*Mike Hanna*	1555 Emerson St, Rochester NY 14606	585-254-4500	R	17*	<.1
302	Stanley M Proctor Co—*John Proctor*	PO Box 446, Twinsburg OH 44087	330-752-4567	R	17*	.1
303	ESA Technology Inc—*Paul Eason*	320 Tesconi Cir Ste J, Santa Rosa CA 95401	707-544-7300	S	17*	<.1
304	Doggett Equipment Services Ltd—*Alan Mcknight*	4001 N Panam Expy, San Antonio TX 78219	210-351-9500	R	17*	.1
305	Engine Power Source Inc—*Steve Couick*	PO Box 36190, Rock Hill SC 29732	704-889-7522	R	17*	.1
306	Harper Shields and Co—*Barton Scowley*	PO Box 2367, Martinez CA 94553	510-653-9119	R	17*	.1
307	California Tool and Welding Supply LLC—*Melody Anderson*	201 Main St, Riverside CA 92501	951-686-7822	R	17*	.1
308	Gulf States Engineering Company Inc—*J Dressel*	17961 Painters Row, Covington LA 70435	985-893-3631	R	17*	<.1
309	Power Great Lakes Inc—*Gary Winemaster*	655 Wheat Ln, Wood Dale IL 60191	630-350-9400	R	17*	.1
310	Robeck Fluid Power Inc—*Peter Becker*	350 Lena Dr, Aurora OH 44202	330-562-1140	R	17*	.1
311	American Equipment Inc—*Kenneth Zimmerman*	451 W 3440 S, Salt Lake City UT 84115	801-269-0896	R	16*	<.1
312	Airdyne Ltd—*Alan Worster*	14910 Henry Rd, Houston TX 77060	281-820-0000	R	16*	.1
313	Allstate Printing Packaging Inc—*Sam Zhong*	791 Paulison Ave Ste 3, Clifton NJ 07011	973-473-0700	R	16*	.1
314	W-B Supply Co—*Ron Hess*	111 Naida St, Pampa TX 79065	806-665-0901	R	16*	.1
315	Global Technology Group Ltd—*Simas Velonskis*	206 E 38th St Fl 2, New York NY 10016	212-490-2186	R	16*	<.1
316	E F Bavis and Associates Inc—*Edward Bavis*	201 Grandin Rd, Maineville OH 45039	513-677-0500	R	16*	<.1
317	Sjf Material Handling Inc—*Frank Sterner*	PO Box 70, Winsted MN 55395	320-485-2824	R	16*	.1
318	Carolina Material Handling Services Inc—*Grady Smith*	PO Box 6, Columbia SC 29202	803-695-0149	R	16*	.1
319	Plnes Manufacturing Inc—*Ian Williamson*	30505 Clemens Rd, Westlake OH 44145	440-835-5553	R	16*	.1
320	Mckinley Equipment Corp—*W Michael Mc Kinl*	17611 Armstrong Ave, Irvine CA 92614	949-261-9222	R	16*	.1
321	Bornquist Inc—*Harry Hultgren*	7050 N Lehigh Ave, Chicago IL 60646	773-774-2800	R	16*	.1
322	Saurer Textile Systems Charlotte Inc—*Helmut Leksa*	PO Box 240828, Charlotte NC 28224	704-394-8111	R	16*	<.1
323	Superior Crane Corp—*Andy Sharp*	PO Box 1464, Waukesha WI 53187	262-542-0099	R	16*	.1
324	Quality Hydraulics and Pneumatics Inc—*John Felsenthal*	1415 Wilhelm Rd, Mundelein IL 60060	847-680-8400	R	16*	<.1
325	Precision Pump and Valve Service Inc—*Barry Kemerer*	PO Box 7027, Charleston WV 25356	304-776-1710	R	15*	.1
326	Mitchell Lewis and Staver Co—*David Brown*	PO Box 621, Wilsonville OR 97070	503-682-1800	R	15*	.1
327	Curry Control Company Inc—*David Curry*	PO Box 5408, Lakeland FL 33807	863-646-5781	R	15*	.1
328	Dilo Company Inc—*Lukas Rothlisberger*	11642 Pyramid Dr, Odessa FL 33556	727-376-5593	R	15*	<.1
329	C and H Distributors LLC—*Phil Areddia*	PO Box 14770, Milwaukee WI 53210	414-443-1700	R	15*	.5
330	New England Industrial Truck Inc—*Robert Krueger*	195 Wildwood Ave, Woburn MA 01801	781-935-9105	R	15*	.1
331	IDG York—*Charles Lingenfelter*	3100 Farmtrail Rd, York PA 17406	717-767-7575	D	15*	.1
332	Turbo Diesel and Electric Systems Inc—*J Roberts*	PO Box 16068, Atlanta GA 30321	404-361-2222	R	15*	.1
333	Global Trading And Sourcing Corp—*Andrew Vandendriessche*	1587 College Pk Bus Ct, Orlando FL 32804	407-532-7600	R	15*	<.1
334	Certified Slings Inc—*Douglas Worswick*	PO Box 180127, Casselberry FL 32718	407-331-6677	R	15*	.1
335	Courreges Pump Company Inc—*Daniel Courreges*	PO Box 821607, Fort Worth TX 76182	512-422-1300	R	15*	<.1
336	Basic Machinery Company Inc—*William Milholen*	PO Box 688, Siler City NC 27344	919-663-2244	R	15*	.1
337	Ace Tank and Equipment Co—*Mike Gray*	6703 E Marginal Way S, Seattle WA 98108	206-281-5000	R	15*	.1
338	Wendt Corp—*Thomas Wendt*	2080 Military Rd, Tonawanda NY 14150	716-873-2211	R	14*	.1
339	HE Tyler Machine Tool Company Inc—*Michael Tyler*	PO Box 396, Seabrook NH 03874	603-474-7730	R	14*	<.1
340	Valtra Inc—*Harry Wong*	7141 Paramount Blvd, Pico Rivera CA 90660	562-949-8625	R	14*	<.1
341	CUESOP Inc—*Alan Morrison*	14 Caldwell Dr Ste 1, Amherst NH 03031	603-889-4071	R	14*	.1
342	E Tech Inc—*Duane Martinson*	1401 W River Rd Ste D, Minneapolis MN 55411	612-722-1366	R	14*	.1
343	Ogden Welding Systems Inc—*Jeffrey Darnell*	372 Division St, Schererville IN 46375	219-322-5252	R	14*	.1
344	Hobbs Iron and Metal Company Inc—*Gene Day*	PO Box 2007, Hobbs NM 88241	575-393-1726	R	14*	.1
345	Cm3 Building Solutions Inc—*Thomas Mcclay*	185 Commerce Dr Ste 1, Fort Washington PA 19034	215-322-8400	R	14*	.1
346	G and W Piedmont Forklift Inc—*Jeff Bradley*	PO Box 16328, Greenville SC 29606	864-297-1330	R	14*	.1
347	Engine Distributors Inc—*Glenn Cummins Jr*	400 University Ct, Blackwood NJ 08012	856-228-7298	R	14*	<.1
348	Productive Products Inc—*Robert Gore*	3020 E Progress Dr Ste, West Bend WI 53095	262-334-5220	R	14*	<.1
349	Fluid System Components Inc—*Jerry Bost*	PO Box 11037, Green Bay WI 54307	920-337-0234	R	14*	.1
350	K and M Newspaper Services Inc—*Mark Jacobs*	45 Gilbert St Ext, Monroe NY 10950	845-782-3817	R	14*	.1
351	Delta Process Equipment Inc—*Wayne Guy*	PO Box 969, Denham Springs LA 70727	225-665-1666	R	14*	.1
352	Miyano Machinery USA Inc—*Tsugio Sasaki*	2316 Touhy Ave, Elk Grove Village IL 60007	630-766-4141	R	14*	<.1
353	JA Cunningham Equipment Inc—*Paul Cunningham*	2025 Trenton Ave, Philadelphia PA 19125	215-426-6650	R	14*	<.1
354	Gill Services Inc—*Mary Gill*	650 Aldine Bender Rd, Houston TX 77060	281-820-5400	R	13*	.1
355	Airflow Systems Inc—*Michael Bodmer*	11221 Pagemill Rd, Dallas TX 75243	214-503-8008	R	13*	.1
356	Linatex Corporation Of America—*Greg Caddle*	1550 Airport Rd, Gallatin TN 37066	615-230-2100	R	13*	.1
357	Spray Equipment and Service Center Inc—*Mark Hammar*	PO Box 3580, Wichita KS 67201	316-264-4349	R	13*	.1
358	Aero Grinding Inc—*Roland Dimattia*	28300 Groesbeck Hwy, Roseville MI 48066	586-774-6450	R	13*	.1
359	Peach State Integrated Technologies Inc—*James Bowes*	3005 Business Park Rd, Norcross GA 30071	678-327-2000	R	13*	.1
360	Florida Clarklift Inc—*Jeff Fischer*	115 S 78th St, Tampa FL 33619	813-621-1000	R	13*	.1
361	Electrodes Inc—*David Dudas*	252 Depot Rd, Milford CT 06460	203-878-7408	R	13*	.1
362	Pro-Am Safety Inc—*Jim DiNardo*	551 Keystone Dr, Warrendale PA 15086	724-776-1818	R	13*	.1
363	General Distributing Co—*Glenn Bliss*	PO Box 2606, Great Falls MT 59403	406-454-1351	R	13*	.1
364	Moore Material Handling Group Inc—*Patrick Moore*	PO Box 32060, San Jose CA 95152	408-998-7100	R	13*	<.1

Rank	Company Name—*Executive Officer*	Address, City, State, Zip	Phone	Type	Fin	Empls
365	Lee Tractor Company Inc	10203 Airline Hwy, Saint Rose LA 70087	504-467-6794	R	13*	<.1
366	Foster F Wineland Inc—*Kim Swindell*	PO Box 227, Martinsburg PA 16662	814-793-3734	R	13*	<.1
367	American Welding and Gas—*Tammy Gran*	PO Box 30118, Billings MT 59107	320-235-4774	R	13*	<.1
368	Vesco Material Handling Equipment Inc—*Vann Williford*	355 Business Park Dr, Winston Salem NC 27107	336-397-5000	R	13*	.1
369	Process Engineering and Equipment Co—*Raymond Vonck*	571 6 Mile Rd Nw, Comstock Park MI 49321	616-784-7636	R	13*	<.1
370	Cisco Air Systems Inc—*William Frkovich*	214 27th St, Sacramento CA 95816	916-287-1435	R	13*	.1
371	Carolina Fluidair Inc—*Russell Hensley*	5100 Reagan Dr Ste 10, Charlotte NC 28206	704-596-5680	R	12*	.1
372	T J Snow Company Inc—*Thomas Snow*	PO Box 22847, Chattanooga TN 37422	423-894-6234	R	12*	.1
373	Liftruck Service Company Inc—*Mary Gayman*	PO Box 3336, Davenport IA 52808	563-322-0983	R	12*	.1
374	Atkinson Electronics Inc—*Gaylen Atkinson*	14 W Vine St, Salt Lake City UT 84107	801-261-3600	R	12*	.1
375	Oil-Air Products LLC—*Roger Schwerin*	PO Box 129, Hamel MN 55340	763-478-8744	R	12*	<.1
376	Lmt USA Inc—*Doug Ewald*	1081 S Northpoint Blvd, Waukegan IL 60085		R	12*	<.1
377	Chickasaw Distributors Inc—*Brad Baker*	800 Bering Dr #330, Houston TX 77057	713-974-2905	R	12*	.1
378	Ana Trading Corporation USA—*Yoshinori Shinagawa*	970 W 190th St Ste 600, Torrance CA 90502	310-329-0211	R	12*	.1
379	APO Holdings Inc—*Ted Mailey*	6607 Chittenden Rd, Hudson OH 44236	330-650-1330	R	12*	.1
380	MIE Corp—*James Andraitis*	PO Box 590, Jackson Center OH 45334	937-596-5511	R	12*	.1
381	Gp Companies Inc—*William Brown*	1174 Northland Dr, Mendota Heights MN 55120	651-454-6500	R	12*	.1
382	Northeast Controls Inc—*David Rizzo*	3 Enterprise Ave, Clifton Park NY 12065	518-664-0230	R	12*	.1
383	Lift Truck Service Center Inc—*Carl Morehead*	7721 Distribution Dr, Little Rock AR 72209	501-568-3330	R	12*	.1
384	Saw Systems Inc—*Natalie Brillhart*	1579 Enterprise Pkwy, Twinsburg OH 44087	330-963-2992	R	11*	<.1
385	Fargo Automation Inc—*Kevin Biffert*	969 34th St N, Fargo ND 58102	701-232-1780	R	11*	.1
386	Pumps Parts and Service Inc—*Ray Miller*	PO Box 7788, Charlotte NC 28241	704-588-6250	R	11*	<.1
387	Tampa Fork Lift Inc—*Gary Mansell*	PO Box 76054, Tampa FL 33675	813-623-5251	R	11*	<.1
388	Us Safetygear Inc—*Tarry Alberini*	PO Box 309, Leavittsburg OH 44430	330-898-1344	R	11*	<.1
389	Hahn Equipment Company Inc—*Margaret Hahn*	5636 Kansas St, Houston TX 77007	713-868-3255	R	11*	<.1
390	G A W Inc—*Gary Wine*	10650 Cloverdale St, Detroit MI 48204	313-933-5890	R	11*	.1
391	Mde Corp—*Robert Nielsen*	14379 Livernois Ave, Detroit MI 48238	313-931-2010	R	11*	.1
392	Horsley Company LLC—*Ian Mctaggart*	1630 S 4800 W Ste D, Salt Lake City UT 84104	801-401-5500	S	11*	.1
393	Horix Manufacturing Company Inc—*Linda Szramowski*	1384 Island Ave, Mc Kees Rocks PA 15136	412-771-1111	R	11*	<.1
394	Kennedy Engine Company Inc—*Thomas Kennedy*	980 Motsie Rd, Biloxi MS 39532	228-392-2200	R	11*	.1
395	Horsley Co—*Michael Malkowski*	1630 S 4800 W Ste D, Salt Lake City UT 84104	801-401-5125	R	11*	.1
396	Allied Industrial Equipment Inc—*Jerry Hatmaker*	1640 Island Home Ave, Knoxville TN 37920	865-573-0995	R	11*	.1
397	Franklin Electrofluid Company Inc—*Richard Franklin*	PO Box 18777, Memphis TN 38181	901-362-7504	R	11*	.1
398	Martin Supply Company Inc—*Victor Lebow*	2740 Loch Raven Rd, Baltimore MD 21218	410-366-1696	R	11*	<.1
399	East Bay Clarklift Inc—*Marshall Cromer*	PO Box 14338, Oakland CA 94614	510-534-6566	R	10*	<.1
400	Bruns Brothers Welding Inc—*Michael Bruns*	PO Box 240, Gray ME 04039	207-657-3111	R	10*	.1
401	Powernail Co—*Tom Anstett*	1300 Rose Rd, Lake Zurich IL 60047	847-634-3000	R	10*	.1
402	Vertique Inc—*Fred Dufour*	115 Vista Blvd, Arden NC 28704	828-654-8900	R	10*	.1
403	Rki Instruments Inc—*Marie Ballentine*	33248 Central Ave, Union City CA 94587	510-441-5656	R	10*	.1
404	Austin International Inc—*Randy Austin*	7 Ross Cannon St, York SC 29745	803-628-0035	R	10*	.2
405	Business Exploration Inc—*Mujeeb Kureshy*	64-03 Roosevelt, Woodside NY 11377	718-247-0224	R	10*	.1
406	Crumpton Welding Supply And Equipment Inc—*Charles Crumpton*	1602 N 34th St, Tampa FL 33605	813-248-8150	R	10*	<.1
407	Tempaco Inc—*Maria Robinson*	1701 Alden Rd, Orlando FL 32803	407-898-3456	R	10*	<.1
408	Deco Tool Supply Co—*Dennis Quinn*	PO Box 3097, Davenport IA 52808	563-386-5970	R	10*	<.1
409	Hi-Tech Pump and Crane Inc—*Paul Reed*	PO Box 24784, Houston TX 77229	281-452-5100	R	10*	<.1
410	Interchange Equipment Inc—*Marc Herrmann*	90 Dayton Ave Ste 120, Passaic NJ 07055	073-473-5005	R	10*	<.1
411	Barry Salee Engineering Inc—*Chris Barry*	116 N Kirkwood Rd, Saint Louis MO 63122	314-821-2525	R	10*	<.1
412	LH Flaherty Company Inc—*Larry Flaherty*	1577 Jefferson Ave SE, Grand Rapids MI 49507	616-245-9266	R	10*	.1
413	Penn West Industrial Trucks LLC	168 Westec Dr, Mount Pleasant PA 15666	724-696-2350	R	10*	.1
414	Dominion Air and Machinery Co—*Richard Bishop*	PO Box 13806, Roanoke VA 24037	540-366-2000	R	10*	.1
415	Viccaro Equipment Corp—*Frank Viccaro*	345 Oser Ave, Hauppauge NY 11788	631-253-2600	R	10*	<.1
416	Carleton Equipment Co—*Phillip Wurtzel*	4704 S 29th St, Kalamazoo MI 49048	269-343-2943	R	10*	.1
417	Warehouse One Inc—*Mary Jacoby*	7800 E 12th St, Kansas City MO 64126	816-483-6999	R	10*	.1
418	Bolzoni Auramo Inc—*Roberto Scotti*	17635 Hoffman Way, Homewood IL 60430	708-957-8809	R	10*	<.1
419	Pennsylvania Sewing Machine Co—*Robert Matusic*	215 Vandale Dr, Houston PA 15342	724-746-8800	R	10*	<.1
420	N-Tech Inc—*Don Nevin*	159 Lafayette Dr, Syosset NY 11791	516-496-7200	R	9*	.1
421	Hallmark Refining Corp—*Anthony Senff*	PO Box 1446, Mount Vernon WA 98273	360-428-5880	R	9*	.1
422	Trico Belting and Supply Co—*John Schafer*	PO Box 62385, Cincinnati OH 45262	513-860-8400	R	9*	<.1
423	B and J Specialty Inc—*John Wicker*	7919 N 100 E, Wawaka IN 46794	260-761-5011	R	9*	.1
424	DC Equipment Inc—*Dan Chadwick*	PO Box 184, Geraldine AL 35974	256-659-4707	R	9*	.1
425	Colorado Compressor Inc—*Alan Pauley*	6030 E 50th Ave, Commerce City CO 80022	303-297-8100	R	9*	.1
426	Eastern Controls Incorporated Of Pennsylvania—*Clifton Mclaughlin*	PO Box 519, Edgemont PA 19028	610-325-4600	R	9*	<.1
427	Eagle Engineering Inc—*Jeff Cook*	PO Box 64, Eldridge IA 52748	563-285-7515	R	9*	.1
428	Conveyor Handling Company Inc—*Jean Rittermann*	6715 Santa Barbara Ct, Elkridge MD 21075	410-379-2700	R	9*	<.1
429	All-Tech Inc—*Bruce Bunker*	1030 58th St Sw, Grand Rapids MI 49509	616-406-0681	R	9*	.1
430	Advantage Controls LLC—*Ted Aukerman*	PO Box 1472, Muskogee OK 74402	918-686-6211	R	9*	.1
431	Associated Electro-Mechanics Inc—*Roland Lebeau*	PO Box 2650, Springfield MA 01101	413-781-4276	R	9*	.1
432	Superior Diesel Inc—*Thomas Umluf*	PO Box 1187, Rhinelander WI 54501	715-365-0500	R	9*	.1
433	Gas Equipment Supply Co—*Skeeter LaDue*	1440 Lakes Pky Ste 300, Lawrenceville GA 30043	770-995-1131	R	9*	.1
434	Welder Services Of Fort Wayne Inc—*Daniel Mulhern*	PO Box 6178, Fort Wayne IN 46896	260-423-4468	R	9*	<.1
435	Elevator Modernization Company Inc—*Robert White*	9101 E Hampton Dr, Capitol Heights MD 20743	301-324-8500	R	9*	<.1
436	Process Solutions and Integration Inc	15000 Bolsa Chica Rd, Huntington Beach CA 92649	714-898-0313	S	9*	<.1
437	Fan Equipment Company Inc—*Timothy Harris*	3925 W Sunset Rd, Las Vegas NV 89118	702-270-8344	R	9*	<.1
438	Paper Handling Solutions Inc—*Don Barbour*	2140 New Market Pkwy S, Marietta GA 30067	770-955-3770	R	9*	<.1
439	Erie Industrial Supply Co—*Dena Zambrzycki*	931 Greengarden Rd, Erie PA 16501	814-452-3231	R	9*	<.1
440	Hisco Pump Inc—*Joseph Montineri*	4 Mosey Dr, Bloomfield CT 06002	860-243-2705	R	9*	.1
441	Reno Forklift Inc—*George Pimpl*	PO Box 50009, Sparks NV 89435	775-329-1384	R	9*	<.1
442	All World Machinery Supply Inc—*Dave Koepp*	1301 W Diggins St, Harvard IL 60033	815-943-9111	R	9*	<.1
443	National Waste Services Inc—*Richard Leone*	1863 Harrison Ave, Bay Shore NY 11706	631-271-5114	R	9*	.1
444	C R Onsrud Inc—*Tom Onsrud*	PO Box 419, Troutman NC 28166	704-508-7000	R	9*	.1
445	Springer Equipment Company Inc—*Annette Springer*	PO Box 100274, Birmingham AL 35210	205-951-3675	R	9*	<.1
446	Leblanc and Associates Inc—*Mervyn Leblanc*	132 Intracoastal Dr, Houma LA 70363	985-876-7982	R	9*	<.1
447	Commonwealth Supply Company Inc—*Mary Shanaman*	PO Box 3790, York PA 17402	717-764-8504	R	9*	<.1
448	Ring Power Lift Trucks—*Catherine Barry*	2700 N Powerline Rd, Pompano Beach FL 33069	954-971-9440	R	9*	.1
449	Tec-Hackett Inc—*Edward Hughes*	PO Box 8830, Fort Wayne IN 46898	260-471-7116	R	9*	<.1
450	Miracle International Corp—*John Chabot*	PO Box 1068, Naugatuck CT 06770	203-723-0928	R	9*	<.1
451	Trio Packaging Corp—*John Bolla*	90 13th Ave Unit 10, Ronkonkoma NY 11779	631-588-0800	R	9*	<.1
452	Delong Equipment Company LLC—*Eddie Freeman*	1216 Zonolite Rd Ne, Atlanta GA 30306	404-607-1234	R	9*	<.1

Note: An asterisk (*) indicates an estimated financial figure. The company type code used is as follows: R = Private, P = Public, S = Private Subsidiary, B = Public Subsidiary, D = Division, J = Joint Venture, I = Investment Fund.

COMPANY RANKINGS BY SALES WITHIN 4-DIGIT SIC

Rank	Company Name—Executive Officer	Address, City, State, Zip	Phone	Type	Fin	Empls
453	B-P Supply Inc—Billy Parnell	PO Box 976, Andrews TX 79714	432-523-5612	R	8*	<.1
454	Wylaco Construction Supply Co—Terry Carpenter	315 Vallejo St, Denver CO 80223	303-778-8201	R	8*	<.1
455	Atlas Manufacturing Company Inc—Larry Crowell	PO Box 1969, Monticello MS 39654	601-587-4511	R	8*	.1
456	Western Power Products Inc—Donald Camp	3000 Gateway Ave, Bakersfield CA 93307	661-397-9155	R	8*	<.1
457	American Environmental Supply LLC—Robin Rohrer	325 Westtown Rd Ste 14, West Chester PA 19382	610-344-0637	R	8*	<.1
458	Dan F Williamson and Company Inc—Dan Williamson	9 Shelter Dr, Greer SC 29650	864-848-1011	R	8*	.1
459	EDL Packaging Engineers Inc—Kenneth Carter	1260 Parkview Rd, Green Bay WI 54304	920-336-7744	R	8*	.1
460	Material Handling Systems Inc—Ronald Fontes	720 Sw 4th Ct, Dania FL 33004	954-921-1171	R	8*	<.1
461	Rod Golden Corp—Alessio Pretto	PO Box 95, Beacon Falls CT 06403	203-723-4400	R	8*	<.1
462	Frain Industries Inc—Richard Frain	9377 Grand Ave, Franklin Park IL 60131	847-288-0258	R	8*	<.1
463	Titanium Holdings Group Inc—Randall K Davis	1023 Morales St, San Antonio TX 78207	210-293-1232	P	8	<.1
464	Rudox Engine And Equipment Co—Edward Rudlinger	PO Box 467, Carlstadt NJ 07072	201-438-0111	R	8*	<.1
465	Carolina Equipment and Supply Company Inc—E Fulmer	PO Box 40907, Charleston SC 29423	843-760-3000	R	8*	<.1
466	Oz Arc/Gas Equipment and Supply Inc—Robert Garner	PO Box 697, Cape Girardeau MO 63702	573-334-2848	R	8*	<.1
467	Duo-Fast Of Knoxville Inc—T Hartman	PO Box 10487, Knoxville TN 37939	865-588-2453	R	8*	<.1
468	A I E Company Inc—David Burke	PO Box 620249, Atlanta GA 30362	770-263-6118	R	8*	<.1
469	Coastal Engineering Corp—Barbara Allbritton	PO Box 23526, New Orleans LA 70183	504-733-8511	S	8*	<.1
470	Oregon Select Inc—Duncan Lean	PO Box 10526, Eugene OR 97440	541-342-5568	R	8*	.1
471	J and W Instruments Inc—Phillip Javinsky	4800 Mustang Cir Ste A, Saint Paul MN 55112	763-784-5708	R	8*	<.1
472	Hgr Industrial Surplus Inc—Paul Betori	20001 Euclid Ave, Cleveland OH 44117	216-486-4567	R	8*	<.1
473	Single Source Technologies Inc—Tony Pekalski	2600 Superior Ct, Auburn Hills MI 48326	248-232-6232	R	8*	<.1
474	Kubat Equipment and Service Co—Gene Hoyer	1070 S Galapago St, Denver CO 80223	303-777-2044	R	8*	<.1
475	Lone Star Fork Lift Inc—Don Swain	4213 Forest Ln, Garland TX 75042	972-494-5438	R	8*	<.1
476	United Dairy Machinery Corp—Steven Sisson	PO Box 257, Buffalo NY 14224	716-674-0500	R	8*	<.1
477	Snk America Inc—Tomohiro Naokawa	1800 Howard St Ste H, Elk Grove Village IL 60007	847-364-0801	R	8*	.1
478	Us Chemical Storage LLC—Steven Lamm	355 Industrial Park Dr, Boone NC 28607	828-264-6032	R	8*	.1
479	Juki Automation Systems Inc—Bob Black	507 Airport Blvd Ste 1, Morrisville NC 27560	919-460-0111	R	8*	<.1
480	Kraft Fluid Systems Inc—Diane Baker	14300 Foltz Pkwy, Strongsville OH 44149	440-238-5545	R	8*	<.1
481	Guy L Warden and Sons—Thomas Pih	16626 Parkside Ave, Cerritos CA 90703	562-926-6682	R	8*	<.1
482	Omni Services Of New York Inc—Bob Mitchell	190 Old Loudon Rd, Latham NY 12110	518-785-8597	R	8*	.1
483	Maryland Industrial Trucks Inc—George Rose	PO Box 64716, Baltimore MD 21264	410-636-1255	R	8*	<.1
484	Pump Pro's Inc—Michael Dunn	7601 Innovation Way, Mason OH 45040	513-860-9771	R	8*	<.1
485	National Machinery Exchange Inc—Joseph Epstein	158 Paris St, Newark NJ 07105	973-344-6100	R	8*	<.1
486	Feeger - Lucas - Wolfe Inc—Andrew Peek	5672 Bolsa Ave, Huntington Beach CA 92649	714-751-7512	R	8*	<.1
487	Capitol Welders Supply Company Inc—Betty Root	PO Box 53304, Baton Rouge LA 70892	225-383-3717	R	8*	<.1
488	Idesco Corp—Andrew Schonzeit	37 W 26th St Fl 10, New York NY 10010	212-889-2530	R	8*	<.1
489	Westec Industries Inc—Ed Christiansen	PO Box 2211, Seattle WA 98111	206-764-4541	R	8*	<.1
490	Tech Quip Inc—R Sellers	PO Box 890649, Houston TX 77289	281-484-4830	R	8*	<.1
491	Hague Equipment Company Of Michigan Inc—Gerald Peal	410 E Dresden St, Kalkaska MI 49646	231-258-9886	R	8*	<.1
492	Ramann Enterprises Inc—James Buck	3134 Marquita Dr, Fort Worth TX 76116	817-560-4222	R	7*	<.1
493	Valley Equipment Co—Roy Robertson	1000 E Main St, Johnson City TN 37601	423-753-3541	R	7*	<.1
494	Diesel Equipment Co—Jerry Harris	PO Box 16066, Greensboro NC 27416	336-373-8331	R	7*	<.1
495	Palmetto Oil Equipment Company Inc—Blake Neal	PO Box 21216, Columbia SC 29221	803-772-5785	R	7*	<.1
496	Scientific Cutting Tools Inc—Dale Christopher	110 W Easy St, Simi Valley CA 93065	805-584-9495	R	7*	<.1
497	Suffolk Iron Works Inc—John Harrell	PO Box 1943, Suffolk VA 23439	757-539-2353	R	7*	<.1
498	Compressor Pump And Service Inc—Eric Nelson	3333 W 2400 S, Salt Lake City UT 84119	801-973-0154	R	7*	<.1
499	Bayliss Machine and Welding Company LLC—Brian Bansant	PO Box 10847, Birmingham AL 35202	205-323-6121	R	7*	<.1
500	Transco Suppliers Corp—Maria Cantu	PO Box 630023, Houston TX 77263	713-779-0909	R	7*	.1
501	Jack Tyler Engineering Of Arkansas Inc—Sherman Eoff	6112 Patterson Rd, Little Rock AR 72209	501-562-2296	R	7*	<.1
502	Bykowski Equipment Co—Richard Largarticha	12360 Eastend Ave, Chino CA 91710	909-902-9400	R	7*	<.1
503	Schutte Msa LLC—Jim Trunk	4055 Morrill Rd, Jackson MI 49201	517-782-3600	R	7*	<.1
504	Machine Tool and Supply Corp—Mark Yates	117 Wright Industrial, Jackson TN 38301	731-424-3400	R	7*	<.1
505	Fugro Geoconsulting Inc—Edwin Houthuijzen	PO Box 740010, Houston TX 77274	713-346-4000	R	7*	<.1
506	Ashland Industries Inc—Randy Rust	1115 Rail Dr, Ashland WI 54806	715-682-4622	R	7*	<.1
507	Green-Tek Inc—Paul Jacobson	3708 Enterprise Dr, Janesville WI 53546	608-754-7336	R	7*	<.1
508	Volunteer International Inc—Billy Cooper	PO Box 2388, Jackson TN 38302	731-422-3411	R	7*	<.1
509	Conroe Welding Supply Inc—Roy Morton	PO Box 1470, Conroe TX 77305	936-539-3124	R	7*	<.1
510	NNT Enterprises Inc—David Nyc	1320 Norwood Ave, Itasca IL 60143	630-875-9600	R	7*	<.1
511	Econo Products Inc—Peter May	PO Box 10458, Rochester NY 14610	585-288-7550	R	7*	<.1
512	US Tech Services Inc—Gary Conlan	3644 Meadow Chase Dr, Marietta GA 30062	770-973-7070	R	7*	.1
513	American Surplus Inc—William Maio	1 Noyes Ave Bldg B, Rumford RI 02916	401-434-4355	R	7*	<.1
514	Timberline International Inc—Don Williams	1967 E Grand Ave, Hot Springs AR 71901	501-623-1665	R	7*	<.1
515	O A Newton and Son Co—Robert Rider	PO Box 397, Bridgeville DE 19933	302-337-8211	R	7*	<.1
516	Universal Equipment Inc—Oliver Carmichael	PO Box 51206, Lafayette LA 70505	337-233-5292	R	7*	<.1
517	Productive Automated Systems Corp—Sandra Elfrink	2600 S Hanley Rd Ste 4, Saint Louis MO 63144	314-781-2212	R	7*	<.1
518	Madden Sales and Services Inc—Eddy Madden	PO Box 3826, Odessa TX 79760	432-335-8503	R	7*	<.1
519	Revenue Markets Inc—Robert Rosakranse	PO Box 10, Accord NY 12404	845-626-8655	R	7*	<.1
520	TCM Progressive Inc—Alan Rice	33900 W 9 Mile Rd, Farmington MI 48335	248-477-0650	R	7*	<.1
521	Dapra Corp—Linda Pilvelis	66 Granby St, Bloomfield CT 06002	860-286-8728	R	7*	<.1
522	Byars Machine Company Inc—Larry Edge	PO Box 1109, Laurens SC 29360	864-682-3146	R	7*	<.1
523	Flagship Automation Inc—Richard Padovano	1 Technology Dr, Uxbridge MA 01569	508-876-9700	R	7*	<.1
524	North - South Machinery Company Inc—James Swartzbaugh	1400 Pioneer St, Brea CA 92821	562-690-7616	R	7*	<.1
525	Washington Crane and Hoist Company Inc—Dale Currie	1334 Thornton Ave Sw, Pacific WA 98047	253-863-6661	R	7*	<.1
526	Joachim Machinery Company Inc—Jane Haley	4627 Independence Sq, Indianapolis IN 46203	317-781-2446	R	7*	.1
527	Allpoints Warehousing Equipment Co—Alan Bridges	5210 Causeway Blvd, Tampa FL 33619	813-246-5800	R	7*	<.1
528	Robert Childs Inc—Robert Childs	PO Box 1431, South Dennis MA 02660	508-398-2556	R	7*	<.1
529	North Light Color Inc—Tom Mittelstadt	5008 Hillsboro Ave N, Minneapolis MN 55428	763-531-8222	R	7*	<.1
530	Key Controls Of Tampa Inc—Robert Munday	5030 Gateway Blvd Ste, Lakeland FL 33811	863-583-0071	R	7*	<.1
531	Central Welding and Industrial Supply Company Inc—Randy Mann	1510 Hawkins Ave, Sanford NC 27330	919-776-0649	R	7*	<.1
532	Ismeca USA Inc—Beat Siegrist	5674 El Camino Real St, Carlsbad CA 92008	760-438-6150	R	7*	<.1
533	Rmh Enterprises Inc—Robert Houston	800 Compton Rd Unit 35, Cincinnati OH 45231	513-522-8340	R	7*	<.1
534	Environmental Control Systems Inc—Sam Hermann	22 Industrial Park Dr, Pelican Rapids MN 56572	218-863-1766	R	6*	<.1
535	Thompson Equipment Company Inc—Chris Wilkins	125 Industrial Ave, Jefferson LA 70121	504-833-6381	R	6*	<.1
536	Pacific Fluid Systems LLC—Tracy Baldwin	12990 Se Hwy 212, Clackamas OR 97015	503-222-3295	R	6*	<.1
537	Preferred Plastics and Packaging Company Inc—Randolph Swickle	681 Main St Ste 42, Belleville NJ 07109	973-759-1510	R	6*	<.1
538	Building Control Technologies Inc—Joel Demoura	100 Delawanna Ave Ste, Clifton NJ 07014	973-633-7730	R	6*	<.1
539	Fillipone Enterprises Inc—Charles Fillipone	2003 E 5th St Ste 1, Tempe AZ 85281	480-966-9311	R	6*	<.1
540	Petro Chem Industries Inc—Clifton Wolf	PO Box 938, Stafford TX 77497	713-645-5024	R	6*	<.1

Rank	Company Name—*Executive Officer*	Address, City, State, Zip	Phone	Type	Fin	Empls
541	Somarakis Inc—*John Somarakis*	PO Box 1948, Vancouver WA 98668	360-573-8542	R	6*	<.1
542	W D Machinery Company Inc—*Manfred Kuhn*	9101 Quivira Rd, Shawnee Mission KS 66215	913-492-9880	R	6*	<.1
543	Craftsman Tool and Mold Co—*Wayne Sikorcin*	2750 Church Rd, Aurora IL 60502	630-851-8700	R	6*	<.1
544	Brabazon Pumpe Company Ltd—*Heath Brabazon*	PO Box 10827, Green Bay WI 54307	920-498-6020	R	6*	<.1
545	Ms Precision Components LLC—*Chris Greck*	895 Garden Ln, Fowlerville MI 48836	517-223-1059	R	6*	<.1
546	Malloy North Carolina Inc—*M Malloy*	PO Box 668804, Charlotte NC 28266	704-364-8771	R	6*	<.1
547	Rusty's Weigh Scales and Service Inc—*Sherrel Jones*	408 N Interstate 27, Lubbock TX 79403	806-747-2912	R	6*	<.1
548	Columbia Southern Inc—*Lj Viotta*	7525 Nw 37th Ave Unit, Miami FL 33147	305-693-4239	R	6*	<.1
549	Osco Inc—*Jesus Osuna-Diaz*	2937 Waterview Dr, Rochester Hills MI 48309	248-852-7310	R	6*	<.1
550	United Industrial Services Inc—*Eugene Reopel*	PO Box 380, Agawam MA 01001	413-789-0896	R	6*	<.1
551	E H Lynn Industries Inc—*John Lynn*	524 Anderson Dr, Romeoville IL 60446	815-328-8800	R	6*	<.1
552	Marling and Associates Inc—*Robert Marling*	20882 Harper Ave, Harper Woods MI 48225	313-886-6210	R	6*	.1
553	Coast Tool and Supply—*Richard Blakley*	2379 Industry St, Oceanside CA 92054	760-757-8525	R	6*	.1
554	Grecon Dimter Inc—*Jeff Davidson*	8658 Huffman Ave, Connellys Springs NC 28612	704-799-0100	R	6*	<.1
555	Capweld Inc—*Dean Dunaway*	PO Box 22562, Jackson MS 39225	601-969-9266	R	6*	<.1
556	Swan Associates Inc—*Robert Mathews*	4680 E 2nd St Ste H, Benicia CA 94510	707-746-1989	R	6*	<.1
557	Independent Components Corp—*Richard Sirow*	528 Hempstead Tpke, West Hempstead NY 11552	516-481-5100	R	6*	<.1
558	General Aire Systems Inc—*Vince Salla*	PO Box 110, Darby PA 19023	610-532-3070	R	6*	<.1
559	G A Fleet Associates Inc—*David Shepard*	PO Box 616, Harrison NY 10528	914-835-4000	R	6*	<.1
560	Imbert International Inc—*William Toth*	7030 N Austin Ave, Niles IL 60714	847-588-3170	R	6*	<.1
561	Advanced Industrial And Marine Services Inc—*Rodney Masters*	1617 Peach Leaf St, Houston TX 77039	281-590-3240	R	6*	<.1
562	Fred Hill and Son Co—*Ken Shaw III*	PO Box 52498, Philadelphia PA 19115	215-698-2200	R	6*	<.1
563	Chicago Electric Co—*Robert E Kaska*	490 Tower Blvd, Carol Stream IL 60188	630-784-0800	R	6*	<.1
564	Berge's Governor Service Inc—*Nils Berge*	302 East D St, Wilmington CA 90744	310-830-4582	R	6	<.1
565	Raeco Inc—*RE Ekstrom*	135 Bernice Dr, Bensenville IL 60106	815-464-6200	R	6*	<.1
566	Advanced Power Services LLC—*John Gribok*	161 Woodford Ave Ste 4, Plainville CT 06062	860-747-8308	R	6*	<.1
567	Smith Engines Inc—*George Smith*	1601 Cross Beam Dr, Charlotte NC 28217	704-392-3100	R	6*	<.1
568	A-1 Air Compressor Corp—*Thomas Hintz*	679 W Winthrop Ave, Addison IL 60101	630-543-2606	R	6*	<.1
569	Midwest Industrial Tools Inc—*Allan Chartier*	PO Box 45206, Omaha NE 68145	402-334-2011	R	6*	<.1
570	Xanthus Inc—*Timothy Kline*	1555 Atlantic Blvd, Auburn Hills MI 48326	248-393-0909	R	6*	<.1
571	Greenville Tractor Company Inc—*Pruitt Toole*	PO Box 2086, Greenville SC 29602	864-232-2463	R	6*	<.1
572	Powerscreen Of Florida Inc—*Dennis Grant*	PO Box 5802, Lakeland FL 33807	863-687-7153	R	6*	<.1
573	Liberty Tool Company Inc—*Ray Wolfe*	2001 Peninsula Dr Ste, Erie PA 16506	610-431-4950	R	6*	<.1
574	Air Systems LLC—*Jim Turner*	4512 Bishop Ln, Louisville KY 40218	502-452-6312	R	6*	<.1
575	Travaini Pumps USA Inc—*Costantino Serpagli*	200 Newman Dr, Yorktown VA 23692	757-988-3930	R	6*	<.1
576	Nickerson Company Inc—*Richard Nickerson*	PO Box 25425, Salt Lake City UT 84125	801-973-8888	R	6*	<.1
577	Nyne Equipment Inc—*Ace Brandt*	1235 Rte 9, Castleton On Hudson NY 12033	518-732-7201	R	6*	<.1
578	Double A Trailer Sales Inc—*Mark Wannemacher*	PO Box 129, Delphos OH 45833	419-692-7626	R	6*	<.1
579	Friskney Equipment Inc—*Gilbert Friskney*	101 Woodhull Dr, Angola IN 46703	260-665-3600	R	6*	<.1
580	Specialty Tool Inc—*Tom Martin*	6925 Trafalgar Dr, Fort Wayne IN 46803	260-493-6351	R	6*	<.1
581	Galaxy Industries Inc—*Joseph Lebar*	231 Jandus Rd, Cary IL 60013	847-639-8580	R	6*	.1
582	Northwest Fuel Systems Inc—*Burl French*	PO Box 94, Kalispell MT 59903	406-755-4343	R	6*	<.1
583	Southwest Materials Handling Company Inc—*Joe Harper*	4719 Almond Ave, Dallas TX 75247	214-630-1375	R	6*	<.1
584	K and K Material Handling Inc—*Le Kaczorowski*	PO Box 10476, Green Bay WI 54307	920-336-3499	R	5*	<.1
585	Hometowne Energy Company Inc—*Chris Andrews*	768 Brooks Ave, Rochester NY 14619	585-436-7503	R	5*	<.1
586	Digital Wave Corp—*Michael Gorman*	13760 E Arapahoe Rd, Centennial CO 80112	303-790-7559	R	5*	<.1
587	General Oil Corp—*Charles Zullo*	1215 Henderson Ave, Washington PA 15301	724-225-8700	R	5*	.1
588	Torgerson's LLC—*Wayne Fisher*	4701 River Dr N, Great Falls MT 59405	406-453-1453	R	5*	<.1
589	Arnold S Welding Service Inc—*Bill Arnold*	1405 Waterless St, Fayetteville NC 28306	910-485-6618	R	5*	<.1
590	Cross Services Inc—*Robert Thompson*	PO Box 3799, Houma LA 70361	985-868-3928	R	5*	<.1
591	W L Walker Company Inc—*Anne Bracket*	330 N Boulder Ave, Tulsa OK 74103	918-583-3109	R	5*	<.1
592	Ams Controls Inc—*Andrew Allman*	12180 Prichard Farm Rd, Maryland Heights MO 63043	314-344-3144	R	5*	<.1
593	Heritage Equipment Co—*Eric Zwirner*	9000 Heritage Dr, Plain City OH 43064	614-873-3941	R	5*	<.1
594	Murphy-Rodgers Inc—*Otto Seeman*	2301 Belgrave Ave, Huntington Park CA 90255	323-587-4118	R	5*	<.1
595	Pmt Forklift Corp—*Pedro Deleon*	275 Great E Neck Rd, West Babylon NY 11704	631-661-5050	R	5*	<.1
596	Trupar LLC—*Jeffrey Carnahan*	PO Box 725377, Berkley MI 48072	248-583-1300	R	5*	<.1
597	B and H Machine Sales Inc—*Richard Bekolay*	PO Box 7340, Dearborn MI 48121	313-843-6720	R	5*	<.1
598	Alaska Pump and Supply Inc—*Terry Gorlick*	261 E 56th Ave Bldg A, Anchorage AK 99518	907-563-3424	R	5*	<.1
599	Parson And Sanderson Inc—*Edmond Parson*	PO Box 958, Metairie LA 70004	504-733-1330	R	5*	<.1
600	Power Clean 2000 Inc—*Candace Chen*	3710 Avalon Blvd, Los Angeles CA 90011	323-235-2000	R	5*	<.1
601	Hi Pressure Inc—*Daryl Payne*	6618 Topper Rdg Ste 1, San Antonio TX 78233	210-637-6700	R	5*	<.1
602	Superior Industrial Sales and Service Inc—*Charles Goostrey*	116 N State St, Jackson MI 49201	517-784-0539	R	5*	<.1
603	Goettsch International Inc—*Eric Goettsch*	9852 Redhill Dr, Blue Ash OH 45242	513-563-6500	R	5*	<.1
604	Hatch and Kirk Inc—*Michael Korotkin*	5111 Leary Ave Nw, Seattle WA 98107	206-783-2766	R	5*	.2
605	Strunk Brothers Inc—*Charles Strunk*	322 Norma Rd, Huntsville TN 37756	423-663-2564	R	5*	.1
606	Alliance Maintenance and Services Inc	3233 W 11th St Ste 100, Houston TX 77008	713-863-0000	R	5*	<.1
607	Henrob Corp—*Keith Jones*	35455 Veronica St, Livonia MI 48150	734-521-3000	R	5*	<.1
608	Southern California Hydraulic Engineering Corp—*Donna Perez*	1130 Columbia St, Brea CA 92821	714-257-4800	R	5*	<.1
609	Global EDM Supplies Inc—*Christopher Frost*	1111 Western Row Rd St, Mason OH 45040	513-573-9918	R	5*	<.1
610	Cross Truck Equipment Company Inc—*M Cross*	PO Box 80509, Canton OH 44708	330-477-8151	R	5*	<.1
611	Energenecs Inc—*Jared Feider*	W59n249 Cardinal Ave, Cedarburg WI 53012	262-377-6360	R	5*	<.1
612	Dickinson Equipment Company LLC	3220 17th Ave W, Seattle WA 98119	206-285-1090	R	5*	<.1
613	Fame Industries Inc—*Jesse Wyka*	51100 Grand River Ave, Wixom MI 48393	248-348-7760	R	5*	<.1
614	Phoenix Installation and Management Co—*Steve Leffler*	397 Haven Hill Rd, Shelbyville KY 40065	502-633-6230	R	5*	<.1
615	Lifco Hydraulics Inc—*Edward Clarke*	100 River Rock Dr Ste, Buffalo NY 14207	716-447-0071	R	5*	<.1
616	Industrial Systems Of Cape Girardeau Inc—*Rodney Norder*	2292 Rusmar St, Cape Girardeau MO 63703	573-334-5766	R	5*	<.1
617	T P Supply Company Inc—*Troy Payne*	PO Box 1543, Mount Airy NC 27030	336-789-2337	R	5*	<.1
618	Midlands Millroom Supply Inc—*Fred Clark*	PO Box 7007, Canton OH 44705	330-453-9100	R	5*	<.1
619	Fabricating and Production Machinery Inc—*Joseph Lowkes*	PO Box 240, Spencer MA 01562	508-885-9973	R	5*	<.1
620	Rodico Inc—*Dieter Neuber*	228 State Rt 17, Upper Saddle River NJ 07458	201-327-6303	R	5*	<.1
621	Service Hydraulic and Supply—*Robert Millan*	615 Airport Dr, Shreveport LA 71107	318-226-1000	R	5*	<.1
622	AW Bohanan Company Inc—*Al Bohanan*	PO Box 1743, Gastonia NC 28053	704-922-9811	R	5*	<.1
623	E P Of Cleveland Inc—*Matt Ontur*	7621 Hub Pkwy, Cleveland OH 44125	216-447-0898	R	5*	<.1
624	Starlift Equipment Company Inc—*Raymond Picarillo*	829 1st Ave, West Haven CT 06516	203-937-8101	R	5*	<.1
625	Beacon Brothers Development Corp—*Timothy Rossetti*	189 Meister Ave, Branchburg NJ 08876	908-231-8077	R	5*	<.1
626	Hassig and Sons Inc—*Arnold Hassig*	5700 Frazho Rd, Warren MI 48091	586-756-7800	R	5*	<.1
627	Herkules Equipment Corp—*Todd Bacon*	2760 Ridgeway Ct, Commerce Township MI 48390	248-960-7100	R	5*	<.1
628	Industrial Air and Hydraulics—*Gary Brown*	111 Gordy Rd, Salisbury MD 21804	410-749-1400	R	5*	<.1
629	Dipaco Incorporated L—*L Walker*	PO Box 11990, Reno NV 89510	775-329-7511	R	5*	<.1
630	Memphis Material Handling Inc—*Russell Caldwell*	3875 Air Park St, Memphis TN 38118	901-947-7225	R	5*	<.1

Note: An asterisk (*) indicates an estimated financial figure. The company type code used is as follows: R = Private, P = Public, S = Private Subsidiary, B = Public Subsidiary, D = Division, J = Joint Venture, I = Investment Fund.

COMPANY RANKINGS BY SALES WITHIN 4-DIGIT SIC

Rank	Company Name—Executive Officer	Address, City, State, Zip	Phone	Type	Fin	Empls
631	Hydraulic Systems And Components Inc—Rassoul Ketabian	725 N Twin Oaks Valley, San Marcos CA 92069	760-744-9350	R	5*	<.1
632	Laser Products Inc—Glenn Rudman	11975 Sw 142nd Ter Ste, Miami FL 33186	305-235-9544	R	5*	<.1
633	International Thermoproducts—Randall Newcomb	11015 Mission Park Ct, Santee CA 92071	619-562-7001	R	5*	.1
634	Specialty Compressor and Engine Company Inc—Roland Ledford	PO Box 783, Borger TX 79008	806-273-9912	R	5*	<.1
635	Universal Chemical And Supply Corp—Marie Smith	PO Box 85217, Hallandale FL 33008	954-454-9731	R	5*	<.1
636	Best and Donovan NA Inc—L Andre	5570 Creek Rd, Blue Ash OH 45242	513-791-9180	R	5*	<.1
637	Flint Machine Tools Inc—Steven Flint	3710 Hewatt Ct, Snellville GA 30039	770-985-2626	R	5*	<.1
638	Iwi Inc—Jeffery Iacco	1399 Rockefeller Rd, Wickliffe OH 44092	440-585-5902	R	5*	<.1
639	John E Fox Inc—Harry Berzack	PO Box 668943, Charlotte NC 28266	704-399-4581	R	5*	<.1
640	Mid-Ohio Forklifts Inc—Art Sherwood	1336 Home Ave, Akron OH 44310	330-633-1230	R	5*	<.1
641	Palatine Welding Co—Dana Piacenza	3848 Berdnick St, Rolling Meadows IL 60008	847-358-1075	R	5*	<.1
642	Techmaster Inc—Michael Radosevic	N94w14376 Garwin Mace, Menomonee Falls WI 53051	262-255-2022	R	5*	<.1
643	Abrasive Tool Specialties—Dave Hellberg	PO Box 25596, Salt Lake City UT 84125	801-978-4420	R	5*	<.1
644	Southeast Industrial Components LLC—Rita Salsbury	PO Box 519, Moncks Corner SC 29461	843-761-6570	R	5*	<.1
645	Baltec Corporation—Fritz Boesch	130 Technology Dr, Canonsburg PA 15317	724-873-5757	R	5*	<.1
646	Key Machine Tool Inc—Thomas Kovalenko	PO Box 1004, Elkhart IN 46515	574-262-1537	R	5*	<.1
647	Texican Turbines and Technology—Ken Blake	7958 Hwy 167 S, Winnfield LA 71483	318-628-4114	R	5*	<.1
648	Menges Roller Company Inc—Matthew Menges	260 Industrial Dr, Wauconda IL 60084	847-487-8877	R	5*	<.1
649	Oliver Equipment Co—Gale Oliver	PO Box 41145, Houston TX 77241	713-856-9206	R	5*	<.1
650	Neff Power Inc—John Murphy	13750 Shoreline Dr, Earth City MO 63045	314-727-6200	R	5*	<.1
651	Mid-Florida Forklift Inc—James Hall	9856 S Orange Ave, Orlando FL 32824	407-859-8750	R	5*	<.1
652	Arr Tech Manufacturing—Tad Marquis	PO Box 10932, Yakima WA 98909	509-966-4300	R	5*	<.1
653	Applied Recovery Systems Inc—Michael Lockman	PO Box 20785, Waco TX 76702	254-666-0144	R	5*	<.1
654	Automotive Precision Machinery Inc—Charles Ratteree	5250 Ga Hwy 85, Forest Park GA 30297	404-768-8830	R	5*	<.1
655	Emrick And Hill Inc—John Adams	4160 Fox St, Denver CO 80216	303-433-7237	R	5*	<.1
656	Mays-Shedd Sales Co—Jeffrey Shroyer	2931 Boulder Ave, Dayton OH 45414	937-277-9451	R	5*	<.1
657	Harris Machine Tools Inc—Jean Harris	14309 Sommermeyer St, Houston TX 77041	713-462-5800	R	5*	<.1
658	Accurate- Superior Scale Co—Mark Hebenstreit	5404 Jedmed Ct, Saint Louis MO 63129	314-845-7778	R	5*	<.1
659	Colliflower Inc—Jim Beachley	11436 Cronridge Dr Ste, Owings Mills MD 21117	410-902-0111	R	4*	<.1
660	Oil Equipment Sales And Service Company Inc—Charles Hubbard	PO Box 5096, Chesapeake VA 23324	757-543-3596	R	4*	<.1
661	Fd Johnson Co—John Robson	31200 Solon Rd Ste 18, Solon OH 44139	440-248-3470	R	4*	<.1
662	Lamco Slings and Rigging Inc—William Lambrecht	4960 41st St Ct, Moline IL 61265	309-764-7400	R	4*	<.1
663	Fluid Power Equipment Inc—Robert Shell	PO Box 40530, Houston TX 77240	713-466-8088	R	4*	<.1
664	Padre Island Brewing Company Inc—Tony Benson	3400 Padre Blvd, South Padre Island TX 78597	956-761-9585	R	4*	<.1
665	SJM Engineering Inc—Stephen Mullen	121 Water St Apt 44, Beverly MA 01915	978-921-2294	R	4*	<.1
666	Konica Minolta Sensing Americas Inc—Hal Yamazaki	101 Williams Dr, Ramsey NJ 07446	201-236-4300	R	4*	<.1
667	Tom Langhals—Tom Langhals	4599 Campbell Rd, Columbus Grove OH 45830	419-659-5629	R	4*	<.1
668	Ogden Forklifts LLC	PO Box 43606, Atlanta GA 30336	404-696-0566	R	4*	<.1
669	Kafco Sales Co—Akira Urakawa	PO Box 58563, Los Angeles CA 90058	323-588-7141	R	4*	<.1
670	Floyd V Wells Inc—Charles Wells	2530 S Broadway Ste C, Santa Maria CA 93454	805-925-8626	R	4*	<.1
671	Malcolm T Gilliland Inc—Malcolm Gilliland	PO Box 2066, Peachtree City GA 30269	770-487-7942	R	4*	<.1
672	Unittool Punch and Die Company Inc—Frank Deni	PO Box 863, Buffalo NY 14240	716-873-8453	R	4*	<.1
673	Summit Pump Inc—Scott Keller	PO Box 12145, Green Bay WI 54307	920-869-4800	R	4*	<.1
674	Cobb Carpet Supply Co—Randall Cobb	1314 Viceroy Dr, Dallas TX 75247	214-634-2622	R	4*	<.1
675	Shanley Pump and Equipment Inc—Larry Shanley	2525 S Clearbrook Dr, Arlington Heights IL 60005	847-439-9200	R	4*	<.1
676	Acme Industrial Sales—John Doucette	1204 E Main St, Stockton CA 95205	209-948-6735	R	4*	<.1
677	Keenline Inc—Peter Kersztyn	1936 Chase Dr, Omro WI 54963	920-685-0365	R	4*	<.1
678	BW D Inc—Merrill Witt	4406 W Wall St, Midland TX 79703	432-697-2241	R	4*	<.1
679	G and F Systems Inc—Frank Salsone	208 Babylon Tpke, Roosevelt NY 11575	516-868-4923	R	4*	<.1
680	Sparling Instruments LLC—Steve Herald	4097 Temple City Blvd, El Monte CA 91731	626-444-0571	R	4*	<.1
681	Chicago Electric Sales Inc—Robert Kaska	490 Tower Blvd, Carol Stream IL 60188	630-495-2900	R	4*	<.1
682	Bayou City Pump Works 1 LP—W Emmons	PO Box 23342, Houston TX 77228	713-631-6451	R	4*	<.1
683	LC Liftpak—Ric Fiedler	4273 Will Rogers Pkwy, Oklahoma City OK 73108	405-947-5100	R	4*	<.1
684	R E Prescott Company Inc—Perrin Prescott	PO Box 339, Exeter NH 03833	603-772-4321	R	4*	<.1
685	Tri-Line Automation Corp—Mark Schiesser	250 Summit Point Dr, Henrietta NY 14467	585-321-9620	R	4*	<.1
686	Inland Printing Company Inc—Edward Lee	PO Box 1574, Springfield MO 65801	417-869-6484	R	4*	<.1
687	Die Cast Press Manufacturing Company Inc—Kasper Smidt	PO Box 268, Paw Paw MI 49079	269-657-6060	R	4*	<.1
688	DIVC O Inc—Sandy Jarvis	2806 N Sheridan Rd, Tulsa OK 74115	918-836-9101	R	4*	<.1
689	Mountain Machine Works—Rebecca Cote	2589 Hotel Rd, Auburn ME 04210	207-783-6680	R	4*	<.1
690	Turbo Dynamics Corp—Mansour Lavi	150 Express St Ste 2, Plainview NY 11803	516-349-8012	R	4*	<.1
691	Industrial Handling Equipment Inc—Tony Fackelmann	PO Box 191, Sparks NV 89432	775-359-3335	R	4*	<.1
692	Bay Verte Machinery Inc—John Krawczyk	975 Parkview Rd Ste 6, Green Bay WI 54304	920-336-7440	R	4*	<.1
693	Powermotion Inc—Jack Carter	90 Robert Jemison Rd, Birmingham AL 35209	205-945-1931	R	4*	<.1
694	West Side Industrial Supply Inc—Thomas Conway	1530 N La Fox St Ste 1, South Elgin IL 60177	847-931-7200	R	4*	<.1
695	Chase-Logeman Corp—Douglas Logeman	303 Friendship Dr, Greensboro NC 27409	336-665-0754	R	4*	<.1
696	International Bag Applications Corp—Peter Allen	PO Box 130880, Spring TX 77393	281-681-0122	R	4*	.1
697	Char-Nor Enterprises Inc—Charles Arnold	PO Box 980, Milan IL 61264	309-787-2427	R	4*	.1
698	Decorating Supplies and Equipment Inc—Paul Carnes	4040 Vogel Rd, Evansville IN 47715	812-473-5050	R	4*	<.1
699	Industrial Packaging Supply Inc—Matt Hogan	122 Main St, Oxford MA 01540	508-499-1600	R	4*	<.1
700	A Liss and Company Inc—Jeffrey Liss	5155 59th Pl, Woodside NY 11377	718-728-0600	R	4*	<.1
701	Petada Company LLC—Jason Larson	2745 Broadway St Ste 1, Cheektowaga NY 14227	716-894-6370	R	4*	<.1
702	Love Machine Company Inc—Richard Love	1645 S 700 W, Salt Lake City UT 84104	801-972-3366	R	4*	<.1
703	Met Pro Supply Inc—Jay Hazen	1550 Centennial Blvd, Bartow FL 33830	863-533-7155	R	4*	<.1
704	Automatic Controls Co—Pierre Grimes	2719 Industrial Row, Troy MI 48084		R	4*	<.1
705	Carlson Dimond and Wright—James L Mousseau	25201 Terra Industrial, Chesterfield MI 48051	586-949-5474	R	4*	<.1
706	John M Allen Co—Frank Whalen	21294 Drake Rd, Strongsville OH 44149	440-238-8700	R	4*	<.1
707	Worldwide Exporters Inc—Scott Manhard	26366 Carmel Rancho Ln, Carmel CA 93923	831-622-5000	R	4*	<.1
708	American ELTEC Inc—Janet Romano Ferris	2401 Windjammer Way, Las Vegas NV 89107	702-878-4085	S	4*	<.1
709	Hardin Tubular Sales Inc—Doc Hardin	PO Box 374, Victoria TX 77902	361-573-2252	R	4*	<.1
710	Plustar Inc—Byron Barlow	2650 Nova Dr, Dallas TX 75229	972-406-1300	R	4*	<.1
711	Robin Hood Supplies Inc—Robin Hood	PO Box 241, Utica MS 39175	601-885-6524	R	4*	<.1
712	Nsrw Inc—Joanne Dinsmore	PO Box 1147, Pelham AL 35124	205-663-1500	R	4*	<.1
713	LR Environmental Equip Company Inc—Richard Fleck	12902 S Spring St, Los Angeles CA 90061	323-770-0634	R	4*	<.1
714	Rankin Automation Company LLC—Joe Blossic	PO Box 190, Broomall PA 19008	610-544-6800	R	4*	<.1
715	General Glass Equipment Co—Victor Plumbo	PO Box 711, Absecon NJ 08201	609-345-7500	R	4*	<.1
716	California Food Technology LLC—Ray Camezon	PO Box 2526, Danville CA 94526	925-736-2784	R	4*	<.1
717	Bo's Hydraulic's Inc—M Thomason	1138 Huell Matthews Hw, South Boston VA 24592	434-575-7506	R	4*	<.1
718	Eastern Lift Truck Inc—Barb Haynes	8001 Penn Randall Pl, Upper Marlboro MD 20772	301-735-7911	R	4*	<.1

Rank	Company Name—*Executive Officer*	Address, City, State, Zip	Phone	Type	Fin	Empls
719	North American Hydraulics Inc—*Bob Lamb*	11549 Sun Belt Ct, Baton Rouge LA 70809	225-751-0500	R	4*	<.1
720	J and S Ventures Inc—*Shawn Chalmers*	705 Sw 10th St Ste 109, Blue Springs MO 64015	816-224-9900	R	4*	<.1
721	Kerley and Sears Inc—*Thomas Sears*	4331 Cement Valley Rd, Midlothian TX 76065	972-775-3902	R	4*	<.1
722	Don Bell Inc—*Bernice Bell*	2808 S Harbor City Blv, Melbourne FL 32901	321-725-8009	R	4*	<.1
723	Fagor Automation Corp—*Fernando D'landa*	2250 Estes Ave, Elk Grove Village IL 60007	847-981-1500	R	4*	<.1
724	Tomahawk Manufacturing Inc—*Bob Tournour*	4716 S Taylor Dr, Sheboygan WI 53081	920-458-8008	R	4*	<.1
725	Yamada America Inc—*Shinji Kameyama*	955 E Algonquin Rd, Arlington Heights IL 60005	847-228-9063	R	4*	<.1
726	EH Walker Supply Company Inc—*Kyle Walker*	45 Derwood Cir, Rockville MD 20850	301-738-6500	R	4*	<.1
727	Expert Crane Inc—*James Doty*	10737 Leuer Ave, Cleveland OH 44108	216-451-9900	R	4*	<.1
728	Sully and Son Hydraulics Inc—*James Sullivan*	PO Box 71270, Bakersfield CA 93387	661-322-2027	R	4*	<.1
729	Arrow Valve and Instrument Inc—*Thomas Balke*	7215 Miller Rd 2, Houston TX 77049	713-672-8423	R	4*	<.1
730	Gt Technology Company Inc—*Thomas Bolz*	3000 Town Ctr Ste 407, Southfield MI 48075	248-358-1030	R	4*	<.1
731	Ohio Graphco Inc—*Christopher Manley*	6563 Cochran Rd, Solon OH 44139	440-248-1700	R	4*	<.1
732	Dennis Design and Manufacturing Inc—*Charles Swanson*	4202 Jessup Rd, Ceres CA 95307	209-632-9956	R	4*	<.1
733	Doering Equipment Company Inc—*Donald Doering*	PO Box N, Franklin MA 02038	508-520-3629	R	4*	<.1
734	Elwood Safety Company Inc—*Peter Gennis*	2180 Elmwood Ave, Buffalo NY 14216	716-877-6622	R	4*	<.1
735	Gk Industrial—*Bruce Gustavason*	3207 C St Ne, Auburn WA 98002	253-735-5543	R	4*	<.1
736	Joe Hill Company Inc—*Joe Hill*	PO Box 6333, Knoxville TN 37914	865-525-1690	R	4*	<.1
737	Powerhouse Diesel Services Inc—*Jim Jones*	4700 E 2nd St, Benicia CA 94510	707-747-6737	R	4*	<.1
738	Triad Tooling Inc—*Robert Vecchiarelli*	7885 W 48th Ave, Wheat Ridge CO 80033	303-424-4280	R	4*	<.1
739	Vance Holdings Inc—*Robin Vance*	809 S Main St, Fredericktown MO 63645	573-783-6334	R	4*	<.1
740	Apparel Machinery and Supply Co—*David Bachrach*	1836 E Ontario St, Philadelphia PA 19134	215-634-2626	R	4*	<.1
741	Spego Inc—*Harvey Spiegel*	21 Old County Home Rd, Asheville NC 28806	828-258-8008	R	4*	<.1
742	Industrial Recovery Service Inc—*Larry Liebgott*	PO Box 5086, York PA 17405	717-854-0316	R	4*	<.1
743	Pentek Inc—*Sheldon Lefkowitz*	1026 4th Ave, Coraopolis PA 15108	412-262-0725	R	4*	<.1
744	Hydro Dynamics Inc—*Robert Newell*	6200 Delfield Dr, Waterford MI 48329	248-623-4700	R	4*	<.1
745	Ralph's Industrial Sewing Machine Company Inc—*Irma Badillo*	PO Box 11307, Denver CO 80211	303-455-6831	R	4*	<.1
746	TEI Engineered Products Inc—*Steve Westmoreland*	PO Box 4611, Englewood CO 80155	303-693-1491	R	4*	<.1
747	David T Olson Inc—*Clinton Olson*	2425 E 25th St, Minneapolis MN 55406	612-722-9523	R	4*	<.1
748	Diesel Engine Parts Inc—*Rick Emmert*	210 Sam Ray Burn Pkwy, Lenoir City TN 37771	865-270-8200	R	4*	<.1
749	Bay Area Oil Supply Inc—*James Lin*	898 E Fremont Ave, Sunnyvale CA 94087	408-738-4838	R	4*	<.1
750	Ink Cupsnow Corp—*Benjamin Adner*	20 Locust St Ste 104, Danvers MA 01923	978-646-8980	R	4*	<.1
751	National Distribution Systems Inc—*Louis Barrett*	8845 First Industrial, Southaven MS 38671	662-393-6522	R	4*	<.1
752	Stewart Instrument Company Inc—*William Stewart*	PO Box 1507, Gonzales LA 70707	225-647-1999	R	4*	<.1
753	Hamar Laser Instruments Inc—*Roderick Hamar*	5 Ye Olde Rd, Danbury CT 06810	203-730-4600	R	4*	<.1
754	M.and L Engine LLC—*Cynthia Naquin*	1212 Saint Charles St, Houma LA 70360	985-857-8000	R	4*	<.1
755	Su America Inc—*Antonio Maccaferri*	5200 Prairie Stone Pkw, Hoffman Estates IL 60192	847-649-1476	R	4*	<.1
756	Capital Engine Co—*Richard Cowher*	97 Cypress St Sw, Reynoldsburg OH 43068	740-964-0089	R	4*	<.1
757	Ver-Tech Inc—*Anthony Vertin*	6801 Bleck Dr, Rockford MN 55373	763-559-2590	R	4*	<.1
758	Pneudralic Power Inc—*Wally Gorka*	3319 Regent Rd, Cleveland OH 44127	216-341-3100	R	4*	<.1
759	Kaltenbach Inc—*Davi Mccorry*	6775 Inwood Dr, Columbus IN 47201	812-342-4471	R	4*	<.1
760	Tech-Energy Co—*John Pickard*	1111 Schneider, Cibolo TX 78108	210-658-0614	R	3*	<.1
761	Bill S Repair Shop Inc—*Barry Cook*	PO Box 1760, Hildebran NC 28637	828-397-6941	R	3*	<.1
762	Imr Environmental Equipment Inc—*Dieter Gromadzki*	3634 Central Ave, Saint Petersburg FL 33711	727-328-2818	R	3*	<.1
763	Mill and Mine Supply Co—*William Steward*	PO Box 15188, Little Rock AR 72231	501-375-0224	R	3*	<.1
764	Air-Oil Systems Inc—*Robert Hicks*	753 Wambold Rd, Mainland PA 19451	215-721-9595	R	3*	<.1
765	Handling Systems Inc—*James Chereskin*	PO Box 626, La Grange IL 60525	708-352-1213	R	3*	<.1
766	Hill Specialty Company Inc—*W Hill*	PO Box 69070, Odessa TX 79769	432-367-9381	R	3*	<.1
767	Koehl Brothers Inc—*James Kafer*	PO Box 286, Fairbury IL 61739	815-692-2326	R	3*	<.1
768	Central Service and Supply Inc—*Dan Abramovich*	1701 Se Hulsizer Rd, Ankeny IA 50021	515-964-8600	R	3*	<.1
769	Mid Oklahoma Coop—*Linda Hill*	115 E Oklahoma, Okarche OK 73762	405-263-7289	R	3*	<.1
770	SC Industrial Resource Group Inc—*David Spencer*	PO Box 473066, Garland TX 75047	972-272-4521	R	3*	<.1
771	Ultra Safe Inc—*Marty Sharp*	2339 N 34th Dr, Phoenix AZ 85009	602-484-7713	R	3*	<.1
772	Horizontal Technology Inc—*John English*	12029 Brittmoore Park, Houston TX 77041	713-774-5594	R	3*	<.1
773	Soltec Inc—*Byron Intire*	PO Box 792, San Fernando CA 91341	818-365-0800	R	3*	<.1
774	Adwood Corp—*Rudolf Stockinger*	PO Box 1195, High Point NC 27261	336-884-1846	R	3*	<.1
775	Bsi Industries Inc—*Vladimir Gokun*	630 Morrison Rd Ste 10, Gahanna OH 43230	614-863-4787	R	3*	<.1
776	Paul O Young Co—*Paul Young*	55 E Cherry Ln, Souderton PA 18964	215-723-4400	R	3*	<.1
777	Supertek USA Corp—*John Shen*	10168 Olney St, El Monte CA 91731	626-350-6362	R	3*	<.1
778	Tps International Inc—*Dean Bentzien*	PO Box 143, Sussex WI 53089	262-246-6110	R	3*	<.1
779	Readco Inc—*Lawrence Read*	725 Venice Blvd, Los Angeles CA 90015	213-749-9451	R	3*	<.1
780	Ritter Manufacturing Inc—*Ase Stornetta*	1300b W 4th St, Antioch CA 94509	925-757-7296	R	3*	<.1
781	Pittsburgh Design Services Inc—*Beth Noonan*	PO Box 469, Carnegie PA 15106	412-276-3000	R	3*	<.1
782	Megatex World Inc—*Elias Nathani*	PO Box 256, Glendale CA 91209	818-548-5394	R	3*	<.1
783	Westport Hardness and Gaging Corp—*Robert Forbes*	510 Montauk Hwy Ste F, West Islip NY 11795	631-321-0160	R	3*	<.1
784	George E Kent Company Inc—*Jonathan Dolan*	PO Box 606, Norwood MA 02062	781-769-1100	R	3*	<.1
785	HD Chasen Company Inc—*Harvey Chasen*	PO Box 170, Somerville MA 02143	617-666-9090	R	3*	<.1
786	Option Iii Inc—*Robert Cann*	10430 J St Ste 1, Omaha NE 68127	402-593-7660	R	3*	<.1
787	Diehl Woodworking Machinery Inc—*Robert Rozman*	PO Box 465, Wabash IN 46992	260-563-2102	R	3*	<.1
788	Ion Technologies Corp—*John Graves*	7494 Muchmore Close, Cincinnati OH 45243	513-561-7660	R	3*	<.1
789	Signal One Fire And Communication LLC—*John Grako*	6100 S Maple Ave Ste 1, Tempe AZ 85283	480-752-1777	R	3*	<.1
790	Crest Supply—*William Rogers*	984 W James Lee Blvd, Crestview FL 32536	850-682-2087	R	3*	<.1
791	Eagle Flo Pumps Inc—*Joe Hamadeh*	306 Orient Way Unit 1, Rutherford NJ 07070	201-438-8595	R	3*	<.1
792	Fanta Equipment Co—*Frank Fanta*	6521 Storer Ave, Cleveland OH 44102	216-281-1515	R	3*	<.1
793	Angel Air Repair and Specialty Company Inc—*Pamela Dore*	705 Hangar Dr, New Iberia LA 70560	337-364-6695	R	3*	<.1
794	Jps Technologies Inc—*Robert Brandner*	11110 Deerfield Rd, Blue Ash OH 45242	513-984-6400	R	3*	<.1
795	Wmh Fluidpower Inc—*Dave Gruss*	862 Lenox Ave, Portage MI 49024	269-327-7011	R	3*	<.1
796	Mid Valley Equipment—*Duane Cotter*	PO Box 8249, Weslaco TX 78599	956-969-0806	R	3*	<.1
797	Springwood Industrial Inc—*Chung Young*	1062 N Kraemer Pl, Anaheim CA 92806	714-632-9701	R	3*	<.1
798	Nu-Meat Technology Inc—*John Sbraga*	PO Box 897, South Plainfield NJ 07080	908-754-3400	R	3*	<.1
799	Edwards Equipment Sales Inc—*James Edwards*	PO Box 19459, Birmingham AL 35219	205-942-8265	R	3*	<.1
800	Pan Pacific Enterprises Inc—*Al Balow*	2822 Juniper St Ste 2, Fairfax VA 22031	703-641-0400	R	3*	<.1
801	Kansas Forklift Inc—*Linda Large*	PO Box 13296, Wichita KS 67213	316-262-1426	R	3*	<.1
802	Raco International LP—*John Piaggesi*	3350 Industrial Blvd, Bethel Park PA 15102	412-835-5744	R	3*	<.1
803	Control Specialists Inc—*Michael Lutterbach*	PO Box 6770, Evansville IN 47719	812-425-9249	R	3*	<.1
804	Mckenzie Handling Systems Inc—*Cooper Mckenzie*	3127 Dublin Ln, Bessemer AL 35022	205-424-4151	R	3*	<.1
805	A G Systems LLC—*Aaron Mckinney*	354 Commerce Ave, New Castle PA 16101	724-657-8100	R	3*	<.1
806	Butler National Services Inc—*Clark D Stewart*	2772 NW 31st Ave, Fort Lauderdale FL 33311	954-733-7511	D	3*	<.1
807	American Monorail Of California LP—*Wendi Baran*	10805 Painter Ave, Santa Fe Springs CA 90670	562-462-1655	R	3*	<.1
808	Blumer USA Inc—*Kevin Coyle*	PO Box 521, Windsor CT 06095	860-688-1589	R	3*	<.1

Note: An asterisk (*) indicates an estimated financial figure. The company type code used is as follows: R = Private, P = Public, S = Private Subsidiary, B = Public Subsidiary, D = Division, J = Joint Venture, I = Investment Fund.

COMPANY RANKINGS BY SALES WITHIN 4-DIGIT SIC

Rank	Company Name—Executive Officer	Address, City, State, Zip	Phone	Type	Fin	Empls
809	Gemini Enterprises Inc—Nezih Zeren	14550 Torrey Chase Blv, Houston TX 77014	281-583-2900	R	3*	<.1
810	Westland International Corp—Casey Westbrook	5000 Hwy 80 E, Jackson MS 39208		R	3*	<.1
811	J Lee Hackett Co—J Lee Juett	5981 E Miller Way, Bloomfield Hills MI 48301	248-593-8589	R	3*	<.1
812	Romark Industries Inc—Alan Greenleaf	20950 Center Ridge Rd, Cleveland OH 44116	440-333-5480	R	3*	<.1
813	Simco Technology Inc—William Simpson	PO Box 1797, Norcross GA 30091	770-729-9100	R	3*	<.1
814	Outside Rms Inc—Aubrey Schultz	PO Box 1000, Westminster MD 21158	410-876-1160	R	3*	<.1
815	I C E S Of Gaston County Inc—Jesse Huffstickler	PO Box 89, Stanley NC 28164	704-263-1418	R	3*	<.1
816	Compumachine Inc—David Shaby	6 Electronics Ave, Danvers MA 01923	978-777-8440	R	3*	<.1
817	Baker-Bohnert Rubber Company Inc—Timothy Baker	PO Box 161238, Louisville KY 40256	502-634-3661	R	3*	<.1
818	Tak Enterprises Inc—Thomas Kunkler	70 Enterprise Dr Ste 1, Bristol CT 06010	860-583-0517	R	3*	<.1
819	Acme Products And Engineering Inc—Neil Falcone	556 39th St, Brooklyn NY 11232	718-851-4200	R	3*	<.1
820	Halsen Enterprises Inc—Tryce Senter	PO Box 877, Belmont MS 38827	662-454-7821	R	3*	<.1
821	Oasis Car Wash Systems Inc—Stephen Wade	1909 E 12th St, Galena KS 66739	620-783-1355	R	3*	<.1
822	Reo Hydraulic and Manufacturing Inc—Robert Obrecht	18475 Sherwood St, Detroit MI 48234	313-891-2244	R	3*	<.1
823	CCBB Inc—Stephen Weiss	850 Pennsylvania Blvd, Feasterville Trevose PA 19053	215-364-5377	R	3*	<.1
824	Advanced Power Systems International Inc—Shayne Murphy	339 Main St, Torrington CT 06790	860-435-2525	R	3*	<.1
825	Millstone Enterprises Inc—John Miller	9800 Fallard Ter, Upper Marlboro MD 20772	301-599-7505	R	3*	<.1
826	Southland Equipment Service Inc—Diane Poston	109 N Shorecrest Rd, Columbia SC 29209	803-783-1171	R	3*	<.1
827	Moore Co—John Moore	800 S Missouri Ave, Marceline MO 64658	660-376-3575	R	3*	<.1
828	Lubromation Inc—Van Dorsey	PO Box 669283, Charlotte NC 28266	704-375-7704	R	3*	<.1
829	Mitchell Instruments Company Inc—Jim Desportes	1570 Cherokee St, San Marcos CA 92078	760-744-2690	R	3*	<.1
830	Portland Pottery Supply—Chris Bruni	8 Fox St, Portland ME 04101	207-772-3273	R	3*	<.1
831	Quixave Technologies Inc—Que Guo	21 Birch St, Westwood MA 02090	781-407-0226	R	3*	<.1
832	Servolift LLC—Marc Kaufman	105 W Dewey Ave Ste 20, Wharton NJ 07885	973-442-7878	R	3*	<.1
833	RT Machine Co—Ronald Boose	201 Boak Ave, Hughesville PA 17737	570-584-2002	R	3*	<.1
834	Spiroflow Systems Inc—Michelle Podevyen	2806 Gray Fox Rd, Monroe NC 28110	704-291-9595	R	3*	<.1
835	Oscar L Foster Inc—Kenneth Forster	PO Box 549, Bremen GA 30110	770-948-3075	R	3*	<.1
836	Allstate Equipment Company Inc—Josephus Terry	1201 Mccloud Rd, Chesapeake VA 23320	757-545-1900	R	3*	<.1
837	Larson Meter-Craft Inc—Gertrud Larson	9328 Wheatlands Rd Ste, Santee CA 92071	619-258-8990	R	3*	<.1
838	Scott-Randall Systems Inc—Walter Prather	5815 Tracy Rd, Sardinia OH 45171	937-446-2293	R	3*	<.1
839	Republic Textile Equipment Company Of South Carolina Inc—Michael Diamond	PO Box 625, York SC 29745	803-684-2321	R	3*	<.1
840	Polymer Machinery Company Inc—Kendall Ashby	154 Potomac Ave Ste B, Tallmadge OH 44278	330-633-5734	R	3*	<.1
841	Robert R Bogaczyk—Robert Bogaczyk	1201 Alexandria Ln, Madison WI 53718	608-223-9387	R	2*	<.1
842	LightbarsCom LLC	527 Rte 303, Orangeburg NY 10962	845-398-7700	R	2*	<.1
843	G W Becker Inc—George Becker	2600 Kirila Blvd, Hermitage PA 16148	724-983-1000	R	2*	<.1
844	Peerless Pumps Sales and Service—Andy Smidth	PO Box 1326, Woodland CA 95776	530-662-2825	R	2*	<.1
845	American Sales and Service—Ben Pool	409 Enterprise Blvd, Hewitt TX 76643	254-666-8181	R	2*	<.1
846	Donamarc Water Systems Co—Donald Mantel	569 E Turkeyfoot Lake, Akron OH 44319	330-494-8366	R	2*	<.1
847	Industrial Tool Services Inc—David Johnson	PO Box 623, Bristol VA 24203	276-669-6571	R	2*	<.1
848	Jakob Mueller Of America Inc—Jakob Mueller	2231 Gateway Blvd, Charlotte NC 28208	704-394-3135	R	2*	<.1
849	Jem Automatics And Tooling Inc—A Garofalo	22845 Hoover Rd, Warren MI 48089	586-755-7300	R	2*	<.1
850	Pampa Machine and Supply Inc—William Robben	PO Box 2558, Pampa TX 79066	806-665-0013	R	2*	<.1
851	American Liba Inc—Karlheinz Liebrandt	3017 Hwy 153, Piedmont SC 29673	864-269-7063	R	2*	<.1
852	Apex Industrial Equipment Inc—Winston Plymale	PO Box 1049, Salem VA 24153	540-387-3880	R	2*	<.1
853	Robert E Mason and Associates Inc—Robert Mason	PO Box 33424, Charlotte NC 28233	704-375-4465	R	2*	<.1
854	Nissan Forklift Trucks—David Hayes	3400 Woodpark Blvd Ste, Charlotte NC 28206	704-509-1900	R	2*	<.1
855	Record Products Of America Inc—Robert Roczynski	700 Sherman Ave, Hamden CT 06514	203-248-6371	R	2*	<.1
856	Fourway Machinery Sales Company Inc—Lynn Hinkley	3215 Gregory Rd, Jackson MI 49202	517-782-9371	R	2*	<.1
857	Orbit Motion Technologies Inc—Jeffrey Oakes	766 Falmouth Rd Ste C1, Mashpee MA 02649	508-539-0100	R	2*	<.1
858	University Research Glassware Company Inc—Cheryl Stone	116 S Merritt Mill Rd, Chapel Hill NC 27516	919-942-2753	R	2*	<.1
859	Digital Site Systems Inc—Farrokh Radjy	5001 Baum Blvd Ste 434, Pittsburgh PA 15213	412-687-2475	R	2*	<.1
860	R and M Associates—Roger Metcalfe	7 Hardin St, Wilmington MA 01887	978-657-7452	R	2*	<.1
861	Green Nerd—Michael Thompson	240 M St Sw Apt 613e, Washington DC 20024	202-257-8844	R	2*	<.1
862	Leeco—Norman Errico	PO Box 34216, Houston TX 77234	281-487-1402	R	2*	<.1
863	Propane Equipment Corp—Mary Vranken	11 Apple St, Tinton Falls NJ 07724	732-747-3795	R	2*	<.1
864	Wmg Enterprises Ii Inc—Max Goodman	PO Box 308, Richmond TX 77406	281-239-6175	R	2*	<.1
865	Air Compressor Products Inc—Charles Becky	PO Box 5385, Jacksonville FL 32247	904-396-5575	R	2*	<.1
866	J Dedoes Enterprises Inc—Billy Wood	28850 Haas Rd, Wixom MI 48393	248-437-3616	R	2*	<.1
867	Metalist International Inc—Edwin Reeser	1159 S Pennsylvania Av, Lansing MI 48912	517-371-2940	R	2*	<.1
868	Rings Battery and Forklift Service Inc—Dave Ring	100 Gordon Commercial, Lagrange GA 30240	706-884-5700	R	2*	<.1
869	Construction and Industrial Supply Company Inc—K Winterowd	2401 Summit St, Kansas City MO 64108	816-842-7777	R	2*	<.1
870	Design Controls LLC—Adrian Reis	9885 Drysdale Ln, Houston TX 77041	713-856-7444	R	2*	<.1
871	Feyenzylstra—Marlan Feyen	210 Front Ave Sw, Grand Rapids MI 49504	616-224-7727	R	2*	<.1
872	TR Encoder Solutions Inc—Todd Warner	PO Box 4448, Troy MI 48099	248-244-2280	R	2*	<.1
873	Firkins Power Motive Inc—Dennis Firkins	1113 N College Ave, Fort Collins CO 80524	970-482-1144	R	2*	<.1
874	Fisher Industries Inc—Raymond Fisher	PO Box 41026, Houston TX 77241	713-937-6838	R	2*	<.1
875	Divesco Inc—Casey Westbrook Westland International Corp	5000 Hwy 80 E, Jackson MS 39208	601-932-1934	S	2*	<.1
876	Henry Servin and Sons Inc—Lupe Servin	2185 Ronald St, Santa Clara CA 95050	408-980-8909	R	2*	<.1
877	Universal Sewing Machine Company Inc—Martin Gopman	2300 Nw 2nd Ave, Miami FL 33127	305-576-0400	R	2*	<.1
878	B-F Sales Engineering Inc—Jeff Hasse	13301 W 43rd Dr Unit 4, Golden CO 80403	303-216-1041	R	2*	<.1
879	International Marketing Specialists Inc—Bill Mathews	1515 N Warson Rd Ste 1, Saint Louis MO 63132	314-423-0052	R	2*	<.1
880	Interstate Tool Corp—Howard Liebing	4538 W 130th St, Cleveland OH 44135	216-671-1077	R	2*	<.1
881	South Shore Packing—Cail Ciocetti	15 Taylor Ave, Brockton MA 02302	508-941-0458	R	2*	<.1
882	Electromatic Equipment Company Inc—David Bromley	600 Oakland Ave, Cedarhurst NY 11516	516-295-4300	R	2*	<.1
883	Geotest Instrument Corp—Peter Bach	828 Davis St Ste 300, Evanston IL 60201	847-869-7645	R	2*	<.1
884	South Coast Controls Corp—Harry Ellis	8065 E Crystal Dr, Anaheim CA 92807	714-998-5656	R	2*	<.1
885	Income Unlimited—Nadine Martin	1155 Mcneil Dr, Blacklick OH 43004	614-220-9161	R	2*	<.1
886	Micro Mini Hydraulics—David Albrecht	534 Township Line Rd, Blue Bell PA 19422	215-542-2198	R	2*	<.1
887	F D Hurka Co—Truman Copeland	PO Box 240695, Charlotte NC 28224	704-552-0008	R	2*	<.1
888	Hardface Alloys Inc—Daren Gansert	1688 Sierra Madre Cir, Placentia CA 92870	714-414-0575	R	2*	<.1
889	Wendells Woodwork Inc—Wendell Long	11223 Blair Rd, Mint Hill NC 28227	704-545-5198	R	2*	<.1
890	HAAS Factory Outlet—Mike Creeg	2650 Baird Rd, Fairport NY 14450	585-641-4227	R	2*	<.1
891	Midwest Fluid Power LLC—Bruce Gonring	5702 Opportunity Dr, Toledo OH 43612	419-478-0015	R	2*	<.1
892	Clearline Inc—Kenneth Storck	810 Dickerson Rd Ste D, North Wales PA 19454	215-699-9292	R	2*	<.1
893	Hazemag USA Inc—Jeffrey Hawker	PO Box 1064, Uniontown PA 15401	724-439-3512	R	2*	<.1
894	Macoser Inc—Diego Cagol	PO Box 667789, Charlotte NC 28266	704-392-0110	R	2*	<.1
895	New Consolidated International Corp—C Meyers	PO Box 118, La Grange IL 60525	773-376-5600	R	2*	<.1
896	Tewl Brothers Machine Inc—Tom Tewell	300 N Parke St, Tuscola IL 61953	217-253-6303	R	2*	<.1

Rank	Company Name—*Executive Officer*	Address, City, State, Zip	Phone	Type	Fin	Empls
897	Presswerx Inc—*Richard Smith*	12070 S Profit Row, Forney TX 75126	972-564-4229	R	2*	<.1
898	Multipli Machinery Corp—*Larry Bennett*	PO Box 550665, Gastonia NC 28055	704-869-6675	R	2*	<.1
899	Kardex Production USA Inc—*Jos Devuyst*	41 Eisenhower Dr, Westbrook ME 04092	207-854-1861	R	2*	<.1
900	Stenner USA Ltd—*Peter Taylor*	284 Maple St, Hopkinton NH 03229	603-746-4793	R	2*	<.1
901	Western Cutterheads Inc—*Kenneth Anselm*	PO Box 599, La Center KY 42056	270-665-5302	R	1*	<.1
902	RF Suering Company Inc—*Richard Seuring*	61 Towns Rd, Levittown PA 19056	215-949-1361	R	1*	<.1
903	Tippman Industrial Products Inc—*Dennis Tippman*	3518 Adams Ctr Rd, Fort Wayne IN 46806	260-441-9603	R	1*	<.1
904	Donald E Savard Company Inc—*Simon Malak*	418 S Pine St, San Gabriel CA 91776	323-283-0504	R	1*	<.1
905	Barnes Holdings Inc—*Gary Barnes*	949 E Main St, Henderson TN 38340	731-989-2224	R	1*	<.1
906	Parts Specialists Inc—*Glenn Duncan*	14639 S Short St, Posen IL 60469	708-371-2444	R	1*	<.1
907	Girard Machine Sales—*Carl Malito*	PO Box 298, Girard OH 44420	330-545-9731	R	1*	<.1
908	Trahide Co—*Juan Traverso*	14355 Sw 139th Ct, Miami FL 33186	305-238-8060	R	1*	<.1
909	EK Hydraulics Inc—*William Kalchik*	2230 N Us Hwy 31, Petoskey MI 49770	231-347-7720	R	1*	<.1
910	A and A Boltless Rack and Shelving—*Liss Campbell*	1124 Santa Anita Ave, South El Monte CA 91733	626-452-1500	R	1*	<.1
911	Waste Minimization and Containment Services Inc—*James Becker*	2140 Scranton Rd, Cleveland OH 44113	216-696-8797	R	1*	<.1
912	RG Egan Equipment Inc—*Ronald Egan*	PO Box 1565, Webster NY 14580	585-671-0465	R	1*	<.1
913	Mq Operating Co—*Eugene Londo*	416 6th St, Calumet MI 49913	906-337-1515	R	1*	<.1
914	A A Jansson Inc—*Alison Mcclellan*	2070 Airport Rd, Waterford MI 48327	248-674-4811	R	1*	<.1
915	Fastener Equipment Corp—*Le Loudermilk*	17531 Ashland Ave, Homewood IL 60430	708-957-5100	R	1*	<.1
916	BA Box Tank and Supply Inc—*Mitchell Box*	PO Box 547, Beeville TX 78104	361-358-1984	R	1*	<.1
917	Paul King Co—*Jim Mainer*	PO Box 580817, Tulsa OK 74158	918-592-5464	R	1*	<.1
918	LR Marketing—*Robert Smith*	4003 Druid Hills Dr St, Dallas TX 75224		R	1*	<.1
919	IPM Precision Inc—*Joe Blechner*	22179 N Pepper Rd, Lake Barrington IL 60010	847-304-7900	R	1*	<.1
920	Vmc Technologies Inc—*Tansel Avci*	1788 Northwood Dr, Troy MI 48084	248-786-3000	R	1*	<.1
921	R R Templeton Corp—*Russell Romey*	PO Box 430, Niles MI 49120	269-684-4440	R	1*	<.1
922	Plastore Inc—*Ingemar Lundh*	1570 Georgetown Rd, Hudson OH 44236	330-653-3047	R	1*	<.1
923	Babbitt International Corp—*Stu Babbitt*	PO Box 70094, Houston TX 77270	713-467-4438	R	1*	<.1
924	Ideal Tool And Machine Company Inc—*Donald Dopkins*	PO Box 213, Stillwater MN 55082	651-439-0654	R	1*	<.1
925	Print Mount Company Inc—*Hugh Neville*	20 Industrial Dr, Smithfield RI 02917	401-232-0096	R	1*	<.1
926	Air Equipment Sales and Service Inc—*Milo Bender*	500 Baldwin St, Elkhart IN 46514	574-262-3591	R	1*	<.1
927	Premium Lift Inc—*Frank O'donnell*	PO Box 730, Levittown PA 19058	215-269-1177	R	1*	<.1
928	Chippewa Systems Ltd—*Darlene Barr*	24574 Beck Ave, Eastpointe MI 48021	586-772-1783	R	1*	<.1
929	Cruz Group Inc—*Jon Cruz*	8280 Clairemont Mesa B, San Diego CA 92111	858-467-9707	R	1*	<.1
930	Rene Swiss Corp—*Rene Wisler*	PO Box 6221, Wolcott CT 06716	203-879-4822	R	1*	<.1
931	Bettcher Industries Inc—*Laurence Bettcher*	PO Box 336, Vermilion OH 44089	440-965-4422	R	1*	.2
932	Ergonomics Inc—*Frances George*	324 2nd St Pke Ste 3, Southampton PA 18966	215-357-5124	R	1*	<.1
933	Liquitrol Co—*Brad Tompkins*	10518 W 148th Ter, Overland Park KS 66221	913-681-5050	R	1*	<.1
934	Control and Automation Inc—*John Hayes*	1039 Goodwin Dr Ste 10, Lexington KY 40505	859-231-0888	R	1*	<.1
935	Anger Associates Inc—*Phillip Deberry*	PO Box 369, Milford MI 48381	248-685-8148	R	1*	<.1
936	Comptus Inc—*Leander Nichols*	342 Lyndeboro Rd, New Boston NH 03070	603-487-5512	R	1*	<.1
937	Burnett Brothers Engineering Inc—*Malcolm Burnett*	PO Box 1224, Fullerton CA 92836	714-526-2448	R	1*	<.1
938	Mbh Engineering Systems—*Mark Heyda*	61 Howard Ave, Lynnfield MA 01940	781-334-2600	R	1*	<.1
939	Avery Manufacturing LLC—*Larry Voris*	312 N Delaware Ave, Springfield MO 65802	417-869-7933	R	<1*	<.1
940	Precision Sharpening Devices Inc—*Mark Mills*	5051 Iroquois Ave, Erie PA 16511	814-899-0796	R	<1*	<.1
941	Industrial Machinery Corp—*James Cvonar*	3741 W National Ave, Milwaukee WI 53215	414-672-5900	R	<1*	<.1
942	Sycron Technologies Inc—*Bradley Thmpson*	8130 Industrial Park D, Grand Blanc MI 48439	810-694-4007	R	<1*	<.1
943	Ansonics Inc—*Anthony Sowers*	PO Box 250, El Prado NM 87529	541-742-7475	R	<1*	<.1
944	Programmable Orienting Systems Inc—*Jerry Goodrich*	1547 Sartwell Creek Rd, Port Allegany PA 16743	814-544-4000	R	<1*	<.1
945	Walther Pilot North America LLC—*Jim Turner*	46890 Continental Dr, Chesterfield MI 48047	586-598-0347	R	<1*	<.1
946	Tool Mate Corporation Inc—*C Brakers*	7293 Swirlwood Ln, Cincinnati OH 45239	513-729-1160	R	<1*	<.1
947	Dale L Quinn—*Dale Quinn*	2439 Industrial Pkwy W, Hayward CA 94545	510-786-0439	R	<1*	<.1
948	Pickard Artistic Blasting Inc—*Bob Pickard*	311 E Main St, Shawnee OK 74801	405-878-9688	R	<1*	<.1
949	Westburne Credit Department—*Dick Attics*	417 Quivas St, Denver CO 80204	303-446-8407	R	<1*	<.1
950	Repair Processes Inc—*Larry Pryor*	5401 N Wood Dr, Okmulgee OK 74447	918-758-0863	R	<1*	<.1
951	MacQueen Equipment Inc—*Dan Gage*	595 Aldine St, Saint Paul MN 55104	651-645-5726	R	N/A	.1

TOTALS: SIC 5084 Industrial Machinery & Equipment
Companies: 951   46,211   85.2

5085 Industrial Supplies

Rank	Company Name—*Executive Officer*	Address, City, State, Zip	Phone	Type	Fin	Empls
1	Freudenberg-Nok GP—*Michael Heidingsfelder*	47690 E Anchor Ct, Plymouth MI 48170	734-451-0200	R	2,954*	4.6
2	McJunkin Red Man Holding Corp—*Andrew Lane*	835 Hillcrest Dr, Charleston WV 25311	304-348-5211	R	2,438*	3.7
3	Motion Industries Inc—*William J Stevens*	PO Box 1477, Birmingham AL 35201	205-956-1122	S	2,250*	5.0
4	Forge Industries Inc—*Carl G James Jr*	4450 Market St, Youngstown OH 44512	330-782-8301	R	1,547*	2.0
5	Hagemeyer North America—*Lisa Mitchell*	1460 Tobias Gadson Blv, Charleston SC 29407	843-745-2400	S	1,021*	2.5
6	Norwood Promotional Products Inc—*Thomas Roller*	10 W Market St Ste 140, Indianapolis IN 46204	317-275-2500	R	860*	1.0
7	Carter Chambers LLC—*Thomas Felter* Desselle-Maggard Corp	PO Box 15705, Baton Rouge LA 70895	225-926-2236	S	826*	.3
8	Kaman Industrial Technologies Inc—*Steven J Smidler*	1 Waterside Crossing, Windsor CT 06095	860-687-5000	S	553*	1.4
9	Industrial Distribution Group Inc—*Charles Lingenfelter*	2100 The Oaks Parkway, Belmont NC 28012		R	538*	1.3
10	Barnes Distribution—*David Nagle*	PO Box 6908, Cleveland OH 44101	216-416-7200	S	534*	3.0
11	National Waterworks Inc—*Harry K Hornish Jr*	1001 Washington Ave, Waco TX 76701	254-772-5355	S	533*	.5
12	Lawson Products Inc—*Thomas J Neri*	1666 E Touhy Ave, Des Plaines IL 60018	847-827-9666	P	315	1.0
13	Hillman Companies Inc (Cincinnati Ohio)—*Max W Hillman*	10590 Hamilton Ave, Cincinnati OH 45231	513-851-4900	R	307*	1.7
14	Berlin Packaging LLC—*Andrew T Berlin*	525 W Monroe St, Chicago IL 60661		R	224*	.2
15	Famous Enterprises Inc—*Jay Blaushild*	PO Box 1889, Akron OH 44309	330-434-5194	R	220*	.7
16	Kaman Aerospace Group Inc—*Neil J Keating*	PO Box 2, Bloomfield CT 06002	860-242-4461	S	219*	.3
17	K-MAX Corp—*Neil J Keating*	1332 Blue Hills Ave, Bloomfield CT 06002	860-243-7100	S	219*	.3
18	Kipper Tool Co—*Jerome Kipper*	PO Box 1750, Gainesville GA 30503	770-532-3232	R	186*	.1
19	J and L Industrial Supply Co—*Michael Wessner*	20921 Lahser Rd, Southfield MI 48033	248-200-4200	S	160*	.5
20	Henry A Petter Supply Co—*Robert Petter*	5110 Charter Oak Dr, Paducah KY 42001	270-443-2441	R	148*	.2
21	Production Tool Supply—*Larry Wolfe*	PO Box 987, Warren MI 48089	586-755-5258	R	143*	.4
22	Precision Industries Inc (Omaha Nebraska)—*Chris Circo*	4611 S 96th St, Omaha NE 68127	402-593-7050	R	142*	.6
23	Bearing and Drives Inc—*Andrew H Nations*	PO Box 4325, Macon GA 31208	478-743-6711	R	119*	.4
24	Macomb Pipe and Supply Company Inc—*William Mcgivern*	34400 Mound Rd, Sterling Heights MI 48310	586-274-4100	R	116*	.2
25	Miller Bearings Inc	17 S Westmoreland Dr, Orlando FL 32805	407-425-9078	R	111*	.1
26	Hi-Line Electric Co—*Mike Sheaffer*	2121 Valley View Ln, Dallas TX 75234		R	107*	.2
27	Industrial Bearing and Transmission Inc—*Stephen R Cloud*	PO Box 2982, Shawnee Mission KS 66201	913-677-3151	R	104*	.4
28	Lydall Industrial Thermal Sales/Service LLC—*Phil Hume*	PO Box 1000, Ossipee NH 03864	603-539-3600	S	104*	.2

Note: An asterisk (*) indicates an estimated financial figure. The company type code used is as follows: R = Private, P = Public, S = Private Subsidiary, B = Public Subsidiary, D = Division, J = Joint Venture, I = Investment Fund.

COMPANY RANKINGS BY SALES WITHIN 4-DIGIT SIC

Rank	Company Name—Executive Officer	Address, City, State, Zip	Phone	Type	Fin	Empls
29	Packwell Inc—Al Duran	10016 Porter Rd, La Porte TX 77571	281-842-5900	R	98*	.2
30	Willamette Valley Co—John Harrison	PO Box 2280, Eugene OR 97402	541-484-9621	R	97*	.3
31	Spencer Industries Incorporated of Seattle—Jean Knowles	19308 68th Ave S, Kent WA 98032	253-796-1100	S	95	.2
32	F and M Mafco Inc—Daniel Kenna	PO Box 11013, Cincinnati OH 45211	513-367-2151	R	83*	.3
33	Munnell and Sherrill Inc—Sam Mangone	975 Wilson St, Eugene OR 97402	541-345-8791	R	72*	.1
34	RG Group Inc—Randall Gross	650 W State St, York PA 17405	717-849-0347	R	62*	.1
35	Lewis-Goetz And Company Inc—Jeffrey Crane	650 Washington Rd Ste, Pittsburgh PA 15228	412-341-7100	R	61*	.9
36	Van Son Holland Ink Corporation Of America—Joseph Bendowski	PO Box 6002, Hauppauge NY 11788	631-715-7000	R	60*	.1
37	Industrial Supply Solutions Inc—Frank Carnazzi	804 Julian Rd, Salisbury NC 28147	704-636-4241	R	59*	.2
38	C L Smith Co—Clarence Smith	1311 S 39th St, Saint Louis MO 63110	314-771-1202	R	59*	.1
39	Black and Co—Brad Kent	PO Box 1160, Decatur IL 62525	217-428-4424	R	59*	.1
40	Diamond P Enterprises Inc—Domingo Perez Jr	PO Box 483, Brownwood TX 76804	325-643-5629	R	59*	.1
41	United Central Industrial Supply Company LLC—Darrell Cole	1241 Volunteer Pkwy St, Bristol TN 37620	423-573-7300	R	58*	.3
42	Mid-States Supply Company Inc—Robert Brown	1716 Guinotte Ave, Kansas City MO 64120	816-842-4290	R	57*	.2
43	Global Flow Technologies—Ray Baker	10600 Corporate Dr, Stafford TX 77477	281-565-1010	R	57*	.1
44	TF Hudgins Inc—Ted Edwards	PO Box 920946, Houston TX 77292	713-682-3651	R	56*	.1
45	Doall Co—Michael Wilkie	1480 S Wolf Rd, Wheeling IL 60090	847-495-6800	R	55*	.8
46	Quality Transmission Components—M Hoffman	125 Railroad Ave, Garden City Park NY 11040	516-437-6700	R	54*	.4
47	Crown Packaging International Inc—Dennis Tilles	8919 Colorado St, Merrillville IN 46410	219-738-1000	R	54*	.2
48	Continental International—Ronald Clem	6723 S Hanna St, Fort Wayne IN 46816	260-447-7000	R	53*	.1
49	Duncan Industrial Solutions Inc—Bill Scheller	3450 S MacArthur Blvd, Oklahoma City OK 73179	405-688-2300	R	52*	.2
50	JF Good Co	166 N Union St, Akron OH 44304	330-535-1811	S	52*	.1
51	Vellano Brothers Inc—Joseph Vellano	7 Hemlock St, Latham NY 12110	518-785-5537	R	50*	.1
52	Drummond American Corp Lawson Products Inc	1666 E Touhy Ave, Des Plaines IL 60018	847-827-0063	S	49*	.1
53	Pioneer Industrial Corp—Bill Pfitzinger	400 Russell Blvd, Saint Louis MO 63104	314-771-0700	R	49*	.1
54	Pacific Echo Inc—Yasuo Ogami	23540 Telo Ave, Torrance CA 90505	310-539-1822	R	49*	.1
55	Ritter Technology LLC—Tim Hall	100 Williams Dr, Zelienople PA 16063	724-452-6000	R	48*	.1
56	Industrial Supply Company Inc (Salt Lake City Utah)—John Richards	PO Box 30600, Salt Lake City UT 84130	801-484-8644	R	47*	.1
57	Sealing Devices Inc—Terry Galanis	4400 Walden Ave, Lancaster NY 14086	716-684-7600	R	47*	.1
58	Rubberlite Inc—J Mayo	2501 Guyan Ave, Huntington WV 25703	304-525-3116	R	45*	.1
59	Gokoh Corp—Shuji Hioki	1280 Archer Dr, Troy OH 45373	937-339-4977	R	44*	<.1
60	New England Newspaper Supply Company Inc—Bradford Beaton	PO Box 847826, Boston MA 02284	508-865-0800	R	43*	.1
61	Multifab Inc—Timothy Smith	3808 N Sullivan Rd Bld, Spokane Valley WA 99216	509-924-6631	R	42*	.1
62	United States Container Corp—Jeffrey Levine	11096 Jersey Blvd Ste, Rancho Cucamonga CA 91730	323-589-1000	R	41*	.1
63	J and B Fasteners LP—Brad Miedke	6121 Griggs Rd, Houston TX 77023	713-645-3480	R	40*	.1
64	Monumental Supply Company Inc—Susan Kirchner	401 S Haven St, Baltimore MD 21224	410-732-9300	R	40*	.1
65	Indiana Supply Corp—Dave Draga	3835 E 21st St, Indianapolis IN 46218	317-359-5451	S	39*	.1
66	NH Bragg and Sons—John W Bragg	PO Box 927, Bangor ME 04402	207-947-8611	R	39*	.1
67	WP and RS Mars Co—Robert S Mars III	215 E 78th St, Bloomington MN 55420	952-884-9388	R	39*	.1
68	GT Sales and Manufacturing Inc—N Onofrio	PO Box 9408, Wichita KS 67277	316-943-2171	R	37*	.2
69	Zatkoff Seals and Packings Co—Gary Zatkoff	23230 Industrial Park, Farmington Hills MI 48335	248-478-2400	R	36*	.1
70	Supply Technologies—Charles Watterson	400 Commerce, Lawrence PA 15055	724-745-7900	S	35*	.2
71	Equipment Valve and Supply Inc—Dan O'Leary	PO Box 722155, Houston TX 77272	281-498-6600	S	35*	<.1
72	Wulco Inc—James Wulfeck	6899 Steger Dr Ste A, Cincinnati OH 45237	513-761-2010	R	35*	.2
73	Standard Die Supply Of Indiana Inc—Charles Wolfred	927 S Pennsylvania St, Indianapolis IN 46225	317-236-6200	R	33*	.1
74	East West Industrial Engineering Co—Dilip Mullick	PO Box 7983, Ann Arbor MI 48107	734-971-6265	R	33*	.2
75	Thg Corp—Carey Rhoten	PO Box 840, Northborough MA 01532	508-393-7660	R	33*	.1
76	Raleigh Mine And Industrial Supply Inc—Stirl Smith	PO Box 72, Mount Hope WV 25880	304-877-5503	R	33*	.6
77	Cornerstone Controls Inc—Kasey Coleman	7131 E Kemper Rd, Cincinnati OH 45249	513-489-2500	R	32*	.1
78	California Industrial Rubber Company Inc—Larry T Cane	2539 S Cherry Ave, Fresno CA 93706	559-268-7321	R	32*	.1
79	Transply Inc—Brain Gross	PO Box 7727, York PA 17404	717-767-1005	R	31*	.1
80	Crowley Associates—David Crowley	3 Overlook Dr, Amherst NH 03031	603-673-7050	R	31*	<.1
81	Carter and Verplanck Inc—Saade Chibani	PO Box 24169, Tampa FL 33623	813-287-0709	R	30*	<.1
82	Quality Mill Supply Company Inc—Mike Baker	2159 Early Ln, Franklin IN 46131	317-489-0600	R	30*	.1
83	American Pipe and Supply Company Inc—Jeffrey Beall	PO Box 11474, Birmingham AL 35202	205-323-0300	R	30*	.1
84	Lemac Packaging Inc—Gerald Lee	PO Box 10788, Erie PA 16514	814-453-7652	R	29*	.1
85	Kaufman Container Co—Ken Slater	1000 Keystone Pkwy Ste, Cleveland OH 44135	216-898-2000	R	28*	.1
86	Reid Supply Co—Paul Reid	2265 Black Creek Rd, Muskegon MI 49444	231-777-3951	R	28*	.1
87	Branham Corp—Doug Branham	PO Box 9286, Louisville KY 40209	502-366-0326	R	28*	.1
88	Bascom-Turner Instruments Inc—A Makrides	111 Downey St, Norwood MA 02062	781-769-9660	R	27*	.1
89	Haun Welding Supply Inc—Mark Haun	5921 Ct St Rd, Syracuse NY 13206	315-463-5241	R	27*	.1
90	Custom Bottle Inc—Barry Lerman	PO Box 979, Naugatuck CT 06770	203-723-6661	R	27*	.2
91	Precision Fitting and Gauge Co—Susie Spanier	1214 S Joplin Ave, Tulsa OK 74112	918-834-5011	R	27*	.1
92	Oliver H Van Horn Company Inc—Stewart Van Horn	PO Box 50427, New Orleans LA 70150		R	26*	.1
93	General Rubber And Plastics Of Paducah Inc—Westman Burnett	PO Box 17204, Louisville KY 40217	502-635-2605	R	26*	.1
94	BW Rogers Co—Rick Rogers	PO Box 1030, Akron OH 44309	330-762-0251	R	25	.1
95	Columbus Paper Company Inc—Michael Greenblatt	807 Joy Rd, Columbus GA 31906		R	25*	.1
96	Schermerhorn Brothers Co—Wayne Rylski	PO Box 668, Lombard IL 60148	630-627-9860	R	25*	<.1
97	Rubber and Gasket Company Of America Inc—James Ghee	3905 E Progress St, North Little Rock AR 72114	501-565-9656	R	25*	.1
98	New England Controls Inc—Thomas Ramundo	PO Box 446, Mansfield MA 02048	508-339-5522	R	25*	.1
99	Inpro/Seal LLC—David Orlowski	PO Box 260, Milan IL 61264	309-787-4971	R	24*	.1
100	Hargis Industries LP—Jim Cater	PO Box 4515, Tyler TX 75712	903-592-2826	R	24*	.2
101	Masters Supply Inc—David Wachtel	PO Box 34337, Louisville KY 40232	502-459-2900	R	24*	.1
102	Aramsco Inc—William Kenworthy	PO Box 29, Thorofare NJ 08086	856-686-7700	R	23*	.1
103	FB Wright Co	PO Box 770, Dearborn MI 48121	313-843-8250	R	23*	.1
104	Cronatron Welding Systems Inc Lawson Products Inc	1666 E Toughy Ave, Des Plaines IL 60018	847-827-9666	S	23*	.1
105	Festo Corp—Gian Arosio	PO Box 18023, Hauppauge NY 11788	631-435-0800	R	23*	.4
106	Victory White Metal Co—Joseph Sturman	6100 Roland Ave, Cleveland OH 44127	216-271-1400	R	23*	.1
107	Uchiyama America Inc—Masatomo Sueki	494 Arrington Bridge R, Goldsboro NC 27530	919-731-2364	R	23*	.1
108	P and I Supply Co—Bruce Stallings	2220 N Fares Ave, Evansville IN 47711	812-423-6256	R	22*	<.1
109	Lewis Supply Company Inc (Memphis Tennessee) Motion Industries Inc	1665 N Pky, Jackson TN 38301	731-424-5656	D	22*	.1
110	Troy Belting Supply Co—Karen Smith	70 Cohoes Rd, Watervliet NY 12109	518-272-4920	R	22*	.1
111	Standard Services Company Inc—Evans Hadden	14694 Airline Hwy, Destrehan LA 70047	985-725-1989	R	22*	<.1

Rank	Company Name—*Executive Officer*	Address, City, State, Zip	Phone	Type	Fin	Empls
112	Fabreeka International Inc—*J Norton*	PO Box 210, Stoughton MA 02072	781-341-3655	R	22*	.1
113	Eads Co—*Steve Albert*	PO Box 36448, Houston TX 77236	713-781-3000	R	22*	.1
114	Walter A Wood Supply Company Inc—*David Henry*	4509 Rossville Blvd, Chattanooga TN 37407	423-867-1033	R	21*	.1
115	Bmf Corp—*Edward Cebulko*	4315 W Oquendo Rd, Las Vegas NV 89118	702-651-9222	R	21*	.1
116	Gulf Coast Seal Ltd—*Cheryl Cortez*	9119 Monroe Rd, Houston TX 77061	713-910-7700	R	21*	.1
117	Lakeside Supply Co—*Kenneth Mathews*	3000 W 117th St, Cleveland OH 44111	216-941-6800	R	21*	<.1
118	Desselle-Maggard Corp—*Joseph Jobe*	PO Box 86630, Baton Rouge LA 70879	225-753-3290	R	20*	.4
119	Reichman Crosby Hays Inc—*Gene Langley*	3150 Carrier St, Memphis TN 38116	901-345-2200	R	20*	.1
120	State Seal Co—*Mike Curtis*	4135 E Wood St, Phoenix AZ 85040	602-437-1532	R	20*	.1
121	Wheeler Consolidated Inc—*David Hoak*	1100 Hoak Dr, West Des Moines IA 50265	515-223-1584	R	20*	.1
122	Novaflex Hose Inc—*Ian Donnelly*	449 Trollingwood Rd, Haw River NC 27258	336-578-2161	R	20*	<.1
123	O Berk Company LLC—*Steven Nussbaum*	PO Box 1690, Union NJ 07083	908-851-9500	R	19*	.1
124	SupplyforceCom LLC—*Wendi Fink*	650 Park Ave Ste 200, King Of Prussia PA 19406	610-239-4300	R	19*	.1
125	Transmission and Fluid Equipment Inc—*Christopher C Hughes*	6912 Trafalgar Dr, Fort Wayne IN 46803	260-493-3223	R	19*	.1
126	Atlas Supply Inc—*John Ittes*	611 S Charlestown St, Seattle WA 98108	206-623-4697	R	19*	<.1
127	BMT Commodity Corp—*Robert Ganz*	530 5th Ave 24th Fl, New York NY 10036	212-302-4200	R	19*	<.1
128	Ziegler Bolt and Parts Co—*William Ziegler*	PO Box 80369, Canton OH 44708	330-478-2542	R	19*	.1
129	Green Rubber-Kennedy Ag LP—*John Green*	PO Box 7488, Spreckels CA 93962	831-753-6100	R	19*	.1
130	Great Western Supply Co—*Mike Gladden*	10616 Hempstead Rd Ste, Houston TX 77092	713-681-4786	R	18*	<.1
131	Reece Supply Company Of Dallas—*Richard Reece*	PO Box 565545, Dallas TX 75356	972-438-3131	R	18*	.1
132	Mancon Empire Industrial Products—*Henry Turner*	3550 Virginia Beach Bl, Norfolk VA 23501	757-222-9200	R	18*	.1
133	Titus Tool Company Inc—*Walter Zabriskie*	800 5th Ave Ste 4100, Seattle WA 98104	253-872-2829	R	18*	.1
134	American Producers Supply Company Inc—*Christopher Brunton*	PO Box 1050, Marietta OH 45750	740-373-5050	R	18*	.1
135	Mine Supply Co—*Jack L Skinner*	PO Box 1330, Carlsbad NM 88220	505-887-2888	R	18*	.1
136	Alloy and Stainless Fasteners Inc—*Garfield Edmonds*	11625 Charles Rd, Jersey Village TX 77041	713-466-3031	R	18*	.1
137	Duncan Co—*Joseph Klick*	425 Hoover St Ne, Minneapolis MN 55413	612-331-1776	R	17*	<.1
138	Delta Rubber Company Inc—*John Wulff*	2648 Teepee Dr, Stockton CA 95205	209-948-0511	R	17*	.1
139	Carolina Filters Inc—*Richard Dwight*	109 E Newberry Ave, Sumter SC 29150	803-773-6042	R	17*	.1
140	Pacemaker Steel And Piping Company Inc—*F Romano*	501 Main St, Utica NY 13501	315-797-2161	R	17*	.1
141	Northern States Supply Inc—*Robert Dols*	PO Box 1057, Willmar MN 56201	320-235-0555	R	16*	.1
142	Arc Fastener Supply and Manufacturing—*Joseph Myers*	8715 Boston Pl, Rancho Cucamonga CA 91730	909-481-8171	R	16*	.1
143	Fort Worth Bolt and Tool Company Inc—*David O'brien*	2822 Bledsoe St, Fort Worth TX 76107	817-335-3361	R	16*	.1
144	Morse Distribution Inc—*Mike Morse*	PO Box 490, Bellingham WA 98227	360-734-2400	R	16*	.1
145	California Glass Co—*Marc Silvani*	155 98th Ave, Oakland CA 94603	510-635-7700	S	16*	.1
146	Colonial Hardware Corp—*Michael O'Connell*	163 Varick St, New York NY 10013	212-741-8989	R	16*	.1
147	Arkansas Packaging Products Inc—*Mark Schaeffer*	PO Box 16202, Little Rock AR 72231	501-945-1400	R	16*	<.1
148	Nmc Group Inc—*Douglas Stephen*	2755 Thompson Creek Rd, Pomona CA 91767	909-451-2290	R	15*	.1
149	Accumetric LLC—*Tim Patterson*	350 Ring Rd, Elizabethtown KY 42701	270-769-3385	R	15*	.1
150	Diamond Blade Warehouse Inc—*Alan Mansfield*	PO Box 5759, Vernon Hills IL 60061	847 388 0200	R	15*	.1
151	Linear Industries Ltd—*Anthony Angelica*	1850 Enterprise Way, Monrovia CA 91016	626-303-1130	R	15*	.1
152	Buckeye Rubber and Packing Co—*Mark Janasek*	23940 Mercantile Rd, Cleveland OH 44122	216-464-8900	R	15*	<.1
153	Interstate Bearing Systems—*Travis Penrod*	2601 E American Blvd, Bloomington MN 55425	952-854-2044	S	15*	<.1
154	Netherland Rubber Company Inc—*Timothy Clarke*	PO Box 62165, Cincinnati OH 45262	513-733-0883	R	15*	<.1
155	Zuckerman-Honickman Inc—*Benjamin Zuckerman*	191 S Gulph Rd, King of Prussia PA 19406	610-962-0100	R	15*	<.1
156	ABA Packaging Corp—*Charles Marchese*	740 Blue Point Rd, Holtsville NY 11742	631-758-4200	R	15*	<.1
157	Grover Corp—*Stuart Banghart*	PO Box 340080, Milwaukee WI 53234	414-384-9472	R	15*	.1
158	Pioneer Supply Company Inc—*James Davis*	1710 N Franklin St, Pittsburgh PA 15233	412-471-5600	R	15*	.1
159	Providence Lacquer and Supply Centre Inc—*Brian Keough*	1155 Park Ave, Cranston RI 02910	401-943-1700	R	15*	<.1
160	Tolco Corp—*William Spengler*	1920 Linwood Ave, Toledo OH 43604	419-241-1113	R	14*	.1
161	US Flange and Fittings Corp—*Michael Maass*	6202 Lumberdale Rd, Houston TX 77092	713-329-5500	R	14*	<.1
162	Strike Force Maintenance Corp—*Stephen Outcault*	648 Middle Country Rd, Saint James NY 11780	631-382-9300	R	14*	.1
163	Tipco Technologies Inc—*Robert Lyons*	11412 Cronhill Dr, Owings Mills MD 21117	410-356-0003	R	14*	<.1
164	IDG Manitowoc—*Charles Lingenfelter* Industrial Distribution Group Inc	4466 W Custer St, Manitowoc WI 54220	920-684-3313	D	14*	<.1
165	Global Industrial Components Inc—*Gerald Toledo*	705 College St, Woodbury TN 37190	615-563-5120	R	14*	<.1
166	George Yardley Company Inc—*Robert Yardley*	3000 W Macarthur Blvd, Santa Ana CA 92704	714-241-7700	R	14*	<.1
167	Packaging Concepts and Design—*Richard Kaspers*	1307-I Allen Rd, Troy MI 48083	248-585-3200	R	14*	.1
168	RL Morrissey and Associates Inc—*James Morrissey*	PO Box 75510, Cleveland OH 44101	440-498-3730	R	13*	.1
169	Gooding Rubber Co—*Dean Goldbeck*	10321 Werch Dr Ste 200, Woodridge IL 60517	630-685-2100	R	13*	.1
170	Swanson-Flosystems Co—*Tom Howe*	151 Cheshire Ln N Ste, Plymouth MN 55441	763-383-4700	R	13*	.1
171	Victory Foam Inc—*Frank Comerford*	2911 Dow Ave, Tustin CA 92780	949-474-0690	R	13*	.1
172	Beemer Precision Inc—*Harold Myer*	PO Box 3080, Fort Washington PA 19034	215-646-8440	R	13*	.1
173	Belting Industries Company Inc—*Webb Cooper*	PO Box 310, Kenilworth NJ 07033	908-272-8591	R	13*	.1
174	Louisiana Safety Systems Inc—*H Bernard*	PO Box 53014, Lafayette LA 70505	337-237-8211	R	13*	.1
175	Erdmann Corp—*James Smith*	PO Box 1269, Louisville KY 40201	502-584-1271	R	12*	<.1
176	Jacon Aircraft Supply Company Inc—*Donald Wientjes*	9539 Vassar Ave, Chatsworth CA 91311	818-700-2901	R	12*	<.1
177	Bluewater Rubber and Gasket Co—*Ronnie Bauve*	PO Box 190, Houma LA 70361	985-851-2400	R	12*	.1
178	Sks Bottle and Packaging Inc—*Paul Horan*	2600 7th Ave, Watervliet NY 12189	518-880-6980	R	12*	<.1
179	Fehr Brothers Industries Inc—*Richard Dooley*	895 Kings Hwy, Saugerties NY 12477	845-246-9525	R	12*	.1
180	Ferguson Thrall Distribution—*Matt Lakko*	4250 McFarland Rd, Loves Park IL 61111		S	12*	<.1
181	Geib Industries Inc—*Michael Zalas*	3220 N Mannheim Rd, Franklin Park IL 60131	847-455-4550	R	12*	<.1
182	Cohn and Gregory Inc—*Scott Mahaffey*	PO Box 7419, Fort Worth TX 76111	817-831-9998	R	12*	.1
183	Nashville Rubber And Gasket Company Inc—*Walter Bates*	PO Box 110357, Nashville TN 37222	615-883-0030	R	11*	.1
184	Saw Daily Service Inc—*Greg Daily*	4481 Firestone Blvd, South Gate CA 90280	323-564-1791	R	11*	.1
185	Bell Pipe and Supply Co—*Franklin Bell*	PO Box 151, Anaheim CA 92815	714-772-3200	R	11*	<.1
186	Allen And Webb—*Charles Swicord*	PO Box 71227, North Charleston SC 29415	843-747-7321	R	11*	<.1
187	Pioneer Fasteners and Tool Inc—*Mary Vantol*	202 S Ector Dr, Euless TX 76040	817-545-0121	R	11*	<.1
188	Pennco Containers Ltd—*David Penny*	4924 Reading St, Dallas TX 75247	214-631-3660	R	11*	.1
189	Specialty Resources Inc—*Richard Procopio*	PO Box 757, Uwchland PA 19480	610-321-0900	R	11*	.1
190	North Coast Bearings LLC—*William Hagy*	1050 Jaycox Rd, Avon OH 44011	440-930-7600	R	11*	.1
191	Pacific Mechanical Supply—*Roger Fowler*	13705 Milroy Pl, Santa Fe Springs CA 90670	562-921-0575	R	11*	<.1
192	Fournier Rubber and Supply Co—*Dennis Davidson*	PO Box 548, Columbus OH 43216	614-294-6453	R	11*	<.1
193	Lane Conveyors and Drives Inc—*Robert Taylor*	PO Box 218, Brewer ME 04412	207-989-4560	R	11*	.1
194	Summers Rubber Co—*Michael Summers*	12555 Berea Rd, Cleveland OH 44111	216-941-7700	R	11*	.1
195	Louis P Canuso Inc—*Joseph Canuso*	PO Box 501, Thorofare NJ 08086	856-845-2700	R	11*	<.1
196	Lutz Sales Company Inc—*William Lutz*	4675 Turnberry Dr, Bartlett IL 60133	630-539-5500	R	10*	.1
197	Allyn Corp—*Charlie Simon*	N106w 13131 Bradley Wa, Germantown WI 53022	262-512-4000	R	10*	.1
198	Mks Pipe and Valve Co—*Pat Adams*	PO Box 412553, Kansas City MO 64141	816-842-6513	R	10*	<.1
199	Affiliated Control Equipment Company Inc—*Mary Lauer*	640 Wheat Ln, Wood Dale IL 60191	630-595-4680	R	10*	.1

Note: An asterisk (*) indicates an estimated financial figure. The company type code used is as follows: R = Private, P = Public, S = Private Subsidiary, B = Public Subsidiary, D = Division, J = Joint Venture, I = Investment Fund.

COMPANY RANKINGS BY SALES WITHIN 4-DIGIT SIC

Rank	Company Name—Executive Officer	Address, City, State, Zip	Phone	Type	Fin	Empls
200	All Star Apparel—Tim Mccallum	6722 Vista Del Mar Ave, La Jolla CA 92037	858-205-7827	R	10*	.1
201	Industrial Safety Supply Co—William F Bonk	PO Box 330720, West Hartford CT 06110	860-233-9881	R	10*	.1
202	Ganister Fasteners—Warren Owens	2301 Patriot Blvd, Glenview IL 60026	224-521-8000	R	10*	<.1
203	Nidec-Shimpo America Corp—Masatoshi Ohnishi	1701 Glenlake Ave, Itasca IL 60143	630-924-7138	R	10*	<.1
204	Jiffy Fastening Systems Inc—Jeff Moss	PO Box 55039, Lexington KY 40555	859-422-1900	R	10*	<.1
205	Dalton Bearing Service Inc—Gerry Lewis	PO Box 1363, Dalton GA 30722	706-278-2804	R	10*	.1
206	M Mauritzon and Company Inc—Steven Karlin	3939 W Belden Ave, Chicago IL 60647	773-235-6000	R	10*	.1
207	Allied High Tech Products Inc—Clayton Smith	PO Box 4608, Compton CA 90224	310-635-2466	R	10*	<.1
208	Ralph A Hiller Co—Randolph Hiller	6005 Enterprise Dr, Export PA 15632	724-325-1200	S	10*	<.1
209	Valve and Actuation Services LLC—Don Poole	1050 Industrial Blvd, Watkinsville GA 30677	706-769-6660	R	10*	.1
210	Ameraflex Rubber and Gasket Company Inc—Cody Cothran	317 Georgia Ave, Deer Park TX 77536	281-476-8500	R	10*	.1
211	Minnesota Flexible Corp—Will Stewart	803 Transfer Rd Ste 1, Saint Paul MN 55114	651-645-7522	R	10*	<.1
212	Epsco International and Companies Inc—Jeff Duncombe	717 Georgia Ave, Deer Park TX 77536	281-476-8100	R	10*	<.1
213	Flex-A-Seal Inc—Hank Slauson	PO Box 184, Essex Junction VT 05453	802-878-8307	R	10*	.1
214	Richmond Supply Co—Levi Hill	PO Box 1727, Augusta GA 30903	706-724-7792	R	9*	<.1
215	Industrial Pipe And Supply Co—Stuart Feinberg	5100 W 16th St, Chicago IL 60804	708-652-7511	R	9*	<.1
216	Electrical Fasteners Company Inc—John Gleason	9860 Clearvue Ct, Mokena IL 60448	708-478-6464	R	9*	<.1
217	Horn International Packaging Inc—David Gomer	44 Dunham Rd, Billerica MA 01821	978-667-8797	R	9*	<.1
218	Madsen and Howell Inc—M Madsen	PO Box 391, Perth Amboy NJ 08862	732-826-4000	R	9*	<.1
219	Binkelman Corp—Daniel Kazmierczak	2601 Hill Ave, Toledo OH 43607	419-537-9333	R	9*	.1
220	Raider Manufacturing Ltd—Breck Colquett	2008 E 50th St, Lubbock TX 79404	806-762-3227	R	9*	.1
221	Valtronics Inc—Kenneth Thompson	PO Box 490, Ravenswood WV 26164	304-273-5356	R	9*	<.1
222	All-Lift Systems Inc—Robert Molitor	2146 W Pershing St, Appleton WI 54914	920-738-0800	R	9*	<.1
223	Complete Drives Inc—Gregory Hale	6419 Discount Dr, Fort Wayne IN 46818	260-489-6033	R	9*	<.1
224	Griffin Supply Inc—Michael Griffin	5026 Columbia Ave, Hammond IN 46327	219-932-2122	R	9*	<.1
225	Chicago Chain and Transmission Co—Harry Schwarz	PO Box 705, La Grange IL 60525	708-482-9000	R	9*	<.1
226	Rubber and Accessories Inc—Harry Robb	PO Box 777, Eaton Park FL 33840	863-665-6115	R	9*	<.1
227	Fairbank Equipment Inc—Cody Wray	PO Box 13237, Wichita KS 67213	316-943-2247	R	9*	<.1
228	Thirty-Three Queen Realty Inc—David Rauch	1 Flexon Plz, Newark NJ 07114	973-824-5527	R	9*	<.1
229	Midwest Rubber Service and Supply Co—H Anderson	14307 28th Pl N, Minneapolis MN 55447	763-559-2551	R	9*	.1
230	Sugino Corp—Hideki Maeda	1380 Hamilton Pkwy, Itasca IL 60143	630-250-8585	R	9*	.1
231	Clean-Seal Inc—Ronald Moore	PO Box 2919, South Bend IN 46680	574-299-1888	R	9*	<.1
232	Commercial Electric Products Corp—Robert Meyer	1738 E 30th St, Cleveland OH 44114	216-241-2886	R	9*	<.1
233	Ohio Drill and Tool Co—Connie Hallman	23255 Georgetown Rd, Homeworth OH 44634	330-525-7717	R	9*	<.1
234	Stritt and Priebe Inc—Joel Scott	37 Clyde Ave, Buffalo NY 14215	716-834-1100	R	9*	<.1
235	Paramount Can Company Inc—Jack Gample	16430 Phoebe Ave, La Mirada CA 90638	714-562-8410	R	8*	<.1
236	General Factory Supplies Company Inc—Teri Stautberg	4811 Winton Rd, Cincinnati OH 45232	513-681-6300	R	8*	<.1
237	Conviber Inc—Frank Pucciarelli	PO Box 301, Springdale PA 15144	724-274-6300	R	8*	<.1
238	Applied Conveyor Technology Inc—Edward Sunseri	14644 El Molino St, Fontana CA 92335	909-350-4703	R	8*	<.1
239	Gardner and Meredith Inc—David Gardner	PO Box 4837, Chattanooga TN 37405	423-756-4722	R	8*	<.1
240	D-S Pipe and Supply Company Inc—Chris Keehner	PO Box 6367, Baltimore MD 21230	410-539-8000	R	8*	<.1
241	Carbide Tools For Industry Inc—Norbert Beadel	2650 S Grand Ave, Santa Ana CA 92705	714-002-0909	R	8*	<.1
242	Hk Aerospace Kirkhill Aircraft Parts Co—Joy Dunning	3098 N California St, Burbank CA 91504	818-559-9783	R	8*	<.1
243	Osha Industrial Products Inc—Gerald Bieber	100 Oak St, East Rutherford NJ 07073	201-935-2577	R	8*	.1
244	Compass Container Group Inc—Ricardo Lacayo	7982 Capwell Dr Fl 2, Oakland CA 94621	510-839-7500	R	8*	<.1
245	Every Supply Company Inc—Enzo Leva	615 S Columbus Ave, Mount Vernon NY 10550	914-667-7713	R	8*	<.1
246	Nuair Filter Company LLC—Jamie Harding	2219 W College Ave, Normal IL 61761	309-888-4331	R	8*	.1
247	West-Specialties Partners—Tanya Esch	20525 Nordhoff St Ste, Chatsworth CA 91311	818-725-7000	R	8*	.1
248	Peer Chain Co—Lawrence Spungen	2300 Norman Dr, Waukegan IL 60085	847-775-4600	R	7*	.1
249	Hydrocarbon Flow Specialist Inc—Nolan Fitch	PO Box 2859, Morgan City LA 70381	985-395-6106	R	7*	<.1
250	Moveable Cubicle Inc—Richard Whelan	6404 Falls Of Neuse Rd, Raleigh NC 27615	919-719-1900	R	7*	<.1
251	Power Products And Services Company Inc—Dominic Medure	5968 Highmarket St, Georgetown SC 29440	843-545-0766	R	7*	<.1
252	Industrial Rubber Company Inc—Peter Dugett	PO Box 359, Elizabeth NJ 07207	908-351-1550	R	7*	<.1
253	Bearing Service Inc—Douglas Savage	12320 Globe St, Livonia MI 48150	734-432-7272	R	7*	<.1
254	Gator Valve Inc—Michael Gillen	115 Thruway Park Rd, Broussard LA 70518	337-837-8228	R	7*	<.1
255	Freund Container—Joseph Freund	4200 Commerce Ct Ste 2, Lisle IL 60532		R	7*	<.1
256	Splawn Belting Inc—Jerry Splawn	PO Box 1299, Burlington NC 27216	336-227-4277	R	7*	<.1
257	Peco Fasteners Inc—Hal Jones	PO Box 43483, Atlanta GA 30336	770-745-1300	R	7*	<.1
258	Able Industrial Products Inc	2006 S Baker Ave, Ontario CA 91761	909-930-1585	R	7*	<.1
259	Gulf Sales And Supply Inc—G Smith	1909 Kenneth Ave, Pascagoula MS 39567	228-762-0268	R	7*	<.1
260	Kanaflex Company Inc—Shigeki Kanao	800 Woodlands Pkwy, Vernon Hills IL 60061	847-634-6100	R	7*	<.1
261	Cgi International LLC—Rick Adams	1215 Henderson Ave, Washington PA 15301	724-225-8700	R	7*	<.1
262	Industrial Finishing Systems Ii LP—Micheal Howell	PO Box 163945, Fort Worth TX 76161	972-563-0037	R	7*	<.1
263	Seal Company Enterprises Inc—John Oldham	1558 N 107th E Ave, Tulsa OK 74116	918-836-0441	R	7*	<.1
264	Braud Co—Lenette Braud	PO Box 127, Geismar LA 70734	225-673-3370	R	7*	<.1
265	Alfred Conhagen Incorporated Of California—Len Cucciare	3900 Oregon St Ste 1, Benicia CA 94510	707-746-4848	R	6*	<.1
266	J W Winco Inc—John Winkler	PO Box 510035, New Berlin WI 53151	262-786-8227	R	6*	<.1
267	Big River Rubber And Gasket Company Inc—Merton Davis	PO Box 369, Owensboro KY 42302	270-926-0241	R	6*	<.1
268	D M and E Corp—W Puckett	PO Box 580, Shelby NC 28151	704-482-8876	R	6*	<.1
269	Mitchell Container Services Inc—Ronnie Mitchell	226 Saraland Blvd S, Saraland AL 36571	251-675-3786	R	6*	<.1
270	Industrial Carbide Saw and Tool Corp—Charles Crush	PO Box 35278, Louisville KY 40232	502-968-8104	R	6*	<.1
271	Clover Group Inc—Genoveva Edmunds	3000 Durazno Ave, El Paso TX 79905	915-590-2525	R	6*	<.1
272	Arnold Supply Inc—William Donahue	67 S Tpke Rd Ste 3, Wallingford CT 06492	203-265-7168	R	6*	<.1
273	S A Day Manufacturing Company Inc—John Martin	1489 Niagara St, Buffalo NY 14213	716-881-3030	R	6*	<.1
274	Panhandle Packing and Gasket Inc—Jay Newton	PO Box 2154, Lubbock TX 79408	806-763-2801	R	6*	<.1
275	Alpine Associates Inc—Mike Ellsworth	3311 Pky Blvd, Salt Lake City UT 84119	801-972-0477	R	6*	<.1
276	Jacon Fasteners and Electronics Inc—Donald Wientjes	9539 Vassar Ave, Chatsworth CA 91311	818-700-2901	R	6*	<.1
277	Transco Northwest Inc—Richard Brown	PO Box 88002, Seattle WA 98138	425-251-5422	R	6*	<.1
278	Pm Fasteners Inc—Jim Spear	PO Box 124, Harleysville PA 19438	215-256-6525	R	6*	<.1
279	John G Shelley Company Inc—H Shelley	PO Box 81250, Wellesley MA 02481	781-237-0900	R	6*	.1
280	Power Tools and Supply Inc—Jeffrey Mcclure	8551 Boulder Ct, Walled Lake MI 48390	248-363-5650	R	6*	<.1
281	Eison Group Inc—Lester Eison	5800 Oakbrook Pkwy, Norcross GA 30093	770-448-7100	R	6*	<.1
282	Allied Purchasing—Brian Janssen	PO Box 1249, Mason City IA 50402	641-423-1824	R	6*	<.1
283	Georgino Industrial Supply Inc—Ron Hetrick	PO Box 300, Penfield PA 15849	814-637-5301	R	6*	<.1
284	Toyo USA Inc—Yutaka Yamada	15415 Katy Fwy Ste 600, Houston TX 77094	281-579-8900	S	6*	<.1
285	Hawks Sales Corp—Harvey Hawks	PO Box 19404, Indianapolis IN 46219	317-898-2511	R	6*	<.1
286	Woodruff Supply Company Inc—Larry Dugger	PO Box 426, Madisonville KY 42431	270-821-3247	R	6*	<.1
287	On Target Marketing—David Neilson	1193 Reads Run, Traverse City MI 49685	231-933-7221	R	6*	<.1
288	Industrial Bearing and Supply Inc—Gordon Brown	PO Box 4629, Dalton GA 30719	706-278-8130	R	6*	<.1
289	Allen Orton LLC—James Alexander	PO Box 2648, Norcross GA 30091	770-986-9999	R	6*	<.1

Rank	Company Name—Executive Officer	Address, City, State, Zip	Phone	Type	Fin	Empls
290	Amerimold Tech Inc—Michael Schon	150 Park Ave, Jackson NJ 08527	732-462-7577	R	6*	<.1
291	Hall Machine And Welding Company Inc—David Hall	102 W Mermod St, Carlsbad NM 88220	575-887-1143	R	6*	<.1
292	Southwest Fastener LLC—Terry Moore	242 E University Dr, Phoenix AZ 85004	602-272-2658	R	6*	<.1
293	Barry And Sewall Industrial Supply Co—Steven Olson	PO Box 50, Minneapolis MN 55440	612-331-6170	R	6*	<.1
294	Myers Brothers Of Kansas City Inc—C Ecton	1210 W 28th St, Kansas City MO 64108	816-931-5501	R	6*	<.1
295	Enviro-Process System Inc—Sam Nakhleh	425 Fairfield Ave, Stamford CT 06902	203-348-1514	R	6*	<.1
296	Williams Oil Filter Service Company Of Tacoma Inc—Larry Hayden	PO Box 2155, Tacoma WA 98401	253-627-8163	R	6*	<.1
297	Boston Pipe and Fittings Company Inc—William Carstensen	12 1st Ave, Somerville MA 02143	617-629-0500	R	6*	<.1
298	Christy Refractories Company LLC—Richard Day	4641 Mcree Ave, Saint Louis MO 63110	314-773-7500	R	5*	<.1
299	Gator Supply Company LLC—Pat Bergeron	PO Box 790, Harvey LA 70059	504-362-0781	R	5*	<.1
300	Dk/Amans Valve Inc—David Kinzler	2385 E Artesia Blvd, Long Beach CA 90805	562-529-8400	R	5*	<.1
301	Waters Industrial Supply Company Inc—James Waters	PO Box 805, Brookfield WI 53008	262-786-1610	R	5*	<.1
302	R M Wright Company Inc—Michael Hamzey	23910 Fwy Park Dr, Farmington Hills MI 48335	248-476-9800	R	5*	<.1
303	Acadiana Rubber and Gasket Co—Grover Dunphy	PO Box 3704, Lafayette LA 70502	337-233-1614	R	5*	<.1
304	Gamer Packaging Inc—Ronald Gamer	330 2nd Ave S Ste 895, Minneapolis MN 55401	612-788-4444	R	5*	<.1
305	BJW Berghorst and Sons Inc—Ford Berghorst	11430 James St Ste A, Holland MI 49424	616-772-2114	R	5*	<.1
306	Coldwell and Company Inc—Kent Weber	1227 Mulberry St, Terre Haute IN 47807	812-232-0276	R	5*	<.1
307	Lake Charles Rubber and Gasket Company LLC—Bryan Vincent	PO Box 3205, Lake Charles LA 70602	337-433-1002	R	5*	<.1
308	Productive Tool Products Inc—Charles Ebert	1075 Headquarters Park, Fenton MO 63026	636-305-1200	R	5*	<.1
309	Hyquip Inc—Eric Jensen	1811 Dolphin Dr, Waukesha WI 53186	262-521-2170	R	5*	<.1
310	Cupp's Industrial Supply Inc—David Timberlin	3101 N 33rd Ave, Phoenix AZ 85017	602-269-2301	R	5*	<.1
311	Viking Tension Products Corp	1790 Swarthmore Ave, Lakewood NJ 08701	732-364-0444	R	5*	.1
312	Mc Neal Industries Inc—Randall Mcneil	835 Richmond Rd, Painesville OH 44077	440-951-7756	R	5*	<.1
313	Atlantic India Rubber Co—Irene Morris	PO Box 460, Hagerhill KY 41222	606-789-9115	R	5*	<.1
314	Delray Sales Inc—Alan Guttman	15345 Lake Wildflower, Delray Beach FL 33484	561-637-6344	R	5*	<.1
315	Dayton Reliable Air-Filter Service Inc—Gary Chrusciel	2294 N Moraine Dr, Moraine OH 45439	937-293-4611	R	5*	<.1
316	Pacific Rubber and Packing Inc—Ashley Burfield	1160 Industrial Rd Ste, San Carlos CA 94070	650-595-5888	R	5*	<.1
317	North American Safety Valve Industries Inc—Allen Tanis	1500 Iron St, Kansas City MO 64116	816-421-7042	R	5*	<.1
318	Minuteman Controls Company Inc—Herbert Morton	PO Box 1559, Wakefield MA 01880	781-245-9550	R	5*	<.1
319	Rahway Steel Drum—Anthony Foglia	202 Elliot St, Avenel NJ 07001	732-382-0113	R	5*	<.1
320	Bennet and Sons Machine and Supply Company Inc—Richard Bennett	PO Box 1642, Muskogee OK 74402	918-682-3357	R	5*	<.1
321	Hose Of South Texas Inc—Hensley Batey	PO Box 9576, Corpus Christi TX 78469	361-884-9335	R	5*	<.1
322	Lubron Bearing Systems—John Fuini	17611 Metzler Ln, Huntington Beach CA 92647	714-841-3007	R	5*	<.1
323	Viking Industrial Center Inc—William Norton	710 Raymond Ave, Saint Paul MN 55114	651-646-6374	R	5*	<.1
324	Sign Source USA Inc—Jeff Pisel	PO Box 776, Lima OH 45802	419-224-1130	R	5*	.1
325	Magary Construction Inc—Larry Dwyer	5550 N Broadway, Saint Louis MO 63147	314-771-1400	R	5*	<.1
326	Amg Forwarding Corp—Flavio Marquez	1474 W Price Rd, Brownsville TX 78520	956-592-1927	R	5*	<.1
327	Cardinal Rubber and Seal Inc—Loren Bruffey	1545 Brownlee Ave Se, Roanoke VA 24014	540-982-0091	R	5*	<.1
328	Iwen Tool Supply Co—Ermin Sallmen	PO Box 604, Bridgeport MI 48722	989-777-7101	R	5*	<.1
329	Dooley Gasket And Seal Inc—James Dooley	PO Box 729, Media PA 19063	610-328-2720	R	5*	<.1
330	Marion Engineering and Technology Inc—James Stengel	PO Box 924, Marion IN 46952	765-662-3894	R	5*	<.1
331	Sup-R-Die Inc—David Palisin	10003 Memphis Ave, Cleveland OH 44144	216-252-3930	R	5*	<.1
332	Abernathy-Thomas Engineering Co—James Ellis	PO Box 1493, Kingsport TN 37662	423-245-6151	R	5*	<.1
333	Shar-Craft Inc—James Craft	1103 33rd St, Bakersfield CA 93301	661-324-4985	R	5*	<.1
334	Cook Iron Store Co—Stephen Wichtowski	128 Saint Paul St, Rochester NY 14604	585-454-5840	R	5*	<.1
335	Bearing Sales Corp—Jim White	4153 N Kostner Ave, Chicago IL 60641	773-282-8686	R	5*	<.1
336	American Quality Tools Inc—Mukesh Aghi	12650 Magnolia Ave Ste, Riverside CA 92503	951-280-4700	R	5*	<.1
337	William Jones and Son Inc—George Williams	238 Liberty St, Camden NJ 08104	856-963-1199	R	5*	<.1
338	Air Filter Service Company Inc—Boykin Sanders	PO Box 1813, Sumter SC 29151	803-773-9321	R	5*	<.1
339	HWEckhardt Corp—John Eckhardt	PO Box 3747, Huntington Beach CA 92605	714-375-4926	R	5*	<.1
340	Louisiana Chemical Pipe Valve and Fitting Inc—Robert De Angelo	PO Box 15485, Baton Rouge LA 70895	225-927-2688	R	5*	<.1
341	Tyler Tool Company Inc—Tyler Harvey	PO Box 272, Tylertown MS 39667	601-876-2145	R	5*	<.1
342	H R S Fastener Inc—Ford Smith	PO Box 6137, Arlington TX 76005	817-640-9991	R	5*	<.1
343	Dante Valve Co—Michael Dante	1324 Ballentine Blvd, Norfolk VA 23504	757-605-6100	R	4*	<.1
344	Capital Industrial Supply Inc—Janette Nieman	2649 R W Johnson Rd Sw, Tumwater WA 98512	360-786-1890	R	4*	<.1
345	East Carolina Supply Company Inc—James Ginn	PO Box 667, Plymouth NC 27962	252-793-2175	R	4*	<.1
346	Western States Tool and Supply Corp—Ralph Rader	PO Box 56574, Hayward CA 94545	510-786-2004	R	4*	<.1
347	Imrie-Gielow Inc—Kenneth Gielow	2823 Papin St, Saint Louis MO 63103	314-772-4200	R	4*	<.1
348	Van Note Supply Inc—Phil Mingus	1403 Hugh Ave Ste B, Louisville KY 40213	502-458-5097	R	4*	<.1
349	Cutter Northern Refractories Inc—C Cutter	10 Micro Dr Ste 500, Woburn MA 01801	781-938-8998	R	4*	<.1
350	Ipaco Inc—Loyal Andersen	555 N 1000 W, Logan UT 84321	435-753-1942	R	4*	<.1
351	C and M Assets LLC—Norm Sherwood	1437 Blowing Rock Blvd, Lenoir NC 28645	828-754-9076	R	4*	<.1
352	Sat Suma Valve and Controls LLC—Candice Faust	PO Box 779, Walker LA 70785	225-664-6502	R	4*	<.1
353	Flex-Ing Inc—Tom Ingram	2828 Fallon Dr, Sherman TX 75090	903-892-8983	R	4*	<.1
354	TEC Industrial Inc—Robert Perry	PO Box 1152, Rochester MN 55903	507-288-9133	R	4*	<.1
355	Mccarthy's Shops Inc—Sean Mccarthy	1845 Daly St, Los Angeles CA 90031	323-581-2001	R	4*	<.1
356	Graff Valve and Fittings Inc—Philip Graff	12345 S Marshfield Ave, Calumet Park IL 60827	708-371-1100	R	4*	<.1
357	Anne Reid Capital Inc—Charles Lehnbeuter	PO Box 210597, Saint Louis MO 63121	314-239-6748	R	4*	<.1
358	RE Mason Company Of The Carolinas—Robert Mason	PO Box 33413, Charlotte NC 28233	704-375-4464	R	4*	<.1
359	Molter Corp—Loretta Molter	PO Box 751, Frankfort IL 60423	708-720-1600	R	4*	<.1
360	Ohio Valley Industrial Services Inc—Thomas Kaminski	530 Moon Clinton Rd St, Moon Township PA 15108	412-269-0020	R	4*	<.1
361	Babbitt Steam Specialty Co—John Babbitt	PO Box 51208, New Bedford MA 02745	508-995-9534	R	4*	<.1
362	Econ-Abrasive Accessories Inc—Barbara Clarkson	PO Box 1628, Frisco TX 75034	972-335-9234	R	4*	<.1
363	North American Seal and Supply Inc—Otis Manis	26820 Fargo Ave, Cleveland OH 44146	216-831-6210	R	4*	<.1
364	F R Blankenstein Co—F Blankenstein	PO Box 986, Natchez MS 39121	601-445-5618	R	4*	<.1
365	Air Filter Sales and Service Of Denver Inc—Jason Boyd	134 Yuma St, Denver CO 80223	303-777-2603	R	4*	<.1
366	Fine Organics Corp	PO Box 2277, Clifton NJ 07015	973-478-1000	R	4	<.1
367	GT Industries Of Oklahoma Inc—Lynn Fesperman	9525 E 55th St Tulsa O, Tulsa OK 74145	918-627-6600	R	4*	<.1
368	Kaufman Company Inc—Dave Kaufman	19 Walkhill Rd, Norwood MA 02062	617-491-5500	R	4*	<.1
369	Mid-Valley Supply LLC—Martin Mayer	106 Commerce Dr, South Point OH 45680	740-377-9700	R	4*	<.1
370	All Appliance Parts Inc—Don Stevic	PO Box 770902, Coral Springs FL 33077	954-714-4009	R	4*	<.1
371	M PT International Corp—Thomas Haffner	PO Box 411244, Charlotte NC 28241	704-588-1091	R	4*	<.1
372	Api Inc—Charles Swenson	616 Powers St, Eugene OR 97402	541-686-9946	R	4*	<.1
373	Atlantic Sales Company LLC	20 Assembly Sq Dr, Somerville MA 02145	617-776-6429	R	4*	<.1
374	Noel's Inc—Gregory Noel	601 Scott Ave, Farmington NM 87401	505-327-3375	R	4*	<.1
375	Konsep Co—Herbert Conrad	PO Box 3327, York PA 17402	717-266-6180	R	4*	<.1

Note: An asterisk (*) indicates an estimated financial figure. The company type code used is as follows: R = Private, P = Public, S = Private Subsidiary, B = Public Subsidiary, D = Division, J = Joint Venture, I = Investment Fund.

COMPANY RANKINGS BY SALES WITHIN 4-DIGIT SIC

Rank	Company Name—*Executive Officer*	Address, City, State, Zip	Phone	Type	Fin	Empls
376	Alabama Industrial LLC—*Deresia Pace*	PO Box 610246, Birmingham AL 35261	205-833-3935	R	4*	<.1
377	Sudmo North America Inc—*Jack Jordan*	1330 Anvil Rd, Machesney Park IL 61115	815-639-0322	R	4*	<.1
378	Carbide Specialties Inc—*Thomas Roth*	3941 Eastern Ave Se, Grand Rapids MI 49508	616-241-1424	R	4*	<.1
379	Colonial Engineering Inc—*Mark Bainbridge*	6400 Corporate Ave, Portage MI 49002	269-323-2495	R	4*	<.1
380	Monroe Rubber and Gasket Company Inc—*Lee Carter*	PO Box 3285, Monroe LA 71210	318-388-4114	R	4*	<.1
381	Jessico—*Jane Kokkinaki*	2240 S Thornburg St, Santa Maria CA 93455	805-922-1311	R	4*	<.1
382	Coca Sales Inc—*Chris Cappe*	PO Box 119, Baker LA 70704	225-775-8700	R	4*	<.1
383	Rockmount Research and Alloys Inc—*Charles Foster*	PO Box 2909, Vancouver WA 98668	360-254-2020	R	4*	<.1
384	Socket Source Inc—*Paul Vittori*	3801 Artesia Ave, Fullerton CA 92833	714-521-2415	R	4*	<.1
385	Tamper-Pruf Screws Inc—*Carmen Melendez*	8808 Somerset Blvd, Paramount CA 90723	562-531-9364	R	4*	<.1
386	Timco Rubber Products Inc—*Robert Kuzmick*	PO Box 35135, Cleveland OH 44135	216-267-6242	R	4*	<.1
387	Uland Supply Co—*James Brown*	500 E Broadway, Louisville KY 40202	502-587-0721	R	4*	<.1
388	Empire Fasteners Inc—*Edward Kessler*	1210 30th Ave, Long Island City NY 11102	718-728-3900	R	4*	<.1
389	R and M Welding Products Inc—*Michael Buckley*	105 Williams Way, Wilder KY 41076	859-572-7474	R	4*	<.1
390	S and J Industrial Supply Corp—*Robert Stuart*	16060 Suntone Dr, South Holland IL 60473	708-339-1708	R	4*	<.1
391	Autobooks Inc—*Scott Koppell*	PO Box 261, Owings Mills MD 21117	410-358-3130	R	4*	<.1
392	MS Rubber Co—*Sandy Lewis*	PO Box 6489, Jackson MS 39282	601-948-2575	R	4*	<.1
393	Mrp Inc—*William Witchger*	2787 S Freeman Rd, Monticello IN 47960	574-583-3464	R	3*	<.1
394	Services For Plastics Inc—*Kurt Begue*	7925 N Clinton St, Fort Wayne IN 46825	260-482-9211	R	3*	<.1
395	SMG Supply Inc—*Brian Gersten*	20 Robert Pitt Dr Ste, Monsey NY 10952	845-352-8600	R	3*	<.1
396	Sunny Sun Glasses Of Miami Inc—*Ja Hsuing Jason Hu*	8900 Nw 33rd St, Doral FL 33172	305-591-3065	R	3*	<.1
397	Symorex Ltd—*Chris Erickson*	683 Airport Blvd Ste 1, Ann Arbor MI 48108	734-971-6000	R	3*	<.1
398	Stanley Kessler and Co—*Jeff Saul*	PO Box 60340, King Of Prussia PA 19406	610-265-3555	R	3*	<.1
399	Mcwilliams Fluid Connectors Inc—*Maureen Mcwilliams*	7375 Convoy Ct, San Diego CA 92111	858-268-4433	R	3*	<.1
400	Nbs Corp—*Don Ou*	3100 E Slauson Ave, Vernon CA 90058	323-923-1627	R	3*	<.1
401	Milwaukee Chaplet Inc—*Robert Rice*	PO Box 510010, New Berlin WI 53151	262-782-3550	R	3*	<.1
402	M N Gumbert Corp—*Michael Gumbert*	10750 Metric Dr, Dallas TX 75243	214-340-0222	R	3*	<.1
403	American Air Filter Snydergeneral Corp—*Bob Densmore*	PO Box 12567, Pittsburgh PA 15241	412-821-8884	R	3*	<.1
404	Trust Drum and Freight—*Carol Benthal*	PO Box 119, Plant City FL 33564	813-754-4255	R	3*	<.1
405	Industrial Diamond Products Co—*Roland Hayes*	PO Box 262158, Houston TX 77207	713-991-1600	R	3*	<.1
406	Automation Center Inc—*David Westerman*	933 Visco Dr, Nashville TN 37210	615-255-2886	R	3*	<.1
407	JE Myles Inc—*J Ed Myles*	310 Executive Dr, Troy MI 48083	248-583-1020	R	3*	<.1
408	Southern Truck and Equipment Inc—*W Spann*	PO Box 1505, Theodore AL 36590	251-653-4716	R	3*	<.1
409	Certified Cylinders Inc—*Reggie Hall*	PO Box 527, Crossville TN 38557	931-484-1521	R	3*	<.1
410	Filpro Corp—*Troy Massack*	PO Box 374, West Point PA 19486	215-646-5800	R	3*	<.1
411	Polyrock Equipment Company Inc—*Jerry Polley*	4763 Murietta St, Chino CA 91710	909-591-4885	R	3*	<.1
412	Sumter Machinery Co—*Henry Killian*	PO Box 700, Sumter SC 29151	803-773-1441	R	3*	<.1
413	Isopur Fluid Technologies Inc—*Raymond Gomes*	183 Prdnc Nw Lndn Tpke, North Stonington CT 06359	860-571-8590	R	3*	<.1
414	Meriden Cooper Corp—*Tom Oberholtzer*	PO Box 692, Meriden CT 06450		R	3*	<.1
415	Uni Global Container Service Corp—*Jamie Chong*	PO Box 2063, El Paso TX 79951	915-760-4425	R	3*	<.1
416	Arkansas Water Products LLC—*Michael Beckman*	8915 Fourche Dam Pke, Little Rock AR 72206	501-490-1244	R	3*	<.1
417	Ector Drum Inc—*Thomas Salmon*	PO Box 1888, Odessa TX 79760	432-366-8352	R	3*	<.1
418	American Blower Supply Inc—*Randall Morrow*	14219 E 10 Mile Rd, Warren MI 48089	586-771-7337	R	3*	<.1
419	Scott Bolt and Screw Company Inc—*Thomas Scott*	PO Box 100872, Nashville TN 37224	615-255-0686	R	3*	<.1
420	Western Rubber and Supply Inc—*Don Ulery*	7888 Marathon Dr Ste F, Livermore CA 94550	925-960-8700	R	3*	<.1
421	Teds Supply Inc—*Teddy Markham*	PO Box 548, Rogersville TN 37857	423-272-9200	R	3*	<.1
422	Procam Controls Inc—*Roy Seibert*	2605 Tech Dr Ste 300, Plano TX 75074	972-881-9797	R	3*	<.1
423	Mosley Tractor And Supply Inc—*Tim Mosley*	2315 Whitestone Rd, Talking Rock GA 30175	706-276-4331	R	3*	<.1
424	FK Bearings Inc—*Frank Fragola*	865 W Queen St, Southington CT 06489	860-628-8722	R	3*	<.1
425	Mile-X Equipment Inc—*Randy Gaerke*	801 N 2nd St, Coldwater OH 45828	419-678-3818	R	3*	<.1
426	Bluewater Rubber and Gasket—*Dennis Combe*	1802 Engineers Rd Ste, Belle Chasse LA 70037	504-392-3001	R	3*	<.1
427	Total Package Systems Ga LLC—*Shaun Reynolds*	2300 Dalton Industrial, Dalton GA 30721	706-270-8635	R	3*	<.1
428	Ash Gear Supply Corp—*Clayton Jerris*	42650 W 9 Mile Rd, Novi MI 48375	248-374-6155	R	3*	<.1
429	Beltrami Industrial Services Inc—*Randy Forseth*	12297 Hwy 2 Nw, Solway MN 56678	218-751-7537	R	3*	<.1
430	Ohio Gear and Transmission Inc—*Carolyn Bauer*	33050 Lakeland Blvd, Willoughby OH 44095	440-951-7576	R	3*	<.1
431	Frazier Machine and Supply Company Inc—*Elmo Frazier*	PO Box 1336, Winnfield LA 71483	318-628-3296	R	3*	<.1
432	Plibrico Sales And Service—*Barry Cox*	1907 Vanderhorn Dr, Memphis TN 38134	901-373-9000	R	3*	<.1
433	Hotflush Inc—*Dennis Hansen*	PO Box 324, New Hampton IA 50659	641-394-6804	R	3*	<.1
434	Pruitt Company Of Ada Inc—*Dexter Pruitt*	3900 N Broadway Ave, Ada OK 74820	580-332-7058	R	3*	<.1
435	PSM Fastener Corp—*Bryan Lind*	12223 C R Koon Hwy 76, Newberry SC 29108	803-321-1300	R	3*	<.1
436	Bin and Storage Authority—*Craig Kates*	3101 Nw 106th St, Miami FL 33147	305-687-2255	R	2*	<.1
437	Greenville Industrial Rubber and Gasket Company Inc—*Frankie Russo*	PO Box 4469, Greenville SC 29608	864-235-2574	R	2*	<.1
438	Metal Finishing Supply Company Inc—*James Choren*	PO Box 526, Brookfield WI 53008	262-782-0555	R	2*	<.1
439	Rcf Technologies Inc—*Dianne Zimnavoda*	320 Commerce Loop, Vidalia GA 30474	912-537-1115	R	2*	<.1
440	Glassautomatic Inc—*Rolf Poeting*	402 E Main St, Mount Pleasant PA 15666	724-547-7500	R	2*	<.1
441	Thomas Losinski—*Tom Losinski*	PO Box 41543, Minneapolis MN 55441	763-208-3373	R	2*	<.1
442	Fischer North America Inc—*Jay Bailey*	119 White Oak Dr, Berlin CT 06037	860-828-0595	R	2*	<.1
443	Delta Flexible Products Inc—*Terence Tollaksen*	1515 16th St Ste 1, Racine WI 53403	262-632-2345	R	2*	<.1
444	Panthera Inc—*Gary Pool*	PO Box 925006, Houston TX 77292	713-939-9939	R	2*	<.1
445	Swift Saw and Tool Supply Company Inc—*Gerald Greenway*	1200 171st St, Hazel Crest IL 60429	708-335-0550	R	2*	<.1
446	RAM Consolidated Industries Inc—*Thomas J Ritter*	642 W Iris Dr, Nashville TN 37204	615-269-7272	R	2*	<.1
447	Little and Company Inc—*Wyatt Smith*	PO Box 1849, Eaton Park FL 33840	863-665-4887	R	2*	<.1
448	Allied Tools Inc—*John Eifer*	PO Box 34367, Louisville KY 40232	502-966-4114	R	2*	<.1
449	Gateway Supply Ltd—*Frederick Colschen*	1930 Roosevelt St, Clinton IA 52732	563-242-7160	R	2*	<.1
450	Kolda Corp—*Felipe Larotta*	2202 Hidden Creek Dr, Kingwood TX 77339	281-448-8995	R	2*	<.1
451	Commercial Janitorial Maintenance—*Laura Mazany*	PO Box 21245, Reno NV 89515	775-358-0422	R	2*	<.1
452	Stiles Enterprises Inc—*Richard Stiles*	PO Box 92, Rockaway NJ 07866	973-625-9660	R	2*	<.1
453	Plastic Depot Inc—*Herb Sutton*	5722 S Flamingo Rd Ste, Cooper City FL 33330	305-944-2190	R	2*	<.1
454	Diamond Eze-Lap Products Inc—*Jack Fletcher*	3572 Arrowhead Dr, Carson City NV 89706	775-888-9500	R	2*	<.1
455	Carolina Color and Chemical Co—*Jack Firpo*	8029 Cedar Glen Dr, Charlotte NC 28212	704-333-5101	R	2*	<.1
456	Cavalier Bolt and Nut Inc—*Garfield Edmonds*	1493 London Bridge Rd, Virginia Beach VA 23453	757-427-6405	R	2*	<.1
457	O-Rings Inc—*Sherin Lee*	PO Box 65675, Los Angeles CA 90065	323-343-9500	R	2*	<.1
458	Cromwell Industries Inc—*Larry Douglas*	23501 Ridge Rte Dr F, Laguna Hills CA 92653	949-680-4061	R	1*	<.1
459	A-1 Babbitt Company Inc—*Brad Rodeheaver*	PO Box 791, Donora PA 15033	724-379-6588	R	1*	<.1
460	Coal Country Industries Inc—*Robert Price*	Off Rte 85, Oceana WV 24870	304-682-6456	R	1*	<.1
461	Data Retrieval Corp—*Nathan Waldman*	13231 Champ Forst Dr S, Houston TX 77069	281-444-5398	R	1*	<.1
462	Winter-Wolff International Inc—*Daniel Weil*	131 Jericho Tpke Ste 2, Jericho NY 11753	516-997-3300	R	1*	<.1
463	Vps Control Systems Inc—*Peter Schaaphok*	PO Box 249, Hoosick NY 12089	518-686-0019	R	1*	<.1
464	Intech Bearing Inc—*W Kroll*	4955 Gulf Fwy, Houston TX 77023	713-926-1136	R	1*	<.1

Rank	Company Name—*Executive Officer*	Address, City, State, Zip	Phone	Type	Fin	Empls
465	Deken Power Inc—*Dennis Hurst*	1402 Ritchey St, Santa Ana CA 92705	714-541-4373	R	1*	<.1
466	Power Parts International Inc—*Roger Shaw*	742 S Indiana Ave, West Bend WI 53095	262-335-2777	R	1*	<.1
467	Instrument Specialists Inc—*Maryann Mcgill*	6126 Stratler St, Salt Lake City UT 84107	801-261-0142	R	1*	<.1
468	Bay Fasteners and Components Inc—*Joseph Greschuk*	604 S Ware Blvd, Tampa FL 33619	813-621-2625	R	1*	<.1
469	Burlingame Builder Inc—*Leonard Burlingame*	3007 W River Rd, Olean NY 14760	716-373-5881	R	1*	<.1
470	Lenser Filtration Inc—*Roberts Iovino*	1215 Rte 70 Ste 1001, Lakewood NJ 08701	732-370-1600	R	1*	<.1
471	Aap International Inc—*David Davis*	PO Box 747, Wofford Heights CA 93285	760-376-4430	R	<1*	<.1
472	Filter Technologies Inc—*Peter Wojnarowicz*	168 Manalapan Rd, Spotswood NJ 08884	732-251-9500	R	<1*	<.1

TOTALS: SIC 5085 Industrial Supplies
     Companies: 472   23,050   56.5

5087 Service Establishment Equipment

Rank	Company Name—*Executive Officer*	Address, City, State, Zip	Phone	Type	Fin	Empls
1	Sally Beauty Holdings Inc (Denton Texas)—*Gary G Winterhalter*	3001 Colorado Blvd, Denton TX 76210	940-898-7500	P	3,269	7.0
2	ABCO Products Inc—*Carlos Albir*	6800 NW 36th Ave, Miami FL 33147	305-694-2226	R	718*	1.8
3	Edward Don and Co—*Steve Don*	2500 S Harlem Ave, North Riverside IL 60546	708-442-9400	R	315*	1.0
4	Clark Foodservice Inc	950 Arthur Ave, Elk Grove Village IL 60007	847-956-1730	S	310*	.8
5	Group One Capital Inc—*Bruce A Olson*	8235 Forsyth Blvd Ste, Saint Louis MO 63105	314-725-4566	R	230*	2.0
6	HP Products Corp—*Bridget Shuel*	PO Box 68310, Indianapolis IN 46268	317-298-9950	R	148*	.4
7	Ferguson Fire and Fabrication Inc—*Leo Klein*	2750 S Towne Ave, Pomona CA 91766	909-517-3085	S	139	.6
8	Aerial Company Inc—*Ryan Hmielewski*	PO Box 197, Marinette WI 54143	715-735-9323	R	128*	.7
9	Beauty Alliance Inc—*Paul Sharnsky*	4555 Danvers Dr Se, Grand Rapids MI 49512	616-942-0060	R	80*	.5
10	P4 Corp—*Robert Cohen*	16001 Trade Zone Ave, Upper Marlboro MD 20774	301-218-1000	R	65*	.2
11	Mikara Corp—*Michael P Hicks*	3109 Louisiana Ave N, Minneapolis MN 55427	763-546-9500	R	65*	.2
12	Hart Intercivic Inc—*Gregg Burt*	PO Box 80649, Austin TX 78708	512-252-6400	R	48*	.1
13	Emiliani Enterprises Inc—*James Emiliani*	600 Green Ln, Union NJ 07083	908-964-6340	R	47*	.3
14	Glory (USA) Inc—*Takashi Mitsi*	10 York Ave, West Caldwell NJ 07006	973-228-4500	R	44*	.3
15	Kellermeyer Co—*Don Kellermeyer*	475 W Woodland Cir, Bowling Green OH 43402	419-255-3022	R	42*	.1
16	Planet Antares Inc—*Dana Bashor*	5700 Buckingham Pkwy S, Culver City CA 90230	310-342-5300	R	42*	.1
17	Phenix Supply Co—*Robbie Freeman*	PO Box 360574, Decatur GA 30036	770-981-2800	R	39*	.1
18	Industrial Soap Co—*Ron Morrison*	722 S Vandeventer Ave, Saint Louis MO 63110	314-241-6363	R	35*	.1
19	Paramount Restaurant Supply Corp—*Steven McGarry*	101 Main St, Warren RI 02885	401-247-6500	R	31*	.1
20	State Service Systems Inc Group One Capital Inc	10405-B E 55th Pl, Tulsa OK 74146	918-627-8000	S	30*	.1
21	OPI Products Inc—*George Schaeffer*	13034 Saticoy St, North Hollywood CA 91605	818-759-2400	R	28*	.5
22	Safety Today—*Ted Cowie*	3287 Southwest Blvd, Grove City OH 43123		R	26*	.1
23	Bermil Industries Corporation Wascomat of America—*Bernard Milch*	461 Doughty Blvd, Inwood NY 11096	516-371-2000	R	25*	.1
24	Kenway Distributors Inc—*Kenneth R Crutcher*	PO Box 14097, Louisville KY 40214	502-367-2201	R	24*	.1
25	Ro-Vic Inc—*Roger Parrott Jr*	146 Sheldon Rd, Manchester CT 06042	860-646-3322	R	24*	.1
26	Adams-Burch Inc—*Dan W Blaylock*	1901 Stanford Ct, Landover MD 20785	301-276-2000	R	23*	.1
27	Ecolab Inc Textile Care Div	370 N Wabasha St, Saint Paul MN 55102	651-293-2233	D	21*	.2
28	Plaza-Ford-Ideal Laundry And Dry Cleaners Inc—*S Eisen*	1305 Virginia Ave, Kansas City MO 64106	816-842-2822	R	21*	.1
29	Firetron Inc—*Billy Corbin*	PO Box 1604, Stafford TX 77497	281-499-1500	R	19*	.1
30	McShane Enterprises Inc—*David R McShane*	PO Box 220, Milltown NJ 08850	732-254-3100	R	19*	.1
31	Kranz Inc—*Jeff Neubauer*	2200 DeKoven Ave, Racine WI 53403	262-638-2200	R	18*	.1
32	SecureUSA Inc—*Carla L Clark*	PO Box 2298, Cumming GA 30028	770-205-0789	R	18*	.1
33	Jeffco Fibres Inc—*Blanche Lonstein*	PO Box 816, Webster MA 01570	508-943-0440	R	18*	.1
34	Standard Companies Inc—*George Bonomo*	2601 S Archer Ave, Chicago IL 60608	312-225-2777	R	16*	.1
35	Sprinkler World Of Arizona Inc—*Richard Wheelock*	2114 E Indian School R, Phoenix AZ 85016	602-954-9022	R	16*	.1
36	Fowler Equipment Company Inc—*Douglas Fowler*	565 Rahway Ave Ste 1, Union NJ 07083	908-686-3400	R	15*	.1
37	Fabriclean Supply—*Shelly Hericks*	8301 Ambassador Row, Dallas TX 75247	214-826-4161	R	15*	.1
38	Tri-State Technical Services Inc—*Matt Stephenson*	912 Francis St, Waycross GA 31503	912 285-9212	R	15*	.1
39	Sanderson Safety Supply Co—*Stephen Spahr*	1101 SE 3rd Ave, Portland OR 97214	503-238-5700	R	14*	.1
40	Cosgrove Enterprises Inc—*R Rogers*	14300 Nw 77th Ct, Miami Lakes FL 33016	305-820-5600	R	14*	.1
41	Olla Beauty Supply Inc—*Marcy Blick*	PO Box 898, Pine Brook NJ 07058	973-575-5260	R	13*	.1
42	Rose Products And Services Inc—*Robert Roth*	545 Stimmel Rd, Columbus OH 43223	614-443-7647	R	13*	.4
43	I Janvey and Sons Inc—*Bruce Janvey*	218 Front St, Hempstead NY 11550	516-489-9300	R	13*	<.1
44	Katzson Brothers Inc—*Richard Right*	960 Vallejo St, Denver CO 80204	303-893-3535	R	12*	<.1
45	Field's Fire Protection Inc—*Glenna Field*	PO Box 1044, Grand Rapids MI 49501	616-453-2200	R	12*	<.1
46	Goldwell Of New York Inc—*Hans Neumaier*	2117 Brghtn Henrta Twn, Rochester NY 14623	585-424-4110	R	12*	<.1
47	Knight Marketing Corporation Of New York—*Stan Peters*	PO Box 780009, Maspeth NY 11378	718-786-8787	R	12*	<.1
48	Callico Distributors Inc—*Mark Callahan*	90 Prince Henry Dr, Taunton MA 02780	508-828-9000	R	11*	.1
49	Binkowsky Inc—*Herbert Binkowsky*	PO Box 88, Sheboygan WI 53082	920-565-4111	R	11*	<.1
50	Mortech Manufacturing Company Inc—*Benny Joseph*	411 N Aerojet Dr, Azusa CA 91702	626-334-1471	R	11*	.1
51	Dongieux's Inc—*John Schemmel*	PO Box 9386, Jackson MS 39286	601-366-2636	R	11*	<.1
52	Fishman Supply Co—*Leland Fishman*	PO Box 750279, Petaluma CA 94975	707-763-8161	R	10*	.1
53	Banner Systems Of Massachusetts Inc—*Frederick Channell*	135 Elliot St, Brockton MA 02302	508-588-1835	R	10*	.1
54	N S Farrington and Co—*David Farrington*	PO Box 12279, Winston Salem NC 27117	336-788-7705	R	10*	<.1
55	Fitch Dustdown Co—*Lynne Kirsner*	2201 Russell St, Baltimore MD 21230	410-539-1953	R	10*	.1
56	Wagner Supply Company Inc—*Paul Wagner*	PO Box 1766, Odessa TX 79760	432-563-9271	R	9*	.1
57	Holtco Inc—*Phillip Consolino*	PO Box 43164, Atlanta GA 30336	404-691-8422	R	9*	<.1
58	Trillium Us Inc—*James Beatty*	13011 Se Jennifer St S, Clackamas OR 97015	503-682-3837	R	9*	.1
59	Western Engravers Supply Inc—*Dennis Trifletti*	17621 N Black Canyon H, Phoenix AZ 85023	602-439-0400	R	9*	.1
60	Windtrax Inc—*Brad Daniels*	6800 Foxridge Dr, Shawnee Mission KS 66202	913-789-9100	R	9*	<.1
61	Bermil Industries Corp—*Neal Milch*	461 Doughty Blvd, Inwood NY 11096	516-371-4400	R	8*	.1
62	Beauty Craft Supply and Equipment Co—*Maximillion Wexler*	11110 Bren Rd W, Hopkins MN 55343	952-935-4420	R	8*	.1
63	Firematic Supply Company Inc—*Michael Hanratty*	PO Box 187, Yaphank NY 11980	631-924-3181	R	8*	<.1
64	Molinari Supply Inc—*David Molinari*	PO Box 2026, Salinas CA 93902	831-424-1928	R	8*	<.1
65	Albany Foam And Supply Inc—*Michael Giacone*	1355 Broadway, Menands NY 12204	518-433-7000	R	8*	.1
66	Cameo Supply Company Inc—*Sylvia Raynor*	335 Merrick Rd, Amityville NY 11701	631-598-1130	R	8*	.1
67	Dish Factory Inc—*Charles Wyatt*	310 S Los Angeles St, Los Angeles CA 90013	213-687-9500	R	8*	<.1
68	Northern Chemical Co—*Charles Hayes*	PO Box 2837, Glendale AZ 85311	623-937-1668	R	8*	<.1
69	Pellerin Laundry Machinery Sales Company Inc—*Curtis Pellerin*	PO Box 1137, Kenner LA 70063	504-467-9593	R	7*	<.1
70	Minnesota Chemical Co—*Michael Baker*	2285 Hampden Ave, Saint Paul MN 55114	651-646-7521	R	7*	<.1
71	Superior International Corp—*Vince Montarosa*	2201 Pinnacle Pkwy, Twinsburg OH 44087	330-405-2644	R	7*	.1
72	Rex Chemical Corp—*Beatrice Granja*	2270 Nw 23rd St, Miami FL 33142	305-634-2471	R	7*	.1
73	Lawton Brothers Inc—*David Lawton*	PO Box 547635, Orlando FL 32854	407-291-2501	R	7*	<.1

Note: An asterisk (*) indicates an estimated financial figure. The company type code used is as follows: R = Private, P = Public, S = Private Subsidiary, B = Public Subsidiary, D = Division, J = Joint Venture, I = Investment Fund.

COMPANY RANKINGS BY SALES WITHIN 4-DIGIT SIC

Rank	Company Name—*Executive Officer*	Address, City, State, Zip	Phone	Type	Fin	Empls
74	Spectrum Paper Company Inc—*A Brown*	27 Concord St, El Paso TX 79906	915-595-0020	R	7*	<.1
75	Greenwood Emergency Vehicles Inc—*Timothy O'neill*	530 John L Dietsch Blv, North Attleboro MA 02763	508-695-7138	R	7*	<.1
76	Mike Horall—*Mike Horall*	906 S 200 W, Salt Lake City UT 84101	801-363-2653	R	7*	.1
77	Carpet Services Inc—*Thor Edman*	PO Box 1128, Kent WA 98035	253-872-0860	R	7*	<.1
78	Alco-Chem Inc—*Anthony Mandala*	45 N Summit St, Akron OH 44308	330-253-3535	R	7*	<.1
79	Don Johns Inc—*Brian Byrne*	1312 W Lake St, Chicago IL 60607	312-666-2210	R	7*	<.1
80	Fire Safety Inc—*Gordon Hill*	PO Box 19, Wood River IL 62095	618-254-2323	R	7*	<.1
81	Cowan Corp—*Steve Cowan*	48 Meadow Ave Ste 2, Joliet IL 60436	815-744-3384	R	7*	<.1
82	L and M Food Service Inc—*Judith Laughlin*	885 Airpark Dr, Bullhead City AZ 86429	928-754-3241	R	6*	<.1
83	Palmer Company Inc—*William Hoffman*	PO Box 737, Waukesha WI 53187	262-547-2246	R	6*	<.1
84	Laundry and Cleaners Supply Inc—*David Eckenrode*	402 S 50th St, Phoenix AZ 85034	602-244-0770	R	6*	<.1
85	Smith Supply Company LLC—*Kelly Simons*	PO Box 3398, Temple TX 76505	254-773-3592	R	6*	<.1
86	Fire-End and Croker Corp—*Paul Sposato*	7 Westchester Plz Ste, Elmsford NY 10523	914-592-3640	R	6*	<.1
87	Nail Emporium—*James George*	1221 N Lakeview Ave, Anaheim CA 92807	714-779-9889	R	6*	.1
88	Tartan Supply Company Inc—*Peter Deverey*	3250 N 126th St Ste 1, Brookfield WI 53005	262-781-2770	R	6*	<.1
89	Brim Laundry Machinery Company Inc—*Mark Brim*	2815 Barge Ln, Dallas TX 75212	214-630-4517	R	6*	<.1
90	Short Company Inc—*James Short*	4222 S Memorial Dr, Tulsa OK 74145	918-663-8841	R	6*	<.1
91	Beauty Towne Inc—*M Deligotti*	147 Delta Dr, Pittsburgh PA 15238	412-963-9871	R	6*	.1
92	Bruco Inc—*Benedict Uselman*	2525 Overland Ave, Billings MT 59102	406-652-1020	R	6*	<.1
93	A and L Sales Inc—*Peter Traigle*	PO Box 74, Belle Chasse LA 70037	504-394-3840	R	6*	<.1
94	JL Wilson Co—*Bill Gallagher*	3800 Lakeside Ave E 10, Cleveland OH 44114	216-431-4040	R	6*	<.1
95	1 Drake Place—*Troy Crawford*	12100 W Ctr Rd Ste 210, Omaha NE 68144	402-933-7253	R	5*	<.1
96	Badgerland Car Wash Equipment Company Inc—*Todd Duthie*	300a E Oak St, Oak Creek WI 53154	414-764-4250	R	5*	<.1
97	Cardinal Novelty Distributing Company Inc—*Daniel Paszkiewicz*	6801 Quad Ave Ste A, Baltimore MD 21237	410-325-2121	R	5*	<.1
98	Pugleasa Company Inc—*Dennis Pietrini*	1253 Connelly Ave, Saint Paul MN 55112	651-636-6442	R	5*	<.1
99	G and H Service Corp—*Don Geddeis*	W7934 Prospect Rd, Beaver Dam WI 53916	920-885-6996	R	5*	.1
100	Restaurant Warehouse Inc—*Roberta Cotton*	3555 N Andrews Ave, Oakland Park FL 33309	954-358-2112	R	5*	<.1
101	Fire Protection Equipment Company Inc—*Robert Leahey*	7206 Impala Dr, Richmond VA 23228	804-262-1594	R	5*	<.1
102	Capital Janitorial Supply and Service LLC	PO Box 88, Midlothian VA 23113	804-897-7910	R	5*	<.1
103	Robinson's Marketing Division Inc—*Melvin Johnson*	PO Box 1464, Janesville WI 53547	608-752-8891	R	5*	.1
104	Ana Molinari—*Ana Molinari*	52 S Palm Ave, Sarasota FL 34236	941-365-1415	R	5*	<.1
105	Rhiel Supply Company Inc—*Toby Mirto*	3735 Oakwood Ave, Austintown OH 44515	330-799-9749	R	5*	<.1
106	VIP Nails and Tans Inc—*Renee Borowy*	15580 King Rd, Riverview MI 48193	734-479-1166	R	5*	.1
107	Exclusive Beauty Supplies Inc—*John Leone*	4750 Oakes Rd Ste O, Davie FL 33314	954-321-6800	R	5*	<.1
108	Ronco Industries Inc—*Ron Morgan*	15401 Cobalt St, Sylmar CA 91342	818-362-1578	R	5*	<.1
109	Lico Chemicals—*Stanley Lichtenstein*	929 5th Ave, Mckeesport PA 15132	412-422-7786	R	5*	<.1
110	Sun Sun Trading Company Inc—*Brandon Lam*	2817 Tyler Ave, El Monte CA 91733	626-575-1500	R	5*	<.1
111	John A Earl Inc—*John Earl*	216 Union St, Hackensack NJ 07601	201-342-2453	R	5*	<.1
112	John M Baxter Sales Company Inc—*Roger Sage*	114 E Niblick St, Longview TX 75604	903-759-2796	R	5*	<.1
113	Metro Fire Protection Inc—*Emanuel Solt*	7526 Deering Ave, Canoga Park CA 91303	818-710-6050	R	5*	<.1
114	Vischer Funeral Supplies Inc—*F Vischer*	1463 Old York Rd, Warminster PA 18974	215-957-9601	R	4*	<.1
115	Odorite Company Of Baltimore Inc—*Gary Lewis*	1111 Maryland Ave, Baltimore MD 21201	410-727-1565	R	4*	<.1
116	Daniels Equipment Company Inc—*Ralph Daniels*	45 Priscilla Ln, Auburn NH 03032	603-641-9487	R	4*	<.1
117	Equipment Concentration Site—*Kim Daniel*	1750 Ontario Ave Ste 1, Watertown NY 13602	315-772-6675	R	4*	.1
118	Progressive Beauty Systems Inc—*Dennis Clarke*	231 Ocean Beach Trl, Vero Beach FL 32963	772-234-6435	R	4*	<.1
119	Nationwide Beauty and Barber LLC—*Witkowski Elizabeth*	PO Box 6169, Syracuse NY 13217	315-446-9026	R	4*	<.1
120	South Tex Beauty Distributors Inc—*Ron Surprise*	211 S Broadway St, Mcallen TX 78501	956-682-4488	R	4*	<.1
121	Dumouchel Paper Company Of Connecticut Inc—*Wayne Sullivan*	PO Box 1185, Waterbury CT 06721	203-756-7261	R	4*	<.1
122	One Way Products Inc—*Isaac Hinkle*	433 E Ransom St, Kalamazoo MI 49007	269-343-3772	R	4*	<.1
123	Topmost Chemical and Paper Corp—*A Proffer*	PO Box 18913, Memphis TN 38181	901-363-7278	R	4*	<.1
124	Marina Shores Beauty Supply—*Wisel Navarro*	6612 E Pacific Coast H, Long Beach CA 90803	562-430-8929	R	4*	.1
125	PI Enterprises Inc—*Liz Christy*	7624 Boone Ave N Ste 2, Brooklyn Park MN 55428	763-447-6600	R	4*	<.1
126	Laun-Dry Supply Company Inc	3800 Durazno Ave, El Paso TX 79905	915-533-8217	R	4*	<.1
127	Car Wash Technologies—*Hank Richard*	716 Thomson Park Dr, Cranberry Township PA 16066	724-742-9000	R	4*	<.1
128	George A Kint Inc—*Brian Kint*	PO Box 60490, Harrisburg PA 17106	717-221-8000	R	4*	.1
129	NVP Hospitality Design Inc—*Gary Eakins*	801 Moreau St, Sainte Genevieve MO 63670	573-883-1002	R	4*	<.1
130	Dundas Systems Inc—*Gary Verdier*	5200 Nw 33rd Ave Ste 2, Fort Lauderdale FL 33309	954-739-0607	R	4*	<.1
131	Quality Beauty Supply Company Inc—*Marcia Strauss*	281 S River Rd, Des Plaines IL 60016	847-299-3388	R	4*	<.1
132	Quality Chemical Co—*Ira Saunders*	1835 Ne 144th St, North Miami FL 33181	305-944-2837	R	4*	<.1
133	AVS Group Inc—*Henry Nwauwa*	PO Box 24, Fayetteville AR 72702	479-443-6791	R	4*	<.1
134	Whitman Vault Inc—*Mark Donavon*	PO Box 308, Whitman MA 02382	781-857-3031	R	4*	<.1
135	Harp Enterprises Inc—*Peggy Harp*	PO Box 12830, Lexington KY 40583	859-253-2601	R	4*	<.1
136	Kamo Manufacturing Company Inc—*Jack Weinstein*	PO Box 1525, Augusta GA 30903	706-724-1488	R	4*	<.1
137	Four Seasons Services Inc—*David Nelson*	636 E 11th St, Albert Lea MN 56007	507-373-9666	R	4*	<.1
138	Protech Service Company LLC—*Michael Melton*	1702 S Hwy 121 Ste 406, Lewisville TX 75067	972-221-1107	R	4*	<.1
139	Kelly Everwear Brush Company Inc—*Glenn Griest*	801 Primos Ave, Folcroft PA 19032	610-583-7960	R	4*	<.1
140	Blackburn Building Services LLC	132 Cross Rd, Waterford CT 06385	860-447-2000	R	3*	<.1
141	Stockton Enterprises Inc—*Steven Gaskin*	PO Box 818, Aberdeen MS 39730	662-369-8338	R	3*	<.1
142	Zim Chemical Company Inc—*Samuel Shonson*	PO Box 13641, Atlanta GA 30324	770-433-8181	R	3*	<.1
143	Gorm Inc—*Morten Riegg*	1501 Hudson St, Ontario CA 91761	909-292-1400	R	3*	<.1
144	Herbert L Flake Management Corp—*Dan Floeck*	5031 Gulf Fwy, Houston TX 77023	713-926-3200	R	3*	<.1
145	Vanguard Salon Systems Inc—*Mark Palermo*	56721 Dwyer St, Slidell LA 70458	985-781-1443	R	3*	<.1
146	Empire Fire Prevention Company Inc—*Kevin Crowley*	3623 Review Ave, Long Island City NY 11101	718-706-8980	R	3*	<.1
147	Stroman Beauty Supply Inc—*Jay Stroman*	1474 Bella Vista Dr, Columbia SC 29223	803-754-1967	R	3*	<.1
148	San-Aid Company Inc—*Larry Shapiro*	PO Box 346, Carlstadt NJ 07072	201-939-4200	R	3*	<.1
149	Heritage Food Services Of Georgia Inc—*R Dye*	2100 Nrcroga Pkwy Ste, Norcross GA 30071	770-368-1465	R	3*	<.1
150	State Beauty Supply Of Louisville Inc—*William Becker*	1226 Gardiner Ln, Louisville KY 40213	502-451-0595	R	3*	<.1
151	Central Products Inc—*Doug Collinsworth*	PO Box 119, Montgomery AL 36101	334-269-4309	R	3*	<.1
152	Hoosier Fire Equipment Inc—*Nick Swartz*	4009 Montdale Park Dr, Valparaiso IN 46383	219-462-1707	R	3*	<.1
153	TWT Distributing Inc—*Thomas Tyree*	11107 S Commerce Blvd, Charlotte NC 28273	704-588-1746	R	3*	<.1
154	Lakeshore Vault Inc—*Claire Mcquestion*	12780 W Lisbon Rd, Brookfield WI 53005	262-781-6262	R	3*	<.1
155	Cen-Tex Fire Protection—*Gail Blue*	1920 Ranch Rd 12, San Marcos TX 78666	512-393-3225	R	3*	<.1
156	Professional Stylist Resource—*Brandi Skirvin*	145 Moore Dr Ste A, Lexington KY 40503	859-276-5151	R	3*	<.1
157	Benco Industrial Supply Inc—*Craig Suverkrup*	4520 Progress Dr, Columbus IN 47201	812-372-3006	R	3*	<.1
158	Fire Master Fire Equipment Inc—*Randy Shelton*	2049 E Division St, Springfield MO 65803	417-865-8713	R	3*	<.1
159	Hawaiian Beauty Products Ltd—*William Kawato*	PO Box 2276, Honolulu HI 96804	808-537-2944	R	3*	<.1
160	Nu-Way Products Company Inc—*Phillip Farmer*	PO Box 1508, West Memphis AR 72303	870-735-4291	R	3*	<.1
161	Styles A E Manufacturing Company Inc—*John Criscuolo*	PO Box 1306, Point Pleasant Beach NJ 08742	732-899-0872	R	3*	<.1

Rank	Company Name—*Executive Officer*	Address, City, State, Zip	Phone	Type	Fin	Empls
162	JR Lambert Enterprises Inc—*James Lambert*	PO Box 1022, Romney WV 26757	304-822-7124	R	3*	<.1
163	Aberdeen Janitorial Service Inc—*John Savage*	40322 Mcduffee Cemeter, Hamilton MS 39746	662-369-2559	R	3*	<.1
164	Core Products Company Inc—*Ed Crawford*	PO Box 669, Canton TX 75103	903-567-1341	R	3*	<.1
165	Manna Inc—*James Majerus*	2060 Overland Ave, Billings MT 59102	406-652-8944	R	3*	<.1
166	Russo Company Inc—*Eddie Demirdjian*	1000 N Western Ave, Los Angeles CA 90029	323-266-3985	R	3*	<.1
167	Wilbert Burial Vault Corp—*George Humberto*	PO Box 130, Grapevine TX 76099	817-481-3577	R	3*	<.1
168	Bergen County Irrigation Inc—*John Carbone*	257 Newark Pompton Tpk, Wayne NJ 07470	201-664-8159	R	3*	<.1
169	Bell Janitorial Supply LLC—*Daren Bell*	4464 W 2100 S Ste A, Salt Lake City UT 84120	801-975-7166	R	3*	<.1
170	Pok Of North America Inc—*Jean-Marc Tasse*	500 Henry St, Cambridge MD 21613	410-901-9900	R	3*	<.1
171	Devere Company Inc—*Cynthia Shackelford*	PO Box 8444, Janesville WI 53547	608-752-0576	R	3*	<.1
172	Chemical Sanitizing Systems Ltd—*John Nobel*	PO Box 156, Le Mars IA 51031	712-546-8185	R	2*	<.1
173	David Distributing Company Inc—*David Stern*	PO Box 7305, Silver Spring MD 20907	301-588-2986	R	2*	<.1
174	Stafford Pluming—*Stafford Law*	12 James Haskell Rd, Wedgefield SC 29168	803-494-5910	R	2*	<.1
175	Campbell Brothers Maintence Inc—*Joe Campbell*	3619 74th Ave Ct Nw, Gig Harbor WA 98335	253-265-3855	R	2*	<.1
176	All State Manufacturing Company Inc—*Jon Ford*	4024 2nd Pkwy, Terre Haute IN 47804	812-466-2276	R	2*	<.1
177	D and S Exports Inc—*Derek Dominici*	24 Broad St, Norwalk CT 06851	203-847-6446	R	2*	<.1
178	H and H Green LLC—*Sherri Haushalter*	13670 Us Hwy 68, Kenton OH 43326	419-674-4152	R	2*	<.1
179	Sanitary Supply and Chemical Company Inc—*Hubert Williams*	1001 7th St, Macon GA 31206	478-746-4827	R	2*	<.1
180	Winner City Shop	PO Box 691, Winner SD 57580	605-842-0931	R	2*	<.1
181	Katcef Sales Inc—*SJ Katcef*	1981 Moreland Pkwy, Annapolis MD 21401	410-268-7877	R	2*	<.1
182	American Industrial Supply—*George Herbst*	519 Potrero Ave, San Francisco CA 94110	415-826-1144	R	2*	<.1
183	Seatronics Inc—*J Ken Deonigi*	16340 SE 376th St, Auburn WA 98092	253-939-6060	R	2*	<.1
184	American Cleaner Inc—*Venon Dye*	1125 Rockingham Rd, Rockingham NC 28379	910-895-1504	R	2*	<.1
185	Santa Fe Beauty Salon—*Sherri Boyce*	1701 S Webster Ave, Green Bay WI 54301	920-435-2242	R	2*	<.1
186	Triad Equipment Services Of Colorado—*Michael Bondi*	2635 S Santa Fe Dr 2a, Denver CO 80223	303-778-9599	R	2*	<.1
187	Supply King Inc—*David Kawut*	PO Box 578, Neptune NJ 07754	732-774-6100	R	2*	<.1
188	Alamana County Maintenance—*Raj Chahal*	2130 Fairmont Dr, San Leandro CA 94578	510-667-4499	R	2*	<.1
189	Craig Allens—*Craig Allens*	10096 E 13th St N Ste, Wichita KS 67206	316-631-3707	R	2*	<.1
190	Venice Trading Company Inc—*Raoul Broth*	1545 Macarthur Blvd, Costa Mesa CA 92626	714-546-6767	R	2*	<.1
191	Irrigation Supply Inc—*Bob Hobar*	4501 Taylor Ln, Cleveland OH 44128	216-831-0095	R	2*	<.1
192	Navico Inc—*Ed Schooling*	3670 Scarlet Oak Blvd, Saint Louis MO 63122	636-861-5500	R	2*	<.1
193	All Nails and More—*Jack Michael*	5169 Mount Alverno Rd, Cincinnati OH 45238	513-451-9170	R	1*	<.1
194	Nichols Oxygen Service Inc—*Raymond Nichols*	1564 Rte 9g, Hyde Park NY 12538	845-229-6041	R	1*	<.1
195	Shoreline Sprinkling Inc—*Rick Lamer*	135 N State St Ste 500, Zeeland MI 49464	616-879-0060	R	1*	<.1
196	Rogersol Inc—*Norman Nichol*	5538 N NW Hwy, Chicago IL 60630	773-735-5100	S	1*	<.1
197	Litz Manufacturing Inc—*Mary Litz*	48056 N Coyote Pass Rd, Phoenix AZ 85087	623-742-0102	R	1*	<.1
198	Aldan Sundries Inc—*Lewis Widoff*	242 E 137th St Fl 3, Bronx NY 10451	718-665-8699	R	<1*	<.1
199	Goodlin Systems Inc—*Rodney Goodlin*	2520 Il Rte 176 Ste 4, Crystal Lake IL 60014	847-854-6725	R	<1*	<.1

TOTALS: SIC 5087 Service Establishment Equipment
Companies: 199   7,003   23.6

5088 Transportation Equipment & Supplies

Rank	Company Name—*Executive Officer*	Address, City, State, Zip	Phone	Type	Fin	Empls
1	Derco Aerospace Inc—*Mark Hoehnen*	8000 W Tower Ave, Milwaukee WI 53223	414-355-3066	S	61,003*	.2
2	Allied Automotive Group—*Guy W Rutland IV*	2302 Parklake Dr Ste 6, Atlanta GA 30345	404-373-4285	S	9,248*	5.0
3	Transdigm Group Inc—*W Nicholas Howley*	1301 E 9th St Ste 3710, Cleveland OH 44114	216-706-2939	P	1,206	3.8
4	Elliott Aviation Inc—*Wynn Elliott*	PO Box 100, Moline IL 61266	309-799-3183	R	667*	.5
5	Banner Aerospace Inc—*Warren D Persavich*	1750 Tysons Blvd Ste 1, McLean VA 22102	703-478-5900	S	420*	.4
6	Kansas City Aviation Center Inc Optica USA Div—*Angelo Fiataruolo*	PO Box 1850, Olathe KS 66063	913-782-0530	R	179*	.1
7	Kellstrom Aerospace LLC—*William Crowe*	3701 S Flamingo Rd, Miramar FL 33027	954-538-2000	R	149*	.2
8	Kellstrom Commercial Aerospace Inc—*Dennis Zalupski* Kellstrom Aerospace LLC	3701 S Flamingo Rd, Miramar FL 33027	954-538-2000	S	149*	.1
9	Diesel Power Equipment Co—*Dan Wells*	13619 Industrial Rd, Omaha NE 68137	402-330-5100	R	149*	.1
10	Willis Lease Finance Corp—*Charles F Willis IV*	773 San Marin Dr Ste 2, Novato CA 94945	415-408-4700	P	148	.1
11	Aero Controls Avionics Inc—*John Titus*	5415 NW 36th St, Miami FL 33166	305-871-1300	R	144*	.1
12	Wiggins Airways Inc	1 Garside Way, Manchester NH 03103	603-629-9191	R	130*	.2
13	GA Telesis LLC—*Abdol Moabery*	5400 NW 49th Ave, Fort Lauderdale FL 33309	954-676-3111	R	120*	.2
14	Fisheries Supply Co—*Carl Sutter*	1900 N Northlake Way S, Seattle WA 98103	206-632-4462	R	119*	.1
15	Argo International Corp—*John Santacroce*	140 Franklin St, New York NY 10013	212-431-1700	R	108*	.3
16	Aerospace Products International—*Kevin Yang*	3778 Distriplex Dr N, Memphis TN 38118	901-365-3470	S	97*	.2
17	ASC International Inc—*Ollin Taylor*	PO Box 200728, Arlington TX 76006	817-640-1300	R	93*	.1
18	Dealers Truck Equipment Company Inc—*Kim Kayser*	PO Box 31435, Shreveport LA 71108	318-635-7567	R	92*	.1
19	Saab Aircraft of America Inc—*Paul Roberts*	21300 Ridgetop Cir, Sterling VA 20166	703-406-7200	S	92*	.1
20	GE SeaCo America LLC—*Robin Lynch*	203 S Ave E 2nd Fl, Westfield NJ 07090	908-232-1187	D	91*	.1
21	Integrated Procurement Technologies Inc—*Etty Yenni*	320 Storke Rd Ste 100, Goleta CA 93117	805-682-0842	R	69*	<.1
22	Yingling Aircraft Inc—*Lynn Nichols*	PO Box 9248, Wichita KS 67209	316-943-3246	R	63*	.1
23	Southern California Aviation Inc—*Craig Garrick*	18438 Readiness St Bld, Victorville CA 92394	760-530-2400	R	62*	.1
24	American General Supplies Inc—*Kassa Maru*	7840 Airpark Rd, Gaithersburg MD 20879	301-590-9200	R	59*	<.1
25	Atlantic Track and Turnout Co—*Peter Hughes*	270 Broad St, Bloomfield NJ 07003	973-748-5885	R	57*	.1
26	Corporate Rotable and Supply Inc—*Armando Leighton Jr*	6701 NW 12th Ave, Fort Lauderdale FL 33309	954-972-2807	R	54*	<.1
27	Paxton Company Inc—*Guy Beale Jr*	PO Box 12103, Norfolk VA 23502	757-853-6781	R	53*	.1
28	Kampi Components Company Inc—*Don Chandler*	88 Canal Rd, Fairless Hills PA 19030	215-736-2000	R	49*	.1
29	Unical Aviation Inc—*Han Tan*	680 S Lemon Ave, City Of Industry CA 91789	626-813-1901	R	48*	.2
30	Avioserv San Diego Inc—*David LeBlanc*	6495 Marindustry Pl, San Diego CA 92121	858-812-9777	S	48*	<.1
31	Irwin International Inc—*James Irwin*	PO Box 4000, Corona CA 92880	951-372-9555	R	45*	.2
32	Birmingham Rail and Locomotive Company Inc—*Carlisle Jones*	PO Box 530157, Birmingham AL 35253	205-424-7245	R	42*	.1
33	Alamo Aircraft Ltd—*Leon Wulfe Jr*	PO Box 37343, San Antonio TX 78237	210-434-5577	R	42*	.1
34	WS Wilson Corp—*W Wilson*	24 Harbor Park Dr, Port Washington NY 11050	516-621-8800	R	42*	<.1
35	Aerodynamics Inc—*Scott Beale*	PO Box 270100, Waterford MI 48327	248-666-3500	S	38*	.1
36	Global Parts Inc—*Troy Palmer*	901 Industrial Rd, Augusta KS 67010	316-733-9240	R	37*	<.1
37	First Wave Inc—*Edward Clark*	5440 S 101st E Ave, Tulsa OK 74146	918-622-0007	R	36*	.1
38	Hopkins-Carter Company Inc—*Parks Masterson*	3300 NW 21st St, Miami FL 33142	305-635-7377	R	34*	<.1
39	FDC/aerofilter Inc—*Andrew Rowen*	8 Digital Dr Ste 104, Novato CA 94949	415-884-0555	R	33*	<.1
40	Artex Aircraft Supplies Inc—*James Hart*	6400 Wilkinson Dr, Prescott AZ 86301	503-678-7929	R	32*	.3
41	Pacific Cornetta Inc—*Alex Liu*	18280 SW 108th Ave, Tualatin OR 97062	503 582 8787	R	31*	<.1
42	Turbo Resources International Inc—*Irving Hoffman*	5780 W Oakland St, Chandler AZ 85226	480-961-3600	R	30*	<.1
43	Marwest LLC—*Jennifer Cianciulli*	1611 17th St, Oakland CA 94607	510-444-7200	R	30*	.1
44	Lewis Marine Supply Inc—*James Lewis*	PO Box 21107, Fort Lauderdale FL 33335	954-523-4371	R	30*	.2
45	Summit Aviation Inc—*Finn Neilsen*	PO Box 258, Middletown DE 19709	302-834-5400	R	28*	.1

Note: An asterisk (*) indicates an estimated financial figure. The company type code used is as follows: R = Private, P = Public, S = Private Subsidiary, B = Public Subsidiary, D = Division, J = Joint Venture, I = Investment Fund.

...PANY RANKINGS BY SALES WITHIN 4-DIGIT SIC

Rank	Company Name—Executive Officer	Address, City, State, Zip	Phone	Type	Fin	Empls
46	Ers Industries Inc—Jeffrey Schmarje	PO Box 363, West Seneca NY 14224	716-675-2040	R	26*	.1
47	Williams and Wells Co—Bruce Margolin	1501 W Blancke St Unit, Linden NJ 07036	908-937-9800	R	26*	.1
48	Martec International Trading—Thomas A Ewig Carl F Ewig Inc	529 Dowd, Elizabeth NJ 07201	908-248-9001	D	24*	.1
49	Iso Group Inc—Kevin Lowdermilk	7700 Technology Dr, West Melbourne FL 32904		R	20*	.1
50	Industry-Railway Suppliers Inc—Ron Hobbs	811 Golf Ln, Bensenville IL 60106	630-766-5708	R	20*	<.1
51	Intermountain Air LLC—Bill Haberstock	301 N 2370 W, Salt Lake City UT 84116	801-322-1645	R	18*	.1
52	Nevada Railroad Materials Inc—Robert Ollendick	917 Country Hills Dr S, Ogden UT 84403	801-621-5544	R	18*	.1
53	Dynatech International Corp—Eric Klar	150 Executive Dr Ste M, Edgewood NY 11717	631-243-1700	R	16*	.1
54	Midland Railway Supply Inc—John Ferenbach	1815 W Delmar Ave, Godfrey IL 62035	618-467-6305	R	16*	.1
55	Tracer Corp—William Morales	1600 W Cornell St, Milwaukee WI 53209	414-875-1234	R	16*	<.1
56	ASC Industries Inc (Arlington Texas)—Ollin Taylor ASC International Inc	PO Box 200728, Arlington TX 76006	817-640-1300	S	15*	.1
57	Boatswain's Locker I Inc—Dan Gribble	931 W 18th St, Costa Mesa CA 92627	949-642-6800	R	15*	<.1
58	Sardello Inc—Ray Sardello	1000 Corporation Dr, Aliquippa PA 15001	724-375-4101	R	15*	.1
59	Aero Toy Store LLC—Susan Gorbel	1710 W Cypress Creek R, Fort Lauderdale FL 33309	954-771-1795	R	15*	<.1
60	Marysville Marine Distributors Inc—Mark Knust	PO Box 126, Marysville MI 48040	810-364-7653	R	14*	.1
61	Cleveland Wheels—Manny Bajakfoujian	1160 Ctr Rd, Avon OH 44011	440-937-5350	R	13*	.1
62	Amacpi Corp—Roscoe Cole	1771 Railroad St, Corona CA 92880	951-272-5858	R	12*	.1
63	Alliance Supply Management Ltd—Bruce Margolin	1830 W 15th St, Houston TX 77008	713-335-2500	R	12*	.1
64	Mr Golf Carts Inc—James Eastmead	PO Box 448, Waynesboro GA 30830	706-554-3617	R	12*	.1
65	Ruston Aviation Inc—James Davison	128 Flightline Dr, Ruston LA 71270	318-251-9098	R	11*	.1
66	Quality Aviation Inc—Sam Nejatian	15042 Whittram Ave, Fontana CA 92335	909-829-3031	R	11*	.1
67	Kovalchick Salvage Co—Joseph Kovalchick	PO Box 279, Indiana PA 15701	724-349-3300	R	11*	.1
68	Mitchell Aircraft Spares Inc—Richard Sebion	1160 Alexander Ct, Cary IL 60013	847-516-3773	R	11*	<.1
69	Jilco Industries Inc—Ken Stoltzfus	PO Box 12, Kidron OH 44636	330-698-0280	R	10*	.1
70	Kitco Inc—J Wood	PO Box 900, Springville UT 84663	801-489-2000	R	10*	.1
71	Med-Craft Inc—Mario Duenas	2450 Nw 110th Ave, Miami FL 33172	305-594-7444	R	10*	<.1
72	Meridian Aerospace Group Ltd—William D Gardner	3796 Vest Mill Rd, Winston Salem NC 27103	336-765-5454	R	10*	<.1
73	Seattle Aero LLC—Roger Ringness	12410 Se 32nd St 1, Bellevue WA 98005	425-643-4224	R	10*	<.1
74	Flite Line Acquisitions Corp—John Biagi	12090 Miramar Pkwy Ste, Miramar FL 33025	954-433-5617	R	10*	<.1
75	Gc Supply Inc—John Lockley	3587 Clover Ln, New Castle PA 16105	724-658-1741	R	10*	<.1
76	Pni Sensor Corp—Becky Oh	133 Aviation Blvd Ste, Santa Rosa CA 95403	707-566-2260	R	9*	<.1
77	Professional Aviation Associates Inc—Glenn McDonald Banner Aerospace Inc	4694 Aviation Pkwy Ste, Atlanta GA 30349	404-767-0282	S	9*	<.1
78	Varga Enterprises Inc—George Varga	2350 S Airport Blvd, Chandler AZ 85286	480-963-6936	R	8*	<.1
79	Associated Aircraft Supply Company Inc—Jason Frazier	PO Box 35788, Dallas TX 75235	214-331-4381	R	8*	<.1
80	International Shipping Partners Inc—Niels-Erik Lund	4770 Biscayne Blvd Pen, Miami FL 33137	305-573-6355	R	8*	<.1
81	Avio-Diepen Inc—Vincent Campen	561 Arport S Pkwy Ste, Atlanta GA 30349	770-996-6430	R	7*	<.1
82	Van Bortel Aircraft Inc—Howard Bortel	4900 S Collins St, Arlington TX 76018	817-468-7788	R	7*	<.1
83	Aviation Brake Services Inc—Andres Posse	7274 Nw 34th St, Miami FL 33122	305-594-4677	R	7*	<.1
84	Air Frame Manufacturing and Supply Company Inc—Yoshi Kawamura	26135 Technology Dr, Valencia CA 91355	661-257-7728	R	7*	<.1
85	Falcon Aerospace Inc—Jerry Bashir	3350 Enterprise Ave St, Weston FL 33331	954-771-9338	R	7*	<.1
86	Shorty's Truck and Railroad Car Parts Inc—Raymond Griffin	PO Box 270, Alexandria AL 36250	256-892-3131	R	7*	<.1
87	Aircraft Instrument And Radio Company Inc—Martin Potash	PO Box 9487, Wichita KS 67277	316-945-0445	R	7*	<.1
88	Tradewinds Engine Services LLC—Dan Musa	4700 Lyons Tech Pkwy, Pompano Beach FL 33073	954-421-2510	R	6*	<.1
89	Kessler International Corp—Kevita Dawson	15946 Derwood Rd, Rockville MD 20855	301-519-3434	R	6*	<.1
90	G and N Aircraft Inc—Paul Goldsmith	1701 E Main St Ste 2, Griffith IN 46319	219-924-7110	R	6*	<.1
91	Daytona Aerospace Inc—Joe Persaud	6101 NW 31st St, Margate FL 33063	954-977-2722	R	5*	<.1
92	Ipeco Holdings Inc—Terry Glover	2275 Jefferson St, Torrance CA 90501	310-783-4700	R	5*	<.1
93	Frank And Jimmie's Propeller Shop Inc—James Harrison	200 Sw 6th St, Fort Lauderdale FL 33301	954-467-7723	R	5*	<.1
94	Capital Aviation Instrument Corp—Pat Colgan	10660 Aviation Ln, Manassas VA 20110	703-369-0500	R	5*	<.1
95	Tec Tran Holding Corp—William Kohler	2215 Airpark Rd, Burlington NC 27215	336-513-0002	R	5*	<.1
96	Lightspeed Aviation Inc—Allan Schrader	6135 Jean Rd, Lake Oswego OR 97035	971-925-5500	R	5*	<.1
97	Aerospace Fasteners Inc—Carole Elfarr	205 E Neches St, Palestine TX 75801	903-723-0693	R	5*	<.1
98	FH Gaskins Company Inc—Robert Gaskins	PO Box 1499, Norfolk VA 23501	757-622-4706	R	5*	<.1
99	Delaware Ship Supply Oldco Inc—Donald Rush	100 Atlantic Ave, Camden NJ 08104	856-338-9100	R	5*	<.1
100	Harbor Marine Maintenance and Supply Inc—Lauren Bivins	1032 W Marine View Dr, Everett WA 98201	425-259-3285	R	4*	<.1
101	East Coast Ship Supply LLC—Jennifer Cinciulli	212 Durham Ave Ste 112, Metuchen NJ 08840	732-205-9790	R	4*	<.1
102	Weems and Plath Inc—Peter Trogdon	214 Eastern Ave Ste B, Annapolis MD 21403	410-263-6700	R	4*	<.1
103	Med Air Inc—Mario Duenas	2450 Nw 110th Ave, Miami FL 33172	305-592-6236	R	4*	<.1
104	Titan Rail Inc—Eric Bachman	1 E Mrchnts Dr Ste 304, Oswego IL 60543	630-892-9020	R	3*	<.1
105	Global Filtration Inc—Rick Caouette	9207 Emmott St, Houston TX 77040	713-856-9800	D	3*	<.1
106	Lcf Systems Inc—Sallie Fitch	7755 E Gelding Dr Ste, Scottsdale AZ 85260	480-247-6303	R	3*	<.1
107	Southern Avionics and Communications Inc—Thomas Greer	2495a Michigan Ave, Mobile AL 36615	251-433-9980	R	3*	<.1
108	J and J Air Parts Inc—Brenda Long	430 N Bryant St, Pleasanton TX 78064	830-569-3892	R	3*	<.1
109	Hammerhead Aviation LLC—William Horvatinovizh	1915 N Marshall Ave 13, El Cajon CA 92020	619-562-6602	R	3*	<.1
110	Charlotte Aircraft Corp—Harold Caldwell	PO Box 25555, Charlotte NC 28229	704-537-0212	R	3*	<.1
111	Bba Project Inc—Junichi Kojima	8 Westchester Plz Ste, Elmsford NY 10523	914-345-3888	R	3*	<.1
112	Marine Propulsion Systems Inc—Ashton Bullard	2185 Nw 34th Ave, Miami FL 33142	305-635-1308	R	2*	<.1
113	Strube Inc—Tom Royer	629 W Market St, Marietta PA 17547	717-426-1906	R	2*	<.1
114	Central Airmotive Inc—Jeff Lowe	805 N 4th St, Clinton MO 64735	660-885-7531	R	2*	<.1
115	Ranger All-Season Corp—Larry Kruse	PO Box 132, George IA 51237	712-475-2811	R	2*	<.1
116	Seafari Marine Group—Robert Restino	3920 Rca Blvd Ste 2004, Palm Beach Gardens FL 33410	561-627-7022	R	2*	<.1
117	Source One Spares Inc—Seth Hall	1818 Memorial Dr Ste 2, Houston TX 77007	281-449-1100	R	2*	<.1
118	Cappsco International Corp—Gary Capps	805 S Park Ave, Tucson AZ 85719	520-903-0822	R	2*	<.1
119	Weedon Engineering Co—James Weedon	5105 Buffalo Ave Ste 1, Jacksonville FL 32206	904-355-8411	R	1*	<.1
120	Carl F Ewig Inc—Thomas Ewig	529 Dowd Ave, Elizabeth NJ 07201	908-248-9001	R	N/A	.1

TOTALS: SIC 5088 Transportation Equipment & Supplies

Companies: 120					76,138	16.6

5091 Sporting & Recreational Goods

1	Academy Sports Outdoors—David Gochman	1800 N Mason Rd, Katy TX 77449	281-646-5200	R	1,636*	10.0
2	Pool Corp—Manuel J Perez de la Mesa	109 Northpark Blvd, Covington LA 70433	985-892-5521	P	1,614	3.2
3	Pool Water Products—Dean Allred	PO Box 17359, Irvine CA 92623	949-756-1666	R	1,249*	.3
4	Specialty Sports Venture—Ken Gart	390 Interlocken Cresce, Broomfield CO 80021	303-399-1970	R	1,065*	2.0
5	AcuSport Corp—William L Fraim	1 Hunter Pl, Bellefontaine OH 43311	937-593-7010	R	191*	.2
6	Life Fitness—Christopher E Clawson	5100 N River Rd, Schiller Park IL 60176		D	190*	1.7
7	Ellett Brothers Inc—Hewitt Grant	PO Box 128, Chapin SC 29036	803-345-3751	R	108*	.3

Rank	Company Name—*Executive Officer*	Address, City, State, Zip	Phone	Type	Fin	Empls
8	Jerry's Sport Center Inc—*Jerry Buffone*	720 Main St, Forest City PA 18421	570-785-9400	R	98*	.2
9	Bridgestone Golf Inc—*Shigeru Nakayama*	14230 Lchridge Blvd St, Covington GA 30014	770-787-7400	R	89*	.2
10	Easton Sports Inc—*Anthony Palma*	7855 Haskell Ave Ste 2, Van Nuys CA 91406	818-782-6445	R	80*	1.5
11	Outdoor Sports Headquarters Inc—*Dick Turner* Jerry's Sport Center Inc	967 Watertower Ln, Dayton OH 45449	937-865-5855	D	78*	.2
12	Henry's Tackle LLC—*R Adrian Holler*	173 Hankison Dr, Newport NC 28570	252-808-3500	R	75	.3
13	RSR Goup Inc—*Bob Steger*	PO Box 4300, Winter Park FL 32793	407-677-1000	R	66*	.2
14	Folsom Corp—*Ed Feldsott*	43 McKee Dr, Mahwah NJ 07430	201-529-3550	R	65*	.2
15	General Pool and SpA Supply Inc—*Philip Gelhaus*	11285 Sunco Dr, Rancho Cordova CA 95742	916-853-2400	R	65*	.1
16	Century LLC—*Jana Carney*	1000 Century Blvd, Oklahoma City OK 73110	405-732-2226	R	59*	.3
17	Rothco—*Howard Somberg*	PO Box 1220, Ronkonkoma NY 11779	631-585-9446	R	53*	.1
18	Simmons Outdoor Corp—*Blake Lipham*	201 Plantation Oak Dr, Thomasville GA 31792		S	52	.1
19	Shimano American Corp	1 Holland, Irvine CA 92618	949-768-5003	S	46*	.1
20	Gym Source	40 E 52nd St, New York NY 10022		R	42*	.1
21	Salomon North America Inc	2030 Lincoln Ave, Ogden UT 84401		R	42*	.1
22	Keys Fitness Products Inc—*Tim W Chen*	PO Box 357, Hughes Springs TX 75656		R	38*	.1
23	G Joannou Cycle Company Inc—*Carine Joannou*	151 Ludlow Ave, Northvale NJ 07647	201-768-9050	R	36*	.1
24	Brownells Inc—*Pete Brownell*	200 S Front St, Montezuma IA 50171	641-623-5401	R	34*	.2
25	Regent Sports Corp—*Carl Farra*	PO Box 11357, Hauppauge NY 11788	631-234-2800	R	32*	.1
26	V F Grace Inc—*Charles Rush*	PO Box 200728, Anchorage AK 99520	907-272-6431	R	29*	.1
27	Hornerxpress Inc—*William Kent*	5755 Powerline Rd, Fort Lauderdale FL 33309	954-772-6966	R	28*	.2
28	Franklin Sports Industries Inc—*Larry J Franklin*	PO Box 508, Stoughton MA 02072	781-344-1111	R	28*	.2
29	Pool and Electrical Products Inc—*Andres Becerra*	1250 E Francis St, Ontario CA 91761	909-673-1160	R	28*	.2
30	2nd Swing Inc—*David Pomije*	3500 Holly Ln, Plymouth MN 55447	763-268-5050	R	26	.1
31	Seabring Marine Industries Inc—*Robert Pita*	1579 Sw 18th St, Williston FL 32696	352-528-2628	R	26*	.2
32	Warrior Custom Golf Inc—*Brendan Flaherty*	15 Mason Ste A, Irvine CA 92618	949-699-2499	R	25*	.2
33	Emsco—*Mark Stoyanoff*	PO Box 360660, Cleveland OH 44136	440-238-2100	R	25*	.1
34	Rand International Leisure Products Ltd—*Allen Goldmeier*	51 Executive Blvd, Farmingdale NY 11735	631-249-6000	R	24*	.1
35	Camfour Inc—*Mike Brown*	65 Westfield Industria, Westfield MA 01085	413-564-2300	R	24*	<.1
36	Quality Pool Supply Co—*Cary Engelhart*	5303 W Vienna Rd, Clio MI 48420	810-686-3010	R	19*	.1
37	Roller Derby Skate Corp—*Walter Frazier*	P O Box 930, Litchfield IL 62056		R	19*	<.1
38	Fuji American Advanced Sports Inc—*Pat Cunnane*	10940 Dutton Rd, Philadelphia PA 19154	215-824-3854	R	19*	.1
39	Country Club Enterprises LLC—*Justin Landry*	PO Box 670, West Wareham MA 02576	508-273-9939	R	18*	.1
40	Bangers LP—*Rick Bestwick*	PO Box 1685, Birmingham AL 35201	205-324-8915	R	18*	<.1
41	Kubic Marketing Inc—*Bob Sayre*	225 S Aviation Blvd, El Segundo CA 90245	310-297-1600	R	16*	.2
42	Lew Horton Distributing Co—*Lew Horton*	PO Box 5023, Westboro MA 01581	508-366-7400	R	16*	<.1
43	Sports South Inc—*Markham Dickson*	PO Box 51367, Shreveport LA 71135	318-797-4848	R	16*	.1
44	Hicks Inc—*John Wise Jr*	PO Drawer 232, Luverne AL 36049	334-335-3311	R	15*	.1
45	National Live Trap Corp—*Gregory Smith*	PO Box 302, Tomahawk WI 54487	715-453-2249	R	15*	<.1
46	Century Sports Inc—*Robert Hellerson*	PO Box 2035, Lakewood NJ 08701	732-905-4422	R	15*	<.1
47	Imtra Corp—*Nat Bishop*	30 Samuel Barnet Blvd, New Bedford MA 02745	508-995-7000	R	14*	<.1
48	Ross Bicycles USA Ltd—*Alan Goldmeier* Rand International Leisure Products Ltd	51 Executive Blvd, Farmingdale NY 11735	631-249-6000	S	14*	<.1
49	Pool World Supplies—*Bruce Johnson*	1310 S Powerline Rd, Deerfield Beach FL 33442	954-596-8781	R	14	.2
50	Kelly's Sports Ltd—*Steven Kelly*	807 S Matlock Ct, West Chester PA 19382	610-436-5458	R	14*	.1
51	Northern Wholesale Supply Inc—*Nick Gargaro*	6800 Otter Lake Rd Ste, Hugo MN 55038	651-429-1515	R	13*	.1
52	Hayden's Sport Center Inc—*Ronald Kruse*	1997 Aucutt Rd, Montgomery IL 60538	630-892-8961	R	13*	<.1
53	Fitness Club Warehouse Inc—*Jim Rosen*	2210 S Sepulveda Blvd, Los Angeles CA 90064	310-235-2040	R	13*	<.1
54	Syndrome Distribution Inc—*David Brown*	1410 Vantage Ct, Vista CA 92081	760-560-0440	R	13*	<.1
55	Barcelona West Inc—*Sam Barcelona*	9999 W Sam Houston Pkw, Houston TX 77064	713-464-8313	R	13*	.1
56	Beretta USA Corp—*Ugo Beretta*	17601 Beretta Dr, Accokeek MD 20607	301-283-2191	R	13*	.3
57	Raleigh America Inc—*Steve Mieneke*	6004 S 190th St Ste 10, Kent WA 98032	253-395-1100	R	13*	.1
58	Dave Bang Associates Inc—*Dave Bang*	PO Box 8760, Mesa AZ 85214	480-892-2266	R	11*	.1
59	Tallgrass Inc—*Gail Ridings*	997 Upper Bear Creek R, Evergreen CO 80439	303-670-4444	R	11*	.1
60	Daiwa Corp—*Tad Suzuki*	PO Box 6600, Cypress CA 90630	562-375-6800	R	11*	.1
61	Normark Corp—*Jorma Kasslin*	10395 Yellow Circle Dr, Minnetonka MN 55343	952-933-7060	R	11*	<.1
62	Efinger Sporting Goods Co—*Thomas Hoey*	PO Box 2003, Bound Brook NJ 08805	732-356-0604	R	11*	<.1
63	Zanders Glenn Fur and Sporting Goods Company Inc—*Dennis Zanders*	PO Box 166, Baldwin IL 62217	618-785-2235	R	11*	.1
64	Lincoln Equipment Inc—*Charles Luecker*	2051 Commerce Ave, Concord CA 94520	925-687-9500	R	11*	<.1
65	Longstreth Sporting Goods LLC—*Richard Heylmun*	PO Box 475, Parker Ford PA 19457	610-495-7022	R	10*	.1
66	Barry Cran Inc—*John Vinton*	PO Box 870, Lynn MA 01903	781-586-0111	R	10*	.1
67	Battle Creek Equipment Co—*John Doty*	307 W Jackson St, Battle Creek MI 49037	269-962-6181	R	10*	.1
68	Carolina Skiff LLC—*Ralph Bufkin*	3231 Fulford Rd, Waycross GA 31503	912-287-0547	R	10*	.3
69	Las Vegas Golf and Tennis Inc—*Steve Puett*	780 Brookline Trace, Alpharetta GA 30022	702-892-9999	R	10*	<.1
70	Gamaliel Shooting Supply Inc—*Goeff Pare*	PO Box 240, Gamaliel KY 42140	270-457-2825	R	10*	<.1
71	Bam Shields Corp—*Patrick Shields*	1100 Rocky Rd, Reading PA 19609	610-288-5030	R	10*	.1
72	Pioneer Althetics—*Doug Schattinger*	4529 Industrial Pkwy, Cleveland OH 44135		S	9*	.1
73	Superior Pool Products LLC—*Manny Perez* Pool Corp	4900 E Landon Dr, Anaheim CA 92807	714-693-8035	S	9*	<.1
74	I and I Sports Supply Co—*Alan Iba*	19751 Figueroa St, Carson CA 90745	310-715-6800	R	9*	.1
75	Tuscarora Corp—*Wayne Gibson*	511 Tarrytown Ctr, Rocky Mount NC 27804	252-443-7041	R	8	.1
76	Baleco International Inc—*Martin Hammersmith*	PO Box 11331, Cincinnati OH 45211	513-353-3000	R	8*	<.1
77	Laux Sporting Goods Inc—*David Laux*	25 Pineview Dr, Amherst NY 14228	716-691-3367	R	8*	.1
78	Sport Dimension Inc—*Joseph Lin*	966 Sandhill Ave, Carson CA 90746	310-320-2023	R	8*	<.1
79	Toledo Physical Education Supply Inc—*Thomas Mcnutt*	5101 Advantage Dr, Toledo OH 43612	419-726-8122	R	8*	<.1
80	Optimus LLC—*Mike Sewell*	3765 Winchester Rd, Memphis TN 38118	901-365-1269	R	7*	<.1
81	Envirotech International Inc—*Susan Currie*	734 Greenview Dr, Grand Prairie TX 75050	972-647-4733	R	7*	<.1
82	South Shore Distributing LC	1999 Tellepsen St, Houston TX 77023	713-926-3295	R	7*	<.1
83	Macsports Inc—*Paul Peng*	2053 Puddingstone Dr, La Verne CA 91750	909-392-8282	R	7*	<.1
84	Winston Trails GCLlc	6101 Winston Trails Bl, Lake Worth FL 33463	561-439-0009	R	7*	<.1
85	FBF Inc—*Fred Baker*	1925 N Macarthur Blvd, Oklahoma City OK 73127	405-789-0530	R	7*	<.1
86	Cue and Case Sales Inc—*James Lucas*	190 Cumberland Park Dr, Saint Augustine FL 32095	904-824-9997	R	7*	<.1
87	Steen Armament Research Company Inc—*Charles Steen*	PO Box 98, Stirling NJ 07980	908-647-3800	R	6*	.1
88	Capital Fitness Xsport Fitness—*Danny Morrscy*	222 Commons Dr, Chicago Ridge IL 60415	708-423-4200	R	6*	.1
89	Advanced Turf Trucking LLC	12840 Ford Dr, Fishers IN 46038	317-596-9600	R	6*	<.1
90	Kinsey's Outdoors Inc—*Rick Kinsey*	1658 Steel Way, Mount Joy PA 17552	717-653-5524	R	6*	<.1
91	New Hankey Company Inc—*Hurley Hankey*	61 Turtle Creek Dr, Jupiter FL 33469	561-746-0061	R	6*	<.1
92	US Kids Golf LLC—*Tom Olsen*	3040 Northwoods Pkwy, Norcross GA 30071	770-441-3077	R	5*	<.1
93	Bobs' Business Inc—*Robert Rehder*	PO Box 35, Red Wing MN 55066	651-388-4742	R	5*	<.1

Note: An asterisk (*) indicates an estimated financial figure. The company type code used is as follows: R = Private, P = Public, S = Private Subsidiary, B = Public Subsidiary, D = Division, J = Joint Venture, I = Investment Fund.

COMPANY RANKINGS BY SALES WITHIN 4-DIGIT SIC

Rank	Company Name—Executive Officer	Address, City, State, Zip	Phone	Type	Fin	Empls
94	Cover Sports USA—Ronald Niffenbaum	5000 Paschall Ave, Philadelphia PA 19143	215-724-3582	R	5*	<.1
95	Rose Industries Inc—Ronald Rose	16742 Stagg St Ste 110, Van Nuys CA 91406	818-988-2823	R	5*	<.1
96	Team Marathon Fitness Inc—Christa Davis	PO Box 17705, Sugar Land TX 77496	281-565-2307	R	5*	<.1
97	Scorpion Sports Inc—Richard Miller	25921 Atlantic Ocean D, Lake Forest CA 92630		R	5*	<.1
98	Petzl America Inc—Mark Rasmussen	PO Box 160447, Clearfield UT 84016	801-926-1500	R	5*	<.1
99	SpA Manufacturing Inc—Bob Magray	6060 Ulmerton Rd, Clearwater FL 33760	727-530-9493	R	5*	<.1
100	Dunkin-Lewis Inc—Charles Dunkin	2552 Rocky Ridge Rd, Vestavia AL 35243	205-822-6104	R	4*	<.1
101	Divers Supply Inc—Ruth Mistretta	PO Box 1663, Gretna LA 70054	504-392-2800	R	4*	<.1
102	Hudalla Associates Inc—Bruce Hudalla	47500 Hwy 51, Perham MN 56573	218-346-2734	R	4*	<.1
103	Swimwise Inc—Manny Smith	1795 W 200 N, Lindon UT 84042	801-785-6490	R	4*	.1
104	Richard Scott Salon and Day SpA—Richard Scott	15 S Moger Ave Ste 1, Mount Kisco NY 10549	914-242-1700	R	4*	<.1
105	Maxium Performance LLC	11481 Snow Creek Ave, Las Vegas NV 89135	479-268-6654	R	4*	<.1
106	Future Dynamics Inc—Barbara Ammirati	1810 Summit Commerce P, Twinsburg OH 44087	330-929-7227	R	4*	<.1
107	Idaho Sporting Goods Co—Pat Brady	PO Box 169, Boise ID 83701	208-344-8448	R	4*	<.1
108	Tohatsu America Corp—Hiroshi Wakayabashi	2005 Valley View Ln St, Dallas TX 75234	214-420-6440	R	4*	<.1
109	S and M Bikes Inc—Chris Moeller	1300 S Lyon St, Santa Ana CA 92705	714-835-3400	R	4*	<.1
110	Tri-County Custom Sports Inc—Robert Von Bargen	1671 Highwood E, Pontiac MI 48340	248-335-6600	R	4*	<.1
111	A1 Stop Non-Stop Scuba Training—Luanda Morris	1800 E 1st St, Santa Ana CA 92705	714-835-5544	R	4*	<.1
112	Fred's Studio Tents and Canopies Inc—Fred Tracy	PO Box 156, Stillwater NY 12170	518-664-4905	R	4*	<.1
113	Houston Marine Supply Inc—Larry Terrell	1707 Velasco St, Houston TX 77003	713-236-8190	R	4*	<.1
114	Athletic Supply Of California—Maureen Grogan	27327 E 201st St S, Haskell OK 74436	918-482-9282	R	4*	<.1
115	Area 51 Snowboards—Specialty Sports	Group Ctr Keystone Rd, Dillon CO 80435	970-496-4911	R	4*	<.1
116	Rehagen Jack Municipal Swimming Pool—Elizabeth Vorbeck	3311 Ashby Rd, Saint Ann MO 63074	314-423-6655	R	4*	<.1
117	USA Gym Supply—Mark Ball	319 Mckinley St, Great Bend KS 67530	620-792-2209	R	4*	<.1
118	Guy E Temple Inc—Robert Norton	1524 6th Ave, Moline IL 61265	309-764-8313	R	4*	<.1
119	York Barbell Company Inc—Bill Irvine	3300 Board Rd, York PA 17406	717-767-6481	R	3*	<.1
120	Western Golf Inc—Robert Wagner	PO Box 970, Thousand Palms CA 92276	760-343-1050	R	3*	<.1
121	Lew Horton Distributing Company Inc—Lewis Horton	PO Box 5023, Westborough MA 01581	508-366-7400	R	3*	<.1
122	SpA At Riverfront LLC	15 W Milwaukee St Ste, Janesville WI 53548	608-741-7848	R	3*	<.1
123	Hornerxpress Worldwide Inc—William Kent	5755 Powerline Rd, Fort Lauderdale FL 33309	954-938-5355	R	3*	<.1
124	Norman Archery Inc—Austin Pugh	PO Box 95029, Oklahoma City OK 73143	405-636-1415	R	3*	<.1
125	Aquaventures LLC—Tom Demery	3912 E Progress St, North Little Rock AR 72114	501-945-4999	R	3*	<.1
126	Visual Impact Products LLC	1150 Shore Rd, Naperville IL 60563	630-544-3520	R	3*	<.1
127	D H Hutson Enterprises Inc—Dan Hutson	PO Box 429, Waxhaw NC 28173	704-843-2251	R	3*	<.1
128	All American Inc—Ronnie Horner	3230 Summer Ave, Memphis TN 38112	901-324-3783	R	3*	<.1
129	Cane Creek Cycling Components Inc—Brad Thorne	355 Cane Creek Rd, Fletcher NC 28732	828-684-3551	R	3*	<.1
130	Home Recreation Center—Frank Mandia	685 Neptune Blvd, Neptune NJ 07753	732-776-8410	R	3*	<.1
131	WEK and Associates Inc—William Knox	PO Box 7818, Marble Falls TX 78657	830-598-1381	R	3*	<.1
132	Hewes Yamaha Outboard Motors Export Inc—Jim Wiborg	12565 Nw 7th Ave, North Miami FL 33168	305-687-7006	R	3*	<.1
133	More Than Bikes Inc—Michael Foley	2221 Las Palmas Dr Ste, Carlsbad CA 92011	760-804-1344	R	3*	<.1
134	Patuxent River Park—Gregory Lewis	16000 Croom Airport Rd, Upper Marlboro MD 20772	301-627-6074	R	2*	<.1
135	Outdoor Products Inc—Kay Barnard	PO Box 270245, Oklahoma City OK 73137	405-943-2191	R	2*	<.1
136	Fit Supply LLC—Jeremy Cervantes	407 113th St, Arlington TX 76011	817-385-8190	R	2*	<.1
137	Vittoria North America LLC—Eugene Riordan	1639 W Sheridan Ave, Oklahoma City OK 73106	405-239-2677	R	2*	<.1
138	Global Adventures LLC—Bernd Laeschke	PO Box 321, Cumming GA 30028	678-947-1262	R	2	<.1
139	Bliss Murski Sales Inc—Mike Murski	9212 Chancellor Row, Dallas TX 75247	214-637-0979	R	2*	<.1
140	Cressi-Sub USA Inc—Antonio Cressi	1 Charles St, Westwood NJ 07675	201-594-1450	R	2*	<.1
141	Any Mountain The Great Outdoor Store—Bud Hoffman	2777 Shattuck Ave, Berkeley CA 94705	510-665-3939	R	2*	<.1
142	Richards Community Pool—Donna Weatherbie	343 Ocean House Rd, Cape Elizabeth ME 04107	207-799-3184	R	2*	<.1
143	American Sporting Systems—Lawrence Burke	365 Westbourne Loop, Burbank WA 99323	509-545-9612	R	2*	<.1
144	Kiva Designs Inc—Tom Koenig	6440 Goodyear Rd, Benicia CA 94510	707-748-1614	R	2*	<.1
145	Weltronics Corp—Amcli Lin	PO Box 80584, San Marino CA 91118	626-799-6396	R	1*	<.1
146	Wissota Manufacturing Co—William Schuessler	865 Hwy 169 N, Minneapolis MN 55441	763-545-1448	R	<1*	<.1
147	Sports Equipment Specialists Inc—Scott Cyran	PO Box 41172, Cleveland OH 44141	216-741-1055	R	<1*	<.1

TOTALS: SIC 5091 Sporting & Recreational Goods
Companies: 147

					8,176	28.0

5092 Toys & Hobby Goods & Supplies

Rank	Company Name—Executive Officer	Address, City, State, Zip	Phone	Type	Fin	Empls
1	Great Planes Model Distributors Co—Wayne Hemming	PO Box 9021, Champaign IL 61826		R	1,683*	.8
2	RC2 Corp—Curtis W Stoelting	1111 W 22nd St Ste 320, Oak Brook IL 60523	630-573-7200	R	437	.8
3	Darice Inc—Mike Catan	13000 Darice Pkwy Park, Strongsville OH 44149	440-238-9150	R	365*	1.0
4	Diamond Comic Distributors Inc—Stephen Geppi	1966 Greenspring Dr St, Timonium MD 21093	410-560-7100	R	305*	.5
5	COKeM International Inc—Chuck Bond	3880 4th Ave E, Shakopee MN 55379	763-545-4500	R	136*	.1
6	BRIO Corp—Tim Oconnor	N 120 W 18485 Freistad, Germantown WI 53022	262-250-3240	D	123*	.1
7	Wm K Walthers Inc—Philip Walthers	5601 W Florist Ave, Milwaukee WI 53218	414-527-0770	R	104*	.2
8	Penn State Industries Inc—Marvin Levy	9900 Global Rd, Philadelphia PA 19115		R	103*	.1
9	Discovery Toys Inc—James Cascino	7364 Marathon Dr Ste A, Livermore CA 94550	925-606-2600	S	93*	.2
10	Shepher Distributors and Sales Corp—Hal Monchik	2300 Linden Blvd, Brooklyn NY 11208	718-649-2525	R	44*	.1
11	Delta Creative Inc—William George	2690 Pellissier Pl, City Of Industry CA 90601	562-695-7969	R	38*	.1
12	International Playthings LLC—Michael Varda	75 D Lackawanna Ave, Parsippany NJ 07054		R	28*	<.1
13	Gamers Factory Inc—Todd Hays	10957 Mccormick Rd, Hunt Valley MD 21031	410-316-9900	R	28*	.1
14	Progressive Balloons Inc—Judy Burns	3100 Industrial Park P, Saint Peters MO 63376	636-240-0444	R	26*	.2
15	RB Howell Co—David Howell	6030 NE 112th Ave, Portland OR 97209	503-255-2001	R	25*	<.1
16	Aqua Superstore—Chris Smith	630 Woodbury Dr, Port Charlotte FL 33954	941-487-2775	R	22*	<.1
17	Annalee Mobilitee Dolls Inc—David Pelletier	71 Nh Rte 104, Meredith NH 03253	603-279-3333	R	21*	<.1
18	Dentt Inc—Gale Hammond	1957 e 4780s, Salt Lake City UT 84117	801-277-7056	R	18*	<.1
19	Kipp Brothers Inc—Bob Glenn	9760 Mayflower Park Dr, Carmel IN 46032	317-704-8120	R	14*	.1
20	Craft Wholesalers Inc—Farley Piper	77 Cypress St Sw, Reynoldsburg OH 43068	740-964-6210	R	12*	.1
21	Toy Wonders Inc—Samuel Su	234 Moonachie Rd, Moonachie NJ 07074	201-229-1700	R	12*	<.1
22	Playmobil USA Inc—Corneilus Nederstight	PO Box 877, Dayton NJ 08810	609-395-5566	R	12*	.1
23	Hobby Products International Inc—Tatsuro Watanabe	70 Icon, El Toro CA 92610	949-753-1099	R	12*	.1
24	Big Bear Fireworks Inc—Bruce Zoldan	8341 Demetre Ave, Sacramento CA 95828	916-388-1479	R	11*	.1
25	M and Y Trading Corp—Lawrence Weiss	37 Hayward Ave, Carteret NJ 07008	732-969-5300	R	11*	.1
26	AW Faber-Castell USA Inc—Jamie Gallagher	9450 Allen Dr, Cleveland OH 44125	216-643-4660	R	10*	.1
27	Atlantic Bingo Supply Inc—Larry Weinstein	1700 Midway Rd, Odenton MD 21113	410-551-2200	R	9*	.1
28	Aqua-Leisure Industries Inc—Steven Berenson	PO Box 239, Avon MA 02322	508-587-5400	R	8*	.1
29	Goffa International Corp—Douglas Song	930 Flushing Ave Ste 2, Brooklyn NY 11206	718-361-8883	R	8*	.1
30	Mod-Ad Agency Inc—Peter Winston	8300 Tonnelle Ave, North Bergen NJ 07047	201-662-8500	R	8*	<.1
31	Nikko America Inc—Yugi Hatori	2801 Summit Ave, Plano TX 75074	972-422-0838	R	8*	<.1
32	Funrise Inc—Arnold Rubin	7811 Lemona Ave, Van Nuys CA 91405	818-883-2400	R	7*	<.1

Rank	Company Name—*Executive Officer*	Address, City, State, Zip	Phone	Type	Fin	Empls
33	Accoutrements—*Mark Pahlow*	PO Box 30811, Seattle WA 98113	425-349-3838	R	7*	<.1
34	GameloftCom Inc—*Gerard Guillemot*	45 W 25th St Fl 9, New York NY 10010	212-993-3000	R	7*	.1
35	Pan De Vida Inc—*Ruben Ulloa*	PO Box 2369, Montclair CA 91763	909-510-5200	R	7*	<.1
36	Consigned Sales Inc—*Evan Palmer*	12105 Grandview Rd, Grandview MO 64030	816-761-8500	R	5*	<.1
37	Superior Amusements and Vending Inc—*Donald Deremer*	333 N Pennsylvania Ave, Wilkes Barre PA 18702	570-824-9994	R	5*	<.1
38	Absorbent Ink—*Lee Eldrige*	4115 Freidrich Ln Ste, Austin TX 78744	512-454-5985	R	5*	<.1
39	Game Source Inc—*Rohollah Ahdoot*	446 Towne Ave, Los Angeles CA 90013	213-683-9700	R	5*	<.1
40	Gordons International Services Inc—*Sam Wong*	4600a Lebanon Rd Ste A, Mint Hill NC 28227	704-545-0382	R	4*	<.1
41	Sale-In-A-Box Inc—*Scott Toland*	1201 Maulhardt Ave, Oxnard CA 93030	805-278-9800	R	4*	<.1
42	Amusement Management Inc—*Alan Putter*	1930 Lansdown Dr, Carrollton TX 75010	972-394-8359	R	4*	<.1
43	Frank Moran and Sons Inc—*Frank Moran*	1404 Rome Rd, Baltimore MD 21227	410-242-6233	R	3*	<.1
44	TableTopics Inc—*Cristy Clarke*	7401 Katelyn Ct Ste A, San Diego CA 92120	510-704-4400	R	3	<.1
45	Hitec Rcd LLC—*Judy Chung*	12115 Paine St, Poway CA 92064	858-748-6948	R	3*	<.1
46	North Central Industries Inc—*Richard Shields*	PO Box 2623, Muncie IN 47307	765-284-7122	R	3*	<.1
47	R And G Enterprises Of Ohio Inc—*Rita Assour*	9213 Harrow Dr, Cleveland OH 44129	440-845-6870	R	3*	<.1
48	Best Bits and Bytes Inc—*Herbert Davis*	12104 Sherman Way, North Hollywood CA 91605	818-764-2442	R	3*	<.1
49	Plush Appeal LLC	PO Box 19965, New Orleans LA 70179	337-667-6866	R	3*	<.1
50	Craftex Wholesale And Distributors Inc—*Henry Langdale*	7215 Ashcroft Dr, Houston TX 77081	713-771-6691	R	2*	<.1
51	Quality Accents Inc—*Marlene Hollencamp*	707 N Main St, Mishawaka IN 46545	574-254-1600	R	2*	<.1
52	X Factory Entertainment LLC—*Nikia Thompson*	621 N Ave Ste C170, Atlanta GA 30308	404-592-3040	R	1*	<.1
53	Knucklestrutz Toys LLC—*Jim Bagley*	PO Box 26513, Salt Lake City UT 84126	801-466-2664	R	1*	<.1
54	Michael's Arts and Crafts—*Laura Cunningham*	5201 N Belt Hwy, Saint Joseph MO 64506	816-676-2945	R	1*	<.1
55	Premier Pyrotechnics Inc—*Matt Setcliss*	124 River Oaks Dr, Madison AL 35758	256-947-0243	R	1*	<.1
56	Maya Group LLC—*Oded Ben-Ezer*	7312 Murdy Cir, Huntington Beach CA 92647	714-375-0100	R	1*	<.1

TOTALS: SIC 5092 Toys & Hobby Goods & Supplies
Companies: 56 — 3,825 — 5.6

5093 Scrap & Waste Materials

Rank	Company Name—*Executive Officer*	Address, City, State, Zip	Phone	Type	Fin	Empls
1	Philip Services Corp—*Bruce Roberson*	5151 San Felipe St Ste, Houston TX 77056	713-623-8777	R	11,539*	5.5
2	Schnitzer Steel Industries Inc—*Tamara L Lundgren*	3200 NW Yeon Ave, Portland OR 97210	503-224-9900	P	3,459	4.1
3	Waste Management Recycle America—*David Steiner*	1001 Fanin Ste 4000, Houston TX 77002	713-512-6200	R	3,145*	1.5
4	NexCycle Inc—*Alex Rankin*	5221 North O'Connor Bl, Irving TX 75039	972-506-7200	R	1,402*	.6
5	OmniSource Corp—*Russell Rinn*	7575 W Jefferson Blvd, Fort Wayne IN 46804	260-422-5541	S	1,178*	2.2
6	Tube City IMS Corp—*Michael Coslov*	PO Box 2000, Glassport PA 15045	412-678-6141	R	1,123*	2.3
7	PSC Metals Inc—*Benjamin Elemker* Philip Services Corp	5875 Landerbrook Dr St, Mayfield Heights OH 44124	440-753-5400	S	1,070*	.5
8	Columbia National Group Inc—*David Miller*	6600 Grant Ave, Cleveland OH 44105	216-883-4972	R	1,048*	.5
9	Fortune Metal Inc—*Norman Ng*	20 Carbon Pl, Jersey City NJ 07305	201-333-3339	S	1,000*	2.0
10	Ferrous Processing And Trading Co—*Howard Sherman*	3400 E Lafayette St, Detroit MI 48207	313-582-2910	R	916*	.4
11	Metalsco Inc—*Sheldon Tauben*	1828 Craig Rd, Saint Louis MO 63146	314-997-5200	R	780*	.1
12	Hugo Neu-Proler Corp—*Jeffrey Neu*	901 New Dock St, Terminal Island CA 90731	310-831-0281	R	549*	.3
13	Universal Steel Co—*David P Miller* Columbia National Group Inc	6600 Grant Ave, Cleveland OH 44105		S	425*	.2
14	ELG Metals—*Simon Merrill*	369 River Rd, McKeesport PA 15132	412-572-9200	R	420*	.2
15	Behr Iron and Steel Inc—*William Bremner*	PO Box 740, Rockford IL 61105	815-987-2700	R	311*	.4
16	Metro Metals Northwest—*Victor Winkler*	5611 NE Columbia Blvd, Portland OR 97218	503-287-8861	R	232*	.1
17	Fox Integrated Technologies Inc—*Robert J Fox*	23194 Foley St, Hayward CA 94545	510-259-1804	R	226*	.1
18	wTe Corp—*M Scott Mellen*	7 Alfred Cir, Bedford MA 01730	781-275-6400	R	192*	.1
19	Cna Metals Ltd—*Hari Agrawal*	10701 Corp Dr Ste 147, Stafford TX 77477	281-494-4940	R	179*	<.1
20	R Freedman and Son Inc—*Maish Freedman*	PO Box 1533, Green Island NY 12183	518-273-1142	R	173*	<.1
21	Sims Metal Management - USA—*Rick Johnson*	600 S 4th St, Richmond CA 94804	510-412-5360	S	166*	.5
22	Winston Brothers Iron and Metal Inc—*Steve Winston*	17384 Conant St, Detroit MI 48212	313-891-4410	R	147*	.1
23	Edman Corp Schnitzer Steel Industries Inc	PO Box 3356, El Centro CA 92244	760-352-2630	S	140*	<.1
24	Grossman Iron and Steel Company Charitable Foundation—*David Grossman*	5 N Market St, Saint Louis MO 63102	314-231-9423	R	138*	.1
25	Metro Metals Corp—*Victor Winkler*	5611 NE Colombia Blvd, Portland OR 97218	503-287-8861	R	136*	.1
26	EKCO Metals—*Ely Keenberg*	2777 E Washington Blvd, Los Angeles CA 90023	323-264-1615	R	133*	.1
27	Huron Valley Steel Corp—*Leonard Fritz*	1650 W Jefferson Ave, Trenton MI 48183	734-479-3500	R	127*	.3
28	Pacific Coast Recycling LLC—*Hajime Ishii*	482 Pier T Ave Berth 1, Long Beach CA 90802	562-628-8100	R	124*	.1
29	Alter Trading Corp—*Robert S Goldstein*	700 Office Pkw, Saint Louis MO 63141	314-872-2400	R	112*	.3
30	Erman Corporation Inc—*Walter L Roth*	21 N Skokie Hwy Ste G7, Lake Bluff IL 60044	847-615-1020	R	110*	.1
31	Southern Holdings Inc—*Joel Dupre*	4801 Florida Ave, New Orleans LA 70117	504-944-3371	R	109*	.2
32	Jack Engle and Co—*Alan Engle*	PO Box 01705, Los Angeles CA 90001	323-589-8111	R	106*	.1
33	South Coast Recycling Inc—*John R Gasparian Sr*	4560 Doran St, Los Angeles CA 90039	323-245-5133	R	106*	.1
34	Thalheimer Brothers Inc—*John Thalheimer*	5550 Whitaker Ave, Philadelphia PA 19124	215-537-5200	R	100*	.1
35	Thermo Fluids Inc—*James Devlin*	8925 E Pima Center Ste, Scottsdale AZ 85258	602-272-2400	S	90*	.2
36	Potential Industries Inc—*Tony Fan*	922 E East St, Wilmington CA 90744	310-549-5901	R	75*	.1
37	Allan Co—*Steve Young*	14620 Joanbridge St, Baldwin Park CA 91706	626-962-4047	R	69*	.2
38	QRS Inc—*Greg Janson*	PO Box 17166, Louisville KY 40217	502-634-8531	R	67*	<.1
39	Utah Metal Works Inc—*Donald Lewon*	PO Box 1073, Salt Lake City UT 84110	801-364-5679	R	65*	<.1
40	Ambit Pacific Recycling Inc—*Roy Abel*	16228 S Figueroa St, Gardena CA 90248	310-538-3798	R	58*	<.1
41	Gdb International Inc—*Sanjeev Bagaria*	1 Home News Row, New Brunswick NJ 08901	732-246-3001	R	57*	.1
42	Empire Recycling Inc	15729 Crabbs Branch Wa, Rockville MD 20855	301-921-9202	R	56*	.2
43	Harmon Associates Corp—*Marc Forman*	2 Jericho Plz Ste 110, Jericho NY 11753	516-997-3400	S	56*	.1
44	MOLAM International Inc—*Nader N Nejad*	7000 Cobb Internationa, Kennesaw GA 30152	770-420-5202	R	55*	<.1
45	Sdr Plastics Inc—*Doug Ritchie*	1 Plastics Ave, Ravenswood WV 26164	304-273-5326	R	50*	.1
46	Pollock Corp—*Mayer Pollock*	PO Box 759, Pottstown PA 19464	610-323-5500	R	44*	.1
47	Cass Inc—*Edward Kangeter*	PO Box 24222, Oakland CA 94623	510-893-6476	R	43*	.1
48	Kirschbaum-Krupp Metal Recycling LLC—*Dusty Gibbs*	PO Box 1863, Fargo ND 58107	612-521-9212	R	43*	<.1
49	Copart Salvage Auto Auctions—*Steven Cohan*	703 Hwy 64 E, Conway AR 72032	501-796-2812	R	38*	<.1
50	Staiman Recycling Corp—*Richard Staiman*	PO Box 1235, Williamsport PA 17703	570-323-9494	R	37*	.1
51	Magnum Steel and Trading Inc—*Paolo Giorgi*	43 Village Way Ste 209, Hudson OH 44236	330-655-9365	R	34*	<.1
52	Somerset Recycling Services Inc—*Steven Keck*	PO Box 1348, Somerset KY 42502	606-274-4170	R	32*	.1
53	Solaris Paper Inc—*Phillip Rundel*	13415 Carmenita Rd, Santa Fe Springs CA 90670	562-376-9717	R	31*	.2
54	Lipsitz Management Company Inc—*Tommy Salome*	PO Box 1175, Waco TX 76703	254-756-6661	R	30*	.2
55	Calbag Metals Co—*Warren Rosenfield*	2495 NW Nicolai, Portland OR 97210	503-226-3441	R	30*	.2
56	Chamlian Enterprises Inc—*Ketty Chamlian*	2360 S Orange Ave, Fresno CA 93725	559-288-8000	R	28*	.1
57	Bollag International Corp—*Mitchel Bollag*	PO Box 99, Newell NC 28126	704-596-2932	R	28*	.1

Note: An asterisk (*) indicates an estimated financial figure. The company type code used is as follows: R = Private, P = Public, S = Private Subsidiary, B = Public Subsidiary, D = Division, J = Joint Venture, I = Investment Fund.

COMPANY RANKINGS BY SALES WITHIN 4-DIGIT SIC

Rank	Company Name—*Executive Officer*	Address, City, State, Zip	Phone	Type	Fin	Empls
58	Galamet Inc—*Richard Galamba*	3005 Manchester Trfy, Kansas City MO 64129	816-861-2700	R	28*	.1
59	Elg Haniel Metals Corp—*Simon Merrills*	369 River Rd, Mckeesport PA 15132	412-672-9200	R	27*	.2
60	Sims Group USA Holdings Corp—*Robert Kelman*	110 5th Ave Fl 7, New York NY 10011	212-604-0710	R	26*	.6
61	Lopez Scrap Metal Inc—*Isidro Lopez*	351 N Nevarez Rd, El Paso TX 79927	915-859-0770	R	26*	.1
62	Prime Materials Recovery Inc—*Bernard Schilberg*	99 E River Dr Fl 8e, East Hartford CT 06108	860-622-7626	R	26*	.1
63	Iron and Metals Inc—*Michael Cohen*	5555 Franklin St, Denver CO 80216	303-292-5555	R	24*	.1
64	Atlas Metal and Iron Corp—*Michael Rosen*	1100 Umatilla St, Denver CO 80204	303-825-7166	R	23*	.1
65	Mid-City Iron and Metal Corp—*George Adams*	2104 E 15th St, Los Angeles CA 90021	213-747-4281	R	22*	.1
66	W Silver Recycling Inc—*Lane Gaddy*	PO Box 307, El Paso TX 79943	915-532-5643	R	21*	.1
67	Batliner Paper Stock Co—*Nick Sterbach*	2501 E Front St, Kansas City MO 64120	816-483-3343	R	21*	.2
68	Agmet LLC—*Steve Jones*	7800 Medusa Rd, Cleveland OH 44146	440-439-7400	R	20*	.1
69	Royal Paper Stock Company Inc—*Michael Radtke*	1300 Norton Rd, Columbus OH 43228	614-851-4714	R	20*	.1
70	Berger and Company Recycling Inc—*Charles Sinel*	126 Front St, Pawtucket RI 02860	401-723-7240	R	20*	<.1
71	MJ Metal Inc—*Jeffrey Dreyer*	201 Hancock Ave, Bridgeport CT 06605	203-334-3484	R	20*	<.1
72	Metro Recycling Company Inc—*Chuck Francis*	2424 Beekman St, Cincinnati OH 45214	513-251-1800	R	20*	<.1
73	Seattle Iron and Metals Corp—*Alan Sidell*	601 S Myrtle St, Seattle WA 98108	206-682-0040	R	19*	.1
74	Arizona Recycling Corp—*Sal Bova*	400 S 15th Ave, Phoenix AZ 85007	602-258-5323	R	19*	<.1
75	Cohen and Green Salvage Company Inc—*Michael Green*	PO Box 510, Fayetteville NC 28302	910-483-1371	R	19*	<.1
76	City Carton Company Inc—*John Ockenfels*	3 E Benton St, Iowa City IA 52240	319-351-2848	R	18*	.2
77	Basic Fibres Inc—*Robert Berg*	6019 S Manhattan Pl St, Los Angeles CA 90047	323-753-3491	R	18*	<.1
78	US Tire Recycling—*Scott Fowler*	6322 Poplar Tent Rd, Concord NC 28027	704-784-1210	R	18*	.1
79	Federal International Inc—*Robbert Van*	7935 Clayton Rd, Saint Louis MO 63117	314-721-3377	R	18*	<.1
80	Garden Street Iron and Metal Incorporated Of SW Florida—*Earl Weber*	3350 Metro Pkwy, Fort Myers FL 33916	239-337-5865	R	18*	.1
81	Schwartzman Company Inc—*John Schwartzman*	2905 N Ferry St, Anoka MN 55303	763-421-1187	R	18*	.1
82	American Iron and Steel Company Inc—*Fred Isaacs*	2800 Pacific St, Minneapolis MN 55411	612-529-9221	R	18*	.1
83	Poly USA Inc—*Trifon Beladakis*	841 N Russell Ave, Aurora IL 60506	630-947-7900	R	18*	<.1
84	Tennessee Valley Recycling LLC—*Jeff Dumes*	PO Box H, Decatur AL 35602	256-353-6351	R	17*	.2
85	I H Schlezinger Inc—*Kenneth Cohen*	1041 Joyce Ave, Columbus OH 43219	614-252-1188	R	17*	<.1
86	Master Fibers Inc—*Sandra Bravo*	1710 E Paisano Dr, El Paso TX 79901	915-544-2299	R	17*	.1
87	Willimantic Waste Paper Company Inc—*Mary Lou De Vivo*	PO Box 239, Willimantic CT 06226	860-423-4527	R	16*	.1
88	Butler Paper Recycling Inc—*James Butler LII*	PO Box 1602, Suffolk VA 23439	757-539-2351	R	15*	.1
89	Freedom Metals Inc—*Bruce Blue*	1401 W Ormsby Ave, Louisville KY 40210	502-637-7657	R	15*	.1
90	Metro Alloys Inc—*Neil Berman*	1024 Sampler Way, Atlanta GA 30344	404-753-6063	R	15*	.1
91	Metal Recycling Services LLC—*Patrick Fuller*	PO Box 812, Monroe NC 28111	704-283-4455	R	15*	.2
92	Great Lakes Paper Stock Corp—*Sanford Rosen*	30700 Edison Dr, Roseville MI 48066	586-779-1310	R	15*	.1
93	M Bloch and Company Inc—*Leo Bloch*	PO Box 24063, Seattle WA 98124	206-763-0200	R	14*	<.1
94	Baltimore Scrap Corp—*David Simon*	3100 Weedon St, Baltimore MD 21226	410-355-4455	R	14*	<.1
95	Patriot Metals Inc—*Pam Nash*	PO Box 300, Gibsonton FL 33534	813-677-1606	R	14*	<.1
96	Herman Strauss Inc—*Carter Strauss*	PO Box 6294, Wheeling WV 26003	304-232-8770	R	14*	.1
97	Langley Recycling Inc—*Greg Bice*	3557 Stadium Dr, Kansas City MO 64129	816-924-8452	R	14*	.1
98	Metals Recycling LLC—*Rob Hueling*	89 Celia St, Johnston RI 02919	401-831-7799	R	13*	.1
99	Bowers Fibers Inc—*H Bowers*	4001 Yancey Rd, Charlotte NC 28217	704-523-5323	R	13*	.1
100	American Metals Company Inc—*Irwin Sheinbein*	740 W Broadway Rd, Mesa AZ 85210	480-834-1923	R	13*	<.1
101	International Rags Ltd—*Amirali Momin*	4800 Blaffer St, Houston TX 77026	713-491-0700	R	13*	.1
102	Shine Brothers Corp—*Toby Shine*	PO Box 737, Spencer IA 51301	712-262-5579	R	13*	.1
103	Universal Scrap Metals Inc—*Philip Zeid*	2500 W Fulton St, Chicago IL 60612	312-666-0011	R	13*	.1
104	A and S Of Modesto Inc—*Stanley Silva*	PO Box 955, Castroville CA 95012	831-633-3379	R	13*	.1
105	Lionetti Associates LLC—*Ed Handle*	450 S Front St, Elizabeth NJ 07202	908-820-8800	R	13*	.1
106	Yank Waste Company Inc—*David Aronson*	PO Box 12024, Albany NY 12212	518-456-2345	R	12*	.1
107	Sutta Co—*Stephen Sutta*	1221 3rd St Ste 2, Oakland CA 94607	510-873-8777	R	12*	.1
108	George Apkin and Sons Inc—*William Apkin*	PO Box 509, North Adams MA 01247	413-664-4936	R	12*	<.1
109	Pascap Company Inc—*Anthony Capasso*	4250 Boston Rd, Bronx NY 10475	718-325-7200	R	12*	.1
110	Hydrocarbon Recovery Services Inc—*Kenneth Cherry*	5800 Farrington Ave, Alexandria VA 22304	703-370-7306	R	12*	.1
111	Recycling Center Inc—*Jack Edelman*	PO Box 2038, Richmond IN 47375	765-966-8295	R	11*	.1
112	Brandywine Recyclers Inc—*Frank Dixon*	328 N 14th St, Lebanon PA 17046	717-272-4655	R	11*	<.1
113	Specialty Fibres LLC—*Simone Jennings*	3201 Dnville Blvd Ste, Alamo CA 94507	925-934-8700	R	11*	.1
114	V and M Corp—*Habib Mamou*	414 E Hudson Ave, Royal Oak MI 48067	248-541-4020	R	11*	.1
115	Southside Recycling Inc—*Greg Jansen*	PO Box 25447, Saint Louis MO 63125	314-631-3400	R	11*	<.1
116	Lasensky Paper Stock Inc—*David Lasensky*	508 E Baltimore Ave, Lansdowne PA 19050	610-623-7772	R	11*	.1
117	Hutcherson Metals Inc—*Wiley Hutcherson*	PO Box 218, Halls TN 38040	731-836-9435	R	11*	.1
118	Riverside Scrap Iron and Metal Corp—*Daniel Frankel*	PO Box 5288, Riverside CA 92517	951-686-2120	R	11*	<.1
119	Schwartz Iron And Metal Co—*Barry Schwartz*	20300 Mount Elliott St, Detroit MI 48234	313-368-3500	R	11*	<.1
120	Ehm Holdings Inc—*Lester Wilson*	PO Box 610, Elizabethton TN 37644	423-543-1991	R	10*	.1
121	Kroot Corp—*Tim Morris*	PO Box 503, Columbus IN 47202	812-372-8203	R	10*	.1
122	Tzeng Long USA Inc—*Bill Chang*	2801 Vail Ave, Commerce CA 90040	323-722-5353	R	10*	<.1
123	Bay Bridge Enterprises LLC—*Vishwas Shaw*	PO Box 7596, Chesapeake VA 23324	757-543-7464	R	10*	.1
124	EG Plastics LLC—*Gabrielle Grossberger*	116 39th St, Brooklyn NY 11232	718-788-3733	R	10*	.1
125	Rocky Mountain Recycling Inc—*Larry Odle*	6510 Brighton Blvd, Commerce City CO 80022	303-287-3681	R	10*	<.1
126	Harding Metals Inc—*Edso Harding*	PO Box 418, Northwood NH 03261	603-942-5574	R	10*	.1
127	Harris Material Exchange Inc—*R Harris*	590 W 500 S, Berne IN 46711	260-589-8965	R	10*	.1
128	Northeast Metal Traders Inc—*Ronald Greller*	7345 Milnor St Ste 1, Philadelphia PA 19136	215-624-7260	R	10*	.1
129	SD Richman Sons Inc—*David Richman*	2435 Wheatsheaf Ln, Philadelphia PA 19137	215-535-5100	R	10*	<.1
130	Chambersburg Waste Paper Company Inc—*Kelly Adams*	PO Box 975, Chambersburg PA 17201	717-264-4890	R	9*	.1
131	Rose Metal Processing Ltd—*Jerry Bailey*	2722 Ctr St, Houston TX 77007	713-880-7000	R	9*	.1
132	Starr Burn Enterprises Inc—*Robert Starr*	PO Box 1388, Saint Joseph MO 64502	816-279-1415	R	9*	<.1
133	Gordon Waste Company Inc—*Robert Gordon*	PO Box 389, Columbia PA 17512	717-684-2201	R	9*	<.1
134	Itronics Metallurgical Inc—*John W Whitney*	6490 S McCarran Blvd S, Reno NV 89509	775-689-7696	S	9*	<.1
135	Mormil Corp—*Chris Gerlitz*	110 SE 5th St, Bend OR 97702	541-382-8471	S	9*	<.1
	Schnitzer Steel Industries Inc					
136	Standard Iron and Metals Co—*Jason Allen*	4525 San Leandro St, Oakland CA 94601	510-535-0222	R	9*	<.1
137	Allegheny Iron and Metal Co—*Charles Dolaway*	2200 Adams Ave, Philadelphia PA 19124	215-743-7759	R	9*	<.1
138	American Compressed Steel Corp—*Larry Byer*	PO Box 1817, Cincinnati OH 45201	513-948-0300	R	9*	<.1
139	Circosta Iron And Metal Inc—*Nick Circosta*	1801 Evans Ave, San Francisco CA 94124	415-282-8568	R	9*	<.1
140	Intercon Solutions Inc—*Brian Brundage*	1001 Washington St, Chicago Heights IL 60411	708-756-9838	R	9*	.1
141	M Hiller and Son Inc—*Leonard Hiller*	1133 Manhattan Ave, Brooklyn NY 11222	718-383-2833	R	8*	.1
142	TerraCycle Inc—*Tom Szaky*	121 New York Ave, Trenton NJ 08638	609-393-4252	R	8*	.1
143	Fpt Schlafer—*Barry Briskin*	1950 Medbury St, Detroit MI 48211	313-925-8200	R	8*	.1
144	Ashley Salvage Co—*Frank Ashely*	4918 Roosevelt Ave, San Antonio TX 78214	210-922-7631	R	8*	<.1
145	Usher Enterprises Inc—*Michael Usher*	9000 Roselawn St, Detroit MI 48204	313-834-7055	R	8*	<.1

Rank	Company Name—*Executive Officer*	Address, City, State, Zip	Phone	Type	Fin	Empls
146	Gann Car Crushing Inc—*Garvin Gann*	PO Box 995, Pembroke GA 31321	912-653-2324	R	8*	<.1
147	Miami Waste Paper Company Inc—*Betty Novas*	PO Box 420854, Miami FL 33242	305-325-0860	R	8*	<.1
148	Cresson Steel Co—*John Calandra*	PO Box 187, Cresson PA 16630	814-886-4121	R	8*	<.1
149	Northstate Recycling Inc—*William Short*	PO Box 720350, Redding CA 96099	530-243-4780	R	8*	<.1
150	Monterrey Iron and Metal Ltd—*Richard Bibb*	PO Box 241509, San Antonio TX 78224	210-927-2727	R	8*	.1
151	Tt and E Iron and Metal Inc—*Ronnie Thompson*	PO Box 554, Garner NC 27529	919-772-9190	R	7*	<.1
152	Sioux City Compressed Steel Inc—*Norman Bernstein*	2600 Blvd Of Champio, Sioux City IA 51111	712-277-4100	R	7*	<.1
153	Accurate Paper Recycling Inc—*Douglas Gardner*	5500 E Giddens Ave, Tampa FL 33610	813-622-7377	R	7*	<.1
154	Delmarva Recycling Inc—*Gregory Stein*	909 Boundary St, Salisbury MD 21801	410-546-1111	R	7*	<.1
155	Beacon Metal Company Inc—*William Smith*	215 Throckmorton St, Freehold NJ 07728	732-462-0543	R	7*	<.1
156	L and D Scrap And Salvage Inc—*Leon Henderson*	2933 Ellisville Blvd, Laurel MS 39440	601-425-9411	R	7*	<.1
157	Steel Processing Inc—*Ellis Rubenstein*	5119 W Bethany Home Rd, Glendale AZ 85301	623-930-1900	R	6*	<.1
158	Bell County Iron and Recycling Company Inc—*Billy Bachmayer*	815 N 14th St, Temple TX 76501	254-773-2700	R	6*	<.1
159	Acme Iron and Metal Company Inc—*Walter Schmider*	PO Box 6605, Albuquerque NM 87197	505-345-2457	R	6*	<.1
160	Can Shed LLC—*Jennifer Pritle*	PO Box 8214, Cedar Rapids IA 52408	319-366-1300	R	6*	<.1
161	Midwest Industrial Metals Corp—*Michael Nanberg*	3030 N Tripp Ave, Chicago IL 60641	773-202-8202	R	6*	<.1
162	Spokane Recycling Products Inc—*John Drew*	3407 E Main Ave, Spokane WA 99202	509-535-0284	R	6*	<.1
163	Energy Answers International Inc—*Patrick F Mahoney*	79 N Pearl St, Albany NY 12207	518-434-1227	R	6*	<.1
164	Emil A Schroth Inc—*Emil Schroth*	PO Box 496, Farmingdale NJ 07727	732-938-5015	R	6*	<.1
165	Madewell and Madewell Inc—*Carmalieta Wells*	PO Box 386, Jones OK 73049	405-399-2201	R	6*	<.1
166	Minnesota Shredding LLC	8400 89th Ave N Ste 43, Minneapolis MN 55445	763-493-3007	R	6*	<.1
167	Brooklyn Resource Recovery Inc—*Robert Rosselli*	741 Rockaway Pkwy, Brooklyn NY 11236	718-531-6606	R	6*	<.1
168	Sol Alman Co—*Larry Alman*	PO Box 1111, Little Rock AR 72203	501-372-5222	R	6*	<.1
169	Hamilton Scrap Processors Inc—*Neil Cohen*	PO Box 446, Hamilton OH 45012	513-863-3474	R	6*	<.1
170	Turner Trucking and Salvage Company Inc—*Harry Turner*	225 Commercial St, Lynn MA 01905	781-595-3741	R	6*	<.1
171	Reliable Environmental Transport Inc—*Jonathon Marks*	PO Box 500, Bridgeport WV 26330	304-623-6490	R	6	<.1
172	Okon Metals Inc—*Louis Okon*	PO Box 151951, Dallas TX 75315	214-426-6566	R	6*	<.1
173	Steel Dust Recycling LLC—*Tom Knepper*	PO Box 819, Millport AL 35576	205-662-8801	R	6*	<.1
174	Integrity Recycling Inc—*Daniel Fangmeyer*	7921 Philadelphia Rd, Baltimore MD 21237	410-866-4000	R	6*	<.1
175	Newco Metals Inc—*E Barber*	7268 S State Rd 13, Pendleton IN 46064	317-485-7721	R	6*	<.1
176	Weiner Iron and Metal Corp—*Steven Field*	PO Box 359, Pottsville PA 17901	570-622-6543	R	6*	<.1
177	Fiber Resources Unlimited Inc—*John Dalton*	3833 Bancroft Dr, Spring Valley CA 91977	619-462-0098	R	5*	<.1
178	H and S Body Works and Towing—*Richard Compton*	314 California Ave, Bakersfield CA 93304	661-324-6703	R	5*	<.1
179	Columbus Scrap Material Company Inc—*Greg Rader*	PO Box 8670, Columbus MS 39705	662-328-8176	R	5*	<.1
180	NH Kelman Inc—*Donald Kelman*	PO Box 103, Cohoes NY 12047	518-237-5133	R	5*	<.1
181	M and M Metals International Inc—*Jerome Mellman*	840 Dellway St, Cincinnati OH 45229	513-221-4411	R	5*	<.1
182	Aluminum Recycling Of Mississippi Inc—*John Bussey*	1819 Valley St, Jackson MS 39204	601-355-5777	R	5*	<.1
183	American Independent Paper Mills Supply Company Inc—*Peter Baselice*	15 S Depot Plz, Tarrytown NY 10591	914-631-8285	R	5*	<.1
184	Elan Trading Inc—*Samuel Waldman*	PO Box 220885, Charlotte NC 28222	704-342-1696	R	5*	<.1
185	Asheville Waste Paper Company Inc—*Thelma Mcmahan*	PO Box 3335, Asheville NC 28802	828-252-6963	R	5*	<.1
186	Joyce Iron and Metal Co—*Paul Garrett*	1283 Joyce Ave, Columbus OH 43219	614-299-4175	R	5*	<.1
187	Lewis-Clark Recyclers Inc—*Mark Armstrong*	PO Box 1687, Lewiston ID 83501	208-746-1187	R	5*	<.1
188	Diver Steel City Auto Crushers Inc—*John Diver*	PO Box 1293, Youngstown OH 44501	330-742-4804	R	5*	<.1
189	Alpha Recycling Inc—*Arthur Yacobozzi*	13314 Satlcoy St, North Hollywood CA 91605	818-982-5800	R	5*	<.1
190	Belton Metal Company Inc—*James Ballard*	PO Box 158, Belton SC 29627	864-338-7426	R	5*	<.1
191	Berlinsky Scrap Corp—*Herbert Glassman*	PO Box 733, Joliet IL 60434	815-726-4334	R	5*	<.1
192	Mednik Wiping Materials Company Inc—*James Mednik*	6740 Romiss Ct, Saint Louis MO 63134	314-524-2200	R	5*	<.1
193	Barry Metals Company Inc—*Howyn Basuk*	3014 N 30th Ave, Phoenix AZ 85017	602-484-7186	R	5*	<.1
194	Sunwest Metals Inc—*Hanan Stanley*	1150 N Anaheim Blvd, Anaheim CA 92801	714-635-0470	R	5*	<.1
195	Metro Environmental Inc—*Shane Roberts*	PO Box 281, Sylacauga AL 35150	256-245-3205	R	5*	<.1
196	A and P Recycling Inc—*William Prescott*	PO Box 2289, Sumter SC 29151	803-775-8383	R	4*	<.1
197	Dimond Scrap Metals Inc—*David Jurman*	PO Box 610, San Jose CA 95106	408-451-9515	R	4*	<.1
198	Ball Trading Corp—*Max Leiter*	266 Freeman St, Brooklyn NY 11222	718-383-2525	R	4*	<.1
199	Silver's Metal Co—*Steven Silverstein*	1401 Woodland St, Detroit MI 48211	313-867-9188	R	4*	<.1
200	Maine Metal Recycling Inc—*David Murphy*	PO Box 1478, Auburn ME 04211	207-786-3531	R	4*	<.1
201	Industrial Recycling Services Inc—*Jack Clevinger*	PO Box 995, Kingsport TN 37662	423-245-5124	R	4*	<.1
202	A and C Auto Parts and Wrecking Company Inc—*Michael Weiss*	3805 Ridge Rd, Cleveland OH 44144	216-961-6840	R	4*	<.1
203	Appertain Corp—*Rod Wells*	PO Box 1010, Pulaski TN 38478	931-363-8284	R	4*	.1
204	Port Iron Ltd—*David Albright*	300 W Rev Dr Ransom Ho, Port Arthur TX 77640	409-983-1641	R	4*	<.1
205	Comal Iron and Metals Inc—*Johnny Rodriguez*	1431 Fm 306, New Braunfels TX 78132	830-625-4920	R	4*	<.1
206	Integrity Iron and Metal—*Russell Fredette*	2674 Cass Rd, Traverse City MI 49684	231-946-3499	R	4*	<.1
207	Strand Inc—*Thomas Quirke*	2649 S Military Hwy, Chesapeake VA 23324	757-545-1500	R	4*	<.1
208	Mullins Max B Auto Parts Salvage Inc—*Max Mullins*	5733 Old Rte 66, Mount Olive IL 62069	217-999-2030	R	4*	<.1
209	Mahzel Metals Inc—*Donald Chaimovitz*	325 N Elizabeth St Fl, Chicago IL 60607	312-733-5500	R	4*	<.1
210	P and T Metals Inc—*Barbara Messinger*	2213 Tyler Ave, South El Monte CA 91733	626-443-6698	R	4*	<.1
211	David Hirschberg Co—*Tom Graham*	PO Box 15815, Cincinnati OH 45215	513-821-0514	R	4*	<.1
212	C and C Paper Recycling—*Craig Sauer*	1957 Railroad Dr Ste A, Sacramento CA 95815	916-920-2673	R	4*	<.1
213	Addlestone International Corp—*Edward Kronsberg*	PO Box 979, Charleston SC 29402	843-577-9300	R	4*	<.1
214	Kuei Tyan LLC	5207 Saint Paul St, Tampa FL 33619	813-626-3283	R	4*	<.1
215	Harry Rock and Company Inc—*James Hubach*	8550 Aetna Rd, Cleveland OH 44105	216-361-2000	R	4*	<.1
216	Fairless Iron and Metal LLC Sims Group USA Holdings Corp	PO Box 5626, Trenton NJ 08638	215-295-6681	S	4*	<.1
217	Bodner Metal And Iron Corp—*Emanuel Bodner*	3660 Schalker Dr, Houston TX 77026	713-223-1148	R	4*	<.1
218	Shoreline Recycling and Supply—*Jeffrey Padnos*	259 Ottawa St, Muskegon MI 49442	231-722-6081	R	4*	<.1
219	Alaska Metal Recycling Co—*Winifred Newell*	9705 King St, Anchorage AK 99515	907-349-4833	R	4*	<.1
220	Atlas Waste Paper Corp—*Bertram Kossis*	2329 Wharton St, Pittsburgh PA 15203	412-431-5329	R	4*	<.1
221	Cousins Metal Industries Inc—*Sheldon Gering*	460 Brown Ct, Oceanside NY 11572	516-536-7755	R	4*	<.1
222	Caracciolo Charles Steel And Metal Yard Inc—*Charles Caracciolo*	PO Box 1924, Altoona PA 16603	814-944-4051	R	3*	<.1
223	Lockamy Scrap Metal Inc—*James Lockamy*	1324 Smith St, Dillon SC 29536	843-774-4171	R	3*	<.1
224	Ritter Disposables Inc—*Mark Pisahl*	PO Box 321, Marion AR 72364	870-735-0744	R	3*	<.1
225	Empire Steel and Metals Corp—*Simon Kahn*	PO Box 754238, Flushing NY 11375	718-268-3607	R	3*	<.1
226	Roy Price Car Crushing Inc—*Roy Price*	PO Box 824, Columbus MS 39703	662-244-3490	R	3*	<.1
227	Andersen Wrecking Co—*James Anderson*	1912 M Ave, Kearney NE 68847	308-237-3163	R	3*	<.1
228	Universal Demolishing and Recycling Inc—*Walter Turner*	PO Box 3455, Lufkin TX 75903	936-637-7300	R	3*	<.1
229	Pasco Auto Wrecking Inc—*Ted Osborne*	3602 E A St, Pasco WA 99301	509-547-7242	R	3*	<.1
230	Tyler Iron and Metal Inc—*Tommy Salome*	PO Box 4536, Tyler TX 75712	903-592-8144	R	3*	<.1
231	Shostak Iron And Metal Company Inc—*Alexander Gold*	700 Kindleberger Rd, Kansas City KS 66115	913-321-9210	R	3*	<.1

Note: An asterisk (*) indicates an estimated financial figure. The company type code used is as follows: R = Private, P = Public, S = Private Subsidiary, B = Public Subsidiary, D = Division, J = Joint Venture, I = Investment Fund.

COMPANY RANKINGS BY SALES WITHIN 4-DIGIT SIC

Rank	Company Name—Executive Officer	Address, City, State, Zip	Phone	Type	Fin	Empls
232	Vangel Paper Inc—Angelos Androutsopoulos	3020 Nieman Ave, Baltimore MD 21230	410-536-4354	R	3*	<.1
233	Arizona Scrap Iron and Metals Inc—Michael Galan	433 S 7th Ave, Phoenix AZ 85007	602-252-8423	R	3*	<.1
234	Arrow Scrap Corp—Nir Shalit	1627 Straight Path, Wyandanch NY 11798	631-491-3061	R	3*	<.1
235	Shapiro Salvage and Supply Co—Stan Shapiro	5617 Natural Bridge Av, Saint Louis MO 63120	314-382-7000	R	3*	<.1
236	State Line Scrap Metal Recycling Inc—Norvelle Simmons	5401 York Hwy, Gastonia NC 28052	704-864-9001	R	3*	<.1
237	Wireless Construction Services Corp—James Bushfield	28051 Camel Heights Ci, Evergreen CO 80439	303-756-2160	R	3*	<.1
238	Pick and Pull Auto Wrecking—Perlen Fein	1625 Prairie Rd, Eugene OR 97402	541-689-2800	R	3*	<.1
239	Atlas Recycling Company Inc—Patricia Shannon	3 Industrial Dr, Sharon Hill PA 19079	610-586-6655	R	3*	<.1
240	Big Island Scrap Metal LLC	91-140 Kaomi Loop, Kapolei HI 96707	808-682-9200	R	3*	<.1
241	King Junk—Dave Raap	538 Pratt Ave N, Schaumburg IL 60193	847-891-2048	R	3*	<.1
242	Universal Metal Corp—Stuart Freilich	PO Box 652, Worcester MA 01613	508-754-6841	R	2*	<.1
243	Kankakee Scrap—Frank Cozzi	1000 N Washington Ave, Kankakee IL 60901	815-933-5011	R	2*	<.1
244	Bristol Metal Company Inc—Angelo Stanzione	PO Box 596, Bristol RI 02809	401-253-4070	R	2*	<.1
245	Silver Harris And Sons Inc—Mark Silver	PO Box 13, Belvidere IL 61008	815-544-9221	R	2*	<.1
246	Bodow Recycling Inc—Andrea Knoller	1925 Park St Ste 2, Syracuse NY 13208	315-422-2552	R	2*	<.1
247	I Broomfield and Sons Inc—David Broomfield	PO Box 72811, Providence RI 02907	401-941-7361	R	2*	<.1
248	Curtis TradeGroup Inc—James M Haberman	PO Box 17575, Sarasota FL 34276	941-927-2333	R	2*	<.1
249	Rosenman's Inc—Tom Hull	PO Box 1002, Ottumwa IA 52501	641-683-1871	R	2*	<.1
250	Midstate Environmental Services LP—William Sturges	PO Box 261180, Corpus Christi TX 78426	361-387-2171	R	2*	<.1
251	Recycling Works Inc—Charles Himes	PO Box 1492, Elkhart IN 46515	574-293-3751	R	1*	<.1

TOTALS: SIC 5093 Scrap & Waste Materials
Companies: 251   33,963   34.1

5094 Jewelry & Precious Stones

Rank	Company Name—Executive Officer	Address, City, State, Zip	Phone	Type	Fin	Empls
1	A-Mark Financial Corp—Steven C Markoff	429 Santa Monica Blvd, Santa Monica CA 90401		R	2,950*	.1
2	Lazare Kaplan International Inc—Leon Tempelsman	19 W 44th St, New York NY 10036	212-972-9700	P	370	.1
3	Gerson Company Inc—Jim Gerson	1450 S Lone Elm Rd, Olathe KS 66061	913-262-7400	R	354*	.2
4	Blue Nile Inc—Diane Irvine	705 5th Ave S Ste 900, Seattle WA 98104	206-336-6700	P	333	.2
5	Chatham Created Gems and Diamonds—Thomas Chatham	360 Post St Ste 701, San Francisco CA 94108	415-397-8450	R	312*	.1
6	Colormasters Gem Corporation of New York—Joseph Marhka	36 W 44th St 5th Fl, New York NY 10036		R	222*	.1
7	Godinger Silver Art Company Ltd (New York New York)—Arnold Godinger	7 W 34th St, New York NY 10001	212-685-5843	R	199*	.1
8	Anaya Gems Inc—Anshul Gandhi	3100 47th Ave Fl 5, Long Island City NY 11101	718-391-7400	R	146*	.1
9	Bulova Corp—Herbet C Hoffman	1 Bulova Ave, Woodside NY 11377	718-204-3300	S	146*	.5
10	Citizen Watch Company of America Inc—Laurence Grunstein	1000 W 190, Torrance CA 90502		R	100*	.3
11	Speidel LLC—John Gugliada	1425 Cranston St, Cranston RI 02920	401-519-2000	R	98*	.1
12	Victorinox Swiss Army Inc—JMerrick Taggart	PO Box 1212, Monroe CT 06468	203-929-6391	S	92*	.3
13	Louis Diamond Glick Corp—Louis Glick	1271 Ave Of The Amrcs, New York NY 10020	212-259-0315	R	91*	.1
14	Frank Mastoloni and Sons Inc—Francis J Mastoloni Sr	415 Madison Ave, New York NY 10017	212-757-7278	R	71*	<.1
15	Disons Gems Inc—Milan Mehta	415 Madison Ave Fl 8, New York NY 10017	212-921-4133	R	60*	<.1
16	A-Mark Precious Metals Inc—Greg Roberts A-Mark Financial Corp	429 Santa Monica Blvd, Santa Monica CA 90401	310-587-1436	S	58*	<.1
17	Stuller Inc—Vicky Blasengain	PO Box 87777, Lafayette LA 70598	337-262-7700	R	56*	1.4
18	Stanley Roberts Inc—Edward Pomeranz	PO Box 686, Lodi NJ 07644	973-778-5900	R	54*	<.1
19	Swiss Watch International Inc—Lior Ben Shmuel	101 S State Rd 7 Ste 2, Hollywood FL 33023	954-985-3827	R	46*	.1
20	Citra Trading Corp—Ari Chitrik	590 Fifth Ave 14th Fl, New York NY 10036	212-354-1000	R	44*	.1
21	Stuckey Diamonds Inc—Michael Tietrangelo	PO Box 79010, Houston TX 77279	713-464-3800	R	30*	<.1
22	Sweda Company LLC—Steven Smith	17411 E Valley Blvd, City Of Industry CA 91744	626-357-9999	R	28*	.2
23	China Pearl Inc—Harold Jabarian	4250 Pennsylvania Ave, La Crescenta CA 91214	818-249-9888	R	21*	.1
24	Leo Wolleman Inc—Todd Wolleman	45 W 45th St Fl 10, New York NY 10036	212-840-1881	R	21*	<.1
25	D M Merchandising Inc—David Marks	835 N Church Ct, Elmhurst IL 60126	630-782-2700	R	20*	.1
26	Corum USA LLC—Paula Hardy	12 Mauchly Ste H, Irvine CA 92618	949-788-6200	R	20*	<.1
27	RDI Trading Inc—Michael Indelicato	5580 LBJ Fwy Ste 525, Dallas TX 75240	972-458-2076	R	20*	<.1
28	Stern/Leach Co—Austin Carr	49 Pearl St, Attleboro MA 02703	508-222-7400	R	18*	.5
29	Trimars Delaware—Victor Weinman	4440 11th St, Long Island City NY 11101	718-706-8814	R	16*	.1
30	Thunderbird Supply Co—Donald Cosper	1907 W Hwy 66, Gallup NM 87301	505-722-4323	R	16*	.1
31	PA J Inc—Felix Chen	18325 Waterview Pkwy F, Dallas TX 75252	214-688-0088	R	15*	.1
32	Gold and Siver Buyers	2200 Main, Houston TX 77002		R	15	.1
33	Denver Merchandise Mart—Darrell Hare	451 E 58th Ave Ste 427, Denver CO 80216	303-292-6278	R	15*	.1
34	B and M Imports Inc—Mois Medine	12 E 46th St Fl 4, New York NY 10017	212-986-5700	R	15*	<.1
35	Designs By FMC Inc—William Nussen	1533 60th St, Brooklyn NY 11219	718-435-0333	R	14*	.2
36	Innovation Specialties Inc—Eddie Blau	11869 Teale St Ste 69, Culver City CA 90230	310-398-8116	R	13*	.1
37	XIV Karats Ltd—Ron Rosenblum	314 S Beverly Dr, Beverly Hills CA 90212	310-551-1212	R	13	<.1
38	Chain N Fantasia Inc—Young Yoo	1239 Broadway Fl 9, New York NY 10001	212-679-2531	R	13*	<.1
39	Art's Elegance Inc—Art Mikaelian	PO Box 307, La Canada CA 91012	626-405-1522	R	11*	.1
40	Gulf Coast Ventures Inc—Ayhan Yuce	10651 Harwin Dr Ste 73, Houston TX 77036	713-777-1000	R	10*	.1
41	Tivoli Jewelers—Frank Palmeri	327 Graham Ave, Brooklyn NY 11211	718-384-1305	R	10*	<.1
42	14 Carats Ltd	314 S Beverly Dr, Beverly Hills CA 90212	310-551-1212	R	9*	.1
43	Sol Savransky Diamonds Inc—Eli Savransky	555 5th Ave Rm 300, New York NY 10017	212-730-4700	R	9*	.1
44	Jewels Connection Inc—Daniel Golshirazin	510 W 6th St Ste 600, Los Angeles CA 90014	213-689-1332	R	8*	<.1
45	Southern Crafts Inc—Arthur De Cesare	PO Box 40471, Baton Rouge LA 70835	225-292-0150	R	7*	.1
46	Jewelry Corner Inc—Chander Buxani	1201 E Elizabeth St, Brownsville TX 78520	956-544-1786	R	7*	<.1
47	S and J Diamond Corp—Milan Mehta	415 Madison Ave Fl 8, New York NY 10017	212-921-8680	R	7*	<.1
48	Harbor Marketing Inc—Isaak Akouka	1960 Ne 118th Rd, North Miami FL 33181	305-949-5900	R	6*	<.1
49	Selco Custom Time Corp—Larry Abels	8909 E 21st St, Tulsa OK 74129	918-622-6100	R	6*	<.1
50	Myron Toback Inc—Myron Toback	25 W 47th St Unit 8, New York NY 10036	212-398-8300	R	6*	<.1
51	SA Kitsinian Inc—Sarkis Kitsinian	6743 Odessa Ave, Van Nuys CA 91406	818-988-9961	R	6*	<.1
52	Stella Golden Inc—Jay Eun	250 Spring St 7n103, Atlanta GA 30303	404-525-4324	R	6*	<.1
53	Crystal Swarovski Components Ltd—Reinhard Mackinger	1 Kenney Dr, Cranston RI 02920	401-463-5136	R	6*	<.1
54	Montechristo Trade Corp—Rafik Oganesian	PO Box 811550, Los Angeles CA 90081	213-629-2958	R	5*	<.1
55	Los Altos Trophy Company Inc—Beverly Rubin	10731 Walker St Ste A, Cypress CA 90630	714-826-4920	R	5*	<.1
56	CJ Environmental Inc—Norm Schneider	101 Hampton Rd, Sharon MA 02067	781-784-2238	R	5*	<.1
57	Pisani Enterprises Inc—Gerald Pisani	350 Ocean Ave, San Francisco CA 94112	415-861-6616	R	5*	<.1
58	Hunt Jack Coin Broker—Clifford Hunt	PO Box 194, Kenmore NY 14217	716-874-7777	R	5*	<.1
59	Rosenthal Jewelers Supply Corp—Raphael Adouth	146 Ne 1st St, Miami FL 33132	305-573-6866	R	5*	<.1
60	Natalia Marketing Inc—Kathy Apacidis	170 High St, Waltham MA 02453	781-693-4900	R	5*	<.1
61	Fernando Originals—Erwin Pearl	184 Woonasquatucket Av, North Providence RI 02911	401-353-2725	R	5*	<.1
62	Maurice Lacroix USA—Stuart Sklar	17835 Ventura Blvd Ste, Encino CA 91316	818-609-8686	R	4*	<.1
63	Boutique Trims Inc—Kevin Williams	21200 Pontiac Trl, South Lyon MI 48178	248-437-2017	R	4*	<.1
64	Rudig Olympic Award Company Inc—Thomas Rudig	580 N 108th Pl, Milwaukee WI 53226	414-773-9000	R	4*	<.1

Rank	Company Name—Executive Officer	Address, City, State, Zip	Phone	Type	Fin	Empls
65	Elite Gold Products Corp—Jan Feld	42 W 48th St Ste 602, New York NY 10036	212-489-5700	R	4*	<.1
66	3sg Inc—Steven Ruggiero	PO Box 1001, Pearl River NY 10965	845-735-7373	R	4*	<.1
67	ItsHotcom—Boris Barshevsky	2 W 46th St Ste 602, New York NY 10036	212-398-3123	R	4	<.1
68	Cine Corp—Allan Robin	6814 Gant Rd Ste 108, Houston TX 77066	281-444-0519	R	4*	<.1
69	Italia Moda Inc—Stefano Vitolo	23852 Pacific Coast Hw, Malibu CA 90265	310-317-9530	R	4*	<.1
70	Roni Casting Inc—Roberto Guanaes	33 W 46th St Fl 7, New York NY 10036	212-869-1432	R	4*	<.1
71	CRP Time Recording Systems Inc—Henry Allen	PO Box 18158, Charlotte NC 28218	704-333-5984	R	3*	<.1
72	Golden Grove Trading Inc—Werner Schulz	854 W Golden Grove Way, Covina CA 91722	626-331-7233	R	3*	<.1
73	Berco Watch And Jewelers Supply Company Inc—Vincent Innocenti	29 E Madison St Ste 55, Chicago IL 60602	312-782-1050	R	3*	<.1
74	M Geller Ltd—Mark Geller	29 E Madison St Ste 18, Chicago IL 60602	312-984-1041	R	3*	<.1
75	Prince International Corp—Kyung Park	1239 Broadway Ste 301, New York NY 10001	212-213-8339	R	3*	<.1
76	SKF International Inc—Sam Koumi	15 W 37th St Fl 7, New York NY 10018	212-719-9094	R	3*	<.1
77	Diaco America Inc—Seymour Pluchenik	1271 Ave Of The Americ, New York NY 10020	212-259-0300	R	3*	<.1
78	Zahntech Advanced Technologies Inc—Muntaser Gaouny	525 N Central Ave Ste, Upland CA 91786	213-627-6925	R	3*	<.1
79	Esslinger and Company Inc—Bill Esslinger	1165 Medallion Dr, Saint Paul MN 55120	651-452-7180	R	3*	<.1
80	Findingkings—Dan O'donnell	3007 N Norfolk, Mesa AZ 85215	480-222-2005	R	3*	<.1
81	La Vie Parisienne Corp—Catherine Popesco	1837 Lincoln Blvd, Santa Monica CA 90404	310-392-8428	R	3*	<.1
82	Barber Coins and Collectibles Inc—Leonard Barber	17305 Cedar Ave S Ste, Lakeville MN 55044	952-997-6410	R	3*	<.1
83	Security Gold Exchange Inc—Bruce Franklin	102 Mill St, Grass Valley CA 95945	530-272-1810	R	2*	<.1
84	Evvtex Company Inc—David Zadeh	551 5th Ave Rm 1901, New York NY 10176	212-754-2626	R	2*	<.1
85	KWJ Wholesale—Kay Wiggins	600 S Tyler Rd Ste W10, Wichita KS 67209	316-941-3755	R	2*	<.1
86	Baroni Designs—Sarah Andrae	1049 Samoa Blvd, Arcata CA 95521	707-822-8067	R	2*	<.1
87	GA Heaton Co—Jerry Heaton	6595 Hwy 49 N, Mariposa CA 95338	209-377-8227	R	2*	<.1
88	Bally Bead Company Inc—Ward Hudspeth	2304 Ridge Rd, Rockwall TX 75087	972-771-4515	R	2*	<.1
89	Killer Beads And Everything Else You Need Inc—David Hamlin	PO Box 18797, Panama City FL 32417	850-234-6361	R	2*	<.1
90	Monster Trendz Inc—Matthew Huusko	1 Washington Unit 5017, Dover NH 03820	603-617-2645	R	1*	<.1
91	Tofa Enterprises Corp—John Chun	269A 7th St, Palisades Park NJ 07650	201-707-2098	R	1	<.1
92	Monsterslayer Inc—John Foutz	PO Box 550, Kirtland NM 87417	505-598-5322	R	1*	<.1
93	Stuffwholesale—Ron Gincastro	250 Shady Valley Rd, Coventry RI 02816	401-603-0309	R	<1	<.1

TOTALS: SIC 5094 Jewelry & Precious Stones
Companies: 93   6,364   7.3

5099 Durable Goods Nec

Rank	Company Name—Executive Officer	Address, City, State, Zip	Phone	Type	Fin	Empls
1	Warner-Elektra-Atlantic Corp—Carl Luttrell	111 N Hollywood Way, Burbank CA 91505	818-843-6311	S	8,333*	1.0
2	Kravet Fabrics Inc—Cary Kravet	225 Central Ave S, Bethpage NY 11714	516-293-2000	R	1,725*	.4
3	CAMAC Group—Kamoru Lawal	1330 Post Oak Blvd Ste, Houston TX 77056	713-965-5100	R	1,620*	.2
4	Alliance Entertainment Corp—Alan Tuchman	4250 Coral Ridge Dr, Coral Springs FL 33065	954-255-4000	S	1,025*	.9
5	Roland Corporation US—Hidekazu Tanaka	5100 S Eastern Ave, Los Angeles CA 90040	323-890-3700	R	940*	.2
6	Mangelsen's—Sherry Kaufman	PO Box 728, Harlan IA 51537	712-755-2184	D	751*	.2
7	Wilton Products Inc—Vince Naccarato	2240 W 75th St, Woodridge IL 60517	630-963-1818	R	492*	.5
8	Franklin Covey Catalog Sales Inc	2200 W Parkway Blvd, Salt Lake City UT 84119	801-817-1776	S	393*	.4
9	Orr Safety Corp—Clark Orr	PO Box 198029, Louisville KY 40259	502-774-5791	R	267*	.2
10	Boulder Canyon Natural Foods Inc—Thomas W Freeze	1898 S Flat Iron Ct St, Boulder CO 80301	303-546-9939	S	192*	.1
11	Arc International North America Inc—Fred Dohn	901 S Wade Blvd, Millville NJ 08332	856-825-5620	S	183*	4.2
12	CMS Communications Inc—Tim Murphy	722 Goddard Ave, Chesterfield MO 63005	636-530-1320	R	179*	.2
13	Reis Environmental Inc—Rudolph L Wise	11022 Linpage Pl, Saint Louis MO 63197	314-426-5600	S	120*	.1
14	Hoshino USA Inc—Bill Reim	1726 Winchester Rd, Bensalem PA 19020	215-638-8670	R	104*	.1
15	VCI Entertainment—Robert Blair	11333 E 60th Pl, Tulsa OK 74146	918-254-6337	D	90*	<.1
16	American Product Distributors Inc—C Ray Kennedy	8350 Arrowridge Blvd, Charlotte NC 28273	704-522-9411	R	85*	<.1
17	LN Curtis and Sons—Paul F Curtis	1800 Peralta St, Oakland CA 94607	510-839-5111	R	84*	.2
18	Reprographics One Inc	36060 Industrial Rd, Livonia MI 48150	734-542-8800	R	84*	.1
19	Caroline Distribution	104 W 29th St 4th Fl, New York NY 10001	212-886-7500	R	68*	.1
20	Blevins Inc—Brad Blevins	PO Box 160387, Nashville TN 37216	615-228-2616	R	65*	.2
21	Rggd Inc—Douglas Song	3359 E 50th St, Vernon CA 90058	323-581-6617	R	61*	.1
22	BMI Gaming Inc—David Young	3500 NW Boca Raton Blv, Boca Raton FL 33431	561-910-0061	R	58*	<.1
23	Ace Mart Restaurant Supply Co—Carl Gustafson	PO Box 18100, San Antonio TX 78218	210-323-4400	R	55*	.3
24	Capcom Entertainment Inc—Kenzo Tsujimoto	800 Concar Dr Ste 300, San Mateo CA 94402	650-350-6500	S	54*	.1
25	United States Brass and Copper Company Inc—Brendan Kavanaugh	1401 Brook Dr Ste A, Downers Grove IL 60515	630-629-9340	R	53*	<.1
26	Bennett Brothers Inc—GK Bennett	30 E Adams St, Chicago IL 60603	312-263-4800	R	50*	.1
27	AKAI Professional—Tommy Moore	200 Scenic View Dr Ste, Cumberland RI 02864	401-658-4032	R	40	.1
28	Global Forestry Management Group—Jeff Fantazia	PO Box 10167, Portland OR 97296	503-228-1950	R	40*	.1
29	Vast Resources Inc—Scott Tucker	PO Box 2488, Chatsworth CA 91313	818-332-4600	R	37*	.3
30	E1 Entertainment US LP—Michael Koch	22 Harbor Park Dr, Port Washington NY 11050	516-484-1000	R	37*	.3
31	Nor-South Corporation Ltd—Vanh Miller	4929 E Paris Ave Se, Grand Rapids MI 49512	616-554-5155	R	35*	<.1
32	Brady Distributing Co—Jon P Brady	PO Box 19269, Charlotte NC 28219	704-357-6284	R	35*	.1
33	New View Gifts and Accessories Ltd—Joseph Narzikul	311 E Baltimore Ave, Media PA 19063	610-627-0190	R	31*	.1
34	SSB Service Inc—Steve Thompson	3060 SE Grimes Blvd St, Grimes IA 50111	515-986-9101	R	30*	.1
35	Accredited Lock and Door Hardware Co—Ronald Weaver	PO Box 1442, Secaucus NJ 07096	201-865-5015	R	24*	<.1
36	Holmes Timber Company Inc—Jerry Holmes	628 West Columbia Ave, Batesburg SC 29006	803-604-8556	R	22*	<.1
37	Select-O-Hits Inc—Sam W Phillips	1981 Fletcher Creek Dr, Memphis TN 38133	901-388-1190	R	20*	<.1
38	American Music and Sound LLC—Janice Gilsig	4325 Executive Dr Ste, Southaven MS 38672	662-342-4010	S	19*	<.1
39	Videotape Products Inc—John Palazzola	2721 W Magnolia Blvd, Burbank CA 91505	818-566-9898	R	19*	<.1
40	Cascio Music Company Inc—Michael Cascio	13819 W National Ave, New Berlin WI 53151	262-786-6249	R	18*	.1
41	Capital Safety USA—Len Barrowclough	3833 Sala Way, Red Wing MN 55066	651-388-8282	R	16*	.5
42	Supply Room Inc—Art Hathorn	PO Box 7277, Oxford AL 36203	256-835-7676	R	15*	.1
43	Coby Electronics Corp—Young Lee	1991 Marcus Ave Ste 30, New Hyde Park NY 11042	718-416-3300	R	15*	.1
44	Smart Carpet—Paul Haney	1913 Atlantic Ave, Manasquan NJ 08736		R	15*	.1
45	Gold Crest Distributing LLC—Mel Toellner	PO Box 157, Mexico MO 65265	573-582-0559	R	15*	<.1
46	Ironclad Performance Wear Corp—Scott Jarus	2201 Park Pl Ste 101, El Segundo CA 90245	310-643-7800	P	15	<.1
47	Martinson-Nicholls—Daniel Ruminski	4910 E 345th St, Willoughby OH 44094	440-951-1312	R	15*	<.1
48	Music City Record Distributors Inc—Bruce Carlock	PO Box 22773, Nashville TN 37202	615-255-7315	R	14*	.1
49	Haip Inc—Husam Alnasr	610 Winters Ave, Paramus NJ 07652	201-487-4871	R	14*	<.1
50	Home Etc Inc—Ronnie Tsao	4535 Mcewen Rd, Dallas TX 75244	972-701-8802	R	14*	.6
51	Avidex Industries LLC—Bent Jakobsen	13555 Bel Red Rd Ste 2, Bellevue WA 98005	425-643-0330	R	14*	.1
52	Reedy International Corp—Michael Reedy	25 E Front St, Keyport NJ 07735	732-264-1777	R	13*	<.1
53	International Wholesale Supply Inc—Jarrett Portz	PO Box 1210, Lake Havasu City AZ 86405	928-764-7777	R	13*	<.1
54	Nancy Sales Company Inc—Stephen Lipkin	22 Willow St, Chelsea MA 02150	617-884-1700	R	13*	.1

Note: An asterisk (*) indicates an estimated financial figure. The company type code used is as follows: R = Private, P = Public, S = Private Subsidiary, B = Public Subsidiary, D = Division, J = Joint Venture, I = Investment Fund.

ANY RANKINGS BY SALES WITHIN 4-DIGIT SIC

Rank	Company Name—Executive Officer	Address, City, State, Zip	Phone	Type	Fin	Empls
55	Decor Moulding Ltd—*Michael Katz*	300 Wireless Blvd, Hauppauge NY 11788	631-231-5959	R	12*	.1
56	Peg Perego USA Inc—*Lucio Perego*	3625 Independence Dr, Fort Wayne IN 46808	260-482-8191	R	12*	.1
57	Davann Inc—*David Orlikowski*	PO Box 124, Riverton IL 62561	217-585-4200	R	12*	<.1
58	LEM Products Inc—*Larry Metz*	109 May Dr, Harrison OH 45030		R	11*	<.1
59	Eufaula Pulpwood Company Inc—*Hal Jones*	PO Box 278, Eufaula AL 36072	334-687-2784	R	11*	.1
60	Prajin 1 Stop Distributors Inc—*Antonio Prajin*	5701 Pacific Blvd 5711, Huntington Park CA 90255	323-588-9323	R	11*	.1
61	AMS Health Sciences Inc—*Gary Hail*	PO Box 12940, Oklahoma City OK 73157	405-842-0131	R	10*	<.1
62	Herbert S Hiller Corp—*Charles Illanne*	401 Commerce Pt, Harahan LA 70123	504-736-0008	R	10*	<.1
63	Spoontiques Inc—*Harold Sawyer*	111 Island St, Stoughton MA 02072	781-344-9530	R	8*	.1
64	Maintenance Builders Supply Inc—*Mark Beatty*	1418 Brittmoore Rd, Houston TX 77043	713-462-8213	R	8*	.1
65	Communications Marketing Southeast Inc—*Jerry Michael Bentley*	442 Cadillac Pkwy, Dallas GA 30157	770-443-9514	R	8*	<.1
66	Aaa Key-Lock Company Inc—*Richard Brown*	PO Box 5851, Hicksville NY 11802	212-840-3939	R	8*	.1
67	Safety Guys LLC—*Raymond Nel*	PO Box 22219, Fort Lauderdale FL 33335	954-463-9811	R	8*	.3
68	Central South Distribution Inc—*Randall Davidson*	3730 Vulcan Dr, Nashville TN 37211	615-833-5960	R	7*	.1
69	Fun Express Inc—*Stephen Frary*	4206 S 108th St, Omaha NE 68137	402-935-5585	R	7*	.1
70	Carolina Safety Sport International LLC—*Debbie Hames*	PO Box 2276, Thomasville NC 27361	336-474-8000	R	7*	.1
71	American Safety Utility Corp—*Buddy Price*	PO Box 1740, Shelby NC 28151	704-482-0601	R	6*	<.1
72	3s Inc—*Matt Euson*	8686 SW Pkwy, Harrison OH 45030	812-656-8045	R	6*	<.1
73	JBS Associates Inc—*James Coppins*	1422 N 44th St Ste 109, Phoenix AZ 85008	602-244-1212	R	6*	<.1
74	Seaver Co—*Dean Seaver*	PO Box 123, Le Sueur MN 56058	507-665-3321	R	6*	.1
75	Meridian Moulding Inc—*George Noor*	330 Cessna Cir, Corona CA 92880	951-279-5220	R	6*	<.1
76	Abco Fire Protection Inc—*Matthew Aloisio*	1391 Frey Rd, Pittsburgh PA 15235	412-373-7730	R	5*	<.1
77	Richard Keldsen—*Richard Keldsen*	PO Box 2841, South San Francisco CA 94083	650-616-7585	R	5*	<.1
78	Fire Extinguisher Sales and Service Of Asheboro Inc—*Chris Baird*	2330 Cragmore Rd, Winston Salem NC 27107	336-629-1381	R	5*	.1
79	Nutmeg Recycling LLC—*Scott Tenny*	300 Rye St, South Windsor CT 06074	860-289-7234	R	5*	<.1
80	Alpha Systems Fire Protection—*Jerry Pivnik*	PO Box 331027, Pacoima CA 91333	323-227-0700	R	5*	.1
81	Air One Equipment Inc—*Sandra Frey*	360 Production Dr, South Elgin IL 60177	847-289-9000	R	5*	<.1
82	Alfa Travelgear Inc—*Tony Ho*	1538 Knowles Ave, Los Angeles CA 90063	323-981-8686	R	5*	<.1
83	Quad City Safety Inc—*Mike Smeaton*	PO Box 1720, Davenport IA 52809	563-445-2170	R	5*	<.1
84	Koetter and Smith Inc—*Sam Smith*	8991 Louis Smith Rd, Borden IN 47106	812-923-5111	R	5*	<.1
85	Woodstock Percussion Inc—*Gary Kvistad*	167 Dubois Rd, Shokan NY 12481	845-657-6000	R	5*	<.1
86	Sunshine Apparel Inc—*Timothy Huffman*	1816 57th St, Sarasota FL 34243	941-351-3308	R	5*	<.1
87	Metro Fire Equipment Inc—*Gary Moody*	63 S Hamilton Pl, Gilbert AZ 85233	480-464-0509	R	5*	<.1
88	Keane Fire and Safety Equipment Company Inc—*Beth Hayes*	1500 Main St, Waltham MA 02451	781-899-6565	R	4*	<.1
89	Squeegee Supply Inc—*Robert Paltz*	703 Elizabeth Ave, Stewartsville NJ 08886	908-454-6222	R	4*	<.1
90	Traffic Safety Service LLC—*Anthony Pecoraro*	PO Box 615, South Plainfield NJ 07080	908-561-4800	R	4*	<.1
91	Squires Timber Co—*Kenneth Thompson*	PO Box 25, Kelly NC 28448	910-862-3533	R	4*	<.1
92	RDD Enterprises Inc—*Ed Diskin*	3200 S Grand Ave, Los Angeles CA 90007	213-742-0020	R	4*	<.1
93	Bacchus Video Releasing—*Mike Johnson*	9718 Glenoaks Blvd Uni, Sun Valley CA 91352	818-768-9101	R	4*	<.1
94	Prosource International Inc—*Ivar Blackner*	5005 S 900 E Ste 200, Salt Lake City UT 84117	801-301-5913	R	4*	<.1
95	Telephonetics Inc—*Stephen Maggs*	2841 Corporate Way, Miramar FL 33025		R	4*	<.1
96	Jefferson Fire and Safety Inc—*Peter Jefferson*	7617 Donna Dr, Middleton WI 53562	608-836-0068	R	4*	<.1
97	Sam Ash Megastores LLC—*David Ash*	PO Box 9047, Hicksville NY 11802	310-214-0340	R	4*	<.1
98	Premiere Hardwoods LLC—*Cindy Conforti*	616 S 55th Ave Ste 103, Phoenix AZ 85043	602-353-8008	R	4*ˑ	<.1
99	Sun Technologies Inc—*Steve Hatly*	PO Box 8928, Johnson City TN 37615	423-477-8857	R	4*	<.1
100	Gasperetti's Distributing Inc—*Fred Gasperetti*	6919 24th St W, Tacoma WA 98466	253-565-2323	R	4*	<.1
101	Thompson Team Inc—*Jon Thompson*	161 Foundation Ave, La Habra CA 90631	714-278-8080	R	4*	<.1
102	Lootens Distributing Inc—*Roy Lootens*	4459 Jordan Rd, Skaneateles NY 13152	315-685-8816	R	3*	<.1
103	Anaba Group Inc—*Ibraham Aboabdo*	1050 W Central Ave Ste, Brea CA 92821	714-990-8900	R	3*	<.1
104	Antique Warehouse Of Arkansas Inc—*Don Keathley*	PO Box 162, Clinton AR 72031	501-745-5842	R	3*	<.1
105	Neal Auction Company Inc—*John Neal*	4038 Magazine St, New Orleans LA 70115	504-899-5329	R	3*	<.1
106	Sun-Rys Distributing Corp—*Gregory Mosley*	1700 W 1st Ave, Coal Valley IL 61240	309-799-7091	R	3*	<.1
107	Wynn Fire Equipment LLC	PO Box 1585, Corbin KY 40702	606-523-9269	R	3*	<.1
108	MA Silva Corks USA LLC—*Rick Lawson*	3433 Westwind Blvd, Santa Rosa CA 95403	707-236-1180	R	3*	<.1
109	Sunbelt USA Inc—*Roy Burchett*	PO Box 2009, Upland CA 91785	909-593-0500	R	3*	<.1
110	Complete Robotics Inc—*Tim Baldwin*	3509 Elizabeth Lake Rd, Waterford MI 48328	248-681-2775	R	3*	<.1
111	Audio-Video Supply Inc—*Clifford Moore*	4575 Ruffner St, San Diego CA 92111	858-565-1101	R	3*	<.1
112	Comspan Communications Inc—*Nataly Scherbakova*	201 Santa Monica Blvd, Santa Monica CA 90401	310-394-0010	R	3	<.1
113	Southwestern Stringed Instruments Inc—*Stephen Shepherd*	1721 S Cherrybell Stra, Tucson AZ 85713	520-624-9390	R	3*	<.1
114	Holland Supply—*Randy Wilde*	1326 Lincoln Ave, Holland MI 49423	616-396-4678	R	3*	<.1
115	Stylemark Inc—*Mark Ascik*	2 Sunshine Blvd, Ormond Beach FL 32174	386-673-4966	R	3*	.6
116	Industrial Wire Products Inc—*Michael Gusdorf*	2005 N Service Rd W, Sullivan MO 63080	573-468-5151	R	3*	<.1
117	Krb Music Companies Inc—*Kenneth Bennett*	134 4th Ave N, Franklin TN 37064	615-794-4033	R	3*	<.1
118	Spin Inc—*Paul Ayers*	35 Sw 12th Ave Ste 105, Dania FL 33004	954-527-2652	R	3*	<.1
119	Agr Of Florida Inc—*George Shami*	PO Box 10158, Jacksonville FL 32247	904-733-9393	R	3*	<.1
120	Western Wood Products Inc—*Ray Levengood*	181 Hwy 555, Raton NM 87740	575-445-1300	R	3*	<.1
121	Amen Packaging Inc—*Bruce Hunt*	PO Box 16342, Denver CO 80216	303-297-8600	R	3*	<.1
122	Fred Harris and Assocs Inc—*Fred Harris*	1395 E 12 Mile Rd Bldg, Madison Heights MI 48071	248-740-9300	R	3*	<.1
123	E and M International Inc—*Edward Vaillancourt*	2820 Vassar Dr Ne, Albuquerque NM 87107	505-883-8955	R	3*	<.1
124	Image Logic Corp—*Woody Landy*	6807 Brennon Ln, Chevy Chase MD 20815	301-907-8891	R	2*	<.1
125	Young Chang Company Ltd—*Jeong Lim*	1432 Main St Ste 1, Waltham MA 02451	781-890-2929	R	2*	<.1
126	Beach Timber Company Inc—*Gary Strickland*	128 Beach Timber Rd, Alma GA 31510	912-632-2800	R	2*	<.1
127	Cellular Products Distributors—*Moris Shemian*	2037 Pontius Ave, Los Angeles CA 90025	310-815-0800	R	2*	<.1
128	Premiere Lock Company LLC—*Matt Hocutt*	8301 E 81st St Ste D, Tulsa OK 74133	918-294-3888	R	2*	<.1
129	Metropolitan Fire Extinguisher Co—*William Davis*	5120 W 65th St, Little Rock AR 72209	501-562-5186	R	2*	<.1
130	Van's Fire and Safety Inc—*Gerald Enkenvort*	PO Box 12055, Green Bay WI 54307	920-494-3346	R	2*	<.1
131	Systematic Impressions Inc—*Jim Hopkins*	373 Rte 347 Rm Ste282, Hauppauge NY 11788	631-293-3877	R	2*	<.1
132	Mortuary Associates Co—*William Potere*	580 S Main St, Northville MI 48167	248-349-0770	R	2*	<.1
133	San Fernando Metals Inc—*Michael Sakajian*	12242 Branford St, Sun Valley CA 91352	818-897-0633	R	2*	<.1
134	Pralay Advanced Supply Chain Solutions LLC—*Prabhakar Veeravalli*	PO Box 303, Medinah IL 60157	630-370-2948	R	2*	<.1
135	Rogue Valley Firewood—*Keith Drevets*	228 Nw B St, Grants Pass OR 97526	541-479-6990	R	2*	<.1
136	Allparts Music Corp—*Steve Wark*	13027 Brittmoore Park, Houston TX 77041	713-466-6414	R	2*	<.1
137	Chemglo USA—*Andre Douglas*	6320 Canoga Ave Ste 15, Woodland Hills CA 91367		R	2*	<.1
138	Southwest Stone Supply Inc—*Larry Woll*	6386 Osage Beach Pkwy, Osage Beach MO 65065	573-302-8855	R	2*	<.1
139	Pr Trading Company Inc—*Minly Sung*	7596 Harwin Dr, Houston TX 77036	713-975-8252	R	2*	<.1
140	Fredriksen and Sons Fire Equipment Company Inc—*Art Staman*	760 Thomas Dr, Bensenville IL 60106		R	2*	<.1

Rank	Company Name—Executive Officer	Address, City, State, Zip	Phone	Type	Fin	Empls
141	Empire Music Group Inc—Robert Stern	195 Steamboat Rd, Great Neck NY 11024	212-580-5959	R	2*	<.1
142	Industrial USA Inc—Chaya Follman	136 Wallabout St Apt 6, Brooklyn NY 11249	718-854-4456	R	2*	<.1
143	Techniche International—Doug Frost	1040 Joshua Way, Carlsbad CA 92008	760-476-0654	R	2*	<.1
144	JBC Safety—Jackson Kuo	3390 Rand Rd Ste A, South Plainfield NJ 07080	908-769-8340	R	1*	<.1
145	Jonathan Paul Eyewear Limited LLP—Preston Jickling	2600 Mchale Ct Ste 175, Austin TX 78758	512-832-6131	R	1*	<.1
146	Wild RecordsCom Inc—Harald Blakeslee	1621 Lakeville Dr Ste, Kingwood TX 77339	281-260-7777	R	1*	<.1
147	Hudson Valley Showcase LLC	591 Beattie Rd, Rock Tavern NY 12575	845-496-9364	R	1*	<.1
148	EconRam Systems—Tigran Kashkarian	8306 Wilshire Blvd Ste, Beverly Hills CA 90211	310-694-8002	R	1*	<.1
149	Specialty Bottle LLC—Dimitri Raisi	3434 4th Ave S, Seattle WA 98134	206-382-1100	R	1*	<.1
150	Mega Sun Inc—Ronald Poe	4515 Miami St, Saint Louis MO 63116	314-772-7000	R	1*	<.1
151	Tesoro Enterprises Inc—Henry J Boucher	26 Cross St, New Canaan CT 06840	203-221-2770	P	1	<.1
152	Environmental Energy Services Inc—A Leon Blaser	3350 Americana Terr St, Boise ID 83706	208-287-4471	R	<1	<.1
153	Phoenix Enterprise Inc—Carol Lant	PO Box 1111, Michigan City IN 46361	219-879-3381	R	<1*	<.1
154	Handleman Co—Albert A Koch	500 Kirts Blvd, Troy MI 48084	248-362-4400	P	<1	<.1
155	Internet Infinity Inc—George Paul Morris	413 Ave G Ste 1, Redondo Beach CA 90277	310-318-2244	P	<1	N/A

TOTALS: SIC 5099 Durable Goods Nec
Companies: 155 — 18,148 — 16.5

5111 Printing & Writing Paper

Rank	Company Name—Executive Officer	Address, City, State, Zip	Phone	Type	Fin	Empls
1	OfficeMax Inc—Matthew Broad	263 Shuman Blvd, Naperville IL 60563	630-438-7800	P	7,121	29.0
2	Unisource Worldwide Inc—Allan Dragone	6600 Governors Lake Pk, Norcross GA 30071		S	5,000	6.0
3	Xpedx—Mary Laschinger	6285 TriRidge Blvd, Loveland OH 45140	513-965-2900	S	4,900*	7.0
4	Maines Paper and Food Service Inc—Chris Mellon	101 Broome Corporate P, Conklin NY 13748	607-779-1200	R	2,800*	2.0
5	Gould Paper Corp—Harry E Gould Jr	11 Madison Ave, New York NY 10010	212-301-0000	R	1,141*	.4
6	Ris Paper Company Inc—James Lenhoff	50 RiverCenter Blvd St, Covington KY 41011	859-292-5000	R	525*	.7
7	xpedx - Kirk Downey—Thomas G Kadien	7500 Amigos Ave, Downey CA 90242	562-803-0550	R	394*	.2
8	Kelly Paper Corp—Ed Pearson	288 Brea Canyon Rd, City of Industry CA 91789	909-859-8200	R	298*	.3
9	Bradner Central Co—Richard S Bull	2300 Arthur Ave, Elk Grove Village IL 60007	847-290-8485	R	297*	.2
10	Cole Papers Inc—R Charles Perkins	PO Box 2967, Fargo ND 58108	701-282-5311	R	263*	.1
11	AT Clayton and Company Inc—Mark Valley Jr	300 Atlantic St 7th Fl, Stamford CT 06901	203-658-1200	R	263*	.1
12	Frank Parsons Paper Co—Michael Lane	1328 Charwood Rd Ste 1, Hanover MD 21076	301-386-5755	R	222*	.3
13	Heartland Paper Co—Dempster Christenson	808 W Cherokee St, Sioux Falls SD 57104	605-336-1190	R	150*	.1
14	Perez Trading Company Inc—John Perez	3490 NW 125th St, Miami FL 33167	305-769-0761	R	143*	.2
15	Jackson Paper Company Inc—Noel Machost	4400-C Mangum Dr, Jackson MS 39207	601-360-9620	R	141*	.2
16	Spicers Paper Inc—Charlie Whitaker	12310 E Slauson Ave, Santa Fe Springs CA 90670	562-698-1199	R	126*	.3
17	Unisource Midwest Inc Unisource Worldwide Inc	PO Box 597, Columbus OH 43216	614 261 7100	S	125*	.3
18	White Rose Paper Co—Mike Lane Frank Parsons Paper Co	1300 Mercedes Dr, Hanover MD 21076	410-247-1900	D	109*	.1
19	Anchor Paper Co—Linda Hartinger	480 Broadway St, Saint Paul MN 55101	651-298-1311	R	77*	.1
20	WCP Solutions—Tom Groves	6703 S 234th StSte 120, Kent WA 98032	253-850-3560	R	76*	.2
21	Clampitt Paper Co—Don Crew	9207 Ambassador Row, Dallas TX 75247	214-638-3300	R	59*	.1
22	CTI Paper Company Inc—Brian J Cowie	1545 Corporate Center, Sun Prairie WI 53590	608-834-9900	R	51*	<.1
23	Gartner Studios Inc—Greg Gartner	220 E Myrtle St, Stillwater MN 55082	651-351-7700	R	46*	.1
24	Websource—Matt Dawley Unisource Worldwide Inc	161 Ave of the America, New York NY 10013	212-255-1600	D	39*	.1
25	Newell Paper Co—Tommy Galyean Jackson Paper Company Inc	PO Box 631, Meridian MS 39301	601-693-1783	D	38*	.1
26	Economy Paper Company of Rochester—Robert Cherry	PO Box 90420, Rochester NY 14609	585-482-5340	R	34*	<.1
27	Hudson Valley Paper Co—Samantha T Jones	PO Box 1988, Albany NY 12201	518-471-5111	S	32*	.1
28	Williamson Printing Corp—Jesse Williamson	PO Box 36622, Dallas TX 75235	214-904-2100	R	25*	.2
29	Lenaro Paper Company Inc—Leonard Aronica	PO Box 9024, Central Islip NY 11722	631-439-8800	R	21*	<.1
30	BCT International Inc—Peter Posk	3000 NE 30th Pl 5th Fl, Fort Lauderdale FL 33306	954-563-1224	R	20*	<.1
31	Carolina Print and Packaging Inc—Sam Davis	1190 Old Beltway, Rural Hall NC 27045	336-642-4170	R	10*	<.1
32	Florida Trade Graphics Inc—Dennis Naney	4305 Ne 11th Ave, Pompano Beach FL 33064	954-786-2000	R	8*	<.1
33	IC Security Printers Incorporated -- Marketing—Dave Jackson	PO Box 25175, Salt Lake City UT 84125	801-265-8100	R	7*	<.1
34	Janway Company USA Inc—Wayne Stebbins	11 Academy Rd, Cogan Station PA 17728	570-494-1239	R	5*	<.1
35	Z-Works—Jeremy Michael	709 W Garfield St, Seattle WA 98119	206-284-5422	R	3*	N/A
36	Progressive Systems Network Inc—Jeff Stangel	1150 S Clinton St, Chicago IL 60607	312-382-8383	R	1*	<.1

TOTALS: SIC 5111 Printing & Writing Paper
Companies: 36 — 24,570 — 48.5

5112 Stationery & Office Supplies

Rank	Company Name—Executive Officer	Address, City, State, Zip	Phone	Type	Fin	Empls
1	United Stationers Inc—Charles Crovtiz	1 Parkway N Blvd Ste 1, Deerfield IL 60015	847-627-7000	P	5,006	6.0
2	Corporate Express USA Inc—Jay Mutschler	1 Environmental Way, Broomfield CO 80021	303-664-2000	S	4,369*	10.0
3	Masterpiece Studios Inc—Dave Humbert	1680 Roe Crest Dr, North Mankato MN 56003	507-388-8788	R	1,171*	.2
4	School Specialty Inc—David J Vander Zanden	PO Box 1579, Appleton WI 54912		P	762	1.9
5	Stationers Inc (Huntington West Virginia)—J Mac Aldridge	1945 5th Ave, Huntington WV 25703	304-528-2780	S	311*	<.1
6	Dade Paper and Bag Co—Irving Genet	9601 NW 112th Ave, Miami FL 33178	305-592-1020	R	271*	.9
7	Paperworks Inc—George H Hill	15477 Woodrow Wilson, Detroit MI 48238	313-867-5600	R	243*	.5
8	Independent Stationers Inc—Michael Gentile	250 E 96th St Ste 510, Indianapolis IN 46240	317-579-1116	R	166*	<.1
9	CM Paula Co—Greg Ionna	6049 Hi Tek Ct, Mason OH 45040	513-336-3100	R	126*	.2
10	Cuna Mutual Business Services Inc—Bill Cheny	5710 Mineral Point Rd, Madison WI 53705	608-231-4000	S	112*	.2
11	Franklin Covey Product Sales Inc	2200 W Parkway Blvd, Salt Lake City UT 84119	801-817-1776	S	98*	.2
12	Staples Business Advantage—Ronald Sargent	500 Staples Dr, Framingham MA 01702		R	91*	.3
13	SP Richards Co—Wayne Beacham	PO Box 1266, Smyrna GA 30081	770-436-6881	S	86*	.3
14	Prime Office Products Inc—Paul J Christians	3841 Green Hills Villa, Nashville TN 37215	615-843-1400	R	80*	.4
15	Katun Corp—Carlyle Singer	10951 Bush Lake Rd Ste, Minneapolis MN 55438	952-941-9505	R	69*	1.1
16	Lindenmeyr Munroe	3 Manhattanville Rd, Purchase NY 10577	914-696-9365	S	61*	.1
17	Pilot Corporation Of America—Dennis Burleigh	3855 Regent Blvd, Jacksonville FL 32224	904-645-9999	R	59*	.3
18	Variety Distributors Inc—Bret Anderson	609 7th St, Harlan IA 51537	712-755-2184	R	55*	.3
19	Supply Room Companies Inc—Patricia W Barber	14140 N Washington Hwy, Ashland VA 23005	804-412-1200	R	53*	.7
20	FM Resources—Fabricio Morales	1 Woodbury Blvd, Rochester NY 14604	585-238-2880	R	39*	.1
21	Pentel Of America Ltd—Isseki Nakayama	2715 Columbia St, Torrance CA 90503	310-320-3831	R	34*	.2
22	World Pac Paper LLC—Edgar L Smith Jr	1821 Summit Rd Ste 370, Cincinnati OH 45237	513-779-9595	R	28	<.1
23	Graphic Systems Inc (Memphis Tennessee)	7200 Goodlet Farms Pky, Cordova TN 38016	901-937-5500	R	27*	.1
24	Modern Business Machines Inc—Fredrick Merizon	PO Box 147, Appleton WI 54912	920-739-4326	R	24*	.1
25	Arctic Office Machine Inc—William Borchardt	PO Box 100083, Anchorage AK 99510	907-276-2322	R	23*	.1
26	Aram Inc—Marjorie Holden	PO Box 832747, Richardson TX 75083	972-690-9793	R	23*	<.1

Note: An asterisk (*) indicates an estimated financial figure. The company type code used is as follows: R = Private, P = Public, S = Private Subsidiary, B = Public Subsidiary, D = Division, J = Joint Venture, I = Investment Fund.

...PANY RANKINGS BY SALES WITHIN 4-DIGIT SIC

Rank	Company Name—*Executive Officer*	Address, City, State, Zip	Phone	Type	Fin	Empls
27	Dominion Solutions Inc—*Dan Sadik*	4721 Starkey Rd, Roanoke VA 24018	540-989-6848	R	22*	.1
28	General Office Products Co—*John Boss*	4521 Hwy 7, Minneapolis MN 55416	952-925-7500	R	21*	.1
29	Custom Data Products Inc—*Richard Dorfman*	PO Box 3650, Culver City CA 90231	310-410-6666	R	20*	.1
30	Louisiana Office Products—*Frank Giovingo*	PO Box 23851, New Orleans LA 70183	504-733-9650	R	20*	<.1
31	Pay-Less Office Products Inc—*James Matgen*	PO Box 390157, Omaha NE 68139	402-891-6210	R	19*	.1
32	Rbo Printlogistix Inc—*James Riley*	2463 Schuetz Rd, Maryland Heights MO 63043	314-432-1636	R	18*	.1
33	Pacific Office Furnishings—*John Stirek*	421 SW 2nd Ave, Portland OR 97204	503-242-4200	R	18*	<.1
34	Officemate International Corp—*Shwu Chen*	PO Box 6680, Edison NJ 08818	732-225-7422	R	17*	.1
35	Yasutomo and Company Inc—*Daniel Egusa*	490 Eccles Ave, South San Francisco CA 94080	650-737-8888	R	17*	<.1
36	Kpaul Properties LLC—*Kevin Paul*	5701 Fortune Circle S, Indianapolis IN 46241	317-270-9501	R	16	.1
37	Hospital Forms and Systems Corp—*Peter Pyhrr*	8900 Ambassador Row, Dallas TX 75247	214-634-8900	R	15*	.1
38	Johnson/Anderson and Associates Inc—*Neil Johnson*	5010 Valley Industrial, Shakopee MN 55379	952-496-6699	R	14*	.1
39	Cliff Weil Inc—*Alvin B Hutzler II*	8043 Industrial Park R, Mechanicsville VA 23116	804-746-1321	R	14*	.1
40	Business Stationery LLC—*Bruce Andrews*	4944 Commerce Pkwy, Cleveland OH 44128	216-514-1277	R	14*	.1
41	Allied Envelope Company Inc—*Robert Royer*	PO Box 6506, Carlstadt NJ 07072	201-440-2000	R	12*	.1
42	American Office Machines Inc—*John Manzella*	PO Box 9429, Metairie LA 70055	504-833-1964	R	10*	<.1
43	Badger Graphics Systems Of Madison Inc—*Gene Davis*	1155 Wilburn Rd, Sun Prairie WI 53590	608-834-3400	R	9*	<.1
44	Printers and Stationers Inc—*Mike Johnson*	PO Box T, Florence AL 35631	256-764-8061	R	8*	.1
45	Zebra Pen Corp—*Clem Restaino*	242 Raritan Center Pkw, Edison NJ 08837	732-225-6310	S	8*	<.1
46	One Stop Shop—*Marx E Acosta-Rubio*	6800 Owensmouth Ave St, Canoga Park CA 91303		R	8*	<.1
47	Mayes Printing Co—*John Phelps*	PO Box 1952, Pensacola FL 32591	850-477-1111	R	8*	.1
48	Wright Business Graphics Of California Inc—*Gene Snitker*	13602 12th St Ste A, Chino CA 91710		R	7*	<.1
49	Odee Co—*James Tatom*	PO Box 550488, Dallas TX 75355	214-340-0415	R	7*	<.1
50	Formost Graphic Communications Inc—*James Feldman*	7564 Standish Pl Ste 1, Rockville MD 20855	301-424-4242	R	7*	<.1
51	Carter Paper and Packaging Inc—*Connie Elling*	PO Box 1349, Peoria IL 61654	309-637-7711	R	7*	<.1
52	Stewart Graphics Inc—*C Stewart*	PO Box 402, Sellersburg IN 47172	812-283-0455	R	6*	<.1
53	S Ruppe Inc—*Edward Ruppe*	PO Box 837, Rutherfordton NC 28139	828-287-4936	R	6*	<.1
54	Seiffert Office Products—*Tom Huldensouser*	3760 Airline Dr, Metairie LA 70001	504-598-4621	R	6*	<.1
55	All-Star Sales Inc—*Michael Seethler*	PO Box 5967, Jacksonville FL 32247	904-396-1653	R	6*	<.1
56	Tabco Business Forms Inc—*Thomas Bilyeu*	PO Box 3400, Terre Haute IN 47803	812-232-4660	R	5*	<.1
57	One Right Business Printing Inc—*Mark Hartnett*	PO Box 438, Lewiston ME 04243	207-784-2419	R	5*	<.1
58	Computer Products Corp—*Jim Volpenhein*	2106 Florence Ave, Cincinnati OH 45206	513-221-0600	R	5*	<.1
59	Advanced Data Capture Corp—*Robert Valleau*	9 Damonmill Sq Ste 1a, Concord MA 01742	978-287-5558	R	5*	<.1
60	Whitlock Business Systems Inc—*Lawrence Werner*	PO Box 71068, Madison Heights MI 48071	248-548-1040	R	5*	<.1
61	Professional Graphic Communications Inc—*Michael Weinzierl*	2260 Big Swckly Creek, Sewickley PA 15143	724-318-1222	R	5*	<.1
62	Brunswick Press Inc—*James Wickman*	9430 Baythorne Dr, Houston TX 77041	713-462-0600	R	4*	<.1
63	Ames Supply Co—*Robert Hildebrandt*	1936 University Ln Ste, Lisle IL 60532	630-964-2440	R	4*	<.1
64	Southern Cross Systems LLC—*Matt Ward*	PO Box 464, Woodstock GA 30188	770-591-5563	R	4*	<.1
65	Data Forms Inc—*Michael Emis*	947 N Main Ave, Fayetteville AR 72701	479-443-0099	R	4*	<.1
66	American Minority Business Forms Inc—*Diane Zavadil*	PO Box 337, Glenwood MN 56334		R	4*	<.1
67	Commercial Office Supply Inc—*John Lewis*	PO Box 1805, Woodinville WA 98072	425-485-6900	R	4*	<.1
68	Pride Products Distributor LLC	673 Morris Ave, Springfield NJ 07081	973-564-6300	R	4*	<.1
69	Story-Wright Inc—*Earl Story*	PO Box 900, Tyler TX 75710	903-595-1991	R	4*	<.1
70	American Binding Company Inc—*Calvin Barlow*	PO Box 829, Kaysville UT 84037	801-927-3020	R	4*	<.1
71	Eaton Forms Corp—*Richard Mullen*	2280 Arbor Blvd, Moraine OH 45439	937-298-3406	R	4*	<.1
72	Automation Graphics Inc—*Joseph Ringelstein*	460 W 34th St Lbby B, New York NY 10001	212-290-8400	R	4*	<.1
73	J Barbour Inc—*Jeffrey Barbour*	1009 Tuckerton Ct, Reading PA 19605	610-926-9850	R	4*	<.1
74	Forms Resource Inc—*George Crump*	10420 Baur Blvd, Saint Louis MO 63132	314-432-7888	R	4*	<.1
75	Topform Data Inc—*Willis Baker*	PO Box 15850, Rio Rancho NM 87174	505-891-9200	R	3*	<.1
76	United Graphics Of Louisville Inc—*Steve Siegwald*	PO Box 3945, Louisville KY 40201	502-584-2488	R	3*	<.1
77	Murray and Heister Inc—*Michael Boyle*	10101 Bacon Dr Ste H, Beltsville MD 20705	301-937-5980	R	3*	<.1
78	Express Printing and Forms Inc—*Russ Mercke*	105 Camille St, Lafayette LA 70503	337-988-0099	R	3*	<.1
79	Intermountain Business Forms Inc—*Jerry Cook*	PO Box 577, Centerville UT 84014	801-292-7971	R	3*	<.1
80	Diamond Business Graphics Inc—*Trent Hake*	PO Box 789, Sheboygan WI 53082	920-458-5595	R	3*	<.1
81	Mountain Advocate Media Inc—*Jay Nolan*	214 Knox St, Barbourville KY 40906	606-546-9225	R	3*	<.1
82	Kemske Paper Co—*James Wittenberg*	PO Box 817, New Ulm MN 56073	507-354-4141	R	3*	<.1
83	Arizona Business Forms Inc—*Scott Williams*	1655 W Drake Dr, Tempe AZ 85283	480-839-1440	R	3*	<.1
84	Dixie Art Supplies Inc—*Keith Marshall*	5005 Bloomfield St, New Orleans LA 70121	504-733-6509	R	3*	<.1
85	Mule-Durel Inc—*Sylvia Hingle*	5813 Plauche St, New Orleans LA 70123	504-733-5707	R	3*	<.1
86	Progressive Business Equipment Inc—*Gerald Clark*	11466 Schenk Dr, Maryland Heights MO 63043	314-298-2887	R	3*	<.1
87	Allan Brooks and Associates Inc—*Deborah Dunne*	413 Park Ave, Lake Villa IL 60046	847-353-5200	R	2*	<.1
88	Service Office Supply and Printing Inc—*Ray Cook*	PO Box 894, Flatwoods KY 41139	606-836-0488	R	2*	<.1
89	Give Something Back Inc—*Mike Hannigan*	7730 Pardee Ln, Oakland CA 94621		R	2*	<.1
90	Laser Line Inc—*Michael White*	2312 Willesden Green R, Toledo OH 43617	419-666-8288	R	2*	<.1
91	Anthony Business Forms Inc—*Katherine Harrah*	PO Box 24754, Dayton OH 45424	937-253-0072	R	2*	<.1
92	Bay Business Forms Inc—*Robert Troop*	1803 W Columbia St, Springfield OH 45504	937-322-3000	R	2*	<.1
93	Media Management And Magnetics Inc—*John Schimberg*	N93w14636 Whittaker Wa, Menomonee Falls WI 53051	262-251-5511	R	2*	<.1
94	Southern Graphics and Systems Inc—*Stan Weaver*	PO Box 818, Cordova TN 38088	901-345-5566	R	2*	<.1
95	Maleport's Sault Printing Company Inc—*Ronald Maleport*	PO Box 323, Sault Sainte Marie MI 49783	906-632-3369	R	2*	<.1
96	Waller Business Forms Inc—*Roger Green*	PO Box 37188, Pensacola FL 32526	850-479-6213	R	1*	<.1
97	Central New York Business Systems Inc—*Wendy Aiello*	502 Ct St Ste 205, Utica NY 13502		R	1*	<.1
98	Buckeye Business Forms Inc—*Ann Patton*	175 E Broadway Ave Ste, Westerville OH 43081	614-882-1890	R	1*	<.1
99	Harpel's Inc—*Richard Harpel*	720 Quentin Rd Ste 1, Lebanon PA 17042	717-272-6687	R	1*	<.1
100	Arya Corp—*Steve Sami*	PO Box 8066, Falls Church VA 22041	703-845-0800	R	1*	<.1

TOTALS: SIC 5112 Stationery & Office Supplies
Companies: 100 — 13,887 — 26.3

5113 Industrial & Personal Service Paper

1	United Stationers Supply Co—*Richard W Gochnauer*	1 Pky North Blvd Ste 1, Deerfield IL 60015	847-627-7000	R	4,832	6.0
2	Central National-Gottesman Inc—*Kenneth L Wallach*	3 Manhattanville Rd, Purchase NY 10577	914-696-9000	R	3,150*	1.1
3	Bunzl Distribution USA—*Patrick Larmon*	701 Emerson Rd Ste 500, Saint Louis MO 63141	314-997-5959	S	1,750*	3.5
4	Associated Packaging Technologies Inc—*Mark Staton*	1 Dickinson Dr Ste 100, Chadds Ford PA 19317	484-785-1120	S	464*	.5
5	Soporcel North America Inc—*Scott Barnard*	40 Richards Ave, Norwalk CT 06854	203-838-5027	R	170*	<.1
6	Dacotah Paper Co—*Matthew Mohr*	3940 15th Ave NW, Fargo ND 58108	701-281-1734	R	138*	.2
7	International Forest Products Corp—*Daniel Moore*	1 Patriot Pl, Foxboro MA 02035	508-698-4600	R	134*	.2
8	M Conley Co—*Richard D Conley*	1312 4th St SE, Canton OH 44707	330-456-8243	R	121*	.1
9	Acme Paper and Supply Company Inc—*Ronald Atman*	PO Box 422, Savage MD 20763	410-792-2333	R	104*	.2
10	Heritage Paper Company Inc—*Robert F Purser Sr*	4011 Morton St, Jacksonville FL 32217	904-737-6603	R	95*	.1
11	Piedmont National Corp—*Gary Marx*	1561 Southland Cir, Atlanta GA 30318	404-351-6130	R	82*	.1
12	Bunzl New Jersey Inc	PO Box 668, Dayton NJ 08810	314-997-5959	D	80*	.3

Rank	Company Name—*Executive Officer*	Address, City, State, Zip	Phone	Type	Fin	Empls
	Bunzl Distribution USA					
13	Calpine Containers Inc—*Walter Tindell*	9499 N Fort Washington, Fresno CA 93730	559-519-7199	R	74*	.2
14	Gem State Paper and Supply Co—*John Anderson*	1801 Highland Ave E, Twin Falls ID 83301	208-733-6081	R	68*	.1
15	Joseph Weil and Sons Inc—*Joseph P Weil*	825 E 26th St, La Grange Park IL 60526	708-579-9585	R	63*	.1
16	Alsco Inc—*Kevin Steiner*	505 E South Temple, Salt Lake City UT 84102	801-328-8831	R	63*	.1
17	K Yamada Distributors Ltd—*Dexter Yamada*	PO Box 29669, Honolulu HI 96820	808-836-3221	R	62*	.1
18	Pacific Packaging Products Inc—*Robert Goldstein*	PO Box 697, Wilmington MA 01887	978-657-9100	R	60*	.2
19	Michael Lewis Co—*Craig Simon*	8900 W 50th St, Mc Cook IL 60525	708-688-2200	R	57*	.3
20	Ernest Packaging Solution—*Timothy G Wilson*	5777 Smithway St, Commerce CA 90040	323-583-6561	R	57*	.2
21	Packaging Concepts Inc—*John Irace*	9832 Evergreen Industr, Saint Louis MO 63123	314-329-9700	R	54*	.3
22	Mooney General Paper Co—*Gary Riemer*	1451 Chestnut Ave, Hillside NJ 07205	973-926-3800	R	49*	.1
23	Maxco Supply Inc—*Max Flaming*	PO Box 814, Parlier CA 93648	559-646-6700	R	45*	.2
24	Paper Products Company Inc—*Dan Lackner*	36 Terminal Way, Pittsburgh PA 15219	412-481-6200	R	45*	.1
25	S Freedman and Sons Inc—*Mark Freedman*	PO Box 1418, Landover MD 20785	301-322-5000	R	45*	.1
26	Elkay Plastics Company Inc—*Louis Chertkow*	PO Box 910968, Los Angeles CA 90091	323-722-7073	R	41*	.2
27	Paper Mart—*Rosemary Martin*	92865-3104, Orange CA 92865	323-726-8200	R	40*	.1
28	Shippers Supply Corp	2428 Crittenden Dr, Louisville KY 40217	502-634-2800	R	40*	.1
29	Leon Korol Co—*Steve Korol*	2050 E Devon Ave, Elk Grove Village IL 60007	847-956-1616	R	37*	.1
30	Garland C Norris Co—*Jimmy King*	PO Box 28, Apex NC 27502	919-387-1059	R	35*	.1
31	Pollock Investments Inc—*Lawrence Pollock*	PO Box 660005, Dallas TX 75266	972-263-2126	R	34*	.5
32	Forman Inc—*JJ Mucha*	2036 Lord Baltimore Dr, Windsor Mill MD 21244	410-298-7500	R	34*	.1
33	Morrisette Paper Company Inc—*William Morrisette*	PO Box 20768, Greensboro NC 27420	336-375-1515	R	34*	.2
34	Unger Co—*Gerald Unger*	12401 Berea Rd, Cleveland OH 44111	216-252-1400	R	33*	<.1
35	Schwarz Paper Co—*Christopher Donnelly*	PO Box 1239, Morton Grove IL 60053	847-966-2550	R	26*	.4
36	Cottingham Paper Co—*Richard S Cottingham*	PO Box 163579, Columbus OH 43216	614-294-6444	S	25*	.1
37	M and R International Inc—*Pedro Belez*	200 Connecticut Ave, Norwalk CT 06854		R	25*	<.1
38	Holt Paper And Chemical Company Inc—*John Holt*	PO Box 3197, Salisbury MD 21802	410-742-7577	R	24*	.1
39	Huff United Paper Co Huff United	4101 Sarellen Rd, Richmond VA 23231	804-226-1936	S	20*	<.1
40	Office Paper Systems Inc—*Ronald Anderson*	7650 Airpark Rd, Gaithersburg MD 20879	301-948-6301	R	20*	.1
41	Vincent Porcaro Inc—*Vincent Porcaro*	PO Box 40220, Providence RI 02940	401-521-6262	R	20*	.1
42	Central Bag Co—*Christopher Klimek*	PO Box 37, Lansing KS 66043	913-250-0325	R	20*	<.1
43	Mansfield Paper Company Inc—*Michael Shapiro*	PO Box 1070, West Springfield MA 01090	413-781-2000	R	17*	.1
44	Baumann Paper Company Inc—*FW Baumann Jr*	PO Box 13022, Lexington KY 40583	859-252-8891	R	17*	.1
45	Runge Paper Company Inc—*Richard Benhart*	2201 Arthur Ave, Elk Grove Village IL 60007	847-593-1788	R	17*	.1
46	Canusa Corp—*Bruce Flemming*	1616 Shakespeare St, Baltimore MD 21231	410-522-0110	R	17*	<.1
47	Queen City Paper Co	PO Box 175708, Covington KY 41017		R	17*	<.1
48	Qualis International Inc—*Kathleen M Gardarian*	23252 Arroyo Vista, Rancho Santa Margarita CA 92688	949-766-6133	R	15	<.1
49	Pkgingcom—*Larry Lackey*	5133 W 66th St, Chicago IL 60638	708-458-7711	R	15*	<.1
50	Mark Anderson And Associates Inc—*Mark Anderson*	PO Box 39, Spring Valley WI 54767	715-778-5822	R	15*	.1
51	C and G Containers Inc—*Gale Breaux*	PO Box 2003, Lafayette LA 70502	337-237-7123	R	13*	.1
52	Textape Inc—*Van Scott*	PO Box 370240, El Paso TX 79937	915-595-1525	R	13*	.1
53	Hollymatic Corp—*James Azzar*	600 E Plainfield Rd, Countryside IL 60525	708-579-3700	R	13*	.1
54	Hudson Paper Co—*Richard Wilk*	1341 W Broad St Ste 4, Stratford CT 06615	203-378-0123	R	12*	<.1
55	Bernard Klein Inc—*Peter Mollo*	PO Box 696, Yonkers NY 10702	914-968-2222	R	12*	<.1
56	American Paper and Supply Co—*Larry Shapiro*	10 Industrial Rd, Carlstadt NJ 07072	201-939-4200	R	10*	<.1
57	St Louis Paper and Box Co—*Robert M Mayer*	PO Box 8260, Saint Louis MO 63156	314-531-7900	R	10*	<.1
58	Foley Distributing Corp—*Mark Foley*	PO Box 99, Rutland VT 05702	802-773-3738	R	9*	<.1
59	Hyman Paper Company Inc—*Robert Hyman*	PO Box 5388, Florence SC 29502	843-395-0215	R	8*	<.1
60	Automatic Bakery Machine Inc—*Omar Aguirre*	2750 S Harbor Blvd Ste, Santa Ana CA 92704	714-540-0994	R	8*	<.1
61	Harris Restaurant Supply Inc—*Anthony Lanza*	25 Abendroth Ave, Port Chester NY 10573	914-937-0404	R	6*	<.1
62	Cox Paper and Printing Company Inc—*Robert Gant*	1160 Carter Rd, Owensboro KY 42301	270-684-1436	R	5*	<.1
63	Advance Paper Co—*Paul Wildenberg*	PO Box 72637, Chattanooga TN 37407	423-622-5126	R	5*	<.1
64	Packaging Distribution Services Inc—*David Lettween*	PO Box 1284, Des Moines IA 50305	515-243-3156	R	5*	<.1
65	Beck Packaging Corp—*David Fredrick*	PO Box 20250, Lehigh Valley PA 18002	610-264-0551	R	5*	<.1
66	Laser Concepts Inc—*Rich Yosha*	6901 W 117th Ave Ste 4, Broomfield CO 80020	303-466-0900	R	5*	<.1
67	Oliner Fibre Company Inc—*Alan Oliner*	2391 Vauxhall Rd, Union NJ 07083	908-688-5800	R	5*	<.1
68	Goff Investment Group LLC—*Adrianne Casey*	980 Lincoln Ave Ste 20, San Rafael CA 94901	415-456-2934	R	4*	<.1
69	AJ Schrafel Paper Corp—*Richard Schrafel*	PO Box 20788, Floral Park NY 11002	516-437-1700	R	4*	<.1
70	Giacona Container Co—*Corrado Giacona*	121 Industrial Ave, New Orleans LA 70121	504-835-5465	R	2*	<.1
71	Packaging Pioneers Inc—*Arthur Lewis*	157 Fisher Ave, Eastchester NY 10709	914-779-6900	R	2*	<.1
72	Shore Manufacturing Co—*William Loughran*	PO Box 214, Manasquan NJ 08736	570-779-4042	R	1*	<.1
73	Huff United—*Paul Burns*	10 Creek Pky, Marcus Hook PA 19061	610-497-5100	R	N/A	.1

TOTALS: SIC 5113 Industrial & Personal Service Paper
Companies: 73   12,656   16.9

5122 Drugs, Proprietaries & Sundries

Rank	Company Name—*Executive Officer*	Address, City, State, Zip	Phone	Type	Fin	Empls
1	McKesson Corp—*John H Hammergren*	1 Post St, San Francisco CA 94104	415-983-8300	P	112,084	36.4
2	AmerisourceBergen Corp—*Steven H Collis*	PO Box 959, Valley Forge PA 19482	610-727-7000	P	80,218	9.4
3	Cardinal Distribution LP—*Kerry Clark*	7000 Cardinal Pl, Dublin OH 43017	614-757-5000	S	37,950*	55.0
4	Omnicare Inc—*John G Figueroa*	1600 RiverCenter II 10, Covington KY 41011	859-392-3300	P	6,183	14.6
5	Kinray Inc—*Stewart Rahr*	152-35 10th Ave Ste 15, Whitestone NY 11357	718-767-1234	R	4,400*	1.0
6	Novo Nordisk Inc—*Jerzy Gruhn*	100 College Rd W, Princeton NJ 08540	609-987-5800	S	3,306*	4.0
7	Anda Inc	2915 Weston Rd, Weston FL 33331		R	2,509*	.5
8	PharMerica Corp—*Gregory S Weishar*	1901 Campus Pl, Louisville KY 40299	502-627-7000	P	2,081	5.9
9	WA Butler Co—*Kevin Vasquez*	5600 Blazer Pky, Dublin OH 43017	614-761-9095	R	1,928*	2.5
10	Quality King Distributors Inc—*Glenn Nussdorf*	2060 9th Ave, Ronkonkoma NY 11779	631-737-5555	R	1,894*	.7
11	Nu Skin International Inc—*Scott E Schwerdt* Nu Skin Enterprises Inc	75 W Center St, Provo UT 84601		S	1,633*	1.6
12	Nu Skin Enterprises Inc—*M Truman Hunt*	75 W Center, Provo UT 84601		P	1,537	3.4
13	Ulta Salon Cosmetics and Fragrance Inc—*Chuck Ruin*	1000 Remington Blvd St, Bolingbrook IL 60440	630-410-4800	P	1,455	11.7
14	Kinney Drugs Inc—*Craig Painter*	520 E Main St, Gouverneur NY 13642	315-287-3600	R	1,395*	1.7
15	BuyCostumescom—*Jalem Getz*	5915 S Moorland Rd, New Berlin WI 53151	262-901-2300	R	1,233*	1.0
16	Marietta Corp—*Donald W Sturdivant*	PO Box 5250, Cortland NY 13045	607-753-6746	R	1,193*	1.2
17	Qualitest Pharmaceuticals Inc—*Mark Fletchor*	130 Vintage Dr NE, Huntsville AL 35811	256-859-4011	S	1,016*	.6
18	HD Smith Wholesale Drug Co—*Henry D Smith Jr*	3063 Fiat Ave, Springfield IL 62703	217-753-1688	R	883*	.8
19	F Dohmen Co—*Cynthia LaConte*	215 N Water St, Milwaukee WI 53202	414-299-4900	R	821*	.3
20	Bellco Drug Corp—*Neal Goldstein*	5500 New Horizons Blvd, Amityville NY 11701	631-789-6900	S	775	.2
21	Darby Group Companies Inc—*Carl Ashkin*	300 Jericho Quadrangle, Jericho NY 11753	516-683-1800	R	670*	1.4

Note: An asterisk (*) indicates an estimated financial figure. The company type code used is as follows: R = Private, P = Public, S = Private Subsidiary, B = Public Subsidiary, D = Division, J = Joint Venture, I = Investment Fund.

COMPANY RANKINGS BY SALES WITHIN 4-DIGIT SIC

Rank	Company Name—Executive Officer	Address, City, State, Zip	Phone	Type	Fin	Empls
22	JM Smith Corp—Tammy Devine	PO Box 1779, Spartanburg SC 29304	864-582-1216	R	600*	1.1
23	Rexall Sundown Inc	90 Orvile Dr, Bohemia NY 11716	561-241-9400	S	531*	1.3
24	Imperial Distributors Inc—Michael Sleeper	33 Sword St, Auburn MA 01501	508-756-5156	R	499*	.7
25	AmeriSource Corp (Paducah Kentucky) AmerisourceBergen Corp	PO Box 330, Paducah KY 42001	270-444-7300	D	453*	.3
26	Lupin Pharmaceuticals Inc—Vinita Gupta	111 S Calvert St 21st, Baltimore MD 21202		S	352*	.3
27	Clarins USA Inc—Jonathan Zrihen	110 E 59th St, New York NY 10022	212-980-1880	R	347*	.4
28	Allion Healthcare Inc—Bill Jones	1660 Walt Whitman Rd S, Melville NY 11747	631-547-6520	P	341	.2
29	Frontier Natural Products Co-Op—Tony Bedard	PO Box 299, Norway IA 52318	319-227-7996	R	255*	.2
30	Knight Distributing Company Inc—Gary Rice	1625 Lakes Pkwy Ste G, Lawrenceville GA 30043		R	246*	.1
31	Airborne Health—Martha A Morfitt	800 Washington Ave N S, Minneapolis MN 55401		R	186*	<.1
32	Bdi Pharma Inc—Edward Stiefel	120 Research Dr, Columbia SC 29203	803-732-1018	R	161*	.1
33	Cesar Castillo Inc—Jose Castillo	PO Box 191149, San Juan PR 00919	787-999-1616	R	156*	.5
34	BMP Sunstone Corp—David (Xiao Ying) Gao	600 W Germantown Pke S, Plymouth Meeting PA 19462	610-940-1675	P	147	1.2
35	BSN Inc—Chris Ferguson	5901 Broken Sound Pkwy, Boca Raton FL 33487	561-994-8335	R	138*	.1
36	Fruit Of The Earth Inc—Thomas Mccurry	3101 High River Rd Ste, Fort Worth TX 76155	817-510-1600	R	130*	.1
37	Diamond Drugs Inc—Joan Zilner	645 Kolter Dr, Indiana PA 15701	724-349-1111	R	121*	.5
38	North Carolina Mutual Wholesale Drug Co—David Moody	PO Box 411, Durham NC 27702	919-596-2151	R	111*	.1
39	Parfums de Coeur Ltd—Mark Laracy	85 Old Kings Hwy N, Darien CT 06820	203-655-8807	R	110*	<.1
40	Richards Products Inc—Scott Greff	1461 SW 32nd Ave, Pompano Beach FL 33069	954-978-0313	R	97*	<.1
41	Sunrx Inc—Timothy Liebmann	815 East Gate Dr Ste 1, Mount Laurel NJ 08054	856-910-7776	R	86*	<.1
42	Mason Distributors—Sonia Rodriquez	15750 NW 59th Ave, Miami Lakes FL 33014	305-624-5557	R	83*	.1
43	ParMed Pharmaceuticals Inc—Daniel H Movens	4220 Hyde Park Blvd, Niagara Falls NY 14305		S	81*	.1
44	Shire Us Inc—Matt Emmens	725 Chesterbrook Blvd, Chesterbrook PA 19087	484-595-8800	R	81*	1.2
45	Reliv' International Inc—Robert L Montgomery	136 Chesterfield Indus, Chesterfield MO 63005	636-537-9715	P	79	.2
46	SST Corp—D Gary Vassallo	PO Box 1649, Clifton NJ 07012	973-473-4300	R	75*	<.1
47	Miami-Luken Inc—Anthony Rattini	265 S Pioneer Blvd, Springboro OH 45066	937-743-7775	R	73*	.1
48	ivpcare Inc—Rebecca M Shanahan	7164 Technology Dr Ste, Frisco TX 75034	214-387-3500	R	68*	.1
49	Florida Infusion Services Inc—Rudy Ciccarello	1053 Progress Ct, Palm Harbor FL 34683		R	61*	<.1
50	Model Imperial Fine Fragrances Inc—Harold Ickovics Quality King Distributors Inc	1061 SW 30th Ave, Deerfield Beach FL 33442	954-418-0097	S	56*	.1
51	Oceana Therapeutics Inc—John T Spitznagel	2035 Lincoln Hwy, Edison NJ 08817	732-318-3800	R	56*	<.1
52	DAVA Pharmaceuticals Inc—John H Klein	400 Kelby St 10th Fl, Fort Lee NJ 07024	201-947-7442	R	53*	<.1
53	PMSI Inc—Eileen Aven AmerisourceBergen Corp	175 Kelsey Ln, Tampa FL 33619	813-626-7788	S	52*	.4
54	Bluebonnet Nutrition Corp—Gary Barrows	12915 Dairy Ashford Rd, Sugar Land TX 77478	281-240-3332	R	50*	.1
55	Genetco Inc—Carol Reinbold	711 Union Pky, Ronkonkoma NY 11779		R	49*	<.1
56	ITG-MEDEV Inc—Alan Dishman	PO Box 320297, San Francisco CA 94132	415-753-9989	R	49*	<.1
57	Golden Neo-Life Diamite International LLC—Roget Uys	PO Box 5012, Fremont CA 94537	510-651-0405	R	43*	.6
58	WF Young Inc—Tyler F Young	302 Benton Dr, East Longmeadow MA 01028	413-526-9999	R	42*	<.1
59	QK Healthcare Inc—Glenn Nussdorf Quality King Distributors Inc	2060 9th Ave, Ronkonkoma NY 11779	631-439-2000	S	36*	.1
60	Pola USA Inc	251 E Victoria St, Carson CA 90746		R	35*	<.1
61	American International Industries—Theresa Cooper	2220 Gaspar Ave, Commerce CA 90040	323-728-2999	R	35*	.7
62	Seacoast Medical LLC—Micheal Hodgkins	13423 Lynam Dr, Omaha NE 68138	402-593-1360	R	34*	<.1
63	Cardinal Pharmaceuticals Inc—Primo Cabral	12035 E Burke St Ste 9, Santa Fe Springs CA 90670	562-696-1954	R	33*	<.1
64	Color Me Beautiful Inc—Steve Di Antonio	7000 Infantry Ridge Rd, Manassas VA 20109	703-471-6400	R	31*	<.1
65	Sportika Export Inc—Richard K White	83 White Oak Dr, Berlin CT 06037	860-828-9000	R	28*	<.1
66	Fragrance International Inc—Brad Levy	398 E Rayen Ave, Youngstown OH 44505	330-747-3341	R	25*	<.1
67	STAT Pharmaceuticals Inc	9545 Pathway St, Santee CA 92071	619-956-4200	R	25*	<.1
68	J R Carlson Laboratories Inc—John Carlson	15 W College Dr, Arlington Heights IL 60004	847-255-1600	R	25*	.1
69	Mechanical Servants Inc—David Baum	2755 Thomas St, Melrose Park IL 60160	708-486-1500	R	25*	<.1
70	Proxycare Inc—Luis Cruz	4700 SW 51st St Ste 21, Fort Lauderdale FL 33314	954-791-5400	S	20*	<.1
71	Robert J Matthews Co—J Matthews	2780 Richville Dr Se, Massillon OH 44646	330-834-3000	R	20*	.1
72	Now Foods—Al Powers	395 S Glen Ellyn Rd, Bloomingdale IL 60108	630-545-9098	R	19*	<.1
73	Armstrong McCall—John Golliher	PO Box 17068, Austin TX 78760	512-444-1757	R	17*	.1
74	Edom Laboratories Inc—Eric Pollack	100 E Jeffryn Blvd Ste, Deer Park NY 11729	631-586-2266	R	17*	<.1
75	Sigma-Tau Pharmaceuticals Inc—Gregg Lapointe	9841 Washingtonian Blv, Gaithersburg MD 20878	301-948-1041	R	17*	.1
76	Allergy Research Group Inc—Stephen Levine	2300 N Loop Rd, Alameda CA 94502	510-263-2000	S	15*	<.1
77	Pound International Corp—David Racklin	800 Brickell Ave, Miami FL 33131	305-530-8702	R	15*	<.1
78	Philosophy Inc—Cristina Carlino	3809 E Watkins St, Phoenix AZ 85034	602-794-8500	R	15*	.1
79	Pacific Nutritional Inc—Chris Taylor	PO Box 820829, Vancouver WA 98682	360-253-3197	R	15*	.1
80	Weleda Inc—Jasper Brakel	1 Closter Rd, Palisades NY 10964	845-268-8599	R	14*	<.1
81	Westbrook Pharmaceutical and Surgical Supply Co—Raymond Westbrook	1910 Cochran Rd, Pittsburgh PA 15220	412-561-6532	R	14*	<.1
82	Adh Health Products Inc—Balram Advani	PO Box 420, Congers NY 10920	845-268-0027	R	13*	.1
83	Xymogen—Brian Blackburn	725 S Kirkman Rd, Orlando FL 32811	407-445-0203	R	12*	.1
84	LEK Pharmaceutical Inc	115 N 3rd St Ste 301, Wilmington NC 28401	910-362-0021	S	12*	<.1
85	Savmart Pharmaceutical Services Inc—Phil Rushing	3545 Midway Dr Ste A, San Diego CA 92110	619-223-9094	R	12*	<.1
86	Gulf Coast Pharmaceuticals Inc—Kenneth Ritchey	995 N Halstead Rd, Ocean Springs MS 39564	228-875-5595	R	12*	<.1
87	Lotus Light Inc—Santosh Krisky	PO Box 1008, Silver Lake WI 53170	262-889-8501	R	11*	.1
88	Midlothian Laboratories—Bryce Harvey	780 Industrial Park Bl, Montgomery AL 36117	334-288-8661	R	11*	<.1
89	Star Nail Products Inc—Anthony Cuccio	29120 Ave Paine, Santa Clarita CA 91355	661-257-7827	R	10*	.1
90	Medisca Inc—Antonio Santos	PO Box 2592, Plattsburgh NY 12901	518-563-4636	R	10*	.1
91	Tri Medica International Inc—Joseph Christy	1895 S Los Feliz Dr, Tempe AZ 85281	480-998-1041	R	8*	.1
92	RG Shakour Inc—Renee Shakour	254 Turnpike Rd Rte 9, Westboro MA 01581	508-870-9571	R	8*	.1
93	HPF LLC—Blaine Applegate	PO Box 1311, Morrisville PA 19067	215-321-8170	R	8*	<.1
94	Keystone Pharmaceuticals Inc—Floyd Benjamin	26072 Merit Cir Ste 10, Laguna Hills CA 92653	949-348-7770	R	8*	<.1
95	Deodorant Stones of America—LW Morris	9420 E Doubletree Ranc, Scottsdale AZ 85258	480-451-4981	R	8*	<.1
96	Beehive Botanicals Inc—Linda Graham	16297 W Nursery Rd, Hayward WI 54843	715-634-4274	R	7*	<.1
97	Flamingo Discount Sales Inc—Jose Goyanes	8275 Nw 36th St, Doral FL 33166	305-591-8373	R	6*	<.1
98	French Transit Ltd—Jerry Rosenblatt	398 Beach Rd, Burlingame CA 94010	650-548-9600	R	6*	<.1
99	Cosmetic Imports International Corp—Hiro Kotchounian	2330 State Rte 11, Mooers NY 12958		R	6*	<.1
100	Audrey Morris Cosmetics International Incorpora—Wayne Morris	1501 Green Rd Ste J, Pompano Beach FL 33064	954-332-2000	R	6*	<.1
101	Reviva Labs Inc—Stephen Strassler	705 Hopkins Rd, Haddonfield NJ 08033	856-428-3885	R	5*	<.1
102	Basic Drugs Inc—Nancy Green	PO Box 412, Vandalia OH 45377	937-898-4010	R	5*	<.1
103	Mid States Paper/Notion Co—Mike Crecelius	810 Cherokee Ave, Nashville TN 37207	615-226-1234	R	5*	<.1
104	Nicole and Andre Pharmaceutical Inc—Odette Khalil	9209 Colima Rd Ste 110, Whittier CA 90605	562-789-5852	R	5*	<.1
105	Quantum Inc—Eve Clure	PO Box 2791, Eugene OR 97402	541-345-5556	R	4*	<.1

Rank	Company Name—*Executive Officer*	Address, City, State, Zip	Phone	Type	Fin	Empls
106	Accurate Chemical and Scientific Corp—*Rudolph Rosenberg*	300 Shames Dr, Westbury NY 11590	516-333-2221	R	4*	<.1
107	Generic Distributors Inc—*Don Couvillon*	1611 Olive St, Monroe LA 71201	318-388-8850	R	4*	<.1
108	Apotheca Inc—*Mitchell Herseth*	1622 N 16th St, Phoenix AZ 85006	602-252-5244	R	4*	<.1
109	Parnell Pharmaceuticals Inc—*Francis Parnell*	PO Box 5130, Larkspur CA 94977	415-256-1800	R	4*	<.1
110	Jace Pharmaceutical Inc—*Franklin Medina*	42 Farview Terr, Paramus NJ 07652	201-226-0601	R	4*	<.1
111	Health Plus Pharmacy Inc—*Dana Nelson*	948 E Foothill Blvd St, San Luis Obispo CA 93405	805-543-5950	R	4*	<.1
112	Helm New York Inc—*Philipp Mangold*	1110 Centennial Ave St, Piscataway NJ 08854	732-981-1160	R	4*	<.1
113	Pharmaceutical Corporation Of America—*Marshall Knieser*	6210 Technology Ctr Dr, Indianapolis IN 46278	317-616-4500	R	3*	<.1
114	Nutrition International Inc—*Robert Lin*	PO Box 50632, Irvine CA 92619	949-854-4855	R	3*	.2
115	Morgan and Sampson USA—*Tom Paalman*	11155 Dana Cir, Cypress CA 90630	714-894-0646	R	3*	<.1
116	JF Lazartigue Inc—*JF Lazartigue*	764 Madison Ave 2nd Fl, New York NY 10021	212-288-2250	R	3*	<.1
117	Wendt Pharmaceuticals Inc—*Harley Blattner*	PO Box 128, Belle Plaine MN 56011	952-873-2288	R	3*	<.1
118	Blankinship Distributors Inc—*G Lawrence Blankinship*	1905 Vine St, Kansas City MO 64108	816-842-6825	R	3*	<.1
119	Aloe Gator Suncare Co—*James D Tehan*	4871 Sharp St, Dallas TX 75247		R	3*	<.1
120	Designer Diagnostics Inc—*Neil Roth*	1930 Village Center Ci, Las Vegas NV 89134	702-233-4804	S	3*	<.1
121	Nectar Pharmaceuticals Inc	25574 Rye Canyon Rd Un, Valencia CA 91355	661-775-1424	R	3*	<.1
122	Reese Pharmaceutical Co—*George W Reese III*	PO Box 1957, Cleveland OH 44106	216-231-6441	R	2*	<.1
123	Action Labs Inc (Placentia California)—*James R Bailey*	2915 E Ricker Way, Anaheim CA 92806	714-630-5941	R	2*	<.1
124	Nest Group Inc—*Amos Heckendorf*	45 Valley Rd, Southborough MA 01772	508-481-6223	R	2*	<.1
125	Hillestad Pharmaceuticals Inc—*Donald Hillestad*	PO Box 1700, Woodruff WI 54568	715-358-2113	R	1	N/A
126	Harvard Drug Group LLC—*Terry Haas*	31778 Enterprise Dr, Livonia MI 48150	734-525-8700	R	1	.4
127	Elite Impex—*Ajit Patel*	PO Box 412, Metuchen NJ 08840	732-906-6637	R	1*	<.1
128	Gemini Cosmetics—*Martha Manha*	1430 Greg St Ste 234, Sparks NV 89431	775-359-3663	R	1*	<.1
129	Martec USA LLC—*Jim Kendel*	9229 Ward Park Ln Ste, Kansas City MO 64114	816-241-4144	R	1*	<.1
130	Marani Brands Inc—*Margrit Eyraud*	13152 Raymer St Ste 1A, North Hollywood CA 91605	818-503-5200	P	<1	<.1
131	Next Pharmaceuticals—*Charles I Kosmont*	360 Espinosa Rd, Salinas CA 93907	831-621-8712	R	<1	<.1
132	Bond Drug Company of Illinois—*Greg D Wasson*	200 Wilmot Rd, Deerfield IL 60015	847-914-2500	S	N/A	6.0
133	Walgreen Arizona Drug Co—*Greg D Wasson*	200 Wilmot Rd, Deerfield IL 60015	847-914-2500	S	N/A	6.0

TOTALS: SIC 5122 Drugs, Proprietaries & Sundries
     Companies: 133   272,071   179.6

5131 Piece Goods & Notions

Rank	Company Name—*Executive Officer*	Address, City, State, Zip	Phone	Type	Fin	Empls
1	Wallis Oil Co—*Lynn Wallis*	106 E Washington, Cuba MO 65453	573-885-2277	R	2,318*	.7
2	Robert Allon Fabrics Inc—*Jeffrey Cordover*	225 Foxboro Blvd, Foxboro MA 02035	508-851-6600	R	942*	.6
3	Daewoo International (America) Corp—*Seok Yoon*	300 Frank W Burr Blvd, Teaneck NJ 07666	201-591-8000	R	500*	<.1
4	Delta Apparel Inc—*Robert W Humphreys*	322 S Main St, Greenville SC 29601	864-232-5200	P	4/5	7.2
5	Barrow Industries Inc—*Stephen Y Barrow*	3 Edgewater Dr, Norwood MA 02062	781-440-2666	R	382*	.3
6	Standard Fiber LLC—*Dellon Chen*	323 Allerton Ave, South San Francisco CA 94080	650-872-6528	R	175*	.3
7	P Kaufman Inc—*Ronald Kaufman*	3 Park Ave, New York NY 10016	212-292-2200	R	150*	.2
8	L and R Distributors Inc—*Maurice Lucas*	9301 Ave D, Brooklyn NY 11236	718-927-2650	R	145*	.4
9	Lucerne Textiles Inc—*Douglas Rimsky*	519 8th Ave, New York NY 10018	212-563-7800	R	125*	.1
10	Jacobson Capital Services Inc—*Alvin Jacobson*	150 Croton Ave, Peekskill NY 10566	914-736-0600	R	122*	.1
11	FH Bonn Co—*Barbara Rossler*	PO Box 1888, Springfield OH 45501	937-323-7024	R	117*	.1
12	Peachtree Fabrics Inc—*Steve Dutson Jr*	1400 English St NW, Atlanta GA 30318	404-351-5400	R	116*	.1
13	EE Schenck Co—*Stanley G Gray*	6000 N Cutter Cir, Portland OR 97217	503-284-4124	R	96*	.1
14	ATD-American Co—*Janet Wischnia*	135 Greenwood Ave, Wyncote PA 19095	215-576-1380	R	91*	.1
15	Symphony Fabrics Corp—*Seymour D Schneiderman*	263 W 38th St, New York NY 10018	212-244-6700	R	85*	.1
16	Kaslen Textiles—*Jack Cook*	6099 Triangle Dr, Commerce CA 90040	323-588-7700	R	82*	.1
17	Schott International Inc—*John C Schott*	PO Box 7152, Akron OH 44306	330-773-7851	R	78*	.1
18	Threadtex Inc—*Kenneth Richman*	1350 6th Ave 10th Fl, New York NY 10019	212-713-1880	R	62*	<.1
19	Raytex Fabrics Inc—*Dan Reich*	130 Crossways Park Dr, Woodbury NY 11797	516-584-1111	R	60*	.1
20	Arthur Sanderson and Sons North America Ltd—*William Wagner*	285 Grand Ave Ste 3, Englewood NJ 07631	201-894-8400	R	52*	<.1
21	Shepherd Products Co—*Joel Shepherd III*	10211 M89, Richland MI 49083	269-629-8001	R	48*	<.1
22	Textile Import LLC—*Stuart Tell*	1410 Broadway 22nd Fl, New York NY 10018	212-354-2200	R	43*	<.1
23	Hoffman California Fabrics—*Philip Hoffman*	25792 Obrero Dr, Mission Viejo CA 92691	949-770-2922	R	42*	.1
24	C and F Enterprises—*Carol S Fang*	819 Blue Crab Rd, Newport News VA 23606	757-873-5688	R	40*	.1
25	Westgate Interiors LLC	418 Chandler Dr, Gaffney SC 29340		R	35*	<.1
26	Charter Fabrics Inc—*Robert Murello*	1430 Broadway, New York NY 10018	212-391-8110	R	34*	<.1
27	Loomcraft Textile and Supply Co—*Ronald Frankel*	2516 Industry Dr, Burlington NC 27215	336-222-0515	R	30*	.1
28	Beckenstein Men's Fabrics Inc—*Neal Boyarsky*	257 W 39th St, New York NY 10018	212-475-6666	R	29*	<.1
29	Keeper Corp—*Kenneth Porter*	6 Industrial Park Rd, North Windham CT 06256	860-456-4151	R	25*	.2
30	Acme Linen Co—*Samuel Bezonsky*	5136 E Triggs St, Commerce CA 90022	323-266-4000	R	25*	<.1
31	Saati Americas Corp—*Alberto Novarese*	247 Rte 100 Ste 123, Somers NY 10589	914-232-7781	R	21*	.1
32	J Robert Scott Inc—*Andrew Frumovitz*	500 N Oak St, Inglewood CA 90302	310-680-4300	R	20*	.1
33	Levcor International Inc—*Robert A Levison*	110 W 40th St, New York NY 10018	212-354-8500	R	19	.1
34	Jim Thompson Silk Co—*Mavis Cahoon*	1694 Chantilly Dr, Atlanta GA 30324	404-325-5004	R	18*	<.1
35	K and R Industries Inc—*Mark Eagen*	PO Box 220690, Chantilly VA 20153	703-631-4200	R	17*	<.1
36	Copland Industries Inc—*Jason Copeland*	PO Box 1208, Burlington NC 27216	336-226-0272	R	17*	.4
37	Aegean Apparel International Inc—*Mehmet Panayirci*	7900 Technology Blvd, Dayton OH 45424	937-531-6900	R	16*	<.1
38	Logantex Inc—*Matt Brennan*	6200 Corporate Park Dr, Browns Summit NC 27214		R	15*	<.1
39	Glick Textiles Inc—*George Levon*	2327 SW Fwy, Houston TX 77098	713-942-8585	R	15*	<.1
40	Kabat Textile Corp—*Arthur Adelman*	247 W 37th St 10th Fl, New York NY 10018	212-398-0011	R	15*	<.1
41	Merrimac Textile—*Stephen Barrow* Barrow Industries Inc	1303 Corporation Dr, Archdale NC 27263	781-440-2666	D	14*	<.1
42	Miroglio Textiles USA Inc—*Frank Iovino*	1430 Broadway Fl 6, New York NY 10018	212-382-2020	D	13*	<.1
43	Custom Labels Inc—*Richard Nicholson*	4924 Hazel Jones Rd, Bossier City LA 71111	318-747-7460	R	13*	<.1
44	Lamont Ltd—*Stephen Fausel*	PO Box 399, Burlington IA 52601	319-753-5131	R	11*	.1
45	Zabin Industries Inc—*Alan Faiola*	PO Box 15218, Los Angeles CA 90015	213-749-1215	R	11*	.1
46	Blumenthal-Lansing Company Inc—*Devi Shaheed* Levcor International Inc	1 Palmer Ter, Carlstadt NJ 07072	201-935-6220	S	10*	.1
47	Houles USA Inc—*Pierre Houles*	8687 Melrose Ave Ste 6, Los Angeles CA 90069	310-652-6171	R	8*	<.1
48	Twin Dragon Marketing Inc—*Dominic Poon*	14600 S Broadway, Gardena CA 90248	310-715-7070	R	8*	<.1
49	Exchange Center Of California Inc—*John Sison*	PO Box 224624, Dallas TX 75222	214-760-7435	H	6*	<.1
50	John Kaldor Fabricmaker USA Ltd—*John Kaldor*	469 7th Ave 12th Fl, New York NY 10018	212-629-9260	D	6*	<.1
51	Martha Pullen Company Inc—*Martha Pullen*	149 Old Big Cove Rd, Brownsboro AL 35741	256-533-9586	R	5*	<.1
52	Eurotextil Inc—*Leonardo Tirado*	307 W 38th St Ste 1412, New York NY 10018	212-221-5324	R	4*	<.1
53	Dana Labels Inc—*Harold Hanes*	1920 Colburn St, Honolulu HI 96819	808-845-3262	R	2*	<.1

Note: An asterisk (*) indicates an estimated financial figure. The company type code used is as follows: R = Private, P = Public, S = Private Subsidiary, B = Public Subsidiary, D = Division, J = Joint Venture, I = Investment Fund.

ANY RANKINGS BY SALES WITHIN 4-DIGIT SIC

Rank	Company Name—*Executive Officer*	Address, City, State, Zip	Phone	Type	Fin	Empls
54	Atlas Thread Gage Inc—*Doug Hamer*	30990 W 8 Mile Rd, Farmington Hills MI 48336	248-477-3230	R	1*	<.1

TOTALS: SIC 5131 Piece Goods & Notions
Companies: 54 — 6,810 — 12.5

5136 Men's/Boys' Clothing

Rank	Company Name—*Executive Officer*	Address, City, State, Zip	Phone	Type	Fin	Empls
1	Ralph Lauren Corp—*Ralph Lauren*	650 Madison Ave, New York NY 10022	212-318-7000	P	5,660	24.0
2	Broder Brothers Co—*Thomas Myers*	6 Neshaminy Interplex, Trevose PA 19053		R	635*	1.2
3	Nautica International Inc—*Richard Anders*	40 W 57th St, New York NY 10019	212-541-5757	S	234*	.2
4	Dorfman-Pacific Company Inc—*Douglas Highsmith*	2615 Boeing Way, Stockton CA 95206		R	102*	.2
5	Scope Imports Inc—*Allan Finkelman*	6300 W Loop S No 100, Bellaire TX 77401	713-688-0077	R	91*	.1
6	Ike Behar Apparel and Design Inc—*Isaac Behar*	13955 NW 60th Ave, Hialeah FL 33014	305-557-5212	R	60*	.2
7	Sportif USA Inc—*John Kirsch*	1415 Greg St Ste 101, Sparks NV 89431	775-359-6400	R	53*	1.0
8	Wise El Santo Company Inc—*Rudolph L Wise*	11000 Linpage Pl, Saint Louis MO 63132	314-428-3100	R	42*	.1
9	Carolina Made Inc—*Jim Cherry*	400 N Indian Trail Rd, Indian Trail NC 28079	704-821-6425	R	40*	.1
10	BUM International Inc—*Stephen Wayne*	42 New Orleans Rd Ste, Hilton Head Island SC 29928		R	38	.7
11	Hat World Corp—*Ken Kocher*	7555 Woodland Dr, Indianapolis IN 46278		S	32*	2.5
12	Keepers International—*Richard Greenberg*	PO Box 4027, Chatsworth CA 91313	818-882-5000	R	28*	.1
13	Swany America Corp—*Yeong C Son*	115 Corporate Dr, Johnstown NY 12095	518-725-3333	R	24*	<.1
14	Jim's Formal Wear Co—*Gary Davis*	PO Box 125, Trenton IL 62293	618-224-9211	R	22*	.3
15	Wayne D Enterprises Inc—*Jim Kirkman*	PO Box 41168, Houston TX 77241	713-896-0300	R	20*	.1
16	Soex West USA LLC—*Anne Guevara*	3294 E 26th St, Vernon CA 90058	323-264-8300	R	18*	.3
17	Ocean Pacific Apparel Corp	1450 Broadway 3rd Fl, New York NY 10018	212-730-0030	S	16*	<.1
18	Heyman Corp—*Lawrence Heyman*	375 N Fairway Dr, Vernon Hills IL 60061	847-247-0909	R	14*	.1
19	Surf Cowboy Inc—*Jeff Shafer*	1001 Main St Ste D, Vancouver WA 98660	360-694-8494	R	13*	<.1
20	Randa Accessories Leather Goods LLC—*Ralph Adams*	2009 W Hastings St, Chicago IL 60608	312-997-2358	R	10*	.1
21	Adidas Golf USA Inc—*Ric Long*	5545 Fermi Ct, Carlsbad CA 92008	760-918-6000	R	10*	<.1
22	Rome Street Apparel Inc—*David Hertzberg*	137 Rome St, Newark NJ 07105	973-466-0082	R	8*	.1
23	Key Industries Inc—*Chris Barnes*	PO Box 389, Fort Scott KS 66701	620-223-2000	R	8*	<.1
24	Image First Professional Apparel—*Joseph Berstein*	42 Lukens Dr Ste 100, New Castle DE 19720	302-656-2774	R	6*	<.1
25	Piramide Imports—*Thomas Fallon*	PO Box 246, Manitou Springs CO 80829	719-685-5912	R	6*	<.1
26	R and N Knitted Headwear Inc—*David Rochlitz*	544 Park Ave Ste 4, Brooklyn NY 11205	718-522-6990	R	3*	<.1
27	Sean John Clothing Inc	1710 Broadway, New York NY 10017	212-500-2200	S	3	.1

TOTALS: SIC 5136 Men's Boys' Clothing
Companies: 27 — 7,195 — 31.5

5137 Women's/Children's Clothing

Rank	Company Name—*Executive Officer*	Address, City, State, Zip	Phone	Type	Fin	Empls
1	BCBG Max Azria Group—*Max Azrie*	2761 Fruitland Ave, Vernon CA 90058	323-589-2224	R	250*	1.2
2	Magla Products LLC—*Andrew Groat*	PO Box 1934, Morristown NJ 07962	973-984-7998	R	229*	.1
3	Magic Kids and Co—*Issac Mizarhi*	8235 Remmet Ave, Canoga Park CA 91304	818-883-3900	R	193*	.3
4	Amerex Group Inc—*Ira Ganger*	512 7th Ave 9th Fl, New York NY 10018	212-609-3000	R	148*	.3
5	Gordon Brothers Wholesale LLC—*Michael Frieze*	101 Huntington Ave, Boston MA 02199		D	146*	.3
6	Spanx Inc—*Lara Ann Goldman*	3391 Peachtree Rd Ste, Atlanta GA 30326	404-321-1608	R	100*	.1
7	Lucy Activewear Inc—*Michael J Edwards*	222 SW Columbia St Ste, Portland OR 97201	503-228-2142	R	77*	.1
8	French Toast—*Samuel Gindi*	3003 Scarlett St Ste 2, Brunswick GA 31520		R	56*	.1
9	Spiegel Brands Inc	711 3rd Ave, New York NY 10017	212-986-2585	S	34*	.2
10	Echo Design Group Inc—*Dorothy Roberts*	10 E 40th St Fl 16, New York NY 10016	212-686-8771	R	34*	.2
11	Bepc Ltd—*Henry Fan*	5352 Irwindale Ave Ste, Irwindale CA 91706	626-804-2100	R	33*	.2
12	Caretek Inc—*Daniel Greene*	9911 E 47th Ave, Denver CO 80238	303-455-2800	R	30*	.1
13	Eveden Inc—*Tracy Lewis*	65 Sprague St Ste 22, Hyde Park MA 02136	617-361-7559	R	30*	.1
14	Sport Obermeyer Ltd—*Klaus Obermeyer*	115 Abc, Aspen CO 81611	970-925-5060	R	25*	.1
15	Topsville Inc—*Mark Nitzberg*	11800 NW 102nd Rd Ste, Medley FL 33178	305-883-8677	D	23*	.1
16	Hartwell Industries Inc—*Charles Sutlief*	PO Box 1399, Hartwell GA 30643	706-856-4900	R	22*	.1
17	Gator Of Florida Inc—*Frank Agliano*	PO Box 4207, Tampa FL 33677	813-877-8267	R	20*	.1
18	Jean Mart Inc—*Helen Yi*	6700 Avalon Blvd, Los Angeles CA 90003	323-752-7775	R	20*	.1
19	Kolonaki—*George Georgiou*	808 Brannan St, San Francisco CA 94103	415-554-8057	R	17*	.4
20	ModCloth Inc—*Eric Koger*	3011 Smallman St, Pittsburgh PA 15201	412-224-5525	R	16*	.1
21	Cabot Hosiery Mills Inc—*Marc Cabot*	PO Box 307, Northfield VT 05663	802-485-6066	R	14*	.1
22	M Foster Associates Inc—*Bonnye N Sherman*	PO Box 420468, Dallas TX 75342	214-631-7732	R	14*	.1
23	Cherry Stix Ltd—*Charles Gammal*	1407 Broadway Rm 1503, New York NY 10018	212-221-5100	R	11*	.1
24	Tyr Sport Inc—*Steve Furniss*	PO Box 1930, Huntington Beach CA 92647	714-897-0799	S	11*	.1
25	Harry J Rashti and Company Inc—*Michael Rashti*	1375 Broadway Fl 20, New York NY 10018	212-594-3733	R	9*	<.1
26	Bennett Jacalyn ES And Co—*Jacalyn Bennett*	45 Water St, Newburyport MA 01950	978-462-1966	R	9*	.1
27	Tea Collection—*Leigh Rawdon*	1 Arkansas St Ste B, San Francisco CA 94107	415-621-9400	R	6*	<.1
28	M and H Enterprises Inc—*Harvey Schiffres*	4200 N 29th Ave, Hollywood FL 33020	954-894-9494	R	5*	<.1
29	Accessory Exchange LLC	1 E 33rd St Fl 6, New York NY 10016	212-931-5000	R	4*	<.1
30	SwaddleDesigns LLC—*Lynette Damir*	4612 Union Bay Pl NE, Seattle WA 98105	206-579-0408	R	4*	<.1
31	Studio Imports Limited Inc—*Elisabeth Mantell*	2252 Hayes St, Hollywood FL 33020	954-920-6880	R	3*	<.1
32	Betmar Hats LLC—*Max Grossman*	411 5th Ave Fl 2, New York NY 10016	212-684-8080	S	3*	<.1
33	France Deco Trading Inc—*Bruno Zerdoun*	8100 Nw 29th St, Doral FL 33122	305-715-9066	R	3*	<.1
34	On Target Promotions—*Keith Schwartz*	18807 Miles Rd, Warrensville Heights OH 44128	216-581-9933	R	3*	<.1
35	Dee Pee Apparel Inc—*Larry Jones*	932 S Whitehall Cir, Florence SC 29501	843-346-5799	R	3*	<.1
36	Cortland Foundations LLC	PO Box 429, Cortland NY 13045	607-756-7566	R	2*	<.1

TOTALS: SIC 5137 Women's Children's Clothing
Companies: 36 — 1,606 — 4.7

5139 Footwear

Rank	Company Name—*Executive Officer*	Address, City, State, Zip	Phone	Type	Fin	Empls
1	Aerogroup International Inc	PO Box 1916, Edison NJ 08818	732-985-6900	R	600*	1.0
2	Birkenstock Footprint Sandals Inc—*Gene Kunde*	PO Box 6140, Novato CA 94948	415-892-4200	R	189*	.3
3	Hi-Tec Sports USA Inc	4801 Stoddard Rd, Modesto CA 95356	209-545-1111	S	188*	.5
4	Iconix Brand Group Inc—*Neil Cole*	1450 Broadway 3rd Fl, New York NY 10018	212-730-0030	P	141	.1
5	Elan-Polo International	2005 Walton Rd, Saint Louis MO 63114	314-655-3300	R	82*	.3
6	Jimlar Corp—*Jim Tarica*	160 Great Neck Rd, Great Neck NY 11021	516-829-1717	R	72	.1
7	Adidas America Inc—*Jim Stutts*	5055 N Greeley Ave, Portland OR 97217	971-234-2300	R	72*	1.0
8	Bostonian Shoe Co	156 Oak St, Newton Upper Falls MA 02464		S	70	<.1
9	Wolff Shoe Co—*Gary Wolff*	1705 Larkin Williams R, Fenton MO 63026	636-343-7170	R	63*	.1
10	Charles David Of California—*Charles Malka*	5731 Buckingham Pkwy, Culver City CA 90230	310-348-5050	R	35*	.2
11	D Myers and Sons Inc—*James M Ries*	4311 Erdman Ave, Baltimore MD 21213	410-522-7500	R	34*	<.1
12	Eastland Shoe Corp—*James Klein*	4 Meetinghouse Rd, Freeport ME 04032	207-865-6314	R	33*	.1
13	Universal Athletic Services Inc—*Larry Aasheim*	PO Box 1620, Bozeman MT 59771	406-587-1220	R	28*	.2

Rank	Company Name—*Executive Officer*	Address, City, State, Zip	Phone	Type	Fin	Empls
14	Cels Enterprises Inc—*Robert Goldman*	3485 S La Cienega Blvd, Los Angeles CA 90016	310-838-2103	R	23*	.1
15	Impo International Inc—*Erik Keeler*	PO Box 639, Santa Maria CA 93456	805-922-7753	R	19*	<.1
16	McCormick's Enterprises Inc—*Ernest Webb*	PO Box 577, Arlington Heights IL 60006	847-398-8680	R	19*	<.1
17	Dvs Shoe Company Inc—*Kevin Dunlap*	955 Francisco St, Torrance CA 90502	310-715-8300	R	19*	.1
18	Inter-Pacific Corp—*Frank Arnsteine*	2257 Colby Ave, Los Angeles CA 90064	310-473-7591	R	18*	<.1
19	Keen Inc—*James Curleigh*	926 Nw 13th Ave Ste 21, Portland OR 97209	503-402-1520	R	16*	.1
20	Superfeet Worldwide LLC—*Ward Collins*	1820 Scout Pl, Ferndale WA 98248	360-384-1820	R	15*	.1
21	LJO Inc—*Leif J Ostberg*	401 Hamburg Tpke Ste 3, Wayne NJ 07470		R	11*	<.1
22	Stevies Inc	211-49 26th Ave, Bayside NY 11360	718-224-4880	S	11	N/A
23	Surefoot LC—*Robert J Shay*	1500 Kearns Blvd Ste A, Park City UT 84060	435-655-8110	R	9	.1
24	TT Group Inc—*James Perivolaris*	PO Box 331, Aurora MO 65605	417-678-2181	S	7*	.1
25	Acorn Products Company LLC—*Suzanne Clark*	2 Cedar St Ste 3, Lewiston ME 04240	207-786-3526	R	3*	<.1
26	Wicked Sportswear/Footwear LLC—*Matt Mahmet*	PO Box 388, Alton NH 03809		R	3*	<.1
27	Footwear Specialties International LLC—*Brian Leckband*	13136 Ne Airport Way, Portland OR 97230	503-287-5070	R	2*	<.1
28	Beacon Shoe Company Inc—*Robert Tucker*	11 Worthington Access, Maryland Heights MO 63043	636-488-5444	R	2*	<.1

TOTALS: SIC 5139 Footwear
  Companies: 28   1,783   4.6

5141 Groceries—General Line

Rank	Company Name—*Executive Officer*	Address, City, State, Zip	Phone	Type	Fin	Empls
1	Wakefern Food Corp—*Joseph Colalillo*	600 York St, Elizabeth NJ 07207	908-527-3300	R	58,068*	50.0
2	C and S Wholesale Grocers Inc—*Rick Cohen*	7 Corporate Dr, Keene NH 03431	603-354-7000	R	20,400	15.0
3	US Foodservice Inc—*John Lederer*	9399 W Higgins Rd, Rosemont IL 60018	847-720-8000	R	18,862	25.0
4	Sysco Atlanta LLC—*Gordon Graham*	2225 Riverdale Rd, College Park GA 30337	404-765-9900	S	18,000	.8
5	CROSSMARK Inc—*John Thompson*	5100 Legacy Dr, Plano TX 75024	469-814-1000	R	15,712*	30.0
6	McLane Company Inc—*Grady Rosier*	4747 McLane Pkwy, Temple TX 76504	254-771-7500	S	12,672*	14.5
7	Performance Food Group Inc—*George Holm*	12500 W Creek Pkwy, Richmond VA 23238	804-484-7700	S	10,306*	10.0
8	McLane Foodservice Inc—*Tom Zatina* McLane Company Inc	2085 Midway Rd, Carrollton TX 75006	972-354-2000	S	7,421	8.0
9	Core-Mark Holding Company Inc—*J Michael Walsh*	395 Oyster Point Blvd, S San Francisco CA 94080	650-589-9445	P	7,267	4.4
10	Gordon Food Service Inc—*Jim Gordon*	PO Box 1787, Grand Rapids MI 49501	616-530-7000	R	6,700*	12.0
11	Tree of Life Inc	405 Golfway West Dr, Saint Augustine FL 32095	904-940-2100	S	6,010*	5.3
12	White Rose Food Inc—*John Annetta*	380 Middlesex Ave, Carteret NJ 07008	732-541-5555	R	5,868*	1.2
13	Nash Finch Co—*Alec C Covington*	PO Box 355, Minneapolis MN 55440	952-832-0534	P	4,807	4.2
14	United Natural Foods Inc—*Steven L Spinner*	313 Iron Horse Way, Providence RI 02908	401-528-8634	P	4,530	6.9
15	SYSCO Food Services of Indianapolis LLC—*Steve Neely*	PO Box 248, Indianapolis IN 46206	317-291-2020	S	3,669*	.8
16	Roundy's Supermarkets Inc—*Robert A Mariano*	PO Box 473, Milwaukee WI 53201	414-231-5000	S	3,646*	17.8
17	Dot Foods Inc—*John Tracy*	PO Box 192, Mount Sterling IL 62353	217-773-4411	R	3,552*	3.3
18	Sysco Food Services Baltimore—*Keith Shapiro*	8000 Dorsey Run Rd, Jessup MD 20794	410-799-7000	D	3,546*	.8
19	McLane Foodservice Distribution McLane Foodservice Inc	2085 Midway Rd, Carrollton TX 75006	972-304-2000	S	3,446	5.0
20	Eastern Region of Supervalu—*Jeff Noddle*	PO Box 26967, Richmond VA 23261	804-746-6000	S	3,412*	5.9
21	SYGMA Network Inc—*Alan Kelso*	5550 Blazer Pky Ste 30, Dublin OH 43017	614-734-2500	S	3,337*	2.8
22	H I Hackney Co—*William B Sansom*	PO Box 238, Knoxville TN 37901	865-546-1291	R	3,130*	3.0
23	Grocers Supply Company Inc—*Max Levit*	PO Box 14200, Houston TX 77221	713-747-5000	R	3,000	10.0
24	KeyImpact Sales and Systems Inc—*Gary Sobkowiak*	255 Colrain St SW, Grand Rapids MI 49548	616-241-3476	R	2,940*	.6
25	Alex Lee Inc—*Boyd L George*	PO Box 800, Hickory NC 28603	828-725-4424	R	2,907*	10.9
26	Bozzuto's Inc—*Michael A Bozzuto*	275 Schoolhouse Rd, Cheshire CT 06410	203-272-3511	R	2,810*	3.2
27	Central Grocers Co-op Inc—*Joe Caccamo*	2600 W Haven Ave, Joliet IL 60433	815-553-8800	R	2,758*	2.3
28	Sysco Food Services of South Florida Inc—*Tim Brown*	12500 NW 112th Ave, Medley FL 33178	305-651-5421	S	2,660*	.6
29	Services Group of America Inc—*Peter K Smith*	PO Box 25109, Scottsdale AZ 85255	480-927-4000	R	2,650*	4.0
30	Spartan Stores Inc—*Dennis Eidson*	PO Box 8700, Grand Rapids MI 49518	616-878-2000	P	2,533	8.6
31	Core-Mark International Inc—*Mike Walsh* Core-Mark Holding Company Inc	395 Oyster Point Blvd, South San Francisco CA 94080	650-589-9445	D	2,476	2.4
32	Smart and Final Inc—*David G Hirtz*	PO Box 2377, Los Angeles CA 90051	323-869-7500	R	2,400*	5.3
33	Ben E Keith Co—*Robert Hallam*	PO Box 2628, Fort Worth TX 76113	817-877-5700	R	2,187*	3.5
34	Martin Brothers Distributing Co—*Brooks Martin*	312 Viking Rd, Cedar Falls IA 50613	319-268-7555	R	1,711*	.4
35	Shamrock Foods Co	2540 N 29th Ave, Phoenix AZ 85009	602-233-6400	R	1,566*	2.5
36	URM Stores Inc—*Dean Sonnenberg*	PO Box 3365, Spokane WA 99220	509-467-2620	R	1,501*	1.9
37	Associated Wholesalers Inc—*J Christopher Michael*	PO Box 67, Robesonia PA 19551	610-693-3161	R	1,483*	1.4
38	Reinhart Institutional Foods Inc—*Mark Drazkowski*	1500 Saint James St, La Crosse WI 54603	608-782-2660	S	1,463*	2.0
39	Topco Associates Inc—*Steven Lauer*	7711 Gross Point Rd, Skokie IL 60077	847-676-3030	R	1,455*	.3
40	Merchants Distributors Inc—*Matt Saunders* Alex Lee Inc	PO Box 2148, Hickory NC 28603		S	1,234*	1.7
41	Purity Wholesale Grocers Inc—*Jeff Levitetz*	5300 Broken Sound Blvd, Boca Raton FL 33487	561-994-9360	R	1,200*	.5
42	Sysco Food Services of San Francisco Inc—*James W Ehlers*	PO Box 60000, San Francisco CA 94160	510-226-3000	S	1,126*	1.0
43	GSC Enterprises Inc—*Michael Baine*	PO Box 638, Sulphur Springs TX 75483	903-885-7621	R	1,050*	1.4
44	AMCON Distributing Co—*Christopher Atayan*	7405 Irvington Rd, Omaha NE 68122	402-331-3727	P	1,042	.9
45	SUPERVALU Champaign Distribution Center—*Mike Guth*	2611 N Lincoln Ave, Urbana IL 61802	217-384-2800	S	1,000*	.9
46	Affiliated Foods Midwest—*Martin Arter*	PO Box 1067, Norfolk NE 68702	402-371-0555	R	916*	.8
47	Foodland Distributors—*Greg Gallis*	PO Box 2886, Livonia MI 48151	734-523-2100	R	910*	1.0
48	Associated Food Stores Inc—*Richard A Parkinson*	PO Box 30430, Salt Lake City UT 84130	801-973-4400	R	907*	1.4
49	Affiliated Foods Inc—*Randy Arceneaux*	PO Box 30300, Amarillo TX 79120	806-372-3851	R	869*	1.2
50	Piggly Wiggly Carolina Company Inc—*David R Schools*	PO Box 118047, Charleston SC 29423	843-554-9880	R	728*	5.2
51	Merchants Grocery Co—*Elvin V Smythers*	PO Box 1268, Culpeper VA 22701	540-825-0786	P	726*	.2
52	Sysco Food Services-Jacksonville Inc—*Walter R Rudisiler*	PO Box 37045, Jacksonville FL 32236	904-786-2600	S	724*	1.0
53	SYSCO Minnesota Inc—*Rick Schnieders*	2400 County Rd J, Saint Paul MN 55112	763-785-9000	S	665*	.6
54	SYSCO Food Services of Metro New York LLC—*Phil Lahm*	20 Theodore Conrad Dr, Jersey City NJ 07305	201-433-2000	S	657*	.5
55	Sysco Food Services of Kansas City Inc—*William J DeLaney*	PO Box 820, Olathe KS 66061	913-829-5555	S	636*	1.0
56	Associated Grocers Inc (Baton Rouge Louisiana)—*Joseph H Campbell Jr*	PO Box 261748, Baton Rouge LA 70826	225-769-2020	R	600*	.8
57	Associated Grocers of Florida Inc—*Christopher Miller*	1141 SW 12th Ave, Pompano Beach FL 33069	954-876-3000	R	547*	.5
58	Sysco Eastern Maryland LLC—*Thomas Lankford*	PO Box 477, Pocomoke City MD 21851	410-677-5555	S	530*	1.0
59	US FoodService Inc Carolina Div—*John Lederer* US Foodservice Inc	125 Fort Mill Pkwy, Fort Mill SC 29715	803-802-6000	S	517*	1.2
60	Hardin's-Sysco Food Services Inc—*William J DeLaney*	4359 BF Goodrich Blvd, Memphis TN 38118	901-795-2300	S	508*	.8
61	SYSCO Food Services Los Angeles Inc—*Daniel S Haag*	20701 E Currier Rd, Walnut CA 91789	909-595-9595	S	500*	1.0
62	Hallsmith-Sysco Food Services—*Fred Casinelli*	380 S Worcester St, Norton MA 02766	508-285-6361	S	491*	1.2
63	Sysco Nashville LLC	1 Hermitage Plz, Nashville TN 37209	615-350-7100	S	490*	1.1
64	I J Tri Cities Inc	2722 S Roan St, Johnson City TN 37601	423-979-1052	D	488*	.1

Note: An asterisk (*) indicates an estimated financial figure. The company type code used is as follows: R = Private, P = Public, S = Private Subsidiary, B = Public Subsidiary, D = Division, J = Joint Venture, I = Investment Fund.

ANY RANKINGS BY SALES WITHIN 4-DIGIT SIC

ank	Company Name—Executive Officer	Address, City, State, Zip	Phone	Type	Fin	Empls
	IJ Co					
65	Systems Services of America—Tim Holland Services Group of America Inc	17600 NE San Rafael St, Portland OR 97230	503-256-4770	S	487*	.1
66	Western Family Foods Inc—Ronald King	PO Box 4057, Portland OR 97208	503-639-6300	R	464*	.1
67	IJ Cos—Mike Devoto	PO Box 51890, Knoxville TN 37950	865-970-7800	R	462*	.4
68	Krasdale Foods Inc—Charles A Krasne	65 W Red Oak Ln, White Plains NY 10604	914-694-6400	R	459*	.6
69	Reinhart Institutional Foods Inc Milwaukee Div Reinhart Institutional Foods Inc	PO Box 395, Oak Creek WI 53154	608-782-2660	D	456*	.2
70	Super Market Services Corp—Sam Martin	2 Paragon Dr, Montvale NJ 07645	201-573-9700	S	425*	.4
71	Sysco Food Services of Baraboo LLC—William J DeLaney	PO Box 90, Baraboo WI 53913	608-356-8711	D	412*	.7
72	Labatt Institutional Supply Company Inc—Blair P Labatt Jr	4500 Industry Park, San Antonio TX 78218	210-661-4216	R	402*	1.0
73	Farm Boy Meats Inc—Robert J Bonenberger	PO Box 996, Evansville IN 47706	812-425-5231	R	388*	.1
74	Sysco Food Services-Chicago Inc—Paul Nasir	250 Wieboldt Dr, Des Plaines IL 60016	847-699-5400	S	370*	.7
75	Kehe Food Distributors Inc—Jerry Kehe	900 N Schmidt Rd, Romeoville IL 60446	630-343-0000	R	359*	.7
76	Laurel Grocery Company Inc—Jim Buchanan	PO Box 4100, London KY 40743	606-878-6601	R	356*	.7
77	FoodSalesWest Inc—Dave Lyons	2900 Collier Canyon Rd, Livermore CA 94551	925-371-0942	R	355*	.1
78	Feesers Inc—Lester Miller	PO Box 4055, Harrisburg PA 17111	717-564-4636	R	345*	.3
79	Associated Grocers of the South Inc—Gerald Totoritis	PO Box 11044, Birmingham AL 35202		R	330*	.4
80	Glazier Foods Co—Bill Mathis	11303 Antoine, Houston TX 77066		R	319*	.5
81	Cento Fine Foods—Rick Ciccotelli	100 Cento Blvd, Thorofare NJ 08086	856-853-5445	R	318*	.1
82	PFG Milton's—George Holm Performance Food Group Inc	3501 Old Oakwood Rd, Oakwood GA 30566	770-532-7779	S	317*	.5
83	Sysco Philadelphia LLC—William Tubb	PO Box 6499, Philadelphia PA 19145	215-463-8200	S	317*	.5
84	Consolidated Companies Inc—Victor J Kurzweg III	PO Box 6096, Metairie LA 70009	504-832-0136	R	313*	.5
85	Sysco Intermountain Food Services Inc—William J DeLaney	PO Box 190, West Jordan UT 84084	801-563-6300	S	303*	.6
86	Sysco Food Service of Seattle Inc—Catherine Kayser	PO Box 97054, Kent WA 98064	206-622-2261	S	302*	.7
87	Goldberg and Solovy Food Inc—Earl Goldberg	5925 S Alcoa Ave, Vernon CA 90058	323-581-6161	R	290*	.3
88	SYSCO/Louisville Food Services Co—Bill DeLaney	PO Box 32470, Louisville KY 40232	502-364-4300	S	288*	.6
89	Mitsubishi International Corp—Seiei Ono	655 3rd Ave, New York NY 10017	212-605-2000	S	288*	.3
90	Foodbuy LLC—Dan Barney	1105 Lakewood Pkwy Ste, Alpharetta GA 30009	678-256-8000	R	281*	.3
91	Federated Group Inc (Arlington Heights Illinois)—David LaPlante	3025 W Salt Creek Ln, Arlington Heights IL 60005	847-577-1200	R	281*	.2
92	Grocery Supply Co—Micheal J Bain GSC Enterprises Inc	PO Box 638, Sulphur Springs TX 75483	903-885-7621	S	262	.6
93	Sysco Food Services of Detroit LLC—Thomas Barnes	41600 Van Born Rd, Canton MI 48188	734-397-7990	S	258*	.7
94	General Trading Company Inc (Carlstadt New Jersey)—George Abad	455 16th St, Carlstadt NJ 07072	201-935-4460	R	256*	.4
95	JT Davenport and Sons Inc—John T Davenport Jr	PO Box 1105, Sanford NC 27330	919-774-9444	R	242*	.3
96	Thoms Proestler Co—Thomas Hoffman Performance Food Group Inc	PO Box 7210, Rock Island IL 61204	309-787-1234	S	238*	.5
97	Real Mex Foods Inc—Rick Dutkiewicz	7150 Village Dr, Buena Park CA 90621	714-523-0031	H	235*	.3
98	IJ Co—Mike Devoto	4721 Singleton Station, Louisville TN 37777	865-970-7800	D	234*	.4
99	Merchants Co—Andrew Mercier	PO Box 1351, Hattiesburg MS 39403	601-583-4351	S	231*	.8
100	Dearborn Wholesale Grocers LP—Bob Krier	2801 S Western Ave, Chicago IL 60608	773-254-4300	R	230*	.5
101	American Foodservice Distributors Inc—Etienne Snollaerts Smart and Final Inc	4343 E Fremont St, Stockton CA 95215	209-948-1814	S	220*	.7
102	Tripifoods Inc—Greg Tripi	PO Box 1107, Buffalo NY 14215	716-853-7400	R	218*	.3
103	HPC Foodservice—Barry Pearson	PO Box 1228, South Windsor CT 06074	860-583-3908	R	217*	.1
104	Alliance Foods Inc—Jim Erickson	605 W Chicago St, Coldwater MI 49036	517-278-2396	R	210*	.4
105	Institutional Sales Associates—Ronald P Koska	PO Box 8938, Houston TX 77249	713-692-7213	R	200*	.1
106	Associated Grocers of Maine Inc—Mark Sprackland	PO Box 1000, Gardiner ME 04345	207-582-6500	R	195*	.3
107	Cross Mark Southern California—John Thompson CROSSMARK Inc	2401 E Katella Ave Ste, Anaheim CA 92806	714-912-8331	D	194*	.5
108	Associated Grocers of New England Inc—Michael Bourgoine	PO Box 6000, Pembroke NH 03275	603-223-6710	R	193*	.3
109	Piggly Wiggly Alabama Distributing Company Inc—Dennis Stewart	2400 J Terrell Wooten, Bessemer AL 35020	205-481-2300	R	191*	.3
110	Co-Sales Co—Don Cox	2700 N 3rd St Ste 1000, Phoenix AZ 85004	602-254-5555	R	189*	.2
111	Shamrock Farms Dairy Div—Norman McClelland Shamrock Foods Co	2228 N Black Canyon Hw, Phoenix AZ 85009	602-272-6721	D	187*	.2
112	AJC International Inc—Gerald L Allison	5188 Roswell Rd NW, Atlanta GA 30342	404-252-6750	R	186*	.1
113	Anderson-DuBose Co—Warren E Anderson	6575 Davis Industrial, Solon OH 44139	440-248-8800	R	185*	.1
114	Sysco Food Services of Austin Inc—William J DeLaney	PO Box 149024, Austin TX 78714	512-388-8000	S	184*	.4
115	Diaz Wholesale and Manufacturing Company Inc—Rene M Diaz	5501 Fulton Industrial, Atlanta GA 30336	404-344-5421	R	182*	.4
116	Long Wholesale Distributors Inc—Randy Long	201 N Fulton Dr, Corinth MS 38834	662-287-2421	R	179*	.2
117	Foodservice Brokerage Company Ltd—Gerald Grieve	PO Box 1127, Renton WA 98057	425-228-3600	R	175*	.1
118	Olean Wholesale Grocery Cooperative Inc—Jim Reed	PO Box 1070, Olean NY 14760	716-372-2020	R	172*	.3
119	Glover Wholesale Inc—David Harris	1333 Cusseta Rd, Columbus GA 31901	706-322-7376	R	172*	.2
120	Key Food Stores Cooperative Inc—Richard Palitto	450 Forest Avenue, Staten Island NY 10314	718-697-8200	S	172*	.2
121	Sysco Lincoln Inc—Tim Peterzen	1700 Center Park Rd, Lincoln NE 68512	402-423-1031	S	166*	.5
122	Millbrook Distribution Services Inc	PO Box 35, Leicester MA 01524	508-892-8711	S	162*	1.3
123	SYSCO Food Services of Grand Rapids LLC—Richard A Johnston	3700 Sysco Ct SE, Grand Rapids MI 49512	616-949-3700	S	161*	.5
124	Alpena Wholesale Grocery Co—Ron Baxter	PO Box 475, Alpena MI 49707	989-356-2281	R	159*	.2
125	Institution Food House Inc—Dave Stansfield Alex Lee Inc	PO Box 2947, Hickory NC 28603	828-323-4500	S	147*	.6
126	Schenck Foods Company Inc—David C Huntsberry	PO Box 2298, Winchester VA 22604	540-869-1870	R	147*	.1
127	Sysco Food Service of Jamestown—Richard Schnieders	2063 Allen St Extensi, Falconer NY 14733	716-665-5620	D	140*	.3
128	Sysco Food Services of Arkansas Inc—Bill DeLaney	PO Box 194060, Little Rock AR 72219	501-562-4111	S	130*	.3
129	Harrison Company Inc—Hal Martin	4801 Viking Dr, Bossier City LA 71112	318-747-0700	R	120*	.1
130	Doerle Food Services LLC—Carolyn Doerle	113 Kol Dr, Broussard LA 70518	337-252-8551	R	119*	.4
131	Sysco Food Services of Central California Inc	136 S Mariposa Rd, Modesto CA 95354	209-527-7700	S	117*	.4
132	Sysco Food Services of Pittsburgh—Len Petrancosta	PO Box 1000, Harmony PA 16037	724-452-2100	S	105*	.3
133	HB Paulk Grocery Inc—Ferris P Youmans	601 Hwy 52 E, Opp AL 36467	334-493-3255	R	105*	.2
134	Yankee Marketers Inc—Brad Johnson	PO Box 370, Middleton MA 01949	978-777-9181	R	104*	<.1
135	NorthCenter Foodservice Corp—George L Holm Performance Food Group Inc	PO Box 2628, Augusta ME 04338	207-623-8451	S	100*	.2
136	Shonfeld's USA Inc—Boaz Shonfeld	3100 S Susan St, Santa Ana CA 92704		R	94*	.1
137	Admiral Exchange Company Inc—Dean L Edwards	1443 Union St, San Diego CA 92101	619-239-2165	R	94*	<.1
138	Heddinger Brokerage Inc—Dave Heddinger	PO Box 65037, West Des Moines IA 50265	515-222-4458	R	91*	<.1

Rank	Company Name—*Executive Officer*	Address, City, State, Zip	Phone	Type	Fin	Empls
139	Bunn Capitol Co—*Robert H Bunn*	PO Box 4227, Springfield IL 62708	217-529-5401	R	90*	.3
140	SYSCO Food Services of Idaho Inc—*Renee Lovejoy*	PO Box 170007, Boise ID 83717	208-345-9500	S	87*	.2
141	Osborn Brothers Inc—*Joel Osborn*	PO Box 649, Gadsden AL 35902	256-547-8601	R	86*	.1
142	Van Eerden Distribution Co—*Dan Van Eerden*	PO Box 3110, Grand Rapids MI 49501	616-452-1426	R	85*	.2
143	Scariano Brothers LLC—*Andrew Czubak*	11052 Scariano Ln, Hammond LA 70403	225-448-0500	R	85*	.1
144	Springfield Grocer Company Inc—*Jefferson McDonald*	PO Box 8500, Springfield MO 65801	417-883-4230	R	83*	.1
145	Economy Cash and Carry Inc—*Paul Dipp*	PO Box 1736, El Paso TX 79949	915-532-2660	R	82*	.1
146	Banta Foods Inc—*Charles T Banta Jr*	PO Box 8246, Springfield MO 65801	417-862-6644	D	81*	.2
147	Banner Wholesale Grocers Inc—*Richard Saltzman*	3000 S Ashland Ave St, Chicago IL 60608	312-421-2650	R	80*	.1
148	Sales Corporation of Alaska—*Bob Galosich*	355 E 76th Ste 104, Anchorage AK 99518	907-522-3057	R	71*	<.1
149	Wilke International Inc—*Wayne Wilke*	14321 W 96th Ter, Lenexa KS 66215	913-438-5544	R	66*	<.1
150	JC Wright Sales Co—*Jack C Wright*	7202 S 212th St, Kent WA 98032	253-395-8799	R	65*	.1
151	Federated Group—*David La Plante* Federated Group Inc (Arlington Heights Illinois)	3025 W Salt Creek Ln, Arlington Heights IL 60005	847-577-1200	S	61*	.3
152	Great Western Meats Inc—*Greg Voorhees*	PO Box 568366, Orlando FL 32856	407-841-4270	R	60*	.1
153	Torn and Glasser Inc—*Robert Glasser*	PO Box 21823, Los Angeles CA 90021	213-627-6496	R	52*	<.1
154	Countryside Foods LLC—*Robert Fishbein*	PO Box 369, Delphos OH 45833	419-695-5015	R	49*	.7
155	WJ Pence Company Inc—*John Pence*	W 227 N 880 Westmound, Waukesha WI 53186	262-524-6300	R	49*	.1
156	Dennis Sales Ltd—*Ryan McLaughlin*	PO Box 4056, Salisbury MD 21803	410-742-1585	R	49*	<.1
157	W Lee Flowers and Company Inc—*Henry Johnson*	127 E W Lee Flowers Rd, Scranton SC 29591	843-389-2731	R	48*	.1
158	Mark Ross and Company International—*Victor Vitlin*	2525 16th St Ste 321, San Francisco CA 94103	415-285-5500	R	48*	<.1
159	Charles C Parks Company Inc—*Crockett Parks III*	500 Belvedere Dr, Gallatin TN 37066	615-452-2406	R	46*	.1
160	Orrell's Food Service Inc—*Tony R Orrell*	9827 S NC Hwy 150, Linwood NC 27299	336-752-2114	R	46*	.1
161	Perkins—*Gary Perkins*	630 John Hancock Rd, Taunton MA 02780	508-824-2800	S	45*	.2
162	Hillcrest Eggs and Cheese Co—*Armin Abraham*	2695 E 40th St, Cleveland OH 44115	216-361-4625	R	45*	.1
163	Knott's Wholesale Foods Inc—*Jerry Knott*	125 N Blakemore, Paris TN 38242	731-642-1961	R	45*	.1
164	Institutional Wholesale Co—*Jimmy W Mackie*	535 Dry Valley Rd, Cookeville TN 38506	931-537-4000	R	43*	.1
165	Synergy Foods LLC—*Sigmund Kramer*	10301 Flora St, Detroit MI 48209	313-849-2900	R	42*	<.1
166	Caro Foods Inc—*Ralph Boudreau* Performance Food Group Inc	2324 Bayou Blue Rd, Houma LA 70364	985-872-1483	S	40*	.2
167	Tusco Grocers Inc—*Jayn Debney*	PO Box 240, Dennison OH 44621	740-922-2223	R	38*	.1
168	Independent Grocers Association Inc—*Mark Batenic*	8725 W Higgins Rd, Chicago IL 60631	773-693-4520	R	36*	<.1
169	Winkler Inc—*Tom Winkler*	PO Box 68, Dale IN 47523	812-937-4421	R	34*	.2
170	Federated Foodservice—*Deb Winter* Federated Group	3025 W Salt Creek Ln, Arlington Heights IL 60005	847-577-1200	D	34*	<.1
171	Allen Foods Inc—*Stanley Allen* US Foodservice Inc	8543 Page Ave, Saint Louis MO 63114	314-426-4100	S	33*	.2
172	Summit Import Corp—*Whiting Wu*	100 Summit Pl, Jersey City NJ 07305	201-985-9800	R	32*	.1
173	Advantage Sales and Marketing LLC—*Sonny King*	18100 Von Karman Ave R, Irvine CA 92612	949-797-2900	R	32*	.1
174	Frank J Catanzaro Sons and Daughters Inc—*Sharon Cantan-zaro Ledonne*	535 Shepherd Ave, Cincinnati OH 45215	513-421-9184	S	31*	.1
175	Gulf Marine and Industrial Supplies—*John Cotsoradis*	5501 Jefferson St Ste, New Orleans LA 70123	504-525-6252	R	31*	.1
176	Brown Food Service—*John F Brown*	PO Box 690, Louisa KY 41230	606-638-1139	R	30*	.1
177	Nichols Foodservice Inc—*JL Nichols III*	PO Box 729, Wallace NC 28466	910-285-3197	R	30*	.1
178	Royal Sausage Company Inc—*Curtis Capps*	PO Box 930, Pell City AL 35125	205-884-1040	R	29*	.2
179	WL Halsey Company Inc—*Cecilia Halsey*	PO Box 6485, Huntsville AL 35813	256-772-9691	R	29*	.1
180	Pocahontas Foods USA Inc—*David Mattews*	PO Box 9729, Richmond VA 23228	804-262-8614	S	28*	.1
181	Union Grocery Company Inc—*Wayne Baquet*	701 Edwards Ave, Elmwood LA 70123	662-534-5089	S	28*	<.1
182	Dunbar Sales Company Inc—*Robert Dunbar*	4616 Montevallo Rd, Birmingham AL 35210	205-956-2121	R	28*	<.1
183	Dennis Beverage Co—*Ronald Dennis*	101 Mecaw Rd, Bangor ME 04401	207-947-0321	R	26*	.1
184	Daffin Mercantile—*John Milton*	PO Box 779, Marianna FL 32447	850-482-4026	R	26*	.1
185	Supreme Foods Inc—*Michael Dilday*	1201 Progress Rd, Suffolk VA 23434	757-538-8000	R	24*	.1
186	Southern Food Concepts Inc—*Jim Finley*	105 Trade Ctr Dr, Birmingham AL 35244	205-403-0375	R	24*	<.1
187	Robin's Food Distribution Inc—*Robin Wold*	PO Box 617617, Chicago IL 60661	312-243-6974	R	24*	<.1
188	Indiana Concession Supply Inc—*Dave Battas*	2402 Shadeland Ave Ste, Indianapolis IN 46219	317-353-1667	R	23*	<.1
189	Koa Trading Co—*Peter Yukimura*	PO Box 1031, Lihue HI 96766	808-245-6961	R	22*	.1
190	Epicurean International Inc—*Alan Wilson*	PO Box 13242, Union City CA 94587	510-675-3025	R	22*	<.1
191	Normans Inc—*Wayne L Norman*	86 S Division St, Battle Creek MI 49017	269-968-6136	R	20*	.1
192	Advantage Food Marketing Corp—*Mitchell Levine*	159 Adams Ave, Hauppauge NY 11788	631-348-8989	R	20*	<.1
193	Blackburn-Russell Company Inc—*Robert B Blackburn*	PO Box 157, Bedford PA 15522	814-623-5181	R	19*	<.1
194	Joseph Antognoli and Co—*JH Antognoli*	1800 N Pulaski Rd, Chicago IL 60639	773-772-1800	R	19*	<.1
195	PRO*ACT LLC—*Steve Grinstead*	24560 Silver Cloud Cou, Monterey CA 93940	831-655-4250	R	18*	<.1
196	Buchy Food Products Inc—*Jim Buchy*	1050 Progress St, Greenville OH 45331		R	18*	<.1
197	Wm H Leahy Associates Inc—*Greg Lojkutz*	2350 Ravine Way Ste 20, Glenview IL 60025	847-498-0240	R	17*	.1
198	Bel Canto Foods Ltd—*Alan Butzbach*	1300 Viele Ave, Bronx NY 10474	718-497-3888	R	14*	.1
199	Food Service Action Inc—*Randy Reid*	1485 Lakes Pkwy, Lawrenceville GA 30043	404-296-2700	R	13*	<.1
200	All Kitchens Inc—*Joe Bodard*	575 E Park Center Blvd, Boise ID 83706	208-336-7003	S	12*	<.1
201	Dependable Food Corp	29 Executive Ave, Edison NJ 08817	732-257-4500	R	12*	<.1
202	Han-D-Pac Products Inc—*Raul Ramos*	PO Box 971456, El Paso TX 79997	915-595-2212	R	11*	<.1
203	Andresen-Ryan Coffee Co—*Donald Andresen*	2206 Winter St, Superior WI 54880	715-392-4771	R	10*	<.1
204	Shimaya Shoten Ltd—*Ichiro Onoye*	710 Kohou St, Honolulu HI 96817	808-845-6691	R	10*	<.1
205	American Foods Inc—*Butch Owens*	131 New Jersey St, Mobile AL 36603	251-433-2528	R	9*	<.1
206	American Outdoor Products Inc—*Rodney Smith*	6350 Gunpark Dr, Boulder CO 80301	303-581-0518	R	9*	<.1
207	Francis-Mustoe and Co—*Vince Schwartz*	3070 Saturn St Ste 201, Brea CA 92821	714-984-4111	R	8*	<.1
208	Phenix Food Service Inc—*Patricia Hardin*	318 Gnral Clin Pwell P, Phenix City AL 36869	334-298-6288	R	8*	<.1
209	Great Lakes Marketing Inc—*Brent Magolan*	16700 W Victor Rd, New Berlin WI 53151	262-754-2780	R	7*	<.1
210	Luzo Maxi Market—*Carl Ribeiro* Hallsmith-Sysco Food Services	PO Box 50370, New Bedford MA 02745	508-999-1771	S	7*	<.1
211	Moctec Enterprises Inc—*Victor Vazquez*	PO Box 905, Lanham MD 20703	301-386-9090	R	7*	<.1
212	Five Star Custom Foods Ltd—*Jeffrey Bledsoe*	3709 E 1st St, Fort Worth TX 76111	817-838-3442	R	6*	<.1
213	Arm National Food Inc—*Armando Rienzi*	1546 Lamberton Rd, Trenton NJ 08611	609-394-0431	R	6*	<.1
214	Joyce Brothers Inc—*Harry Joyce*	PO Box 888, Winston Salem NC 27102	336-765-6927	R	6*	<.1
215	Switzers Inc—*Carolyn Switzer Hundley*	575 N 20th St, East Saint Louis IL 62205	618-271-6336	R	5*	<.1
216	Strohmeyer and Arpe Co—*Charles Kocot*	106 Allen Rd, Basking Ridge NJ 07920	908-580-9100	R	5*	<.1
217	Liberty Gold Fruit Co	500 Eccles Ave, South San Francisco CA 94080	650-583-4700	R	5*	<.1
218	Halling Co—*Dan Halling*	37475 Schoolcraft Rd, Livonia MI 48150	734-591-0805	R	5*	<.1
219	Rocky Mountain Foods Inc—*David Greenhouse*	13105 E 38th Ave Unit, Denver CO 80239	303-371-3511	R	4*	<.1
220	Smith and Sons Foods Inc—*James A Smith III*	PO Box 4688, Macon GA 31208	478-745-4759	R	4	.9
221	Chin's Import Export Company Inc—*Keith Lee*	PO Box 83035, Portland OR 97283	503-224-4082	R	4*	<.1
222	Kleen Supply Co—*Carlos Pena*	710 9th St N, Texas City TX 77590	409-762-0140	R	4*	<.1

Note: An asterisk (*) indicates an estimated financial figure. The company type code used is as follows: R = Private, P = Public, S = Private Subsidiary, B = Public Subsidiary, D = Division, J = Joint Venture, I = Investment Fund.

COMPANY RANKINGS BY SALES WITHIN 4-DIGIT SIC

Rank	Company Name—Executive Officer	Address, City, State, Zip	Phone	Type	Fin	Empls
223	Dawson Sales Co—Diane L Dawson	2015 Spring Rd Ste 275, Oak Brook IL 60523	630-203-8174	R	4*	<.1
224	Monroe and Associates Inc—Dennis Monroe	23533 Mercantile Rd, Cleveland OH 44122	216-464-9222	R	4*	<.1
225	B Del Toro and Sons Inc—Michael Deltoro	393 Harris Ave, Providence RI 02909	401-421-5820	R	3*	<.1
226	Mutual Trading Company Inc—Noritoshi Kanai	431 Crocker St, Los Angeles CA 90013	213-626-9458	R	3*	.1
227	Apple Food Sales Company Inc—Alan S Applebaum	117 Fort Lee Rd, Leonia NJ 07605	201-592-0277	R	3*	<.1
228	JL Henderson and Co—James L Henderson	PO Box 21352, Bakersfield CA 93390	661-664-4636	R	3*	<.1
229	Pro-Fac Cooperative Inc—Steve Wright	PO Box 274, Fairport NY 14450	585-218-4210	R	3	<.1
230	Amir Foods Inc—Butch Rassi	4422 Mayfield Rd, Cleveland OH 44121	216-291-1800	R	3*	<.1
231	Arnone and Sons—Anthony Arnone	1711 Cherry St, Erie PA 16502	814-453-5197	R	2*	<.1
232	Egerstrom Inc—Paul Egerstrom	10012 E 64th St, Kansas City MO 64133	816-358-3025	R	2*	<.1
233	S3 Investments Company Inc—Jim Bickel	4115 Blackhawk Plz Cir, Danville CA 94506	925-648-2080	P	2	<.1
234	Tombstone Exploration Corp—Alan Brown	6529 E Fries Dr, Scottsdale AZ 85254	520-457-3066	P	<1	<.1
235	LP Shanks Co—Scot Shanks	624 Industrial Blvd, Crossville TN 38555	931-484-5155	R	N/A	.2

TOTALS: SIC 5141 Groceries— General Line
Companies: 235 — 302,653 — 347.1

5142 Packaged Frozen Foods

Rank	Company Name—Executive Officer	Address, City, State, Zip	Phone	Type	Fin	Empls
1	SYSCO Corp—William J DeLaney	1390 Enclave Pkwy, Houston TX 77077	281-584-1390	P	39,324	46.0
2	Unified Grocers Inc—Alfred A Plamann	5200 Sheila St, Los Angeles CA 90040	323-264-5200	R	3,848	3.0
3	Citrosuco North America Inc—Nick Emanuel	PO Box 3950, Lake Wales FL 33859	863-696-6077	S	806*	.2
4	Burris Foods Inc—Robert D Burris	PO Box 219, Milford DE 19963	302-422-4531	R	644*	1.7
5	Beaver Street Fisheries Inc—Benjamin Frisch	PO Box 41430, Jacksonville FL 32203	904-354-8533	R	443*	.2
6	J Kings Food Service Professionals Inc—John King	700 Furrows Rd, Holtsville NY 11742	631-289-8401	R	382*	.3
7	Southeast Frozen Food Co—Rich Bauer	18770 NE 6th Ave, Miami FL 33179	305-652-4622	R	337*	.5
8	Sherwood Food Distributors—Earl Ishbia	12499 Evergreen Rd, Detroit MI 48228	313-659-7300	R	268*	.7
9	Monogram Food Solutions LLC—Don Brunson	930 S White Station Rd, Memphis TN 38117	901-685-7167	R	174*	.8
10	Schwan's Consumer Brands North America Inc—Mark Dalrymple	8500 Normandale Lake B, Bloomington MN 55437	952-832-4300	R	171*	3.1
11	Trafon Group Inc—Carlos Trapaga	Garden Hills Plz Pmb, Guaynabo PR 00966	787-783-0011	R	150*	.4
12	Roberts Sysco Foods Inc—Dean Robert Jr SYSCO Corp	P O Box 620, Lincoln IL 62656	217-735-7700	S	115*	.1
13	Rainbow Inc (Pearl City Hawaii)—William Prideaux	98-715 Kuahao Pl, Pearl City HI 96782	808-487-6455	R	103*	.1
14	Norpac Food Sales—Mike Woods	4350 SW Galewood St, Lake Oswego OR 97035	503-635-9311	R	89*	.1
15	Mile Hi Frozen Food Co—Tony Taddanio	4770 E 51rst Ave, Denver CO 80216	303-399-6066	R	77*	.2
16	International Food Group Inc—Berry Wright SYSCO Corp	2401 Williamette Dr St, Plant City FL 33566	813-707-6161	S	68*	<.1
17	Wilcox Frozen Foods Inc—Robert C Smith	2200 Oakdale Ave, San Francisco CA 94124	415-282-4116	R	62*	<.1
18	VIP Sales Company Inc	2395 American Ave, Hayward CA 94545		S	60*	<.1
19	King Provision Corp—Edward Hicks	220 Ponte Vedra Park D, Ponte Vedra Beach FL 32082	904-543-7074	R	59*	<.1
20	Kaelbel Wholesale Inc—Eddie Kaelbel	2501 SW 31st St, Fort Lauderdale FL 33312	954-797-7789	R	42*	<.1
21	Marketfare Foods Inc—Al Carfora	2512 E Magnolia St, Phoenix AZ 85034	602-275-5509	R	38*	.6
22	Travis Meats Inc—William Travis	PO Box 670, Powell TN 37849	865-938-9051	R	29*	.2
23	Superior Foods Inc—Mateo Lettunich	275 Westgate Dr, Watsonville CA 95076	831-728-3691	R	23*	.1
24	Lincoln Provision Inc—James Stevens	824 W 38th Pl, Chicago IL 60609	773-254-2400	R	23*	.1
25	Maryland Hotel Supply Company Inc—Russell Niller	701 W Hamburg St, Baltimore MD 21230	410-539-7055	R	21*	.1
26	Foodsources Inc	2913 Saturn St Ste A-B, Brea CA 92821	714-996-7350	R	21*	<.1
27	Preferred Foods Martin LP—Charles Poirier	2011 Silver St, Houston TX 77007	713-869-6191	R	18*	.3
28	American Fish and Seafood Inc—Lowell Bialick	5501 Opportunity Ct, Hopkins MN 55343	952-935-3474	R	16*	.1
29	Harvest Farms Inc—Andrew Mccluskey	45000 Yucca Ave, Lancaster CA 93534	661-945-3636	R	15*	.1
30	Bakalars Sausage Company Inc—Michael Bakalars	PO Box 1943, La Crosse WI 54602	608-784-0384	R	12*	.1
31	J And J Wall Baking Company Inc—John Wall	8806 Fruitridge Rd, Sacramento CA 95826	916-381-1410	R	11*	.1
32	Buzz Products Inc—Dickinson Gould	4818 Kanawha Blvd E St, Charleston WV 25306	304-925-4781	R	10*	.1
33	Miami Beef Company Inc—Michael Young	4870 Nw 157th St, Hialeah FL 33014	305-621-3252	R	10*	<.1
34	Chipwich Inc—Samuel Metzer	105 Shad Row, Piermont NY 10968	845-359-1440	R	9*	<.1
35	Leelanau Fruit Co—Allen Steimel	2900 S W Bay Shore Dr, Suttons Bay MI 49682	231-271-3514	R	8*	.1
36	Mcgreevy's Midwest Meat Co—Tim Mcgreevy	230 N W St, Wichita KS 67203	316-946-5522	R	8*	<.1
37	Hahn Brothers Inc—William Redmer	PO Box 395, Westminster MD 21158	410-848-4200	R	6*	<.1
38	Seacoast Seafoods Sales Inc—Vincent Bertolino	PO Box 909, Hampton NH 03843	978-462-8127	R	5*	<.1
39	Baja Foods LLC—Cheryl Canning	636 W Root St, Chicago IL 60609	773-376-9030	R	4*	<.1
40	Turner New Zealand Inc—Noel Turner	PO Box 8919, Newport Beach CA 92658	949-622-6181	R	4*	<.1
41	Angy's Food Products Inc—May Fu	77 Servistar Industria, Westfield MA 01085	413-572-1010	R	4*	<.1
42	Florida Veal Processors Inc—Richard Nusman	6712 State Rd 674, Wimauma FL 33598	813-634-5545	R	2*	<.1
43	Pecan Point Food Products Inc—Julius Lister	729 Pecan Point Rd, Norfolk VA 23502	757-461-2731	R	2*	<.1
44	Mary Kate Foods—Russell Burch	1641 N 8th St, Colton CA 92324	909-825-8542	R	2*	<.1

TOTALS: SIC 5142 Packaged Frozen Foods
Companies: 44 — 47,522 — 59.3

5143 Dairy Products Except Dried or Canned

Rank	Company Name—Executive Officer	Address, City, State, Zip	Phone	Type	Fin	Empls
1	Vistar/VSA Corp—Patrick T Hagerty	12650 E Arapahoe Rd, Centennial CO 80112	303-662-7234	R	2,252*	3.1
2	Maryland And Virginia Milk Producers Cooperative Association Inc—Steve Graybeal	1985 Isaac Newton Sq W, Reston VA 20190	703-742-6800	R	1,219*	.6
3	Associated Milk Producers Inc—Ed Welch	PO Box 455, New Ulm MN 56073	507-354-8295	R	876*	1.7
4	Pierre's Ice Cream Co—Rochelle Roth	6200 Euclid Ave, Cleveland OH 44103	216-432-1144	S	500*	.1
5	Rockview Dairies Inc—Egbert Groot	PO Box 668, Downey CA 90241	562-927-5511	R	375*	.3
6	Dairylea Cooperative Inc—Gregory I Wickham	PO Box 4844, Syracuse NY 13221	315-433-0100	R	352*	.1
7	Challenge Dairy Products Inc—John Whetten	PO Box 2369, Dublin CA 94568	925-828-6160	S	278*	.2
8	Norseland Inc—David Brohel	1290 E Main St, Stamford CT 06902	203-324-5620	R	156*	<.1
9	Mid Valley Dairy Company-Turlock—Jay Simon	2600 Spengler Way, Turlock CA 95380	209-668-2100	R	150*	.2
10	Independent Procurement Alliance Program LLC—Kathy Geenen	1650 Tri Park Way Ste, Appleton WI 54914	920-832-1100	R	150*	<.1
11	DeConna Ice Cream Inc—Vince DeConna	PO Box 39, Orange Lake FL 32681	352-591-1530	R	121*	.1
12	Carvel Corp—Steve Romaniello	200 Glnrdg Point Pkwy, Atlanta GA 30342	404-255-3250	R	117*	.1
13	Heluva Good LLC—Mary Hughs	PO Box 410, Sodus NY 14551	315-483-6971	R	100*	.2
14	Western Dairy Products Inc—Graeme Honeyfield	3625 Westwind Blvd, Santa Rosa CA 95403	707-524-6770	S	90	<.1
15	Dairy Fresh Food Inc—Alan Must	21405 Trolley Industri, Taylor MI 48180	313-295-6300	R	89*	.2
16	Bassett Dairy Products Inc—Jay Boosinger	680 Industrial Park Dr, Perry FL 32348	850-584-5149	R	89	<.1
17	Prairie Farms Dairy Inc Ice Cream Specialties Div	PO Box 19766, Saint Louis MO 63144	314-962-2550	D	70*	.1
18	Sure Winner Foods Inc—Keith Benoit	PO Box 430, Saco ME 04072	207-282-1258	R	54*	.1
19	Cacique Distributors US—Gilbert De Cardenas	PO Box 91330, City Of Industry CA 91715	626-937-3593	R	54*	.2
20	Sunrise AG Coop—Danny Popp	P O Box 458, Buckman MN 56317	320-468-6433	R	53*	<.1

Rank	Company Name—*Executive Officer*	Address, City, State, Zip	Phone	Type	Fin	Empls
21	Swiss Valley Farms Coop—*Don Boelens*	PO Box 4493, Davenport IA 52808	563-468-6600	R	49*	.8
22	Dairyland Inc	PO Box 4387, Macon GA 31208	478-742-6461	S	45*	<.1
23	Dairy Fresh Of Alabama LLC—*Suzanne Holston*	PO Box 10457, Prichard AL 36610	251-456-3381	R	43*	.7
24	Reilly Dairy and Food Co—*Gerald Reilly*	PO Box 19217, Tampa FL 33686	813-839-8458	R	36*	.1
25	Kickapoo Valley Cheese Corp—*James Leytus*	9285 3rd St, Milladore WI 54454	715-652-2173	R	35*	.1
26	Hautly Cheese Company Inc—*Alan C Hautly*	251 Axminister Dr, Fenton MO 63026	636-533-4400	R	34*	<.1
27	John R White Company Inc—*Donald Patton*	PO Box 10043, Birmingham AL 35202	205-595-8381	R	30*	<.1
28	Los Altos Food Products Inc—*Raul Andrade*	450 Baldwin Park Blvd, City Of Industry CA 91746	626-330-6555	R	21*	.1
29	Bliss Brothers Dairy Inc—*David Bliss*	PO Box 2288, Attleboro MA 02703	508-222-0787	R	20*	.1
30	Dairyfood USA Inc—*Daniel Culligan*	2819 County Rd F, Blue Mounds WI 53517	608-437-5598	R	19*	.1
31	Farmers Cooperative Dairy Inc—*John Moisey*	104 Rotery Dr, Hazleton PA 18202	570-453-0203	D	15*	<.1
32	Brown's Ice Cream Co—*Tim Nelson*	3501 Marshall St NE St, Minneapolis MN 55418	612-378-1075	R	14*	<.1
33	C F Burger Creamery Co—*Lawrence Angott*	8101 Greenfield Rd, Detroit MI 48228	313-584-4040	R	13*	.1
34	Yancey's Fancy Inc—*Wayne Henry*	857 Main Rd, Corfu NY 14036	585-599-4448	S	12*	.1
35	Williams Cheese Co—*Michael Williams*	PO Box 249, Linwood MI 48634	989-697-4492	R	10*	.1
36	Lone Elm Sales Inc—*Glen D Dedow*	9695 N Van Dyne Rd, Van Dyne WI 54979	920-688-2338	R	10*	<.1
37	Getchell Brothers Inc—*Douglas Farnham*	PO Box 8, Brewer ME 04412	207-989-7335	R	10*	<.1
38	Abbott's Premium Ice Cream Inc—*Charles S Marshall*	PO Box 411, Center Conway NH 03813	603-356-2344	R	9*	<.1
39	Wades Dairy Inc—*Douglas H Wade Jr*	1316 Barnum Ave, Bridgeport CT 06610	203-579-9233	R	8*	<.1
40	Pleasant View Dairy Corp—*E Leep*	PO Box 1949, Highland IN 46322	219-838-0155	R	8*	<.1
41	Dairy-Mix Inc—*Edward J Coryn*	3020 46th Ave N, Saint Petersburg FL 33714	727-525-6101	R	7*	<.1
42	Z and R Corp—*Richard Rzeszotarski*	260 Forest Ave, Amsterdam NY 12010	518-842-4940	R	6*	<.1
43	Gordon Food Company Inc—*Michael Gordon*	PO Box 41534, Memphis TN 38174	901-454-4100	R	6*	<.1
44	Harry C Wenzel and Sons Inc—*Russell Wenzel*	PO Box 357, Marshfield WI 54449	715-387-1218	R	5*	<.1
45	Marque Foods Inc—*Ramon Canova*	322 Littlefield Ave, South San Francisco CA 94080	650-583-4114	R	4*	<.1
46	Scott's Inc—*Holly Cremer*	PO Box 1, Madison WI 53701	608-837-8020	R	3*	<.1
47	Sentry Refrigeration Inc—*Andrew Crivaro*	1001 Lower Landing Rd, Blackwood NJ 08012	856-853-1967	R	2*	<.1

TOTALS: SIC 5143 Dairy Products Except Dried or Canned
Companies: 47 — 7,617 — 9.8

5144 Poultry & Poultry Products

Rank	Company Name—*Executive Officer*	Address, City, State, Zip	Phone	Type	Fin	Empls
1	Sutherland Foodservice Inc—*Gene Sutherland Sr*	PO Box 786, Forest Park GA 30298	404-366-8550	R	250*	.2
2	Lincoln Poultry and Egg Co—*Richard Evnen*	800 Cattail Rd, Lincoln NE 68521	402-477-3757	R	224*	.6
3	Cagle's Farms Inc—*J Douglas Cagle*	1385 Collier Rd NW, Atlanta GA 30318	404-355-2820	S	200*	.2
4	North South Foods Group Inc—*Ron Bateman*	3373 Sterling Ridge Ct, Longwood FL 32779	407-805-3290	R	177*	<.1
5	Sonstegard Foods Co—*Philip Sonstegard*	1911 W 57th St Ste 102, Sioux Falls SD 57108	605-338-4642	R	150*	.4
6	Crystal Farms Refrigerated Distribution Co—*Mark Anderson*	301 Carlson Pkwy Ste 4, Hopkins MN 55305	952-544-8101	S	147*	.4
7	Pennfield Corp—*Ernest Horn*	PO Box 4366, Lancaster PA 17604	717-299-2561	R	141*	.3
8	Rose Acre Farms Inc—*Lois Rust*	PO Box 1250, Seymour IN 47274	812-497-2557	R	137*	1.8
9	Troyer Foods Inc—*Paris Ball-Miller*	PO Box 608, Goshen IN 46527	574-533-0302	R	129*	.2
10	Dutt and Wagner of Virginia Inc—*Rodney Wagner*	PO Box 519, Abingdon VA 24212	276-628-2116	R	70*	.2
11	Metropolitan Poultry and Seafood Company Inc—*Brian C Willard*	1920 Stanford Ct, Landover MD 20785	301-772-0060	R	70*	.2
12	Nulaid Foods Inc—*David Crockett*	200 W 5th St, Ripon CA 95366	209-599-2121	R	66*	.1
13	Ohio Fresh Eggs LLC—*Julie Hilton*	PO Box 247, Croton OH 43013	740-893-7200	R	55*	.3
14	Poultry Products Company Inc—*Julian Stogniew*	11 Bemis Rd, Hooksett NH 03106	603-263-1600	R	41*	.2
15	Will Poultry Company Inc—*Donald Will*	PO Box 1146, Buffalo NY 14240	716-853-2000	R	19*	.1
16	United Egg Marketing Corp—*Jacques Klempf*	PO Box 649, Blackshear GA 31516	912-449-4466	R	16*	.1
17	Lehman's Egg Service Inc—*Ron Kissel*	PO Box 99, Greencastle PA 17225	717-375-2261	R	16*	.1
18	Villa Ranch—*Dolores Hoover*	33700 Wildwood Canyon, Yucaipa CA 92399	909-795-2527	R	14*	<.1
19	Houston Poultry and Egg Company Inc—*Ronnie Bennett*	PO Box 16027, Houston TX 77222	713-699-3585	R	10*	<.1
20	New Stockton Poultry Inc—*John Luu*	PO Box 2129, Stockton CA 95201	209-466-9503	R	9*	.1
21	Scruggs Poultry Inc—*Anderson Holt*	PO Box 305, Rocky Mount NC 27802	252-442-9400	R	8*	<.1
22	Intra-Coastal Packing Inc—*Jerrald Duthler*	3222 S Military Trl, Lake Worth FL 33463	561-964-6020	R	8*	<.1
23	Johnson County Egg Farm—*Moses Rodriguez*	1275 Se Y Hwy, Knob Noster MO 65336	660-563-2775	R	8*	.1
24	Squab Producers Of Calif Inc—*Robert Shipley*	409 Primo Way, Modesto CA 95358	209-537-4744	R	7*	.1
25	Pet Poultry Products Inc—*Robert Hunsberger*	PO Box 128, Bridgeville DE 19933	302-337-8223	R	6*	<.1
26	Comer Packing Company Inc—*Jimmy Comer*	PO Box 33, Aberdeen MS 39730	662-369-9325	R	6*	<.1
27	Joseph Trenk and Sons—*David Trenk*	171 Thomas St, Newark NJ 07114	973-589-5778	R	5*	<.1
28	G And H Forty-Niners Inc—*Don Weaver*	PO Box 37, Fredericksburg PA 17026	717-865-2597	R	4*	<.1
29	Brown Brothers Produce Co—*John Brown*	9647 Idot Shed Rd, Nashville IL 62263	618-327-8154	R	4*	<.1
30	Norbest Inc—*John Hall*	PO Box 890, Moroni UT 84646		S	3*	<.1
31	David Mitchell Inc—*David Mitchell*	210 Park Dr, Voorhees NJ 08043	856-429-2610	R	3*	<.1
32	American Poultry International Ltd—*Gerry Holaday*	5420 I 55 N Ste A, Jackson MS 39211	601-956-1715	R	3*	<.1

TOTALS: SIC 5144 Poultry & Poultry Products
Companies: 32 — 2,006 — 5.7

5145 Confectionery

Rank	Company Name—*Executive Officer*	Address, City, State, Zip	Phone	Type	Fin	Empls
1	Ferrero U S A Inc—*Bernard Kreilmann*	600 Cottontail Ln, Somerset NJ 08873	732-764-9300	R	9,238*	.5
2	Burklund Distributors Inc—*Jon Burklund*	2500 N Main St Ste 3, East Peoria IL 61611	309-694-1900	R	164*	.2
3	Los Angeles Nut House—*Donald Presant*	1601 E Olympic Blvd St, Los Angeles CA 90021	213-623-2541	R	51*	<.1
4	Fritz Company Inc—*Elizabeth Fritz*	1912 Hastings Ave, Newport MN 55055	651-459-9751	R	48*	.1
5	Score Acquisitions Corp—*Reid Chase*	200 Corporate Dr, Blauvelt NY 10913	845-353-1251	R	47*	<.1
6	Perfetti Van Melle USA Inc—*Ronald Korenhof*	PO Box 18190, Erlanger KY 41018	859-283-1234	R	46*	.2
7	Kar Nut Products Co—*Ernest Nicolay*	1200 E 14 Mile Rd Ste, Madison Heights MI 48071	248-588-1903	R	40*	.1
8	SWD Corp—*Carl Berger*	PO Box 340, Lima OH 45802	419-227-2436	R	38*	.1
9	Peanut Processors Inc—*Houston Brisson*	PO Box 160, Dublin NC 28332	910-862-2136	R	34*	<.1
10	R W Garcia Company Inc—*Robert Garcia*	PO Box 8290, San Jose CA 95155	408-287-4616	R	20*	.1
11	Abdallah Inc—*Steven Hegedus*	3501 County Rd 42 W, Burnsville MN 55306	952-890-4770	R	18*	.1
12	Candyrific LLC—*Rob Auerbach*	3738 Lexington Rd, Louisville KY 40207	502-893-3626	R	17*	<.1
13	Edward A Berg and Sons—*Harry Berg*	75 W Century Rd, Paramus NJ 07652	201-845-8200	R	16*	.2
14	Queen City Wholesale Inc	PO Box 1083, Sioux Falls SD 57101	605-336-3215	R	16*	<.1
15	Ohio Hickory Harvest Brand Products Inc—*Darlene Swiatkowski*	90 Logan Pkwy, Akron OH 44319	330-644-6266	R	11*	<.1
16	Kennedy Wholesale Inc—*Al Paulus*	PO Box 2426, Irwindale CA 91706	818-241-9977	R	11*	<.1
17	John F Trompeter Co—*Dave Nash*	637 E Main St, Louisville KY 40202	502-585-5852	R	10*	<.1
18	BBG Management Group—*R Burkle*	12164 California St, Yucaipa CA 92399	909-790-1876	R	8*	.1
19	Lavin Candy Company Inc—*Irvin C Reid*	4989 S Catherine St, Plattsburgh NY 12901	518-563-4630	R	8*	.1
20	Santa Clara Nut Co—*James Pusateri*	1590 Little Orchard St, San Jose CA 95110	408-298-2425	R	7*	<.1

Note: An asterisk (*) indicates an estimated financial figure. The company type code used is as follows: R = Private, P = Public, S = Private Subsidiary, B = Public Subsidiary, D = Division, J = Joint Venture, I = Investment Fund.

COMPANY RANKINGS BY SALES WITHIN 4-DIGIT SIC

Rank	Company Name—Executive Officer	Address, City, State, Zip	Phone	Type	Fin	Empls
21	Davidson's Of Dundee—Tom Davidson	PO Box 800, Dundee FL 33838	863-439-1698	R	7*	<.1
22	Ramsey Popcorn Company Inc—Wilfred Sieg	5645 Clover Valley Rd, Ramsey IN 47166	812-347-2441	R	6*	<.1
23	Black Bear Bottling Group LLC—Peter Caruso	2025 W S Branch Blvd, Oak Creek WI 53154	414-302-5660	R	6*	<.1
24	Powers Candy And Nut Co—John Cooley	PO Box 6525, Spokane WA 99217	509-489-1955	R	6*	<.1
25	Poppee's Popcorn Inc—Tom Mcguire	38727 Taylor Pkwy, North Ridgeville OH 44035	440-327-0775	R	6*	<.1
26	Rocky Peanut Company Inc—Joseph Russo	1525 Wanda St, Ferndale MI 48220	248-545-3540	R	5*	<.1
27	Pez Candy Inc—Joseph Vittoria	35 Prindle Hill Rd, Orange CT 06477	203-795-0531	R	5*	<.1
28	International Commodity Distributors Inc—Justin Lewis	7260 Acacia Ave, Garden Grove CA 92841	714-799-9822	R	5*	<.1
29	Midwest-Northern Inc—Laure Rockman	3105 Columbia Ave Nw, Minneapolis MN 55418	612-781-6596	R	5*	<.1
30	Dayton Nut Specialties Inc—Stanley Maschino	919 N Main St, Dayton OH 45405	937-223-3225	R	5*	<.1
31	Stichler Products Inc—Martin Deutschman	1800 N 12th St Ste 1, Reading PA 19604	610-921-0211	R	4*	<.1
32	Laymon Candy Company Inc—Kenneth Laymon	276 Commercial Rd, San Bernardino CA 92408	909-825-4408	R	4*	<.1
33	Nut Bar Co—David Weidenfeller	4050 Roger B Chaffee Av, Grand Rapids MI 49548	616-241-3489	R	4*	<.1
34	Revonah Pretzel LLC—Kevin Biddelspach	1250 York St, Hanover PA 17331	717-632-4477	R	4*	<.1
35	Select Drink Inc—Susan Kinsella	5757 N Lindbergh Blvd, Hazelwood MO 63042	314-731-4500	R	4*	<.1
36	Victor Products Corp—Mitchell Zinder	PO Box 7910, Richmond VA 23223	804-643-9091	R	4*	<.1
37	BW Clifford Inc—Ronald Bernstein	90 Elm St, Morristown NJ 07960	908-829-0007	R	3*	<.1
38	Asbury Syrup Company Inc—Anthony Sammarco	904 Sunset Ave Ste 1, Asbury Park NJ 07712	732-774-5746	R	3*	<.1
39	Hillson Nut Co—Richard Hillson	PO Box 602038, Cleveland OH 44102	216-961-4477	R	2*	<.1
40	Fort Fudge Shop Inc—Robert Heilman	PO Box 340, Mackinaw City MI 49701	231-436-8931	R	1*	<.1
41	Thomas P Wilbur—Thomas Wilbur	174 Lower Main St, Freeport ME 04032	207-865-6506	R	1*	<.1

TOTALS: SIC 5145 Confectionery
Companies: 41 — — 9,935 2.4

5146 Fish & Seafoods

Rank	Company Name—Executive Officer	Address, City, State, Zip	Phone	Type	Fin	Empls
1	Inland Seafood Corp—Joel Knox	1651 Montreal Cir, Tucker GA 30084	404-350-5850	R	230*	.3
2	Atalanta Corp—George Gellert	1 Atalanta Plz, Elizabeth NJ 07206	908-351-8000	R	208*	.1
3	Stavis Seafoods Inc—Richard Stavis	212 Northern Ave Ste 3, Boston MA 02210	617-482-6349	R	192*	.1
4	Empress International Ltd—Tim McLellan	5 Dakota Dr Ste 303, Lake Success NY 11042	516-740-4100	S	180*	.1
5	Ore-Cal Corp—William Shinbane	634 S Crocker St, Los Angeles CA 90021	213-680-9540	R	97*	.2
6	Robert Wholey and Company Inc—James Wholey	1711 Penn Ave, Pittsburgh PA 15222		R	74*	.2
7	Progressive Companies Inc—Larry Stoller	PO Box B, Spirit Lake IA 51360	712-336-1750	R	47*	<.1
8	Floribbean Wholesale Inc—Mike Black	5151 NW 17th St, Margate FL 33063	954-968-4091	R	34*	<.1
9	Mazzetta Co—Tom Mazzetta	PO Box 1126, Highland Park IL 60035	847-433-1150	R	32*	<.1
10	Louis Foehrkolb Inc—Louis Foehrkolb	7901 Oceano Ave, Jessup MD 20794		R	29*	<.1
11	Isf Trading Inc—Atsshi Tamaki	PO Box 772, Portland ME 04104	207-879-1575	R	29*	.2
12	Ruggiero Seafood Inc—Rocco Ruggiero	PO Box 5369, Newark NJ 07105	973-589-0524	R	28*	.2
13	Slade Gorton and Company Inc—Kimberly Gorton	225 Southampton St, Boston MA 02118	617-442-5800	R	28*	.1
14	East Coast Seafood Inc—Michael Tourkistas	PO Box 790, Lynn MA 01903	781-593-1737	R	28*	.2
15	United Shellfish Company Inc—George Pappas	PO Box 146, Grasonville MD 21638	410 827-0171	R	26*	.1
16	Pacific Pride Seafoods Inc—Frank Dulcich	4520 107th St Sw, Mukilteo WA 98275	425-347-7994	R	22*	.1
17	Lund's Fisheries Inc—Jeff Reichle	PO Box 830, Cape May NJ 08204	609-884-7600	R	21*	.1
18	Morley Sales Company Inc—Gary R Slavik	119 N 2nd St, Geneva IL 60134	630-845-8750	R	20*	<.1
19	Ipswish Shellfish Company Inc—Chrissi Pappas	PO Box 550, Ipswich MA 01938	978-356-4371	R	19*	.1
20	Eastern Fisheries Inc—Ronald Enoksen	200 Herman Melville Bl, New Bedford MA 02740	508-993-5300	R	18*	.1
21	Bama Sea Products Inc—John Stephens	756 28th St S, Saint Petersburg FL 33712	727-327-3474	R	18*	.1
22	Southeast Alaska Smoked Salmon Company Inc—Giovanni Gallizio	550 S Franklin St, Juneau AK 99801	907-463-4617	R	16*	<.1
23	Annette Island Co—Freeman Mcgilton	PO Box 10, Metlakatla AK 99926	907-886-4661	R	16*	.1
24	Casey's Seafood Inc—Jim Casey	807 Jefferson Ave, Newport News VA 23607	757-928-1979	R	16*	.1
25	B and J Seafood LLC	PO Box 3321, New Bern NC 28564	252-637-1552	R	13*	.1
26	Race Street Foods Inc—Gino Barsanti	PO Box 28385, San Jose CA 95159	408-294-6161	R	12*	.1
27	Little River Seafood Inc—Gregory Lewis	440 Rock Town Rd, Reedville VA 22539	804-453-3670	R	12*	.1
28	International Shell Inc—Nancy Arnold	PO Box 609, Camden TN 38320	731-584-7747	R	12*	<.1
29	Bornstein Seafood Inc—Colin Bornstein	PO Box 188, Oak Harbor WA 98277	360-734-7990	R	11*	.2
30	Bristol Seafood Inc—Ray Swenton	PO Box 486, Portland ME 04112	207-761-4251	R	11*	.1
31	LD Amory and Company Inc—Charles Amory Jr	PO Box 518, Hampton VA 23669	757-722-1915	R	10*	<.1
32	North Landing Limited LLC—Terry Bautista	610 Brighton Rd, Clifton NJ 07012	973-249-5300	R	10*	.1
33	Quality Crab Company Inc—William Barclift	177 Knobbs Creek Dr, Elizabeth City NC 27909	252-338-0808	R	10*	.1
34	AML International Inc—Louis Juillard	7 Conway St, New Bedford MA 02740	508-979-1200	R	9*	.1
35	Sea Pearl Seafood Company Inc—Joseph Ladnier	PO Box 649, Bayou La Batre AL 36509	251-824-2129	R	9*	.1
36	Garland F Fulcher Seafood Company Inc—Sherrill Styron	PO Box 100, Oriental NC 28571	252-249-1341	R	8*	<.1
37	International C-Food Marketing—William Millerstrom	PO Box 2213, Florence OR 97439	541-997-7978	R	8*	.1
38	Ngc Inc—Noah Clark	PO Box 608, Narragansett RI 02882	401-789-2200	R	8*	<.1
39	York River Seafood Company Inc—John Shackelford	PO Box 239, Hayes VA 23072	804-642-2151	R	7*	.1
40	Seapac Of Idaho Inc—Ken Ashley	PO Box 546, Buhl ID 83316	208-326-3100	R	7*	.1
41	Wilfred's Sea Food Inc—Gary Machowski	805 Cumberland Hill Rd, Woonsocket RI 02895	401-769-6260	R	7*	.1
42	Metompkin Bay Oyster Company Inc—Casey Todd	PO Box 671, Crisfield MD 21817	410-968-0660	R	7*	.1
43	Stokes Fish Co—Beryl Stokes	PO Box 490298, Leesburg FL 34749	352-787-4335	R	6*	.1
44	Paul Piazza and Son Inc—Kristen Baumer	PO Box 52049, New Orleans LA 70152	504-524-6011	R	6*	.1
45	Sierra Seafood Specialties LLC—Joe Sweat	PO Box 235, Oakhurst CA 93644	559-683-3479	R	6*	.1
46	George Braun Oyster Company Inc—Kenneth Homan	PO Box 971, Cutchogue NY 11935	631-734-6700	R	6*	.1
47	Blanchard's Seafood Inc—Linda Blanchard	1348 Bayou Alexander H, Saint Martinville LA 70582	337-394-6907	R	6*	.1
48	Deep Creek Custom Packing Inc—Jeff Berger	PO Box 39229, Ninilchik AK 99639	907-567-3980	R	6*	.1
49	Acadiana Fisherman's Company Op—James Blanchard	1020 Devillier St, Breaux Bridge LA 70517	337-228-7503	R	5*	.1
50	South Pier Fish Company Inc—Paul Barbera	PO Box 5310, Wakefield RI 02880	401-783-6611	R	5*	.1
51	Shore Seafood Inc—Greg Linton	19424 Saxis Rd, Saxis VA 23427	757-824-5517	R	5*	.1
52	James E Headley Oyster Co—James Headley	565 Gardys Mill Rd, Callao VA 22435	804-529-7169	R	5*	.1
53	Rome Packing Company Inc—Albert Greca	2266 Pawtucket Ave, East Providence RI 02914	401-228-7170	R	5*	.1
54	Raffield Fisheries Inc—William Raffield	PO Box 309, Port Saint Joe FL 32457	850-229-8229	R	5*	.1
55	Service Smoked Fish Corp—Jay Wiener	54 Throop Ave, Brooklyn NY 11206	718-388-4067	R	4*	.1
56	P and G Trading Company Inc—Gary Davis	2 Ott St, Trenton NJ 08638	609-394-5177	R	4*	.1
57	Weyand Fisheries Inc—David Blume	600 Biddle Ave, Wyandotte MI 48192	734-284-0402	R	4*	.1
58	Harlon's L A Fish LLC—Michelle Konnicker	PO Box 486, Kenner LA 70063	504-467-3809	R	4*	.1
59	Amende and Schultz Corp—Matt Garaway	PO Box 788, South Pasadena CA 91031	323-682-3806	R	4*	.1
60	Fresher Then Fresh Inc—Ronald H Wrenn	700 Tulip Dr, Gastonia NC 28052	704-867-1818	R	4*	.1
61	Mendocino Sea Vegetable Co—John Lewallen	PO Box 455, Philo CA 95466	707-895-2996	R	4*	.1
62	Gulf Pride Enterprises Inc—Janet Seymour	PO Box 355, Biloxi MS 39533	228-432-2488	R	4*	<.1
63	Vincent Piazza Jr and Sons Seafood Inc—Vincent Piazza	PO Box 10325, New Orleans LA 70181	504-734-0012	R	4*	<.1
64	Guidry's Catfish Inc—Bobby Guidry	1093 Henderson Hwy, Breaux Bridge LA 70517	337-228-7545	R	3*	<.1

Rank	Company Name—*Executive Officer*	Address, City, State, Zip	Phone	Type	Fin	Empls
65	Mill Cove Lobster Pound Co—*Jeffrey Lewis*	PO Box 280, Boothbay Harbor ME 04538	207-633-3340	R	3*	<.1
66	Ocean Crest Seafoods Inc—*Anthony P Parco Sr*	PO Box 1183, Gloucester MA 01931	978-281-0232	R	3*	<.1
67	Shores and Ruark Seafood Inc—*Rufus Ruark*	PO Box 567, Urbanna VA 23175	804-758-5640	R	3*	<.1
68	Mount Pleasant Seafood Co—*Rial Fitch*	1 Seafood Dr, Mount Pleasant SC 29464	843-884-4122	R	3*	<.1
69	LN White and Company Inc—*David White*	225 W 34th St, New York NY 10122	212-239-7474	R	3*	<.1
70	Catfish Wholesale Inc—*James Rich*	PO Box 759, Abbeville LA 70511	337-643-6700	R	3*	.1
71	Carolina Seafoods Inc—*Rutledge Leland*	PO Box 396, Mc Clellanville SC 29458	843-887-3713	R	2*	<.1
72	Clayton's Crab Company Inc—*Clayton Korecky*	5775 Us Hwy 1, Rockledge FL 32955	321-636-6673	R	2*	<.1
73	Purcell's Seafood Inc—*Richard Harding*	PO Box 7, Burgess VA 22432	804-453-3300	R	2*	<.1
74	Martin Fish Company Inc—*J Martin*	12929 Harbor Rd, Ocean City MD 21842	410-213-2195	R	2*	<.1
75	Keyser Brother's Inc—*Robert Keyser*	965 Honest Point Rd, Lottsburg VA 22511	804-529-6837	R	2*	<.1
76	Sau-Sea Foods Inc—*Antonio Estadella*	PO Box 1380, Water Mill NY 11976	631-726-0269	R	1*	<.1
77	Fishhawk Fisheries Inc—*Steve Fick*	PO Box 715, Astoria OR 97103	503-325-5252	R	1*	<.1

TOTALS: SIC 5146 Fish & Seafoods
Companies: 77 — 1,730 — 4.4

5147 Meats & Meat Products

Rank	Company Name—*Executive Officer*	Address, City, State, Zip	Phone	Type	Fin	Empls
1	Boar's Head Provisions Company Inc—*Van Ayvazian*	1819 Main St Ste 800, Sarasota FL 34236	941-955-0994	R	2,382*	.1
2	JAO Meat Packing Company Inc—*James Ortenzio*	565 W St, New York NY 10014	212-243-1121	R	1,910*	.5
3	Colorado Boxed Beef Co—*John J Rattigan Jr*	302 Progress Rd, Auburndale FL 33823	863-967-0636	R	1,088*	.6
4	Maverick Ranch Natural Meats—*Roy Moore*	5360 N Franklin St, Denver CO 80216	303-294-0146	R	405*	.1
5	Omaha Steaks International—*Tod Simon*	PO Box 3300, Omaha NE 68103	402-331-1010	R	376*	2.3
6	Porky Products Inc—*Jonathan Ewig*	400 Port Carteret Dr, Carteret NJ 07008	732-541-0200	R	374*	.3
7	Agar Supply Inc—*Karen Bressler*	225 John Hancock Rd My, Taunton MA 02780	508-821-2060	R	343*	.3
8	Earp Distribution—*Steve Hewlett*	6550 Kansas Ave, Kansas City KS 66111	913-287-3311	R	267*	.3
9	Dole and Bailey Inc—*Nancy Matheson-Burns*	PO Box 2405, Woburn MA 01888	781-935-1234	R	196*	.2
10	United Meat Company Inc—*Philip Gee Jr*	1040 Bryant St, San Francisco CA 94103	415-864-2118	R	195*	.1
11	Foodcomm International—*Greg Bourke*	4260 El Camino Real, Palo Alto CA 94306	650-813-1300	R	168*	<.1
12	Aas Holding Co—*Curtis Pohl*	PO Box 4796, Portland OR 97208	503-284-3314	R	155*	.1
13	Dan's Prize Inc—*Mark Morey*	930 Interstate Ridge D, Gainesville GA 30501	770-503-1881	R	150*	.3
14	Halperns' Steak And Seafood Co—*Kirk Halpern*	4685 Welcome All Rd Sw, Atlanta GA 30349	404-767-9229	R	150*	.2
15	Tony's Fine Foods—*Karl Berger*	PO Box 1501, West Sacramento CA 95605		R	133*	.4
16	Pancho's Management Inc—*Brenda Berger O'Brien*	2855 Lamb Pl, Memphis TN 38118	901-362-9691	R	129*	.1
17	Midamar Corp—*Bill Aossey*	PO Box 218, Cedar Rapids IA 52406	319-362-3711	R	128*	<.1
18	D'Artagnan Inc—*George Faison*	280 Wilson Ave, Newark NJ 07105		R	125*	.1
19	K Heeps Inc—*James Heeps*	5239 W Tilghman St, Allentown PA 18104	610-530-8010	R	108*	.1
20	Waco Meat Service Inc—*Dana Harrell*	PO Box 7249, Waco TX 76714	254-772-5644	R	105*	<.1
21	Sierra Meat Company Inc—*Armando Flocchini Jr*	1330 Capital Blvd, Reno NV 89502	775-322-4073	R	86*	.1
22	DeBragga and Spitler Inc—*Marc John Sarrazin*	826-D Washington St, New York NY 10014	212-924-1311	R	58*	.1
23	H C Schau and Son Inc—*Charles Schau*	10350 Argonne Dr Ste 4, Woodridge IL 60517	630-783-1000	R	55*	.2
24	Trim-Rite Food Corporation Inc—*James Jendruczek*	801 Commerce Pkwy, Carpentersville IL 60110	847-649-3400	R	55*	.2
25	Patterson Brothers Meat Co—*Micheal Schirato*	PO Box 710505, Dallas TX 75371	214-821-3300	R	48*	.1
26	Mcfarling Foods Inc—*Michael Mc Farling*	PO Box 2207, Indianapolis IN 46206	317-635-2633	R	48*	.2
27	Rochester Meat Co—*Scott Hudspeth*	1825 7th St Nw, Rochester MN 55901	507-529-4700	R	43*	.2
28	Julian Freirich Food Products Inc—*Jeff Freirich*	PO Box 1529, Salisbury NC 28145	704-636-2621	R	35*	<.1
29	White Apron Inc—*Eugene Schlessinger*	340 Cliffwood Park St, Brea CA 92821	714-255-8560	R	35*	.2
30	Ferris-Stahl-Meyer Packing Corp—*Eli Hochman*	PO Box 5000, Bronx NY 10460	718-328-0059	R	34*	.2
31	Glen Rose Meat Services Inc—*Glen Rose*	4561 Loma Vista Ave, Vernon CA 90058	323-589-3393	R	32*	<.1
32	Star Food Products Inc—*Norman Mabry*	2050 Willow Spring Ln, Burlington NC 27215	336-227-4079	R	31*	.1
33	Jensen Meat Company Inc—*Robert Jensen*	2525 Birch St, Vista CA 92081	760-727-6700	R	26*	.1
34	Buedel Food Products Co—*Kristyn Benson*	7661 S 78th Ave Unit A, Bridgeview IL 60455	708-496-3500	R	25*	.1
35	S S Logan Packing Co—*Nester Logan*	PO Box 5658, Huntington WV 25703	304-525-7625	R	24*	.1
36	Calumet Diversified Meats Inc—*Lawrence Becker*	10000 80th Ave, Pleasant Prairie WI 53158	262-947-7200	R	24*	.1
37	Tri-City Meats Inc—*Randy Hetrick*	1346 N Hickory Ave, Meridian ID 83642	208-884-2600	R	24*	.1
38	Three Sons Inc—*Ronald Day*	PO Box 6, Pico Rivera CA 90660	562-801-4100	R	23*	.1
39	Greentree Packing Inc—*Michael Waters* JAO Meat Packing Company Inc	PO Box 386, Passaic NJ 07055	973-473-1305	S	22*	.1
40	Interstate Meat Distributors Inc—*Jerry Meng*	PO Box 298, Clackamas OR 97015	503-656-0633	R	22*	.1
41	Amity Packing Company Inc—*Richard Samuel*	210 N Green St, Chicago IL 60607	312-942-0270	R	21*	.1
42	Columbia Packing Company Inc—*Joseph Ondrusek*	2807 E 11th St, Dallas TX 75203	214-946-8171	R	20*	.1
43	Omaha Beef Company Inc—*Brian Street*	PO Box 339, Danbury CT 06813	203-748-2651	R	20*	<.1
44	Smith Dale T And Sons Meat Packing Corp—*Dale Smith*	PO Box 479, Draper UT 84020	801-571-3611	R	20*	.1
45	Quality Boneless Beef Company Inc—*Cary Wetzstein*	PO Box 337, West Fargo ND 58078	701-282-0202	R	19*	.1
46	Deen Meats and Cooked Foods—*Danny Deen*	PO Box 4155, Fort Worth TX 76164	817-335-2257	R	19*	.1
47	Thompson Packers Inc—*Mary Thompson*	550 Carnation St, Slidell LA 70460	985-641-6640	R	18*	.1
48	Heartland Meat Company Inc—*Joseph Stidman*	3461 Main St, Chula Vista CA 91911	619-407-3668	R	18*	.1
49	Mike Hudson Distributing Inc—*Jim Davis*	PO Box 808033, Petaluma CA 94975	707-763-7388	R	18*	.1
50	Consumers Packing Company Inc—*William Schutz*	1301 Carson Dr, Melrose Park IL 60160	708-345-6780	R	18*	.1
51	Ditta Meat Co—*Sammy Ditta*	PO Box 5623, Pasadena TX 77508	281-487-2010	R	18*	.1
52	Red Bird Farms Distribution Co—*Mareo Torito*	PO Box 1197, Englewood CO 80150	303-934-2200	R	17*	.1
53	Cambridge Packing Company Inc—*Bruce Rodman*	41 Food Mart Rd, Boston MA 02118	617-269-6700	R	17*	.1
54	Erla's Inc—*Clarence Erla*	PO Box 68, Cass City MI 48726	989-872-2191	R	16*	.1
55	Boyle Meat Co	1638 St Louis Ave, Kansas City MO 64101	816-842-5852	R	16*	.1
56	James Calvetti Meats Inc—*James C Calvetti*	4240 S Morgan St, Chicago IL 60609	773-927-9242	R	16*	<.1
57	West Trading Co—*John Wehba*	3517 Conway St, Fort Worth TX 76111	817-831-0051	R	16*	.1
58	Tillamook Country Smoker Inc—*A Smith*	PO Box 3120, Bay City OR 97107	503-377-2222	R	16*	.3
59	Ray's Wholesale Meats Inc—*Ray Shuel*	PO Box 9875, Yakima WA 98909	509-575-0729	R	15*	.1
60	Smith Packing Company Inc—*Wesley Smith*	PO Box 520, Utica NY 13503	315-732-5125	R	15*	.1
61	Casing Associates Inc—*Phillip Schwartz*	1120 Close Ave, Bronx NY 10472	718-842-7151	R	15*	<.1
62	Cameco Inc—*Jerome Perl*	PO Box 209, Verona NJ 07044	973-239-2700	R	13*	.1
63	R and R Provision Co—*Richard Rogers*	PO Box 889, Easton PA 18044	610-258-5366	R	13*	.1
64	Jemm Wholesale Meat Company Inc—*Daniel Goldman*	4649 W Armitage Ave, Chicago IL 60639	773-523-8161	R	13*	.1
65	O'steen Meat Specialties Inc—*Jim Steen*	2126 N Broadway Ave, Oklahoma City OK 73103	405-236-1952	R	13*	.1
66	Dutch Prime Foods Inc—*Bernard Kennedy*	PO Box 660, Long Branch NJ 07740	732-222-0910	R	13*	.1
67	Poston Packing Company Of Florence Inc—*Aubrey Poston*	5810 Pamplico Hwy, Florence SC 29505	843-662-1376	R	13*	.1
68	Portillo's Food Service Inc—*Richard Portillo*	1751 W Armitage Ct, Addison IL 60101	630-620-0460	R	12*	.1
69	Miami Purveyors Inc—*Rick Rosenberg*	7350 Nw 8th St, Miami FL 33126	305-262-6170	R	12*	.1
70	Berry Veal Corp—*Alan Gioia*	1421 Neptune Dr, Boynton Beach FL 33426	561-736-1993	R	12*	.1
71	Fairway Packing Inc—*Eugene Baratta*	PO Box 7097, Detroit MI 48207	313-832-2711	R	12*	<.1

Note: An asterisk (*) indicates an estimated financial figure. The company type code used is as follows: R = Private, P = Public, S = Private Subsidiary, B = Public Subsidiary, D = Division, J = Joint Venture, I = Investment Fund.

ank	Company Name—*Executive Officer*	Address, City, State, Zip	Phone	Type	Fin	Empls
72	Great Western Beef Co—*John Wilkinson*	4044 S Halsted St, Chicago IL 60609	773-927-3790	R	12*	.1
73	Pritzlaff Wholesale Meats Inc—*Bruce Pritzlaff*	17025 W Glendale Dr, New Berlin WI 53151	262-786-1151	R	11*	.1
74	Tyler Meat Co—*James Jaffe*	PO Box 9296, Toledo OH 43697	419-244-6200	R	11*	.1
75	Lone Star Food Service Co—*Franklin Hall*	1403 E 6th St, Austin TX 78702	512-478-3161	R	11*	<.1
76	Habbersett Sausage Inc	103 S Railroad Ave, Bridgeville DE 19933	610-532-9973	S	11*	<.1
77	Columbia Empire Meat Company Inc—*Cecilia Lux*	3820 Se Milwaukie Ave, Portland OR 97202	503-234-9926	R	11*	<.1
78	Goodnight Brothers Produce Company Inc—*Bill Goodnight*	PO Box 287, Boone NC 28607	828-264-8892	R	10*	<.1
79	Bunting's Wholesale Market Inc—*Robert Winn*	2250 Lone Star Dr, Dallas TX 75212	214-634-0456	R	10*	<.1
80	L and C Meat Inc—*Gerald Likely*	PO Box 46, Independence MO 64051	816-796-6100	R	10*	<.1
81	Ideal Meats and Provision—*Lawrence Vad*	18425 Parthenia Pl, Northridge CA 91325	818-886-9733	R	9*	<.1
82	Tulsa Beef and Provision Inc—*Larry Compston*	1537 E 7th St, Tulsa OK 74120	918-587-5197	R	9*	<.1
83	Grant Park Packing Company Inc—*Joe Maffei*	842 W Lake St, Chicago IL 60607	312-421-4096	R	9*	<.1
84	O'jacks Inc—*Steven Slavin*	PO Box 245, Eldred PA 16731	814-225-4755	R	9*	<.1
85	Mineola Packing Co—*Johnie Henderson*	PO Box 928, Mineola TX 75773	903-569-5355	R	8*	.1
86	Rinehart's Meat Processing Inc—*Jack Harris*	PO Box 6880, Branson MO 65615	417-334-2044	R	8*	<.1
87	Slovacek Foods LLP—*Laura Doskocil*	PO Box 220, Snook TX 77878	979-272-8625	R	8*	<.1
88	S and S Meat Company Inc—*John Stilka*	637 Prospect Ave, Kansas City MO 64124	816-241-4700	R	8	<.1
89	Blue Mountain Meats Inc—*Scott Frost*	333 S 2nd E, Monticello UT 84535	435-587-2289	R	8*	<.1
90	Burger Maker Company Inc—*David Schweid*	666 16th St, Carlstadt NJ 07072	201-939-4747	R	8*	<.1
91	Yoakum Packing Co—*Glen Kusak*	PO Box 192, Yoakum TX 77995	361-293-3541	R	8*	<.1
92	SP Wholesale Meat Co—*Charlie Ryan*	2331 Nw 23rd Ave, Portland OR 97210	503-234-0579	R	8*	<.1
93	Carriage House Foods Inc—*Jerry Grauf*	1131 Dayton Ave, Ames IA 50010	515-232-2273	R	7*	<.1
94	ALS Inc—*Thomas Lampe*	3730 Westlake Ct, West Lafayette IN 47906	765-497-4750	R	7*	.1
95	Economy Locker Storage Company Inc—*Thomas Kubinsky*	324 Worthington Ln, Muncy PA 17756	570-546-2241	R	7*	<.1
96	A To Z Portion Control Meats Inc—*Lee Kagy*	201 N Main St, Bluffton OH 45817	419-358-2926	R	7*	<.1
97	Kelly Corned Beef Company Of Chicago—*Marvin Eisenberg*	3531 N Elston Ave, Chicago IL 60618	773-588-2882	R	7*	<.1
98	Manger Packing Corp—*Alvin Manger*	124 S Franklintown Rd, Baltimore MD 21223	410-233-0126	R	7*	<.1
99	Walker Meats Corp—*Donald Walker*	821 Tyus Carrollton Rd, Carrollton GA 30117	770-834-8171	R	7*	<.1
100	Cornbelt Beef Corp—*Samuel Flatt*	PO Box 8132, Detroit MI 48208	313-237-0087	R	7*	<.1
101	New City Packing Company Inc—*Marvin Fagel*	PO Box 128, North Aurora IL 60542		R	7*	<.1
102	Cypress Provision Co—*Steve Scully*	PO Box 70688, Houston TX 77270	713-862-6328	R	6*	<.1
103	Lori Holding Co—*Joseph Siemer*	1400 Commerce Dr, New Lexington OH 43764	740-342-3230	R	6*	<.1
104	El Toro Meat Packing Corp—*Hortensia Rodriguez*	738 Nw 72nd St, Miami FL 33150	305-836-4461	R	6*	<.1
105	Omni Custom Meats Inc—*Curtis Sullivan*	151 Vanderbilt Ct, Bowling Green KY 42103	270-796-6664	R	6*	<.1
106	Sharon Packing Company Inc—*Arthur Mogg*	101 Broadway Ave, Farrell PA 16121	724-346-5574	R	6*	<.1
107	Frozen Food Service Corp—*Jerry Clellan*	PO Box 542, Salem IN 47167	812-883-2196	R	6*	<.1
108	Tomcyndi Inc—*Thomas Summers*	PO Box 09083, Chicago IL 60609	773-847-5400	R	5*	<.1
109	Pontrelli and Laricchia Limited A California LP—*Dominic Pontrelli*	6080 Malburg Way, Vernon CA 90058	323-583-6690	R	5*	<.1
110	Harvin Choice Meats Inc—*Sep Harvin*	PO Box 939, Sumter SC 29151	803-775-9367	R	5*	.1
111	YMBD Inc—*Ron Butler*	841 Watson Ave, Wilmington CA 90744	310-549-4992	R	5*	<.1
112	Plains Meat Company Ltd—*John Adams*	812 Ave G, Lubbock TX 79401	806-765-5595	R	5*	<.1
113	John Garner Meats Inc—*John Garner*	PO Box 625, Van Buren AR 72957	479-474-6894	R	5*	<.1
114	Liberty Bell Steak Co—*John Bellios*	PO Box 12728, Philadelphia PA 19134	215-537-4797	R	5*	<.1
115	Troutman Brothers Inc—*Glenn L Troutman*	PO Box 73, Klingerstown PA 17941	570-425-2341	R	5*	<.1
116	Krusinski John—*John Krusinski*	6300 Heisley Ave, Cleveland OH 44105	216-441-0100	R	5*	<.1
117	Canal Fulton Provision Inc—*George Mizarek*	2014 Locust St S, Canal Fulton OH 44614	330-854-3502	R	5*	<.1
118	International Meat Company Inc—*Joseph Bomprezzi*	7107 W Grand Ave, Chicago IL 60707	773-622-1400	R	4*	<.1
119	Lindsay Foods Inc—*Gary Lindsay*	PO Box 4403, Milwaukee WI 53204	414-649-2500	R	4*	<.1
120	Mcdonald's Meats Inc—*David Mcdonald*	PO Box 117, Clear Lake MN 55319	320-743-2311	R	4*	<.1
121	Malcolm's Meat Service Inc—*Barbara Lane*	PO Box 1239, Bristol VA 24203	276-669-1107	R	4*	<.1
122	Royal Meats Inc—*Greg Arnoldy*	464 Forest St, Wyandotte MI 48192	734-285-1410	R	4*	<.1
123	Prime Smoked Meats Inc—*Steven Sacks*	220 Alice St, Oakland CA 94607	510-832-7167	R	4*	<.1
124	Schroedl's Brothers Inc—*Dennis Schroedl*	N3705 State Rd 89, Jefferson WI 53549	920-674-3760	R	4*	<.1
125	P and N Packing Inc—*Walter Newton*	RR Box 180, Wyalusing PA 18853	570-746-1974	R	4*	<.1
126	George G Ruppersberger and Sons Inc—*John Ruppersberger*	2639 Pennsylvania Ave, Baltimore MD 21217	410-669-2600	R	4*	<.1
127	Cable Meat Center Inc—*Tom Wheat*	PO Box 527, Marlow OK 73055	580-658-6646	R	4*	<.1
128	Lee's Sausage Company Inc—*Walter Lee*	1054 Neeses Hwy, Orangeburg SC 29115	803-534-5517	R	3*	<.1
129	Southern Provision Company Inc—*Scott Mchenry*	1944 Rossville Ave, Chattanooga TN 37408	423-267-3894	R	3*	<.1
130	Boesl Packing Company Inc—*Jeffrey Burton*	2322 Belair Rd, Baltimore MD 21213	410-675-1071	R	3*	<.1
131	Martin's Specialty Sausage Co—*Martin Guinta*	150 Harmony Rd, Mickleton NJ 08056	856-423-4000	R	3*	<.1
132	Natural Meat Specialties—*Dave Johnston*	2065 Rockhurst, Colorado Springs CO 80918	719-548-1735	R	3*	<.1
133	Crest Meat Company Inc—*Mark Tubre*	134 Brookhollow Esplan, New Orleans LA 70123	985-345-6845	R	3*	<.1
134	Munsee Meats Inc—*E Selvey*	PO Box 2843, Muncie IN 47307	765-288-3645	R	3*	<.1
135	Rocko Meats—*James Fraley*	12623 Catoctin Furnace, Thurmont MD 21788	301-271-7030	R	3*	<.1
136	Burdick Packing Company Inc—*Michael Burdick*	PO Box 1601, Battle Creek MI 49016	269-962-5111	R	3*	<.1
137	Sculli Brothers Inc	1114 S Front St, Philadelphia PA 19147	215-336-1223	R	3*	<.1
138	Kewaskum Frozen Foods Inc—*Paul Ries*	PO Box 510, Kewaskum WI 53040	262-626-2181	R	2*	<.1
139	Glenwood Smoked Products Inc—*Clark Scott*	4491 N Haroldsen Dr, Idaho Falls ID 83401	208-529-9851	R	2*	<.1
140	Kern Meat Company Inc—*H Kern*	2225 Cherokee St, Saint Louis MO 63118	314-664-4467	R	2*	<.1
141	Chicago Beef Co—*Mary Daskas*	1939 Adelaide St, Detroit MI 48207		R	2*	<.1
142	North American Halal Food Industries Inc—*Jalal Aossey*	900 66th Ave Sw, Cedar Rapids IA 52404	319-366-8327	R	2*	<.1
143	Chip Steak and Provision Co—*Michael Miller*	232 Dewey St, Mankato MN 56001	507-388-6277	R	2*	<.1
144	Mishler Packing Company Inc—*Paul Mishler*	5680 W 100 N, Lagrange IN 46761	260-768-4156	R	2*	<.1
145	Kruse Meat Products Inc—*Jeanne Hutchison*	2100 Kruse Loop, Alexander AR 72002	501-316-2110	R	2*	<.1
146	Champlain Beef Company Inc—*Barton Cuomo*	9679 State Rte 4, Whitehall NY 12887	518-499-1895	R	2*	<.1
147	Old Fashioned Meat Company Inc—*Roberto Casmilo*	920 W Fulton Market, Chicago IL 60607	312-421-4555	R	1*	<.1
148	Amato International Inc (Miami Florida)—*Claudette Touzard*	407 Lincoln Rd Ste 12C, Miami FL 33139	305-675-1001	R	1*	<.1

TOTALS: SIC 5147 Meats & Meat Products
Companies: 148   10,565   12.6

5148 Fresh Fruits & Vegetables

1	RD Offutt Co—*Ronald D Offutt*	PO Box 7160, Fargo ND 58106	701-237-6062	R	2,171*	1.6
2	SKH Management Co—*Paul W Stauffer*	PO Box 1500, Lititz PA 17543		R	1,356*	1.0
3	FreshPoint Inc—*Brian M Sturgeon*	1390 Enclave Pkwy, Houston TX 77077		S	732*	2.5
4	Sunkist Growers Inc—*Russell L Hanlin*	PO Box 7888, Van Nuys CA 91409	818-986-4800	R	463*	.4
5	Melissa's/World Variety Produce Inc	PO Box 21127, Los Angeles CA 90021		R	425*	.3
6	DiMare Homestead Inc—*Paul J Dimare*	PO Box 900460, Homestead FL 33090	305-245-4211	R	270*	.2
7	ProPacific Fresh—*Bruce Parks*	PO Box 1069, Durham CA 95938	530-893-0596	R	267*	.2
8	Standard Fruit and Vegetable Company Inc—*Larry Crowley*	PO Box 225027, Dallas TX 75222	214-428-3600	R	243*	.5

Rank	Company Name—*Executive Officer*	Address, City, State, Zip	Phone	Type	Fin	Empls
9	DiMare Florida—*Paul Dimare* DiMare Homestead Inc	PO Box 11128, Tampa FL 33680	813-238-7981	D	239*	.1
10	Bland Farms Inc—*Delbert Bland*	PO Box 2299, Reidsville GA 30453	912-654-1426	R	225*	.1
11	DNE World Fruit Sales Inc—*Greg Nelson* Bernard Egan and Co	1900 Old Dixie Hwy, Fort Pierce FL 34946	772-465-7555	S	202*	.1
12	Freshway Foods Inc—*Phil Gilardi*	601 Stolle Ave, Sidney OH 45365	937-498-4664	R	201*	.5
13	Sanson Co—*Jeffrey Sanson*	3716 Croton Ave, Cleveland OH 44115	216-431-8560	R	191*	.1
14	Fresh Point Inc—*Brian Sturgeon*	1245 W Fairbanks Ave S, Winter Park FL 32789	407-857-3930	S	169*	.3
15	Albert's Organics Inc—*Kurt Luttecke*	PO Box 624, Bridgeport NJ 08014	856-241-9090	R	165*	.5
16	Produce Alliance LLC—*Michael Mccollum*	100 Lexington Dr Ste 2, Buffalo Grove IL 60089	847-808-3030	R	149*	<.1
17	Cherry Central Cooperative Inc—*Richard Bogard*	PO Box 988, Traverse City MI 49685	231-946-1860	R	136*	.1
18	Food Source Inc—*Pete Schaffer*	653 Swedesford Rd, Frazer PA 19355	610-540-0300	R	136*	.1
19	VIP Foodservice—*Nelson Okumura*	PO Box 517, Kahului HI 96733	808-877-5055	R	132*	.1
20	John H Burrows Inc—*John H Burrows*	PO Box 604, Sparks NV 89432	775-358-2442	R	131*	.1
21	Costa Fruit and Produce Co—*Manuel R Costa*	PO Box 290574, Boston MA 02129	617-241-8007	R	105*	.2
22	H Smith Packing Corp—*Greg Smith*	99 Fort Rd Ste 1, Presque Isle ME 04769		R	103*	.1
23	Paramount Export Co—*Nick Kukulan*	175 Filbert St Ste 201, Oakland CA 94607	510-839-0150	R	98*	.1
24	Jac Vandenberg Inc—*David Schiro*	100 Corporate Blvd, Yonkers NY 10701	914-964-5900	R	90*	<.1
25	Andrew and Williamson Sales Co—*Fred L Williamson*	9940 Marconi Dr, San Diego CA 92154	619-661-6000	R	80*	.1
26	FreshPoint Southern California—*Brian M Sturgeon* FreshPoint Inc	5301 Rivergrade Rd, Irwindale CA 91706	626-813-5600	S	74*	.3
27	Giumarra Brothers Fruit Co—*Donald J Corsaro*	PO Box 21218, Los Angeles CA 90021	213-627-2900	D	74*	.2
28	Nor-Cal Produce Inc—*Dan Achondo*	PO Box 980188, West Sacramento CA 95798	916-373-0830	R	66*	.1
29	Lee Ray-Tarantino Company Inc—*Paul Tarantino* FreshPoint Inc	PO Box 2408, South San Francisco CA 94083	650-871-4323	S	55*	.1
30	J Hellman Produce Inc—*Bryce Hellman*	1601 E Olympic Blvd St, Los Angeles CA 90021	213-243-9105	R	53*	<.1
31	Progressive Produce Co—*James K Leimkuhler*	5790 Peachtree St, Los Angeles CA 90040	323-890-8100	R	50*	.2
32	Hickenbottom and Sons Inc—*Jerry Hickenbottom*	301 Warehouse Ave, Sunnyside WA 98944	509-837-4100	R	49*	<.1
33	Flavor 1st Growers and Packers Inc—*Brian Rose*	PO Box 609, Horse Shoe NC 28742	828-890-3630	R	48*	.2
34	Consumers Produce Co—*Alan Siger*	1 21st St, Pittsburgh PA 15222	412-281-0722	R	47*	.1
35	Earth Brothers Ltd—*Steve Birge*	Po Box 489, North Springfield VT 05150	802-230-4800	R	42*	.1
36	Muir Enterprises—*Phil Muir*	951 S 3600 W, Salt Lake City UT 84104	801-908-6091	R	41*	.1
37	Garden Fresh Salad Company Inc—*Ismaele D'alleva*	11-20 Neng Prod Ctr, Chelsea MA 02150	617-889-1580	R	41*	<.1
38	Hearn Kirkwood—*Peter Gilbert*	7251 Standard Dr, Hanover MD 21076	410-712-6000	R	37*	.1
39	Hollar and Greene Produce Co—*Dale Greene*	PO Box 3500, Boone NC 28607	828-264-2177	R	36*	.1
40	D'Arrigo Brothers of Massachusetts Inc—*Peter A D'Arrigo Jr*	105 New England Produc, Chelsea MA 02150	617-884-1800	R	34*	<.1
41	Goodson Farms Inc—*Don Goodson*	PO Box 246, Balm FL 33503	813-634-2164	R	34*	<.1
42	General Produce Company Ltd—*Thomas Chan*	PO Box 308, Sacramento CA 95812	916-441-0431	R	32*	.3
43	Chiquita Fresh North America—*Richard Continelli*	3403 Macintosh Rd, Fort Lauderdale FL 33316	954-527-7816	R	31*	.1
44	DiMare Brothers Inc—*Charles Dolan*	84 New England Produce, Chelsea MA 02150	617-889-3800	R	31*	.1
45	Custom Cuts Fresh LLC—*Michael Jennaro*	2842 S 5th Ct, Milwaukee WI 53207	414-483-0491	R	30*	.2
46	Gilbert Foods Inc—*Charles Gilbert*	7251 Standard Dr, Hanover MD 21076	410-712-6000	R	30*	.2
47	Frieda's Inc—*Karen B Caplan*	PO Box 58488, Los Angeles CA 90058	714-826-6100	R	30*	.1
48	Federal Fruit and Produce Co—*Stan Kouba*	1890 E 58th Ave, Denver CO 80216	303-292-1303	R	30*	.1
49	Mission Produce Inc—*Steve Barnard*	PO Box 5267, Oxnard CA 93031	805-981-3650	R	28*	.1
50	Casey Woodwyk Inc—*Jim Woodwyk*	PO Box 9, Hudsonville MI 49426	616-669-1700	R	26*	<.1
51	Black Gold Potato Sales Inc—*Gregg Halverson*	4575 32nd Ave S Ste 2A, Grand Forks ND 58201	701-772-2620	R	25*	<.1
52	Gargiulo Inc—*Christian Leleu*	15000 Old Hwy 41 N, Naples FL 34110	239-597-3131	R	23*	.4
53	Paragon Wholesale Foods Corp—*Elaine Bellin*	55 36th St, Pittsburgh PA 15201	412-621-2626	R	22*	.1
54	Bernard Egan and Co—*Bernard A Egan*	1900 Old Dixie Hwy, Fort Pierce FL 34946		R	20*	.1
55	If and P Foods Inc—*Michael Mascari*	4501 Massachusetts Ave, Indianapolis IN 46218	317-546-2425	R	20*	.4
56	Garden-Fresh Foods Inc—*Thomas Hughes*	726 S 12th St, Milwaukee WI 53204	414-645-1000	R	19*	.1
57	Leroy Smith Inc—*Elson Smith*	PO Box 716, Vero Beach FL 32961	772-567-3421	R	19*	.1
58	Vinyard Fruit And Vegetable Company Inc—*Roy Vinyard*	PO Box 2778, Oklahoma City OK 73101	405-272-0339	R	19*	.1
59	Johnson Foods Inc—*George Johnson*	PO Box 916, Sunnyside WA 98944	509-837-4214	R	19*	.1
60	Country Fresh Mushroom Co—*James Howard*	PO Box 489, Avondale PA 19311	610-268-3033	R	18*	.1
61	Meyer LLC—*Bob Meyer*	PO Box 1944, Nogales AZ 85621	520-281-9754	R	18*	.5
62	Adams Produce Co—*Scott Grinstead*	300 Union Hill Dr Ste, Homewood AL 35209	205-397-9300	R	17*	.1
63	Del Monte Fresh Produce NA Inc—*Hani Naffy*	14 Stuart Dr, Kankakee IL 60901	815-936-7400	R	17*	.1
64	Sunny Dell Foods Inc—*Gary Caligiuri*	135 N 5th St, Oxford PA 19363	610-932-5164	R	15*	.1
65	William George Company Inc—*Randy George*	1002 Mize St, Lufkin TX 75904	936-634-7738	R	15*	.2
66	Moody Creek Produce Inc—*Bart Webster*	PO Box 329, Sugar City ID 83448	208-356-9447	R	15*	.1
67	Oneonta Trading Corp—*Dalton Thomas*	PO Box 549, Wenatchee WA 98807	509-663-2631	R	15*	<.1
68	Van Solkema Produce Co—*Jerry Van Solkema*	PO Box 308, Byron Center MI 49315	616-878-1508	R	14*	<.1
69	AJ Rinella and Company Inc—*Peter Rinella*	381 Broadway Ste 6, Albany NY 12204	518-465-4581	R	10*	<.1
70	Home Style Foods Inc—*Mike Kadian*	5163 Edwin St, Detroit MI 48212	313-874-3250	R	9*	<.1
71	Hop Kee Inc—*Thomas Lam*	2425 S Wallace St, Chicago IL 60616	312-791-9111	R	8*	<.1
72	Vanguard International Inc—*Craig Stauffer*	22605 Se 56th St Ste 2, Issaquah WA 98029	425-557-8250	R	8*	<.1
73	Associated Potato Growers Inc—*Paul Dolan*	2001 N 6th St, Grand Forks ND 58203	701-775-4614	R	7*	<.1
74	Minnesota Produce Inc—*Paul Piazza*	2801 Wayzata Blvd, Minneapolis MN 55405	612-377-6790	R	7*	<.1
75	Michigan Celery Promotion Co-Operative Inc—*Duane Frens*	PO Box 306, Hudsonville MI 49426	616-669-1250	R	7*	<.1
76	Jack Brown Produce Inc—*John Schaefer*	8035 Fruit Ridge Ave N, Sparta MI 49345	616-887-9568	R	7*	.1
77	S and M Food Service Inc	12935 Lake Charles Hwy, Leesville LA 71446	337-537-3588	R	6*	<.1
78	G and S Packing Company Inc—*Earl Scales*	PO Box 157, Weirsdale FL 32195	352-821-2251	R	5*	<.1
79	Mixon Fruit Farms Inc—*William P Mixon Jr*	2525 27th St E, Bradenton FL 34208	941-748-5829	R	5*	.1
80	Krisp Pak Company Inc—*Paul Battaglia*	PO Box 1093, Virginia Beach VA 23451	757-622-8440	R	5*	.1
81	Grower Shipper Potato Co—*Kris Miner*	PO Box 432, Monte Vista CO 81144	719-852-3569	R	5*	.1
82	A and L Potato Co—*Randy Boushey*	PO Box 193, East Grand Forks MN 56721	218-773-0123	R	5*	<.1
83	Ritchey Produce Company Inc—*Nadim Ritchey*	PO Box 1416, Zanesville OH 43702	740-454-0545	R	5*	<.1
84	Peninsula Fruit Exchange Inc—*Jim Horton*	2955 Kroupa Rd, Traverse City MI 49686	231-223-4282	R	4*	<.1
85	Mary's Salads And Produce LLC—*Randall Hendrix*	349 Austin Springs Rd, Johnson City TN 37601	423-282-4831	R	3*	<.1
86	William P Hearne Produce Co—*William P Hearne Jr*	160 Farmers Market Rd, Salisbury MD 21804	813-633-8910	R	3*	<.1
87	Hard-E Foods Inc—*Judith Rutz*	3228 N Broadway, Saint Louis MO 63147	314-533-2211	R	3*	<.1
88	WR Foods—*Bryan Wagner*	PO Box 217, Jonesboro AR 72403	870-932-6688	R	3*	<.1
89	Jackson Produce Co—*Gerald Jackson*	3226 McKelvey Rd, Bridgeton MO 63044	314-291-1080	R	3*	<.1
90	Jk Packing Co—*Joseph Korelko*	PO Box 1231, Uniontown PA 15401	724-437-9801	R	2*	<.1
91	Mascot Pecan Shelling Company Inc—*Kenny Tarver*	PO Box 760, Glennville GA 30427	912-654-2195	R	2*	<.1
92	Seald-Sweet Growers Inc—*Mayda Sotomayor*	1991 74th Ave, Vero Beach FL 32966	772-569-2244	R	N/A	<.1

TOTALS: SIC 5148 Fresh Fruits & Vegetables
Companies: 92   9,980   15.0

Note: An asterisk (*) indicates an estimated financial figure. The company type code used is as follows: R = Private, P = Public, S = Private Subsidiary, B = Public Subsidiary, D = Division, J = Joint Venture, I = Investment Fund.

COMPANY RANKINGS BY SALES WITHIN 4-DIGIT SIC

Rank	Company Name—*Executive Officer*	Address, City, State, Zip	Phone	Type	Fin	Empls
	5149 Groceries & Related Products Nec					
1	Reyes Holdings LLC—*Gregory Nickele*	6250 N River Rd Ste 90, Rosemont IL 60018	847-227-6500	R	13,000*	11.0
2	Perrier Group of America Inc—*Kim Jaffrey*	777 W Putnam Ave, Greenwich CT 06830		S	7,472*	4.5
3	MBM Corp—*Jerry L Wordsworth*	3134 Industry Dr, North Charleston SC 29418		R	4,066*	3.0
4	Distribution Plus Inc (Wilmette Illinois)—*Jim DeKeyser*	1007 Church St Ste 314, Evanston IL 60201	847-492-8036	R	1,712*	1.0
5	Manischewitz Co—*David L Yale*	80 Ave K, Newark NJ 07105	201-553-1100	R	602*	1.8
6	Surf City Squeeze Inc	9311 E Via de Ventura, Scottsdale AZ 85258	480-362-4800	S	497*	.4
7	Roma Food Enterprises Inc—*Joe Davi*	1 Roma Blvd, Piscataway NJ 08854	732-463-7662	R	491*	.4
8	Niagara Water—*Andrew Peykoff*	2560 E Philadelphia St, Ontario CA 91761	909-758-5300	R	382*	.3
9	Best Brands Corp—*Scott Humphrey*	111 Cheshire Ln Ste 10, Saint Paul MN 55121	952-404-7500	S	362*	1.0
10	Bi Rite Foodservice Distributors—*Bill Barulich*	123 S Hill Dr, Brisbane CA 94005	415-656-0187	R	355*	.3
11	High Grade Beverage—*Joseph DeMarco*	PO Box 7092, North Brunswick NJ 08902	732-821-7600	R	264*	.3
12	Reliv' World Corp—*Robert L Montgomery*	PO Box 405, Chesterfield MO 63006	636-537-9715	S	247*	.2
13	Dairy Fresh Products Co—*Dan Madsen* Distribution Plus Inc (Wilmette Illinois)	601 Rockefeller Ave, Ontario CA 91761	909-975-1019	S	232*	.5
14	Schiff Nutrition International Inc—*Tarang Amin*	2002 S 5070 W, Salt Lake City UT 84104	801-975-5000	B	214	.4
15	H and H Meat Products Company Inc—*Liborio Hinojosa Sr*	PO Box 358, Mercedes TX 78570	956-565-6363	R	210*	1.0
16	Sovena USA Inc—*Luis Gato*	1 Olive Grove St, Rome NY 13441	315-797-7070	R	186*	.2
17	JFC International Inc—*Hiroyuka Enomoto*	7101 East Slauson Ave, Los Angeles CA 90040	323-721-6100	S	166	.4
18	Pan-O-Gold Baking Co—*Howard Alton*	PO Box 848, Saint Cloud MN 56302	320-251-9361	R	164*	1.1
19	Jarritos Inc—*Ramon Carrasco*	500 W Overland Ave Ste, El Paso TX 79901	915-594-1618	R	162*	.2
20	Atlantic Premium Brands Ltd—*Thomas M Dalton*	1033 Skokie Blvd Ste 6, Northbrook IL 60062	847-412-6200	P	130	.5
21	Bakemark Ingredients USA—*Jim Howard*	7351 Crider Ave, Pico Rivera CA 90660	562-949-1054	R	129*	.2
22	Pepsi-Cola Bottling Company of Rochester—*Fritz Truax*	1307 Valley High Dr NW, Rochester MN 55901	507-288-3772	S	123*	.1
23	Tom Cat Bakery—*Matthew Reich*	4305 10th St, Long Island City NY 11101	718-786-4224	R	120*	.1
24	Freedman's Bakery Inc—*Herbert Freedman*	803 Main St Ste 1, Belmar NJ 07719	732-681-2334	R	120*	.2
25	L and E Bottling Company Inc—*Brian Charneski*	PO Box 11159, Olympia WA 98508	360-357-3812	R	116*	.1
26	Mitsui Foods Inc—*Evan Hyman*	35 Maple St, Norwood NJ 07648	201-750-0500	S	110	.1
27	Southern Beverage Company Inc—*Theo Costas Jr*	1939 Davis Johnson Dr, Richland MS 39218	601-933-6900	R	108*	.2
28	Crystal Bottling Company Inc—*Hayes Johnson*	8631 Younger Creek Dr, Sacramento CA 95828	916-568-3300	S	107*	.1
29	Minges Bottling Group—*Jeffrey M Minges*	PO Box 520, Ayden NC 28513	252-746-9700	R	101*	.2
30	Joseph's Lite Cookies Inc—*Joseph Semprevivo*	3700 J St SE, Deming NM 88030	505-546-2839	R	100	.1
31	Imperial Commodities Corp—*John Morley*	17 Battery Pl, New York NY 10004	212-837-9400	S	100*	<.1
32	Fox River Foods Inc—*Ken Nagel*	5030 Baseline Rd, Montgomery IL 60538	630-896-1991	R	97*	.3
33	Essex Grain Products Inc—*Luke Palante*	9 Lee Blvd, Frazer PA 19355	610-647-3800	S	96	<.1
34	Bruno Scheidt Inc—*Charles E Scheidt*	71 W 23rd St, New York NY 10010	212-741-8290	R	83*	.1
35	Veronica Foods Co—*Veronica Bradley*	PO Box 2225, Oakland CA 94621	510-535-6833	R	78*	.1
36	NutriCology Inc—*Manfred Salomon*	2300 N Loop Rd, Alameda CA 94502	510-263-2000	S	75*	.1
37	Svenhard's Swedish Bakery—*Ronny Svenhard*	335 Adeline St, Oakland CA 94607	510-834-5035	R	72*	.3
38	Crystal Rock Holdings Inc—*Peter K Baker*	1050 Buckingham St, Watertown CT 06795		P	72	.4
39	Spice World Inc—*Andrew Caneza*	8101 Presidents Dr, Orlando FL 32809	407-851-9432	R	69*	.1
40	JA Vassilaros and Sons Inc—*John Vassilaros*	29-05 120th St, Flushing NY 11354	718-886-4140	R	68*	<.1
41	Atkins Nutritionals Inc—*Christopher Smith*	1050 17th St Ste 1000, Denver CO 80265	303-633-2840	R	67*	.1
42	Frullati Cafe and Bakery Inc	9311 E Via de Ventura, Scottsdale AZ 85258	480-362-4800	S	62*	.1
43	Attitude Drinks Inc—*Roy Warren*	10415 Riverside Dr Ste, Palm Beach Gardens FL 33410	561-799-5053	P	61	<.1
44	Jim L Shetakis Distributing Co—*Lloyd Meher*	PO Box 14987, Las Vegas NV 89114	702-735-8985	R	58*	.2
45	Sunflower Restaurant Supply Inc—*Leroy A Baumberger*	PO Box 1277, Salina KS 67402	785-823-6394	R	58*	<.1
46	Tipp Enterprises Inc—*Ramon Carrasco*	500 W Overland Ste 300, El Paso TX 79901	915-594-1618	R	56*	.2
47	Ira Higdon Grocery Company Inc—*Larry Higdon*	PO Box 488, Cairo GA 39828	229-377-1272	R	51*	.1
48	Bryan Baking Inc—*Fred Bauer*	600 Phil Gramm Blvd, Bryan TX 77807	979-778-6600	R	51*	.3
49	Sugar Foods Corp—*Donald G Tober*	950 3rd Ave 21st Fl, New York NY 10022	212-753-6900	R	50*	.3
50	J Sosnick and Son Inc—*Jeff Sosnick*	258 Littlefield Ave, South San Francisco CA 94080	650-952-2226	R	50*	<.1
51	Greco and Sons Inc—*Pasquale Greco*	1550 Hecht Dr, Bartlett IL 60103	630-837-9900	R	50*	.2
52	Noble Americas Corp—*Stephen Brown*	107 Elm St Ste 4, Stamford CT 06902	203-324-8555	R	48*	.6
53	Springfield Pepsi-Cola Bottling Co—*Mike Bartell*	PO Box 4146, Springfield IL 62708	217-522-8841	R	47*	.1
54	Pure Beverage Inc—*Jim Klein*	1835 Stout Field West, Indianapolis IN 46241	317-375-9925	R	47*	<.1
55	Jackson Coca-Cola Bottling Co—*Robert Wadlaw*	1421 Hwy 80 W, Jackson MS 39204	601-355-6487	S	45*	.3
56	Vitality Foodservice Inc—*Gary Viljoen*	400 N Tampa St Ste 150, Tampa FL 33602	813-301-4600	R	45*	.7
57	Primo Water Corp—*Billy D Prim*	104 Cambridge Plz Dr, Winston-Salem NC 27104	336-331-4000	P	45	.1
58	JF Braun and Sons—*Gerald Vogel*	PO Box 6061, Elizabeth NJ 07207	516-997-2200	R	44*	<.1
59	Canada Dry of Delaware Valley	8275 Rte 130, Pennsauken NJ 08110	856-662-6767	R	40*	.3
60	Neri's Bakery Products Inc—*Dominick Neri*	31 Pearl St 37, Port Chester NY 10573	914-939-3311	R	40*	.2
61	Central States Coca-Cola (Springfield Illinois)—*Jay Concardia*	3495 E Sangamon Ave, Springfield IL 62707	217-544-4891	D	37*	.1
62	Essential Baking Company Inc—*Tom Campanile*	5601 1st Ave S, Seattle WA 98108	206-545-3804	R	37*	.2
63	Trinidad/Benham Corp—*Carl Hartman*	PO Box 378007, Denver CO 80237	303-220-1400	R	36*	.5
64	National Distributors Inc—*Jeffery D Kane*	116 Wallace Ave, South Portland ME 04106	207-773-1719	R	36*	.1
65	Alabama Coca-Cola Bottling Co—*Frank Harrison*	PO Box 1687, Decatur AL 35602	256-353-9211	S	35*	<.1
66	Lee Kum Kee USA Inc—*David Lee*	14841 Don Julian Rd, City Of Industry CA 91746	626-709-1888	R	34*	<.1
67	FoodScience Corp—*Dale Metz*	20 New England Dr, Essex Junction VT 05452	802-878-5508	R	32*	.2
68	Elki Corp—*Elizabeth Lie*	2215 Merrill Creek Pkw, Everett WA 98203	425-261-1002	R	32*	.1
69	Cloverleaf Farms Distributors Inc—*Michael Bailey*	13835 Kostner Ave, Midlothian IL 60445	708-597-2200	R	32*	<.1
70	Lar-Par Inc—*Edison R Lara Sr*	PO Box 649, South Gate CA 90280	323-566-2304	R	31	.1
71	Peninsula Bottling Company Inc—*Jeffrey Hinds*	311 S Valley St, Port Angeles WA 98362	360-457-3383	R	31*	<.1
72	Tropical Nut and Fruit Co—*John Bauer*	PO Box 7507, Charlotte NC 28241	704-588-0400	R	30*	.2
73	Wolfson Casing Corp—*Montague Wolfson*	700 S Fulton Ave, Mount Vernon NY 10550	914-668-9000	R	29*	.1
74	Mays Meats Inc—*Jimmy Mays*	541 E Main Ave, Taylorsville NC 28681	828-632-2034	R	28*	.1
75	Hagen Pet Foods Inc—*Rolf Hagen*	PO Box 29, Waverly NY 14892	607-565-3497	R	28*	.1
76	Goglanian Bakeries Inc—*George Goglanian*	3710 S Susan St, Santa Ana CA 92704	714-444-3500	R	28*	.4
77	Ginsburg Bakery Inc—*John Mulloy*	300 N Tennessee Ave, Atlantic City NJ 08401	609-345-2265	R	27*	.1
78	Pepe's Wholesale Pizza Co—*Ron Gall*	6821 Eastgate Blvd, Lebanon TN 37090	615-443-0999	R	27*	<.1
79	AD Huesing Corp—*Bud Helpenstell*	PO Box 6880, Rock Island IL 61204	309-788-5652	R	26*	.1
80	Palermo Villa Inc—*Giacomo Fallucca*	3301 W Canal St, Milwaukee WI 53208	414-643-0919	R	25*	.4
81	Setton Pistachio Of Terra Bella Inc—*Joshua Setton*	PO Box 11089, Terra Bella CA 93270	559-535-6050	S	24*	.1
82	Farm Fresh Foods Inc—*Gregg Ostrander*	3840 N Civic Center Dr, North Las Vegas NV 89030	702-643-5238	S	24*	.1
83	Wet Planet Beverage Co—*CJ Rapp*	PO Box 25107, Rochester NY 14625	585-381-3560	R	24*	<.1
84	Ellis Coffee Co—*Eugene Kestenbaum*	2835 Bridge St, Philadelphia PA 19137	215-537-9500	R	24*	.1
85	Pepsi Bottling Ventures LLC—*Keith Reimer*	4141 Parklake Ave Ste, Raleigh NC 27612	919-865-2300	S	22*	.2
86	Harlan Bakeries-Avon LLC—*Chris Taylor*	7597 E Us Hwy 36, Avon IN 46123	317-272-3600	R	21*	.4
87	Clofine Dairy and Food Products Inc—*Fred Smith*	PO Box 335, Linwood NJ 08221	609-653-1000	R	21	<.1

Rank	Company Name—*Executive Officer*	Address, City, State, Zip	Phone	Type	Fin	Empls
88	Bobak Sausage Co—*Stanley Bobak*	5275 S Archer Ave, Chicago IL 60632	773-735-5334	R	21*	.1
89	Portland Specialty Baking LLC—*Cathy Richardson*	3423 Ne 172nd Pl, Portland OR 97230	503-228-4975	R	20*	.1
90	Daystar Desserts LLC—*Kevin Clarke*	10440 Leadbetter Rd, Ashland VA 23005	804-550-7660	R	20*	.1
91	Prince of Peace Enterprises Inc—*Kenneth Yeung*	3536 Arden Rd, Hayward CA 94545	510-887-1899	R	20*	.1
92	Milner Milling Inc—*Charles Stout*	PO Box 2247, Chattanooga TN 37409	423-265-2313	R	20*	.1
93	Cadillac Coffee Co—*John Gehlert*	1801 Michael St, Madison Heights MI 48071	248-545-2266	R	20*	.1
94	Foodcraft Inc—*Ernest Lieblich*	1625 Riverside Dr, Los Angeles CA 90031	323-223-2381	R	19*	.1
95	Northwest Distribution Tools for Schools Inc	PO Box 277, Emmett ID 83617	208-365-1445	S	18*	<.1
96	Pepsi-Cola of Siouxland—*Indra K Nooyi*	400 W Colonial Dr, South Sioux City NE 68776	402-494-3023	S	18*	<.1
97	Shatila Food Products Inc—*Riad Shatila*	8505 W Warren Ave, Dearborn MI 48126	313-934-1520	R	17*	.1
98	Tyler Mountain Water Company Inc—*Richard Merrill*	159 Harris Dr, Poca WV 25159	304-755-8400	R	16*	.3
99	Jonesboro Coca-Cola Bottling Co—*Billy Skaggs*	PO Box 19189, Jonesboro AR 72402	870-932-6601	S	16*	.1
100	Starwest Botanicals Inc—*Van Joerger*	11253 Trade Ctr Dr A, Rancho Cordova CA 95742	916-638-8100	R	15*	.1
101	BakeMark-Youngstown OH—*Doug Townsend*	9401 Le Saint Dr, Fairfield OH 45014	513-870-0880	S	15	<.1
102	Pacific Spice Company Inc—*Akiba Schlussel*	6430 E Slauson Ave, Commerce CA 90040	323-726-9190	R	14*	.1
103	Apollo Ship Chandlers Inc—*Rafael A Ordonez*	1775 NW 70th Ave, Miami FL 33126	305-592-8790	R	14*	.1
104	Excelso Coffee Co—*Geoffrey Paul*	6700 Dawson Blvd, Norcross GA 30093	770-449-8140	R	14*	.1
105	Protano and Sons Inc—*Pat Protano*	2301 N 22nd Ave, Hollywood FL 33020	954-925-3474	R	14*	.1
106	Dipasa USA Inc—*Cesar Coello*	6600 Fm 802 Ste B, Brownsville TX 78526	956-831-4072	R	13*	<.1
107	Magnetic Springs Water Co—*James Allison*	PO Box 182076, Columbus OH 43218	614-421-1780	R	13*	.1
108	Semifreddi's Inc—*Thomas Frainier*	1980 N Loop Rd, Alameda CA 94502	510-596-9930	R	13*	.1
109	Swire Coca-Cola—*Jack Pelo*	PO Box 86, Twin Falls ID 83303	208-733-3833	S	13*	<.1
110	A Camacho Inc—*Raphael Comacho Alvarez*	2502 Walden Woods Dr, Plant City FL 33566	813-305-4534	R	13*	<.1
111	Mille Lacs Gourmet Foods—*David Mckee*	PO Box 217, Sun Prairie WI 53590	608-837-8535	R	13*	.1
112	Stapleton - Spence Packing Co—*M Stapleton*	1530 The Alameda Ste 3, San Jose CA 95126	408-297-8815	R	13*	.1
113	Just Bagels Manufacturing Inc—*Charles Contreras*	527 Casanova St, Bronx NY 10474	718-328-9700	R	12*	.1
114	Penta International Corp—*Grace Volpe*	PO Box 1448, Caldwell NJ 07007	973-740-2300	R	12*	.1
115	Coca-Cola Aberdeen—*Jeff Erezden*	221 N Main St, Aberdeen SD 57401	605-225-6780	D	12*	<.1
116	Morris J Golombeck Inc—*Hy Golombeck*	960 Franklin Ave, Brooklyn NY 11225	718-284-3505	R	12*	.1
117	Kikkoman Sales USA Inc—*Ken Saito*	50 California St Ste 3, San Francisco CA 94111	415-956-7750	R	12*	.1
118	Presto Delivery Inc—*Joe Press*	67 Lyell Ave, Rochester NY 14608	585-454-5231	R	11*	.1
119	Cedars Mediterranean Foods Inc—*Charles Hanna*	PO Box 8277, Haverhill MA 01835	978-372-8010	R	11*	.1
120	Masada Bakery Inc—*Koby Stein*	1500 Oakbrook Dr Ste B, Norcross GA 30093	770-295-0012	R	10*	.1
121	La Ronga Bakery and Delicatessen—*Michael Ronga*	599 Somerville Ave, Somerville MA 02143	617-625-8600	R	10*	.1
122	Suncoast Coffee Inc—*Rick Hubbard*	1114 E 52nd St, Indianapolis IN 46205	513-369-0357	R	10*	.1
123	Melita Corp—*Emanuel Darmanin*	828 E 144th St, Bronx NY 10454	718-392-7280	R	10*	.2
124	Gourmet Kitchens Inc—*Micheal Lacey*	1238 Corlies Ave, Neptune NJ 07753	732-775-5222	R	10*	.1
125	Seven-Up Bottling Co (Watertown Wisconsin)—*William Kwapil*	410 S 1st St, Watertown WI 53094	920-261-5254	R	10*	<.1
126	GD Mathews and Sons Inc—*David Mathews*	521 Medford St, Charlestown MA 02129	617-242-1770	R	10*	<.1
127	John E Koerner and Company Inc—*Tim Koerner*	PO Box 10218, New Orleans LA 70181	504-734-1100	R	10*	<.1
128	Idaho Beverages Inc—*Gary Prasil*	2108 1st Ave N, Lewiston ID 83501	208-743-6535	R	10*	.1
129	Glorybee Natural Sweeteners Inc—*Richard Turanski*	PO Box 2744, Eugene OR 97402	541-689-0913	R	10*	.1
130	Mediterranean Gyros Products Inc—*Vasilios Memmos*	1102 38th Ave, Long Island City NY 11101	718-786-3399	R	9*	.1
131	Virginia Beach Beverages—*Jay Jones*	1400 Air Rail, Virginia Beach VA 23455	757-464-1771	R	9*	.1
132	Figueroa International Inc—*Gregory P Figueroa*	151 Regal Row Ste 128, Dallas TX 75247	214-351-9060	R	9*	<.1
133	Cerenzia Foods Inc—*Joe Annunziato*	8585 White Oak Ave, Rancho Cucamonga CA 91730	909-989-4000	R	9*	<.1
134	Grapevine Trading Inc—*Sandra VanVaorhis*	59 Maxwell Ct, Santa Rosa CA 95401	707-576-3950	R	9*	<.1
135	BW Dyer and Co—*Chip Dyer*	PO Box 197, Telluride CO 81435	970-728-9393	R	9*	<.1
136	Eldorado Artesian Springs Inc—*Douglas A Larson*	PO Box 445, Eldorado Springs CO 80025	303-499-1316	P	9	.1
137	Brolite Products Inc—*Virgil Ghingaro*	1900 S Park Ave, Streamwood IL 60107	630-830-0340	R	9*	.1
138	Specialty Baking Inc—*Antonio Escobar*	1365 N 10th St, San Jose CA 95112	408-298-6919	R	8*	.1
139	Lenox-Martell Inc—*James Lerner*	89 Heath St, Boston MA 02130	617-442-7777	R	8*	.1
140	Grand Strand Sandwich Co—*Lee Dreyfous*	8910 Hwy 90, Longs SC 29568	843-399-2999	R	8*	.1
141	Pocono Springs Co—*Michael Melnic*	PO Box 787, Mount Pocono PA 18344	570-839-2837	R	8*	.1
142	Baker Maid Products Inc—*Darryl Sorenson*	PO Box 50424, New Orleans LA 70150	504-827-5500	R	8*	.1
143	Tarrier Foods Corp—*Timothy Tarrier*	3915 Zane Trace Dr, Columbus OH 43228	614-876-8595	R	8*	<.1
144	Carl's Donuts Inc—*Amiel Curnutt*	6350 Sunset Corporate, Las Vegas NV 89120	702-382-6138	R	7*	.1
145	Classic Delights Inc—*Darl Harkleroad*	PO Box 367, Saint Marys OH 45885	419-394-7955	R	7*	.1
146	Sun Ten Labs Liquidation Co—*Charleson Hsu*	9250 Jeronimo Rd, Irvine CA 92618	949-587-0509	R	7*	.1
147	Latina Inc—*Robert Kolb*	230 Cannon Blvd, Staten Island NY 10306	718-351-1400	R	7*	<.1
148	Aladdin's Baking Company Inc—*Carl Nahra*	1301 Carnegie Ave, Cleveland OH 44115	216-861-0317	R	7*	<.1
149	Skally's Old World Bakery Inc—*Odette Skally*	1933 W Galbraith Rd, Cincinnati OH 45239	513-931-1411	R	7*	<.1
150	Niitakaya USA Inc—*Hideo Nakagawa*	1801 Gage Rd, Montebello CA 90640	323-720-5050	R	7*	<.1
151	Widoffs Modern Bakery Inc—*Jerry Ducas*	129 Water St, Worcester MA 01604	508-752-7200	R	7*	.1
152	Bodacious Breads Inc—*James Amaral*	PO Box 1800, Wells ME 04090	207-641-8800	R	7*	.1
153	Wyoming Beverages Inc—*Forrest Clay*	PO Box 18, Worland WY 82401	307-347-4231	R	6*	<.1
154	Spiceco Inc—*Andy Barna*	6c Terminal Way, Avenel NJ 07001	732-499-9070	R	6*	<.1
155	Tampico Spice Company Inc—*Jesus Martinez*	PO Box 1229, Los Angeles CA 90001	323-235-3154	R	6*	.1
156	Gregory's Foods Inc—*Gregory Helland*	1301 Trapp Rd, Saint Paul MN 55121	651-454-0277	R	6*	<.1
157	Toudouze Market Inc—*Charles Toudouze Jr*	PO Box 7449, San Antonio TX 78207	210-224-1891	R	6*	<.1
158	Lorann Oils Inc—*John Grettenberger*	PO Box 22009, Lansing MI 48909	517-882-0215	R	6*	<.1
159	Minardi Baking Company Inc—*Thomas Minardi*	125 Grand St, Paterson NJ 07501	973-742-1107	R	6*	<.1
160	Allen and Cowley Urban Trading Company LLC—*Karen Chengelis*	625 S 5th St 1, Phoenix AZ 85004	602-272-9500	R	6*	<.1
161	Apple Baking Company Inc—*Matt Deboer*	380 Apple Rd, Salisbury NC 28147	704-637-6800	R	6*	<.1
162	K And B Company Inc—*Edward Bischoff*	PO Box 28, Gallup NM 87305	505-863-9347	R	6*	.1
163	Rdk Corp—*Mike Heyer*	2529 Golf Ave, Racine WI 53404	262-633-1819	R	6*	.1
164	Log House Foods Inc—*Josh Kasdan*	700 Berkshire Ln N, Minneapolis MN 55441	763-546-8395	R	6*	<.1
165	Bascom Maple Farms Inc—*Bruce Bascom*	56 Sugar House Rd, Alstead NH 03602	603-835-2230	R	6*	<.1
166	Varda International Inc—*Varda Shamban*	41 S Spring St, Elizabeth NJ 07201	908-354-9090	R	6*	<.1
167	Berardi's Fresh Roast Inc—*Patrick Leneghan*	12029 Abbey Rd, North Royalton OH 44133	440-582-4303	R	5*	<.1
168	Stahl's Bakery Inc—*Max Plante*	51021 Washington St, New Baltimore MI 48047	586-716-8500	R	5*	<.1
169	Staunton Foods LLC—*Robert Anders*	PO Box 569, Staunton VA 24402	540-885-1214	R	5*	<.1
170	McLendon Co—*William J McLendon*	2100 N Stemmons Fwy St, Dallas TX 75207	214-748-1555	R	5*	<.1
171	I Wanna Distribution Company Inc—*Susan B Sullivan*	2540 Shader Rd, Orlando FL 32804	407-292-0299	R	5*	<.1
172	Laurel Farms—*Betsy Pryor*	PO Box 2896, Sarasota FL 34230	941-351-2233	R	5*	<.1
173	Terranetti's Italian Bakery—*Terrence Mahon*	844 W Trindle Rd, Mechanicsburg PA 17055	717-697-5434	R	5*	.1
174	Dallis Brothers Inc—*Herbert Dallis*	10030 Atlantic Ave, Ozone Park NY 11416	718-845-3010	R	5*	<.1
175	New Carbon Company Inc—*Rick Mckeel*	4101 Wlliam Richardson, South Bend IN 46628	574-247-2270	R	4*	<.1
176	Walton Feed Inc—*Lamar Clement*	PO Box 307, Montpelier ID 83254	208-847-0465	R	4*	<.1

Note: An asterisk (*) indicates an estimated financial figure. The company type code used is as follows: R = Private, P = Public, S = Private Subsidiary, B = Public Subsidiary, D = Division, J = Joint Venture, I = Investment Fund.

RANKINGS BY SALES WITHIN 4-DIGIT SIC

	Company Name—*Executive Officer*	Address, City, State, Zip	Phone	Type	Fin	Empls
177	Valdez Corp—*Glenora Valdez*	1808 Monetary Ln Ste 1, Carrollton TX 75006	972-242-7660	R	4*	<.1
178	Victory Foods Inc—*Sondra Frost*	3417 Dundalk Ave, Baltimore MD 21222	410-282-2910	R	4*	<.1
179	Sun Drop Bottling Company Of Concord—*John King*	PO Box 305, Concord NC 28026	704-786-1165	R	4*	<.1
180	Italian French Baking Co—*Richard Pinocci*	1501 Grant Ave, San Francisco CA 94133	415-421-3796	R	4*	<.1
181	Neiman Brothers Company Inc—*William Neiman*	3322 W Newport Ave, Chicago IL 60618	773-463-3000	R	4*	<.1
182	Capricorn Coffees Inc—*Craig Edwards*	353 10th St, San Francisco CA 94103	415-621-8500	S	4*	<.1
183	J Weil and Co—*Bill Tippetts*	5907 Clinton St, Boise ID 83704	208-377-0590	R	4*	<.1
184	Hernandez and Solis Inc—*Sabrina Vrooman*	2249 Memorial Blvd, Port Arthur TX 77640	409-983-4006	R	4*	<.1
185	New York Bakeries Inc—*Sarah Zimmerman*	261 W 22nd St, Hialeah FL 33010	305-882-1355	R	4*	<.1
186	Henderson Coffee Corp—*Mark Plaster*	PO Box 175, Muskogee OK 74402	918-682-8751	R	4*	<.1
187	Clover Club Bottling Co—*Joseph Troy*	356 N Kilbourn Ave, Chicago IL 60624	773-261-7100	R	4*	<.1
188	White Rock Products Corp—*Alfred Morgan*	14107 20th Ave Ste 403, Whitestone NY 11357	718-746-3400	R	3*	<.1
189	Amin Food Inc—*Tony Leung*	525 E Walnut St, Garland TX 75040	972-272-8079	R	3*	<.1
190	La Criolla Inc—*Carmen Maldonado*	907 W Randolph St Ste, Chicago IL 60607	312-243-8882	R	3*	<.1
191	Sabroso Foods—*Clem Sanchez*	1019 Sunset Rd Sw, Albuquerque NM 87105	505-842-5579	R	3*	<.1
192	White Cloud Mountain Company Inc—*Jerome Eberharter*	5125 N Sawyer Ave, Garden City ID 83714	208-322-1166	R	3*	<.1
193	Becharas Brothers Coffee Co—*Nicholas Becharas*	14501 Hamilton Ave, Detroit MI 48203	313-869-4700	R	3*	<.1
194	Rising Dough Bakery—*Colette Jamet*	8135 Elder Creek Rd, Sacramento CA 95824	916-387-9700	R	3*	<.1
195	Great Gourmet Inc—*Kim Scott*	5115 Clark Cannon Hous, Federalsburg MD 21632	410-754-8800	R	3	<.1
196	Sarolo Bagel Restaurant Corp—*Louis Borenstein*	3202 E Greenway Rd Ste, Phoenix AZ 85032	602-971-8010	R	3*	.1
197	Flanigan Farms Inc—*Patsy Flanigan*	PO Box 347, Culver City CA 90232	310-838-4998	R	3*	<.1
198	SD Enterprises Inc—*Stephen Dirtzu*	PO Box A, Peshtigo WI 54157	715-582-3736	R	3*	<.1
199	Kozlowski Farms A Corp—*Perry Kozlowski*	5566 Hwy 116, Forestville CA 95436	707-887-1587	R	3*	<.1
200	Twenty-Six Juice Inc—*James Bradley*	5917 Liberty Rd, Baltimore MD 21207	410-298-1114	R	3*	<.1
201	Piemonte Bakery Company Inc—*Steve Keever*	1122 Rock St, Rockford IL 61101	815-962-4833	R	3*	<.1
202	Bay Beyond Inc—*Pamela Barefoot*	29368 Atlantic Dr, Melfa VA 23410	757-787-3602	R	3*	<.1
203	Grabill Country Meat 1 Inc—*Patrick Fonner*	PO Box 190, Grabill IN 46741	260-627-3691	R	3*	<.1
204	Gulinello's Towne and Country Inc—*Frances Gulinello*	7 Dock St, Hudson NY 12534	518-828-1506	R	3*	<.1
205	Mazzarelli's Bakery Inc—*John Rush*	229 Central St, Milford MA 01757	508-473-1175	R	3*	<.1
206	Sunkist Bakery Company Inc—*Robert Kolar*	4607 Morningside Ave, Sioux City IA 51106	712-276-9422	R	3*	<.1
207	Cold Hollow Cider Mill Inc—*Paul Brown*	PO Box 420, Waterbury Center VT 05677	802-244-8771	R	3*	<.1
208	Easton Spring Inc—*William Bertarelli*	PO Box 328, South Easton MA 02375	508-238-2741	R	3*	<.1
209	New Moon Noodle Inc—*Lee Lum*	909 Stanley Dr, Battle Creek MI 49037	269-962-8820	R	2*	<.1
210	Golden Crust Bakeries Inc—*Albert Mouawad*	25170 Anza Dr, Santa Clarita CA 91355	661-294-9750	R	2*	.1
211	Klein Smoked Meats LLC	1800 S Congress Ave, Austin TX 78704	512-445-6611	R	2*	<.1
212	Ferrell Industries Inc—*Frank Ferell*	136 E Chapel Hill St, Durham NC 27701	919-286-0303	R	2*	<.1
213	United Noodles—*Lee Tran*	2015 E 24th St, Minneapolis MN 55404	612-721-6677	R	2*	<.1
214	Adventure in Food Trading Company Inc—*Eric Guenther*	381 Broadway, Menands NY 12204	518-436-7603	R	2*	<.1
215	Spindler Co—*David Kittoe*	4430 Portage St NW, North Canton OH 44720	330-499-2560	R	2*	<.1
216	Dough-To-Go Inc—*Elizabeth Lee*	3535 De La Cruz Blvd, Santa Clara CA 95054	408-727-4094	R	2*	<.1
217	Chuck's Bakery—*Lola Vanderstelt*	2105 Calumet Ave, Valparaiso IN 46383	219-464-1511	R	2*	<.1
218	Apicellas Bakery Inc—*Alphonse Cimino*	365 Grand Ave, New Haven CT 06513	203-865-6204	R	2*	<.1
219	Kona Pacific Farmers Coop—*Brenda Mundo*	PO Box 309, Captain Cook HI 96704	808-328-2411	R	2*	<.1
220	Alakef Coffee Roasters Inc—*Nessim Bohbot*	1330 E Superior St Ste, Duluth MN 55805	218-724-6849	R	2*	<.1
221	Brookfield's Great Water Inc—*Arthur D Brookfield II*	2500 W Pennway, Kansas City MO 64108	913-648-1234	R	1*	<.1
222	Crown Beverage Co—*Clancy Kenck*	216 Commerce St, Missoula MT 59808	406-728-8100	R	1*	<.1
223	Mila Kofman—*Mila Kofman*	PO Box 691, Thiensville WI 53092	262-242-1404	R	1*	<.1
224	Asplund Coffee LLC—*Elizabeth Saust*	1002 1st St Ne, Buffalo MN 55313	763-682-6633	R	1*	<.1
225	Herbologics Ltd—*Cathryn Caton*	4580 S Hwy 181, Kenedy TX 78119	830-583-3761	R	<1*	<.1

TOTALS: SIC 5149 Groceries & Related Products Nec
Companies: 225

					35,676	44.1

5153 Grain & Field Beans

	Company Name—*Executive Officer*	Address, City, State, Zip	Phone	Type	Fin	Empls
1	ADM/Growmark River Systems Inc—*Patricia A Woertz*	PO Box 1470, Decatur IL 62525	217-424-5200	S	12,877*	22.8
2	DeBruce Grain Inc—*Paul DeBruce*	PO Box 34621, Kansas City MO 64116	816-421-8182	S	5,760*	.6
3	Scoular Co—*Chuck Elsea*	2027 Dodge St, Omaha NE 68102	402-342-3500	R	4,900	.7
4	Andersons Inc—*Michael J Anderson*	PO Box 119, Maumee OH 43537	419-893-5050	P	4,576	3.0
5	Consolidated Grain and Barge	PO Box 249, Mandeville LA 70470	985-867-3500	R	2,573*	1.2
6	Bruce Oakley Inc—*Dennis Oakley*	PO Box 17880, North Little Rock AR 72117	501-945-0875	R	2,332*	.2
7	ADM Grain—*Mark A Bemis*	4666 E Faries Pky, Decatur IL 62526	217-424-5200	S	1,662*	1.2
8	Connell Co—*Grover Connell*	200 Connell Dr, Berkeley Heights NJ 07922	908-673-3700	R	1,546*	.2
9	Farmers Cooperative Co (Dayton Iowa)—*Roger Koppen*	2321 N Loop Dr Ste 220, Ames IA 50010	515-817-2100	R	1,401*	.8
10	Countryside Coop—*George Rude*	PO Box 250, Durand WI 54736	715-672-8947	R	1,223*	.2
11	Countrymark Cooperative Inc—*Charlie Smith*	225 S East St Ste 144, Indianapolis IN 46202	317-692-8500	R	1,083*	.9
12	ConAgra Mills—*Joan Chow*	11 ConAgra Dr, Omaha NE 68102	402-595-4368	D	1,080	1.3
13	ADM Farmland Grain—*Pete Goetzmann*	8000 W 110th St Ste 22, Overland Park KS 66210	913-266-6300	S	1,060*	.4
14	West Central Coop—*Jeff Stroburg*	PO Box 68, Ralston IA 51459	712-667-3200	R	700*	.2
15	Heartland Co-Op—*Larry Petersen*	PO Box 71399, Des Moines IA 50325	515-225-1334	R	667*	.3
16	Interstate Commodities Inc—*Greg Oberting*	PO Box 607, Troy NY 12181	518-272-7212	R	540*	.1
17	Collingwood Grain Inc—*Patricia A Woertz*	PO Box 2657, Overland Park KS 66225		S	488	.5
18	Pendleton Grain Growers Inc—*Allen Waggoner*	PO Box 1248, Pendleton OR 97801	541-276-7611	R	391*	.2
19	Skyland Grain LLC—*David Cron*	PO Box 280, Johnson KS 67855	620-492-6210	R	390*	.1
20	Gold-Eagle Coop—*William Cruise*	PO Box 280, Goldfield IA 50542	515-825-3161	R	303*	.2
21	Champaign Landmark Inc—*John Dunbar*	PO Box 828, Urbana OH 43078	937-652-2135	R	285*	.1
22	Farmers Cooperative Society—*Ken Ehrp*	317 3rd St Nw, Sioux Center IA 51250	712-722-2671	R	249*	.2
23	Premier Cooperative—*Roger Miller*	2104 W Park Crt, Champaign IL 61821	217-355-1983	R	213*	<.1
24	Demeter Inc—*JoAnn Brouillette*	PO Box 506, Fowler IN 47944	765-884-9320	R	210*	<.1
25	Frontier Cooperative Co—*Randy Robeson*	PO Box 379, David City NE 68632	402-367-3019	R	187*	.1
26	Huskers Coop—*Rich Richey*	PO Box 1129, Columbus NE 68601	402-563-3636	R	187*	.1
27	Provico Inc—*Lee Braun*	PO Box 579, Botkins OH 45306	937-693-2411	S	184*	.2
28	Harvest Land Coop—*Gordy Jenfcm*	PO Box 278, Morgan MN 56266	507-249-3196	R	183*	.2
29	Ag Partners LLC—*Troy Upah*	PO Box 38, Albert City IA 50510	712-843-2291	J	181*	.2
30	Wheeler Brothers Grain Company Inc—*Mike Mahoney*	PO Box 29, Watonga OK 73772	580-623-7223	R	180*	.1
31	Mid Iowa Coop—*Cliss Kitzman*	PO Box 80, Beaman IA 50609	641-366-2740	R	178*	.1
32	New Vision Coop—*Frank McDowell*	38438 210th St, Brewster MN 56119	507-842-2001	R	174*	.1
33	Trc Group Inc—*Jay Kapila*	3721 Douglas Blvd Ste, Roseville CA 95661	916-784-7745	R	174*	3.0
34	Prairie Lakes Coop—*Brad Manderschied*	PO Box 580, Starbuck MN 56381	320-239-2226	D	163*	.1
35	Southwest Grain Div—*Morris Jacobs*	315 1st St E, Lemmon SD 57638	605-374-3301	D	146	.1
36	Johnston Enterprises Inc—*Butch Meibergen*	411 W Chestnut Ave, Enid OK 73701	580-233-5800	R	140*	.3
37	Gulf Pacific Rice Company Inc—*Fred Brenchkman*	12010 Taylor Rd, Houston TX 77041	713-464-0606	R	125*	.1

Rank	Company Name—Executive Officer	Address, City, State, Zip	Phone	Type	Fin	Empls
38	Madison Farmers Elevator Co—Mark Stoller	PO Box 228, Madison SD 57042	605-256-4584	R	119*	<.1
39	Perryton Equity Exchange—Doug Mitchell	PO Box 889, Perryton TX 79070	806-435-4016	R	110*	.1
40	East Central Iowa Coop—Mark Grove	PO Box 300, Hudson IA 50643	319-988-3257	R	109*	.1
41	Progressive Ag Cooperative—Ron Balek	PO Box 227, Northwood IA 50459	641-324-2753	R	107*	<.1
42	Ag Partners Cooperative Inc—Mitch Williams	708 S 10th St, Hiawatha KS 66434	785-742-2196	R	102*	<.1
43	Ritzville Warehouse Co—Grant Miller	201 E 1st Ave, Ritzville WA 99169	509-659-0130	R	90*	.1
44	FJ Krob and Co—Mark Krob	1705 Dows St, Ely IA 52227	319-848-4161	R	84*	.1
45	Farmers Cooperative Association (Brule Nebraska)—Tom Struckman	PO Box 127, Brule NE 69127	308-287-2304	R	82*	<.1
46	Andale Farmers Cooperative Co—Steve Shaver	PO Box 18, Andale KS 67001	316-444-2141	R	80*	<.1
47	Rock River Lumber and Grain Co—Joe Rosengren	PO Box 68, Prophetstown IL 61277	815-537-5131	R	78*	.1
48	JaGee Holdings LLP—Richard F Garvey	2918 Wingate St, Fort Worth TX 76107	817-335-5881	R	74*	.2
49	Midwest Cooperatives—Milt Handcock	1919 E Souix Ave, Pierre SD 57501	605-224-5935	R	74*	.1
50	Heart of Iowa Coop—Bob Finch	13585 620th Ave, Roland IA 50236	515-388-4341	R	72*	.1
51	Fredericksburg Farmers Coop—James Erickson	PO Box 261, Fredericksburg IA 50630	563-237-5324	R	71*	<.1
52	United Farmers Coop (Shelby Nebraska)—Tom Redman	PO Box 310, Shelby NE 68662	402-527-5511	R	71*	<.1
53	Dunkerton Cooperative Elevator—Bill Beirschmidtt	PO Box 286, Dunkerton IA 50626	319-822-4291	R	69*	<.1
54	United Farmers Coop (Lafayette Minnesota)—Jeff Nielsen	PO Box 4, Lafayette MN 56054	507-647-6600	R	68*	.1
55	Ludlow Cooperative Elevator Company Inc—Bruce Bastert	PO Box 155, Ludlow IL 60949	217-396-4111	R	68*	<.1
56	Garden City Co-Op Inc—John McClelland	PO Box 838, Garden City KS 67846	620-275-6161	R	66*	.1
57	Osage Cooperative Elevator—Tracy Funk	PO Box 358, Osage IA 50461	641-732-3768	R	66*	<.1
58	Colusa Elevator Company Inc—Dale Griffiths	2531 N County Rd, Colusa IL 62329	217-755-4221	R	60*	<.1
59	Decatur Cooperative Association—Rod Bryant	PO Box 68, Oberlin KS 67749	785-475-2234	R	59*	.1
60	Chem Gro Of Houghton Inc—Harold Dyer	PO Box 76, Houghton IA 52631	319-469-2611	R	57*	<.1
61	Sunray Coop—Ray Stipe	PO Box 430, Sunray TX 79086	806-948-4121	R	56*	.1
62	Anthony Farmers Cooperative and Elevator Co—Dan Cashier	PO Box 111, Anthony KS 67003	620-842-5181	R	54*	<.1
63	Alliance Grain Co—Robert Landau	PO Box 546, Gibson City IL 60936	217-784-4284	R	53*	<.1
64	Two Rivers Coop—Tracy Gathman	109 South St, Pella IA 50219		R	52*	<.1
65	Elkhart Cooperative Equity Exchange—Karen Hill	PO Box 210, Elkhart KS 67950	620-697-2135	R	50*	.1
66	Olton Grain Cooperative Inc—Greg Allen	PO Box 1083, Olton TX 79064	806-285-2638	R	49*	<.1
67	Lowes Pellets And Grain Inc—Don Lowe	2372 W State Rd 46, Greensburg IN 47240	812-663-7863	R	49*	<.1
68	Leroy Cooperative Association Inc—Rick Crooks	PO Box 248, Le Roy KS 66857	620-964-2225	R	48*	<.1
69	North Central Grain Coop—Lynnette Berg	PO Box 8, Bisbee ND 58317	701-656-3263	R	48*	.1
70	Cassel Farms—David Cassel	5626 Tupper Lake Rd, Sunfield MI 48890	517-566-8031	R	48*	<.1
71	Deshler Farmers Elevator Company Inc—Mark Sunderman	PO Box 226, Deshler OH 43516	419-278-3015	R	47*	<.1
72	Fessenden Cooperative Association—Mark Hovland	PO Box 126, Fessenden ND 58438	701-547-3291	R	46*	.1
73	Spokane Seed Co—Peter Johnstone	PO Box 11007, Spokane WA 99211	509-535-3671	R	46*	.1
74	Watertown Cooperative Elevator Association	811 Burlington Norther, Watertown SD 57201	605-886-3039	R	46*	.1
75	Arizona Grain Inc—Eric Wilkey	601 E Main Ave, Casa Grande AZ 85122	520-836-8228	R	45*	.1
76	Right Cooperative Association—Kyle Eberlee	PO Box 38, Wright KS 67882	620-227-8611	R	45*	<.1
77	Cooperative Country Farmer's Elevator—Craig Hebrink	PO Box 604, Renville MN 56284		R	43*	<.1
78	AGP Grain Coop—Marty Reagan	770 County Rd DD, Farwell TX 79325	806-825-2565	R	43*	<.1
79	Fulton-Marshall Coop—Barry Day	1496 N Meridian Rd, Rochester IN 46975	574-224-2667	R	42*	.1
80	Chesapeake Grain Co—Frank T Williams	5500 Dainbridge Blvd, Chesapeake VA 23320	757-543-2041	R	42*	.1
81	Michigan Agricultural Commodities—Dave Geers	PO Box 96, Blissfield MI 49228	517-486-2131	R	41*	<.1
82	Farmers Cooperative of Pilger—Walene Heermann	PO Box 326, Pilger NE 68768	402-396-3414	R	41*	<.1
83	Heartland Co-op (Trumbull Nebraska)—Kaye Doane	647 Hartford St, Trumbull NE 68980	402-743-2381	R	38*	<.1
84	Metamora Grain—Dupree Hoge Andersons Inc	PO Box G, Metamora OH 43540	419-644-4711	S	38*	<.1
85	Carrollton Farmers Elevator Company Inc—Rick Steinacher	PO Box 264, Carrollton IL 62016	217-942-6922	R	38*	<.1
86	Mercer Landmark Inc—Louis Mcintire	PO Box 328, Celina OH 45822	419-586-2303	R	36*	.2
87	Kelley Bean Company Inc—Robert Kelley	PO Box 2488, Scottsbluff NE 69363	308-635-6438	R	36*	.2
88	Plains Grain and Agronomy LLC—Gary Lindermann	109 3rd Ave, Enderlin ND 58027	701-437-2400	R	35*	<.1
89	VH Associates Inc—Roger Oliver	PO Box 380, Cerro Gordo IL 61818	217-677-2131	R	34*	<.1
90	New Cooperative Inc—Bob Dobson	PO Box 818, Fort Dodge IA 50501	515-955-2040	R	30*	.2
91	Prairie Grain Partners LLC—Scott Mauch	1220 Prairie Grain Rd, Clarkfield MN 56223	320-669-7501	R	30*	<.1
92	Minier Cooperative Grain Co—Duane Haning	PO Box 650, Minier IL 61759	309-392-2424	R	28*	<.1
93	Gateway Co-Op	PO Box 125, Galva IL 61434	309-932-2081	R	27*	.1
94	Trainor Grain and Supply Co—John A Trainor	13201 N 2753 East Rd, Forrest IL 61741	815-832-5512	R	27*	<.1
95	Agfirst Farmers Coop (Brookings South Dakota)—Terry Knudson	PO Box 127, Brookings SD 57006		R	27*	<.1
96	Hopkinsville Elevator Co—Jerry Good	PO Box 767, Hopkinsville KY 42241	270-886-5191	R	26*	<.1
97	Coshocton Grain Co—Rhoda Crown	PO Box 606, Coshocton OH 43812	740-622-0941	R	26*	<.1
98	Great Bend Cooperative Association—Frank Riedll	PO Box 68, Great Bend KS 67530	620-793-3531	R	25*	.1
99	Northeast Coop—Tom Ortmeier	445 S Main St, West Point NE 68788	402-372-5081	R	25*	<.1
100	Lawrence County Exchange—Gene Pickens	12955 Alabama Hwy 157, Moulton AL 35650	256-974-9214	R	25*	<.1
101	Farmers Cooperative Co (Readlyn Iowa)—Bruce Buxton	PO Box 339, Readlyn IA 50668	319-279-3396	R	25*	<.1
102	New Horizons AG Services—Jerry Kramer	PO Box 230, Herman MN 56248	320-677-2251	R	25*	<.1
103	Nomura and Company Inc—George Okamoto	40 Broderick Rd, Burlingame CA 94010	650-692-5457	R	25*	<.1
104	Lake Elbow Co-Op Grain—Scott Tyberg	PO Box 68, Elbow Lake MN 56531	218-685-5331	R	24*	<.1
105	Tama-Benton Cooperative Co—Mel Campbell	PO Box 459, Dysart IA 52224	319-476-3666	R	23*	<.1
106	Terre Haute Grain Co—Dustin Toberman	200 W Voorhees St, Terre Haute IN 47802	812-232-1044	R	23*	<.1
107	Stonington Cooperative Grain Co—Bruce Briggs	PO Box 350, Stonington IL 62567	217-325-3211	R	23*	<.1
108	Hoople Farmers Grain Co—Guy M Phelps	PO Box 140, Hoople ND 58243	701-894-6116	R	23*	<.1
109	Plains Equity Exchange—Stacey McVey	PO Box 157, Plains KS 67869	620-563-7269	R	22*	<.1
110	Graymont Cooperative Association Inc—Matt Jacobs	PO Box 98, Graymont IL 61743	815-743-5321	R	22*	<.1
111	McGeary Organics Inc—David Poorbaugh	PO Box 299, Lancaster PA 17608	717-394-6843	R	22*	<.1
112	Farmers Cooperative Co (Dows Iowa)—Mike Wilson	304 Ellsworth St, Dows IA 50071	515-852-4136	R	22*	<.1
113	Assumption Cooperative Grain Co—Scott Durbin	104 W North St, Assumption IL 62510	217-226-3213	R	21*	<.1
114	Central Grain Co—Robert R Mickey	1140 W Locust St, Belvidere IL 61008	815-544-3455	R	21*	<.1
115	Geneva Elevator Co—Moury Hyde	PO Box 49, Geneva IA 50633	641-458-8145	R	21*	<.1
116	Meadowland Farmers Coop—Jack Reiner	PO Box 338, Lamberton MN 56152	507-752-7352	R	21*	.1
117	Ag Partners LLC—Cathy Lode	PO Box 128, Sheldon IA 51201	712-324-2548	R	20*	.1
118	Sublette Cooperative Inc—Lynn Leonard	PO Box 340, Sublette KS 67877	620-675-2297	R	20*	<.1
119	Oberbeck Grain Co—Robert Luitjohan	PO Box 145, Highland IL 62249	618-654-2387	R	20*	<.1
120	Farmers Elevator and Supply Co—Doug Vandernyde	301 E Market St, Morrison IL 61270	815-772-4029	R	19	<.1
121	Halstad Elevator Co—Robin Stene	PO Box 87, Halstad MN 56548	218-456-2135	R	19*	<.1
122	Gulf Pacific Inc—Friedrich Brenckmann	12010 Taylor Rd, Houston TX 77041	713-464-0606	R	19*	.1
123	FGDI LLC Agrex Inc	PO Box 4887, Des Moines IA 50306	515-223-7400	S	18*	<.1

Note: An asterisk (*) indicates an estimated financial figure. The company type code used is as follows: R = Private, P = Public, S = Private Subsidiary, B = Public Subsidiary, D = Division, J = Joint Venture, I = Investment Fund.

COMPANY RANKINGS BY SALES WITHIN 4-DIGIT SIC

Rank	Company Name—*Executive Officer*	Address, City, State, Zip	Phone	Type	Fin	Empls
124	Yale Farmers Coop—*Gary Doering*	PO Box 128, Yale SD 57386	605-599-2911	R	18*	<.1
125	Grain Store Elevators—*MJ Anderson*	PO Box 629, Galesburg IL 61402	309-342-2112	R	18*	<.1
126	Juergens Produce and Feed Co—*Ron Juergens*	PO Box 1027, Carroll IA 51401	712-792-3506	R	18*	.1
127	FS Gateway Inc—*Ronald Fehr*	PO Box 100, Red Bud IL 62278	618-282-4000	R	17*	.1
128	Hereford Grain Corp—*Joe Perrin*	PO Box 910, Hereford TX 79045	806-364-3755	R	17*	<.1
129	Nathan Segal and Company Inc—*Barbara Segal Goldfield*	PO Box 272189, Houston TX 77277	713-621-2000	R	17*	<.1
130	Farmers Grain Company of Chestnut—*Phile Seaman*	PO Box 139, Chestnut IL 62518	217-796-3513	R	17*	<.1
131	Jesse C Stewart Co—*Robert Danik*	360 Broadmoor Ave, Pittsburgh PA 15228	412-343-0600	R	17*	<.1
132	Tri Central Co-op—*David Pratt*	PO Box 176, Ashkum IL 60911	815-698-2327	R	17*	<.1
133	Farmers Elevator Cooperative Of Rock Valley Iowa—*Keith Boer*	PO Box 37, Rock Valley IA 51247	712-476-5321	R	17*	.1
134	Western Iowa Coop—*John Cronin*	PO Box 106, Hornick IA 51026	712-874-3211	R	17*	.1
135	Aurora Cooperative Elevator Co—*George Hohwieler*	605 12th St, Aurora NE 68818	402-694-2106	R	16*	.3
136	Odessa Trading Company Inc—*HP Carstensen* Ritzville Warehouse Co	PO Box 277, Odessa WA 99159	509-982-2661	S	16*	<.1
137	Berthold Farmers Elevator Co—*Keith Neshem*	1 Main St S, Berthold ND 58718	701-453-3431	R	16*	<.1
138	Progressive Ag Center LLC—*Ronald Nelson* All-American Co-Op	PO Box 125, Stewartville MN 55976	507-533-4222	S	16*	<.1
139	Farmers Coop (Carmen Oklahoma)—*Kendall Poland*	PO Box 100, Carmen OK 73726	580-987-2234	R	15*	<.1
140	Donovan Farmers Cooperative Elevator Inc	PO Box 159, Donovan IL 60931	815-486-7325	R	15*	<.1
141	Earlville Farmers Coop—*Jim Sutton*	PO Box 479, Earlville IL 60518	815-246-8461	R	15*	<.1
142	Hunter Grain Co—*Paul Skarnagel*	PO Box 97, Hunter ND 58048	701-874-2112	R	15*	<.1
143	Union Elevator and Warehouse Co	PO Box 370, Lind WA 99341	509-677-3441	R	15*	<.1
144	Farmers Cooperative Elevator Co (Halstead Kansas)—*Dale Dick*	302 W 1st St, Halstead KS 67056	316-835-2261	R	15	<.1
145	Farmers Cooperative Mill Elevator—*Lee Partridge*	PO Box 69, Carnegie OK 73015	580-654-1016	R	14*	<.1
146	Farm Chemicals Inc—*Alfred Leach*	PO Box 667, Raeford NC 28376	910-875-4277	R	14*	<.1
147	Atherton Grain Co—*Roy A Atherton*	PO Box 366, Walnut IL 61376	815-379-2177	R	13*	<.1
148	Tri Valley Coop—*Cort Walberg*	4713 1st St Ste 110, Pleasanton CA 94566	925-417-7600	R	13*	<.1
149	Cissna Park Cooperative Inc—*Charles Schmidt*	PO Box 98, Cissna Park IL 60924	815-457-2181	R	13*	<.1
150	Morrisonville Farmers Coop—*Dan Litteken*	PO Box 17, Morrisonville IL 62546	217-526-3123	R	13*	<.1
151	Ellsworth Coop—*Alan Doubrava*	PO Box 397, Ellsworth KS 67439	785-472-3261	R	13*	<.1
152	Sunrise Cooperative Inc—*George Secor*	PO Box 870, Fremont OH 43420	419-332-6468	R	13*	.1
153	Old Dominion Grain Corp—*Don Mennel*	PO Box 816, West Point VA 23181	804-843-2922	R	12*	<.1
154	Topflight Grain Co—*Scot Docherty*	PO Box 69, Cisco IL 61830	217-669-2141	R	12*	<.1
155	Five Star Coop (Joice Iowa)—*Wayne Steven*	355 410th St, Joice IA 50446	641-592-2552	R	11*	<.1
156	Co-Op Country Farmers Elevator—*Craig Hebrink*	PO Box 604, Renville MN 56284	320-329-8377	R	11*	.1
157	Farmers Cooperative Association (Gillette Wyoming)—*Daryl Meyer*	1206 S Douglas Hwy, Gillette WY 82716	307-682-4468	R	11*	.1
158	Producers Grain Co—*Greg Reynolds*	1200 S Main St, El Dorado Springs MO 64744	417-876-2422	R	11*	<.1
159	St Francis Mercantile Equity Exchange—*Karol Lohman*	PO Box 545, Saint Francis KS 67756	785-332-2113	R	11*	<.1
160	Dakota Prairie AG—*Marv Schulz*	PO Box 8, Edgeley ND 58433	701-493-2481	R	11*	<.1
161	Rosholt Farmers Cooperative Elevator Co—*Bruce Luick*	PO Box 16, Rosholt SD 57260	605-537-4236	R	11*	<.1
162	Danvers Farmers Elevator Co—*Jim Vierling*	200 S West St, Danvers IL 61732	309-963-4305	R	11*	<.1
163	Delphos Cooperative Association Inc—*Kent Baldock*	PO Box 308, Delphos KS 67436	785-523-4213	R	10*	<.1
164	Ittner Bean and Grain Inc—*Oscar Ittner*	301 Park Ave, Auburn MI 48611	989-662-4461	R	9*	<.1
165	Minooka Grain Lumber and Supply Co—*Bernard Bols*	PO Box 100, Minooka IL 60447	815-467-2232	R	9*	<.1
166	Farmers Feed and Grain Co—*Steve Eastman*	PO Box 291, Riceville IA 50466	641-985-2147	R	9*	<.1
167	Sand Seed Service Inc—*Gene Andrews*	4765 Hwy 143, Marcus IA 51035	712-376-4135	R	8*	.1
168	Farmers Union Cooperative Business Association Of St Marys Kan—*Jeff Overmeyer*	PO Box 218, Saint Marys KS 66536	785-437-2984	R	8*	<.1
169	Farmer's Mill and Elevator Company Inc—*D Knight*	PO Box 1086, Dexter GA 31019	478-875-3107	R	8*	<.1
170	Country Partners Co-Op Elevators—*Lonny Clausen*	PO Box 208, Ord NE 68862	308-728-3254	R	8*	<.1
171	Moweaqua Farmers Cooperative Grain Co—*ER Harper*	PO Box 146, Moweaqua IL 62550	217-768-4416	R	8*	<.1
172	Grainland Coop—*Jeff Brooks*	927 County Hwy 3, Eureka IL 61530	309-467-2355	R	8*	<.1
173	Ursa Farmers Cooperative Company Inc—*Gerald Jenkins*	PO Box 8, Ursa IL 62376	217-964-2111	R	8*	<.1
174	Moss Peoples Gin Company Inc—*Jeff Benhard*	PO Box 68, Palmetto LA 71358	337-623-4294	R	8*	.1
175	All-American Co-Op—*Mickeal Hims*	PO Box 125, Stewartville MN 55976	507-533-4222	R	7*	<.1
176	Farmers Gin Company Inc—*Kenny Ward*	Cotton Gin Rd, Clinton KY 42031	270-653-2731	R	7*	<.1
177	Rugby Farmers Union Elevator Co—*Steve Danielson*	PO Box 286, Rugby ND 58368	701-776-5214	R	7*	<.1
178	Beardsley Farmers Elevator Co—*Ken Kellen*	PO Box 297, Beardsley MN 56211	320-265-6933	R	7*	<.1
179	Northwest Pea and Bean Co—*Joe Hulett*	PO Box 11973, Spokane Valley WA 99211	509-534-3821	R	7*	.1
180	Beaumont Rice Mills Inc—*Louis Broussard*	PO Box 3111, Beaumont TX 77704	409-832-2521	R	7*	<.1
181	Madison Service Co—*Sharon Coyne*	PO Box 137, Alhambra IL 62001	618-488-2265	R	7*	<.1
182	Farmers Cooperative Grain Co—*Robert Johnston*	PO Box 191, Caldwell KS 67022	620-845-6441	R	7*	<.1
183	Farmers Co-Op Association—*Eriq Anderson*	PO Box 307, New Hartford IA 50660	319-983-2259	R	6*	<.1
184	Prinz Grain and Feed Inc—*Dave Prinz*	575 S Main St, West Point NE 68788	402-372-2495	R	6*	<.1
185	Rumbold and Kuhn Inc—*Mike Rumbold*	20014 N Rice Rd, Princeville IL 61559	309-385-4361	R	6*	<.1
186	Danforth-Gilman Grain Co—*Jason Risley*	117 W 3rd St, Gilman IL 60938		R	6*	<.1
187	Hub Grain Company Inc—*Howard Fleming*	1452 Hwy 214, Friona TX 79035	806-265-3215	R	6*	<.1
188	Bee Agricultural Co—*Fred Schauer*	PO Box 1208, Beeville TX 78104	361-358-3470	R	6*	<.1
189	Pettisville Grain Co—*Neil Rupt*	PO Box 53009, Pettisville OH 43553	419-446-2547	R	5*	<.1
190	Countyline Co-Op Inc—*Donald Kline*	PO Box C, Pemberville OH 43450	419-287-3241	R	5*	<.1
191	Ypsilanti Equity Elevator Company Inc—*Keith Larsen*	204 Front Ave N, Ypsilanti ND 58497	701-489-3379	R	5*	<.1
192	Agrisource Inc—*Bill Mendenhal*	PO Box 1000, Burley ID 83318	208-678-2286	R	5*	<.1
193	Hayes Food Products Inc—*Bill Francis*	PO Box 121, Greenville SC 29602	864-244-4841	R	5*	<.1
194	Harmony Agri Services Inc—*Jeffrey Soma*	25 Second St Ne, Harmony MN 55939	507-886-6062	R	4*	<.1
195	Albright's Mill LLC	PO Box 195, Kempton PA 19529	610-756-6022	R	4*	<.1
196	Custer Grain Company Inc—*Wayne Custer*	2006 County Rd 48, Garrett IN 46738	260-357-5432	R	4*	<.1
197	Tietje Mullet and Klink Inc—*Larry Tietje*	PO Box 278, Sugarcreek OH 44681	330-852-4681	R	4*	<.1
198	Farmers Elevator Grain And Supply—*Dennis Niese*	PO Box 249, New Bavaria OH 43548	419-653-4132	R	3*	<.1
199	David W Reed Co—*Charles Reed*	PO Box 380, Sylvania GA 30467	912-564-7473	R	3*	<.1
200	North Iowa Cooperative Elevator—*Spotts Marcus*	19856 Main St, Mason City IA 50401	641-423-5311	R	3*	<.1
201	Farmers Elevator Company Of Pelican Rapids—*Dean Johnson*	PO Box 631, Pelican Rapids MN 56572	218-863-1551	R	3*	<.1
202	S and S Farm Center—*Bill Mathews*	302 S Beard St, Shawnee OK 74801	405-273-6907	R	3*	<.1
203	Clearbrook Elevator Association—*Glen Nelson*	PO Box 9, Clearbrook MN 56634	218-776-3511	R	2*	<.1
204	Ohio Grain Co—*Richard Swanson*	PO Box 67, Ohio IL 61349	815-376-2411	R	2*	<.1
205	Kragnes Farmers Elevator—*Todd Dravland*	PO Box 157, Dilworth MN 56529	218-287-2379	R	N/A	<.1

TOTALS: SIC 5153 Grain & Field Beans
Companies: 205   53,439   46.0

Rank	Company Name—*Executive Officer*	Address, City, State, Zip	Phone	Type	Fin	Empls
5154 Livestock						
1	Prairie Livestock LLC—*James D Bryan*	PO Box 636, West Point MS 39773	662-494-5651	R	260*	<.1
2	United Producers Inc—*W Dennis Bolling*	PO Box 29800, Columbus OH 43229	614-890-6666	R	130*	.1
3	Coharie Hog Farm Inc—*Nelson Waters*	PO Box 1391, Clinton NC 28329	910-592-0105	R	75*	.2
4	Bales Continental Commission Co—*Alan Bales*	PO Box 1337, Huron SD 57350	605-352-8682	R	25*	<.1
5	Sharn Veterinary Inc	10008 N Dale Mabry Hwy, Tampa FL 33618	813-962-6664	S	4*	<.1
6	Philip Livestock Auction—*Jerry Roseth*	PO Box 875, Philip SD 57567	605-859-2685	R	3*	.1
7	Kingsport Livestock Auction Corp—*James Dobyns*	PO Box 322, Kingsport TN 37662	423-378-3254	R	3*	<.1
TOTALS: SIC 5154 Livestock						
Companies: 7					**500**	**.4**
5159 Farm-Product Raw Materials Nec						
1	Universal Corp—*George C Freeman III*	PO Box 25099, Richmond VA 23260	804-359-9311	P	2,572	26.0
2	Dunavant Enterprises Inc—*William B Dunavant Jr*	3797 New Getwell Rd, Memphis TN 38118	901-369-1500	R	2,272*	3.0
3	Alliance One International Inc—*Mark W Kehaya*	PO Box 2009, Morrisville NC 27560	919-379-4300	P	2,094	3.3
4	Staplcotn Cooperative Association—*Woods E Eastland*	PO Box 547, Greenwood MS 38935	662-453-6231	R	1,499*	.5
5	Sunrise AG Service Co—*Rich Vanderpool*	PO Box 108, Virginia IL 62691	217-452-7751	R	846*	.3
6	Calcot Ltd—*Jarral T Neeper*	PO Box 259, Bakersfield CA 93302	661-327-5961	R	272*	.1
7	Birdsong Corp—*Jeff Johnson*	PO Box 1400, Suffolk VA 23439	757-539-3456	R	252*	.7
8	Hail and Cotton Inc—*Warren Corbin*	PO Box 638, Springfield TN 37172	615-384-9576	R	235*	.1
9	Cargill Cotton Inc—*Gary Taylor*	7101 Goodlett Farms Pk, Cordova TN 38016	901-937-4500	S	110*	.3
10	Hog Inc—*Dave Conrady*	RR 2 Box 8, Greenfield IL 62044		R	104*	<.1
11	McClesky Mills Inc—*Jerry M Chandler*	PO Box 98, Smithville GA 31787	229-846-2003	R	95*	.1
12	ABJ Enterprises Inc—*Alsey B Johnson*	PO Box 428, Dunn NC 28335	910-892-1357	R	75*	<.1
13	Commodity Specialists Co—*Philip J Lindau Jr*	920 2nd Ave S Ste 850, Minneapolis MN 55402	612-330-9889	R	70*	.1
14	Weil Brothers-Cotton Inc—*Robert S Weil II*	PO Box 20100, Montgomery AL 36116	334-244-1800	S	70*	.1
15	Ohsman and Sons Co—*Michael Ohsman*	PO Box 1196, Cedar Rapids IA 52406	319-365-7546	R	68*	<.1
16	Pioneer Growers Co-Op—*Gene Duff*	227 NW Ave L, Belle Glade FL 33430	561-996-5211	R	50	.1
17	Thomas Monahan Co—*Thomas Monahan*	PO Box 250, Arcola IL 61910	217-268-4955	R	40	.2
18	Severn Peanut Company Inc—*Dallas Barnes*	PO Box 710, Severn NC 27877	252-585-0838	R	34*	.2
19	Texoma Peanut Co—*Allen Ortloff*	PO Box 310, Madill OK 73446	580-795-5555	R	32*	.2
20	Western District Warehousing Corp—*Bruce Langley*	PO Box 336, Shelbyville KY 40066	502-633-1345	R	20*	.2
21	Dollins Pecan Company Inc—*Hubert Dollins*	308 S Houston St, Comanche TX 76442	325-356-5291	R	20*	.1
22	CA Perry and Son Inc—*Sidney Perry*	4033 Virginia Rd, Hobbsville NC 27946	252-221-4463	R	13*	.1
23	Damascus Peanut Co—*JW Willis*	PO Box 526, Arlington GA 39813	229-725-3353	R	12*	.1
24	Whaley Pecan Company Inc—*Robert Whaley*	PO Box 609, Troy AL 36081	334-566-3504	R	9*	.1
25	AM Bickley Inc—*James Liipfert*	PO Box 91, Marshallville GA 31057	478-967-2291	R	9*	<.1
26	HJ Bergeron Pecan Shelling Plant Inc—*Lester Bergeron*	10003 False River Rd, New Roads LA 70760	225-638-9626	R	5*	<.1
27	Coley Farm Services—*Ronnie Coley*	PO Box 232, Ashburn GA 31714	229-567-9661	R	4*	<.1
28	Millstadt Rendering Co—*Robert Kostelac*	3151 Cloverleaf School, Belleville IL 62223	618-538-5312	R	4*	<.1
29	Orangeburg Pecan Company Inc—*Frederick Felder*	PO Box 38, Orangeburg SC 29116	803-534-4277	R	3*	<.1
30	Southern Tier Hide and Tallow Inc—*Roy Slusser*	3385 Lwer Maple Ave St, Elmira NY 14901	607-734-3661	R	2*	<.1
31	Luckett Holdings Inc—*Caroline Owre*	2000 Warrington Way St, Louisville KY 40222	502-561-0070	R	2*	<.1
32	Louisville Pecan Company Inc—*Homer Henson*	PO Box 38, Louisville AL 36048	334-266-5388	R	2*	<.1
33	Wonalancet Co—*James J Dunn*	1130 Senoia Rd Ste A2, Tyrone GA 30290	770-774-2821	R	2*	<.1
34	Appalachian Root And Herb Co—*T Thomas*	PO Box 649, Rainelle WV 25962	304-438-5211	R	2*	<.1
TOTALS: SIC 5159 Farm Product Raw Materials Nec						
Companies: 34					**10,899**	**35.9**
5162 Plastics Materials & Basic Shapes						
1	H Muehlstein and Company Inc—*J Kevin Donohue*	800 Connecticut Ave, Norwalk CT 06854	203-855-6000	R	875*	.4
2	Woodbridge Sales and Engineering Inc—*Bob Magee*	1515 Equity Dr, Troy MI 48084	248-288-0100	R	722*	.1
3	Harrington Industrial Plastics Inc—*William C McCollum*	14480 Yorba Ave, Chino CA 91710	909-597-8641	R	600*	.6
4	Gruber Systems Inc—*John Hoskinson*	25636 Ave Stanford, Valencia CA 91355	682-518-7400	R	322*	.3
5	Best Vinyl Inc—*John Morrell*	62 N 1020 W, American Fork UT 84003	801-409-0442	S	245*	.2
6	Bunzl Philadelphia	10814 Northeast Ave, Philadelphia PA 19116	215-969-0600	D	203*	.3
7	Mitsui Plastics Inc—*Hiroshi Ogawa*	11 Martine Ave Ste 117, White Plains NY 10606	914-287-6800	S	163*	.1
8	Mexichem America Inc—*Ricardo Utierrez*	PO Box 69, Tennent NJ 07763	732-577-7900	R	149*	<.1
9	Curbell Inc—*Shuhartha Ghose*	7 Cobham Dr, Orchard Park NY 14127	716-667-3377	R	142*	.4
10	Regal Plastic Supply Co—*Richard Cull*	111 E 10th Ave, Kansas City MO 64116	816-421-6290	R	128*	.2
11	Ryan Herco Products Corp—*Frank Gibbs*	PO Box 588, Burbank CA 91503		R	96*	.3
12	Modern Plastics Inc—*James Carbone*	678 Howard Ave, Bridgeport CT 06605	203-333-3128	R	64*	.1
13	Bay Polymer Corp—*John Fountain*	44530 Grimmer Blvd, Fremont CA 94538	510-490-1791	R	57*	.1
14	TricorBraun—*Keith Strope*	10330 Old Olive St Rd, Saint Louis MO 63141	314-569-3633	R	54*	.1
15	Laird Plastics Inc—*Mark Cramer*	6800 Broken Sound Pkwy, Boca Raton FL 33487	561-443-9100	S	49*	.4
16	Ribelin Sales Inc—*Michael Ribelin*	3857 Miller Park Dr, Garland TX 75042	972-272-1594	R	33*	<.1
17	Advanced Plastics Inc—*Roy Abner*	7360 Cockrill Bend Blv, Nashville TN 37209	615-350-6500	R	32*	.1
18	Port Plastics Inc—*Keith Eitzen*	15325 Fairfield Ranch, Chino Hills CA 91709	909-393-5984	R	31*	.1
19	Aetna Plastics Corp—*Gary P Davis*	1702 Saint Clair Ave, Cleveland OH 44114	216-781-4421	R	31*	<.1
20	Kyowa America Corp—*Sumito Furuya*	14600 Hoover St, Westminster CA 92683	714-889-6600	R	27*	.4
21	Ohio Valley Supply Co—*Kenneth Shear*	3512 Spring Grove Ave, Cincinnati OH 45223	513-681-8300	R	25*	.1
22	Sundance Products Inc—*Larry Parmet*	615 Colonial Park Dr S, Roswell GA 30075	678-318-9000	R	25*	.1
23	Midland Plastics Inc—*Mark Hense*	PO Box 510055, New Berlin WI 53151	262-938-7000	R	23*	.1
24	Cleret Inc—*Alan Hansen*	11705 SW 68th Ave, Portland OR 97223	503-222-9227	R	23*	<.1
25	Cope Plastics Inc—*Jane Saale*	PO Box 129, Godfrey IL 62035	618-466-0221	R	22*	.4
26	H Sattler Plastics Company Inc—*John Sattler*	5410 W Roosevelt Rd, Chicago IL 60644	312-733-2900	R	22*	<.1
27	Regal Plastic Supply Co—*Charles Wade*	PO Box 59977, Dallas TX 75229	972-484-0741	R	21*	.1
28	Unlimited Flexible Plastics Inc—*Effia Starovisky*	13017 Artesia Blvd Ste, Cerritos CA 90703	323-460-6436	R	21*	.2
29	Corr Tech Inc—*James E Gottesman*	4545 Homestead Rd, Houston TX 77028	713-674-7887	R	20*	.1
30	Lainiere De Picardie Inc—*John Huss*	180 Wheeler Ct Ste A, Langhorne PA 19047	215-702-9090	R	19*	<.1
31	Cytex Plastics Inc—*David Burg*	12955 Emmett Rd, Houston TX 77041	713-937-1300	R	18*	.1
32	Housechem Inc—*Lee Fantone*	21-25 Industrial Park, Waldwick NJ 07463	201-445-8808	R	18*	.1
33	Thermoplastic Services Inc—*Eddie Wade*	1700 W 4th St, Dequincy I A 70633	337-786-7022	R	16*	.1
34	Agri-Nutrients Company Inc—*Ben Wilson*	4813 County Dr, Disputanta VA 23842	804-732-6884	R	15*	<.1
35	Parkland Plastics Inc—*Charles Yoder*	PO Box 339, Middlebury IN 46540	574-825-4336	R	14*	<.1
36	Acrilex Inc—*Steve Sullivan*	230 Culver Ave, Jersey City NJ 07305	201-333-1500	R	13*	.1
37	Matrixx Group Inc—*Michael Fitzpatrick*	15000 Hwy 41 N, Evansville IN 47725	812-421-3600	R	13*	.2
38	Orange County Industrial Plastics Inc—*Robert Robinson*	4811 E La Palma Ave, Anaheim CA 92807	714-632-9450	R	12*	<.1

Note: An asterisk (*) indicates an estimated financial figure. The company type code used is as follows: R = Private, P = Public, S = Private Subsidiary, B = Public Subsidiary, D = Division, J = Joint Venture, I = Investment Fund.

COMPANY RANKINGS BY SALES WITHIN 4-DIGIT SIC

Rank	Company Name—Executive Officer	Address, City, State, Zip	Phone	Type	Fin	Empls
39	C Bamberger Molding Compounds Inc—Claude P Bamberger	PO Box 67, Carlstadt NJ 07072	201-933-6262	R	12*	<.1
40	Consolidated Plastics Corp—Jean Bouris	14954 La Palma Dr, Chino CA 91710	909-393-8222	R	11*	.1
41	Northeast Plastic Supply Company Inc—Louis Altomari	3021 Darnell Rd, Philadelphia PA 19154	215-637-2221	R	11*	<.1
42	Plastic Products Inc—Jay Raxter	PO Box 188, Bessemer City NC 28016	704-739-7463	R	9*	<.1
43	Adapt Plastics Inc—Larry Phippen	7949 Forest Hills Rd, Loves Park IL 61111	815-633-9263	R	8*	<.1
44	Merit Paper Co—Maurice H Sussman	555 Broadhollow Rd Ste, Melville NY 11747	631-454-1560	R	8*	<.1
45	Delmar Products Inc—Stephen Mugno	PO Box 504, Berlin CT 06037	860-828-6501	R	7*	<.1
46	Lake Country Corp—Richard Gillette	PO Box 231, Mayville WI 53050	920-387-4110	R	7*	<.1
47	Channel Prime Alliance Inc—Tom Irvine	1803 Hull Ave, Des Moines IA 50313	515-265-4110	R	7*	<.1
48	SP Morell Co—Samuel P Morell	PO Box 147, Armonk NY 10504	914-273-0300	R	7*	<.1
49	Crown Plastics Inc—Thomas Beusekom	12615 16th Ave N, Minneapolis MN 55441	763-557-6000	R	7*	<.1
50	Trident Plastics Inc—Ronald Cadic	1029 Pulinski Rd, Warminster PA 18974	215-672-5582	R	7*	<.1
51	Ohio Valley Plastics Inc—Gary Smith	PO Box 6964, Evansville IN 47719	812-425-8544	R	6*	<.1
52	Ability Plastics Inc—Michael Nuzzo	8721 Industrial Dr, Justice IL 60458	708-458-4480	R	6*	<.1
53	Albis Plastics Corp—Michael Gray	19901 SW Fwy, Sugar Land TX 77479	281-207-5466	R	5*	<.1
54	Allpak Co—Burt Levy	1010 Lake St, Oak Park IL 60301	708-383-7200	R	4*	<.1
55	CIMS Corp—Mike Peeples	2204 Industrial S Rd, Dalton GA 30721	706-277-9059	R	3*	<.1
56	Rutgers Pressure Forming Company Inc—Greg Horowitz	617 Little Britain Rd, New Windsor NY 12553	914-968-8866	R	3*	<.1
57	Hammer Plastics Inc—Michael Hammer	PO Box 446, Mishawaka IN 46546	574-255-7230	R	3*	<.1
58	Rummel Industries Inc—Peter Rummel	PO Box 1326, Union NJ 07083	908-688-6600	R	3*	<.1
59	Trans World Services Inc—Thomas Ford	72 Stone Pl Ste 1, Melrose MA 02176	781-665-9200	R	3*	<.1
60	Signum Inc—Peter Joyce	PO Box 391437, Solon OH 44139	440-543-8000	R	3*	<.1
61	El-Mar Plastics Inc—Allen Schor	109 W 134th St, Los Angeles CA 90061	310-327-3180	R	3*	<.1
62	Amerifilm Converters LLC—Robert Oreilly	85 Lincoln Hwy, Kearny NJ 07032	973-690-5900	R	3*	<.1
63	Plastic Sales Southern Inc—James R Quinn	6490 Fleet St, Los Angeles CA 90040	323-728-8309	R	2*	<.1
64	Angus-Campbell Inc—Stuart Campbell	4417 S Soto St, Vernon CA 90058	323-587-1236	R	2*	<.1
65	A 1 Packaging Products Inc—Norman Rabenstein	3608 Review Ave, Long Island City NY 11101	718-392-2444	R	2*	<.1
66	Nordic Co—Donald Kaercher	PO Box 405, Gibsonia PA 15044	724-443-6840	R	2*	<.1
67	Epi Systems Inc—Bobby Wright	PO Box 4085, Huntsville AL 35815	256-533-5966	R	2*	<.1
68	Eire Ltd—Dennis O'brien	1041 Glassboro Rd Ste, Williamstown NJ 08094	856-728-0500	R	1*	<.1
69	Frelab Plastic Products Inc—Freddi Barrett	PO Box 165, Deerfield IL 60015	847-816-8888	R	1*	<.1
70	Aztec Supply Co—Eric Berge	954 N Batavia St, Orange CA 92867	714-771-6580	R	1*	<.1
71	American Renolit Corp—Richard Sternthal	1207 E Lincolnway, La Porte IN 46350	219-324-6886	S	1*	<.1
72	RCV Industries—Rod Vonder Reith	PO Box 2539, Canyon Country CA 91386	661-251-9986	R	1*	<.1

TOTALS: SIC 5162 Plastics Materials & Basic Shapes
Companies: 72   **4,524**   **6.2**

5169 Chemicals & Allied Products Nec

Rank	Company Name—Executive Officer	Address, City, State, Zip	Phone	Type	Fin	Empls
1	Brenntag Great Lakes LLC—Michael Arrichiello	PO Box 444, Butler WI 53007	262-252-3550	R	6,940*	.2
2	RR Plumbing Services Corp—Arthur V Tucker Jr	225 E 5th St, Cincinnati OH 45202	513-762-6690	S	5,403*	4.0
3	Brenntag Mid-South Inc—Joel Hopper	PO Box 20, Henderson KY 42419	270-830-1200	R	5,379*	.2
4	Airgas Inc—Peter McCausland	259 N Radnor-Chester R, Radnor PA 19087	610-687-5253	P	4,252	14.0
5	Ecolab Inc Institutional Div—Jack Schaefers	Ecolab Center 370 N Wa, Saint Paul MN 55102	651-293-2233	D	3,149*	23.0
6	Univar Inc—John J Zillmer	17425 NE Union Hill Rd, Redmond WA 98052	425-889-3400	R	3,116*	4.0
7	Brenntag North America Inc—William A Fidler	PO Box 13788, Reading PA 19612	610-926-4151	S	2,580*	4.3
8	Waxie Sanitary Supply—Charles Wax	9353 Waxie Way, San Diego CA 92123	858-292-8111	R	2,524*	.5
9	Sigma-Aldrich Corp—Rakesh Sachdev	3050 Spruce St, Saint Louis MO 63103	314-771-5765	P	2,271	7.9
10	Wacker Chemical Corp—Rudolf Staudigl	3301 Sutton Rd, Adrian MI 49221	517-264-8500	S	2,029*	.5
11	CHEMCENTRAL Corp—John Maher	PO Box 730, Bedford Park IL 60499	708-594-7000	R	1,375	1.1
12	Rosen's Diversified Inc—Ivan Wells	1631 NE Broadway Ste 6, Portland OR 97232	507-238-4201	R	1,200*	2.2
13	Amway International Inc—Douglas Devos	PO Box 513, Ada MI 49301	616-787-6000	R	910*	10.0
14	Coyne Chemical Company Inc—Thomas H Coyne	3015 State Rd, Croydon PA 19021	215-785-3000	R	550*	.1
15	Solvay Solexis Inc—Laird Mcbeth	10 Leonard Ln, West Deptford NJ 08086	856-853-8119	R	503*	.3
16	Aceto Corp—Albert Eilender	4 Tri Harbor Ct, Port Washington NY 11050	516-627-6000	P	412	.2
17	Farwest Corrosion Control Co—Gordon Rankin	1480 W Artesia Blvd, Gardena CA 90248	310-532-9524	R	405*	.1
18	Interplastic Corp—James Wallenfelsz	1225 Willow Lake Blvd, Saint Paul MN 55110	651-481-6860	R	400*	.5
19	Pressure Vessel Service Inc—James Nicholson	10900 Harper Ave, Detroit MI 48213	313-921-1200	R	357*	.8
20	Ucb Chemicals Corp—Larry Golen	2000 Lake Park Dr Se, Smyrna GA 30080	770-434-6188	R	350*	.4
21	JLM Industries Inc—John L Macdonald	8675 Hidden River Pkwy, Tampa FL 33637	813-632-3300	R	334*	.2
22	Meherrin Agricultural and Chemical Co—Dallas Barnes	413 Main St, Severn NC 27877	252-585-1744	R	300*	.7
23	Merichem Co—Kenneth F Currie	5455 Old Spanish Trail, Houston TX 77023	713-428-5000	R	298*	.2
24	Hawkins Inc—John H Hawkins	3100 E Hennepin Ave, Minneapolis MN 55413	612-331-6910	P	298	.3
25	Harcros Chemicals Inc—Kevin Mirner	PO Box 2930, Kansas City KS 66110	913-321-3131	R	282*	.5
26	Harris and Ford LLC—Tim Harris	9307 E 56th St, Indianapolis IN 46216	317-591-0000	R	261*	<.1
27	Ecolab Inc Professional Products Div	370 N Wabasha St, Saint Paul MN 55102	651-293-2233	D	249*	1.8
28	Seaforth Mineral and Ore Company Inc—Gary McClurg	3690 Orange Pl Ste 495, Cleveland OH 44122	216-292-5820	R	249*	.1
29	Chemical Associates Inc—Nicholas Berchtold	1270 S Cleveland Massi, Copley OH 44321	330-666-5200	R	218*	.1
30	Mays Chemical Company Inc—William G Mays	5611 E 71st St, Indianapolis IN 46220	317-842-8722	R	185*	.2
31	Shrieve Chemical Co—James Shrieve	1755 Woodstead Ct, Spring TX 77380	281-367-4226	R	174*	.1
32	Flint Hills Resources LLC—David Robertson	PO Box 2917, Wichita KS 67201	316-828-3477	R	170*	2.1
33	Marubeni Specialty Chemicals Inc—Yoshihiro Ono	10 Bank St Ste 740, White Plains NY 10606	914-428-8900	R	163*	<.1
34	Loos and Dilworth Inc—Richard G Campbell	61 E Green Ln, Bristol PA 19007	215-785-3591	S	143*	<.1
35	Brenntag Latin America Inc—Peter Startjes	PO Box 701069, Houston TX 77270	713-880-5400	R	142*	.1
36	NuCo2 Inc—Michael DeDomenico	2800 SE Market Pl, Stuart FL 34997	772-221-1754	S	130	.7
37	Kraft Chemical Co—Rick Kraft	1975 N Hawthorne Ave, Melrose Park IL 60160	708-345-5200	R	122*	<.1
38	Detroit Div	17191 Chrysler Fwy, Detroit MI 48203	248-244-8455	D	119*	<.1
39	Coastal Chemical Company LLC—Randy King Brenntag North America Inc	3520 Veterans Memorial, Abbeville LA 70510	337-898-0001	S	105*	.3
40	Memphis Chemical Janitorial Supply Inc—Laurita Jackson	2717 Huntley Dr, Memphis TN 38132	901-521-1612	R	103*	<.1
41	Nubiola—Mary Lane	6369 Peachtree St, Norcross GA 30071	770-277-8819	S	100*	<.1
42	Pro Products LLC—Joel Harder	7201 Engle Rd, Fort Wayne IN 46804	260-490-5970	R	96*	.1
43	Berryman Products Inc—Maurice Blankenship	3800 E Randol Mill Rd, Arlington TX 76011	817-640-2376	R	92*	.2
44	Mel Chemicals Inc—Alan Foster	500 Point Breeze Rd, Flemington NJ 08822	908-782-5800	R	90*	.1
45	Benetech Inc—Ronald Pircon	2245 Sequoia Dr, Aurora IL 60506	630-844-0064	R	88*	.1
46	John R Hess and Company Inc—Peter Hess	PO Box 3615, Cranston RI 02910	401-785-9300	R	87*	<.1
47	ET Horn Co—Jeff Martin	16050 Canary Ave, La Mirada CA 90638	714-523-8050	R	86*	.1
48	Progas Service Inc—Ben Winke	1674 Green Bay Rd, Wever IA 52658	319-372-1062	R	79*	<.1
49	Ecolab Inc Food and Beverage Div	370 N Wabasha St, Saint Paul MN 55102	651-293-2233	D	74*	.5
50	Ulrich Chemical Inc—Edward M Pitkin Brenntag Great Lakes LLC	3111 N Post Rd, Indianapolis IN 46226	317-898-8632	D	74*	.2

Rank	Company Name—*Executive Officer*	Address, City, State, Zip	Phone	Type	Fin	Empls
51	Goldsmith and Eggleton Inc—*Michael Fagan*	300 1st St, Wadsworth OH 44281	330-336-6616	R	71*	.1
52	Brandt Technologies Inc—*T R Brandt*	231 W Grand Ave Ste 20, Bensenville IL 60106	630-787-1800	R	71*	<.1
53	Seward Sales Corporation LLC—*Ken Schmidt*	6620 Binford Medical D, Indianapolis IN 46220	317-578-3700	S	71*	<.1
54	Valley National Gases Inc—*Michael Ziegler*	200 W Beau St Ste 200, Washington PA 15301	724-228-3000	S	70*	.3
55	D W Dickey And Son Inc—*Timothy Dickey*	PO Box 189, Lisbon OH 44432	330-424-1441	R	67*	.2
56	Automotive International Inc—*Rick Hallberg*	8855 Blue Ash Rd, Cincinnati OH 45242	513-489-7883	R	64*	<.1
57	A Daigger and Company Inc	620 Lakeview Pky, Vernon Hills IL 60061	847-816-5060	R	62*	.2
58	LCI Ltd—*David Messerlie*	415 Pablo Ave N Ste 20, Jacksonville Beach FL 32250	904-241-1200	R	62*	<.1
59	Tulstar Products Inc—*Mark Nagle*	5510 S Lewis Ave, Tulsa OK 74105	918-749-9060	R	62*	<.1
60	Humco Holding Group Inc—*Greg Pulido*	7400 Alumax Dr, Texarkana TX 75501	903-334-6200	R	61*	.1
61	Mozel Inc EMCO Chemical Distributors Inc	1900 Westgate Dr, Columbia IL 62236	618-281-3040	S	58*	.1
62	Brody Chemical Company Inc—*Jon Liddiard*	6125 Double Eagle Cir, Salt Lake City UT 84118	801-963-2436	R	57*	.1
63	EMCO Chemical Distributors Inc—*Edward Polen*	PO Box 1030, North Chicago IL 60064	847-689-2200	R	55*	.2
64	Savol Bleach Co—*Ken Camello*	91 Prestige Park Cir U, East Hartford CT 06108	860-282-0878	R	55*	<.1
65	Holston Gases Inc—*William Baxter*	PO Box 27248, Knoxville TN 37927	865-573-1917	R	52*	.2
66	Chemical Solvents Inc—*Edward Pavlish*	3751 Jennings Rd, Cleveland OH 44109	216-741-9310	R	52*	.1
67	TRInternational Trading Company Inc—*Anthony Ridnell*	1218 Third Ave Ste 210, Seattle WA 98101	206-505-3500	R	50*	<.1
68	Machine and Welding Supply Co—*Emmett C Aldredge Jr*	PO Box 1708, Dunn NC 28335	910-892-4016	R	46*	.2
69	Ellsworth Corp—*Paul Ellsworth*	PO Box 1002, Germantown WI 53022	262-253-8600	R	43*	.2
70	Fitz Chem Corp—*Robert C Becker*	450 E Devon Ste 175, Itasca IL 60143	630-467-8383	R	40*	<.1
71	ChemSol LLC—*Derek Staloch*	601 Carlson Pkwy Ste 4, Minnetonka MN 55305	952-807-7460	R	38*	<.1
72	Phoenix Products Co—*John Haase*	55 Container Dr, Terryville CT 06786	860-589-7502	R	36*	<.1
73	Dpc Industries Inc—*S Morian*	PO Box 130468, Houston TX 77219	713-863-1947	R	36*	.2
74	San Esters Corp—*Cakashi Mamemura*	55 E 59th St 19th Fl, New York NY 10022	212-223-0020	S	35*	<.1
75	Allied Universal Corp—*Robert Namoff*	3901 Nw 115th Ave, Doral FL 33178	305-888-2623	R	33*	.2
76	Haviland Products Co—*E Haviland*	421 Ann St Nw, Grand Rapids MI 49504	616-361-6691	R	30*	.1
77	Ideal Chemical and Supply Co—*Sam Block Jr*	4025 Air Park St, Memphis TN 38118	901-363-7720	R	28*	.1
78	S J Smith Company Inc—*Richard Smith*	3707 W River Dr, Davenport IA 52802	563-324-5237	R	28*	.1
79	Iq Products Co—*Yohanne Gupta*	16212 State Hwy 249, Houston TX 77086	281-444-6454	R	28*	.2
80	Connell Brothers Company Ltd—*Herbert Tully*	345 California St 27 F, San Francisco CA 94104	415-772-4000	S	27*	.1
81	Textile Rubber And,Chemical Company Inc—*Frederick Howalt*	1300 Tiarco Dr Sw, Dalton GA 30721	706-277-1300	R	27*	.5
82	Maine Oxy-Acetylene Supply Co—*Bruce Albiston*	22 Albiston Way, Auburn ME 04210	207-784-5788	R	27*	.1
83	Hubbard-Hall Inc—*Andrew Skipp*	PO Box 790, Waterbury CT 06720	203-756-5521	R	26*	.1
84	Resource One Inc—*Duncan Yull*	PO Box 1990, Largo FL 33779	727-584-2163	R	26*	<.1
85	National Refrigerants Inc—*John Reilly*	PO Box 820103, Philadelphia PA 19182	215-698-9100	R	25*	.1
86	Keystone Aniline Corp—*Arthur J Andrews*	2501 W Fulton St, Chicago IL 60612	312-666-2015	R	25*	.1
87	GJ Chemical Company Inc—*Diane Colonna*	370-376 Adams St, Newark NJ 07114	973-589-1450	R	25*	<.1
88	K A Steel Chemicals Inc—*Robert Steel*	PO Box 729, Lemont IL 60439	630-257-3900	R	24*	.1
89	EE Zimmerman Co—*E Zimmerman*	PO Box 111254, Pittsburgh PA 15238	412-963-0949	R	24*	<.1
90	Citrus And Allied Essences Ltd—*Richard Pisano*	3000 Marcus Ave Ste 3e, New Hyde Park NY 11042	516-354-1200	R	23*	.1
91	Houghton Chemical Corp—*Bruce Houghton*	PO Box 307, Allston MA 02134	617-254-1010	R	22*	.1
92	Inolex Chemical Co—*Robert Paganelli*	2101 S Swanson St, Philadelphia PA 19148	215-271-0800	R	22*	.1
93	Newport Adhesives And Composites Inc—*Chiaki Suematsu*	1822 Reynolds Ave, Irvine CA 92614	949-253-5680	R	21*	.1
94	Warsaw Chemical Company Inc—*Kenneth Bucher*	PO Box 858, Warsaw IN 46581	574-267-3251	R	21*	.1
95	Interstate Chemical Company Inc—*Albert Puntureri*	PO Box 1600, Hermitage PA 16148	724-981-3771	R	21*	.3
96	Berje Inc—*Kim Bleimann*	5 Lawrence St Ste 3, Bloomfield NJ 07003	973-748-8980	R	21*	.1
97	Water Tech Inc—*Ken Farris*	7215 Hwy 271 S, Fort Smith AR 72908	479-649-7447	R	20*	.1
98	Western International Gas and Cylinders Inc—*Dan Hord*	PO Box 668, Bellville TX 77418	979-865-5991	R	19*	.1
99	Stein's Inc—*Kevin Stein*	PO Box 248, Moorhead MN 56561	218-233-2727	R	18*	<.1
100	Sierra Chemical Co—*Stanley Kinder*	PO Box 50730, Sparks NV 89435	775-358-0888	R	17*	.1
101	N Jonas and Company Inc—*Stephan Jonas*	PO Box 425, Bensalem PA 19020	215-639-8071	R	17*	.1
102	Weiler Welding Company Inc—*Herbert Weiler*	324 E 2nd St, Dayton OH 45402	937-222-8312	R	16*	.1
103	Alpha Dyno Nobel—*Bradley Langner*	PO Box 310, Lincoln CA 95648	916-645-3377	R	16*	.1
104	KRAnderson CoInc—*Dennis Wagner*	18330 Sutter Blvd, Morgan Hill CA 95037	408-825-1800	R	16*	.1
105	Doe and Ingalls Inc—*John Hollenbach*	2520 Meridian Pky Ste, Durham NC 27713	919-598-1986	R	16*	<.1
106	St Lawrence Explosives Corp—*Julie Pecori*	PO Box 230, Adams Center NY 13606	315-583-5432	R	15*	.1
107	Clark Foam Products Corp—*James Clark*	655 Remington Blvd, Bolingbrook IL 60440	630-226-5900	R	15*	.1
108	Surpass Chemical Company Inc—*Irwin Smith*	PO Box 4165, Albany NY 12204	518-434-8101	R	15*	.1
109	Lynde Co—*Jim Timberg*	1300 Sylvan St, Saint Paul MN 55117	651-487-7665	R	15*	<.1
110	Welco Gases Corp—*Robert D'alessandro*	425 Ave P, Newark NJ 07105	973-589-7895	R	15*	.1
111	Rowell Chemical Corp—*Nat Rowell*	15 Salt Creek Ln Ste 2, Hinsdale IL 60521	630-920-8833	R	15*	.1
112	North American Hoganas Holdings Inc—*Avinash Gore*	111 Hoganas Way, Hollsopple PA 15935	814-479-2551	R	14*	.3
113	Milport Enterprises Inc—*Warren Greisch* Rowell Chemical Corp	2829 S 5th Ct, Milwaukee WI 53207	414-769-7350	S	14*	.1
114	Cameron Welding Supply—*Elizabeth Perry*	PO Box 266, Stanton CA 90680	714-530-9353	R	14*	.1
115	Carroll Service Co—*Floyd Heller*	505 W IL Rt 64, Lanark IL 61046	815-493-2181	R	12*	.1
116	BJ Chemical Services—*Andy O'Donnell*	4601 Westway Park Blvd, Houston TX 77041	713-462-4239	S	12*	<.1
117	SOS Gases Inc—*Steve DeFilipps*	1100 Harrison Ave, Kearny NJ 07032	201-998-7800	R	12*	<.1
118	Cherokee Chemical Company Inc—*Denny Criswell*	3540 E 26th St, Vernon CA 90058	323-265-1112	R	12*	.1
119	Monson Companies Inc—*Charles Walkovich*	154 Pioneer Park, Leominster MA 01453	978-534-1425	R	11*	.1
120	Pur-O-Zone Inc—*Mark Elzea*	PO Box 727, Lawrence KS 66044	785-843-0771	R	11*	<.1
121	Merritt Company Inc—*Bob Merritt*	PO Box 3657, Urbandale IA 50323	515-252-7322	R	11*	.1
122	Sanolite Corp—*Norman Lubin*	PO Box 818, Elizabeth NJ 07207	908-355-8745	R	11*	.1
123	National Ammonia Co—*Stephen B Tanner*	735 Davisville Rd 3rd, Southampton PA 18966	215-322-1238	D	10*	<.1
124	Nolmar Corp—*Robyn Marshall*	PO Box 850275, New Orleans LA 70185	504-486-7681	R	10*	<.1
125	Schibley Chemicals Company Inc—*Kris Schibley*	1570 Lowell St, Elyria OH 44035	440-322-1350	R	10*	<.1
126	Andrews Paper and Chemical Co—*Harold Kroez*	PO Box 509, Port Washington NY 11050	516-767-2800	R	10*	<.1
127	Marsh-Armfield Of Newton Inc—*George Armfield*	PO Box 227, Conover NC 28613	828-464-3818	R	10*	.1
128	Columbus Chemical Industries Inc—*Richard Sheard*	PO Box 8, Columbus WI 53925	920-623-2140	R	9*	<.1
129	Amalgamet Inc—*R Seibel*	222 Bloomingdale Rd, White Plains NY 10605	914-683-5809	S	9*	<.1
130	Shesam Inc—*Sam Bramande*	PO Box 870, Cumberland MD 21501	301-729-2515	R	9*	<.1
131	Tci America—*Masatoshi Isono*	9211 N Harborgate St, Portland OR 97203	503-283-1681	R	9*	<.1
132	Usr Optonix Inc—*John Daforno*	PO Box 151, Washington NJ 07882	908-835-0010	R	8*	<.1
133	E Weinberg Supply Company Inc—*David Weinberg*	7434 W 27th St, Minneapolis MN 55426	952-920-0888	R	8*	<.1
134	F-Matic Inc—*Haruo Miyagi*	299 S Millpond Dr, Lehi UT 84043	801-768-2000	R	8*	<.1
135	Soil Stabilization Products Company Inc—*Robert Randolph*	PO Box 2779, Merced CA 95344	209-383-3296	R	8*	<.1
136	Green Earth Technologies Inc—*William J (Jeff) Marshall*	10 Bank St Ste 680, White Plains NY 10606		P	8	<.1
137	M and P Industries Inc—*Pete Mastrangelo*	PO Box 187, Lesage WV 25537	304-736-4046	R	7*	<.1
138	Gateway Proclean Inc—*Thomas Wohlgemuth*	2081 Exchange Dr, Saint Charles MO 63303	636-947-9191	R	7*	<.1

Note: An asterisk (*) indicates an estimated financial figure. The company type code used is as follows: R = Private, P = Public, S = Private Subsidiary, B = Public Subsidiary, D = Division, J = Joint Venture, I = Investment Fund.

COMPANY RANKINGS BY SALES WITHIN 4-DIGIT SIC

Rank	Company Name—*Executive Officer*	Address, City, State, Zip	Phone	Type	Fin	Empls
139	Rainbow Technology Corp—*Neal Schmidt*	PO Box 26445, Birmingham AL 35260	205-733-0333	R	7*	<.1
140	Plant Health Care Inc—*John Brady*	285 Kappa Dr Ste 100, Pittsburgh PA 15238	412-826-5488	R	7*	<.1
141	Boren Explosives Company Inc—*Russell Boren*	8425 Hwy 269, Parrish AL 35580	205-686-5095	R	7*	<.1
142	Gamay Foods Inc—*Aly Gamay*	2770 S 171st St, New Berlin WI 53151	262-789-5104	R	6*	<.1
143	Cci Manufacturing Illinois Corp—*Tetsuya Okabe*	PO Box 339, Lemont IL 60439	630-739-0606	R	6*	<.1
144	Pacifica Chemical Inc—*Hussain Shaikh*	935 E Artesia Blvd, Carson CA 90746	310-464-8900	R	6*	<.1
145	Sentry Industries Inc—*Stephen Sidelko*	PO Box 470667, Miami FL 33247	305-638-0800	R	5*	<.1
146	Specialty Gases Inc—*Louis Wright*	PO Box 21007, Louisville KY 40221	502-635-7531	R	5*	<.1
147	Allchem Services Inc—*Richard Robinson*	PO Box 7746, Pasadena TX 77508	713-796-8000	R	5*	.1
148	John Scoggins Company Inc—*Dan Scoggins*	PO Box 1388, Sallisaw OK 74955	918-775-2748	R	5*	<.1
149	Komp Equipment Company Inc—*George P Komp*	PO Box 1489, Hattiesburg MS 39403	601-582-8215	R	5*	<.1
150	Maintenance Engineering Corp—*Brad Hance*	PO Box 1729, Houston TX 77251	713-222-2351	R	5*	<.1
151	Avebe America Inc—*Robert Jackson*	45 Gunning Ln, Langhorne PA 19047	215-741-4705	R	5*	<.1
152	Correlated Products Inc—*Gary King*	PO Box 42387, Indianapolis IN 46242	317-243-3248	R	5*	<.1
153	Techwood Industrial Gases LLC	3230 Hopeland Industri, Powder Springs GA 30127	770-439-7454	R	5*	<.1
154	Tricon Chemical Corp—*Ira Moss*	8140 Cryden Way, Forestville MD 20747	301-420-8506	R	4*	<.1
155	Dominion Chemical Co—*Wilson Ferrell*	2050 Puddledock Rd, Petersburg VA 23803	804-733-7628	R	4*	<.1
156	William/Reid Ltd—*Reid Snedaker*	PO Box 397, Germantown WI 53022	262-255-5420	R	4*	<.1
157	Nashville Chemical and Equipment Company Inc—*James Mulloy*	PO Box 90246, Nashville TN 37209	615-350-7070	R	4*	<.1
158	Capitol Scientific Inc—*Felix Ware*	2500 Rutland Dr, Austin TX 78758	512-836-1167	R	4*	<.1
159	D W Davies and Company Inc—*David Davies*	PO Box 1497, Racine WI 53401	262-637-6133	R	4*	.1
160	US Chemicals Inc—*Carol Piccaro*	280 Elm St Fl 2, New Canaan CT 06840	203-966-8777	R	3*	<.1
161	Sto-Cote Products Inc—*James Stoller*	PO Box 310, Genoa City WI 53128	262-279-6000	R	3*	<.1
162	Pepin-Ireco Inc—*Joseph Pepin*	PO Box 8, Ishpeming MI 49849	906-486-4473	R	3*	<.1
163	Blue Wave Ultrasonics Inc—*Roger Stoneking*	PO Box 4347, Davenport IA 52808	563-322-0144	R	3*	<.1
164	American Distillation Inc—*Andrew Simmons*	PO Box 400, Leland NC 28451	910-371-0993	R	3*	<.1
165	Unisource Group Inc—*Jack Rubens*	3021 W Harrison St, Chicago IL 60612	773-267-9000	R	3*	<.1
166	Cedar Rapids Welding Supply Inc—*Greg VasekEllis*	PO Box 453, Cedar Rapids IA 52406	319-365-1466	R	3*	<.1
167	Caap International Corp—*Carmen Pierola*	5575 Nw 74th Ave, Medley FL 33166	305-885-1177	R	3*	<.1
168	Courtesy Sanitary Supply Inc—*Robert Nasierowski*	33533 Mound Rd, Sterling Heights MI 48310	586-979-8010	R	3*	<.1
169	Crisci Food Equipment Company Inc—*Sally Firmi*	315 W Midlothian Blvd, Youngstown OH 44511	330-782-0022	R	3*	<.1
170	Trusty-Cook Inc—*John Trusty*	10530 E 59th St, Indianapolis IN 46236	317-823-6821	R	3*	<.1
171	Mothers Polishes Waxes Cleaners Inc—*Barbara Holloway*	5456 Industrial Dr, Huntington Beach CA 92649	714-891-3364	R	3*	<.1
172	Enequist Chemical Company Inc—*Walter Schwartz*	100 Varick Ave, Brooklyn NY 11237	718-497-1200	R	2*	<.1
173	Chargar Corp—*Bertram Frankenberger*	PO Box 4367, Hamden CT 06514	203-562-9948	R	2*	<.1
174	Environmental Chemical Corp—*Richard Morena*	PO Box 20110, Canton OH 44701	330-453-5200	R	2*	<.1
175	Colfran Industrial Sales Inc—*Carl Stevens*	38127 Ecorse Rd, Romulus MI 48174	734-595-8920	R	2*	<.1
176	Florida Chemical Supply Inc—*Marilyn Exum*	6810 E Chelsea St, Tampa FL 33610	813-623-1274	R	2*	<.1
177	Industrial Motor Supply Inc—*Michael Nelson Jr*	PO Box 4128, Harrisburg PA 17111	717-564-0550	R	2*	<.1
178	JTS Enterprises Inc—*Forrest Henson Jr*	4600 Post Oak Pl Ste 1, Houston TX 77027	713-621-6740	R	2*	<.1
179	Deveco Corp—*William Ifkovits*	424 Fairview St, Belvidere IL 61008	815-544-9797	R	1*	<.1
180	Champion Chemical CoOf Calif—*David Ellis*	PO Box 5429, Whittier CA 90607	562-945-1456	R	1*	<.1
181	High Valley Products Inc—*Gene Hadley*	PO Box 69, Centerville UT 84014	801-295-9591	R	1*	<.1
182	Burlington Chemical Company LLC—*Vickie Edwards*	8646 W Market St Ste 1, Greensboro NC 27409	336-584-0111	R	1*	<.1
183	Georgia Steel and Chemical Co—*Thomas G O'Neill*	10820 Guilford Rd Ste, Annapolis Junction MD 20701	301-317-5502	R	1*	<.1
184	Dealer Chemical—*Rose Parsons*	PO Box 460462, Saint Louis MO 63146		R	1*	<.1
185	Octel Starreon LLC—*J Mark McPherson*	8375 S Willow St, Littleton CO 80124	303-792-5554	S	N/A	<.1

TOTALS: SIC 5169 Chemicals & Allied Products Nec
Companies: 185

					51,562	91.1

5171 Petroleum Bulk Stations & Terminals

Rank	Company Name—*Executive Officer*	Address, City, State, Zip	Phone	Type	Fin	Empls
1	Warren Equities Inc—*Herbert Kaplan*	27 Warren Way, Providence RI 02905	401-781-9900	R	8,630*	2.0
2	Global Partners LP—*Eric Slifka*	PO Box 9161, Waltham MA 02454	781-894-8800	P	7,802	.3
3	Oxbow Corp—*William I Koch*	1601 Forum Pl Ste 1400, West Palm Beach FL 33401	561-697-4300	R	4,909*	1.2
4	Bell Gas Inc—*Eugene Bell*	PO Box 490, Roswell NM 88202	575-622-4800	R	4,140*	.5
5	Genesis Energy LP—*Grant E Sims*	919 Milam Ste 2100, Houston TX 77002	713-860-2500	P	3,090	.7
6	US Oil Company Petroleum Operation—*John Schmidt*	425 S Washington St, Combined Locks WI 54113	920-739-6101	R	2,190	1.2
7	Martin Oil Co—*Thomas Martin*	528 N 1st St, Bellwood PA 16617	814-742-8438	R	1,626*	.2
8	Roland J Robert Distributors Inc—*Gayle T Robert*	5423 Hwy 44, Gonzales LA 70737		R	1,613*	.2
9	Truman Arnold Companies Inc—*Gregory Arnold*	PO Box 1481, Texarkana TX 75504	903-794-3835	R	1,205*	.5
10	RKA Petroleum Companies Inc—*Kaye Albertie*	28340 Wick Rd, Romulus MI 48174	734-946-2199	R	1,081*	.1
11	Martin Midstream Partners LP—*Ruben S Martin*	4200 Stone Rd, Kilgore TX 75662	903-983-6200	P	912	N/A
12	Colonial Oil Industries Inc—*Robert H Demere*	PO Box 576, Savannah GA 31402	912-236-1331	S	739*	.2
13	Illini FS Inc—*Roger Read*	1509 E University St, Urbana IL 61802	217-384-8300	R	668*	.1
14	Dilmar Oil Company Inc—*OC Lane Jr*	PO Box 5629, Florence SC 29502	843-662-4179	R	629*	.1
15	Veach Oil Co—*John Veach*	PO Box 68, Vienna IL 62995	618-658-2581	R	581*	.1
16	Bowen Petroleum—*Stephen Moore*	PO Box 2012, Pocatello ID 83206	208-232-1326	S	452*	.1
17	Midwest Oil Co—*Brad Dyar*	615 E 8th St, Sioux Falls SD 57103	605-336-3337	R	314*	<.1
18	J D Streett and Company Inc—*Newell Baker*	144 Weldon Pkwy, Maryland Heights MO 63043	314-432-6600	R	313*	.3
19	McCall Oil and Chemical Co—*Jim Charriere*	5480 NW Front Ave, Portland OR 97210	503-221-6400	R	278*	.1
20	Richland Partners LLC—*Douglas Woosnam*	PO Box 302, Mount Joy PA 17552	717-653-1411	R	255*	.2
21	Reeder Distributors Inc—*Gary M Reeder*	5450 Wilbarger St, Fort Worth TX 76119	817-429-5957	R	246*	.1
22	JH Williams Oil Company Inc—*Hulon Williams III*	PO Box 439, Tampa FL 33601	813-228-7776	R	214*	<.1
23	Jacobus Energy Inc—*CD Jacobus*	11815 W Bradley Rd, Milwaukee WI 53224	414-359-0700	R	198	.3
24	Rebel Oil Company Inc—*Jack Cason*	2200 S Highland Dr, Las Vegas NV 89102	702-382-5866	R	184*	<.1
25	H Wolf Edward And Sons Inc—*Craig Wolf*	PO Box 348, Slinger WI 53086	262-644-5030	R	177*	.1
26	Midland 66 Oil Company Inc—*Randall Stevens*	1612 Garden City Hwy, Midland TX 79701	432-682-9404	R	166*	<.1
27	Service Oil Inc—*Steven D Lenthe*	1718 Main Ave E, West Fargo ND 58078	701-277-1050	R	165*	.3
28	Petroleum Marketers Inc—*Ron Hare*	PO Box 12203, Roanoke VA 24023	540-772-4900	R	151*	.7
29	EO Habhegger Company Inc—*Ken Hagman*	460 Penn St, Yeadon PA 19050	610-622-1977	R	147*	<.1
30	Beck Suppliers Inc—*Douglas L Beck*	PO Box 808, Fremont OH 43420	419-332-5527	R	140*	.3
31	Webb's Oil Corp—*Janice Webb*	8223 Resevoir Rd, Roanoke VA 24019	540-362-3795	R	132*	<.1
32	District Petroleum Products Inc—*Scott Stipp*	1814 River Rd Ste 100, Huron OH 44839	419-433-8373	R	131*	.2
33	Hopkins-Gowen Oil Company Inc—*Harold Gowen*	3693 Main St, Folkston GA 31537	912-496-2331	R	107*	<.1
34	St Martin Oil and Gas Inc—*Jimmy Poirier*	2040 Terrace Hwy, Saint Martinville LA 70582	337-394-3163	R	98*	<.1
35	Glover Oil Company Inc—*Joseph Glover III*	3109 S Main St, Melbourne FL 32901	321-723-3953	R	88*	<.1
36	Julian W Perkins Inc—*P Brine*	40657 Butternut Ridge, Elyria OH 44035	440-458-5125	R	82*	<.1
37	Sioux Valley Energy—*Don Marker*	PO Box 216, Colman SD 57017	605-534-3535	R	67*	.1
38	Thaler Oil Company Inc—*Steve Thaler*	310 S Main St, Chippewa Falls WI 54729	715-723-2822	R	58*	<.1

Rank	Company Name—*Executive Officer*	Address, City, State, Zip	Phone	Type	Fin	Empls
39	G and M Oil Company Inc—*Jerry Garland*	76 Old 25 E, Barbourville KY 40906	606-546-3909	R	56*	.2
40	Star Oil Company Inc—*Chris Kellerman*	228 Rockdale Ave, New Bedford MA 02740		R	54*	<.1
41	Boncosky Oil Co—*Kevin McCarter*	739 N State St, Elgin IL 60123	847-741-2577	S	52*	.1
42	Nittany Oil Co—*James O Martin*	1540 Martin St, State College PA 16803	814-237-4859	R	45*	.3
43	Stuarts' Petroleum Corp—*John Stuart Jr*	11 E 4th St, Bakersfield CA 93307	661-325-6320	R	44*	<.1
44	Johnson Oil Company of Gaylord—*Don Elgas*	PO Box 629, Gaylord MI 49734	989-732-2451	R	42*	.1
45	Farmers Union Oil Coop—*Dan Belohavek*	219 N 20th, Bismarck ND 58501	701-223-8707	R	36*	.1
46	Midway Oil Co—*David Requet*	PO Box 4540, Rock Island IL 61201	309-788-4549	R	36*	<.1
47	Phibro LLC—*Andrew Hall*	500 Nyala Farms, Westport CT 06880	203-221-5800	S	35	.1
48	FOF Inc—*Marla Gardner*	471 N Curtis Rd, Boise ID 83706	208-377-0024	R	35*	<.1
49	Kentucky Oil And Refining Co—*Dale Tomlinson*	156 Ky Oil Village, Betsy Layne KY 41605	606-478-9501	R	31*	.2
50	G and B Oil Company Inc—*Jeff Edison*	PO Box 811, Elkin NC 28621	336-835-3607	R	31*	.1
51	Jefferson City Oil Company Inc—*Tom Kolb*	PO Box 576, Jefferson City MO 65102	573-634-2025	R	29*	<.1
52	Yoder Oil Company Inc—*Kent Yoder*	PO Box 1097, Elkhart IN 46515	574-264-2107	R	28*	.1
53	Alpena Oil Company Inc	235 Water St, Alpena MI 49707	989-356-1098	R	24*	<.1
54	Barney Holland Oil Co—*Barney Holland Jr*	PO Box 1260, Fort Worth TX 76101	817-834-6600	R	24*	<.1
55	Ampride—*Tracy Blon*	300 Sd Hwy 44, Chancellor SD 57015	605-647-2700	R	24*	<.1
56	HC Lewis Oil Co—*HC Lewis Jr*	PO Box 649, Welch WV 24801	304-436-2148	R	23*	.1
57	Home Oil Co—*Tim Shirley*	5744 East US 84, Cowarts AL 36321	334-793-1544	R	18*	<.1
58	Acorn Petroleum Inc—*Harlan Ochs*	529 Sahwatch St, Colorado Springs CO 80903	719-634-8874	R	16*	<.1
59	Porter Oil Company Inc—*Martin Porter*	306 S Motel Blvd, Las Cruces NM 88007	575-524-8666	R	14*	.1
60	Prairie Pride Coop—*Al Steffes*	1100 E Main St, Marshall MN 56258	507-532-9686	R	13*	.1
61	Cowboy Oil Co—*DG Geisler*	PO Box L, Pocatello ID 83205	208-232-7814	R	13*	.1
62	Black Oil Company Inc—*J Burton Black*	PO Box 159, Monticello UT 84535	435-587-2215	R	13*	<.1
63	Lakeside Oil Company Inc—*William Elliott*	555 W Brown Deer Rd, Milwaukee WI 53217	414-540-4000	R	12*	<.1
64	McCracken Oil and Propane Co—*Bob Leene*	600 S Main St Ste A, Rolesville NC 27571	919-556-9018	R	11*	.1
65	Fapp Brothers Petroleum Inc—*Keith Crandall*	9915 S 148th St, Omaha NE 68138	402-895-2202	R	11*	.1
66	Cooperative Gas and Oil Company Inc—*Roger Fedders*	PO Box 137, Sioux Center IA 51250	712-722-2501	R	11*	<.1
67	Wooten Oil Co—*SD Wooten Jr*	PO Box 1277, Goldsboro NC 27533	919-734-1357	R	10*	<.1
68	Merlin Petroleum Company Inc—*Terri Ignozzi-Little*	235 Post Rd W, Westport CT 06880	203-227-3200	R	10*	<.1
69	Lone Star Company Inc—*Al M Heringer III*	PO Box 2067, Jonesboro AR 72402	870-932-6679	S	8*	<.1
70	Kohler Oil and Propane Co—*Robert Kohler*	PO Box 573, Brown City MI 48416	810-346-2820	R	8*	<.1
71	Northern Cooperative Services (Lake Mills Iowa)	107 W Main St Ste 41, Lake Mills IA 50450	641-592-0011	S	8*	<.1
72	C and S Inc—*Mike Stratton*	300 W 1st St, Portales NM 88130	505-356-4496	R	7*	<.1
73	Reece Oil Co—*Jack Reece*	PO Box 3195, Terre Haute IN 47803	812-232-6621	R	7*	<.1
74	Blackwater Midstream Corp—*Michael D Suder*	660 Labauve Dr, Westwego LA 70094	504-340-3000	P	7	<.1
75	Wheat Energy Services—*Doug Wheat*	PO Box 367, Winters TX 79567	325-754-4555	R	6*	<.1
76	Hightower Oil and Petroleum Company Inc—*Kenny Shipp*	PO Box 36, Plumerville AR 72127	501-354-4780	R	5*	<.1
77	A and W Oil Company Inc—*Brad Arterbury*	PO Box 180100, Fort Smith AR 72918	479-646-0595	R	5*	<.1
78	Morris Oil Inc—*Bradley Morris*	PO Box 1029, Columbia MS 39429	601-736-2634	R	5*	<.1
79	Delta Oil Company Inc—*Mark E Holt III*	PO Box 829, Petersburg VA 23803	804-733-3582	R	4*	.1
80	Consumers Cooperative Oil Co—*Lynn Pistorius*	PO Box 76, Rosholt SD 57260	605-537-4216	R	3*	<.1
81	Duck Island Terminal Inc—*Don Waldman*	1463 Lamberton Rd, Trenton NJ 08611	609-393-6899	R	3*	<.1
82	James Oil Co—*Hobert James*	PO Box 328, Carlisle IA 50047	515-989-3314	R	3*	<.1
83	Central Dakota Frontier Com—*Dan Vetter*	PO Box U, Napoleon ND 58561	701-754-2252	R	2*	<.1
84	Raymond Oil Co—*EH Erling*	PO Box 142, Huron SD 57350	605-352-8711	R	2*	<.1
85	Barkus Oil Corp—*Frank Baxley*	3501 Pearl St, Boulder CO 80301	303-442-6000	R	2*	<.1
86	Thompson Oil Co—*Alfred Bendell III*	PO Box 589, Waynesboro PA 17268	717-762-3011	R	2*	<.1

TOTALS: SIC 5171 Petroleum Bulk Stations & Terminals
Companies: 86 — 44,866 — 12.2

5172 Petroleum Products Nec

Rank	Company Name—*Executive Officer*	Address, City, State, Zip	Phone	Type	Fin	Empls
1	World Fuel Services Corp—*Paul H Stebbins*	9800 NW 41st St Ste 40, Miami FL 33178	305-428-8000	P	19,131	1.5
2	Castrol North America Holdings Inc—*Peter Meola*	1500 Valley Rd, Wayne NJ 07470	973-633-2200	S	7,489*	2.0
3	Apex Oil Company Inc—*Anthony Novelly*	8235 Forsyth Blvd Ste, Clayton MO 63105	314-889-9600	R	6,200*	.5
4	Southern Maryland Oil—*John Combs*	PO Box 2810, La Plata MD 20646	301-932-3600	R	4,341*	.3
5	Gulf Oil LP—*Joseph H Petrowski*	100 Crossing Blvd, Framingham MA 01702	508-270-8300	R	4,268*	.4
6	Dead River Co—*P Andrews Nixon*	PO Box 1427, Bangor ME 04402	207-947-8641	R	3,749*	1.0
7	Atlantic Aviation—*Louis T Pepper*	PO Box 20718 AMF, Atlanta GA 30320	404-765-1300	R	2,508*	.4
8	Adams Resources and Energy Inc—*K S Adams Jr*	PO Box 844, Houston TX 77001	713-881-3600	P	2,212	.7
9	Paraco Gas Corp—*Joe Armentano*	800 Westchester Ave St, Rye Brook NY 10573	914-250-3700	R	2,173*	.2
10	Crosstex Energy Inc—*Barry E Davis*	2501 Cedar Springs Rd, Dallas TX 75201	214-953-9500	P	2,014	.5
11	FL Roberts and Company Inc—*Steven Roberts*	93 W Broad St, Springfield MA 01105	413-781-7444	R	1,887*	.5
12	Mitchell Supreme Fuel Co—*Deborah Fineman*	532 Freeman St, Orange NJ 07050	973-678-1800	R	1,704*	.1
13	Ever-Ready Oil Co—*Charles L Ochs*	PO Box 25845, Albuquerque NM 87125	505-842-6121	R	1,481*	.3
14	Texor Petroleum Co World Fuel Services Corp	3340 S Harlem Ave, Riverside IL 60546	708-447-1999	S	1,404*	.1
15	Gray Oil Company Inc—*Tina Powell*	804 Denver Ave, Fort Lupton CO 80621	303-857-2288	R	1,264*	.1
16	Tauber Oil Co—*David W Tauber*	PO Box 4645, Houston TX 77210	713-869-8700	R	1,196*	.1
17	Grays Petroleum Inc—*Ron Moore*	PO Box 1010, De Queen AR 71832	870-642-2234	R	1,179*	.1
18	On-Site Fuel Service Inc—*Greg Nethery*	1089 Old Fannin Rd Ste, Brandon MS 39047		R	1,151*	.1
19	Harbor Enterprises Inc—*RJ Reierson*	PO Box 389, Seward AK 99664	907-224-3190	R	1,135*	.3
20	Sprague Energy Corp—*David Glendon*	2 International Dr Ste, Portsmouth NH 03801	603-431-1000	R	1,050*	.4
21	Delgasco Inc—*Glenn Jennings*	3617 Lexington Rd, Winchester KY 40391	859-744-6171	S	840*	.2
22	Getty Petroleum Marketing Inc	1500 Hempstead Tpke, East Meadow NY 11554	516-542-5025	R	767*	.6
23	EnergyNorth Propane Inc—*Kevin Bayley*	75 Regional Dr, Concord NH 03301	603-225-6660	S	742*	.1
24	Western Petroleum Co—*Rick Neville*	Po Box 9429, Minneapolis MN 55440		R	640*	.1
25	Sturdy Oil Company Inc—*Jon P Fanoc*	1511 Abbott St, Salinas CA 93901		R	633*	<.1
26	Bob Harris Oil Co—*David Harris*	PO Box 691, Cleburne TX 76033	817-641-9749	R	541	<.1
27	GEO Drilling Fluids Inc—*Jim Clifford*	1431 Union Ave, Bakersfield CA 93305	661-325-5919	R	539*	.1
28	Lank Oil Co—*William C Lank Jr*	420 W McNab Rd, Fort Lauderdale FL 33309	954-979-4070	R	515*	<.1
29	Mercury Air Group Inc—*Joseph A Czyzyk*	5456 McConnell Ave, Los Angeles CA 90066	310-827-2737	R	506*	1.4
30	Trans-Tec Services Inc—*Paul H Stebbins* World Fuel Services Corp	9800 NW 41st St Ste 40, Miami FL 33178	305-428-8000	S	429*	.1
31	Brewer Oil Co—*Jay Lamberth*	2701 Candelaria NE, Albuquerque NM 87107	505-884-2040	R	396*	.5
32	Petroleum Service Co—*RW Simms*	454 S Main St, Wilkes Barre PA 18701	570-822-1151	R	380*	.1
33	Russell Petroleum Corp—*Wayne Russell*	PO Box 250330, Montgomery AL 36125	334-834-3750	R	374*	.1
34	Scullin Oil Co—*RK Scullin*	PO Box 350, Sunbury PA 17801	570-286-4519	R	362*	.1
35	Winters Oil Partners LP—*William Winters*	PO Box 1637, Corsicana TX 75151	903-872-4166	R	358*	<.1

Note: An asterisk (*) indicates an estimated financial figure. The company type code used is as follows: R = Private, P = Public, S = Private Subsidiary, B = Public Subsidiary, D = Division, J = Joint Venture, I = Investment Fund.

COMPANY RANKINGS BY SALES WITHIN 4-DIGIT SIC

Rank	Company Name—*Executive Officer*	Address, City, State, Zip	Phone	Type	Fin	Empls
36	Fannon Petroleum Services Inc—*Chester W Fannon*	PO Box 989, Alexandria VA 22313	703-468-2060	R	355*	<.1
37	Consumer Cooperative Oil Co—*Joel Wyttenbach*	740 Phillips Blvd, Sauk City WI 53583	608-643-3301	R	319*	.1
38	Keystops LLC—*Rex Hazelip*	PO Box 2809, Franklin KY 42135	270-586-8283	R	315*	.3
39	Dilmar Oil Company Inc (Wilmington North Carolina)	1325 Castle Hayne Rd, Wilmington NC 28401	910-762-0312	S	272*	<.1
40	Swift Aviation Services Inc—*Steve Silvestro*	2710 E Old Tower Rd, Phoenix AZ 85034	602-273-3770	R	264*	.1
41	Vanguard Petroleum Corp—*Tom Garner*	1111 N Loop W Ste 1100, Houston TX 77008	713-802-4242	R	260*	<.1
42	SMF Energy Corp—*Richard E Gathright*	200 W Cypress Creek Rd, Fort Lauderdale FL 33309	954-308-4200	P	236	.2
43	Heritage FS Inc—*Gary Boehrnsen*	PO Box 339, Gilman IL 60938		R	232*	.1
44	Metalworking Lubricants Co—*Keith Johnson*	PO Box 214379, Auburn Hills MI 48321	248-332-3500	R	227*	.2
45	Whitaker Oil Co—*Bart Whitaker*	1557 Marietta Rd NW, Atlanta GA 30318	404-355-8220	R	225*	.1
46	North Central Cooperative Inc—*Darrell Smith*	PO Box 299, Wabash IN 46992	260-563-8381	R	224*	.3
47	Drew Oil Corp—*Christopher Drew*	31 Calder St, Cranston RI 02920	401-942-5470	R	217*	<.1
48	Ownbey Enterprises Inc—*Rodney Ownbey*	PO Box 1146, Dalton GA 30722	706-278-3019	R	215*	<.1
49	MercFuel Inc—*Eric Beelar* Mercury Air Group Inc	5456 McConnell Ave, Los Angeles CA 90066	310-827-2737	S	203	<.1
50	Romanelli and Son Inc—*Marty Romanelli*	PO Box 544, Lindenhurst NY 11757	631-956-1201	R	191*	<.1
51	Surner Heating Company Inc—*Bruce Montague*	60 Shumway St, Amherst MA 01002	413-253-5999	R	186*	<.1
52	Alliance Energy Services LLC	PO Box 100, Murdock MN 56271	320-875-2641	R	172*	<.1
53	TransMontaigne Product Services Inc	PO Box 5660, Denver CO 80217	303-626-8200	S	171*	.2
54	ISO Industries Inc—*Robert Powell*	5353 E Princess Anne R, Norfolk VA 23502	757-855-0900	R	171*	<.1
55	Woroco Management LLC	40 Woodbridge Ave Ste, Sewaren NJ 07077	732-855-7720	R	170*	<.1
56	Gresham Petroleum Co—*WW Gresham Jr*	PO Box 690, Indianola MS 38751	662-887-2160	R	167*	<.1
57	King Fuels Inc—*Zaki Niazi*	14825 Willis St, Houston TX 77039	281-449-9975	R	163*	<.1
58	Agland Inc—*Mitch Anderson*	PO Box 338, Eaton CO 80615	970-454-3391	R	160*	.2
59	NOCO Energy Corp—*James D Newman*	2440 Sheridan Dr, Tonawanda NY 14150	716-833-6626	R	157*	.6
60	Miller Oil Co—*Gus Miller*	1000 E City Hall Ave, Norfolk VA 23504	757-623-6600	R	156*	.4
61	Hightowers Petroleum Co—*Stephen Hightower*	3577 Commerce Dr, Franklin OH 45005	513-423-4272	R	154*	<.1
62	Enterprise Oil Co—*Lee Hamby*	651 Joe Frank Harris P, Cartersville GA 30120	770-382-4804	R	150*	.1
63	Vesco Oil Corp—*Donald Epstein*	PO Box 525, Southfield MI 48037	248-557-1600	R	147*	.2
64	Gas Land Petroleum Inc—*Majed Nesheiwat*	785 Broadway Ste 1, Kingston NY 12401	845-331-7545	R	144*	<.1
65	C and P Oil Inc—*Ted Groff*	PO Box 157, Millersburg IN 46543	574-642-3823	R	143*	<.1
66	Cole Chemical and Distributing Inc—*Donna Fujimoto Cole*	1500 Dairy Ashford Ste, Houston TX 77077	713-465-2653	R	135*	<.1
67	Red Rock Distributing Co—*Steven M Brown*	PO Box 18755, Oklahoma City OK 73154	405-677-3373	R	135*	<.1
68	Eden Oil Company Inc—*Ried Teague*	124 N Fieldcrest Rd, Eden NC 27288	336-635-3311	R	133*	<.1
69	Agriland FS Inc—*Robert Adkins*	421 N 10th St, Winterset IA 50273	515-462-5353	S	132*	.1
70	Northville Industries Corp—*Jay Bernstein*	PO Box 2937, Melville NY 11747	631-293-4700	S	123*	<.1
71	Rex Oil Company Inc (Thomasville North Carolina)—*Harold S Kennedy*	PO Box 1050, Thomasville NC 27360	336-472-3000	R	112*	<.1
72	River City Petroleum Inc—*Leonard D Robinson*	PO Box 235, West Sacramento CA 95691	916-371-4960	R	111*	<.1
73	MO Dion and Sons Inc	1543 W 16th St, Long Beach CA 90813	562-432-3946	R	104*	.1
74	Kimber Petroleum Corp—*Warren S Kimber III*	545 Martinsville Rd, Liberty Corner NJ 07938	908-903-9600	R	102*	.2
75	Mallory Propane—*Stan Mallory*	1677 S US Hwy 69, Mineola TX 75773	903-569-3837	S	101*	<.1
76	Silvas Oil Company Inc—*Charles E Silvas*	PO Box 1048, Fresno CA 93714	559-233-5171	R	98*	.1
77	Red-Kap Sales Inc—*Fred Kaplan*	1806 Erie Blvd, Schenectady NY 12308	518-377-6431	R	94*	<.1
78	Rite Way Oil and Gas Company Inc—*Rex E Ekwall*	PO Box 27049, Omaha NE 68127	402-331-6400	R	93*	.3
79	Retif Oil and Fuel Inc—*Milton Retif*	527 Destrehan Ave, Harvey LA 70058	504-349-9000	R	86*	.1
80	Drake Petroleum Company Inc—*David Preeble*	PO Box 866, North Grosvenordale CT 06255	860-935-5200	S	83*	<.1
81	Nelson Petroleum Inc—*Mark Nelson*	1125 80th Ave SW, Everett WA 98203	425-355-1240	R	81*	<.1
82	Kingston Oil Supply Corp—*Barry Motzkin*	PO Box 760, Port Ewen NY 12466	845-331-0770	S	80*	.2
83	Grimes Oil Company Inc—*Calvin M Grimes Jr*	PO Box 276, West Tisbury MA 02575	617-825-1200	R	78*	<.1
84	Menomonie Farmers Union Coop—*Paul Diemert*	PO Box 438, Menomonie WI 54751	715-232-6200	R	75*	.1
85	Jax Inco—*Eric Peter*	W134n5373 Campbell Dr, Menomonee Falls WI 53051	262-781-8850	R	68*	.1
86	PS Energy Group Inc—*Livia Whisenhunt*	PO Box 29399, Atlanta GA 30359	404-321-5711	R	67*	<.1
87	Tbm Inc—*Robin Vance*	PO Box 142489, Saint Louis MO 63114	314-721-2888	R	67*	.1
88	Specialized Services Inc—*David E Joseph*	23077 Greenfield Rd St, Southfield MI 48075	248-557-1030	R	66*	<.1
89	Carson Oil Company Inc—*Terry Mohr*	PO Box 10948, Portland OR 97296	503-224-8500	R	60*	.1
90	Campbell Oil Company Inc	611 Erie St S, Massillon OH 44646	330-833-8555	R	60*	.1
91	Farmers Union Oil Co (Devils Lake North Dakota)—*Terry Borstad*	600 Highway 2 W, Devils Lake ND 58301	701-662-4014	D	58*	.1
92	Condon Oil Company Inc—*Kraig Bauman*	PO Box 184, Ripon WI 54971	920-748-3186	R	57*	.2
93	Humboldt Petroleum Inc—*Robert Wotherspoon*	PO Box 131, Eureka CA 95502	707-443-3069	R	56*	.1
94	Pinnacle Petroleum Inc—*Liz McKinley*	7911 Professional Cir, Huntington Beach CA 92648	714-841-8877	R	54*	<.1
95	Region Oil—*Bill Olivier*	15 Richboynton, Dover NJ 07801	973-366-3100	S	52*	.1
96	Phoenix Petroleum Co—*Steve Wang*	122 E Lancaster Ave St, Wayne PA 19087	610-687-1666	R	52*	<.1
97	Avfuel Corp—*Craig R Sincock*	PO Box 1387, Ann Arbor MI 48106	734-663-6466	R	48*	.1
98	Stockton Oil Co—*Dan Stockton Jr*	PO Box 1756, Billings MT 59103	406-245-6376	R	48*	<.1
99	ET Lawson and Son—*Donald B Allen Jr*	PO Box 249, Hampton VA 23669	757-722-1928	R	45*	.1
100	Luther P Miller Inc—*Troy Miller*	PO Box 714, Somerset PA 15501	814-443-6569	R	44*	.1
101	Country Pride Coop—*Carl Dickinson*	648 W 2nd St, Winner SD 57580	605-842-2711	R	43*	.2
102	Marcello Distributors/Thibaut Oil Co—*Frank Marcello*	PO Box 302, Donaldsonville LA 70346	225-473-1300	R	42*	<.1
103	Triton Marketing Inc—*James Patton*	8255 Dunwoody Pl, Atlanta GA 30350	770-992-7088	R	38*	.2
104	Stahl Oil Company Inc—*Ernest E Stahl*	659 Berlin Plank Rd, Somerset PA 15501	814-443-2615	R	38*	<.1
105	Siegel Oil Co—*Donald Siegel*	PO Box 40567, Denver CO 80204	303-893-3211	R	37*	<.1
106	Van Zeeland Oil Company Inc—*Chuck Van Zeeland*	PO Box 7777, Appleton WI 54912	920-738-3520	R	35*	.2
107	Chapman Inc—*Andrew Olmstead*	622 E Lamar St, Sherman TX 75090	903-893-9106	R	35*	<.1
108	Riggins Inc—*Paul Riggins*	3938 S Main Rd, Vineland NJ 08360	856-825-7600	R	34*	.1
109	Keltner Enterprises Inc—*Kurt Keltner*	2829 S Scenic Ave, Springfield MO 65807	417-882-8844	S	32*	.1
110	Mansfield Oil Company of Gainesville Inc—*Michael F Mansfield Sr*	1025 Airport Pky SW, Gainesville GA 30501	770-532-6266	R	32*	.1
111	Western States Oil Company Inc—*Steve Lopes*	PO Box 1307, San Jose CA 95109	510-895-1037	R	31*	<.1
112	Mid-Valley Grain Coop—*Robert Staehnke*	PO Box 398, Crookston MN 56716	218-281-2881	R	27*	<.1
113	Massey Wood and West Inc—*Gerard W Bradley*	PO Box 5008, Richmond VA 23220	804-355-1721	R	25*	.1
114	Western States Petroleum Inc—*Robert F Kec*	450 S 15th Ave, Phoenix AZ 85007	602-252-4011	R	24*	<.1
115	Home Oil and Gas Company Inc—*Sara Crafton*	PO Box 397, Henderson KY 42419	270-826-3925	R	23*	<.1
116	Maytag Aircraft Corp—*Joseph Czyzyk* Mercury Air Group Inc	6145 Lehman Dr Ste 300, Colorado Springs CO 80918	719-593-1600	S	21*	.6
117	Newsom Oil Company Inc—*David J Newsom*	1503 W 10th St, Roanoke Rapids NC 27870	252-537-3587	R	21*	.1
118	Battenfeld Management Inc—*John Bellanti*	PO Box 728, North Tonawanda NY 14120	716-695-2100	R	21*	.1
119	John E Jones Oil Company Inc—*Eugene Westhusing*	1016 S Cedar St, Stockton KS 67669	785-425-6746	R	20*	<.1
120	AMEN Properties Inc—*Kris Oliver*	300 N Coit Rd Ste 1150, Richardson TX 75080	972-664-1610	P	20	<.1

Rank	Company Name—*Executive Officer*	Address, City, State, Zip	Phone	Type	Fin	Empls
121	Kirby Oil Co—*Caroline Kirby*	2026 E Front St, Tyler TX 75702	903-592-3841	R	19*	.1
122	M Spiegel and Sons Oil Corp—*Richard Spiegel*	PO Box 833, Tuxedo NY 10987	845-351-4700	R	18*	<.1
123	Central Oil Company Inc—*Ruben S Martin*	1001 McCloskey Blvd, Tampa FL 33605	813-248-2105	S	18*	<.1
124	NHC Inc—*David J Newsom*	1503 W 10th St, Roanoke Rapids NC 27870	252-537-3587	R	17*	.1
125	Harper Oil Products Inc—*Steve Harper*	PO Box 6325, Florence KY 41022	859-283-1001	R	17*	<.1
126	Pen-Fern Oil Co—*Jay H May*	640 Main Rd, Dallas PA 18612	570-675-5731	R	17*	<.1
127	Tulco Oils Inc—*Rick McCleer*	PO Box 582410, Tulsa OK 74158	918-838-3354	R	17*	<.1
128	Gull Industries Inc—*Douglas L True*	PO Box 24687, Seattle WA 98124	206-624-5900	R	16*	<.1
129	Quogue Sinclair Fuel Inc—*Chester Sinclair*	PO Box 760, Hampton Bays NY 11946	631-728-1066	R	15*	<.1
130	UniSource Energy Inc—*Ken Gansmann*	40 Shuman Blvd, Naperville IL 60563	630-470-6030	R	15*	<.1
131	Advance Petroleum Distributing Company Inc—*Kyle Kirby*	2451 Great Southwest P, Fort Worth TX 76106	817-626-5458	R	15*	<.1
132	Vulcan Energy Corp—*John T Raymond*	333 Clay St Ste 1600, Houston TX 77002	713-646-4100	R	15*	<.1
133	Atlanta Fuel Company Inc—*Carol Waters*	PO Box 93586, Atlanta GA 30377	404-792-9888	R	14*	<.1
134	Central Oil of Virginia Corp—*Don Thacker*	PO Box 587, Rocky Mount VA 24151	540-483-5342	R	13*	<.1
135	Chronister Oil Co—*Grady Chronister*	2026 N Republic Ave, Springfield IL 62702	217-523-5050	R	12*	.1
136	Dickey Transport—*Dave Dickey*	PO Box 809, Packwood IA 52580	319-695-3601	R	12*	<.1
137	Rose's Oil Service Inc—*Timothy Rose*	PO Box 1346, Gloucester MA 01931	978-283-3334	R	11*	<.1
138	Blanchardville Cooperative Oil Association—*David Erickson*	PO Box 88, Blanchardville WI 53516	608-523-4294	R	11*	.1
139	Southern LNG Inc—*William A Smith*	PO Box 2563, Birmingham AL 35202	205-325-7410	S	10	<.1
140	Truck Towne Plaza—*David Dearth*	47016 SD Hwy 46, Beresford SD 57004		R	10*	<.1
141	Liberty Oil Company Inc	801 Bridge St, Lehighton PA 18235	610-377-0635	R	9*	<.1
142	Addington Oil Corp—*James Addington*	PO Box 125, Gate City VA 24251	276-386-3961	R	8*	<.1
143	American Chemical Technologies Inc—*Kevin Kovanda*	485 E Van Riper Rd, Fowlerville MI 48836	517-223-0300	R	8*	<.1
144	Pollard-Swain Inc—*Dale Swain*	218 E Meats Ave, Orange CA 92865	714-637-1531	R	7*	<.1
145	Danville Gasoline and Oil Company Inc—*WT Leverenz*	201 W Main St, Danville IL 61832	217-442-0049	R	7*	<.1
146	Warren E and P Inc—*Norman Swanton*	100 Oceangate Ste 950, Long Beach CA 90802	562-590-0909	R	7*	<.1
147	Central Energy Partners LP—*Imad K Anbouba*	8150 N Central Express, Dallas TX 75206	214-360-7480	P	6	<.1
148	Heetco Inc—*Phillip Murfin*	PO Box 188, Lewistown MO 63452	573-497-2295	R	6*	.1
149	Rosebud Farmers Union Cooperative Associates Inc—*Ken Dooley*	209 W Hwy 18, Gregory SD 57533	605-835-9656	R	6*	<.1
150	Kennedy Oil Company Inc—*Harold R Ridge*	1203 Courtesy Rd, High Point NC 27260	336-885-5184	R	6*	<.1
151	Oil Chem Inc—*Robert Massey*	711 W 12th St, Flint MI 48503	810-235-3040	R	5*	<.1
152	Reinauer Petroleum Co—*BF Reinauer III*	3 University Plz Ste 6, Hackensack NJ 07601	201-489-9700	R	5*	<.1
153	Home Oil Company of Sikeston Inc—*Leven Cox*	838 E Malone Ave, Sikeston MO 63801	573-471-5141	R	5*	<.1
154	Achates International Inc—*Alexander Liu*	15200 Shady Grove Rd, Rockville MD 20850	301-670-2836	R	5*	<.1
155	Holmes Oil Co—*Edward Holmes Jr*	100 Europa Dr Ste 450, Chapel Hill NC 27514	919-929-9979	R	4*	<.1
156	Supreme Oil Company Inc—*Matt Sexton*	PO Box 62, New Albany IN 47151	812-945-5266	R	3*	<.1
157	Farmers Union Oil Co (Rolla North Dakota)—*Myron Jacobson*	104 W Main Ave, Rolla ND 58367	701-477-3127	R	2*	<.1
158	Keller Oil Inc—*Mary Keller*	PO Box 147, Saint Marys PA 15857	814-781-1507	R	2*	<.1
159	Green Star Products Inc—*Joseph R LaStella*	858 3rd Ave, Chula Vista CA 91911		P	2	N/A
160	Delta Petroleum Products—*Anthony Igwe*	13342 Cedar Creek Pt, Sugar Land TX 77478	713-266-5566	R	1	<.1
161	Largo Vista Group Ltd—*Deng Shan*	4570 Campus Dr, Newport Beach CA 92660	949-252-2180	P	<1	<.1
162	Merit Energy Co—*Terry Gottberg*	13727 Noel Rd Ste 500, Dallas TX 75240	972-701-8377	R	N/A	.5

TOTALS: SIC 5172 Petroleum Products Nec
Companies: 162

					85,576	22.1

5181 Beer & Ale

Rank	Company Name—*Executive Officer*	Address, City, State, Zip	Phone	Type	Fin	Empls
1	Quality Beverage Inc—*Conrad Wetterau*	525 Myles Standish Blv, Taunton MA 02780	508-822-6200	R	1,430*	.1
2	Topa Equities Ltd—*John E Anderson*	1800 Avenue of the Sta, Los Angeles CA 90067	310-203-9199	R	1,166*	2.1
3	Wirtz Corp—*Rocky Wirtz*	680 N Lakeshore Dr Ste, Chicago IL 60611	312-943-7000	R	1,045*	2.0
4	Andrews Distributing Company of North Texas—*Barry Andrews*	2730 Irving Blvd, Dallas TX 75207	214-525-9400	R	876*	1.0
5	Heineken USA Inc—*Don J Blaustein*	360 Hamilton Ave Ste 1, White Plains NY 10601	914-681-4100	S	733*	.2
6	Georgia Crown Distributing Co—*Don Leebern III*	100 Georgia Crown Dr, McDonough GA 30253	770-302-3000	R	702*	1.6
7	Manhattan Beer Distributors LLC	400 Walnut Ave, Bronx NY 10454	718-292-9300	R	593	1.2
8	General Beverage Sales Co—*Daniel Weinstein*	PO Box 44326, Madison WI 53744	608-271-1234	R	421*	.5
9	Gold Coast Beverage Distributors Inc—*Eric Levin*	3325 NW 70th Ave, Miami FL 33122	305-591-9800	R	405*	.7
10	Martignetti Cos—*Carmine A Martignetti*	975 University Ave, Norwood MA 02062	781-278-2000	R	390*	1.2
11	Labatt USA Inc—*GLen Walter*	50 Fountain Plz Ste 90, Buffalo NY 14220		S	300*	.5
12	Atlanta Beverage Co—*Mark Pirrung*	PO Box 44008, Atlanta GA 30336	404-699-6700	R	222*	.2
13	Jordanos Inc—*Peter Jordano*	550 S Patterson Ave, Santa Barbara CA 93111		R	211*	.5
14	Hand Family Beverage—*JR Hand*	45 EH Crump Blvd W, Memphis TN 38106	901-948-4543	R	182*	.2
15	Clare Rose Inc—*Lisa Rose*	72 Clare Rose Blvd, Patchogue NY 11772	631-475-1840	R	180	.3
16	Blue Ridge Beverage Company Inc—*Bob Archer*	4446 Barley Dr, Salem VA 24153	540-380-2000	R	180*	.2
17	Columbia Distributing Co—*Edward L Maletis*	6840 N Cutter Cir, Portland OR 97217	503-289-9600	R	176*	.6
18	Powers Distributing Company Inc—*Gerald Powers*	3700 Giddings Rd, Orion MI 48359	248-393-3700	R	169*	.2
19	Maloof Distributing LLC—*Greg Brous*	PO Box 27821, Albuquerque NM 87125	505-243-2293	R	146*	2.3
20	Hartford Distributors Inc—*Ross Hollander*	PO Box 8400, Manchester CT 06040	860-643-2337	R	137*	.2
21	Mt Hood Beverage Co / Columbia Distributing Co	3601 NW Yeon Ave, Portland OR 97210	503-274-0990	S	130*	.6
22	Crest Beverage LLC—*Steve S Sourapas*	8870 Liquid Ct, San Diego CA 92121	858-452-2300	R	125*	.3
23	Gate City Beverage Distributors—*Leona Aronoff*	2505 Steel St, San Bernardino CA 92408	909-799-1600	S	124*	.4
24	DET Distributing Co—*Fred Dettwiller*	301 Great Circle Rd, Nashville TN 37228	615-244-4113	R	112*	.2
25	De Luca Liquor and Wine Ltd / Wirtz Corp	1849 Cheyenne, North Las Vegas NV 89032	702-735-9141	S	107*	.4
26	General Wholesale Co—*William D Young Sr*	1271-A Tacoma Dr, Atlanta GA 30318	404-351-3626	R	107*	.3
27	Markstein Beverage Company of Sacramento—*Hayden Markstein*	60 Main Ave, Sacramento CA 95838	916-920-9070	R	107*	.1
28	McLaughlin and Moran Inc—*Terence Moran*	PO Box 20217, Cranston RI 02920	401-463-5454	R	107*	.1
29	Halo Distributing Co—*Don Gallian*	200 Lombrano St, San Antonio TX 78207	210-735-1111	R	102*	.3
30	Buck Distributing Company Inc—*Elizabeth Buck*	PO Box 1490, Upper Marlboro MD 20773	301-952-0400	R	96*	.1
31	Commercial Distributing Co—*Richard C Placek*	PO Box 1476, Westfield MA 01086	413-562-9691	R	92*	.1
32	Wisconsin Distributors Inc—*Pierre McCormick*	900 Progress Way, Sun Prairie WI 53590	608-834-2337	R	91*	.1
33	Nevada Beverage Co—*Pat Clark*	PO Box 93538, Las Vegas NV 89193	702-739-9474	R	89*	.3
34	Bob Hall Inc—*Evalina S Mitchell*	5600 SE Crain Hwy, Upper Marlboro MD 20772	301-627-1900	R	89*	.1
35	Pearlstine Distributors Inc—*Larry Lipov*	1600 Charleston Region, Charleston SC 29492	843-388-6800	R	82*	.2
36	East Side Beverage Co	1260 Grey Fox Rd, Arden Hills MN 55112	651-482-1133	S	79*	.2
37	B Olinde and Sons Company Inc—*Thomas Olinde*	9536 Airline Hwy, Baton Rouge LA 70815	225-926-3380	R	71*	.2
38	General Distributing Co—*Micheal P Brennan*	PO Box 221210, Salt Lake City UT 84122	801-531-7895	R	71*	.1
39	Wright Wisner Distributing Corp—*Claude H Wright*	3165 Brighton Henriett, Rochester NY 14623	585-427-2880	R	69*	.2

Note: An asterisk (*) indicates an estimated financial figure. The company type code used is as follows: R = Private, P = Public, S = Private Subsidiary, B = Public Subsidiary, D = Division, J = Joint Venture, I = Investment Fund.

RANKINGS BY SALES WITHIN 4-DIGIT SIC

nk	Company Name—Executive Officer	Address, City, State, Zip	Phone	Type	Fin	Empls
40	Grantham Distributing Company Inc—H Varley Grantham	2685 Hansrob Rd, Orlando FL 32804	407-299-6446	R	63*	.1
41	DBI Beverage Inc—Robert Stahl	2225 Jerrold Ave, San Francisco CA 94124	415-643-9900	R	61*	.2
42	Bonanza Beverage Co—William Gialketsis	6333 S Ensworth St, Las Vegas NV 89119	702-361-4166	R	60*	.2
43	RH Barringer Distributing Company Inc—Jasie Barringer	1620 Fairfax Rd, Greensboro NC 27407	336-854-0555	R	60*	.2
44	Miller-Brands-Milwaukee LLC	1400 N 113th St, Wauwatosa WI 53226	414-443-2337	R	60*	.2
45	Grey Eagle Distributors Inc—David Stokes	2340 Millpark Dr, Maryland Heights MO 63043	314-429-9100	R	59*	.2
46	Pacific Beverage Company Inc—Peter Jordano Jordanos Inc	5305 Ekwill St, Santa Barbara CA 93111	805-964-0611	S	51*	.2
47	Beechwood Distributors Inc—John Sheehan	5350 S Emmer Dr, New Berlin WI 53151	262-717-2831	R	50*	.2
48	Frank B Fuhrer Wholesale Co—Frank B Fuhrer III	3100 E Carson St, Pittsburgh PA 15203	412-488-8844	R	50*	.2
49	Muller Inc—John Janosko	2800 Grant Ave, Philadelphia PA 19114	215-676-7575	R	49*	.2
50	Coastal Beverage Company Inc—Lewis T Nunnelee III	301 Harley Rd, Wilmington NC 28405	910-799-3011	R	48*	.2
51	Hubert Distributors Inc—Robert Gustafson	1200 Auburn Rd, Pontiac MI 48342	248-858-2340	R	43*	.1
52	Beloit Beverage Company Inc—Don Morello	4059 W Bradley Rd, Milwaukee WI 53209	414-362-5000	R	42*	.1
53	Kramer Beverage Company Inc—Mark Kramer	PO Box 470, Hammonton NJ 08037	609-704-7000	R	40*	.1
54	Dutchess Beer Distributors Inc—Dennis J Capillino	5 Laurel St, Poughkeepsie NY 12601	845-452-0940	R	40*	.1
55	Tri County Beverage Co—Walter Wolpin	14301 Prospect Ave, Dearborn MI 48126	313-584-7100	R	40*	.1
56	Beck's North America Inc	1 Station Pl Ste 4, Stamford CT 06902	203-388-2325	S	39*	.1
57	Premium Distributors of Washington DC LLC—Jimmy Reyes	3500 Fort Lincoln Dr N, Washington DC 20018	202-526-3900	S	38*	.1
58	McBride Distributing Co—Bob McBride	PO Box 1403, Fayetteville AR 72702	479-521-2500	R	38*	<.1
59	H Dennert Distributing Corp—Ronald J Plattner	351 Wilmer Ave, Cincinnati OH 45226	513-871-7272	R	37	.1
60	Saratoga Eagle—Jeff Vukelic	PO Box 315, Glens Falls NY 12801	518-792-3112	R	36*	.1
61	Markstein Beverage Co—Hayden Markstein	PO Box 6902, San Marcos CA 92079	760-744-9004	R	36*	.1
62	Merrimack Valley Distributing Company Inc—Richard Tatelman	PO Box 417, Danvers MA 01923	978-777-2213	R	36*	.1
63	Moon Distributors Inc—Harry Hastings	2800 Vance St, Little Rock AR 72206	501-375-8291	R	36*	.1
64	Wayne Densch Performing Arts Center—Sarah Reece	201-203 S Magnolia Ave, Sanford FL 32771	407-321-8111	R	36*	.1
65	House of Schwan Inc—Barry Schwan	3636 N Comotara St, Wichita KS 67226	316-636-9100	R	36*	.1
66	Burke Beverages Inc—Kevin Burke	4900 S Vernon, McCook IL 60525	708-688-2000	R	35*	.1
67	Wilsbach Distributors Inc—Frank R Sourbeer	905 Katie Ct, Harrisburg PA 17109	717-561-3760	R	35*	.1
68	Maple City Ice Co—Patricia Hipp	371 Cleveland Rd, Norwalk OH 44857	419-668-2531	R	30*	.1
69	Greene Beverage Company Inc—Spencer Burchfield	6000 Grover Burchfield, Tuscaloosa AL 35401	205-345-6950	R	30*	.1
70	Central Distributors Inc—Fernand J Barriault	PO Box 1936, Lewiston ME 04241	207-784-4026	R	30*	.1
71	Skokie Valley Beverage Co—Kenneth Schirmang	199 Shepard Ave, Wheeling IL 60090	847-541-1500	R	30*	.1
72	Virginia Distributing Company Inc—S Kime Patsel	PO Box 4210, Roanoke VA 24015	540-342-3105	R	29*	.1
73	Gambrinus Co—Carlos Alvarez	14800 San Pedro Ave St, San Antonio TX 78232	210-490-9128	R	27*	.4
74	Bissman Company Inc—Ben F Bissman IV	30 W 5th St, Mansfield OH 44902	419-524-2337	R	27*	<.1
75	Clarke Distributors Inc—Jeffery A Clarke	PO Box 624, Keene NH 03431	603-352-0344	R	26*	.1
76	Lake Beverage Corp—Bernard Schroeder	900 John St, West Henrietta NY 14586	585-427-0090	R	26*	.1
77	Cunningham Wholesale Company Inc—Thomas E Cunningham	PO Box 32651, Charlotte NC 28232	704-392-8371	R	25*	.1
78	Classic City Beverages Inc—Robert L O'Rear	530 Calhoun Dr, Athens GA 30601	706-353-1650	R	24*	.1
79	North Shore Bottling Company Inc—Marilyn Miller	1900 Linden Blvd, Brooklyn NY 11207	718-272-8900	R	22*	.1
80	Metz Beverage Company Inc—Diana Roberts	PO Box 828, Sheridan WY 82801	307-672-5848	R	22*	.1
81	Iron City Distributing Company Inc—Robert Chapman KMC Corp	2670 Commercial Ave, Mingo Junction OH 43938	740-598-4171	S	22*	<.1
82	Henry A Fox Sales Co—Henry A Fox Jr	4494 36th St SE, Grand Rapids MI 49512	616-949-1210	R	21*	.1
83	Savannah Distributing Company Inc—Henry Monsees	PO Box 1388, Savannah GA 31402	912-233-1167	R	20*	.1
84	Beauchamp Distributing Co—Patrick L Beauchamp	1911 Santa Fe Ave, Compton CA 90221	310-639-5320	R	18*	.1
85	Five Star Distributing Inc—Stan Zihbrl	4055 E Parl 30 Dr, Columbia City IN 46725	260-244-3775	R	18*	<.1
86	V Santoni and Co—Chuck Santoni	PO Box 1236, Woodland CA 95776	530-666-4447	R	15*	.1
87	KMC Corp—Michael Bellas	2670 Commercial Ave, Mingo Junction OH 43938	740-598-4171	R	14*	.1
88	Rudisill Enterprises Inc—Ben Rudisill	2733 E Ozark Ave, Lowell NC 28098	704-824-9597	R	13*	<.1
89	Girardi Distributors Corp—George R Girardi Jr	PO Box 967, Athol MA 01331	978-249-3581	R	12*	<.1
90	Carolina Beer Company Inc—William L Lyles Jr	PO Box 938, Anderson SC 29622	864-225-1668	R	11	<.1
91	Carenbauer Wholesale Corp—Carl Carenbauer	1900 Jacob St, Wheeling WV 26003	304-232-3000	R	10*	<.1
92	Warsteiner Importers Agency Inc—Geoffery Westapher	9359 Allen Rd, West Chester OH 45069	513-942-9872	S	10*	<.1
93	City Beverage—John Caruso	1105 E Lafayette St, Bloomington IL 61701	309-662-1373	R	9*	<.1
94	Dwan and Company Inc—William J Sweetman	PO Box 96, Torrington CT 06790	860-489-3149	R	9*	<.1
95	Blach Distributing Co—Patrick Blach	131 Main St, Elko NV 89801	775-738-7111	R	9*	<.1
96	Carter Distributing Co—Blair Carter	PO Box 349, Chattanooga TN 37401	423-266-0056	R	8*	.1
97	Northern Eagle Beverages Inc—Louis B Hagger	7 Railroad Ave, Oneonta NY 13820	607-432-0400	R	8*	<.1
98	Haubrich Enterprises Inc—Tony Haubrich	1901 Seminary Rd, Quincy IL 62301	217-223-1183	R	8*	<.1
99	Mautino Distributing Company Inc—Tony Mautino	PO Box 190, Spring Valley IL 61362	815-663-4000	R	7*	<.1
100	Allentown Beverage Company Inc—Samuel Daurkot	1249 N Quebec St, Allentown PA 18103	610-432-4581	R	6*	.1
101	Boisset Family Estates—Jean-Charles Boisset	849 Zinfandel Ln, St Helena CA 94574		R	6*	<.1
102	Chatham Imports Inc—Joseph J Magliocco	245 5th Ave, New York NY 10016	212-473-1100	R	4*	<.1
103	Phoenix Imports Ltd—George Saxon	19010 70th Ave E, Bradenton FL 34211		R	4*	<.1
104	Madison Bottling Co—Tim Roth	PO Box 68, Madison MN 56256	320-598-7573	R	3*	<.1
105	Merchant du Vin Corp—Rich Hamilton	18200 Olympic Ave S, Tukwila WA 98188	253-656-0320	R	3*	<.1
106	Gusto Brands Inc—LA Haralson	PO Box 278, LaGrange GA 30241	706-882-2573	R	2*	.1
107	Thames America Trading Company Ltd—Jeffrey House	3100 Gravenstein Hwy N, Sebastopol CA 95472	707-829-1101	R	2*	<.1
108	B United International Inc—Matthias Neidhart	PO Box 661, Redding CT 06896	203-938-0713	R	1*	<.1
109	Capital Beverage Corp—Carmine N Stella	2209 Sulphur Spring Rd, Baltimore MD 21227	410-242-7404	P	<1	<.1

TOTALS: SIC 5181 Beer & Ale

Companies: 109					13,389	26.1

5182 Wines & Distilled Beverages

	Company Name—Executive Officer	Address, City, State, Zip	Phone	Type	Fin	Empls
1	Southern Wine and Spirits of America Inc—Harvey R Chaplin	1600 NW 163rd St, Miami FL 33169	305-625-4171	R	7,424*	11.0
2	Republic National Distributing Co—Tom Cole	8045 Northcourt Rd, Houston TX 77040	832-782-1000	R	5,000*	5.0
3	Glazer's Wholesale Drug Company Inc—Sheldon Stein	PO Box 809013, Dallas TX 75380	972-392-8200	R	3,164*	5.8
4	National Wine and Spirits Inc—James E LaCrosse	PO Box 1602, Indianapolis IN 46206	317-636-6092	R	1,819*	1.6
5	Young's Market Company LLC—Chris Underwood	2164 N Batavia St, Orange CA 92865	714-283-4933	R	1,323*	1.7
6	Johnson Brothers Co (St Paul Minnesota)—Michael Johnson	1999 Shepard Rd, Saint Paul MN 55116	651-649-5800	R	1,277*	1.1
7	Fedway Associates Inc—Richard Leventhal	Po Box 519, Kearny NJ 07032	973-624-6444	R	715*	.5
8	National Distributing Company Inc (Atlanta Georgia)—Jay Davis	PO Box 44127, Atlanta GA 30336	404-696-9440	R	608*	1.0
9	Republic National Distributing Co (Louisville Kentucky)—Tom Cole	2300 Stanley Gault Pky, Louisville KY 40223	502-254-8600	R	504*	.2
10	Alabama Crown Distributing Co—Greg Raines	PO Box 19068, Birmingham AL 35219	205-941-1155	D	334*	.1
11	Remy Cointreau USA Inc—Tom Jenson	1290 Ave of the Americ, New York NY 10104	212-399-4200	S	301*	.3

Rank	Company Name—*Executive Officer*	Address, City, State, Zip	Phone	Type	Fin	Empls
12	United Liquors Ltd—*Mark Fisher*	175 Campanelli Dr, Braintree MA 02184		S	195*	.7
13	Major Brands Inc—*Todd Epsten*	550 E 13th Ave, Kansas City MO 64116	816-221-1070	R	170*	.5
14	Western Distributing Co—*Vieri Gaines*	PO Box 5542, Denver CO 80217	303-388-5755	R	160*	.7
15	Kronheim Company Inc—*Pat Vogel*	8201 Stayton Dr, Jessup MD 20794	410-724-3300	R	160*	.3
16	R and R Marketing LLC—*Jon Maslin*	10 Patton Dr, West Caldwell NJ 07006	973-228-5100	R	151	.3
17	WineCommune LLC—*Michael Stajer*	7305 Edgewater Dr Ste, Oakland CA 94621	510-632-5300	R	120*	.1
18	Olinger Distributing Co—*Jim Oliver* Glazer's Wholesale Drug Company Inc	PO Box 681008, Indianapolis IN 46268	317-876-1188	D	114*	.4
19	NKS Distributors Inc—*Christopher J Tigani*	399 Churchman Rd, New Castle DE 19720	302-322-1811	R	88*	.3
20	Badger West Wine and Spirits LLC—*Ronald Sadoff*	PO Box 869, Eau Claire WI 54702	715-836-8600	R	60*	.1
21	Standard Beverage Corp—*Leslie Rudd*	PO Box 968, Wichita KS 67201	316-838-7707	R	56*	.2
22	Wirtz Beverage Distribution Nevada—*W Rockwell Wirtz*	100 Distribution Dr, Sparks NV 89441	775-331-3400	S	56*	.1
23	Admiral Wine and Liquor Co—*Michael Zeiger*	74 Sand Park Rd, Cedar Grove NJ 07009	973-857-2100	R	53*	<.1
24	M S Walker Inc—*Harvey Allen*	20 3rd Ave, Somerville MA 02143	617-776-6700	R	46*	.2
25	Koerner Distributors Inc—*Paul Koerner*	PO Box 67, Effingham IL 62401		R	43*	.1
26	Badger Liquor Company Inc—*Ronald Sadoff*	850 S Morris St, Fond du Lac WI 54937	920-923-8160	R	42*	.2
27	Horizon Wine and Spirits—*Thomas E Bernard*	3851 Industrial Pkwy, Nashville TN 37209	615-320-7292	R	31*	.1
28	Click Wine Group—*Peter Click*	315 2nd Ave S Fl 2, Seattle WA 98104	206-443-1996	S	27*	<.1
29	JW Costello Beverage and SW Vending Service—*JW Costello*	4370 S Valley View Blv, Las Vegas NV 89102	702-876-4000	R	23*	.1
30	Maisons Marques and Domaines USA Inc—*Gregory Balogh*	383 4th St Ste 400, Oakland CA 94607	510-286-2000	S	23*	<.1
31	Sterling Distributing Co—*Gene Pace*	4433 S 96th St, Omaha NE 68127	402-339-2300	R	22*	.1
32	Fine Wine Brokers Inc—*Phil Bernstein*	4621 N Lincoln Ave, Chicago IL 60625	773-989-8166	R	20*	<.1
33	Federal Wine and Liquor Co—*Richard Leventhal* Fedway Associates Inc	PO Box 519, Mt Laurel NJ 08054	973-624-6444	S	18*	.1
34	Ed Phillips and Sons Co (Fargo North Dakota)—*Rob Hansen*	PO Box 9095, Fargo ND 58106	701-277-1499	R	16*	.1
35	Phillips Distributing Corp—*Marvin J Levy*	PO Box 7725, Madison WI 53707	608-222-9177	R	16*	<.1
36	Cameron Hughes Wine—*Cameron Hughes*	444 De Haro St Ste 101, San Francisco CA 94107	415-495-1350	R	16*	<.1
37	Major Brands-Columbia—*Todd Epsten* Major Brands Inc	1502 Business Loop 70, Columbia MO 65202	573-443-3169	D	15*	.1
38	Vintwood International Ltd—*Frank A Gentile*	40 Prospect St, Huntington NY 11743	631-424-9777	R	15*	<.1
39	Greenfield Wine Co—*Tony Cartlidge*	205 Jim Oswalt Way Ste, Vallejo CA 94503	707-552-5199	R	11*	<.1
40	Total Beverage Solution and Vino Importers—*Dave Pardus*	1671 Belle Isle Ave St, Mount Pleasant SC 29464	843-881-0761	R	9*	<.1
41	Royale International Beverage Company Inc—*Joe Colombari*	5315 Tremont Ave Ste A, Davenport IA 52807	563-386-5222	R	6*	<.1
42	Cushman Winery Corp—*Brook Williams*	PO Box 899, Los Olivos CA 93441	805-688-9339	R	6*	<.1
43	Humboldt Group—*Patrick O'Dell*	PO Box 690, Fortuna CA 95540	707-725-6661	R	5*	.1
44	Julien Chateau Inc—*Robert Brower*	PO Box 221775, Carmel CA 93922	831-624-2600	R	4*	<.1
45	Carriage House Imports Ltd—*Steven Karp*	99 Morris Ave, Springfield NJ 07081	973-467-9646	R	4*	<.1
46	Winesellers Ltd—*Yale Sager*	7520 N Caldwell Ave, Niles IL 60714	847-647-1100	R	2*	<.1
47	Wine Country Chef LLC—*Chef Harold*	PO Box 1416, Hidden Valley Lake CA 95461	707-322-0406	R	2*	<.1
48	Maggiore Public Salt Co—*Salvatore V Maggiore Jr*	2927 Harrisburg Rd NE, Canton OH 44705	330-454-7913	R	1*	<.1

TOTALS: SIC 5182 Wines & Distilled Beverages
Companies: 48   **24,276**   **33.0**

5191 Farm Supplies

Rank	Company Name—*Executive Officer*	Address, City, State, Zip	Phone	Type	Fin	Empls
1	Transammonia Inc—*Ronald P Stanton*	320 Park Ave, New York NY 10022	212-223-3200	R	8,947*	.4
2	GROWMARK Inc—*Jeff Solberg*	1701 Towanda Ave, Bloomington IL 61701	309-557-6000	R	8,597	6.5
3	Wilbur-Ellis Co—*John Thacher*	345 California St 27th, San Francisco CA 94104	415-772-4000	R	3,608*	3.5
4	Helena Chemical Co—*Mike McCarty*	225 Schilling Blvd Ste, Collierville TN 38017	901-761-0050	R	2,632*	.2
5	Southern States Cooperative Inc—*Tom Scribner*	PO Box 26234, Richmond VA 23260	804-281-1000	R	1,330*	5.0
6	Syngenta Seeds Incorporated - NK—*Michael Mack*	PO Box 959, Minneapolis MN 55440	612-656-8600	S	1,044*	1.3
7	Yara North America Inc—*Peter Valesares*	100 N Tampa St Ste 320, Tampa FL 33602	813-222-5700	S	880*	.2
8	Rockingham Cooperative Inc—*Richard J Morris*	101 W Grace St, Harrisonburg VA 22801	540-434-3856	R	674*	.1
9	Animal Health Holdings Inc—*James C Robinson*	7 Village Cir Ste 200, Westlake TX 76262	817-859-3000	P	669	.9
10	AgriPride FS Inc—*Ron Hejlik*	PO Box 329, Nashville IL 62263	618-327-3046	R	563*	.1
11	New Horizons Supply Coop—*Randy Heins*	770 Lincoln Ave, Fennimore WI 53809	608-822-3217	R	461*	.1
12	Craighead Farmers Coop—*Mike Eaton*	3617 Coop Dr, Bono AR 72416	870-932-3623	R	380*	.1
13	Stanislaus Farm Supply Co—*Sam Bettencourt*	624 E Service Rd, Modesto CA 95358	209-538-7070	R	343*	.1
14	Farmers Cooperative Association (Jackson Minnesota)—*Jerry Svoboda*	PO Box 228, Jackson MN 56143	507-847-4160	R	305*	.1
15	Ceres Solutions LLP—*Dennis Foster*	PO Box 432, Crawfordsville IN 47933	765-362-6700	R	285*	.1
16	Rabo AgriFinance	6919 Chancellor Dr, Cedar Falls IA 50613	319-277-0261	S	282*	.2
17	Horizon—*Jim Ross*	5214 S 30th St, Phoenix AZ 85040	602-305-6046	R	280*	.5
18	Ag-Valley Co-op—*Ron Hunter*	PO Box 68, Edison NE 68936	308-927-3681	R	273*	.3
19	Phosphate Holdings Inc—*Robert E Jones*	100 Webster Cir Ste 4, Madison MS 39110	601-898-9004	P	261	.2
20	Agri-Sales Associates Inc—*Jerry Bellar*	209 Louise Ave, Nashville TN 37203	615-329-1141	R	243*	<.1
21	Maplehurst Farms Inc (Rochelle Illinois)—*James Carmichael*	936 S Moore Rd, Rochelle IL 61068	815-562-8723	R	241*	.1
22	Watonwan Farm Services—*Todd Ludwig*	PO Box 68, Truman MN 56088	507-776-2831	R	208*	.3
23	Mid-County Coop—*Ron Hillmann*	660 E Seward St, Shawano WI 54166	715-526-3197	R	193*	<.1
24	Van Diest Supply Co—*Robert Diest*	PO Box 610, Webster City IA 50595	515-832-2366	R	191*	.5
25	Accelerated Genetics—*Joel Groskreutz*	E 10890 Penny Ln, Baraboo WI 53913	608-356-8357	R	174*	.3
26	Southern States Holdings Inc—*Tom Scribner*	PO Box 26234, Richmond VA 23260	804-281-1206	S	167*	3.0
27	Independent Agribusiness Professionals Cooperative Inc—*Bob Higby*	6177 N Thesta St Ste 1, Fresno CA 93710	559-440-1980	R	144*	<.1
28	AL Gilbert Co—*David Gilbert*	PO Box 38, Oakdale CA 95361	209-847-1721	R	138*	.2
29	Fruit Growers Supply Co—*Nazir Khan*	14130 Riverside Dr, Sherman Oaks CA 91423	818-986-6480	R	135*	.2
30	Hopkins Agricultural Chemical Co—*Jim Herbert*	PO Box 7190, Madison WI 53707	920-326-5141	S	126*	.4
31	Adams Fairacre Farms	765 Dutchess Turnpike, Poughkeepsie NY 12603	845-454-4330	R	114	.6
32	Frenchman Valley Farmer's Cooperative Inc—*Jim Chism*	PO Box 578, Imperial NE 69033	308-882-3200	R	91*	.2
33	Medford Cooperative Inc	160 Medford Plz, Medford WI 54451	715-748-2056	R	89*	.1
34	Rosen's Inc—*Ivan Wells*	PO Box 933, Fairmont MN 56031	507-238-4201	R	82*	.1
35	Abell Corp—*Dixon Abell*	2500 Sterlington Rd, Monroe LA 71203	318-343-7565	R	81*	.1
36	DeLong Company Inc—*David D DeLong*	PO Box 552, Clinton WI 53525	608-676-2255	R	80*	.1
37	Prosource One—*Bob Lee*	5387 Pleasant View Rd, Memphis TN 38134	901-383-2524	S	80*	<.1
38	Good Earth Organics Corp—*Guenter Burkhardt*	PO Box 266, Lancaster NY 14086	716-684-8111	R	78*	.1
39	Co-op Country Partners	N7160 Raceway Rd, Beaver Dam WI 53916	920-887-1756	S	72*	.3
40	Battle Creek Farmers Coop—*Dean Thernes*	PO Box 10, Battle Creek NE 68715		R	72*	.1
41	Posey County Farm Bureau Cooperative Association Inc—*Thomas Weilbrenner*	PO Box 565, Mount Vernon IN 47620	812-838-4468	R	71*	.1
42	Gibson Farmers Coop—*Tommy Townsend*	PO Box 497, Trenton TN 38382	731-855-1891	R	65*	.1

Note: An asterisk (*) indicates an estimated financial figure. The company type code used is as follows: R = Private, P = Public, S = Private Subsidiary, B = Public Subsidiary, D = Division, J = Joint Venture, I = Investment Fund.

COMPANY RANKINGS BY SALES WITHIN 4-DIGIT SIC

Rank	Company Name—*Executive Officer*	Address, City, State, Zip	Phone	Type	Fin	Empls
43	Osborne Distributing Company Inc—*Connie Duffie*	PO Box 2100, Vernon TX 76385	940-552-7711	R	62*	.1
44	Lucky Farmers Inc—*John Bergman*	PO Box 217, Woodville OH 43469	419-849-2711	R	59*	.1
45	California Ammonia Co—*Bob Brown*	PO Box 280, French Camp CA 95231	209-982-1000	R	59*	<.1
46	Winona River and Rail Inc—*Jeff Kuhn*	1000 E 3rd St, Winona MN 55987	507-452-9205	S	57*	<.1
47	Harvey Fertilizer And Gas Co—*Herbert Rouse*	PO Box 189, Kinston NC 28502	252-523-9090	R	56*	.2
48	Western Reserve Farm Cooperative Inc—*Michael Eastlake*	PO Box 339, Middlefield OH 44062	440-632-0271	R	55*	.1
49	Mauston Farmers Cooperative Association	310 Prairie St, Mauston WI 53948	608-847-5679	R	54*	.1
50	Tennessee Farmers Cooperative Inc—*Vernon Glover*	PO Box 3003, La Vergne TN 37086	615-793-8011	R	53*	.7
51	Martrex Inc	PO Box 1709, Minnetonka MN 55345	952-933-5000	R	51*	<.1
52	Whatcom Farmers Co-Op—*Richard Stipe*	PO Box 611, Lynden WA 98264	360-354-2108	R	50*	.3
53	FM Brown's Sons Inc—*Franklin Brown*	PO Box 2116, Reading PA 19608	610-678-2838	R	50*	.2
54	Southern Agricultural Insecticides Inc—*John Diem*	PO Box 218, Palmetto FL 34220	941-722-3285	R	50*	.1
55	Door County Cooperative Inc—*Trent Allen*	317 Green Bay Rd, Sturgeon Bay WI 54235	920-743-6555	R	48*	.1
56	Moyer and Son Inc—*John Moyer*	PO Box 64198, Souderton PA 18964	215-723-6000	R	47*	.3
57	Shipman Elevator Co—*Bart Baker*	PO Box 349, Shipman IL 62685	618-729-9009	R	46*	<.1
58	Northwest Wholesale Inc—*Jim Standerford*	PO Box 1649, Wenatchee WA 98807	509-662-2141	R	45*	.1
59	Twomey Co—*J Craig Twomey*	PO Box 158, Smithshire IL 61478	309-325-7100	R	43*	.1
60	Frontier FS Coop—*Perry Goetsch*	PO Box 359, Jefferson WI 53549	920-674-7000	R	38*	.1
61	Kettle-Lakes Coop—*Mark Mentink*	430 1st St, Random Lake WI 53075	920-994-4316	R	38*	.1
62	Mountain View Coop—*Bruce Clark*	2200 Old Havre Hwy, Black Eagle MT 59414	406-453-5900	R	35*	<.1
63	Agland Cooperative Inc—*Jeffrey Osentoski*	364 Lisbon St, Canfield OH 44406	330-533-5551	R	33*	.1
64	Research Seeds Inc—*Mark McCaslin*	PO Box 339, Nampa ID 83653	208-466-3568	R	33*	<.1
65	Frontier FS Coop—*Perry Goetsch* GROWMARK Inc	16119 Hwy 81 W, Darlington WI 53530	608-776-4600	S	32*	.1
66	Seedway—*Donald Wertman* GROWMARK Inc	PO Box 250, Hall NY 14463		D	32*	<.1
67	Traylor Chemical and Supply Co—*William Traylor*	PO Box 547937, Orlando FL 32854	407-422-6151	R	31*	.1
68	Beattie Farmers Union Cooperative Association—*Gary Fischer*	PO Box 79, Beattie KS 66406	785-353-2237	R	31*	<.1
69	Culpeper Farmers' Cooperative Inc—*Gregory Smith*	PO Box 2002, Culpeper VA 22701	540-825-2200	R	30*	.1
70	Stratton Seed Co—*Windell Stratton*	PO Box 1088, Stuttgart AR 72160	870-673-4433	R	30*	.1
71	Bingham Cooperative Inc—*Lance Gardener*	PO Box 887, Blackfoot ID 83221	208-785-3440	R	30*	.1
72	River Country Coop—*Bruce Misna*	1080 W River St, Chippewa Falls WI 54729	715-723-2828	R	29*	.2
73	Cooperative Grain and Supply (Hillsboro Kansas)—*Lyman Adams*	135 N Main, Hillsboro KS 67063	620-947-3917	R	29*	.1
74	Dairyland Seed Company Inc—*Tom Strachota*	PO Box 958, West Bend WI 53095	262-626-3080	R	28*	<.1
75	White Cloud Grain Company Inc—*Warren Beavers*	PO Box 276, Hiawatha KS 66434	785-742-3000	R	28*	<.1
76	John Taylor Fertilizers Co—*Daniel Vradenburg*	PO Box 15289, Sacramento CA 95851	916-991-4451	R	25*	.1
77	Ohigro Inc—*Jerry Ward*	6720 Gillette Rd, Waldo OH 43356	740-726-2429	R	25*	<.1
78	Van Zyverden Inc—*Jacqueline Van Zyverden Hogan*	PO Box 550, Meridian MS 39302	601-679-8274	R	25*	.3
79	Jackson-Jennings Farm Bureau Coop—*Robert Marley*	PO Box 304, Seymour IN 47274	812-522-4911	R	25*	.1
80	Equity Elevator And Trading Co—*Paul Frank*	PO Box 69, Wood Lake MN 56297	507-485-3153	R	25*	<.1
81	Warner Fertilizer Company Inc—*C Warner*	PO Box 796, Somerset KY 42502	606-679-8484	R	25*	.1
82	First Cooperative Association—*Jim Carlson*	PO Box 60, Cherokee IA 51012	712-225-5400	R	23*	.1
83	Maine Potato Growers Inc—*Joseph Lallande*	PO Box 271, Presque Isle ME 04769	207-764-3131	R	23*	.1
84	Jimmy Sanders Inc—*Michael Sanders*	PO Box 1169, Cleveland MS 38732	662-843-3626	R	23*	.1
85	Monterey Chemical Company Inc—*Jay Irvine*	PO Box 35000, Fresno CA 93745	559-499-2100	R	22*	<.1
86	Co-Alliance LLP—*Mark Patman*	PO Box 560, Danville IN 46122	317-745-4491	R	22*	.3
87	Belle Plaine Coop—*John Nagel*	820 E Main St, Belle Plaine MN 56011	952-873-4244	R	21*	<.1
88	Cal-West Seeds Inc—*Paul Frey*	PO Box 1428, Woodland CA 95776	530-666-3331	R	21*	.1
89	Customer One Coop—*Andy Altenhofen*	PO Box 215, Marathon WI 54448	715-443-2241	R	21*	.1
90	Certis USA LLC—*Loan Vu*	9145 Guilford Rd Ste 1, Columbia MD 21046	301-604-7340	R	21*	.1
91	Big Horn Cooperative Market Association Inc—*Louis Pistulka*	PO Box 591, Greybull WY 82426	307-765-9656	R	20*	.1
92	Richardson Seeds Inc—*Larry Richardson*	PO Box 60, Vega TX 79092		R	20*	<.1
93	Town And Country Coop—*Al Holdren*	813 Clark Ave, Ashland OH 44805	419-281-2153	R	20*	<.1
94	Farmers Union Oil Company Inc—*Robert Hjeldness*	PO Box 67, Oslo MN 56744	218-695-2511	R	20*	<.1
95	Farmers Commission Co—*Eric Parthemore*	PO Box 59, Upper Sandusky OH 43351	419-294-2371	R	19*	.1
96	Stateline Coop—*Larry Sterk*	PO Box 67, Burt IA 50522	515-924-3555	R	19*	.1
97	Ridgeland Chetek Coop—*Carl Vernes*	PO Box 155, Ridgeland WI 54763	715-949-1165	R	18*	.1
98	AgVantage FS Inc—*Gaylan Brunssen*	PO Box 828, Waverly IA 50677	319-483-4900	R	18	.1
99	F Henry Michell Co—*Henry Michell*	PO Box 60160, King Of Prussia PA 19406	610-265-4200	R	17*	.1
100	Terral Riverservice Inc—*Thomas Gattle*	10100 Hwy 65 S, Lake Providence LA 71254	318-559-1500	R	17*	.1
101	Christian County Farmers Supply Co—*Mike Builta*	PO Box 377, Taylorville IL 62568		R	16*	<.1
102	Mer-Roc FS Inc—*Steve Swanstrom*	PO Box 129, Aledo IL 61231	309-582-7271	R	16*	.1
103	Forage Genetics International—*Mark McCaslin*	PO Box 339, Nampa ID 83653	208-466-3568	R	16*	<.1
104	Keystone Mills—*Harold Kurtz*	309 Martindale Rd, Ephrata PA 17522	717-354-4616	R	16*	<.1
105	Pestcon Systems Inc—*Manford Voight*	1808 Firestone Pky, Wilson NC 27893	252-237-7923	R	16*	<.1
106	Urwiler Oil and Fertilizer Inc—*Greg Urwiler*	301 Hwy 15 W, Laurel NE 68745	402-256-3177	R	16*	<.1
107	Seed Resource Inc—*Gary Regner*	PO Box 326, Tulia TX 79088	806-995-3882	R	16*	<.1
108	E B Stone and Son Inc—*Bradford Crandall*	PO Box 550, Suisun City CA 94585	707-426-2500	R	16*	.1
109	O'neal's Feeders Supply Inc—*Hollis Neal*	PO Box 307, Deridder LA 70634	337-463-8665	R	16*	.1
110	Northeast Texas Farmers Co-Op—*Brad Johnson*	PO Box 489, Sulphur Springs TX 75483	903-885-3143	R	14*	.1
111	Mwp LLC—*Lyle Jefferson*	4212 S Hwy 191, Rexburg ID 83440	208-356-4571	R	14*	.1
112	Kova Fertilizer Inc—*Richard Reed*	1330 N Anderson St, Greensburg IN 47240	812-663-5081	R	14*	.1
113	Cochran Oil Mill and Ginnery—*Leo Phillips*	PO Box 192, Cochran GA 31014	478-934-6204	R	14*	<.1
114	Peterson's North Branch Mill Inc—*Jerome Peterson*	PO Box 218, North Branch MN 55056	651-674-4425	R	13*	.1
115	Ottawa Cooperative Association Inc—*Adrian Derousseau*	PO Box 680, Ottawa KS 66067	785-242-5170	R	13*	<.1
116	Farm Depot—*Dennis Pierce*	42 Office Park Dr, Hattiesburg MS 39402	601-582-3545	R	13*	.1
117	Chokio Equity Exchange Inc—*Doug Olson*	PO Box 126, Chokio MN 56221	320-324-2477	R	13*	.1
118	Southeast Cooperative Service Co—*CD Stewart*	PO Box 340, Advance MO 63730	573-722-3522	R	12*	<.1
119	Calarco Inc—*George Fuller*	PO Box 727, Corcoran CA 93212	559-992-3127	R	12	<.1
120	Bolivar Farmers Exchange—*John Samek*	PO Box 27, Bolivar MO 65613	417-326-5231	R	12*	.1
121	Livengood Feeds Inc—*Burt Livengood*	PO Box 1080, Lockhart TX 78644	512-398-2351	R	12*	.1
122	Red Lake County Cooperative Inc—*Gary Weiss*	PO Box 37, Brooks MN 56715	218-698-4271	R	11*	.1
123	Blount Farmers Coop—*Doyle Broome*	1514 W Broadway Ave, Maryville TN 37801	865-982-2761	R	11*	.1
124	Bulloch Fertilizer Company Inc—*Mike Anderson*	PO Box 1447, Statesboro GA 30459	912-764-9084	R	11*	<.1
125	Harmony Country Coop—*Ronald Schmidt*	702 S Division St, Colby WI 54421	715-223-2306	R	11*	.1
126	Midwest Supply and Distributing—*Rob Jamison*	PO Box 426, Saint Cloud MN 56302	320-363-4700	R	11*	<.1
127	Esco Industries Inc—*Sheldon Sturgis*	PO Box 7126, Saint Cloud MN 56302	320-259-9470	R	10*	.1
128	Bouldin Corp—*Mark Brown*	PO Box 7116, Mcminnville TN 37111	931-815-8520	R	10*	.1
129	Agbest Cooperative Inc—*John Bauer*	PO Box 392, Muncie IN 47308	765-288-5001	R	10*	<.1

Rank	Company Name—*Executive Officer*	Address, City, State, Zip	Phone	Type	Fin	Empls
130	Redi-Gro Corp—*Dennis Chan*	8909 Elder Creek Rd, Sacramento CA 95828	916-381-6063	R	10*	<.1
131	Clunette Elevator Company Inc—*John Anglin*	4316 W 600 N, Leesburg IN 46538	574-858-2281	R	10*	<.1
132	Hunt and Behrens Inc—*Dan Figone*	PO Box 2040, Petaluma CA 94953	707-762-4594	R	10*	<.1
133	Central Connecticut Co-Operative Farmers Association Inc—*Daniel Logue*	PO Box 8500, Manchester CT 06040	860-649-4523	R	10*	<.1
134	Husch and Husch Inc—*L Husch*	PO Box 160, Harrah WA 98933	509-848-2951	R	9*	<.1
135	Chemgro Fertilizer Company Inc—*Carl Funk*	PO Box 218, East Petersburg PA 17520	717-569-3296	R	9*	<.1
136	Rockbridge Farmers Coop—*Wilson Whitmore*	645 Waddell St, Lexington VA 24450	540-463-7381	R	9*	.1
137	Tu-Co Peat—*Raymond Tubbs*	PO Box 1158, Avon Park FL 33826	863-382-2043	R	8*	<.1
138	Lawrence D Oliver Seed Company Inc—*William Nichols*	PO Box 156, Milton VT 05468	802-893-4628	R	8*	<.1
139	Cold Spring Cooperative Creamery—*Dave Regnier*	PO Box 423, Cold Spring MN 56320	320-685-8651	R	8*	<.1
140	Farmers Cooperative Grain and Seed—*Gary Anderson*	PO Box 525, Thief River Falls MN 56701	218-681-6281	R	8*	<.1
141	Poet Nutrition Inc—*Jeff Broin*	851 Washington St, Scotland SD 57059	605-583-2258	R	8*	.1
142	Kentucky Fertilizer LLC—*S Caudill*	303 Hill St, Winchester KY 40391	859-744-3759	R	8*	<.1
143	Pennfield Oil Co—*Willis Winstrom*	14040 Industrial Rd, Omaha NE 68144	402-330-6000	R	7*	<.1
144	Dykes Dairyman Supplier Inc—*Brian Dykes*	35504 Hwy 16, Montpelier LA 70422	225-777-4350	R	7*	<.1
145	Cooperative Farmer"s—*Vincent Smith*	PO Box 188, Weatherford OK 73096	580-772-3334	R	7*	<.1
146	PL Rohrer and Brother Inc—*Douglas Rohrer*	PO Box 250, Smoketown PA 17576	717-299-2571	R	7*	<.1
147	John J Hoober Inc—*Mark Wagner*	PO Box 39, Gordonville PA 17529	717-768-3216	R	6*	<.1
148	X-Cel Feeds Inc—*John Wriglesworth*	PO Box 9157, Tacoma WA 98490	253-474-0531	R	6*	<.1
149	Merschman Seeds Inc—*Joseph Merschman*	PO Box 67, West Point IA 52656	319-837-6111	R	6*	<.1
150	Bemidji Cooperative Association—*R Lewis*	PO Box 980, Bemidji MN 56619	218-751-4260	R	6*	.1
151	Florida Fertilizer Company Inc—*Edgar Davis*	PO Box 1087, Wauchula FL 33873	863-773-4159	R	6*	<.1
152	Onate Feed Company LLC—*Ginger Washburn*	8000 Broadway Blvd Se, Albuquerque NM 87105	505-877-0410	R	6*	<.1
153	Rolla Farmers Exchange—*Robert Miers*	PO Box 98, Rolla MO 65402	573-364-1874	R	6*	<.1
154	Valley Farmers Coop (Natchitoches Louisiana)—*John Aaron*	PO Box 2116, Natchitoches LA 71457	318-352-6426	R	6*	<.1
155	Helena Chemical Company Hughes Helena Chemical Co	225 Schilling Blvd Ste, Collierville TN 38017	901-761-0050	D	6*	<.1
156	Rivard's Quality Seeds Inc—*Glenn Rivard*	102 E 3rd St, Argyle MN 56713	218-437-6638	R	6*	<.1
157	Laurel Aggregates Inc—*James Laurita*	300 Dents Run Rd, Morgantown WV 26501	304-296-7501	R	5*	<.1
158	Melrose Farm Service Inc—*Rodney Draeger*	PO Box 295, Melrose WI 54642	608-488-6661	R	5*	<.1
159	Schlessman Seed Co—*Daryl Deering*	11513 Us Hwy 250 N, Milan OH 44846	419-499-2572	R	5*	<.1
160	Hennepin Cooperative Seed Exchange—*David Worth*	11810 Brockton Ln N, Maple Grove MN 55369	763-428-0134	R	5*	<.1
161	J B Feed Fertilizer and Farm Service Inc—*Jack Berry*	PO Box 146, Stephenville TX 76401	254-965-3194	R	5*	<.1
162	Leaf River Ag Service—*Scott Dau*	PO Box 511, Wadena MN 56482	218-385-2366	R	5*	<.1
163	Light Milling Co—*Roy Light*	PO Box 309, Abingdon VA 24212	276-628-7361	R	5*	<.1
164	Sauder Feeds Inc—*Jerry Sauder*	PO Box 130, Grabill IN 46741	260-627-2196	R	5*	<.1
165	Evangeline Farmers Coop—*Dennis Thompson*	521 Lithcote Rd, Ville Platte LA 70586	337-363-1046	R	4*	<.1
166	Farmers Coop (Fort Smith Arkansas)—*Gene Bruick*	201 S 10th St, Fort Smith AR 72901	479-783-8959	R	4*	<.1
167	Farmers Elevator and Exchange Inc—*Rod Fisher*	PO Box 65, Wapello IA 52653	319-523-5351	R	4*	<.1
168	Paramount Feed and Supply Inc—*Darrell Martin*	19310 Longmeadow Rd, Hagerstown MD 21742	301-733-8150	R	4*	<.1
169	Surefed Ltd—*David Barksdale*	PO Box 711, Brady TX 76825	325-792-0102	R	4*	<.1
170	Eatonton Cooperative Feed Company Inc—*Ernest Turk*	PO Box 4371, Eatonton GA 31024	706-485-6423	R	3*	<.1
171	Eckroat Seed Co—*Robert Eckroat*	PO Box 17610, Oklahoma City OK 73136	405-427-2484	R	3*	<.1
172	Salamonie Mills Inc—*Kevin Grayer*	PO Box 416, Warren IN 46792	260-375-2200	R	3*	<.1
173	Thompsons Farm Supply Inc—*Roy Herrington*	PO Box 130, Baxley GA 31515	912-367-7723	R	3*	<.1
174	Rutherford Farmers Coop—*Jerry Ray*	PO Box 1296, Murfreesboro TN 37133	615-898-8800	R	3*	.1
175	O K Co-Operative Grain and Mercantile Co—*Ron Hansen*	PO Box 144, Kiowa KS 67070	620-825-4212	R	3*	<.1
176	Fieldcrest Fertilizer Co—*Kevin Tollefson*	210 5th Ave S, Madison MN 56256	320-598-7567	R	3*	<.1
177	Madison County Coop—*James Foy*	PO Box 587, Canton MS 39046	601-859-1271	R	3*	<.1
178	B and W Farm Center Inc—*Beverly McCay*	1502 S 6th St, Cordele GA 31015	229-273-3398	R	3*	<.1
179	Ingredient Resource Corp—*James W Ford*	2401 Lower Hunters Trc, Louisville KY 40216	502-448-4480	R	3*	<.1
180	Quality Rock Inc—*Jan Storey*	PO Box 1406, Idabel OK 74745	580-286-7178	R	3*	<.1
181	Mattocks Five Inc—*Richard Mattocks*	133 Pine St, Meadville PA 16335	814-333-8421	R	3*	<.1
182	Erie Growers Exchange Coop—*George Peters*	PO Box 312, Union City PA 16438	814-438-2411	R	3*	<.1
183	Saddle Barn Tack Distributors—*Marc Andrus*	PO Box 2465, Roswell NM 88202	575-622-9344	R	3*	<.1
184	Platt's Mill Inc—*Scott Morton*	PO Box 197, Spartansburg PA 16434	814-654-7814	R	3*	<.1
185	Clifton and Quigg Fertilizer Service Inc—*Jay Clifton*	PO Box 197, Linden IN 47955	765-339-7278	R	3*	<.1
186	Garden Valley Coop—*Joel Fenbobach*	PO Box 338, Alma WI 54610	608-685-4481	R	2*	<.1
187	Lake Valley Seed Company Inc—*Richard Roen*	5717 Arapahoe Ave Ste, Boulder CO 80303	303-449-4882	R	2*	<.1
188	Pratt Feed and Supply Co—*Jerry Schinkle*	5237 W Glendale Ave, Glendale AZ 85301	623-939-3326	R	<1*	<.1

TOTALS: SIC 5191 Farm Supplies

Companies: 188					**37,369**	**35.1**

5192 Books, Periodicals & Newspapers

Rank	Company Name—*Executive Officer*	Address, City, State, Zip	Phone	Type	Fin	Empls
1	Follett Corp (River Grove Illinois)—*Charles Follett*	2233 West St, River Grove IL 60171	708-583-2000	R	2,855*	10.0
2	Baker and Taylor Inc—*Tom Morgan*	2550 W Tyvola Rd Ste 3, Charlotte NC 28217	704-998-3100	R	2,260	3.8
3	Kable News Export Ltd—*Michael Duloc*	16 S Wesley Ave, Mount Morris IL 61054	815-734-4151	S	861*	1.5
4	Kable News International Inc—*Michael P Duloc*	16 S Wesley Ave, Mount Morris IL 61054	815-734-4151	S	861*	1.5
5	MBS Textbook Exchange Inc—*Robert Pugh*	2711 W Ash St, Columbia MO 65203	573-445-2243	R	696*	.8
6	Levy Home Entertainment LLC—*Howard Reese*	1375 N Weber Rd, Romeoville IL 60446	815-306-2900	R	503*	3.0
7	Kable Media Services Inc—*Michael Duloc*	16 S Wesley Ave, Mount Morris IL 61054	815-734-4151	S	364*	1.5
8	Blackwell's Delaware Inc—*Andrew Hutching*	6024 SW Jean Rd Bldg G, Lake Oswego OR 97035	503-684-1140	R	195*	.3
9	Nebraska Book Company Inc—*Mark Oppegard*	4700 S 19th St, Lincoln NE 68512	402-421-7300	R	171*	2.0
10	Btac Holding Corp—*Tom Morgan*	2550 W Tyvola Rd Ste 3, Charlotte NC 28217	704-998-3100	R	166*	3.6
11	Ascend Media—*Cameron Bishop*	7015 College Blvd Ste, Overland Park KS 66211	913-469-1110	R	162*	.2
12	Weston Presidio Capital Ii LP—*Mark Oppegard*	200 Clarendon St Fl 50, Boston MA 02116	617-988-2500	R	150*	3.5
13	Nbc Holdings Corp—*Mark Oppegard* Weston Presidio Capital Ii LP	4700 S 19th St, Lincoln NE 68512	402-421-7300	S	141*	3.0
14	Blackwell's Book Services—*Andrew Hutchings* Blackwell's Delaware Inc	6024 Jean Rd Bldg G, Lake Oswego OR 97035	503-684-1140	S	133*	.4
15	Imagine Nation Books Ltd—*Earl Kaplan*	282 Century Pl Ste 200, Louisville CO 80027	303-516-3400	R	112*	.1
16	Spring Arbor Distribution Company Inc—*Janet McDonald*	1 Ingram Blvd, La Vergne TN 37086		R	107*	.5
17	Publishers Group West Inc—*Rich Freese*	1700 4th St, Berkeley CA 94710	510-809-3700	R	102*	.3
18	Kable Distribution Services Inc Kable Media Services Inc	16 S Wesley Ave, Mount Morris IL 61054	815-734-4151	S	92*	.2
19	Distribution Systems of America Inc—*Paul Fleishman*	235 Pinelawn Rd, Melville NY 11747	631-843-4000	S	47*	.2
20	PBD Inc—*Scott A Dockter*	1650 Bluegrass Lakes P, Alpharetta GA 30004	770-442-8633	R	46*	.2
21	Educational Development Corp—*Randall W White*	PO Box 470663, Tulsa OK 74147	918-622-4522	P	40	.1

Note: An asterisk (*) indicates an estimated financial figure. The company type code used is as follows: R = Private, P = Public, S = Private Subsidiary, B = Public Subsidiary, D = Division, J = Joint Venture, I = Investment Fund.

COMPANY RANKINGS BY SALES WITHIN 4-DIGIT SIC

Rank	Company Name—*Executive Officer*	Address, City, State, Zip	Phone	Type	Fin	Empls
22	Hertzberg-New Method Inc—*James Orr*	617 E Vandalia Rd, Jacksonville IL 62650	217-243-5451	R	35*	.6
23	Whitaker Corp—*Robert Whitaker*	1030 Hunt Valley Cir, New Kensington PA 15068	724-334-7000	R	27*	.1
24	Chicago Review Press Inc—*Curtis Matthews*	814 N Franklin St Fl 1, Chicago IL 60610	312-337-0747	R	25*	.1
25	Mississippi Safety Services Inc—*John Brodbeck*	PO Box 1379, Clinton MS 39060	601-924-7815	R	18*	<.1
26	Periodical Management Group Inc—*Bill Salomon*	1011 N Frio St 2nd Fl, San Antonio TX 78207	210-226-6820	R	17*	.1
27	Quality Books Inc—*Rob Zimmers*	1003 W Pines Rd, Oregon IL 61061		S	14*	<.1
28	Lectorum Publications Inc—*Teresa Mlawer*	205 Chubb Ave, Lyndhurst NJ 07071		S	12*	.1
29	Thieme Medical Publishers Inc—*Brian Scanlan*	333 7th Ave Rm 500, New York NY 10001	212-760-0888	R	10*	.1
30	Caxton Printers Ltd—*David Gipson*	312 Main St, Caldwell ID 83605	208-459-7421	R	10*	<.1
31	Marco Book Company Inc—*Stuart Penn*	PO Box 695, Lodi NJ 07644	973-458-0485	R	7*	.1
32	Consortium Book Sales and Distribution Inc—*Randall Beck*	34 13th Ave NE Ste 101, Saint Paul MN 55112	612-746-2600	R	7	<.1
33	Western Livestock Reporter Inc—*Patrick Goggins*	PO Box 30758, Billings MT 59107	406-259-4589	R	6*	.1
34	21st Century Christian Inc—*Barry Brewer*	PO Box 40526, Nashville TN 37204	615-383-3842	R	6*	<.1
35	Booklegger—*Robert Kraut*	PO Box 2626, Grass Valley CA 95945	530-272-1556	R	4*	<.1
36	Hulbert Financial Digest—*Mark Hulbert*	5051-B Backlick Rd, Annandale VA 22003	703-750-9060	S	4*	<.1
37	Css Publishing Company Inc—*Wesley Runk*	5450 N Dixie Hwy, Lima OH 45807	419-227-1818	R	4*	<.1
38	Improper Publications Inc—*Marion Semonian*	142 Berkeley St Ste 3, Boston MA 02116	617-859-1400	R	3*	<.1
39	Gallopade International Inc—*Carole Marsh*	PO Box 2779, Peachtree City GA 30269	770-631-4222	R	2*	<.1
40	Metroland—*John Matthews*	419 Madison Ave, Albany NY 12210	518-463-2500	R	2*	<.1
41	Beeman Jorgensen Inc—*Brett Johnson*	7510 Allisonville Rd S, Indianapolis IN 46250	317-841-7677	R	2*	<.1
42	CD Stampley Enterprises Inc—*Crews Walden*	PO Box 33172, Charlotte NC 28233	704-333-6631	R	1*	<.1
43	Story Teller Too LLC—*Donita Boulter*	PO Box 921, Salem UT 84653	801-423-2560	R	1*	<.1
44	Hudson News Co—*Joseph DiDomizio*	1 Meadowlands Plz Ste, East Rutherford NJ 07073	201-939-5050	R	<1	2.0
45	Sunday News—*John Buckwalker*	PO Box 1328, Lancaster PA 17608	717-291-8788	R	<1*	<.1

TOTALS: SIC 5192 Books, Periodicals & Newspapers
Companies: 45

					10,281	39.9

5193 Flowers & Florists' Supplies

1	Color Spot Nurseries Inc—*Michael Vukelich*	PO Box 849, Fallbrook CA 92088	760-695-1430	R	206*	2.5
2	Bailey Nurseries Inc—*Gordon Bailey Jr*	1325 Bailey Rd, Newport MN 55055	651-459-9744	R	194*	.4
3	John Deere Landscapes—*Dave Werning*	5610 McGinnis Ferry Rd, Alpharetta GA 30005	770-442-8881	D	165*	.6
4	Ball Horticultural Co—*Anna Caroline Ball*	622 Town Rd, West Chicago IL 60185	630-231-3600	R	90*	.5
5	Manatee Fruit Co—*Walter Preston*	1320 33rd St W, Palmetto FL 34221	941-722-3279	R	74*	.3
6	Metrolina Greenhouses Inc—*Tom Van Wingerden*	16400 Huntersville Con, Huntersville NC 28078	704-875-1371	R	64*	.6
7	Pennock Co—*Robert Billings*	2711 Penn Ave, Pittsburgh PA 15222	412-471-8461	R	62*	.4
8	L and L Nursery Supply Inc—*Tom Medhurst*	2552 Shenandoah Way, San Bernardino CA 92407	909-591-0461	R	52*	.3
9	Roy Houff and Co—*Roy A Houff*	6200 S Oak Park Ave, Chicago IL 60638	773-586-8118	R	45*	.3
10	Wetsel Inc—*Floyd Grigsby*	PO Box 791, Harrisonburg VA 22803	540-434-6753	R	36*	.2
11	New England Pottery Co—*Lawrence D Gitlitz*	1000 Washington St, Foxboro MA 02035	508-543-7700	R	32*	.2
12	Greenleaf Wholesale Florists—*Scott Kitayama*	PO Box 537, Brighton CO 80601	303-659-8000	R	27*	.3
13	Holmberg Farms Inc—*Douglas Holmberg*	13430 Hobson Simmons R, Lithia FL 33547	813-689-3601	R	26*	.2
14	Valley Crest Tree Co—*Burton S Sperber*	24151 Ventura Blvd, Calabasas CA 91302	818-223-8500	S	22*	.4
15	Mid American Growers—*Nick Van Wingerden*	14240 Greenhouse Ave, Granville IL 61326	815-339-6881	R	12*	.2
16	Zieger and Sons Inc—*Stephen Zieger*	6215 Ardleigh St, Philadelphia PA 19138	215-438-7060	R	9*	.1
17	Danken Inc—*Ken Gemerden*	9201 Roe St, Pensacola FL 32514	850-484-3225	R	2*	<.1
18	Arty Imports Inc—*Don Rosenbaum*	111 Regal Row, Dallas TX 75247	214-741-1289	R	1*	<.1
19	International Decoratives Company Inc—*RE Russell*	PO Box 777, Valley Center CA 92082	760-749-2682	R	1	<.1

TOTALS: SIC 5193 Flowers & Florists' Supplies
Companies: 19

					1,121	7.2

5194 Tobacco & Tobacco Products

1	Eby-Brown Company LLC—*Richard W Wake*	PO Box 3067, Naperville IL 60566	630-778-2800	R	4,500	2.0
2	Harold Levinson Associates Inc—*Edward Berro*	21 Banfi Plz, Farmingdale NY 11735	631-962-2400	R	984*	.4
3	Imperial Trading Co—*John Georges*	PO Box 23508, New Orleans LA 70183	504-733-1400	R	882*	.3
4	S Abraham and Sons Inc—*Alan Abraham*	PO Box 1768, Grand Rapids MI 49501	616-453-6358	R	632*	.5
5	800-JR Cigar Inc—*Lewis Rothman*	2589 Eric Ln, Burlington NC 27215		S	544*	1.0
6	Seminole Tribe Of Florida Inc—*Mitchell Cypress*	3107 N State Rd 7, Hollywood FL 33021	954-966-6300	R	165*	2.1
7	Miller Distributing Inc—*William Miller*	PO Box 6, Saint Clair PA 17970	570-429-1191	R	92*	<.1
8	Albert H Notini and Sons Inc—*Robert Notini*	PO Box 299, Lowell MA 01853	978-459-7151	R	88*	.2
9	BTC Wholesale Distributers Inc—*Frank P Damico III*	100 Airview Ln, Alabaster AL 35007	205-324-2581	R	88*	.2
10	Wiemuth and Son Company Inc—*Robert A Wiemuth*	1500 Wabash Ave, Terre Haute IN 47807	812-232-3384	R	72*	<.1
11	Kaiser Wholesale Inc—*JR Kaiser*	PO Box 1115, New Albany IN 47150	812-945-2651	R	50*	<.1
12	Axton Candy and Tobacco Co—*Paul Myers*	PO Box 32219, Louisville KY 40232	502-634-8000	R	41*	.1
13	Albert Guarnieri Company Inc—*Albert Guarnieri III*	PO Box 927, Warren OH 44482	330-394-5636	R	41*	<.1
14	Pine Lesser and Sons Inc—*Allan G Lesser*	PO Box 1807, Clifton NJ 07015	973-478-3310	R	32*	<.1
15	Keilson-Dayton Co—*GT Wellinghoff*	PO Box 1457, Dayton OH 45401	937-236-1070	R	29*	<.1
16	FB McFadden Wholesale Company Inc—*EH McFadden*	415 Railroad Ave, Rock Springs WY 82901	307-362-5441	R	26*	<.1
17	Montano Cigarettes Candy and Tobacco Inc—*Gary Montano*	290 Boston Post Rd, Milford CT 06460	203-877-0341	R	23*	<.1
18	AW Marshall Co—*Bill Marshall*	437 N 500 W, Salt Lake City UT 84116	801-328-4713	R	18*	<.1
19	Atlas Merchandising Co—*Rose Kiski*	138 McKean Ave, Charleroi PA 15022		R	15*	<.1
20	Republic Tobacco LP—*Donald Levin*	PO Box 98, Glenview IL 60025	847-832-9700	R	10*	.1
21	Franklin Supply Inc—*Keith A Landen*	PO Box 1151, Franklin LA 70538	337-828-3208	R	9*	<.1
22	Governor's Distributing LLC—*Manny Balani*	8803 NW 23rd St, Miami FL 33172	305-597-1501	R	9*	<.1
23	Boyd-Bluford Company Inc—*Bruce Melchor*	2359 E Virginia Beach, Norfolk VA 23504	757-455-6042	R	2*	<.1
24	Shealy Sales and Vending Inc—*G Shealy*	PO Box 4926, Columbia SC 29240	803-754-9101	R	1*	<.1

TOTALS: SIC 5194 Tobacco & Tobacco Products
Companies: 24

					8,353	7.1

5198 Paints, Varnishes & Supplies

1	FinishMaster Inc—*JA Lacy*	54 Monument Cir 8th Fl, Indianapolis IN 46204	317-237-3678	S	404*	1.4
2	Brewster Home Fashions—*Kenneth Grandberg*	67 Pacella Park Dr, Randolph MA 02368	781-963-4800	R	132*	.5
3	Westgate Fabrics Inc—*Mark Knight*	418 Chandler Dr, Gaffney SC 29340		S	71*	.1
4	Seven's Paint and Wallpaper Co—*Tom Seven*	3070 29th St SE, Grand Rapids MI 49512	616-942-2020	R	60*	.1
5	JC Licht Company Inc—*John Vanderpool*	320 W Fullerton Ave, Carol Stream IL 60188	630-351-0400	D	55*	.4
6	Stroheim and Romann Inc—*Julian Grauer*	3000 47th Ave Ste 701, Long Island City NY 11101	718-706-7000	R	36*	.2
7	DesignTex Group Inc—*Tom Hamilton*	200 Varick St 8th Fl, New York NY 10014	212-886-8110	S	32*	.1
8	Lansco Colors—*Donald Greenwald*	PO Box 1685, Pearl River NY 10965		R	19*	<.1
9	Dunbar Sales Company Inc—*Stephen Rubinstein*	PO Box 8, Bayonne NJ 07002	201-437-6500	R	16*	<.1
10	Induron Coatings Inc—*David Hood*	PO Box 2371, Birmingham AL 35201	205-324-9584	R	10*	<.1
11	American Standox Inc—*William Kregel*	47802 W Anchor Ct, Plymouth MI 48170	734-454-4556	R	6*	.1

Rank	Company Name—*Executive Officer*	Address, City, State, Zip	Phone	Type	Fin	Empls
12	Industrial Finishing Products Inc—*Steven Galgano*	465 Logan St, Brooklyn NY 11208	718-277-3333	R	5*	<.1
13	Exterior Performance Coatings Inc—*George Carson*	1165 Hull Ct, Aurora IL 60504	630-675-4509	R	3*	<.1
14	Circle Aviation Inc—*Adrian Glanner*	1144 Ashwaubenon St, Green Bay WI 54304	920-336-7772	R	1*	<.1
15	Perma-Glaze Inc—*Dale R Young*	1638 S Research Loop R, Tucson AZ 85710	520-722-9718	R	1*	<.1
16	Xiom Corp—*James Weber*	78 Lamar St, West Babylon NY 11704	631-643-4400	S	1	<.1

TOTALS: SIC 5198 Paints, Varnishes & Supplies
Companies: 16   851   3.0

5199 Nondurable Goods Nec

Rank	Company Name—*Executive Officer*	Address, City, State, Zip	Phone	Type	Fin	Empls
1	Golden State Foods Corp—*Mark S Wetterau*	18301 Von Karman Ave S, Irvine CA 92612	949-252-2000	R	4,000	4.0
2	Central Garden and Pet Co—*William E Brown*	1340 Treat Blvd Ste 60, Walnut Creek CA 94597	925-948-4000	P	1,629	3.9
3	Elmo Leather Inc—*Nalle Johansson*	505 Thornall St Ste 30, Edison NJ 08837	732-549-5151	R	395*	<.1
4	Central Pet Supply—*Jeff Sutherland*	301 Island Rd, Mahwah NJ 07430	201-529-5050	R	361*	.4
5	Enesco LLC—*Basil Elliott*	225 Windsor Dr, Itasca IL 60143	630-875-5300	R	244	1.2
6	Knox Nursery Inc—*Bruce R Knox*	940 Avalon Rd, Winter Garden FL 34787	407-654-1972	R	225*	.2
7	HC Accents and Associates Inc—*Jan Murley* Boyds Collection Ltd	350 S St, McSherrystown PA 17344	717-633-9898	S	210*	.2
8	Nikken International Inc—*Kurt Fulle*	52 Discovery, Irvine CA 92618	949-789-2000	R	168*	.5
9	Shims Bargain Inc—*Kenny Suh*	2600 S Soto St, Vernon CA 90058	323-881-0099	R	152*	.3
10	Halo Branded Solutions Inc—*Marc Simon*	PO Box 657, Sterling IL 61081	815-625-0980	R	150*	.2
11	Roman Inc—*Dan Loughman*	472 Brighton Dr, Bloomingdale IL 60108	630-705-4600	R	149*	.2
12	Clarence House Imports Ltd—*Robert Appelbaum*	979 3rd Ave Ste 205, New York NY 10022	212-752-2890	R	141*	.1
13	FFR-DSI Inc—*Gerald A Conway*	PO Box 635696, Cincinnati OH 45263	440-505-6919	R	119*	.3
14	Sergeant's Pet Care Products Inc—*Bob Scharf*	PO Box 50399, Omaha NE 68154	402-938-7000	R	89*	.1
15	Tharperobbins Company Inc—*G Tharpe*	PO Box 1719, Statesville NC 28687	704-872-5231	R	85*	.3
16	Kurt S Adler Inc—*Howard Adler*	7 W 34th St, New York NY 10010	212-924-0900	R	80*	.2
17	Boyds Collection Ltd—*Jan L Murley*	350 South St, McSherrystown PA 17344	717-633-9898	R	79	.4
18	Texas Art Supply Co—*Louis K Adler*	2001 Montrose Blvd, Houston TX 77006	713-526-5221	R	67*	.1
19	Jacob Stern and Sons Inc—*Phillip Bernstein*	PO Box 50740, Santa Barbara CA 93150	805-565-1411	R	66*	.3
20	Sullivans—*Marian Sullivan*	PO Box 5361, Sioux Falls SD 57117	605-339-4274	R	64*	.1
21	NAPCO Marketing Corp—*James McCann*	7800 Bayberry Rd, Jacksonville FL 32256	904-737-8500	R	63*	.1
22	United Pacific Pet LLC—*Maureen Costello*	12060 Cabernet Dr, Fontana CA 92337	951-360-8550	R	62*	.1
23	Storming Media LLC—*Jock Friedly*	1375 Maryland Ave NE L, Washington DC 20002	202-360-4172	R	61*	.1
24	Grand Rapids Foam Technologies Inc—*Richard Amann*	2788 Remico St Sw, Wyoming MI 49519	616-726-1677	R	59*	.3
25	Vernon Co—*Chris Vernon*	PO Box 600, Newton IA 50208	641-792-9000	R	59*	.9
26	Nygala Corp—*Wendy Shen*	698 Rt 46 W, Teterboro NJ 07608	201-288-6400	R	57*	.1
27	Sun Coast Merchandise Corp—*Kumar Bhavnani*	6315 Bandini Blvd, Commerce CA 90040	323-720-9700	R	50*	.3
28	Specialty Merchandise Corp—*Mark Schwartz*	996 Flower Glen St, Simi Valley CA 93065		R	48*	.3
29	Maxco Inc—*Max A Coon*	1005 Charlevoix Dr, Grand Ledge MI 48837	517-627-1734	R	47	.3
30	Hair U Wear—*Michael R Napolitano*	5900 Equitable Rd, Kansas City MO 64120	816-231-3700	R	44*	<.1
31	Fresh Beginnings Inc—*Judith Hathcock*	4001 Coleman Rd N, Valdosta GA 31602	229-242-0237	R	44*	.3
32	Myron Corp—*Donald Adler*	205 Maywood Ave, Maywood NJ 07607	201-843-6464	R	42*	.7
33	Foam Products of San Antonio Inc—*David Jakobeit*	1119 N Mesquite St, San Antonio TX 78202	210-228-0033	R	42*	<.1
34	Buxton Acquisition Inc—*Russell Whiteford*	PO Box 1650, Springfield MA 01102	413-734-5900	R	40*	.1
35	Scott Pet Products Inc—*Michael Bassett*	PO Box 168, Rockville IN 47872	765-569-4636	R	37*	.1
36	Atlanco Inc—*Carl Zaglin*	1125 Hayes Industrial, Marietta GA 30062	770-427-1334	R	37*	.1
37	Mary Maxim Inc—*Larry Phedrain*	PO Box 5019, Port Huron MI 48061	810-987-2000	R	37*	.2
38	William Barnet and Son LLC—*Diane Holzworth*	PO Box 131, Arcadia SC 29320	864-576-7154	R	36*	.6
39	Midwest Quality Gloves Inc—*Stephen Franke*	PO Box 260, Chillicothe MO 64601	660-646-2165	R	36*	.2
40	Stump Printing Company Inc—*N Moyle*	PO Box 305, South Whitley IN 46787	260-723-5171	R	35*	.2
41	D Franklin Packaging Inc—*David Franklin*	9350 Bay Plz Blvd Ste, Tampa FL 33619	813-684-6080	R	35*	.1
42	SaltWorks Inc—*Naomi Novotny*	15000 Wood-Red Rd NE S, Woodinville WA 98072	425-885-7258	R	31*	<.1
43	Gatewaycdi Inc—*Chuck Fandos*	909 N 20th St, Saint Louis MO 63106	314-535-1888	S	30*	.1
44	Presence Incorporated Corporate—*Jeffrey Sehgal*	19 W 21st St Rm 301, New York NY 10010	212-989-6446	R	30*	.1
45	RBC Life Sciences Inc—*Clinton Howard*	2301 Crown Ct, Irving TX 75038	972-893-4000	P	28	.1
46	Corporate ImageWorks—*Gerold Stephens*	10375 Star Rt 43, Streetsboro OH 44241	216-292-8800	R	28*	<.1
47	Choice Products USA LLC—*Pete Garza*	PO Box 307, Eau Claire WI 54702	715-833-8761	R	26*	.2
48	Speciality Incentives Inc—*Tina Montgomery*	PO Box 19430, Denver CO 80219	303-934-5755	R	25*	.1
49	Fotofolio Inc—*Juliette Galant*	561 Broadway Ste 2bc, New York NY 10012	212-226-0923	R	24*	<.1
50	Miller Manufacturing Company Inc—*Ban Ferrise*	2600 Eagan Woods Dr St, Saint Paul MN 55121	651-982-5100	R	24*	.2
51	C And S Sales Inc—*Terry Storms*	12947 Chadron Ave, Hawthorne CA 90250	310-538-1219	R	24*	<.1
52	Natural Health Trends Corp—*Chris Sharng*	751 Canyon Dr Ste 150, Coppell TX 75019	972-241-4080	P	24	.1
53	Johnson Brothers Rubber Company Inc—*Lawrence Cooke*	PO Box 812, West Salem OH 44287	419-853-4122	R	22*	.1
54	Linzer Products Corp—*Brent Swenson*	248 Wyandanch Ave, West Babylon NY 11704	631-253-3333	R	21*	.4
55	Bufkor Inc—*Leslie Unger*	PO Box 17226, Clearwater FL 33762	727-572-9991	R	21*	<.1
56	Hanchett Paper Co—*David Shorr*	PO Box 6800, Aurora IL 60598	630-978-1000	R	18*	.1
57	Recycled Wood Products—*Chris Kiralla*	1313 E Philip Blvd, Pomona CA 91766	909-868-6882	R	17*	<.1
58	Nalpac Enterprises Ltd—*Ralph Caplan*	1111 E 8 Mile Rd Ste 1, Ferndale MI 48220	248-541-1140	R	16*	.1
59	Mpc Promotions LLC—*Sean Cooper*	PO Box 34336, Louisville KY 40232	502-451-4900	R	16*	.1
60	Gail Pittman Inc—*Gail Pittman*	PO Box 779, Ridgeland MS 39158	601-856-5646	R	14*	.1
61	Nationwide Advertising Specialty Inc—*John Newbern*	PO Box 928, Arlington TX 76004	817-275-2678	R	14*	<.1
62	Mele Companies Inc—*Michael Valentine*	PO Box 6538, Utica NY 13504	315-733-4600	R	14*	.1
63	Soul Co—*Jerry Flatt*	4322 Pet Ln, Lutz FL 33559	813-907-6000	R	14*	.1
64	Goldner Associates Inc—*James Straus*	231 Venture Cir, Nashville TN 37228	615-244-3007	R	13*	.1
65	Foam Factory and Upholstery Inc—*Salvatore Baladomente*	22800 Hall Rd, Clinton Township MI 48036	586-627-3626	R	13	<.1
66	Albinson Reprographics LLC—*Paul Karpinko*	1401 Glenwood Ave, Minneapolis MN 55405	612-374-1120	R	12*	.1
67	Comade Inc—*Chris A Schaller*	1920 E Warner Ave Ste, Santa Ana CA 92705	714-389-9600	R	12*	<.1
68	USA Scientific Inc—*Robert Declerk*	PO Box 3565, Ocala FL 34478	352-237-6288	R	12*	.1
69	Katherine's Collections At Silver Lake Inc—*Katherine Kleski*	370 Falls Commerce Pkw, Cuyahoga Falls OH 44224	330-572-2780	R	11*	.1
70	Executive Trading Company Ltd—*Abraham Spetner*	4929 30th Pl, Long Island City NY 11101	718-707-0800	R	11*	.1
71	Ben S Loeb Inc—*Benjamin Goldstein*	25 Pier Ln W Ste 1, Fairfield NJ 07004	973-882-9022	R	11*	.1
72	Brandvia Alliance Inc—*James Childers*	2159 Bering Dr, San Jose CA 95131	408-955-0500	R	11*	<.1
73	Keltner and Associates Inc—*Eric Keltner*	520 W Carmel Dr, Carmel IN 46032	317-574-1058	R	10*	<.1
74	A-Roo Company LLC—*Phil Basak*	PO Box 360050, Strongsville OH 44136	440-238-8850	R	9*	<.1
75	Acme Sponge and Chamois Company Inc—*James Cantonis*	PO Box 339, Tarpon Springs FL 34688	727-937-3222	R	9*	<.1
76	Charles River BRF Inc—*Raj Bhalla*	305 Almeda-Genoa Rd, Houston TX 77047	713-433-5846	S	9*	<.1
77	Scarborough Specialties Inc—*Jack Scarborough*	10501 Indiana Ave, Lubbock TX 79423	806-792-9925	R	9*	<.1
78	Carimex International Trading Inc—*Andy Yoon*	4601 S Soto St, Vernon CA 90058	323-582-8333	R	9*	<.1
79	Webb Sunrise Inc—*Lawrence Webb*	5390 Napa St, San Diego CA 92110	619-220-7050	R	8*	.1

Note: An asterisk (*) indicates an estimated financial figure. The company type code used is as follows: R = Private, P = Public, S = Private Subsidiary, B = Public Subsidiary, D = Division, J = Joint Venture, I = Investment Fund.

RANKINGS BY SALES WITHIN 4-DIGIT SIC

	Company Name—Executive Officer	Address, City, State, Zip	Phone	Type	Fin	Empls
80	Accento Plastics Inc—Joe Cotton	PO Box 1517, Tarpon Springs FL 34688	727-938-2464	R	8*	.1
81	Rocket Jewelry Box Inc—Michael Kaplan	PO Box 597, Bronx NY 10451	718-292-5370	R	8*	.1
82	Prime Packaging Corp—Arnold Kohn	1290 Metropolitan Ave, Brooklyn NY 11237	718-417-3000	R	7*	<.1
83	Art Phoenix Group Inc—Harriet Hiburn	4125 N 14th St, Phoenix AZ 85014	602-241-1060	R	7*	.1
84	Gordon Bernard Company Inc—Robert Sherman	22 Whitney Dr, Milford OH 45150	513-248-7600	R	7*	<.1
85	Adams Foam Rubber Co—Lonny Gold	4737 S Christiana Ave, Chicago IL 60632	773-523-5252	R	7*	<.1
86	Gem Specialty Companies Inc—Michael Shulkin	5610 W Bloomingdale Av, Chicago IL 60639	773-237-3000	R	7*	<.1
87	Titan Textile—Stephen Wener	PO Box Ae, Paterson NJ 07509	973-684-1600	R	7*	<.1
88	Power Sales And Advertising Inc—David Roberts	801 N Meadowbrook Dr, Olathe KS 66062	913-324-4900	R	7*	<.1
89	Adams Apple Distributing LP—Don Levin	2301 Ravine Way, Glenview IL 60025	847-832-9900	R	6*	.1
90	Universal Rubber and Plastics Corp—Bobbie Tilton	PO Box 516, Tallmadge OH 44278	330-633-1666	R	6*	<.1
91	Scafa-Tornabene Art Publishing Company Inc—John Bridgewater	165 Chubb Ave Ste 4, Lyndhurst NJ 07071	201-842-8500	R	6*	<.1
92	Innovative Marketing Consultants—Shane J Erickson	4284 Shoreline Dr, Spring Park MN 55384	952-252-1254	R	6*	<.1
93	Karol Western Corp—Gary Zoss	PO Box 3060, Bell CA 90202	323-832-8885	R	6*	<.1
94	Davco Advertising Inc—Jerry Esh	PO Box 288, Kinzers PA 17535	717-442-4155	R	6*	<.1
95	Anheuser Marketing Inc—L Anheuser	6941 Peachtree Industr, Norcross GA 30092	770-441-1704	R	6*	<.1
96	Food Market Merchandising Inc—Jon Tollefson	6401 W 106th St Ste 20, Minneapolis MN 55438	952-894-0110	R	6*	<.1
97	Libra Inc—Ziv Liberman	3310 N 2nd St, Minneapolis MN 55412	612-522-2600	R	6*	<.1
98	Greenwich Workshop Inc—Scott Usher	PO Box 231, Seymour CT 06483	203-881-3336	R	5*	<.1
99	Kid Stuff Marketing Inc—Joe Tindall	PO Box 19235, Topeka KS 66619	785-862-3707	R	5*	<.1
100	Star Sales Company Of Knoxville Inc—Neil Foster	PO Box 1503, Knoxville TN 37901	865-524-0771	R	5*	<.1
101	New Products International Inc—Giora Tamir	1 Alpine Ct, Chestnut Ridge NY 10977	845-352-9700	R	5*	<.1
102	Phase One Graphic Resources Inc—Larry Underkoffler	315 Market St, Sunbury PA 17801	570-286-1111	R	5*	<.1
103	Nucon International Inc—J Kovach	PO Box 29151, Columbus OH 43229	614-846-5710	R	5*	<.1
104	Southern Link Of Georgia Inc—Frederick Rosenkampff	230 Spring St Nw Ste 1, Atlanta GA 30303	404-523-6225	R	5*	<.1
105	Central Shippee Inc—Eric Hubner	PO Box 135, Bloomingdale NJ 07403	973-838-1100	R	4*	<.1
106	Badge-A-Minit Ltd—Cindy Kurkowski	345 N Lewis Ave, Oglesby IL 61348	815-883-8822	R	4*	<.1
107	Wbt Group LLC—Luis Padilla	831 Monterey Pass Rd, Monterey Park CA 91754	323-735-1201	R	4*	<.1
108	Martexport Inc—Martin Kalkstein	155 E 55th St Ste 4E, New York NY 10022	212-935-0300	R	4*	<.1
109	Accesories That Matter—Roy Kean	320 5th Ave Ste 609, New York NY 10001	212-947-3012	R	4*	<.1
110	Map Supply Inc—Al Cleveland	PO Box 1748, Welcome NC 27374	336-731-3230	R	4*	<.1
111	Circle Creations Inc—Theresa Carollo	4600 W 72nd St, Chicago IL 60629	773-284-3650	R	4*	<.1
112	7th Sense Inc—Darren Lisiten	PO Box 644, Merrick NY 11566	516-868-7199	R	3*	<.1
113	JM Wechter and Associates Inc—Janet Wechter	569 Main St, Monroe CT 06468	203-452-0063	R	3*	<.1
114	Medina Farmers Exchange Co—James Duffy	320 S Ct St, Medina OH 44256	330-723-3607	R	3*	<.1
115	Martin Universal Design Inc—Dennis Kapp	4444 Lawton St, Detroit MI 48208	313-895-0700	R	3*	<.1
116	Small Wonder Inflatables Inc—Mark Bachman	1810 Gillespie Way Ste, El Cajon CA 92020	619-258-4466	R	3*	<.1
117	Lawrence Enterprises Inc—John S Lawrence II	PO Box 6284, Louisville KY 40206		R	3*	<.1
118	Restoration Preservation Conservation—Dennis Blaine	6819 SE Sleepy Hollow, Stuart FL 34997	772-219-0436	R	3*	<.1
119	Twism Promotions Inc—Richard Pellegrino	500 Executive Blvd, Ossining NY 10562	845-623-9258	R	3*	<.1
120	M S Plastics And Packaging Company Inc—Al Saraisky	10 Park Pl Bldng2 1a 2, Butler NJ 07405	973-492-2400	R	3*	<.1
121	Chest LLC—Brenda Eddington	2 Pauwels Dr, Washington MO 63090	636-239-7411	R	3*	<.1
122	Regency House Pictures And Frames Inc—Robert Estes	2344 Lawrenceville Hwy, Decatur GA 30033	404-633-1789	R	3*	<.1
123	Worrell Brothers Inc—Louise Worrell	PO Box 1823, Shreveport LA 71166	318-227-2727	R	3*	<.1
124	Bud's Bulk Ice Service Inc—Leonard Wesson	PO Box 6010, Phoenix AZ 85005	602-268-0292	R	2*	<.1
125	Seawall Specialty Company Inc—Jen Marie	1411 W Alabama St, Houston TX 77006	713-522-9064	R	2*	<.1
126	Major World Wide Ltd—Arthur Rosenberg	19706 53rd Ave, Fresh Meadows NY 11365	718-224-7023	R	2*	<.1
127	Xit Activewear Inc—Frank Gizatullin	430 Allentown Dr, Allentown PA 18109	610-435-9222	R	2*	<.1
128	Atlanta Ice Company Inc—Mike Basaric	1587 Taylor Ave, Atlanta GA 30344	404-762-0139	R	2*	<.1
129	Bells Advertising Inc—Terrence Wilt	109 Denson Dr Ste D, Austin TX 78752	512-454-9663	R	2*	<.1
130	Great Promotions—Scott Larsen	PO Box 1194, Tacoma WA 98401	253-396-1984	R	2*	<.1
131	Isi Inc—Guy Driggers	1212 E Michigan St, Indianapolis IN 46202	317-631-7980	S	2*	<.1
132	Nuzzolese Brothers Ice Corp—Vincent Nuzzolese	68 E Marie St, Hicksville NY 11801	516-931-4687	R	2*	<.1
133	Forget Me Knot Ltd—Nike Akindahunsi	16 New Jersey St, Dix Hills NY 11746	631-242-9119	R	2*	<.1
134	Metro Ice Inc—Howard Watkins	5911 Gateway Industria, Belleville IL 62223	618-234-3080	R	2*	<.1
135	FotimaUSA Inc—Anne Keating	7401 Katelyn Ct, San Diego CA 92120	858-549-6687	R	2	<.1
136	C X and B United Corp—Fenton Mitchell	1301 253rd St, Harbor City CA 90710	310-530-2102	R	1*	<.1
137	PJ Marketing Services Inc—Jeffrey Kuroski	20950 Ireland Rd, South Bend IN 46614	574-259-8843	R	1*	<.1
138	Thymes Ltd—Stephanie Shopa	629 9th St SE, Minneapolis MN 55414	612-338-4471	R	1*	<.1
139	Art Colbar Inc—Ovidiu Colea	3503 Bradley Ave, Long Island City NY 11101	718-786-0980	R	1*	<.1
140	American Lecithin Co—Matthias Rebmann	115 Hurley Rd Ste 2b, Oxford CT 06478	203-262-7100	R	1*	<.1
141	House Of Specialties Inc—Danny Sirmon	5451 Able Ct, Mobile AL 36693	251-438-2422	R	1*	<.1
142	Howell D Buster—Doug Buster	PO Box 2350, Selma AL 36702	334-872-0226	R	1*	<.1
143	American Packaging Products Inc—Yvonne Bruns	140 Prairie Lake Rd, East Dundee IL 60118	847-426-8888	R	1*	<.1
144	Seacoast Imprint—Richard Colucci	5613 Lakeview Mews Ct, Boynton Beach FL 33437	561-385-3486	R	<1	<.1

TOTALS: SIC 5199 Nondurable Goods Nec
Companies: 144   10,334   22.1

5211 Lumber & Other Building Materials

	Company Name—Executive Officer	Address, City, State, Zip	Phone	Type	Fin	Empls
1	The Home Depot Inc—Frank S Blake	2455 Paces Ferry Rd NW, Atlanta GA 30339	770-433-8211	P	67,997	321.0
2	Lowe's Companies Inc—Robert A Niblock	PO Box 1000, Mooresville NC 28117	704-758-1000	P	48,815	234.0
3	Lowe's Home Centers Inc—Robert A Niblock Lowe's Companies Inc	PO Box 1111, North Wilkesboro NC 28659	704-757-9210	S	46,927*	210.0
4	Menard Inc—John R Menard Jr	5101 Menard Dr, Eau Claire WI 54703	715-876-5911	R	7,895*	40.0
5	Fastenal Co—Willard D Oberton	2001 Theurer Blvd, Winona MN 55987	507-454-5374	P	2,269	13.3
6	84 Lumber Co—Joe Hardy	PO Box 8484, Eighty Four PA 15330	724-228-8820	R	1,382*	3.7
7	Interline Brands Inc—Michael J Grebe	801 West Bay St, Jacksonville FL 32204	904-421-1400	P	1,250	3.6
8	Sutherland Lumber Company LP—Steven Scott	4000 Main St, Kansas City MO 64111	816-756-3000	R	1,180*	2.3
9	Carter Lumber Co—Neil Sackett	601 Tallmadge Rd, Kent OH 44240	330-673-6100	R	942*	3.5
10	United Building Centers—Thomas Hetzel	3560 N Service Dr, Winona MN 55987	507-452-3384	D	750*	6.0
11	Building Materials Holding Corp—Peter C Alexander	720 Park Blvd Ste 200, Boise ID 83712	208-331-4300	R	646*	4.0
12	Foxworth-Galbraith Lumber Co	4965 Preston Park Blvd, Plano TX 75093	972-665-2400	R	641*	2.5
13	Lumber Liquidators Holdings Inc—Robert M Lynchy	3000 John Deere Rd, Toano VA 23168	757-259-4280	B	620	1.2
14	Meeks Building Centers—Bill Meeks	1651 Response RdSte 20, Sacramento CA 95815	916-576-3042	R	614*	1.0
15	Marvins—Al Cohn	PO Box 1110, Leeds AL 35094	205-702-7305	R	404*	.6
16	McCoy Corp—Brian McCoy	1350 IH-35 N, San Marcos TX 78666		R	370*	1.3
17	National Lumber Co (Mansfield Massachusetts)—Steven Kaitz	PO Box 9032, Mansfield MA 02048	508-339-8020	R	307*	.5
18	Ridout Lumber Cos—Wayne Ridout	125 Henry Farrar Dr, Searcy AR 72143	501-268-3929	R	303*	.5
19	EC Barton and Co—Niel Crowson	PO Box 16360, Jonesboro AR 72403	870-932-6673	R	300*	1.2

Rank	Company Name—*Executive Officer*	Address, City, State, Zip	Phone	Type	Fin	Empls
20	Carter Jones Lumber Company Inc—*Neil Sackett* Carter Lumber Co	601 Tallmadge R, Kent OH 44240	330-673-6100	S	290*	4.0
21	Meek's - The Builder's Choice—*Terry O Meek*	PO Box 1746, Springfield MO 65801	417-521-2801	R	260*	1.0
22	Hayward Lumber Company Inc—*William Hayward*	10 Ragsdale Dr Ste 100, Monterey CA 93940	831-643-1900	R	250*	.3
23	Big C Lumber Company Inc—*Matt Magor*	PO Box 176, Granger IN 46530	574-277-4550	R	202*	.3
24	Dixieline Lumber Co—*Joe Lawrence*	3250 Sports Arena Blvd, San Diego CA 92110	619-224-4120	R	189*	1.0
25	Crane Johnson Company Inc—*Wylie Briggs*	PO Box 9139, Fargo ND 58106	701-235-3131	R	188*	.3
26	Seigle's Home and Building Centers Inc	1331 Davis Rd, Elgin IL 60123	708-742-2000	R	151	.7
27	Vidalia Naval Stores Co—*Hugh Peterson Jr*	325 Commerce Loop, Vidalia GA 30474	912-537-8964	R	142*	.5
28	Ganahl Lumber Co—*Peter Ganahl*	1220 E Ball Rd, Anaheim CA 92805	714-772-5444	R	138*	.6
29	Strober Organization Inc—*Paul Hylbert*	40 21st St, Brooklyn NY 11232	718-875-9700	R	128*	.7
30	Central Valley Builders Supply—*Stephen Patterson*	1100 Vintage Ave, Saint Helena CA 94574	707-963-3622	R	116*	.2
31	HW Jenkins Lumber Co—*HW Jenkins Jr*	PO Box 18347, Memphis TN 38181	901-363-7641	R	114*	.1
32	Stones Inc—*Joe M Higdon*	PO Box 986, Bainbridge GA 39818	229-246-2929	R	110*	.2
33	Scherer Brothers Lumber Co—*Peter L Scherer*	9401 73rd Ave N Ste 40, Brooklyn Park MN 55428	612-379-9633	R	108*	.4
34	Probuild Company LLC—*Bart Roberts*	7595 Tech Way Ste 500, Denver CO 80237	303-262-8500	R	107*	2.0
35	Curtis Lumber Company Inc—*Jay Curtis*	885 State Rt 67, Ballston Spa NY 12020	518-885-5311	R	105*	.4
36	Leaman Building Materials LP—*Lee Leaman*	7555 FM 762, Sugar Land TX 77469	281-238-1100	R	102*	.5
37	Ro-Mac Lumber and Supply Inc—*Dan Robuck Jr*	700 E Main St, Leesburg FL 34788	352-787-4545	R	90*	.4
38	Hammond Lumber Co—*Donald Hammond*	PO Box 500, Belgrade ME 04917	207-495-3303	R	90*	.3
39	RP Lumber Company Inc—*Robert L Plummer*	514 E Vandalia St, Edwardsville IL 62025	618-656-1514	R	80*	.5
40	Busy Beaver Building Centers Inc—*Frank Filmeck*	3130 William Pitt Way, Pittsburgh PA 15238	412-828-2323	R	79*	.4
41	Barr Lumber Company Inc—*John Shirley*	111 E Mill St, San Bernardino CA 92408	909-884-4744	R	79*	.3
42	Lezzer Lumber Inc—*Mike Lezzer*	PO Box 217, Curwensville PA 16833	814-236-0220	R	78*	.3
43	Big Creek Lumber Co—*Bud McCrary*	3564 Hwy 1, Davenport CA 95017	831-457-5024	R	69*	.2
44	WT Harvey Lumber Co—*WE Gross Jr*	PO Box 310, Columbus GA 31902	706-322-8204	R	69*	.2
45	National Lumber Co (Warren Michigan)—*Marvin Rosenthal*	24595 Groesbeck Hwy, Warren MI 48089	586-775-8200	R	68*	.1
46	Riverhead Building Supply Corp—*Edgar Goodale*	1093 Pulaski St, Riverhead NY 11901	631-727-1400	R	66*	.3
47	Star Lumber and Supply Company Inc—*CJ Goebel*	PO Box 7712, Wichita KS 67277	316-942-2221	R	64*	.5
48	FE Wheaton Lumber Co (Yorkville Illinois)—*Jeff Brown*	204 W Wheaton Ave, Yorkville IL 60560	630-553-8300	R	63*	.2
49	Wilson Lumber Company Inc	4818 Meridian St N, Huntsville AL 35811		R	62*	.2
50	Lakeville Lumber—*Fenton Hord*	63 B Bedfort St, Lakeville MA 02347	508-923-2900	S	60*	.2
51	Lummus Supply Co—*William L Lummus*	1554 Bolton Rd NW, Atlanta GA 30331	404-794-1501	R	59*	.2
52	Wright Do It Center—*Ted Huntoon*	208 S Williams St, Murphysboro IL 62966	618-687-1702	R	59*	.1
53	Standard Companies Inc—*Timothy O Rottschafer*	1535 Kalamazoo Ave SE, Grand Rapids MI 49507	616-243-3653	R	58*	.2
54	TH Rogers Lumber Co—*John M Kennedy*	PO Box 5770, Edmond OK 73083	405-330-2181	R	57*	.2
55	Zuern Building Products Inc—*Jenny Zuern*	426 Hwy W, Allenton WI 53002	262-629-5551	R	57*	.1
56	Millard Lumber Inc—*G Richard Russell*	PO Box 45445, Omaha NE 68145	402-896-2800	R	55*	.2
57	Champion Lumber Co—*George Champion*	1313 Chicago Ave, Riverside CA 92507	051 684 5670	R	55*	.1
58	Gaster Lumber and Hardware Inc—*O Raymond Gaster Jr*	15010 Abercorn Expy, Savannah GA 31419	912-925-1100	S	55*	.1
59	Stenerson Brothers Lumber Co—*Leslie G Stenerson*	1702 1st Ave N, Moorhead MN 56560	218-233-2754	R	54*	.1
60	Jackson Lumber And Millwork Company Inc—*Alfred Torrisi*	PO Box 449, Lawrence MA 01842	978-686-4141	R	53*	.1
61	Gilcrest/Jewett Lumber Co—*Philip S Worth*	PO Box 1000, Waukee IA 50263	515-987-3600	R	53*	.2
62	Cofer Brothers Inc—*Chip Cofer*	PO Box 200, Tucker GA 30085	770-938-3200	R	53*	.1
63	Rowley Building Products Corp—*RB Rowley*	40 Golf Links Rd, Middletown NY 10940	845-343-6515	R	52*	.2
64	Pine Tree Lumber Co—*Jerry Stubblefield*	707 N Andreasen Dr, Escondido CA 92029	760-745-0411	R	50*	.1
65	Chelsea Lumber Co—*Bob Daniels*	Old Barn Cir, Chelsea MI 48118	734-475-9126	R	50*	.1
66	Big L Corp—*James Perry*	PO Box 134, Sheridan MI 48884	989-291-3232	R	48*	.3
67	Higginbotham-Bartlett Co—*Michael King*	2211 Lubbock Hwy, Lamesa TX 79331	806-872-8321	R	47*	.1
68	Krempp Lumber Co—*Andy Krempp*	216 Main St, Jasper IN 47546		R	46*	.2
69	Lavalley Building Supply Inc—*Lawrence Huot*	PO Box 267, Newport NH 03773	603-863-1050	R	46*	.2
70	Dykes Lumber Company Inc—*Charles Kreyer*	1218 Rte 34, Aberdeen NJ 07747	732-290-9960	R	43*	.2
71	Jewett-Cameron Trading Company Ltd—*Donald M Boone*	PO Box 1010, North Plains OR 97133	503-647-0110	P	42	<.1
72	Lyon and Billard Co—*Edd Goralnik*	38 Gypsy Ln, Meriden CT 06450	203-235-4487	R	40*	.1
73	Nickerson Lumber Co—*Douglas B Bohannon*	15 Main St, Orleans MA 02653	508-255-0200	R	39*	.2
74	JT Lumber—*Patrick Rooney*	PO Box 484, Newport RI 02840	401-846-2220	R	39*	.2
75	Tindell's Inc—*Johann van Tilburg*	7751 Norris Fwy, Knoxville TN 37938	865-922-7751	R	39*	.2
76	Cape Cod Lumber Company Inc—*Harvey Hurvitz*	PO Box 2013, Abington MA 02351	781-878-0715	R	38*	.2
77	Ellsworth Builders Supply Inc	261 State St, Ellsworth ME 04605	207-667-7134	R	37*	.2
78	Morgan Buildings and Spas Inc—*Guy Morgan*	PO Box 660280, Dallas TX 75266	972-864-7300	R	36*	.4
79	Lee Lumber and Building Materials Corp	3250 N Kedzie Ave, Chicago IL 60618	773-509-6700	R	36*	.1
80	Matt's Cash and Carry Building Materials—*Danny Smith*	PO Box 900, Pharr TX 78577	956-787-5561	R	35*	.1
81	Raymond Building Supply Corp—*Brian Martin*	7751 Bayshore Rd, Fort Myers FL 33917	239-731-8300	R	34*	.2
82	Jaeger Lumber Co—*Lowell E Jaeger*	PO Box 126, Union NJ 07083	908-686-0073	R	34*	.1
83	Arlington Coal and Lumber Co—*Robert Mc Namara*	41 Park Ave, Arlington MA 02476	781-643-8100	R	33*	<.1
84	Nassau Suffolk Lumber and Supply Corp—*William H Van Tuyl III*	2000 Ocean Ave, Ronkonkoma NY 11779	631-467-2020	R	33*	.2
85	FE Wheaton Lumber Co (Wheaton Illinois)—*Jeff Brown* FE Wheaton Lumber Co (Yorkville Illinois)	703 W Wesley St, Wheaton IL 60187	630-668-1400	D	32*	.2
86	Lafata Cabinet Shop—*Peter Fata*	50905 Hayes Rd, Shelby Township MI 48315	586-247-1140	R	32*	.1
87	Elk Supply Company Inc—*James Browning*	103 E Gary Blvd, Clinton OK 73601	580-323-1250	R	32*	.1
88	M and G Building Materials Corp—*Allen Grothues*	2651 SW Military Dr, San Antonio TX 78224	210-924-5131	R	31*	.1
89	Crosslin Supply Company Inc—*Kenneth W Victory*	111 Enon Springs Rd W, Smyrna TN 37167	615-459-2854	R	31*	.1
90	Contractor Yard Inc—*Hal King* Strober Organization Inc	2717 Patterson St, Greensboro NC 27407	336-292-5693	S	31*	.1
91	Whelan's Inc—*Ted Huntoon*	PO Box 1340, Topeka KS 66601	785-357-0321	R	30	.2
92	Hughes Lumber Co—*Robert L Hughes*	5611 Bird Creek Ave, Catoosa OK 74015	918-266-9180	R	30*	.1
93	INR Beatty Lumber Co—*Robert B Beatty*	2001 Cherry Hill Rd, Joliet IL 60433	815-724-0001	R	30*	.1
94	Sunnyvale Lumber Inc—*Rick Roberts*	870 W Evelyn Ave, Sunnyvale CA 94086	408-736-5411	R	30*	.1
95	Norwood Sash and Door Manufacturing Company Inc—*Stephen Klekamp*	PO Box 8460, Cincinnati OH 45208	513-531-5700	R	29*	.1
96	Florida Lumber Co—*Martin Perez*	2431 NW 20th St, Miami FL 33142	305-635-6412	R	28*	.1
97	Hancock Lumber Company Inc—*Kevin Hancock*	PO Box 299, Casco ME 04015	207-627-4201	R	28*	.6
98	Sterling Lumber and Investment Co—*Marvin L Steele*	9101 Harlan St, Westminster CO 80031	303-427-9661	R	26*	.1
99	Truitt and White Lumber Co—*Warren White*	642 Hearst Ave, Berkeley CA 94710	510-841-0511	R	25*	.1
100	Prestige Lumber and Supplies Inc—*Stephen Rominger*	PO Box 1538, Sanford FL 32772	407-323-5662	R	24*	.1
101	Higginbotham Brothers and Co—*Rufus Ducan Jr*	PO Box 392, Comanche TX 76442	325-356-3456	R	24*	.2
102	Suwannee Lumber Manufacturing Co—*Frank Faircloth*	PO Box 5090, Cross City FL 32628	352-498-3363	R	24*	.3
103	Hamshaw Lumber Inc—*Douglas Hamshaw*	PO Box 725, Keene NH 03431	603-352-6506	R	22*	.1
104	Orgain Building Supply Co—*William Orgain*	PO Box 969, Clarksville TN 37041	931-647-1567	R	22*	.2

Note: An asterisk (*) indicates an estimated financial figure. The company type code used is as follows: R = Private, P = Public, S = Private Subsidiary, B = Public Subsidiary, D = Division, J = Joint Venture, I = Investment Fund.

COMPANY RANKINGS BY SALES WITHIN 4-DIGIT SIC

Rank	Company Name—*Executive Officer*	Address, City, State, Zip	Phone	Type	Fin	Empls
105	JF Johnson Holdings Inc—*Robert Johnson*	PO Box 248, Millersville MD 21108	410-987-5200	R	22*	.1
106	Mathew Hall Lumber Co—*Loran Hall*	PO Box 128, Saint Cloud MN 56302	320-252-1920	R	21*	.1
107	Gbs Lumber Inc—*Olin Mc Neely*	PO Box 159, Mauldin SC 29662	864-288-3627	R	21*	.1
108	Marling Lumber Company Inc—*John Marling*	PO Box 7668, Madison WI 53707	608-244-4777	R	21*	.1
109	Porter's Building Center Inc—*Kim Miller*	PO Box 1330, Kearney MO 64060	816-628-6111	R	20*	.1
110	Allen Lumber Company Inc—*Gary Allen*	502 N Main St, Barre VT 05641	802-476-4156	R	20*	.1
111	Plainfield Lumber and Hardware Co—*Steve Van Vliet*	3669 Plainfield Ave NE, Grand Rapids MI 49525	616-363-9021	R	20*	.1
112	Wheelwright Lumber Co—*Paul Wheelwright*	3127 Midland Dr, Ogden UT 84401	801-627-0850	R	19*	.1
113	Brunsell Brothers Ltd—*Craig Brunsell*	4611 W Beltline Hwy, Madison WI 53711	608-275-7171	R	19*	.1
114	Kleet Lumber Company Inc—*Howard Kleet*	777 Park Ave, Huntington NY 11743	631-427-7060	R	19*	.1
115	Construction Supply—*Jim Lindquist*	PO Box 1080, Farmington NM 87499	505-325-2871	R	19*	<.1
116	Geis Building Products Inc—*Dan Hinkes*	20520 Enterprise Ave, Brookfield WI 53045	262-784-4250	R	19*	<.1
117	Jimmy Whittington Lumber Co—*Jimmy Whittington*	3637 Jackson Ave, Memphis TN 38108	901-386-2800	R	18*	<.1
118	East Coast Lumber And Building Supply Company Inc—*Christine Morse*	PO Box 530, East Hampstead NH 03826	603-329-5322	R	18*	.1
119	Willamette Graystone Inc—*DW Jones*	3700 Franklin Blvd, Eugene OR 97403	541-726-7666	R	17*	.1
120	Lumberjack Building Center Inc—*Gordon Birgbauer III*	3470 Pointe Tremble Rd, Algonac MI 48001	810-794-4921	R	17*	.1
121	Len-Co Lumber Corp—*Stephen M Coppola*	1445 Seneca St, Buffalo NY 14210	716-822-0243	R	17*	.1
122	Brookside Lumber and Supply Co—*Bruce Edwards*	PO Box 327, Bethel Park PA 15102	412-835-7610	R	17*	.1
123	Warner Robins Supply Company Inc—*Mark Bayer*	PO Box 2268, Warner Robins GA 31099	478-953-4100	R	16*	.3
124	Carhart Lumber Co—*Scott Carhart*	PO Box 430, Wayne NE 68787	402-375-2110	R	16*	.1
125	Mazer's Discount Home Centers Inc—*Michael Mazer*	816 Green Springs Hwy, Homewood AL 35209	205-942-2744	R	16*	.1
126	Marson and Marson Lumber Inc—*Ken Marson Jr*	PO Box 218, Leavenworth WA 98826	509-548-5829	R	16*	.1
127	Schoeneman Brothers Co—*Al Schoeneman*	305 E 8th St, Sioux Falls SD 57103	605-336-2440	R	16*	.1
128	Sanford and Hawley Inc—*Robert Sanford*	PO Box 545, Unionville CT 06085	860-673-3213	R	16*	.1
129	Belair Road Supply Company Inc—*Thurston Adams Jr*	7750 Pulaski Hwy, Baltimore MD 21237	410-687-4200	R	16*	.1
130	Junior's Building Materials Inc—*Otto Boehm*	7574 Battlefield Pkwy, Ringgold GA 30736	706-937-3400	R	15*	<.1
131	Olshan Lumber Co—*Richard Ledermann*	PO Box 1274, Houston TX 77251	713-225-5551	R	15*	.1
132	American Building Supply Inc—*Mark Ballentyne*	8360 Elder Creek Rd, Sacramento CA 95828	916-503-4100	R	15*	<.1
133	Heartland Building Center Inc—*Curt Pfannenstiel*	PO Box 39, Hays KS 67601	785-625-6554	R	14*	.1
134	Alamo Lumber Co	PO Box 17258, San Antonio TX 78217	210-352-1300	R	14*	.1
135	Pierson Building Center Inc—*Bill Pierson*	4100 Broadway, Eureka CA 95503	707-441-2700	R	14*	.1
136	Kimal Lumber Co—*Al Bavry*	PO Box 1177, Nokomis FL 34274	941-484-9721	R	14*	.1
137	Standale Lumber and Supply Co—*Kenneth L Holtvluwer Jr*	2971 Franklin Ave SW, Grandville MI 49418	616-530-8200	R	14*	.1
138	Construction Materials Inc—*Bill Francis*	6725 Oxford St, Minneapolis MN 55426	952-929-0431	R	14*	.1
139	Gobble-Fite Lumber Company Inc—*James E Hurst*	PO Box 1808, Decatur AL 35602	256-353-5713	R	14*	.1
140	MSI-PRO Co—*Donald M Boone*	PO Box 1009, North Plains OR 97133	503-647-7351	S	14*	<.1
141	Dunn Lumber Company Inc—*Edward Dunn*	PO Box 45550, Seattle WA 98145	206-632-2129	R	14*	.2
142	Farmer's Building Supply Inc—*Leon Stutzman*	1741 Dowell Rd, Grants Pass OR 97527	541-476-0851	R	14*	<.1
143	Sierra Point Lumber And Plywood Company Inc—*Lee Nobmann*	601 Tunnel Ave, Brisbane CA 94005	415-468-1000	R	14*	.1
144	New England Building Materials LLC—*Louis Westfall*	PO Box P, Sanford ME 04073	207-324-3350	R	13*	.3
145	United Farmers Mercantile Coop—*John Pruss*	203 W Oak St, Red Oak IA 51566	712-623-5453	R	13*	.1
146	Barrons Enterprises Inc—*James E Davis*	23 W Diamond Ave, Gaithersburg MD 20877	301-948-6600	R	13*	<.1
147	Queen Anne Window and Door Inc—*Chad Hovde*	2233 1st Ave S, Seattle WA 98134	206-352-2672	R	13*	<.1
148	Beckerle Lumber Supply Company Inc—*Laurence Beckerle*	PO Box 649, Spring Valley NY 10977	845-356-1600	R	13*	.1
149	Spahn and Rose Lumber Co—*J Hannan*	PO Box 149, Dubuque IA 52004	563-582-3606	R	13*	.2
150	Reisterstown Lumber Co—*Richard Forbes*	PO Box 337, Reisterstown MD 21136	410-833-1300	R	12*	.1
151	Tum-A-Lum Lumber Co—*James W Crawford*	PO Box 5008, Bend OR 97708	541-382-0957	R	12*	.1
152	Deer Park Lumber Company Inc—*Jeff Lawther*	PO Box 430, Deer Park TX 77536	281-479-2326	R	12*	.1
153	Dillman And Upton Inc—*Brad Upton*	607 Woodward Ave, Rochester MI 48307	248-651-9411	R	12*	<.1
154	Kitchen Guild—*Jim McCoy*	1011 King St, Alexandria VA 22314	703-518-5006	R	12*	<.1
155	Allensville Planing Mill Inc—*Karl Westover*	PO Box 177, Allensville PA 17002	717-483-6386	R	12*	.2
156	Causeway Lumber Company Inc—*Michael Whiddon*	PO Box 21088, Fort Lauderdale FL 33335	954-763-1224	R	12*	.2
157	Century Everglades LLC—*Evelio Ortesa*	6991 Sw 8th St, Miami FL 33144	305-261-1155	R	11*	.2
158	Stanford Lumber Company Inc—*Carl Piekarski*	2001 Rte 286, Pittsburgh PA 15239	724-327-6800	R	11*	.1
159	Beverly Lumber Co—*John Dowd*	PO Box 9038, Riverside MO 64168	816-741-3061	R	11*	<.1
160	Schmuck Lumber Co—*Gregory Livelsberger*	PO Box 414, Hanover PA 17331	717-637-6616	R	11*	<.1
161	Nu-Sash Of Indianapolis Inc—*Ron Mckee*	5350 W 84th St, Indianapolis IN 46268	317-874-2780	R	11*	.1
162	Timberland Home Center Inc—*Sam Emmert*	PO Box 193, Brazil IN 47834	812-446-2397	R	11*	.1
163	Barry County Lumber Company Inc—*James Wiswell*	225 Industrial Park Dr, Hastings MI 49058	269-945-3431	R	11*	.1
164	RK Miles Inc—*Josiah Miles*	PO Box 1125, Manchester Center VT 05255	802-362-1952	R	10*	.2
165	Portal Service Co—*Douglas Johnson*	PO Box 67, Lignite ND 58752	701-933-2314	R	10*	.1
166	Honor Hardware And Building Supply Inc—*Lynn Hopkins*	PO Box 128, Honor MI 49640	231-325-4551	R	10*	<.1
167	National Lumber (Berlin Massachusetts)—*Manny Pina* National Lumber Co (Mansfield Massachusetts)	PO Box 190, Berlin MA 01503	978-838-2491	D	10*	<.1
168	Timber Holdings Intl—*Brian Lotz*	600 E Vienna Ave, Milwaukee WI 53212	414-445-8989	R	10*	<.1
169	Spenard Builders Supply Inc—*Ed Waite*	840 K St Ste 200, Anchorage AK 99501	907-261-9105	S	10*	<.1
170	East Coast Lumber and Supply Company Inc—*William Osteen*	308 Ave A, Fort Pierce FL 34950	772-466-1700	R	10*	.3
171	Anchor Lumber Company Inc—*James Alexander Mc Ge*	1505 1st Ave, Silvis IL 61282	309-792-0050	R	10*	.1
172	Dresser-Hull Co—*Richard Shields*	PO Box 670, Lee MA 01238	413-243-1400	R	10*	<.1
173	Viola Brothers Inc—*Brian Viola*	180 Washington Ave, Nutley NJ 07110	973-667-7000	R	9*	<.1
174	Builders Station Land LLC—*Ron Free*	PO Box 798, Carrollton GA 30112	770-832-0114	R	9*	.1
175	Cbs Builders Supply Inc—*Robert Ryan*	PO Box 120158, Clermont FL 34712	352-394-2116	R	9*	.1
176	Woods Lumber Of Independence Ks Inc—*Mark Woods*	PO Box 528, Independence KS 67301	620-331-4900	R	9*	<.1
177	Hopewell Builders Supply Inc—*James R Jones*	PO Box 939, Hopewell VA 23860	804-458-6356	R	9*	<.1
178	Chase Lumber and Fuel Company Inc—*David Chase*	PO Box 45, Sun Prairie WI 53590	608-837-5101	R	9*	<.1
179	Christmas Lumber Company Inc—*John H Smith*	10519 Kingston Pke, Knoxville TN 37922	865-693-2571	R	9*	<.1
180	Diebolt Lumber and Supply Inc—*Don Diebolt*	2661 Nebraska Rd, La Harpe KS 66751	620-496-2222	R	9*	<.1
181	Texas Door and Trim Inc—*Lonnie Messenger*	PO Box 551326, Dallas TX 75355	214-342-9393	R	8*	.1
182	Rossi Building Materials Inc—*Robert Rossi*	835 Stewart St, Fort Bragg CA 95437	707-964-4086	R	8*	<.1
183	High Brothers Inc—*Michael High*	PO Box 818, Camdenton MO 65020	573-346-5663	R	8*	<.1
184	Louies Home Center Inc—*Edward Louie*	1855 W Williams Ave, Fallon NV 89406	775-423-7008	R	8*	<.1
185	Burnett and Sons Planing Mill And Lumber Co—*James Miller*	PO Box 1646, Sacramento CA 95812	916-442-0493	R	8*	.1
186	Botello Lumber Company Inc—*Paul Botello*	26 Bowdoin Rd, Mashpee MA 02649	508-477-3132	R	8*	.1
187	Professional Garage Door Systems Inc—*Andrew Biddle*	6030 Gateway Dr, Plainfield IN 46168	317-204-2702	R	8*	.1
188	Barker Lumber Co—*Ron Kastein*	PO Box 503, Delavan WI 53115	262-728-9193	R	8*	.1
189	Gulf Stream Builders Supply Inc (Boynton Beach Florida)—*Steven Graves*	1481 W 15th St, Boynton Beach FL 33435	561-472-9220	R	8*	.1
190	Siwek Lumber and Millwork Inc—*Joseph Siwek*	2536 Marshall St Ne, Minneapolis MN 55418	612-781-3333	R	8*	<.1

Rank	Company Name—*Executive Officer*	Address, City, State, Zip	Phone	Type	Fin	Empls
191	Alternative Energy Store LLC—*Sascha Deri*	43 Broad St Ste A408, Hudson MA 01749	978-562-5858	R	8*	<.1
192	Valley Lumber and Building Supply Inc—*Dan Graves*	8525 Old Dairy Rd, Juneau AK 99801	907-789-7500	R	8*	<.1
193	Sampson Lumber Company Inc—*Donald Sampson*	PO Box 1149, Pembroke MA 02359	781-294-8033	R	8*	<.1
194	Sallisaw Lumber Company Inc—*Jerry Hetherington*	PO Box 220, Sallisaw OK 74955	918-775-6246	R	8*	<.1
195	Metro Stairs Inc—*Gerald Atkinson*	3420 Dalworth St, Arlington TX 76011	817-572-9410	R	7*	.1
196	Midway Building Supply Inc—*Stan Bettis*	Atlanta Hwy, Alpharetta GA 30004	770-475-7067	R	7*	<.1
197	Squires-Belt Material Co—*Bradley Benson*	PO Box 152047, San Diego CA 92195	619-266-6100	R	7*	.1
198	Fanelli's Windowpros Inc—*Marty Fanelli*	103 Glenworth Rd, Pottsville PA 17901	570-628-9111	R	7*	.1
199	Lincoln Contractors Supply Inc—*Norm Knief*	PO Box 270168, Milwaukee WI 53227		R	7*	<.1
200	Sonoma Overhead Doors—*David Nisenson*	21600 8th St E, Sonoma CA 95476		R	7*	<.1
201	Bob Hill Enterprises Inc—*Robert Hill*	1301 E Main St, Havelock NC 28532	252-447-1880	R	7*	.1
202	Cliff Buzick Inc—*Susan Elmore*	PO Box 2244, Bardstown KY 40004	502-348-5953	R	7*	<.1
203	Krystal Gravel Company Inc—*John Sojourner*	113 Bo Bo Dr, Crystal Springs MS 39059	601-892-6200	R	7*	<.1
204	Von Tobel Lumber and Home Center Inc—*Ken Pylipow*	PO Box 2068, Michigan City IN 46361	219-879-8484	R	7*	<.1
205	Devine Brothers Inc—*Michael Devine*	PO Box 189, Norwalk CT 06852	203-866-4421	R	7*	<.1
206	Doyle Lumber Company Inc—*Gregory Doyle*	43 River Rd, Andover MA 01810	978-688-4099	R	7*	<.1
207	Fuller Building Supply Company Inc—*Bruce Fuller*	PO Box 1464, Selma AL 36702	334-872-7409	R	6*	<.1
208	Applewood Lumber Co—*Vincent Tague*	405 Bridge St, Phoenixville PA 19460	610-933-5858	R	6*	.1
209	Hadlock Building Supply Inc—*E Lovato*	PO Box 869, Port Hadlock WA 98339	360-385-1771	R	6*	.1
210	Millwood Industries LLC—*Holly Cohen*	PO Box 265, Millwood NY 10546	914-941-2171	R	6*	<.1
211	Hlx Inc—*Donald Hoida*	PO Box 5907, De Pere WI 54115	920-983-4200	R	6*	.1
212	Triangle Building Supplies And Services Inc—*Allen Mattern*	1076 E Bishop St, Bellefonte PA 16823	814-355-5885	R	6*	<.1
213	Weston Builders Supply Co—*Bill Greuel*	PO Box 5568, Lancaster CA 93539	661-949-9468	R	6*	<.1
214	Cash and Carry Building Supply Inc—*William Mc Bryde*	PO Box 2404, Columbus MS 39704	662-328-5776	R	6*	<.1
215	Greenwood Products Inc—*Donald M Boone* Jewett-Cameron Trading Company Ltd	PO Box 249, Portland OR 97207	503-670-9663	S	6*	<.1
216	Boulder Lumber Co—*Craig Bandemoer*	PO Box 57, Boulder CO 80306	303-443-0582	R	6*	<.1
217	BPD Inc—*Edward Findley*	PO Box 548, Edwardsburg MI 49112	269-663-3615	R	6*	.1
218	Naples Lumber and Supply Company Inc—*Ronald Labbe*	3828 Radio Rd, Naples FL 34104	239-643-7000	R	6*	<.1
219	Boyce Lumber Co—*Bob Boyce*	PO Box 4825, Missoula MT 59806	406-728-7100	R	6*	<.1
220	Fulton Lumber and Home Center Inc—*Yaakov Gross*	2360 Fulton St, Brooklyn NY 11233	718-385-2262	R	6*	<.1
221	RP Johnson and Son Inc—*Stephen Johnson*	10 Mill Rd, Andover NH 03216	603-735-5544	R	6*	<.1
222	Eagle Lumber Inc—*Andrew P Craig*	PO Box 7246, Warwick RI 02887	401-737-0400	R	6	<.1
223	HN Hinckley and Sons Inc—*Wayne Guyther*	PO Box 578, Vineyard Haven MA 02568	508-693-0075	R	5*	<.1
224	Kelsey Vel Lumber And Supply Co—*Robert Borthesani*	PO Box 370, Kelseyville CA 95451	707-279-4297	R	5*	.1
225	Russell-Moore Lumber Inc—*Randy Russell*	PO Box 7520, Monroe LA 71211	318-325-3164	R	5*	<.1
226	TK W Inc—*Ansley Whatley*	PO Box 8009, Dothan AL 36304	334-792-1131	R	5*	<.1
227	Champion Window Company Of Toledo—*Toby Tokes*	6214 Monclova Rd, Maumee OH 43537	419-841-0154	R	5*	<.1
228	S And W Lumber Co—*John Saunders*	720 Camden Ave, Campbell CA 95008	408-378-5231	R	5*	<.1
229	Shaw Lumber Company Inc—*James Hyman*	PO Box 7, Florence SC 29503	843-662-3289	R	5*	<.1
230	Heines Insulators Incorporated Of Jersey—*Steven Raia*	419 Franklin Ave Ste 2, Rockaway NJ 07866	973-586-2911	R	5*	<.1
231	Heeby's Surplus Inc—*Kevin Heebner*	1164 Park Rd, Reading PA 19605	610-926-0944	R	5*	<.1
232	Tk Pacific Inc—*Terry Krausgrill*	PO Box 2265, Bakersfield CA 93303	661-325-5878	R	5*	<.1
233	L Sweet Lumber Company Inc—*Edward Angell*	PO Box 3300, Providence RI 02909	401-521-3800	R	5*	<.1
234	Mayfair Lumber Co—*Len B Koenen*	4825 W Lawrence Ave, Chicago IL 60630	773-283-3300	R	5*	<.1
235	Premier Builder Supply Inc—*Mostafa Ezzelgot*	1111 Horan Dr Ste F, Fenton MO 63026	636-349-6055	R	5*	<.1
236	Bryant W-D and Son Inc—*Lee Bryant*	372 S 5th St, Williamsburg KY 40769	606-549-2385	R	5*	<.1
237	Best Building and Supply Lumber Corp—*Isaac Saidmehr*	PO Box 222140, Great Neck NY 11022	631-325-2000	R	5*	<.1
238	Dilly Door Co—*Gary Konst*	1640 Baltimore St, Defiance OH 43512	419-782-1181	R	5*	<.1
239	Pamlico Home Builder and Supply Company Inc—*Lane Parrott*	PO Box 69, Alliance NC 28509	252-745-4111	R	5*	<.1
240	Rose and Walker Supply Inc—*Ronald Rose*	3974 N Indianapolis Rd, Columbus IN 47201	812-372-8181	R	5*	<.1
241	Dufrene Building Materials Inc—*Paul Dufrene*	PO Box 338, Cut Off LA 70345	985-632-6828	R	5*	<.1
242	Lee Builder Mart Inc—*Tony Lett*	1000 N Horner Blvd, Sanford NC 27330	919-775-5555	R	5*	<.1
243	Paul Feed and Supply Co—*Martin Paul*	PO Box 307, Garrettsville OH 44231	330-527-4301	R	5*	<.1
244	Gill Window Company Inc—*Nick Gill*	1813 Pacific Ave, Cheyenne WY 82007	307-778-3037	R	5*	<.1
245	Onancock Building Supply Inc—*Wayne Greene*	PO Box 219, Onancock VA 23417	757-787-2000	R	5*	<.1
246	Lawrence Gravel Inc—*Everett Lawrence*	21265 E Darwin Ferry R, West Union IL 62477	217-826-2800	R	4*	<.1
247	Express Enterprises Inc—*Anthony Willis*	PO Box 1936, Weaverville NC 28787	828-645-3000	R	4*	<.1
248	Gainey's Concrete Products Inc—*Lisa Chandler*	28021 Coker Vail Rd, Holden LA 70744	225-567-2700	R	4*	<.1
249	Spanish Tiles Ltd—*Manuel Gasch*	525 N State Rd, Briarcliff Manor NY 10510	914-923-4295	R	4*	<.1
250	Jim's Lumber and Building Supply Inc—*Rick Meer*	1390 W 6th S, Mountain Home ID 83647	208-587-3342	R	4*	<.1
251	Tarheel Lumber Company Inc—*C Boan*	735 Monroe St, Statesville NC 28677	704-873-1794	R	4*	<.1
252	White Hardware Company Inc—*Hoyt Anderson*	PO Box 679, La Jara CO 81140	719-274-5857	R	4*	<.1
253	C and M Building Materials Inc—*Carl Tiedeman*	PO Box 518, Cathedral City CA 92235	760-328-6543	R	4*	<.1
254	State Stone Corporation Inc—*Keith Mackay*	4640 S 300 W, Salt Lake City UT 84107	801-262-9323	R	4*	<.1
255	Adkins Co—*Richard G Holland Sr*	PO Box 156, Berlin MD 21811	410-641-2200	R	4*	<.1
256	ES Adkins and Co—*William Turner*	PO Box 1779, Salisbury MD 21802	410-749-7731	R	4	<.1
257	Cagle Lumber and Pallet—*Paul Cagle*	PO Box 867, South Houston TX 77587	713-946-7582	R	4*	<.1
258	Clement Lumber Company Inc—*William Hambrick*	PO Box 3145, Spartanburg SC 29304	864-582-8722	R	4*	<.1
259	Long Barn Inc—*Charles Long*	223 Mini Mall Rd Ste 1, Ebensburg PA 15931	814-472-9122	R	4*	<.1
260	Paramus Building Supply Company Inc—*Kevin Behnke*	PO Box 587, Paramus NJ 07653	201-262-1818	R	4*	<.1
261	Rankin's Inc—*Lisa Burgess*	PO Box 636, Camden ME 04843	207-236-3275	R	4*	<.1
262	Rose Brick and Materials Inc—*Boyd Harwood*	918 Oliver Plow Ct, South Bend IN 46601	574-234-2133	R	4*	<.1
263	Shannon Lumber Co—*Edward Shannon*	4540 W Belmont Ave, Chicago IL 60641	773-286-4512	R	4*	<.1
264	Don Murphy Door Specialties Inc—*Michael Murphy*	805 US Hwy 50, Milford OH 45150	513-771-6087	R	4*	<.1
265	Armstrong Lumber Co—*Robert Litchfield*	PO Box 4168, Corpus Christi TX 78469	361-882-6513	R	4*	<.1
266	Halsey Myers Inc—*Robert Myers*	2890 S Main St, Middletown OH 45044	513-423-4601	R	4*	<.1
267	Meek's Inc—*Michael Meek*	PO Box 255749, Sacramento CA 95865	916-576-3042	R	4*	<.1
268	Sports Health Home Care Corp—*William Mc Gilivray*	PO Box 302, Randolph MA 02368	781-961-1232	R	4*	<.1
269	Hometown Lumber And Hardware Inc—*Thomas Knollmeyer*	PO Box 650, Linn MO 65051	573-897-2276	R	4*	<.1
270	E J Stephens Co—*Hugh Stephens*	PO Box 330, New Albany MS 38652	662-534-4793	R	4*	<.1
271	Modern Builders Supply Company Inc—*Buddy Bolin*	1402 E Main St, Mountain View AR 72560	870-269-5091	R	4*	<.1
272	Breland Building Supply Inc—*James Price*	PO Box 56, Philadelphia MS 39350	601-656-5541	R	4*	<.1
273	Casey's Color Center Inc—*Robert Gondek*	219 E Fourth St, Winslow AZ 86047	928-289-4311	R	4*	<.1
274	Lewis Lumber And Supply LLC	PO Box 879, Benton AR 72018	501-315-6444	R	4*	<.1
275	Gladieux Lumber and Supply Company Inc—*Ronald Gladieux*	PO Box 167437, Oregon OH 43616	419-693-0601	R	4*	<.1
276	Superior Moulding Inc—*Eric Kalman*	5953 Sepulveda Blvd, Van Nuys CA 91411	818-376-1415	R	3*	<.1
277	Mid-America Lumber Inc—*Randy Smith*	PO Box 2005, Lawton OK 73502	580-353-3828	R	3*	<.1
278	Orange Coast Hardware and Lumber Company Inc—*John Hormuth*	2727 S Main St, Santa Ana CA 92707	714-556-1774	R	3*	<.1

Note: An asterisk (*) indicates an estimated financial figure. The company type code used is as follows: R = Private, P = Public, S = Private Subsidiary, B = Public Subsidiary, D = Division, J = Joint Venture, I = Investment Fund.

COMPANY RANKINGS BY SALES WITHIN 4-DIGIT SIC

Rank	Company Name—*Executive Officer*	Address, City, State, Zip	Phone	Type	Fin	Empls
279	Bruder Inc—*Robert Bruder*	9005 Woodland Ave, Cleveland OH 44104	216-791-9800	R	3*	<.1
280	Carr-Trumbull Lumber Co—*William Trumbull*	PO Box 139, Scottsbluff NE 69363	308-632-2143	R	3*	<.1
281	Friends Lumber Inc—*Eleanor Peters*	1870 Hamburg St, Schenectady NY 12304	518-372-5476	R	3*	<.1
282	Croft Lumber Co—*Warren Croft*	101 Spring St, Sayre PA 18840	570-888-2364	R	3*	<.1
283	Topanga Lumber and Hardware Company Inc—*Dennis Contis*	PO Box 1058, Topanga CA 90290	310-455-2047	R	3*	<.1
284	Berlin G Myers Lumber Corp—*Berlin Myers*	PO Box 965, Summerville SC 29484	843-873-2010	R	3*	<.1
285	J T White Hardware And Lumber Company LLC—*Judy Bishop*	915 E Parker Rd, Jonesboro AR 72404	870-932-7411	R	3*	<.1
286	Oconto County Lumber Inc—*John Dingeldein*	PO Box 147, Oconto Falls WI 54154	920-846-2307	R	3*	<.1
287	Bruce Kennedy Sand and Gravel Co—*Gloria Kennedy*	PO Box 5457, Texarkana TX 75505	903-838-3377	R	3*	<.1
288	Minnesota Rusco Inc—*Melvin Hazelwood*	5558 Smetana Dr, Hopkins MN 55343	952-935-9669	R	3*	<.1
289	Central Builder Supplies Of Gainesville Inc—*C Veley*	6800 Nw 22nd St, Gainesville FL 32653	352-372-1111	R	3*	<.1
290	Adobe Lumber Inc—*Michael Simoni*	PO Box 10098, Vallejo CA 94503	707-647-2100	R	3*	<.1
291	Coldwater Lumber Co—*Jeff Wenning*	PO Box 98, Coldwater OH 45828	419-678-2306	R	3*	<.1
292	Louis A Jammer Company Inc—*Louis Jammer*	2850 Us Hwy 1 Ste 1, Trenton NJ 08648	609-883-0900	R	3*	<.1
293	Midwood Quarry and Construction Inc—*William Smallwood*	200 Tolland St, East Hartford CT 06108	860-289-1414	R	3*	<.1
294	Thermo Door Co—*Eric Harr*	7508 Triple Lakes Rd, East Carondelet IL 62240	618-234-9338	R	3*	<.1
295	Central Building Supply Inc—*O Lamm*	PO Box 473, Rocky Mount NC 27802	252-977-2277	R	3*	<.1
296	H and M Lumber Company Inc—*Walter Morris*	PO Box 3318, West Helena AR 72390	870-572-3777	R	3*	<.1
297	Colwich Lumber and Supply Inc—*David Fisher*	PO Box 75009, Wichita KS 67275	316-796-1115	R	3*	<.1
298	Coleman's Lumber Yard Inc—*Jack Coleman*	302 N College St, Harrodsburg KY 40330	859-734-4334	R	3*	<.1
299	MR Lee Building Materials Inc—*Mel Lee*	12630 S Hamlin Ct, Alsip IL 60803	708-396-8000	R	3*	<.1
300	Roofing Supply Of Charlotte LLC—*David Merck*	1600 Westinghouse Blvd, Charlotte NC 28273	704-332-8440	R	3*	<.1
301	Virgil and Brothers Inc—*Anthony Godhino*	149 Pineda St, Longwood FL 32750	407-831-4123	R	3*	<.1
302	Baldridge Lumber and Supply Inc—*Roger Baldridge*	PO Box 813, Dalton GA 30722	706-278-2263	R	3*	<.1
303	Caron Building Center Inc—*Michael Caron*	39 Union St, Berlin NH 03570	603-752-1500	R	3*	<.1
304	Hughes' Lumber Plus—*Ralph Hughes*	PO Box 744, Fairfield TX 75840	903-389-2152	R	3*	<.1
305	Railroad Yard Inc—*William Anderson*	PO Box 2283, Stillwater OK 74076	405-377-8763	R	3*	<.1
306	Gene Stringfield Building Materials Co—*Mark Stringfield*	PO Box 2707, Eugene OR 97402	541-689-8014	R	3*	<.1
307	Cedaredge Lumber Co—*John Lindsey*	200 Sw 2nd St, Cedaredge CO 81413	970-856-3185	R	2*	<.1
308	Pawlik Supply Company Inc—*James Pawlik*	PO Box 1040, George West TX 78022	361-449-1576	R	2*	<.1
309	Whitman Truss and Lumber Inc—*Bill Rodman*	315 W 2nd St, Weiser ID 83672	208-414-0206	R	2*	<.1
310	Bobby J Smith—*Bobby Smith*	PO Box 1333, Conway SC 29528	843-235-9653	R	2*	<.1
311	Farney's Incorporated Home And Building Center—*Vincent Farney*	PO Box 189, Carthage NY 13619	315-493-3500	R	2*	<.1
312	Fountain Building and Supply Company Inc—*Sidney Howard*	731 20th St N, Bessemer AL 35020	205-428-4173	R	2*	<.1
313	East End Lumber Co—*Thomas Croyle*	544 E 3rd St, Williamsport PA 17701	570-323-9437	R	2*	<.1
314	Watertown Door and Windows Inc—*Michael Belcher*	217 High St, Watertown NY 13601	315-788-1500	R	2*	<.1
315	Broadhead Building Supplies Inc—*Larry Broadhead*	PO Box 67, Mendenhall MS 39114	601-847-3320	R	2*	<.1
316	Southeastern Sash and Door Inc—*William Peacock*	94 Ready Ave Nw Unit D, Fort Walton Beach FL 32548	850-664-5252	R	2*	<.1
317	Henderson Lumber Company Inc—*David Pigg*	PO Box 99, Tarboro NC 27886	252-823-2138	R	2*	<.1
318	KTU Worldwide Inc—*Dave Haglund*	813 Cir Dr, Aberdeen SD 57401	605-225-4049	R	2*	<.1
319	Villa Lagoon Tile—*Lundy Wilder*	15342 Fort Morgan Rd, Gulf Shores AL 36542	251-968-3375	R	2*	<.1
320	Robinson Builders-Mart Of Newton Inc—*Cecil Robinson*	PO Box 345, Newton NC 28658	828-464-7700	R	2*	<.1
321	Cashway West Inc—*Jim Ward*	2601 N County Rd W, Odessa TX 79763	432-333-3137	R	2*	<.1
322	Trinidad Builders Supply Inc—*Scott Sandlin*	PO Box 787, Trinidad CO 81082	719-846-9211	R	2*	<.1
323	E and E Lumber Inc—*Gilbert Emory*	1364 State Ave, Marysville WA 98270	360-659-7661	R	2*	<.1
324	J and M Service Inc—*Mike Sieve*	11532 Anabel Ave, Garden Grove CA 92843	714-530-3325	R	2*	<.1
325	CFI Inc—*Dale Grant*	2063 Newport Hwy, Sevierville TN 37876	865-774-7441	R	1*	<.1
326	Gennett Lumber Co—*Philip Gennett*	PO Box 5088, Asheville NC 28813	828-253-3626	R	1*	<.1
327	Bridgeport Lumber—*William Finn*	1460 Barnum Ave, Bridgeport CT 06610	203-334-5556	R	1*	<.1
328	Steelmaster Buildings Inc—*Rhae Adams*	1023 Laskin Rd Ste 109, Virginia Beach VA 23451	757-422-6800	R	<1*	<.1

TOTALS: SIC 5211 Lumber & Other Building Materials
Companies: 328

					191,163	886.0

5231 Paint, Glass & Wallpaper Stores

Rank	Company Name—*Executive Officer*	Address, City, State, Zip	Phone	Type	Fin	Empls
1	Vista Paint Corp—*Eddie Fischer*	2020 E Orangethorpe Av, Fullerton CA 92831	714-680-3800	R	342*	.5
2	N Siperstein Inc—*Steven Siperstein*	415 Montgomery St, Jersey City NJ 07302	201-333-2215	R	67*	.3
3	Seabrook Wallcoverings Inc—*James Seabrook Jr*	1325 Farmville Rd, Memphis TN 38122	901-320-3611	R	50*	.1
4	Contract Wallcoverings Inc—*Marc Moss*	2786 Industrial Row Dr, Troy MI 48084	248-280-5888	R	10*	<.1
5	Haley Paint Co—*Robert Haley*	1595 Paoli Pke Ste 200, West Chester PA 19380	484-947-5854	R	9*	.2
6	DL Couch Wallcoverings Inc—*Dennis Couch*	PO Box 570, New Castle IN 47362		R	8*	.1
7	Dyco Paints Inc—*Maxie Quinn*	5850 Ulmerton Rd, Clearwater FL 33760	727-536-6560	R	5*	.1
8	Daly's Inc—*Herbert Paulson*	3525 Stone Way N, Seattle WA 98103	206-633-4200	R	5*	.1
9	Color and Supply Company Inc—*Joseph Deifel*	921 National Ave, Lexington KY 40502	859-254-3836	R	3*	<.1
10	Singer Showroom—*Lee Davidson*	PO Box 7017, La Vergne TN 37086	513-621-3081	R	2*	<.1
11	Glass Merchants Inc—*Randy Sylvester*	PO Box 16091, Duluth MN 55816	218-722-2030	R	2*	<.1
12	Paint Supply Co (Hampton Virginai)—*Robert Wood*	2528 W Pembroke Ave, Hampton VA 23661	757-247-6651	R	1*	<.1

TOTALS: SIC 5231 Paint, Glass & Wallpaper Stores
Companies: 12

					504	1.2

5251 Hardware Stores

Rank	Company Name—*Executive Officer*	Address, City, State, Zip	Phone	Type	Fin	Empls
1	Do It Best Corp—*Mike Altendorf*	PO Box 868, Fort Wayne IN 46801	260-748-5300	R	2,038	1.4
2	Orchard Supply Hardware Corp—*Rob Lynch*	PO Box 49027, San Jose CA 95161	408-281-3500	S	1,493*.	7.0
3	Airgas Incorporated Nor-Pac North—*Peter McCausland*	11900 NE 95th St Ste 4, Vancouver WA 98682	503-283-2295	S	428*	.2
4	WE Aubuchon Company Inc—*William Aubuchon III*	95 Aubuchon Dr, Westminster MA 01473	978-874-0521	R	233*	1.1
5	H and S Hardware—*David Snow*	5416 Preston Hwy, Louisville KY 40213	502-969-1337	R	210*	.1
6	Van Lott Inc—*Van D Lott III*	3464 Sunset Blvd, West Columbia SC 29169	803-794-9340	R	190*	.1
7	AL Damman Co—*Rick Damman*	29235 Stephenson Hwy, Madison Heights MI 48071	248-399-5080	R	124*	.5
8	Dodge City Cooperative Exchange—*Scott Mcnair*	PO Box 610, Dodge City KS 67801	620-225-4193	R	117*	.1
9	McLendon Hardware Inc—*Gail McLendon*	440 Rainer Ave S, Renton WA 98057	425-235-3555	R	93*	.5
10	All American Home Center Inc—*Leonard Gertler*	7201 E Firestone Blvd, Downey CA 90241	562-927-8666	R	56*	.3
11	Woodcraft Supply LLC—*Bryan J Katchur*	PO Box 1686, Parkersburg WV 26102		R	50*	.3
12	Marc Paul Inc—*Ken Kaplan*	1756 Lacassie Ave Ste, Walnut Creek CA 94596	925-947-0705	R	41*	.2
13	Miller Hardware Co (Harrison Arkansas)—*TM Miller*	2 E Necessity Ave, Harrison AR 72601	870-741-3493	R	41*	.1
14	Short and Paulk Supply Co—*Jordan Short IV*	910 S Main St, Tifton GA 31794	229-382-2314	R	38*	.1
15	Bass Security Services Inc—*Dale Bass*	26701 Richmond Rd, Cleveland OH 44146		R	33*	.1
16	Kabelin Hardware Company Inc—*Jerry Kabelin*	432 Saint John Rd, Michigan City IN 46360	219-872-5431	S	32*	.2
17	Bering Home Center Inc—*August C Bering IV*	6102 Westheimer Rd, Houston TX 77057	713-785-6400	R	31*	.2
18	Imperial Hardware Co—*Phillip P Heald*	PO Box 3010, El Centro CA 92244	760-353-1120	R	30*	.3
19	Elliott's Ace Hardware—*Ray Griffith*	15360 Watertown Plank, Elm Grove WI 53122	262-782-9000	R	28*	.3

Rank	Company Name—*Executive Officer*	Address, City, State, Zip	Phone	Type	Fin	Empls
20	Placerville Hardware—*David Fausel*	441 Main St, Placerville CA 95667	530-622-1151	R	20*	<.1
21	Rockler Companies Inc—*Ann Jackson*	4365 Willow Dr, Hamel MN 55340	763-478-8201	R	20*	.5
22	Bluestem Farm and Ranch Supply Inc—*Lee Nelson*	2611 W Hwy 50, Emporia KS 66801	620-342-5502	R	18*	.1
23	Elliott's Hardware Inc—*Kyle Walters*	2049 Coit Rd, Plano TX 75075	972-312-0700	R	16*	.1
24	Yardville Supply Co—*George Smith*	PO Box 8427, Hamilton NJ 08650	609-585-5000	R	14*	.1
25	McQueeny-Lock Co—*Jeff Fisher*	520 W Pennway, Kansas City MO 64108	816-842-3503	R	13*	<.1
26	Steve's Wholesale Distributors Inc—*Richard Cupit*	PO Box 892456, Oklahoma City OK 73189	405-631-1001	R	12*	.1
27	County Home Improvement Center Inc—*David Hendrix*	PO Box 490, Saint Peters MO 63376	636-278-5080	R	12*	<.1
28	Westlake Hardware Inc—*George Smith*	14000 Marshall Dr, Lenexa KS 66215	913-888-0808	R	11*	1.5
29	Channel-Track and Tube-Way Industries Inc—*Max West*	PO Box 70067, Houston TX 77270	713-864-2551	R	10*	.1
30	Drillspotcom—*Paul Lin*	5603 Arapahoe Ave Ste, Boulder CO 80303	720-204-3660	R	10*	<.1
31	Owt Industries Inc—*Horst Pudwill*	PO Box 35, Pickens SC 29671	864-878-6331	R	10*	.2
32	Colony Hardware Supply Company Inc—*Michael Weiner*	15 Stiles St, New Haven CT 06512	203-466-5252	R	9*	.1
33	Cas Enterprises Inc—*Todd Sommerfeld*	201 Campus Dr, Huxley IA 50124	515-597-6400	R	6*	.1
34	Designer Plumbing Outletcom—*Eric Strand*	PO Box 9150, Jupiter FL 33468		R	6*	<.1
35	Nicholson Inc—*Paul Nicholson*	PO Box 1718, Rockford IL 61110	815-963-4821	R	6*	<.1
36	US Airweld Inc—*J Boccaccio*	PO Box 62555, Phoenix AZ 85082	602-437-3070	R	5*	.1
37	Coast To Coast Security Services Inc—*Brian Kervick*	32242 Paseo Adelanto A, San Juan Capistrano CA 92675	949-493-3957	R	5*	<.1
38	Tom Scott Lumber Yard Inc—*Larry Scott*	PO Box 558, Mount Vernon TX 75457	903-588-2397	R	4*	<.1
39	Gale General Co—*Martin Gale*	PO Box 60, Keyport NJ 07735	732-264-2000	R	4*	<.1
40	E M Hundley Hardware Co—*Grant Hundley*	617 Bryant St, San Francisco CA 94107	415-777-5050	R	3*	<.1
41	Colonial Saw Inc—*Paul Ravinski*	PO Box A, Kingston MA 02364	781-585-4364	R	3*	<.1
42	Manhattan Wire Products	711 Lidgerwood Ave, Elizabeth NJ 07202	908-925-8000	S	3*	<.1
43	Computer Revolution—*John Paul*	19450 Business Ctr Dr, Northridge CA 91324	818-407-4800	R	2*	<.1
44	Paitson Brothers Ace Hardware—*Ron Day*	2700 Wabash Ave, Terre Haute IN 47803	812-232-1864	R	2*	<.1
45	Emory Enterprises Inc—*Max Emery*	4402 Us Hwy 17 N, Brunswick GA 31525	912-265-2190	R	2*	<.1
46	M and W Equipment Company Inc—*Rhonda Sharp*	11607 Memorial Pkwy Sw, Huntsville AL 35803	256-880-7188	R	2*	<.1
47	B3O EnviroTek—*Julie Cosens*	695 Nashville Pike No, Gallatin TN 37066	615-989-1576	R	2	<.1
48	Hughes Lumber and Building Supply Company Inc—*Edward Burn*	82 Mary St, Charleston SC 29403	843-577-6671	R	2*	<.1
49	Lewiston Hardware And Lumber Inc—*Gary Haas*	4421 Hanson Ave, Lewiston MI 49756	989-786-2388	R	2*	<.1
50	C and C Machinery Inc—*David Corbin*	2120 E 2nd St, Russellville AR 72801	479-968-7144	R	1*	<.1
51	Cal-Ore Carbide Inc—*Jack Adams*	2919 N Pacific Hwy, Medford OR 97501	541-772-2293	R	1*	<.1
52	Poultry Plus Corp—*Sam Gaerner*	1009 E Coke Rd, Winnsboro TX 75494	903-342-7788	R	1*	<.1
53	Grande Hardware Company Inc—*John Bouska*	PO Box 967, Virginia MN 55792	218-741-5240	R	1*	<.1
54	Danmar Industries Inc—*Mukund Patel*	11952 Challenger Ct, Moorpark CA 93021	805-529-3788	R	1*	<.1
55	Big John Manufacturing Company Inc—*James Fritz*	PO Box 456, Osmond NE 68765	402-748-3860	R	1*	<.1
56	Ed's Mower and Saw Shoppe Inc—*Judy Herrmann*	17635 Se Mcloughlin Bl, Portland OR 97267	503-652-2711	R	1*	<.1

TOTALS: SIC 5251 Hardware Stores
Companies: 56

					5,548	16.2

5261 Retail Nurseries & Garden Stores

Rank	Company Name—*Executive Officer*	Address, City, State, Zip	Phone	Type	Fin	Empls
1	Tractor Supply Co—*James F Wright*	200 Powell Pl, Brentwood TN 37027	615-366-4600	P	4,233	16.4
2	Calloway's Nursery Inc—*James C Estill*	4200 Airport Fwy Ste 2, Fort Worth TX 76117	817-222-1122	R	280*	.3
3	Earl May Seed and Nursery LP—*Bill Shaw*	208 N Elm St, Shenandoah IA 51601	712-246-1020	R	211*	.5
4	George W Park Seed Company Inc—*Chase Fox*	1 Parkton Ave, Greenwood SC 29647	864-223-8555	R	103*	.2
5	Hinsdale Nurseries Inc—*Richard Theidel*	7200 S Madison Rd, Willowbrook IL 60527	630-323-1411	R	72*	.1
6	Stein Garden and Gifts—*Jack Stein*	5400 S 27th St, Milwaukee WI 53221	414-761-5400	R	50*	1.0
7	Barnes Nursery Inc—*Robert W Barnes*	3511 W Cleveland Rd, Huron OH 44839	419-433-5525	R	48*	.2
8	Cornelius Nurseries Inc—*James Estill* Calloway's Nursery Inc	2233 Voss Rd, Houston TX 77257		S	33*	.1
9	Dakota Plains Coop—*Ken Astrup*	151 9th Ave NW, Valley City ND 58072	701-845-0812	D	28*	.1
10	Mahoney's Rocky Ledge Farm Nursery—*Paul Mahoney*	242 Cambridge St, Winchester MA 01890	781-729-5900	R	25*	.3
11	Miles Farm Supply LLC—*Philip Franz*	PO Box 22879, Owensboro KY 42304	270-926-2420	R	16*	.5
12	Revels Tractor Company Inc—*Charles Revels Jr*	PO Box 339, Fuquay Varina NC 27526	919-552-5697	R	16*	.1
13	Valley Farmers Coop—*Jonathan Pierce*	PO Box 888, Athens TN 37303	423-745-0443	R	13*	.1
14	Western Cooperative Co—*David Briggs*	PO Drawer H, Alliance NE 69301	308-762-3112	R	9*	.1
15	White's Old Mill Garden Center—*Norman White*	3133 Old Mill Rd, Chesapeake VA 23323	757-487-2300	R	8*	<.1
16	American Soil Products Inc—*Lou Truesdell*	2121 San Joaquin St, Richmond CA 94804	510-292-3000	R	7*	<.1
17	Waukeenah Fertilizer And Farm Supply Inc—*Sloan Walker*	9643 Waukeenah Hwy, Monticello FL 32344	850-997-4460	R	7*	<.1
18	Memphis New Holland Inc—*David Sax*	3849 New Getwell Rd, Memphis TN 38118	901-362-9200	R	5*	<.1
19	Flowerwood Garden Center Inc—*Gary Siegmeier*	PO Box 217, Crystal Lake IL 60039	815-459-6200	R	5*	.1
20	Cactus Sands Nursery and Garden Center	1533 Hwy 17 S, North Myrtle Beach SC 29582	843-272-5314	R	3*	<.1
21	Coos Grange Supply Co—*Ed Kreutzer*	1085 S 2nd St, Coos Bay OR 97420	541-267-7051	R	3*	<.1
22	Elizabeth Ryan Floral Designs—*Elizabeth Ryan*	178 Norfolk St, New York NY 10002	212-995-1111	R	3*	<.1
23	Small Engine Warehouse Inc—*Roy Padgett*	2347 S 800 E, Dunkirk IN 47336	765-768-6725	R	3*	<.1
24	Elkhart Farmers Co-Op Association Inc—*George Beeler*	PO Box 903, Elkhart TX 75839	903-764-2298	R	2*	<.1

TOTALS: SIC 5261 Retail Nurseries & Garden Stores
Companies: 24

					5,181	20.1

5271 Mobile Home Dealers

Rank	Company Name—*Executive Officer*	Address, City, State, Zip	Phone	Type	Fin	Empls
1	Bropfs Manufactured Homes Inc—*Mike Bross*	PO Box 857, Saint Charles MO 63302	636-946-6399	R	94*	.1
2	Steenberg Homes Inc—*Bill Steenberg*	PO Box 1257, Fond du Lac WI 54936	920-922-3166	R	42*	.2
3	George R Pierce Inc—*Ron Pierce*	PO Box 80707, Billings MT 59108	406-655-8000	R	41*	.2
4	Mobile Homes Central	6383 10th Ave N Ste B-, Lake Worth FL 33463	561-967-9195	R	30*	<.1
5	Cutting Systems Inc—*Tony Johnson*	774 Zeb Rd, Union Grove NC 28689	704-592-2451	R	16*	.1
6	Frontier Homes Inc—*Fred Fogleman*	412 Main St, Summersville WV 26651	304-872-3271	R	6*	.1

TOTALS: SIC 5271 Mobile Home Dealers
Companies: 6

					229	.5

5311 Department Stores

Rank	Company Name—*Executive Officer*	Address, City, State, Zip	Phone	Type	Fin	Empls
1	Target Corp—*Gregg Steinhafel*	1000 Nicollet Mall, Minneapolis MN 55403	612-304-6073	P	67,390	355.0
2	Sears Roebuck and Co—*W Bruce Johnson*	3333 Beverly Rd, Hoffman Estates IL 60179	847-286-2500	S	30,030	247.0
3	Macy's Inc—*Terry J Lundgren*	7 W 7th St, Cincinnati OH 45202	513-579-7000	P	25,003	166.0
4	Neiman Marcus Co—*Karen W Katz* Neiman Marcus Inc	1618 Main St, Dallas TX 75201	214-741-6911	D	18,436*	17.0
5	Kohl's Corp—*Kevin Mansell*	N56 W17000 Ridgewood D, Menomonee Falls WI 53051	262-703-1440	P	18,391	136.0
6	JC Penney Company Inc—*Ron Johnson*	6501 Legacy Dr, Plano TX 75024	972-431-1000	P	17,759	156.0
7	Gayfer Montgomery Fair Co—*William Dillard II* Dillard's Inc	1600 Cantrell Rd, Little Rock AR 72201	501-376-5200	S	7,207	N/A

Note: An asterisk (*) indicates an estimated financial figure. The company type code used is as follows: R = Private, P = Public, S = Private Subsidiary, B = Public Subsidiary, D = Division, J = Joint Venture, I = Investment Fund.

COMPANY RANKINGS BY SALES WITHIN 4-DIGIT SIC

Rank	Company Name—*Executive Officer*	Address, City, State, Zip	Phone	Type	Fin	Empls
8	Dillard's Inc—*William Dillard II*	PO Box 486, Little Rock AR 72203	501-376-5200	P	6,121	38.9
9	Macyscom Inc—*Terry J Lundgren*	151 W 34th St, New York NY 10001	212-695-4400	S	4,943*	33.2
	Macy's Inc					
10	Kohl's Department Stores Inc—*Kevin Mansell*	N95 W18000 Appleton Av, Menomonee Falls WI 53051	262-251-9075	S	4,557*	43.0
	Kohl's Corp					
11	Neiman Marcus Inc—*Karen W Katz*	1 Marqus Sq 1618 Main, Dallas TX 75201	214-743-7600	S	4,002	14.9
12	Macy's West Inc—*Terry L Lundgren*	170 OFarrell St, San Francisco CA 94102	415-397-3333	S	3,748	31.0
	Macy's Inc					
13	Belk Inc—*Thomas M Belk Jr*	2801 W Tyvola Rd, Charlotte NC 28217	704-357-1000	R	3,513	24.0
14	Bon-Ton Stores Inc—*Bud Bergren*	2801 E Market St, York PA 17402	717-757-7660	P	2,981	26.5
15	Belk Brothers Co—*Tim Belk*	PO Box 190238, Charlotte NC 28201		R	2,842*	29.0
16	Saks Inc—*Stephen I Sadove*	12 E 49th St, New York NY 10017	212-753-4000	P	2,786	12.9
17	Harcourt Inc—*Brian J Knez*	6277 Sea Harbor Dr, Orlando FL 32887	407-345-2000	S	2,408	13.2
18	ShopKo Stores Operating Co LLC—*W Paul Jones*	PO Box 19060, Green Bay WI 54307	920-497-2211	S	2,200	16.0
19	Lord and Taylor—*Brendan L Hoffman*	424 5th Ave, New York NY 10018	212-391-3344	D	1,155*	10.0
20	Schottenstein Stores Corp—*Jay L Schottenstein*	1800 Moler Rd, Columbus OH 43207	614-221-9200	R	1,009*	8.1
21	Macys Inc—*Marna Whittington*	1601 3rd Ave, Seattle WA 98101	206-344-2121	S	975	6.9
	Macy's Inc					
22	Boscov's Department Stores Inc—*Albert Boscov*	PO Box 4116, Reading PA 19606	610-779-2000	R	879*	9.2
23	Shopko Operating—*W Paul Jones*	PO Box 19060, Green Bay WI 54307	920-429-2211	R	758*	.7
24	Bon-Ton Department Stores Inc	PO Box 2821, York PA 17405	717-757-7660	S	711	9.7
	Bon-Ton Stores Inc					
25	Variety Wholesalers Inc—*James A Pope*	218 S Garnett St, Henderson NC 27536	252-430-2600	R	694*	7.2
26	Elder-Beerman Operations LLC—*Byron L Bergren*	PO Box 1448, Dayton OH 45401	937-296-2700	S	665*	6.0
	Bon-Ton Stores Inc					
27	Maidenform Brands Inc—*Maurice S Reznik*	485 Rte1 S Bldg F, Iselin NJ 08830	732-621-2300	P	557	1.2
28	Gordmans Stores Inc—*Jeffrey J Gordman*	12100 W Center Rd Ste, Omaha NE 68144	402-691-4000	P	517	4.2
29	Savers Inc—*Ken Alterman*	PO Box 808, Bellevue WA 98009	425-462-1515	R	500*	10.0
30	Dillard Department Stores Inc Fort Worth Div—*David Smith*	4501 N Beach St, Fort Worth TX 76137	817-831-5111	D	432*	.4
	Dillard's Inc					
31	Peebles Inc—*Andy Hall*	10201 Main St, Houston TX 77025	434-447-5200	S	411*	2.2
32	Bloomingdale's Inc—*Michael Gould*	1000 3rd Ave, New York NY 10022	212-705-2000	S	401*	3.0
	Macy's Inc					
33	Filene's Basement Corp—*Mark Shulman*	25 Corporate Dr Ste 40, Burlington MA 01803	617-348-7000	S	389*	3.0
34	Dillard Inc St Louis Div—*Joe Brennan*	145 Crestwood Plz, Saint Louis MO 63126	314-301-6890	D	216*	.2
	Dillard's Inc					
35	JC Penney Mexico Inc—*Mike Ullman*	6501 Legacy Dr, Plano TX 75024	972-431-1000	S	166*	3.5
36	Century 21 Inc—*Abraham Gindi*	700 SECAUCUS ROAD, Secaucus NJ 07094	212-227-9092	R	163*	2.5
37	Bon-Ton National Corp—*Byron Bergren*	2801 E Market St, York PA 17402	717-757-7660	S	148*	.5
	Bon-Ton Stores Inc					
38	Macy's Florida Welfare Benefits Trust	7 W 7th St, Cincinnati OH 45202	513-579-7000	R	147*	<.1
39	Adir International LLC—*Inna Illson*	1605 W Olympic Blvd St, Los Angeles CA 90015	213-386-4412	R	140*	2.2
40	Von Maur Inc—*James D von Maur*	6565 Brady St, Davenport IA 52806	563-388-2200	R	113*	1.2
41	El-Bee Receivables Corp	PO Box 2821, York PA 17405	717-757-7660	S	69*	.1
	Bon-Ton Stores Inc					
42	Elder-Beerman Holdings Inc	PO Box 2821, York PA 17405	717-757-7660	S	69*	.1
	Bon-Ton Stores Inc					
43	Elder-Beerman Indiana LP	PO Box 2821, York PA 17405	717-757-7660	S	69*	.1
	Bon-Ton Stores Inc					
44	Elder-Beerman Operations LLC	PO Box 2821, York PA 17405	717-757-7660	S	69*	.1
	Bon-Ton Stores Inc					
45	Apex at Home LLC—*Andrew Gates*	100 Main St, Pawtucket RI 02860		R	62*	.8
46	Skagway Department Stores—*Bill Martin*	620 W State St, Grand Island NE 68801	308-384-8222	R	52*	.5
47	Halls Merchandising Inc—*Robert Leitstein*	200 E 25th St, Kansas City MO 64108	816-274-8111	S	39*	.4
48	Dillard Incorporated Southeast Div	6990 Tyrone Sq 3rd Fl, Saint Petersburg FL 33710	727-341-6000	D	33*	.2
	Dillard's Inc					
49	Allen's of Hastings Inc—*Robert M Allen*	PO Box 987, Hastings NE 68901	402-463-5633	R	17*	.2
50	Silverman Brothers Inc—*Alan Silverman*	6601 Harvard Ave, Cleveland OH 44105		R	14*	.2
51	Langston Co—*M Barber*	2034 NW 7th St, Oklahoma City OK 73106	405-235-9536	R	12*	.1
52	Northern Lakes Co-op Inc—*Mike Kaveli*	PO Box 985, Hayward WI 54843	715-634-3211	R	11*	.2
53	Annie Sez	80 Enterprise Ave S, Secaucus NJ 07094	201-601-4278	R	4*	.1

TOTALS: SIC 5311 Department Stores
Companies: 53　　　　　　　　　　　　　　　　　　　　　　　　　　　　　　235,982　　1,454.1

5331 Variety Stores

Rank	Company Name—*Executive Officer*	Address, City, State, Zip	Phone	Type	Fin	Empls
1	Wal-Mart Stores Inc—*Michael T Duke*	702 SW 8th St, Bentonville AR 72716	479-273-4000	P	418,952	2,100.0
2	Costco Wholesale Corp—*James D Sinegal*	PO Box 34331, Seattle WA 98124	425-313-8100	P	87,048	161.0
3	Kmart Corp—*W Bruce Johnson*	3333 Beverly Rd, Hoffman Estates IL 60179	248-643-1000	S	16,219*	8.5
4	Dollar General Corp—*Richard W Dreiling*	100 Mission Rdg, Goodlettsville TN 37072	615-855-4000	P	13,035	85.9
5	Family Dollar Stores Inc—*Howard R Levine*	PO Box 1017, Charlotte NC 28201	704-847-6961	P	8,548	31.0
6	Dollar Tree Inc—*Bob Sasser*	500 Volvo Pkwy, Chesapeake VA 23320		P	5,882	63.9
7	Big Lots Inc—*Steven S Fishman*	PO Box 28523, Columbus OH 43228	614-278-6800	P	4,952	35.6
8	Sheetz Inc—*Stanton R Sheetz*	5700 6th Ave, Altoona PA 16602	814-946-3611	R	2,658*	11.5
9	Fred's Inc—*Bruce A Efird*	4300 New Getwell Rd, Memphis TN 38118	901-365-8880	P	1,842	9.9
10	Retail Ventures Inc—*James A McGrady*	4150 E 5th Ave, Columbus OH 43219	614-238-4148	S	1,822	10.5
11	PriceSmart Inc—*Jose Luis Laparte*	9740 Scranton Rd, San Diego CA 92121	858-404-8800	P	1,714	5.5
12	99 Cents Only Stores—*Eric Schiffer*	4000 Union Pacific Ave, Commerce CA 90023	323-980-8145	P	1,424	12.0
13	Cost-U-Less Inc—*Rex A Wilhelm*	3633 136th Pl SE Ste 1, Bellevue WA 98006	425-945-0213	S	222	.6
14	CSN Stores LLC—*Niraj Shah*	800 Boylston St Ste 16, Boston MA 02199	617-880-8593	R	213*	.4
15	Frost Motors Inc—*Thomas R Keery II*	399 Washington St, Newton MA 02458	617-630-3000	R	49*	.1
16	Greetings and Readings Inc—*Steve Baum*	118-AA Shawan Rd, Hunt Valley MD 21030	410-471-3022	R	12*	.2
17	Masotta Variety and Deli—*Catino Masotta*	313 Main St, Woburn MA 01801	781-935-2648	R	1*	<.1

TOTALS: SIC 5331 Variety Stores
Companies: 17　　　　　　　　　　　　　　　　　　　　　　　　　　　　　　564,594　　2,536.4

5399 Miscellaneous General Merchandise Store

Rank	Company Name—*Executive Officer*	Address, City, State, Zip	Phone	Type	Fin	Empls
1	Defense Commissary Agency—*Joseph H Jeu*	1300 E Ave, Fort Lee VA 23801	804-734-8000	R	18,500	18.0
2	Alon Brands Inc—*Kyle C McKeen*	7616 LBJ Fwy Ste 300, Dallas TX 75251	972-367-3600	S	1,274*	2.0
3	Marden Discount Store Inc—*Harold Marden*	458 Kennedy Memorial D, Waterville ME 04901	207-873-6112	R	442*	.9

Rank	Company Name—*Executive Officer*	Address, City, State, Zip	Phone	Type	Fin	Empls
4	Pamida Inc—*Ken Seipel*	8800 F St, Omaha NE 68127	402-339-2400	S	300*	2.5
5	ZV Pate Inc—*David L Burns*	PO Box 159, Laurel Hill NC 28351	910-462-2122	R	196*	1.0
6	Schaeperkoetter Sales and Service	PO Box 37, Mount Sterling MO 65062	573-943-6323	R	127*	<.1
7	Industriaplex Inc—*Jason Gries*	11810 Wills Rd Bld 100, Alpharetta GA 30004	678-990-7868	R	105*	.1
8	Pandigital—*Dean Finnegan*	6375 Clark Ave Ste 100, Dublin CA 94568	925-833-7898	R	103*	.1
9	Atwood Distributing Inc—*Gary Atwood*	5400 Owen K Garriott R, Enid OK 73703	580-233-3700	R	66*	.9
10	Toolbarncom—*Dan Williams*	7820 L St, Omaha NE 68127	402-331-5550	R	61*	<.1
11	Four Seasons Coop—*David Van Schamel*	PO Box 148, Britton SD 57430	605-448-2231	R	40*	.1
12	Millionaire Corp—*Jim Bounce*	2375 S Jones Blvd Ste, Las Vegas NV 89146	702-948-8522	R	40*	<.1
13	Hammer and Wikan Inc—*Gainhart Samuelson*	PO Box 249, Petersburg AK 99833	907-772-4811	R	34*	.1
14	Richards Brothers Supermarket Inc—*Wells E Richards*	PO Box 866, Mountain Grove MO 65711	417-926-4168	R	23*	<.1
15	One Way Shopping LLC—*Anderson Koibita*	1441 Fortune Retail Ct, Kissimmee FL 34744	407-574-2505	R	22*	.1
16	Pierre Part Store Inc—*Gerald St Germain*	PO Box 10, Pierre Part LA 70339	985-252-6261	R	13*	.1
17	Mid-Wood Inc—*Tom Dorman*	12818 E Gypsy Ln, Bowling Green OH 43402	419-352-5231	R	12*	.1
18	Carco International Inc—*Dan Greenfield*	2721 Midland Blvd, Fort Smith AR 72904	479-441-3270	R	11*	<.1
19	Floyd's Stores Inc—*Jan Meyer*	2020 S Chester Ave, Bakersfield CA 93304		R	10	.2
20	Deters Dairy—*Rich Deters*	3024 Broadway, Quincy IL 62301	217-221-8950	R	7*	<.1
21	Kane Industries Corp—*Jim Zimring*	1250 Graves Ave, Oxnard CA 93030	805-988-3904	R	6*	<.1
22	Harold L Keay and Son—*Kevin G Keay*	58 Main St, Albion ME 04910	207-437-2540	R	6*	<.1
23	Susquehanna Glass Co—*Walter Rowen*	731 Ave H, Columbia PA 17512	717-684-2155	R	5*	.1
24	T-Mart Enterprises Inc—*Anthony Fernandez*	3137 E Seminary Dr, Fort Worth TX 76119	817-534-7709	R	4*	<.1
25	Gb Instruments Inc—*Maurice Rochman*	1143 W Newport Ctr Dr, Deerfield Beach FL 33442	954-596-5000	R	4*	<.1
26	RAC Enterprise LLC—*Rocco Ciavarella Jr*	175 Lions Dr, Hazleton PA 18202	570-606-0729	R	2*	<.1

TOTALS: SIC 5399 Miscellaneous General Merchandise Store
Companies: 26   21,412   26.3

5411 Grocery Stores

Rank	Company Name—*Executive Officer*	Address, City, State, Zip	Phone	Type	Fin	Empls
1	Kroger Co—*David B Dillon*	1014 Vine St, Cincinnati OH 45202	513-762-4000	P	82,189	338.0
2	Safeway Inc—*Steven A Burd*	PO Box 99, Pleasanton CA 94566	925-467-3000	P	41,050	180.0
3	Albertson's LLC—*Robert Miller* SUPERVALU Inc	PO Box 20, Boise ID 83726	208-395-6200	S	40,358	234.0
4	SUPERVALU Inc—*Craig R Herkert*	11840 Valley View Rd, Eden Prairie MN 55344	952-828-4000	P	37,534	142.0
5	Publix Super Markets Inc—*William E Crenshaw*	PO Box 407, Lakeland FL 33802	863-688-1188	R	26,967	152.0
6	Ahold USA Inc—*Dick Boer*	1385 Hancock St, Quincy MA 02169	781-380-8000	S	26,252*	170.0
7	Food Maxx—*Paul Laurell*	8065 Watt Ave, Elverta CA 95626	916-348-3425	S	25,515*	22.3
8	Dominick's Finer Foods Dominick's Supermarkets Inc	711 Jorie Blvd Ste 1, Oak Brook IL 60523	630-891-5000	S	18,497*	18.0
9	Meijer Inc—*Hank Meijer*	2929 Walker Ave NW, Grand Rapids MI 49544	616-453-6711	R	14,803*	75.0
10	E-Z Mart Stores Inc—*Sonya Hubbard*	PO Box 1426, Texarkana TX 75504	903-832-6502	R	14,461*	2.0
11	Rosauer's Supermarkets Inc—*Jeff Philipps*	PO Box 9000, Spokane WA 99209	509-326-8900	R	13,086*	2.5
12	BJ's Wholesale Club Inc—*Laura J Sen*	PO Box 9601, Natick MA 01760		P	10,877	24.8
13	Whole Foods Market Inc—*John P Mackey*	550 Bowie St, Austin TX 78703		P	10,108	64.2
14	HE Butt Grocery Co—*Charles C Butt*	PO Box 839999, San Antonio TX 78283	210-938-8000	R	9,926*	45.0
15	The Stop and Shop Supermarket Co—*Carl Schlicker* Ahold USA Inc	PO Box 55888, Boston MA 02205	781-380-8000	S	9,642*	59.0
16	Giant Eagle Inc—*Laura Shapira Karet*	101 Kappa Dr, Pittsburgh PA 15238	412-963-6200	R	9,300*	36.0
17	Food Lion LLC—*Rick Anicetti*	PO Box 1330, Salisbury NC 28145	704-633-8250	S	8,099*	73.0
18	Great Atlantic and Pacific Tea Company Inc—*Sam Martin*	2 Paragon Dr, Montvale NJ 07645	201-573-9700	B	8,079	39.0
19	Martin and Bayley Inc—*Frank Bayley*	1311 W Main Rm A, Carmi IL 62821	618-382-2334	R	7,879*	1.5
20	Kwik Trip Inc—*Don Zieplow*	PO Box 2107, La Crosse WI 54602	608-781-8988	R	7,849*	8.7
21	QuikTrip Corp—*Chester Cadieux*	PO Box 3475, Tulsa OK 74101	918-615-7900	R	7,796*	12.0
22	Scolari's Food and Drug Co—*Joey Scolari*	PO Box 5070, Reno NV 89513	775-331-7700	R	7,318*	1.4
23	Hy-Vee Inc—*Richard N Jurgens*	5820 Westown Pkwy, West Des Moines IA 50266	515-267-2800	R	7,300	60.0
24	Winn-Dixie Stores Inc—*Peter L Lynch*	5050 Edgewood Ct, Jacksonville FL 32254	904-783-5000	P	6,881	47.0
25	Ralphs Grocery Co—*Dave Hirz* Food Maxx	PO Box 54143, Los Angeles CA 90054	310-884-9000	S	6,403*	35.0
26	Circle K Corp—*Brian Hannasch*	PO Box 52085, Phoenix AZ 85072	602-728-8000	S	6,257*	36.0
27	Circle K Stores Inc—*Robert Lavinia*	PO Box 52085, Phoenix AZ 85072	602-728-8000	S	6,257*	36.0
28	Casey's General Stores Inc—*Robert J Myers*	PO Box 3001, Ankeny IA 50021	515-965-6100	P	5,635	2.3
29	Dillon Companies Inc—*Joseph Grieshaber Jr* Kroger Co	PO Box 1608, Hutchinson KS 67501		S	5,610*	47.3
30	Food 4 Less of Southern California Inc—*David B Dillon* Ralphs Grocery Co	PO Box 54143, Los Angeles CA 90054		S	5,500*	28.0
31	Giant Food Inc—*John Rishton*	8301 Professional Pl S, Landover MD 20785	301-341-4100	S	5,289*	35.0
32	United Supermarkets LLC—*Dan Sanders*	7830 Orlando Ave, Lubbock TX 79493	806-791-0220	R	5,220*	6.7
33	Vons Companies Inc—*Thomas Keller* Safeway Inc	618 Michillinda Ave, Arcadia CA 91007	626-821-7000	S	5,071	30.0
34	Trader Joe's Co—*Dan Bane*	PO Box 5049, Monrovia CA 91017	626-599-3700	R	5,000*	4.5
35	United Dairy Farmers Inc—*Brad Lindner*	3955 Montgomery Rd, Cincinnati OH 45212	513-396-8700	R	4,878*	3.0
36	Four B Corp—*David Ball*	5300 Speaker Rd, Kansas City KS 66106	913-321-4223	R	4,633*	4.0
37	Shaw's Supermarkets Inc SUPERVALU Inc	750 W Center St, West Bridgewater MA 02379		S	4,436*	30.0
38	Wawa Inc—*Howard Stoeckel*	260 W Baltimore Pike, Wawa PA 19063	610-358-8000	R	4,430*	16.0
39	Harris Teeter Inc—*Fred J Morganthall II* Ruddick Corp	PO Box 10100, Matthews NC 28106	704-844-3100	S	4,400*	24.5
40	Ruddick Corp—*Thomas W Dickson*	301 S Tryon St Ste 180, Charlotte NC 28282	704-372-5404	P	4,286	24.5
41	Pathmark Stores Inc—*John T Standley* Great Atlantic and Pacific Tea Company Inc	2 Paragon Dr, Montvale NJ 07645	732-499-3000	S	4,058*	26.0
42	Wegmans Food Markets Inc—*Danny Wegman*	PO Box 30844, Rochester NY 14603	585-328-2550	R	4,009*	35.0
43	Stater Brothers Markets—*Jack H Brown*	301 S Tippecanoe Ave, San Bernardino CA 92408	909-783-5000	S	3,983*	18.0
44	Ingles Markets Inc—*Robert P Ingle*	PO Box 6676, Asheville NC 28816	828-669-2941	P	3,560	19.6
45	Golub Corp—*Neil M Golub*	461 Nott St, Schenectady NY 12308	518-355-5000	R	3,300*	24.0
46	Giant Food Stores Inc—*Sander van der Laan* Ahold USA Inc	PO Box 249, Carlisle PA 17013	717-249-4000	S	3,200*	23.0
47	Raley's Inc—*Michael J Teel*	500 W Capitol Ave, West Sacramento CA 95605	916-373-3333	R	3,200	13.4
48	Better Val-U Supermarkets Inc—*Frank Bokoff*	657 Norwich Rd, Plainfield CT 06374		R	3,167*	.6
49	Save Mart Supermarkets—*Robert M Piccinini*	PO Box 4278, Modesto CA 95352	209-577-1600	R	2,914*	12.0
50	Martin's Super Markets Inc—*Robert Bartels Jr*	PO Box 2709, South Bend IN 46680	574-234-5848	R	2,883*	3.0
51	BI-LO Holdings LLC—*Michael Byars*	PO Box 99, Mauldin SC 29662	864-234-1600	R	2,722*	15.0

Note: An asterisk (*) indicates an estimated financial figure. The company type code used is as follows: R = Private, P = Public, S = Private Subsidiary, B = Public Subsidiary, D = Division, J = Joint Venture, I = Investment Fund.

COMPANY RANKINGS BY SALES WITHIN 4-DIGIT SIC

Rank	Company Name—Executive Officer	Address, City, State, Zip	Phone	Type	Fin	Empls
52	DeMoulas Super Markets Inc—Arthur S Demoulas	875 East St, Tewksbury MA 01876	978-851-8000	R	2,712*	15.5
53	WinCo Foods Inc—William D Long	PO Box 5756, Boise ID 83705	208-377-0110	R	2,681*	9.4
54	Dominick's Supermarkets Inc Safeway Inc	711 Jorie Blvd Ste 1, Oak Brook IL 60523	630-891-5000	S	2,658*	20.0
55	Weis Markets Inc—David J Hepfinger	PO Box 471, Sunbury PA 17801	570-286-4571	P	2,620	17.7
56	Randall's Food Markets Inc—Steven Burd Safeway Inc	3663 Briarpark Dr, Houston TX 77042	713-268-3500	S	2,585*	14.0
57	Cumberland Farms Inc—Ari Haseotes	100 Crossing Blvd, Framingham MA 01702	508-270-1400	R	2,571*	6.0
58	Schnuck Markets Inc—Scott Schnuck	PO Box 46928, St Louis MO 63146	314-994-4400	R	2,564*	16.0
59	Houchens Industries Inc—Jim Gipson	PO Box 90009, Bowling Green KY 42102	270-843-3252	R	2,500*	16.0
60	Shaw's Supermarkets Inc Northern Div—Paul Gannon Shaw's Supermarkets Inc	PO Box 600, East Bridgewater MA 02333		D	2,446*	3.1
61	Jay C Food Stores—James McCoy Kroger Co	PO Box 1004, Seymour IN 47274	812-522-1374	D	2,356*	2.0
62	Brookshire Grocery Co—Rick Rayford	PO Box 1411, Tyler TX 75701	903-534-3000	R	2,134*	12.7
63	Kum and Go LLC—Kyle Krause Krause Gentle Corp	6400 Westown Pkwy, West Des Moines IA 50266	515-226-0128	S	2,000*	4.0
64	King Soopers Inc—Russ Dispense Dillon Companies Inc	PO Box 5567, Denver CO 80217	303-778-3100	S	1,895*	14.5
65	K-Va-T Food Stores Inc—Steven C Smith	PO Box 1158, Abingdon VA 24212	276-628-5503	R	1,806*	12.0
66	Bruno's Supermarkets Inc—Dean Cohagen Ahold USA Inc	PO Box 2486, Birmingham AL 35201	205-916-5220	S	1,744*	14.5
67	Tops Markets Inc—Frank Curci	PO Box 1027, Buffalo NY 14240	716-635-5000	S	1,699*	13.0
68	Todd Holding Co—Mick Todd	2313 17th St, Greeley CO 80634	970-352-4980	R	1,616*	.3
69	Bashas' Inc—Eddie Basha Jr	22402 S Basha Rd, Chandler AZ 85248	480-895-9350	R	1,370*	10.5
70	Dahl's Foods Inc—David Sinnwell	4343 Merle Hay Rd, Des Moines IA 50310	515-276-4845	R	1,360*	1.5
71	Lauers Supermarket Inc—Ed Lauer	8095 Edwin Raynor Blvd, Pasadena MD 21122	410-255-0070	R	1,307*	.3
72	Village Super Market Inc—James Sumas	PO Box 7812, Edison NJ 08818	201-467-2200	P	1,299	5.7
73	Shopper's Food Warehouse Corp—Dick Bergman SUPERVALU Inc	4600 Forbes Blvd, Lanham MD 20706	301-306-8600	S	1,288*	7.0
74	Saker Shoprites Inc—Richard J Saker	922 Hwy 33 Bldg 6 Ste, Freehold NJ 07728	732-462-4700	R	1,260*	6.9
75	Big Y Foods Inc—Donald D'Armour	PO Box 7840, Springfield MA 01102	413-784-0600	R	1,252*	8.9
76	Holiday Companies Inc—Ronald A Erickson	PO Box 1224, Minneapolis MN 55440	952-830-8700	R	1,250*	6.0
77	Kash n' Karry Food Stores Inc—Shelly Broader Food Lion LLC	6422 Harney Rd, Tampa FL 33610	813-621-0200	S	1,240*	9.0
78	JB Sullivan Inc—John Sullivan	PO Box 387, Savanna IL 61074	815-273-4511	R	1,198*	1.4
79	Heinen's Inc—Jeff Heinen	4540 Richmond Rd, Bedford Heights OH 44128		R	1,179*	1.3
80	Quality Food Centers Inc	10116 NE 8th St, Bellevue WA 98004		S	1,110*	6.5
81	Brookshire Brothers Ltd—Jerry Johnson	PO Box 1688, Lufkin TX 75902	936-633-4774	R	1,100	5.6
82	Highland Park Market Inc—Timothy J Devanney	317 Highland St, Manchester CT 06040	860-646-4277	R	1,085*	.2
83	Genuardi's Family Markets LP Safeway Inc	301 E Germantown Pike, Norristown PA 19401	610-277-6000	D	1,062*	7.4
84	Marsh Supermarkets Inc—Frank Lazaran	333 S Franklin Rd, Indianapolis IN 46219	317-594-2100	R	1,054*	9.0
85	Lowe's Food Stores Inc—Dennis G Hatchell	PO Box 24968, Winston Salem NC 27114	336-659-0180	S	1,040*	8.0
86	Sweetbay Supermarket—Shelley Broader	3801 Sugar Palm Dr, Tampa FL 33619	813-620-1139	S	1,000*	10.0
87	Thorntons Inc—Matt Thornton	10101 Linn Station Rd, Louisville KY 40223		R	1,000*	2.5
88	Minyard Food Stores Inc—Ron McDearmon	PO Box 518, Coppell TX 75019	972-393-8700	R	918*	4.1
89	Save-A-Lot Ltd—Santiago Roces	100 Corporate Office D, Earth City MO 63045	314-592-9100	R	903*	5.0
90	Inserra Supermarkets Inc—Lawrence R Inserra	20 Ridge Rd, Mahwah NJ 07430	201-529-5900	R	901*	3.5
91	Penn Traffic Co—Gregory Young	1200 State Fair Blvd, Syracuse NY 13209	315-453-7284	P	872	6.2
92	Fareway Stores Inc—F William Beckwith	2300 E 8th St, Boone IA 50036	515-432-2623	R	842*	6.5
93	Leever's Foods Inc—Robert Leever	2195 N Hwy 83 Ste AA, Franktown CO 80116	701-662-8646	R	816*	.8
94	Newcomb Oil Co—Jack Newcomb	1360 E John Rowan Blvd, Bardstown KY 40004	502-348-3961	R	814*	.8
95	Stormans Inc—Ken Stormans	1932 E 4th Ave, Olympia WA 98506	360-754-2203	R	789	.2
96	Food Market Northwest Inc—Terry Halverson	4025 Delridge Way SW S, Seattle WA 98106	206-923-0740	R	768*	.8
97	Ream's Food Stores—Carl Willoby	160 E Claybourne Ave, Salt Lake City UT 84115	801-485-8451	R	737*	.8
98	King Kullen Grocery Company Inc—Bernard D Kennedy	185 Central Ave, Bethpage NY 11714	516-733-7100	R	736*	4.5
99	Piggly Wiggly Co—Richard Taggart	255 McGregor Plz, Platteville WI 53818	608-348-2345	R	687*	.8
100	Autry Greer and Sons Inc—Bartee Greer Jr	2850 W Main St, Mobile AL 36612	251-457-8655	R	678*	.7
101	Carrs/Safeway—Greg Sparks Safeway Inc	6401 A St, Anchorage AK 99518	907-561-1944	S	658*	3.5
102	Fiesta Mart Inc—Louis Katopodis	5235 Katy Fwy, Houston TX 77007	713-869-5060	R	640	5.9
103	Ukrop's Super Markets Inc—Robert S Ukrop	2001 Maywill St Ste 10, Richmond VA 23230	804-340-3004	R	619*	6.0
104	Haggen Inc—Jim Donald	PO Box 9704, Bellingham WA 98227	360-733-8720	R	616*	3.7
105	C and K Market Inc—Doug Nidfiffer	615 Fifth St, Brookings OR 97415	541-469-3113	R	616*	2.9
106	Redner's Markets Inc—Richard Redner	3 Quarry Rd, Reading PA 19605	610-926-3700	R	585*	3.8
107	Fitzgerald Food Store Inc—Bryan Devoe	710 Hopmeadow St, Simsbury CT 06070	860-658-2271	R	576*	.1
108	Fred Meyer Marketplace	3800 SE 22nd Ave, Portland OR 97202		S	520*	4.0
109	Gristede's Foods Inc—John A Catsimatidis	823 11th Ave, New York NY 10019	212-956-5803	S	514*	4.0
110	Piggly Wiggly Midwest—Paul Butera	PO Box 419, Sheboygan WI 53082	920-457-4433	R	502*	1.8
111	Coborn's Inc—Chris Coborn	1445 E Hwy 23 Bldg A, Saint Cloud MN 56304	320-252-4222	R	499*	4.6
112	Marvelous Market Inc—Lisa Bourven	505 Huntmar Park Dr St, Herndon VA 20170	703-964-5500	R	493*	.5
113	HP Nemenz Food Stores Inc—HP Nemenz	70 W Mckinley Way Ste, Youngstown OH 44514	330-757-8940	R	483*	.5
114	Camellia Food Stores Inc—Scott Beavers	1300 Diamond Springs R, Virginia Beach VA 23455	757-855-3371	R	470*	.8
115	City Market Inc Dillon Companies Inc	555 Sandhill Ln, Grand Junction CO 81505		S	462*	3.7
116	D and W Food Centers Inc—Doug Blease	3001 Orchard Vista Dr, Grand Rapids MI 49588	616-940-3580	R	455*	3.5
117	Yucaipa Cos—Ronald W Burkle	9130 W Sunset Blvd, Los Angeles CA 90069	310-789-7200	R	443*	3.3
118	Harp's Food Stores Inc—Roger Collins	918 S Gutensohn Rd, Springdale AR 72762	479-751-7601	R	440	3.2
119	Nugget Markets—Eric Stille	168 Court St, Woodland CA 95695		R	431*	.9
120	Arden Group Inc—Bernard Briskin	PO Box 2256, Los Angeles CA 90051	310-638-2842	P	417	2.1
121	Western Beef Inc—Peter Castellana Jr	47-05 Metropolitan Ave, Ridgewood NY 11385	718-417-3770	R	415*	2.5
122	Gelson's Markets—Bob Stiles Arden-Mayfair Inc	PO Box 1802, Encino CA 91426	818-906-5700	S	406*	2.3
123	Food Giant Super Markets Inc—Ron Watkins	120 Industrial Dr, Sikeston MO 63801	573-471-3500	R	398*	4.0
124	Norrenberns Foods Inc—Donald T Norrenberns	205 E Harnett St, Mascoutah IL 62258	618-566-7010	R	396*	.4
125	Hannaford Brothers Co—Ronald C Hodge	PO Box 1000, Portland ME 04104	207-883-2911	S	366*	26.0
126	Macey's Inc	7850 S 1300 East, Sandy UT 84094	801-255-4888	R	364*	2.0
127	Pay and Save Inc—Roger Lowe Jr	1804 Hall Ave, Littlefield TX 79339	806-385-3366	R	364*	2.0
128	Harmon City Inc—Dean Peterson	3540 S 4000 W Ste 500, Salt Lake City UT 84120	801-969-8261	R	362*	2.0

Rank	Company Name—Executive Officer	Address, City, State, Zip	Phone	Type	Fin	Empls
129	Roche Brothers Supermarkets—Ed Roche	70 Hastings St, Wellesley Hills MA 02481	781-235-9400	R	360*	3.0
130	Forks Prairie Mart Inc—Bert W Paul	PO Box 1429, Forks WA 98331	360-374-6161	R	340*	.1
131	Niemann Foods Inc—Richard H Niemann Jr	1501 N 12th St, Quincy IL 62301	217-221-5600	R	333*	3.0
132	Busch's Valu Land—John Busch	2240 S Main St, Ann Arbor MI 48103	734-998-2666	R	333*	.4
133	Baker's Supermarkets—Phillip Farmer Dillon Companies Inc	11126 Q St, Omaha NE 68137	402-397-4321	S	325*	1.8
134	UR West Linn Thriftway Inc	6433 SE Lake Rd, Portland OR 97222	503-833-1288	R	302*	.1
135	Village Pantries LLC—Dan Cross Marsh Supermarkets Inc	9800 Crosspoint Blvd, Indianapolis IN 46256	317-594-2100	S	292*	2.2
136	G and G Supermarket Inc—Lee Gong	1211 W College Ave, Santa Rosa CA 95401	707-546-6877	R	289*	.3
137	Schmuckal Oil Co—Paul Schmuckal	1516 Barlow St, Traverse City MI 49686	231-946-2800	R	285*	.3
138	Kwik-Way Inc—Theresa Jenkins	PO Box 20799, Billings MT 59104	406-656-6310	R	263*	.1
139	Acme Stores Inc—F Steven Albrecht	PO Box 1910, Akron OH 44309	330-733-2263	R	259*	2.0
140	Zallie Supermarkets Inc—Joseph Colalillo	PO Box 7812, Edison NJ 08818	856-627-6501	R	257*	1.9
141	Plaid Pantries Inc—WC Girard	10025 SW Allen Blvd, Beaverton OR 97005	503-646-4246	R	250*	1.0
142	Handy Andy Supermarkets—Terry Warren	1500 S Zarzamora St St, San Antonio TX 78207	210-227-8755	R	242*	2.5
143	Atlantic Food Mart Inc—AJ Rubin	30 Haven St, Reading MA 01867	781-944-0054	R	241*	.2
144	MWS Enterprises Inc—Mark Sidebottom	5701 Transit Rd, East Amherst NY 14051	716-689-0600	R	221*	.2
145	Quick Chek Food Stores Inc—Dean Durling	PO Box 600, Whitehouse Station NJ 08889	908-534-2200	R	216*	1.7
146	Dorignac's Food Center Inc—Tony Fasullo	710 Veterans Blvd, Metairie LA 70005	504-837-4650	R	206*	.3
147	G and R Felpausch Co—Mark Felpausch	127 S Michigan Ave, Hastings MI 49058	269-945-3485	R	206	1.9
148	D'Agostino Supermarkets Inc—Nicholas D'Agostino Jr	1385 Boston Post Rd, Larchmont NY 10538	914-833-4000	R	202*	1.1
149	Food Circus Super Markets Inc—Joseph Azzolina Sr	PO Box 278, Middletown NJ 07748	732-671-2220	R	200*	1.4
150	Valley Markets Inc—Doug Driscoll	1315 Columbia Rd S, Grand Forks ND 58201	701-772-7283	R	200*	.8
151	Jerry Lee's Grocery Inc—Mark Lee	1804 Ingalls Ave, Pascagoula MS 39567	228-762-5292	R	198*	.2
152	Bonnie Be-Lo Markets Inc—Ed Dery Camellia Food Stores Inc	1300 Diamond Springs R, Virginia Beach VA 23455	757-855-3371	S	187*	1.4
153	Par Mar Oil Co—Sandra Warner	114 Westview Ave Unit, Marietta OH 45750	740-373-1380	R	180*	.5
154	Nice N Easy Grocery Shoppes Inc—John Macdougall	7840 Oxbow Rd, Canastota NY 13032	315-697-2287	R	179*	.7
155	Berat Corp—George Zallie	1230 Blckwood Clmenton, Clementon NJ 08021	856-627-6501	R	179*	2.1
156	Convenience Retailers LLC—Mike Cruz	PO Box 3290, San Ramon CA 94583	925-884-0800	R	177*	2.3
157	Fast Fare Inc—Henry Rosenberg	PO Box 1168, Baltimore MD 21203	410-539-7400	R	176*	1.9
158	Arden-Mayfair Inc—Robert Stiles Arden Group Inc	PO Box 512256, Los Angeles CA 90051	310-638-2842	S	175*	2.2
159	Rosauers Supermarkets Inc—Jeffery Philipps	PO Box 9000, Spokane WA 99209	509-326-8900	R	170*	1.7
160	B and R Stores Inc—Pat Raybould	PO Box 5824, Lincoln NE 68505	402-464-6297	R	169*	2.2
161	Woodman's Food Market Inc—Phillip Woodman	2631 Liberty Ln, Janesville WI 53545	608-754-8382	R	169*	2.0
162	Danny and Clyde's Food Store Inc—Chris Rittiner	2301 N Hullen Ste 100, Metairie LA 70001	504-833-5438	R	167*	.2
163	CL Thomas Inc—Cliff Thomas	PO Box 1876, Victoria TX 77902	361-573-7662	R	163*	2.0
164	VG's Food Center Inc—Lisa Gilder	209 S Alloy Dr, Fenton MI 48430	810-629-1383	R	162*	2.0
165	Exit 76 Corp—Jerry Hop	2696 Chicago Dr Sw, Grand Rapids MI 49519	616-534-2181	R	161*	.5
166	Dash In Food Stores Inc—Mel Strine	PO Box 2310, La Plata MD 20646	301-932-3600	R	161*	.4
167	Town and Country Food Stores Inc—Alvin New	PO Box 9036, Corpus Christi TX 78469	325-655-0676	R	158*	2.0
168	Pro's Market Inc—Mike Provenzano	1700 S De Soto Pl Ste, Ontario CA 91761	909-930-9552	R	157*	1.6
169	Homeland Stores Inc—Daryl Fitzgeralds	2016 NW 39th St, Oklahoma City OK 73105	405-521-1890	R	155*	1.5
170	Foodmaster Super Markets Inc—John A DeJesus	100 Everett Ave Ste 12, Chelsea MA 02150	617-660-1300	R	148*	1.5
171	Fairplay Inc—Richard Goodrich	4640 S Halsted St, Chicago IL 60609	773-247-3077	R	147*	.8
172	I sf5 Cavalier Investmonto Inc Star Gatewood	PO Box 7467, Charlottesville VA 22906	434-979-1380	I	140*	.3
173	United Supermarkets of Oklahoma Inc—HD Snell	1520 N Main St, Altus OK 73521	580-482-7260	R	140*	1.1
174	Lees Supermarket—Albert Lees III	PO Box 3329, Westport MA 02790	508-636-3348	R	138*	.1
175	PDQ Food Stores Inc—Jerry Archer	PO Box 620997, Middleton WI 53562	608-836-3335	R	135*	.7
176	Sherm's Thunderbird Markets Inc—Sherman M Olsrud	PO Box 1400, Medford OR 97501	541-857-0850	R	128*	.6
177	Rice Epicurean Markets—Gary Friendlander	PO Box 159, Bellaire TX 77402	713-662-7700	R	127*	1.0
178	Gerland Corp—Kevin P Doris	3131 Pawnee, Houston TX 77054	713-746-3600	R	127*	.9
179	Andronico's Market—Bill Andronico	1109 Washington Ave, Albany CA 94706	510-559-2800	R	125*	1.0
180	Riesbeck Food Markets Inc—Richard L Riesbeck	48661 National Rd, Saint Clairsville OH 43950	740-695-7050	R	112*	1.3
181	Cressler's Marketplace—Norman Rich Weis Markets Inc	1075 W King St, Shippensburg PA 17257	717-532-2161	S	111*	.1
182	Draeger's Supermarkets Inc—James Draeger	291 Utah Ave, South San Francisco CA 94080	650-244-6500	R	106	.6
183	Stewart's Shops Corp—Gary Dake	PO Box 435, Saratoga Springs NY 12866	518-581-1200	R	105*	4.0
184	Treasure Island Foods Inc—Christ Kamberos	3460 N Broadway, Chicago IL 60657	773-327-4265	R	100	.8
185	Bristol Farms Inc—Kevin Davis Albertson's LLC	915 E 230th St Ste 100, Carson CA 90745	310-233-4700	S	88*	1.3
186	Pioneer Super Market—Leonard Franzblau	289 Columbus Ave, New York NY 10023	212-874-1882	R	87*	.1
187	Quillin's Inc—Phil Quillin	700 3rd St N Ste 105, La Crosse WI 54601	608-785-1424	R	85*	.7
188	Cub Foods—Keith Wyche SUPERVALU Inc	PO Box 9, Stillwater MN 55082	651-439-7200	S	85*	.2
189	Tidyman's LLC	PO Box 19186, Spokane WA 99219	509-928-7480	S	84*	1.1
190	Richland Market—GS Pallios	PO Box 156, Ceres CA 95307	209-538-3000	R	78*	.4
191	Mad Butcher Inc—Jerry Ward	629 Hwy 65 S, Dumas AR 71639	870-382-5161	R	72*	.4
192	D'Onofrio Inc—Joe D'Onofrio	1749 N Hermitage Rd, Hermitage PA 16148	724-962-9538	R	64*	.1
193	Remke Markets Inc—William Remke	1299 Cox Ave, Erlanger KY 41018	859-594-3400	R	62*	.8
194	PCC Natural Markets—Tracy Wolpert	4201 Roosevelt Way NE, Seattle WA 98105	206-547-1222	R	62*	.7
195	HG Hill Realty Group LLC—James W Granberry	3011 Armory Dr Ste 130, Nashville TN 37204	615-252-8100	R	62*	.3
196	Dean and DeLuca Inc—Mark Daley	4115 E Harry, Wichita KS 67218	316-821-3200	R	60	.8
197	Moo and Oink Inc—Barry Levy	7158 S Stony Island Av, Chicago IL 60649	773-420-2000	R	58	.3
198	Dierbergs Markets Inc—Greg Dierberg	PO Box 1070, Chesterfield MO 63017	636-532-8884	R	57*	.5
199	American Frozen Foods Inc—William Rappoport	155 Hill St Ste 4, Milford CT 06460	203-378-7900	R	56*	.7
200	Hegedorns Inc—B Hegedorn	964 Ridge Rd, Webster NY 14580		R	56*	.2
201	Western Supermarkets Inc—Ken Hubbard	2614 19th St S, Birmingham AL 35209	205-879-3471	R	54*	.4
202	Lil' Thrift Food Marts Inc—Chris Neal	1007 Arsenal Ave, Fayetteville NC 28305	910-433-4490	R	54*	.3
203	Haleiwa Supermarket Ltd—Roy Sakai	62-595 Kamehameha Hwy, Haleiwa HI 96712	808-637-5004	R	52*	.1
204	Lunardi's Super Market Inc	432 N Canal St Unit 22, South San Francisco CA 94080	650-588-7507	R	50*	.4
205	Sunshine Inc—Lisa Colonna	1492 Hwy 315, Wilkes Barre PA 18702	570-829-1392	R	50	.2
206	Oleson's Food Stores	PO Box 72, Traverse City MI 49685	231-947-6510	R	50*	.2
207	Quik Stop Markets Inc—Ron Stewart Dillon Companies Inc	4567 Enterprise St, Fremont CA 94538	510-657-8500	S	47*	.1
208	Dan Incorporated Oregon—Craig T Danielson	PO Box 2200, Oregon City OR 97045	503-655-9141	R	47*	<.1
209	Wesselmans Div—George Brandt	5011 Washington Ave St, Evansville IN 47715	812-479-0993	D	46*	.4
210	Angeli's Central Market—Alfred Angeli	PO Box 312, Iron River MI 49935	906-265-5107	R	45*	.4

Note: An asterisk (*) indicates an estimated financial figure. The company type code used is as follows: R = Private, P = Public, S = Private Subsidiary, B = Public Subsidiary, D = Division, J = Joint Venture, I = Investment Fund.

COMPANY RANKINGS BY SALES WITHIN 4-DIGIT SIC

Rank	Company Name—*Executive Officer*	Address, City, State, Zip	Phone	Type	Fin	Empls
211	Deweese Enterprises Inc—*Doug Deweese*	PO Box 5338, Meridian MS 39302	601-483-8291	R	45*	.3
212	Hy LaBonne and Son Inc—*Robert LaBonne Jr*	PO Box 448, Woodbury CT 06798	203-263-1940	R	45*	.3
213	Kroger Co Atlanta Div—*Bruce Lucia* Kroger Co	2175 Park Lake Dr, Atlanta GA 30345	770-496-7400	D	45*	.3
214	Calhoun Enterprises Inc—*Gregory B Calhoun*	4155 Lomac St Ste G, Montgomery AL 36106	334-272-4400	R	43*	.4
215	Rainwater Gas and Oil Company Inc—*Rick Rainwater*	PO Box 430, Florence SC 29501	843-662-1525	R	42*	.2
216	Sure Save Supermarket Ltd	16-586 Old Volcano Rd, Keaau HI 96749	808-966-9009	R	40*	.4
217	Thruway Food Market and Shopping Center	78 Oak St, Walden NY 12586	845-778-3535	R	39*	.4
218	Bill Martin's Cee Bee Food Stores—*WL Martin Jr*	1105 Fatherling St, Nashville TN 37206	615-228-8971	R	37*	.2
219	Wills Group Inc—*Lock Wills Jr*	6355 Crain Hwy, LaPlata MD 20646	301-932-3600	R	36*	.3
220	Grand Food Center—*Christopher Barber*	606 Green Bay Rd, Winnetka IL 60093	847-446-6707	R	35*	.1
221	Hyde Park Cooperative Society Inc—*Claudia Fegan*	1526 E 55th St, Chicago IL 60615	773-667-1444	R	34*	.3
222	American Consumers Inc—*Paul Cook*	PO Box 2328, Fort Oglethorpe GA 30742	706-861-3347	P	33	.2
223	Consun Food Industries Inc—*Dennis Walter*	123 N Gateway Blvd, Elyria OH 44035	440-322-6301	R	30*	.2
224	Wallace and Owens Store Inc	PO Box 55, Alton MO 65606	417-778-6155	S	30*	.3
225	Mary Lawrence Corp—*Larry Rothwell*	25 Rte 31 S Ste X, Pennington NJ 08534	609-737-0058	R	30*	.2
226	Cooke's Food Stores Inc—*Dan S Cooke*	3400 Keith St, Cleveland TN 37312	423-479-8208	R	28*	.2
227	Quik Mart Inc—*J Wes Little*	8351 E Broadway Blvd, Tucson AZ 85710	520-298-8929	R	27*	.2
228	Hi Nabor Supermarket Inc—*Sam Crifasi*	7201 Winbourne Ave, Baton Rouge LA 70805	225-357-1448	R	26*	.3
229	O'Neil's Markets Inc (St Louis Missouri)—*Dave O'Neil*	248 S Florissant Rd, Ferguson MO 63135	314-972-1114	R	26*	.2
230	Ralph's Foods—*Tim Forth*	501 N Carol Malone Blv, Grayson KY 41143	606-474-5522	S	26*	.1
231	New Seasons Market—*Mark Feuenborn*	1954 SE Division St, Portland OR 97202	503-292-1987	R	25*	.9
232	Grace Foods Inc—*Lowell A Peters*	PO Box 1114 B, Indianapolis IN 46206	317-780-5070	R	25*	.4
233	Grocery Outlets—*Bob Tiernan*	2000 5th St, Berkeley CA 94710	510-845-1999	R	25*	.3
234	Straub's Markets—*Jack Straub Jr*	8282 Forsyth Blvd, Clayton MO 63105	314-725-2121	R	25*	.2
235	Bruceton Farm Service Inc—*Marshall Bishop*	1768 Mileground Rd, Morgantown WV 26505	304-291-6980	R	25*	.4
236	Pinny Food Center and HWI Hardware—*Martin V Hornacek*	PO Box 597, Pinconning MI 48650	989-879-3313	R	22*	.2
237	FT Reynolds Company Inc—*John K Reynolds*	1014 W Bell St, Glendive MT 59330	406-377-2174	R	22*	.1
238	Jack Young Super Market Inc—*Kenneth Young*	3513 W Walnut Ave, Visalia CA 93277	559-625-0135	R	20*	.3
239	Vicente Foods Inc—*Michael Adams*	12027 San Vicente Blvd, Los Angeles CA 90049	310-472-5215	R	20*	.1
240	Tatsuda's IGA—*Bill Tatsuda Jr*	633 Stedman St, Ketchikan AK 99901	907-225-4125	R	20*	<.1
241	Tom's Food Markets Inc—*Dan Deering*	1201 S Division St, Traverse City MI 49684	231-946-4115	R	19*	.5
242	IGA Martins and Frozen Food Centers Inc—*L Newlin Martin*	101 S Merchant St, Effingham IL 62401	217-347-7191	R	19*	.2
243	FJ Mahar Service Store Inc—*Francis J Mahar Jr*	112 N 13th St, Olean NY 14760	716-372-6928	R	19*	.2
244	B and B Corporate Holdings Inc—*J Andrew Bever*	927 S US Hwy 301, Tampa FL 33619	813-621-6411	R	19*	.2
245	Byerly's Foods Of Illinois Inc—*Dale Riley*	4100 W 50th St Ste 100, Minneapolis MN 55424	952-831-3601	R	19*	.4
246	Abel's Quik Shops—*Mark M Abel*	PO Box 532, Louisiana MO 63353	573-754-5595	R	18*	.2
247	Hillcrest Foods Inc—*Chris Barkyoumb*	104 Huntville Rd, Fairfax VT 05454	802-849-6586	R	18*	.1
248	Bethel Food Market Inc—*Anthony Caraluzzi Jr*	98 Greenwood Ave, Bethel CT 06801	203-748-3547	R	17*	.1
249	Shavers Inc—*Dennis Shaver*	705 S 8th St, Boise ID 83702	208-344-2553	R	16*	.2
250	Eikenberrys Super Value Inc—*Niles Eikenberry*	1120 Sweitzer St, Greenville OH 45331	937-548-9214	R	15*	.2
251	Corti Brothers Market—*Darrell Corti*	PO Box 191358, Sacramento CA 95819	916-736-3800	R	14*	.1
252	Burns Enterprises Inc—*Tommy Burns Jr*	1631 W Hill St, Louisville KY 40210	502-585-4548	R	14*	<.1
253	Capri Foods Inc—*Randy Kamman*	224 E Harris, Greenville IL 62246	618-664-0022	R	13*	.1
254	Claiborne's Thriftway Supermarket—*Jess Claiborne*	710 N 4th St, Lamesa TX 79331	806-872-7011	R	12*	.1
255	Rozier Mercantile Co—*James Lottes*	PO Box 150, Perryville MO 63775	573-547-6521	R	12*	.1
256	Ferri Supermarkets Inc—*John Ferri*	3913 Old William Penn, Murrysville PA 15668	724-327-0822	R	11*	.1
257	Guaranteed Foods Inc	7700 Wedd St, Overland Park KS 66204	913-888-5000	R	10*	<.1
258	V Richard's Market Inc—*John Nehring*	17165a W Bluemound Rd, Brookfield WI 53005	262-784-8300	R	9*	.1
259	Baines Management Corp—*Henry T Baines Sr*	200 S Arlington Ave St, Baltimore MD 21223	410-783-8180	R	9*	.1
260	Anchor Gasoline Corp—*Betty Mockley*	114 E 5th St, Tulsa OK 74103	918-584-5291	R	9*	.1
261	El Burrito Market Inc—*Mary Silva*	175 Cesar Chavez St St, Saint Paul MN 55107	651-227-2192	R	8*	.1
262	Morasch Meats Inc—*Michael Morasch*	PO Box 30028, Portland OR 97294	503-257-9821	R	8*	.1
263	Kwik Shop Inc—*Jeff Parker* Dillon Companies Inc	PO Box 1927, Hutchinson KS 67504	620-669-8504	S	8*	.1
264	Ulbrich's IGA Super Market—*Barbara Ulbrich*	PO Box 1494, Piqua OH 45356	937-773-4073	R	8*	<.1
265	Kilroy's Wonder Market Inc—*Janis Kilroy*	288 Rock Rd, Glen Rock NJ 07452	201-444-5151	R	7*	.1
266	City Market Burleson Tx—*Curt Jaeger*	PO Box 70, Burleson TX 76097	817-295-1051	R	7*	.1
267	Son's Supermarket Inc—*Jimmy Lee*	400 9th Ave N, Jasper AL 35501	205-384-6066	R	7*	<.1
268	Real Good Food Store Inc—*Jim Dixon*	833 SE Main, Portland OR 97214	503-222-5658	R	6*	.1
269	Springboro IGA Inc—*Homer L Preston*	15 N Main St, Springboro OH 45066	937-748-2867	R	6*	.1
270	Johnny's Super Market Inc—*John Loeffelman*	11555 Gravois Rd, Saint Louis MO 63126	314-843-5760	R	6*	.1
271	Bruno Specialty Foods Inc—*Louis D'agrosa*	208 Cherry Ave, West Sayville NY 11796	631-589-1700	R	4*	<.1
272	Rines Market Inc—*James Rines*	15500 Sw Trl Dr, Indiantown FL 34956	772-597-3535	R	4*	<.1
273	Mentor Family Foods—*Bob Campbell*	7294 Lakeshore Blvd, Mentor OH 44060	440-946-3788	R	4*	<.1
274	Barrick Enterprises—*Robert Barrick*	4307 Delemere Ct, Royal Oak MI 48073	248-549-3737	R	4*	<.1
275	Harold W Pelton Co—*Sandra Keel*	418 S Town St, Fostoria OH 44830		R	4*	<.1
276	Kai Paalaa Market Inc—*Roy Sakai*	PO Box 519, Waialua HI 96791	808-637-9795	R	4*	<.1
277	Juan Don Foods Inc—*Arturo Bautista*	PO Box 580449, Modesto CA 95358	209-538-0817	R	3*	<.1
278	Bales for Food Inc—*Robin Thomas*	12675 NW Cornell Rd, Portland OR 97229	503-646-9635	R	3*	.1
279	Churchill's Super Markets Inc—*Lynn Colwell*	2845 W Central Ave, Toledo OH 43606	419-473-1461	R	3*	<.1
280	Foodtown International Inc—*Frank Jaber*	PO Box 532, Edison NJ 08818	732-287-2400	R	3*	<.1
281	Kelly's Super Market—*David Kelly*	PO Box 27, Torrington WY 82240	307-532-3113	R	3*	<.1
282	Burke's Bakery and Delicatessen Inc—*Joe Burke*	121 W Main St, Danville KY 40422	859-236-5661	R	3*	<.1
283	Anderson's Grocery A Family Tradition Inc—*Kari Beedle*	711 S Clark Ave, Republic WA 99166	509-775-3378	R	3*	<.1
284	Weikel Enterprises Inc—*James Weikel*	2247 W State Hwy 71, La Grange TX 78945	979-968-9413	R	3*	<.1
285	Bodies Dairy Markets Company Inc—*Al Patel*	208 N Bedford St, Georgetown DE 19947	302-856-7014	R	2*	<.1
286	Winegars Supermarkets Inc—*Don Matthews*	3371 S Orchard Dr, Bountiful UT 84010	801-292-0178	R	2*	<.1
287	Mangia Pasta LLC—*David Bermeister*	3145 S Grand Blvd, Saint Louis MO 63118	314-664-8585	R	2*	<.1
288	Sophie's Choice Inc—*Chris Zebrowski*	4617 Turney Rd, Cleveland OH 44125	216-341-5910	R	2*	<.1
289	Brandon Meats and Sausage Inc—*Alan Feucht*	PO Box 382, Brandon WI 53919	920-346-2227	R	1*	<.1
290	Albertsons LLC—*Robert Miller* SUPERVALU Inc	250 Parkcenter Blvd, Boise ID 83706	208-395-6200	S	1	1.0
291	Food Emporium—*Cheryl Palmer* Great Atlantic and Pacific Tea Company Inc	42 W 39th St 18th Fl, New York NY 10018	212-915-2202	S	N/A	6.5
292	Krause Gentle Corp—*Kyle Krause*	6400 Westown Pkwy, West Des Moines IA 50266	515-226-0128	R	N/A	3.6
293	Winn-Dixie Louisiana Inc—*Joey Medina* Winn-Dixie Stores Inc	3925 Hwy 190 W Ste 9, Hammond LA 70401	985-549-6700	S	N/A	.1

TOTALS: SIC 5411 Grocery Stores
Companies: 293   670,990   2,894.1

Rank	Company Name—*Executive Officer*	Address, City, State, Zip	Phone	Type	Fin	Empls
5421 Meat & Fish Markets						
1	French Market Foods Of Louisiana LLC	3935 Ryan St, Lake Charles LA 70605	337-477-5499	R	25*	.1
2	Ham Honeybaked Co—*Craig Kurz*	11935 Mason Montgomery, Cincinnati OH 45249	513-583-9700	R	15*	.4
3	Tony's Seafood Ltd—*Bill Pizzolato*	5215 Plank Rd, Baton Rouge LA 70805	225-357-9669	R	8*	.2
4	Merkley and Sons Inc—*James Merkley*	3994 W 180n, Jasper IN 47546	812-482-7020	R	6*	<.1
5	Laudermilch Meats Inc—*Lee Laudermilch*	PO Box 154, Annville PA 17003	717-867-1251	R	6*	.1
6	Miesfeld's Triangle Market Inc—*Charles Miesfeld*	4811 Venture Dr, Sheboygan WI 53083	920-565-6328	R	5*	<.1
7	J W Treuth and Sons Inc—*Vernon Treuth*	PO Box 3288, Baltimore MD 21228	410-465-4650	R	5*	<.1
8	Patti Joe Seafood Co—*Frank Patti*	PO Box 12567, Pensacola FL 32591	850-432-3315	R	4*	.1
9	Lee Williams Meats Inc—*Barry Williams*	3002 131st St, Toledo OH 43611	419-729-3893	R	4*	<.1
10	Groff Meats Inc—*John Groff*	33 N Market St, Elizabethtown PA 17022	717-367-1246	R	4*	<.1
11	High Summit Distribution Inc—*Ken Pocress*	PO Box 17513, Denver CO 80217	303-252-9491	R	3*	<.1
12	Dewig Brothers Packing Company Inc—*Thomas Dewig*	PO Box 186, Haubstadt IN 47639	812-768-6208	R	3*	<.1
13	Marshallville Packing Company Inc—*Frank Tucker*	PO Box 276, Marshallville OH 44645	330-855-2871	R	3*	<.1
14	Quality Meat Inc—*David Schoenemann*	205 W Hwy 21, Caldwell TX 77836	979-567-3511	R	3*	<.1
15	Weber Processing Plant Inc—*Norman Weber*	725 N Jackson St, Cuba City WI 53807	608-744-2159	R	2*	<.1
16	Maplewood Packing Inc—*Roger Hemelryk*	4663 Milltown Rd, Green Bay WI 54313	920-865-7901	R	2*	<.1
17	Kasper's Meat Market Inc—*Maurice Kasper*	119 E Post Office St, Weimar TX 78962	979-725-8227	R	2*	<.1
18	Bringhurst Brothers Inc—*Ralph Bringhurst*	38 W Taunton Rd, Berlin NJ 08009	856-767-0110	R	2*	<.1
19	Rosa Brothers Inc—*Jamie Rosa*	1100 Nw 22nd St, Miami FL 33127	305-324-1510	R	2*	<.1
20	Manley Meats Inc—*Roger Manley*	302 S 400 E, Decatur IN 46733	260-592-7313	R	2*	<.1
21	Boone's Abattoir Inc—*Luel Gboone*	100 Old Bloomfield Pke, Bardstown KY 40004	502-348-3668	R	2*	<.1
22	Buddy's Seafood Inc—*Buddy Daisy*	120 N Hollywood Rd, Houma LA 70364	985-872-6472	R	1*	<.1
23	Bernthal Packing Inc—*Herbert Bernthal*	9378 Junction Rd, Frankenmuth MI 48734	989-652-2648	R	1*	<.1
24	Portier Fine Foods Inc—*Sean Portier*	436 Waverly Ave, Mamaroneck NY 10543	914-698-7700	R	1*	<.1
25	Bichelmeyer Meats A Corp—*James Bichelmeyer*	704 Cheyenne Ave, Kansas City KS 66105	913-342-5945	R	1*	<.1
26	Josephson's Smokehouse and Dock—*Michael Josephson*	106 Marine Dr, Astoria OR 97103	503-325-2190	R	1*	<.1
27	Duma's Meats Inc—*Dave Duma*	PO Box 54, Mogadore OH 44260	330-628-3438	R	1*	<.1
TOTALS: SIC 5421 Meat & Fish Markets						
	Companies: 27				115	1.4
5431 Fruit & Vegetable Markets						
1	Norman Brothers Produce—*David Nelson*	7621 SW 87th Ave, Miami FL 33173	305-274-9363	R	46*	.1
2	J-M Foods Inc—*Terry Jurgensmeyer*	6995 S Hwy 69 A, Miami OK 74354	918-540-2437	R	1*	<.1
3	Northville Cider Mill Inc—*Diane Jones*	714 Baseline Rd, Northville MI 48167	248-349-3181	R	<1*	.1
TOTALS: SIC 5431 Fruit & Vegetable Markets						
	Companies: 3				48	.2
5441 Candy, Nut & Confectionery Stores						
1	Sweet Factory Inc—*David Kim*	5900 Katella Ave Ste A, Cypress CA 90630	562-391-2410	R	80*	1.1
2	Gorant Chocolatier LLC—*Michael Handel*	PO Box 9068, Youngstown OH 44513	330-726-8821	R	76*	.6
3	Fannie May Confections Inc	8550 W Bryn Mawr Ave S, Chicago IL 60631	312-453-0010	S	13*	.3
4	Malley's Candies Inc—*William Malley*	1685 Victoria Ave, Lakewood OH 44107	216-325-5570	R	12*	.2
5	Koeze Co—*Jeffrey Koeze*	PO Box 9470, Grand Rapids MI 49509	616-724-2621	R	9*	<.1
6	James Candy Company Inc—*Frank Glaser*	1519 Boardwalk, Atlantic City NJ 08401	609-344-1519	R	8*	.1
7	Dylan's Candy Bar LLC—*Dylan Lauren*	1011 3rd Ave, New York NY 10065	646-735-0078	R	5*	.2
8	Van Rian Corp—*Sean Gilronan*	PO Box 10384, Portland OR 97296	503-227-1927	R	3*	.1
9	Boehm's Candies Inc—*Helen Shafer*	255 Ne Gilman Blvd, Issaquah WA 98027	425-392-6652	R	3*	.1
10	Hoffman Commercial Group Inc—*Fredrick Meltzer*	5190 Lake Worth Rd, Greenacres FL 33463	561-967-2213	R	3*	.1
11	Beerntsen's Confectionery Inc—*Dean Schadrie*	108 N 8th St, Manitowoc WI 54220	920-684-9616	R	2*	.1
12	Dinstuhl's Fine Candy Company Inc—*Rebecca Dinstuhl*	5280 Pleasant View Rd, Memphis TN 38134	901-377-2639	R	2*	<.1
13	Home Of The Hebert Candies Inc—*Ronald Hebert*	47 Sugar Rd, Bolton MA 01740	978-779-6586	R	2*	<.1
14	Candy Kitchen Shoppes Inc—*Bruce Leiner*	5301 Coastal Hwy, Ocean City MD 21842	410-524-6002	R	2*	<.1
15	Peterbrooke Chocolatier Inc—*Phyllis Lockwood*	2024 San Marco Blvd, Jacksonville FL 32207	904-398-2488	R	2*	<.1
16	Callie's Candy Kitchens Inc—*Gretchen Reisenwitz*	PO Box 126, Mountainhome PA 18342	570-595-2280	R	1*	<.1
17	Hubbard Peanut Company Inc—*Lynne Rabil*	PO Box 94, Sedley VA 23878	757-562-4081	R	1*	<.1
18	Dolle's Candyland Inc—*Rudolph Dolle*	PO Box 105, Ocean City MD 21843	410-289-6000	R	1*	<.1
19	Candy Express Franchising Inc—*Joel Rosenberg*	3320 Greencastle Rd, Burtonsville MD 20866	301-384-5889	R	1*	<.1
20	Melt Inc—*Clive Barwin*	31556 Loma Linda St, Temecula CA 92592	310-601-7907	P	1	<.1
21	Kris Kandy Inc—*Todd Davis*	1412 W 3rd Ave, Spokane WA 99201	509-624-1969	R	1*	<.1
22	Paul L Henry—*Paul Henry*	13237 Broadway St, Alden NY 14004	716-937-3400	R	<1*	<.1
23	Plantation Pecan and Gift Inc—*Harrison Miller*	503 Hwy 571, Waterproof LA 71375	318-749-5421	R	<1*	<.1
TOTALS: SIC 5441 Candy, Nut & Confectionery Stores						
	Companies: 23				229	3.0
5451 Dairy Products Stores						
1	Heritage's Dairy Stores Inc—*Jack Heritage*	376 Jessup Rd, Thorofare NJ 08086	856-845-2855	R	155*	.4
2	WH Braum Inc—*W Bostwick*	PO Box 25429, Oklahoma City OK 73125	405-478-1656	R	25*	.6
3	Royal Crest Dairy Inc—*Lynn Miller*	350 S Pearl St, Denver CO 80209	303-777-2227	R	21*	.5
4	Ritchey's Dairy—*Reid Ritchey*	2130 Cross Cove Rd, Martinsburg PA 16662	814-793-2157	R	8*	.1
5	Vella Cheese Company Of California Inc—*Ignazio Vella*	PO Box 191, Sonoma CA 95476	707-938-3232	R	1*	<.1
TOTALS: SIC 5451 Dairy Products Stores						
	Companies: 5				209	1.5
5461 Retail Bakeries						
1	Cinnabon Inc—*Kat Cole*	200 Glenridge Point Pk, Atlanta GA 30342	404-255-3250	S	155*	4.5
2	Abp Corp—*Susan Morelli*	1 Au Bon Pain Way Fl 2, Boston MA 02210	617-423-2100	R	77*	1.5
3	Crumbs Bake Shop—*Jason Bauer*	110 W 40th St Ste 2100, New York NY 10018		P	36*	.6
4	Felix's Caketeria—*Felix Papadakis*	5 W Washington Ave, Newtown PA 18940	215-860-2444	R	14*	<.1
5	Byrnes and Kiefer Company Inc—*Edward Byrnes*	131 Kline Ave, Callery PA 16024	724-538-5200	R	11*	<.1
6	Busken Bakery Inc—*D Busken*	2675 Madison Rd, Cincinnati OH 45208	513-871-5330	R	10*	.2
7	Just Desserts Inc—*Ira Haber*	550 85th Ave, Oakland CA 94621	510-567-2900	R	10*	.3
8	Tarheel Bagels Inc—*Nordahl Brue*	100 Dominion Dr Ste 10, Morrisville NC 27560	919-462-9470	R	10*	.3
9	La Gloria Foods Corp—*Maria De Luz Vera*	3455 E 1st St, Los Angeles CA 90063	323-262-0410	R	6*	.1
10	Chaves Bakery Ii Inc—*John Chaves*	1365 State St Ste 1, Bridgeport CT 06605	203-333-6254	R	5*	.1
11	BAB Operations Inc—*Michael W Evans*	500 Lake Cook RdSte475, Deerfield IL 60015		S	5*	<.1
12	Janie's Cookie Co—*Cindy Gade*	3365 36th St Se, Grand Rapids MI 49512	616-956-5603	R	4*	.1
13	Mozzicato Pastry and Bake Shop Inc—*Luigi Mozzicato*	329 Franklin Ave, Hartford CT 06114	860-296-0426	R	4*	<.1

Note: An asterisk (*) indicates an estimated financial figure. The company type code used is as follows: R = Private, P = Public, S = Private Subsidiary, B = Public Subsidiary, D = Division, J = Joint Venture, I = Investment Fund.

COMPANY RANKINGS BY SALES WITHIN 4-DIGIT SIC

Rank	Company Name—*Executive Officer*	Address, City, State, Zip	Phone	Type	Fin	Empls
14	Firehook Bakers Ltd—*Pierre Abushacra*	14701 Flint Lee Rd, Chantilly VA 20151	703-519-8020	R	4*	.1
15	Henri's Bakery Inc—*Madeline Leonard*	61 Irby Ave Nw, Atlanta GA 30305	404-237-0202	R	3*	<.1
16	Deising's Bakery and Pastry Shop Inc—*Eric Deising*	109 N Front St Ste 117, Kingston NY 12401	845-338-7503	R	3*	.1
17	Di Camillo Baking Company Inc—*David Camillo*	811 Linwood Ave, Niagara Falls NY 14305	716-282-2341	R	2*	.1
18	National Bakery Inc—*Anthony Vitaletti*	1100 Capouse Ave, Scranton PA 18509	570-343-1609	R	2*	<.1
19	Calandra Italian and French Bakery Inc—*Luciano Calandra*	204 1st Ave, Newark NJ 07107	973-484-5598	R	2*	.1
20	Strossner's Bakery Inc—*Richard Strossner*	21 Roper Mountain Rd, Greenville SC 29607	864-233-3996	R	2*	.1
21	A and M Donuts Inc—*Chris Swanson*	384 Tenney Mountain Hw, Plymouth NH 03264	603-536-7622	R	2*	.1
22	Dudley's Bakery Inc—*Melvin Ashley*	PO Box 67, Santa Ysabel CA 92070	760-765-0488	R	2*	<.1
23	Paddycake Bakery—*Patrick Connolly*	4763 Liberty Ave, Pittsburgh PA 15224	412-621-4477	R	2*	<.1
24	King Of Pita Bakery Inc—*Antoine Tahan*	6460c General Green Wa, Alexandria VA 22312	703-941-8999	R	2*	<.1
25	Gardner Baking Company Inc—*Wayne Kindig*	5555 N 7th St Ste 116, Phoenix AZ 85014	602-264-4874	R	2*	<.1
26	Scott's Bakeries Inc—*Vann Scott*	2916 18th St S, Birmingham AL 35209	205-871-4901	R	2*	<.1
27	Yamazaki California Inc—*Kazumasa Tsugita*	123 Jpanese Village Pl, Los Angeles CA 90012	213-624-2773	R	2*	<.1
28	Edgar's Old Style Bakery—*Terry Smith*	3439 Colonnade Pkwy, Birmingham AL 35243	205-968-0150	R	2*	<.1
29	Papas Bakery Inc—*George Papas*	6055 S Howell Ave, Milwaukee WI 53207	414-483-9003	R	2*	<.1
30	Rizen LLC—*Craig Foster*	14595 Southfield Rd, Allen Park MI 48101	313-388-3699	R	2*	<.1
31	Solvang Bakery—*Susan Halme*	460 Alisal Rd, Solvang CA 93463	805-688-4939	R	2*	<.1
32	Laufers Pastries Inc—*Richard Laufer*	1717 Ne Broadway St, Portland OR 97232	503-287-1251	R	2*	<.1
33	Lacascia's Bakery Inc—*Fred Moscaritolo*	418 Main St, Medford MA 02155	781-396-5041	R	2*	<.1
34	Braschler's Bakery Inc—*Robert Braschler*	410 W 3rd St, Red Wing MN 55066	651-388-1589	R	1*	.1
35	James J Tuzzi Jr—*James Tuzzi*	504 Washington St, Berwick PA 18603	570-752-2704	R	1*	<.1
36	Pacific Cookie Company Inc—*Lawrence Pearson*	303 Potrero St Ste 40, Santa Cruz CA 95060	831-429-9709	R	1*	<.1
37	Concord Teacakes Etcetera Inc—*Judy Fersch*	PO Box 1427, Concord MA 01742	978-369-2409	R	1*	<.1
38	New York Bagel Baking Co—*Harvey Goldsmith*	23316 Woodward Ave, Ferndale MI 48220	248-548-2580	R	1*	<.1
39	Achenbach's Pastry Inc—*John Burkeholder*	375 E Main St, Leola PA 17540	717-656-6671	R	1*	<.1
40	Leonard's Bakery Ltd—*Lennie Rego*	933 Kapahulu Ave, Honolulu HI 96816	808-737-5591	R	1*	<.1
41	CMT Ii Investments Inc—*Haridermos Papas*	4100 Pelham Rd, Greenville SC 29615	864-627-4300	R	1*	<.1
42	Los Bagels Inc—*Dennis Rael*	1061 I St Ste 101, Arcata CA 95521	707-822-3150	R	1*	<.1
43	Daubes Bakery Inc—*Cynthia Daube*	1310 5th Pl Nw, Rochester MN 55901	507-289-3095	R	1*	<.1
44	Tulsa Baking Inc—*Larry Merritt*	3202 E 15th St, Tulsa OK 74104	918-747-2301	R	1*	<.1
45	Italian Bakery Inc—*Joseph Prebonich*	205 1st St S, Virginia MN 55792	218-741-3464	R	1*	<.1
46	BM M Inc—*Charles Bauer*	1222 S Park Ctr, Strongsville OH 44136	440-572-9722	R	1*	<.1
47	Almira's Bakery—*Frank Vantil*	2635 169th St, Hammond IN 46323	219-844-4334	R	1*	<.1
48	Bagels and Blenderz—*Lang Chhan*	8200 Stockdale Hwy Ste, Bakersfield CA 93311	661-833-6644	R	1*	<.1
49	Kretchmar Bakery Inc—*Henry Kretchmar*	664 3rd St, Beaver PA 15009	724-774-2324	R	1*	<.1
50	Tag's Bakery Inc—*Gregory Vetter*	2010 Central St, Evanston IL 60201	847-328-1200	R	1*	<.1
51	Larsen Bakery Inc—*Donald Hutshinson*	3311 Washington Ave, Racine WI 53405	262-633-4298	R	1*	<.1
52	Weinrich Bakery—*Edward Weinrich*	55 Easton Rd, Willow Grove PA 19090	215-659-7062	R	1*	<.1
53	Snowhite Bakery—*Sandy Davis*	155 Sayles Blvd, Abilene TX 79605	325-677-5981	R	1*	<.1
54	George Dolan—*George Dolan*	706 Brookline Blvd, Pittsburgh PA 15226	412-531-5322	R	1*	<.1
55	Ann's Bakery Inc—*Sharon Pollock*	7 N Harvard Ave, Tulsa OK 74115	918-834-2345	R	1*	<.1
56	Elite Sweets Inc—*Dan Miller*	33471 8 Mile Rd, Livonia MI 48152	248-476-3600	R	1*	<.1
57	Fishers' Bakery Of Ellicott City—*Chris Sikora*	8143 Main St, Ellicott City MD 21043	410-461-9275	R	<1*	<.1

TOTALS: SIC 5461 Retail Bakeries
Companies: 57   412   9.4

5499 Miscellaneous Food Stores

Rank	Company Name—*Executive Officer*	Address, City, State, Zip	Phone	Type	Fin	Empls
1	7-Eleven Inc—*Joseph M DePinto*	PO Box 711, Dallas TX 75221	972-828-7011	S	62,700	400.0
2	Pantry Inc—*Edward J Holman*	305 Gregson Dr, Cary NC 27511	919-774-6700	P	8,139	13.9
3	DS Waters of America Inc—*Stewart E Allen*	5660 New Northside Dr, Atlanta GA 30328	770-933-1400	R	5,539*	4.5
4	General Nutrition Centers Inc—*Joseph Fortunato*	300 6th Ave Ste 2, Pittsburgh PA 15222	412-288-4600	S	1,822*	13.1
5	GNC Holdings Inc—*Joseph Fortunato*	300 6th Ave, Pittsburgh PA 15222		P	1,822	13.1
6	Fresh Market Inc—*Craig Carlock*	628 Green Valley Rd St, Greensboro NC 27408	336-272-1338	P	974*	7.3
7	Diedrich Coffee Inc—*J Russell Phillips*	28 Executive Pk Ste 20, Irvine CA 92614	949-260-1600	S	62	.2
8	Agostino Passanante Brothers—*AJ Passanante*	PO Box 604, Bristol PA 19007		R	48*	<.1
9	Natural Grocers by Vitamin Cottage Inc	12612 Alameda Pkwy, Lakewood CO 80228	303-986-4600	R	35*	.2
10	Belmont Springs Water Company Inc DS Waters of America Inc	36 Country Club Ln, Belmont MA 02478	617-489-4752	S	32*	.2
11	Green Beans Coffee Company Inc—*Jason Araghi*	900 Larkspur Landing C, Larkspur CA 94939	415-461-4023	R	27*	.4
12	The Fresh Diet—*Zalmi Duchman*	9429 Harding Ave Ste 3, Surfside FL 33154		R	18	.2
13	Willow Tree Poultry Farm Inc—*Chester Cekala*	997 S Main St, Attleboro MA 02703	508-222-2479	R	15*	.1
14	Tadin Inc—*Jose Gonzalez*	PO Box 2968, Huntington Park CA 90255	323-728-5100	R	14*	.1
15	Bucks County Coffee Co—*Rodger Owen*	2250 W Cabot Blvd, Langhorne PA 19047	215-741-1855	R	13*	.4
16	Standard Process Inc—*Charles Du Bois*	PO Box 904, Palmyra WI 53156	262-495-2122	R	10*	.2
17	DS Waters of America LP	1761 Newport Rd, Ephrata PA 17522	717-859-6500	R	7*	.1
18	Hickory Farms Inc—*Mark Rodriguez*	PO Box 219, Maumee OH 43537	419-893-7611	R	6*	.1
19	Coffee Beanery Ltd—*Joanne Shaw*	3429 Pierson Pl, Flushing MI 48433	810-733-1020	R	4*	.1
20	P and S Ravioli Co—*Secondo Digiacomo*	2001 S 26th St, Philadelphia PA 19145	215-465-7744	R	2*	<.1
21	Amante Marketing Corp—*Philip Russo*	2770 29th St Se, Grand Rapids MI 49512	616-942-2980	R	1*	<.1
22	HealthE Goods—*Benjamin Lynch*	1708 Kentucky St, Bellingham WA 98229	360-306-8749	R	1*	<.1
23	Advanced Nutrient Science LLC	10540 72nd St Ste 603, Largo FL 33777	727-547-5222	R	1*	<.1

TOTALS: SIC 5499 Miscellaneous Food Stores
Companies: 23   81,291   454.2

5511 New & Used Car Dealers

Rank	Company Name—*Executive Officer*	Address, City, State, Zip	Phone	Type	Fin	Empls
1	AutoNation Inc—*Mike Jackson*	200 SW 1st Ave Ste 160, Fort Lauderdale FL 33301		P	12,461	19.0
2	Penske Automotive Group Inc—*Roger S Penske*	2555 Telegraph Rd, Bloomfield Hills MI 48302	248-648-2500	P	10,714	14.8
3	Ricart Chrysler Plymouth—*Fred Ricart*	4255 S Hamilton Rd, Groveport OH 43125	614-836-5321	R	9,600*	.8
4	CarMax Inc—*Thomas J Folliard*	12800 Tuckahoe Creek P, Richmond VA 23238	804-747-0422	P	8,976	15.6
5	Sonic Automotive Inc—*O Bruton Smith*	6415 Idlewild Rd, Charlotte NC 28212	704-566-2400	P	7,871	9.2
6	Automotive Investment Group Inc (Phoenix Arizona)	PO Box 16460, Phoenix AZ 85011	602-264-2332	P	7,349*	127.6
7	Group 1 Automotive Inc—*Earl J Hesterberg*	800 Gessner Ste 500, Houston TX 77024	713-647-5700	P	6,080	8.3
8	VT Inc—*Larry Van Tuyl*	Po Box 795, Mission KS 66201	913-432-6400	R	4,300*	6.0
9	Asbury Automotive Group Inc—*Craig T Monaghan*	2905 Premiere Pkwy Ste, Duluth GA 30097	770-418-8200	P	4,277	6.8
10	Hendrick Automotive Group—*Rick Hendrick*	6000 Monroe Rd Ste 100, Charlotte NC 28212	704-568-5550	R	3,711*	5.0
11	Kinsel Ford Inc—*Joe B Kinsel Jr* Kinsel Motors Inc	PO Box 2470, Beaumont TX 77704	409-899-4000	S	3,340*	.1
12	Lithia Motors Inc—*Sidney B DeBoer*	360 E Jackson St, Medford OR 97501		P	2,699	4.4
13	Larry H Miller Group—*Larry H Miller*	9350 S 150 E Ste 1000, Sandy UT 84070	801-563-4100	R	2,550*	6.0

Rank	Company Name—*Executive Officer*	Address, City, State, Zip	Phone	Type	Fin	Empls
14	Holman Enterprises—*Malinda K Holman*	573 Rt 38W, Maple Shade NJ 08052	856-235-8902	R	2,043*	2.6
15	Phil Long Automotive Group Inc—*Jay Cimino*	1212 Motor City Dr, Colorado Springs CO 80906		R	1,772*	3.5
16	Major Automotive Group Inc—*Bruce Bendell*	43-40 Northern Blvd, Long Island City NY 11101	718-937-3700	S	1,299*	.5
17	Compass Dodge Inc Major Automotive of New Jersey Inc	200 Central Ave, Orange NJ 07050	973-676-3000	S	1,249*	.5
18	Compass Lincoln-Mercury Inc—*Bruce Bendell* Major Automotive of New Jersey Inc	200 Central Ave, Orange NJ 07050	973-676-3000	S	1,249*	.5
19	Major Chevrolet Inc	43-40 Northern Blvd, Long Island City NY 11101	718-937-3700	S	1,249*	.5
20	Major Chrysler Jeep Dodge of Long Island City Inc—*Bruce Bendell*	4601 Northern Blvd, Long Island City NY 11101	718-786-2100	S	1,249*	.5
21	Major Kia Inc	55-19 Northern Blvd, Woodside NY 11377	718-777-1800	S	1,249*	.5
22	Major Orange Properties LLC Major Automotive Companies Inc	43-40 Northern Blvd, Long Island City NY 11101	718-937-3700	S	1,249*	.5
23	Hempstead Mazda Inc—*Bruce Bendell* Major Automotive Companies Inc	179 N Franklin St, Hempstead NY 11550	516-486-1200	S	1,248*	.5
24	Serra Automotive Inc—*Joseph O Serra*	3118 E Hill Rd, Grand Blanc MI 48439	810-694-1720	R	1,232*	1.5
25	Jim Koons Management Co—*James E Koons*	2000 Chain Bridge Rd, Vienna VA 22182	703-356-0400	R	1,135*	1.4
26	Allen Samuels Auto Group—*Jeff A Wooley*	301 Owen Ln, Waco TX 76710	254-761-6800	R	984*	1.2
27	Galpin Motors Inc—*Bert Boeckmann*	15505 Roscoe Blvd, North Hills CA 91343	818-787-3800	R	956*	1.2
28	Ed Morse Automotive Group—*Edward Morse*	6363 NW 6th Way Ste 40, Fort Lauderdale FL 33309	954-351-0055	R	938*	2.0
29	Tuttle-Click Automotive Group of Dealerships—*James Click*	38 Auto Center Dr, Irvine CA 92618	949-472-7400	R	931*	2.1
30	Coggin Automotive Corp—*Luther Coggin*	11003 Atlantic Blvd, Jacksonville FL 32225	904-565-8800	R	905*	2.0
31	Jeff Wyler Dealer Group—*Jeff Wyler*	829 Eastgate S Dr, Cincinnati OH 45245	513-752-7450	R	882*	1.0
32	Lou Fusz Automotive Network Inc—*Lou Fusz Jr*	925 N Lindbergh Blvd, Saint Louis MO 63141	314-994-1500	R	818*	1.1
33	Herb Chambers Cos—*Herbert G Chambers*	259 McGrath Hwy, Somerville MA 02143	617-666-8333	R	800*	1.0
34	Nalley Automotive Group—*CV Nalley III* Asbury Automotive Group Inc	87 W Paces Ferry Rd, Atlanta GA 30305	404-261-3130	S	794*	1.7
35	Courtesy Acura Isuzu—*Terry Dixon*	7590 S Broadway, Littleton CO 80122	303-795-7800	R	791*	1.1
36	Russ Darrow Group Inc—*Phil Harrington*	W 133 N 8569 Executive, Menomonee Falls WI 53051	262-250-9600	R	769*	.8
37	Sheehy Auto Stores—*Vincent Sheehy*	2950 Crain Hwy, Waldorf MD 20601	703-802-3480	R	716*	1.2
38	Flow Automotive Cos—*Don Flow*	1425 Plaza Dr, Winston Salem NC 27103	336-760-7030	R	698*	.9
39	Prestige Automotive Group—*Gregory Jackson*	20200 E Nine Mile Rd, St Clair Shores MI 48080	586-773-2369	R	656*	.3
40	Rosenthal Automotive Group—*Don Bavely*	1100 Glebe Rd, Arlington VA 22201	703-553-4300	R	644*	1.6
41	Cutter Management Co—*Nick Cutter*	1100 Alakea St PH 2, Honolulu HI 96813	808-529-2000	R	638*	.9
42	George R Norris Inc—*Bill Vowels*	901 Merritt Blvd, Dundalk MD 21222	410-285-0200	R	596*	2.0
43	Sam Swope Automotive Group Inc—*Richard Swope*	Swope Auto Center Dr, Louisville KY 40299	502-499-4600	R	588*	.7
44	Scott-McRae Automotive Group—*David C Hodges*	701 Riverside Park Pl, Jacksonville FL 32204	904-354-4000	R	573*	.9
45	Fletcher Jones Management Group—*Fletcher Jones Jr*	7300 W Sahara Ave, Las Vegas NV 89117	702-364-2700	R	567*	.8
46	Planet Ford—*Shawn Burns*	20403 Interstate 45 N, Spring TX 77388		R	562*	.7
47	Richardson and Partners—*Dennis Snyder*	8601 Lomas Blvd NE, Albuquerque NM 87112	505-292-0000	R	548*	.6
48	Earnhardt Ford Sales Co—*Hal Earnhardt*	777 E Baseline Rd, Tempe AZ 85283	480-813-9009	S	540*	1.5
49	Ourisman Chevrolet Company Inc—*Mandell J Ourisman*	4400 Branch Ave, Marlow Heights MD 20748	301-423-4000	R	522*	1.0
50	Spitzer Management Inc—*Alan Spitzer*	150 E Bridge St, Elyria OH 44035	440-323-4671	R	500*	1.0
51	Braman Management Association—*Norman Braman*	2060 Biscayne Blvd 2nd, Miami FL 33137	305-576-1889	R	500*	.8
52	Lupient Automotive Group—*James Lupient*	7100 Wayzata Blvd, Golden Valley MN 55426	763-546-2222	R	494*	1.0
53	Ancira Enterprises Inc—*Ernesto Ancira Jr*	PO Box 29719, San Antonio TX 78229	210-681-4900	R	490*	.6
54	Sanderson Ford Inc—*David Kimmerle*	6400 N 51st Ave, Glendale AZ 85301	623-842-8600	R	440*	.5
55	Curry Corp (Scarsdale New York)—*Bernard F Curry III*	728 Central Ave, Scarsdale NY 10583		R	439*	.5
56	Ed Voyles Honda—*Valery Boyles-Singleton*	2103 Cobb Pky, Marietta GA 30067	770-951-2211	R	432*	.6
57	Toresco Enterprises Inc—*Donald Toresco*	170 Rte 22 E, Springfield NJ 07081	973-467-2900	R	432*	.6
58	Elder Automotive Group—*Irma Elder*	777 John R Rd, Troy MI 48083	248-585-4000	R	417*	.2
59	Major Automotive Companies Inc—*Bruce Bendell*	43-40 Northern Blvd, Long Island City NY 11101	718-937-3700	R	397	.5
60	Charlie Thomas Ford Ltd—*Bob Zweig* AutoNation Inc	12227 Gulf Fwy, Houston TX 77034	713-371-4300	S	396*	.5
61	America's Car-Mart Inc—*William H Henderson*	802 SE Plz Ave Ste 200, Bentonville AR 72712	479-464-9944	P	379	1.0
62	New Country Motor Car Group Inc—*Michael Cantanucci*	358 Broadway, Saratoga Springs NY 12866	518-584-7700	R	366*	.6
63	Chapman Chevrolet Isuzu—*John Chapman*	1717 E Baseline Rd, Tempe AZ 85283	480-752-1525	R	353*	.4
64	Bommarito Automotive Group—*Frank Bommarito*	15736 Manchester Rd, Ellisville MO 63011	636-391-7200	R	352*	.4
65	S Woods Enterprises Inc—*Sanford L Woods*	PO Box 76037, Tampa FL 33675	813-620-4300	R	345*	.4
66	Gunn Chevrolet Inc—*Curtis C Gunn* Curtis C Gunn Inc	12602 IH-35 N, San Antonio TX 78233	210-599-5000	S	329*	.7
67	Ancira Winton Chevrolet Inc—*Ernesto Ancira Jr* Ancira Enterprises Inc	6111 Bandera Rd, San Antonio TX 78238	210-681-4900	S	329*	.3
68	Reedman Toll Auto World—*Bruce Toll*	1700 E Lincoln Hwy, Langhorne PA 19047	215-757-4961	R	328*	.5
69	Burt Automotive Network—*Angelo Chavez*	5200 S Broadway, Englewood CO 80113	303-761-0333	R	323*	1.2
70	Geo Byers and Sons Inc—*George Byers*	PO Box 16513, Columbus OH 43216	614-228-5111	R	314*	.6
71	Ron Tonkin Chevrolet Co—*Ron Tonkin*	203 NE 122nd Ave, Portland OR 97230	503-255-4100	R	313*	.9
72	Curtis C Gunn Inc—*Curtis C Gunn*	227 Broadway St, San Antonio TX 78205	210-472-2501	R	300*	.9
73	Arrow Truck Sales Inc—*Ed Justis*	3200 Manchester Traffi, Kansas City MO 64129	816-923-5000	R	300*	.3
74	Porter Auto Group—*Cory Porter*	414 E Cleveland Ave, Newark DE 19711	302-453-6800	R	298*	.4
75	Heiser Automobile Dealership Inc—*Steve Sadek*	1700 W Silver Spring D, Milwaukee WI 53209	414-355-7401	R	293*	.4
76	Plaza Motors Co—*Rick Steinberg* Asbury Automotive Group Inc	11830 Olive Blvd, Creve Coeur MO 63141	314-301-1718	S	290*	.3
77	Drew Ford/Hyundai/Volkswagon—*Bill Drew*	8850 Grossmont Bouleva, La Mesa CA 91942	619-464-7777	R	286*	.4
78	Johnson Automotive Group Inc—*David Johnson*	5839 Capital Blvd, Raleigh NC 27616	919-877-1800	R	283*	.4
79	LuJack Auto Plaza—*Tom Pospisil*	3700 N Harrison St, Davenport IA 52806	563-386-1511	R	281*	.4
80	Guaranty Chevrolet-Pontiac-Oldsmobile—*Shannon Nill*	PO Box 279, Junction City OR 97448		R	278*	.5
81	Ferman Automotive Group—*James L Ferman Jr*	1306 W Kennedy Blvd, Tampa FL 33606	813-251-2765	R	273*	.6
82	Martin Automotive Group Inc—*Chadwick A Martin*	1065 Ashley St Ste 100, Bowling Green KY 42103	270-783-8080	R	269*	.5
83	CarsDirectcom Inc	909 Sepulveda Blvd 11t, El Segundo CA 90245		S	266*	.3
84	Barrier Motors Inc—*Jimmy Barrier*	11950 Bellevue Redmond, Bellevue WA 98005	425-455-8535	R	265*	.3
85	Damerow Beaverton Ford—*Dan Mkaiser*	12325 SW Canyon Rd, Beaverton OR 97005	503-644-1131	R	265*	.3
86	Ted Britt Ford—*Gardner Britt*	11165 Fairfax Blvd, Fairfax VA 22030	703-591-8484	R	264*	.3
87	Napleton Auto Group—*Bill Napleton*	200 N Northwest Hwy, Park Ridge IL 60068	847-825-1800	R	258*	.3
88	Pacifico Group—*Kerry Pacifico*	6701 Essington Ave, Philadelphia PA 19153	215-492-1700	R	254*	.2
89	Jim Keras Chevrolet Memphis—*Penelli Keras*	2000 Covington Pike, Memphis TN 38128	901-387-2000	R	247*	.3
90	Capitol Auto Group—*Scott Casebeer*	2711 Mission St SE, Salem OR 97302		R	244*	.3
91	Folsom Lake Ford—*Chuck Peterson*	12755 Folsom Blvd, Folsom CA 95630	916-353-2000	R	243*	.3
92	Holmes Tuttle Ford Inc—*James H Click*	660 W Auto Mall Dr, Tucson AZ 85705		R	242*	.3
93	Roundtree Automotive Group LLC—*Frank Stinson*	910 Pierremont Rd Ste, Shreveport LA 71106	318-798-6500	R	234*	.5

Note: An asterisk (*) indicates an estimated financial figure. The company type code used is as follows: R = Private, P = Public, S = Private Subsidiary, B = Public Subsidiary, D = Division, J = Joint Venture, I = Investment Fund.

RANKINGS BY SALES WITHIN 4-DIGIT SIC

Rank	Company Name—Executive Officer	Address, City, State, Zip	Phone	Type	Fin	Empls
94	Joe Myers Ford Inc—Bill Tennant	16634 Northwest Fwy, Houston TX 77040	713-482-5060	R	233*	.5
95	O'Brien Auto Park—Gary Matern	3801 W Wabash Ave, Springfield IL 62711		R	232	.5
96	Berge Ford Inc—Craig Berge	PO Box 4008, Mesa AZ 85211	480-497-1111	R	232*	.3
97	David McDavid Honda of Irving—David McDavid Jr	3700 W Airport Fwy, Irving TX 75062		S	228*	.4
	Asbury Automotive Group Inc					
98	Capistrano Toyota—Marc J Spizzirri	33395 Camino Capistran, San Juan Capistrano CA 92675	949-493-4100	R	227*	.3
99	Beechmont Investments Inc—William Woeste Jr	PO Box 54366, Cincinnati OH 45254	513-388-3700	R	226*	.3
100	Shamrock Chevrolet Geo Inc—Tommy Stallings	PO Box 65210, Lubbock TX 79464	806-747-3211	R	223*	.3
101	Herson's Inc	15525 Frederick Rd, Rockville MD 20855	301-279-8600	R	221*	.3
102	King Auto Mall—Clay King	700 E Sunrise Blvd, Fort Lauderdale FL 33304	954-764-2122	R	220*	.3
103	Lithia Of Sioux Falls	4200 W 12th St, Sioux Falls SD 57107	605-336-1700	S	218*	.3
104	Norm Reeves Honda Superstore Inc—Brad Mugg	18500 Studebaker Rd, Cerritos CA 90703		R	212*	.3
105	Dorschel Automotive Group—Rick Dorschel	3817 W Henrietta Rd, Rochester NY 14623	585-334-9440	R	211*	.5
106	North Park Lincoln-Mercury—Clarence Kahlig	9207 San Pedro Ave, San Antonio TX 78216	210-341-8841	R	207*	.2
107	Wendle Motors Inc—Chud Wendle	9000 N Division St, Spokane WA 99218	509-991-2852	R	204*	.3
108	Camp Chevrolet—Scott Hushen	101 E Montgomery Ave, Spokane WA 99207	509-456-7890	S	203*	.3
	Lithia Motors Inc					
109	Jim Click Ford Inc—Jim Click	6244 E 22nd St, Tucson AZ 85711		R	203*	.3
110	McDonald Automotive Group—Doug McDonald	6040 S Broadway, Littleton CO 80121	303-795-1100	R	203*	.3
111	John Sullivan Dealerships—John Sullivan	700 Automall Dr, Roseville CA 95661	916-782-1243	R	202*	.3
112	Mercedes-Benz of Pompano—RA Kirland	350 W Copans Rd, Pompano Beach FL 33064	954-943-5000	R	201*	.3
113	Darlings—Jay Darling	96 Pky S, Brewer ME 04412	207-941-1240	R	194*	.3
114	Ricart Automotive—Rhett C Ricart	PO Box 27130, Columbus OH 43227	614-836-5321	R	189*	.3
115	Midway Ford Truck Center Inc—Donald C Ahnger	PO Box 12656, Kansas City MO 64116	816-455-3000	R	189*	.2
116	Jerry Seiner Chevrolet—Jerry Seiner	1530 S 500 W, Salt Lake City UT 84115	801-952-5700	R	187*	.4
117	Mac Haik Ford Inc—Mac Haik	10333 Katy Fwy, Houston TX 77024	713-932-5000	R	186*	.4
118	Martin Cadillac Company Inc—Tim Tate	12101 W Olympic Blvd, Los Angeles CA 90064	310-622-9334	R	186*	.3
119	Miller Auto Company Inc—Joe Cicotte	13 Labombard Rd, Lebanon NH 03766	603-448-3500	R	186*	.3
120	Valley Dodge Inc (Van Nuys California)	6110 Van Nuys Blvd, Van Nuys CA 91401	818-787-0900	R	186*	.3
121	Yark Automotive Group—Jim Yark	6019 W Central Ave, Toledo OH 43615	419-842-7900	R	180*	.3
122	Maita Automotive Group—Vincent Maita	2500 Auburn Blvd, Sacramento CA 95821	916-473-7890	R	180*	.2
123	Jack Ingram Motors Inc—C Ingram	PO Box 240309, Montgomery AL 36124	334-277-5700	R	180*	.2
124	Hyatt Automotive LLC—Buddy Hyatt	1887 Hwy 501, Myrtle Beach SC 29577	843-626-3657	R	180*	.1
125	Blackwell Baldwin Chevrolet Geo Oldsmobile Cadillac Inc—Harry Blackwell	621 S Westwood Blvd, Poplar Bluff MO 63901	573-785-0893	R	180*	.1
126	Fred Beans Holdings Inc—Fred W Beans	835 N Easton Rd, Doylestown PA 18902	215-348-2901	R	179*	.5
127	Friendly Ford—Edward J Olliges	660 N Decatur Blvd, Las Vegas NV 89107	702-870-7221	R	179*	.4
128	Town and Country Ford Inc—O Bruton Smith	5401 E Independence Bl, Charlotte NC 28212		S	176*	.2
129	Hubler Chevrolet Inc—Howard Hubler	8220 US 31 S, Indianapolis IN 46227	317-882-4389	R	176*	.2
130	John L Sullivan Chevrolet—John L Sullivan	350 Automall Dr, Roseville CA 95661	916-782-1243	D	176*	.2
	John Sullivan Dealerships					
131	Performance Chevrolet—John McMichael	4811 Madison Ave, Sacramento CA 95841	916-331-6777	R	176*	.2
132	Schaumburg Toyota Inc—Chris Haley	875 W Golf Rd, Schaumburg IL 60194	847-882-1800	R	176*	.2
133	Schlossman's Honda City—Robert L Schlossmann	3450 S 108th St, Milwaukee WI 53227	414-320-3500	R	176*	.2
134	Scott Robinson Honda—Jeff Robinson	20340 Hawthorne Blvd, Torrance CA 90503	310-371-3521	R	176*	.2
135	Neely Coble Company Inc—Neely Coble III	319 Fesslers Ln, Nashville TN 37210	615-244-8900	R	175*	.2
136	Reeves Import Motorcars Inc—Vivian Reeves	11333 N Florida Ave, Tampa FL 33612	813-933-2811	R	175*	.2
137	Pulliam Motor Co—Bob Pulliam	PO Box 908, Columbia SC 29202	803-254-4000	R	174*	.3
138	Courtesy Chevrolet (Phoenix Arizona)—William Gruwell	PO Box 7709, Phoenix AZ 85011	602-274-8000	R	172*	.4
139	Apple Ford (Lynchburg Virginia)—Nancy Huften	2113 Lakeside Dr, Lynchburg VA 24501	434-385-5012	R	170	.3
140	Russell Chevrolet-Geo-Honda Inc—Bob Russell	6100 Landers Rd, Sherwood AR 72117	501-835-8300	R	167*	.2
141	Al Piemonte Ford Sales Inc—Alex Piemonte	2500 W N Ave, Melrose Park IL 60160	708-345-9300	R	166*	.1
142	Lanphere Enterprises Inc—Bob Lanphere Jr	10760 SW Canyon Rd, Beaverton OR 97005	503-643-5577	R	166*	.6
143	Frank Kent Motor Co—Will Churchill	3535 W Loop 820 S, Fort Worth TX 76116	817-244-9600	R	163*	.4
144	Lujack's Northpark Auto Plaza—Tom Pospisil	3700 N Harrison St, Davenport IA 52806	563-386-1511	S	163*	.4
	LuJack Auto Plaza					
145	Warnock Automotive Group Inc—Tim Ryan	175 State Rte 10, East Hanover NJ 07936	973-884-2100	R	163*	.2
146	Holler Chevrolet—Elmer Shifflett	1970 State Rd 436, Winter Park FL 32792	407-645-1234	R	162*	.2
147	Bud Clary Chevrolet Oldsmobile Subaru Jeep Eagle Inc—James Clary	PO Box 127, Longview WA 98632	360-423-2130	R	162*	.2
148	Mac Haik Chevrolet Inc—Mac Haik	11711 Katy Fwy, Houston TX 77079	281-509-9085	R	161*	.2
149	32 Ford Mercury Inc—Vauni Blaut	610 W Main St, Batavia OH 45103		R	161*	.1
150	Jim Click Inc—Christopher Cotter	780 W Competition Rd, Tucson AZ 85705	520-884-4100	R	161*	.8
151	Superior Automotive Group—Mike McGinley	8300 Shawnee Mission P, Merriam KS 66202	913-384-1550	R	159*	.2
152	ADESA Birmingham Inc—Tom Caruso	804 Sollie Dr, Moody AL 35004	205-640-1010	S	158*	.3
153	Frank Parra Autoplex—George Davey	1000 E Airport Fwy, Irving TX 75062	972-721-4300	R	154*	.3
154	Marc Miller Pontiac GMC Inc—Marc Miller	4700 S Memorial Dr, Tulsa OK 74145	918-663-4700	R	153*	.2
155	Miller Automotive Group Inc—Michael Miller	5425 Van Nuys Blvd, Sherman Oaks CA 91401	818-787-8400	R	151*	.7
156	Capital Ford Inc—Tim Michael	4900 Capital Blvd, Raleigh NC 27616	919-790-4600	R	151*	.3
157	Seidle Enterprises Inc—William Seidle	2900 Nw 36th St, Miami FL 33142	305-635-8000	R	150*	.3
158	Austin Mac Haik Ford Lincoln Mercury Ltd—Ralph Werchan	PO Box 710, Georgetown TX 78627	512-930-3673	R	150*	.2
159	Toyota Of Melbourne—Kevin Brodsky	24 N Harbor City Blvd, Melbourne FL 32935	321-254-8888	R	150*	.2
160	Maroone Chevrolet Inc—Mike Jackson	PO Box 848480, Pembroke Pines FL 33084		S	149*	.5
	AutoNation Inc					
161	Sunrise Chevrolet—Dan Kurtz	414 E North Ave, Glendale Heights IL 60139		R	149*	.2
162	Bob Moore Auto Group LLC—Michael Womble	101 N Robinson Ave Ste, Oklahoma City OK 73102	405-605-2350	R	149*	.8
163	United Ford LLC	PO Box 470210, Tulsa OK 74147	918-280-6500	S	148*	.3
	Penske Automotive Group Inc					
164	Champion Toyota of Corpus Christi	6672 S Padre Island Dr, Corpus Christi TX 78412		S	147*	.2
	AutoNation Inc					
165	Mercedes-Benz of Houston Greenway—Jeff Quisenberry	3900 Southwest Fwy, Houston TX 77027	713-986-6400	S	147*	.2
	AutoNation Inc					
166	Niello Co—Rick Niello	1481 River Park Dr, Sacramento CA 95815	916-643-7300	R	147*	.2
167	Briarwood Ford Inc—Eddie L Hall Jr	7070 E Michigan Ave, Saline MI 48176	734-429-5478	R	147*	.2
168	Green Chevrolet Hummer Inc—Mark Tondi	8017 N Knoxville Ave, Peoria IL 61615		R	146*	.2
169	Wilde Of West Allis Inc—Justin Parish	3225 S 108th St, Milwaukee WI 53227	414-545-8010	R	145*	.2
170	Linhart Corp—Ted Linhart	12050 W Broad St, Richmond VA 23233	804-451-1488	R	145*	.2
171	Jim Burke Automotive—JJ Burke Jr	1409 5th Ave N, Birmingham AL 35203	205-324-3371	R	145*	.2
172	Carr Chevrolet Inc—Wally Preble	15005 Tualatin Valley, Beaverton OR 97006	503-520-4101	R	144*	.3
173	Bobby Murray Chevrolet Inc—Bobby L Murray Jr	1820 Capital Blvd, Raleigh NC 27604		R	144*	.2

Rank	Company Name—Executive Officer	Address, City, State, Zip	Phone	Type	Fin	Empls
174	Beck and Masten Pontiac-Gmc Inc—James Masten	11300 Fm 1960 Rd W, Houston TX 77065	281-469-5222	R	143*	.1
175	Jardine Hawaii Motor Holdings Ltd—Fletcher Jones	818 Kapiloni Blvd, Honolulu HI 96813	808-592-5600	R	142*	.1
176	Broadway Ford and Jeep	PO Box 11567, Green Bay WI 54307		R	142*	.2
177	Al Serra Chevrolet Inc—Joe Serra	6167 S Saginaw St, Grand Blanc MI 48439	810-694-5440	R	141*	.3
178	Paul Miller Ford-Mazda Inc—John Paul Miller	981 Beasley St, Lexington KY 40509	606-255-4242	R	141*	.2
179	Future Ford Inc	650 Auto Mall Dr, Roseville CA 95661	916-786-3673	R	140*	.4
180	Huffines Chevrolet Company Inc—Ray Huffines	PO Box 338, Lewisville TX 75067	972-221-8686	R	140*	.3
181	Bruckner Truck Sales Inc—Ben Bruckner Jr	9471 I 40 E, Amarillo TX 79118	806-235-8194	R	139*	.2
182	McRee Ford Inc—William Dale	2800 Gulf Fwy, Dickinson TX 77539	281-337-1529	R	139*	.2
183	Bill Currie Ford—Bill Currie	5815 N Dale Mabry Hwy, Tampa FL 33614	813-872-5555	R	136*	.3
184	Meade Group Inc—Gary Brinin	PO Box 189010, Utica MI 48318	586-726-7900	R	136*	.3
185	Keeler Motor Car Co—Alexander Keeler	1111 Troy-Schenectady, Latham NY 12110	518-785-4197	R	136*	.2
186	Mercedes-Benz of Buckhead—Gregory T Baranco	2799 Piedmont Rd, Atlanta GA 30305		R	135*	.2
187	Gerry Lane Enterprises Inc—Gerald L Lane	6505 Florida Blvd, Baton Rouge LA 70806	225-926-4600	R	134*	.3
188	BMW Center—Jack Guenther	8434 Airport Blvd, San Antonio TX 78216	210-732-7121	R	134*	.2
189	Kuni Enterprises Inc—Greg Goodwin	10999 SW Canyon Rd, Beaverton OR 97005	503-643-1543	R	133*	.4
190	Mercedes-Benz of Ft Pierce—Terry Robinson Coggin Automotive Corp	4500 S US Hwy 1, Fort Pierce FL 34982		S	133*	.2
191	Courtesy Chevrolet (San Jose California)—John Anderson	3640 Stevens Creek Blv, San Jose CA 95117	408-533-8484	R	132*	.2
192	Holmes Automotive—Max H Holmes	11344 Hickman Rd, Des Moines IA 50325	515-253-3000	R	130*	.2
193	Tamaroff Buick Honda Isuzu—Marvin M Tamaroff	28585 Telegraph Rd, Southfield MI 48034	248-353-1300	R	130*	.2
194	WW Wallwork Inc—Alex Newson	900 35th St NW, Fargo ND 58102	701-476-7000	R	129*	.3
195	Don Rasmussen Co—Greg Rasmussen	1605 SW Naito Pky, Portland OR 97201	503-228-8351	R	129*	.2
196	Sons Acura	7060 Jonesboro Rd, Morrow GA 30260		R	128*	.3
197	Rickenbaugh Cadillac/Volvo—Mary Pacifico-Valley	777 Broadway, Denver CO 80203	303-573-7773	R	128*	.1
198	Mike Shaw Automotive—Mike Shaw	1080 S Colorado Blvd, Denver CO 80246	303-757-6161	R	126*	.4
199	Hoselton Chevrolet Inc—Drew Hoselton	909 Fairport Rd, East Rochester NY 14445	585-586-7373	R	126*	.3
200	Village Ford Inc—Jim Seavitt	23535 Michigan Ave, Dearborn MI 48124	313-565-3900	R	126*	.2
201	Walker Ford Company Inc—Frank A Walker	17556 Us Hwy 19 N, Clearwater FL 33764	727-535-3673	R	126*	.2
202	Ewald Automotive Group Inc—Craig Ewald	36883 E Wisconsin Ave, Oconomowoc WI 53066	262-569-6500	R	124*	.4
203	Glockner Chevrolet Company Inc—Andrew M Glockner	2867 US 23 N, Portsmouth OH 45662	740-354-3255	R	124*	.3
204	Baierl Chevrolet Inc—Jeff Pepper	10430 Perry Hwy, Wexford PA 15090	724-935-3711	R	124*	.3
205	Reliable Chevrolet Inc (Springfield Missouri)	3655 S Campbell St, Springfield MO 65807	417-887-5800	R	123*	.2
206	Joe Basil Chevrolet Inc—Joe Basil	5111 Transit Rd, Depew NY 14043	716-683-6800	R	123*	.2
207	Southern States Buick Dodge Mazda	2511 Wake Forest Rd, Raleigh NC 27609	919-839-7481	R	123*	.2
208	Woody Anderson Ford Inc—Cathy Anderson	PO Box 11400, Huntsville AL 35814	256-539-9441	R	123*	.2
209	Connell Chevrolet—Wayne Doddridge	2828 Harbor Blvd, Costa Mesa CA 92628	714-546-1200	R	123*	.2
210	Wolfchase Toyota—Jeff Field Penske Automotive Group Inc	2201 N Germantown Pky, Cordova TN 38016	901-377-8000	S	123*	.2
211	Town East Ford Sales Inc—Mike Ward	18411 LBJ Frwy, Mesquite TX 75150	972-270-6441	R	122*	.2
212	Bale Chevrolet Geo Co—John H Bale Jr	13101 Chenal Pkwy, Little Rock AR 72211	501-859-6262	R	122*	.2
213	Fuller Ford Inc—Doug G Fuller	560 Auto Park Dr, Chula Vista CA 91911		R	122*	.2
214	Atzenhoffer Chevrolet Company Inc—Milton S Greeson Jr	PO Box 2509, Victoria TX 77902	361-578-0181	R	121*	.2
215	Lexus Santa Monica Inc	1501 Santa Monica Blvd, Santa Monica CA 90404	310-453-9900	R	121*	.2
216	Schumacher European Ltd—Werner Schumacher	18530 N Scottsdale Rd, Phoenix AZ 85054		R	120*	.2
217	House of Imports Inc—Pat Lustig AutoNation Inc	6862 Auto Center Dr, Buena Park CA 90621	714-562-1100	S	119*	.2
218	Denny Menholt Frontier Chevrolet Inc	3000 King Ave W, Billings MT 59102		R	119*	.2
219	Smythe European Inc—Mark Akbar AutoNation Inc	4500 Stevens Creek Blv, San Jose CA 95129	408-983-5200	S	118*	.3
220	Burt Toyota Inc—Lloyd Chavez Jr	5460 S Broadway, Englewood CO 80113	303-761-3222	R	117*	.3
221	Don Davis Auto Group—Robert Howard	PO Box 1587, Arlington TX 76004	817-461-1000	R	117*	.3
222	Allen Samuels Chevrolet Inc—Bryan Johnson Allen Samuels Auto Group	7000 SW Fwy, Houston TX 77074	713-272-3600	S	117*	.1
223	Sheehy Ford Inc—Vincent Sheehy IV	10601 Midlothian Tpk, Richmond VA 23235	804-794-0500	R	116*	.2
224	Bob Johnson Auto Group—David Foringer	1271 Ridge Rd W, Rochester NY 14615	585-663-4040	R	116	.2
225	Bill Perkins Automotive Group—Mark Montante	13801 S Telegraph Rd, Taylor MI 48180	734-250-6220	R	115*	.1
226	Crown Ford Inc—Charlie Coats	646 Thompson Ln, Nashville TN 37204	615-244-3615	R	115*	.1
227	Don Allen Automotive Group—David Voelker	5315 Baum Blvd, Pittsburgh PA 15224	412-681-4800	R	114*	.1
228	San Francisco Ford Lincoln Mercury—Teddy Stephens	1595 Van Ness Ave, San Francisco CA 94109	415-861-6000	R	114*	.1
229	Brown Automotive Group Inc—Robert Brown	5625 W Central Ave, Toledo OH 43615	419-531-0151	R	113*	.1
230	Pundmann Ford Inc—Ed Pundmann	2727 W Clay St, Saint Charles MO 63301		R	112*	.2
231	Stumpf Motor Company Inc—Les Stumpf	PO Box 1737, Appleton WI 54913	920-731-5211	R	112*	.2
232	Trapp Cadillac Chevrolet Inc—Heinke Trepp Jr	200 S Hollywood Rd, Houma LA 70360	985-876-6570	R	112*	.2
233	Nimnicht Chevrolet Co—Bill N Nimnicht III	PO Box 14000, Jacksonville FL 32210	904-425-6311	R	111*	.2
234	BMW of Sterling—Thomas A Moorehead	21826 Pacific Blvd, Sterling VA 20166	571-434-1944	R	111*	.1
235	Fairway Chevrolet Co—Greg Heinrich	3100 E Sahara Ave, Las Vegas NV 89104	702-641-1525	R	110*	.2
236	Lindsay Automotive Group—Charles T Lindsay Jr	1525 Kenwood Ave, Alexandria VA 22302		R	110*	.1
237	Chapman's Las Vegas Dodge	3175 E Sahara Ave, Las Vegas NV 89104		R	110*	.1
238	Downtown Ford Sales Inc—Ray Enos	525 N 16th St, Sacramento CA 95814	916-442-6931	R	110*	.1
239	Barnett Auto Group—Carl L Barnett Sr	10200 Hartsook St, Houston TX 77034	281-287-7000	R	109	.1
240	Leif Johnson Ford Inc—Robert Johnson	501 E Koenig Ln, Austin TX 78751		R	107	.3
241	Family Ford Sales Inc—Richard L Thigpen	1602 Florence Blvd, Florence AL 35630	256-764-3351	R	107*	.1
242	Montgomery Chevrolet—Brian Caldwell	5325 Preston Hwy, Louisville KY 40213	502-968-6111	R	106*	.1
243	Adamson Motors Inc—Bill Adamson	4800 Hwy 52 N, Rochester MN 55901	507-289-4004	R	106*	.1
244	Demontrond Auto Group—George A DeMontrond III	14101 North Fwy, Houston TX 77090	281-377-6347	R	105*	.2
245	Edwards Chevrolet Company Inc—Leon Edwards	1400 3rd Ave N, Birmingham AL 35203	205-716-3300	R	105*	.1
246	Quirk Auto Park—Jack Quirk Jr	PO Box 1386, Bangor ME 04402	207-299-1600	R	104*	.3
247	Avis Ford Inc—Walter E Douglas Sr	29200 Telegraph Rd, Southfield MI 48034	248-355-7500	R	104*	.1
248	Joe Holland Chevrolet Inc—Joe B Holland	210 SW MacCorkle Ave, South Charleston WV 25303	304-553-0695	R	104*	.1
249	Thompson Sales Company Inc—Milton B Thompson	1555 E Independence, Springfield MO 65804	417-866-6611	R	104*	.1
250	Bryan Chevrolet Inc—Jay Bryan Jr	8213 Airline Dr, Metairie LA 70003	504-273-7066	R	101*	.1
251	Dick Dyer and Associates Inc—Steve Dyer	5825 Two Notch Rd, Columbia SC 29223	803-786-8888	R	101*	.1
252	Mullinax Ford North Canton—Charles Mullinax AutoNation Inc	5900 Whipple Ave, North Canton OH 44720	440-984-2431	S	101*	.1
253	Northgate Lincoln Mercury Inc—Terry Mullane	10505 N Florida Ave, Tampa FL 33612	813-235-4936	R	101*	.1
254	1 Cochran Inc—Robert E Cochran	4520 William Penn Hwy, Monroeville PA 15146	412-373-3333	R	100*	.4
255	Bill Ussery Motors Inc—Robert Brockway	300 Almeria Ave, Coral Gables FL 33134	305-445-8593	R	100*	.2
256	Wes Lasher Acura/Isuzu Inc—Wesley B Lasher	925 South St, Sacramento CA 95838	916-392-1400	R	100*	.1
257	Tallahassee Motors Inc—John Craig	243 N Magnolia Dr, Tallahassee FL 32301	850-877-1171	R	99*	.2

Note: An asterisk (*) indicates an estimated financial figure. The company type code used is as follows: R = Private, P = Public, S = Private Subsidiary, B = Public Subsidiary, D = Division, J = Joint Venture, I = Investment Fund.

RANKINGS BY SALES WITHIN 4-DIGIT SIC

Rank	Company Name—Executive Officer	Address, City, State, Zip	Phone	Type	Fin	Empls
258	Tropical Ford Inc—Hamilton W Massey	9900 S Orange Blossom, Orlando FL 32837	407-851-3800	R	99*	.2
259	LaMarque Dodge Inc—Ronnie LaMarque	3101 Williams Blvd, Kenner LA 70065	504-443-2500	R	99*	.1
260	Peterson Autoplex—Marvin Peterson	9101 W Fairview, Boise ID 83704	208-378-5980	R	99*	.2
261	Kenneth Nieman—John Nieman	2111 Morena Blvd, San Diego CA 92110	619-276-6171	R	98*	.3
262	Bankston Chevrolet Dallas—Larry Farrington AutoNation Inc	6411 E Northwest Hwy, Dallas TX 75231	214-363-8341	S	98*	.2
263	Cable-Dahmer Chevrolet Inc—Marty Dahmer	1834 S Noland Rd, Independence MO 64055	816-254-3860	R	98*	.2
264	Fette Ford and Imports—John Fette	1137 Rte 46, Clifton NJ 07013	973-779-7000	R	98*	.1
265	Lexus of Memphis Inc—Stefan Smith	2600 Ridgeway Rd, Memphis TN 38119	901-326-8833	R	98*	.1
266	Sutton Ford Inc—Nathaniel K Sutton	21315 Central Ave, Matteson IL 60443	708-720-8000	R	98*	.1
267	Rick Hendrick Toyota Jeep Eagle—Tom Costello	1969 Skibo, Fayetteville NC 28314	910-213-3371	R	97*	.1
268	Bob Saks Motor Mall—Kevin Mechigian	35080 Grand River Ave, Farmington Hills MI 48335	248-478-0500	R	96*	.2
269	Bert Wolfe Ford Porsche Audi Toyota Inc—Parke Wolfe	1900 Patrick St Plz, Charleston WV 25330	304-344-1601	R	96*	.2
270	Bert Smith Oldsmobile Inc—EW Smith Jr	3800 34th St N, Saint Petersburg FL 33714	727-527-1111	R	96*	.1
271	Fitzpatrick Dealership Group—Ed Fitzpatrick	4369 McHenry Ave, Modesto CA 95356	209-575-0269	R	95*	.1
272	Wade Ford Inc—Steve Ewing	3860 S Cobb Dr, Smyrna GA 30080	770-436-1200	R	95*	.1
273	Coulter Cadillac Inc—William Coulter	1188 E Camelback Rd, Phoenix AZ 85014	602-714-3112	R	94*	.2
274	Fitzgerald Auto Mall—Dorothy Fitzgerald	11411 Rockville Pike, Kensington MD 20895	301-881-4000	R	94*	.2
275	Landmark Ford Inc—Jim Corliss	PO Box 23970, Tigard OR 97281	503-639-1131	R	94*	.2
276	Mike Castrucci Ford Sales Inc—Mike Castrucci	1020 State Rt 28, Milford OH 45150	513-831-7010	R	94*	.2
277	Nichols Ford Inc—Mike Jackson AutoNation Inc	2401 E I-20, Fort Worth TX 76119	817-536-1725	S	94*	.2
278	Ron Carter Automotive Group—Cary Wilson	3005 FM 528, Alvin TX 77511	281-331-3111	R	94*	.2
279	Wentworth Chevrolet Subaru—Bob Wentworth	107 SE Grand Ave, Portland OR 97214	503-232-2000	R	94*	.2
280	Sinclair Buick-GMC Trucks Inc—John Sinclair	5655 S Lindbergh Blvd, Saint Louis MO 63123	314-842-4200	R	94*	.1
281	Harris Chevrolet Inc—Richard Martorana	15015 Florida Blvd, Baton Rouge LA 70819	225-272-6500	R	93*	.2
282	Mike Smith Auto Plaza—Mike Smith	1515 I-10 S, Beaumont TX 77701	409-833-7100	R	93	.2
283	New Country Volkswagon Of Greenwich—Michael Basta	200 W Putnam Ave, Greenwich CT 06830	203-869-4600	R	93*	.2
284	Victory Layne Chevrolet Inc—Jaime Layne	3980 Fowler St, Fort Myers FL 33901	239-936-8561	R	93*	.2
285	Weston Buick GMC—Jim Weston	22555 SE Stark St, Gresham OR 97030	503-665-2166	R	93*	.2
286	Earnhardt Toyota	6136 E Auto Loop Ave, Mesa AZ 85206	480-218-2513	R	93*	.2
287	Dick Norris Buick Pontiac GMC Inc—Richard Norris	30777 US Hwy 19 N, Palm Harbor FL 34684	727-787-8663	R	93*	.1
288	Mel Rapton Honda—Katrina Rapton	2820 Fulton Ave, Sacramento CA 95821	916-482-5400	R	93*	.1
289	Advantage Chevrolet Inc—Desmond A Roberts	9510 W Joliet Rd, Hodgkins IL 60525		R	93*	.1
290	Greiner Motor Company Inc—Philip Schmidt	3333 CY Ave, Casper WY 82604	307-266-1680	R	93*	.1
291	Lee-Smith Inc—Less Lee	2600 8th Ave, Chattanooga TN 37407	423-622-4161	R	92*	.2
292	McCluskey Chevrolet-Geo Inc—Mike Kelsey	435 E Galbraith Rd, Cincinnati OH 45215	513-761-1111	R	92*	.2
293	Colonial Chevrolet—Don Williams Hendrick Automotive Group	6252 E Virginia Beach, Norfolk VA 23502	757-455-4500	D	92*	.2
294	Frank Motors Inc (National City California)—Ron Fornaca	3150 National City Blv, National City CA 91950	619-474-5502	R	91*	.2
295	Broadway Chevrolet Oldsmobile Inc—Keven J Cuene	PO Box 28437, Green Bay WI 54324	855-395-2131	R	90*	.2
296	Bill Jacobs of Joliet—Brad Wise	2001 W Jefferson St, Joliet IL 60435	815-725-7110	R	90*	.2
297	DeFouw Chevrolet-BMW Inc—Dennis Gernhardt	PO Box 4907, Lafayette IN 47903	765-449-2800	R	90*	.1
298	Betts Auto Campus—Rich Willis	2121 NW 100 St, Des Moines IA 50325	515-253-9600	R	90*	.1
299	Steven's Creek Buick Pontiac BMC	4201 Stevens Creek Blv, Santa Clara CA 95051	408-983-5308	R	90*	.1
300	Gaudin Motor Co—Gary Ackerman	2121 E Sahara Ave, Las Vegas NV 89104		R	89*	.2
301	Sands Chevrolet—Jerry Moore	5418 NW Grand Ave, Glendale AZ 85301		R	89*	.2
302	Crossroads Ford Inc (Raleigh North Carolina)	2333 Walnut St, Angier NC 27501	919-460-5601	R	89*	.2
303	Holz Motors Inc—Jerry Holz	5961 S 108 Pl, Hales Corners WI 53130	414-377-4532	R	89*	.2
304	Vista Ford—Jon Shuken	21501 Ventura Blvd, Woodland Hills CA 91364	818-884-7600	R	89*	.2
305	Jim Reed Chevrolet Co—Jim H Reed IV	1512 Broadway, Nashville TN 37203	615-369-2098	R	89*	.2
306	Mike Riehl's Chrysler Plymouth Jeep—Mike Riehl	25800 Gratiot Ave, Roseville MI 48066	586-859-2500	R	89*	.1
307	Nationwide Autoworld Infiniti—Brandon Schaefer	22 W Timonium Rd, Timonium MD 21093	410-252-8000	R	89*	.1
308	Performance Chrysler Jeep and Dodge LLC—Steve Loehr	4240 W Glendale Ave, Phoenix AZ 85051	623-247-4444	R	89*	.1
309	Westlie Motor Co—Steve Blasing	500 S Broadway, Minot ND 58701	701-852-1354	R	89*	.1
310	Lindsay Ford of Wheaton—Jim Davie	11250 Viers Mill Rd, Wheaton MD 20902	301-949-4060	R	89*	.1
311	Harbor Chevrolet Corp—Randy Johnson	3770 Cherry Ave, Long Beach CA 90807	562-264-0939	R	89*	.1
312	Lithia Ford Lincoln Mercury of Grand Forks	2273 32nd Ave S, Grand Forks ND 58201	701-746-6411	R	89*	.1
313	Weseloh Chevrolet Co—Charles B Weseloh Jr	5335 Paseo Del Norte, Carlsbad CA 92008	760-438-1001	R	89*	.1
314	Iten Chevrolet Co—Marty Iten	6701 Brooklyn Blvd, Minneapolis MN 55429	763-561-9220	R	88*	.2
315	Murray's Ford-Lincoln-Mercury Inc—Greg Murray	Rte 119 S, Du Bois PA 15801	814-371-6600	R	88*	.1
316	Art Moehn Chevrolet Co—John M Kudner	2200 Seymour Rd, Jackson MI 49201	517-787-7700	R	88*	.1
317	Bianchi Motors Inc—Louis J Porreco	8430 Peach St, Erie PA 16509	814-868-9678	R	88*	.1
318	Hall Chevrolet Company Inc—Don Frohmader	11011 W N Ave, Milwaukee WI 53226	414-778-1500	R	88*	.1
319	Harry's On The Hill—Patricia P Grimes	819 Patton Ave, Asheville NC 28806	828-248-0616	R	88*	.1
320	Kelly Chevrolet-Cadillac Inc—Mike Kelly	252 Pittsburgh Rd, Butler PA 16002	724-287-2701	R	88*	.1
321	Kimnach Ford Inc—Jay Council	6401 East Virginia Bea, Norfolk VA 23502	757-461-6401	R	88*	.1
322	Knapp Chevrolet—Robby Knapp	815 Houston Ave, Houston TX 77007		R	88*	.1
323	Nissan of San Bernardino	735 W Showcase Dr S, San Bernardino CA 92408		R	88*	.1
324	O'Hare Auto Group—Kevin Mize	1533 S River Rd, Des Plaines IL 60018	847-824-3141	R	88*	.1
325	Rico Motor Company Inc—Marty Menapace	220 S 5th St, Gallup NM 87301	505-722-2271	R	88*	.1
326	Town and Country Chrysler Jeep—Ralph Martinez	16800 SE McLoughlin Bl, Milwaukie OR 97267		R	88*	.1
327	Mountain View Ford Inc—Clay Watson	301 E 20th St, Chattanooga TN 37408	423-756-1331	R	87*	.2
328	Walker Automotive—Foster Walker III	1616 MacArthur Dr, Alexandria LA 71301	318-445-6421	R	87*	.1
329	MK Smith Chevrolet Inc—Marc Smith	12845 Central Ave, Chino CA 91710	909-628-8961	R	87*	.1
330	Overland Park Jeep Inc—Frank Thompson	8775 Metcalf, Overland Park KS 66212	913-381-8100	R	87*	.1
331	Progressive Chevrolet Co—Daniel C Sanders	8000 Hills and Dales R, Massillon OH 44646	330-833-8564	R	87*	.1
332	DSU Peterbilt and GMC Truck Inc—Wally Yost	PO Box 3486, Portland OR 97208	503-285-7771	R	86*	.2
333	Arrow Ford Inc—Seaton Higginbotham	4001 S 1st St, Abilene TX 79605		R	86*	.2
334	Goudy Honda—Gordon H Goudy	1400 W Main St, Alhambra CA 91801	323-283-7336	R	86*	.2
335	James Corlew Chevrolet Inc—James L Corlew	722 College St, Clarksville TN 37040		R	86*	.1
336	Don Seelye Ford Inc—Duane Davis	3820 Stadium Dr, Kalamazoo MI 49008	269-375-3820	R	85*	.1
337	Bob Moore Cadillac Inc—Robert Stalnacker	13000 N Broadway Ext, Oklahoma City OK 73114	405-749-9000	R	85*	.1
338	BMW/Mini of Sterling—Tony Moorehead	21826 Pacific Blvd, Sterling VA 20166	571-434-1944	R	85*	.1
339	Don McGill Toyota Inc—Don McGill	11800 Old Katy Rd, Houston TX 77079	281-496-2000	R	84*	.3
340	Charles Gabus Ford Inc—Gene Gabus	4545 Merle Hay Rd, Des Moines IA 50310	515-270-0707	R	84*	.2
341	Worthington Ford Inc—Cal Worthington	2950 Bellflower Blvd, Long Beach CA 90815	562-420-3333	R	84*	.2
342	Roy Robinson Chevrolet Subaru—Roy Robinson	PO Box 168, Marysville WA 98270	360-659-6236	R	84*	.1
343	Kistler Ford Inc—Bobby Jorgensen	5555 W Central Ave, Toledo OH 43615	419-531-9911	R	83*	.1
344	Park Place Motor Cars—Robert Morris	6113 Lemmon Ave, Dallas TX 75209		R	82	.2

Rank	Company Name—*Executive Officer*	Address, City, State, Zip	Phone	Type	Fin	Empls
345	Dan Perkins Group—*Dan Perkins*	734 Bridgeport Ave, Milford CT 06460	203-878-4621	R	82*	.2
346	Royal Oak Ford Sales Inc—*Eddie Hall Jr*	27550 Woodward Ave, Royal Oak MI 48067	248-548-4100	R	82*	.2
347	Mirak Chevrolet Inc—*Edward Mirak*	1125 Massachusetts Ave, Arlington MA 02474	339-368-6193	R	82*	.1
348	Camelback Ford Lincoln—*Gerie L Clayton*	1330 E Camelback Rd, Phoenix AZ 85014	602-264-1611	R	82*	.1
349	Hopkins Ford Inc—*John Mackenzie*	1650 The Fairway, Jenkintown PA 19046	215-886-5900	R	82*	.1
350	Royal Gate Dodge Chrysler—*Mark Winstead*	15502 Manchester Rd, Ellisville MO 63011		R	82*	.1
351	Selman Chevrolet—*Walter Motley*	1001 N Weir Canyon Blv, Anaheim Hills CA 92807	714-283-5400	R	82*	.1
352	Snider Motors Inc—*Blake Snider*	9640 West Stockton Blv, Elk Grove CA 95757	916-391-1511	R	81*	.2
353	Carl Burger Dodge—*Paul McKenna*	8333 Hercules St, La Mesa CA 91942		R	81	.1
354	Cherry Creek Dodge Inc	2727 S Havana St, Denver CO 80014		R	81*	.1
355	Coast Cadillac Co—*Vance Dickinson*	2200 Bee Ridge Rd, Sarasota FL 34239	941-922-1571	R	81*	.1
356	Crescent Ford Inc—*Owen Bertschi*	100 Old Winston Rd, High Point NC 27265	336-869-2181	R	81*	.1
357	Davis Automotive Group Inc—*Jeffrey S Davis*	6135 Kruse Dr, Solon OH 44139	440-542-0600	R	81*	.1
358	Edmark Auto Inc—*Jim E Chalfant*	15700 Idaho Center Blv, Nampa ID 83687	208-442-2717	R	81*	.1
359	El Cajon Ford—*Paul F Leader*	1595 E Main St, El Cajon CA 92021	619-579-8888	R	81*	.1
360	Fowler Buick-GMC Inc—*Tom Hudson*	PO Box 2538, Jackson MS 39207	601-519-4306	R	81*	.1
361	Freeman Pontiac Buick GMC—*James Freeman*	501 W State Hwy 114, Grapevine TX 76051	817-410-5000	R	81*	.1
362	Gary Force Inc—*Gary Force*	PO Box 90000, Bowling Green KY 42102	270-843-4321	R	81*	.1
363	Mercedes Benz of Austin—*Harvey Dyer*	6757 Airport Blvd, Austin TX 78752	512-454-6821	R	81*	.1
364	Southgate Automotive Group Inc—*Walter Olben Jr*	PO Box 1423, Southgate MI 48195	734-282-3636	R	81*	.1
365	Sterling BMW—*Thomas Moorehead*	3000 West Coast Hwy, Newport Beach CA 92663	949-645-5900	R	81*	.1
366	Capitol Chevrolet Inc—*Dean Vette*	PO Box 36, Montgomery AL 36101	334-272-8700	R	80*	.2
367	Gates Automotive Group—*Larry Gates*	636 W McKinley Ave, Mishawaka IN 46545	574-807-9438	R	80*	.2
368	Mike Daugherty Chevrolet Inc—*Michael D Daugherty*	2341 Fulton Ave, Sacramento CA 95825	916-482-1600	R	80*	.2
369	Moss Brothers Dodge—*Glenn Moss*	8151 Auto Dr, Riverside CA 92504	951-688-6200	R	80*	.2
370	DeMontrond Auto Country Inc—*George DeMontrond III*	888 I 45 S, Conroe TX 77304	281-443-2500	R	80*	.1
371	De Paula Chevrolet Inc—*Anthony J De Paula*	781 Central Ave, Albany NY 12206	518-489-5551	R	80*	.1
372	Dick Masheter Ford Inc—*Bob Masheter*	1090 S Hamilton Rd, Columbus OH 43227	614-861-7150	R	80*	.1
373	Faulkner Harrisburg Inc—*Don Perry*	PO Box 2861, Harrisburg PA 17105	717-238-7324	R	80*	.1
374	Ramey Chevrolet Inc—*James C Ramey Sr*	PO Box 100, Tazewell VA 24651	276-988-6526	R	80*	.1
375	Jim Fresard GMC-Oldsmobile—*Mike Dersa*	21800 Woodward Ave, Ferndale MI 48220	248-399-3200	R	79*	.1
376	Red River Motor Co—*James N Fritze*	221 Traffic St, Bossier City LA 71111	318-549-7500	R	78*	.1
377	Loehmann-Blasius Chevrolet Inc—*Frederick Blasius Sr*	90 Scott Rd, Waterbury CT 06705	203-437-4141	R	78*	.1
378	Tracy Auto LLC—*Keena Turner*	2895 N Naglee Rd, Tracy CA 95304	209-834-1111	R	78*	.1
379	Coffman Truck Sales Inc—*Mark Coffman*	PO Box 151, Aurora IL 60507	630-892-7093	R	78*	.1
380	Schilling Enterprises—*Harry L Smith*	PO Box 172079, Memphis TN 38117	901-261-5412	R	77*	.2
381	Walt Sweeney Automotive Inc—*Walt Sweeney*	5400 Glenway Ave, Cincinnati OH 45238	513-922-4500	R	77*	.2
382	Sweeney Buick GMC Truck Co—*Doug Sweeney*	PO Box 3847, Youngstown OH 44513	330-726-2277	R	77*	.1
383	The Ford Store San Leandro-Lincoln Mercury—*Robert Knezevich*	1111 Marina Blvd, San Leandro CA 94577	510-347-4177	R	77*	.1
384	Felix Chevrolet—*Jonathon Lange*	3330 S Figueroa St, Los Angeles CA 90007	213-748-6141	R	76*	.2
385	Fairway Ford of Augusta—*Perry Osman*	4333 Washington Rd, Evans GA 30809	706-854-9200	R	76*	.1
386	Findlay Automotive Inc—*Cliff Findlay*	310 N Gibson Rd, Henderson NV 89014	702-630-4210	R	76*	.1
387	Kinsel Motors Inc—*Joe B Kinsel*	PO Box 2470, Beaumont TX 77704	409-899-4000	R	75*	.3
388	Jim Coleman Cadillac—*James Coleman*	10400 Auto Park Ave, Bethesda MD 20817	301-469-6600	R	75*	.2
389	Young Ford Inc—*Tim McKinney*	5411 N Tryon St, Charlotte NC 28213		R	75*	.2
390	Andrew Automotive Inc—*Andrew Schlesinger*	1500 W Silver Spring D, Milwaukee WI 53209		R	75*	.2
391	Westfall GMC Truck Inc—*Jane O'dell*	3915 NE Randolph Rd, Kansas City MO 64161		R	75*	.2
392	Karl Malone Toyota—*Karl Malone*	11453 South Lone Peak, Draper UT 84020		R	75*	.2
393	Lakewood Fordland—*Robert L Liedel*	11595 West Colfax, Lakewood CO 80215		R	75*	.1
394	Rohrich Cadillac Inc—*Tom Rohrich*	2116 W Liberty Ave, Pittsburgh PA 15226	412-344-6000	R	75*	.1
395	Rapid Chevrolet-Cadillac—*Kevin Randell*	2090 Deadwood Ave N, Rapid City SD 57702	605-343-1282	R	75*	.1
396	Purvis Ford Inc—*R Eli Patrick*	PO Box 3489, Fredericksburg VA 22402	540-898-3000	R	75*	.1
397	Elder Ford of Tampa—*Erma Elder*	9545 N Florida Ave, Tampa FL 33612	813-840-3981	R	74*	.2
398	Mansfield Truck Sales and Service Inc—*Rod Rafael*	PO Box 1516, Mansfield OH 44901	419-522-9811	R	74*	.2
399	Bob Hall Chevrolet—*Bob Hall*	1700 E Yakima Ave, Yakima WA 98901	509-248-7600	R	74*	.1
400	Dutch Miller Chevrolet-Hyundai Inc—*Matt Miller*	1100 Washington Ave, Huntington WV 25704	304-529-2301	R	74*	.1
401	Freedom Lincoln Mercury—*James Church*	1765 S Military Hwy, Chesapeake VA 23320	757-424-1100	R	74*	.1
402	Hoskins Chevrolet Inc—*Richard Hoskins*	175 N Arlington Hts Rd, Elk Grove Village IL 60007	847-354-4871	R	74*	.1
403	O'Rielly Chevrolet Inc—*Jerry Lauer*	6160 E Broadway Blvd, Tucson AZ 85711	520-829-4400	R	74*	.1
404	Reed Lallier Chevrolet Inc—*Michael G Lallier*	4500 Raeford Rd, Fayetteville NC 28304		R	74*	.1
405	Sport Chevrolet Company Inc—*Gerry Ryan*	3101 Automobile Blvd, Silver Spring MD 20904	301-890-6000	R	74*	.1
406	Sport Honda—*Robert Fogarty*	3201 Automobile Blvd, Silver Spring MD 20904	301-890-4700	R	74*	.1
407	Stillwater Motor Company Inc—*Daniel Raduenz*	PO Box 337, Stillwater MN 55082	651-439-4333	R	74*	.1
408	Story Oldsmobile Inc—*Leo Jerome*	3165 E Michigan Ave, Lansing MI 48912	517-351-0400	R	74*	.1
409	Wray Ford Inc—*Greg Snelling*	2851 Benton Rd, Bossier City LA 71111	318-686-7300	R	74*	.1
410	Champion Toyota—*Kim Eddy*	11711 Gulf Fwy, Houston TX 77034	713-943-9900	R	74*	.1
411	Rydell Chevrolet Olds Cad Inc—*Wesley Rydell*	PO Box 13398, Grand Forks ND 58208	701-772-7211	R	73*	.2
412	Bruce Lowrie Chevrolet Inc—*Bruce Lowrie*	711 SW Loop 820, Fort Worth TX 76134	817-293-5811	R	73*	.1
413	Pompano Honda—*Judy Manderson*	5381 N Federal Hwy, Pompano Beach FL 33064	954-427-4744	R	73*	.1
414	Wilde Automotive Group—*Mark Wilde*	1603 E Moreland Blvd, Waukesha WI 53186	262-542-0771	R	73*	.1
415	Power Nissan South Bay AutoNation Inc	14610 Hindry Ave, Hawthorne CA 90250	310-536-4000	S	73*	.1
416	Robberson Ford Sales Inc—*Jeff Robberson*	2100 NE 3rd St, Bend OR 97701	541-382-4521	R	73*	.1
417	Salinas Valley Ford Sales Inc—*Ron Frieberg*	1100 Auto Center Cir, Salinas CA 93907	831-444-4444	R	73*	.1
418	Tom Endicott Buick Inc—*Tom Endicott*	1345 S Federal Hwy, Pompano Beach FL 33062	954-781-7700	R	73*	.1
419	Five Star International LLC—*Scott Rumberger*	PO Box 1747, Harrisburg PA 17105	717-986-1500	R	72*	.2
420	Capitol Toyota—*Jerry G Brassfield*	775 W Capitol Expy Aut, San Jose CA 95136	408-267-0500	R	72*	.2
421	Hub City Ford Inc—*Jarvis Fortier*	PO Box 90670, Lafayette LA 70509	337-233-4500	R	72*	.2
422	Tipton Motors Inc—*Jim Tipton*	3840 N Expy, Brownsville TX 78526	956-350-5600	R	72*	.1
423	Courtesy Chevrolet Center—*Chad Hubler*	PO Box 33283, San Diego CA 92163	619-297-4321	R	71*	.2
424	Jones Ford Inc—*David M Walters*	PO Box 62829, North Charleston SC 29419	843-744-3311	R	71*	.2
425	McCarthy Morse Chevrolet Inc—*Mitch Morse*	9201 Metcalf Ave, Overland Park KS 66212	913-649-6000	R	71*	.2
426	Service Chevrolet Inc—*Jesse Luquette*	4313 Cameron St, Lafayette LA 70506	337-234-9411	R	71*	.2
427	Bowen Scarff Ford Sales Inc—*Mark Scarff*	1157 Central Ave N, Kent WA 98032	253-852-1480	R	71*	.1
428	Dick Huvaere's Richmond Chrysler/Dodge/Jeep/Ram Inc—*Richard Huvaere*	67567 S Main St, Richmond MI 48062	586-727-7577	R	71*	.1
429	LP Safford Inc—*Raymond MacAnanny*	3110 Automobile Blvd, Silver Spring MD 20904		R	71*	.1
430	Jaguar of Novi—*John Oraha*	24295 Haggerty Rd, Novi MI 48375		R	71*	.1
431	Carl Black Chevrolet—*Carl Black*	535 Murfreesboro Rd, Murfreesboro TN 37127	615-748-8500	R	70*	.2

Note: An asterisk (*) indicates an estimated financial figure. The company type code used is as follows: R = Private, P = Public, S = Private Subsidiary, B = Public Subsidiary, D = Division, J = Joint Venture, I = Investment Fund.

COMPANY RANKINGS BY SALES WITHIN 4-DIGIT SIC

Rank	Company Name—*Executive Officer*	Address, City, State, Zip	Phone	Type	Fin	Empls
432	Duval Ford	1616 Cassat Ave, Jacksonville FL 32210	904-381-6599	R	70*	.2
433	Great Valley Auto—*Dick Keil*	2329 Fulton Ave, Sacramento CA 95825	916-973-3200	R	70*	.2
434	Koons Ford Annapolis Inc—*Joseph Koons*	2540 Riva Rd, Annapolis MD 21401		R	70*	.2
435	Mike Shad Ford at the Avenues—*James Lampke* AutoNation Inc	10720 Phillips Hwy, Jacksonville FL 32256	904-292-3325	S	70*	.2
436	Moran Art Pontiac-GMC Inc—*Tom Moran*	29300 Telegraph Rd, Southfield MI 48034	248-353-9000	R	70*	.2
437	Nalley Nissan—*Charles R Oglesby*	1625 Church St, Decatur GA 30033	404-292-3853	R	70*	.2
438	Quantrell Inc—*Bill Bridges*	1490 E New Circle Rd, Lexington KY 40509	859-266-2161	R	70*	.2
439	Rydell Chevrolet Mitsubishi Inc—*Jeff Smock*	1325 E San Marnan Dr, Waterloo IA 50702	319-234-4601	R	70*	.2
440	Scott Clark's Toyota City—*Scott Clark*	13000 E Independence B, Matthews NC 28105	704-535-1972	R	70*	.2
441	Sears Imported Autos Inc—*Don Davidson*	13500 Wayzata Blvd, Minnetonka MN 55305		R	70*	.2
442	Team Chevrolet Oldsmobile Geo Inc—*Jeremy Gump*	3003 E Colorado Blvd, Pasadena CA 91107	626-449-3333	R	70*	.2
443	Weber Chevrolet Co—*Nelson Leder*	12015 Olive Blvd, Creve Coeur MO 63141	314-567-3300	R	70*	.2
444	Westgate Chevrolet Inc—*Gary Morganflash* AutoNation Inc	7300 W I-40, Amarillo TX 79106	806-356-5600	S	70*	.2
445	Superior-Brookdale Ford Inc—*Tom Rabiola*	9700 56th Ave N, Plymouth MN 55442	763-559-9111	R	70*	.1
446	Automaster Motor Company Inc—*Jack DuBrul*	3328 Shelburne Rd, Shelburne VT 05482	802-985-8411	R	70*	.1
447	Dealer Management Agency Inc—*Diane Musson-Kyle*	PO Box 12210, New Iberia LA 70562	337-365-3411	R	70*	.1
448	Van Dyke Dodge Inc—*Frank Galeana*	PO Box 1539, Warren MI 48090	586-573-4000	R	70*	.1
449	Don Bulluck Chevrolet Cadillac Inc—*DO Bulluck Jr*	PO Box 1100, Rocky Mount NC 27802		R	70*	.1
450	Krenzen Cadillac Pontiac Inc—*Howie Krenzen*	2500 Mall Dr, Duluth MN 55811	218-727-2905	R	70*	.1
451	Joe Lunghamer Chevrolet Inc—*Joseph E Lunghamer*	PO Box 430090, Pontiac MI 48343	248-683-7100	R	70*	.1
452	Toyota of North Hollywood—*Chris Ashworth*	4606 Lankershim Blvd, N Hollywood CA 91602		R	69	.1
453	Bergstrom Automotive—*Dick Bergstrom*	PO Box 549, Neenah WI 54956	920-722-1111	R	68*	.2
454	Lamarque Motor Co—*Ronnie Lamarque*	3101 Williams Blvd, Kenner LA 70065	504-443-2500	R	68*	.2
455	Thane Hawkins Polar Chevrolet Inc—*Thane Hawkins*	1801 County Rd E Ste F, White Bear Lake MN 55110	651-429-7791	R	68*	.2
456	Fairway Ford Inc (Greenville South Carolina)—*Foster McKissick III*	2323 Laurens Rd, Greenville SC 29607	864-242-5060	R	68*	.1
457	Saturn of Orlando South—*Roland Daniels*	2725 S Hwy 17-92, Casselberry FL 32707	407-767-2022	R	68*	.1
458	Sonny Hancock Chevrolet Olds Cadillac Inc—*Martin L Hancock III*	PO Box 1926, Gastonia NC 28053	704-824-2000	R	68*	.1
459	Jerry Gleason Chevrolet Inc—*Michael J Jackson* AutoNation Inc	110 SE 6th St, Fort Lauderdale FL 33301	954-769-6100	S	68*	.1
460	Vogler Ford Lincoln Mercury—*Dennis Rathjen*	1170 E Main St, Carbondale IL 62901	618-457-8135	R	68*	.1
461	Deery Brothers Inc—*Brad Deery*	PO Box 1, West Burlington IA 52655	319-752-6000	R	67*	.2
462	Mercedes Benz of Sacramento—*James Crowley*	1810 Howe Ave, Sacramento CA 95825		R	67*	.1
463	Carmichael Honda	6151 Auburn Blvd, Citrus Heights CA 95621	916-723-6151	R	67*	.1
464	Five Star Ford—*Owen McCumber*	7100 E McDowell Rd, Scottsdale AZ 85257	480-946-3900	R	67*	.1
465	Toyota of Orange Inc—*David Wilson*	1400 N Tustin St, Orange CA 92867	714-639-6750	R	67*	.1
466	Texas Motors Ford—*J Clifford Johnson*	300 West Loop 820 S, Fort Worth TX 76108	817-935-7000	R	67*	.1
467	Republic Ford Lincoln Inc—*Bob Beine*	1740 US Hwy 60 E, Republic MO 65738	417-732-2626	R	67*	.1
468	Barlow Chevrolet and Oldsmobile Inc—*Ed Barlow Jr*	6057 Rte130 S and Fair, Delran NJ 08075	856-461-8400	R	67*	.1
469	Dave Syverson Inc—*Dave Syverson*	2310 E Main St, Albert Lea MN 56007	507-373-1438	R	67*	.1
470	Bob Howard Chevrolet Inc—*Hal Steinke*	PO Box 14508, Oklahoma City OK 73113	405-936-8800	R	67*	.1
471	Richmond Motor Company Inc—*Ron Kody*	4600 W Broad St, Richmond VA 23230	804 358 5521	R	66*	.2
472	Dyerly Ford Inc—*JR Daunhauer Jr*	4041 Dixie Hwy, Louisville KY 40216	502-448-1661	R	66*	.1
473	Bob Ross Buick Inc—*Norma J Ross*	85 Loop Rd, Centerville OH 45459	937-401-2037	R	66*	.1
474	Landers Auto Sales Inc—*Steve Landers* Penske Automotive Group Inc	PO Box 1649, Little Rock AR 72209	501-568-5800	S	66*	.1
475	Bill Sullivan Pontiac Inc—*Ariel Szwec*	777 W Dundee Rd, Arlington Heights IL 60004		R	66*	.1
476	De Lillo Chevrolet Co—*David De Lillo*	PO Box 908, Huntington Beach CA 92648	714-847-6087	R	66*	.1
477	Honda of Tiffany Springs—*Gerald Bentley* John Chezik Holding Company Inc	9200 NW Prairie View R, Kansas City MO 64153	816-452-7000	S	66*	.1
478	Kenworth Northwest Inc—*Marshall Cymbaluk*	PO Box 98967, Seattle WA 98198	206-433-5911	R	66*	.1
479	International Truck Sales Of Richmond Inc—*Thomas Thayer*	PO Box 1450, Ashland VA 23005	804-353-5555	R	65*	.1
480	Huntington Chevrolet Inc—*Gregory M Williams Sr*	370 Oakwood Rd, Huntington Station NY 11746	631-427-0900	R	65*	.1
481	Diver Chevrolet Inc—*Richard Diver*	2101 Pennsylvania Ave, Wilmington DE 19806	302-575-0161	R	65*	.1
482	Johnny Londoff Chevrolet—*John Londoff*	1375 Dunn Rd, Florissant MO 63031	314-262-4526	R	65*	.1
483	Crown Chrysler Jeep Inc—*Mark Wigler*	6350 Perimeter Loop Rd, Dublin OH 43017	614-761-2360	R	65*	.1
484	Concours Motors Inc—*Karl Wuesthoff*	1400 W Silver Spring D, Milwaukee WI 53209	414-290-1400	R	64*	.2
485	Corley Automotive Group—*Eddie B Corley Sr*	1870 W Santa Fe, Grants NM 87020	505-285-4595	R	64*	.2
486	Lakeside Toyota—*Anthony Gullo*	3701 N Causeway Blvd, Metairie LA 70002	504-833-3311	R	64*	.1
487	Hedrick's Hallowell Chevrolet Co—*WL Hedrick*	961 W Shaw Ave, Clovis CA 93612	559-291-7711	R	64*	.1
488	Ed Voyles Chrysler Jeep Dodge—*Drew Tutton*	789 Cobb Pky SE, Marietta GA 30060		R	63*	.1
489	Ed Shults Chevrolet Inc—*Ed Shults Jr*	300 Fluvanna Ave, Jamestown NY 14701	716-664-0101	R	63*	.1
490	Hank Graff Chevrolet—*Hank Graff*	PO Box 430, Davison MI 48423		R	63*	.1
491	Jim Culligan's Inc—*Jim Culligan*	8129 Main St, Williamsville NY 14221	716-633-4000	R	63*	.1
492	Ford of Kirkland—*Jim Walen*	11800 124th Ave NE, Kirkland WA 98034	425-821-6611	R	63*	.1
493	Mid-Tenn Ford Truck Sales Inc—*Bick Boyte*	1319 Foster Ave, Nashville TN 37210	615-259-2050	R	63*	.1
494	Midway Motors Inc—*George Lamb*	3737 Beverly Blvd, Los Angeles CA 90004	213-385-1411	R	63*	.1
495	Huntsville Dodge Inc—*Ellenae Fairhurst*	6580 University Dr, Huntsville AL 35806	256-824-8050	R	63*	.1
496	John Nolan Auto Service—*Robert Nolan*	3250 Highland Ave, Cincinnati OH 45213	513-631-2000	R	63*	.1
497	Ace Auto Lease Inc—*Rob Henry*	9650 Atlantic Blvd, Jacksonville FL 32225	904-723-6110	R	62*	.2
498	Ellis Brooks Automotive—*Marie Brooks*	1395 Van Ness Ave, San Francisco CA 94109	415-776-2400	R	62*	.1
499	Erhard Motor Sales Inc—*Scott Appleford*	4065 W Maple St, Bloomfield Hills MI 48301	248-642-6565	R	62*	.1
500	Cole Chevrolet-Cadillac Inc—*Tom Cole*	PO Box 688, Bluefield WV 24701	304-327-8116	R	62*	.1
501	North Hills Lincoln-Mercury Sales Inc—*Kenon Jones*	401 NE Loop 820, Hurst TX 76053	817-595-4488	R	62*	.1
502	Wharton Jeep	1225 7th St, Parkersburg WV 26101	304-485-7511	R	62*	.1
503	Hidy Motors Inc—*David Hidy*	2300 Hller Drv Beaver, Dayton OH 45434	937-426-9564	R	62*	.1
504	Bell Honda—*Robby Motz*	701 W Bell Rd, Phoenix AZ 85023	602-789-9771	R	61*	.1
505	Bill Black Chevrolet Cadillac—*Bill Black III*	601 E Bessemer Ave, Greensboro NC 27405	336-275-9641	R	61*	.1
506	Grande Truck Center Inc—*Richard S Kane*	PO Box 201210, San Antonio TX 78220	210-661-4121	R	61*	.1
507	Dean Sellers Ford Co—*Liz Sellers*	2600 W Maple Rd, Troy MI 48084	248-643-7500	R	61*	.1
508	Peachtree Ford—*Cindy Killingsworth*	5675 PeachTree Industr, Atlanta GA 30341	770-455-7673	R	61*	.1
509	Don Brown Chevrolet Buick Inc—*Don Brown*	2244 S Kingshighway Bl, Saint Louis MO 63110	314-450-7169	R	61*	.1
510	Halladay Motors Inc—*Tim Joannides*	2100 Westland Rd, Cheyenne WY 82001	307-634-1511	R	61*	.1
511	Jim Keim Ford Inc—*James R Keim*	5575 Keim Cir, Columbus OH 43228	614-888-3333	R	61*	.1
512	John Chezik Holding Company Inc—*Robert Hennessey*	9200 NW Prairie View R, Kansas City MO 64153	816-452-7000	R	61*	.1
513	Libertyville Chevrolet—*Brad Williams*	1001 S Milwaukee Ave, Libertyville IL 60048		R	61*	.1
514	Louis Lakis Ford Inc—*Louis Lakis*	2201 W Main, Galesburg IL 61401	309-342-1121	R	61*	.1

Rank	Company Name—*Executive Officer*	Address, City, State, Zip	Phone	Type	Fin	Empls
515	Randy Reed Nissan—*Randy Reed*	9600 NW Prairie View R, Kansas City MO 64153	816-801-8634	R	61*	.1
516	Kirkwood Motors Inc—*Gene Pointkowski*	3807 Kirkwood Hwy, Wilmington DE 19808	302-998-2271	R	61*	.1
517	Medved Brutyn Ford Lincoln and Mercury Inc—*Bob Brutyn*	1404 S Wilcox St, Castle Rock CO 80104	303-872-9778	R	61*	.1
518	Folsom Buick-Pontiac-GMC Inc—*Steve J Jackson*	12640 Auto Mall Cir, Folsom CA 95630	916-358-8963	R	61*	.1
519	Rothrock Motor Sales Inc	Rte 22 and 15th St, Allentown PA 18104	610-439-8485	R	60*	.2
520	Rimrock Cadillac GMC—*John Soares*	PO Box 80208, Billings MT 59108	406-651-5000	R	60*	.2
521	Bob Richards Chevrolet Company Inc—*JR Richards*	2031 Gordon Hwy, Augusta GA 30909	706-550-1359	R	60*	.2
522	Harrold Ford—*Dave Hellinge*	1535 Howe Ave, Sacramento CA 95825		R	60*	.2
523	Palmer Auto Group—*Gary Huffman*	4545 E 96th St, Indianapolis IN 46240	317-846-5555	R	60*	.2
524	Marvin K Brown Auto Center Inc—*James E Brown*	1441 Camino Del Rio S, San Diego CA 92108	619-291-2040	R	60*	.1
525	Central Ford Center Inc—*Roger Penske* Penske Automotive Group Inc	4600 S University Ave, Little Rock AR 72204	501-562-3673	S	60*	.1
526	Ziems Ford Corners Inc—*Rich Cross*	5700 E Main St, Farmington NM 87402		R	60*	.1
527	Cobb Parkway Chevrolet—*Patrick Decuir*	2155 Cobb Pky, Smyrna GA 30080	770-953-0100	R	60*	.1
528	O'Neill Automotive Plaza—*Rick O'Neil*	7979 Metcalf Ave, Overland Park KS 66204	913-648-5400	R	60*	.1
529	Valley Cadillac Corp	3100 Winton Rd S, Rochester NY 14623		R	60*	.1
530	Gustman Chevrolet Sales Inc—*Steve Gustman*	PO Box 800, Kaukauna WI 54130	920-766-3581	R	60*	.1
531	Central Chevrolet Inc—*Todd Volk*	675 Memorial Ave, West Springfield MA 01089	413-781-3400	R	60*	.1
532	Allen Samuels Chevrolet Mercedes—*Allen Samuels* Allen Samuels Auto Group	1625 N Valley Mills Dr, Waco TX 76710	254-772-8850	S	59*	.2
533	Mercedes-Benz of Calabasas—*David Peterson* Sonic Automotive Inc	24181 Calabasas Rd, Calabasas CA 91302	818-591-2377	S	59*	.2
534	Rippy Cadillac Oldsmobile Inc—*JF Rippy III*	4951 New Centre Dr, Wilmington NC 28403	910-799-2421	R	59*	.1
535	Ed Hicks Imports—*Ed Hicks*	3026 S Padre Island, Corpus Christi TX 78415	361-854-1955	R	59*	.1
536	Braley and Graham Buick Pontiac and GMC Truck	2200 Fulton Ave, Sacramento CA 95825		R	59*	.1
537	Glenn E Thomas Co—*Glenn Thomas*	2100 E Spring St, Signal Hill CA 90755	562-426-5111	R	59*	.1
538	Thomson MacConnell Cadillac Inc—*Chris MacConnell*	2820 Gilbert Ave, Cincinnati OH 45206	513-221-5600	R	59*	.1
539	Powell Chevrolet Oldsmobile Inc—*John H Powell Jr*	8008 Marvin D Love Fwy, Dallas TX 75237	972-298-4911	R	59*	.1
540	Red McCombs Automotive Center Inc—*Red McCombs*	8333 IH-10 W, San Antonio TX 78230	210-349-4949	S	58*	.4
541	Leo Hoffman Chevrolet Inc—*Thomas L Hoffman*	15432 E Nelson Ave, City of Industry CA 91744	626-968-8411	R	58*	.2
542	Fladeboe Automotive Group—*Ray Fladeboe*	20 Auto Center Dr, Irvine CA 92618	949-830-7600	R	58*	.2
543	Maita Toyota—*Vince Maita*	2500 Auburn Blvd, Sacramento CA 95821	916-473-7890	R	58*	.2
544	Friendly Ford Inc (Springfield Missouri)	3241 S Glenstone Ave, Springfield MO 65804	417-883-4330	R	58*	.1
545	Green Chevrolet Chrysler Inc—*Ric Zillmer*	1703 Ave of the Cities, East Moline IL 61244	309-792-1550	R	58*	.1
546	Hollingsworth-Richards Inc—*Mark Hollingsworth*	7787 Florida Blvd, Baton Rouge LA 70806	225-927-5555	R	58*	.1
547	Lockhart Cadillac Inc—*Marc Lockhart*	5550 N Keystone Ave, Indianapolis IN 46220	317-644-2817	R	58*	.1
548	Hamilton Chevrolet Inc—*Michael Boguth*	5800 14 Mile Rd, Warren MI 48092	586-264-1400	R	58*	.1
549	Martin Chevrolet Chrysler—*Bill Martin*	8800 Gratiot Rd, Saginaw MI 48609	989-781-4590	R	58*	.1
550	LaRich Chevrolet Cadillac—*John LaRiche*	215 E Main Cross St, Findlay OH 45840		R	58*	.1
551	Barry Bunker Chevrolet Cadillac—*Barry Bunker*	1307 N Wabash Ave, Marion IN 46952	765-664-1275	R	58*	.1
552	Williamson Cadillac Co—*Tommy Williamson*	7815 SW 104th St, Miami FL 33156	305-670-7100	R	57	.1
553	Kuehn Motor Inc—*Charles Kuehn*	5020 Hwy 52 N, Rochester MN 55901	507-282-7700	R	57*	.1
554	Paul Harvey Ford Sales Inc—*Jerry Harvey*	5252 W 38th St, Indianapolis IN 46254	317-298-8814	R	57*	.1
555	Crevier Motors Inc—*Don Crevier*	1500 Auto Mall Dr, Santa Ana CA 92705	714-835-3171	R	56*	.2
556	Brown and Brown Nissan AutoNation Inc	1701 W Broadway, Mesa AZ 85202		S	56*	.1
557	Cavender Buick Company Inc—*Robert Cavender*	17811 San Pedro Ave, San Antonio TX 78232	210-807-9089	R	56*	.1
558	De Nooyer Leasing Inc—*Joel Denooyer*	127 Wolf Rd, Colonie NY 12205	518-458-7700	R	56*	.1
559	Ed Rinke Chevrolet Inc—*Ray Stemple*	PO Box 3377, Center Line MI 48015	586-754-7000	R	56*	.1
560	Townsend Ford Inc—*Charles J Townsend*	5801 McFarland Blvd E, Tuscaloosa AL 35405	205-752-0401	R	56*	.1
561	Dewey Ford Inc—*Daniel Boettcher*	3055 SE Delaware Ave, Ankeny IA 50021	515-289-4949	R	56*	.1
562	Fred Martin Chevrolet—*Fred Martin*	333 E Market St, Akron OH 44304	330-535-4161	R	56*	.1
563	Underriner Motors—*William Underriner*	1830 4th Ave N, Billings MT 59101	406-255-2350	R	56*	.1
564	Gault Chevrolet Company Inc—*Robert Gault*	2507 North St, Endicott NY 13760	607-748-8244	R	56*	.1
565	Hampton Automotive Inc—*Sam Jones*	3700 Fernandina Rd, Columbia SC 29210	803-667-4937	R	56*	.1
566	Chevy Chase Cars Inc—*John F Bowis*	7725 Wisconsin Ave, Bethesda MD 20814	301-656-9200	R	55*	.2
567	John Hine Pontiac Mazda Dodge—*John Hine*	1545 Camino Del Rio S, San Diego CA 92108	619-297-4251	R	55*	.2
568	Crown Buick-GMC Truck Inc—*Larry Oggz*	2121 Clearview Pkwy, Metairie LA 70001	504-455-6666	R	55*	.1
569	Bob Fisher Chevrolet Geo	4111 Pottsville Pike, Reading PA 19605	610-370-6683	R	55*	.1
570	Gladstone Dodge Inc—*Andy Foster*	5610 N Oak Trafficway, Gladstone MO 64118	816-455-3500	R	55*	.1
571	Green Gifford Motor Corp—*Michael Galloway*	2747 N Military Hwy, Norfolk VA 23518	757-855-2277	R	54*	.2
572	Bonander Pontiac Inc—*Jerry Russell*	231 S Center St, Turlock CA 95380	209-632-8871	R	54*	.1
573	RE Barber Ford Inc (Holland Michigan)—*Larry Meister*	640 E 8th St, Holland MI 49423	616-396-2361	R	54*	.1
574	Delaware Motor Sales Inc—*Michael Uffner*	1606 Pennsylvania Ave, Wilmington DE 19806	302-656-3100	R	54*	.1
575	Capital Automobile Co—*William Bridges*	2210 Cobb Pkwy S, Smyrna GA 30080	770-952-2277	R	54*	.1
576	Gwatney Mazda of Germantown—*Russell Gwatney* Jim Keras Chevrolet Memphis	7300 Winchester Rd, Memphis TN 38125	901-751-7300	S	54*	.1
577	Cambria Truck Center—*Trevor Cambria*	136 Talmadge Rd, Edison NJ 08817	732-985-6500	R	54*	.1
578	General Truck Sales and Service Inc—*Jim McCulloch*	PO Box 161202, Memphis TN 38186	901-345-3270	R	54	.1
579	Bewley Allen Cadillac—*Ted Hwang*	801 E Main St, Alhambra CA 91801	626-289-5203	R	54*	.1
580	McCoy-Mills Ford Inc—*James Miller*	700 W Commonwealth Ave, Fullerton CA 92832	714-526-5501	R	53*	.3
581	Sopp Chevrolet—*Randy Sopp*	6400 S Atlantic Blvd, Bell CA 90201		R	53*	.1
582	Libertyville Lincoln Mercury Sales Inc—*Julius Marks*	941 S Milwaukee Ave, Libertyville IL 60048	847-367-1700	R	53*	.1
583	Jim Bradley Pontiac Buick GMC Inc—*Todd Burt*	3500 Jackson Rd, Ann Arbor MI 48103	734-769-1200	R	53*	.1
584	Colonial Cadillac-Hyundai Inc—*Jeffrey Feldman*	1655 N Olden Ave, Trenton NJ 08638	609-883-3500	R	53*	.1
585	Delaney Chevrolet Inc—*John J Delaney*	626 Water St, Indiana PA 15701	724-349-3000	R	53*	.1
586	Elm Chevrolet Company Inc—*Robert B McKinnon*	301 E Church St, Elmira NY 14901	607-734-4141	R	53*	.1
587	Harvey Cadillac Co—*John M Leese*	2600 28th St SE, Grand Rapids MI 49512	616-949-1140	R	53*	.1
588	Bubba Oustalet Ford Lincoln-Mercury Toyota—*Richard Oustalet*	PO Box 260, Jennings LA 70546	337-824-3673	R	53*	.1
589	Neil Huffman VW Inc Neil Huffman Automotive Group	4926 Dixie Hwy, Louisville KY 40216	502-448-6666	S	53*	.1
590	Rector Motor Car Co—*E James Hannay*	1010 Cadillac Way, Burlingame CA 94010	650-348-0111	R	53*	.1
591	Roto Lincoln-Mercury and Subaru Leasing Inc	1555 E Rand Rd, Arlington Heights IL 60004	847-255-5700	R	53*	.1
592	Sheppard Motors Ltd—*John Sheppard*	PO Box 2807, Eugene OR 97402	541-343-8811	R	53*	.1
593	Spradley Barr of Greeley—*Mark Cook*	4901 29th St, Greeley CO 80634	970-506-3600	R	53*	.1
594	Jerry's Chevrolet/Buick Inc—*Jerry Durant*	PO Box 839, Weatherford TX 76086	817-596-8088	R	52*	.1
595	Mercedes-Benz Of Cincinnati—*Dana C Hackney*	8727 Montgomery Rd, Cincinnati OH 45236	513-984-9000	R	52*	.1
596	Island Lincoln-Mercury Inc—*Jim Cavanaugh*	1850 E Merritt Island, Merritt Island FL 32952	321-452-9220	R	52*	.1
597	Patson Inc—*Doug Cayce*	4000 Mannheim Rd, Franklin Park IL 60131	847-671-7100	R	52*	.1

Note: An asterisk (*) indicates an estimated financial figure. The company type code used is as follows: R = Private, P = Public, S = Private Subsidiary, B = Public Subsidiary, D = Division, J = Joint Venture, I = Investment Fund.

ANY RANKINGS BY SALES WITHIN 4-DIGIT SIC

nk	Company Name—Executive Officer	Address, City, State, Zip	Phone	Type	Fin	Empls
598	Vic Canever Chevrolet Co—Richard Canever	3000 Owen Rd, Fenton MI 48430	810-629-3350	R	52*	.1
599	Hennessy River View Ford Inc—John Hennessey	2200 US Hwy 30, Oswego IL 60543	630-897-8900	R	52*	.1
600	Krieger Motor Company Inc—Douglas Krieger	501 W Bypass 61, Muscatine IA 52761	563-263-5432	R	52*	.1
601	MacMulkin Chevrolet Geo Inc—Bernard J Thompson Sr	3 Marmon Dr, Nashua NH 03060	603-888-1121	R	52*	.1
602	McDaniel Motor Co—Michael J McDaniel	1111 Mount Vernon Ave, Marion OH 43302	740-389-2355	R	52*	.1
603	Sharp Chevrolet Inc	PO Box 1654, Watertown SD 57201		R	52*	.1
604	South Tacoma Honda—Ron Loper	7802 S Tacoma Way, Tacoma WA 98409	253-472-2300	R	52*	.1
605	University Motors Ltd	60 Don Knotts Blvd, Morgantown WV 26508	304-296-4401	R	52*	.1
606	World Wide Motors Inc—Paul A C Pettenaro	3900 E 96th St, Indianapolis IN 46240	317-580-6800	R	52*	.1
607	Elder Ford Inc—Irma Elder Elder Automotive Group	777 John R Rd, Troy MI 48083	248-585-4000	D	52*	.1
608	Jackson Acura—Harvey L Jackson	10900 Alpharetta Hwy, Roswell GA 30076		R	52*	.1
609	Hale Trailer Brake and Wheel Inc—Barry Hale	PO Box 1400, Voorhees NJ 08043	856-768-1330	R	52*	.2
610	Dan Vaden Chevrolet Inc—Dan M Vaden Jr	9393 Abercorn St, Savannah GA 31406	912-925-9393	R	51*	.1
611	Ivan Leonard Chevrolet Inc—John Wolfe	1620 Montgomery Hwy, Hoover AL 35216	205-588-4411	R	51*	.1
612	Pat Clark Pontiac GMC—Pat Clark Jr	2575 E Sahara Ave, Las Vegas NV 89104	702-457-2111	R	51*	.1
613	Union Park Buick GMC—John Smith	1704 Pennsylvania Ave, Wilmington DE 19806	302-353-1636	R	51*	.1
614	Jimmy Walker Auto Group—Jimmy Walker	2018 Hwy 15 N, Laurel MS 39440	601-649-4511	R	51*	.1
615	Key Cadillac Oldsmobile—Adam Stanzak	6825 York Ave S, Minneapolis MN 55435	952-920-4300	R	51*	.1
616	Superior Buick Cadillac—Louis Faller	1151 W 104th St, Kansas City MO 64114		R	51*	.1
617	Legacy Automotive Inc (McDonough Georgia)—Emanuel Jones	413 Industrial Blvd, McDonough GA 30253	770-914-2800	R	51*	.1
618	BMW of the Hudson Valley—Buddy Hill	2068 South Rd, Poughkeepsie NY 12601		R	51*	.1
619	Royal Automotive—Greg Belcher	3010 Columbiana Rd, Vestavia Hills AL 35216	205-823-3100	R	50*	.1
620	Colonial Ford Truck Sales Inc—Rob Brown	1833 Commerce Rd, Richmond VA 23224	804-232-6700	R	50*	.1
621	Bobby Layman Chevrolet-Geo—Robert A Layman	3900 W Broad St, Columbus OH 43228		R	50*	.1
622	Kerry Ford Inc—Arthur Hendrixson	155 W Kemper, Springdale OH 45246	513-671-6400	R	50*	.1
623	Malcolm Cunningham Automotive Group Inc—Malcolm A Cunningham	5675 Peachtree Industr, Atlanta GA 30341	770-621-0200	R	50*	.1
624	Bohn Brothers Inc—Donald B Bohn Jr	3611 Lapalco Blvd, Harvey LA 70058	504-341-3300	R	50	.1
625	Herb Gordon Autoworld Inc	3131 Automobile Blvd, Silver Spring MD 20904	301-890-3000	R	50*	.1
626	Griffin Ford Inc—Ken Alderson	1710 North Expy, Griffin GA 30223	770-229-1600	R	50*	.1
627	Lucas Ford Inc—Chris Lucas	1360 Greely Chapel Rd, Lima OH 45804	419-224-3673	R	50*	.1
628	Plattner Automotive Group	6100 NW 167th St, Hialeah FL 33014	305-362-7283	R	50*	.1
629	Yokem Toyota Inc—Hoyt Yokem	1199 E Bert Kouns Indu, Shreveport LA 71105	318-798-3773	R	50*	.1
630	Saccucci Lincoln-Mercury-Honda Inc—Cora Saccucci	1350 W Main Rd, Middletown RI 02842	401-847-4737	R	50*	.1
631	Lexus of Mishawaka—Perry Watson IV	4325 N Grape Rd, Mishawaka IN 46545	574-243-7700	R	50*	.1
632	Frontier Ford—James Landes	3701 Stevens Creek Blv, Santa Clara CA 95051	408-241-1800	R	49*	.2
633	Jerry Biggers Chevrolet Inc—James Leichter	1385 E Chicago St, Elgin IL 60120	847-742-9000	R	49*	.1
634	Giant Auto Group of Ashland—Sim E Fryson	2565 Winchester Ave, Ashland KY 41101	606-329-2288	R	49*	.1
635	Master Pontiac Buick GMC Inc—William L Schafer III	PO Box 204688, Augusta GA 30917	706-855-9400	R	49*	.1
636	Paradise Ford Inc—Wayne Martin	1360 W King St, Cocoa FL 32922	321-632-2222	R	49*	.1
637	Lou LaRiche Chevrolet Inc—LH La Riche	40875 Plymouth Rd, Plymouth MI 48170	734-453-4600	R	49*	.1
638	Butler County Motor Company Inc—Cathy Glasgow	PO Box 1028, Butler PA 16003	724-287-2766	R	49*	.1
639	Ferrario Ford Inc—Don Ferrario	2472 Corning Rd, Elmira NY 14903	607-734-1681	R	49*	.1
640	Gilleland Chevrolet Inc—Duane Gilleland	3019 W Division St, Saint Cloud MN 56301	320-281-4290	R	49*	.1
641	Girard Motors Inc—Robbie Tasca	425 Goldstar Hwy, Groton CT 06340	860-448-0050	R	49*	.1
642	Jordan Automotive Group—Craig Kapson	920 E Jefferson Blvd, Mishawaka IN 46545	574-259-1981	R	49*	.1
643	Snethkamp Chrysler Jeep Inc—Mark Snethkamp	11600 Telegraph Rd, Redford MI 48239	313-255-2700	R	49*	.1
644	Stone Mountain Chrysler Jeep Dodge—Darryl Ford	5054 E Hwy 78, Stone Mountain GA 30087		R	49*	.1
645	BMW Northwest Inc—Manfred Scharmach	4011 20th St E, Fife WA 98424	253-922-8700	R	49*	.1
646	Taylor Chevrolet Inc—Milton J Taylor	2510 N Memorial Dr, Lancaster OH 43130	740-653-2091	R	48*	.2
647	Volkswagen Santa Monica Inc—Mike Sullivan	2440 Santa Monica Blvd, Santa Monica CA 90404		S	48*	.2
648	Tommie Vaughn Motors—Tommie Vaughn	1145 N Shepherd Dr, Houston TX 77008	713-869-4661	R	48*	.1
649	Palmetto Ford Inc—Graham Eubank	1625 Savannah Hwy, Charleston SC 29407	843-571-3673	R	48*	.1
650	Phil Smart Inc—Phil M Smart Jr	600 E Pike St, Seattle WA 98122	206-324-5959	R	48*	.1
651	Bo Beuckman Ford Inc—Fred Beuckman Jr	15675 Manchester Rd, Ellisville MO 63011	636-227-5700	R	48*	.1
652	Varsity Ford Lincoln Mercury Inc—Anthony Majors	1351 Earl Rudder Fwy, College Station TX 77845	979-694-2022	R	48*	.1
653	Steve Hopkins Inc—Scott Hopkins	2459 Auto Mall Pkwy, Fairfield CA 94533	707-427-1000	R	48*	.1
654	Neil Huffman Automotive Group—Neil Huffman	100 Oxmoor Ct, Louisville KY 40222	502-426-8048	R	48*	.1
655	Reichard Buick Inc—Gene Reichard	161 Salem Ave, Dayton OH 45406	937-401-2034	R	48*	.1
656	Whaling City Ford—Romano Primus	475 Broad St, New London CT 06320	860-443-8361	R	48*	.1
657	Allen Samuels Dodge Hyundai—Thomas Hervey Allen Samuels Auto Group	7740 NE Loop 820, Fort Worth TX 76180	817-276-7763	S	47*	.1
658	Auburn Buick Pontiac GMC—David Palaca	2725 Grass Valley Hwy, Auburn CA 95603	530-823-6111	R	47*	.1
659	Bill Penney Toyota Company Inc—Jerre F Penney	4808 University Dr NW, Huntsville AL 35816	256-837-1111	R	47*	.1
660	Bob Davidson Ford Lincoln Mercury Inc—Bruce Schundler	1845 E Joppa Rd, Baltimore MD 21234	410-661-6400	R	47*	.1
661	Bob Dunn Ford Inc—Robert C Dunn Jr	801 E Bessemer Ave, Greensboro NC 27405	336-275-9761	R	47*	.1
662	Cavender Cadillac—William B Cavender Jr	PO Box 419, San Antonio TX 78215	210-226-7221	R	47*	.1
663	Guaranty Chevrolet Motors—Robert J Long	PO Box 11566, Santa Ana CA 92711	714-973-1711	R	47*	.1
664	Hansel Prestige Inc—Tyler Whetsel	2800 Corby Ave, Santa Rosa CA 95407	707-545-6602	R	47*	.1
665	Huntington Beach Dodge—Clay James	16555 Beach Blvd, Huntington Beach CA 92647		R	47*	.1
666	ig Burton and Company Inc—Charles Burton	793 Bay Rd, Milford DE 19963	302-422-3041	R	47*	.1
667	Joe Self Chevrolet Inc—Joe Self Jr	8801 E Kellog Dr, Wichita KS 67207	316-684-6521	R	47*	.1
668	Mike McGrath Auto Center—Pat McGrath	4610 Center Point Rd N, Cedar Rapids IA 52402	319-393-4610	R	47*	.1
669	Musson-Patout Automotive Group Inc—Diane Musson Kyle Dealer Management Agency Inc	214 W Hwy 90, New Iberia LA 70560	337-367-0488	S	47*	.1
670	Patriot Buick GMC—Bill Cliewer	4600 E Central Texas E, Killeen TX 76543	254-247-3395	R	47*	.1
671	Plaza Motors Inc—Andrew T Jessup	68111 E Palm Canyon Dr, Cathedral City CA 92234	760-904-0525	R	47*	.1
672	Ray Skillman Auto Center	8424 US Hwy 31 S, Indianapolis IN 46227	317-888-9500	S	47*	.1
673	Round Rock Auto Group—Don Tamburro	2301 N IH-35, Round Rock TX 78664	512-244-9000	R	47*	.1
674	Scholfield Pontiac GMC—Scott Hatchett	7633 E Kellogg Dr, Wichita KS 67207	316-768-4950	R	47*	.1
675	Shadyside Honda—Alvin Shuman	5121 Liberty Ave, Pittsburgh PA 15224	412-683-3800	R	47*	.1
676	Sovereign Motor Cars Ltd—Alan Feldman	1800 Shore Pky, Brooklyn NY 11214	718-258-5100	R	47*	.1
677	Cunningham Motors Inc—Calvin Cothron	2516 Memorial Blvd, Springfield TN 37172	615-212-2263	R	47*	.1
678	Park Circle Motor Co—Jeffrey A Legum	1829 Reisterstown Rd S, Baltimore MD 21208	410-484-0600	R	47*	.1
679	Pat Patterson Motor Sales Inc—JM Patterson	2085 Covington Pike, Memphis TN 38128	901-373-3000	R	47*	.1
680	Boggus Ford—Bob Boggus	PO Box 2318, McAllen TX 78502	956-686-7411	R	46	.1
681	Chapman Automotive Group LLC—Eddie Davault	PO Box 11550, Scottsdale AZ 85271	480-970-0740	R	46*	.1
682	Brewbaker Motors Inc—W Brewbaker Jr	300 Eastern Blvd, Montgomery AL 36117	334-279-0174	R	46*	.1
683	Carl Black Of Orlando—Mike Bowsher	11500 E Colonial Dr, Orlando FL 32817	407-849-0610	R	46*	.1

Rank	Company Name—Executive Officer	Address, City, State, Zip	Phone	Type	Fin	Empls
684	Community Motors Inc—Harry McCall	8325 W 159th St 8425, Tinley Park IL 60477	708-377-3851	R	46*	.1
685	Ed Napleton Honda—Mark Rahn	4780 N Service Rd, Saint Peters MO 63376	636-928-1155	S	46*	.1
	Honda of Tiffany Springs					
686	Fairway Ford Sales Inc (Placentia California)—Dave Patton	1350 E Yorba Linda Blv, Placentia CA 92870	714-579-3857	R	46*	.1
687	Herb Easley Motors Corp—Brad Lawson	1125 Central Fwy, Wichita Falls TX 76306	940-228-4402	R	46*	.1
688	Jim McKay Chevrolet Inc—Kathy McKay-Olsick	3509 University Dr, Fairfax VA 22030	703-591-4800	R	46*	.1
689	Mossy Nissan Houston—David L Mossy	12150 Katy Fwy, Houston TX 77079		R	46*	.1
690	Parks Chevrolet Inc—James Berry	611 Edgewood St, Kernersville NC 27284	336-993-2102	R	46*	.1
691	Sam Johnson Cross Creek Lincoln—Sam Johnson Jr	PO Box 43805, Fayetteville NC 28309	910-864-5240	R	46*	.1
692	Mike Pruitt Honda—Dave Kinion	43 Pruitt Blvd, Akron OH 44310	330-633-6060	R	46*	.1
693	DMR Automotive Group LLC—Pamela E Rodgers	23755 Allen Rd, Woodhaven MI 48183	734-676-9600	R	46*	.1
694	Kuni Honda on Arapahoe—Herm Brocksmith	10750 E Arapaho Rd, Centennial CO 80112	303-800-1352	R	45*	.2
695	Freeway Motors Inc—Robert I Will Jr	4701 11th Ave NE, Seattle WA 98105	206-634-3322	R	45*	.1
696	Harry Green Chevrolet Inc—Harry L Green Jr	PO Box 1527, Clarksburg WV 26302	304-624-6304	R	45*	.1
697	Newins Bay Shore Ford Inc—Charles Stickney	219 W Main St, Bay Shore NY 11706	631-665-1300	R	45*	.1
698	Noble Automotive Group—Steve Westra	PO Box 579, Indianola IA 50125	515-961-8151	R	45*	.1
699	Ratigan Motor Center Inc—John Elliott	PO Box 386, Missouri Valley IA 51555	712-642-4731	R	45*	.1
700	Long-McArthur Inc—North McArthur	3450 S 9th St, Salina KS 67401	785-823-2237	R	45*	.1
701	Anoka Motors LLC—Franf Wrzos	10401 Woodcrest Dr, Coon Rapids MN 55433	763-427-1120	R	45*	.1
702	Frank Z Chevrolet Company Inc—Nick Monk	442 N Main St, Dayton OH 45405	937-224-2600	R	45*	.1
703	Matthews-Hargreaves Chevrolet Co—Walter Tutak	2000 E 12 Mile Rd, Royal Oak MI 48067	248-398-8800	R	45*	.1
704	Capitol Mazda—Nick Corini	909 W Capitol Expy Aut, San Jose CA 95136	408-723-8800	R	45*	.1
705	Rairdon's Chrysler Jeep of Kirkland—Craig Rairdon	12828 NE 124th St, Kirkland WA 98034		R	45*	.1
706	Tennessee Motor Co—Micheal B Kidd	207 Princeton Rd, Johnson City TN 37601	423-282-3000	R	45*	.1
707	UHL Truck Sales Inc—Mike Shireman	4300 Poplar Level Rd, Louisville KY 40213	502-451-8360	R	45*	.1
708	Toyota of Bedford—Jed Hunter	18151 Rockside Rd, Bedford OH 44146	440-439-8600	R	45*	.1
709	White's Frontier Motors—Tim White Sr	444 Skyline Dr, Gillette WY 82718	307-257-6808	R	45*	.1
710	Gate City Motor Company Inc—Bruce Beaton	PO Box 20600, Greensboro NC 27420	336-274-0195	R	45*	.1
711	Burd Ford Inc—Richard Burd	10320 E Pendleton Pke, Indianapolis IN 46236	317-545-8551	R	45*	.1
712	R and H Motor Cars Ltd—Rick Astarita	9727 Reisterstown Rd, Owings Mills MD 21117	410-363-3900	R	44*	.2
713	Korum Motors Inc—Jerry M Korum	PO Box 538, Puyallup WA 98371	253-845-6600	R	44*	.2
714	Viva Chevrolet—JA Dick	5915 Montana Ave, El Paso TX 79925	915-613-2017	R	44*	.1
715	Crown Motors Inc	555 W Cypress, Redding CA 96001	530-241-4321	R	44*	.1
716	Jeff Schmitt Auto Group—Jeff Schmitt	PO Box 152, Fairborn OH 45324	937-878-3471	R	44*	.1
717	Norman Frede Chevrolet Co—Joan McKinney	16801 Feathercraft Ln, Houston TX 77058	281-486-2200	R	44*	.1
718	Chino Hills Ford Sales Inc—Charlie Grosso	4480 Chino Hills Pky, Chino CA 91710	909-203-5700	S	44*	.1
719	Falore Chrysler/Plymouth/Jeep and Eagle—Joseph Falore	680 E El Camino Real, Sunnyvale CA 94087	408-735-6888	R	44*	.1
720	Stoddard Imported Cars Inc—Pat DiCesare	38845 Mentor Ave, Willoughby OH 44094	440-951-1040	R	44*	.1
721	Douglas Infiniti—Edward English	430 Morris Ave, Summit NJ 07901	908-522-7300	R	44*	.1
722	Fiehrer Motors Inc—Robert Fiehrer	2531 Dixie Hwy, Hamilton OH 45015	513-863-8111	R	44*	.1
723	Ken Garff Motors—Robert Garff	405 S Main St, Salt Lake City UT 84111	801-955-7448	R	44*	.1
724	Sanborn Chevrolet Inc—Dennis Calton	1210 S Cherokee Ln, Lodi CA 95240	209-642-4954	R	44*	.1
725	Bird-Kultgen Inc—Peter Kultgen	1701 W Loop 340, Waco TX 76712	254-666-2473	R	43*	.1
726	Kenyon Dodge Inc	110 SE 6th St, Fort Lauderdale FL 33301	954-769-6000	S	43	.1
	AutoNation Inc					
727	Mercedes-Benz of Encino—John M Hansell	16721 Ventura Blvd, Encino CA 91436		R	43*	.1
728	Piehler Buick GMC—Michael Piehler	755 Ridge Rd, Webster NY 14580	585-347-2086	R	43*	.1
729	McClinton Chevrolet Company Inc—James McClinton Jr	712 Liberty St, Parkersburg WV 26101	304-099-2478	R	43*	.1
730	Sioux City Ford Lincoln Mercury—Rob Brooks	3601 Singing Hills Blv, Sioux City IA 51106	712-277-8420	R	43*	.1
731	Blake Utter Ford—Blake Utter	215 Hwy 75 N, Denison TX 75020	903-465-5671	R	43*	.1
732	BMW South Atlanta—Henry L Aaron Sr	4171 Jonesboro Rd, Union City GA 30291	770-969-0755	R	43*	.1
733	Lexus of Dayton Inc—Jeff Pizza	8111 Yankee St, Centerville OH 45458	937-438-3800	R	43*	.1
734	Woody Sander Ford Inc—William Sander	235 W Mitchell Ave, Cincinnati OH 45232	513-541-5586	R	43*	.1
735	East Tulsa Dodge Inc—Yvonne Hovell	4627 S Memorial Dr, Tulsa OK 74145	918-663-6343	R	43*	.1
736	Marquette Public Service Garage—John S Veiht	919 W Baraga Ave, Marquette MI 49855	906-226-3592	R	43*	<.1
737	Modern Chevrolet Co—Fred Fowler	5955 University Pkwy, Winston Salem NC 27105	336-722-4191	R	42*	.2
738	Bickford Motors Inc—Mike Bickford	PO Box 1119, Snohomish WA 98291	360-568-2122	R	42*	.1
739	Freeman Honda—Jerry Freeman	39670 I-20 East, Dallas TX 75237	214-800-6500	R	42*	.1
740	Riverton Motors Inc—Christopher B Page	10770 S Automall Dr, Sandy UT 84070	801-576-4600	R	42*	.1
741	Larry H Miller Honda—Eric Rosner	4646 S State St, Murray UT 84107	801-262-3331	S	42*	.1
	Larry H Miller Group					
742	Daniels Long Chevrolet—Elizabeth Daniels	670 Automotive Dr, Colorado Springs CO 80906	719-632-5591	R	42*	.1
743	Chapman Ford of Lancaster—Ray Garraffa	5201 Manheim Pke, East Petersburg PA 17520	717-299-4331	R	42*	.1
744	Drew Hyundai—Bill Drew	PO Box 188, La Mesa CA 91944	619-668-7756	R	42*	.1
745	Midwest Super Store—Eldon Estes	1100 E 30th, Hutchinson KS 67502	620-662-6631	R	42*	.1
746	Pugmire Lincoln Mercury Inc—Richard H Pugmire	1865 Cobb Pky S, Marietta GA 30062	770-952-2261	R	42*	.1
747	R and R Inc—Dan Ralich	44 Victoria Rd, Youngstown OH 44515	330-799-1536	R	42*	.1
748	Sharpe Buick and BMW Inc—George Sharpe	1010 28th St SE, Grand Rapids MI 49508	616-452-5101	R	42*	.1
749	Finish Line Ford Inc—William Pearson	2100 W Pioneer Pkwy, Peoria IL 61615	309-693-2525	R	42*	.1
750	Universal Ford Inc—Harry Harris	10751 W Broad St, Glen Allen VA 23060	804-273-9700	R	42*	.1
751	Lang Chevrolet Co—Dick F Lang	635 Orchard Ln, Beavercreek OH 45434	937-458-3161	R	42*	.1
752	Gulfgate Dodge—James H Davis	7250 Gulf Fwy, Houston TX 77017		R	42*	.1
753	JK Chevrolet Isuzu—Robert Turner	1451 Hwy 69, Nederland TX 77627	409-527-4142	R	42*	.1
754	Lexus of Huntsville—Ellenae Fairhurst	6580 University Dr, Huntsville AL 35806	880-721-9560	R	42*	.1
755	Bosak Motor Sales Inc—Cary Bosak	3111 W Lincoln Hwy, Merrillville IN 46410	219-738-2323	R	42*	<.1
756	Casey Chevrolet Corp	11700 Jefferson Ave, Newport News VA 23606	757-591-1100	S	41*	.2
	Casey Auto Group Inc					
757	Brookdale Ford Inc—Tom Rabiola	9700 56th Avenue N, Plymouth MN 55442	763-561-5500	R	41*	.1
758	Gus Johnson ford Inc—Gus Johnson	8300 E Sprague Ave, Spokane Valley WA 99212	509-924-1000	R	41*	.1
759	Jackson Automotive Inc—James L Jackson Jr	4781 Riverside Dr, Macon GA 31210	478-477-4858	R	41*	.1
760	Vista Lexus—Tori Shuken	21611 Ventura Blvd, Woodland Hills CA 91364	818-888-2777	R	41*	.1
761	Winslow BMW—Phil A Winslow	730 N Circle Dr, Colorado Springs CO 80909	719-473-1373	R	41*	.1
762	BMW Of Darien	140 Ledge Rd, Darien CT 06820	203-656-1804	R	41*	.1
763	Broome Oldsmobile-Cadillac Inc—Paul Broome	11911 E 40 Hwy, Independence MO 64055	816-358-2500	R	41*	.1
764	Circle Chevrolet Co—Thomas J Defelice	641 Shrewsbury Ave, Shrewsbury NJ 07702	732-741-3130	R	41*	.1
765	Coastal Lincoln—Brian Kelledy	4411 Interstate 10 E, Baytown TX 77521	281-839-9900	R	41*	.1
766	Mack Massey Motors Inc—Agustin Vasquez	950 Crockett St, El Paso TX 79922		R	41*	.1
767	Roundtree Ford Lincoln Mercury—Ken Shapen	8770 Business Pk Dr, Shreveport LA 71105	318-798-3673	D	41*	.1
	Roundtree Automotive Group LLC					
768	Taylor Cos—Andy Bryant	PO Box 3008, Arlington WA 98223	360-659-0886	R	41*	.1

Note: An asterisk (*) indicates an estimated financial figure. The company type code used is as follows: R = Private, P = Public, S = Private Subsidiary, B = Public Subsidiary, D = Division, J = Joint Venture, I = Investment Fund.

RANKINGS BY SALES WITHIN 4-DIGIT SIC

	Company Name—Executive Officer	Address, City, State, Zip	Phone	Type	Fin	Empls
769	Don Ayres Pontiac Inc—Don Ayres	4740 Lima Rd, Fort Wayne IN 46808	260-484-0551	R	40*	.1
770	Alaska Sales and Service Inc—Dianna Pfeiffer	1300 E 5th Ave, Anchorage AK 99501	907-279-9641	R	40*	.1
771	David Wilson Ford of Orange—Michael Kitzmiller	1350 W Katella Ave, Orange CA 92867	714-633-6731	R	40*	.1
772	Dayton Andrews Inc—Alfred Andrews	2388 Gulf to Bay Blvd, Clearwater FL 33765	727-799-4539	R	40*	.1
773	Dimmitt Chevrolet—Lawrence H Dimmitt III	25485 US Hwy 19 N, Clearwater FL 33763		R	40*	.1
774	Edwards Subaru Hyundai—David Edwards	1029 32nd Ave, Council Bluffs IA 51501	712-366-9411	R	40*	.1
775	Hubacher Cadillac Inc—Bob Foster	1 Cadillac Dr, Sacramento CA 95825		R	40*	.1
776	Huntington Beach Ford—Robert Levenstein	18255 Beach Blvd, Huntington Beach CA 92648	714-842-6611	R	40*	.1
777	Moore Cadillac Company Inc—Frank Perrone	9177 W Broad St, Richmond VA 23294		R	40*	.1
778	Orange Coast Jeep-Chrysler Inc—Johnathan Gray	2929 Harbor Blvd, Costa Mesa CA 92626	714-549-8023	R	40*	.1
779	Orange Motor Company Inc—Carl Touhey	799 Central Ave, Albany NY 12206	518-489-5414	R	40*	.1
780	Piercey Toyota—Art Wicker	950 Thompson St, Milpitas CA 95035		R	40*	.1
781	Swope Motors Inc—Sam Swope	1100 N Dixie Hwy, Elizabethtown KY 42701	270-765-2181	R	40*	.1
782	Uebelhor and Sons Inc—Anthony Uebelhor	PO Box 630, Jasper IN 47547	812-482-2222	R	40*	.1
783	Good Chevrolet Inc—Howard Sheridan	PO Box 935, Renton WA 98057	425-235-2000	R	40	.1
784	Benzel-Busch Motor Car Corp—Joseph Agresta	28 Grand Ave, Englewood NJ 07631	201-567-1400	R	40*	.1
785	Frankel Cadillac Land Rover—Robert Frankel	201 Reisterstown Rd, Owings Mills MD 21117	410-484-8800	R	40*	.1
786	Wallace Buick Jeep—Joseph L Breslin	3434 NE Sandy Blvd, Portland OR 97232	503-234-9441	R	40*	.1
787	Dodge City of McKinney—Charles W Sutton	700 S Central Expy, McKinney TX 75070	214-504-2101	R	40*	.1
788	Luther Brookdale Chrysler Jeep Dodge Inc—David Luther	8188 Brooklyn Blvd, Brooklyn Park MN 55445	763-535-5200	R	40*	.1
789	Powers-Swain Chevrolet Inc—WC Powers	PO Box 35845, Fayetteville NC 28303	910-864-9500	R	40*	.1
790	McLarty Auto Mall—Thomas F McLarty III	PO Box 1228, Texarkana TX 75504	903-792-7121	R	40*	.1
791	Courtesy Ford-Lincoln-Mercury—JR Fregia	231 W Main St, Danville IL 61832	217-442-1840	R	40*	.1
792	De Nooyer Chevrolet—William T DeNooyer	5800 Stadium Dr, Kalamazoo MI 49009	269-372-3040	R	40*	.1
793	Eisenhauer Nissan-Saab—Pete Eisenhauer	6345 Penn Ave Rte 422, Wernersville PA 19565	610-678-8071	R	40*	.1
794	Elk Grove Pontiac Buick GMC—Tony Stevens	8450 Laguna Grove Dr, Elk Grove CA 95757	916-400-2782	R	40*	.1
795	Giuffre Buick Inc—Roger Sables	1030 S Dirksen Pkwy, Springfield IL 62703	217-953-4820	R	40*	.1
796	Henderson Automotive Family—Randy Henderson	810 Ridge Rd, Webster NY 14580	585-787-1700	R	40*	.1
797	Infiniti of Chantilly—Ken Smith	4145 Auto Park Cir, Chantilly VA 20151	703-322-3600	R	40*	.1
798	Massey Automotive Group—Jerry E Massey	1706 Massey Blvd, Hagerstown MD 21740	301-739-6756	R	40*	.1
799	Peterbilt Of Louisville Inc—Glenn Larson	4415 Hamburg Pke, Jeffersonville IN 47130	812-288-8007	R	40*	.1
800	Sunnyside Motor Company Inc—DJ Harrington Jr	PO Box 74, Holden MA 01520	508-829-4333	R	40*	.1
801	Cowles Parkway Ford Inc—Steven Cowles	13779 Noblewood Plz, Woodbridge VA 22193		R	39*	.2
802	Chapman Ford Sales Inc—Joseph Chapman	1255 Columbus Ave, Marysville OH 43040	937-642-0015	R	39*	.1
803	Lafayette Motor Company Inc	1515 Jefferson St, Lafayette LA 70501		R	39*	.1
804	Carl Beasley Ford Inc—Edward Baker	PO Box 3115, York PA 17402	717-755-2911	R	39*	.1
805	Freysinger Pontiac Inc—Tom Freysinger	6251 Carlisle Pike, Mechanicsburg PA 17050	717-766-8422	R	39*	.1
806	Len Lyall Chevrolet Company Inc—Dan Johnson	14500 E Colfax Ave, Aurora CO 80011	303-344-7186	R	39*	.1
807	River Oaks Chrysler Dodge Jeep Ram—Jack Helfman	4807 Kirby Dr, Houston TX 77098	713-524-3801	R	39*	.1
808	Dick Keffer Pontiac GMC Truck—Ken Reed	1001 Tyvola Rd, Charlotte NC 28217	704-525-7650	R	39*	.1
809	ORR Chevrolet Searcy—Greg Orr	PO Box 237, Searcy AR 72143	501-268-2423	R	39*	.1
810	Cross Motors Corp—Joe D Cross	PO Box 34067, Louisville KY 40232	502-459-9900	R	39*	.1
811	Nissan-Mitsubishi-Kia of Lake Charles—John F Stelly	1700 Siebarth Dr, Lake Charles LA 70615	337-439-9955	R	39*	.1
812	New Country Pontiac GMC Buick and Oldsmobile—Michael Cantanucci	205 Rt 146, Mechanicville NY 12118	518-664-9861	R	39*	.1
813	Classic Ford Lincoln Mercury—Stan Lovejoy	1698 Booker Dairy Rd, Smithfield NC 27577	919-934-6500	R	39*	.1
814	HE McGonigals Inc—Ivan Gingerich	1220 E Blvd, Kokomo IN 46902	765-459-0381	R	39*	.1
815	Smokey Point Buick GMC—Anderson B Bryant Jr	16632 Smokey Point Blv, Arlington WA 98223	360-659-0886	R	39*	.1
816	Peach State Truck Centers—Tom Reynolds	PO Box 808, Norcross GA 30091	770-449-5300	R	39*	.2
817	RE Barber Ford Inc (Ventura California)—Gail Alcalla	3440 E Main St, Ventura CA 93003	805-642-6701	R	38*	.1
818	Trader Bud's Westside Dodge Sonic Automotive Inc	4000 W Broad St, Columbus OH 43228		S	38*	.1
819	Outten Chevrolet Inc—Willy Outten	1701 W Tilghman St, Allentown PA 18104	610-434-4201	R	38*	.1
820	Broadway Ford Truck Sales Inc—Eli R Linton	1506 S 7th St, Saint Louis MO 63104	314-241-9140	R	38*	.1
821	Brown Nissan Pontiac and Subaru Inc—William Schuiling	3200 Columbia Pike, Arlington VA 22204	703-486-3200	R	38*	.1
822	Cassens and Sons Inc—Allen Cassens	3333 S Hwy 159, Glen Carbon IL 62034	618-656-6070	S	38*	.1
823	Plaza Ford Inc (Bel Air Maryland)—Thomas Walls	1701 Bel Air Rd, Bel Air MD 21014	410-838-3100	R	38*	.1
824	Tyrrell-Doyle Auto Centers—David A Doyle	2142 W Lincolnway, Cheyenne WY 82001	307-634-2540	R	38*	.1
825	Whitman Ford Company Inc—Jon Whitman	7555 Lewis Ave, Temperance MI 48182	734-847-3673	R	38*	.1
826	Witham Truck Center	2343 Biddle Rd, Medford OR 97504	541-773-6293	R	38*	.1
827	Champion Ford Lincoln Mercury—Bruce Brubaker	140 Southtown Blvd, Owensboro KY 42303	270-684-1441	R	38*	.1
828	Superstition Springs Chrysler Jeep Inc—Wayne Martin	6130 E Auto Park Dr, Mesa AZ 85206		R	38*	<.1
829	Ukiah Ford-Lincoln-Mercury Inc—Huxley Richardson	1170 S State St, Ukiah CA 95482	707-468-0091	R	38*	<.1
830	Beck Imports Inc—Ed Keady	5141 E Independence Bl, Charlotte NC 28212		R	37*	.1
831	Bill Page Honda—William Page III	6715 Arlington Blvd, Falls Church VA 22042	703-533-9700	R	37*	.1
832	Bud Wolf Chevrolet Inc—Charlie Fraker	5350 N Keystone Ave, Indianapolis IN 46220	317-257-4481	R	37*	.1
833	Champion Ford Katy—Mike Johnson AutoNation Inc	20777 Katy Fwy, Katy TX 77450		S	37*	.1
834	Dudley Martin Chevrolet Inc—Michael C Martin	8000 Sudley Rd, Manassas VA 20109	703-659-0458	R	37*	.1
835	Murray Chevrolet Co—Stephen Murray	1999 E Powell Blvd, Gresham OR 97080	503-661-2222	R	37*	.1
836	Parkway Chevrolet—Jean Durdin	25500 State Hwy 249, Tomball TX 77375	281-351-8211	R	37*	.1
837	Rudy Luther Imports Inc—Rudy Luther	7801 Lyndale Ave S, Bloomington MN 55420	952-881-6200	R	37*	.1
838	Suburban Chevrolet Cadillac Ann Arbor—David T Fischer	3515 Jackson Rd, Ann Arbor MI 48103	734-663-3321	R	37*	.1
839	Tom Naquin Chevrolet Nissan Inc—J Phad Naquin	2500 W Lexington Ave, Elkhart IN 46514	574-293-8621	R	37*	.1
840	Town Motors Inc—Robert Siebold	135 S Dean St, Englewood NJ 07631	201-568-5200	R	37*	.1
841	Wally McCarthy's Cadillac Inc—Wally McCarthy	2325 N Prior Ave, Saint Paul MN 55113	651-925-2666	R	37*	.1
842	Whitaker Buick Jeep Eagle Co—Steve Whitaker	131 19th St SW, Forest Lake MN 55025	651-645-7781	R	37*	.1
843	Gene Butman Ford Sales Inc—Ken Butman	2105 Washtenaw Ave, Ypsilanti MI 48197	734-482-8581	R	37*	.1
844	Continental BMW of Darien—Felix F Callari BMW Of Darien	140 Ledge Rd, Darien CT 06820	203-656-1804	D	37*	.1
845	Ganley Chevrolet Inc—Jim Helton	15315 Lorain Ave, Cleveland OH 44111	216-671-1620	R	37*	.1
846	Johnson Motor Sales Inc—Curt Johnson	620 Deere Dr, New Richmond WI 54017		R	37*	.1
847	Phil Waterfords Manteca Ford Mercury—Phil Waterford	555 N Main St, Manteca CA 95336	209-239-3561	R	37*	.1
848	Suburban Cadilac Buick Inc—David Fischer	PO Box 909, Troy MI 48099	248-643-0070	R	37*	.1
849	Arnie Bauer Cadillac-GMC Trucks Co—Dennis Bauer	5525 Miller Circle Dr, Matteson IL 60443		R	37*	<.1
850	Crest Cadillac Inc—William Hartigan	12800 W Capital Dr, Brookfield WI 53005	262-781-2800	R	37*	<.1
851	Balise Motor Sales Co—James E Balise Jr	1399 Riverdale St, West Springfield MA 01089	413-734-8795	R	36*	.8
852	Pat Milliken Ford Inc—Bruce Godfrey	9600 Telegraph Rd, Redford MI 48239	313-255-3100	R	36*	.1
853	DeSoto Auto Mall Enterprise—Mark Schlundt	PO Box 190, Arcadia FL 34265	863-494-4848	R	36*	.1
854	Jim Ellis Auto Dealership Inc—Jim Ellis	5901 Peachtree Industr, Atlanta GA 30341	770-458-6811	R	36*	.1

Rank	Company Name—*Executive Officer*	Address, City, State, Zip	Phone	Type	Fin	Empls
855	Normandin Chrysler-Plymouth-Jeep-Eagle—*Mark Normandin*	900 Capitol Expwy Auto, San Jose CA 95136	408-266-9500	R	36*	.1
856	Orange Buick-GMC Truck Co—*Raj Lally*	3883 W Colonial Dr, Orlando FL 32808	407-295-8100	R	36*	.1
857	Rydell Automotive Group Inc—*Jim Lynch*	18600 Devonshire St, Northridge CA 91324	818-832-1600	R	36*	.1
858	Holman Cadillac Co—*Tom Murphy*	1200 Rte 73 S, Mount Laurel NJ 08054	856-778-1000	R	36*	.1
859	Jack Griffin Ford Inc—*John Griffin*	1940 E Main St, Waukesha WI 53186	262-542-5781	R	36*	.1
860	Jones Chevrolet Inc—*John T Jones Jr*	PO Box 458, Sumter SC 29151	803-469-2515	R	36*	.1
861	JL Freed and Sons Inc—*Donald J Franks*	685 Bethlehem Pike, Montgomeryville PA 18936	215-368-1840	R	36*	.1
862	Van Campen Motors Inc—*George Wurster*	601 W 3rd St, Williamsport PA 17701	570-326-0567	R	36*	.1
863	Nelson Ford-Lincoln-Mercury Inc—*Laurel Nelson*	2228 College Way, Fergus Falls MN 56537	218-739-4401	R	36*	<.1
864	Volvo of Westport—*Raymond Kearns* BMW Of Darien	556 Post Rd E, Westport CT 06880	203-222-1122	S	36*	<.1
865	Armen of Ardmore—*Armen Filippo*	125 E Lancaster Ave, Ardmore PA 19003	610-726-1499	R	36*	<.1
866	Ford Richmond LLC—*Conrad Irons*	PO Box 11145, Richmond VA 23230	804-358-5521	R	35*	.2
867	Paddock Chevrolet Inc—*Duane Paddock*	3232 Delaware Ave, Kenmore NY 14217	716-803-6241	R	35*	.1
868	Reeder Chevrolet Co	4301 Clinton Hwy, Knoxville TN 37912		R	35*	.1
869	Young Chevrolet Oldsmobile Cadillac Inc—*Tony Young*	1500 E Main St, Owosso MI 48867	989-725-2184	R	35*	.1
870	Westway Ford Inc—*Barton Hankins*	801 W Airport Fwy, Irving TX 75062	972-659-0333	R	35*	.1
871	Regal Ford Inc—*Lucian H Neal*	PO Box 20725, Winston Salem NC 27120	336-722-2593	R	35*	.1
872	North Florida Lincoln-Mercury Inc—*Tom Lynch*	4620 Southside Blvd, Jacksonville FL 32216	904-642-4100	R	35*	.1
873	Joe Hall Ford—*Joe Hall*	PO Box 606, Lewiston ID 83501	208-746-2391	R	35*	.1
874	Ryan Chevrolet Inc—*Kathy Gaddie*	1800 S Broadway, Minot ND 58701	701-852-3571	R	35*	.1
875	Leson Chevrolet—*Donald R Trapp*	1501 Westbank Expy, Harvey LA 70058	504-366-4381	R	35*	.1
876	Armstrong Ford Inc—*Bill Armstrong*	1241 Hwy 70 E, Hickory NC 28602	828-328-2221	R	35*	.1
877	Bill Ray Nissan—*William D Ray*	2724 N US Hwy 17-92, Longwood FL 32750	407-831-1318	R	35*	.1
878	Conlon and Collins Ford Jeep Eagle Inc	5213 Northwest Hwy, Crystal Lake IL 60014	815-459-8200	R	35*	.1
879	John Stuckey Ford Inc—*Matt Stuckey*	500 Broad St, Hollidaysburg PA 16648	814-695-9863	R	35*	.1
880	Kilgore Ford	1615 Hwy 259 N, Kilgore TX 75662	903-984-2006	R	35*	.1
881	Sanders Ford Inc—*Mat C Raymond III*	1135 Lejeune Blvd, Jacksonville NC 28540	910-455-1911	R	35*	.1
882	Sommer's Inc—*Walter Sommer*	7211 W Mequon Rd, Mequon WI 53092		R	35*	.1
883	Dick Smith Automotive Group Inc—*Calvin F Legette*	2800 Two Notch Rd, Columbia SC 29204	803-254-4000	R	35*	<.1
884	Paul Heuring Motors Inc—*David Heuring*	720 N Hobart Rd, Hobart IN 46342	219-942-2143	R	35*	<.1
885	Beechmont Motors Inc—*Bill Woeste* Beechmont Investments Inc	8660 Beechmont Ave, Cincinnati OH 45255	513-388-3700	S	35*	<.1
886	George R Gibson Chevrolet Inc—*Jim Gibson*	1533 E 162nd St, South Holland IL 60473	708-339-7400	R	35*	<.1
887	Strieter Motor Co—*David Strieter*	520 W Kimberly Rd, Davenport IA 52806	563-391-1500	R	35*	<.1
888	Superior Ford Lincoln Mercury (Morgantown West Virginia)—*Jared Hartsock*	1351 Earl L Core Rd, Morgantown WV 26505	304-296-4477	R	35*	<.1
889	Melloy Brothers Enterprises Inc—*Robert E Melloy*	7707 Lomas Blvd NE, Albuquerque NM 87110	505-265-7701	R	34*	.2
890	Lou Bachrodt Auto Mall—*Patrick Bachrodt*	7070 Cherryvale N Blvd, Rockford IL 61112	815-332-3000	R	34*	.1
891	Triad Freightliner of Greensboro Inc—*Larry Tysinger*	6420 Burnt Poplar Rd, Greensboro NC 27409	336-668-0911	R	34*	.1
892	Paul Moak Pontiac Inc—*Paul G Moak Jr*	450 Steed Rd, Ridgeland MS 39157	601-707-8097	R	34*	.1
893	Perry Buick Co—*Jamie Perry*	6633 E Virginia Beach, Norfolk VA 23502	757-333-0906	R	34*	.1
894	Zimmerman Ford Inc—*Michael Zimmerman*	2525 E MAIN St, Saint Charles IL 60174	630-584-1800	R	34*	.1
895	Carl Cannon Chevrolet-Cadillac—*James Cannon*	299 Carl Cannon Blvd, Jasper AL 35501		R	34*	.1
896	Johnson Motors Inc—*Robert Johnson*	RR 1 Box 122, Du Bois PA 15801	814-371-4444	R	34*	.1
897	David Self Ford Lincoln Mercury Inc—*David Self*	1601 Green Ave, Orange TX 77630		R	34*	.1
898	Northeast Acura Inc—*Jim Higgins*	PO Box 366, Latham NY 12110	518-785-4105	R	34*	<.1
899	Capital City International Trucks Inc—*Bruce Nederveld*	1700 N Grand River Ave, Lansing MI 48900	517 487 5908	R	34*	.1
900	Valley Stream Motors Inc—*Joel Lieberman*	709 W Merrick Rd, Valley Stream NY 11580	516-204-4030	R	34	.1
901	Webb Automotive Group Inc (Farmington New Mexico)—*Perry M Webb*	3911 E Main St, Farmington NM 87402	505-325-1911	R	33*	.1
902	Millennium Ford Inc—*Frank Wilcher*	14500 1st Ave S, Burien WA 98168		R	33*	.1
903	Don Drennen Motor Company Inc—*Don Drennen*	1626 Montgomery Hwy, Hoover AL 35216	205-823-5220	R	33*	.1
904	Ed Morse Honda Inc—*Michael Scaglione*	3790 W Blue Heron Blvd, Riviera Beach FL 33404		R	33*	.1
905	Independence Lincoln Mercury Inc—*Joe Messner*	3225 S Noland Rd, Independence MO 64055	816-833-4700	R	33*	.1
906	Midway Motors Supercenter	PO Box 1625, Hutchinson KS 67504	620-662-4421	R	33*	.1
907	Mike Haggarty Pontiac GMC Truck and Volkswagen Inc—*Michael D Haggerty*	9301 S Cicero Ave, Oak Lawn IL 60453	708-423-5000	R	33*	.1
908	Robert Green Chevrolet Oldsmobile Inc—*Robert Green*	PO Box 8002, Rock Hill NY 12775	845-794-6161	R	33*	.1
909	Team Motor Sales Inc—*Bill Smith*	1215 Scalp Ave, Johnstown PA 15904	814-266-8611	R	33*	.1
910	Tom Matson Dodge Inc—*Thomas Matson*	2925 Auburn Way N, Auburn WA 98002		R	33*	.1
911	Don Davis Auto World Inc—*John Davis*	2277 Niagara Falls Blv, Amherst NY 14228	716-691-7800	R	33*	.1
912	Service Motors Inc—*Jeff Alexander*	24 E Scott St, Fond du Lac WI 54935	920-921-2120	R	33*	<.1
913	Bozeman Motors Inc—*David Wallin*	2900 N 19th St, Bozeman MT 59718	406-587-1221	R	33*	<.1
914	Thomas Chevrolet Subaru Cadillac Inc—*Mark Thomas*	PO Box 165, Bedford PA 15522	814-623-8131	R	32*	.1
915	Stamford Motors Inc—*Dominic Franchella*	212 Magee Ave, Stamford CT 06902	203-357-0357	R	32*	.1
916	Summit City Chevrolet—*Jane De Haven*	5200 Illinois Rd, Fort Wayne IN 46804	260-432-0677	R	32*	.1
917	Faulkner Collision—*Joseph Faulkner*	9802 Haldeman Ave, Philadelphia PA 19115	215-698-8700	R	32*	.1
918	Barton Birks Chevrolet Cadillac—*Ronald Barton*	800 Auto Park Pl, Newburgh NY 12550	845-234-4731	R	32*	.1
919	Chapman Ford Lincoln Mercury Nissan—*Randy Chapman*	2001 Cumberland St, Lebanon PA 17042	717-272-7671	R	32*	.1
920	Crestview Cadillac Corp—*Brian Barr*	717 W Genesee St, Syracuse NY 13201	315-422-2231	R	32*	.1
921	Crossroads Chevrolet Cadillac—*Seth Knighton*	4630 E 32nd St, Joplin MO 64804	417-624-3600	R	32*	.1
922	Hare Pontiac Buick GMC—*John Hopkins*	5336 Pike Plz, Indianapolis IN 46254	317-299-5555	R	32*	.1
923	Smith Motors of Hammond Inc—*Jarvis Roper*	6405 Indianapolis Blvd, Hammond IN 46320		R	32*	.1
924	Laurel Ford Lincoln Mercury Inc—*Jimmy Walker*	2018 Hwy 15 N, Laurel MS 39440	601-649-4511	R	32*	.1
925	Santa Maria Ford—*Randy Renforow*	PO Box 1188, Santa Maria CA 93456	805-925-2445	R	32*	.1
926	Shelton Pontiac-Buick Inc—*Russell Shelton*	855 S Rochester Rd, Rochester Hills MI 48307		R	32*	.1
927	BMW of Corpus Christi—*Calvin Miller*	4225 S Staples St, Corpus Christi TX 78411	361-991-5555	R	32*	<.1
928	Eskridge Honda Co—*Ed Eskridge*	1030 SW 74th St, Oklahoma City OK 73139	405-631-4444	R	32*	<.1
929	Garber Management Group Inc—*Richard J Garber Jr*	999 S Washington Ste1, Saginaw MI 48602	989-790-9090	R	32*	<.1
930	H and N Chevrolet-Buick Co—*J Douglas Hart*	PO Box 451, Spencer IA 51301	712-262-3230	R	32*	<.1
931	Reganis Auto Center Inc—*Timothy Reganis*	PO Box 1245, Scottsbluff NE 69363	308-632-8200	R	31*	.1
932	Garber Buick Co—*Norman F Geyer* Garber Management Group Inc	5925 State St, Saginaw MI 48603		S	31*	.1
933	Bob Thomas Cheverolet Cadillac Honda—*Robert S Thomas*	345 NE 3rd St, Bend OR 97701	541-382-2911	R	31*	.1
934	City Motor Company Inc—*Robert Oakland*	3900 10th Ave S, Great Falls MT 59405	406-761-4900	R	31*	.1
935	Western Slope Auto Inc—*Vern Engbar*	2264 Hwy 6 and 50, Grand Junction CO 81505	970-243-0843	R	31*	.1
936	Courtesy Ford—*Keith Palmer*	1830 W Grand River Ave, Okemos MI 48864	517-347-1830	R	31*	.1
937	Roberts Motors Inc—*Samuel H Roberts*	4350 Alby St, Alton IL 62002		R	31*	.1
938	Lively Cadillac-GMC—*Gordon Lively Jr*	400 Spur 63 N, Longview TX 75601	903-757-6600	R	31*	.1

Note: An asterisk (*) indicates an estimated financial figure. The company type code used is as follows: R = Private, P = Public, S = Private Subsidiary, B = Public Subsidiary, D = Division, J = Joint Venture, I = Investment Fund.

COMPANY RANKINGS BY SALES WITHIN 4-DIGIT SIC

Rank	Company Name—*Executive Officer*	Address, City, State, Zip	Phone	Type	Fin	Empls
939	Somerset Buick GMC Truck Inc—*John Fowler*	1850 W Maple Rd, Troy MI 48084	248-566-6471	R	31*	.1
940	Carriage Enterprises Ltd—*Norm Tompkins*	4040 Stevens Creek Blv, San Jose CA 95129	408-246-7600	R	31*	<.1
941	Sonnen Enterprises Inc—*Amir Bahkatiari*	740 Francisco Blvd W, San Rafael CA 94901	415-460-4100	R	31*	<.1
942	Freeway Ford Truck Sales Inc—*Mary Dolan*	8445 W 45th St, Lyons IL 60534	708-442-9000	R	31*	<.1
943	Mack Pontiac Buick GMC (Hicksville New York)—*Martin Nix*	330 W Old Country Rd, Hicksville NY 11801	516-931-0900	R	31*	<.1
944	Winchester Ford Mazda Subaru Inc—*Jim Mitchell*	1911 Valley Ave, Winchester VA 22601	540-664-3314	S	30*	.1
945	Pat McGrath Chevrolet Inc—*Pat McGrath* McGrath ChevyLand	1600 51st St NE, Cedar Rapids IA 52402	319-393-6300	S	30*	.1
946	O'Connor Chevrolet Inc—*Mark O'Connor*	3850 W Henrietta Rd, Rochester NY 14623	585-359-1300	R	30*	.1
947	Prostrollo Motor Co—*Pat Prostrollo*	18573 Pennington Rd, Madison SD 57042	605-256-9111	R	30*	.1
948	Voss Village Cadillac—*John E Voss*	650 State Rte 725 Rd, Centerville OH 45459	937-428-2300	R	30*	.1
949	Acura of Bellevue—*Robert Sesnon*	13424 NE 20th St, Bellevue WA 98005		R	30*	.1
950	Andy Mohr Truck Center	1301 S Holt Rd, Indianapolis IN 46241	317-244-6811	R	30*	.1
951	Fuson Buick Cadillac and GMC Inc—*Emily Hogan*	PO Box 10039, Terre Haute IN 47801	812-232-2364	R	30*	.1
952	Mark Chevrolet Inc—*Charlie Cabana*	33200 Michigan Ave, Wayne MI 48184	734-629-4964	R	30*	.1
953	Miller Brothers Chevrolet Inc—*John Miller*	9035 Baltimore Nat'l P, Ellicott City MD 21042	443-364-9007	R	30*	.1
954	Morrie's Cadillac/Saab—*Charles York*	7400 Wayzata Blvd, Golden Valley MN 55426	763-449-4200	R	30*	.1
955	Mountain States Motors Co—*Tim Van Binsbergen*	201 W 70th Ave, Denver CO 80221	303-302-6562	R	30*	.1
956	Pierson Chevrolet Inc—*Brent Ellison*	PO Box 589, Gadsden AL 35902	256-546-3391	R	30*	.1
957	Reed Motors Inc—*Raymond Reed*	3776 W Colonial Dr, Orlando FL 32808	407-297-7333	R	30*	.1
958	Rainbow Westbank—*Lloyd Guillot*	1700 West Bank Expy, Harvey LA 70058	504-367-1700	R	30*	.1
959	Sycamore Chevrolet Nissan Inc—*Dennis Meng*	4444 US Hwy 41 S, Terre Haute IN 47802	812-234-6661	R	30*	.1
960	Springdale Ford Inc	2259 N Thompson, Springdale AR 72764	479-751-5766	R	30*	.1
961	Southwest Ford Lincoln-Mercury Inc—*Eddie Hinojoza*	4001 Interstate 30, Greenville TX 75403	903-455-7222	R	30*	.1
962	Tustin Cars Inc—*Len Knott*	50 Auto Center Dr, Tustin CA 92782	714-734-2400	R	30*	.1
963	Bob Rohrman Indy Susuki Inc—*Bob Rohrman*	7101 E Washington St, Indianapolis IN 46219	317-613-7000	S	30*	<.1
964	Middletown Ford Inc—*Robinson Roosevelt*	PO Box 505, Middletown OH 45042	513-420-8700	R	30*	<.1
965	Westborough Buick Pontiac GMC Inc—*Michael Bates*	88 Turnpike Rd, Westborough MA 01581	508-366-8787	R	30*	<.1
966	Highland Park Lincoln Mercury Sales Inc—*Al Frisch*	1333 Park Ave West, Highland Park IL 60035		R	30*	<.1
967	TH Evans Enterprises Inc—*Thomas Evans*	1510 US Hwy 29 N, Athens GA 30601	706-548-8888	R	30*	<.1
968	Nabors Inc—*Neal Draper*	621 Desoto Ave, Clarksdale MS 38614	662-624-2585	R	30*	<.1
969	Crossroads Ford Truck Sales Inc—*John Hogan*	PO Box 6548, Springfield IL 62708	217-528-0770	R	29*	.1
970	Barnett Chrysler-Plymouth-Jeep-Kia—*Jack Mayeron*	3610 Hwy 61 N, White Bear Lake MN 55110	651-429-3391	R	29*	.1
971	Fairfield Ford/Volkswagen/Hyundai/Mitsubishi Inc—*William Manos*	PO Box 308, Montoursville PA 17754	570-368-8121	R	29*	.1
972	John Watson Chevrolet Inc—*John L Watson*	3535 Wall Ave, Ogden UT 84401	801-394-2611	R	29*	.1
973	Osborne-McCann Cadillac Inc	6411 20th St E, Fife WA 98424		S	29*	.1
974	Daniels Cadillac BMW Inc—*Gary Daniels*	4600 Crackersport Rd, Allentown PA 18104	610-820-2950	R	29*	.1
975	Efird Chrysler Jeep Dodge Inc—*Howard Efird*	1711 W Lucas St, Florence SC 29501	843-669-1881	R	29*	.1
976	Simpson Buick Pontiac GMC—*David Simpson*	6600 Auto Center Dr, Buena Park CA 90621	714-690-6200	R	29*	.1
977	Vision Ford Lincoln Mercury Inc—*Chris Taylor*	1500 S White Sands Blv, Alamogordo NM 88310	505-434-4800	R	29*	.1
978	Daigle and Houghton Inc—*Gary Daigle*	PO Box 191, Fort Kent ME 04743	207-834-6186	R	29*	<.1
979	Summerville Ford Mercury Inc—*Sam Johnson*	9700 Dorchester Rd, Summerville SC 29485	843-873-3550	R	29*	<.1
980	Elliott Chevrolet Inc—*William J Elliott IV*	1100 Greenville Ave, Staunton VA 24401	540-885-1584	R	29*	<.1
981	Borton Volvo Inc—*Kjell Bergh*	5428 Lyndale Ave S, Minneapolis MN 55419	612-827-3666	R	28*	.1
982	Southern States Imports Inc—*Wayne Miracle*	2421 Wake Forest Rd, Raleigh NC 27608	919-828-0901	R	28*	.1
983	Capital Ford Lincoln Mercury—*Mark Roberts*	2012 Stone Ross Dr, Rocky Mount NC 27804	252-977-1234	R	28*	.1
984	Jim Ellis Chevrolet Inc—*Jim Ellis*	5900 Peachtree Industr, Atlanta GA 30341	770-457-8211	R	28*	.1
985	Superior Motors Inc (Orangeburg South Carolina)—*James Guthrie*	PO Box 649, Orangeburg SC 29116	803-534-1123	R	28*	.1
986	Brown's Buick Inc—*Daniel Legge*	10501 Midlothian Tpke, Richmond VA 23235	804-379-7283	R	28*	.1
987	Colussy Chevrolet Inc—*Timothy Colussy*	3073 Washington Pike, Bridgeville PA 15017	412-221-1600	R	28*	.1
988	Doenges Ford Company Inc—*Robert S Doenges*	1901 SE Washington Blv, Bartlesville OK 74006	918-333-0900	R	28*	.1
989	Fairfield Volkswagon Inc	6065 Dixie Hwy, Fairfield OH 45014	513-874-3740	R	28*	.1
990	Ford Lincoln Mercury of Bellevue—*Jimmy Barrier* Barrier Motors Inc	411 116th Ave NE, Bellevue WA 98004	425-454-9585	S	28*	.1
991	Kenworth of Indianapolis Inc—*Eldon Palmer*	2929 S Holt Rd, Indianapolis IN 46241	317-247-8421	R	28*	.1
992	Pleasantville Ford Inc—*Jim Borelli*	47 Pleasantville Rd, Pleasantville NY 10570	914-769-1800	R	28*	.1
993	RJ Chevrolet Inc—*David Foringer*	1271 Ridge Rd W, Rochester NY 14615	585-663-4040	R	28*	.1
994	Toyota of Fort Worth—*John Easley* Sonic Automotive Inc	9001 Camp Bowie W, Fort Worth TX 76116	817-560-1500	D	28*	.1
995	Devereaux Motor Sales Inc—*PS Devereaux*	230 Buffalo St, Freeport PA 16229	724-295-2171	R	28*	<.1
996	Natchitoches Ford Lincoln Mercury Inc—*Calvin W Braxton Sr*	7501 Hwy 1 Bypass, Natchitoches LA 71457		R	28*	<.1
997	Spirit Ford Inc—*Cliff Cicotte*	4402 Ann Arbor Rd, Dundee MI 48131	734-529-5521	R	28*	<.1
998	Spreen Saturn Inc—*Gregory Spreen*	PO Box 1096, Loma Linda CA 92354	909-799-9900	R	28*	.1
999	Baker Chevrolet—*Alfred E Baker*	914 E 4th Ave, Red Springs NC 28377	910-843-5168	R	27*	.1
1000	Ed Martin Nissan—*Ed W Martin*	802 N Shadeland Ave, Indianapolis IN 46219		R	27*	.1
1001	Jerry Hamm Chevrolet Inc—*Jerry Hamm*	3494 Phillips Hwy, Jacksonville FL 32207	904-398-3036	R	27*	.1
1002	Boand Automotive Group Inc—*JF Boand*	100 S San Gabriel Blvd, San Gabriel CA 91776	626-287-6184	R	27*	.1
1003	Performance Motors—*Jay Steibleman*	1700 E San Juan Blvd, Farmington NM 87401	505-327-4851	R	27*	.1
1004	Racette Ford of Oshkosh—*Ralph A Racette*	3355 Jackson St, Oshkosh WI 54901	920-231-1610	R	27*	.1
1005	Ferris Chevrolet Inc—*Tom Ferris*	634 Wabash Ave NW, New Philadelphia OH 44663	330-343-7761	R	27*	.1
1006	Courtesy Ford Lincoln Mercury—*Kim Leggett*	101 Hwy 411 E, Rome GA 30161	706-235-4453	R	27*	.1
1007	Ewald's Hartford Ford Lincoln Mercury—*Glenn Leirnen* Ewald Automotive Group Inc	5788 Hwy 60 E, Hartford WI 53027	262-673-9400	D	27*	.1
1008	Ford of Montebello Inc—*James Ross Sr*	2747 Via Campo, Montebello CA 90640	323-838-6920	R	27*	.1
1009	Robert Brogden Pontiac Buick—*Robert Brogden*	1500 E Santa Fe Dr, Olathe KS 66061	913-712-9347	R	27*	.1
1010	WI Simonson Inc—*Hamlet Karapetian* Sonic Automotive Inc	1626 Wilshire Blvd, Santa Monica CA 90403		S	27*	.1
1011	Sexton Chevrolet Co—*William C Sexton*	PO Box 1328, Manteca CA 95336	209-823-3167	R	27*	<.1
1012	Freedom Ford Lincoln-Mercury Inc—*Bobby H Dawson*	151 Woodland Dr, Wise VA 24293	276-328-2686	R	27*	<.1
1013	Monte Shelton Motor Co—*Monte Shelton*	1638 W Burnside, Portland OR 97209	503-224-3232	R	27*	<.1
1014	Nationwide Lift Trucks Inc—*Arthur Conte*	3900 N 28th Ter, Hollywood FL 33020	954-922-4645	R	27*	.1
1015	Beall Transport Equipment Co—*Jerry Beall*	8801 N Vancouver Ave, Portland OR 97217	503-735-2110	S	26*	.1
1016	Chicago International Trucks (Joliet Illinois)	103 S Larkin Ave, Joliet IL 60436	815-741-7500	R	26*	.2
1017	Castriota Chevrolet Inc—*Anthony Castriota*	1701 W Liberty Ave, Pittsburgh PA 15226	412-343-2100	R	26*	.1
1018	Harvey Chevrolet Corp—*George M Harvey Jr*	PO Box 972, Radford VA 24141	540-639-3923	R	26*	.1
1019	Gene Beltz Shadeland Dodge—*Gene Beltz*	1630 N Shadeland Ave, Indianapolis IN 46219	317-357-8001	R	26*	.1
1020	Napleton Cadillac Saab—*Jeff feinblatt* Napleton Auto Group	505 N Perryville Rd, Rockford IL 61107	815-398-0505	S	26*	.1

Rank	Company Name—*Executive Officer*	Address, City, State, Zip	Phone	Type	Fin	Empls
1021	Valley Honda Madza Volkswagen—*Bob Navarre*	4173 Ogden Ave, Aurora IL 60504	630-851-5700	R	26*	.1
1022	Jim Barnard Chevrolet Geo Inc—*Allyn G Barnard*	7101 Buffalo Rd, Churchville NY 14428	585-293-8061	R	26*	.1
1023	Saturn of Memphis Inc—*ZaK Imam* Jim Keras Chevrolet Memphis	2420 Covington Pike, Memphis TN 38128	901-385-8700	S	26*	.1
1024	Auto Mall Inc—*Christian McCaulley*	800 Putney Rd, Brattleboro VT 05301	802-257-4510	R	26*	<.1
1025	Nick Crivelli Ford LLC—*Nick Crivelli*	2085 Brodhead Rd, Aliquippa PA 15001	724-857-0400	R	26*	<.1
1026	Sud's Motor Car Company Inc—*Gian C Sud*	1430 E Fort Jesse Rd, Normal IL 61761	309-454-1101	R	26*	<.1
1027	Automobile Consumer Services Inc—*Tarry Shebesta*	6249 Stewart Rd, Cincinnati OH 45227	513-527-7700	R	26*	<.1
1028	Rudolph Chevrolet Inc—*Dennis Neessen*	5625 S Desert Blvd, El Paso TX 79932	915-317-5956	R	25*	.1
1029	Lafferty Chevrolet Inc—*Jack Lafferty*	829 W Street Rd, Warminster PA 18974	215-259-5817	R	25*	.1
1030	Jim Price Automotive	2150 Seminole Trl, Charlottesville VA 22901	434-817-1881	R	25*	.1
1031	Mankato Motors—*Dale Schmitt*	1815 Madison Ave, Mankato MN 56001	507-625-5641	R	25*	.1
1032	Tri-County Ford-Mercury Inc—*Gary Haupt*	5101 W Hwy 146, Buckner KY 40010	502-241-7333	R	25*	.1
1033	Barberino Brothers Inc—*Tom Barberino*	505 N Colony Rd, Wallingford CT 06492	203-265-1611	R	25*	.1
1034	Dave Sinclair Mid Rivers Lincoln Mercury Inc—*James Sinclair*	4760 N Service Rd, Saint Peters MO 63376	636-441-4400	R	25*	<.1
1035	Dartmouth Motors Sales Inc—*Marshall Friedman*	PO Box 6, Newport NH 03773	603-863-2800	R	25*	<.1
1036	Colerain Ford—*YunHee Jang*	8571 Colerain Ave, Cincinnati OH 45251	513-385-1414	R	24*	.1
1037	Cross Creek Lincoln-Mercury Inc—*Sam Johnson Sr*	497 N Mcpherson Church, Fayetteville NC 28303	910-864-5240	R	24*	.1
1038	Preston Hood Chevrolet Inc—*A Preston Hood*	PO Box 370, Fort Walton Beach FL 32549		R	24*	.1
1039	Commercial Motor Co—*Ronnie Boehnke*	160 S Commercial St, Aransas Pass TX 78336	361-758-5361	R	24*	.1
1040	Corwin-Churchill Motors Inc—*Bruce Whittey*	PO Box 1078, Bismarck ND 58502	701-223-1170	R	24*	.1
1041	Don Gooley Cadillac Inc—*Don Gooley*	PO Box 509, Saint Clair Shores MI 48080	586-772-8200	R	24*	.1
1042	Landmark Lincoln Mercury Inc—*Tom Daniels*	5000 S Broadway, Englewood CO 80113	303-761-1560	R	24*	.1
1043	Rod Baker Ford Inc—*Monica Utter*	16101 S Lincoln Hwy, Plainfield IL 60586	815-436-5681	R	24*	.1
1044	Strong Inc—*Blake Strong*	1070 S Main St, Salt Lake City UT 84101		R	24*	<.1
1045	Donovan Auto and Truck Center—*Robert Donovan*	PO Box 12326, Wichita KS 67277	316-678-4891	R	24*	<.1
1046	Snyder Chevrolet Oldsmobile—*Bill Snyder*	524 N Perry St, Napoleon OH 43545	419-599-1015	R	24*	<.1
1047	John Rogin Buick Inc—*John Rogin*	30500 Plymouth Rd, Livonia MI 48150	734-525-0900	R	24*	<.1
1048	Scott Motors Inc—*C Bradford Scott*	777 Taunton Ave, East Providence RI 02914	401-438-5555	R	24*	<.1
1049	Signature Automotive Group—*Gene E Moon*	680 E Napier Ave, Benton Harbor MI 49022		R	24*	<.1
1050	Columbus Truck and Equipment Company Inc—*Ray Mason*	PO Box 83250, Columbus OH 43203	614-252-3111	R	23*	.1
1051	Smith Chevrolet Cadillac Co—*John Smith Jr*	1215 Hwy 71 S, Fort Smith AR 72901	479-646-7301	R	23*	.1
1052	Courtesy Ford Inc—*Todd Mixon*	1410 W Pine St, Hattiesburg MS 39401	601-544-8111	R	23*	.1
1053	Levis Chevrolet Cadillac—*Keith Williams*	316 Howze Beach Rd, Slidell LA 70461	985-643-1800	R	23*	.1
1054	Mossy Motors Inc—*Joe Mossy*	1331 S Broad St, New Orleans LA 70125	504-708-2978	R	23*	.1
1055	Crosby Cadillac GMC Truck Inc	447 State St, Waycross GA 31501	912-816-4793	R	23*	.1
1056	Gillman Honda—*Stacey Gillman Wimbish*	10595 W Sam Houston Pk, Houston TX 77099		R	23*	.1
1057	Highland Park Ford Sales Inc—*Bob Lee*	1333 Park Ave W, Highland Park IL 60035		R	23*	.1
1058	Jorgensen Ford Sales Inc—*Milton Brandenberg*	8333 Michigan Ave, Detroit MI 48210	313-584-2250	R	23*	.1
1059	Marin Acura Inc—*Debi Steven-Byrnes*	5860 Paradise Dr, Corte Madera CA 94925	415-924-5100	R	23*	.1
1060	Middleton Motors Inc—*Hobert WL Hudson*	PO Box 620525, Middleton WI 53562	608-831-7725	R	23*	.1
1061	Motor Inn Co—*Dave Christensen*	2114 E Main St, Albert Lea MN 56007	507-369-2362	R	23*	.1
1062	Reichert Chevrolet and Buick Sales Inc	5220 Northwest Hwy, Crystal Lake IL 60014	815-261-0121	R	23*	.1
1063	Scottsbluff Motor Company Inc—*Kent Holub*	2014 E 20th Pl, Scottsbluff NE 69361	308-632-2173	R	23*	.1
1064	Sunshine Buick Pontiac GMC—*Tom Jenson*	5200 San Mateo Blvd NE, Albuquerque NM 87109	505-908-9068	R	23*	.1
1065	Franchini Chevrolet Inc—*Robert Franchini*	2 Passaic St, Garfield NJ 07026	973-472-9200	R	23*	<.1
1066	Holmes Auto Group Inc—*Charlton Holmes*	PO Box 52417, Shreveport LA 71135	318-861-3500	R	23*	<.1
1067	Kristal Auto Mall Inc—*Lilaahar Bical*	5200 Kings Hwy, Brooklyn NY 11234	718-307-6384	R	23*	<.1
1068	Beltway International LLC	1800 Sulphur Spring Rd, Baltimore MD 21227	410-247-5700	R	23*	<.1
1069	Orlando Dodge Inc—*Mike Smith*	4101 W Colonial Dr, Orlando FL 32808	407-299-1120	R	22*	.1
1070	Laurel Mercedes-Benz	200 E Ogden Ave, Westmont IL 60559	630-537-0313	R	22*	.1
1071	Ken Wilson Chevrolet Inc—*Ken Wilson Jr*	2545 Vestal Pky E, Vestal NY 13850	607-729-6266	R	22*	.1
1072	Parsons Buick Co—*Stephen Parsons*	151 East St, Plainville CT 06062		R	22*	.1
1073	Team Mazda Hyundai—*Michael Drinker*	301 Auto Mall Pky, Vallejo CA 94591	707-643-9000	R	22*	.1
1074	Seaside Buick Inc—*Lloyd Lickert*	6435 Miramar Rd, San Diego CA 92121	858-597-1111	R	22*	.1
1075	Fargo Freightliner Inc—*Ron Ristvedt*	Box 11057, Fargo ND 58106	701-293-9133	R	22*	.1
1076	Central Chevrolet Co (Jonesboro Arkansas)—*Doyle Yarbrough*	3207 Stadium Blvd, Jonesboro AR 72404	870-935-5575	R	22*	.1
1077	Davenport Auto Park—*Neill Nelson*	PO Box 4323, Rocky Mount NC 27804	252-937-8500	R	22*	.1
1078	Saginaw Valley Ford Lincoln - Mercury—*Gilbert S Johnson*	4201 Bay Rd, Saginaw MI 48603	989-792-1700	R	22*	.1
1079	Griffin Motor Company Inc—*Bruce Griffin*	PO Box 1699, Monroe NC 28110	704-288-0210	R	22*	<.1
1080	Grubbs Infiniti—*George Grubbs Jr*	1661 Airport Fwy, Euless TX 76040	817-318-1200	R	22*	<.1
1081	Heiser Chevrolet and Geo Inc—*Brian Crandall* Heiser Automobile Dealership Inc	10200 W Arthur Ave, West Allis WI 53227	414-327-2300	S	22*	<.1
1082	Metro Ford Truck Sales Inc—*Jim Metford*	4000 Irving Blvd, Dallas TX 75247	214-631-2050	R	22*	<.1
1083	Eastern Horizons Inc—*Philip Noonan*	405 Industrial Ave, Cheshire CT 06410	203-250-8000	R	22*	<.1
1084	Godfrey Chevrolet-Buick Inc—*Joe Godfrey*	1701 N Mitchell St, Cadillac MI 49601		R	22*	<.1
1085	Anthony Underwood Automotive—*Anthony Underwood*	4006 Bessemer Super Hw, Bessemer AL 35020	205-424-4033	R	22*	<.1
1086	Hunterdon BMW—*Gailon McGowen*	655 Route 202/206, Bridgewater NJ 08807	908-236-6302	R	22*	<.1
1087	Metropolitan Cadillac Inc—*Max Stephenson*	10221 W Arthur Ave, Milwaukee WI 53227	414-455-1104	R	22*	<.1
1088	Sharp Honda—*Steve Matukewicz*	1818 S Topeka Blvd, Topeka KS 66612	785-249-2719	R	22*	<.1
1089	Sunderland Chevrolet—*Lloyd Sunderland*	1601 S State St, Jerseyville IL 62052	618-498-2123	R	22*	<.1
1090	Van Bortel Motorcar Inc—*Kitty Van Bortel*	6327 Rte 96, Victor NY 14564	585-924-5230	R	22*	<.1
1091	Marshall Ford Lincoln Mercury—*John Shelton*	4200 E End Blvd S, Marshall TX 75672	903-935-0665	R	22*	<.1
1092	Prestige Auto Corp—*Don Mattoon*	5500 Freideck Rd, Eau Claire WI 54701	715-833-0177	R	22*	<.1
1093	Freightliner Of Hartford Inc—*Lindy Bigliazzi*	222 Roberts St, East Hartford CT 06108	860-289-0201	R	22*	<.1
1094	Transource Inc—*James Bland*	PO Box 446, Kernersville NC 27285	336-996-6060	R	21*	.1
1095	Groth Brothers Oldsmobile Inc—*Robin Groth-Hill*	59 S L St, Livermore CA 94550	925-344-4207	R	21*	.1
1096	Mullahey Fullerton Chevrolet—*Tim Mullahey*	600 W Commonwealth Ave, Fullerton CA 92832	714-871-9110	R	21*	.1
1097	VIP Honda—*Adam Kucynski*	700 US Hwy 22 E, N Plainfield NJ 07060	908-753-1500	R	21	.1
1098	Friendly Buick and Honda—*James Riehl*	18900 Hall Rd, Clinton Township MI 48038	586-412-9600	R	21*	.1
1099	Prestige Ford—*Randall Reed*	3601 S Shiloh, Garland TX 75041	972-864-3673	R	21*	.1
1100	Grieger Motor Sales Inc—*David Rodgers*	1756 W Hwy 30, Valparaiso IN 46385	219-462-4117	R	21*	.1
1101	Bird Chevrolet Co—*Chris Muir*	PO Box 57, Dubuque IA 52004	563-583-9121	R	21*	<.1
1102	Butch Oustalet Chevrolet Cadillac—*Butch Oustalet*	4012 14th St, Pascagoula MS 39567	228-762-2711	R	21*	<.1
1103	Cawood Auto Company Inc—*Charles E Barrett*	2516 Pine Grove Ave, Port Huron MI 48060	810-987-3030	R	21*	<.1
1104	Dave Sinclair Ford Inc—*John Sinclair*	7466 S Lindbergh, Saint Louis MO 63125	314-892-2600	R	21*	<.1
1105	Horace G Ilderton Inc—*Brian Monk*	PO Box 350, High Point NC 27261	336-841-6100	R	21*	<.1
1106	Mike Young Motor Co—*Mike Young*	PO Box 146, Winnie TX 77665	409-296-2121	R	21*	<.1
1107	Larsen Chevrolet Oldsmobile Aurora Inc—*R R Kriesel Jr*	1420 Ogden Ave, Superior WI 54880		R	21*	<.1
1108	Plaza Ford-Lincoln-Mercury Inc	98 New Hwy 64 W, Lexington NC 27295		R	21*	<.1

Note: An asterisk (*) indicates an estimated financial figure. The company type code used is as follows: R = Private, P = Public, S = Private Subsidiary, B = Public Subsidiary, D = Division, J = Joint Venture, I = Investment Fund.

NKINGS BY SALES WITHIN 4-DIGIT SIC

	Company Name—Executive Officer	Address, City, State, Zip	Phone	Type	Fin	Empls
1109	Astoria Ford Inc—Dane Gouge	710 W Marine Dr, Astoria OR 97103	503-325-6411	R	21*	<.1
1110	Overseas Military Sales Corp Ltd—Thomas Pisano	175 Crossways Park Dr, Woodbury NY 11797	516-921-2800	R	21*	<.1
1111	Greenway Ford Inc—Frank Rodriquez	9001 E Colonial Dr, Orlando FL 32817	407-275-3200	R	21*	<.1
1112	Legacy Ford	1225 N Autoplex Way, Pasco WA 99301	509-544-8000	S	21*	<.1
1113	Venus Ford Sales Inc—Sue James	2727 E Layton Ave, Cudahy WI 53110	414-481-8500	R	20*	.1
1114	Kenyon-Peck Inc—Donald A Peck	800 N Glebe Rd, Arlington VA 22203	703-522-9000	R	20*	.1
1115	Latham Motors Inc—Robert J Selkis	637 Columbia St Rte 9R, Latham NY 12110		R	20*	.1
1116	Courtesy Chevrolet—Paul Heflin	3161 Madison Rd, Cincinnati OH 45209	513-549-3952	R	20*	.1
1117	McCaddon Cadillac Buick GMC Truck—Mark McCaddon	PO Box 1618, Boulder CO 80306	303-442-3160	R	20*	.1
1118	Satcher Motor Co—Richard Heath	1850 Jefferson Davis H, Graniteville SC 29829	803-593-3700	R	20*	.1
1119	Gentry Ford Subaru Inc—Ryan Gentry	PO Box 598, Ontario OR 97914	541-889-9694	R	20*	.1
1120	John Deery Motor Co—John G Deery Jr	6823 University Ave, Cedar Falls IA 50613	319-277-6200	R	20*	.1
1121	Kenworth of Mid-Iowa Inc	4111 Delaware Ave, Des Moines IA 50313	515-265-8111	D	20*	.1
1122	Lakeshore Utility Trailer Inc—Charles Pfeffer	PO Box 338, Taylor MI 48180	734-285-4560	R	20*	.1
1123	Martin Chevrolet Inc (Torrance California)—Bill Martin	23505 Hawthorne Blvd, Torrance CA 90505		R	20*	.1
1124	Milo Gordon Auto Mall—Todd Wyatt	5221 NW Cache Rd, Lawton OK 73505	580-354-2277	R	20*	.1
1125	Modern Auto Company Inc—Alex Straatmann	6224 Hwy 100, Washington MO 63090	636-239-6777	R	20*	<.1
1126	Brasher Motor Company of Weimar Inc—Thomas F Brasher	PO Box 975, Weimar TX 78962	979-725-8515	R	20*	<.1
1127	Johnson Motor Co—Steven Lust	801 Auto Plaza Dr, Aberdeen SD 57401	605-225-8920	R	20*	<.1
1128	Patterson Chevrolet Inc—Glenn West	200 Renaissance Blvd, Lawrenceville NJ 08648	609-587-1599	R	20*	<.1
1129	Joe Hotze Ford Inc—Joseph Hotze	PO Box 340, Salem IL 62881	618-548-1711	R	20*	<.1
1130	Thompsons Toyota of Placerville—Ron Thompson Thompsons Auto Centers	140 Forni Rd, Placerville CA 95667	530-622-6232	S	20*	<.1
1131	Bert Ogden Motors Inc—Robert C Vackar	602 W Jackson St, Harlingen TX 78550	956-622-4257	R	19*	.1
1132	Schukei Chevrolet Inc—Steven R Schukei	721 S Monroe Ave, Mason City IA 50401	641-423-5402	R	19*	.1
1133	Graham Ford L and M Inc—Jay Graham	1717 Hwy 46 S, Dickson TN 37055	615-446-2308	R	19*	<.1
1134	Bob Frensley Chrysler Plymouth Isuzu Inc—Robert O Frensley	2210 N Gallatin Pike N, Madison TN 37115	615-859-0000	R	19*	<.1
1135	Carriker Ford Inc—Todd Carriker	1201 S 17th St, Oskaloosa IA 52577	641-673-8373	R	19*	<.1
1136	Cronin KIA—Michael Monroe	10700 New Haven Rd, Harrison OH 45030	513-202-5821	R	19*	<.1
1137	Dearth Motors Inc—Charles J Dearth	520 8th St, Monroe WI 53566	608-325-3181	R	19*	<.1
1138	Mack Housby Inc—Kelly Housby	4747 Ne 14th St, Des Moines IA 50313	515-266-2666	R	19*	.1
1139	Steele Truck Center Inc—Theodore Steele	2150 Rockfill Rd, Fort Myers FL 33916	239-334-7300	R	18*	.1
1140	H L Gage Sales Inc—Gary Hans	PO Box 5170, Albany NY 12205	518-456-8871	R	18*	.1
1141	Fritts Ford—Duane Pratt	8000 Auto Dr, Riverside CA 92504	951-687-2121	R	18*	.2
1142	Fox and James Inc—Thomas James	3690 Rte 30, Latrobe PA 15650	724-539-3561	R	18*	.1
1143	Cooley Motors Corp—Erik Cooley	401 N Greenbush Rd Rt, Rensselaer NY 12144		R	18*	.1
1144	Coyle Chevrolet Inc—Mike Coyle	1801 Broadway, Clarksville IN 47129	812-218-1100	R	18*	.1
1145	Ford World of Roselle Park—Joe Catena	158 E Westfield Ave, Roselle Park NJ 07204	908-245-6100	R	18*	.1
1146	Sound Ford Inc—Richard Snyder	101 SW Grady Way, Renton WA 98057	425-235-1000	R	18*	.1
1147	Cramer Motors Inc—Phillip Cramer	PO Box 430, North East PA 16428		R	18*	<.1
1148	Music Carter Chevrolet Buick—Wes Blackburn	713 S Lake Dr, Prestonsburg KY 41653	606-263-1636	R	18*	<.1
1149	Green Chevrolet-Buick-Pontiac Inc—Gerry Heaton	1700 W Morton Rd, Jacksonville IL 62650	217-245-4117	R	18*	<.1
1150	Frontier Ford Lincoln-Mercury Inc—Jim Bailes	200 Military Ave, Dodge City KS 67801	620-227-3171	R	18*	<.1
1151	Garbo Motor Sales Inc—Jack Garbo	3077 Douglas, Racine WI 53402	262-639-4154	R	18	<.1
1152	Martens Cars of Washington Inc—Harry Martens	4800 Wisconsin Ave NW, Washington DC 20016	202-537-3000	R	17*	.1
1153	Damascus Motor Company Inc—HD Warfield Jr	26100 Woodfield Rd, Damascus MD 20872	301-253-2151	R	17*	.1
1154	Kelly Cadillac Inc—Patrick Kelly	2110 Chapman Rd, Chattanooga TN 37421	423-267-1104	R	17*	<.1
1155	Bob Brock Ford Inc—Robert W Brock	500 W 4th St, Big Spring TX 79720	432-267-7424	R	17*	<.1
1156	Maplewood Imports—Doug Mulder	2780 N Hwy 61, Maplewood MN 55109	651-483-2681	R	17*	<.1
1157	CF Schwartz Motor Company Inc—Robert A Schwartz	PO Box 755, Dover DE 19903	302-734-5748	R	17*	<.1
1158	Culberson Stowers Inc—Dan Culberson	PO Box 1542, Pampa TX 79066	806-665-1665	R	17*	<.1
1159	Northern Motor Co—Stephen J Rosemurgy	1419 Ludington St, Escanaba MI 49829	906-786-1130	R	17*	<.1
1160	Bayview Ford Lincoln-Mercury Inc—Damon Wickware	27180 Hwy 98, Daphne AL 36526	251-626-7777	R	17*	<.1
1161	Ultimate Pontiac Buick GMC Isuzu—Randall Harris	5150 Jefferson Davis H, Fredericksburg VA 22408		R	17*	<.1
1162	Centralia Ford Lincoln-Mercury Inc—Leonard Taylor	848 E Noleman, Centralia IL 62801	618-532-4733	R	17*	.1
1163	Freightliner Of San Antonio Ltd—Paul Kane	PO Box 200410, San Antonio TX 78220	210-666-6665	R	17*	.1
1164	Shealy's Truck Center Inc—Bruce Shealy	1340 Bluff Rd, Columbia SC 29201	803-771-0176	R	16*	.1
1165	Baskin Auto Truck And Tractor Inc—Donald Baskin	1844 Hwy 51 S, Covington TN 38019	901-476-2626	R	16*	.1
1166	Hudspeth Motors Inc—Shain Satterwhite	PO Box 370, Harrison AR 72602	870-743-3200	R	16*	<.1
1167	Place Motor Inc—Steven Place	19 Thompson Rd, Webster MA 01570	508-943-8012	R	16*	<.1
1168	Charleston Lincoln Mercury Inc—Rob Hart	321 Virginia St W, Charleston WV 25302	304-346-9441	R	16*	<.1
1169	Randy Curnow Buick/GMC—Randy Curnow	7707 State Ave, Kansas City KS 66112	913-334-1166	R	16*	<.1
1170	Orr Cadillac-Pontiac Inc—Sandy Orr	10 Mill St, Springfield MA 01108	413-781-1677	R	16*	<.1
1171	Park Place Dealerships—Stephen James	4422 W Plano Pky, Plano TX 75093	972-769-2000	R	16*	<.1
1172	Edwards Automotive Inc—Dale Edwards	PO Box 40, Iron Mountain MI 49801	906-828-3093	R	16*	<.1
1173	Landers McLarty Dodge Chrysler Jeep Ram—Jordan Frazier	5080 Academy Ln, Bessemer AL 35022		R	16*	<.1
1174	Jim Bilton Ford Inc—Steve Bilton	PO Box 98, Saint George SC 29477	843-563-2341	R	16*	<.1
1175	MTC Kenworth Inc—Frank Casagrande	239 Bergen Tpke, Ridgefield Park NJ 07660	201-641-4440	R	16*	<.1
1176	Capital Chevrolet and Imports—David Miles Sonic Automotive Inc	111 Newland Rd, Columbia SC 29229	803-254-1431	S	15*	.1
1177	Lawson Chevrolet	545 Hwy 515 S, Jasper GA 30143	706-692-3441	R	15*	.1
1178	Fairway Ford Inc—Barney Rubin	301 US Hwy 79 S, Henderson TX 75654	903-657-2566	R	15*	<.1
1179	Joe Van Horn Chevrolet Geo Inc—Theresa Van Horn	PO Box 238, Plymouth WI 53073	920-893-6361	R	15*	<.1
1180	Sport Mitsubishi—Scot Davis	3772 W Colonial Dr, Orlando FL 32808		R	15*	<.1
1181	Schmit Ford Mercury Corp—Thomas Schmit	PO Box 8, Thiensville WI 53092	262-242-1100	R	15*	<.1
1182	Jasper Ford Lincoln Mercury—Robert E Allison Jr	PO Box 1510, Jasper TX 75951	409-384-3411	R	15*	<.1
1183	Advantage Ford—Ty Viger	13040 I-10 Service Rd, New Orleans LA 70128	504-246-2010	R	14*	.1
1184	East Bay Ford Truck Sales Inc—Ernest Speno	333 Filbert St, Oakland CA 94607	510-272-4400	R	14*	.1
1185	Roberts Motor Sales Inc—John Roberts	200 E 18th St, Owensboro KY 42303		R	14*	<.1
1186	Andco Inc—Jack Anderson	170 Amaral St, East Providence RI 02915	401-434-5900	R	14*	<.1
1187	Parker Auto Collection—Tom Parker	5105 Warden Rd, North Little Rock AR 72116	501-771-1700	R	14*	<.1
1188	Wylie Musser Chevrolet Oldsmobile Cadillac—Wylie Musser	1212 W Moore, Terrell TX 75160	972-524-2663	R	14*	<.1
1189	West Virginia-Ohio Motor Sales Inc—Robert Mendenhall	PO Box 71, Wheeling WV 26003	304-232-7517	R	14*	<.1
1190	Golling Pontiac Gmc Truck Inc—A Golling	1491 S Lapeer Rd, Lake Orion MI 48360	248-693-5900	R	14*	<.1
1191	Burr Truck and Trailer Sales Inc—Melvin Burr	2901 Vestal Rd, Vestal NY 13850	607-729-2211	R	13*	<.1
1192	Herrin-Gear Chevrolet Inc—Jack Herrin	PO Box 329, Jackson MS 39205	601-354-3882	R	13*	.2
1193	Silsbee Ford Lincoln Mercury Inc	1211 US Hwy 96, Silsbee TX 77656	409-895-3800	R	13*	<.1
1194	Lake Forest Sportscars Ltd—Rick Mancuso	990 North Shore Dr, Lake Bluff IL 60044	847-295-6560	R	13*	<.1
1195	Maxton Motors Inc—Bobbie Gaunt	114 W Main St, Butler IN 46721	260-868-2195	R	13*	<.1
1196	Rozum Motor Co—Jim Rozum	2300 N Main St, Mitchell SD 57301	605-996-5614	R	13*	<.1

Rank	Company Name—*Executive Officer*	Address, City, State, Zip	Phone	Type	Fin	Empls
1197	Miller's Dodge—*Bob Miller Jr*	300 Baltimore Pike, Springfield PA 19064	610-544-5300	R	13*	<.1
1198	Bezema Auto Body Inc—*Eric Bezema*	401 Providence Hwy, Norwood MA 02062	781-769-2440	R	12*	<.1
1199	Bob Gillingham Ford Inc—*David Zudell*	8383 Brookpark Rd, Parma OH 44129	216-398-1300	R	12*	.1
1200	Turnpike Ford Inc—*Steve Parsons*	PO Box 1328, Huntington WV 25714	304-529-2200	R	12*	<.1
1201	Wright Motors Inc—*Robert Wright*	4500 Division St, Evansville IN 47715	812-479-3131	R	12*	<.1
1202	Billco Motors Inc—*Gregg Semel*	PO Box 488, Wexford PA 15090	724-940-1000	R	12*	<.1
1203	Jim Murphy Pontiac Buick GMC—*James A Murphy*	3000 Walden Ave, Depew NY 14043	716-684-8900	R	12*	<.1
1204	Martin Chevrolet Inc—*John E Martin Jr*	1315 Reese St, Breaux Bridge LA 70517	337-332-2132	R	12*	<.1
1205	Straub Honda Hyundai—*Bryan Fato*	200 Straub Dr, Triadelphia WV 26059		R	12*	<.1
1206	Jack Morris Ford Lincoln Mercury Inc—*Jack Morris*	PO Box 740, Plainview TX 79073	806-293-2511	R	12*	<.1
1207	Asbury Automotive Group LLC—*Charles R Oglesby* Asbury Automotive Group Inc	622 3rd Ave 37th Fl, New York NY 10017	212-885-2500	S	12*	<.1
1208	Langdale Chevrolet-Pontiac—*Chris Jessee*	1006 W Franklin St, Sylvester GA 31791	706-846-2125	R	12*	<.1
1209	Goodman Truck and Tractor Company Inc—*Charles Goodman*	PO Box 166, Amelia Court House VA 23002	804-561-2141	R	12*	<.1
1210	Mack Tidewater Inc—*John Doub*	301 Bulldog Dr, Chesapeake VA 23320	757-547-7151	R	12*	<.1
1211	Anchor Subaru LLC—*Chris Benoit*	949 Eddie Dowling Hwy, North Smithfield RI 02896	401-769-1199	R	11*	<.1
1212	McMahon Ford Inc—*William J Schicker*	3295 S Kingshighway, Saint Louis MO 63139	314-664-4100	R	11*	.1
1213	Burroughs Diesel Inc—*Robert Burroughs*	PO Box 4451, Laurel MS 39441	601-649-3062	R	11*	<.1
1214	Kings Nissan of Cincinatti—*Don Riley*	9819 Kings Auto Mall R, Cincinnati OH 45249		R	11*	<.1
1215	Sherwood Automotive Group Inc	215 S Euclid St, Anaheim CA 92802	714-991-3100	R	11*	<.1
1216	Goode Motor Inc—*Garth Williams*	1096 E Main St, Burley ID 83318		R	11*	<.1
1217	Al Asher and Sons Inc—*James Asher*	5301 Valley Blvd, Los Angeles CA 90032	323-225-2295	R	11*	<.1
1218	Clevenger Ford—*Truman Clevenger*	701 N Main St, Porterville CA 93257	559-784-6000	R	10*	<.1
1219	Utility Sales And Service Inc—*William Loehrke*	412 Randolph Dr, Appleton WI 54913	920-788-2699	R	10*	<.1
1220	Jim Riehls Friendly Automotive Group—*Jim Riehl*	1515 S Lepeer Rd, Lapeer MI 48446	810-664-2900	R	10*	<.1
1221	Joyce Buick GMC—*Mike Joyce*	1860 Colorado Ave, Lorain OH 44052	440-288-1288	R	10*	<.1
1222	Williams Service Inc—*Rodney Williams*	PO Box 147, Florence KS 66851	620-878-4225	R	10*	<.1
1223	Classic East Inc—*Jim Brown*	6300 N Ridge Rd, Madison OH 44057	440-951-1116	R	9*	<.1
1224	Vic Bailey Imports—*Vic Bailey III*	501 E Daniel Morgan Av, Spartanburg SC 29302	864-582-1200	R	9*	<.1
1225	Trenor Motor Co—*Edward A Tehan III*	4701 Urbana Rd, Springfield OH 45502	937-399-9900	R	9*	<.1
1226	Ervin N Baker Inc—*Karl Behnken*	2604 W DeYoung, Marion IL 62959	618-364-4741	R	9*	<.1
1227	Harbin Ford Lincoln Mercury—*Tom Vosen*	564 Micah Way, Scottsboro AL 35768	256-574-1819	R	9*	<.1
1228	North Coast Nissan Inc—*Jacob Studor*	7168 Pearl Rd, Cleveland OH 44130	440-884-7800	R	9*	<.1
1229	Meyer Sales Company Inc—*Fred Meyer*	PO Box 279, Cameron WI 54822	715-458-2838	R	9*	<.1
1230	Hubler Brothers Inc—*Keith Billotte*	PO Box 1319, Clearfield PA 16830	814-765-7400	R	8*	<.1
1231	Classic Automobiles Inc—*Arthur Miller*	541 White Plains Rd, Eastchester NY 10709	914-779-2020	R	8*	<.1
1232	Hollingsworth Mazda—*Mike Hollingsworth*	7787 Florida Blvd, Baton Rouge LA 70806	225-272-2900	R	8*	<.1
1233	Compact Cars Inc—*John Apostolakis*	3156 Elm Rd Ne, Cortland OH 44410	330-638-3060	R	7*	<.1
1234	Gordon Rountree Motors Ltd—*Richard Carr*	PO Box 1667, Waco TX 76703	254-756-4461	R	7*	<.1
1235	Ford Lincoln of Cookville—*Mike Cass*	1600 Interstate Dr, Cookeville TN 38501	931-526-3325	R	7*	<.1
1236	Ultimate Automotive Group LLC—*Chris Rathol*	185 Commonwealth Ct, Winchester VA 22602	540-868-1300	R	7*	<.1
1237	All Points Equipment Inc—*James Veit*	12851 Prospect St, Dearborn MI 48126	313-584-6879	R	6*	<.1
1238	Dealer Operating Control Services Inc—*Andrew L Breech*	2120 Wilshire Blvd Ste, Santa Monica CA 90403	310-828-4748	R	6*	<.1
1239	Paul Snider Enterprises—*Paul H Snider*	5150 Madison Ave, Sacramento CA 95841	916-334-7397	R	5*	<.1
1240	Ams Vans Inc—*Kip Crum*	5555 Pkwy Ste 555, Norcross GA 30093	770-729-9400	R	5*	<.1
1241	Stevinson Automotive—*Kent Stevenson*	1546 Cole Blvd Ste 100, Golden CO 80401	303-232-2006	R	4*	.1
1242	Tunmore Auto Center—*Roger Tunmore*	2677 Delaware Ave, Buffalo NY 14216	716-877-1500	R	4*	<.1
1243	R and R Truck Sales Inc—*George Ralich*	PO Box 7309, Akron OH 44306	330-794-9304	R	4*	<.1
1244	Chenoweth Ford Inc—*Allen Chenoweth*	PO Box 1640, Clarksburg WV 26302	304-623-6501	R	3*	.1
1245	WindyCityJay Truck Sales—*Jason DeSanto*	11 S 183 Madison St, Burr Ridge IL 60527		R	3*	<.1
1246	Caravan Trailer LLC—*David Smith*	PO Box 12595, Kansas City MO 64116	816-781-1701	R	3*	.1
1247	Auto Locator	167 Lambert St, Oxnard CA 93030	805-988-0884	R	2	<.1
1248	John Hall Motors Inc—*John Hall*	2825 N 48th St, Lincoln NE 68504		R	1*	<.1
1249	Major Automotive of New Jersey Inc Major Automotive Companies Inc	43-0 Northern Blvd, Long Island City NY 11101	718-937-3700	S	N/A	.5
1250	Cox Chevrolet Inc	2900 Cortez Rd W, Bradenton FL 34207	941-749-2699	R	N/A	.2
1251	Ralph Schomp Automotive Inc—*Mark Wallace*	5700 S Broadway, Littleton CO 80121	303-797-8801	R	N/A	.2
1252	Matthews Automotive Group—*Irving J Matthews*	966 W International Sp, Daytona Beach FL 32114	386-255-6412	R	N/A	.2
1253	Thompsons Auto Centers—*Ron Thompson*	55 Placerville Dr, Placerville CA 95667		R	N/A	.2
1254	Red Holman Pontiac Co—*Mark Kowalski*	35100 Ford Rd, Westland MI 48185	734-423-1007	R	N/A	.1
1255	Trans Power Inc—*TC Cannon*	2702 Palmyra Rd, Albany GA 31707	229-883-6550	S	N/A	.1
1256	Devan Lowe Inc—*Devan Lowe*	801 Grand Ave, Rainbow City AL 35906	256-399-4843	R	N/A	<.1

TOTALS: SIC 5511 New & Used Car Dealers
Companies: 1,256

					201,496	412.2

5521 Used Car Dealers

Rank	Company Name—*Executive Officer*	Address, City, State, Zip	Phone	Type	Fin	Empls
1	DriveTime Automotive Group Inc—*Ray Fidel*	4020 E Indian School R, Phoenix AZ 85018	602-852-6600	R	1,154*	2.4
2	Joe Myers Automotive Inc—*Cecil Tuyl*	19010 NW Fwy, Jersey Village TX 77065	281-890-8700	R	172*	.2
3	Kruse International	5540 County Rd 11A, Auburn IN 46706	260-925-5600	R	125*	.1
4	David Taylor Cadillac Co—*David W Taylor Jr*	PO Box 36428, Houston TX 77236	713-777-7151	R	39*	.2
5	Elliff Motors Inc—*Bill Elliff*	1307 W Harrison St, Harlingen TX 78550	956-423-3434	R	13*	<.1
6	Hulbert Auto Park—*Steve Hulbert*	1100 Plum St SE, Olympia WA 98501	360-754-3900	R	12*	<.1
7	Big Joe Lift Trucks Inc—*James Kiefus*	1112 E Dominguez St, Carson CA 90746	310-637-6000	R	6*	<.1
8	H and H Chief Sales Inc—*Lance Sullivan*	PO Box 456, Carthage MS 39051	601-267-9643	R	4*	<.1
9	Massop Electric Inc—*Steve Massop*	1409 Silver St E, Mapleton MN 56065	507-524-3726	R	4*	<.1

TOTALS: SIC 5521 Used Car Dealers
Companies: 9

					1,529	3.0

5531 Automobile & Home Supply Stores

Rank	Company Name—*Executive Officer*	Address, City, State, Zip	Phone	Type	Fin	Empls
1	Advance Auto Parts Inc—*Darren Jackson*	5008 Airport Rd, Roanoke VA 24012	540-362-4911	P	5,925	49.0
2	O'Reilly Automotive Inc—*Greg Henslee*	233 S Patterson Ave, Springfield MO 65802	417-829-5727	P	5,398	47.1
3	Pep Boys-Manny Moe and Jack—*Michael R Odell*	3111 W Allegheny Ave, Philadelphia PA 19132	215-430-9000	P	1,989	18.3
4	Discount Tire Co—*Tom Englert*	20225 N Scottsdale Rd, Scottsdale AZ 85255	480-606-6000	R	1,622*	10.0
5	Les Schwab Tire Co—*Dick Borgman*	PO Box 5350, Bend OR 97708	541-447-4136	R	1,167*	7.0
6	CSK Auto Corp—*Lawrence N Mondry* O'Reilly Automotive Inc	645 E Missouri Ave Ste, Phoenix AZ 85012	602-265-9200	S	836	15.1
7	Morgan Tire and Auto—*Jim Curley*	2021 Sunnydale Blvd, Clearwater FL 33765	727-441-3727	S	807*	6.5
8	JC Whitney and Co—*Thomas M West*	PO Box 8410, Chicago IL 60680	312-431-6000	R	286*	.5
9	Tire Kingdom Inc—*Orland Wolford*	823 Donald Ross Rd, Juno Beach FL 33408	561-383-3000	S	276*	.4

Note: An asterisk (*) indicates an estimated financial figure. The company type code used is as follows: R = Private, P = Public, S = Private Subsidiary, B = Public Subsidiary, D = Division, J = Joint Venture, I = Investment Fund.

RANKINGS BY SALES WITHIN 4-DIGIT SIC

	Company Name—Executive Officer	Address, City, State, Zip	Phone	Type	Fin	Empls
10	Hwashin America Corp—Milton Park	661 Montgomery Hwy, Greenville AL 36037	334-382-1100	R	264*	.2
11	Jack Williams Tire Company Inc—Bill Williams	PO Box 3655, Scranton PA 18505		R	206*	.3
12	Tire Warehouse Inc—Robert Dabrowski	PO Box 486, Keene NH 03431	603-352-4478	R	197*	.3
13	Sullivan Investment Company Inc—Robert Sullivan	41 Accord Park Dr, Norwell MA 02061	781-982-1550	R	174*	1.0
14	Strauss Discount Auto—Glenn Langberg	7C Brick Plant Rd, South River NJ 08882	732-390-9000	R	130*	1.2
15	Solideal USA Inc—Paul Gaines	PO Box 410888, Charlotte NC 28241	704-374-9700	R	119*	.4
16	Big 10 Tire Co—Don Kennemer	3938A Government Blvd, Mobile AL 36693	251-666-9938	S	87*	.8
17	Peerless Tyre Co—Samuel E Forbes	5000 Kingston St, Denver CO 80239	303-371-4300	R	62*	.3
18	Clark Tire and Auto Supply Company Inc—John D Clark	220 S Center St, Hickory NC 28602	828-322-2303	R	50*	.3
19	Hesselbein Tire Company Inc—Denny King	3004 Lynch St, Jackson MS 39209	601-352-3611	R	47*	.1
20	Technicar Inc—Charles Mesa	4421 Annete St Ste 11, West Palm Beach FL 33409	561-615-4002	R	45*	.2
21	Year One Inc—Kevin King	P O Box 521, Braselton GA 30517	706-658-2140	R	39*	.2
22	Stratham Tire Inc—Lionel Labonte	355 Rte 125, Brentwood NH 03833	603-679-2232	R	33*	.2
23	Western Tire Centers Inc—John Furrier	PO Box 26911, Tucson AZ 85726	520-748-1700	R	28*	.2
24	Midwest Acoust-A-Fiber Inc—Jerry Wolf	PO Box 1279, Delaware OH 43015	740-369-3624	R	23*	.2
25	Johnson's Tire Service Inc—Jim Johnson	3330 Denali St, Anchorage AK 99503	907-562-7090	R	20*	.1
26	MFS Supply Inc	31100 Solon Rd Ste 16, Solon OH 44139	440-248-5300	R	18	<.1
27	Winfield Consumer Products Inc—Robert D Tyler	PO Box 839, Winfield KS 67156	620-221-2268	R	17*	.1
28	Power Train Service Company Inc—Joe Leffel	PO Box 42911, Indianapolis IN 46242	317-241-9393	R	17*	.2
29	Leonard Aluminum Utility Buildings Inc—Sandra Leonard	PO Box 1728, Mount Airy NC 27030	336-789-5018	R	15*	.2
30	Campbell Supply Company Inc—David Campbell	1526 N Industrial Ave, Sioux Falls SD 57104	605-331-5470	R	14*	.2
31	Gem-Top Manufacturing Inc—Janet Deim	36600 Industrial Way, Sandy OR 97055	503-826-1801	R	11*	.2
32	Benny's Inc—Malcolm Bromberg	340 Waterman Ave, Esmond RI 02917	401-231-1000	R	11*	.1
33	Nu-Way Auto Parts—Eli N Futerman	415 Main St, Rochester NY 14608	585-235-1595	S	11*	<.1
34	National Auto Parts—Phil Payne	7249 Hwy 85, Riverdale GA 30274	770-997-5757	R	10*	<.1
35	Stellar Distribution LLC—Jeff Hickman	2000 Dogwood Dr Se, Conyers GA 30013	770-918-6130	R	10*	.1
36	Bert Williams And Sons Inc—Herbert Williams	525 Northbay Dr, Napa CA 94559	707-255-0969	R	10*	<.1
37	Myrmo and Sons Inc—Eric Myrmo	PO Box 3215, Eugene OR 97403	541-747-4561	R	9*	.1
38	Rayside Truck and Trailer Inc—Charles Rayside	2983 S Military Trl, West Palm Beach FL 33415	561-965-7950	R	8*	<.1
39	General Auto Repair Inc—Timothy Gerrity	4425 International Blv, Oakland CA 94601	510-533-3333	R	7*	.1
40	Spring Tampa Co—John Messina	8820 N Brooks St, Tampa FL 33604	813-933-2805	R	6*	<.1
41	M and G Distributors Inc—Marc Faigus	2440 W McDowell Rd, Phoenix AZ 85009	602-269-5769	R	6*	<.1
42	KN Kaminaka Inc—Kenneth Kaminaka	94-099 Leokane St, Waipahu HI 96797	808-871-7668	R	6*	<.1
43	Dencompany LLC—Karen Sick	PO Box 441, Manlius NY 13104	315-682-8834	R	5*	<.1
44	Sbd Holding Company LLC—Bernice Parks	90 Harts Ln, Albany NY 12204	518-449-7171	R	5*	.1
45	Royal Battery Distributors Inc—Ed Safee	2580 N Orange Blossom, Kissimmee FL 34744	407-846-4466	R	5*	<.1
46	Intercon Truck Equipment Inc—Gerald Southern	591 Meetinghouse Rd, Upper Chichester PA 19061	610-364-9500	R	5*	<.1
47	Saylor Electric Products Corp—Gregory Westhooven	17484 Saylor Ln, Grand Rapids OH 43522	419-832-2125	R	4*	.1
48	Vance C Francis Enterprises Inc—Larry Francis	2420 W Ave M, Temple TX 76504	254-778-5223	R	4*	<.1
49	Monterey Auto Supply Inc—Ronald Ferguson	2320 Del Monte Ave C1, Monterey CA 93940	831-372-4553	R	4*	<.1
50	Jack Lyons Truck Parts Inc—John Lyons	8482 Nw 96th St, Medley FL 33166	305-884-4222	R	4*	<.1
51	Toce Brothers Inc—Dominic Toce	143 E Main St, Torrington CT 06790	860-496-2080	R	4*	<.1
52	Area Diesel Service Inc—Val Leefers	PO Box 115, Carlinville IL 62626	217-854-2641	R	4*	<.1
53	Burton Auto Parts Inc—Michael Winston	G4523 S Saginaw St, Burton MI 48529	810-742-5240	R	3*	<.1
54	J and J Amusements Incorporated An Oregon Corp—Leon Wilbanks	4897 Indian School Rd, Salem OR 97305	503-304-8899	R	3*	<.1
55	Tri-County Parts and Equipment—Clifford Tugh	PO Box 945, Crossville TN 38557	931-484-6168	R	3*	<.1
56	Arizona Auto and Truck Parts Inc—Michael Pierson	2021 W Buckeye Rd, Phoenix AZ 85009	602-253-5111	R	3*	<.1
57	Star Blue Auto Stores Inc—David Lass	2001 S State St, Chicago IL 60616	312-225-7174	R	3*	<.1
58	Stan The Tire Man Inc—Dale Lowery	1213 Broadway St, Mount Vernon IL 62864	618-242-6400	R	3*	<.1
59	Crookston Welding Machine Co—Larry Altringer	PO Box 377, Crookston MN 56716	218-281-6911	R	3*	<.1
60	Trailer Sales Of Tennessee Inc—James Huffaker	PO Box 100894, Nashville TN 37224	615-259-3301	R	3*	<.1
61	Barnes Motor and Parts Company Inc—Henry Walston	PO Box 1207, Wilson NC 27894	252-243-2161	R	2*	.3
62	Lightning Rv Supply Inc—Brad Green	PO Box 448, Thonotosassa FL 33592	813-986-3442	R	2*	<.1
63	AAC Enterprises LLC	4401 Division St, Metairie LA 70002	504-835-0055	R	2	<.1
64	L D Willcox and Son Inc—Newell Willcox	233 Elmira Rd, Ithaca NY 14850	607-273-6310	R	2*	<.1
65	AutoAccessoriesGaragecom—Steve Therriault	7450 Duvan Dr, Tinley Park IL 60477	708-444-2580	R	2*	<.1
66	Finn Auto Parts—Eli N Futerman	30 Muar St, Canandaigua NY 14424	585-394-3370	S	2*	<.1
67	AccessoRize 4 Less—Rick Lillard	4509 Cherry St, Pearland TX 77581	281-485-0000	R	2*	<.1
68	American Taximeters and Communications Inc—Antonio Martinez	2146 44th Dr, Long Island City NY 11101	718-937-4600	R	1*	<.1
69	Battery Factory S/W Divn Inc—Johnny White	2552 N Oracle Rd, Tucson AZ 85705	520-882-8598	R	1*	<.1
70	Continental Contact and Supply Inc—John Majewski	1832 Mearns Rd, Warminster PA 18974	215-443-0558	R	<1*	<.1

TOTALS: SIC 5531 Automobile & Home Supply Stores
Companies: 70   20,096   161.7

5541 Gasoline Service Stations

	Company Name—Executive Officer	Address, City, State, Zip	Phone	Type	Fin	Empls
1	Pilot Flying J—James A Haslam III	5508 Lonas Dr, Knoxville TN 37909	865-588-7487	R	28,935*	13.0
2	Speedway SuperAmerica LLC—Tony Kenney	PO Box 1500, Springfield OH 45501	937-864-3000	S	20,560*	1.9
3	Pilot Corp—James A Haslam III	PO Box 10146, Knoxville TN 37939	865-588-7487	R	11,800*	13.0
4	BP Oil Co—Lord Browne	150 W Warrenville Rd, Naperville IL 60563	630-420-5111	R	10,525*	11.9
5	Petro Stopping Centers LP	24601 Center Ridge RdS, Westlake OH 44145	404-808-9100	S	7,878*	4.2
6	RaceTrac Petroleum Inc—Carl E Bolch Jr	PO Box 105035, Atlanta GA 30348	770-431-7600	R	5,393*	5.6
7	Susser Holdings Corp—Sam L Susser	4525 Ayers St, Corpus Christi TX 78415	361-884-2463	P	3,931	7.2
8	Love's Travel Stops and Country Stores Inc—Tom Love	PO Box 26210, Oklahoma City OK 73126	405-751-9000	R	3,636*	6.7
9	Petro Stopping Centers Holdings LP—Jack A Cardwell Sr	24601 Center Ridge Rd, Westlake OH 44145	440-808-9100	R	2,147*	4.2
10	Gas America Services Inc—Stephanie White	2700 W Main St, Greenfield IN 46140	317-468-2515	R	1,447*	.8
11	Nella Oil Co—Thomas W Dwelle	2360 Lindberg St, Auburn CA 95602	530-885-0401	R	642*	.5
12	Kocolene Oil Corp—Robert R Myers Kocolene Marketing LLC	PO Box 448, Seymour IN 47274	812-522-2224	S	640*	.5
13	AT Williams Oil Co—Walter L Williams	5446 University Pkwy, Winston-Salem NC 27105		R	552*	2.5
14	Gate Petroleum Co—Herbert Peyton	PO Box 23627, Jacksonville FL 32241	904-737-7220	R	538*	3.5
15	Olympian Co—Alan Breese	999 Bayhill Dr Ste 135, San Bruno CA 94066	650-873-8200	R	430*	.4
16	Maverik Country Stores Inc—Michael Call	PO Box 8008, Afton WY 83110	307-885-3861	R	375*	2.5
17	American Pride Coop—Gary Morrison	55 W Bromley Ln, Brighton CO 80601	303-659-1230	R	299*	.1
18	Shirley Oil and Supply Company Inc—Chuck Beeler	PO Box 17, Mc Lean IL 61754	309-874-2323	R	212*	.5
19	Gibbs Oil Co—Gary Kaneb	PO Box 9151, Chelsea MA 02150	617-660-7520	S	187*	.4
20	South Tennessee Oil Company Inc—Jonathan Edwards	PO Box 807, Lawrenceburg TN 38464	931-762-9600	R	178*	.4
21	Jamieson-Hill A General Partnership—W Hill	PO Box 82515, Bakersfield CA 93380	661-393-7000	R	171*	.1
22	Town Pump Incorporated and Affiliates—Thomas Kenneally	PO Box 6000, Butte MT 59702	406-497-6700	R	170*	1.8

Rank	Company Name—*Executive Officer*	Address, City, State, Zip	Phone	Type	Fin	Empls
23	Kocolene Marketing LLC—*Robert R Myers*	PO Box 448, Seymour IN 47274	812-522-2224	R	169*	.4
24	Spartan Stores Fuel LLC	850 76th St Sw, Grand Rapids MI 49518	616-878-2000	R	150*	.1
25	Jaco Oil Co—*Tom J Jamison*	3101 State Rd, Bakersfield CA 93308	661-393-7000	R	148*	.4
26	Herndon Oil Corp—*David Herndon*	22164 US Hwy 98, Foley AL 36535	251-971-2225	R	129*	.1
27	Premium Oil Co—*Paul S Callister*	2005 S 300 W, Salt Lake City UT 84115	801-487-4721	R	106*	.2
28	Miller and Holmes Inc—*Gerald Peterson*	2311 O'Neil Rd, Hudson WI 54016	715-377-1730	R	103*	.3
29	J and H Oil Co—*Jerry Hop*	PO Box 9464, Wyoming MI 49509	616-534-2181	R	96*	.5
30	Greenway Co-Operative Service—*David Eickdoff*	PO Box 6878, Rochester MN 55903	507-289-4086	R	96*	.2
31	Silco Oil Co—*Sue Vanderburg*	181 E 56th Ave, Denver CO 80216	303-292-0500	R	70*	.4
32	Freedom Oil—*Michael Owens*	PO Box 3697, Bloomington IL 61702	309-828-7750	R	67*	.3
33	Lassus Brothers Oil Co—*Jon F Lassus*	1800 Magnavox Way, Fort Wayne IN 46804	260-436-1415	R	63*	.3
34	Kent Cos—*Bill Kent*	PO Box 908001, Midland TX 79708	432-520-4000	R	52*	.3
35	Jubitz Corp—*Fred Jubitz*	10210 N Vancouver Way, Portland OR 97217	503-283-1111	R	42*	.3
36	Leathers Oil Co—*Lila Leathers-Fitz*	22300 SE Stark St, Gresham OR 97030	503-661-1244	R	42*	.2
37	Monte Vista Cooperative Inc—*Matt Seger*	1901 E Hwy 160, Monte Vista CO 81144	719-852-5181	R	38*	.1
38	Walla Walla Farmers Co-op Inc—*Barry Chabre*	111 N 9th Ave, Walla Walla WA 99362	509-525-6690	R	36*	.1
39	Polk County Farmers Coop—*Steve Danner*	9055 Rickreall Rd, Rickreall OR 97371	503-363-2332	R	31*	.1
40	Bowlin Travel Centers Inc—*Michael L Bowlin*	150 Louisiana NE, Albuquerque NM 87108	505-266-5985	P	26	.1
41	O'Connell Oil Associates Inc—*Mchael R Sobon*	545 Merrill Rd, Pittsfield MA 01201	413-499-4800	R	24*	.2
42	Bay Oil Co—*Link C Smith*	PO Box 1367, Dickinson TX 77539	281-337-4671	R	21*	.1
43	Cannon Oil Corp—*Frank Weathers*	PO Drawer 6307, Dothan AL 36302	334-794-2776	R	21*	.1
44	Friends Enterprises—*John O'Neill*	PO Box 2708, Morgan City LA 70381	985-384-1610	R	21*	.1
45	Farmers Union Oil Co (Ellendale North Dakota)—*Robert Carlson*	PO Box 2136, Jamestown ND 58401	701-349-3280	R	21*	<.1
46	Gay Johnson's Inc—*Bert Johnson*	PO Box 1829, Grand Junction CO 81502	970-242-3021	R	19*	.1
47	Country Pride Services Coop—*Kevin Jackson*	144 9th St, Bingham Lake MN 56118	507-831-2580	R	19*	<.1
48	Tucson Truck Terminal Inc—*Frank B Jakubik*	5451 E Benson Hwy, Tucson AZ 85706	520-574-0050	R	17*	.2
49	Central Valley Coop—*Dave Seykora*	900 30th Place NW, Owatonna MN 55060	507-451-1230	R	17*	.1
50	NE Jones Oil Company Inc—*Gary Jones*	PO Box 5070, Texarkana TX 75505	903-838-8541	R	17*	.1
51	Dunlap Oil Company Inc—*Kenneth T Dunlap*	759 S Haskell Ave, Willcox AZ 85643	520-586-7178	R	17*	<.1
52	Farmers Union Oil Company of Kenmare—*Kevin Williams*	PO Box 726, Kenmare ND 58746	701-385-4222	R	17*	<.1
53	G and G Oil Company Of Indiana Inc—*Scott Arrington*	PO Box 71, Muncie IN 47308	765-288-7795	R	15*	.2
54	Roy Motors Inc—*Martin A Roy Jr*	PO Box 520, Opelousas LA 70571	337-942-9701	R	15*	<.1
55	Lewis Entertainment Group—*Sherman Lewis III*	3333 W Alabama St, Houston TX 77098	713-850-1300	R	12*	<.1
56	I-74 Auto Truck Plaza—*Kenna Saadosf*	PO Box 39, Oakwood IL 61858	217-354-2181	R	11*	<.1
57	TOC Holdings Co—*H Roger Holliday*	PO Box 24447, Seattle WA 98124	206-285-2400	R	11*	<.1
58	Global Energy of Hutchinson	707 N Main St, South Hutchinson KS 67505	620-663-6300	R	10*	<.1
59	Consumer Oil and Supply Co—*Wayne Leamer*	PO Box 38, Braymer MO 64624	660-645-2215	R	9*	<.1
60	Waco Scaffoldng—*Marty Cughlin*	676 Moss St, Chula Vista CA 91911	619-591-2300	R	9*	.1
61	Southwest Energy Distributors Inc—*Clay Wood*	13718 W Hwy 80 E, Odessa TX 79765	432-332-1301	R	7*	<.1
62	Farmers Union Oil Coop (Watford City North Dakota)—*Tony Volski*	PO Box 624, Watford City ND 58854	701-444-3639	R	5*	<.1
63	Key Oil Co—*Peter S Wareing*	3355 W Alabama Ste 630, Houston TX 77098	713-355-6767	R	5*	<.1
64	Dave's Emergency Roadside—*David Mulzet*	PO Box 90375, Allentown PA 18109	610-849-2328	R	2*	<.1

TOTALS: SIC 5541 Gasoline Service Stations
Companies: 64

					102,453	87.0

5551 Boat Dealers

Rank	Company Name—*Executive Officer*	Address, City, State, Zip	Phone	Type	Fin	Empls
1	West Marine Inc—*Geoff Eisenberg*	PO Box 50070, Watsonville CA 95077	831-728-2700	P	623	3.3
2	MarineMax Inc—*William H McGill Jr*	18167 US 19 Hwy N Ste, Clearwater FL 33764	727-531-1700	P	481	1.2
3	Jefferson Beach Marina Inc—*Greg Krueger*	24400 E Jefferson Ave, Saint Clair Shores MI 48080	586-778-7600	R	25*	.1
4	Bassett Boat Co—*Diane Bassett-Zable* MarineMax Inc	121 West St, Springfield MA 01104	413-739-4745	S	20*	<.1
5	Boat Center Inc—*Darryl Smith*	49 Douglas St, Savannah GA 31406	912-355-0025	R	17*	<.1
6	Howell Laboratories Inc—*Paul Wescott*	PO Box 389, Bridgton ME 04009	207-647-3327	R	13*	.1
7	Argonaut Inflatable Research And Engineering Inc—*Greg Ramp*	PO Box 186, Meridian ID 83680	208-888-1772	R	5*	<.1
8	D and R Boats Inc—*Robert Barone*	271 US HIGHWAY 22, Green Brook NJ 08812	732-968-2600	R	4*	<.1
9	Boater's World Marine Centers—*Fred Lerner*	2010 Main St, Irvine CA 92614		D	3*	<.1
10	Valiant Yachts—*Richard Worstell*	500 Harbour View Rd, Gordonville TX 76245	903-523-4899	R	1*	<.1

TOTALS: SIC 5551 Boat Dealers
Companies: 10

					1,192	4.7

5561 Recreational Vehicle Dealers

Rank	Company Name—*Executive Officer*	Address, City, State, Zip	Phone	Type	Fin	Empls
1	Camping World Inc—*Mark Lemonis*	PO Box 90018, Bowling Green KY 42102	270-781-2718	S	950*	1.0
2	Lazydays—*John Horton*	6130 Lazy Days Blvd, Seffner FL 33584		R	750*	.7
3	National Powersport Auctions—*Cliff Clifford*	13175 Gregg St, Poway CA 92064	858-513-1500	R	139*	.2
4	Cruise America Inc—*Randall Smalley Jr*	11 W Hampton Ave, Mesa AZ 85210	480-464-7300	R	131*	.4
5	Poulsbo RV Inc—*Ken Wakazuru*	19705 Viking Ave NW, Poulsbo WA 98370		R	80*	.2
6	McClain's RV Inc—*Larry McClain*	PO Box 969, Lake Dallas TX 75065	940-497-1000	R	73*	.2
7	Robert Crist and Company RV—*Paul Skogebo*	2025 E Main St, Mesa AZ 85213	480-834-9410	R	68*	.1
8	Tom Raper Inc—*Douglas Peters*	2250 Williamsburg Pke, Richmond IN 47374	765-966-8361	R	64*	.2
9	La Mesa RV Center Inc—*James R Kimbrell*	7430 Copley Park Pl, San Diego CA 92111	858-874-8000	R	58*	.5
10	Holiday World of Dallas Ltd	4630 Interstate 30, Mesquite TX 75150	214-328-4151	R	38*	.1
11	Hansel Ford—*Justin Hansel*	PO Box 610, Santa Rosa CA 95402	707-543-7300	R	30*	.1
12	Reines RV Center Inc—*Lindsey Reines*	10850 Balls Ford Rd, Manassas VA 20109	703-392-1100	R	22*	<.1
13	Bad Boy Enterprises LLC—*Jim Willard*	PO Box 19087, Natchez MS 39122		R	22	.1
14	Stoltzfus Trailer Sales Inc—*Earl Stoltzfus*	1335 Wilmington Pike, West Chester PA 19382	610-399-0628	R	18*	.1
15	L and H Manufacturing Co—*Donald Helbling*	PO Box 639, Mandan ND 58554	701-663-9821	R	15*	.1
16	Blaine Jensen and Sons RV Centers of Utah—*Craig Jensen*	780 N 900 W, Kaysville UT 84037	801-544-4298	R	15*	.1
17	Tom Stinnett RV Freedom Center—*Tom Stinnett*	520 Marriott Dr, Clarksville IN 47129	812-282-7718	R	15*	.1
18	JH Global Services Inc—*Jane Zhang*	52 Pelham Davis Cir, Greenville SC 29615	864-297-8833	R	10*	<.1
19	Dean's RV Superstore Inc—*Randy Coy*	9955 E 21st St, Tulsa OK 74129	918-664-3333	R	8*	<.1
20	Seven O's Inc—*Hearld E Oot*	7917 DeVaul Rd, Kirkville NY 13082	315-687-7777	R	8*	<.1
21	Wheeler's Las Vegas RV—*Marlene Wheeler*	13175 Las Vegas Blvd S, Las Vegas NV 89124	702-896-9000	S	8*	<.1
22	Charlie's RV and Camping Center Inc—*Charles L Widerman*	10100 Liberty Rd, Randallstown MD 21133	410-655-5200	R	6*	<.1

TOTALS: SIC 5561 Recreational Vehicle Dealers
Companies: 22

					2,528	3.9

Note: An asterisk (*) indicates an estimated financial figure. The company type code used is as follows: R = Private, P = Public, S = Private Subsidiary, B = Public Subsidiary, D = Division, J = Joint Venture, I = Investment Fund.

COMPANY RANKINGS BY SALES WITHIN 4-DIGIT SIC

Rank	Company Name—*Executive Officer*	Address, City, State, Zip	Phone	Type	Fin	Empls
5571 Motorcycle Dealers						
1	Kolbe Cycle Sales—*Andrew R Kolbe*	22123 Ventura Blvd, Woodland Hills CA 91364	818-348-7865	R	58*	.1
2	Chester's Harley-Davidson Inc—*Craig Chester*	922 S Country Club Dr, Mesa AZ 85210	480-894-0404	R	56*	.1
3	North Country Harley-Davidson Inc—*Troy Reynolds*	3099 N Belfast Ave, Augusta ME 04330	207-622-7994	R	39*	<.1
4	Destination Harley-Davidson—*Ed Wallace Jr*	2302 Pacific Hwy E, Tacoma WA 98424	253-922-3700	R	34*	.1
5	Honda of Houston—*Dave Martin*	12655 West Rd, Houston TX 77041		R	34*	<.1
6	Dudley Perkins Co—*Tom Perkins*	333 Corey Way S, South San Francisco CA 94080	650-737-5467	R	28*	.1
7	Lambretta South Inc—*David Bamdas*	3671 N Dixie Hwy, Pompano Beach FL 33064	954-785-4820	R	21*	.1
8	Bost Harley-Davidson of Nashville—*Mike Bost*	4600 Delaware Ave, Nashville TN 37209	615-297-7500	R	16*	<.1
9	Ashworth's Inc—*Ken Mc Cormick*	3797 Robert C Byrd Dr, Beckley WV 25801	304-252-9775	R	5*	<.1
10	Monster Scooter Parts—*Kevin Alvey*	26262 Three Notch Rd U, Mechanicsville MD 20659		R	3	<.1
11	Bangor Motor Sports Inc—*Kurt Thomas*	34 Banair Rd, Bangor ME 04401	207-942-4444	R	2*	<.1
12	Malott's Honda and Yamaha—*Tim Tingey*	1780 Yosemite Rd, Manteca CA 95336	209-823-7181	R	<1	<.1

TOTALS: SIC 5571 Motorcycle Dealers
Companies: 12 — 296 — .5

Rank	Company Name—*Executive Officer*	Address, City, State, Zip	Phone	Type	Fin	Empls
5599 Automotive Dealers Nec						
1	Rush Enterprises Inc—*W M Rusty Rush*	555 IH-35 S Ste 500, New Braunfels TX 78130	830-626-5200	P	1,498	3.0
2	Thompson Lift Truck Co—*Mike Thompson*	PO Box 10367, Birmingham AL 35202	205-841-8601	R	1,316*	1.4
3	Copart Inc—*A Jayson Adair*	4665 Business Center D, Fairfield CA 94534	707-639-5000	P	872	2.8
4	Hitchcock Automotive Resources Inc—*Fredrick E Hitchcock Jr*	PO Box 8610, City of Industry CA 91748	626-839-8401	R	665*	.8
5	Holt of California—*Ken Monroe*	PO Box 324, Sacramento CA 95812	916-921-8800	R	281*	.5
6	Cummins Intermountain Inc—*Bill Wolpert*	PO Box 25428, Salt Lake City UT 84125	801-355-6500	S	261*	.3
7	Cutter Aviation Inc—*William Cutter*	2802 E Old Tower Rd, Phoenix AZ 85034	602-273-1237	R	97*	.2
8	Woodland Aviation Inc—*Thomas Grant*	25170 Aviation Ave, Davis CA 95616	530-383-2505	R	83*	.1
9	Elliott/Wilson Capitol Trucks LLC—*George Wilson III*	8300 Ardwick-Ardmore R, Landover MD 20785	301-341-5500	R	70*	.1
10	Sun State International Trucks LLC—*Oscar J Horton*	6020 Adamo Dr, Tampa FL 33619	813-621-1331	R	69*	.2
11	Utility Trailer Sales Company of Arizona—*George Cravens*	1402 N 22 Ave, Phoenix AZ 85009	602-254-7213	R	37*	.1
12	Midwest Recreational Clearinghouse LLC—*Brian Livingston*	6352 320th St Way, Cannon Falls MN 55009	507-263-9234	R	31	<.1
13	Central Flying Service Inc—*Dick Holbert*	1501 Bond St, Little Rock AR 72202	501-375-3245	R	26*	.2
14	Stafford Equipment Co—*Kevin Belflower*	PO Box 808, Tifton GA 31793	229-382-4400	D	26*	<.1
15	Mid-Continent Aircraft Corp—*Richard Reade*	PO Box 540, Hayti MO 63851	573-359-0500	R	23*	<.1
16	Kermit K Kistler Inc—*Trent Bliss*	7886 Kings Hwy, New Tripoli PA 18066	610-298-2011	R	11*	<.1
17	La Pine Truck Sales Inc—*Mel Morris*	3131 E Royalton Rd, Cleveland OH 44147	440-526-6363	R	8*	<.1
18	Slowboy Racing Inc—*Michael Huml*	PO Box 471448, Lake Monroe FL 32747	321-304-4907	R	8*	<.1
19	Kamp Implement Co—*Tom Kamp*	PO Box 629, Belgrade MT 59714	406-388-4295	R	7*	<.1
20	R A Adams Enterprises Inc—*Marybeth Adams*	2600 W Il Rte 120, Mchenry IL 60051	815-385-2600	R	4*	<.1
21	Gotham Dream Cars LLC—*Noah Lehmann-Haupt*	241 William St, Englewood NJ 07631	212-957-4400	R	3*	<.1
22	Austin Jet Corp—*Jerry Edwards*	8729 Copano Dr, Austin TX 78749	512-292-7088	R	3*	<.1
23	Meridian Jet Prop Inc—*William D Gardner*	3796 Vest Mill Rd, Winston Salem NC 27103	336-765-5454	S	3*	<.1
24	C and P Machine Company Inc—*Pedro Agreda*	100 Commerce Way, South Windsor CT 06074	860-289-2520	R	3*	<.1
25	Mcdermott Associates Inc—*Bernard Mc Dermott*	PO Box 29617, Dallas TX 75229	972-247-7146	R	1*	<.1

TOTALS: SIC 5599 Automotive Dealers Nec
Companies: 25 — 5,406 — 9.9

Rank	Company Name—*Executive Officer*	Address, City, State, Zip	Phone	Type	Fin	Empls
5611 Men's & Boys' Clothing Stores						
1	Nordstrom Inc—*Blake Nordstrom*	PO Box 21986, Seattle WA 98111	206-628-2111	P	9,310	52.0
2	Brooks Brothers Inc—*Claudio Vecchio*	346 Madison Ave, New York NY 10017	212-682-8800	R	7,868*	3.5
3	Hanesbrands Inc—*Richard Noll*	1000 E Hanes Mill Rd, Winston Salem NC 27105	336-519-4400	P	4,637	53.0
4	Urban Outfitters Inc—*Richard A Hayne*	5000 S Broad St, Philadelphia PA 19112	215-454-5500	P	2,274	16.0
5	Men's Wearhouse Inc—*Douglas S Ewart*	6380 Rogerdale Rd, Houston TX 77072	713-776-7000	P	2,103	16.6
6	Eddie Bauer Holdings Inc—*Neil Fiske*	10401 NE 8th St Ste 50, Bellevue WA 98004	425-755-6544	R	1,023	7.4
7	Eddie Bauer LLC—*Neil Fiske*	PO Box 219, Bellevue WA 98009	425-755-6100	S	950*	8.0
8	Pacific Sunwear of California Inc—*Gary Schoenfeld*	3450 E Miraloma Ave, Anaheim CA 92806	714-414-4000	P	930	11.5
9	K and G Men's Center Inc—*George Zimmer* Men's Wearhouse Inc	1225 Chattahoochee Ave, Atlanta GA 30318	404-351-7987	S	288*	1.3
10	Bachrach Clothing Inc—*Sheila Arnold*	323 W 39th St FL11, New York NY 10018	212-354-4927	S	235*	.6
11	Conway Stores Inc—*Abe Cohen*	39 W 37th St, New York NY 10018	212-967-5300	R	181*	1.2
12	UpAgainstthe Wallcom—*Chuck Rendelman*	1420 Wisconsin Ave NW, Washington DC 20007	202-337-6610	R	175*	.3
13	Grace Holmes Inc—*Millard Drexler*	770 Broadway S, New York NY 10003	212-209-2500	R	156*	3.0
14	Rochester Big and Tall Clothing Corp—*Robert L Sockolov*	555 Turnpike St, Canton MA 02021	415-982-6455	S	124*	.3
15	Metropark USA Inc	5750 Grace Place, Los Angeles CA 90022	323-622-3600	R	100	2.0
16	Pacific Sunwear Stores Corp Pacific Sunwear of California Inc	3450 E Miraloma Ave, Anaheim CA 92806	714-414-4000	S	76*	.5
17	Paul Stuart Inc—*Clifford Grodd*	Madison Ave and 45th S, New York NY 10017	212-682-0320	R	71*	.2
18	Sharpe Dry Goods Co—*Louis Sharpe IV*	200 N Broadway St, Checotah OK 74426	918-473-2233	R	60*	.4
19	Mark Shale Co—*Scott Baskin*	10441 Beaudin Blvd Ste, Woodridge IL 60517	630-427-1100	R	47*	.4
20	Stamor Corp—*Mitchell Fine*	1164 Azalea Garden Rd, Norfolk VA 23502	757-857-6813	R	31*	.3
21	Lithgow Industries Inc—*Howart Vogt*	4938 Brownsboro Rd, Louisville KY 40222	502-753-7633	R	16*	<.1
22	Gushner Brothers Inc—*Gerald Gushner*	1818 Chestnut St, Philadelphia PA 19103	215-564-9000	R	15*	.2
23	Alfred Dunhill of London Inc—*Danny Taubenfeld*	450 Park Ave, New York NY 10022	212-888-4003	S	11	.1
24	Burtons (Cumberland Maryland)—*RW Burton*	800 Frederick St, Cumberland MD 21502	301-777-3866	R	11	<.1
25	Norton Ditto Inc—*Dick Hite*	2425 W Alabama St, Houston TX 77098	713-688-9800	R	9*	.1
26	Miltons Inc—*Dana Katz*	250 Granite St Ste 208, Braintree MA 02184	781-848-1880	R	6*	.1
27	Rubenstein Brothers Inc—*David Rubenstein*	102 St Charles Ave, New Orleans LA 70130	504-581-6666	R	6*	.1
28	Bijan Corp (Beverly Hills California)—*Bijan Pakzad*	420 N Rodeo Dr, Beverly Hills CA 90210	310-273-6544	R	6*	<.1
29	Custom Shop Clothiers—*Mike Smith*	6475 Wheatstone Ct, Maumee OH 43537	419-861-2400	R	5*	<.1
30	Marlin Holdings Co—*Harry Kraly*	1701 Pearl St Ste 4, Waukesha WI 53186	262-549-5100	R	5*	.1
31	Gus Mayer—*Jeff Pizitz*	225 Summit Blvd Ste700, Birmingham AL 35243	205-870-3300	R	3*	<.1
32	Imprinted Sportswear Shop Inc—*Randy Anderson*	4225 N Elizabeth St, Pueblo CO 81008	719-544-4777	R	2*	<.1
33	C and C Partners Inc—*Donald Clark*	64 Fairbanks, Irvine CA 92618	949-252-8810	R	2*	<.1

TOTALS: SIC 5611 Men's & Boys' Clothing Stores
Companies: 33 — 30,736 — 179.2

Rank	Company Name—*Executive Officer*	Address, City, State, Zip	Phone	Type	Fin	Empls
5621 Women's Clothing Stores						
1	Old Navy Inc—*Tom Wyatt*	1 Harrison St, San Francisco CA 94105	650-952-4400	S	6,856*	8.0
2	Ascena Retail Group Inc—*David R Jaffe*	30 Dunnigan Dr, Suffern NY 10901		P	2,914	31.0
3	Catocorpcom LLC Cato Corp	8100 Denmark Rd, Charlotte NC 28273	704-554-8510	S	2,830*	8.0

Rank	Company Name—*Executive Officer*	Address, City, State, Zip	Phone	Type	Fin	Empls
4	Charming Shoppes Inc—*Anthony M Romano*	450 Winks Ln, Bensalem PA 19020	215-245-9100	P	2,062	27.0
5	ANN INC—*Kay Krill*	7 Times Sq 15th Fl, New York NY 10036	212-541-3300	P	1,980	19.4
6	Express Inc—*Michael Weiss*	1 Express Dr, Columbus OH 43230	614-474-7000	P	1,906*	16.0
7	Chico's FAS Inc—*David Dyer*	11215 Metro Pkwy, Fort Myers FL 33966	239-277-6200	P	1,905	18.9
8	Talbots Inc—*Trudy F Sullivan*	1 Talbots Dr, Hingham MA 02043	781-749-7600	P	1,213	9.1
9	Catherines Stores Corp	450 Winks Ln, Bensalem PA 19020	215-245-9100	S	1,027*	3.2
	Charming Shoppes Inc					
10	New York and Company Inc—*Gregory Scott*	450 W 33rd St 5th Fl, New York NY 10001	212-884-2000	P	1,022	20.4
11	Coldwater Creek Inc—*Dennis Pence*	1 Coldwater Creek Dr, Sandpoint ID 83864	208-263-2266	P	981	9.2
12	Lane Bryant Inc—*Brian P Woolf*	3344 Morse Crossing, Columbus OH 43219	614-463-5200	D	934*	.2
	Charming Shoppes Inc					
13	Cato Corp—*John P Derham Cato*	8100 Denmark Rd, Charlotte NC 28273	704-554-8510	P	926	9.6
14	Charlotte Russe Holding Inc—*Jenny Ming*	575 Florida St, San Francisco CA 94110	415-820-6400	R	900	10.0
15	Wet Seal Inc—*Susan P McGalla*	26972 Burbank, Foothill Ranch CA 92610	949-699-3900	P	581	7.0
16	Destination Maternity Corp—*Edward M Krell*	456 N 5th St, Philadelphia PA 19123	215-873-2200	P	545	4.5
17	Maurices Inc—*David Jaffe*	105 W Superior St, Duluth MN 55802	218-727-8431	S	510*	3.5
	Ascena Retail Group Inc					
18	United Retail Group Inc—*Raphael Benaroya*	365 W Passaic St, Rochelle Park NJ 07662	201-845-0880	S	462	5.5
19	Christopher and Banks Corp—*Larry Barenbaum*	2400 Xenium Ln N, Plymouth MN 55441	763-551-5000	P	448	6.4
20	Big M Inc—*Lawrence Mandelbaum*	12 Vreeland Ave, Totowa NJ 07512	973-890-0021	R	448*	4.3
21	Bergdorf Goodman Inc—*James Gold*	754 5th Ave, New York NY 10019	212-753-7300	S	392*	2.0
22	Loehmann's Holdings Inc—*Robert N Friedman*	2500 Halsey St, Bronx NY 10461	718-409-2000	S	365	1.8
23	Deb Shops Inc—*Marvin Rounick*	9401 Blue Grass Rd, Philadelphia PA 19114	215-676-6000	R	325	3.5
24	Body Central Corp—*B Allen Weinstein*	6225 Powers Ave, Jacksonville FL 32217	904-737-0811	P	243	2.4
25	Cache Inc—*Thomas E Reinckens*	1440 Broadway 5th Fl, New York NY 10018	212-575-3200	P	207	2.2
26	Windsor Fashions Inc—*Leon Zekaria*	4533 Pacific Blvd, Vernon CA 90058	323-282-9000	R	164*	.5
27	Catherines Inc—*Diane Paccione*	450 Winks Ln Ste 100, Bensalem PA 19020	215-245-9100	R	150*	2.5
28	Appleseed's Holding Inc—*Brenda Koskinen*	30 Tozer Rd, Beverly MA 01915	978-922-2040	R	122*	.3
29	Draper's and Damon's—*Brad Farmer*	PO Box 57088, Irvine CA 92619	949-784-3000	R	105*	.7
30	Henri Bendel Inc—*Leslie H Wexner*	712 5th Ave, New York NY 10019	212-247-1100	S	94	N/A
31	Vanity Shop of Grand Forks Inc—*Rick Weinstein*	1001 25th St N, Fargo ND 58102		R	90	1.3
32	Betsey Johnson Inc—*Betsey Johnson*	498 7th Ave 21st Fl, New York NY 10018	212-244-0843	R	72*	.2
33	White House / Black Market—*Donna Noce*	11215 Metro Pkwy, Fort Myers FL 33966	239-277-6200	S	68*	.7
	Chico's FAS Inc					
34	Tootsies Inc—*Michael Rosmarin*	4045 Westheimer, Houston TX 77027	713-629-9990	R	67*	.2
35	Avenue Inc (Troy Ohio)—*Raphael Benaroya*	One United Retail Plz, Troy OH 45373		S	27*	.1
	United Retail Group Inc					
36	Vouge Body Shop Inc—*Jerrold Rosenbaum*	6225 Powers Ave, Jacksonville FL 32217	904-737-0811	R	27*	.1
37	Seal and Co—*Bert Model*	410 Springfield Ave, Summit NJ 07901	908-277-1777	R	23*	.3
38	Lady Grace Stores Inc—*Steve Berson*	5 Commonwealth Ave Ste, Woburn MA 01801	781-569-0727	R	15*	.2
39	Griffin 88 Store Inc—*Todd Griffin*	PO Box 88, Polkton NC 28135	704-272-8021	R	15*	.1
40	Escada Inc (New York New York)—*Bruno Salzar*	1412 Broadway, New York NY 10018	201-462-6000	S	11*	.1
41	Topson Downs Of California Inc—*John Boyer*	3840 Watseka Ave, Culver City CA 90232	310-558-0300	R	5*	.1
42	Bringing Up Baby Inc—*Corky Harvey*	2415 Wilshire Blvd, Santa Monica CA 90403	310-998-1981	R	2*	<.1
43	Coplon's—*Hank Greenburg*	6235 River Rd, Richmond VA 23229	804-288-3699	R	2*	<.1
44	Shop For Bags Inc—*Katie Messersmith*	PO Box 59645, Dallas TX 75229	214-637-5300	R	2*	<.1
45	Zaxwear—*Andrea Zax*	37 Poole Rd, Belchertown MA 01007	617-771-2348	R	1*	<.1
46	Dan Howard Industries Inc—*Edward Krell*	456 N 5th St, Philadelphia PA 19123	215-873-2000	S	N/A	.1
	Destination Maternity Corp					

TOTALS: SIC 5621 Women's Clothing Stores
Companies: 46

					33,043	240.5

5632 Women's Accessory & Specialty Stores

Rank	Company Name—*Executive Officer*	Address, City, State, Zip	Phone	Type	Fin	Empls
1	Victoria's Secret Stores LLC—*Lori Greeley*	4 Limited Pky E, Reynoldsburg OH 43068	614-577-7000	S	3,222	29.0
2	Claire's Stores Inc—*Eugene S Kahn*	3 SW 129th Ave, Pembroke Pines FL 33027	954-433-3900	S	1,413*	18.4
3	Hot Topic Inc—*Lisa Harper*	18305 San Jose Ave, City of Industry CA 91748	626-839-4681	P	708	8.9
4	rue21 inc—*Robert N Fisch*	800 Commonwealth Dr St, Warrendale PA 15086	724-776-9780	P	635	7.2
5	Juicy Couture Inc—*LeAnn Nealz*	12723 Wentworth St, Arleta CA 91331	818-767-0849	S	500*	<.1
6	Claire's Boutiques Inc—*Nancy Rich*	2400 W Central Rd, Hoffman Estates IL 60192	847-765-1100	S	440	6.5
	Claire's Stores Inc					
7	Frederick's of Hollywood Inc—*Linda LoRe*	6608 Hollywood Blvd, Los Angeles CA 90028	602-760-2111	R	176	.1
8	A and E Stores Inc—*Alan A Ades*	1000 Huyler St, Teterboro NJ 07608	201-393-0600	R	125*	1.5
9	Louis Vuitton NA Inc—*Thomas O'Neal*	19 E 57th St, New York NY 10022	917-281-2000	S	100*	.4
10	Bakers Jewelry and Gifts—*Theodore Baker*	PO Box 11065, Norfolk VA 23517	757-625-2529	R	38*	<.1
11	Saks Jandel—*Peter Marx*	5510 Wisconsin Ave, Chevy Chase MD 20815	301-652-2250	R	15*	.1
12	MidCenturyJewelrycom—*Audrey Chapline*	PO Box 515, Milford OH 45150	513-317-7693	R	5*	<.1
13	Fashionphile—*Sarah Davis*	9551 Wilshire Blvd, Beverly Hills CA 90212	310-279-1136	R	4	<.1

TOTALS: SIC 5632 Women's Accessory & Specialty Stores
Companies: 13

					7,381	72.2

5641 Children's & Infants' Wear Stores

Rank	Company Name—*Executive Officer*	Address, City, State, Zip	Phone	Type	Fin	Empls
1	Babies "R" Us	1 Geoffrey Way, Wayne NJ 07470	973-617-3500	D	3,874*	5.0
2	Tween Brands Inc	8323 Walton Pkwy, New Albany OH 43054	614-775-3500	S	995	12.2
3	OshKosh B'Gosh Retail Inc	112 Otter Ave, Oshkosh WI 54901	920-231-8800	S	250*	2.1
4	Hartstrings LLC—*Peggy Earle*	270 E Conestoga Rd, Wayne PA 19087	610-687-6900	R	203*	.4
5	Children's Place LLC (Roanoke Virginia)—*Charles Crovitz*	4802 Valley View Blvd, Roanoke VA 24012	540-362-4888	S	9*	<.1
6	GapKids—*Glen Murphy*	2 Folsom St, San Francisco CA 94105	650-952-4400	D	8*	.1
7	See Kai Run—*Cause Haun*	5809 238th St SE Ste7, Woodinville WA 98072		R	5	<.1
8	Cotton Tails Inc—*Miki Brugge*	389 Perkins Rd Ext, Memphis TN 38117	901-685-8417	R	1*	<.1

TOTALS: SIC 5641 Children's & Infants' Wear Stores
Companies: 8

					5,345	19.8

5651 Family Clothing Stores

Rank	Company Name—*Executive Officer*	Address, City, State, Zip	Phone	Type	Fin	Empls
1	TJX Companies Inc—*Carol Meyrowitz*	770 Cochituate Rd, Framingham MA 01701	508-390-1000	P	21,942	166.0
2	Gap Inc—*Glenn K Murphy*	2 Folsom St, San Francisco CA 94105		P	14,664	134.0
3	Limited Brands Inc—*Leslie H Wexner*	PO Box 16000, Columbus OH 43216	614-415-7000	P	9,613	96.5
4	Ross Stores Inc—*Michael Balmuth*	4440 Rosewood Dr, Pleasanton CA 94588	925-965-4400	P	7,866	49.5
5	Burlington Coat Factory Warehouse Corp—*Thomas A Kingsbury*	1830 Rte 130, Burlington NJ 08016	609-387-7800	S	3,701	31.4

Note: An asterisk (*) indicates an estimated financial figure. The company type code used is as follows: R = Private, P = Public, S = Private Subsidiary, B = Public Subsidiary, D = Division, J = Joint Venture, I = Investment Fund.

RANKINGS BY SALES WITHIN 4-DIGIT SIC

	Company Name—Executive Officer	Address, City, State, Zip	Phone	Type	Fin	Empls
6	Abercrombie and Fitch Co—Michael S Jeffries	6301 Fitch Path, New Albany OH 43054	614-283-6500	P	3,469	85.0
7	American Eagle Outfitters Inc—Christopher Fiore	77 Hot Metal St, Pittsburgh PA 15203	412-432-3300	P	2,968	39.9
8	Saks Holdings Inc	12 E 49th St, New York NY 10017	212-753-4000	S	2,418	15.6
9	Children's Place Retail Stores Inc—Jane Elfers	500 Plaza Dr, Secaucus NJ 07094	201-558-2400	P	1,674	20.8
10	Stage Stores Inc—Andrew Hall	10201 Main St, Houston TX 77025	713-667-5601	P	1,471	13.5
11	Finish Line Inc—Glenn S Lyon	3308 N Mitthoeffer Rd, Indianapolis IN 46235	317-899-1022	P	1,229	11.5
12	Stein Mart Inc—David H Stovall Jr	1200 Riverplace Blvd, Jacksonville FL 32207	904-346-1500	P	1,182	11.5
13	Specialty Retailers Inc—James Scarborough Stage Stores Inc	10201 Main St, Houston TX 77025	713-667-5601	S	1,000*	10.0
14	Buckle Inc—Dennis H Nelson	PO Box 1480, Kearney NE 68848		P	950	7.6
15	Hermes of Paris Inc—Robert Chavez	55 E 59th St, New York NY 10022	212-759-7585	S	484*	.2
16	Syms Corp—Marcy Syms	1 Syms Way, Secaucus NJ 07094	201-902-9600	P	445	2.5
17	Casual Male Retail Group Inc—David A Levin	555 Turnpike St, Canton MA 02021	781-828-9300	P	394	2.5
18	Beall's Department Stores Inc—Stephen Knopik	PO Box 25207, Bradenton FL 34206	941-747-2355	R	150*	3.0
19	J and M Sales Inc—Michael Fallas	15001 S Figueroa St, Gardena CA 90248	310-324-9962	R	146*	2.5
20	Barney's New York—Mark Lee	1201 Valley Brook Ave, Lyndhurst NJ 07071	212-222-7639	S	146*	1.4
21	Urban Outfitters Wholesale Inc—Richard A Hayne	5000 S Broad St, Philadelphia PA 19112		S	134	N/A
22	Dawahares Inc—Richard Harding	1801 Alexandria Dr Ste, Lexington KY 40504	859-278-0422	R	120*	.5
23	Glik Stores—Jeffrey W Glik	3248 Nameoki Rd, Granite City IL 62040	618-876-6717	R	34*	.5
24	Foursome Inc—Gordon Engel	3570 Vicksburg Lane N, Plymouth MN 55447	952-473-4667	R	29*	.1
25	CNRG Apparel LLC—David A Levin Casual Male Retail Group Inc	555 Turnpike St, Canton MA 02021	781-828-9300	S	23	.1
26	Crescent Retail JV—Crawford Brock	500 Crescent Ct Ste 10, Dallas TX 75201	214-871-3600	S	20*	.1
27	Bob's Stores Inc—David Farrell TJX Companies Inc	160 Corporate Ct, Meriden CT 06450	203-235-5775	S	18*	.2
28	Banana Republic—Jack Calhoun Gap Inc	5900 N Meadows Dr, Grove City OH 43123		S	11	N/A
29	Saba's Western Stores—Roger Saba Sr	3270 N Colorado St Ste, Chandler AZ 85225	480-833-0753	R	9*	.1
30	Puritan Clothing Company of Cape Cod Inc—Richard Penn	PO Box 730, Hyannis MA 02601	508-775-2400	R	9*	.1
31	Luskey's/Ryons Inc—Jerry Doty	3402 Catclaw Dr, Abilene TX 79606	325-793-9953	R	6*	<.1

TOTALS: SIC 5651 Family Clothing Stores
Companies: 31 — 76,324 — 706.6

5661 Shoe Stores

1	Foot Locker Inc—Ken C Hicks	112 W 34th St, New York NY 10120	212-720-3700	P	5,049	38.0
2	Collective Brands Inc—Michael J Massey	3231 SE 6th Ave, Topeka KS 66607	785-233-5171	P	3,376	29.0
3	DSW Inc—Michael R MacDonald	810 DSW Dr, Columbus OH 43219	614-237-7100	P	1,822	10.5
4	Genesco Inc—Robert J Dennis	PO Box 731, Nashville TN 37202	615-367-7000	P	1,790	15.2
5	Famous Footwear—Richard M Ausick	7010 Mineral Point Rd, Madison WI 53717	608-829-3668	D	1,500	10.0
6	Eurostar Inc—Eric Alon	13425 S Figueroa St, Los Angeles CA 90061	310-715-9300	R	934*	.6
7	Shoe Carnival Inc—Timothy T Baker	7500 E Columbia St, Evansville IN 47715	812-867-6471	P	739	4.3
8	Athlete's Foot Group Inc—Robert J Corliss	1346 Oakbrook Dr Ste 1, Norcross GA 30093	770-514-4500	R	248	3.5
9	Bakers Footwear Group Inc—Peter A Edison	2815 Scott Ave, St Louis MO 63103	314-621-0699	P	186	2.5
10	Cavender's Boot City—James Cavender	7820 S Broadway Ave, Tyler TX 75702	903-509-9509	R	168*	.8
11	Steve Madden Retail Inc	211-49 26th Ave, Bayside NY 11360	718-224-4880	S	79	N/A
12	Birkenstock USA LP	6 Hamilton Landing Ste, Novato CA 94949	415-884-3200	S	75	.1
13	Tradehome Shoe Stores Inc—Patrick Teal	8300 97th St S, Cottage Grove MN 55016	651-459-8600	R	40*	.4
14	Saxon Shoes Inc—Gary Weiner	11800 W Broad St Ste 2, Richmond VA 23233	804-285-3473	R	23*	.1
15	White's Boots Inc—Gary March	4002 E Ferry Ave, Spokane WA 99202	509-535-2422	R	10*	.1
16	Shoe Metro—David Duong	8960 Carroll Way Ste 1, San Diego CA 92121		R	9*	<.1
17	Cowtown Boot Co—Paul Calcattera	PO Box 26428, El Paso TX 79926	915-593-2565	R	7*	.1
18	Schnee's Inc—Jon Edward	PO Box 6069, Bozeman MT 59771	406-587-0981	R	6*	.1
19	RunTex Inc—Paul Carrozza	422 W Riverside Dr, Austin TX 78704	512-472-3254	R	4*	<.1
20	Thomas Hardware Co—Todd Jones	18680 Mack Ave, Grosse Pointe MI 48236	313-886-6094	R	1*	<.1
21	Footstar Inc—Jonathan M Couchman	933 MacArthur Blvd, Mahwah NJ 07430	201-934-2000	P	<1	<.1

TOTALS: SIC 5661 Shoe Stores
Companies: 21 — 16,066 — 115.3

5699 Miscellaneous Apparel & Accessory Stores

1	Aeropostale Inc—Karin Hirtler Garvey	112 W 34th St 22nd Fl, New York NY 10120	646-485-5410	P	2,400	4.2
2	Gander Mountain Co—David Pratt	180 E 5th St Ste1300, Saint Paul MN 55101	651-325-4300	R	1,065	5.6
3	Jos A Bank Clothiers Inc—R Neal Black	PO Box 1000, Hampstead MD 21074	410-239-2700	P	858	5.0
4	Citi Trends Inc—R David Alexander	104 Coleman Blvd, Savannah GA 31408	912-443-4903	P	623	5.0
5	Zumiez Inc—Richard M Brooks	6300 Merrill Creek Pky, Everett WA 98203	425-551-1500	P	479	4.8
6	Fairchild Corp—Phillip S Sassower	1750 Tysons Blvd Ste 5, McLean VA 22102	703-478-5800	P	355	.8
7	Walking Company Holdings Inc—Andrew D Feshbach	121 Gray Ave, Santa Barbara CA 93101	805-963-8727	P	233	1.1
8	Sheplers Inc—Mark Syrstad	6501 W Kellogg, Wichita KS 67209	316-946-3600	S	183*	1.2
9	Crazy Shirts Inc—Mark Hollander	99-969 Iwaena St, Aiea HI 96701	808-486-1212	R	169*	.5
10	511 Inc	4300 Spyres Way, Modesto CA 95356	209-527-4511	R	82*	.1
11	Swim 'N Sport—Mark Sidel	2396 NW 96th Ave, Miami FL 33172	305-593-5071	R	66*	.2
12	Smartphone Experts Inc—Marcus Adolfsson	3151 E Thomas St, Inverness FL 34453	352-400-4400	R	20*	<.1
13	Working Person's Store—Eric Deniger	1608 Commerce Dr, South Bend IN 46628		R	14*	<.1
14	Oak Hall Industries LP—Martha Anderson	PO Box 1078, Salem VA 24153	540-387-0000	R	14*	.4
15	Costume Craze LLC—Kathryn Maloney	350 W Center St, Pleasant Grove UT 84062	801-796-1053	R	11*	<.1
16	Sportek International Inc—Benhoor Hanas	820 Gladys Ave, Los Angeles CA 90021	231-239-6700	R	6*	<.1
17	Defenshield Inc—Collins White	14 Corporate Cir Ste 8, East Syracuse NY 13057	315-448-0252	R	5*	<.1
18	Kimro Manufacturing Inc—Roy Dibiney	PO Box 190, Trezevant TN 38258	731-669-3933	R	3*	.1
19	Some's Uniforms Inc—Jerome Some	PO Box 68, Hackensack NJ 07602	201-843-1199	R	2*	<.1
20	Allisa's Bridal	888 E 59th St, Brooklyn NY 11234	718-531-0608	R	1*	<.1
21	Embroidery Boulevard Inc—Duane Brower	82 S Federal Inc, Denver CO 80219	303-742-0639	R	<1	<.1
22	Lost Arrow Corp—Casey Sheahan	PO Box 150, Ventura CA 93002	805-643-8616	R	N/A	1.1

TOTALS: SIC 5699 Miscellaneous Apparel & Accessory Stores
Companies: 22 — 6,589 — 30.2

5712 Furniture Stores

1	Aaron's Inc—Ron Allen	309 E Paces Ferry Rd N, Atlanta GA 30305	404-231-0011	P	2,024	11.2
2	Farmers Home Furniture—S Fountain	PO Box 1140, Dublin GA 31040	478-272-4000	R	1,961*	1.4
3	Rooms To Go Inc—Jeffrey Seaman	11540 Hwy 92 E, Seffner FL 33584	813-623-5400	R	1,596*	6.5
4	Pier 1 Imports Inc—Alex W Smith	100 Pier 1 Pl, Fort Worth TX 76102	817-252-8000	P	1,397	17.0
5	Restoration Hardware Inc—Gary Friedman	15 Koch Rd Ste J, Corte Madera CA 94925	415-924-1005	P	722	1.9

Rank	Company Name—*Executive Officer*	Address, City, State, Zip	Phone	Type	Fin	Empls
6	Haverty Furniture Companies Inc—*Steven G Burdette*	780 Johnson Ferry Rd N, Atlanta GA 30342	404-443-2900	P	620	3.1
7	Levin Furniture—*Robert Levin*	609 W Main St, Mount Pleasant PA 15666	724-872-2050	R	557*	.4
8	Lack Valley Stores Ltd—*Lee Aaronson*	1300 San Patricia Dr, Pharr TX 78577	956-702-3361	R	543*	.7
9	Steinhafels Inc—*Gary Steinhafel*	W231N1013 Hwy F, Waukesha WI 53186		R	481*	.6
10	Art Van Furniture Inc—*Art Van Elslander*	6500 E 14 Mile Rd, Warren MI 48092	586-939-0800	R	455*	3.0
11	Nebraska Furniture Mart Inc—*Irvin Blumkin*	PO Box 2335, Omaha NE 68103	402-397-6100	S	405*	2.7
12	RC Willey Home Furnishings—*Scott L Hymas*	2301 S 300 W, Salt Lake City UT 84115	801-461-3900	S	347*	1.8
13	Gallery Furniture Inc—*Jim McIngvale*	6006 N Fwy, Houston TX 77076	713-694-5570	R	342*	.4
14	IKEA North America LLC—*Anders Dahlvig*	420 Alan Wood Rd, Conshohocken PA 19428	610-834-0180	S	305*	2.6
15	Dearden's Inc—*Raquel Bensimon*	700 S Main St, Los Angeles CA 90014	213-362-9600	R	294*	.5
16	Grand Furniture Discount Stores Corp—*John Heinz*	5129 Va Beach Blvd, Virginia Beach VA 23462	757-497-4891	R	276*	.4
17	Raymour and Flanigan Furniture Co—*Neil Goldberg*	7230 Morgan Rd, Liverpool NY 13090	315-652-3711	R	258*	3.8
18	Jordan's Furniture Inc—*Barry Tattelman*	450 Revolutionary Dr, East Taunton MA 02718	508-828-4000	S	214*	1.4
19	Mattress Giant Corp—*Michael L Glazer*	14665 Midway Rd Ste 10, Addison TX 75001	972-392-2202	R	196*	.8
20	Design Within Reach Inc—*John Edelman*	225 Bush St 20th Fl, San Francisco CA 94104	415-676-6500	P	179	.4
21	Office Resources Inc—*Kevin Barbary*	374 Congress St, Boston MA 02210	617-423-9100	R	175*	.2
22	Interior Investments LLC—*Steve Rice*	625 Heathrow Dr, Lincolnshire IL 60069	847-325-1000	R	150*	.1
23	Elmhult LP—*Laurie Helm*	601 Sw 41st St, Renton WA 98057	425-656-2980	R	143*	.6
24	Rotman's—*Steve Rotman*	725 Southbridge St, Worcester MA 01610	508-755-5276	R	135*	.2
25	Lacks Stores Inc—*M Lack*	200 S Ben Jordan St, Victoria TX 77901	361-578-3571	R	117	1.0
26	Western Contract Furnishers of Sacramento—*Don Turner*	11455 Folsom Blvd, Rancho Cordova CA 95742	916-638-3338	R	112*	.2
27	Porter Of Racine—*HR Waters*	301 6th St, Racine WI 53403	262-633-6363	R	110*	.1
28	BKM Enterprises Inc—*Donald Griesdorn*	300 E River Dr, East Hartford CT 06108	860-528-9981	R	108*	.4
29	Goodman's Inc (Phoenix Arizona)—*Murray Goodman*	1400 E Indian School R, Phoenix AZ 85014	602-263-1110	R	105*	.1
30	Goldberg's Furniture—*Michael Ergort*	506 S Main St, N Syracuse NY 13212		R	103*	.1
31	Miskelly Furniture—*Oscar Miskelly Jr*	101 Airport Rd, Jackson MS 39208	601-939-6288	R	89*	.4
32	Grand Home Furnishings—*George B Cartledge Jr*	4235 Electric Rd SW, Roanoke VA 24018	540-776-7000	R	87*	.7
33	Schewel Furniture Company Inc—*Marc A Schewel*	PO Box 6120, Lynchburg VA 24505	434-845-2326	R	86*	.7
34	Big Sandy Furniture Inc (South Point Ohio)—*John C Stewart Jr*	45 County Rd 407, South Point OH 45680	740-894-4242	R	80*	.5
35	Granite Furniture Company Inc—*Jim Taggart*	1475 W 9000 S, West Jordan UT 84088	801-566-4444	R	77*	.4
36	Jennifer Convertibles Inc—*Harley J Greenfield*	417 Crossways Park Dr, Woodbury NY 11797	516-496-1900	P	76	.4
37	El Dorado Furniture Co—*Manuel Capo*	4200 NW 167th St, Miami FL 33054	305-624-2400	R	70*	.3
38	Jerome's Furniture Warehouse—*Jim Navarra*	16960 Mesamint St, San Diego CA 92127		R	64*	.4
39	Sam Levitz Furniture Co—*Sam R Levitz*	3430 E 36th St, Tucson AZ 85713	520-624-7443	R	62*	.5
40	Marlo Furniture Company Inc—*Neal Glickfield*	725 Rockville Pke, Rockville MD 20852	301-738-9000	R	59*	.3
41	Welcome Home Inc—*Thomas H Quinn*	309-D Raleigh St, Wilmington NC 28412	910-791-4312	S	57	.3
42	Complete Office—*Rick Israel*	11521 E Marginal Way S, Seattle WA 98168	206-628-0059	R	51*	.2
43	Kimbrell's Furniture Distributors Inc—*Henry L Johnson*	PO Box 11117, Charlotte NC 28220	704-523-7693	R	50*	.6
44	Room and Board Inc—*John Gabbert*	4600 Olson Memorial Hw, Minneapolis MN 55422	763-588-7525	R	50*	.4
45	Arenson Office Furnishings Inc—*Carl Milianta*	1115 Broadway Fl 6, New York NY 10010	212-633-2400	R	48*	.2
46	RH Kuhn Co—*Michael R Kuhn*	2250 Roswell Dr, Pittsburgh PA 15205	412-444-2300	R	46*	.4
47	Darvin Furniture and Appliances Inc—*Steven Darvin*	15400 S La Grange Rd, Orland Park IL 60462	708-460-4100	R	45*	.3
48	DeKalb Office Environments—*John Rasper*	1320 Ridgeland Pky, Alpharetta GA 30004	770-360-0200	R	41*	.1
49	Cabot House Inc—*Robert Bendeston*	220 Worcester Rd, Framingham MA 01702	508-872-5900	R	40*	.2
50	Baers Furniture Company Inc—*Alan Baer*	1025 S Federal Hwy, Dania Beach FL 33004	954-927-0237	R	39*	.3
51	Scott Rice of Kansas City Inc—*Ed Wills*	PO Box 419380, Kansas City MO 64141	913-888-7600	R	37*	.1
52	Royals Inc—*GL Royal Jr*	225 W Canal St N, Belle Glade FL 33430	561-996-7646	R	35	.6
53	Office Pavilion Inc (Houston Texas)—*Steve Marnoy*	10030 Bent Oak Dr, Houston TX 77040	713-803-0000	S	34*	.1
54	Meadows Office Furniture Co—*Rosalie Stackman-Edson*	71 W 23rd St, New York NY 10010	212-741-0333	R	33*	<.1
55	Rothman Furniture Stores Inc—*Dale Steinbeck*	2101 E Terra Ln, O Fallon MO 63366	636-978-3500	R	32	.2
56	Olum's of Binghamton Inc—*Keith Solomon*	3701 Vestal Pky E, Vestal NY 13850	607-729-5775	R	32*	.2
57	Carol House Furniture Inc—*Brook Dubman*	2332 Millpark Dr, Maryland Heights MO 63043	314-427-4200	R	30*	.1
58	CS Wo and Sons Ltd—*Bob Wo*	702 S Beretania St, Honolulu HI 96813	808-543-5388	R	26*	.3
59	LFD Home Furnishings—*Greg Thrash*	1602 S 23rd St, McAllen TX 78503	956-682-1441	R	26*	.3
60	Hurwitz-Mintz Furniture Co—*Mitchell Mintz*	1751 Airline Dr, Metairie LA 70001	504-568-9555	R	26*	.2
61	Weir's Furniture Village—*Dan Weir*	PO Box 600125, Dallas TX 75360	214-528-0321	R	26*	.1
62	JC White Office Furniture and Interiors—*Irwin Kirsner*	3501 Commerce Pky, Miramar FL 33025	954-499-6677	R	25*	.1
63	Carter's Furniture Co—*Allen E Carter Jr*	410 N Vine StSte 1, Urbana IL 61802	217-367-4066	R	23*	<.1
64	Gorman's Inc—*Bernard Moray*	29145 Telegraph Rd, Southfield MI 48034	248-353-9880	R	21*	.1
65	Royal Furniture Co—*Richard Faber*	PO Box 3784, Memphis TN 38173	901-527-6407	R	20*	.1
66	Commercial Office Furniture Co—*Alan Einstein*	2200 N American St, Philadelphia PA 19133	215-291-4648	R	19*	.1
67	Ivan Allen Workspace LLC—*Jackie Parker*	1000 Marietta St NW St, Atlanta GA 30318	404-760-8700	R	17*	<.1
68	Stevens Office Interiors—*Thomas Maugeri*	1449 Erie Blvd E, Syracuse NY 13210	315-479-5595	R	17*	<.1
69	SmithCFI—*Tom McDougal*	620 NE 19th Ave, Portland OR 97232	503-226-4151	R	17*	<.1
70	Dunk and Bright Furniture Company Inc—*Jim Bright*	2648 S Salina St, Syracuse NY 13205	315-475-2000	R	16*	.1
71	Smulekoff Furniture Company Inc—*Abbott Lipsky*	PO Box 74090, Cedar Rapids IA 52406	319-362-2181	R	16*	.1
72	Stoess Manor—*Clayton Stoess*	6541 W Hwy 22, Crestwood KY 40014	502-241-8494	R	16*	<.1
73	Hinson Galleries Inc—*Robert Hinson Jr*	1208 13th Ave, Columbus GA 31901	706-327-3671	R	16*	<.1
74	Interior Office Solutions Inc—*Jesse Bagley*	17800 Mitchell N, Irvine CA 92614	949-724-9444	R	16*	<.1
75	Wholesale Interiors Inc—*Chuck Tanner*	794 Golf Ln, Bensenville IL 60106	630-238-8877	R	14*	<.1
76	Seattle Office Furniture LLC—*Cheryl Thompson*	3035 1st Ave, Seattle WA 98121	206-728-5710	R	14*	<.1
77	Havertys Credit Services Inc—*Clarence H Smith* Haverty Furniture Companies Inc	1501 Riverside Dr, Chattanooga TN 37406	423-624-1969	S	13*	.1
78	Everything2gocom LLC—*David Widsma*	250 E Wisconsin Ave, Milwaukee WI 53202	414-765-1100	R	13*	<.1
79	FurnitureFIND Corp	177 Huntington Ave Ste, Boston MA 02115	617-502-7813	R	12*	.1
80	OneWayFurniturecom—*Mitch Lieberman*	535 Broadhollow Rd Ste, Melville NY 11747		R	12*	<.1
81	Kittle's Home Furnishings—*Jim Kittle*	8600 Allisonville Rd, Indianapolis IN 46250	317-849-5300	R	11*	.1
82	Interior Concepts Inc—*Arlene Critzos*	2560 Riva Rd, Annapolis MD 21401	410-224-7366	R	11*	.1
83	Greenbaum Interiors LLC	101 Washington St, Paterson NJ 07505	973-279-3000	R	10*	.1
84	Dakota Kitchen and Bath Inc—*Don Miller*	4101 N Hainje Ave, Sioux Falls SD 57104	605-334-9727	R	10*	.1
85	Levitz Furniture (New York New York)—*Tom Baumlin*	300 Crossways Park Dr, Woodbury NY 11797	516-496-9560	S	9*	.1
86	Gibson McDonald Furniture Stores Inc—*H Clay Gibson*	PO Box 1848, Waycross GA 31502	912-490-1001	R	8*	.1
87	Grindstaff's Interior Inc—*Boyce F Grindstaff*	1007 W Main St, Forest City NC 28043	828-245-4263	R	8*	<.1
88	Solid Comfort Inc—*Jason Larkin*	3931 37th Ave S, Fargo ND 58104	701-282-4900	R	8*	.1
89	Moser Corp—*Harley Moser*	PO Box 1984, Rogers AR 72757	479-636-3481	R	8*	.1
90	A Diamond Production Inc—*Suzanne Diamond*	2150 Cesar Chavez, San Francisco CA 94124	415-920-6800	R	8*	<.1
91	Pompanoosuc Mills Corp—*Dwight Sargent*	PO Box 238, East Thetford VT 05043	802-785-4851	R	7*	.2
92	Garrison's Custom Cabinets Inc—*Kathy Garrison*	2045 First Commercial, Southaven MS 38671	662-393-7010	R	6*	<.1
93	Miller's Carpet One—*Andrew L Miller*	500 W Basin Rd, New Castle DE 19720	302-322-5452	R	6*	<.1
94	Star Furniture Co—*Dwayne Johnson*	16666 Barker Springs R, Houston TX 77084		S	6*	<.1

Note: An asterisk (*) indicates an estimated financial figure. The company type code used is as follows: R = Private, P = Public, S = Private Subsidiary, B = Public Subsidiary, D = Division, J = Joint Venture, I = Investment Fund.

COMPANY RANKINGS BY SALES WITHIN 4-DIGIT SIC

Rank	Company Name—Executive Officer	Address, City, State, Zip	Phone	Type	Fin	Empls
95	Fleischmann Office Interiors Inc—Christy Jones	1215 4th Ave Ste1125, Seattle WA 98161	206-623-4300	D	6*	<.1
96	Perers Enterprises Inc—Robert Perers	PO Box 2048, Melbourne FL 32902	321-723-5003	R	6*	<.1
97	R/W Bowman Corp—Wanda Bowman	3299 Del Ray Blvd, Las Cruces NM 88012	575-523-3933	R	5*	<.1
98	Recycled Systems Furniture Inc—Ron Morris	401 E Wilson Bridge Rd, Worthington OH 43085	614-880-9110	R	5*	<.1
99	Contemporary Galleries of Kentucky Inc—Charles Mason	220 N Hurstbourne Ln, Louisville KY 40222	502-426-2406	R	5*	<.1
100	Autrey Furniture Manufacturing Inc—John Edwards	PO Box 1821, Moultrie GA 31776	229-891-2319	R	4*	<.1
101	Hopkins Furniture Inc—David Hopkins	1509 NW 28th St, Fort Worth TX 76164	817-624-8444	R	4*	<.1
102	Heritage Enterprise Inc—Sharon Perkins	2850 Broad St, Sumter SC 29150	803-469-7283	R	4*	<.1
103	Salem Village Craftsmen Inc—Richard Dabrowski	14 S Pleasant St, Ashburnham MA 01430	978-827-9900	R	4*	<.1
104	Charles Ritter Company Inc—Gordon Pepper	PO Box 215, Mansfield OH 44901	419-522-1911	R	4*	<.1
105	Lindsey Office Furnishings Inc—Robert Lindsey	2223 1st Ave N, Birmingham AL 35203	205-251-9088	R	3*	<.1
106	Kammer Furniture Inc—Max Kammer	400 Bland St, Bluefield WV 24701	304-327-6917	R	3*	<.1
107	Jmj Corporation Warehouse—John Massad	6031 Nine Mile Rd, Richmond VA 23223	804-328-6220	R	2*	<.1
108	Ducky's Office Furniture Inc—Russ Windebaum	970 Denny Way, Seattle WA 98109	206-623-7777	R	2*	<.1
109	EOI Inc—Randy Reicheneach	8377 Green Meadow Dr N, Lewis Center OH 43035	740-201-3300	R	2*	<.1
110	Sheid's Corp—Carl Sheid	PO Box 2668, Mountain Home AR 72654	870-425-5165	R	2*	<.1
111	Ducky's Office Furniture	1910 132nd Ave NE, Bellevue WA 98005	425-747-5577	R	2*	<.1
112	Maurice Vaughan Inc—F Vaughan	610 E Stuart Dr, Galax VA 24333	276-236-9781	R	2*	<.1
113	Herrick and Ashcraft Interiors and Furniture Co—Phyllis Herrick-Ashcraf	5641 Sw Foxcrost S 102, Topeka KS 66614	785-271-8910	R	2*	<.1
114	Acacia Home and Garden Inc—Alex Te	PO Box 426, Conover NC 28613	828-465-1700	R	1*	<.1

TOTALS: SIC 5712 Furniture Stores
Companies: 114 — — — — 16,482 75.3

5713 Floor Covering Stores

1	Flooring America—Evan Hackel	284 Rt 101, Bedford NH 03110	603-325-4139	S	763	3.3
2	ABC Carpet Company Inc	888 Broadway, New York NY 10003	212-473-3000	R	73*	.5
3	Buddy's Carpet Inc—Ben Goodyear	1480 E Second St, Franklin OH 45005	937-743-7700	R	61*	.2
4	Hagopian World of Rugs—Edmond Hagopian Hagopian and Sons Inc	850 S Old Woodward, Birmingham MI 48009	248-646-7847	D	59*	.2
5	Carpeteria Inc—Mel Markarian	1933 Davis St, San Leandro CA 94577		R	57*	.2
6	Grossman's Kensington Home Furnishings Center—Michael Grossman	200 Tilton Rd, Northfield NJ 08225	609-241-0807	R	57*	.2
7	Hagopian and Sons Inc—Edmond Hagopian	14000 W 8 Mile Rd, Oak Park MI 48237	248-546-7847	R	51*	.2
8	Donald E McNabb Co—Douglas McNabb	PO Box 448, Milford MI 48381	248-437-8146	R	33*	.1
9	Carpet King Inc—William Bailey	1815 W River Rd N, Minneapolis MN 55411	612-588-9999	R	25*	.1
10	Elite Flooring and Design Inc—Sean McCarthy	3480 Green Pointe Pky, Norcross GA 30092	770-409-8228	R	22*	.1
11	Miller's Interiors Inc—William W Miller	PO Box 1116, Lynnwood WA 98046	425-329-7783	R	14*	.1
12	Hessler's Inc—Carl Hessler	1788 Fowler St, Fort Myers FL 33901	239-334-1537	R	9*	.1
13	Cloud Carpet and Draperies Inc—Ed Sotelo	7351 W Lake Mead Blvd, Las Vegas NV 89103	702-798-0798	R	8*	.1
14	MMM Carpets Unlimited Inc—Steve Boardman	3100 Molinero St, Santa Clara CA 95054	408-988-4661	R	6*	<.1
15	Hopkins Carpet Co—Nick Hopkins	2323 Hwy 67, Festus MO 63028	636-937-2400	R	6*	<.1
16	All Teriors Floor Covering Inc—Dexter Rose	1104 W Geneva Dr, Tempe AZ 85282	480-921-8419	R	5*	<.1
17	O'Krent Floor Covering Co—Sam O'Krent	2075 N Loop 1604 E, San Antonio TX 78232	210-227-7387	R	4*	<.1
18	Greenwell Interiors—Carmen Choi	14950 N 83rd Pl Sto 2, Scottsdale AZ 05260	480-483-1241	H	2*	<.1
19	Jbp International Inc—Bill Boukalis	3100 22nd Ave N, Saint Petersburg FL 33713	727-322-5757	R	2*	<.1
20	CHC Inc—William G Franey	8 W Main St, Plano IL 60545	630-552-3400	R	2*	<.1
21	Hagopian Rug Outlet Inc—Edmond Hagopian Hagopian and Sons Inc	14000 W 8 Mile Rd, Oak Park MI 48237	248-546-7847	D	1*	<.1
22	South Cypress Floors—Drew Goneke	2818 Government Blvd, Mobile AL 36606		R	1*	<.1

TOTALS: SIC 5713 Floor Covering Stores
Companies: 22 — — — — 1,261 5.3

5714 Drapery & Upholstery Stores

1	Allied Realty Co—Lake Polan III	PO Box 1700, Huntington WV 25717	304-525-9125	R	31*	.1
2	No Brainer Inc—Jay Steinfeld	4660 Beechnut 3 Braine, Houston TX 77096	713-666-9992	R	20*	<.1
3	Sunshine Drapery Company Inc—Bruce Bernstein	11800 Adie Rd, Maryland Heights MO 63043	314-569-2980	R	14*	.1
4	Calico Corners—Bert Kerstetter	203 Gale Ln Walnut Bus, Kennett Square PA 19348	610-444-9700	D	11*	.1
5	Pomona Textile Inc—Abraham Reichbach	8105 Frankford Ave, Philadelphia PA 19136	215-335-9494	R	2*	<.1
6	Nitsa's Custom Draperies Inc—Nitsa Avouris	28983 Little Mack Ave, Saint Clair Shores MI 48081	586-772-1196	R	1*	<.1
7	Design 24 Inc—Jim Konen	23 W Lawrence, Pontiac MI 48342	248-335-6677	R	1	<.1

TOTALS: SIC 5714 Drapery & Upholstery Stores
Companies: 7 — — — — 81 .4

5719 Miscellaneous Home Furnishings Stores

1	Bed Bath and Beyond Inc—Steven H Temares	650 Liberty Ave, Union NJ 07083	908-688-0888	P	8,759	45.0
2	Williams-Sonoma Inc—Laura J Alber	3250 Van Ness Ave, San Francisco CA 94109	415-421-7900	P	3,504	28.0
3	Pottery Barn Inc—Laura Alber Williams-Sonoma Inc	3250 Van Ness Ave, San Francisco CA 94109	415-421-7900	S	2,531*	5.3
4	Euromarket Designs Inc—Barbara Turf	1250 Techny Rd, Northbrook IL 60062	847-272-2888	S	2,215*	7.0
5	Cost Plus World Market Inc—Barry J Feld	200 4th St, Oakland CA 94607	510-893-7300	P	917	5.9
6	Container Store Inc—Kip Tindell	500 Freeport Pkwy, Coppell TX 75019	972-538-6000	R	555*	4.0
7	Lamps Plus Inc—Dennis Swanson	20250 Plummer St, Chatsworth CA 91311	818-886-5267	R	453*	1.0
8	Anna's Linen Co	3550 Hyland Ave, Costa Mesa CA 92626		R	391*	2.8
9	California Acrylic Industries Inc—Casie Lloyd	1462 E 9th St, Pomona CA 91766	909-623-8781	R	342*	1.0
10	Cost Plus Management Services Inc Cost Plus World Market Inc	200 4th St, Oakland CA 94607	510-893-7300	S	315	2.8
11	Janovic Plaza Inc—Paul Renn	3025 Thomson Ave, Long Island City NY 11101	718-392-3999	R	176*	.3
12	Sur La Table Inc—Jack Schwefel	PO Box 34626, Seattle WA 98124	206-613-6000	R	174*	3.0
13	Del Mar Designs Inc—Colby Harris	301 Division Ave Unit, Ormond Beach FL 32174	386-767-1997	R	153*	<.1
14	Appliance Recycling Centers of America Inc—Edward R Cameron	7400 Excelsior Blvd, Minneapolis MN 55426	952-930-9000	P	108	.4
15	Marsh Pottery LLC—Tim Marsh	3775 Ave of the Caroli, Fort Mill SC 29708	803-936-1447	R	105*	.3
16	Dallas Market Center Company Ltd—Bill Winsor	2100 Stemmons Fwy, Dallas TX 75207	214-655-6100	R	97*	.2
17	Princess House Inc—Timothy Brown	470 Myles Standish Blv, Taunton MA 02780	508-823-0711	R	76*	.2
18	3 Day Blinds Inc—Michael Bush	25 Technology Dr Ste B, Irvine CA 92618	714-634-4600	R	67*	1.0
19	Market Antiques and Homefurnishings Inc—JT Campbell Jr	5470 W Lovers Ln Ste 3, Dallas TX 75209	214-352-1220	R	66*	.1
20	Seattle Lighting Fixtures Co	26 South Hanford St, Seattle WA 98134	206-622-1962	R	40*	.2
21	Altmeyer Home Stores Inc—Rod Altmeyer Sr	6515 Rte 22, Delmont PA 15626	724-468-3434	R	30*	.1

Rank	Company Name—*Executive Officer*	Address, City, State, Zip	Phone	Type	Fin	Empls
22	Uppercase Living LLC—*Jeff Wilson*	9350 S 150 East Ste 70, Sandy UT 84070	801-619-5000	R	21*	.1
23	Design Toscano Inc—*Michael Stopka*	1400 Morse Ave, Elk Grove Village IL 60007	847-255-6760	R	19*	.1
24	Progressive Lighting Inc—*Randy Parole*	PO Box 491750, Lawrenceville GA 30043	770-476-8537	R	15*	.1
25	Function Junction Inc—*Steve Eberman*	2450 Grand Blvd Ste 31, Kansas City MO 64108	816-471-4300	R	12*	<.1
26	Platypus Inc—*Jeffrey Schulman*	PO Box 118, Hopewell NJ 08525	732-274-9500	R	9*	.1
27	Darboy Stone Inc—*Greg Schuh*	W3277 Creekview Ln, Appleton WI 54915	920-734-2882	R	5*	<.1
28	Knife Company Inc—*Goldie Russell*	1920 N 26th St, Lowell AR 72745	479-631-0055	R	4*	<.1
29	Brooke Pottery Inc—*Kammi Newberry*	223 N Kentucky Ave, Lakeland FL 33801	863-688-6844	R	4*	<.1
30	Adams and Co—*Timothy A Hutchinson*	3022 Trenton Rd, Santa Rosa CA 95401	707-546-9588	R	4*	<.1
31	LL and T Inc—*William Hurd*	2198 Wilkinson Blvd, Charlotte NC 28208	704-372-7305	R	3*	<.1
32	Home Office Solutions Inc—*Marc Levin*	720 landwehr Rd, Northbrook IL 60062	847-826-2272	R	3*	<.1
33	Llsco LLC—*J Barger*	780 S Floyd Rd, Richardson TX 75080	972-480-9700	R	3*	<.1
34	Buffalo Light and Supply Corp—*Greg Speicher*	1546 Walden Ave, Buffalo NY 14225	716-895-7300	R	2*	<.1
35	Arrelle Fine Linens Inc—*Robert Rosenberg*	445 N Wells St, Chicago IL 60654	312-321-3696	R	2*	<.1
36	Pclt Corp—*David Potter*	3971 Eastern Ave SE, Grand Rapids MI 49508	616-451-0000	R	2*	<.1
37	B and B Lighting Supply Inc—*Sharon Bradford*	PO Box 68084, Baltimore MD 21215	410-523-7300	R	1*	<.1
38	Kitchen Collection Inc—*Gregory H Trepp*	71 E Water St, Chillicothe OH 45601	740-774-0561	S	N/A	1.0

TOTALS: SIC 5719 Miscellaneous Home Furnishings Stores
Companies: 38

					21,182	110.2

5722 Household Appliance Stores

Rank	Company Name—*Executive Officer*	Address, City, State, Zip	Phone	Type	Fin	Empls
1	hhgregg Inc—*Dennis L May*	4151 E 96th St, Indianapolis IN 46240	317-848-8710	P	2,078	4.9
2	BrandsMart USA—*Michael Perlman*	3200 SW 42nd St, Hollywood FL 33312	954-797-4000	R	1,040*	2.6
3	Conn's Inc—*Theodore M Wright*	3295 College St, Beaumont TX 77701	409-832-1696	P	791	2.6
4	PC Richard and Son—*Gary H Richard*	150 Price Pky, Farmingdale NY 11735	631-843-4300	R	610*	2.5
5	Ed Marling Stores Inc—*Mark Marling*	2950 SW McClure Rd, Topeka KS 66614	785-273-6970	R	174*	.1
6	Dan's Fan City Inc—*Dan Hibbeln Jr*	300 Dunbar Ave, Oldsmar FL 34677	813-855-7384	R	173*	.1
7	Pieratt's Inc—*Bruce W Pieratt*	110 S Mt Tabor Rd, Lexington KY 40517	859-268-6000	R	134*	.1
8	Vann's Inc—*George Manlove*	3623 Brooks St, Missoula MT 59801	406-541-6000	R	106*	.2
9	Barbeques Galore Inc—*Jeffery R Sears*	2173 Salk Ave Ste 150, Carlsbad CA 92008		S	102*	.6
10	BGE Home Products and Services Inc—*Kevin Klages*	7161 Columbia Gateway, Columbia MD 21046		S	79*	.5
11	Adray Appliance and Photo Center Inc—*Debra Adray*	20219 Carlysle, Dearborn MI 48124	313-274-9500	R	70*	.1
12	Gerhard's Inc—*Charles Gerhard*	290 N Keswick Ave, Glenside PA 19038	215-884-8650	R	33*	.1
13	Southeast Steel Sales Co—*Staurt Kimball*	63 W Amelia St, Orlando FL 32801	407-423-7654	R	18*	<.1
14	DeSears Appliances Inc—*John Rice*	6430 14th St W, Bradenton FL 34207	941-751-7525	R	11*	.1
15	Hupp Electric Motors Inc—*Kevin Hupp*	275 33rd Ave Sw, Cedar Rapids IA 52404	319-366-0761	R	10*	.2
16	Appliance Zone Inc—*Jim Allen*	500 N Capitol Ave, Corydon IN 47112		R	9*	<.1
17	Robertson Airtech International Inc—*Stephen Robertson*	PO Box 5646, Charlotte NC 28299	704-377-3939	R	8*	.1
18	Rensen House Of Lights Inc—*Thomas Rensenhouse*	9212 Marshall Dr, Lenexa KS 66215	913-888-0888	R	4*	<.1
19	Albee Appliances Inc—*Solomon Seferadi*	6305 Wilshire Blvd, Los Angeles CA 90048	323-651-0620	R	4*	<.1
20	Sozio Corp—*Louis Sozio*	61 Squire Rd, Revere MA 02151	781-284-4363	R	3*	<.1
21	Fairfax Kitchen and Bath Inc—*Hamid Sharifi*	14325 Willard Rd Ste H, Chantilly VA 20151	703-817-1977	R	3*	<.1
22	Hubbard and Hoke Inc—*George Hubbard*	401 W Main St, Blytheville AR 72315	870-763-4409	R	2*	<.1
23	Mid-South Sewing Machine Sales Inc—*Earl Witcher*	4296 Cowan Rd, Tucker GA 30084	770-939-3195	R	1*	<.1
24	Europa Company Inc—*Fred Schmidt*	11289 Slater Ave, Fountain Valley CA 92708	714-432-0112	R	1*	<.1
25	Amay Inc—*Albert Rivero*	8822 Sw 131st St, Miami FL 33176	305-251-1623	R	<1*	<.1

TOTALS: SIC 5722 Household Appliance Stores
Companies: 25

					5,463	14.9

5731 Radio, Television & Electronics Stores

Rank	Company Name—*Executive Officer*	Address, City, State, Zip	Phone	Type	Fin	Empls
1	Best Buy Company Inc—*Brian J Dunn*	PO Box 9312, Minneapolis MN 55440	612-291-1000	P	50,272	180.0
2	Circuitcitycom Inc—*Richard Leeds*	7795 W Flagler St Ste, Miami FL 33144		S	11,744	43.0
3	RadioShack Corp—*James F Gooch*	300 RadioShack Cir, Fort Worth TX 76102		P	4,378	34.0
4	Fry's Electronics Inc—*John Fry*	600 E Brokaw Rd, San Jose CA 95112	408-487-4500	R	3,045*	14.0
5	American Television and Appliance of Madison Inc	2404 W Beltline Hwy, Madison WI 53713	608-271-1000	R	1,496*	1.9
6	ABC Appliance Inc—*Gordon Hartunian*	PO Box 436001, Pontiac MI 48343	248-335-4222	R	1,330*	1.8
7	Tweeter Home Entertainment Group Inc—*Joseph G McGuire*	40 Pequot Way, Canton MA 02021	781-830-3000	P	775	3.2
8	Ultimate Electronics Inc—*Bruce Giesbrecht*	321 W 84th Ave Ste A, Thornton CO 80260	303-657-5880	R	718*	3.5
9	D L Cole and Associates Inc—*Daniel Cole*	3407 Bridgeland Dr, Bridgeton MO 63044	314-291-3139	R	372*	.2
10	Rex American Resources Corp—*Stuart Rose*	2875 Needmore Rd, Dayton OH 45414	937-276-3931	P	302	<.1
11	Car Toys Inc—*Dan Brettler*	20 W Galer St, Seattle WA 98119	206-443-0980	R	236*	1.2
12	Paul's TV - King Of The Big Screen—*Paul Goldenberg*	2660 Barranco Pkwy, Irvine CA 92606	949-596-8899	R	221*	.1
13	Myer-Emco Inc—*Jonathan Myer*	PO Box 98, Orlean VA 20128	301-921-0700	R	140*	.2
14	Star West Satellite Inc—*Pete Sobrepena*	580 Pronghorn Trl, Bozeman MT 59718	406-522-8402	R	131*	.2
15	Magnolia Audio Video—*Jim Tweten* Best Buy Company Inc	180 University Ave, Palo Alto CA 94301	650-838-0547	S	129*	.2
16	Let's Talk Cellular and Wireless Inc—*Delly Tamer*	410 Townsend St Ste 10, San Francisco CA 94107		R	123	1.0
17	Audio Craft Company Inc—*Wayne Puntel*	3915 Carnegie Ave, Cleveland OH 44115	216-431-7300	R	109*	.1
18	Audiovisual Inc—*Joe Stoebner*	9675 W 76th St Ste 200, Eden Prairie MN 55344	952-949-3700	R	78*	.3
19	Queen City Audio Video and Appliances—*Woodrow Player Jr*	2430 Queen City Dr, Charlotte NC 28208	704-391-6000	R	59*	.2
20	Comtran Associates Inc—*Leonard Knigin*	1961 Utica Ave, Brooklyn NY 11234	718-531-7676	R	54*	<.1
21	Audio Ethics Inc—*Donnie Haulk*	PO Box 668065, Charlotte NC 28266		R	52*	<.1
22	Kaleidescape Inc—*Michael Malcolm*	440 Potrero Ave, Sunnyvale CA 94085	650-625-6100	R	47	.1
23	County TV and Appliance LOS Corp—*Lester Cohn*	2770 Summer St, Stamford CT 06905	203-327-2630	R	34*	<.1
24	Arjay Telecom—*Arun Bhumitra*	23215 Hawthorne Blvd, Torrance CA 90505	310-791-3300	R	31*	.2
25	Ed Kellum and Son Appliance Co—*Pat Kellum*	4533 Cole Ave, Dallas TX 75205	214-526-1717	R	30*	.1
26	Central Audio Visual Inc—*D Robert Schwartz*	1212 S Andrews Ave, Fort Lauderdale FL 33316	954-522-3796	R	25*	.1
27	Schaefer's TV and Appliance Center Inc—*Ron Romero*	PO Box 30184, Lincoln NE 68503	402-464-8888	R	23*	.1
28	JJR Enterprises Inc—*Dan Reilly*	10491 Old Placerville, Sacramento CA 95827	916-363-2666	R	22*	.1
29	Baton Rouge Car Audio Inc—*Brenda Saltz*	6275 Siegen Ln, Baton Rouge LA 70809	225-292-5050	R	19*	<.1
30	Creve Coeur Camera and Video Inc—*Stephen Weiss*	11615 Olive Blvd, Creve Coeur MO 63141	314-567-3456	R	18*	.2
31	WHP Electronics Inc—*Bill Pelfery*	1600 Shorter Ave, Rome GA 30165	706-235-7941	R	16*	.1
32	Creative Communications Sales and Rentals Inc—*Scott Weisenburger*	3332 E Broadway Rd, Phoenix AZ 85040	602-955-8405	R	16*	.1
33	Markey's Rental and Staging—*Chuck Markey*	2365 Enterprise Park P, Indianapolis IN 46218	317-783-1155	R	15*	.2
34	Amateur Electronic Supply LLC—*Gary Burk*	5710 W Good Hope Rd, Milwaukee WI 53223	414-358-0333	R	15*	.1
35	Thompson Communications and Electronics—*Bill Fribley*	PO Box 465, New Castle IN 47362	765-529-6737	R	11*	<.1
36	South Sales Liquidations Inc—*Timothy Rock*	446 Crompton St, Charlotte NC 28273	704-969-9000	R	10*	<.1
37	Valeo Radar Systems Inc—*Roland Lartigue*	150 Stephenson Hwy, Troy MI 48083	248-619-8563	R	10*	.1

Note: An asterisk (*) indicates an estimated financial figure. The company type code used is as follows: R = Private, P = Public, S = Private Subsidiary, B = Public Subsidiary, D = Division, J = Joint Venture, I = Investment Fund.

...NKINGS BY SALES WITHIN 4-DIGIT SIC

	Company Name—Executive Officer	Address, City, State, Zip	Phone	Type	Fin	Empls
	Overseas Connection Inc—Surendra Jain	7886 Deering Ave, Canoga Park CA 91304	818-884-8444	R	10*	<.1
39	Sky Blue Satellite Services Inc—David Bennett	2116 Delaware St Ste A, Lawrence KS 66046	785-331-3444	R	10*	.2
40	Hello Inc—Edward L Smith	2315 W Broad St, Richmond VA 23220	804-353-5566	R	9*	.1
41	RCA Home Theater Showcase Inc—Glenn Midet	9115 Galleria Ct, Naples FL 34109	239-594-8845	R	9*	<.1
42	Discountcell Inc—Craig King	350 W 500 S, Provo UT 84601	801-235-9809	R	9*	<.1
43	Home Video Library Electronics—Harold Ward	16544 Se Division St, Portland OR 97236	503-760-6488	R	8*	<.1
44	OAP Inc—Michael O'Rourke	PO Box 3309, Suwanee GA 30024	770-945-1028	R	8*	<.1
45	S and S Buying Service Inc—Jack Lichaa	PO Box 799, New York NY 10108	212-575-0210	R	8*	<.1
46	American Satellite and Entertainment Inc—Todd Toler	40 Terrill Park Dr Uni, Concord NH 03301	603-228-8815	R	7*	.1
47	FireFold—Chris Grouse	2701 Derita Rd, Concord NC 28027	704-979-7100	R	7*	<.1
48	Gogotech Inc—Uri Cohen	1410 Broadway Fl 20, New York NY 10018	212-386-7192	R	6*	.1
49	Crescom Engineering Company Inc—David Thomas	944 Searcy Way, Bowling Green KY 42103	270-781-7076	R	6*	<.1
50	DICE Electronics LLC—Laszlo Barabas	2650 Gundry Ave, Signal Hill CA 90755		R	6*	<.1
51	Sound Components Inc—Mark Goldman	1536 S Dicksy Hwy, Coral Gables FL 33146	305-665-4299	R	6*	<.1
52	Audiophile Systems Inc—Karen Richardson	PO Box 50710, Indianapolis IN 46250	317-849-5880	R	6*	<.1
53	Matter of Fax—Jonathan Sheldon	105 Harrison Ave, Harrison NJ 07029	973-482-3700	R	6*	<.1
54	H and H Service Store Inc—Laurie Watson	100 Glynn Isle, Brunswick GA 31525	912-265-8100	R	6*	<.1
55	Satellite Solutions LLC	37878 State Rd 78, Durant OK 74701	580-924-3234	R	6*	<.1
56	Camcor Inc—Raymond Bailey	PO Box 1899, Burlington NC 27216	336-228-0251	R	6*	.1
57	Rockingham Corp—David Lane	40 Jay Scutti Blvd, Rochester NY 14623	585-272-1792	R	6*	<.1
58	Innovation USA Trading Inc—Patricia Lopez	1408 Water Lilly Ln, Kissimmee FL 34744	407-348-9054	R	5*	.1
59	Electronic Express Inc—Sam Yazdian	2627 Grandview Ave, Nashville TN 37211	615-259-2031	R	5*	.1
60	CAM Audio Inc—Dean Harrison	2210 Executive Dr, Garland TX 75041	972-271-2800	R	5*	<.1
61	Greenville Tv and Appliance Inc—Malcolm Williams	200 Greenville Blvd Se, Greenville NC 27858	252-756-2616	R	5*	<.1
62	Solid Signal LLC—Jerry Chapman	25225 Regency Dr, Novi MI 48375	248-896-8587	R	5	<.1
63	Barretts Inc—Joe Barrett	576 S Rte 59, Naperville IL 60540	630-898-2850	R	5*	<.1
64	Houston 2-Way Radio—Alan Van Velkinburgh	5805 Central Crest, Houston TX 77092	713-681-2525	R	5*	<.1
65	Focus Electronics Inc—Ann Singer	4509 13th Ave, Brooklyn NY 11218	718-436-4646	R	5*	<.1
66	Wellman and Griffith Inc—Jeffrey Saari	22765 Lorain Rd, Cleveland OH 44126	440-734-2322	R	5*	<.1
67	Starpower Home Entertainment Systems Inc—David Pidgeon	15340 Dallas Pkwy Ste, Dallas TX 75248	972-503-6000	R	5*	<.1
68	Gifford Tv and Electronics Inc—Kenneth Gifford	1493 W S Loop, Stephenville TX 76401	254-968-2112	R	5*	<.1
69	Ken's Stereo-Video Junction Inc—J Jones	3677 Mercer University, Macon GA 31204	478-474-2324	R	5*	<.1
70	Daddy's Discount Stereo Inc—Ron Moore	10343 Atlantic Blvd, Jacksonville FL 32225	904-641-3100	R	4*	<.1
71	Don's Tv and Appliance Inc—Don Thedford	6714 S Broadway Ave, Tyler TX 75703	903-561-1151	R	4*	<.1
72	San Francisco Stereo Inc—Kerry Blessing	7 Beaconsfield Ct, Orinda CA 94563	925-376-2126	R	4*	<.1
73	Electronics Expo LLC—Levent Cemiz	38 Fairfield Pl, Caldwell NJ 07006	973-808-8838	R	4*	<.1
74	Noralph Inc—Ralph Tarnofsky	182 Essex St, Millburn NJ 07041	973-467-1950	R	4*	<.1
75	Metro Video Systems Inc—Robert L Weir	1220 E Imperial Ave, El Segundo CA 90245	310-640-9250	R	4*	<.1
76	AVAC of Myrtle Beach Inc—Harold R Ferrell	1850 Mr Joe Whire Ave, Myrtle Beach SC 29577	843-626-6996	R	4*	<.1
77	Les Wallen USA Inc—Jerry Hirsch	219 California Dr, Williamsville NY 14221	716-634-0634	D	4*	<.1
	Hirsch Sales Corp					
78	Band Pro Film and Digital Inc—Amnon Band	3403 W Pacific Ave, Burbank CA 91505	818-841-9655	R	4*	<.1
79	Sound Room Ii Inc—David Young	1661 Clarkson Rd, Chesterfield MO 63017	636-537-0404	R	4*	<.1
80	Audio Xcellence Inc—Ron Canosa	2301 E Sunset Rd Ste 4, Las Vegas NV 89119	702-214-3650	R	4*	<.1
81	Supreme Radio Communications Inc—Dale Tripp	4017 N Prospect Rd, Peoria IL 61616	309-682-0831	R	4*	<.1
82	GP Systems Inc—Russell Maynard	2350 S Bascom Ave, Campbell CA 95008	408-371-9177	R	4*	<.1
83	Crumpton Tv Audio and Video Center—Dale Crumpton	8602 Wesley St, Greenville TX 75402	903-455-2043	R	4*	<.1
84	Gately Communications Inc—Joseph Gately	PO Box 9188, Hampton VA 23670	757-826-8216	R	3*	<.1
85	Spinitar—Doug Chew	3659 Depot Rd, Hayward CA 94545	510-266-0300	R	3*	<.1
86	Stargatemobile LLC—Johnny Cooper	6070 S Saginaw Rd, Grand Blanc MI 48439	810-694-9300	R	3*	<.1
87	New York Camera and Video Inc—Frank Cundari	1139 St Rd, Southampton PA 18966	215-364-6583	R	3*	<.1
88	JP Jenkins Inc—Jay Jenkins	5811 34th St Ste B, Lubbock TX 79407	806-795-5823	R	3*	<.1
89	Triangle Communications Inc—Roy Smoker	940 W Main St, New Holland PA 17557	717-656-2211	R	3*	<.1
90	Eklund Appliance and TV—Calvin Eklund	1007 Central Ave W, Great Falls MT 59404	406-761-3430	R	3*	<.1
91	Granite Electronics Inc—Andrew Faith	535 31st Ave N, Saint Cloud MN 56303	320-252-1887	R	3*	<.1
92	Dyckman Electronics Center Inc—Avraham Oz	151 Dyckman St, New York NY 10040	212-304-2000	R	3*	<.1
93	Trotter's Of Alexandria Inc—Gregory Trotter	PO Box 7999, Alexandria LA 71306	318-487-8978	R	3*	<.1
94	Trevose Electronics Inc—David Funk	4033 Brownsville Rd, Trevose PA 19053	215-357-1400	R	3*	<.1
95	Marketing Products Inc—James Alexander	18174 Mohawk Dr, Spring Lake MI 49456	616-846-4905	R	3*	<.1
96	Two-Way Radio Service Inc—John Hutter	PO Box 299, Cumberland MD 21501	301-777-2692	R	3*	<.1
97	Suncoast Communications and Electronics Inc—Lawrence Garuti	3195 Tech Dr N, Saint Petersburg FL 33716	727-571-1110	R	3*	<.1
98	Coast Satellite Inc—Ryan Evans	PO Box 2860, Atascadero CA 93423	805-461-1522	R	3*	<.1
99	Protech E2 Inc—John Forrer	PO Box 372846, Key Largo FL 33037	305-453-0010	R	3*	<.1
100	Dish Tv Inc—James Jugon	PO Box 90535, Houston TX 77290	281-821-1994	R	3*	.1
101	Integrated Electronics Inc—Keith Axe	9847 Lackman Rd, Shawnee Mission KS 66219	913-663-3366	R	3*	<.1
102	Centre Communications Inc—Karl Hosterman	PO Box 119, Bellefonte PA 16823	814-234-2345	R	3*	<.1
103	Big Dog Satellite LLC	1310 Yellowstone Ave, Pocatello ID 83201	208-232-5483	R	3*	<.1
104	CM City Inc—Phil Taylor	153 Northside Dr E Ste, Statesboro GA 30458	912-764-7343	R	3*	<.1
105	Residential Systems Inc—Kenneth Karnes	4885 Ward Rd Ste 500, Wheat Ridge CO 80033	303-277-9983	R	3*	<.1
106	Radio Service Company Inc—Danny Smith	PO Box 11570, El Dorado AR 71730	870-862-3475	R	3*	<.1
107	Contemporary Sounds Of Oklahoma City Inc—Richard Ades	2940 Nw 149th St, Oklahoma City OK 73134	405-755-0795	R	3*	<.1
108	Stereoland—Mel Sutterhome	8743 Columbine Rd, Eden Prairie MN 55344	952-829-9700	R	3*	<.1
109	Audio Installation Company LLC—Lyndia Thompson	476 E Riverside Dr Ste, Saint George UT 84790	435-656-2452	R	3*	<.1
110	Buy-Global Inc—Jeff Mansbach	530 Eagle Ave, West Hempstead NY 11552	516-565-9500	R	2*	<.1
111	Hillson Group Inc—Max Hillson	195 Libbey Industrial, Weymouth MA 02189	781-335-0062	R	2*	<.1
112	Computer King Inc—Lyle Richins	3145 Stockton Hill Rd, Kingman AZ 86401	928-753-4466	R	2*	<.1
113	Custom Sound Of Athens Inc—Benjamin Murray	PO Box 327, Bogart GA 30622	706-549-4844	R	2*	<.1
114	Tri County Communications Inc—Frederick Muller	6 Keith St, Oneonta NY 13820	607-432-1125	R	2*	<.1
115	Desco Electronics Corp—Richard Scott	2306 Harrison Ave Nw, Olympia WA 98502	360-943-1393	R	2*	<.1
116	Mid-Shore Electronics Inc—Frank Daringer	205 Trenton St, Cambridge MD 21613	410-228-7335	R	2*	<.1
117	Liquidation Station Inc—Bartholomew Brown	109 Gateway Dr, North Sioux City SD 57049	605-242-5028	R	2*	<.1
118	Video Max Inc—Todd Corwin	2511 W Edgewood Dr Ste, Jefferson City MO 65109	573-893-5006	R	2*	<.1
119	Tjm Electronics West Inc—Thomas Mccarthy	2640 W Medtronic Way, Tempe AZ 85281	480-446-3150	R	2*	<.1
120	Curt A Barad Audio-Video Inc—Curt Barad	3585 Lawson Blvd, Oceanside NY 11572	516-763-4144	R	2*	<.1
121	Servex Electronic Distributing Inc—Gregory Sens	2050 Marion Mt Gilead, Marion OH 43302	740-389-4686	R	2*	<.1
122	Rykel Global Inc—Ryan Argenta	1435 Centennial Blvd, Colorado Springs CO 80919	719-210-4533	R	2*	<.1
123	Tmv Properties Inc—Jamie Stephens	2306 Clydesdale Dr, Bismarck ND 58503	701-258-1032	R	2*	<.1
124	Schagby Inc—James Schillinger	325 E Betteravia Rd B1, Santa Maria CA 93454	805-928-0533	R	2*	<.1
125	Heydlauff's Inc—Matt Heydlauff	113 N Main St, Chelsea MI 48118	734-475-1221	R	2*	<.1

Rank	Company Name—*Executive Officer*	Address, City, State, Zip	Phone	Type	Fin	Empls
126	Sun Communication Technologies Inc—*Ruben Nunez*	4350 Airport Rd Ste 6, Santa Fe NM 87507	505-424-7223	R	2*	.1
127	Insight Satellite—*Thomas Rice*	10829 Tineville Rd Ste, Pineville NC 28134	704-889-7989	R	2*	<.1
128	Space Connections Inc—*John Axley*	2903 Hwy 411 Ste 1, Madisonville TN 37354	423-442-5080	R	2*	<.1
129	Audio Connection Inc—*David Bran*	1735 E Joppa Rd Ste 4, Baltimore MD 21234	410-768-1580	R	2*	<.1
130	Audio Visions South Inc—*George Liu*	3655 Henderson Blvd, Tampa FL 33609	813-871-2989	R	2*	<.1
131	Boyer Automotive Center Inc—*Cory Boyer*	345 Elk Ridge Dr, Payson UT 84651	801-423-2332	R	2*	<.1
132	Yourchouk's Hardware Video—*Joseph Yourchuck*	24537 State Rd 35, Siren WI 54872	715-349-5200	R	2*	<.1
133	Audio Encounters Inc—*Peggy Deem*	4271 W Dublin Granvill, Dublin OH 43017	614-766-4434	R	2*	<.1
134	Big Apple Of New Hartford LLC—*Peter Bolos*	8441 Seneca Tpke, New Hartford NY 13413	315-732-4162	R	2*	<.1
135	Hi Fidelity of Lubbock Inc—*Chad Waller*	7619 University Ave, Lubbock TX 79423	806-794-4507	R	2*	<.1
136	James A Smith—*James Smith*	2439 Boundary St, Beaufort SC 29906	843-524-5238	R	2*	<.1
137	Master Media Systems Inc—*Don Snede*	8555 W 123rd St, Savage MN 55378	952-941-0474	R	2*	<.1
138	All Star Audio-Video Inc—*Percy Lawless*	4009 Richmond Ave, Houston TX 77027	713-464-8203	R	2*	<.1
139	Auto Sounds—*Paul Polizzi*	5841 Hollister Ave, Goleta CA 93117	805-964-3366	R	2*	<.1
140	Raskin Jerry Needle Doctor Inc—*Jerry Raskin*	419 14th Ave Se, Minneapolis MN 55414	612-378-0543	R	2*	<.1
141	Agm Entertainment Inc—*Anthony Marney*	7027 Belgold St, Houston TX 77066	281-440-3607	R	2*	<.1
142	Special Electronics Inc—*Kush Samtani*	316 Convent Ave, Laredo TX 78040	956-722-5557	R	2*	<.1
143	R F Ltd—*Samuel Lewis*	PO Box 445, Issaquah WA 98027	425-295-0390	R	2*	<.1
144	Autosound and Security Inc—*Dan Friz*	1322 S State Hwy 121, Lewisville TX 75067	972-219-9700	R	2*	<.1
145	Cable Unlimited Inc—*Darwin Huett*	3540 S Westwood Blvd, Poplar Bluff MO 63901	573-778-1031	R	2*	<.1
146	Comtech Vipersat Networks Inc—*Fred Morris*	3215 Skyway Ct, Fremont CA 94539	510-252-1462	R	2*	<.1
147	Ams Car Stereo Inc—*Yoo Kim*	3910 Stevens Creek Blv, San Jose CA 95129	408-248-1111	R	2*	<.1
148	Saturday Audio Exchange Inc—*Andy Zimmerman*	1021 W Belmont Ave, Chicago IL 60657	773-935-8733	R	2*	<.1
149	Empress Of Ocean Springs Inc—*William Seal*	PO Box 240, Pascagoula MS 39568	228-769-7802	R	2*	<.1
150	K-T Enterprises Inc—*Kenneth Kupp*	7620 E 42nd Pl, Tulsa OK 74145	918-627-1400	R	2*	<.1
151	Mo-Ark Communications And Electronics Inc—*Stephen Hubbard*	PO Box 987, Blytheville AR 72316	870-763-9441	R	2*	<.1
152	Sound and Vision Of Orland Park Inc—*Eric Schmidt*	530 Executive Dr, Willowbrook IL 60527	630-242-4600	R	2*	<.1
153	Wee Bee Audio Of Lancaster Inc—*Kerry Schanz*	1305 Manheim Pke, Lancaster PA 17601	717-399-9926	R	2*	<.1
154	Sound Shop Inc—*Lawrence Powers*	7 E Cimarron St, Colorado Springs CO 80903	719-636-1684	R	2*	<.1
155	Crystal Smr Inc—*David Hernandez*	1601 Neptune Dr, San Leandro CA 94577	510-895-9500	R	2*	<.1
156	Fowler's Tv Inc—*Mark Fowler*	1301 E Spring St, Saint Marys OH 45885	419-394-5312	R	2*	<.1
157	Electronic Home Systems Inc—*Bernie Kattner*	3701 Hwy 16, Eagle ID 83616	208-286-9262	R	2*	<.1
158	Radio Shop Inc—*Tim Bennett*	1711 S Division Ave, Orlando FL 32805	407-423-8561	R	2*	<.1
159	Wild West Sound Company Inc—*Brad Bolotin*	8060 Double R Blvd Ste, Reno NV 89511	775-853-4600	R	2*	<.1
160	M and A Electronics Inc—*Dean Schneider*	2705 Calumet Ave, Manitowoc WI 54220	920-684-3393	R	2*	<.1
161	Rand's Camera And Hi-Fi Inc—*Saul Rand*	1841 Hooper Ave, Toms River NJ 08753	732-255-3213	R	2*	<.1
162	Lincoln-Way Electronics—*William Lander*	26118 Simotes Ln, Wilmington IL 60481	815-476-6462	R	2*	<.1
163	Videoconferencing Center—*Andrew Martin*	3 Riverway Ste 250, Houston TX 77056	713-888-0632	R	2*	<.1
164	Breakers Mobile Electronics Inc—*Erica Papadaki*	465 N Oxnard Blvd, Oxnard CA 93030	805-486-8307	R	2*	<.1
165	Satellites Unlimited Inc—*Charles Stubblefield*	715 Poplar Ave, Nashville TN 37210	615-254-5238	R	2*	<.1
166	Duluth Audio Distributing and Service—*Peter Prudden*	4940 Matterhorn Dr, Duluth MN 55811	218-727-3053	R	2*	<.1
167	Avalon Acoustics Inc—*Neil Patel*	2800 Wilderness Pl Ste, Boulder CO 80301	303-440-0422	R	2*	<.1
168	Denco Electronics Inc—*Yoni Kernezi*	953 E 11th St, Los Angeles CA 90021	213-629-2444	R	2*	<.1
169	Digital Interiors Inc—*Ron Rimawi*	5935 Shiloh Rd E Ste 3, Alpharetta GA 30005	770-844-5800	R	2*	<.1
170	Karaoke Kandy Store Inc—*Charles Polidori*	5361 Pearl Rd, Parma OH 44129	216-929-1022	R	2*	<.1
171	Powers News Inc—*Paul Dunigan*	101 Gorham St, Lowell MA 01852	978-452-8693	R	2*	<.1
172	Sound Ideas Inc—*Keith Belman*	3671 Karl Rd, Columbus OH 43224	614-263-3720	R	2*	<.1
173	Soundquest Inc—*Rony Reckelbus*	6800 Gateway Blvd E St, El Paso TX 79915	915-779-5421	R	2*	<.1
174	Video Systems and Security Inc—*Maurice Siakaly*	586 Seiberling St, Akron OH 44306	330-784-7500	R	2*	<.1
175	Car Audio Specialist Inc—*Sam Allwer*	177 Hamakua Dr, Kailua HI 96734	808-262-9940	R	2*	<.1
176	Mc Lelland Tv Inc—*Douglas Lelland*	302 Broadway Dr, Hattiesburg MS 39401	601-583-0542	R	2*	<.1
177	Dnsllc Irmo SC Inc—*Charlie Ergon*	1108 Lykes Ln Ste C, Irmo SC 29063	803-732-0115	R	2*	<.1
178	B and L Sound Inc—*Mary Edger*	207 W Mitchell St, Petoskey MI 49770	231-347-6810	R	2*	<.1
179	Collier2way Communications Inc—*Helen Lynch*	3900 Mannix Dr Ste 107, Naples FL 34114	239-354-0600	R	2*	<.1
180	Elite Communications Inc—*Amit Bennoun*	7009 Austin St Ste 4, Forest Hills NY 11375	718-263-8466	R	2*	<.1
181	Metro Audio Dynamics Inc—*John Henry*	7710 L St, Omaha NE 68127	402-537-1966	R	2*	<.1
182	Audio Vision Inc—*William Dotson*	521 Hwy 105 Ext Ste 1, Boone NC 28607	828-264-5713	R	2*	<.1
183	Brilliant Store Inc—*Guangpeng Liu*	933 Corporate Way, Fremont CA 94539	510-668-0398	R	2*	<.1
184	Graybill Electronics Inc—*Kevin Graybill*	305 Miller Rd, Hiawatha IA 52233	319-393-5456	R	2*	<.1
185	Pascual J And L Of Santa Fe Inc—*Leonard Pascual*	502 Cerrillos Rd, Santa Fe NM 87501	505-983-5509	R	2*	<.1
186	Johnson and Walee Inc—*Walee Gon*	1507 Ocean Ave, San Francisco CA 94112	415-594-0029	R	2*	<.1
187	Sobe Electronics—*Adil Danjellooun*	1059 Collins Ave Ste 1, Miami Beach FL 33139	305-532-0039	R	2*	<.1
188	Xcable Company Corp—*Steve Hammon*	PO Box 120008, Arlington TX 76012	817-261-3733	R	1*	<.1
189	Redco Communications Inc—*Donald Nolde*	570 Windy Point Dr, Glendale Heights IL 60139	630-858-5212	R	1*	<.1
190	Action Communications Inc—*William Baxter*	2816 N Stone Ave, Tucson AZ 85705	520-792-0326	R	1*	<.1
191	Alpha Sound International Inc—*Cliff Youn*	1039 Commercial St, San Jose CA 95112	408-451-9035	R	1*	<.1
192	Home Media Stores LC—*Cathy Downs*	1111 Alverser Dr, Midlothian VA 23113	804-379-0900	R	1*	<.1
193	Pro Audio Services Inc—*Christopher Bertler*	3195 Commerce Pkwy Uni, North Port FL 34289	941-876-3386	R	1*	<.1
194	Kinder Guard LLC—*Trey Matula*	1308 Dealers Ave, New Orleans LA 70123	504-736-9187	R	1*	<.1
195	Bell and Bates Inc—*Mark Bates*	PO Box 1038, Quincy FL 32353	850-627-6115	R	1*	<.1
196	K and M Satellite Inc—*Darrel Knight*	30 Sw E Ave, Lawton OK 73501	580-357-5040	R	1*	<.1
197	Digital Video Group Inc—*Alex Martin*	8529 Meadowbridge Rd S, Mechanicsville VA 23116	804-559-8850	R	1*	<.1
198	Technical Assistance Inc—*Bill Kelley*	PO Box 1545, Orangeburg SC 29116	803-516-0005	R	1*	<.1
199	Billy Jack Hardware and Electronics—*Billy Walters*	905 W Central Ave, Moultrie GA 31768	229-985-0013	R	1*	<.1
200	Canfield Systems Inc—*Lynn Brady*	PO Box 898, Scarborough ME 04070	207-883-4110	R	1*	<.1
201	Coastal Sound Shop Inc—*Steve Knight*	1102 New Rd, Northfield NJ 08225	609-646-6282	R	1*	<.1
202	Huntsville Radio Service Inc—*Beverly Boylan*	2402 Clinton Ave W, Huntsville AL 35805	256-534-4232	R	1*	<.1
203	Selma Communications Service—*Allen Williams*	1605 W Highland Ave, Selma AL 36701	334-874-8375	R	1*	<.1
204	Texas Communications Of Brownwood Inc—*Toney Prather*	PO Box 3307, Brownwood TX 76803	325-646-0972	R	1*	<.1
205	Electronic Design Group Inc—*George Veile*	10120 Sw Nimbus Ave C1, Portland OR 97223	503-598-7380	R	1*	<.1
206	Audio Direct LLC—*Paul Greaeme*	460 W Roger Rd Ste 105, Tucson AZ 85705	520-292-6112	R	1*	<.1
207	Long Island Sound Services Inc—*Dan Orza*	16 Rocklyn Ave, Lynbrook NY 11563	516-887-7170	R	1*	<.1
208	Main Street Trading Company Inc—*Randy Moore*	908 E Pioneer Pkwy, Arlington TX 76010	817-548-1992	R	1*	<.1
209	Sound Designs Inc—*Jack Schroeder*	6310 W Donges Bay Rd, Mequon WI 53092	262-242-5599	R	1*	<.1
210	Sound Waves Audio Video Interiors Inc—*Jeff Beyers*	3049 Drane Feld Rd Ste, Lakeland FL 33811	863-619-7734	R	1*	<.1
211	Valley Satellite—*Ola Tucker*	PO Box 523, Patten ME 04765	207-528-2829	R	1*	<.1
212	Multicomm Inc—*Jerry Cox*	201 Wayne St, Hollidaysburg PA 16648	814-696-7929	R	1*	<.1
213	Custom Tv and Stereo Inc—*Steven Setzer*	3250 Dale Rd Ste A, Modesto CA 95356	209-529-6231	R	1*	<.1
214	Larry's Northern Electronics Inc—*Larry Derosa*	PO Box 1609, Havre MT 59501	406-265-5568	R	1*	<.1

Note: An asterisk (*) indicates an estimated financial figure. The company type code used is as follows: R = Private, P = Public, S = Private Subsidiary, B = Public Subsidiary, D = Division, J = Joint Venture, I = Investment Fund.

COMPANY RANKINGS BY SALES WITHIN 4-DIGIT SIC

Rank	Company Name—Executive Officer	Address, City, State, Zip	Phone	Type	Fin	Empls
215	Allegiance Inc—Jonathan Trumble	1833 Us Hwy 1, Vero Beach FL 32960	772-562-9001	R	1*	<.1
216	Audio Images Corp—Ron Timmons	735 Bryant St, San Francisco CA 94107	415-957-9131	R	1*	<.1
217	Select Communications Inc—Tim Millican	7653c Fullerton Rd, Springfield VA 22153	703-569-4400	R	1*	<.1
218	Electronics Depot Inc—Scott Davis	830 Burkemont Ave, Morganton NC 28655	828-433-7000	R	1*	<.1
219	Audiovisual Consultations Inc—Thomas Mackay	3584 Rocking J Rd, Round Rock TX 78665	512-255-8678	R	1*	<.1
220	Audio Video Lifestyles Inc—Todd Freeland	7107 W Jefferson Blvd, Fort Wayne IN 46804	260-436-4669	R	1*	<.1
221	Theatre Vision Inc—Gerald Bessell	5550 Nicholson Ln, Rockville MD 20852	301-816-0300	R	1*	<.1
222	Screening Room LLC—Craig Miller	10311 Clayton Rd, Saint Louis MO 63131	314-991-5999	R	1*	<.1
223	Mel Quale's Electronics Inc—Mel Quale	1730 Kimberly Rd, Twin Falls ID 83301	208-733-4910	R	1*	<.1
224	Lucid Audio Video Inc—Arthur Chitikian	PO Box 5476, Englewood NJ 07631	201-233-6653	R	1*	<.1
225	Central Communications Corp—Francis Hull	PO Box 950, Londonderry NH 03053	603-432-4313	R	1*	<.1
226	Entertainment Systems Inc—James O'riley	2309 Sw Us Hwy 40 C, Blue Springs MO 64015	819-229-9930	R	1*	<.1
227	Flower City Communications LLC	1848 Lyell Ave, Rochester NY 14606	585-458-5350	R	1*	<.1
228	Hirsch Sales Corp—Rick Hirsch	219 California Dr, Williamsville NY 14221	716-632-1189	R	1*	<.1
229	Twoway Communications Inc—Brian Cordes	35473 Us Hwy 212, Olivia MN 56277	320-523-5682	R	1*	<.1
230	Audio Video Caribe Inc—Arnaldo Hernandez	7640 Nw 25th St Ste 11, Miami FL 33122	305-717-0902	R	1*	<.1
231	Action Radio and Communications Inc—Mike Dyer	11133 86th Ave N, Maple Grove MN 55369	763-391-6611	R	1*	<.1
232	American Cable Inc—Roy Helm	PO Box 620, Jamestown KY 42629	270-343-2177	R	1*	<.1
233	Commline Inc—James Jun	5563 Sepulveda Blvd St, Culver City CA 90230	310-390-8003	R	1*	<.1
234	D and H Electronics Inc—Sam Hofstatter	5215 13th Ave Ste A, Brooklyn NY 11219	718-633-4000	R	1*	<.1
235	Sanders Satellite Systems—Allen Sanders	2901 S Western St, Amarillo TX 79109	806-353-6706	R	1*	<.1
236	Victory Sound Communications Inc—Joseph Yeargain	PO Box 1743, Whitehouse TX 75791	903-839-1095	R	1*	<.1
237	Apex Industry Service Inc—Virginia Lee	5011 Blum Rd Ste 6, Martinez CA 94553	925-370-9660	R	1*	<.1
238	England Audio Inc—Murnard England	760 Charnelton St, Eugene OR 97401	541-687-2927	R	1*	<.1
239	Hi-Tech Audio Systems Inc—Louis Adamo	471 Littlefield Ave, South San Francisco CA 94080	650-742-9166	R	1*	<.1
240	Satellite TV Supermarket—Ron Moore	2924 North Ave, Grand Junction CO 81504	970-243-7237	R	1	<.1
241	Henshaw Electronics—Joe Henshaw	7622 Wornall Rd, Kansas City MO 64114	816-444-3434	R	1*	<.1
242	C Depot Ii—Brian Bangs	8639 Loch Raven Blvd, Baltimore MD 21286	410-663-5720	R	1*	<.1
243	CP Electronics Inc—Charles Parks	220 I 45 S, Huntsville TX 77340	936-295-0833	R	1*	<.1
244	Sound Image Audio and Video Design Group Ltd—Anthony Militello	3330 Earhart Dr Ste 10, Carrollton TX 75006	972-503-4434	R	1*	<.1
245	Audio Video International Ltd—David Dessing	1117 N Baldwin Ave, Marion IN 46952	765-662-9344	R	1*	<.1
246	Electronic Home Inc—Terry Massey	349 Peachtree Hils Ave, Atlanta GA 30305	404-231-0504	R	1*	<.1
247	Audio Elite Inc—Monica Houlihan	3330 E Hammer Ln Ste A, Stockton CA 95212	209-473-4100	R	1*	<.1
248	Dealer Electronic Services Inc—David Sykes	3325 N Hwy 17, Mount Pleasant SC 29466	843-881-6693	R	1*	<.1
249	Speaker Shop Inc—Edward Sullivan	3604 Main St, Amherst NY 14226	716-837-1557	R	1*	<.1
250	TV Woods Inc—Tycho Wood	PO Box 390, Mount Airy NC 27030	336-786-4191	R	1*	<.1
251	Stereotypes Inc—Carlos Gonzalez	550 N Nova Rd, Daytona Beach FL 32114	386-253-7093	R	1*	<.1
252	Global Interactive Solutions LLC—Claudia Kraft	1751 Fair Oak Way, Mableton GA 30126	404-699-2002	R	1*	<.1
253	Max Optical LLC—Leslie Kavanaugh	862 Horseshoe Pke, Downingtown PA 19335	610-269-7033	R	1*	<.1
254	Cpeck Inc—Mark Harris	6537 Market Dr, Gloucester VA 23061	804-695-1825	R	1*	<.1
255	CTL Electronics Inc—Chi-Tien Lui	45 Murray St, New York NY 10007	212-233-0754	R	1*	<.1
256	Wilson Entertainment Inc—Randy Wilson	6130 Melvin Ave, Tarzana CA 91356	818-783-7625	R	1*	<.1
257	C and C Communications—Cartis Carpenter	873 E Laurel Rd, London KY 40741	606-878-2658	R	1*	<.1
258	Soundwerks—Don Cikrduloo	2001 N Scottsdale Rd F, Scottsdale AZ 85257	480-303-0033	R	1*	<.1
259	Wireless Technologies Inc—Brad Toliver	3158 S 108th Ave Ste 2, Tulsa OK 74146	918-665-1244	R	1*	<.1
260	Sound Minds LLC	1800 Texas Ave, Shreveport LA 71103	318-869-0081	R	1*	<.1
261	Morgan Communications Inc—Michael Morgan	115 Greenwood Ave, Belle Vernon PA 15012	724-929-8422	R	1*	<.1
262	Audio Video Communication Store Inc—Arnaldo Hernandez	7500 Nw 25th St Unit 1, Miami FL 33122	305-717-0902	R	1*	<.1
263	Finchers Inc—Ben Fincher	520 N Main St, South Boston VA 24592	434-572-8966	R	1*	<.1
264	RF Applications Inc—Bruce Knox	9000 Tyler Blvd, Mentor OH 44060	440-974-1961	R	1*	<.1
265	Skeoch Waron Inc—Sean Waron	1720 W Elliot Rd Ste 1, Gilbert AZ 85233	480-926-1448	R	1*	<.1
266	King Antenna Inc—Henry Langan	6502 6th Ave, Brooklyn NY 11220	718-745-8200	R	1*	<.1
267	Suite Sounds Inc—Derek Smith	51 Bullet Hill Rd Ste, Southbury CT 06488	203-267-3008	R	<1*	<.1
268	Vital Communication Inc—David Asplin	PO Box 528, Marshfield WI 54449	715-387-1970	R	<1*	<.1
269	Expertech LLC	303 Quail Cir, West Bend WI 53095	262-306-8539	R	<1*	<.1
270	Expert Satellite Inc—Patrick Hudgin	150 Blackstone River R, Worcester MA 01607	508-752-7230	R	<1*	<.1
271	Burk Electronics—Wayne Burk	35 N Kensington Ave, La Grange IL 60525	708-482-9310	R	<1*	<.1
272	Li Hao—Hao Li	9600 Bellaire Blvd Ste, Houston TX 77036	713-988-5200	R	<1*	<.1
273	Smarthome Solutions Inc—Jeffrey Binette	86 York St Ste 1, Kennebunk ME 04043	207-985-9770	R	<1*	<.1
274	Knitec Inc—Eric Christiansen	140 Llokalani Ave Ste, Honolulu HI 96815		R	<1*	<.1
275	Mwa Speaker Parts Inc—Robert Hanshaw	PO Box 687, Vail AZ 85641	520-647-7193	R	<1*	<.1
276	Sharp Attitude Corp—Renato Viana	6025 NW 87th Ave, Miami FL 33178	305-717-3555	R	<1*	<.1
277	StereoVision Entertainment Inc—Jack Honour	15452 Cabrito Rd Ste 2, Van Nuys CA 91406	818-326-6018	P	<1	<.1

TOTALS: SIC 5731 Radio, Television & Electronics Stores

	Companies: 277				76,670	290.7

5734 Computer & Software Stores

Rank	Company Name—Executive Officer	Address, City, State, Zip	Phone	Type	Fin	Empls
1	GameStop Corp—J Paul Raines	625 Westport Pkwy, Grapevine TX 76051	817-424-2000	P	9,474	68.0
2	CompUSA Inc—Roman Ross	14951 N Dallas Pkwy, Dallas TX 75254	972-982-4000	S	3,340*	14.0
3	Electronics Boutique Holdings Corp GameStop Corp	625 Westport Pkwy, Grapevine TX 76051	817-424-2000	S	1,984	11.8
4	Micro Electronics Inc—Rick M Mershad	4119 Leap Rd, Hilliard OH 43026	614-850-3000	R	1,036*	2.6
5	Quill Computer Div—Mike Patriarca	100 Schelter Rd, Lincolnshire IL 60069		D	1,000*	.8
6	Tranzon Asset Strategies—Michael Walters	9980 Irvine Center Dr, Irvine CA 92618	949-398-6480	R	312	<.1
7	Gamestop—R Richard Fontaine GameStop Corp	625 Westport Pkwy, Grapevine TX 76051	817-424-2000	S	253*	3.5
8	Solunet Inc—Philip O'Reilly	7703 Technology Dr Ste, West Melbourne FL 32904	321-676-7947	S	166*	.1
9	Commercial Data Systems Inc—Mark Wong	50 S Beretania St C208, Honolulu HI 96813	808-527-2000	R	84*	.1
10	Technical Communities Inc—Peter Ostrow	1000 Cherry Ave Ste 10, San Bruno CA 94066	650-624-0525	R	72*	<.1
11	HarrisData—Lane Nelson	13555 Bishops Ct Ste 3, Brookfield WI 53005	262-784-9099	R	70*	.2
12	Print Inc—Charlene Malone	3015 112 Ave NE Ste 10, Bellevue WA 98004	425-822-6130	R	63*	.2
13	Computer Tech—Ming Chung	3910 FM1960 Rd W, Houston TX 77068	281-444-5566	R	58*	.2
14	Electronic Maintenance Company Inc—Janice H Pellar	8900 S Choctaw Dr, Baton Rouge LA 70815	225-925-8900	R	44*	.1
15	Baillio's Electronic and Appliance Connection—Jack Baillio	5301 Menaul Blvd NE, Albuquerque NM 87110	505-883-7511	R	41*	.1
16	Ross Capital Finance LLC	2710 W Lake St, Minneapolis MN 55416	612-929-9222	R	40*	<.1
17	PClaptops LLC—Dan Young	745 S State St, Salt Lake City UT 84111	801-596-7283	R	34*	.1
18	E-Max Group Inc—Anindya Seal	12070 Miramar Pkwy, Miramar FL 33025	954-843-0483	R	33*	.1
19	Resource One Computer Systems Inc—Stampp Corbin	1159 Dublin Rd, Columbus OH 43215	614-485-4800	R	31*	.1
20	Blizzard Digital Corp	64 Sailors Dr, Ellijay GA 30540	706-635-3703	R	30*	.1

Rank	Company Name—*Executive Officer*	Address, City, State, Zip	Phone	Type	Fin	Empls
21	TDX Tech—*David A Duhaime*	5735 Old Shakopee Rd W, Bloomington MN 55437	952-936-9280	R	30*	.1
22	Nexum—*David Lesser*	190 S LaSalle St, Chicago IL 60603	312-726-6900	R	30*	<.1
23	Calypso Technology Inc—*Charles Marston*	595 Market St, San Francisco CA 94105	415-817-2400	R	26*	.1
24	VoIP Supply LLC—*Benjamin P Sayer*	454 Sonwil Dr, Buffalo NY 14225	716-630-1555	R	25*	.1
25	Complete Computing Inc—*Dan Harpool*	400 W 7th St, Little Rock AR 72201	501-372-3379	R	25*	<.1
26	Alpha Computers Inc	14725 SW 72nd Ave, Tigard OR 97224	503-684-1111	R	24*	.1
27	Api Systems Inc—*Thomas Boller*	3117 State Rte 10 Ste, Denville NJ 07834	973-328-3328	R	24*	.3
28	Volusion Inc—*Kevin Sproles*	4100 Guardian St Ste 1, Simi Valley CA 93063		R	22*	.1
29	Creative Business Concepts Inc—*Gregg Stempson*	130 Vantis Ste 160, Aliso Viejo CA 92656	949-727-3104	R	22*	<.1
30	Ewiz Express Corp—*Ruiting Rao*	2079 N Capitol Ave, San Jose CA 95132	408-934-2500	R	20*	.1
31	Fogle Computing Corp—*John B Fogle*	PO Box 1045, Hendersonville NC 28793	828-697-9080	R	20*	<.1
32	Laser Printing Technologies Inc—*Sean Carey*	2500 Lexington Ave S, Mendota Heights MN 55120	952-888-7375	R	19*	.1
33	Netsolace Inc—*Tariq Farid*	95 Barnes Rd Ste 103, Wallingford CT 06492	203-907-4601	R	19*	<.1
34	Electronic Discount Sales Inc—*Randy Moore*	908 E Pioneer Pky, Arlington TX 76010	817-548-1992	R	18*	<.1
35	EBC Computers LLC—*Eduardo A Bedoya*	2698 S Redwood Rd Unit, Salt Lake City UT 84119	801-886-0100	R	18	.1
36	iCore Networks Inc—*Stephen G Canton*	7900 Westpark Dr Ste A, McLean VA 22102	703-673-1350	R	17*	.1
37	Midwest Technology Connection Inc—*Brett Littrell*	410 W 5th St, Kansas City MO 64105	816-471-3553	R	16*	.1
38	Pj Systems Inc—*Pei-Lin Tsai*	25 Drydock Ave Fl 6, Boston MA 02210	617-951-4650	R	15*	<.1
39	Stallard Technologies Inc—*James Stallard*	16041 Marty Cir, Overland Park KS 66085	913-851-2260	R	15*	<.1
40	Pashupati Ltd—*Vipin Jain*	7377 Convoy Ct Ste A, San Diego CA 92111	858-268-7370	R	15*	<.1
41	BESCO Computer Centers—*Dan Besco*	6205 Goddard, Shawnee KS 66203	913-268-7633	R	15*	<.1
42	Iatric Systems Inc—*Joel Berman*	27 Great Pond Dr, Boxford MA 01921	978-805-4101	R	14*	.2
43	Spectrum Computer Corp	12611 Hoover St, Garden Grove CA 92841	714-799-7345	R	14*	<.1
44	Desktop Darkroom Inc—*Joe Luter*	2916 University Blvd W, Jacksonville FL 32217	904-398-9934	R	13	<.1
45	Nextround Inc—*Vipul Minocha*	1881 Worcester Rd Ste, Framingham MA 01701	508-665-5200	R	13*	<.1
46	Pogo Linux Corp—*Jonathan Holmes*	8675 154th Ave Ne, Redmond WA 98052	425-898-2200	R	12*	<.1
47	Ignify Inc—*Sandeep Walia*	10900 183rd St Ste 285, Cerritos CA 90703	562-219-2000	R	11*	.1
48	Marketware Inc—*Darryl Johnson*	3840 Rosin Ct Ste 100, Sacramento CA 95834	916-925-3337	R	10*	<.1
49	Databranch—*David L Prince*	213 Prescott Ave, Elmira Heights NY 14903	607-733-8550	R	10*	<.1
50	Way Technology LLC—*Brian Way*	655 Leffingwell Ave, Saint Louis MO 63122	314-856-4020	R	10*	<.1
51	K2 Network Inc—*Joshua Hong*	6440 Oak Canyon Ste 20, Irvine CA 92618	949-870-3126	R	10*	.2
52	Connecting Point Inc—*Richard Mandell*	545 Stevens St, Medford OR 97504	541-773-9861	R	9*	.2
53	Metro Business Systems Inc—*Jeffrey Lorusso*	PO Box 4920, Stamford CT 06907	203-967-3435	R	9	<.1
54	Weird Stuff Inc—*Chuck W Schuetz*	384 W Caribbean Dr, Sunnyvale CA 94089	408-743-5650	R	9*	<.1
55	Computer 1 Products Of America Inc—*Elsa Argumedo*	11135 Rush St Ste A, South El Monte CA 91733	626-213-2400	R	9*	<.1
56	Anakam Inc—*Allan Camaisa*	1010 N Glebe Rd Ste 50, Arlington VA 22201	703-888-4600	S	8	<.1
57	Ultimate Technical Solutions—*David St Etienne*	651 Leson Ct, Harvey LA 70058	504-367-4957	R	8*	<.1
58	Neocomp Systems Inc—*James L Bailey*	21541 Nordhoff St Ste, Chatsworth CA 91311	818-700-8722	R	8*	<.1
59	Net Systems	1 Peters Canyon Ste 10, Irvine CA 92606	949-752-5100	R	8*	<.1
60	Hi and Low Computers Inc—*Walter Lin*	74 Hillside Ave, Williston Park NY 11596	516-349-8088	R	8*	<.1
61	Accountants World LLC—*Melvin Amir*	140 Fell Ct Ste 201, Hauppauge NY 11788	631-232-2669	R	7*	.1
62	Realage Inc—*Richard Benci*	5375 Mira Sorrento Pl, San Diego CA 92121	858-200-7171	R	7*	.1
63	Automotive Business Management Consultants Inc—*Bruce Weaver*	30500 State Hwy 181st, Spanish Fort AL 36527	251-626-8383	R	7*	.1
64	Grupocomp LLC	5225 E 22nd St, Tucson AZ 85711	520-546-2363	R	7*	<.1
65	Syracuse Computer Store Inc—*Thomas Karkowski*	6891 E Genesee St, Fayetteville NY 13066	315-446-5005	R	7*	<.1
66	A2Z Cables Inc—*Tetsuji Nakayama*	PO Box 283, Syracuse NY 13206	315-433-1200	R	7*	<.1
67	PC Treasures Inc—*Brian Austin*	1795 N Lapeer Rd, Oxford MI 48371	240-960 7800	R	7*	<.1
68	Workshare Technology Inc—*Alan Fraser*	208 Utah St Ste 350, San Francisco CA 94103	415-901-9022	R	7*	.1
69	Teammark International Inc—*Faye Rona*	PO Box 641204, San Jose CA 95164	408-428-0900	R	6*	<.1
70	LogicalsolutionsNet Inc—*James Salviski*	1100 Pittsford Victor, Pittsford NY 14534	585-244-9930	R	6*	.1
71	Dalet Digital Media Systems USA Inc—*Stephane Guez*	110 Wall St Lbby 2, New York NY 10005	212-269-6700	R	6*	.1
72	AudiomidiCom—*Russ Jones*	9240 Deering Ave, Chatsworth CA 91311	818-993-0772	R	6*	<.1
73	Atiam Technologies LP—*Jeffery Brocco*	1510 Chester Pke Ste 1, Eddystone PA 19022	610-872-6800	R	6*	.1
74	Right Ascension Inc—*John D'arcangelo*	2140 Woodland Rd, Warrendale PA 15086	724-625-0299	R	6*	.1
75	PowerON Services Inc—*Brent Kelley*	8801 Washington Blvd S, Roseville CA 95678	916-677-6227	R	6*	<.1
76	DI-NO Computers Inc—*Sal Cordaro*	2091 E Colorado Blvd, Pasadena CA 91107	626-795-6674	R	6*	<.1
77	Computer Supply Supermarket—*Sandra Seltzer*	21540 Prairie St Unit, Chatsworth CA 91311	818-407-1555	R	6*	<.1
78	DavTech Computer Center—*Michael Simanian*	914 S Victory Blvd, Burbank CA 91502	213-977-9000	R	6*	<.1
79	Envoy Data Corp—*Sandra Ciraulo*	1310 W Boxwood Ave, Gilbert AZ 85233	480-829-6565	R	6*	<.1
80	EIMS Ltd—*Peter Vigliano*	14121 W Hwy 290 Bldg 4, Austin TX 78737	512-858-7622	R	6*	<.1
81	CA 2000—*Carlo Boscaino*	82 Wall St Ste 1105, New York NY 10005	212-271-2235	R	6*	.1
82	Prine Systems Inc—*Jeremy Prine*	140 Stockton St, Jacksonville FL 32204	904-854-9283	R	6*	<.1
83	Computer SI Corp—*Gerard Manna*	22 High St, Norwalk CT 06851	203-855-0101	R	6*	.1
84	Mike Collins and Associates Inc—*Thomas Collins*	6048 Century Oaks Dr, Chattanooga TN 37416	423-892-8899	R	6*	.1
85	Tech Depot Inc—*Don Greece*	1433 Hooper Ave Ste 13, Toms River NJ 08753	732-557-7575	R	6*	.1
86	Teres Solutions Inc—*Tim Kelly*	12365 Riata Trce B, Austin TX 78727	512-218-4200	R	6*	.1
87	Document Imaging Dimensions Inc—*Sylvia Underhill*	1213 S Bridge St, Yorkville IL 60560	630-553-3131	R	6*	<.1
88	Dc Consultants Inc—*Greg Herting*	2025 E Dorothy Ln, Dayton OH 45420	937-643-2667	R	6*	<.1
89	Superlative Technologies Inc—*Tk Gil*	45195 Research Pl, Ashburn VA 20147	703-821-3732	R	5*	.1
90	FrozencpuCom Inc—*Mark Friga*	311 E Chestnut St, East Rochester NY 14445	585-218-0120	R	5*	<.1
91	Nieto Computer Services LLC—*Luis Nieto*	6 N Chantsong Cir, Spring TX 77382	281-362-7218	R	5*	.1
92	Health Solutions Plus Inc—*John Buser*	130 Maple Ave Ste 7b, Red Bank NJ 07701	732-758-1666	R	5*	<.1
93	Computer Data Inc—*James T Weyand*	29229 Franklin Rd, Southfield MI 48034	248-544-9900	R	5*	<.1
94	E-Convergence Solutions LLC	15023 Greymont Dr 100, Centreville VA 20120	703-815-8828	R	5*	<.1
95	Dv Warehouse Inc—*Mohsen Joukar*	747 Seward St, Los Angeles CA 90038	323-463-5005	R	5*	<.1
96	Colossus Technology Inc—*David Taheri*	1012 W Beverly Blvd St, Montebello CA 90640	323-838-5599	R	5*	<.1
97	Holland Computers Inc—*William Holland*	483 N Abbe Rd, Elyria OH 44035	440-365-9906	R	5*	.1
98	KSI Computer Centers—*Michael Setz*	610 B Bidwell St, Folsom CA 95630	916-984-1941	R	5*	<.1
99	Custom Computer Inc—*Reid Meyers*	1501 W Main St Ste B, Ephrata PA 17522	717-733-2231	R	5*	<.1
100	CyberWarehouse—*Robert S Beckit*	896-J Plaza Blvd, Lancaster PA 17601	717-391-8220	R	5*	.1
101	Macwest Associates Inc—*William Gates*	481 W Sopris Creek Rd, Basalt CO 81621	970-927-4541	R	5*	<.1
102	Ncal Computer Source Inc—*Jose Olivera*	4825 Hopyard Rd Ste 18, Pleasanton CA 94588	925-460-0580	R	5*	<.1
103	Tech Advanced Computers Inc—*Chiu Tan*	1508 Creighton Rd, Pensacola FL 32504	850-479-9227	R	5*	<.1
104	Tec Electronic Component Inc—*Thomas Leong*	1134 49th Ave, Long Island City NY 11101	212-627-8008	R	5*	<.1
105	Eastern Computer Exchange Inc—*Brendan Lynch*	105 Cascade Blvd, Milford CT 06460	203-877-4334	R	5*	<.1
106	Teogas Inc—*David Browning*	15265 Alton Pkwy Ste 3, Irvine CA 92618	949-777-0400	R	5*	<.1
107	RC Electronics International Inc—*Rudolph Corrales*	1590 N Lakeview Ave, Anaheim CA 92807	714-379-3632	R	5*	<.1
108	Alpha Data Systems Inc—*Charles Bond*	2001 Thomasville Rd, Tallahassee FL 32308	850-385-7000	R	5*	<.1
109	Information Networks Inc—*Robert Sloat*	21 Charles St Fl 3, Westport CT 06880	203-226-3367	R	5*	.1

Note: An asterisk (*) indicates an estimated financial figure. The company type code used is as follows: R = Private, P = Public, S = Private Subsidiary, B = Public Subsidiary, D = Division, J = Joint Venture, I = Investment Fund.

COMPANY RANKINGS BY SALES WITHIN 4-DIGIT SIC

Rank	Company Name—Executive Officer	Address, City, State, Zip	Phone	Type	Fin	Empls
110	Tameran Graphic Systems Inc—Mark Wise	30340 Solon Industrial, Solon OH 44139	440-349-7100	R	5*	.1
111	Argon Office Supplies—Tina Mark	1731 Adrian Rd Ste 2, Burlingame CA 94010	650-552-9965	R	5*	<.1
112	Showroom Solutions Inc—Mark Bellissimo	1819 Denver W Dr Ste 4, Lakewood CO 80401	303-788-9970	R	4*	<.1
113	Mary Thureson—Chris Booth	1902 Hoquiam Pl Ne, Renton WA 98059	425-271-9818	R	4*	.1
114	Benecom Computer Company Inc—David Benedic	4140 Poche Ct W, New Orleans LA 70129	504-254-1441	R	4*	<.1
115	Tcw Computer Systems Inc—Lamar Weaver	254 S Esbenshade Rd, Manheim PA 17545	717-653-2700	R	4*	<.1
116	Porter Lee Corp—Tim Smith	1901 Wright Blvd, Schaumburg IL 60193	847-985-2060	R	4*	<.1
117	Specialty Enterprise Inc—Jon Cohen	720 W 121st Ave, Westminster CO 80234	303-252-1997	R	4*	<.1
118	One Point Solutions Inc—Ron Flannery	43422 W Oaks Dr Ste 29, Novi MI 48377	248-887-8470	R	4*	<.1
119	H 2 Computers Inc—James Habel	739 N Easton Rd Ste 20, Doylestown PA 18902	215-345-4411	R	4*	<.1
120	Radio Adventures Corp—Lisa Groner	2803 State Rte 257, Seneca PA 16346	814-677-2447	R	4*	<.1
121	1099 Pro—Raymond Stewart	23901 Calabasas Rd Ste, Calabasas CA 91302	818-876-0200	R	4*	<.1
122	Swift Office Solutions Inc—Edward Swift	2429 W 12th St Ste 6, Tempe AZ 85281	480-966-2100	R	4*	<.1
123	LA Computer Center—Harry Neman	463 N Oak St, Inglewood CA 90302		R	4*	<.1
124	Nothing But NET—Robert Cox	4500 S Lakeshore Dr, Tempe AZ 85282	480-222-6020	R	4*	<.1
125	Singular Solutions Inc—Steve Klein	448 S Santa Anita Ave, Pasadena CA 91107	626-792-9567	R	4*	<.1
126	Today's Technology—Rodney Kay	1126 S Ash St, Buffalo MO 65622	417-345-8810	R	4*	<.1
127	Digital Entertainment Systems Inc—Kevin Lambidonis	2349 W Hudson Rd, Rogers AR 72756	479-621-8889	R	4*	<.1
128	US Micro PC Inc—John Lotzkar	13600 Ne 20th St Ste C, Bellevue WA 98005	425-462-7300	R	4*	<.1
129	cyberLaptopscom—Cristina Fandino	1636 R St NW Fl 2, Washington DC 20009	202-462-7195	R	4*	<.1
130	ThePowerXChange LLC—Cyndie Shaffstall	PO Box 2049, Wheat Ridge CO 80034	303-940-0600	R	4*	<.1
131	Twin Cities Digital Inc—Bob Leach	3550 W 145th St, Burnsville MN 55306	952-895-0522	R	4*	<.1
132	Dti Integrated Business Solutions Inc—Charles White	PO Box 18254, Greensboro NC 27419	336-346-1580	R	4*	<.1
133	Southwest Business Machines Inc—Kevin Stockert	564 23rd Ave E, Dickinson ND 58601	701-225-3213	R	4*	<.1
134	ValleycomputerNet - LLC—Brian Nunn	1830 W Caldwell Ave St, Visalia CA 93277	559-627-8324	R	4*	<.1
135	Sunnking Inc—Duane Beckett	4 Owens Rd, Brockport NY 14420	585-637-8365	R	4*	<.1
136	T and K Holdings Inc—Tim Riddle	1201 N Watson Rd Ste 1, Arlington TX 76006	817-640-0016	R	4*	<.1
137	Pcfs 2000 Inc—Robert Cota	259 S Randolph Ave Ste, Brea CA 92821	714-674-0009	R	4*	<.1
138	Tristar Inc—Pat Maderia	3740 E La Salle St, Phoenix AZ 85040	602-333-1600	R	4*	<.1
139	Qlvs Inc—Alan Cox	3910 S Georgia St, Amarillo TX 79109	806-355-7466	R	4*	<.1
140	Computer Performance Inc—Martin Bodo	2695 Walsh Ave, Santa Clara CA 95051	408-588-1110	R	4*	<.1
141	Dps Infrastructure Monitoring Systems Inc—Robert Kent	PO Box 1268, Oxford GA 30054	770-498-9622	R	4*	<.1
142	Aque Computers Inc—Floyd Jones	2156 W 108th St, Los Angeles CA 90047	213-447-1174	R	4*	<.1
143	PC Products and Services Inc—Amar Nuggehalli	25w217 Lake St, Roselle IL 60172	630-307-7600	R	4*	<.1
144	TcsnNet Inc—Arnie Fitton	1306 Pine St Ste B, Paso Robles CA 93446	805-237-2271	R	4*	<.1
145	Wayne Reaves Computer Systems Inc—Wayne Reaves	6211 Thomaston Rd, Macon GA 31220	478-474-8779	R	4*	<.1
146	Coffman Computer Consultants—Paul Coffman	Rr 1 Box 327, Cookville TN 75558	903-572-1322	R	3*	.1
147	Computer Works Of Arkansas Inc—Pat Wilson	PO Box 2620, Conway AR 72033	501-329-9144	R	3*	<.1
148	Mcr Technologies Inc—Thomas Speropolous	6 Greenwood St, Wakefield MA 01880	781-245-6644	R	3*	<.1
149	Connectwise Inc—Arnold Bellini	2803 W Busch Blvd Ste, Tampa FL 33618	813-935-7100	R	3*	<.1
150	Computer Warranty Services LLC—Bill Crawford	PO Box 1953, Leander TX 78646	214-224-0440	R	3*	.1
151	X Inc—Marx Acosta-Rubio	6800 Owensmouth Ave St, Canoga Park CA 91303	818-703-6111	R	3*	<.1
152	Microworks Pos Solutions Inc—Scott Paratore	2112 Empire Blvd Ste 2, Webster NY 14580	585-787-2058	R	3*	<.1
153	Westwind Computing Inc—Michael Koidahl	PO Box 27859, Seattle WA 98165	206-522-3530	R	3*	<.1
154	Bader Corp—Tina Bader	8780 Big Bend Blvd Ste, Saint Louis MO 03119	314-918-7600	R	3*	<.1
155	Diversified Imaging Supplies Inc—Alexis Denholtz	1740 Skyway Dr Ste B, Longmont CO 80504	303-554-9551	R	3*	<.1
156	Sirenic Inc—G Vachon	2109 Landings Dr, Mountain View CA 94043	650-691-1512	R	3*	<.1
157	Rogers Software Development Inc—Matt Rogers	1292 Sadler Way 2nd Fl, Fairbanks AK 99701	907-458-1001	R	3*	.1
158	Complete Tablet Solutions Ltd—James Bainter	3290 E Spring St, Long Beach CA 90806	562-216-7170	R	3*	<.1
159	Sendouts LLC—Cynthia Brand	200 S Hanley Rd Ste 71, Saint Louis MO 63105	314-862-6883	R	3*	<.1
160	Vanguard Computers Inc—Deborah Smith	13100 W Lisbon Rd Ste, Brookfield WI 53005	262-317-1900	R	3*	<.1
161	Medical Data Information Services Inc—Stephen Fosnot	417 Caredean Dr Ste E, Horsham PA 19044	215-672-9367	R	3*	<.1
162	Computer Gate International—Glen Shih	2995 Gordon Ave Ste A, Santa Clara CA 95051	408-730-0673	S	3*	<.1
163	Morse Micro Solutions Inc—Robert Morse	16106 Jewel Ave, Fresh Meadows NY 11365	207-807-4424	R	3*	<.1
164	Pembroke's Inc—Mike Pembroke	47 S Orange St Rm A-8, Salt Lake City UT 84116	801-521-0450	R	3*	<.1
165	Abacus 24-7 LLC—Jason Zaffron	2990 E Northern Ave St, Phoenix AZ 85028	602-787-1223	R	3*	<.1
166	Quick Electronics Inc—Joyce Kozz	10800 76th Ct N, Largo FL 33777	727-546-9299	R	3*	<.1
167	New Age Electronics—Jim Edwards	420 S 10th Ave, Sterling CO 80751	970-522-2763	R	3*	<.1
168	Mac Guys—Mike Siegrist	670 W 17th St Unit G1, Costa Mesa CA 92627	949-645-4022	R	3*	<.1
169	Borough Park Computer Center Inc—Stanley Furst	5404 New Utrecht Ave S, Brooklyn NY 11219	718-686-0909	R	3*	<.1
170	Rodbard and Associates—Larry S Robdard	723 Pleasant Hill Rd, Ellicott City MD 21043	410-461-1022	R	3*	<.1
171	Dial Sound Data Systems—Dan Lavi	45554 Industrial Pl Un, Fremont CA 94538	510-656-9788	R	3*	<.1
172	Doty Computers—Debbie Doty	309 A Ave E, Oskaloosa IA 52577	641-673-4173	R	3*	<.1
173	AGO Insurance Software Inc—Larry Martin	200 Valley Rd Ste 208, Mount Arlington NJ 07856	973-770-3200	R	3*	<.1
174	Bsc Supply LLC—Jaime Macfall	411 Waverley Oaks Rd S, Waltham MA 02452	781-893-1299	R	3*	<.1
175	California Computer Center Corp—Kaveh Jebeli	3930 Broadway Pl, Los Angeles CA 90037	213-689-0808	R	3*	<.1
176	Medtech Inc—Dan Kloepper	180 S Weidman Rd Ste 1, Ballwin MO 63021	636-207-0277	R	3*	<.1
177	Trimark Computer Systems Inc—James Berger	5250 W Century Blvd St, Los Angeles CA 90045	310-417-8651	R	3*	<.1
178	Potentials Management Corp—Mary Lou Mc Call	PO Box 96, Delmar NY 12054	518-439-1158	R	3*	<.1
179	Los Altos PC Inc—Wilson Ng	334 State St Ste 109, Los Altos CA 94022	650-949-3451	R	3*	<.1
180	Taxware Systems Inc—King Dalton	924 W 9th St, Upland CA 91786	909-931-3131	R	3*	<.1
181	Integra Consulting and Computer Services Inc—David Antar	1490 N Clinton Ave, Bay Shore NY 11706	631-969-2500	R	3*	<.1
182	Softpacific—Don Taylor	27265 Darlene Dr, Moreno Valley CA 92555	951-242-0454	R	3*	<.1
183	Brandsway International Inc—Zia Khwaja	19 Harbor Park Dr, Port Washington NY 11050	516-484-7600	R	3*	<.1
184	Mediasouth Computer Supplies Inc—John Dress	6021 Live Oak Pkwy, Norcross GA 30093	770-242-6200	R	3*	<.1
185	Educational Learning Systems Inc—Ken Hodges	2874 Remington Green C, Tallahassee FL 32308	850-386-3708	R	3*	<.1
186	Brighten Technologies LLC—Yusuf Duzgun	11000 S Wilcrest Dr, Houston TX 77099	281-495-2004	R	3*	<.1
187	Atlantic Digital Inc—Mark Mcclain	PO Box 2138, Ann Arbor MI 48106	734-995-8989	R	3*	<.1
188	Capture 3d Inc—Richard White	3505 Cadillac Ave Ste, Costa Mesa CA 92626	714-546-7278	R	3*	<.1
189	Turnkey Computer Systems Inc—Steve Myers	PO Box 51630, Amarillo TX 79159	806-372-1200	R	3*	<.1
190	Newleads Inc—John Hasbrouck	5740 Ralston St Ste 30, Ventura CA 93003	805-658-3330	R	3*	<.1
191	Florida Medical Computers Inc—Gary Kurstin	1650 S Powerline Rd St, Deerfield Beach FL 33442	954-426-8002	R	3*	<.1
192	PC Enterprises Inc—Kirk Birrell	138 Memorial Ave Ste 3, West Springfield MA 01089	413-736-2112	R	3*	<.1
193	Bundy Typewriter Co—Arnold Foley	1809 Chestnut St, Philadelphia PA 19103	215-567-2500	R	3*	<.1
194	Netscada Inc—Dave Dixon	108 Kol Dr, Broussard LA 70518	337-839-1020	R	3*	<.1
195	Mirabilis Design Inc—Deepak Shankar	798 S Bernardo Ave Ste, Sunnyvale CA 94087	408-245-8552	R	3*	<.1
196	Dan Pedone Inc—Dan Pedone	110 N Main St, Victoria TX 77901	361-575-6886	R	3*	<.1
197	Definiens Inc—Thomas Heydler	1719 State Rt 10 Ste 1, Parsippany NJ 07054	973-457-7150	R	3*	<.1
198	Ics Service Of Miami Florida Corp—Francisco Herreo	7120 Nw 72nd Ave, Miami FL 33166	305-888-3007	R	3*	<.1
199	Cimcorp USA LLC—Hamilton Fonte	8215 Nw 64th St Unit 5, Miami FL 33166	305-392-9923	R	3*	<.1

Rank	Company Name—Executive Officer	Address, City, State, Zip	Phone	Type	Fin	Empls
200	Big Huge Games Inc—Brian Reynolds	1954 Greenspring Dr St, Lutherville Timonium MD 21093	410-842-0033	R	2*	<.1
201	Advanced Computer Products Inc—David Freeman	3621 W Warner Ave, Santa Ana CA 92704	714-558-8822	R	2*	<.1
202	Mahrenholtz Inc—Al Prosuk	271 Grove Ave Ste G, Verona NJ 07044	973-239-3147	R	2*	<.1
203	V Tech Industrial Corp—Yuko Takano	17 Leslie Ct, Whippany NJ 07981	973-887-1447	R	2*	<.1
204	Mark Bolles—Mark Bolles	PO Box 926, Pflugerville TX 78691	512-990-1188	R	2*	<.1
205	Action Computers Inc—Alain Breyer	2890 S Colorado Blvd S, Denver CO 80222	303-759-1668	R	2*	<.1
206	Ztrace Inc—Alexander Kesler	411 Waverley Oaks Rd S, Waltham MA 02452	781-891-1328	R	2*	<.1
207	Counterpoint Systems—Scott Herring	11835 W Olympic Blvd S, Los Angeles CA 90064	310-473-0200	R	2*	<.1
208	Algorithmic Implementations Inc—David Wu	PO Box 669, Manchester Center VT 05255	802-362-3612	R	2*	<.1
209	Data Staff Inc—Kevin Weiss	152 Lorraine Dr, Lake Zurich IL 60047	312-683-1144	R	2*	<.1
210	Madison Computer Corp—Michael Yao	310 5th Ave Fl 2, New York NY 10001	212-679-1088	R	2*	<.1
211	Delta Management and Distribution Inc—Mike Kell	445 Park Ave Ste 1000, New York NY 10022	917-254-0400	R	2*	<.1
212	Telemach Information International Inc—Emanuel Fourakis	830 E Cub Hunt Ln, West Chester PA 19380	610-429-2962	R	2*	<.1
213	Digital Innovation Inc—John Kutcher	134 Industry Ln Ste 3, Forest Hill MD 21050	410-838-4034	R	2*	<.1
214	Computer Direct Outlet LLC—Tad Dodds	2382 Laurens Rd, Greenville SC 29607	864-288-8680	R	2*	<.1
215	Data Seek Corp—Frank Jarzombek	PO Box 791138, San Antonio TX 78279	210-308-0202	R	2*	<.1
216	Nationwide Electronics Inc—Kim Yung	PO Box 5177, West Covina CA 91791	714-529-7801	R	2*	<.1
217	Kiernan Consulting Inc—David Kiernan	120 N Fraternity Ln, Whitewater WI 53190	262-473-1064	R	2*	<.1
218	Progressive Computer Service Inc—Ralph Hirsch	6229 Olentangy River R, Worthington OH 43085	614-880-4466	R	2*	<.1
219	LA Data Systems LLC—Tom Duke	1825 Surveyor Ave Ste, Simi Valley CA 93063	805-526-1603	R	2*	<.1
220	Nintex USA LLC—Mark Mcdermott	600 106th Ave Ne Ste 2, Bellevue WA 98004	425-201-5840	R	2*	<.1
221	Integration Systems LLC—Derek Keene	350 Fairway Dr Ste 110, Deerfield Beach FL 33441	954-725-0006	R	2*	<.1
222	Fredricdorf John—John Fredricdorf	7218 Joy Marie Ln, Waterford WI 53185	262-662-3735	R	2*	<.1
223	Reality Digital Inc—Cynthia Francis	49 Stevenson St Ste 80, San Francisco CA 94105	415-644-4601	R	2*	<.1
224	Total Computer Systems Inc—Stafford Jones	PO Box 12665, Gainesville FL 32604	352-377-4145	R	2*	<.1
225	Wolfe Rf And Associates Inc—S Blackerby	2152 Springdale Rd, Bessemer AL 35022	205-425-8158	R	2*	<.1
226	Powel Inc—Jesse Houser	720 Main St Ste 201, Mendota Heights MN 55118	651-251-3005	R	2*	<.1
227	Universal Data Inc—Charles Phyle	4150 Grange Hall Rd, Holly MI 48442	248-634-4000	R	2	<.1
228	FairCom Corp—Ray A Brown	6300 W Sugar Creek Dr, Columbia MO 65203	573-445-6833	R	2*	<.1
229	Accunet Solutions Inc—Alan Dumas	20 Park Plz Ste 444, Boston MA 02116	617-867-0281	R	2*	<.1
230	Debco Electronics Inc—Debra Case	3931 Edwards Rd, Cincinnati OH 45209	513-531-4499	R	2*	<.1
231	Bmi Associates Inc—Boyd Mortensen	475 N 300 W Ste 5, Kaysville UT 84037	801-546-7462	R	2*	<.1
232	Wong's Advanced Technologies Inc—Shing Wong	1340 Poydras St Ste 34, New Orleans LA 70112	504-962-2000	R	2*	<.1
233	Geek City Electronics Inc—Brad Jones	418 3rd St Ste 2, Fairbanks AK 99701	907-455-7281	R	2*	<.1
234	PCW Computer—Jc Chang	565 Boston Post Rd, Orange CT 06477	203-799-0431	R	2*	<.1
235	Ireland Technologies Inc—Gary Voss	PO Box 25, Cedar Falls IA 50613	319-268-8324	R	2*	<.1
236	Brocomp Inc—Lynn Breaux	PO Box 9166, New Iberia LA 70562	337-364-4777	R	2*	<.1
237	Practical Vision LLC	4398 Cove Island Dr Ne, Marietta GA 30067	678-560-2468	R	2*	<.1
238	A-2-Z Solutions Inc—Larry Garroway	5982 Las Colinas Cir, Lake Worth FL 33463	561-967-4646	R	2*	<.1
239	Bootsector Industries Inc—Pete Rizzo	171 Unit B Eads St, West Babylon NY 11704	631-249-2700	R	2*	<.1
240	Ink Solutions LLC Eduardo Seyffert	1212 N Yarbrough Dr St, El Paso TX 79925	915-591-2423	R	2*	<.1
241	Laptops Plus Inc—Richard D Conner	955 S Orlando Ave, Winter Park FL 32789	407-740-7587	R	2*	<.1
242	MicroQuill Software Publishing Inc—Scott Kralik	10512 NE 68th St Ste 1, Kirkland WA 98033	425-827-7200	R	2*	<.1
243	BC Technologies—Benjamin Shaw	1 N Main St, Mansfield PA 16933	570-662-7990	R	2*	<.1
244	Hardin Computers—Louis Hardin	4000 Five Points Blvd, Arlington TX 76018	817-572-2775	R	2*	<.1
245	ASYM Technologies—Jacques Couture	924 Carl Rd, Lafayette CA 94549	925-943-6157	R	2*	<.1
246	Cajun Computers—Michael Richard	625 Front St Ste B, Evanston WY 82930	307-789-8145	R	2*	<.1
247	East Coast Computers—Frank P Cirillo Jr	400 N DuPont Hwy Ste G, Dover DE 19901	302-674-4537	R	2*	<.1
248	Nmedia Systems Inc—Jenny Chen	5051 Stone Canyon Dr, Castro Valley CA 94552	510-886-6338	R	2*	<.1
249	Direct Technology Group Inc—Frazer Langley	5101 Nw 21st Ave Ste 1, Fort Lauderdale FL 33309	954-739-4700	R	2*	<.1
250	Northeast Laser Image Of New England Inc—Wilfred Johnson	PO Box 41449, Providence RI 02940	401-431-5233	R	2*	<.1
251	American Information Technology Solutions LLC	420 Ctr St, Wallingford CT 06492	203-269-1900	R	2*	<.1
252	Strategy 7 Corp—Joseph Rodriguez	3306 Wiley Post Rd Ste, Carrollton TX 75006	972-560-9201	R	2*	<.1
253	Forest Scientific Corp—John Martincic	408 Emert Rd, Tionesta PA 16353	814-463-5006	R	2*	<.1
254	Handheld4me Inc—Mike Enkerlin	12265 World Trade Dr B, San Diego CA 92128	858-385-1976	R	2*	<.1
255	Kiwi Tek LLC—Mark Wagner	11611 N Meridian St St, Carmel IN 46032	317-571-3440	R	2*	<.1
256	Traeger Inc—Raymond Traeger	4202 Glenmore Ave, Baltimore MD 21206	410-254-0283	R	2*	<.1
257	Max Glide Inc—Denton Meier	11 Spokane St Ste 100, Wenatchee WA 98801	509-663-7082	R	2*	<.1
258	Rose Systems Corp—Sergio Monarrez	11450 Rojas Dr Ste D6, El Paso TX 79936	915-772-4994	R	2*	<.1
259	Brick Street Software Inc—Christopher Maeda	215 S Broadway 241, Salem NH 03079	603-912-0046	R	2*	<.1
260	Gnd Systems—Greg Delong	PO Box 1004, Nashville IN 47448	812-988-2125	R	2*	<.1
261	Pcretro Inc—Robert Sergant	6901 Distribution Dr, Beltsville MD 20705	301-937-8440	R	2*	<.1
262	Sarga Solutions Inc—Madhu Kumar	2515 Isham Randolph Dr, Herndon VA 20171	703-793-5911	R	2*	<.1
263	Jsc Global Solutions Inc—Naresh Jain	24w500 Maple Ave Ste 2, Naperville IL 60540	630-961-5246	R	2*	<.1
264	Mac Pro Systems and Software—Mike Ajlouny	3585 Stevens Creek Blv, San Jose CA 95117	408-554-0555	R	2*	<.1
265	Computer Software Plus Inc—Ike Abady	1722 Kings Hwy, Brooklyn NY 11229	718-645-1880	R	2*	<.1
266	Byteside Computer Services—Reine Mcintosh	PO Box 231, Kiester MN 56051	763-684-3908	R	2*	<.1
267	Dahl Robins and Associates Inc—Kevin Dahl	1560 S 5th Ave, Yuma AZ 85364	928-819-0825	R	2*	<.1
268	Greenprint Technologies LLC—Hayden Hamilton	115 NW 1st Ave Ste 200, Portland OR 97209	503-241-0818	R	2*	<.1
269	Softmems LLC	2391 Nobili Ave, Santa Clara CA 95051	408-426-4301	R	2*	<.1
270	Herman Street—Jerry Ropelato	181 S 600 W, Ogden UT 84404		R	2*	<.1
271	Intuitive Computers Inc—Craig Hirai	4709 Chase Ave, Bethesda MD 20814	301-907-0300	R	2*	<.1
272	Cherry And Cherry Games Inc—Jerry Cherry	4465 Nw 50th St, Oklahoma City OK 73112	405-942-6610	R	2*	<.1
273	Harvest Solutions Inc—Sidney Lejfer	1050 Winter St Ste 100, Waltham MA 02451	781-530-3736	R	2*	<.1
274	Vermont Panurgy Corp—Curtis Trousdale	21 Gregory Dr Ste 3, South Burlington VT 05403	802-658-7788	R	2*	<.1
275	Fastcam Inc—Mathew Fagen	8700 W Bryn Mawr Ave, Chicago IL 60631	312-715-1535	R	2*	<.1
276	Atr Distributing Inc—James Murray	PO Box 85, Cleves OH 45002	513-353-1800	R	2*	<.1
277	T and T Int'l Inc—Kenneth Reabdean	81 Sheltingham Box C, Schenectady NY 12306	518-356-4381	R	2*	<.1
278	Computer Customware Inc—Randy Verble	5757c Atlanta Hwy, Montgomery AL 36117	334-271-0179	R	2*	<.1
279	Knowtions Inc—Karl Rauch	6 Forest Ave Ste 6b, Paramus NJ 07652	201-334-0332	R	2*	<.1
280	New England Electronics and Technology Corp—Victoria Lin	15 Highland St, Tyngsboro MA 01879	978-649-9580	R	2*	<.1
281	HL Computer Inc—Henry Nuyen	1525 E Park Pl Blvd St, Stone Mountain GA 30087	770-879-7989	R	2*	<.1
282	Host Engineering Inc—Robert Oglesby	593 Aa Deakins Rd, Jonesborough TN 37659	423-913-2587	R	2*	<.1
283	International Systems Management Inc—Tom Kuipers	5824 Peachtree Cors E, Norcross GA 30092	770-840-8994	R	2*	<.1
284	J and B Technologies Ltd—John Kistler	180 Weldon Pkwy, Maryland Heights MO 63043	314-993-5528	R	2*	<.1
285	Rvf Investments Group Inc—Rich Flieger	7254 N Oracle Rd, Tucson AZ 85704	520-888-8100	R	2*	<.1
286	Tab Consulting Inc—Tony Berendes	3200 E Trent Ave Ste 3, Spokane WA 99202	509-232-4040	R	2*	<.1
287	Mass Computer Systems Inc—Ronald Stodden	306 S 4th St, Effingham IL 62401	217-342-4976	R	2*	<.1
288	Penn Systems Group Inc—Stephen Brooks	PO Box 417, Edgemont PA 19028	610-353-3800	R	2*	<.1
289	Pc-N-U Inc—Hsia Huang	2154 County Line Rd, Huntingdon Valley PA 19006	215-396-8968	R	2*	<.1

Note: An asterisk (*) indicates an estimated financial figure. The company type code used is as follows: R = Private, P = Public, S = Private Subsidiary, B = Public Subsidiary, D = Division, J = Joint Venture, I = Investment Fund.

RANKINGS BY SALES WITHIN 4-DIGIT SIC

	Company Name—Executive Officer	Address, City, State, Zip	Phone	Type	Fin	Empls
290	S and Z Enterprises Inc—Jim Stewart	1686 S Lost Trl Dr, Walnut CA 91789	909-923-6124	R	2*	<.1
291	Mpak Technologies Inc—Michael Kornblum	9260 Isaac St Ste D, Santee CA 92071	619-749-6437	R	2*	<.1
292	Teck Solutions Inc—Teck Khor	PO Box 221, Iron Mountain MI 49801	906-774-8808	R	2*	<.1
293	Option Technologies Inc—James Mclaughlin	2404 Northline Industr, Maryland Heights MO 63043	314-991-6000	R	2*	<.1
294	Michiana Accounting Solutions Inc—Stuart Phillips	PO Box 15612, Fort Wayne IN 46885	260-748-4866	R	2*	<.1
295	Sunops Inc—Henry Faris	6985 Via Del Oro Ste B, San Jose CA 95119	408-445-1455	R	2*	<.1
296	Ace Computers and Telecom Inc—Lyle Simon	6 Commercial Blvd Ste, Novato CA 94949	415-883-9264	R	2*	<.1
297	Qc Plus Computer Inc—Nani Wu	1411 E Campbell Rd Ste, Richardson TX 75081	972-644-7536	R	2*	<.1
298	Finta Corp—Szabolcs Finta	4060 Peachtree Rd Ste, Atlanta GA 30319	678-618-8196	R	2*	<.1
299	Linda Sue Sandidge—Linda Sandidge	PO Box 6594, Carmel CA 93921	831-626-6885	R	2*	<.1
300	Vast Data Systems Inc—Sheryl Bell	6136 Frisco Sq Blvd, Frisco TX 75034	214-227-8735	R	2*	<.1
301	Roger Shaw and Associates—Roger Shaw	423 Woodland Dr, Lewisville TX 75077	940-241-2808	R	2*	<.1
302	Csp Enterprises—Brian Vesper	8709 Reichs Ford Rd, Frederick MD 21704	301-695-9517	R	1*	<.1
303	AB Computer LLC—Nelson Cecilee	7324 Union Park Ave St, Midvale UT 84047	801-565-9199	R	1*	<.1
304	Delasoft Inc—Satish Bola	2200 S Main St Ste 302, Lombard IL 60148	630-620-8188	R	1*	<.1
305	Strategic Reporting Systems Inc—Phil Adams	83 Pine St Section D, Peabody MA 01960	978-531-0905	R	1*	<.1
306	Data Processing Consultants Inc—David Parker	1116 Woodbern Ln, Tallahassee FL 32304	850-575-0745	R	1*	<.1
307	Interlink Computers Inc—Jason Ellis	PO Box 120627, Newport News VA 23612	757-827-0999	R	1*	<.1
308	Dmd Data Systems Inc—Dave Sevigny	2288 Savannah Ln, Lexington KY 40513	859-296-5780	R	1*	<.1
309	Strategic Solutions Inc—Robert Breilh	PO Box 3593, Bellevue WA 98009	425-827-3727	R	1*	<.1
310	Schat Dot Net—Aaron Schat	174 N Main St, Bishop CA 93514	760-873-4377	R	1*	<.1
311	Sterling Computer Sales LLC—Nancy Brunke	11 Laetitia Ln, Landenberg PA 19350	610-255-0198	R	1*	<.1
312	Virtual World Technologies—Jason Bellflowers	2935 N Ashley St Ste 1, Valdosta GA 31602	229-253-8000	R	1*	<.1
313	Haley Technologies Inc—Paul Haley	16321 Westwoods Bus Pa, Ellisville MO 63021	636-527-5924	R	1*	<.1
314	Kki Corp—Ken Iwahashi	3460 Oakdale Rd Ste E, Modesto CA 95355	209-551-8623	R	1*	<.1
315	Crazy Computers Inc—Cezary Eliminowicz	176 Child St Unit 3, Warren RI 02885	401-247-9791	R	1*	<.1
316	Communication And Data System Consultants Inc—Joy Sporle-der	111 E Joliet St, Schererville IN 46375	219-322-3004	R	1*	<.1
317	Micro-Star Computer Services Inc—Ray Margarit	9420 Lazy Ln Ste D11, Tampa FL 33614	813-876-8900	R	1*	<.1
318	Mms Inc—Darrell Harrell	1006 Hillcrest Pkwy St, Dublin GA 31021	478-274-0024	R	1*	<.1
319	Cosmic Computers Inc—Hasmukh Parikh	181 Main St, Norwalk CT 06851	203-849-0298	R	1*	<.1
320	Edgerton/Irium Americas Inc—Robert Walters	22560 Lunn Rd, Strongsville OH 44149	440-268-0000	R	1*	<.1
321	Fraternal Business Service Inc—Sanjay Chudasama	108 Duane St, New York NY 10007	212-374-1008	R	1*	<.1
322	Intellinetics Inc—Matthew Chretien	2190 Dividend Dr, Columbus OH 43228	614-921-8170	R	1*	<.1
323	Sun Management Inc—James Vanderzon	2000 14th St N Ste 540, Arlington VA 22201	703-778-3796	R	1*	<.1
324	Castle Computers Inc—Mark Bogossian	1143 Sacandaga Rd, Schenectady NY 12302	518-399-8668	R	1*	<.1
325	Miami Computer Distributors Inc—Nestor Quispez-Asin	8013 Nw 29th St, Doral FL 33122	305-591-4025	R	1*	<.1
326	Townsend Assets Group Inc—Peter Gilberd	35 Reed Blvd Ste A, Mill Valley CA 94941	415-626-4231	R	1*	<.1
327	PC Solutions Inc—H Drodge	2969 E High St, Pottstown PA 19464	610-323-3351	R	1*	<.1
328	Word Processing Supplies Inc—Shelley Lamoureaux	3417 Oakcliff Rd Ste 1, Atlanta GA 30340	770-454-9054	R	1*	<.1
329	A-Trac Computer Sales and Service Inc—David Burnside	332 2nd Ave, Waltham MA 02451	781-891-6930	R	1*	<.1
330	World-Wide Power Co—Cyndie Klofenstein ThePowerXChange LLC	PO Box 2049, Wheat Ridge CO 80034	303-940-0600	D	1*	<.1
331	Computer Condiments Inc—Cary Scheck	7618 Woodman Ave Ste 6, Panorama City CA 91402	818-904-9222	R	1*	<.1
332	Tec Tec Inc—Kashif Humayun	2000 Bering Dr Ste 265, Houston TX 77057	832-576-0635	R	1*	<.1
333	Sunshine Software Sales Inc—Gary Scotto	956 Ne 62nd St, Fort Lauderdale FL 33334	954-493-5047	R	1*	<.1
334	1 Stop Electronics Center Inc—Albert Fourti	1100 Coney Island Ave, Brooklyn NY 11230	718-249-1201	R	1*	<.1
335	First Network Group Inc—Stephen Walter	PO Box 1662, Wapakoneta OH 45895	419-739-9240	R	1*	<.1
336	Web Plus Inc—Victor Tong	416 Production St, Aberdeen SD 57401	605-229-0307	R	1*	<.1
337	Computer Renaissance Of Wisconsin LLC	2262 W Mason St, Green Bay WI 54303	920-494-3054	R	1*	<.1
338	Computer Services Industry—Disera Desselles	6009 Allen Rd, Ocean Springs MS 39565	228-872-9618	R	1*	<.1
339	City Computer Corp—David Saul	816 S Aiken Ave, Pittsburgh PA 15232	412-621-2222	R	1*	<.1
340	Compuwiz Enterprises Inc—Jan Lin	2442 Rte 38 38, Cherry Hill NJ 08002	856-482-9099	R	1*	<.1
341	Seagil Software Co—D Tilford	6020 Pky N Dr Ste 900, Cumming GA 30040	770-844-1140	R	1*	<.1
342	It Services Of Utah Inc—Mark Stauffer	1080 E Tabernacle St, Saint George UT 84770	435-673-1655	R	1*	<.1
343	Business Suppliers Inc—Ralph Ditchie	13333 Cicero Ave, Crestwood IL 60445	708-389-0234	R	1*	<.1
344	Cinesys Inc—Michael Windelmann	5104 Lillian St, Houston TX 77007	713-272-0732	R	1*	<.1
345	Eduware Inc—William Stevens	24 Bellemeade Ave Ste, Smithtown NY 11787	631-421-9783	R	1*	<.1
346	Lasercharge Holdings LLC	20350 Empire Ave Ste A, Bend OR 97701	541-388-1797	R	1*	<.1
347	Northeast Computer Systems Inc—Joan King	PO Box 1059, Lyndonville VT 05851	802-626-1050	R	1*	<.1
348	Plug-In Storage Systems Inc—Ralf Maroney	PO Box 928, Stratford CT 06615	203-937-0887	R	1*	<.1
349	Wycomp Technology Inc—Derrick Wyatt	PO Box 20866, Tuscaloosa AL 35402	205-758-5292	R	1*	<.1
350	American Business Networking Inc—Leon Shaffer	14107 Cellini Dr, Cypress TX 77429	713-895-8877	R	1*	<.1
351	Bi-Tech Enterprises Inc—Al Rosen	855 S 1st St Ste C, Ronkonkoma NY 11779	631-737-5300	R	1*	<.1
352	Computers and Telephones Inc—Susan Blum	140 Washington Ave Uni, Cedarhurst NY 11516	516-295-0300	R	1*	<.1
353	Neo Technologies Inc—Ronald Curry	2901 Druid Park Dr C10, Baltimore MD 21215	410-728-9104	R	1*	<.1
354	Mr Ink Jet Inc—Donna Knauss	125 Topeka Dr Ste D an, Waco TX 76712	254-399-9736	R	1*	<.1
355	Gatekeepers Internet Marketing Inc—Wavely Veney	1654 33rd St Nw, Washington DC 20007	202-554-2444	R	1*	<.1
356	Equinox Computer Systems Inc—John Mahoney	1433 Heather Ln Ste A, Charlotte NC 28209	704-375-0047	R	1*	<.1
357	Computer Solution LLC—Wayne Perego	3806 Brookhaven Ln, Odessa TX 79762	432-362-9494	R	1*	<.1
358	Vontronics Inc—Eric Leue	779 92nd Ave N Ste 101, Naples FL 34108	239-597-0001	R	1*	<.1
359	Lanscape Inc—Erich Krauss	847 S Randall Rd Ste 4, Elgin IL 60123	847-760-9282	R	1*	<.1
360	Laserlink International Inc—Pradeep Singh	1310 63rd St, Emeryville CA 94608	510-652-8000	R	1*	<.1
361	Leopard Enterprises Inc—Larry Eppard	4406 Bluffview Blvd, Dallas TX 75209	214-352-5006	R	1*	<.1
362	Altico Advisors LLC—Carol Abate	225 Cedar Hill St Ste, Marlborough MA 01752	508-485-5588	R	1*	<.1
363	Advanced National Electronic Technologies 1 Inc—Clyde Case	205 W Main St Ste G, Havelock NC 28532	252-447-7019	R	1*	<.1
364	Bijan Computers Inc—Mostapha Bijan	1614 W I 240 Service R, Oklahoma City OK 73159	405-685-4100	R	1*	<.1
365	Concord Information Systems LLC—Jennifer Mead	165 Middlesex Tpke Ste, Bedford MA 01730	781-863-7200	R	1*	<.1
366	Expercom of Utah Inc—Roger Smith	PO Box 265, Hyde Park UT 84318	435-563-6112	R	1*	<.1
367	North Bay Networks Inc—Michael Panico	5750 Hollis St, Emeryville CA 94608	510-903-8999	R	1*	<.1
368	Physic Systems Inc—David Lieberman	4424 Technology Dr, Fremont CA 94538	510-824-0252	R	1*	<.1
369	Shore Consultants Ltd—Richard Bruno	179 W Chestnut Hill Rd, Newark DE 19713	302-737-3375	R	1*	<.1
370	Sterling Office Systems—Anthony Bellotto	23939 Research Dr, Farmington Hills MI 48335	248-426-6200	R	1*	<.1
371	Super Software Inc—Kevin Fraley	829 Smoky Bay Way, Homer AK 99603	907-235-8500	R	1*	<.1
372	Gulfstream Digital Solutions Inc—Chris McDaniel	2825 Business Center B, Melbourne FL 32940	321-757-3488	R	1*	<.1
373	Computer Ware Inc—David Sahl	1801 Tully Rd Ste E, Modesto CA 95350	209-578-9739	R	1*	<.1
374	Country Systems—David Myers	709 Washington St, Huntingdon PA 16652	814-643-6341	R	1*	<.1
375	Pro Systems Inc (Charlotte North Carolina)—Gary S Hutchins	PO Box 620490, Charlotte NC 28262	704-849-0400	R	1*	<.1
376	Nakra Labs Inc—Jahangir Nakra	PO Box 894, North Andover MA 01845	978-975-2071	R	1*	<.1
377	Rayco Supply Inc—Katherine Thompson	808 Executive Park Dr, Mobile AL 36606	251-476-2224	R	1*	<.1

Rank	Company Name—*Executive Officer*	Address, City, State, Zip	Phone	Type	Fin	Empls
378	SurpluseqCom Inc—*Daniel Parsons*	329 W Melinda Ln, Phoenix AZ 85027	623-581-9777	R	1*	<.1
379	Comco Inc (Bettendorf Iowa)—*Brian Gillette*	PO Box 349, Bettendorf IA 52722	563-355-1212	R	1*	<.1
380	Compunet USA—*Josan Fajer*	9051 Siempre Viva Rd G, San Diego CA 92154	619-407-7220	R	1*	<.1
381	Datasplice LLC—*Rick Hessdorfer*	414 E Oak St, Fort Collins CO 80524	970-484-0841	R	1*	<.1
382	Lexicom Computer Systems LLC—*Kay Penton*	PO Box 240156, Montgomery AL 36124	334-215-4500	R	1*	<.1
383	Net Engineers Inc—*Chris Rowe*	PO Box 825, Sullivan MO 63080	573-860-6388	R	1*	<.1
384	Stine Enterprises Inc—*Paula Larson*	1606 Evers Dr, Mc Lean VA 22101	703-556-0458	R	1*	<.1
385	Bromley Engineering Inc—*Peter Bromley*	668 Main St Unit 12, Wilmington MA 01887	978-658-8477	R	1*	<.1
386	Dunco Enterprises Inc—*Steven Dunlap*	1896 Corporate Sq Blvd, Jacksonville FL 32216	904-724-1935	R	1*	<.1
387	Jesre Inc—*James Spoerndle*	6730 Wise Ave Nw, Canton OH 44720	330-244-1595	R	1*	<.1
388	Microsphere Inc—*Donald Thompson*	1550 Ne Williamson Blv, Bend OR 97701	541-388-1194	R	1*	<.1
389	Computer Spectrum Inc—*Patrick Creed*	908 S 8th St Ste 100, Louisville KY 40203	502-585-8866	R	1*	<.1
390	Millenium Computer Solutions LLC	PO Box 661, South Windsor CT 06074	860-289-3632	R	1*	<.1
391	Welch PA Inc—*Peter Welch*	80 Belden Rd Ste 3, Rutland VT 05701	802-775-5113	R	1*	<.1
392	Atric Technology Inc—*Kevin Chou*	9659 Las Tunas Dr, Temple City CA 91780	626-537-4111	R	1*	<.1
393	Sunridge Corp—*Tony Su*	2500 E Foothill Blvd S, Pasadena CA 91107	626-535-1780	R	1*	<.1
394	Usakd Enterprise Inc—*Phu Tran*	10825 Garland Rd, Dallas TX 75218	214-320-2849	R	1*	<.1
395	Integrity Office Solutions Inc—*Gerry Hamontree*	PO Box 606, Argyle TX 76226	817-491-3900	R	1*	<.1
396	Jwj Electronics Inc—*Jon Myers*	5038 Trl Lake Dr, Fort Worth TX 76133	817-361-8847	R	1*	<.1
397	PC Menu Inc—*Ira Poorsh*	2190 Pimmit Dr Ste 204, Falls Church VA 22043	703-734-1800	R	1*	<.1
398	PC Supply Co—*Greg Worrel*	23953 W 9 Mile Rd, Southfield MI 48033	248-353-0351	R	1*	<.1
399	T and C Systems Inc—*Tom Brower*	315 Commercial Dr Ste, Savannah GA 31406	912-355-2568	R	1*	<.1
400	Briartec Consulting Corp—*Dennis Travers*	618 Broad Cove Rd, Hopkinton NH 03229	603-746-6000	R	1*	<.1
401	Computer Shak Inc—*Steven Fore*	8675 9th Ave, Port Arthur TX 77642	409-729-7425	R	1*	<.1
402	G and H Computer Company Inc—*Andrew F Glunt*	10621 N May Ave, Oklahoma City OK 73120	405-748-6608	R	1*	<.1
403	AG Computer Center Inc—*Steve Dritschel*	PO Box 872, Westwood NJ 07675	201-666-6290	R	1*	<.1
404	AZ Used Computers Inc—*Edward Rich*	167 Lamp And Lantern V, Chesterfield MO 63017	314-428-2221	R	1*	<.1
405	Chicotec Inc—*Ken Liao*	473 Sapena Ct Ste 2, Santa Clara CA 95054	408-988-6066	R	1*	<.1
406	Port Computers—*Martin Samuelson*	2887 Krafft Rd Ste 700, Port Huron MI 48060	810-987-1668	R	1*	<.1
407	Allied Electronics Trading Inc—*Ruben Jaramillo*	2736 NW 29th Ter, Fort Lauderdale FL 33311	954-358-8200	R	1*	<.1
408	Aramedia Group—*Tom Lick*	61 Adams St, Braintree MA 02184	781-849-0021	R	1*	<.1
409	Communications Resource Corp—*J Joyner*	PO Box 7707, Gulfport MS 39506	228-863-4170	R	1*	<.1
410	Doheny PC—*Todd Miller*	1046 Calle Recodo Ste, San Clemente CA 92673		R	1*	<.1
411	E-Town Computers—*Janice Foltz*	1638 S Market St, Elizabethtown PA 17022	717-361-8255	R	1*	<.1
412	Customervision Inc—*Cindy Rockwell*	515 N 2nd St, Carlisle IA 50047		R	1*	<.1
413	Computer Systems Of Algona Inc—*Patty Rusch*	107 E State St, Algona IA 50511	515-295-2236	R	1*	<.1
414	Buffaloe Com Inc—*Greg Buffaloe*	205 N Wilson Ave, Dunn NC 28334	910-891-4658	R	1*	<.1
415	CMH Software Inc—*Robert Hosea*	254 Taylor Rd, Libby MT 59923	406-293-4977	R	1*	<.1
416	Information Computer Inc—*Kerry Couch*	277 Wilson Pke Cir Ste, Brentwood TN 37027	615-377-0054	R	1*	<.1
417	Internet Business Enterprises And Marketing Inc—*Peter Rosati*	5 Crystal Pond Rd, Southborough MA 01772	508-429-9400	R	1*	<.1
418	Micom Systems—*Ayman Mahmoud*	300 White Bridge Pke A, Nashville TN 37209	615-356-3884	R	1*	<.1
419	Newocean Micro LLC	1604 Nw 84th Ave, Doral FL 33126	305-717-9993	R	1*	<.1
420	Openspot LLC	285 Lowell St, Lexington MA 02420	781-863-2082	R	1*	<.1
421	Valcom Technology—*Larry Vrchoticky*	1009 N 9th St, Fort Dodge IA 50501	515-576-1889	R	1*	<.1
422	Lsi Computers Inc—*Mehran Vahabzadeh*	9111 Katy Fwy Ste 210, Houston TX 77024	713-789-7788	R	1*	<.1
423	PC People Inc—*Catalin Gaitanaru*	534 Abrego St, Monterey CA 93940	831-649-5900	R	1*	<.1
424	Teledata Inc—*Ed Hawley*	900 E Ocean Blvd Ste 2, Stuart FL 34994	772-219-4661	R	1*	<.1
425	Dualex Office Products Inc—*Rosemary Addeo*	2531 Union Rd, Cheektowaga NY 14227	716-668-5401	R	1*	<.1
426	Software Expression Inc—*Roger Gersonde*	14380 W Capitol Dr, Brookfield WI 53005	262-827-7080	R	1*	<.1
427	Statimate Systems Inc—*Edgar Hammer*	139 S Pennsylvania Ave, Greensburg PA 15601	724-832-8440	R	1*	<.1
428	Business Computing—*Mike Joukhajian*	3100 E Foothill Blvd S, Pasadena CA 91107	818-243-3666	R	1*	<.1
429	Machollywood Inc—*Bryan Murray*	6605 W Sunset Blvd, Los Angeles CA 90028	323-957-9557	R	1*	<.1
430	Ormsby's Computer Store Inc—*Bradley Ormsby*	12 Keith Ave, Barre VT 05641	802-476-1414	R	1*	<.1
431	Computer Marketing Group Inc—*John Meadows*	8225 Tower Point Dr, Charlotte NC 28227	704-841-2233	R	1*	<.1
432	Nuritech Inc—*Yang Ahn*	1451 W Artesia Blvd St, Gardena CA 90248	310-324-5525	R	1*	<.1
433	California Computer Aided Design Solutions Inc—*Raymond Kinser*	PO Box 4779, Modesto CA 95352	209-578-5580	R	1*	<.1
434	Bow Management—*Kevin Wang*	11911 Clark St Ste C, Arcadia CA 91006	626-303-8885	R	1*	<.1
435	Creative Data Systems Inc—*Patrick Higgins*	PO Box 1352, Cape Girardeau MO 63702	573-335-1520	R	1*	<.1
436	Intersight—*Paul Mcgavin*	1001 Bridgeway Ste 150, Petaluma CA 94952	415-382-4040	R	1*	<.1
437	Stratatech Group LLC—*Tony Boccanfuso*	92 Wall St, Norwalk CT 06850	203-299-0222	R	1*	<.1
438	Bgsg Inc—*Brian Ginsberg*	28562 Oso Pkwy Ste D, Rcho Sta Marg CA 92688	949-580-3790	R	1*	<.1
439	Jathco Inc—*Tracey Heller*	609 S Main St Stop 1, Conrad MT 59425	406-271-7889	R	1*	<.1
440	Rick's Computers Inc—*Robert Hamers*	4482 Hwy 175, Danbury IA 51019	712-883-2444	R	1*	<.1
441	Rm Business Solutions Inc—*Renny Staab*	3300 Irvine Ave Ste 12, Newport Beach CA 92660	949-261-5556	R	1*	<.1
442	Custom Words Inc—*Bobby Hamby*	2304 Gault Ave N, Fort Payne AL 35967	256-997-9765	R	1*	<.1
443	Nytex LLC	101 N Victory Blvd, Burbank CA 91502	310-526-6998	R	1*	<.1
444	Entre Computer Center—*Steve Curtis*	395 W Wesmark Blvd, Sumter SC 29150	803-905-1111	R	1*	<.1
445	Nadrich Corp—*Randy Nadrich*	PO Box 12, Camilla GA 31730	229-336-5233	R	1*	<.1
446	Unique Computer Inc—*Lynn Toole*	325 1st Ave, Sterling IL 61081	815-625-5018	R	1*	<.1
447	Inex Technologies LLC—*Chuck Bartlomeo*	10870 Murdock Dr, Knoxville TN 37932	865-671-1400	R	1*	<.1
448	Metric Halo Laboratories Inc—*Joseph Buchalter*	5 Donovan Dr, Hopewell Junction NY 12533	845-223-6112	R	1*	<.1
449	Phld Inc—*Tuan Vu*	2607 N Macarthur Blvd, Oklahoma City OK 73127	405-787-7767	R	1*	<.1
450	Solvent Systems Inc—*Dennis Moore*	13118 Maple Dr Ste 1, Saint Louis MO 63127	314-822-9958	R	1*	<.1
451	Comsources USA Inc—*Viguen Mangasarian*	9829 Korman Ct, Potomac MD 20854	301-765-1118	R	1*	<.1
452	Golubitsky Corp—*Leo Golubitsky*	4364 Cranwood Pkwy, Cleveland OH 44128	216-663-5880	R	1*	<.1
453	Pcps Inc—*Ron Lager*	7676 Fm 1960 Rd W, Houston TX 77070	281-807-4646	R	1*	<.1
454	Pdr Inc—*Mark Donegan*	17505 N 79th Ave Ste 4, Glendale AZ 85308	623-879-8222	R	1*	<.1
455	Futuristic Computers—*Larry Shonselt*	396 Northgate Rd, Lindenhurst IL 60046	847-833-6864	R	1*	<.1
456	Cutting Edge Design—*Ronald Fiedler*	167 Albatross Ave, Manahawkin NJ 08050	609-597-0335	R	1*	<.1
457	Peach Systems—*James Ezzell*	2712 Pky Dr, Raleigh NC 27603	919-773-9000	R	1*	<.1
458	World Of Cd-Rom—*John Turcott*	4026 S Westnedge Ave D, Kalamazoo MI 49008	269-382-3766	R	1*	<.1
459	Belland and Son's Edp and Network—*Francis Belland*	313 Green Reed Rd, Debary FL 32713	386-668-0359	R	1*	<.1
460	Pg Computers—*Kim Aubuchon*	150 Mar Vista Dr Ste B, Monterey CA 93940	831-655-8799	R	1*	<.1
461	Bbs Computing—*Ron Bess*	3400 W Ridge Rd Ste 6, Rochester NY 14626	585-723-3360	R	1*	<.1
462	Blue Print Data—*Bob Bahlstrom*	2002 San Marco Blvd St, Jacksonville FL 32207	904-398-1911	R	1*	<.1
463	TSH Inc—*Jerry Wyrick*	3507 S 3rd Pl, Terre Haute IN 47802	812-232-7754	R	1*	<.1
464	Beach Financial Corp—*Walter Seidel*	701 Enterprise Rd E St, Safety Harbor FL 34695	727-725-2500	R	1*	<.1
465	Cellsys Inc—*George Uyesuti*	14931 Califa St Ste D, Van Nuys CA 91411	818-786-0420	R	1*	<.1
466	Laptops and Bags Matter Inc—*Jerry Yonga*	10200 73rd Ave N Ste 1, Maple Grove MN 55369	763-425-7084	R	1*	<.1

Note: An asterisk (*) indicates an estimated financial figure. The company type code used is as follows: R = Private, P = Public, S = Private Subsidiary, B = Public Subsidiary, D = Division, J = Joint Venture, I = Investment Fund.

COMPANY RANKINGS BY SALES WITHIN 4-DIGIT SIC

Rank	Company Name—Executive Officer	Address, City, State, Zip	Phone	Type	Fin	Empls
467	Recycled Micro Inc—John Kwilosz	4312 E University Dr, Phoenix AZ 85034	602-437-1413	R	1*	<.1
468	Poseidon Computer Systems Inc—Cliff Kirk	913 E Gonzalez St, Pensacola FL 32503	850-469-9117	R	1*	<.1
469	Ken Akins—Ken Akins	8229 Morven Rd, Hahira GA 31632	229-794-2261	R	1*	<.1
470	APC Upgrades and Services Inc—Craig Collins	PO Box 1314, Owings Mills MD 21117	410-602-9981	R	1*	<.1
471	Printer Solutions—Bill Cody	3302 4th Ave Sw, Fargo ND 58103	701-526-0313	R	1*	<.1
472	All That Ink and Computer Produc—Michael Wheeler	1251 Sepulveda Blvd St, Torrance CA 90502	310-373-4468	R	1*	<.1
473	Crystal Communications LLC—Daniel Whitaker	304 E 5th St S, Big Stone Gap VA 24219	276-523-6311	R	1*	<.1
474	Fallsnet LLC—Joel Larson	62 E Broadway, Little Falls MN 56345	320-616-2166	R	1*	<.1
475	Pixel USA Computer LLC—Tracy Bui	3229 Stevens Creek Blv, San Jose CA 95117	408-293-8333	R	1*	<.1
476	Right Solutions Inc—Laurence Parsons	PO Box 191046, Boise ID 83719	208-343-3200	R	1*	<.1
477	Union Computer International—Noel Shu	152 Cherry St, Kent OH 44240	330-673-5155	R	<1*	<.1
478	Compudirect Holding Company Inc—Leland Pinkstaff	6175 Hickory Flat Hwy, Canton GA 30115	770-516-3591	R	<1*	<.1
479	Kraytec Business Solutions Inc—Arthur Clark	PO Box 8663, Chattanooga TN 37414	423-304-8054	R	<1*	<.1
480	Prairie Company LLC	885 W 3rd Ave, Springfield CO 81073	719-523-6919	R	<1*	<.1
481	Merchant Expo LLC	7065 W Ann Rd Ste 130, Las Vegas NV 89130	702-655-4072	R	<1*	<.1
482	Dcs Technologies—Dean Berryman	2090 Ctr Ave, Payette ID 83661	208-642-9099	R	<1*	<.1
483	Information Works Inc—William Ryan	550 Morgan Cir, Northville MI 48167	248-347-4841	R	<1*	<.1
484	New Image Computers—Tommy Thorinton	110 Magnolia Dr S, Tifton GA 31794	229-382-3004	R	<1*	<.1
485	MJM Programming Consultants—Micheal Menzies	15375 Barranca Pkwy B2, Irvine CA 92618	949-753-8595	R	<1*	<.1
486	CsitechnologyCom—Roy Sheppard	PO Box 650, Jamestown ND 58402	701-252-1835	R	<1*	<.1
487	Daktronix Computer Inc—Dana Kinsey	19501 E Parker Sq Dr, Parker CO 80134	720-851-5555	R	<1	<.1
488	Global Software Solutions—Ron Rasmussen	20301 70th St E, Sumner WA 98391	253-862-6303	R	<1*	<.1
489	KpekNet Inc—Paul Insana	9510 Glen Dr, Brecksville OH 44141	440-838-8300	R	<1*	<.1
490	Matrix Computers—Steve Guarino	204 N Main St, Franklin KY 42134	270-598-9898	R	<1*	<.1
491	Red Rock Computer—Todd Barton	6105 S Pke Dr, Larkspur CO 80118	303-681-3924	R	<1*	<.1
492	TrianglecablesCom LLC	18735 E Clnl Dr Ste 11, Orlando FL 32820	407-369-4015	R	<1*	<.1

TOTALS: SIC 5734 Computer & Software Stores
Companies: 492 — Fin: 19,732 — Empls: 111.0

5735 Record & Prerecorded Tape Stores

Rank	Company Name—Executive Officer	Address, City, State, Zip	Phone	Type	Fin	Empls
1	Trans World Entertainment Corp—Robert J Higgins	38 Corporate Cir, Albany NY 12203	518-452-1242	P	652	4.7
2	Hastings Entertainment Inc—John H Marmaduke	PO Box 35350, Amarillo TX 79120	806-351-2300	P	521	5.8
3	Kingdom Tapes and Electronics—Johnny Berguson	719 Lambs Creek Rd, Mansfield PA 16933	570-662-7515	R	78*	.2
4	Schmitt Music Co—Tom Schmitt	2400 Freeway Blvd, Brooklyn Center MN 55430	763-566-4560	R	46*	.4
5	Newbury Comics Inc—Mike Dreese	5 Guest St, Brighton MA 02135	617-254-1666	R	44*	.3
6	CD Warehouse Finance Co—Christopher M Salyer PrePlayed Entertainment	900 N Broadway, Oklahoma City OK 73102	405-236-8742	S	34*	.1
7	Compact Disc Management Inc—Christopher M Salyer PrePlayed Entertainment	900 N Broadway, Oklahoma City OK 73102	405-236-8742	S	34*	.1
8	PrePlayed Entertainment—Christopher M Salyer	900 N Broadway Ave, Oklahoma City OK 73102	405-297-9968	R	27	.3
9	Video Depot Inc—John Booth	41865 Boardwalk Ste 10, Palm Desert CA 92211	760-346-3492	R	23*	.1
10	Music Millenium Inc—Terry Courier	3158 E Burnside St, Portland OR 97214	503-231-8926	R	16*	.1
11	Sound of Market Street—Daryl King	15 S 11th St 2nd Fl, Philadelphia PA 19107	215-925-3150	R	10*	<.1
12	Zia Enterprises Inc—Barry Barton	21002 N 19th Ave Ste 1, Phoenix AZ 85027	623-580 4942	R	8*	.2
13	CD Universe Inc—Charles Beilman	101 N Plains Industria, Wallingford CT 06492	203-294-1648	R	8*	<.1
14	Worth Love Finding Inc—Adrian Rogers	PO Box 38300, Germantown TN 38183	901-382-7900	R	7*	<.1
15	Central South Music Inc—Randall Davidson	3730 Vulcan Dr, Nashville TN 37211	615-833-5960	R	5*	<.1
16	Candyman Ltd—Mathew Schwartzman	851 St Michael's Dr, Santa Fe NM 87501	505-983-9309	R	5*	<.1
17	CheckOutStore Inc—Lee Chen	319 37th St, Brooklyn NY 11232		R	3	<.1
18	Mill Creek Entertainment LLC—Robert Zakheim	244 Nevada Ave N, Golden Valley MN 55427	763-512-1000	R	3*	<.1
19	Pendleton Corp—Gaines Campbell	PO Box 3718, Cleveland TN 37320	423-473-8050	R	1*	<.1
20	Shelby Singleton Enterprises Inc—John Singleton	PO Box 120711, Nashville TN 37212	615-385-1960	R	1*	<.1

TOTALS: SIC 5735 Record & Prerecorded Tape Stores
Companies: 20 — Fin: 1,526 — Empls: 12.4

5736 Musical Instruments Stores

Rank	Company Name—Executive Officer	Address, City, State, Zip	Phone	Type	Fin	Empls
1	Guitar Center Inc—Greg A Trojan	5795 Lindero Canyon Rd, Westlake Village CA 91362	818-735-8800	R	2,021*	9.5
2	Sam Ash Music Corp	PO Box 9047, Hicksville NY 11802		R	599*	1.8
3	Numark Industries LP—Jay Schlabs	200 Scenic View Dr Ste, Cumberland RI 02864	401-658-3131	R	150*	.1
4	Music and Arts Center Inc—Ken O'Brien Guitar Center Inc	4626 Wedgewood Blvd, Frederick MD 21703	301-620-4040	S	113*	1.7
5	Jeffers Handbell Supply Inc—Thomas Jeffers	PO Box 1728, Irmo SC 29063	803-781-0555	R	108*	<.1
6	Jordan-Kitt Music Inc—Rick Grant	9520 Baltimore Blvd, College Park MD 20740	301-345-3310	R	52*	.3
7	Fletcher Music Centers Inc—John Riley	3966 Airway Cir, Clearwater FL 33762		R	38*	.2
8	JW Pepper and Son Inc—Greg Burtch	2480 Industrial Blvd, Paoli PA 19301	610-648-0500	R	28*	.2
9	Manny's Music—Ian Goldrich	156 W 48th St, New York NY 10036	212-819-0576	R	26*	.1
10	Chuck Levins Washington Music Sales Center Inc	11151 Veirs Mill Rd, Wheaton MD 20902	301-946-8808	R	25*	.1
11	Sherman Clay and Co—Eric Schwartz	1111 Bayhill Dr Ste 45, San Bruno CA 94066		R	22*	.1
12	Piano and Organ Distributors Inc—Bill Boyce	2403 New Raleigh Hwy, Durham NC 27703	919-596-2105	R	6*	<.1
13	West LA Music—Rick Waite	11345 Santa Monica Blv, Los Angeles CA 90025	310-477-1945	R	6*	<.1
14	Southern Music Company Inc—Arthur Gurwitz	PO Box 329, San Antonio TX 78292	210-226-8167	R	5*	<.1
15	EE Forbes and Sons Piano Company Inc—French Forbes Jr	3048 Montgomery Hwy, Homewood AL 35209	205-879-4154	R	4*	<.1
16	Gand Music and Sound Inc—Gary Gand	780 W Frontage Rd, Northfield IL 60093	847-446-4263	R	3*	<.1
17	Day Music Co—Robert C Day	5516 SE Foster Rd, Portland OR 97206	503-775-4351	R	2*	<.1
18	Paragon Music Center Inc	2119 W Hillsborough Av, Tampa FL 33603	813-876-3459	R	2*	<.1
19	Matt Umanov Guitars—Matt Umanov	273 Bleecker St, New York NY 10014	212-675-2157	R	2*	<.1
20	Consignment Music—Joe Nathan	4040 Park Ave, Memphis TN 38111	901-458-2094	R	2*	<.1
21	Kolenick Corp—Samantha Olenick	3075 Peters Way, San Diego CA 92117	858-274-1237	R	1*	<.1

TOTALS: SIC 5736 Musical Instruments Stores
Companies: 21 — Fin: 3,215 — Empls: 14.3

5812 Eating Places

Rank	Company Name—Executive Officer	Address, City, State, Zip	Phone	Type	Fin	Empls
1	McDonald's Corp—Jose Armario	2111 McDonald's Dr, Oak Brook IL 60523	630-623-3000	P	24,075	400.0
2	Bob Evans Restaurants Inc—Steven A Davis	5190 28th St SE, Grand Rapids MI 49512	616-942-0190	S	17,571*	42.0
3	Subway Restaurants—Frederick A Deluca	325 Bic Dr, Milford CT 06461	203-877-4281	R	16,200	1.0
4	HMSHost Corp—Elie W Maalouf	6905 Rockledge Dr, Bethesda MD 20817	240-694-4100	S	14,741*	34.0
5	ARAMARK Corp—Joseph Neubauer	1101 Market St, Philadelphia PA 19107	215-238-3000	R	13,082	250.0
6	Starbucks Corp—Howard Schultz	PO Box 3717, Seattle WA 98124	206-447-1575	P	11,700	149.0
7	Yum! Brands Inc—David C Novak	1441 Gardiner Ln, Louisville KY 40213	502-874-8300	P	11,343	378.0
8	Compass Group USA Inc—Gary Green	2400 Yorkmont Rd, Charlotte NC 28217	704-329-4000	S	10,265*	175.0

Rank	Company Name—*Executive Officer*	Address, City, State, Zip	Phone	Type	Fin	Empls
9	Morrison Management Specialists Inc—*Scott MacLellan*	5801 Peachtree Dunwood, Atlanta GA 30342	404-845-3330	S	7,600*	18.0
10	Darden Restaurants Inc—*Clarence Otis Jr*	PO Box 695011, Orlando FL 32869	407-245-4000	P	7,500	178.5
11	Houlihan's Restaurant Group Inc—*Bob Hartwell*	8700 State Line Rd Ste, Leawood KS 66206	913-901-2500	R	6,575*	8.3
12	Taco Bell Corp—*Greg Creed* Yum! Brands Inc	1 Glen Bell Way, Irvine CA 92618	949-863-4500	S	6,200	100.0
13	Pizza Hut Inc—*Scott O Bergren* Yum! Brands Inc	7100 Corporate Dr, Plano TX 75024	972-338-7700	S	4,978*	140.0
14	Guckenheimer Enterprises Inc—*Jeanie S Ritchie*	3 Lagoon Dr Ste 325, Redwood City CA 94065	650-592-3800	R	3,809*	4.2
15	OSI Restaurant Partners LLC—*Elizabeth Smith*	2202 N West Shore Blvd, Tampa FL 33607	813-282-1225	R	3,629	96.0
16	Family Sports Concepts Inc—*Chris Elliott*	5510 W LaSalle St Ste, Tampa FL 33607	813-226-2333	R	2,896*	7.0
17	Mimi's Cafe—*Russ Bendel* Bob Evans Farms Inc	17852 E 17th St S Ste, Tustin CA 92780	714-544-4826	S	2,846*	7.5
18	Brinker International Inc—*Douglas H Brooks*	6820 LBJ Fwy, Dallas TX 75240	972-980-9917	P	2,761	60.3
19	Red Lobster Div—*Kim Lopdrup* Darden Restaurants Inc	5900 Lake Ellenor Dr, Orlando FL 32809	407-245-4000	S	2,694*	75.0
20	Quality Dining Inc—*Daniel B Fitzpatrick*	4220 Edison Lakes Pkwy, Mishawaka IN 46545	574-271-4600	R	2,610*	7.2
21	Burger King Holdings Inc—*Bernardo Hees*	5505 Blue Lagoon Dr, Miami FL 33126	305-378-3000	R	2,574*	40.0
22	Cracker Barrel Old Country Store Inc—*Michael A Woodhouse*	PO Box 787, Lebanon TN 37088	615-444-5533	P	2,434	67.0
23	Wendy's Co—*Emil Brolick*	1 Dave Thomas Blvd, Dublin OH 43017	614-764-3100	P	2,431	42.8
24	Olive Garden Restaurants Div—*David Pickens* Darden Restaurants Inc	PO Box 592037, Orlando FL 32859		D	2,431*	100.0
25	Bon Appetit Management Co—*Fedele Bauccio*	100 Hamilton Ave Ste 3, Palo Alto CA 94301	650-798-8000	R	2,407*	8.0
26	Carlson Restaurants Worldwide Inc—*Nick Shepherd*	4201 Marsh Ln, Carrollton TX 75007	972-662-5400	S	2,400	28.0
27	Chipotle Mexican Grill Inc—*Steven Ells*	1401 Wynkoop St Ste 50, Denver CO 80202	303-595-4000	P	2,270	30.9
28	Delaware North Companies Inc—*Jeremy M Jacobs Sr*	40 Fountain Plz, Buffalo NY 14202	716-858-5000	R	2,244*	55.0
29	Jack in the Box Inc—*Linda A Lang*	9330 Balboa Ave, San Diego CA 92123	858-571-2121	P	2,193	25.7
30	PJ United—*Doug Stevens*	2300 Resource Dr, Birmingham AL 35242	205-981-2800	S	1,971*	5.2
31	Panera Bread Co—*William W Moreton*	6710 Clayton Rd, Richmond Heights MO 63117	314-633-7100	P	1,822	18.0
32	Thomas and King Inc—*Mike Scanlon*	249 E Main St Ste 101, Lexington KY 40507	859-254-2180	R	1,784*	6.0
33	Cheesecake Factory Inc—*David Overton*	26901 Malibu Hills Rd, Calabasas Hills CA 91301	818-871-3000	P	1,758	32.2
34	Bob Evans Farms Inc—*Steven A Davis*	PO Box 07863, Columbus OH 43207		P	1,677	44.8
35	Domino's Pizza Inc—*J Patrick Doyle*	PO Box 997, Ann Arbor MI 48106	734-930-3030	R	1,652	10.0
36	Landry Group—*Tilman J Fertitta*	1510 W Loop S, Houston TX 77027	713-850-1010	R	1,636*	15.0
37	K-Mac Enterprises Inc—*Sam Fiori*	PO Box 6538, Fort Smith AR 72906	479-646-2053	R	1,600*	5.0
38	Consolidated Restaurant Operations Inc	12200 Stemmons Fwy Ste, Dallas TX 75234	972-241-5500	R	1,583*	5.5
39	ARAMARK Healthcare Support Services Inc—*Joseph Neubauer* ARAMARK Corp	Aramark Tower 1101 Mar, Philadelphia PA 19107	215-238-5943	S	1,558*	2.0
40	Ilitch Holdings Inc—*Christopher Ilitch*	2211 Woodward Ave, Detroit MI 48201	313-983-6600	R	1,480*	17.0
41	Burger King Corp Burger King Holdings Inc	5505 Blue Lagoon Dr, Miami FL 33126		S	1,475*	37.0
42	Carl Karcher Enterprises Inc—*Andrew F Puzder*	6307 Carpinteria Ave, Carpinteria CA 93013	805-745-7500	S	1,419	21.3
43	Buffets Holdings Inc—*Michael Andrews*	1020 Discovery Rd Ste, Eagan MN 55121	651-994-8608	R	1,388*	23.0
44	Chick-fil-A Inc—*Truett Cathy*	5200 Buffington Rd, Atlanta GA 30349	404-765-8038	R	1,373	.6
45	Buffets Inc—*R Michael Andrews*	1460 Buffet Way, Eagan MN 55121	651-994-6808	S	1,353*	33.0
46	Bistro Management Company Inc—*Jeff Ritson*	5803 Mariemont Ave, Mariemont OH 45227	513-271-2349	R	1,269*	3.5
47	Ruby Tuesday Inc—*Sandy Beall*	150 W Church Ave, Maryville TN 37801	865-379-5700	P	1,265	40.5
48	PF Chang's China Bistro Inc—*Robert T Vivian*	7676 E Pinnacle Peak R, Scottsdale AZ 85255	480-888-3000	P	1,239	26.0
49	Buffet Partners LP—*Greg Buchanan*	2701 E Plano Pky Ste 2, Plano TX 75074	214-291-2900	R	1,221*	3.2
50	Papa John's International Inc—*John H Schnatter*	PO Box 99900, Louisville KY 40269	502-261-7272	P	1,218	16.5
51	Hardee's Food Systems Inc—*Andy Puzder* Carl Karcher Enterprises Inc	100 N Broadway Ste 120, Saint Louis MO 63102	314-259-6200	S	1,215*	40.0
52	ARAMARK Refreshment Services Inc—*Joseph Neubauer* ARAMARK Corp	1101 Market St, Philadelphia PA 19107	215-238-3000	S	1,169*	1.5
53	Little Caesar Enterprises Inc—*Dave Scrivano* Ilitch Holdings Inc	2211 Woodward Ave, Detroit MI 48201	313-983-6000	S	1,160*	86.0
54	Applebee's International Inc	11201 Renner Blvd, Lenexa KS 66219	913-967-4000	S	1,149*	28.0
55	Hard Rock Cafe International Inc—*Hamish Dodds*	6100 Old Park Ln, Orlando FL 32835	407-445-7625	R	1,138*	3.0
56	Texas Roadhouse Inc—*Scott Colosi*	6040 Dutchmans Ln Ste, Louisville KY 40205	502-426-9984	P	1,109	33.0
57	Peter Piper Inc—*Joseph Luongo Jr*	950 W Behrend Dr Ste 1, Phoenix AZ 85027	480-609-6400	P	1,092*	1.4
58	Landry's Restaurants Inc—*Tilman J Fertitta*	1510 W Loop S, Houston TX 77027	713-850-1010	R	1,060	19.9
59	Back Bay Restaurant Group Inc—*Charles F Sarkis*	284 Newbury St, Boston MA 02115	617-536-2800	R	1,035*	2.5
60	Eateries Inc—*Vincent F Orza Jr*	1220 S Santa Fe Ave, Edmond OK 73003	405-705-5000	R	1,029*	3.0
61	Rare Hospitality International Inc—*David George* Darden Restaurants Inc	8215 Roswell Rd Bldg 6, Atlanta GA 30350	770-399-9595	S	987	19.8
62	Lackmann Culinary Services—*Matthew Lackmann* Compass Group USA Inc	303 Crossways Park Dr, Woodbury NY 11797	516-364-2300	S	951*	1.2
63	Phillips Foods Inc—*Steve Phillips*	1215 E Fort Ave, Baltimore MD 21223	443-263-1200	R	951*	1.2
64	Red Robin Gourmet Burgers Inc—*Stephen Carley*	6312 S Fiddlers Green, Greenwood Village CO 80111	303-846-6000	P	915	22.3
65	Holland Inc—*Tom Mears*	109 W 17th St, Vancouver WA 98660	360-694-1521	R	908*	1.2
66	NPC International Inc—*James K Schwartz*	7300 W 129th St, Overland Park KS 66213	913-327-5555	R	845*	17.0
67	Restaurant Associates Corp—*Dick Cattani* Compass Group USA Inc	330 5th Ave, New York NY 10001	212-613-5500	S	842*	7.7
68	Perkins Family Restaurants LP—*Joseph Trungale*	6075 Poplar Ave Ste 80, Memphis TN 38119	901-766-6400	S	832*	25.0
69	O'Charley's Inc—*David W Head*	3038 Sidco Dr, Nashville TN 37204	615-256-8500	P	826	22.0
70	CEC Entertainment Inc—*Michael H Magusiak*	PO Box 152077, Irving TX 75015	972-258-8507	P	821	17.3
71	Ruby's Diner Inc—*Douglas S Cavanaugh*	557 Wald, Irvine CA 92618	949-644-7829	R	807*	1.1
72	Buffalo Wild Wings Inc—*Sally J Smith*	5500 Wayzata Blvd Ste, Minneapolis MN 55416	952-593-9943	P	785	21.0
73	Carrols Restaurant Group Inc—*Alan Vituli*	968 James St, Syracuse NY 13203	315-424-0513	P	751	16.3
74	Rod Fraser Enterprises—*Rick Fraser*	1320 N Manzanita St, Orange CA 92867	714-633-7844	R	744*	1.0
75	Centerplate Inc—*Des Hague*	2187 Atlantic St, Stamford CT 06902		S	741	29.1
76	J Alexander's Restaurants Inc J Alexander's Corp	2609 W End Ave, Nashville TN 37203	615-269-1900	S	718*	2.5
77	Biglari Holdings Inc—*Sadar Biglari*	175 East Houston St St, San Antonio TX 78205	210-344-3400	P	709	21.0
78	ARAMARK Sports and Entertainment Services Inc—*Joseph Neubauer* ARAMARK Corp	Aramark Tower 1101 Mar, Philadelphia PA 19107	215-238-3000	S	700*	.7
79	Lone Star Steakhouse and Saloon Inc	5055 W Park Blvd Ste 5, Plano TX 75093	972-295-8600	R	669	19.8
80	California Pizza Kitchen Inc—*GJ Hart*	6053 W Century Blvd St, Los Angeles CA 90045	310-342-5000	S	642	14.0
81	Culver Franchising System Inc—*Craig C Culver*	1240 Water St, Prairie du Sac WI 53578	608-643-7980	R	636*	.1

Note: An asterisk (*) indicates an estimated financial figure. The company type code used is as follows: R = Private, P = Public, S = Private Subsidiary, B = Public Subsidiary, D = Division, J = Joint Venture, I = Investment Fund.

COMPANY RANKINGS BY SALES WITHIN 4-DIGIT SIC

Rank	Company Name—Executive Officer	Address, City, State, Zip	Phone	Type	Fin	Empls
82	White Castle System Inc—Edgar Ingram	PO Box 1498, Columbus OH 43216	614-228-5781	R	631*	11.5
83	BJ's Restaurants Inc—Jerry Deitchle	7755 Center Ave Ste 30, Huntington Beach CA 92647	714-500-2400	P	621	14.2
84	CulinArt Inc—Joseph H Pacifico	175 Sunnyside Blvd, Plainview NY 11803	516-437-2700	R	614*	.8
85	Hurricane Food Inc	800 E Thompson Rd, Indianapolis IN 46227	317-789-4000	R	614*	.8
86	TGI Friday's Inc—Richard Snead Carlson Restaurants Worldwide Inc	4201 Marsh Ln, Carrollton TX 75007	972-662-5400	S	600*	20.7
87	Azteca Restaurant Enterprises Inc—Jose Ramos	133 SW 158th St, Burien WA 98166	206-243-7021	R	592*	1.4
88	Ivar's Inc—Bob Donegan	1001 Alaskan Way Pier, Seattle WA 98104	206-587-6500	R	586*	.8
89	Denny's Corp—John Miller	203 E Main St P-8-6, Spartanburg SC 29319	864-597-8000	P	549	11.5
90	Dave and Buster's Holdings Inc—Stephen M King	2481 Manana Dr, Dallas TX 75220	214-357-9588	R	536	8.2
91	Friendly Ice Cream Corp—Harsha V Agadi	1855 Boston Rd, Wilbraham MA 01095	413-731-4000	R	532	12.8
92	Long John Silver's Inc Yum! Brands Inc	1900 Colonel Sanders L, Louisville KY 40213	502-874-3000	S	525*	14.0
93	Papa Gino's Inc—Tom Galligan	600 Providence Hwy, Dedham MA 02026	781-461-1200	R	511*	5.0
94	First Watch Restaurants Inc—Ken Pendery	9027 Town Center Pkwy, Bradenton FL 34202	941-907-9800	R	509*	1.4
95	RPM Pizza Inc—Richard Mueller	15384 5th St, Gulfport MS 39503	228-832-4000	R	507*	8.0
96	Real Mex Restaurants Inc—Richard E Rivera	5660 Katella Ave Ste 1, Cypress CA 90630	562-346-1200	S	501*	12.1
97	Villa Enterprises Ltd—Biagio Scotto	25 Washington St, Morristown NJ 07960	973-285-4800	R	501*	1.4
98	Uno Restaurant Holdings Corp—Frank W Guidara	100 Charles Park Rd, Boston MA 02132	617-323-9200	R	500	8.2
99	Whataburger Inc—Tom Dobson	300 Concord Plz, San Antonio TX 78216	210-476-6000	R	498*	15.5
100	Shoney's North America Corp—David Davoudpour	1717 Elm Hill Pke Ste, Nashville TN 37210		S	488*	11.0
101	Ram International Ltd—Jeff Iverson	PO Box 99010, Lakewood WA 98496	253-588-1788	R	480*	1.6
102	Old Spaghetti Factory—Chris Dussin	0715 SW Bancroft St, Portland OR 97239	503-225-0433	R	460*	4.2
103	Montgomery Inn—Tom Gregory	9440 Montgomery Rd, Montgomery OH 45242		R	458*	.6
104	Chin Chin Inc—Bob Mandler	3710 S Robertson Blvd, Culver City CA 90232	310-237-7013	R	453*	.5
105	Boddie-Noell Enterprises Inc—Willaim L Boddie	PO Box 1908, Rocky Mount NC 27802	252-937-2000	R	438*	12.5
106	Sizzler Restaurants International Inc—Kerry Kramp	6101 W Centinela Ave, Culver City CA 90230	310-846-8750	R	436	8.2
107	Popeyes Inc—Cheryl Bachelder AFC Enterprises Inc	5555 Glenridge Connect, Atlanta GA 30342	404-459-4450	S	427*	6.2
108	Ninfa's Inc	2704 Navigation Blvd, Houston TX 77003	713-228-1175	R	427*	3.1
109	Dunkin' Brands Group Inc—Kate Lavelle	130 Royall St, Canton MA 02021	781-737-5200	P	427*	1.1
110	Einstein Noah Restaurant Group Inc—Jeffrey J O'Neill	555 Zang St Ste 300, Lakewood CO 80228	303-568-8000	P	412	6.8
111	Sonic Corp—J Clifford Hudson	300 Johnny Bench Dr, Oklahoma City OK 73104	405-225-5000	P	411	12.1
112	Waffle House Inc—Joe Rogers	5986 Financial Dr, Norcross GA 30071	770-729-5700	R	410*	16.5
113	Rebecca's Commissary Inc—Michael McAdam	99 S Bedford St, Burlington MA 01803	781-272-0539	D	379*	.5
114	Valley Innovative Management Services Inc—Jim Walt	PO Box 5454, Jackson MS 39288	601-664-3100	R	369*	2.7
115	Ruth's Hospitality Group Inc—Michael P O'Donnell	1030 W Canton Ave Ste, Winter Park FL 32789	407-333-7440	P	368	5.7
116	Krispy Kreme Doughnuts Inc—James H Morgan	PO Box 83, Winston Salem NC 27102	336-725-2981	P	362	3.7
117	McCormick and Schmick Holdings LLC—William T Freeman	1414 NW Northrup Ste 7, Portland OR 97209	503-226-3440	P	351	6.6
118	Johnny's Pizza House Inc—Bruce Jackson	189 Chappel Rd, Fayetteville GA 30215	404-729-4900	R	349*	.5
119	Luby's Inc—Christopher J Pappas	13111 NW Freeway Ste 6, Houston TX 77040	713-329-6800	P	349	7.3
120	Bravo Brio Restaurant Group Inc—Saed Mohseni	777 Goodale Blvd Ste 1, Columbus OH 43212	614-326-7944	P	343	8.0
121	Phillips Crab House Inc—Mark Sneed Phillips Foods Inc	1215 E Fort Ave, Baltimore MD 21230	443-263-1200	S	341*	2.5
122	Ruth's Chris Steak House Inc—Craig S Miller Ruth's Hospitality Group Inc	500 International Pky, Heathrow FL 32746	407-333-7440	S	340*	5.0
123	Sbarro Inc—Peter Beaudrault	401 Broadhollow Rd, Melville NY 11747	631-715-4100	R	339*	7.5
124	Catalina Restaurant Group Inc—Kazumasa Ogawa	2200 Faraday Ave St 25, Carlsbad CA 92008	760-804-5750	S	330*	10.0
125	Qdoba Restaurant Corp—Gary J Beister Jack in the Box Inc	4865 Ward Rd, Wheat Ridge CO 80033	720-898-2300	S	330*	.9
126	Benihana Inc—Richard C Stockinger	8685 NW 53rd Ter, Miami FL 33166	305-593-0770	P	326	6.7
127	Manna Inc (Louisville Kentucky)—Ulysses Bridgeman Jr	1903 Stanley Gault Pky, Louisville KY 40223	502-254-7130	R	325*	11.0
128	Sysco Food Services of Cleveland Inc—Alan E Hasty	4747 Grayton Rd, Cleveland OH 44135	216-201-3000	S	325*	.8
129	Palomino Euro Bistro—Per Cummings Restaurants Unlimited Inc	1420 5th Ave Ste 350, Seattle WA 98101	206-623-1300	D	320*	.4
130	Frisch's Restaurants Inc—Craig F Maier	2800 Gilbert Ave, Cincinnati OH 45206	513-961-2660	P	304	8.4
131	Captain D's LLC—David Head	1717 Elm Hill Pike Ste, Nashville TN 37210	615-391-5461	R	300	6.6
132	Golden Corral Corp—Ted Fowler	PO Box 29502, Raleigh NC 27626	919-781-9310	S	299*	10.0
133	Morton's Restaurant Group Inc—Christopher J Artinian	325 N LaSalle St Ste 5, Chicago IL 60654	312-923-0030	P	296	4.2
134	Elmer's Pancake and Steak Inc—Dennis Waldron Elmer's Restaurants Inc	11802 SE Stark St, Portland OR 97216	503-252-1485	S	290*	.8
135	Chevys Inc—Fred Wolfe	1890 Powell St, Emeryville CA 94608	510-653-8210	R	285*	9.0
136	Caribou Coffee Company Inc—Michael Tattersfield	3900 Lakebreeze Ave N, Minneapolis MN 55429	763-592-2200	P	284	5.8
137	Pacific Coast Restaurants Inc—Alan A Fleenor Restaurants Unlimited Inc	7165 SW Fir Loop Ste 2, Portland OR 97223	503-684-2803	S	283*	2.2
138	MCL Cafeterias Inc—Casey McGaughey	2730 E 62nd St, Indianapolis IN 46220	317-257-5425	R	280*	1.8
139	EPL Intermediate Inc—Steve Carley	3535 Harbor Blvd Ste 1, Costa Mesa CA 92626	714-599-5000	S	278	.2
140	Harper's Restaurants Inc—Tom Sasser	1228 E Morehead St Ste, Charlotte NC 28204	704-375-9715	R	277*	.6
141	Specialty Restaurants Corp	8191 E Kaiser Blvd, Anaheim CA 92808	714-279-6100	R	272*	5.0
142	Piccadilly Restaurants LLC—David Green	PO Box 2467, Baton Rouge LA 70821	225-293-9440	R	268*	6.0
143	Potbelly Sandwich Works LLC—Aylwin Lewis	222 Merchandise Mart P, Chicago IL 60654		R	260*	3.0
144	DeRosa Corp—Joseph DeRosa	7613 W State St, Milwaukee WI 53213	414-771-3100	R	254*	.7
145	Elmer's Restaurants Inc—Bruce N Davis	PO Box 16595, Portland OR 97292	503-252-1485	R	252*	.7
146	Buca Inc Planet Hollywood International Inc	1300 Nicollet Mall Ste, Minneapolis MN 55403	612-225-3400	S	246*	5.7
147	Boston Market Corp—F Lane Cardwell Jr	PO Box 4086, Golden CO 80401	303-278-9500	S	245*	.3
148	El Pollo Loco Inc—Stephen Carley	3535 Harbor Blvd Ste 1, Costa Mesa CA 92626	714-599-5000	S	237	4.3
149	SWH Corp—Russell W Bendel Bob Evans Farms Inc	17852 E 17th St Ste 10, Tustin CA 92780	714-544-4826	S	234*	7.5
150	Rainforest Cafe Inc—Tilman Fertitta Landry's Restaurants Inc	5015 Westheimer Rd Ste, Houston TX 77056	713-840-1088	S	229*	6.0
151	Bertucci's Corp—David G Lloyd	155 Otis St, Northborough MA 01532	508-351-2500	R	227*	8.5
152	Rock Bottom Restaurants Inc—Frank Day	248 Centennial Pkwy St, Louisville CO 80027	303-664-4000	R	223*	6.7
153	Pollo Tropical—James Tunnessen Carrols Restaurant Group Inc	7300 N Kendall 8th Fl, Miami FL 33156	305-670-7696	S	222*	3.0
154	Garden Fresh Restaurant Corp—Michael P Mack	15822 Bernardo Ctr Dr, San Diego CA 92127	858-675-1600	R	221	5.4
155	Saxton Pierce Restaurant Corp—Kelly Saxton	8117 Preston Rd, Dallas TX 75225	214-373-3400	R	220*	.3
156	Mad Anthony's Inc—Herbert Gould	10502 NE 37th Cir Bldg, Kirkland WA 98033	425-455-0732	R	219*	2.0
157	Marco's Inc—Jack Butorac	5254 Monroe St, Toledo OH 43623	419-885-4844	R	218*	1.6
158	International Theatres Corp—Michael Brindisi	501 W 78th St, Chanhassen MN 55317	952-934-1525	S	209*	.3

Rank	Company Name—*Executive Officer*	Address, City, State, Zip	Phone	Type	Fin	Empls
159	K-M Concessions Inc—*T Kevin McNicholas*	4699 Marion St, Denver CO 80216	303-322-3031	R	207*	.5
160	Guardian Corp—*Leon A Dunn Jr*	PO Box 7397, Rocky Mount NC 27804	252-443-4101	R	205*	1.5
161	Davco Acquisition Holding Inc—*Harvey Rothstein*	1657 Crofton Blvd, Crofton MD 21114	410-721-3770	R	204*	5.9
162	Five Guys Enterprises LLC—*Jerry Murrell*	10440 Furnace Rd Ste 2, Lorton VA 22079	703-339-9500	R	200*	.1
163	Champps Entertainment Inc—*Steve Johnson* Fox and Hound Restaurant Group	1551 N Waterfront Pkwy, Wichita KS 67206	303-804-1333	S	198	5.4
164	Heart of America Group—*Mike Whalen*	1501 River Dr, Moline IL 61265	309-797-9300	R	197*	1.8
165	Fox and Hound Restaurant Group—*Steven M Johnson*	PO Box 782558, Wichita KS 67278	316-634-0505	R	193*	4.8
166	Papa Gino's Holdings Corp—*Rick Wools*	600 Providence Hwy, Dedham MA 02026	781-461-1200	R	192*	5.0
167	Hornblower Dining Yachts Inc—*Terry MacRae*	Pier 3 On the Embarcad, San Francisco CA 94111	415-394-8900	R	190*	.5
168	Guest Services Inc—*Gerard T Gabrys*	3055 Prosperity Ave, Fairfax VA 22031	703-849-9300	R	189*	3.5
169	Rubio's Restaurants Inc—*Marc Simon*	1902 Wright Pl Ste 300, Carlsbad CA 92008	760-929-8226	R	189	3.8
170	Jackmont Hospitality Inc—*Daniel Halpern*	100 Peachtree St Ste 2, Atlanta GA 30303	404-523-5744	R	188*	.5
171	Myriad Restaurant Group Inc—*Drew Nieporent*	249 W Broadway Ste2E, New York NY 10013	212-219-9500	R	182*	.5
172	Mcdonald's Restaurants Of Michigan Inc—*Allan Feldman*	1 Mcdonalds Plz, Oak Brook IL 60523	630-623-3000	R	180*	7.3
173	Sbarro America Inc—*Michael Odonnell*	401 Broadhollow Rd Fl, Melville NY 11747	631-864-0200	R	178*	3.0
174	Lettuce Entertain You Too Inc—*Kevin Brown*	5419 N Sheridan Rd Ste, Chicago IL 60640	773-878-7340	R	177*	5.0
175	Max and Erma's Restaurants Inc—*Rob Lindeman*	739S Third Street, Columbus OH 43206	614-431-5800	R	175	1.7
176	Fazoli's Restaurants LLC—*Carl Howard*	2470 Palumbo Dr, Lexington KY 40509	859-268-1668	R	173*	5.5
177	Concord Hospitality Inc—*Maggie Stine*	1701 Windhoek Dr, Lincoln NE 68512	402-421-2551	R	172*	5.0
178	Furr's Restaurant Group Inc—*William Snyder* Buffet Partners LP	2701 E Plano Pkwy Ste, Plano TX 75074		S	171*	4.7
179	Bubba Gump Shrimp Company Restaurant and Market Inc	209 Avenida Fabricante, San Clemente CA 92672	949-366-6260	R	170*	.5
180	James Original Coney Island Inc—*Darrin Straughan*	11111 Katy Fwy Ste 700, Houston TX 77079	713-932-1500	R	170*	.5
181	Thompson Hospitality Corporation Inc—*Warren M Thompson*	505 Huntmar Park Dr St, Herndon VA 20170	703-964-5500	R	165*	2.5
182	Bertucci's Restaurant Corp Bertucci's Corp	155 Otis St, Northborough MA 01532	508-351-2500	S	162*	6.0
183	Noodles and Company Inc—*Kevin Reddy*	520 Zang St, Broomfield CO 80021	720-214-1900	R	162*	4.0
184	Lunan Corp—*Gregory Schulson*	414 N Orleans St Ste 4, Chicago IL 60654	312-645-9898	R	162*	1.2
185	Briad Main Street Inc—*Brad Honigfeld*	78 Okner Pkwy, Livingston NJ 07039	973-597-6433	R	161*	7.0
186	Mcdonald's Restaurants Of Florida Inc—*James Skinner*	1 Mcdonalds Plz, Hinsdale IL 60523	630-623-3000	R	161*	6.7
187	Delaware North Companies Travel Hospitality Services Inc— *Matt King*	40 Fountain Plz Ste 17, Buffalo NY 14202	716-858-5000	R	161*	5.0
188	Bj Holdings Corp—*Eric Newman* Bojangles' Holdings Inc	PO Box 240239, Charlotte NC 28224	704-527-2675	S	161*	4.5
189	Nath Minnesota Franchise Group Inc—*Mahendra Nath*	900 E 79th St Ste 300, Minneapolis MN 55420	952-853-1400	R	160*	1.3
190	Frisch's Ohio Inc—*Craig Maier*	2800 Gilbert Ave, Cincinnati OH 45206	513-961-2660	R	160*	.1
191	Mccormick and Schmick Holding Corp—*William Mc Cormick*	720 Sw Washington St S, Portland OR 97205	503-226-3440	R	158*	4.3
192	On The Border Corp—*Stephen Clark*	6820 Lyndon B Johnson, Dallas TX 75240	972-980-9917	R	157*	6.0
193	Bojangles' Restaurants Inc—*Randy Kibler*	PO Box 240239, Charlotte NC 28224	704-527-2675	R	154*	4.5
194	Latour Management Inc—*Joumna Touhia*	2945 S Kansas St, Wichita KS 67216	316-524-2290	R	153*	.2
195	Bojangles Restaurants Inc—*Randy Kibler*	9432 Southern Pine Blv, Charlotte NC 28273	704-527-2675	R	152*	4.5
196	Interfoods Of America Inc—*Cheryl Bachelder*	5555 Glenridge Connect, Atlanta GA 30342	305-670-0746	R	152*	3.6
197	Del Frisco's Restaurant Group LLC—*Mark S Mednansky*	224 E Douglas Ste 700, Wichita KS 67202	316-264-8899	R	152*	2.3
198	Bojangles' Holdings Inc—*Joe Drury*	PO Box 240239, Charlotte NC 28224	704-527-2675	R	151*	4.5
199	Sammy's Woodfired Pizza—*Sami Ladoki*	565 Pearl St Ste 225, La Jolla CA 92037	858-456-8018	R	151*	.5
200	Miami Subs Corp—*Don Perlyn* Nathan's Famous Inc	6300 NW 31st Ave, Fort Lauderdale FL 33309	954-973-0000	S	150*	.5
201	J Alexander's Corp—*Lonnie J Stout II*	3401 West End Ave Ste, Nashville TN 37203		P	149	2.8
202	Famous Dave's of America Inc—*Christopher O'Donnell*	12701 Whitewater Dr St, Minnetonka MN 55343	952-294-1300	P	148	3.2
203	Osf International Inc—*Chris Dussin*	0715 Suthwest Bancroft, Portland OR 97239	503-225-0433	R	148*	3.7
204	Shari's Management Corp	9400 SW Gemini Dr, Beaverton OR 97008	503-605-4299	R	148*	4.5
205	Pepper Dining Inc—*John Mcglone*	11600 N Cmnity House R, Charlotte NC 28277	704-943-5276	R	147*	6.0
206	AFC Enterprises Inc—*Cheryl Bachelder*	5555 Glendridge Connec, Atlanta GA 30342	404-459-4450	P	146	1.2
207	Caterair Holdings Corp—*Donald West*	524 E Lamar Blvd, Arlington TX 76011	817-792-2100	S	145*	6.0
208	Breads Of The World LLC—*Clay Vratny*	2433 S Hanley Rd, Saint Louis MO 63144	314-644-6226	R	144*	2.8
209	Sybra LLC—*Susan Kaplis*	1155 Perimetr Ctr W St, Atlanta GA 30338	678-514-4100	S	143*	4.3
210	Thomas And King Of Arizona Inc—*Michael Scanlon*	249 E Main St Ste 101, Lexington KY 40507	859-254-2180	R	141*	4.0
211	Ark Restaurants Corp—*Nancy Alvarez*	85 5th Ave 14th Fl, New York NY 10003	212-206-8800	P	139	2.0
212	Zarda Development Company Inc—*Michael Zarda*	214 N 7 Hwy, Blue Springs MO 64014	816-229-9999	R	138*	.2
213	Taco Cabana Inc—*Stephen Clark* Carrols Restaurant Group Inc	8918 Tesoro Dr, San Antonio TX 78217	210-804-0990	R	137*	4.0
214	Grotto Pizza Inc—*Dominick Pulieri*	20376 Coastal Hwy, Rehoboth Beach DE 19971	302-227-3567	R	136*	1.0
215	Canterbury Park Concessions Inc	1100 Canterbury Rd, Shakopee MN 55379	952-445-7223	S	136*	.4
216	Brown's Chicken and Pasta Inc—*Toni Portillo*	55 E Park Blvd, Villa Park IL 60181	630-359-5358	R	133*	.4
217	Parrish Mcdonald's Restaurants Ltd—*Roland Parrish*	12300 Lake June Rd, Mesquite TX 75180	972-286-7673	R	131*	.4
218	Restaurants Unlimited Inc—*Steve Stoddard*	1818 N Northlake Way, Seattle WA 98103		R	130*	4.0
219	Mitzel's American Kitchen Inc—*Dennis Waldron* Elmer's Restaurants Inc	22330 84th Ave S, Kent WA 98032	425-355-3383	S	130*	1.2
220	El Chico Restaurants Inc—*John Harkey* Consolidated Restaurant Operations Inc	12200 Stemmons Fwy Ste, Dallas TX 75234	972-241-5500	S	128*	3.2
221	Ark Operating Corp—*Michael Weinstein* Ark Restaurants Corp	85 5th Ave 14th Fl, New York NY 10003	212-206-8800	R	125*	1.4
222	Smith and Wollensky Restaurant Group Inc—*Nick Valenti*	260 Franklin St Ste 24, Boston MA 02110	617-600-3500	R	125*	1.7
223	Palm Management Corp—*Bruce Bozzi Sr*	1730 Rhode Island Ave, Washington DC 20036	202-775-7256	R	125*	1.6
224	DavCo Restaurants Inc—*Harvey Rothstein*	1657 Crofton Blvd, Crofton MD 21114	410-721-3770	R	123*	4.5
225	Il Fornaio America Corp—*Michael Beatrice*	770 Tamalpais Dr Ste 4, Corte Madera CA 94925	415-945-0500	R	122*	3.0
226	Morton's of Chicago Inc Morton's Restaurant Group Inc	325 N LaSalle St Ste 5, Chicago IL 60654	847-413-8771	S	120*	2.0
227	Grandmother's Inc—*Dean Rasmussen*	5310 S 84th St Ste 200, Omaha NE 68127	402-334-1007	R	115*	.3
228	Fazoli's System Management—*Carl Howard*	2470 Palumbo Dr, Lexington KY 40509	859-268-1668	S	113*	4.2
229	Donatos Pizzeria Corp—*Jane Grote Abell*	935 Taylor Station Rd, Columbus OH 43230	614-416-7700	R	113*	3.8
230	Cosi Inc—*James F Hyatt*	1751 Lake Cook Rd 6th, Deerfield IL 60015	847-597-8880	P	110	2.0
231	Krystal Co—*James Exum Jr*	1 Union Sq, Chattanooga TN 37402	423-757-1550	R	104*	3.2
232	Tacala Inc—*Don Ghareeb*	4268 Cahaba Heights Ct, Birmingham AL 35243	205-443-9600	R	102	3.0
233	Port-of-Subs Inc—*John R Larsen*	5365 Mae Anne Ave Ste, Reno NV 89523	775-747-0555	R	101*	.1
234	Agro Land and Cattle Company Inc—*Daniel Bates*	6541 E Tanque Verde Rd, Tucson AZ 85715	520-296-5442	R	98*	.3
235	Gordon Biersch Brewery Restaurant Group Inc—*Dan Gordon*	2001 Riverside Dr, Chattanooga TN 37406	423-424-2000	S	97*	2.1
236	Morgan's Foods Inc—*Leonard R Stein-Sapir*	4829 Galaxy Pky Ste S, Cleveland OH 44128	216-359-9000	P	90	1.7
237	Granite City Food and Brewery Ltd—*Steven J Wagenheim*	5402 Parkdale Dr Ste 1, Saint Louis Park MN 55416	952-215-0660	P	89	2.3

Note: An asterisk (*) indicates an estimated financial figure. The company type code used is as follows: R = Private, P = Public, S = Private Subsidiary, B = Public Subsidiary, D = Division, J = Joint Venture, I = Investment Fund.

ANKINGS BY SALES WITHIN 4-DIGIT SIC

	ny Name—*Executive Officer*	Address, City, State, Zip	Phone	Type	Fin	Empls
38	Kona Grill Inc—*Michael A Nahkunst*	7150 E Camelback Rd St, Scottsdale AZ 85251	480-922-8100	P	88	2.0
239	Fuddruckers Inc—*Peter Large*	5700 Mopac Expwy S, Austin TX 78749	512-891-1300	R	87	3.8
240	BR Associates Inc—*Robert Ruckriegel*	4201-A Manheim Rd, Jasper IN 47546	812-482-3212	R	87*	2.6
241	Halo Burger—*Lou Dortch*	800 S Saginaw St, Flint MI 48502	810-238-4607	R	85*	.2
242	Fresh Enterprises Inc—*David Kim*	5900 Katella Ave Ste 1, Cypress CA 90630	562-391-2400	R	78	2.2
243	Star Buffet Inc—*Robert E Wheaton*	1312 N Scottsdale Rd, Scottsdale AZ 85257	480-425-0397	P	78	1.8
244	Taco John's International Inc—*Barry Sims*	PO Box 1589, Cheyenne WY 82003	307-635-0101	R	78*	.3
245	Iron Horse	20 Washington Ave, Westwood NJ 07675	201-666-9682	R	76*	.1
246	Lindley Food Services—*Gilbert Rossomondo*	201 Wallace St, New Haven CT 06511	203-777-3598	S	75*	.2
247	Flanigan's Enterprises Inc—*Joseph G Flanigan*	5059 NE 18th Ave, Fort Lauderdale FL 33334	954-377-1961	P	72	1.1
248	Bridgeman Foods Inc—*Ulysses L Bridgeman Jr*	2025 W South Branch Bl, Oak Creek WI 53154	414-302-5650	R	72*	2.5
249	Jerry's Famous Deli Inc—*Guy Starkman*	12711 Ventura Blvd Ste, Studio City CA 91604	818-766-8311	R	72*	1.5
250	Meritage Hospitality Group Inc—*Robert E Schermer Jr*	3310 Eagle Run Dr NE S, Grand Rapids MI 49525	616-776-2600	R	70	1.7
251	Union Square Hospitality Group	24 Union Square East, New York NY 10003	212-228-3585	R	70	<.1
252	Sonic Restaurants Inc—*Omar Janjua* Sonic Corp	300 Johnny Bench Dr, Oklahoma City OK 73104	405-225-5000	S	69*	.2
253	Empire Resorts Inc—*Joseph D'Amato*	PO Box 5013, Monticello NY 12701	845-807-0001	P	68	.3
254	CA Muer Corp Landry's Restaurants Inc	1510 W Loop South, Houston TX 77027	713-850-1010	S	66*	2.0
255	A and W Restaurants Inc—*Roger Eaton* Yum! Brands Inc	1900 Colonel Sanders L, Louisville KY 40213	502-874-3000	S	66	1.3
256	Carisch Inc—*Fred Stauber*	641 E Lake St Ste 226, Wayzata MN 55391	952-473-4291	R	66*	.6
257	Mexican Restaurants Inc—*Curt Glowacki*	12000 Aerospace Ave, Houston TX 77034	832-300-5858	P	66	2.0
258	Nutrition Inc—*Edward Caswell*	580 Wendel Rd Ste 100, Irwin PA 15642	724-978-2100	R	64*	2.0
259	America's Incredible Pizza Co—*Scott Axon*	2772 S Campbell Ave, Springfield MO 65807	417-890-1408	R	64	1.2
260	Spaghetti Warehouse Inc	5525 Mac Arthur Blvd S, Irving TX 75038	972-536-2002	R	64*	3.4
261	Bickford's Family Restaurants—*Alexander Milley* ELXSI Corp	37 Oak St, Brockton MA 02301	617-782-4010	S	62*	2.6
262	Pancho's Mexican Buffet Inc—*Marty Adler*	3500 Noble Ave, Fort Worth TX 76111	817-838-1424	R	62*	2.2
263	Kings Family Restaurants—*Hartley C King*	1180 Long Run Rd, McKeesport PA 15131	412-751-0700	R	60*	3.0
264	Pappa's Bar-B-Que—*Chris Pappas*	PO Box 41567, Houston TX 77241		S	60*	.1
265	Rainforest Cafe Inc (Overland Park Kansas)—*Jim Anderson* Landry's Restaurants Inc	11327 W 95th St, Overland Park KS 66214	913-438-7676	S	59*	.2
266	Abigail Kirsch at Tappan Hill Inc—*Jim Kirsh*	81 Highland Ave, Tarrytown NY 10591	914-631-3030	R	59*	.1
267	Nathan's Famous Inc—*Eric Gatoff*	1 Jericho Plaza 2nd Fl, Jericho NY 11753	516-338-8500	P	57	.3
268	Romacorp Inc—*John Morgan*	1700 Alma Dr Ste 400, Plano TX 75075	214-343-7800	R	57*	1.7
269	Buckhead Life Restaurant Group—*Pano Karatassos*	265 Pharr Rd NE, Atlanta GA 30305	404-237-2060	R	57*	.2
270	Schlotzsky's Inc—*Kelly Roddy*	301 Congress Ave Ste 1, Austin TX 78701	512-236-3600	S	56	1.1
271	Kahunaville Management Inc—*David Tuttleman*	3300 Las Vegas Blvd, Las Vegas NV 89109	702-894-7111	R	55*	3.3
272	Marcus Restaurants Inc—*Larry Flam*	100 E Wisconsin Ave St, Milwaukee WI 53202	414-905-1000	S	55*	2.5
273	Cassano's Inc—*Vic Cassano Jr*	1700 E Stroop Rd, Kettering OH 45429	937-294-8400	R	55*	.4
274	Lauraine Murphy Jericho Inc—*Bruce Murphy*	585 N Broadway, Jericho NY 11753	516-931-2201	R	55*	.4
275	Panera LLC Panera Bread Co	6710 Clayton Rd, Richmond Heights MO 63117	314-633-7100	S	54*	.2
276	K-Paul's Louisiana Enterprises Inc—*Paul Prudhomme*	416 Chartres St, New Orleans LA 70130	504-524-7394	R	54*	.1
277	ELXSI Corp—*Alexander M Milley*	3600 Rio Vista Ave Ste, Orlando FL 32805	407-849-1090	P	52	2.4
278	Grandy's Inc—*Ward Olgreen*	401 S Stemmons Fwy, Lewisville TX 75067	972-434-9225	R	52*	1.8
279	Johnny Rockets Group Inc—*Lee Sanders*	20 Enterprise Dr Ste 3, Aliso Viejo CA 92656	949-643-6100	R	51*	2.3
280	RLW Inc (Las Vegas Nevada)—*Jackie L Robinson*	6325 Harrison Dr Ste 1, Las Vegas NV 89120	702-798-3696	R	51*	2.1
281	Daniel (New York New York)—*Daniel Boulud*	60 E 65th St, New York NY 10021	212-288-0033	R	51*	.2
282	Jean-Georges Enterprises LLC	111 Prince St 2nd Fl, New York NY 10012	212-358-0688	R	50*	2.0
283	Planet Hollywood International Inc—*David Crabtree*	6052 Turkey Lake Rd, Orlando FL 32819	407-903-5500	R	50*	1.0
284	HLW Fast Track Inc—*Herbert L Washington*	4900 Market St, Youngstown OH 44512	330-783-5659	R	50*	1.0
285	Fog Cutter Capital Group Inc—*Andrew A Wiederhorn*	301 Arizona Ave Ste 20, Santa Monica CA 90401	310-319-1850	P	50	.9
286	D and B Holding Inc—*Stephen King* Dave and Buster's Holdings Inc	2481 Manana Dr, Dallas TX 75220	214-357-9588	S	49*	1.3
287	Dave and Buster's of Georgia Inc—*Steve King* Dave and Buster's Holdings Inc	2215 D And B Dr SE, Marietta GA 30067	770-951-5554	S	49*	.2
288	Wall Street Deli Inc—*Jeffrey Bernstein* TruFoods LLC	14 Penn Plz Ste 1305, New York NY 10122	212-359-3600	S	48*	.9
289	Back Yard Burgers Inc—*C Stephen Lynn*	500 Church St Ste 200, Nashville TN 37219	615-620-2300	S	45	1.0
290	Fresh Choice Inc—*Tim G O'Shea*	485 Cochrane Cir, Morgan Hill CA 95037		R	44*	1.1
291	Lou Malnati's Pizzeria—*Marc Malnati*	3685 Woodhead Dr, Northbrook IL 60062	847-562-1814	R	41*	.1
292	Mr Gatti's Inc—*Mike Mrlik II*	5912 Balcones Dr Ste 2, Austin TX 78731	512-459-4796	R	40*	1.5
293	Fili Enterprises Inc—*George Katakalidis*	6125 Cornerstone Crt S, San Diego CA 92121		R	40*	.5
294	Sirloin Saloon Inc—*David Melincoff*	8057 Raytheon Rd Ste 1, San Diego CA 92111	858-874-1846	R	40*	.4
295	Alexander's Restaurants of Texas Inc—*Raul Soria* J Alexander's Corp	255 E Basse Rd Ste1300, San Antonio TX 78209	210-824-0275	S	39*	.1
296	Chesapeake Bay Seafood House Associates LP	1960 Gallows Rd Ste 20, Vienna VA 22182	703-827-0320	R	38*	1.5
297	Logan's Roadhouse Inc—*Tom Vogel*	PO Box 291047, Nashville TN 37229	615-885-9056	R	38*	1.2
298	Hilltop Steak House Inc—*Don Doward*	855 Broadway, Saugus MA 01906	781-233-7700	S	38*	.3
299	Typhoon Inc—*Bo Kline*	720 SW Washington Ste, Portland OR 97205	503-222-7991	R	38*	.1
300	Big Boy Restaurants International LLC—*Debra Murphy*	4199 Marcy St, Warren MI 48091	586-759-6000	R	38*	1.5
301	Hasslocher Enterprises Inc—*Robert Hasslocher*	8520 Crownhill Blvd, San Antonio TX 78209	210-828-1493	R	37*	1.3
302	Maid-Rite Corp—*Bradley L Burt*	2951 86th St, Des Moines IA 50322	515-276-5448	R	35*	.1
303	Sylvia's Food Products Inc—*Sylvia Woods*	328 Lennox Ave, New York NY 10027	212-996-0660	R	35*	.1
304	Dynamic Management Company LLC—*Robert M Langford*	313 E Main St Ste 1, Hendersonville TN 37075	615-277-1234	R	35*	<.1
305	Cafe Rio Inc—*Bob Nilsen*	2825 E Cottonwood Pky, Salt Lake City UT 84121	801-930-6000	R	34*	.6
306	Premier and Carriage Trade Inc—*Patricia Karetas*	7966 Arjons Dr, San Diego CA 92126	858-621-5151	R	33*	.3
307	On A Roll Sales Inc—*Alan Leppo*	121 Liberty St, Brockton MA 02301	508-586-8418	R	33*	.1
308	Silver Diner Inc—*Bob Giaimo*	12276 Rockville Pike, Rockville MD 20852	301-770-0333	R	32*	1.0
309	Culinary Ventures Vending—*Joseph Cirillo*	1835 Burnet Ave, Union NJ 07083	908-624-9940	R	32*	.1
310	Gastronomy Inc—*John Williams*	48 W Market St Ste 250, Salt Lake City UT 84101	801-322-2020	R	31*	.9
311	Cousins Submarines Inc—*William Specht*	N 83 W 13400 Leon Rd, Menomonee Falls WI 53051	262-253-7700	R	30*	.8
312	Anthony's Seafood Group—*Richard A Ghio*	215 Bay Blvd, Chula Vista CA 91910	619-651-2345	R	30*	.6
313	Fox and Hound of Michigan Inc—*Ellis King* Fox and Hound Restaurant Group	22091 Michigan Ave, Dearborn MI 48124	313-277-3212	S	30*	.1
314	Fox and Hound of Missouri Inc (Springfield Missouri)—*Betsy Bridgers* Fox and Hound Restaurant Group	2035 E Independence St, Springfield MO 65804	417-890-6289	S	30*	.1

Rank	Company Name—*Executive Officer*	Address, City, State, Zip	Phone	Type	Fin	Empls
315	Kahala-Cold Stone Corp—*Kevin Blackwell*	9311 E Via De Ventura, Scottsdale AZ 85258	480-443-0200	R	29*	.4
316	J Alexander's Restaurants of Kansas Inc	11471 Metcalf Ave, Overland Park KS 66210	913-469-1995	S	29*	.1
	J Alexander's Corp					
317	PA Menard Inc—*Michael F Menard*	PO Box 50158, New Orleans LA 70150	504-523-6882	R	29*	.1
318	Native New Yorker Inc	2110 S Gilber Rd, Chandler AZ 85286	480-782-0840	R	29*	N/A
319	Skyline Chili Inc—*Kevin Mc Donnell*	4180 Thunderbird Ln, Fairfield OH 45014	513-874-1188	R	28*	1.0
320	Blimpie International Inc—*Jeffrey K Endervelt*	180 Interstate N Pky S, Atlanta GA 30339		S	28*	.1
321	CA One Services Inc—*Nick Ellen*	40 Fountain Plz, Buffalo NY 14202	716-858-5000	S	27*	3.0
	Delaware North Companies Inc					
322	Italianni's—*Brett Russell*	1601 Precinct Line Rd, Hurst TX 76054	817-498-6770	R	27*	.5
323	Crab House Inc	8291 International Dr, Orlando FL 32819	407-352-6140	S	27*	.1
	Landry's Restaurants Inc					
324	Landry's Seafood House (Birmingham Alabama)—*Jay Allan*	139 State Farm Pky, Birmingham AL 35209	205-916-0777	S	27*	.1
	Landry's Restaurants Inc					
325	Heartland Brewery—*John Bloostein*	35 Union Sq W, New York NY 10003	212-645-3400	R	27*	.1
326	Good Times Drive Thru Inc—*Scott G LeFever*	601 Corporate Cir, Golden CO 80401	303-384-1400	S	26	.1
	Good Times Restaurants Inc					
327	Fox and Hound of Houston No 2 Ltd—*Tim Myers*	12802 Gulf Fwy, Houston TX 77034	281-481-0068	S	26*	.1
	Fox and Hound Restaurant Group					
328	Fox and Hound of Virginia Inc—*Kevin Garrison*	7502 W Broad St, Richmond VA 23294	804-755-6800	S	26*	.1
	Fox and Hound Restaurant Group					
329	O'Charley's Sports Bar Inc—*Gregory L Burns*	1709 Fulton Rd, Fultondale AL 35068	205-849-6401	S	26*	.1
	O'Charley's Inc					
330	Martin's Caterers Inc—*Wayne Resnick*	6817 Dogwood Rd, Baltimore MD 21244	410-944-9433	R	25*	.8
331	Columbia Restaurant Group Inc—*Richard Gonzmart*	2025 E 7th Ave, Tampa FL 33605	813-248-3000	R	25*	.7
332	Grand Traverse Pie Co—*Michael Busley*	525 W Front St, Traverse City MI 49684	231-922-7437	R	25*	N/A
333	Preferred Meal Systems Inc—*Joseph Bistritzky*	5240 Saint Charles Rd, Berkeley IL 60163	708-318-2500	R	25*	1.0
334	Fox and Hound of Pennsylvania Inc—*Jim Smith*	2002 N Way Mall, Pittsburgh PA 15237	412-364-1885	S	24*	.1
	Fox and Hound Restaurant Group					
335	Fox and Hound of Richardson Ltd—*Todd Creeknur*	112 W Campbell Rd, Richardson TX 75080	972-437-4225	S	24*	.1
	Fox and Hound Restaurant Group					
336	Libby Hill Seafood Restaurants Inc	4517 W Market St, Greensboro NC 27407	336-294-0505	R	24*	<.1
337	Boston Restaurant Associates Inc—*Robert C Taft*	6 Kimball Ln Ste 210, Lynnfield MA 01940	339-219-0466	R	24	.4
338	Bazaar Del Mundo Inc—*Diane Powers*	4133 Taylor St, San Diego CA 92110	619-296-3161	R	23*	.7
339	Fast Eddie's Bon Air—*Eddie Scholar Sr*	1530 E 4th St, Alton IL 62002	618-462-5532	R	23*	.1
340	Chefs International Inc—*Robert Lombardi*	62 Broadway, Point Pleasant Beach NJ 08742	732-295-0350	R	22	.6
341	Pizzaco Inc—*Carol Schroeder*	121 W Marlin Ste 300, McPherson KS 67460	620-241-5588	S	22*	.1
	Pizza Hut Inc					
342	Original Pete's Pizza Pasta Grill Inc—*Allen Rosenberg*	5005 Foothills Blvd, Roseville CA 95747	916-786-2154	R	22*	<.1
343	Dunkin' Donuts Inc—*Will Kussell*	130 Royall St, Canton MA 02021	781-737-3000	S	21*	.7
	Dunkin' Brands Group Inc					
344	Bravo Restaurants Inc—*Jeffrey Himmel*	600 W Jackson 2nd Fl, Chicago IL 60661	312-463-1239	R	21*	.5
345	Le Colonial Corp—*Jean Goutal*	149 E 57th St, New York NY 10022	212-752-0808	R	21*	.1
346	Good Times Restaurants Inc—*Boyd E Hoback*	601 Corporate Cir, Golden CO 80401	303-384-1400	P	21	.4
347	Culinaire International Inc—*Richard N Gussoni*	2100 Ross Ave Ste 3100, Dallas TX 75201	214-754-1880	R	20*	1.1
348	Aloha Restaurants Inc—*Steve Moyer*	17320 Redhill Ave Ste1, Irvine CA 92614	949-250-0331	R	20	.8
349	El Gallo Giro Inc—*Carlos Bonaparte*	8141 2nd St Ste 414, Downey CA 90241	562-904-7088	R	20*	.3
350	Nutrition Management Services Co—*Joseph V Roberts*	2071 Kimberton Rd, Kimberton PA 19442	610-935-2050	P	20	.3
351	Quizno's Corp—*Rick Schaden*	1001 17th St Ste 200, Denver CO 80202	720-359-3300	R	20*	.2
352	Del Frisco's Double Eagle Steak House—*Jamie Coulter*	5251 Spring Valley Rd, Dallas TX 75254	972-490-9000	D	20*	.2
	Lone Star Steakhouse and Saloon Inc					
353	Concession Services Inc—*Edith Leonian*	1723 S Michigan Ave, Chicago IL 60616	312-987-9500	R	20*	.1
354	Fox and Hound of Kansas Inc—*Jennifer O'Dell*	10428 Metcalf Ave, Overland Park KS 66212	913-649-1700	S	19*	.1
	Fox and Hound Restaurant Group					
355	MEG Restaurant Enterprises Ltd	102 E 22nd St, New York NY 10010		R	19*	<.1
356	Western Sizzlin Corp—*Sardan Biglari*	PO Box 12167, Roanoke VA 24023		S	17	.3
	Biglari Holdings Inc					
357	Fox and Hound of Lewisville Ltd—*Fernando Varela*	1640 S Stemmons Fwy, Lewisville TX 75067	972-221-8346	S	17*	.1
	Fox and Hound Restaurant Group					
358	Izzy's Franchise Systems Inc—*D Fred Jansen*	PO Box 1689, Albany OR 97321	541-926-8693	R	16*	.6
359	Aunt Sarahs LLC—*John Dankos*	PO Box 9504, Richmond VA 23228	804-264-9189	R	16*	.5
360	Along Came Mary Productions Inc—*Mary Micucci*	5265 W Pico Blvd, Los Angeles CA 90019	323-931-9082	R	16*	.1
361	Fox and Hound of Indiana Inc—*Nathan Smith*	4901 E 82nd St Ste 900, Indianapolis IN 46250	317-913-1264	S	16*	.1
	Fox and Hound Restaurant Group					
362	Fox and Hound of Tennessee Inc—*Joe Clark*	819 Exocet Dr, Cordova TN 38018	901-624-9060	S	16*	.1
	Fox and Hound Restaurant Group					
363	Organic to Go Food Corp—*Jason Brown*	PO Box 1040, Mercer Island WA 98040		R	16	.3
364	Dick Clark Restaurants Inc—*Orly Adelson*	2900 Olympic Blvd, Santa Monica CA 90404	310-255-4600	S	15	.5
365	Wynkoop Brewing Co—*Lee Driscoll*	1634 18th St, Denver CO 80202	303-297-2700	R	15*	.5
366	TruFoods LLC—*Andy Unanue*	14 Penn Plz Ste 1305, New York NY 10122	212-359-3600	R	15*	.2
367	Fox and Hound of Louisiana Inc—*Anthony Chapman*	5246 Corporate Blvd, Baton Rouge LA 70808	225-926-1444	S	15*	<.1
	Fox and Hound Restaurant Group					
368	Jimmy John's Inc—*James Liautaud*	2212 Fox Dr, Champaign IL 61820	217-356-9900	R	15*	<.1
369	Claim Jumper Restaurants—*Robert Ott*	16721 Millikan Ave, Irvine CA 92606	949-756-9001	R	14*	5.0
370	VIPS Industries Inc—*T J Sullivan*	201 Liberty Street Sou, Salem OR 97301	503-779-1606	R	13*	.5
371	Huddle House Inc—*Ken keymer*	PO Box 906, Scottdale GA 30079	770-325-1300	R	13*	.1
372	Fox and Hound of Houston Ltd—*Patrick Lerma*	11470 Westheimer Rd, Houston TX 77077	281-589-2122	S	13*	<.1
	Fox and Hound Restaurant Group					
373	Fox and Hound of Lubbock Ltd—*Mitchell Jones*	4210 82nd St Unit 240, Lubbock TX 79423	806-791-1526	S	13*	<.1
	Fox and Hound Restaurant Group					
374	Fox and Hound of Nebraska Inc—*Jessica Ulrich*	506 N 120th St Western, Omaha NE 68154	402-964-9074	S	13*	<.1
	Fox and Hound Restaurant Group					
375	Fox and Hound of San Antonio Ltd—*Sean Gillispie*	12651 Vance Jackson Rd, San Antonio TX 78230	210-690-1356	S	13*	<.1
	Fox and Hound Restaurant Group					
376	Papa John's USA Inc	2002 Papa John's Blvd, Louisville KY 40299	502-261-7272	S	13*	<.1
	Papa John's International Inc					
377	Mr Goodcents Franchise Systems Inc—*Dave Goebel*	8997 Commerce Dr, De Soto KS 66018	913-583-8400	R	13*	<.1
378	Busler Enterprises Inc—*George W Busler*	PO Box 23610, Evansville IN 47724	812-424-7511	R	12*	.1
379	Happy Chef Systems Inc—*Thomas P Frederick Sr*	PO Box 3328, Mankato MN 56002	507-345-4671	R	11*	.2
380	Schmidt's Restaurants and Catering—*Andrew Schmidt*	240 E Kossuth St Germa, Columbus OH 43216	614-444-5908	R	11*	.1

Note: An asterisk (*) indicates an estimated financial figure. The company type code used is as follows: R = Private, P = Public, S = Private Subsidiary, B = Public Subsidiary, D = Division, J = Joint Venture, I = Investment Fund.

COMPANY RANKINGS BY SALES WITHIN 4-DIGIT SIC

Rank	Company Name—Executive Officer	Address, City, State, Zip	Phone	Type	Fin	Empls
381	Fox and Hound of Ohio Inc—Chris King Fox and Hound Restaurant Group	667 Lyons Rd Washingto, Dayton OH 45459	937-432-9904	S	11*	<.1
382	Papachinos Franchise Corp—Mary Manos	2650 Via De La Valle, Del Mar CA 92014	858-481-7171	R	10*	.3
383	Caspers Co—Blake Casper	4908 W Nassau St, Tampa FL 33607	813-287-2231	R	10*	.1
384	Fox and Hound of Fort Worth Ltd Fox and Hound Restaurant Group	6051 SW Loop 820 Ste 3, Fort Worth TX 76132	817-423-3600	S	10*	<.1
385	F and H Restaurant of Georgia Inc—Joe Kolegue Fox and Hound Restaurant Group	2500 Cobb Pl Ln NW Ste, Kennesaw GA 30144	770-794-4444	S	10*	<.1
386	Mansion on Turtle Creek—Duncan Graham	2821 Turtle Creek Blvd, Dallas TX 75219	214-559-2100	S	9*	.3
387	Coleman's Authentic Irish Pub—Peter J Coleman	100 S Lowell Ave, Syracuse NY 13204	315-476-1933	R	9*	.1
388	Rollerz Kahala-Cold Stone Corp	9311 E Via de Ventura, Scottsdale AZ 85258	480-362-4800	S	9*	<.1
389	Betty A Jones Catering Inc—Julie Schamel	1801 Beechwood Ave, New Albany IN 47150	812-944-3640	R	9*	<.1
390	BR Guest Inc—Stephen Hanson	206 Spring St, New York NY 10012	212-529-0900	R	9*	<.1
391	Northwest Florida Facility Management Inc—Saras Taveprung- senuku	137 Eglin Pkwy Se, Fort Walton Beach FL 32548	850-244-2388	R	9*	.3
392	White Coffee Pot Family Inns Inc—Robert J Katz	137 S Warwick Ave, Baltimore MD 21223	410-233-8600	R	8*	.1
393	LDB Corp—Lloyd D Brinkman	444 Sidney Baker St S, Kerrville TX 78028	830-257-2100	R	8*	<.1
394	Ruth Meric Catering—Ruthee Meric	3030 Audley St, Houston TX 77098	713-522-1448	R	8*	<.1
395	Noble Roman's Inc—Paul W Mobley	1 Virginia Ave Ste 300, Indianapolis IN 46204	317-634-3377	P	7	<.1
396	SoDel Concepts—Matt Haley	PO Box 31, Bethany Beach DE 19930	302-228-3786	R	7*	.2
397	Grand Havana Enterprises Inc—Stanley Shuster	1990 Westwood Blvd 3rd, Los Angeles CA 90025	310-475-5600	R	7*	.1
398	Bailey Co—David Bailey	601 Corporate Cir, Golden CO 80401	303-384-0200	R	7*	.1
399	Jake's Pizza Enterprises John Flowers	1931 Rohlwing Rd Ste B, Rolling Meadows IL 60008	847-368-1990	R	7*	<.1
400	Manchester Creamery LLC—Raymond Boucher	46 Milford St, Manchester NH 03102	603-623-7242	R	7*	.2
401	Reggio's Pizza Inc—John Clark	340 W 83rd St, Chicago IL 60620	773-488-1411	R	6*	.2
402	Cici's Enterprises Inc—Michael R Shumsky	1080 W Bethel Rd, Coppell TX 75019	972-745-4200	R	6*	.3
403	Jody Maroni's Sausage Kingdom—Roberto Dias	PO Box 1487, Burbank CA 91507	310-822-5639	R	6*	<.1
404	Breadeaux Pizza Inc—Matthew G Gilliland	PO Box 6158, Saint Joseph MO 64506		R	6*	<.1
405	Sarris Candies Inc—Frank Sarris	511 Adams Ave, Canonsburg PA 15317	724-745-4042	R	6*	.3
406	Mangia Pizza and Pasta Inc—David White	PO Box 364, Clinton NY 13323	315-853-8698	R	6*	.2
407	In-N-Out Burgers—Lynski Martinez	4199 Campus Dr 9th Fl, Irvine CA 92612	949-509-6200	R	5*	.2
408	OOC Inc—Todd Parent	1062 Folsom St, San Francisco CA 94103	415-703-8122	R	5*	.2
409	Papa Romanos Inc—Moe Sermour	8101 Richardson Rd Ste, Commerce Township MI 48390	248-888-7272	S	5*	<.1
410	Bickford's Holding Company Inc—Sandy Milley Bickford's Family Restaurants	37 Oak St Ext, Brockton MA 02301	617-782-4010	S	5*	<.1
411	Fowler Card Club Inc	4735 S Durango Dr Ste, Las Vegas NV 89147	702-227-9800	S	5*	<.1
412	Young's Jersey Dairy Inc—C Young	6880 Springfield Xenia, Yellow Springs OH 45387	937-325-0629	R	5*	.3
413	Ufood Restaurant Group Inc—George Naddaff	255 Washington St Ste, Newton MA 02458	617-787-6000	P	5	<.1
414	123 E Doty Corp—Eliot Butler	123 E Doty St Ste 1, Madison WI 53703	608-284-0000	R	5*	.1
415	Spicy Pickle Franchising Inc—Mark Laramie	90 Madison St Ste 700, Denver CO 80206	303-297-1902	P	5	.1
416	Buscemi's International Inc—Anthony P Buscemi	30362 Gratiot Ave, Roseville MI 48066	586-296-5560	R	4	.1
417	Zpizza International Inc—Sid Fanarof	19712 MacArthur Blvd S, Irvine CA 92612	949-222-5600	R	4*	.1
418	Schirf Brewing Co—J Schirf	250 Main St, Park City UT 84060	435-645-9500	R	4*	.1
419	Deli Management Inc—Joe V Tortorice	2400 Broadway, Beaumont TX 77702	409-838-1976	R	4*	<.1
420	Little Rock Back Yard Burgers Inc—Stephen Lynn Back Yard Burgers Inc	305 N Shackleford Rd, Little Rock AR 72211	501-227-5998	S	4*	<.1
421	Faultline Brewing Company Inc—Steven Geiszler	1235 Oakmead Pkwy, Sunnyvale CA 94085	408-736-2739	R	4*	.1
422	Marin Brewing Company Inc—Chris Heajek	1809 Larkspur Landing, Larkspur CA 94939	415-461-4677	R	3*	.1
423	Sourdough Mining Company An Alaska Restaurant Inc— Michael Johnson	5200 Juneau St, Anchorage AK 99518	907-562-2434	R	3*	.1
424	Zoup Fresh Soup Co	29177 Northwestern Hwy, Southfield MI 48034	248-799-2800	R	3*	.1
425	Marble Slab Creamery Inc—Chris Dull	1346 Oakbrook Dr Ste 1, Norcross GA 30093	770-514-4500	S	3*	<.1
426	Le Streghe—Maria Pezzella	331 W Broadway, New York NY 10013	212-343-2080	R	3*	<.1
427	EAJ PHL Airport Inc—Joseph Fiore Eat at Joe's Ltd	8500 Essington Ave, Philadelphia PA 19153	215-937-5141	S	3*	<.1
428	Denver Food System Inc—Bennett Shotwell	3538 Peoria St Ste 508, Aurora CO 80010	303-792-3088	R	3*	<.1
429	Comarco Products Inc—Thomas Hoversen	501 Jackson St, Camden NJ 08104	856-342-7557	R	3*	.1
430	Dixie Chili Inc—Spiros Sarakatsannis	733 Monmouth St, Newport KY 41071	859-291-5337	R	3*	.1
431	uWink Inc—Peter F Wilkniss	6801 Hollywood Blvd St, Los Angeles CA 90028	323-466-1800	P	3	<.1
432	Hideaway Restaurant Inc—Richard Dermer	230 S Knoblock St, Stillwater OK 74074	405-372-4777	R	2*	.1
433	Shelter Harbor Inn Inc—James Dey	10 Wagner Rd, Westerly RI 02891	401-322-8883	R	2*	.1
434	La Baguette Bakery Inc—Namatallah Jazzar	620 N Berry Rd, Norman OK 73069	405-329-4910	R	2*	.1
435	Renault Winery Inc—Joseph Milza	72 N Bremen Ave, Egg Harbor City NJ 08215	609-965-2111	R	2*	.1
436	Taco Via Franchise Systems Inc—Steve Throneberry	1221 NE Rice Rd, Lees Summit MO 64086	816-554-2121	R	2*	.1
437	V's Italiano Ristorante—Greg Hunsucker	10819 E Hwy 40, Independence MO 64055	816-353-1241	R	2*	.1
438	Stuckey's Corp—WS Stuckey Jr	8555 16th St Ste 850, Silver Spring MD 20910	301-913-9800	R	2*	.1
439	Las Vegas America Corp—Michael Weinstein Ark Restaurants Corp	85 5th Ave 14th Fl, New York NY 10003	212-206-8800	S	2*	<.1
440	Emmett's Tavern and Brewing Co—Andrew Burns	128 W Main St, West Dundee IL 60118	847-428-4500	R	2*	.1
441	Miller's Shady Oaks Inc—Jerry Miller	144 Ken Rose Ln, Cave Junction OR 97523	541-592-3556	R	2*	.1
442	Brown's Brewing Co—Garrett Brown	417 River St Ste 417, Troy NY 12180	518-273-2337	R	2*	<.1
443	Ice Cream Club Inc—Richard Draper	1580 High Ridge Rd, Boynton Beach FL 33426	561-731-3331	R	2*	.1
444	Olympia Candy Kitchen—Will Pananes	43 S Main St, Chambersburg PA 17201	717-263-3282	R	2*	<.1
445	Carnegie Management Group LLC	1288b Teaneck Rd, Teaneck NJ 07666	201-833-2265	R	1*	.1
446	Andre Bollier Ltd—Marcel Bollier	5018 Main St, Kansas City MO 64112	816-561-3440	R	1*	.1
447	Damons Management Inc—Shannon Foust	9500 Diamond Centre Dr, Mentor OH 44060	440-358-1847	R	1*	.1
448	Psf Management—Paul Schmidt	9614 Winter Gardens Bl, Lakeside CA 92040	619-390-2706	R	1*	<.1
449	Eat at Joe's Ltd—Joseph Fiore	PO Box 500, Yonkers NY 10703	914-725-2700	P	1	<.1
450	EH Higgins and Son Inc—Glenn Higgins	1216 S Talbot St, Saint Michaels MD 21663	410-745-5056	R	1*	<.1
451	Lancaster Brewing Co—Irene Keares	302 N Plum St, Lancaster PA 17602	717-391-6258	R	1*	<.1
452	V and J Holding Companies Inc—Valerie Daniels-Carter	6933 W Brown Deer Rd, Milwaukee WI 53223	414-365-9003	R	1*	.1
453	World of Good Tastes Inc—Trong D Nguyen	8109-1 Fruitridge Rd, Sacramento CA 95820	916-387-1515	S	1*	<.1
454	Alpine Wurst and Meathouse Inc—Mark Eifert	1106 Texas Palmyra Hwy, Honesdale PA 18431	570-253-5899	R	1*	<.1
455	Chiles Catering Inc—Roger Artman	5181 Falcon Rd, Rockford IL 61109	815-484-9648	R	1*	<.1
456	Anthony's Caribbean Cafe Inc—Tony Martin	2001 E 7th St, Charlotte NC 28204	704-608-9031	R	1*	<.1
457	Bridgemans Ice Cream—Steve Lampi	6201 Brooklyn Blvd, Brooklyn Center MN 55429	763-971-2947	R	1*	<.1
458	Pumpernick's Restaurant and Delicatessen—Paul Kline	917 Bethlehem Pke, North Wales PA 19454	215-393-5800	R	1*	<.1
459	Matt Prentice Restaurant Group—Matthew Prentice	1380 E Jefferson Ave, Detroit MI 48207	248-646-0370	R	1	<.1
460	Roosters Bar and Grill—Bill Gray	7585 S Northshore Dr, Knoxville TN 37919	865-691-3938	R	1*	<.1

Rank	Company Name—*Executive Officer*	Address, City, State, Zip	Phone	Type	Fin	Empls
461	Gray's Ice Cream Inc—*Marilyn Dennis*	16 E Rd, Tiverton RI 02878	401-624-4500	R	1*	<.1
462	Huckleberry Patch—*Jackie Watkins*	PO Box 190001, Hungry Horse MT 59919	406-387-5000	R	1*	<.1
463	Coeur D'alene Brewing Co—*Gage Strombert*	209 E Lakeside Ave, Coeur D Alene ID 83814	208-664-2739	R	1*	<.1
464	Giggles N' Hugs Inc—*Tracie Hadama*	1000 N Green Valley Pk, Henderson NV 89074	702-879-8565	P	<1	N/A
465	Lansdowne Security Inc—*David Roff*	16970 Dallas Pky Ste 4, Dallas TX 75248	972-931-9237	R	<1	N/A
466	Ale House Management Inc—*John Miller*	612 N Orange Ave, Jupiter FL 33458	561-744-3111	R	N/A	3.0
467	KFC Corp—*David Novak* Yum! Brands Inc	1441 Gardiner Ln, Louisville KY 40213	502-874-8300	S	N/A	2.0

TOTALS: SIC 5812 Eating Places
Companies: 467   300,802   4,148.3

5813 Drinking Places

Rank	Company Name—*Executive Officer*	Address, City, State, Zip	Phone	Type	Fin	Empls
1	Rick's Cabaret International Inc—*Eric Langan*	10959 Cutten Rd, Houston TX 77066	281-820-1181	P	83	1.2
2	Mcmenamins Inc—*Mike Menamin*	430 N Killingsworth St, Portland OR 97217	503-223-0109	R	78*	1.4
3	Big Night Entertainment Group Inc—*Ed Kane*	3 Boylston Pl 3rd Fl, Boston MA 02116	617-338-4343	R	17	.2
4	Southern Entertainment USA Inc—*Richy Hasting*	5100 Poplar Ave Ste 21, Memphis TN 38137	901-767-5786	R	16*	.5
5	Blues Alley—*Harry Schnipper*	1073 Wisconsin Ave NW, Washington DC 20007	202-337-4141	R	7*	<.1
6	Salt Lake Brewing Company LC—*Amy Coady*	147 W Broadway, Salt Lake City UT 84101	801-328-2329	R	4*	.2
7	Oaken Barrel Brewing Company Inc—*William Fulton*	50 Airport Pkwy Ste L, Greenwood IN 46143	317-887-2287	R	2*	<.1
8	River City Brewery Inc—*Ty Issa*	150 N Mosley St, Wichita KS 67202	316-263-2739	R	2*	.1
9	Rattlesnake Mountain Brewing Co—*Doug Ryder*	2696 N Columbia Ctr Bl, Richland WA 99352	509-783-5747	R	2*	.1
10	Pennsylvania Brewing Co—*Thomas Pastorius*	800 Vinial St Ste 1, Pittsburgh PA 15212	412-237-9400	R	2*	<.1
11	Cedar Brewing Co—*Rebecca Mumaw Smith*	500 Blairs Ferry Rd Ne, Cedar Rapids IA 52402	319-378-9090	R	1*	<.1

TOTALS: SIC 5813 Drinking Places
Companies: 11   214   3.8

5912 Drug Stores & Proprietary Stores

Rank	Company Name—*Executive Officer*	Address, City, State, Zip	Phone	Type	Fin	Empls
1	CVS Caremark Corp—*Larry J Merlo*	1 CVS Dr, Woonsocket RI 02895	401-765-1500	P	96,413	201.0
2	Walgreen Co—*Gregory D Wasson*	200 Wilmot Rd, Deerfield IL 60015	847-914-2500	P	67,400	244.0
3	Medco Health Solutions Inc—*David B Snow Jr*	PO Box 800, Franklin Lakes NJ 07417	201-269-3400	P	64,889	23.4
4	CVS Pharmacy Inc—*Larry J Merlo* CVS Caremark Corp	1 CVS Dr, Woonsocket RI 02895		S	50,947*	110.0
5	SAM'S Club—*Brian Cornell*	2101 SE Simple Savings, Bentonville AR 72716		D	46,700	36.0
6	Express Scripts Inc—*George Paz*	1 Express Way, St Louis MO 63121	314-996-0900	P	44,973	13.2
7	Rite Aid Corp—*John T Standley*	PO Box 3165, Harrisburg PA 17105	717-761-2633	P	25,215	91.8
8	Fred Meyer Inc—*Mike Ellis*	PO Box 42121, Portland OR 97242	503-797-3830	D	14,900	92.0
9	Bioscrip Inc—*Stephen B Cichy*	100 Clearbrook Rd, Elmsford NY 10523	914-460-1600	P	1,639	2.6
10	Duane Reade Holdings Inc—*John A Lederer* Walgreen Co	440 9th Ave, New York NY 10001	212-273-5700	S	1,575*	6.0
11	Marc Glassman Inc—*Kevin Yaugher*	5841 W 130th St, Parma OH 44130	216-265-7700	R	1,083*	7.0
12	Thrifty Drug Stores—*Robert Narveson*	6901 E Fish Lake Rd St, Maple Grove MN 55369	763-513-4300	R	641*	1.3
13	VS Holdings Inc—*Thomas A Tolworthy*	2101 91st St, North Bergen NJ 07047	201-868-5959	R	627*	3.4
14	Discount Drug Mart Inc—*Parviz Boodjeh*	211 Commerce Dr, Medina OH 44256	330-725-2340	R	533*	2.8
15	Kerr Drug Inc—*Anthony N Civello*	3220 Spring Forest Rd, Raleigh NC 27616	919-544-3896	R	493*	2.3
16	Perfumania Holdings Inc—*Michael W Katz*	35 Sawgrass Dr Ste 2, Bellport NY 11713	631-866-4100	P	485	2.0
17	Astrup Drug Inc—*Leonard B Astrup*	PO Box 658, Austin MN 55912	507-433-7447	R	480*	.2
18	Lewis Drug Inc—*Mark E Griffin*	2701 S Minnesota Ave S, Sioux Falls SD 57105	605-367-2000	R	466*	1.0
19	drugstorecom Inc—*Dawn G Lepore* Walgreen Co	411 108th Ave NE Ste 1, Bellevue WA 98004	425-372-3200	S	457	.9
20	May's Drug Stores Inc—*Gerald Heller*	1437 S Boulder Ave Ste, Tulsa OK 74119	918-592-6297	S	396*	.9
21	Diplomat Specialty Pharmacy—*Phil Hagerman*	4100 S Saginaw St, Flint MI 48507	810-768-9000	R	378*	.4
22	Medicap Pharmacies Inc—*Terry Burnside*	1 Rider Trail Plaza Dr, Earth City MO 63045	314-993-6000	S	359*	.1
23	Navarro Discount Pharmacies Inc—*Steve Kaczynski*	9400 NW 104th St, Medley FL 33178	305-633-3000	S	309*	2.0
24	RxAmerica LLC CVS Caremark Corp	221 N Charles Lindberg, Salt Lake City UT 84116	801-961-6000	S	305*	.7
25	PetMed Express Inc—*Menderes Akdag*	1441 SW 29th Ave, Pompano Beach FL 33069	954-979-5995	P	232	.2
26	Happy Harry's Inc Walgreen Co	200 Wilmot Rd, Deerfield IL 60015	847-940-2500	S	200*	1.6
27	Quidsi—*Marc Lore*	PO Box 483, Jersey City NJ 07303		R	182*	.2
28	Bartell Drug Co—*George D Bartell*	4727 Denver Ave S, Seattle WA 98134	206-763-2626	R	170*	1.7
29	Lynnfield Drug Inc—*Kim Rondeau*	12 Kent Way Ste 120, Byfield MA 01922	978-499-1400	R	165*	.2
30	Big A Drug Stores Inc—*Edward Dallal*	12030 S Garfield Ave, South Gate CA 90280	562-633-9578	R	115*	.3
31	Smith's Food and Drug Centers Inc—*James Hallsey* Fred Meyer Inc	1550 S Redwood Rd, Salt Lake City UT 84104		S	101*	.2
32	IHT Health Products Inc—*Robert L Erwin*	225 Long Ave Bldg 15, Hillside NJ 07205	973-926-0816	S	97*	.1
33	Commcare Pharmacy—*Nicholas M Saraniti*	2817 E Oakland Park Bl, Fort Lauderdale FL 33306	954-332-6170	R	72	.1
34	Fruth Pharmacy Inc—*Lynne Fruth*	PO Box 332, Point Pleasant WV 25550	304-675-1612	R	66*	.5
35	Mast Drug Company Inc—*William Mast*	1910 Ross Mill Rd, Henderson NC 27536	252-438-3112	R	56*	.1
36	Metro Drugs Inc—*Joe Tawil*	931 Lexington Ave, New York NY 10065	212-627-2300	R	47*	.1
37	Accredo's Hemophilia Health Services Inc	201 Great Circle Rd, Nashville TN 37228	615-352-2500	D	44*	.1
38	Parkway Drugs Inc—*Edward Fox*	7366 N Lincoln Ave Ste, Lincolnwood IL 60712	847-673-2424	R	42*	.1
39	Doc's Drugs Ltd—*Anthony Sartoris*	455 E Reed St, Braidwood IL 60408	815-458-6104	R	33*	.3
40	Discount Drugs Wisconsin Inc—*Roy Rodman*	4301 Randolph Rd, Wheaton MD 20906	301-942-9210	R	30*	.3
41	Wall Drug Store Inc—*Ted Hustead*	PO BOX 401, Wall SD 57790	605-279-2175	R	27*	.1
42	Abington Pharmacy Inc—*Richard D Barbieri*	1460 Old York Rd, Abington PA 19001	215-884-2767	R	22*	.1
43	Marra's Pharmacy Inc—*Barbara McDonald*	217 Remsen St Ste I, Cohoes NY 12047	518-237-2110	R	18*	<.1
44	Serv-U Pharmacies	6107 W Greenfield Ave, West Allis WI 53214	414-771-1350	R	15*	.1
45	People's Pharmacy Inc—*Joe Graedon*	3801 S Lamar Ste C, Austin TX 78704	512-459-9090	R	14*	.1
46	Rinderer's Drug Stores Inc—*Matt Carlisle*	1053 Cave Springs Rd, Saint Peters MO 63376	636-928-3957	R	14*	.1
47	Jim Myers Drug Inc—*Roger Meyers*	3325 University Blvd E, Tuscaloosa AL 35404	205-556-3800	R	14*	.1
48	Degen-Berglund Inc—*Dan Reckase*	4000 Mormon Coulee Rd, La Crosse WI 54601	608-775-8500	R	11*	.1
49	Northwest Hills Pharmacy and Florist Corp—*Tom Sansing*	3801 N Capital of TX H, Austin TX 78746	512-329-8667	R	11*	.1
50	Dougherty's Pharmacy Inc—*David Bowe*	5959 Royal Ln STE 515, Dallas TX 75230	214-373-5300	S	11*	<.1
51	Corner Homecare Inc—*James Knauff*	PO Box 607, Princeton KY 42445	270-365-3903	R	10*	.1
52	Ralston Drug Stores Inc—*Rick R Zapp*	3147 Southmore Blvd, Houston TX 77004	713-524-3045	R	9*	.1
53	Madison Pharmacy Associates/Bajamar Women's Health-Care—*Matt Wanderer*	PO Box 259690, Madison WI 53725	608-833-7046	R	9*	.1
54	Foss Co—*Robert Lowry*	1224 Washington Ave, Golden CO 80401	303-279-3373	R	6*	.1
55	Healthwarehousecom Inc—*Lalit Dhadphale*	7107 Industrial Rd, Florence KY 41042	513-618-0911	P	6	<.1

Note: An asterisk (*) indicates an estimated financial figure. The company type code used is as follows: R = Private, P = Public, S = Private Subsidiary, B = Public Subsidiary, D = Division, J = Joint Venture, I = Investment Fund.

COMPANY RANKINGS BY SALES WITHIN 4-DIGIT SIC

Rank	Company Name—*Executive Officer*	Address, City, State, Zip	Phone	Type	Fin	Empls
56	Santa Monica Homeopathic Pharmacy Inc—*Robert Litvak*	629 Broadway, Santa Monica CA 90401	310-395-1131	R	5*	<.1
57	Rite Aid Pharmacy Atlanta—*J Stephen Anderson*	2345 Peachtree Rd NE, Atlanta GA 30305	404-233-2101	R	5*	<.1
58	Halpin's Pharmacy Inc—*Rick Erickson*	11406 E Sprague Ave, Spokane WA 99206	509-928-9500	R	5*	<.1
59	Mother Nature Inc—*R Whitney Anderson*	322 7th Ave 3rd Fl, New York NY 10001		R	5*	<.1
60	Ascend Pharmaceuticals Inc—*Majid Seraj*	1849 W Redlands Blvd, Redlands CA 92373	909-793-2205	R	5*	<.1
61	Pro-Med Pharmacies Inc—*Don Chrysler Jr*	701 N Taylor St, Amarillo TX 79107	806-379-7126	R	4*	<.1
62	Lincoln Pharmacy	232 North Ave, Pittsburgh PA 15209	412-821-2379	R	4*	<.1
63	Crosby's Drugs Inc—*Sherrie Cohen Merchant*	2609 N High St, Columbus OH 43202	614-263-9424	R	4*	<.1
64	Faast Pharmacy—*Lisa Faast*	3400 Calloway Dr Ste 7, Bakersfield CA 93312	661-410-7979	R	4*	<.1
65	Standard Drug Co (St Charles Missouri)—*Gerald W Roberts*	1 Westbury Dr Bldg B S, Saint Charles MO 63301	636-946-6557	R	3*	<.1
66	Evans Drug Company Inc	1106 W Willow St, Enid OK 73703	580-234-5494	R	3*	<.1
67	Keasling's Drug Store—*H Wesley Brown*	1414 Main St, Keokuk IA 52632	319-524-5436	R	3*	<.1
68	Chemique Pharmaceuticals Inc—*Phil Millman*	13306 Whittier Blvd, Whittier CA 90602	562-698-0921	R	3*	<.1
69	Rite Time Pharmaceuticals Inc—*Soji Akanwo*	PO Box 390415, Anza CA 92539	951-763-7670	R	3*	<.1
70	Budget Drug—*Charlotte Lopacki*	1137 Bustleton Pike, Feasterville Trevose PA 19053	215-322-4048	R	3*	<.1
71	Consumer Discount Drug Store Inc—*Ted N Turner*	6542 Hollywood Blvd, Hollywood CA 90028	323-461-3606	R	2*	<.1
72	Medicine Shop—*Maria Costas*	110 Main St, Park Ridge IL 60068	847-698-3323	R	2*	<.1
73	Jorge's Pharmacy—*Jorge Monteagudo*	1701 Coral Way, Miami FL 33145	305-856-1250	R	2*	<.1
74	Advantage Pharmaceuticals Inc—*Art Whitney*	4351 Pacific St, Rocklin CA 95677	916-630-4960	R	2*	<.1
75	HomeMed Channel Inc—*Ryan O'Rouke*	6210 Technology Center, Indianapolis IN 46278		R	2*	<.1
76	Cambridge Chemists Inc	855 Lexington Ave, New York NY 10065	212-734-5678	R	1*	<.1
77	Vetline Larson Labs Inc—*Ken Larson*	425 John Deere Rd, Fort Collins CO 80524	970-484-1900	R	1	<.1
78	Weber and Judd Company Inc—*Dean Weir*	1814 15th St NW, Rochester MN 55901	507-289-6368	R	N/A	.1

TOTALS: SIC 5912 Drug Stores & Proprietary Stores
Companies: 78

					423,582	852.4

5921 Liquor Stores

Rank	Company Name—*Executive Officer*	Address, City, State, Zip	Phone	Type	Fin	Empls
1	ABC Fine Wine and Spirits—*Charles E Bailes III*	PO Box 593688, Orlando FL 32859	407-851-0000	R	2,754*	1.9
2	21st Amendment Inc	1158 W 86th St, Indianapolis IN 46260	317-846-1678	R	270*	.1
3	Spec's Family Partner's—*John Rydman*	2410 Smith St, Houston TX 77006	713-526-8787	R	80*	.3
4	Gold Standard Enterprises Inc—*Michael Binstein*	5100 W Dempster, Skokie IL 60077	847-581-3186	R	60*	.3
5	Total Wine and More—*David Trone*	11325 7 Locks Rd Ste 2, Potomac MD 20854	301-795-1080	R	54*	.2
6	David Briggs Enterprises Inc—*David A Briggs Jr*	641 Papworth Ave, Metairie LA 70005	504-831-9415	R	53*	.5
7	Sam's Wine and Spirits	1925 N Clybourn Ste 30, Chicago IL 60614	773-296-2604	R	43*	.2
8	Sherry-Lehmann Corp—*Chris Adams*	505 Park Ave, New York NY 10022	212-838-7500	R	42*	.1
9	Martin Wine's Ltd—*Dave Gladden*	3500 Magazine St, New Orleans LA 70115	504-899-7411	R	38*	.2
10	V Sattui Winery—*Daryl Sattui*	1111 White Ln, Saint Helena CA 94574	707-963-7774	R	25*	.1
11	Berbiglia Inc—*Jack C Bondon*	1114 W 103 Rd, Kansas City MO 64114	816-942-0070	R	19*	.1
12	Oliver Wine Company Inc—*William Oliver*	8024 N State Rd 37, Bloomington IN 47404	812-876-5800	R	10*	.1
13	Kings Liquor Inc—*Jack Labovitz*	6659 Camp Bowie Blvd, Fort Worth TX 76116	817-732-8091	R	8*	<.1
14	Sinskey Vineyards Inc—*Robert Sinskey*	6320 Silverado Trl, Napa CA 94558	707-944-9090	R	6*	<.1
15	Wine Club Inc—*Ron Loutherback*	2110 E McFadden Ave St, Santa Ana CA 92705	714-835-6485	R	6*	<.1
16	Trefethen Vineyards Winery—*Susan Vowell*	PO Box 2460, Napa CA 94558	707-255-7700	R	6*	.1
17	Chaddsford Winery Ltd—*Eric Miller*	632 Baltimore Pke, Chadds Ford PA 19317	610-388-6221	R	4*	<.1
18	Peju Province Winery Ltd—*Astrid Buchanan*	PO Box 478, Rutherford CA 94573	707-963-3600	R	4*	<.1
19	JFilippi Vintage Co—*Joseph Filippi*	12467 Baseline Rd, Rancho Cucamonga CA 91739	909-899-5755	R	4*	<.1
20	Goody-Goody Liquor Store Inc—*Albert Sanchez*	10301 Harry Hines Blvd, Dallas TX 75220		R	2*	<.1

TOTALS: SIC 5921 Liquor Stores
Companies: 20

					3,488	4.2

5932 Used Merchandise Stores

Rank	Company Name—*Executive Officer*	Address, City, State, Zip	Phone	Type	Fin	Empls
1	EZCORP Inc—*Paul Rothamel*	1901 Capital Pkwy, Austin TX 78746	512-314-3400	P	869	5.6
2	First Cash Financial Services Inc—*Rick Wessel*	690 E Lamar Blvd Ste 4, Arlington TX 76011	817-460-3947	P	521	5.3
3	Intechra Group LLC—*Michael Profit*	PO Box 3226, Ridgeland MS 39158		S	64*	.2
4	Buffalo Exchange—*Kerstin Block*	PO Box 40488, Tucson AZ 85717	520-622-2711	R	43*	N/A
5	Winmark Corp—*John L Morgan*	605 Hwy 169 N Ste 400, Minneapolis MN 55441	763-520-8500	P	41	.1
6	Just My Carlaz Thing—*Michelle'l Lee*	1000 W Century Blvd, Los Angeles CA 90044	323-759-8939	R	37*	<.1
7	Ohio Valley Goodwill Industries Rehabilitation Center Inc—*Joseph Byrom*	10600 Springfield Pke, Cincinnati OH 45215	513-771-4800	R	34*	.7
8	Phoenician Stone—*Joseph Sage*	3034 East Coast Hwy, Corona del Mar CA 92625	949-759-6944	R	24	.3
9	Federal Equipment Co—*Larry Kadis*	8200 Bessemer Ave, Cleveland OH 44127	216-271-3500	R	13*	<.1
10	Skinner Inc—*Karen M Keane*	274 Cedar Hill St, Marlborough MA 01752	508-970-3000	R	8*	.1
11	Lotus Fixture LLC	401 S Webster St, Seattle WA 98108	206-390-1204	R	5*	<.1
12	Sunrise Enterprises Of Roseburg—*Dan Clark*	4880 Grange Rd PMB 51, Roseburg OR 97471	541-673-0195	R	4*	.2
13	Compression Source Inc—*Steve Wylder*	28338 Constellation Rd, Valencia CA 91355	661-257-8000	R	3*	<.1
14	Didier Aaron Inc—*Herve Aaron*	32 E 67th St, New York NY 10021	212-988-5248	R	2*	<.1
15	1st Rate Fixtures—*Leah Himmel*	1108 E 53rd St, Austin TX 78723	512-420-9262	R	2*	<.1
16	Cash America Incorporated of Oklahoma—*Daniel R Feehan*	904 W Broadway St, Muskogee OK 74401	918-683-2646	S	2*	<.1
17	EZPAWN Colorado Inc EZCORP Inc	12415 E Mississippi Av, Aurora CO 80012	303-367-9075	S	2*	<.1
18	Access Information Technologies Inc—*Allyn Vineberg*	422 Conklin St Ste 1, Farmingdale NY 11735	631-756-2700	R	1*	<.1
19	Boss Unlimited—*Cynthia Wright*	10 S Broadway, Denver CO 80203	303-871-0373	R	1*	<.1
20	Maverick Machinery Company Inc—*WR Ellenwood*	PO Box 661, Atkinson IL 61235	309-936-7731	R	1*	<.1
21	KZ Store Fixtures—*Daniel Eveland*	1019 Schuster St, Kalamazoo MI 49009	269-978-8589	R	<1	<.1

TOTALS: SIC 5932 Used Merchandise Stores
Companies: 21

					1,679	12.5

5941 Sporting Goods & Bicycle Shops

Rank	Company Name—*Executive Officer*	Address, City, State, Zip	Phone	Type	Fin	Empls
1	Dick's Sporting Goods Inc—*Edward W Stack*	345 Court St, Coraopolis PA 15108		P	4,872	26.0
2	Sports Authority Inc—*Darrell Webb*	1050 W Hampden Ave, Englewood CO 80110	303-200-5050	R	2,818*	15.0
3	Cabela's Inc—*Thomas L Millner*	1 Cabela Dr, Sidney NE 69160	308-254-5505	R	2,811	14.8
4	Bass Pro Shops Inc—*James Hagale*	2500 E Kearney, Springfield MO 65803	417-873-5000	R	2,456*	12.0
5	Dunham's Athleisure Corp—*Jeff Lynn*	5000 Dixie Hwy, Waterford MI 48329	248-626-9595	R	1,830*	2.0
6	Fila USA Inc—*Gene Yoon*	PO Box 3000, Sparks MD 21152	410-773-3000	S	1,757	2.9
7	Recreational Equipment Inc—*Sally Jewell*	6750 S 228th St, Kent WA 98032	253-891-2500	R	1,455*	10.0
8	Academy Ltd—*David Gochman*	1800 N Mason Rd, Katy TX 77449		R	1,007*	7.0
9	Big 5 Sporting Goods Corp—*Steven G Miller*	2525 E El Segundo Blvd, El Segundo CA 90245	310-536-0611	P	897	8.9
10	Bass Pro Inc—*James Hagale*	2500 E Kearney St, Springfield MO 65898	417-873-5000	R	829*	12.0
11	Hibbett Sports Inc—*Jeffry O Rosenthal*	451 Industrial Ln, Birmingham AL 35211	205-942-4292	P	665	6.1

Rank	Company Name—*Executive Officer*	Address, City, State, Zip	Phone	Type	Fin	Empls
12	Sport Chalet Inc—*Craig L Levra*	1 Sport Chalet Dr, La Canada CA 91011	818-949-5300	P	362	3.1
13	Retail Concepts Inc—*Barry Goldware*	10560 Bissonnet St St, Houston TX 77099	281-340-5000	R	354*	.4
14	Sportsman's Guide Inc—*Gregory R Binkley*	411 Farwell Ave, South Saint Paul MN 55075	651-451-3030	R	285	.6
15	Scheels All Sports Inc—*Steve D Scheel*	1551 45th St S, Fargo ND 58103	701-298-2918	R	250*	3.0
16	Performance Inc—*Gary Snook*	PO Box 2741, Chapel Hill NC 27515	919-933-9113	R	232*	1.6
17	Michigan Sporting Goods Distributors Inc—*Bruce Ullery*	3070 Shaffer Ave SE, Grand Rapids MI 49512	616-942-2600	R	200*	2.5
18	Olympia Sports Center	5 Bradley Dr, Westbrook ME 04092	207-854-2794	R	191	1.9
19	Saucony Inc—*John H Fisher*	Po Box 9191, Lexington MA 02420	617-824-6000	S	166*	.3
20	Sports Endeavors Inc—*Mike Moylan*	431 Us Hwy 70a E, Hillsborough NC 27278	919-644-6800	R	150*	.8
21	Ron Jon Surf Shop—*Debbie Harvey*	4151 N Atlantic Ave, Cocoa Beach FL 32931	321-799-8888	R	142*	.4
22	Eastern Mountain Sports Inc—*Mitchell Johnson*	1 Vose Farm Rd, Peterborough NH 03458	603-924-9571	R	104*	.2
23	Dover Saddlery Inc—*Stephen L Day*	PO Box 1100, Littleton MA 01460		P	78	.5
24	Perfect Fitness—*Alden Mills*	1400 Raff Rd SW, Canton OH 44750		R	64*	<.1
25	Bullrich Corp—*Keith Van Velkinburgh*	875 Parfet St, Lakewood CO 80215	303-237-6321	R	49*	.4
26	Aspen Sports Inc—*Ernest Frywald*	408 E Cooper Ave, Aspen CO 81611	970-925-6331	R	43*	.1
27	US Fitness Products	5912 Oleander Dr, Wilmington NC 28403	910-790-2029	R	42*	.1
28	Kevin Inc—*Kevin Adams*	PO Box 904, Kittery ME 03904	207-439-2700	R	40*	.3
29	Paragon Sporting Goods Corp—*Bruce Blank*	867 Broadway, New York NY 10003	212-255-8889	R	36*	.5
30	Bike Pedlar—*Bill Perkins*	144 Franklin Rd, Brentwood TN 37027	615-373-4700	R	21*	<.1
31	Pro Golf Discount Inc—*Randy Silver*	13405 SE 30th St Ste 1, Bellevue WA 98005	425-957-3626	R	20*	.1
32	Island Water Sports Inc	1985 NE 2nd St, Deerfield Beach FL 33441	954-427-4929	R	17*	.1
33	RockBottomGolf.Com—*Tom Rath*	601 State Fair Blvd, Syracuse NY 13209		R	16*	<.1
34	Promaxima Manufacturing Ltd—*Bob Leppke*	5310 Ashbrook Dr, Houston TX 77081	713-667-9606	R	12*	.2
35	Mel Cottons Sporting Goods—*Steve Zehring*	1266 W San Carlos St, San Jose CA 95126	408-287-5994	R	11*	.1
36	Dive Shop Inc—*Gene McNeese*	999 S Yates Rd, Memphis TN 38119	901-763-3483	R	10*	<.1
37	Outdoor Adventures Unlimited Inc—*Richard Mcnatt*	5208 Mercer University, Macon GA 31210	478-474-6790	R	7*	<.1
38	Hansen Surfboards Inc—*Donald Hansen*	1105 S Coast Hwy 101, Encinitas CA 92024	760-753-6595	R	5*	<.1
39	Cole Sport Ski Shops—*Gary E Cole*	PO Box 3509, Park City UT 84060	435-649-4806	R	5*	<.1
40	Carter's Shooting Center Inc—*William O Carter*	6231 Treschwig Rd, Spring TX 77373	281-443-8393	R	3*	.1
41	Crosslake Sales Inc—*Thomas Maschhoff*	PO Box 524, Crosslake MN 56442	218-297-0747	R	3*	<.1
42	Sports Mania—*John Smith*	924 N 3rd St, Jacksonville Beach FL 32250	904-242-0640	R	2*	<.1
43	Special Tee Golf of Florida Inc—*Jack Hazen*	620 E Altamonte Dr, Altamonte Springs FL 32701	407-834-1900	R	2*	<.1
44	Distant Replays Inc—*Andy Hyman*	2980 Cobb Pkwy Ste 103, Atlanta GA 30339	770-953-2722	H	2*	<.1
45	Dive Station—*Keith A Mattson*	3465 Edgewater Dr, Orlando FL 32804	407-843-3483	R	2*	<.1
46	Vegas Golf Inc—*Lance Cangey*	4860 W Desert Inn Ste2, Las Vegas NV 89102	702-873-8077	R	2*	<.1
47	Frank's Shoe Fitting and Sporting Goods Inc—*Frank Giannino*	747 Rt 211E, Middletown NY 10941	845-692-9225	R	2*	<.1
48	Live Bait Boat The—*Burt Korpela*	2670 Bird Ave, Coconut Grove FL 33133		R	2*	<.1
49	Walter Craig Inc—*Len Hale*	1201 N Eastern Blvd, Montgomery AL 36117	334-396-5297	R	2*	<.1
50	Long's Amusement Co—*Anthony Long*	PO Box 1025, Newport News VA 23601	757-599-3661	R	1*	<.1

TOTALS: SIC 5941 Sporting Goods & Bicycle Shops
Companies: 50 — 24,333 — 134.0

5942 Book Stores

1	Borders Inc—*Micheal Edwards* Borders Group Inc	100 Phoenix Dr, Ann Arbor MI 48108	734-477-1100	S	14,201*	10.0
2	Barnes and Noble Inc—*William J Lynch Jr*	PO Box 111, Lyndhurst NJ 07071		P	6,999	35.0
3	Follett College Stores Co—*Christopher Traut*	2233 West St, River Grove IL 60171	708-583-2000	R	3,796*	10.0
4	Borders Group Inc—*Glen Tomaszewski*	100 Phoenix Dr, Ann Arbor MI 48108	734-477-1100	P	2,253	16.4
5	Barnes and Noble College Booksellers Inc—*Max Roberts*	120 Mountain View Blvd, Basking Ridge NJ 07920	908-991-2665	S	1,930	14.4
6	Follett Higher Education Group Inc—*Thomas Christopher*	1818 Swift Dr, Oak Brook IL 60523	630-279-2330	R	671*	8.5
7	Books-A-Million Inc—*Clyde Anderson*	PO Box 19768, Birmingham AL 35219	205-942-3737	P	495	5.3
8	B Dalton Bookseller Inc—*Leonard Riggio* Barnes and Noble Inc	122 5th Ave, New York NY 10011	212-633-3300	S	426*	12.0
9	Barnesandnoble.com Inc—*William J Lynch Jr* Barnes and Noble Inc	122 5th Ave, New York NY 10011	212-633-3300	S	394*	1.0
10	ASM International—*Mark F Smith*	9639 Kinsman Rd, Materials Park OH 44073	440-338-5151	R	179*	.1
11	Davis-Kidd Booksellers Inc	The Mall at Green Hill, Nashville TN 37215	615-385-2645	S	112*	.6
12	Berean Christian Stores—*Joseph Gimelli*	9415 Meridian Way, West Chester OH 45069		R	108*	.7
13	Shakespeare and Co—*Bill Spath*	939 Lexington Ave, New York NY 10021	212-570-0201	R	69*	.1
14	Praxis Bookstore Group LLC	PO Box 3160, Ann Arbor MI 48103		R	68*	<.1
15	Half Price Books Records Magazines Inc	5803 E NW Hwy, Dallas TX 75231		R	63*	1.0
16	Voertman's—*Michelle Dellis*	1314 W Hickory, Denton TX 76201	940-387-1313	R	55*	<.1
17	NorAm International Partners—*Kellie DuGally*	22 Hampshire Dr, Hudson NH 03051	603-881-3151	R	51	.2
18	University Book Store Inc—*Bryan Pearce*	4326 University Way NE, Seattle WA 98105	206-634-3400	R	49*	.3
19	Books Inc—*Michael Tucker*	1501 Vermont St, San Francisco CA 94107	415-643-3400	R	45*	.2
20	Powell's Books Inc—*Michael Powell*	7 NW 9th Ave, Portland OR 97209	503-228-4651	R	41*	.5
21	Chegg Inc—*Dan Rosensweig*	2350 Mission College B, Santa Clara CA 95054		R	39*	.1
22	Little Professor Book Center—*John Glazer* Praxis Bookstore Group LLC	PO Box 3160, Ann Arbor MI 48103		S	34*	<.1
23	Student Book Corp—*Joanna Koliba*	700 Ne Thatuna St, Pullman WA 99163	509-332-2537	R	33*	.2
24	Eastern National—*George Minnucci*	470 Maryland Dr Ste 1, Fort Washington PA 19034	215-283-6900	R	28*	.5
25	University Cooperative Society Inc—*George Mitchell*	2246 Guadalupe St, Austin TX 78705	512-476-7211	R	24*	.1
26	University Book Store—*Carol Good*	711 State St, Madison WI 53703	608-257-3784	R	20*	.3
27	Tattered Cover Book Store Inc—*Joyce Meskis*	1628 16th St, Denver CO 80202	303-436-1070	R	10*	.2
28	White Wing Resource Centre—*Perry Gillum*	3750 Keith St Nw, Cleveland TN 37312	423-559-5217	R	8*	.1
29	Storyopolis—*Lori Abramowitz*	16740 Ventura Blvd, Encino CA 91436	818-509-5600	R	6*	<.1
30	Page One Inc (Albuquerque New Mexico)—*Steve Stout*	11018 Montgomery Blvd, Albuquerque NM 87111		R	6*	<.1
31	Gospel Advocate Co—*Kerry Anderson*	1006 Elm Hill Pke, Nashville TN 37210	615-254-8781	R	5*	<.1
32	Watermark Books—*Sarah Bagby*	4701 E Douglas, Wichita KS 67218	316-682-1181	R	5*	<.1
33	Brian's Books Inc—*Matt Schleede*	4282 Pierce St, Allendale MI 49401	616-892-4170	R	5*	<.1
34	Barbour Publishing Inc—*Tim Martins*	PO Box 719, Uhrichsville OH 44683	740-922-6045	R	4*	.1
35	Home Tech Inc—*Henry Reynolds*	5161 River Rd Ste 104, Bethesda MD 20816	301-654-8380	R	2*	<.1
36	Eso Won Books—*James Fugate*	4331 Degnan Blvd, Los Angeles CA 90008	323-290-1048	R	1*	<.1

TOTALS: SIC 5942 Book Stores
Companies: 36 — 32,234 — 117.9

5943 Stationery Stores

1	Staples Inc—*Brian Light*	PO Box 2312, Framingham MA 01703	508-253-5000	P	24,545	89.0
2	Office Depot Inc—*Neil R Austrian*	6600 N Military Trl, Boca Raton FL 33496		P	11,633	40.0

Note: An asterisk (*) indicates an estimated financial figure. The company type code used is as follows: R = Private, P = Public, S = Private Subsidiary, B = Public Subsidiary, D = Division, J = Joint Venture, I = Investment Fund.

RANKINGS BY SALES WITHIN 4-DIGIT SIC

	Company Name—Executive Officer	Address, City, State, Zip	Phone	Type	Fin	Empls
	WB Mason Co	59 Centre St, Brockton MA 02303	508-586-3434	R	430*	.9
4	Factory Card and Party Outlet Corp—Gary W Rada	2727 W Diehl Rd, Naperville IL 60563	630-579-2000	S	244*	2.5
5	ComDoc Inc—Riley Lochridge	PO Box 908, Akron OH 44309	330-899-8000	S	176*	.6
6	Smith and Butterfield Inc—James Butterfield	2800 Lynch Rd, Evansville IN 47711	812-422-3261	S	33	<.1
7	Diecuts with a View—Nancy M Hill	2250 N University Pkwy, Provo UT 84604	801-224-6766	R	15*	.1
8	American Trading and Production Corp Hazel Div—Tim Orewe	1100 Stafford St Ste 2, Washington MO 63090	636-239-2781	S	14*	.1
9	Solution One—John Kuchta	7407 O St, Lincoln NE 68510	402-476-8833	R	12*	<.1
10	Today's Office Inc—Rhonda Bradley	717 W 7th St, Little Rock AR 72201	501-375-5050	R	10*	<.1
11	Midwest Commercial Interiors—Marshall Tate	987 SWTemple, Salt Lake City UT 84101	801-505-4288	R	9*	.1
12	Newport Stationers Inc—Barry West	17681 Mitchell N Rm 12, Irvine CA 92614	949-863-1200	R	8*	.1
13	Spellbinders Paper Arts LLC—Jeff Caron	1125 W Pinnacle Peak R, Phoenix AZ 85027	602-385-7700	R	8*	<.1
14	Vip Office Furniture And Supply Inc—Dianne Horton	PO Box 1190, Hinesville GA 31310	912-368-3339	R	6*	<.1
15	Crittenden Publishing Co—Alexander Coulter	PO Box 459, West Memphis AR 72303	870-735-1010	R	6*	.1
16	Forms Management Inc—Walter Haley	PO Box 4004, Tallahassee FL 32315	850-576-0171	R	6*	<.1
17	Quality Printing and Supply Inc—Thomas Sykes	PO Box 1765, Mobile AL 36633	251-479-3587	R	5*	.1
18	One Point Inc—Patrick Mcmahon	101 Poplar St Unit 2, Scranton PA 18509	570-342-0737	R	5*	.1
19	Advantage Laser Products Inc—Brian Chaney	1840 Marietta Blvd Nw, Atlanta GA 30318	404-351-2700	R	5*	<.1
20	Firmin Printing and Office Equipment Co—Chuck Firmin	PO Box 951, Texarkana TX 75504	903-793-5566	R	4*	<.1
21	Ogden Brothers Inc—Stephen Ogden	1833 Columbia Ave, Folcroft PA 19032	215-925-5232	R	4*	<.1
22	Ray-Block Stationery Company Inc—Arthur Bloch	3 Plainfield Ave, Floral Park NY 11001	516-437-2222	R	4*	<.1
23	Bodemuller The Printer Inc—Murphy Carriere	PO Box 27, Opelousas LA 70571	337-942-5712	R	4*	<.1
24	Ives Business Forms Inc—Peter Ives	1009 Camp St, New Orleans LA 70130	504-561-8811	R	4*	.1
25	Cay Industries Inc—Bob Keshigian	1721 N Federal Hwy, Fort Lauderdale FL 33305	954-563-0775	R	4*	<.1
26	ABC School Supply Inc—Gloria Lewis	PO Box 369, Landisville PA 17538	717-653-7568	S	3*	<.1
27	Paper Place—Betsy Hendricks	4130 N Marshall Way, Scottsdale AZ 85251	480-941-2858	R	3*	<.1
28	Jackpine Press Inc—Jeff Trucks	76 Filer St, Manistee MI 49660	231-723-8344	R	3*	<.1
29	Attaway Inc—Andrew Patrick	PO Box 302, Anderson SC 29622	864-225-1286	R	3*	<.1
30	Jason Office Products Inc—Harriett Novatt	140 W 31st St Frnt 1, New York NY 10001	212-279-7455	R	3*	<.1
31	Dan Cooks Inc—Wallace Cook	PO Box C, Camden AR 71711	870-836-5018	R	2*	<.1
32	Hadley's Office Products Inc—Mark Hadley	PO Box 1326, Wausau WI 54402	715-842-5651	R	2*	<.1
33	Butler's Office Equipment and Supply Inc—Barry Butler	1900 E Hwy 66 Ste 3, Gallup NM 87301	505-722-6661	R	2*	<.1
34	Insta-Copy Printing Office Supply Inc—E Lyon	PO Box 2274, Las Cruces NM 88004	575-526-6602	R	2*	<.1
35	El Dorado Printing and Stationery Company Inc—Donald Harrell	332 S Washington Ave, El Dorado AR 71730	870-863-5173	R	2*	<.1
36	Unity Printing Company Inc—James Ernette	5848 State Rte 981, Latrobe PA 15650	724-537-5800	R	2*	<.1
37	Central Office Systems Corp—Perry Bartkiewizz	2238 Bluemount Rd Ste, Waukesha WI 53186	262-784-9698	R	2*	<.1
38	Stuart's of Eldorado Inc—Richard Stuart	3213 Northwest Ave, El Dorado AR 71730	870-862-3484	R	2*	<.1
39	GC Office Supply—Ann Keil	2224 Stringtown Rd, Grove City OH 43123	614-875-2363	R	2*	<.1
40	Northwest Print Strategies Inc—Ken Wong	8175 Sw Nimbus Ave Ste, Beaverton OR 97008	503-641-5156	R	2*	<.1
41	Southern Accounting Systems Inc—Robert Joiner	PO Box 3299, Muscle Shoals AL 35662	256-383-2029	R	2*	<.1
42	Ward's Systems Inc—George Ward	PO Box 124, Morrisville VT 05661	802-888-4163	R	2*	<.1
43	Dan's Printing and Office Supplies Inc—Caroline Vaclav	14800 Cicero Ave Ste 1, Oak Forest IL 60452	708-687-3055	R	1*	<.1
44	Decoupage Supply Centre Inc—Claude Vance	26650 County Rd 46A, Sorrento FL 32776	352-383-3883	R	1*	<.1
45	B and B Office Supply Inc—Conrad Magouirk	622 W Texas Ave, Baytown TX 77520	281-422-8151	R	1*	<.1

TOTALS: SIC 5943 Stationery Stores
Companies: 45   37,236   134.2

5944 Jewelry Stores

	Company Name—Executive Officer	Address, City, State, Zip	Phone	Type	Fin	Empls
1	Tiffany and Co—Michael J Kowalski	727 Fifth Ave, New York NY 10022	212-755-8000	P	3,085	9.2
2	Sterling Jewelers Inc—Mark Light	375 Ghent Rd, Akron OH 44333	330-668-5000	S	2,744	N/A
3	Zale Corp—Theo Killion	901 W Walnut Hill Ln, Irving TX 75038	972-580-4000	P	1,743	12.6
4	Samuels Jewelers Inc—Randy N McCullough	2914 Montopolis Dr Ste, Austin TX 78741	512-369-1400	R	1,056*	.8
5	Finlay Enterprises Inc—Arthur E Reiner	529 5th Ave, New York NY 10017	212-808-2800	P	754	9.7
6	Helzberg's Diamond Shops Inc—Beryl Raff	1825 Swift Ave, N Kansas City MO 64116	816-842-7780	S	333*	2.5
7	Gordon's Div—Neil Goldberg Zale Corp	901 W Walnut Hill Ln, Irving TX 75038	972-580-4000	D	262*	2.8
8	Fortunoff Fine Jewelry and Silverware Inc—Arnold Orlick	PO Box 1550, Westbury NY 11590	516-832-9000	R	250*	2.5
9	Bailey Banks and Biddle—Charles Fieramosca Zale Corp	901 W Walnut Hill Ln, Irving TX 75038	972-580-4000	D	197	1.8
10	Sterling Of Ohio Inc—Mark Light	375 Ghent Rd, Fairlawn OH 44333	330-668-5000	R	173*	3.0
11	Ben Bridge Jeweler Inc—Herb Bridge	PO Box 1908, Seattle WA 98111	206-239-6802	S	162*	.9
12	Ultra Stores Inc—Daniel Marks	122 S Michigan Ave, Chicago IL 60603	312-922-3800	R	146*	1.0
13	Kobold Watch Company LLC—Michael Kobold	1817 Parkway View Dr, Pittsburgh PA 15205	412-722-1277	R	121*	<.1
14	Piercing Pagoda Inc—Mary Forte Zale Corp	901 W Walnut Hill Ln, Irving TX 75038	972-580-4000	S	104*	2.0
15	Reeds Jewelers Inc—Alan M Zimmer	PO Box 2229, Wilmington NC 28402	910-350-3100	R	102*	.7
16	DGSE Companies Inc—William Oyster	11311 Reeder Rd, Dallas TX 75229	972-484-3662	P	83	.1
17	Borsheim's Jewelry Company Inc—Susan Jacques	120 Regency Pkwy, Omaha NE 68114	402-391-0400	S	60*	.4
18	Stella and Dot—Jessica Herrin	1860 El Camino Real St, Burlingame CA 94010			33*	<.1
19	Albert S Smyth Company Inc—Thomas A Smyth	2020 York Rd, Timonium MD 21093	410-252-6666	R	31*	.2
20	Harry Ritchie's Jeweler Inc—Donald Ritchie	956 Willamette St, Eugene OR 97401	541-686-1787	R	22*	.3
21	S Joseph and Sons Inc—William Baum	320 6th Ave, Des Moines IA 50309	515-283-1961	R	20*	.1
22	Schwarzschild Jewelers Inc—Peter Boone	11800 West Broad St St, Richmond VA 23233	804-644-1941	R	15*	.1
23	Richemont North America Inc—Callum Barton	645 5th Ave 5th Fl, New York NY 10022		R	10*	.1
24	Pala International Inc—William Larson	912 S Live Oak Park Rd, Fallbrook CA 92028	760-728-9121	R	10*	<.1
25	Robert W Johnson Inc—R Johnson	6280 Sawmill Rd, Dublin OH 43017	614-336-4545	R	10*	.1
26	Elegant Illusions Inc—James Cardinal	542 Lighthouse Ave Ste, Pacific Grove CA 93950	831-649-1814	R	8*	.1
27	Collector—Jeanne Larson Pala International Inc	912 S Live Oak Park Rd, Fallbrook CA 92028	760-728-9121	D	8*	<.1
28	Fusion Holdings LLC—David Lindmeir	265 N Main St Ste D-24, Kaysville UT 84037	801-299-9282	R	7	<.1
29	Tappins Inc—Frank F Goodman	452 Pompton Ave Ste 2C, Cedar Grove NJ 07009	973-239-6201	R	7*	.1
30	Las Savell Jewelry Inc—Las Savell	61 S McLean Blvd, Memphis TN 38104	901-725-4200	R	6*	<.1
31	Hoover's Jewelers Inc—Linda Griffiths	2106 Central Ave, Kearney NE 68847	308-234-3592	R	5*	<.1
32	RAI Technology Inc—Ron Henricksn	1244 State St Ste 358, Lemont IL 60439	630-243-0430	R	4*	<.1
33	Randolph Jewelers—Charles Stephens	375 Main St, Placerville CA 95667	530-622-3787	R	3*	<.1
34	Frank Adams Jewelers Inc—David F Adams	1475 Western Ave Ste 2, Albany NY 12203	518-435-0075	R	2*	<.1
35	Baker Jewelers of Virginia Beach Inc—George Baker	972 Laskin Rd, Virginia Beach VA 23451	757-422-5522	S	1*	<.1
36	Kirk Root Designs—C Kirk Root	10000 Research Blvd St, Austin TX 78759	512-346-1780	R	1*	<.1
37	Elizabeth Locke Jewels—Elizabeth Locke	PO Box 315, Millwood VA 22646	540-837-2215	R	1*	<.1
38	Carpenter's Time Center Inc—Nathan Carpenter	7090 College St, Beaumont TX 77707	409-838-5410	R	<1*	<.1

Rank	Company Name—*Executive Officer*	Address, City, State, Zip	Phone	Type	Fin	Empls
39	Morgan Clock Co—*Daniel Morgan*	815 Century Dr Ste 2, Dubuque IA 52002	563-583-2220	R	<1*	<.1
40	Odimo Inc—*Amerisa Kornblum*	9858 Clint Moore Rd, Boca Raton FL 33496	954-993-4703	P	<1	N/A

TOTALS: SIC 5944 Jewelry Stores
Companies: 40   11,580   51.1

5945 Hobby, Toy & Game Shops

Rank	Company Name—*Executive Officer*	Address, City, State, Zip	Phone	Type	Fin	Empls
1	Toys "R" Us Inc—*Gerald L Storch*	1 Geoffrey Way, Wayne NJ 07470	973-617-3500	S	13,864	71.0
2	Michaels Stores Inc—*Brian C Cornell*	PO Box 619566, Dallas TX 75261	972-409-1300	R	4,031	40.5
3	Hobby Lobby Stores Inc—*David Green*	7707 SW 44th St, Oklahoma City OK 73179	405-745-1100	R	2,200*	19.0
4	KB Holdings LLC—*Gregory R Staley*	100 West St, Pittsfield MA 01201	413-496-3000	S	1,500*	15.0
5	AC Moore Arts and Crafts Inc—*Joseph A Jeffries*	130 AC Moore Dr, Berlin NJ 08009	856-768-4930	P	448	4.4
6	Build-A-Bear Workshop Inc—*Maxine K Clark*	1954 Innerbelt Busines, Saint Louis MO 63114	314-423-8000	P	401	5.5
7	AC Moore Inc—*Joseph A Jeffries* AC Moore Arts and Crafts Inc	130 AC Moore Dr, Berlin NJ 08009	856-228-6700	S	345*	1.3
8	Otc Holdings Corp—*Stephen Frary*	4206 S 108th St, Omaha NE 68137	402-331-5511	S	153*	2.6
9	Grdg Holdings LLC	19411 Atrium Pl Ste 17, Houston TX 77084	281-578-2334	R	149*	3.5
10	RightStartcom Inc—*Mike Wagner*	4643 S Ulster St Ste 1, Denver CO 80237	720-974-8198	S	113*	.3
11	Dreams Inc—*Ross Tannenbaum*	2 S University Dr Ste, Plantation FL 33324	954-377-0002	P	111	.4
12	S and S Worldwide Inc (Colchester Connecticut)—*Stephen Schwartz*	PO Box 513, Colchester CT 06415	860-537-3451	R	43	.3
13	Memories and More Inc	515 W 2600 S Colonial, Bountiful UT 84010		R	13	.2
14	The Elf on the Shelf—*Carol Aebersold*	1174 Hayes Industrial, Marietta GA 30062		R	6*	<.1
15	Oompa Enterprises Inc—*Milanie Cleere*	1311 W Badger Rd, Madison WI 53713	608-260-2620	R	4	<.1
16	Fame (USA) ProductsInc—*John Yen*	7556 Sand St, Fort Worth TX 76118	817-284-2032	R	<1*	<.1

TOTALS: SIC 5945 Hobby, Toy & Game Shops
Companies: 16   23,383   164.0

5946 Camera & Photographic Supply Stores

Rank	Company Name—*Executive Officer*	Address, City, State, Zip	Phone	Type	Fin	Empls
1	Ritz Camera Centers Inc—*Fred H Lerner*	6711 Ritz Way, Beltsville MD 20705	301-419-0000	S	1,150	10.2
2	Waterhouse Inc—*Scott Whiting*	670 Queen St Ste 200, Honolulu HI 96813	808-592-4800	R	60*	.2
3	Dodd Camera and Video—*Mark Leonard*	2077 E 30th St, Cleveland OH 44115	216-361-6811	R	33*	.1
4	Inkley's Inc—*Fred H Lerner* Ritz Camera Centers Inc	6711 Ritz Way, Beltsville MD 20705		S	24*	<.1
5	Ritz Interactive Inc—*Scott Neamand*	2010 Main St Ste 550, Irvine CA 92614	949-442-0202	R	22*	<.1
6	Focus Camera Inc—*Anthony Z Berkowitz*	905 McDonald Ave, Brooklyn NY 11218	718-437-8810	R	16*	<.1
7	Filmtools Inc—*Stan Mcclain*	1400 W Burbank Blvd, Burbank CA 91506	818-845-8066	R	10*	<.1
8	Samy's Camera Inc—*Samy Kamienowizz*	431 S Fairfax Ave, Los Angeles CA 90036	323-938-2420	R	8*	.1
9	Wright Images—*Michael Wright*	3340 Monroe Ave Ste 2, Rochester NY 14618	585-586-3250	R	8*	<.1
10	Comgraphics Inc—*Denise Kretzer*	329 W 18th St 10th Fl, Chicago IL 60616	312-226-0900	R	7*	.1
11	Visual Sound Inc—*John Bogosian*	485 Park Way, Broomall PA 19008	610-544-8700	R	6*	.1
12	Consolidated Purchasing Corp—*Jonathan Sweetwood*	123 Us Hwy 46, Fairfield NJ 07004	973-377-5555	R	5*	.1
13	Liska Imaging Inc—*Christopher Leclear*	2202 E Mcdowell Rd, Phoenix AZ 85006	602-273-0927	R	4*	<.1
14	Harold Tymer Company Inc—*William Tymer*	8005 Nw 17th Ave, Vancouver WA 98665	360-573-6053	R	3*	<.1
15	Mike Crivello's Camera Centers Inc—*S Crivello*	18110 W Bluemound Rd S, Brookfield WI 53045	262-782-4303	R	2*	<.1
16	Alan Gordon Enterprises Inc—*Grant Loucks*	5625 Melrose Ave, Hollywood CA 90038	323-466-3561	R	1*	<.1

TOTALS: SIC 5946 Camera & Photographic Supply Stores
Companies: 16   1,359   10.9

5947 Gift, Novelty & Souvenir Shops

Rank	Company Name—*Executive Officer*	Address, City, State, Zip	Phone	Type	Fin	Empls
1	Arango Inc—*David Russell*	7519 SW 88th St, Miami FL 33156	305-661-4229	R	1,180*	<.1
2	Duty Free Shoppers Group Ltd (San Francisco California)—*Ed Brennan*	525 Market St, San Francisco CA 94105	415-977-2700	R	1,158*	3.2
3	Kirlins Hallmark Inc—*Brad Kirlin*	PO Box 3097, Quincy IL 62305	217-224-8953	R	477*	2.0
4	Disney Store Inc—*Tara Poseley*	2148 Glendale Galleria, Glendale CA 91210	818-247-0222	S	304*	3.6
5	Paradies Shops Inc—*Greg Paradies*	5950 Fulton Industrial, Atlanta GA 30336	404-344-7905	R	297*	3.3
6	Thirty-One Gifts LLC—*Heather Yakes*	3425 Morse Xing, Columbus OH 43219	614-414-4300	R	180*	1.4
7	Discovery Channel Retail Div—*Greg Shealey*	PO Box 788, Florence KY 41022		D	176*	2.2
8	Calendar Club LLC—*Mike Hejny*	6411 Burleson Rd, Austin TX 78744	512-386-7220	S	106*	.2
9	Long's Jewelers Ltd—*Bob Rottenberg*	60A South Ave, Burlington MA 01803	781-272-5400	R	101*	.1
10	iParty Corp—*Sal Perisano*	270 Bridge St Ste 301, Dedham MA 02026	781-329-3952	P	81	.9
11	Hazelwood Enterprises Inc—*Richard Hazelwood*	402 N 32nd St, Phoenix AZ 85008	602-275-7709	R	48*	.1
12	Celebrate Express—*Gregory Maffei*	11232 120th Ave NE Ste, Kirkland WA 98033	425-250-1064	S	23*	.3
13	Index Notion Company Inc—*Susie Bowles*	887 W Carmel Dr, Carmel IN 46032	317-573-3990	S	23*	.2
14	Canzoniero Corp—*Daniel Canzoniero*	7413 Pulaski Hwy, Baltimore MD 21237	410-866-4700	R	17*	.3
15	GourmetGiftBasketscom—*Ryan Abood*	34 Londonderry Rd, Londonderry NH 03053	603-606-5269	R	12	.1
16	General Novelty Ltd—*Greg Walker*	420 E 58th Ave, Denver CO 80216	303-292-5537	R	10*	.3
17	Arribas Brothers Company Inc—*Alfonso Arribas*	1500 Live Oak Ln, Lake Buena Vista FL 32830	407-828-4840	R	8*	.1
18	LaserGifts—*David Mudrick*	PO Box 10035, Prescott AZ 86304	928-776-4430	R	7	.1
19	Clines Corners Operating Co—*CC Blair*	1 Yacht Club Dr, Clines Corners NM 87070	575-472-5488	R	6*	.1
20	West Coast Event Productions Inc—*Duane Smith*	1400 NW 15th Ave, Portland OR 97209	503-294-0412	R	6*	.1
21	Rod's Pawz LLC—*Nini Casey*	PO Box 496, Newmarket NH 03857	603-659-1070	R	5*	<.1
22	Wendell August Forge Inc—*V Knecht*	PO Box 109, Grove City PA 16127	724-458-8360	R	4*	.1
23	Shell Factory Museum Inc—*Tom Cronin*	2787 N Tamiami Trail, Fort Myers FL 33903	239-995-2141	R	4*	.1
24	M-G Novelty Co—*Mike Dillon*	PO Box 270606, Oklahoma City OK 73137	405-948-1234	R	4*	.1
25	Riegseckers Inc—*Mel Riegsecker*	PO Box 220, Shipshewana IN 46565	260-768-4725	R	3*	.1
26	Big Top Party Shop Inc—*David Kiedider*	536 Industrial Park Dr, Newport News VA 23608	757-875-0505	R	3*	<.1
27	Jett Racing And Sales Inc—*Wolf Hofman*	1301 Lincoln St, Laredo TX 78040	956-722-3102	R	2*	.1
28	General Novelty Ltd Coach House Gifts Div—*Craig J Walker* General Novelty Ltd	1609 Golden Aspen Dr S, Ames IA 50010	515-232-3580	D	2*	.1
29	Balloonatics Inc—*Connie Curry*	180 Dillon Ave, Campbell CA 95008	408-866-8206	R	2*	<.1
30	Chittenden Cider Mill—*Robert Chittenden*	1580 Dorset St, South Burlington VT 05403	802-862-4602	R	1*	<.1

TOTALS: SIC 5947 Gift, Novelty & Souvenir Shops
Companies: 30   4,250   18.9

5948 Luggage & Leather Goods Stores

Rank	Company Name—*Executive Officer*	Address, City, State, Zip	Phone	Type	Fin	Empls
1	Meenan Oil Company Inc—*Elena Zazzera*	3020 Burns Ave, Wantagh NY 11793	516-783-1000	S	166*	.2
2	Colorado Baggage Co—*Peter Paradise*	2433 Curtis St, Denver CO 80205	303-292-0020	R	10*	.1
3	Latina Niagara Importing Co—*Charles Marrazo*	2299 Military Rd, Tonawanda NY 14150	716-693-9999	R	9*	.1

Note: An asterisk (*) indicates an estimated financial figure. The company type code used is as follows: R = Private, P = Public, S = Private Subsidiary, B = Public Subsidiary, D = Division, J = Joint Venture, I = Investment Fund.

COMPANY RANKINGS BY SALES WITHIN 4-DIGIT SIC

Rank	Company Name—*Executive Officer*	Address, City, State, Zip	Phone	Type	Fin	Empls
4	Ohio Gas and Appliance Co—*Irik P Sevin*	56 S Limestone St, Jamestown OH 45335	937-675-5251	S	7*	<.1

TOTALS: SIC 5948 Luggage & Leather Goods Stores
Companies: 4 — 192 — .4

5949 Sewing, Needlework & Piece Goods

Rank	Company Name—*Executive Officer*	Address, City, State, Zip	Phone	Type	Fin	Empls
1	Jo-Ann Stores Inc—*Travis Smith*	5555 Darrow Rd, Hudson OH 44236	330-656-2600	R	2,079	21.5
2	Everfast Inc—*Roy B Simpson Jr*	203 Gale Ln, Kennett Square PA 19348	610-444-9700	R	788*	2.0
3	Renfro Corp—*Warren Nichols*	PO Box 908, Mount Airy NC 27030	336-719-8000	R	376*	6.0
4	HF Merchandising Inc—*Jane F Aggers*	One Fashion Way, Baldwyn MS 38824	662-842-2834	S	123*	.3
5	HF Resources Inc—*Jane F Aggers*	One Fashion Way, Baldwyn MS 38824	662-842-2834	S	101*	.2
6	HF Enterprises Inc—*Jane F Aggers*	103 Foulk Rd, Wilmington DE 19803	302-425-4993	S	85*	.2
7	hancockfabricscom Inc—*Jane F Aggers*	One Fashion Way, Baldwyn MS 38824	662-842-2834	S	76*	.2
8	HFM Interiors LLC—*Glenda Kirby*	PO Box 888, Cheshire CT 06410	203-272-3529	R	6*	<.1
9	Yarn Sellar Inc—*Dawn Morlan*	6114 E Riverside Blvd, Loves Park IL 61111	815-637-9666	R	3*	<.1

TOTALS: SIC 5949 Sewing, Needlework & Piece Goods
Companies: 9 — 3,637 — 30.3

5961 Catalog & Mail-Order Houses

Rank	Company Name—*Executive Officer*	Address, City, State, Zip	Phone	Type	Fin	Empls
1	Dell Inc—*Michael S Dell*	1 Dell Way, Round Rock TX 78682	512-728-4100	P	61,494	103.3
2	Amazoncom Inc—*Jeffrey P Bezos*	PO Box 81226, Seattle WA 98108	206-266-1000	P	34,204	33.7
3	CDW Corp—*Thomas E Richards*	200 N Milwaukee Ave, Vernon Hills IL 60061	847-465-6000	R	9,400	6.6
4	QVC Inc—*Mike George*	1200 Wilson Dr, West Chester PA 19380	484-701-1000	S	7,288*	17.0
5	Lands' End Inc—*Edgar Huber*	1 Lands End Ln, Dodgeville WI 53595	608-935-9341	D	6,723*	6.0
6	Brylane Inc—*Peter Canzone*	463 7th Ave, New York NY 10018	212-613-9500	S	5,316*	6.4
7	Insight Enterprises Inc—*Kenneth Lamneck*	6820 S Harl Ave, Tempe AZ 85283		P	5,287	5.4
8	BandNcom Holding Corp—*Leonard Riggio*	76 Ninth Ave, New York NY 10011	212-414-6000	S	4,223	1.0
9	Systemax Inc—*Richard Leeds*	11 Harbor Park Dr, Port Washington NY 11050	516-608-7000	P	3,590	5.6
10	HSN Inc—*Mindy F Grossman*	1 HSN Dr, Saint Petersburg FL 33729	727-872-1000	P	3,177	5.1
11	J Jill Direct Inc—*Paula Bennett*	PO Box 2006, Tilton NH 03276	603-266-2600	S	2,845*	3.5
12	Patagonia Inc—*Casey Sheahan*	259 W Santa Clara St, Ventura CA 93001	805-643-8616	S	2,403*	1.0
13	Roll Global LLC—*Stewart A Resnick*	11444 W Olympic Blvd, Los Angeles CA 90064	310-966-5700	R	2,204*	4.0
14	PC Connection Inc—*Timothy McGrath*	730 Milford Rd Rte 101, Merrimack NH 03054	603-683-2000	P	2,103	1.9
15	Chadwick's of Boston—*Kevin Doyle*	500 Bic Dr Bldg 4, Milford CT 06461	508-583-8110	D	2,071*	2.0
16	Scientifics—*Randy Burkard*	60 Pearce Ave, Tonawanda NY 14150	716-874-9091	R	2,038*	.5
17	J Crew Group Inc—*Millard S Drexler*	770 Broadway, New York NY 10003		B	1,722	12.7
18	Fingerhut Companies Inc—*Jeffrey Sherman*	6509 Flying Cloud Dr, Eden Prairie MN 55344	952-656-3700	S	1,694*	10.0
19	America's Collectibles Network Inc—*Tim Matthews*	10001 Kingston Pike, Knoxville TN 37922	865-692-6000	R	1,611*	2.0
20	Miles Kimball Co—*Stan Krangel*	250 City Center, Oshkosh WI 54906	920-231-3800	S	1,446*	.6
21	LL Bean Inc—*Chris McCormick*	15 Casco St, Freeport ME 04033	207-865-4761	R	1,400	4.5
22	PC Mall Inc—*Frank F Khulusi*	2555 W 190th St Ste 20, Torrance CA 90504	310-354-5600	P	1,368	2.7
23	eMachines Inc—*J Edward Coleman*	7565 Irvine Center Dr, Irvine CA 92618	949-471-7000	S	1,153*	.2
24	Columbia House Co	PO Box 91601, Rantoul IL 61866	212-596-2000	R	1,136*	2.5
25	Lillian Vernon International Ltd Lillian Vernon Corp	2600 International Pkw, Virginia Beach VA 23452		S	1,136*	1.2
26	Plow and Hearth Inc—*Peter G Rice*	1107 Emmet St N Ste C, Charlottesville VA 22903	434-977-3707	S	1,096*	.5
27	Victoria's Secret Direct LLC—*Mindy Meads*	PO Box 16589, Columbus OH 43216	614-337-5000	S	939	N/A
28	Zapposcom Inc—*Tony Hsieh*	2280 Corporate Cir Ste, Henderson NV 89074	702-943-7688	R	840*	1.3
29	Heritage Capital Corp—*Steve Ivy*	3500 Maple Ave 17th Fl, Dallas TX 75219	214-528-3500	R	802*	.3
30	Redcats USA Inc—*Sylvain Desjonqures*	463 7th Ave, New York NY 10018	212-613-9500	R	735*	9.7
31	Zones Inc—*Firoz H Lalji*	1102 15th St SW Ste 10, Auburn WA 98001	253-205-3000	R	680	.7
32	Boston Proper Inc	6500 Park of Commerce, Boca Raton FL 33487	561-241-1700	R	635*	.3
33	Northern Tool and Equipment Catalog Co—*Donald L Kotula*	2800 Southcross Dr W, Burnsville MN 55306	952-894-9510	R	625*	2.0
34	ValueVision Media Inc—*Keith R Stewart*	6740 Shady Oak Rd, Eden Prairie MN 55344	952-943-6000	P	562	.9
35	NutriSystem Inc—*Joseph M Redling*	300 Welsh Rd Bldg 1 St, Horsham PA 19044	215-706-5300	P	510	.6
36	BUYCOM Inc—*Neel Grover*	85 Enterprise Dr Ste 1, Aliso Viejo CA 92656	949-389-2000	R	482*	.2
37	Provell Inc—*George S Richards*	855 Village Center Dr, North Oaks MN 55127	952-258-2000	R	460*	.5
38	J Jill Group Inc—*Paula Bennett*	4 Batterymarch Pk, Quincy MA 02169	617-376-4300	S	450*	1.4
39	Swets Blackwell North America—*David Main*	PO Box 1459, Runnemede NJ 08078	856-312-2690	D	446*	.8
40	Harry and David Holdings Inc—*Kay Hong*	2500 S Pacific Hwy, Medford OR 97501	541-864-2362	R	427*	1.0
41	Hanover Direct Inc—*Wayne P Garten*	1500 Harbor Blvd, Weehawken NJ 07086	201-863-7300	R	416*	2.0
42	McMaster-Carr Supply Co—*Robert Delaney Jr*	PO Box 4355, Chicago IL 60680	630-834-9600	R	413*	1.0
43	Orchard Brands Corp—*Neale Attenborough*	130 Conant St 3rd Fl, Beverly MA 01915	978-922-2040	R	392*	6.4
44	Alloy Entertainment Inc Alloy Inc	151 W 26th St 11th Fl, New York NY 10001	212-244-4307	S	373*	.3
45	Publishers Clearing House—*Andy Goldberg*	382 Channel Dr, Port Washington NY 11050	516-883-5432	R	366*	.5
46	AmeriMark Direct LLC—*Gary L Geisler*	6864 Engle Rd, Cleveland OH 44130	440-826-1900	R	353*	.7
47	SmartBargains Inc—*Ben Fischman*	20 Channel Center St, Boston MA 02210	617-695-7300	R	347*	.4
48	NM Direct—*Gerald Barnes*	111 Customer Way, Irving TX 75039	972-401-6300	S	341	1.5
49	Wal-Martcom USA LLC	7000 Marina Blvd, Brisbane CA 94005	650-837-5000	S	327*	.3
50	JW Jung Seed Company Inc—*Richard J Zondag*	335 S High St, Randolph WI 53956	920-326-5672	R	300*	.3
51	National Product Sales Inc—*Kelly Farmer*	1600 S Empire Rd, Salt Lake City UT 84104	801-972-4132	R	296*	.4
52	TigerDirect Inc—*Gilbert Fiorentino* Systemax Inc	7795 W Flagler St Ste, Miami FL 33144		S	285*	.5
53	Gilt Groupe Inc—*Kevin Ryan*	2 Park Ave 4th Fl, New York NY 10016		R	283*	.3
54	RxUSA Inc—*Robert Drucker*	81 Seaview Blvd, Port Washington NY 11050	516-467-2500	R	259*	<.1
55	Sport Supply Group Inc—*Adam Blumenfeld*	1901 Diplomat Dr, Dallas TX 75234	972-484-9484	R	250*	.8
56	Campmor Inc	PO Box 680, Mahwah NJ 07430	201-335-9064	R	250*	.3
57	Vermont Country Store—*Lyman Orton*	PO Box 6993, Rutland VT 05702		R	243*	.3
58	Movies Unlimited Inc—*Ava Leas*	3015 Darnell Rd, Philadelphia PA 19154	215-637-4444	R	243*	.1
59	Lillian Vernon Fulfillment Services Inc Lillian Vernon Corp	2600 International Pkw, Virginia Beach VA 23452		S	228	1.2
60	LVC Retail Corp Lillian Vernon Corp	2600 International Pkw, Virginia Beach VA 23452		S	228	1.2
61	Long Motor Corp—*Leo W Long*	PO Box 14991, Lenexa KS 66285		R	227*	.3
62	Delia's Inc—*Walter Killough*	50 W 23rd St, New York NY 10010	212-590-6200	P	221	2.6
63	Vitacostcom Inc—*Jeffrey J Horowitz*	5400 Broken Sound Blvd, Boca Raton FL 33487	561-982-4180	P	221	.4
64	PFSweb Retail Connect Inc	1940 E Mariposa Ave, El Segundo CA 90245	310-658-5000	S	210*	.3
65	Ross-Simons Jewelers Inc—*Darrell S Ross*	9 Ross Simons Dr, Cranston RI 02920	401-463-3100	R	207*	.5
66	Alloy Inc—*Matthew C Diamond*	151 W 26th St 11th Fl, New York NY 10001	212-244-4307	R	205	.6
67	Lillian Vernon Corp—*Michael Muoio*	2600 International Pky, Virginia Beach VA 23452		R	198*	1.0

Rank	Company Name—*Executive Officer*	Address, City, State, Zip	Phone	Type	Fin	Empls
68	Peapod LLC—*Andrew Parkinson*	9933 Woods Dr, Skokie IL 60077	847-583-9400	S	196*	1.8
69	Etsy Inc	55 Washington St Ste 5, Brooklyn NY 11201	718-855-7955	R	181	.1
70	Plow and Hearth LLC—*Scoot Wood*	PO Box 5000, Madison VA 22727	540-948-2272	R	180*	.4
71	US Cavalry Inc	2855 Centennial Ave, Radcliff KY 40160	270-351-1164	R	178*	.1
72	Eastbay Inc—*Dowe Tillema*	PO Box 8066, Wausau WI 54402	715-845-5538	S	177*	1.5
73	Hammacher Schlemmer and Company Inc—*Richard W Tinberg*	147 E 57th St, New York NY 10022	212-421-9000	R	152*	.2
74	Stores Online International Inc—*Brandon Lewis*	754 Technology Ave, Orem UT 84097	801-227-0004	R	150*	.3
75	Lab Safety Supply Inc—*Larry J Loizzo*	PO Box 1368, Janesville WI 53547	608-754-7160	R	147*	.8
76	Homeclick LLC—*Michael Golden*	245 Belmont Dr, Somerset NJ 08873		R	147*	.2
77	Taymark Inc—*Troy Ethan*	4875 White Bear Pkwy, Saint Paul MN 55110	651-426-1667	R	134*	.4
78	Allpetscom Inc—*Niloofar Howe*	1 Maplewood Dr, Hazleton PA 18202	570-384-5555	D	121*	.1
79	Forestry Suppliers Inc—*John R Gwaltney*	PO Box 8397, Jackson MS 39284	601-354-3565	R	116*	.1
80	Alps Electric USA Inc—*Masataka Kataoka*	910 E Hamilton Ave Ste, Campbell CA 95008	408-361-6400	D	112*	.1
81	Replacements Ltd—*Bob Page*	PO Box 26029, Greensboro NC 27420	336-697-3000	R	102*	.6
82	Norm Thompson Outfitters Inc—*D Sorensen*	PO Box 126, Jessup PA 18434		S	100*	.3
83	Specialty Catalog Corp—*Jon Bernstein*	400 Manley St, W Bridgewater MA 02379	508-638-7000	S	100*	.1
84	Anco Fine Foods—*Alan Voss*	149 New Dutch Ln, Fairfield NJ 07004	973-575-9120	R	91*	.2
85	BabyCenter LLC—*Tina Sharkey*	163 Freelon St, San Francisco CA 94107	415-537-0900	S	90*	.2
86	Bluefly Inc—*Melissa Payner-Gregor*	42 W 39th St 9th Fl, New York NY 10018	212-944-8000	P	89	.1
87	TicketsNowcom—*Shawn Freeman*	620 N Rte 31, Crystal Lake IL 60012	815-444-9800	R	86*	.2
88	Stampscom Inc—*Kenneth McBride*	12959 Coral Tree Pl, Los Angeles CA 90066	310-482-5800	P	86	.2
89	Brigade Quartermasters Ltd—*Mitchell WerBell*	177 Georgia Ave, Providence RI 02905		R	83*	.1
90	NASCO International Inc NASCO West Div	PO Box 3837, Modesto CA 95352		R	80*	.4
91	Crutchfield Corp—*Bill Crutchfield*	1 Crutchfield Pk, Charlottesville VA 22911	434-817-1000	R	79*	.5
92	Real Goods Solar Inc—*Bill Yearsley*	833 W South Boulder Rd, Louisville CO 80027		B	77	.3
93	SkyMall Inc—*Christine Aguilera*	1520 E Pima St, Phoenix AZ 85034	602-254-9777	S	76*	.2
94	Levenger Co—*Steven Leveen*	420 S Congress Ave, Delray Beach FL 33445	561-274-0904	R	75*	.4
95	Seta Corp—*Joe Seta*	6400 E Rogers Cir, Boca Raton FL 33499	561-994-2660	R	75*	.1
96	Hello Direct Inc—*Jorn Kildegaard*	77 Northeastern Blvd, Nashua NH 03062	603-579-5300	S	74*	.2
97	Mason Companies Inc—*Daniel Hunt*	1251 1st Ave, Chippewa Falls WI 54729	715-723-1871	R	73*	.4
98	PHE Inc—*Phil D Harvey*	302 Meadowlands Dr, Hillsborough NC 27278		R	73*	.4
99	Title 9 Sports Inc	6201 Doyle St, Emeryville CA 94608	510-653-9949	R	68*	.2
100	PC Parts Inc—*George Crist Jr*	1800 Paxton St, Harrisburg PA 17104	717-233-6650	R	63*	.1
101	G Neil Direct Mail Inc—*Tina Sanchez*	PO Box 450939, Sunrise FL 33345		S	62*	.4
102	IBuyDigitalcom Inc—*Elliot Antebi*	2931 Ave S, Brooklyn NY 11229		R	61	N/A
103	Alloy Marketing and Promotions—*Gary Colen* Alloy Inc	77 N Washington St, Boston MA 02114	617-723-8929	S	57*	.1
104	Mid America Motorworks—*Michael D Yager*	PO Box 1368, Effingham IL 62401	217-540-4200	R	55*	.1
105	Sundance Catalog Company Ltd—*Steven Gordon*	3865 W 2400 S, Salt Lake City UT 84120	801-973-2711	R	54*	.3
106	Allied Marketing Group Inc—*David Ybarra*	1555 Regal Row, Dallas TX 75247	214-915-7000	R	54*	.3
107	Piragis Northwoods Co—*Steve Piragis*	105 N Central Ave, Ely MN 55731	218-365-6745	R	54*	<.1
108	Bedford Fair Industries—*Steve Whiteman*	360 Greenwich Ave, Greenwich CT 06830	203-629-2020	S	53*	<.1
109	Forestfarm—*Ray Pragg*	990 Tetherow Rd, Williams OR 97544	541-846-7269	R	51*	<.1
110	Smooth Corp—*Steve Simonson*	17616 West Valley Hwy, Tukwila WA 98188	425-460-4700	R	48*	.1
111	Sunnyland Farms—*Jane Willson*	2314 Wilson Rd, Albany GA 31705	229-436-5654	R	46*	.1
112	SC Direct—*Ron Fabbro* Specialty Catalog Corp	400 Manloy St, West Bridgewater MA 02379	508-638-7000	S	44*	.3
113	Highsmith Inc—*Duncan Highsmith*	PO Box 7820, Madison WI 53707		S	44*	.2
114	Professional Cutlery Direct LLC—*Terri S Alpert*	242 Branford Rd, North Branford CT 06471		R	44*	<.1
115	Kaplan Co—*Hal Kaplan*	1310 Lewisville Clemmo, Lewisville NC 27023	336-766-7374	R	43*	.2
116	Jameco Electronics Inc—*James Farrey*	1355 Shoreway Rd, Belmont CA 94002	650-592-8097	R	43*	.1
117	Chef's Catalog Inc	5070 Centennial Blvd, Colorado Springs CO 80919		R	42*	.1
118	KVM Switches Online LLC—*Alan Manane*	12202 Airport Way, Broomfield CO 80021		R	42*	<.1
119	Autotest Co—*Robert Cox*	5347 Dietrich Rd, San Antonio TX 78219	210-661-8661	R	42*	<.1
120	Eastwood Co—*Curt Strohacker*	263 Shoemaker Rd, Pottstown PA 19464		R	41*	.1
121	Thomas Direct Sales Inc—*Nancy D'Andrea*	33 Plymouth St, Montclair NJ 07042	973-777-6500	R	41*	.1
122	Bluestem Brands Inc—*John Damrow*	6509 Flying Cloud Dr, Eden Prairie MN 55344	952-656-3700	R	39*	.8
123	McFeely's Co—*Jim Ray*	PO Box 44976, Madison WI 53744		R	38*	<.1
124	Calyx and Corolla Inc—*Andrew W Williams*	3975 20th St Rm 2, Vero Beach FL 32960	772-299-1377	R	36*	<.1
125	Hanna Andersson Corp—*Adam Stone*	1010 NW Flanders Blvd, Portland OR 97209	503-242-0920	R	34*	.2
126	LexJet Corp—*Ronald Simkins*	1605 Main St Ste 400, Sarasota FL 34236	941-330-1210	R	34*	<.1
127	Leadman Electronics—*Frank Fu*	2995 Gordon Ave, Santa Clara CA 95051	408-738-1751	R	33*	<.1
128	Winetastingcom—*Chris Edwards*	2545 Napa Valley Corpo, Napa CA 94558		S	28	.1
129	Newbridge Communications Inc—*Georg Richter*	333 E 38th St 10th Fl, New York NY 10016	212-455-5000	R	26*	.2
130	Indiana Botanic Gardens Inc—*Timothy Cleland*	PO Box 5, Hammond IN 46325	219-947-4040	R	25*	.2
131	Headsetscom Inc—*Mike Faith*	1 Daniel Burnham Ct St, San Francisco CA 94109		R	25*	<.1
132	Alibris Inc—*Brian Elliott*	1250 45th St Ste 100, Emeryville CA 94608	510-594-4500	R	23*	<.1
133	iboats Inc—*Bruno Vassel III*	170 West Election Rd S, Draper UT 84020	801-571-0071	R	21*	.1
134	eXpansys Inc—*Roger Butterworth*	1702 GE Rd Ste 6, Bloomington IL 61704	309-834-0323	S	20*	<.1
135	Brian's Toys—*Brian Semling*	W 730 Hwy 35, Fountain City WI 54629	608-687-7572	R	19*	<.1
136	Nashbar and Associates Inc—*Eric Nashbar*	6103 State Rte 446, Canfield OH 44406	330-533-1989	R	18*	.2
137	eCompanyStore—*Craig Callaway*	5945 Cabot Pkwy Bldg 2, Alpharetta GA 30005		R	16*	.1
138	Diligence Inc—*Bob Lowe*	110 Leawood Dr, New Century KS 66031	913-254-0500	R	16*	<.1
139	Deep Surplus—*Kelly McGranahan*	27671 La Paz Rd Ste 10, Laguna Niguel CA 92677	949-643-5004	R	16*	<.1
140	Country Home Products Inc—*Joe Perrotto*	PO Box 25, Vergennes VT 05491	802-877-1201	R	15*	.2
141	America's Gardening Resource Inc—*William Raap*	128 Intervale Rd, Burlington VT 05401	802-660-3500	R	14*	.1
142	Databit Inc—*Shlomie Morganstern*	200 State Rt 17, Mahwah NJ 07430	201-529-8050	S	12*	<.1
143	Fabulous Furs—*Donna Salyers*	25 W Robbins St, Covington KY 41011	859-291-3300	R	12*	<.1
144	Johns Computer Depot Inc—*John Deshiro*	2119 10th St Ste 8, Baker City OR 97814	541-523-6185	R	12*	<.1
145	Simply Certificates Inc—*Matthew Esler*	1 Crossgates Mall Rd S, Albany NY 12203	518-869-6986	R	12*	<.1
146	FeelGood for Life Inc	6864 Engle Rd, Cleveland OH 44130		R	11	<.1
147	Best Computer Supplies Inc—*Tim Crosson*	895 E Patriot Blvd Ste, Reno NV 89511	775-850-2600	R	11*	<.1
148	Applied Computer Online Services—*Sam Chan*	2901 Moorpark Ave Ste, San Jose CA 95128	408-248-8811	R	10*	<.1
149	SemWare Corp	730 Elk Cove Ct, Kennesaw GA 30152	678-355-9810	R	10*	<.1
150	Prudent Publishing Company Inc—*Bernard D'avella*	PO Box 360, Ridgefield Park NJ 07660	201-641-7900	R	10*	<.1
151	Parke-Bell Limited Inc—*Frederick Bell*	PO Box 237, Huntingdon IN 46750	812-683-3707	R	10*	.2
152	SkyBox Inc—*Paul V Gartlan*	1900 NW 97th Ave, Doral FL 33172	786-265-4880	R	9*	<.1
153	Usedroutercom Inc—*Ben Nelson*	5335 S Campbell Ste D, Springfield MO 65810	417-887-7724	R	9*	<.1
154	Real Estate Image Inc—*Ty Mcmillin*	1415 S Acacia Ave, Fullerton CA 92831	714-502-3900	R	9*	.1

Note: An asterisk (*) indicates an estimated financial figure. The company type code used is as follows: R = Private, P = Public, S = Private Subsidiary, B = Public Subsidiary, D = Division, J = Joint Venture, I = Investment Fund.

RANKINGS BY SALES WITHIN 4-DIGIT SIC

	Name—Executive Officer	Address, City, State, Zip	Phone	Type	Fin	Empls
	Voice Of God Recording Inc—Joseph Branham	PO Box 950, Jeffersonville IN 47131	812-256-1177	R	9*	.1
156	Hobbytroncom—Tim Gibson	24700 Ave Rockefeller, Santa Clarita CA 91355	818-675-9000	R	8*	.1
157	Smart Office Services LLC—Steven Myer	810 Cromwell Park Dr S, Glen Burnie MD 21061	410-787-2521	R	8*	<.1
158	Backcountry Store Inc—Jim Holland	2607 South 3200 W Ste, West Valley City UT 84119	801-973-4553	R	8*	<.1
159	Headset Zone	406 164th St SW Ste A, Lynnwood WA 98087		R	8*	<.1
160	Protocol Ii Inc—Devin Kimura	11901 137th Ave Ct Kpn, Gig Harbor WA 98329	253-857-2372	R	8*	.1
161	Roman Research Inc—Dale Southworth	800 Franklin St, Hanson MA 02341	781-447-3411	R	7*	.1
162	HearthSong Inc—Sydney R Klevatt	PO Box 1050, Madison VA 22727		R	7*	<.1
163	Williamsport Barber and Beauty Corp—John G Incitti Jr	1231 Sheridan St, Williamsport PA 17701	570-323-7772	D	6*	<.1
164	DVDCITY Inc—Sidney D Davis III	2020 Howell Mill Rd NW, Atlanta GA 30318	404-352-0151	R	6*	<.1
165	Kids Stuff Inc—William L Miller	7090 Whipple Ave NW, North Canton OH 44720	330-492-8090	R	6*	<.1
166	Time Passages Ltd—Scott Anderson	PO Box 65596, W Des Moines IA 50265	515-223-5105	R	6*	<.1
167	S B Machining Inc—Bhal Shah	1340 S Allec St, Anaheim CA 92805	714-772-9011	R	5*	<.1
168	Quilt In A Day Inc—Eleanor Burns	1955 Diamond St, San Marcos CA 92078	760-591-0929	R	5*	<.1
169	Gold Medal Hair Products Inc—Richard Laban	1 Bennington Ave, Freeport NY 11520	516-378-6900	R	5*	<.1
170	Texas Coffee Company Inc—Carlo Busceme	PO Box 31, Beaumont TX 77704	409-835-3434	R	5*	<.1
171	Sauna Warehouse Inc—Dave Dickerson	6 Orchard Ste 201, Lake Forest CA 92630	949-609-2202	R	4*	<.1
172	One Source Plus Inc—Darrin M King	11535 Carmel Commons B, Charlotte NC 28226	704-341-0876	R	4*	<.1
173	UsedLaptopsCom Inc—Marc LeBaron	958 San Leandro Ave St, Mountain View CA 94043	408-779-5599	R	4*	<.1
174	Tri-State Camera Exch Inc—Michael Beilush	150 Sullivan St, Brooklyn NY 11231	212-633-2454	R	4*	<.1
175	Ablenet Inc—David Binczik	2625 Patton Rd, Saint Paul MN 55113	612-379-0956	R	4*	<.1
176	Connecticut Valley Biological Supply Company Inc—Robert Lohr	PO Box 326, Southampton MA 01073	413-527-4030	R	3*	<.1
177	Sun Groves Inc—Michelle Urbanski	3393 State Rd 580, Safety Harbor FL 34695	727-726-8484	R	3*	.1
178	Sunelco—Tom Bishop	2086 US Hwy 93 N Ste 1, Victor MT 59875	406-642-6422	R	3*	<.1
179	Commint Inc—Keith Kelley	12337 Jones Rd Ste 450, Houston TX 77070	281-558-2433	J	3*	<.1
180	floppydiskcom—Tom E Persky	2620 Walnut Ave Unit D, Tustin CA 92780	714-669-8301	R	3*	<.1
181	Falcon Northwest Computer Systems Inc—Kelt Reeves	2015 Commerce Dr, Medford OR 97504	541-858-5660	R	3*	<.1
182	Heaton Pecan Farm—John Rheaton	309 Sunrise Blvd, Clanton AL 35045	205-755-8654	R	3*	<.1
183	Kaufmann's Streamborn Inc—Lance Kaufmann	8861 SW Commercial St, Tigard OR 97223	503-639-6400	R	2*	<.1
184	Hearlihy And Co—Harvey R Dean	PO Box 1747, Pittsburg KS 66762		R	2*	<.1
185	Gallery of History Direct—Todd M Axelrod	3601 W Sahara Ave, Las Vegas NV 89102	702-364-1000	D	2*	<.1
186	Total Medical Systems Inc—Michael Hanik	PO Box 1661, Rockville MD 20849		R	2*	<.1
187	Imaginethis—Steve Kirsch	4002 Doney St, Columbus OH 43213	614-231-7766	R	2*	<.1
188	Interconnect West	6239 South Highland Dr, Salt Lake City UT 84121	801-277-4429	R	2*	<.1
189	Smartsoft Software Inc—Sean Campbell Hanna	10885 Kalama River Ave, Fountain Valley CA 92708	714-963-2332	R	2*	<.1
190	Wilderness Inspirations—Dorothy Keeler	PO Box 433, Emigrant MT 59027	406-333-4366	R	2*	<.1
191	Featherspring International Corp—Peter Rothschild	712 N 34th St, Seattle WA 98103	206-545-8585	R	2*	<.1
192	Anacondabookscom—Howard Karno	PO Box 2100, Valley Center CA 92082	760-749-2304	R	1	<.1
193	Industrial Instruments and Supplies Inc—Christine Walter	PO Box 416, Southampton PA 18966	215-396-0822	R	1*	<.1
194	Sormani Calendars—Judith S Jenkins	PO Box 6059, Chelsea MA 02150		R	1*	<.1
195	Apason Distributors—Vadim Dubrovin	250 Sycamore Cir, Langhorne PA 19053	215-322-0331	R	1*	<.1
196	Communication Concepts Inc—Rodger Southworth	508 Mill Stone Dr, Beavercreek OH 45434	937-426-8600	R	1*	<.1
197	RST Engineering—Gail Allinson	13993 Downwind Ct, Grass Valley CA 95945	530-272-2203	H	<1*	<.1

TOTALS: SIC 5961 Catalog & Mail-Order Houses
Companies: 197   189,857   300.7

5962 Merchandising Machine Operators

	Name—Executive Officer	Address, City, State, Zip	Phone	Type	Fin	Empls
1	Canteen Service Co—Joe O'Connor	3755 Broadmoor Ave SE, Grand Rapids MI 49512	616-956-5066	S	120	.8
2	Glacier Water Services Inc—Brian H McInerney	1385 Park Center Dr, Vista CA 92081	760-560-1111	P	100	.3
3	Calderon Brothers Vending Company Inc—Steven Calderon	PO Box 29099, Indianapolis IN 46229	317-899-1234	R	51*	.3
4	Sanese Services Inc—Ralph Sanese	6465 Busch Blvd, Columbus OH 43229	614-436-1234	R	42*	.9
5	Advanced Vending Systems Inc—Dennis Thornton	PO Box 987, Ringgold GA 30736	706-866-6044	R	40*	.2
6	Ace Coffee Bar Inc—Bernard Cavitt	601 E Lake St, Streamwood IL 60107	630-233-2800	R	33*	.5
7	Atlas Food Systems And Services Inc—Alex Kiriakides	205 Woods Lake Rd, Greenville SC 29607	864-232-1885	R	32*	.3
8	RE Services LLC—Stan Ledbetter	1853 W North Main St, La Fayette GA 30728	706-638-3366	R	29*	.4
9	Zaug's Inc—Allen Zaug	PO Box 2335, Appleton WI 54912	920-734-9881	R	29*	.1
10	J B Vending Company Inc—Kendall Jackson	31 International Plz C, Saint Ann MO 63074	314-423-3993	R	23*	.2
11	United Bank Card Inc—Donald Isaacman	PO Box 4006, Clinton NJ 08809	908-730-6102	R	19*	.1
12	Konop Companies Inc—Thomas J Konop	1725 Industrial Dr, Green Bay WI 54302	920-468-8517	R	18*	.2
13	Burch Food Services Inc—Bill Burch	PO Box 1667, Sikeston MO 63801	573-471-3003	R	10*	.2
14	Patton Music Company Inc—James B Reed	811 Kearney Ave, Modesto CA 95350	209-574-1101	R	10*	.1
15	Refreshments Inc—Kenneth Williams	PO Box 240, Corinth MS 38835	662-286-6051	R	8*	.1
16	Black Tie Services LLP—Scott Meskin	4813 Benson Ave, Baltimore MD 21227	410-247-8255	R	5*	<.1
17	Food Services Inc—James Weeks	PO Box 670, Opp AL 36467	334-493-4505	R	4*	<.1
18	Greater Tri-Cities Services LLC—Ken Frohlich	2029 Brookside Ln, Kingsport TN 37660	423-578-8188	R	4*	<.1
19	South Peninsula Sales Inc	6907 Rockton Ave, San Jose CA 95119	408-225-1001	R	4*	<.1
20	First Choice Food Service Inc—Clarence Barnette	2102 Industrial Park D, Wilson NC 27893	252-291-7733	R	3*	<.1
21	Tri State Vending—Don Gill	PO Box 591, Thorofare NJ 08086	856-384-0440	R	3*	<.1
22	Hvp Inc—Dennis Jorganson	PO Box 382, Morrison IL 61270	815-772-4035	R	3*	<.1
23	Terminal Amusement Co—George Hamilton Jr	301 W Clinton Ave, Oaklyn NJ 08107	856-854-2100	R	2*	<.1
24	WaterPure International Inc—Paul Lipschutz	2944 NW 27th St Bldg 1, Oakland Park FL 33311	954-731-2002	P	<1	<.1

TOTALS: SIC 5962 Merchandising Machine Operators
Companies: 24   592   4.7

5963 Direct Selling Establishments

	Name—Executive Officer	Address, City, State, Zip	Phone	Type	Fin	Empls
1	Alticor Inc—Steve Van Andel	7575 Fulton St E, Ada MI 49355	616-787-1000	R	6,892*	14.0
2	Amway Corp—Doug DeVos Alticor Inc	PO Box 513, Ada MI 49301	616-787-6000	S	5,293*	13.0
3	Mary Kay Inc—David B Holl	PO Box 799045, Dallas TX 75379	972-687-6300	R	2,500	4.5
4	Forever Living Products International Inc—Rex Maughan	7501 E McCormick Ranch, Scottsdale AZ 85258	480-998-8888	R	1,580*	4.0
5	Herbalife International Inc	PO Box 80210, Los Angeles CA 90080	310-410-9600	S	1,337*	2.6
6	Amyway North America—Doug Devos Alticor Inc	7575 Fulton St East, Ada MI 49355	616-787-6000	S	705*	.6
7	SCOOTER Store Inc—Doug Harrison	PO Box 310709, New Braunfels TX 78131	830-626-5660	R	476*	2.0
8	Cutco Corp—James Stitt	PO Box 810, Olean NY 14760	716-372-3111	P	252*	.8
9	Lens Express Inc—Jonathan C Coon	350 SW 12th Ave, Deerfield Beach FL 33442		R	212	N/A
10	UndercoverWear Inc—Tiffany James	30 Commerce Way Ste 2, Tewksbury MA 01876	978-851-8580	R	100*	.1
11	Tastefully Simple Inc—Jill Blashack Strahan	PO Box 3006, Alexandria MN 56308	320-763-0695	R	99*	.3
12	4Life Research LC—David Lisonbee	9850 S 300 W, Sandy UT 84070	801-562-3600	R	77*	.2

Rank	Company Name—*Executive Officer*	Address, City, State, Zip	Phone	Type	Fin	Empls
13	Eos International Inc—*James Cascino*	73 Turning Mill Ln, New Canaan CT 06840	203-652-2525	R	72	.6
14	Rena Ware Int'l—*Russel Zylstra*	8383 158th Ave NE, Redmond WA 98052	425-881-6171	R	53*	.1
15	Douglas Communications Corporation II—*Douglas H Dittrick*	317 Godwin Ave, Midland Park NJ 07432	201-444-1700	R	51*	.1
16	American Liquid Packaging Systems Inc—*Saeed Amidhozour*	440 N Wolfe Rd, Sunnyvale CA 94085	408-524-7474	R	35*	.6
17	5Linx Enterprises Inc—*Craig Jerabeck*	275 Kenneth Dr Ste 100, Rochester NY 14623	585-334-2600	R	35*	.2
18	Method Home Products—*Eric Ryan*	637 Commercial St, San Francisco CA 94111	415-931-3947	R	34*	<.1
19	Guthy-Renker Corp—*Bill Guthy*	41-550 Eclectic St Ste, Palm Desert CA 92260	760-773-9022	R	33*	.1
20	National Trade Supply LLC—*Todd Anthony*	5340 S Harding St, Indianapolis IN 46217	317-536-7445	R	20*	<.1
21	Waiters on Wheels Inc—*Takis Zarikas*	5425 Mission St, San Francisco CA 94112	415-452-6600	R	16	.2
22	Courtesy Products Co—*Matt Schwarz*	PO Box 17488, Saint Louis MO 63178	314-592-5100	S	16*	<.1
23	Country Home Collection Co—*Gerald Henn*	1001 Country Way Sw, Warren OH 44481	330-824-2575	R	15*	.2
24	CableOrganizercom Inc—*Valerie Holstein*	5610 NW 12th Ave Ste 2, Fort Lauderdale FL 33309	954-861-2000	R	11*	<.1
25	Ics Investment Inc-Gabreil Group—*Michael Peterson*	3190 Rider Trl S, Saint Louis MO 63146	314-713-5100	R	4*	.1
26	Dean's Water Service Inc—*Richard Dean*	950 Jessop Pl, Washington PA 15301	724-225-1002	R	3*	<.1
27	Cheesecake Factory Inc—*Steven Mager*	3300 Menaul Blvd Ne, Albuquerque NM 87107	505-884-1777	R	3*	.1
28	Rdm Technologies Inc—*David Kemp*	3650 Kennesaw 75 Pkwy, Kennesaw GA 30144	770-427-7757	R	2*	.1
29	Soski S Piroeff Inc—*S Piroeff*	PO Box 877, Malvern PA 19355	610-648-0100	R	2*	<.1
30	Fischer and Herron Inc—*Greg Fischer*	1636 N Brian St, Orange CA 92867	714-921-2660	R	1*	<.1
31	Hybond Inc—*Hanns Lindberg*	330 State Pl, Escondido CA 92029	760-746-7105	R	1*	<.1
32	Holden Landmark Corp—*Kirk Davis*	PO Box 546, Holden MA 01520	508-829-5981	R	1*	<.1
33	Slumber Parties By Cari—*Cari Frazier*	3825 Birdsville Rd, Davidsonville MD 21035	240-274-3713	R	N/A	<.1

TOTALS: SIC 5963 Direct Selling Establishments

Companies: 33					19,932	44.7

5983 Fuel Oil Dealers

Rank	Company Name—*Executive Officer*	Address, City, State, Zip	Phone	Type	Fin	Empls
1	Petro Holdings Inc—*Daniel Donovan*	2187 Atlantic St, Stamford CT 06902	203-325-5400	S	1,105*	3.0
2	Griffith Energy Services Inc—*Randy Groft*	2510 Schuster Dr, Cheverly MD 20781	301-322-3111	S	544*	.4
3	Quality Oil Company LLC—*Graham Bennett*	PO Box 2736, Winston Salem NC 27102	336-722-3441	R	470*	.6
4	Castle Oil Corp—*Michael Romita*	440 Mamaroneck Ave 4th, Harrison NY 10528	914-381-6600	R	462*	.3
5	Able Energy Inc—*Gregory D Frost*	1140 Ave of the Americ, New York NY 10036	212-835-0200	P	276	.5
6	LaForgia Fuel Oil Co—*Frank LaForgia*	1640 McDonald Ave, Brooklyn NY 11230	718-627-5100	R	156*	.1
7	Santa Fuel Inc—*Peter S Russell*	154 Admiral St, Bridgeport CT 06605		R	135*	.2
8	Team Schierl Cos—*William Schierl*	PO Box 308, Stevens Point WI 54481	715-345-5060	R	119*	.5
9	Irving Oil Corp—*Arthur Irving*	190 Commerce Way, Portsmouth NH 03801	603-559-8736	R	92*	.1
10	Norbert E Mitchell Company Inc—*Norbert E Mitchell Jr*	PO Box 186, Danbury CT 06813	203-744-0600	R	62*	.1
11	Forward Corp—*Terry McTaggart*	219 N Front St, Standish MI 48658	989-846-4501	R	57*	.6
12	Larsen Cooperative Company Inc—*Leroy Peterson*	PO Box 308, New London WI 54961	920-982-1111	R	50*	.1
13	Madison Oil Co—*Bill Carroll*	30 Scotland Ave, Madison CT 06443	203-245-2239	R	46*	<.1
14	JW Pierson Co—*James W Pierson*	89 Dodd St, East Orange NJ 07017	973-673-5000	R	39*	.1
15	Woodruff Energy Co—*Robert A Woodruff Jr*	PO Box 777, Bridgeton NJ 08302	856-455-1111	R	38*	.1
16	Robison Oil Corp—*Fran Singer*	500 Executive Blvd, Elmsford NY 10523	914-345-5700	R	30*	.2
17	Tri-City Fuel and Heating Company Inc—*Richard Shull*	640 N 12th St, West Columbia SC 29171	803-450-0874	R	29*	<.1
18	Brinker's Fuels Inc—*Michael Anton*	PO Box 816, Doylestown PA 10901	215 343 0660	R	21*	.1
19	AC and T Company Inc—*Adna Fulton*	PO Box 4217, Hagerstown MD 21741	301-582-2700	R	20*	.1
20	SW Rawls Inc—*W Elliott Whitfield*	PO Box 777, Franklin VA 23851	757-562-3115	R	19*	.1
21	First Call Heating And Cooling Co—*Kevin Kelly*	1650 Ne Lombard St, Portland OR 97211	503-231-3311	R	18*	.1
22	Lawes Coal Company Inc—*Donald E Lawes Jr*	PO Box 258, Shrewsbury NJ 07702	732-741-6300	R	18*	.1
23	Rocket Oil Inc—*Douglas Lawrence*	2477 Main St NW, Coon Rapids MN 55448	763-755-4930	R	15*	.1
24	Holcomb Fuel Company Inc—*Steven Lant*	PO Box 486, Newtown CT 06470	203-426-5804	R	10*	<.1
25	Clickable Enterprises Inc—*Nicholas Cirillo Jr*	2 Madison Ave Ste 209, Larchmont NY 10538	914-833-9125	P	8	<.1
26	Seaboard Service Inc—*Glen Kruman*	PO Box 248, Oakhurst NJ 07755	732-775-5900	R	8*	<.1
27	Globe Petroleum Inc—*Patrick Mazzucca*	9 Central Ave, Red Bank NJ 07701	732-747-1023	R	8*	<.1
28	Ackner Fuels Inc—*Harry Ackner*	2692 NY 43, Averill Park NY 12018	518-674-3812	R	4*	<.1
29	Herrin Brothers Coal and Ice Co—*Marshall Herrin*	PO Box 5291, Charlotte NC 28299	704-332-2193	R	2*	<.1
30	AJ Petrunis Inc—*Michael Petrunis*	173 Water St, Bridgeton NJ 08302	856-451-7558	R	2*	<.1
31	Jet Fuel Oil Co—*Anthony Lineberger*	PO Box 819, Saint Petersburg FL 33731	727-824-8909	R	2*	<.1
32	Native American Energy Group Inc—*Joseph D'Arrigo*	108-18 Queens Blvd Ste, Forest Hills NY 11375	718-408-2323	P	<1	<.1
33	Webber Oil Co—*Michael Shea*	700 Main St, Bangor ME 04401	207-942-5501	R	N/A	.6

TOTALS: SIC 5983 Fuel Oil Dealers

Companies: 33					3,866	7.9

5984 Liquefied Petroleum Gas Dealers

Rank	Company Name—*Executive Officer*	Address, City, State, Zip	Phone	Type	Fin	Empls
1	AmeriGas Propane Parts and Service Inc—*Eugene VN Bissell*	PO Box 965, Valley Forge PA 19482	610-337-7000	S	4,860*	6.0
2	Titan Propane—*Bill Corbin*	432 Westridge Dr, Watsonville CA 95076	831-724-1921	R	2,479*	1.3
3	Ferrellgas Partners LP—*Stephen L Wambold*	7500 College Blvd Ste, Overland Park KS 66210	913-661-1500	P	2,423	3.6
4	Star Gas Partners LP—*Daniel P Donovan*	2187 Atlantic St, Stamford CT 06902	203-328-7300	P	1,591	2.7
5	Suburban Propane LP—*Michael J Dunn*	PO Box 206, Whippany NJ 07981	973-887-5300	S	1,495*	3.4
6	Heritage Operating LP—*William Powers*	8801 S Yale Ave St 31, Tulsa OK 74137	918-492-7272	S	716*	2.4
7	Ferrellgas LP—*Stephen L Wambold* Ferrellgas Partners LP	7500 College Blvd Ste, Overland Park KS 66210	913-661-1500	S	244*	.3
8	Patterson Oil Co	100 Lincoln Ave, Torrington CT 06790	860-489-9271	R	202*	.2
9	Cvc Holding Company Inc—*Charles Clement*	PO Box 1800, Rochester NH 03866	603-332-2080	R	147*	.3
10	Three Rivers Fs Co—*David Kirsch*	PO Box 248, Earlville IA 52041	563-923-2315	R	75*	.1
11	AmeriGas Eagle Parts and Service Inc—*Eugene VN Bissell*	460 N Gulph Rd, King of Prussia PA 19406	610-337-7000	S	61*	.1
12	Gas Equipment Co—*Jack LaDue*	11616 Harry Hines Blvd, Dallas TX 75229		R	42*	.3
13	Hocon Gas Inc—*David Gable*	33 Rockland Rd, Norwalk CT 06854	203-853-1500	R	34*	.1
14	Jenkins Gas Company Inc—*John Robert Mattocks*	PO Box 156, Pollocksville NC 28573	252-224-8911	S	33*	.2
15	Guilford Gas Service Inc—*Daniel Welles*	710 Patton Ave, Greensboro NC 27406	336-274-8449	S	33*	<.1
16	Sharp Energy Inc—*S Robert Zola*	648 Ocean Hwy, Pocomoke City MD 21851	410-957-1501	S	22*	.1
17	Southern LP Gas Inc—*Ron Moore*	PO Box 1010, De Queen AR 71832	870-642-2234	R	21*	.1
18	Como Oil Company Inc—*John Heino*	PO Box 16108, Duluth MN 55816	218-722-6666	R	16*	<.1
19	Mutual Liquid Gas and Equipment Company Inc	17117 S Broadway St, Gardena CA 90248	323-321-3771	R	15*	.1
20	Gas Inc—*Kendrick Mattox Jr*	77 Jefferson Pkwy, Newnan GA 30263	770-502-8800	R	14*	.1
21	Litter Quality Propane—*Matthew Litter*	PO Box 297, Chillicothe OH 45601	740-773-2196	R	13*	.1
22	TriCounty Farm Service Inc—*Joe Fesser*	PO Box 367, Jerseyville IL 62052	618-498-5534	R	12*	<.1
23	Highland Propane Co—*Sam Hodges*	PO Box 19683, Roanoke VA 24019	540-777-7928	S	9*	<.1
24	Glaser Gas Inc—*Edwin Glaser*	215 Auburn Dr, Colorado Springs CO 80909	719-596-4765	R	5*	<.1
25	Range Cooperatives Inc—*John Briski*	102 S Hoover Rd, Virginia MN 55792	218-741-7393	R	5*	<.1
26	CAP Propane Plus Inc—*Bruce Munter*	PO Box 38, Kettle River MN 55757		R	5	<.1

Note: An asterisk (*) indicates an estimated financial figure. The company type code used is as follows: R = Private, P = Public, S = Private Subsidiary, B = Public Subsidiary, D = Division, J = Joint Venture, I = Investment Fund.

COMPANY RANKINGS BY SALES WITHIN 4-DIGIT SIC

Rank	Company Name—*Executive Officer*	Address, City, State, Zip	Phone	Type	Fin	Empls
27	Stem Brothers Inc	PO Box 619, Milford NJ 08848	908-995-4825	R	4*	<.1
28	Western Natural Gas Co—*Henry C Baker*	2960 Strickland St, Jacksonville FL 32254	904-387-3511	R	4*	<.1
29	Overpeck Gas Co—*Carl Duncan*	PO Box 77, Marshall IN 47859	765-597-2201	R	4*	<.1
30	Boulden Inc—*Urie Boulden*	540 Old Barksdale Rd, Newark DE 19711	302-368-2553	R	3*	<.1

TOTALS: SIC 5984 Liquefied Petroleum Gas Dealers
Companies: 30   **14,587**   **21.6**

5989 Fuel Dealers Nec

Rank	Company Name—*Executive Officer*	Address, City, State, Zip	Phone	Type	Fin	Empls
1	Inergy LP—*John J Sherman*	2 Brush Creek Blvd Ste, Kansas City MO 64112	816-842-8181	P	2,154	2.9
2	General Finance Corp—*Ronald F Valenta*	39 E Union St, Pasadena CA 91103	626-584-9722	P	388	.4
3	Federated Co-Ops Inc—*Tom Rausch*	502 S 2nd St Ste 2, Princeton MN 55371	763-389-2582	R	108*	.3
4	Refron Inc—*Jay Kestenbaum*	38-18 33rd St, Long Island City NY 11101	718-392-8002	D	100*	.1
5	Hinsbrook Bank and Trust—*Eugene C Ognibene*	6262 S Rte 83, Willow Brook IL 60527	630-920-2700	R	97*	<.1
6	Solar Liberty—*Adam Rizzo*	6225 Sheridan Dr Ste 1, Williamsville NY 14221	716-634-3780	R	16*	<.1

TOTALS: SIC 5989 Fuel Dealers Nec
Companies: 6   **2,862**   **3.7**

5992 Florists

Rank	Company Name—*Executive Officer*	Address, City, State, Zip	Phone	Type	Fin	Empls
1	1-800 FLOWERS Team Services Inc 1-800-Flowerscom Inc	1 Old Country Rd Ste 5, Carle Place NY 11514	516-237-6000	S	2,416*	1.8
2	Cactus and Tropicals Inc—*Scott Pynes*	2735 S 2000 E, Salt Lake City UT 84109	801-485-2542	R	2,035*	.1
3	1-800-Flowerscom Inc—*James F McCann*	1 Old Country Rd Ste 5, Carle Place NY 11514	516-237-6000	P	690	2.3
4	FTD Group Inc—*Rob Apatoff*	3113 Woodcreek Dr, Downers Grove IL 60515	630-719-7800	S	646*	1.0
5	P and H LP—*James F McCann* 1-800-Flowerscom Inc	1 Old Country Rd Ste 5, Carle Place NY 11514	516-237-6000	S	410*	.4
6	Conroy's Inc 1-800-Flowerscom Inc	12901 Victory Blvd, North Hollywood CA 91606	818-840-9191	S	405*	.3
7	Amlings Flowerland—*Brian J McCarthy*	331 N York, Elmhurst IL 60126	630-850-5000	R	33*	.4
8	Lloyd's Florist	9215 Preston Hwy, Louisville KY 40229	502-968-5428	R	30*	<.1
9	Stems and Vines—*Jan Belisle*	917 Grand Ave, St Paul MN 55105	651-228-1450	R	16*	.1
10	Susan's Florist Inc—*Amy Streeter*	2731 Preston Hwy, Louisville KY 40217	502-635-6351	R	8*	<.1
11	Payne and Morrison Florists—*Michael Bailey*	7146 N 35th Ave, Phoenix AZ 85051	602-841-7890	R	7*	<.1
12	Ronsley Inc—*Michael Leventhal*	1200 N N Branch St, Chicago IL 60642	312-649-0777	R	7*	.1
13	Tillie's Flower Shop—*Kenneth Denton*	3701 E Harry St, Wichita KS 67218	316-687-0630	R	4*	<.1
14	Blossoms Inc—*Dale Morgan*	33866 Woodward Ave, Birmingham MI 48009	248-644-4411	R	4*	<.1
15	Harper's Nurseries and Flower Shops—*Jay Harper*	2529 N Hayden Rd, Scottsdale AZ 85257	480-946-3481	R	2*	<.1
16	Freda's Fancy Florist Antiques Inc—*Freda Chapman*	11517 Main St, Louisville KY 40243	502-245-8720	R	1*	<.1
17	Country Squire Florist—*Dick Wellum*	10310 Shelbyville Rd, Louisville KY 40223	502-425-1530	R	1*	<.1

TOTALS: SIC 5992 Florists
Companies: 17   **6,715**   **6.5**

5993 Tobacco Stores & Stands

Rank	Company Name—*Executive Officer*	Address, City, State, Zip	Phone	Type	Fin	Empls
1	International Cigar Bar of Tampa—*Bill Davies*	17506 Brighton Avenue, Port Charlotte FL 33954	941-429-7997	R	2	<.1
2	Social Smoke Inc—*Sayyid Nadimi*	PO Box 121002, Arlington TX 76012	817-633-6300	R	2*	<.1
3	Johnny Ravioli Cigars *Burwell Noyes*	251B San Marco Ave, St Augustine FL 32084	904-687-5058	R	2*	<.1

TOTALS: SIC 5993 Tobacco Stores & Stands
Companies: 3   **6**   **<.1**

5994 News Dealers & Newsstands

Rank	Company Name—*Executive Officer*	Address, City, State, Zip	Phone	Type	Fin	Empls
1	Healy News Store Inc—*Freeman A Healy Jr*	231 Robinson St, Wakefield RI 02879	401-789-9566	R	2*	<.1
2	Iowa State Daily—*Annette Forbes*	108 Hamilton Hl Ia St, Ames IA 50011	515-294-4120	R	1*	<.1

TOTALS: SIC 5994 News Dealers & Newsstands
Companies: 2   **3**   **<.1**

5995 Optical Goods Stores

Rank	Company Name—*Executive Officer*	Address, City, State, Zip	Phone	Type	Fin	Empls
1	Eye Care Centers of America Inc—*David L Holmberg*	175 E HOuston Street, San Antonio TX 78205	210-340-3531	S	4,568*	5.6
2	Cole National Corp—*Larry Pollock*	4000 Luxottica Pl, Mason OH 45040	513-765-6000	S	1,202	13.7
3	Davis Vision Inc—*Steve Holden*	159 Express St, Plainview NY 11803	516-932-9500	R	390*	5.0
4	1-800 CONTACTS Inc—*Jonathan C Coon*	66 E Wadsworth Park Dr, Draper UT 84020	801-924-9800	R	172*	.3
5	US Vision Inc—*William Schwartz*	1 Harmon Dr, Glendora NJ 08029	856-228-1000	R	171*	3.0
6	Lombart Instruments US—*Rick Lombart*	5358 Robin Hood Rd, Norfolk VA 23513	757-853-8888	R	125*	.1
7	Sterling Optical Emerging Vision Inc	520 Eighth Ave Fl 23, New York NY 10018		S	87*	.1
8	Rosin Eyecare—*James Rosin*	6233 W Cermak Rd, Berwyn IL 60402	708-749-2020	R	82*	.1
9	Spectera Inc—*David Hall*	6220 Old Dobbin Ln Ste, Columbia MD 21045	410-265-6033	S	74*	.7
10	Emerging Vision Inc—*Glenn Spinna*	520 8th Ave 23rd Fl, New York NY 10018	646-737-1500	P	55	.2
11	Nationwide Vision Center PC—*Mark Hechtman*	220 N Mckemy Ave, Chandler AZ 85226	480-961-1865	R	26*	.5
12	Sterling Vision Kenoha Inc—*Christopher Payan* Emerging Vision Inc	7532 Pershing Blvd, Kenosha WI 53142	262-694-2400	S	25*	<.1
13	Cummins Charles M Od And Elliot L Shack Od PA—*Elliot Shack*	1255 Broad St, Bloomfield NJ 07003	973-338-8886	R	15*	.2
14	Sunland Optical Company Inc—*Gordon Bishop*	1156 Barranca Dr, El Paso TX 79935	915-591-9483	R	12*	.3
15	Sterling Vision Westminster Inc Emerging Vision Inc	400 N Center St, Westminster MD 21157	410-857-4200	S	11*	<.1
16	Cooperative Optical Services Inc—*Jackee Smith*	2424 E 8 Mile Rd, Detroit MI 48234	313-366-5100	R	7*	.1
17	CVK Corp—*Lois Copple*	3725 Ingersoll Ave, Des Moines IA 50312	515-255-5533	R	7*	.1
18	Clark Appler and Optical—*Thomas Appler*	7301 York Rd Ste 2, Baltimore MD 21204	410-825-4454	R	5*	<.1
19	San Luis Obisbo Eye Associates A Me—*Cindi Cole*	234 Heather Ct Ste 1, Templeton CA 93465	805-434-5970	R	4*	<.1
20	Prescription Optical Inc—*Kevin Reimer*	311 28th Ave S, Waite Park MN 56387	320-252-3113	R	4*	<.1
21	Sunstar Optical Inc—*Ron Steffey*	5960 Edmond St, Las Vegas NV 89118	702-739-8880	R	3*	<.1
22	General Optical Co—*James Moore*	1235 S Ctr Rd Ste 16, Burton MI 48509	810-744-1950	R	2*	<.1
23	Western Ophthalmics Corp—*Pete D'Amico*	19019 36th Ave W Ste G, Lynnwood WA 98036	425-672-9332	R	N/A	<.1

TOTALS: SIC 5995 Optical Goods Stores
Companies: 23   **7,045**   **29.9**

5999 Miscellaneous Retail Stores Nec

Rank	Company Name—*Executive Officer*	Address, City, State, Zip	Phone	Type	Fin	Empls
1	Energy Transfer Equity LP—*Kelcy L Warren*	3738 Oak Lawn Ave, Dallas TX 75219	214-918-0700	P	8,241	2.5
2	PETsMART Inc—*Robert F Moran*	19601 N 27th Ave, Phoenix AZ 85027	321-309-9065	P	5,694	47.0
3	AmeriGas Partners LP—*Eugene V N Bissell*	PO Box 965, Valley Forge PA 19482	610-337-7000	P	2,538	5.8

Rank	Company Name—*Executive Officer*	Address, City, State, Zip	Phone	Type	Fin	Empls
4	Aki Inc—*Debra Leipman-Yale*	PO Box 60088, Chattanooga TN 37406	212-541-2600	R	2,520*	.5
5	Bath and Body Works Inc—*Diane Neal*	7 Limited Pky E, Reynoldsburg OH 43068	614-856-6000	S	2,374*	20.0
6	Petco Animal Supplies Inc—*James M Myers*	9125 Rehco Rd, San Diego CA 92121	858-453-7845	R	2,230*	20.0
7	Cash America International Inc—*Daniel R Feehan*	1600 W 7th St, Fort Worth TX 76102	817-335-1100	P	1,541	6.0
8	Konica Minolta Business Solutions—*Bill Troxil*	100 Williams Dr, Ramsey NJ 07446	727-825-4000	S	1,200*	20.0
9	Suburban Propane Partners LP—*Michael J Dunn Jr*	PO Box 206, Whippany NJ 07981	973-887-5300	P	1,191	2.4
10	Vitamin Shoppe Inc—*Anthony N Truesdale*	2101 91st St, North Bergen NJ 07047	201-868-5959	B	857	3.9
11	Sunglass Hut International Inc	4000 Luxottica Pl, Mason OH 45040	513-765-6000	S	682*	9.2
12	Party City Corp—*Gerald C Rittenberg*	25 Green Pond Rd Ste 1, Rockaway NJ 07866	973-983-0888	D	553*	4.5
13	PETsMARTcom Inc—*Philip L Francis* PETsMART Inc	19601 N 27th Ave, Phoenix AZ 85027	623-580-6100	S	551*	.7
14	National Vision Inc—*L Reade Fahs*	296 Grayson Hwy, Lawrenceville GA 30045	770-822-3600	S	450*	5.0
15	Brookstone Inc—*Ronald D Boire*	1 Innovation Way, Merrimack NH 03054	603-880-9500	R	430*	3.2
16	Kirkland's Inc—*Robert E Alderson*	2501 McGavock Pke Ste, Nashville TN 37214	615-872-4800	P	415	3.9
17	Scentsy Inc—*Orville Thompson*	3698 E Lanark, Meridian ID 83642	208-855-0617	R	382	.7
18	Hancock Fabrics Inc—*Steven R Morgan*	1 Fashion Way, Baldwyn MS 38824	662-365-6000	P	276	4.3
19	Blue Rhino Corp—*Tod D Brown*	470 W Hanes Mill Rd St, Winston Salem NC 27105		D	258*	.4
20	Defender Direct Inc—*Dave Lindsey*	3750 Priority Way S Dr, Indianapolis IN 46240	317-810-4720	R	256*	1.3
21	Body Shop Inc—*Peter Saunders*	5036 One World Way, Wake Forest NC 27587	919-554-4900	S	173*	2.6
22	Gcp California Fund LP—*Leonard Green*	11111 Santa Monica Blv, Los Angeles CA 90025	310-954-0444	R	153*	3.2
23	US Home Systems Inc—*Murray Gross*	405 State Hwy 121 Bypa, Lewisville TX 75067	214-488-6300	P	146	.9
24	Bare Escentuals Beauty Inc—*Leslie Blodgett*	71 Stevenson St Fl 22, San Francisco CA 94105	415-489-5000	R	143*	2.7
25	Al Friedman—*Jim White*	44 W 18th St, New York NY 10011	212-243-9000	R	134*	.2
26	Knot Inc—*David Liu*	462 Broadway 6th Fl, New York NY 10013	212-219-8555	P	113	.6
27	JT Sports—*John Robinson*	PO Box 1956, Rogers AR 72757	479-464-8700	S	105*	.1
28	Duty Free Americas Inc—*Jerome Falic*	6100 Hollywood Blvd 7t, Hollywood FL 33024	954-986-7700	R	93*	.1
29	Diaperscom—*Marc Lore*	PO Box 483, Jersey City NJ 07303		R	89*	.1
30	Littleton Coin Company Inc—*David Sundman*	1309 Mount Eustis Rd, Littleton NH 03561	603-444-3571	R	88*	.4
31	Celebrate Express Inc	5915 S Moorland Rd, New Berlin WI 53151	262-901-2000	S	85*	.3
32	Fossil Stores II Inc	2280 N Greenville Ave, Richardson TX 75082	972-234-2525	S	83*	.1
33	Merle Norman Cosmetics Inc—*Arthur Armstrong*	9130 Bellanca Ave, Los Angeles CA 90045	310-641-3000	R	79*	.6
34	Zagg Inc—*Robert G Pedersen II*	3855 S 500 West Ste B, Salt Lake City UT 84115	801-263-0099	P	76	.2
35	Arjay Telecommunications Inc—*Ajay Bhumitra*	300 Denton Ave, New Hyde Park NY 11040	212-581-4800	R	73*	.1
36	Successories Inc	1040 Holland Dr, Boca Raton FL 33487		R	65*	.1
37	Sharpe Business Systems Corp—*Dale Wedge*	8670 Argent St, Santee CA 92071	619-258-1400	R	64*	.1
38	Wabash Valley Services Co—*Todd Neibel*	909 N Ct St, Grayville IL 62844	618-375-2311	R	52*	.2
39	PawnMart Inc Xponential Inc	6400 Atlantic Blvd Ste, Norcross GA 30071	678-720-0660	S	52*	.1
40	Grange Cooperative Supply Association—*Barry Robino*	PO Box 3637, Central Point OR 97502	541-664-1261	R	50*	.2
41	William Doyle Galleries Inc—*Kathleen M Doyle*	175 E 87th St, New York NY 10128	212-427-2730	R	49*	.1
42	Corporate Safe Specialists Inc—*Edward Mcgunn*	14800 S Mckinley Ave, Posen IL 60469	708-371-4200	R	48*	.1
43	Leslie's Poolmart Inc—*Lawrence H Hayward*	3925 E Broadway Rd Ste, Phoenix AZ 85040		R	45*	2.2
44	Edward Tyler Nahem Fine Art—*Edward Nahem*	37 W 57th St Ste 200, New York NY 10019	212-517-2453	R	45*	.1
45	Syndero—*Brad Klaus*	800 Market St 7th Fl, San Francisco CA 94102	415-655-8000	R	43	N/A
46	A and A Jewelry Supply—*John Adem*	319 W 6th St, Los Angeles CA 90014		R	39*	.1
47	Floral Supply Syndicate	PO Box 1305, Camarillo CA 93010	805-389-1141	R	35*	.1
48	Pinch-A-Penny—*John Thomas*	PO Box 6025, Clearwater FL 33758	727-531-8913	R	33*	.2
49	Niche Retail	2240 Greer Blvd, Sylvan Lake MI 48320	248-738-6200	R	32*	.1
50	FragranceNetcom Inc—*Dennis M Apfel*	931 Grand Blvd, Deer Park NY 11729	631-582-5204	P	32	<.1
51	Zachys—*Jeff Zacharia*	16 E Pkwy, Scarsdale NY 10583	914-723-0241	R	31*	.1
52	America Hears Inc—*Henry C Smith*	806 Beaver St, Bristol PA 19007		R	31*	.1
53	Xponential Inc—*Jeffrey A Cummer*	6400 Atlantic Blvd Ste, Norcross GA 30071	678-720-0660	P	30	N/A
54	Foothills Farmers Coop—*Tom Mccall*	1514 W Broadway Ave, Maryville TN 37801	865-982-2761	R	27*	.1
55	Offiserve Inc—*Michael W Dixon*	1430-K Village Way, Santa Ana CA 92705	714-547-9567	R	26*	<.1
56	Chicago Communications LLC	200 Spangler Ave, Elmhurst IL 60126	630-832-3311	R	25*	.1
57	Spectrum Financial System Inc—*Larry Nicholson*	163 McKenzie Rd, Mooresville NC 28115	704-663-4466	R	24*	.2
58	Brooks Tractor Inc—*Lewis P Brooks*	PO Box 9, Sun Prairie WI 53590	608-837-5141	R	23*	<.1
59	ACE Business Solutions Inc—*John Baron*	6599 Granger Rd, Cleveland OH 44131	216-642-9555	R	22*	.1
60	Source Inc—*David Potter*	14060 Proton Rd, Dallas TX 75244	972-371-2600	R	22*	.1
61	CPO Commerce Inc—*Rob Tolleson*	120 W Bellevue Dr, Pasadena CA 91105	626-585-3600	R	22*	.1
62	Jackson-Lee-Pearson Inc—*William Pearson*	PO Box 27, Flora IN 46929	574-967-4164	R	22*	<.1
63	Tri-Parish Co-Operative—*John Thompson*	PO Box 89, Slaughter LA 70777	225-654-2727	R	21*	<.1
64	Farmers Supply Association Inc—*Roger Tohlner*	16240 Hwy 14 E, Harrisburg AR 72432	870-578-2468	R	21*	.1
65	Daniel Smith Artist Materials—*John Cogley*	PO Box 84268, Seattle WA 98124	206-223-9599	R	20*	.1
66	Entrepreneurial Ventures Inc—*Matt Fidiam*	590 Division St, Campbell CA 95008	408-866-8255	R	20*	.4
67	Bridgevine Inc—*Vinnie Olmstead*	2770 Indian River Blvd, Vero Beach FL 32960	772-564-9871	R	19*	.1
68	Franklin Feed and Supply Co—*Carl Flohr*	1977 Philadelphia Ave, Chambersburg PA 17201	717-264-6148	R	18*	.1
69	Office Peeps—*Joel Vockdrodt*	807 S Broadway St, Watertown SD 57201	605-886-6488	R	18*	<.1
70	Falmouth Co-Operative Company Inc—*Wes Edington*	PO Box 85, Falmouth MI 49632	231-826-3301	R	18*	<.1
71	Klingensmith Inc—*David Knepshield*	PO Box 151, Ford City PA 16226	724-763-8889	R	17*	.2
72	Allied Fire and Security Inc—*Jay Hunt*	425 W 2nd Ave, Spokane WA 99201	509-624-3152	R	17*	.1
73	Home Care United Inc—*Richard Bourne*	2802 Walton Commons W, Madison WI 53718	608-242-1516	R	17*	.1
74	Greenway Medical Technologies Inc—*W Thomas Green*	121 Greenway Blvd, Carrollton GA 30117	770-836-3100	R	16*	.1
75	Morse Communications Inc—*Annette Costello*	395 E Dr, Melbourne FL 32904	321-259-8469	R	16*	.1
76	Express Business Service LLC—*Robert Lafon*	160 Alameda Plz, Butler PA 16001	724-283-6033	R	15*	.1
77	TAP Plastics Inc—*David Freeberg*	7176 Regional St, Dublin CA 94568	925-828-7744	R	15*	.2
78	Lionudakis Firewood—*Phil Lionudakis*	25071 E Jones Rd, Escalon CA 95320	209-838-8150	R	15*	.1
79	Stacks—*Lawrence Stack*	123 W 57th St, New York NY 10019	212-582-2580	R	15*	<.1
80	The Art of Framing—*Albert Griffinger*	13450 Baltimore Ave Ste, Laurel MD 20707	301-210-3404	R	15*	<.1
81	Cutler-Dickerson Co—*Jack Patterson*	PO Box 867, Adrian MI 49221	517-265-5191	R	14*	<.1
82	Cmc Rescue Inc—*James Frank*	PO Box 6870, Santa Barbara CA 93160	805-961-1641	R	13*	.1
83	Wild Birds Unlimited Inc—*James Carpenter*	11711 N College Ave St, Carmel IN 46032		R	13	<.1
84	Diversified Business Solutions Inc—*Jeff Theilacker*	9765 Clairemont Mesa B, San Diego CA 92124	858-565-2737	R	13*	<.1
85	Southwest Ag Inc—*Dennis Hillyer*	39927 Us Hwy 160, Bayfield CO 81122	970-884-4101	R	13*	<.1
86	Woodford Feed Company Inc—*Robert Cleveland*	PO Box 116, Versailles KY 40383	859-873-4811	R	13*	<.1
87	Johnson Implement Company Of Belzoni—*J Johnson*	PO Box 926, Greenwood MS 38935	662-453-6525	R	13*	<.1
88	Allied Home Medical Inc—*Kirk Caskey*	3075 Poplar Grove Rd, Cookeville TN 38506	931-528-6199	R	12*	<.1
89	Fax Plus Inc—*Richard Kramer*	1011 Arlington Blvd, Arlington VA 22209	703-807-1000	R	12*	<.1
90	ReStockItcom—*Matt Kuttler*	101 S State Rd 7 Ste 2, Hollywood FL 33023		R	12*	<.1
91	Sun Devil Fire Equipment Inc—*Randy Simmers*	2929 W Clarendon Ave, Phoenix AZ 85017	623-245-0636	R	12*	.1

Note: An asterisk (*) indicates an estimated financial figure. The company type code used is as follows: R = Private, P = Public, S = Private Subsidiary, B = Public Subsidiary, D = Division, J = Joint Venture, I = Investment Fund.

KINGS BY SALES WITHIN 4-DIGIT SIC

	Company Name—*Executive Officer*	Address, City, State, Zip	Phone	Type	Fin	Empls
92	Champaign Telephone Co—*Mike Hosier*	1300 S Neil St, Champaign IL 61820	217-359-4282	R	12*	.1
93	J D Young Company Inc—*Robert Stuart*	PO Box 3368, Tulsa OK 74101	918-582-9955	R	11*	.2
94	Hyatt's Graphic Supply Company Inc—*Gregory C Hyatt*	910 Main St, Buffalo NY 14202	716-884-8900	R	11*	.1
95	Granville Milling Co—*Phillip Watts*	PO Box 393, Granville OH 43023	740-587-0221	R	10*	<.1
96	Cel-Net Communications Inc—*Daniel Gazal*	1111 44th Dr, Long Island City NY 11101	718-609-0135	R	10*	.2
97	Valley Fertilizer And Chemical Company Inc—*Orville Smoot*	PO Box 816, Mount Jackson VA 22842	540-477-3121	R	10*	<.1
98	B L Makepeace Inc—*William Joyce*	125 Guest St, Boston MA 02135	617-782-3800	R	10*	<.1
99	Northern Business Machines Inc—*William Tracia*	24 Terry Ave, Burlington MA 01803	781-272-2034	R	9*	.1
100	All Copy Products Inc—*Scott Dewar*	4141 Colorado Blvd, Denver CO 80216	303-295-0741	R	9*	.1
101	Batteries Plus LLC—*Russ Reynolds*	925 Walnut Ridge Dr St, Hartland WI 53029	262-912-3000	R	9*	.2
102	BabyEarth—*James Bendle*	21 Cypress Blvd Ste 11, Round Rock TX 78665	512-275-6935	R	9*	<.1
103	Continental Coin Corp—*Missim Edri*	5627 Sepulveda Blvd, Van Nuys CA 91411	818-781-4232	R	9*	<.1
104	BackJoy Orthotics—*Bing Howenstein*	25852 McBean Pky Ste 5, Valencia CA 91355		R	9	.1
105	Superior Water And Air Inc—*Gerald Lamborne*	3536 S 1950 W, Salt Lake City UT 84119	801-974-9090	R	9*	<.1
106	Triangle Blueprint Co—*Joseph Teti*	3175 Princeton Pke, Lawrenceville NJ 08648	609-896-4100	S	8*	.1
107	Nelson White Systems Inc—*Arlene Wilder*	PO Box 20389, Baltimore MD 21284	410-668-9628	R	8*	.1
108	Kwik-Kopy Corp—*Steven Hammerstien*	PO Box 777, Cypress TX 77410	281-256-4100	R	8*	.1
109	Digital Telecommunications Corp—*Gordon Maccani*	7733 Lemona Ave, Van Nuys CA 91405	818-951-5300	R	8*	<.1
110	Pettit Machinery Inc—*Brody Pettit*	PO Box 5976, Ardmore OK 73403	580-223-7722	R	8*	.1
111	Dick's Home Care Inc—*Randy Dick*	401 Maple Ave, Altoona PA 16601	814-949-6764	R	8*	.1
112	Public Safety Center Inc—*Rick Montoya*	PO Box 2370, Eugene OR 97402	541-344-4434	R	8*	.1
113	Portland Saturday Market—*Paul Verhoeven*	108 W Burnside, Portland OR 97209	503-222-6072	R	8*	<.1
114	Royal Riders—*Janet Graham*	120-A Mast St, Morgan Hill CA 95037	408-779-1997	R	8*	<.1
115	Scope Orthotics and Prosthetics Inc—*Loren Saxton*	7720 Cardinal Ct, San Diego CA 92123	858-292-7448	R	8*	.1
116	Cellular Air Inc—*Travis Crane*	109 Interstate Blvd St, Anderson SC 29621	864-231-0023	R	8*	.1
117	National Seating and Mobility Inc—*Mike Ballard*	5959 Shallowford Rd St, Chattanooga TN 37421	423-756-2268	R	8*	.6
118	Dankmeyer Inc—*Barbara Lorenzo*	825 N Hammonds Ferry R, Linthicum Heights MD 21090	410-636-8114	R	8*	.1
119	American Alarm Systems Inc—*M Beale*	PO Box 10520, Santa Ana CA 92711	714-547-7474	R	7*	.1
120	Unicover Corp—*James Willms*	3001 E Pershing Blvd, Cheyenne WY 82001	307-771-3000	R	7*	.1
121	Kaat's Water Conditioning Inc—*Jeff Kaat*	PO Box 598, Plymouth WI 53073	920-893-5967	R	7*	.1
122	D and G Equipment Inc—*Elden Gustafson*	2525 E Grand River Rd, Williamston MI 48895	517-655-4606	R	7*	.1
123	New England Communications Inc—*Eric Nason*	480 Riverside St, Portland ME 04103	207-878-7585	R	7*	<.1
124	Northwestern Publishing House—*Jerome Loeffel*	1250 N 113th St, Milwaukee WI 53226	414-475-6600	R	7*	.1
125	Pyrosignal and Suppression Inc—*Greg Montgomery*	4032 216th St, Bayside NY 11361	718-279-3473	R	7*	.1
126	Utility Communications Inc—*Edward Abrams*	920 Sherman Ave, Hamden CT 06514	203-287-1306	R	7*	<.1
127	William A Fraser Inc—*William Fraser*	PO Box 7, Reading PA 19603	610-378-0101	R	7*	.1
128	Coastal Tractor—*Francis Rianda*	10 Harris Pl, Salinas CA 93901	831-757-4101	R	6*	<.1
129	GEE Communications Inc—*Kohn Poole*	4166 Legacy Pkwy, Lansing MI 48911		R	6*	.1
130	Leo's Professional Audio Inc—*Rosemary Rodd*	5447 Telegraph Ave, Oakland CA 94609	510-653-1000	R	6*	<.1
131	All Poolside Services Inc—*Robert Anderson*	121 County Rd C E, Saint Paul MN 55117	651-483-6600	R	6*	.1
132	Tri Electronics Inc—*Thomsas Donovan*	PO Box 4310, Hammond IN 46324	219-931-6850	R	6*	<.1
133	Artemis Woman LLC—*Ann Buivid*	767 Post Rd, Darien CT 06820		R	6*	<.1
134	Thomas Investigative Publications Inc—*Ralph Thomas*	PO Box 82148, Austin TX 78708	512-719-3595	R	6*	<.1
135	Sharpe Images Properties Inc—*David Sharpe*	PO Box 5716, Winston Salem NC 27113	336-724-2871	R	6*	.1
136	Telmex USA LLC—*Miguel Garcia*	3350 Sw 148th Ave Ste, Miramar FL 33027	954-517-7301	R	6*	.1
137	Z and M Enterprises LLC	9525 Berger Rd Ste P, Columbia MD 21046	443-539-1400	R	6*	<.1
138	Security Sentry Inc—*Robert Helstrom*	PO Box 3407, Lacey WA 98509	360-352-2509	R	5*	.1
139	Memphis Communications Corp—*Dean Berry*	PO Box 770389, Memphis TN 38177	901-725-9271	R	5*	.1
140	Dinn Brothers Inc—*Paul Dinn*	PO Box 111, Holyoke MA 01041	413-750-3466	R	5*	.1
141	Datamation Systems Inc—*Jerome Raymond*	125 Louis St, South Hackensack NJ 07606	201-329-7200	R	5*	<.1
142	Prime Service Center—*Dina Rotundo*	2015 Hamburg St, Schenectady NY 12304	518-347-1141	R	5*	.1
143	Yankee Medical Inc—*John Ficociello*	PO Box 276, Burlington VT 05402	802-863-4591	R	5*	.1
144	Boll Medical Inc—*C Boll*	PO Box 11810, Charleston WV 25339	304-345-2944	R	5*	<.1
145	Arkansas Copier Center Inc—*Ralph Thompson*	PO Box 192464, Little Rock AR 72219	501-562-8297	R	5*	<.1
146	Canvas On Demand—*Joe Schmidt*	10700 World Trade Blvd, Raleigh NC 27617		S	5*	<.1
147	Police Equipment Worldwide Inc—*Anne Anderson*	11155 Lu Wista Ln, Brooksville FL 34601	352-544-1049	R	5*	<.1
148	Rocky Mountain Business Systems Inc—*Sophie Gonzales*	PO Box 4204, Santa Fe NM 87502	505-983-1181	R	5*	.1
149	All West Utah Inc—*Tony Distefano*	50 W 100 N, Kamas UT 84036	435-783-4371	R	5*	.1
150	Syracuse Blueprint Company Inc—*Andrew Nye*	825 E Genesee St, Syracuse NY 13210	315-476-4084	R	5*	<.1
151	Capitol Foam Products Inc—*Bart Krupp*	PO Box 7564, East Rutherford NJ 07073	201-933-5277	R	5*	.1
152	Defelicecare Inc—*Leslie Defelice*	PO Box 6442, Wheeling WV 26003	304-232-4210	R	5*	.1
153	Hackworth Reprographics Inc—*Dorothy Hackworth*	PO Box 5037, Chesapeake VA 23324	757-545-7675	R	4*	<.1
154	Accurate Telecom Inc—*Ken Jones*	16108 Covello St, Van Nuys CA 91406	818-997-6700	R	4*	<.1
155	Integra NeuroSupplies Inc	311 Enterprise Dr, Plainsboro NJ 08536	905-632-7888	S	4*	N/A
156	Hollywood Media Corp—*Mitchell Rubenstein*	2255 Glades Rd Ste 221, Boca Raton FL 33431	561-998-8000	P	4	.1
157	LE Sommer and Sons Inc—*Donald Sommer*	PO Box 230, Kidron OH 44636	330-857-2031	R	4*	<.1
158	Duluth/Superior Communications Inc—*Dale Thompson*	711 Hammond Ave, Superior WI 54880	715-392-2911	R	4*	<.1
159	Fps Inc—*Mike Fleenor*	10446 Cogdill Rd, Knoxville TN 37932	865-966-5507	R	4*	<.1
160	Conco Co's—*Rob Baird*	333 Park Central E Ste, Springfield MO 65806	417-863-2000	R	4*	.1
161	Kahn Tractor and Equipment Inc—*James Beckwith*	PO Box 38, North Franklin CT 06254	860-642-7596	R	4*	<.1
162	Communications Of Fort Smith LLC	PO Box 10467, Fort Smith AR 72917	479-452-4800	R	4*	<.1
163	Cardinal Pools Of Oklahoma Inc—*Jerry Shipley*	6500 Nw 10th St, Oklahoma City OK 73127	405-495-2570	R	4*	<.1
164	Tele-Tector Of Maryland Inc—*William Emshwiller*	6935 Okland Mlls Rd St, Columbia MD 21045	410-290-5600	R	4*	<.1
165	Chase Enterprises Inc—*Roy Chappell*	412 N Rockwell Ave, Oklahoma City OK 73127	405-495-1722	R	4*	<.1
166	Dandridge Equipment Inc—*W Dandridge*	11495 Us Hwy 64, Somerville TN 38068	901-465-9811	R	4*	<.1
167	Prescott's Limbs and Braces—*Gary Prescott*	6715 San Pedro Ave, San Antonio TX 78216	210-224-0726	R	4*	.1
168	Sunshine Wireless Inc—*Janice Thompson*	110 Rollinwood Dr, Tarboro NC 27886	252-717-8691	R	4*	<.1
169	Central Security Systems Inc—*Gary Edwards*	6831 E 32nd St Ste 100, Indianapolis IN 46226	317-543-1300	R	4*	<.1
170	Tri Tel Inc—*Chris Davidson*	405 S 4th, Basin WY 82410	307-568-2445	R	4*	<.1
171	Ed M Feld Equipment Company Inc—*John Feld*	PO Box 625, Carroll IA 51401	712-792-3143	R	4*	<.1
172	All Star Awards and Ad Specialties Inc—*Charles Vogt*	835 W 39th St, Kansas City MO 64111	816-531-3635	R	4*	<.1
173	Cavin S Business Solutions Inc—*Randy Gainer*	PO Box 53964, Fayetteville NC 28305	910-485-5151	R	4*	<.1
174	Gardner-Watson Inc—*Charles Watson*	PO Box 1704, Tupelo MS 38802	662-842-2661	R	4*	<.1
175	Mohawk Dental Supply Company Inc—*Alan Braverman*	PO Box 6369, Syracuse NY 13217	315-437-2255	R	4*	<.1
176	Cook's Communications Corp—*Robert Cook*	160 N Broadway St, Fresno CA 93701	559-233-8818	R	4*	<.1
177	Summits 7 Inc—*Charles Siegel*	450 Weaver St Ste 1, Winooski VT 05404	802-658-0424	R	4*	<.1
178	C And S Enterprises Inc—*James Schulz*	1801 Commerce Ct, Columbia MO 65202	573-874-6147	R	3*	<.1
179	Northeast Photocopy Company Inc—*Nora Schulz*	PO Box 1757, Appleton WI 54912	920-733-5059	R	3*	<.1
180	Automatic Pool Covers Inc—*Michael Shebek*	9001 133rd Pl, Fishers IN 46038	317-579-2000	R	3*	<.1
181	Wireless One World—*Barry Casoli*	1360 N Hamilton Rd, Columbus OH 43230	614-337-1588	R	3*	<.1

Rank	Company Name—Executive Officer	Address, City, State, Zip	Phone	Type	Fin	Empls
182	Compu-Phone Inc—Abraham Lemmer	328 Grand Ave, Brooklyn NY 11238	718-230-9292	R	3*	<.1
183	Seaena Inc—Kevin Ryan	1181 Grier Dr Ste B, Las Vegas NV 89119	702-740-4616	P	3	.1
184	Fast Page Radio Inc—Brad Greene	1027 Union Blvd, Allentown PA 18109	610-770-6656	R	3*	.1
185	Aztec Capital LLC—Karl Blasavage	5 Connair Rd, Orange CT 06477	203-795-9317	R	3*	<.1
186	Learning Labs Inc—David Richardson	PO Box 1419, Calhoun GA 30703	706-629-4624	R	3*	<.1
187	Blue Ridge Copiers Inc—Paul Story	PO Box 866, Salem VA 24153	540-389-4400	R	3*	<.1
188	C R Newton Company Ltd—David Newton	PO Box 11689, Honolulu HI 96828	808-949-8389	R	3*	<.1
189	Fourroux Orthotics And Prosthetics Inc—Marvin Fourroux	2743 Bob Wallace Ave S, Huntsville AL 35805	256-534-8672	R	3*	<.1
190	JB Equipment Specialists Inc—Judith Bjorn	PO Box 490667, Leesburg FL 34749	352-787-7607	R	3*	<.1
191	R J Lillis Enterprises Inc—Richard Lillis	3890 Washington St Ste, Boston MA 02131	617-524-6852	R	3*	<.1
192	Ranger Joe's International—Albert Davis	4030 Victory Dr Ste B, Columbus GA 31903	706-689-3455	R	3*	<.1
193	O'gallerie Inc—Thomas Grady	228 Ne 7th Ave, Portland OR 97232	503-238-0202	R	3*	<.1
194	Harvey Milling Company Inc—Michael Crackin	PO Box 189, Carson City MI 48811	989-584-3466	R	3*	<.1
195	Mcclain S Stone Company Inc—Stacey Mcclain	PO Box 585, Tunkhannock PA 18657	570-836-5035	R	3*	<.1
196	Fletcher Chicago Inc—Archie Fletcher	1000 N N Branch St, Chicago IL 60642	312-932-2700	R	3*	<.1
197	Silex Interiors Inc—Eric English	1140 S Joplin, Tulsa OK 74112	918-836-5454	R	3*	<.1
198	EcoTech Marine—Tim Marks	1349 Lynn Ave, Bethlehem PA 18015	610-954-8480	R	3*	<.1
199	Illustration House Inc—Roger T Reed	110 W 25th St, New York NY 10001	212-966-9444	R	3*	<.1
200	Sigel Feed and Grain Inc—Dale Adkins	PO Box 36, Effingham IL 62401	217-844-3311	R	3*	<.1
201	Tekno Books Inc—Marty Greenburg Hollywood Media Corp	840 Challenger Dr, Green Bay WI 54311	920-437-6711	S	3*	<.1
202	Dusson	2020 Hollywood Blvd, Hollywood FL 33020	954-925-3003	R	3*	<.1
203	Gift Globally LLC—Joseph Mendoza	209 Summit N Dr NE, Atlanta GA 30324	404-254-1578	R	3	<.1
204	Southern Retail Systems LLC—Darryl Thompson	PO Box 2288, London KY 40743	606-878-8647	R	3*	<.1
205	Digitec Office Solutions Inc—Bill Patsouras	12550 Reed Rd Ste 200, Sugar Land TX 77478	281-565-1100	R	3*	<.1
206	Trinity Video Communications Inc—Barry Sawayer	11400 Decimal Dr, Louisville KY 40299	502-240-6100	R	3*	<.1
207	Upstate Network Solutions Inc—Tolga Soyata	3760 W Henrietta Rd St, Rochester NY 14623	585-321-9999	R	3*	<.1
208	Peach Net Communications Inc—Robert Gilstrap	PO Box 2203, Cartersville GA 30120	770-606-1379	R	3*	<.1
209	A and B Communication Inc—Arturo Velasco	2530 Main St Ste A, Chula Vista CA 91911	619-424-9555	R	3*	<.1
210	Wheelchairs Plus Inc—Thomas Mcenany	PO Box 66149, Orange Park FL 32065	904-644-6220	R	3*	<.1
211	Custom Marketing Company Inc—Bruce Halland	1126 Main Ave W, West Fargo ND 58078	701-281-0493	R	3*	<.1
212	Warren Fire Equipment Inc—Robert Malone	6880 Tod Ave Sw, Warren OH 44481	330-824-3523	R	3*	<.1
213	Intermessage Communications Inc—Robert Schimmelpfennig	7745 Mentor Ave, Mentor OH 44060	440-942-1555	R	3*	<.1
214	Document Business Solutions LLC	PO Box 42668, Baltimore MD 21284	410-298-4900	R	3*	<.1
215	GR Mccoy Inc—G Randy Mc Coy	604 College St, Jacksonville FL 32204	904-353-7551	R	3*	<.1
216	Southeastern Cellular Inc—Jerry Calhoun	208 Battle St E, Talladega AL 35160	256-362-5500	R	3*	<.1
217	Colortone Camera Inc—Marvin Lederman	PO Box 128, Elmsford NY 10523	914-592-4151	R	3*	<.1
218	USA Digital Inc—Phil Mcclendon	PO Box 2, Gadsden AL 35902	205-824-0331	R	3*	<.1
219	Capricon Enterprises Inc—Shahana Zafar	1164 Broadway Unit 4, New York NY 10001	212-447-4400	R	3*	<.1
220	Shuman Healthcare Of Waycross Inc—Roy Shuman	2015 Tebeau St, Waycross GA 31501	912-285-5272	R	3*	<.1
221	B Com Wireless Inc—Gary Emerick	1122 Chestnut Ridge Rd, Humble TX 77339	281-358-2589	R	3*	<.1
222	Mastor Telecom Equipment Inc—Thomas Ortbal	11999 Borman Dr, Saint Louis MO 63146	314-993-2324	R	3*	<.1
223	Dialink Corp—Jeff Klapper	1660 S Amphlett Blvd, San Mateo CA 94402	650-691-9330	R	3*	<.1
224	Meehan Corp—Tim Meehan	220 Great Cir Rd Ste 1, Nashville TN 37228	615-256-3838	R	3*	<.1
225	Walker Brothers Inc—Thomas Walker	PO Box 1045, Lexington SC 29071	803-359-2839	R	3*	<.1
226	Nova Cellular West Inc—Kevin Mcallister	PO Box 230987, Encinitas CA 92023	760-944-3434	R	3*	<.1
227	Engineered Communication Systems Inc—Kurt Krupp	PO Box 3218, Idaho Falls ID 83403	208-529-9400	R	3*	<.1
228	Small World Wireless—Kevin Crump	111 Drum Hill Rd, Chelmsford MA 01824	978-446-2661	R	2*	<.1
229	Towers Fire Apparatus Company Inc—Brad Towers	502 S Richland St, Freeburg IL 62243	618-539-3863	R	2*	<.1
230	Copy Graphics Inc—Ron Doebler	130 J M Tatum Industri, Hattiesburg MS 39401	601-264-3939	R	2*	<.1
231	Classic Ventures Diversified Inc—Douglas Sinclair	1461 Banks Rd, Margate FL 33063	954-968-1908	R	2*	<.1
232	Blickman Casework and Design Corp—Alfred Palma	3 Michael Ct, Hamburg NJ 07419	973-827-2247	R	2*	<.1
233	B-E Hospital Equipment Company Inc—Pamela Ellersick	1917 Rutger St, Saint Louis MO 63104	314-241-0855	R	2*	<.1
234	Advance Sign Company LLC—Susan Campolo	1010 Saw Mill Run Blvd, Pittsburgh PA 15226	412-481-6990	R	2*	<.1
235	Fiberglass Fabricators Inc—Anthony Capo	PO Box 17068, Smithfield RI 02917	401-231-3552	R	2*	<.1
236	Grand Stage Lighting Co—Glenn Becker	630 W Lake St, Chicago IL 60661	312-332-5611	R	2*	<.1
237	Dynatel Radio Access Inc—David Shaw	15705 Arrow Hwy Ste 1, Irwindale CA 91706	626-334-1799	R	2*	<.1
238	Orthopedic Service Company Of Raleigh Inc—William Wendt	2521 Noblin Rd, Raleigh NC 27604	919-878-7183	R	2*	<.1
239	Automated Business Products Inc—Robert Mahalik	PO Box 368, Hackensack NJ 07602	201-489-1440	R	2*	<.1
240	Berlin and Ocean City Ice—Ed Bramble	305 Washington St, Berlin MD 21811	410-641-0747	R	2*	<.1
241	Leimkuehler Inc—Robert Leimkuehler	4625 Detroit Ave, Cleveland OH 44102	216-651-7788	R	2*	<.1
242	Sanders Gallery—Edward Sanders	107 E Belding St, Hot Springs AR 71901	501-525-2420	R	2*	<.1
243	Woodbury Products Inc—Robert Jablonski	PO Box 250, Island Park NY 11558	516-594-8100	R	2*	<.1
244	Bi-State Machinery Co—Dwayne Wallin	2235 E Mulberry St, Fort Collins CO 80524	970-482-0400	R	2*	<.1
245	Fiberglass Structures Inc—Robert Harris	PO Box 206, Laurel MT 59044	406-628-8208	R	2*	<.1
246	All-American SportPark Inc—Ronald S Boreta	6730 S Las Vegas Blvd, Las Vegas NV 89119	702-798-7777	P	2	<.1
247	Prime Materials Corp—Russell Western	PO Box 678, Batavia NY 14021	585-815-0400	R	2*	<.1
248	Just Mobile Inc—Victor Setton	575 Madison Ave Frnt B, New York NY 10022	212-572-9888	R	2*	<.1
249	Lighthouse Communications—William Zeyen	501 Joan St, La Habra CA 90631	714-990-8877	R	2*	<.1
250	Party Fair Inc—David Silverstein	4345 US Hwy 9, Freehold NJ 07728	732-780-1110	R	2*	<.1
251	Wcs Communications Inc—Larry Saunders	PO Box 5159, San Angelo TX 76902	325-949-3000	R	2*	<.1
252	Guilford Fabricators Inc—Don Payne	PO Box 7245, High Point NC 27264	336-434-3163	R	2*	<.1
253	Roth Cash Register Company Inc—Paul Roth	1600 Saw Mill Run Blvd, Pittsburgh PA 15210	412-884-5700	R	2*	<.1
254	3 S Industries—Greg Srmabekian	25321 Rye Canyon Rd, Valencia CA 91355	661-295-1078	R	2*	<.1
255	Hawkins Hawkins Company Inc—Norman Hawkins	1255 Eastshore Hwy, Berkeley CA 94710	510-525-8500	R	2*	<.1
256	Peet Brothers Co	31 E 17th St, Saint Cloud FL 34769	321-206-6214	R	2*	<.1
257	Walpole Feed And Supply Co—Edwin Walpole	PO Box 1723, Okeechobee FL 34973	863-763-6905	R	2*	<.1
258	Copy-All Of Brevard Inc—Harold Kemper	1100 E Strawbridge Ave, Melbourne FL 32901	321-723-9229	R	2*	<.1
259	Barclay Enterprises Inc—Christopher Barclay	2275 La Crcae Ave Ste, Colton CA 92324	909-783-9091	R	2*	<.1
260	Cellular Concepts II Inc—Ayman Khader	4600 Durham Chpl Hl Bl, Durham NC 27707	919-489-2929	R	2*	<.1
261	Fitness Plus Equipment Services Inc—John Jacobs	108 Hamilton Industria, Wentzville MO 63385	636-634-2202	R	2*	<.1
262	Airmall—Mark R Knight	PO Box 12318, Pittsburgh PA 15231	412-472-5180	S	2*	<.1
263	EasySeat—David Evans	747 Farmington Ave, New Britain CT 06053	860-348-0676	R	2*	<.1
264	Future Cellular Communications—Michael Bennett	979 Concord Pkwy N, Concord NC 28027	704-786-8734	R	2*	<.1
265	Rueschhoff Corp—David Rueschhoff	3727 W 6th St, Lawrence KS 66049	785-841-0111	R	2*	<.1
266	Atic LLC—Lisa Matthews	1070 Saint Andrews Blv, Charleston SC 29407	843-571-0000	R	2*	<.1
267	Fineline Imprints Inc—Robert Kessler	516 State St, Zanesville OH 43701	740-453-1083	R	2*	<.1
268	Go Wireless Inc—Kevin Elder	27617 Commerce Ctr Dr, Temecula CA 92590	951-326-1410	R	2*	<.1
269	Olairos Investments Inc—Guillermo Olaizola	7195 Old Alxndria Frry, Clinton MD 20735	301-856-0693	R	2*	<.1
270	Regency Telecommunications Corp—Larry Stanton	2014 Commonwealth St, Houston TX 77006	713-622-8800	R	2*	<.1

Note: An asterisk (*) indicates an estimated financial figure. The company type code used is as follows: R = Private, P = Public, S = Private Subsidiary, B = Public Subsidiary, D = Division, J = Joint Venture, I = Investment Fund.

RANKINGS BY SALES WITHIN 4-DIGIT SIC

	Company Name—*Executive Officer*	Address, City, State, Zip	Phone	Type	Fin	Empls
271	Thompson Telephone Inc—*David Thompson*	10 Atkinson Dr, Doylestown PA 18901	215-348-1588	R	2*	<.1
272	Comtel Group Inc—*Robert Schubert*	3195 Airport Loop Dr S, Costa Mesa CA 92626	714-435-8000	R	2*	<.1
273	Louisiana Moulding and Supply—*Leo Waddell*	PO Box 6772, Shreveport LA 71136	318-868-5322	R	2*	<.1
274	Executive Telephony Solutions Inc—*Richard Holliday*	1309 Worthington St, Grapevine TX 76051	972-233-2287	R	2*	<.1
275	Manta-Ray Inc—*William Peters*	PO Box 796, West Unity OH 43570	419-924-2328	R	2*	<.1
276	HCI Enterprises Inc—*Lilia Juga*	7903 Santa Monica Blvd, West Hollywood CA 90046	323-848-2000	R	2*	<.1
277	Speaking Roses International Inc—*Alan K Farrell*	1536 North Woodland Pa, Layton UT 84041	801-807-0106	P	2	<.1
278	San Diego Stage and Lighting Supply Inc—*Denise Doyle*	2203 Verus St, San Diego CA 92154	619-299-2300	R	2*	<.1
279	J and R Electronics Inc—*James Lemm*	14817 W Hwy 53, Rathdrum ID 83858	208-687-0700	R	2*	<.1
280	Aleev Inc—*David Shanks*	816 Secretary Dr, Arlington TX 76015	817-265-0333	R	2*	<.1
281	Peck Water Systems Inc—*Philip Peckinpaugh*	4720 Everhard Rd Nw, Canton OH 44718	330-499-1333	R	2*	<.1
282	Acura SpA Systems Inc—*Joseph Elnar*	2954 Rubidoux Blvd, Riverside CA 92509	951-684-6667	R	2*	<.1
283	Bunkie Trinite Trophies Inc—*Samuel Trinite*	12 E Grace St, Richmond VA 23219	804-648-2416	R	2*	<.1
284	Nanotek Machines LLC—*Dwayne Comeger*	227 Bellevue Way Ne 29, Bellevue WA 98004	425-269-0742	R	2*	<.1
285	Craft Mobile Tel—*Pam Craft*	671 S Seguin Ave, New Braunfels TX 78130	830-629-7466	R	1*	<.1
286	Mid America Telephone Systems—*Mark Sanders*	11643 S Austin Ave, Alsip IL 60803	708-396-8821	R	1*	<.1
287	Carolina Koolers LLC—*Richard Brown*	PO Box 2909, Matthews NC 28106	704-847-7911	R	1*	<.1
288	Columbus Wireless Communications—*Kermit Anderson*	4228 Buena Vista Rd, Columbus GA 31907	706-561-6050	R	1*	<.1
289	Lima Elevator Company Inc—*Frank Sherman*	PO Box 157, Howe IN 46746	260-562-2113	R	1*	<.1
290	A-Com Telephone Company Inc—*Ronnie Knoles*	PO Box 700, Fortson GA 31808	706-322-1870	R	1*	<.1
291	Tssco Inc—*William Bradley*	25 Deforest St, Amityville NY 11701	631-842-4800	R	1*	<.1
292	Jordan Group—*Lawrence Jordan*	319 W N Ave, Milwaukee WI 53212	414-431-0100	R	1*	<.1
293	Middleton Holdings LLC—*Ken Brown*	PO Box 293, Hainesport NJ 08036	609-261-1336	R	1*	<.1
294	SCR Inc—*Rodney Boles*	150 S Orchard Ave, Vacaville CA 95688	707-447-2377	R	1*	<.1
295	RGP Orthopedic Appliance Inc—*Thomas Guth*	6147 University Ave, San Diego CA 92115	619-582-3871	R	1*	<.1
296	Alert Communications—*Louis Hahn*	2516 Hampton Rd Ste 4, Erie PA 16502	814-452-4111	R	1*	<.1
297	Oberlander Communication Systems Inc—*Joyce Oberlander*	2415 N University St S, Peoria IL 61604	309-688-4766	R	1*	<.1
298	Msi Security Systems Inc—*Marvin Schnapper*	1 E Centre St, Nutley NJ 07110	973-562-9500	R	1*	<.1
299	Industrial and Commercial Security Systems Inc—*Steven Berniklau*	2400 Comanche Rd Ne, Albuquerque NM 87107	505-888-2954	R	1*	<.1
300	Incentium LLC—*Richard Char*	328 Cherokee Blvd, Chattanooga TN 37405	423-785-2200	R	1*	.1
301	Imperial Copy Products Inc—*Brian Abrams*	961 State Rte 10 1ee, Randolph NJ 07869	973-927-5500	R	1*	<.1
302	Ascend Technologies Inc—*Gerald Williams*	PO Box 80007, Conyers GA 30013	770-788-8089	R	1*	<.1
303	Premier Lighting—*Linda Pavletich*	4300 Ashe Rd Ste 118, Bakersfield CA 93313	661-835-8500	R	1*	<.1
304	Advanced Battery Systems Inc—*Brian Kmito*	516 Bedford St, East Bridgewater MA 02333	508-378-2284	R	1*	<.1
305	TonerStore Inc—*Richard Streets*	1990 W Iliff Ave, Englewood CO 80110	303-935-2791	R	1*	<.1
306	United Digital Integrators Inc—*Kevin Cleary*	13463 State Rd 23, Granger IN 46530	574-273-9039	R	1*	<.1
307	Apache Rental LLC—*Nancy Piraquiva*	3910 W Magnolia Blvd, Burbank CA 91505	818-842-9944	R	1*	<.1
308	Warp 9 Inc—*William E Beifuss*	6500 Hollister Ave Ste, Santa Barbara CA 93117	805-964-3313	P	1	<.1
309	Priority Systems Inc—*Andrew Orons*	PO Box 4240, Harrisburg PA 17111	717-939-2700	R	1*	<.1
310	Abc Orthotics and Prosthetics Inc—*Stephen Mullins*	3616 7th Ct S, Birmingham AL 35222	205-324-2461	R	1*	<.1
311	TCS Tele Communication Systems Inc—*G Jackson*	350 W Gregson Ave, Salt Lake City UT 84115	801-486-3600	R	1*	<.1
312	Asi Systems—*Troy Baumert*	12054 Roberts Rd, La Vista NE 68128	402-334-4844	R	1*	<.1
313	Al Lasher Electronics—*Ellen Lasher*	1734 University Ave, Berkeley CA 94703	510-843-5915	R	1*	<.1
314	New Orleans Bourbon French Perfume Co—*Mary Behlar*	805 Royal St, New Orleans LA 70116	504-522-4480	R	1*	<.1
315	Caribbean Whirlpools—*Robert Fuchs*	141 E Omaha St, Rapid City SD 57701	605-341-0815	R	<1*	<.1
316	Aqua Sun Ozone International—*Edward Otero*	605 S Williams Rd, Palm Springs CA 92264	760-320-8500	R	<1*	<.1
317	Hiron's Memorial Works Inc—*Ronald Hirons*	14950 Us Hwy 68, Mount Orab OH 45154	937-444-2917	R	<1*	<.1
318	Odell Electronics Cleaning Stations—*John Koniarczyk*	1061 Bradley Rd, Westlake OH 44145	440-365-5910	R	<1*	<.1
319	Shadow Box Theatre Inc—*Sandra Robbins*	325 W End Ave Apt 12b, New York NY 10023	212-724-0677	R	<1*	<.1
320	Penco Graphic Supply Inc—*Conrad Segal*	718 Washington Ave N, Minneapolis MN 55401	612-333-3330	R	N/A	<.1

TOTALS: SIC 5999 Miscellaneous Retail Stores Nec
Companies: 320   36,532   188.3

6011 Federal Reserve Banks

	Company Name—*Executive Officer*	Address, City, State, Zip	Phone	Type	Fin	Empls
1	Federal Reserve Bank of New York—*Denis M Hughes*	33 Liberty St, New York NY 10045	212-720-5000	R	199,305*	3.3
2	Federal Reserve Bank of Richmond—*Jeffrey Lacker*	PO Box 27622, Richmond VA 23261	804-697-8000	R	45,459*	2.6
3	Federal Reserve Bank of Chicago—*Charles Evans*	230 S LaSalle St Ste 1, Chicago IL 60604	312-322-5322	R	39,594*	1.3
4	Federal Reserve Bank of Philadelphia—*Charles I Plosser*	10 Independence Mall, Philadelphia PA 19106	215-574-6000	R	37,993	1.3
5	Federal Reserve Bank of San Francisco—*John C Williams*	PO Box 7702, San Francisco CA 94120	415-974-2000	R	37,489*	1.6
6	Federal Reserve Bank of Cleveland—*Sandra Pianalto*	PO Box 6387, Cleveland OH 44101	216-579-2000	R	33,519*	1.4
7	Federal Reserve Bank of Dallas—*Richard W Fisher*	PO Box 655906, Dallas TX 75265	214-922-6000	R	21,666*	1.6
8	Federal Reserve Bank of Boston—*Eric S Rosengren*	PO Box 55882, Boston MA 02205	617-973-3000	R	19,104*	1.2
9	Federal Reserve Bank of Kansas City—*Thomas M Hoenig*	1 Memorial Dr, Kansas City MO 64108	816-881-2000	R	14,276*	1.7
10	Federal Reserve Bank of Minneapolis—*Gary H Stern*	90 Hennepin Ave, Minneapolis MN 55401	612-204-5000	R	5,633*	1.0
11	Wayne Savings Community Bank—*Phillip E Becker*	151 N Market St, Wooster OH 44691	330-264-5767	S	340*	.1
12	First Federal of Charleston—*A Thomas Hood*	34 Broad St, Charleston SC 29401	843-724-0800	S	268*	<.1

TOTALS: SIC 6011 Federal Reserve Banks
Companies: 12   454,646   17.0

6019 Central Reserve Depository Nec

	Company Name—*Executive Officer*	Address, City, State, Zip	Phone	Type	Fin	Empls
1	Federal Home Loan Bank of San Francisco—*Dean Schultz*	PO Box 7948, San Francisco CA 94120	415-616-1000	R	192,862	.3
2	Federal Home Loan Bank of Atlanta—*Wesley McMullan*	PO Box 105565, Atlanta GA 30348	404-888-8000	S	190,841*	.4
3	Federal Home Loan Bank of Cincinnati—*David H Hehman*	PO Box 598, Cincinnati OH 45254	513-852-7500	R	87,532*	.2
4	Federal Home Loan Bank of Chicago—*Matt Feldman*	200 E Randolph Dr, Chicago IL 60601	312-565-5700	R	86,714*	.2
5	Federal Home Loan Bank of Topeka—*Andrew J Jetter*	PO Box 176, Topeka KS 66601	785-233-0507	R	84,382*	.2
6	Federal Home Loan Bank of New York—*Alfred A DelliBovi*	101 Park Ave, New York NY 10178	212-681-6000	R	81,703*	.2
7	Federal Home Loan Bank of Pittsburgh—*Winthrop Watson*	601 Grant St, Pittsburgh PA 15219	412-288-2826	R	65,291*	.3
8	Federal Home Loan Bank of Boston—*Michael A Jessee*	PO Box 990411, Boston MA 02199	617-292-9600	R	62,487*	.2
9	Federal Home Loan Bank of Seattle—*Michael L Wilson*	1501 4th Ave Ste 1800, Seattle WA 98101	206-340-2300	R	51,100	.2
10	Federal Home Loan Bank of Indianapolis—*Milton J Miller*	PO Box 60, Indianapolis IN 46206	317-465-0200	R	46,869*	.2
11	Federal Home Loan Bank of Des Moines—*Richard Swanson*	801 Walnut St Ste 200, Des Moines IA 50309	515-281-1000	R	42,041	N/A
12	Federal Home Loan Bank of Dallas—*Terry Smith*	PO Box 619026, Dallas TX 75261	214-441-8500	R	27,825*	.2

TOTALS: SIC 6019 Central Reserve Depository Nec
Companies: 12   1,019,647   2.4

6021 National Commercial Banks

	Company Name—*Executive Officer*	Address, City, State, Zip	Phone	Type	Fin	Empls
1	Bank of America Corp—*Charles O Holliday Jr*	PO Box 34153, Charlotte NC 28234	704-386-5681	P	2,439,602	288.0
2	Citibank NA—*William R Rhodes*	399 Park Ave, New York NY 10022	212-627-3999	S	262,500	74.3

Rank	Company Name—*Executive Officer*	Address, City, State, Zip	Phone	Type	Fin	Empls
3	PNC Bank NA—*James Rohr*	249 5th Ave Ste 30, Pittsburgh PA 15222	412-762-2000	S	127,760*	20.5
4	KeyBank NA—*Henry Meyers*	127 Public Sq, Cleveland OH 44114	216-689-5580	R	107,855*	15.8
5	Branch Banking and Trust Co—*Robert Greene*	PO Box 1250, Winston Salem NC 27102	336-733-2500	S	100,500	N/A
6	First National Bank (Ames Iowa)—*Scott T Bauer*	PO Box 607, Ames IA 50010	515-232-5561	S	52,342	.1
7	Zions Bancorp—*Harris H Simmons*	1 S Main St 15th Fl, Salt Lake City UT 84133	801-524-4787	P	51,035	10.5
8	Key Bank USA NA KeyBank NA	127 Public Sq, Cleveland OH 44114	216-689-6300	S	46,967*	10.0
9	Union Bank of California NA—*Masashi Oka*	400 California St, San Francisco CA 94104	415-765-0400	S	43,212*	10.0
10	Synovus Financial Corp—*Kessel D Stelling Jr*	PO Box 120, Columbus GA 31902	706-649-2311	P	31,966	6.1
11	Huntington National Bank	41 S High St Huntingto, Columbus OH 43215	614-480-8300	S	31,022*	9.7
12	Wells Fargo Bank Ltd—*John Stumpf*	420 Montgomery St, San Francisco CA 94104		S	28,373*	120.0
13	Associated Bank Green Bay NA—*Philip B Flynn*	PO Box 19006, Green Bay WI 54307	920-433-3200	S	25,480*	4.9
14	City National Bank—*Russell Goldsmith*	PO Box 1141, Beverly Hills CA 90210	310-888-6000	S	16,900*	2.9
15	Commerce Bank NA (Wichita Kansas)—*David W Kemper*	PO Box 419248, Kansas City MO 64141	316-261-4700	S	14,424*	N/A
16	First Tennessee Bank NA	PO Box 84, Memphis TN 38101		S	14,400*	5.0
17	TCF National Bank (Wayzata Minnesota)—*Lynn Nagorske*	200 Lake St E, Wayzata MN 55391	612-661-6500	S	11,512*	7.0
18	Rabobank NA—*James W Lokey*	PO Box 580, Arroyo Grande CA 93421	805-473-6804	S	10,649*	1.7
19	Fulton Bank NA—*Randy Taylor*	PO Box 520, Georgetown DE 19947	302-855-2406	S	9,619*	1.4
20	United Missouri Bank NA—*J Mariner Kemper*	PO Box 419226, Kansas City MO 64141	816-860-7000	S	8,660*	3.5
21	NewAlliance Bank—*CGene Kirby*	195 Church St, New Haven CT 06510	203-787-1111	S	8,286	1.1
22	Webster Bank NA—*James C Smith*	145 Bank St, Waterbury CT 06702	203-578-2230	S	8,154*	2.2
23	Bank of Oklahoma NA—*Stanley Lybarger*	PO Box 2300, Tulsa OK 74102	918-588-6010	D	8,137	3.1
24	United Missouri Bank of St Louis NA—*W Thomas Chulick*	PO Box 66919, Saint Louis MO 63166	314-621-1000	S	8,124*	2.7
25	Trustmark National Bank—*Richard Hickson*	PO Box 291, Jackson MS 39205		S	7,579*	2.6
26	Household Bank NA—*Bobby Mehta*	1441 Schilling Pl, Salinas CA 93901	831-754-1450	S	7,540*	1.5
27	INTRUST Bank NA	PO Box 1, Wichita KS 67201	316-383-1111	S	7,017*	1.1
28	Whitney National Bank—*John Hope*	PO Box 61260, New Orleans LA 70161	504-586-7168	S	6,571*	2.4
29	Frost National Bank	PO Box 1600, San Antonio TX 78296	210-220-4011	S	6,425*	1.8
30	First National Bank of Omaha—*Bruce Lauritzen*	PO Box 2490, Omaha NE 68103		S	6,351*	4.0
31	First Merchants Bank NA—*Mike Baker*	200 E Jackson St, Muncie IN 47305	765-747-1382	S	6,047*	1.2
32	Pacific Western Bank—*Michael J Purdue*	2602 El Camino Real, Carlsbad CA 92008	760-434-3344	S	5,514	.9
33	Mercantil Commercebank NA—*J Guillermo Villar*	220 Alhambra Cr 12th F, Coral Gables FL 33134	305-629-1200	S	5,232*	.9
34	Pacific Capital Bank NA—*George S Leis*	30343 Canwood St Ste 1, Agoura Hills CA 91301	805-564-6405	S	5,041*	1.3
35	PlainsCapital Bank Corp	2323 Victory Ave, Dallas TX 75219	214-252-4100	S	4,890*	1.5
36	First National Bank of Pennsylvania—*Stephen J Gurgovits*	166 Main St, Greenville PA 16125	724-588-6770	S	4,798*	.8
37	Commerce Bank NA (St Louis Missouri)	PO Box 11573, Saint Louis MO 63105	314-746-8787	S	4,624*	1.4
38	Amcore Bank NA—*William McManaman*	PO Box 1537, Rockford IL 61110	815-968-2241	S	4,500	.4
39	Sterling National Bank—*John C Millman*	650 5th Ave, New York NY 10019	212-757-3300	S	4,091*	.5
40	Northern Trust Bank of Florida NA—*Frederick H Waddell*	700 Brickell Ave, Miami FL 33131	305-372-1000	S	3,500	1.0
41	Commerce Bank NA (Kansas City Missouri)	PO Box 13686, Kansas City MO 64199	816-234-2000	S	3,405	1.6
42	First Financial Bank NA—*Norman L Lowery*	643-645 Wabash Ave, Terre Haute IN 47808	812-238-6000	S	3,229*	1.0
43	Community Trust Bancorp Inc—*Jean R Hale*	PO Box 2947, Pikeville KY 41502	606-432-1414	P	3,220	1.0
44	National Bank of Arizona—*Keith Maio* Zions Bancorp	6001 N 24th St, Phoenix AZ 85016	602-235-6000	S	2,930*	.1
45	Hampton Roads Bancshares Inc—*Douglas J Glenn*	999 Waterside Dr Ste 2, Norfolk VA 23510	757-217-1000	P	2,900	.8
46	First National Bank Alaska—*Daniel H Cuddy*	PO Box 100720, Anchorage AK 99510	907-777-4362	P	2,726	.6
47	Sandy Spring Bank	17801 Georgia Ave, Olney MD 20832	301-774-6400	S	2,687*	.9
48	City National Bank of Florida—*Jorge Gonzalez*	25 W Flaglor St, Miami FL 33130	305-577-7333	S	2,565*	.4
49	First National Bank (Fort Collins Colorado)—*Jack Wolfe*	PO Box 578, Fort Collins CO 80521	970-482-4861	S	2,500	.7
50	First United Bank and Trust	PO Box 9, Oakland MD 21550	301-334-9471	S	2,448*	.4
51	First National Bank Anchorage—*Kimberly Srensley* First National Bank Alaska	PO Box 100720, Anchorage AK 99501	907-276-6300	S	2,437	.7
52	Bancorp Inc—*Betsy Z Cohen*	409 Silverside Rd Ste, Wilmington DE 19809	302-385-5000	P	2,396	.4
53	CoBiz Financial Inc—*Steven Bangert*	821 17th St, Denver CO 80202	303-312-2265	P	2,395	.6
54	Camden National Corp—*Gregory A Dufour*	PO Box 310, Camden ME 04843	207-236-8821	P	2,303	.4
55	Bank of Texas Lake Worth—*Norman Baqwell*	PO Box 136699, Fort Worth TX 76136	817-498-4035	S	2,274	N/A
56	Trustco Bank NA—*Robert J McCormick*	PO Box 1082, Schenectady NY 12305	518-377-3311	S	2,268*	.5
57	US Trust Company of Texas NA—*William Goodwin*	2001 Ross Ave Ste 2700, Dallas TX 75201	214-754-1200	S	2,251*	.1
58	National Penn Bank—*Glen Moyer*	PO Box 547, Boyertown PA 19512	610-705-9101	S	2,248*	.9
59	BNC Bancorp—*W Swope Montgomery*	1226 Eastchester Dr, High Point NC 27265	336-476-9200	P	2,150	.4
60	Intervest Bancshares Corp—*Lowell Dansker*	1 Rockefeller Plz Ste, New York NY 10020	212-218-2800	P	2,071	.1
61	Tower Bank—*Andrew S Samuel*	PO Box 8, Greencastle PA 17225	717-597-2137	S	2,061*	.3
62	Fifth Third Bank of Northwestern Ohio NA—*Bruce Lee*	PO Box 1868, Toledo OH 43603	419-259-7890	S	2,056*	.8
63	Mission Oaks National Bank—*Gary W Votapka*	41530 Enterprise Circl, Temecula CA 92590	951-719-1200	S	2,022*	.3
64	Canandaigua National Bank and Trust Co—*George W Hamlin IV*	72 S Main St, Canandaigua NY 14424	585-394-4260	R	1,872*	.3
65	Emprise Bank—*Thomas Page*	PO Box 2970, Wichita KS 67201	316-383-4400	S	1,840*	.5
66	Centerstate Banks Inc—*Ernest S Piner*	42745 US Hwy 27, Davenport FL 33837	863-419-7750	P	1,837	.6
67	First National Bank of Central California—*D Vernon Horton*	307 Main St, Salinas CA 93901	831-757-4900	S	1,811*	.3
68	Huntington National Bank of Indiana—*Aaron Jones*	PO Box 249, Noblesville IN 46061	317-776-4212	S	1,790*	.3
69	Rockville Financial Inc—*William J McGurk*	25 Park St, Rockville CT 06066	860-291-3600	P	1,680	.2
70	Community Bank NA—*Sanford A Belden*	5790 Widewaters Pky, DeWitt NY 13214	315-445-2282	S	1,634	.7
71	Far East National Bank—*Stan Siao*	977 N Broadway, Los Angeles CA 90012	213-687-1300	S	1,581*	.3
72	Camden National Bank—*Gregory A Dufour* Camden National Corp	PO Box 310, Camden ME 04843	207-236-8821	S	1,566*	.2
73	National Cooperative Bank—*Charles E Snyder*	2001 Pennsylvania Ave, Washington DC 20006	202-349-7444	R	1,558*	.3
74	American National Bank of Texas—*Robert A Halsey*	PO Box 40, Terrell TX 75160		R	1,547*	.6
75	Horizon Bank NA—*Craig M Dwight*	515 Franklin Sq, Michigan City IN 46360	219-879-0211	S	1,508*	.3
76	Suffolk County National Bank	PO Box 9000, Riverhead NY 11901	631-208-2350	S	1,469	.4
77	PremierWest Bancorp—*James M Ford*	PO Box 40, Medford OR 97501	541-618-6020	P	1,411	.5
78	Stearns Bank NA—*Norm Skalicky*	4191 2nd St S, St Cloud MN 56301	320-253-6607	R	1,355*	.2
79	Woodforest Financial Group Inc—*Robert E Marling Jr*	PO Box 7889, The Woodlands TX 77387	832-375-2000	R	1,353*	1.2
80	Wells Fargo (New Boston Texas)	PO Box 608, New Boston TX 75570	903-223-1470	S	1,337	.4
81	First Mid-Illinois Bank and Trust—*John Hedges*	1515 Charleston Ave, Mattoon IL 61938	217-258-0653	S	1,324*	.4
82	Pacific Western Bank (San Diego California)—*Robert Borgman*	401 W A St, San Diego CA 92101	619-233-5588	S	1,318*	.3
83	Park National Bank—*C Daniel DeLawder*	PO Box 3500, Newark OH 43058	740-349-8451	S	1,295*	.5
84	Amboy National Bank—*George E Scharpf*	PO Box 1076, Old Bridge NJ 08857	732-591-8700	R	1,279*	.2
85	Bank Midwest NA—*Tom Metzger*	1111 Main St, Kansas City MO 64105	816-471-9800	S	1,260	.5
86	Guaranty Bond Bank—*Ty Abston*	100 W Arkansas, Mount Pleasant TX 75455	903-572-9881	S	1,260*	.3
87	First NA—*Hoppy Cole* First Bancshares Inc (Hattiesburg Mississippi)	PO Box 15549, Hattiesburg MS 39404	601-268-8998	S	1,259*	.2

Note: An asterisk (*) indicates an estimated financial figure. The company type code used is as follows: R = Private, P = Public, S = Private Subsidiary, B = Public Subsidiary, D = Division, J = Joint Venture, I = Investment Fund.

COMPANY RANKINGS BY SALES WITHIN 4-DIGIT SIC

Rank	Company Name—*Executive Officer*	Address, City, State, Zip	Phone	Type	Fin	Empls
88	Citizens First National Bank—*Thomas C Ogard*	606 S Main St, Princeton IL 61356	815-875-4444	S	1,194*	.2
89	Wilber National Bank (Oneonta New York)	PO Box 430, Oneonta NY 13820	607-432-1700	S	1,193*	.2
90	First Security Group Inc—*Ralph E Coffman Jr*	531 Broad St, Chattanooga TN 37402	423-266-2000	P	1,169	.3
91	Union Center National Bank	2455 Morris Ave, Union NJ 07083	908-688-9500	S	1,148	N/A
92	First Citizens National Bank—*Jeffrey Dean Agee*	PO Box 370, Dyersburg TN 38025	731-285-4410	S	1,134*	.2
93	First National Bank of Northern California—*Thomas McGraw*	975 El Camino Real, South San Francisco CA 94080	650-583-8450	S	1,129*	.2
94	Commercial Bank of Texas NA—*Scott Bowyer*	215 E Main St, Nacogdoches TX 75961	936-715-4100	R	1,116*	.2
95	Centrue Financial Corp—*Kurt Stevenson*	7700 Bonhomme Ave Ste, Saint Louis MO 63105	314-505-5500	P	1,100	.3
96	Farmers Capital Bank Corp—*Lloyd Hillard Jr*	PO Box 309, Frankfort KY 40602	502-227-1668	P	1,085	.5
97	Seacoast National Bank—*Dennis S Hudson III*	PO Box 9012, Stuart FL 34994	772-569-4000	S	1,081	.3
98	Savannah Bancorp Inc—*John C Helmken II*	PO Box 188, Savannah GA 31402	912-629-6486	P	1,048	.2
99	Bridgehampton National Bank—*Kevin M O'Connor*	PO Box 3005, Bridgehampton NY 11932	631-537-1000	S	1,029	.2
100	Regions Bank Nashville Tn—*C Dowd Ritter*	PO Box 198958, Nashville TN 37219	615-244-0571	S	1,023*	.3
101	CommunityOne Bank—*Michael C Miller*	PO Box 1328, Asheboro NC 27204	336-626-8300	S	1,000*	.2
102	Bridge Capital Holdings—*Dan Myers*	55 Almaden Blvd Ste 20, San Jose CA 95113	408-423-8500	P	1,000	.2
103	Broadway National Bank—*James D Goudge*	PO Box 17001, San Antonio TX 78217	210-283-6500	S	978	.4
104	Middleburg Financial Corp—*Gary R Shook*	PO Box 5, Middleburg VA 20117	540-687-6377	P	966	.4
105	Commerce Bank NA (Omaha Nebraska)—*David R Kemper*	3930 S 147th St, Omaha NE 68144	402-691-7800	S	964*	.2
106	Bridge Bank NA—*Dan Myers* Bridge Capital Holdings	55 Almaden Blvd, San Jose CA 95113	408-423-8500	S	954*	.1
107	CoBiz Insurance Inc CoBiz Financial Inc	821 17th St, Denver CO 80202	303-988-0446	S	952*	.2
108	First National Bank of Jasper—*L Gwaltney McCollum Jr* Synovus Financial Corp	PO Box 31, Jasper AL 35501	205-221-3121	S	946*	.1
109	Harris Bank Palatine NA—*Jack Lloyd*	50 N Brockway, Palatine IL 60078	847-359-1070	S	941*	.1
110	UMB Bank Colorado NA (Denver Colorado)—*Jon Robinson*	1670 Broadway, Denver CO 80202	816-860-5607	S	940	.2
111	Patriot National Bank (Stamford Connecticut)—*Charles F Howell*	900 Bedford St, Stamford CT 06901	203-324-7500	S	933*	.2
112	First National Bank of Olathe—*Brain L Roby*	PO Box 1500, Olathe KS 66051	913-782-3211	S	919*	.2
113	PremierWest Bank PremierWest Bancorp	PO Box 40, Medford OR 97501	541-440-2600	S	914*	<.1
114	American National Bank—*Steve Ritzman*	PO Box 2139, Omaha NE 68103		S	906*	.3
115	American National Bank and Trust Co (Danville Virginia)—*Charles H Majors* American National Bankshares Inc	PO Box 191, Danville VA 24543	434-792-5111	S	906*	.3
116	Albany Bank and Trust Company NA	3400 W Lawrence Ave, Chicago IL 60625	773-267-7300	S	895*	.2
117	Central National Bank and Trust Co—*RS Baker Jr*	PO Box 3448, Enid OK 73702	580-233-3535	R	894*	.2
118	Hometown Bancorp Ltd—*Tim McFarlen*	80 Sheboygan St, Fond du Lac WI 54935	920-907-0788	R	894*	.2
119	Farmers National Bank of Canfield—*John S Gulas*	PO Box 555, Canfield OH 44406	330-533-3341	S	879*	.3
120	NexTier Bank—*Margaret Irvine Weir*	PO Box 350, Evans City PA 16033	724-538-9808	R	876*	.3
121	Wells Fargo Bank Northwest NA—*Robert Joss* Wells Fargo Bank Ltd	299 S Main St 12th Fl, Salt Lake City UT 84111	801-246-5630	S	864	.4
122	American National Bankshares Inc—*Charles H Majors*	PO Box 191, Danville VA 24543	434-792-5111	P	834	.2
123	National Bank of Indianapolis—*Morri Maurer*	107 N Pennsylvania St, Indianapolis IN 46204	317-261-9000	R	808*	.2
124	Montgomery Bank—*Jeff Sutton*	PO Box 948, Sikeston MO 63801	573-471-2275	R	779*	.1
125	First National Bank of St Louis—*S Bryan Cook*	7707 Forsythe Blvd, Clayton MO 63105	314-862-8300	S	769*	.2
126	Baker Boyer National Bank—*Megan Clubb*	PO Box 1796, Walla Walla WA 99362	509-525-2000	S	747*	.2
127	Spirit Bank—*Paul Cornell*	601 N Main St, Bristow OK 74010	918-367-3311	S	730*	.3
128	Britton and Koontz First National Bank	PO Box 1407, Natchez MS 39121	601-445-5576	S	728*	.1
129	First National Bank of Durango—*Steve Short*	PO Box 2910, Durango CO 81302	970-247-3020	R	715*	.1
130	Heritage Savings Bank—*Brian Vance*	201 5th Ave SW, Olympia WA 98501	360-943-1500	S	711*	.2
131	Access National Bank—*Michael W Clarke*	1800 Robert Fulton Dr, Reston VA 20191	703-871-2100	S	701	.3
132	Boone County National Bank—*RB Price*	PO Box 678, Columbia MO 65205	573-874-8535	S	698*	.4
133	First National Bank of Long Island	10 Glen Head Rd, Glen Head NY 11545	516-671-4900	S	696*	.2
134	Ballston SpA National Bank—*Christopher R Dowd*	PO Box 70, Ballston Spa NY 12020	518-885-6781	S	679*	.1
135	National Exchange Bank and Trust—*Peter E Stone*	130 S Main St, Fond du Lac WI 54935	920-921-7700	S	673*	.3
136	Beach First National Bancshares Inc—*W Swope Montgomery Jr*	3751 Robert M Grissom, Myrtle Beach SC 29577	843-626-2265	P	669	.2
137	Community Capital Corp—*Jerry C Cherry*	1402C Hwy 72 W, Greenwood SC 29649	864-941-8200	S	656	.2
138	One National Bank—*Layton Stuart*	300 W Capitol, Little Rock AR 72201	501-370-4400	R	654*	.1
139	Milford National Bank and Trust Co (Milford Massachusetts)—*Kristen Carvalho*	300 E Main St, Milford MA 01757	508-634-4100	R	653*	.1
140	LCNB National Bank—*Stephen P Wilson*	2 N Broadway, Lebanon OH 45036	513-932-1414	S	650*	.2
141	First National Bank of Damariscotta—*Daniel R Daigneault*	PO Box 940, Damariscotta ME 04543	207-563-3195	S	647*	.1
142	Baraboo National Bank—*Merlin E Zitner*	101 3rd Ave, Baraboo WI 53913	608-356-7703	S	640*	.1
143	Valley Bank (Roanoke Virginia)	PO Box 2740, Roanoke VA 24001	540-342-2265	S	639*	.1
144	UMB National Bank of America—*J Mariner Kemper*	1010 Grand Blvd, Kansas City MO 64106	816-860-7000	S	638*	.1
145	First-Knox National Bank of Mount Vernon—*Gordon E Yance*	PO Box 1270, Mount Vernon OH 43050	740-399-5500	S	627*	.2
146	Graystone Tower Bank and Mortgage Co—*Kevin C Quinn*	PO Box 523, West Chester PA 19381	484-881-4000	S	626*	.1
147	Fairfield National Bank—*Steve Wells* Park National Bank	143 W Main St, Lancaster OH 43130	740-653-7242	D	614*	.2
148	Metro Bank—*Gary Nalbandian*	3801 Paxton St, Harrisburg PA 17111	717-412-6621	S	610*	.5
149	South Carolina Bank and Trust NA—*Robert Hill*	2770 Main Hwy, Bamberg SC 29003	803-245-2416	S	607*	.1
150	Harris Bank Barrington NA—*William Downe*	201 S Grove Ave, Barrington IL 60010	847-381-4000	S	606*	.2
151	Colonial Financial Services Inc—*Edward J Geletka*	2745 S Delsea Dr, Vineland NJ 08360	856-451-5800	P	590	.1
152	Alliance Bank NA	PO Box 90, Oneida NY 13421		S	582*	.3
153	First Victoria National Bank—*M Russell Marshall*	PO Box 1338, Victoria TX 77902		S	582*	.3
154	Falcon International Bank—*Adolfo E Gutierrez*	5219 McPherson Rd, Laredo TX 78041	956-723-2265	R	578*	.2
155	Hudson Valley Bank—*James L Landy*	21 Scarsdale Rd, Yonkers NY 10707	914-961-6100	S	578*	.2
156	First Financial Bank—*Ron D Butler*	400 Pine St, Abilene TX 79601	325-627-7200	S	577*	.3
157	Sabadell United Bank—*Mario Trueba*	5901 Miami Lakes Dr E, Miami Lakes FL 33014	305-825-9500	S	575*	.1
158	First National Bank of Griffin—*John Charles Copland*	318 S Hill St, Griffin GA 30224	770-227-2251	S	574*	.1
159	Progressive Bank NA	PO Box 4075, Wheeling WV 26003	304-277-1100	S	574*	.1
160	Conway National Bank—*W Jennings Duncan*	PO Box 320, Conway SC 29528	843-248-4008	R	573*	.2
161	Tidelands Bancshares Inc—*Thomas H Lyles*	875 Lowcountry Blvd, Mount Pleasant SC 29464	843-388-8433	P	571	.1
162	OneUnited Bank—*Kevin Cohee*	100 Franklin St, Boston MA 02110		R	561	.2
163	Lorain National Bank—*Daniel Klimas*	457 Broadway, Lorain OH 44052	440-244-7185	S	543*	.3
164	First National Bank (Paragould Arkansas)—*Donald Guinn*	PO Box 700, Paragould AR 72451	870-239-8521	S	542*	.2
165	Security National Bank Springfield Ohio—*Bill Fralick*	40 S Limestone St, Springfield OH 45502	937-324-6800	S	533	.3

Rank	Company Name—*Executive Officer*	Address, City, State, Zip	Phone	Type	Fin	Empls
166	First Place Bank (Southfield Michigan)—*Steven Lewis*	PO Box 5006, Southfield MI 48086	248-358-4710	S	533	N/A
167	First National Bank of Central Florida—*J Lamar Roberts*	PO Box 913900, Longwood FL 32791	407-774-3000	R	519	N/A
168	Commerce National Bank—*Jennifer Griffith*	3650 Olentangy River R, Columbus OH 43214	614-583-2200	S	511*	.1
169	Commercial Bank and Trust of Pennsylvania—*Greg Hunter*	PO Box 429, Latrobe PA 15650	724-539-3501	S	511*	.1
170	First Bancshares Inc (Hattiesburg Mississippi)—*Ray Cole Jr*	6480 Hwy 98 W Ste A, Hattiesburg MS 39402	601-268-8998	P	503	.2
171	First National Bank of Chester County—*Andrew S Samuel*	PO Box 523, West Chester PA 19381	484-881-4010	S	496*	.2
172	Community Bancorp—*Stephen P Marsh*	PO Box 259, Derby VT 05829	802-334-7915	P	492	N/A
173	International Bank of Miami NA—*Alba Prestamo*	121 Alhambra Plz, Coral Gables FL 33134	305-854-8800	S	482*	.2
174	Mainline National Bank—*JoAnne Brinzey*	PO Box 660, Ebensburg PA 15931	814-472-5400	R	482*	.1
175	Emclaire Financial Corp—*William C Marsh*	PO Box D, Emlenton PA 16373	724-867-2311	P	482	.1
176	BankTrust (Brewton Alabama)—*W Bib Lamar Jr*	227 Belleville Ave, Brewton AL 36426	251-867-3231	S	480*	.1
177	Evans National Bank—*David Nasca*	14 N Main St, Angola NY 14006	716-549-1120	S	474*	.1
178	Herald National Bank—*Raymond Nielson*	623 5th Ave 11th Fl, New York NY 10022		P	470	.1
179	First National Bank of Wynne—*Harold Hardwick*	PO Box 129, Wynne AR 72396	870-238-2361	S	466*	.1
180	Commercial National Bank (Texarkana Arkansas)—*Julia Mobley*	PO Box 1998, Texarkana AR 71854	870-773-4561	R	462*	.1
181	Northern Trust Bank/Lake Forest NA—*Arthur Wood*	265 E Deerpath Rd, Lake Forest IL 60045	847-234-5100	S	461*	.1
182	Zions First National Bank—*Scott Anderson* Zions Bancorp	1 S Main St, Salt Lake City UT 84133	801-524-2330	S	458*	2.5
183	Millennium Bank NA Millennium Bankshares Corp	11414 Washington Plz, Reston VA 20190	703-467-3401	S	451*	.2
184	Old Second National Bank of Aurora—*Jim Eccher*	37 S River St, Aurora IL 60506	630-892-6565	S	449*	.3
185	Bradford Bank—*Dallas R Arthur*	6910 York Rd, Baltimore MD 21212	410-377-9610	S	448*	.1
186	Cornerstone Bancshares Inc—*Nathaniel F Hughes*	6401 Lee Hwy Ste B, Chattanooga TN 37421	423-385-3000	P	442	.1
187	First National Bank and Trust Company of McAlester—*Roy Nelson*	PO Box 948, McAlester OK 74502	918-426-0211	R	439	N/A
188	Delta National Bank—*Warren E Wegge*	PO Box 1900, Manteca CA 95336		S	438*	.1
189	First National Bank of Santa Fe—*Greg Ellena*	PO Box 609, Santa Fe NM 87504	505-992-2000	S	433*	.2
190	First American Bank (Naples Florida)—*Ken Aschom*	3701 Tamiami Trail N, Naples FL 34103	239-403-0076	S	432*	.1
191	MidSouth Bank NA—*CR Cloutier*	PO Box 3745, Lafayette LA 70502	337-237-8343	S	428*	.1
192	Coastal Banking Company Inc—*Michael Sanchez*	PO Box 1899, Beaufort SC 29901	843-522-1228	P	427	.1
193	First National Bank of Illinois—*Gilbert Rynberk*	3256 Ridge Rd, Lansing IL 60438	708-474-1300	R	427*	.1
194	Glens Falls National Bank and Trust—*Thomas Hoy*	250 Glen St, Glens Falls NY 12801	518-793-4121	S	423*	.2
195	National Bank of Blacksburg—*James G Rakes*	PO Box 90002, Blacksburg VA 24062	540-951-6226	S	422*	.2
196	Marquette National Bank—*George S Moncada*	10000 W 151st St, Orland Park IL 60462	773-476-5100	S	407*	.1
197	FundsXpress Financial Network—*Brent Warrington*	11950 Jollyville Rd, Austin TX 78759	512-493-2500	S	404*	.1
198	Security National Bank of Sioux City Iowa—*William C Fralick*	PO Box 147, Sioux City IA 51102	712-277-6500	S	400*	.2
199	Klein Bank (Waconia Minnesota)—*Doug Hile*	PO Box 85, Waconia MN 55387	952-442-2265	S	393*	.1
200	First National Bank of North Platte—*LH Kolkman*	PO Box 10, North Platte NE 69103	308-532-1000	S	391*	.2
201	FCB Services Inc—*G Anthony Busseni* Farmers Capital Bank Corp	PO Box 309, Frankfort KY 40602	502-227-1668	S	388*	.1
202	Hanmi Bank—*Jay S Yoo*	3660 Wilshire Blvd Ste, Los Angeles CA 90010	213-382-2200	S	386*	.1
203	Seaway Bank and Trust Co—*Walter E Grady*	645 E 87th St, Chicago IL 60619	773-487-4800	S	386	.2
204	Quakertown National Bank—*Dave Freeman*	PO Box 9005, Quakertown PA 18951	215-538-5600	S	381*	.2
205	Farmers Citizens Bank—*David G Dostal*	105 Washington Sq, Bucyrus OH 44820	419-562-7040	S	376*	.1
206	Farmers National Bank of Emlenton—*William C Marsh* Emclaire Financial Corp	PO Drawer D, Emlenton PA 16373	724-867-2311	S	374*	.1
207	BankFinancial—*James Russ*	5140 Main St, Downers Grove IL 60515	630-968-6300	S	374*	.1
208	Merchants National Bank of Winona—*Rod Nelson*	PO Box 248, Winona MN 55987	507-457-1100	S	364*	.2
209	First Citizens National Bank of Upper Sandusky—*Mark G Johnson*	100 N Sandusky Ave, Upper Sandusky OH 43351	419-294-2351	R	364*	.1
210	Heartland Capital Trust I	1398 Central Ave, Dubuque IA 52001	563-589-2100	S	363	N/A
211	FNB Bank NA—*Richard A Grafmyre*	PO Box 279, Danville PA 17821	570-275-3740	S	361*	.1
212	San Benito Bank—*Ed Stephenson*	PO Box 1786, Salinas CA 93902		S	359*	.1
213	Cheviot Financial Corp—*Thomas J Linneman*	3723 Glenmore Ave, Cheviot OH 45211	513-661-0457	P	358	.1
214	CommerceWest Bank NA—*Ivo Tjan*	2111 Business Center D, Irvine CA 92612	949-251-6959	P	350	.1
215	American Bank Inc—*Mark W Jaindl*	4029 W Tilghman St, Allentown PA 18104	610-366-1800	P	344	.1
216	Sovereign Bank NA—*Roy J Salley*	17950 Preston Rd, Dallas TX 75252	214-242-1900	R	344*	.1
217	First National Bank in Alamogordo—*Pete Cook*	PO Box 9, Alamogordo NM 88311	575-437-4880	S	343*	.1
218	Rancho Santa Fe National Bank—*Don Schempp* Pacific Western Bank	PO Box 2388, Rancho Santa Fe CA 92067	858-756-3023	S	341*	.2
219	Oak Ridge Financial Services Inc—*Ronald O Black*	PO Box 2, Oak Ridge NC 27310	336-644-9944	P	338	.1
220	Mars National Bank—*Jim Dionise*	PO Box 927, Mars PA 16046	724-625-1555	R	337*	.1
221	National Bank of California—*Barry W Uzel*	145 S Fairfax Ave, Los Angeles CA 90036	323-655-6001	S	334*	.1
222	First National Bank of AltaVista—*Robert Gilliam Jr*	PO Box 29, Altavista VA 24517	434-369-3000	S	332	.1
223	Downingtown National Bank—*William S Latoff*	4 Brandywine Ave, Downingtown PA 19335	610-269-1040	S	331*	.1
224	Metlife Bank NA—*Donnalee A DeMaio*	PO Box 6892, Bridgewater NJ 08807		S	330*	.1
225	PBI Bank—*Maria L Bouvette*	PO Box 436029, Louisville KY 40253	502-499-4800	S	323*	.1
226	Bank of Oak Ridge—*Ronald O Black* Oak Ridge Financial Services Inc	2211 Oak Ridge Rd, Oak Ridge NC 27310	336-644-9944	S	320*	.1
227	First National Bank of South Miami—*Drew A Dammeier*	PO Box 431000, South Miami FL 33243		S	318*	.1
228	1ST Century Bancshares Inc—*Alan I Rothenberg*	1875 Century Park E St, Los Angeles CA 90067	310-270-9500	P	308	<.1
229	Terrabank NA—*Antonio Uribe*	PO Box 140460, Miami FL 33114	305-448-4898	S	307	.1
230	Commercial Bank (Alma Michigan)—*Jeffrey S Barker*	PO Box 638, Alma MI 48801	989-463-2185	S	307*	.1
231	Northern Trust Bank of California NA—*Andrew Chou*	206 E Anapamu St, Santa Barbara CA 93101	805-965-6200	S	306*	.3
232	Hawaii National Bank—*Warren KK Luke*	45 N King St, Honolulu HI 96817	808-528-7711	S	304*	.3
233	Southern Bancorp—*Walter Smiley*	PO Box 160, Helena AR 72342	870-816-1111	S	298*	.1
234	Pascack Bancorp Inc—*Bruce M Meisel*	21 Jefferson Ave, Westwood NJ 07675	201-722-4722	P	298	N/A
235	Madison National Bank—*Daniel L Murphy*	2222 Merrick Rd, Merrick NY 11566	516-632-1600	P	297	<.1
236	Saratoga National Bank and Trust Co—*Raymond O'Connor*	171 S Broadway, Saratoga Springs NY 12866	518-583-3114	S	295	<.1
237	UPS Capital Business Credit	35 Glenlake Pky Ste 50, Atlanta GA 30328		S	293*	.2
238	1st Colonial Bancorp Inc—*Gerard M Banmiller*	1040 Haddon Ave, Collingswood NJ 08108	856-858-1100	P	291	<.1
239	First National Bank of Muscatine—*Scott Ingstad*	PO Box 539, Muscatine IA 52761	563-263-4221	S	287*	.1
240	Security Bank of Kansas City—*James S Lewis*	1300 N 78th St, Kansas City KS 66112	913-281-3165	R	283*	.1
241	Huntington National Bank West Virginia—*Clayton Rice*	PO Box 633, Charleston WV 25322	304-348-5000	S	280*	.2
242	Enterprise National Bank of Palm Beach—*Tim Terry*	11811 US Hwy 1, North Palm Beach FL 33410	561-624-4400	R	276*	<.1
243	Harford Bank—*Charles Jacob Jr*	PO Box 640, Aberdeen MD 21001	410-272-5000	R	274*	.1
244	City National Bank of West Virginia—*Charles R Hageboeck*	3601 MacCorkle Ave SE, Charleston WV 25304	304-926-3308	S	271*	.1
245	Swineford National Bank—*Michael R Wimer*	227 E Main St, Middleburg PA 17842	570-837-1881	S	269*	.1
246	Two River Community Bank—*William D Moss*	1250 Hwy 35 S, Middletown NJ 07748	732-706-9009	S	268*	<.1

Note: An asterisk (*) indicates an estimated financial figure. The company type code used is as follows: R = Private, P = Public, S = Private Subsidiary, B = Public Subsidiary, D = Division, J = Joint Venture, I = Investment Fund.

...KINGS BY SALES WITHIN 4-DIGIT SIC

	...y Name—Executive Officer	Address, City, State, Zip	Phone	Type	Fin	Empls
...8	Sturgis Bancorp Inc—Eric L Eishen	PO Box 600, Sturgis MI 49091	269-651-9345	R	267*	.1
...8	Carolina Trust Bank—J Michael Cline	901 E Main St, Lincolnton NC 28092	704-735-1104	P	266	<.1
249	First National Bank of Barry—John C Shover	PO Box 156, Barry IL 62312	217-335-2393	R	264*	<.1
250	Merchants Bank of California	1 Civic Plz Dr, Carson CA 90745	310-549-4350	R	263*	<.1
251	First National Bank (Ronceverte West Virginia)—Benny Williams	PO Box 457, Ronceverte WV 24970	304-647-4500	R	262*	<.1
252	First National Bank (Orrville Ohio)—David C Vernon	112 W Market St, Orrville OH 44667	330-682-1010	S	261*	.1
253	National Capital Bank of Washington—Richard A Didden	316 Pennsylvania Ave S, Washington DC 20003	202-546-8000	R	259	<.1
254	Commerce National Bank (Fullerton California)—Mark E Simmons	4040 MacArthur Blvd St, Newport Beach CA 92660	949-474-1020	P	256	<.1
255	National Bank of Texas at Fort Worth—George Bradford	PO Box 161969, Fort Worth TX 76161	817-625-5511	R	256*	<.1
256	First National Bank of Jeffersonville—Wayne V Zanetti	PO Box 398, Jeffersonville NY 12748	845-482-4000	S	252*	.1
257	Low Country National Bank—Randy Kohn Coastal Banking Company Inc	36 Sea Island Pky, Beaufort SC 29907	843-522-1228	S	250*	<.1
258	Continental National Bank of Miami—Guillermo Diaz-Rousslet	1801 SW 1st St, Miami FL 33135	305-642-2440	R	249*	.1
259	Citizens National Bank of Elkins West Virginia—William Johnson	PO Box 1519, Elkins WV 26241	304-636-4095	S	246	N/A
260	First National Bank of Pulaski	PO Box 289, Pulaski TN 38478	913-363-2585	S	245*	.2
261	City National Bank of New Jersey—Louis E Prezeau	900 Broad St, Newark NJ 07102	973-624-0865	S	243*	.1
262	First National Bank of De Queen—Tony Bob Ray	PO Box 980, De Queen AR 71832	870-642-2212	R	242*	<.1
263	Citywide Bank of Aurora—Marty Schmitz	10660 E Colfax Ave, Aurora CO 80010	303-365-3640	S	241*	.1
264	Farmers National Bank of Buhl—Mike Hamilton	PO Box 392, Buhl ID 83316	208-543-4351	R	240*	.1
265	Highland Bank	2100 Ford Pkwy, Saint Paul MN 55116	651-698-2471	S	239*	.1
266	US Bank Trust Company NA	800 Nicollet Mall, Minneapolis MN 55402	612-973-1111	S	238	N/A
267	Hometown Bank NA—Jimmy Rasmussen	PO Box 3909, Galveston TX 77552	409-763-1271	R	234*	.1
268	Security Business Bank of San Diego—Paul F Rodeno	701 B St Ste 100, San Diego CA 92101	619-231-8500	P	233	<.1
269	FPB Bancorp Inc—David W Skiles	1301 SE Port St Lucie, Port Saint Lucie FL 34952	722-225-5930	P	232	.1
270	Millennium Bankshares Corp—John F Novak	21430 Cedar Dr Ste 200, Sterling VA 20164	703-464-0100	P	231	<.1
271	Mid City Bank Inc—James G Fitl	304 S 42nd St, Omaha NE 68131	402-558-8000	R	230*	.1
272	Oak Ridge Capital Group Inc—Marc Kozberg	701 Xenia Ave S Ste100, Golden Valley MN 55416	763-923-2200	R	227	.1
273	Community Capital Bancshares Inc—Luke Flatt	PO Drawer 71269, Albany GA 31707	229-446-2265	P	224	.1
274	First National Bank of Midwest City—Robert H Croak	PO Box 10600, Midwest City OK 73140	405-732-4571	S	222*	.2
275	First National Bank in Montevideo—Doug Hile	PO Box 468, Montevideo MN 56265	320-269-6454	S	222*	<.1
276	Sabine State Bank and Trust Co—Lee H McCann	121 University, Leesville LA 71446	337-239-1000	R	220*	.3
277	First National Bank of Bar Harbor—Daniel Daigneault	102 Main St, Bar Harbor ME 04609	207-288-3341	S	220	N/A
278	Broadway Bank—James D Goudge	2302 Stanley Rd, San Antonio TX 78234	210-227-7131	S	217*	.1
279	Cadence Bank NA (Memphis Tennessee)	6075 Poplar Ave Ste 12, Memphis TN 38119	901-312-3522	S	214*	.1
280	American National Bank (Oakland Park Florida)—Ginger Martin	4301 N Federal Hwy Ste, Oakland Park FL 33308	954-491-7788	R	214*	<.1
281	First National Bank Eastland—Tom Barrow	PO Box 788, Eastland TX 76448	254-629-6100	S	212*	<.1
282	Independent Bancshares Inc—Mark Imes	60 SW 17th St, Ocala FL 34478	352-622-2377	R	211	.1
283	National Bank of Arkansas—James Renk	PO Box 837, North Little Rock AR 72115	501-771-4000	S	209*	.1
284	Commerce First Bancorp Inc—Richard J Morgan	1804 West St Ste 200, Annapolis MD 21401	410-280-6695	P	207	<.1
285	Commonwealth National Bank—Tyrone Fenderson	PO Box 2326, Mobile AL 36652	251-476-5938	R	207*	<.1
286	First National Bank of Polk County—Laron Maloney	PO Box 228, Cedartown GA 30125	770-748-1750	R	207*	<.1
287	Mission Community Bancorp—James W Lockey	3380 S Higuera St, San Luis Obispo CA 93401	805-782-5000	P	205	.1
288	Security National Bank of Enid—Bill Athey	PO Box 1272, Enid OK 73702	580-234-5151	S	204*	.1
289	First Pioneer National Bank—Keith E Waggoner	PO Box 96, Wray CO 80758	970-332-4824	R	204*	.1
290	Canon National Bank—Dan Tanner	816 Royal Gorge Blvd, Canon City CO 81212	719-276-9153	R	203*	.1
291	Progressive Bank NA (Bellaire Ohio)—Sylvan J Dlesk	426 34th St, Bellaire OH 43906	740-676-3141	R	203*	<.1
292	BNC National Bank—Greg Cleveland	PO Box 4050, Bismarck ND 58502	701-250-3000	S	202*	.1
293	Mission National Bank—Owen J Erickson	3060 16th St, San Francisco CA 94141	415-826-3627	R	202*	<.1
294	Clarkston Financial Corp—J Grant Smith	6600 Highland Rd Ste 2, Waterford MI 48327	248-886-0086	P	201	.1
295	Hometown Bank Hometown Bancorp Ltd	80 Sheboygan St, Fond du Lac WI 54935	920-907-0788	S	201*	.1
296	Pelican Financial Inc—Ken Aschom	811 Anchor Rode Dr, Naples FL 34103	239-403-0076	S	199	.1
297	National Bank of Middlebury—G Kenneth Perine	PO Box 189, Middlebury VT 05753	802-388-4982	R	198	N/A
298	Bank of McKenney—Richard M Liles	PO Box 370, McKenney VA 23872	804-478-4433	P	192	.1
299	Harris Bank Aurora - Branch—Ellen M Castello	2412 Indian Trail Rd, Aurora IL 60506	630-801-7700	S	191	<.1
300	First National Bank of Holdrege—D Scott Latter	PO Box 800, Holdrege NE 68949	308-995-4411	S	191*	<.1
301	First National Bank of Huntsville—Sam H Burris Jr	1300 11th St, Huntsville TX 77340	936-295-5701	R	190*	.1
302	Pacific Commerce Bank NA—Brian H Kelley	420 E 3rd St Ste 1010, Los Angeles CA 90013	213-617-0082	P	189	<.1
303	Bank of Fayetteville—Marybeth Brooks	1 S Block St, Fayetteville AR 72701	479-444-4444	R	189*	.1
304	Great Southern National Bank—Bill Abbey	PO Box 1271, Meridian MS 39302	601-693-5141	S	184*	.2
305	Los Angeles National Bank—Johnson M Tsai	7025 Orangethorpe Ave, Buena Park CA 90621	714-670-2400	R	182*	<.1
306	Bank of Southern California (San Diego California)—Nathan L Rogge	12265 El Camino Real S, San Diego CA 92130	858-847-4700	P	180	N/A
307	Commerce Bank of Washington NA—Stanley Savage	601 Union St Ste 3600, Seattle WA 98101	206-292-4500	S	177*	.1
308	FirstBank of South Jeffco—Pam Lorenz	PO Box 620219, Littleton CO 80162	303-763-2664	S	176	.1
309	Western Springs National Bank and Trust—Jerry F Miceli	4456 Wolf Rd, Western Springs IL 60558	708-246-2200	R	176*	.1
310	Old Second National Bank—Latanya Simonton	4080 Fox Valley Ctr Dr, Aurora IL 60504	630-499-4330	R	176*	<.1
311	First National Bank (Waverly Iowa)—Jeff Plagge	316 E Bremer Ave, Waverly IA 50677	319-352-1340	R	174*	.1
312	Weatherford National Bank—Scott Dueser	PO Box 1299, Weatherford TX 76086	817-598-2500	S	174	.1
313	Adams National Bank—Kathleen Walsh-Carr	1130 Connecticut Ave N, Washington DC 20036	202-772-3600	R	173*	.1
314	Cayuga Lake National Bank—G William Ryan	PO Box 512, Union Springs NY 13160	315-889-7358	R	172*	<.1
315	First National Bank and Trust Co (Ardmore Oklahoma)—Curtis Davidson	405 W Main, Ardmore OK 73401	580-223-1111	R	171*	.1
316	Unity Bank Crosby Minnesota—Dean E Davidson	PO Box 157, Crosby MN 56441	218-546-5153	R	171*	<.1
317	Ohio Legacy Corp—Rick Hull	600 S Main St, North Canton OH 44720	330-499-1900	P	171	.1
318	JPMorgan Chase Bank NA (New York New York)—James Dimon	1 Chase Manhattan Plz, New York NY 10081	212-270-6000	S	170	N/A
319	Scbt NA—Mike Evans	950 John C Calhoun Dr, Orangeburg SC 29115	803-897-2121	R	169*	N/A
320	Pioneer Bankshares Inc—Thomas R Rosazza	PO Box 10, Stanley VA 22851	540-778-2294	P	168	.1
321	Eastside Commercial Bank NA—Maryann Nelson	3326 160th Ave SE Ste, Bellevue WA 98008	425-373-0400	R	165*	<.1
322	Oregon Pacific Bancorp—Jim Clark	PO Box 22000, Florence OR 97439	541-997-7121	P	164	.1
323	Bridge Street Financial Inc—Gregory J Kreis	300 State Rte 104, Oswego NY 13126	315-343-4100	R	163*	.1
324	Kearney Commercial Bank—Larry Ellington	100 W 92 Hwy, Kearney MO 64060	816-628-6050	R	160*	<.1
325	Premier Bank and Trust—Rick L Hull Ohio Legacy Corp	PO Box 959, Wooster OH 44691	330-263-1955	S	158*	.1
326	Hillsdale County National Bank—Craig Conner	1 S Howell St, Hillsdale MI 49242	517-439-4300	R	156*	.1
327	American Bank of Oklahoma—Joe A Landon	PO Box 7009, Muskogee OK 74402	918-686-7000	R	156*	.1

Rank	Company Name—*Executive Officer*	Address, City, State, Zip	Phone	Type	Fin	Empls
328	Centennial Bank (Fountain Valley California)—*Ron Robertson*	18837 Brookhurst St St, Fountain Valley CA 92708	714-964-9111	R	156*	<.1
329	First National Bank of Ipswich—*Bruce Macdonald*	PO Box 31, Ipswich MA 01938	978-356-3700	S	155*	.1
330	First Financial Bank of Cleburne—*Matt Reynolds*	403 North Main, Cleburne TX 76033	817-556-5000	S	152*	<.1
331	JGB Bank—*Didier Fabelo*	8200 NW 33rd St Ste 40, Miami FL 33102	305-418-6000	S	151*	.1
332	Virginia Commerce Bank—*Peter Converse*	5350 Lee Hwy, Arlington VA 22207	703-534-0700	R	151*	.1
333	First National Bank of Berryville—*William Hudspeth III*	PO Box 367, Berryville AR 72616	870-423-6601	R	150*	.1
334	1st Colonial National Bank—*Gerard Banmiller* 1st Colonial Bancorp Inc	1040 Haddon Ave, Collingswood NJ 08108	856-858-1100	S	150*	<.1
335	Capitol National Bank—*Paula D Cunningham*	200 N Washington Sq, Lansing MI 48933	517-484-5080	S	146*	<.1
336	Premier Commercial Bank NA—*Kenneth J Cosgrove*	2400 E Katella Ave Ste, Anaheim CA 92806	714-978-2400	S	146*	<.1
337	Pacific Coast National Bancorp—*Bob R Adkins*	905 Calle Amanecer Ste, San Clemente CA 92673	949-361-4300	P	143	<.1
338	Central Kentucky Savings and Loan Service Corp—*William H Johnson*	340 W Main St, Danville KY 40422	859-236-4181	S	141*	<.1
339	Santa Clara Valley Bank NA—*Ralph de Leon*	PO Box 191, Santa Paula CA 93061	805-525-1999	P	140	<.1
340	Banco Popular NA	6001 E Washington Blvd, Commerce CA 90040	323-724-8800	S	140	.1
341	Community National Bancorp—*T Brinson Brock*	PO Box 2619, Ashburn GA 31714	229-567-9686	R	139	.1
342	First National Bank of Canton—*Ben Shirey*	PO Box 517, Canton TX 75103	903-567-4184	R	135*	.1
343	First National Bank (Antlers Oklahoma)—*Steve Burrage*	PO Box 458, Antlers OK 74523	580-298-3368	R	129*	<.1
344	First National Bank and Trust Company of Weatherford—*Herschel Brewster*	PO Box 311, Weatherford OK 73096	580-772-5574	R	127*	<.1
345	Northway Bank—*William J Woodward*	9 Main St, Berlin NH 03570	603-752-1171	S	125	.1
346	First National Bank of Canadian—*George Briant*	PO Box 97, Canadian TX 79014	806-323-6455	R	124*	<.1
347	First National Bank of Montana (Libby Montana)—*Joe Kesler*	PO Box 1550, Libby MT 59923	406-293-0280	R	123*	<.1
348	First Financial Bank (Sweetwater Texas)—*Kirby Andrews*	201 Elm, Sweetwater TX 79556	325-235-6600	S	121*	<.1
349	Woodhaven National Bank—*Ronnie Casey*	6750 Bridge St, Fort Worth TX 76112	817-496-6700	R	119*	<.1
350	New York National Bank—*James J Landy*	369 E 149th St, Bronx NY 10455	718-402-1195	R	116*	.1
351	First National Bank of Southern California—*Don Murray*	1110 San Marino Dr, San Marcos CA 92078	760-471-1051	R	111*	<.1
352	First National Bank of Beardstown—*Scott Musch*	300 Washington St, Beardstown IL 62618	217-323-4105	R	110*	<.1
353	Old Second Bank-Yorkville—*William B Skoglund*	26 W Countryside Pky, Yorkville IL 60560	630-553-4230	S	109*	<.1
354	City National Securities Inc—*Russell Goldsmith*	400 N Roxbury Dr, Beverly Hills CA 90210	310-888-6000	S	108*	<.1
355	Bank of Napa NA—*Tom LeMasters*	2007 Redwood Rd Ste 10, Napa CA 94558	707-257-7777	P	106	<.1
356	Capital Bank NA—*Scot Browning*	1 Church St Ste 100, Rockville MD 20850	240-283-0416	S	106	<.1
357	Inland Empire National Bank (Riverside California)—*Candace H Wiest*	3727 Arlington Ave Ste, Riverside CA 92506	909-788-2265	R	102	<.1
358	First Merchants Bank of Central Indiana—*Mike Stewart*	33 W 10th St, Anderson IN 46016	765-622-9773	S	101*	<.1
359	Native American Bank NA—*David M Gilman*	999 18th St Ste 2460, Denver CO 80202	303-988-2727	R	100	N/A
360	First National Bank in Mena—*Gary Newcomb*	PO Box 1049, Mena AR 71953	479-394-3552	R	97*	<.1
361	Community Trust Bank Inc (Pikeville Kentucky) Community Trust Bancorp Inc	PO Box 2947, Pikeville KY 41502	606-432-1414	S	95*	.9
362	First National Bank of Brundidge—*James T Ramage III*	137 S Main St, Brundidge AL 36010	334-735-2351	R	94*	<.1
363	Midland National Bank—*Ronald R Lang*	527 N Main St, Newton KS 67114	316-283-1700	R	92*	.1
364	First National Bank in Fairfield—*Pat Hurley*	PO Box 1007, Fairfield IA 52556	641-472-4121	S	92*	<.1
365	Bank of Manhattan NA—*Deepak Kumar*	2141 E Rosecrans Ave, El Segundo CA 90245	310-606-8000	S	92*	<.1
366	Bessemer Trust Company NA—*John Hilton*	630 5th Ave, New York NY 10111	212-708-9100	S	91*	.7
367	First Interstate Bank of Alaska NA—*Ron Kukes*	PO Box 92360, Anchorage AK 99509	907-561-5258	R	91*	<.1
368	FirstBank of Tech Center	5105 DTC Pky Ste 100, Greenwood Village CO 80111	303-694-1000	S	87*	<.1
369	South Valley National Bank Pacific Capital Bank NA	PO Box 1786, Salinas CA 93902		S	86*	<.1
370	First National Bank of Izard County—*Kenny Thornton*	PO Box 609, Calico Rock AR 72519	870-297-3711	S	85*	<.1
371	First Cherokee State Bank	PO Box 1238, Woodstock GA 30188	770-591-9000	S	83	<.1
372	Commerce Bank of Hannibal NA—*David Kemper*	100 Huck Finn Shopping, Hannibal MO 63401	573-221-0103	S	77*	<.1
373	Bank of the Rockies NA—*Michael E Grove*	PO Box 709, White Sulphur Springs MT 59645	406-547-3331	S	76*	<.1
374	United Bank of Philadelphia—*Evelyn F Smalls*	30 S 15th St Ste 1200, Philadelphia PA 19102	215-351-4600	S	73	<.1
375	First National Bank in Tremont—*Jim Shafer*	PO Box 23, Tremont IL 61568	309-925-2121	R	73*	<.1
376	Clear Creek National Bank—*Leo Bradley*	PO Box 337, Georgetown CO 80444	303-569-9700	R	73*	<.1
377	Simmons First National Bank—*J Thomas May*	PO Box 7009, Pine Bluff AR 71601	870-541-1000	S	71*	.5
378	Twin River National Bank—*Jody Servatius*	PO Box 1324, Lewiston ID 83501	208-746-4848	S	71*	<.1
379	City National Financial Services Inc—*Russell Goldsmith*	400 N Roxbury Dr, Beverly Hills CA 90210	310-888-6000	S	71*	<.1
380	Mainsource Bank of Illinois—*Archie M Brown*	216 S 4th St, Watseka IL 60970	815-432-3977	S	66*	<.1
381	American West Bank NA—*John J Feldman*	16861 Ventura Blvd, Encino CA 91436	818-501-2265	R	62	<.1
382	State National Bank and Trust—*David R Ley*	PO Box 130, Wayne NE 68787	402-375-1130	S	61*	<.1
383	Merchants Bank (Cannon Falls Minnesota)—*Paul H Bringgold*	300 W Main St, Cannon Falls MN 55009	507-263-4281	S	58*	<.1
384	Duetche Bank—*James Zahringer*	350 Royal Palm Way, Palm Beach FL 33480	561-659-8820	D	58*	<.1
385	Central Valley Bank NA	PO Box 70, Toppenish WA 98948	509-865-2511	S	56*	<.1
386	Klein National Bank of Madison	PO Box 127, Madison MN 56256	320-598-7591	S	55*	<.1
387	First National Bank of Floydada—*Thomas K Farris Jr*	PO Box 550, Floydada TX 79235	806-983-3717	R	55*	<.1
388	Borrego Springs Bank NA—*William P Ruhlman*	7777 Alvarado Rd Ste 5, La Mesa CA 91942	619-668-5159	R	52*	.1
389	First National Bank of the Lakes—*David J Delaney Jr*	PO Box 0123, Navarre MN 55392	952-471-0111	S	50*	<.1
390	InterContinental National Bank—*Steven J Pritchard*	6810 Military Dr W, San Antonio TX 78227	210-645-3710	R	50*	<.1
391	Excel National Bank—*Brian Carlson*	9701 Wilshire Blvd, Beverly Hills CA 90212	310-362-2000	R	48*	<.1
392	Alpine Banks of Colorado—*J Robert Young*	PO Box 2040, Telluride CO 81435	970-728-5050	R	34*	<.1
393	Bank of Laramie—*Nancy Stutzman*	PO Box 1027, Laramie WY 82073	307-745-3619	S	27*	<.1
394	Bank of America Texas NA Bank of America Corp	901 Main St, Dallas TX 75202	214-209-1370	S	27*	<.1
395	M and T Bank NA	54 Main St, Oakfield NY 14125	585-948-5232	S	25*	<.1
396	First Keystone Community Bank—*J Gerald Bazewicz*	111 W Front St, Berwick PA 18603	570-752-3671	S	21*	.1
397	First National Bank (Independence Kansas)—*Brad W Oakes*	PO Box 868, Independence KS 67301	620-331-2265	R	21*	<.1
398	First National Bank of Marquette—*John D Ferguson*	PO Box 39, Marquette NE 68854	402-854-2221	S	21*	<.1
399	Chester National Bank of Missouri	1010 N Main St, Perryville MO 63775	573-547-7611	R	21*	<.1
400	National Bank and Trust Co (Norwich New York)	PO Box 351, Norwich NY 13815	607-337-2265	S	19*	.5
401	First National Bank of Jefferson—*Mayo Kasling*	PO Box 799, Jefferson TX 75657	903-665-2535	R	15*	<.1
402	Amegy Bank NA—*Scott McLean*	PO Box 4837, Houston TX 77210	713-235-8800	S	11	N/A
403	Independent National Bank (Ocala Florida)—*Mark Imes* Independent Bancshares Inc	60 SW 17th St, Ocala FL 34471	352-622-2377	S	6*	.1

TOTALS: SIC 6021 National Commercial Banks
Companies: 403

					3,767,757	682.2

6022 State Commercial Banks

| 1 | Union Bank (Kansas City Missouri)—*Jeffrey J Jernigan* | 9300 Blue Ridge Blvd, Kansas City MO 64138 | 816-763-4400 | R | 563,711 | N/A |

Note: An asterisk (*) indicates an estimated financial figure. The company type code used is as follows: R = Private, P = Public, S = Private Subsidiary, B = Public Subsidiary, D = Division, J = Joint Venture, I = Investment Fund.

KINGS BY SALES WITHIN 4-DIGIT SIC

	Company Name—*Executive Officer*	Address, City, State, Zip	Phone	Type	Fin	Empls
	Bank of New York—*Gerald L Hassell*	1 Wall St, New York NY 10005	212-530-1784	S	56,154	15.1
3	Bank of the West—*Michael J Shepherd*	180 Montgomery St, San Francisco CA 94104	925-942-8300	S	55,158*	10.4
4	State Street Bank and Trust Co—*Ronald Logue*	PO Box 5501, Boston MA 02111	617-786-3000	S	43,995*	10.0
5	HSBC Bank USA NA—*Irene Dorner*	PO Box 2013, Buffalo NY 14225		S	29,724*	9.5
6	Harris Trust and Savings Bank—*Ellen Costello*	PO Box 755, Chicago IL 60690	312-461-2121	S	28,000*	6.5
7	Discover Bank—*Christina Favilla*	502 E Market St, Greenwood DE 19950	302-323-7110	S	23,662	1.2
8	Capital One Bank—*Richard Fairbank*	PO Box 5038, Glen Allen VA 23058	804-747-7200	S	22,613*	3.7
9	East West Bancorp Inc—*Dominic Ng*	135 N Los Robles Ave 7, Pasadena CA 91101	626-799-5700	P	20,701	2.1
10	Fifth Third Bank (Cincinnati Ohio)	38 Fountain Sq Plz, Cincinnati OH 45202	513-579-5203	S	15,747*	5.0
11	First BanCorp—*Aurelio Aleman-Bermudez*	PO Box 9146, San Juan PR 00908	787-729-8200	P	15,593	2.5
12	Banco Popular de Puerto Rico	PO Box 362708, San Juan PR 00936	787-765-9800	S	14,877*	5.3
13	State Bank and Trust Co—*Stephen McGill*	1025 6th St, Nevada IA 50201	515-382-2191	S	14,144	<.1
14	Boone Bank and Trust Co—*Jeffrey K Putzier*	PO Box 428, Boone IA 50036	515-432-6200	S	12,968	<.1
15	PrivateBancorp Inc—*Larry D Richman*	120 S LaSalle St, Chicago IL 60603	312-683-7100	P	12,417	1.0
16	Westamerica Bank	1108 5th Ave, San Rafael CA 94901	415-257-8057	S	11,632*	1.8
17	First Citizens Bank and Trust Co—*Frank B Holding Jr*	PO Box 27131, Raleigh NC 27611	919-716-2692	S	10,944*	5.0
18	Citizens Bank of Rhode Island—*Ellen Alemany*	1 Citizens Dr, Riverside RI 02915	401-456-7000	S	10,570*	1.7
19	California Bank and Trust—*David Blackford*	11622 El Camino Real S, San Diego CA 92130	858-793-7400	S	10,000*	2.0
20	Prosperity Bancshares Inc—*David Zalman*	4295 San Felipe, Houston TX 77027	281-269-7199	P	9,823	1.7
21	Citizens Bank of Michigan	328 S Saginaw St, Flint MI 48502	810-766-7500	S	9,044*	1.4
22	Randall-Story State Bank—*Richard Schreier*	PO Box 278, Story City IA 50248	515-733-4396	S	8,809	<.1
23	Umpqua Bank—*Raymond P Davis*	PO Box 1820, Roseburg OR 97470	541-440-3961	S	8,599	1.6
24	First Bank (Creve Coeur Missouri)—*Terrance McCarthy*	11901 Olive Blvd, Creve Coeur MO 63141	314-995-8700	S	8,480*	1.9
25	Great Western Bank (Watertown South Dakota)—*Ken Karels*	35 1st Ave NE, Watertown SD 57201	605-765-2491	S	8,203	1.5
26	Oriental Financial Group Inc—*Jose Rafael Fernandez*	997 San Roberto St Pro, San Juan PR 00926	787-771-6800	P	7,313	.7
27	First Hawaiian Bank—*Donald G Horner*	PO Box 3200, Honolulu HI 96847	808-525-7000	S	6,665*	2.1
28	Prosperity Bank—*David Zalman* Prosperity Bancshares Inc	PO Drawer G, El Campo TX 77437	979-543-2200	S	6,358	1.4
29	Central Pacific Bank—*Ronald Miqita*	PO Box 3590, Honolulu HI 96811	808-544-0500	S	6,269*	1.0
30	Cathay Bank—*Dunson K Cheng*	777 N Broadway, Los Angeles CA 90012	213-625-4700	S	6,100*	.8
31	CapitalSource Bank—*Tad Lowrey*	633 W 5th St Ste 3300, Los Angeles CA 90071	213-443-7700	S	5,884*	.3
32	Johnston Bank—*Helen Johnson-Leipold*	555 Main St, Racine WI 53403	262-619-2700	S	5,692*	.9
33	Commerce Bank (Laredo Texas)	2120 Saunders Ave, Laredo TX 78040	956-724-1616	S	5,628*	1.6
34	United States Trust Company of New York—*Keith Banks*	114 W 47th St, New York NY 10036	212-852-1000	S	5,607*	1.9
35	First Security Bank (Searcy Arkansas)—*Reynie Rutledge*	PO Box 1009, Searcy AR 72145	501-279-3400	S	5,599*	.9
36	Citizens Business Bank—*Christopher D Myers*	701 N Haven Ave, Ontario CA 91764	909-980-4030	S	5,417	.7
37	Bank of America (Phoenix Arizona)	51 E Camelback Rd, Phoenix AZ 85012	602-248-4823	S	5,165*	6.7
38	Branch Banking and Trust Company of South Carolina—*Robert Greene*	PO Box 408, Greenville SC 29602	864-242-8026	S	4,900	1.0
39	Brown Brothers Harriman and Co—*Robert G Bergman*	140 Broadway, New York NY 10005	212-483-1818	R	4,753*	4.0
40	East West Bank—*Irene Oh* East West Bancorp Inc	135 N Los Robles Ave 7, Pasadena CA 91101	626-768-6000	S	4,706*	.9
41	Columbia Banking System Inc—*Melanie J Dressel*	PO Box 2156, Tacoma WA 98401	253-305-1900	P	4,509	1.3
42	First Mariner Bank	3301 Boston St, Baltimore MD 21224	410-558-4375	S	4,416*	.7
43	First Interstate Bank—*Lyle R Knight*	PO Box 30918, Billings MT 59116	406-255-5000	S	4,376*	2.5
44	1st Source Corp—*Christopher J Murphy III*	PO Box 1602, South Bend IN 46634	574-235-2000	P	4,374	1.2
45	People's United Bank (Burlington Vermont)	PO Box 820, Burlington VT 05402	802-658-4000	S	4,328*	.7
46	First Bank (Troy North Carolina)—*Jerry Ocheltree*	PO Box 508, Troy NC 27371	910-576-2265	S	4,271*	.7
47	Farmers and Merchants Bank of Long Beach—*Henry Walker*	PO Box 1370, Long Beach CA 90801	562-437-0011	P	4,262	.7
48	PNC Bank Delaware—*Calvert A Morgan Jr*	PO Box 791, Wilmington DE 19801	302-429-1361	S	4,249*	.7
49	Bank Leumi USA—*Uzi Rosen*	579 5th Ave, New York NY 10170	917-542-2343	S	4,123*	.4
50	TowneBank—*Robert Aston Jr*	5716 High St, Portsmouth VA 23703	757-638-7500	P	4,082	.6
51	Fulton Bank—*Craig Roda*	1 Penn Sq, Lancaster PA 17602	717-291-2411	S	4,000*	.9
52	Heartland Financial USA Inc—*Lynn B Fuller*	PO Box 778, Dubuque IA 52004	563-589-2100	P	4,000	1.1
53	Santa Barbara Bank and Trust—*George S Leis*	PO Box 60839, Santa Barbara CA 93160		S	3,864*	1.4
54	Home BancShares Inc—*C Randall Sims*	PO Box 966, Conway AR 72033	501-328-4715	P	3,763	.7
55	Chemical Bank and Trust Co	PO Box 231, Midland MI 48640	989-631-9200	S	3,760*	1.6
56	Carter Bank and Trust—*Worth Harris Carter Jr*	1300 Kings Mountain Rd, Martinsville VA 24112	276-656-1776	P	3,706	N/A
57	Brotherhood Bank and Trust Co—*Calvin T Roberts*	756 Minnesota Ave, Kansas City KS 66101	913-321-4242	S	3,702*	.2
58	Sterling Bancorporation Inc—*J Downey Bridgwater*	PO Box 40333, Houston TX 77240	713-466-8300	S	3,336	1.0
59	Israel Discount Bank of New York	511 5th Ave, New York NY 10017	212-551-8500	S	3,240*	.5
60	BancFirst—*David E Rainbolt*	PO Box 26788, Oklahoma City OK 73126	405-270-1000	S	3,229*	.5
61	Berkshire Bank—*Michael Daly*	24 North St, Pittsfield MA 01201	413-443-5601	S	3,225*	.5
62	Atlantic Bank—*Thomas O'Brien*	615 Merrick Ave, Westbury NY 11590		D	3,182	.3
63	First Defiance Service Inc	PO Box 248, Defiance OH 43512	419-782-5015	S	3,069*	.5
64	Parkway Bank and Trust Co—*ROco Suspenzi*	4800 N Harlem Ave, Harwood Heights IL 60706	708-867-6600	R	2,992*	.4
65	Wilshire Bancorp Inc—*Jae Whan Yoo*	3200 Wilshire Blvd, Los Angeles CA 90010	213-387-3200	P	2,971	.4
66	First State Community Bank—*Matt Sebastian*	201 E Columbia St, Farmington MO 63640	573-756-4547	S	2,732*	.5
67	Vectra Bank Colorado—*Bruce Alexander*	2000 S Colorado Blvd S, Denver CO 80222	720-947-7700	S	2,715*	.8
68	1st Source Bank—*Christopher Murphy III* 1st Source Corp	PO Box 1602, South Bend IN 46660	574-235-2000	S	2,713*	1.0
69	Pulaski Service Corp—*Gary W Douglass* Pulaski Bank	12300 Olive Blvd, Creve Coeur MO 63141	314-878-2210	S	2,694*	.4
70	BBCN Bank NA—*Min Kim*	3731 Wilshire Blvd Ste, Los Angeles CA 90010	213-639-1700	S	2,669*	.4
71	American Express Retirement Services—*Ward Armstrong*	PO Box 489, Minneapolis MN 55440	612-671-2992	S	2,631*	.9
72	Oritani Financial Corp—*Kevin J Lynch*	PO Box 1329, Township of Washington NJ 07676	201-664-5400	P	2,587	.2
73	First Security Bank (Mountain Home Arkansas)—*Larry Nelson*	PO Box 1906, Mountain Home AR 72654	870-425-2166	S	2,500	N/A
74	Enterprise Financial Services Corp—*Peter F Benoist*	150 N Meramec Ave, Clayton MO 63105	314-725-5500	P	2,456	.3
75	Hancock Bank of Louisiana	1 American Pl 591, Baton Rouge LA 70821		S	2,447*	.4
76	Green Bankshares Inc—*Stephen Rownd*	100 N Main St, Greeneville TN 37743	423-639-5111	P	2,406	.7
77	Washington Trust Co—*Joseph J MarcAurele*	23 Broad St, Westerly RI 02891	401-348-1200	S	2,398	.4
78	Union Bank and Trust Co (Lincoln Nebraska)—*Angie Muhleisen*	PO Box 82535, Lincoln NE 68506	402-323-1828	S	2,385*	.7
79	Ironstone Bank—*Frank B Holding*	10865 Haynes Bridge Rd, Alpharetta GA 30022	770-777-8960	S	2,340*	<.1
80	S and T Bank—*James Mill*	PO Box 190, Indiana PA 15701	724-349-1800	S	2,290*	.8
81	Cole Taylor Bank—*Mark A Hoppe*	9550 W Higgins Rd, Rosemont IL 60018	847-653-7978	S	2,262*	.5
82	Great Lakes Bank NA—*Ron Shropshire*	13057 S Western Ave, Blue Island IL 60406	708-503-0400	S	2,104*	.3
83	Eagle Bancorp Inc—*Ronald Paul*	7815 Woodmont Ave, Bethesda MD 20814	301-986-1800	P	2,089	.3
84	NewBridge Bank—*Pressley A Ridgill*	38 W 1st Ave, Lexington NC 27292	336-248-6500	S	2,074*	.5
85	German American Bank—*Mark Schroeder*	PO Box 810, Jasper IN 47547	812-482-1314	S	2,073*	.3

Rank	Company Name—*Executive Officer*	Address, City, State, Zip	Phone	Type	Fin	Empls
86	First Commonwealth Bank—*Thomas Michael Price*	PO Box 400, Indiana PA 15701	724-463-8555	S	2,018*	.6
87	Ocean National Bank—*Dianne Mercier*	PO Box 627, Keene NH 03431	603-352-1600	S	2,008*	.3
88	Bank Mutual—*Michael T Crowley Jr*	4949 W Brown Deer Rd, Brown Deer WI 53223	414-354-6886	S	2,000	.7
89	Yadkin Valley Financial Corp—*Joseph Towell*	209 N Bridge St, Elkin NC 28621	336-526-6300	P	1,993	.5
90	Cardinal Bank—*Bernard H Clineburg*	8270 Greensboro Dr Ste, McLean VA 22102	703-584-3500	S	1,976	N/A
91	Bankers Trust Co (Des Moines Iowa)—*Suku Radia*	PO Box 897, Des Moines IA 50304	515-245-2919	R	1,920*	.3
92	First Community Bank NA	PO Box 989, Bluefield VA 24605	276-322-5487	S	1,894*	.7
93	BankWest of Nevada—*Bruce Hendricks*	2700 W Sahara Ave, Las Vegas NV 89102	702-248-4200	S	1,893*	.3
94	Hillcrest Bank (Overland Park Kansas)—*Jeff Wheeler*	11111 W 95th St, Overland Park KS 66214	913-492-7500	S	1,882*	.3
95	Fidelity Southern Corp—*James B Miller Jr*	PO Box 105075, Atlanta GA 30348	404-639-6500	P	1,880	.6
96	First Financial Bank (Celina Ohio)—*Sam Munafo*	PO Box 170, Celina OH 45822	419-586-5121	S	1,831*	.3
97	Pacific Continental Bank	111 W 7th Ave, Eugene OR 97401	541-686-8685	S	1,823*	.3
98	EagleBank Eagle Bancorp Inc	7815 Woodmont Ave, Bethesda MD 20814	301-986-1800	S	1,806	<.1
99	Columbus Bank and Trust Co—*Stephen A Melton*	PO Box 120, Columbus GA 31902	706-649-4900	S	1,794*	3.0
100	HBC Insurance Group Inc	515 Franklin Sq, Michigan City IN 46360	219-879-0211	S	1,744*	.3
101	Legacy Bank of Texas—*Phil Dyer*	PO Box 869111, Plano TX 75024	972-461-1300	R	1,700	N/A
102	TIB Bank—*Michael Carrigan*	599 9th St N Ste 100, Naples FL 34102	239-263-3344	S	1,697*	.4
103	Pacific Coast Bankers Bank—*Steven A Brown*	340 Pine St, San Francisco CA 94104	415-399-1900	S	1,653*	.2
104	Mercantile Bank Corp—*Michael H Price*	310 Leonard St NW, Grand Rapids MI 49504	616-406-3000	P	1,632	.3
105	STAR Financial Bank New Castle—*Tom Marcuccilli*	403 Parkview Dr, New Castle IN 47362	765-593-5100	S	1,605	.7
106	Centier Bank—*Michael Schrage*	600 E 84th Ave, Merrillville IN 46410	219-756-2265	R	1,597*	.7
107	Macatawa Bank Corp—*Ronald Hahn*	10753 Macatawa Dr, Holland MI 49424	616-820-1444	P	1,578	.4
108	West Coast Bank	5335 Meadows Rd Ste 20, Lake Oswego OR 97035		S	1,573*	.6
109	Orrstown Bank—*Kenneth Shoemaker* Orrstown Financial Services Inc	77 E King St, Shippensburg PA 17257	717-532-6114	S	1,557*	.3
110	Great Florida Bank—*M Mehdi Ghomeshi*	15050 NW 79th Ct Ste 2, Miami Lakes FL 33016	305-514-6900	P	1,556	.2
111	Kitsap Bank—*James E Carmichael*	PO Box 9, Port Orchard WA 98366		R	1,551*	.3
112	Waukesha State Bank—*Ty Taylor*	PO Box 648, Waukesha WI 53187	262-549-8500	R	1,535*	.3
113	Georgia Bank and Trust Company of Augusta—*R Daniel Blanton*	PO Box 15367, Augusta GA 30919	706-738-6990	S	1,524*	.3
114	Exchange Bank—*William R Schrader*	PO Box 403, Santa Rosa CA 95402	707-524-3000	P	1,521	.4
115	Orrstown Financial Services Inc—*Thomas R Quinn Jr*	PO Box 250, Shippensburg PA 17257	717-530-3521	P	1,512	N/A
116	Washington Trust Bank—*Peter Stanton*	PO Box 2127, Spokane WA 99210	509-353-4204	S	1,485*	.9
117	Mutual Bank (MuncieIndiana)	110 E Charles St, Muncie IN 47305	765-747-2898	S	1,482*	.2
118	Tristate Capital Bank—*James F Getz*	301 Grant St Ste 2700, Pittsburgh PA 15219	412-304-0304	R	1,429*	.1
119	Merchants and Farmers Bank of Kosciusko—*Hugh Potts*	134 W Washington St, Kosciusko MS 39090	662-289-5121	S	1,421*	.6
120	Enterprise Bancorp Inc—*John Clancey Jr*	222 Merrimack St, Lowell MA 01852	978-459-9000	P	1,397	.3
121	Bank of Hampton Roads—*A B Davies Jr*	999 Waterside Dr Ste 2, Norfolk VA 23510	757-217-1000	S	1,391*	.5
122	Peapack-Gladstone Bank—*Frank A Kissel*	PO Box 700, Bedminster NJ 07921	908-234-0700	S	1,380	.2
123	Tompkins Trust Co—*Gregory J Hartz*	PO Box 460, Ithaca NY 14851	607-273-3210	S	1,375*	.2
124	Pulaski Bank—*Gary W Douglass*	12300 Olive Blvd, Creve Coeur MO 63141	314-878-2210	S	1,362*	.4
125	Glacier Bank of Whitefish	319 F 2nd St, Whitefish MT 59937	406-863-6300	S	1,332	.3
126	American State Bank—*William R Collier*	PO Box 1401, Lubbock TX 79408	806-767-7000	S	1,326*	.6
127	Republic Bank and Trust Co (Louisville Kentucky)—*Steve Trager*	601 W Market St, Louisville KY 40202	502-584-3600	R	1,320*	.6
128	Quad City Bank and Trust Co—*John H Anderson* QCR Holdings Inc	PO Box 395, Bettendorf IA 52722	563-344-0600	S	1,311*	.2
129	West Bancorporation Inc—*David D Nelson*	PO Box 65020, West Des Moines IA 50265	515-222-2300	P	1,306	.2
130	Fifth Third Bank of Indiana	251 N Illinois St, Indianapolis IN 46204	317-383-2300	S	1,300*	.3
131	Hawthorn Bank (Jefferson City Missouri)—*James E Smith*	PO Box 688, Jefferson City MO 65102	573-761-6100	S	1,280	.2
132	Square 1 Bank—*Doug Bowers*	406 Blackwell St Ste 2, Durham NC 27701	919-314-3040	R	1,273*	.2
133	Wilshire State Bank—*Joann Kim* Wilshire Bancorp Inc	3200 Wilshire Blvd Ste, Los Angeles CA 90010	213-368-7700	S	1,266*	.2
134	Manufacturers Bank (Los Angeles California)—*Mitsugu Serizawa*	PO Box 556000, Los Angeles CA 90055	213-489-6200	S	1,258*	.4
135	Preferred Bank (Los Angeles California)—*Li Yu*	601 S Figueroa St 29th, Los Angeles CA 90017	213-891-1188	P	1,257	.1
136	China Trust Bank USA—*William Hon*	22939 Hawthorne Blvd, Torrance CA 90505	310-791-2868	R	1,254*	.3
137	Timberland Bank—*Michael R Sand*	PO Box 697, Hoquiam WA 98550	360-533-4747	S	1,251*	.2
138	Heritage Commerce Corp—*Walter T Kaczmarek*	150 Almaden Blvd, San Jose CA 95113	408-947-6900	P	1,246	.2
139	Allegheny Valley Bank of Pittsburgh—*Andrew W Hasley*	5137 Butler St, Pittsburgh PA 15201	412-781-0318	S	1,244*	.2
140	Independent Bank of McKinney Texas—*David R Brooks*	1600 Redbud Blvd, McKinney TX 75069	972-548-5910	R	1,243*	.2
141	Fifth Third Bank of Northern Kentucky Inc—*Kevin Kabat*	8100 Burlington Pke, Florence KY 41042	859-283-8222	S	1,231*	.2
142	Bank of Marin Bancorp—*Russell A Colombo*	PO Box 2039, Novato CA 94948	415-763-4520	P	1,208	.2
143	Mountain West Bank (Coeur d'Alene Idaho)—*Jon W Hippler*	P O Box 1059, Coeur D Alene ID 83816	208-765-0284	S	1,199	.4
144	Central Bank and Trust Co—*Luther Deaton*	PO Box 1360, Lexington KY 40588	859-253-6222	S	1,173*	.4
145	Mellon 1st Business Corp—*Joseph Otting*	601 W 5th St, Los Angeles CA 90071	213-489-1000	S	1,151*	.2
146	Farmers Bank and Capital Trust Co—*Rick Harp*	PO Box 309, Frankfort KY 40602	502-227-1600	S	1,130*	.2
147	Premier Financial Bancorp Inc—*Robert W Walker*	2883 5th Ave, Huntington WV 25702	304-525-1600	P	1,124	.4
148	Interaudi Bank—*Joseph G Audi*	19 E 54th St, New York NY 10022	212-833-1000	R	1,120*	.1
149	Eastern Virginia Bankshares Inc—*Joe A Shearin*	PO Box 1455, Tappahannock VA 22560	804-443-8400	P	1,119	.3
150	Bank of Sturgeon Bay Building Corp—*Thomas Herlache* Baylake Bank	217 N 4th Ave, Sturgeon Bay WI 54235	920-743-5551	S	1,119*	.4
151	Kewaunee County Banc-Shares Inc—*Thomas Herlache*	217 N 4th Ave, Sturgeon Bay WI 54235	920-743-5551	S	1,119*	.4
152	Fremont Bank—*Bradford Anderson*	PO Box 5101, Fremont CA 94538	510-792-2300	S	1,115*	.6
153	Bankers Trust (Wilmington Delaware)—*Edward Reznick*	1011 Centre Rd Ste 200, Wilmington DE 19805	302-636-3000	S	1,113*	<.1
154	Heritage Financial Group Inc—*O Leonard Dorminey*	PO Box 5728, Albany GA 31703	229-420-0000	P	1,090	.3
155	Tri Counties Bank—*Richard P Smith*	146 W East Ave, Chico CA 95926	530-898-0380	S	1,084*	.5
156	Panhandle State Bank—*Curt Hecker*	PO Box 967, Sandpoint ID 83864	208-263-0505	S	1,082	.4
157	Central Bank (Jefferson City Missouri)—*Sam B Cook*	PO Box 779, Jefferson City MO 65102	573-634-1234	S	1,080*	.3
158	Bank of Essex—*George M Longest Jr*	PO Box 965, Tappahannock VA 22560	804-443-4343	S	1,079	.2
159	Bank of Rockbridge—*George Longest* Bank of Essex	744 N Lee Hwy, Lexington VA 24450	540-464-9884	D	1,076*	.2
160	First State Bank (Waynesboro Mississippi)—*Joel C Clements*	PO Box 506, Waynesboro MS 39367	601-735-3124	R	1,071*	.2
161	Farmers and Merchants Bank of Central California—*Kent Steinwert*	121 W Lodi Ave, Lodi CA 95240	209-367-2300	S	1,062*	.2
162	Cape Bancorp—*Michael D Devlin*	225 N Main St, Cape May Court House NJ 08210	609-465-5600	P	1,061	.2
163	Standard Bank and Trust Co—*Lawrence P Kelley*	2400 W 95th St, Evergreen Park IL 60805	708-499-2000	S	1,051*	.5
164	Dubuque Bank and Trust Co—*Douglas J Horstmann* Heartland Financial USA Inc	PO Box 778, Dubuque IA 52004	563-589-2000	S	1,041	.3

Note: An asterisk (*) indicates an estimated financial figure. The company type code used is as follows: R = Private, P = Public, S = Private Subsidiary, B = Public Subsidiary, D = Division, J = Joint Venture, I = Investment Fund.

COMPANY RANKINGS BY SALES WITHIN 4-DIGIT SIC

Rank	Company Name—*Executive Officer*	Address, City, State, Zip	Phone	Type	Fin	Empls
165	Lake City Bank	PO Box 1387, Warsaw IN 46581	574-267-6144	S	1,039*	.5
166	First Bank of Georgia—*Remer Y Brinson III* Georgia-Carolina Bancshares Inc	PO Box 15148, Augusta GA 30919	706-731-6600	S	1,038*	.2
167	Fidelity Bank—*Richard Spencer*	1009 Perry Hwy, Pittsburgh PA 15237	412-364-3200	S	1,036*	.2
168	American Business Bank (Los Angeles California)—*Donald P Johnson*	523 W 6th St Ste 900, Los Angeles CA 90014	213-430-4000	P	1,010	.1
169	North Dallas Bank and Trust Co—*Mike Shipman*	PO Box 679001, Dallas TX 75367	972-387-1300	P	1,000	N/A
170	F and M Financial Corp—*Dan Williams*	221 N Main St, Salisbury NC 28144	704-633-1772	R	995*	.2
171	Bar Harbor Bank and Trust Co—*Joseph M Murphy*	PO Box 400, Bar Harbor ME 04609	207-288-3314	S	978*	.2
172	WesBanco Bank Wheeling	1 Bank Plaza, Wheeling WV 26003	304-234-9000	S	972*	.4
173	Citizens and Northern Bank—*Todd Coolidge*	PO Box 58, Wellsboro PA 16901	570-724-3411	S	971*	.3
174	Totalbank—*Bill Heffernan*	2720 Coral Way, Miami FL 33145	305-448-6500	R	971*	.3
175	Westfield Savings Bank	141 Elm St, Westfield MA 01085	413-568-1911	S	965*	.2
176	Four Oaks Fincorp Inc—*Ayden R Lee Jr*	PO Box 309, Four Oaks NC 27524	919-963-2177	P	948	.2
177	Bank of Commerce Holdings—*Patrick J Moty*	1951 Churn Creek Rd, Redding CA 96002	530-224-3333	P	939	.3
178	Bank of Marin—*Russell Colombo* Bank of Marin Bancorp	504 Redwood Blvd, Novato CA 94947	415-763-4520	S	934	.2
179	Croghan Colonial Bank—*Rick Robertson*	323 Croghan St, Fremont OH 43420	419-332-7301	S	933*	.2
180	First Community Financial Partners Inc—*Patric Roe*	2801 Black Rd, Joliet IL 60435	815-725-0123	P	930	N/A
181	Citizens Banking Co (Sandusky Ohio)	100 E Water St, Sandusky OH 44870	419-625-4121	S	927*	.3
182	Columbia Bank (Tacoma Washington)—*Melanie Dressel* Columbia Banking System Inc	PO Box 2156, Tacoma WA 98401		S	923*	.4
183	Glenview State Bank—*Paul A Jones*	800 Waukegan Rd Ste 1, Glenview IL 60025	847-729-1900	S	920	.2
184	Guaranty Bank and Trust Co (Denver Colorado)—*Daniel M Quinn*	PO Box 5847, Denver CO 80217	303-296-9600	S	912*	.3
185	Enterprise Bank and Trust Co—*John P Clancy* Enterprise Bancorp Inc	222 Merrimack St, Lowell MA 01852	978-459-9000	S	910*	.2
186	C and F Financial Corp—*Larry G Dillon*	PO Box 391, West Point VA 23181	804-843-2360	P	904	.5
187	Southern Community Bank and Trust (Pilot Mountain North Carolina)—*F Scott Bauer*	PO Box 1368, Pilot Mountain NC 27041	336-368-5334	S	896*	.3
188	AMTRUST Inc—*Nicholas J Schrup III*	PO Box 938, Dubuque IA 52004	563-582-1841	R	896*	.3
189	Citizens Bank of Mukwonago—*Doug Bruins*	PO Box 223, Mukwonago WI 53149	262-363-6500	S	893*	.1
190	Southern Michigan Bank and Trust—*John Castle*	51 W Pearl St, Coldwater MI 49036	517-279-5500	S	892*	.1
191	Carrollton Bank—*Robert A Altieri* Carrollton Bancorp	PO Box 1391, Baltimore MD 21203	410-536-4600	S	886*	.1
192	People's United Bank (Portland Maine)—*William Lucy*	467 Congress St, Portland ME 04104	207-828-3000	S	863*	.1
193	North Valley Bank—*Michael Cushman*	300 Park Marina Cir, Redding CA 96001	530-226-0500	S	855*	.3
194	Stonegate Bank—*David Seleski*	PO Box 4678, Ft Lauderdale FL 33338	954-315-5500	P	855	<.1
195	DL Evans Bank—*John V Evans Jr*	PO Box 1188, Burley ID 83318	208-678-9076	R	850	.2
196	Bank of Utah—*James Anderson*	PO Box 231, Ogden UT 84402	801-409-5000	R	848*	.3
197	Saehan Bank—*Dong Il Kim*	3580 Wilshire Blvd Ste, Los Angeles CA 90010	213-389-5550	S	843*	.1
198	East Carolina Bank—*Dwight Utz*	PO Box 337, Engelhard NC 27824	252-925-9411	S	842	.2
199	Peoples Financial Corp (Biloxi Mississippi)—*Chevis C Swetman*	152 Lameuse St, Biloxi MS 39530	228-435-5511	P	840	.2
200	Citizens Bank (Flint Michigan)—*Cathleen Nash*	328 S Saginaw St, Flint MI 48502		S	838*	.1
201	Monarch Financial Holdings Inc *Brad Schwartz*	1101 Executive Blvd, Chesapeake VA 23320	757-389-5111	P	826	.5
202	Citizens Holding Co—*Greg L McKee*	PO Box 209, Philadelphia MS 39350	601-656-4692	P	818	N/A
203	Citizens Bank of Farmington—*Sam J Butler*	PO Box 4140, Farmington NM 87499	505-599-0100	R	815*	.1
204	Bank of the Commonwealth—*Edward J Woodard Jr*	PO Box 1177, Norfolk VA 23501	757-446-6920	S	807*	.2
205	Horizon Trust and Investment Management—*Craig M Dwight*	515 Franklin Sq, Michigan City IN 46360	219-874-9318	S	802*	.3
206	Community Bank Shares of Indiana Inc—*James D Rickard*	PO Box 939, New Albany IN 47151	812-981-7345	P	802	.2
207	Juniata Valley Bank	PO Box 66, Mifflintown PA 17059	717-436-8211	S	801*	.3
208	Boston Private Bank and Trust Co—*Mark Thompson*	Ten Post Office Sq, Boston MA 02109	617-912-1900	S	796*	.3
209	Central Valley Community Bancorp—*Daniel J Doyle*	7100 N Financial Dr, Fresno CA 93720	559-298-1775	P	778	.2
210	Oxford Bank and Trust (Addison Illinois)—*Bruce Glawe*	PO Box 129, Addison IL 60101	630-629-5000	S	777*	.2
211	Associated Bank Milwaukee—*Phillip B Flynn*	401 E Kilbourn Ave, Milwaukee WI 53202	414-271-1786	S	767	N/A
212	West Des Moines State Bank	PO Box 65020, West Des Moines IA 50265	515-222-2300	S	766*	.1
213	Auburn National Bancorporation Inc—*EL Spencer Jr*	PO Drawer 3110, Auburn AL 36831	334-821-9200	P	764	.2
214	North Community Bank—*Peter A Fasseas*	3639 N Broadway, Chicago IL 60613	773-244-7000	S	762*	.1
215	Consumers National Bank	PO Box 256, Minerva OH 44657	330-868-7701	S	758*	.1
216	Parke Bancorp Inc—*Vito S Pantilione*	PO Box 40, Sewell NJ 08080	856-256-2500	P	757	.1
217	California United Bank—*David I Rainer*	15821 Ventura Blvd Ste, Encino CA 91436	818-257-7700	P	756	.1
218	Lebanon Citizens National Bank—*Steve P Foster*	PO Box 59, Lebanon OH 45036	513-932-1414	S	751*	.3
219	Bank of Lancaster—*Austin L Roberts III*	PO Box 1869, Kilmarnock VA 22482	804-435-1171	R	748*	.1
220	Meridian Bank—*Scott Schafer*	PO Box 6630, Peoria AZ 85385	602-636-4939	R	747*	.1
221	Jefferson Bank and Trust Co (St Louis Missouri)—*John L Dulle*	2301 Market St, Saint Louis MO 63103	314-621-0100	S	742*	.1
222	Texas Independent Bank—*Michael O'rourke*	PO Box 560528, Dallas TX 75356	972-650-6000	R	736*	.3
223	First Commercial Bank (Birmingham Alabama)—*Nelson Bean*	800 Shades Creek Pkwy, Birmingham AL 35209	205-868-4954	S	734*	.3
224	Bank of the Orient—*Ernet Go*	PO Box 2489, San Francisco CA 94126	415-338-0831	S	732*	.3
225	Washington First International Bank—*W Elizabeth Huang*	9709 3rd Ave NE, Seattle WA 98115	206-525-8118	R	717*	.1
226	Athens First Bank and Trust Co—*J William Douglas*	150 W Hancock Ave, Athens GA 30601	706-357-7070	S	716*	.3
227	First Independent Bank—*William J Firstenburg*	PO Box 8904, Vancouver WA 98668	360-699-4200	S	699*	.4
228	Carolina Bank Holdings Inc—*Robert T Braswell*	PO Box 10209, Greensboro NC 27404	336-288-1898	P	696	.2
229	Columbia Bank (Columbia Maryland)—*John M Bond Jr*	7168 Columbia Gateway, Columbia MD 21046	410-730-5000	S	695*	.3
230	Community National Bank (Derby Vermont)	PO Box 259, Derby VT 05829	802-334-7915	S	684*	.1
231	Jersey Shore State Bank—*Richard A Grafmyre*	300 Market St, Williamsport PA 17701	570-322-1111	S	676	N/A
232	Community Partners Bancorp—*William D Moss*	1250 Hwy 35 S, Middletown NJ 07748	732-706-9009	P	675	.1
233	Bank of Wisconsin Dells—*Jon B Bernander*	PO Box 490, Wisconsin Dells WI 53965	608-253-1111	R	672*	.1
234	American Bank of St Paul	1578 University Ave W, Saint Paul MN 55104	651-628-2661	R	668*	.2
235	NorStates Bank—*Fred Abdula*	PO Box 39, Waukegan IL 60079	847-244-6000	S	666	N/A
236	Banknorth Connecticut—*John Patrick*	2461 Main St, Glastonbury CT 06033	860-652-3232	D	663*	.1
237	WesBanco Bank South Hills—*Paul Limbert*	PO Box 2574, Charleston WV 25329	304-345-0670	D	660*	.1
238	Kentucky Bancshares Inc—*Louis Prichard*	PO Box 157, Paris KY 40362	859-987-1795	P	659	.2
239	Bank of the Sierra	PO Box 1930, Porterville CA 93257	559-782-4900	S	650	.3
240	Busey Bank—*Van Dukeman*	PO Box 17430, Urbana IL 61803	217-365-4544	S	649*	.3
241	Hawthorn Bank (Clinton Missouri)—*James E Smith*	PO Box 646, Clinton MO 64735	660-885-2241	S	648*	.1
242	Baylake Bank—*Michale Gilson* Kewaunee County Banc-Shares Inc	PO Box 9, Sturgeon Bay WI 54235	920-743-5551	S	646	.1
243	Bank of the Pacific—*John VanDijk*	PO Box 1826, Aberdeen WA 98520	360-533-8870	S	644*	.2
244	First State Bank of East Detroit—*David Harris*	24300 Little Mack Ave, Saint Clair Shores MI 48080	586-775-5000	S	644*	.2

Rank	Company Name—*Executive Officer*	Address, City, State, Zip	Phone	Type	Fin	Empls
245	International Bank of Commerce—*Dennis Nixon*	1200 San Bernardo Ave, Laredo TX 78042	956-722-7611	S	642*	.2
246	Albany Bank and Trust NA	2815 Meredyth Dr, Albany GA 31707	229-446-2265	S	642*	.1
247	Graystone Tower Bank	PO Box 8, Greencastle PA 17225	717-597-2137	S	641*	.1
248	Mid Penn Bancorp Inc—*Rory G Ritrievi*	349 Union St, Millersburg PA 17061	717-692-2133	P	638	.2
249	Tamalpais Bank—*Mark Garwood*	630 Las Gallinas Ave, San Rafael CA 94903	415-454-1212	S	636*	.1
250	Commerce Bank and Trust Co (Worcester Massachusetts)—*Brian W Thompson*	PO Box 15020, Worcester MA 01615	508-797-6842	R	627*	.2
251	New Century Bancorp Inc—*William L Hedgepeth II*	PO Box 1988, Dunn NC 28335	910-892-7080	P	627	.1
252	Rome Savings Bank—*Charles M Sprock*	100 W Dominick St, Rome NY 13440	315-336-7300	S	623*	.1
253	MetroBank NA (Houston Texas)—*George M Lee*	9600 Bellaire Blvd Ste, Houston TX 77036	713-776-3876	S	622*	.1
254	PSB Holdings Inc—*Peter W Knitt*	PO Box 1686, Wausau WI 54401	715-842-2191	P	621	.1
255	Heritage Bank (Longview Washington)	PO Box 1518, Longview WA 98632	360-423-9800	D	619*	.1
256	Sunwest Bank—*Glen Gray*	17542 E 17th St Ste 20, Tustin CA 92780	714-730-4441	P	617	.1
257	Platte Valley State Bank and Trust Co—*Mark Sutko*	PO Box 430, Kearney NE 68848	308-234-2424	S	615*	.1
258	CCFNB Bancorp Inc—*Lance O Diehl*	232 East St, Bloomsburg PA 17815	570-784-4400	P	614	.2
259	Truman Bank—*Robert J Minkler Sr*	8151 Clayton Rd, Saint Louis MO 63117	314-383-5555	R	614*	.1
260	United Bank and Trust Co (Versailles Kentucky)—*Paul Edwards*	PO Box 89, Versailles KY 40383		S	614	<.1
261	Associated Bank	130 E Randolph St Bldg, Chicago IL 60601	312-861-1000	S	612*	.1
262	Chemung Canal Trust Co—*Ronald Bentley*	PO Box 1522, Elmira NY 14902	607-737-3711	S	607*	.1
263	Bank of Marion—*Raymond Altmix*	300 Tower Sq, Marion IL 62959	618-997-4341	R	603*	.1
264	Fauquier Bankshares Inc—*Randy Kent Ferrell*	PO Box 561, Warrenton VA 20188	540-347-2700	P	598	.2
265	Private Bank of California—*David R Misch*	10100 Santa Monica Blv, Los Angeles CA 90067	310-286-0710	P	597	<.1
266	Union Planters Bank of Louisiana—*Danny Montichello*	PO Box 2710, Baton Rouge LA 70821	225-763-2411	S	594*	.2
267	Village Bank and Trust Financial Corp—*Thomas W Winfree*	15521 Midlothian Tnpk, Midlothian VA 23113	804-897-3900	P	592	.2
268	Jefferson State Bank (San Antonio Texas)—*Richard Petitt*	PO Box 5190, San Antonio TX 78201	210-734-4311	R	590*	.2
269	First Internet Bancorp—*David B Becker*	9200 Keystone Crossing, Indianapolis IN 46240		P	585	.1
270	Fidelity Deposit and Discount Bank—*Daniel Santaniello*	101 S Blakely St, Dunmore PA 18512	570-342-8281	S	575*	.2
271	Alliance Bank Corp—*Thomas A Young Jr*	12735 Shoppes Ln, Fairfax VA 22033	703-631-6411	S	572*	.1
272	Community Bank of Florida—*Robert L Epling*	PO Box 900400, Homestead FL 33090	305-245-2211	R	569*	.2
273	Northeast Bank—*Thomas Beck*	77 Broadway St NE, Minneapolis MN 55413	612-379-8811	S	562*	.1
274	Rockland Trust Co—*Christopher Oddleifson*	8 N Main St Ste 301, Attleboro MA 02703	508-223-3318	S	559*	.2
275	Waccamaw Bankshares Inc—*Geoffrey Hopkins*	PO Box 2009, Whiteville NC 28472	910-641-0044	P	559	N/A
276	Citizens Bank of Clovis—*Kent Carruthers*	PO Box 1629, Clovis NM 88102	575-769-1911	R	554*	.1
277	Lafayette Bank and Trust Co (Lafayette Indiana)—*Tony Albrecht*	PO Box 1130, Lafayette IN 47902	765-423-7170	S	553*	.2
278	Nexity Bank—*Greg L Lee*	3500 Blue Lake Dr Ste, Birmingham AL 35243		S	552*	.1
279	Liberty Bank and Trust Co—*Alden J McDonald Jr*	PO Box 60131, New Orleans LA 70160	504-240-5149	S	550	.2
280	Cedar Rapids Bank and Trust Co—*Larry J Helling* QCR Holdings Inc	500 1st Ave NE Ste 100, Cedar Rapids IA 52401	319-862-2728	S	550	.1
281	New Washington State Bank—*Patrick Glotzback*	402 E Main St, New Washington IN 47162	812-293-3321	R	546*	.1
282	Coastal Bank and Trust—*Thomas Carter*	PO Box 12966, Pensacola FL 32591	850-436-7800	S	544*	.2
283	Vectra Bank—*Bruce Alexander*	2000 S Colorado Blvd S, Denver CO 80222		S	543*	.2
284	Diméco Inc—*Gary C Beilman*	PO Box 509, Honesdale PA 18431	570-253-1902	P	542	.1
285	Dime Bank—*Gary C Beilman* Dimeco Inc	PO Box 509, Honesdale PA 18431	570-253-1902	S	542	.1
286	Norwood Financial Corp—*Lewis J Critelli*	PO Box 269, Honesdale PA 18431	570-253-1455	P	537	.1
287	First Capital Bancorp Inc (Glen Allen Virginia)—*John Presley*	4222 Cox Rd Ste 200, Glen Allen VA 23060	804-273-1160	P	536	.1
288	Mercantile Trust and Savings Bank—*Ted Awerkant*	PO Box 3455, Quincy IL 62305	217-223-7300	S	529*	.2
289	First Community Bank of Joliet First Community Financial Partners Inc	2801 Black Rd, Joliet IL 60435	815-725-0123	S	529*	.1
290	Premier Valley Bank—*J Mike McGowan*	8355 N Fresno St Ste 1, Fresno CA 93720	559-438-2002	P	522	<.1
291	Big Sky Western Bank—*Don J Chery*	4150 Valley Commons Dr, Bozeman MT 59718	406-587-2922	S	522*	.1
292	PrimeSouth Bank—*Nick Taylor*	3473 Hwy 84 W, Blackshear GA 31516	912-449-6685	R	522*	.1
293	Union Bankshares Inc—*Kenneth Gibbons*	PO Box 667, Morrisville VT 05661	802-888-6600	P	514	.2
294	Atlantic Capital Bank—*Douglas L Williams*	3280 Peachtree Rd Ste, Atlanta GA 30305	404-995-5846	R	513*	.1
295	First Guaranty Bank—*Mike Sharp*	PO Box 2009, Hammond LA 70404	985-345-7685	R	512*	.2
296	Empire Bank—*Mike Williamson*	1800 S Glenstone, Springfield MO 65804	417-881-3100	S	511	.3
297	Mid-Wisconsin Financial Services Inc—*James F Warsaw*	PO Box 90, Medford WI 54451	715-748-8300	P	509	.2
298	Community First Bancorp—*Frederick D Shepherd Jr*	3685 Blue Ridge Blvd, Walhalla SC 29691	864-638-2105	P	506	.1
299	First Internet Bank of Indiana—*David B Becker* First Internet Bancorp	PO Box 80508, Indianapolis IN 46280	317-532-7900	S	502	.1
300	FirstBank Southwest—*Donald Ellis*	PO Box 32552, Amarillo TX 79120	806-355-9661	S	501*	.2
301	First Farmers Bank and Trust—*Gene Miles*	PO Box 690, Converse IN 46919	765-395-3316	S	500*	.2
302	Mid Penn Bank Mid Penn Bancorp Inc	349 Union St, Millersburg PA 17061	717-692-5000	S	499*	.1
303	Libertyville Bank and Trust Co—*J Bert Carstens*	1200 South Milwaukee A, Libertyville IL 60048	847-367-6800	R	499*	.1
304	American Security Bank—*David Blankenhorn*	1401 Dove St Ste 100, Newport Beach CA 92660	949-440-5200	R	497*	.1
305	WesBanco Bank (Fairmont West Virginia)—*Paul M Limbert*	PO Box 115, Fairmont WV 26555		S	496	.3
306	First Banking Center-Burlington—*John Smith*	400 Milwaukee Ave, Burlington WI 53105	262-763-3581	S	496*	.2
307	Georgia-Carolina Bancshares Inc—*Remer Y Brinson III*	PO Box 15148, Augusta GA 30919	706-731-6600	P	495	.2
308	Wheatland Bank (Naperville Illinois)—*Michael Sykes*	2244 95th St, Naperville IL 60564	630-848-8080	R	491	<.1
309	Clinton Savings Bank—*Robert J Paulhus Jr*	200 Church St, Clinton MA 01510	978-365-3700	S	487*	.1
310	Iowa State Bank and Trust Co—*Michael Hubbard*	PO Box 1700, Iowa City IA 52244	319-356-5800	S	486*	.2
311	Southern Commercial Bank—*Vince Coleman*	5515 S Grand Blvd, Saint Louis MO 63111	314-481-6800	S	481*	.2
312	ChoiceOne Financial Services Inc—*James A Bosserd*	PO Box 186, Sparta MI 49345	616-887-7366	P	481	.2
313	Rocky Mountain Bank—*Danny Skarda* Heartland Financial USA Inc	2615 King Ave W, Billings MT 59102	406-656-3140	S	477*	.4
314	Bank of Nashville—*William Nigh*	PO Box 198986, Nashville TN 37219	615-271-2000	S	477*	.1
315	Southeastern Bank—*R Daniel Blanton*	PO Box 455, Darien GA 31305	912-437-4141	S	473*	.2
316	Peoples Bank (Newton North Carolina)—*Tony W Wolfe*	PO Box 467, Newton NC 28658	828-466-1765	S	469	.2
317	First Bank and Trust—*James Dierberg*	11901 Olive Blvd, Creve Coeur MO 63141	314-995-8700	S	469*	.2
318	Chemical Bank Key State—*David B Ramaker*	PO Box 820, Owosso MI 48867	989-723-6767	S	469*	.1
319	First State Bank of Rush City—*Rachel Goodell*	PO Box 604, Rush City MN 55069	320-358-3600	R	465*	.1
320	InterBank (Oklahoma City Oklahoma)—*John Osborne*	PO Box 12669, Oklahoma City OK 73157	405-782-4200	R	461*	.1
321	SMB and T Financial Services Inc—*John H Castle* Southern Michigan Bank and Trust	51 W Pearl St, Coldwater MI 49036	517-279-5500	S	458*	.1
322	Bank of St Petersburg—*Susan Martinez*	777 Pasadena Ave S, Saint Petersburg FL 33707	727-347-3132	R	458*	.1
323	CSB Bancorp Inc—*Eddie Steiner*	PO Box 232, Millersburg OH 44654	330-674-9015	P	457	.1
324	Central Valley Comunity Bank—*Daniel Doyle* Central Valley Community Bancorp	600 Pollasky Ave, Clovis CA 93612	559-323-3480	S	457*	.1

Note: An asterisk (*) indicates an estimated financial figure. The company type code used is as follows: R = Private, P = Public, S = Private Subsidiary, B = Public Subsidiary, D = Division, J = Joint Venture, I = Investment Fund.

COMPANY RANKINGS BY SALES WITHIN 4-DIGIT SIC

Rank	Company Name—*Executive Officer*	Address, City, State, Zip	Phone	Type	Fin	Empls
325	Trust One Bank—*Terence Lewis*	1715 Aaron Brenner Dr, Memphis TN 38120	901-759-3500	D	457*	.1
326	Plaza Bank—*Peter Fasseas*	7460 W Irving Park Rd, Norridge IL 60634	708-456-3440	R	456*	.1
327	Virginia Heritage Bank—*David P Summers*	11166 Fairfax Blvd Ste, Fairfax VA 22030	703-359-4100	P	453	N/A
328	Cambridge Trust Co—*Joseph V Roller II*	1336 Massachusetts Ave, Cambridge MA 02138	617-876-5500	S	453*	.2
329	Citizens Bank of Northern California	305 Railroad Ave Ste 1, Nevada City CA 95959	530-478-6000	S	452*	.1
	Citizens Bancorp (Nevada City California)					
330	Skagit State Bank—*Cheryl R Bishop*	PO Box 285, Burlington WA 98233	360-755-0411	R	450*	.2
331	Firstbank-West Branch—*Thomas R Sullivan*	502 W Houghton Ave, West Branch MI 48661	989-345-7900	S	449*	.1
332	Jackson County Bank (Seymour Indiana)—*David M Geis*	125 S Chestnut St, Seymour IN 47274	812-522-3607	S	445*	.2
333	Artisan's Bank—*Stephen C Nelson*	2961 Centerville Rd, Wilmington DE 19808	302-658-6881	R	445*	.2
334	First South Bank (Spartanburg South Carolina)—*Joyce Miller*	1450 John B White Sr B, Spartanburg SC 29306	864-595-0455	S	443*	.1
335	Idaho Independent Bank—*Jack W Gustavel*	401 W Front St, Boise ID 83702	208-947-1160	P	442	.2
336	Nevada State Bank—*Dallas Haun*	PO Box 990, Las Vegas NV 89125	702-383-0009	R	440	.3
337	BankTennessee—*Jim Rout*	1125 W Poplar Ave, Collierville TN 38017	901-854-0854	R	438*	.1
338	St Johns Bank and Trust Co—*Jack Burleson*	8924 Saint Charles Roc, Saint Louis MO 63114	314-428-1000	R	436*	.2
339	Farmers and Merchants Trust Co—*William E Snell Jr*	20 S Main St, Chambersburg PA 17201	717-264-6116	S	433*	.2
340	Peoples Bank and Trust of Lincoln County—*David Thompson*	PO Box G, Troy MO 63379	636-528-7001	R	430*	.2
341	Whidbey Island Bank—*Jack Wagner*	450 SW Bayshore Dr, Oak Harbor WA 98277	360-679-3121	S	426*	.1
342	Bank of Walnut Creek	PO Box 8080, Walnut Creek CA 94596	925-932-5353	S	425*	.2
343	River City Bank—*Steve Fleming*	2485 Natomas Park Dr, Sacramento CA 95833	916-567-2600	S	420*	.2
344	Bank of Louisiana—*G Harrison Scott*	300 St Charles Ave, New Orleans LA 70130	504-592-0600	R	417	.1
345	State Bank of Cross Plains—*Jan Hogan*	PO Box 218, Cross Plains WI 53528	608-798-3961	R	416	N/A
346	WesBanco of Parkersburg—*Paul Limbert*	PO Box 1427, Parkersburg WV 26102		S	413*	.2
347	Centenial Bank (Conway Arkansas)	620 Chestnut St, Conway AR 72032	501-328-4663	S	413*	.1
	Home BancShares Inc					
348	Penn Security Bank and Trust Co—*Craig W Best*	150 N Washington Ave, Scranton PA 18503	570-346-7741	S	408*	.2
349	Casey State Bank—*BRAD WOLFE*	PO Box 337, Casey IL 62420	217-932-2136	R	408*	.1
350	Harris Trust Bank of Arizona	6720 N Scottsdale Rd S, Scottsdale AZ 85255	480-951-4900	S	407*	.1
	Harris Trust and Savings Bank					
351	Marine Bank—*Charles J Ponicki*	2323 N Mayfair Rd, Wauwatosa WI 53226	414-607-6000	S	404*	.1
352	Citizens Bancorp(Corvalis Oregon)—*WIlliam V Humpreys*	PO Box 30, Corvallis OR 97339	541-752-5161	R	404	N/A
353	Richland Trust Co—*David Gooch*	3 N Main St, Mansfield OH 44902	419-525-8700	S	402*	.1
354	Farmers Bank and Trust Co (Blytheville Arkansas)—*Randy Scott*	PO Box 688, Blytheville AR 72316	870-763-8101	S	402*	.1
355	First Arkansas Bank and Trust Co—*Larry Wilson*	600 W Main, Jacksonville AR 72076	501-982-4511	R	401	.2
356	Flagship Bank and Trust Co—*Jim Garvey*	120 Front St, Worcester MA 01608	508-890-5199	S	400*	.1
357	Lafayette Ambassador Bank—*Gerald A Nau*	PO Box 25091, Lehigh Valley PA 18002	610-250-2350	S	398*	.2
358	First United Security Bank (Thomasville Alabama)—*R Terry Phillips*	131 W Front St, Thomasville AL 36784	334-636-5424	S	396*	.2
359	Pascack Community Bank—*Bruce M Meisel*	21 Jefferson Ave, Westwood NJ 07675	201-722-4722	S	396*	.1
360	BankAnnapolis Inc	1000 Bestgate Rd, Annapolis MD 21401	410-224-4455	S	395	.1
361	Citizens Deposit Bank and Trust Co—*James Hay*	10 2nd St, Vanceburg KY 41179	606-796-3001	S	392*	.1
	Premier Financial Bancorp Inc					
362	First Northern Bank of Dixon—*Owen Onsum*	11 W Court St Rm A, Woodland CA 95695	530-661-6000	S	390*	.1
363	Redlands Centennial Bank	218 E State St, Redlands CA 92373	909-798-3611	S	388*	.1
364	Carrollton Bancorp—*Robert A Altieri*	7151 Columbia Gateway, Columbia MD 21046	410-312-5400	P	387	.1
365	PrivateBank—*Larry Richman*	1401 S Brentwood Blvd, Saint Louis MO 63144	314-301-2200	S	385*	.1
	PrivateBancorp Inc					
366	Bay Bank and Trust Co—*Clay Lewis*	PO Box 59350, Panama City FL 32412	850-769-3333	R	382*	.1
367	Citizens Bank—*William Humphreys Sr*	PO Box 30, Corvallis OR 97339	541-752-5161	S	381	N/A
	Citizens Bancorp(Corvalis Oregon)					
368	North Jersey Community Bank—*Frank Sorrentino III*	301 Sylvan Ave, Englewood Cliffs NJ 07632	201-816-8900	R	378*	.1
369	Premier Bank (Maplewood Minnesota)—*Mark Novitzki*	2866 White Bear Ave N, Maplewood MN 55109	651-777-7700	R	371*	.1
370	PremierWest Bank (Elk Grove California)	9340 E Stockton Blvd, Elk Grove CA 95624	916-685-6546	S	370*	.1
371	Calvin B Taylor Banking Co—*Raymond M Thompson*	24 N Main St, Berlin MD 21811	410-641-1700	R	369*	.1
372	First Century Bank—*Frank Wilkinson*	PO Box 1559, Bluefield WV 24701	304-325-8181	S	367*	.3
373	United Security Bank (Fresno California)—*Dennis Woods*	2126 Inyo St, Fresno CA 93721	559-248-4930	S	367	.1
374	WSB Financial Group Inc—*Donald F Cox Jr*	607 Pacific Ave, Bremerton WA 98337	360-876-7834	P	365	.1
375	Bank of Georgia (Peachtree Georgia)	100 Westpark Dr, Peachtree City GA 30269	770-631-9488	S	363	.1
376	Metcalf Bank—*Thomas B Fitzsimmons*	609 N 291 Hwy, Lee's Summit MO 64086	816-525-5300	S	359*	.1
377	Benchmark Community Bank—*Michael O Walker*	PO Box 569, Kenbridge VA 23944	434-676-8444	S	356*	.1
378	World's Foremost Bank—*Joseph M Friebe*	1 Cabela Dr, Sidney NE 69160	308-254-5505	S	354*	.3
379	Independent Bank South Michigan—*Edward B Swanson*	PO Box 536, Leslie MI 49251	517-589-8222	S	353*	.1
380	Summit State Bank—*Thomas Duryea*	PO Box 6188, Santa Rosa CA 95406	707-568-6000	P	351	.1
381	American Banking Co—*Ronnie Marchant*	225 S Main St, Moultrie GA 31768	229-985-2222	S	348*	.1
382	Citizens Bank (Kilgore Texas)—*Sammy York*	PO Box 1700, Kilgore TX 75663	903-984-8671	S	340*	.1
383	Atlantic Stewardship Bank—*Paul Van Ostenbridge*	630 Godwin Ave, Midland Park NJ 07432	201-444-7100	S	340*	.1
384	United Bank and Trust (Tecumseh Michigan)—*Joe Williams*	PO Box 248, Tecumseh MI 49286	517-423-8373	S	339*	.2
385	Commonwealth Business Bank—*Joanne Kim*	5055 Wilshire Blvd Ste, Los Angeles CA 90036	323-988-3000	P	336	N/A
386	Bank of Agriculture and Commerce—*William R Trezza*	2001-2021 W March Ln, Stockton CA 95207	209-473-6800	R	336*	.1
387	National Bank and Trust Co—*John Limbert*	PO Box 711, Wilmington OH 45177	937-382-1441	S	336*	.1
388	Citizens Trust Bank—*James E Young*	PO Box 4485, Atlanta GA 30302	404-575-8400	S	332*	.2
389	Antelope Valley Bank—*Jack Seefus*	831 W Lancaster Blvd, Lancaster CA 93534	661-945-4511	D	331*	.2
	California Bank and Trust					
390	Somerset Hills Bancorp—*Stewart E McClure Jr*	155 Morristown Rd, Bernardsville NJ 07924	908-221-0100	P	329	.1
391	STAR Financial Bank Columbia City—*David Smith*	105 Frontage Rd, Columbia City IN 46725	260-248-6063	S	328*	.1
392	Citizens Bancorp (Nevada City California)—*Gary D Gall*	PO Box 1420, Nevada City CA 95959	530-478-6000	P	327	.1
393	Plumas Bank—*Douglas Biddle*	35 S Lindan Ave, Quincy CA 95971	530-283-7305	R	326*	.2
394	American Bank and Trust Co—*Ronnie Lashute*	PO Box 1819, Opelousas LA 70571	337-948-3056	R	324*	.1
395	MainSource Bank—*Archie M Brown*	201 N Broadway, Greensburg IN 47240	812-663-4711	S	321*	.2
396	Bank of Springfield—*Tom Marantz*	2600 Stevenson Dr, Springfield IL 62703	217-529-5555	R	321*	.1
397	Bank of Charles Town—*Robert F Baronner Jr*	PO Box 906, Charles Town WV 25414	304-725-8431	S	321*	.1
	Potomac Bancshares Inc					
398	Bank of Washington—*LB Eckelkamp Jr*	PO Box 377, Washington MO 63090	636-239-7831	R	321	.1
399	Firstbank-Mount Pleasant—*Thomas P Sullivan*	102 S Main St, Mount Pleasant MI 48858	989-773-2600	S	321*	.1
400	United American Bank—*John C Schrup*	101 S Ellsworth Ave, San Mateo CA 94401	650-579-1500	P	321	<.1
401	Sonoma Valley Bank—*Sean Cutting*	202 W Napa St, Sonoma CA 95476	707-935-3200	S	318*	.1
402	Commercial and Savings Bank of Millersburg Ohio—*Rick L Ginther*	PO Box 232, Millersburg OH 44654	330-674-9015	S	317	.1
	CSB Bancorp Inc					

Rank	Company Name—*Executive Officer*	Address, City, State, Zip	Phone	Type	Fin	Empls
403	Redding Bank of Commerce—*Patrick J Moty*	1951 Churn Creek Rd, Redding CA 96002	530-224-3333	S	316*	.1
404	Marine Bank Springfield—*Roger Chandler*	3120 Robbins Rd, Springfield IL 62704	217-726-0600	R	314*	.2
405	California Republic Bank—*Jon Wilcox*	1400 Newport Center Dr, Newport Beach CA 92660	949-270-9700	P	314	<.1
406	Bryn Mawr Trust Co—*Joyce Johnson*	801 W Lancaster Ave, Bryn Mawr PA 19010	610-581-4910	S	313*	.2
407	Peoples Community Bank—*Robert K Bailey III*	PO Box 306, Montross VA 22520	804-493-8031	R	313*	.1
408	M and F Bancorp Inc—*Kim D Saunders*	PO Box 19322, Durham NC 27702	919-687-7800	P	312	.1
409	Chemical Bank West—*David B Ramaker*	PO Box 569, Midland MI 48640		S	312*	.1
410	Madison Bohemian Savings Bank—*Lawrence Williams*	1920 Rock Spring Rd, Forest Hill MD 21050	410-420-9600	R	311*	.1
411	Mason State Bank—*Timothy Gaylord*	322 S Jefferson St, Mason MI 48854	517-676-0500	S	311*	.1
412	Enfield Federal Savings and Loan Assoc—*David J O'Connor*	PO Box 1279, Enfield CT 06083	860-253-5200	S	308	.1
413	Beach Business Bank—*Robert M Franko*	1230 Rosecrans Ave Ste, Manhattan Beach CA 90266	310-536-2260	P	305	<.1
414	Industrial Bank NA—*B Doyle Mitchell Jr*	4812 Georgia Ave NW, Washington DC 20011	202-722-2000	S	304*	.2
415	Potomac Bancshares Inc—*Robert F Baronner Jr*	PO Box 906, Charles Town WV 25414	304-725-8431	P	304	.1
416	Habersham Bank	1151 Washington St N, Clarkesville GA 30523	706-778-1000	S	304*	.1
417	Killbuck Savings Bank—*Luther E Proper*	PO Box 407, Killbuck OH 44637	330-276-4881	S	304*	.1
418	Little Bank Inc—*Rob Jones*	804 Carey Rd, Kinston NC 28501	252-939-3900	P	299	.1
419	Harris Bank Woodstock—*Ellen M Costello*	PO Box 729, Woodstock IL 60098	815-338-3131	S	297*	<.1
420	First National Bank of Colorado—*Mark Driscoll*	PO Box 9032, Boulder CO 80301	303-443-9090	S	296*	.2
421	Bank of North Dakota—*Eric Hardmeyer*	PO Box 5509, Bismarck ND 58506	701-328-5600	R	294*	.1
422	Inland Bank and Trust—*Dan Goodwin*	2225 S Wolf Rd, Hillside IL 60162		S	294*	<.1
423	Pueblo Bank and Trust Co—*Bill Tandy*	PO Box 639, Pueblo CO 81002	719-545-1834	R	293*	.2
424	Commercial Bank (Thomasville Georgia)—*Tom Callaway*	101 S Crawford St, Thomasville GA 31792	229-226-3535	S	293*	.1
425	First Bank of San Luis Obispo—*George Leis*	995 Higuera St, San Luis Obispo CA 93406		S	293*	.1
426	NewDominion Bank—*C John Hipp III*	PO Box 37389, Charlotte NC 28237	704-943-5700	R	291	N/A
427	Callaway Bank—*Bruce T Harris*	PO Box 10, Fulton MO 65251	573-642-3322	R	291*	.1
428	First Bank (McComb Mississippi)—*James W Covington*	100 S Broadway, McComb MS 39648	601-684-2231	S	291*	.1
429	First Bank (Florissant Missouri)—*Terrance M McCarthy* First Bank and Trust	4090 N Hwy 67, Florissant MO 63034	314-837-9032	S	291*	<.1
430	Syringa Bank—*Scott Gibson*	1299 N Orchard, Boise ID 83706	208-322-6363	S	290*	.1
431	County Bank Corp—*Bruce J Cady*	PO Box 250, Lapeer MI 48446	810-664-2977	P	289	.1
432	Bank of Castile—*James Fulmer*	PO Box 129, Castile NY 14427	585-493-2576	S	288*	.2
433	IBERIABANK fsb—*Daryl G Byrd*	5800 R St, Little Rock AR 72207	501-661-7700	S	287*	.2
434	First Southern Bank (Florence Alabama)—*Jack Johnson*	PO Box 777, Florence AL 35631		S	287*	<.1
435	Skylands Community Bank—*Steve Miller*	PO Box 507, Hackettstown NJ 07840	908-850-9010	S	285*	.1
436	Summit Bank (Oakland California)—*Shirley W Nelson*	2969 Broadway, Oakland CA 94611	510-839-8800	S	285*	.1
437	First State Bank and Trust Co—*David Durland*	3650 Inner Perimeter R, Valdosta GA 31602	229-242-5725	D	283*	.1
438	First State Bank and Trust Company Inc—*Gordan Waller*	PO Box 18, Caruthersville MO 63830	573-333-1700	R	281*	.1
439	Connecticut Bank and Trust Co—*David A Lentini*	58 State House Sq, Hartford CT 06103	860-246-5200	P	281	.1
440	Heritage Bankshares Inc (Norfolk Virginia)—*Michael S Ives*	150 Granby St Ste 150, Norfolk VA 23510	757-648-1700	P	280	.1
441	Alpine Bank of Illinois—*Bill Roop*	PO Box 6086, Rockford IL 61125	815-398-6500	R	277*	.1
442	Farmers and Savings Bank—*James S Lingenfielder*	120 N Water St, Loudonville OH 44842	419-994-4115	D	277*	.1
443	Portage Commerce Bank—*Paul Ballard*	PO Box 727, Portage MI 49081	269-323-2200	S	275*	<.1
444	Jefferson Security Bank—*K Stephen Morris*	PO Box 35, Shepherdstown WV 25443	304-876-9000	P	275	.1
445	Farmers and Merchants Bank (Granite Quarry North Carolina)—*Paul Fisher* F and M Financial Corp	PO Box 307, Granite Quarry NC 28072	704-279-7291	S	274*	.1
446	Premier Bank—*David W Caffrey*	15301 W 87th St Pkwy, Lenexa KS 66219	913-888-8490	R	269*	.1
447	Hopewell Valley Community Bank—*James Hyman*	4 Rte 31 S, Pennington NJ 08534	609-466-2900	P	265	<.1
448	Bank of Alameda—*Stephen G Andrews*	PO Drawer F, Alameda CA 94501	510-748-8000	S	264	.1
449	Burke Group Inc—*Patrick Burke*	10 East St, Honeoye Falls NY 14472	585-624-5500	S	260*	.1
450	Harbor Bank of Maryland—*Joseph Haskins Jr*	25 W Fayette St, Baltimore MD 21201	410-528-1801	S	257*	.1
451	First Bank of Missouri—*Kenneth W Hollander*	7001 N Oak Trfy, Gladstone MO 64118	816-436-1900	R	255*	.1
452	Alliance Bank of Arizona—*Jim Lundy*	4646 E Van Buren St St, Phoenix AZ 85008	602-797-3600	S	253*	.1
453	Xenith Bankshares Inc—*T Gaylon Layfield III*	One James Center 901 E, Richmond VA 23219	804-433-2200	P	251	.1
454	Bank of Tuscaloosa—*Mark S Sullivan*	PO Box 2508, Tuscaloosa AL 35403	205-345-4033	S	251*	.1
455	California Community Bank—*Larry D Hartwig*	800 W Valley Pkwy Ste, Escondido CA 92025	760-888-1100	P	250	<.1
456	Cardinal Bankshares Corp—*R Leon Moore*	PO Box 215, Floyd VA 24091	540-745-4191	P	249	.1
457	Bank of Landisburg—*Thomas Cook*	PO Box 179, Landisburg PA 17040	717-789-3213	R	247*	<.1
458	Mayflower Bancorp Inc—*Edward M Pratt*	PO Box 311, Middleboro MA 02346	508-947-4343	P	247	.1
459	Four Oaks Bank and Trust Co—*Ayden R Lee* Four Oaks Fincorp Inc	PO Box 309, Four Oaks NC 27524	919-963-2177	S	245*	<.1
460	Buffalo FSB—*Paul Brunkhorst*	PO Box 1020, Buffalo WY 82834	307-684-5591	S	244*	<.1
461	First State Bank (Brazil Indiana)—*Donald E Smith*	18 N Walnut St, Brazil IN 47834	812-448-3357	S	244*	<.1
462	Park Avenue Bank (Valdosta Georgia)	PO Box 3730, Valdosta GA 31604	229-242-7758	S	243*	.1
463	BankTrust—*W Bibb Lamar Jr*	100 Saint Joseph St, Mobile AL 36602	251-431-7800	S	240*	.1
464	First Community Bank of Tifton—*John M Davis*	PO Box 8, Tifton GA 31793	229-382-3321	S	240*	<.1
465	Community Bank (Lancaster Ohio)—*Timothy L Kelly*	PO Box 280, Lancaster OH 43130	740-654-0900	D	239	<.1
466	Bank of O'Fallon—*Richard J Thoman*	PO Box 1626, O Fallon IL 62269	618-632-3595	R	239*	.1
467	Community Shores Bank Corp—*Heather D Brolick*	1030 W Norton Ave, Muskegon MI 49441	231-780-1800	P	238	.1
468	First Parke State Bank—*Donald E Smith*	1311 N Lincoln Rd, Rockville IN 47872	765-569-3171	S	238*	<.1
469	Heartland Bancshares Inc—*Steven L Bechman*	PO Box 469, Franklin IN 46131	317-738-3915	P	233	.1
470	Bank and Trust - Del Rio—*Sid Cauthorn*	PO Box 4010, Del Rio TX 78841	830-774-2555	R	233*	.1
471	Harris Bank Westchester—*Ellen Costello*	10500 W Cermak Rd, Westchester IL 60154	708-562-3100	S	233*	<.1
472	Independent Bankers' Bank of Florida—*James McKillop III*	615 Crescent Executive, Lake Mary FL 32746	407-541-1620	R	232*	.1
473	Advance Bank (Baltimore Maryland)—*John Hamilton*	4801 Seton Dr, Baltimore MD 21215	410-358-1700	R	231*	.1
474	Bank of Idaho—*Park Price*	399 N Capital Ave, Idaho Falls ID 83402	208-524-5500	R	228*	.1
475	Circle Bank—*Arthur Chatham*	1400A Grant Ave, Novato CA 94945	415-898-5400	S	227	<.1
476	Peoples Exchange Bank of Beattyville Kentucky—*Claude E Bentley*	P O Box 127, Beattyville KY 41311	606-464-3631	R	227*	.1
477	Renasant Bank—*Jack Johnson*	2177 Germantown, Germantown TN 38138	901-312-4000	S	226	.1
478	Firstbank of Alma—*Dale Peters*	311 Woodworth Ave, Alma MI 48801	989-463-3131	S	226	.2
479	Ireland Bank	PO Box 186, Malad City ID 83252	208-766-2211	S	226	.1
480	Heritage Community Bank—*Tim Jones*	1000 W Screven St, Quitman GA 31643	229-263-7525	S	226*	<.1
481	Pinnacle Bank (Jasper Alabama)—*Robert B Nolen Jr*	1811 2nd Ave, Jasper AL 35501	205-221-4111	S	225	.1
482	First Crawford State Bank—*Donald E Smith*	108 W Main St, Robinson IL 62454	618-544-8666	S	225*	<.1
483	Galena State Bank and Trust Co—*Andrew E Townsend* Heartland Financial USA Inc	PO Box 317, Galena IL 61036	815-777-0663	S	223*	.1
484	Puget Sound Bank—*Jim Mitchell*	10500 NE 8th St Ste 15, Bellevue WA 98004	425-455-2400	P	222	<.1
485	North Side Bank and Trust Co—*John A Coors*	4125 Hamilton Ave, Cincinnati OH 45223	513-542-7800	R	221*	.1

Note: An asterisk (*) indicates an estimated financial figure. The company type code used is as follows: R = Private, P = Public, S = Private Subsidiary, B = Public Subsidiary, D = Division, J = Joint Venture, I = Investment Fund.

COMPANY RANKINGS BY SALES WITHIN 4-DIGIT SIC

Rank	Company Name—*Executive Officer*	Address, City, State, Zip	Phone	Type	Fin	Empls
486	Commercial Bank (West Liberty Kentucky)—*Hank L Allen*	PO Box 635, West Liberty KY 41472	606-743-3195	R	219*	<.1
487	Grand Haven Bank—*Thomas Creswell*	333 Washington Ave, Grand Haven MI 49417	616-846-1930	S	219*	<.1
488	Union Bank Co—*Shawn McFarland*	PO Box 67, Columbus Grove OH 45830		S	218*	<.1
489	Simsbury Bank and Trust Co—*Martin J Geitz*	PO Box 248, Simsbury CT 06070	860-658-2265	S	217	.1
490	First American Bank (Vincennes Indiana)—*Mark A Schroeder*	101 N 3rd St, Vincennes IN 47591	812-882-4528	S	217*	.1
491	Colony Management Services Inc—*Paul W Williams*	PO Box 989, Fitzgerald GA 31750	229-426-6000	S	217*	<.1
492	Greenfield Banking Co—*James W Miller*	PO Box 587, Greenfield IN 46140	317-462-1431	S	216*	.1
493	Piedmont Community Bank—*R Drew Hulsey Jr*	110 Bill Conn Pkwy, Gray GA 31032	478-986-5900	R	214*	<.1
494	Redwood Capital Bank—*John E Dalby*	402 G St, Eureka CA 95501	707-444-9800	P	213	<.1
495	Charter Bank and Trust Co	PO Box 120, Columbus GA 31902	770-751-4780	S	213*	.1
496	Mesa Bank—*Gail Grace*	63 E Main St Ste 100, Mesa AZ 85201	480-649-5100	S	213*	<.1
497	VSB Bancorp Inc—*Raffaele Branca*	4142 Hylan Blvd, Staten Island NY 10308	718-979-1100	P	213	.1
498	Sea Island Bank—*D Wayne Akins Jr*	PO Box 30458, Sea Island GA 31561	912-489-8661	S	212*	.1
499	Bank of Santa Clarita—*James D Hicken*	23780 Magic Mountain P, Santa Clarita CA 91355	661-362-6000	P	210	<.1
500	Freedom Bank of Virginia—*Craig S Underhill*	502 Maple Ave W, Vienna VA 22180	703-667-4170	P	208	<.1
501	Wheatland Bank—*Susan Pittman Horton*	PO Box 960, Davenport WA 99122	509-725-0211	R	207*	.1
502	Centerbank (Milford Ohio)—*Stewart M Greenlee*	744 State Rte 28, Milford OH 45150	513-965-8505	R	206*	<.1
503	American Exchange Bank—*Donald Wells*	510 W Main St, Henryetta OK 74437	918-652-3321	R	206*	<.1
504	Alden State Bank—*Richard D Koelbl*	PO Box 238, Alden NY 14004	716-937-3381	R	205	.1
505	Orange County Business Bank NA—*JP Gough*	4675 MacArthur Ct Ste, Newport Beach CA 92660	949-221-0001	P	204	<.1
506	San Diego Trust Bank—*Michael Perry*	2550 5th Ave Ste 1010, San Diego CA 92103	619-230-6521	P	203	<.1
507	Cache Valley Bank—*J Gregg Miller*	101 N Main St, Logan UT 84321	435-753-3020	R	202*	<.1
508	Mechanics and Farmers Bank—*Kim D Saunders* M and F Bancorp Inc	2634 Durham Chapel Hil, Durham NC 27707	919-687-7800	S	201*	.1
509	Generations Bank—*Larry Goddard*	PO Box 26467, Overland Park KS 66225		S	201*	<.1
510	Redwood Bank—*Fred Jensen*	PO Box 2359, San Francisco CA 94126	415-788-3700	S	200	.1
511	M and I Bank South Central—*Mark Furlong*	205 N 2nd St, Watertown WI 53094	920-261-7102	S	198*	.1
512	Commercial Bank and Trust Company of Troup County—*Robert L Carmichael Jr*	200 N Greenwood St, LaGrange GA 30240	706-880-2200	S	195*	.1
513	Security Bank of California—*James A Robinson*	3403 10th St Ste 830, Riverside CA 92501		S	194*	.1
514	Valley State Bank—*Jim H Davis*	PO Box 1234, Russellville AL 35653	256-332-3600	R	194*	<.1
515	Phelps County Bank—*Bill Marshall*	718 N Pine St, Rolla MO 65401	573-364-5202	S	193*	.1
516	Royal Bank of Pennsylvania—*Robert Tabas*	732 Montgomery Ave, Narberth PA 19072	610-668-4700	S	193*	.1
517	Lake Forest Bank and Trust Co—*David Lee*	727 North Bank Ln, Lake Forest IL 60045	847-234-2882	S	193*	<.1
518	First Commercial Bank (Huntsville Alabama)—*Charles E Kettle*	PO Box 040002, Huntsville AL 35804	256-551-3300	S	192*	.1
519	Southwest Georgia Bank—*DeWitt Drew*	201 1st St SE, Moultrie GA 31768	229-985-1120	S	192*	.1
520	Pennsylvania State Bank—*Joseph Guyaux*	PO Box 487, Camp Hill PA 17011	717-730-1080	R	192	N/A
521	Capitol City Bank and Trust Co—*George G Andrews*	562 Lee St SW, Atlanta GA 30310	404-752-6067	S	189*	.1
522	Cornerstone Community Bank—*Paul A Foy*	2090 Wisconsin Ave, Grafton WI 53024	262-375-9150	R	187*	<.1
523	Blackhawk Bank and Trust—*W Gerard Huiskamp*	PO Box 1100, Milan IL 61264	309-787-4451	R	186*	.1
524	Eagle Bank (Glenwood Minnesota)—*Erick A Gandrud*	PO Box 217, Glenwood MN 56334	320-634-4545	R	185*	<.1
525	Central Virginia Bank	PO Box 39, Powhatan VA 23139	804-403-2000	S	184*	.1
526	Bayonne Community Bank—*Donald Mindiak*	104-110 Ave C, Bayonne NJ 07002	201-823-0700	S	183	<.1
527	Conestoga Bank—*Richard A Elko*	165 Pottstown Pike, Chester Springs PA 19425		R	183*	<.1
528	First South Bank (Washington North Carolina)—*Thomas A Vann*	PO Box 2047, Washington NC 27889	252-946-4178	S	183*	<.1
529	Paragon Bank and Trust—*Mark J Dewitt*	240 E 8th St, Holland MI 49423	616-394-9600	S	183*	<.1
530	Regions Bank Marion—*Mike Mathis*	402 S Washington St, Marion IN 46953	765-668-8111	S	182	.1
531	Professional Business Bank—*Mary Lynn Lenz*	199 S Los Robles Ave S, Pasadena CA 91101	626-395-7000	R	182*	<.1
532	Christiana Bank and Trust Co—*Zissimos A Frangopoulos*	3801 Kennett Pke, Greenville DE 19807	302-421-5800	D	181	.1
533	QCR Holdings Inc—*Douglas M Hultquist*	3551 7th St, Moline IL 61265	309-736-3584	P	180	.4
534	Peoples Bank (Mount Washington Kentucky)—*David Thurman*	PO Box 95, Mount Washington KY 40047	502-538-7301	S	180*	.1
535	Citizens Independent Bank—*Bradly Bakken*	5000 W 36th St, Saint Louis Park MN 55416	952-926-6561	R	180*	.1
536	Harris Bank of Oakbrook Terrace—*Mary Klingenberger*	17 W 695 Roosevelt Rd, Oakbrook Terrace IL 60181	630-495-3100	S	178*	<.1
537	First Security Bancorp—*Reynie Rutledge*	PO Box 1009, Searcy AR 72145	501-279-3400	R	177*	.5
538	Coastal Bank of Georgia—*Wayne Johnson*	1500 Newcastle St, Brunswick GA 31520	912-262-5200	S	177*	.1
539	Lea County State Bank—*Samuel S Spencer Jr*	PO Box 400, Hobbs NM 88241	575-397-4511	R	177*	.1
540	First Independence National Bank—*Donald Davis*	44 Michigan Ave, Detroit MI 48226	313-256-8400	S	176*	.1
541	Clarkston State Bank	15 S Main St, Clarkston MI 48346	248-625-8585	S	176*	.1
542	BancoPopular Illinois	1700 W Lake St, Melrose Park IL 60160	708-681-8600	S	175	.1
543	Liberty Bell Bank—*Kevin L Kutcher*	145 N Maple Ave, Marlton NJ 08053	856-830-1130	P	174	<.1
544	Columbia State Bank—*Melanie Dressel*	PO Box 2156, Tacoma WA 98401	253-305-1900	R	171*	.5
545	Washington Trust Company Of Westerly—*John Treanor*	PO Box 512, Westerly RI 02891	401-348-1200	R	171*	.5
546	Citizens First Bank (Rome Georgia)—*Angela W Lewis*	701 Broad St, Rome GA 30162	706-291-9772	S	171*	.1
547	New Resource Bank—*Vincent Siciliano*	405 Howard St Ste 110, San Francisco CA 94105	415-995-8100	P	171	<.1
548	Valley Community Bank—*Rick Loupe*	465 Main St, Pleasanton CA 94566	925-484-5400	R	168*	<.1
549	The Ohio State Bank—*Shawn Keller* Ohio State Bank Inc	111 S Main St, Marion OH 43302	740-387-2265	S	166*	.1
550	Heartland Bank (Leawood Kansas)—*Mark Fitzpatrick*	4801 Town Center Dr, Leawood KS 66211	913-663-5656	S	166*	<.1
551	Patterson Bank—*William Hughes*	PO Drawer 15, Patterson GA 31557	912-647-5332	S	165*	.1
552	Bank of Belle Glade—*Stephen Prielozny*	PO Box 790, Belle Glade FL 33430	561-996-6711	R	165*	<.1
553	Citizens Bank Of Connecticut—*Joe Marcaurel*	63 Eugene Oneill Dr, New London CT 06320	860-444-6300	R	164*	.2
554	Monogram Credit Card Bank Of Georgia—*C Shave*	7840 Roswell Rd 100, Atlanta GA 30350	770-353-2300	R	164*	.3
555	Independent Bank East Michigan—*Michael M Magee Jr*	305 E Huron Ave, Bad Axe MI 48413	989-269-6471	S	164*	.1
556	State Bank of Viroqua—*James Hohfelder*	101 N Main, Viroqua WI 54665	608-637-3127	S	164*	<.1
557	Bay Commercial Bank—*George J Guarini*	1280 Civic Dr Ste 100, Walnut Creek CA 94596	925-476-1800	P	163	N/A
558	Citizens Bank (Morehead Kentucky)—*Robert D Neff*	114 W Main St, Morehead KY 40351	606-780-0000	S	162*	.1
559	Randolph Bank and Trust Co—*Micheal Whitehead Jr*	175 N Fayetteville St, Asheboro NC 27203	336-625-1000	R	161*	.1
560	UMB Oklahoma Bank—*Royce Hammons*	PO Box 82427, Oklahoma City OK 73148	405-239-5800	S	160*	.1
561	Southern Bancorp—*Scott Fife*	6764 Hwy 7, Bismarck AR 71929	501-865-2909	S	160*	.1
562	Boone County Bank Inc—*Emma Bernstein* Premier Financial Bancorp Inc	300 State St, Madison WV 25130	304-369-2407	S	160*	.1
563	Valley Republic Bank—*Bruce Jay*	5000 California Ave St, Bakersfield CA 93309	661-371-2000	R	160*	<.1
564	American Momentum Bank—*Donald A Adam*	4830 W Kennedy Blvd St, Tampa FL 33609	813-549-4742	S	159	.1
565	Bank of Floyd—*Leon Moore* Cardinal Bankshares Corp	PO Box 215, Floyd VA 24091	540-745-4191	S	158	.1
566	PNC National Bank of Delaware—*James Gorman*	300 Bellevue Pkwy Ste, Wilmington DE 19809	302-479-4529	S	158*	.5
567	Pan American Bank—*Jesse Torres*	3626 E 1st St, Los Angeles CA 90063	323-264-3310	R	157*	<.1
568	Eastern Michigan Bank—*Timothy Ward*	65 N Howard Ave, Croswell MI 48422	810-679-2500	S	156*	.1
569	Bank of Coweta—*Anne B Bell*	PO Box 1218, Newnan GA 30264	770-254-7931	S	156*	.1

Rank	Company Name—*Executive Officer*	Address, City, State, Zip	Phone	Type	Fin	Empls
570	Carver State Bank—*Robert E James*	701 Martin Luther King, Savannah GA 31415	912-447-4200	R	156*	<.1
571	Premier Service Bank—*Kerry L Pendergast*	3637 Arlington Ave Ste, Riverside CA 92506	951-274-2400	P	156	<.1
572	First Citizens National Bank of Mansfield—*Daniel K Fitzpatrick*	525 William Penn Pl, Pittsburgh PA 15219	412-867-2000	S	155	N/A
573	Siuslaw Valley Bank—*Johan Mehlum*	PO Box 280, Florence OR 97439	541-997-3486	S	155*	.1
574	Zavala County Bank—*Tammy Ritchie*	PO Box 810, Crystal City TX 78839	830-374-5866	R	155*	<.1
575	State Bank of Cochran—*J S Helms*	PO Box 539, Cochran GA 31014	478-934-4501	R	155*	<.1
576	First Mountain Bank—*John G Briner*	PO Box 6868, Big Bear Lake CA 92315	909-866-5861	S	154*	<.1
577	Industrial State Bank—*James S Lewis*	PO Box 6007, Kansas City KS 66106	913-831-2000	S	154*	<.1
578	Cohutta Banking Co—*Mike M Sarvis*	800 Market St Ste 100, Chattanooga TN 37402	423-648-2265	S	153*	.1
579	Citizens Bank and Trust Co (Springhill Louisiana)—*G Kent Gibson*	PO Box 760, Springhill LA 71075	318-539-5656	R	153*	.1
580	Yosemite Bank—*J Mike McGowen* Premier Valley Bank	PO Box 1267, Mariposa CA 95338		D	153*	.1
581	People's Community Bank—*Robert Buzzo* First Community Bank NA	300 Sunset Dr, Johnson City TN 37604	423-915-2200	D	153*	<.1
582	Lakeland Bank—*Tom Shara*	250 Oak Ridge Rd, Oak Ridge NJ 07438	973-697-2000	R	153*	.5
583	Security Federal Savings Bank (McMinnville Tennessee)—*Joe H Pugh*	PO Box 7027, McMinnville TN 37111	931-473-4483	S	153	<.1
584	First American Bank and Trust (Vacherie Louisiana)—*Frank Bourgeois*	PO Box 550, Vacherie LA 70090	225-265-2265	S	152*	.1
585	Northern Trust Bank/DuPage—*David C Blowers*	1 Oakbrook Ter, Oakbrook Terrace IL 60181	630-691-2200	S	152*	<.1
586	Camelback Community Bank—*Gail Grace*	2777 E Camelback Rd St, Phoenix AZ 85016	602-224-5800	S	152*	<.1
587	Bank Of Tokyo Mitsubishi Ufj Ltd—*Minoru Shimada*	1251 Ave Amercs C3 Ste, New York NY 10020	212-782-4000	R	151*	.1
588	Bank of Akron—*E Peter Forrestel III*	46 Main St, Akron NY 14001	716-542-5401	R	151*	.1
589	American Chartered Bank—*Daniel Miller* American Chartered Bancorp Inc	1199 E Higgins Rd, Schaumburg IL 60173	847-517-5400	S	151*	.4
590	Easton Bancorp Inc—*Mike Menzies*	PO Box 629, Easton MD 21601	410-819-0300	R	150*	.1
591	Farmers State Bank and Trust Co—*Joy Becker*	200 W State St, Jacksonville IL 62650	217-479-4000	S	149*	.1
592	American Chartered Bancorp Inc—*Daniel Miller*	1199 E Higgins Rd, Schaumburg IL 60173	847-517-5400	R	148*	.4
593	Ozark Mountain Bank—*Craig Richards*	PO Box 130, Branson MO 65615	417-334-4125	S	148*	.1
594	Nashville Bank and Trust Co—*Thomas Snyder*	4525 Harding Rd Ste 30, Nashville TN 37205	615-515-1700	R	148	<.1
595	Bank Of Nevada—*Robert Sarver*	PO Box 26237, Las Vegas NV 89126	702-248-4200	R	148*	.2
596	Desert Commercial Bank—*Tony J Swartz*	44-801 Village Court D, Palm Desert CA 92260	760-340-7595	P	148	<.1
597	Alliance Bank and Trust Co—*Daniel C Ayscue*	292 W Main Ave, Gastonia NC 28052	704-867-5828	S	147	<.1
598	Ohio State Bank Inc—*Shawn Keller*	PO Box 1818, Marion OH 43301	740-387-2265	R	147	<.1
599	First State Bank (Tell City Indiana)—*Mark A Schroeder*	645 Main St, Tell City IN 47586	812-547-7025	S	145*	<.1
600	Habersham Bank (Canton Georgia)—*David Stovall*	PO Box 351, Canton GA 30114	770-479-2111	S	143*	<.1
601	Cortland Savings and Banking Co—*Rodger W Platt*	194 W Main St, Cortland OH 44410	330-637-8040	S	142*	.1
602	Bank of Arizona	2398 East Camelback Rd, Phoenix AZ 85016	602-808-5349	S	142*	<.1
603	America California Bank—*Stuart O Keirle*	417 Montgomery St, San Francisco CA 94104	415-986-5678	R	142*	<.1
604	Tidelands Bank—*Robert Coffee*	875 Lowcountry Blvd, Mount Pleasant SC 29464	843-388-8433	R	142*	<.1
605	Genoa Banking Co—*Martin P Sutter*	PO Box 98, Genoa OH 43430	419-855-8381	S	141*	.1
606	Bank of Zachary—*Harry Morris Jr*	4743 Main St, Zachary LA 70791	225-654-2701	S	141*	<.1
607	River Valley Community Bank—*John I Jelavich*	1629 Colusa Ave, Yuba City CA 95993	530-755-0418	P	141	<.1
608	Legacy Bank (Wiley Colorado)—*David Esgar*	PO Box 400, Wiley CO 81092	719-829-4811	R	140*	<.1
609	American Riviera Bank—*Jeffrey B DeVine*	PO Box 329, Santa Barbara CA 93102	805-965-5942	P	140	<.1
610	First Kansas Bank and Trust Co—*James Christiansen*	PO Box 67, Gardner KS 66030	913-856-7715	S	139	.1
611	Sunshine Savings Bank—*Louis O Davis Jr*	1400 E Park Ave, Tallahassee FL 32301	850-219-7200	R	137*	.1
612	HNB Bank—*Dan S Dugan*	PO Box 378, Perry MO 63462	573-565-2221	S	136*	.1
613	Signature Group Holdings Inc—*Craig Noell*	15303 Ventura Blvd Ste, Sherman Oaks CA 91403	805-409-4340	P	136	<.1
614	OptimumBank	10197 Cleary Blvd, Plantation FL 33324	954-452-9501	S	135	<.1
615	Victory State Bank—*Raffaelle M Branca* VSB Bancorp Inc	4142 Hylan Blvd, Staten Island NY 10308	718-979-1100	S	135*	<.1
616	Heartland Bank—*Tiney M McComb*	850 N Hamilton Rd, Gahanna OH 43230	614-337-4605	R	135	.1
617	University Bancorp Inc—*Stephen L Ranzini*	2015 Washtenaw Ave, Ann Arbor MI 48104	734-741-5858	P	134	.2
618	Mercantile Bank of Boca Raton	21845 Powerline Rd, Boca Raton FL 33433	561-368-6300	S	134*	<.1
619	Tri-State Bank Of Memphis—*Jesse H Turner Jr*	180 S Main St, Memphis TN 38103	901-525-0384	R	133*	.1
620	Morris Bank—*Spence N Mullis*	301 Bellevue Ave, Dublin GA 31021	478-272-5202	R	132*	<.1
621	Peoples Southern Bank—*Richard Moore Jr*	PO Box 269, Clanton AL 35046	205-755-2240	S	131*	.1
622	Presidio Bank—*Stephen G Heitel*	1 Montgomery St Ste 23, San Francisco CA 94104	415-229-8400	R	131	<.1
623	Community Bank and Trust of Southeast Alabama—*Lamar Loftin*	901 Boll Weevil Cir, Enterprise AL 36330	334-347-0081	S	130*	.1
624	Centennial Bank of Mountain View Ar—*Ron Sims*	PO Box 1228, Mountain View AR 72560	870-269-3815	S	130*	<.1
625	Seacoast Commerce Bank—*Richard M Sanborn*	678 3rd Ave Ste 101, Chula Vista CA 91910	619-476-7776	P	130	<.1
626	Illini Bank—*Ed Hart*	3200 W Iles Ave, Springfield IL 62711	217-787-5111	S	129*	.1
627	Brighton Bank—*Bruce L Hunt*	7101 S Highland Dr, Salt Lake City UT 84121	801-943-6500	S	128*	.1
628	CB Technology Inc—*Fe Bocoboc*	201 Merchant St, Honolulu HI 96813	808-546-3909	S	128*	<.1
629	Goshen Community Bank—*Doug Johnston*	511 W Lincoln Ave, Goshen IN 46526	574-533-2006	S	128*	<.1
630	CB and T Bank of Middle Georgia—*Eddie Norris*	PO Box 2107, Warner Robins GA 31099	478-929-1004	S	126*	.1
631	Catskill Hudson Bank—*Glenn Sutherland*	PO 855, Rock Hill NY 12775	845-794-9203	R	125	.1
632	First City Bank of Fort Walton Beach—*John C McGee*	PO Box 2977, Fort Walton Beach FL 32549	850-244-5151	R	125*	.1
633	Incommons Bank—*Greg Stubbs*	301 E Commerce St, Mexia TX 76667	254-562-3821	R	125*	<.1
634	South Carolina Community Bank—*Clente Fleming*	PO Box 425, Columbia SC 29202	803-733-8100	R	125*	<.1
635	Bank of Little Rock—*Pete Maris*	200 N State St, Little Rock AR 72201	501-376-0800	R	124*	<.1
636	First United Bank (San Diego California)—*Mitchell W Kitayama*	7320 Clairemont Mesa B, San Diego CA 92111	858-496-3800	S	124*	<.1
637	New Frontier Bank—*Joe Crenshaw*	1771 Zumbehl Rd, Saint Charles MO 63303	636-940-8740	S	123*	<.1
638	Davison State Bank—*Holly J Pingatore*	625 S State Rd, Davison MI 48423	810-658-2265	S	123*	<.1
639	Albina Community Bank—*Cheryl Cebula*	2002 NE Martin Luther, Portland OR 97212	503-287-7537	S	122	N/A
640	Southside Bank—*BG Hartley*	PO Box 1079, Tyler TX 75710	903-531-7111	S	122*	.6
641	First National Bank South Dakota—*Randall A Johnson*	PO Box 670, Yankton SD 57078	605-665-9611	S	122*	<.1
642	Bank of Las Vegas—*Thomas Mangione*	10000 W Charleston Blv, Las Vegas NV 89135	702-948-7500	S	122*	<.1
643	Bank of Naples—*Robert Guididas*	4099 Tamiami Trl N Ste, Naples FL 34103	239-430-2500	R	122*	<.1
644	Black Mountain Community Bank—*Tom Magione*	1700 W Horizon Ridge P, Henderson NV 89012	702-990-5900	S	122*	<.1
645	First Midwest Bank of Poplar Bluff—*Joey McLane*	PO Box 160, Poplar Bluff MO 63901	573-785-8461	R	122*	<.1
646	Michigan Commerce Bank (Grand Rapids Michigan)—*John Smythe*	4505 Cascade Rd SE Ste, Grand Rapids MI 49546	616-974-0200	S	122*	<.1
647	Sunrise Bank of Arizona—*Gail Grace*	4350 E Camelback Rd St, Phoenix AZ 85018	480-624-2630	S	122*	<.1
648	State Bank of Faribault—*John R Carlander*	PO Box 429, Faribault MN 55021	507-332-7401	R	121*	.1
649	Bank of Commerce and Trust Co (Wellington Kansas)—*JC Long*	PO Box 529, Wellington KS 67152	620-326-7471	R	121*	<.1

Note: An asterisk (*) indicates an estimated financial figure. The company type code used is as follows: R = Private, P = Public, S = Private Subsidiary, B = Public Subsidiary, D = Division, J = Joint Venture, I = Investment Fund.

COMPANY RANKINGS BY SALES WITHIN 4-DIGIT SIC

Rank	Company Name—Executive Officer	Address, City, State, Zip	Phone	Type	Fin	Empls
650	First Security Bank of Clarksville—Reynie Rutledge	PO Box 288, Clarksville AR 72830	479-754-2020	S	120*	<.1
651	Union Bank and Trust Co (Pottsville Pennsylvania)—Bruce Hart	25 S Centre St, Pottsville PA 17901	570-622-3011	R	119*	.1
652	Community Business Bank (West Sacramento California)—John A DiMichele	1550 Harbor Blvd Ste 2, West Sacramento CA 95691	916-830-3597	P	119	N/A
653	Citizens Security Bank—Lawton Bassett	PO Box 249, Tifton GA 31793	229-382-7311	S	118*	<.1
654	Promerica Bank—John Quinn	888 Figueroa St Ste 10, Los Angeles CA 90017	213-613-5000	P	117	<.1
655	Pacific Alliance Bank—Robert Oehler	8400 E Valley Blvd, Rosemead CA 91770	626-773-8888	P	117	<.1
656	AltaPacific Bancorp—Charles O Hall	3725 Westwind Blvd Ste, Santa Rosa CA 95403	707-236-1500	P	115	<.1
657	Bank of Sacramento—William J Martin	1750 Howe Ave Ste 100, Sacramento CA 95825	916-648-2100	S	115	N/A
658	AmeriServ Trust and Financial Services Co—Ronald W Virag	PO Box 520, Johnstown PA 15907	814-533-5147	S	115*	<.1
659	City National Bank (Mineral Wells Texas)—Ken Williamson	1900 E Hubbard St, Mineral Wells TX 76067	940-327-5400	S	115*	<.1
660	Broward Bank of Commerce—Keith Costello	101 NE 3rd Ave 21st Fl, Fort Lauderdale FL 33301	954-761-4900	R	115*	<.1
661	Community Bank of the Bay—Brian K Garrett	1750 Broadway, Oakland CA 94612	510-433-5400	P	115	N/A
662	Business Bank (Vienna Virginia)—Harold C Rauner	PO Box 2459, Vienna VA 22183	703-938-2500	S	114*	<.1
663	Edens Bank—Peter A Fasseas	3245 W Lake Ave, Wilmette IL 60091	847-256-5105	R	114*	<.1
664	Citizens Bank of Pagosa Springs—Curtis Miller	PO Box 1508, Pagosa Springs CO 81147	970-264-2235	R	113*	<.1
665	Harris Bank Hoffman-Schaumburg—Terry Jenkins	1100 N Roselle Rd, Schaumburg IL 60193	847-885-5858	S	112	<.1
666	Green Lake Bank (Green Lake Wisconsin)—Terrence Williamson	PO Box 186, Green Lake WI 54941	920-294-3369	S	112*	<.1
667	Citizens Bank of Florida—Richard H Lee	PO Box 620729, Oviedo FL 32762	407-365-6611	R	111*	.1
668	Minden Exchange Bank and Trust Co—Rich Armstrong	PO Box 179, Minden NE 68959	308-832-1600	R	111*	<.1
669	Bank of Clarke County—John R Milleson	PO Box 391, Berryville VA 22611	540-955-2510	S	110*	.1
670	Independent Bank West Michigan—Michael M Magee Jr	PO Box 441, Rockford MI 49341	616-866-4471	S	110*	<.1
671	Sterling Bank (Montgomery Alabama)—W Alan Worrell	PO Box 230849, Montgomery AL 36123	334-244-4437	S	110*	<.1
672	Arrowhead Community Bank—Gail Grace	17235 N 75th Ave Ste B, Glendale AZ 85308	623-776-0800	S	110*	<.1
673	Southern Arizona Community Bank—John P Lewis	6400 N Oracle Rd, Tucson AZ 85704	520-219-5000	S	110*	<.1
674	University Bank—Stephen Ranzini University Bancorp Inc	2015 Washtenaw Ave, Ann Arbor MI 48104	734-741-5858	S	109*	<.1
675	CB and T Bank of East Alabama—Wade Burford	PO Box 2400, Phenix City AL 36868	334-297-7000	S	108*	.1
676	Hyde Park Bank—Tim Goodsell	1525 E 53rd St, Chicago IL 60615	773-752-4600	R	108*	.1
677	Rivergreen Bank	36 Portland Rd, Kennebunk ME 04043	207-985-9222	S	108*	<.1
678	Banesco USA—Rafael Saldana	150 Alhambra Cir Ste 1, Coral Gables FL 33134	786-552-0524	R	108	<.1
679	Peoples Bank of Commerce—Kenneth D Trautman	750 Biddle Rd, Medford OR 97504	541-776-5350	P	106	<.1
680	Michigan Commerce Bank—Richard G Dorner	2950 South State St, Ann Arbor MI 48104	734-887-3100	S	105*	.3
681	Republic Bank and Trust Co—Steven E Trager	1700 Scottsville Rd, Bowling Green KY 42104	270-782-9111	S	105*	<.1
682	Firstbank-Lakeview—William Benear	PO Box 409, Lakeview MI 48850	989-352-7271	S	102*	.1
683	Intervest National Bank—Keith A Olsen	625 Court St, Clearwater FL 33756	727-442-2551	D	102*	<.1
684	Central Bank and Trust (Lander Wyoming)—Carl Huhnke	285 Main St, Lander WY 82520	307-332-4730	S	102*	<.1
685	Marine Trust Company of Carthage—Dan S Dugan	PO Box 190, Carthage IL 62321	217-357-3151	S	102*	<.1
686	Golden Valley Bank—Mark Francis	190 Cohasset Rd Ste 17, Chico CA 95926	530-894-1000	P	102	<.1
687	Bank of the West (Thomas Oklahoma)—Richie Johnston	101 S Main, Thomas OK 73669	580-661-3541	S	101*	<.1
688	Magic Valley Bank—Curt Hecker	113 Main Ave W, Twin Falls ID 83301	208-736-2400	S	100*	<.1
689	Bankers Bank (Oklahoma City Oklahoma)—Ricki Sonders	3015 United Founders B, Oklahoma City OK 73112	405-848-8877	S	100*	<.1
690	Hereford State Bank—Mike Mauldin	PO Box 272, Hereford TX 79045	806-364-3456	S	99*	<.1
691	Bank of Jamestown—Don J Cooper	PO Box 6, Jamestown KY 42629	270-343-3186	R	99*	<.1
692	First Texas Bank—Mike Adams	PO Box 671, Lampasas TX 76550	512-556-3691	R	99*	<.1
693	Stellar Business Bank—Timothy P Walbridge	PO Box 2519, Covina CA 91722	626-214-1760	P	98	N/A
694	Highland Community Bank—Dennis J Irvin	1701 W 87th St, Chicago IL 60620	773-881-6800	S	98*	<.1
695	North Milwaukee State Bank—Erbert C Johnson	5630 W Fond du Lac Ave, Milwaukee WI 53216	414-466-2344	R	98*	<.1
696	Central Arizona Bank—Frank Shelton	7001 N Scottsdale Rd S, Scottsdale AZ 85253	480-596-0883	S	98*	<.1
697	Village Bank and Trust—Guy Eisenhuth	234 W Northwest Hwy, Arlington Heights IL 60004	847-670-1000	R	97*	<.1
698	Ohio River Bank—Jody Rowe-Collins Premier Financial Bancorp Inc	221 Railroad St, Ironton OH 45638	740-533-4505	S	97*	<.1
699	Cairo Banking Co—Don Monk	PO Box 240, Cairo GA 39828	229-377-1110	S	97*	<.1
700	Delaware Place Bank—James W Aldrich	190 E Delaware Pl, Chicago IL 60611	312-280-0360	R	96*	<.1
701	BFC Capital Trust—Jane Dickson	101 N Broadway Ave Ste, Oklahoma City OK 73102	405-270-1086	S	96*	<.1
702	Northwest Bank (Lake Oswego Oregon)—Karen Fornshell	4900 SW Meadow Rd Ste, Lake Oswego OR 97035	503-906-3939	R	96*	<.1
703	Associated Bank Gladstone-Norwood	5200 N Central Ave, Chicago IL 60630	773-792-0440	S	94*	<.1
704	First Community Bank of Plainfield—Donn Domico First Community Financial Partners Inc	14150 S Rt 30, Plainfield IL 60544	815-436-6300	S	94*	<.1
705	Heritage Oaks Bank—Lawrence P Ward	PO Box 7012, Paso Robles CA 93447	805-369-5206	S	93	.1
706	Valley Business Bank—Donald A Gilles	200 S Ct St, Visalia CA 93291	559-622-9000	S	93*	<.1
707	Bank of Georgetown—Michael P Fitzgerald	1001 Wisconsin Ave NW, Washington DC 20007	202-965-1717	R	92*	<.1
708	Treasure State Bank Inc—James A Salisbury	3660 Mullan Rd, Missoula MT 59808	406-543-8700	P	92	N/A
709	TPB Holdings Inc—Russell Goldsmith	400 N Roxbury Dr, Beverly Hills CA 90210	310-888-6000	S	91*	<.1
710	Hastings State Bank—Thomas Fausch	PO Box 2178, Hastings NE 68902	402-463-0505	S	89*	<.1
711	Republic Capital Trust—Steven E Trager	601 W Market St, Louisville KY 40202	502-584-3600	S	89*	<.1
712	Union Bank NA—Ken McIlhaney	4921 N May Ave, Oklahoma City OK 73112	405-782-4200	S	88*	<.1
713	Oregon Pacific Banking Co—Jim Clark	PO Box 22000, Florence OR 97439	541-997-7121	S	87	<.1
714	Community Valley Bank—Robert E Hahn	PO Box 1808, El Centro CA 92244	760-352-7777	P	87	<.1
715	State Bank of Long Island—Thomas M O'Brien	699 Hillside Ave, New Hyde Park NY 11040		S	86*	.3
716	Home Bank (Seagoville Texas)—JT McDonald	PO Box 909, Seagoville TX 75159	972-287-2030	R	85*	.1
717	Keokuk Savings Bank and Trust Co—Joseph Steil	501 Main, Keokuk IA 52632	319-524-2944	R	85*	<.1
718	Bank of Willits—Richard M Willoughby	PO Box 98, Willits CA 95490	707-459-5533	R	85*	<.1
719	Liberty Bank of Arkansas—John Freeman	300 E Drew Ave, Monette AR 72447	870-486-5493	R	85*	<.1
720	Southland Bank—Edwin Hortman	3299 Ross Clark Cir NW, Dothan AL 36303	334-671-4000	S	84*	.1
721	Farmers State Bank of Western Illinois—Bret Robinson	PO Box 369, Alpha IL 61413	309-629-4361	S	84*	.1
722	Bank of Amador—David Taber	PO Box 908, Jackson CA 95642	209-223-2320	S	84*	<.1
723	City National Asset Management Inc—Russell Goldsmith	400 N Roxbury Dr, Beverly Hills CA 90210	310-888-6000	S	84*	<.1
724	RiverWood Bank	PO Box 458, Bemidji MN 56619	218-751-5120	S	84*	<.1
725	First Community Bank of Homer Glen and Lockport—Patrick Roe First Community Financial Partners Inc	13963 S Bell Rd, Homer Glen IL 60491	708-301-5900	S	84*	<.1
726	Northrim Bank—Marc Langland	PO Box 241489, Anchorage AK 99524	907-562-0062	S	84	N/A
727	Stock Yard Bank and Trust Co—David P Heintzman	PO Box 32890, Louisville KY 40232	502-582-2571	S	83*	<.1
728	Signature Bank of Arkansas—Gus Rusher	PO Box 727, Brinkley AR 72021	870-734-3133	R	82*	<.1
729	Treynor State Bank	PO Box A, Treynor IA 51575	712-487-3000	S	81*	<.1
730	Mahopac National Bank—Gerald J Klein Jr	1441 Rt 22, Brewster NY 10509	845-628-3500	S	81	N/A
731	Associated Bank Madison—Philip Flynn	PO Box 2016, Madison WI 53701	608-259-2000	S	79*	.1
732	Michigan Community Bancorp Ltd—Ronald Reed	43850 Schoenherr Rd, Sterling Heights MI 48313	586-532-8000	R	78	<.1

Rank	Company Name—*Executive Officer*	Address, City, State, Zip	Phone	Type	Fin	Empls
733	First Tuskegee Bank—*James W Wright*	301 N Elm St, Tuskegee AL 36083	334-727-2560	R	78*	<.1
734	Bank of Blue Valley—*Robert D Regnier*	11935 Riley St, Overland Park KS 66213	913-338-1000	S	78	.2
735	Summit Bank and Trust—*John P Carmichael* Heartland Financial USA Inc	2002 E Coalton Rd, Louisville CO 80027	303-460-4700	S	78	N/A
736	First Bank Muleshoe—*Tommy Gunstream*	PO Box 565, Muleshoe TX 79347	806-272-4515	R	77*	<.1
737	Capitol Valley Bank—*Ray Davis*	PO Box 1190, Roseville CA 95661	916-783-8999	S	77	N/A
738	First Utah Bank—*David L Brown*	3826 S 2300 E, Salt Lake City UT 84109	801-272-9454	R	75*	.1
739	InvestorsBank—*Emily Schonath*	W239 N1700 Busse Rd, Waukesha WI 53188	262-523-1000	R	75*	<.1
740	Global Commerce Bank—*Samuel Chin*	PO Box 47500, Doraville GA 30362	770-457-5858	R	74*	<.1
741	First National Bank of South Georgia—*Don Monk*	PO Box 71787, Albany GA 31708	229-888-5600	S	74*	<.1
742	Concord Bank—*Dennis J Geoghegan*	12040 Tesson Ferry Rd, Saint Louis MO 63128	314-843-7770	S	74*	<.1
743	Tallahassee State Bank—*Sharon Weeden*	3471 Thomasville Rd, Tallahassee FL 32309	850-576-1182	S	72*	.1
744	Bank of Delmarva NA—*Edward M Thomas*	9550 Ocean Hwy, Delmar MD 21875	410-896-9041	S	72*	<.1
745	Farmers and Merchants Bank of St Clair—*David Hoffman*	PO Box 635, Saint Clair MO 63077	636-629-2225	R	72	<.1
746	Simmons First Bank of Jonesboro—*Barry Ledbetter*	1720 S Caraway, Jonesboro AR 72401	870-933-8000	S	72*	<.1
747	Bank of Choice (Denver Colorado)—*Darrell McAllister*	3780 West 10th St, Greeley CO 80634	970-352-6400	R	68*	.4
748	Merchants and Farmers Bank—*John C Mosely*	109 W Third St, Donalsonville GA 39845	229-524-2112	S	67*	<.1
749	Sunrise Bank of Albuquerque—*Steve Marcum*	219 Central Ave NW Ste, Albuquerque NM 87102	505-244-8000	S	67*	<.1
750	Union Bank and Trust Co (Minneapolis Minnesota)—*Greg Payne*	312 Central Ave SE, Minneapolis MN 55414	612-379-3222	R	66*	<.1
751	Glenwood State Bank—*Peter Nelson*	PO Box 197, Glenwood MN 56334	320-634-5111	R	65*	<.1
752	Bank of Northumberland Inc Eastern Virginia Bankshares Inc	PO Box 9, Heathsville VA 22473	804-580-3621	S	65*	<.1
753	Cass Commerce Bank—*Lawrence A Collett*	13001 Hollenberg Dr, Bridgeton MO 63044	314-506-5500	S	62*	.8
754	Chemical Bank Shoreline (Marshall Michigan)—*Becky Vettel*	115 West Dr S, Marshall MI 49068	269-781-6880	S	61*	<.1
755	Citizens Bank of Cochran—*Chip Benton*	PO Box 427, Cochran GA 31014	478-934-6277	S	61*	<.1
756	Stone City Bank of Bedford Indiana—*Joe Dedman*	1502 I St Ste 100, Bedford IN 47421	812-279-6604	S	60	<.1
757	SY Bancorp Capital Trust I—*David Heintzman*	1040 E Main St, Louisville KY 40206	502-582-2571	S	58*	<.1
758	Signature Bank (Chicago Illinois)—*Michael O'Rourke*	6400 Northwest HwySte, Chicago IL 60631	773-467-5600	R	58*	<.1
759	US Bank (Woodland California)—*Richard K Davis*	PO Box 1050, Woodland CA 95776	530-661-1333	S	58*	<.1
760	Peoples Bank NA—*Blaise Adams*	138 Putnam St, Marietta OH 45750	740-373-3155	S	56	.3
761	Logan County Bank—*Joe Fritsche*	PO Box 85, Scranton AR 72863	479-938-7300	R	56*	<.1
762	International Bank of Commerce Zapata	PO Box 1030, Zapata TX 78076	956-765-8361	S	56*	<.1
763	Union State Bank (Kewaunee Wisconsin)—*Jeffrey W Kleiman*	223 Ellis St, Kewaunee WI 54216	920-388-3466	R	55	<.1
764	Castle Bank NA—*Tim Struthers*	121 W Lincoln Hwy, Dekalb IL 60115	815-758-2411	S	55*	<.1
765	Brown County State Bank—*Dan Dugan*	PO Box 32, Mount Sterling IL 62353	217-773-3327	S	55*	<.1
766	Consolidated Bank and Trust Co—*Joseph Williams*	PO Box 26823, Richmond VA 23261	804-771-5200	R	54*	<.1
767	Spectrum Bank—*William H Baribault* Professional Business Bank	2417 W Whittier Blvd, Montebello CA 90640	323-726-1411	S	51*	<.1
768	Bank of Hazlehurst—*Leonard Bateman*	PO Box 628, Hazlehurst GA 31539	912-375-4228	R	51*	<.1
769	Northern Star Bank—*Tom Stienessen*	1650 E Madison Ave, Mankato MN 56001	507-387-2265	S	51*	<.1
770	Northway State Bank	480 W Center St, Grayslake IL 60030	847-543-7900	S	51*	<.1
771	Union State Bank (Arkansas City Kansas)—*William R Docking*	PO Box 928, Arkansas City KS 67005	620-442-5200	R	50*	<.1
772	First State Bank of Kansas City—*David L Herndon*	650 Kansas Ave, Kansas City KS 66105	913-371-1242	S	49*	<.1
773	Community Business Bank—*Debra R Lins*	PO Box 636, Sauk City WI 53583	608-643-6300	S	49*	<.1
774	Bodcaw Bank—*Scott Hultberg*	PO Box 8, Stamps AR 71860	870-533-4486	R	49*	<.1
775	Hamler State Bank—*Richard L Kuhbander*	PO Box 358, Hamler OH 43524	419-274-3955	R	47*	<.1
776	Home Savings Bank (Salt Lake City Utah)—*John G Sorensen*	PO Box 526155, Salt Lake City UT 84152	801-487-0811	R	47*	<.1
777	First State Bank (Tabor Iowa)—*Randel Smith*	PO Box 130, Tabor IA 51653	712-629-2435	R	47*	<.1
778	AmeriServ Financial Bank—*Alan Denison*	PO box 520 216 Frankli, Johnstown PA 15901	814-533-5300	S	47	.4
779	Heritage Bank (Phoenix Arizona)	4222 E Camelback Rd St, Phoenix AZ 85018	602-840-3400	S	46*	<.1
780	Western Bank (Alamogordo New Mexico)—*Dion Kidd Johnson*	500 9th St, Alamogordo NM 88311	505-443-5000	R	46*	<.1
781	Farmers State Bank of Hamel—*DJ Dorweiler*	PO Box 236, Hamel MN 55340	763-478-6611	R	46*	<.1
782	Golden State Bank—*Dan S Dugan*	PO Box 216, Golden IL 62339	217-696-4423	S	46*	<.1
783	Midwest Independent Bank—*Eric McClure*	PO Box 104180, Jefferson City MO 65110	573-636-9555	S	44*	<.1
784	Bank of Grain Valley—*Allen L Lefko*	14801 E 40 Hwy, Kansas City MO 64136	816-373-1905	R	44*	<.1
785	Republic Financial Services—*Steven E Trager* Republic Bank and Trust Co	601 W Market St, Louisville KY 40202	502-584-3600	S	44*	<.1
786	Isabella Bank and Trust—*Richard J Barz*	PO Box 100, Mount Pleasant MI 48804	989-772-9471	R	43*	.3
787	New York Commercial Bank—*Joseph Ficalora*	615 Merrick Ave, Westbury NY 11590		S	42	N/A
788	Independent Bankers of Colorado—*Jennifer Lusk*	1900 Grant St Ste1120, Denver CO 80203	303-832-2000	R	40*	<.1
789	Home Bank and Trust Co	PO Box 620, Eureka KS 67045	620-583-5516	S	38	<.1
790	First Financial Bank (San Angelo Texas)—*Michael L Boyd*	PO Box 5291, San Angelo TX 76902	325-659-5900	S	38	N/A
791	First Ridge Farm State Bank—*Norman Lowery*	11 S State St, Ridge Farm IL 61870	217-247-2126	S	37*	<.1
792	Meramec Valley Bank—*William H Jones Jr*	199 Clarkson Rd, Ellisville MO 63011	636-230-3500	R	36*	<.1
793	First Delta Bank—*Chris Lehman*	PO Box 395, Tyronza AR 72386	870-487-2161	S	36*	<.1
794	Interchange Bank	Park 80 W Plz 2, Saddle Brook NJ 07663	201-368-2241	S	35*	.2
795	Peoples Bank (Lynden Washington)—*Charles LeCocq*	PO Box 233, Lynden WA 98264	360-354-4044	S	33*	<.1
796	Global Trust Bank	700 E El Camino Real S, Mountain View CA 94040	650-810-9400	S	33*	<.1
797	Desert Community Bank—*Ronald L Wilson* East West Bancorp Inc	PO Box 1346, Victorville CA 92393	760-243-2140	D	32	.2
798	Better Bank—*Bob Mowrer Jr*	PO Box 230, Wyoming IL 61491	309-695-2831	R	32*	<.1
799	Sound Banking Co—*Jim Bisceglia*	PO Box 98719, Tacoma WA 98498	253-588-0100	R	32*	<.1
800	Great American Bank—*L Travis Hicks* Enterprise Financial Services Corp	33050 W 83rd St, De Soto KS 66018	913-585-1131	S	31*	<.1
801	Coconut Grove Bank—*Robert Coords*	PO Box 330227, Miami FL 33233	305-858-6666	R	30*	.1
802	State Bank of Ledyard—*Richard Baxter*	210 Edmond St, Ledyard IA 50556	515-646-2035	S	28	<.1
803	First State Bank of Winchester Illinois—*Scott Musch*	PO Box 137, Winchester IL 62694	217-742-3134	S	27*	<.1
804	Union Planters Bank of North Central Tennessee—*Carl E Jones*	4774 E Main St, Erin TN 37061	931-289-4224	S	25*	<.1
805	City Holding Capital Trust	PO Box 7520, Charleston WV 25356	304-769-1100	S	24*	<.1
806	City Holding Capital Trust II	3601 MacCorkle SE, Charleston WV 25304	304-926-3380	S	24*	<.1
807	Union Planters (Monticello Iowa)—*Carla Kohler*	202 W 1st St, Monticello IA 52310	319-465-3505	S	23*	<.1
808	United Bank (Arlington Virginia)—*James Consagra*	3801 Wilson Blvd, Arlington VA 22203	703-525-1501	S	23*	<.1
809	PrivateBank and Trust Co—*Larry Richman* PrivateBancorp Inc	120 S LaSalle St, Chicago IL 60603	312-564-2000	S	23	N/A
810	Great Lakes Bankers Bank—*Charlotte Martin*	1182 Claycraft Rd, Gahanna OH 43230	614-864-3883	R	22*	<.1
811	Hopeton State Bank—*Scott Ware*	PO Box 118, Hopeton OK 73746	580-435-2221	R	20*	<.1
812	Bank of Wonewoc—*Merlin Zitner*	226 Center St, Wonewoc WI 53968	608-464-3201	S	19*	<.1
813	Farmington State Bank—*Jerry Klossner*	PO Box 67, Farmington WA 99128	509-287-2041	R	19*	<.1

Note: An asterisk (*) indicates an estimated financial figure. The company type code used is as follows: R = Private, P = Public, S = Private Subsidiary, B = Public Subsidiary, D = Division, J = Joint Venture, I = Investment Fund.

RANKINGS BY SALES WITHIN 4-DIGIT SIC

	Company Name—*Executive Officer*	Address, City, State, Zip	Phone	Type	Fin	Empls
814	Lapeer County Bank and Trust Co—*Bruce J Cady* County Bank Corp	PO Box 250, Lapeer MI 48446	810-245-2950	S	17	<.1
815	Farmers Bank of Gower—*Keith Bodenhausen*	PO Box 197, Gower MO 64454	816-424-6476	R	16*	<.1
816	Tri-Valley Bank—*David P Greiner*	2404 San Ramon Valley, San Ramon CA 94583	925-791-4340	P	15	<.1
817	Signature Bank—*Joseph J DePaolo*	565 5th Ave, New York NY 10017	646-822-1500	P	15	.6
818	Roundbank—*Larry Thompson*	PO Box 667, Waseca MN 56093	507-835-4220	R	14*	<.1
819	Susquehanna Bank	8000 Sagemore Ave, Marlton NJ 08053	856-983-4000	S	14	N/A
820	Hall Community Bank—*Ricky Pugh*	311 Green St NE Ste 10, Gainesville GA 30501	770-532-9700	R	13*	<.1
821	First Commercial Bank (Bloomington Minnesota)—*Jeffrey A Betchwars*	8500 Normandale Lake B, Bloomington MN 55437	952-903-0777	R	13	<.1
822	Bonneville Bank	PO Box 400, Provo UT 84603	801-374-9505	S	12*	<.1
823	Southern Bank—*J Grey Morgan*	PO Box 729, Mount Olive NC 28365	919-658-7000	S	12	.1
824	Fifth Third Holdings LLC—*Kevin T Kabat*	38 Fountain Sq Plz, Cincinnati OH 45263	513-579-5300	S	11*	<.1
825	Umpqua Bank (Arcata California)—*Sharon Cissa*	1063 G St, Arcata CA 95521	707-269-7329	D	8*	<.1
826	Arvest Holdings Inc—*Jim C Walton*	PO Box 1229, Bentonville AR 72712	479-271-1253	R	8*	<.1
827	GNB Management LLC—*Kevin T Kabat*	38 Fountain Sq Plz, Cincinnati OH 45263	513-579-5300	S	8*	<.1
828	Record Press Inc—*Hugh Wilmot*	229 W 36th St Fl 8, New York NY 10018	212-619-4949	R	6*	<.1
829	Young Americans Bank—*Richard Martinez*	3550 E 1st Ave, Denver CO 80206	303-321-2265	R	3*	.1
830	First Business Financial Services Inc—*Corey A Chambas*	PO Box 44961, Madison WI 53744	608-238-8008	P	1	.1
831	The State Bank and Trust Co—*Mark Klein*	401 Clinton St, Defiance OH 43512	419-783-8950	S	N/A	.2
832	Pacific City Bank—*Jung C Chang*	3701 Wilshire Blvd Ste, Los Angeles CA 90010	213-210-2000	R	N/A	<.1

TOTALS: SIC 6022 State Commercial Banks
Companies: 832 ... 1,567,400 ... 234.0

6029 Commercial Banks Nec

	Company Name—*Executive Officer*	Address, City, State, Zip	Phone	Type	Fin	Empls
1	Capmark Bank—*Steven J Nielsen*	6955 Union Park Ctr St, Midvale UT 84047	801-304-2900	S	10,585*	<.1
2	FirstMerit Bank NA—*Paul Greig*	106 S Main St Ste C, Akron OH 44308	330-996-6025	S	10,369	N/A
3	Univest National Bank and Trust Co—*K Leon Moyer*	PO Box 64197, Souderton PA 18964	215-721-2400	S	9,623*	.5
4	Investors Savings Bank—*Kevin Cummings*	101 JFK Pkwy, Short Hills NJ 07078	973-924-5100	S	9,602	.8
5	Doral Financial Corp—*Glen Wakeman*	1451 Franklin D Roosev, San Juan PR 00920	787-474-6700	P	8,646	1.4
6	Santander International Bank	207 Ponce de Leon Ave, San Juan PR 00917	787-759-7070	S	7,001*	1.4
7	Sagent Advisors Inc—*Herald L Ritch*	299 Park Ave 9th Fl, New York NY 10171	212-904-9400	R	4,226*	.2
8	Sun National Bank—*Thomas X Geisel*	226 Landis Ave, Vineland NJ 08360	856-691-7700	S	3,329	.8
9	Mitsubishi UFJ Financial Group Inc—*Nobuo Kuroyanagi*	1251 Ave of the Americ, New York NY 10020		P	2,577	80.4
10	Firstrust Savings Bank—*Richard J Green*	15 E Ridge Pike, Conshohocken PA 19428		R	2,345*	.5
11	Boenning and Scattergood Inc—*Harold F Scattergood Jr*	4 Tower Bridge 200 Bar, West Conshohocken PA 19428	610-832-1212	R	1,924*	.1
12	First Chicago Bank and Trust—*J Mikesell Thomas*	1145 N Arlington Heigh, Itasca IL 60143	603-250-9500	R	1,039*	.1
13	Bank of Belton	PO Box 770, Belton MO 64012	816-331-4888	S	845*	<.1
14	Bank of Internet USA—*Gregory Garrabrants*	PO Box 919008, San Diego CA 92191	858-350-6200	S	563*	<.1
15	Galen Capital Group LLC—*William P Danielczyk*	8300 Greensboro Dr Ste, McLean VA 22102	703-893-0021	R	507*	<.1
16	Wisconsin Community Bank (Cottage Grove Wisconsin)—*Rick Cushman*	PO Box 410, Cottage Grove WI 53527	608-839-5171	S	430	N/A
17	Milestone Merchant Partners LLC—*Eugene S Weil*	1775 Eye St NW Ste 800, Washington DC 20006	202-367-3000	R	385*	<.1
18	Bryan Bank and Trust—*Jimmy Burnsed*	9971 Ford Ave, Richmond Hill GA 31324	912-756-4444	S	259	N/A
19	Riverside Community Bank—*Steven Ward*	6855 E Riverside Blvd, Rockford IL 61114	815-637-7000	S	245	N/A
20	First NLC Financial Services Inc—*Neil S Henschel*	4680 Conference Way S, Boca Raton FL 33431	561-962-9000	S	227*	.8
21	Bank of Virginia—*Jack Zoeller*	PO Box 5658, Midlothian VA 23112	804-744-7576	P	209	.1
22	Bank of Eastern Oregon—*Jeff Bailey*	250 NW Gale, Heppner OR 97836	541-676-9125	S	158*	.1
23	Pinnacle Bank (Gilroy California)—*Susan K Black*	7597 Monterey St, Gilroy CA 95020	408-842-8200	P	155	<.1
24	Community 1st Bank—*Robert C Haydon*	PO Box 670, Roseville CA 95661	916-724-2424	P	155	<.1
25	Crestmark Bank—*W David Tull*	5480 Corporate Dr Ste, Troy MI 48098	248-641-5100	R	134*	.1
26	First Community Bank FSB—*James Hankes*	320 Concert St, Keokuk IA 52632	319-524-6921	S	123	N/A
27	California Business Bank—*Cole W Minnick Jr*	800 W 6th St Ste 1000, Los Angeles CA 90017	213-688-9668	P	115	<.1
28	Americas United Bank—*Adriana M Boeka*	801 N Brand Blvd Ste 1, Glendale CA 91203	818-637-7000	P	114	<.1
29	Capital Bank (San Juan Capistrano California)—*J Michael Justice Jr*	31351 Rancho Viego Rd, San Juan Capistrano CA 92675	949-489-4200	P	94	N/A
30	Western Commercial Bank—*Carl W Raggio III*	21550 Oxnard St, Woodland Hills CA 91367	818-449-7700	S	91	N/A
31	Altapacific Bank (Santa Rosa California)—*Charles O Hall*	3725 Westwind Blvd Ste, Santa Rosa CA 95403	707-236-1500	S	84	<.1
32	Pacific West Bank—*Steve Gray*	2040 8th Ave, West Linn OR 97068	503-905-2222	P	58	<.1
33	Financial Supermarkets Inc—*Aubrey Motz*	PO Box 1450, Cornelia GA 30531		S	12*	<.1
34	Moelis and Co—*Kenneth D Moelis*	399 Park Ave 5th Fl, New York NY 10022	212-883-3800	R	<1	.5

TOTALS: SIC 6029 Commercial Banks Nec
Companies: 34 ... 76,228 ... 88.1

6035 Federal Savings Institutions

	Company Name—*Executive Officer*	Address, City, State, Zip	Phone	Type	Fin	Empls
1	World Savings Bank FSB—*Robert Steel*	1901 Harrison St, Oakland CA 94612	510-446-3420	S	106,800	9.7
2	USAA FSB—*Josue Robles*	9800 Fredricksburg Rd, San Antonio TX 78240	210-456-8000	S	99,450*	22.0
3	Sovereign Bank—*Jorge Moran*	PO Box 841003, Boston MA 02284	610-320-8400	S	59,503*	8.5
4	Home Federal Bank Sioux Falls South Dakota—*Curtis L Hage*	PO Box 5000, Sioux Falls SD 57117		S	50,000*	.3
5	E*TRADE Financial Corp—*Frank Petrilli*	1271 Avenue of the Ame, New York NY 10020	646-521-4300	P	46,373	3.0
6	ING Bank FSB—*Arkadi Kuhlmann*	802 Deleware Ave, Wilmington DE 19801	302-255-3750	S	34,051*	.7
7	People's United Financial Inc—*John Barnes*	PO Box 7001, Bridgeport CT 06601	203-338-7171	P	25,037	5.2
8	OneWest Bank FSB—*Joseph Otting*	888 E Walnut St, Pasadena CA 91101		S	20,912*	3.0
9	Sovereign Bank FSB—*Joseph P Campanelli*	PO Box 12646, Reading PA 19612	610-320-8400	S	18,667*	3.5
10	Astoria Financial Corp—*Monte E Redman*	1 Astoria Federal Plz, Lake Success NY 11042	516-327-3000	P	17,022	1.6
11	BankAtlantic FSB—*Jarett S Levan*	PO Box 8608, Fort Lauderdale FL 33310	954-760-5429	S	16,000*	3.0
12	Charter One Bank NA—*Randy Stickler*	1215 Superior Ave, Cleveland OH 44114	216-566-5300	S	14,193*	2.6
13	Doral Bank—*Edwin Arrroyo*	1451 Franklin D Roose, San Juan PR 00920	787-474-6200	S	14,060	2.5
14	Flagstar Bancorp Inc—*Joseph Campanelli*	5151 Corporate Dr, Troy MI 48098	248-312-2000	P	13,644	3.3
15	Guaranty Federal Bank FSB (Dallas Texas)	8333 Douglas Ave, Dallas TX 75225	214-360-3360	S	13,214*	.4
16	Astoria Federal SLA—*George L Engelke Jr* Astoria Financial Corp	1 Astoria Federal Plz, Lake Success NY 11042	516-327-3000	S	10,949*	1.5
17	TFS Financial Corp—*Marc Stefanski*	7007 Broadway Ave, Cleveland OH 44105	216-441-6000	P	10,893	N/A
18	Third Federal Savings and Loan Association of Cleveland—*Marc A Stefanski*	7007 Broadway Ave, Cleveland OH 44105	216-441-6000	R	8,979*	1.1
19	MB Financial Bank NA—*Mitchell Feiger*	800 W Madison St, Chicago IL 60607		S	8,802	1.3
20	Washington Federal Savings (Seattle Washington)	425 Pike St, Seattle WA 98101	206-624-7930	S	7,394*	.9
21	Doral Bank FSB—*Glen R Wakeman*	1451 Franklin D Roosev, San Juan PR 00920	787-474-6700	S	7,176*	1.2
22	Everbank—*Robert M Clements*	501 Riverside Ave, Jacksonville FL 32202	904-623-3837	S	7,047	1.5
23	TCF National Bank—*William A Cooper*	801 Marquette Ave S, Minneapolis MN 55402	612-823-2265	S	7,008*	1.2

Rank	Company Name—*Executive Officer*	Address, City, State, Zip	Phone	Type	Fin	Empls
24	Ocwen Federal Bank FSB—*Ronald Faris*	1675 Palm Beach Lakes, West Palm Beach FL 33416	561-682-8000	S	6,800	N/A
25	MidFirst Bank—*Jeff Records* Midland Financial Co	PO Box 26750, Oklahoma City OK 73126	405-767-7000	S	6,730*	1.8
26	Eastern Bank Corp—*Stanley J Lukowski*	265 Franklin St, Boston MA 02110	617-897-1100	R	6,614*	1.7
27	Midland Financial Co—*George J Records*	501 NW Grand Blvd, Oklahoma City OK 73118	405-840-7600	R	5,096*	1.3
28	Beneficial Mutual Bancorp Inc—*Gerald P Cuddy*	510 Walnut St, Philadelphia PA 19106	215-864-6000	P	4,929	1.0
29	First Federal Savings and Loan Association of Charleston—*A Thomas Hood*	2440 Mall Dr 1st Fl, Charleston SC 29406	843-529-5800	S	4,455*	.8
30	Flushing Financial Corp—*John R Buran*	1979 Marcus Ave Ste E1, Lake Success NY 11042	718-961-5400	P	4,325	.4
31	Dime Community Bancshares Inc—*Vincent F Palagiano*	209 Havemeyer St, Brooklyn NY 11211	718-782-6200	P	4,040	.4
32	Liberty Savings Bank (Wilmington Ohio)	PO Box 1000, Wilmington OH 45177		S	4,015*	.7
33	Capitol FSB—*John Dicus*	PO Box 3505, Topeka KS 66601	785-235-1341	S	3,899*	.7
34	American Savings Bank FSB (Honolulu Hawaii)—*Constance Lau*	PO Box 2300, Honolulu HI 96804	808-627-6900	S	3,799*	1.0
35	Scottrade Bank—*Joseph Pope*	12800 Corporate Hill D, Des Peres MO 63131	314-965-1555	R	3,691	<.1
36	First Federal Bank—*James L Rohrs*	PO Box 248, Defiance OH 43512	419-782-5130	S	3,605*	.5
37	First Defiance Loan Servicing Co First Federal Bank	PO Box 248, Defiance OH 43512	419-782-5015	S	3,416*	.5
38	First Place Financial Corp (Warren Ohio)—*Steven R Lewis*	PO Box 551, Warren OH 44482	330-373-1221	P	3,153	.9
39	Home Savings and Loan Company of Youngstown Ohio	275 W Federal St, Youngstown OH 44503	330-742-0500	S	2,397*	.6
40	North Shore Bank FSB—*James McKenna*	15700 W Bluemound Rd, Brookfield WI 53005		R	2,055*	.5
41	TCF Bank Wisconsin FSB—*Timothy P Bailey*	PO Box 170995, Milwaukee WI 53217	414-352-4080	S	2,048*	.4
42	ESB Bank FSB—*Pam Zikeli*	600 Lawrence Ave, Ellwood City PA 16117	724-758-5584	S	1,968*	.3
43	Dime Savings Bank of Williamsburgh—*Vincent F Palagiano* Dime Community Bancshares Inc	209 Havemeyer St, Brooklyn NY 11211	718-782-6200	S	1,962*	.3
44	Roma Financial Corp—*Peter A Inverso*	2300 Rt 33, Robbinsville NJ 08691	609-223-8300	P	1,819	.2
45	Waterstone Financial Inc—*Douglas S Gordon*	11200 W Plank Ct, Wauwatosa WI 53226	414-761-1000	P	1,809	.6
46	E*Trade Bank—*Robert V Burton* E*TRADE Financial Corp	PO Box 1542, Merrifield VA 22116	678-624-6210	S	1,705*	.5
47	Bank of Kentucky Financial Corp—*Robert W Zapp*	PO Box 17510, Crestview Hills KY 41017	859-371-2340	P	1,665	.4
48	Viewpoint Bank—*Gary Base*	1309 W 15th St, Plano TX 75075	972-578-5000	S	1,658	.5
49	Capital One Bank (Lynbrook New York)—*John Adam Kanas*	303 Merrick Rd, Lynbrook NY 11563	631-844-1000	S	1,620	.4
50	United Financial Bancorp Inc—*Richard B Collins*	95 Elm St, West Springfield MA 01089	413-787-1700	P	1,585	.3
51	BankFinancial Corp—*F Morgan Gasior*	15W060 N Frontage Rd, Burr Ridge IL 60527	708-747-2000	P	1,531	.3
52	Nationwide Bank—*Steve Rasmussen*	PO Box 182049, Columbus OH 43218		S	1,516	.1
53	Principal Financial Services Inc	711 High St, Des Moines IA 50392		S	1,514	.1
54	West Suburban Bank—*Kevin J Acker*	711 S Meyers Rd, Lombard IL 60148	630-652-2000	S	1,431*	.7
55	Think Mutual Bank—*Paul Mackin*	5200 Members Pky NW, Rochester MN 55901		R	1,431*	.3
56	Glacier Bank FSB—*Nick Brodnick*	PO Box 27, Kalispell MT 59903	406-756-4200	S	1,419*	.3
57	Northfield Bank—*John W Alexander*	1731 Victory Blvd, Staten Island NY 10314	718-448-1000	S	1,387	N/A
58	Riverview Community Bank—*Ron Wysaske*	900 Washington St Ste, Vancouver WA 98660	360-693-7086	S	1,353*	.2
59	New South Bancshares Inc—*Hob Couch*	2000 Crestwood Blvd, Birmingham AL 35210	205-951-4000	R	1,348*	.4
60	Pulaski Financial Corp—*Gary Douglass*	PO Box 419033, Creve Coeur MO 63141	314-878-2210	P	1,309	.4
61	Stillwater National Bank and Trust Co	PO Box 1988, Stillwater OK 74076	405-372-4762	S	1,305*	.4
62	Encore Bank (Houston Texas)—*Preston M Moore*	9 Greenway Pl Ste 1000, Houston TX 77046	713-787-3100	S	1,186*	.3
63	Flushing Savings Bank FSB—*John R Buran* Flushing Financial Corp	144-51 Northern Blvd, Flushing NY 11354	718-961-5400	S	1,180*	.2
64	North American Savings Bank FSB—*David H Hancock*	12498 S 71 Hwy, Grandview MO 64030	816-765-2200	S	1,176*	.4
65	Gibraltar Bank FSB—*Steven D Hayworth*	220 Alhambra Cir 5th F, Coral Gables FL 33134	305-476-1982	R	1,167*	.2
66	First Federal Savings Bank of Elizabethtown—*Keith Johnson*	PO Box 5006, Elizabethtown KY 42702	270-765-2131	S	1,159*	.3
67	Safra National Bank of New York—*Jacob Safra*	546 5th Ave, New York NY 10036	212-704-5500	R	1,142*	.2
68	First Federal Bank of Tuscaloosa—*Charles Wolbach*	PO Box 1910, Tuscaloosa AL 35403	205-391-6700	R	1,135*	.2
69	Kentucky Bank—*Louis Prichard*	PO Box 157, Paris KY 40362	859-987-1795	S	1,135*	.2
70	Crescent State Bank—*Michael Carlton*	PO Box 5809, Cary NC 27513	919-460-7770	S	1,110*	.2
71	Savings Bank of Maine—*Willard Soper*	PO Box 190, Gardiner ME 04345	207-582-5550	R	1,096*	.3
72	Fox Chase Bancorp Inc—*Thomas M Petro*	4390 Davisville Rd, Hatboro PA 19040	215-682-7400	P	1,096	.1
73	American FSB (East Grand Forks Minnesota)—*Randy Moore-hart*	PO Box 638, East Grand Forks MN 56721	218-773-9711	S	1,050*	.2
74	Beacon Federal Bancorp Inc—*Ross J Prossner*	PO Box 186, East Syracuse NY 13057	315-433-0111	P	1,033	.1
75	Charter Financial Corp—*Robert Johnson*	600 3rd Ave, West Point GA 31833	706-645-1391	R	1,022*	.2
76	Teragon Financial Corp—*Kent C Lufkin*	3 Penns Trl, Newtown PA 18940	215-579-4000	S	1,001	.2
77	Ocean Shore Holding Co—*Steven E Brady*	1001 Asbury Ave, Ocean City NJ 08226	609-399-0012	P	995	.1
78	First Federal Bank of Arkansas FA—*Dabbs Cavin*	PO Box 550, Harrison AR 72602	870-741-7641	S	987*	.3
79	Atlantic Southern Financial Group Inc—*William A Fickling III*	1701 Bass Rd, Macon GA 31210	478-476-2170	P	948	.2
80	FirstFed Bancorp Inc—*B K Goodwin III*	PO Box 340, Bessemer AL 35021	205-428-8472	R	935*	.1
81	First Security Bank of Missoula—*Dale Bouchee*	PO Box 4506, Missoula MT 59806	406-728-3115	S	935	.2
82	Home FSB—*Brad Krehbiel*	1016 Civic Center Dr N, Rochester MN 55901	507-535-1200	S	928*	.2
83	SI Financial Group Inc—*Rheo Brouillard*	803 Main St, Willimantic CT 06226	860-423-4581	P	926	.2
84	Park View FSB—*Robert King*	34400 Aurora Rd, Solon OH 44139	440-542-6070	S	894*	.2
85	Colonial Savings FA—*James E DuBose*	PO Box 2988, Fort Worth TX 76113	817-390-2000	R	863*	.6
86	Lake Sunapee Bank FSB—*Stephen W Ensign*	PO Box 29, Newport NH 03773	603-863-5772	S	812*	.2
87	Atlantic Coast Federal Corp—*G Thomas Frankland*	505 Haines Ave, Waycross GA 31501		P	789	.2
88	Clifton Savings Bank SLA—*Walter Celuch*	PO Box 2149, Clifton NJ 07015	973-473-2200	S	785*	.1
89	Third Federal Bank—*Kent C Lufkin*	950 Newtown-Yardley Rd, Newtown PA 18940	215-968-4444	S	774*	.2
90	Beneficial Savings Bank (Burlington New Jersey) Beneficial Mutual Bancorp Inc	3 Sunset Rd & Rte 541, Burlington NJ 08016	609-387-2728	S	772*	.4
91	Cenlar FSB—*Gregory S Tornquist*	425 Phillips Blvd, Ewing NJ 08618	609-883-3900	S	759*	.4
92	Carver Bancorp Inc—*Deborah C Wright*	75 W 125th St, New York NY 10027	718-230-2900	P	709	.1
93	Carver Federal Savings Bank—*Deborah C Wright* Carver Bancorp Inc	75 W 125th St, New York NY 10027	212-230-2900	S	709	.1
94	OceanFirst Bank—*John R Garbarino*	975 Hooper Ave, Toms River NJ 08753	732-240-4500	S	701*	.1
95	United Western Bank—*Scot T Wetzel*	700 17th St Ste 100, Denver CO 80202	720-956-6500	S	700*	.1
96	Abacus FSB—*Thomas Sung*	6 Bowery, New York NY 10013	212-285-4770	R	675*	.1
97	Naugatuck Valley Savings and Loan SB	333 Church St, Naugatuck CT 06770	203-720-5000	S	671*	.1
98	Ocean City Home Bank—*Steven Brady* Ocean Shore Holding Co	1001 Asbury Ave, Ocean City NJ 08226	609-927-7722	S	670*	.2
99	Country Trust Bank—*John D Blackburn*	PO Box 2901, Bloomington IL 61702	309-557-3222	S	667*	.1
100	Maspeth Federal Savings—*Kenneth Rudzewick*	56-18 69th St, Maspeth NY 11378	718-335-1300	R	648*	.2
101	1st Constitution Bancorp—*Robert F Mangano*	PO Box 634, Cranbury NJ 08512	609-655-4500	P	644	<.1
102	Great Southern Bank—*Joseph W Turner*	PO Box 9009, Springfield MO 65808	417-887-4400	S	637*	.6

Note: An asterisk (*) indicates an estimated financial figure. The company type code used is as follows: R = Private, P = Public, S = Private Subsidiary, B = Public Subsidiary, D = Division, J = Joint Venture, I = Investment Fund.

COMPANY RANKINGS BY SALES WITHIN 4-DIGIT SIC

Rank	Company Name—*Executive Officer*	Address, City, State, Zip	Phone	Type	Fin	Empls
103	BCSB Bancorp Inc—*Joseph J Bouffard*	4111 E Joppa Rd Ste 30, Baltimore MD 21236	410-256-5000	P	625	.2
104	Newport FSB—*Kevin McCarthy*	PO Box 210, Newport RI 02840	401-847-5500	S	624*	.1
105	Park Sterling Bank Inc—*James C Cherry*	1043 E Morehead St Ste, Charlotte NC 28204	704-716-2134	P	616	.1
106	Baltimore County Savings Bank—*Joseph J Bouffard* BCSB Bancorp Inc	4111 E Joppa Rd, Baltimore MD 21236	410-256-5000	S	602*	.2
107	Peoples Federal Savings Bank of DeKalb County—*Maurice F Winkler III*	PO Box 231, Auburn IN 46706	260-925-2500	S	587*	.1
108	Sound Community Bank—*Laura Stewart* Sound Financial Inc	2005 5th Ave Ste 200, Seattle WA 98121		S	583*	<.1
109	Salisbury Bancorp Inc—*Richard J Cantele Jr*	5 Bissell St, Lakeville CT 06039	860-435-9801	P	576	.1
110	First Clover Leaf Financial Corp—*Dennis M Terry*	300 St Louis St, Edwardsville IL 62025	618-656-6122	P	575	.1
111	Jefferson Bancshares Inc—*Anderson L Smith*	120 Evans Ave, Morristown TN 37814	423-586-8421	P	561	.1
112	Community Valley Bancorp—*John Coger*	1360 E Lassen Ave, Chico CA 95973	530-899-2344	P	539	.3
113	First Savings Financial Group Inc—*Larry Myers*	501 E Lewis and Clark, Clarksville IN 47129	812-283-0724	P	537	.1
114	Citizens Community Bancorp Inc—*Edward H Schaefer*	2174 Eastridge Ctr, Eau Claire WI 54701	715-836-9994	P	537	.2
115	Community Financial Corp (Staunton Virginia)—*P Douglas Richard*	38 N Central Ave, Staunton VA 24401	540-886-0796	P	530	.2
116	RSI Bank—*D Russell Taylor*	PO Box 1003, Rahway NJ 07065	732-388-1800	R	525*	.1
117	Magyar Bancorp Inc—*John Fitzgerald*	400 Somerset St, New Brunswick NJ 08901	732-342-7600	P	524	.1
118	Northwest Bank (Spencer Iowa)—*Bill Orrison*	PO Box 80, Spencer IA 51301	712-262-4100	R	520*	.2
119	Citizens Community Federal—*James G Cooley* Citizens Community Bancorp Inc	PO Box 218, Altoona WI 54720	715-836-9994	S	518*	.2
120	Brooklyn FSB—*Gregg J Wagner* Brooklyn Federal Bancorp Inc	81 Court St, Brooklyn NY 11201	718-855-8500	S	488	.1
121	Cecil Bancorp Inc—*Mary B Halsey*	PO Box 568, Elkton MD 21922	410-398-1650	P	487	.1
122	Sterling Bank and Trust FSB—*Tom St Dennis*	1 Towne Sq Ste 165, Southfield MI 48076	248-351-3442	R	475*	.2
123	United Community Bancorp—*Robert Narmont*	92 Walnut St, Lawrenceburg IN 47025	812-537-4822	P	473	.1
124	First Community Bank Corporation of America—*Kenneth P Cherven*	9001 Blecher Rd, Pinellas Park FL 33782	727-520-0987	P	471	<.1
125	Alliance Bancorp Incorporated of Pennsylvania—*Dennis D Cirucci*	541 Lawrence Rd, Broomall PA 19008	610-353-2900	P	470	.1
126	Northeast Community Bancorp Inc—*Kenneth A Martinek*	325 Hamilton Ave, White Plains NY 10601	914-684-2500	P	466	.1
127	Brooklyn Federal Bancorp Inc—*Gregg J Wagner*	81 Court St, Brooklyn NY 11201	718-855-8500	P	459	.1
128	BankLiberty—*Brent Giles*	16 W Franklin, Liberty MO 64068	816-781-4822	S	458	.1
129	First Federal Savings Bank of Iowa—*David M Bradley*	825 Central Ave, Fort Dodge IA 50501	515-576-7531	S	452*	.1
130	Cecil Service Corp—*Mary B Halsey*	PO Box 469, Elkton MD 21922	410-398-1650	S	448*	.1
131	LaPorte Bancorp Inc—*Lee A Brady*	710 Indiana Ave, La Porte IN 46350	219-362-7511	P	444	.1
132	Jefferson Federal Bank—*Anderson Smith* Jefferson Bancshares Inc	PO Box 1198, Morristown TN 37816	423-586-8421	S	444*	.1
133	Northeast Community Bank—*Kenneth A Martinek* Northeast Community Bancorp Inc	325 Hamilton Ave, White Plains NY 10601	914-684-2500	S	443*	.1
134	Washington Savings Bank FSB—*Phillip C Bowman*	4201 Mitchellville Rd, Bowie MD 20716	301-352-3100	S	437*	.1
135	Pacific Premier Bank FSB—*Steven R Gardner*	1600 Sunflower Ave, Costa Mesa CA 92626	714-431-4000	S	426*	.1
136	DD and T Correspondent Lending—*George Malloy*	3720 Davinci Ct Ste 15, Norcross GA 30092	770-936-3250	S	418*	.1
137	Century National Bank (Zanesville Ohio)—*Thomas M Lyall*	14 S 5th St, Zanesville OH 43701	740-454-2521	S	400*	.2
138	Federal Trust Bank	312 W 1st St, Sanford FL 32771	407-323-1833	S	389*	.1
139	Broadway Federal Bank FSB—*Paul C Hudson*	4800 Wilshire Blvd, Los Angeles CA 90010	323-634-1700	S	378*	.1
140	Provident Savings Bank FSB	3756 Central Ave, Riverside CA 92506	909-686-6060	S	370*	.1
141	Silvergate Bank—*Alan J Lane*	4275 Executive Sq, La Jolla CA 92037	858-362-6300	S	363*	<.1
142	Elmira Savings Bank FSB—*Michael P Hosey*	333 E Water St, Elmira NY 14901	607-734-3374	P	359*	.1
143	Olympia Federal SLA—*Wayne E Staley*	PO Box 1338, Olympia WA 98507	360-754-3400	R	359*	.1
144	First Bancorp of Indiana Inc—*Michael H Head*	5001 Davis Lant Dr, Evansville IN 47715	812-492-8100	P	356	.1
145	MSB Financial Corp—*Gary T Jolliffe*	1902 Long Hill Rd, Millington NJ 07946	908-647-4000	P	350	.1
146	Community Financial Shares Inc—*Scott W Hamer*	357 Roosevelt Rd, Glen Ellyn IL 60137	630-545-0900	P	347	.1
147	Finance and Thrift Co—*Robert Hughes*	39 E Cleveland, Porterville CA 93257	559-784-1780	S	342*	.1
148	Lafayette Savings Bank FSB—*Randolph F Williams*	PO Box 1628, Lafayette IN 47902	765-742-1064	S	341*	.1
149	Washington Savings Bank—*James Hogan*	30 Middlesex St, Lowell MA 01852	978-458-7999	R	338*	.1
150	Sound Financial Inc—*Laura Stewart*	2005 5th Ave Ste 200, Seattle WA 98121	206-448-0884	P	335	.1
151	Nittany Bank—*Scott V Fainor*	116 E College Ave, State College PA 16801	814-234-7320	S	332*	.1
152	OBA Federal Savings and Loan—*Charles E Weller*	20300 Seneca Meadows P, Germantown MD 20876	301-528-9900	R	318*	.1
153	River Valley Financial Bank—*Matthew P Forrester*	PO Box 1590, Madison IN 47250	812-273-4949	S	315*	.1
154	CenterState Bank Central Florida NA (Winter Haven Florida)—*Ernest S Pinner*	1101 1st St South Ste, Winter Haven FL 33880	863-291-3900	S	300*	.1
155	Polonia Bancorp—*Anthony J Szuszczewicz*	3993 Huntingdon Pke, Huntingdon Valley PA 19006	215-938-8800	P	299	.1
156	Queen City FSB—*Kevin E Pietrini*	PO Box 1147, Virginia MN 55792	218-741-2040	S	296*	<.1
157	Citizens National Bank of Urbana—*Jeff Darding*	PO Box 351, Urbana OH 43078	937-653-1200	S	295*	.1
158	Sonabank NA—*Georgia S Derrico*	1770 Timberwood Blvd S, Charlottesville VA 22911	434-973-5242	S	292*	.1
159	American Savings Bank FSB (Portsmouth Ohio)—*Robert M Smith* AMB Financial Corp	PO Box 1583, Portsmouth OH 45662	740-354-3177	S	286*	.1
160	First FSB (Monessen Pennsylvania)—*Patrick G O'Brien*	577 Donner Ave, Monessen PA 15062	724-684-6800	S	284*	.1
161	Patapsco Bank—*Michael Dee*	1301 Merritt Blvd, Dundalk MD 21222	410-285-1010	S	258*	.1
162	UmbrellaBank FSB	6000 Legacy Dr, Plano TX 75024		S	250	<.1
163	Century Bank FSB—*Mike Warren*	PO Box 1507, Santa Fe NM 87504	505-995-1200	R	248*	.1
164	First Trade Union Savings Bank FSB—*Bill Butler*	1 Harbor St, Boston MA 02210	617-439-3118	R	245*	.1
165	Citizens Federal Savings and Loan Association of Bellefontaine Ohio—*Charles R Earick*	110 N Main St, Bellefontaine OH 43311	937-593-0015	R	237*	<.1
166	United Fidelity Bank FSB—*Brian Davis*	PO Box 1347, Evansville IN 47706	812-424-0921	S	236	.1
167	Severn Savings Bank FSB—*Alan J Hyatt*	200 Westgate Cir Ste 2, Annapolis MD 21401	410-841-6925	S	235	N/A
168	Kentucky First Federal Bancorp—*Tony D Whitaker*	479 Main St, Hazard KY 41701	606-436-3860	P	226	<.1
169	BANK'34—*Jill Gutierrez*	500 E 10th St, Alamogordo NM 88310	575-437-9334	R	223*	<.1
170	First Robinson Saving Bank NA—*Rick Catt*	501 E Main St, Robinson IL 62454	618-544-8621	S	223*	.1
171	Park FSB	5400 S Pulaski Rd, Chicago IL 60632	773-582-8200	S	220*	.1
172	Weststar Financial Services Corp—*Randall C Hall*	PO Box 1285, Asheville NC 28802	828-575-4608	P	219	.1
173	American Bank (Silver Spring Maryland)—*Phillip Bowman*	8630 Georgia Ave, Silver Spring MD 20910	240-485-0520	R	219*	<.1
174	Newport Federal Bank—*Chris Triplett*	PO Box 249, Newport TN 37822	423-623-6088	R	218*	<.1
175	First Federal of Northern Michigan—*Mike Mahler*	100 S Second Ave, Alpena MI 49707	989-356-9041	S	216	.1
176	Equitable Financial Corp—*Richard Harbaugh*	PO Box 160, Grand Island NE 68802	308-382-3136	P	207	.1
177	Peoples Federal SLA—*Douglas Stewart*	PO Box 727, Sidney OH 45365	937-492-6129	S	203*	<.1
178	United Labor Bank—*Malcohm Hotchkiss*	100 Hegenberger Rd Ste, Oakland CA 94621	510-567-6900	S	202*	<.1

Rank	Company Name—*Executive Officer*	Address, City, State, Zip	Phone	Type	Fin	Empls
179	Resource Capital Trust I—*R Scott Smith*	PO Box 61009, Virginia Beach VA 23452	757-463-2265	S	200*	<.1
180	First National Bank of Pasco—*Robert D Sumner*	13315 US Hwy 301, Dade City FL 33525	352-521-0141	S	196*	<.1
181	Gouverneur Savings and Loan Association—*Richard F Bennett*	42 Church St, Gouverneur NY 13642		S	196*	<.1
182	Ottawa Savings Bancorp Inc—*Jon L Kranov*	925 La Salle St Ste 1, Ottawa IL 61350	815-433-2525	P	195	<.1
183	Mid-Southern Savings Bank FSB—*Michael W Smith*	PO Box 545, Salem IN 47167	812-883-2639	P	193	<.1
184	Alaska Pacific Bank—*Craig E Dahl*	2094 Jordan Ave, Juneau AK 99801	907-789-4484	S	192*	.1
185	Polonia Bank—*Anthony J Szuszczewicz* Polonia Bancorp	3993 Huntingdon Pike, Huntingdon Valley PA 19006	215-938-8688	S	189*	<.1
186	First Savings Bank—*Mark Richards* Advantage Bank	P O Box 250, Washington Court House OH 43160	740-335-3771	D	187*	.1
187	Franklin Templeton Bank and Trust	Box 17406, Salt Lake City UT 84117		R	186*	.1
188	AMB Financial Corp—*Michael Mellon*	8230 Hohman Ave, Munster IN 46321	219-836-5870	P	181	<.1
189	Diamond Bank—*Matthew Gambs*	1051 Perimeter Dr, Schaumburg IL 60173	847-427-7800	R	181*	.1
190	FPB Financial Corp—*Ronnie Fugarino*	1300 W Morris Ave, Hammond LA 70403	985-345-1880	P	174	<.1
191	Home Town Bank—*Dean Toft*	PO Box 317, Redwood Falls MN 56283	507-637-1000	R	173*	<.1
192	American FSB—*Larry A Dreyer*	PO Box 4999, Helena MT 59604	406-442-3080	S	167*	<.1
193	Commerce Bank—*David Kemper*	PO Box 1323, Columbia MO 65205		S	167*	<.1
194	Stockgrowers State Bank—*Keith Randall*	PO Box 458, Ashland KS 67831		R	167*	<.1
195	First Place Bank—*Steven Lewis*	PO Box 551, Warren OH 44482	330-373-1221	R	165*	.9
196	Fpc Financial FSB—*Jim Meegh*	8402 Excelsior Dr, Madison WI 53717	608-821-2000	R	161*	.2
197	Osage Bancshares Inc—*Mark S White*	239 E Main St, Pawhuska OK 74056	918-287-2919	P	158	<.1
198	Preferred Bank—*Howard Farr*	11757 Katy Fwy Ste100, Houston TX 77079	281-556-6443	R	158*	<.1
199	Bay-Vanguard Federal Savings Bank—*Caroline Mroz* BV Financial Inc	7114 N Point Rd, Baltimore MD 21219	410-799-1909	S	157*	<.1
200	Logansport Savings Bank FSB—*David G Wihebrink*	PO Box 569, Logansport IN 46947	574-722-3855	S	157*	<.1
201	Independence FSB—*Robert B Isard*	1301 9th St NW, Washington DC 20001	202-628-5500	P	157	<.1
202	Centerbank of Jacksonville NA—*Raymond K Mason Jr*	1325 Hendricks Ave, Jacksonville FL 32207	904-348-3100	R	156*	<.1
203	First Federal Savings and Loan Association Independence—*James Mitchell*	PO Box 947, Independence KS 67301	620-331-1660	S	156*	<.1
204	American Savings FSB—*Ginger Watts* AMB Financial Corp	8230 Hohman Ave, Munster IN 46321	219-836-5870	S	155*	<.1
205	InvestorsBancorp Inc—*George R Schonath*	PO Box 337, Waukesha WI 53188	262-523-1000	R	153*	<.1
206	MetaBank—*J Tyler Haahr*	PO Box 98, Brookings SD 57006	605-692-2314	S	150*	<.1
207	Frankfort First Bancorp Inc—*Clay Hulette* Kentucky First Bancorp	PO Box 535, Frankfort KY 40602	502-223-1638	S	149*	<.1
208	First Federal Savings Bank of Dover—*Trent Troyer*	321 N Wooster Ave, Dover OH 44622	330-364-7777	S	148*	<.1
209	Second National Bank—*C Daniel Delawder*	PO Box 130, Greenville OH 45331	937-548-2122	S	147*	<.1
210	BV Financial Inc—*Carolyn M Mroz*	7114 N Point Rd, Baltimore MD 21219	410-799-1909	P	147	<.1
211	CFG Community Bank—*Daniel E Mackew*	500 York Rd, Towson MD 21204	410-823-0500	S	146	<.1
212	First Federal Savings Bank of Champaign-Urbana—*George R Rouse*	1311 S Neil St, Champaign IL 61824	217-356-2265	S	145*	.1
213	Southfirst Bank—*Sandra Stevens*	PO Box 167, Sylacauga AL 35150	256-245-4365	S	145*	.1
214	Florida Parishes Bank—*Ronnie Fugarino* FPB Financial Corp	1300 W Morris Ave, Hammond LA 70403	985-345-1880	S	142*	<.1
215	Cornerstone Bank NA—*David Grist*	54 S Main St, Lexington VA 24450	540-463-2222	R	141*	<.1
216	First Federal Savings Bank of Frankfort—*R Clay Hulette* Frankfort First Bancorp Inc	PO Box 535, Frankfort KY 40602	502-223-1638	S	139*	<.1
217	United Bank NA—*Donald R Stone*	401 S Sandusky Ave, Bucyrus OH 44820	419-562-3040	S	139*	<.1
218	Wedbush Bank—*R Scott Racusin*	PO Box 60058, Los Angeles CA 90060		R	137*	<.1
219	First Federal Savings and Loan Association of Middletown—*Margaret Smith*	PO Box 2023, Middletown NY 10940	845-343-1401	R	135*	<.1
220	Walden Federal Savings and Loan Assoc—*Thomas F Gibney*	12 Main St, Walden NY 12586	845-778-2171	S	133*	.1
221	Illinois Service Federal Savings and Loans Association—*Norman J Williams*	4619 S King Dr, Chicago IL 60653	773-624-2000	R	129*	.1
222	Midland Capital Holdings Corp—*Paul M Zogas*	8929 S Harlem Ave, Bridgeview IL 60455	708-598-9400	P	125	<.1
223	Community Investors Bancorp Inc—*Phillip W Gerber*	PO Box 749, Bucyrus OH 44820	419-562-7055	P	125	<.1
224	Brattleboro Savings and Loan Association FA—*George S Haines*	PO Box 1010, Brattleboro VT 05302	802-254-5333	R	121*	<.1
225	Provident Financial Corp—*Craig Blunden* Provident Savings Bank FSB	3756 Central Ave, Riverside CA 92506	951-686-6060	S	111*	<.1
226	First Federal Community Bank of Bucyrus—*Phil Gerber* Community Investors Bancorp Inc	119 S Sandusky Ave, Bucyrus OH 44820	419-562-7055	S	109*	<.1
227	Alliance FSB—*Lawrence H Chlum*	4800 S Pulaski Rd, Chicago IL 60632	773-376-3800	S	106*	<.1
228	WPS Community Bank FSB—*John Hecht*	5900 Gisholt Dr, Madison WI 53713	608-224-5500	R	106*	<.1
229	Central Kentucky FSB—*William Johnson*	340 W Main St, Danville KY 40422	859-236-4181	S	97*	<.1
230	MetaBank—*Tyler Haahr*	PO Box 1307, Storm Lake IA 50588	712-732-4117	S	96*	<.1
231	Southern Bank Co—*Gates Little Jr*	221 S 6th St, Gadsden AL 35901	256-543-3860	R	87*	<.1
232	Central Valley Bank	116 W Main St, Ottumwa IA 52501	641-682-8355	S	85*	<.1
233	Home Building Savings Bank—*Mike Head* First Bancorp of Indiana Inc	200 E VanTrees St, Washington IN 47501	812-254-2641	S	85*	<.1
234	First Federal Savings Bank of Boston—*Peter Frazier*	19 School St, Boston MA 02108		S	79*	.2
235	Salisbury Bank and Trust Co—*John RH Blum* Salisbury Bancorp Inc	5 Bissell St, Lakeville CT 06039	860-435-9801	S	78*	<.1
236	Advantage Bank—*James E Huston*	814 Wheeling Ave, Cambridge OH 43725	740-435-2020	S	72*	<.1
237	Desjardins Bank—*James Long*	1001 E Hallandale Beac, Hallandale FL 33009	954-454-1001	R	68*	<.1
238	Profed Mortgage Inc—*Craig Blunden* Provident Savings Bank FSB	3756 Central Ave, Riverside CA 92506		S	67*	<.1
239	First Iowa Mortgage Inc First Federal Savings Bank of Iowa	825 Central Ave, Fort Dodge IA 50501	515-576-7531	S	63*	<.1
240	First Iowa Title Services Inc First Federal Savings Bank of Iowa	825 Central Ave, Fort Dodge IA 50501	515-576-7531	S	63*	<.1
241	Gulfstream Community Bank—*Philip H Chesnut*	PO Box 220, Port Richey FL 34668	727-846-0066	S	61	<.1
242	Boulevard Bank—*C R Butler*	PO Box 369, Neosho MO 64850	417-451-0429	R	60*	<.1
243	First Federal Savings and Loan Association of Bloomington—*Albert F Knight*	532 Court St, Pekin IL 61554	309-347-3106	S	58*	<.1
244	SFB Bancorp Inc—*Peter W Hampton*	632 E Elk Ave, Elizabethton TN 37643	423-543-1000	P	55	<.1
245	Wilmington Trust FSB—*Sandra Fleming*	800 SE Monterey Common, Stuart FL 34996	772-286-3686	S	54	<.1
246	Security FSB (Elizabethton Tennessee)—*Peter W Hampton* SFB Bancorp Inc	632 E Elk Ave, Elizabethton TN 37643	423-543-1000	S	53*	<.1
247	Texas Bank and Trust—*Rogers Pope Jr*	PO Box 3188, Longview TX 75606	903-237-5500	R	48*	<.1

Note: An asterisk (*) indicates an estimated financial figure. The company type code used is as follows: R = Private, P = Public, S = Private Subsidiary, B = Public Subsidiary, D = Division, J = Joint Venture, I = Investment Fund.

COMPANY RANKINGS BY SALES WITHIN 4-DIGIT SIC

Rank	Company Name—*Executive Officer*	Address, City, State, Zip	Phone	Type	Fin	Empls
248	First Federal Bank FSB (Kansas City Missouri)—*Clarence Zugelter*	PO Box 419194, Kansas City MO 64141	816-241-7800	R	41*	.2
249	Southern Missouri Bank and Trust Co—*Greg A Steffens*	PO Box 520, Poplar Bluff MO 63901	573-778-1800	S	39	.1
250	Guardian Savings Bank—*James R Seiz*	3800 Nameoki Rd, Granite City IL 62040	618-876-5544	R	38*	<.1
251	First Federal Investments Inc First Federal Savings Bank of Iowa	825 Central Ave, Fort Dodge IA 50501	515-576-7531	S	35*	<.1
252	First Federal Savings and Loan Association of Olathe—*Mitch Ashlock*	700 E Santa Fe, Olathe KS 66061	913-782-0026	R	34*	<.1
253	Argentine Federal Savings—*Mark Rielley*	PO Box 6269, Kansas City KS 66106	913-831-2004	R	32*	<.1
254	Bank of Fayette County—*H McCall Wilson*	PO Box 277, Moscow TN 38057	901-877-6891	R	28	<.1
255	Hometown Insurors Inc—*Curtis L Hage* Home Federal Bank Sioux Falls South Dakota	PO Box 5048, Sioux Falls SD 57110	605-336-2470	S	28*	<.1
256	TCF National Bank Illinois—*William Cooper*	800 Burr Ridge Pkwy, Hinsdale IL 60521	630-986-4900	S	26	2.0
257	First FSB (Huntington Indiana)—*Stephen E Zahn*	648 N Jefferson St, Huntington IN 46750	260-356-3311	S	19*	.1
258	Capitol Funds Inc—*John B Dicus* Capitol FSB	PO Box 3505, Topeka KS 66601	785-235-1341	S	18*	<.1
259	Back and Middle River Savings and Loan—*Daniel Hubers*	1520 Old Eastern Ave, Essex MD 21221	410-687-1600	R	18*	<.1
260	Shelby County Bank	29 E Washington St, Shelbyville IN 46176	317-398-9721	S	11*	.1
261	American Loan and Savings Association—*Joseph C Raible*	105 N Maple Ave, Hannibal MO 63401	573-221-4306	R	8*	<.1
262	Liberty Bank (Middletown Connecticut)—*Chandler J Howard*	315 Main St, Middletown CT 06457	860-638-2922	R	3*	.6
263	Wilmington Savings Fund Society FSB—*Mark Turner*	500 Delaware Ave, Wilmington DE 19801	302-792-6000	S	N/A	.5
264	Security Federal Bank—*Timothy W Simmons*	PO Box 810, Aiken SC 29802	803-641-3000	S	N/A	.2

TOTALS: SIC 6035 Federal Savings Institutions
Companies: 264   799,718   120.2

6036 Savings Institutions Except Federal

Rank	Company Name—*Executive Officer*	Address, City, State, Zip	Phone	Type	Fin	Empls
1	New York Community Bancorp Inc—*Joseph R Ficalora*	615 Merrick Ave, Westbury NY 11590	516-683-4100	P	41,191	3.9
2	Citizens Bank of Massachusetts—*Ellen Alemany*	28 State St, Boston MA 02109	617-725-5500	S	34,000	12.0
3	First Republic Bank—*James H Herbert II*	111 Pine St, San Francisco CA 94111	415-392-1400	B	11,634*	.5
4	BankUnited Inc—*John A Kanas*	14817 Oak Ln, Miami Lakes FL 33016	786-313-1010	P	11,322	1.4
5	Hudson City Savings Bank	W 80 Century Rd, Paramus NJ 07652	201-967-0950	S	10,200*	1.0
6	Northwest Savings Bank—*William J Wagner*	PO Box 128, Warren PA 16365	814-723-9696	S	7,233*	1.5
7	Emigrant Savings Bank Executive Offices—*Howard Milstein*	5 E 42nd St, New York NY 10017		R	6,851*	1.3
8	Sterling Savings Bank—*Ezra Echardt*	111 N Wall St, Spokane WA 99201	509-458-2711	S	5,697*	2.5
9	Provident New York Bancorp—*Jack L Kopnisky*	PO Box 600, Montebello NY 10901	845-369-8040	P	3,137	.6
10	AnchorBank FSB—*Mark Timmerman*	25 W Main St, Madison WI 53703	608-252-8827	S	3,113*	.8
11	Citibank Texas NA—*Jorge A Bermudez*	201 S Texas Ave, Bryan TX 77803	979-260-4350	S	2,978	.9
12	Berkshire Hills Bancorp Inc—*Michael P Daly*	24 North St, Pittsfield MA 01201	413-443-5601	P	2,881	.7
13	Provident Savings Bank—*Paul M Pantozzi*	830 Bergen Ave, Jersey City NJ 07306	201-333-1000	S	2,610*	.6
14	Salem Five Cents Savings Bank—*Joseph M Gibbons*	210 Essex St, Salem MA 01970	978-745-5555	R	2,544*	.4
15	Community Bank (Pasadena California)—*David P Malone*	790 E Colorado Blvd, Pasadena CA 91101	626-577-1700	R	2,440	.3
16	Cambridge Savings Bank—*Robert Wilson*	PO Box 380206, Cambridge MA 02238	617-864-8700	R	2,415*	.4
17	TELACU Industries Inc—*Michael D Lizarraga*	5400 E Olympic Blvd St, Commerce CA 90022	323-721-1655	R	2,155*	.4
18	Iberiabank—*Daryl G Dyrd*	PO Box 12440, Now Iberia LA 70562	318-365-2361	S	1,950*	.8
19	Parkvale Savings Bank—*Robert J McCarthy Jr*	4220 William Penn Hwy, Monroeville PA 15146	412-373-7200	S	1,902*	.5
20	Meridian Interstate Bancorp Inc—*Richard Gavegnano*	10 Meridian St, East Boston MA 02128	617-567-1500	P	1,836	.4
21	El Dorado Savings Bank—*Thomus C Meuser*	4040 El Dorado Rd, Placerville CA 95667	530-622-1492	R	1,600*	.3
22	Ridgewood Savings Bank—*William C McGarry*	PO Box 141, Ridgewood NY 11385	718-240-4778	R	1,584*	.5
23	Bank Rhode Island—*Merrill W Sherman*	PO Box 9488, Providence RI 02940	401-456-5000	S	1,528	.3
24	Heritage Financial Corp—*Brian L Vance*	PO Box 1578, Olympia WA 98507	360-943-1500	P	1,368	.3
25	Home Trust Bank—*Dana L Stonestreet*	PO Box 10, Asheville NC 28802	828-254-8144	D	1,220*	.2
26	First Financial Northwest Inc—*Victor Karpiak*	201 Wells Ave S, Renton WA 98057	425-225-4400	P	1,194	.1
27	Savings Institute Bank and Trust	PO Box 95, Willimantic CT 06226	860-423-4581	S	1,184*	.2
28	Pacific Union Bank—*David B Warner Jr*	3530 Wilshire Blvd 18t, Los Angeles CA 90010	213-385-0909	S	1,136	N/A
29	Fairfield County Bank—*Gary C Smith*	PO Box 2050, Ridgefield CT 06877	203-438-6518	R	1,130*	.3
30	Amalgamated Bank of Chicago—*Eugene P Heytow*	1 W Monroe St, Chicago IL 60603	312-822-3000	R	1,077*	.2
31	Hingham Institution for Savings—*Robert Gaughen Jr*	55 Main St, Hingham MA 02043	781-749-2200	P	1,018	.1
32	Waterstone Bank—*Douglas S Gordon*	11200 W Plank Ct, Wauwatosa WI 53226		R	998*	.1
33	First County Bank—*Richard E Taber*	117 Prospect St, Stamford CT 06901	203-462-4200	R	919*	.2
34	Boiling Springs Savings Bank—*Robert Stillwell*	25 Orient Way, Rutherford NJ 07070	201-939-5000	R	899*	.2
35	Androscoggin Bank—*Steve A Clossen*	30 Lisbon St, Lewiston ME 04240	207-376-3618	R	853*	.2
36	Essa Bank and Trust—*Gary S Olson*	200 Palmer St, Stroudsburg PA 18360	570-421-0531	S	845	.2
37	Camco Financial Corp—*James E Huston*	814 Wheeling Ave, Cambridge OH 43725	740-435-2020	P	815	.2
38	Brookline Savings Bank—*Richard P Chapman*	PO Box 470469, Brookline MA 02447		S	724*	.1
39	First Savings Bank of Renton—*Victor Karpiak*	PO Box 360, Renton WA 98057	425-255-4400	R	689*	.1
40	Country Bank for Savings—*Paul Scully*	75 Main St, Ware MA 01082	413-967-6221	R	684*	.2
41	Malvern Federal Bancorp Inc—*Ronald Anderson*	42 E Lancaster Ave, Paoli PA 19301	610-644-9400	P	667	.1
42	Oneida Financial Corp—*Michael R Kallet*	182 Main St, Oneida NY 13421	315-363-2000	P	662	.3
43	Milford Bank—*Robert Macklin*	33 Broad St, Milford CT 06460	203-783-5700	R	657*	.1
44	Abington Saving Bank (Jenkintown Pennsylvania)—*Robert W White*	180 Old York Rd, Jenkintown PA 19046	215-886-8280	S	653*	.1
45	Chesapeake Bank Corp—*Jeffery M Szyperski*	97 N Main St, Kilmarnock VA 22482	804-435-1181	S	634*	.1
46	Malaga Bank SSB—*Randy Bowers*	2514 Via Tejon Rd, Palos Verdes Estates CA 90274	310-375-9000	S	623*	.1
47	Chicopee Savings Bank—*William J Wagner*	70 Center St, Chicopee MA 01013	413-594-6692	S	622*	.1
48	Bridgewater Savings Bank—*Keith Graveline*	14 Main St, Bridgewater MA 02324	508-697-6908	R	592*	.1
49	Hingham Securities Corp—*Robert H Gaughen Jr* Hingham Institution for Savings	55 Main St, Hingham MA 02043	781-749-2200	S	572*	.1
50	Guaranty Bank SSB—*Douglas S Levy*	4000 W Brown Deer Rd, Milwaukee WI 53209	414-362-4000	R	571*	1.0
51	Northfield Savings Bank—*Thomas Pelletier*	PO Box 347, Northfield VT 05663	802-485-5871	R	571*	.1
52	First South Bank Inc—*Thomas A Vann*	PO Box 2047, Washington NC 27889	252-946-4178	S	566*	.2
53	Greene County Bancorp Inc—*Donald E Gibson*	PO Box 470, Catskill NY 12414	518-943-2600	P	548	.1
54	Standard Bank PaSB—*Timothy K Zimmerman*	PO Box 114, Murrysville PA 15668	724-327-0010	S	538*	.1
55	Chicago Community Bank—*Peter A Fasseas*	1110 W 35th St, Chicago IL 60609	773-927-6200	R	525*	.1
56	Hampden Bank—*Thomas R Burton*	19 Harrison Ave, Springfield MA 01103	413-736-1812	S	494*	.1
57	Northwestern Savings Bank and Trust—*Scrub Calcutt*	PO Box 809, Traverse City MI 49685	231-947-5490	R	489*	.4
58	Great Midwest Bank SSB—*Dennis Doyle*	15900 W Bluemound Rd, Brookfield WI 53005	262-784-4400	R	478*	.1
59	Prudential Savings Bank (Philadelphia Pennsylvania)—*Thomas A Vento*	1834 W Oregon Ave, Philadelphia PA 19145	215-755-1500	S	447*	.1
60	Savings Bank (Wakefield Massachusetts)—*Brian McCoubrey*	357 Main St, Wakefield MA 01880	781-224-5341	R	442*	.2
61	Northwest Community Bank (Winsted Connecticut)	PO Box 1019, Winsted CT 06098	860-379-7561	R	432*	.1

Rank	Company Name—*Executive Officer*	Address, City, State, Zip	Phone	Type	Fin	Empls
62	Ameriana Bank and Trust SB—*Joanie Roberts*	2118 Bundy Ave, New Castle IN 47362	765-529-2230	S	417*	.2
63	Equitable Bank SSB—*John P Matter*	2290 N Mayfair Rd, Wauwatosa WI 53226	414-476-6434	R	417*	.2
64	Clover Leaf Bank—*Kathy Wehling*	2143 S State Rt 157, Edwardsville IL 62025	618-692-9900	S	416*	.1
65	Savings Institute Bank and Trust Co—*Rheo Brouillard*	803 Main St, Willimantic CT 06226	860-423-4581	S	384*	.1
66	Oxford Bank Corp—*Randall Fox*	60 S Washington St, Oxford MI 48371	248-628-2533	R	363*	.1
67	First BancTrust Corp—*Jack R Franklin*	PO Box 880, Paris IL 61944	217-465-6381	P	362	.1
68	United Community Bank—*William F Ritzmann*	92 Walnut St, Lawrenceburg IN 47025	812-537-4822	S	355*	.1
69	First Savings Bank of Perkasie—*Fred Schea*	PO Box 176, Perkasie PA 18944	215-257-5035	R	351*	.1
70	Citizens Savings Bank (Martins Ferry Ohio)—*Scott A Everson*	201 S 4th St, Martins Ferry OH 43935	740-633-0445	S	336*	.1
71	KS Bank Inc—*Harold T Keen*	200 N Church St, Kenly NC 27542	919-284-1017	S	325	.1
72	Louisiana Bancorp Inc—*Lawrence J LeBon III*	1600 Veterans Blvd, Metairie LA 70005	504-834-1190	P	321	.1
73	Shore Bank (Onley Virginia)—*Scott C Harvard*	PO Box 920, Onley VA 23418	757-787-1335	S	318*	.1
74	Provident Bank—*George Strayton* Provident New York Bancorp	400 Rella Blvd, Montebello NY 10901	845-369-8040	S	270*	.1
75	Jacksonville Savings Bank—*Richard A Foss*	PO Box 880, Jacksonville IL 62651	217-245-4111	S	267*	.1
76	Marquette Savings Bank (Erie Pennsylvania)—*Michael Edwards*	920 Peach St, Erie PA 16501	814-455-4481	R	267*	<.1
77	Bank of Greene County Greene County Bancorp Inc	PO Box 470, Catskill NY 12414	518-943-2600	S	260	.1
78	Oneida Savings Bank—*Michael R Kallet* Oneida Financial Corp	182 Main St, Oneida NY 13421	315-363-2000	S	257*	.1
79	CMS Bancorp Inc—*John E Ritacco*	123 Main St Ste 750, White Plains NY 10601	914-422-2700	P	254	.1
80	Nantucket Bank—*Hourihan Hourihan*	PO Box 988, Nantucket MA 02554	508-228-0580	S	253*	.1
81	West View Savings Bank—*David J Bursic*	9001 Perry Hwy, Pittsburgh PA 15237	412-364-1911	S	245*	.1
82	Bank of Glen Burnie—*F William Kuethe Jr*	PO Box 70, Glen Burnie MD 21060	410-766-3300	S	234*	.1
83	College Savings Bank—*Gilbert S Johnson*	PO Box 3769, Princeton NJ 08540	609-987-3700	S	231*	<.1
84	Home Savings Bank of Albemarle SSB—*Carl M Hill*	103 N 2nd St, Albemarle NC 28001	704-982-9184	S	221	<.1
85	Georgetown Bancorp Inc—*Robert E Balletto*	2 E Main St, Georgetown MA 01833	978-352-8600	P	212	<.1
86	Guaranty Savings Bank—*Stephen E Wessel*	3798 Veterans Memorial, Metairie LA 70002	504-457-6220	S	209*	<.1
87	First Community Bank of Mercer County Inc	PO Box 989, Bluefield VA 24605	276-326-9000	S	194*	.1
88	Florida Community Bank—*Daniel Healy*	1400 N 15th St, Immokaloe FL 34142	239-657-3171	S	168*	<.1
89	St Casimirs Savings Bank—*Ronald D Jasion*	2703 Foster Ave, Baltimore MD 21224	410-276-0894	R	154*	<.1
90	East Dubuque Savings Bank—*Steven J Bonnet*	PO Box 259, East Dubuque IL 61025	815-747-3173	S	145*	.1
91	Willamette Valley Bank—*Neil D Grossnicklaus*	101 High St NE, Salem OR 97301	503-485-2222	P	144	N/A
92	Turnberry SLA—*Roark Young*	20295 NE 29th Pl, Aventura FL 33180	305-931-7100	R	132*	<.1
93	Litchfield Bancorp—*Mark E Macomber*	PO Box 997, Litchfield CT 06759	860-567-9401	R	126*	<.1
94	Owen Community Bank SB	279 E Morgan St, Spencer IN 47460	812-829-2095	S	125*	<.1
95	Foundation Savings Bank—*Joseph Hughes*	25 Garfield Pl, Cincinnati OH 45202	513-721-0120	R	123*	<.1
96	Marine Bank FSB—*Katie Chruchill*	15030 N Hayden Rd Ste, Scottsdale AZ 85260	480-368-2600	S	96	<.1
97	Germantown Trust and Savings Bank—*Dale C Deiters*	PO Box 246, Germantown IL 62245	618-523-4202	S	89*	<.1
98	Quaint Oak Bank—*Robert T Strong*	607 Lakeside Dr, Southampton PA 18966	215-364-4059	S	84*	<.1
99	Collinsville Building and Loan Association—*Susan Hemker*	701 Belt Line Rd, Collinsville IL 62234	618-344-3172	R	83*	<.1
100	Citizens First Bank Inc	1805 Campbell Ln, Bowling Green KY 42104	270-393-0700	S	78*	<.1
101	Buffalo Savings Bank—*James A Matthys*	120 Washington St, Buffalo IA 52728	563-381-3150	R	62*	<.1
102	Peoples Savings Bank (Rhineland Missouri)—*Mark Laune*	PO Box 489, Rhineland MO 65069	573-236-4414	R	57*	<.1
103	American Trust and Savings Bank—*Fred White*	PO Box 938, Dubuque IA 52004	563-582-1841	S	46*	.3
104	Granite Savings Bank—*Norman S Seppala*	PO Box 180, Rockport MA 01900	978-546-7185	H	46*	<.1
105	Columbia SLA (Milwaukee Wisconsin)—*George Gary*	2020 W Fond Du Lac Ave, Milwaukee WI 53205	414-374-0486	S	41*	<.1
106	Citizens Savings Bank and Trust Co—*Deborah A Cole*	1917 Heiman Street, Nashville TN 37208	615-327-9787	R	26*	<.1
107	First Home Savings Bank (Mountain Grove Missouri)—*R Bradley Weaver*	PO Box 807, Mountain Grove MO 65711	417-926-5151	S	N/A	.1
108	Home Savings and Loan Association of Oklahoma City—*Alvin Harrell*	3301 S Western Ave, Oklahoma City OK 73109	405-634-1445	R	N/A	<.1

TOTALS: SIC 6036 Savings Institutions Except Federal
Companies: 108   200,898   41.1

6061 Federal Credit Unions

Rank	Company Name—*Executive Officer*	Address, City, State, Zip	Phone	Type	Fin	Empls
1	GreenStone Farm Credit Services—*David B Armstrong*	3515 West Rd, East Lansing MI 48823		R	42,300*	.5
2	Orange County Teachers Federal Credit Union—*Rudy Hanley*	PO Box 11547, Santa Ana CA 92711	714-258-4000	R	5,000	N/A
3	Navy Federal Credit Union—*Cutler Dawson*	PO Box 3000, Merrifield VA 22119	703-255-8000	R	4,605*	7.0
4	Southwest Corporate Federal Credit Union—*John Cassidy*	6801 Parkwood Blvd, Plano TX 75024	214-703-7500	R	3,959*	.2
5	Desert Schools Federal Credit Union—*Susan C Frank*	PO Box 2942, Phoenix AZ 85062	602-433-7000	R	3,200	1.2
6	Pentagon Federal Credit Union—*James Quinn*	Box 1432, Alexandria VA 22313	703-739-3600	R	2,626*	1.0
7	Suncoast Schools Federal Credit Union—*Tom Dorety*	PO Box 11904, Tampa FL 33680	813-621-7511	R	2,566*	.8
8	Wescom Credit Union—*Darren Williams*	PO Box 7058, Pasadena CA 91109	626-535-1000	R	2,449	N/A
9	Grow Financial Federal Credit Union	PO Box 89909, Tampa FL 33689	813-837-2451	R	1,777*	.4
10	Fort Knox Federal Credit Union—*William J Rissel*	PO Box 900, Radcliff KY 40159	502-942-0254	R	1,704*	.6
11	Community America Credit Union—*Dennis E Pierce*	9777 Ridge Dr, Lenexa KS 66219	913-905-7000	R	1,700	.5
12	Affinity Federal Credit Union—*John Fenton*	73 Mountain View Blvd, Basking Ridge NJ 07920		R	1,475*	.4
13	South Carolina Federal Credit Union—*Scott Woods*	PO Box 190012, North Charleston SC 29419	843-797-8300	R	1,452*	.5
14	State Employees Federal Credit Union—*Michael Castellana*	700 Patroon Creek Blvd, Albany NY 12206	518-452-8183	R	1,364	N/A
15	SAFE Credit Union—*Henry Wirz*	PO Box 1057, North Highlands CA 95660	916-979-7233	R	1,340	N/A
16	Kinecta Federal Credit Union—*Simone Lagomarsino*	PO Box 10003, Manhattan Beach CA 90266	310-643-5400	R	1,192*	.5
17	San Antonio Federal Credit Union—*Franklin W Burk*	PO Box 1356, San Antonio TX 78295	210-258-1414	R	1,128*	.6
18	Fairwinds Credit Union—*Larry Tobin*	3087 N Alafaya Trail, Orlando FL 32826	407-277-5045	R	1,106*	.5
19	Police and Fire Federal Credit Union—*John LaRosa*	901 Arch St, Philadelphia PA 19107	215-931-0300	R	1,106*	.4
20	Space Coast Credit Union—*Steven C McGill*	3700 Lakeside Dr, Miramar FL 33027	305-882-5000	R	1,058*	.4
21	DFCU Financial—*Mark Shobe*	400 Town Center Dr, Dearborn MI 48126	313-336-2700	R	1,051*	.4
22	Travis Credit Union—*Patsy Van Ouwwerk*	PO Box 2069, Vacaville CA 95696	707-449-4000	R	1,049*	.4
23	GTE Federal Credit Union—*Bucky Sebastian*	PO Box 172599, Tampa FL 33672	813-871-2690	R	1,034*	.4
24	OmniAmerican Federal Credit Union—*Tim Carter*	PO Box 150098, Fort Worth TX 76108	817-335-6664	R	934*	.5
25	Indiana Members Credit Union—*Ron Collier*	PO Box 47769, Indianapolis IN 46247	317-248-8556	R	920*	.4
26	Truliant Federal Credit Union—*Marcus Schaefer*	3200 Truliant Way, Winston Salem NC 27103	336-659-1955	R	900	.3
27	Mission Federal Credit Union—*Debra Schwartz*	PO Box 919023, San Diego CA 92191	858-524-2850	R	888*	.3
28	Randolph-Brooks Federal Credit Union—*Randy Smith*	PO Box 2097, Universal City TX 78148	210-945-3300	R	830*	.4
29	Polish and Slavic Federal Credit Union—*Bogdan Chmielewski*	140 Greenpoint Ave, Brooklyn NY 11222	718-383-6268	R	800	N/A
30	Premier America Credit Union—*John M Merlo*	PO Box 2178, Chatsworth CA 91313	818-772-4000	R	741*	.2
31	Provident Central Credit Union—*Wayne Bunker*	PO Box 8007, Redwood City CA 94065	650-508-0300	R	717*	.3
32	Los Angeles Federal Credit Union—*Steven McDiffett*	PO Box 53032, Los Angeles CA 90053	818-242-8640	R	707*	.1

Note: An asterisk (*) indicates an estimated financial figure. The company type code used is as follows: R = Private, P = Public, S = Private Subsidiary, B = Public Subsidiary, D = Division, J = Joint Venture, I = Investment Fund.

COMPANY RANKINGS BY SALES WITHIN 4-DIGIT SIC

Rank	Company Name—Executive Officer	Address, City, State, Zip	Phone	Type	Fin	Empls
33	Elevations Credit Union—Gerry Agnes	PO Box 9004, Boulder CO 80301	303-443-4672	R	700*	.2
34	Central Florida Educators' Federal Credit Union—Wenday Mayer	PO Box 785005, Orlando FL 32878	407-896-9411	R	692	N/A
35	Keesler Federal Credit Union—DS Broome	2602 Pass Rd, Biloxi MS 39531	228-385-5500	R	687*	.2
36	Vantage West Credit Union—Robert D Ramirez	PO Box 15115, Tucson AZ 85708	520-298-7882	R	672*	.3
37	Arkansas Federal Credit Union—Larry Biernabki	PO Box 9, Jacksonville AR 72078	501-982-1000	R	671*	.3
38	Los Angeles Police Federal Credit Union—Stephen M Endaya	PO Box 10188, Van Nuys CA 91410	818-787-6520	R	590*	.1
39	A Federal Credit Union—Kerry Parker	PO Box 14807, Austin TX 78723	512-302-6800	R	543*	.2
40	Arizona Federal Credit Union—Ron Westad	PO Box 60070, Phoenix AZ 85082	602-683-1234	R	526*	.2
41	Genisys Credit Union	PO Box 436034, Pontiac MI 48343	248-322-9800	R	515	.1
42	Hanscom Federal Credit Union—David P Sprague	1610 Eglin St, Hanscom AFB MA 01731	781-698-2000	R	467	N/A
43	Fort Worth Community Credit Union—Richard Howdeshell	PO Box 210848, Bedford TX 76095	817-835-5000	R	459*	.2
44	Park Federal Credit Union—David Eib	PO Box 18630, Louisville KY 40261	502-968-3681	R	443*	.2
45	Centra Credit Union—Loretta M Burd	PO Box 789, Columbus IN 47202	812-376-9771	R	435*	.2
46	Heritage Trust Federal Credit Union—James McDaniel Sr	PO BOX 118000, Charleston SC 29423	843-832-2600	R	430	.2
47	Government Employees Credit Union—Harriet May	PO Box 20998, El Paso TX 79998	915-778-9221	R	427*	.4
48	Numerica Credit Union—Dennis Cutter	PO Box 4000, Spokane WA 99217	509-535-7613	R	408*	.2
49	Campus Federal Credit Union—John W Milazzo Jr	PO Box 98036, Baton Rouge LA 70898	225-769-8841	R	405*	.1
50	New Orleans Firemen's Federal Credit Union—Donald Brock	PO Box 689, Metairie LA 70004	504-889-9090	R	401*	.1
51	Finance Center Federal Credit Union—Kevin Ryan	PO Box 26501, Indianapolis IN 46226	317-916-7700	R	392*	.1
52	Airforce Federal Credit Union—Robert Glenn	1560 Cable Ranch Rd St, San Antonio TX 78245	210-673-5610	R	385*	.1
53	Power Financial Credit Union—Allan M Prindle	2020 NW 150 Ave, Pembroke Pines FL 33028	954-538-4441	R	376	N/A
54	Evansville Teachers Federal Credit Union—Michael Phipps	PO Box 5129, Evansville IN 47716	812-477-9271	R	367*	.2
55	Pacific Northwest Federal Credit Union—Thomas Griffith	12106 NE Marx St, Portland OR 97220	503-256-5858	R	362*	.1
56	Centra Credit Union (New Albany Indiana)—Loretta Burd	710 Pillsbury Ln, New Albany IN 47150	812-944-1325	R	350*	.3
57	Merrimack Valley Federal Credit Union—Peter Matthews Jr	PO Box 905, North Andover MA 01845	978-975-4095	R	332*	.1
58	Missoula Federal Credit Union—Carl Rummel	3600 Brooks St, Missoula MT 59801	406-523-3300	R	330*	.1
59	Stanford Federal Credit Union—John R Davis	PO Box 10690, Palo Alto CA 94303	650-723-2509	R	325*	.1
60	First Financial Federal Credit Union—Richard Ghysels	PO Box 90, West Covina CA 91793	626-814-4611	R	317*	.1
61	Kitsap Credit Union—Elliot E Gregg	PO Box 990, Bremerton WA 98337	360-662-2000	R	314*	.1
62	Rockland Federal Credit Union—Thomas White	241 Union St, Rockland MA 02370	781-878-0232	R	313*	.2
63	Topline Federal Credit Union—Harry Carter	9353 Jefferson Hwy, Maple Grove MN 55369	763-391-9494	R	300*	.1
64	Georgia United Credit Union—Warren Butler	6705 Sugarloaf Pky, Duluth GA 30097	770-493-4328	R	293*	.2
65	Cornerstone Community Federal Credit Union—Ann M Brittin	6485 S Transit Rd, Lockport NY 14094	716-434-2290	R	292	.1
66	Eli Lilly Federal Credit Union—Lisa Schlehuber	PO Box 7123, Indianapolis IN 46207	317-276-2105	R	291*	.1
67	First City Savings Federal Credit Union—Terry Osteen	717 W Temple St4th FL, Los Angeles CA 90012	213-482-3477	R	290*	.1
68	Seattle Metropolitan Credit Union—Bob Harvey	PO Box 780, Seattle WA 98111	206-340-4500	R	290*	.1
69	Northeast Arkansas Federal Credit Union—Steve Purpee	PO Box 467, Blytheville AR 72316	870-763-1111	R	289*	<.1
70	Quorum Federal Credit Union—Bruno Sementilli	2 Manhattanville Rd St, Purchase NY 10577	914-641-3700	R	285*	.1
71	Communication Federal Credit Union	4141 NW Expwy Ste 200, Oklahoma City OK 73116		R	279*	.1
72	Park Community Federal Credit Union—David Eib	PO Box 18630, Louisville KY 40261	502-968-3681	R	279*	.1
73	Cascade Federal Credit Union—Dale Kerslake	18020 80th Ave S, Kent WA 98032	425-251-8888	R	274*	.1
74	Verity Credit Union—William Hayes	PO Box 75974, Seattle WA 98175	206-440-9000	R	274*	.1
75	Watermark Federal Credit Union—Sharon Sanford	800 Stewart St, Seattle WA 98101	206-382-7000	R	274*	.1
76	AltaOne Federal Credit Union—Robert M Boland	PO Box 1209, Ridgecrest CA 93556	760-371-7000	R	260*	.1
77	Mid-Atlantic Corporate Federal Credit Union—Jay R Murray	1201 Fulling Mill Rd, Middletown PA 17057	717-985-3300	R	254*	.1
78	Carolinas Telco Federal Credit Union—Roger Shelor	PO Box 668467, Charlotte NC 28266	704-391-5600	R	228*	.1
79	Premier Members Federal Credit Union—Thomas Evers	5495 Arapahoe Ave, Boulder CO 80303	303-449-9600	R	210*	.1
80	Dade County Federal Credit Union—George Joseph	1500 NW 107 Ave, Miami FL 33172	305-471-5080	R	209*	.1
81	Direct Federal Credit Union—David C Breslin	PO Box 9123, Needham Heights MA 02494	781-455-6500	R	209*	.1
82	Credit Union of Southern California—David Gunderson	PO Box 200, Whittier CA 90608	562-698-8326	R	189*	.1
83	Florida Commerce Credit Union—Ronald Fye	PO Box 6416, Tallahassee FL 32314	850-488-0035	R	188*	.1
84	Continental Federal Credit Union—Tom Martin	111 W Rio Salado Pkwy, Tempe AZ 85281	480-642-6480	R	187*	.1
85	GenFed Federal Credit Union—Joyce R Jones	85 Massillon Rd, Akron OH 44312	330-784-5451	R	185*	.1
86	Genisys Credit Union (Troy Michigan)—Jackie Buchanan	PO Box 436034, Pontiac MI 48343	248-322-9800	R	174*	.1
87	Family First Federal Credit Union—Kent W Moore	PO Box 1750, Orem UT 84059	801-225-6080	R	168	N/A
88	Capital Educators Federal Credit Union—Todd Erickson	PO Box 570, Meridian ID 83680	208-884-0150	R	167*	.1
89	Greater Texas Federal Credit Union—Tommy D Seargeant	6411 N Lamar Blvd, Austin TX 78752	512-458-2558	R	166*	.2
90	Bay Gulf Federal Credit Union—William DeMare	PO Box 271990, Tampa FL 33688	813-932-1301	R	159*	.1
91	First New York Federal Credit Union—Rachele Granka	1776 Union St, Schenectady NY 12309	518-393-1325	R	157*	.1
92	Jefferson County Federal Credit Union—Carl F Hicks Jr	PO Box 22289, Louisville KY 40252	502-429-4955	R	151*	.1
93	Lockheed Federal Credit Union—David Styler	PO Box 11269, Burbank CA 91510	818-565-2000	R	142*	.4
94	LOC Federal Credit Union—Jim Dickenson	22981 Farmington Rd, Farmington MI 48336	248-474-2200	R	137*	.1
95	Sharefax Credit Union Inc—Arthur J Kremer	1147 Old State Rt 74, Batavia OH 45103	513-753-2440	R	137*	.1
96	First Eagle Federal Credit Union—Lois Profili	PO Box 1585, Owings Mills MD 21117	410-548-8003	R	132*	.1
97	Unity One Credit Union—Gary Williams	6701 Burlington Blvd, Fort Worth TX 76131	817-306-3100	R	132*	.1
98	CinFed Employees Federal Credit Union—Christine J Kunnen	830 Main St, Cincinnati OH 45202	513-333-3800	R	130*	.1
99	Cornerstone Community Financial—Heidi Kassab	2955 University Dr, Auburn Hills MI 48326	248-340-9310	R	130	N/A
100	Excel Federal Credit Union—Gary R Nalley	5070 Peachtree Industr, Norcross GA 30071	770-441-9235	R	113*	<.1
101	Family Trust Federal Credit Union—Lee C Gardner Jr	PO Box 10233, Rock Hill SC 29731	803-367-4100	R	112*	.1
102	Cuna and Affiliates	PO Box 431, Madison WI 53701	608-231-4000	D	110*	.4
103	Carolina Cooperative Credit Union—Paris Aranguiz	6502 McMahon Dr, Charlotte NC 28226	704-543-8901	R	107*	<.1
104	Lusitania Savings Bank—Augusto Gomez	107 Pulaski St, Newark NJ 07105	973-344-5125	R	105*	<.1
105	Powerco Federal Credit Union—Tony Videtto	241 Ralph McGill Blvd, Atlanta GA 30308	404-506-3750	R	104*	<.1
106	1st Patriots Federal Credit Union—Diane Catoe	PO Box 2893, Rock Hill SC 29732	803-366-6148	R	102*	<.1
107	CTCE Federal Credit Union—Glenn Potteiger	PO Box 13385, Reading PA 19612	610-376-6639	R	94*	<.1
108	AutoTruck Federal Credit Union—J Huston Reinle	PO Box 18890, Louisville KY 40261	502-459-8981	R	91*	<.1
109	Tremont Credit Union—Leonard Broderick	PO Box 850649, Braintree MA 02185	781-843-5626	R	91*	<.1
110	JetStream Federal Credit Union—Jeanne Kucey	PO Box 5487, Miami Lakes FL 33014	305-821-7060	R	88*	.1
111	Pocatello Railroad Federal Credit Union—Clay Baden	PO Box 1450, Pocatello ID 83204	208-232-5746	R	87*	<.1
112	First Carolina Corporate Credit Union—David Brehmer	PO Box 49379, Greensboro NC 27419		R	83*	<.1
113	People's Community Credit Union—Ed Siedenberg	7403 NE Hazel Dell Ave, Vancouver WA 98665	360-695-5121	R	81	<.1
114	USE Federal Credit Union—Russell Newshaunder	PO Box 44000, Oklahoma City OK 73144	405-685-6200	R	81*	<.1
115	First US Community Credit Union—Richard Cochran	580 University Ave, Sacramento CA 95825	916-576-5700	R	79*	<.1
116	Coosa Pines Federal Credit Union—Brant Malone	PO Box 407, Childersburg AL 35044	256-378-5559	R	78*	<.1
117	Forum Credit Union—Gary Irvin	PO Box 50738, Indianapolis IN 46250	317-558-6000	R	71*	.3
118	Beacon Community Credit Union—Jeff Roberts	7910 National Tpke, Louisville KY 40214	502-366-6022	R	67*	<.1
119	Miramar Federal Credit Union—Max R Paul	PO Box 261370, San Diego CA 92196	858-695-9494	R	67*	<.1
120	Community Resource Federal Credit Union—Elizabeth U Kindlon	20 Wade Rd Ste 2, Latham NY 12110	518-783-2211	R	56*	<.1

Rank	Company Name—*Executive Officer*	Address, City, State, Zip	Phone	Type	Fin	Empls
121	Louisiana Federal Credit Union—*Rhonda Hotard*	PO Box 1956, La Place LA 70069	985-652-4990	R	55*	.1
122	Owensboro Federal Credit Union—*Stephen B Sharp*	PO Box 1189, Owensboro KY 42302	270-683-1054	R	55*	<.1
123	49er Federal Credit Union—*Judy A Hinz*	PO Box 1147, Placerville CA 95667	530-621-5878	R	55*	<.1
124	Idaho Advantage Credit Union—*Bo Burns*	PO Box 190899, Boise ID 83719	208-327-3445	R	54*	<.1
125	Carolina Federal Credit Union—*Donna Berringer*	PO Box 1088, Cherryville NC 28021	704-435-0186	R	53*	<.1
126	Class Act Federal Credit Union—*Lynn Huether*	3620 Fern Valley Rd, Louisville KY 40219	502-964-7575	R	52	N/A
127	Pine Bluff Cotton Belt Federal Credit Union—*Joe Spardoni*	1703 River Pines Blvd, Pine Bluff AR 71601	870-535-6365	R	41*	<.1
128	Anne Arundel County Employee Federal Credit Union—*Richard Stoll*	PO Box 1385, Millersville MD 21108	410-222-7283	R	35*	<.1
129	Bison Federal Credit Union—*Tony Thompson*	2 W MacArthur St, Shawnee OK 74804	405-275-5014	R	35*	<.1
130	Columbine Federal Credit Union—*Dion Martinez*	2305 E Arapahoe Rd Ste, Centennial CO 80122	720-283-2346	R	35*	<.1
131	Tyco Electronics Federal Credit Union—*Christine L Brown Petro*	PO Box 3449, Redwood City CA 94064	650-361-3090	R	33*	<.1
132	Central Florida Postal Credit Union—*John Blount*	301 E Michigan St, Orlando FL 32806	407-425-2561	R	31*	<.1
133	Affiliated Bank—*Gary Graham*	PO Box 210069, Bedford TX 76095	817-285-6195	R	30*	<.1
134	Credit Union West (Sun City Arizona)	19436 N RH Johnson Blv, Sun City West AZ 85375	623-975-2100	R	30	<.1
135	Louisville Medical Center Federal Credit Union—*Edward Dusch*	234 E Gray St Ste 130, Louisville KY 40202	502-629-3716	R	28*	<.1
136	Denver Fire Department Federal Credit Union—*Scott Simpson*	2201 Federal Blvd, Denver CO 80211	303-228-5300	R	28*	<.1
137	Oklahoma City Thrift Federal Credit Union—*Carol Underhill*	PO Box 25125, Oklahoma City OK 73125	405-475-3680	R	28*	<.1
138	Edwards Federal Credit Union—*Jan Fourr*	10 S Muroc Dr, Edwards CA 93524	661-952-5945	R	27	<.1
139	Mount Zion First Baptist Federal Credit Union—*Harold Foster*	333 Martin Luther King, San Antonio TX 78203	210-533-7132	R	27*	<.1
140	Oklahoma Federal Credit Union—*Tim Delise*	517 NE 36th St, Oklahoma City OK 73105	405-524-6467	R	27	N/A
141	Gulf States Credit Union—*Gary Teramae*	PO Box 945110, Maitland FL 32794	407-831-8844	R	24	<.1
142	School Systems Federal Credit Union—*Mark A Hatfield*	150 Defreest Dr, Troy NY 12180	518-286-1611	R	22*	<.1
143	Simplot Employees Credit Union—*Donna Burge*	PO Box 1059, Caldwell ID 83606	208-454-4286	R	22*	<.1
144	ANG Federal Credit Union—*Horace Hulsey*	PO Box 170204, Birmingham AL 35217	205-841-4525	R	22	<.1
145	Western Corporate Federal Credit Union—*Philip R Perkins*	PO Box 9024, San Dimas CA 91773	909-394-6300	R	21	N/A
146	Family 1st of Texas Federal Credit Union	3501 Western Center Bl, Fort Worth TX 76137	817-847-8992	R	21*	<.1
147	Integris Federal Credit Union—*Michael D Davenport*	4900 N Portland Ave St, Oklahoma City OK 73112	405-947-3730	R	20*	<.1
148	AllWealth Federal Credit Union—*Rudolph Rattman*	309 Court St, Hamilton OH 45011	513-868-5881	R	19*	<.1
149	Marisol Federal Credit Union—*Robin Romano*	721 N 3rd St, Phoenix AZ 85004	602-252-6831	R	18*	<.1
150	California Feminist Federal Credit Union—*Christine Youngs*	PO Box 16587, San Diego CA 92176	619-298-7283	R	14*	<.1
151	Clark County Indiana Teachers Federal Credit Union—*Wanda Holdaway*	1410 Charlestown New A, Jeffersonville IN 47130	812-282-1207	R	13*	<.1
152	Deer Valley Federal Credit Union—*Rob Scott*	16215 N 28th Ave, Phoenix AZ 85053	602-375-7300	R	12*	.1
153	Georgia Florida United Methodist Federal Credit Union—*Keith Pritchard*	PO Box 6448, Marietta GA 30065	770-565-3794	R	12*	.1
154	Community Financial Members Federal Credit Union—*Bill Lawton*	PO Box 8050, Plymouth MI 48170	734-453-1200	R	10*	.1
155	Rarin Federal Credit Union—*Cindy Hodson*	218 McCloy Ave, Stockton CA 95203	209-933-9275	R	8*	<.1
156	Reading Federal Credit Union—*Ken Cornelius*	2110 E Galbraith Rd, Cincinnati OH 45237	513-948-7778	R	7*	<.1
157	Century Employees' Savings Fund Credit Union—*Lola G Bumbarger*	PO Box 608, Hickory NC 28603	828-326-8512	R	6*	<.1
158	SEI-US Employees Credit Union—*Rob North*	PO Box 1466, Pocatello ID 83204	208-233-4395	R	6*	<.1
159	Federal and State Inspectors Federal Credit Union—*Brenda Dunham*	PO Box 71787, Albany GA 31708	229-435-5889	R	5*	<.1
160	St Monica/St Martin Federal Credit Union—*Randy Trimm*	13623 Rockside Rd, Garfield Heights OH 44125	216-663-6800	R	4*	<.1
161	Local 142 Federal Credit Union—*Marsha Burleson*	PO Box 12067, San Antonio TX 78212	210-226-4536	R	2*	<.1
162	American Airlines Employees Federal Credit Union—*Angie Owens*	PO Box 619001, Dallas TX 75261	817-952-4500	R	1*	.6
163	Patterson-Kelley Employees Federal Credit Union—*Ernest Lesloin*	PO Box 348, East Stroudsburg PA 18301	570-424-1523	R	<1*	<.1
164	La Capitol Federal Credit Union—*Susan Parry Leake*	PO Box 3398, Baton Rouge LA 70821	225-342-5055	R	N/A	.1

TOTALS: SIC 6061 Federal Credit Unions
Companies: 164   118,137   29.8

6062 State Credit Unions

Rank	Company Name—*Executive Officer*	Address, City, State, Zip	Phone	Type	Fin	Empls
1	North Carolina State Employees' Credit Union—*Jim Blaine*	PO Box 29606, Raleigh NC 27611	919-839-5472	R	28,457*	2.0
2	Lion's Share Credit Union—*John P McGrail*	PO Box 278, Salisbury NC 28145	704-636-0643	R	21,425*	<.1
3	Healthcares Cooperative Credit Union—*Maury Pilver*	9790 Touchton Rd, Jacksonville FL 32246	904-296-1292	R	8,300	N/A
4	Golden 1 Credit Union—*Teresa A Halleck*	PO Box 15966, Sacramento CA 95852	916-732-2900	R	7,277*	1.3
5	State Employee's Credit Union—*Jim Blaine*	1000 Wade Ave, Raleigh NC 27605	919-839-5003	R	6,946*	2.8
6	Veridian Credit Union—*Jean Trainor*	PO Box 6000, Waterloo IA 50704	515-289-1822	R	5,861*	.4
7	US Central—*Francois G Henriquez II*	9701 Renner Blvd Ste 1, Lenexa KS 66219	913-227-6000	R	4,336	N/A
8	First Community Credit Union—*Glen Barks*	15715 Manchester Rd, Ellisville MO 63011	636-728-3333	R	3,417*	.2
9	OnPoint Community Credit Union—*Robert Stuart*	PO Box 3750, Portland OR 97208	503-228-7077	R	2,841	.3
10	Delta Community Credit Union—*Rick Foley*	1025 Virginia Ave, Atlanta GA 30354	404-715-4725	R	2,500	N/A
11	Patelco Credit Union—*Andrew Hunter*	PO BOx 2227, Merced CA 95344	415-442-6200	R	2,086*	.4
12	Whatcom Educational Credit Union—*Wayne Langei*	PO Box 9750, Bellingham WA 98227	360-676-1168	R	2,079*	.1
13	Credit Union ONE—*Gary Moody*	400 E 9 Mile Rd, Ferndale MI 48220	248-398-1210	R	1,899*	.3
14	Neighborhood Credit Union—*Chet Kimmell*	PO Box 224444, Dallas TX 75222	214-748-9393	R	1,890*	1.0
15	TruWest Credit Union—*Dan Desmond*	PO Box 3489, Scottsdale AZ 85271	480-441-5900	R	1,827*	.1
16	Washington School Employees Credit Union—*Sandy Kurack*	PO Box 576, Seattle WA 98111	206-628-4010	R	1,464*	.1
17	Financial Center Credit Union—*Michael Duffy*	PO Box 208005, Stockton CA 95208	209-948-6024	R	1,458*	.1
18	Educators Credit Union—*Eugene Szymczak*	1400 N Newman Rd, Racine WI 53406		R	1,453*	.3
19	Pacific Service Federal Credit Union—*Steve Punch*	PO Box 8191, Walnut Creek CA 94596	925-296-6200	R	1,430*	.1
20	AurGroup Financial Credit Union—*Tim Boellner*	8811 Holden Blvd, Fairfield OH 45014	513-942-4422	R	1,421*	.1
21	Rhode Island State Employees Credit Union—*David B Suvall*	160 Francis St, Providence RI 02903	401-751-7440	R	1,418*	.1
22	St Anne's Credit Union—*Ross Upton*	286 Oliver St, Fall River MA 02724	508-324-7300	R	1,264*	.7
23	Corporate Central Credit Union Inc—*Robert Fouch*	PO Box 469, Hales Corners WI 53130	414-425-5555	R	1,251*	.1
24	Granite State Credit Union—*Denise Caristi*	PO Box 6420, Manchester NH 03108	603-668-2221	R	1,223*	.1
25	North Coast Credit Union—*Thom Kroll*	1100 Dupont Plz, Bellingham WA 98225	360-733-3982	R	1,185*	.1
26	Weokie Credit Union—*Brent Taylor*	PO Box 26090, Oklahoma City OK 73126	405-235-3030	R	1,109*	.2
27	Freedom Credit Union—*Barry Crosby*	PO Box 3009, Springfield MA 01101	413-739-6961	R	1,097*	.1
28	NW Priority Credit Union—*Mark Turnham*	PO Box 16640, Portland OR 97292	503-760-5304	R	1,066*	.1
29	Baxter Credit Union—*Michael G Valentine*	PO Box 8133, Vernon Hills IL 60061	847-522-8600	R	1,013*	.2
30	Arsenal Credit Union—*Linda Allen*	3780 Vogel Rd, Arnold MO 63010	314-962-6363	R	937*	.1
31	Eagle Legacy Credit Union—*Sundie Seefried*	PO Box 1346, Arvada CO 80001	303-422-6221	R	887*	.1
32	FAA Credit Union—*Steve Rasmussen*	PO Box 26406, Oklahoma City OK 73126	405-682-1990	R	868*	.2

Note: An asterisk (*) indicates an estimated financial figure. The company type code used is as follows: R = Private, P = Public, S = Private Subsidiary, B = Public Subsidiary, D = Division, J = Joint Venture, I = Investment Fund.

COMPANY RANKINGS BY SALES WITHIN 4-DIGIT SIC

Rank	Company Name—Executive Officer	Address, City, State, Zip	Phone	Type	Fin	Empls
33	Community First Credit Union of Florida—John Hirabayashi	PO Box 2600, Jacksonville FL 32232	904-354-8537	R	855*	.3
34	State Employees Credit Union of Maryland Inc—Rodney H Staatz	971 Corporate Blvd, Linthicum MD 21090	410-487-7328	R	850*	.4
35	Valley Credit Union—Anthony D Jones	670 Lincoln Ave, San Jose CA 95126	408-955-1300	R	843*	.2
36	St Mary's Bank La Caisse Populaire Ste-Marie—Ronald Rioux	PO Box 990, Manchester NH 03105	603-669-4600	R	837*	.2
37	Landmark Credit Union—Ron Kase	2400 N Grandview Blvd, Waukesha WI 53188	262-796-4500	R	811*	.4
38	Coast Central Credit Union—Joyce Jury	2650 Harrison Ave, Eureka CA 95501	707-445-8801	R	795*	.1
39	United Cooperative Bank—Richard Collins	95 Elm St, West Springfield MA 01089	413-787-1700	R	772*	.1
40	MilePost Credit Union—Daniel Fiorino	PO Box 8700, Tacoma WA 98418	253-474-9000	R	712*	<.1
41	Christian Financial Credit Union—Roger Quitter	18441 Utica Rd, Roseville MI 48066	586-772-6330	R	711*	.1
42	Hawthorne Credit Union—Carl Sorgatz	1519 N Naper Blvd, Naperville IL 60563	630-369-4070	R	683*	<.1
43	Meriwest Credit Union—Christopher Owen	PO Box 530953, San Jose CA 95153		R	671*	.2
44	Tapco Credit Union—John Bechtholt	PO Box 64369, Tacoma WA 98464	253-565-9895	R	669*	<.1
45	Space Coast Credit Union—Doug Samuels	PO Box 419002, Melbourne FL 32941	321-752-2222	R	611*	.4
46	TwinStar Credit Union—Marshal Ellison	PO Box 718, Olympia WA 98507	360-357-9917	R	586*	.2
47	Credit Union of Denver—Keith Cowling	PO Box 261420, Lakewood CO 80226	303-234-1700	R	564*	.1
48	Telhio Credit Union Inc—Leslie Bumbarner	96 N Fourth St, Columbus OH 43215	614-221-3233	R	534*	.1
49	HarborOne Credit Union—James W Blake	PO Box 720, Brockton MA 02301	508-895-1000	R	521*	.3
50	Firstmark Credit Union—Leon Ewing	PO Box 701650, San Antonio TX 78270	210-342-8484	R	515	.2
51	KeyPoint Credit Union—Tim Kramer	2805 Bowers Ave, Santa Clara CA 95051	408-731-4100	R	511*	.2
52	Directions Credit Union (Mansfield Ohio)—Patrick McGrady	PO Box 216, Mansfield OH 44901	419-522-0309	D	507*	.1
53	Charlotte Postal Credit Union—Joy Watts	3601 Mulberry Church R, Charlotte NC 28208	704-392-3418	R	494*	<.1
54	Central Communications Credit Union—Philip Weber	17811 E US Hwy 40, Independence MO 64055	816-842-0727	R	450*	<.1
55	Unitus Community Credit Union—Patricia Smith	PO Box 1937, Portland OR 97207	503-227-5571	R	449*	.1
56	Associated Credit Union—Jack Click	PO Box 9004, League City TX 77574	281-479-3441	R	435*	<.1
57	University and State Employees Credit Union—Jim Harris	10120 Pacific Heights, San Diego CA 92121	858-795-6100	R	427*	.2
58	Water and Power Community Credit Union—Carl E Stewart	1053 W Sunset Blvd, Los Angeles CA 90012	213-580-1600	R	418	N/A
59	First Class Credit Union—Kent Strawn	303 Euclid Ave, Des Moines IA 50313	515-282-7363	R	409*	<.1
60	E1 Financial Credit Union—Lynn Bowers	1155 Corporate Center, Monterey Park CA 91754	323-981-4000	R	403*	.1
61	Workers' Credit Union—Frederick D Healey	PO Box 900, Fitchburg MA 01420	978-345-1021	R	400*	.1
62	Anheuser-Busch Employees Credit Union—David Osborn	1001 Lynch St, Saint Louis MO 63118	314-771-7700	R	386*	.2
63	Red Canoe Credit Union—Bob Kane	PO Box 3020, Longview WA 98632	360-425-2130	R	374*	.2
64	Sacramento Credit Union—Jerrold A Kinlock	PO Box 2351, Sacramento CA 95812	916-444-6070	R	335	.1
65	Boulder Valley Credit Union—Rick Allen	5505 Arapahoe Ave, Boulder CO 80303	303-442-8850	R	331*	.1
66	Smart Financial Credit Union—Gary Tuma	PO Box 920719, Houston TX 77292	713-850-1600	R	315*	.2
67	Webster First Federal Credit Union	1 N Main St, Webster MA 01570		R	306*	.1
68	Pinnacle Credit Union—Susan M Jackson	536 N Ave NE, Atlanta GA 30308	404-888-1648	R	302*	<.1
69	Michigan First Credit Union—Michael D Poulos	27000 Evergreen Road, Lathrup Village MI 48076	248-443-4600	R	286*	.1
70	Oklahoma RE and T Employees Credit Union—Chris Meyers	PO Box 54309, Oklahoma City OK 73154	405-478-0046	R	268*	<.1
71	Coors Credit Union—Brian Resch	816 Washington Ave, Golden CO 80401	303-279-6414	R	232*	<.1
72	Dupaco Community Credit Union—Robert W Hoefer	PO Box 179, Dubuque IA 52004	563-557-7600	R	231*	.1
73	Raytown-Lee's Summit Community Credit Union—Donna Bunton	10021 E 66th Ter, Raytown MO 64133	816-356-0791	R	230*	<.1
74	Louisville Gas and Electric Company Credit Union—Heather D Simler	PO Box 32040, Louisville KY 40232	502-627-3140	R	228*	<.1
75	American's Christian Credit Union—Mendell L Thompson	PO Box 5100, Glendora CA 91740	626-208-5400	R	223*	.1
76	First South Credit Union—W Craig Esreal	6471 Stage Rd, Bartlett TN 38134	901-380-7400	R	221	N/A
77	Listerhill Credit Union—Brad Green	PO Box 566, Sheffield AL 35660	256-383-9204	R	200*	.1
78	Prevail Credit Union—Tom Graves	801 2nd Ave Ste 100, Seattle WA 98104	206-382-1888	R	200	.1
79	Corning Cable Systems Credit Union—Mark Jacobson	PO Box 489, Hickory NC 28603	828-901-5290	R	185*	<.1
80	Co-op Services Credit Union—Anthony Carnarvon	29550 Five Mile Rd, Livonia MI 48154	734-522-3700	R	180*	.1
81	Community First Credit Union—Roger Gieseke	PO Box 55909, Shoreline WA 98155	206-367-7328	R	166*	<.1
82	Group Health Credit Union—Joseph W Veneziani	PO Box 19340, Seattle WA 98109	206-298-9394	R	161*	.1
83	METRO Credit Union—Deidra M Williams	6611 Chicago Rd, Warren MI 48092	586-276-3000	R	160*	.1
84	Horizon Credit Union—Roy Meythaler	1931 Grove Ave, Racine WI 53405	262-633-5302	R	158*	<.1
85	Self-Help Credit Union—Martin Eakes	PO Box 3619, Durham NC 27702	919-956-4400	R	154*	.1
86	Brewery Credit Union—Jim Schrimpf	1351 Dr Martin Luther, Milwaukee WI 53212	414-273-3170	R	142*	<.1
87	Oklahoma Employees Credit Union—Mark W Kelly	PO Box 24027, Oklahoma City OK 73124	405-602-6328	R	124*	.1
88	Municipal Employees Credit Union of Oklahoma City—Agnes C Berkenbile	101 N Walker Ave, Oklahoma City OK 73102	405-297-2995	R	122*	.1
89	Telecommunity Credit Union—Jack Sarver	2500 N Turkeyfoot Rd, Akron OH 44319	330-645-2700	R	119*	<.1
90	CommScope Credit Union—Barry Graham	PO Box 199, Catawba NC 28609	828-241-6048	R	119*	<.1
91	Craftsman Credit Union—Margie L Wilkes	2444 Clark St, Detroit MI 48209	313-554-9300	R	116*	<.1
92	First Service Credit Union—John Urdave	333 N 35th St, Milwaukee WI 53208	414-342-7680	R	113*	<.1
93	Kemba Cincinnati Credit Union—Stephen G Behler	PO Box 14090, Cincinnati OH 45250	513-762-5070	R	104*	<.1
94	Firefighters Community Credit Union Inc—Ben Laurendeau	2300 St Clair Ave, Cleveland OH 44114	216-621-4644	R	98*	<.1
95	1st Financial Federal Credit Union—Frank Nelson	1232 Wentzville Pkwy, Wentzville MO 63385	636-916-8300	R	91	.1
96	BSE Credit Union Inc—Drema Braun	19249 Bagley Rd, Middleburg Heights OH 44130	440-243-9180	R	91*	<.1
97	First Educators Credit Union—George S Nix	PO Box 36489, Hoover AL 35236	205-581-8800	R	85*	<.1
98	Cincinnati Central Credit Union—William Herring	1717 Western Ave, Cincinnati OH 45214	513-241-2050	R	81*	.1
99	Arrow Pointe Federal Credit Union—Tim Lyda	5298 Cureton Ferry Rd, Catawba SC 29704	803-324-1124	R	72*	<.1
100	Secure First Credit Union—Jordan Sullivan	PO Box 170070, Birmingham AL 35217	205-520-2115	R	69*	<.1
101	Fort Worth City Credit Union—Ron Fox	PO Box 100099, Ft Worth TX 76185	817-732-2803	R	65*	<.1
102	Charlotte Fire Department Credit Union—Debbie Trotter	2100 Commonwealth Ave, Charlotte NC 28205	704-375-3950	R	62*	<.1
103	Blue Flame Credit Union—Ben Hill	PO Box 33068, Charlotte NC 28233	704-523-0075	R	61*	<.1
104	Courier-Journal and Times Credit Union Inc—Linda Parish	525 W Broadway, Louisville KY 40202	502-582-4530	R	57*	<.1
105	Wisconsin Education Association Credit Union—Mark k Schrimpf	PO Box 8003, Madison WI 53708	608-274-9828	R	56*	<.1
106	Louisville Federal Credit Union—Howard E Jackson	PO Box 33303, Louisville KY 40232	502-458-2681	R	48	<.1
107	Campus Credit Union—Michael Wayne	PO Box 65, Wichita KS 67260	316-978-3666	R	40*	<.1
108	USAgencies Credit Union—James Lumpkin	95 SW Taylor St, Portland OR 97204	503-275-0300	R	36*	<.1
109	Midwest Regional Credit Union—Lloyd D Nugent	PO Box 12217, Kansas City KS 66112	913-334-4200	R	33*	<.1
110	Peoples Credit Union—Thomas E Ribel	680 NE 124th St, North Miami FL 33161	305-893-4880	R	32*	<.1
111	First Class American Credit Union—Nancy Croix-Stroud	PO Box 162539, Fort Worth TX 76161	817-834-9777	R	31*	<.1
112	SPCO Credit Union—Joanne Staley	9800 Northwest Fwy Ste, Houston TX 77092	713-520-5060	R	31*	<.1
113	Sacramento District Postal Employees Credit Union Co—Valorie Pruitt	1485 River Park Dr, Sacramento CA 95815	916-921-5050	R	26*	<.1
114	First Legacy Community Credit Union—Saundra Scales	431 Beatties Ford Rd, Charlotte NC 28216	704-375-5781	R	25*	N/A
115	Michigan Educational Credit Union—William Brunton	9200 N Haggerty Rd, Plymouth MI 48170	734-455-9200	R	24*	.1
116	Baptist Credit Union—Nick Holguin	5815 IH 10 W, San Antonio TX 78201	210-525-0100	R	19*	.1

Rank	Company Name—*Executive Officer*	Address, City, State, Zip	Phone	Type	Fin	Empls
117	Brown-Forman Employees Credit Union—*Paul Varga*	850 Dixie Hwy, Louisville KY 40210	502-774-7636	S	18*	<.1
118	Health Credit Union—*Brian Debrow*	1400 6th Ave S, Birmingham AL 35233	205-930-1213	R	17*	<.1
119	BrightStar Credit Union—*Raffael Crockett*	PO Box 8966, Fort Lauderdale FL 33310	954-486-2728	R	15*	<.1
120	Auto Parts Employees Credit Union—*Charlotte Douglas*	1216 Everman Pky, Fort Worth TX 76140	817-293-8412	R	12*	<.1
121	Michigan Services Credit Union—*Elizabeth J Morehouse*	27650 Franklin Rd, Southfield MI 48034	248-440-6790	R	9*	<.1
122	Public Employees Credit Union—*Linda Chatfield*	1410 N Government Way, Coeur D Alene ID 83814	208-667-7722	R	8*	<.1
123	Louisville Metro Police Officer Credit Union—*Virginia Adcock*	1402 Burghard St, Louisville KY 40210	502-635-6458	R	3*	<.1
124	Cadmus Credit Union Inc—*James Winkler*	2901 Byrdhill Rd, Richmond VA 23228	804-264-2711	R	<1*	<.1
125	Jeanne D'Arc Credit Union—*Mark S Cochran*	PO Box 1238, Lowell MA 01853	978-452-5001	R	N/A	.2
126	Oklahoma Educators Credit Union—*Floyd Atha*	PO Box 22222, Oklahoma City OK 73123	405-722-2234	R	N/A	<.1

TOTALS: SIC 6062 State Credit Unions
Companies: 126   **147,234**   **18.4**

6091 Nondeposit Trust Facilities

Rank	Company Name—*Executive Officer*	Address, City, State, Zip	Phone	Type	Fin	Empls
1	Gain Capital Group LLC—*Glenn Stevens*	135 US Hwy 202/206 Ste, Bedminster NJ 07921	908-731-0700	R	11,322*	.4
2	Glenmede Trust Co—*Al Piscopo*	1 Liberty Pl 1650 Mark, Philadelphia PA 19103	215-419-6000	R	4,001*	.3
3	Huntington National Bank-Private Financial Group—*Daniel Benhase*	41 S High St, Columbus OH 43215		S	4,001*	.3
4	Laird Norton Tyee—*Robert Moser*	801 2nd Ave Ste 1600, Seattle WA 98104	206-464-5100	S	1,763*	.1
5	Lincoln Trust Co—*Bob Beriault*	717 17th St Ste 2200, Denver CO 80202	303-658-3000	S	1,545*	.1
6	Custodial Trust Co—*Ben J Szwalbenest*	101 Carnegie Ctr, Princeton NJ 08540	609-951-2300	S	1,489*	.1
7	Happy State Bank and Trust Co—*Judy Shipman*	PO Box 68, Happy TX 79042	806-558-2265	S	1,478*	.1
8	Harris Bank	501 7th St, Rockford IL 61104	815-969-1500	S	1,323*	.1
9	BancOklahoma Mortgage Corp—*Ben Cowen*	7060 S Yale Ave Ste 20, Tulsa OK 74136	918-488-7140	S	1,293*	.1
10	Pennsylvania Trust Co—*Richardson T Merriman*	5 Radnor Corporate Ctr, Radnor PA 19087	610-975-4300	S	1,051*	<.1
11	Austin Trust Co—*William Hudspeth*	336 S Congress Ave Ste, Austin TX 78704	512-478-2121	R	715*	<.1
12	PennFirst Capital Trust I	600 Lawrence Ave Ste 7, Ellwood City PA 16117	724-654-7781	S	645	.1
13	Capital Guardian Trust Co—*Robert Ronus*	333 S Hope St 55nd Fl, Los Angeles CA 90071	213-486-9200	S	640*	.3
14	Northern Trust International Banking Corp—*James H Peterson*	103 2nd St Ste 1401, Jersey City NJ 07302	201-793-4900	S	412*	<.1
15	Capital Crossing Bank—*Demetrios (Jim) Kyrios*	101 Summer St, Boston MA 02110	617-880-1000	D	116*	.1
16	Raymond James Trust Company West—*David Ness*	PO Box 1221, Tacoma WA 98401	253-572-5339	S	71*	<.1
17	AmalgaTrust Company Inc—*Robert Wrobel*	1 W Monroe St 3rd Fl, Chicago IL 60603	312-822-3000	S	53*	<.1
18	Marshall and Ilsley Trust Co—*Mark Furlong*	111 E Kilbourn Ave 2nd, Milwaukee WI 53202	414-287-8700	S	47*	.3
19	Bank of Texas Trust Company NA—*Stanley A Lybarger*	5956 Sherry Ln Ste 110, Dallas TX 75225	817-427-7400	S	30*	<.1
20	Chicago Trust Company of California	3900 5th Ave Ste 280, San Diego CA 92103	619-239-3091	S	4*	<.1
21	First Midwest Trust Company NA—*Michael Scudder*	2801 W Jefferson St, Joliet IL 60435	815-727-5222	S	2*	.1
22	First Trust of MidAmerica—*Kevin R Ingram*	605 Cherry St Ste 304, Belton MO 64012	816-348-6988	S	1*	<.1
23	UW Trust Co—*D Mark Spencer*	PO Box 2526, Waco TX 76702	254-751-1505	S	1	N/A

TOTALS: SIC 6091 Nondeposit Trust Facilities
Companies: 23   **32,003**   **2.5**

6099 Functions Related to Deposit Banking

Rank	Company Name—*Executive Officer*	Address, City, State, Zip	Phone	Type	Fin	Empls
1	BancorpSouth Capital Trust I	PO Box 789, Tupelo MS 38802	662-680-2000	S	30,860*	4.5
2	Pay-O-Matic Corp—*Rich Gaccioni*	160 Oak Dr, Syosset NY 11791	516-496-4900	R	5,793*	.9
3	Western Union Co—*Hikmet Ersek*	PO Box 6992, Greenwood Village CO 80155	720-332-1000	P	5,193	7.0
4	First Data Merchant Services Corp—*Michael Capellas*	6200 S Quebec St, Greenwood Village CO 80111	303-488-8000	S	4,100	3.0
5	Cardservice International Inc (Simi Valley California)—*Joe Forehand*	PO Box 5180, Simi Valley CA 93062		S	3,988*	.9
6	Concord EFS Inc—*Edward A Labry III*	5565 Glenridge Connect, Atlanta GA 30342	901-371-8000	S	2,528	2.6
7	Public Currency Inc—*Jay B Shipowitz* ACE Cash Express Inc	1231 Greenway Dr Ste 6, Irving TX 75038	972-550-5000	S	2,112*	.3
8	QC and G Financial Inc—*Jay B Shipowitz* ACE Cash Express Inc	1231 Greenway Dr Ste 6, Irving TX 75038	972-550-5000	S	2,112*	.3
9	Bofl Holding Inc—*Gregory Garrabrants*	12777 High Bluff Dr St, San Diego CA 92130	858-350-6200	P	1,940	.2
10	Dollar Financial Corp—*Jeffrey A Weiss*	1436 Lancaster Ave Ste, Berwyn PA 19312	610-296-3400	P	1,663	5.4
11	Litton Loan Servicing LP—*Larry Litton Sr*	4828 Loop Central Dr, Houston TX 77081	713-960-9676	P	1,370*	1.2
12	Euronet Worldwide Inc—*Michael Brown*	3500 College Blvd, Leawood KS 66211	913-327-4200	P	1,038	3.1
13	ONB Finance Inc—*Robert Jones*	1 Main St, Evansville IN 47708	812-464-1434	S	883*	.2
14	PennFirst Financial Services Inc	600 Lawrence Ave Ste 7, Ellwood City PA 16117	724-758-5584	S	676*	.1
15	Prebon Yamane Inc USA—*Arthur Hughes*	101 Hudson St, Jersey City NJ 07302	201-557-5000	R	636	.5
16	Fx Solutions Inc—*Michael Cairns*	1 Rte 17 S Ste 260, Saddle River NJ 07458	201-345-2210	R	573*	.1
17	ACE Cash Express Inc—*Jay B Shipowitz*	1231 Greenway Dr Ste 6, Irving TX 75038	972-550-5000	R	512*	4.0
18	GAIN Capital Holdings Inc—*Glenn H Stevens*	135 US Hwy 202/206 Ste, Bedminster NJ 07921	908-731-0700	P	443	.3
19	Cross Check Inc—*J David Siembieda*	PO Box 6008, Petaluma CA 94955	707-665-2100	R	367*	.1
20	Euro Brokers Inc—*Howard Lutnick*	1 Seaport Plz 19th Fl, New York NY 10038	646-346-7000	R	360*	.3
21	HFF Inc—*John H Pelusi Jr*	1 Oxford Ctr 301 Grant, Pittsburgh PA 15219	412-281-8714	P	333	.4
22	Moneygram Payment Systems Inc—*Tony Ryan*	3940 S Teller St, Lakewood CO 80235	952-591-3000	S	295	.5
23	Global eTelecom Inc—*Chris Brundage*	73 Eglin Pkwy NE Ste 3, Fort Walton Beach FL 32548		R	281*	<.1
24	Southern Telecheck Inc—*Charlie Fote*	5251 Westheimer Rd Ste, Houston TX 77056	713-331-7600	S	173*	2.5
25	Cu Cooperative Systems Inc—*Stanley Hollen*	9692 Haven Ave, Rancho Cucamonga CA 91730	909-948-2500	R	155*	.3
26	Star System Inc—*Ronald V Congemi*	401 W A St Ste 600, San Diego CA 92101	619-234-4774	S	117*	.1
27	ECS Prepaid LLC—*Derran Winfrey*	1615 S Ingram Mill B, Springfield MO 65804		R	81	<.1
28	First Southeast Fiduciary and Trust Services Inc	34 Broad St, Charleston SC 29401	843-724-0800	S	57*	<.1
29	Payments Resource One—*Holly Merrill*	4000 N Central Ave Ste, Phoenix AZ 85012	602-340-1320	R	56*	<.1
30	Legacy Capital Management Inc—*Joe Milam*	3741 Douglas Blvd Ste, Roseville CA 95661	916-783-6200	R	31*	<.1
31	National Payment Corp—*Jefferson Harkins*	PO Box 577, Tampa FL 33606		R	16*	<.1
32	National Cash Processors Inc—*Bruce Korman*	1434 W 11th St, Los Angeles CA 90015	213-745-2000	S	6	.2
33	Money Centers of America Inc—*Christopher Wolfington*	601 S Henderson Rd Ste, King of Prussia PA 19406	610-354-8888	R	6	<.1
34	Payment Data Systems Inc—*Michael R Long*	12500 San Pedro Ste 12, San Antonio TX 78216	210-249-4100	P	2	<.1
35	United eSystems Inc—*Walter Reid Green Jr*	2150 N Hwy 190, Covington LA 70433	985-590-5396	R	2*	<.1

TOTALS: SIC 6099 Functions Related to Deposit Banking
Companies: 35   **68,758**   **39.0**

6111 Federal & Federally-Sponsored Credit

Rank	Company Name—*Executive Officer*	Address, City, State, Zip	Phone	Type	Fin	Empls
1	Federal National Mortgage Association Fannie Mae—*Michael J Williams*	3900 Wisconsin Ave NW, Washington DC 20016	202-752-7000	P	3,221,972	7.3
2	Freddie Mac—*Charles E 'Ed' Haldeman Jr*	8200 Jones Branch Dr, McLean VA 22102	703-903-2000	P	2,261,780	5.3
3	IBC Trading Co	1200 San Bernardo Ave, Laredo TX 78040	956-722-7611	S	104,575*	1.6
4	CoBank ACB—*Robert Engel*	PO Box 5110, Denver CO 80217	303-740-4000	R	79,889*	.6

Note: An asterisk (*) indicates an estimated financial figure. The company type code used is as follows: R = Private, P = Public, S = Private Subsidiary, B = Public Subsidiary, D = Division, J = Joint Venture, I = Investment Fund.

COMPANY RANKINGS BY SALES WITHIN 4-DIGIT SIC

Rank	Company Name—*Executive Officer*	Address, City, State, Zip	Phone	Type	Fin	Empls
5	Farm Credit Bank of Texas—*Larry R Doyle*	PO Box 202590, Austin TX 78720	512-465-0400	R	26,082*	.2
6	Farm Credit Bank of Omaha—*Doug Stark*	PO BOX 2409, Omaha NE 68103		R	20,647*	.8
7	AGFirst Farm Credit Bank—*F Andrew Lowrey*	PO Box 1499, Columbia SC 29202	803-799-5000	R	9,881*	.3
8	AgriBank FCB—*Billy York*	PO Box 64949, Saint Paul MN 55164	651-282-8800	R	2,129*	.3
9	Missouri Higher Education Loan Authority—*Raymond Bayer*	633 Spirit Dr, Chesterfield MO 63005	636-532-0600	R	180*	.2
10	Lumina Foundation For Education Inc—*Jamie Merisotis*	PO Box 1806, Indianapolis IN 46206	317-951-5300	R	172*	<.1
11	Great Lakes Higher Education Corp	PO Box 7860, Madison WI 53707	608-246-1700	R	171*	1.2
12	Great Lakes Educational Loan Services Inc—*Paul Thornburgh*	2401 International Ln, Madison WI 53704	608-246-1800	R	145*	.7
13	Federal Agricultural Mortgage Corp—*Michael A Gerber*	1999 K St NW 4th Fl, Washington DC 20036	202-872-7700	P	10	.1

TOTALS: SIC 6111 Federal & Federally-Sponsored Credit
Companies: 13

					5,727,632	18.5

6141 Personal Credit Institutions

Rank	Company Name—*Executive Officer*	Address, City, State, Zip	Phone	Type	Fin	Empls
1	General Electric Capital Corp—*Michael A Neal*	901 Main Ave, Norwalk CT 06851	203-357-4000	B	553,662	55.0
2	SLM Corp—*Albert L Lord*	12061 Bluemont Way, Reston VA 20190	703-810-3000	P	205,307	7.6
3	Ally Financial Inc—*Michael A Carpenter*	PO Box 200, Detroit MI 48265	313-656-6278	R	172,306	18.8
4	Ford Motor Credit Company LLC—*Michael E Bannister*	PO Box 1732, Dearborn MI 48121	313-322-3000	S	117,344*	8.0
5	HSBC Finance Corp—*Niall SK Booker*	2700 Sanders Rd, Prospect Heights IL 60070	224-514-2000	S	97,861*	32.0
6	Toyota Motor Credit Corp—*George Borst*	19001 S Western Ave, Torrance CA 90501	310-787-1310	S	81,193	3.3
7	Discover Financial Services—*David W Nelms*	2500 Lake Cook Rd, Riverwoods IL 60015	224-405-0900	P	60,785	10.3
8	Wells Fargo Financial Inc—*David Kvamme*	800 Walnut St, Des Moines IA 50309	515-243-2131	S	58,941*	18.0
9	City Financial Corp—*Harry Goff*	300 St Paul Pl, Baltimore MD 21202	410-332-3000	R	54,726*	18.0
10	Student Loan Corp—*Michael J Reardon* Discover Financial Services	PO Box 6151, Sioux Falls SD 57117	203-975-6320	S	31,018	.2
11	Nelnet Inc—*Michael S Dunlap*	PO Box 82561, Lincoln NE 68501	402-458-2370	P	25,894	2.2
12	Citicorp Diners Club Inc—*BVictoria Cook*	8430 W Bryn Mawr Ave, Chicago IL 60631	773-380-5160	S	25,008*	3.5
13	Beneficial Corp—*Finn M Caspersen* HSBC Finance Corp	2700 Sanders Rd, Prospect Heights IL 60070	847-564-5000	S	17,645	10.2
14	American General Financial Services—*Frederick R Geissinger*	PO Box 59, Evansville IN 47701	812-424-8031	S	13,295*	8.0
15	First Marblehead Corp—*Daniel Meyers*	800 Boylston St 34th F, Boston MA 02199	617-638-2000	P	7,652	.3
16	Springleaf Finance Corp—*Frederick Geissinger*	PO Box 3662, Evansville IN 47735	812-424-8031	S	7,646*	6.5
17	World Finance Corporation of Kentucky Inc—*A Alexander McLean III* World Acceptance Corp	PO Box 753, Hopkinsville KY 42241	270-885-8100	S	6,237*	2.1
18	Transamerica Financial Services—*John Beckett*	1150 S Olive St, Los Angeles CA 90015	213-742-4141	S	4,977*	2.5
19	Triad Financial Corp—*Daniel Leonard*	7711 Center Ave Ste 10, Huntington Beach CA 92647	714-373-8300	S	4,249*	1.3
20	World Omni Financial Corp—*Louis R Feagles*	PO Box 8544, Deerfield Beach FL 33443	954-363-6285	S	4,111*	.8
21	Education Lending Group Inc—*Robert deRose*	12680 High Bluff Dr St, San Diego CA 92130	858-617-6080	S	3,584	.1
22	CenterOne Financial Services LLC—*Colin Brown* World Omni Financial Corp	190 Jim Moran Blvd, Deerfield Beach FL 33442		S	3,276*	1.0
23	Amalgamated Bank—*Derrick Cephas*	275 7th Ave, New York NY 10001		R	2,500*	.3
24	Aegis Lending Corp	10049 N Reiger Rd, Baton Rouge LA 70809		S	1,850	3.5
25	Credit Acceptance Corp—*Brett A Roberts*	25505 W Twelve Mile Rd, Southfield MI 48034	248-353-2700	P	1,759	1.0
26	Academic Management Services Corp—*Albert L Lord* SLM Corp	1 AMS Pl 463 Swansea M, Swansea MA 02777	508-532-2900	S	1,583*	.3
27	CompuCredit Corp—*David G Hanna* CompuCredit Holdings Corp	5 Concourse Pkwy Ste 4, Atlanta GA 30328	770-828-2000	S	1,527	3.5
28	Origen Financial LLC—*Ronald Klein* Origen Financial Inc	27777 Franklin Rd Ste, Southfield MI 48034	248-746-7000	S	1,284*	.3
29	AmeriCredit Financial Services Inc—*Daniel Berce*	801 Cherry St Ste 3500, Fort Worth TX 76102	817-302-7000	S	1,140*	3.0
30	Bank of America Speciality Group—*Kenneth Lewis*	19601 Yorda Linda Blvd, Yorba Linda CA 92886		S	1,111	N/A
31	PennantPark Investment Corp—*Arthur H Penn*	590 Madison Ave 15th F, New York NY 10022	212-905-1000	P	929	N/A
32	CompuCredit Holdings Corp—*David G Hanna*	5 Concourse Pky Ste 40, Atlanta GA 30328	770-828-2000	P	881	1.6
33	Foothill Capital Corp—*John Stumpf*	2450 Colorado Ave Ste, Santa Monica CA 90404	310-453-7300	S	750*	.1
34	Origen Financial Inc—*Ronald Klein*	27777 Franklin Rd Ste, Southfield MI 48034	248-746-7000	P	744	<.1
35	World Acceptance Corp—*A Alexander McLean III*	PO Box 6429, Greenville SC 29606	864-298-9800	P	666	3.3
36	Ameristar Financial Co—*Charles F Wonderlic*	1795 N Butterfield Rd, Libertyville IL 60048	847-247-2600	R	551*	.3
37	Advance America Cash Advance Centers Inc—*J Patrick O'Shaughnessy*	135 N Church St, Spartanburg SC 29306	864-342-5600	P	525	5.8
38	Genesis Financial Solutions Inc—*Irving Levin*	PO Box 4865, Beaverton OR 97076	503-350-4300	R	518*	.2
39	Onyx Acceptance Corp—*John W Hall*	27051 Towne Centre Dr, Foothill Ranch CA 92610	949-465-3900	S	419*	.9
40	First Investors Financial Services Group Inc—*Tommy A Moore Jr*	675 Bering Dr, Houston TX 77057		P	394	.2
41	Harley-Davidson Financial Services Inc—*Keith E Wandell*	222 W Adams St Ste 200, Chicago IL 60606	312-368-9501	S	381*	.5
42	Check Into Cash Inc	PO Box 550, Cleveland TN 37364		R	356*	3.0
43	1st Franklin Financial Corp—*Virginia Herring*	PO Box 880, Toccoa GA 30577	706-886-7571	R	323*	.9
44	World Acceptance Corporation of Missouri Inc—*A Alexander McLean III* World Acceptance Corp	1303 N Washington St, Chillicothe MO 64601	660-707-1349	S	294	2.1
45	World Finance Corporation of Georgia Inc—*A Alexander McLean III* World Acceptance Corp	1104 N Westover Blvd S, Albany GA 31707	229-436-6576	S	294	2.1
46	World Finance Corporation of Illinois Inc—*A Alexander McLean III* World Acceptance Corp	3214 E Broadway Ste B, Alton IL 62002	618-465-9330	S	294	2.1
47	World Finance Corporation of Louisiana Inc—*A Alexander McLean III* World Acceptance Corp	2500 Louisville Ave, Monroe LA 71201	318-323-3626	S	294	2.1
48	World Finance Corporation of New Mexico Inc—*A Alexander McLean III* World Acceptance Corp	1508 N Prince St, Clovis NM 88101	505-762-1211	S	294	2.1
49	World Finance Corporation of Tennessee Inc—*A Alexander McLean III* World Acceptance Corp	420 Market St Ste 8, Dayton TN 37321	423-570-0772	S	294	2.1
50	World Finance Corporation of Texas Inc—*A Alexander McLean III* World Acceptance Corp	1713 Troup Hwy, Tyler TX 75701	903-597-8393	S	294	2.1
51	Security National Automotive Acceptance Corp—*Ted Catino*	6951 Cintas Blvd, Mason OH 45040	513-459-8118	R	289*	.1
52	Cash and Go Management LLC	690 E Lamar Blvd Ste 4, Arlington TX 76011	817-460-3947	S	268*	.1
53	Kropp Holdings Inc—*Linda Kropp*	4 North Park Dr Ste 41, Hunt Valley MD 21030	410-771-2701	R	222*	.1

Rank	Company Name—Executive Officer	Address, City, State, Zip	Phone	Type	Fin	Empls
54	General Motors Financial Company Inc—Daniel Berce	801 Cherry St Ste 3500, Fort Worth TX 76102	817-302-7000	R	170*	3.0
55	Brazos Higher Education Authority Inc—Murray Watson	PO Box 1308, Waco TX 76703	254-753-0915	R	156*	.2
56	Imperial Holdings Inc—Antony Mitchell	701 Park of Commerce B, Boca Raton FL 33487	561-995-4200	P	153	.1
57	Ge Capital Montgomery Ward—Marc Sheinbaum	260 Long Ridge Rd, Stamford CT 06927	203-357-4000	R	145*	2.3
58	White River Capital Inc—John M Eggemeyer III	PO Box 9876, Rancho Santa Fe CA 92067	858-997-6740	P	142	.1
59	Marquette Commercial Finance Inc—Daniel Karas	5910 N Central Expy St, Dallas TX 75206	214-389-5900	R	140*	.1
60	Union Acceptance Corp—Lee N Ervin White River Capital Inc	250 N Shadeland Ave, Indianapolis IN 46219	317-231-6400	S	117	.6
61	CDC Small Business Finance Corp—Kurt Chilcott	2448 Historic Decatur, San Diego CA 92106	619-291-3594	R	82*	<.1
62	Aqp Holdings LP—Matthew Clary	425 N Martingale Rd St, Schaumburg IL 60173	847-240-4300	R	64*	<.1
63	Southern California Grading Inc—Robert Cuttler	16291 Construction Cir, Irvine CA 92606	949-551-6655	R	42*	<.1
64	Shelter Financial Bank—Ron Wheeling	1817 W Broadway, Columbia MO 65218	573-214-4219	S	23*	<.1
65	BWC Real Estate—Andrea Head	1400 Civic Dr, Walnut Creek CA 94596	925-932-5353	S	18*	<.1
66	Creditguard Of America Inc—Roger Costa	5300 Broken Sound Blvd, Boca Raton FL 33487	561-948-7961	R	11*	.1
67	FastBucks	1650 Rio Rancho Blvd S, Rio Rancho NM 87124		R	11*	.1
68	Susque-Bancshares Leasing Company Inc—Richard M Cloney	PO Box 1000, Lititz PA 17543	717-626-4721	S	5*	<.1
69	Interact Holdings Group Inc—William Yates	2854 Johnson Ferry Rd, Marietta GA 30062	678-388-9857	P	4	N/A
70	Royal Premium Budget Inc—Allen Kaufman	PO Box 257, Southfield MI 48037	248-932-9020	S	1*	<.1
71	PrepaYd Inc—Bruce Berman	20271 SW Acacia St Ste, Newport Beach CA 92660	949-553-9044	P	1	<.1
72	Trycera Financial Inc—Ray Smith	18200 Von Karman Ave S, Irvine CA 92612	949-263-1800	P	<1	N/A

TOTALS: SIC 6141 Personal Credit Institutions
Companies: 72   1,581,028   260.2

6153 Short-Term Business Credit

Rank	Company Name—Executive Officer	Address, City, State, Zip	Phone	Type	Fin	Empls
1	Key Equipment Finance—Adam D Warner	1000 S McCaslin Blvd, Superior CO 80027		S	16,296*	1.1
2	Sears Roebuck Acceptance Corp	3711 Kennett Pike, Greenville DE 19807	302-656-9971	S	12,010*	<.1
3	Direct Capital Corp—James Broom	155 Commerce Way, Portsmouth NH 03801		R	4,788*	.3
4	BankUnited Capital—John A Kanas	255 Alhambra Cir, Coral Gables FL 33134	305-569-0327	S	3,681*	.3
5	BankUnited Capital II—John A Kanas	255 Alhambra Cir, Coral Gables FL 33134	305-569-0327	S	3,681*	.3
6	BankUnited Capital III—John A Kanas	255 Alhambra Cir, Coral Gables FL 33134	305-569-0327	S	3,681*	.3
7	Premium Financing Specialists Inc—Mike Gallagher	13520 Wyandotte St, Kansas City MO 64145	816-942-6336	R	2,493*	.2
8	Nicholas Financial Inc (Clearwater Florida)—Peter L Vosotas Nicholas Financial Inc	2454 McMullen-Booth Rd, Clearwater FL 33759	727-726-0763	S	1,846*	.1
9	Rosenthal and Rosenthal Inc—Stephen J Rosenthal	1370 Broadway, New York NY 10018	212-356-1400	R	1,702*	.2
10	Leaf Financial Corp—Crit S DeMent	2005 Market St 15th Fl, Philadelphia PA 19103		S	1,563*	.1
11	FleetCor Technologies Inc—Ronald F Clarke	655 Engineering Dr Ste, Norcross GA 30092	770-449-0479	P	1,123	2.1
12	Wells Fargo Foothill LLC—Peter E Schwab	2450 Colorado Ave Ste, Santa Monica CA 90404		S	1,000*	.2
13	Barnes Financing LLC—Gregory F Milzcik	PO Box 489, Bristol CT 06011	860-583-7070	S	859*	.1
14	Barnes Group Finance Co—Gregory F Milzcik	PO Box 489, Bristol CT 06011	860-583-7070	S	859*	.1
15	AMGRO Inc—Mike Gallagher Premium Financing Specialists Inc	PO Box 15089, Worcester MA 01615	508-757-1628	S	857*	.1
16	Encore Capital Group Inc—J Brandon Black	8875 Aero Dr Ste 200, San Diego CA 92123	858-560-2600	P	813	2.2
17	Capital Business Credit LLC—Andrew Tananbaum	1799 West Oakland Park, Fort Lauderdale FL 33311	954-730-2900	R	786*	.3
18	Metro Financial Services—Peter Cooney	PO Box 38604, Dallas TX 75238	214-363-4557	S	598*	<.1
19	ABN AMRO Inc—Mark Fisher	540 W Madison St, Chicago IL 60661	312-855-6000	D	528*	<.1
20	Plumas Bancorp—Andrew Ryback	35 S Lindan Ave, Quincy CA 06971	530-283-7305	P	500	.2
21	Mesirow Financial Holdings Inc—Richard Price	353 N Clark St, Chicago IL 60654	312-595-6000	R	403*	1.2
22	Arkansas Capital Corp—Sam Walls	200 S Commerce Ste 400, Little Rock AR 72201	501-374-9247	R	352	<.1
23	Midtown Partners and Company LLC—John R Clarke	380 Lexington Ave Ste, New York NY 10168	212-972-8390	R	332*	<.1
24	Merchant Factors Corp—Adam Winters	1430 Broadway 18th Fl, New York NY 10018	212-840-7575	R	315*	<.1
25	LawFinance Group Inc—Alan Zimmerman	1401 Los Gamos Dr Ste, San Rafael CA 94903	415-446-2300	R	271*	<.1
26	American Express Credit Corp—Chris Formo	200 Vesey St 31st Fl, New York NY 10285		S	264*	<.1
27	Asta Funding Inc—Gary Stern	210 Sylvan Ave, Englewood Cliffs NJ 07632	201-567-5648	P	248	.1
28	Nicholas Financial Inc—Cathy L Braswell	2454 McMullen Booth Rd, Clearwater FL 33759	727-726-0763	P	244	.3
29	Mazon Associates Inc—John Mazon	PO Box 166858, Irving TX 75016	972-554-6967	R	212*	<.1
30	PACCAR Financial Services Corp—Mark Pigott	PO Box 1518, Bellevue WA 98004	425-468-7400	S	180*	.3
31	Premium Payment Plan—Joe Klimas	PO Box 668, Hudson NY 12534	518-828-5504	R	175*	<.1
32	Bay Area Development Co—Jim Baird	1801 Oakland Blvd Ste, Walnut Creek CA 94596	925-926-1020	R	175*	<.1
33	Pseg Energy Holdngs LLC—Stephen Byrd	80 Park Plz Ste 3, Newark NJ 07102	973-430-7000	R	166*	2.8
34	Consumer Portfolio Services Inc—Charles E Bradley Jr	PO Box 57071, Irvine CA 92619	949-753-6800	P	155	.4
35	Td Auto Finance LLC—Thomas Gilman	PO Box 9217, Farmington Hills MI 48333	248-427-6800	S	141*	2.3
36	Thermo Credit LLC—James Lynch	639 Loyola Ave Ste 256, New Orleans LA 70113	504-620-3100	S	92*	<.1
37	Cash Systems Inc—Michael D Rumbolz	7350 Dean Martin Dr St, Las Vegas NV 89139	702-987-7169	S	69	.3
38	BluePay Processing LLC—John Rante	184 Shuman Blvd Ste 35, Naperville IL 60563		R	60*	.1
39	Frost Capital Group—Dick Evans	1010 Lamar St Ste 700, Houston TX 77002	713-759-9070	D	42*	<.1
40	Center Capital Corp—Walter Greenfield	3 Farm Glen Blvd, Farmington CT 06032		S	40*	<.1
41	First e-Solutions LLC—Julio A Omana	2805 E Oakland Park Bl, Fort Lauderdale FL 33306		R	30*	<.1
42	Xerox Financial Services Inc—Anne Mulcahy	PO Box 4505, Norwalk CT 06856	203-968-3000	S	20*	<.1
43	GK Financing LLC	4 Embarcadero Center S, San Francisco CA 94111	415-788-5300	S	20*	<.1
44	Remitstream Solution LLC—Tammy Pruitt	350 N Orleans St 8, Chicago IL 60654	312-660-5100	R	12*	.3
45	Entrust Bankcard LLC—Nathan Reis	1255 W Baseline Rd Ste, Mesa AZ 85202		R	9	.2
46	Braintree Inc—Bryan Johnson	464 Bourbon Ln, Naperville IL 60565		R	5	<.1
47	Timepayment Corp—Richard Latour	10 M Commerce Way, Woburn MA 01801	781-994-4870	S	1*	.1
48	Milberg Factors Inc—David J Milberg	99 Park Ave 21st Fl, New York NY 10016	212-697-4200	R	<1	.1

TOTALS: SIC 6153 Short Term Business Credit
Companies: 48   63,696   16.8

6159 Miscellaneous Business Credit Institutions

Rank	Company Name—Executive Officer	Address, City, State, Zip	Phone	Type	Fin	Empls
1	General Electric Capital Services Inc—Jeffrey R Immett	201 High Ridge Rd, Stamford CT 06905	203-316-7550	S	370,000*	23.0
2	GMAC Commercial Credit LLC—Jay Craig	1290 Ave of the Americ, New York NY 10104		S	337,652*	27.0
3	GE Capital—Michael Neal	260 Long Ridge Rd, Stamford CT 06902	203-357-4000	S	172,736	N/A
4	CIT Group Inc—John A Thain	1 CIT Dr, Livingston NJ 07039	973-740-5000	S	50,958	3.8
5	PPL Global LLC—Rick L Klingensmith	2 N 9th St, Allentown PA 18101	610-774-5418	S	33,471*	2.4
6	Volvo Finance North America Inc—Anthony Nicolosi	PO Box 914, Rockleigh NJ 07647		S	33,320*	1.9
7	Ford International Capital Corp—William Ford Jr	1 American Rd, Dearborn MI 48126	313-322-3000	S	33,309*	1.9
8	Morgan Stanley—James P Gorman	1585 Broadway, New York NY 10036	212-761-4000	P	31,622	62.5
9	John Deere Capital Corp—Samuel R Allen John Deere Credit Co	1 E 1st St Ste 600, Reno NV 89501	775-786-5527	S	22,512*	1.7
10	Caterpillar Financial Services Corp—Kent Adams	PO Box 340001, Nashville TN 37203	615-341-1000	S	21,428*	1.2

Note: An asterisk (*) indicates an estimated financial figure. The company type code used is as follows: R = Private, P = Public, S = Private Subsidiary, B = Public Subsidiary, D = Division, J = Joint Venture, I = Investment Fund.

COMPANY RANKINGS BY SALES WITHIN 4-DIGIT SIC

Rank	Company Name—*Executive Officer*	Address, City, State, Zip	Phone	Type	Fin	Empls
11	National Rural Utilities Cooperative Finance Corp—*Sheldon C Petersen*	2201 Cooperative Way, Herndon VA 20171	703-709-6700	I	20,983	.2
12	Wells Fargo Financial Leasing Inc	800 Walnut St, Des Moines IA 50309	515-557-4000	S	16,003*	.4
13	John Deere Credit Co—*Robert Lane*	1 John Deere Pl, Moline IL 61265	309-765-8000	S	11,241*	1.6
14	Nuvell Credit Corp—*Tom Pritchard*	PO Box 1700, Little Rock AR 72223	501-821-5252	S	11,170*	1.6
15	Textron Financial Corp—*Warren Lyons*	PO Box 6687, Providence RI 02940	401-621-4200	S	9,383	1.2
16	CapitalSource Inc—*John K Delaney*	5404 Wisconsin Ave 2 F, Chevy Chase MD 20815	301-841-2700	P	8,300	.6
17	Boeing Capital Corp—*Walt Skowronski*	500 Naches Ave SW 3rd, Seattle WA 98124	206-655-2121	S	8,155*	.2
18	Lender's Service Inc—*Ron Fraizer*	700 Cherrington Pkwy, Coraopolis PA 15108	412-299-4000	S	7,476*	.6
19	Private Export Funding Corp—*Don B Taggart*	280 Park Ave Ste 4W, New York NY 10017	212-916-0300	R	6,604*	<.1
20	Automotive Finance Corp	13085 Hamilton Crossin, Carmel IN 46032	317-815-9645	S	5,641*	.5
21	Barclays American Mortgage Corp—*Robert Diamond*	200 Park Ave, New York NY 10166	212-412-4000	S	4,990*	2.9
22	Hyundai Motor Finance Co—*Michael Buckingham*	10550 Talbert Ave, Fountain Valley CA 92708		S	4,317*	.3
23	Bombardier Capital—*Pierre Beaudoin*	261 Mountain View Dr 4, Colchester VT 05446	904-288-1000	S	4,248*	.2
24	Bombardier Capital Rail Inc—*Andre Navarri*	261 Mountain View Dr 4, Colchester VT 05446	904-288-1000	S	4,248*	.2
25	Farm Credit Services of Mid-America—*Donnie Winters*	PO Box 34390, Louisville KY 40232	502-420-3700	R	4,210*	.7
26	Wells Fargo Equipment Finance Inc—*John M McQueen*	733 Marquette Ave Ste, Minneapolis MN 55402	612-667-9876	S	3,800*	.3
27	Baylake Investments Inc—*Thomas Herlache*	217 N 4th Ave, Sturgeon Bay WI 54235	920-743-5551	S	3,248*	.4
28	FedFirst Corp—*Brian Turnau*	3661 W Oakland Park Bl, Lauderdale Lakes FL 33311	954-581-9893	R	3,168*	.2
29	No Red Tape Mortgage—*Blake Scheifele*	11150 W Olympic Blvd S, Los Angeles CA 90064		R	2,570*	.2
30	Freeman Spogli and Co—*Bradford M Freeman*	11100 Santa Monica Blv, Los Angeles CA 90025	310-444-1822	R	2,000	<.1
31	Navistar Financial Corp—*David Johanneson*	425 N Martingale Rd, Schaumburg IL 60173	630-753-4000	S	1,908*	.4
32	First American Equipment Finance—*William Verhelle*	PO Box 96, Fairport NY 14450	585-598-0900	R	1,634*	.1
33	People's United Equipment Finance Corp—*Paul R Sinsheimer*	1300 Post Oak Blvd, Houston TX 77056	713-439-1177	S	1,548	.2
34	JMP Securities LLC—*Joseph Jolson*	600 Montgomery St Ste, San Francisco CA 94111	415-835-8900	R	1,469*	.1
35	Farm Credit Leasing Services Corp—*Russ Nelson*	600 Hwy 169 S Ste 300, Minneapolis MN 55426	952-417-7800	S	1,463*	.2
36	Rental Car Finance Corp	5330 E 31st St, Tulsa OK 74135	918-669-2550	S	1,424	8.3
37	Loop Capital Markets LLC—*James Reynolds Jr*	200 W Jackson Blvd Ste, Chicago IL 60606	312-913-4900	R	1,143*	.1
38	BNP US Funding LLC	787 7th Ave, Manhattan NY 10019	212-841-2000	S	1,043	N/A
39	Financial Federal Credit Inc—*John Golio* People's United Equipment Finance Corp	1300 Post Oak Blvd Ste, Houston TX 77056	713-439-1177	S	898*	.1
40	Manufacturers Community Development Corp—*Mitch Feiger*	800 W Madison St, Chicago IL 60607		S	784	N/A
41	First South Production Credit Association—*Stephen L Rochelle*	PO Box 6008, Ridgeland MS 39158	601-977-8394	R	702*	.2
42	Philip Morris Capital Corp—*William Gifford*	225 High Ridge Rd Ste, Stamford CT 06905		S	626*	.1
43	Priority Leasing—*Robert D Glendon*	174 Green St, Melrose MA 02176	781-321-8778	R	572*	<.1
44	1st Farm Credit Services ACA—*Gary Ash*	2005 Jacobssen Dr Ste, Normal IL 61761	309-268-0327	R	500	.1
45	Orchard First Source—*Kathi Inorio*	2850 W Golf Rd 5th Fl, Rolling Meadows IL 60008	847-734-2000	R	496*	<.1
46	Taycor Financial—*Bob Skibinski*	6100 Center Dr Ste 710, Los Angeles CA 90045	310-568-9900	R	491*	<.1
47	Global Cash Access Holdings Inc—*Scott H Betts*	3525 E Post Rd Ste 120, Las Vegas NV 89120	702-855-3000	P	458	.4
48	Main Street Capital Corp—*Vincent D Foster*	1300 Post Oak Blvd Ste, Houston TX 77056	713-350-6000	P	449	<.1
49	Ruan Transportation Management Systems—*Steve Chapman*	3200 Ruan Ctr, Des Moines IA 50309	515-245-2500	R	440*	4.4
50	Evercore Partners Inc—*Ralph Schlosstein*	55 E 52nd St, New York NY 10055	212-857-3100	P	431	.8
51	SNS Investment Co—*Peter Dunn*	36 S Pennsylvania St, Indianapolis IN 46204	317-633-4100	S	413*	.1
52	Alpha Card Services Inc—*Lazaros Kalemis*	475 Veit Rd, Huntingdon Valley PA 19006		R	397*	<.1
53	PDS Gaming Corp—*Johan P Finley*	6280 Annie Oakley Dr, Las Vegas NV 89120	702-736-0700	R	386*	<.1
54	Inter-American Investment Corp—*Jacques Rogozinski*	1350 New York Ave NW, Washington DC 20005	202-623-3790	R	310*	.1
55	Mercantile Capital Corp—*Christopher G Hurn*	940 Centre Cir Ste 300, Altamonte Springs FL 32714	407-786-5040	R	286*	<.1
56	Cravey Green and Wahlen Inc—*Richard L Cravey*	3060 Peachtree Rd Ste, Atlanta GA 30305	404-816-3255	R	283*	<.1
57	Kohlberg Capital Corp—*Dayl W Pearson*	295 Madison Ave 6th Fl, New York NY 10017	212-455-8300	P	280	<.1
58	Siebert Brandford Shank and Company LLC—*Suzanne Shank*	1999 Harrison St Ste 2, Oakland CA 94612	510-645-2245	R	206*	<.1
59	Financial Pacific Co—*Paul J Menzel*	PO Box 4568, Federal Way WA 98063	253-568-6000	S	199*	.1
60	Aimbridge Group—*Steve Bentley*	116 Inverness Dr E Ste, Englewood CO 80112	303-695-1005	R	194*	<.1
61	Amerisource Funding Inc—*Michael Monk*	7225 Langtry St, Houston TX 77040	713-863-8300	R	189*	.1
62	CSA Financial Corp—*J Frank Keohane*	343 Commercial St, Boston MA 02109	617-357-1700	R	183*	<.1
63	Oak Council Investment Corp—*Kent Faison*	101 N Broadway Ave Ste, Oklahoma City OK 73102	405-270-1000	R	170*	<.1
64	Vna Holding Inc—*Ava Persson*	7825 National Service, Greensboro NC 27409	336-393-4890	R	161*	3.7
65	Fidelity National Capital Inc—*Alan Stinson*	7701 France Ave S Ste, Edina MN 55435	952-224-5880	S	156*	.1
66	Equipment Finance Corp—*Michael Begg*	219 Roswell St Ste 125, Alpharetta GA 30009	678-319-0333	R	150*	<.1
67	New York Business Development Corp—*Patrick J MacKrell*	PO Box 738, Albany NY 12201	518-463-2268	R	144*	<.1
68	MicroFinancial Inc—*Richard F Latour*	16 New England Executi, Burlington MA 01803	781-994-4800	P	144	.1
69	Leviathan Corp—*Brian Cohn*	20 Jay St Ste 356, Brooklyn NY 11201	718-701-5718	R	141*	<.1
70	Alpha Equipment Leasing—*Jim Buckingham*	3707 Grand Way Ste409, Minneapolis MN 55416		R	129*	<.1
71	Premier Finance Co—*James Ford*	10415 SE Stark St Ste, Portland OR 97216	503-262-9880	S	116*	<.1
72	PremierWest Investment Services Inc	PO Box 40, Medford OR 97501	541-618-6020	S	116*	<.1
73	City Capital Corp (Metairie Louisiana)—*John C McNamarra II*	111 Veterans Blvd Ste, Metairie LA 70005	504-831-5252	R	112*	<.1
74	MidCap Business Credit—*Richard Mount*	433 S Main St, West Hartford CT 06110		R	104*	<.1
75	Atalanta/Sosnoff Capital Corp—*Martin T Sosnoff*	101 Park Ave 6th Fl, New York NY 10178	212-867-5000	R	103*	<.1
76	Manufacturers Leasing Services Corp—*Roger Marce*	818 E Osborn Rd Ste 20, Phoenix AZ 85014	602-944-4411	R	103*	<.1
77	Jules and Associates Inc—*Jules Buenabenta*	515 S Figueroa St Ste, Los Angeles CA 90071	213-362-5600	R	93*	<.1
78	Meridian Venture Partners—*Robert E Brown Jr*	201 King of Prussia Rd, Radnor PA 19087	610-254-2999	J	79*	<.1
79	Telogy Inc—*Gary B Phillips*	3200 Whipple Rd, Union City CA 94587	510-675-9500	R	62*	.2
80	LendingTree Inc—*Douglas R Lebda*	11115 Rushmore Dr, Charlotte NC 28277	704-541-5351	S	51*	.4
81	Massachusetts Community Development Finance Corp—*Charles Grigsby*	155 Federal St Rm 202, Boston MA 02110	617-523-6262	R	49*	<.1
82	Summit Funding Group Inc—*Richard Ross*	11500 Northlake Dr Ste, Cincinnati OH 45249	513-489-1222	R	45*	<.1
83	Protective Capital Structures Corp—*Randall G Burton*	PO Box 271, Wilmington DE 19899	302-824-7064	P	45	<.1
84	Allied Financial Corp—*Andre Danesh*	188 Mason Ter, Brookline MA 02446	617-734-7771	R	38*	<.1
85	MCC Aviation Services Inc—*Frederick Dibble*	6867 Elm St Ste 101, Mc Lean VA 22101	703-847-6595	R	32*	<.1
86	Phoenix American Inc—*Gus Constantin*	2401 Kerner Blvd, San Rafael CA 94901	415-485-4500	R	25*	.3
87	Reyna Capital Corp—*Finbarr O'neil*	PO Box 1474, Dayton OH 45401	937-485-2955	S	22	<.1
88	Automated Installment Systems—*Diane Wood*	955 Executive Pkwy Ste, Saint Louis MO 63141	314-576-0007	R	8*	<.1
89	Armco Financial Services Corp—*Tony Madoskey*	1500 Graham Ave, Windber PA 15963	814-467-4421	S	7*	<.1
90	First Connecticut Capital Corp—*Bernard Zimmerman*	200 Connecticut Ave, Norwalk CT 06854	203-855-7700	R	4*	<.1
91	Chicago Deferred Exchange Corporation of California—*Mary Cunningham*	333 H St Ste 5052, Chula Vista CA 91910	619-497-2490	S	3*	<.1
92	United Leasing Corp—*Edward Shield*	PO Box 2260, Mechanicsville VA 23116	804-730-9500	R	3*	<.1
93	Nortia Capital Partners Inc—*William J Bosso*	400 Hampton View Ct, Alpharetta GA 30004	770-777-6795	P	2	<.1
94	Heritage Partners Inc—*Mark J Jrolf*	800 Boylston St Ste 15, Boston MA 02199	617-439-0688	R	1*	<.1
95	Southern Dallas Development Corp—*Charles McElrath*	400 Zang Blvd Ste 1210, Dallas TX 75208	214-948-7800	R	1*	<.1
96	Cooper Leasing Inc—*Russell Laing*	PO Box 58205, Raleigh NC 27658	919-878-3901	R	<1*	<.1

Rank	Company Name—*Executive Officer*	Address, City, State, Zip	Phone	Type	Fin	Empls
97	Stratford Financial Group Ltd—*Michael Caska*	300 Park Ave, New York NY 10022	212-705-4201	P	<1	<.1

TOTALS: SIC 6159 Miscellaneous Business Credit Institutions
Companies: 97   **1,272,985**   **158.7**

6162 Mortgage Bankers & Correspondents

Rank	Company Name—*Executive Officer*	Address, City, State, Zip	Phone	Type	Fin	Empls
1	Countrywide Financial Corp—*David Bigelow*	4500 Park Granada, Calabasas CA 91302	818-225-3000	S	211,730*	50.6
2	Rock Financial Corp—*William Emerson*	20555 Victor Pky, Livonia MI 48152	734-805-5000	S	160,000	N/A
3	Mercury Companies Inc—*Jerry Hauptman*	1515 Arapaho St, Denver CO 80202	303-233-9090	R	100,159*	5.3
4	Everhome Mortgage Co—*Robert Clements*	Po Box 2167, Jacksonville FL 32232	904-281-6380	R	46,959*	1.6
5	SunTrust Mortgage Inc—*Sterling Edmunds Jr*	Mail Code HDQ 4109 PO, Richmond VA 23285	804-291-0740	S	45,750*	2.5
6	Select Portfolio Servicing Inc	PO Box 65250, Salt Lake City UT 84165	801-293-1883	S	40,026*	2.0
7	Option One Mortgage Corp—*Bob Dubrish*	3 Ada, Irvine CA 92618	949-790-3600	S	35,850*	2.2
8	Great Southern Bank One LLC—*Joseph W Turner*	PO Box 9009, Springfield MO 65808	417-887-4400	S	31,717*	.9
9	Doral Bank (Catano Puerto Rico)—*Glen Wakeman*	163 Barbosa Ave, Catano PR 00962	787-474-6119	S	28,976*	1.0
10	Pulte Mortgage LLC—*Debra Still*	7475 S Joliet St, Englewood CO 80112	303-740-8800	S	18,835*	.8
11	Champion Mortgage Co NationStar Mortgage	350 Highland Dr, Lewisville TX 75067		D	16,191*	1.0
12	Capstead Mortgage Corp—*Andrew F Jacobs*	8401 N Central Expy St, Dallas TX 75225	214-874-2323	P	12,845	<.1
13	Centex Financial Services Inc—*Richard Dugas*	2728 N Harwood St, Dallas TX 75201	214-981-5000	S	12,453*	.4
14	Accredited Home Lenders Holding Co—*James A Konrath*	PO Box 502480, San Diego CA 92150		R	11,495	2.8
15	Impac Lending Co—*Bill Ashmore*	19500 Jamboree Rd, Irvine CA 92612	949-475-3600	R	10,287*	.4
16	Prudential Mortgage Capital Co—*David A Twardock*	100 Mulberry St, Newark NJ 07102	973-367-1051	S	9,745*	.6
17	First Franklin Financial Corp—*Andrew Pollock*	2150 N 1st St, San Jose CA 95131	408-964-6000	S	9,372*	.4
18	Countrywide Home Loans Inc—*Oscar Robertson* Countrywide Financial Corp	2 N Lake Ave Ste 100, Pasadena CA 91101	626-405-9448	S	8,658	4.8
19	Gateway Funding Diversified Mortgage Services LP—*Regina Lowrie*	300 Welsh Rd Bldg 5, Horsham PA 19044	215-591-0222	R	8,205*	.5
20	Plaza Home Mortgage Corp—*Kevin Parra*	5090 Shoreham Pl Ste 2, San Diego CA 92122	858-346-1208	R	8,047*	.2
21	Coldwell Banker Burnet—*Mary Baymler*	7550 France Ave S Ste, Edina MN 55435	952-844-6000	S	8,017*	.5
22	Saxon Capital Inc	4880 Cox Rd, Glen Allen VA 23060	804-967-7400	S	7,232	1.1
23	Seattle Mortgage Co—*Patrick F Patrick*	190 Queen Anne Ave N S, Seattle WA 98109	206-281-1500	R	7,167*	.5
24	Impac Mortgage Holdings Inc—*Joseph R Tomkinson*	19500 Jamboree Rd, Irvine CA 92612	949-475-3600	P	6,154	.4
25	Bell Mortgage Co—*Gary V Kirt*	1000 Shelard Pkwy Ste, Saint Louis Park MN 55426	952-591-1880	D	5,785*	.2
26	Rurban Mortgage Co—*Mark Klein*	401 Clinton St, Defiance OH 43512	419-783-8905	S	5,349*	.1
27	BankUnited Mortgage Corp—*John A Kanas*	255 Alhambra Cir, Coral Gables FL 33134	305-569-0327	S	4,564*	.3
28	First Mortgage Corp—*Clement Ziroli*	PO Box 4500, Diamond Bar CA 91765	909-595-1996	R	4,342*	.1
29	First Financial Services—*Donald Landgraff*	6230 Fairview Rd Ste 4, Charlotte NC 28210	704-365-3097	R	3,580*	.1
30	Doral Money Inc—*Paul Mak*	623 5th Ave 13th Fl, New York NY 10022	212-447-9000	S	3,573*	.2
31	Accredited Home Lenders Inc—*James M Moran* Accredited Home Lenders Holding Co	15253 Ave of Science B, San Diego CA 92128	858-676-2100	S	3,501	2.1
32	Merrill Lynch Credit Corp—*Larry Washington*	4804 Deer Lake Dr E 5t, Jacksonville FL 32246	904-218-6000	S	3,216*	1.4
33	Saxon Mortgage Services Inc	PO Box 161489, Fort Worth TX 76161		R	2,982*	.2
34	First Eastern Mortgage Corp—*Richard F Kalagher*	100 Brickstone Sq, Andover MA 01810	978-749-3100	S	2,217*	.1
35	Universal Lending Corp—*Pete Lansing*	6775 E Evans Ave, Denver CO 80224	303-758-4969	R	2,066*	.1
36	Municipal Mortgage and Equity LLC—*Michael L Falcone*	621 E Pratt St Ste 300, Baltimore MD 21202	443-263-2900	P	2,060	<.1
37	HomeAmerican Mortgage Corp—*Robert Hathaway*	7595 Technology WaySte, Denver CO 80237	303-770-1155	S	1,950*	.1
38	ARCS Commercial Mortgage Company LP—*Timothy White*	26901 Agoura Rd Ste 20, Calabasas Hills CA 91301	818-880-3300	R	1,848*	.1
39	Guaranty Home Equity Inc—*Joe Mundwiler*	4000 W Brown Deer Rd, Milwaukee WI 53209	414-365-6945	S	1,803*	.1
40	Broadway Service Corp—*Wayne Kent Bradshaw*	4800 Wilshire Blvd, Los Angeles CA 90010	323-634-1700	S	1,748*	.1
41	McMillin Mortgage—*Mark McMillin*	4210 Bonita Rd Ste B, Bonita CA 91902	619-477-4117	S	1,719*	.1
42	CapLease Inc—*Paul H McDowell*	1065 Ave of the Americ, New York NY 10018	212-217-6300	P	1,642	<.1
43	Home Trust Co—*Lynn Nunez*	5353 W Alabama Ste 500, Houston TX 77056	713-369-4000	R	1,528*	.1
44	GFI Mortgage Bankers Inc—*Allen Gross*	50 Broadway 4th Fl, New York NY 10004	212-668-1444	S	1,289*	.1
45	Genworth Mortgage Insurance Corp—*Kevin G Schneider*	6601 Six Forks Rd, Raleigh NC 27615	919-846-4100	S	1,092*	1.0
46	CountryPlace Mortgage Ltd—*Larry Keener*	15305 Dallas Pkwy Ste, Addison TX 75001	972-991-2422	S	1,034*	.1
47	Republic Mortgage Home Loans LLC—*L Scott Leishman*	5241 S State St Ste 2, Murray UT 84107	801-288-9400	R	1,000	N/A
48	Fireside Bank—*Fred Reichelt*	5050 Hopyard Rd, Pleasanton CA 94588		S	900	N/A
49	Commerce Mortgage Corp	922 Walnut St Ste 1100, Kansas City MO 64106	816-234-2990	S	894*	.1
50	Mississippi Home Corp—*Diane Bolen*	PO Box 23369, Jackson MS 39225	601-718-4642	R	780*	<.1
51	Fullerton Mortgage and Escrow Co—*Eric Hartman*	PO Box 27, Oceanside CA 92049	714-870-4411	R	758*	<.1
52	Community Mortgage Corp—*Pat Sandlin*	142 Timber Creek Dr, Cordova TN 38018	901-759-4400	R	752*	<.1
53	Ryland Mortgage Co—*Larry T Nicholson*	3011 Townsgate Rd Ste, Westlake Village CA 91361	805-367-3800	S	743*	.1
54	Flagstar Bank FSB—*Jay Hansen*	2600 Telegraph Rd, Bloomfield Hills MI 48302	248-338-7700	S	642*	.4
55	Industry Mortgage Associates LLC—*Jeff Toland*	25283 Cabot Rd Ste 101, Laguna Hills CA 92653	949-583-9918	R	641*	<.1
56	Circle Mortgage Corp—*David Levitt*	6600 Taft St 4th Fl, Hollywood FL 33024	954-981-6800	R	573*	<.1
57	Delmar Financial Co—*Matt Levison*	1066 Executive Pky Ste, Saint Louis MO 63141	314-434-7000	R	572*	<.1
58	Mission Mortgage of Texas Inc—*LeeAnn McCoy*	901 S Mopac Bldg V Ste, Austin TX 78746	512-328-0400	R	537*	<.1
59	Franklin Credit Holding Corp—*Thomas Axon*	101 Hudson St 25th Fl, Jersey City NJ 07302	201-604-1800	P	518	.1
60	Alambry Funding Inc	3333 Street Rd Ste 150, Bensalem PA 19020	215-638-7300	S	445*	<.1
61	HomeBanc Mortgage Corp—*Patrick Flood*	5555 Glenridge NE Ste, Atlanta GA 30342	404-459-7400	S	430*	1.2
62	Simmons First Mortgage Co	8315 Cantrell Rd Ste 1, Little Rock AR 72227	501-223-4200	S	410*	<.1
63	intervest Mortgage Investment Com—*Campbell S O'Neill*	2030 Franklin St 5th F, Oakland CA 94612	510-622-8500	S	395*	.1
64	AMRESCO Commercial Finance Inc	412 E Parkcenter Blvd, Boise ID 83706	208-333-2000	S	392*	.5
65	Independent Mortgage Co-South Michigan—*Mike MaGee Jr*	PO Box 536, Leslie MI 49251	517-589-8222	S	336*	<.1
66	Bryco Funding Inc—*Bryce Angell*	580 California St 8th, San Francisco CA 94104		R	334*	.1
67	Guild Mortgage Co—*Martin L Gleich*	5898 Copley Dr, San Diego CA 92111	858-560-6330	R	326*	.3
68	Mission Hills Mortgage Bankers—*Ron Tarbell*	1403 N Tustin Ave Ste, Santa Ana CA 92705		R	320*	.3
69	Sterling National Mortgage Company Inc—*Michael Bizenov*	98 Cuttermill Rd Ste 2, Great Neck NY 11021	516-487-0018	S	309*	<.1
70	Pergolis-Swartz Associates Inc—*Richard Pergolis*	12 W 37th St 8th Fl, New York NY 10018	212-643-5663	R	309*	<.1
71	Marquest Financial Inc—*Edward M Graca*	3800 American Blvd W, Bloomington MN 55431	952-857-2500	R	304*	<.1
72	M Robert Goldman and Company Inc—*Kenneth Goldman*	100 Jericho Quadrangle, Jericho NY 11753	516-487-5100	R	298*	<.1
73	SBT Bancorp Inc—*Martin J Geitz*	PO Box 248, Simsbury CT 06070	860-408-5493	P	296	<.1
74	Town and Country Mortgage Co—*Kevin McGinnis*	36 Four Seasons Ctr St, Chesterfield MO 63017	314-909-5700	R	287*	<.1
75	Franklin American Mortgage Co—*Daniel G Crockett*	501 Corporate Center D, Franklin TN 37067	615-778-1000	R	266*	.9
76	Citizens Bank Mortgage Co—*Cathy Nash*	328 S Saginaw St, Flint MI 48502	810-766-7500	S	243*	<.1
77	Independent Mortgage Co-East Michigan—*Michael M Magee Jr*	PO Box 69, Caro MI 48723	989-673-5656	S	241*	<.1
78	Dwyer-Curlett and Co—*Shelley Magoffin*	1880 Century Park E St, Los Angeles CA 90067	310-226-2700	R	216*	<.1
79	Coastal States Mortgage Corp—*Richard Higgins*	600 Corporate Dr Ste 6, Fort Lauderdale FL 33334	954-964-3200	R	214*	<.1

Note: An asterisk (*) indicates an estimated financial figure. The company type code used is as follows: R = Private, P = Public, S = Private Subsidiary, B = Public Subsidiary, D = Division, J = Joint Venture, I = Investment Fund.

COMPANY RANKINGS BY SALES WITHIN 4-DIGIT SIC

Rank	Company Name—Executive Officer	Address, City, State, Zip	Phone	Type	Fin	Empls
80	Aztec Group Inc—Ezra Katz	2665 S Bayshore Dr PH-, Miami FL 33133	305-854-5000	R	211*	<.1
81	BMIC Mortgage Inc—Gary Schiller	5640 Nicholson Ln Ste, Rockville MD 20852	301-231-5770	R	187*	<.1
82	City National Mortgage Co—Russell Goldsmith	400 N Roxbury Dr, Beverly Hills CA 90210	310-888-6000	S	182*	<.1
83	Shelter Mortgage Corp—Jill Levy Belconis	4000 W Brown Deer Rd, Milwaukee WI 53209	414-362-4000	S	170*	.2
84	First Manhattan Funding LLC	261 E 300 S Ste 255, Salt Lake City UT 84111	801-643-3022	R	160*	.1
85	CMax LLC—Stephen Kass	1555 Palm Beach Lakes, West Palm Beach FL 33401	561-352-2200	R	158	<.1
86	Bay Network Funding—Patricia Goyeau	1845 Hamilton Ave, San Jose CA 95125	408-369-7800	R	158*	<.1
87	ditechcom—Timothy Montgomery	1100 Virginia Dr, Ft Washington PA 19034	714-800-5800	S	150*	.4
88	Mortgage Source LLC—Jennifer Weisman	600 Old Country Rd Rm, Garden City NY 11530	516-487-3111	R	150*	.1
89	Continental Mortgage Bankers—Walter Stashin	1025 Old Country Rd St, Westbury NY 11590	516-876-8500	R	150*	.1
90	Mid-Valley Services Inc—Larry Korth	7644 N Palm Ave, Fresno CA 93711	559-432-8221	R	150*	<.1
91	Platinum Mortgage Inc—Terry Clark	103b Spenryn Dr, Madison AL 35758	256-461-8677	R	148*	.1
92	First Security Mortgage Home Loans Inc—Sylvia C Rios	3914 Murphy Canyon Rd, San Diego CA 92123	858-565-4466	R	147*	<.1
93	CUNA Mutual Mortgage Corp—Jeff Post	5910 Mineral Point Rd, Madison WI 53705	608-238-5851	S	146*	1.6
94	Thomas D Wood and Co—Thomas D Wood Jr	95 Merrick Way Ste 360, Coral Gables FL 33134	305-447-7820	R	144*	<.1
95	Arbor Commercial Mortgage LLC—Ivan Kaufman	333 Earle Ovington Blv, Uniondale NY 11553	516-832-8002	R	137*	.1
96	Cherry Creek Mortgage Company Inc—Jeff Mey	7600 E Orchard Rd Ste, Greenwood Village CO 80111	303-320-4040	R	135*	.5
97	Urban Lending Solutions—Charles Sanders	1001 Liberty Ave Ste 1, Pittsburgh PA 15222	412-325-7046	R	127	.7
98	Century Mortgage—Alan Gandall	110 Newport Center Dr, Newport Beach CA 92660	949-759-3610	R	119*	<.1
99	Kaufman and Broad Mortgage Co—Richard Powers	10990 Wilshire Blvd 9t, Los Angeles CA 90024	310-893-7300	S	114*	.1
100	Franklin Mortgage Co—Mark Purcell	4222 E Camelback Rd St, Phoenix AZ 85018	602-224-5995	R	110*	<.1
101	Premier Mortgage Co	139 Del Norte Ave, Denham Springs LA 70726		R	101*	<.1
102	Carteret Mortgage Corp—Eric Weinstein	3514 Rawdon Dr, Durham NC 27713		R	100*	2.1
103	Dominion Capital Inc—Thomas Chewning	PO Box 26543, Richmond VA 23290	804-257-4725	S	100*	.1
104	George Mason Mortgage Corp—Ed Dean	4100 Monument Corner D, Fairfax VA 22030	703-273-2600	S	99*	.1
105	Bay Finance Company Inc—Bob Hamilton	1 Corporate Dr Ste 300, Wausau WI 54401		S	99*	<.1
106	First Tennessee Capital Assets Corp—Jerry Hubbard	845 Crossover Ln Ste 1, Memphis TN 38117	901-435-8080	S	98*	<.1
107	Action Mortgage Co—Jim Kirshbaum	111 N Wall, Spokane WA 99201	509-458-2373	S	94*	.1
108	M and T Mortgage Corp—Mark Czarnecki	4949 SW Meadows Rd Ste, Lake Oswego OR 97035	503-603-2555	S	75*	.1
109	Crowder Mortgage Corp—James Crowder	3445 Penrose Pl Ste 24, Boulder CO 80301	303-444-1545	R	74*	<.1
110	NVR Mortgage Finance Inc—William J Inman	11700 Plz American Dr, Reston VA 20190	703-956-4000	R	62*	.5
111	Globe Mortgage America LLC—Lisa Lopez	475 Grand Ave, Englewood NJ 07631	201-816-5900	R	58*	<.1
112	Hamilton Carter Smith and Company Inc—Herman Churchwell	8500 Wilshire Blvd, Beverly Hills CA 90211	310-289-9181	R	58*	<.1
113	Gross Mortgage Finance Inc—Allan Gross	3325 S University Dr S, Davie FL 33328	954-475-7784	R	57*	<.1
114	MortgageAmerica Inc—John Johnson	1800 International Par, Birmingham AL 35243	205-970-3000	R	55*	.1
115	CBRE Capital Markets—Brian Stoffers	2800 Post Oak Blvd Ste, Houston TX 77056	713-787-1900	S	50*	.4
116	Amtrust Mortgage Corp—Steve B Whipple III	100 Glenridge Point Pk, Atlanta GA 30342		R	46*	.2
117	Ncb Management Services Inc—Marcelo Aita	1 Allied Dr, Trevose PA 19053	215-244-4200	R	38*	.3
118	Legacy Financial Group Inc—C Chad Bates	1205 W Abram, Arlington TX 76013	817-860-3232	R	38*	<.1
119	Americor Mortgage Inc—Thomas S Balames	255 E Brown St, Birmingham MI 48009	248-816-7245	R	29*	<.1
120	Family First Mortgage Corp—Gregory Hill	33 Old Kings Rd N Ste, Palm Coast FL 32137	386-246-6955	R	24*	.6
121	First Residential Mortgage Network Inc—Saul Pohn	9500 Ormsby Station Rd, Louisville KY 40223	502-315-4750	R	24*	.4
122	James B Nutter and Co—James Nutter Jr	4153 Broadway, Kansas City MO 64111	816-531-2345	R	21*	.2
123	Gold Star Mortgage Financial Group LLC—Daniel Milstein	3879 Packard Rd, Ann Arbor MI 48108		R	15	.3
124	National Fidelity Mortgage Inc—David Silverman	505 Progress Dr, Linthicum MD 21090	443-451-3199	R	15*	.2
125	Homebuilders Financial Network Inc—Jeffrey P Mouhalis	7900 Miami Lakes Dr W, Miami Lakes FL 33016	305-820-3980	R	15*	.1
126	Vestin Group Inc—Michael V Shustek	6149 S Rainbow Blvd, Las Vegas NV 89118	702-227-0965	R	14	<.1
127	Capstead Inc—Andrew F Jacobs Capstead Mortgage Corp	8401 N Central Expy St, Dallas TX 75225	214-874-2323	S	12	<.1
128	Southwest Funding LP—Don Yount	8848 Greenville Ave, Dallas TX 75243	214-221-5215	R	12*	.2
129	FirsTrust Mortgage—Mark McDougald	4501 College Blvd Ste, Leawood KS 66211	913-312-2000	R	10*	<.1
130	OneCap—Vincent Hesser	5440 W Sahara Ave 3rd, Las Vegas NV 89146	702-948-8800	R	9	<.1
131	AAA Financial Inc—Dave DiNatale	9600 W Sample Rd, Coral Springs FL 33065	954-344-2530	R	8*	<.1
132	George Elkins Mortgage Banking Co—Jeffrey Hudson	12100 Wilshire Blvd St, Los Angeles CA 90025	310-207-3456	R	6*	.1
133	Republic State Mortgage Co—Robert Wagnon	2715 Bissonnet Ste 102, Houston TX 77005	713-520-7791	R	6*	<.1
134	Signature Mortgage—Bob Caitlin	4790 Douglas Cir NW, Canton OH 44718	330-305-1996	R	6*	<.1
135	Princeton Financial Corp—Don Zivitz	6085 Lake Forrest Dr N, Atlanta GA 30328	404-252-7868	R	5*	N/A
136	AGM Financial Services Inc—Margaret Allen	20 N Charles St Ste 10, Baltimore MD 21201	410-727-2111	R	4*	<.1
137	Aasent Mortgage Corp	100 Galleria Pkwy Ste9, Atlanta GA 30339	770-988-7000	R	4	.1
138	Stancorp Mortgage Investors LLC—J Gregory Ness	1100 SW 6th Ave, Portland OR 97204		S	3*	.1
139	Pagasus Claims Service Inc—Chuck Orapeza	910 W 17th St Ste A, Santa Ana CA 92706	714-647-6200	R	3*	<.1
140	Renet Financial Corp—Keith Gellar	1182 N Tustin St, Orange CA 92867	805-445-7544	R	3	<.1
141	Malcap Mortgage LLC—Joshua Malnofski	115 East Park Dr Ste 2, Brentwood TN 37027	615-324-5200	R	2	<.1
142	Reliance Inc—Stacey Jones	3940 10th Ave N, Lake Worth FL 33461	561-967-5066	R	2	<.1
143	Coratolo Carrieri Associates LLC—Michael V Coratolo	18 North Central Ave S, Hartsdale NY 10530	914-681-1300	R	2*	<.1
144	PSM Holdings Inc—Ron Hanna	1112 N Main St, Roswell NM 88201	575-624-4170	P	1	.1
145	Fisher Mortgage Company Inc—Todd Fisher	333 E Il Rte 83, Mundelein IL 60060	847-573-1234	R	1*	<.1
146	Business West Mortgage Co—Dan Wood	5152 Katella Ave Rm 10, Los Alamitos CA 90720		R	1*	<.1
147	Heritage Group LLC—Josh Hoecherl	1460 Moon River Dr, Provo UT 84604	801-655-1600	R	1*	<.1
148	Complete Care Medical Inc—JP Monteverde III	5353 W Sam Houston Pky, Houston TX 77041	281-619-2050	P	1	N/A
149	Metrocities Mortgage LLC—Paul Wylie	15301 Ventura Blvd Ste, Sherman Oaks CA 91403		R	N/A	1.4
150	NationStar Mortgage—Tony Barone	350 Highland Dr, Lewisville TX 75067	469-549-2000	R	N/A	1.4
151	Cornerstone Mortgage Co—Marc Laird	1177 W Loop S Ste 200, Houston TX 77027	713-621-4663	R	N/A	.1

TOTALS: SIC 6162 Mortgage Bankers & Correspondents
Companies: 151   935,153   104.9

6163 Loan Brokers

Rank	Company Name—Executive Officer	Address, City, State, Zip	Phone	Type	Fin	Empls
1	Capmark Financial Group Inc—Jay N Levine	116 Welsh Rd, Horsham PA 19044	215-328-4622	S	23,264	3.0
2	MortgageIT Holdings Inc—Gary Bierfriend	33 Maiden Ln, New York NY 10038	212-651-7700	S	7,653*	2.1
3	EMC Mortgage Corp—John Vella	P O Box 293150, Lewisville TX 75029		S	5,281*	1.0
4	Collegiate Funding Services LLC—J Barry Morrow	10304 Spotsylvania Ave, Fredericksburg VA 22408		R	5,043	.8
5	ESB Financial Services Inc	600 Lawrence Ave, Ellwood City PA 16117	724-758-5584	S	1,960*	.3
6	HD Vest Mortgage Services Inc	6333 N State Hwy 161 4, Irving TX 75038	972-870-6000	S	1,590*	.1
7	Blackrock Kelso Capital Corp—James R Maher	40 E 52nd St 21st Fl, New York NY 10022	212-810-5800	P	701	N/A
8	Florida First Capital Finance Corp—Todd G Kocourek	1351 N Gadsden St, Tallahassee FL 32303	850-681-3601	R	678*	<.1
9	Meridian Capital Group LLC—Ralph Herzka	1 Battery Park Plaza, New York NY 10004	212-972-3600	R	646*	.1
10	Prime Lending Inc—Todd Salmans	18111 Preston Rd Ste 9, Dallas TX 75252	972-248-7866	R	562*	.1
11	Walker and Dunlop Inc—William Walker	7501 Wisconsin Ave Ste, Bethesda MD 20814	301-215-5500	P	486	.2
12	Manhattan Mortgage Co—Melissa Cohn	750 Lexington Ave, New York NY 10022	212-593-4343	S	379*	.1
13	American Family Financial Services Inc	6000 American Pkwy, Madison WI 53783	608-249-2111	S	375*	.1

Rank	Company Name—*Executive Officer*	Address, City, State, Zip	Phone	Type	Fin	Empls
14	Berthel Fisher and Co—*Thomas J Berthel*	PO Box 609, Marion IA 52302	319-447-5700	R	347*	.1
15	Bankers Small Business Community Development Corp—*Kurt Chilcott*	2448 Historic Decatur, San Diego CA 92106	619-291-3594	R	304*	<.1
16	BellGroup Financial Services Inc—*Carl W Bell*	16980 Dallas Pkwy, Dallas TX 75248	972-581-4800	R	301*	.1
17	Synergy Direct Mortgage—*Don Scioli*	9 Peddlers Village, Newark DE 19702	302-613-0763	R	283*	.1
18	PMC Funding Corp—*Lance Rosemore*	17950 Preston Rd Ste 6, Dallas TX 75252	972-349-3200	S	250*	.1
19	Taylor Bean and Whitaker Mortgage Corp—*Paul R Allen*	315 NE 14th St, Ocala FL 34470	352-351-1109	R	229*	<.1
20	Hilco Capital LP—*Jeffrey Hecktman*	5 Revere Dr Ste 206, Northbrook IL 60062	847-509-1100	S	182*	<.1
21	Academy Mortgage Corp—*Adam Kessler*	1218 E 7800 S Ste 100, Sandy UT 84094	801-233-3700	R	163*	1.3
22	Consumer Home Mortgage Inc—*Robert Standfast*	115 Broadhollow Rd, Melville NY 11747	631-547-6840	R	160*	.2
23	Martha's Vineyard Mortgage Company LLC	PO Box 2697, Vineyard Haven MA 02568	508-696-1801	R	160*	<.1
24	QC Holdings Inc—*Don Early*	9401 Indian Creek Pkwy, Overland Park KS 66210	913-234-5000	P	138	1.7
25	Elite Financial Group Inc—*Dodi Handy*	4701 N Federal Hwy Ste, Pompano Beach FL 33064	954-537-7775	R	106*	<.1
26	Southside Financial Group LLC—*Steve Burke*	PO Box 3538, Arlington TX 76007	817-461-8100	S	103*	<.1
27	Sotheby's Financial Services Inc—*William Ruprecht*	1334 York Ave, New York NY 10021	212-894-2355	S	65*	<.1
28	CW Capital—*Michael Berman*	1 Charles River Pl 63, Needham MA 02494	781-707-9300	R	57*	<.1
29	LeadFlashcom—*Jeffrey Kleiman*	6700 Broken Sound Pkwy, Boca Raton FL 33487	561-499-3329	R	51	<.1
30	Regency Finance Co—*Charles Moore*	8600 E Market St Ste 8, Warren OH 44484	330-856-9900	S	50*	<.1
31	Mortgage Resources Inc—*Steven Carrico*	425 S Woodsmill Ste 10, Chesterfield MO 63017	314-576-5577	R	39*	<.1
32	Mercury Equipment Finance Group—*Barry Lyon*	28562 Oso Pkwy Ste D14, Rancho Santa Margarita CA 92688	949-218-8700	R	27*	<.1
33	Atlantic Bay Mortgage Group LLC—*Brian K Holland*	613 Lynnhaven Pkwy, Virginia Beach VA 23452	757-498-6789	R	22*	.3
34	P/R Mortgage and Investment Corp—*Michael Petrie*	11711 N Meridian St St, Carmel IN 46032	317-569-7420	R	18*	<.1
35	Awp Copperfield Inc—*Ann Walker*	8514 Hwy 6 N, Houston TX 77095	281-856-0808	R	17*	.1
36	Mortgage Research Center—*Nathan Long*	2101 Chapel Hill Plz, Columbia MO 65203		R	15*	.1
37	Baltimore Financial LLC—*R Joseph Moore*	31 Commercial Blvd Ste, Novato CA 94949	415-883-1593	R	15*	<.1
38	Specialty Group—*Ned Sokoloff*	3205 McKnight E Dr, Pittsburgh PA 15237	412-369-1555	R	9*	<.1
39	Vantage Point Mortgage—*Rick Lee*	5800 Jameson Ct Ste 10, Carmichael CA 95608	916-482-0541	R	9*	<.1
40	Royal Mortgage Corp—*Richard Nacht*	3490 US Hwy 1, Princeton NJ 08540	609-452-1730	S	7*	.1
41	Gallatin Mortgage Co—*Jeffrey R Gallatin*	409 S Division, Ann Arbor MI 48104	734-994-1202	R	7*	<.1
42	USA Lending Group—*Brian Goodman*	10542 S Jordan Gtwy St, South Jordan UT 84095	801-676-1200	R	5*	.1
43	Lendio Inc—*Brock Blake*	3630 W South Jordan Pk, South Jordan UT 84095	855-853-6346	R	5*	.1
44	London Financial Capital LLC—*Hunter Herbert*	12745 S Saginaw, Grand Blanc MI 48439	248-807-8767	R	5	<.1
45	Data Select Systems Inc	2829 Townsgate Rd Ste, Westlake Village CA 91361	805-446-2090	R	4*	<.1
46	Healthient Inc—*Katherine West*	15132 Park of Commerce, Jupiter FL 33478		P	2	<.1
47	Living Water Funding—*Paul Lufkin*	PO Box 210671, Bedford TX 76095	817-875-4524	R	1	<.1
48	Treecom Inc—*Douglas Lebda*	11115 Rushmore Dr, Charlotte NC 28277	704-541-5351	P	<1	.9

TOTALS: SIC 6163 Loan Brokers
Companies: 48   51,773   13.4

6211 Security Brokers & Dealers

Rank	Company Name—*Executive Officer*	Address, City, State, Zip	Phone	Type	Fin	Empls
1	American Express Co—*Kenneth I Chenault*	200 Vesey St, New York NY 10285	212-640-2000	P	144,209	61.0
2	Charles Schwab Corp—*Walter W Bettinger II*	211 Main St, San Francisco CA 94105	415-636-7000	P	92,568	12.4
3	Lehman Brothers Holdings Inc—*Richard S Fuld Jr*	1271 Ave of the Americ, New York NY 10020	646-285-9000	P	59,003	28.6
4	MF Global Ltd—*Laurie R Ferber*	717 5th Ave 9th Fl, New York NY 10022	212-589-6200	P	50,966	3.2
5	Goldman Sachs Group Inc—*Lloyd C Blankfein*	200 West St 29th Fl, New York NY 10282	212-902-1000	P	39,161	35.7
6	Babcock and Brown Holdings LP—*Phil Green*	2 Harrison St 6th Fl, San Francisco CA 94105	415-512-1515	I	29,333*	.5
7	Citigroup Global Markets Holdings Inc—*Vikram S Pandit*	388 Greenwich St, New York NY 10013	212-816-6000	S	20,722	39.0
8	JP Morgan Securities LLC—*Michael Cavanagh*	60 Wall St Fl 46, New York NY 10005	212-483-2323	S	18,110	15.5
9	Calvert Group—*Barbara J Krumsiek*	4550 Montgomery Ave St, Bethesda MD 20814	301-951-4800	D	15,420*	.2
10	FMR LLC—*Edward C Johnson III*	82 Devonshire St, Boston MA 02109	617-563-7000	R	14,029*	46.4
11	DE Shaw and Company LP—*David E Shaw*	1166 Ave of the Americ, New York NY 10036	212-478-0000	R	9,864*	1.3
12	BlackRock Inc—*Laurence D Fink*	55 E 52nd St Park Aven, New York NY 10055	212-810-5300	P	8,612	9.1
13	AIM Management Group Inc—*Philip Taylor*	PO Box 4739, Houston TX 77210	713-626-1919	S	8,058*	2.5
14	UBS Financial Services Inc—*Mark B Sutton*	PO Box 766, Union City NJ 07087	212-713-2000	S	7,823*	19.6
15	IBC Capital Corp	1200 San Bernardo Ave, Laredo TX 78040	956-722-7611	S	7,102*	1.6
16	Nuveen Investments LLC—*John P Amboian*	333 W Wacker Dr, Chicago IL 60606	312-917-7700	S	7,069*	.5
17	Credit Suisse First Boston Inc—*Oswald J Grubel*	11 Madison Ave, New York NY 10010	212-325-2000	S	6,070	15.5
18	Fiduciary Trust Company International—*James Goodfellow*	600 Fifth Ave, New York NY 10020	212-632-3000	S	5,678*	.7
19	Brandywine Brokerage Services LLC—*Gerald Sweeney*	555 E Lancaster Ave St, Wayne PA 19087	610-325-5600	S	4,913*	.6
20	AIM Investment Services Inc—*Phil Taylor* AIM Management Group Inc	PO Box 4739, Houston TX 77210	713-626-1919	S	4,645*	.6
21	NYSE Euronext—*Duncan L Niederauer*	11 Wall St, New York NY 10005	212-656-3000	P	4,425	3.0
22	Bear Stearns Companies Inc—*Alan D Schwartz*	1 Metrotech N 9th Fl, Brooklyn NY 11201	212-272-2000	D	4,363*	14.2
23	Edward Jones Ltd—*James D Weedle*	12555 Manchester Rd, St Louis MO 63131	314-515-2000	S	4,163	37.0
24	Investcorp International Inc—*Nemir A Kirdar*	280 Park Ave, New York NY 10017	212-599-4700	R	4,123*	.3
25	Schwab Holdings Inc—*Charles R Schwab* Charles Schwab Corp	101 Montgomery St, San Francisco CA 94104	415-627-7000	S	3,945	18.1
26	Carlyle Group—*Daniel D'Aniello*	1001 Pennsylvania Ave, Washington DC 20004	202-729-5626	R	3,859*	.5
27	Raymond James and Associates Inc—*Dennis W Zank*	880 Carillon Pky, Saint Petersburg FL 33716	727-567-1000	S	3,760*	1.5
28	Bernard L Madoff Investment Securities LLC—*Bernard L Madoff*	885 3rd Ave, New York NY 10022	212-230-2434	R	3,744*	.4
29	Cowen and Company LLC—*David M Malcom*	1221 Ave of The Americ, New York NY 10020	646-562-1000	S	3,726*	3.0
30	Bank of America Securities LLC	600 Montgomery St, San Francisco CA 94111	415-627-2000	S	3,669*	1.5
31	Mesirow Financial Inc—*James C Tyree*	350 N Clark St, Chicago IL 60610	312-595-6000	S	3,576*	1.1
32	Moors and Cabot Inc—*Daniel M Joyce*	111 Devonshire St, Boston MA 02109	617-426-0500	R	3,475*	.5
33	FBR Investment Services Inc—*Richard J Hendrix*	1001 19th St N, Arlington VA 22209	703-312-9500	S	3,407*	.7
34	Euro Brokers Investment Corp	1 Seaport Plz 19th Fl, New York NY 10038	646-346-7000	R	3,160*	.3
35	Wunderlich Securities Inc—*Gary Wunderlich*	6000 Poplar Ave Ste 15, Memphis TN 38119	901-251-1330	R	3,062*	.4
36	Broadpoint Descap—*Lee Fensterstock* Gleacher and Company Inc	One Penn Plz 42nd Fl, New York NY 10119	212-546-6001	S	3,030*	.3
37	Jefferies Group Inc—*Richard B Handler*	520 Madison Ave 10th F, New York NY 10022	212-284-2300	P	2,797	3.1
38	TD AmeriTrade Holding Corp—*Tom Bradley*	PO Box 3288, Omaha NE 68103	402-331-7856	P	2,763	5.5
39	Linsco/Private Ledger Corp	9785 Town Centre Dr, San Diego CA 92121	858-450-9606	S	2,748*	2.5
40	TransMarket Group LLC—*Jim McCormick*	550 W Jackson Blvd Rm, Chicago IL 60661	312-284-5500	R	2,724*	.4
41	Toronto Dominion Securities Inc—*W Edmund Clark*	31 W 52nd St, New York NY 10019	212-827-7700	S	2,700	2.4
42	Morgan Stanley and Company Inc—*David Sidwell*	1585 Broadway, New York NY 10036	212-761-4000	S	2,658	N/A
43	Cerberus Capital Management LP—*John W Snow*	299 Park Ave, New York NY 10171	212-891-2100	R	2,392*	.3
44	T Rowe Price Group Inc—*James AC Kennedy*	100 E Pratt St, Baltimore MD 21202	410-345-2000	P	2,367	5.1
45	Arcapita Inc—*Atif A Abdulmalik*	75 14th St 24th Fl, Atlanta GA 30309	404-920-9000	S	2,341*	.3

Note: An asterisk (*) indicates an estimated financial figure. The company type code used is as follows: R = Private, P = Public, S = Private Subsidiary, B = Public Subsidiary, D = Division, J = Joint Venture, I = Investment Fund.

COMPANY RANKINGS BY SALES WITHIN 4-DIGIT SIC

Rank	Company Name—*Executive Officer*	Address, City, State, Zip	Phone	Type	Fin	Empls
46	Oppenheimer and Company Inc—*Sherri Castner*	125 Broad St Fl 16, New York NY 10004	212-668-8000	S	2,160*	3.0
47	TF Investments Corp—*Ken C Lufkin*	3 Penns Trl, Newtown PA 18940	215-579-4000	S	1,920*	.2
48	First Financial Bancorp Service Corp—*Rex A Hockmeyer*	4400 Lewis St, Middletown OH 45044	513-705-4400	S	1,919*	.2
49	Anderson and Strudwick Inc—*Tod Newton*	707 E Main St 20th Fl, Richmond VA 23219	804-643-2400	R	1,863*	.2
50	Stephens Inc—*Warren A Stephens*	111 Center St, Little Rock AR 72201	501-377-2000	R	1,835*	.8
51	Needham and Company LLC—*George A Needham*	445 Park Ave, New York NY 10022	212-371-8300	S	1,756*	.2
52	David A Noyes and Co—*John Bouckart*	209 S LaSalle St, Chicago IL 60604	312-782-0400	R	1,753*	.2
53	Sandler O'Neill and Partners LP—*James Dunne*	919 3rd Ave 6th Fl, New York NY 10022	212-466-7800	R	1,728*	.2
54	GMS Group LLC—*John Feeney* Ryan Beck and Company Inc	5 N Regent St Ste 513, Livingston NJ 07039	973-535-5000	S	1,609*	.2
55	Detwiler Fenton and Co—*Peter Fenton*	100 High St Ste 2800, Boston MA 02110	617-451-0100	P	1,520*	.2
56	Merriman Curhan Ford and Co—*D Jonathan Merriman* Merriman Holdings Inc	600 California St 9th, San Francisco CA 94108	415-248-5600	S	1,493*	.2
57	Stifel Financial Corp—*Ronald Kruszewski*	501 N Broadway 1 Finan, Saint Louis MO 63102	314-342-2000	P	1,417	5.1
58	Smith Barney Inc—*Todd Thomson* Citigroup Global Markets Holdings Inc	388 Greenwich St, New York NY 10013	212-816-1880	D	1,407*	12.5
59	Knight Capital Group Inc—*Thomas M Joyce*	545 Washington Blvd, Jersey City NJ 07310	201-222-9400	P	1,405	1.4
60	Imperial Capitol LLC—*Jason W Reese*	2000 Ave of Stars 9th, Los Angeles CA 90067	310-246-3700	R	1,318*	.2
61	Huntleigh Securities Corp—*Robert L Chambers*	7800 Forsyth Blvd 5th, Saint Louis MO 63105	314-236-2400	R	1,310*	.2
62	Spear Leeds and Kellogg LP—*John Lauto* Goldman Sachs Group Inc	120 Broadway 21st Fl, New York NY 10271	212-433-7060	S	1,300*	2.5
63	GFI Group Inc—*Michael A Gooch*	55 Water St, New York NY 10041	212-968-4100	P	1,271	2.0
64	Scott and Stringfellow Inc—*Walter Robertson III* Scott and Stringfellow Financial Inc	PO Box 1575, Richmond VA 23218	804-643-1811	S	1,238	N/A
65	BGC Partners Inc—*Howard Lutnick*	499 Park Ave, New York NY 10022	646-346-7000	P	1,229	1.3
66	Waddell and Reed Financial Inc—*Henry J Herrmann*	PO Box 29217, Shawnee Mission KS 66201	913-236-2000	P	1,195	1.6
67	Instinet Inc—*Anthony Abenante*	3 Times Square Ste 8, New York NY 10036	212-310-9500	S	1,187	1.0
68	Gilford Securities Inc—*Ralph Worthington*	777 3rd Ave, New York NY 10017	212-888-6400	R	1,152*	.2
69	Capital Institutional Services Inc—*Kristi Wetherington*	1601 Elm St 39th Fl, Dallas TX 75201	214-720-0055	R	1,081*	.1
70	Wedbush Corp—*Edward W Wedbush*	1000 Wilshire Blvd, Los Angeles CA 90017	213-688-8000	R	1,069*	.6
71	Morgan Keegan and Company Inc—*John Carson Jr*	50 N Front St 17th Fl, Memphis TN 38103	901-524-4100	S	1,067*	4.4
72	Unified Management Corp—*Lynn E Wood*	PO Box 6110, Indianapolis IN 46206	317-917-7100	S	1,067*	.1
73	Interactive Brokers Group Inc—*Thomas Peterffy*	1 Pickwick Plz, Greenwich CT 06830	203-618-5800	P	988	.9
74	First Albany Corp—*Lee Fensterstock* Gleacher and Company Inc	677 Broadway, Albany NY 12207	518-447-8200	S	988*	.4
75	Nollenberger Capital Partners Inc—*Bruce Nollenberger*	101 California St Ste, San Francisco CA 94111	415-402-6000	R	980*	.1
76	Bank of America Investment Services Inc—*Timothy Maloney*	900 W Trade St, Charlotte NC 28202	704-386-6333	S	974*	.3
77	Westrock Group Inc—*Don Hunter*	230 Park Ave Ste 934, New York NY 10169	212-220-7551	R	973*	.1
78	MuniServices LLC—*Marc Herman*	7335 N Palm Bluffs Ave, Fresno CA 93711		S	963*	.1
79	Jefferies Fixed Income—*Richard B Handler* Jefferies Group Inc	520 Madison Ave 10th F, New York NY 10022	212-284-2300	D	962*	.1
80	SEI Investments Co—*Alfred P West Jr*	1 Freedom Valley Dr, Oaks PA 19456	610-676-1000	P	930	2.4
81	Front Royal Inc—*Mark Watson*	10101 Reunion Pl Ste 5, San Antonio TX 78216	210-321-8400	S	911*	.1
82	Home Equity of America Inc—*Kevin T Kabat*	38 Fountain Sq Plz, Cincinnati OH 45202	513-579-5300	S	901*	.1
83	Morgan Stanley Capital International Inc—*Henry A Fernandez*	88 Pine St, New York NY 10005	212-804-3990	B	901	2.4
84	Gleacher Partners LLC—*Eric Gleacher*	660 Madison Ave, New York NY 10021	212-418-4200	R	879*	.1
85	Broadview Associates LLC—*Alec Ellison*	1050 Winter St, Waltham MA 02451	781-522-8400	R	878*	.1
86	First Allied Securities Inc—*Mark Dransfield*	655 W Broadway 12 Fl, San Diego CA 92101	619-702-9600	S	878*	.1
87	Bain Capital LLC—*Gregory Why*	111 Huntington Ave, Boston MA 02199	617-516-2000	R	868*	.2
88	National Financial Services Corp—*Sanjiv Mirchandani*	200 Liberty St NY4F, New York NY 10281	212-335-5000	S	763*	.6
89	Kohlberg Kravis Roberts and Co—*Henry R Kravis*	9 W 57th St Ste 4200, New York NY 10019	212-750-8300	P	724	.9
90	Aware Security Corp	40 Middlesex Tpke, Bedford MA 01730	781-276-4000	S	720*	.2
91	McAdams Wright Ragen Inc—*Scott McAdams*	925 4th Ave, Seattle WA 98104	206-664-8850	R	694*	.1
92	MJ Whitman Holding Corp—*Martin J Whitman*	622 3rd Ave, New York NY 10017	212-888-2290	R	679*	.1
93	MJ Whitman Inc—*Martin J Whitman* MJ Whitman Holding Corp	622 Third Ave, New York NY 10017	212-888-2290	S	679*	.1
94	Central Securities Corp—*William H Kidd*	630 5th Ave, New York NY 10111	212-698-2020	P	642	<.1
95	Stone and Youngberg LLC—*Ken Williams*	1 Ferry Bldg, San Francisco CA 94111	415-445-2300	R	622*	.2
96	Goldsmith Agio Helms and Co—*Mike McFadden*	225 S 6th St 46th Fl, Minneapolis MN 55402	612-339-0500	R	617*	.1
97	Duff and Phelps Management Co—*Noah Gottdiener*	311 South Wacker Dr St, Chicago IL 60606	312-697-4600	S	610*	.1
98	WR Hambrecht and Co—*William Hambrecht*	539 Bryant St Ste 100, San Francisco CA 94107	415-551-8600	R	594*	<.1
99	Cantor Fitzgerald LP—*Howard W Lutnick*	499 Park Ave, New York NY 10022	212-938-5000	R	589*	1.0
100	Dougherty and Company LLC—*Gerald Kraut*	90 S 7th St Ste 4300, Minneapolis MN 55402	612-376-4000	R	574*	.2
101	Creditex Inc—*Grant Biggar*	875 3rd Ave 29th Fl, New York NY 10022	212-323-8500	S	573*	.1
102	Huntington Holdings Inc—*Jack Corwin*	2150 N Lincoln St, Burbank CA 91504	213-617-1500	R	554*	.6
103	Wachovia Securities Inc—*Danny Ludeman*	1 N Jefferson, St Louis MO 63103	336-725-2961	S	548*	.3
104	Liquidnet Holdings Inc—*Seth Merrin*	498 7th Ave 15th Fl, New York NY 10018	646-674-2000	S	546*	.6
105	Estrada Hinojosa and Company Inc—*Noe Hinojosa*	100 W Houston St Ste 1, San Antonio TX 78205	210-223-4888	S	543*	.1
106	Harold C Brown and Company Inc—*Charles McCollum*	1 HSBC Center Ste 3800, Buffalo NY 14203	716-854-2500	R	538*	.1
107	EarlyBirdCapitalcom Inc—*Steven Levine*	275 Madison Ave Ste 27, New York NY 10016	212-661-0200	R	510*	.1
108	Greenhill and Company Inc—*Scott L Bok*	300 Park Ave, New York NY 10022	212-389-1500	P	509	.3
109	Detwiler Fenton and Company Inc—*Peter Fenton* Detwiler Fenton and Co	225 Franklin St 20th F, Boston MA 02110	617-451-0100	S	506*	.1
110	DMC Financial Services Detwiler Fenton and Company Inc	225 Franklin St 20th F, Boston MA 02110	617-451-0100	S	506*	.1
111	HD Vest Investment Securities Inc HD Vest Inc	6333 N State Highway 1, Irving TX 75038	972-870-6000	S	502*	.3
112	Greenwich Capital Markets Inc—*Ben Carpenter*	600 Steamboat Rd, Greenwich CT 06830	203-625-2700	S	499*	.5
113	Craig-Hallum Capital Group LLC—*Brad Baker*	222 S 9th St Ste 350, Minneapolis MN 55402	612-334-6300	R	495*	.1
114	Pioneer Funds Distributor Inc—*Osbert Hood*	PO Box 55014, Boston MA 02205	617-742-7825	S	485*	.5
115	John Hancock Funds LLC—*Keith F Harstein*	PO Box 55913, Boston MA 02205	617-375-1500	S	475*	.5
116	Independent Community Bankers of America—*Camden R Fine*	1615 L St NW Ste 900, Washington DC 20036	202-659-8111	R	461*	.2
117	Piper Jaffray Companies Inc—*Andrew S Duff*	800 Nicollet Mall Ste, Minneapolis MN 55402	612-303-6000	P	458	1.0
118	John Hsu Capital Group Inc—*John Hsu*	747 3rd Ave 26th Fl, New York NY 10017	212-223-7515	R	457*	<.1
119	BTI Financial Group—*Joseph M Murphy*	82 Main St, Bar Harbor ME 04609	207-288-0354	S	452*	.1
120	E*TRADE Securities Inc—*Donald H Layton*	PO Box 1542, Merrifield VA 22116	703-247-3700	S	450	.4
121	Southwest Securities Group Inc—*James Ross*	1201 Elm St Ste 3500, Dallas TX 75270	214-859-1800	P	422	1.1
122	Saratoga Investment Corp—*Christian L Oberbeck*	535 Madison Ave, New York NY 10022	212-906-7800	P	416	N/A
123	Charterhouse Group International Inc—*Merril M Halpern*	535 Madison Ave 28th F, New York NY 10022	212-584-3200	R	412*	<.1
124	Duff and Phelps Corp—*Noah Gottdiener*	55 E 52nd St 31st Fl, New York NY 10055	212-871-2000	P	397	1.0

Rank	Company Name—*Executive Officer*	Address, City, State, Zip	Phone	Type	Fin	Empls
125	Bids Trading LP—*Tim Mahoney*	111 Broadway Ste 1603, New York NY 10006	212-618-2060	R	388*	.1
126	Riverstone Holdings LLC—*David Leuschen*	712 5th Ave 51st Fl, New York NY 10019	212-993-0076	I	388*	.1
127	Saybrook Capital LLC—*Jonathan Rosenthal*	401 Wilshire Blvd, Santa Monica CA 90401	310-899-9200	R	387*	<.1
128	Frazier Healthcare Ventures—*Thomas Hodge*	601 Union St Ste 3200, Seattle WA 98101	206-621-7200	R	380*	.1
129	Diversified Private Equity Corp—*Scott L Mathis*	135 5th Ave 10th Fl, New York NY 10010	212-739-7650	R	379*	.1
130	Thinkorswim Inc—*Lee Barba* TD AmeriTrade Holding Corp	600 W Chicago Ave Ste, Chicago IL 60654	773-435-3210	S	372	.7
131	INVEST Financial Corp—*Steve Dowden*	8745 Henderson Rd Ste, Tampa FL 33634	813-289-0722	S	359*	.1
132	US Global Brokerage Inc—*Frank E Holmes*	7900 Callaghan Rd, San Antonio TX 78229	210-308-1234	S	354*	.1
133	Main Street Management Co—*William E Hayek*	8 N Main St, Dover PA 17315	717-292-7440	R	340*	<.1
134	Nomura Securities International Inc—*Kenichi Watanabe*	2 World Financial Ctr, New York NY 10281	212-667-9300	S	336*	1.2
135	KeyBanc Capital Markets Inc—*Yank Heisler*	127 Public Square, Cleveland OH 44114	216-443-2300	S	333	1.5
136	Auerbach Grayson and Company Inc—*Johnathan Auerbach*	25 W 45th St, New York NY 10036	212-557-4444	R	330*	<.1
137	Gulfstar Group I Ltd—*Colt Luedde*	700 Louisiana St Ste 3, Houston TX 77002	713-300-2020	S	329*	<.1
138	Gulfstar Group II Ltd—*Colt Luedde*	700 Louisiana St Ste 3, Houston TX 77002	713-300-2020	S	329*	<.1
139	George K Baum Holdings Inc—*Jonathan E Baum*	4801 Main St Ste 500, Kansas City MO 64112	816-474-1100	R	325*	.3
140	ALPS Fund Services Inc—*Edmund Burke*	1290 Broadway Ste 1100, Denver CO 80203	303-623-2577	R	320*	.3
141	Commonwealth Financial Network—*Wayne Bloom*	29 Sawyer Rd, Waltham MA 02453	781-736-0700	R	300*	.5
142	First Continental Trading Inc—*Roger E Carlsson*	150 S Wacker Dr Ste 80, Chicago IL 60606	312-424-3030	R	287*	.1
143	Kohlberg and Co—*Samuel P Frieder*	111 Radio Cir Dr, Mount Kisco NY 10549	914-241-7430	R	285*	<.1
144	Gleacher and Company Inc—*Thomas Hughes*	1290 Ave of the Americ, New York NY 10104	212-273-7178	P	282	.4
145	Harland Financial Solutions Inc—*Raj M Shivdasani*	605 Crescent Executive, Lake Mary FL 32746	503-274-7280	S	279*	1.4
146	Clark Capital Management Group—*Harry J Clark*	1 Liberty Pl 1650 Mark, Philadelphia PA 19103	215-569-2224	R	271*	<.1
147	Citistreet Retirement Services LLC—*Tom Kuhn*	2 Tower Ctr, East Brunswick NJ 08816	732-514-2000	R	265*	1.0
148	Janney Montgomery Scott LLC (Philadelphia Pennsylvania)— *Tomothy C Scheve*	1801 Market St 8th Fl, Philadelphia PA 19103	215-665-6000	S	265*	1.5
149	KBW Inc—*John G Duffy*	The Equitable Bldg 787, New York NY 10019	212-887-7777	P	265	.5
150	Goelzer Investment Management Inc—*Gregory Goelzer*	111 Monument Cir Ste 5, Indianapolis IN 46204	317-264-2600	R	264*	<.1
151	Gain Securities—*Sherry Bruce*	27600 Chagrin Blvd, Cleveland OH 44122		R	263*	<.1
152	Bessemer Securities LLC—*John Hilton* Bessemer Group Inc	630 5th Ave, New York NY 10111	212-708-9100	S	260*	.7
153	Coastal Securities LP—*D Ann Komar*	5555 San Felipe St Ste, Houston TX 77056	713-435-4300	R	259*	.1
154	Sunset Financial Services Inc—*Bruce Olberding*	3520 Broadway, Kansas City MO 64111	816-753-7000	S	254*	<.1
155	Dominick and Dominick LLC—*Michael J Campbell*	150 E 52nd St 3rd Fl, New York NY 10022	212-558-8800	R	251*	.1
156	RS Investments—*Matthew H Scanlan*	388 Market St Ste 1700, San Francisco CA 94111	415-591-2700	R	249*	.2
157	FBR and Co—*Richard J Hendrix*	1001 19th St N 18th Fl, Arlington VA 22209	703-312-9500	P	247	.5
158	Cowen Group Inc—*Peter A Cohen* Cowen and Company LLC	599 Lexington Ave, New York NY 10022	646-562-1000	B	234	.6
159	optionsXpress Holdings Inc—*David A Fisher* Charles Schwab Corp	PO Box 2197, Chicago IL 60606	312-630-3300	S	231	.4
160	ICBA Securities Corp—*Jim Reber* Independent Community Bankers of America	775 Ridge Lake Blvd, Memphis TN 38120		S	224*	.2
161	T Stephen Johnson and Associates—*T Stephen Johnson*	3650 Mansell Rd Ste 49, Alpharetta GA 30022	770-998-6491	R	219*	<.1
162	Seattle-Northwest Securities Corp—*Maud Dauden*	1420 5th Ave Ste 4300, Seattle WA 98101	206-628-2882	R	216*	.1
163	ABRY Partners LLC—*Royce Yudkoff*	111 Huntington Ave, Boston MA 02199	617-859-2959	R	213*	<.1
164	Schwab Capital Markets LP	677 Washington Blvd, Stamford CT 06901	212-804-3389	S	209*	.3
165	Seaport Group LLC—*Stephen Smith*	360 Madison Ave 22nd F, New York NY 10017	212-616-7700	R	205*	<.1
166	Financial Service Corp—*Joseph Gruber*	2300 Windy Ridge Pky S, Atlanta GA 30339		S	200*	.2
167	US Sterling Capital Corp—*Herbert A Orr Jr*	1393 Veterans Memorial, Hauppauge NY 11788		R	198*	<.1
168	Barrington Associates	11755 Wilshire Blvd St, Los Angeles CA 90025	310-479-3500	D	196*	.1
169	William Blair and Company LLC—*John Ettelson*	222 W Adams St, Chicago IL 60606	312-236-1600	R	195*	.8
170	Ladenburg Thalmann Financial Services Inc—*Richard Lampen*	4400 Biscayne Blvd 12t, Miami FL 33137	305-572-4100	P	195	.2
171	Hold Brothers On-Line Investment Services Inc—*Gregory F Hold*	525 Washington Blvd St, Jersey City NJ 07310	201-499-8741	S	192*	.5
172	Howard Weil Inc—*Paul E Pursley*	1100 Poydras St Ste 35, New Orleans LA 70163	504-582-2500	R	190*	.2
173	WY Campbell and Co—*William CampbellDuffy*	1 Woodward Ave, Detroit MI 48226	313-496-9000	S	185*	<.1
174	Houlihan Lokey Howard and Zukin Inc—*Scott Beiser*	1930 Century Pk W, Los Angeles CA 90067	310-553-8871	R	176*	.8
175	BB and T Investment Services Inc	200 S College St 8th F, Charlotte NC 28202	704-954-1150	S	176*	.1
176	Ingalls and Snyder LLC—*Lawton S Lamb*	61 Broadway 31st Fl, New York NY 10006	212-269-7800	R	175*	.1
177	Cain Brothers and Company LLC—*Robert J Fraiman*	360 Madison Ave 5th Fl, New York NY 10017	212-869-5600	R	173*	<.1
178	Scott and Stringfellow Financial Inc—*Walter S Robertson III*	PO Box 1575, Richmond VA 23218	804-643-1811	S	170*	1.0
179	Royal Alliance Associates Inc—*Art Tambaro*	1 World Financial Ctr, New York NY 10281	212-551-5100	S	170*	.2
180	Vero Group—*Mark Fehrs Haukohl*	811 Dallas St Ste 1025, Houston TX 77002	713-655-0071	R	170*	.1
181	Edelman Financial Group Inc—*George L Ball*	5800 JPMorgan Chase Tw, Houston TX 77002	713-993-4610	P	169	.5
182	Palladium Equity Partners Iii LP—*Thomas Mastrobuorni*	1270 Ave Of The Ste 22, New York NY 10020	212-218-5150	R	166*	3.1
183	HD Vest Inc—*Roger Ochs*	6333 N State Hwy 161 4, Irving TX 75038	972-870-6000	S	165*	.3
184	Beal Bank—*Andy Beal*	6000 Legacy Dr, Plano TX 75024	469-467-5000	S	165*	.1
185	AEA Investors Inc—*John Garcia*	666 5th Ave 36th Fl, New York NY 10103	212-644-5900	R	163*	.1
186	Jefferies Quarterdeck LLC—*Richard Handler* Jefferies Group Inc	520 Madison Ave 12th F, New York NY 10022	212-284-2300	S	162*	<.1
187	Beringea LLC—*David Eberly*	32330 W 12 Mile Rd, Farmington Hills MI 48334	248-489-9000	R	161*	<.1
188	Network 1 Financial Securities Inc—*Richard Hunt*	2 Bridge Ave Ste 241, Red Bank NJ 07701	732-758-9001	S	161*	<.1
189	Walnut Street Securities Inc—*Richard Lee*	1095 Ave of the Americ, New York NY 10036	212-578-0594	S	160*	.1
190	Eaton Vance Distributors Inc—*Matthew J Witkos*	255 State St, Boston MA 02109	617-482-8260	S	159	.7
191	Thayer Capital Partners LP—*Matthew Mcnabb*	1455 Penn Ave Nw Ste 3, Washington DC 20004	202-371-0150	R	159*	3.1
192	Mbna Consumer Services Inc—*John Hewes*	1100 N King St, Wilmington DE 19884	302-453-9930	R	155*	3.0
193	Northern Trust Securities Inc—*Lloyd Wennlund*	50 S La Salle St Ste 1, Chicago IL 60603	312-630-6000	S	153*	.1
194	Stifel Nicolaus and Company Inc—*Ken Schuman* Stifel Financial Corp	501 N Broadway, Saint Louis MO 63102	314-342-2000	S	151	.9
195	Hilliard Lyons—*James W Allen*	500 W Jefferson St, Louisville KY 40202	502-588-8400	R	150*	1.3
196	Knight Execution and Clearing Services LLC—*Christy Oeth*	545 Washington Blvd, Jersey City NJ 07310	201-222-9400	R	150*	.1
197	First Tenn Brokerage—*Paul Mann*	4990 Poplar Ave Fl 3, Memphis TN 38117	901-818-6000	R	150*	<.1
198	RAF Industries Inc—*Robert A Fox*	165 Township Line Rd S, Jenkintown PA 19046	215-572-0738	R	150*	<.1
199	SBK Brooks Investment Corp—*Eric L Small*	820 Terminal Twr 50 Pu, Cleveland OH 44113	216-861-6950	R	146*	<.1
200	JMP Group Inc—*Joseph A Jolson*	600 Montgomery St Ste, San Francisco CA 94111	415-835-8900	P	145	.2
201	Mellon Financial Markets LLC—*Steve Cobain*	1 Mellon Bank Ctr Ste, Pittsburgh PA 15258	412-234-6086	S	141*	.1
202	Loring Ward Advisor Services—*Alex Potts*	3055 Olin Ave Ste 2000, San Jose CA 95128	408-260-3100	R	129*	<.1
203	National Holdings Corp—*Mark A Goldwasser*	120 Broadway 27th Fl, New York NY 10271	212-417-8000	P	127	1.0
204	Vining-Sparks IBG LP—*Mark Medford*	775 Ridge Lake Blvd, Memphis TN 38120	901-766-3000	R	126*	.3
205	Mutual of Omaha Investor Services Inc—*Daniel Neary*	Mutual of Omaha Plz 5t, Omaha NE 68175	402-351-5770	S	124*	<.1

Note: An asterisk (*) indicates an estimated financial figure. The company type code used is as follows: R = Private, P = Public, S = Private Subsidiary, B = Public Subsidiary, D = Division, J = Joint Venture, I = Investment Fund.

COMPANY RANKINGS BY SALES WITHIN 4-DIGIT SIC

Rank	Company Name—*Executive Officer*	Address, City, State, Zip	Phone	Type	Fin	Empls
206	Hellman and Friedman LLC—*Brian Powers*	1 Maritime Plz Ste 120, San Francisco CA 94111	415-788-5111	R	123*	.1
207	Leucadia Financial Corp—*Joseph Steinberg*	529 E South Temple, Salt Lake City UT 84102	801-521-5400	S	115*	.1
208	Lehman Brothers Bank FSB—*Henry Kaufman* Lehman Brothers Holdings Inc	10350 Park Meadows Dri, Littleton CO 80124		S	114*	7.0
209	RBC Capital Markets—*Todd I Braff*	414 Walnut St Ste 300, Cincinnati OH 45202	513-621-2000	S	113*	<.1
210	Granum Securities LLC—*Walter F Harrison III*	126 E 56th St Fl 25, New York NY 10022		I	110*	<.1
211	Invemed Associates Inc—*Kenneth Lengone*	375 Park Ave Ste 2205, New York NY 10152	212-421-2500	R	105*	<.1
212	Wedbush Morgan Securities Inc—*Edward Wedbush* Wedbush Corp	PO Box 30014, Los Angeles CA 90030	213-688-8000	S	102*	.5
213	Meridian Investments—*John F Boc*	10220 River Rd Ste 115, Potomac MD 20854	301-983-5000	R	102*	<.1
214	LaSalle National Bank Broker-Dealer Services—*Patrick Kelley*	327 Plz Real Ste 225, Boca Raton FL 33432	561-361-1100	S	101*	.1
215	Securities Research Inc—*Thad Cook*	3055 Cardinal Dr Ste 1, Vero Beach FL 32963	772-231-6689	R	101*	<.1
216	Burnham Securities Inc—*Jon M Burnham*	1325 Ave of the Americ, New York NY 10019	212-262-3100	R	101	N/A
217	Ramirez and Company Inc—*Samuel A Ramirez*	61 Broadway Ste 2924, New York NY 10006	855-726-4739	R	98*	.1
218	Baird Patrick and Company Inc—*Stuart K Patrick*	Harborside Financial C, Jersey City NJ 07311	201-680-7300	R	98*	<.1
219	LJR Recapture Services Inc—*Joseph Velli*	1633 Broadway 48th Fl, New York NY 10019	212-497-1509	S	97*	<.1
220	Global Forex Trading Ltd—*Gary Tilkin*	618 Kenmoor Ave SE, Grand Rapids MI 49546	616-956-9273	R	88*	.2
221	Fletcher Asset Management Inc—*Alphonse Fletcher*	48 Wall St 5th Fl, New York NY 10005	212-284-4800	R	88*	<.1
222	Grace Brothers Ltd—*Bradford Whitmore*	1560 Sherman Ave Ste 9, Evanston IL 60201	847-733-1230	R	88*	<.1
223	Wells Fargo Private Bank—*Greg Bronstein*	999 3rd Ave Ste 4000, Seattle WA 98104	206-343-5000	S	86*	.3
224	Forsyth Securities Inc—*Hugh Murray*	243 N Lindbergh Blvd, Saint Louis MO 63141	314-997-7488	R	86*	<.1
225	Royal Securities Co—*William Kapteyn Jr*	PO Box 509, Grandville MI 49468	616-538-2550	R	86*	<.1
226	Davenport and Company LLC—*Coleman Wortham III*	PO Box 85678, Richmond VA 23285	804-780-2000	R	84*	.5
227	Rodman and Renshaw Capital Group Inc—*Edward Rubin*	1251 Ave of the Americ, New York NY 10020	212-356-0500	P	84	.1
228	Fox-Pitt Kelton Cochran Caronia Waller LLC—*John Waller*	420 5th Ave 5th Fl, New York NY 10018	212-687-1105	R	82*	.2
229	TR Winston and Co—*John Galuchie* Kent Financial Services Inc	PO Box 74, Bedminster NJ 07921	908-234-0300	S	81*	<.1
230	First Trust Portfolios LP—*Richard Lebrun*	120 E Liberty Dr Ste 4, Wheaton IL 60187	630-765-8000	R	80*	.2
231	Knox and Co—*Paul K Kelly*	33 Riverside Ave 5th F, Westport CT 06880	203-226-6288	R	80*	<.1
232	Ladenburg Thalmann and Company Inc—*David Rosenberg* Ladenburg Thalmann Financial Services Inc	369 Lexington Ave 18th, New York NY 10017	212-409-2000	S	77*	.3
233	Wedgewood Partners Inc	9909 Clayton Rd, Saint Louis MO 63124	314-567-6407	R	77*	<.1
234	Daiwa Securities America Inc—*Hironon Oka*	32 Old Slip Rd 14th Fl, New York NY 10005	212-612-7000	S	76*	.3
235	Vrolyk and Company LLC—*AnneK Vrolyk*	527 Howard St 2nd Fl, San Francisco CA 94105	415-538-8400	R	73*	<.1
236	First Southwest Co—*Hill A Feinberg*	325 N Saint Paul St St, Dallas TX 75201	214-953-4000	R	72*	.4
237	Barnwell Hawaiian Properties—*Morton H Kinzler*	1100 Alakea St Ste 290, Honolulu HI 96813	808-531-8400	S	72*	<.1
238	JB Hanauer and Co—*Jeffrey Wolf*	4 Gatehall Dr, Parsippany NJ 07054	973-829-2100	R	70*	.5
239	Northeast Capital and Advisory Inc—*Arthur Loomis II*	7 Airport Park Blvd Fl, Latham NY 12110	518-426-0100	R	70*	<.1
240	Calumet Investment Corp—*Joseph F Kruy*	850 Library Ave, Newark DE 19711	302-738-9640	S	68*	<.1
241	Ziegler Companies Inc—*Tom Paprocki*	200 S Wacker Dr Ste 20, Chicago IL 60606	312-263-0110	P	68	.3
242	Commerzbank Capital Markets Corp—*Gerry McCaughey*	1251 Ave of the Americ, New York NY 10020	212-703-4000	R	67*	.2
243	Bodell Overcash Anderson and Company Inc—*Daniel R Overcash*	PO Box 1237, Jamestown NY 14702	716-484-7141	R	67*	<.1
244	Bessemer Group Inc—*John A Hilton Jr*	630 5th Ave 6th Fl, New York NY 10111	212-708-9100	R	63*	.3
245	First Honolulu Securities Inc—*Frank Irizarry*	900 Fort St Mall Ste 9, Honolulu HI 96813	808-523-9422	R	63*	<.1
246	Summit Financial Services Group Inc—*Marshalll T Leeds*	595 S Federal Hwy Ste, Boca Raton FL 33432		P	63	.1
247	Sowell and Co—*James Sowell*	1601 Elm St 3rd Fl Tha, Dallas TX 75201		R	62*	<.1
248	Liberty Partners—*Michael Stakias*	485 Lexington Ave 2nd, New York NY 10017	212-541-7676	R	61*	<.1
249	Buckingham Research Group Inc—*David B Keidan*	750 Third Ave, New York NY 10017	212-922-5500	R	60*	.1
250	Securities Service Network Inc—*Wade Wilkinson*	9729 Cogdill Rd, Knoxville TN 37932		R	60*	.1
251	Stonington Partners Inc—*Alexis P Michas*	600 Madison Ave16th Fl, New York NY 10022	212-339-8500	R	58*	<.1
252	Diamond Hill Investment Group Inc—*Roderick H Dillon*	325 John H McConnell B, Columbus OH 43215	614-255-3333	P	57	.1
253	Roth Capital Partners LLC—*Byron Roth*	24 Corporate Plz Dr, Newport Beach CA 92660	949-720-5700	R	56*	.2
254	Allen C Ewing Mortgage and Realty—*David W Jackson*	50 N Laura St Ste 3625, Jacksonville FL 32202	904-354-5573	S	55*	<.1
255	Conning and Co—*Salvatore Correnti*	1 Financial Plz, Hartford CT 06103	860-299-2000	S	52*	.2
256	Silicon Valley Bank—*Ken Wilcox*	3003 Tasman Dr, Santa Clara CA 95054	408-654-7400	S	52	N/A
257	Cadaret Grant and Company Inc—*Arthur Grant*	1 Lincoln Crt 5th Fl, Syracuse NY 13202	315-471-2191	R	51*	.1
258	FA Technology Ventures Corp—*Gregory Hulecki* Gleacher and Company Inc	100 High St Ste 1105, Boston MA 02110	617-757-3880	S	51*	<.1
259	Santa Monica Partners—*Lawrence Goldstein*	1865 Palmer Ave, Larchmont NY 10538	914-833-0875	R	49*	<.1
260	National Securities Corp—*Mark Goldwasser* National Holdings Corp	1001 4th Ave Ste 2200, Seattle WA 98154	206-622-7200	S	48*	.4
261	East West Securities Co—*Charles Chen*	100 Pine St Ste500, San Francisco CA 94111	415-397-3400	R	46*	<.1
262	George K Baum and Co—*Jonathan E Baum* George K Baum Holdings Inc	4801 Main St Ste 500, Kansas City MO 64112	816-474-1100	S	45*	.3
263	Prudential Annuities—*David Odenath*	1 Corporate Dr Ste 800, Shelton CT 06484	203-926-1888	R	43*	.9
264	PMB Securities Corp—*Gary D Cohee*	4630 Campus Dr Ste 101, Newport Beach CA 92660	949-467-2200	S	43*	<.1
265	AssetExchange Inc—*Willie Koo*	1221 SW Yamhill St Ste, Portland OR 97205	503-220-0007	R	43*	<.1
266	Blum Capital Partners—*N Colin Lind*	909 Montgomery St, San Francisco CA 94133	415-434-1111	R	42*	<.1
267	Meridian Capital LLC—*Chuck Wilke*	1809 7th Ave Ste 1209, Seattle WA 98101	206-623-4000	R	42*	<.1
268	Gilman Ciocia Inc—*Michael P Ryan*	11 Raymond Ave, Poughkeepsie NY 12603	845-471-8600	P	42	.2
269	Brown Gibbons Lang and Company LP—*Scott Lang*	1111 Superior Ave Ste, Cleveland OH 44114	216-241-2800	R	41*	<.1
270	Franklin Templeton Distributors Inc—*Charles B Johnson*	1 Franklin Pky Bldg 97, San Mateo CA 94403	650-312-2000	S	40*	1.1
271	Miramar Securities Inc—*Julio Gonzales*	12600 Deerfield Pkwy S, Alpharetta GA 30004	404-230-9317	R	39*	<.1
272	American Heritage Securities Inc—*Edgar G Ingraham*	655 W Market St, Akron OH 44303	330-535-0881	R	39*	<.1
273	Fairydust Lending and Investments Inc—*Audrey Patton*	1668 S State Rd 267, Avon IN 46123	317-348-0732	R	39*	<.1
274	Falkenberg Capital Corp—*Bruce Falkenberg*	600 S Cherry St Ste 11, Denver CO 80246	303-320-4800	R	39*	<.1
275	Interbank FX LLC—*Todd Crosland*	3165 E Millrock Dr Ste, Salt Lake City UT 84121		R	38*	.2
276	Allen C Ewing Financial Services Inc—*Benjamin Bishop*	50 N Laura St Ste 3625, Jacksonville FL 32202	904-354-5573	R	38*	<.1
277	Federally Insured Savings Network—*Thomas M Cohn*	4800 Montgomery Ln Ste, Bethesda MD 20814	240-497-0400	R	38*	<.1
278	Hamilton Cos—*Frederic C Hamilton*	1560 Broadway Ste 2200, Denver CO 80202	303-863-3000	R	38*	<.1
279	Jesup and Lamont Inc—*Steven Rabinovici*	2170 W State Rd 434 St, Longwood FL 32779	407-774-1300	P	37	.2
280	Sterne Agee and Leach Inc—*James S Holbrook Jr*	800 Shades Creek Pky S, Birmingham AL 35209	205-949-3500	R	36*	.3
281	Ryan Beck and Company Inc—*Ben A Plotkin*	18 Columbia Tpke, Florham Park NJ 07932	973-549-4100	S	36*	.2
282	Questar Capital Corp—*Michael Jorgensen*	PO Box 59177, Minneapolis MN 55459		R	36*	<.1
283	Paulson Investment Company Inc—*Trent D Davis* Paulson Capital Corp	811 SW Naito Pky Ste 2, Portland OR 97204	503-243-6000	S	35*	.1
284	Interpacific Investors Services Inc—*Arthur Levitt*	2623 2nd Ave, Seattle WA 98121	206-269-5050	R	35*	<.1
285	FMS Bonds Inc—*James A Klotz*	PO Box 3024, Boca Raton FL 33431	561-368-5284	R	34*	.1
286	TradeStar Investments Inc—*Nancy Sympson*	1900 St James Pl Ste 1, Houston TX 77056		S	34*	.1

Rank	Company Name—*Executive Officer*	Address, City, State, Zip	Phone	Type	Fin	Empls
287	Pacific Crest Securities Inc—*Scott E Sandbo*	111 SW 5th Ave 42nd Fl, Portland OR 97204	503-248-0721	R	33*	.1
288	Affiliated Financial Services Inc—*Richard Graham*	7840 E Berry Pl, Greenwood Village CO 80111	303-770-4429	R	33*	<.1
289	BMO Capital Markets (Chicago Illinois)—*Thomas V Milroy*	115 S LaSalle St, Chicago IL 60603	312-441-2500	R	32*	.1
290	Benedetto Gartland and Co—*William Benedetto*	1180 Ave of the Americ, New York NY 10036	212-424-9700	R	32*	<.1
291	Nutmeg Securities Ltd—*Matt Rochlin*	257 Riverside Ave, Westport CT 06880	203-255-3838	R	32*	<.1
292	Merriman Holdings Inc—*Jonathan Merriman*	600 California St 9th, San Francisco CA 94108	415-248-5600	P	31	.1
293	Wayne Hummer Wealth Management—*Eric Munger*	300 S Wacker Dr Ste 15, Chicago IL 60606	312-431-1700	S	28*	.2
294	Beaconsfield Financial Services Inc—*King Rainier*	160 Technology Dr Ste, Canonsburg PA 15317		R	28*	<.1
295	Berkery Noyes and Company LLC—*Joseph W Berkery*	1 Liberty Plz 13th Fl, New York NY 10006	212-668-3022	R	26*	<.1
296	Koonce Securities Inc—*Scott Koonce*	6550 Rock Springs Dr S, Bethesda MD 20817	301-897-9700	R	26*	<.1
297	Carver Financial Services Inc—*Randy Carver*	7473 Center St, Mentor OH 44060	440-974-0808	R	26*	<.1
298	Southbrook Corp—*Alan Joelson*	9701 Wilshire Blvd Ste, Beverly Hills CA 90212	310-275-9821	R	26*	<.1
299	Blount Parrish and Company Inc—*William Blount*	PO Box 5212, Montgomery AL 36103	334-264-8410	R	26*	<.1
300	Morgen Evan and Company Inc—*Mark J Lerner*	80 Wall St, New York NY 10005	212-480-4511	R	26*	<.1
301	Shields and Company Inc—*Thomas J Shields*	890 Winter St Ste 160, Waltham MA 02451	781-890-7033	R	25*	<.1
302	Sterling Financial Investment Group Inc—*Charles Garcia*	1200 N Federal Hwy Ste, Boca Raton FL 33432	561-886-2200	R	24*	.3
303	NW Financial Group—*Daniel C Mariniello*	10 Exchange Pl 17th Fl, Jersey City NJ 07302	201-656-0115	R	24*	<.1
304	Corby North Bridge Securities Inc—*Michael J Reilly*	99 Bedford St, Boston MA 02111	617-482-8780	R	24*	<.1
305	Richland Gordon and Co—*Alan Gordon*	233 S Wacker Dr Ste 93, Chicago IL 60606	312-382-9330	R	24*	<.1
306	Tejas Inc—*Kurt Rechner*	8226 Bee Caves Rd, Austin TX 78746	512-306-8222	P	23	<.1
307	Updata Capital Inc—*Ira D Cohen*	379 Thornall St, Edison NJ 08837	732-945-1000	R	23*	<.1
308	Law Offices of David A Carter PA—*David Carter*	1900 Glades Rd Ste 401, Boca Raton FL 33431	561-807-6804	R	23*	<.1
309	Miller and Schroeder Financial Inc—*James F Dlugosch*	PO Box 789, Minneapolis MN 55440	612-376-1500	R	21*	.1
310	Siebert Financial Corp—*Muriel F Siebert*	885 3rd Ave 17th Fl, New York NY 10022	212-644-2400	P	21	.1
311	Seidler Companies Inc—*Roland Seidler Jr*	515 S Figueroa St Ste, Los Angeles CA 90071	213-683-4580	R	20*	.1
312	Barington Capital Group LP—*James A Mitarotonda*	888 7th Ave 17th Fl, New York NY 10106	212-974-5700	R	20*	<.1
313	Gardner Rich and Co—*Christopher P Gardner*	401 S Financial Pl, Chicago IL 60605	312-922-3333	R	20*	<.1
314	Hefren-Tillotson Inc—*Kim Tillotson-Fleming*	308 7th Ave, Pittsburgh PA 15222	412-434-0990	R	19*	.2
315	Silicon Valley Securities Inc—*Paul Magnuson*	4880 Stevens Creek Blv, San Jose CA 95129	408-243-6801	R	19*	<.1
316	Lauber CFOs—*John G Lauber*	6737 W Washington St S, Milwaukee WI 53214	414-273-8060	R	19*	<.1
317	MS Howells and Co—*Mark S Howells*	20555 N Pima Rd Ste 10, Scottsdale AZ 85255	480-563-2000	R	19*	<.1
318	Peninsular Securities Co—*Rob Peel*	333 Bridge St NW Ste 1, Grand Rapids MI 49504	616-233-8700	S	19*	<.1
319	Paulson Capital Corp—*Trent D Davis*	811 SW Naito Pkwy Ste, Portland OR 97204	503-243-6000	P	18	.1
320	City Securities Corp—*Michael E Bosway*	30 S Meridian St Ste 6, Indianapolis IN 46204	317-634-4400	R	18*	.1
321	Grigsby and Associates Inc—*Alvin Boutte Jr*	311 California St Ste, San Francisco CA 94104	415-392-4800	R	17*	.1
322	Vestar Capital Partners LP—*Daniel O'Connell*	245 Park Ave 41st Fl, New York NY 10167	212-351-1600	R	16*	.1
323	Howe Barnes Hoefer and Arnett—*Dan Coughlin*	555 Market St 18th Fl, San Francisco CA 94105	415-538-5700	R	16*	.1
324	Macaluso Group—*Joe Macaluso*	271 Rte 46 W Bldg B 2n, Fairfield NJ 07004	973-244-9110	R	16*	<.1
325	Muriel Siebert and Company Inc—*Muriel F Siebert* Siebert Financial Corp	885 3rd Ave 17th Fl, New York NY 10022	212-644-2400	S	15*	.1
326	Watermill Ventures Ltd—*Steven Karol*	One Cranberry Hill 750, Lexington MA 02421	781-891-6660	S	15*	<.1
327	Atlantic Securities Inc—*Morris Wexler*	920 Providence Rd Ste, Baltimore MD 21286	410-296-0470	R	15*	<.1
328	Kirkpatrick Pettis Inc—*Randal Peck*	10250 Regency Cir Ste, Omaha NE 68114	402-397-5797	D	14*	.1
329	Pacific Growth Equities Inc—*Stephen J Massocca*	1 Bush St Ste 1700, San Francisco CA 94104	415-274-6800	R	14*	.1
330	Mark Boyar and Co—*Mark Boyar*	35 E 21st St Ste 8E, New York NY 10010	212-995-8300	R	14*	<.1
331	Starshak Winzenburg—*Joseph B Starshak*	55 W Monroe St, Chicago IL 60603	312-444-9367	R	14*	<.1
332	Innovaro Inc—*Asa Lanum*	2109 E Palm Ave, Tampa FL 33605	813-754-4330	P	13	<.1
333	Prospera Financial Services—*David Stringer*	5429 LBJ Frwy Ste 400, Dallas TX 75240	972-581-3000	R	13*	.1
334	Leonard Green and Partners LP—*John G Danhakl*	11111 Santa Monica Blv, Los Angeles CA 90025	310-954-0444	R	13*	<.1
335	Ferrell Capital Management—*William G Ferrell*	9 Greenwich Office Pk, Greenwich CT 06831	203-862-9500	R	12*	<.1
336	First Capital Equities Ltd—*David Schwartz*	80 Cutter Mill Rd Ste, Great Neck NY 11021	516-487-8220	R	12*	<.1
337	Take Charge Financial—*Joan Perry*	315 University Ave, Los Gatos CA 95030	408-399-6600	R	12*	<.1
338	Lewis Hollingsworth LP—*John P Lewis*	13355 Noel Rd Ste 1750, Dallas TX 75240	972-702-7390	R	12*	<.1
339	Maine Securities Corp—*Brad McCurtain*	15 Monument Square Ste, Portland ME 04101	207-775-0800	R	12*	<.1
340	Thompson Group Inc—*James A Thompson*	244 Westchester Ave, West Harrison NY 10604	914-997-9229	R	12*	<.1
341	Avalon Group Ltd—*Lynda Davey*	1375 Broadway, New York NY 10018	212-764-5610	R	11*	<.1
342	Thornhill Securities Inc—*Felder Thornhill*	336 S Congress, Austin TX 78704	512-472-7171	S	11*	<.1
343	Mizuho Securities USA Inc—*Makoto Fukuda*	111 River St 11th Fl, Hoboken NJ 07030	212-209-9300	S	10*	.1
344	Meyers Associates LP—*Bruce Meyers*	45 Broadway 2nd Fl, New York NY 10006	212-742-4200	R	10*	.1
345	GX Clarke and Co	10 Exchange Pl Ste 100, Jersey City NJ 07302	201-200-3600	R	10*	.1
346	Dimeling Schreiber and Park—*Richard R Schreiber*	1629 Locust St, Philadelphia PA 19103	215-546-8585	R	10*	<.1
347	Butler Capital Corp—*Gilbert Butler*	745 5th Ave, New York NY 10151	212-980-0606	R	10*	<.1
348	Ostrowski and Co—*Peter J Ostrowski*	1150 Raritan Rd, Cranford NJ 07016	908-497-0049	R	10*	<.1
349	Windmill Group Inc—*John Maceranka*	PO Box 295, Somers NY 10589	914-277-2700	R	10*	<.1
350	Smith Moore and Co—*Jim Deutsch*	7777 Bonhomme Ave Ste, Clayton MO 63105	314-727-5225	R	9*	.1
351	Performance Capital Management LLC—*David Caldwell*	PO Box 6266, Buena Park CA 90622	714-736-3790	R	8*	.1
352	Financial West Investment Group Inc—*Tad Mellelo*	4510 E Thousand Oaks B, Westlake Village CA 91362	805-497-9222	R	8*	.4
353	Neidiger Tucker Bruner Inc—*Charles C Bruner*	1331 17th St Rm 400, Denver CO 80202	303-825-1825	R	8*	.1
354	Parker/Hunter—*James W Wolitarsky*	600 Grant St Ste 3100, Pittsburgh PA 15219	412-562-8000	R	8*	.1
355	Ameritas Investment Corp—*Salene Hitchcock-Gear*	PO Box 5507, Lincoln NE 68501	402-466-4565	S	8*	<.1
356	Bentley Associates LP—*Oliver D Cromwell*	250 Park Ave Ste 1101, New York NY 10177	212-972-8700	R	8*	<.1
357	Kellner DiLeo Cohen and Co—*George A Kellner*	900 3rd Ave Ste 1000, New York NY 10022	212-350-0244	R	8*	<.1
358	Anderson Pacific Corp—*Kenneth D Anderson*	875 N Michigan Ave 31s, Chicago IL 60611	312-951-8500	R	8*	<.1
359	BOSC Agency Inc (Dallas Texas)—*Stanley L Lybarger*	5956 Sherry Ln, Dallas TX 75225	817-427-7400	S	8*	<.1
360	Brady Investment Co—*Frank M Jaehnert*	PO Box 571, Milwaukee WI 53201	414-438-6918	S	8*	<.1
361	Wilson-Davis and Co—*Paul N Davis*	236 S Main St, Salt Lake City UT 84101	801-532-1313	R	7*	<.1
362	Summit Brokerage Services Inc—*Marshall T Leeds* Summit Financial Services Group Inc	595 S Federal Hwy, Boca Raton FL 33432	561-338-2600	S	7*	<.1
363	Massachusetts Lumber Co—*Eliot I Snider*	929 Massachusetts Ave, Cambridge MA 02139	617-354-6000	R	7*	<.1
364	AdVentures—*Brent Beshore*	3500 Buttonwood Dr, Columbia MO 65203		R	7	.1
365	Signal Securities Inc—*Jerry Singleton*	700 Throckmorton St, Fort Worth TX 76102	817-877-4256	R	6	.1
366	Scarborough Group Inc—*Mike Scarborough*	441 Defense Hwy Ste E, Annapolis MD 21401	410-573-5700	R	6*	<.1
367	Fortune Group LLC—*Paul C Schnoebelen III*	7701 Forsyth Blvd Ste, Saint Louis MO 63105	314-862-8500	R	6*	<.1
368	Warwick Group Inc—*R Paul Sprague*	70 Main St 2nd Fl, New Canaan CT 06840	203-966-7447	R	6*	<.1
369	JA Glynn and Co—*Norman Conley III*	9841 Clayton Rd, Saint Louis MO 63124	314-997-1277	R	5*	<.1
370	Indiana Bond Bank—*Richard Mourdock*	2980 Market Tower 10 W, Indianapolis IN 46204	317-233-0888	R	5*	<.1
371	SN Phelps and Co—*Stanford N Phelps*	8 Sound Shore Dr, Greenwich CT 06830	203-622-4880	R	5*	<.1
372	Diamond Hill Securities Inc—*RH Dillon* Diamond Hill Investment Group Inc	375 N Front St Ste 300, Columbus OH 43215	614-255-3333	S	4	<.1
373	Perkins Investment Management LLC—*Peter Q Thompson*	311 S Wacker Ste 6000, Chicago IL 60606	312-922-0355	R	4*	<.1

Note: An asterisk (*) indicates an estimated financial figure. The company type code used is as follows: R = Private, P = Public, S = Private Subsidiary, B = Public Subsidiary, D = Division, J = Joint Venture, I = Investment Fund.

COMPANY RANKINGS BY SALES WITHIN 4-DIGIT SIC

Rank	Company Name—*Executive Officer*	Address, City, State, Zip	Phone	Type	Fin	Empls
374	UVEST Financial Services Group Inc—*Dan Arnold*	2810 Coliseum Centre D, Charlotte NC 28217	704-375-0484	R	3*	<.1
375	Porter White and Company Inc—*James H White III*	PO Box 12367, Birmingham AL 35202	205-252-3681	R	3*	<.1
376	Gates Capital Corp—*Robert DeMonbrun*	100 Park Ave Fl 22, New York NY 10017	212-661-8686	R	3*	<.1
377	JH Chapman Group LLC—*John W Loeb*	9700 W Higgins Rd Ste, Rosemont IL 60018	773-693-4800	R	3*	<.1
378	Frazer Lanier Company Inc—*Clifford Lanier*	PO Box 5190, Montgomery AL 36103	334-265-8483	R	3*	<.1
379	Northtown Capital Strategies—*David E Hitchcock* Cadaret Grant and Company Inc	1071 County Hwy 10 NE, Minneapolis MN 55432	763-786-2813	D	3*	<.1
380	DS Kennedy and Co—*Donald Kennedy*	1 Montgomery St Ste 33, San Francisco CA 94104	415-392-0422	R	3*	<.1
381	Vermont Municipal Bond Bank—*Robert Giroux*	PO Box 564, Montpelier VT 05601	802-223-2717	R	3*	<.1
382	First Midwest Securities Inc—*Terry Buffalo*	207 W Jefferson St, Bloomington IL 61701	309-888-2788	R	2*	.1
383	Quest Securities Inc—*Robert Schoen*	8080 Madison Ave Ste 1, Fair Oaks CA 95628		R	2*	.1
384	Conners and Company Inc—*Robert L Conners*	1 W 4th St Ste 2800, Cincinnati OH 45202	513-421-0606	R	2*	<.1
385	Concord Securities Corp—*Henry Feldman*	150 S Wacker Dr Ste 35, Chicago IL 60606	312-236-1166	R	2*	<.1
386	GeoCapital Corp—*Gena Flaherty*	747 3rd Ave 24 floor, New York NY 10022	212-486-4455	R	2*	<.1
387	Brimberg and Co—*Douglas Z Brimberg*	45 Rockefeller Plz Ste, New York NY 10111	212-332-4440	R	2*	<.1
388	MacAllaster Pitfield MacKay Inc—*David MacAllaster*	30 Broad St 26th Fl, New York NY 10004	212-422-9250	R	2*	<.1
389	Broad Street Financial Co—*William E Arthur*	37 W Broad St Ste1100, Columbus OH 43215	614-228-0326	R	2*	<.1
390	Duncan Smith Co—*Craig S Wilson*	711 Navarro Ste 740, San Antonio TX 78205	210-223-8907	R	2*	N/A
391	Evision International Inc—*Tony TW Chan*	1999 Broadway Ste 2270, Denver CO 80202	303-894-7971	P	2	<.1
392	Horizon Mortgage and Investment Co—*Douglas Huntington*	15 Oregon Ave Ste 307, Tacoma WA 98409	253-471-0292	R	1*	<.1
393	Allen C Ewing and Co—*David W Jackson*	50 N Laura St Ste 3625, Jacksonville FL 32202	904-354-5573	S	1*	<.1
394	Cutter and Company Brokerage Inc—*William Meyer*	15415 Clayton Rd, Ballwin MO 63011	636-537-8770	R	1*	<.1
395	MASI Ltd—*S Jack Campbell*	800 Hart Rd Ste 120, Barrington IL 60010	847-948-7300	R	1*	<.1
396	Founders Equity Inc—*Warren Haber*	711 5th Ave 5th Fl, New York NY 10022	212-829-0900	R	1*	<.1
397	Kaufman and Co—*Sumner Kaufman*	101 Federal St Ste 131, Boston MA 02110	617-426-0444	R	1*	<.1
398	Lamaute Capital Inc—*Daniel Lamaute*	1940 Duke St, Alexandria VA 22314	202-726-1662	R	1*	<.1
399	Omega Securities Inc—*Joseph E Hardgrove*	309 W 7th St Ste 900, Fort Worth TX 76102	817-335-5739	R	1*	<.1
400	Sims Financial Group Inc—*Charles Sims Jr*	6373 Quail Hollow Rd S, Memphis TN 38120	901-682-2410	R	1*	<.1
401	Raymond James Financial Services—*Paul Reilly*	880 Carillon Pky, Saint Petersburg FL 33716	727-567-1000	S	1*	<.1
402	Wachtel and Company Inc—*Bonnie K Wachtel*	1101 14th St NW 8th Fl, Washington DC 20005	202-898-1144	R	1*	<.1
403	Woodward Financial Corp—*Thomas Fanning*	1050 Webster, Birmingham MI 48009	248-644-3358	R	1*	<.1
404	Eagle Ventures Inc—*Melvin Pirchesky*	400 S Highland Ave, Pittsburgh PA 15206	412-683-3400	R	1*	<.1
405	Montague Partners—*Jeanne A Montague*	601 Montgomery St, San Francisco CA 94111	415-928-2183	R	1*	<.1
406	Kent Financial Services Inc—*Paul Koether*	211 Pennbrook Rd, Far Hills NJ 07931	908-766-7221	P	<1	<.1
407	Merrill Lynch and Company Inc—*Thomas K Montag*	4 World Financial Ctr, New York NY 10080	212-449-1000	S	<1	38.7
408	Blaylock Robert Van LLC—*Eric Van Standifer*	600 Lexington Ave 3rd, New York NY 10022	212-715-6600	R	N/A	.1
409	Forstmann Little and Co—*Theodore J Forstmann*	767 5th Ave 45th Fl, New York NY 10153	212-355-5656	R	N/A	<.1

TOTALS: SIC 6211 Security Brokers & Dealers
Companies: 409   735,033   546.0

6221 Commodity Contracts Brokers & Dealers

1	ICAP Energy LLC—*Denis Crum*	9931 Corporate Campus, Louisville KY 40223	502-327-1400	S	9,051*	2.8
2	Rosenthal Collins Group LP—*Scott Gordon*	216 W Jackson Blvd Ste, Chicago IL 60606		R	1,268*	.6
3	Hold Brothers Inc—*Gregory F Hold*	1177 Avenue of the Ame, New York NY 10036	212-792-0900	R	1,063*	.3
4	Rand Financial Services Inc—*Joni Malpede*	141 W Jackson Ste 1950, Chicago IL 60604	312-559-8800	R	361*	.1
5	FXCM Inc—*Dror (Drew) Niv*	32 Old Slip Financial, New York NY 10005	212-897-7660	P	360	.8
6	Glencore Ltd—*Ivan Streisberg*	301 Tresser Blvd 14th, Stamford CT 06901	203-328-4900	S	208*	.2
7	Seam—*Phillip C Burnett*	6055 Primacy Pky Ste 1, Memphis TN 38119	901-374-0374	R	60*	<.1
8	Barex World Trade Corp—*Steven Rothschild*	10 New King St, West Harrison NY 10604	914-285-1300	R	32*	<.1
9	General Cocoa Company Inc—*Tom P Hogan*	110 Wall St 25th Fl, New York NY 10005	212-422-7520	R	25*	<.1
10	Volcot America Inc—*Andrew Smith*	2020 N Central Ave Ste, Phoenix AZ 85004	602-307-9290	R	25*	<.1
11	ADM Investors Services Inc—*Richard Dodson*	141 W Jackson Blvd Ste, Chicago IL 60604	312-435-7000	R	24*	.2
12	McKeany-Flavell Company Inc—*Ray Washmera*	11 Embarcadero W Ste 2, Oakland CA 94607	510-832-2866	R	24*	<.1
13	Vincent Commodities Corp—*Ronald M Vincent*	PO Box 620481, Middleton WI 53562	608-831-4447	R	13*	<.1
14	APB Financial LLC—*Dennis Crum* ICAP Energy LLC	9931 Corporate Campus, Louisville KY 40223	502-327-1400	S	8*	.1
15	Commodities Resource Corp—*George Kleinman*	PO Box 8700, Incline Village NV 89450		R	8*	<.1
16	RWA Financial Services Inc—*Randy Allen*	11149 Calavar Dr, Austin TX 78726	512-336-1754	R	3*	<.1

TOTALS: SIC 6221 Commodity Contracts Brokers & Dealers
Companies: 16   12,533   5.1

6231 Security & Commodity Exchanges

1	Nasdaq OMX Group Inc—*H Furlong Baldwin*	1 Liberty Plz 165 Broa, New York NY 10006	212-401-8700	P	3,197	2.4
2	Securian Financial Group Inc—*Robert L Senklar*	400 Robert St N, Saint Paul MN 55101	651-665-3500	R	3,057	5.0
3	CME Group Inc—*Terrence Duffy*	20 S Wacker Dr, Chicago IL 60606	312-930-1000	P	3,004	2.6
4	NYMEX Holdings Inc—*Jsmes E Newsome* CME Group Inc	1 N End Ave, New York NY 10282	212-299-2000	S	673*	.4
5	CBOE Holdings Inc—*William J Brodsky*	400 S Lasalle St, Chicago IL 60605	312-786-5600	P	508	.6
6	International Securities Exchange Holdings Inc—*Gary Katz*	60 Broad St, New York NY 10004	212-943-2400	S	404*	.2
7	Nasdaq OMX PHLX Inc—*Thomas Whittman* Nasdaq OMX Group Inc	1900 Market St, Philadelphia PA 19103	215-496-5000	S	246*	.1
8	Jesup and Lamont Securities Corp—*James Fellus*	650 5th Ave 3rd Fl, New York NY 10019	212-307-2660	S	175*	.1
9	Minneapolis Grain Exchange—*Mark Bagan*	400 S 4th St, Minneapolis MN 55415	612-321-7101	R	116	<.1
10	American Stock Exchange Inc—*Duncan L Niederauer*	86 Trinity Pl, New York NY 10006	212-306-1000	S	89*	.4
11	Chicago Board Options Exchange Inc—*William J Brodsky*	400 S LaSalle St, Chicago IL 60605	312-786-5600	R	55	.9
12	Chicago Stock Exchange Inc—*David A Herron*	440 S LaSalle St, Chicago IL 60605	312-663-2222	R	45*	.2
13	Cincinnati Stock Exchange—*Jacob Mulaikal*	440 S LaSalle St Ste 2, Chicago IL 60605	312-786-8713	R	9*	<.1

TOTALS: SIC 6231 Security & Commodity Exchanges
Companies: 13   11,578   12.9

6282 Investment Advice

1	Gulf Stream Asset Management—*Mark Mahoney*	The Rotunda Bldg 4201, Charlotte NC 28209		S	3,300,000	<.1
2	US Trust Bank of America Private Wealth Management—*Keith Banks*	114 W 47th St, New York NY 10036		S	102,000	2.3
3	TCW Group Inc—*Marc I Stern*	865 S Figueroa St Ste, Los Angeles CA 90017	213-244-0000	S	49,254*	.6
4	Putnam Investment Management Inc—*Charles E Haldeman*	PO Box 8383, Boston MA 02266	617-292-1000	S	39,551*	5.6
5	Royce and Associates LLC—*Charles M Royce* Legg Mason Inc	745 5th Ave, New York NY 10151	212-500-4500	S	26,400	N/A
6	Frank Russell Co—*Len Brennin*	1301 Second Ave Fl 18, Seattle WA 98101	253-572-9500	S	26,254*	2.0

Rank	Company Name—*Executive Officer*	Address, City, State, Zip	Phone	Type	Fin	Empls
7	John Hancock Subsidiaries Inc—*Arthur R Sawchuk*	PO Box 111, Boston MA 02117	617-572-6000	S	18,491*	9.2
8	AIG SunAmerica Inc—*Jay S Wintrob*	21650 Oxnard St, Woodland Hills CA 91367	310-772-6000	S	12,900*	1.6
9	Jefferies Advisers Inc—*Richard B Handler*	520 Madison Ave 10th F, New York NY 10022	212-284-2300	S	11,250*	1.4
10	New York Life Investment Management LLC—*John Kim*	51 Madison Ave, New York NY 10010	212-576-7000	S	10,937*	1.4
11	Ameriprise Financial Inc—*James M Cracchiolo*	PO Box 1661, Minneapolis MN 55440	612-671-3131	P	10,046	10.5
12	Clarke Lanzen Skalla Investment Firm Inc—*W Patrick Clarke*	4020 South 147th st, Omaha NE 68137	402-493-3313	R	9,233*	1.5
13	Boston Company Inc—*Robert P Kelly*	1 Boston Pl, Boston MA 02108	617-722-7000	S	9,200*	4.5
14	Cadence Capital Management Corp—*Michael J Skillman* Allianz Global Investors	265 Franklin St, Boston MA 02110	617-624-3500	S	7,357*	<.1
15	Franklin Resources Inc—*Gregory E Johnson*	1 Franklin Pkwy Bldg 9, San Mateo CA 94403		P	7,140	8.5
16	Stern Agee—*Jim Holbrook*	800 Shades Creek Pkwy, Birmingham AL 35209	205-949-3500	R	6,366*	1.0
17	American Capital Ltd—*Malon Wilkus*	2 Bethesda Metro Ctr 1, Bethesda MD 20814	301-951-6122	P	5,961	.2
18	Rubicon Financial Inc—*Joseph Mangiapane Jr*	18872 MacArthur Blvd 1, Irvine CA 92612	949-798-7220	P	5,233	<.1
19	TCW Funds Management Inc—*Marc Stern* TCW Group Inc	865 S Figueroa St Ste, Los Angeles CA 90017	213-244-0000	S	4,033*	.6
20	Loomis Sayles and Company LP—*Robert J Blanding*	1 Financial Ctr, Boston MA 02111	617-482-2450	S	3,293*	.4
21	Primerica Financial Services Inc—*John Addison Jr*	3120 Breckinridge Blvd, Duluth GA 30099		S	3,286*	1.7
22	AEGON USA Realty Advisors Inc—*David L Blankenship*	4333 Edgewood Rd NE, Cedar Rapids IA 52499	355-369-2300	S	3,266*	2.3
23	Blackstone Group LP—*Stephen Schwarzman*	345 Park Ave 31st Fl, New York NY 10154	212-583-5000	P	3,253	1.6
24	Grantham Mayo Van Otterloo and Co—*Mark Mayer*	40 Rowes Wharf, Boston MA 02110	617-330-7500	R	3,188*	.5
25	Oriental Financial Services Corp	996 Professional Offic, Rio Piedras PR 00927	787-474-0474	S	3,172*	.4
26	Nicholas-Applegate Capital Management—*Marna C Whittington*	600 W Broadway, San Diego CA 92101	619-687-8000	R	2,866*	.5
27	Legg Mason Inc—*Mark R Fetting*	PO Box 1496, Baltimore MD 21203	410-539-0000	P	2,784	3.4
28	AllianceBernstein Holding LP—*Peter S Kraus*	1345 Ave of the Americ, New York NY 10105	212-969-2301	B	2,752	3.8
29	AXA Roseberg Investment Management LLC—*Martha Clark*	4 Orinda Way Bldg E, Orinda CA 94563	925-254-6464	R	2,548*	.4
30	Man Investments Div—*Peter Clarke*	123 N Wacker Dr Ste 28, Chicago IL 60606	312-881-6800	D	2,520*	1.8
31	PFM Asset Management LLC—*F John White*	One Keystone Plz Ste 3, Harrisburg PA 17101	717-231-6200	R	2,484*	.4
32	Credit Suisse Asset Management Ltd—*Brady W Dougan*	11 Madison Ave, New York NY 10010	212-325-2000	S	2,421*	.3
33	Oxford Realty Services Corp—*Randall McCombs*	7200 Wisconsin Ave Ste, Bethesda MD 20814	301-654-3100	R	2,255*	1.6
34	Broadridge Financial Solutions Inc—*Richard J Daly*	1981 Marcus Ave, Lake Success NY 11042	516-472-5400	P	2,167	5.9
35	Affiliated Managers Group Inc—*Sean M Healey*	600 Hale St, Prides Crossing MA 01965	617-747-3300	P	1,705	2.0
36	Alamo Capital Inc—*Ronald A Robinson*	1627 E Walnut St, Seguin TX 78155	830-379-1480	S	1,585*	.2
37	Torch Energy Advisors Inc—*J P Bryan*	1331 Lamar St Ste 1450, Houston TX 77010	713-650-1246	S	1,585*	.2
38	Highland Capital Management LP—*James Dondero*	Nexbank Tower13455 Noe, Dallas TX 75240	972-628-4100	R	1,534*	.3
39	CBIZ Financial Solutions Inc—*Christopher T Matthews*	44 Baltimore St, Cumberland MD 21502	301-777-1500	S	1,505*	.2
40	Heitman LLC—*Maury Tognarelli*	191 N Wacker Dr Ste 25, Chicago IL 60606	312-855-5700	S	1,425*	.2
41	Barclays Global Investors—*Laurence D Fink*	45 Fremont St, San Francisco CA 94105	415-597-2000	R	1,399*	.7
42	Newland Communities—*Robert McLeod*	9820 Towne Centre Dr, San Diego CA 92121	858-455-7503	R	1,308*	.1
43	Eaton Vance Corp—*Thomas E Faust*	PO Box 9653, Providence RI 02940	617-482-8260	P	1,260	1.2
44	Brown Advisory—*Michael D Hankin*	901 S Bond St Ste 400, Baltimore MD 21231	410-537-5400	R	1,222*	.2
45	American Capital Financial Services—*Malon Wilkus* American Capital Ltd	2 Bethesda Metro Cente, Bethesda MD 20814	301-951-6122	S	1,107*	.1
46	Franklin Advisers Inc—*Gregory Johnson* Franklin Resources Inc	PO Box 7777, San Mateo CA 94403	650-312-3200	S	1,000*	5.0
47	Janus Capital Group Inc—*Richard M Weil*	151 Detroit St, Denver CO 80206	303-333-3863	P	982	1.1
48	Brandes Investment Partners Inc—*Glenn R Carlson*	PO Box 919048, San Diego CA 02191	858-755-0239	R	973*	.5
49	Canaccord Adams Inc—*Kevin Dunn*	99 High St Ste 1200, Boston MA 02110	617-371-3900	S	907*	.4
50	Federated Investors Inc—*J Christopher Donahue*	Federated Investors Tw, Pittsburgh PA 15222	412-288-8141	P	895	1.5
51	APS Asset Management Inc—*John Lindquist*	1301 S Capital of Texa, Austin TX 78746	512-328-0888	S	886*	.1
52	Aeltus Investment Management Inc—*Michel Tilmant*	10 State House Sq, Hartford CT 06103	860-275-3720	S	866	N/A
53	SunAmerica Asset Management Corp—*Dan Chung* AIG SunAmerica Inc	PO Box 219186, Kansas City MO 64121		S	862*	.1
54	Fortress Investment Group LLC—*Daniel H Mudd*	1345 Avenue of the Ame, New York NY 10105	212-798-6100	P	859	1.0
55	JMB Realty Corp—*Neil G Bluhm*	900 N Michigan Ave Ste, Chicago IL 60611	312-915-2000	R	855*	.5
56	Templeton Investment Counsel Inc—*Charles B Johnson* Templeton Worldwide Inc	500 E Broward Blvd Ste, Fort Lauderdale FL 33394	954-527-7500	D	846*	.5
57	Ziegler Asset Management Inc	250 E Wisconsin Ave St, Milwaukee WI 53202	414-978-6400	S	834*	.4
58	Payden and Rygel—*Joan A Payden*	333 S Grand Ave Ste 32, Los Angeles CA 90071	213-625-1900	R	831*	.1
59	Nuveen Investments Inc—*John P Amboian*	333 W Wacker Dr, Chicago IL 60606	312-917-7700	R	818*	1.0
60	Pacific Investment Management Co—*Mohamed El-Erian* Allianz Global Investors	840 Newport Center Dr, Newport Beach CA 92660	949-720-6000	S	797*	1.5
61	First Pacific Advisors LLC—*Robert L Rodriguez*	11400 W Olympic Blvd S, Los Angeles CA 90064	310-473-0225	S	788*	.1
62	Fischer Francis Trees and Watts Inc—*Michel C Anastassiades*	200 Park Ave 46th Fl, New York NY 10166	212-681-3000	S	761*	.1
63	Interactive Data Corp—*Mason Slaine*	32 Crosby Dr, Bedford MA 01730	781-687-8500	S	757	2.5
64	Principal Financial Advisors Inc	PO Box 407, Jefferson IA 50129	515-386-3519	S	711	N/A
65	Tremont Partners Inc Tremont Capital Management Inc	555 Theodore Fremd Ave, Rye NY 10580	914-925-1140	S	706*	.1
66	Moneta Group LLC—*Gene Diederich*	100 S Brentwood Blvd S, Clayton MO 63105	314-726-2300	R	703*	.1
67	Neuberger Berman Inc—*George Walker*	605 3rd Ave, New York NY 10158	212-476-9000	S	662*	1.3
68	American Century Companies Inc—*Jonathan S Thomas*	PO Box 419200, Kansas City MO 64141	816-531-5575	R	650*	2.0
69	Cohen Financial—*Jack Cohen*	2 N LaSalle St Ste 800, Chicago IL 60602	312-346-5680	R	637*	.1
70	Van Kampen Investment Advisory Corp—*Jerry Miller* Van Kampen Investments Inc	1 Parkview Plz, Oakbrook Terrace IL 60181	630-684-6000	S	633*	.5
71	Morningstar Inc—*Joe Mansueto*	22 W Washington St, Chicago IL 60602	312-696-6000	P	631	3.5
72	Broyhill Asset Management—*M Hunt Broyhill*	PO Box 500, Lenoir NC 28645	828-758-6100	R	631*	.1
73	Bryn Mawr Brokerage Company Inc—*Frederick Peters*	801 Lancaster Ave, Bryn Mawr PA 19010	610-687-4268	S	630*	.3
74	Och-Ziff Capital Management Group LLC—*Daniel S Och*	9 W 57th St 39th Fl, New York NY 10019	212-790-0041	P	616	.4
75	HIG Capital Management Inc—*Sami Mnaymneh*	1001 Brickell Bay Dr 2, Miami FL 33131	305-379-2322	R	612*	.1
76	TCW Management Co—*Marc I Stern* TCW Group Inc	865 S Figueroa St Ste, Los Angeles CA 90017	213-244-0000	S	600*	.6
77	Tiger Management Corp—*Julian H Robertson Jr*	101 Park Ave 48th Fl, New York NY 10178	212-867-4350	R	600*	.2
78	Putnam Investments Inc—*Robert L Reynolds*	100 Financial Park, Franklin MA 02038	617-292-1000	S	588*	5.3
79	Tecolote Research Inc—*James Y Takayesu*	420 S Fairview AveSte, Goleta CA 93117	805-571-6366	R	588*	.5
80	Voyageur Asset Management Inc—*Dexter Dodge* Eaton Vance Corp	100 S 5th St Ste 2300, Minneapolis MN 55402	612-376-7000	S	580*	.1
81	Kennedy Associates Inc—*Gary Whitelaw*	1215 4th Ave Ste 2400, Seattle WA 98161	206-623-4739	R	555*	.1
82	Vantage Financial Group Inc—*Marty Uhle*	PO Box 318082, Cleveland OH 44131	216-642-7878	R	554*	.1
83	Silvercrest Asset Management Group LLC—*G Moffett Cochran*	1330 Ave of the Americ, New York NY 10019	212-649-0600	R	534*	.1
84	First Southwest Asset Management Inc—*Scott Mcintyre*	325 N St Paul Ste 800, Dallas TX 75201	214-953-4000	S	531*	.3
85	Earnest Partners LLC—*Paul E Viera*	1180 Peachtree St Ste, Atlanta GA 30309	404-815-8772	R	524*	.1

Note: An asterisk (*) indicates an estimated financial figure. The company type code used is as follows: R = Private, P = Public, S = Private Subsidiary, B = Public Subsidiary, D = Division, J = Joint Venture, I = Investment Fund.

COMPANY RANKINGS BY SALES WITHIN 4-DIGIT SIC

Rank	Company Name—*Executive Officer*	Address, City, State, Zip	Phone	Type	Fin	Empls
86	Haverford Trust Co—*Joseph J McLaughlin Jr*	3 Radnor Corporate Ctr, Radnor PA 19087	610-995-8700	R	507*	.1
87	Fenimore Asset Management Inc—*David Pollitzer*	384 N Grand St, Cobleskill NY 12043	518-234-4393	R	486*	<.1
88	FCCI Investment Group Inc—*GW Jacobs*	6300 University Pkwy, Sarasota FL 34240	941-907-3224	S	482*	.7
89	First Atlantic Capital Ltd—*Roberto Buaron*	135 E 57th St 29th Fl, New York NY 10022	212-207-0300	R	480	N/A
90	4086 Advisors Inc—*Eric Johnson*	535 N College Dr, Carmel IN 46032	317-817-4086	S	469*	.1
91	Massachusetts Financial Services Co—*Robert Manning*	500 Boylston St, Boston MA 02116	617-954-5000	S	468*	1.8
92	Robert W Baird and Company Inc—*Paul E Purcell*	PO Box 0672, Milwaukee WI 53201	414-765-3500	R	456*	2.2
93	J and W Seligman and Company Inc—*William C Morris*	100 Park Ave, New York NY 10017	212-850-1864	R	439*	.3
94	Navellier and Associates Inc—*Louis G Navellier*	1 E Liberty St 3rd Fl, Reno NV 89501	775-785-2300	R	430*	.1
95	Private Capital Management Inc—*Gregg J Powers* Legg Mason Inc	8889 Pelican Bay Blvd, Naples FL 34108	239-254-2500	S	430*	.1
96	Gregory FCA Communications Inc—*Gregory Matusky*	27 W Athens Ave Ste 20, Ardmore PA 19003	610-642-8253	R	418*	.1
97	Kinder Lydenberg Domini and Company Inc—*Peter D Kinder*	121 High St 4th Fl, Boston MA 02110	617-426-5270	R	395*	.1
98	Callan Associates Inc—*Ronald Peyton*	101 California St Ste, San Francisco CA 94111	415-974-5060	R	389*	.2
99	H and R Block Financial Advisors Inc—*Mark Ernst*	719 Griswold Ste 140, Detroit MI 48226		S	387*	4.0
100	Public Financial Management Inc—*F John White*	2 Logan Sq Ste 1600 18, Philadelphia PA 19103	215-567-6100	S	384*	.2
101	RNC Genter Capital Managmnt—*Daniel J Genter*	11601 Wilshire Blvd 25, Los Angeles CA 90025	310-477-6543	R	383*	.1
102	Bartlett and Co (Cincinnati Ohio)—*Kelley J Downing* Legg Mason Inc	600 Vine St Ste 2100, Cincinnati OH 45202	513-621-4612	S	379*	.1
103	Van Kampen Investments Inc—*Jerry Miller*	PO Box 5555, Oakbrook Terrace IL 60181	630-684-6000	S	377*	1.3
104	Dreyfus Corp—*Jon Baum*	200 Park Ave 7th Fl, New York NY 10166	212-922-6000	S	360*	2.0
105	Arden Asset Management LLC—*Averell H Mortimer*	375 Park Ave 37th Fl, New York NY 10152	212-751-5252	R	356*	.1
106	Weiss Group Inc—*Martin Weiss PhD*	15430 Endeavour Dr, Jupiter FL 33478	561-627-3300	R	322*	<.1
107	Castle Harlan Inc—*John K Castle*	150 E 58th St, New York NY 10155	212-644-8600	R	319*	.1
108	Landmark Partners Inc—*Francisco Borges*	10 Mill Pond Ln, Simsbury CT 06070	860-651-9760	R	319*	.1
109	Wedge Capital Management LLP—*Richard Hodde*	301 S College St, Charlotte NC 28202	704-334-6475	R	319*	.1
110	Sterling Capital Management Co—*Alex McCalister*	4064 Colony Rd Ste 300, Charlotte NC 28211	704-372-8670	R	311*	<.1
111	B Riley and Company Inc—*Tom Kelleher*	11100 Santa Monica Blv, Los Angeles CA 90025	310-966-1444	R	307*	.1
112	MR Beal and Co—*Bernard Beal*	110 Wall St 6th Fl, New York NY 10005	212-983-3930	R	307*	<.1
113	GLG Partners Inc—*Noam Gottesman*	390 Park Ave 20th Fl, New York NY 10022	212-224-7200	S	301	.4
114	Ehrenkrantz King Nussbaum Inc—*Anthony Ottimo*	201 Old Country Rd, Melville NY 11747	516-396-1234	R	288*	.2
115	Anchor Capital Advisors LLC—*William P Rice*	1 Post Office Sq Ste 3, Boston MA 02109	617-338-3800	R	287*	<.1
116	Phoenix Investment Partners Ltd—*Donna D Young*	1 American Row, Hartford CT 06103	860-403-5000	S	287	.7
117	Gamco Investors Inc—*Mario Gabelli*	1 Corporate Ctr, Rye NY 10580	914-921-5100	P	280	.2
118	Artio Global Investors Inc—*Richard Pell*	330 Madison Ave, New York NY 10017	212-297-3600	P	276	.2
119	Brenner Group Inc—*Richard M Brenner*	19200 Stevens Creek Bl, Cupertino CA 95014	408-873-3400	R	274*	<.1
120	Eagle Asset Management Inc—*Richard K Riess*	PO Box 10520, Saint Petersburg FL 33733	727-573-2453	S	270*	.2
121	Budros Ruhlin and Roe Inc—*Peggy Ruhlin*	1801 Watermark Dr Ste, Columbus OH 43215	614-481-6900	R	270*	<.1
122	Babson Capital Management LLC—*Tom Finke*	470 Atlantic Ave, Boston MA 02210	617-225-3800	S	262*	.9
123	Fund Evaluation Group LLC—*Scott B Harsh*	201 East 5th St Ste 16, Cincinnati OH 45202	513-977-4400	S	260*	.1
124	Eastover Group of Cos—*David H Hoster II*	PO Box 22728, Jackson MS 39225	601-354-3555	R	256*	.1
125	Moore Capital Management LP—*Louis Moore Bacon*	1251 Ave of the Americ, New York NY 10020	212-782-7000	R	254*	.2
126	BTS Asset Management Inc—*Matthew Pasts*	PO Box 9178, Lexington MA 02420		R	254*	<.1
127	Delaware Investments—*Patrick P Coyne*	2005 Market St 30th Fl, Philadelphia PA 19103	215-255-1200	R	252*	.8
128	GCG Wealth Management Inc—*Dennis Howe*	9115 Harris Corners Pk, Charlotte NC 28269	704-372-4491	R	251*	<.1
129	UCM Partners—*Gregory Parsons*	52 Vanderbilt Ave Four, New York NY 10017	212-612-9101	R	245*	<.1
130	Capital Research and Management Co—*Larry Clemmensen*	333 S Hope St 53rd Fl, Los Angeles CA 90071	213-486-9200	R	241*	.8
131	Fayez Sarofim and Co—*Fayez Sarofim*	2 Houston Ctr Ste 2907, Houston TX 77010	713-654-4484	R	240*	.1
132	Kennedy Capital Management Inc—*Randall Kirkland*	10829 Olive Blvd, Saint Louis MO 63141	314-432-0400	R	240*	<.1
133	APS Financial Corp—*John Lindquist*	1301 S Capital of Texa, Austin TX 78746	512-314-4375	S	238*	<.1
134	Norwest Venture Capital Management Inc—*John E Lindahl*	80 S 8th St Ste 3600, Minneapolis MN 55402	612-215-1600	S	237*	<.1
135	Fox Asset Management LLC—*William E Dodge* Eaton Vance Corp	331 Newman Springs Rd, Red Bank NJ 07701	732-747-6345	S	234*	<.1
136	World Business Brokers Inc—*Dean Sena*	9516 S Dixie Hwy, Miami FL 33156	305-670-6565	R	232*	.1
137	Goldner Hawn Johnson and Morrison Inc—*Darren Achenson*	3700 Wells Fargo Ctr 9, Minneapolis MN 55402	612-338-5912	R	224*	<.1
138	Renaissance Investment Management—*Michael E Schroer*	625 Eden Park Dr Ste 1, Cincinnati OH 45202	513-723-4500	R	224*	<.1
139	Peninsula Asset Management Inc—*William E Middlebrooks Jr*	1111 3rd Ave W Ste 340, Bradenton FL 34205	941-748-8680	R	222*	<.1
140	Prime Advisors Inc—*Duane Castles*	22635 NE Market Pl Dr, Redmond WA 98053	425-202-2000	R	218*	<.1
141	BKF Asset Management Inc—*Gregory Rogers*	1 Rockefeller Plz, New York NY 10020	212-332-8400	R	214*	.2
142	Equus Capital Corp—*Jon Hardy*	2727 Allen Pky 13th Fl, Houston TX 77019	713-529-0900	R	214*	<.1
143	Munder Capital Management—*James V Fitzgerald*	480 Pierce St, Birmingham MI 48009	248-647-9200	R	211*	.1
144	Legend Advisory Services Inc—*Glen Ferris*	4600 E Park Dr Ste 300, Palm Beach Gardens FL 33410	561-694-0110	R	211*	.1
145	AR Schmeidler and Company Inc—*Stephen Burke*	500 5th Ave 14th Fl, New York NY 10110	212-687-9800	R	210*	<.1
146	Roffman Miller Associates Inc—*Marvin Roffman*	1835 Market St Ste 500, Philadelphia PA 19103	215-981-1030	R	204*	<.1
147	Forex Club LLC—*Peter Tatarnikov*	120 Wall St 16th Fl, New York NY 10005		R	202*	.5
148	FH Prince and Company Inc—*Frederick H Prince*	303 W Madison Ste 1900, Chicago IL 60606	312-419-9500	R	200*	.1
149	Duke Management Co—*Thruston B Morton III*	2200 W Main St Ste 100, Durham NC 27705	919-286-6605	R	199*	<.1
150	Johnson Capital Group Inc—*Guy K Johnson*	2603 Main St Ste 200, Irvine CA 92614	949-660-1999	R	193*	.1
151	LJ Altfest and Company Inc—*Lewis J Altfest*	425 Park Ave 24th Fl, New York NY 10022	212-406-0850	R	191*	<.1
152	New England Pension Consultants Inc—*Richard M Charlton*	1 Main St 8th Fl, Cambridge MA 02142	617-374-1300	R	185*	.1
153	CMS Companies Inc—*Paul Silberberg*	1926 Arch St, Philadelphia PA 19103	215-246-3000	R	183*	.1
154	Mount Lucas Management Corp—*Timothy J Rudderow*	47 Hulfish St Ste 510, Princeton NJ 08542		R	183*	<.1
155	Goldentree Asset Management LP—*Steven Tananbaum*	300 Park Ave Ste 21, New York NY 10022	212-847-3500	R	180*	.2
156	Meyer Handelman Co—*Donald Handelman*	4 International Dr, Port Chester NY 10573	914-939-4060	R	180*	<.1
157	Towneley Capital Management Inc—*Wesley G McCain*	23197 La Cadena Dr Ste, Laguna Hills CA 92653		R	178*	<.1
158	FOLIOfn Inc—*Steven M H Wallman*	8000 Towers Crescent D, Vienna VA 22182	703-245-4000	R	177*	.1
159	RMH Associates Inc—*Richard Hannafin*	PO Box 91, South Orleans MA 02662	508-255-9355	R	177*	<.1
160	Dalbar Financial Services Inc—*Louis Harvey*	600 Atlantic Ave, Boston MA 02210	617-723-6400	R	172*	<.1
161	Muhlenkamp and Company Inc—*Ronald H Muhlenkamp*	5000 Stonewood Dr Ste, Wexford PA 15090	724-935-5520	R	172*	<.1
162	Delaware Management Holdings Inc—*Patrick Coyne*	2005 Market St, Philadelphia PA 19103	215-255-2300	S	170*	.6
163	Winmill and Company Inc—*Thomas B Winmill*	11 Hanover Sq, New York NY 10005	212-785-0900	P	170*	<.1
164	Intrepid Capital Management Inc—*Mark F Travis* Intrepid Capital Corp	1400 Marsh Landing Pkw, Jacksonville Beach FL 32250	904-246-3433	S	162*	<.1
165	Diamond Hill Capital Management Inc	325 John H McConnell B, Columbus OH 43215	614-255-3333	S	161*	<.1
166	Oberweis Asset Management Inc—*Jim Oberweis Jr*	3333 Warrenville Road, Lisle IL 60532	630-577-2300	R	161*	<.1
167	PanAgora Asset Management Inc—*Eric Sorensen*	470 Atlantic Ave 8th F, Boston MA 02210	617-439-6300	R	160*	<.1
168	Gateway Investment Advisers LP—*Patrick Rogers*	312 Walnut St 35th Fl, Cincinnati OH 45202	513-719-1100	S	160*	<.1
169	Russell Investments—*Len Brennan*	1301 2nd Ave Fl 18, Seattle WA 98101	206-505-7877	R	160*	2.5
170	Wall Street Strategies Inc—*Charles Payne*	61 Broadway, New York NY 10006	212-514-9500	R	159*	<.1
171	Renaissance Capital LLC—*William K Smith*	165 Mason St, Greenwich CT 06830	203-622-2978	R	159*	<.1

Rank	Company Name—*Executive Officer*	Address, City, State, Zip	Phone	Type	Fin	Empls
172	Fiduciary Management Inc—*Ted D Kellner*	100 E Wisconsin Ave St, Milwaukee WI 53202	414-226-4545	R	159*	<.1
173	Portola Group Inc—*Bob Fitzwilson*	3000 Sand Hill Rd Ste, Menlo Park CA 94025	650-854-7550	R	158*	<.1
174	American Capital Partners LLC—*Michael Karfunkel*	205 Oser Ave, Hauppauge NY 11788	631-851-0918	R	158*	3.8
175	Cooke and Bieler Inc—*Samuel H Ballam III*	1700 Market St Ste 322, Philadelphia PA 19103	215-567-1101	R	155*	<.1
176	Capital Advisors Inc—*Keith C Goddard*	2200 S Utica Pl Ste 15, Tulsa OK 74114	918-599-0045	R	155*	<.1
177	Angelo Gordon and Company LP—*Michael Chang*	245 Park Ave Fl 26, New York NY 10167	212-692-2000	R	154*	2.7
178	Boyd Watterson Asset Management LLC—*Brian Gevry*	1801 E 9th St Ste 1400, Cleveland OH 44114	216-771-3450	R	153*	<.1
179	Weiss Research Inc—*Martin WeissPhD* Weiss Group Inc	15430 Endeavour Dr, Jupiter FL 33478	561-354-4400	S	153*	<.1
180	Harris Associates LP—*John Raitt*	2 N LaSalle St Ste 500, Chicago IL 60602	312-621-0600	S	152*	.2
181	SMH Capital Advisors Inc—*George Ball*	4800 Overton Plz Ste 3, Fort Worth TX 76109	817-731-4308	S	146*	<.1
182	Pax World Management Corp—*Joe Keefe*	30 Penhallow St Ste 40, Portsmouth NH 03801	603-431-8022	R	145*	<.1
183	Baring Asset Management Inc—*Michael Brown*	470 Atlantic Ave Indep, Boston MA 02210	617-946-5200	S	142*	.1
184	Miller/Russell and Associates Inc—*Dennis H Miller*	2701 E Camelback Rd St, Phoenix AZ 85016	602-468-1232	S	141*	<.1
185	Ryan Labs Inc—*Sean McShea*	500 Fifth Ave Ste 2520, New York NY 10110	212-635-2300	R	140*	<.1
186	Diesslin and Associates Inc—*David H Diesslin*	303 Main St Ste 200, Fort Worth TX 76102	817-332-6122	R	140*	<.1
187	CT Realty Corp—*James Watson*	65 Enterprise Ste 150, Aliso Viejo CA 92656	949-330-5770	R	139*	<.1
188	AdMedia Partners Inc—*Seith Alpert*	3 Park Ave 31st Fl, New York NY 10016	212-759-1870	R	137*	<.1
189	Wellington Management Company LLP—*Perry Traquina*	75 State St Ste 2108, Boston MA 02109	617-951-5000	R	136*	1.0
190	Robeco Investment Managemnet—*Mark E Donovan*	1 Beacon St 30th Fl, Boston MA 02108	617-832-8200	S	136*	.1
191	Premier Trust of Nevada—*Mark Dreschler*	2700 W Sahara Ste 300, Las Vegas NV 89102	702-507-0750	S	133*	<.1
192	Rice Hall James and Associates—*Thomas McDowell*	600 W Broadway Ste 100, San Diego CA 92101	619-239-9005	R	130*	<.1
193	Intrepid Capital Corp—*Mark F Travis*	1400 Marsh Landing Pky, Jacksonville Beach FL 32250	904-246-3433	P	130*	<.1
194	Kayne Anderson Rudnick Investment Management LLC— *Richard A Kayne*	1800 Ave of Stars 2nd, Los Angeles CA 90067	310-556-2721	R	128*	.1
195	Investment Counselors of Maryland LLC—*William V Heaphy*	803 Cathedral St, Baltimore MD 21201	410-539-3838	R	128*	<.1
196	Peak6 Investments LP—*Matt Hulsizer*	141 W Jackson Blvd Ste, Chicago IL 60604	312-362-2401	R	127*	.1
197	First Republic Investment Management—*Bob Thornton*	111 W Micheltorena St, Santa Barbara CA 93101	805-963-5963	R	127*	<.1
198	Great Point Investors LLC—*Joe Versaggi*	2 Center Plaza Ste 410, Boston MA 02108	617-526-8800	R	127*	<.1
199	Harbor Capital Management Company Inc—*David G Van Hoo-ser*	PO Box 804660, Chicago IL 60680		R	126*	<.1
200	Rothschild/Pell Rudman Inc—*John S Markwalter*	100 E Pratt St Ste 255, Baltimore MD 21202	410-539-4660	R	125*	<.1
201	Dresdner RCM Global Investors LLC—*Udo Frank*	4 Embarcadero Ctr Ste, San Francisco CA 94111	415-954-5400	R	122*	.4
202	Driehaus Capital Management LLC—*Richard H Driehaus*	25 E Erie St, Chicago IL 60611	312-587-3800	R	122*	.1
203	WCM Investment Management—*Kurt Winrich*	281 Brooks St, Laguna Beach CA 92651	949-380-0200	R	118*	<.1
204	Van Eck Global Corp—*Jan van Eck*	335 Madison Ave 19th F, New York NY 10017	212-687-5200	R	117*	.1
205	NFJ Investment Group—*Chris Najork* Allianz Global Investors	2100 Ross Ave Ste 700, Dallas TX 75201	214-754-1780	S	115*	<.1
206	First Equity Development Inc—*Aaron P Hollander*	15 Riverside Ave, Westport CT 06880	203-291-7700	R	115*	<.1
207	Kensington Realty Advisors Inc—*James Smith*	100 N Riverside Plaza, Chicago IL 60606	312-993-7800	R	113*	<.1
208	Strategic Investment Group—*Hilda Ochoa Brillembourg*	1001 19th St N 16th Fl, Arlington VA 22209	703-243-4433	R	111*	.1
209	Elkins/McSherry LLC—*James Bryson*	225 Liberty St 2 World, New York NY 10281	917-790-4611	S	110*	<.1
210	Templeton Worldwide Inc Franklin Resources Inc	500 E Broward Blvd Ste, Fort Lauderdale FL 33394	954-527-7500	S	106*	.6
211	McGlinn Capital Management Inc—*Michael J McGlinn*	PO 6158, Wyomissing PA 19610	610-374-5125	R	106*	<.1
212	Campbell Group Inc—*John Gilleland*	1 SW Columbia St Ste 1, Portland OR 97258	503-275-9675	R	105*	.1
213	Berkshire Partners LLC—*Brad Bloom*	200 Clarendon St, Boston MA 02116	617-227-0050	R	105*	<.1
214	Demer IR Counsel Inc—*Deborah B Demer*	3527 Mt Diablo Blvd St, Lafayette CA 94549	925-938-2678	R	103*	<.1
215	L and B Realty Advisors LLP—*G Andrews Smith*	8750 N Central Expy St, Dallas TX 75231	214-989-0800	R	102*	.1
216	Arnold Investment Counsel Inc—*Lilli Gust*	3960 Hillside Dr Ste 2, Delafield WI 53018	262-303-4850	R	102*	<.1
217	Myerberg and Company LP—*Marsha Myerberg*	780 3rd Ave 19th Fl, New York NY 10017	212-750-3939	R	101*	<.1
218	Cramer Rosenthal and McGlynn Inc—*Jay B Abramson*	520 Madison Ave 32 Fl, New York NY 10022	212-326-5300	R	99*	.1
219	Envestnet Inc—*Judson Bergman*	35 E Wacker Dr 24th Fl, Chicago IL 60601	312-827-2800	P	98	.5
220	Hencorp Becstone LC—*Raul Henriquez*	777 Brickell Ave Ste 1, Miami FL 33131	305-373-9000	R	97*	.1
221	Madison Investment Advisors Inc—*Frank E Burgess*	550 Science Dr, Madison WI 53711	608-274-0300	R	97*	.1
222	Capstone Partners LLC—*John Ferrara*	176 Federal St, Boston MA 02110	617-619-3300	R	97*	<.1
223	Hottinger US Inc—*Philippe Comby*	1270 Ave of the Americ, New York NY 10020	212-332-7930	R	96*	<.1
224	Beacon Financial Group Inc—*Randy Landsman*	101 Town Center Dr Ste, Warren NJ 07059	908-769-4333	R	96*	<.1
225	Wilshire Asset Management—*Dennis Tito* Wilshire Associates Inc	1299 Ocean Ave, Santa Monica CA 90401	310-451-3051	D	95*	.4
226	Bindley Capital Partners—*Thomas J Salentine*	8909 Purdue Rd Ste 500, Indianapolis IN 46268	317-704-4162	R	94*	<.1
227	Dean Investment Associates Div CH Dean and Associates Inc	3500 Pentagon BlvdSte, Beavercreek OH 45431	937-222-9531	D	92*	.1
228	Davidson Cos—*William A Johnstone*	PO Box 5015, Great Falls MT 59403	406-727-4200	R	90*	.9
229	Dubin and Swieca Capital Management LLC—*Ronald Resnick*	9 W 59th St 27th Fl, New York NY 10153	212-751-4510	R	90*	.1
230	Clinton Group Inc—*George Hall*	9 W 57th St 26th Fl, New York NY 10019	212-825-0400	R	88*	<.1
231	Principal Global Investors LLC—*James P McCaughan*	801 Grand Ave, Des Moines IA 50309	515-247-6582	S	87*	1.0
232	CL King and Associates Inc—*Candace King Weir*	9 Elk St, Albany NY 12207	518-431-3500	R	86*	.1
233	Dwight Asset Management Co—*David Thompson*	100 Bank St Ste 800, Burlington VT 05401	802-862-4170	S	86*	.1
234	Oechsle International Advisers LP—*Walter Oechsle*	1 International Pl 23r, Boston MA 02110	617-330-8810	D	85*	.1
235	Vector Wealth Management—*Thomas G Fee*	43 Main St SE Ste 236, Minneapolis MN 55414	612-378-7560	R	83*	<.1
236	Imperial Capital Group LLC—*Jason W Reese*	2000 Avenue of the Sta, Los Angeles CA 90067	310-246-3700	R	82*	.2
237	Winslow Management Co—*Jackson W Robinson* Canaccord Adams Inc	99 High St, Boston MA 02110	617-788-1600	D	82*	<.1
238	Pioneer Group Inc—*Osbert Hood*	60 State St, Boston MA 02109	617-742-7825	S	80*	.7
239	WealthTrust Inc—*M Rush Benton*	102 Woodmount Blvd Ste, Nashville TN 37205	615-297-6884	R	80*	<.1
240	Atlanta Capital Management Company LLC—*Kelly Williams* Eaton Vance Corp	1075 Peachtree StNE St, Atlanta GA 30309	404-876-9411	S	79*	<.1
241	Essex Investment Management Company LLC—*Christopher P McConnell*	125 High St 29th Fl, Boston MA 02110	617-342-3200	R	78*	.1
242	Peoples Financial Services Inc—*Charles Sulerzyski*	PO Box 231, Auburn IN 46706	260-925-2500	S	78*	<.1
243	Kunath Karren Rinne and Atkin Inc—*Michael Kunath*	1000 2nd Ave Ste 4000, Seattle WA 98104	206-621-7400	R	78*	<.1
244	Pzena Investment Management Inc—*Richard S Pzena*	120 W 45th St 20th Fl, New York NY 10036	212-355-1600	P	78	.1
245	AppIntelligence Inc—*Stephen Gott*	17 Research Park Dr St, Weldon Spring MO 63304	636-300-2500	R	77*	<.1
246	Hotchkis and Wiley Capital Management—*George H Davis Jr*	725 S Figueroa St Ste, Los Angeles CA 90017	213-430-1000	R	75*	.1
247	Emkay Inc—*Greg Tepas*	805 W Thorndale Ave, Itasca IL 60143	630-250-7400	R	75*	<.1
248	Tom Johnson Investment Management Inc—*Richard H Parry*	201 Robert S Kerr Ave, Oklahoma City OK 73102	405-236-2111	R	75*	<.1
249	ARA Portfolio Management Company LLC—*A R Arulpragasam*	195 Church St, New Haven CT 06510	203-497-8700	R	74*	<.1
250	Prime Buchholz and Associates Inc—*Jon L Prime*	273 Corporate Dr, Portsmouth NH 03801	603-433-1143	R	72*	<.1
251	Clarion Capital Partners LLC—*Marc A Utay*	110 E 59th St Ste 2100, New York NY 10022	212-821-0111	R	72*	<.1

Note: An asterisk (*) indicates an estimated financial figure. The company type code used is as follows: R = Private, P = Public, S = Private Subsidary, B = Public Subsidary, D = Division, J = Joint Venture, I = Investment Fund.

COMPANY RANKINGS BY SALES WITHIN 4-DIGIT SIC

Rank	Company Name—Executive Officer	Address, City, State, Zip	Phone	Type	Fin	Empls
252	Westchester Capital Management Inc—John W Rogers	801 N 96th St, Omaha NE 68114	402-392-2418	R	72*	<.1
253	Aris Corporation Spectrum Financial Network—John S Battaglia Jr	PO Box 1318, State College PA 16804	814-231-2292	R	71*	.1
254	Morgan Investments Inc—Raymond P Morgan	PO Box 372, Greenville SC 29602	864-235-4196	R	71*	.1
255	Rainer Investment Management Inc—Leonard P Brennan	601 Union St Ste 2801, Seattle WA 98101	206-464-0400	R	71*	.1
256	DePrince Race and Zollo Inc—Gregory M DePrince	250 Park Ave S Ste 250, Winter Park FL 32789	407-420-9903	R	70*	.1
257	Marvin and Palmer Associates Inc—Stanley Palmer	1201 N Market St Ste 2, Wilmington DE 19801	302-573-3570	R	70*	.1
258	Cambiar Investors Inc—Brian Barish	2401 E 2nd Ave Ste 500, Denver CO 80206	303-302-9000	R	70*	<.1
259	St Johns Investment Management Co—Albert J Toole III	10060 Skinner Lake Dr, Jacksonville FL 32246	904-399-0662	S	70*	<.1
260	Berkeley Capital Management—Kevin Cuccias	One Bush St 12th Fl, San Francisco CA 94111	415-393-0300	S	69*	.1
261	Alare Capital Partners LLC—Kent Petzold	14861 N Scottsdale Rd, Scottsdale AZ 85254	480-951-9200	R	69*	<.1
262	Peachtree Capital Corp—Jim Terlizzi	3060 Peachtree Rd NW S, Atlanta GA 30305	404-364-2100	R	68*	<.1
263	Fred Alger Management Inc—Daniel C Chung	PO Box 8480, Boston MA 02266		R	67*	.2
264	Garrison Bradford Inc—William G Garrison	122 E 42nd St Ste 3500, New York NY 10168	212-557-7440	R	66*	<.1
265	Tudor Investment Corp—Paul Tudor Jones	1275 King St, Greenwich CT 06831	203-863-6700	S	65*	.3
266	OAM Avatar LLC—Ned Babbitt	575 Lexington Ave 8th, New York NY 10022	212-624-1900	R	65*	.1
267	Clover Capital Management Inc—Michael Jones	400 Meridian Centre St, Rochester NY 14618	585-385-6090	R	64*	<.1
268	Advent Capital Management LLC—Tracy V Maitland	1271 Ave of the Americ, New York NY 10020	212-482-1600	R	64*	<.1
269	Fiduciary Capital Management Inc—Peter E Bowles	PO Box 80, Wallingford CT 06492	203-269-0440	S	64*	<.1
270	Patterson Capital Corp—Joseph Patterson	2029 Century Park E St, Los Angeles CA 90067	310-556-2496	R	64*	<.1
271	Friess Associates—Foster Friess	PO Box 4166, Greenville DE 19807	302-656-3017	R	63*	.1
272	Brown Capital Management Inc—Eddie C Brown	1201 N Calvert St, Baltimore MD 21202	410-837-3234	R	63*	<.1
273	Barrington Research Associates Inc—Alexander Paris	161 N Clark St Ste 295, Chicago IL 60601	312-634-6000	R	62*	<.1
274	Oppenheimer Capital LP—Marra Whittington Allianz Global Investors	1633 Broadway, New York NY 10019		S	61	.3
275	Bailard Biehl and Kaiser Inc—Peter M Hill	950 Tower Ln Ste 1900, Foster City CA 94404	650-571-5800	R	61*	.1
276	Wasmer Schroeder and Company Inc—Martin Wasmer	600 5th Ave S Ste 210, Naples FL 34102	239-263-6877	R	61*	<.1
277	AEW Capital Management LP—Jefferey Furber	2 Seaport Ln, Boston MA 02110	617-261-9000	S	60*	.3
278	American Growth Fund Inc—Robert Brody	110 16th St Ste 1400, Denver CO 80202	303-626-0600	R	60*	<.1
279	Kornitzer Capital Management Inc—John Kornitzer	5420 W 61st Pl, Shawnee Mission KS 66205	913-677-7778	R	59*	<.1
280	Joel Isaacson and Company Inc—Joel Scott Isaacson	546 5th Ave 20th Fl, New York NY 10036	212-302-6300	R	59*	<.1
281	Tunstall Consulting Inc—Gordon Tunstall	13153 N Dale Mabry Hwy, Tampa FL 33618	813-968-4461	R	59*	<.1
282	Clifford Associates Inc—Linda Davis Taylor	200 S Los Robles Ave S, Pasadena CA 91101	626-792-2228	R	59*	<.1
283	Badgley Phelps—Steven C Phelps	1420 5th Ave Ste 3200, Seattle WA 98101	206-623-6172	R	58*	<.1
284	Columbia Management Co—Kenneth Lewis	1 Financial Ctr, Boston MA 02111		S	57*	.2
285	Congress Asset Management Co—Daniel A Lagan	2 Seaport Ln, Boston MA 02210	617-737-1566	R	57*	<.1
286	Flexible Plan Investments Ltd—Jerry Wagner	3883 Telegraph Rd Ste, Bloomfield Hills MI 48302	248-642-6640	R	57*	<.1
287	Mercer Capital Management Inc—Christopher Mercer	5100 Poplar Avenue Sui, Memphis TN 38137	901-685-2120	R	57*	<.1
288	Westwood Holdings Group Inc—Brian O Casey	200 Crescent Ct Ste 12, Dallas TX 75201	214-756-6900	P	55	.1
289	LifePlans Inc—Marc Cohen	51 Sawyer Rd Ste 340, Waltham MA 02453	781-893-7600	R	55*	.2
290	Ruane Cunniff and Company Inc—Robert D Goldfarb	767 Fifth Ave Ste 4701, New York NY 10153	212-832-5280	R	55*	<.1
291	Caliber Advisors—Kenneth Nunes	514 Via De La Valle St, Solana Beach CA 92075	858-792-8990	R	55*	<.1
292	Mohetta Financial Services Inc—Robert S Bacarella	1776A S Naperville Rd, Wheaton IL 60189	630-462-9800	R	55*	<.1
293	Saber Partners LLC—Joseph S Fichera	44 Wall St, New York NY 10005	212-401-2370	R	55*	<.1
294	Safra Asset Management Corp—Joseph Safra	546 5th Ave, New York NY 10036	212-704-7600	S	54*	<.1
295	Smith Graham and Company Investment Advisors LP—Gerald B Smith	600 Travis St Ste 6900, Houston TX 77002	713-227-1100	R	53*	<.1
296	UBS Asset Management Inc	51 W 52nd St, New York NY 10019	212-821-3000	S	52*	.2
297	Investment Counsel Co	255 S Orange Ave Ste 9, Orlando FL 32801	914-246-3433	R	51*	<.1
298	Westpeak Investment Advisors LP—Kal Ghayur	1470 Walnut St Ste 300, Boulder CO 80302	303-786-7700	R	51*	<.1
299	Beekman Capital Management Ltd—Nedim Hamarat	PO Box 31116, Santa Fe NM 87501	505-984-2944	R	51*	<.1
300	Kopp Investment Advisors Inc—Lee Kopp	8400 Normandale Lake B, Bloomington MN 55437	952-841-0400	R	51*	<.1
301	Mellon Capital Management—Charles J Jacklin	50 Fremont St Ste 3900, San Francisco CA 94105	415-546-6056	S	50*	.4
302	Motley Fool Inc—David Gardner	2000 Duke St 4th Fl, Alexandria VA 22314	703-838-3665	R	50*	.2
303	Appleton Partners Inc—Douglas C Chamberlain	45 Milk St 8th Fl, Boston MA 02109	617-338-0700	R	50*	<.1
304	Convergent Capital Management LLC—Richard Adler	190 S LaSalle St Ste 2, Chicago IL 60603	312-444-6000	S	50*	<.1
305	JVB Financial Group LLC—Vincent W Butkevits III	2700 N Military Tr Ste, Boca Raton FL 33431	561-416-5876	R	50*	<.1
306	Jacobs Levy Equity Management Inc—Bruce Jacobs	PO Box 650, Florham Park NJ 07932	973-410-9222	R	49*	<.1
307	William D Witter Inc—Michael D Witter	153 E 53rd St 51st Fl, New York NY 10022	212-753-7878	R	49*	<.1
308	Burney Co—Lowell D Pratt	121 Rowell Ct, Falls Church VA 22046	703-241-5611	R	49*	<.1
309	Matrix Asset Advisors Inc—David A Katz	747 3rd Ave 31st Fl, New York NY 10017	212-486-2004	R	49*	<.1
310	Sterling Resources Inc—Peter Demmer	6 Forest Ave, Paramus NJ 07652	201-843-6444	R	49*	<.1
311	Neuenschwander Asset Management LLC—Roy Neuenschwander	4722 Farwell St, Mc Farland WI 53558	608-838-3330	R	49*	<.1
312	Value Line Inc—Howard A Brecher	220 E 42nd St, New York NY 10017	212-907-1500	P	49	.2
313	United Retirement Plan Consultants Inc—John Davis	485 Metro Pl S Ste 275, Dublin OH 43017	614-923-8822	S	48	.3
314	Nomura Capital Management Inc—Yasushi Suzuki	2 World Financial Ctr, New York NY 10281	212-667-1414	S	48*	<.1
315	Armstong MacIntyre and Severns Inc—Alexandra Armstrong	1850 M St NW Ste 250, Washington DC 20036	202-887-8135	R	48*	<.1
316	Concord Asset Management LLC—Henry A Feldman Jr Madison Investment Advisors Inc	150 S Wacker Dr Ste 35, Chicago IL 60606	312-236-1166	S	48*	<.1
317	Insight Capital Research and Management Inc—Jim Collins	2121 N California Blvd, Walnut Creek CA 94596	925-274-5000	R	47*	<.1
318	Castle Group Inc—Rick Wall	3 Waterfront Plz 500 A, Honolulu HI 96813	808-524-0900	R	46*	1.2
319	The Ellman Cos—Steve Ellman	2850 E Camelback Rd St, Phoenix AZ 85016	602-840-3000	R	46*	<.1
320	Gifford Fong Associates—H Gifford Fong	3658 Mt Diablo Blvd St, Lafayette CA 94549	925-299-7800	R	43*	<.1
321	Bahl and Gaynor Investment Council Inc—Vere W Gaynor	212 E 3rd St Ste 200, Cincinnati OH 45202	513-287-6100	R	42*	<.1
322	Clifton Group—Orison Chaffee	3600 Minnesota Dr Ste, Edina MN 55435	612-870-8800	R	42*	<.1
323	HLM Management Co—Edward Cahill	222 Berkeley St 21st F, Boston MA 02116	617-266-0030	R	42*	<.1
324	Omega Advisors Inc—Leon Cooperman	88 Pine St 31st Fl, New York NY 10005	212-495-5200	R	42*	<.1
325	Quantitative Financial Strategies Inc—Sanford Grossman	10 Glenville St, Greenwich CT 06831	203-983-5600	R	42*	<.1
326	Stratford Advisory Group Inc—Thomas H Dodd	500 W Madison St Ste 2, Chicago IL 60661	312-798-3200	R	42*	<.1
327	US Global Investors Inc—Frank E Holmes	PO Box 781234, San Antonio TX 78278	210-308-1234	P	42	.1
328	WisdomTree Investments Inc—Jonathan L Steinberg	380 Madison Ave 21st F, New York NY 10017	212-918-4580	R	42	.1
329	300 North Capital LLC	300 N Lake Ave Ste 112, Pasadena CA 91101	626-449-8500	S	41*	.1
330	Heartland Capital Management Inc—Thomas F Maurath	251 N Illinois St Ste, Indianapolis IN 46204	317-383-2000	R	41*	<.1
331	Aronson and Partners—Theodore Arnson	230 S Broad St 20th Fl, Philadelphia PA 19102	215-546-7500	R	40*	<.1
332	Abbott Capital Management Inc—Jonathan D Roth	1211 Ave of the Americ, New York NY 10036	212-757-2700	R	40*	<.1
333	RRE Ventures LLC—Stuart J Ellman	130 E 59th, New York NY 10022	212-418-5100	R	40*	<.1
334	JMC Financial Corp—Rob Jeffords James Mitchell and Co	9710 Scranton Rd Ste 1, San Diego CA 92121	858-450-0055	S	40*	<.1
335	JMC Insurance Services Corp—Rob Jeffords James Mitchell and Co	9710 Scranton Rd Ste 1, San Diego CA 92121	858-450-0055	S	40*	<.1
336	Fieldman Rolapp and Associates—Thomas M DeMars	19900 MacArthur Blvd S, Irvine CA 92612	949-660-7300	R	39*	<.1

Rank	Company Name—*Executive Officer*	Address, City, State, Zip	Phone	Type	Fin	Empls
337	Cedar Hill Associates Inc—*Joel H Jastromb*	120 S LaSalle St Ste 1, Chicago IL 60603	312-445-2900	R	39*	<.1
338	Consulting Services Group LLC—*E Lee Giovannetti*	6075 Poplar Ave Ste 70, Memphis TN 38119	901-761-8080	R	38*	.1
339	Wurts and Associates Inc—*Jeffery MacLean*	999 3rd Ave Ste 4200, Seattle WA 98104	206-622-3700	R	38*	<.1
340	Howland Capital Management Inc—*Weston Howland*	75 Federal St Ste1100, Boston MA 02110	617-357-9110	R	38*	<.1
341	InterSec Research Corp—*Marc William Libby*	2 Ave de Lafayette 6th, Boston MA 02111	617-664-8987	R	38*	<.1
342	Capital Advantage Inc—*John Sterrett Hayman*	Post Office Box 789, Lafayette CA 94549	925-299-1500	R	38*	<.1
343	Carnegie Investment Counsel—*Richard L Alt*	25550 Chagrin Blvd Ste, Beachwood OH 44122		R	38*	<.1
344	Creative Capital Management Inc—*Peg Eddy*	8880 Rio San Diego Dr, San Diego CA 92108	619-298-3993	R	38*	<.1
345	LB Capital Inc—*Carin M Barth*	PO Box 56048, Houston TX 77256	713-627-2600	R	38*	<.1
346	Portfolio Capital Management Inc—*Mark Durica*	5950 Fairview Rd Ste 6, Charlotte NC 28210	704-552-0073	R	38*	<.1
347	CH Dean and Associates Inc—*Dennis Dean*	3500 Pentagon Blvd Ste, Beavercreek OH 45431	937-222-9531	R	37*	<.1
348	KNW Public Finance—*David Brodsly*	1333 Broadway Ste 1000, Oakland CA 94612	510-839-8200	D	37*	<.1
349	Dalton Greiner Hartman Maher and Co—*Bruce H Geller*	565 5th Ave Ste 2101, New York NY 10017	212-557-2445	R	37*	<.1
350	Graybill Bartz and Associates Ltd—*Steven Bartz*	568 S Spring Rd, Elmhurst IL 60126	630-941-9460	R	37*	<.1
351	Goldin Associates LLC—*Harrison J Goldin*	350 5TH AVE, New York NY 10118	212-593-2255	R	36*	<.1
352	Cohen Klingenstein and Marks Inc—*George Cohen*	2109 Broadway Ste 207, New York NY 10023	212-799-4880	R	36*	<.1
353	Cornerstone Equity Investors LLC—*Mark Rossi*	281 Tresser Blvd Fl 12, Stamford CT 06901	212-753-0901	R	36*	<.1
354	McConnell Budd and Romano Inc—*Thomas Romano*	119 Littleton Rd, Parsippany NJ 07054	973-402-0300	R	36*	<.1
355	Advisor Group Inc—*Marc A Canovali*	3000 McKnight E Dr, Pittsburgh PA 15237	412-931-3900	R	35*	<.1
356	LCG Associates Inc—*Edward F Johnson*	400 Galleria Pky Ste 1, Atlanta GA 30339	770-644-0100	R	35*	<.1
357	Seaward Management Corp—*Christopher T Barrow*	265 Franklin St 20th F, Boston MA 02110		R	35*	<.1
358	Fiduciary Management Associates Inc—*Kathryn Vorisek*	55 W Monroe St Ste 255, Chicago IL 60603	312-334-0253	R	35*	<.1
359	Marlin Equity Partners—*David McGovern*	2121 Rosecrans Ave Ste, El Segundo CA 90245	310-364-0100	R	34	.2
360	Brandywine Global Investment Management LLC—*Stephen S Smith* Legg Mason Inc	2929 Arch St 8th Fl, Philadelphia PA 19104	215-609-3500	S	34*	.1
361	Hyperion Brookfield Asset Management Inc—*Bruce Flatt*	200 Vesey St 10th Fl, New York NY 10281	212-549-8400	S	34*	.1
362	Brouwer and Janachowski—*Stephen Janachowski*	1831 Tiburon Blvd, Tiburon CA 94920	415-435-8330	R	34*	<.1
363	Travelers Investment Management Co—*Jay S Fishman*	1 Tower Sq, Hartford CT 06183	860-277-0111	S	34*	<.1
364	Olson Research Associates Inc—*Brad Olson*	10290 Old Columbia Rd, Columbia MD 21046	410-290-6999	R	34*	<.1
365	Asset Preservation Inc—*Javier Vande Steeg*	1420 Rocky Ridge Dr St, Roseville CA 95661	916-791-5991	S	32*	<.1
366	James M Davidson and Co—*James M Davidson*	20 N Waterloo Rd, Devon PA 19333	610-687-6540	R	32*	<.1
367	Plancorp Inc—*J Christopher Kerckhoff Jr*	540 Maryville Centre D, Saint Louis MO 63141	636-532-7824	R	32*	<.1
368	Eagle Boston Investment Management Inc—*David Adams*	880 Carillon Pkwy, Saint Petersburg FL 33716		S	32*	<.1
369	Swarthmore Group Inc—*Paula R Mandle*	1717 Arch St Ste 3810, Philadelphia PA 19103	215-557-9300	R	32*	<.1
370	Alan B Lancz and Associates Inc—*Alan B Lancz*	2400 N Reynolds Rd, Toledo OH 43615	419-536-5200	R	32*	<.1
371	Bane Barham and Holloway Assets Management Inc—*William G Barham*	25195 SW Parkway Ave S, Wilsonville OR 97070	503-582-9500	R	32*	<.1
372	LRG Capital Group LLC—*Lawrence Goldfarb*	80 E Sir Francis Drake, Larkspur CA 94939	415-834-4600	R	32*	<.1
373	Sadoff's Investment Management LLC—*Ronald Sadoff*	250 W Coventry Ct Ste, Milwaukee WI 53217	414-352-8460	R	32*	<.1
374	Offutt Securities Inc—*R Bentley Offutt*	PO Box 559, Cockeysville MD 21030	410-429-4462	R	32*	<.1
375	Argus Research Group Incorporated Del—*Fern Dorsey*	61 Broadway Rm 1700, New York NY 10006	212-425-7500	R	31*	.1
376	Oxxford Information Technologies Ltd—*Raymond Greenhill*	1461 Perth Rd, Hagaman NY 12086	518-882-9393	R	31*	<.1
377	Ewing Asset Management Inc—*David W Jackson* Intrepid Capital Corp	50 N Laura St Ste 3625, Jacksonville FL 32202	904-354-5573	S	31*	<.1
378	FundQuest Inc—*Robert Del Col*	1 Winthrop Square 5th, Boston MA 02110	617-526-7300	R	30*	.1
379	Legend Group—*LiuChuan Zhi*	4600 E Park Dr Ste 300, Palm Beach Gardens FL 33410	561-694-0110	R	30*	.1
380	Russell Investment Management Co—*Lynn L Anderson* Frank Russell Co	1301 2nd Ave 18th Fl, Seattle WA 98101	206-505-7877	S	29*	.1
381	Mercator Asset Management Inc—*John Thompson*	5200 Town Center Cir S, Boca Raton FL 33486	561-361-1079	R	29*	<.1
382	Gannett Welsh and Kotler Inc—*Harold G Kotler*	222 Berkeley St 15th F, Boston MA 02116	617-236-8900	S	28*	<.1
383	Ardsley Partners—*George Gorman*	262 Harbor Dr 4th Fl, Stamford CT 06902		R	28*	<.1
384	Pacific Corporate Group Inc—*Christopher Bower*	1200 Prospect St Ste 2, La Jolla CA 92037	858-456-6000	S	28*	<.1
385	Cullinan Associates Inc—*R Keith Cullinan*	1406 Browns Ln, Louisville KY 40207	502-893-0300	R	28*	<.1
386	Great Lakes Advisors Inc—*Raymond O Wicklander Jr*	123 N Wacker Dr Ste 23, Chicago IL 60606	312-553-3700	R	28*	<.1
387	Howe and Rusling Inc—*Craig Cairns*	120 E Ave, Rochester NY 14604	585-325-4140	R	28*	<.1
388	Ariston Capital Management Corp—*Richard B Russell*	227 Bellevue Way NE St, Bellevue WA 98004	425-454-1600	R	28*	<.1
389	Taplin Canida and Habacht Inc—*Tere Alvarez Canida*	1001 Brickell Bay Dr S, Miami FL 33131	305-379-2100	R	27*	<.1
390	Madison Management Corp—*Huong Nguyen*	1156 15th St NW Ste 30, Washington DC 20005	202-223-4545	R	26*	<.1
391	Edward O Thorp and Associates LP—*Edward O Thorp*	610 Newport CenterSte, Newport Beach CA 92660	949-720-0130	R	26*	<.1
392	Securities Management and Research Inc—*Michael W Mc-Croskey*	2450 S Shore Blvd Ste, League City TX 77573	281-334-2469	S	25*	.1
393	Simms Capital Management Inc—*Thomas L Melly*	177 Broad St Ste 1000, Stamford CT 06901		R	25*	<.1
394	Edgar Lomax Co—*Randall R Eley*	6564 Loisdale Ct Ste 3, Springfield VA 22150	703-719-0026	R	25*	<.1
395	Contrarian Group—*Peter Ueberroth*	5 San Joaquin St, Newport Beach CA 92660	949-720-9646	R	25*	<.1
396	Lang Asset Management Inc—*Robert B Lang*	5605 Glenridge Dr Ste, Atlanta GA 30342	404-256-4100	R	25*	<.1
397	Pitcairn Trust Co—*Dirk Junger*	165 Township Line Rd S, Jenkintown PA 19046	215-887-6700	R	24*	.1
398	Wentworth Hauser and Violich—*Judith Stevens*	301 Battery St Ste 400, San Francisco CA 94111	415-981-6911	R	24*	.1
399	Fairmount Capital Advisors Inc—*Don Kligerman*	1500 JFK Blvd Ste 1150, Philadelphia PA 19102	215-717-2299	R	24*	<.1
400	Moody Aldrich Partners LLC—*William B Moody*	18 Sewall St, Marblehead MA 01945	781-639-2750	R	24*	<.1
401	Knott Partners LP—*David M Knott*	485 Underhill Blvd Ste, Syosset NY 11791	516-364-0303	R	23*	<.1
402	Cornerstone Financial Inc—*Donald M Dusick*	275 14th St NW, Atlanta GA 30318	404-874-3111	R	23*	<.1
403	Sit Investment Associates Inc—*Roger J Sit*	80 S Eighth St Ste 330, Minneapolis MN 55402	612-332-3223	R	22*	<.1
404	Analytic Investors Inc—*Harindra de Silva*	555 West Fifth Street, Los Angeles CA 90013		R	22*	.1
405	QCI Asset Management Inc—*Kevin Gavagan*	40A Grove St, Pittsford NY 14534		R	22*	<.1
406	FCM Investments—*T Montgomery Jones*	2200 Ross Ave Ste 4600, Dallas TX 75201	214-665-6900	R	22*	<.1
407	Arnhold and S Bleichroeder Advisers LLC—*John P Arnhold*	1345 Aveof the America, New York NY 10105	212-698-3000	R	21*	.2
408	Resource Services Inc—*Carl W Hefton*	5151 Belt Line Rd Ste, Dallas TX 75254	214-866-7500	R	21*	.1
409	Davis/Dinsmore Management Co—*Thomas H Dinsmore*	65 Madison Ave, Morristown NJ 07960	973-631-1177	R	21*	<.1
410	Paragon Investment Management Inc—*Shari Burns*	1420 5th Ave Ste 3020, Seattle WA 98101	206-583-8300	R	21*	<.1
411	Nottingham Advisors—*Thomas Quealy*	500 Essjay Rd Ste 220, Buffalo NY 14221	716-633-3800	R	21*	<.1
412	Capital Management LLC—*Larry Powell*	10801 Mastin Blvd Ste, Overland Park KS 66210	913-345-2766	R	21*	<.1
413	Pugh Capital Management Inc—*Mary E Pugh*	520 Pike St Ste 2900 5, Seattle WA 98101	206-322-4985	R	21*	<.1
414	Baxter Financial Corp—*Donald H Baxter*	1200 N Federal Hwy Ste, Boca Raton FL 33432	561-395-2155	R	21*	<.1
415	Jacoway Financial Corp—*M Doak Jacoway*	8055 E Tafts Ave Ste 1, Denver CO 80237	303-793-9395	R	21*	<.1
416	Denver Mining Finance Co—*Tony Jensen*	1660 Wynkoop St Ste 10, Denver CO 80202	303-575-6504	S	20*	<.1
417	Thomson Horstmann and Bryant Inc—*William W Bryant*	501 Main Ave, Norwalk CT 06851	203-653-7060	S	20*	<.1
418	Killen Group Inc—*Robert E Killen*	1189 Lancaster Ave, Berwyn PA 19312	610-296-7222	R	20*	<.1
419	WESCAP Management Group Inc—*Joel Edstrom*	303 N Glenoaks Blvd St, Burbank CA 91502	818-563-5170	R	20*	<.1
420	Cincinnati Asset Management Inc—*William Sloneker*	4350 Glendale-Milford, Cincinnati OH 45242	513-554-8503	R	20*	<.1

Note: An asterisk (*) indicates an estimated financial figure. The company type code used is as follows: R = Private, P = Public, S = Private Subsidiary, B = Public Subsidiary, D = Division, J = Joint Venture, I = Investment Fund.

COMPANY RANKINGS BY SALES WITHIN 4-DIGIT SIC

Rank	Company Name—Executive Officer	Address, City, State, Zip	Phone	Type	Fin	Empls
421	LR Horn Capital Concepts Inc—Linda Horn	9676 Dry Fork Rd, Harrison OH 45030	513-367-1793	R	20*	<.1
422	Ambassador Capital Management Inc—Brian T Jeffries	500 Griswold St, Detroit MI 48226	313-961-3111	R	20*	<.1
423	GE Investment Management Inc—Ronald Pressman	3003 Summer St, Stamford CT 06905	203-326-2300	S	19*	.2
424	Acadian Asset Management LLC—Churchill G Franklin	1 Post Office Sq 20th, Boston MA 02109	617-850-3500	S	19*	<.1
425	Trust Company of Lehigh Valley—G Allen Weiss	1620 Pond Rd Ste 301, Allentown PA 18104	610-366-9934	R	19*	<.1
426	Suffolk Capital Management—Donald M Gilbert	810 7th Ave Ste 3600, New York NY 10019	212-247-2160	R	19*	<.1
427	Rosenblum-Silverman-Sutton SF Inc—Barbara G Rosenblum	1388 Sutter St Ste 725, San Francisco CA 94109	415-771-2631	R	19*	<.1
428	Bauer Financial Reports Inc—Paul A Bauer	Box 143520, Coral Gables FL 33134	305-445-9500	S	19*	<.1
429	Schuylkill Capital Management Ltd—James W Lewis	1631 Locust St 3rd Fl, Philadelphia PA 19103	215-735-0299	R	19*	<.1
430	Cano and Co—Alfonzo Cano	4438 Center View Ste11, San Antonio TX 78228	210-731-6613	R	19*	<.1
431	Hamilton Advisors Inc—Deborah Hamilton	373 Stanwich Rd, Greenwich CT 06830	203-629-1112	R	19*	<.1
432	Creative Planning Inc—Peter Mallouk	3400 College Blvd, Leawood KS 66211	913-338-2727	R	18*	.1
433	First Reserve Corp—William E Macaulay	1 Lafayette Pl, Greenwich CT 06830	203-661-6601	R	18*	<.1
434	Keeley Asset Management Corp—John Keeley	401 S LaSalle St Ste 1, Chicago IL 60605		R	18*	<.1
435	Parker Carlson and Johnson Inc—Kathleen Carlson	120 W 3rd St Ste 300, Dayton OH 45402	937-223-0600	R	18*	<.1
436	Ameritas Investment Advisors Inc—William Lester	390 N Cotner Blvd, Lincoln NE 68505	402-467-6962	S	18	N/A
437	Barrow Hanley Mewhinney and Strauss Inc—James P Barrow	2200 Ross Ave 31st Fl, Dallas TX 75201	214-665-1900	S	17*	.1
438	Abner Herrman and Brock Inc—Howard J Abner	Harborside Financial C, Jersey City NJ 07311	201-484-2000	R	17*	<.1
439	Orleans Capital Management Corp—Louis F Crane	PO Box 1750, Mandeville LA 70470	985-674-1367	R	17*	<.1
440	Cordillera Asset Management Inc—Michael Barela	4175 Harlan St Ste 200, Wheat Ridge CO 80033	303-572-6888	R	17*	<.1
441	Tremont Capital Management Inc—Rupert Allan	555 Theodore Fremd Ave, Rye NY 10580	914-925-1140	S	16	.1
442	Allegheny Financial Group Ltd—James Browne	811 Camp Horne Rd, Pittsburgh PA 15237	412-367-3880	R	16*	.1
443	Progress Investment Management Co—Thurman V White Jr	33 New Montgomery St 1, San Francisco CA 94105	415-512-3480	R	16*	.1
444	Segall Bryant and Hamill Investment Counsel—C Alfred Bryant	10 S Wacker Dr Ste 350, Chicago IL 60606	312-474-1222	R	16*	.1
445	Mitchell Group—Rodney B Mitchell	1100 Louisiana St Ste, Houston TX 77002	713-759-2071	R	16*	<.1
446	Chase Investment Counsel Corp—Derwood S Chase Jr	300 Preston Ave Ste 50, Charlottesville VA 22902	434-293-9104	R	16*	<.1
447	Willis Financial Planning Services Inc—D Vernon Willis	4 W 4th Ave, San Mateo CA 94402	650-579-0162	R	16*	<.1
448	Greenwich Alternative Investments—Thomas B Whelan	4 High Ridge Pk, Stamford CT 06905	203-487-6180	R	15*	<.1
449	Branson Fowlkes/Russell Inc—Jay Branson	3300 Chimney Rock Ste, Houston TX 77056	713-780-0606	R	15*	<.1
450	Dover Partners Inc—Jack Newell	476 Windsor Park Dr, Dayton OH 45459	937-299-4105	R	15*	<.1
451	Legacy Wealth Management Inc—James J Isaacs	6800 Poplar Ave Ste 10, Memphis TN 38138	901-758-9006	R	14*	<.1
452	Caldwell and Orkin Funds Inc—Michael B Orkin	6200 The Corners Pkwy, Norcross GA 30092	678-533-7850	R	14*	<.1
453	Finial Investment Corp	600 Travis St, Houston TX 77002	713-222-6868	R	14*	<.1
454	Renaissance Capital Group Inc—Russell Cleveland	8080 N Central Expy St, Dallas TX 75206	214-891-8294	R	14*	<.1
455	Resource Investments Advisory Inc—Stephen Woods	9115 SW Oleson Ste 303, Portland OR 97223	503-245-3110	R	14*	<.1
456	Sachs Investment Group—Gerald T Case	1346 S 3rd St, Louisville KY 40208	502-637-1949	R	14*	<.1
457	Lynch Investment Co—Harry H Lynch	1845 Woodall Rodgers F, Dallas TX 75201	214-871-2400	R	14*	<.1
458	TH Fitzgerald and Co—Tom Fitzgerald	180 Church St, Naugatuck CT 06770	203-729-1200	R	14*	<.1
459	JD Martin and Co—Michael Beckman	615 Griswold Ste 408, Detroit MI 48226	313-961-1117	R	14*	<.1
460	Cosmos Partners LP—Phillip Maisano	200 Connecticut Ave St, Norwalk CT 06854	203-854-7000	R	13*	.1
461	Hamilton Lane Advisors Inc—Mario Giannini	1 Presidential Blvd 4t, Bala Cynwyd PA 19004	610-934-2222	R	13*	.2
462	MPPW Consultants Information Systems LLC—Douglas Mueller	7733 Forsyth Blvd Ste, Saint Louis MO 63105	314-862-2070	R	13*	.1
463	Guidant Financial Group Inc—David Nilssen	1120 112th Ave NE Ste, Bellevue WA 98004		R	13*	.1
464	Security Ballew Inc—Brooks Mosley	PO Box 14888, Jackson MS 39236	601-368-3500	R	13*	<.1
465	Southeastern Asset Management Inc—Staley Cates	6410 Poplar Ave Ste 90, Memphis TN 38119	901-761-2474	R	13*	<.1
466	Becker Capital Management Inc—Janeen McAninch	1211 SW 5th Ave Ste 21, Portland OR 97204	503-223-1720	R	13*	<.1
467	Gratry and Co—Jerome Gratry	20600 Chagrin Blvd 320, Shaker Heights OH 44122	216-283-8423	R	13*	<.1
468	Investment Trust Co—John A Benson	3200 Cherry Creek Sout, Denver CO 80209	303-778-6800	R	13*	<.1
469	Brookfield and Co—Julie Curd	5050 Poplar Ave Ste 14, Memphis TN 38157	901-681-9000	R	13*	<.1
470	Thompson Co—Dean Renkes	12225 Greenville Ave S, Dallas TX 75243	972-699-8451	R	13*	<.1
471	Denby Brandon Organizations Inc—Ray Brandon	5101 Wheelis Rd Ste 11, Memphis TN 38117	901-324-6600	R	13*	<.1
472	Bond-Tech Inc—Roger A Cox	PO Box 192, Englewood OH 45322	937-836-3991	R	13*	<.1
473	Preferred Yield Inc—Fred H Vollbeer	19 E Main St, Dahlonega GA 30533	404-266-8702	R	13*	<.1
474	Wilshire Associates Inc—Dennis A Tito	1299 Ocean Ave Ste 700, Santa Monica CA 90401	310-451-3051	R	13	N/A
475	Aris Corporation of America Inc—John Battaglia	PO Box 1318, State College PA 16804	814-231-3710	R	12*	.2
476	Batterymarch Financial Management Inc—William Elcock Legg Mason Inc	200 Clarendon St, Boston MA 02116	617-266-8300	S	12*	.1
477	Needelman Asset Management Inc—Chet Needelman	111 Pacifica Ste 140, Irvine CA 92618	949-453-1333	R	12*	<.1
478	SKBA Capital Management—Kenneth J Kaplan	44 Montgomery St Ste 3, San Francisco CA 94104	415-989-7852	R	12*	<.1
479	Summit Private Investments—Jeffrey Karp	47 Maple St Ste 301, Summit NJ 07901	908-522-1414	R	12*	<.1
480	Burke Marketgrowth International Ltd—Joseph P Burke	2905 Piedmont Rd NE, Atlanta GA 30305	404-231-3181	R	12*	<.1
481	Heritage Capital Management Inc—George Rooks	63 Franklin St, Boston MA 02110	617-423-0379	S	12*	<.1
482	Siphron Capital Management—David C Siphron	280 S Beverly Dr Ste 4, Beverly Hills CA 90212	310-858-7281	R	12*	<.1
483	Spectrum Asset Management Inc (Newport Beach California)—Ryan Kelly	1301 Dove St Ste 970, Newport Beach CA 92660	949-717-3400	R	12*	<.1
484	Whitcom Partners Inc—Edward Barlow	375 Park Ave Ste 3800, New York NY 10152	212-582-2300	R	12*	<.1
485	Brynavon Group—George B Lemmon Jr	PO Box 160, Villanova PA 19085	610-525-2102	R	12*	<.1
486	D Hoover and Associates Investments Inc—Lawrence D Hoover	3443 N Central Ave Ste, Phoenix AZ 85012	602-266-2440	R	12*	<.1
487	Harbor Capital Advisors Inc—David Van Hoover	PO Box 804660, Chicago IL 60680	312-443-4400	S	11*	.1
488	Marco Consulting Group—Richard E Graf	550 W Washington Blvd, Chicago IL 60661	312-575-9000	R	11*	.1
489	Smith Breeden Associates Inc—Eugene Flood Jr	280 S Mangum St Ste 30, Durham NC 27701	919-967-7221	R	11*	.1
490	Resurgence Financial LLC—H Josh Chaet	4100 Commercial Ave, Northbrook IL 60062	847-656-2200	R	11*	.1
491	Coburn and Meredith Inc—Barry Coburn	225 Asylum St 15th Fl, Hartford CT 06103	860-522-7171	R	11*	<.1
492	Parametric Portfolio Associates Inc—Brian Langstraat Eaton Vance Corp	1151 Fairview Ave N, Seattle WA 98109	206-694-5575	S	11*	<.1
493	Univest Financial Group Inc—William S Aichele	PO Box 64197, Souderton PA 18964	215-721-2400	R	11	<.1
494	WH Reaves and Company Inc—Ronald J Sorenson	10 Exchange Pl 18th Fl, Jersey City NJ 07302	201-332-4596	R	11*	<.1
495	Heartland Advisors Inc—William J Nasgovitz	PO Box 177, Denver CO 80201	414-347-7777	R	11*	<.1
496	First Financial Network Inc—Bliss A Morris	9211 Lake Hefner Pkwy, Oklahoma City OK 73120	405-748-4100	R	11*	<.1
497	Equinox Capital Management LLC—Ronald Ulirch	590 Madison Ave Fl 41, New York NY 10022	212-207-1100	R	11*	<.1
498	Adviso Group Ltd—Lauren M Miralia	50 Main St Ste 1000, White Plains NY 10606	914-682-2073	R	11*	<.1
499	Capital Investment Counsel Inc—Richard Bryant	17 Glenwood Ave, Raleigh NC 27603	919-831-2370	S	11*	<.1
500	Duncker Streett and Company LLC—Kelly B Sullivan	8000 Maryland Ave Ste, Saint Louis MO 63105	314-726-2600	R	11*	<.1
501	Greenhaven Associates Inc—Edgar Wachenheim III	3 Manhattanville Rd, Purchase NY 10577	914-253-9350	R	11*	<.1
502	Van Cleef Jordan and Wood Inc—Gary Reetz	370 Lexington Ave Ste, Troy NY 12181	212-986-2600	R	11*	<.1
503	Imlay Investments Inc—John P Imlay Jr	945 E Paces Ferry Rd S, Atlanta GA 30326	404-239-1799	R	11*	<.1

Rank	Company Name—*Executive Officer*	Address, City, State, Zip	Phone	Type	Fin	Empls
504	Builder Investment Group Inc—*Allen Builder*	3340 Peachtree Rd NE S, Atlanta GA 30326	404-233-9341	R	11*	<.1
505	Laura Waller Advisors Inc—*Laura Waller*	100 N Tampa St Ste 215, Tampa FL 33602	813-221-1956	R	11*	<.1
506	Allianz Global Investors—*Nicholas Applegate*	PO Box 8050, Boston MA 02266		S	10*	.1
507	Rodney Square Management Corp—*Charlotta Nielson*	1100 N Market St, Wilmington DE 19801	302-651-8344	R	10	.1
508	Trivest Partners LP—*Earl W Powell*	2665 S Bayshore Dr Ste, Miami FL 33133	305-858-2200	R	10*	<.1
509	JM Hartwell LP—*William C Miller IV*	515 Madison Ave, New York NY 10022	212-308-3355	R	10*	<.1
510	Murphy Capital Management Inc—*John J Murphy*	PO Box 718, Gladstone NJ 07934	908-719-6430	R	10*	<.1
511	REMY Investors and Consultants Inc—*Mark S Siegel*	1801 Century Park E St, Los Angeles CA 90067	310-843-0050	R	10*	<.1
512	Thomas P Reynolds Securities Inc—*Thomas P Reynolds*	45 Broadway 31st Fl, New York NY 10006	212-742-1616	R	10*	<.1
513	PenTrust Real Estate Advisory Services Inc—*James E Noland*	333 Baldwin Rd Ste 200, Pittsburgh PA 15205	412-279-4100	R	10*	<.1
514	Asset Strategies Portfolio Services Inc—*George H Vitta*	2635 Lapeer Rd, Auburn Hills MI 48326	248-373-9900	R	10*	<.1
515	Charter Investment Advisors Inc—*Terry Rogers*	5956 Turkey Lake Rd St, Orlando FL 32819	407-226-1112	R	10*	<.1
516	Harvest Investment Consultants LLC—*Stephen S Duklewski Jr*	2345 York Rd Ste 300, Timonium MD 21093	410-561-9040	R	10*	<.1
517	Accrued Equities Inc—*David Schoenwald*	150 Broadhollow Rd PH, Melville NY 11747	516-423-7373	R	10*	<.1
518	Brownlie and Braden LLC—*James Braden*	301 Commerce St, Fort Worth TX 76102	817-339-8822	R	10*	<.1
519	Weinstein Associates Ltd—*Stanley H Weinstein*	One Biscayne Twr Ste 2, Miami FL 33131	305-371-8701	R	10*	<.1
520	Fulton Breakefield Broenniman LLC—*Mitchel Schlesinger*	4326 Montgomery Ave, Bethesda MD 20814	301-657-8870	R	9*	<.1
521	Rock Capital Management—*Jo Ann Rock*	PO Box 549, Millbrae CA 94030	650-697-9054	R	9*	<.1
522	Yacktman Funds Inc—*Donald A Yacktman*	6300 Bridgepoint Pkwy, Austin TX 78730	512-767-6700	R	9*	<.1
523	Structured Finance Advisors Inc—*Joseph A Lorusso*	30 Avon Meadow Ln, Avon CT 06001	860-409-7171	R	9*	<.1
524	JL Bainbridge and Company Inc—*Jerry L Bainbridge*	1582 Main St, Sarasota FL 34236	941-365-3435	R	9*	<.1
525	Fred Alger and Company Inc—*Daniel C Chung* Fred Alger Management Inc	P O Box 8480, Boston MA 02266	212-806-8800	S	8*	.1
526	Westport Resources Management Inc—*John Adams Vaccaro*	315 Post Rd W, Westport CT 06880	203-226-0222	R	8*	.1
527	First Quadrant Corp—*Tim Meckel*	800 E Colorado Blvd, Pasadena CA 91101	626-795-8220	R	8*	.1
528	Canterbury Consulting Inc—*Poorvi Parekh*	660 Newport Center Dr, Newport Beach CA 92660	949-721-9580	R	8*	<.1
529	Flippin Bruce and Porter Inc—*John Flippin*	PO Box 6138, Lynchburg VA 24505	434-845-4900	R	8*	<.1
530	Morley Financial Services Inc—*Tim Stumpff*	1300 SW 5th Ave Ste 33, Portland OR 97201	503-484-9300	S	8*	<.1
531	Bridgeway Capital Management Inc—*John Montgomery*	5615 Kirby Dr Ste 518, Houston TX 77005	713-661-3500	R	8*	<.1
532	Robert Harrell Inc—*Robert L Harrell*	8310 N Capital of Texa, Austin TX 78731	512-795-9100	R	8*	<.1
533	Winslow Capital Management Inc—*Clark J Winslow* Nuveen Investments Inc	80 S 8th St, Minneapolis MN 55402	612-376-9100	S	8*	<.1
534	Account Management Corp—*Peter DeRoetlh*	17 Arlington St Ste 3, Boston MA 02116	617-236-4200	R	8*	<.1
535	CE Walters and Associates Inc—*Charles E Walters*	PO Box 556, Glen Echo MD 20812	301-320-0628	R	8*	<.1
536	NSB Public Finance—*Andrew Artusa*	230 Las Vegas Blvd Ste, Las Vegas NV 89101	702-796-7080	D	8*	<.1
537	Waycross Investment Management Co—*Michael F Ryan*	PO Box 1618, Bellingham WA 98227	360-671-0148	R	8*	<.1
538	North American Capital Management Co—*Robert McElwain*	PO Box 6728, Leawood KS 66206	913-381-8401	R	8*	<.1
539	Driehaus Securities LLC—*Richard Driehaus*	25 E Erie St, Chicago IL 60611	312-587-3800	R	7*	.1
540	SSI Investment Management Inc—*Amy Jo Gottfurcht*	9440 Santa Monica Blvd, Beverly Hills CA 90210	310-595-2000	R	7*	<.1
541	Yanni Partners Inc—*James Yanni*	310 Grant St Ste 3000, Pittsburgh PA 15219	412-232-1000	R	7*	<.1
542	Bartlett Fund Management Co—*Alvery A Bartlett Jr*	8182 Maryland Ave Ste, Saint Louis MO 63105	314-725-2000	R	7*	<.1
543	Capital Investment Strategies—*John Ryan*	PO Box39, Wood Dale IL 60191	630-932-4100	R	7*	<.1
544	Contravisory Research Corp—*William Noonan*	99 Derby St Ste 302, Hingham MA 02043	781-740-1786	R	7*	<.1
545	Marshfield Associates—*Christopher M Niemczewski*	21 Dupont Cir NW Ste 5, Washington DC 20036	202-828-6200	R	7*	<.1
546	Peirce Park Group—*Michael Shone*	300 S High St, West Chester PA 19382	610-719-0300	R	7*	<.1
547	Strategic Financial Designs Inc—*Ellen Rogin*	1780 Ash St Ste 200, Northfield IL 60093	847-441-8700	R	7*	<.1
548	Clean Yield Asset Management Inc—*Ryan Fried*	PO Box 117 Garvin Hill, Greensboro VT 05841	802-526-2525	R	7*	<.1
549	Thompson/Rubinstein Investment Management Inc—*Richard Rubinstein*	715 SW Morrison St Ste, Portland OR 97205	503-224-1488	R	7*	<.1
550	Thompson Plumb Funds Inc—*John W Thompson*	PO Box 701, Milwaukee WI 53201	608-827-5700	R	6*	.1
551	Froley Revy Investment Company Inc—*Andrea Revy O'Connell*	10900 Wilshire Blvd, Los Angeles CA 90024	310-208-4938	S	6*	<.1
552	Sunrise Financial Group Inc—*Nathan Low*	641 Lexington Ave 25th, New York NY 10022	212-421-1616	R	6*	<.1
553	Capital Investment Services of America Inc—*Paul Muzzey*	700 N Water St Ste 325, Milwaukee WI 53202	414-278-7744	R	6*	<.1
554	Shott Capital Management Inc—*George Shott*	601 California St Ste, San Francisco CA 94108	415-394-7271	R	6*	<.1
555	Hines Interests Realty Advisers LP—*Jeffrey C Hines*	2800 Post Oak Blvd Ste, Houston TX 77056	713-621-8000	S	6*	<.1
556	Brooks Montague and Associates Inc—*J Brooks*	735 Broad St Ste 306, Chattanooga TN 37402	423-756-8628	R	6*	<.1
557	Yon-Drake and Associates Inc	914 Richland St Ste C2, Columbia SC 29201	803-256-1212	R	6*	<.1
558	Brode Management Group Ltd—*David B Brode*	49 Estate Dr, Glencoe IL 60022	847-242-0494	R	6*	<.1
559	Partnership Capital Growth Advisors—*Brent Knudsen*	1 Embarcadero Ctr Ste, San Francisco CA 94111	415-705-8008	R	5	<.1
560	Wanger Asset Management—*Ralph Wanger* Columbia Management Co	227 W Monroe St Ste 30, Chicago IL 60606	312-634-9200	S	5*	.1
561	Miles Capital—*David Miles*	1415 28th St Ste 200, West Des Moines IA 50266	515-244-5426	S	5*	.1
562	Kane McKenna and Associates Inc—*Philip R McKenna*	150 N Wacker Dr Ste 16, Chicago IL 60606	312-444-1702	R	5*	<.1
563	Knightsbridge Advisers Inc—*Joel Romines*	122 SW Frank Phillips, Bartlesville OK 74003	918-336-0978	R	5*	<.1
564	Thomas J Herzfeld Advisors Inc—*Thomas J Herzfeld*	PO Box 161465, Miami FL 33116	305-271-1900	R	5*	<.1
565	Holland Capital Management LLC—*Monica L Walker*	1 N Wacker Dr Ste 700, Chicago IL 60606	312-553-4830	R	5*	<.1
566	Nelson Capital Management Inc—*Scott Benner*	1860 Embarcadero Rd St, Palo Alto CA 94303	650-493-1000	S	5*	<.1
567	Strategic Fixed Income LP—*Kenneth A Windheim*	1001 19th St N Ste 140, Arlington VA 22209	703-812-8300	R	5*	<.1
568	Atco Investment Co—*Edward J Crawford III*	333 Texas St Ste 2300, Shreveport LA 71101	318-222-2161	R	5*	<.1
569	Commonwealth Group Inc—*David A Kipp*	465 California St Ste, San Francisco CA 94104	415-391-4687	R	5*	<.1
570	Finley Colmer and Co—*Peter W Colmer* Finley Group Inc	3091 Governors Lake Dr, Norcross GA 30071	770-668-0637	S	5*	<.1
571	Rutland Dickson Asset Management Inc—*Barbara Dickson*	1901 N Akard St 2nd Fl, Dallas TX 75201	214-969-7088	R	5*	<.1
572	Bhirud Associates Inc—*Suresh Bhirud*	6 Thorndal Cir Ste 5, Darien CT 06820	203-662-6659	R	5*	<.1
573	Economic Analysis Associates Inc—*Susan M Sterne*	5 Glen Ct, Greenwich CT 06830	203-869-9667	R	5*	<.1
574	Investors Advisory Services Inc—*Ron Goldberg*	7007 College Blvd Ste, Overland Park KS 66211	913-345-8108	R	5*	<.1
575	Southern Trust Securities Holding Corp—*Robert Escobio*	145 Almeria, Coral Gables FL 33134	305-446-4800	P	5	<.1
576	Northern Trust Global Advisors Inc—*Joe Mcinerny*	300 Atlantic St Ste 40, Stamford CT 06901	203-977-7000	S	4*	.1
577	John G Ullman and Associates Inc—*John G Ullman*	PO Box 1424, Corning NY 14830	607-936-3785	R	4*	<.1
578	David White and Associates Inc—*David White*	3150 Crow Canyon Pl St, San Ramon CA 94583	925-277-2600	R	4*	<.1
579	Foxhall Capital Management Inc—*Paul G Dietrich*	35 Old Tavern Rd, Orange CT 06477	203-891-8377	R	4*	<.1
580	Bjurman Berry and Associates—*G Andrew Bjurman*	2049 Century Park E St, Los Angeles CA 90067	310-553-6577	R	4*	<.1
581	Haberer Registered Investment Advisor Inc—*Edward M Haberer*	201 E 5th St Ste 1100, Cincinnati OH 45202	513-381-8200	R	4*	<.1
582	Gruppo Levey and Co—*Antonia Ness*	122 E 46th Fl, New York NY 10168	212-697-5753	R	4*	<.1
583	Capital Market Risk Advisors Inc—*Leslie Rahl*	600 Lexington Ave 30th, New York NY 10022	212-404-6100	R	4*	<.1
584	Connors Investor Services Inc—*Peter J Connors*	1210 Broadcasting Rd S, Wyomissing PA 19610	610-376-7418	R	4*	<.1
585	Granahan Investment Management Inc—*Jane White*	275 Wyman St Ste 270, Waltham MA 02451	781-890-4412	R	4*	<.1
586	Parnassus Investments—*Jerome Dodson*	1 Market St Steuart Tw, San Francisco CA 94105	415-778-0200	R	4*	<.1
587	Alpha Investment Consulting Group LLC—*Robert Bukowski*	111 E Kilbourne Ave St, Milwaukee WI 53202	414-319-4100	R	4*	<.1

Note: An asterisk (*) indicates an estimated financial figure. The company type code used is as follows: R = Private, P = Public, S = Private Subsidiary, B = Public Subsidiary, D = Division, J = Joint Venture, I = Investment Fund.

COMPANY RANKINGS BY SALES WITHIN 4-DIGIT SIC

Rank	Company Name—Executive Officer	Address, City, State, Zip	Phone	Type	Fin	Empls
588	Balestra Capital Management—James L Melcher	58 W 40th St 12th Floo, New York NY 10018	212-768-9000	R	4*	<.1
589	Desai Capital Management Inc—Rohit Desai	410 Park Ave, New York NY 10022	212-838-9191	R	4*	<.1
590	Ganucheau Capital Management—Frank Ganucheau III	301 Commerce St Ste 14, Fort Worth TX 76102	817-332-9915	R	4*	<.1
591	Alexander Law Firm PC—Hugh Alexander	1580 Lincoln St Ste 70, Denver CO 80203	303-825-7307	R	4*	<.1
592	Paragon Asset Management—Mike Ryan	120 Lawndale Ave, Wilmette IL 60091	847-256-6700	R	4*	<.1
593	JP Morgan Invest LLC—James Dimon	1 Beacon St, Boston MA 02108	617-742-2600	S	4	N/A
594	Sagient Research Systems Inc—Robert F Kyle	3655 Nobel Dr Ste 540, San Diego CA 92122	858-623-1600	R	3	<.1
595	Mid-Continent Capital LLP—John Mabie	150 W Wacker Dr Ste 40, Chicago IL 60606	312-551-8200	R	3	<.1
596	Dunham and Associates Investment Counsel Inc—Jeffrey A Dunham	10251 Vista Sorrento P, San Diego CA 92121	858-964-0500	S	3*	<.1
597	American Express Investment Advisors—Paul Yurachek Ameriprise Financial Inc	6400 Goldsboro Rd Ste, Bethesda MD 20817	301-320-0500	D	3	<.1
598	Christian Podlesko and van Musschenbroek Ltd—Jeffrey M Christian	30 Broad St 37th Fl, New York NY 10004	212-785-8320	R	3*	<.1
599	Equus Capital Management Corp Equus Capital Corp	8 Greenway Plaza Ste 9, Houston TX 77046	713-529-0900	S	3*	<.1
600	Garcia Hamilton and Associates—Jake Hamilton	1401 McKinney St Ste 1, Houston TX 77010	713-853-2322	R	3*	<.1
601	Kirr Marbach and Co—Mickey Kim	PO Box 1729, Columbus IN 47202	812-376-9444	R	3*	<.1
602	3W Internet Corp—Joe E Winegardner	PO Box 209, Morrisville PA 19067	215-736-1107	R	3*	<.1
603	Cambridge Capital Management Corp—Jean Wojtowicz	4181 E 96th St Ste 200, Indianapolis IN 46240	317-843-9704	R	3*	<.1
604	EMC Capital Management Inc—Elizabeth M Chevel	2201 Waukegan Rd Ste W, Bannockburn IL 60015	847-267-8700	R	3*	<.1
605	HD Vest Advisory Services Inc—Roger Ochs	6333 N State Hwy 161 S, Irving TX 75038	972-870-6000	S	3	<.1
606	Bollinger Capital Management Inc—John Bollinger	PO Box 3358, Manhattan Beach CA 90266	310-798-8855	R	3*	<.1
607	Dolan Capital Management—John K Dolan	635 Bryant St, Palo Alto CA 94301	650-327-8100	R	3*	<.1
608	AMAS Securities—Shrichand Hinduja	535 Madison Ave 12th F, New York NY 10022	212-471-8684	S	3*	<.1
609	Dane Falb Stone and Co—Edward N Dane	15 Broad St Ste 406, Boston MA 02109	617-742-0666	R	3*	<.1
610	Kenneth J Gerbino and Co—Kenneth J Gerbino	9595 Wilshire Blvd Ste, Beverly Hills CA 90212	310-550-6304	R	3*	<.1
611	O'Herron and Co—Kennedy C O'Herron	2424 Gelnwood Ave Ste1, Raleigh NC 27608	919-571-7722	R	3*	<.1
612	Wakley and Roberton Inc—Neil Wakley	500 108th Ave NE Ste17, Bellevue WA 98004	425-455-4875	R	3*	<.1
613	Intercontinental Asset Management Group Ltd—John Kauth III	300 Convent St Ste 135, San Antonio TX 78205	210-271-7947	R	3	<.1
614	Guardian Asset Management Corp—Dennis J Manning	7 Hanover Sq, New York NY 10004	212-598-8000	S	2*	.1
615	Cumberland Advisors—David R Kotok	PO Box 1419, Sarasota FL 34236		S	2*	<.1
616	Zevenbergen Capital Investments LLC—Nancy Zevenbergen	601 Union St Ste 4600, Seattle WA 98101	206-682-8469	R	2*	<.1
617	L/G Research—Jeremy Degroot	4 Orinda Way Ste 200D, Orinda CA 94563	925-254-8999	R	2*	<.1
618	Design Capital Planning Group Inc—Albert F Coletti	PO Box 728, Smithtown NY 11787	631-979-6161	R	2*	<.1
619	Affinity Wealth Management—Donald Kalil	1702 Lovering Ave, Wilmington DE 19806	302-652-6767	R	2*	<.1
620	Eclipse Capital Management Inc—Thomas W Moller	7700 Bonhomme Ave Ste, Saint Louis MO 63105	314-725-2100	R	2*	<.1
621	Norris Perne and French LLP—Ford C Perne	40 Pearl St NW Ste 300, Grand Rapids MI 49503	616-459-3421	R	2*	<.1
622	Snavely King Majoros O'Connor and Lee Inc—Charles W King	1111 14th St NW Ste 30, Washington DC 20005	202-371-1111	R	2*	<.1
623	Access Financial Services Inc—Stephen E Kairies	1650 W 82nd St Ste 850, Minneapolis MN 55431	952-885-2700	R	2*	<.1
624	Bornhoft Group Inc—Richard E Bornhoft	1775 Sherman St Ste 25, Denver CO 80203	303-572-1000	R	2*	<.1
625	Capital Z Investment Partners—Laurence W Cheng	230 Park Ave S 11th Fl, New York NY 10003		R	2*	<.1
626	Financial Management Solutions Inc—Walter M Scott	1720 Windward Condours, Alpharetta GA 30005	770-619-3443	R	2*	<.1
627	Income Property Finance Corp—Thomas Rowland	77 Fayerweather St, Cambridge MA 02138	617-661-1654	R	2*	<.1
628	Safian Investment Research Inc—Kenneth Safian	96 Brook Hills Circle, White Plains NY 10605	914-697-9700	S	2*	<.1
629	Finley Group Inc—Robert R Dunn	6100 Fairview Rd Ste 1, Charlotte NC 28210	704-375-7542	R	2*	<.1
630	Tukman Grossman Capital Management Inc—Melvin Tukman	60 E Sir Francis Drake, Larkspur CA 94939	415-461-6833	R	2*	<.1
631	Eastover Capital Management Inc—Will Mackey	5605 Carnegie Blvd Ste, Charlotte NC 28209	704-336-6818	R	2*	<.1
632	AG Bisset and Company Inc—Ulf Lindahl	71 Rowayton Ave, Rowayton CT 06853	203-866-3540	R	2*	<.1
633	Aster Investment Management Company Inc—Richard F Aster Jr	60 E Sir Francis Drake, Larkspur CA 94939	415-461-8770	R	2*	<.1
634	ESOP Services Inc—Ronald J Gilbert	251 Albevanna Ln, Scottsville VA 24590	434-286-3130	R	2*	<.1
635	Messner and Smith—John Messner	530 B St Ste 300, San Diego CA 92101	619-239-9049	R	2*	<.1
636	Regency Investment Advisors Inc—Daniel Ray	970 West Alluvial Ste, Fresno CA 93711	559-438-2640	R	2*	<.1
637	Econoclast Inc—Michael H Cosgrove	3419 Westminster Ste 2, Dallas TX 75205	214-890-7877	R	2*	<.1
638	Fischer Investment Group—Robert Fischer	400 Andrew St, Rochester NY 14604	585-325-0900	R	2*	<.1
639	Parks Capital Management Inc—Nicholas Parks	230 Park Ave, New York NY 10169	212-986-6633	R	2*	<.1
640	Whelan Capital Management—Gabe Whelan	261 Hamilton Ave Ste 2, Palo Alto CA 94301	650-833-7880	R	2*	<.1
641	Shaw Management—Ralph Shaw	400 SW Sixth Ave Ste 1, Portland OR 97204	503-228-4888	R	2*	<.1
642	Business Valuations Inc—David O McCoy	PO Box 53458, Cincinnati OH 45253	513-522-1300	R	2*	<.1
643	Copley Financial Services Corp—Irving Levine	PO Box 3287, Fall River MA 02722	508-674-8459	R	2*	<.1
644	Fuqua Ventures LLC—John J Huntz	1201 W Peachtree St NW, Atlanta GA 30309	404-815-4500	R	2*	<.1
645	JSB Research and Analysis Company Inc—JS Brandenburger	1611 Borel Pl Ste 5, San Mateo CA 94402	650-572-7192	R	2*	<.1
646	Mercer Inc—Mark Coler	20 River Terrace Ste 5, New York NY 10279	212-334-6212	R	1*	<.1
647	Orix USA Corp—Christopher Smith	1717 Main St Ste 900, Dallas TX 75201	214-237-2000	S	1*	1.3
648	Transamerica Investment Services Inc—John Riazzi	1150 S Olive St, Los Angeles CA 90015	213-742-2111	S	1*	.1
649	CS McKee LP—Eugene M Natali	1 Gateway Ctr Fl 8, Pittsburgh PA 15222	412-566-1234	R	1*	<.1
650	Todd Investment Advisors Inc—Curt Scott	101 S 5th St, Louisville KY 40202	502-585-3121	S	1*	<.1
651	Sharkey Howes and Javer Inc—Joel Javer	720 S Colorado Blvd St, Denver CO 80246	303-639-5100	R	1*	<.1
652	Ambs Investment Counsel LLC—Barbara DeMoor Convergent Capital Management LLC	1241 E Beltline Ave NE, Grand Rapids MI 49525	616-949-8160	S	1*	<.1
653	LM Capital Management Inc—Luis Maizel	401 B St Ste 920, San Diego CA 92101	619-814-1401	R	1*	<.1
654	Dale K Ehrhart Inc—Michael T Hartley	101 W Venice Ave Ste 1, Venice FL 34285	941-485-8220	R	1*	<.1
655	Hourglass Capital Management Inc—Kenneth A Moffett	4409 Montrose Blvd Ste, Houston TX 77006		R	1*	<.1
656	Kelman-Lazarov Inc—Ronald Lazarov	5100 Poplar Ave Ste 31, Memphis TN 38137	901-685-8284	R	1*	<.1
657	Westport Consulting Group Inc—John Laurino	606 Post Rd E Ste 727, Westport CT 06880	203-226-1600	R	1*	<.1
658	Flaherty and Crumrine Inc—Donald F Crumrine	301 E Colorado Blvd St, Pasadena CA 91101	626-795-7300	R	1*	<.1
659	Marshall and Sullivan Inc—Ronald Marshall	1109 1st Ave Ste 200, Seattle WA 98101	206-621-9014	R	1*	<.1
660	Rayner Associates Inc—Arno A Rayner	655 Redwood Hwy Ste 37, Mill Valley CA 94941	415-332-7433	R	1*	<.1
661	Seger-Elvekrog Inc—Scott Horsburgh	39555 Orchard Hill Pla, Novi MI 48375	248-380-1700	R	1*	<.1
662	Steven Charles Capital Ltd—C Braverman	1st Federal Plz 28 E M, Rochester NY 14614	585-325-1870	R	1*	<.1
663	Bourne StenstromLent Asset Management Inc—Clare M Stenstrom	7 Penn Plaza Ste 310, New York NY 10001	212-643-1098	R	1*	<.1
664	Hughes Capital Management Inc—Frankie D Hughes	916 Prince St 3rd Fl, Alexandria VA 22314	703-684-7222	R	1*	<.1
665	Barnett and Company Inc—Warren M Barnett	1300 Broad St Ste 303, Chattanooga TN 37402	423-756-0125	R	1*	<.1
666	Campbell Newman Asset Management Inc—Mary C Brown	12080 N Corporate Pkwy, Mequon WI 53092	262-243-7000	R	1*	<.1
667	Consolidated Financial Investments Inc—Alan Stiffelman	222 N Meramec Ave, Clayton MO 63105	314-727-1177	R	1*	<.1
668	Mills and Partners Inc—James N Mills	8235 Forsyth Blvd Ste, Saint Louis MO 63105	314-727-1701	R	1*	<.1
669	MPI Investment Management Inc—David W Pequet	15 Salt Creek Ln Ste 4, Hinsdale IL 60521	630-325-6900	R	1*	<.1
670	Northern Oak Capital Management—Mark Zellmer	250 E Wisconsin Ave St, Milwaukee WI 53202	414-278-0590	R	1*	<.1

Rank	Company Name—*Executive Officer*	Address, City, State, Zip	Phone	Type	Fin	Empls
671	Perritt Capital Management Inc—*Gerald W Perritt*	300 S Wacker Dr Ste 28, Chicago IL 60606	312-669-1650	R	1*	<.1
672	Spectrum Advisory Services Inc—*Marc S Heilweil*	1050 Crown Pointe Pkwy, Atlanta GA 30338	770-393-8725	R	1*	<.1
673	Tanaka Capital Management Inc—*Graham Tanaka*	369 Lexington Ave, New York NY 10017	212-490-3380	R	1*	<.1
674	Murphy and Partners—*John J Murphy Jr*	45 Rockefeller Ctr Ste, New York NY 10111	917-847-0628	R	1*	<.1
675	Barrow Investment Management Inc—*Alston M Barrow*	3800 Bay to Bay Blvd S, Tampa FL 33629	813-831-4191	R	1*	<.1
676	Leylegian Investment Management Inc—*George A Leylegian*	PO Box 1028, Menlo Park CA 94026	650-322-8900	R	1*	<.1
677	James Pappas Investment Counsel—*James Pappas*	PO Box 475, Redding Ridge CT 06876	203-938-8916	R	1*	<.1
678	Calamos Asset Management Inc—*John P Calamos*	2020 Calamos Ct, Naperville IL 60563	630-245-7200	P	1	.3
679	Western Asset Management Co—*Nicholas Dalmaso* Legg Mason Inc	385 E Colorado Blvd, Pasadena CA 91101	626-844-9400	S	<1	.4
680	Kibble and Prentice Holding Co—*Arnie Prentice*	2 Union Sq 601 Union S, Seattle WA 98101	206-441-6300	R	<1	.2
681	Schwartz Investment Counsel Inc—*George Schwartz*	3707 W Maple Rd, Bloomfield Hills MI 48301	248-644-8500	R	N/A	<.1

TOTALS: SIC 6282 Investment Advice
Companies: 681 — 3,789,816 — 167.5

6289 Security & Commodity Services Nec

Rank	Company Name—*Executive Officer*	Address, City, State, Zip	Phone	Type	Fin	Empls
1	Pershing LLC—*Brian Shea*	1 Pershing Plz, Jersey City NJ 07399	201-413-2000	S	15,619*	3.7
2	TETRA Financial Services Inc—*Stuart M Brightman*	24955 I-45 N, The Woodlands TX 77380	281-367-1983	S	6,777*	1.7
3	SWS Financial Services Inc—*James Ross*	1201 Elm St Ste 3500, Dallas TX 75270	214-859-5519	S	4,288*	1.0
4	Transfirst Holdings Inc—*John Shlonsky*	5950 Berkshire Ln Ste, Dallas TX 75225	214-453-7700	R	2,880*	.8
5	TD Ameritrade Inc—*John Bunch*	4211 S 102nd St, Omaha NE 68127		S	1,804*	2.6
6	BUFC Financial Services Inc—*John A Kanas*	255 Alhambra Cir, Coral Gables FL 33134	305-569-0327	S	1,662*	.3
7	American Stock Transfer and Trust Co—*Michael Karfunkel*	59 Maiden Ln Plz Level, New York NY 10038	212-936-5100	R	1,622*	.4
8	Depository Trust and Clearing Corp—*Donald F Donahue*	55 Water St, New York NY 10041		R	1,279	2.5
9	ASC Securities Corp—*Gregory J Yurek*	64 Jackson Rd, Devens MA 01434	978-842-3000	S	1,259*	.3
10	UNX Inc—*Thomas Kim*	175 E Olive Ave 2nd Fl, Burbank CA 91502		R	396*	.1
11	T Rowe Price Investment Services Inc—*James Kennedy*	100 E Pratt St, Baltimore MD 21202	410-345-2000	S	382	1.9
12	RJ O'Brien and Associates Inc—*Gerald F Corcoran*	222 S Riverside Plz St, Chicago IL 60606	312-373-5000	S	300*	.3
13	ITG Inc—*Robert Gasser*	380 Madison Ave, New York NY 10017		S	290*	.5
14	Putnam Investments LLC—*Robert L Reynolds*	PO Box 8383, Boston MA 02266	617-292-1000	S	215*	.1
15	GMAC Financial Services LLC—*Michael Carpenter*	PO Box 200, Detroit MI 48231	313-556-5000	S	190	26.7
16	Options Clearing Corp—*Wayne P Luthringshausen*	1 N Wacker Dr Ste 500, Chicago IL 60606	312-322-6200	R	105*	.3
17	Georgeson Shareholder Communications Inc—*Alexander B Miller*	199 Water St 26th Fl, New York NY 10038	212-440-9800	R	83*	.5
18	Emerson Investment Management Inc—*Bradford A Gardner*	30 Federal St, Boston MA 02110	617-695-1516	R	71*	<.1
19	Hansen Quality Loan Services LLC	9339 Carroll Park Dr S, San Diego CA 92121	858-909-4300	S	55*	<.1
20	Keller Enterprises Inc—*Frank Keller*	1514 Main St, Northampton PA 18067	610-262-3975	R	39*	<.1
21	SecondMarket Holdings Inc—*Barry E Silbert*	26 Broadway 12th Fl, New York NY 10004	212-668-5920	R	35*	.1
22	Track Data Corp—*Marty Kaye*	95 Rockwell Pl, Brooklyn NY 11217	718-522-7373	P	31	.1
23	Newedge USA LLC—*John Fay*	220 Bush St Ste 650, San Francisco CA 94104	415-733-3000	R	24*	.1
24	Cambex Securities Corp—*Joseph F Kruy*	115 Flanders Rd, Westborough MA 01581	508-983-1200	S	14	<.1
25	Investment Property Exchange Service Inc—*Radah Butler*	50 California St Ste 3, San Francisco CA 94111	415-399-1590	S	13*	.1
26	Atalanta/Sosnoff Management Corp—*Martin T Sosnoff*	101 Park Ave 6th Fl, New York NY 10178	212-867-5000	S	13*	<.1
27	TradeMaven Group LLC—*Jeffrey C Ganis*	141 W Jackson Blvd, Chicago IL 60604	312-521-7300	R	11*	<.1
28	Woodstock Corp—*Paul D Simpson*	27 School St Sto 300, Boston MA 02108	617-227-0600	R	8*	<.1
29	Pink OTC Inc—*R Cornwell Coulson*	304 Hudson St 2nd Fl, New York NY 10013	212-896-4400	R	7*	<.1
30	Market Profile Theorems Inc—*Michael Painchaud*	4 Wilson St, Topsham ME 04086	207-406-2314	R	4*	<.1
31	Stocktrans Inc—*Jonathan E Miller*	44 W Lancaster Ave, Ardmore PA 19003	610-649-7300	R	4*	<.1
32	Illinois Stock Transfer Co—*Robert Pearson*	209 W Jackson Bvd Ste, Chicago IL 60606	312-427-2953	R	3*	<.1
33	Fitch Ratings—*Stephen W Joynt*	One State St Plz, New York NY 10004	212-908-0500	S	1*	2.0
34	Fidelity Transfer Co—*Kevin Kopaunik*	8915 South 700 E Ste 1, Sandy UT 84070	801-562-1300	R	1*	<.1
35	Hicks Acquisition Company II Inc—*Christina Weaver Vest*	100 Crescent Ct Ste 12, Dallas TX 75201	214-615-2300	P	<1	N/A

TOTALS: SIC 6289 Security & Commodity Services Nec
Companies: 35 — 39,485 — 46.2

6311 Life Insurance

Rank	Company Name—*Executive Officer*	Address, City, State, Zip	Phone	Type	Fin	Empls
1	Provident Life and Casualty Insurance Co—*Tom Watjen* Unum Group	1 Fountain Sq, Chattanooga TN 37402	423-294-1011	S	635,700*	13.0
2	Prudential Financial Inc—*John R Strangfeld*	751 Broad St, Newark NJ 07102	973-802-6000	P	539,854	41.0
3	AXA Financial Inc—*Anthony Sages*	1290 Ave of the Americ, New York NY 10104	212-554-1234	S	370,874*	9.5
4	Allstate Life Insurance Co	3100 Sanders Rd Ste K1, Northbrook IL 60062		S	365,392*	39.0
5	Lincoln National Corp—*Dennis R Glass*	150 N Radnor Chester R, Radnor PA 19087	484-583-1400	P	193,824	8.3
6	Northwestern Mutual Life Insurance Co—*John E Schlifske*	720 E Wisconsin Ave, Milwaukee WI 53202	414-271-1444	R	180,038	5.0
7	Principal Financial Group Inc—*Rex Auyeung*	PO Box 10423, Des Moines IA 50306		P	145,631	13.6
8	State Farm Life Insurance Co—*Edward B Rust Jr*	1 State Farm Plz, Bloomington IL 61701	309-766-2311	S	145,117*	15.0
9	Massachusetts Mutual Life Insurance Co—*Roger W Crandall*	1295 State St, Springfield MA 01111	413-744-8411	R	141,102	19.0
10	Aetna Life Insurance Company of America—*John W Rowe*	151 Farmington Ave, Hartford CT 06101	860-273-0123	S	135,054*	28.0
11	Nationwide Life Insurance Co—*Mark Thresher* Nationwide Financial Services Inc	One Nationwide Plz, Columbus OH 43215	614-249-7111	S	119,412	36.0
12	Nationwide Financial Services Inc—*Kirt A Walker*	1 Nationwide Plz, Columbus OH 43215		S	119,207	4.8
13	Pacific Life Insurance Co—*James T Morris*	PO Box 9000, Newport Beach CA 92658	949-219-3011	R	115,992	3.1
14	Teachers Insurance and Annuity Assoc College Retirement Equities Fund—*Roger W Ferguson Jr*	730 3rd Ave, New York NY 10017		R	113,939	7.0
15	Genworth Financial Inc—*Michael D Fraizer*	6620 W Broad St, Richmond VA 23230	804-484-3821	P	112,400	6.0
16	Jackson National Life Insurance Co—*Mike Wells*	PO Box 24068, Lansing MI 48909	517-381-5500	S	107,000	.6
17	Equitable Life Assurance Society of the United States—*Anthony Sages* AXA Financial Inc	1290 Ave of the Americ, New York NY 10104	212-554-1234	S	73,728*	16.5
18	Canada Life Assurance Co	8515 E Orchard Rd, Greenwood Village CO 80111	303-737-3037	D	72,826*	.7
19	Allianz Life Insurance Company of North America—*Gary C Bhojwani*	PO Box 1344, Minneapolis MN 55459		S	62,270*	2.0
20	Transamerica Corp—*Donald J Shepard*	600 Montgomery St Ste, San Francisco CA 94111	415-983-4000	S	58,503	9.2
21	Unum Group—*Thomas J Watjen*	1 Fountain Sq, Chattanooga TN 37402	423-294-1011	P	57,308	9.5
22	Zurich North America—*Mario Vitale*	1400 American Ln, Schaumburg IL 60196	847-605-6000	S	55,820*	11.7
23	WellPoint Inc—*Angela F Braly*	120 Monument Cir, Indianapolis IN 46204	317-532-6000	P	50,167	37.5
24	GenAmerica Financial Corp	PO Box 396, Saint Louis MO 63166	314-231-1700	S	49,359*	4.7
25	Protective Life Corp—*John D Johns*	PO Box 12687, Birmingham AL 35202	205-268-1000	P	47,563	2.3
26	CIGNA Corp—*David M Cordani*	2 Liberty Pl 1601 Ches, Philadelphia PA 19192	215-761-1000	P	45,682	30.6
27	American General Life Insurance Co—*Mary Jane Fortin*	PO Box 4373, Houston TX 77210	713-522-1111	S	38,425*	4.0

Note: An asterisk (*) indicates an estimated financial figure. The company type code used is as follows: R = Private, P = Public, S = Private Subsidiary, B = Public Subsidiary, D = Division, J = Joint Venture, I = Investment Fund.

RANKINGS BY SALES WITHIN 4-DIGIT SIC

	Company Name—Executive Officer	Address, City, State, Zip	Phone	Type	Fin	Empls
28	Western and Southern Financial Group—John F Barrett	400 Broadway Mail Stat, Cincinnati OH 45202		R	37,498	54.0
29	Dairyland Insurance Co—Dale Schuh	1800 Northpoint Dr, Stevens Point WI 54481	715-346-6000	S	36,869*	3.9
30	United of Omaha Life Insurance Co—Daniel Neary	Mutual of Omaha Plz, Omaha NE 68175	402-342-7600	S	33,591*	5.0
31	Guardian Life Insurance Company of America—Deanna M Muligan	7 Hanover Sq Ste H-26-, New York NY 10004	212-598-8000	R	33,178	5.0
32	CNO Financial Group Inc—C James Prieur	11825 N Pennsylvania S, Carmel IN 46032		P	31,900	3.7
33	Transamerica Occidental Life Insurance Co—Jim Bowman	1100 Walnut St, Kansas City MO 64106	816-855-5100	R	30,000	2.7
34	Sun Life Assurance Company of Canada US—Wesley Thompson	PO Box 9106, Wellesley Hills MA 02481	781-237-6030	S	29,240*	4.0
35	RGA Reinsurance Co—A Greig Woodring	1370 Timberlake Manor, Chesterfield MO 63017	636-736-7000	S	29,100	1.5
36	Life Re Corp—Jacques E Dubois	175 King St, Armonk NY 10504		S	27,349*	.9
37	Minnesota Life Insurance Co—Robert L Senkler	400 N Robert St, Saint Paul MN 55101	651-665-3500	S	26,644	5.0
38	American Equity Investment Life Holding Co—Wendy C Waugaman	PO Box 71216, Des Moines IA 50325	515-221-0002	P	26,427	N/A
39	Sammons Enterprises Inc—David C Bratton	5949 Sherry Ln Ste 190, Dallas TX 75225	214-210-5000	R	26,191*	3.8
40	Symetra Financial Corp—Thomas M Marra	PO Box 34690, Seattle WA 98124	425-256-8000	P	25,637	1.1
41	Lincoln National Life Insurance Co—Dennis R Glass Lincoln National Corp	1300 S Clinton St, Fort Wayne IN 46802		S	25,000	3.7
42	Conseco Variable Insurance Co—Glenn Hillard CNO Financial Group Inc	11825 N Pennsylvania S, Carmel IN 46032	317-817-6100	S	23,250*	2.2
43	Alfa Life Insurance Corp—Jerry Newby	PO Box 11000, Montgomery AL 36191		S	22,531*	2.5
44	Ohio National Financial Services—David B O'Maley	PO Box 237, Cincinnati OH 45201	513-794-6100	R	21,760*	.8
45	American Family Life Assurance Company of Columbus— Daniel P Amos	1932 Wynnton Rd, Columbus GA 31999	706-323-3431	S	21,534*	3.4
46	American National Insurance Co—Robert L Moody	PO Box 1896, Galveston TX 77553	409-763-4661	P	21,413	3.3
47	New York Life Insurance Co—Theodore A Mathas	PO Box 922, New York NY 10159	212-576-7000	R	19,964	17.0
48	National Life Group—Mehran Assadi	1 National Life Dr, Montpelier VT 05604	802-229-3333	R	19,411	.9
49	Keyport Life Insurance Co—Jon A Boscia Sun Life Assurance Company of Canada US	PO Box 9133, Wellesley Hills MA 02481	781-237-6030	S	19,360*	4.0
50	Monumental Life Insurance Co—Henry G Hagan AEGON USA Inc	4333 Edgewood Rd NE, Cedar Rapids IA 52499	319-355-8511	S	19,261*	2.3
51	Zurich Kemper Life Insurance Co—Gale K Caruso	1 Kemper Dr, Long Grove IL 60049	847-550-5658	S	18,300	1.1
52	Great-West Life and Annuity Insurance Co—Mitchell TG Graye	PO Box 1700, Denver CO 80201		S	17,935*	3.1
53	American United Mutual Insurance Holding Co—Dayton Molendorp	PO Box 368, Indianapolis IN 46206	317-285-1111	R	17,606	N/A
54	Ameritas Life Insurance Corp—JoAnn Martin UNIFI Mutual Holding Co	5900 O St, Lincoln NE 68501	402-467-1122	S	17,269*	1.0
55	Trustmark Life Insurance Co	400 Field Dr, Lake Forest IL 60045	847-615-1500	S	17,000	N/A
56	American Family Mutual Insurance Co—David R Anderson	6000 American Pkwy, Madison WI 53777	608-242-4100	R	16,788	7.8
57	People's Benefit Life Insurance Co—Marilyn Carp AEGON USA Inc	4333 Edgewood Rd NE, Cedar Rapids IA 52499	319-398-8511	S	15,496	.3
58	CUNA Mutual Group—Jeff Post	PO Box 391, Madison WI 53701	608-238-5851	R	15,300	5.5
59	Hartford Life Insurance Co Hartford Life Inc	200 Hopmeadow St, Simsbury CT 06089		S	14,948*	3.1
60	Penn Mutual Life Insurance Co—Robert E Chappell	PO Box 178, Philadelphia PA 19105	215-956-8000	R	14,082*	2.0
61	Trustmark Insurance Co—David McDonough	400 Field Dr, Lake Forest IL 60045	847-615-1500	S	14,047*	1.5
62	Mutual of America Life Insurance Co—Thomas J Moran	320 Park Ave, New York NY 10022		R	13,662	1.1
63	Great American Financial Resources Inc—S Craig Lindner	PO Box 5420, Cincinnati OH 45201	513-333-5300	S	13,335	1.0
64	New England Financial—Brian Breneman	501 Boylston St, Boston MA 02116	617-578-2000	S	10,569*	4.4
65	AEGON USA Inc—Patrick S Baird	433 Edgewood Road NE, Cedar Rapids IA 52499	319-355-8511	S	10,182*	13.0
66	Primerica Inc—D Richard Williams	3120 Breckinridge Blvd, Duluth GA 30099	770-381-1000	P	9,999	2.0
67	Country Investors Life Assurance Co—John D Blackburn Country Financial (Bloomington Illinois)	1705 Towanda Ave, Bloomington IL 61701	309-557-3000	S	9,997*	2.0
68	Colonial Life and Accident Insurance Co—Randall Horn Unum Group	PO Box 1365, Columbia SC 29202		S	9,545*	1.0
69	National Penn Life Insurance Co	PO Box 547, Boyertown PA 19512	610-705-9101	S	9,023*	1.2
70	National Western Life Insurance Co—Robert L Moody	850 E Anderson Ln, Austin TX 78752	512-836-1010	P	8,774	.3
71	State Life Insurance Co—Dayton H Molendorp	PO Box 368, Indianapolis IN 46206	317-285-2300	S	8,451*	1.7
72	FBL Financial Group Inc—James W Hohmann	5400 University Ave, West Des Moines IA 50266	515-225-5400	P	8,226	1.7
73	Kemper Corp—Donald G Southwell	1 E Wacker Dr, Chicago IL 60601	312-661-4600	P	8,086	7.2
74	USLIFE Corp—Donald W Britton	125 Maiden Ln Ste 6, New York NY 10038	212-709-6000	S	7,880	2.2
75	John Hancock Financial Services Inc—James Boyle	PO Box 111, Boston MA 02117	617-572-6000	S	7,827	3.9
76	Conseco Annuity Assurance Co—James Prieur CNO Financial Group Inc	11815 N Pennsylvania S, Carmel IN 46032	317-817-6100	S	7,747*	2.0
77	ING America Life Corp—Thomas McInerney ING America Insurance Holdings Inc	PO Box 105006, Atlanta GA 30348	770-980-5100	S	7,253*	1.5
78	Bankers Life Insurance Company of Illinois—Edward Berube CNO Financial Group Inc	222 Merchandise Mart P, Chicago IL 60654	312-396-6000	S	7,006*	1.5
79	Kemper Investors Life Insurance Co—Diane Davis Zurich Kemper Life Insurance Co	1400 American Ln, Schaumburg IL 60196	206-232-8400	S	6,893	N/A
80	EMC National Life Co—Bruce G Kelley	PO Box 9202, Des Moines IA 50306		S	6,842	N/A
81	Genworth Financial Service—Pam Schutz Genworth Financial Inc	6620 W Broad St, Richmond VA 23230	804-281-6000	S	6,720*	1.0
82	Fidelity and Guaranty Life Insurance Co—Lee Launer	PO Box 1137, Baltimore MD 21203	410-895-0100	S	6,500*	.2
83	AGC Life Insurance Co—Jim Mallon	PO Box 305940, Nashville TN 37230	615-749-1000	S	6,062*	.9
84	ING America Insurance Holdings Inc—R Glenn Hilliard	PO Box 105006, Atlanta GA 30348		S	6,049*	.9
85	First Allmerica Financial Life Insurance Co—Frederick H Eppinger	440 Lincoln St, Worcester MA 01653	508-855-1000	S	5,704*	4.4
86	ULLICO Inc—Edward M Smith	1625 Eye St NW, Washington DC 20006	202-682-0900	R	5,600	N/A
87	Farmers New World Life Insurance Co—Paul Patsis	3003 77th Ave SE, Mercer Island WA 98040	206-232-8400	S	5,311*	.5
88	Western-Southern Enterprises—John F Barrett Western and Southern Life Insurance Co	400 Broadway, Cincinnati OH 45202	513-629-1800	S	5,133*	2.0
89	Illinois Agricultural Holding Co—John Blackburn	PO Box 2020, Bloomington IL 61702	309-557-2111	R	5,077*	.4.2
90	Pekin Life Insurance Co—Gordon Walker	2505 Court St, Pekin IL 61558	309-346-1161	R	4,960*	.8
91	Protective Life Insurance Co Protective Life Corp	PO Box 2606, Birmingham AL 35202	205-268-1000	S	4,821*	.8
92	ING North America Insurance Corp—Thomas McInerney ING America Insurance Holdings Inc	5780 Powers Ferry Rd N, Atlanta GA 30327	770-980-5100	S	4,767*	2.1
93	Banknorth Insurance Agency Inc/MA—William Ryan	1 Griffin Brook Dr Ste, Methuen MA 01844	978-983-6900	S	4,527*	.4
94	Kansas City Life Insurance Co—R Philip Bixby	PO Box 219139, Kansas City MO 64121	816-753-7000	P	4,398	.4

Rank	Company Name—*Executive Officer*	Address, City, State, Zip	Phone	Type	Fin	Empls
95	Western and Southern Life Insurance Co Western and Southern Financial Group	400 Broadway St, Cincinnati OH 45202	513-629-1800	S	4,285*	1.7
96	Fort Dearborn Life Insurance Co—*Anthony Trani*	20445 Emerald Pkwy Ste, Cleveland OH 44135		S	3,917*	.4
97	Reliance Standard Life Insurance Co—*Lawrence E Daurelle* Delphi Financial Group Inc	2001 Market St Ste 150, Philadelphia PA 19103	267-256-3500	S	3,910	.5
98	Presidential Life Corp—*Donald L Barnes*	69 Lydecker St, Nyack NY 10960		P	3,902	.1
99	NIA Group LLC—*Steve Grossberg*	66 N Rte 17, Paramus NJ 07652		S	3,742*	.4
100	Universal American Corp—*Richard A Barasch*	6 International Dr, Rye Brook NY 10573	914-934-5200	P	3,656	1.8
101	Midland National Life Insurance Co—*Steve Palmitier* Sammons Enterprises Inc	1 Sammons Plz, Sioux Falls SD 57193		S	3,353*	.5
102	Colony Insurance Co—*Michael Warfield*	PO Box 85122, Richmond VA 23285	804-560-2000	S	3,158*	.3
103	Beneficial Life Insurance Co—*Kent H Cannon*	PO Box 45654, Salt Lake City UT 84136	801-933-1100	R	3,093*	.3
104	United Insurance Company of America—*Donald Reyster* Kemper Corp	1859 W 87th St, Chicago IL 60620	713-779-7300	S	2,920*	8.5
105	Country Financial (Bloomington Illinois)—*John D Blackburn*	1711 General Electric, Bloomington IL 61704		R	2,880*	.5
106	Golden Rule Financial Corp—*John M Whelan*	7440 Woodland Dr, Indianapolis IN 46278	618-943-8000	R	2,830*	1.3
107	Presidential Life Insurance Co—*Herbert Kurz* Presidential Life Corp	69 Lydecker St, Nyack NY 10960	845-358-2300	S	2,781*	.1
108	Shenandoah Life Insurance Co—*Robert W Clark*	PO Box 12847, Roanoke VA 24029	540-985-4400	R	2,697*	.3
109	Liberty National Life Insurance Co—*Anthony L McWhorter*	PO Box 2612, Birmingham AL 35202	205-325-4979	S	2,693	4.4
110	Country Financial—*John D Blackburn*	1701 N Towanda Ave, Bloomington IL 61701		R	2,601*	4.5
111	North American Company for Life and Health Insurance—*Michael Masters*	525 W Van Buren, Chicago IL 60607	312-648-7600	R	2,408*	.3
112	Family Life Insurance Co Americo Life Inc	PO Box 410288, Kansas City MO 64105	816-391-2800	S	2,400*	.4
113	Harleysville Mutual Insurance Co—*David V McDonnell*	355 Maple Ave, Harleysville PA 19438	215-256-5000	S	2,355*	1.9
114	Forethought Life Insurance Co—*John Graf* Forethought Financial Services Inc	1 Forethought Ctr, Batesville IN 47006	812-934-7139	D	2,100	.2
115	Penn Treaty Network America Life Insurance Co—*Eugene Woznicki*	3440 Lehigh St, Allentown PA 18103	610-965-2222	S	2,051*	.4
116	Security Mutual Life Insurance Company of New York—*Bruce W Boyea*	PO Box 1625, Binghamton NY 13902	607-723-3551	R	2,041*	.3
117	Illinois Mutual Life Insurance Co—*Michel A McCord*	300 SW Adams St, Peoria IL 61602	309-674-8255	R	2,037*	.2
118	United Fidelity Life Insurance Co—*Gary Muller* Americo Life Inc	PO Box 410288, Kansas City MO 64141	816-391-2000	S	1,926*	.2
119	Pan-American Life Insurance Co—*Jose S Suquet*	601 Poydras St, New Orleans LA 70130		R	1,914	1.1
120	Delphi Financial Group Inc—*Robert Rosenkranz*	PO Box 8985, Wilmington DE 19899	302-478-5142	P	1,900	2.0
121	Pruco Life Insurance Co—*Scott D Kaplan* Prudential Financial Inc	213 Washington St 9th, Newark NJ 07102	973-802-6000	S	1,882*	.2
122	National Guardian Life Insurance Co—*John D Larson*	PO Box 1191, Madison WI 53701		R	1,845*	.2
123	GMAC Insurance—*Mary Hennesey*	PO Box 3199, Winston Salem NC 27102	336-770-2000	S	1,788*	1.0
124	United Life Insurance Co—*John A Rife*	PO Box 73909, Cedar Rapids IA 52407	319-399-5700	S	1,719*	.4
125	United States Life Insurance Company in the City of New York—*David Dietz* American General Life Insurance Co	1 World Financial Cnt, New York NY 10281		S	1,708*	<.1
126	Forethought Financial Services Inc—*John Graf*	1 Forethought Ctr, Batesville IN 47006	812-933-6600	R	1,693*	.3
127	Guaranty Corp (Baton Rouge Louisiana)—*George Foster*	929 Government St, Baton Rouge LA 70802	225-383-0355	R	1,689*	.2
128	Horace Mann Life Insurance Co—*Peter H Heckman*	1Horace Mann Plz, Springfield IL 62715	217-789-2500	S	1,678*	2.3
129	Sentry Life Insurance Co—*Dale R Schuh*	1800 North Point Dr, Stevens Point WI 54481	715-346-6000	S	1,588	N/A
130	Nationwide Corp—*Keith Eckel*	1 Nationwide Plz, Columbus OH 43215	614-249-7111	S	1,570	36.0
131	Cincinnati Life Insurance Co—*David H Popplewell*	PO Box 145496, Cincinnati OH 45250	513-870-2000	S	1,517*	.2
132	BMI Financial Group—*Anthony F Smith*	1320 S Dixie Hwy 6th F, Coral Gables FL 33146	305-443-2898	R	1,467*	.2
133	InterContinental Life Corp—*RF Mitte*	PO Box 149138, Austin TX 78714	512-404-5500	R	1,451*	.4
134	Western Reserve Life Assurance Company of Ohio—*Ronald F Wagley* AEGON USA Inc	570 Carillon Pkwy, St Petersburg FL 33716	727-299-1800	S	1,421*	1.2
135	New ERA Life Insurance Co—*Bill Chen*	PO Box 4884, Houston TX 77210	281-368-7200	R	1,391*	.3
136	Independence Holding Co (Stamford Connecticut)—*Roy TK Thung*	96 Cummings Point Rd, Stamford CT 06902	203-358-8000	P	1,362	.7
137	MML Pension Insurance Co—*Stuart Reese* Massachusetts Mutual Life Insurance Co	1295 State St, Springfield MA 01111	413-788-8411	S	1,251	N/A
138	Booker T Washington Insurance Co	PO Box 697, Birmingham AL 35201	205-328-5454	S	1,189*	.1
139	Lincoln Benefit Life Co—*Lawrence W Dahl* Allstate Life Insurance Co	PO Box 80469, Lincoln NE 68501	402-475-4061	S	1,185*	1.0
140	Texas Life Insurance Co—*Steven T Cates* MetLife Insurance Co	PO Box 830, Waco TX 76703	254-752-6521	S	1,171*	.1
141	Investors Life Insurance Company of North America—*Bill Marden* InterContinental Life Corp	PO Box 700, Jacksonville IL 62651		S	1,085	N/A
142	Northwestern Mutual Financial Network—*John Ertz* Northwestern Mutual Life Insurance Co	1801 E 9th St Ste 800, Cleveland OH 44114	216-241-5840	S	1,066*	.1
143	Aviva Life and Annuity—*Thomas C Godlasky*	7700 Mills Civic Pkwy, West Des Moines IA 50266		S	1,016	.2
144	Investors Heritage Life Insurance Co—*HL Waterfield II* Investors Heritage Capital Corp	PO Box 717, Frankfort KY 40602	502-223-2361	S	1,002*	.1
145	William Penn Life Insurance Company of New York—*David Lenaburg*	100 Quentin Roosevelt, Garden City NY 11530	516-794-3700	S	1,000*	.1
146	Folksamerica Holding Co—*Dwight Evans*	1 Liberty Plz 19th Fl, New York NY 10006	212-312-2500	S	992*	.2
147	Peachtree Planning Corp—*Robert E Mathis*	5040 Roswell Rd, Atlanta GA 30342	404-260-1600	R	990*	.1
148	Financial Industries Corp—*William Prouty*	Po Box 149138, Austin TX 78714	512-404-5180	R	988	.1
149	FPIC Insurance Group Inc—*Richard E Anderson*	1000 Riverside Ave Ste, Jacksonville FL 32204	904-354-2482	S	986	.2
150	MetLife Investors Insurance Co—*Mike Ferrell*	5 Park Plaza Ste 1900, Irvine CA 92614		S	965*	.1
151	Americo Financial Life and Annuity Insurance Co—*Gary Muller* Americo Life Inc	PO Box 410288, Kansas City MO 64179	816-391-2000	S	964*	.2
152	Liberty Life Insurance Co	PO Box 1389, Greenville SC 29602	864-609-8111	S	964*	.2
153	Eastern Life And Insurance Co Security Life Insurance Company of America	PO Box 83149, Lancaster PA 17603	717-397-2751	S	958*	.2
154	McCamish Systems LLC—*J Gordon Beckham Jr*	6425 Powers Ferry Rd, Atlanta GA 30339		R	954*	.1
155	Columbian Mutual Life Insurance Co—*Thomas Rattman*	PO Box 1381, Binghamton NY 13902	607-724-2472	R	940*	.3
156	Mutual Trust Life Insurance Co—*Gary L Eisenbarth*	1200 Jorie Blvd, Oak Brook IL 60523	630-990-1000	R	918*	.1

Note: An asterisk (*) indicates an estimated financial figure. The company type code used is as follows: R = Private, P = Public, S = Private Subsidiary, B = Public Subsidiary, D = Division, J = Joint Venture, I = Investment Fund.

COMPANY RANKINGS BY SALES WITHIN 4-DIGIT SIC

Rank	Company Name—Executive Officer	Address, City, State, Zip	Phone	Type	Fin	Empls
157	Amalgamated Life Insurance Co—David J Walsh	333 Westchester Ave, White Plains NY 10604	212-539-5000	R	918*	.1
158	BCS Life Insurance Co—Scott Beacham	2 Mid America Plaza St, Oakbrook Terrace IL 60181	630-472-7700	R	901*	.1
159	Baltimore Life Insurance Co—David K Ficca Baltimore Life Co	10075 Red Run Blvd, Owings Mills MD 21117	410-581-6600	S	859*	.4
160	Boston Mutual Life Insurance Co—Paul Petry	120 Royall St, Canton MA 02021	781-828-7000	R	842*	.3
161	Security Benefit Group of Companies Inc	1 SW Security Benefit, Topeka KS 66606	785-295-3000	R	793*	.1
162	Federated Life Insurance Co—Jeffrey Fetters	PO Box 328, Owatonna MN 55060	507-455-5200	S	735*	.1
163	Savings Bank Life Insurance Co—Robert K Sheridan	1 Linscott Rd, Woburn MA 01801	781-938-3500	R	723*	.2
164	KeyCorp Insurance Agency USA Inc—Paul A Larkins	127 Public Sq, Cleveland OH 44114	216-443-2685	S	712*	.2
165	Reliable Life Insurance Company of Missouri—Don M Royster United Insurance Company of America	12115 Lackland Rd, Saint Louis MO 63146	314-819-4300	S	695*	1.3
166	American Heritage Life Insurance Co—David A Bird	1776 American Heritage, Jacksonville FL 32224	904-992-3507	S	687*	.6
167	Employers Mutual Casualty Co—Bruce G Kelley	PO Box 712, Des Moines IA 50306	515-280-2511	R	683*	2.1
168	American Income Life Insurance Co—Roger Smith	PO Box 2608, Waco TX 76702	254-761-6400	S	679	.3
169	The Meltzer Group—Alan Meltzer	6500 Rock Spring Dr, Bethesda MD 20817	301-581-7300	R	655*	.1
170	MetLife Insurance Company of Connecticut	1 City Place, Hartford CT 06103	860-650-3000	S	646*	1.4
171	Old American Insurance Co—Walter Bixby Kansas City Life Insurance Co	PO Box 218573, Kansas City MO 64121	816-753-4900	S	646*	.6
172	Oxford Life Insurance Co—Mark Haydukovich	2721 N Central Ave, Phoenix AZ 85004	602-263-6666	S	641*	.2
173	Monarch Life Insurance Co—Kevin McAdoo	1 Monarch Pl, Springfield MA 01144	413-784-2000	R	633*	.1
174	Baltimore Life Co—David K Ficca	10075 Red Run Blvd, Owings Mills MD 21117	410-581-6600	R	615*	.2
175	Globe Life and Accident Insurance Co—Charles Hudson	204 N Robinson 5th Fl, Oklahoma City OK 73184	405-270-1400	S	590*	.3
176	Alliant Resources Group—Thomas Corbett	1301 Dove St Ste 200, Newport Beach CA 92660	949-809-1422	R	539*	.1
177	Americo Life Inc—Gary Muller	PO Box 410288, Kansas City MO 64141	816-391-2000	R	529*	.3
178	Forrest Sherer Inc—John Lukens	PO Box 506, Terre Haute IN 47808	812-232-0441	S	524*	.1
179	Standard Security Life Insurance Company of New York—Roy TK Thung Independence Holding Co (Stamford Connecticut)	485 Madison Ave 6th Fl, New York NY 10022	212-355-4141	S	520*	.1
180	Management Financial Group—Fred H Jonske	1125 NW Couch St Ste 9, Portland OR 97209	503-232-6960	R	517*	.1
181	Coventry First LLC—Alan H Buerger	7111 Valley Green Rd, Fort Washington PA 19034	215-233-5100	R	485*	.2
182	CNL Financial Corp—J R Miller	PO Box 6097, Macon GA 31208	478-477-0400	S	471*	.1
183	Security National Financial Corp—George R Quist	PO Box 57250, Salt Lake City UT 84157	801-264-1060	P	466	.8
184	Independence American Insurance Co—Roy TK Thung	485 Madison Ave, New York NY 10022	212-355-4141	R	462*	.1
185	Londen Insurance Group Inc—Jack Londen	PO Box 29045, Phoenix AZ 85038	602-957-1650	R	453*	.1
186	UTG Inc—Jesse T Correll	PO Box 5147, Springfield IL 62705	217-241-6300	P	442	.1
187	Investors Heritage Capital Corp—Harry Lee Waterfield II	PO Box 717, Frankfort KY 40602	502-223-2361	P	431	N/A
188	Frost Insurance Agency—RJ Waldt	3707 Richmond Ave, Houston TX 77046	713-388-1250	S	416*	<.1
189	Life Insurance Company of the Southwest—Wayde H Mayo National Life Group	PO Box 569080, Dallas TX 75356	214-638-7100	S	412*	.1
190	Southern National Life Insurance Co—Mike Reitz	PO Box 98029, Baton Rouge LA 70809	225-295-2525	S	408*	.1
191	United Home Life Insurance Co—Michael Giddings	PO Box 7192, Indianapolis IN 46207	317-692-7979	S	392*	<.1
192	Madison National Life Insurance Company Inc—Larry R Graber Independence Holding Co (Stamford Connecticut)	PO Box 5008, Madison WI 53705	608-830-2000	S	389*	.2
193	Standard Life and Accident Insurance Co—Richard Ferdinandt-sen American National Insurance Co	1 Moody Plz, Galveston TX 77550		S	382*	.3
194	Sunset Life Insurance Company of America—Robert Bixby Kansas City Life Insurance Co	PO Box 219532, Kansas City MO 64121	816-753-7000	S	381*	.1
195	Guaranty Income Life Insurance—George A Foster Jr Guaranty Corp (Baton Rouge Louisiana)	PO Box 2231, Baton Rouge LA 70821	225-383-0355	S	374*	.1
196	West Coast Life Insurance Co Protective Life Insurance Co	2801 Hwy 280 S, Birmingham AL 35223		S	368*	.1
197	Union Labor Life Insurance Co—Edward McElroy ULLICO Inc	1625 Eye St NW, Washington DC 20006	202-682-0900	S	354*	N/A
198	United Insurance Group—Chuck Westover	4778 N 300 W, Provo UT 84604	801-226-2662	R	313*	<.1
199	Lifewise Assurance Co—Jeff Roe	PO Box 2272, Seattle WA 98111	425-918-4575	S	310*	<.1
200	Best Meridian Insurance Co—Anthony F Sierra BMI Financial Group	8950 SW 74th Ct, Miami FL 33156	305-443-2898	S	304*	.1
201	Universal Guaranty Life Insurance Co—James P Rousey UTG Inc	PO Box 5147, Springfield IL 62705	217-241-6300	S	291*	.1
202	GuideOne Mutual Insurance Co—Brian Hughes	1111 Ashworth Rd, West Des Moines IA 50265		R	284*	.8
203	Cotton States Life Insurance Co—John D Blackburn Country Financial	244 Perimeter Center P, Atlanta GA 30346	770-391-8966	S	284	.1
204	CB Financial Services Inc—Cathy Nash	328 S Saginaw St, Flint MI 48502	810-766-7500	S	282*	<.1
205	Atlantic American Corp—Hilton H Howell Jr	4370 Peachtree Rd NE, Atlanta GA 30319	404-266-5500	P	278	.1
206	CSI Brokerage Services Inc—J Ridley Howard Cotton States Life Insurance Co	244 Perimeter Center P, Atlanta GA 30346		S	272*	<.1
207	Standard Life Insurance Company of Indiana—Ronald D Hunter	10689 N Pennsylvania S, Indianapolis IN 46280	317-574-6201	S	268*	<.1
208	Funeral Directors Life Insurance Co—Kris Seale Directors Holding Corp	PO Drawer 5649, Abilene TX 79608	325-695-3412	S	267*	.1
209	Forever Enterprises Inc—Brent D Cassity	10 S Brentwood 5th Fl, Saint Louis MO 63105	314-726-3371	R	263*	.2
210	MetLife Insurance Co—Robert Henrikson	200 Park Ave, New York NY 10166	212-578-2211	R	255*	1.7
211	Mutual Savings Life Insurance Co—C Larimore Whitaker	1420 5th Ave SE, Decatur AL 35601	256-353-1031	R	245*	1.0
212	Unity Mutual Life Insurance Co—Patrick Mannion	PO Box 5000, Syracuse NY 13250	315-448-7000	R	240*	.1
213	MML Bay State Life Insurance Co—Robert J O'Connell Massachusetts Mutual Life Insurance Co	1295 State St, Springfield MA 01111	413-788-8411	S	214	N/A
214	Erie Family Life Insurance Co—Terrence W Cavanaugh	100 Erie Insurance Pl, Erie PA 16530	814-451-5000	S	208	N/A
215	Doty Agency Inc—Anthony Cochran	518 E Main St, Petersburg IN 47567	812-354-8888	S	206*	<.1
216	Brown and Brown of Washington Inc—John Folsom	PO Box 1718, Tacoma WA 98401	253-396-5500	S	205*	<.1
217	Atlanta Life Financial Group Inc—William Taggart	100 Auburn Ave NE 300, Atlanta GA 30303	404-659-2100	R	202	N/A
218	Security Life Insurance Company of America—Gil C Rohde	10901 Red Cir Dr, Minnetonka MN 55343	952-544-2121	S	181*	<.1
219	National Foundation Life Insurance Co—Patrick J Mitchell	3100 Burnett Pl Unit 3, Fort Worth TX 76102		S	178*	.5
220	Germania Farm Mutual Insurance Association—David Sommer	PO Box 645, Brenham TX 77834	979-836-5224	R	170*	.4
221	Lafayette Life Insurance Co—Jerry B Stillwell Western and Southern Financial Group	400 Broadway, Cincinnati OH 45202	513-362-4900	S	169	.2
222	Ilona Financial Group Inc—Peter Fitzpatrick	1807 S Wshngtn St Pmb, Naperville IL 60565	630-699-6147	R	158*	.2
223	Professional Life Underwriters Services Inc—Lloyd West	2155 Butterfield Dr St, Troy MI 48084	248-356-7587	S	153*	<.1
224	Scottish Re (US) Inc—Meredith Ratajczak	14120 Ballantyne Ste, Charlotte NC 28277	704-542-9192	R	151*	.2
225	Catholic Order Of Foresters Inc—David Huber	PO Box 3012, Naperville IL 60566	630-983-4900	S	148*	.2

Rank	Company Name—*Executive Officer*	Address, City, State, Zip	Phone	Type	Fin	Empls
226	LeadersLife Insurance Co—*Burt B Holmes*	PO Box 35768, Tulsa OK 74153	918-254-0200	R	147*	<.1
227	American Life Insurance Co—*Edwin Betz*	PO Box 2226, Wilmington DE 19899	302-594-2000	R	142*	3.0
228	Pyramid Life Insurance Co—*Aubrey Ryan*	1001 Heathrow Park Ln, Lake Mary FL 32746		S	142*	.1
229	National Security Group Inc—*William Brunson*	PO Box 703, Elba AL 36323		P	137	.1
230	Alliance Underwriters AP Benefits Div—*Lynn Jennings*	120 International Pkwy, Lake Mary FL 32746	407-333-0024	R	119*	<.1
231	North Carolina Mutual Life Insurance Co—*James H Speed Jr*	411 W Chapel Hill St M, Durham NC 27701	919-682-9201	R	112*	.1
232	CSE Insurance Group—*Pierre Bize*	2121 N California Blvd, Walnut Creek CA 94596	925-817-6300	R	109*	.2
233	Susque-Bancshares Life Insurance Co—*Robert Bolinger*	PO Box 1000, Lititz PA 17543	717-626-4721	S	98*	<.1
234	Electronic Insurance Office Inc—*Ken Curtis*	PO Box 157, Mount Holly NJ 08060	609-267-1992	R	96*	<.1
235	Parker Services LLC—*David Schuh*	1800 Northpoint Dr, Stevens Point WI 54481		S	95*	<.1
236	ICC Insurance Agency Inc—*Peter Acciavatti*	230 Broadway E, Lynnfield MA 01940	781-593-8565	S	94*	<.1
237	USAble Life Inc—*Jason Mann*	PO Box 1650, Little Rock AR 72203	501-375-7200	S	90*	.1
238	Central States Health and Life Company of Omaha—*T Edward Kizer*	PO Box 34350, Omaha NE 68134	402-397-1111	R	88*	.2
239	Macduff Underwriters Inc—*Phil Adams*	1717 N Clyde Morris Bl, Daytona Beach FL 32117	386-366-6300	S	85*	<.1
240	North Central Life Insurance Co—*Christopher Chapman* American General Life and Accident Insurance Co	PO Box 4373, Houston TX 77210	732-922-7000	S	83*	.1
241	American General Life Insurance Company of New York—*Rodney O Martin Jr* United States Life Insurance Company in the City of New York	PO Box 4373, Houston TX 77210		S	82*	<.1
242	Point West Insurance Associates—*Stuart Nelson*	PO Box 255647, Sacramento CA 95865	916-925-5155	R	78*	<.1
243	Southern Security Life Insurance Co—*George R Quist* Security National Financial Corp	PO Box 57220, Salt Lake City UT 84151		S	78	N/A
244	United World Life Insurance Co—*Jack Weekly* United of Omaha Life Insurance Co	Mutual of Omaha Plz, Omaha NE 68175	402-342-7600	S	78	N/A
245	Global Preferred Holdings Inc—*Edward F McKernan*	PO Box 1561, Suwanee GA 30024	770-248-3311	R	74*	<.1
246	Directors Holding Corp—*B Kris Seale*	955 S Virginia St Ste, Reno NV 89502	775-329-9031	R	70	.1
247	Life Partners Holdings Inc—*Brian Pardo*	PO Box 20034, Waco TX 76702		P	66	.1
248	Sagicor Life Insurance Co—*Dodridge Miller*	4343 N Scottsdale Rd S, Scottsdale AZ 85251		R	63*	.1
249	Champions Life Insurance Co—*William H Lewis*	PO Box 833879, Richardson TX 75082	972-699-2770	S	60*	.2
250	Day Deadrick and Marshall Inc—*Caroline Day Scruggs*	PO Box 1840, Beltsville MD 20705	301-937-1500	R	59*	<.1
251	Banc of America Insurance Services Inc—*Kenneth Lewis*	PO Box 21848, Greensboro NC 27420		S	57*	<.1
252	Jack Rice Insurance Inc—*Jack Rice*	13080 S Belcher Rd Ste, Largo FL 33773	727-530-0684	R	53*	<.1
253	Bankers Fidelity Life Insurance Co—*Eugene Choate* Atlantic American Corp	4370 Peachtree Rd NE, Atlanta GA 30319	404-266-5500	S	52*	.1
254	Life and Health Underwriters Inc—*George Holland*	2001 6th Ave Ste 2550, Seattle WA 98121	206-728-1314	R	52*	<.1
255	Transamerica Financial Life Insurance Co—*Robert Rubinstein* Transamerica Corp	4 Manhattanville Rd, Purchase NY 10577	914-697-8300	S	50*	<.1
256	CS Marketing Resources Inc—*J Ridley Howard* Cotton States Life Insurance Co	244 Perimeter Center P, Atlanta GA 30346		S	48	.1
257	Savers Marketing Corp—*Jerry Francis*	635 W 4th St Ste 201, Winston Salem NC 27101	336-759-3888	R	47*	<.1
258	Pacific Guardian Life Insurance Company Ltd—*Yogi Nakamura*	1440 Kapiolani Blvd St, Honolulu HI 96814	808-955-2236	S	44*	.1
259	Physicians Insurance Company of Ohio—*John R Hart*	1 Easton Oval Ste 530, Columbus OH 43219	614-475-3178	S	40*	<.1
260	Lincoln Heritage Life Insurance Co—*Tom Londen* Londen Insurance Group Inc	PO Box 29045, Phoenix AZ 85038	602-957-1650	S	29	.1
261	Hartford Life Inc	200 Hopmeadow St, Simsbury CT 06089	860-547-5000	S	22*	4.0
262	Companion Life Insurance Co—*John W Weekly* United of Omaha Life Insurance Co	Mutual of Omaha Plz, Omaha NE 68175	402-342-7600	S	19	N/A
263	Central Security Life Insurance Corp—*James Lewis* Champions Life Insurance Co	PO Box 833879, Richardson TX 75083	972-699-2770	S	17*	.1
264	UNIFI Mutual Holding Co—*JoAnn M Martin*	PO Box 40888, Cincinnati OH 45240		R	17	N/A
265	Cherokee National Life Insurance Co—*Chris Green*	PO Box 6097, Macon GA 31208		S	16*	.1
266	Advance Insurance Co—*Beryl Lowery-Born*	1133 SW Topeka Blvd, Topeka KS 66629	785-273-9804	S	16*	<.1
267	Viatical Settlements Inc—*Bill Crust*	PO Box 151, Liberty MO 64069		R	14*	<.1
268	Winnfield Life Insurance Company Inc—*Charles B Henderson Sr*	PO Box 816, Natchitoches LA 71458	318-352-8346	R	13*	.1
269	Reliable Life Insurance Co (Monroe Louisiana)—*Joseph H Miller Jr* Kemper Corp	2932 Renwick St, Monroe LA 71201	318-387-1000	S	12*	.1
270	Principal Life Insurance Co Principal Financial Group Inc	711 High St, Des Moines IA 50392	515-247-5111	S	11	<.1
271	Trans World Assurance Co—*Charles Royals*	PO Box 5009, San Mateo CA 94402	650-348-2300	R	7*	<.1
272	Gertrude Geddes Willis Life Insurance Co—*Joseph O Misshore III*	2120 Jackson Ave, New Orleans LA 70113	504-522-2525	R	6*	<.1
273	Exceptional Risk Advisors LLC—*Edward Tafaro*	1 International Blvd S, Mahwah NJ 07495	201-512-0110	R	5*	<.1
274	Assurity Life Insurance Co—*Thomas E Henning*	PO Box 85233, Lincoln NE 68501	402-476-6500	R	2*	.2
275	Insurance Network—*Brenda Ayala*	7551 Callaghan Rd Ste, San Antonio TX 78229	210-424-2378	R	1*	<.1
276	NCIA Insurance Agency Delaware—*Tim Constantine*	PO Box 8737, Wilmington DE 19899	302-421-8962	S	1*	<.1
277	American General Life and Accident Insurance Co—*Jim Mallon*	American General Ctr M, Nashville TN 37250	615-749-1000	S	N/A	4.0
278	Pennsylvania Life Insurance Co—*Gary Bryant* Universal American Corp	1001 Heathrow Park Ln, Lake Mary FL 32746	407-995-8000	S	N/A	.3
279	PSA Insurance and Financial Services—*Trevor Lewis*	11311 McCormick Rd, Hunt Valley MD 21031	410-821-7766	R	N/A	.1

TOTALS: SIC 6311 Life Insurance

	Companies: 279				5,337,836	710.4

6321 Accident & Health Insurance

Rank	Company Name—*Executive Officer*	Address, City, State, Zip	Phone	Type	Fin	Empls
1	CIGNA Group Insurance—*David M Cordani*	2 Liberty Pl 1601 Ches, Philadelphia PA 19192	215-761-1000	R	207,186*	30.6
2	Health Care Service Corporation A Mutual Legal Reserve Co—*Patricia A Hemingway Hall*	300 E Randolph St, Chicago IL 60601	312-653-6000	R	110,179*	16.0
3	AFLAC Inc—*Daniel P Amos*	1932 Wynnton Rd, Columbus GA 31999	706-323-3431	P	101,039	7.9
4	Reinsurance Group of America Inc—*A Greig Woodring*	1370 Timberlake Manor, Chesterfield MO 63017	636-736-7000	P	29,082	1.5
5	Blue Cross and Blue Shield of North Carolina—*J Bradley Wilson*	PO Box 2291, Durham NC 27702	919-489-7431	R	29,036*	4.6
6	Assurant Inc—*Robert B Pollock*	1 Chase Manhattan Plz, New York NY 10005	212-859-7000	P	26,397	14.0
7	Blue Cross and Blue Shield of Georgia Inc	PO Box 9907, Columbus GA 31908	404-842-8000	S	19,168*	3.0
8	StanCorp Financial Group Inc—*J Greg Ness*	1100 SW 6th Ave, Portland OR 97204	971-321-7000	P	18,434	3.0
9	Wisconsin Physicians Service Insurance Corp—*James Riordan*	PO Box 8190, Madison WI 53708	608-221-4711	R	12,519*	4.0
10	Blue Cross and Blue Shield of Kansas—*Andrew Corbin*	1133 SW Topeka Blvd, Topeka KS 66629	785-291-4180	R	9,351*	1.5

Note: An asterisk (*) indicates an estimated financial figure. The company type code used is as follows: R = Private, P = Public, S = Private Subsidiary, B = Public Subsidiary, D = Division, J = Joint Venture, I = Investment Fund.

COMPANY RANKINGS BY SALES WITHIN 4-DIGIT SIC

Rank	Company Name—*Executive Officer*	Address, City, State, Zip	Phone	Type	Fin	Empls
11	UNUM Holding Co—*Thomas R Watjen*	2211 Congress St, Portland ME 04122	207-575-2211	S	9,242	4.0
12	EmblemHealth Inc—*Anthony Watson*	55 Water St, New York NY 10041	646-447-5000	R	8,610	5.4
13	Aon Corp—*Gregory C Case*	200 E Randolph St, Chicago IL 60601	312-381-1000	P	8,512	59.0
14	Blue Cross and Blue Shield of Delaware Inc CareFirst BlueCross BlueShield	800 Delaware Ave, Wilmington DE 19801	302-421-3000	S	5,723*	.9
15	Arkansas Blue Cross and Blue Shield—*P Mark White*	PO Box 2181, Little Rock AR 72203	501-378-2000	R	5,632*	2.2
16	Highmark Blue Cross Blue Shield—*Kenneth R Milani*	PO Box 226, Pittsburgh PA 15230		R	4,830	N/A
17	CareFirst BlueCross BlueShield	10455 Mill Run Cir, Owings Mills MD 21117	410-581-3000	S	4,500*	6.0
18	Blue Cross and Blue Shield of Alabama—*Phillip Pope*	450 Riverchase Pky E, Birmingham AL 35244	205-220-2100	R	3,709*	3.0
19	Independence Blue Cross—*Joseph A Frick*	1901 Market St, Philadelphia PA 19103	215-241-2400	R	3,605*	6.0
20	Employers Holdings Inc—*Douglas D Dirks*	10375 Professional Cir, Reno NV 89521		P	3,482	.7
21	Physicians Mutual Insurance Co—*Robert Reed*	PO Box 3313, Omaha NE 68103	402-633-1000	R	3,411*	1.3
22	Horizon Healthcare Services Inc—*Robert A Marino*	PO Box 820, Newark NJ 07101	973-466-4000	R	3,023*	4.7
23	Blue Cross and Blue Shield of Western New York—*Joseph Castiglia*	PO Box 80, Buffalo NY 14240	716-884-2800	R	2,939*	1.1
24	HealthMarkets Inc—*Phillip J Hildebrand*	9151 Blvd 26, North Richland Hills TX 76180	817-255-5200	R	2,876*	2.0
25	Definity Health Corp—*Tony Miller*	1600 Utica Ave S Ste 9, Saint Louis Park MN 55416	952-277-5500	S	2,740*	.5
26	Combined Insurance Company of America—*Doug Wendt* Aon Corp	1000 N Milwaukee Ave, Glenview IL 60025	847-953-2025	S	2,668	N/A
27	Group Health Inc—*Frank J Branchini*	441 9th Ave, New York NY 10001	212-615-0000	R	2,578*	2.4
28	Medical Mutual of Ohio—*Rick Chiricosta*	2060 E 9th St, Cleveland OH 44115	216-687-7000	R	2,299*	3.0
29	Blue Cross and Blue Shield of Michigan—*Daniel Loepp*	600 E Lafayette Blvd, Detroit MI 48226	313-225-9000	R	2,197*	7.5
30	Chesapeake Life Insurance Co—*David W Fields* HealthMarkets Inc	1331 W Memorial Rd Ste, Oklahoma City OK 73114	405-848-0179	S	2,121	N/A
31	Cerulean Companies Inc—*JL Laboon Jr*	3350 Peachtree Rd NE, Atlanta GA 30326	404-842-8000	S	2,034	2.9
32	Blue Cross and Blue Shield of Vermont—*Don George*	PO Box 186, Montpelier VT 05601		R	1,861*	.3
33	National American Insurance Co—*W Brent Lagere*	1010 Manvel Ave, Chandler OK 74834	405-258-0804	R	1,377*	.2
34	Penn Treaty American Corp—*Eugene J Woznicki*	3440 Lehigh St, Allentown PA 18103	610-965-2222	P	1,315	.4
35	Washington National Insurance Co—*William S Kirsch*	11825 N Pennsylvania S, Carmel IN 46032	317-817-4180	S	1,142	N/A
36	Capital Blue Cross—*William Lehr Jr*	PO Box 774611, Harrisburg PA 17177	717-541-7000	R	1,100*	2.0
37	American Health and Life Insurance Co—*Dava Sherill Carson*	PO Box 2548, Fort Worth TX 76113	817-348-7500	R	1,075*	.4
38	Blue Cross and Blue Shield of Minnesota—*Mark Banks*	PO Box 64560, Saint Paul MN 55164	651-662-5200	R	948	N/A
39	Safety National Casualty Corp—*Terrence Schoeninger*	1832 Schuetz Rd, Saint Louis MO 63146	314-995-5300	S	929*	.2
40	Healthmarket Inc—*William Gedwed* HealthMarkets Inc	20 Glover Ave 5th Fl, Norwalk CT 06850	203-229-1000	S	828*	.1
41	PartnerRe USA—*Tad Walker*	1 Greenwich Plz, Greenwich CT 06830	203-485-4200	S	805*	.1
42	United American Insurance Co—*Vern D Herbel*	PO Box 8080, McKinney TX 75070	972-529-5085	S	764*	.5
43	Acuity Mutual Insurance Co—*Ben Salzman*	PO Box 58, Sheboygan WI 53082	920-458-9131	R	741*	.9
44	Blue Cross and Blue Shield of Rhode Island—*James E Purcell*	500 Exchange St, Providence RI 02903	401-459-5795	R	674*	1.1
45	Transguard General Insurance Agency Inc—*Larry Writ*	215 Shuman Blvd, Naperville IL 60563		R	619*	.1
46	Philadelphia American Life Insurance—*Bill S Chen*	PO Box 4884, Houston TX 77210		R	616*	.2
47	Willis Faber North America Inc—*Peter Hearn*	5420 Millstream Rd, Mc Leansville NC 27301	336-574-8800	R	614*	.1
48	Blue Cross and Blue Shield United of Wisconsin—*Stuart K Campbell*	401 W Michigan St, Milwaukee WI 53203	414-226-5000	S	550*	2.2
49	American Public Life Insurance Co—*Jim Pate*	PO Box 925, Jackson MS 39205	601-936-6600	R	537*	.1
50	Bravo Health Insurance Company Inc	3601 O'Donnell St, Baltimore MD 21224		S	533*	1.0
51	Berkshire Hathaway Homestate Insurance Co	PO Box 2048, Omaha NE 68103		S	480*	.1
52	MedAdvantage Inc—*John B Witty*	11301 Corp Blvd Ste 30, Orlando FL 32817	407-282-5131	S	466*	.1
53	Paul Revere Corp	1 Fountain Sq, Chattanooga TN 37402	423-755-1011	S	420*	.3
54	Louisiana Health Service and Indemnity Co—*Mike Reitz*	PO Box 98029, Baton Rouge LA 70898	225-295-3307	R	379*	1.7
55	First Nonprofit Insurance Co—*Philip R Warth Jr*	111 N Canal St Ste 801, Chicago IL 60606		R	310*	.1
56	Medico Insurance Co—*Timothy J Hall*	1515 S 75th St, Omaha NE 68124	402-391-6900	R	287*	.2
57	Blue Cross and Blue Shield of Arizona Inc—*Richard L Boals*	PO Box 13466, Phoenix AZ 85002		R	270*	1.6
58	LifeWise Health Plan of Oregon Inc—*Majd El-Azma*	2020 SW 4th Ave Ste 10, Portland OR 97201	503-295-6707	S	245*	.2
59	LDG Management Company Inc—*Peter Recka*	401 Edgewater Pl Ste 4, Wakefield MA 01880	781-245-2220	S	240*	.1
60	Avon-Dixon Agency LLC—*Terry Meade*	28969 Information Ln, Easton MD 21601	410-822-0506	S	221*	<.1
61	PreferredOne Administrative Services Inc—*Marcus Merz*	PO Box 59212, Minneapolis MN 55459	763-847-4477	R	210*	.3
62	Patriot Risk Management Inc—*Steven M Mariano*	401 E Las Olas Blvd St, Fort Lauderdale FL 33301	954-670-2900	R	175*	.2
63	Ace Property And Casualty Insurance Co—*Gerald Isom*	2 Liberty Pl 2 Liberty, Philadelphia PA 19102	215-761-1000	R	170*	3.3
64	Bcbsm Inc—*Mark Banks*	PO Box 64560, Saint Paul MN 55164	651-662-8000	R	167*	3.7
65	HealthScope Benefits—*Joe Edwards*	8800 Lyra Dr Ste 650, Columbus OH 43240	614-797-5200	R	153*	.3
66	USHEALTH Group Inc—*Benjamin M Cutler*	801 Cherry St Ste 33, Fort Worth TX 76102	817-878-3300	R	151*	.2
67	Continental General Insurance Co—*Mike Abbott*	PO Box 2650, Omaha NE 68103		R	146*	.2
68	Conseco Medical Insurance Co	11825 N Pennsylvania S, Carmel IN 46032	317-817-6100	S	130*	2.6
69	Arista Insurance Co—*Stanley S Mandel*	116 John St, New York NY 10038	212-964-2150	S	108*	<.1
70	BB and T Insurance Services Inc—*Wade Reece*	3605 Glenwood Ave Ste, Raleigh NC 27612		S	107*	<.1
71	Brown and Associates LLC—*Keith W Brown*	1407 Union Ave Ste 100, Memphis TN 38104	901-725-4500	R	30*	<.1
72	American Network Insurance Co—*William W Hunt Jr* Penn Treaty American Corp	3440 Lehigh St, Allentown PA 18103	610-965-2222	S	19	<.1
73	Financial Pacific Insurance Co—*Robert T Kingsley*	PO Box 45376, San Francisco CA 94145		S	19*	.1
74	Kansas Medical Mutual Insurance Co—*David Ross*	623 SW 10th Ave, Topeka KS 66612	785-232-2224	R	10*	<.1
75	Willis of New Hampshire Inc—*Joseph J Plumeri*	1 New Hampshire Ave St, Portsmouth NH 03801	603-334-6668	D	8*	.1
76	Hartville Group Inc—*Dennis Rushovich*	3840 Greentree Ave SW, Canton OH 44706	330-484-8166	P	7	.1
77	Affordable Health Insurance Inc—*Gary R Harrell*	2340 S Arlington Heigh, Arlington Heights IL 60005	847-437-1113	R	6*	.1
78	Fiesta Insurance Franchise Corp—*John Rost*	16162 Beach Blvd Ste 1, Huntington Beach CA 92647	714-842-5420	R	6*	<.1
79	Anthem Blue Cross Blue Shield (Richmond Virginia)—*Thomas Snead*	PO Box 27401, Richmond VA 23261	804-354-7000	S	2	N/A
80	Assurant Health—*Don Hamm* Assurant Inc	PO Box 3050, Milwaukee WI 53201	414-299-8800	D	2	N/A
81	Progress Sharing Co—*Frederick A Prince*	605 US Rt 1 Box 5, Scarborough ME 04074	207-883-9164	R	1*	<.1

TOTALS: SIC 6321 Accident & Health Insurance

	Companies: 81				671,093	224.0

6324 Hospital & Medical Service Plans

Rank	Company Name—*Executive Officer*	Address, City, State, Zip	Phone	Type	Fin	Empls
1	UnitedHealth Group Inc—*Stephen J Hemsley*	PO Box 1459, Minneapolis MN 55440		P	63,063	87.0
2	Aetna Inc—*Mark T Bertolini*	151 Farmington Ave, Hartford CT 06156	860-273-0123	P	37,739	34.0
3	BayCare Healh System Inc—*Stephen R Mason*	16255 Bay Vista Dr, Clearwater FL 33760	727-799-3335	R	21,310*	18.0
4	Sisters of Providence Health of Washington—*John Koster*	1801 Lind Ave SW #9016, Renton WA 98057		R	18,667*	33.9
5	PacifiCare Health Systems Inc—*Howard G Phanstiel* UnitedHealth Group Inc	PO Box 6006, Cypress CA 90630	714-952-1121	S	16,185*	9.8

Rank	Company Name—*Executive Officer*	Address, City, State, Zip	Phone	Type	Fin	Empls
6	Humana Inc—*Michael B McCallister*	500 W Main St, Louisville KY 40202	502-580-1000	P	16,103	35.2
7	Highmark Inc—*Kenneth Melani*	120 5th Ave, Pittsburgh PA 15222	412-544-7000	R	13,351*	19.5
8	Blue Cross and Blue Shield of South Carolina—*David Pankau*	PO Box 100300, Columbia SC 29202	803-788-0222	R	11,077*	15.0
9	AtlantiCare Health System—*George F Lynn*	1401 Atlantic Ave, Atlantic City NJ 08401	609-572-6030	R	9,571*	5.8
10	Coventry Health Care Inc—*Allen F Wise*	6705 Rockledge Dr Ste, Bethesda MD 20817	301-581-0600	P	8,495	14.0
11	Anthem Insurance Companies Inc—*Larry C Glasscock*	120 Monument Cir, Indianapolis IN 46204	317-488-6000	S	5,785*	15.0
12	First Health Group Corp—*Dale Wolf* Coventry Health Care Inc	3200 Highland Ave, Downers Grove IL 60515	630-737-7900	S	5,542*	6.0
13	Centene Corp—*Michael F Neidorff*	7700 Forsythe Blvd, Saint Louis MO 63105	314-725-4477	P	5,341	5.3
14	Regence Group—*Mark B Ganz*	PO Box 1071, Portland OR 97207	503-225-5221	R	4,968*	6.5
15	Vanguard Health Systems Inc—*Charles N Martin Jr*	20 Burton Hills Blvd S, Nashville TN 37215	615-665-6000	P	4,896	38.6
16	Health Net Inc—*Jay M Gellert*	21650 Oxnard St, Woodland Hills CA 91367	818-676-6000	P	4,132	8.2
17	Kaiser Foundation Health Plan of the Northwest	500 NE Multnomah St St, Portland OR 97232	503-813-2000	S	3,866*	8.2
18	Health Net of California Inc Health Net Inc	21650 Oxnard St, Woodland Hills CA 91367	818-676-6000	S	3,800	3.5
19	Oxford Health Plans LLC—*Charles G Berg* UnitedHealth Group Inc	48 Monroe Tpk, Trumbull CT 06611	203-459-6000	S	3,375*	5.0
20	Anthem Blue Cross of California—*David S Helwig*	4553 Latienda Dr, Thousand Oaks CA 91362	805-557-6655	S	3,126*	7.0
21	Delta Dental Plan of California—*Gary D Radine*	PO Box 997330, Sacramento CA 95899	415-972-8300	R	2,709*	3.6
22	WellCare Health Plans Inc—*Alec R Cunningham*	PO Box 31372, Tampa FL 33631	813-290-6200	P	2,488	4.0
23	HealthSpring Inc—*Herbert Fritch*	9009 Carothers Pkwy St, Franklin TN 37067	615-291-7000	P	2,349	3.2
24	Amerigroup Corp—*James G Carlson*	PO Box 62509, Virginia Beach VA 23462	757-490-6900	P	2,283	4.5
25	Health Insurance Plan of Greater New York Inc—*David S Aber-nethy*	55 Water St, New York NY 10041	646-447-5000	R	1,951*	2.0
26	Medica—*David Tilford*	PO Box 9310, Minneapolis MN 55440	952-992-2900	D	1,854*	1.1
27	ING Financial Advisers LLC—*Tom McInerney*	151 Farmington Ave, Hartford CT 06156		S	1,847*	2.0
28	University of Pennsylvania Health System—*Ralph W Muller*	3400 Spruce St, Philadelphia PA 19104	215-662-4000	R	1,754*	3.5
29	Premera Blue Cross—*Brereton Gubby Barlow*	7001-220th St SW Bldg, Mountlake Terrace WA 98043	425-918-4000	R	1,493*	2.8
30	Gateway Health Plan—*Michael Blackwood*	US Steel Tower 600 Gra, Pittsburgh PA 15219	412-255-4640	R	1,200*	.4
31	American Physicians Capital Inc—*Richard Anderson*	PO Box 1471, East Lansing MI 48826	517-351-1150	P	945	1.0
32	Blue Cross and Blue Shield of Kansas City—*David Gentile*	1 Pershing Sq 2301 Mai, Kansas City MO 64108	816-395-2222	R	909*	1.0
33	University Health Plans Inc—*Alexander McLean*	550 Broad St 17th Fl, Newark NJ 07102	973-623-8700	R	906*	1.0
34	AvMed Health Plans—*Michael P Gallagher*	4300 NW 89th Blvd, Gainesville FL 32606	352-372-8400	R	844*	.8
35	Kaiser Foundation Health Plan of Colorado—*Donna Lynne*	2500 S Havana St, Aurora CO 80014	303-338-4545	S	836*	3.8
36	Mid Atlantic Medical Services Inc—*Thomas P Barbera* UnitedHealth Group Inc	4 Taft Ct, Rockville MD 20850	301-762-8205	S	773*	3.3
37	Multiplan Inc—*Mark Tabak*	115 5th Ave, New York NY 10003	212-780-2000	S	734*	1.0
38	Crozer Keystone Health System—*Joan Richards*	190 W Sproul Rd 3rd Fl, Springfield PA 19064	610-338-8200	R	700*	4.0
39	Excel Health—*David S Gallatin*	532 W Pittsburgh St, Greensburg PA 15601	724-832-4000	R	678*	1.6
40	USA Workers' Injury Network Inc—*George Bogle* USA Managed Care Organization Inc	916 Capitol of Texas H, Austin TX 78746	512-306-0201	S	644*	.4
41	Kaiser Foundation Health Plan of Georgia Inc	3495 Piedmont Rd NE, Atlanta GA 30305	404-279-4636	S	601*	1.3
42	Keystone Health Plan Central	PO Box 774611, Harrisburg PA 17177		S	600*	.5
43	Oregon Dental Service Inc—*Robert Gootee*	PO Box 40384, Portland OR 97240		R	530*	.7
44	ODS Health Plan Inc—*Robert Gootee* Oregon Dental Service Inc	PO Box 40384, Portland OR 97240	503-228-6554	S	504*	.7
45	HealthPlus of Michigan Inc—*Bruce Hill*	PO Box 1700, Flint MI 48501	810-230-2000	R	497*	.3
46	Wellness Plan—*Anthony V King*	2888 W Grand Blvd, Detroit MI 48202	313-875-4200	R	432*	.9
47	CIGNA Healthcare Mid-Atlantic Inc—*David Cordani*	9700 Patuxent Woods Dr, Columbia MD 21046	410-720-5800	S	424*	1.0
48	Omni Care Health Plan Inc—*Dale B Wolfe* Coventry Health Care Inc	6705 Rockledge Dr, Bethesda MD 20817	301-581-7828	S	414*	.3
49	Health Alliance Plan of Michigan—*William Alvin*	2850 W Grand Blvd, Detroit MI 48202	313-872-8100	S	411*	.9
50	American Medical Security Group Inc—*Steve DeRaleau* PacifiCare Health Systems Inc	PO Box 19032, Green Bay WI 54307	920-661-1111	S	400*	1.3
51	Preferred Care Partners Inc—*Joseph L Caruncho*	9100 S Dadeland Blvd S, Miami FL 33156	305-670-8432	R	385*	.3
52	CIGNA HealthCare of Arizona Inc—*Kurt A Weimer*	11001 N Black Canyon H, Phoenix AZ 85029	602-942-4462	S	355*	2.5
53	Rocky Mountain Health Plans—*Steve ErkenBrack*	PO Box 10600, Grand Junction CO 81502	970-244-7800	R	352*	.4
54	Tufts Associated Health Plans Inc—*James Roosevelt*	705 Mt Auburn St, Watertown MA 02472	617-972-9400	R	323*	2.5
55	AmeriChoice Corp—*Stephen J Hemsley* UnitedHealth Group Inc	PO Box 1459, Minneapolis MN 55440		S	319*	.9
56	Priority Health Managed Benefits Inc—*Kimberly K Horn*	1231 E Beltline Ave NE, Grand Rapids MI 49525	616-942-0954	R	270*	.6
57	AMERIGROUP Florida Inc—*James G Carlson* Amerigroup Corp	4200 W Cypress St Ste, Tampa FL 33607	813-830-6900	S	268*	.4
58	CompBenefits of Georgia Inc—*Kirk Rothrock* Humana Inc	100 Mansell Ct E Ste 4, Roswell GA 30076	770-552-7101	S	252	.7
59	CIGNA Dental Health—*David M Cordani*	1571 Sawgrass Corporat, Sunrise FL 33323	954-514-6600	S	219*	.4
60	Cofinity—*Kelly Wright*	28588 Northwestern Hwy, Southfield MI 48034	303-691-2200	R	217*	.4
61	HCC Benefits—*Craig Kelbel*	225 Townpark Dr Ste 14, Kennesaw GA 30144		S	185*	.2
62	Blue Cross And Blue Shield Of Texas—*Rogers Coleman*	PO Box 655730, Dallas TX 75265	972-766-6900	R	178*	4.3
63	Health First Health Plans Inc—*Jerry Senne*	6450 Us Hwy 1, Rockledge FL 32955	321-434-5600	R	174*	.2
64	USA Managed Care Organization Inc—*George Bogle*	7301 N 16th St Ste 201, Phoenix AZ 85020	602-371-3860	R	174*	.2
65	Universal Care Inc—*Howard Davis*	1600 E Hill St, Signal Hill CA 90755	562-424-6200	R	173*	.4
66	Sharp Health Plan—*Kathlyn Mead*	4305 University Ave St, San Diego CA 92105	619-228-2300	R	172*	.1
67	Wilmington Health Associates PA—*Jeff James*	1202 Medical Center Dr, Wilmington NC 28401	910-341-3300	R	170*	.4
68	Blue Cross and Blue Shield Of Rochester—*Scott Ellsworth*	165 Ct St, Rochester NY 14647	585-454-1700	R	169*	4.0
69	Shields MRI—*Tom Shields*	265 Westgate Dr, Brockton MA 02301	508-580-6482	R	159*	.4
70	Senior Whole Health LLC—*John Baackes*	58 Charles St, Cambridge MA 02141	617-494-5353	R	159*	.2
71	Arizona Dental Insurance Service Inc—*Bernard Glossy*	5656 W Talavi Blvd, Glendale AZ 85306	602-938-3131	R	151*	.1
72	Georgia West Medical Center Inc—*Jerry Folks*	1514 Vernon Rd, Lagrange GA 30240	706-882-1411	R	150*	1.5
73	Private Medical-Care Inc—*Robert Elliott*	12898 Towne Ctr Dr, Cerritos CA 90703	562-924-8311	R	144*	.4
74	Inter-Valley Health Plan Inc—*Ronald Bolding*	PO Box 6002, Pomona CA 91769	909-623-6333	R	143*	.1
75	Unity Health Plans Insurance Corp—*Terry Bolz*	840 Carolina St, Sauk City WI 53583	608-643-2491	S	131*	.2
76	AmeriChoice of Pennsylvania Inc—*Anthony Welters* AmeriChoice Corp	100 Penn Sq E Ste 900, Philadelphia PA 19107	215-832-4500	S	126*	.3
77	CIGNA Healthcare of Florida Inc—*David Cordani*	2701 North Rocky Point, Tampa FL 33607	813-637-1200	S	121	.6
78	AtlantiCare Health Plans—*Pat Koolling* AtlantiCare Health System	2500 English Creek Ave, Egg Harbor Township NJ 08234	609-407-2300	S	111*	.1
79	United Health Care of Arizona—*Benton Davis* UnitedHealth Group Inc	3141 N 3rd Ave Ste 100, Phoenix AZ 85013	602-664-5003	S	103*	.8
80	Nationwide Healthplan—*Joe Sanfilippo*	1 Nationwide Plz, Columbus OH 43215		S	103*	.3

Note: An asterisk (*) indicates an estimated financial figure. The company type code used is as follows: R = Private, P = Public, S = Private Subsidiary, B = Public Subsidiary, D = Division, J = Joint Venture, I = Investment Fund.

COMPANY RANKINGS BY SALES WITHIN 4-DIGIT SIC

Rank	Company Name—*Executive Officer*	Address, City, State, Zip	Phone	Type	Fin	Empls
81	Health New England Inc—*Peter F Straley*	1 Monarch Pl Ste 1500, Springfield MA 01144	413-233-3178	S	97	.2
82	Health Net Health Plan of Oregon—*Jay Gellert*	PO Box 286, Clackamas OR 97015	503-802-7000	R	92*	.1
83	Pacific Medical Clinics—*Harvey Smith*	1200 - 12th Ave S, Seattle WA 98144		R	91*	.1
84	Devon Health Services Inc—*John A Bennett*	1100 1st Ave Ste 100, King of Prussia PA 19406	610-757-4166	R	88*	.1
85	Delta Dental Plan of Kentucky—*Cliff Maesaka*	PO Box 242810, Louisville KY 40224	502-736-5000	R	86*	.1
86	Luke and Associates Inc—*Jim Barfield*	775 E Merritt Island C, Merritt Island FL 32952	321-452-4601	R	86	.9
87	Olympus Managed Health Care Inc—*Steven W Jacobson*	777 Brickell AveSte 41, Miami FL 33131	305-530-8600	R	83*	.1
88	AMERIGROUP New Jersey Inc—*Peter Haytaian* Amerigroup Corp	399 Thornall St Ste 9, Edison NJ 08818	732-452-6000	S	76*	.1
89	Safeguard Health Enterprises Inc—*Steven Baker*	95 Enterprise Ste 200, Aliso Viejo CA 92656	949-425-4300	S	71*	.4
90	First Choice Health Network Inc—*Kenneth A Hamm*	PO Box 12659, Seattle WA 98111	206-667-8062	R	71*	.2
91	International Healthcare Services Inc—*Martin Kane*	333 Earl Ovington Blvd, Uniondale NY 11553	516-794-3000	S	68*	.2
92	Best Life and Health Insurance Co—*Donald R Lawrenz*	2505 McCabe Way, Irvine CA 92614	949-253-4080	R	62*	.1
93	MEDEX Global Group Inc—*Tim Mitchell*	PO Box 19056, Baltimore MD 21284	410-453-6300	R	59*	.1
94	QualChoice Health Plan Inc—*Thomas Sullivan*	6000 Parkland Blvd, Mayfield Heights OH 44124	440-460-0093	R	42*	.3
95	Health Advantage—*David Bridges*	PO Box 8069, Little Rock AR 72203	501-221-1800	D	42*	.1
96	Extend Health Inc—*Bryce Williams*	2929 Campus Dr Ste 400, San Mateo CA 94403	650-288-4800	R	37*	.4
97	Humana/ChoiceCare—*Michael McCallister* Humana Inc	500 W Main St, Louisville KY 40202	513-784-5200	S	32*	.5
98	Dental Network of America Inc—*John Doyle*	701 E 22nd St, Lombard IL 60148	630-691-1133	S	32*	.4
99	WellCare of New York Inc—*Marc Russo* WellCare Health Plans Inc	280 Broadway, Newburgh NY 12550	845-440-2400	S	32*	.1
100	Doral Dental USA LLC—*Gregory Borca*	12121 N Corporate Pky, Mequon WI 53092	262-241-7140	S	31*	.3
101	AMERIGROUP Illinois Inc—*James Carlson* Amerigroup Corp	4425 Corporation Ln, Virginia Beach VA 23462	757-490-6900	S	25*	<.1
102	Texas True Choice Inc—*Michael Wilson*	5080 Spectrum Dr Ste 6, Addison TX 75001	214-267-3300	R	23*	<.1
103	Dimension Health Inc—*Charles A Lindgren*	5881 NW 151st St Ste 2, Hialeah FL 33014		R	23*	<.1
104	WellCare Management Group Inc—*Heath Schiesser* WellCare Health Plans Inc	PO Box 31372, Tampa FL 33631		S	23	<.1
105	Sagamore Health Network Inc	11555 N Meridian St St, Carmel IN 46032	317-573-2900	S	20*	.1
106	Benecon Group Inc—*Samuel N Lombardo*	PO Box 5406, Lancaster PA 17606	717-723-4600	R	19*	<.1
107	San Luis Valley HMO Inc—*Cynthia Palmer*	700 Main St Ste 100, Alamosa CO 81101	719-589-3696	R	18*	<.1
108	WPPA Inc—*Karen Cox*	1102 S Hillside St, Wichita KS 67211	316-683-4111	R	16*	<.1
109	Comprehensive Care Corp—*Clark A Marcus*	3405 W Dr Martin Luthe, Tampa FL 33607	813-288-4808	P	15	.1
110	Medical Advantage Group—*Charlie Carpenter* American Physicians Capital Inc	1305 Abbott Rd, East Lansing MI 48823	517-336-1400	S	14*	<.1
111	American Dental Professional Services LLC—*Gregory Serrao*	9052 N Deerbrook Trl, Milwaukee WI 53223		S	12*	<.1
112	Audigy Group LLC—*Brandon Dawson*	11201 NE 9th St Ste 30, Vancouver WA 98684		R	11	.1
113	Healthcare Management Inc—*Robert West*	155 Franklin Rd Ste 10, Brentwood TN 37027	615-661-5145	R	11*	<.1
114	Professional Credential Verification Services Inc—*Charlie Carpenter* American Physicians Capital Inc	1305 Abbott Rd, East Lansing MI 48823	517-336-5715	S	10*	<.1
115	International Managed Care Strategies Inc—*Richard D Rostowsky*	1385 Kemper Meadow Dr, Cincinnati OH 45246	513-772-8866	R	7*	.1
116	Select Benefits Group Inc—*Brent Williams*	5373 S Green St Ste 40, Salt Lake City UT 84123	801-495-3000	R	7*	.1
117	America's Choice Healthplans Inc—*Clelland Green*	PO Box 922043, Houston TX 77292	610-962-1985	R	7	.1
118	Eye Care Network Inc	PO Box 25209, Santa Ana CA 92799	415-362-7771	R	6*	.1
119	Managed Care Consultants Inc—*William Coleman*	8920 Canyon Falls, Twinsburg OH 44087	440-442-0002	R	5*	<.1
120	Cypress Dental Administrators—*Chuck Richardson*	7510 Shoreline Dr Ste, Stockton CA 95219	209-478-4808	R	4*	<.1
121	Highland Campus Health Group LLC—*Mike Wood*	PO Box 168007, Irving TX 75016	325-437-8300	R	4*	<.1
122	CareAdvantage Inc—*Dennis J Mouras*	485-A Rte 1 S 2nd Fl S, Iselin NJ 08830	732-362-5000	P	4	<.1
123	Araz Group—*Nazie Eftekhari*	7201 W 78th St, Bloomington MN 55439	952-896-1200	R	3*	<.1
124	Pacific Health Alliance—*Lawrence Cappel*	1350 Bayshore Hwy, Burlingame CA 94010	650-375-5800	R	2*	<.1
125	Healthdent of California Inc—*Richard White*	10604 Trademark Pkwy S, Rancho Cucamonga CA 91730	909-483-8310	S	2*	<.1
126	HealthEos—*Bruce Lefco* Multiplan Inc	PO Box 6090, De Pere WI 54115		S	2*	<.1
127	Sun Health Medison Inc—*Sohn Won-gihl*	13632 N 99th Ave Ste B, Sun City AZ 85351	623-974-7430	R	1	<.1
128	SelectCare Inc—*Roman Kulch*	2401 W Big Beaver Rd S, Troy MI 48084	248-637-5300	R	N/A	.5
129	Union Health Services Inc	1634 W Polk St, Chicago IL 60612	312-423-4200	R	N/A	.1

TOTALS: SIC 6324 Hospital & Medical Service Plans
Companies: 129   300,628   457.1

6331 Fire, Marine & Casualty Insurance

Rank	Company Name—*Executive Officer*	Address, City, State, Zip	Phone	Type	Fin	Empls
1	Citigroup Inc—*Vikram Pandit*	399 Park Ave, New York NY 10022	212-559-1000	P	1,913,902	260.0
2	Berkshire Hathaway Inc—*Warren E Buffett*	3555 Farnam St Ste 144, Omaha NE 68131	402-346-1400	P	372,229	260.0
3	Hartford Financial Services Group Inc—*Liam E McGee*	1 Hartford Plz, Hartford CT 06155	860-547-5000	P	318,346	26.8
4	Allstate Insurance Co—*Judy Greffin*	2775 Sanders Rd, Northbrook IL 60062	847-402-5000	R	262,609*	35.7
5	St Paul Fire and Marine Insurance Co	385 Washington St, Saint Paul MN 55102	651-310-7911	S	159,811*	37.0
6	Nationwide Mutual Insurance Co—*Stephen S Rasmussen*	1 Nationwide Plz, Columbus OH 43215	614-249-7111	R	148,702	32.7
7	Farmers Insurance Exchange	PO Box 2478, Los Angeles CA 90051	323-932-3200	S	134,866*	17.6
8	Allstate Corp—*Michele Coleman Mayes*	2775 Sanders Rd, Northbrook IL 60062	847-402-5000	P	130,874	35.0
9	American General Corp—*Matt Winter*	PO Box 3247, Houston TX 77253	713-522-1111	S	120,094	15.9
10	Liberty Mutual Insurance Co—*Edmund F Kelly*	175 Berkeley St, Boston MA 02116	617-357-9500	S	112,400	45.0
11	National Indemnity Co—*Donald F Wurster* Berkshire Hathaway Inc	3024 Harney St, Omaha NE 68131	402-916-3000	S	111,645	.7
12	State Farm Mutual Automobile Insurance Co—*Edward B Rust Jr*	1 State Farm Plz, Bloomington IL 61710	309-766-2311	R	106,988	68.0
13	United Services Automobile Association Inc—*Josue Robles Jr*	9800 Fredricksburg Rd, San Antonio TX 78288	210-498-2211	R	94,262	22.6
14	Loews Corp—*James S Tisch*	667 Madison Ave, New York NY 10065	212-521-2000	P	76,277	18.4
15	State Farm Fire and Casualty Co—*Gerald M Czarnecki* State Farm Mutual Automobile Insurance Co	1 State Farm Plz, Bloomington IL 61710	309-766-2311	S	72,389*	68.0
16	Hartford Steam Boiler Inspection and Insurance Co—*Douglas Elliot* HSB Group Inc	PO Box 5024, Hartford CT 06101	860-722-1866	S	64,117*	2.0
17	XL Environmental Inc—*Jacob Rosengarten*	505 Eagleview Blvd, Exton PA 19341	610-968-9500	S	57,767	N/A
18	CNA Financial Corp—*Thomas F Motamed* Loews Corp	333 S Wabash, Chicago IL 60604	312-822-5000	B	55,179	7.6
19	Chubb Corp—*John D Finnegan*	15 Mountain View Rd, Warren NJ 07059	908-903-2000	P	50,249	10.1
20	GEICO General Insurance Co Government Employees Insurance Co	1 Geico Plz, Washington DC 20076	301-986-2500	S	45,584*	4.0

Rank	Company Name—*Executive Officer*	Address, City, State, Zip	Phone	Type	Fin	Empls
21	21st Century Casualty Co—*Robert Woudstra* 21st Century Insurance Co	6301 Owensmouth Ave, Woodland Hills CA 91367	818-704-3700	S	35,189*	3.1
22	American Financial Group Inc—*Carl H Lindner III*	1 E 4th St, Cincinnati OH 45202	513-579-2121	P	32,454	5.1
23	Bitco Corp—*Greg Ator* Old Republic International Corp	320 18th St, Rock Island IL 61201	309-786-5401	S	31,500*	.5
24	Federal Insurance Co—*John D Finnegan* Chubb Corp	PO Box 1615, Plainfield NJ 07061	908-903-2000	S	30,153	N/A
25	Mercury Insurance Co—*Gabe Tirador* Mercury General Corp	PO Box 1150, Brea CA 92821	714-671-6600	S	29,021*	4.0
26	Government Employees Insurance Co—*Tony Nicely* Berkshire Hathaway Inc	1 Geico Plz, Washington DC 20076	301-986-3000	S	28,000	26.0
27	Ohio Casualty Insurance Co—*Mike Winner* Ohio Casualty Corp	9450 Seward Rd, Fairfield OH 45014	513-603-2600	S	27,183*	3.0
28	Mutual of Omaha Insurance Co—*Daniel P Neary*	Mutual of Omaha Plz, Omaha NE 68175	402-342-7600	R	26,900	6.6
29	General Re Corp—*Franklin Montross IV* Berkshire Hathaway Inc	PO Box 10351, Stamford CT 06904	203-328-5000	S	26,789*	2.5
30	Infinity Select Insurance Co—*James Gober* Infinity Insurance Co	PO Box 830693, Birmingham AL 35283	205-803-8406	S	23,060*	2.3
31	Alfa Insurance Corp—*Jerry Newby* Alfa Corp	PO Box 11000, Montgomery AL 36191	334-613-4363	S	22,634*	2.5
32	Alfa General Insurance Corp—*Jerry Newby* Alfa Corp	PO Box 11000, Montgomery AL 36191	334-288-3900	S	22,627*	2.5
33	Progressive Corp—*Glenn M Renwick*	6300 Wilson Mills Rd, Mayfield Village OH 44143	440-461-5000	P	21,150	24.6
34	Federated Service Insurance Co—*Jeffrey Fretters* Federated Mutual Insurance Co	PO Box 328, Owatonna MN 55060	507-455-5200	S	19,674*	2.6
35	Continental Casualty Co—*Thomas F Montamed* CNA Financial Corp	333 S Wabash Ave, Chicago IL 60685	312-822-5000	S	19,512	N/A
36	General Casualty—*Peter Christen* General Casualty Insurance Cos	1 General Dr, Sun Prairie WI 53596	608-837-4440	S	18,786*	1.7
37	Geico Indemnity Co—*Olza M Nicely* Government Employees Insurance Co	1 Gcico Plz, Washington DC 20076	301-986-2500	S	18,210*	2.5
38	ALLIED Group Inc—*Kurt Walker* Nationwide Mutual Insurance Co	1100 Locust St, Des Moines IA 50391	515-280-4211	S	17,765*	2.4
39	Horace Mann Lloyds—*Peter H Heckman* Horace Mann Educators Corp	1 Horace Mann Plz, Springfield IL 62715	217-789-2500	S	17,720*	2.3
40	Horace Mann Insurance Co—*Peter H Heckman* Horace Mann Educators Corp	1 Horace Mann Plz, Springfield IL 62715	217-789-2500	S	17,680*	2.3
41	WR Berkley Corp—*William R Berkley*	475 Steamboat Rd, Greenwich CT 06830	203-629-3000	P	17,529	6.3
42	SRM Insurance Brokerage LLC Selective Way Insurance Co	40 Wantage Ave, Branchville NJ 07890	973-948-3000	S	16,963*	2.2
43	Wantage Avenue Holding Company Inc Selective Insurance Group Inc	40 Wantage Ave, Branchville NJ 07890	973-948-3000	S	16,963*	2.2
44	Infinity Insurance Co Infinity Property and Casualty Corp	PO Box 830693, Birmingham AL 35283		S	16,685*	2.3
45	Infinity National Insurance Co—*James Gober* Infinity Insurance Co	PO Box 830693, Birmingham AL 35283		S	16,685*	2.3
46	Lawley Service Insurance—*William J Lawley Jr*	361 Delaware Ave, Buffalo NY 14202	716-849-8618	R	16,457*	.2
47	Old Republic International Corp—*Aldo C Zucaro*	307 N Michigan Ave, Chicago IL 60601	312-346-8100	P	15,882	8.0
48	Transatlantic Holdings Inc—*Robert F Orlich*	80 Pine St, New York NY 10005	212-365-2200	B	15,705	.6
49	CNA Insurance	333 S Wabash, Chicago IL 60604		S	15,621*	.5
50	Cincinnati Financial Corp—*Kenneth W Stecher*	PO Box 145496, Cincinnati OH 45250	513-870-2000	P	15,095	4.1
51	State Auto Mutual Insurance Co—*Robert P Restrepo Jr*	518 E Broad St, Columbus OH 43215	614-464-5000	R	14,673*	2.0
52	FM Global—*Shivan S Subramaniam*	PO Box 7500, Johnston RI 02919	401-275-3000	R	14,258	5.0
53	White Mountains Insurance Group Ltd—*Raymond Barrette*	80 S Main St, Hanover NH 03755	603-640-2200	P	14,064	1.8
54	Risk Enterprise Management Ltd—*Mike Riney*	2540 Rte130 Ste109, Cranbury NJ 08512	609-495-0001	S	13,985*	.5
55	Indiana Insurance—*Richard T Bell*	6281 Tri-Ridge Blvd, Loveland OH 45140	513-576-2300	R	13,980*	.5
56	Commerce Holdings Inc—*Arthur J Remillard Jr* Commerce Insurance Co	211 Main St, Webster MA 01570	508-943-9000	S	13,786*	1.8
57	Fireman's Fund Insurance Co—*Michael LaRocco*	777 San Marin Dr, Novato CA 94945	415-899-2000	S	13,534*	9.0
58	Zurich—*Mike Foley*	7045 College Blvd, Overland Park KS 66211	913-339-1000	S	13,417*	1.5
59	Nationwide Agribusiness Nationwide Mutual Insurance Co	1100 Locust St, Des Moines IA 50391	515-508-3300	S	13,122*	4.0
60	SAFECO Corp—*Michael Hughes*	1001 4th Ave, Seattle WA 98154	206-545-5000	S	12,640	7.1
61	Hanover Insurance Group Inc—*Frederick H Eppinger*	440 Lincoln St, Worcester MA 01653	508-855-1000	P	12,624	5.1
62	GMAC Insurance Holdings Inc—*William B Muir*	13736 River Port Dr St, Maryland Heights MO 63043	314-493-8000	S	12,465*	3.8
63	Markel Corp—*Alan I Kirshner*	4521 Highwoods Pkwy, Glen Allen VA 23060	804-747-0136	P	11,532	5.4
64	Odyssey Re Holdings Corp—*Brian D Young*	300 First Stamford Pl, Stamford CT 06902	203-977-8000	S	10,700	.7
65	Sentry Insurance Group—*Dale R Schuh*	PO Box 8022, Stevens Point WI 54481		R	10,465	3.8
66	HCC Insurance Holdings Inc—*John N Molbeck Jr*	13403 Northwest Fwy, Houston TX 77040	713-690-7300	P	9,625	1.9
67	FM Global Insurance Co—*Ruud Bosman*	PO Box 7500, Johnston RI 02919	401-275-3000	R	9,560*	5.0
68	Crum and Forster Holdings Inc—*Douglas Libby*	PO Box 1973, Morristown NJ 07962	973-490-6600	S	8,901*	1.2
69	Kemper Insurance Cos—*Doug Sean Andrews*	1 Kemper Dr, Long Grove IL 60049	847-320-2000	R	8,881*	9.0
70	Great Central Insurance Co—*William T Meisen* Argonaut Great Central Insurance Co	PO Box 807, Peoria IL 61652	309-688-8571	S	8,653*	1.1
71	Munich Reinsurance America Inc—*Anthony J Kuczinski*	PO Box 5241, Princeton NJ 08543	609-243-4200	S	8,371*	1.5
72	EMC Underwriters LLC—*Bruce Kelley*	PO Box 712, Des Moines IA 50306	515-280-2511	R	8,117*	1.1
73	Columbia Insurance Co—*Donald F Wurster* Berkshire Hathaway Inc	3024 Harney St, Omaha NE 68131	402-536-3000	S	7,637	N/A
74	Penn National Insurance—*Douglas Shutts*	PO Box 2361, Harrisburg PA 17105	717-234-4941	R	7,489*	1.0
75	Horace Mann Educators Corp—*Peter Heckman*	1 Horace Mann Plz, Springfield IL 62715	217-789-2500	P	7,484	1.4
76	Star Insurance Co—*Robert Cubbin* Meadowbrook Insurance Group Inc	26255 American Dr, Southfield MI 48034	248-358-1100	S	7,422*	.7
77	Peerless Insurance Co—*Dwight Bowie* Liberty Mutual Insurance Co	62 Maple Ave, Keene NH 03431	603-352-3221	S	7,332*	1.0
78	State Compensation Insurance Fund—*Tom Rowe*	PO Box 420807, San Francisco CA 94142	415-565-1234	R	6,831*	6.0
79	Country Mutual Insurance Co—*John Blackburn*	PO Box 2020, Bloomington IL 61702	309-821-3000	R	6,564*	2.0
80	AMEX Assurance Co	PO Box 19054, Green Bay WI 54307	920-330-5100	S	6,068*	.6
81	Transatlantic Reinsurance Co—*Robert Orloch* Transatlantic Holdings Inc	80 Pine St 7th Fl, New York NY 10005	212-770-2000	S	5,790*	.4
82	Gates McDonald and Co—*Bill Evans* Nationwide Mutual Insurance Co	PO Box 182032, Columbus OH 43218	614-854-8577	S	5,759*	.8

Note: An asterisk (*) indicates an estimated financial figure. The company type code used is as follows: R = Private, P = Public, S = Private Subsidiary, B = Public Subsidiary, D = Division, J = Joint Venture, I = Investment Fund.

COMPANY RANKINGS BY SALES WITHIN 4-DIGIT SIC

Rank	Company Name—*Executive Officer*	Address, City, State, Zip	Phone	Type	Fin	Empls
83	Selective Insurance Group Inc—*Gregory E Murphy*	40 Wantage Ave, Branchville NJ 07890	973-948-3000	P	5,736	2.0
84	Ohio Casualty Corp—*Mike Winner*	9450 Seward Rd, Fairfield OH 45014	513-603-2400	S	5,699*	2.1
85	Automobile Club of Michigan—*Charles Podowski*	1 Auto Club Dr, Dearborn MI 48126	313-336-1234	R	5,697*	3.9
86	New Jersey Manufacturers Insurance Co—*Anthony G Dickson*	301 Sullivan Way, West Trenton NJ 08628	609-883-1300	R	5,666*	1.5
87	Bituminous Casualty Corp—*Greg Ator* Bitco Corp	320 18th St, Rock Island IL 61201	309-786-5401	S	5,100*	.7
88	Bogart and Brownell of Maryland Inc—*John Seguin*	7529 Standish Pl Ste 3, Rockville MD 20855	301-444-4500	R	5,080*	<.1
89	ProAssurance Corp—*W Stancil Starnes*	100 Brookwood Pl Ste 3, Birmingham AL 35209	205-877-4400	P	4,999	.7
90	Hartford Accident and Indemnity Co—*Ramani Ayer* Hartford Financial Services Group Inc	One Hartford Plz, Hartford CT 06115	860-547-5000	S	4,956	N/A
91	Republic Underwriters Insurance Co—*Parker Rush*	5525 LBJ Fwy, Dallas TX 75240	972-788-6001	S	4,940*	.6
92	General Casualty Insurance Cos—*Pete Christen*	1 General Dr, Sun Prairie WI 53590	608-837-4440	R	4,681*	1.8
93	Progressive Casualty Insurance Co—*Glenn M Renwick* Progressive Corp	6300 Wilson Mills Rd, Mayfield Village OH 44143	440-461-5000	S	4,549*	13.9
94	Farm Family Casualty Insurance Co Farm Family Holdings Inc	PO Box 656, Albany NY 12201	518-431-5000	S	4,524*	.5
95	Great American Insurance Co—*Carl H Linder III* American Financial Group Inc	580 Walnut St, Cincinnati OH 45202	513-369-5000	S	4,429*	4.0
96	Covanta Holding Corp—*Anthony J Orlando*	59 Maiden Lane, New York NY 10038	862-345-5000	P	4,385	3.7
97	National Fire and Marine Insurance Co—*Donald Wurster* Berkshire Hathaway Inc	3024 Harney St, Omaha NE 68131	402-536-3000	S	4,259	N/A
98	Tower Group Inc—*Michael H Lee*	120 Broadway 31st Fl, New York NY 10271	212-655-2000	P	4,214	1.4
99	Amtrust Financial Services Inc—*Barry D Zyskind*	59 Maiden Ln 6th Fl, New York NY 10038	212-220-7120	P	4,183	1.4
100	Amica Mutual Insurance Co—*Robert DiMuccio*	PO Box 9128, Providence RI 02940		R	4,112	3.2
101	Mercury General Corp—*Gabriel Tirador*	4484 Wilshire Blvd, Los Angeles CA 90010	323-937-1060	P	4,070	4.5
102	Motors Insurance Corp—*Gary Kuzumi* GMAC Insurance Holdings Inc	PO Box 66937, Saint Louis MO 63166		S	3,849*	2.2
103	Argonaut Group Inc	10101 Reunion Pl Ste 5, San Antonio TX 78216	281-640-7912	S	3,722*	1.1
104	Navigators Group Inc—*Stanley A Galanski*	6 International Dr, Rye Brook NY 10573	914-934-8999	P	3,670	.5
105	Allianz Insurance Co	PO Box 1344, Minneapolis MN 55440	818-260-7500	S	3,617	.4
106	Golden Eagle Insurance Co—*Pete McPartland* Liberty Mutual Insurance Co	PO Box 85826, San Diego CA 92186	619-744-6000	S	3,610*	1.1
107	Federated Mutual Insurance Co—*Jeffrey Fetter*	PO Box 328, Owatonna MN 55060	507-455-5200	R	3,542*	2.6
108	Nationwide Mutual Fire Insurance Co Nationwide Mutual Insurance Co	One Nationwide Plz, Columbus OH 43215		S	3,367*	35.0
109	American Hardware Mutual Insurance Co—*John Bishop*	PO Box 435, Minneapolis MN 55440		R	3,344*	.5
110	Royal and SunAlliance USA—*John Tighe*	PO Box 1000, Charlotte NC 28201	704-522-2000	S	3,305*	1.5
111	Harleysville Group Inc—*Michael L Browne*	355 Maple Ave, Harleysville PA 19438	215-256-5000	P	3,278	1.7
112	Amerisure Insurance Co—*Richard Russell* Amerisure Inc	26777 Halsted Rd Ste 2, Farmington Hills MI 48331		S	3,274*	.4
113	Cincinnati Insurance Co Cincinnati Financial Corp	PO Box 145496, Cincinnati OH 45250	513-870-2000	S	3,087*	2.6
114	Lexington Insurance Co—*David J Bresnahan* National Union Fire Insurance Company of Pittsburgh Pennsylvania	100 Summer St, Boston MA 02110	617-330-1100	S	3,074*	.4
115	Hilb Rogal and Hobbs Company Pittsburgh LLC—*Martin Vaughan*	4951 Lake Brook Dr Ste, Glen Allen VA 23060	804-747-0200	S	3,056*	.4
116	Hagerty Insurance Agency—*McKeel Hagerty*	PO Box 1303, Traverse City MI 49685	231-947-6868	R	3,040*	.4
117	United Fire and Casualty Co—*Randy A Ramlo*	PO Box 73909, Cedar Rapids IA 52407	319-399-5700	P	3,007	.7
118	Commerce Insurance Co	211 Main St, Webster MA 01570	508-943-9000	S	2,970*	1.8
119	State Auto Financial Corp—*Robert P Restrepo Jr* State Auto Mutual Insurance Co	PO Box 182738, Columbus OH 43218	614-464-5000	B	2,722	2.5
120	Protective Insurance Co Baldwin and Lyons Inc	PO Box 7099, Indianapolis IN 46207	317-636-9800	S	2,672*	.4
121	Alfa Corp—*Jerry A Newby*	PO Box 11000, Montgomery AL 36191	334-288-3900	R	2,642	N/A
122	Florida Farm Bureau Insurance Cos—*John Hoblick*	PO Box 147030, Gainesville FL 32614	352-378-1321	R	2,623*	.3
123	Continental Insurance Co—*Thomas E Motamed* CNA Financial Corp	333 S Wabash, Chicago IL 60604	312-822-5000	S	2,535	24.7
124	Zenith National Insurance Corp—*Stanley R Zax*	21255 Califa St, Woodland Hills CA 91367	818-713-1000	S	2,438	1.4
125	Pacific Specialty Insurance Co	3601 Haven Ave, Menlo Park CA 94025		S	2,400*	<.1
126	Liberty Mutual Fire Insurance Co—*Edmund F Kelly*	175 Berkeley St, Boston MA 02116	617-357-9500	S	2,365	N/A
127	PMA Companies Inc—*Vincent T Donnelly* Old Republic International Corp	380 Sentry Pkwy, Blue Bell PA 19422	610-397-5298	S	2,363*	1.4
128	Baylake Insurance Agency Inc—*Thomas Herlache*	217 N 4th Ave, Sturgeon Bay WI 54235	920-743-5551	S	2,304*	.4
129	Unigard Insurance Co	PO Box 90701, Bellevue WA 98008		S	2,288*	.3
130	Arrowpoint Capital Corp—*John Tighe*	PO Box 1000, Charlotte NC 28201	704-522-2000	R	2,273*	.3
131	Merastar Insurance Co—*Timothy Bruns*	PO Box 181101, Chattanooga TN 37414	423-296-7700	S	2,267*	.2
132	Discover Re Managers Inc—*Arthur W Wright*	5 Batterson Park, Farmington CT 06032	860-674-2660	S	2,210*	.3
133	HSB Group Inc—*Anthony J Kuczinski* Munich Reinsurance America Inc	PO Box 5024, Hartford CT 06102	860-722-1866	S	2,198*	2.4
134	Meadowbrook Insurance Group Inc—*Robert S Cubbin*	26255 American Dr, Southfield MI 48034	248-358-1100	P	2,178	1.0
135	Wesco-Financial Insurance Co—*Donald F Wurster* Wesco Financial LLC	3024 Harney St, Omaha NE 68131	402-536-3000	S	2,116	N/A
136	Utica Mutual Insurance Co—*Jerry Hartman*	PO Box 530, Utica NY 13503	315-734-2000	R	2,036*	1.5
137	Mahoney Group—*Glendon D Nelson*	PO Box 15001, Casa Grande AZ 85230	520-836-7483	R	1,972*	.2
138	Farmers Alliance Mutual Insurance Co—*L Keith Birkhead*	PO Box 1401, McPherson KS 67460	620-241-2200	R	1,968*	.3
139	21st Century Insurance Co—*Bruce W Marlow*	PO Box 2000, Woodland Hills CA 91367	818-704-3700	S	1,952	2.9
140	Infinity Property and Casualty Corp—*James R Gober*	3700 Colonnade Pky, Birmingham AL 35243	205-870-4000	P	1,852	1.8
141	Philadelphia Insurance Cos—*James J Maguire Jr*	231 St Asaph's Rd Ste, Bala Cynwyd PA 19004	610-617-7900	S	1,819	.2
142	FCCI Mutual Insurance Co—*G W Jacobs*	6300 University Pkwy, Sarasota FL 34240	941-907-3224	R	1,791*	.7
143	Odyssey America Reinsurance Corp—*Brian D Young* Odyssey Re Holdings Corp	300 First Stamford Pl, Stamford CT 06902	203-977-8000	S	1,736*	.2
144	Farm Family Holdings Inc—*Timothy A Walsh*	PO Box 656, Albany NY 12201	518-431-5000	S	1,695*	.6
145	Motorists Mutual Insurance Co—*Robert Rabold*	471 E Broad St Ste 200, Columbus OH 43215	614-232-1700	R	1,672	.9
146	Erie Insurance Company of New York	PO Box 22840, Rochester NY 14623	585-214-5800	S	1,581*	.2
147	Rockhill Holding Co—*Terry Younganz*	700 W 47th St Ste 350, Kansas City MO 64112	816-412-2865	S	1,567*	.2
148	MEEMIC Holdings Inc—*Lynn M Kalinowski*	PO Box 217019, Auburn Hills MI 48321	248-373-5700	S	1,559*	.2
149	Firemen's Insurance Company of Washington DC—*Kevin Nat-trass* Berkley Insurance Co	4820 Lake Brook Dr Ste, Glen Allen VA 23060	804-285-2700	S	1,511*	.2

Rank	Company Name—*Executive Officer*	Address, City, State, Zip	Phone	Type	Fin	Empls
150	National Interstate Corp—*David W Michelson*	3250 Interstate Dr, Richfield OH 44286	330-659-8900	P	1,489	.5
151	Pacific Compensation Insurance Co—*James E Little*	PO Box 5043, Thousand Oaks CA 91359	818-575-8500	R	1,467*	.2
152	Selective Insurance Company of America—*Gregory E Murphy* Selective Insurance Group Inc	40 Wantage Ave, Branchville NJ 07826	973-948-3000	S	1,429*	2.0
153	Encore Insurance Group LLC—*Jerry Vollmer*	201 N Broadway St, Greensburg IN 47240	812-663-5151	R	1,394*	.2
154	Indiana Farmers Mutual Insurance Co—*Daniel E Stone*	PO Box 527, Indianapolis IN 46206	317-846-4211	R	1,394*	.2
155	Integon Corp—*Gary Kusumi* GMAC Insurance Holdings Inc	PO Box 3199, Winston Salem NC 27102	336-435-2000	S	1,357*	2.3
156	Michigan Millers Mutual Insurance Co—*Thomas Lindell*	PO Box 30060, Lansing MI 48909	517-482-6211	R	1,334*	.2
157	Donegal Group Inc—*Donald H Nikolaus*	PO Box 302, Marietta PA 17547	717-426-1931	P	1,291	.4
158	Georgia Casualty and Surety—*Hilton H Howell Jr*	4370 Peachtree Rd NE S, Atlanta GA 30319	404-266-5500	S	1,246*	<.1
159	Fire Insurance Exchange—*Martin Feinstein*	PO Box 2478, Los Angeles CA 90051	208-239-8400	S	1,195	N/A
160	EMC Insurance Group Inc—*Bruce G Kelley*	PO Box 712, Des Moines IA 50303	515-280-2511	B	1,188	N/A
161	Republic Indemnity Company of America—*Dwayne Marioni* Great American Insurance Co	PO Box 20036, Encino CA 91416	818-990-9860	S	1,142*	.2
162	Amerisure Mutual Insurance Co—*Richard F Russell*	26777 Halsted Rd, Farmington Hills MI 48331	248-615-9000	R	1,140*	.7
163	AMERISAFE Inc—*C Allen Bradley Jr*	2301 Hwy 190 W, DeRidder LA 70634		P	1,128	.4
164	Sequoia Insurance Co—*Rick Quaglaroli*	31 Upper Ragsdale Dr, Monterey CA 93940	831-333-9880	S	1,127*	.1
165	Safety Insurance Group Inc—*David F Brussard*	20 Custom House St, Boston MA 02110	617-951-0600	P	1,121	.6
166	Williamsburg National Insurance Co—*Meadowbrook Insurance Group Inc*	12461 E 166th St, Cerritos CA 90703	562-926-6163	S	1,114	N/A
167	American Modern Insurance Group Inc—*John W Hayden*	PO Box 5323, Cincinnati OH 45201	513-943-7200	S	1,074*	1.1
168	SeaBright Insurance Holdings Inc—*John G Pasqualetto*	1501 4th Ave Ste 2600, Seattle WA 98101	206-269-8500	P	1,027	.3
169	Foremost Insurance Co—*Steve Boshoven*	PO Box 2450, Grand Rapids MI 49501		S	988*	2.5
170	Bliss and Glennon Inc—*Corinne Jones*	435 N Pacific Coast Hw, Redondo Beach CA 90277		R	977*	.1
171	United Heartland Inc—*Stephan Cooper*	PO Box 3026, Milwaukee WI 53201	262-798-7700	R	966*	.1
172	Bristol West Insurance Group—*Bob Sadler*	PO Box 229080, Hollywood FL 33022	954-316-5200	S	945	1.2
173	Viking Insurance Co—*Joe Metz* Sentry Insurance Group	PO Box 88315, Milwaukee WI 53288	608-836-3000	S	922*	.1
174	New Hampshire Insurance Co—*Martin Sullivan* National Union Fire Insurance Company of Pittsburgh Pennsylvania	70 Pine St, New York NY 10270	212-770-7000	S	920*	1.0
175	RLI Corp—*Jonathan E Michael*	9025 N Lindbergh Dr, Peoria IL 61615	309-692-1000	P	912	.7
176	Commerce West Insurance Co Commerce Insurance Co	PO Box 8006, Pleasanton CA 94588	925-734-1700	S	877*	.1
177	Direct General Corp—*William C Adair Jr*	1281 Murfreesboro Rd, Nashville TN 37217	615-399-0600	R	851*	2.4
178	American Empire Surplus Lines Insurance Co—*Frederick J Woebse* Great American Insurance Co	580 Walnut St 10th Fl, Cincinnati OH 45202	513-369-3000	S	845*	.1
179	Baldwin and Lyons Inc—*Joseph J DeVito*	PO Box 7099, Indianapolis IN 46207		P	838	.3
180	Westfield Group—*Bob Joyce*	PO Box 5001, Westfield Center OH 44251	330-887-0101	R	819*	2.0
181	Rockwood Casualty Insurance Co—*John P Yediny* Argonaut Group Inc	654 Main St, Rockwood PA 15557	814-926-4661	S	806*	.1
182	Consolidated Insurance Co—*Greg Gennett*	9333 N Meridian St Ste, Indianapolis IN 46260	317-846-5805	R	782*	<.1
183	State Auto Property and Casualty Insurance Co State Auto Financial Corp	112 S Main St, Greer SC 29650	864-877-3311	S	771*	.1
184	Wesco Financial LLC—*Charles T Munger* Berkshire Hathaway Inc	301 E Colorado Blvd St, Pasadena CA 91101	626-585-6700	S	766	N/A
185	American Empire Insurance Co—*Frederick J Woebse* American Empire Surplus Lines Insurance Co	PO Box 5370, Cincinnati OH 45202	513-369-3000	S	765*	.1
186	Interboro Mutual Indemnity Insurance Co—*Peter Resnick*	155 Mineola Blvd, Mineola NY 11501	516-248-1100	R	762*	.1
187	Hylant of Indianapolis LLC—*Richard Hylant*	811 Madison Ave, Toledo OH 43624	419-255-1020	R	760*	.1
188	Shelter Mutual Insurance Co—*J Dave Moore*	1817 W Broadway, Columbia MO 65218	573-445-8441	R	752*	1.6
189	Affirmative Insurance Holdings Inc—*Gary Kusumi*	4450 Sojourn Dr Ste 50, Addison TX 75001	972-728-6300	P	746	1.3
190	Cotton States Mutual Insurance Co—*Ridley Howard*	PO Box 105303, Atlanta GA 30348	770-391-8600	R	739*	.3
191	Grinnell Mutual Reinsurance Co—*Steven R Crawford*	PO Box 790, Grinnell IA 50112		R	738*	.7
192	Philadelphia Contributionship Insurance Co—*Robert Whitlock Jr*	210 S 4th St, Philadelphia PA 19106	215-627-1752	R	735*	.1
193	First Insurance Company of Hawaii Ltd—*Allen Uyeda*	PO Box 2866, Honolulu HI 96803	808-527-7777	J	732*	.3
194	Insurance Company of the West—*Kevin Prior*	PO Box 85563, San Diego CA 92186	858-350-2400	R	727*	.7
195	Republic Companies Group Inc—*Parker W Rush*	5525 LBJ Fwy, Dallas TX 75240	972-788-6001	S	707*	.3
196	HRH Financial Institutions Group Inc	600 Grant St Ste 5500, Pittsburgh PA 15219	412-281-3353	S	694*	.1
197	SCOR Reinsurance Co—*Henry Klecan Jr*	199 Water St Ste 2100, New York NY 10038	212-480-1900	S	690	.1
198	RLI Insurance Co—*Jonathan E Michael* RLI Corp	9025 N Lindbergh Dr, Peoria IL 61615	309-692-1000	S	683*	.5
199	Mid-Continent Casualty Co—*Mike Coon* Great American Insurance Co	PO Box 1409, Tulsa OK 74101	918-587-7221	S	645	.3
200	Putnam Reinsurance Co—*Robert F Orlich* Transatlantic Reinsurance Co	80 Pine St 7th Fl, New York NY 10005	212-770-2000	S	625*	.3
201	Atlantic Mutual Insurance Co—*Klaus G Dorfi*	100 Wall St, New York NY 10005	212-943-1800	R	610*	1.8
202	Mercer Insurance Group Inc—*Andrew R Speaker* United Fire and Casualty Co	PO Box 278, Pennington NJ 08534		B	604	.2
203	Church Mutual Insurance Co—*Mike Ravn*	PO Box 357, Merrill WI 54452	715-536-5577	R	579*	.8
204	ProAssurance Casualty Co	PO Box 150, Okemos MI 48805	517-349-6500	S	544*	.1
205	Admiral Insurance Co—*Scott Baraclough* WR Berkley Corp	PO Box 5725, Cherry Hill NJ 08034	856-429-9200	S	539*	.1
206	Mt Hawley Insurance Co—*Jonathan E Michael* RLI Insurance Co	9025 N Lindbergh Dr, Peoria IL 61615	309-692-1000	S	498*	.8
207	National Grange Mutual Insurance Co—*Tom Van Berkel*	55 West St, Keene NH 03431	603-352-4000	R	491*	1.0
208	Zenith Insurance Co Zenith National Insurance Corp	21255 Califa St, Woodland Hills CA 91367	818-713-1000	S	482*	1.1
209	Stifel Nicolaus Insurance Agency Inc—*Scott McCauig*	501 N Broadway, Saint Louis MO 63102	314-342-2000	S	471*	<.1
210	Unitrin Specialty Lines Insurance—*John Mullen*	PO Box 10360, Van Nuys CA 91410	818-313-8500	S	462*	.8
211	Hamilton Insurance Agency—*Alan Zuccari*	4100 Monument Corner D, Fairfax VA 22030	703-359-8100	R	460*	.1
212	State Automobile Insurance Co—*Robert Restrepo Jr* State Auto Financial Corp	518 E Broad St, Columbus OH 43215	614-464-5000	S	455*	1.2
213	Specialty Underwriters Alliance Inc—*Courtney C Smith* Tower Group Inc	222 S Riverside Pl, Chicago IL 60606	312-277-1600	S	455	.1
214	Travelers Indemnity Co (Hartford Connecticut)	1 Tower Sq, Hartford CT 06183	860-277-0111	S	452	N/A

Note: An asterisk (*) indicates an estimated financial figure. The company type code used is as follows: R = Private, P = Public, S = Private Subsidiary, B = Public Subsidiary, D = Division, J = Joint Venture, I = Investment Fund.

COMPANY RANKINGS BY SALES WITHIN 4-DIGIT SIC

Rank	Company Name—*Executive Officer*	Address, City, State, Zip	Phone	Type	Fin	Empls
215	United Automobile Insurance Co—*Richard Parrillo*	PO Box 694140, Miami FL 33269	305-932-7096	R	444*	.2
216	Clements International—*Jon B Clements*	1 Thomas Cir 8th Fl, Washington DC 20005	202-872-0060	R	436*	.1
217	Glencoe US Holdings Ltd—*David A Heatherly*	5801 Tennyson Pkwy Ste, Plano TX 75024	972-664-7000	S	426*	.1
218	National Liability and Fire Insurance Co—*Donald F Wurster* Berkshire Hathaway Inc	3024 Harney St, Omaha NE 68131	402-536-3000	S	410	N/A
219	State Auto Insurance Co State Auto Financial Corp	6993 Pearl Rd, Middleburg Heights OH 44130	440-842-6200	S	385*	.1
220	NOVA Casualty Co—*Marita Zuraitis* NOVA American Group Inc	726 Exchange St Ste 10, Buffalo NY 14210	716-856-3722	S	384*	.1
221	Ranger Insurance Co—*Marc Adee*	PO Box 2807, Houston TX 77252	713-954-8100	S	381	.3
222	SAIF Corp—*Brenda Rocklin*	400 High St SE, Salem OR 97312	971-242-5001	R	378*	.8
223	Amerisure Inc—*Richard F Russell* Amerisure Mutual Insurance Co	26777 Halsted Rd, Farmington Hills MI 48331	248-615-9000	S	375*	.3
224	Selective Way Insurance Co Selective Insurance Group Inc	40 Wantage Ave, Branchville NJ 07826	973-948-3000	S	374*	.8
225	State Farm General Insurance Co—*Jairon L Wills* State Farm Mutual Automobile Insurance Co	1 State Farm Plz, Bloomington IL 61701	309-766-2311	S	374*	.1
226	American National Property and Casualty Co—*Gregory V Ostergren*	1949 E Sunshine St, Springfield MO 65804	417-887-0220	S	369*	.6
227	Seibels Bruce and Co—*Michael Culbertson* Seibels Bruce Group Inc	PO Box 1, Columbia SC 29202	803-748-2000	S	369*	.2
228	AOPA Insurance Agency Inc—*Brenda Jennings*	PO Box 9170, Wichita KS 67277	316-942-2223	D	368*	.1
229	Cumbre Inc—*Ruben Medina*	3333 Concours Ste 5100, Ontario CA 91764	909-484-2456	R	368*	.1
230	USI Insurance Services LLC—*Michael J Sigard*	470 Park Avenue South, New York NY 10016	212-689-7200	S	354*	3.2
231	First Mercury Financial Corp—*Richard H Smith*	29110 Inkster Rd Ste 1, Southfield MI 48034	248-358-4010	R	344	.4
232	Hallmark Insurance Co—*Mark Morrison*	777 Main St Ste 1000, Fort Worth TX 76102	817-348-1600	R	329*	.1
233	Berkley Insurance Co—*William Berkley* WR Berkley Corp	475 Steamboat Rd, Greenwich CT 06830	203-542-3800	S	326*	.1
234	Federated National Insurance Co—*Mike Braun*	3661 W Oakland Park Bl, Lauderdale Lakes FL 33311	954-581-9993	S	326*	.1
235	Mendota Insurance Co—*David L Pickard*	PO Box 64586, Saint Paul MN 55164		R	323*	<.1
236	Eastern Insurance Holdings Inc—*Michael L Boguski*	25 Race Ave, Lancaster PA 17603		P	323	.2
237	Preferred Employers Group Inc—*Mel Harris*	10800 Biscayne Blvd 10, Miami FL 33161		S	317*	<.1
238	Central Mutual Insurance Co—*FW Purmort*	PO Box 351, Van Wert OH 45891	419-238-1010	R	315*	.5
239	Farmers Casualty Insurance Co State Auto Financial Corp	1300 Woodland Ave, West Des Moines IA 50265	515-223-9488	S	308*	<.1
240	Pennsylvania Manufacturers' Association Insurance Co—*Frederick W Anton III*	225 State St, Harrisburg PA 17101	717-232-0737	S	304	.9
241	First Acceptance Corp—*Stephen J Harrison*	3813 Green Hills Villa, Nashville TN 37215	615-327-4888	P	296	1.0
242	NOVA American Group Inc—*Stephen Mulready*	180 Oak St, Buffalo NY 14203	716-856-3722	R	296*	.1
243	Continental Western Insurance Co—*Bradley Kuster* Berkley Insurance Co	PO Box 1594, Des Moines IA 50322	515-473-3000	S	292*	.3
244	Granada Insurance Co—*Juan Diaz Padron*	4075 SW 83rd Ave, Miami FL 33155	305-554-0353	R	291*	<.1
245	Twin City Fire Insurance Co—*David Zwiener*	PO Box 14209, Lexington KY 40512	860-547-5000	S	289	7.0
246	Northland Insurance Cos—*Randall Dean Jones*	PO Box 64816, Saint Paul MN 55164		S	288*	.6
247	Columbia Casualty Co—*Thomas F Motamed* CNA Financial Corp	333 S Wabash, Chicago IL 60604	312-822-5000	S	288*	<.1
248	Atlantic States Insurance Co Donegal Group Inc	1195 River Rd, Marietta PA 17547	717-426-1931	S	288	.4
249	Florida Family Insurance Services LLC—*Rick Hardy*	PO Box 136001, Bonita Springs FL 34136	239-495-4700	R	285*	<.1
250	Acceptance Insurance Companies Inc—*John E Martin*	300 W Broadway Ste 160, Council Bluffs IA 51503	712-329-3600	P	279	<.1
251	Arch Reinsurance (USA) Co—*Timothy J Olson*	PO Box 1988, Morristown NJ 07962	973-898-9575	S	279*	<.1
252	Navigators Insurance Co Navigators Group Inc	6 International Dr, Rye Brook NY 10573	914-934-8999	S	278*	.1
253	Safe Auto Insurance Group Inc—*Ari Deshe*	4 Easton Oval, Columbus OH 43213	614-231-0200	R	274*	1.0
254	Hastings Mutual Insurance Co—*William H Wallace*	404 E Woodlawn Ave, Hastings MI 49058	269-945-3405	R	273*	.4
255	AXA Art Insurance Corp—*Christiane Fischer-Harling*	3 W 35th St, New York NY 10001	212-415-8400	S	271*	<.1
256	Carolina Casualty Insurance Co—*Douglas J Powers* WR Berkley Corp	PO Box 2575, Jacksonville FL 32203	904-363-0900	S	264*	.2
257	Gateway Insurance Comp—*Daniel J Boxell*	1401 S Brentwood Blvd, Saint Louis MO 63144	314-373-3333	R	259*	<.1
258	Leucadia Properties Inc—*Joseph S Steinberg*	315 Park Ave S, New York NY 10010	212-460-1900	S	254*	<.1
259	Ohio Indemnity Co—*John Sokol* Bancinsurance Corp	250 E Broad St 10th Fl, Columbus OH 43215	614-228-2800	S	250*	<.1
260	GAINSCO Inc—*Glenn W Anderson*	PO Box 199023, Dallas TX 75219	972-629-4301	P	242	.4
261	White Mountains Holdings Inc—*Raymond Barette* White Mountains Insurance Group Ltd	80 S Main St, Hanover NH 03755	603-640-2200	S	240*	.4
262	Merchants Insurance Company of New Hampshire Inc—*Robert M Zak* Merchants Group Inc	250 Main St, Buffalo NY 14202	716-849-3333	S	236*	.3
263	PICOM Claims Services Corp—*W Stancil Starnes* ProAssurance Casualty Co	2600 Professionals Dr, Okemos MI 48864	517-349-6500	S	233*	<.1
264	Willis HRH Upstate New York—*Joseph J Plumeri*	344 Delaware Ave, Buffalo NY 14202	716-856-1100	S	232*	<.1
265	Merchants Group Inc—*Robert Vak*	250 Main St, Buffalo NY 14202	716-849-3333	R	231*	.3
266	Harleysville Insurance Company of New Jersey—*John Iannello* Harleysville Group Inc	112 W Park Dr, Mount Laurel NJ 08054	856-642-9779	S	230*	2.0
267	Nautilus Insurance Co—*Tom Kuzma* Admiral Insurance Co	7233 E Butherus Dr, Scottsdale AZ 85260	480-951-0905	S	224*	.1
268	Willis HRH Illinois—*Joseph J Plumeri*	2200 52nd Ave, Moline IL 61265	309-764-9666	S	218*	<.1
269	Canal Insurance Co—*Charles M Timmons Jr*	PO Box 7, Greenville SC 29602	864-242-5365	R	214*	.3
270	National Indemnity Company of Mid-America—*Donald F Wurster* Berkshire Hathaway Inc	3024 Harney St, Omaha NE 68131	402-536-3000	S	214	N/A
271	NI Acquisition Corp—*Thomas F Motamed*	333 S Wabash Ave, Chicago IL 60685	312-822-5000	S	205*	<.1
272	Transcontinental Insurance Co—*Thomas F Motamed* CNA Financial Corp	333 S Wabash, Chicago IL 60685	312-822-5000	S	205*	<.1
273	EG Bowman Company Inc—*Harry Ennevol*	97 Wall St, New York NY 10005	212-425-8150	R	193*	<.1
274	American Country Insurance Co—*Roger Beck*	150 NW Point Blvd Ste, Elk Grove Village IL 60007	847-472-6700	S	192*	.2
275	Valley Forge Life Insurance Co—*Thomas F Motamed* CNA Financial Corp	100 CNA Blvd, Nashville TN 37214	615-886-3300	S	192*	<.1
276	Allianz of America Inc—*Jan Carendi*	PO Box 5160, Westport CT 06881	203-221-8500	S	189*	<.1

Rank	Company Name—*Executive Officer*	Address, City, State, Zip	Phone	Type	Fin	Empls
277	Galloway-Chandler McKinney Insurance Agency Inc—*Jimmy Galloway*	PO Box 9670, Columbus MS 39705	662-328-0492	R	185*	<.1
278	Allied Specialty Insurance Inc—*Rick D Aprile*	10451 Gulf Blvd, Treasure Island FL 33706	727-367-6900	R	182*	.1
279	American Fire and Casualty Co—*Terrence Bachr*	9450 Seward Rd, Fairfield OH 45014	513-843-6446	R	176*	N/A
280	Bituminous Fire and Marine Insurance Co—*Dan Noe* Bitco Corp	320 18th St, Rock Island IL 61201	309-788-9361	S	175*	<.1
281	White Mountains Capital Inc—*Reid Campbell*	265 Franklin St Ste 50, Boston MA 02110	617-725-7122	R	170*	5.1
282	ISU Insurance Services of Colorado Inc—*Pamela Adams*	950 17th St Ste 1000, Denver CO 80202	303-534-2133	S	170*	<.1
283	Rhode Island Joint Reinsurance Assoc—*John Golembeski*	2 Ctr Plz, Boston MA 02108	617-723-3800	R	163*	.1
284	Kramer-Wilson Company Inc—*Kevin Wilson*	PO Box 3999, North Hollywood CA 91609	818-760-0880	R	162*	.4
285	North Carolina Insurance Underwriting Association—*Dewey Meshaw*	PO Box 8009, Cary NC 27512	919-821-1299	R	162*	.1
286	Bancinsurance Corp—*John S Sokol*	250 E Broad St 7th Fl, Columbus OH 43215	614-220-5200	R	161	<.1
287	Munich-American Holding Corp—*John Phelan*	PO Box 5241, Princeton NJ 08543	609-243-4200	R	159*	3.9
288	International Financial Group Inc—*Robert Linton*	238 International Rd, Burlington NC 27215	336-586-2500	R	158*	.3
289	Workers Compensation Fund—*Ray Pickup*	PO Box 57929, Salt Lake City UT 84157	385-351-8000	R	155*	.4
290	Monterey Insurance Co	401 Fremont St Ste 100, Monterey CA 93940	831-373-4925	S	154*	<.1
291	Stateco Financial Services Inc—*Robert P Restrepo* State Auto Financial Corp	518 E Broad St, Columbus OH 43215	614-464-5000	S	154*	<.1
292	Seibels Bruce Group Inc—*Michael Culbertson*	PO Box 1, Columbia SC 29201	803-748-2000	R	152*	.3
293	Columbia Insurance Group Inc—*Robert J Wagner*	PO Box 618, Columbia MO 65205	573-474-6193	R	145*	.3
294	Farmland Mutual Insurance Company Inc—*Kim Austen*	1100 Locust St, Des Moines IA 50391	515-508-3300	R	144*	.2
295	California Capital Insurance Co—*Peter M Cazzolla*	PO Box 3110, Monterey CA 93942	831-233-5500	S	144	.3
296	Argonaut Great Central Insurance Co—*William Meisen* Argonaut Group Inc	PO Box 807, Peoria IL 61652	309-688-8571	S	144*	.1
297	Penn Independent Corp—*Matt Scott*	3 Bala Plz E Ste 300, Bala Cynwyd PA 19004		D	144*	.1
298	Louisiana Workers' Compensation Corp—*Kristen Wall*	2237 S Acadian Thruway, Baton Rouge LA 70808	225-924-7788	R	143*	.3
299	North Star Mutual Insurance Company Inc—*Jeffrey Mauland*	269 Barstad Rd S, Cottonwood MN 56229	507-423-6262	R	143*	.2
300	Union Standard Insurance Co—*Craig Sparks* Berkley Insurance Co	PO Box 152180, Irving TX 75015	972-719-2400	S	141*	.2
301	Homeowners Choice Inc—*Paresh Patel*	5300 W Cypress St Ste, Tampa FL 33607	813-405-3600	P	141	.1
302	Houston Casualty Co—*John Molbeck* HCC Insurance Holdings Inc	13403 Northwest Fwy, Houston TX 77040	713-462-1000	S	140*	.2
303	United Property and Casualty Insurance Co—*Don Cronin*	PO Box 1011, Saint Petersburg FL 33731	727-895-7737	R	140*	<.1
304	Blue Chip Stamps—*Jeff Jacobson* Berkshire Hathaway Inc	PO Box 831, Pasadena CA 91102	626-585-6714	S	137*	<.1
305	Hilltop Holdings Inc—*Jeremy B Ford*	PO Box 1330, Dallas TX 75201	214-855-2177	P	132	.1
306	AssuranceAmerica Corp—*Guy W Millner*	PO Box 723128, Atlanta GA 31139		P	128	.3
307	Indiana Lumbermens Mutual Insurance Co—*John F Wolf*	PO Box 68600, Indianapolis IN 46268	317-875-3600	R	123*	.1
308	Penn-America Insurance Co—*Larry Frakes*	3 Bala Plz, Bala Cynwyd PA 19004	610-664-1500	S	119*	.1
309	Professional Practice Insurance Brokers Inc—*Joseph J Plumeri*	100 Marine Parkway Ste, Redwood City CA 94065	650-369-5900	S	115*	<.1
310	Colonial Claims Corp—*Doug Branham*	2200 Bayshore Blvd, Dunedin FL 34698	727-738-1366	R	114*	<.1
311	Preserver Group Inc—*Patrick J HaveronGilbert* Tower Group Inc	PO Box 931, Paramus NJ 07653	201-291-2000	S	113*	.1
312	Occidental Fire and Casualty Company of North Carolina—*Sephen L Stephano*	PO Box 10800, Raleigh NC 27605	919-833-1600	R	112*	.2
313	Lincoln General Insurance Co—*Scott Wollney*	PO Box 3709, York PA 17402	717-757-0000	S	111*	.1
314	Navigators Insurance Services of Texas Inc—*John Jones* Navigators Group Inc	2121 Sage Ste 145, Houston TX 77056	713-629-5480	S	110*	<.1
315	E Kinker and Co—*Samuel W Tuten*	7750 Montgomery Rd, Cincinnati OH 45236	513-891-6615	R	109*	<.1
316	Odyssey Reinsurance Corp—*Brian Young*	17 State St 29 FL, New York NY 10004	212-978-2700	S	107	N/A
317	TITAN Insurance Co—*David Arango* Nationwide Mutual Insurance Co	901 Wilshire Dr Ste 55, Troy MI 48084	248-244-9770	S	101*	.2
318	Access Group Inc—*Tammy Simmons*	2830 Dresden Dr, Atlanta GA 30341	770-234-3600	R	100*	.2
319	AVEMCO Insurance Co—*Jim Lauerman* HCC Insurance Holdings Inc	411 Aviation Way Ste 1, Frederick MD 21701	301-694-5700	S	100	.1
320	National Union Fire Insurance Company of Pittsburgh Pennsylvania—*Robin Betza*	625 Liberty Ave, Pittsburgh PA 15222	412-288-2160	S	98*	<.1
321	Weaver Brothers Insurance Associates Inc—*Robert Moltz*	7315 Wisconsin Ave Ste, Bethesda MD 20814	301-986-4400	R	98*	<.1
322	ME Wilson Company Inc—*Doug Wilson*	300 W Platt St, Tampa FL 33606	813-229-8021	R	96*	<.1
323	AAA Auto Club South—*Thomas O'Brien*	1515 N Westshore Blvd, Tampa FL 33607	813-289-5000	R	90*	3.0
324	National Indemnity Company of the South—*Donald F Wurster* Berkshire Hathaway Inc	3024 Harney St, Omaha NE 68131	402-536-3000	S	90	N/A
325	Berg-Berry Associates Inc—*Kenneth Berry*	1127 Fehl lane, Cincinnati OH 45230	513-221-7711	R	87*	<.1
326	Union Insurance Co Berkley Insurance Co	PO Box 80439, Lincoln NE 68501	402-423-7688	S	86	.2
327	IMT Insurance Company Mutual—*Richard Keith*	PO Box 1336, Des Moines IA 50305	515-327-2777	R	84*	.2
328	Mutual Assurance Agency of Ohio Inc—*W Stancil Starnes*	100 Brookwood Pl Ste 3, Birmingham AL 35209	205-877-4400	S	84*	<.1
329	Victoria Financial Corp—*Kathy Mabe* Nationwide Mutual Insurance Co	5915 Landerbrook Dr St, Cleveland OH 44124	440-461-3461	S	83	.2
330	Rural Mutual Insurance Cos—*Peter Pelizza*	PO Box 5555, Madison WI 53705	608-836-5525	R	80	.2
331	Allied Insurance—*W G Jurgensen* ALLIED Group Inc	1100 Locust St, Des Moines IA 50391		S	74	N/A
332	Gramercy Insurance Co—*Joan Hammer*	3109 Crossing Park Rd, Norcross GA 30071		R	73*	<.1
333	Navigators Insurance Services of Washington Inc—*Stanley Galanski* Navigators Group Inc	2101 4th Ave Ste 910, Seattle WA 98121	206-728-2315	S	73*	<.1
334	Allianz Underwriters Insurance Co—*Wolfgang Schlink* Allianz of America Inc	PO Box 7780, Burbank CA 91505	818-260-7500	S	70*	.4
335	American Indemnity Financial Corp—*J Fellman Seinsheimer III* United Fire and Casualty Co	PO Box 1259, Galveston TX 77553	409-766-4600	S	69	.2
336	Armed Forces Insurance Exhange—*Thomas Dials*	PO Box G, Fort Leavenworth KS 66027	913-727-5500	R	67*'	.2
337	Illinois Farmers Insurance Co—*Clinton Gardner*	2245 Sequoia Dr, Aurora IL 60506	630-907-0030	S	66*	.5
338	Hortica Insurance and Employee Benefits—*Mona Haberer*	PO Box 428, Edwardsville IL 62025	618-656-4240	R	66*	.2
339	Motor Club of America Insurance Co—*Stephen A Gilbert* Preserver Group Inc	95 S State Rte 17 Ste, Paramus NJ 07652	201-291-2100	S	63*	.1
340	Fidelity National Insurance Co (Omaha Nebraska)—*Steve Jensen* Mutual of Omaha Insurance Co	3316 Farnam St, Omaha NE 68175	402 342 3326	S	62*	.1
341	Utica First Insurance Co—*Richard J Zick*	PO Box 851, Utica NY 13503	315-736-8211	R	62*	.1

Note: An asterisk (*) indicates an estimated financial figure. The company type code used is as follows: R = Private, P = Public, S = Private Subsidiary, B = Public Subsidiary, D = Division, J = Joint Venture, I = Investment Fund.

COMPANY RANKINGS BY SALES WITHIN 4-DIGIT SIC

Rank	Company Name—*Executive Officer*	Address, City, State, Zip	Phone	Type	Fin	Empls
342	Frederick Mutual Insurance Co—*Kevin R Filler*	57 Thomas Johnson Dr, Frederick MD 21702	301-663-9522	R	62*	<.1
343	American Physicians Service Group Inc—*Kenneth S Shifrin* ProAssurance Corp	1301 S Capital of Texa, Austin TX 78746	512-328-0888	S	62	N/A
344	Clark-Prout Insurance Agency Inc—*Arthur J Remillard Jr* Commerce Insurance Co	400 S Main St, Webster MA 01570	508-943-0058	S	58*	<.1
345	Preserver Insurance Co—*Michael Lee* Preserver Group Inc	PO Box 931, Paramus NJ 07653	201-291-2000	S	55*	.1
346	First Metro Insurance Agency—*Tim D'Angelo*	1810 Barataria Blvd, Marrero LA 70072	504-348-3131	R	53*	<.1
347	Seneca Insurance Inc—*Gary Dubois*	160 Water St 16th Fl, New York NY 10038	212-344-3000	R	50*	.1
348	Jacobs Company Inc—*Frank Jacobs*	7164 Columbia Gateway, Columbia MD 21046	410-995-6611	R	50*	<.1
349	Unifax Insurance Systems Inc—*Cary Cheldin*	23251 Mulholland Dr, Woodland Hills CA 91364	818-591-9800	S	48	.1
350	Commonwealth Mutual Insurance Company of America—*Thomas J Calleri*	3450 Ellicott Center D, Ellicott City MD 21043	410-889-2500	R	46*	<.1
351	Cumberland Technologies Inc—*Joseph M Williams*	4311 W Waters Ave Ste, Tampa FL 33614	813-885-2112	R	41*	<.1
352	Grain Dealers Mutual Insurance Co—*Donald L Malcom*	PO Box 1747, Indianapolis IN 46206	317-388-4500	R	39*	.1
353	Harleysville Insurance Company of New York—*Dennis Otmaskin* Harleysville Group Inc	215 Washington St Ste, Watertown NY 13601	315-782-1160	S	36*	.1
354	Columbia Lloyds Insurance Co—*Bob Sullivan*	PO Box 540307, Houston TX 77254	713-528-6686	R	36*	<.1
355	Kingsway Amigo Insurance Co—*Roberto Espin*	3155 NW 77th Ave, Doral FL 33122	305-716-6000	S	30*	<.1
356	Motor Ways Inc—*Patrick J Storey*	PO Box 42308, Urbandale IA 50322	515-266-1113	R	24*	<.1
357	Crowe Paradis Services Corp—*Ken Paradis*	400 Riverpark Dr Ste 4, North Reading MA 01864		R	21*	.1
358	Burns and Wilcox of San Francisco—*Alan Jay Kaufman*	100 Pine St 23rd Fl, San Francisco CA 94111	415-421-4244	S	15*	<.1
359	Capitol County Mutual Fire Insurance Co—*Mike Rassder*	PO Box 428, Converse TX 78109	210-658-6393	R	15*	<.1
360	Eagle West Insurance Co—*Peter M Cazzolla* California Capital Insurance Co	2300 Garden Rd, Monterey CA 93940	831-233-5500	S	14	<.1
361	Mariemont Insurance Co—*Clifford M Clemons*	5725 Dragon Way, Cincinnati OH 45227	513-271-4060	R	13*	<.1
362	Hodge Hart and Schleifer Inc—*David Hodge*	8401 Connecticut Ave S, Chevy Chase MD 20815	240-644-6000	R	9*	<.1
363	Marysville Mutual Insurance Co—*Trent Moser*	PO Box 151, Marysville KS 66508	785-562-2379	R	7*	<.1
364	Great Northwest Insurance Company Inc—*Stephen Doucette*	1161 W River St Ste 31, Boise ID 83702	208-336-7851	R	7*	<.1
365	Inner-City Underwriting Agency Inc—*Matthew H Cooper*	1631 S Michigan Ste 1, Chicago IL 60616	312-341-9080	R	6*	<.1
366	Ohio Security Insurance Co Ohio Casualty Corp	9450 Seward Rd, Fairfield OH 45014	513-867-3000	S	4	N/A
367	Fulmont Mutual Insurance Co—*Marlene A Benton*	PO Box 487, Johnstown NY 12095	518-762-3171	R	3*	<.1
368	Kansas Mutual Insurance Co—*R Dan Scott*	PO Box 1247, Topeka KS 66601	785-354-8452	R	3*	<.1
369	Direct Insurance Co—*Charlotte Maroon* Direct General Corp	1128 Murfreesboro Rd S, Nashville TN 37217	615-361-4507	S	3	<.1
370	Changemyratecom—*Jackie Graves*	4320 Atlantic Ave, Long Beach CA 90807	562-988-7700	R	2	<.1
371	Teachers Insurance Co—*Peter H Heckman* Horace Mann Educators Corp	1 Horace Mann Plz, Springfield IL 62701	217-789-2500	S	<1	1.7
372	Swiss Re Underwriters—*Judy Mann*	26050 Mureau Rd, Calabasas CA 91302	818-878-9500	S	N/A	.1
373	GHS Property and Casualty Insurance Co—*Russell Angell*	PO Box 60545, Oklahoma City OK 73146	405-841-9555	S	N/A	<.1

TOTALS: SIC 6331 Fire, Marine & Casualty Insurance
Companies: 373   5,680,211   1,406.0

6351 Surety Insurance

Rank	Company Name—*Executive Officer*	Address, City, State, Zip	Phone	Type	Fin	Empls
1	MBIA Inc—*Jay Brown*	113 King St, Armonk NY 10504	914-273-4545	P	32,279	.4
2	AMBAC Financial Group Inc—*David W Wallis*	1 State St Plz, New York NY 10004	212-668-0340	P	29,047	.2
3	Assured Guaranty—*Dominic J Frederico*	31 W 52nd St, New York NY 10019	212-826-0100	S	26,117*	.4
4	MBIA Insurance Corp MBIA Inc	113 King St, Armonk NY 10504	914-273-4545	S	16,467*	.7
5	Financial Security Assurance Inc—*Robert P Cochran* Assured Guaranty	31 W 52nd St, New York NY 10019	212-826-0100	S	11,600	.2
6	American Skandia Life Assurance Corp	1 Corporate Dr, Shelton CT 06484	203-926-1888	S	8,802*	.8
7	Mortgage Guaranty Insurance Corp—*Curt S Culver* MGIC Investment Corp	PO Box 488, Milwaukee WI 53201	414-347-6480	S	7,879*	1.2
8	Radian Group Inc—*SA Ibrahim*	1601 Market St, Philadelphia PA 19103	215-231-1000	P	6,657	.7
9	Mortgage Guaranty Investment Corp—*Curt Culver*	PO Box 488, Milwaukee WI 53201	414-347-6480	R	6,488*	.7
10	PMI Group Inc—*L Stephen Smith*	3003 Oak Rd, Walnut Creek CA 94597	925-658-7878	P	4,219	.7
11	Financial Guaranty Insurance Co—*John S Dubel*	125 Park Ave, New York NY 10017	212-312-3000	S	4,164*	.2
12	Amwest Surety Insurance Co—*John E Savage*	8300 N Hayden Rd Ste A, Scottsdale AZ 85258	480-367-6925	R	3,438*	.5
13	Pennsylvania Manufacturers Indemnity Co—*Vincent T Donnelly*	PO Box 3031, Blue Bell PA 19422	610-397-5000	S	2,356*	.4
14	Penn-America Group Inc—*Joseph F Morris*	3 Bala Plz East Ste 30, Bala Cynwyd PA 19004	610-664-1500	S	2,207*	.6
15	Home Buyers Warranty Corp—*Scott Cronney*	3587 Parkway Ln, Norcross GA 30092	770-496-4970	R	1,889*	.4
16	CNA Surety Corp—*John F Welch*	333 S Wabash Ave 41st, Chicago IL 60604		S	1,838	.7
17	Assured Guaranty Corp—*Robert Bailenson*	31 W 52nd St, New York NY 10019	212-974-0100	S	1,688*	.1
18	MGIC Investment Corp—*Curt S Culver*	PO Box 488, Milwaukee WI 53201		P	1,504	.9
19	Physicians' Reciprocal Insurers—*Anthony Bonomo*	1800 Northern Blvd, Roslyn NY 11576	516-365-6690	R	1,245*	.3
20	Roanoke Companies Inc—*Bond Clerk*	1475 E Woodfield Rd St, Schaumburg IL 60173		R	1,122*	.2
21	Professionals Advocate Insurance Co—*Jeffrey M Poole* Medical Mutual Liability Insurance Society of Maryland	225 International Cir, Hunt Valley MD 21030	410-785-0050	S	1,017*	.1
22	Triad Guaranty Inc—*Kenneth W Jones*	101 S Stratford Rd, Winston Salem NC 27104	336-723-1282	P	992	.1
23	Medical Mutual Liability Insurance Society of Maryland—*Jeffrey M Poole*	PO Box 8016, Cockeysville MD 21030	410-785-0050	R	977*	.1
24	Darwin Professional Underwriters Inc—*W Gordon Knight*	9 Farm Springs Rd, Farmington CT 06032	860-284-1300	S	827	.2
25	American Physicians Assurance Corp	PO Box 1471, East Lansing MI 48826	517-351-1150	S	750*	.3
26	PMI Mortgage Insurance Co—*L Stephen Smith* PMI Group Inc	3003 Oak Rd, Walnut Creek CA 94597		S	670	.7
27	United Guaranty Residential Insurance Co—*William Nutt Jr*	PO Box 21567, Greensboro NC 27420	336-373-0232	S	602*	.4
28	Lamberson Koster and Co—*Doug Bowring*	580 California St Ste, San Francisco CA 94104	415-391-1500	S	462*	.1
29	Victor O Schinnerer and Company Inc—*John F Shettle Jr*	Two Wisconsin Cir, Chevy Chase MD 20815	301-961-9800	S	442*	.3
30	Old Kent Mortgage Services Inc—*Kevin T Kabat*	38 Fountain Sq Plz, Cincinnati OH 45263	513-579-5300	S	421*	.1
31	Manufacturers Alliance Insurance Co—*Vincent T Donnelly*	PO Box 3031, Blue Bell PA 19422	610-397-5298	S	329*	.4
32	CMG Mortgage Insurance Co—*Kiimberly Shaul*	22 4th St Fl 13, San Francisco CA 94103	415-284-2500	J	326*	<.1
33	Medical Assurance—*Victor Adamo*	PO Box 590009, Birmingham AL 35259	205-877-4400	S	322	N/A
34	Triad Guaranty Insurance Corp Triad Guaranty Inc	101 S Stratford Rd, Winston Salem NC 27104	336-723-1282	S	274*	.2
35	JW Terrill Inc—*Andy Thome*	825 Maryville Centre D, Chesterfield MO 63017	314-594-2700	R	254*	.2
36	Crusader Insurance Co	23251 Mulholland Dr, Woodland Hills CA 91364	818-591-9800	S	203*	.1
37	Freberg Environmental Inc—*Michael J Hill*	1451 Larimer St Ste 20, Denver CO 80202	303-534-1171	R	185*	<.1

Rank	Company Name—*Executive Officer*	Address, City, State, Zip	Phone	Type	Fin	Empls
38	USI Affinity—*Douglas Kreitzberg*	120 Broadway Ste 11C, New York NY 10005	917-551-8500	S	184*	.1
39	RVI Services Company Inc—*Douglas May* RVI Guaranty Company Ltd	177 Broad St 9th Fl, Stamford CT 06901	203-975-2100	S	180	<.1
40	EULER American Credit Indemnity—*Paul Overeem*	800 Red Brook Blvd, Owings Mills MD 21117		S	167*	.4
41	Kindred Operating Incorporated Benefit Trust	680 S 4th St, Louisville KY 40202	502-596-7300	R	163*	<.1
42	First American Home Buyers Protection Corp—*Martin Wool*	PO Box 267, Santa Ana CA 92702	818-781-5050	R	161*	.8
43	International Fidelity Insurance Co—*Francis Mitterhoff*	1 Newark Ctr Fl 20, Newark NJ 07102	973-624-7200	R	143*	.2
44	RVI Guaranty Company Ltd—*Douglas May*	177 Broad St, Stamford CT 06901	203-975-2100	S	112	N/A
45	ERJ Insurance Group Inc—*Tony Wanderon*	PO Box 660960, Miami Springs FL 33266	305-885-4216	S	108*	<.1
46	ACMAT Corp—*Henry W Nozko Jr*	PO Box 2350, New Britain CT 06050	860-229-9000	P	102	<.1
47	First Southeast Insurance Services Inc	2430 Mall Dr Ste 280, Charleston SC 29406	843-529-5470	S	86*	<.1
48	Property and Casualty Insurance Guaranty Corp—*Joseph Petr*	305 Washington Ave Ste, Baltimore MD 21204	410-296-1820	R	71*	<.1
49	Exstar Financial Corp—*Steve Shinn*	PO Box 678, Solvang CA 93463	805-688-4995	R	57*	<.1
50	Savers Property and Casualty Insurance Co	11880 College Blvd Ste, Overland Park KS 66210	913-339-5000	S	55*	.1
51	Wilshire Insurance Co—*Stephen L Stephano*	PO Box 10800, Raleigh NC 27605	919-833-1600	R	51*	<.1
52	Safe Passage International LLC—*Jon Gerlach*	3609 S Wadsworth Blvd, Lakewood CO 80214	303-988-9626	R	49*	<.1
53	Surety Group Inc—*Sam H Newberry*	1900 Emery St NW Ste 1, Atlanta GA 30318	404-352-8211	R	41*	<.1
54	Texas Lawyers Insurance Exchange—*John Randolph*	900 Congress Ste 500, Austin TX 78701	512-480-9074	R	38*	<.1
55	JP Everhart and Co—*Doug Burkert*	1840 N Greenville Ave, Richardson TX 75081	972-808-9001	R	8*	.1
56	Acstar Holdings Inc ACMAT Corp	PO Box 2350, New Britain CT 06051	860-224-2000	S	7*	<.1
57	Acstar Insurance Co—*Henry W Nozko Jr* Acstar Holdings Inc	233 Main St, New Britain CT 06051	860-224-2000	S	7*	<.1

TOTALS: SIC 6351 Surety Insurance

Companies: 57					**181,849**	**15.4**

6361 Title Insurance

Rank	Company Name—*Executive Officer*	Address, City, State, Zip	Phone	Type	Fin	Empls
1	Fidelity National Financial Inc—*George Scanlon*	601 Riverside Ave, Jacksonville FL 32204		P	7,888	18.2
2	Alleghany Corp—*Weston M Hicks*	7 Times Square Twr, New York NY 10036	212-752-1356	P	6,478	.8
3	Fidelity National Title Insurance Co—*Don DuBois* Fidelity National Financial Inc	1300 Dove St Ste 300, Newport Beach CA 92660	949-250-0473	S	5,520*	6.0
4	Lawyers Title Insurance Corp Fidelity National Financial Inc	601 Riverside Ave, Jacksonville FL 32204		S	3,471*	3.8
5	First American Financial Corp—*Dennis J Gilmore*	1 First American Way, Santa Ana CA 92707	714-250-3000	P	3,110	5.5
6	First American Title Insurance Co—*Parker Kennedy* First American Financial Corp	PO Box 267, Santa Ana CA 92702	714-250-3000	S	2,063	14.3
7	Stewart Title Company of Houston—*Stewart Morris Jr* Stewart Information Services Corp	1980 Post Oak Blvd Ste, Houston TX 77056	713-625-8100	S	1,174*	6.3
8	Stewart Information Services Corp—*Matt Morris*	PO Box 2029, Houston TX 77252	713-625-8100	P	1,141	5.7
9	Stewart Title Guaranty Co—*Michael B Skalka* Stewart Information Services Corp	1980 Post Oak Blvd Ste, Houston TX 77056	713-625-8100	S	1,082	4.8
10	Attorneys Title Insurance Fund Inc—*G Thomas Smith*	6545 Corporate Centre, Orlando FL 32822		R	966*	.7
11	Investors Title Accommodation Corp—*Carol Hayden* Investors Title Co	PO Box 2687, Chapel Hill NC 27514	919-968-2200	S	409*	.3
12	Investors Title management Services Inc Investors Title Co	PO Box 2687, Chapel Hill NC 27514	919-968-2200	S	409*	.3
13	First American Title Insurance Agency Incorporated Utah—*Brenden Faber* First American Title Insurance Co	1 First American Way, Santa Ana CA 92707	714-250-3000	S	345*	.3
14	Ticor Title Insurance Co	493 State Rd 436 Ste 1, Casselberry FL 32707	407-831-3455	S	297*	.4
15	Monroe Title Insurance Corp—*Thomas Podsiadlo* Stewart Title Company of Houston	47 W Main St, Rochester NY 14614	585-232-2070	S	275*	.2
16	Old Republic Title Insurance Group Inc—*Rande K Yeagar*	400 2nd Ave S, Minneapolis MN 55401	612-371-1111	S	271*	.3
17	Attorney's Title Guaranty Fund Inc—*Peter J Birnbaum*	2102 Windsor Pl, Champaign Il 61820	217-359-2000	R	210*	.2
18	Stewart Title Company of California Inc—*Salley Leimbach* Stewart Title Guaranty Co	7676 Hazard Center Dr, San Diego CA 92108	619-692-1600	S	208*	.2
19	Old Republic Title Co—*R Wayne Shupe* Old Republic Title Insurance Group Inc	275 Battery St Ste 150, San Francisco CA 94111	510-465-0500	S	190*	1.2
20	Investors Title Co—*J Allen Fine*	PO Drawer 2687, Chapel Hill NC 27515	919-968-2200	P	154	.2
21	Fidelity National Title Insurance Company of Dallas County—*Darryl Tyson* Fidelity National Title Insurance Co	600 E John Carpenter F, Irving TX 75062	972-550-8666	S	139*	.2
22	Baton Rouge Title Company Inc—*Mark Schoen*	10500 Coursey Blvd, Baton Rouge LA 70816	225-291-1111	S	108*	.1
23	Spokane County Title Insurance Co—*John Schreiner*	1010 N Normandie St St, Spokane WA 99201	509-326-2626	R	93*	.1
24	Fidelity National Title Insurance Company of New York—*Patrick F Stone* Fidelity National Title Insurance Co	1 Park Ave Ste 1402, New York NY 10016	212-481-5858	S	80*	.1
25	Rattikin Title Co—*Jack Rattikin III*	201 Main St Ste 800, Fort Worth TX 76102	817-332-1171	R	73*	.1
26	Old Republic National Title Insurance Co Old Republic Title Insurance Group Inc	400 2nd Ave S, Minneapolis MN 55401	612-371-1111	S	69*	.3
27	North America Title Co—*Bill Bond*	PO Box 1130, Waukegan IL 60079	847-249-4041	S	56*	.2
28	Inter-County title Company of El Dorado—*Tom Chandler*	596 Main St, Placerville CA 95667	530-622-3135	R	19*	<.1
29	Transunion Title Insurance Co—*William L Exeter*	4250 Executive Sq Ste, La Jolla CA 92037	858-658-8908	S	18	.3
30	Security Union Title Insurance Co	601 Riverside Ave, Saint Augustine FL 32092	904-854-5000	S	14*	<.1
31	Lawyers Title of Arizona Inc Lawyers Title Insurance Corp	3131 E Camelback Rd St, Phoenix AZ 85016	602-257-2600	S	13*	.2
32	First American Title Insurance Company of Oregon—*Dennis J Gilmore* First American Title Insurance Co	1 First American Way, Santa Ana CA 92707	714-800-3000	S	12*	.2
33	Land Title Services Inc—*Harvey Pollack*	7700 W Bluemound Rd, Wauwatosa WI 53213	414-259-5060	R	12*	<.1
34	Prominent Title Insurance Agency Inc—*Karina Pol*	827 Cypress Pkwy, Kissimmee FL 34759	407-343-1560	S	12*	<.1
35	AmeriPoint Title Inc—*Jack Rogers*	10101 Reunion Pl Ste 2, San Antonio TX 78216	210-340-2921	R	12*	<.1
36	Bay Title and Abstract Inc—*John May*	345 S Monroe Ave, Green Bay WI 54301	920-431-6100	R	11*	.1
37	Investors Title Co (Glendale California)—*Chris White*	700 N Brand Blvd Rm 11, Glendale CA 91203	818-476-4000	R	11*	.1
38	Fidelity National Title Company of Washington Inc—*Chet Hodgson* Fidelity National Title Insurance Co	3500 188th St SW Ste 3, Lynnwood WA 98037	425-771-3031	S	10*	.1
39	Old Republic Title Company of Conroe—*Gary Griffith* Old Republic National Title Insurance Co	PO Box 2119, Conroe TX 77305	936-441-3121	S	6*	<.1

Note: An asterisk (*) indicates an estimated financial figure. The company type code used is as follows: R = Private, P = Public, S = Private Subsidiary, B = Public Subsidiary, D = Division, J = Joint Venture, I = Investment Fund.

COMPANY RANKINGS BY SALES WITHIN 4-DIGIT SIC

Rank	Company Name—*Executive Officer*	Address, City, State, Zip	Phone	Type	Fin	Empls
40	Neshaminy Abstract Co—*John Croke*	22 S Main St, Doylestown PA 18901	215-348-1848	R	6*	<.1
41	Investors Title Insurance Co (Columbia South Carolina)—Investors Title Co	PO Box 4900, Columbia SC 29240	803-799-8650	S	2*	<.1

TOTALS: SIC 6361 Title Insurance
Companies: 41 — 36,436 — 71.4

6371 Pension, Health & Welfare Funds

Rank	Company Name—*Executive Officer*	Address, City, State, Zip	Phone	Type	Fin	Empls
1	AIG American General—*Mary Jane B Fortin*	PO Box 4373, Houston TX 77210	713-522-1111	S	276,268*	11.3
2	Pioneer America Income Trust Fund—*Kenneth Taubes*	60 State St, Boston MA 02109	617-742-7825	I	104,675*	2.3
3	Kentucky Employees Retirement System—*Robert Burnside*	1260 Louisville Rd, Frankfort KY 40601	502-696-8800	R	15,474	N/A
4	Integrity Life Insurance Co—*John Lindholm*	PO Box 5720, Cincinnati OH 45201	502-582-7900	R	9,900*	.3
5	Public Employees' Retirement System of Mississippi—*Pat Robertson*	429 Mississippi St, Jackson MS 39201	601-359-3589	R	5,940*	.1
6	Firemen's Annuity Benefit Fund of Chicago—*Kenneth Kaczmarz*	20 S Clarke St Ste 140, Chicago IL 60603	312-726-5823	R	1,237	N/A
7	Placemark Investments Inc—*Lee Chertavian*	16633 Dallas Pky Ste 7, Addison TX 75001	972-404-8100	R	1,124*	.1
8	Epic Advisors Inc—*James M Genthner*	150 State St Ste 200, Rochester NY 14614		S	867*	<.1
9	Orange County Employees Retirement System—*Steve Delaney*	2223 E Wellington Ave, Santa Ana CA 92701	714-558-6200	R	452*	<.1
10	Freedom Health Inc—*Kiran Patel*	PO Box 151137, Tampa FL 33684		R	396*	.5
11	Wyoming Retirement System—*Thomas Williams*	6101 Yellowstone Rd St, Cheyenne WY 82009	307-777-7691	R	360*	<.1
12	Stage Hands Local 2 Retirement Plan—*Daniel K Kerins*	216 S Jefferson St Ste, Chicago IL 60661	312-705-2020	R	228*	<.1
13	Allied Partners Inc—*Eric Hadar*	770 Lexington Ave 17th, New York NY 10021	212-935-4900	R	109*	<.1
14	Welfare and Pension Administration Service Inc—*Mike Parmelee*	PO Box 34203, Seattle WA 98124	206-441-7574	R	16*	.2
15	Healthcare Strategies Inc—*Janice Albert*	9841 Broken Land Pkwy, Columbia MD 21046	410-423-9400	R	16*	.1
16	Next Generation Enrollment Inc—*Bradley Taylor*	PO Box 527, Ada MI 49301		R	3	<.1

TOTALS: SIC 6371 Pension, Health & Welfare Funds
Companies: 16 — 417,065 — 15.0

6399 Insurance Carriers Nec

Rank	Company Name—*Executive Officer*	Address, City, State, Zip	Phone	Type	Fin	Empls
1	Federal Deposit Insurance Corp—*Sheila Bair*	550 17th St NW, Washington DC 20429	202-898-6993	R	31,286*	7.3
2	Assurant Solutions—*Craig Lemasters*	260 Interstate N Cir S, Atlanta GA 30339	770-763-1000	S	10,868*	2.0
3	American Fidelity Group—*William Cameron*	PO Box 25523, Oklahoma City OK 73125	405-523-2000	R	6,685*	2.2
4	Allied Solutions LLC—*Chris Hilger*	1320 City Ctr Dr, Carmel IN 46032	317-706-7600	R	3,428*	.8
5	Automobile Protection Corp—*Larry Dorfman*	6010 Atlantic Blvd, Norcross GA 30071		R	2,218*	.5
6	FirstComp Insurance Co—*Luke Yeransian*	PO Box 3009, Omaha NE 68103	402-926-0099	R	930*	.6
7	CNA National Warranty Corp—*Joan Saunders*	PO Box 2840, Scottsdale AZ 85252	480-941-1626	S	846*	.2
8	Hallmark Financial Services Inc—*Mark J Morrison*	777 Main St Ste 1000, Fort Worth TX 76102	817-348-1600	P	737	.4
9	Doctors Co—*Richard E Anderson*	185 Greenwood Rd, Napa CA 94558		R	673*	.1
10	Albert G Ruben and Company Inc—*Gregory C Case*	15303 Ventura Blvd Ste, Sherman Oaks CA 91403	818-742-1400	S	616*	.2
11	Mutual Insurance Company of Arizona—*James F Carland*	PO Box 33180, Phoenix AZ 85067	602-956-5276	R	590*	.1
12	Wallace Welch and Willingham Inc—*Scott Gramling*	300 1st Ave S 5th Fl, Saint Petersburg FL 33701	727-522-7777	R	390*	.1
13	Medical Liability Mutual Insurance Co—*Robert A Menotti*	2 Park Ave Rm 2500, New York NY 10016	212-576-9800	R	388*	.1
14	Pioneer Mutual Life Insurance Co—*Dayton Molendrop*	101 N 10th St, Fargo ND 58102	701-297-5700	S	297*	.1
15	Risk Services Corp—*Chris Sternberg*	2002 Papa John's Blvd, Louisville KY 40299	502-261-7272	S	241*	.1
16	Standard Casualty Co—*Larry Keener*	100 Northwoods Dr, New Braunfels TX 78132	830-629-6111	S	227*	<.1
17	Standard Insurance Agency Inc—*Larry Keener*	100 Northwoods Dr, New Braunfels TX 78132		S	227*	<.1
18	First Harrison Financial Services Inc—*Samuel Uhl*	220 Federal Dr NW, Corydon IN 47112	812-738-2198	R	215*	<.1
19	Delos Insurance Group—*William Davis*	120 W 45th St 36th Fl, New York NY 10036	212-702-3700	S	187*	<.1
20	Insurance Exchange Inc—*Joseph E Brown*	9713 Key West Ave Ste, Rockville MD 20850	301-279-5500	R	138*	<.1
21	NationsBuilders Insurance Services	2859 Paces Ferry Rd, Atlanta GA 30339	770-257-1121	R	96*	.1
22	Veterinary Pet Insurance Co—*Dennis P Drent*	PO Box 2344, Brea CA 92822	714-989-0555	R	85*	.1
23	Kansas Bankers Surety Co—*Don Towle*	PO Box 1654, Topeka KS 66601	785-228-0000	S	58*	<.1
24	American Feed Industry Insurance Co—*Dan Carlisle*	4685 Merle Hay Rd Ste, Des Moines IA 50322	515-254-0400	R	32*	<.1
25	Safeware Inc (Columbus Ohio)—*Mark Gannaway*—Assurant Solutions	6500 Busch Blvd Ste 23, Columbus OH 43229	614-781-1492	S	31*	<.1
26	New South Agency Inc—*Robert M Couch*	1900 Crestwood Blvd, Birmingham AL 35210	205-951-1052	S	20*	<.1
27	Frontier Adjusters of America Inc—*John M Davies*	7100 E Pleasant Valley, Independence OH 44131	216-674-0645	R	13*	<.1
28	Preferred Warranties Inc—*Wayne Herring*	PO Box 278, Orwigsburg PA 17961	570-366-1146	R	8*	.1
29	Ensurity Group LLC—*Modesto Flores*	1001 N Hampton Blvd, Desoto TX 75115		R	4*	<.1
30	Kirk Horse Insurance Inc—*Ronald K Kirk*	129 Walton Ave, Lexington KY 40508	859-231-0838	R	3*	<.1
31	Elite Marketing Group—*Thomas Archer*	800 Bering Dr Ste 105, Houston TX 77057	713-507-1000	R	2*	<.1

TOTALS: SIC 6399 Insurance Carriers Nec
Companies: 31 — 61,539 — 15.0

6411 Insurance Agents, Brokers & Service

Rank	Company Name—*Executive Officer*	Address, City, State, Zip	Phone	Type	Fin	Empls
1	Group Health Cooperative of South Central Wisconsin—*Larry Zanoni*	PO Box 44971, Madison WI 53744	608-828-4853	R	147,335	.7
2	Hub Internationall Midwest Ltd—*Martin P Hughes*—Hub International Ltd	55 E Jackson Blvd, Chicago IL 60604	312-922-5000	S	58,904*	3.2
3	Aon Group Inc—*Gregory C Case*	200 E Randolph St, Chicago IL 60601	312-381-1000	S	43,716*	36.0
4	Marsh Inc—*Peter Zaffino*—Marsh and McLennan Companies Inc	1166 Ave of the Americ, New York NY 10036	212-345-6000	S	28,125*	25.0
5	Aon Risk Services Companies Inc—*Richard A Riley*	200 E Randolph St, Chicago IL 60601	312-381-1000	S	18,214*	15.0
6	Auto-Owners Insurance Co—*Jeffrey F Harrold*	PO Box 30660, Lansing MI 48909	517-323-1200	R	12,831	41.1
7	Marsh and McLennan Companies Inc—*Brian Duperreault*	PO Box 4974, New York NY 10185	212-345-5000	P	10,550	51.0
8	CNA—*Thomas F Motamed*	333 S Wabash Ave, Chicago IL 60604	312-822-5000	S	10,000*	10.0
9	Insurance Services Office Inc—*Frank Coyne*	545 Washington Blvd, Jersey City NJ 07310	201-469-2000	R	9,131*	3.5
10	AXA Equitable Life Insurance Co—*Henri de Castries*	1290 Avenue of the Ame, New York NY 10104	212-554-1234	S	8,558*	5.8
11	Flagship Group Inc (Norfolk Virginia)—*Richard Freebourn Jr*—Brown and Brown Inc	500 E Main St Ste 600, Norfolk VA 23510	757-625-0938	S	5,759*	4.0
12	Catalyst Health Solutions Inc—*David T Blair*	800 King Farm Blvd, Rockville MD 20850	301-548-2900	P	5,330	1.4
13	SXC Health Solutions Corp—*Mark Thierer*	2441 Warrenville Rd St, Lisle IL 60532	630-577-3100	P	4,976	1.4
14	Erie Indemnity Co—*Terrence W Cavanaugh*	PO Box 13002, Erie PA 16514	814-870-2000	P	4,890	4.2
15	Broadspire LLC—*Ken Martino*—Crawford and Co	1001 Summit Blvd, Atlanta GA 30319		S	3,517*	2.5
16	ING Institutional Plan Services—*Philip Lussier*	1 Heritage Dr, North Quincy MA 02171		S	2,982*	2.5
17	CoreSource Inc—*Nancy Eckrich*	400 N Field Dr, Lake Forest IL 60045	847-604-9200	R	2,746*	1.6

Rank	Company Name—*Executive Officer*	Address, City, State, Zip	Phone	Type	Fin	Empls
18	Bankers Life and Casualty Co—*Scott Perry*	600 W Chicago Ave, Chicago IL 60654	312-396-6000	S	2,532*	1.5
19	Acadia Insurance Co—*Douglas M Nelson*	PO Box 9010, Westbrook ME 04098	207-772-4300	S	2,482*	.4
20	Arthur J Gallagher and Co—*J Patrick Gallagher Jr*	2 Pierce Pl, Itasca IL 60143	630-773-3800	P	2,135	12.4
21	Great Western Life Insurance Co—*Mitchell T Graye*	PO Box 1700, Denver CO 80201	303-737-3000	R	2,028*	3.1
22	General Casualty Cos—*Peter Christen*	1 General Dr, Sun Prairie WI 53596	608-837-4440	D	1,816*	1.3
23	Trustmark Mutual Holding Co—*David M McDonough*	400 Field Dr, Lake Forest IL 60045	847-615-1500	R	1,700*	3.5
24	National Electronics Warranty Corp—*Tony Nader*	PO Box 1340, Sterling VA 20167	703-318-7700	R	1,660*	3.0
25	McGraw Group Of Affiliated Cos—*Michael McGraw*	3601 Haven Ave, Menlo Park CA 94025	650-780-4800	R	1,490*	.1
26	Grange Mutual Casualty Co—*Thomas H Welch*	PO Box 1218, Columbus OH 43216		R	1,300*	2.0
27	American Safety Insurance Holdings Ltd—*Stephen R Crim*	100 Galleria Pky Ste 7, Atlanta GA 30339	770-916-1908	P	1,221	.2
28	Interline Insurance Services Inc	12461 E 166th St, Cerritos CA 90703	562-926-5061	S	1,212*	.7
29	Crawford and Co—*Jeffrey T Bowman*	PO Box 5047, Atlanta GA 30302	404-300-1000	P	1,211	8.7
30	Harrington Services Corp—*Jay Anliker*	675 Brooksedge Blvd, Westerville OH 43081	614-212-7000	S	1,165*	.9
31	Eagan Insurance Agency Inc—*Marc F Eagan Jr*	2629 N Causeway Blvd, Metairie LA 70002	504-836-9600	R	1,002*	.1
32	Citizens Inc—*Harold E Riley*	400 E Anderson Ln, Austin TX 78752	512-837-7100	P	987	.3
33	Brown and Brown Inc—*J Powell Brown*	PO Box 2412, Daytona Beach FL 32114	386-252-9601	P	973	5.3
34	Newport Group—*Peter S Cahall*	300 International Pkwy, Heathrow FL 32746	407-333-2905	R	863*	.5
35	Lockton Cos—*John T Lumelleau*	444 W 47 St Ste 900, Kansas City MO 64112	816-960-9000	R	836	4.1
36	Aon Services Group Inc—*Michael D Rice* Aon Group Inc	200 E Randolph, Chicago IL 60601	312-381-1000	S	801*	.6
37	Willis of Virginia Inc	PO Box 1220, Glen Allen VA 23060		S	800	4.2
38	Flagship Maritime Adjusters Inc—*Richard Freebourn Jr* Flagship Group Inc (Norfolk Virginia)	500 E Main St Ste 600, Norfolk VA 23510	757-625-0938	S	786	4.0
39	Arthur J Gallagher and Company of Mississippi Inc—*Jim Gault* Arthur J Gallagher and Co	PO Box 16447, Jackson MS 39236	601-956-5810	S	735*	<.1
40	Horace Mann Service Corp—*Louis G Lower*	1 Horace Mann Plz, Springfield IL 62701	217-789-2500	S	714*	2.5
41	Wells Fargo Insurance Services of California—*Kevin Kenney*	45 Freemont Ste 800, San Francisco CA 94105	415-541-7900	S	704*	9.6
42	Crump Group Inc—*John Howard*	105 Eisenhower Pky, Roseland NJ 07068		R	574*	.4
43	Alamo Title Holding Co—*Larry King*	10010 San Pedro Ste 70, San Antonio TX 78216	210-340-0456	R	561*	1.1
44	I lub International Ltd—*Martin P Hughes*	55 E Jackson Blvd 14A, Chicago IL 60604	312-922-5000	S	544	3.8
45	USI Holdings Corp—*Michael J Sicard*	555 Pleasantville Rd S, Briarcliff Manor NY 10510	914-749-8500	S	530*	2.9
46	Guy Carpenter and Company Inc—*Alex Moczarski* Marsh and McLennan Companies Inc	1166 Ave of the Americ, New York NY 10036	917-937-3000	S	502	1.5
47	Near North Insurance Brokerage Inc	875 N Michigan Ave Ste, Chicago IL 60611	312-280-5600	R	469*	.4
48	Merriwether and Williams Insurance Service Inc—*Ingrid Merri-wether*	550 Montgomery St Ste, San Francisco CA 94111	415-986-3999	R	462*	<.1
49	Unigard Insurance Group—*Peter Christen*	PO Box 90701, Bellevue WA 98009	425-641-4321	D	453*	.4
50	Wells Fargo Insurance Services—*Neal Aton*	150 N Michigan Ave Ste, Chicago IL 60601	312-423-2500	S	437*	4.5
51	Alamo Title Co—*Don Walker* Alamo Title Holding Co	10010 San Pedro Ave St, San Antonio TX 78216	210-340-0456	S	429*	.3
52	Baylake Capital Trust I—*Thomas Herlache*	217 N 4th Ave, Sturgeon Bay WI 54235	920-743-5551	S	425*	.4
53	AmeriServ Life Insurance Co	PO Box 520, Johnstown PA 15901	814-533-5300	B	416*	.3
54	Insurance Counsellors of Bryn Mawr Inc	801 Lancaster Ave, Bryn Mawr PA 19010	610-525-1700	S	394*	.3
55	AXA Distributors LLC—*Andrew McMahon*	1290 Ave of the Americ, New York NY 10104	212-314-2968	S	384*	.2
56	Horton Group—*Glen Horton*	10320 Orland Pksy, Orland Park IL 60467	708-845-3000	R	375*	.3
57	Wells Fargo Insurance Services of North Carolina—*Steve Smith* Wells Fargo Insurance Services	PO Box 411, Chapel Hill NC 27516	336-223-0073	S	347	N/A
58	Burns and Wilcox Ltd—*Alan Kaufman* HW Kaufman Financial Group Inc	30833 Northwestern Hwy, Farmington MI 48334	248-932-9000	S	340*	.7
59	Berkely Group—*Claire Rosenzweig*	PO Box 9022, Jericho NY 11753		R	306*	.3
60	Superior Adjusting Inc—*Brian Turnau*	3661 W Oakland Park Bl, Lauderdale Lakes FL 33311	954-581-9893	R	302*	.2
61	Lovitt and Touche Inc—*Charles A Touche*	PO Box 32702, Tucson AZ 85751	520-722-3000	R	287*	.2
62	CorVel Corp—*Daniel J Starck*	2010 Main St Ste 600, Irvine CA 92614	949-851-1473	P	275	3.0
63	Creative Financial Group—*Dominic Nappi Jr*	16 Campus Blvd Ste 200, Newtown Square PA 19073	610-325-6100	R	234*	.2
64	GENEX Services Inc—*Peter C Madeja*	440 E Swedesford Rd St, Wayne PA 19087	610-964-5100	S	233*	2.0
65	World Access Service Corp—*Jonathan M Ansell*	2805 N Parham Rd Ste 1, Richmond VA 23294	804-285-3300	R	230*	.5
66	Wells Fargo Insurance Services Southeast Inc—*Tom Longhta* Wells Fargo Insurance Services	2502 N Rocky Point Dr, Tampa FL 33607		S	226*	.2
67	Parker Smith and Feek Inc—*Greg Collins*	2233 112th Ave NE, Bellevue WA 98004	425-709-3600	R	225*	.2
68	Seitlin and Co—*Thomas M Cornish*	9800 NW 41st Ste 300, Miami FL 33178	305-591-0090	R	224*	.2
69	Norcal Mutual Insurance Co—*Scott Diener*	560 Davis St Ste 200, San Francisco CA 94111	415-397-9700	R	222*	.2
70	AON Re Inc—*Michael G Bungert* Aon Re Worldwide Inc	200 E Randolph, Chicago IL 60601	312-381-1000	S	218*	.4
71	International Medical Group Inc—*Joe Brougher*	2960 N Meridian St, Indianapolis IN 46208	317-655-4500	R	214*	.2
72	Fortegra Financial Corp—*Richard S Kahlbaugh*	10151 Deerwood Park Bl, Jacksonville FL 32256	904-416-1539	P	204	.5
73	Travel Insurance Services—*Kevin O'Neal* USI Holdings Corp	2950 Camino Diablo Ste, Walnut Creek CA 94596	925-932-1387	S	203*	.1
74	HCC Underwriters—*Frank J Bramanti*	13403 Northwest Fwy, Houston TX 77040	713-690-7300	S	200*	.2
75	Aon Re Worldwide Inc—*Michael Bungert* Aon Group Inc	200 E Randolph St16th, Chicago IL 60601	312-381-0171	S	197*	.4
76	eHealth Inc—*Gary Lauer*	440 E Middlefield Rd, Mountain View CA 94043		P	187	.6
77	Seabury and Smith Inc—*Michael Cherkasky* Marsh and McLennan Companies Inc	1255 23rd Street NW St, Washington DC 20037	202-367-5035	S	180*	1.5
78	CL Frates and Co—*Rodman Frates*	PO Box 26967, Oklahoma City OK 73126	405-290-5600	R	180*	.2
79	First Acceptance Insurance Company Inc—*James Dickson*	PO Box 23410, Nashville TN 37202	615-327-4888	R	180*	.3
80	Holmes Murphy and Associates Inc—*James S Swift*	3001 Westown Pkwy, West Des Moines IA 50266	515-223-6800	R	179*	.3
81	NIP Group Inc—*Richard Augustyn*	PO Box 39, Woodbridge NJ 07095		R	173*	.1
82	Tml Intergovernmental Risk Pool—*Marvin Townsend*	PO Box 149194, Austin TX 78714	512-491-2300	R	171*	.2
83	INAMAR Insurance Underwriting Agency Inc	55 Haddonfield Rd, Cherry Hill NJ 08002	856-755-6000	S	170*	.2
84	American Safety Casualty Insurance Co—*Stephen R Crim* American Safety Insurance Holdings Ltd	100 Galleria Pky Ste 7, Atlanta GA 30339	770-916-1908	S	169*	.1
85	American Safety Indemnity Co—*Stephen R Crim* American Safety Insurance Holdings Ltd	100 Galleria Pkwy Ste, Atlanta GA 30339	770-916-1908	S	169*	.1
86	American Safety Insurance Services Inc—*Stephen R Crim* American Safety Insurance Holdings Ltd	100 Galleria Pkwy Ste, Atlanta GA 30339	770-916-1908	S	169*	.1
87	Nationwide Insurance Company Of Florida—*David Meyer*	2 Nationwide Plz, Columbus OH 43215	614-249-7111	R	166*	N/A
88	Warranty Direct Inc—*Chester Luby*	333 Earle Ovington Blv, Uniondale NY 11553		S	165*	.1
89	Neace Lukens—*John Neace*	2305 River Rd, Louisville KY 40206	502-894-2100	S	165*	.1
90	Seashore Insurance And Associates Inc—*W Mills*	827 Gum Branch Rd, Jacksonville NC 28540	910-455-7576	R	165*	.1

Note: An asterisk (*) indicates an estimated financial figure. The company type code used is as follows: R = Private, P = Public, S = Private Subsidiary, B = Public Subsidiary, D = Division, J = Joint Venture, I = Investment Fund.

COMPANY RANKINGS BY SALES WITHIN 4-DIGIT SIC

Rank	Company Name—*Executive Officer*	Address, City, State, Zip	Phone	Type	Fin	Empls
91	Laborers-Employers Benefit Plan Collection Trust	905 16th St Nw, Washington DC 20006	202-393-7344	R	164*	<.1
92	SAFECO Financial Institution Solutions Inc—*Paula Reynolds*	2677 N Main St Ste 600, Santa Ana CA 92705	714-571-3900	S	162*	.1
93	Riggs Counselman Micheals and Downes Inc—*Albert R Counselman*	555 Fairmount Ave, Baltimore MD 21286	410-339-7263	R	161*	.3
94	Trident Insurance Services LLC—*Hilbert Schenck*	PO Box 460729, San Antonio TX 78246	210-342-8808	S	159*	.1
95	Shps Holdings Inc—*Rishabh Mehrotra*	9200 Shelbyville Rd St, Louisville KY 40222	502-267-4900	R	156*	2.0
96	Hartford Insurance Company Of Illinois—*David Zwiener*	690 Asylum Ave, Hartford CT 06115	860-547-5000	R	155*	5.0
97	Sedgwick Claims Management Services Inc—*David North*	PO Box 171865, Memphis TN 38187	901-415-7400	R	154*	4.3
98	ARAG Group—*David Murray*	400 Locust St Ste 480, Des Moines IA 50309	515-246-1200	R	152*	.1
99	Cei Group Inc—*Wayne Smolda* Csi Holdings Inc	4850 E St Rd Ste 200, Feasterville Trevose PA 19053	215-364-5600	S	151*	.2
100	Ups Capital Trade Protection Services Inc—*Mike Tobin*	35 Glenlake Pkwy Ne, Atlanta GA 30328	404-828-8385	R	150*	.1
101	Christian Brothers Employee Benefit Trust	1205 Windham Pkwy, Romeoville IL 60446	630-378-2900	R	150*	<.1
102	North Star General Insurance Co—*Jeff Mauland*	269 Barstad Rd S, Cottonwood MN 56229	507-423-6262	R	147*	.1
103	New Jersey Property Liability Insurance Guaranty Association—*Holly Bakke*	222 Mount Airy Rd, Basking Ridge NJ 07920	908-953-9533	R	146*	<.1
104	Crouse And Associates Insurance Brokers Inc—*William Crouse*	100 Pine St Ste 2500, San Francisco CA 94111	415-982-3870	R	145*	<.1
105	Employee Welfare Benefit Plans Trust Of Fpl Group	700 Universe Blvd, Juno Beach FL 33408	561-691-2254	R	144*	<.1
106	Stephen Chelbay Co—*Robert J Bradley*	1120 S Bascom Ave, San Jose CA 95128		R	143*	.1
107	American Wholesale Insurance Group Inc—*M Steven DeCarlo*	4725 Piedmont Row Dr S, Charlotte NC 28210	704-749-2700	R	142	.9
108	Capital Partners—*Brian D Fitzgerald*	8 Greenwich Office Pk, Greenwich CT 06831	203-625-0770	R	142*	1.4
109	Hbw Insurance Services LLC—*Sam Kitty*	4501 Circ 75 Pkwy Sef6, Atlanta GA 30339	678-742-6300	R	142*	.1
110	Fluor Employee Benefit Trust	6700 Las Colinas Blvd, Irving TX 75039	469-398-7000	R	140*	<.1
111	Triple-S Propiedad Inc—*Eva Salgado*	PO Box 70313, San Juan PR 00936	787-749-4600	R	140*	.2
112	Aon Risk Services Incorporated of Florida—*Gregory Case* Aon Risk Services Companies Inc	1001 Brickell Bay Dr S, Miami FL 33131	305-372-9950	S	135*	.1
113	American Independence Corp—*Roy TK Thung*	485 Madison Ave, New York NY 10022	212-355-4141	P	133	.1
114	American Country Underwriting Agency Inc	150 NW Point Blvd Ste, Elk Grove Village IL 60007	847-700-8200	S	131*	.1
115	PSA Professional Liability Inc—*Craig English*	11311 McCormick Rd, Hunt Valley MD 21031	410-821-7766	S	130*	.1
116	PULIC Insurance Services Inc—*Stephen D Freedman*	1888 Century Park East, Los Angeles CA 90067	310-571-0730	S	127	N/A
117	Bank of Hawaii Insurance Services Inc—*Allan Landon*	130 Merchant St Ste 19, Honolulu HI 96813	808-538-4599	R	127*	.1
118	Arthur J Gallagher and Company of Oklahoma Inc—*Wally Bryce* Arthur J Gallagher and Co	PO Box 3142, Tulsa OK 74101	918-584-1433	S	127*	.1
119	Gallagher Bassett Services Inc—*Peter Durkalski* Arthur J Gallagher and Co	2 Pierce Pl, Itasca IL 60143	630-773-3800	S	126	1.3
120	GNW-Evergreen Insurance Services LLC—*Andrew Forchelli*	16030 Ventura Blvd Ste, Encino CA 91436	818-257-7400	R	121*	.1
121	DCAP Management Corp Kingstone companies Inc	1158 Broadway, Hewlett NY 11557	516-374-7600	S	119*	.1
122	FA Richard and Associates Inc—*M Todd Richard*	1625 W Causeway Approa, Mandeville LA 70471	985-624-8383	R	118*	.1
123	TOPA Insurance Co—*Nosh Marfatia*	1800 Ave of the Stars, Los Angeles CA 90067	310-201-0451	S	112*	.1
124	Willis of Wisconsin Inc—*Joseph Plumeri*	330 E Kilbourn Ave Ste, Milwaukee WI 53202	414-271-9800	S	110	N/A
125	Pacific Premier Financial Insurance Services Inc	1600 Sunflower Ave, Costa Mesa CA 92626	714-431-4000	S	109*	.1
126	Ceridian Benefits Services Inc—*Kathryn Marinello* ABR Information Services Inc	3201 34th St S, Saint Petersburg FL 33711	727-864-3300	S	108*	2.0
127	Andreini and Co—*John Andreini*	220 W 20th Ave, San Mateo CA 94403	650-573-1111	R	105*	.2
128	Berkley Risk Administrators Company LLC—*Mike Foley*	222 S 9th St Ste 1300, Minneapolis MN 55402	612-766-3000	S	100*	.3
129	Stonington Insurance Co—*William Ashley*	5080 Spectrum Dr Ste 9, Addison TX 75001	972-664-7000	S	97*	.1
130	WorldNet Services Corp—*Felisse Pinsky*	3050 Universal Blvd St, Weston FL 33331		S	97*	.1
131	Tompkins Insurance Agencies Inc—*James Hardie*	14 Market St, Attica NY 14011	585-591-0262	S	97*	.1
132	HealthPlan Services Inc—*Jeff Bak*	PO Box 30098, Tampa FL 33630	813-289-1000	S	94*	.7
133	Aon Risk Services Central Inc—*Stephen P McGill* Aon Risk Services Companies Inc	3000 Town Center Ste 3, Southfield MI 48075	248-936-5200	S	94*	.2
134	Rampart Group—*Gary Morris*	1983 Marcus Ave Ste C1, Lake Success NY 11042	516-538-7000	R	87*	.2
135	ACE Tempest Re USA Inc—*Jacques Q Bonneau*	281 Tresser Blvd Ste 5, Stamford CT 06901	203-328-7000	S	87*	.1
136	US Risk Insurance Group Inc—*Randall Goss*	10210 N Central Expy S, Dallas TX 75231	214-265-7090	R	86*	.2
137	Huval Insurance Agency of Abbeville Inc—*Tommy Huval*	102 Asma Blvd Ste 300, Lafayette LA 70508	337-893-4964	S	86*	.1
138	Huval Insurance Agency of Arnaudville Inc—*Tommy Huval*	102 Asma Blvd Ste 300, Lafayette LA 70508	337-234-5111	S	86*	.1
139	Huval Insurance Agency of Church Point Inc—*Tommy Huval*	102 Asma Blvd Ste 300, Lafayette LA 70508		S	86*	.1
140	Huval Insurance Agency of Grand Coteau-Sunset Inc—*Tommy Huval*	102 Asma Blvd Ste 300, Lafayette LA 70508	337-234-5111	S	86*	.1
141	Huval Insurance Agency of Lafayette Inc—*Tommy Huval*	102 Asma Blvd Ste 300, Lafayette LA 70508	337-234-5111	S	86*	.1
142	Huval Insurance Agency of Loreauville Inc—*Tommy Huval*	102 Asma Blvd Ste 300, Lafayette LA 70508	337-234-5111	S	86*	.1
143	Huval Insurance Agency of Opelousas Inc—*Tommy Huval*	102 Asma Blvd Ste 300, Lafayette LA 70598	337-234-5111	S	86*	.1
144	Insurance Programs Inc—*J Powell Brown*	102 Asma Blvd Ste 300, Lafayette LA 70508	337-234-0815	S	86*	.1
145	Signature Insurance Group	28202 Cabot Rd Ste 600, Laguna Niguel CA 92677		R	85*	.1
146	ESIS Inc—*David Patterson*	PO Box 1000, Philadelphia PA 19106		S	85	N/A
147	Selective Insurance Company of South Carolina	3426 Toringdon Way Ste, Charlotte NC 28277	704-341-7474	S	82*	.1
148	HW Kaufman Financial Group Inc—*Alan Jay Kaufman*	PO Box 2090, Southfield MI 48037	248-932-9030	R	81*	.7
149	Gallagher Benefit Services of Kansas City Inc—*James W Durkin* Gallagher Benefit Services Inc	2345 Grand Blvd Ste 80, Kansas City MO 64108	816-421-7788	S	78*	.1
150	Entertainment Brokers International—*Jack Cave*	10940 Wilshire Blvd 17, Los Angeles CA 90024	310-954-3950	R	76*	.1
151	ABR Information Services Inc—*Ronald L Turner*	34125 US Hwy 19 N, Palm Harbor FL 34684	727-785-2819	S	75	.6
152	Aon Consulting Washington DC	1120 20th St NW Ste 60, Washington DC 20036	202-223-0673	S	73*	.1
153	Gallagher Benefit Services of Colorado Inc—*Les Kohn* Gallagher Benefit Services Inc	6399 S Fiddlers Green, Greenwood Village CO 80111	303-220-7575	S	73*	.1
154	Ringler Associates Inc—*Michael J Casey*	27422 Aliso Creek Rd S, Aliso Viejo CA 92656	949-425-5400	R	69*	.1
155	Southern Health Services Inc—*Michael Pervan*	9881 Mayland Dr Ste 20, Richmond VA 23233	804-747-3700	S	67*	.1
156	Brown and Brown Insurance of Arizona Inc—*Michael Paschke* Brown and Brown Inc	2800 N Central Ave Ste, Phoenix AZ 85004	602-277-6672	S	66*	.1
157	Bottrell Insurance Agency Inc—*Jerry Veazey*	PO Box 1490, Jackson MS 39215	601-960-8200	S	65*	.1
158	Willis of Texas Inc—*Loyd Esler*	1 Riverway Ste 2200, Houston TX 77056	713-961-3800	S	64*	.1
159	Keller Stonebraker Insurance Inc—*Jim Talbott*	PO Box 609, Hagerstown MD 21741	301-733-2530	R	64*	<.1
160	Crawford and Company HealthCare Management Inc—*Heather Matthews* Crawford and Co	PO Box 5047, Atlanta GA 30302	519-578-5540	S	63*	<.1
161	Halcyon Underwriters Inc—*Paul Lyons* Brown and Brown Inc	2600 Lake Lucien Dr St, Maitland FL 32751		S	62*	<.1
162	Haas and Wilkerson Inc—*Ryan Wilkerson*	4300 Shawnee Mission P, Fairway KS 66205	913-432-4400	R	61*	.1

Rank	Company Name—*Executive Officer*	Address, City, State, Zip	Phone	Type	Fin	Empls
163	Brown and Brown Insurance Services of Texas Inc—*J Powell Brown* Brown and Brown Inc	10700 North Fwy Ste 30, Houston TX 77037	281-260-2000	S	61*	.1
164	John L Wortham and Sons LLP—*Bob Hixon*	2727 Allen Pky, Houston TX 77019	713-526-3366	R	60*	.5
165	United Agencies Insurance Group—*James E Cogan*	1422 Euclid Ave Ste 90, Cleveland OH 44115	216-696-8044	R	60*	.1
166	Walter P Dolle Insurance Agency Inc—*Robert D Lang*	201 E 5th St Ste 1000, Cincinnati OH 45202	513-421-6515	R	60*	.1
167	Crump Insurance Services Inc—*John Jennings*	7557 Rambler Rd Ste 40, Dallas TX 75231	214-265-2660	S	58*	.5
168	Potomac Basin Group Associates Inc—*John Gardiner*	PO Box 1330, Beltsville MD 20704		R	58*	.1
169	APPCO Premium Finance Inc	3155 NW 77th Ave, Miami FL 33122	305-716-6000	S	58*	<.1
170	GemGroup—*Leonard Spencer*	401 Liberty Ave Ste 12, Pittsburgh PA 15222	412-471-2885	R	55*	.1
171	Advantage Insurers Inc	282 Historic 441 Hwy, Cornelia GA 30531	706-778-1000	S	53*	<.1
172	Diversified Group Administrators Inc—*Daniel Riston*	1910 Cochran Rd Ste 60, Pittsburgh PA 15220	724-746-8700	R	52*	<.1
173	SouthGroup Insurance and Financial Services—*Ronnie Tudertini*	795 Woodlands Pkwy Ste, Ridgeland MS 39157	601-914-3220	R	52*	<.1
174	Gallagher Benefit Services of New York Inc—*James Durkin Jr* Gallagher Benefit Services Inc	770 Lexington Ave, New York NY 10002	212-755-0800	S	51*	<.1
175	Brown and Brown of Lehigh Valley Inc—*Richard Knudson* Brown and Brown Inc	3001 Emrick Blvd Ste 1, Bethlehem PA 18020	610-974-9490	S	51*	<.1
176	Independent Insurance Associates Inc—*Gordon Clay*	1555 Poydras St Ste 17, New Orleans LA 70112	504-586-1000	R	49*	<.1
177	National Service Contract Insurance Company Risk Retention Group Inc	333 Earle Ovington Blv, Uniondale NY 11553	516-228-8600	S	48*	<.1
178	Arthur A Watson and Company Inc—*Tom Willsey*	PO Box 290230, Wethersfield CT 06129	860-563-8111	R	44*	.1
179	James D Collier and Company Inc—*Stuart Collier Jr*	606 S Mendenhall Rd, Memphis TN 38117	901-529-2900	R	43*	<.1
180	Gallagher Benefit Services of Washington DC—*Curt Dyckman* Gallagher Benefit Services Inc	1015 A StSte 800, Tacoma WA 98402	253-627-7183	S	43*	<.1
181	Gallagher Benefit Services of Michigan Inc—*Bryan Hirn* Gallagher Benefit Services Inc	22930 9 Mile Rd, Saint Clair Shores MI 48080	586-774-5300	S	42*	<.1
182	American Southern Insurance Co—*Scott G Thompson*	PO Box 723030, Atlanta GA 31139	404-266-9599	S	40*	<.1
183	Gallagher Captive Services Inc—*Patrick J Gallagher* Arthur J Gallagher and Co	2 Pierce Pl Ste 100, Itasca IL 60143	630-773-3800	S	40*	<.1
184	Hayes Utley and Hedgspeth—*Kenton Hayes*	PO Box 991069, Louisville KY 40269	502-493-2777	R	40*	<.1
185	Gregory and Appel Insurance Inc—*Daniel C Appel*	1402 N Capitol AveSte, Indianapolis IN 46202	317-634-7491	R	39*	.1
186	Empire Financial Services Inc—*Robert M Burgio*	5214 Main St 2nd Fl, Williamsville NY 14221	716-635-6800	S	38*	<.1
187	Epoch Group LC—*Paul Stucky*	2020 W 89th St, Leawood KS 66206	913-362-0040	S	37*	.3
188	Wells Fargo Insurance Inc—*John G Stumpf*	600 S Hwy 169 12th Fl, Saint Louis Park MN 55426	612-667-5600	S	36*	.1
189	Gallagher Benefit Services Inc—*James Durkin JR* Arthur J Gallagher and Co	2 Pierce Pl, Itasca IL 60143	630-773-3800	S	36*	<.1
190	Kinney Agency Inc Wells Fargo Insurance Services	320 Osuna Rd NE SET G-, Albuquerque NM 87107	505-262-2621	S	36*	<.1
191	Harris Holdings Inc (Manassas Virginia)—*Pattysue Rauh* Brown and Brown Inc	11220 Asset Loop Ste 3, Manassas VA 20109		S	35*	<.1
192	Robert J Hanafin Inc—*R Martin Hanafin*	PO Box 509, Endicott NY 13761	607-754-3500	R	33*	.1
193	Homeland HealthCare Inc—*Steven Jones*	825 Market St Ste 300, Allen TX 75013	214-871-2118	R	31*	.1
194	Babb Inc—*Ronald B Livingston Sr*	850 Ridge Ave, Pittsburgh PA 15212	412-237-2020	R	31*	.1
195	Murray and MacDonald Insurance Services Inc—*Douglas D MacDonald*	550 MacArthur Blvd, Bourne MA 02532	508-540-2400	S	31*	<.1
196	Anchor Investment Services Inc—*Chris Boyce*	302 N Midvale Blvd, Madison WI 53705	608-231-5252	S	31*	<.1
197	Sitehawk—*Mark Perlstein*	8500 Keystone Crossing, Indianapolis IN 46240	317-844-5313	R	30*	<.1
198	Alliant Insurance Services Inc—*Thomas W Corbett*	701 B St 6th Fl, San Diego CA 92101	619-238-1828	S	29*	.2
199	Brown and Brown of Colorado Inc—*Jim Triplone* Brown and Brown Inc	101 N Cascade Ave Ste, Colorado Springs CO 80903	714-471-0262	S	29*	<.1
200	Manifold Capital Corp—*Raymond J Brooks Jr*	600 5th Ave 2nd Fl, New York NY 10020	212-375-2000	P	29	.1
201	Daniel and Henry Co—*Jeffrey Mentel*	1001 Highlands Plz Dr, Saint Louis MO 63110	314-421-1525	R	28*	.3
202	Prestige Insurance Services Inc—*Terry Trexler*	PO Box 1659, Ocala FL 34474	352-732-5157	S	28*	<.1
203	Westwood Insurance Agency—*John Flynn*	8407 Fallbrook Ave Ste, West Hills CA 91304		R	28*	<.1
204	AFC Insurance Inc—*Jane Gordon* Brown and Brown Inc	3101 Emrick Blvd Ste 3, Bethlehem PA 18020	610-866-0401	S	28*	<.1
205	Woodruff-Sawyer and Co—*Charles Rosson*	220 Bush St 7th Fl, San Francisco CA 94104	415-391-2141	R	27*	.2
206	Van Zandt Emrich and Cary Inc—*Paul G Franz*	PO Box 99565, Louisville KY 40269	502-456-2001	R	27*	<.1
207	Gallagher Benefit Services of the Carolinas Inc—*John Tournet* Gallagher Benefit Services Inc	4064 Colony Rd Ste 450, Charlotte NC 28211	704-643-7005	S	27*	<.1
208	LD O'Mire Inc—*LD O'Mire*	PO Box 1110, Ridgeland MS 39158	601-957-3841	R	27*	<.1
209	National Catastrophe Adjusters—*Dave Ross*	9725 Windermere Blvd, Fishers IN 46037	317-915-8888	R	26*	.2
210	Micheletti Inc—*David Micheletti*	99 Almaden Blvd Ste 80, San Jose CA 95113	408-292-4900	R	26*	<.1
211	Nationair Insurance—*Dave McCoy*	1525 Kautz Rd Ste 100, West Chicago IL 60185	630-584-7552	R	26*	<.1
212	Ascension Insurance Services Inc—*Bob Underwood*	87 E Green St Ste 206, Pasadena CA 91105	626-844-7100	R	24*	.1
213	Brown and Brown of Missouri Inc—*Dan Daly* Brown and Brown Inc	9666 Olive Blvd Ste 20, Saint Louis MO 63132	314-692-0300	S	24*	<.1
214	Brown and Brown of South Carolina Inc—*Todd Tyler* Brown and Brown Inc	PO Box 62588, N Charleston SC 29419	843-572-4567	S	24*	<.1
215	McKinnon and Mooney Inc—*Steve Randall* Brown and Brown Inc	2353 S Linden Rd, Flint MI 48532	810-230-1613	S	24*	<.1
216	MVI Administrators Inc—*George McGregor*	1011 Camino Del Rio S, San Diego CA 92108	619-260-2660	R	24*	<.1
217	Herbert H Landy Insurance Agency Inc—*Betsy Magnuson*	75 2nd Ave Ste 410, Needham MA 02494		R	23*	<.1
218	Retirement System Consultants Inc—*Robert C Albanese*	108 Corporate Park Dr, White Plains NY 10604	212-503-0100	S	22*	.1
219	Brown and Brown Insurance Services of El Paso Inc—*Robert Olguin* Brown and Brown Inc	440 Raynolds, El Paso TX 79905	915-772-8881	S	22*	<.1
220	Arthur J Gallagher and Company of Kentucky Inc—*John Nelson* Arthur J Gallagher and Co	2000 Envoy Cir Ste 200, Louisville KY 40299	502-491-7752	S	22*	<.1
221	Byrne Insurance Agency Inc—*Johnny Byrne*	PO Box 1505, Natchez MS 39121	601-442-2511	R	22*	<.1
222	Kingstone companies Inc—*Barry B Goldstein*	1154 Broadway, Hewlett NY 11557	516-374-7600	P	22	<.1
223	Marketing Alliance Inc (St Louis Missouri)—*Timothy M Klusas*	111 W Port Plz Ste 101, Saint Louis MO 63146	314-275-8713	P	22	N/A
224	Wachovia Insurance—*John Stumpf*	PO Box 220748, Charlotte NC 28222	704-366-8834	S	21*	.3
225	Peachtree Special Risk Brokers LLC—*Tony Strianese* Brown and Brown Inc	303 Corporate Center D, Stockbridge GA 30281	770-506-6373	S	21*	<.1
226	Health Design Plus Inc—*M Ruth Coleman*	1755 Georgetown Rd, Hudson OH 44236	330-656-1072	R	20*	.1
227	GamePlan Financial Marketing LLC	300 ParkBrooke Pl Ste, Woodstock GA 30189		R	20*	.1
228	QuoteWizard—*Scott Peyree*	157 Yesler Way Ste 400, Seattle WA 98104		R	20	<.1

Note: An asterisk (*) indicates an estimated financial figure. The company type code used is as follows: R = Private, P = Public, S = Private Subsidiary, B = Public Subsidiary, D = Division, J = Joint Venture, I = Investment Fund.

COMPANY RANKINGS BY SALES WITHIN 4-DIGIT SIC

Rank	Company Name—*Executive Officer*	Address, City, State, Zip	Phone	Type	Fin	Empls
229	Gould and Lamb LLC—*John Williams*	101 Riverfront Blvd St, Bradenton FL 34205		R	19*	.2
230	Gebco Insurance Associates Inc—*Thomas J Woods*	11350 McCormick Rd, Hunt Valley MD 21031	410-527-1820	R	19*	.1
231	Dietrich and Associates Inc—*Kurt Dietrich*	1000 Germantown Pk Ste, Plymouth Meeting PA 19462	610-279-9455	R	19*	<.1
232	Pagnotti Enterprises Inc—*Charles Parente*	46 Public Sq Ste 600, Wilkes Barre PA 18701	570-825-8700	R	19*	.5
233	Anderson and Murison Inc—*James M McCarthy*	PO Box 41911, Los Angeles CA 90041	323-255-2333	R	18*	<.1
234	Brown and Brown Agency of Insurance Professionals Inc—*Lance O'Rourke* Brown and Brown Inc	208 N Mill, Pryor OK 74361	918-825-3295	S	18*	<.1
235	Rumson Capital LP—*Robert Meyer*	261 Old York Rd, Jenkintown PA 19046	215-886-8433	R	18*	<.1
236	RT Nelson and Associates Ltd—*R T Nelson*	903 Commerce Dr Ste 15, Oak Brook IL 60523	630-990-4220	R	17*	<.1
237	Healthplex Inc—*Martin Kane*	333 Earle Ovington Blv, Uniondale NY 11553	516-542-2200	R	16	.1
238	Heiden and Garland Inc—*Doug Garland*	548 Keyway Dr, Flowood MS 39232	601-932-5700	R	16*	<.1
239	Roger Bouchard Insurance Inc—*Doug Bishop*	101 Starcrest Dr, Clearwater FL 33765	727-447-6481	S	15*	.1
240	Lawson Hawks Insurance Associates—*John Miller*	1091 N Shoreline Blvd, Mountain View CA 94043	650-964-8000	R	15*	<.1
241	CGA Associates Inc—*Nicholas Campanella*	34 W Main St, Freehold NJ 07728		R	15*	<.1
242	Marchetti Robertson Brickell Insurance Inc—*John Marchetti*	PO Box 3348, Ridgeland MS 39158	601-605-4082	R	14*	<.1
243	United Administrative Services Co—*David Andresen* Stephen Chelbay Co	1120 S Bascom Ave, San Jose CA 95128	408-288-4400	S	13*	.1
244	Snyder Insurance Agency Inc—*John P Snyder III*	100 S Main St, Oconomowoc WI 53066	262-567-0288	R	13*	<.1
245	Spencer and Associates Inc—*Catherine Fiasconaro* Brown and Brown Inc	7341 Office Park Place, Melbourne FL 32940		S	13*	<.1
246	Wood Snodgrass Inc—*William M Wood*	12980 Metcalf Ave Ste, Overland Park KS 66213	913-681-2200	R	13*	<.1
247	Concentra Network Services—*Tom Bartlett*	720 Cool Springs Blvd, Franklin TN 37067	615-778-4000	R	12*	.2
248	Insurance and Risk Management—*Jim Van Dike*	PO Box 1705, Fort Wayne IN 46801	260-436-1676	R	12*	.2
249	InsurMark Inc—*Steve Kerns*	820 Gessner Ste 970, Houston TX 77024	713-973-7575	R	12*	<.1
250	Yates Insurance Agency Inc—*Jason Yates* Brown and Brown Inc	201 E Reynolds Dr, Ruston LA 71270	318-251-9559	S	12*	<.1
251	Wright and Kimbrough/Cotton	2150 Douglas Blvd Ste, Roseville CA 95661	916-751-7682	R	12*	<.1
252	Forest Products Supply—*Henry Hinman*	PO Box 20429, Sarasota FL 34276	941-922-0731	R	12*	.3
253	Integrity Capital Partners LLC—*Robert E Finfer*	6701 Democracy Blvd St, Bethesda MD 20817		R	11	<.1
254	Wells Fargo Insurance Services of Ohio LLC	PO Box 3499, Youngstown OH 44513	330-726-8861	S	11*	<.1
255	Smith and Bell Insurance Agency—*James W Bobe*	PO Box 925, Vincennes IN 47591	812-882-2900	R	11*	<.1
256	Hathaway Agency Inc—*William R Fiedler*	P O Box 951, Gloversville NY 12078	518-773-7981	S	11*	<.1
257	Csi Holdings Inc—*Wayne Smolda*	4850 E St Rd Ste 230, Feasterville Trevose PA 19053	215-357-4400	R	11*	.4
258	National Health Insurance Agency Inc—*Gene Stracener*	2119 W Brandon Blvd, Brandon FL 33511	813-689-2583	R	10*	<.1
259	Arthur J Gallagher and Company of Michigan Inc—*Jim Gault* Arthur J Gallagher and Co	PO Box 7007, Troy MI 48007	248-528-6630	S	9	.1
260	Mississippi Insurance Services Inc—*Harper Young*	PO Box 958, Greenville MS 38702	662-378-5200	R	9*	<.1
261	Prime Tempus Inc—*Craig Koenig*	27310 Ranch Rd 12, Dripping Springs TX 78620	512-894-3705	R	9*	<.1
262	Insurance Information Institute—*Gordon Stewart*	110 William St Fl 24, New York NY 10038	212-669-9200	R	9*	<.1
263	John Mullen and Company Inc—*J Terrance Mullen*	PO Box 2096, Honolulu HI 96805	808-531-9733	R	8*	.1
264	Willis Management Vermont Ltd—*Joseph J Plumeri*	40 Main St Ste 200, Burlington VT 05401	802-658-4600	D	8*	<.1
265	M Barrington Corp—*Keith Miller*	12080 Corporate Pkwy S, Mequon WI 53092	262-478-2000	R	8*	<.1
266	Gill Insurance—*Jim Gill*	PO Box 4040, Rock Hill SC 29732	803-324-5300	R	8*	<.1
267	North Star Agency Inc—*Julius Eirich*	3663 Pontchartrain Dr, Slidell LA 70458	985-643-7977	R	8*	<.1
268	Wells Fargo Insurance Services of Michigan Inc—*Kevin Kenney*	4000 Town Ctr Ste 800, Southfield MI 48075	248-353-5800	S	7*	.1
269	First Bank Insurance Services Inc—*Jerry L Ocheltree*	PO Box C, Troy NC 27371	910-572-3761	S	7*	<.1
270	Louisiana Cos—*George D Nelson Jr*	PO Box 991, Baton Rouge LA 70821	225-383-4761	R	6*	.1
271	Old Kentucky Insurance Inc—*Howard Meyer*	PO Box 20887, Louisville KY 40250	502-451-8800	R	5*	<.1
272	Schmidt Insurance Agency Inc—*Leonard Schmidt*	7410 New Lagrange Rd S, Louisville KY 40222	502-429-0477	R	5*	<.1
273	Retirement Planning Associates Inc	265 N Main St, Wallingford CT 06492	203-269-8018	S	5*	<.1
274	MBA Holdings Inc—*Gaylen M Brotherson*	PO Box 4800, Scottsdale AZ 85261	480-860-2288	P	5	<.1
275	Health Cost Solutions Inc—*William Beeler*	PO Box 1439, Hendersonville TN 37077	615-822-0483	R	5*	<.1
276	NII Brokerage LLC—*Matt Grossberg*	1285 Avenue of the Ame, New York NY 10019	201-476-1000	R	5	.1
277	Esurance Inc—*Gary C Tolman*	650 Davis St, San Francisco CA 94111	415-875-4500	S	4*	.1
278	Arista Investors Corp—*Stanley S Mandel*	116 John St, New York NY 10038	212-964-2150	R	4*	<.1
279	Welch Graham and Ogden Insurance Agency—*Thomas L Welch*	7896 Donegan Dr, Manassas VA 20109		R	4*	<.1
280	Mercury Adjustment Bureau Investigations Ltd—*Lisa Anne Hugasian*	26 Charter Ave Ste 1, Huntington Station NY 11746	516-997-3338	R	4*	<.1
281	Phoenix Loss Prevention Inc—*Paul Moore*	PO Box 1180, Fayetteville GA 30214	770-460-5659	R	4*	<.1
282	Nexia Holdings Inc—*Richard D Surber*	59 W 100 S 2nd Fl, Salt Lake City UT 84101	801-575-8073	R	3	<.1
283	RTI Insurance Services of Florida Inc—*John A Folino*	6311 Atrium Dr Ste 200, Bradenton FL 34202	941-328-4487	R	3*	<.1
284	Qestrel Claims Management Inc—*David Graft*	7201 Haven Ave Rm E 32, Rancho Cucamonga CA 91701	626-440-9100	R	3*	<.1
285	UMC Healthcare Solutions—*Pete Seaman*	200 N Cuyler St, Pampa TX 79065	806-661-4209	R	3	<.1
286	AA Adjustment Company Inc—*Dale Krauss*	PO Box 130, Woodbine MD 21797	410-252-9575	R	3*	<.1
287	Benefit Design Group—*Bill Charter*	5340 College Blvd, Overland Park KS 66211	913-338-2525	R	2*	<.1
288	Franklin Financial Group Inc—*Kevin Ary*	755 Maidstone Ct, Cincinnati OH 45230	513-231-4927	R	2*	<.1
289	Ovation Health and Life Services Inc—*Daniel LaBroad*	6315 Crested Butte Dr, Dallas TX 75252	972-407-9959	R	1*	<.1
290	Hi-Q Products Inc—*Todd Mills*	PO Box 50618, Santa Barbara CA 93150	626-308-4400	R	1*	<.1
291	Peoples Insurance Agency Inc	416 Hart St, Marietta OH 45750	740-373-3994	S	<1	.3
292	US Bancorp Insurance Services—*William Benjamin*	809 S 60th St, West Allis WI 53214		S	<1	<.1
293	Quasar Aerospace Industries Inc—*Joseph Canouse*	9300 Normandy Blvd Ste, Jacksonville FL 32221	904-378-3259	P	<1	<.1
294	MedBillsAssist—*Katalin Goencz*	1127 High Ridge Rd Ste, Stamford CT 06905	203-569-7610	R	<1	<.1

TOTALS: SIC 6411 Insurance Agents, Brokers & Service
Companies: 294 — 433,761 — 340.9

6512 Nonresidential Building Operators

Rank	Company Name—*Executive Officer*	Address, City, State, Zip	Phone	Type	Fin	Empls
1	Icahn Enterprises LP—*Daniel A Ninivaggi*	767 5th Ave 47th Fl, New York NY 10153	212-702-4300	P	21,338	42.7
2	Major Automotive Realty Corp	43-40 Northern Blvd, Long Island City NY 11101	718-937-3700	S	4,112*	.5
3	Rogue Valley Manor—*Kevin McLoughlin*	1200 Mira Mar Ave, Medford OR 97504	541-857-7214	S	3,040*	.5
4	SABC Realty Inc	1625 Central Pky, Cincinnati OH 45214	513-412-3210	R	2,214*	.4
5	Dial Properties Co—*TL Clauff*	11506 Nicholas St Ste, Omaha NE 68154	402-493-2800	S	1,616*	.2
6	Brookfield Office Properties Inc—*Richard B Clark*	3 World Financial Ctr, New York NY 10281	212-417-7000	R	1,326	2.2
7	Forest City Enterprises Inc—*David J LaRue*	50 Public Sq Terminal, Cleveland OH 44113	216-621-6060	P	1,178	2.9
8	Inland Real Estate Corp—*Mark E Zalatoris*	2901 Butterfield Rd, Oak Brook IL 60523		P	1,160	.1
9	Madison Square Garden Inc—*Hank J Ratner*	2 Penn Plz, New York NY 10121	212-465-6000	P	1,157	1.3
10	Gibraltar Trade Center Inc—*James Koester*	15525 Racho Rd, Taylor MI 48180	734-287-2000	R	970*	.2
11	Deseret Management Corp—*Mark Willis*	60 E South Temple Ste, Salt Lake City UT 84111	801-538-0651	R	954*	4.0

Rank	Company Name—*Executive Officer*	Address, City, State, Zip	Phone	Type	Fin	Empls
12	Forest City Commercial Group Inc—*Charles Ratner* Forest City Enterprises Inc	50 Public Square Ste 1, Cleveland OH 44113	216-621-6060	S	900*	4.1
13	Konover and Associates Inc—*Jim Ainsworth*	135 South Rd, Farmington CT 06032	860-284-7200	R	665*	.3
14	Mericle Commercial Real Estate Group Inc—*Robert K Mericle*	East Mountain Corporat, Wilkes Barre PA 18702	570-823-1100	R	648*	.1
15	FranklinCovey (Salt Lake City Utah)—*Robert Whitman*	2200 Pkwy Blvd, Salt Lake City UT 84119	801-817-1776	S	547	3.5
16	Forest City Management Inc—*David J LaRue* Forest City Enterprises Inc	50 Public Sq Ste 750, Cleveland OH 44113	216-621-6060	S	461*	1.0
17	Perry Brothers Inc (Lufkin Texas)—*Charles Acklen*	PO Box 28, Lufkin TX 75902	936-634-6686	R	450*	.9
18	MPG Office Trust Inc—*David L Weinstein*	355 S Grand Ave Ste 33, Los Angeles CA 90071	213-626-3300	P	407	.1
19	Combined Properties Inc—*Ronald Haft*	1255 22nd St NW Ste 60, Washington DC 20037	202-293-4500	R	282*	.1
20	Carlson Real Estate Co—*Matt Van Slooten*	301 Carlson Pkwy Ste 1, Hopkins MN 55305	952-404-5000	S	282*	<.1
21	Atco Properties and Management Inc—*Dale Hemmerdinger*	555 5th Ave 16th Fl, New York NY 10017	212-687-5154	R	261*	<.1
22	INFOMART-Dallas LP—*Suzanne Glen*	1950 Stemmons Fwy Ste, Dallas TX 75207	214-800-8000	R	220*	<.1
23	Vornado/Charles E Smith Realty—*Michael Schear*	2345 Crystal Dr Ste 10, Arlington VA 22202	703-920-8200	S	202*	1.4
24	Genco Of Lebanon Inc—*Herbert Shear*	100 Papercraft Park, Pittsburgh PA 15238	412-820-3747	R	169*	6.5
25	Insignia/Esg Hotel Partners Inc—*Mary Tighe*	11150 Santa Monica Blv, Los Angeles CA 90025	310-765-2600	S	163*	5.8
26	Real Capital Solutions—*Marcel Arsenault*	1450 Infinite Dr Ste E, Louisville CO 80027	303-466-2500	R	156*	<.1
27	Kato Kagaku Company Ltd—*Shoichi Kato*	151 E Wacker Dr, Chicago IL 60601	312-565-1234	R	146*	1.3
28	Rockefeller Group Inc—*Kevin Hackett*	1221 Ave of the Americ, New York NY 10020	212-282-2000	S	145*	1.0
29	Ramco-Gershenson Properties LP—*Dennis Gershenson*	31500 Nw Hwy Ste 300, Farmington Hills MI 48334	248-350-9900	R	142*	.1
30	Palace Sports and Entertainment—*Tom Gores*	6 Championship Dr, Auburn Hills MI 48326	248-377-0100	R	137*	.3
31	Lloyd Center—*Wanda Rosenbarger*	2201 Lloyd Ctr, Portland OR 97232	503-282-2511	D	122*	.1
32	PIER 39 LP—*Robert C MacIntosh*	PO Box 193730, San Francisco CA 94119	415-705-5500	R	115*	.3
33	Mission West Properties Inc—*Carl E Berg*	10050 Bandley Dr, Cupertino CA 95014	408-725-0700	P	99	<.1
34	Shamrock Industrial Fastener Corp—*Sam Waichulis*	1475 Industrial Dr, Itasca IL 60143	630-595-6260	R	95*	<.1
35	O'Brien and Gere Ltd—*James A Fox*	5000 Brittonfield Pkwy, East Syracuse NY 13057	315-437-6100	R	89*	.9
36	Parc Presentations Inc—*James Nederlander Jr*	6233 Hollywood Blvd St, Los Angeles CA 90028	323-468-1700	R	80*	.2
37	L and B Realty Advisors Inc—*G Andrews Smith*	8750 N Central Expy St, Dallas TX 75231	214-989-0800	R	75*	.1
38	Property One Inc—*Quentin Dastugue*	4141 Veterans Memorial, Metairie LA 70002	504-681-3400	R	68*	<.1
39	Westfield Group USA—*Peter S Lowy*	11601 Wilshire Blvd, Los Angeles CA 90025	310-478-4456	S	63*	.5
40	Linder Group Inc—*Steve Delaney*	8500 Keystone Crossing, Indianapolis IN 46240	317-844-5313	R	56*	<.1
41	Washington SuperMall Interest LP—*Greg Fleser*	1101 Supermall Way Ste, Auburn WA 98001	253-833-1790	S	56*	<.1
42	Herrick Company Inc—*Norton Herrick*	2295 Corp Blvd NW, Boca Raton FL 33431	561-241-9880	R	50*	.1
43	Eton Centers Co—*Louis Brause*	52 Vanderbilt Ave, New York NY 10017	212-697-5454	R	49*	<.1
44	Time Equities Inc—*Robert Kantor*	55 5th Ave 15th Fl, New York NY 10003	212-206-6000	R	46*	.1
45	Vehicle Safety Manufacturing LLC—*Rebecca Krishman*	61 Morris Ave, Newark NJ 07103	973-643-3000	R	44*	.2
46	Fredman Brothers Furniture Company Inc—*Carmin Fredman*	PO Box 512, Collinsville IL 62234	314-426-3999	R	43*	.4
47	Milestone Properties Inc—*Leonard S Mandor*	200 Congress Park Dr, Delray Beach FL 33445	561-394-9533	R	43*	<.1
48	Ifp Inc—*Feephi Eyal*	2125 Airport Dr, Faribault MN 55021	507-334-2730	R	39*	.1
49	Benderson Development Company Inc—*Nathan Benderson*	8441 Cooper Creek Blvd, University Park FL 34201	941-359-8303	R	38*	.3
50	Jacksonville Holdings Inc—*Carey Webb*	1 Imeson Park Blvd Bld, Jacksonville FL 32218	904-696-3407	R	34*	<.1
51	Bel-Art Products Inc—*David Landsberger*	6 Industrial Rd, Pequannock NJ 07440	973-694-0500	R	32*	.3
52	New Valley LLC—*Howard Lorber*	100 SE 2nd St, Miami FL 33131	305-579-8000	S	27	<.1
53	Weitzman Group—*Herbert D Weitzman*	3102 Maple Ave Ste 350, Dallas TX 75201	214-954-0600	R	26*	.1
54	Jujamcyn Theaters Corp—*Jordan Roth*	246 W 44th St, New York NY 10036	212-840-8181	R	24	.5
55	Tower Properties Co—*Thomas R Willard*	1000 Walnut Dr Ste 900, Kansas City MO 64106	816-421-8255	R	24	.1
56	Stoltz Management of Delaware Inc—*Keith Stoltz*	725 Conshohocken State, Bala Cynwyd PA 19004	610-667-5800	R	23*	.1
57	Underground Atlanta Inc—*William Ciccaglione*	50 Upper Alabama St St, Atlanta GA 30303	404-523-2311	R	23*	<.1
58	Glenborough LLC—*Andrew Batinovich*	400 S El Camino Real, San Mateo CA 94402	650-343-9300	S	17*	.4
59	JW Mays Inc—*Lloyd J Shulman*	9 Bond St, Brooklyn NY 11201	718-624-7400	P	15	<.1
60	Scholle Custom Packaging Inc—*William Scholle*	200 W N Ave, Northlake IL 60164	708-562-7290	S	12*	.5
61	New England Development—*Stephen R Karp*	1 Wells Ave, Newton MA 02459	617-965-8700	R	10*	.1
62	Landau and Heyman Inc—*Patrick Oleary*	120 S Riverside Plz St, Chicago IL 60606	312-780-1933	R	9*	.3
63	NSP Ventures—*Sadao Tsunoda*	750 N St Paul Dr Ste16, Dallas TX 75201	214-740-0090	R	7*	<.1
64	Universal Veneer Mill Corp—*Klaus Krajewski*	1776 Tamarack Rd, Newark OH 43055	740-522-1147	R	6*	.2
65	Iowa National Properties LLC—*Raymond Di Paglia*	4500 Merle Hay Rd, Des Moines IA 50310	515-278-1132	R	6*	<.1
66	Donatelle Properties—*Charles Donatelle*	501 County Rd E2 Ext, Saint Paul MN 55112	651-633-4200	R	6*	.1
67	Gyrodyne Company of America Inc—*Stephen V Maroney*	1 Flowerfield Ste 24, Saint James NY 11780	631-584-5400	P	6	<.1
68	Jazzy Electronics Corp—*Zigmond Brach*	1600 63rd St, Brooklyn NY 11204	718-236-8000	R	5*	.1
69	Alexander's of Brooklyn Inc—*Steve Roth*	210 Rt 4 E, Paramus NJ 07652	201-587-8541	S	5	N/A
70	Gehring Corp—*Robert Dermolen*	24800 Drake Rd, Farmington Hills MI 48335	248-478-8060	R	5*	.1
71	Hailwood Inc—*Glywn Chase*	PO Box 1272, Oxnard CA 93032	805-487-4981	R	5*	<.1
72	Equity Office—*Tom August*	2 N Riverside Plaza, Chicago IL 60606	312-466-3300	D	5*	<.1
73	Sarnia Corp—*Charles Judkins*	6850 Versar Ctr, Springfield VA 22151	703-642-6800	S	4*	.1
74	Saint Andrews Hall Inc—*Blair Gowan*	431 E Congress St, Detroit MI 48226	313-961-8961	R	4*	.1
75	Graham Group Inc—*George Milligan*	505 5th Ave Ste 200, Des Moines IA 50309	515-244-0387	R	3*	<.1
76	James C White Co—*Stephen White*	PO Box 5495, Greenville SC 29606	864-288-4692	R	2*	<.1
77	Canal Capital Corp—*Michael E Schultz*	490 Wheeler Rd, Hauppauge NY 11788	631-234-0140	P	2	<.1
78	Vallco Fashion Park—*Mike Rohde* Westfield Group USA	10123 N Wolfe Rd, Cupertino CA 95014	408-255-5660	S	2*	<.1
79	National Contracting Group Ltd	6740 Huntley Rd Unit A, Columbus OH 43229	614-436-6001	R	2*	<.1
80	Hawks Electrics Inc—*Donald Hawkes*	PO Box 1489, Shelton WA 98584	360-426-9955	R	2*	<.1
81	Lockwood Inc—*Michael Lockwood*	PO Box 53466, Houston TX 77052	713-675-8186	R	2*	<.1
82	Earl's Manufacturing Company Inc—*Earl Beard*	PO Box 939, Crockett TX 75835	936-544-5521	R	1*	<.1
83	ONEOK Leasing Co	PO Box 871, Tulsa OK 74102	918-588-7000	S	1*	<.1
84	Erl Properties Inc—*Larry Wilkins*	2560 Charlestown Rd, New Albany IN 47150	812-948-8484	R	1*	<.1
85	Cambridge Holdings Ltd—*Gregory S Pusey*	106 S University Blvd, Denver CO 80209	303-722-4008	P	1	<.1
86	Advanced Oxygen Technologies Inc—*Robert E Wolfe*	PO Box 189, Randolph VT 05060	212-727-7085	P	1	<.1
87	Hunt-Wilde Corp—*Kenneth Hunt*	2835 Overpafl Rd Ste 1, Tampa FL 33619	813-623-2461	R	1*	<.1
88	Afco Electronics—*Sandy Gross*	471 Roland Way, Oakland CA 94621	510-635-7000	R	<1*	<.1
89	Mo-Pa Enterprise Inc—*Eric Moscahlaidis*	13600 Snow Rd, Cleveland OH 44142	216-676-8500	R	<1*	<.1
90	Ambase Corp—*Richard A Bianco*	100 Putnam Green 3rd F, Greenwich CT 06830	203-532-2000	P	<1	<.1

TOTALS: SIC 6512 Nonresidential Building Operators

Companies: 90					47,077	88.1

6513 Apartment Building Operators

Rank	Company Name—*Executive Officer*	Address, City, State, Zip	Phone	Type	Fin	Empls
1	Related Companies LP—*Stephen M Ross*	60 Columbus Cir, New York NY 10023	212-421-5333	R	15,000	2.0
2	Wilmac Corp—*Karen McCormack*	PO Box 5047, York PA 17405	717-854-7857	R	4,832*	1.0
3	Prometheus Real Estate Group Inc—*Jackie Safier*	1900 S Norfolk St Ste, San Mateo CA 94401	650-931-3400	R	3,698*	.7

Note: An asterisk (*) indicates an estimated financial figure. The company type code used is as follows: R = Private, P = Public, S = Private Subsidiary, B = Public Subsidiary, D = Division, J = Joint Venture, I = Investment Fund.

COMPANY RANKINGS BY SALES WITHIN 4-DIGIT SIC

Rank	Company Name—*Executive Officer*	Address, City, State, Zip	Phone	Type	Fin	Empls
4	Campus Apartment Inc—*David J Adelman*	4043 Walnut St, Philadelphia PA 19104	215-243-7000	R	3,134*	.6
5	140 North Beacon LP New England Realty Associates LP	39 Brighton Ave, Allston MA 02134	617-783-0039	S	2,361*	.2
6	345 Franklin LLC New England Realty Associates LP	39 Brighton Ave, Allston MA 02134	617-783-0039	S	2,361*	.2
7	Brookside Associates LP New England Realty Associates LP	39 Brighton Ave, Allston MA 02134	617-783-0039	S	2,361*	.2
8	Clovelly Apartments LP New England Realty Associates LP	39 Brighton Ave, Allston MA 02134	617-783-0039	S	2,361*	.2
9	River Drive LP New England Realty Associates LP	39 Brighton Ave, Allston MA 02134	617-783-0039	S	2,361*	.2
10	Fath Properties Inc—*Harry Fath*	255 E 5th St Ste 2300, Cincinnati OH 45202	513-721-4070	R	1,818*	.3
11	Holiday Retirement Corp—*William E Colson*	2250 McGilchrist St SE, Salem OR 97302		R	1,027	7.5
12	John Knox Village Inc—*Daniel Rexroth*	1001 NW Chipman Rd, Lees Summit MO 64081	816-251-8000	R	861*	1.0
13	America First Properties Management Company LLC—*Niles Andersen*	1004 Farnam St, Omaha NE 68102	402-444-1630	S	790*	.1
14	Erickson Living—*R Alan Butler*	701 Maiden Choice Ln, Catonsville MD 21228	410-242-2880	R	778*	12.0
15	Reading International Inc—*James J Cotter*	500 Citadel Dr Ste 300, Commerce CA 90040	213-235-2240	P	230	2.1
16	Gull Creek Center Inc—*Margaret White*	1 Meadow St, Berlin MD 21811	410-641-3171	R	210*	<.1
17	Stone Brook	1616 Lifesearch Way, Denison TX 75020	903-465-5051	R	208*	8.0
18	Intergroup Corp—*John V Winfield*	10940 Wilshire Blvd St, Los Angeles CA 90024	310-889-2500	P	154	<.1
19	Focus Group Inc—*Michael Blonder*	3423 Piedmont Rd Ste 2, Atlanta GA 30305	404-816-6300	R	105*	<.1
20	Arizona Coral Point Apartments LP—*Jack Brown*	2343 W Main St, Mesa AZ 85201	480-844-4000	S	105*	<.1
21	Brookdale Living Communities Inc	330 N Wabash Ave Ste 1, Chicago IL 60611	312-977-3800	S	96*	2.0
22	Bresler and Reiner Inc—*Charles Bresler*	6010 Executive Blvd St, Rockville MD 20852	301-945-4300	P	93	N/A
23	Campus Crest Communities Inc—*Ted Rollins*	2100 Rexford Rd Ste 41, Charlotte NC 28211	704-496-2500	P	88	.5
24	Fifteen Asset Management LLC—*Mark Sanders*	1680 Michigan Ave Ste, Miami Beach FL 33139	305-938-4300	R	87*	<.1
25	Oakwell Farms LP—*Thomas Wilkerson*	1800 Oakwell Farms Ln, Hermitage TN 37076	615-885-0300	S	79*	<.1
26	Auger Enterprises Inc—*Ulysses Auger*	1232 22nd St NW Fl 6, Washington DC 20037	202-331-7850	R	72*	.5
27	Patterson-Erie Corp—*William L Patterson Jr*	1250 Tower Ln, Erie PA 16505	814-455-8031	R	62*	1.8
28	Vintage at Plantation Bay Apartments LLC The—*William S Friedman*	7740 Plantation Bay Dr, Jacksonville FL 32244	904-771-7576	S	46*	<.1
29	Prime Property Investors Ltd—*Michael H Zaransky*	333 Skokie Blvd Ste 11, Northbrook IL 60062	847-562-1800	R	41*	<.1
30	New England Realty Associates LP—*Ronald Brown*	39 Brighton Ave, Allston MA 02134	617-783-0039	P	33	N/A
31	Carlyle Tower National Associates LP	23300 Providence Dr, Southfield MI 48075	248-559-2111	S	31*	<.1
32	University City Housing Co—*Michael Karp*	3418 Sansom St, Philadelphia PA 19104	215-222-2000	R	30*	.1
33	Panorama City Corp—*Joseph J Di Santo*	1751 Circle Ln SE, Lacey WA 98503	360-456-0111	R	28*	.4
34	Jonas Equities Inc—*Terry Bernstein*	725 Church Ave, Brooklyn NY 11218	718-871-6020	R	21*	<.1
35	South Dakota Achieve—*Anne Rieck-Mcfarland*	4100 S Western Ave, Sioux Falls SD 57105	605-336-7100	R	18*	.5
36	Regent Circle LLC—*William S Friedman*	423 W 55th St, New York NY 10019	212-949-5000	S	16*	<.1
37	Lyon Capital Ventures—*Frank T Suryan Jr*	4901 Birch St, Newport Beach CA 92660	949-252-9101	S	14*	.2
38	Park Trace Apartments LP—*Shanterian Franklin*	700 Atlanta Ave, Decatur GA 30030	404-371-0887	R	12*	<.1
39	Park at Countryside LP—*Joan Newman*	958 Village Trl, Port Orange FL 32127	386-756-2877	S	10*	<.1
40	Wilchiro Entorpricoc Inc—*S Wilzig Izak*	100 Eaglo Rook Avo Sto, Eaot Hanovor NJ 07036	201 420 2706	R	0	<.1
41	Park at Fifty Eight LP—*MaryAnn Clark*	4827 Jersey Pk, Chattanooga TN 37416	423-855-2860	S	8*	<.1
42	Beal Group—*Stewart Beal*	221 Felch St Ste 7, Ann Arbor MI 48103	734-662-6133	R	6	.1
43	Residential Plaza At Blue Lagoon Inc—*Mauro Hernandez*	5617 Nw 7th St, Miami FL 33126	305-267-2700	R	5*	.1
44	Salem Senior Housing—*William G Benton*	1105 Brookstown Ave, Winston Salem NC 27101	336-724-1000	P	3	.1
45	Crown Pointe Div	2820 S 80th St, Omaha NE 68124	402-391-7555	D	1*	<.1
46	Wisconsin Ear Mold Co—*Walter Kolb*	1703 Pearl St, Waukesha WI 53186	262-524-2424	R	1*	<.1
47	Littlestone LLC—*Teresa Ray*	1008 Village Green Xin, Gallatin TN 37066	615-451-1500	S	N/A	<.1
48	Oakhurst Apartments LP—*Mary NA*	3001 SE Lake Weir Ave, Ocala FL 34471	352-867-7373	R	N/A	<.1

TOTALS: SIC 6513 Apartment Building Operators
Companies: 48   45,663   42.7

6514 Dwelling Operators Except Apartments

Rank	Company Name—*Executive Officer*	Address, City, State, Zip	Phone	Type	Fin	Empls
1	Shee Atika Inc—*Elliott Wimberly*	315 Lincoln St Ste 300, Sitka AK 99835	907-747-3534	R	147*	<.1
2	Aegis Assisted Living—*Dwayne J Clark*	17602 NE Union Hill Rd, Redmond WA 98052		R	48*	1.0

TOTALS: SIC 6514 Dwelling Operators Except Apartments
Companies: 2   195   1.0

6515 Mobile Home Site Operators

Rank	Company Name—*Executive Officer*	Address, City, State, Zip	Phone	Type	Fin	Empls
1	Rancho Carlsbad	5200 El Camino Real, Carlsbad CA 92008	760-438-0237	R	44*	<.1
2	Outdoor Resorts of America Inc	101 S California Ave, Beaumont CA 92223		R	15*	.1

TOTALS: SIC 6515 Mobile Home Site Operators
Companies: 2   59   .1

6517 Railroad Property Lessors

Rank	Company Name—*Executive Officer*	Address, City, State, Zip	Phone	Type	Fin	Empls
1	Pioneer Resources Inc—*Michael Carr*	1318 S Johanson Rd, Peoria IL 61607	309-697-1400	S	5*	<.1

6519 Real Property Lessors Nec

Rank	Company Name—*Executive Officer*	Address, City, State, Zip	Phone	Type	Fin	Empls
1	A and P Properties Ltd—*Christian Haub*	2 Paragon Dr, Montvale NJ 07645	201-573-9700	S	167,519*	78.0
2	Carlson Hospitality Worldwide Procurement Group Inc—*Marilyn C Nelson*	701 Carlson Pkwy, Minnetonka MN 55305	763-212-5000	S	19,253*	163.6
3	Lightstone Group LLC—*Stephen Hamrick*	1985 Cedar Bridge Ave, Lakewood NJ 08701	732-367-0129	R	3,260*	1.2
4	American Realty Investors Inc—*Daniel J Moos*	1603 Lyndon B Johnson, Dallas TX 75234	469-522-4200	P	1,557	N/A
5	U-Store-It Trust—*Dean Jernigan*	460 E Swedesford Rd St, Wayne PA 19087	610-293-5700	P	1,479	1.2
6	Trammell Crow Co—*Robert E Sulentic*	2001 Ross Ave Ste 3400, Dallas TX 75201	214-863-4101	R	802*	6.0
7	Bay Holdings Inc—*John A Kanas*	255 Alhambra Cir, Coral Gables FL 33134	305-569-0327	S	640*	.3
8	CRE Properties Inc—*John A Kanas*	255 Alhambra Cir, Coral Gables FL 33134	305-569-0327	S	640*	.3
9	Tand D Properties South Florida Inc—*John A Kanas*	255 Alhambra Cir, Coral Gables FL 33134	305-569-0327	S	640*	.3
10	Miller-Valentine Group—*William H Krul II*	PO Box 744, Dayton OH 45401	937-293-0900	R	397*	.1
11	California Market Center—*Bill Winsor*	110 E 9th St Ste A727, Los Angeles CA 90079	213-630-3600	R	287*	.1
12	WP Carey and Company LLC—*Trevor P Bond*	50 Rockefeller Plz, New York NY 10020	212-492-1100	P	274	.2
13	CoreSite Realty Corp—*Thomas M Ray*	1050 17th St Ste 800, Denver CO 80265	303-405-1000	P	173	.2
14	Glimcher Dayton Mall Inc—*Dave Duebber*	2700 Miamisburg Center, Dayton OH 45459	937-433-9834	S	156*	.1
15	Amerco Real Estate Co—*Carlos Vizcarro*	2721 N Central Ave Ste, Phoenix AZ 85004	602-263-6555	S	113*	<.1
16	Aeroterm—*John Cammett*	201 West St Ste 200, Annapolis MD 21401	410-280-1100	R	110*	<.1
17	EACO Corp—*Glen F Ceiley*	1500 N Lakeview Ave, Anaheim Hills CA 92807	714-876-2490	P	104	.1

Rank	Company Name—*Executive Officer*	Address, City, State, Zip	Phone	Type	Fin	Empls
18	Pocahontas Land Corp—*Daniel D Smith*	PO Box 1517, Bluefield WV 24701	304-324-2400	S	62*	<.1
19	Nevada Land and Resource Company LLC—*John R Hart*	3480 GS Richards Blvd, Carson City NV 89703	775-885-5000	S	59*	<.1
20	HomeFed Communities Inc—*Paul Borden* Homefed Corp	1903 Wright Pl Ste 220, Carlsbad CA 92008	760-918-8200	S	37*	<.1
21	Tejon Ranch Co—*Robert A Stine*	PO Box 1000, Lebec CA 93243	661-248-3000	P	37	.1
22	Homefed Corp—*Paul J Borden*	1903 Wright Pl Ste 220, Carlsbad CA 92008	760-918-8200	P	34	<.1
23	Hinkson Development Corp—*Craig E Hinkson*	PO Box 955, Ouray CO 81427		R	21*	<.1
24	Aura Energy Corp—*Andre Williams*	PO Box 20712, Boulder CO 80308	303-449-7656	R	14*	.3
25	Property Solutions International Inc—*David Bateman*	1656 S East Bay Blvd, Provo UT 84606	801-375-5522	R	7*	.1
26	Gaston Co—*William P Gaston*	PO Box 10085, Austin TX 78766	512-458-2444	R	7*	<.1
27	Hillery Holding Co—*Terry Hillery*	260 W Broadway, Boston MA 02127	617-765-4456	R	7*	<.1
28	e-Tenants LLC—*Gerard Sweeney*	401 Plymouth Rd Ste 50, Plymouth Meeting PA 19462	610-832-5634	S	5*	<.1
29	BGI Inc—*William F Schwartz*	13091 Pond Springs Rd, Austin TX 78729	512-335-0065	P	2*	<.1
30	Country Estate Products—*Rex German*	PO Box 45, Cozad NE 69130	308-784-2500	R	1*	<.1
31	Ntm Properties Inc—*William Zeus*	100 124 N 12 St, Kenilworth NJ 07033	908-276-7601	R	<1*	<.1
32	Columbia Beverage Co—*Phil Isle*	PO Box 11039, Olympia WA 98508	360-357-9090	R	<1*	<.1
33	Circle Entertainment Inc—*Robert FX Sillerman*	650 Madison Ave, New York NY 10022	212-838-3100	P	<1	<.1

TOTALS: SIC 6519 Real Property Lessors Nec
Companies: 33

					197,697	252.5

6531 Real Estate Agents & Managers

Rank	Company Name—*Executive Officer*	Address, City, State, Zip	Phone	Type	Fin	Empls
1	John L Scott Real Estate—*JLennox Scott*	1700 NW Gilman Blvd St, Issaquah WA 98027	425-392-1211	R	12,356*	4.5
2	BT Commercial Real Estate—*C Michael Kamm*	1650 Technology Dr Ste, San Jose CA 95110	408-436-8000	R	9,664*	2.5
3	Coldwell Banker Real Estate Corp—*Jim Gillespie*	1 Campus Dr, Parsippany NJ 07054	973-407-5466	S	7,681*	2.0
4	NDC LLC—*Gary Kaufman*	6312 S 27 St, Oak Creek WI 53154	414-761-2040	R	6,775*	2.0
5	Keyes Company Realtors—*Michael Pappas*	2121 SW 3rd Ave, Miami FL 33129	305-371-3592	R	6,000*	1.8
6	Long and Foster Real Estate Inc—*P Wesley Foster Jr*	14501 George Carter Wa, Chantilly VA 20151	703-653-8500	R	5,570*	2.1
7	Reece and Nichols—*Jerry Reece*	11500 Granada Ln, Leawood KS 66211	913-945-3704	R	5,357*	2.0
8	Keyes Asset Management Inc—*Michael Pappas*	2121 SW 3rd Ave, Miami FL 33129	305-371-3592	R	5,098*	1.5
9	Real Estate Ono Inc—*Dick Staunton*	25800 Northwestern Hwy, Southfield MI 48075	248-304-6700	R	4,724*	2.0
10	TETRA Real Estate LLC—*Stuart M Brightman*	24955 I-45 N Ste 600, The Woodlands TX 77380	281-367-1983	S	4,309*	2.0
11	Sperry Van Ness—*Kevin Maggiacomo*	18881 Von Karman Ste 7, Irvine CA 92612	949-250-4100	R	4,022*	1.5
12	HHHunt Corp—*David E Reemsnyder II*	800 Hethwood Blvd, Blacksburg VA 24060	540-552-3515	R	3,992*	1.5
13	West USA Commercial Realty Inc—*Clay Fouts*	16150 N Arrowhead Foun, Peoria AZ 85382	602-942-4200	R	3,958*	1.5
14	Prudential Connecticut Realty—*Peter G Helie*	520 Cromwell Ave, Rocky Hill CT 06067	860-571-7000	R	3,928*	1.6
15	TRI Realtors—*Tom Martindale* TRI Commercial Real Estate Services Inc	1 California St Ste 20, San Francisco CA 94111	415-268-2200	S	3,768*	1.1
16	Prudential Gardner Realtors—*Barbara Blades*	3332 N Woodlawn, Metairie LA 70006	504-887-7588	R	3,605*	1.3
17	Jones Lang LaSalle Inc—*Colin Dyer*	200 E Randolph Dr, Chicago IL 60601	312-782-5800	P	3,585	45.5
18	Mac Haik Realty Corp—*Mac Haik*	11757 Katy Fwy Ste 150, Houston TX 77079	281-496-7788	R	3,442*	1.3
19	2020 Properties LLC	226 Landis Ave, Vineland NJ 08360	856-691-7700	S	3,329	.8
20	Highwoods Properties Inc (Raleigh North Carolina)—*Edward J Fritsch*	3100 Smoketree Ct Ste, Raleigh NC 27604	919-872-4924	P	3,181	.4
21	SunCor Development Co—*Steve Betts*	80 E Rio Salado Pkwy S, Tempe AZ 85281	480-317-6800	S	2,927*	.8
22	Nationwide Housing Properties LP	2450 S Shore Blvd Ste, League City TX 77573	281-334-9700	S	2,893*	.7
23	Transwestern Commercial Services—*Larry P Heard*	1900 W Loop S Ste 1300, Houston TX 77027	713-270-7700	R	2,860*	1.4
24	Gene B Glick Company Inc—*David Glick*	PO Box 40177, Indianapolis IN 46240	317-469-0400	R	2,608*	.6
25	Cohen-Esrey Real Estate Services Inc—*Lee Harris*	6800 West 64th St, Overland KS 66202	913-671-3300	R	2,585*	.8
26	Sovran Acquisition LP—*Robert J Attea*	6467 Main St, Williamsville NY 14221	716-633-1850	S	2,466	1.1
27	Riverbay Corp—*Othelia Jones*	2049 Bartow Ave, Bronx NY 10475	718-320-3300	R	2,366*	1.0
28	Weichert REO Services—*James Weichert* Weichert Realtors Inc	1625 Rte 10 E, Morris Plains NJ 07950	973-267-7777	D	2,271*	1.0
29	Amli Residential Properties LP—*Gregory Mutz*	200 W Monroe St, Chicago IL 60606	312-283-4700	S	2,100*	.9
30	Jack Conway and Company Inc—*Richard F Cahill*	137 Washington St, Norwell MA 02061	781-871-0080	R	2,072*	.6
31	LEDIC Management Group—*Pierce Ledbetter*	2650 Thousand Oaks Blv, Memphis TN 38118	901-435-7700	R	2,027*	.6
32	Habitat Co—*Mark Segal*	350 W Hubbard St Ste 5, Chicago IL 60610	312-527-5400	R	2,004*	.9
33	Stirling Properties Inc—*Martin Mayer*	109 Northpark Blvd Ste, Covington LA 70433	985-898-2022	R	1,988*	.4
34	Prudential New Jersey Properties Inc—*Bill Keleher*	220 Davidson Ave, Somerset NJ 08873		R	1,665*	.5
35	HER Realtors Inc	77 E Nationwide Blvd, Columbus OH 43215	614-459-7400	S	1,622*	.6
36	Cushman and Wakefield Inc—*Glen J Rufrano*	1290 Avenue of the Ame, New York NY 10104	212-841-7500	S	1,548*	13.0
37	Glimcher Properties LP—*Michael Glimcher*	180 E Broad St, Columbus OH 43215	614-621-9000	S	1,512*	.4
38	Tri-City Rentals—*Morris Massry*	255 Washington Ave Ext, Albany NY 12205	518-862-6600	R	1,415*	.4
39	Polinger Shannon and Luchs Inc—*Arnold Polinger*	5530 Wisconsin Ave Ste, Chevy Chase MD 20815	301-657-3600	R	1,339*	.5
40	Kidder Mathews Inc—*Jeffrey S Lyon*	601 Union St Ste 4720, Seattle WA 98101	206-296-9600	R	1,333*	.4
41	CB Richard Ellis Services Inc CB Richard Ellis Inc	990 W 190th St Ste 100, Torrance CA 90502	310-516-2300	S	1,324	9.6
42	Taubman Company LP (Bloomfield Hills Michigan)—*Robert S Taubman*	PO Box 200, Bloomfield Hills MI 48303	248-258-6800	S	1,295*	.4
43	Prudential Fox and Roach Inc—*Lawerence Flick IV*	1401 Rte 70 E, Cherry Hill NJ 08034	856-428-8000	R	1,216*	.4
44	CB Richard Ellis Inc—*Brett White*	11150 Santa Monica Blv, Los Angeles CA 90025	212-984-6515	S	1,171*	9.7
45	Phillips Real Estate LLC—*Louie Micheli*	223 Taylor Ave N Ste 2, Seattle WA 98109	206-622-8600	R	1,167*	.4
46	Heritage Texas Properties—*Lynn S Zarr*	1177 W Loop S Ste 1200, Houston TX 77027	713-965-0812	R	1,162*	.3
47	Prudential Kansas City Realty—*David Cooper*	8101 College Blvd, Overland Park KS 66210	913-661-8500	R	1,098*	.4
48	Re/Max International Inc—*Margaret Kelley*	5075 S Syracuse St, Denver CO 80237	303-770-5531	R	1,082*	.4
49	Grady Management Inc—*John Grady*	8630 Fenton St Ste 625, Silver Spring MD 20910	301-587-3330	R	1,077*	.4
50	Tenant Advisors Inc—*David Ven Horst*	1501 E Woodfield Rd, Schaumburg IL 60173	847-843-2460	R	1,000	<.1
51	Younan Properties Inc—*Zaya S Younan*	5959 Topanga Canyon Bl, Woodland Hills CA 91367	818-703-9600	R	978*	.1
52	Coldwell Banker Residential Brokerage—*Kate Rossi* NRT LLC	360 Main St Ste 4, Ridgefield CT 06877	781-684-6300	S	970*	.3
53	Ruffin Cos—*Phil Ruffin*	1522 S Florence St, Wichita KS 67209	316-942-7940	R	966*	.4
54	Keller Williams Realty Inc—*Mark Willis*	807 Las Cimas Pkwy Ste, Austin TX 78746	512-327-3070	R	948*	46.2
55	Charles Dunn Co—*Patrick J Conn*	800 W 6th St 6th Fl, Los Angeles CA 90017	213-683-0500	R	945*	.4
56	Fortune International Realty—*Gerry O Hara D*	328 Crandon Blvd Ste 1, Key Biscayne FL 33149	305-361-1720	R	942*	.4
57	Draper and Kramer Inc—*Forrest D Bailey*	33 W Monroe St 19th Fl, Chicago IL 60603	312-346-8600	R	910*	1.8
58	YaSheng Group—*Zhou Chang Sheng*	805 Veterans Blvd Ste, Redwood City CA 94063	650-363-8345	P	850	15.0
59	Clear Capital—*Duane Andrews*	10875 Pioneer Trl, Truckee CA 96161	530-550-2500	R	835*	.3
60	The Randall Group Inc	9500 SW Barbur Blvd St, Portland OR 97219	503-245-1131	R	835*	.3
61	Lautrec Aquisition Co—*Spencer Partich*	31550 Northwestern Hwy, Farmington Hills MI 48334	248-851-7700	R	812*	.4
62	Tarantino Properties Inc—*Anthony Tarantino*	7887 San Felipe St Ste, Houston TX 77063	713-974-4292	R	803*	.3

Note: An asterisk (*) indicates an estimated financial figure. The company type code used is as follows: R = Private, P = Public, S = Private Subsidiary, B = Public Subsidiary, D = Division, J = Joint Venture, I = Investment Fund.

COMPANY RANKINGS BY SALES WITHIN 4-DIGIT SIC

Rank	Company Name—*Executive Officer*	Address, City, State, Zip	Phone	Type	Fin	Empls
63	Shorenstein Company LP—*Douglas W Shorenstein*	235 Montgomery St 16th, San Francisco CA 94104	415-772-7000	R	744*	.3
64	Towne Realty Inc—*Arthur Wigchers*	710 N Plankinton Ave, Milwaukee WI 53203	414-273-2200	R	734*	.2
65	Coldwell Banker Gundaker—*Gordon A Gundaker Jr*	2458 Old Dorsett Rd St, Maryland Heights MO 63043	314-298-5000	R	689*	.2
66	Public Investment Corp—*DT Alphson*	528 Arizona Ave Ste 20, Santa Monica CA 90401	310-451-5227	R	688*	.3
67	Shorenstein Realty Services LP—*Douglas W Shorenstein* Shorenstein Company LP	235 Montgomery St 16th, San Francisco CA 94104	415-772-7000	S	672*	.3
68	Situs Cos—*Keith Johnson*	4665 Southwest Fwy Ste, Houston TX 77027	713-328-4400	R	662*	.3
69	Colliers Arnold Management Inc—*Lee Arnold*	311 Park Place Blvd St, Clearwater FL 33759	727-442-7184	R	633*	.2
70	Kohner Properties Inc—*Jon Pyzyk*	1034 S Brentwood Ste 1, Saint Louis MO 63117	314-862-5955	R	628*	.3
71	Cencor Realty Services—*Herbert D Weitzman*	4200 N Lamar Blvd Ste, Austin TX 78756		R	622*	.2
72	NRT LLC—*Bruce Zipf*	1 Campus Dr, Parsippany NJ 07054	973-407-2000	S	612*	8.0
73	Allen Tate Company Inc—*Allen Tate Jr*	6700 Fairview Rd, Charlotte NC 28210	704-365-6910	R	600	N/A
74	Grubb and Ellis Co—*Thomas P D'Arcy*	1551 N Tustin Ave Ste, Santa Ana CA 92705	714-667-8252	P	576	4.5
75	Cornish and Carey Commercial—*Charles E Seufferlein*	2804 Mission College B, Santa Clara CA 95054	408-727-9600	R	549*	.2
76	Heitman Advisory Corp—*Maury Tognarelli*	191 N Wacker Dr Ste 25, Chicago IL 60606	312-855-5700	R	548*	.2
77	Thomas Properties Group Inc—*James A Thomas*	515 S Flower St 6th Fl, Los Angeles CA 90071	213-613-1900	P	540	.2
78	Mall of America Co—*Dave Hazelman*	60 E Broadway, Bloomington MN 55425	952-883-8800	R	526*	1.0
79	Arlington Properties Inc—*William C Hulsey*	2117 2nd Ave N, Birmingham AL 35203	205-328-9600	R	501*	.2
80	Morton G Thalhimer Inc—*Paul F Silver*	1313 E Main St Ste 400, Richmond VA 23219	804-648-5881	R	490*	.1
81	Colliers International USA—*Thomas J Hynes Jr*	160 Federal St 11th FL, Boston MA 02110	617-722-0221	R	478*	.1
82	Prudential Carruthers Realtors—*J Thomas Carruthers Jr*	3050 Chain Bridge Rd, Fairfax VA 22030	703-934-1400	R	464*	.1
83	MLG Commercial—*Timothy J Wallen*	13400 Bishops Ln Ste 1, Brookfield WI 53005	262-797-9400	R	421*	.2
84	Janet McAfee Inc—*Ted W Thornhill*	9889 Clayton Rd, Saint Louis MO 63124	314-997-4800	R	412*	.1
85	American Realty Investors—*Fausto Rusca*	11811 North Fwy Ste 30, Houston TX 77060	281-820-0747	S	397*	.2
86	Merin Hunter Codman Inc—*Jay M Grossman*	1601 Forum Pl Ste 200, West Palm Beach FL 33401	561-471-8000	R	384*	.1
87	Charles E Smith Residential Realty Inc—*James D Rosenberg*	2345 Crystal Dr 11th F, Arlington VA 22202	703-920-8500	D	383	2.7
88	Metropolitan Properties of America—*Jeffrey J Cohen*	175 Federal St, Boston MA 02110	617-603-7000	R	371*	.2
89	Sheldon Good and Co—*John J Cuticelli Jr*	333 W Wacker Dr Ste 40, Chicago IL 60606	312-346-1500	R	366*	.1
90	Bluegreen Corp—*John Maloney Jr*	4960 Conference Way N, Boca Raton FL 33431	561-912-8000	P	366	3.8
91	Koenig and Strey Incorporated Realtors—*Nancy Nagy*	1940 N Clark St, Chicago IL 60614	312-642-1400	R	356*	.2
92	Beeler Property Inc—*Carl Beeler*	7500 San Felipe St Ste, Houston TX 77063	713-785-8200	R	351*	.1
93	Atlantic Realty Companies Inc—*David Ross*	8150 Leesburg Pike Ste, Vienna VA 22182	703-760-9500	R	350*	.1
94	Dilbeck Realtors—*Mark Dilbeck*	4766 Park Granada Ste, Calabasas CA 91302	818-703-6100	R	346*	.1
95	Kiemle and Hagood Co—*Tom Quigley*	601 W Main Ave Ste 400, Spokane WA 99201	509-838-6541	R	343*	.1
96	Reeder Management Inc—*Brian P Reeder*	PO Box 99250, Lakewood WA 98496	253-584-6732	R	341*	.2
97	Schuler Bauer Real Estate Services—*Barbara Popp*	4206 Charlestown Rd, New Albany IN 47150	812-948-2888	R	339*	.2
98	Macklowe Properties Inc—*Harry Macklowe*	767 5th Ave, New York NY 10153	212-265-5900	R	334*	.1
99	Targa Real Estate Services Inc—*Tom Petramalo*	PO Box 4508, Federal Way WA 98003	253-815-0393	R	333*	.1
100	Cushman and Wakefield of Georgia Inc—*Bruce Mosler* Cushman and Wakefield Inc	55 Ivan Allen Jr Blvd, Atlanta GA 30308	404-875-1000	D	327*	.1
101	American Invsco Realty Corp—*Kimberly Binkowski*	111 E Chestnut St Ste, Chicago IL 60611	312-621-4100	R	322*	.2
102	Voit Cos—*Robert D Voit*	101 Shipyard Way, Newport Beach CA 92663	818-593-6330	R	315*	.6
103	FNC Realty Corp—*David B Henry*	3333 New Hyde Park Rd, New Hyde Park NY 11042	516-869-9000	S	311	3.9
104	Prime Retail LP—*Robert A Brevenik*	217 E Redwood St 20th, Baltimore MD 21202	410-234-0782	R	306	1.1
105	Lyon and Associates Realtors—*Michael Lyon*	3640 American River Dr, Sacramento CA 95864	916-484-5444	R	288*	.1
106	Transwestern Commercial Services (Bethesda Maryland)—*Eric Mockler*	6700 Rockledge Dr Ste, Bethesda MD 20817	301-571-0900	R	284*	.1
107	Rubloff Inc—*James W Kinney*	80 W Harrison St, Chicago IL 60605	312-980-5100	R	271*	.1
108	SAFECO Properties Inc—*Michael Hughes*	1001 4th Ave, Seattle WA 98154	206-545-5000	S	268*	.1
109	Colliers Macaulay Nicolls International—*Dylan Taylor* Colliers International USA	601 Union St Ste 5300, Seattle WA 98101	206-223-0866	D	260*	.1
110	Unico Properties LLC—*Quentin Kuhrau*	1215 4th Ave Ste 600, Seattle WA 98161	206-628-5050	R	258*	.1
111	Planned Residential Communities Inc—*Robert M Kaye*	PO Box 70, West Long Branch NJ 07764	732-222-2000	R	236*	.1
112	NAI Partners Commercial—*Jon Silberman*	1900 West Loop S Ste 5, Houston TX 77027	713-629-0500	J	234*	.1
113	Moody Rambin Interests—*Howard Rambin III*	1455 W Loop S Ste 700, Houston TX 77027	713-773-5500	R	230*	.1
114	Scalzo Realty Inc—*Paul Scalzo*	2 Stony Hill Rd Ste 20, Bethel CT 06801	203-790-7077	R	230*	.1
115	Silverleaf Resorts Inc—*Robert E Mead*	1221 River Bend Dr Ste, Dallas TX 75247	214-631-1166	P	226	1.1
116	Centro Watt—*Tony Torney*	One Fayette St Ste 300, Conshohocken PA 19428	610-825-7100	R	221*	.1
117	Abbey Co—*Donald G Abbey*	310 Golden Shore Ste 3, Long Beach CA 90802	562-435-2100	R	213*	.1
118	Bowen Real Estate Group—*Walter Bowen*	1800 SW 1st Ave, Portland OR 97201	503-227-4000	R	211*	.1
119	Sunburst Hospitality Corp—*Kevin Hanley*	10770 Columbia Pike St, Silver Spring MD 20901	301-592-3800	R	210*	4.3
120	Post Apartment Homes LP	4401 Northside Pkwy St, Atlanta GA 30327	404-846-5000	S	208*	1.4
121	Revel Companies Inc—*Rory J Underwood*	7050 E 116th St, Fishers IN 46038	317-684-3333	R	208*	.1
122	Eliason Inc—*Brian Eliason*	PO Box 219, Saint Germain WI 54558		R	205*	<.1
123	Jack Christensen Inc—*Jack Christensen*	1475 W Big Beaver Rd S, Troy MI 48084	248-649-6800	R	204*	.2
124	Suhrco Residential Properties—*E Craig Suhrbier*	2010 156th Ave NE Ste, Bellevue WA 98007	425-455-0900	R	200*	.2
125	H Pearce Real Estate Co—*Barbara Pearce*	393 State St, North Haven CT 06473	203-281-3400	R	197*	.1
126	Bradford Realty Services Inc—*Kevin J Santaularia*	9400 N Central Expy St, Dallas TX 75231	972-776-7000	R	193*	.1
127	Move Inc—*Steven Berkowitz*	910 E Hamilton Ave 6th, Campbell CA 95008	805-557-2300	P	192	.9
128	Arthur J Rogers and Co—*William G Schmitz*	3170 Des Plains Ave, Des Plaines IL 60018	847-297-2200	R	188*	.2
129	Core Realty Holdings LLC—*Douglas Moorehead*	1600 Dove St Ste 450, Newport Beach CA 92660	949-863-1031	R	186*	.1
130	Corcoran Group Inc—*Pamela Liebman* NRT LLC	660 Madison Ave, New York NY 10021	212-355-3550	S	182	9.0
131	Rio Rico Realty Inc—*Gerald D Kelfer* Avatar Properties Inc	275 Rio Rico Dr, Rio Rico AZ 85648	520-281-8451	S	181*	.1
132	Prudential Blake Atlantic Realtors—*Jeffrey Christiana*	8 Airline Drive, Albany NY 12203	518-464-0870	R	181*	<.1
133	Four Corners Financial Corp—*William S Gagliano*	370 E Ave, Rochester NY 14604	585-454-2263	R	180*	.1
134	Tenth City LLC Koeppel Companies LLC	575 Lexington Ave Fl 2, New York NY 10022	212-344-2150	S	178*	.1
135	Dayton Mall Venture LLC—*Dave Duebber* Glimcher Properties LP	2700 Miamisburg-Center, Dayton OH 45459	937-433-9834	S	177*	.1
136	Ferland Corp—*A Austin Ferland*	558 Smithfield Avenue, Pawtucket RI 02860	401-728-4000	R	177*	.1
137	Olde Town Brokers Inc—*Phillip Rampy*	11 N Summerlin Ave Ste, Orlando FL 32801	407-425-5069	R	175*	<.1
138	Palm Harbor Marketing Inc—*Larry Keener*	605 S Frontage Rd Ste, Plant City FL 33566		S	172*	<.1
139	Collier Enterprises—*Tom Flood*	2550 Goodlette Rd Rm 1, Naples FL 34103	239-261-4455	R	171*	.1
140	Army Hawaii Family Housing LLC—*Leslie Dalzell*	215 Duck Rd Bldg 950, Schofield Barracks HI 96857	808-275-3100	R	170*	.3
141	Garden Properties Corp—*Leonard Wilf*	820 Morris Tpke Ste 10, Short Hills NJ 07078	973-467-5000	R	170*	5.0
142	Visionary Enterprises Inc—*Bryan Mills*	7330 Shadeland Sta Ste, Indianapolis IN 46256	317-621-7400	R	170*	1.6
143	Walsh Manning Corp—*Leonard Barnes*	60 E 42nd St Ste 1166, New York NY 10165	212-875-7742	R	168*	<.1
144	Smith and Associates Realtors Inc—*Robert Glaser*	3801 Bay to Bay Blvd, Tampa FL 33629	855-292-6556	R	167*	.1

Rank	Company Name—*Executive Officer*	Address, City, State, Zip	Phone	Type	Fin	Empls
145	Halpin Smith and Christian Real Estate Services Inc	3101 Western Ave Ste 4, Seattle WA 98121	206-282-5200	S	166*	.1
146	Orion Real Estate Services Inc—*Gene R Blevins*	1455 W Loop S Ste 800, Houston TX 77027	713-622-5844	R	165*	.1
147	United Commercial Realty Co—*Micky Ashmore*	7001 Preston Rd Ste 22, Dallas TX 75205	214-526-6262	R	164*	.1
148	Dunes Properties Of Charleston Inc—*Randolph Walker*	PO Box 524, Isle Of Palms SC 29451	843-886-5600	R	163*	.1
149	Central Management Inc—*Victor E Vacek*	820 Gessner Ste 1525, Houston TX 77024	713-961-9777	R	163*	<.1
150	William L Lyon and Associates Inc—*Larry Knapp*	3640 American River Dr, Sacramento CA 95864		R	160*	.1
151	MS Management Associates Inc (Indianapolis Indiana)—*David Simon*	PO Box 7033, Indianapolis IN 46207	317-636-1600	R	160*	5.0
152	LandSafe Inc—*Michael J Faine*	6400 Legacy Dr, Plano TX 75024		S	159	1.0
153	Sgs North America Inc—*Christian Jilch*	201 State Rt 17 Fl 7, Rutherford NJ 07070	201-508-3000	R	158*	4.5
154	PM Realty Group LP—*Rick V Kirk*	1000 Main St Ste 2400, Houston TX 77002	713-209-5800	R	157*	1.1
155	Peabody Hotel Group—*Martin S Belz*	5118 Park Ave Ste 245, Memphis TN 38117	901-762-5400	S	155*	2.8
156	Hawkins Inc—*OE Hawkins*	2033 Portage Rd, Wooster OH 44691	330-262-4023	R	154*	<.1
157	Unlimited Horizons Inc—*Richard Rager*	11480 Sunset Ste 120, Reston VA 20190	703-435-0776	R	152*	.1
158	Fischer and Co—*Clifford R Fischer*	13455 Noel Rd Ste 1900, Dallas TX 75240	972-980-7100	R	149*	.1
159	Value Group Inc—*Andrew B Abramson*	1122 Clifton Ave, Clifton NJ 07013	973-473-2800	R	148*	.1
160	Beal Cos—*Robert Beal*	177 Milk St, Boston MA 02109	617-451-2100	R	146*	.1
161	Avatar Properties Inc—*Jon M Donnell*	201 Alhambra Cir 12th, Coral Gables FL 33134	305-442-7000	S	145*	.1
162	New Water Street Corp—*Harry Bridgewood*	55 Water St Ste Conc6, New York NY 10041	212-747-9120	R	143*	<.1
163	Merritt Properties LLC—*Laurie Dettamer*	2066 Lord Baltimore Dr, Baltimore MD 21244	410-298-2600	R	140*	.2
164	Baird and Warner Inc—*Stephen W Baird*	120 S Lasalle St Ste 2, Chicago IL 60603	312-857-9654	R	139*	1.8
165	Real Estate Mart of Tennessee Inc	7836 Church St, Millington TN 38053	901-872-8888	R	136*	<.1
166	Cutler/GMAC Inc—*Bud Marting*	2800 W Market St, Akron OH 44333	330-836-9141	R	131*	<.1
167	Corus Realty Holdings Inc—*Michael T Gorman*	6726 Curran St, McLean VA 22101	703-827-0075	R	129*	<.1
168	Prudential Slater James River Realtors—*Earl M Jackson*	2737 McRae Rd, Richmond VA 23235	804-320-1391	R	128*	.1
169	Beitler Commercial Realty Services—*Barry Beitler*	825 S Barrington Ave, Los Angeles CA 90049	310-820-2955	R	125*	<.1
170	Richard Bowers and Co—*Richard E Bowers*	260 Peachtree St Ste 2, Atlanta GA 30303	404-816-1600	R	123*	.1
171	Greystar Management Services LP—*Robert Faith*	18 Broad St 3rd Fl, Charleston SC 29401	843-579-9400	R	121*	.1
172	ZipRealty Inc—*Lanny Baker*	2000 Powell St Ste 300, Emeryville CA 94608	510-735-2600	P	119	.2
173	Divaris Real Estate Inc—*Micheal Divaris*	One Columbus Ctr Ste 7, Virginia Beach VA 23462	757-497-2113	R	116*	.1
174	Terranomics Retail Services LP—*Matthew Kircher* BT Commercial Real Estate	1350 Bayshore Hwy Ste, Burlingame CA 94010	650-348-2400	D	116*	.1
175	US Realty Consultants Inc—*Robert J Feeley*	492 S High St Ste 200, Columbus OH 43215	614-221-9494	R	114*	<.1
176	Hayman Co—*Steven P Hayman*	5700 Crooks Rd Ste 400, Troy MI 48098	248-879-7777	R	111*	<.1
177	Louisiana Chemical Equipment Co—*Stephen Rotenberg*	PO Box 65064, Baton Rouge LA 70896	225-923-3602	R	111*	<.1
178	Ben Carter Properties Inc—*Paisley Boney*	3050 Peachtree Rd Ste, Atlanta GA 30305	404-869-2800	R	110*	<.1
179	Betz Cos—*Raymond R Betz*	10940 W Sam Houston Pk, Houston TX 77064	281-873-4444	R	107*	<.1
180	Demmer Engineering and Machine Co—*William Demmer*	PO Box 12030, Lansing MI 48901	517-321-3600	R	106*	.7
181	Glimcher Lloyd Center LLC—*Wanda Rosenbarger* Glimcher Properties LP	2201 Lloyd Ctr, Portland OR 97232	503-282-2511	S	106*	<.1
182	Tic Properties LLC—*Barry L Gruebbel*	101 N Main St Ste 1203, Greenville SC 29601	864-672-4842	R	106*	<.1
183	Stevensen and Neal Realtors—*Mark Stevenson*	116 E Campbell Ave Ste, Campbell CA 95008	408-370-1020	R	105*	<.1
184	Koeppel Companies LLC—*Caleb Koeppel*	575 Lexington Ave 29th, New York NY 10022	212-344-2150	R	104*	<.1
185	Moison Investment Co—*Jerry E Moison*	350 2nd St Ste 7, Los Altos CA 94022	650-949-9310	R	104*	<.1
186	Grubb and Ellis Realty Advisers Inc—*Thomas P D'Arcy* Grubb and Ellis Co	1551 N Tustin Ave Ste, Santa Ana CA 92705	312-698-6700	S	102*	.1
187	Davis Group LLP—*Michael Davis*	Down Town Business Dis, Los Angeles CA 90010	310-202-4333	R	100*	.3
188	Carlsberg Management Co—*William Geary*	PO Box 92006, Los Angeles CA 90009	310-258-9000	R	100*	.1
189	Ross Realty Investments Inc—*Barry Ross*	3325 S University Dr S, Davie FL 33328	954-452-5000	R	100*	<.1
190	Carlson GMAC Real Estate—*John Zerrden*	1847 Memorial Dr, Chicopee MA 01020	413-532-1418	S	100*	<.1
191	Kappes Miller Management—*Walter Berninger*	1500 112th NE, Bellevue WA 98004	425-688-2042	R	100	<.1
192	Team Resources Inc—*David Cantor*	210 Clay Ave, Lyndhurst NJ 07071	201-438-1177	R	100*	<.1
193	American Appraisal Associates Inc—*Joseph P Zvesper*	411 E Wisconsin Ave St, Milwaukee WI 53202	414-271-7240	R	99*	.9
194	Milan Properties—*Amy Rubenstein*	5369 W Pico Blvd 2nd F, Los Angeles CA 90019	323-850-4900	R	99*	<.1
195	Coldwell Banker Crossroads Realtors Coldwell Banker Real Estate Corp	1158 NW Cache Rd, Lawton OK 73507	580-248-8460	S	96*	<.1
196	Harrison and Lear Inc—*Thomas T Thompson*	2310 Tower Pl Ste 105, Hampton VA 23666	757-825-9100	R	93*	<.1
197	Lakes Mall LLC—*Michael Hagen*	5600 Harvey St, Muskegon MI 49444	231-798-7104	S	91*	<.1
198	Getty Realty Corp—*David B Driscoll*	125 Jericho Tpke Ste 1, Jericho NY 11753	516-478-5400	P	88	<.1
199	Westmont Hospitality Group—*Al Richards*	5847 San Felipe Ste 46, Houston TX 77057	713-782-9100	R	87*	<.1
200	TCDFW Inc—*Adam Saphier*	2001 Ross Ave Ste 3400, Dallas TX 75201	214-863-4101	S	85*	.2
201	Colliers Arnold—*Lee E Arnold Jr*	311 Park Pl Blvd Ste 6, Clearwater FL 33759	727-442-7184	R	84*	.2
202	Slifer Smith and Frampton Real Estate—*Jim Flaum*	PO Drawer 2820, Avon CO 81620	970-845-2000	R	84*	<.1
203	NAI Southern Real Estate Inc—*Caldwell R Rose*	PO Box 35309, Charlotte NC 28235	704-375-1000	R	83*	<.1
204	Nitze-Stagen and Company Inc—*Frank Stagen*	2401 Utah Ave S Ste 30, Seattle WA 98134	206-467-0420	R	83*	<.1
205	United Marketing Inc (Bellevue Washington)—*Tom Anderson*	13400 NE 20th St Ste 3, Bellevue WA 98005	425-562-1200	R	83*	<.1
206	Freeport Center Associates—*Betty Parker*	PO Box 160466 Bldg A-1, Clearfield UT 84016	801-825-9741	R	80*	<.1
207	PropSys Real Estate Management Inc—*Susan Bosse*	PO Box 660, Lewiston ME 04243	207-784-0142	R	78*	<.1
208	Morgan Stanley Real Estate Fund—*Amy Wissmann*	1999 Ave of the Stars, Los Angeles CA 90067	310-788-2000	R	77*	<.1
209	Grubb and Ellis Management Services Inc—*Thomas P D'Arcy* Grubb and Ellis Co	500 W Monroe St Ste 29, Chicago IL 60661	312-698-6700	S	75*	<.1
210	LK Wood Realty Inc—*LK Wood Jr*	4604 Butler Bend Court, Saint Louis MO 63128	314-351-4444	R	74*	.1
211	Barclay's International Realty Inc—*Shirley Wyner*	249 Peruvian Ave, Palm Beach FL 33480	561-659-0000	R	74*	<.1
212	Mesirow Stein Real Estate Inc—*James C Tyree*	350 N Clark St, Chicago IL 60610	312-595-6200	S	73*	.7
213	Grubb and Ellis Consulting Services Co—*Thomas P D'Arcy* Grubb and Ellis Co	1551 N Tustin Ave Ste, Santa Ana CA 92705	312-698-6700	S	73*	<.1
214	Old Hickory Mall Venture—*Tommy White*	2021 N Highland Ave, Jackson TN 38305	731-664-5319	S	73*	<.1
215	Steele Realty and Investment Company Inc—*Michael Steele*	8900 Grant Line Rd, Elk Grove CA 95624	916-686-6500	R	70*	<.1
216	Campi Properties Inc—*Gary Campi*	195 S San Antonio Rd, Los Altos CA 94022	650-941-4300	R	69*	<.1
217	Gibson Brokers Inc—*Ray Gibson*	PO Box 310, Englewood OH 45322	937-836-5600	R	69*	<.1
218	Imperial Realty Co—*Larry Klairmont*	4747 W Peterson Ave St, Chicago IL 60646	773-736-4100	R	68*	.1
219	Cornell and Associates Inc—*J Blake Cornell*	2633 Eastlake Ave E St, Seattle WA 98102	206-329-0085	R	67*	<.1
220	Corporate Realty—*Russell Palmer*	201 St Charles Ave Ste, New Orleans LA 70170	504-581-5005	R	67*	<.1
221	Queenstowne Realty Inc—*David Pliner*	10015 Park Cedar Dr S, Charlotte NC 28210	704-543-6046	R	67*	<.1
222	Starboard TCN Worldwide Real Estate Services—*Doron Baruth*	33 New Montgomery St S, San Francisco CA 94105	415-765-6900	R	67*	<.1
223	The Property Group of Connecticut Inc—*Sylvan Ponerantz*	25 Crescent St, Stamford CT 06906	203-967-8337	R	67*	<.1
224	Yates Wood and MacDonald Inc—*Nancy Darlington*	425 Pontius Ave N Ste, Seattle WA 98109	206-268-3300	R	67*	<.1
225	Flatley Co—*John J Flatley*	35 Braintree Hill Offi, Braintree MA 02184	781-848-2000	R	66*	.6
226	Talbot Realty Group—*Bobby Talbot*	747 Magazine St Unit 7, New Orleans LA 70130	504-525-9763	R	66*	<.1
227	Brookfield Square JV—*Lori Boinski*	95 N Moorland Rd, Brookfield WI 53005	262-797-7245	S	66*	<.1

Note: An asterisk (*) indicates an estimated financial figure. The company type code used is as follows: R = Private, P = Public, S = Private Subsidiary, B = Public Subsidiary, D = Division, J = Joint Venture, I = Investment Fund.

COMPANY RANKINGS BY SALES WITHIN 4-DIGIT SIC

Rank	Company Name—*Executive Officer*	Address, City, State, Zip	Phone	Type	Fin	Empls
228	Grubb and Ellis Utah Realty—*Robert Osbrink* Grubb and Ellis Co	2215 Sanders Road Ste4, Northbrook IL 60062		S	63	N/A
229	Marcus and Millichap Real Estate Investment Brokerage Co—*John J Kerin*	16830 Ventura Blvd Ste, Encino CA 91436	818-212-2700	R	62*	1,2
230	King Group Inc (Cleveland Ohio)—*Donald M King*	25550 Chagrin Blvd Ste, Beachwood OH 44122	216-831-9330	R	62*	<.1
231	Century 21 Evans Realtors—*LD Evans*	2250 Morriss Rd Ste 20, Flower Mound TX 75028	972-539-8877	R	61*	.1
232	Grubb and Ellis Affiliates Inc—*Thomas P D'Arcy* Grubb and Ellis Co	1551 N Tustin Ave Ste, Santa Ana CA 92705		S	61*	<.1
233	Ukpeagvik Inupiat Corp—*Anthony Edwardson*	PO Box 890, Barrow AK 99723		R	60*	.2
234	Meridian Mall Company Inc—*Larry Parsons*	1982 Grand River Ave, Okemos MI 48864	517-349-2031	S	59*	<.1
235	Re/Max North Realtors—*Margaret Kelly*	870 High St, Worthington OH 43085	614-431-0300	R	57*	<.1
236	Stroud Mall LLC—*Kevin Dixon*	454 Stroud Mall, Stroudsburg PA 18360	570-424-2770	S	55*	<.1
237	Jenny Pruitt and Associates Inc—*Dan Parmer*	4848 Ashford Dunwoody, Atlanta GA 30338	770-394-2131	S	54*	.1
238	Comey and Shepherd Realtors—*Scott Nelson*	6901 Wooster Pike, Cincinnati OH 45227	513-561-5800	S	52*	.3
239	HW Allen Co—*Phillip Allen*	4835 S Peoria Ave, Tulsa OK 74105	918-747-8700	R	52*	<.1
240	Vallone and Associates—*Vincent Vallone Jr*	1937 W Gray Ste 200, Houston TX 77019	713-524-9131	R	52*	<.1
241	Keystone Property Group—*William Glazer*	1 Presidential Blvd St, Bala Cynwyd PA 19004	610-980-7000	R	51*	.1
242	Kevin F Donohoe Company Inc—*Kevin F Donohoe*	Bell Atlantic Tower 17, Philadelphia PA 19103	215-988-0440	R	51*	<.1
243	Kennedy-Wilson Holdings Inc—*William J McMorrow*	9701 Wilshire Blvd Ste, Beverly Hills CA 90212	310-887-6400	P	51	.3
244	Andover Company Inc—*Dave Baumer*	415 Baker Blvd Ste 200, Tukwila WA 98188	206-244-0770	R	50*	<.1
245	Performa Entertainment Real Estate Inc—*John A Elkington*	615 Oakleaf Ln, Memphis TN 38117	901-526-0110	R	50*	<.1
246	Potter-Taylor and Co—*Timothy Taylor*	1792 Tribute Rd Ste 20, Sacramento CA 95815	916-923-0200	R	50*	<.1
247	Realty Asset Advisors LLC—*Timothy B Johnson*	1311 N Westshore Blvd, Tampa FL 33607	813-574-2200	R	50*	<.1
248	Grubb and Ellis Institutional Properties Inc—*Thomas P D'Arcy* Grubb and Ellis Co	1551 N Tustin Ave Ste, Santa Ana CA 92705		S	49*	<.1
249	Crane Real Estate Group—*Roger Crane*	PO Box 14054, Spokane WA 99214	509-921-2121	R	47*	.1
250	Beauchamp Enterprises Inc—*Richard Beauchamp*	151 Kalmus Dr Ste B150, Costa Mesa CA 92626	949-851-8087	R	46*	<.1
251	First Properties of The Carolinas Inc—*Julie VanSlanbrook*	2222 Gold Hill Rd, Fort Mill SC 29715	803-548-0131	R	46*	<.1
252	Realty Trac Inc—*James Saccacio*	1 Venture Plaza Ste 30, Irvine CA 92618	949-502-8300	R	45*	.1
253	Grubb and Ellis Asset Services Co—*Thomas P D'Arcy* Grubb and Ellis Co	1551 N Tustin Ave Ste, Santa Ana CA 92705		S	45*	<.1
254	CROWN Management Corp—*Robert Locke*	1702 Macy Dr, Roswell GA 30076	770-998-9300	R	45*	<.1
255	Whittle Realty—*Mahlon Whittle*	520 Cottonwood St Ste, Woodland CA 95695	530-666-1925	R	45*	<.1
256	Carter and Associates LLC—*Bob Peterson*	171 17th St NW Ste 120, Atlanta GA 30363	404-888-3000	R	44*	.4
257	Greystar Realty Services—*Bob Faith*	18 Broad St 3rd Fl, Charleston SC 29401	602-522-1200	R	44*	.4
258	Fayette Plaza LLC—*Myron Worley*	3401 Nicholasville Rd, Lexington KY 40503	859-272-3493	S	44*	<.1
259	Allied Group Inc (Bellevue Washington)—*Gregory Anderson*	221 Wells Ave S Ste 10, Renton WA 98057	425-226-5150	R	43*	<.1
260	Max J Derbes Inc—*David Quinn*	5440 Mounes St Ste 100, New Orleans LA 70123	504-733-4555	R	43*	<.1
261	Three Seasons Corp	8014 SW 135th St Rd, Ocala FL 34473	352-347-2322	S	43*	<.1
262	Residential Properties Management Inc	1105 Brookstown Ave, Winston Salem NC 27101	336-724-1000	S	42*	<.1
263	Albert D Phelps Inc—*John P Crosby*	401 Merritt 7, Norwalk CT 06851	203-847-8087	R	42*	<.1
264	Gladstone Commercial Corp—*David Gladstone*	1521 Westbranch Dr Ste, McLean VA 22102	703-287-5893	P	42	N/A
265	Schweitzer Real Estate Inc—*Paul Schweitzer*	3555 E 14 Mile Rd, Sterling Heights MI 48310		R	41*	.1
266	Studley Inc—*Mitchell S Steir*	300 Park Ave Ste 3, New York NY 10022	212-326-1029	R	40*	.4
267	CSX Real Property Inc—*Stephen A Crosby*	500 Water St, Jacksonville FL 32202	904-359-3200	S	40*	.1
268	HA Gill and Son Inc—*John W Gill Sr*	1722 Wisconsin Ave NW, Washington DC 20007	202-338-5000	R	40*	<.1
269	Western Development Corp—*Herbert S Miller*	3255 Grace St NW, Washington DC 20007	202-338-5200	R	40*	<.1
270	Stiles Realty Co	301 E Las Olas Blvd, Fort Lauderdale FL 33301	954-627-9400	D	40*	<.1
271	Parkway Place Inc—*Lucinda Hawthorn*	2801 Memorial Pkwy S, Huntsville AL 35801	256-533-0700	S	40*	<.1
272	Post Oak Mall—*Jack Love*	1500 Harvey Rd, College Station TX 77840	979-764-0060	S	40*	<.1
273	AMSCO Inc	600 Lawrence Ave Ste 7, Ellwood City PA 16117	724-758-5584	S	40	N/A
274	Glimcher SuperMall Venture LLC—*Greg Fleser* Glimcher Properties LP	1101 SuperMall Way Ste, Auburn WA 98001	253-833-1790	S	39*	<.1
275	Five Points Title Services Company Inc	8014 SW 135th St Rd, Ocala FL 34473	352-347-2322	S	38*	<.1
276	State Wide Investors Inc—*Roy Hearrean*	5000 E Spring St Ste 7, Long Beach CA 90815	562-984-3500	R	37*	.1
277	Parkdale Mall Associates—*Kurt Lundgreen*	6155 Eastex Fwy Ste 20, Beaumont TX 77706	409-898-2222	S	37*	<.1
278	Portsmouth Square Inc—*John V Winfield*	820 Moraga Dr, Los Angeles CA 90049	310-889-2500	B	36	<.1
279	Gerald A Teel Company Inc—*Gerald A Teel*	974 Campbell Rd Ste 20, Houston TX 77024	713-467-5858	R	36*	<.1
280	PRM Realty Group LLC—*David M Glickman*	150 N Wacker Dr, Chicago IL 60606	312-704-0400	R	35	.3
281	Patterson-Schwartz and Associates Inc—*Richard T Christopher*	7234 Lancaster Pke Ste, Hockessin DE 19707	302-239-3000	R	35*	.5
282	Fourmidable Group—*J Ronald Slavik*	32500 Telegraph Rd Ste, Bingham Farms MI 48025	248-593-4600	R	35*	.4
283	Grubb and Ellis New York Inc—*Thomas P D'Arcy* Grubb and Ellis Co	1177 Ave of the Americ, New York NY 10036	212-759-9700	S	35*	<.1
284	Terminella and Associates—*Tom Terminella*	123 N College, Fayetteville AR 72701	479-973-9777	R	35*	<.1
285	MacLaughlin and Co—*Jim MacLaughlin*	1401 Shore St, West Sacramento CA 95691	916-371-9021	R	34*	<.1
286	United Systems Integrators Corp—*Alex Molinaroli*	281 Tresser Blvd 2 Sta, Stamford CT 06901	203-327-7272	R	33*	.2
287	Maui Condominium and Home Realty Inc—*James S Olin*	1819 S Kihei Rd Ste D1, Kihei HI 96753	808-879-5445	S	33*	<.1
288	Fox and Bubela Inc—*John Fox*	9977 W Sam Houston Pky, Houston TX 77064	281-477-7889	R	33*	<.1
289	Solid Source Realty Inc—*Michele Velcheck*	10900 Crabapple Rd, Roswell GA 30075	770-475-1130	R	32*	2.4
290	Frederick Ross Co—*John P Box*	717 17th St Ste 2000, Denver CO 80202	303-892-1111	R	32*	.3
291	Robert L Bradley and Associates Inc—*Robert Bradley*	10200 Richmond Ave Ste, Houston TX 77042	713-954-2088	R	32*	<.1
292	Deltona Marketing Corp	8014 SW 135th St Rd, Ocala FL 34473	352-347-2322	S	31*	<.1
293	Colliers Pinkard Colliers International USA	100 Light St Ste 1400, Baltimore MD 21202	410-752-4285	S	30*	.3
294	Sunbelt Title Agency and Lending Services—*E Coley Tooke*	300 S Park Pl Ste 150, Clearwater FL 33759	727-723-8880	R	30*	.1
295	Bridgewater Properties—*Robert Bridgewater*	5612 Jefferson Hwy, New Orleans LA 70123	504-733-9638	R	30*	<.1
296	Crane Realty Services Inc—*Thomas P D'Arcy*	5430 LBJ Frwy Ste 1400, Dallas TX 75240	972-450-3300	S	29*	<.1
297	Twin Peaks Mall Associates Ltd—*Sandra O'Clock* Jones Lang LaSalle Inc	1250 S Hover Rd, Longmont CO 80501	303-651-6454	S	29*	<.1
298	Westgate Mall LP—*Ron Thomas*	205 W Blackstock Rd St, Spartanburg SC 29301	864-574-0264	S	29*	<.1
299	Amurcon Corp—*Gilbert Silverman*	32100 Telegraph Rd Ste, Bingham Farms MI 48025	248-646-0202	R	28*	.3
300	PWS Inc—*Morton Pollack*	6500 Flotilla St, Los Angeles CA 90040	323-721-8832	R	28*	.1
301	Major Properties Realtors Corp—*Bradley Luster*	1200 W Olympic Blvd, Los Angeles CA 90015	213-747-4151	R	28*	<.1
302	Don Randon Real Estate Inc—*Don Randon*	600 Carondelet St Ste, New Orleans LA 70130	504-581-1111	R	28*	<.1
303	REVAC Inc—*William C Forrest*	PO Box 219029, Houston TX 77218	281-496-2388	R	28*	<.1
304	Realty One Group Inc—*Kuba Jewgieniew*	1333 N Buffalo Dr Unit, Las Vegas NV 89128	702-898-6111	R	27*	<.1
305	Grubb and Ellis Mortgage Services Inc—*Thomas P D'Arcy* Grubb and Ellis Co	500 W Monroe St Ste 29, Chicago IL 60661	312-698-6700	S	27*	<.1
306	Landauer Securities Inc—*Thomas P D'Arcy* Grubb and Ellis Consulting Services Co	1551 N Tustin Ave Ste, Santa Ana CA 92705	312-698-6700	S	27*	<.1

Rank	Company Name—*Executive Officer*	Address, City, State, Zip	Phone	Type	Fin	Empls
307	Lechner Realty Group Inc—*Steven B Lechner*	13421 Manchester Rd St, Saint Louis MO 63131	314-909-8100	R	27*	<.1
308	Alliance Management Inc—*Linden Larson*	801 2nd Ave Ste 1501, Seattle WA 98104	206-903-2480	R	27*	<.1
309	Brown Stevens Elmore and Sparre—*Fritz Brown*	5 Park Center Dr Ste 1, Sacramento CA 95825	916-929-0262	R	27*	<.1
310	Katz Properties Inc—*Daniel Katz*	614 W Brown Deer Rd St, Bayside WI 53217	414-332-8080	R	27*	<.1
311	Fredericks Commercial—*Brent Fredericks*	2537 S Gessner Rd Ste, Houston TX 77063	713-789-0890	R	27*	<.1
312	HomeVestors of America Inc—*John P Hayes*	8500 Greenville Ave St, Dallas TX 75206	972-761-0046	R	27*	N/A
313	Landauer Hospitality International Inc—*Thomas P D'Arcy* Grubb and Ellis Consulting Services Co	1551 N Tustin Ave Ste, Santa Ana CA 92705		S	27	N/A
314	Russ Lyon Realty Co—*Deems Dickinson*	7135 E Camelback Rd St, Scottsdale AZ 85259	480-287-5200	R	26*	.4
315	San Francisco Design Center—*Bill R Poland*	2 Henry Adams St Ste 4, San Francisco CA 94103	415-490-5800	R	26*	.1
316	Shorenstein Asset Services East LP—*Douglas W Shorenstein* Shorenstein Realty Services LP	850 3rd Ave 17th Fl, New York NY 10022	212-986-2100	S	26*	.1
317	Aequus Property Management Co—*Thomas P D'Arcy* Grubb and Ellis Co	1551 N Tustin Ave Ste, Santa Ana CA 92705	714-667-8252	S	26*	<.1
318	Grubb and Ellis of Nevada Inc—*Thomas P D'Arcy* Grubb and Ellis Co	3930 Howard Hughes Pkw, Las Vegas NV 89169	702-733-7500	S	26*	<.1
319	Select Properties Ltd—*Leon Giorgio*	PO Box 75010, Metairie LA 70033	504-833-0044	R	26*	<.1
320	Chelsea Moore Co—*Daniel W Mawer*	8940 Glendale-Milford, Loveland OH 45140	513-561-5454	R	26*	<.1
321	Barletta and Associates Inc—*Phillip F Barletta*	1313 Campbell Rd Ste F, Houston TX 77055	713-464-7700	R	26*	<.1
322	Scott Stephens and Associates Inc—*Scott Stephens*	12723 Woodforest Blvd, Houston TX 77015	713-451-3600	R	26*	<.1
323	Steinbauer Associates Inc—*John R Steinbauer*	7875 NW 12th, Miami FL 33126	305-629-9740	R	26*	<.1
324	Valuation Management Group—*Vicky Thompson*	1640 Powers Ferry Rd B, Marietta GA 30067	678-483-4420	R	25	.1
325	Cole-Layer-Trumble Co—*John S Marr*	3199 Klepinger Rd, Dayton OH 45406	937-276-5261	S	25*	.5
326	First Realty Management Corp—*Jan Brandin*	151 Tremont St, Boston MA 02111	617-423-7000	R	25*	.2
327	Commerce CRG LLC—*Mike Lawson*	170 S Main St Ste 1600, Salt Lake City UT 84101	801-322-2000	R	25*	<.1
328	Oak Creek Housing Properties LP	2450 S Shore Blvd Ste, League City TX 77573	281-334-9710	S	25*	<.1
329	Price Brothers Realty Co	12721 Metcalf Ave Ste, Overland Park KS 66213	913-381-2280	R	25	<.1
330	Market Leader Inc—*Ian Morris*	11332 NE 122nd Way Ste, Kirkland WA 98034	425-952-5500	P	24	.2
331	AMC Inc—*Frank McDowell*	10540 Talbert Ave Ste, Fountain Valley CA 92708	714-754-6262	R	24*	.2
332	Avatar Realty Inc—*Susan M Buscaglia* Avatar Properties Inc	896 Cypress Pkwy, Poinciana FL 34759	407-944-4600	S	24*	<.1
333	Belfry Development Corp—*William Battjes*	3777 Sparks Dr SE Ste, Grand Rapids MI 49546	616-942-1930	R	23*	<.1
334	Johnson-Rast and Hays Company Inc—*Robert E Reed*	2501 20th Pl S Ste 425, Birmingham AL 35223	205-871-6364	R	23*	<.1
335	Woods Management Corporation of Florida—*Richard Goldberg*	2740 W 5th Ave, Hialeah FL 33010	305-887-9801	R	23*	<.1
336	JB Goodwin Residential Corp—*JB Goodwing*	3933 Steck Ave Ste B10, Austin TX 78759	512-502-7804	R	22*	.2
337	JM Jayson and Company Inc—*Joseph Jayson*	2350 N Forest Rd Ste, Getzville NY 14068	716-636-9090	R	22*	.2
338	Taggart Management and Real Estate Services LLC	3780 Fishinger Blvd, Hilliard OH 43026	614-876-4848	R	22*	<.1
339	Grubb and Ellis Mortgage Group Inc—*Thomas P D'Arcy* Grubb and Ellis Co	1551 N Tustin Ave Ste, Santa Ana CA 92705		S	22*	<.1
340	Grubb and Ellis of Oregon Inc—*Thomas P D'Arcy* Grubb and Ellis Co	1120 NW Couch Ste 350, Portland OR 97209	503-241-1155	S	22*	<.1
341	Page Mill Properties—*David Taran*	480 Cowper St 2nd Fl, Palo Alto CA 94301	650-833-3800	R	22*	<.1
342	Agree LP—*Richard Agree*	31850 Northwestern Hwy, Farmington Hills MI 48334	248-737-4190	S	22*	<.1
343	Foothills Mall Inc—*JoAnn King*	197 Foothills Dr, Maryville TN 37801	865-982-3613	S	22*	<.1
344	Muselli Commercial Realtors—*Vincent C Muselli*	1513 6th St Ste 201, Santa Monica CA 90401	310-458-4100	R	22*	<.1
345	Faulk and Foster Real Estate Inc—*John Perry*	PO Box 2568, Monroe LA 71207	318-325-4666	R	22*	.1
346	Benjamin E Sherman and Sons Inc—*David A Sherman*	500 Lake Cook Rd Ste 2, Deerfield IL 60015	847-374-2700	R	21*	.2
347	Grubb and Ellis of Michigan Inc—*Thomas P D'Arcy* Grubb and Ellis Co	300 Ottawa Ave Ste 400, Grand Rapids MI 49503	616-774-3500	S	21*	<.1
348	Gerber/Somma Associates Inc—*Harold Gerber*	210 River St Ste 33, Hackensack NJ 07601	201-646-1234	R	21*	<.1
349	Vacation Internationale Ltd—*Roy Fraser*	1417 116th Ave NE, Bellevue WA 98004	425-454-3065	R	20	.2
350	Colliers Bennett and Kahnweiler Inc—*Thomas J Hynes Jr*	160 Federal St Ste 11t, Boston MA 02110		R	20*	<.1
351	Valleyfair Realty Co—*Rich Shulman*	1975 Hamilton Ave Ste, San Jose CA 95125	408-371-4415	R	20*	<.1
352	Texas Pacific Land Trust—*Roy Thomas*	1700 Pacific Ave Ste 1, Dallas TX 75201	214-969-5530	P	20	<.1
353	Brawley and Associates Inc—*Reid Brawley*	PO Box 221037, Charlotte NC 28222	704-364-5222	R	20*	<.1
354	Premier/GMAC Real Estate—*Jim Pitts*	8206 Louisiana Blvd NE, Albuquerque NM 87113	505-798-6300	R	20*	<.1
355	Project Management Inc—*Thomas G Neutzling*	10411 Old Placerville, Sacramento CA 95827	916-366-0486	R	19*	<.1
356	Jack Tyrrell and Co—*Jack Tyrrell*	1288 Ala Moana Blvd St, Honolulu HI 96814	808-532-3330	R	19*	<.1
357	Goldstar Group Inc—*Michael Brodsky*	4630 Montgomery Ave St, Bethesda MD 20814	301-657-8848	R	19*	<.1
358	Greater Houston Group—*Jerry Ashmore*	8203 Willow Pl Dr S, Houston TX 77070	281-469-0092	R	19*	<.1
359	Rentalscom Inc—*Jamie Clymer*	3585 Engineering Dr St, Norcross GA 30092		S	19	<.1
360	Vordermeier Management Co—*Alan Vordermeier Sr*	2132 E Oakland Park Bl, Fort Lauderdale FL 33306	954-566-1661	R	18*	<.1
361	Centex Homes Realty Co—*Richard J Dugas Jr*	3700 Douglas Blvd Ste, Roseville CA 95661	916-771-9000	S	18*	<.1
362	Insight Realty Group Inc—*Emory Tedders*	4446 Hendricks Ave Ste, Jacksonville FL 32207	904-634-8800	R	17*	<.1
363	Majestic Properties—*Jeff Morr*	1682 Jefferson Ave, Miami Beach FL 33139	305-398-7888	R	17*	<.1
364	Rebman Properties Inc—*Roger Rebman*	1014 W Fairbanks Ave, Winter Park FL 32789	407-875-8001	R	17*	<.1
365	Belle Haven Realty Co—*Joseph Greenback*	801 Brewster Ave Ste 1, Redwood City CA 94063	650-364-1533	R	17*	<.1
366	Farmers National Co—*Jim Farrell*	11516 Nicholas St Ste, Omaha NE 68154	402-496-3276	R	16*	.2
367	Cushman and Wakefield of Illinois Inc—*Glenn Rufrano* Cushman and Wakefield Inc	200 S Wacker Dr Ste 28, Chicago IL 60606	312-470-1800	S	16*	.2
368	SRSA Commercial Real Estate Inc—*Barry Spizer*	2555 Severn Ave Ste 20, Metairie LA 70002	504-831-2363	R	16*	<.1
369	Growth Properties—*Ronald Gilbert*	1329 Bristol Pike, Bensalem PA 19020	215-546-5980	R	15*	.3
370	Colliers Meredith and Grew Inc—*Thomas J Hynes Jr*	160 Federal St, Boston MA 02110	617-330-8000	R	15*	<.1
371	Lewis Realty Advisors—*Kim M Kobriger*	7600 W Tidwell Ste 205, Houston TX 77040	713-461-1466	R	15*	<.1
372	Hunington Properties Inc—*Sanford P Aron*	109 N Post Oak Ln Ste, Houston TX 77024	713-623-6944	R	15*	<.1
373	Meyer-Manz Real Estate Inc—*Vicky Manz*	11100 Bonita Beach Rd, Bonita Springs FL 34135	239-947-1044	R	15*	<.1
374	D'Agostino and Associates—*Ken D'Agostino*	1348 Fruitville Rd Ste, Sarasota FL 34236	941-320-0044	R	15*	<.1
375	Michael Stevens Interests Inc—*Eileen Subinsky*	8582 Katy Fwy Ste 201, Houston TX 77024	281-496-4141	R	14*	.2
376	Desmond Virgulak Brown Commercial Realty Inc—*Robert Virgulak*	16 River St, Norwalk CT 06850	203-855-8050	R	14*	<.1
377	Phoenician Properties Realty—*Joseph B Scarp*	5111 N Scottsdale Rd, Scottsdale AZ 85250	480-663-1400	R	14*	< 1
378	Thomas Bearden Co—*Bruce Ripper*	4950 Terminal St, Bellaire TX 77401	713-660-9500	R	14*	<.1
379	Barrister Executive Suites Inc—*Vince H Otte*	9841 Airport Blvd Ste, Los Angeles CA 90045	310-258-8000	R	13*	.1
380	TRI Commercial Real Estate Services Inc—*Peter Meier*	1 California St Ste200, San Francisco CA 94111	415-268-2200	R	12*	.3
381	AHM Graves Company Incorporated Realtors—*Thomas S Osborne*	12220 N Meridian St St, Carmel IN 46032	317-575-8010	R	12*	.1
382	Wolohan Capital Strategies—*James L Wolohan*	1740 Midland Rd, Saginaw MI 48603	989-793-4532	R	12*	<.1
383	Village Square Realty Inc—*Lawrence Baldasano*	15575 Los Gatos Blvd B, Los Gatos CA 95032	408-399-3418	R	12*	<.1
384	Foram Management and Leasing Inc—*Loretta H Cockrum*	600 Brickell Ave Ste14, Miami FL 33131	305-358-9807	R	12*	<.1
385	Southside Mall LLC—*Jessica Dombrowski*	5006 State Hwy 23, Oneonta NY 13820	607-432-5478	R	12*	<.1

Note: An asterisk (*) indicates an estimated financial figure. The company type code used is as follows: R = Private, P = Public, S = Private Subsidiary, B = Public Subsidiary, D = Division, J = Joint Venture, I = Investment Fund.

COMPANY RANKINGS BY SALES WITHIN 4-DIGIT SIC

Rank	Company Name—Executive Officer	Address, City, State, Zip	Phone	Type	Fin	Empls
386	Westbridge Realty—Aki Moezzi	17328 Ventura Blvd No, Encino CA 91316	818-371-7117	R	12*	<.1
387	Marshall and Stevens Inc—Mark W Santarsiero	355 S Grand Ave Ste 17, Los Angeles CA 90071	213-612-8000	R	11*	.2
388	Cassidy Turley—Mark Burkhart	2600 Grand Blvd Ste 10, Kansas City MO 64108	816-221-2200	R	11*	.1
389	Kagan Realty Investors—Lawrence Kayan	8801 Knight Rd, Houston TX 77054	713-748-2000	R	10*	<.1
390	Strategic Capital Resources Inc—David Miller	1801 N Military Trl St, Boca Raton FL 33431	561-391-6117	R	10*	<.1
391	Gateway Co—Chris Ksidakis	1601 Response Rd Ste 3, Sacramento CA 95815	916-920-1500	R	10*	<.1
392	Santana Property Group Inc—Mercedes Santana	350 5th Ave 59th Fl, New York NY 10118	212-268-9322	R	10*	<.1
393	Bullitt-Hutchins Inc—Kevin O'Connor	5555 West Loop S Ste 2, Bellaire TX 77401	713-464-7705	R	10*	<.1
394	Whalen/Stoddard Inc—Debbie Stoddard	1100 Poydras Ste 1806, New Orleans LA 70163	504-524-2700	R	10*	<.1
395	Owners' Resorts And Exchange Inc—Neil Hutchinson	1521 E 3900 S, Salt Lake City UT 84124	801-278-9629	R	10*	.2
396	Mountain Lake Corp—John Delcamp	PO Box 832, Lake Wales FL 33859	863-676-3494	R	10*	.1
397	Solvern Innovations Inc—Andre Gudger	5523 Research Park Dr, Baltimore MD 21228	443-543-5760	R	9	.1
398	Trillium Management Inc—James Cumming	84 Peachtree St NW Ste, Atlanta GA 30303	404-659-1440	R	9*	<.1
399	DCC Corp—Steven G Deuble	PO Box 2288, North Canton OH 44720	330-494-0494	R	9*	<.1
400	Garden Confederate Point LP—Ted P. Stokely	4455 Confederate Point, Jacksonville FL 32210	904-772-8663	S	9*	<.1
401	Michael and Sons Real Estate Inc—Jay Michael	965 University Ave Ste, Sacramento CA 95825	916-646-6492	R	9*	<.1
402	Holiday Fenoglio and Fowler LP—Scott Galloway	9 Greenway Plz, Houston TX 77046	713-852-3500	S	8*	.1
403	Hacienda Escrow Corp—Bryan Forno	1131 W 6th St Ste 210, Ontario CA 91762	909-444-5700	S	8*	<.1
404	Columbine Management Company Inc—Colin V Reed	PO Box 2590, Dillon CO 80435	970-468-9137	S	8*	<.1
405	Fiur Organization Inc—Leslie Fiur	469 W 83rd St, Hialeah FL 33014	305-557-7770	R	8*	<.1
406	Luedemann and Associates—Waldo Luedemann	5555 W Loop S Ste 615, Bellaire TX 77401	713-935-9935	R	8*	<.1
407	Stan Creech Properties—Stan Creech	1800 St James Pl Ste 4, Houston TX 77056	713-840-1671	R	8*	<.1
408	Northwest Corporate Real Estate Inc—Steve M Harris	337 4th St NE, Auburn WA 98002	253-852-5800	R	8*	<.1
409	Parker Stevenson Brokerage Co—Mark Stevenson Sr	4030 Truxel Rd Ste D, Sacramento CA 95834	916-928-3800	R	8*	<.1
410	Sittema-Bullock Realty Partners—Mike Bullock	5445 DTC Pky Ste P4, Englewood CO 80111	303-770-7275	R	8*	<.1
411	Blue Ridge Real Estate Co—Patrick M Flynn	PO Box 707, Blakeslee PA 18610	570-443-8433	P	8	<.1
412	Cushman and Wakefield of Arizona Inc—Bruce Mosler Cushman and Wakefield Inc	2525 E Camelback Rd St, Phoenix AZ 85016	602-253-7900	S	7*	.1
413	Nexcore Healthcare Capital Corp—Greg Venn	1621 18th St Ste 250, Denver CO 80202	303-244-0700	P	7	<.1
414	Cushman and Wakefield of Florida Inc—Glenn Rufrano Cushman and Wakefield Inc	1 Tampa City Center St, Tampa FL 33602	813-223-6300	S	6*	.1
415	Yancey-Hausman and Associates—Craig Hausman	13333 Northwest Fwy St, Houston TX 77040	713-462-8802	R	6*	.1
416	ZKS Real Estate Partners LLC—Rick Stephens	1660 Olympic Blvd Ste, Walnut Creek CA 94596	925-932-0181	S	6*	<.1
417	Buyer's Resource Southeast Ltd—Russ Murray	6900 E Belleview Ave S, Greenwood Village CO 80111	303-721-1100	R	6*	<.1
418	RA Reynolds Appraisal Service Inc—John Stauffer	117 E Washington Row, Sandusky OH 44870	419-627-4543	S	6*	<.1
419	Crg Management LLC—Linda Morgan	744 Broad St Fl 4, Newark NJ 07102	212-582-6688	R	6*	<.1
420	Rampart Capital Corp—Charles W Janke	16401 Country Club Dr, Crosby TX 77532	713-223-4610	R	6	.1
421	Millstein Industries—Mark Allison	Armbrust Rd, Youngwood PA 15697	724-925-1300	R	5*	.1
422	HG Fenton Co—Mike Neal	7577 Mission Valley Rd, San Diego CA 92108	619-400-0120	R	5*	<.1
423	Resource Properties Inc	1845 Walnut St 10th Fl, Philadelphia PA 19103	215-546-5005	R	5*	<.1
424	Northwest Multiple Listing Service Inc—Tom Hurdelbrink	PO Box 2519, Kirkland WA 98083	425-820-9200	R	5*	.1
425	Howard Hanna Real Estate Services—Howard W Hanna III	4141 Rockside Rd 4th F, Seven Hills OH 44131	216-447-4477	R	4*	.2
426	Cushman and Wakefield of Colorado Inc—Patrick Devereaux Cushman and Wakefield Inc	1050 17th St Ste 1400, Denver CO 80265	303-813-6400	S	4*	<.1
427	Tucson Realty and Trust Co—George Amos	335 N Wilmot Rd Ste 50, Tucson AZ 85711	520-577-7000	R	4*	<.1
428	Otis Warren Real Estate Services Inc—Otis Warren	10 S Howard St Ste 110, Baltimore MD 21201	410-539-1070	R	4*	<.1
429	Platinum Realty—Scott DeNeve	9225 Indian Creek Pky, Overland Park KS 66210	913-227-0798	R	4*	<.1
430	Atlantic Companies Inc—Greg Finnican	4525 Hedgemore Dr, Charlotte NC 28209	704-525-5565	R	4*	<.1
431	Office Buildings of Houston Inc—Jerry Ray	6910 Bellaire Blvd, Houston TX 77074	713-772-2929	R	4*	<.1
432	Woody Nelson and Company Inc—Woody Nelson	14011 Park Dr, Tomball TX 77375	281-351-8140	R	4*	<.1
433	Donaldson Group LLC	15245 Shady Grove Rd S, Rockville MD 20850	301-251-8980	R	4*	.1
434	Prudential Preferred Properties (Lynnwood Washington)—Roger Vallo	20115 44th Ave W, Lynnwood WA 98036	425-744-8286	R	3*	.1
435	GetMyHomesValuecom—Steve Young	221 Rohrerstown Rd, Lancaster PA 17603		R	3	.1
436	Sitehawk Retail Real Estate—Mark Perlstein	8500 Keystone Crossing, Indianapolis IN 46240	317-844-5313	S	3*	<.1
437	Real Property Management LLC—Kirk McGary	579 Heritage Park Blvd, Layton UT 84041	801-546-4200	R	3*	<.1
438	Northeast Land Co—Patric Flynn Blue Ridge Real Estate Co	PO Box 707, Blakeslee PA 18610	570-443-8433	S	3*	<.1
439	RealNet Equities LLC—Scott D Fouser	10260 SW Greenburg Rd, Portland OR 97223	503-274-6201	R	3*	<.1
440	Mccoun and Associates Inc—Phillip Mccoun	8402 E 116th St, Fishers IN 46038	317-842-5744	R	3*	.1
441	Hoffman Management LLC—Anita Nelson	PO Box 8034, Appleton WI 54912	920-731-2322	R	2*	.1
442	Shorewood Realtors Inc—Arnold Goldstein	3300 Highland Ave, Manhattan Beach CA 90266	310-546-7561	R	2*	.2
443	Rauch Weaver Norfleet Kurtz and Co—Kenneth Kurtz	5300 Federal Hwy N, Fort Lauderdale FL 33308	954-771-4400	R	2*	<.1
444	HomePointe Property Management Inc—Robert A Machado	5896 S Land Park Dr, Sacramento CA 95822	916-429-1205	R	2*	<.1
445	Vasquez Group Inc—Virgilio Vasquez	688 Spring St, Herndon VA 20170		R	2*	<.1
446	Foremark Ltd—Clark Knippers	8235 Douglas Ave Ste 9, Dallas TX 75225	214-561-6500	R	2*	<.1
447	First West Capital Corp—Robert Gilroy	2151 Michaelson Ste 19, Irvine CA 92612	949-752-7890	R	2*	<.1
448	Maritime Beach Club—Carson Ray	400 N Ocean Blvd, North Myrtle Beach SC 29582	843-249-3414	R	2*	<.1
449	Fairfield Avenue Leasing Co—James Reichard	338 S Main St, Columbiana OH 44408	330-482-5511	R	2*	<.1
450	Hyatt Vacation Ownership Inc—Douglas Geoga	450 Carillon Pkwy Ste, Saint Petersburg FL 33716	727-803-9400	R	2*	<.1
451	Poinciana Vacation Villas—Denise Latiak	500 Cypress Pkwy, Kissimmee FL 34759	407-933-0700	R	1*	<.1
452	WHY USA Financial Group Inc—James Kylstad	2801 S Wayzata Blvd St, Minneapolis MN 55405		P	1	<.1
453	Iowa Realty Company Inc—Michael Knapp	3501 Westown Pkwy, West Des Moines IA 50266	515-224-6222	S	1*	.2
454	Cottingham-Chalk and Associates Inc—Linda Dudley	6846 Morrison Blvd, Charlotte NC 28211	704-364-1700	R	1*	<.1
455	Diane Moser Properties Inc—Diane Moser	7700 San Felipe St Ste, Houston TX 77063	713-827-8017	R	1*	<.1
456	Atoll Holdings Inc—H Harbers	PO Box 3259, San Luis Obispo CA 93403	805-544-8203	R	1*	<.1
457	Ecosystem Inc—Graham Bell	PO Box 1893, Thomasville GA 31799	229-228-6888	R	1*	<.1
458	Teco Corp—Nina Gardner	976 New Hampton Rd, Sanbornton NH 03269	603-731-8569	R	<1*	<.1
459	ILX Resorts Inc—Joseph P Martori	2111 E Highland Ave St, Phoenix AZ 85016	602-957-2777	R	<1	.5
460	BNS Holdings Inc—Terry Gibson	49 Stanton Ave, Riverside RI 02915	401-848-6300	P	<1	<.1
461	Integra Realty Resources Inc—Jeffrey Rogers	1133 Avenue of the Ame, New York NY 10036	212-255-7858	R	N/A	.6
462	Secure Collateral LLC—Jim Dammerich	7910 Baymeadows Way, Jacksonville FL 32256	904-733-1701	R	N/A	.1
463	South Kohala Management Corp—Thomas Hagen	62-1210 Waiemi Pl, Kamuela HI 96743	808-883-8500	R	N/A	<.1

TOTALS: SIC 6531 Real Estate Agents & Managers
Companies: 463   210,513   290.9

6541 Title Abstract Offices

1	Public Abstract Corp	1 First American Corpo, Santa Ana CA 92707	714-250-3000	S	1,214*	.3
2	North American Title Group Inc—Beverly McReynolds	700 NW 107th Ave Ste 3, Miami FL 33172	305-552-1102	S	483*	1.0
3	THF Inc	600 Lawrence Ave Ste 7, Ellwood City PA 16117	724-654-7781	S	462*	.2

Rank	Company Name—*Executive Officer*	Address, City, State, Zip	Phone	Type	Fin	Empls
4	Great American Title Agency—*Bruce Beverly*	7720 North 16th St Ste, Phoenix AZ 85020	602-445-5525	R	327*	.2
5	First American Title Company of Alaska Inc—*Terry E Bryan*	3035 C St, Anchorage AK 99503	907-561-1844	S	256*	.1
6	Land Records of Texas Inc—*Jay Jacobs*	1945 W Walnut Hill Ln, Irving TX 75038	972-580-8575	S	246*	<.1
7	Fountainhead Title Group Corp—*Edward Brush*	10025 Governor Warfiel, Columbia MD 21044	410-381-5300	R	240*	.2
8	MGE Power LLC—*Gary Wolter*	PO Box 1231, Madison WI 53701	608-252-7000	S	137*	.3
9	Universal Land Title of Colorado Inc Universal Land Title Inc	10700 E Geddes Ave Ste, Englewood CO 80112	303-338-0433	S	109*	.2
10	Universal Land Title Inc—*Michael Glass*	1555 Palm Beach Lakes, West Palm Beach FL 33401	561-689-8200	S	108*	.2
11	Service Link LP—*Jeff Coury*	345 Rouser Rd, Coraopolis PA 15108		R	95*	.8
12	Universal Land Title of the Palm Beaches Ltd—*Michael Glass* Universal Land Title Inc	1555 Palm Beach Lakes, West Palm Beach FL 33401	561-689-8200	S	93*	.1
13	Beach Abstract and Guaranty Co—*Brett Pitts*	PO Box 2580, Little Rock AR 72203	501-376-3301	R	64*	<.1
14	Equity Title Co—*Neil Gulley*	2112 E 4th St Ste 100, Santa Ana CA 92705	714-972-4200	S	39*	.1
15	Guaranty Abstract Co—*John C Kirkpatrick*	PO Box 3048, Tulsa OK 74101	918-587-6621	R	39*	.1
16	Houston Title Co—*Rande K Yeager*	777 Post Oak Blvd Ste, Houston TX 77056	713-626-9220	S	34*	.1
17	Community Title and Escrow Inc—*Mark Hord*	5400 Independence Pky, Plano TX 75023	972-867-3449	R	20*	<.1
18	Old Republic Title Company of St Louis—*Rande K Yeager*	9645 Clayton Rd 2nd Fl, Ladue MO 63124	314-692-8565	S	14*	.1
19	iMortgage Services LLC—*Brian Uffelman*	PO Box 62276, Pittsburgh PA 15241	412-220-7330	R	13*	.1
20	Property Title Inc—*Sidney D Torres III*	8301 W Judge Perez Dr, Chalmette LA 70043	504-278-2000	S	12*	<.1
21	Stewart Santa Fe Abstract Ltd—*Matthew Miles*	433 Paseo de Peralta, Santa Fe NM 87501	505-982-5582	S	11*	<.1
22	Stewart Title of Louisiana—*John Costello*	700 Camp St, New Orleans LA 70130	504-525-1491	S	7*	<.1
23	Stewart Title of Pinellas Inc—*Karen Price*	PO Box 12046, Saint Petersburg FL 33733	727-895-3664	S	5*	.1
24	United General Financial Services—*John Dwyer*	999 18th St Ste 3400, Denver CO 80202	303-291-1010	R	2*	<.1
25	Camco Title Insurance Agency	PO Box 700, Cambridge OH 43725	740-432-6363	S	2*	<.1
26	Fast Appraisals Inc—*Alan Zielinski*	38 Lakeview Dr, Lake Barrington IL 60010	847-382-6890	R	2*	<.1

TOTALS: SIC 6541 Title Abstract Offices
Companies: 26   4,034   4.0

6552 Subdividers & Developers Nec

Rank	Company Name—*Executive Officer*	Address, City, State, Zip	Phone	Type	Fin	Empls
1	C/N Group Inc—*Ravi Chopra*	114 E 90th Dr, Merrillville IN 46410	219-736-2700	R	13,539*	<.1
2	Ritz Carlton Hotel Company LLC—*Herve Humler*	4445 Willard Ave Ste 8, Chevy Chase MD 20815	301-547-4700	S	8,075*	38.0
3	Starwood Vacation Ownership Inc—*Fritz Van-Paasschen*	9002 San Marco Ct, Orlando FL 32819	407-903-4640	S	7,714*	4.3
4	Corporex Development Services Inc—*William P Butler*	100 E RiverCenter Blvd, Covington KY 41011	859-292-5500	R	5,338*	3.0
5	Shell Vacations Inc—*Sheldon Ginsburg*	40 Skokie Blvd Ste 350, Northbrook IL 60062	847-564-4600	R	4,350*	2.5
6	Broe Companies Inc—*Pat Broe*	252 Clayton St 4th Fl, Denver CO 80206	303-393-0033	R	3,495*	2.0
7	Lefrak Organization Inc—*Richard S LeFrak*	9777 Queens Blvd Ste 1, Rego Park NY 11374	718-459-9021	R	2,784*	16.2
8	Corporex Companies Inc—*Thomas E Banta*	100 E Rivercenter Blvd, Covington KY 41011	859-292-5500	R	2,079*	3.0
9	Chevron Real Estate Management Co—*Hap Payne*	2613 Camino Ramon, San Ramon CA 94583	925-842-1000	D	1,912*	.4
10	CSM Corp—*Gary Holmes*	500 Washington Ave S S, Minneapolis MN 55415	612-395-7000	R	1,467*	2.0
11	Panattoni Development Co—*Dudley Mitchell*	8775 Folson Blvd Ste 2, Sacramento CA 95826	916-381-1561	R	1,400*	.2
12	Chelsea Piers Management Inc—*Tom A Bernstein*	Pier 62 Ste 300, New York NY 10011	212-336-6800	R	1,333*	1.0
13	Crescent Resources LLC—*Todd Mansfield*	227 W Trade St Ste 100, Charlotte NC 28202	980-321-6000	S	1,308*	.4
14	Peoples First Properties Inc—*Raymond Powell*	1022 W 23rd St, Panama City FL 32402	850-770-7000	R	1,167*	1.0
15	Burroughs and Chapin Company Inc—*James Apple*	PO Box 2095, Myrtle Beach SC 29578	843-448-5123	R	1,133*	.6
16	Lowe Enterprises Inc—*Robert J Lowe*	11777 San Vicente Blvd, Los Angeles CA 90049	310-820-6661	R	1,103*	8.0
17	Sun Lakes of Robson Communities—*Steve Robson*	9532 E Riggs Rd, Sun Lakes AZ 85248	480-895-9200	R	1,102*	1.5
18	JPI—*Mark Bryant*	600 E Las Colinas Blvd, Irving TX 75039	972-556-1700	R	1,087*	1.5
19	DiVosta and Company Inc—*Chuck Hathaway*	4500 PGA Blvd Ste 400, Palm Beach Gardens FL 33418	561-627-2112	D	933*	1.4
20	Universal Paragon Corp—*Denn Hu*	150 Executive Park Blv, San Francisco CA 94134	415-468-6676	R	913*	.4
21	Hartz Group Inc—*Leonard N Stern*	667 Madison Ave, New York NY 10021	212-308-3336	R	870*	.5
22	Helmsley Enterprises Inc Helmsley-Spear Inc	230 Park Ave, New York NY 10169	212-679-3600	S	833*	2.5
23	New Community Corp—*William Linder*	233 W Market St, Newark NJ 07103	973-623-2800	R	757*	1.0
24	Whitebirch Enterprises Inc—*Robert Spizzo*	9252 Breezy Point Dr, Breezy Point MN 56472	218-562-4204	R	696*	.4
25	Prime Group Realty Trust—*Jeffrey A Patterson*	330 N Wabash Ave Ste 2, Chicago IL 60611		S	676*	.1
26	Kraus-Anderson Capital LLC—*Dave Olsen*	525 S 8th St, Minneapolis MN 55404	612-305-2934	S	673*	.4
27	Ryan Companies US Inc—*Jim Ryan*	50 S 10th St Ste 300, Minneapolis MN 55403	612-492-4000	R	624*	.9
28	Westcor Partners—*Wayne Silberschlag*	11411 N Tatum Blvd, Phoenix AZ 85028	602-953-6200	S	597*	.8
29	Corky McMillin Cos—*Mark McMillin*	2750 Womble Rd, San Diego CA 92106	619-477-4117	R	574*	.7
30	Daniel Corp—*Charlie Tickle*	3660 Grandview Pkwy St, Birmingham AL 35243	205-443-4500	R	568*	.3
31	Semonin Realtors—*Brad Devries*	4967 US Hwy 42 Ste 100, Louisville KY 40222	502-425-4760	S	560*	.8
32	Cafaro Co—*Anthony M Cafaro Sr*	PO Box 2186, Youngstown OH 44504	330-747-2661	R	558*	.8
33	Mericle Commercial Real Estate Group Inc - Logistics Div	100 Baltimore Dr, Wilkes Barre PA 18702	570-823-1100	D	557*	.3
34	Irvine Company Inc—*Donald Bren*	PO Box 6370, Newport Beach CA 92658	949-720-2000	R	547*	.3
35	Portman Holdings LP—*Ambrish Baisiwala*	303 Peachtree Center A, Atlanta GA 30303	404-614-5252	R	545*	.7
36	Van Metre Cos—*Albert G Van Metre Jr*	5252 Lyngate Ct, Burke VA 22015	703-425-2600	R	537*	.3
37	Jonathan's Landing Inc—*Raymond P Caraballo*	16823 Captain Kirle Dr, Jupiter FL 33477	561-746-2561	R	536*	.3
38	Castle and Cooke Inc—*David H Murdock*	10900 Wilshire Blvd St, Los Angeles CA 90024	310-208-3636	R	496*	1.5
39	Ford Motor Land Development Corp—*Donna Inch*	330 Town Ctr Dr Ste 11, Dearborn MI 48126	313-323-3100	S	473*	.3
40	Kiawah Resort Associates—*Charles Darby*	PO Box 12001, Charleston SC 29422	843-768-3400	R	448*	.6
41	Crown Power and Redevelopment Corp—*Bill Lucas*	2450 Grand Blvd Ste 20, Kansas City MO 64108	816-274-8444	S	438*	.2
42	Hines Interests LP—*Jeffrey C Hines*	2800 Post Oak Blvd, Houston TX 77056	713-621-8000	R	435*	2.9
43	Newhall Land and Farming Co—*Gary Cusumano*	25124 Springfield Ct S, Valencia CA 91355	661-255-4000	S	411*	.3
44	Joseph F Sexton Co—*Joseph F Sexton*	9001 N Meridian St, Indianapolis IN 46260	317-846-4444	R	373*	.2
45	Sares-Regis Group—*John S Hagestad*	18802 Bardeen Ave, Irvine CA 92612	949-756-5959	R	371*	.6
46	Druker Company Ltd—*Ronald M Druker*	50 Federal St Ste 1000, Boston MA 02110	617-357-5700	R	368*	.5
47	JMB Properties Co—*Neil Bluhm*	900 N Michigan Ave 19t, Chicago IL 60611	312-440-4900	R	368*	.5
48	Millennium Partners—*Christoper M Jeffries*	1995 Broadway, New York NY 10023	212-875-4900	R	359*	.2
49	Rockrose Development Corp—*Henry Elghanayan*	666 5th Ave 5th Fl, New York NY 10103	212-847-3700	R	340*	.5
50	Donohoe Companies Inc—*John J Donohoe Jr*	2101 Wisconsin Ave NW, Washington DC 20007	202-333-0880	R	333*	.5
51	Turnberry Associates—*Jeffrey Soffer*	19501 Biscayne Blvd St, Aventura FL 33180	305-937-6200	R	285*	.4
52	Buzz Oates Group of Cos—*Marvin L 'Buzz' Oates*	8615 Elder Creek Rd, Sacramento CA 95828	916-379-3800	R	277*	.2
53	Centex Development Company LP—*Timothy Eller*	PO Box 199000, Dallas TX 75219	214-981-5000	S	276*	.2
54	Carabetta Companies—*Joseph F Carabetta*	PO Box C-1011, Meriden CT 06450	203-237-7400	R	270*	.4
55	American Land Development US Inc—*Alan Shearer* American Community Properties Trust	10400 O'Donnell Pl Ste, Saint Charles MD 20603	301-843-8600	S	267*	.2
56	American Rental Management Co—*Alan Shearer* American Community Properties Trust	222 Smallwood Village, Saint Charles MD 20602	301-843-8600	S	267*	.2
57	Schostak Brothers and Company Inc—*Steven Fisher*	17800 Laurel Park Dr N, Livonia MI 48152	248-262-1000	R	260*	.2

Note: An asterisk (*) indicates an estimated financial figure. The company type code used is as follows: R = Private, P = Public, S = Private Subsidiary, B = Public Subsidiary, D = Division, J = Joint Venture, I = Investment Fund.

COMPANY RANKINGS BY SALES WITHIN 4-DIGIT SIC

Rank	Company Name—Executive Officer	Address, City, State, Zip	Phone	Type	Fin	Empls
58	Helmerich and Payne Properties Inc	1437 S Bolder Ave, Tulsa OK 74119	918-742-5531	S	256*	.2
59	Mauna Lani Resort Inc	68-1400 Mauna Lani Dr, Kohala Coast HI 96743	808-885-6622	R	254*	1.2
60	Shawnee Development Inc—Robert A Shebelsky	PO Box 93, Shawnee on Delaware PA 18356	570-421-1500	R	243*	.4
61	NTS Corp—Brian Lavin	10172 Linn Station Rd, Louisville KY 40223	502-426-4800	R	238*	.4
62	Stiles Corp—Terry Stiles	301 E Las Olas Blvd, Fort Lauderdale FL 33301	954-627-9300	R	238*	.4
63	DeMatteis Organizations—Richard Dematteis	820 Elmont Rd, Elmont NY 11003	516-285-5500	R	227*	.1
64	Helmsley-Spear Inc—Kent M Swig	770 Lexington Ave, New York NY 10065	212-396-8100	R	224*	.3
65	Tishman Speyer Properties LP—Jerry Speyer	45 Rockefeller Plz, New York NY 10011	212-715-0300	R	224*	.3
66	Ball Homes Inc—Ray Ball	PO Box 12950, Lexington KY 40583	859-268-1191	R	224*	.1
67	Peebles Corp—R Donahue Peebles	1 Alhambra Plz Ste 140, Coral Gables FL 33134	305-442-4342	R	222*	.3
68	Woodlands Operating Company LP—Thomas J D'Alesandro IV	2201 Timberloch Pl, The Woodlands TX 77380	281-719-6100	R	217*	.3
69	Grandbridge Real Estate Capital—Thomas Dennard	227 W Trade St Ste 400, Charlotte NC 28202	704-379-6900	S	212*	.2
70	Urban Settlement Services LLC—Charles Sanders	4 Allegheny Center E C, Pittsburgh PA 15212	412-325-7046	R	197*	.1
71	Rose Associates Inc—Adam Rose	200 Madison Ave, New York NY 10016	212-210-6666	R	186*	.1
72	George D Zamias Developer—George D Zamias	300 Market St, Johnstown PA 15901	814-535-3563	R	174*	.1
73	Rotterdam Ventures Inc—Francesco Galesi	695 Rotterdam Industri, Schenectady NY 12306	518-356-4445	R	172*	.8
74	Charles W Davidson Co—Charles Davidson	255 W Julian St Ste 20, San Jose CA 95110	408-295-9162	R	169*	.1
75	Lake Nona Corp	9801 Lake Nona Rd, Orlando FL 32827	407-851-9091	R	160*	.1
76	HSA Commercial Real Estate—Daniel F Miranda	233 S Wacker Dr Ste 35, Chicago IL 60606	312-332-3555	R	146*	.2
77	The St Joe Co—Park Brady	PO Box 1380, Jacksonville FL 32201	904-301-4200	P	145	.1
78	Standard Pacific Of Orange County Inc—Kenneth L Campbell	26 Technology Dr, Irvine CA 92618	949-789-1600	S	144*	.1
79	Gentry Development Co—Norman Gentry	560 N Nimitz Hwy Ste 2, Honolulu HI 96817	808-599-5558	R	142*	.1
80	Hillwood Development Corp—Todd L Platt Perot Group	5430 LBJ Fwy Ste 800, Dallas TX 75240		S	138*	.2
81	Heritage Development Group Inc—Henry Paparazzo	PO Box 873, Southbury CT 06488	203-264-8291	R	137*	.2
82	Richmond American Homes of Colorado Inc—Larry A Mizel	3600 S Yosemite St, Denver CO 80237	303-773-1100	S	129*	.3
83	Mountain Development Corp—L Robert Lieb	3 Garret Mountain Plaz, Woodland Park NJ 07424	973-279-9000	R	125*	.1
84	Sembler Co—Greg S Sembler	5858 Central Ave, St Petersburg FL 33707	727-384-6000	R	121*	.1
85	HJ Russell and Co—Michael B Russell	504 Fair St SW, Atlanta GA 30313	404-330-1000	R	118*	.5
86	Shopping Center Group Inc—Sam Latone	300 Galleria Pkwy 12th, Atlanta GA 30339	770-955-2434	R	118*	.2
87	Zaremba Group LLC—Walter Zaremba	14600 Detroit Ave, Cleveland OH 44107	216-221-6600	R	115*	.1
88	TA Association Realty—Michael A Ruane	28 State St 10th Fl, Boston MA 02109	617-476-2700	R	114*	.1
89	Forbes Trinchera Ranch—Louis Moore Bacon	24492 Trinchera Ranch, Fort Garland CO 81133	719-379-3263	D	113*	.1
90	JJ Gumberg Co—Ira J Gumberg	1051 Brinton Rd, Pittsburgh PA 15221	412-244-4000	R	107*	.5
91	Centex Commercial Development LP—Richard Dugas Centex Development Company LP	2728 N Harwood St, Dallas TX 75201	214-981-5000	S	107*	.1
92	Centex Multi-Family Development Co—Richard Dugas Centex Development Company LP	2728 N Harwood St, Dallas TX 75201	214-981-5000	S	107*	.1
93	MCZ Development—Michael Lerner	1555 N Sheffield, Chicago IL 60642	312-573-1122	R	104*	.1
94	Peterson Companies LC—Milt Peterson	12500 Fair Lakes Cir S, Fairfax VA 22033	703-227-2000	R	103*	.2
95	Manekin LLC—Richard Alter	8601 Robert Fulton Dr, Columbia MD 21046	410-290-1400	R	102*	.2
96	Forestar Group Inc—Jim DeCosmo	6300 Bee Cave Rd Bldg, Austin TX 78746	512-433-5200	P	101	.1
97	John Akridge Co—Matthew J Klein	601 13th St NW Ste 300, Washington DC 20005	202-638-3000	R	101*	.2
98	Belz Enterprises—Jack A Belz	100 Peabody Pl Ste 140, Memphis TN 38103	901-260-7348	R	100*	3.0
99	Double Diamond Inc—R Mike Ward	5495 Belt Line Rd, Dallas TX 75254	214-706-9801	R	100*	.5
100	Classic Residence by Hyatt—Penny Pritzker	71 S Wacker Dr Rm 900, Chicago IL 60606	312-803-8800	S	100*	.2
101	Triangle Real Estate Services Inc—Trey Giller	470 Old Worthington Rd, Westerville OH 43082	614-540-2400	R	100*	.1
102	Berkley Group Inc—Becky Foster	3015 N Ocean Blvd Ste, Fort Lauderdale FL 33308	954-563-2444	R	99*	.2
103	Howard Hughes Corp—Kevin T Orrock	10000 W Charleston Blv, Las Vegas NV 89135	702-791-4500	S	99*	.2
104	Anastasi Development Company LLC—Wayne Anastasi	511 Torrance Blvd 2nd, Redondo Beach CA 90277	310-376-8077	R	99*	.1
105	Greenbriar Homes Co—Mike Meyer	43160 Osgood Rd, Fremont CA 94539	510-497-8200	R	95*	.1
106	Kravco Simon Co—Jon R Powell	PO Box 1528, King of Prussia PA 19406	610-768-6300	R	90*	.1
107	Hofmann Co	1380 Galaxy Way, Concord CA 94520	925-682-4830	R	89*	.1
108	MAF Developments Inc	24118 W Chicago St Ste, Plainfield IL 60544	815-577-3800	R	89*	.1
109	McL Cos—Daniel E McLean	505 E Illinois St Ste, Chicago IL 60611	312-321-8900	R	88*	.1
110	Perini Land and Development Co—Ronald Tutor	73 Mt Wayte Ave, Framingham MA 01701	508-628-2000	S	87*	.1
111	American Community Properties Trust—Alan Shearer	222 Smallwood Village, Saint Charles MD 20602	301-843-8600	R	83*	.2
112	Stanley Martin Companies Inc—Steven Alloy	11111 Sunset Hills Rd, Reston VA 20190	703-964-5000	R	83*	.1
113	Winchester Homes Inc—Alan E Shapiro	6905 Rockledge Dr Ste, Bethesda MD 20817	301-803-4800	S	80*	.4
114	Hadler Cos—William N Hadler	2000 W Henderson Rd St, Columbus OH 43220	614-457-6650	R	78*	<.1
115	Hearthside Homes Inc—Raymond J Pacini	6 Executive Cir Ste 25, Irvine CA 92614	949-250-7700	S	76*	<.1
116	KiSKA Construction Corporation - USA—Erden Arkan	1034 44th Dr 2nd Fl Ll, Long Island City NY 11101	718-943-0400	S	76*	<.1
117	Broadbent Company Inc—George P Broadbent	117 E Washington St Rm, Indianapolis IN 46204	317-237-2900	R	75*	.1
118	Hogan Group Inc—Michael D Hogan	16506 Pointe Village D, Lutz FL 33558	813-274-8000	R	75*	.1
119	Bay West Group—Tim Tready	2 Henry Adams St Ste 4, San Francisco CA 94103	415-490-5800	R	74*	.1
120	Bowen Property Management—Walter Bowen	1800 SW 1st Ave Ste 18, Portland OR 97223		S	74*	.1
121	William A Hazel Inc—Jay Keyser	4305 Hazel Park Ct, Chantilly VA 20151	703-378-8300	R	74*	.1
122	Boyle Investment Co—Henry Morgan	5900 Poplar Ave, Memphis TN 38119	901-767-0100	R	73*	.1
123	National Realty and Development Corp—Robert C Baker	3 Manhattanville Rd, Purchase NY 10577		R	73*	<.1
124	Berwind Property Group Ltd—Daniel M DiLella	1500 Market St, Philadelphia PA 19102	215-563-2800	S	73*	<.1
125	Village Homes of Colorado Inc—John Osborn	6000 Greenwood Plz Blv, Greenwood Village CO 80111	303-795-1976	R	72*	.1
126	Breslin Realty Development Corp—Wilber F Breslin	500 Old Country Rd Ste, Garden City NY 11530	516-741-7400	R	70*	<.1
127	Senterra Real Estate Group LLC—Douglas W Schnitzer	12 Greenway Plz Ste 31, Houston TX 77006	713-965-2900	R	70*	<.1
128	Capital Development Co—Larry Blume	PO Box 3487, Olympia WA 98509	360-491-6850	R	69*	.1
129	Charles S Pefley And Associates Realtors—Charles Pefley	1808 Arctic Ave Ste A, Virginia Beach VA 23451		R	69*	.1
130	DR Horton Incorporated - Torrey—Donald Tomnitz	8200 Roberts Dr Ste 40, Atlanta GA 30350	770-730-7900	S	69*	.1
131	DMB Associates Inc—Eneas Kane	7600 E Doubletree Ranc, Scottsdale AZ 85258	480-367-7000	R	68*	.1
132	Kimco Development Corp—David B Henry	1111 Burlington Ave St, Lisle IL 60532	630-322-9200	S	67*	<.1
133	EJM Development Co—Jerry Monkarsh	9061 Santa Monica Blvd, Los Angeles CA 90069	310-278-1830	R	66*	.1
134	Highridge Partners—John Long	400 Continental Blvd S, El Segundo CA 90245	310-648-7600	R	66*	.1
135	Suarez Housing Corp—Robert Suarez	9950 Princess Palm Ave, Tampa FL 33619	813-664-1100	R	65*	<.1
136	Spectrum Properties Inc—Darryl Dewberry	201 S Tryon St Ste 550, Charlotte NC 28202	704-358-1000	R	62*	.1
137	Lauth Property Group Inc—Robert L Lauth	11595 N Meridian St, Carmel IN 46032	317-848-6500	R	61*	.1
138	Selig Enterprises Inc—Steve Selig	1100 Spring St NW Ste, Atlanta GA 30309	404-876-5511	R	60*	.8
139	Quadrant Corp (Bellevue Washington)—Ken Krivanec	14725 SE 36th St, Bellevue WA 98006	425-562-4005	S	58*	.1
140	Allen Morris Co—W Allen Morris	121 Alhambra Plz Ph 1, Coral Gables FL 33134	305-443-1000	R	57*	<.1
141	Pizzuti Cos—Ronald A Pizzuti Pizzuti Inc	2 Miranova Pl Ste 800, Columbus OH 43215	614-280-4000	S	56*	.1
142	Irgens Development Partners—Mark Irgens	10700 Research Dr Ste, Milwaukee WI 53226	414-443-0700	S	56*	.1
143	Ellicott Development Co—William Paladino	295 Main St Ste 210, Buffalo NY 14203	716-854-0060	R	55*	.3

Rank	Company Name—*Executive Officer*	Address, City, State, Zip	Phone	Type	Fin	Empls
144	Korman Residential—*John Korman*	2 Neshaminy Interplex, Trevose PA 19053		R	55*	.1
145	Live Oak Gottesman LLC—*Rob Golding*	300 W 6th St Ste 1900, Austin TX 78701	512-472-5000	R	54*	<.1
146	JBG Cos—*Benjamin Jacobs*	4445 Willard Ave Ste 4, Chevy Chase MD 20815	240-333-3600	R	54*	<.1
147	Mercer Companies Inc—*William Bantz*	13000 S Tryon St Ste F, Charlotte NC 28278	518-434-1311	R	54*	<.1
148	Hans Hagen Homes Inc—*Hans T Hagen Jr*	941 NE Hillwind Rd Ste, Fridley MN 55432	763-528-2756	R	53*	<.1
149	Hilco Real Estate LLC—*Jeffrey B Hecktman*	5 Revere Dr Ste 300, Northbrook IL 60062	847-509-1100	S	51*	<.1
150	ScanlanKemperBard Companies Inc—*Peter Stott*	810 NW Marshall St Ste, Portland OR 97209	503-220-2600	R	51*	<.1
151	Horning Brothers—*Joseph F Horning*	1350 Connecticut Ave N, Washington DC 20036	202-659-0700	R	50*	.1
152	LCOR Inc—*Peter P DiLullo*	850 Cassatt Rd Ste 300, Berwyn PA 19312	610-251-9110	R	49*	.2
153	Carl M Freeman Associates Inc—*Thomas M Aiello*	18330 Village Ctr Dr S, Olney MD 20832	240-779-8000	R	47*	.1
154	Jack Parker Corp—*Adam Glick*	1700 Broadway 34th Fl, New York NY 10019	212-333-3353	R	47*	.1
155	Butters Construction and Development Inc—*Mark Butters*	6820 Lyons Technology, Coconut Creek FL 33073	954-312-2400	R	47	<.1
156	NLS Group—*Jim Riley*	PO Box 137, Danbury NH 03230		R	45*	<.1
157	DCG Development Co—*Donald Greene*	240 Clifton Corp Pky, Clifton Park NY 12065	518-383-0059	R	44*	.1
158	MB Real Estate—*Peter E Ricker*	181 W Madison St Ste 3, Chicago IL 60602	312-726-1700	R	44*	.1
159	Sachs Properties Inc—*Kathleen Higgins*	400 Chesterfield Ctr S, Chesterfield MO 63017	636-537-1000	R	44*	<.1
160	Wright Runstad and Co—*Gregory Johnson*	1201 Third Ave Ste 270, Seattle WA 98101	206-447-9000	R	43*	.1
161	Kickerillo Building Co—*Jim A Miller*	1306 S Fry Blvd, Katy TX 77450	713-951-0666	R	43*	<.1
162	Phillips Property Management Inc—*Robert M Arnold*	6106 MacArthur Blvd St, Bethesda MD 20816	301-320-0422	R	42*	.1
163	Florida Southeast Development Corp—*Kenneth Mamula*	3816 W Linebaugh Ave S, Hialeah FL 33018	813-968-8230	R	42*	<.1
164	Chase Enterprises—*David Chase*	225 Asylum St, Hartford CT 06103	860-549-1674	R	41*	.1
165	Ackerman and Co—*Vivian Barnes*	10 Glenlake Pkwy Ste 1, Atlanta GA 30328	770-913-3900	R	40*	.1
166	Pizzuti Inc—*Ronald A Pizzuti*	2 Miranova Pl Ste 800, Columbus OH 43215	614-280-4000	R	40*	.1
167	Rancon Financial Corp—*Mike Dial*	27740 Jefferson Ave St, Temecula CA 92590	951-676-5736	R	38*	.1
168	Perot Group—*H Ross Perot*	PO Box 269014, Plano TX 75026	972-577-6165	R	38*	.1
169	Ponderosa Homes Inc—*Dick Baker*	6671 Owens Dr, Pleasanton CA 94588	925-460-8900	R	37*	.1
170	McKeough Land Company Inc—*Michael A McKeough*	229 Washington Ave, Grand Haven MI 49417	616-847-1995	R	37	<.1
171	Neighborhood Development Co—*AdrianG Washington*	4110 Kansas Ave NW, Washington DC 20011	202-722-6002	R	37*	<.1
172	Donahue Schriber—*Patrick S Donahue*	200 E Baker St Ste 100, Costa Mesa CA 92626	714-545-1400	R	36*	.4
173	Kaiser Ventures LLC—*Richard E Stoddard*	3633 E Inland Empire B, Ontario CA 91764	909-483-8500	R	36*	<.1
174	Chelsea Investment Corp—*James J Schmld*	5993 Avenida Encinas S, Carlsbad CA 92008	760-456-6000	R	35*	.1
175	Podolsky Northstar Realty Partners LLC—*John R Homsher*	2610 Lake Cook Rd Ste, Riverwoods IL 60015	847-444-5700	R	35*	.1
176	Miller Real Estate Investments—*Steven A Shoflick*	850 Englewood Pkwy Ste, Englewood CO 80110	303-799-6300	R	35*	<.1
177	Narragansett Improvement Co—*John Everson*	223 Allens Ave, Providence RI 02903	401-331-7420	R	35*	.1
178	Alexander Company Inc—*Randall Alexander*	145 E Badger Rd Ste 20, Madison WI 53713	608-258-5580	R	34*	.1
179	McKee Group—*Frank J McKee*	940 W Sproul Rd Ste 30, Springfield PA 19064	610-604-9800	R	33*	.2
180	Lennar Homes of California Inc—*Stuart Miller*	24800 Chrisanta Dr, Mission Viejo CA 92691	949-455-2596	S	33	.1
181	Investec—*Ken P Slaught*	200 E Carrillo St Ste, Santa Barbara CA 93101	805-962-8989	R	33*	<.1
182	Hollingsworth Capital Partners LLC—*Trey Hollingsworth*	2 Centre Plz, Clinton TN 37716	865-457-3601	R	33	<.1
183	David Hocker and Associates Inc—*David E Hocker*	1901 Frederica St, Owensboro KY 42301	270-926-2616	R	32*	.2
184	John Buck Co—*John A Buck*	1 N Wacker Dr Ste 2400, Chicago IL 60606	312-993-9800	R	32*	.2
185	MJ Peterson Real Estate Inc—*Victor L Peterson Jr*	501 John James Audubon, Amherst NY 14228	716-688-1234	R	30*	.1
186	Al Neyer Inc—*John Handelsman*	302 W 3rd St Ste 800, Cincinnati OH 45202	513-271-6400	R	30*	.1
187	Security Properties Inc—*John M Orehek*	1201 3rd Ave Ste 5400, Seattle WA 98101	206-622-9900	R	29*	<.1
188	MBK Real Estate Ltd—*Stefan Markowitz*	175 Technology Dr Ste2, Irvine CA 92618	949-789-8300	S	28*	.1
189	Held Properties—*Robert D Held*	1880 Century Park E St, Los Angeles CA 90067	310-300-2200	R	28*	<.1
190	Mika Co—*Rick Barreca*	837 Traction Ave Ste 4, Los Angeles CA 90013	213-680-1230	R	27*	<.1
191	Sabre Realty Management Inc—*Denny Holman*	16475 Dallas Pky Ste 8, Addison TX 75001	972-931-7400	R	27*	<.1
192	United Commercial Development Inc—*David Dunning*	7001 Preston Rd Ste 50, Dallas TX 75205	214-224-4600	R	27*	<.1
193	Deltona Corp—*Antony Gram*	8014 SW 135 St Rd, Ocala FL 34473	352-307-8100	R	26*	.1
194	Magi Realty Inc—*J Rick Rodriguez*	10010 San Pedro Ste 45, San Antonio TX 78216	210-545-2181	R	26*	<.1
195	Edwards Cos—*Richard Kirk*	500 S Front St Ste 770, Columbus OH 43215	614-241-2070	R	25*	.1
196	J Loew and Associates Inc—*Jack Loew*	55 Country Club Dr Ste, Downingtown PA 19335	610-873-5585	R	25*	<.1
197	Meruelo Maddux Properties Inc—*Richard Meruelo*	761 Terminal St Bldg 1, Los Angeles CA 90021	213-291-2800	P	24	.1
198	Preit-Rubin Inc—*Ronald Rubin*	200 S Broad St 3rd Fl, Philadelphia PA 19102	215-875-0700	S	24*	.1
199	Kikiaola Land Company Ltd—*Peter Herdon*	PO Box 367, Waimea HI 96796	808-338-1900	R	24*	<.1
200	Olympus Real Estate Corp—*David Deniger*	5080 Spectrum Dr Ste 1, Addison TX 75001	972-980-2200	R	24*	<.1
201	Pacific International Equities Inc—*Michael Bedzow*	20803 Biscayne Blvd St, Aventura FL 33180	305-891-7987	R	24*	<.1
202	Transdevelopment Corp—*John MacGregor*	2701 NW Vaughn St Ste, Portland OR 97210	503-241-1551	R	24*	<.1
203	Alliance Land Co—*Ken Vagts*	19550 Michael Ave, Hastings MN 55033	651-438-9333	S	24*	<.1
204	Continental Development Corp—*Richard C Lundquist*	2041 Rosecrans Ave Ste, El Segundo CA 90245	310-640-1520	R	23*	<.1
205	Russell Lands Inc—*Ben Russell*	2544 Willow Point Rd, Alexander City AL 35010		R	22*	.3
206	Richmond American Homes of Nevada Inc—*David D Mandarich*	7770 S Dean Martin Dr, Las Vegas NV 89139	702-617-8464	S	22*	.1
207	Hon Development Co—*Barry Hon*	27422 Portola Pky Ste, Foothill Ranch CA 92610	949-586-4400	R	22*	<.1
208	Mann Properties—*Brian Mann*	6925 E 96th St Ste 200, Indianapolis IN 46250	317-849-0452	R	22*	<.1
209	Taylor Properties—*Lux Taylor*	1792 Tribute Rd Ste 27, Sacramento CA 95815	916-923-0200	D	22*	<.1
210	Elm Street Development Inc—*William A Moran*	1355 Beverly Rd Ste 24, McLean VA 22101	703-734-9730	R	21*	<.1
211	Zamagias Properties—*Michael G Zamagias*	336 4th Ave, Pittsburgh PA 15222	412-391-7887	R	21*	<.1
212	Indigo Group Inc	PO Box 10809, Daytona Beach FL 32120	386-274-2202	S	21*	<.1
213	Indigo International Inc	PO Box 10809, Daytona Beach FL 32120	386-274-2202	S	21*	<.1
214	JCC Homes—*Jack Cameron*	2632 W 237th St Ste 20, Torrance CA 90505	310-539-1788	R	21*	<.1
215	American Fidelity Property Co—*Bill Cameron*	PO Box 25523, Oklahoma City OK 73125		S	20*	<.1
216	Leggat McCall Properties LLC—*Eric Sheffels*	10 Post Office Sq, Boston MA 02109	617-422-7000	R	20*	<.1
217	Dial Realty Corp—*Bob Welspead*	11506 Nicholas St Ste, Omaha NE 68154	402-493-2800	S	19*	<.1
218	Elan Development LP—*Michael Manners*	211 Highland Crossing, Houston TX 77073	281-821-5556	R	19*	<.1
219	Tate Development Corp—*J Kenneth Tate*	1175 NE 125th St Ste 1, North Miami FL 33161	305-891-1107	R	18*	.1
220	Cappelli Development Corp—*Louis Cappelli*	115 Stevens Ave, Valhalla NY 10595	914-769-6500	R	18*	<.1
221	Parkside Management Services LLC—*Michael S McCarthy*	5215 Old Orchard Rd St, Skokie IL 60077	847-779-8500	R	18*	<.1
222	Realty Investment Company Ltd—*Richard Henderson*	PO Box 747, Hilo HI 96721	808-961-5252	R	18*	<.1
223	Sam Rodgers Enterprises Inc—*Sam R Rodgers*	PO Box 558, Venice FL 34284	941-497-0254	R	17*	<.1
224	South Shore Harbour Development Ltd—*Thomas Brooker*	PO Box 2152, League City TX 77574	281-334-7501	S	17*	<.1
225	Southeast Shopping Centers Corp—*Gerald Higier*	7284 W Palmetto Park R, Boca Raton FL 33433	561-347-0888	R	17*	<.1
226	Savoy Corp—*Andrew A Pansini*	170 Columbus Ave Ste 3, San Francisco CA 94133		R	17*	<.1
227	Watkins Associated Developers Inc—*Neal Freeman*	1946 Monroe Dr NE, Atlanta GA 30324	404-872-8666	R	17*	<.1
228	Republic Properties Corp—*Steven Grigg*	1280 Maryland Ave SW S, Washington DC 20024	202-552-5300	R	17*	<.1
229	Carillon Properties—*Barbara Leland*	4100 Carillon Point, Kirkland WA 98033	425-822-1700	R	17*	<.1
230	Interstate Waste Technologies Inc—*Mark Augenblick*	17 Mystic Ln, Malvern PA 19355	610-644-1665	S	17*	<.1
231	Westerra Management LLC—*Walter Nelson*	3030 LBJ Fwy Ste 1450, Dallas TX 75234	972-443-7200	R	16*	.2
232	Castle and Cooke Properties Inc—*Harry Saunders*	100 Kahelu Ave 2nd Fl, Mililani HI 96789	808-548-4811	S	16*	.1

Note: An asterisk (*) indicates an estimated financial figure. The company type code used is as follows: R = Private, P = Public, S = Private Subsidiary, B = Public Subsidiary, D = Division, J = Joint Venture, I = Investment Fund.

COMPANY RANKINGS BY SALES WITHIN 4-DIGIT SIC

Rank	Company Name—Executive Officer	Address, City, State, Zip	Phone	Type	Fin	Empls
	Castle and Cooke Inc					
233	Intracorp Real Estate LLC—Mike Miller	419 Occidental Ave S S, Seattle WA 98104	206-625-9226	R	16*	.1
234	CV Perry and Co—Carlyle V Perry Jr	370 S 5th St, Columbus OH 43215	614-221-4131	R	16*	<.1
235	Marina LP—Allen E Rosenberg Sr	11691 Fall Creek Rd, Indianapolis IN 46256	317-845-0270	R	15*	<.1
236	Killearn Properties Inc—JT Williams	300 Lester Mill Rd Rm, Locust Grove GA 30248	770-389-2020	R	15*	<.1
237	Randall Davis Co—Stephen Swan	1210 W Clay St, Houston TX 77019	713-526-3222	R	15*	<.1
238	Residential Development Group Inc—Jim Berg	800 S McHenry Ave Ste, Crystal Lake IL 60014	815-459-5500	R	15*	<.1
239	Chadmar Group—Charles Lande	2716 Ocean Park Blvd S, Santa Monica CA 90405	310-314-2590	R	15*	<.1
240	Goldberg Companies Inc—Larry Goldberg	25101 Chagrin Blvd, Beachwood OH 44122	216-831-6100	R	14*	<.1
241	Robert B Aikens and Associates—Jeffery P Thompson	350 N Old Woodward Ave, Birmingham MI 48009	248-283-1071	R	14*	<.1
242	Western Select Properties LP—Louis Norry	2525 N Shadeland Ave, Indianapolis IN 46219	317-357-7000	R	14*	<.1
243	Acquest Development LLC—William Huntress	80 Curtwright Dr Ste 5, Buffalo NY 14221	716-204-3570	R	13*	<.1
244	Harich-Tahoe Developments—Sharon Cary	PO Box 5790, Stateline NV 89449	775-588-3553	R	13*	.3
245	WESTGROUP Management LLC—Gerald T Halpin	1600 Anderson Rd, Mc Lean VA 22102	703-356-2400	R	12*	<.1
246	Kitchell Development Co	1707 E Highland Ave St, Phoenix AZ 85016	602-264-4411	S	12*	<.1
247	Federal Business Centers—Peter Viseglia	PO Box 7815, Edison NJ 08818	732-225-2200	R	11	.1
248	Southwest Diversified Inc—William Foote	3 San Joaquin Plz, Newport Beach CA 92660	949-720-3600	R	11*	.1
249	Richard E Jacobs Group LLC	25425 Center Ridge Rd, Cleveland OH 44145	440-871-4800	R	11*	.1
250	Page Properties Corp—William L Page	PO Drawer 9012, Woodland Park CO 80866	719-687-3085	R	11*	<.1
251	Saxton Inc—Thomas Saxton	600 3rd St SE Ste 300, Cedar Rapids IA 52401	319-365-6967	R	10*	<.1
252	Kardon Industries Inc—Robert Kardon	1201 Chestnut St, Philadelphia PA 19107	215-665-9600	R	10*	<.1
253	Amcal Group of Cos—Percival Vaz	30141 Agura Rd Ste 100, Agoura Hills CA 91301	818-706-0694	R	10*	<.1
254	Corum Real Estate Group Inc—Michael Komppa	600 S Cherry St Ste 62, Denver CO 80246	303-796-2000	R	10*	<.1
255	Florida Rock Properties Inc	155 E 21st St, Jacksonville FL 32206	904-355-1781	D	10*	<.1
256	Robert C Rhein Interests Inc—Bob Rhein	7265 Kenwood Rd Ste 22, Cincinnati OH 45236	513-891-1100	R	10*	<.1
257	Landar Corp—Kevin Robins	1110 N Post Oak Rd Ste, Houston TX 77055	713-951-9600	R	10*	<.1
258	HCV Pacific Partners—Randall J Verrue	222 Kearny St, San Francisco CA 94108	415-882-0900	R	10*	<.1
259	Stratus Properties Inc—William H Armstrong III	212 Lavaca St Ste 300, Austin TX 78701	512-478-5788	P	9	<.1
260	Rancho Mission Viejo—Anthony R Moiso	PO Box 1209, San Juan Capistrano CA 92693	949-240-3363	R	9*	<.1
261	Hoppe Inc—John Hoppe Jr	PO Box 6035, Lincoln NE 68506	402-437-9200	R	9*	<.1
262	Lomas Santa Fe Group—Theodore E Gildred III	265 Santa Helena Ste 2, Solana Beach CA 92075	858-755-5572	R	9*	<.1
263	Indianapolis Economic Development Corp—Ron Gifford	111 Monument Cir Ste 1, Indianapolis IN 46204	317-236-6262	R	9*	<.1
264	Koustas Realty Inc—Gus Koustas	2696 S Colorado Blvd S, Denver CO 80222	303-757-4100	R	9*	<.1
265	Maroon Development Inc—William S Maroon	1400 W Fairbanks Ave S, Winter Park FL 32789	407-774-7083	R	9*	<.1
266	Zaepfel Development Company Inc—James Zaepfel	5505 Main St Ste A, Williamsville NY 14221	716-632-7230	R	8*	<.1
267	Alexander Communities—Guy Alexander Jr	3184 Airway Ave Ste H, Costa Mesa CA 92626	714-850-1919	R	8*	<.1
268	Artery Group LLC—Henry Goldberg	7200 Wisconsin Ave, Bethesda MD 20814	301-961-8000	R	8*	<.1
269	Flying Dutchman Management Inc—Carol Van Curler	2008 Hogback Rd Ste 6, Ann Arbor MI 48105	734-971-4000	R	8*	<.1
270	Lankford and Associates Inc—Robert V Lankford	655 W Broadway Ste 145, San Diego CA 92101	619-702-5655	R	7*	<.1
271	Capeletti Brothers Inc—Joe Capeletti	PO Box 4944, Miami Lakes FL 33014	305-823-9500	R	7*	<.1
272	McGranahan Carlson and Co—Robert Carlson	2271 W Malvern Ave Ste, Fullerton CA 92833		R	7*	<.1
273	United States Construction Corp—Gregory L Spatz	2785 SE 11th St, Pompano Beach FL 33062	954-785-6085	R	7*	<.1
274	Stanford Ranch I LLC—Larry Kelley	2210 Plaza Dr Ste 300, Rocklin CA 95765	916-624-0613	R	6*	.1
275	Orchard Properties Inc—Joe Lewis	2055 Laurelwood Rd Ste, Santa Clara CA 95054	408-955-1414	R	6*	<.1
276	Echelon Development LLC—Darryl A LeClair	235 3rd St S Ste 300, Saint Petersburg FL 33701	727-803-8200	R	6*	<.1
277	Meadow Park Land Co—William L Page	PO Drawer 9012, Woodland Park CO 80866	719-687-7670	S	5*	<.1
	Page Properties Corp					
278	La Caze Development Co—Norman R LaCaze	2601 Airport Dr Ste 30, Torrance CA 90505	310-534-0411	R	5*	<.1
279	Prestige Properties and Development Company Inc—Joseph Comparretto	546 5th Ave 15th Fl, New York NY 10036	212-944-0444	R	5*	<.1
280	Geifman Food Stores Inc—Steve Geifman	2550 Middle Rd Ste 600, Bettendorf IA 52722	563-323-2626	R	5*	<.1
281	Charles Skinner Co—Charles Skinner	10175 Fortune Pky Ste, Jacksonville FL 32256	904-519-8002	R	5*	<.1
282	Future Estates Inc—Cris Di Ruggiero	357 E Carson St Ste 20, Carson CA 90745	310-549-2511	R	5*	<.1
283	Minnesota Financial Development Corp—James Klung	401 N 3rd St Ste 160, Minneapolis MN 55401	612-455-4020	R	5	<.1
284	Sea Ranch Properties Inc	312 SE 17th St Ste 300, Fort Lauderdale FL 33316	954-527-0880	S	5*	<.1
285	Mediterra Gatehouse—Doug Keeperton	15715 Corso Mediterra, Naples FL 34110	239-254-3080	R	4*	.1
286	Allen and O'Hara Inc—Paul O Bower	530 Oak Ct Dr Ste 300, Memphis TN 38117	901-259-2500	R	4*	.1
287	Fineberg Management Inc—Gerald Fineberg	1 Washington St Ste 40, Wellesley MA 02481	781-239-1480	R	4*	<.1
288	Kaupulehu Developments Inc—Morton H Kinzler	1100 Alakea St Ste 290, Honolulu HI 96813	808-531-8400	S	4*	<.1
289	Indigo Development Inc—William H McMunn	PO Box 10809, Daytona Beach FL 32120	386-274-2202	S	4*	<.1
290	George Kessel Associates—George Kessel	PO Box 39, Bergenfield NJ 07621	201-384-0098	R	4*	<.1
291	Rilea Group Inc—Alan Ojeda	1450 Brickell Ave Ste, Miami FL 33131	305-371-5254	R	4*	<.1
292	Pointe Vista Development LLC	PO Box 1009, Kingston OK 73439	580-564-2581	R	4	.1
293	Springfield Underground Inc—Louis Griesemer	PO Box 2240, Springfield MO 65801	417-874-1400	R	4*	<.1
294	Robert Weiler Co—Robert Weiler	10 N High St Ste 401, Columbus OH 43215	614-221-4286	R	3*	<.1
295	Crown Community Development—Marvin Bailey	1751A W Diehl Rd, Naperville IL 60563	630-851-5490	S	3*	<.1
296	WCB Properties—Michael R Chase	450 Newport Center Dr, Newport Beach CA 92660	949-640-6900	R	3*	<.1
297	Shorebank Development Corp—Mary Houghton	5100 W Harrison St, Chicago IL 60644	773-420-5150	S	3*	<.1
298	Boone Fetter Associates—Blaine Fetter	602 E Huntington Dr St, Monrovia CA 91016	626-305-5530	R	3*	<.1
299	Tipton Interests Inc—William Woodward	424 Wards Corner Rd, Loveland OH 45140	513-576-0060	R	3*	<.1
300	Winrock Enterprises Inc—Russell B McDonough Jr	1501 N University Ave, Little Rock AR 72207	501-663-5340	R	3*	<.1
301	Duffel Financial and Construction Co—Joseph A Duffel	1430 Willow Pass Rd St, Concord CA 94520	925-603-8444	R	3*	<.1
302	Hope Communities Inc—Larry Fullerton	2543 California St, Denver CO 80205	303-860-7747	R	2*	<.1
303	Heartland Properties Inc—John Stoneman	2418 Crossroads Dr Ste, Madison WI 53718	608-310-6900	S	1*	<.1
304	BF Enterprises Inc—Brian P Burns	100 Bush St Ste 1250, San Francisco CA 94104	415-989-6580	R	1*	<.1
305	Abrams Properties Inc—Mathew Abrams	1945 The Exchange SE, Atlanta GA 30339	770-953-1777	S	1*	<.1
306	Russell Development Company Inc—John W Russell	200 SW Market St Ste 1, Portland OR 97201	503-228-2500	R	1*	<.1
307	Washington Services Inc—Robert M Whitehead	425 Pike St, Seattle WA 98101	206-624-7930	D	1	N/A
308	Dage Enterprises Inc—Arthur Sterling	701 N Roeske Ave, Michigan City IN 46360	219-872-5514	R	<1*	<.1
309	Falcon Ridge Development Inc—Fred M Montano	5111 Juan Tabo Blvd NE, Albuquerque NM 87111	505-856-6043	P	<1	N/A

TOTALS: SIC 6552 Subdividers & Developers Nec
Companies: 309   93,379   132.9

6553 Cemetery Subdividers & Developers

Rank	Company Name—Executive Officer	Address, City, State, Zip	Phone	Type	Fin	Empls
1	StoneMor Partners LP—Lawrence Miller	311 Veterans Hwy Ste B, Levittown PA 19056	215-826-2800	P	197	2.6
2	Forest Lawn Memorial Parks and Mortuaries—John Llewellyn	1712 S Glendale Ave, Glendale CA 91205	323-254-3131	R	66*	.8
3	Skylawn Corp—Andy Bryant	PO Box 5070, San Mateo CA 94402	650-349-4411	S	43*	.3
4	Memorial Estates Inc—George Quist	PO Box 57250, Salt Lake City UT 84157	801-268-8771	S	28*	<.1
5	Memory Gardens Management Corp—Robert Nelms	PO Box 441009, Indianapolis IN 46244	317-923-5474	R	16*	<.1
6	Cunningham Memorial Park Inc—Everett N Kendrick	815 Cunningham Ln, Saint Albans WV 25177	304-727-4349	S	2*	<.1

Rank	Company Name—*Executive Officer*	Address, City, State, Zip	Phone	Type	Fin	Empls
7	Parklawn Inc—*John Johnson*	12800 Veirs Mill Rd, Rockville MD 20853	301-881-2151	S	1*	<.1

TOTALS: SIC 6553 Cemetery Subdividers & Developers
Companies: 7   353   3.8

6712 Bank Holding Companies

Rank	Company Name—*Executive Officer*	Address, City, State, Zip	Phone	Type	Fin	Empls
1	JPMorgan Chase and Co—*James Dimon*	270 Park Ave, New York NY 10017	212-270-6000	P	2,117,605	239.8
2	Wells Fargo and Co—*John G Stumpf*	PO Box 63750, San Francisco CA 94163	612-667-1234	P	1,258,128	272.2
3	Wachovia Corp—*John G Stumpf* Wells Fargo and Co	420 Montgomery St, San Francisco CA 94104		D	782,896*	121.9
4	US Bancorp—*Richard K Davis*	800 Nicollet Mall, Minneapolis MN 55402	651-446-3000	P	340,122	62.5
5	PNC Financial Services Group Inc—*James E Rohr*	249 5th Ave 1 PNC Plz, Pittsburgh PA 15222	412-762-2000	P	264,284	50.8
6	Bank of New York Mellon Corp—*Robert P Kelly*	1 Wall St, New York NY 10005	212-495-1784	P	247,259	48.0
7	Capital One Financial Corp—*Richard D Fairbank*	1680 Capital One Dr, McLean VA 22102	703-720-1000	P	197,503	27.8
8	SunTrust Banks Inc—*William H Rogers Jr*	PO Box 4418, Atlanta GA 30302	404-588-7711	P	172,375	29.1
9	State Street Corp—*Joseph L Hooley*	PO Box 5501, Boston MA 02206	617-786-3000	P	160,505	28.7
10	BB and T Corp—*Kelly S King*	200 W 2nd St, Winston-Salem NC 27101	336-733-2000	P	157,081	31.4
11	HSBC USA Inc—*Paul Lawrence*	PO Box 2013, Buffalo NY 14240	716-525-6110	R	153,900	15.0
12	Regions Financial Corp—*O B Grayson Hall Jr*	1900 5th Ave N, Birmingham AL 35203	205-944-1300	P	132,351	27.8
13	Charter One Financial Inc—*Steven Hester* Citizens Financial Group Inc	1215 Superior Ave E, Cleveland OH 44114		S	126,619*	22.7
14	Fifth Third Bancorp—*Kevin Kabat*	PO Box 4444, Cincinnati OH 45263		P	111,007	20.8
15	KeyCorp—*Beth E Mooney*	127 Public Sq, Cleveland OH 44114	216-689-6300	P	91,834	15.6
16	UnionBanCal Corp—*Masaaki Tanaka*	PO Box 7104, San Francisco CA 94120	415-765-2000	S	85,598*	10.0
17	Santandar Holdings USA Inc—*Gabriel Jaramillo*	75 State St, Boston MA 02109	617-346-7200	S	82,953	10.6
18	Northern Trust Corp—*Frederick H Waddell*	50 S LaSalle St, Chicago IL 60603	312-630-6000	P	70,373	12.8
19	HNB Corp—*Frank Techar*	111 W Monroe St Ste 12, Chicago IL 60603	312-461-2121	R	68,700*	6.5
20	M and T Bank Corp—*Robert G Wilmers*	PO Box 1288, Buffalo NY 14240	716-842-5445	P	68,380	13.4
21	Hudson City Bancorp Inc—*Ronald E Hermance Jr*	W 80 Century Rd, Paramus NJ 07652	201-967-1900	P	61,166	1.6
22	Marshall and Ilsley Corp—*Mark F Furlong*	770 N Water St, Milwaukee WI 53202	414-765-7801	S	54,429	9.1
23	Huntington Bancshares Inc—*Stephen D Steinour*	Huntington Center 41 S, Columbus OH 43215	614-480-8300	P	53,820	11.3
24	Comerica Inc—*Ralph W Babb Jr*	1717 Main St, Dallas TX 75201	214-462-6831	P	53,667	9.4
25	BancWest Corp—*J Michael Shepherd*	180 Montgomery St, San Francisco CA 94104	925-942-8300	S	44,217*	12.0
26	Harris Bankcorp Inc—*Ellen Costello*	PO Box 755, Chicago IL 60690	312-461-2121	S	41,741*	9.7
27	TD Banknorth Inc—*Bharat B Masrani*	PO Box 9540, Portland ME 04112	207-761-8500	R	40,159	8.7
28	Compass Bancshares Inc	15 S 20th St, Birmingham AL 35233	205-297-3000	S	39,300*	10.0
29	Popular Inc—*Richard L Carrion*	P O Box 362708 209 Ave, San Juan PR 00918	787-765-9800	P	38,723	8.3
30	RBC Bank—*Jim Westlake*	PO Box 1220, Rocky Mount NC 27802	252-454-4400	S	26,000	5.0
31	First Horizon National Corp—*D Bryan Jordan*	165 Madison Ave, Memphis TN 38103	901-523-4444	P	24,699	5.4
32	Midland States Bancorp Inc—*Leon J Holschbach*	133 W Jefferson St, Effingham IL 62401	217-342-2141	R	24,500*	.1
33	OneAmerica Financial Partners Inc—*Dayton H Molendorp*	PO Box 368, Indianapolis IN 46206	317-285-1111	S	24,359	1.7
34	BOK Financial Corp—*Stanley A Lybarger*	PO Box 2300, Tulsa OK 74102	918-588-6000	P	23,942	4.5
35	Associated Banc-Corp—*Philip B Flynn*	PO Box 13307, Green Bay WI 54307	920-491-7000	P	21,786	4.9
36	Old National Bank—*Robert G Jones* Old National Bancorp	One Main St, Evansville IN 47708	812-464-1200	S	21,728*	2.5
37	City National Corp—*Russell Goldsmith*	555 S Flower St, Los Angeles CA 90071	310-888-6000	P	21,350	3.2
38	First Niagara Financial Group Inc—*John Koelmel*	PO Box 514, Lockport NY 14095	716-625-7500	P	21,084	3.8
39	First Citizens BancShares Inc (Raleigh North Carolina)—*Frank Holding*	4300 Six Forks Rd, Raleigh NC 27609	919-716-7000	P	20,807	4.4
40	Cullen/Frost Bankers Inc—*Richard W Evans Jr*	PO Box 1600, San Antonio TX 78296	210-220-4011	P	20,317	3.8
41	Great Western Securities Inc—*Ken Karels*	6015 NW Radial Hwy, Omaha NE 68104	402-293-7426	R	20,242*	1.5
42	SVB Financial Group—*Greg Becker*	3005 Tasman Dr, Santa Clara CA 95054	408-654-7400	P	19,969	1.5
43	Hancock Holding Co—*Carl J Chaney*	PO Box 4019, Gulfport MS 39502	228-868-4727	P	19,774	4.7
44	TCF Financial Corp—*William A Cooper*	200 Lake St E, Wayzata MN 55391	612-661-6500	P	18,979	7.1
45	Central Bancompany Inc—*Bryan Cook*	238 Madison St, Jefferson City MO 65101	573-634-1111	R	18,755*	1.5
46	Webster Financial Corp—*Daniel H Bley*	145 Bank St, Waterbury CT 06702	203-465-4364	P	18,714	3.0
47	Commerce Bancshares Inc—*David W Kemper*	PO Box 419248, Kansas City MO 64141	816-234-2000	P	18,502	5.0
48	First National of Nebraska—*Bruce Lauritzen*	PO Box 2490, Omaha NE 68103	402-341-0500	P	18,000	7.5
49	Guaranty Financial Group Inc—*Dennis Faulkner*	1300 MoPac Expwy S, Austin TX 78746	512-434-1000	P	16,796	2.3
50	Fulton Financial Corp—*R Scott Smith Jr*	PO Box 4887, Lancaster PA 17604	717-291-2411	P	16,371	3.5
51	Wintrust Financial Corp—*Edward J Wehmer*	727 N Bank Ln, Lake Forest IL 60045	847-615-4096	P	15,894	2.9
52	W Holding Company Inc—*Frank C Stipes*	PO Box 1180, Mayaguez PR 00681	787-834-8000	P	15,283	1.4
53	BankUnited Financial Corp—*John A Kanas*	255 Alhambra Cir, Coral Gables FL 33134	305-569-2000	P	15,046	1.5
54	Plains Capital Corp—*Allan B White*	2323 Victory Ave Ste 1, Dallas TX 75219	214-252-9100	R	15,003*	1.2
55	Susquehanna Bancshares Inc—*William J Reuter*	26 N Cedar St, Lititz PA 17543	717-626-4721	P	14,975	3.1
56	FirstMerit Corp—*Paul G Greig*	3 Cascade Plz 7th Fl, Akron OH 44308	330-996-6300	P	14,442	3.2
57	Valley National Bancorp—*Gerald H Lipkin*	1455 Valley Rd, Wayne NJ 07470	973-305-8800	P	14,270	2.8
58	UMB Financial Corp—*J Mariner Kemper*	1010 Grand Blvd, Kansas City MO 64106	816-860-7889	P	13,541	3.4
59	Washington Federal Inc—*Roy M Whitehead*	425 Pike St, Seattle WA 98101	206-624-7930	P	13,423	1.2
60	HomeStreet Bank Inc—*Mark K Mason*	601 Union St Ste 2000, Seattle WA 98101	206-389-6309	R	13,009	.4
61	BancorpSouth Inc—*Aubrey B Patterson Jr*	1 Mississippi Plz 201, Tupelo MS 38804	662-680-2000	P	12,996	4.2
62	Bank of Hawaii Corp—*Peter S Ho*	130 Merchant St, Honolulu HI 96813		P	12,415	2.4
63	Great Western Bancorporation Inc—*Jeff Erickson*	100 N Phillips Ave, Sioux Falls SD 57104	605-334-2548	R	12,378*	1.5
64	First Security Bancorp Inc (Searcy Arkansas)—*Reynie Rutledge*	PO Box 1009, Searcy AR 72145	501-279-3400	R	11,790*	.9
65	IBERIABANK Corp—*Daryl G Byrd*	200 W Congress St, Lafayette LA 70501	337-521-4003	P	11,758	2.6
66	International Bancshares Corp—*Dennis E Nixon*	1200 San Bernardo Ave, Laredo TX 78042	956-722-7611	P	11,740	3.0
67	Umpqua Holdings Corp—*Raymond P Davis*	1 SW Colombia St Ste 1, Portland OR 97258	503-727-4100	P	11,563	2.3
68	Superior Financial Corp—*Marvin Scott*	7167 S Mingo Rd, Tulsa OK 74133	918-250-2135	S	10,783*	.9
69	Valley National Bank (Wayne New Jersey)—*Gerald H Lipkin* Valley National Bancorp	1445 Valley Rd, Wayne NJ 07470	973-305-8800	S	10,763*	2.0
70	Investors Bancorp Inc—*Kevin Cummings*	101 JFK Pkwy, Short Hills NJ 07078	973-924-5100	P	10,702	1.0
71	Cathay General Bancorp—*Dunson K Cheng*	777 N Broadway, Los Angeles CA 90012	213-625-4700	P	10,645	1.0
72	Banner Bank—*Mark Grescovich* Banner Corp	PO Box 907, Walla Walla WA 99362	509-527-3636	S	9,922*	.8
73	MB Financial Inc—*Mitchell Feiger*	800 W Madison St, Chicago IL 60607	312-421-7600	P	9,833	1.7
74	Trustmark Corp—*Gerard Host*	PO Box 291, Jackson MS 39205	601-208-5111	P	9,727	2.5
75	Citizens Republic Bancorp Inc—*Cathleen H Nash*	328 S Saginaw St, Flint MI 48502	810-766-7500	P	9,463	2.0
76	Sterling Financial Corp—*J Gregory Seibly*	111 N Wall St, Spokane WA 99201	509-458-3711	P	9,193	2.5
77	FNB Corp—*Stephen Gurgovits*	1 FNB Blvd, Hermitage PA 16148	724-981-6000	P	8,960	2.7

Note: An asterisk (*) indicates an estimated financial figure. The company type code used is as follows: R = Private, P = Public, S = Private Subsidiary, B = Public Subsidiary, D = Division, J = Joint Venture, I = Investment Fund.

COMPANY RANKINGS BY SALES WITHIN 4-DIGIT SIC

Rank	Company Name—*Executive Officer*	Address, City, State, Zip	Phone	Type	Fin	Empls
78	Old National Bancorp—*Robert G Jones*	PO Box 718, Evansville IN 47705	812-464-1434	P	8,610	2.6
79	Capitol Federal Financial—*John B Dicus*	PO Box 3505, Topeka KS 66601	785-235-1341	P	8,487	.8
80	National Penn Bancshares Inc—*Scott Fainor*	PO Box 547, Boyertown PA 19512	610-369-6128	P	8,486	1.8
81	First Banks Inc—*Terrance M McCarthy*	135 N Meramec Ave, Clayton MO 63105	314-854-4600	R	8,480	1.9
82	United Bankshares Inc—*Richard M Adams*	300 United Ctr 500 Vir, Charleston WV 25301	304-424-8704	P	8,452	1.6
83	Amarillo National Bank Inc—*Martin King*	PO Box 1, Amarillo TX 79105	806-378-8000	R	8,383*	.6
84	Fidelity Bankshares Mutual Holding Co—*Vince A Elhilow*	PO Box 989, West Palm Beach FL 33402	561-659-9900	R	8,149*	.8
85	Northwest Bancshares Inc (Warren Pennsylvania)—*William J Wagner*	PO Box 128, Warren PA 16365	814-726-2140	P	7,958	2.1
86	FirstBank Holding Company of Colorado—*John Ikard*	12345 W Colfax Ave, Lakewood CO 80215	303-232-3000	R	7,900	2.2
87	First Midwest Bancorp Inc—*Michael Scudder*	PO Box 459, Itasca IL 60143	630-875-7450	P	7,848	1.8
88	Compass Bank Inc—*Garrett R Hegel* Compass Bancshares Inc	505 N 20th St, Birmingham AL 35203		S	7,806*	2.8
89	Credit One Bank—*Robert DeJong*	PO Box 98873, Las Vegas NV 89193	702-269-1000	R	7,599*	.7
90	Amegy Corp—*Scott McLean*	PO Box 4837, Houston TX 77210	713-235-8810	S	7,506	2.1
91	United Community Banks Inc—*Jimmy C Tallent*	PO Box 398, Blairsville GA 30514	706-781-2265	P	7,443	1.8
92	First Interstate Bancsystem Inc—*Lyle R Knight*	PO Box 30918, Billings MT 59107	406-255-5390	P	7,326	1.7
93	Glacier Bancorp Inc—*Michael J Blodnick*	49 Commons Loop, Kalispell MT 59901	406-756-4200	P	7,188	1.7
94	Park National Corp—*Charles Daniel DeLawder*	PO Box 3500, Newark OH 43058	740-349-8451	P	6,972	1.9
95	Provident Financial Services Inc (Jersey City New Jersey)—*Christopher Martin*	239 Washington St, Jersey City NJ 07302	732-590-9200	P	6,825	1.0
96	IBC Subsidiary Corp International Bancshares Corp	1200 San Bernardo Ave, Laredo TX 78040	956-722-7611	S	6,802*	1.6
97	Santander BanCorp—*Juan Moreno Blanco*	PO Box 362589, San Juan PR 00936	787-777-4100	S	6,766	1.8
98	First Financial Bancorp—*Claude E Davis*	PO Box 476, Hamilton OH 45012		P	6,672	1.7
99	Johnson International Inc—*Richard A Hansen*	555 Main St Ste 400, Racine WI 53403	262-681-4620	S	6,568*	.8
100	CVB Financial Corp—*Christopher D Myers*	701 N Haven Ave Ste 35, Ontario CA 91764	909-980-4030	P	6,506	.8
101	Community Bank System Inc—*Mark E Tryniski*	5790 Widewaters Pky, DeWitt NY 13214	315-445-2282	P	6,488	1.9
102	Texas Capital Bancshares Inc—*George Jones Jr*	2000 McKinney Ave Ste, Dallas TX 75201	214-932-6600	P	6,446	.7
103	Boston Private Financial Holdings Inc—*Clayton Deutsch*	10 Post Office Sq, Boston MA 02109	617-912-3799	P	6,138	.9
104	Pacific Capital Bancorp—*Carl Webb*	PO Box 60839, Santa Barbara CA 93160	805-564-6405	P	6,086	1.0
105	First Commonwealth Financial Corp—*John Dolan*	PO Box 400, Indiana PA 15701	724-349-7220	P	5,841	1.6
106	BFC Financial Corp—*Alan B Levan*	2100 W Cypress Creek R, Fort Lauderdale FL 33309	954-940-4900	P	5,813	5.1
107	Bremer Financial Corp—*Stan K Dardis*	445 Minnesota St, Saint Paul MN 55101	651-227-7621	R	5,573*	1.8
108	WesBanco Inc—*Paul M Limbert*	1 Bank Plz, Wheeling WV 26003	304-234-9000	P	5,536	1.4
109	PacWest Bancorp—*Matthew P Wagner*	401 West A St, San Diego CA 92101	619-744-7200	P	5,529	.9
110	NBT Bancorp Inc—*Martin A Dietrich*	PO Box 351, Norwich NY 13815	607-337-2265	P	5,446	1.6
111	Chemical Financial Corp—*David B Ramaker*	PO Box 569, Midland MI 48640	989-839-5350	P	5,340	1.4
112	Whitaker Bank Corp—*Elmer Whitaker*	PO Box 14037, Lexington KY 40512	859-299-9200	R	5,266*	.4
113	Sterling Bancshares Inc—*J Downey Bridgwater*	PO Box 40333, Houston TX 77240	713-466-8300	P	5,192	.9
114	BancFirst Corp—*David E Rainbolt*	101 N Broadway Ave Ste, Oklahoma City OK 73102	405-270-1086	P	5,060	1.5
115	Westamerica Bancorp—*David L Payne*	1108 Fifth Ave, San Rafael CA 94901	415-257-8000	P	5,042	1.0
116	Irwin Financial Corp—*William Miller*	PO Box 929, Columbus IN 47202	812-376-1909	P	4,914	.9
117	Pinnacle Financial Partners Inc—*M Terry Turner*	150 3rd Ave S Ste 900, Nashville TN 37201	615-744-3700	P	4,909	.8
118	Ocwen Financial Corp—*Ronald M Faris*	PO Box 24737, West Palm Beach FL 33416	561-682-8000	P	4,737	5.1
119	Independent Bank Corp (Rockland Massachusetts)—*Christopher Oddleifson*	288 Union St, Rockland MA 02370	781-878-6100	P	4,696	.9
120	BankAtlantic Bancorp Inc—*Alan B Levan*	PO Box 8608, Fort Lauderdale FL 33310	954-940-5000	P	4,509	1.4
121	Taylor Capital Group Inc—*Mark A Hoppe*	9550 W Higgins Rd, Rosemont IL 60018	847-653-7978	P	4,484	.6
122	Banner Corp—*Mark J Grescovich*	PO Box 907, Walla Walla WA 99362	509-527-3636	P	4,406	1.1
123	Renasant Corp	PO Box 709, Tupelo MS 38802	662-680-1001	P	4,297	1.0
124	First Merchants Corp—*Michael C Rechin*	PO Box 792, Muncie IN 47305	765-747-1500	P	4,272	1.2
125	Gold Banc Corporation Inc Marshall and Ilsley Corp	11301 Nall Ave, Leawood KS 66211	913-451-8050	S	4,230	.7
126	First Financial Bankshares Inc—*F Scott Dueser*	PO Box 701, Abilene TX 79604	325-627-7155	P	4,120	1.0
127	S and T Bancorp Inc—*Todd D Brice*	PO Box 190, Indiana PA 15701	724-349-1800	P	4,114	.9
128	Huntington Preferred Capital Inc—*Donald Kimble*	41 S High St, Columbus OH 43215	614-480-8300	P	4,113	N/A
129	CommerceBank Holding Corp—*J Guillermo Villar*	220 Alhambra Cir, Coral Gables FL 33134	305-468-8701	S	4,111	N/A
130	Central Pacific Financial Corp—*John C Dean*	PO Box 3590, Honolulu HI 96811	808-544-0500	P	4,100	.9
131	WSFS Financial Corp—*Mark A Turner*	500 Delaware Ave, Wilmington DE 19801	302-792-6000	P	3,954	.7
132	FVNB Corp—*MRussell Marshall*	PO Box 1338, Victoria TX 77902	361-573-6321	R	3,747*	.3
133	TrustCo Bank Corporation of New York—*Robert J McCormick*	PO Box 1082, Schenectady NY 12301	518-377-3311	P	3,689	.7
134	Republic Bancorp Inc (Louisville Kentucky)—*Steven E Trager*	601 W Market St, Louisville KY 40202	502-584-3600	P	3,623	.7
135	SCBT Financial Corp—*Robert R Hill Jr*	PO Box 1030, Columbia SC 29201	803-771-2265	P	3,595	1.0
136	Capitol Bancorp Ltd—*Joseph D Reid*	200 Washington Sq N Ca, Lansing MI 48933	517-487-6555	P	3,540	1.0
137	Sandy Spring Bancorp Inc—*Daniel J Schrider*	17801 Georgia Ave, Olney MD 20832	301-774-6400	P	3,519	.7
138	Sun Bancorp Inc—*Thomas X Geisel*	226 Landis Ave, Vineland NJ 08360	856-691-7700	P	3,418	.6
139	Great Southern Bancorp Inc—*Joseph W Turner*	PO Box 9009, Springfield MO 65808	417-887-4400	P	3,412	1.1
140	First Busey Corp—*Van A Dukeman*	PO Box 123, Urbana IL 61801	217-365-4516	P	3,402	.9
141	Anchor BanCorp Wisconsin Inc—*Chris Bauer*	PO Box 7933, Madison WI 53707	608-252-8700	P	3,395	.8
142	First Bancorp (Troy North Carolina)—*Jerry Ocheltree*	PO Box 508, Troy NC 27371	910-576-6171	P	3,291	.8
143	Bank of the Ozarks Inc—*George Gleason*	PO Box 8811, Little Rock AR 72231	501-978-2265	P	3,274	.9
144	Dickinson Financial Corp—*Paul P Holewinski*	PO Box 26158, Kansas City MO 64196	816-472-5244	R	3,262*	.3
145	Superior Bancorp—*C Marvin Scott*	17 N 20th St, Birmingham AL 35203	205-326-2265	P	3,222	.8
146	First Financial Holdings Inc—*R Wayne Hall*	34 Broad St Ste 10, Charleston SC 29401	843-529-5931	P	3,206	.9
147	Tompkins Financial Corp—*Stephen S Romaine*	PO Box 460, Ithaca NY 14851	607-274-7299	P	3,192	.8
148	Simmons First National Corp (Pine Bluff Arkansas)—*J Thomas May*	PO Box 7009, Pine Bluff AR 71611	870-541-1000	P	3,134	1.1
149	First Independent Group—*William J Firstenberg*	PO Box 8904, Vancouver WA 98668	360-699-4293	R	3,103*	.2
150	Washington Trust Bancorp Inc—*Joseph J MarcAurele*	23 Broad St, Westerly RI 02891	401-348-1200	P	3,064	.5
151	Southside Bancshares Inc—*BG Hartley*	PO Box 1079, Tyler TX 75710	903-531-7111	P	3,000	.6
152	Ameris Bancorp—*Edwin Hortman Jr*	PO Box 3668, Moultrie GA 31776	229-890-1111	P	2,994	.7
153	StellarOne Corp—*OR Barham Jr*	590 Peter Jefferson Pk, Charlottesville VA 22911	434-964-2211	P	2,977	.8
154	ViewPoint Financial Group—*Mark Hord*	1309 W 15th St, Plano TX 75075	972-578-5000	P	2,942	.6
155	Hanmi Financial Corp—*Jay S Yoo*	3660 Wilshire Blvd Pen, Los Angeles CA 90010	213-382-2200	P	2,907	.5
156	Kearny Financial Corp—*Craig L Montanaro*	120 Passaic Ave, Fairfield NJ 07004	973-244-4500	P	2,904	.4
157	State Bank Financial Corp—*Joseph W Evans*	PO Box 4748, Macon GA 31208	478-722-6200	P	2,829	.5
158	Southwest Bancorp Inc (Stillwater Oklahoma)—*Rick J Green*	PO Box 1988, Stillwater OK 74076	405-377-4762	P	2,821	.4
159	Lakeland Bancorp Inc—*Thomas J Shara*	250 Oak Ridge Rd, Oak Ridge NJ 07438	973-697-2000	P	2,793	.5
160	City Holding Co—*Charles R Hageboeck*	PO Box 7520, Charleston WV 25356	304-769-1100	P	2,777	.8

Rank	Company Name—*Executive Officer*	Address, City, State, Zip	Phone	Type	Fin	Empls
161	MainSource Financial Group Inc—*Archie M Brown Jr*	2105 N State Rd 3 Bypa, Greensburg IN 47240	812-663-6734	P	2,769	.9
162	Pacific Coast Bankers Bancshares—*Steven A Brown*	340 Pine St Ste 401, San Francisco CA 94104	415-399-1900	R	2,756*	.3
163	Tower Bancorp Inc—*Andrew S Samuel* Susquehanna Bancshares Inc	112 Market St, Harrisburg PA 17101	717-231-2700	B	2,747	.9
164	Century Bancorp Inc—*Barry R Sloane*	400 Mystic Ave, Medford MA 02155	781-391-4000	P	2,743	.4
165	Virginia Commerce Bancorp Inc—*Peter A Converse*	5350 Lee Hwy, Arlington VA 22207	703-534-0700	P	2,742	.3
166	Brookline Bancorp Inc—*Paul A Perrault*	160 Washington St, Brookline MA 02445	617-730-3500	P	2,721	.3
167	Hudson Valley Holding Corp—*James J Landy*	21 Scarsdale Rd, Yonkers NY 10707	914-961-6100	P	2,669	.5
168	Lakeland Financial Corp—*Michael L Kubacki*	PO Box 1387, Warsaw IN 46581	574-267-6144	P	2,653	.5
169	INTRUST Financial Corp—*Charles Q Chandler III*	PO Box 1, Wichita KS 67201	316-383-1111	R	2,635*	1.0
170	Capital City Bank Group Inc—*William G Smith Jr*	PO Box 900, Tallahassee FL 32302	850-671-0300	P	2,622	1.0
171	Bank Mutual Corp—*Michael T Crowley Jr*	4949 W Brown Deer Rd, Milwaukee WI 53224	414-354-1500	P	2,592	.8
172	City National Bancshares Inc—*Leonard Abess*	25 W Flagler St, Miami FL 33130		S	2,565*	.4
173	Independent Bank Corp (Ionia Michigan)—*Michael M Magee Jr*	PO Box 491, Ionia MI 48846	616-527-9450	P	2,535	1.2
174	First American Bank—*Frank J Bourgeois*	PO Box 550, Vacherie LA 70090	225-265-2265	R	2,510*	.2
175	First State Financial Corp—*Gene Lovell*	16100 E Nine Mile Rd, Eastpointe MI 48021	586-775-5000	R	2,480*	.2
176	First Financial Corp (Terre Haute Indiana)—*Norman L Lowery*	PO Box 540, Terre Haute IN 47808	812-238-6000	P	2,451	.8
177	West Coast Bancorp—*Robert D Sznewajs*	5335 Meadows Rd Ste 20, Lake Oswego OR 97035	503-684-0884	P	2,430	.7
178	Old Second Bancorp Inc—*William B Skoglund*	37 S River St, Aurora IL 60506	630-892-0202	P	2,426	.5
179	Integra Bank Corp—*Michael J Alley*	PO Box 868, Evansville IN 47705	812-464-9677	P	2,421	.5
180	OceanFirst Financial Corp—*John R Garbarino*	975 Hooper Ave, Toms River NJ 08753	732-240-4500	P	2,251	.4
181	Northfield Bancorp—*John W Alexander*	1410 St Georges Ave, Avenel NJ 07001	732-499-7200	P	2,247	.4
182	Sterling Bancorp (New York New York)—*Louis J Cappelli*	650 Fifth Ave, New York NY 10019	212-757-3300	P	2,245	.6
183	Huntington Bancshares West Virginia Inc—*Stephen Steinoyer* Huntington Bancshares Inc	1 Huntington Sq, Charleston WV 25301	304-348-5000	S	2,240*	1.2
184	Metro Bancorp Inc—*Gary L Nalbandian*	PO Box 4999, Harrisburg PA 17111	717-412-6301	P	2,235	1.0
185	Financial Institutions Inc—*Peter G Humphrey*	220 Liberty St, Warsaw NY 14569	585-786-1100	P	2,214	.6
186	United Community Financial Corp—*Patrick W Bevack*	PO Box 1111, Youngstown OH 44501	330-742-0500	P	2,197	.6
187	Security National Corp—*Douglas Rice*	PO Box 147, Sioux City IA 51102	712-277-6500	R	2,195*	.3
188	Emprise Financial Corp—*Thomas A Page*	PO Box 2970, Wichita KS 67201	316-383-4301	R	2,192*	.5
189	TriCo Bancshares—*Richard P Smith*	63 Constitution Dr, Chico CA 95973	530-898-0300	P	2,190	.7
190	First Community Bancshares Inc—*John M Mendez*	PO Box 989, Bluefield VA 24605	276-326-9000	P	2,165	.6
191	BancTrust Financial Group Inc—*W Bibb Lamar Jr*	PO Box 3067, Mobile AL 36652	251-431-7800	P	2,158	.5
192	Norway Bancorp Inc—*Robert Harmon*	PO Box 347, Norway ME 04268	207-743-7986	R	2,127*	.3
193	Univest Corporation of Pennsylvania—*William S Aichele*	PO Box 64197, Souderton PA 18964	215-721-2400	P	2,093	.6
194	Cardinal Financial Corp—*Bernard H Clineburg*	8270 Greensboro Dr Ste, McLean VA 22102	703-584-3400	P	2,072	.4
195	First Defiance Financial Corp—*William J Small*	601 Clinton St, Defiance OH 43512	419-782-5015	P	2,036	.5
196	Seacoast Banking Corporation of Florida—*Dennis S Hudson III*	PO Box 9012, Stuart FL 34995	772-287-4000	P	2,016	.4
197	Shorebank Corp—*George Surgeon*	7936 S Cottage Grove A, Chicago IL 60619	773-288-1000	R	2,000*	.4
198	SY Bancorp Inc—*David P Heintzman*	PO Box 32890, Louisville KY 40232	502-582-2571	P	1,960	.5
199	ESB Financial Corp—*Charlotte A Zuschlag*	600 Lawrence Ave, Ellwood City PA 16117	724-758-5584	P	1,914	.3
200	Arrow Financial Corp—*Thomas L Hoy*	250 Glen St, Glens Falls NY 12801	518-745-1000	P	1,908	.4
201	WTB Financial Corp—*Peter F Stanton*	PO Box 2127, Spokane WA 99210	509-353-2265	R	1,908*	.8
202	FNB United Corp—*Brian Simpson*	PO Box 1328, Asheboro NC 27203	336-626-8300	P	1,902	.5
203	Guaranty Bancorp—*Paul W Taylor*	1331 17th St Ste 300, Denver CO 80202	303-293-5563	P	1,900	.4
204	German American Bancorp Inc—*Mark A Schroeder*	PO Box 810, Jasper IN 47546	812-482-1314	P	1,874	.4
205	Farmers and Merchants Bancorp—*Kent A Steinwert*	111 W Pine St, Lodi CA 95240	209-367-2300	P	1,842	.3
206	Devon Bancorp—*Richard Loundy*	6445 N Western Ave, Chicago IL 60645	773-465-2500	R	1,820*	.1
207	First California Financial Group Inc—*CG Kum*	3027 Townsgate Rd Ste, Westlake Village CA 91361	805-322-9655	P	1,813	.2
208	NewBridge Bancorp—*Pressley A Ridgill*	1501 Highwoods Blvd St, Greensboro NC 27410	336-369-0905	P	1,807	.5
209	Parkvale Financial Corp—*Robert J McCarthy Jr*	4220 William Penn Hwy, Monroeville PA 15146	412-373-7200	P	1,800	.4
210	Peoples Bancorp Inc—*David L Mead*	PO Box 738, Marietta OH 45750	740-373-3155	P	1,794	.5
211	Cenlar Capital Corp—*Gregory Tornquist*	425 Phillips Blvd, Ewing NJ 08618	609-883-3900	R	1,791*	.4
212	Bryn Mawr Bank Corp—*Frederick C Peters II*	801 Lancaster Ave, Bryn Mawr PA 19010	610-525-1700	P	1,775	.3
213	TIB Financial Corp—*R Eugene Taylor*	599 9th St N Ste 100, Naples FL 34102	239-263-3344	P	1,757	.4
214	Porter Bancorp Inc—*Maria L Bouvette*	PO Box 436029, Louisville KY 40253	502-499-4800	P	1,724	.3
215	First American Bank Group Ltd—*Thomas Schnurr* Stark Bank Group Ltd	1207 Central Ave, Fort Dodge IA 50501	515-573-2154	S	1,721*	.2
216	Cascade Bancorp—*Patricia Moss*	PO Box 369, Bend OR 97709	541-617-3500	P	1,717	.4
217	First of Long Island Corp—*Michael N Vittorio*	10 Glen Head Rd, Glen Head NY 11545	516-671-4900	P	1,711	.2
218	Washington Banking Co—*John L Wagner*	450 SW Bayshore Dr, Oak Harbor WA 98277	360-679-3121	P	1,705	.4
219	Stark Bank Group Ltd—*Ken Aschom*	1207 Central Ave, Fort Dodge IA 50501	515-573-2154	R	1,700*	.2
220	First United Corp—*William B Grant*	PO Box 9, Oakland MD 21550	301-334-9471	P	1,696	.5
221	AmericanWest Bancorp—*Patrick J Rusnak*	41 W Riverside Ave Ste, Spokane WA 99201	509-467-6993	P	1,656	.5
222	Southern Community Financial Corp—*F Scott Bauer*	PO Box 26134, Winston-Salem NC 27114	336-768-8500	P	1,653	.3
223	Suffolk Bancorp—*J Gordon Huszaph*	PO Box 9000, Riverhead NY 11901	631-727-5667	P	1,618	.4
224	Southeastern Bank Financial Corp—*R Daniel Blanton*	3530 Wheeler Rd, Augusta GA 30909	706-738-6990	P	1,607	.3
225	First M and F Corp—*Hugh S Potts Jr*	134 W Washington St, Kosciusko MS 39090	662-289-5121	P	1,604	.5
226	Bancorp Rhode Island Inc—*Merrill W Sherman*	1 Turks Head Pl, Providence RI 02903	401-456-5000	P	1,604	.2
227	CNB Financial Corp (Clearfield Pennsylvania)—*Joseph Bower Jr*	PO Box 42, Clearfield PA 16830	814-765-9621	P	1,602	.3
228	Klein Financial Inc—*Dougl Hile*	PO Box 37, Chaska MN 55318	952-448-2350	R	1,600*	.3
229	Virginia Financial Group Inc—*OR Barham Jr*	PO Box 71, Culpeper VA 22701	540-829-1633	P	1,595	.5
230	State Bancorp Inc—*Thomas M O'Brien*	Two Jericho Plaza, Jericho NY 11753	516-437-1000	P	1,590	.3
231	Capital Bank Corp—*R Eugene Taylor*	333 Fayetteville St St, Raleigh NC 27601	919-645-6400	B	1,586	.4
232	MidWestOne Financial Group Inc—*Charles N Funk*	PO Box 1700, Iowa City IA 52244	319-356-5800	P	1,581	.4
233	First Bank Southwest (Perryton Texas)—*Larry Orman*	PO Box 32552, Amarillo TX 79120		R	1,572*	.1
234	West Alabama Capital Corp—*Brenda Manning*	PO Box 310, Reform AL 35481	205-375-6261	R	1,567*	.1
235	Metrocorp Bancshares Inc—*George M Lee*	9600 Bellaire Blvd Ste, Houston TX 77036	713-776-3876	P	1,559	.3
236	Albank Corp—*Martin L Gecht*	3400 W Lawrence Ave, Chicago IL 60625	773-267-7300	R	1,532*	.2
237	Merchants Bancshares Inc—*Michael R Tuttle*	PO Box 1009, Burlington VT 05402	802-658-3400	P	1,488	.3
238	Encore Bancshares Inc—*Preston M Moore*	9 Greenway Plz Ste 100, Houston TX 77046	713-787-3100	P	1,480	.3
239	Summit Financial Group Inc—*H Charles Maddy III*	PO Box 179, Moorefield WV 26836	304-530-1000	P	1,470	.2
240	First Mid-Illinois Bancshares Inc—*William S Rowland*	1515 Charleston Ave, Mattoon IL 61938	217-234-7454	P	1,468	.4
241	Firstbank Corp—*Thomas R Sullivan*	PO Box 1029, Alma MI 48801	989-463-3131	P	1,458	.4
242	Tennessee Commerce Bancorp Inc—*Michael Sapp*	381 Mallory Station Rd, Franklin TN 37067	615-599-2274	P	1,453	.1
243	VIST Financial Group—*Robert D Davis*	PO Box 6219, Wyomissing PA 19610	610-208-0966	P	1,425	.3
244	Alliance Financial Corp—*Jack H Webb*	PO Box 5430, Cortland NY 13045	315-475-4478	P	1,409	.3
245	MutualFirst Financial Inc—*David W Heeter*	PO Box 551, Muncie IN 47305	765-747-2800	P	1,407	.4
246	Horizon Bancorp—*Craig M Dwight*	515 Franklin Sq, Michigan City IN 46360		P	1,401	.3

Note: An asterisk (*) indicates an estimated financial figure. The company type code used is as follows: R = Private, P = Public, S = Private Subsidiary, B = Public Subsidiary, D = Division, J = Joint Venture, I = Investment Fund.

COMPANY RANKINGS BY SALES WITHIN 4-DIGIT SIC

Rank	Company Name—*Executive Officer*	Address, City, State, Zip	Phone	Type	Fin	Empls
247	Liberty Capital Inc—*James R Powell*	PO Box 1000, Wilmington OH 45177	937-382-1000	R	1,400*	.7
248	First National Community Bancorp Inc—*Gerard A Champi*	102 E Drinker St, Dunmore PA 18512	570-346-7667	P	1,395	.3
249	First Bancorp Inc (Damariscotta Maine)—*Daniel R Daigneault*	PO Box 940, Damariscotta ME 04543	207-563-3195	P	1,394	.2
250	1N Bank—*John A Featherman III* Susquehanna Bancshares Inc	PO Box 523, West Chester PA 19381	484-881-4010	S	1,377	.7
251	Chemical Bank Shoreline—*Len Amat* Chemical Financial Corp	823 Riverview Dr, Benton Harbor MI 49022	269-927-2251	S	1,377*	.3
252	Southern Bancshares NC Inc—*J Grey Morgan*	PO Box 729, Mount Olive NC 28365	919-658-7000	P	1,372	.4
253	Arvest Bank—*Kelly Brander* Arvest Bank Group Inc	PO Box 55500, Oklahoma City OK 73155	405-677-8711	S	1,362*	.3
254	Peapack-Gladstone Financial Corp—*Frank A Kissel*	PO Box 700, Bedminster NJ 07921	908-234-0700	P	1,352	.3
255	Citywide Banks of Colorado Inc—*Kevin Quinn*	1800 Larimer St Ste 20, Denver CO 80202	303-365-3600	R	1,344*	.2
256	First Financial Service Inc—*B Keith Johnson*	PO Box 5006, Elizabethtown KY 42702	270-765-2131	P	1,321	.3
257	Provident Financial Holdings Inc—*Craig G Blunden*	3756 Central Ave, Riverside CA 92506	951-686-6060	P	1,315	.4
258	Citizens and Northern Corp—*Charles H Updegraff Jr*	90-92 Main St Ste 92, Wellsboro PA 16901	570-724-3411	P	1,313	.3
259	First Mariner Bancorp—*Edwin F Hale Sr*	1501 S Clinton St, Baltimore MD 21224	410-558-4200	P	1,310	.7
260	PAB Bankshares Inc—*Donald J Torbert Jr*	PO Box 3460, Valdosta GA 31604	229-241-2775	P	1,307	.3
261	West Texas National Bank—*Keith Moore*	6 Desta Dr Ste 2400, Midland TX 79705	432-685-6500	S	1,305*	.1
262	Sierra Bancorp—*James C Holly*	PO Box 1930, Porterville CA 93258	559-782-4900	P	1,287	.4
263	Colony Bankcorp Inc—*Al Ross*	115 S Grant St, Fitzgerald GA 31750	229-426-6000	P	1,276	.3
264	Meta Financial Group Inc—*J Tyler Haahr*	PO Box 1307, Storm Lake IA 50588	712-732-4117	P	1,276	.4
265	MBT Financial Corp—*H Douglas Chaffin*	102 E Front St, Monroe MI 48161	734-241-3431	P	1,259	N/A
266	Delmar Bancorp—*Edward M Thomas*	9550 Ocean Highway, Delmar MD 21875	410-896-9041	R	1,255*	.1
267	NASB Financial Inc—*David H Hancock*	12498 S Hwy 71, Grandview MO 64030	816-765-2200	P	1,254	.4
268	Westfield Financial Inc—*James Hagen*	141 Elm St, Westfield MA 01086	413-568-1911	P	1,240	.2
269	Commonwealth Bankshares Inc—*Chris E Beisel* First Community Bancshares Inc	PO Box 1177, Norfolk VA 23501	757-446-6900	B	1,221	.2
270	Pacific Continental Corp—*Hal M Brown*	PO Box 10727, Eugene OR 97440	541-686-8685	P	1,210	.3
271	Center Bancorp Inc—*Anthony C Weagley*	2455 Morris Ave, Union NJ 07083	908-688-9500	P	1,207	.2
272	Hawthorn Bancshares Inc—*David T Turner*	PO Box 688, Jefferson City MO 65102	816-347-8100	P	1,200	.4
273	HF Financial Corp—*Stephen M Bianchi*	PO Box 5000, Sioux Falls SD 57117	605-333-7620	P	1,191	.3
274	First Miami Bancorp Inc—*Drew A Dammeier*	PO Box 431000, South Miami FL 33143	305-667-5511	R	1,188*	.1
275	Home Federal Bancorp Inc (Nampa Idaho)—*Len E Williams*	500 12th Ave S, Nampa ID 83651	208-466-4634	P	1,177	.4
276	West Suburban Bancorp Inc—*Kevin Acker*	711 S Meyers Rd, Lombard IL 60148	630-629-4200	R	1,174*	.5
277	Southern Bancshares Inc—*Vince Coleman*	5515 S Grand Blvd, Saint Louis MO 63111	314-481-6800	R	1,170*	.2
278	Rabobank (El Centro California)—*Ronald Block*	1448 Main St, El Centro CA 92243	760-337-3200	S	1,168*	.4
279	Bar Harbor Bankshares—*Joseph M Murphy*	PO Box 400, Bar Harbor ME 04609	207-288-3314	P	1,168	.2
280	Broadway Bancshares Inc—*James D Goudge*	PO Box 17001, San Antonio TX 78217	210-283-6500	R	1,162*	.6
281	Banterra Corp—*Everett D Knight*	PO Box 291, Eldorado IL 62930	618-273-2242	R	1,160*	.3
282	Wilkinson Banking Corp—*Stanhope Wilkinson*	PO Box 610, Greenwood AR 72936	479-996-4171	R	1,153*	.1
283	LNB Bancorp Inc—*Daniel E Klimas*	457 Broadway, Lorain OH 44052	440-244-6000	P	1,153	.3
284	American State Financial Corp—*Frank P Keogh*	PO Box 1401, Lubbock TX 79408	806-767-7000	R	1,132*	.5
285	Cambridge Bancorp—*Joseph V Roller II*	PO Box 380186, Cambridge MA 02238	617-876-5500	P	1,131	.2
286	Shore Bancshares Inc—*W Moorhead Vermilye*	18 E Dover St, Easton MD 21601	410-763-7800	P	1,130	.3
287	Clifton Savings Bancorp Inc—*Walter Celuch*	1433 Van Houten Ave, Clifton NJ 07013	973-473-2200	P	1,123	.1
288	CFS Bancorp Inc—*Thomas F Prisby*	707 Ridge Rd, Munster IN 46321	219-836-5500	P	1,122	.3
289	Community Bankers Trust Corp—*Rex Smith III*	4235 Innslake Dr Ste 2, Glen Allen VA 23060	804-934-9999	P	1,116	.3
290	Virginia Commonwealth Trust Co—*Ed Barham*	102 S Main St, Culpeper VA 22701	540-825-4800	R	1,107*	.2
291	BCB Bancorp Inc—*Donald Mindiak*	104-110 Ave C, Bayonne NJ 07002	201-823-0700	P	1,107	.2
292	Marquette National Corp—*Paul M McCarthy*	10000 W 151st St, Orland Park IL 60462	773-476-5100	R	1,103*	.4
293	First Citizens Banc Corp—*James O Miller*	PO Box 5016, Sandusky OH 44871	419-625-4121	P	1,101	N/A
294	Essa Bancorp Inc—*Gary S Olson*	PO Box 1, Stroudsburg PA 18360	570-421-0531	P	1,098	.2
295	Princeton National Bancorp Inc—*Thomas D Ogaard*	606 S Main St, Princeton IL 61356	815-875-4444	P	1,097	N/A
296	American Founders Bancorp Inc—*John T Taylor*	318 E Main St, Lexington KY 40507	859-367-3700	R	1,093*	.1
297	Capital Bancorp Ltd—*Joseph D Reid* Capitol Bancorp Ltd	2777 E Camelback Rd, Phoenix AZ 85016	602-955-6100	S	1,092*	.2
298	Steel Partners Holdings LP—*Terry Gibson*	590 Madison Ave 32nd F, New York NY 10022	212-520-2300	P	1,092	<.1
299	Tri City Bankshares Corp—*Ronald K Puetz*	6400 S 27th St, Oak Creek WI 53154	414-761-1610	P	1,087	.5
300	Baylake Corp—*Robert J Cera*	PO Box 9, Sturgeon Bay WI 54235	920-743-5551	P	1,087	.3
301	Terrabank Holding Corp	PO Box 140460, Miami FL 33114	305-448-4898	R	1,086*	.1
302	HopFed Bancorp Inc—*John E Peck*	PO Box 537, Hopkinsville KY 42241	270-887-2999	P	1,083	.3
303	Alerus Financial Corp—*Randy L Newman*	401 DeMers Ave, Grand Forks ND 58201	701-795-3200	P	1,079	.5
304	Peoples Bancorp of North Carolina Inc—*Tony W Wolfe*	518 W C St, Newton NC 28658	828-464-5620	P	1,078	.3
305	CCB Corp—*Paul Thompson*	414 Nichols Rd, Kansas City MO 64112	816-931-4060	R	1,075*	.2
306	Farmers National Banc Corp—*John Gulas*	PO Box 555, Canfield OH 44406	330-533-3341	P	1,068	N/A
307	Denmark Bancshares Inc—*Jill Feller*	PO Box 130, Denmark WI 54208	920-863-2161	R	1,067*	.1
308	Citizens South Banking Corp—*Kim S Price*	PO Box 2249, Gastonia NC 28053	704-868-5200	P	1,065	.2
309	Indiana Community Bancorp—*John K Keach Jr*	501 Washington St, Columbus IN 47201	812-522-1592	P	1,043	.2
310	City National Bancshares Corp—*Louis E Prezeau*	900 Broad St, Newark NJ 07102	973-624-0865	R	1,040*	.1
311	NEB Corp—*Tony Johnson*	PO Box 988, Fond du Lac WI 54936	920-921-7700	R	1,033*	<.1
312	Bridge Bancorp Inc—*Kevin M O'Connor*	PO Box 3005, Bridgehampton NY 11932	631-537-1001	P	1,028	.2
313	First Eastern Bankshares Corp—*Richard Kalagher*	100 Brickstone Sq, Andover MA 01810	978-748-3100	R	1,027*	.1
314	Pacific Mercantile Bancorp—*Raymond E Dellerba*	949 S Coast Dr Ste 300, Costa Mesa CA 92626	714-438-2500	P	1,025	.3
315	National Bankshares Inc—*James G Rakes*	PO Box 90002, Blacksburg VA 24062	540-951-6300	P	1,022	.2
316	Fidelity BancShares NC Inc—*Mike Whitley*	PO Box 8, Fuquay Varina NC 27526	919-552-2242	R	1,013*	.4
317	Codorus Valley Bancorp Inc—*Larry J Miller*	PO Box 2887, York PA 17405	717-846-1970	P	1,012	.2
318	Northrim BanCorp Inc—*Joseph Beedle*	PO Box 241489, Anchorage AK 99524	907-562-0062	P	1,011	.2
319	Colorado State Bank and Trust—*Bill Sullivan* BOK Financial Corp	1600 Broadway, Denver CO 80202	303-861-2111	S	1,008*	.2
320	Intermountain Community Bancorp—*Curt Hecker*	PO Box 967, Sandpoint ID 83864	208-263-0505	P	1,005	.3
321	MidSouth Bancorp Inc—*CR Cloutier*	PO Box 3745, Lafayette LA 70502	337-237-8343	P	1,002	.4
322	New Hampshire Thrift Bancshares Inc—*Stephen W Ensign*	PO Box 9, Newport NH 03773	603-863-0886	P	995	.2
323	Bank of Granite Corp—*R Scott Anderson*	PO Box 128, Granite Falls NC 28630	828-496-2000	P	988	.2
324	Heritage Oaks Bancorp—*Simone F Lagomarsino*	1222 Vine St, Paso Robles CA 93446	805-239-5200	P	983	.3
325	Eastern Michigan Financial Corp—*Timothy Ward*	PO Box 139, Croswell MI 48422	810-679-2500	R	982*	.1
326	Royal Bancshares of Pennsylvania Inc—*Robert R Tabas*	732 Montgomery Ave, Narberth PA 19072	610-668-4700	P	981	.2
327	Metropolitan Bank Group—*Peter Fasseas*	2201 W Cermak Rd, Chicago IL 60608		R	978*	.1
328	Crescent Financial Corp—*Michael G Carlton*	PO Box 5809, Cary NC 27512	919-460-7770	P	973	.2
329	Adams County National Bank—*Thomas A Ritter*	PO Box 3129, Gettysburg PA 17325	717-334-3161	P	969	.3
330	Ames National Corp—*Thomas H Pohlman*	PO Box 846, Ames IA 50010	515-232-6251	P	963	.2

Rank	Company Name—*Executive Officer*	Address, City, State, Zip	Phone	Type	Fin	Empls
331	Severn Bancorp Inc—*Alan J Hyatt*	PO Box 6679, Annapolis MD 21401	410-260-2000	P	963	.1
332	Chemung Financial Corp—*Ronald M Bentley*	PO Box 1522, Elmira NY 14902	607-737-3711	P	958	.3
333	Franklin Financial Services Corp—*William E Snell Jr*	PO Box 6010, Chambersburg PA 17201	717-264-6116	P	952	.3
334	AmeriServ Financial Inc—*Glenn Wilson*	PO Box 430, Johnstown PA 15907	814-533-5300	P	949	.4
335	East Texas Financial Corp—*Sammy York*	PO Box 1700, Kilgore TX 75662	903-984-8671	R	947*	.1
336	Ireland Bancorp Ltd—*R Blair Hawkes*	PO Box 186, Malad City ID 83252	208-766-2211	R	945*	.1
337	Security Federal Corp—*Timothy W Simmons*	238 Richland Ave W, Aiken SC 29801	803-641-3000	P	934	.2
338	Mercantile Bancorp Inc (Quincy Illinois)—*Lee R Keith*	PO Box 3455, Quincy IL 62305	217-223-7300	P	929	.3
339	ECB Bancorp Inc—*A Dwight Utz*	PO Box 337, Engelhard NC 27824	252-925-9411	P	920	.2
340	Penseco Financial Services Corp—*Craig W Best*	150 N Washington Ave S, Scranton PA 18503	570-346-7741	P	916	.2
341	Dearborn Bancorp Inc—*Michael J Ross*	1360 Porter St, Dearborn MI 48124	313-565-5700	P	916	.2
342	STAR Financial Group Inc—*Thomas M Marcuccilli*	PO Box 11409, Fort Wayne IN 46858	219-479-2500	R	907	.5
343	Old Point Financial Corp—*Robert F Shuford Sr*	1 W Mellen St, Hampton VA 23663	757-728-1200	P	887	.3
344	North Valley Bancorp—*Michael J Cushman*	300 Park Marina Cir, Redding CA 96001	530-226-2900	P	885	.3
345	HMN Financial Inc—*Bradley C Krehbiel*	PO Box 6057, Rochester MN 55903	507-535-1200	P	881	.2
346	Standard Bancshares Inc—*Lawrence P Kelley*	7800 W 95th St, Hickory Hills IL 60457	708-598-7400	R	878*	.5
347	Republic First Bancorp Inc—*Harry D Madonna*	50 S 16th St Ste 2400, Philadelphia PA 19102	215-735-4422	P	876	.2
348	Unity Bancorp Inc—*James A Hughes*	64 Old Hwy 22, Clinton NJ 08809	908-730-7630	P	869	.2
349	BNCCORP Inc—*Gregory K Cleveland*	PO Box 4050, Bismarck ND 58502	701-250-3040	P	868	.2
350	First PacTrust Bancorp Inc—*Gregory A Mitchell*	610 Bay Blvd, Chula Vista CA 91910	619-691-1519	P	862	.1
351	Riverview Bancorp Inc—*Patrick Sheaffer*	PO Box 872290, Vancouver WA 98687	360-693-6650	P	859	.2
352	Kaiser Federal Financial Group Inc—*Dustin Luton*	1359 N Grand Ave, Covina CA 91724	626-339-9663	P	856	.1
353	Ohio Valley Banc Corp—*Jeffrey E Smith*	PO Box 240, Gallipolis OH 45631	740-446-2631	P	852	.3
354	Citizens Financial Group Inc—*James Connolly*	1 Citizens Plz, Providence RI 02903	401-456-7000	S	844*	.2
355	First National Bank and Trust (Atmore Alabama)—*Shepard Marsh*	PO Box 27, Atmore AL 36504	251-368-3148	R	840*	.1
356	Harleysville Savings Financial Corp—*Ronald Geib*	271 Main St, Harleysville PA 19438	215-256-8828	P	836	.1
357	Access National Corp—*Michael W Clarke*	1800 Robert Fulton Dr, Reston VA 20191	703-871-2100	P	832	.3
358	Pacific Premier Bancorp Inc—*Steven R Gardner*	1600 Sunflower Ave 2nd, Costa Mesa CA 92626	714-431-4000	P	827	.1
359	Portales National BancShares Inc—*David Stone*	PO Box 888, Portales NM 88130	575-356-6601	R	819*	.1
360	First Keystone Corp—*Matthew P Prosseda*	PO Box 289, Berwick PA 18603	570-752-3671	P	819	.2
361	First Citizens Bancorporation Inc—*Jim B Apple*	1230 Main St, Columbia SC 29201	803-733-2020	P	815	1.4
362	Hemet Bancorp—*Kevin Farrenkopf*	3715 Sunnyside Dr, Riverside CA 92506	951-248-2000	R	815*	.2
363	Malaga Financial Corp—*Randy C Bowers*	2514 Via Tejon Rd, Palos Verdes Estates CA 90274	310-375-9000	P	814	<.1
364	QNB Corp—*Thomas J Bisko*	PO Box 9005, Quakertown PA 18951	215-538-5600	P	809	.2
365	First South Bancorp Inc (Washington North Carolina)—*Thomas A Vann*	PO Box 2047, Washington NC 27889	252-946-4178	P	797	.3
366	International Bancorp of Miami Inc—*Alba Prestamo*	121 Alhambra Plz, Coral Gables FL 33134	305-854-8800	R	797*	.2
367	United PanAm Financial Corp—*Jim Vagim*	18191 Von Karman Ave S, Irvine CA 92612	949-224-1917	R	795	.7
368	Teche Holding Co—*Patrick O Little*	1120 Jefferson Terrace, New Iberia LA 70560	337-560-7151	P	793	.3
369	LCNB Corp—*Stephen P Wilson*	2 N Broadway St, Lebanon OH 45036	513-932-1414	P	792	.2
370	PVF Capital Corp—*Robert J King Jr*	30000 Aurora Rd, Solon OH 44139	440-248-7171	P	787	.2
371	River City Bank (Sacramento California)—*Steve Fleming*	PO Box 15247, Sacramento CA 95851	916-567-2899	R	786*	.2
372	Central Bancshares Inc (Lexington Kentucky)—*Luther Deaton Jr*	PO Box 1360, Lexington KY 40588	859-253-6222	R	785*	.3
373	Patriot National Bancorp Inc—*Michael A Carrazza*	900 Bedford St, Stamford CT 06901	203-324-7500	P	784	.2
374	Carlsbad Bancorporation Inc—*Jim Renfrow*	202 W Stevens St, Carlsbad NM 88220	575-234-2500	R	782*	.1
375	Baraboo Bancorporation Inc—*Merlin E Zitzner*	101 3rd Ave, Baraboo WI 53913	608-356-7703	P	775	.1
376	Benchmark Bankshares Inc—*Mike Walker*	PO Box 569, Kenbridge VA 23944	434-676-8444	R	768*	.1
377	Valley Financial Corp—*Ellis L Gutshall*	PO Box 2740, Roanoke VA 24001	540-342-2265	P	768	.1
378	Commerce Bancorp (Seattle Washington)—*Stanley Savage*	601 Union St Ste 3600, Seattle WA 98101	206-292-3900	R	749*	.1
379	Bank of Southside Virginia—*J Peter Clements*	PO Box 40, Carson VA 23830	434-246-5211	R	746*	.1
380	Greenville First Bancshares Inc—*R Arthur Seaver Jr*	100 Verdae Blvd Ste 10, Greenville SC 29607	864-679-9000	P	743	.1
381	Timberland Bancorp Inc—*Michael R Sand*	624 Simpson Ave, Hoquiam WA 98550	360-533-4747	P	738	.3
382	First Northern Community Bancorp—*Jeffrey R Adamski*	PO Box 547, Dixon CA 95620	707-678-3041	P	737	.2
383	Marion County Bancshares Inc—*Austin H Adkins*	PO Box 99, Hamilton AL 35570	205-921-7435	R	737*	.1
384	Blue Valley Ban Corp—*Robert D Regnier*	PO Box 26128, Overland Park KS 66225	913-338-1000	P	723	.2
385	Union Bankshares Inc (Kansas City Missouri)—*Jeffrey Jernigan*	9300 Blue Ridge Blvd, Kansas City MO 64138	816-763-4400	R	720*	.1
386	FNB Bancorp—*Tom McGraw*	975 El Camino Real 3rd, South San Francisco CA 94080	650-588-6800	P	715	.2
387	TF Financial Corp—*Kent C Lufkin*	3 Penns Trl, Newtown PA 18940	215-579-4000	P	710	.2
388	Hillcrest Bancshares Inc—*Thomas J Davies*	11111 W 95th St, Overland Park KS 66214	913-492-7500	R	707*	.1
389	Tamalpais Bancorp—*Mark Garwood*	630 Las Gallinas Ave, San Rafael CA 94903	415-454-1212	R	703	.1
390	Home Bancorp Inc—*John W Bordelon*	503 Kaliste Saloom Rd, Lafayette LA 70508	337-237-1960	P	700	.1
391	CNB Financial Corp (Taylor Texas)—*Andrew Littlejohn*	PO Box 1099, Taylor TX 76574	512-671-2265	R	700*	.1
392	Country Club Bank (Leavenworth Kansas)—*Sean Doherty*	PO Box 189, Leavenworth KS 66048	913-682-0001	R	692*	.1
393	Penns Woods Bancorp Inc—*Richard A Grafmyre*	PO Box 967, Williamsport PA 17703	570-322-1111	P	692	.2
394	NB and T Financial Group Inc—*John J Limbert*	PO Box 711, Wilmington OH 45177	937-382-1441	P	691	.2
395	Southern Missouri Bancorp Inc—*Jennifer Harmon*	531 Vine St, Poplar Bluff MO 63901	573-778-1800	P	688	.2
396	Stewardship Financial Corp—*Paul Van Ostenbridge*	630 Godwin Ave, Midland Park NJ 07432	201-444-7100	P	688	.1
397	Guaranty Federal Bancshares Inc—*Shaun Burke*	1341 W Battlefield St, Springfield MO 65807	417-520-4333	P	683	.2
398	New England Bancshares Inc—*David J O'Connor*	855 Enfield St, Enfield CT 06082	860-253-5200	P	682	.1
399	Hopkins Financial Corp—*Jack Hopkins*	PO Box 1246, Mitchell SD 57301	605-996-7775	R	680*	.2
400	United Security Bancshares Inc—*Dennis Woods*	2126 Inyo St, Fresno CA 93721	559-248-4943	P	678	.1
401	BPC Corp—*David Williamson*	140 S Jefferson Ave, Cookeville TN 38501	931-528-5441	R	678*	.1
402	Community West Bancshares—*Lynda J Nahra*	445 Pine Ave, Goleta CA 93117	805-692-1862	P	677	.1
403	Fremont Bancorp—*Bradford L Anderson*	39150 Fremont Blvd, Fremont CA 94538	510-505-5226	R	675*	.5
404	Union Savings Bank (Cincinnati Ohio)—*Sarah Miller* US Bancorp	8534 E Kemper Rd, Cincinnati OH 45249	513-247-0300	S	675*	.2
405	Clackamas County Bank—*Kathy Proctor*	PO Box 38, Sandy OR 97055	503-668-5501	R	672*	.1
406	First Paragould Bankshares Inc—*William E Brewer*	PO Box 700, Paragould AR 72451	870-239-8521	R	671*	.1
407	Fidelity Bancorp Inc—*Richard G Spencer*	1009 Perry Hwy, Pittsburgh PA 15237	412-367-3300	P	667	.2
408	Rurban Financial Corp—*Mark A Klein*	PO Box 467, Defiance OH 43512	419-783-8950	P	660	.2
409	Saehan Bancorp—*Chung hoon Youk*	3580 Wilshire Blvd Ste, Los Angeles CA 90010	213-388-5550	R	660	N/A
410	Total Bancshares Corp—*Jorge Rossell*	2720 Coral Way, Miami FL 33145	305-448-6500	R	660*	.3
411	Tower Financial Corp—*Michael D Cahill*	116 E Berry St, Fort Wayne IN 46802	260-427-7000	P	660	.1
412	Cardinal Bancorp Inc—*David Bentele*	7305 Manchester, Saint Louis MO 63143	314-645-0666	R	659*	.1
413	Germantown Bancorp—*Dale G Deiters*	601 Main St, Germantown IL 62245	618-523-4202	R	655*	.1
414	Jacksonville Bancorp Inc—*Price W Schwenck*	100 N Laura St Ste 100, Jacksonville FL 32202	904-421-3040	P	652	.1
415	Northwest Indiana Bancorp—*David A Bochnowski*	9204 Columbia Ave, Munster IN 46321	219-853-7575	P	652	.2
416	Northway Financial Inc—*William J Woodward*	9 Main St, Berlin NH 03570	603-752-1171	R	651	.2

Note: An asterisk (*) indicates an estimated financial figure. The company type code used is as follows: R = Private, P = Public, S = Private Subsidiary, B = Public Subsidiary, D = Division, J = Joint Venture, I = Investment Fund.

COMPANY RANKINGS BY SALES WITHIN 4-DIGIT SIC

Rank	Company Name—*Executive Officer*	Address, City, State, Zip	Phone	Type	Fin	Empls
417	New Mexico Banquest Corp—*Greg Ellena*	PO Box 609, Santa Fe NM 87504	505-992-2000	R	650*	.2
418	Evans Bancorp Inc—*David J Nasca*	1 Grimsby Dr, Hamburg NY 14075	716-926-2000	P	647	.2
419	Pacific Financial Corp—*Dennis A Long*	1101 S Boone St, Aberdeen WA 98520	360-533-8870	P	644	.2
420	First Federal Bancorp	PO Box 458, Bemidji MN 56619	218-751-5120	R	644*	.1
421	Wilber Corp—*Douglas Gulotty*	245 Main St, Oneonta NY 13820		R	643*	.2
422	Chesapeake Financial Shares Inc—*Jeffrey M Szyperski*	PO Box 1419, Kilmarnock VA 22482	804-435-1181	P	638	.2
423	Treynor Bancshares Inc—*Michael Guttau*	PO Box A, Treynor IA 51575	712-487-3000	R	634*	<.1
424	United Security Bankshares Inc—*Richard Key*	PO Box 249, Thomasville AL 36784	334-636-5424	P	627	N/A
425	United Bancshares Inc (Columbus Grove Ohio)—*Daniel W Schutt*	100 S High St, Columbus Grove OH 45830	419-659-2141	P	625	.2
426	Johnson Bank—*Scott Cornellius*	3131 E Camelback Rd St, Phoenix AZ 85016	602-381-2100	R	609*	.1
427	Slade's Ferry Bancorp—*Mary Lynn D Lenz*	PO Box 390, Somerset MA 02726	508-675-2121	S	608	.1
428	DNB Financial Corp—*William S Latoff*	4 Brandywine Ave, Downingtown PA 19335	610-269-1040	P	602	.1
429	DG Bancorp Inc	5140 Main St, Downers Grove IL 60515	630-968-6300	R	601*	.1
430	First Federal Bancshares of Arkansas Inc—*W Dabbs Cavin*	PO Box 550, Harrison AR 72602	870-741-7641	P	600	.2
431	First Community Corp—*Michael C Crapps*	5455 Sunset Blvd, Lexington SC 29072	803-951-2265	P	599	.1
432	Northeast Bancorp—*Richard Wayne*	500 Canal St, Lewiston ME 04240	207-786-3245	P	596	.2
433	Southern National Bancorp of Virginia Inc—*Georgia S Derrico*	6830 Old Dominion Dr, McLean VA 22101	703-893-7400	P	591	.1
434	First Banking Center Inc—*Brantley Chappell*	PO Box 660, Burlington WI 53105	262-763-3581	R	585*	.2
435	Federal Trust Corp—*Dennis T Ward*	PO Box 1867, Sanford FL 32772	407-323-1121	S	585	.1
436	American River Bankshares—*David T Taber*	3100 Zinfandel Dr Ste, Rancho Cordova CA 95670	916-851-0123	P	579	.1
437	Chicopee Bancorp Inc—*William J Wagner*	PO Box 300, Chicopee MA 01014	413-594-6692	P	574	.1
438	Hampden Bancorp—*Thomas R Burton*	19 Harrison Ave, Springfield MA 01103	413-736-1812	P	573	.1
439	Naugatuck Valley Financial Corp—*John C Roman*	333 Church St, Naugatuck CT 06770	203-720-5000	P	568	.1
440	Industrial Bancshares Inc—*James Lewis*	PO Box 6007, Kansas City KS 66106	913-831-2000	R	567*	.1
441	Fidelity D and D Bancorp Inc—*Daniel J Santaniello*	101 N Blakely St, Dunmore PA 18512	570-342-8281	P	562	.2
442	Landmark Bancorp Inc—*Patrick L Alexander*	701 Poyntz Ave, Manhattan KS 66502	785-565-2000	P	562	.2
443	Eagle Financial Services Inc—*John R Milleson*	PO Box 391, Berryville VA 22611	540-955-2510	P	559	.2
444	Cowlitz Bancorp—*Richard J Fitzpatrick*	PO Box 1518, Longview WA 98632	360-423-9800	P	552	.1
445	Castle BancGroup Inc—*Tim Struthers*	121 W Lincoln Hwy, Dekalb IL 60115	815-758-7007	D	552*	.2
446	Marshall and Ilsley Bank—*Dennis J Kuester* Marshall and Ilsley Corp	1245 Main St, Stevens Point WI 54481	715-344-5100	S	550*	.1
447	Farmers Bank (Frankfort Indiana)—*Karen I Miller*	PO 129, Frankfort IN 46041	765-654-8731	R	549*	.2
448	Oxford Financial Corp—*Jeffrey M Davidson*	PO Box 129, Addison IL 60101	630-629-5000	R	548*	.2
449	First National Corporation of Wynne—*Harold Hardwick*	PO Box 129, Wynne AR 72396	870-238-2361	R	547*	.1
450	Peoples Bancorporation Inc—*Lillian P Ballentine*	PO Box 1989, Easley SC 29641	864-859-2265	P	547	.1
451	Rock Bancshares Inc—*L Walter Quinn*	2300 Andover Crt, Little Rock AR 72227	501-664-8722	R	546*	.1
452	First National Corp (Strasburg Virginia)—*Dennis A Dysart*	112 W King St, Strasburg VA 22657	540-465-9121	P	545	.2
453	Blackhawk Bancorp Inc—*R Richard Bastian III*	PO Box 719, Beloit WI 53512	608-364-8911	P	540	.2
454	F and M Bank Corp—*Dean W Withers*	PO Box 1111, Timberville VA 22853	540-896-8941	P	539	.1
455	Alliance Bankshares Corp—*William E Doyle Jr*	14200 Park Meadow Dr S, Chantilly VA 20151	703-814-7200	P	539	.1
456	Huntington Bancshares Kentucky Inc—*Don Castro* Huntington Bancshares Inc	540 Madison Ave, Covington KY 41011	859-292-7610	S	532*	.3
457	Midwest Independent Bancshares Inc—*Michael Wasson*	910 Weathered Rock Rd, Jefferson City MO 65110	573-636-9555	R	525*	<.1
458	Delta Bancshares—*Michael J Ross*	2301 Market St, Saint Louis MO 63103	314-621-0100	R	524*	.1
459	Brannen Banks of Florida Inc—*H Wayne Oswald*	320 Hwy 41 S, Inverness FL 34450	352-726-1221	R	521*	.3
460	Seaway Bancshares Inc—*Jory Luster*	645 E 87th St, Chicago IL 60619	773-487-4800	S	516	.3
461	Southcoast Financial Corp—*L Wayne Pearson*	PO Box 1561, Mount Pleasant SC 29465	843-884-0504	P	515	N/A
462	West Bank (West Des Moines Iowa)—*Brad L Winterbottom*	PO Box 65020, West Des Moines IA 50265	515-222-2300	S	511*	.1
463	First Olathe Bancshares—*Brian L Roby*	PO Box 1500, Olathe KS 66051	913-782-3211	R	506*	.1
464	Cortland Bancorp—*James M Gasior*	194 W Main St, Cortland OH 44410	330-637-8040	P	500	.2
465	Associated Bank-Chicago Associated Banc-Corp	130 E Randolph St, Chicago IL 60601	312-861-1000	S	500*	<.1
466	Prudential Bancorp Incorporated of Pennsylvania—*Thomas A Vento*	1834 Oregon Ave, Philadelphia PA 19145	215-755-1500	P	500	.1
467	Croghan Bancshares Inc—*Rick Robertson*	323 Croghan St, Fremont OH 43420	419-332-7301	P	490	.2
468	Central Bancorp Inc—*John D Doherty*	399 Highland Ave, Somerville MA 02144	617-628-4000	P	488	.1
469	Broadway Financial Corp—*Paul C Hudson*	4800 Wilshire Blvd, Los Angeles CA 90010	323-634-1700	P	484	.1
470	Lake Shore Bancorp Inc—*Daniel P Reininga*	125 E 4th St, Dunkirk NY 14048	716-336-4070	P	479	.1
471	Mackinac Financial Corp—*Paul Tobias*	130 S Cedar St, Manistique MI 49854	906-341-8401	P	479	.1
472	Southern Michigan Bancorp Inc—*John H Castle*	PO Box 309, Coldwater MI 49036	517-279-5500	P	478	.1
473	Republic Bancorp (Oak Brook Illinois)—*Bill Sperling*	2221 Camden Ct, Oak Brook IL 60523	630-928-1505	R	477*	.1
474	Sussex Bancorp—*Anthony Labozzetta*	200 Munsonhurst Rd, Franklin NJ 07416	973-827-2914	P	474	.1
475	Peoples Bancorp (Auburn Indiana)—*Maurice F Winkler III*	PO Box 231, Auburn IN 46706	260-925-2500	P	473	.1
476	Bridgeview Bancorp—*Bill Conaghan*	7940 S Harlem Ave, Bridgeview IL 60455	708-594-7400	R	472*	<.1
477	Merchants Financial Group Inc—*Rodney Nelson*	PO Box 248, Winona MN 55987	507-457-1100	R	470*	.1
478	Baker Boyer Bancorp—*Megan Clubb*	PO Box 1796, Walla Walla WA 99362	509-525-2000	P	466	.2
479	Northern States Financial Corp—*Scott Yelvington*	1601 N Lewis Ave, Waukegan IL 60085	847-244-6000	P	463	.1
480	PSB Group Inc—*Henry R Thiemann*	1800 E 12 Mile Rd, Madison Heights MI 48071	248-548-2900	P	462	.1
481	Liberty Bancorp Inc (Liberty Missouri)—*Brent M Giles*	16 W Franklin St, Liberty MO 64068	816-781-4822	P	458	.1
482	Habersham Bancorp—*David D Stovall*	PO Box 1980, Cornelia GA 30531	706-778-1000	P	456	.1
483	PSB Bancshares Inc—*Leland P Howard Jr*	PO Box 269, Clanton AL 35046	205-755-2240	R	456*	.1
484	Newport Bancorp Inc—*Kevin M McCarthy*	PO Box 210, Newport RI 02840	401-847-5500	P	453	.1
485	North Central Bancshares Inc—*David Bradley*	825 Central Ave, Fort Dodge IA 50501	515-576-7531	P	452	.1
486	First National Bank (Sioux Falls South Dakota)—*WL Baker*	PO Box 5186, Sioux Falls SD 57117	605-335-5200	R	450*	.3
487	The Bank of Harlan—*Edward Parsons*	201 E Central St, Harlan KY 40831	606-573-1202	R	444*	<.1
488	Stockmens Financial Corp—*Greg Hunter*	805 5th St, Rapid City SD 57701	605-718-8300	R	442*	.2
489	Delta National Bancorp—*Warren E Wegge*	PO Box 1900, Manteca CA 95336		R	438*	.1
490	Shorebank (Bellwood Illinois) Shorebank Corp	219 S Mannheim Rd, Bellwood IL 60104		S	437*	<.1
491	Juniata Valley Financial Corp—*Marcie A Barber*	PO Box 66, Mifflintown PA 17059	717-436-8211	P	436	.1
492	American National Corp (Omaha Nebraska)—*John F Kotouc*	8990 W Dodge Rd, Omaha NE 68114	402-399-5000	R	435*	.3
493	Premier Commercial Bancorp—*Ken Cosgrove*	2400 E Katella Ave Ste, Anaheim CA 92806	714-978-2400	P	433	.1
494	Ameriana Bancorp—*Jerome J Gassen*	PO Box H, New Castle IN 47362	765-529-2230	P	433	.2
495	Annapolis Bancorp—*Richard Lerner*	1000 Bestgate Rd Ste 4, Annapolis MD 21401	410-224-4455	P	432	.1
496	Home FSB (Marshalltown Iowa)—*Brad Krehbiel* HMN Financial Inc	303 W Main St, Marshalltown IA 50158	641-754-6000	S	431*	<.1
497	Jeffersonville Bancorp—*Wayne V Zanetti*	PO Box 398, Jeffersonville NY 12748	845-482-4000	P	431	.1
498	Southeastern Banking Corp—*Cornelius P Holland III*	PO Box 455, Darien GA 31305	912-437-4141	P	428	.1
499	Orient Bancorp—*Ernest L Go*	233 Sansome St, San Francisco CA 94104	415-338-0843	R	427*	.2

Rank	Company Name—*Executive Officer*	Address, City, State, Zip	Phone	Type	Fin	Empls
500	Fentura Financial Inc—*Donald L Grill*	PO Box 725, Fenton MI 48430	810-750-8725	P	424	.1
501	CCF Holding Co—*Leonard A Mooreland*	PO Box 935, Jonesboro GA 30237	770-478-8881	P	423	.1
502	Metrocorp Inc—*Gary D Andersen*	1523 8th St, East Moline IL 61244	309-755-0871	R	417*	.3
503	Iowa First Bancshares Corp—*D Scott Ingstad*	300 E 2nd St, Muscatine IA 52761	563-263-4221	P	417	.1
504	Capital Directions Inc—*Timothy P Gaylord*	PO Box 130, Mason MI 48854	517-676-0500	P	415*	<.1
505	Security California Bancorp—*James A Robinson*	3403 10th St Ste 830, Riverside CA 92501	951-368-2265	P	413	N/A
506	Central Virginia Bankshares Inc—*Herbert E Marth Jr*	PO Box 39, Powhatan VA 23139	804-403-2000	P	409	.1
507	Allegheny Valley Bancorp Inc—*Andrew W Hasley*	5137 Butler St, Pittsburgh PA 15201	412-781-1464	P	409	.2
508	Provident Community Bancshares Inc—*Dwight V Neese*	2700 Celanese Rd, Rock Hill SC 29732	803-325-9400	P	409	.1
509	First Century Bankshares Inc—*Frank W Wilkinson*	PO Box 1559, Bluefield WV 24701	304-325-8181	P	408	.2
510	Wayne Savings Bancshares Inc—*Rod C Steiger*	151 N Market St, Wooster OH 44691	330-264-5767	P	408	.1
511	Greater Sacramento Bancorp—*William J Martin*	1750 Howe Ave Ste 100, Sacramento CA 95825	916-648-2100	P	408	<.1
512	Central Trust Co—*Bill Vonholtum*	285 Main St, Lander WY 82520	307-332-4730	R	406*	<.1
513	Killbuck Bancshares Inc—*Craig Lawhead*	PO Box 407, Killbuck OH 44637	330-276-4881	P	405	.1
514	Old Line Bancshares Inc—*James Cornelsen*	1525 Pointer Ridge Pl, Bowie MD 20716	301-430-2500	P	402	.1
515	Hills Bank and Trust Co—*Dwight O Seegmiller*	PO Box 70, Hills IA 52235	319-679-2291	R	400*	.1
516	Lenox Wealth Management Inc—*John C Lame*	8044 Montgomery Rd Ste, Cincinnati OH 45236	513-618-7080	P	400	N/A
517	Highlands Bankshares Inc—*Samuel L Neese*	PO Box 929, Petersburg VA 26847	276-628-9811	P	400	.1
518	WSB Holding Inc—*Phillip C Bowman*	4201 Mitchellville Rd, Bowie MD 20716	301-352-3120	P	396	.1
519	Ledyard Financial Group Inc—*Kathryn G Underwood*	2 Maple St, Hanover NH 03755	603-640-2666	P	395	N/A
520	Ohnward Bancshares Inc—*Brigham Tubbs*	107 E Quarry St, Maquoketa IA 52060	563-652-7822	R	394*	.2
521	National Banking Corp—*Jim Renk*	PO Box 837, North Little Rock AR 72115	501-771-4000	P	393*	.1
522	Citizens Bancshares Corp (Atlanta Georgia)—*James E Young*	PO Box 4485, Atlanta GA 30302	404-659-5959	P	388	.1
523	River Valley Bancorp—*Matthew P Forrester*	PO Box 1590, Madison IN 47250	812-273-4949	P	387	.1
524	Ballston SpA Bancorp Inc—*Christopher Dowd*	PO Box 70, Ballston Spa NY 12020	518-885-6781	P	386	.1
525	Commercial National Financial Corp (Ithaca Michigan)—*Jeffrey S Barker*	PO Box 280, Ithaca MI 48847	989-875-4144	P	385	.1
526	Middlebury National Corp—*G Kenneth Perine*	PO Box 189, Middlebury VT 05753	802-388-4982	R	383*	.1
527	Brotherhood Bancshares Inc—*Cal Roberts*	756 Minnesota Ave, Kansas City KS 66101	913-321-4242	R	382*	.2
528	NCAL Bancorp—*Henry Homsher*	145 S Fairfax Ave, Los Angeles CA 90048	310-882-4800	P	381	N/A
529	Cornerstone Bank NA—*CG Holthus*	PO Box 69, York NE 68467	402-363-7411	R	376*	<.1
530	Britton and Koontz Capital Corp—*W Page Ogden*	PO Box 1407, Natchez MS 39121	601-445-5576	P	375	.1
531	National Bancshares Corp—*David Vernon*	PO Box 57, Orrville OH 44667	330-682-1010	P	374	.1
532	LSB Financial Corp—*Randolph F Williams*	101 Main St, Lafayette IN 47901	765-742-1064	P	372	.1
533	Hyden Citizens Bancorp Inc—*WFred Brashear*	PO Box 948, Hyden KY 41749	606-672-2344	R	370*	<.1
534	Hastings Bancorp Inc—*Thomas Thomas*	PO Box 2178, Hastings NE 68902	402-463-0505	R	369*	<.1
535	First South Bancorp Inc (Spartanburg South Carolina)—*Barry L Slider*	1450 John B White Sr B, Spartanburg SC 29306	864-595-0455	P	365	.1
536	National Bank of Sallisaw—*Michael Neer*	PO Box 549, Sallisaw OK 74955	918-775-5501	R	362*	<.1
537	SCB Bancorp Inc—*Leon M Hinton*	455 N Main St, Decatur IL 62523	217-428-7781	R	360*	.2
538	Sonoma Valley Bancorp—*Sean Cutting*	202 W Napa St, Sonoma CA 95476	707-935-3200	P	358	.1
539	Commercial National Financial Corp (Latrobe Pennsylvania)—*Gregg E Hunter*	PO Box 429, Latrobe PA 15650	724-539-3501	P	356	.1
540	Georgia Bancshares Inc—*Ira P Shepherd III*	100 Westpark Dr, Peachtree City GA 30269	770-631-9488	P	353	.1
541	Citizens First Corp—*Todd Kanipe*	1805 Campbell Ln, Bowling Green KY 42104	270-393-0700	P	350	.1
542	Glen Burnie Bancorp—*Michael G Livingston*	101 Crain Hwy SE, Glen Burnie MD 21061	410-766-3300	P	347	.1
543	First Citizens Bancshares Inc (Dyersburg Tennessee)—*Jeff Agee*	PO Box 370, Dyersburg TN 38025	731-285-4410	R	344*	.2
544	FedFirst Financial Corp—*Patrick G O'Brien*	565 Donner Ave, Monessen PA 15062	724-684-6800	P	343	.1
545	Valley Commerce Bancorp—*Allan W Stone*	701 W Main St, Visalia CA 93291	559-622-9000	P	341	.1
546	Perry Bancshares Inc—*Zach Hall*	PO Box 797, Perry OK 73077	580-336-5531	R	340*	.1
547	Security National Bank (Enid Oklahoma)—*Bill Athey*	201 W Broadway Ave, Enid OK 73701	580-234-5151	R	340	.1
548	First Alamogordo Bancorp of Nevada Inc—*Pete Cook*	PO Box 9, Alamogordo NM 88311	575-437-4880	R	338*	.1
549	Regions Bank (New Orleans Louisiana)—*Scott Howard*	400 Poydras St Rm 100, New Orleans LA 70130	504-838-4533	R	338*	.1
550	Pinnacle Bankshares Corp—*Aubrey Hall III*	622 Broad St, Altavista VA 24517	434-369-3000	P	337	.1
551	CIB Marine Bancshares LLC—*John Hickey*	1930 W Bluemound Rd St, Waukesha WI 53186	262-695-6010	P	337*	.1
552	Hawaii National Bancshares Inc—*Warren K Luke*	45 N King St, Honolulu HI 96817	808-528-7711	R	336*	.3
553	KS Bancorp Inc—*Harold T Keen*	PO Box 661, Smithfield NC 27577	919-938-3101	P	336	.1
554	First National Bank of Waverly—*Richard Carlson*	316 E Bremer Ave, Waverly IA 50677	319-352-1340	R	334*	.1
555	First Ipswich Bancorp—*Russell G Cole*	31 Market St, Ipswich MA 01938	978-356-3700	R	333*	.1
556	Eagle Bancorp Montana Inc—*Peter J Johnson*	PO Box 4999, Helena MT 59604	406-442-3080	B	331	.1
557	Citizen Bank Holding Inc—*Francis Wagner*	PO Box 223, Mukwonago WI 53149	262-363-6500	R	329*	.1
558	United Bancorp Inc (Martins Ferry Ohio)—*James W Everson*	PO Box 10, Martins Ferry OH 43935	740-633-0445	P	324	N/A
559	Howard Bancorp Inc—*Mary Ann Scully*	6011 University Blvd S, Ellicott City MD 21043	410-750-0020	P	323	.1
560	FFW Corp—*Roger K Cromer*	PO Box 259, Wabash IN 46992	260-563-3185	P	323	.1
561	Drexel Bancshares Inc—*Joe Balentine*	PO Box 710, Belton MO 64012	816-322-1239	R	316*	<.1
562	First Holdrege Bancshares Inc—*Scott Latter*	PO Box 800, Holdrege NE 68949	308-995-4411	R	306*	<.1
563	South Street Financial Corp—*R Ronald Swanner*	PO Box 489, Albemarle NC 28002	704-982-9184	P	306	<.1
564	SE Financial Corp—*Pamela Cyr*	1901-03 E Passyunk Ave, Philadelphia PA 19148	215-468-1700	P	305	<.1
565	Commercial Bancshares Inc (Upper Sandusky Ohio)—*Robert E Beach*	118 S Sandusky Ave, Upper Sandusky OH 43351	419-294-5781	P	304	.1
566	LifeStore Financial Group—*Robert E Washburn*	PO Box 26, West Jefferson NC 28694	336-246-4344	P	301	.1
567	Consumers Bancorp Inc—*Ralph J Lober*	PO Box 256, Minerva OH 44657	330-868-7701	P	300	.1
568	Siuslaw Financial Group Inc—*Johan Mehlum*	PO Box 280, Florence OR 97439	541-997-3486	R	300	N/A
569	Nittany Financial Corp—*David Z Richards Jr*	1300 N Atherton St, State College PA 16803	814-238-2620	R	299*	.1
570	Southwest Georgia Financial Corp—*DeWitt Drew*	201 1st St SE, Moultrie GA 31768	229-985-1120	P	296	.1
571	American Federal Corp—*Steven Worwa*	PO Box 2946, Fargo ND 58108	701-461-5900	R	294*	.2
572	Bancorp of Southern Indiana—*David M Geis*	125 S Chestnut St, Seymour IN 47274	812-522-3607	R	290*	.1
573	Twin River Financial Corp—*Jody Servatius*	PO Box 1324, Lewiston ID 83501	208-746-4848	R	290*	<.1
574	Nova Financial Holdings Inc—*Brian M Hartline*	1420 Locust St, Philadelphia PA 19102	215-545-6500	P	289*	.1
575	Overland Bancorp Inc—*James F Blair III*	PO Box 770, Belton MO 64012	816-331-4888	R	288*	<.1
576	United Bank (Atmore Alabama)—*Robert R Jones III*	PO Box 8, Atmore AL 36504	251-368-2525	R	286*	.2
577	Peoples Bancorp (Lynden Washington)—*Charles LeCocq*	418 Grover St, Lynden WA 98264	360-354-4044	R	283*	.2
578	Citizens Financial Corp (Elkins West Virginia)—*Robert J Schoonover*	PO Box 1519, Elkins WV 26241	304-636-4095	P	283	.1
579	Bank of South Carolina Corp—*Hugh C Lane Jr*	PO Box 538, Charleston SC 29402	843-724-1500	P	281	.1
580	First West Virginia Bancorp Inc—*Sylvan J Dlesk*	1701 Warwood Ave, Wheeling WV 26003	304-277-1100	P	278	<.1
581	Central Federal Corp—*Eloise L Mackus*	2923 Smith Rd, Fairlawn OH 44333	330-666-7979	P	275	.1
582	Farmers Holding Co—*Joy French Becker*	200 W State St, Jacksonville IL 62650	217-479-4000	R	273*	.1
583	First National Corp (Pulaski Tennessee)—*Mark A Hayes*	206 S 1st St, Pulaski TN 38478	931-363-2585	R	268*	.2

Note: An asterisk (*) indicates an estimated financial figure. The company type code used is as follows: R = Private, P = Public, S = Private Subsidiary, B = Public Subsidiary, D = Division, J = Joint Venture, I = Investment Fund.

COMPANY RANKINGS BY SALES WITHIN 4-DIGIT SIC

Rank	Company Name—*Executive Officer*	Address, City, State, Zip	Phone	Type	Fin	Empls
584	Blue River Bancshares Inc—*Russell Breeden III*	29 E Washington St, Shelbyville IN 46176	317-398-9721	P	267	.1
585	Patapsco Bancorp Inc—*Michael J Dee*	1301 Merritt Blvd, Dundalk MD 21222	410-285-1010	P	265	.1
586	Northeast Indiana Bancorp Inc—*Michael S Zahn*	PO Box 70, Huntington IN 46750	260-356-3311	P	262	.1
587	Genoa Bank—*Martin Sutter*	PO Box 98, Genoa OH 43430	419-855-8381	R	259*	.1
588	HFB Financial Corp—*David B Cook*	1602 Cumberland Ave, Middlesboro KY 40965	606-248-1095	R	258*	.1
589	Monarch Community Bancorp Inc—*Richard J DeVries*	375 N Willowbrook Rd, Coldwater MI 49036	517-278-4566	P	257	.1
590	NorCal Community Bancorp—*Stephen G Andrews*	1701 Harbor Bay Pky St, Alameda CA 94502	510-748-8450	P	256	.1
591	BEO Bancorp—*Jeff Bailey*	PO Box 39, Heppner OR 97836	541-676-0201	P	252	N/A
592	FNS Bancshares Inc—*Randy Giles*	PO Box 130, Scottsboro AL 35768	256-259-6000	R	250*	.1
593	Peoples Exchange Bancorp—*Claude Bentley*	PO Box 127, Beattyville KY 41311	606-464-3631	R	249*	<.1
594	First ULB Corp—*Malcolm Hotchkiss*	100 Hegenberger Rd Ste, Oakland CA 94621	510-567-6900	R	245*	<.1
595	Bancshares of Gleason Inc—*Curtis Mayo*	PO Box 231, Gleason TN 38229	731-648-5506	R	244*	<.1
596	Winnsboro State Bank and Trust Co—*Michael L Woods*	PO Box 970, Winnsboro LA 71295	318-435-7535	R	243*	<.1
597	Lizton Financial Corp—*Leslie J Mongell*	PO Box 170, Lizton IN 46149	317-994-5115	R	240	.1
598	Wells Financial Corp—*Lonnie R Trasamar*	53 1st St SW, Wells MN 56097	507-553-3151	P	238	.1
599	Merchants and Manufacturers Bancorp—*James Bomberg*	19105 W Capitol Dr, Brookfield WI 53045	262-790-2120	R	238	.2
600	First National Bank—*Kieth Hughes*	PO Box 913, Hutchinson KS 67504	620-663-1521	R	238*	.1
601	Illini Corp—*Gaylon E Martin*	3200 W Iles Ave, Springfield IL 62711	217-787-5111	R	238	.2
602	First CB Corp—*Ward Billhartz*	PO Box 809, Collinsville IL 62234	618-346-9000	R	236*	.1
603	WVS Financial Corp—*David J Bursic*	9001 Perry Hwy, Pittsburgh PA 15237	412-364-1911	P	229	<.1
604	Syringa Bancorp—*Scott Gibson*	999 W Main St Ste 100, Boise ID 83702	208-336-6865	P	228	N/A
605	IBW Financial Corp—*Clinton W Chapman*	4812 Georgia Ave NW, Washington DC 20011	202-722-2000	R	225*	.2
606	AJS Bancorp Inc—*Thomas R Butkus*	14757 S Cicero Ave, Midlothian IL 60445	708-687-7400	P	223	.1
607	First National Bank (Midwest City Oklahoma)—*Robert H Croak*	PO Box 10600, Midwest City OK 73140	405-732-4571	R	222*	.2
608	South Banking Co—*Lawrence Bennett*	PO Box 1988, Alma GA 31510	912-632-8631	R	217*	.1
609	LoLyn Financial Corp—*William R McDaniel*	PO Box 200, Raymore MO 64083	816-322-2100	R	217*	<.1
610	First Federal of Northern Michigan Bancorp Inc—*Michael Mahler*	100 S 2nd Ave, Alpena MI 49707	989-356-9041	P	216	.1
611	FFD Financial Corp—*Trent B Troyer*	PO Box 38, Dover OH 44622	330-364-7777	P	216	.1
612	Redding Bancorp—*Michael C Mayer*	1951 Churn Creek Rd, Redding CA 96002	530-224-3333	R	212*	.1
613	Park Bancorp Inc—*David A Remijas*	5400 S Pulaski Rd, Chicago IL 60632	773-582-8616	P	212	.1
614	FC Banc Corp—*Coleman J Clougherty*	PO Box 567, Bucyrus OH 44820	419-562-7040	P	211	N/A
615	First Bancshares Inc (Mountain Grove Missouri)—*R Bradley Weaver*	142 E 1st St, Mountain Grove MO 65711	417-926-5151	P	210	.1
616	US Bank—*John Jones*	891 Feehanville Dr, Mount Prospect IL 60056	847-299-9550	R	208*	<.1
617	First Capital Bank Holding Corp—*Michael G Sanchez*	1891 S 14th St, Fernandina Beach FL 32034	904-321-0400	R	206*	<.1
618	United Financial Banking Companies Inc—*Harold C Rauner*	PO Box 2459, Vienna VA 22183	703-938-2500	P	206	.1
619	First Robinson Financial Corp—*Rick L Catt*	501 E Main St, Robinson IL 62454	618-544-8621	P	205	.1
620	Fidelity Federal Bancorp—*Donald R Neel*	PO Box 1347, Evansville IN 47706	812-424-0921	R	201*	.1
621	Pinnacle Bancshares Inc—*Robert B Nolen Jr*	1811 2nd Ave, Jasper AL 35501	205-221-4111	P	201	.1
622	Harbor Bankshares Corp—*Joseph Haskins Jr*	25 W Fayette St, Baltimore MD 21201	410-342-4563	R	198*	.1
623	Northwest Bank and Trust Co—*Joe B Slavens*	PO Box 8001, Davenport IA 52806		R	198*	.1
624	Brighton Bancorp—*Howard Holt*	PO Box 71309, Salt Lake City UT 84171	801-943-6500	R	197*	.1
625	First Farmers Financial Corp—*Gene Miles*	PO Box 690, Converse IN 46919	765-395-3316	R	197*	.1
626	Patterson Bancshares Inc—*William E Hughes*	PO Drawer 15, Patterson GA 31557	912-647-5332	R	194*	<.1
627	First Cherokee Bancshares Inc—*Carl C Hames Jr*	9860 Hwy 92, Woodstock GA 30188	770-591-9000	R	193*	.1
628	OptimumBank Holdings Inc—*Richard L Browdy*	2477 E Commercial Blvd, Fort Lauderdale FL 33308	954-776-2332	P	190	<.1
629	First Southwest Corp—*James W Covington*	100 S Broadway, McComb MS 39648	601-684-2231	R	190*	.2
630	High Country Bancorp Inc—*Larry D Smith*	PO Box 309, Salida CO 81201	719-539-2516	P	187	.1
631	Home Federal Bancorp Incorporated of Louisiana—*Daniel R Herndon*	624 Market St, Shreveport LA 71101	318-222-1145	P	185	<.1
632	Summit Bancshares Inc (Oakland California)—*Shirley W Nelson*	2969 Broadway, Oakland CA 94611	510-839-8800	P	185	<.1
633	First Independence Corp—*Larry Spencer*	PO Box 947, Independence KS 67301	620-331-1660	P	184	<.1
634	Valley Community Bancshares Inc—*David H Brown*	PO Box 578, Puyallup WA 98371	253-848-2316	R	182*	.1
635	Cherokee Banking Co—*Dennis W Burnette*	PO Box 4250, Canton GA 30114	770-479-3400	P	181	<.1
636	AB and T Financial Corp—*Daniel C Ayscue*	292 W Main Ave, Gastonia NC 28052	704-867-5828	P	175	<.1
637	Alaska Pacific Bancshares Inc—*Craig E Dahl*	2094 Jordan Ave, Juneau AK 99801	907-789-4844	P	174	.1
638	Great Southern Capital Corp—*Leslie Usher*	PO Box 1271, Meridian MS 39302	601-693-5141	R	173*	.2
639	Capitol City Bancshares Inc—*George G Andrews*	562 Lee St, Atlanta GA 30310	404-752-6067	R	172*	.1
640	First Utah Bancorp—*David L Brown*	3826 S 2300 E, Salt Lake City UT 84109	801-272-9454	R	171*	.1
641	Phelps County Bancshares Inc—*Bill C Marshall*	718 N Pine St, Rolla MO 65401	573-364-5202	R	169*	.1
642	Bainum Bancorp—*Tim Bainum*	PO Box 800, Glenwood AR 71943	870-356-2121	R	168*	<.1
643	Holton National Bank—*Kenneth Glennon*	PO Box 229, Holton KS 66436	785-364-2166	R	165*	<.1
644	Northeast Securities Corp—*Thomas M Beck*	77 Broadway St NE, Minneapolis MN 55413	612-379-8811	R	164*	.1
645	Roebling Financial Corporation Inc—*Frank J Travea III*	Rte 130 S and Delaware, Roebling NJ 08554	609-499-9400	P	164	<.1
646	Stearns Financial Services Inc—*Norman Skalicky*	PO Box 7338, Saint Cloud MN 56302	320-253-6607	R	163*	.3
647	Home Loan Financial Corp—*Robert C Hamilton*	401 Main St, Coshocton OH 43812	740-622-0444	P	162	<.1
648	Security Bancorp Inc (McMinnville Tennessee)—*Joe H Pugh*	PO Box 7027, Mc Minnville TN 37111	931-473-4483	P	162	<.1
649	North Penn Bancorp Inc—*Frederick Hickman*	216 Adams Ave, Scranton PA 18503	570-344-6113	P	161	<.1
650	Great American Bancorp Inc—*George R Rouse*	PO Box 1010, Champaign IL 61824	217-356-2265	P	158	.1
651	Crazy Woman Creek Bancorp Inc—*Paul M Brunkhorst*	PO Box 1020, Buffalo WY 82834	307-684-5591	P	157	<.1
652	Valley Bank and Trust—*Suzette Coecke*	30 N 4th Ave, Brighton CO 80601	303-659-5450	R	156*	.1
653	Commonwealth Bancshares Inc (Shelbyville Kentucky)—*Ann Cowley Wells*	PO Box 249, Shelbyville KY 40066	502-633-1000	R	156	.1
654	Mission Oaks Bancorp—*Gary W Votapka*	41530 Enterprise Circl, Temecula CA 92590	951-719-1200	P	155	N/A
655	Hometown Bancorp Inc—*Thomas F Gibney*	12 Main St, Walden NY 12586	845-778-2171	P	155	.1
656	Manhattan Bancorp—*Terry Robinson*	2141 E Rosecrans Ave S, El Segundo CA 90245	310-606-8000	R	153	.1
657	Trans Pacific National Bank Corp—*David Funkhouser*	55 2nd St Ste 100, San Francisco CA 94105	415-543-3377	R	152*	<.1
658	Brunswick Bancorp—*Roman Gumina*	439 Livingston Ave, New Brunswick NJ 08901	732-247-5800	P	152	<.1
659	Logansport Financial Corp—*David G Wihebrink*	723 E Broadway, Logansport IN 46947	574-722-3855	P	151	<.1
660	Home City Financial Corp—*J William Stapleton*	PO Box 1288, Springfield OH 45501	937-390-0470	P	146	<.1
661	Bangor Bancorp Mhc—*David Carlisle*	PO Box 930, Bangor ME 04402	207-942-5211	R	145*	<.1
662	Eagle National Holding Co—*Robert Brooks*	PO Box 012281, Miami FL 33101	305-418-6000	R	144*	<.1
663	Intown Holding Company LLC	2727 Paces Fery Rd 2 1, Atlanta GA 30339	770-799-5000	R	144*	<.1
664	Gouverneur Bancorp Inc—*Charles C Van Vleet*	42 Church St, Gouverneur NY 13642	315-287-2600	P	144	<.1
665	First Mountain Bancorp—*John G Briner*	3070 Rasmussen Rd Ste, Park City UT 84098	435-658-4979	P	144	N/A
666	Community Business Bancshares Inc—*Debra R Lins*	PO Box 636, Sauk City WI 53583	608-643-6300	R	138*	<.1
667	Peoples-Sidney Financial Corp—*Douglas Stewart*	PO Box 727, Sidney OH 45365	937-492-6129	P	136	<.1
668	Banco Popular Inc—*Richard Carrion*	717 N Michigan Ave Ste, Chicago IL 60611	312-440-3000	R	136*	<.1

Rank	Company Name—*Executive Officer*	Address, City, State, Zip	Phone	Type	Fin	Empls
669	Global Bancorp—*Robert Sweeney*	700 E El Camino Real S, Mountain View CA 94040	650-810-9400	R	135*	<.1
670	United Bancshares Inc—*Evelyn F Smalls* Wells Fargo and Co	30 S 15th St Ste 1200, Philadelphia PA 19102	215-351-4600	S	134*	.1
671	First National Security Co—*John Hendix*	PO Box 980, De Queen AR 71832	870-642-2212	R	134*	<.1
672	Sun Road Interprises—*Aaron Feldman*	4435 Eastgate Mall Ste, San Diego CA 92121	858-558-5627	R	134*	<.1
673	East Dubuque Bancshares Inc—*Steven J Bonnet*	PO Box 259, East Dubuque IL 61025	815-747-3173	R	131	<.1
674	CKF Bancorp Inc—*William H Johnson*	PO Box 400, Danville KY 40423	859-236-4181	P	131	<.1
675	Mountain View Bancshares Inc—*C Randall Sims*	PO Box 1228, Mountain View AR 72560	870-269-3815	S	130*	<.1
676	SouthFirst Bancshares Inc—*Sandra H Stephens*	PO Box 167, Sylacauga AL 35150	256-245-4365	P	129	.1
677	Tri-State 1st Banc Inc—*Stephen R Sant*	PO Box 796, East Liverpool OH 43920	330-385-9200	P	125	.1
678	Albina Community Bancorp—*Cheryl Cebula*	2002 NE Martin Luther, Portland OR 97212	503-287-7537	R	122*	.1
679	First Independence Corp (Detroit Michigan)—*Donald Davis*	44 Michigan Ave, Detroit MI 48226	313-256-8400	R	121*	.1
680	Riverside Bancshares Inc—*Robert Dudley*	1001 W Markham St, Little Rock AR 72201	501-614-6161	R	117*	<.1
681	Terme Bancorp Inc—*John G Yedinak*	1100 W Cermak Rd, Chicago IL 60608	312-268-2424	P	117	N/A
682	Liberty Financial Services Inc (New Orleans Louisiana)—*Alden J McDonald Jr*	PO Box 60131, New Orleans LA 70160	504-240-5288	R	115	.1
683	Chester Bancorp Inc—*Edward Collins*	PO Box 327, Chester IL 62233	618-826-5038	P	114	<.1
684	Bankers Bancorp—*Donald Abernathy Jr*	9020 N May Ave Ste 200, Oklahoma City OK 73120	405-848-8877	R	114*	<.1
685	Westwood Homestead Financial Corp—*Richard Baylor*	3002 Harrison Ave, Cincinnati OH 45211	513-661-5735	S	112*	<.1
686	Treaty Oak Bancorp—*Ronald W Simpson*	101 Westlake Dr, West Lake Hills TX 78746	512-617-3600	P	110	N/A
687	Lexington B and L Financial Corp—*E Steva Vialle*	PO Box 190, Lexington MO 64067	660-259-2247	R	107*	<.1
688	First Southern Bancshares Inc—*B Jack Johnson*	PO Box 777, Florence AL 35631	256-718-4200	R	103*	.1
689	Quaint Oak Bancorp Inc—*Robert T Strong*	607 Lakeside Dr, Southampton PA 18966	215-364-4059	P	102	<.1
690	Highland Community Co—*Dennis J Irvin*	1701 W 87th St, Chicago IL 60620	773-881-6800	R	102*	<.1
691	First Boaz Bancorp—*Ricky Ray*	PO Box 757, Boaz AL 35957	256-593-8670	R	100	<.1
692	First Niles Financial Inc—*Lawrence Safarek*	55 N Main St, Niles OH 44446	330-652-2539	P	99	.1
693	Highland Bancshares Inc—*Rick Wall*	2100 Ford Pky, Saint Paul MN 55116	651-698-2471	R	96*	.1
694	Webster City Federal Bancorp—*Phyllis A Murphy*	PO Box 638, Webster City IA 50595	515-832-3071	P	93	<.1
695	WCB Holdings Inc—*Carl W Raggio III*	21550 Oxnard St Ste 10, Woodland Hills CA 91367	818-449-7700	R	91	N/A
696	Crossroads Bancorp Inc—*David Thurman*	PO Box 95, Mount Washington KY 40047	502-538-7301	R	91*	.1
697	BancWest Inc—*Donald McNeil*	101 S Main, Thomas OK 73669	580-661-3541	R	91*	<.1
698	Banc Affiliated Inc—*Garry J Graham*	500 Harwood Rd, Bedford TX 76021	817-285-6195	P	80	<.1
699	First State Bank (Kansas City Kansas)—*David Herndon*	650 Kansas Ave, Kansas City KS 66105	913-371-1242	R	77	<.1
700	Lafayette Community Bancorp—*Bradley Marley*	2 N 4th St, Lafayette IN 47901	765-429-7200	R	77	<.1
701	Dacotah Bank (Rolla North Dakota)—*Richard Westra*	PO Box 789, Rolla ND 58367	701-477-3175	R	75*	<.1
702	Home Financial Bancorp—*Kurt D Rosenberger*	279 E Morgan St, Spencer IN 47460	812-829-2095	P	75	<.1
703	Bank of Marquette—*John D Ferguson*	PO Box 39, Marquette NE 68854	402-854-2221	R	74*	<.1
704	Montana Community Banks Inc—*Donald E Olsson Jr*	63239 US Hwy 93, Ronan MT 59864	406-676-4600	R	70*	<.1
705	Tyronza Bancshares—*Chris Lehman*	PO Box 635, Marked Tree AR 72365	870-358-6000	R	69*	<.1
706	Oceanic Bank Holding Inc—*Chris Leong*	PO Box 2968, San Francisco CA 94126	415-392-0642	R	68*	<.1
707	Garfield County Bancshares Inc—*Rex Phipps*	PO Box 6, Jordan MT 59337	406-557-2201	R	67*	<.1
708	Southern Community Bancshares Inc—*William R Faulk*	PO Box 249, Cullman AL 35056	256-734-4863	R	64*	<.1
709	Countri Corp—*Michael E Grove*	PO Box 709, White Sulphur Springs MT 59645	406-547-3331	R	63*	<.1
710	Alpha Banco Inc—*Bruce Robinson*	PO Box 369, Alpha IL 61413	309-629-4361	R	62*	<.1
711	Arrowhead Co—*Will Moursand*	PO Box 1, Round Mountain TX 78663	830-825-3233	R	61*	<.1
712	State National Bancshares—*David R Ley*	PO Box 130, Wayne NE 68787	402-375-1130	R	61*	<.1
713	Wilson Bancshares Inc—*Theodore S Wilson*	PO Box 8, Wooton MO 64008	816-640-5252	H	60*	<.1
714	Longview Capital Corp—*John Albin*	PO Box 377, Newman IL 61942		R	59*	<.1
715	First Weatherford Bancshares Inc—*Lin Bearden*	PO Box 730, Weatherford TX 76086	817-594-7481	R	58*	<.1
716	Surety Capital Corp—*John H Mackey*	PO Box 1778, Fort Worth TX 76101	817-335-5955	P	50	<.1
717	Greenwood County Financial Services Inc—*Richard D Rucker*	PO Box 620, Eureka KS 67045	620-583-5516	R	49*	<.1
718	Centennial Bank of Omaha—*John Sorrell*	9003 S 145th St, Omaha NE 68138	402-891-0003	R	45*	<.1
719	Northern Star Financial Inc—*Thomas P Stienessen*	1650 Madison Ave Ste 5, Mankato MN 56001	507-387-2265	P	45	<.1
720	First Capital Bancshares Inc—*Charles O Rivers*	209 Hwy 15-401 Bypass, Bennettsville SC 29512	843-454-9337	R	44*	<.1
721	Orono Financial Inc—*David J Delaney*	PO Box 123, Navarre MN 55392	952-471-0111	R	44	<.1
722	Granville Bancshares Inc—*Philip Carlson*	PO BOX 344, Granville IL 61326	815-339-2222	R	41*	<.1
723	Guaranty Bancshares Inc—*Tyson T Abston*	PO Box 1158, Mount Pleasant TX 75456	903-572-9881	R	34*	.2
724	Belvedere Capital Partners LLC—*Anthony M Frank*	1 Maritime Plz Ste 825, San Francisco CA 94111	415-434-1236	R	34*	<.1
725	Globe Bancorp Inc—*Mae H Leaveau*	4051 Veterans Blvd Ste, Metairie LA 70002	504-887-0057	R	30*	<.1
726	Cox and Powers Insurance Agency Inc—*Charles Courtney*	207 W Main St, Carthage MS 39051	601-267-6166	R	26*	<.1
727	Bonneville Bancorp—*Douglas Christensen*	PO Box 400, Provo UT 84603	801-374-9505	R	25	<.1
728	First Western Financial Inc—*Scott C Wylie*	1200 17th St Ste 2650, Denver CO 80202	303-531-8100	R	21	.2
729	Greenfield Bancshares Inc—*James W Miller*	1920 N State St, Greenfield IN 46140	317-462-1431	R	17*	.1
730	Mount Victory State Bank—*Robert L Temple*	PO Box 67, Mount Victory OH 43340	937-354-3171	R	17*	<.1
731	Queen City Federal Bancorp Inc—*Kevin E Pietrini*	PO Box 1147, Virginia MN 55792	218-741-2040	R	11	<.1
732	Central Bancshares Inc (Golden Valley Minnesota)—*John M Morrison*	945 Winnetka Ave N Ste, Golden Valley MN 55427	763-545-9005	R	6*	.1
733	Ridgestone Financial Services Inc—*Bruce W Lammers*	13925 W North Ave, Brookfield WI 53005	262-789-1011	R	4	<.1
734	Patriot Bancshares Inc—*William Ellis*	7500 San Felipe St Ste, Houston TX 77063	713-400-7100	R	1	N/A
735	HEI Diversified Inc—*Robert F Clarke*	PO Box 730, Honolulu HI 96808	808-543-5662	S	N/A	1.3

TOTALS: SIC 6712 Bank Holding Companies
Companies: 735   8,733,212   1,480.6

6719 Holding Companies Nec

1	MetLife Inc—*Steven A Kandarian*	200 Park Ave, New York NY 10166	212-578-2211	P	730,906	66.0
2	American International Group Inc—*Robert H Benmosche*	180 Maiden Ln, New York NY 10038	212-770-7000	P	683,443	63.0
3	Liberty Mutual Group Inc—*Edmund F Kelley*	175 Berkeley St, Boston MA 02116	617-357-9500	R	104,316	40.0
4	Cardinal Health Inc—*George S Barrett*	7000 Cardinal Pl, Dublin OH 43017	614-757-5000	P	102,644	22.6
5	Farmers Group Inc—*Bob Woudstra*	4680 Wilshire Blvd, Los Angeles CA 90010	208-239-8400	S	49,592*	29.0
6	Sears Holdings Corp—*Louis J D'Ambrosio*	3333 Beverly Rd, Hoffman Estates IL 60179	847-286-2500	P	43,326	280.0
7	GMAC Residential Holding Corp—*David Applegate*	100 Witmer Rd, Horsham PA 19044	215-682-1000	S	35,927*	27.0
8	United Continental Holdings Inc—*Jim Compton*	PO Box 66919, Chicago IL 60666	312-997-8000	P	23,229	86.0
9	Green Tree Servicing LLC—*Neal S Cohen*	345 St Peter St 11th F, Saint Paul MN 55102	651-293-3400	R	22,228	1.2
10	Phoenix Companies Inc—*James D Wehr*	PO Box 5056, Hartford CT 06102	860-403-5000	P	21,077	.7
11	IDEX Holdings Inc—*Andrew K Silvernail*	1925 W Field Ct, Lake Forest IL 60045	847-498-7070	S	11,755*	4.2
12	CS Tech-Fab Holding Inc—*David L Berges*	281 Tresser Blvd 2 Sta, Stamford CT 06901	203-969-0666	S	11,431*	4.1
13	OSI Group—*Sheldon Lavin*	1225 Corporate Blvd, Aurora IL 60505	630-851-6600	R	8,372*	9.2
14	Jones Financial Companies LLLP—*James D Weddle*	12555 Manchester Rd, Saint Louis MO 63131	314-515-2000	R	8,241	40.5
15	Murdock Holding Co—*David H Murdock*	10900 Wilshire Blvd St, Los Angeles CA 90024	310-208-3636	R	7,900*	90.2

Note: An asterisk (*) indicates an estimated financial figure. The company type code used is as follows: R = Private, P = Public, S = Private Subsidiary, B = Public Subsidiary, D = Division, J = Joint Venture, I = Investment Fund.

COMPANY RANKINGS BY SALES WITHIN 4-DIGIT SIC

Rank	Company Name—*Executive Officer*	Address, City, State, Zip	Phone	Type	Fin	Empls
16	NCI Holding Corp	PO Box 692055, Houston TX 77269	281-897-7788	S	7,609*	3.8
17	Investors Management Corp—*Theodore M Fowler*	PO Box 29502, Raleigh NC 27626	919-781-9310	R	7,053*	9.0
18	TECO Diversified Inc	702 N Franklin St, Tampa FL 33602	813-228-4111	S	6,765	4.3
19	CalsonicKansei North America Inc—*Kiyoto Shinohara*	1 Calsonic Way, Shelbyville TN 37160	931-684-4490	S	6,668*	3.3
20	Virgin Media Inc—*Neil Berkett*	909 3rd Ave Ste 2863, New York NY 10022	212-906-8440	P	6,276	12.4
21	Western Alliance Bancorp—*Robert G Sarver*	One E Washington St St, Phoenix AZ 85004	602-389-3500	P	6,194	.9
22	TravelCenters of America LLC—*Thomas M O'Brien*	24601 Center Ridge Rd, Westlake OH 44145	440-808-9100	P	5,963	15.2
23	Apple Bank for Savings—*Alan Shamoon*	122 E 42nd St, New York NY 10017	212-224-6400	R	5,930	.8
24	CB Richard Ellis Group Inc—*Brett White*	11150 Santa Monica Blv, Los Angeles CA 90025	310-405-8900	P	5,115	31.0
25	Laboratory Corporation of America Holdings—*David P King*	PO Box 2240, Burlington NC 27216	336-229-1127	P	5,004	31.0
26	EADS North America—*Sean O'Keefe*	2550 Wasser Ter Ste 90, Herndon VA 20171	703-466-5600	S	4,962*	3.0
27	UIL Holdings Corp—*James P Torgerson*	PO Box 1564, New Haven CT 06506	203-499-2000	P	4,745	1.9
28	Charmer Sunbelt Group—*Charles Merinoff*	60 E 42nd St Ste 1915, New York NY 10165	212-699-7000	R	4,600*	7.0
29	Philadelphia Consolidated Holding Corp—*James J Maguire Jr*	231 St Asaph's Rd Ste, Bala Cynwyd PA 19004		R	4,100	1.3
30	Stater Brothers Holdings Inc—*Jack H Brown*	301 S Tippecanoe Ave, San Bernardino CA 92408	909-733-5000	R	3,693	16.5
31	LSB Holdings Inc—*Jack Golsen*	16 S Pennsylvania Ave, Oklahoma City OK 73107	405-235-4546	S	3,546*	1.3
32	Prime Holdings Corp—*Jack Golsen*	16 S Pennsylvania Ave, Oklahoma City OK 73107	405-235-4546	S	3,546*	1.3
33	Raymond James Financial Inc—*Paul Reilly*	880 Carillon Pkwy, Saint Petersburg FL 33716	727-567-1000	P	3,400	7.6
34	Clark Enterprises Inc—*A James Clark*	7500 Old Georgetown Rd, Bethesda MD 20814	301-657-7100	R	3,258*	4.3
35	Aspen Manufacturing Inc—*David Piccione*	373 Atascocita Rd, Humble TX 77396	281-441-6500	R	3,173*	.1
36	Sabre Holdings Corp—*Sam Gilliland*	3150 Sabre Dr, Southlake TX 76092	682-605-1000	R	3,138*	10.0
37	Maxcor Inc—*Mo Meidar*	60 E 42nd St Ste 2330, New York NY 10165	212-400-2655	R	2,907*	1.4
38	Vanguard Car Rental Group Inc—*William E Lobeck*	6929 N Lakewood Ave St, Tulsa OK 74117	918-401-6000	S	2,891	12.6
39	TMS International Corp—*Joseph Curtain*	12 Monongahela Ave, Glassport PA 15045	412-678-6141	P	2,662	4.0
40	CIC Group Inc—*Michael Bytnar*	530 Maryville Centre D, Saint Louis MO 63141	314-682-2900	R	2,243*	1.1
41	DeVry Inc—*Daniel Hamburger*	3005 Highland Pkwy, Downers Grove IL 60515	630-571-7700	P	2,182	12.6
42	Heico Companies LLC—*EA Roskovensky*	5600 - 3 First Nationa, Chicago IL 60602	312-419-8220	R	2,170*	8.0
43	Tokyo Electron US Holdings Inc	2400 Grove Blvd, Austin TX 78741	512-424-1000	S	2,148*	1.0
44	Major Acquisition Corp	43-40 Northern Blvd, Long Island City NY 11101	718-937-3700	S	2,141*	.8
45	ASI Investments Holding Co	3550 W Market St, Fairlawn OH 44333	330-666-3751	S	2,013*	1.0
46	Raytheon Aircraft Holdings Inc—*William H Swanson*	870 Winter St, Waltham MA 02451	781-522-3000	S	2,003	N/A
47	Frank Consolidated Enterprises—*Jim Frank*	666 Garland Pl, Des Plaines IL 60016	847-699-7000	R	2,000*	.6
48	NewStar Financial Inc—*Timothy J Conway*	500 Boylston St Ste 12, Boston MA 02116	617-848-2500	P	1,975	.1
49	California Physicians' Service—*Bruce Bodaken*	PO Box 272540, Chico CA 95927		R	1,472*	3.7
50	Packerland Holdings Inc—*Richard V Vesta*	PO Box 23000, Green Bay WI 54305	920-468-4000	S	1,400*	4.0
51	Atlas Air Worldwide Holdings Inc—*William Flynn*	2000 Westchester Ave, Purchase NY 10577	914-701-8000	P	1,398	1.7
52	Prosperity Holdings Inc—*David Zalman*	4295 San Felipe, Houston TX 77027	713-693-9400	S	1,387*	.7
53	Focus Brands Inc—*Russ Umphenour*	200 Glenridge Point Pk, Atlanta GA 30342	404-255-3250	S	1,339*	.6
54	SF Holdings Group Inc—*Robert M Korzenski*	373 Park Ave S, New York NY 10016	212-779-7448	S	1,308*	7.4
55	Redi-Direct Marketing Inc—*Thomas Buckley*	5 Audry Pl, Fairfield NJ 07004	973-808-4500	R	1,263*	.7
56	IntercontinentalExchange Inc—*Jeffrey C Sprecher*	2100 RiverEdge Pkwy St, Atlanta GA 30328	770-857-4700	P	1,150	.9
57	Barnes Group Inc—*Gregory F Milzcik*	123 Main St, Bristol CT 06010	860-583-7070	P	1,016*	4.4
58	LPL Holdings Inc—*Mark Cassidy*	1 Beacon St 22nd Fl, Boston MA 02108		R	1,004*	2.2
59	Primoris Service Corp—*Brain Pratt*	26000 Commercentre Dr, Lake Forest CA 92630	949-598-9242	P	942	4.0
60	Avalon Global Group Inc—*Fred Lynn*	2350 34th St N, Saint Petersburg FL 33713	727-321-6352	R	844*	.4
61	S and P Co—*Brian Kovalchuk*	PO Box 792627, San Antonio TX 78279	210-226-0231	R	770	.3
62	MCI Sales and Service Center—*Tom Sorrells*	1700 East Golf Rd Ste, Schaumburg IL 60173		S	700	4.2
63	Magellan Terminals Holdings LP—*Michael N Mears*	PO Box 22186, Tulsa OK 74121	918-574-7000	S	695*	1.0
64	PICO Holdings Inc—*John R Hart*	7979 Ivanhoe Ave Ste 3, La Jolla CA 92037	858-456-6022	P	684	.1
65	Investment Technology Group Inc—*Robert Gasser*	380 Madison Ave, New York NY 10017	212-588-4000	P	572	1.1
66	Buckingham Capital Partners—*Shail Sheth*	950 3rd Ave Fl 19, New York NY 10022	212-752-0500	R	558*	2.1
67	Wicks Group of Companies LLC—*Craig Klosk*	405 Park Ave Ste 702, New York NY 10022	212-838-2100	R	542*	<.1
68	Associated Materials Holdings Inc—*Jerry Burris*	PO Box 2010, Akron OH 44309	330-929-1811	S	518*	5.0
69	MSCO Inc—*Gordon Ruggles*	200 Appleton Ave, Sheffield AL 35660	256-383-3131	R	491*	.2
70	Tremont LLC	5430 LBJ Fwy, Dallas TX 75240	972-233-1700	S	487	2.4
71	Hiland Holdings GP LP—*Joseph L Griffin*	205 W Maple Ste 1100, Enid OK 73701	580-242-6040	R	436	.1
72	Doane Pet Care Enterprises Inc	210 Westwood Pl S Ste, Brentwood TN 37027	615-373-7774	S	425*	.2
73	INTL FCStone Inc—*Sean O'Connor*	708 3rd Ave 15th Fl, New York NY 10017	212-485-3500	P	423	.9
74	Latshaw Enterprises Inc—*John Latshaw*	2533 South West St, Wichita KS 67217		R	423*	.4
75	Heckmann Corp—*Richard J Heckmann*	75080 Frank Sinatra Dr, Palm Desert CA 92211	760-341-3606	P	401	1.1
76	Calgon Carbon Investments Inc—*John S Stanik*	PO Box 717, Pittsburgh PA 15230	412-787-6700	S	400*	.3
77	Everett Smith Group Ltd—*J Douglas Gray*	330 Kilbourn Ave Ste 7, Milwaukee WI 53202	414-223-1560	R	394*	3.1
78	Ziff Davis Holdings Inc—*Jason Young*	28 E 28th St, New York NY 10016	212-503-3500	S	389*	1.0
79	Teco Holdings USA Inc—*H Meng*	5100 Ih 35 N Ste N, Round Rock TX 78681	512-255-4141	R	352*	.4
80	Atlas World Group Inc—*Glen E Dunkerson*	1212 St George Rd, Evansville IN 47711	812-424-2222	R	328*	.5
81	Nash Engineering Company Inc—*Mark Nordenson*	9 Trefoil Dr, Trumbull CT 06611	203-459-3900	R	312*	.1
82	C and D Charter Holdings Inc—*Jeffrey Graves*	P O Box 3053, Blue Bell PA 19422	215-619-2700	S	303*	.1
83	Servco Pacific Inc—*Mark H Fukunaga*	2850 Pukoloa St Ste 30, Honolulu HI 96819		S	297*	.9
84	SilkRoad Equity LLC—*Andrew Filipowski*	111 N Chestnut St Ste, Winston-Salem NC 27101	336-201-5100	R	296*	.2
85	Charys Holding Company Inc—*Michael Oyster*	1117 Perimeter Center, Atlanta GA 30338	678-443-2300	R	291	.9
86	Hirschfeld Holdings LP—*Dennis Hirschfeld*	PO Box 3768, San Angelo TX 76902	325-486-4201	R	283*	.9
87	Cohen and Steers Inc—*Martin Cohen*	280 Park Ave, New York NY 10017	212-832-3232	P	278	.2
88	Muzak Holdings LLC—*Stephen Villa*	3318 Lakemont Blvd, Fort Mill SC 29708	803-396-3000	R	247	N/A
89	Lynden Inc—*Jim H Jansen*	18000 International Bl, Seattle WA 98188	206-241-8778	R	240	1.5
90	Plastipak Holdings Inc—*William C Young*	41605 Ann Arbor Rd, Plymouth MI 48170	734-455-3600	R	235*	3.0
91	Total Apparel Group Inc—*Janon Costley*	230 W 39th St Ste 600, New York NY 10018	646-895-8988	P	231	N/A
92	SCP Private Equity Partners—*Winston J Churchill*	1200 Liberty Ridge Dr, Wayne PA 19087	610-995-2900	R	208*	.1
93	B Braun Of America Inc—*Caroll Neubauer*	PO Box 4027, Bethlehem PA 18018	610-691-5400	R	190*	4.1
94	21st Century Holding Co—*Michael H Braun*	PO Box 25220, Tamarac FL 33320	954-581-9993	P	184	.1
95	Centerline Holding Co—*Robert L Levy*	625 Madison Ave, New York NY 10022	212-317-5700	P	180	.2
96	Sun Suites Interests LLLP—*Jeff Brashear*	4770 S Atlanta Rd Se, Smyrna GA 30080	404-350-9990	R	179*	3.6
97	Caliber Holdings Corp—*Steve Grimshaw*	17771 Cowan Ave Ste 10, Irvine CA 92614	949-224-0300	R	175*	1.6
98	Trans National Group Services LLC—*Steve Belkin*	2 Charlesgate W, Boston MA 02215	617-262-9200	R	175*	.2
99	Rhc Holdings LP—*Paul Foster*	6500 Trowbridge Dr, El Paso TX 79905	915-881-0008	R	166*	3.4
100	Packaging Dynamics Corp—*Roger M Prevot*	3900 W 43rd St, Chicago IL 60632	773-843-8000	R	160*	1.1
101	Bsg Int'l LLC	PO Box 316, Archbold OH 43502	419-446-2711	R	159*	3.5
102	Unico American Corp—*Cary L Cheldin*	23251 Mulholland Dr, Woodland Hills CA 91364	818-591-9800	P	158	.1
103	Chimes International Ltd—*Terry Perl*	4815 Seton Dr, Baltimore MD 21215	410-358-6400	R	156*	N/A
104	CU Cos—*S Bradley Crandall*	500 Main St, New Brighton MN 55112	651-631-3111	R	151*	.1
105	Princeton Insurance Co—*Bill Mcdonough*	PO Box 5322, Princeton NJ 08543	609-452-9404	R	148*	.2

Rank	Company Name—*Executive Officer*	Address, City, State, Zip	Phone	Type	Fin	Empls
106	Circle B Enterprises Holding Company Inc—*Brad Bedell*	PO Box 1210, Sikeston MO 63801	573-471-1276	R	145*	2.8
107	Uci Acquisition Holdings (No1) Corp—*Bruce Zorich*	14601 Hwy 41 N, Evansville IN 47725	812-867-4156	R	143*	3.9
108	Legrand Holding Inc—*John Selldorff*	60 Woodlawn St, West Hartford CT 06110	860-233-6251	S	143*	2.3
109	Cfhs Holdings Inc—*Fred Hunter*	4650 Lincoln Blvd, Marina Del Rey CA 90292	310-823-8911	R	142*	2.8
110	Pii Inc—*Tom Kellim*	17 Research Park Dr, Saint Charles MO 63304	636-685-1047	R	141*	3.3
111	Cherokee Nation Businesses LLC—*David Stewart*	777 W Cherokee St Bldg, Catoosa OK 74015	918-384-7474	R	140*	3.1
112	World-Wide Holdings Corp—*Victor Elmaleh*	150 E 58th St 39th Fl, New York NY 10155	212-486-2000	R	137*	<.1
113	Ho-Chunk Inc—*Lance Morgan*	1 Mission Dr, Winnebago NE 68071	402-878-2809	R	136*	.5
114	Alliance Holdings Inc—*David Fenkell*	1021 Old York Rd Ste 3, Abington PA 19001	215-706-0873	R	135*	.3
115	Canopy Group Inc—*Ron Heinz*	333 S 520 W Ste 300, Lindon UT 84042	801-229-2223	R	129*	.1
116	Armstrong Holdings	4508 SW 97th Ter, Gainesville FL 32608	352-336-0045	R	128*	.2
117	Ranger Aerospace LLC—*Steve Townes*	Parkway Plz 125 The Pa, Greenville SC 29615	864-329-9000	R	120*	.6
118	Quadion Corp—*James Lande*	1100 Xenium Ln N, Plymouth MN 55441	952-927-1400	R	117*	1.1
119	Swisher International Inc—*J Ryan*	20 Thorndal Cir, Darien CT 06820	203-656-8000	R	112*	1.6
120	Hoenig and Company Inc—*Alan Herzog* Investment Technology Group Inc	4 International Dr, Rye Brook NY 10573	914-312-2300	S	109*	.1
121	Progressive Group Alliance—*David Matthews*	PO Box 9729, Richmond VA 23228	804-262-8614	R	109*	.1
122	Bristol Bay Native Corp—*Jason Metrokin*	111 W 16th Ave Ste 400, Anchorage AK 99501	907-278-3602	R	108*	.2
123	Westway Holdings Corp—*Jim Jenkins*	365 Canal St Ste 2900, New Orleans LA 70130	504-525-9741	S	105*	.1
124	LICT Corp—*Mario J Gabelli*	401 Theodore Fremd Ave, Rye NY 10580	914-921-8821	P	92	.4
125	Ripplewood Holdings LLC—*Timothy C Collins*	1 Rockefeller Plz 32nd, New York NY 10020	212-582-6700	R	92*	.1
126	Dunham Holdings Inc—*Jeffrey A Dunham*	10251 Vista Sorrento P, San Diego CA 92121	858-964-0500	R	89*	<.1
127	Takara Holding Co	708 Addison St, Berkeley CA 94710	510-540-8250	S	87*	<.1
128	SPL Holdings Inc	1751 Lake Cook Rd Arbo, Deerfield IL 60015	847-945-5591	R	85*	.1
129	Sonic Financial Corp—*O Bruton Smith*	5401 E Independence Bl, Charlotte NC 28212	704-566-2400	R	70*	.2
130	PLATO Learning Inc—*Vin Riera*	5600 W 83rd St Ste 300, Bloomington MN 55437	952-832-1000	R	65	.3
131	Berwind Natural Resources Corp—*Bryan Rorke*	1500 Market St Ste 300, Philadelphia PA 19102	215-563-2800	S	63*	<.1
132	KRG Capital Partners LLC—*Mark M King*	1515 Arapahoe St Ste 1, Denver CO 80202	303-390-5001	R	61*	<.1
133	Hilco Trading Company Inc—*Jeffrey Hecktman*	5 Revere Dr Ste 300, Northbrook IL 60062	847-509-1100	R	59*	<.1
134	Entrade Inc—*Peter R Harvey*	500 Central Ave, Northfield IL 60093	847-441-6650	R	57	.3
135	Thayer Capital Partners—*Frederic V Malek*	1455 Pennsylvania Ave, Washington DC 20004	202-371-0150	R	55*	<.1
136	Atlas Industries Holdings LLC—*Andrew M Bursky*	One Sound Shore Dr Ste, Greenwich CT 06830	203-622-9138	R	53*	<.1
137	Energy USA - TPC—*Val Trinkley*	233 East 84th Drive, Merrillville IN 46410		S	51*	<.1
138	Franchise Services Inc—*Don Lowe*	26722 Plaza Dr, Mission Viejo CA 92691	949-348-5000	D	46*	.1
139	New Henley Holdings Inc—*Raymond J Pacini*	6 Executive Cir Ste 25, Irvine CA 92614	949-250-7700	S	45*	<.1
140	Tanner Companies LLC—*David Owens*	PO Box 1139, Rutherfordton NC 28139	828-287-4205	R	43*	.3
141	Benton Offshore China Holding Co	1177 Enclave Pky Ste 3, Houston TX 77077	281-899-5700	S	42*	<.1
142	Orepac Holding Co—*Sandy Bodak*	30170 Sw Orepac Ave, Wilsonville OR 97070	503-685-5499	R	41*	.8
143	Andlinger and Company Inc—*Merrick G Andlinger*	520 White Plains Rd St, Tarrytown NY 10591	914-332-4900	R	38*	<.1
144	Olympus Partners—*Robert S Morris*	1 Station Pl, Stamford CT 06902	203-353-5900	R	37*	<.1
145	Odyssey Investment Partners LLC—*Brian Kwait*	280 Park Ave 38th Fl W, New York NY 10017	212-351-7900	R	36*	<.1
146	Silver Lake Partners—*Jim Davidson*	2775 Sand Hill Rd Ste, Menlo Park CA 94025	650-233-8120	R	31*	<.1
147	Cmc Group Inc—*Al Caperna*	12836 S Dixie Hwy, Bowling Green OH 43402	419-354-2591	R	31*	.3
148	Burcham and McCune Inc—*Joanna McCune*	5300 District Blvd, Bakersfield CA 93313	661-397-5300	R	28*	<.1
149	McNish Corp—*Jim McNish*	840 N Russell Ave, Aurora IL 60506	630-892-7921	R	27*	.2
150	Westminster Capital Inc—*William Belzberg*	9665 Wilshire Blvd Ste, Beverly Hills CA 90212	310-278-1930	R	27*	.1
151	Saratoga Partners III LP—*Christian Oberbeck*	535 Madison Ave, New York NY 10022	212-906-7800	R	27*	<.1
152	Heartland Enterprises Inc—*Jay Dunsing*	1401 Branding Ln Ste 3, Downers Grove IL 60515	630-786-1055	R	26*	.4
153	Pivotal Group Inc—*F Francis Najafi*	3200 East Camelback Rd, Phoenix AZ 85018	602-956-7200	R	26*	<.1
154	Stave Island LP—*Debbie Howard*	PO Box 600, Colchester VT 05446	802-863-6376	R	25*	.2
155	POWDR Corp—*John Cumming*	PO Box 4646, Park City UT 84060	435-658-5820	R	24*	<.1
156	Peavey Corp—*Doug Peavey*	PO Box 14100, Lenexa KS 66285	913-888-0600	R	21	.1
157	Atw Companies Inc—*Peter Frost*	55 Service Ave, Warwick RI 02886	401-739-0740	R	20*	.4
158	Xebec Corp—*Rick Thompson*	5612 Brighton Ter, Kansas City MO 64130	816-444-9700	R	19*	.1
159	Devco Corp—*William Durnan*	PO Box 176, Wyckoff NJ 07481	973-781-0200	R	16*	.5
160	Vista Equity Partners—*Robert F Smith*	150 California St 19th, San Francisco CA 94111	415-765-6500	R	16*	.1
161	Parallax Capital Partners LLC—*James Hale*	23332 Mill Creek Dr St, Laguna Hills CA 92653	949-296-4800	R	16*	<.1
162	Brazos Private Equity Partners LLC—*Jeff S Fronterhouse*	100 Crescent Ct Ste 17, Dallas TX 75201	214-756-6500	R	13*	<.1
163	Ambath LLC—*Georgina Medrano*	421 W Alameda Dr 105, Tempe AZ 85282	480-844-2596	R	13*	.1
164	Environmental Capital Holdings Inc—*Gianni Arcaini*	6622 Southpoint Dr Ste, Jacksonville FL 32216	904-296-2800	R	12*	.1
165	Gateway International Holdings Inc—*George Colin*	2672 Dow Ave, Tustin CA 92780	714-630-6253	R	12	.1
166	Bromberg Holdings Inc—*Frederick Bromberg*	123 20th St N, Birmingham AL 35203	205-252-0221	R	11*	.1
167	DeGol Organization—*Donald A DeGol*	3229 Pleasant Valley B, Altoona PA 16602	814-941-7777	R	11*	<.1
168	UniFirst Holdings Inc—*Ron D Croatti*	68 Jonspin Rd, Wilmington MA 01887	978-658-8888	S	11	N/A
169	Menlo Acquisition Corp—*Richard S Greenberg*	PO Box 5430, Parsippany NJ 07054	973-560-1400	R	9	<.1
170	Sgf Holdings Inc—*Peter Emmons*	PO Box 4116, Atlanta GA 30302	404-609-9300	R	7*	<.1
171	Metaltech Investments Inc—*Edwin Gott*	2400 2nd Ave, Pittsburgh PA 15219	412-464-5000	R	7*	.1
172	Southern Perfection Fabrication Holdings Inc—*Gordon Hale*	PO Box 628, Byron GA 31008	478-956-4442	R	6*	.1
173	Broaster Co—*James Cipra*	2855 Cranston Rd, Beloit WI 53511	608-365-0193	R	6*	.1
174	North American Filtration Inc	PO Box 306, Denmark SC 29042	803-793-0340	R	5*	<.1
175	Lingate Financial Group Inc—*Michael P Hannon*	8301 Golden Valley Rd, Minneapolis MN 55427	763-546-8201	R	5*	<.1
176	Wickland Oil Co—*John A Wickland Jr*	3610 American River Dr, Sacramento CA 95864	916-978-2400	R	5*	<.1
177	Delhaize America Inc—*Kathy Green*	PO Box 1330, Salisbury NC 28145	704-633-8250	S	5	109.0
178	Alta Industries Limited LP—*Robert Michaelis*	1887 S 700 W, Salt Lake City UT 84104	801-972-8160	R	5*	.1
179	Del Ozone Holding Company Inc—*Dennis Lavelle*	PO Box 4509, San Luis Obispo CA 93403	805-541-1601	R	5*	.1
180	United American Corporation Inc—*Benoit Laliberte*	3273 E Warm Springs Rd, Las Vegas NV 89120	212-738-0009	P	4	<.1
181	Vmi Americas Inc—*Auke Diaster*	4485 Allen Rd, Stow OH 44224	330-929-6800	R	4*	<.1
182	Myllykoski North America Inc—*Bob Olah*	PO Box 129, Madison ME 04950	207-696-3307	R	4*	.3
183	Heather Ridge Inc—*Anthony Besthoff*	1492 High Ridge Rd Ste, Stamford CT 06903	203-329-7000	R	3*	<.1
184	Contran Corp—*Harold C Simmons*	5430 LBJ Fwy Ste 1700, Dallas TX 75240	972-233-1700	R	3*	<.1
185	Reserve Group—*Mark Hamlin*	3560 W Market St Ste 3, Akron OH 44333	330-665-2900	R	3*	<.1
186	Mayline Group—*Paul Simons*	PO Box 728, Sheboygan WI 53082	920-457-5537	R	3*	<.1
187	Cd Holdings Inc—*Dean Stroh*	1343 Miami St, Toledo OH 43605	419-698-2900	R	3*	<.1
188	ML Holdings Inc—*John Lees*	110 Herman Melville Bl, New Bedford MA 02740	508-991-6026	R	2*	<.1
189	Beta Industries Corp—*Arnold Serchuk*	707 Commercial Ave, Carlstadt NJ 07072	201-939-2400	R	2*	<.1
190	PSI Corp—*Eric Kash*	7222 Commerce Center D, Colorado Springs CO 80919	914-371-2441	P	1	<.1
191	Inland Industries Inc—*Brian D Murray*	PO Box 15999, Lenexa KS 66215	913-492-9050	R	1*	.3
192	Spare Backup Inc—*Cery B Perle*	990 Iron Wood Dr, Minden NV 89423	775-392-2180	P	1	<.1
193	Eaglecom Real Estate LLC—*Peter Baird*	2900 Hilton Rd, Ferndale MI 48220	248-541-3700	R	1*	<.1
194	JT Holding Co—*Ralph Griffin*	3400 Peachtree Rd NE S, Atlanta GA 30326	404-240-0139	R	1*	<.1

Note: An asterisk (*) indicates an estimated financial figure. The company type code used is as follows: R = Private, P = Public, S = Private Subsidiary, B = Public Subsidiary, D = Division, J = Joint Venture, I = Investment Fund.

COMPANY RANKINGS BY SALES WITHIN 4-DIGIT SIC

Rank	Company Name—*Executive Officer*	Address, City, State, Zip	Phone	Type	Fin	Empls
195	Options Media Group Holdings Inc—*Scott Frohman*	123 NW 13th St Ste 300, Boca Raton FL 33432	561-368-5967	P	1	<.1
196	National Diversified Co—*S Brown*	PO Box 8739, Waco TX 76714	254-776-2632	R	1*	<.1
197	United American Healthcare Corp—*John Fife*	303 E Wacker Dr Ste 12, Chicago IL 60601	313-393-4571	P	<1	<.1
198	Leadership Software Corp—*Roger Seiler*	PO Box 725, Nyack NY 10960	845-358-0406	R	<1*	<.1
199	Domark International Inc—*R Thomas Kidd*	1809 East Broadway Ste, Oviedo FL 32765		P	<1	<.1
200	Air Transport Group Holdings Inc—*Arnold Leonora*	7453 Woodruff Way, Stone Mountain GA 30087	404-671-9253	P	<1	N/A
201	Lindquist Investment Co—*Steven E Lindquist*	3917 Airport Rd, Ogden UT 84405	801-399-4532	R	<1	N/A

TOTALS: SIC 6719 Holding Companies Nec
Companies: 201   2,030,538   1,191.9

6722 Management Investment—Open-End

Rank	Company Name—*Executive Officer*	Address, City, State, Zip	Phone	Type	Fin	Empls
1	Oakmark Fund—*Bill Nygren*	PO Box 219558, Kansas City MO 64121	617-483-3250	I	2,500,000	N/A
2	Vanguard Group Inc—*F William McNabb III*	PO Box 2600, Valley Forge PA 19482	610-669-1000	R	105,000*	13.0
3	Vanguard Fixed Income-Short Term Fund Vanguard Group Inc	PO Box 1110, Valley Forge PA 19482	610-669-1000	D	96,000	N/A
4	TGI Fund I LC—*Nancy M Taylor*	1100 Boulders Pky, Richmond VA 23225	804-330-1000	S	90,344*	3.0
5	Thrivent Investment Management Inc—*Brad Hewitt*	4321 N Ballard Rd, Appleton WI 54919	920-734-5721	S	83,248*	2.8
6	American Funds Capital Inc Builder 529F—*James Lovelace*	333 S Hope St, Los Angeles CA 90071		I	78,300	N/A
7	Fidelity Contrafund—*William Danoff*	82 Devonshire St, Boston MA 02109		I	54,250	N/A
8	American Balanced Fund—*John Smet*	PO Box 25065, Santa Ana CA 92799	415-421-9360	I	51,000	N/A
9	Putnam Diversified Income Trust—*Partice Tirado*	PO Box 8383, Boston MA 02114	617-292-1000	R	40,851*	1.5
10	American Funds EuroPacific Gr A—*Stephen Bepler*	333 S Hope St 55th Fl, Los Angeles CA 90071	213-486-9200	I	40,620	N/A
11	Dodge and Cox Stock Fund—*John Gunn*	555 California St 40th, San Francisco CA 94104		I	38,200	N/A
12	American Funds Washington Mutual A—*James Dunton*	PO Box 6007, Indianapolis IN 46206		I	37,300	N/A
13	Nomura Pacific Basin Fund Inc—*Kenichi Watanabe*	2 World Financial Cent, New York NY 10281	212-667-9100	R	37,233*	1.2
14	American Funds Bond Fund of Amer 529A—*Abner D Goldstine*	333 S Hope St 53nd Fl, Los Angeles CA 90071	213-486-9200	I	36,600	N/A
15	American Funds SMALLCAP World A—*Gordon Crawford*	333 S Hope St 55th Fl, Los Angeles CA 90071		I	35,170	N/A
16	Van Kampen Reserve Fund—*Michael Kiley*	PO Box 5555, Oakbrook Terrace IL 60181	630-684-6774	I	26,722*	.5
17	Advanced Equities Financial Corp—*Dwight Badger*	311 S Wacker Dr Ste 61, Chicago IL 60606	312-377-5300	R	26,617*	.9
18	American Funds Investment Company of America A—*James B Lovelace*	333 S Hope St, Los Angeles CA 90071		I	26,120	N/A
19	Virtus Insight Money Market Fund—*George Aylward*	PO Box 8301, Boston MA 02266	415-677-1570	I	25,400	N/A
20	Rockefeller Financial—*Austin V Shapard*	10 Rockefeller Plz, New York NY 10020	212-549-5100	R	25,000	.2
21	Fidelity Low-Priced Stock Fund—*Joel Tillinghast*	82 Devonshire St, Boston MA 02109		I	24,150	N/A
22	Dodge and Cox Income Fund—*Dana Emery*	555 California St 40th, San Francisco CA 94104	415-981-1710	I	24,100	N/A
23	American Funds AMCAP A—*Timothy D Armour*	333 S Hope St 52nd Fl, Los Angeles CA 90071	213-486-9200	I	22,800	N/A
24	Fidelity Magellan Fund—*Harry Lange*	82 Devonshire St, Boston MA 02109		I	21,210	N/A
25	Vanguard GNMA Portfolio—*Thomas Pappas*	PO Box 2600, Valley Forge PA 19482		I	17,790	N/A
26	Putnam Voyager Fund—*Robert L Reynolds*	30 Dan Rd, Canton MA 02021	617-292-1000	R	16,996	N/A
27	Schwab Government Money Fund—*Karen Wiggan*	101 Montgomery St, San Francisco CA 94104	415-627-7000	I	16,300	N/A
28	CREF Money Market Fund—*Roger W Ferguson Jr*	730 3rd Ave, New York NY 10017	212-490-9000	I	15,130	N/A
29	Vanguard Wellington Fund Inc—*F William McNabb III*	PO Box 1100, Valley Forge PA 19482	610-648-6000	I	15,130	N/A
30	PPM America Capital Partners LLC—*Bruce D Gorchow*	225 W Wacker Dr Ste 12, Chicago IL 60606	312-634-2500	S	13,576*	.3
31	Franklin California Tax Free Income Fund Inc—*Christopher Sperry*	PO Box 997152, Sacramento CA 95899		I	13,109	N/A
32	Dodge and Cox Balanced Fund—*John Gunn*	555 California St 40th, San Francisco CA 94104		I	13,000	N/A
33	American Funds American Mutual A—*James Dunton*	333 S Hope St 55th Fl, Los Angeles CA 90071	213-486-9200	I	12,700	N/A
34	American Funds Tax-Exempt Bond A—*Neil L Langberg*	333 S HOPE St, Los Angeles CA 90071		I	12,340	N/A
35	Angelo Gordon and Co—*John M Angelo*	245 Park Ave, New York NY 10167	212-692-2000	R	12,277*	.2
36	Fidelity Investments—*Edward C Johnson III*	82 Devonshire St, Boston MA 02109	617-563-7000	R	11,979*	39.0
37	Longleaf Partners Fund—*O Mason Hawkins*	6410 Poplar Ave Ste 90, Memphis TN 38119	901-761-2474	R	10,966*	<.1
38	American High-Income Trust—*Abner D Goldstine*	333 S Hope St, Los Angeles CA 90071	213-486-9200	I	10,800	N/A
39	Oaktree Capital Management LP—*Bruce Karsh*	333 S Grand Ave 28th F, Los Angeles CA 90071	213-830-6300	R	10,675*	.2
40	Fidelity Blue Chip Growth Fund—*Sonu Kalra*	82 Devonshire St, Boston MA 02109		I	10,450	N/A
41	Vanguard STAR Fund—*F William McNabb III*	PO Box 2600, Valley Forge PA 19482	610-669-1000	I	10,428	N/A
42	Capital Group Companies Inc—*Philip de Toledo*	333 S Hope St 53 Fl, Los Angeles CA 90071	213-486-9200	R	8,668*	7.5
43	Janus Twenty Fund—*Ronald Sachs*	151 Detroit St, Denver CO 80206	303-333-3863	I	8,600	N/A
44	Janus T Fund—*Daniel Riff*	151 Detroit St, Denver CO 80206		I	8,370	N/A
45	Rydex SGI—*Richard M Goldman*	805 King Farm Blvd Ste, Rockville MD 20850	301-296-5100	R	8,075*	.3
46	TD Banknorth Wealth Management Group—*Bharat B Masrani*	PO Box 1180, South Yarmouth MA 02664	508-394-1300	D	8,000*	.5
47	Fidelity Value Fund—*Richard B Fentin*	82 Devonshire St, Boston MA 02109		I	7,350	N/A
48	Van Kampen Emerging Growth Fund—*David Linton*	1 Parkview Plz, Oakbrook Terrace IL 60181		R	7,219	N/A
49	Vanguard Short Term Treasury Fund—*David Glocke*	PO Box 2600, Valley Forge PA 19482	610-669-1000	I	6,880	N/A
50	AIM Constellation Fund—*Eric Voss*	PO Box 4739, Houston TX 77210	713-626-1919	I	6,859	N/A
51	Vanguard Energy Fund—*Karl Bandtel*	PO Box 2600 V26, Valley Forge PA 19482		I	6,540	N/A
52	Warburg Pincus Emerging Growth Fund—*Charles Kaye*	450 Lexington Ave, New York NY 10017	212-878-0600	R	6,511*	.2
53	Fidelity Overseas Fund—*Ian Hart*	82 Devonshire St, Boston MA 02109	617-563-7000	I	6,410	N/A
54	Franklin US Government Secs A—*Jack Lemein*	PO Box 7777, San Mateo CA 94403	650-312-2000	I	6,400	N/A
55	T Rowe Price Growth Stock Fund Inc—*James Kennedy*	PO Box 89000, Baltimore MD 21289	410-345-2000	I	6,254	N/A
56	T Rowe Price International Stock Fund—*Robert Smith*	PO Box 89000, Baltimore MD 21289		I	5,870	N/A
57	Vanguard High Yield Corporate Portfolio—*Michael Hong*	PO Box 2600, Valley Forge PA 19482		I	5,730	N/A
58	American Funds Intermediate Bond Fund of America—*John Smet*	333 S Hope St, Los Angeles CA 90021		I	5,700	N/A
59	T Rowe Price New Horizons Fund Inc—*James Kennedy*	PO Box 89000, Baltimore MD 21289	410-345-2000	I	5,640	N/A
60	Marmon Group LLC—*Frank S Ptak*	181 W Madison St 26th, Chicago IL 60602	312-372-9500	S	5,591*	15.0
61	Franklin High Yield Tax-Free Income Fund—*John Wiley*	PO Box 7777, San Mateo CA 94403	650-312-2000	I	5,390	N/A
62	Vanguard Morgan Growth Fund—*James Stetler*	PO Box 2600, Valley Forge PA 19482	610-669-1000	I	5,240	N/A
63	Fidelity OTC Fund—*Gavin Baker*	82 Devonshire St, Boston MA 02109		I	5,130	N/A
64	T Rowe Price New Era Fund Inc—*James Kennedy*	PO Box 17630, Baltimore MD 21297	410-345-2000	I	5,060	N/A
65	American Funds Group US Government Securities Fund—*John Smet*	PO Box 7650, San Francisco CA 94120	213-486-9200	I	4,470	N/A
66	Oakmark International Fund I—*David Herro*	PO Box 219558, Kansas City MO 64121	617-483-8327	I	4,350	N/A
67	Janus Growth and Income Fund—*Marc Pinto*	PO Box 173375, Denver CO 80217	303-333-3863	I	3,810	N/A
68	FPA New Income—*Thomas Atteberry*	11400 W Olympic Blvd S, Los Angeles CA 90064	310-473-0225	I	3,800	N/A
69	Janus Balanced Fund—*Augustus Cheh*	151 Detroit St, Denver CO 80206		I	3,690	N/A
70	American Century Growth Investors—*Gregory Woodhams*	PO Box 419200, Kansas City MO 64141	816-340-7010	I	3,650	N/A
71	Fidelity Independence Fund—*Robert C Bertelson*	82 Devonshire St, Boston MA 02109		I	3,610	N/A
72	Janus Flexible Income Fund—*Darrell Watters*	151 Detroit St, Denver CO 80206	303-333-3863	I	3,560	N/A
73	Thrivent Money Market Fund—*Brad Hewitt*	625 4th Ave S, Minneapolis MN 55415		I	3,503	N/A
74	Sun Capital Partners Inc—*Rodger Krouse*	5200 Town Center Cir S, Boca Raton FL 33486	561-394-0550	R	3,500*	26.5

Rank	Company Name—Executive Officer	Address, City, State, Zip	Phone	Type	Fin	Empls
75	Advent International Financial Service Inc—Peter A Brooke	75 State St 29th Fl, Boston MA 02109	617-951-9400	S	3,133*	.1
76	Offitbank Investment Group—John Stumpf	520 Madison Ave 27th F, New York NY 10022	212-758-9600	S	3,108*	.1
77	Fidelity Real Estate Investment—Bary Greenfield	82 Devonshire St, Boston MA 02109	617-563-7000	I	3,106	N/A
78	Janus Research Fund—James P Goff	PO Box 55932, Boston MA 02205		I	3,090	N/A
79	Vanguard Short-Term Tax Ex fund—Pam Wisehaupt-Tynan	PO Box 2600, Valley Forge PA 19482		I	3,040	N/A
80	Putnam New Opportunities Fund—Kevin Divney	1 Post Office Sq, Boston MA 02109		I	2,974	N/A
81	Franklin Income Fund A—Edward D Perks	3355 Data Dr, Rancho Cordova CA 95670		I	2,962	N/A
82	Insight Capital Inc—Michael S Willner	810 7th Ave, New York NY 10019	917-286-2300	S	2,830*	.1
83	Fidelity Inversters—S Joseph Wickwire	82 Devonshire St, Boston MA 02109		I	2,660	N/A
84	Providence Equity Partners LLC—Jonathan M Nelson	50 Kennedy Plz 18th Fl, Providence RI 02903	401-751-1700	R	2,548*	.1
85	Vanguard Short-Term Federal Portfolio—Ronald Reardon	PO Box 2600, Valley Forge PA 19482		I	2,540	N/A
86	Equity One Inc—Jeffrey Olson	1600 NE Miami Garden D, North Miami Beach FL 33179	305-947-1664	I	2,452	.2
87	Wells Fargo Advantage Municipal Bond Fund Inc—Lyle Fitterer	525 Market St, San Francisco CA 94105		I	2,442	N/A
88	Apollo Advisors LP—Anthony Ressler	2 Manhattanville Rd, Purchase NY 10577	914-694-8000	R	2,428*	.1
89	T Rowe Price Science and Technology Fund Inc—James Kennedy	PO Box 89000, Baltimore MD 21289	410-345-2000	I	2,404	N/A
90	Eaton Vance Limited Duration Income Fund—Payson Swaffield	255 State St, Boston MA 02109	617-482-8260	I	2,340	N/A
91	Fidelity Convertible Securities Fund—Thomas Soviero	265 Franklin St, Boston MA 02110	617-570-7000	I	2,330	N/A
92	Janus Worldwide Fund—George Maris	151 Detroit St, Denver CO 80206		I	2,300	N/A
93	NWD Investment Management Inc—John H Grady	1200 River Rd, Conshohocken PA 19428	484-530-1310	R	2,263*	.1
94	Franklin Growth Fund A—Jerry Palmieri	1 Franklin Pkwy, San Mateo CA 94403		I	2,250	N/A
95	AIM Weingarten Fund—Lanny Sachnowitz	PO Box 4739, Houston TX 77210	713-626-1919	I	2,100	N/A
96	Putnam OTC Emerging Growth Fund	PO Box 8383, Boston MA 02266	617-292-1000	R	1,991	N/A
97	Wells Fargo Advantage Opportunity Fund—Ann Miletti	525 Market St, San Francisco CA 94163		I	1,976	N/A
98	WinWholesale Inc—Richard W Schwartz	3110 Kettering Blvd, Dayton OH 45439	937-294-5331	R	1,920*	4.8
99	Franklin Money Fund A—Shawn Lyons	PO Box 997152, Sacramento CA 95899		I	1,891	N/A
100	Franklin California Insured Tax-Free Income Fund—John Wiley	PO Box 7777, San Mateo CA 94403	650-312-2000	I	1,860	N/A
101	Midas Special Equities Fund Inc—Thomas B Winmill	PO Box 6110, Indianapolis IN 46206		R	1,811	N/A
102	Franklin Utilities Fund—John Kohli	PO Box 997152, Sacramento CA 95899	650-312-2000	I	1,800	N/A
103	Fidelity Growth Strategies—Steve Calhoun	82 Devonshire St, Boston MA 02109		I	1,780	N/A
104	Pax World Balanced Fund Inc—Christopher Brown	PO Box 9824, Providence RI 02940		I	1,770	N/A
105	Twentieth Century Vista Investors—Brandley Eixmann	PO Box 419200, Kansas City MO 64141		I	1,700	N/A
106	Vanguard Asset Allocation Fund Inc—Bill McNabb	PO Box 2600, Valley Forge PA 19482	610-669-1000	I	1,700	N/A
107	American Funds Tax-Exempt Fund CA A—Neil Langberg	333 S Hope St, Los Angeles CA 90071		I	1,641	N/A
108	Janus Enterprise Fund—Brian Demain	PO Box 55932, Boston MA 02205		I	1,640	N/A
109	American Century Select Investors—Keith Lee	PO Box 419200, Kansas City MO 64141	816-531-5575	I	1,620	N/A
110	Veronis Suhler Stevenson Partners LLC—Jeffrey T Stevenson	Park Ave Plz 55 E 52nd, New York NY 10055	212-935-4990	R	1,593*	.1
111	Franklin Adjustable US Government Securities Fund—Paul Varunok	PO Box 7777, San Mateo CA 94403	650-312-2000	I	1,590	N/A
112	AIM Summit Fund Inc—Mark H Williamson	PO Box 4739, Houston TX 77210	713-626-1919	S	1,491*	1.6
113	Janus Short-Term Bond Fund—Augustus Cheh	151 Detroit St, Denver CO 80206		I	1,480	N/A
114	Vanguard Equity Income Fund Inc	PO Box 2600, Valley Forge PA 19482		I	1,480	N/A
115	Eaton Vance Income Fund of Boston—Michael Weilheimer	255 State St, Boston MA 02109	617-482-8260	I	1,430	N/A
116	Neuberger and Berman Partners Fund Inc—S Basu Mullick	605 3rd Ave 2nd Fl, New York NY 10158		I	1,430	N/A
117	Columbia Mid Cap Value A Fund—Lori Ensinger	1 Financial Ctr, Boston MA 02111		I	1,410	N/A
118	Pennsylvania Mutual Fund Inc—Charles M Royce	745 Fifth Ave, New York NY 10151		I	1,320	N/A
119	FPA Capital Fund Inc—Robert L Rodriguez	11400 W Olympic Blvd S, Los Angeles CA 90064	310-473-0225	I	1,300	N/A
120	Franklin New Jersey Tax-Free Income Fund—Stella Wong	PO Box 7777, San Mateo CA 94403		I	1,220	N/A
121	Williams Capital Group LP—Christopher Williams	650 5th Ave 11th Fl, New York NY 10019	212-830-4500	R	1,197*	<.1
122	Golden Gate Capital—David Dominik	1 Embarcadero Ctr 39th, San Francisco CA 94111	415-983-2700	R	1,176*	<.1
123	Franklin Florida Tax-Free Income Fund—Stella Wong	PO Box 7777, San Mateo CA 94403	650-312-3200	I	1,140	N/A
124	George Putnam Fund of Boston A—Raman Srivastava	PO Box 8383, Boston MA 02114		I	1,120	N/A
125	Putnam Tax Exempt Income Fund—Thalia Meehan	PO Box 41203, Providence RI 02940	617-292-1000	I	1,120	N/A
126	Fairport Asset Management LLC—Scott Roulston	3636 Euclid Ave Ste 30, Cleveland OH 44115	216-431-3000	R	1,114*	<.1
127	Putnam NY Tax Exempt Income A—Thalia Meehan	PO Box 8383, Boston MA 02114	617-292-1100	I	1,060	N/A
128	Thompson Street Capital Partners—James A Cooper	120 S Central Ave Ste, Saint Louis MO 63105	314-727-2112	R	1,059*	<.1
129	Neuberger and Berman Focus Fund—Robet B Corman	605 3rd Ave 36th Fl, New York NY 10158	212-476-8800	I	1,044	N/A
130	T Rowe Price Growth and Income Fund Inc—James Kennedy	PO Box 89000, Baltimore MD 21289	410-345-2000	I	1,040	N/A
131	Franklin Pennsylvania Tax-Free Income Fund—Stella Wong	PO Box 997152, Sacramento CA 95899	650-312-2000	I	995	N/A
132	Fidelity Worldwide Fund—William Kennedy	82 Devonshire St, Boston MA 02109	617-563-7000	I	992	N/A
133	Spectrum Equity Investors—William P Collatos	1 International Pl 29t, Boston MA 02110	617-464-4600	R	986*	<.1
134	Franklin Arizona Tax-Free Income Fund—Carrie Higgins	PO Box 997152, Sacramento CA 95899	650-312-2000	I	974	N/A
135	Franklin Oregon Tax-Free Income Fund—Chris Sperry	PO Box 7777, San Mateo CA 94403	650-312-2000	I	940	N/A
136	Franklin North Carolina Tax-Free Income Fund—Stella Wong	PO Box 7777, San Mateo CA 94403	650-312-3200	I	907	N/A
137	Neuberger Berman Cash Reserves—Robert Conti	PO Box 8403, Boston MA 02266	212-476-8800	I	905	N/A
138	Republic Financial Corp—W Randall Dietrich	3300 S Parker Rd Ste 5, Aurora CO 80014	303-751-3501	R	905*	.1
139	Pegasus Capital Advisors LP—Craig Cogut	99 River Rd, Cos Cob CT 06807	203-869-4400	R	904*	<.1
140	Twentieth Century Giftrust Investors—James Stowers Jr	PO Box 419200, Kansas City MO 64141	816-531-5570	I	903	<.1
141	Dean Witter American Value Fund—John J Mack	1585 Broadway, New York NY 10036	212-761-4000	R	899	N/A
142	Lydian Trust Co—Andy Putterman	2000 PGA Blvd, Palm Beach Gardens FL 33410	561-776-8860	R	871*	.8
143	AllianceBernstein Global Thematic Growth Fund—Catherine Wood	1345 Avenue of the Ame, New York NY 10105	212-969-1000	I	859	N/A
144	Thrivent Small Cap Stock A—Brad Hewitt	625 4th Ave S, Minneapolis MN 55415		I	851	N/A
145	Franklin Missouri Tax-Free Income Fund—Carrie Higgins	PO Box 7777, San Mateo CA 94403	650-312-2000	I	848	N/A
146	Van Kampen Government Securities A Fund—Jaidip Singh	522 Fifth Ave, New York NY 10020		I	790	N/A
147	JLL Partners Inc—Paul S Levy	450 Lexington Ave 31st, New York NY 10017	212-286-8600	R	789*	<.1
148	Fidelity Trend Fund—Jeffrey Feingold	82 Devonshire St, Boston MA 02109	617-439-1706	I	780	N/A
149	Calera Capital—James Farrell	580 California St Ste, San Francisco CA 94104	415-632-5200	R	740*	<.1
150	Thermo Cos—James Monroe III	1735 19th St Ste 200, Denver CO 80202	303-294-0690	R	724*	<.1
151	Vanguard Convertible Securities Fund Inc—F William McNabb III	PO Box 2600, Valley Forge PA 19482	610-669-6295	I	716	N/A
152	AIM Energy Fund—Andrew Lees	11 Greenway Plz Ste 10, Houston TX 77046		I	699	N/A
153	US Global Investors Global Resources Fund—Frank E Holmes	PO Box 781234, San Antonio TX 78278	210-308-1222	I	684	N/A
154	Putnam American Government Income Fund—Robert Bloemker	1 Post Office Sq, Boston MA 02109	617-292-1000	I	680	N/A
155	Vanguard Pennsylvania Long Term Tax-Exempt Fund	PO Box 2600, Valley Forge PA 19482		I	670	N/A
156	Franklin Virginia Tax-Free Income Fund—Stella Wong	PO Box 7777, San Mateo CA 94403	650-312-3200	I	666	N/A
157	Wells Fargo Advantage Short-Term—Jay Mueller	525 Market St, San Francisco CA 94163		I	652	N/A
158	Columbia High Yield Municipal Fund—Chad Farrington	1 Financial Center, Boston MA 02111		I	644	N/A
159	Van Kampen Corporate Bond A—Joseph Mehlman	522 5th Ave, New York NY 10036		I	636	N/A

Note: An asterisk (*) indicates an estimated financial figure. The company type code used is as follows: R = Private, P = Public, S = Private Subsidiary, B = Public Subsidiary, D = Division, J = Joint Venture, I = Investment Fund.

NKINGS BY SALES WITHIN 4-DIGIT SIC

	Company Name—Executive Officer	Address, City, State, Zip	Phone	Type	Fin	Empls
	Fidelity Stock Selector—Chris Sharpe	82 Devonshire St, Boston MA 02109		I	614	N/A
	Putnam Classic Equity Fund—Ronald J Bukovac	1 Post Office Sq, Boston MA 02109	617-292-1000	I	608	N/A
162	Fidelity Select Defense and Aerospace Fund—John Sheehy	82 Devonshire St, Boston MA 02109		I	586	N/A
163	Franklin Convertible Securities A—Alan Muschott	PO Box 7777, San Mateo CA 94403	650-312-2000	I	583	N/A
164	Eos Private Equity—Steven M Friedman	320 Park Ave 9th Fl, New York NY 10022	212-832-5800	R	576*	<.1
165	Lovell Minnick Partners LLC—Jeffrey D Lovell	2141 rosecrans Ave Ste, El Segundo CA 90245	310-414-6160	R	572*	<.1
166	Putnam Utilities Growth and Income Fund—Robert Reynolds	PO Box 8383, Boston MA 02114	617-760-7529	R	562	N/A
167	Fidelity Select Brokerage and Investment Management Fund—Benjamin Hesse	82 Devonshire St, Boston MA 02109	617-563-1413	I	559	N/A
168	Franklin Colorado Tax-Free Income Fund—Carrie Higgins	PO Box 7777, San Mateo CA 94403	650-312-2000	I	558	N/A
169	Gabelli Growth Fund—Howard Ward	One Corporate Ctr, Rye NY 10580	914-921-5100	I	533	N/A
170	Franklin DynaTech A—Matthew Moberg	1 Franklin Pkwy Fl 1 B, San Mateo CA 94403	231-632-2301	I	515	N/A
171	Franklin Maryland Tax-Free Income Fund—John Pomeroy	PO Box 7777, San Mateo CA 94403	650-312-2000	I	504	N/A
172	Fidelity Select Computers Fund—Heather Lawrence	82 Devonshire St, Boston MA 02109		I	477	N/A
173	American Century Balanced Investors—Brian Howell	PO Box 419200, Kansas City MO 64141	816-340-7010	I	470	N/A
174	Franklin Connecticut Tax-Free Income Fund—Stella Wong	PO Box 997152, Sacramento CA 95899	650-312-2000	I	469	N/A
175	AllianceBernstein Balanced Shares A—Aryeh Glatter	1345 Avenue of the Ame, New York NY 10105	212-969-1000	I	469	N/A
176	US Global Investors Eastern European Fund—Frank Holmes	PO Box 781234, San Antonio TX 78278	210-308-1234	I	463	N/A
177	Trinity Ventures—Patricia Nakache	3000 Sand Hill Rd Bldg, Menlo Park CA 94025	650-854-9500	R	460*	<.1
178	Profit Investment Management LLC—Eugene Profit	8401 Colesville Rd Ste, Silver Spring MD 20910	301-650-0059	R	449*	<.1
179	Pension Associates Inc—Tom Erickson	PO Box 8100, Wausau WI 54402	715-843-8835	R	410*	.1
180	Hambrecht and Quist Capital Management LLC—Daniel R Omstead	2 Liberty Sq 9th Fl, Boston MA 02109	617-772-8500	I	408	<.1
181	Fidelity Select Chemicals Fund—Matthew Schuldt	82 Devonshire St, Boston MA 02109		I	396	N/A
182	TIAA-CREF Social Choice Eq Retire—Anne Sapp	730 3rd Ave, New York NY 10017		I	388	N/A
183	AMA Capital Partners—Paul M Leand Jr	405 Lexington Ave 67th, New York NY 10174	212-682-3344	R	388*	<.1
184	Franklin NY Insured Tax-Free A Fund—John Pomeroy	PO Box 7777, San Mateo CA 94403	650-312-2000	I	380	N/A
185	American Funds Tax-Exempt Fund of Virginia—Brenda S Ellerin	1101 Vermont Ave NW, Washington DC 20005		I	365	N/A
186	Franklin Georgia Tax-Free Income Fund—John Pomeroy	PO Box 7777, San Mateo CA 94403	650-312-3200	I	361	N/A
187	Putnam Tax-Free Income Insured Fund—Thalia Meehan	1 Post Office Sq, Boston MA 02109	617-292-1000	I	351	N/A
188	AllianceBernstein Small/Mid Cap Growth A—Bruce Aronow	1345 Avenue of the Ame, New York NY 10105	212-969-1000	I	327	N/A
189	Eaton Vance California Municipals Fund—Thomas Faust	2 International Pl, Boston MA 02110	617-482-8260	I	326	N/A
190	Franklin Louisiana Tax-Free Income Fund—John Wiley	PO Box 7777, San Mateo CA 94403	650-312-2000	I	325	N/A
191	Neuberger and Berman Genesis Fund Inc—Judith Vale	605 3rd Ave 2nd Fl, New York NY 10158		I	322	N/A
192	TCW Investment Funds Inc—Marc I Stein	865 S Figueroa St Ste, Los Angeles CA 90017	213-244-0000	I	321	N/A
193	FPA Paramount Fund Inc—Eric S Ende	11400 W Olympic Blvd S, Los Angeles CA 90064	310-473-0225	I	287	N/A
194	FPA Perennial Fund Inc—Eric S Ende	11400 W Olympic Blvd S, Los Angeles CA 90064	310-473-0225	I	278	N/A
195	Putnam International Value A—Darren Jaroch	P O Box 8383, Boston MA 02114	617-292-1000	I	276	N/A
196	Questor Management Company LLC—Jay Alix	700 E Maple Rd 4th Fl, Birmingham MI 48009	248-593-1930	R	249*	<.1
197	Franklin Alabama Tax-Free Income Fund—John Pomeroy	PO Box 7777, San Mateo CA 94403	650-312-3200	I	244	N/A
198	AIM Charter Fund C—Ron Sloan	11 Greenway Plz Ste 10, Houston TX 77046	713-626-1919	I	244	N/A
199	Gladstone Investment Corp—David Gladstone	1521 Westbranch Dr Ste, McLean VA 22102	703-287-5893	P	241	N/A
200	Templeton Foreign Smaller Companies Fund—Martin Cobb	PO Box 2258, Rancho Cordova CA 95741	916-463-1500	I	230	N/A
201	CommonFund—Vern Sedlacek	15 Old Danbury Rd, Wilton CT 06897	203-563-5000	R	227*	.2
202	US Global Investors Gold and Precious Metals Fund—Frank E Holmes	PO Box 781234, San Antonio TX 78278	210-308-1222	I	208	N/A
203	Invesco Distributors Inc—Martin Flanagan	11 Greenway Plz Ste 10, Houston TX 77046	713-626-1919	I	208	N/A
204	NCM Capital Management Group Inc—Maceo K Sloan	2634 Durham-Chapel Hil, Durham NC 27707	919-688-0620	R	201*	<.1
205	Neuberger and Berman Government Money Fund—Eric Hiatt	605 3rd Ave 2nd Fl, New York NY 10158	212-476-8800	I	192	N/A
206	American Century Target Mat 2010—Robert Gahagan	4500 Main St, Kansas City MO 64111		I	183	N/A
207	AIM Global Growth B Fund—Barrett K Sides	PO Box 4739, Houston TX 77210		I	182	N/A
208	Thrivent Large Cap Value Fund—Brad Hewitt	625 4th Ave S, Minneapolis MN 55415		I	181	N/A
209	UrbanAmerica Advisors LLC—Richmond S McCoy	30 Broad St 31st Fl, New York NY 10004	212-612-9100	R	180*	<.1
210	United Enterprise Fund LP—Jeffrey Scott Keys	30 Broad St 21st Fl, New York NY 10004	212-635-2303	R	179*	<.1
211	American Century Target Mat 2020—Robert Gahagan	4500 Main St, Kansas City MO 64111	816-340-4200	I	178	N/A
212	Franklin Kentucky Tax-Free Income Fund—Carrie Higgins	PO Box 997152, Sacramento CA 95899	650-312-2000	I	175	N/A
213	Aig Global Asset Management Holdings Corp—Bob Benmosche	599 Lexington Ave, New York NY 10022	212-709-6100	R	166*	3.0
214	Eaton Vance National Municipals Income B—David C McCabe	PO Box 9653, Providence RI 02940	617-482-8260	I	165	N/A
215	Pioneer Europe Select Equity Fund—Andrew Arbuthnott	PO Box 55014, Boston MA 02205	617-422-4947	I	155	N/A
216	Insight Equity Holdings LLC—Kevin Slaton	1400 Civic Pl Ste 250, Southlake TX 76092	817-488-7775	R	153*	4.0
217	Falconhead Capital LLC—Ali Beller	450 Park Ave Fl 3, New York NY 10022	212-634-3304	R	153*	2.9
218	Yacktman Fund—Donald A Yacktman	303 W Madison St, Chicago IL 60606		I	153	N/A
219	Fidelity Select Automotive Fund—Michael Weaver	82 Devonshire St, Boston MA 02109	617-563-1413	I	146	N/A
220	Atlas Copco USA Holdings Inc—Mark Cohen	PO Box 2028, Pine Brook NJ 07058	973-439-3412	R	143*	3.1
221	AIM Financial Services Fund—Meggan M Walsh	PO Box 4739, Houston TX 77210		I	134	N/A
222	Scout Bond—Bruce Fernandez	803 W Michigan St, Milwaukee WI 53233	414-271-5885	I	134	N/A
223	Information Services Group Inc (Stamford Connecticut)—Michael P Connors	281 Tresser Blvd, Stamford CT 06901	203-517-3100	P	132	.4
224	Eaton Vance Greater India B—Christopher Darling	255 State St 7th Fl, Boston MA 02109	617-482-8260	I	126	N/A
225	Putnam Global Income Trust—D William Kohli	1 Post Office Sq, Boston MA 02109	617-292-1000	I	124	N/A
226	Dreyfus Discovery A Fund—B Randall Watts	210 University Blvd St, Denver CO 80206		I	123	N/A
227	Thrivent Large Cap Growth Fund—Brad Hewitt	625 4th Ave, Minneapolis MN 55415		I	122	N/A
228	Oberweis Emerging Growth Fund—James Oberweis	3333 Warrenville Rd St, Lisle IL 60532	630-577-2300	I	114	N/A
229	Alliance California Municipal Income Fund Inc—Peter Kraus	1345 Avenue of the Ame, New York NY 10105	212-486-5800	I	111	N/A
230	RBC Enterprise S Fund—Lance James	100 S 5th St Ste 2300, Minneapolis MN 55402	816-376-7090	I	107	N/A
231	AIM US Government B Fund—Brian Schneider	PO Box 4739, Houston TX 77210	713-626-1919	I	105	N/A
232	Franklin Global Health Care Fund—Matthew Willey	PO Box 7777, San Mateo CA 94403	650-312-3000	I	103	N/A
233	American Funds Incorporated Fund of Amer 529B—Abner Goldstine	PO Box 7650, San Francisco CA 94120		I	100	N/A
234	Goode Investment Management Inc—Bruce T Goode	1700 Terminal Tower, Cleveland OH 44113	216-771-9000	R	94*	<.1
235	Fidelity Select Construction and Housing Fund—Daniel Kelley	82 Devonshire St, Boston MA 02109		I	92	N/A
236	Philadelphia Fund Inc—Donald H Baxter	PO Box 6110, Indianapolis IN 46206	561-395-2155	I	86	N/A
237	Asset Management Associates—Charles Holmes	PO Box 250, Rutherford NJ 07070	201-531-9250	R	80*	<.1
238	Neuberger Berman Short Duration Bond Fund—Thomas Sontag	PO Box 8403, Boston MA 02114	212-476-8800	I	71	N/A
239	Stratton Monthly Dividend Shares Inc—James Beers	610 W Germantown Pike, Plymouth Meeting PA 19462	610-941-0888	I	71	N/A
240	Putnam Convertible Income-Growth Y—Robert Salvin	PO Box 8383, Boston MA 02114	617-292-1000	I	70	N/A
241	Fidelity Select Multimedia Portfolio—Kristina Salen	82 Devonshire St, Boston MA 02109		I	69	N/A

Rank	Company Name—*Executive Officer*	Address, City, State, Zip	Phone	Type	Fin	Empls
242	Alliance New York Municipal Income Fund—*Peter Kraus*	1345 Avenue of the Ame, New York NY 10105	212-486-5800	I	66	N/A
243	Clark Holdings Inc—*Skip Fischer*	121 New York Ave, Trenton NJ 08638	609-396-1100	R	65	.2
244	Hennessy Funds Inc—*Neil Hennessey*	7250 Redwood Blvd Ste, Novato CA 94945	415-899-1555	R	61*	<.1
245	AIM Basic Balanced B Fund—*Brett Stanley*	PO Box 4739, Houston TX 77210	713-626-1919	I	61	N/A
246	AIM International Growth B Fund—*Barrett K Sides*	PO Box 4739, Houston TX 77210	713-626-1919	I*	59	N/A
247	Elk Associates Funding Corp—*Gary Granoff* Ameritrans Capital Corp	747 3rd Ave Ste 4C, New York NY 10017	212-355-2449	S	57*	<.1
248	American Funds Capital World G/I A—*Mark Denning*	333 S Hope St 55th Fl, Los Angeles CA 90071	714-671-7000	I	57	N/A
249	Graham Group (York Pennsylvania)—*William Kerlin*	PO Box 1104, York PA 17405	717-849-4001	R	54*	.1
250	US Global Investors China Reg Opp—*Frank E Holmes*	PO Box 781234, San Antonio TX 78278	210-308-1222	I	52	N/A
251	Putnam High Yield Y—*Paul Scanlon*	PO Box 41203, Providence RI 02940		I	51	N/A
252	AIM High Yield Fund—*Peter Ehret*	PO Box2190780, Kansas City MO 64121	713-626-1919	I	43	N/A
253	Neuberger and Berman Municipal Securities Trust—*Bobby Conti*	605 3rd Ave 36th Fl, New York NY 10158	212-476-8800	S	42	N/A
254	RBC Small Cap Core S—*Lance James*	100 S 5th St Ste 2300, Minneapolis MN 55402		I	42	N/A
255	WB Capital Bond—*Laurie Mardis*	1415 28th St Ste 200, West Des Moines IA 50266		I	39	N/A
256	Rand Capital Corp—*Allan F (Pete) Grum*	2200 Rand Bldg, Buffalo NY 14203	716-853-0802	P	35	<.1
257	Wynnchurch Capital Ltd—*Charles B Grace*	6250 N River Rd Ste 10, Rosemont IL 60018	847-604-6100	R	32*	<.1
258	Vanguard Index Trust Inc—*Bill McNabb* Vanguard Group Inc	PO Box 2600, Valley Forge PA 19482	610-669-1000	D	32	N/A
259	Ameritrans Capital Corp—*Michael Feinsod*	830 3rd Ave Ste 830, New York NY 10022	212-355-2449	P	30	<.1
260	Sorrento Capital Inc—*Robert Knohl*	7505 Irvine Ctr Dr Ste, Irvine CA 92618	910-573-8150	R	30*	.4
261	Putnam US Government Income M—*Robert L Bloemker*	P O Box 8383, Boston MA 02114	617-292-1000	I	30	N/A
262	Ariel Capital Management LLC—*John W Rogers Jr*	200 E Randolph Dr Ste, Chicago IL 60601	312-726-0140	R	28*	.1
263	MassMutual Premier International Bond S—*Dagmar Dvorak*	1295 State St, Springfield MA 01111		I	27	N/A
264	AIM Income Fund—*Darren Hughes*	PO Box 4739, Houston TX 77210	713-626-1919	I	24	N/A
265	US Global Investors Near-Term Tax Free Fund—*John Derrick*	PO Box 781234, San Antonio TX 78278	210-308-1222	I	23	N/A
266	US Global Investors Tax Free Fund—*Frank Holmes*	PO Box 781234, San Antonio TX 78278	210-308-1222	I	22	N/A
267	Cash Management Trust of America—*Abner D Goldstine*	333 S Hope St 52nd Fl, Los Angeles CA 90021	213-486-9200	I	19	N/A
268	Invesco Utilities Fund—*Meggan Walsh*	PO Box 4739, Houston TX 77210	713-626-1919	I	17	N/A
269	US Global Investors All American Equity Fund—*Frank Holmes*	PO Box 781234, San Antonio TX 78278	210-308-1234	I	16	N/A
270	Leerink Swann and Company Inc—*Jeffrey A Leerink*	1 Federal St 37th Fl, Boston MA 02110	617-248-1601	R	15*	.1
271	Managers Funds LP	800 Connecticut Ave, Norwalk CT 06854	203-299-3500	S	14*	<.1
272	AIM Municipal Bond B Fund—*Richard A Berry*	PO Box 4739, Houston TX 77210	713-626-1919	I	14	N/A
273	Nicholas Limited Edition Inc—*Albert O Nicholas*	615 E Michigan St 3rd, Milwaukee WI 53202	414-272-6133	R	13	N/A
274	Putnam Pennsylvania Tax Exempt Income Fund—*Thalia Meehan*	1 Post Office Sq, Boston MA 02109	617-292-1000	I	12	N/A
275	Hansberger Global Investors Inc—*Ron Holt*	401 E Las Olas Blvd St, Fort Lauderdale FL 33301	954-522-5150	R	10*	.1
276	MACC Private Equities Inc—*David R Schroder*	580 2nd St Ste 102, Encinitas CA 92024	760-479-5080	P	10	N/A
277	Putnam California Tax Exempt Money Market Fund—*George Putnam*	PO Box 8383, Boston MA 02266	617-292-1000	R	9	N/A
278	Eaton Vance Government Obligations R Fund—*Susan Schiff*	2 International Pl, Boston MA 02110		I	7	N/A
279	Tuxis Corp—*Mark C Winmill*	3814 Rte 44, Millbrook NY 12545	845-677-2700	P	7	<.1
280	Eaton Vance Connecticut Municipals Fund—*David C McCabe*	PO Box 9653, Providence RI 02940	617-482-8260	I	7	N/A
281	Rhumbline Advisers Corp—*Wayne T Owen*	30 Rowes Wharf Ste 420, Boston MA 02110	617-345-0434	R	4*	<.1
282	Vontobel USA Inc—*Henry Schlegel*	1540 Broadway 38th Fl, New York NY 10036	212-415-7000	S	3*	<.1
283	Snyder Capital Management—*Walter Niemasik*	1 Market Plz Ste 1200, San Francisco CA 94105	415-392-3900	S	2*	<.1
284	Randolph Capital Management—*Jay R Holiday*	77 Musiker Ave, Randolph NJ 07869	973-895-2625	R	N/A	<.1

TOTALS: SIC 6722 Management Investment—Open-End

Companies: 284					5,114,210	135.8

6726 Investment Offices Nec

Rank	Company Name—*Executive Officer*	Address, City, State, Zip	Phone	Type	Fin	Empls
1	Busey Group—*Phil G Busey*	4747 Gaillardia Pky St, Oklahoma City OK 73142	405-721-7776	R	14,111*	.2
2	Anworth Mortgage Asset Corp—*Joseph Lloyd McAdams*	1299 Ocean Ave 2nd Fl, Santa Monica CA 90401	310-255-4493	I	7,790	<.1
3	Ares Capital Corp—*Michael J Arougheti*	245 Park Ave 44th Fl, New York NY 10167	212-710-2100	P	5,387	.5
4	Caxton-Iseman Capital Inc—*Frederick J Iseman*	500 Park Ave, New York NY 10012	212-752-1850	R	4,521*	<.1
5	Gleacher Investment Corp—*Lee Fensterstock*	660 Madison Ave, New York NY 10021	212-418-4200	S	3,583*	.1
6	Guggenheim Funds Distribution Inc—*David C Hooten*	2455 Corporate West Dr, Lisle IL 60532	630-505-3700	P	3,024*	<.1
7	JW Childs Associates LP—*John W Childs*	111 Huntington Ave Ste, Boston MA 02199	617-753-1100	R	3,012*	<.1
8	DNP Select Income Fund Inc—*Nathan Partain*	200 S Wacker Dr Ste 50, Chicago IL 60606	312-368-5510	I	2,549	N/A
9	Aberdeen Asia Pacific Income Fund Inc—*Martin Gilbert*	800 Scudders Mill Rd, Plainsboro NJ 08536		I	2,378	N/A
10	Venture Capital Fund of New England—*Jack Stewart*	30 Washington St, Wellesley MA 02481	781-431-8400	R	2,066*	<.1
11	Nuveen Insured Municipal Opportunity Fund—*Gifford Zimmerman*	333 W Wacker Dr, Chicago IL 60606	312-917-7700	I	2,049	N/A
12	Nuveen Municipal Value Fund Inc—*Thomas C Spalding Jr*	333 W Wacker Dr, Chicago IL 60606	312-917-7800	I	1,945	N/A
13	Paradigm Asset Management Company LLC—*James E Francis*	445 Hamilton Ave, White Plains NY 10601	212-771-6100	R	1,875*	<.1
14	AllianceBernstein Income Fund Inc—*Gershon Distenfeld*	1345 Avenue of the Ame, New York NY 10105	212-969-1000	I	1,820	N/A
15	Tortoise Energy Infrastructure Corp—*Terry Matlack*	11550 Ash St Ste 300, Leawood KS 66211	913-981-1020	P	1,552	<.1
16	Fort Dearborn Income Securities Inc—*Mark E Carver*	1285 Ave of the Americ, New York NY 10019	212-713-2000	P	1,317	N/A
17	Nuveen Performance Plus Municipal Fund Inc—*Thomas Spalding*	333 W Wacker Dr, Chicago IL 60606		I	1,302	N/A
18	Nuveen Premium Income Municipal Fund Inc—*Paul Brennan*	333 W Wacker Dr, Chicago IL 60606		I	1,286	N/A
19	Tri-Continental Corp—*Patrick Bannigan*	100 Park Ave 3th Fl, New York NY 10017	212-850-1864	I	1,180	N/A
20	Gabelli Equity Trust Inc—*Mario J Gabelli*	1 Corporate Center Dr, Rye NY 10580	914-921-5100	I	1,024	N/A
21	BlackRock Income Trust Inc—*Laurence Fink*	100 Bellevue Pkwy, Wilmington DE 19809	302-797-2000	I	1,014	N/A
22	General American Investors Company Inc—*Spencer Davidson*	100 Park Ave 35th Fl, New York NY 10017		I	986	<.1
23	Nuveen Municipal Market Opportunity Fund Inc—*Thomas Spalding*	333 W Wacker Dr, Chicago IL 60606	312-917-8200	I	974	N/A
24	Putnam Premier Income Trust—*Charles Reynolds*	1 Post Office Sq Fl 12, Boston MA 02109	617-292-1000	I	874	N/A
25	Invesco Van Kampen Municipal Trust—*Colin Meadows*	1555 Peachtree St NE, Atlanta GA 30309	713-626-1919	I	862	N/A
26	MFS Intermediate Income Trust—*Robert J Manning*	PO BOX 55824, Boston MA 02205	617-954-5000	I	813	N/A
27	China Fund Inc—*Jamie Skinner*	PO Box 5049, Boston MA 02206		P	785	N/A
28	Western Asset Managed Municipals Fund Inc—*Jay Gerken*	125 Broad St 10th Fl, New York NY 10004		I	780	N/A
29	Petroleum and Resources Corp—*Douglas G Ober*	7 St Paul St Ste 1140, Baltimore MD 21202		P	765	<.1
30	John Hancock Patriot Premium Div Fund II—*Gregory K Phelps*	601 Congress St, Boston MA 02210	617-663-4497	I	740	N/A
31	Nuveen Investment Quality Municipal Fund Inc—*Christopher Drahan*	333 W Wacker Dr, Chicago IL 60606		I	729	N/A
32	Liberty ALL-STAR Equity Fund—*William Parmentier Jr*	1290 Broadway Ste 1100, Denver CO 80203	303-623-2577	I	676	N/A

Note: An asterisk (*) indicates an estimated financial figure. The company type code used is as follows: R = Private, P = Public, S = Private Subsidiary, B = Public Subsidiary, D = Division, J = Joint Venture, I = Investment Fund.

COMPANY RANKINGS BY SALES WITHIN 4-DIGIT SIC

Rank	Company Name—*Executive Officer*	Address, City, State, Zip	Phone	Type	Fin	Empls
33	Van Kampen High Income Trust II—*Edward Wood*	522 Fifth Ave, New York NY 10036	212-762-7400	I	641	N/A
34	MFS Charter Income Trust—*Robert J Manning*	PO Box 55824, Boston MA 02205	617-954-5000	I	629	N/A
35	Newgate LLC—*Sonia Rosenbaum*	1 Sound Shore Dr, Greenwich CT 06830	203-661-0700	R	614*	<.1
36	Medallion Financial Corp—*Alvin M Murstein*	437 Madison Ave 38th F, New York NY 10022	212-328-2100	P	550	.1
37	Nuveen New York Select Quality Municipal Fund Inc—*Scott Romans*	333 W Wacker Dr, Chicago IL 60606		I	513	N/A
38	Duff and Phelps Utility and Corporate Bond Trust—*Nathan I Partain*	200 S Wacker Dr Ste 50, Chicago IL 60606		I	509	N/A
39	Putnam Managed Municipal Income Trust—*Jeffrey Sacknowitz*	PO Box 41203, Providence RI 02940	617-292-1000	I	498	N/A
40	Patriot Premium Dividend Fund I—*Keith Hartstein*	1 John Hancock Way Ste, Boston MA 02117		I	488	N/A
41	Pacific Office Properties Trust Inc—*James R Ingebritsen*	10188 Telesis Crt Ste, San Diego CA 92121	858-882-9500	P	468	.1
42	Nuveen Premier Insured Municipal Income Fund Inc—*Timothy Schwertger*	333 W Wacker Dr, Chicago IL 60606	312-917-7800	I	459	N/A
43	Nuveen New Jersey Investment Quality Municipal Fund—*Paul Brennan*	333 W Wacker Dr, Chicago IL 60606	312-917-7800	I	435	N/A
44	Banyan Rail Services Inc—*Gary O Marino*	2255 Glades Rd Ste 342, Boca Raton FL 33431	216-737-5000	I	415*	<.1
45	Mexico Fund Inc—*Jose Luis Gomez Pimienta*	1775 I St NW, Washington DC 20006	202-261-7941	P	399	N/A
46	BlackRock Income Opportunity Trust—*James Keenan*	100 Bellevue Pkwy, Wilmington DE 19809	302-797-2000	I	379	N/A
47	Nuveen Premier Municipal Income Fund—*Tim Schwertseger*	333 W Wacker Dr, Chicago IL 60606	312-917-7700	I	377	N/A
48	Nuveen New York Performance Plus Municipal Fund Inc—*Scott Romans*	333 W Wacker Dr, Chicago IL 60606	312-917-7700	I	375	N/A
49	Nuveen Pennsylvania Investment Quality Municipal Fund—*Paul L Brennen*	333 W Wacker Dr, Chicago IL 60606	312-917-7800	I	350	N/A
50	Van Kampen California Value Municipal Income Trust—*Jerry Miller*	522 5th Ave, New York NY 10036	212-762-4000	I	340	N/A
51	New Germany Fund Inc—*Michael Clark*	345 Park Ave, New York NY 10154	617-443-6918	I	298	N/A
52	Nuveen California Investment Quality Municipal Fund Inc—*Scott Romans*	333 W Wacker Dr, Chicago IL 60606		I	284	N/A
53	Nuveen California Performance Plus Municipal Fund Inc—*Scot Romans*	333 W Wacker Dr, Chicago IL 60606		I	272	N/A
54	Nuveen New Jersey Premium Income Municipal Fund Inc—*Cathryn Steeves*	333 W Wacker Dr, Chicago IL 60606	312-917-7700	I	267	N/A
55	MFS High Yield Municipal Trust—*Gary Lasman*	500 Boylston St, Boston MA 02111	617-426-3750	I	258	N/A
56	Nuveen Insured California Premium Income Municipal Fund 2 Inc—*Scott Romans*	333 W Wacker Dr, Chicago IL 60606	312-917-7700	I	257	N/A
57	Western Asset Managed High Income Fund Inc	PO Box 55214, Boston MA 02205		I	246	N/A
58	Nuveen Select Tax-Free Income Portfolio—*Thomas Spalding*	333 W Wacker Dr, Chicago IL 60606	312-917-8200	I	235	N/A
59	MFS Government Markets Income Trust—*Robert J Manning*	PO Box 55824, Boston MA 02205	617-954-5000	I	235	N/A
60	Nuveen California Municipal Value Fund Inc—*Gifford Zimmerman*	333 W Wacker Dr, Chicago IL 60606	312-917-7800	I	231	N/A
61	Nuveen Ohio Quality Income Municipal Fund Inc (Chicago Illinois)—*Dan Close*	333 W Wacker Dr, Chicago IL 60606	312-917-7700	I	230	N/A
62	John Hancock Investors Trust—*Keith Hartstein*	PO box 55913, Boston MA 02205	617-663-2844	I	226	N/A
63	Aberdeen Australia Equity Fund Inc—*Hugh Young*	800 Scudders Mill Rd, Plainsboro NJ 08536		I	211	N/A
64	Nuveen Texas Quality Income Municipal Fund Inc—*Dan Close*	333 W Wacker Dr, Chicago IL 60606		I	204	N/A
65	Boulder Growth and Income Fund Inc—*Stewart Horejsi*	2344 Spruce St Ste A, Boulder CO 80302	303-442-2156	I	200	N/A
66	Audax Group LP—*Edward Feuerstein*	101 Huntington Ave Ste, Boston MA 02199	617-859-1500	R	160*	2.9
67	Nuveen Maryland Premium Income Municipal Fund—*Thomas C Spalding*	333 W Wacker Dr, Chicago IL 60606	312-917-7700	I	157	N/A
68	Nuveen Michigan Quality Income Municipal Fund Inc—*Dan Close*	333 W Wacker Dr, Chicago IL 60606	312-917-8200	I	157	N/A
69	Nuveen New York Municipal Value Fund Inc—*Scott Romans*	333 W Wacker Dr, Chicago IL 60606		I	148	N/A
70	Transamerica Income Shares Inc—*John Carter*	570 Carillon Pkwy, Saint Petersburg FL 33716	727-299-1800	I	139	N/A
71	Van Kampen Ohio Quality Municipal Trust—*Edward Wood*	1221 Avenue of the Ame, New York NY 10036	212-762-7400	I	138	N/A
72	Nuveen Virginia Premium Income Municipal Fund—*Thomas C Spalding*	333 W Wacker Dr, Chicago IL 60606	312-917-7700	I	133	N/A
73	Singapore Fund Inc—*Ikuo Mori*	1 Evertrust Plz, Jersey City NJ 07302	201-915-3054	I	132	N/A
74	Chile Fund Inc—*Christian Pittard*	11 Madison Ave, New York NY 10010	212-325-2000	I	121	N/A
75	Nuveen California Municipal Marketing Opportunity Fund Inc—*Scott Romans*	333 W Wacker Dr, Chicago IL 60606	312-917-7800	I	114	N/A
76	Putnam High Income Securities Fund—*Charles Haldeman*	PO Box 8383, Boston MA 02114	617-760-7529	I	112	N/A
77	Nuveen Florida Quality Income Municipal Fund—*Dan Close*	333 W Wacker Dr, Chicago IL 60606		I	108	N/A
78	Ellsworth Fund Ltd—*Thomas Dinsmore*	65 Madison Ave Ste 550, Morristown NJ 07960	973-631-1177	I	106	N/A
79	Flaherty and Crumine Preferred Income Opportunity Fund Inc—*Donald Crumrine*	301 E Colorado Blvd St, Pasadena CA 91101	626-795-7300	I	105	N/A
80	Nuveen Massachusetts Premium Income Municipal Fund—*John Peter Amboian*	333 W Wacker Dr, Chicago IL 60606	312-917-7700	I	103	N/A
81	European Equity Fund Inc—*Michael Colon*	31 W 52nd St, New York NY 10019	212-469-7052	I	99	N/A
82	Jardine Fleming China Region Fund Inc—*Simon James Crinage*	PO Box 43010, Providence RI 02940		I	99	N/A
83	Templeton Russia and East European Fund Inc—*Charles Johnson*	500 Broward Blvd Ste 2, Fort Lauderdale FL 33394	954-527-7500	I	91	N/A
84	Daiwa Securities Trust Co—*Hideo Tanaka*	1 Evertrust Plz 9th Fl, Jersey City NJ 07302	201-915-3054	I	87	N/A
85	Nuveen Municipal Income Fund Inc—*Christopher Drahn*	333 W Wacker Dr, Chicago IL 60606		I	86	N/A
86	Hartford Income Shares Fund Inc—*Mark Niland*	690 Asylum Ave, Hartford CT 06105	860-547-5000	I	81	N/A
87	Nuveen California Premium Income Municipal Fund—*Scott Romans*	333 W Wacker Dr, Chicago IL 60606	312-917-7810	I	81	N/A
88	MFS Intermediate High Income Fund—*Maria Dwyer*	500 Boylston St, Boston MA 02116	617-954-5000	I	79	N/A
89	RENN Global Entrepreneurs Fund Inc—*Russell Cleveland*	8080 N Central Expwy S, Dallas TX 75206	214-891-8294	I	72*	<.1
90	Asia Tigers Fund Inc—*Prakash Melwani*	53 State St, Boston MA 02109	617-598-2000	I	71	N/A
91	Cornerstone Strategic Value Fund Inc—*Raplh W Bradshaw*	260 Madison Ave 8th Fl, New York NY 10016	646-881-4985	I	66	N/A
92	Turkish Investment Fund Inc—*Randy Takian*	522 Fifth Ave, New York NY 10036		I	56	N/A
93	Van Kampen Merritt California Municipal Trust—*Ed Wood*	1 Park View Plz, Villa Park IL 60181	630-684-6000	I	55	N/A
94	Indonesia Fund Inc—*Christian Pittard*	11 Madison Ave, New York NY 10010	212-325-2000	I	48	N/A
95	BlackRock Insured Municipal Term Trust Inc—*Theodore Jaeckel*	100 Bellvue Pkwy, Wilmington DE 19809		I	48	N/A
96	MFS Special Value Trust—*Richard J Manning*	PO BOX 55824, Boston MA 02205	617-954-5000	I	47	N/A
97	Gobal Income Fund Inc—*Thomas B Winmill*	PO Box 922, New York NY 10269	212-344-6310	I	29	N/A
98	Eagle Capital Growth Fund Inc—*Luke Sims*	205 E Wisconsin Ave, Milwaukee MI 53202	414-765-1107	I	27	N/A
99	Waterside Capital Corp—*Franklin (Lin) P Earley*	3092 Brickhouse Rd, Virginia Beach VA 23452	757-626-1111	P	26	<.1

Rank	Company Name—*Executive Officer*	Address, City, State, Zip	Phone	Type	Fin	Empls
100	Firstmark Corp—*H William Coogan Jr*	PO Box 29669, Richmond VA 23242	804-320-8001	P	17	N/A
101	Delaware Corporate Bond R Fund—*Roger Early*	2005 Market St, Philadelphia PA 19103	215-255-1200	I	13	N/A
102	EnerCorp Inc—*William Salatino*	3509 Auburn Rd, Auburn Hills MI 48326	248-683-4600	P	<1	N/A

TOTALS: SIC 6726 Investment Offices Nec
Companies: 102 — 89,069 — 4.1

6733 Trusts Nec

Rank	Company Name—*Executive Officer*	Address, City, State, Zip	Phone	Type	Fin	Empls
1	Thrivent Financial for Lutherans—*Brad Hewitt*	4321 N Ballard Rd, Appleton WI 54919	920-734-5721	R	46,723	2.9
2	America's Drive-in Trust—*J Clifford Hudson*	300 Johnny Bench Dr, Oklahoma City OK 73104	405-225-5000	S	3,897*	.3
3	Houston Trust Co—*William McCain*	1001 Fannin St Ste 700, Houston TX 77002	713-651-9400	R	2,400*	<.1
4	Trust For The Employee Welfare Benefi	435 N Michigan Ave, Chicago IL 60611	312-222-4857	R	180*	<.1
5	1199seiu Greater Ny Benefit Fund	PO Box 842, New York NY 10108	646-473-6030	R	163*	<.1
6	Kpmg LLP Health Plans Trust	PO Box 456, Pittsburgh PA 15230	212-635-1520	R	160*	<.1
7	Cnh Welfare Benefit Trust	700 State St, Racine WI 53404	262-636-6004	R	158*	<.1
8	Meijer Employee Benifits Plan and Trust	PO Box 2281, Grand Rapids MI 49501	616-453-5711	R	154*	<.1
9	Jpmorgan Chase Veba Trust For Retiree	1 Chase Pl Fl 13, New York NY 10005	212-552-2992	R	150*	<.1
10	Western Conference Of Teamsters Pension Trust Fund—*Chris Hughes*	2323 Eastlake Ave E, Seattle WA 98102	206-329-4900	R	149*	<.1
11	Teachers Health Trust—*Peter Albert*	2950 E Rochelle Ave, Las Vegas NV 89121	702-866-6133	R	149*	<.1
12	Episcopal Church Clergy And Employees Benefit Trust	445 5th Ave, New York NY 10016	212-592-1800	R	147*	<.1
13	Strategic Value Partners LLC—*Craig Klein*	100 W Putnam Ave, Greenwich CT 06830	203-618-3500	R	144*	.2
14	Environmental Capital Partners LLC—*Robert L Egan*	6 E 43rd St 20th Fl, New York NY 10017	917-262-5240	R	122*	<.1
15	Van Kampen Limited Duration A—*Jaidip Singh*	522 Fifth Ave, New York NY 10020		I	53	N/A
16	Dominion Resources Black Warrior Trust—*Ron E Hooper*	PO Box 830650, Dallas TX 75283	214-209-2400	P	17	N/A

TOTALS: SIC 6733 Trusts Nec
Companies: 16 — 54,766 — 3.4

6792 Oil Royalty Traders

Rank	Company Name—*Executive Officer*	Address, City, State, Zip	Phone	Type	Fin	Empls
1	Hugoton Royalty Trust—*Louis G Baldwin*	PO Box 830650, Dallas TX 75283		P	119	N/A
2	Tripower Resources Inc—*John D Gibbs*	PO Box 849, Ardmore OK 73402	580-226-6700	R	22*	<.1
3	Martin Franchises Inc—*Anthony Strike*	422 Wards Corner Rd, Loveland OH 45140	513-351-6211	R	20*	<.1
4	Eastern American Natural Gas Trust—*Mike Ulrich*	c/o The Bank of New Yo, Austin TX 78701		P	16	N/A
5	Dr Seuss Enterprises LP—*Audrey Geisel*	1200 Prospect St Ste 7, La Jolla CA 92037	858-459-9744	R	15*	<.1
6	Mesa Royalty Trust—*Mike Ulrich*	919 Congress Ave 5th F, Austin TX 78701	512-236-6599	I	7	N/A
7	North European Oil Royalty Trust—*John R Van Kirk*	PO Box 456, Red Bank NJ 07701	732-741-4008	P	6	<.1
8	Sabine Royalty Trust—*Ron E Hooper*	PO Box 830650, Dallas TX 75283	214-209-2400	P	5	N/A
9	Williams Coal Seam Gas Royalty Trust Inc—*Ron Hooper*	PO Box 830650, Dallas TX 75283	214-209-2400	R	5	N/A
10	Central Natural Resources Inc—*Phelps C Wood*	911 Main St Ste 1710, Kansas City MO 64105	816-842-2430	P	4	<.1
11	Tidelands Royalty Trust B—*Ron E Hooper*	901 Main St 17th Fl, Dallas TX 75202	214-508-1792	P	1	N/A
12	LL and E Royalty Trust—*Mike Ulrich*	919 Congress Ave, Austin TX 78701		P	1	N/A

TOTALS: SIC 6792 Oil Royalty Traders
Companies: 12 — 221 — <.1

6794 Patent Owners & Lessors

Rank	Company Name—*Executive Officer*	Address, City, State, Zip	Phone	Type	Fin	Empls
1	Century 21 Real Estate Corp—*Thomas Kunz*	1 Campus Dr, Parsippany NJ 07054		S	76,714*	100.0
2	Avis Budget Group Inc—*Ronald L Nelson*	6 Sylvan Way, Parsippany NJ 07054		P	10,327	21.0
3	Merry Maids LP—*Michael Isakson*	1650 Shelby Oaks drive, Memphis TN 38134	901-259-5005	S	9,383*	8.0
4	BE Intellectual Property Inc—*Amin Khoury*	1400 Corporate Center, Wellington FL 33414	561-791-5000	S	2,858*	3.5
5	DineEquity Inc—*Julia A Stewart*	450 N Brand Blvd, Glendale CA 91203	818-240-6055	P	2,857	17.7
6	Mazzio's Corp—*Gregory Lippert*	4441 S 72nd E Ave, Tulsa OK 74145	918-663-8880	R	1,956*	37.8
7	Elliott Foreign Sales Corp—*Tony Casillo*	901 N Fourth St, Jeannette PA 15644	724-527-2811	S	1,633*	2.0
8	Jiffy Lube International Inc—*Rick Altizer*	PO Box 4427, Houston TX 77210	713-546-4100	S	1,408*	26.0
9	Valenti Mid South Management LLC—*Darrell J Valenti*	1775 Mariah Woods Ste, Memphis TN 38117	901-684-1211	R	1,282*	2.0
10	Fox's Pizza Den Inc—*Jim Fox*	4425 William Penn Hwy, Murrysville PA 15668	724-733-7888	R	1,170*	2.0
11	InterDigital Inc—*William J Merritt*	781 3rd Ave, King of Prussia PA 19406	610-878-7800	P	997	.3
12	Corbis Corp—*Gary Shenk*	710 2nd Ave Ste 200, Seattle WA 98104	206-373-6000	R	939*	1.0
13	Marvel Entertainment LLC	417 5th Ave, New York NY 10016	212-576-4000	S	938	.3
14	Blue Cross and Blue Shield Association—*Scott P Serota*	225 N Michigan Ave, Chicago IL 60601	312-297-6000	R	811*	.9
15	Nautica Enterprises Inc—*John Vartos*	40 W 57th St, New York NY 10019	212-541-5757	S	694*	3.3
16	Nautica Apparel Inc—*Christopher Heyn* Nautica Enterprises Inc	11 W 19th St 11th Fl, New York NY 10011	212-206-7000	S	580	.5
17	Coverall Cleaning Concepts—*Laura J Hendricks*	5201 Congress Ave Ste2, Boca Raton FL 33487	561-922-2500	R	500*	.5
18	International Dairy Queen Inc	7505 Metro Blvd, Minneapolis MN 55439	952-896-8696	S	460*	.7
19	Fired Up Inc—*Creed Ford*	7500 Rialto Blvd Ste 2, Austin TX 78735	512-263-0800	R	450*	.4
20	VICORP Restaurants Inc—*Hazem Ouf*	400 W 48th Ave, Denver CO 80216	303-296-2121	R	395	N/A
21	GNC Franchising Inc—*Joseph Fortunato*	300 6th Ave, Pittsburgh PA 15222	412-338-2503	S	362*	.6
22	Acacia Research Corp—*Paul Ryan*	500 Newport Center Dr, Newport Beach CA 92660	949-480-8300	P	353	.1
23	Jackson Hewitt Tax Services Inc—*Philip Sanford*	3 Sylvan Way Ste 301, Parsippany NJ 07054	973-630-1040	R	346	.3
24	Tower Cleaning Systems—*Ivan Dubow*	PO Box 2468, Southeastern PA 19399	610-278-9000	R	290*	.4
25	Broadcast Music Inc—*Del Bryant*	10 Music Sq E, Nashville TN 37203	615-401-2000	R	289*	.5
26	Tass Enterprises Inc—*Steve Nelson*	808 13th St Ste 3, West Des Moines IA 50265	515-224-4646	R	274*	.3
27	Sonic Industries Inc (Oklahoma City Oklahoma)	300 Johnny Bench Dr St, Oklahoma City OK 73104	405-280-7654	S	207*	.3
28	Copyright Clearance Center Inc—*Tracey L Armstrong*	222 Rosewood Dr, Danvers MA 01923	978-750-8400	R	197*	.2
29	Fed USA Inc—*Michael Braun*	8960 Taft St, Pembroke Pines FL 33024	954-581-9893	R	193*	.2
30	Carlcin Restaurants—*Cindy Grimm*	448 Lakeshore Pkwy Ste, Rock Hill SC 29730	803-329-5180	R	188*	.3
31	Valvoline Instant Oil Change Franchising Inc	3499 Blazer Pky, Lexington KY 40509		D	185*	4.0
32	Prudential Real Estate Affiliates Inc—*John R Strangfeld Jr*	3333 Michelson Dr Ste, Irvine CA 92612	949-794-7900	S	172*	.2
33	EMI Christian Music Group—*Bill Hern*	PO Box 5084, Brentwood TN 37024	615-371-4300	S	156*	.2
34	Clark Brands LLC—*Pat Enright*	1601 Bond St Ste 103, Naperville IL 60563	630-355-8918	R	144*	3.2
35	Arby's Restaurant Group Inc—*Hala Moddelmog*	1155 Perimeter Ctr W 1, Atlanta GA 30338	678-514-4100	S	142*	.2
36	Big O Tires Inc (Englewood Colorado)—*John Adams*	12650 E Briarwood Ave, Englewood CO 80112	303-728-5500	S	125*	.5
37	Strings Inc—*Al DeCaprio*	11344 Coloma Rd, Gold River CA 95670	916-635-6465	R	113*	.2
38	NBC Universal Network Television	100 Universal City Plz, Universal City CA 91608	818-840-4444	D	105*	.1
39	Realty Executives International Inc—*Richard A Rector*	7600 N 16th St Ste 100, Phoenix AZ 85020	602-957-0747	R	105*	.1
40	Cotton Inc—*J Berrye Worsham III*	6399 Weston Pkwy, Cary NC 27513	919-678-2220	R	103*	.2
41	Clockwork Home Services Inc—*Jim Abrams*	50 Central Ave Ste 920, Sarasota FL 34236	941-366-9692	R	103*	.1
42	Supercuts Inc—*Jackie Lang*	7201 Metro Blvd, Minneapolis MN 55439	952-947-7777	D	101*	5.0
43	Papa Murphy's Pizza—*John Barr*	8000 NE Pkwy Dr Ste 35, Vancouver WA 98662	360-260-7272	R	100*	.1
44	Jazzercise Inc—*Judi Sheppard-Missett*	2460 Impala Dr, Carlsbad CA 92010	760-476-1750	R	96	.2

Note: An asterisk (*) indicates an estimated financial figure. The company type code used is as follows: R = Private, P = Public, S = Private Subsidiary, B = Public Subsidiary, D = Division, J = Joint Venture, I = Investment Fund.

RANKINGS BY SALES WITHIN 4-DIGIT SIC

	Company Name—*Executive Officer*	Address, City, State, Zip	Phone	Type	Fin	Empls
	SESAC Inc—*Stephen Swid*	55 Music Sq E, Nashville TN 37203	615-320-0055	R	95	.1
46	Great Clips Inc—*Rhoda Olsen*	7700 France Ave S Ste, Minneapolis MN 55435	952-893-9088	R	94*	.1
47	ePlus Content Services Inc—*Phillip Norton*	13595 Dulles Technolog, Herndon VA 20171	703-984-8400	S	83	.1
48	Raving Brands Inc—*Martin Sprock*	1801 Peachtree Rd Ste, Atlanta GA 30309	404-355-5400	R	67*	.1
49	OCH International Inc—*John E Shepanek*	1200 NW Naito Pkwy Ste, Portland OR 97209	503-243-6311	R	66*	.1
50	1800mattresscom—*Napoleon Barragan*	3110 48th Ave, Long Island City NY 11101		R	65	.3
51	Meineke Car Care Centers Inc—*Kenneth D Walker*	128 S Tryon St Ste 900, Charlotte NC 28202	704-377-8855	R	63*	.1
52	Steak-Out Franchising Inc—*Donald Harkleroad*	6801 Governors Lake Dr, Norcross GA 30071		R	61	2.2
53	ePlus Systems Inc—*Phillip Norton*	13595 Dulles Technolog, Herndon VA 20171	703-984-8400	S	58	.1
54	UniShippers Association Inc—*Dan Lockwood*	746 E Winchester St, Salt Lake City UT 84107	801-708-5800	R	58*	.1
55	TVT Records Inc	23 E 4th St 3rd Fl, New York NY 10003	212-979-6410	S	57*	.1
56	Budget Blinds Inc—*Chad Haddock*	1927 N Glassell St, Orange CA 92865	714-637-2100	R	56*	.1
57	Choice Capital Corp—*Stephen P Joyce*	10750 Columbia Pke, Silver Spring MD 20901	301-592-5000	S	55*	.1
58	Hungry Howie's Pizza and Subs Inc—*Steve Jackson*	30300 Stephenson Hwy, Madison Heights MI 48071	248-414-3300	R	54*	.1
59	Dwyer Group Inc—*Dina Dwyer-Ownes*	PO Box 3146, Waco TX 76707	254-745-2400	S	53*	.3
60	Melting Pot Restaurants Inc—*Mike Lester*	8810 Twin Lakes Blvd, Tampa FL 33614	813-881-0055	R	43*	.1
61	Pizza Inn Inc—*Charles Morrison*	3551 Plano Pky, The Colony TX 75056	469-384-5000	P	41	.2
62	Warner Brothers Records Inc—*Barry Meyer*	3300 Warner Blvd, Burbank CA 91505	818-846-9090	S	40*	.4
63	Medicine Shoppe International Inc—*Terry Burnside*	1 Rider Trl Pl Dr Ste3, Earth City MO 63045	314-993-6000	S	38*	.2
64	Music Theatre International—*Freddie Gershon*	421 W 54th St, New York NY 10019	212-541-4684	R	38*	.1
65	Fantastic Sams—*Scott Colabuono*	50 Dunham Rd 3rd Fl, Beverly MA 01915	978-232-5626	R	38*	.1
66	Payless Car Rental System Inc—*Richard L Stevens*	PO Box 66609, Saint Petersburg FL 33713	727-321-6352	S	37*	.1
67	Sport Clips Inc—*Gordon Logan*	110 Briarwood Dr, Georgetown TX 78628	512-930-5111	R	35*	<.1
68	American Leak Detection Inc—*Stan Berenbaum*	PO Box 1701, Palm Springs CA 92263	760-320-9991	S	34*	<.1
69	Convenient Food Mart Inc—*John Call*	467 N State St, Painesville OH 44077	440-354-5500	R	32	.3
70	Leros Associates Inc—*John Nichols*	6 Skyline Dr, Hawthorne NY 10532	914-747-2300	R	32*	<.1
71	Rounder Records Corp—*Marian Leighton-Levy*	1 Rounder Way, Burlington MA 01803	617-354-0700	R	31*	.1
72	Harris Research Inc—*Robert Harris*	1530 N 1000 W, Logan UT 84321	435-755-0099	R	31*	.1
73	4Kids Entertainment Inc—*Samuel R Newborn*	53 W 23rd St, New York NY 10010	212-758-7666	P	29	.1
74	Christian Dior Inc—*Patricia Malone*	712 5th Ave, New York NY 10019	212-582-0500	S	29*	.1
75	Brewster's Franchise Corp—*Michael W Evans*	500 Lake Cook Rd Ste 4, Deerfield IL 60015	847-948-7520	S	29*	<.1
76	Abbey Carpet Co—*Phillip Gutierrez*	3471 Bonita Bay Blvd, Bonita Springs FL 34134	239-948-0900	R	28*	<.1
77	Capitol Nashville Inc—*Mike Dungan*	3322 W End Ave, Nashville TN 37203	615-269-2000	S	27*	<.1
78	Pepe's Inc—*Robert Ptak*	1325 W 15th St, Chicago IL 60608	312-733-2500	R	23*	<.1
79	Maids International Inc—*Daniel J Bishop*	4820 Dodge St, Omaha NE 68132	402-558-5555	R	21*	.2
80	Sir Speedy Inc—*Don Lowe*	26722 Plz Dr, Mission Viejo CA 92691	949-348-5000	S	21*	.1
81	Choice Systems Inc—*Cathy Marcum*	9960 Corporate Campus, Louisville KY 40223	502-357-6300	R	21*	<.1
82	Amerimac Cal-West Financial—*Phillip Pitts*	1725 S Bascom Ave Ste1, Campbell CA 95008	408-559-4444	R	20*	<.1
83	Hobby Town USA—*Merlin Hayes*	6301 S 58th St, Lincoln NE 68516		R	19*	<.1
84	Physicians Weight Loss Centers of America Inc—*Charles E Sekeres*	83 N Miller Rd Ste 101, Fairlawn OH 44333	330-666-7952	R	19*	<.1
85	HME Providers Inc—*Surinder Guliani*	2320 E Little Creek Rd, Norfolk VA 23518	757-588-1487	R	18*	<.1
86	Colortyme Inc—*Robert Bloom*	5000 Legacy Dr Ste 210, Plano TX 75024	972-403-4900	S	18*	<.1
87	Jersey Mike's Franchise Systems Inc—*Peter Cancro*	2251 Landmark Pl, Manasquan NJ 08736	732-223-4044	R	18*	<.1
88	Mamma Ilardo's Corp—*Harry Ilardo*	28 Allegheny Ave Ste 1, Towson MD 21204	410-296-9104	R	18*	<.1
89	BAB Systems Inc—*Michael W Evans*	500 Lake Cook Rd Ste 4, Deerfield IL 60015	847-948-7520	S	17*	<.1
90	Inland Homebuilding Group Inc—*James R Clark*	6522 Gunn Hwy, Tampa FL 33625	813-886-2433	R	17*	<.1
91	Fastframe USA Inc—*Brian Harper*	1200 Lawrence Dr Ste 3, Newbury Park CA 91320	805-498-4463	R	17*	<.1
92	United Media Licensing Co—*Douglas Stern*	200 Madison Ave 4th Fl, New York NY 10016	212-293-8500	D	16*	.2
93	Gold's Gym International Inc	125 E John Carpenter F, Irving TX 75062	214-296-5062	R	16*	<.1
94	Barbizon International Inc—*Debra Hall*	3111 N University Dr S, Coral Springs FL 33065	954-345-4140	R	15*	<.1
95	Escape Enterprises Ltd—*Mark Turner*	222 Nielston St, Columbus OH 43215	614-224-0300	R	15*	<.1
96	Shanachie Entertainment Corp—*Richard Nevins*	37 E Clinton St, Newton NJ 07860		R	15*	<.1
97	NeuMedia Inc (Los Angeles California)—*Peter Adderton*	4751 Wilshire Blvd 3rd, Los Angeles CA 90010	310-601-2500	B	14	.2
98	HouseMaster of America Inc—*Kenneth T Austin*	421 W Union Ave, Bound Brook NJ 08805	732-469-6565	R	14*	<.1
99	Shakey's Inc—*Joe Remsa*	2200 W Valley Blvd, Alhambra CA 91803	626-576-0616	R	14*	<.1
100	U-Save Auto Rental of America Inc—*Tom McDonnell*	4780 I-55 N Ste 300 Le, Jackson MS 39211	601-713-4333	R	13*	<.1
101	Wetzel's Pretzels LLC—*William Phelps*	35 Hugus Alley Ste 300, Pasadena CA 91103	626-432-6900	R	13*	<.1
102	Cherry Lane Music Publishing Company Inc—*Peter Primont*	6 E 32nd St Fl 11, New York NY 10016	212-561-3000	R	12*	.1
103	Golden Southern Chicken Corp—*Mike Jensen*	11488 Luna Rd, Dallas TX 75234	972-831-0911	R	12*	.1
104	Heel Quik Inc—*Raymond Margiano*	2359 Windy Hill Rd Ste, Marietta GA 30067	770-951-9440	R	12*	.1
105	Rico's Pizza Inc—*Daniel E Ryhal*	171 W Main St, Woodland CA 95695	530-666-7809	R	12*	<.1
106	Wild Bird Centers of America Inc—*Henrik Lehmann*	7370 MacArthur Blvd, Glen Echo MD 20812	301-229-9585	R	12*	<.1
107	Double F Foods LLC—*Murry Gast*	302 Shelley St Ste 2, Springfield OR 97477	541-744-1093	R	11*	.1
108	Minuteman Press International Inc—*Robert Titus*	61 Executive Blvd, Farmingdale NY 11735	631-249-1370	R	11*	.1
109	Chiropractic USA Inc—*Michael Gelmon*	1925 Century Pk E Ste, Los Angeles CA 90067		S	11*	<.1
110	Monday Morning America Inc—*Suzanne Schmidt*	276 White Oak Ridge Rd, Bridgewater NJ 08807	908-668-6840	R	11*	<.1
111	Omni Optical Lab—*Gregory Segall*	4925 W Cardinal Dr, Beaumont TX 77705	409-842-4113	R	10*	.1
112	Environmental Biotech Inc—*William F Hadley*	4693 19th St Ct E, Bradenton FL 34203	941-757-2591	R	10*	<.1
113	United States Arbitration and Mediation Inc—*Diane McGaha*	600 University St, Seattle WA 98101	206-467-0793	R	10*	<.1
114	Tubby's Inc—*Robert Paganes*	18357 E 14 Mile Rd, Fraser MI 48026	586-293-5099	R	10	.1
115	Microtel Inns and Suites—*Ted Torres*	22 Sylvan Way, Parsippany NJ 07054	973-753-6000	S	9*	.2
116	Steamatic Inc—*Bill Sims*	3333 Quorum Dr Ste 280, Fort Worth TX 76137	817-332-1575	S	9*	<.1
117	Nancy Bailey and Associates Inc—*Nell Roney*	1403 Macy Dr, Roswell GA 30076	678-352-1000	S	9*	<.1
118	Dollar Rent A Car Systems Inc—*Gary L Paxton*	PO Box 35985, Tulsa OK 74135		S	8	N/A
119	Oil Express National Inc—*Arthur Lukowski*	15 Spinning Wheel Rd S, Hinsdale IL 60521	630-325-8666	R	8*	.1
120	Fleet Feet Inc—*Tom Raynor*	PO Box 789, Carrboro NC 27510	919-942-3102	R	8*	<.1
121	Golden Franchising Corp—*Mark S Parmerlee* Golden Southern Chicken Corp	1131 Rockingham Ste250, Richardson TX 75080	972-831-0911	S	8*	<.1
122	US Franchise Systems Inc—*Michael A Leven*	13 Corporate Sq Ste250, Atlanta GA 30329	404-321-4045	S	7*	.1
123	Round Table Franchise Corp—*Jim Fletcher*	1320 Willow Pass Rd St, Concord CA 94520	925-969-3900	R	7*	.1
124	Fiducial Century Small Business Solutions Inc	1370 Ave of the Americ, New York NY 10019	212-207-4700	S	7*	.1
125	Hydromer Inc—*Manfred F Dyck*	35 Industrial Pky, Branchburg NJ 08876	908-722-5000	P	7	<.1
126	Sugar Hill Records Inc—*Barry Poss*	PO Box 55300, Durham NC 27717		R	7*	.1
127	Dominion Entertainment Inc—*Philip Kives*	2491 Xenium Ln N, Plymouth MN 55441	763-559-5566	S	6*	.1
128	Ralph Lauren Home—*Ralph Lauren*	650 Madison Ave, New York NY 10022	212-642-8700	D	6*	.1
129	ADTI Media LLC—*James P Martindale*	42230 Zevo Dr, Temecula CA 92590	951-795-4446	R	6	<.1
130	LubePro's International Inc—*Dave Carbonell*	1740 S Bell School Rd, Cherry Valley IL 61016	815-332-9200	R	5*	.1
131	Contours Express Inc—*Bill Helton*	156 Imperial Way, Nicholasville KY 40356	859-241-2230	R	5*	<.1
132	Sanford Rose Associates (Akron Ohio)—*Richard L Carter*	265 S Main St, Akron OH 44308	330-762-0279	R	5*	<.1

Company Rankings by Sales within 4-Digit SIC

Rank	Company Name—Executive Officer	Address, City, State, Zip	Phone	Type	Fin	Empls
	El Centro Foods Inc—Robert Ohanian	6930 1/2 Tujunga Ave, North Hollywood CA 91605	818-766-4395	R	5*	<.1
137	Competitive Technologies Inc—Johnnie D Johnson	1375 Kings Hwy, Fairfield CT 06824	203-368-6044	P	5	<.1
138	Beach Franchising Corp—Stephen Smith	5145 Taravella Rd, Marrero LA 70072	504-361-5550	R	4	<.1
139	Marvest Franchising Inc—Mike Ferretti	28 S Montana St, Dillon MT 59725	406-683-6842	R	4*	<.1
140	Bag Onction and Consulting Services	626 Jacksonville Rd, Warminster PA 18974	215-953-9200	R	4*	<.1
141	Rent-A-Whitters LP—John Clark	8002 E Brainerd Rd, Chattanooga TN 37421		R	4*	<.1
142	Bay State Cho Michael Haith	5445 DTC Pkwy Ste 1050, Greenwood Village CO 80111	303-781-7800	R	4*	<.1
143	N-Viro International Ono	110 W 79th St, New York NY 10024	212-595-5537	R	4	<.1
144	Carlin America Inc—Fic Inc—Kenneth L Blum Sr	105 Main St, Laurel MD 20707	240-581-1350	R	4*	<.1
145	Duraclean International Inc—Richard Lamattina	101 Phoenix Ave, Lowell MA 01852	978-970-1144	P	3	<.1
146	Arthur Murray International Inc	3450 W Central Ave Ste, Toledo OH 43606	419-535-6374	R	3*	<.1
147	Virginia Tech Intellectual Properties Marello	126 E 38th St, New York NY 10016	212-779-7977	R	3*	<.1
148	World Gym Licensing Ltd—Michael Urems	220 W Campus Dr Ste A, Arlington Heights IL 60004	847-704-7100	R	3*	<.1
149	Creative Licensing Corp—Rand Marlis Coburn	1077 Ponce De Leon Blv, Coral Gables FL 33134	305-445-9645	R	3*	<.1
150	Stark Encapsulation Inc—J Norman Stark	2200 Kraft Dr Ste 1050, Blacksburg VA 24060	540-951-9374	R	3*	<.1
151	Rex Fine Foods—John Adams	3223 Washington Blvd, Marina Del Rey CA 90292	310-827-7705	R	3*	<.1
152	Bonjour Group Ltd—Charles Dayan	2551 S Bundy Dr, Los Angeles CA 90064	310-479-6777	R	3*	.1
153	Amailcenter Franchise Corp—Michael Sawitz	1310 E 49th St, Cleveland OH 44114	216-426-8400	R	3*	.1
154	Dr Vinyl and Associates Ltd—Tom Buckley Jr	PO Box 1726, Gonzales TX 78629	504-602-9487	R	3*	.1
155	Stewart's Restaurants Supply—Jerry Stewart	1441 Broadway 26th Fl, New York NY 10018	212-398-1000	R	2*	<.1
156	Western Design Center Inc—William Mensch	2050 D Rockfield Blvd, Irvine CA 92618	949-837-4151	R	2*	<.1
157	Moxie Java International Inc—Rick Dean	PO Box Victoria Dr, Lees Summit MO 64086	816-525-6060	R	2*	<.1
158	MGW Group Inc—Gwen Willhite	2166 E Brs, Hot Springs AR 71902	501-623-9299	R	2*	<.1
159	Kirin Pharma USA Inc—Junichi Koumegawa	4990 W Chind Rd, Mesa AZ 85213	480-962-4545	R	2*	<.1
160	Bliss House Inc—Jerome L Houle III	1865 Summit Avd St, Boise ID 83714	208-246-8500	S	1*	<.1
161	Lorie Line Music Inc—Lorie Line	9420 Athena Cir, La 60, Plano TX 75074	972-398-9536	R	1	<.1
162	New Albion Records Inc	785 Williams St Ste 22, CA 92037	858-952-7000	S	1	<.1
163	Micro Identification Technologies Inc—Michael W Brennan	222 Minnetonka Ave S, Wayzmeadow MA 01106		R	1*	<.1
		22 Friendship St, Tivoli NY 1258, MN 55391	952-474-1000	R	1*	<.1
164	SaviCorp—Serge Monros	970 Calle Amanecer Ste, San Clemente CA 92673	518-755-4609	R	1*	<.1
		2530 S Birch St, Santa Ana CA 92707	949-388-4546	P	<1	<.1
			714-312-5352	P	<1	N/A

TOTALS: SIC 6794 Patent Owners & Lessors
Companies: 164

					123,166	253.5

6798 Real Estate Investment Trusts

Rank	Company Name—Executive Officer	Address, City, State, Zip	Phone	Type	Fin	Empls
1	MFS Investment Management—Robert Manning	PO Box 55824, Boston MA 02205	617-954-5000	I	172,000	2.3
2	INVESCO Mortgage Capital Inc—Richard J King	1360 Peachtree St NE, Atlanta GA 30309	404-892-0896	S	106,383*	.3
3	Home Properties Fentil Inc—Ed J Pettinella, Home Properties Inc	850 Clinton Sq, Rochester NY 14604	585-546-4900	S	90,773*	2.0
4	Annaly Capital Management Inc—Michael A J Farrell	1211 Avenue of the Ame, New York NY 10036	212-696-0100	I	83,027	.1
5	Hudson City Preferred Funding Corp—Ronald E Hermance Jr	W 80 Century Rd, Paramus NJ 07652	201-967-1900	S	73,624*	1.5
6	GE Capital Real Estate—Mark Begor	901 Main Ave, Norwalk CT 06851		S	52,881*	1.1
7	General Growth Properties Inc—Sandeep Mathrani	110 N Wacker Dr, Chicago IL 60606	312-960-5000	P	32,367	2.8
8	Home Properties Southern Meadows LLC, Home Properties Inc	850 Clinton Sq, Rochester NY 14604	585-546-4900	S	30,772*	.7
9	Simon Property Group Inc—David Simon	225 W Washington St, Indianapolis IN 46204	317-636-1600	P	27,192	5.9
10	Hometown America—Richard Cline	150 North Wacker Dr St, Chicago IL 60606	312-604-7500	R	21,394*	.5
11	Centerline Capital Group—Marc D Schnitzer	625 Madison Ave, New York NY 10022	212-317-5700	S	20,992*	.5
12	Vornado Realty Trust—Michael D Fascitelli	888 7th Ave, New York NY 10019	212-894-7000	P	20,500	4.8
13	Schnitzer Investment Corp—Robert Phillip	1211 SW 5th Ave Ste 22, Portland OR 97204	503-595-8100	R	19,182*	.4
14	Hatteras Financial Corp—Michael R Hough	110 Oakwood Dr Ste 340, Winston-Salem NC 27103	366-760-9331	P	18,587	N/A
15	Arborview LLC—Thomas Herlache	217 N 4th Ave, Sturgeon Bay WI 54235	920-743-5551	S	17,458*	.4
16	Equity Residential—David J Neithercut	2 N Riverside Plz Ste, Chicago IL 60606	312-474-1300	P	16,184	4.0
17	AERC Oak Bend Inc, Associated Estates Realty Corp	1 AEC Pky, Richmond Heights OH 44143	216-261-5000	S	15,461*	.4
18	ProLogis—Hamid R Moghadam	Pier 1 Bay 1, San Francisco CA 94133	415-394-9000	P	14,903	1.1
19	Weingarten Properties Trust—Andrew M Alexander, Weingarten Realty Investors	PO Box 924133, Houston TX 77292	713-866-6000	S	14,566*	.3
20	American Capital Agency Corp—Malon Wilkus	2 Bethesda Metro Ctr 1, Bethesda MD 20814	301-968-9300	P	14,476	N/A
21	Boston Properties Inc—Mortimer B Zuckerman	800 Boylston St, Boston MA 02199	617-236-3300	P	13,348	.7
22	Archstone-Smith Trust—R Scot Sellers	9200 E Panorama Cir St, Englewood CO 80112	303-708-5959	R	13,259	2.7
23	Arden Realty Inc—Joaquin DeMonet	11601 Wilshire Blvd St, Los Angeles CA 90025	310-966-2600	S	13,065*	.3
24	MFA Financial Inc—Stewart Zimmerman	350 Park Ave 21st Fl, New York NY 10022	212-207-6400	P	11,751	<.1
25	SL Green Realty Corp—Marc Holliday	420 Lexington Ave, New York NY 10170	212-594-2700	P	11,300	1.0
26	ProLogis First GP LLC, ProLogis	4545 Airport Way, Denver CO 80239	303-567-5000	S	11,033*	.2
27	Kimco Realty Corp—David B Henry	3333 New Hyde Park Rd, New Hyde Park NY 11042	516-869-9000	I	9,833	.4
28	CYS Investments Inc—Kevin E Grant	890 Winter St, Waltham MA 02451	617-639-0440	P	9,518	<.1
29	Public Storage—Ronald L Havner Jr	PO Box 25050, Glendale CA 91221	818-244-8080	P	9,495	4.9
30	Health Care REIT Inc—George L Chapman	4500 Dorr St, Toledo OH 43615	419-247-2800	I	9,452	.3
31	HRT of Alabama Inc—David R Emery, Healthcare Realty Trust Inc	3310 West End Ave Ste, Nashville TN 37203	615-269-8175	S	9,198*	.2
32	KKR Financial Holdings LLC—William C Sonneborn	555 California St 50th, San Francisco CA 94104	415-315-3620	P	8,647	N/A
33	Two Harbors Investment Corp—Thomas Siering	601 Carlson Pky Ste 15, Minnetonka MN 55305	612-629-2500	P	8,100	N/A
34	Macerich Co—Arthur M Coppola	401 Wilshire Blvd Ste, Santa Monica CA 90401	310-394-6000	P	7,939	1.4
35	AvalonBay Communities Inc—Bryce Blair	671 N Glebe Rd Ste 800, Arlington VA 22203	703-329-6300	P	7,822	2.0
36	Equity Office Properties Trust—Tom August	2 N Riverside Plz, Chicago IL 60606	312-466-3300	S	7,539*	.7
37	iStar Financial Inc—Jay Sugarman	1114 Ave of the Americ, New York NY 10036	212-930-9400	P	7,518	.2
38	Developers Diversified Realty Corp—Daniel B Hurwitz	3300 Enterprise Pkwy, Beachwood OH 44122	216-755-5500	P	7,469	.6
39	CommonWealth REIT—Adam D Portnoy	2 Newton Pl 255 Washin, Newton MA 02458	617-332-3990	P	7,447	N/A
40	Apartment Investment and Management Co—Terry Considine	4582 S Ulster St Ste11, Denver CO 80237	303-757-8101	P	7,379	3.1
41	Duke Realty Corp—Dennis D Oklak	600 E 96th St Ste 100, Indianapolis IN 46240	317-808-6000	P	7,004	.9
42	HomeBanc Corp—Kevin Race	2002 Summit Blvd Ste 1, Atlanta GA 30319	404-303-4000	R	6,823	1.2
43	CBL and Associates Properties Inc—Stephen D Lebovitz	2030 Hamilton Pl Blvd, Chattanooga TN 37421	423-855-0001	P	6,719	.9
44	Alexandria Real Estate Equities Inc—Joel S Marcus	385 E Colorado Blvd St, Pasadena CA 91101	626-396-4828	P	6,574	.2
45	National Golf Properties Inc—Paul Major	2951 28th St Ste 3001, Santa Monica CA 90405	310-664-4000	R	6,312*	.1
46	Douglas Emmett Inc—Jordan L Kaplan	808 Wilshire Blvd 2nd, Santa Monica CA 90401	310-255-7700	P	6,232	.5
47	Digital Realty Trust Inc—Michael F Foust	560 Mission St Ste 290, San Francisco CA 94105	415-738-6500	P	6,099	.5

Note: An asterisk (*) indicates an estimated financial figure. The company type code used is as follows: R = Private, P = Public, S = Private Subsidiary, B = Public Subsidiary, D = Division, J = Joint Venture, I = Investment Fund.

RANKINGS BY SALES WITHIN 4-DIGIT SIC

	Company Name—Executive Officer	Address, City, State, Zip	Phone	Type		
48	Ventas Inc—Debra A Cafaro	111 S Wacker Dr Ste 48, Chicago IL 60606			.5	
49	Redwood Trust Inc—Martin S Hughes	1 Belvedere Pl Ste 300, Mill Valley CA 94941	312-660-3800		5,492	.1
50	Gramercy Capital Corp—Roger M Cozzi	420 Lexington Ave, New York NY 10170	415-389-737		5,214*	.1
51	AERC Broker of Texas Inc—Jeffrey Friedman	1 AEC Pkwy, Richmond Heights OH 44143	212-297-1	I	5,133	1.4
	Associated Estates Realty Corp		216-260			
52	United Dominion Realty Trust Inc—Thomas W Toomey	1745 Shea Center Dr, Highlands Ranch CO 80129		P	4,893	.1
53	CIFC Corp—Peter Gleysteen	250 Park Ave 5th Fl, New York NY 10177	-6000	P	4,588	.4
54	Weingarten Realty Investors—Andrew M Alexander	PO Box 924133, Houston TX 77292	325-5600	P	4,558	.4
55	Brandywine Realty Trust—Gerard H Sweeney	555 E Lancaster Ave St, Radnor PA 19087	770-418-8800	P	4,448	.1
56	Piedmont Office Realty Trust—Donald A Miller	11695 Johns Creek Pky, Duluth GA 30097	858-485-9840	P	4,429	.2
57	BioMed Realty Trust Inc—Alan D Gold	17190 Bernardo Center, San Diego CA 92128	760-741-2111	P	4,419	.1
58	Realty Income Corp—Tomas A Lewis	600 La Terraza Blvd, Escondido CA 92025	617-796-8350	P	4,383	N/A
59	Senior Housing Properties Trust—David J Hegerty	2 Newton Pl 255 Washin, Newton MA 024	732-590-1000	P	4,296	.4
60	Mack-Cali Realty Corp—Mitchell E Hersh	PO Box 7817, Edison NJ 08818	585-546-4900	P	4,153	1.1
61	Home Properties Inc—Edward J Pettinella	850 Clinton Sq, Rochester NY 1460 2202	904-598-7000	P	3,974	.4
62	Regency Centers Corp—Martin E Stein Jr	One Independent Dr Ste, Jacks	312-443-1477	R	3,871*	.9
63	Amli Residential Properties Trust—Gregory T Mutz	125 S Wacker Dr Ste 31, Chi d MD 21046	443-285-5400	P	3,868	.4
64	Corporate Office Properties Trust Inc—Randall M Griffin	6711 Columbia Gateway, ngeles CA 90025	310-478-4456	S	3,830	N/A
65	Westfield America Inc—Peter Lowry	11601 Wilshire Blvd 12, 10022	212-810-3333	P	3,827	N/A
66	Anthracite Capital Inc—Chris A Milner	40 E 52nd St, New York 92606	949-856-8300	D	3,780	.7
67	ECC Capital Corp—Shabi S Asghar	1833 Alton Pkwy, Irvine York NY 10022	212-547-2600	P	3,722	.1
68	NorthStar Realty Finance Corp—David T Hamamoto	399 Park Ave 18te 40, Chicago IL 60606	312-344-4300	S	3,663*	.1
69	First Industrial Florida Finance Corp—Bruce Duncan	311 S Wacker				
	First Industrial Realty Trust Inc	erson St, Rockville MD 20852	301-998-8100	P	3,660	.4
70	Federal Realty Investment Trust—Donald Wood	1626 e of the Americ, New York NY 10105	212-798-6100	P	3,613	N/A
71	Newcastle Investment Corp—R Edens	134 Riverside Plz Ste, Chicago IL 60606	312-279-1400	P	3,496	3.5
72	Equity Lifestyle Properties Inc—Thomas P Heneghan	180 N Michigan Ave Ste, Chicago IL 60601	312-726-9622	R	3,459*	.1
73	M and J Wilkow Ltd—Mark R Wilkow	525 Market St 4th Fl, San Francisco CA 94105	415-445-6530	P	3,353	.7
74	BRE Properties Inc—Constance B Moore	2101 6th Ave N Ste 750, Birmingham AL 35203	205-250-8700	P	3,259	1.0
75	Colonial Properties Trust—Thomas H Lowder	11620 Wilshire Blvd10t, Los Angeles CA 90025	310-470-2600	R	3,095*	.1
76	SCI Real Estate Investments LLC—Marc Paul	200 S Broad St, Philadelphia PA 19102	215-875-0700	I	3,080	.7
77	Pennsylvania Real Estate Investment Trust—Ronald Rubin	1 Penn Plz Ste 4015, New York NY 10119	212-692-7200	P	3,078	.1
78	Lexington Realty Trust—T Wilson Eglin	805 Las Cimas Pkwy Ste, Austin TX 78746	512-732-1000	P	3,009	2.4
79	American Campus Communities Inc—William C Bayless Jr	1004 Farnam St, Omaha NE 68102	402-444-1630	S	3,006*	.1
80	Agribusiness Management Company LLC—Robert Peyton					
	Burlington Capital Group					
81	Shurgard Storage Centers Inc—David K Grant	1155 Valley St Ste 400, Seattle WA 98109	206-624-8100	S	2,957*	2.3
	Public Storage					
82	RAIT Financial Trust—Scott F Schaeffer	Cira Ctr 2929 Arch St, Philadelphia PA 19104	215-243-9000	P	2,903	.4
83	DCT Industrial Trust Inc—Phillip L Hawkins	518 17th St Fl 8, Denver CO 80202	303-228-2200	R	2,850	N/A
84	LaSalle Hotel Properties—Michael D Barnello	3 Bethesda Metro Ctr S, Bethesda MD 20814	301-941-1500	P	2,833	<.1
85	Entertainment Properties Trust—David Brain	909 Walnut St Ste 200, Kansas City MO 64106		I	2,803*	<.1
86	Spirit Finance Corp—Christopher H Volk	14631 N Scottsdale Rd, Scottsdale AZ 85254	480-606-0820	R	2,787*	<.1
87	First Industrial Realty Trust Inc—Bruce Duncan	311 S Wacker Dr Ste 40, Chicago IL 60606	312-344-4300	P	2,667	.2
88	National Retail Properties—Craig Macnab	450 S Orange Ave Ste 9, Orlando FL 32801	407-265-7348	I	2,591	.1
89	Dynex Capital Inc—Thomas B Akin	4991 Lake Brook Dr Ste, Glen Allen VA 23060	804-217-5800	P	2,582	<.1
90	Omega Healthcare Investors Inc—C Taylor Pickett	200 International Cir, Hunt Valley MD 21030	410-427-1700	P	2,557	<.1
91	Taubman Centers Inc—Robert S Taubman	PO Box 200, Bloomfield Hills MI 48303	248-258-6800	P	2,547	.6
92	Mid-America Apartment Communities Inc—H Eric Bolton Jr	6584 Poplar Ave, Memphis TN 38138	901-682-6600	P	2,531	1.4
93	Extra Space Storage Inc—Spencer F Kirk	2795 E Cottonwood Pkwy, Salt Lake City UT 84121	801-562-5556	P	2,485	2.1
94	National Penn Investors Trust Co—James King	2201 Ridgewood Rd Ste, Wyomissing PA 19610	610-372-6414	S	2,484*	.1
95	DiamondRock Hospitality Co—Mark W Brugger	3 Bethesda Metro Cente, Bethesda MD 20814	240-744-1150	P	2,415	<.1
96	FelCor Lodging Trust Inc—Richard A Smith	545 E John Carpenter F, Irving TX 75062	972-444-4900	P	2,359	.1
97	Healthcare Realty Trust Inc—David R Emery	3310 West End Ave Ste, Nashville TN 37203	615-269-8175	P	2,357	.2
98	HEI Investment Inc—Constance H Lau	PO Box 730, Honolulu HI 96808	808-543-5662	S	2,357*	.1
99	Ellington Financial LLC—Laurence Penn	53 Forest Ave, Old Greenwich CT 06870	203-409-3575	P	2,334	N/A
100	Saul QRS Inc	7501 Wisconsin Ave Ste, Bethesda MD 20814	301-986-6200	S	2,181*	.1
	Saul Centers Inc					
101	Capital Automotive REIT—Thomas D Eckert	8270 Greensboro Dr Ste, McLean VA 22102	703-288-3075	R	2,158*	<.1
102	Post Properties Inc—David P Stockert	4401 Northside Pkwy St, Atlanta GA 30327	404-846-5000	P	2,139	.6
103	Strategic Hotel Capital Inc—Laurence G Geller	200 W Madison St Ste 1, Chicago IL 60606	312-658-5000	R	2,080*	<.1
104	Chelsea Property Group Inc—John Klein	105 Eisenhower Pky, Roseland NJ 07068	973-228-6111	S	1,970*	.9
	Simon Property Group Inc					
105	Resource Capital Corp—Jonathan Z Cohen	712 5th Ave 10th Fl, New York NY 10019	212-506-3899	P	1,934	N/A
106	Burlington Capital Group—Lisa Y Roskens	1004 Farnam St Ste 400, Omaha NE 68102	402-444-1630	P	1,914*	<.1
107	Glimcher Realty Trust—Michael P Glimcher	180 E Broad St, Columbus OH 43215	614-621-9000	P	1,861	1.1
108	Arbor Realty Trust Inc—Ivan Kaufman	333 Earle Ovington Blv, Uniondale NY 11553	516-832-8002	P	1,731	<.1
109	Alexander's Inc—Steven Roth	210 Rte 4 E, Paramus NJ 07652	212-894-7000	P	1,679	.1
110	Cedar Shopping Centers Inc—Bruce J Schanzer	44 S Bayles Ave, Port Washington NY 11050	516-767-6492	P	1,623	.1
111	Investors Real Estate Trust—Timothy P Mihalick	PO Box 1988, Minot ND 58702	701-837-4738	P	1,615	.4
112	Acadia Realty Trust—Kenneth F Bernstein	1311 Mamaroneck Ave St, White Plains NY 10605	914-288-8100	P	1,525	.1
113	Charlesbank Capital Partners LLC—Michael Thonis	200 Clarendon St 54th, Boston MA 02216	617-619-5400	R	1,515*	<.1
114	EastGroup-LNH Corp—David H Hoster II	PO Box 22728, Jackson MS 39225	601-354-3555	R	1,420*	<.1
115	Realty Finance Corp—Richard Koenigsberger	75 2nd Ave Ste 620, Needham MA 02494	781-514-1638	P	1,403	<.1
116	Glenborough Realty Trust Inc—Andrew Batinovich	400 S El Camino Real S, San Mateo CA 94402	650-343-9300	S	1,402*	.1
117	First Potomac Realty Trust—Douglas J Donatelli	7600 Wisconsin Ave 11t, Bethesda MD 20814	301-986-9200	P	1,397	.1
118	Transcontinental Realty Investors Inc—Daniel J Moos	1800 Valley View Ln St, Dallas TX 75234	469-522-4200	P	1,385	N/A
119	Government Properties Income Trust—David M Blackman	255 Washington St Two, Newton MA 02458	617-219-1440	P	1,369	N/A
120	Sun Communities Inc—Gary A Schiffman	27777 Franklin Rd Ste, Southfield MI 48034	248-208-2500	P	1,368	.7
121	Capital Trust Inc—Stephen D Plavin	410 Park Ave 14th Fl, New York NY 10022	212-655-0220	P	1,366	<.1
122	Medical Properties Trust Inc—Edward K Aldag Jr	1000 Urban Center Dr S, Birmingham AL 35242	205-969-3755	P	1,349	<.1
123	Cousins Properties Inc—Larry L Gellerstedt III	191 Peachtree St NE St, Atlanta GA 30303	404-407-1000	P	1,236	.3
124	Tanger Factory Outlet Centers Inc—Steven B Tanger	3200 Northline Ave Ste, Greensboro NC 27408	336-292-3010	P	1,217	.4
125	Plum Creek Timber Company Inc—Rick R Holley	999 3rd Ave Ste 4300, Seattle WA 98104	206-467-3600	P	1,167	1.2
126	Kite Realty Group Trust—John A Kite	30 S Meridian St Ste 1, Indianapolis IN 46204	317-577-5600	P	1,133	.1
127	American Assets Trust Inc—John Chamberlain	11455 El Camino Real S, San Diego CA 92130	858-350-2600	P	1,117	.1
128	Innkeepers USA Trust—Tim Walker	340 Royal Poinciana Wa, Palm Beach FL 33480	561-835-1800	P	1,102	<.1
129	CW Capital Inc—Barry S Blattman	11200 Rockville Pke, Rockville MD 20852	301-255-4700	R	1,070	.1
130	Forest Investment Associates—L Michael Kelly	15 Piedmont Ctr Ste 12, Atlanta GA 30305	404-261-9575	R	1,052*	<.1
131	Associated Estates Realty Corp—Jeffrey I Friedman	1 AEC Pkwy, Richmond Heights OH 44143	216-261-5000	P	1,018	.4

Rank	Company Name—*Executive Officer*	Address, City, State, Zip	Phone	Type	Fin	Empls
132	Saul Centers Inc—*B Francis Saul II*	7501 Wisconsin Ave Ste, Bethesda MD 20814	301-986-6200	P	1,014	.1
133	Hudson Pacific Properties Inc—*Victor J Coleman*	11601 Wilshire Blvd St, Los Angeles CA 90025	310-445-5700	P	1,005	.1
134	CreXus Investment Corp—*Kevin Riordan*	1211 Avenue of the Ame, New York NY 10036	646-829-0160	P	993	N/A
135	Arlington Asset Investment Corp—*Eric F Billings*	1001 19th St N, Arlington VA 22209	703-373-0200	P	955	<.1
136	Inland American Real Estate Trust Inc—*Robert D Parks*	2901 Butterfield Rd, Oak Brook IL 60523	603-218-8800	R	866	N/A
137	Ladder Capital Finance LLC—*Brian R Harris*	600 Lexington Ave 23rd, New York NY 10022	212-715-3170	I	744*	<.1
138	Education Realty Trust Inc—*Randy Churchey*	530 Oak Court Dr Ste 3, Memphis TN 38117	901-259-2500	P	737	1.1
139	Blue Gem Inc—*Alan W Cone*	PO Box 29346, Greensboro NC 27429	336-275-0756	R	710*	<.1
140	Citinational Real Estate Inc—*Russell Goldsmith*	400 N Roxbury Dr, Beverly Hills CA 90210	310-888-6000	S	691*	<.1
141	Excel Trust Inc—*Gary B Sabin*	17140 Bernardo Center, San Diego CA 92128	858-613-1800	P	688	<.1
142	Argosy Capital—*Kirk Griswold*	950 W Valley Rd Ste 29, Wayne PA 19087	610-971-9685	R	671*	<.1
143	LTC Properties Inc—*Wendy Simpson*	2829 Townsgate Rd, Westlake Village CA 91361	805-981-8655	P	647	<.1
144	Cogdell Spencer Inc—*Raymond W Braun*	4401 Barclay Downs Dr, Charlotte NC 28209	704-940-2900	P	633	.4
145	American Spectrum Realty Inc—*William J Carden*	2401 Fountain View Dr, Houston TX 77057	713-706-6200	P	618	.2
146	Lanhold Investments Inc—*David Singer*	PO Box 32368, Charlotte NC 28232	704-554-1421	S	600*	4.3
147	First Washington Realty Trust Inc—*William J Wolfe*	4350 East-West Highway, Bethesda MD 20814	301-907-7800	R	583*	.1
148	National Health Investors Inc—*J Justin Hutchens*	222 Robert Rose Dr, Murfreesboro TN 37129	615-890-9100	P	580	N/A
149	Kurisu and Fergus—*Duane Kurisu*	1000 Bishop St Ste 810, Honolulu HI 96813	808-523-5644	R	571*	<.1
150	Urstadt Biddle Properties Inc—*Charles J Urstadt*	321 Railroad Ave, Greenwich CT 06830	203-863-8200	I	557	<.1
151	CenterPoint Properties Corp—*Paul S Fisher*	1808 Swift Dr, Oak Brook IL 60523	630-586-8000	R	555*	.1
152	AllCapital/GPT Properties LLC—*Thomas D Peschio*	13625 California St, Omaha NE 68154	402-391-0010	R	531	N/A
153	Colbalt Holdings Group LLC—*Zachery H Pashel*	1442 Market St Ste 200, Denver CO 80202	303-993-7130	R	521	<.1
154	Potlatch Corp—*Michael J Covey*	601 W Riverside Ave St, Spokane WA 99201	509-835-1500	P	497	.9
155	Winthrop Realty Trust—*Michael L Ashner*	PO Box 9507, Boston MA 02114	617-570-4614	I	493	N/A
156	Summit Hotel Properties Inc—*Daniel P Hansen*	2701 S Minnesota Ave S, Sioux Falls SD 57105	605-361-9566	P	493	<.1
157	Eagle Hospitality Properties Trust Inc—*J William Blackham*	100 E RiverCenter Blvd, Covington KY 41011	859-581-5900	R	462	<.1
158	Regency Realty Corp—*Martin E Stein Jr*	1 Independent Dr St 11, Jacksonville FL 32202	904-598-7000	R	459*	.2
159	First Republic Preferred Capital Corp—*James H Herbert II*	111 Pine St 2nd Fl, San Francisco CA 94111	415-392-1400	P	459	N/A
160	Berkshire Income Realty Inc—*Douglas Krupp*	1 Beacon St Ste 1500, Boston MA 02108	617-523-7722	P	457	N/A
161	One Liberty Properties Inc—*Patrick J Callan Jr*	60 Cutter Mill Rd Ste, Great Neck NY 11021	516-466-3100	P	445	<.1
162	Berkshire Property Advisors LLC	1 Beacon St Ste 1550, Boston MA 02108	617-646-2300	R	442*	.5
163	American Land Lease Inc—*David B Lentz*	380 Park Place Blvd St, Clearwater FL 33759	727-726-8868	R	437	.2
164	Sterling Investment Partners LP—*William Macey Jr*	285 Riverside Ave Ste, Westport CT 06880	203-226-8711	R	421*	<.1
165	Trident Investments Inc—*Bruce Berreth*	12505 Bel-Red Rd Ste 2, Bellevue WA 98005		R	398*	<.1
166	New York Mortgage Trust Inc—*Steven R Mumma*	52 Vanderbilt Ave Ste, New York NY 10017	212-792-0107	P	374	<.1
167	Thompson National Properties LLC—*Tony Thompson*	1900 Main St Ste 700, Irvine CA 92614	949-858-8252	R	332*	<.1
168	Institutional Financial Markets Inc—*Daniel G Cohen*	2929 Arch St 17th Fl, Philadelphia PA 19104	215-701-9555	P	307	.1
169	Sizeler Property Investors Inc—*Mark Tanz*	2542 Williams Blvd, Kenner LA 70062	504-471-6200	R	302	.2
170	AmREIT Inc—*H Kerr Taylor*	8 Greenway Plz Ste 100, Houston TX 77046	713-850-1400	P	294	<.1
171	Whitestone REIT—*James C Mastandrea*	2600 S Gessner Ste 500, Houston TX 77063	713-827-9595	P	274	.1
172	Terreno Realty Corp—*W Blake Baird*	16 Maiden Ln 5th Fl, San Francisco CA 94108	415-655-4580	P	267	<.1
173	Agree Realty Corp—*Richard Agree*	31850 Northwestern Hwy, Farmington Hills MI 48334	248-737-4190	I	257	<.1
174	PIMCO Commercial Mortgage Securities Trust Inc—*Mohamed El-Erian*	840 Newport Center Dr, Newport Beach CA 92660	949-720-6000	R	246*	1.3
175	First Real Estate Investment Trust of New Jersey—*Robert S Hekemian*	PO Box 667, Hackensack NJ 07602	201-488-6400	P	243	<.1
176	Universal Health Realty Income Trust—*Alan B Miller*	PO Box 61558, King of Prussia PA 19406	610-265-0688	I	229	N/A
177	PMC Commercial Trust—*Lance B Rosemore*	17950 Preston Rd Ste 6, Dallas TX 75252	972-349-3200	I	228	<.1
178	Chatham Lodging Trust—*Jeffrey H Fisher*	50 Cocoanut Row Ste 20, Palm Beach FL 33480	561-802-4477	P	222	<.1
179	JER Investors Trust Inc—*Joseph Robert Jr*	7950 Jones Branch Dr S, McLean VA 22107	703-714-8000	P	211	N/A
180	MHI Hospitality Corp—*Andrew M Sims*	410 W Francis St, Williamsburg VA 23185	757-229-5648	P	210	<.1
181	Tarragon Corp—*William S Friedman*	423 W 55th St, New York NY 10019	212-949-5000	P	206	.5
182	Jameson Inns Inc—*Dan Burdakin*	4770 S Atlanta Rd, Smyrna GA 30080	404-350-9990	R	204	1.5
183	Midland Loan Services Inc—*Douglas Danforth Jr*	PO Box 25965, Shawnee Mission KS 66225	913-253-9000	S	183*	.4
184	Winston Hotels Inc—*Robert W Winston III* Inland American Real Estate Trust Inc	2626 Glenwood Ave Ste, Raleigh NC 27608	919-500-6010	S	175	N/A
185	Care Investment Trust Inc—*Salvatore V Riso Jr*	780 Third Ave 21st FL, New York NY 10017	212-446-1410	R	167	<.1
186	Corporate Property Associates 14 Inc—*Gino Sabatini*	50 Rockefeller Plz, New York NY 10020	212-492-1100	R	157*	<.1
187	Bimini Capital Management Inc—*Robert E Cauley*	3305 Flamingo Dr, Vero Beach FL 32963	772-231-1400	P	157	N/A
188	UMH Properties Inc—*Samuel A Landy*	3499 Rte 9 Ste 3C, Freehold NJ 07728	732-577-9997	I	148	.1
189	Archstone Communities LLC—*R Sellers*	9200 E Panorama Cir St, Englewood CO 80112	303-708-5959	R	143*	2.7
190	Webster Preferred Capital Corp—*James C Smith*	145 Bank St, Waterbury CT 06702	203-465-4366	P	132	<.1
191	Income Opportunity Realty Investors Inc—*Daniel J Moos*	1603 Lyndon B Johnson, Dallas TX 75234	469-522-4200	P	117	N/A
192	Sentinel Real Estate Corp—*John H Streicker*	1251 Ave of the Americ, New York NY 10020	212-408-2920	R	115*	.5
193	Vestin Realty Mortgage II Inc—*Michael V Shustek*	8880 W Sunset Rd Ste 2, Las Vegas NV 89148	702-227-0965	P	112	N/A
194	Semele Group Inc—*Gary D Engle*	200 Nyala Farms Rd, Westport CT 06880	203-341-0555	R	93	<.1
195	Rosebriar Holdings Corp—*William Hanks*	PO Box 541208, Dallas TX 75354	214-902-2287	P	87*	<.1
196	DVL Inc—*Michael P Murphy*	115 Sinclair Rd, Bristol PA 19007	215-785-5950	P	69	N/A
197	US Federal Properties Trust Inc—*Richard Baier*	4705 Central St, Kansas City MO 64112	816-531-2082	R	68*	<.1
198	Roberts Realty Investors Inc—*Charles S Roberts*	450 Northridge Pkwy St, Atlanta GA 30350	770-394-6000	P	50	<.1
199	HMG/Courtland Properties Inc—*Maurice Wiener*	1870 S Bayshore Dr, Coconut Grove FL 33133	305-854-6803	I	41*	<.1
200	Harley Stanfield Inc—*Cedric J Franklin*	1725 I St NW Ste 300, Washington DC 20006	202-349-3822	R	38	<.1
201	NovaStar Financial Inc—*W Lance Anderson*	2114 Central St Ste 60, Kansas City MO 64108	816-237-7000	P	38	.3
202	InnSuites Hospitality Trust—*James F Wirth*	InnSuites Hotel Ctr 16, Phoenix AZ 85020	602-944-1500	P	28	.4
203	Presidential Realty Corp—*Jeffrey F Joseph*	180 S Broadway, White Plains NY 10605	914-948-1300	I	28	<.1
204	Vestin Realty Mortgage I Inc—*Michael V Shustek*	8880 W Sunset Rd Ste 2, Las Vegas NV 89148	702-227-0965	P	24	N/A
205	DASCO Medical Properties Trust—*Malcom S Sina*	11360 Jog Rd, Palm Beach Gardens FL 33418	561-691-9900	R	19*	.1
206	Atlantic American Properties Trust—*David Murdock* Brandywine Realty Trust	PO Box 28, Kannapolis NC 28082	704-932-0141	S	11*	.1
207	Middleton Doll Co—*Salvatore L Bando*	615 W 131st St, New York NY 10027	301-895-4793	R	11	.1
208	National Penn Investment Co—*Scott V Fainor*	PO Box 547, Boyertown PA 19512	610-705-9101	S	10*	1.2
209	Mainstreet Property Group LLC—*Paul Ezekiel Turner*	PO Box 767, Cicero IN 46034	317-420-0205	R	10	.1
210	Pacific Property Assets—*Michael J Stewart*	2600 Michelson Dr Ste, Irvine CA 92612	949-488-9400	R	7*	<.1
211	Investment Directions Inc—*Chris Bauer*	25 W Main St Ste 789, Madison WI 53703	608-252-8700	S	7	N/A
212	Camden Property Trust—*Richard J Campo*	3 Greenway Plz Ste 130, Houston TX 77046	713-354-2500	I	5	1.8
213	WedBush Securities—*Thomas Hislop*	2999 N 44th St Ste 100, Phoenix AZ 85018	602-952-6800	S	4	N/A
214	Starwood Property Trust *Barry S Sternlicht*	591 W Putnam Ave, Greenwich CT 06830	203-422-8100	P	3	N/A
215	Winreal Operating Company LP—*Larry Bell*	5220 Pcf Concourse Dr, Los Angeles CA 90045	310-727-9589	R	2*	<.1
216	Simpson Organization Inc—*A Boyd Simpson*	1401 Peachtree St NE, Atlanta GA 30309	404-872-3990	R	2*	<.1
217	Pebblebrook Hotel Trust—*Jon E Bortz*	2 Bethseda Metro Ctr S, Bethesda MD 20814	240-507-1300	P	1	<.1

Note: An asterisk (*) indicates an estimated financial figure. The company type code used is as follows: R = Private, P = Public, S = Private Subsidiary, B = Public Subsidiary, D = Division, J = Joint Venture, I = Investment Fund.

COMPANY RANKINGS BY SALES WITHIN 4-DIGIT SIC

Rank	Company Name—Executive Officer	Address, City, State, Zip	Phone	Type	Fin	Empls
218	CMG Holdings Inc—Alan Morell	5601 Biscayne Blvd, Miami FL 33137	305-751-1667	P	1	<.1
219	Feldman Mall Properties Inc—Bruce E Moore	1065 Avenue of the Ame, New York NY 10018	212-221-2620	P	1	.2
220	Colony Financial Inc—Richard B Saltzman	2450 Broadway 6th Fl, Santa Monica CA 90404	310-282-8820	I	<1	N/A
221	Paragon Real Estate Equity and Investment Trust—James C Mastandrea	1240 Huron Rd, Cleveland OH 44115	216-430-2700	P	<1	<.1
222	Apollo Commercial Real Estate Finance Inc—Joseph F Azrack	9 W 57th St, New York NY 10019	212-515-3200	P	<1	N/A
223	Durham Medical Office Building Inc—David Emery Healthcare Realty Trust Inc	3310 West End Ave Ste, Nashville TN 37203	615-269-8175	S	N/A	.2

TOTALS: SIC 6798 Real Estate Investment Trusts
Companies: 223 ⟶ 1,359,235   103.5

6799 Investors Nec

Rank	Company Name—Executive Officer	Address, City, State, Zip	Phone	Type	Fin	Empls
1	OpenGate Capital—Andrew Nikou	1999 Avenue of the Sta, Los Angeles CA 90067	310-432-7000	R	63,035*	1.9
2	TPG Capital—John Viola	301 Commerce St Ste 33, Fort Worth TX 76102	817-871-4000	R	50,000	.1
3	Madison Dearborn Partners LLC—Paul Finnegan	3 First National Plz S, Chicago IL 60602	312-895-1000	R	44,778*	4.2
4	Harbour Group—Jeffrey L Fox	7701 Forsyth Blvd Ste, Saint Louis MO 63105	314-727-5550	R	17,275*	3.3
5	Tektronix Development Co—Rick Willis	PO Box 500, Beaverton OR 97077	503-627-7111	S	16,628*	1.5
6	Northwest Capital Corp—Jack Golsen Prime Financial Corp	16 S Pennsylvania Ave, Oklahoma City OK 73107	405-235-4546	S	13,580*	1.2
7	Prime Financial Corp—Jack Golsen	16 S Pennsylvania Ave, Oklahoma City OK 73107	405-235-4546	S	13,580*	1.2
8	Madison Capital Partners Corp—Larry W Gies Jr	500 W Madison Ste 3890, Chicago IL 60661	312-277-0156	R	11,230*	1.0
9	Thoma Cressey Bravo—Bryan Cressey	300 N LaSalle St Ste 4, Chicago IL 60654	312-254-3300	R	10,770*	1.0
10	Chimera Investment Corp—Paul Donlin	1211 Ave of the Americ, New York NY 10036	212-696-0100	P	8,074	N/A
11	Wexford Capital LLC—Joseph Jacobs	411 W Putnam Ave Wexfo, Greenwich CT 06830	203-862-7000	R	7,000*	.1
12	Apprise Media LLC—Charles G McCurdy	PO Box 306, Mill Neck NY 11765	516-723-9060	R	5,469*	.2
13	Nelson Communications—Lorraine Pastore	41 Madison Ave, New York NY 10010	212-684-9470	R	5,444*	1.0
14	Platinum Equity LLC—Tom T Gores	360 N Crescent Dr, Beverly Hills CA 90210	310-712-1850	R	4,939*	35.0
15	Ares Management LLC—Michael Arougheti	1999 Ave of the Stars, Los Angeles CA 90067	310-201-4100	R	4,735*	.2
16	Pulte Financial Companies Inc—Richard J Dugas	100 Bloomfield Hills P, Bloomfield Hills MI 48304	248-647-2750	S	4,564*	.1
17	Cohen Brothers and Co—Chris Ricciardi	2929 Arch St 17th Fl, Philadelphia PA 19104	215-701-9555	R	4,340*	.1
18	Cohen and Company LLC—Chris Ricciardi	2929 Arch St 17th Fl, Philadelphia PA 19104	215-701-9555	R	4,325*	.1
19	Preferred Unlimited Inc—Michael G O'Neill	1001 E Hector St Ste 1, Conshohocken PA 19428	610-834-1969	R	4,166*	.1
20	Consumer Capital Partners LLC—Rick Schaden	1515 Arapahoe St Twr 1, Denver CO 80202	303-592-3800	R	3,227*	.1
21	Forsch Corp—Kenneth V Madren Jr	1000 Abernathy Rd NE S, Atlanta GA 30328	678-292-6592	R	3,218*	.6
22	Apollo Investment Corp—James C Zelter	9 W 57th St, New York NY 10019	212-515-3450	P	3,149	N/A
23	Grove Street Advisors LLC—Clint Harris	20 William St Ste 230, Wellesley MA 02481	781-263-6100	R	2,758*	.1
24	Hampshire Equity Partners—Gregory Flynn	45 E Putnam Ave Ste 11, Greenwich CT 06830	203-769-5601	R	2,758*	.1
25	Harbourvest—D Brooks Zug	One Financial Center 4, Boston MA 02111	617-348-3707	R	2,457*	.2
26	Fort Washington Capital Partners—Maribeth S Rahe	303 Broadway Ste 1200, Cincinnati OH 45202	513-361-7600	R	2,322*	.1
27	Peachtree Settlement Funding—Deborah Benaim	3301 Quantum Blvd 2nd, Boynton Beach FL 33426		R	2,249*	.2
28	Rothschild Realty Inc—John McGurk	1251 Ave of the Americ, New York NY 10020	212-403-3500	R	2,210*	.2
29	Sierra Ventures—Jeffrey M Drazan	2884 Sand Hill Rd Ste, Menlo Park CA 94025	650-854-1000	R	2,200*	<.1
30	Pequot Capital Management—Arthur Samberg	500 Nyala Farm Rd, Westport CT 06880	203-429-2200	R	2,154*	.2
31	Caris and Company Inc—Darren J Caris	12671 high Bluff Dr St, San Diego CA 92130	858-704-0300	R	2,013*	.1
32	American Beverage Corp—Antonino Battaglia	1 Daily Way, Verona PA 15147	412-828-9020	S	1,790*	.4
33	Soave Enterprises LLC—Yale Levin	3400 E Lafayette St, Detroit MI 48207	313-567-7000	R	1,670*	2.5
34	Oak Hill Capital Partners—Ted Dardani	One Stamford Plz 263 T, Stamford CT 06901	203-328-1600	R	1,653*	.1
35	Prospect Capital Corp—John Francis Barry III	10 E 40th St 44th Fl, New York NY 10016	212-448-0702	P	1,549	N/A
36	TL Ventures—Robert E Keith Jr	435 Devon Park Dr Bldg, Wayne PA 19087	610-971-1515	R	1,400*	.1
37	Vulcan Ventures Inc—Jody Allen	505 5th Ave S Ste 900, Seattle WA 98104	206-342-2000	R	1,376*	.3
38	Fairview Capital Partners Inc—Rebecca S Connolly	75 Isham Rd Ste 200, West Hartford CT 06107	860-674-8066	R	1,232*	<.1
39	Friedman Fleischer and Lowe LLC—Tully M Friedman	1 Maritime Plz 22nd Fl, San Francisco CA 94111	415-402-2100	R	1,230*	<.1
40	Draper Fisher Jurvetson—Timothy C Draper	2882 Sand Hill Rd Ste, Menlo Park CA 94025	650-233-9000	R	1,201*	<.1
41	Warburg Pincus LLC—Charles R Kaye	466 Lexington Ave, New York NY 10017	212-878-0600	R	1,175*	.3
42	Rampart Investment Management Company Inc—Ronald M Egalka	1 International Pl 14t, Boston MA 02110	617-342-6900	R	1,161*	<.1
43	Adams Express Co—Douglas G Ober	7 St Paul St Ste 1140, Baltimore MD 21202		P	1,125	<.1
44	Kelso and Company LP—Frank T Nickell	320 Park Ave 24th Fl, New York NY 10022	212-751-3939	R	1,105*	<.1
45	Pamlico Capital—Thomas W Jones	150 N College St Ste 2, Charlotte NC 28202	704-414-7150	R	1,101*	<.1
46	Frontenac Co—Martin J Koldyke	135 S La Salle St Ste, Chicago IL 60603	312-368-0044	R	1,090*	<.1
47	Levine Leichtman Capital Partners—Lauren B Leichtman	335 N Maple Dr Ste 130, Beverly Hills CA 90210	310-275-5335	R	1,077*	.1
48	Black Enterprise Greenwich Street Corporate Growth Partners LP—Earl Graves Jr	130 5th Ave 10th Fl, New York NY 10011	212-242-8000	R	1,075*	.1
49	Hilton Capital Inc—Sam Hilton	31151 Old Trail Crl, Murrieta CA 92563	951-834-6523	R	1,000	.1
50	Atlantic-Pacific Capital Inc—James E Manley	50 California St Ste 1, San Francisco CA 94111	415-291-8199	R	971*	<.1
51	Rainwater Inc—Richard Rainwater	777 Main St, Fort Worth TX 76102	817-820-6600	R	923*	<.1
52	Goldman Sachs Private Equity Group—Lloyd Blankfein	200 West St, New York NY 10282	212-902-1000	R	913*	.1
53	MCG Capital Corp—Richard W Neu	1100 Wilson Blvd Ste 3, Arlington VA 22209	703-247-7500	P	891	<.1
54	Avondale Partners LLC—Richard Henderson	3102 West End Ave Ste, Nashville TN 37203	615-467-3500	R	872*	.1
55	Natixis Global Asset Management—John Hailer	399 Boylston St, Boston MA 02116	617-449-2507	R	869	N/A
56	MSD Capital LP—Glenn R Fuhrman	645 Fifth Ave 21st Fl, New York NY 10022	212-303-1650	R	862*	.1
57	ComVest Investment Partners—Michael S Falk	830 3rd Ave 8th Fl, New York NY 10022	212-829-5800	R	781*	<.1
58	Hissong Group Inc—Robert E Hissong	PO Box 495, Bath OH 44210	330-659-4481	R	761*	.2
59	Stonehenge Partners—David Meuse	191 W Nationwide Blvd, Columbus OH 43215	614-246-2500	R	754*	.1
60	C and B Capital—Edward S Croft III	4200 Northside Pkwy NW, Atlanta GA 30327	404-841-3131	R	747*	<.1
61	TH Lee Putnam Ventures—Thomas Lee	200 Madison Ave Ste 19, New York NY 10016	212-951-8600	J	694*	<.1
62	eSecLendingcom LLC—Christopher R Jaynes	175 Federal St, Boston MA 02110	617-204-4500	S	692*	.1
63	Advent International Corp—Jeff Case	75 State St, Boston MA 02109	617-951-9400	R	691*	.3
64	Communications Equity Associates—J Patrick Michaels Jr	101 E Kennedy Blvd Ste, Tampa FL 33602	813-226-8844	R	691*	<.1
65	Endeavor Capital Partners—Anthony Buffa	49 Richmondville Ave S, Westport CT 06880	203-341-7788	R	691*	<.1
66	Golub Capital—Lawrence Golub	551 Madison Ave, New York NY 10022	212-750-6060	R	690*	<.1
67	MidOcean Capital—Ted Virtue	320 Park Ave Ste 1600, New York NY 10022	212-497-1400	R	689*	<.1
68	MESBIC Ventures Holding Co—Donald Lawhorne	2435 N Central Expy St, Richardson TX 75080	972-991-1597	R	684*	<.1
69	Prudential Capital Group—Allen A Weaver	Two Prudential Plaza 1, Chicago IL 60601	312-540-4235	R	646*	.1
70	Paul Capital Partners—Richard Chow	50 California St Ste30, San Francisco CA 94111	415-283-4300	R	644*	.1
71	Audax Management Company LLC—Geoffrey S Rehnert	101 Huntington Ave, Boston MA 02199	617-859-1500	R	642*	<.1
72	Pharos Capital Group LLC—Bob Crants	300 Crescent Ct Ste 13, Dallas TX 75201	214-855-0194	R	642*	<.1
73	Matrix Management Corp—Paul J Ferri	1000 Winter St Ste 450, Waltham MA 02451	781-890-2244	R	625*	<.1
74	Gallagher Enterprises LLC—KC Gallagher	1400 Wewatta St Ste 91, Denver CO 80202	303-595-7700	R	622*	<.1
75	Brockway Moran and Partners Inc—Michael E Moran	225 NE Mizner Blvd Ste, Boca Raton FL 33432	561-750-2000	R	608*	<.1

Rank	Company Name—Executive Officer	Address, City, State, Zip	Phone	Type	Fin	Empls
76	Sandler Capital Manager...	711 Fifth Ave 15th Fl, New York NY 10022	212-754-8100	R	605*	<.1
77	One Equity Partners—Dic...ndrew Sandler	320 Park Ave 18th Fl, New York NY 10022	212-277-1500	R	590*	.1
78	Equity Group Investments In...	2 N Riverside Plz6th F, Chicago IL 60606	312-454-0100	R	566*	.1
79	Great Hill Partners LLC—Chr...ald Liebentrigt	1 Liberty Sq, Boston MA 02109	617-790-9400	R	560*	.1
80	WM Sprinkman Corp—Robert S,S Gaffney	PO Box 390, Franksville WI 53126	262-835-2390	R	554*	.1
81	Intercontinental Television Group Ian	1990 S Bundy Dr Ste 85, Los Angeles CA 90025	310-478-1818	R	552*	.1
82	VMG Equity Partners—David G Barloy Beindorf	39 Mesa St, San Francisco CA 94129	415-632-4200	R	550*	<.1
83	W Capital Partners—Robert J Miglion...	One E 52 St, New York NY 10022	212-561-5240	R	550*	<.1
84	Western Technology Investments—Maun...erdegar	2010 N 1st St Ste 310, San Jose CA 95131	408-436-8577	R	550*	<.1
85	Capital Southwest Corp—Gary L Martin	12900 Preston Rd Ste 7, Dallas TX 75230	972-233-8242	P	543	<.1
86	Jackson Securities LLC—Reuben McDaniel	100 Auburn Ave, Atlanta GA 30303	404-522-5766	S	542*	.1
87	Azalea Capital—Patrick A Duncan	1 Liberty Sq 55 Beatti, Greenville SC 29601	864-235-0201	R	540*	.1
88	TowerBrook Capital Partners—Neal Moszkowsk...	65 E 55th St, New York NY 10022		R	536*	.1
89	LJC Investments Inc—Raymond J Pacin...	6 Executive Cir Ste 25, Irvine CA 92614	949-250-7700	S	535*	.1
90	UNC Partners Inc—Edward Dugger III	54 Burroughs St, Boston MA 02130	617-522-2160	R	521*	<.1
91	GTCR Golder Rauner LLC—Craig A Bondy	300 N LaSalle St Ste 5, Chicago IL 60654	312-382-2200	R	511*	<.1
92	Cypress Group LLC (New York New York)	437 Madison Ave 33rd F, New York NY 10022	212-705-0150	R	503*	<.1
93	Forward Ventures—Standish M Fleming	9393 Towne Centre Dr S, San Diego CA 92121	858-677-6077	R	500*	<.1
94	Aquiline Capital Partners LLC—Jeffrey W Greenbe...	535 Madison Ave 27th F, New York NY 10022	212-624-9500	R	498*	<.1
95	Nautic Partners LLC—Bernie Buonanno	50 Kennedy Plz 12th Fl, Providence RI 02903	401-278-6770	R	497*	<.1
96	Quadrangle Group LLC—Michael Huber	375 Park Ave, New York NY 10152	212-418-1700	R	488*	<.1
97	Elevation Partners—Roger McNamee	70 E 55th St 12th Fl, New York NY 10022	212-317-6555	R	484*	<.1
98	Mayfield Fund—James Beck	2800 Sand Hill Rd, Menlo Park CA 94025	650-854-5560	R	482*	<.1
99	Key Principal Partners LLC—John Sinnenberg	800 Superior Ave 10th, Cleveland OH 44114	216-828-8125	R	481*	<.1
100	GenNx360 Capital Partners—Arthur H Harper	...0 Madison Ave 27th F, New York NY 10022		R	478*	<.1
101	Meritage Private Equity Funds—Tracey Kerr	...0 Wynkoop Ste 300, Denver CO 80202	303-352-2040	R	470*	.3
102	FirstCity Financial Corp—James T Sartain	181... Imperial Dr, Waco TX 76712	254-751-1750	P	460	.3
103	eRT Investment Corp	...arket St Ste 100, Philadelphia PA 19103	215-972-0420	S	458*	<.1
104	Ascent Venture Partners—Brian Girvan	255 St...e St 5th Fl, Boston MA 02109	617-720-9400	R	451*	<.1
105	Stepstone LLC—Monte Brem	4350 La...lla Village D, San Diego CA 92122	858-558-9700	R	447*	<.1
106	Domain Associates LLC—James C Blair	12481 Hig... Bluff Dr St, San Diego CA 92130	858-480-2400	R	440*	<.1
107	Lexington Partners—Brent R Nicklas	660 Madison Ave 23rd F, New York NY 10065	212-754-0411	R	429*	<.1
108	Softbank Inc—Kabir Misra	38 Glen Ave, Newton MA 02459	617-928-9300	S	426*	<.1
109	Prime Cable—William Glascow	600 Congress Ave Ste 2, Austin TX 78701	512-476-7888	R	424	.8
110	Idealab Capital Partners LP—Bill Gross	130 W Union St, Pasadena CA 91103	626-585-6900	R	424*	.1
111	Resource America Inc—Jonathan Z Cohen	712 Fifth Ave 10th Fl, New York NY 10019	212-506-3899	P	423	.3
112	Francisco Partners—David Stanton	1 Letterman Dr Bldg C, San Francisco CA 94129	415-418-2900	R	419*	<.1
113	Avista Capital Holdings LP—Thompson Dean	65 E 55th St 18th Fl, New York NY 10022	212-593-6900	R	415*	<.1
114	Inverness Capital Partners LP—Kenneth Graham	3811 W Chester Pk Bldg, Newtown Square PA 19073	610-722-0300	R	415*	<.1
115	Gordon Brothers Corp—Michael Frieze	101 Huntington Ave 10t, Boston MA 02199	617-426-3233	R	405*	.2
116	Softbank Capital Partners Inc—Ronald Fisher	1188 Centre St, Newton Center MA 02459	617-928-9300	R	381*	<.1
117	InterWest Partners LLC—Stephen Holmes	2710 Sand Hill Rd Ste, Menlo Park CA 94025	650-854-8585	R	375*	<.1
118	Healthcare Ventures LLC	44 Nassau St, Princeton NJ 08542	609-430-3900	R	348*	<.1
119	TH Lee Putnam Ventures LP—Jim Brown	200 Madison Ave Ste 19, New York NY 10016	212-951-8600	R	347*	.1
120	Roark Capital Group—Jeffrey Keenan	1180 Peachtree St NE S, Atlanta GA 30309	404-591-5200	R	345*	<.1
121	Capital Resource Partners—Robert C Ammerman	31 State St 6th Fl, Boston MA 02109	617-478-9600	R	342*	<.1
122	Enterprise Partners Venture Capital—Carl Eibl	2223 Avendia de la Pla, La Jolla CA 92037	858-454-8833	R	333*	<.1
123	Forrest Binkley and Brown—Gregory J Forrest	19800 MacArthur Blvd S, Irvine CA 92612	949-222-1987	R	332*	<.1
124	NTS Realty Holdings LP—Brian F Lavin	10172 Linn Station Rd, Louisville KY 40223	502-426-4800	P	329	N/A
125	Hilco Equity LLC—John W Tornes	5 Revere Dr Ste 300, Northbrook IL 60062	847-509-1100	S	326*	<.1
126	Rice Financial Products Co—J Donald Rice Jr	17 State St 40th Fl, New York NY 10004	212-908-9200	R	324*	<.1
127	Milestone Venture Partners LLC—Richard J Dumler	551 Madison Ave 7th Fl, New York NY 10022	212-223-7400	R	318*	<.1
128	TICC Capital Corp—Jonathan H Cohen	8 Sound Shore Dr Ste 2, Greenwich CT 06830	203-983-5275	P	318	N/A
129	Atlas Venture—Alexander Bruhl	25 1st St Ste 303, Cambridge MA 02141	781-622-1700	R	317*	.1
130	Silver Creek Technology Investors—Mark Masur	5949 Sherry Ln, Dallas TX 75225	214-265-2020	R	311*	<.1
131	Stone Point Capital—Charles A Davis	20 Horseneck Ln, Greenwich CT 06830	203-862-2900	R	302*	<.1
132	Gores Technology Group—Alec E Gores	10877 Wilshire Blvd 18, Los Angeles CA 90024	310-209-3010	S	300*	1.0
133	NGP Capital Resources Co—Stephen Gardner	1221 McKinney St Ste 2, Houston TX 77010	713-752-0062	P	292	N/A
134	Shawmark Group—Jon M Stout	PO Box 343, Middleburg VA 20118	540-687-3870	R	290*	<.1
135	Generation Partners—John Hawkins	1 Greenwich Office Par, Greenwich CT 06831	203-422-8200	R	289*	<.1
136	Financo Inc—Colin Welch	645 Madison Ave, New York NY 10022	212-553-9000	R	280*	<.1
137	Monitor Clipper Partners—Michael Bell	Two Canal Park 4th Fl, Cambridge MA 02141	617-252-2200	R	279*	<.1
138	Sevin Rosen Funds—Dave McLean	13455 Noel Rd Ste 1670, Dallas TX 75240	972-702-1100	R	276*	<.1
139	Westview Capital Partners—Carlo A von Schroeter	125 High St, Boston MA 02110	617-261-2050	R	275*	<.1
140	Marketing Services Inc—Stacey Girt	140 Terry Dr Ste 103, Newtown PA 18940	978-657-7000	R	270*	.1
141	Prairie Capital—C Bryan Daniels	191 N Wacker Dr Ste 80, Chicago IL 60606	312-360-1133	R	269*	<.1
142	Sutter Hill Ventures—William H Younger Jr	755 Page Mill Rd, Palo Alto CA 94304	650-493-5600	R	269*	<.1
143	Diamond Castle Holdings LLC—Stephen M Bassford	280 Park Ave 25th Fl, New York NY 10017	212-300-1900	R	268*	<.1
144	Lightyear Capital LLC—Donald B Marron	375 Park Ave 11th Fl, New York NY 10152	212-328-0555	R	267*	<.1
145	Jazz Semiconductor Inc—Russell Ellwanger	4321 Jamboree Rd, Newport Beach CA 92660	949-435-8000	S	266*	.7
146	Ascend Venture Group LLC—Darryl Wash	1500 Broadway 14th Fl, New York NY 10036	212-324-2222	R	260*	.1
147	Damon's International Inc—Carl T Howard	4645 Executive Dr, Columbus OH 43220	614-442-7900	R	250*	.1
148	Property Markets Group—Kevin P Maloney	5 E 17th St 2nd Fl, New York NY 10003	212-610-2800	R	250*	.1
149	Fenway Partners Inc—Peter Lamm	152 W 57th St 59th Fl, New York NY 10019	212-698-9400	R	248*	.1
150	Nobelmen Group LLC—David J Ferran	3614 Harvard Ave, Dallas TX 75205	858-699-5338	R	248*	<.1
151	Smart Balance Inc—Stephen B Hughes	115 W Century Rd Ste 2, Paramus NJ 07652	201-421-3970	P	242	<.1
152	America First Tax Exempt Investors LP—Mark A Hiatt	1004 Farnam St, Omaha NE 68102	402-444-1630	P	242	N/A
153	Clayton Dubilier and Rice Inc—Donald J Gogel	375 Park Ave 18th Fl, New York NY 10152	212-407-5200	R	241*	.1
154	Sterling Partners—Eric Becker	650 S Exeter St Ste 10, Baltimore MD 21202	443-703-1700	R	232*	.1
155	Western Water Co—James Sherman	705 Mission Ave Rm 200, San Rafael CA 94901	415-256-8800	R	231*	<.1
156	Vector Capital Group—Alexander R Slusky	456 Montgomery St 19th, San Francisco CA 94104	415-293-5000	R	224*	<.1
157	Red Diamond Capital Inc—Mark Kammert	655 3rd Ave, New York NY 10017	212-605-2300	R	223*	<.1
158	Venture Investors LLC—Roger H Ganser	505 S Rosa Rd Ste 201, Madison WI 53719	608-441-2700	R	223*	<.1
159	Piedmont Investment Advisors LLC—Isaac H Green	300 W Morgan St, Durham NC 27701	919-688-8600	R	222*	<.1
160	Smith Whiley and Co—Gwendolyn Smith Iloani	242 Trumbull St, Hartford CT 06103	860-548-2513	R	219*	<.1
161	Shee Atika Inc—Elliott Wimberly	315 Lincoln St Ste 300, Sitka AK 99835	907-747-3534	R	218*	<.1
162	North Castle Partners LLC—Charles F Baird Jr	183 E Putnam Ave, Greenwich CT 06830	203-862-3200	R	217*	<.1
163	Royal Gold Inc—Tony Jensen	1660 Wynkoop St Ste 10, Denver CO 80202	303-573-1660	P	216	<.1
164	Paladin Capital Group—Michael R Steed	2020 K St NW, Ste 400, Washington DC 20006	202-293-5590	R	215*	<.1
165	Riverside Partners LLC—David Belluck	1 Exeter Plaza 699 Boy, Boston MA 02116	617-351-2800	R	215*	<.1

Note: An asterisk (*) indicates an estimated financial figure. The company type code used is as follows: R = Private, P = Public, S = Private Subsidiary, B = Public Subsidiary, D = Division, J = Joint Venture, I = Investment Fund.

...Y RANKINGS BY SALES WITHIN 4-DIGIT SIC

	Company Name—Executive Officer	Address, City, State, Zip	...one	Type	Fin	Empls
166	Swander Pace Capital—Andrew Richards	100 Spear St Ste 1900, San Francisco CA 94105	415-477-8500	R	215*	<.1
167	Florida Capital Partners Inc—Peter Franz	500 N Westshore Blvd S, Tampa FL 33609	813-222-8000	R	215*	<.1
168	Capstar Partners LLC—R Steven Hicks	1703 W 5th St, Austin TX 78703	512-340-7800	R	214*	<.1
169	Linsalata Capital Partners Inc—Frank N Linsalata	5900 Landerbrook Dr St, Mayfield Heights OH 44124	440-684-1400	R	210*	<.1
170	TSG Consumer Partners—Charles H Esserman	600 Montgomery St Ste, San Francisco CA 94111	415-217-2300	R	210*	<.1
171	Compass Technology Partners Inc—David Arscott	261 Hamilton Ave Ste 2, Palo Alto CA 94301	650-322-7595	R	209*	<.1
172	Tortoise North American Energy Corp—Terry Matlack	11550 Ash St Ste 300, Leawood KS 66211	913-981-1020	P	208	N/A
173	Bank Street Telecom Funding Corp—Peter A Rust	201 Broad St 4th Fl, Stamford CT 06901	203-252-2800	R	205*	<.1
174	Accel-KKR—Tom Barnds	2500 Sand Hill Rd Ste, Menlo Park CA 94025	650-289-2460	R	204*	<.1
175	Twin Bridge Capital Partners—Patrick Lanigan	30 S Wacker Dr Ste 174, Chicago IL 60606	312-284-5600	R	202*	<.1
176	G and L Realty Corp—Daniel Gottlieb	439 N Bedford Dr, Beverly Hills CA 90210	310-273-9930	R	195*	<.1
177	ACI Capital—Kevin S Penn	666 3rd Ave 29th Fl, New York NY 10017	212-634-3333	R	182*	<.1
178	Childs Jw Equity Partners LP—John Childs	111 Huntington Ave Ste, Boston MA 02199	617-753-1100	R	178*	3.1
179	Court Square Capital Partners—John D Weber	55 E 52nd St 34th Fl, New York NY 10055	212-752-6110	R	177*	<.1
180	New Enterprise Associates—Louis Citron	1954 Greenspring Dr St, Timonium MD 21093	410-842-4000	R	171*	.1
181	Greylock Management Corp—Henry McCance	880 Winter St Ste 300, Waltham MA 02451	781-622-2200	R	170*	<.1
182	Vesbridge Partners LLC—Zenas Hutcheson	601 Edgewater Dr Ste 3, Wakefield MA 01880	508-475-2300	R	169*	<.1
183	21st Century Group LLC—John L Ware	200 Crescent Ct Ste 16, Dallas TX 75201.626	214-965-7999	R	167*	<.1
184	Westar Capital LLC—John W Clark	949 S Coast Dr Ste 170, Costa Mesa CA 20910	714-481-5160	R	166*	<.1
185	SYNCOM Venture Partners—Herbert Wilkins Jr	8515 Georgia Ave Ste 7, Silver Spring 111	301-608-3203	R	164*	<.1
186	Riverside Co—Bela Szigethy	630 5th Ave Ste 2400, New York NY 10611	212-265-6575	R	163*	.1
187	Mansur and Co—E Barry Mansur	875 N Michigan Ave Ste, Chicago 10011	312-263-2400	R	163*	<.1
188	Three Cities Research Inc—J William Uhrig	37 W 20th St Ste 908, New York 10104	212-838-9660	R	161*	<.1
189	Versa Capital Management—Ira M Lubert	2929 Arch St, Philadelphia PA 19104	215-609-3400	R	161*	<.1
190	Acoustic Ventures LLC—Alex Cranberg	1775 Sherman St Ste 23, Denver CO 80203	303-573-7011	R	160*	.1
191	SV Investment Partners—Phillip Cole	505 Fifth Ave 28th Fl, New York NY 10017	212-735-0700	S	160*	<.1
192	Rockwood Service Corp—Ken Stankievech	43 Arch St, Greenwich CT 06830	203-869-6734	R	159*	2.6
193	Sequoia Capital—Donald T Valentine	3000 Sand Hill Rd Ste, Menlo Park CA 94025	650-854-3927	R	158*	<.1
194	Investment Centers of America Inc—Greg Gunderson	PO Box 2796, Bismarck ND 58502	701-250-3300	R	158*	<.1
195	Leeds Equity Partners—Jeffrey T Leeds	350 Park Ave 23rd Fl, New York NY 10022	212-835-2000	R	157*	<.1
196	De Novo Ventures—Frederick J Dotzler	2180 Sand Hill Rd, Menlo Park CA 94025	650-329-1999	R	157*	<.1
197	Dbd Investors V LLC—Daniel D'aniello	1001 Penn Ave Nw Ste 2, Washington DC 20004	202-729-5626	R	156*	3.9
198	Aurora Capital Group—William coughlin	10877 Wilshire Blvd, Los Angeles CA 90024	310-551-0101	R	151*	<.1
199	Weeden Investors LP—Weeden Corp	145 Mason St, Greenwich CT 06830	203-861-7600	R	150*	.2
200	Davis Tuttle Venture Partners LP—Barry M Davis	110 W 7th St Ste 1000, Tulsa OK 74119	918-584-7272	R	150*	<.1
201	Brera Capital Partners LLC	244 5th Ave, New York NY 10001	212-835-1350	R	150*	3.4
202	Harris and Harris Group Inc—Douglas W Jamison	1450 Broadway 24th Fl, New York NY 10018	212-582-0900	P	149	<.1
203	Versa Capital Management Inc—Gregory Segall	2929 Arch St Ste 1650, Philadelphia PA 19104	215-609-3400	R	148*	3.0
204	SCF Partners—LE Simmons	600 Travis St Ste 6600, Houston TX 77002	713-227-7888	R	146*	<.1
205	Institutional Venture Partners—Reid Dennis	3000 Sand Hill Rd Bldg, Menlo Park CA 94025	650-854-0132	R	144*	<.1
206	Pfingsten Partners LLC—Thomas S Bagley	300 N LaSalle St Ste 5, Chicago IL 60654	312-222-8707	R	144*	<.1
207	Lend Lease Inc (New York New York)—Peter Marchetto	200 Park Ave Fl 9, New York NY 10166	212-592-6700	R	141*	3.1
208	Comvest Investment Partners Iii LP—Geoffrey Alexander	525 Okeechobee Blvd St, West Palm Beach FL 33401	561-727-2000	R	141*	3.1
209	Euclid SR Partners Inc—Frank Lin	45 Rockefeller Plz Ste, New York NY 10111	212-218-6880	R	140*	<.1
210	RWI Group—Donald Lucas	2440 Sand Hill Rd Ste, Menlo Park CA 94025	650-543-3300	R	139*	<.1
211	Centennial Ventures—Steve Halstedt	1125 17th St Ste 740, Denver CO 80202	303-405-7500	R	138*	<.1
212	Empire Investment Holdings LLC—David F Alfonso	703 Waterford Way Ste, Miami FL 33126	305-403-1111	R	135*	.8
213	Morgenthaler Ventures—David Morgenthaler	2710 Sand Hill Rd Ste, Menlo Park CA 94025	650-388-7600	R	130*	<.1
214	Quadrangle Capital Partners—Michael Huber Quadrangle Group LLC	375 Park Ave 14th Fl, New York NY 10152	212-418-1700	S	129*	<.1
215	FocalPoint Partners LLC—Daniel Conway	11766 Wilshire Blvd St, Los Angeles CA 90025	310-405-7000	R	128*	<.1
216	Ground Swell Equity Partners—Robert P Bennett	910 Stratford Ct, Del Mar CA 92014		R	128*	<.1
217	Edelson Technology Partners—Harry Edelson	300 Tice Blvd, Woodcliff Lake NJ 07677	201-930-9898	R	125*	<.1
218	Canaan Partners—Mark Biestman	2765 Sand Hill Rd Ste, Menlo Park CA 94025	650-854-8092	R	123*	<.1
219	Code Hennessy and Simmons LLC—Andrew Code	10 S Wacker Dr Ste 317, Chicago IL 60606	312-876-1840	R	123*	<.1
220	Menlo Ventures—H Dubose Montgomery	3000 Sand Hill RdBldg, Menlo Park CA 94025	650-854-8540	R	123*	<.1
221	Centre Partners Management LLC—Lester Pollack	30 Rockefeller Plz 50t, New York NY 10112	212-332-5800	R	121*	<.1
222	Century Park Capital Partners—Martin Sarafa	10250 Constellation BI, Los Angeles CA 90067	310-867-2210	R	119*	<.1
223	Toussaint Capital Partners LLC—Avery F Byrd Sr	110 Wall St 2nd Fl, New York NY 10005	212-328-1800	R	111*	<.1
224	Wingate Partners LP—Fred Hegi Jr	750 N St Paul St Ste 1, Dallas TX 75201	214-720-1313	R	111*	<.1
225	PNC Equity Management Corp—Jack C Glover	2 PNC Plz 620 Liberty, Pittsburgh PA 15222	412-762-8892	S	110*	<.1
226	Mobius Venture Capital—Brad Feld	1050 Walnut St Ste 210, Boulder CO 80302	303-642-4000	R	110*	<.1
227	Garnett and Helfrich Capital—Terry Garnett	1200 Park Pl Ste 200, San Mateo CA 94403	650-234-4200	R	108*	<.1
228	ICV Capital Partners LLC—LLoyd Metz	299 Par Ave Fl 34, New York NY 10171	212-455-9600	R	108*	<.1
229	NewWest Mezzanine—David L Henry	8110 E Union Ave Ste 1, Denver CO 80237	303-764-9678	R	108*	<.1
230	Steelpoint Capital Partners LP—Jim Caccavo	333 Hudson St 9th Fl, New York NY 10013	212-912-3800	R	108*	<.1
231	Black Canyon Capital—Michael Hooks	2000 Avenue of the Sta, Los Angeles CA 90067	310-272-1800	R	107*	<.1
232	Desco Capital Partners—Arnold B Siemer	150 East Campus View B, Columbus OH 43235	614-888-8855	R	107*	<.1
233	Gemini Partners Inc—Matthew Johnson	10900 Wilshire Blvd St, Los Angeles CA 90024	310-696-4001	R	107*	<.1
234	Saugatuck Capital Company LP—Frank Hawley Jr	187 Danbury Rd, Wilton CT 06897	203-348-6669	R	104*	<.1
235	Alta Communications Inc—Tim Dibble	28 State St Ste 1801, Boston MA 02109	617-262-7770	R	103*	<.1
236	Marwit Capital—Chris Britt	100 Bayview Cir Ste 55, Newport Beach CA 92660	949-861-3636	R	97*	<.1
237	Genstar Capital LLC—Jean-Pierre Conte	4 Embarcadero Ctr Ste, San Francisco CA 94111	415-834-2350	R	96*	<.1
238	Transportation Resource Partners LP—Roger S Penske	2555 Telegraph Rd, Bloomfield Hills MI 48302	248-648-2101	R	96*	<.1
239	Sprout Group (New York New York)—Robert Finzi	11 Madison Ave 13th Fl, New York NY 10010	212-538-3600	S	93*	<.1
240	Arch Venture Partners—Clinton W Bybee	8725 W Higgins Rd Ste, Chicago IL 60631	773-380-6600	R	92*	<.1
241	Dominion Ventures Inc—Peter Aquino	1646 N California Blvd, Walnut Creek CA 94596	925-280-6300	R	92*	<.1
242	Cambridge Ventures LP—Jean Wojtowicz	4181 E 96th St Ste 200, Indianapolis IN 46240	317-843-9704	R	88*	<.1
243	MidMark Capital LLC—Wayne L Clevenger	177 Madison Ave, Morristown NJ 07960	973-971-9960	R	87*	<.1
244	Kirtland Capital Corp—John Nestor	3201 Enterprise Pkwy S, Beachwood OH 44122	216-593-0100	R	86*	<.1
245	Ranieri and Company Inc—Lewis Ranieri	50 Charles Lindbergh B, Uniondale NY 11553	516-745-6644	R	85*	<.1
246	Clearlight Partners LLC—Michael S Kaye	100 Bayview Cir Ste 50, Newport Beach CA 92660	949-725-6610	R	84*	<.1
247	Heartland Industrial Partners LP—Daniel Tredwell	177 Broad St 10th Fl, Stamford CT 06901	203-327-1202	R	84*	<.1
248	Hummer Winblad Venture Partners—John Hummer	1 Lombard St Ste 300, San Francisco CA 94107	415-979-9600	R	83*	<.1
249	Galen Associates—David Jahns	680 Washington Blvd 11, Stamford CT 06901	203-653-6400	R	82*	<.1
250	Advanced Technology Ventures—Steve Baloff	1000 Winter St Ste 370, Waltham MA 02451	781-290-0707	R	80*	<.1
251	Arlington Capital Partners—Jeffrey H Freed	5425 Wisconsin Ave Rm, Chevy Chase MD 20815	202-337-7500	R	76*	<.1
252	Haas Wheat and Partner LP—Robert Haas	300 Crescent Ct Ste 17, Dallas TX 75201	214-871-8300	R	75*	<.1
253	TMB Industries—Jeffrey L Elmer	980 N Michigan Ave Ste, Chicago IL 60611	312-280-2565	R	75*	<.1
254	Trident Capital LP—Donald R Dixon	505 Hamilton Ave, Palo Alto CA 94301	650-289-4400	R	72*	<.1

Rank	Company Name—Executive Officer	Address, City, State, Zip	Phone	Type	Fin	Empls
255	Smith Affiliated Capital Corp—Matthew J Smith	800 Third Ave 12th Fl, New York NY 10022	212-644-9440	R	72*	<.1
256	Santa Fe Financial Corp—John V Winfield	10940 Wilshire Blvd St, Los Angeles CA 90024	310-889-2500	P	67	<.1
257	Lombard Inc—Thomas Smith	3 Embarcadero Ctr Ste, San Francisco CA 94111	415-397-5900	R	67*	<.1
258	American Industrial Partners—Nate Belden	535 5th Ave 32nd Fl, New York NY 10017	212-627-2360	R	66*	<.1
259	Riverlake Partners LLC—Erik Krieger	1000 SW Broadway Ste 1, Portland OR 97205	503-228-7100	R	64*	<.1
260	Mason Wells—John T Byrnes	411 E Wisconsin Ave St, Milwaukee WI 53202	414-727-6400	R	63*	<.1
261	Signalert Corp—Gerald Appel	150 Great Neck Rd Ste, Great Neck NY 11021	516-829-6444	R	63*	<.1
262	Kleiner Perkins Caufield and Byers—Brook Byers	2750 Sand Hill Rd, Menlo Park CA 94025	650-233-2750	R	62*	.1
263	Boston Ventures Management Inc—Barry Baker	125 High St 17th Fl, Boston MA 02110	617-350-1500	R	62*	<.1
264	Gollust Management—Keith Gollust	645 Madison Ave, New York NY 10022	212-758-7220	R	62*	<.1
265	Sanderling Ventures—Robert McNeil	400 S El Camino Real S, San Mateo CA 94402	650-401-2000	R	57*	<.1
266	CEO Venture Fund—James Colker	1 N Shore Ctr Ste 201, Pittsburgh PA 15212	412-322-2572	R	57*	<.1
267	Baker Nye Investments LP—Richard Nye	477 Madison Ave, New York NY 10022	212-826-3030	R	56*	<.1
268	American Pacific Financial Corp—Larry Polhill	22365 Barton Rd Ste 21, Grand Terrace CA 92313	909-387-0800	R	56*	<.1
269	Charter Venture Capital—Barr Dolan	525 University Ave Ste, Palo Alto CA 94301	650-325-6953	R	56*	<.1
270	Kinetic Ventures LLC—Jake Tarr	2 Wisconsin Cir Ste 62, Chevy Chase MD 20815	301-652-8066	R	55*	<.1
271	Nazem and Co—Fred Nazum	570 Lexington Ave 15th, New York NY 10022	212-371-7900	R	55*	<.1
272	Hecla Ventures Corp	6500 N Mineral Dr Ste, Coeur D Alene ID 83815	208-769-4100	S	55	N/A
273	Lovett Miller and Co—W Radford Lovett II	One Independent Dr Ste, Jacksonville FL 32202	813-222-1477	R	54*	<.1
274	MCG Global LLC—Vincent A Wasik	1 Morningside Dr N Ste, Westport CT 06880	203-226-7664	R	54*	<.1
275	Equus Total Return Inc—John A Hardy	8 Greenway Plz Ste930, Houston TX 77046		P	53	N/A
276	Alpha Capital Partners Ltd—Andrew H Kalnow	122 S Michigan Ave Ste, Chicago IL 60603	312-322-9800	R	51*	<.1
277	GFI Energy Ventures LLC—Lawrence Gilson	11611 San Vicente Blvd, Los Angeles CA 90049	310-442-0542	S	51*	<.1
278	The Transition Cos—Gene Sartin	5080 Spectrum Dr Ste 3, Addison TX 75001	972-450-3100	R	50*	.1
279	ABS Ventures—Bill Burgess	950 Winter St Ste 2600, Waltham MA 02451	781-250-0400	R	50	<.1
280	Brynwood Partners LP—Hendrick Hartong	8 Sound Shore Dr Ste 2, Greenwich CT 06830	203-622-1790	R	50*	<.1
281	Technology Partners—Ira Ehran Preis	550 University Ave, Palo Alto CA 94301	650-289-9000	R	50*	<.1
282	Veritas Capital Fund LP—Robert B McKeon	590 Madison Ave 41st F, New York NY 10022		R	50*	<.1
283	Accel Management Company Inc—Kevin Efrusy	428 University Ave, Palo Alto CA 94301	650-614-4800	R	49*	<.1
284	Woodworth Capital Inc—Jeffrey Woodworth	3110 Ruston Way Ste D, Tacoma WA 98402	253-383-3585	R	49*	<.1
285	Ampersand Ventures Management Corp—Richard Charpie	55 William St Ste 240, Wellesley MA 02481	781-239-0700	R	49*	<.1
286	Whitney and Company LLC—Robert Q Berlin	130 Main St, New Canaan CT 06840	203-716-6100	R	48*	.1
287	Apex Venture Partners—Wayne T Boulals	225 W Washington Ste 1, Chicago IL 60606	312-857-2800	R	47*	<.1
288	Hoak Capital Corp—Eric D Van den Brqanden	500 Crescent Ct Ste 22, Dallas TX 75201	972-960-4848	R	46*	<.1
289	Massachusetts Capital Resource Co—William Torpey Jr	420 Boylston St, Boston MA 02116	617-536-3900	R	45*	<.1
290	Naylor Capital Corp—John B Naylor	92 E Washington St, Chagrin Falls OH 44022	440-247-1400	R	45*	<.1
291	Hillman Co—Joe Mansinger	310 Grant St Ste 1900, Pittsburgh PA 15219	412-281-2620	R	43*	.1
292	TSG Equity Partners LLC—Thomas R Shepherd	636 Great Rd, Stow MA 01775	978-461-9900	R	43*	<.1
293	Fuji Industries Corp—Junji Yamada	600 3rd Ave 8th Fl, New York NY 10016	212-986-1890	R	41*	<.1
294	Capital For Business Inc—Stephen Broun	11 S Meramec Ave Ste 1, Saint Louis MO 63105	314-746-7427	S	40*	<.1
295	Cordova Ventures—Gerald F Schmidt	2500 Northwinds Pkwy S, Alpharetta GA 30009	678-942-0300	R	40*	<.1
296	Pennington Partners—Kelvin J Pennington	30 N LaSalle St Ste 16, Chicago IL 60602	312-346-1800	R	38*	<.1
297	Bexil Corp—Thomas B Winmill	11 Hanover Sq, New York NY 10005	212-785-0400	P	37	<.1
298	Phillips-Smith-Machens Venture Partners—Donald J Phillips	25 Highland Park Villa, Dallas TX 75205	972-387-0725	R	35*	<.1
299	Entrepreneur Venture Capital Inc—John Locker	2415 E 4th St, Duluth MN 55812	218-724-9773	R	34*	<.1
300	Northstar Industries Inc (Wayzata Minnesota)—Thomas C O'Connell	1001 Twelve Oaks Cente, Wayzata MN 55391	952-835-2000	R	33*	<.1
301	Yucaipa Capital Partners LP—Ron Burkle	9130 W Sunset Blvd, Los Angeles CA 90069	310-789-7200	S	32*	<.1
302	River Capital Inc (Atlanta Georgia)—Jerry Wethington	4200 Northside PkwyNW, Atlanta GA 30327	404-873-2166	R	32	<.1
303	Kansas Venture Capital Inc—Marshall D Parker	10601 Mission Rd Ste 2, Leawood KS 66206	913-262-7117	R	32*	<.1
304	Stoudt Co—William Stoudt	1618 Judson Rd, Longview TX 75601	903-753-7239	R	32*	<.1
305	Two Rivers Associates LLC—John S McCarthy	8000 Maryland Ave, Saint Louis MO 63105	314-721-5707	R	31*	<.1
306	Boston Capital Ventures—Johan von der Goltz	84 State St Ste 320, Boston MA 02109	617-227-6550	R	30*	<.1
307	Stanford Ranch Capital Corp—Larry Kelley	2210 Plz Dr, Rocklin CA 95765	916-624-0613	S	30*	<.1
308	Opportunity Capital Partners—J Peter Thompson	2201 Walnut Ave Ste 21, Fremont CA 94538	510-795-7000	R	29*	<.1
309	Heico Acquisitions Co—Micheal E Heisley	3 First National Plz, Chicago IL 60602	312-419-8220	R	28*	<.1
310	Kidd and Company LLC—William Kidd	10 Glenville St, Greenwich CT 06831	203-661-0070	R	28*	<.1
311	Brookwood Investments Inc—Paul Gaston	575 Lexington Ave Ste, New York NY 10022	212-644-3880	R	28*	<.1
312	Head and Co—John C Head	1330 Ave of the Americ, New York NY 10019	212-258-5250	R	27*	<.1
313	Wand Partners LP—Bruce W Schnitzer	1 Union Sq W, New York NY 10003	212-909-2620	R	27*	<.1
314	Siegfried Companies Inc—Phil Frohlich	1924 S Utica Ave Ste 1, Tulsa OK 74104	918-747-3411	R	26*	<.1
315	Millennium India Acquisition Company Inc—F Jacob Cherian	330 E 38th St, New York NY 10016	212-681-6763	P	26	<.1
316	American International Industries Inc—Daniel Dror	601 Cien St Ste 235, Kemah TX 77565	281-334-9479	P	24	<.1
317	SR One Ltd—Christoph Westphal	161 Washington St Ste, Conshohocken PA 19428	610-567-1000	S	24*	<.1
318	Massey Burch Capital Corp—Donald M Johnston	4007 Hillsboro Rd Ste, Nashville TN 37215	615-665-3227	R	24*	<.1
319	Jabara Ventures Group—Harvey Jabara	PO Box 782050, Wichita KS 67278	316-636-1266	R	22*	<.1
320	Citizens Capital Inc	28 State St, Boston MA 02109	617-725-5636	S	22*	<.1
321	RBC Ventures Inc—Todd Smith	2627 E 21st St, Tulsa OK 74114	918-743-2993	S	21*	<.1
322	Great Northern Iron Ore Properties—Joseph S Micallef	332 Minnesota St W 129, Saint Paul MN 55101	651-224-2385	P	21	<.1
323	Coral Group Inc—Yural Almog	60 S 6th St Ste 2210, Minneapolis MN 55402	612-335-8666	R	20*	<.1
324	Service Financial LLC—John Michael Stevens	PO Box 170186, Milwaukee WI 53217	414-273-0300	R	20*	<.1
325	Malaco Records Inc—Thomas J Couch	PO Box 9287, Jackson MS 39286	601-982-4522	R	19*	.1
326	BRRE Holdings Inc—Eldon Dietterick	PO Box 707, Blakeslee PA 18610	570-443-8433	S	19*	.1
327	Investors Capital Holdings Ltd—Timothy B Murphy	230 Broadway E, Lynnfield MA 01940		P	19	.1
328	Multimedia Broadcast Investment Corp—Walter L Threadgill	3101 South St NW, Washington DC 20007	202-293-1166	R	18*	<.1
329	Campus Habitat Corp—Maximus Yaney	145 Madison Ave, New York NY 10016		R	16*	<.1
330	Alliance Technology Ventures LP—Michael A Henos	2400 Lakeview Pky Ste, Alpharetta GA 30009	678-336-2000	R	16*	<.1
331	Massachusetts Technology Development Corp—Robert Crowley	40 Broad St Ste 230, Boston MA 02109	617-723-4920	R	16*	<.1
332	Integrity Asset Management LLC—Matthew G Bevin	18500 Lake Rd Ste 300, Rocky River OH 44116	216-920-5001	R	16	<.1
333	Oak Investment Partners Inc—Ed Glassmeyer	1 Gorham Island, Westport CT 06880	203-226-8346	R	14*	<.1
334	Kinship Venture Management LLP—Edward F Tuck	100 N Barranca St Ste9, West Covina CA 91791	626-966-6235	R	13*	<.1
335	NEPA Venture Fund LP—Frederick Beste	125 Goodman Dr, Bethlehem PA 18015	610-865-6550	R	12*	<.1
336	Marquette Venture Partners—Lloyd D Ruth	PO Box 1609, Vail CO 81658		R	10*	<.1
337	Horizon Partners Ltd—Robert M Feerick	3838 Tamiami Trl N Ste, Naples FL 34103	239-261-0020	R	9*	<.1
338	Flagship Ventures—Noubar Afoyan	1 Memorial Dr 7th Fl, Cambridge MA 02142	617-868-1888	R	8*	<.1
339	Mohr Davidow Ventures—William Davidow	3000 Sand Hill Rd Ste, Menlo Park CA 94025	650-854-7236	R	7*	<.1
340	Primus Capital Funds—Loyal W Wilson	5900 Landerbrook Dr St, Cleveland OH 44124	440-684-7300	R	7*	<.1
341	Berkeley International Capital Corp—Arthur Trueger	650 California St 26th, San Francisco CA 94108	415-249-0450	R	7*	<.1
342	Uchida Enterprises Inc—Yoshihiro Uchida	95 S Market St Ste 520, San Jose CA 95113	408-298-7551	R	7*	<.1

Note: An asterisk (*) indicates an estimated financial figure. The company type code used is as follows: R = Private, P = Public, S = Private Subsidiary, B = Public Subsidiary, D = Division, J = Joint Venture, I = Investment Fund.

RANKINGS BY SALES WITHIN 4-DIGIT SIC

	Company Name—Executive Officer	Address, City, State, Zip	Phone	Type	Fin	Empls
343	CoConnect Inc—Bradly M Bingham Esq	1133 6th Ave, San Diego CA 92101	760-804-8844	P	7	N/A
344	Delta Seaboard International Inc—Daniel Dror	601 Cien St Ste 235, Kemah TX 77565	713-782-1468	B	6	<.1
	American International Industries Inc					
345	Littlejohn and Company LLC—Angus C Littlejohn Jr	8 Sound Shore Dr Ste 3, Greenwich CT 06830	203-552-3500	R	5*	<.1
346	Gen Cap America Inc—Barney D Byrd	40 Burton Hills Blvd S, Nashville TN 37215	615-256-0231	R	5*	<.1
347	Thompson Clive Inc—Greg Ennis	4620 White Chapel Way, Raleigh NC 27615	919-846-1061	R	5	<.1
348	HIIFinance Corp—Samia Farouki	8075 Leesburg Pike Ste, Vienna VA 22182	703-442-8668	S	5*	<.1
349	American Research and Development Corp—Francis J Hughes	85 Devonshire St, Boston MA 02109	617-423-7500	R	4	<.1
350	Harvest Partners Inc—Harvey P Mallement	280 Park Ave 25th Fl, New York NY 10017	212-599-6300	R	3*	<.1
351	Rockies Fund Inc—Stephen G Calandrella	5373 N Union Blvd Ste, Colorado Springs CO 80918	719-590-4900	R	3	<.1
352	Central Arizona Farming Inc—Stephen Martori	7332 E Butherus Dr Ste, Scottsdale AZ 85260	480-998-1444	R	3*	<.1
353	We Buy Houses Home Services LLC—Arthur Veal	430 E 162nd St Ste 305, South Holland IL 60473	708-339-8951	R	3	<.1
354	Brantley Partners (Beachwood Ohio)—Robert P Pinkas	3550 Lander Rd Ste 300, Pepper Pike OH 44124	216-464-8400	R	2*	<.1
355	Hamilton Robinson LLC—Scott I Oakford	281 Tresser Blvd Ste 1, Stamford CT 06901	203-602-0011	R	2*	<.1
356	Milestone Growth Fund Inc—Richard Venegar	527 Marquette Ave Ste, Minneapolis MN 55402	612-838-0090	R	2*	<.1
357	NTC Group Inc—Thomas C Foley	3 Pickwick Plz, Greenwich CT 06830	203-862-2850	R	2	<.1
358	UAN Cultural and Creative Company Ltd—Parsh Patel	1021 Hill St Ste 200, Three Rivers MI 49093	586-530-5605	P	1	<.1
359	Spartan Ultrasonics Inc—Richard Maheu	1663 Fenton Business P, Fenton MO 63026	636-343-8300	R	1*	<.1
360	CVF Technologies Corp—Jeffrey I Dreben	8604 Main St Ste 1, Williamsville NY 14221	716-565-4711	P	1	.1
361	PennyMac Mortgage Investment Trust—Stanford L Kurland	6101 Condor Dr, Moorpark CA 93021	818-224-7442	P	1	N/A
362	Mvoc LLC—Chuck Russitano	208 Ave Of The Est, Cary NC 27518	919-791-2387	R	<1*	<.1
363	Lake Capital—Paul Yovovich	676 N Michigan Ave Ste, Chicago IL 60611	312-640-7050	R	<1	<.1
364	Long Point Capital—Gerry Boylan	26700 Woodward Ave, Royal Oak MI 48067	248-591-6000	R	<1	<.1
365	Horizon Holdings—James M Shorin	1 Bush St Ste 650, San Francisco CA 94104	415-788-2000	R	<1	<.1
366	Arbor EnTech Corp—Brad Houtkin	7100 Island Blvd Slip, Aventura FL 33160	305-466-6988	P	<1	N/A
367	Bear Lake Recreation Inc—Wayne Bassham	4685 S Highland Dr Ste, Salt Lake City UT 84117	801-278-9424	P	<1	N/A
368	Fuse Science Inc—Adam Adler	20900 NE 30th Ave 8th, Miami FL 33180	305-503-3873	P	<1	N/A
369	Pinnacle West—Donald E Brandt	PO Box 53999 Mail Sta, Phoenix AZ 85072	602-250-1000	S	N/A	<.1
370	Advanced Technologies Group Ltd—Abel Raskas	331 Newman Springs Rd, Red Bank NJ 07701	732-784-2801	S	N/A	<.1

TOTALS: SIC 6799 Investors Nec
Companies: 370   416,030   92.0

7011 Hotels & Motels

	Company Name—Executive Officer	Address, City, State, Zip	Phone	Type	Fin	Empls
1	Marriott International Inc—JW Marriott Jr	10400 Fernwood Rd, Bethesda MD 20817	301-380-3000	P	11,691	129.0
2	Hilton Worldwide—Christopher J Nassetta	7930 Jones Branch Dr S, McLean VA 22102	703-883-1100	S	10,105*	130.0
3	Radisson Hotels and Resorts—Hubert Joly	11340 Blondo St Rm 100, Omaha NE 68164	763-212-5000	S	9,585*	72.1
	Carlson Companies Inc					
4	Extended Stay Hotels—Gary A DeLapp	100 Dunbar St, Spartanburg SC 29306	864-573-1600	R	8,951*	7.6
5	Bellagio LLC—Bill McBeath	PO Box 7700, Las Vegas NV 89177	702-693-7111	S	8,185*	8.5
	Mirage Resorts Inc					
6	MGM Resorts International—James J Murren	3600 Las Vegas Blvd S, Las Vegas NV 89109	702-693-8077	P	7,849	61.0
7	Las Vegas Sands Corp—Sheldon G Adelson	3355 Las Vegas Blvd S, Las Vegas NV 89109	702-414-1000	P	6,853	34.0
8	Bally's Park Place Inc—Loveman Greg	Park Pl and Boardwalk, Atlantic City NJ 08401	609-340-2000	S	5,314*	4.3
9	Starwood Hotels and Resorts Worldwide Inc—Frits van Paasschen	1111 Westchester Ave, White Plains NY 10604	914-640-8100	P	5,071	145.0
10	Hilton International Co—Chris Nassetta	901 Ponce de Leon Blvd, Coral Gables FL 33134	305-444-3444	S	4,565*	40.0
11	Carlson Companies Inc—Hubert Joly	701 Carlson Pky, Minnetonka MN 55305	763-212-4000	R	4,500*	170.0
12	Host Hotels and Resorts Inc—W Edward Walter	6903 Rockledge Dr Ste1, Bethesda MD 20817	240-744-1000	P	4,437	.2
13	Barcelo Crestline Corp—Bruce Wardinski	3950 University Dr Ste, Fairfax VA 22030	571-529-6000	S	4,431*	3.7
14	H Group Holding Inc—John Stellato	71 S Wacker 39th Fl, Chicago IL 60606	312-873-4900	R	3,994*	80.0
15	Wyndham Worldwide Corp—Stephen P Holmes	22 Sylvan Way, Parsippany NJ 07054	973-753-6000	P	3,851	26.4
16	Little America Hotels and Resorts—R Earl Holding	PO Box 30825, Salt Lake City UT 84130	801-524-2700	D	3,819*	7.0
17	Hyatt Hotels Corp—Mark S Hoplamazian	71 S Wacker Dr, Chicago IL 60606	312-750-1234	B	3,698	50.0
	H Group Holding Inc					
18	Trump Hotels and Casino Resorts Holdings LP	15 S Pennsylvania Ave, Atlantic City NJ 08401	609-449-6515	S	3,619*	4.0
	Trump Entertainment Resorts Inc					
19	Davidson Hotel Company Inc—John Belden	3340 Players Club Pkwy, Memphis TN 38125	901-761-4664	R	3,471*	3.9
20	Shilo Corporation Management Offices—Mark S Hemstreet	11600 SW Shilo Ln, Portland OR 97225	503-641-6565	R	3,463*	2.5
21	Shilo Inns Co—Mark S Hemstreet	11600 SW Shilo Ln, Portland OR 97225		S	3,088*	2.5
	Shilo Corporation Management Offices					
22	Super 8 Motels Inc—John Valletta	1 Sylvan Way, Parsippany NJ 07054	973-428-9700	S	2,850*	25.0
23	Richfield Holdings Inc—Bill Lenahand	7600 East Orchard Ste, Greenwood Village CO 80111	303-220-2000	R	2,827*	2.0
24	Stratosphere Corp—Frank Riolo	2000 Las Vegas Blvd S, Las Vegas NV 89104	702-380-7777	R	2,534*	2.2
25	Sunstone Hotel Investors Inc—Ken Cruse	120 Vantis Ste 350, Aliso Viejo CA 92656	949-369-4000	P	2,436	<.1
26	Country Inns and Suites	701 Carlson Pky, Minnetonka MN 55305	763-212-1342	S	2,408*	3.0
	Carlson Hotels Worldwide					
27	Horseshoe Casino and Hotel—Gary Loveman	711 Horseshoe Blvd, Bossier City LA 71111	318-742-0711	D	2,353*	2.0
28	Trump Taj Mahal Casino Resort—Mark Juliano	1000 Boardwalk, Atlantic City NJ 08401	609-449-1000	S	2,231	N/A
	Trump Entertainment Resorts Inc					
29	Caesars Entertainment Corp—Gary W Loveman	1 Caesars Palace Dr, Las Vegas NV 89109	702-407-6000	R	2,172	69.0
30	Amway Hotel Corp—Joe Tomaselli	187 Monroe Ave, Grand Rapids MI 49503	616-776-6417	S	2,119*	1.5
31	Fiesta Station Inc—Frankfort Fertitta III	1505 S Pavillion Cente, Las Vegas NV 89135	702-631-7000	S	1,836*	1.3
	Station Casinos Inc					
32	Harrah's Operating Co—Gary Loveman	1 Caesars Palace Dr, Las Vegas NV 89109	702-407-6000	S	1,619*	23.0
	Caesars Entertainment Corp					
33	Pinehurst Co—Pat Corso	PO Box 4000, Pinehurst NC 28374	910-295-6811	S	1,586*	2.0
34	Mohegan Tribal Gaming Authority—Mitchell Grossinger Etess	1 Mohegan Sun Blvd, Uncasville CT 06382	860-862-8000	R	1,572	10.3
35	Station Casinos Inc—Frank J Fertitta III	1505 S Pavilion Center, Las Vegas NV 89102	702-495-3000	R	1,330*	14.5
36	Castle Resorts and Hotels Inc—Rick Wall	3 Waterfront Plz 500 A, Honolulu HI 96813	808-545-3510	S	1,231*	1.0
37	Seven Springs Mountain Resort—Eric Mauck	777 Waterwheel Dr, Champion PA 15622	814-352-7777	R	1,014*	.9
38	Castle Group (Honolulu Hawaii)—Rick Wall	3 Waterfront Plz Ste 5, Honolulu HI 96813	808-524-0900	R	964*	.8
39	Gaylord Entertainment Co—Stephen G Buchanan	1 Gaylord Dr, Nashville TN 37214	615-316-6000	P	952	10.4
40	Carlson Hotels Worldwide—Hubert Joly	PO Box 59159, Minneapolis MN 55459	763-212-5000	S	920*	.8
	Carlson Companies Inc					
41	Lane Industries Inc (Northbrook Illinois)—Forrest M Schneider	1200 Shermer Rd Ste 40, Northbrook IL 60062	847-498-6789	R	900*	.9
42	Quorum Hotels and Resorts—Tony Farris	5429 LBJ Frwy, Garland TX 75040	972-458-7265	R	871*	2.2
43	Sunstone Hotel Properties Inc—Ken Cruse	120 Vantis Ste 350, Aliso Viejo CA 92656	949-330-4000	R	865*	.9
44	Mt Bachelor Inc—Dave Rathbun	PO Box 1000, Bend OR 97709	541-382-2442	S	851*	.9
45	Trump Entertainment Resorts Inc—Mark Juliano	1000 Boardwalk, Atlantic City NJ 08401	609-449-5866	P	792	5.5
46	Interstate Hotels and Resorts Inc—Thomas F Hewitt	4501 N Fairfax Dr, Arlington VA 22203	703-387-3100	P	780	19.0

Rank	Company Name—*Executive Officer*	Address, City, State, Zip	Phone	Type	Fin	Empls
47	Gaylord Entertainment Co Entertainment Div—*Colin Reed* Gaylord Entertainment Co	1 Gaylord Dr, Nashville TN 37214	615-316-6000	D	768*	6.0
48	Hart Hotels Inc—*David P Hart*	617 Dingens St Ste 4, Buffalo NY 14206	716-893-6551	R	741*	.8
49	TRT Holdings Inc—*James Caldwell*	420 Decker Dr Ste 200, Irving TX 75062	972-730-6664	R	714*	10.5
50	Pointe Hilton Resorts Inc—*Teri Agosta* Hilton Worldwide	7677 N 16th St, Phoenix AZ 85020	602-997-2626	S	698*	.5
51	Best Western International Inc—*David T Kong*	6201 N 24th Pky, Phoenix AZ 85016	602-957-4200	R	696*	1.2
52	John Q Hammons Hotels Inc—*Jaqueline Dowdy*	300 John Q Hammons Pkw, Springfield MO 65806	417-864-4300	R	646*	9.0
53	JW Marriott Ihilani Resort and SpA—*Dan Banchiu*	92-1001 Olani St, Kapolei HI 96707	808-679-0079	R	606*	.5
54	Stratton Corp—*Alex Wasilov*	5 Village Lodge Rd, Stratton Mountain VT 05155	802-297-4000	S	597*	1.0
55	Choice Hotels International Inc—*Stephen P Joyce*	10750 Columbia Pike, Silver Spring MD 20901	301-592-5000	P	596	1.5
56	LQ Management LLC—*Wayne B Goldberg*	PO Box 2636, San Antonio TX 78299	214-492-6600	R	585*	9.0
57	Adam's Mark Hotels and Resorts—*Fred S Kummer*	PO Box 419039, Saint Louis MO 63141	314-567-9000	D	581*	.4
58	Grand Traverse Resort and SpA—*Donald Ponniah*	PO Box 404, Acme MI 49610	231-534-6000	R	572*	.7
59	JHM Hotels Inc—*Hasmukh P Rama*	60 Point Cir, Greenville SC 29615	864-232-9944	R	568*	1.0
60	Loews Ventana Canyon Resort—*Brian Johnson*	7000 N Resort Dr, Tucson AZ 85750	520-299-2020	S	553*	.5
61	Destination Hotels and Resorts Inc	10333 E Dry Creek Rd S, Englewood CO 80112	303-799-3830	S	542*	6.5
62	DJONT Operations LLC	545 E John Carpenter F, Irving TX 75062	972-444-4900	S	535	N/A
63	Pioneer Hotel and Gambling Hall—*Margaret Gabaldon*	2200 S Casino Dr, Laughlin NV 89029	702-298-2442	S	519*	.6
64	Outrigger Enterprises Inc—*David P Carey III*	2375 Kuhio Ave, Honolulu HI 96815		R	514*	3.0
65	Opry Mills—*Jad Murphy*	433 Opry Mills Dr, Nashville TN 37214	615-514-1100	S	513*	4.0
66	Mirage Resorts Inc MGM Resorts International	3400 S Las Vegas Blvd, Las Vegas NV 89109	702-791-7111	S	497*	6.0
67	Harrison Group (Ocean City Maryland)—*Hale Harrison*	PO Box 160, Ocean City MD 21843	410-289-5182	R	496*	.8
68	Evans Hotels—*Grace Evans Cherashore*	998 W Mission Bay Dr, San Diego CA 92109	858-488-0551	R	493*	1.3
69	Naples Registry Resort—*Hunter Hansen*	475 Seagate Dr, Naples FL 34103	239-597-3232	S	477*	.8
70	Charter One Hotels and Resorts Inc—*John W Balliett*	2032 Hillview St, Sarasota FL 34239	941-364-9224	R	417*	.8
71	Rio Hotel and Casino Inc—*Ralph Horn* Caesars Entertainment Corp	3700 W Flamingo Rd, Las Vegas NV 89103		S	392	5.0
72	Kyo-Ya Company Ltd—*Kelly Sanders*	2255 Kalakaua Ave, Honolulu HI 96815	808-931-8600	S	384*	3.0
73	Marcus Corp—*Gregory S Marcus*	100 E Wisconsin Ave St, Milwaukee WI 53202	414-905-1000	P	377	6.2
74	Red Roof Inns Inc—*Joseph Wheeling*	121 E Nationwide Blvd, Columbus OH 43215	614-744-2600	S	371*	5.8
75	Fairmont Copley Plaza Hotel Corp—*Bill Fatt* Fairmont Hotel And Resorts US/Mexico Div	138 St James Ave, Boston MA 02116	617-267-5300	S	371*	.3
76	Atlantic City Showboat Inc—*Jay Snowden* Caesars Entertainment Corp	PO Box 840, Atlantic City NJ 08404	609-343-4000	S	357*	3.6
77	Sundance Enterprises—*Mike Washburn*	8841 N Alpine Loop Rd, Sundance UT 84604	801-225-4107	R	357*	.4
78	Barton's Club 93 Inc—*TW Barton*	PO Box 523, Jackpot NV 89825	775-755-2341	R	350*	.3
79	Harveys Casino Resorts—*Gary Loveman* Caesars Entertainment Corp	PO Box 128, Stateline NV 89449	775-588-2411	S	340*	5.1
80	Fortune Valley Hotel and Casino—*Lisa Boyer*	321 Gregory St, Central City CO 80427	303-582-0800	R	338*	2.7
81	Crowne Plaza Downtown Columbus—*Catherine Burton*	3 Ravinia Dr Ste 100, Atlanta GA 30346	770-604-2000	D	324	.4
82	Skytop Lodges Inc—*Ed Mayotte*	1 Skytop Lodge, Skytop PA 18357		R	312*	.4
83	Noble Investment Group LLC—*Mitesh Shah*	3424 Peachtree Rd Ste, Atlanta GA 30326	404-262-9660	R	309*	.3
84	Rainbow Hotel Casino—*Robert L Miodunski*	PO Box 820768, Vicksburg MS 39182	601-636-7575	S	297*	.5
85	Great Wolf Resorts Inc—*Kimberly K Schaefer*	122 W Washington Ave, Madison WI 53703	608-661-4700	P	297	6.7
86	New York-New York Hotel and Casino LLC MGM Resorts International	3790 Las Vegas Blvd S, Las Vegas NV 89109	702-650-7565	S	294*	2.3
87	Benchmark Hospitality International—*Burt Cabanas*	4 Waterway Sq Ste 300, The Woodlands TX 77380	281-367-5757	R	286*	5.0
88	Inns of America—*Horace D'Angelo*	5010 Avenida Encinas, Carlsbad CA 92008	760-438-6661	R	268*	.3
89	HLC Hotels Inc—*Charley Aimone*	PO Box 13069, Savannah GA 31416	912-352-4493	R	265*	.3
90	Fairmont Hotel And Resorts US/Mexico Div—*William Fatt*	650 California St 12th, San Francisco CA 94108	415-772-7800	R	258*	5.0
91	Tempe Mission Palms Destination Hotels and Resorts Inc	60 E 5th St, Tempe AZ 85281	480-894-1400	D	247*	.3
92	Morgans Hotel Group Co—*Michael Gross*	475 10th Ave, New York NY 10018	212-277-4100	P	236	4.6
93	Hilton Hawaiian Village—*Jerry Gibson* Hilton Worldwide	2005 Kalia Rd, Honolulu HI 96815	808-949-4321	S	230*	1.8
94	Lodgian Inc—*Dana M Ciraldo*	2002 Summit Blvd Ste 3, Atlanta GA 30319	404-364-9400	S	205	2.4
95	Mount Snow Ltd—*Kelly Pawlak*	PO Box 2810, West Dover VT 05356	802-464-3333	R	204*	.5
96	Primadonna Company LLC—*Michael Starr* MGM Resorts International	31700 S Las Vegas Blvd, Primm NV 89019	702-382-1212	S	199*	2.7
97	RLJ Lodging Trust—*Thomas Baltimore*	3 Bethesda Metro Ctr S, Bethesda MD 20814	301-280-7777	P	197	.1
98	ResortQuest International Inc—*Mark Fioravanti* Gaylord Entertainment Co	8955 Hwy 98 W Ste 203, Destin FL 32550	850-278-4000	S	190	5.0
99	Glenwood Hot Springs Lodge and Pool Inc—*Henry A Bosco*	PO Box 308, Glenwood Springs CO 81602	970-945-6571	R	181*	.2
100	Gasparilla Inn Inc—*Jack G Damioli*	PO Box 1088, Boca Grande FL 33921		R	179*	.4
101	Victoria Partners—*Alisson May*	3770 Las Vegas Blvd S, Las Vegas NV 89109		R	176*	3.0
102	Rahn Bahia Mar Ltd—*H Wayne Huizenga*	801 Seabreeze Blvd, Fort Lauderdale FL 33316	954-764-2323	S	174*	.1
103	Ramparts Inc—*Glen Schaffer*	3950 Las Vegas Blvd S, Las Vegas NV 89119	702-734-0410	R	173*	3.1
104	Canyon Ranch	8600 E Rockcliff Rd, Tucson AZ 85750	520-749-9000	R	172*	1.0
105	Marina Associates Ltd—*Timothy Wilmott*	777 Harrahs Blvd, Atlantic City NJ 08401	609-441-5000	R	172*	2.9
106	Monarch Casino and Resort Inc—*John Farahi*	3800 S Virginia St, Reno NV 89502	775-335-4600	P	171	1.8
107	Choctaw Resort Development Enterprises—*Paul Harvey*	PO Box 6048, Choctaw MS 39350	601-650-1234	R	164*	4.0
108	Red Lion Hotels Corp—*Jon E Eliassen*	201 W North River Dr S, Spokane WA 99201	509-459-6100	P	163	2.5
109	Allegro Resorts Market Corp—*Benny Guevara*	6303 Blue Lagoon Dr St, Miami FL 33921	305-261-3450	S	160*	6.0
110	Driftwood Hospitality Management LLC—*Dee Osborne*	11780 Us Hwy 1 Ste 400, North Palm Beach FL 33408	561-207-2700	R	158*	3.0
111	Primm Valley Resort And Casino—*Rene West*	31900 Las Vegas Blvd S, Jean NV 89019	702-679-5160	R	156*	3.0
112	HI Development Corp—*David Callen*	111 W Fortune St, Tampa FL 33602	813-229-6686	R	154*	1.2
113	Squaw Valley Ski Corp	PO Box 2007, Olympic Valley CA 96146	530-583-6985	S	153*	1.2
114	Cypress Hotel Management Company Inc—*Larry Walker*	2250 N Orange Blossom, Orlando FL 32804	407-839-3939	R	152*	2.5
115	Riviera Operating Corp—*William L Westerman* Riviera Holdings Corp	2901 Las Vegas Blvd S, Las Vegas NV 89109	702-734-5110	O	151*	2.1
116	InnLink LLC—*Kristin Intress*	130 Maple Dr N, Hendersonville TN 37075		R	148*	.1
117	Trump Marina Hotel And Casino Inc—*Donald Trump*	Brigantine Blvd Huron, Atlantic City NJ 08401	609-441-8440	R	145*	2.7
118	Loews Hotels Holding Corp—*Jonathan Tisch*	667 Madison Ave, New York NY 10065	212-521-2000	R	143*	2.5
119	Peppermill Casinos Inc—*Bill Paganitti*	90 W Grove St Ste 600, Reno NV 89509	775-689-8900	R	141*	2.5
120	Deluxe Motel—*Sam Patel*	2700 N Main St, Sumter SC 29153	803-469-0236	R	140*	<.1
121	Procaccianti Az Ii LP—*Jeff Blott*	6333 N Scottsdale Rd O, Scottsdale AZ 85250	480-948-7750	R	140*	N/A
122	Recreational Enterprises Inc—*Donald Carano*	PO Box 3399, Reno NV 89505	775-786-5700	R	140*	2.4
123	Lane Hospitality Inc—*Bill DeForrest* Lane Industries Inc (Northbrook Illinois)	1200 Shermer Rd, Northbrook IL 60062	847-498-6650	S	134*	2.5

Note: An asterisk (*) indicates an estimated financial figure. The company type code used is as follows: R = Private, P = Public, S = Private Subsidiary, B = Public Subsidiary, D = Division, J = Joint Venture, I = Investment Fund.

COMPANY RANKINGS BY SALES WITHIN 4-DIGIT SIC

Rank	Company Name—*Executive Officer*	Address, City, State, Zip	Phone	Type	Fin	Empls
124	InTown Suites Management Inc—*Mark S Ticotin*	2727 Paces Ferry Rd, Atlanta GA 30339	770-799-5000	R	133*	.1
125	Jackson Hole Mountain Resort—*Jerry M Blann*	PO Box 290, Teton Village WY 83025	307-733-2292	R	128*	1.0
126	Gaston's White River Resort—*Jim Gaston*	1777 River Rd, Lakeview AR 72642	870-431-5202	R	124*	.2
127	Riviera Holdings Corp—*Andy Choy*	2901 Las Vegas Blvd S, Las Vegas NV 89109	702-734-5110	P	119	.9
128	Camberley Associates Inc—*Ian Lloyd-Jones*	4405 Northside Pky NW, Atlanta GA 30327	404-261-9600	R	112*	.7
129	Midamerica Hotels Corp—*Dan Drury*	105 S Mount Auburn Rd, Cape Girardeau MO 63703	573-334-0546	R	103*	.8
130	Ski Roundtop Operating Corp—*Ron Hawks* Snow Time Inc	925 Roundtop Rd, Lewisberry PA 17339	717-432-9631	S	103*	.8
131	Sedona Resort Management Inc—*George Lidicker*	200 Farmbrook Ct, Atlanta GA 30350	678-579-0770	R	102	.8
132	Waterville Valley Resort Inc—*Chris Sununu*	PO Box 540, Waterville Valley NH 03215	603-236-8311	R	102*	.8
133	Grand Teton Lodge Co—*John Rutter*	PO Box 250, Moran WY 83013	307-543-2811	S	100*	.8
134	Sunday River Skiway Corp—*John Diller*	PO Box 4500, Newry ME 04261	207-824-3000	R	97*	1.8
135	Doral Arrowwood—*Howard Kaskel*	975 Andersonhill Rd, Rye Brook NY 10573	914-939-5500	R	90	.8
136	Sandy Beach Resort—*Tony Volpe*	201 S Ocean Blvd, Myrtle Beach SC 29577	843-448-5522	R	88*	.1
137	Mt Mansfield Co—*Robert McEleney*	5781 Mountain Rd, Stowe VT 05672	802-253-3500	S	86*	.5
138	Imperial Palace Inc Caesars Entertainment Corp	3535 Las Vegas Blvd S, Las Vegas NV 89109	702-731-3311	S	84*	2.2
139	Ralph Williams and Associates—*Ralph Williams*	1800 N Wabash Rd Ste 3, Marion IN 46952	765-668-7561	R	82*	.1
140	Bennett Enterprises Inc—*David Bennett*	PO Box 670, Perrysburg OH 43552	419-874-3111	R	81*	1.5
141	Renaissance Chicago Downtown Hotel—*Paige Koerbel* Marriott International Inc	One W Wacker Dr, Chicago IL 60601	312-372-7200	S	81*	.5
142	Aspen Skiing Co—*Pat O'Donnell*	PO Box 1248, Aspen CO 81612	970-925-1220	R	80*	2.5
143	Sahara Nevada Corp—*Al Hummel*	2535 Las Vegas Blvd S, Las Vegas NV 89109	702-737-2111	S	80*	1.5
144	White Lodging Services Corp—*Bruce White*	701 E 83rd Ave, Merrillville IN 46410	219-472-2900	R	80*	.8
145	Travelodge Hotels Inc—*Ken Greene*	7 Sylvan Way, Parsippany NJ 07054	973-428-9700	S	78*	2.0
146	Breakers Palm Beach Inc—*Paul Leone* Flagler System Inc	1 S County Rd, Palm Beach FL 33480	561-655-6611	S	78*	1.7
147	AmericInn International LLC—*Arnold A Angeloni*	250 Lake Dr E, Chanhassen MN 55317	952-294-5000	S	78*	.1
148	VCA Tucson Inc Varsity Clubs of America Inc	3855 E Speedway Blvd, Tucson AZ 85716	520-318-3777	S	77*	<.1
149	Concord Hospitality Enterprises Co—*Mark G Laport*	8601 Six Forks Rd Ste, Raleigh NC 27615	919-455-2900	R	76*	2.0
150	Coastal Hotel Group Inc—*Yogi Hutsen*	18525 36th Ave S, Seattle WA 98188	206-388-0400	R	76*	.6
151	Sonesta International Hotels Corp—*Stephanie Sonnabend*	116 Huntington Ave, Boston MA 02116	617-421-5400	P	72	.7
152	Golden Road Motor Inn Inc—*David Hyday* Monarch Casino and Resort Inc	3800 S Virginia St, Reno NV 89502	775-335-4600	S	71*	2.0
153	Rosewood Hotels and Resorts Inc—*Radha Arura*	500 Crescent Ct Ste 30, Dallas TX 75201	214-880-4200	S	71*	.6
154	Chase Resorts Inc—*Mark Brown*	PO Box 215, Lake Ozark MO 65049	573-365-3000	R	68*	.6
155	Balsams Corp—*Stephen Barba*	100 Cold Spring Rd, Colebrook NH 03576	603-255-3400	R	68*	.4
156	Wailea Golf LLC—*Barry Helle*	4050 Kalai Waa St, Kihei HI 96753	808-879-4471	R	68*	.1
157	Hampton Inns Inc Hilton Worldwide	755 Crossover Ln, Memphis TN 38117	901-374-5000	S	65*	1.5
158	Pebble Beach Co—*Bill Perocchi*	PO Box 567, Pebble Beach CA 93953	831-624-3811	R	64*	1.6
159	Kapalua Land Company Ltd—*Tom Juliano*	200 Village Rd, Lahaina HI 96761	808-669-5622	S	64*	.4
160	Resort at Squaw Creek—*Charles Peck*	P O Box 3333, Olympic Valley CA 96146	530-583-6300	R	63*	.5
161	Mammoth Mountain Ski Area—*Rusty Gregory*	PO Box 24, Mammoth Lakes CA 93546	760-934-2571	R	62*	2.5
162	ILX Bell Rock Inc	6246 Hwy 179, Sedona AZ 86351	928-282-4161	S	59*	<.1
163	Boomtown Hotel and Casino Inc	PO Box 399, Verdi NV 89439	775-345-6000	S	57*	1.0
164	Brown Palace Hotel Company Inc—*Tony Farris*	321 17th St, Denver CO 80202	303-297-3111	R	56*	.4
165	Dry Pocket Road Hotel Development LLC—*Stephen P Joyce* Choice Hotels International Inc	10750 Columbia Pke, Silver Spring MD 20901	301-592-5000	S	54*	.1
166	Camelback Ski Corp—*Samuel Newman*	PO Box 168, Tannersville PA 18372	570-629-1661	R	53*	.4
167	Seagate Hospitality Group—*E Anthony Wilson*	601 N Congress Ave Ste, Delray Beach FL 33445	561-665-4800	R	51	1.5
168	Madison Hotel Inc—*Jonathan M Tisch*	1177 15th St NW, Washington DC 20005	202-862-1600	S	51*	.4
169	Killington Ltd—*Chris Nyberg*	4763 Killington Rd, Killington VT 05751	802-422-6200	R	49*	1.5
170	Premier Resorts Inc—*Barbara Zimonja*	PO Box 4800, Park City UT 84060	435-655-4800	R	48*	1.2
171	Waimea Plantation Cottages	PO Box 367, Waimea HI 96796	808-338-1625	D	46*	.1
172	Callaway Gardens Resort Inc—*Robert Mceleney*	PO Box 2000, Pine Mountain GA 31822	706-663-2281	R	45*	1.0
173	Outrigger Lodging Services	16000 Ventura Blvd Ste, Encino CA 91436	818-905-8280	R	45*	1.0
174	Barton Creek Conference Resort Inc—*James Walsh* Pinehurst Co	8212 Barton Club Dr, Austin TX 78735	512-329-4000	S	44*	.8
175	Saddlebrook Resorts Inc—*Thomas L Dempsey*	5700 Saddlebrook Way, Wesley Chapel FL 33543	813-973-1111	R	41*	.8
176	Hawk's Cay Resort and Marina—*Sheldon Suga*	61 Hawks Cay Blvd, Duck Key FL 33050	305-743-7000	R	39*	.4
177	Vagabond Inns Inc—*Bruce Weitzman*	50 Glenlake Parkway St, Atlanta GA 30328	770-393-2662	R	38*	.9
178	Lake Powell Resorts and Marinas—*Joseph Neubauer*	PO Box 1597, Page AZ 86040	928-645-1083	D	37*	1.2
179	Lake Mountain Co—*Melanie Murphy* Big Boulder Corp	PO Box 1539, Blakeslee PA 18610	570-443-8433	S	36	<.1
180	Best Value Inn—*Parish Patel*	822 S Cumberland St, Lebanon TN 37087	615-449-5781	S	36*	<.1
181	Peek 'N Peak Recreation Inc—*Paul Kiebler*	PO Box 360, Findley Lake NY 14736	716-355-4141	R	32*	.7
182	Robert M Goff and Associates—*RM Goff*	PO Box 29, Little Rock AR 72203	501-664-3332	R	32*	.6
183	Gurneys Inn Resort and SpA—*Ingrid Lemme*	290 Old Montauk Hwy, Montauk NY 11954	631-668-2345	R	30*	.3
184	Big Bear Mountain Resort—*Richard C Kun*	PO Box 77, Big Bear Lake CA 92315	909-866-5766	R	28*	1.0
185	Grand Cypress Florida Inc—*Mark Cox* Kyo-Ya Company Ltd	1 N Jacaranda, Orlando FL 32836	407-239-4700	S	28*	.5
186	Sunriver Resorts—*Tom Luersen*	PO Box 3609, Sunriver OR 97707	541-593-1000	R	27*	.5
187	Sun Valley Company Inc—*Wallace Huffman*	1 Sun Valley Rd, Sun Valley ID 83353	208-622-2001	S	26*	.2
188	Windmill Inns of America Inc—*John Cauvin*	15455 N Greenway-Hayde, Scottsdale AZ 85260	480-443-0909	R	24*	<.1
189	Fort William Henry Corp—*Robert Black Sr*	48 Canada Street, Lake George NY 12845	518-668-3081	R	23	.6
190	Grand Hotel Co—*RD Musser*	PO Box 286, Mackinac Island MI 49757	906-847-3331	R	22*	.5
191	Kemmons Wilson Inc—*Spence L Wilson*	8700 Trail Lake Dr W S, Memphis TN 38125	901-346-8800	R	22*	.3
192	Smiley Brothers Inc—*Albert K Smiley*	1000 Mountain Rest Rd, New Paltz NY 12561	845-255-1000	R	20*	.7
193	Cooper Hotel Group Inc—*Pace Cooper*	1661 Aaron Brenner Dr, Memphis TN 38120	901-322-1400	R	20*	.4
194	Sierra Summit Mountain Resort Inc—*RC Kun* Big Bear Mountain Resort	PO Box 236, Lakeshore CA 93634	559-233-2500	S	18*	.4
195	Long Lines Ltd—*Craig Cavey*	501 4th St, Sergeant Bluff IA 51054	712-271-4000	R	18	.3
196	Brentwood Boulevard Hotel Development LLC—*Stephen P Joyce* Choice Hotels International Inc	10750 Columbia Pke, Silver Spring MD 20901	301-592-5000	S	18*	<.1
197	Rosewood Property Co—*John Scott*	500 Crescent Ct Ste 30, Dallas TX 75201	214-880-4200	S	18*	<.1
198	Titan Global Distribution—*Daniel Kelly*	1100 Corporate Sq Dr, Saint Louis MO 63132	314-817-0051	S	18*	<.1

Rank	Company Name—Executive Officer	Address, City, State, Zip	Phone	Type	Fin	Empls
190	The STAR Group—Linda Rosanio	220 Laurel Rd, Cherry Hill NJ 08002	856-782-7000	R	57*	.1
191	Intermark Communications Inc—Timothy McCallan	311 Crossways Park Dr, Woodbury NY 11797	631-719-1250	R	57*	<.1
192	M J Brunner Inc—Michael Brunner	11 Stanwix St Fl 5, Pittsburgh PA 15222	412-995-9500	R	57*	.2
193	API Advertising—Mike Brown	4471 Nicole Dr, Lanham MD 20706	301-731-6100	R	56*	.1
194	MarketSense LLC—Andrew Mahler	7020 High Grove Blvd, Burr Ridge IL 60527	630-654-0170	R	56*	.1
195	Media Logic—David Schultz	1 Park Pl, Albany NY 12205	518-456-3015	S	55*	.1
196	Charles Tombras Advertising—Charles Tombras Jr	PO Box 15151, Knoxville TN 37901	865-524-5376	R	55*	.1
197	Pavone—Michael R Pavone	1006 Market St, Harrisburg PA 17101	717-234-8886	R	55*	.1
198	Mintz and Hoke Inc—Kris Knopf	40 Tower Ln, Avon CT 06001	860-678-0473	R	55*	.1
199	GlynnDevins Inc—George Devins	11230 College Blvd, Overland Park KS 66210	913-491-0600	R	54*	.1
200	Montgomery Zukerman Davis Inc—Allan Zukerman	1800 N Meridian St Ste, Indianapolis IN 46202	317-924-6271	R	54*	.1
201	Lehman Millet Inc—Bruce Lehman	2 Atlantic Ave, Boston MA 02110	617-722-0019	R	54*	.1
202	Hitchcock Fleming and Associates Inc—Jack S DeLeo	500 Wolf Ledges Pkwy, Akron OH 44311	330-376-2111	R	53*	.1
203	Shaker Advertising Agency Inc—Joseph G Shaker	1100 Lake St, Oak Park IL 60301	708-383-5320	R	53*	.1
204	the bounce agency—Carlos Jimenez	201 Riverplace Ste 400, Greenville SC 29607	864-271-8340	R	52*	.1
205	Tri-Media Inc—Gary Jordan	305 Washington Ave Ste, Baltimore MD 21204	410-825-1800	R	52*	.1
206	Anderson Communications Inc—Al Anderson	2245 Godby Rd, Atlanta GA 30349	404-766-8000	R	52*	<.1
207	Laughlin/Constable Inc—Karen Duffy	207 E Michigan St, Milwaukee WI 53202	414-272-2400	R	51*	.1
208	One Technologies—Mark Henry	8144 Walnut Hill Ln St, Dallas TX 75231	469-916-1700	R	51*	.1
209	Mason Inc—Charlie Mason	23 Amity Rd, Bethany CT 06524	203-393-1101	R	50*	.1
210	Zoran Advertising and Design Inc—Zoran Marinkovich	2092 Appaloosa Ct W, Wheaton IL 60189	630-682-9534	R	50*	.1
211	Ovation Marketing Inc—Ralph S Heath III	201 Main St Ste 601, La Crosse WI 54601	608-785-1520	R	50*	.1
212	Sigma Group—Vladimir Chronis	690 Kinderkamack Rd, Oradell NJ 07649	201-261-1123	R	50*	.1
213	Soloman Friedman Advertising LLC—William Eubanks	40900 Woodward Ave Ste, Bloomfield Hills MI 48304	248-540-0660	R	50*	.1
214	PGR Media—Pattie Garrahy	34 Farnsworth St 2nd F, Boston MA 02210	617-502-8400	R	50*	<.1
215	RTC Relationship Marketing—Barry Kessel WPP Group USA Inc	1055 Thomas Jefferson, Washington DC 20007	202-625-2111	S	49*	.1
216	DGWB Inc—Mike Weisman	217 N Main St Ste 200, Santa Ana CA 92701	714-881-2300	R	49*	.1
217	Dalton Agency—Jim Dalton	140 W Monroe St Ste 20, Jacksonville FL 32202	904-398-5222	R	49*	.1
218	Schafer Condon Carter—Tim Condon	1029 W Madison, Chicago IL 60607	312-464-1666	R	49*	.1
219	Gyro Inc—Adryanna Sutherland	7755 Montgomery Rd Ste, Cincinnati OH 45236	513-671-3811	R	49*	.1
220	Archer/Malmo Advertising Inc—Russ Williams	65 Union Ave 5th Fl, Memphis TN 38103	901-523-2000	R	48*	.1
221	Cranford Johnson Robinson Woods—Wayne Woods	303 W Capitol Ave, Little Rock AR 72201	501-975-6251	R	47*	.1
222	Del Rivero Messianu Advertising—Eduardo Del Rivero	770 S Dixie Hwy Ste 10, Coral Gables FL 33146	305-666-2101	R	46*	<.1
223	Seiter and Miller Advertising Inc—Livingston Miller	460 Park Ave 5th Fl, New York NY 10016	212-843-9900	R	46*	<.1
224	IMM Interactive—Michael Krongel	135 Crossways Park Dr, Woodbury NY 11797	631-719-1250	R	46*	.1
225	Moroch and Associates—Pat Kempf	3625 N Hall Ste 1100, Dallas TX 75219	214-520-9700	R	45*	.1
226	Spike/DDB LLC—Spike Lee	55 Washington St Ste 6, Brooklyn NY 11201	718-596-5400	R	45*	<.1
227	Stevens Baron Communications Inc—Ed Stevens	1991 Crocker Rd, Westlake OH 44145	440-617-0100	R	45*	<.1
228	Barnhart—William Schumacher	1732 Champa St, Denver CO 80202	303-626-7200	R	45*	<.1
229	Sherry Matthews Advocacy Marketing Inc—Sherry Matthews	200 S Congress Ave, Austin TX 78704	512-478-4397	R	45*	<.1
230	Fraser/White Inc—Renee Fraser	1631 Pontius Ave, Los Angeles CA 90025	310-319-3737	R	44*	<.1
231	EMI Strategic Marketing Inc—Campbell Edlund	15 Broad St, Boston MA 02109	617-224-1101	R	44*	.1
232	RJ Dale Advertising and Public Relations Inc—Robert J Dale	211 E Ontario St Ste 2, Chicago IL 60611	312-644-2316	R	44*	<.1
233	MOST Brand Development and Advertising—John G Most	25 Enterprise Ste 250, Aliso Viejo CA 92656	949-475-4050	R	43	<.1
234	Lopez Negrete Communications Inc—Alex Lopez Negrete	3336 Richmond Ave Ste, Houston TX 77098	713-877-8777	R	43*	<.1
235	Paradigm/Lord Lasker—Chris Howell	5301 Cypress St Ste 10, Tampa FL 33607	813-287-0028	R	42*	.1
236	Cronin and Company Inc—Steve Wolfberg	50 Nye Rd, Glastonbury CT 06033	860-659-0514	R	42*	.1
237	Nelson and Schmidt Inc—Dan Nelson Sr	600 E Wisconsin Ave, Milwaukee WI 53202	414-224-0210	R	42*	.1
238	Register Tapes Unlimited Inc—Edward Endsley	17015 Park Row, Houston TX 77084	281-206-2500	R	41*	.6
239	Hyper Interactive Media LLC—Frank Suwalski	11778 S Election Rd St, Draper UT 84020	801-307-3300	R	41	<.1
240	Marion Montgomery Inc—Cindy Marion	2412 South Blvd, Houston TX 77098	713-523-7900	R	41*	.1
241	FKQ Advertising Inc	15351 Roosevelt Blvd, Clearwater FL 33760	727-539-8800	R	41*	.1
242	Jeffrey/Scott Advertising Inc—Bruce Batti	670 P St, Fresno CA 93721	559-268-9741	R	41*	<.1
243	Alexander Marketing Services Inc—Steve Schmieder	801 Broadway Ave NW, Grand Rapids MI 49504	616-957-2000	R	40*	.1
244	Kovel/Fuller Advertising and Marketing—John Fuller	9925 Jefferson Blvd, Culver City CA 90232	310-841-4444	R	40*	<.1
245	VML Inc—Matt Anthony	250 Richards Rd, Kansas City MO 64116	816-283-0700	S	39*	.3
246	Fletcher Martin Ewing—Andy Fletcher	303 Peachtree Center A, Atlanta GA 30303	404-221-1188	R	39*	.1
247	Jamison McKay LLP—David Jamison	335 Powell St 14th Fl, San Francisco CA 94102	415-398-2848	R	39*	.1
248	Phoenix Creative Co—Matt O'Neill	611 N 10th St Ste 700, Saint Louis MO 63101	314-421-5646	R	39*	.1
249	Stephan and Brady Inc—George Whitely	1850 Hoffman St, Madison WI 53704	608-241-4141	R	39*	.1
250	Thompson and Company Inc—Michael Thompson	50 Peabody Pl, Memphis TN 38103	901-527-8000	R	38*	.1
251	Griffin York and Krause—Travis York	121 River Front Dr, Manchester NH 03102	603-625-5713	R	38*	.1
252	Phelps and Associates Inc—Joe Phelps	901 Wilshire Blvd, Santa Monica CA 90401	310-752-4400	R	38*	.1
253	Avenue A/NYC LLC—Clark Kokich	162 5th Ave 7th Fl, New York NY 10010	212-462-4662	S	38*	<.1
254	O2 Ideas Inc—Shelly Stewart Worldwide Partners Inc	600 University Park Pl, Birmingham AL 35209	205-949-9494	S	38*	<.1
255	Borders Perrin and Norrander Inc—Michael O'Rourke	818 SW 1rst Ave, Portland OR 97204	503-227-2506	R	37*	.1
256	Clarity Coverdale Fury Advertising Inc—Tim Clarity	120 S 6th St Ste 1300, Minneapolis MN 55402	612-339-3902	R	37*	.1
257	Rawle-Murdy Associates Inc—Bruce D Murdy	2 Beaufain St, Charleston SC 29401	843-577-7327	R	37*	.1
258	Young and Laramore Corp—Tom Denari	407 N Fulton St, Indianapolis IN 46202	317-264-8000	R	37*	<.1
259	Bandy Carroll Hellige Advertising—Susan Bandy	307 W Muhammad Ali Blv, Louisville KY 40202	502-589-7711	R	36*	<.1
260	Quest Business Agency Inc—Alan D Vera	2150 W 18th St Ste 202, Houston TX 77008	713-956-6569	R	36*	<.1
261	Luquire George Andrews Inc—Steve Luquire	4201 Congress St Ste 4, Charlotte NC 28209	704-552-6565	R	35*	<.1
262	EGC Media Group Inc—Ernest G Canadeo	1175 Walt Whitman Rd, Melville NY 11747	516-935-4044	R	35*	<.1
263	Anita Santiago Advertising Inc—Anita Santiago	2448 Main St, Santa Monica CA 90405	310-396-8846	R	35*	<.1
264	Meyer and Wallis Inc—Bob Meyer	731 N Jackson St 7th F, Milwaukee WI 53202	414-224-0212	R	35*	<.1
265	Adcom Communications Inc—Joe Kubic	1370 W 6th St 3rd Fl, Cleveland OH 44113	216-574-9100	R	34*	<.1
266	Clear Channel Spectacolor LLC—Harry Coghan	1501 Broadway Ste 450, New York NY 10036	212-221-3100	S	34*	<.1
267	Morrison Agency Inc—Robert B Morrison	3365 Piedmont Rd NE St, Atlanta GA 30305	404-233-3405	R	34*	<.1
268	All-Ways Advertising Co—Robert Jay Lieberman	1442 Broad St, Bloomfield NJ 07003	973-338-0700	R	33*	.2
269	Bailey Lauerman—Jim Lauerman	1248 O St Ste 900, Lincoln NE 68508	402-475-2800	R	33*	.1
270	Hunter Hamersmith and Associates Inc—Cheryl Hamersmith	725 NE 125th St, North Miami FL 33161	305-895-8430	R	33*	<.1
271	Pace Advertising—Milton Bagley	1065 Ave of the Americ, New York NY 10018	212-818-0100	S	33*	<.1
272	Keiler and Co—Wilford Smith	304 Main St, Farmington CT 06032	860-677-8821	R	32*	<.1
273	AdBrite Inc—Iggy Fanlo	731 Market St 5th Fl, San Francisco CA 94103		R	32*	<.1
274	Posner Advertising—Peter Posner	30 Broad St 9th Fl, New York NY 10004	212-867-3900	R	32*	.1
275	Jay Advertising Inc—F Jay Smith	170 Linden Oaks, Rochester NY 14625	585-264-3600	R	32*	<.1
276	Hamilton Communications Group—Jim Lee	20 N Wacker Dr Ste 196, Chicago IL 60606	312-321-5000	R	32*	<.1
277	Prime Access Inc—Howard Buford	345 7th Ave, New York NY 10001	212-868-6800	R	32*	<.1

Note: An asterisk (*) indicates an estimated financial figure. The company type code used is as follows: R = Private, P = Public, S = Private Subsidiary, B = Public Subsidiary, D = Division, J = Joint Venture, I = Investment Fund.

COMPANY RANKINGS BY SALES WITHIN 4-DIGIT SIC

Rank	Company Name—*Executive Officer*	Address, City, State, Zip	Phone	Type	Fin	Empls
278	Smith Kaplan Allen and Reynolds Advertising Agency Inc—*Joleen David*	111 S 108th Ave, Omaha NE 68154	402-330-0110	R	32*	<.1
279	TG Madison Inc—*Lauren Genkinger*	3340 Peachtree Rd Ste, Atlanta GA 30326	404-262-2623	R	32*	<.1
280	Powers and Associates Inc—*Charles W Powers*	1 W 4th St, Cincinnati OH 45202	513-721-5353	R	32*	<.1
281	Barker Campbell and Farley—*Art Webb*	4500 Main St, Virginia Beach VA 23462	757-497-4811	R	31*	<.1
282	Glenn Group—*Valerie Glenn*	50 Washington St, Reno NV 89503	775-686-7777	R	31*	<.1
283	McCormick Advertising Agency—*Mark Perrin*	1201 NW Briarcliff Pky, Kansas City MO 64116	816-584-8444	R	30*	<.1
284	Rieches Baird Advertising—*Ryan Rieches*	1 Wrigley, Irvine CA 92618	949-586-1200	R	30*	<.1
285	Williams-Helde Inc—*Marc Williams*	711 6th Ave N Ste 200, Seattle WA 98106	206-285-1940	R	30*	<.1
286	CPO Inc—*Norm Golding*	736 N Western Ave Rm 1, Lake Forest IL 60045	847-735-7365	R	30	.1
287	Anderson Marketing Group—*Chuck Anderson*	7420 Blanco Rd Ste 200, San Antonio TX 78216	210-223-6233	R	29*	<.1
288	Littlefield Marketing and Advertising Inc—*David Littlefield*	1350 S Boulder Ave Ste, Tulsa OK 74119	918-295-1000	R	29*	<.1
289	Grafica Inc—*Debra A Taeschler*	525 E Main St, Chester NJ 07930	908-879-2169	R	29*	<.1
290	949 Web Presence Management—*Brian Schraff*	19071 Live Oak Canyon, Trabuco Canyon CA 92679	949-216-6000	R	29*	<.1
291	Adworks Inc (Washington DC)—*Marc Greenspun*	1225 19th St NW Ste 50, Washington DC 20036	202-342-5585	R	29*	<.1
292	Dale Pon Advertising Inc—*Dale Pon*	155 Ave of the America, New York NY 10013	212-675-4200	R	29*	<.1
293	Houser and Hennesee Advertising Corp—*Clifford R Houser*	PO Box 658, Bridgeport MI 48722	989-921-1172	R	29*	<.1
294	Kleber and Associates Advertising—*Steven L Kleber*	1215 Hightower Trl Bld, Atlanta GA 30350	770-518-1000	R	29*	<.1
295	Barker Specialty Co—*Gerald Barker*	Caller Box 222, Cheshire CT 06410		R	28*	.1
296	Sides and Associates Inc—*Larry Sides*	PO Box 3267, Lafayette LA 70502	337-233-6473	R	28*	<.1
297	Mckee Wallwork Cleveland LLC—*Steve Mckee*	1030 18th St W, Albuquerque NM 87104	505-821-2999	R	28*	<.1
298	Princeton Partners Inc—*Thomas Sullivan*	205 Rockingham Row, Princeton NJ 08540	609-452-8500	R	28*	<.1
299	San Jose Group—*George L San Jose*	233 N Michigan Ave 24t, Chicago IL 60601	312-565-7000	R	28*	<.1
300	Stein and Partners—*Thomas Stein*	432 Park Ave S, New York NY 10016	212-213-1112	R	28*	<.1
301	Stoner Bunting Advertising—*Dan Nguyen*	210 W Grant St, Lancaster PA 17603	717-291-1491	R	28*	<.1
302	iContact Corp—*Ryan PM Allis*	5221 Paramount Pky Ste, Morrisville NC 27560	919-968-3996	R	27*	.2
303	Just Marketing International—*Zak Brown*	10960 Bennett Pkwy, Zionsville IN 46077	317-344-1900	R	27*	.1
304	Wirestone (Boise Idaho)—*Dan Lynch*	913 W River St Ste 200, Boise ID 83702	208-343-2868	S	27*	.1
305	eBridge Advertising—*Mark Cave*	16133 Ventura Blvd, Encino CA 91436	323-525-3900	R	27*	.1
306	Diccicco Battista Communications—*Michael Diccicco*	1200 River Rd Ste 300E, Conshohocken PA 19428	484-342-3600	R	27*	<.1
307	Matthews Marks—*John Hartman*	523 W 24th St, New York NY 10011	212-243-0200	R	27*	<.1
308	Agencysacks—*Andrew Sacks*	345 Seventh Ave Ste 7, New York NY 10001	212-826-4004	R	27*	<.1
309	Brushfire Inc—*John Leonardi*	2 Wing Dr, Cedar Knolls NJ 07927	973-871-1700	R	27*	<.1
310	Glass/McClure Inc—*Gregory J Glass*	2700 J St 2nd Fl, Sacramento CA 95816	916-448-6956	R	27*	<.1
311	CRC Marketing Solutions—*Michael Lundeby*	6321 Bury Dr Ste 10, Eden Prairie MN 55346	952-937-6000	R	27*	<.1
312	Public Relations Advertising Co—*Nechie Hall*	6 N Tejon St Ste 400, Colorado Springs CO 80903	719-473-0704	R	27*	.1
313	Diditcom LLC—*Kevin Lee*	330 Old Country Rd Ste, Mineola NY 11501	516-255-0500	R	26*	.1
314	Freedman Gibson and White Inc—*Kim Allan Sharp*	100 E Business Way, Cincinnati OH 45241	513-241-3900	R	26*	<.1
315	Bisig Impact Group—*Larry Bisig*	640 S 4th St Ste 400, Louisville KY 40202	502-583-0333	R	26*	<.1
316	Intelligent Beauty Inc—*Adam Goldenberg*	2301 Rosecrans Ave Ste, El Segundo CA 90245	310-683-0940	R	26*	<.1
317	Pearson McMahon Fletcher England—*Ronald Pearson*	3755 E 82nd St Ste 350, Indianapolis IN 46240	317-842-0700	R	26*	<.1
318	Cavanaugh Marketing Network Inc—*Patrick Cavanaugh*	101 Bellevue Rd, Pittsburgh PA 15229	412-939-3399	R	26*	<.1
319	Kilgannon—*Rena Kilgannon*	1360 Peachtree St Ste, Atlanta GA 30309	404-876-2800	R	26*	<.1
320	Interlex Communications—*Rudy Ruiz*	4005 Broadway, San Antonio TX 78209	210-930-3339	R	26*	<.1
321	Dimassimo Carr Brand Advertising—*Lee Goldstein*	220 E 23rd St, New York NY 10010	212-253-7500	R	25*	.1
322	Fogarty Klein Monroe Agency—*Tom Monroe*	1800 W Loop S Ste 2100, Houston TX 77027	713-862-5100	R	25	<.1
323	Images USA Inc—*Robert McNeil*	1320 Ellsworth Industr, Atlanta GA 30318	404-892-2931	R	25*	<.1
324	Advance Notice Inc—*John Ivester*	PO Box 593, Peabody MA 01960	978-531-6722	R	25*	<.1
325	Penny Ohlmann Neiman Inc—*Walter Ohlmann*	1605 N Main St, Dayton OH 45405	937-278-0681	R	25*	<.1
326	Nelson and Gilmore—*Wayne Nelson*	1604 Aviation Blvd, Redondo Beach CA 90278	310-376-0296	R	24*	<.1
327	Storandt Pann Margolis Inc—*Gary Storandt*	15 W Harris Ave Ste 30, La Grange IL 60525	708-246-7700	R	24*	.1
328	E Morris Communications Inc—*Eugene Morris*	820 N Orleans Ste 402, Chicago IL 60610	312-943-2900	R	23*	.1
329	Clayton-Davis and Associates Inc—*Jennifer Davis Jermak*	230 S Bemiston Ave Ste, Saint Louis MO 63105	314-862-7800	R	23*	<.1
330	Lindsay Stone and Briggs Inc—*Marsha Lindsay*	100 State St, Madison WI 53703	608-251-7070	R	23*	<.1
331	Rhythm NewMedia—*Ujjal Kohli*	800 W El Camino Real S, Mountain View CA 94040	650-961-9024	R	23*	<.1
332	Williams Group (Grand Rapids Michigan)—*Bob Tobin*	70 Ionia Ave SW, Grand Rapids MI 49503	616-222-3600	R	23*	<.1
333	Core-Create Inc—*Ken Ribotsky*	100 Franklin Sq Dr Ste, Somerset NJ 08873	732-748-0433	R	23*	<.1
334	Gard Communications—*Brian Gard*	711 SW Alder St 4th Fl, Portland OR 97205	503-221-0100	R	23*	<.1
335	Hickman and Associates Inc—*Melissa Hickman*	11350 N Meridian St St, Carmel IN 46032	317-816-9780	R	23*	<.1
336	Katz Dochtermann and Epstein Inc—*Erik Dochtermann*	129 W 27th St 11th Fl, New York NY 10001	212-686-0006	R	23*	<.1
337	Oden Marketing and Design—*Bill Carkeet*	119 S Main St Rm 300, Memphis TN 38103	901-578-8055	R	23	<.1
338	Bamko—*Philip Koosed*	110 E 9th St Ste C1069, Los Angeles CA 90079	310-470-5859	R	23	.1
339	Lawrence and Schiller Inc—*Paul Schiller*	3932 S Willow Ave, Sioux Falls SD 57105	605-338-8000	R	22*	.1
340	Msi Marketing Inc—*Richard Harshaw*	2140 E Southlake Blvd, Southlake TX 76092	817-416-4333	R	22*	.1
341	Boelter and Lincoln—*Jill Brzeski*	222 E Erie St 4th Fl, Milwaukee WI 53202	414-271-0101	R	22*	<.1
342	Creative Civilization—*Al Aguilar*	106 Auditorium Cir 2nd, San Antonio TX 78205	210-227-1999	R	22*	<.1
343	Quinn Fable Advertising Inc—*Kathy Fable*	115 E 55th St, New York NY 10022	212-974-8700	R	22*	<.1
344	Translation LLC *Interpublic Group of Companies Inc*	145 W 45th St 12th Fl, New York NY 10036	212-299-5505	S	22*	<.1
345	William Mills and Associates Inc—*William E Mills III*	300 W Wieuca Rd Bldg 1, Atlanta GA 30342	678-781-7200	R	22*	<.1
346	Lou Beres and Associates Inc—*Carrie Strieter*	175 E Delaware Place, Chicago IL 60611	312-720-7347	R	22*	<.1
347	Omni Media Group—*Thomas O'Toole*	2518 Spring Grove Ave, Cincinnati OH 45250	513-381-5000	R	22*	<.1
348	Linett and Harrison Inc—*Caryl Linett*	2500 Morris Ave, Union NJ 07083	908-686-0606	R	22*	<.1
349	Green Advertising Associates Inc—*Phyllis Green*	7301 N Federal Hwy Stu, Boca Raton FL 33487	561-989-9550	D	22*	<.1
350	GL Nemirow Inc—*Grant Nemirow*	2550 N Hollywood Way, Burbank CA 91505	818-562-9433	R	21*	.1
351	Chandler Ehrlich and Company Inc—*Robert Chandler*	6750 Lenox Center Ct S, Memphis TN 38115	901-761-5748	R	21*	<.1
352	Creative Marketing Alliance Inc—*Jeffrey E Barnhart*	191 Clarksville Rd, Princeton Junction NJ 08550	609-799-6000	R	21*	<.1
353	The Way ? Group—*Nick Shore*	180 Varick St, New York NY 10014	212-209-1194	R	21*	<.1
354	Grady Britton Advertising—*Frank Grady*	107 SE Washington St S, Portland OR 97214	503-228-4118	R	21*	<.1
355	Martz and Associates Inc—*Carrie A Martz*	7077 E Marilyn Bldg 2, Scottsdale AZ 85254	480-998-3154	R	20*	.1
356	Richter7—*Dave Newbold*	280 S 400 W Ste 200, Salt Lake City UT 84101	801-521-2903	R	20*	<.1
357	Brandtrust Inc—*Daryl Travis*	875 N Michigan Ave Ste, Chicago IL 60611	312-440-1833	R	20*	<.1
358	Beckerman Public Relations—*Michael D Beckerman*	1 University Plz Ste 5, Hackensack NJ 07601	201-465-8000	R	20*	<.1
359	Cruz/Kravetz Ideas Inc	11858 LaGrange Ave 2nd, Los Angeles CA 90025	310-312-3630	R	20	<.1
360	Meyocks Group—*Donna Jeskee*	6800 Lake Dr Ste150, West Des Moines IA 50266	515-225-1200	S	20*	<.1
361	rVue Inc—*Jason Kates*	100 NE 3rd Ave Ste 200, Fort Lauderdale FL 33301		R	20*	<.1
362	Freebairn and Co—*John Freebairn*	3475 Lenox Rd Ste 900, Atlanta GA 30326	404-237-9945	R	20*	<.1
363	Nowak Associates Inc—*Tim Nowak*	6075 E Molloy Rd, Syracuse NY 13211	315-463-1001	R	20*	<.1
364	Nemer Fieger and Associates Inc—*Jim Fieger*	6250 Excelsior Blvd St, Minneapolis MN 55416	952-925-4848	R	19*	<.1
365	Altus Group Inc (Phildadelphia Pennsylvania)—*David Jefferys*	211 N 13th St, Philadelphia PA 19107	215-977-9900	R	19*	<.1

Rank	Company Name—*Executive Officer*	Address, City, State, Zip	Phone	Type	Fin	Empls
366	Blass Communications LLC—*Kenneth Blass*	17 Drowne Rd, Old Chatham NY 12136	518-766-2222	R	19*	<.1
367	Coakley Heagerty Companies Ltd—*Tom Zazueta*	1165 N 1st St Ste 201, San Jose CA 95112	408-275-9400	R	19*	<.1
368	Devine and Pearson Communications—*John Pearson*	300 Congress St, Quincy MA 02169	617-472-2700	R	19*	<.1
369	Evolution Bureau—*Daniel Stein*	1596 Howard St, San Francisco CA 94103	415-281-3950	R	19*	<.1
370	Kelley Swofford Roy Inc—*Susan P Kelley*	50 NE 29th, Miami FL 33137	305-444-0004	R	19*	<.1
371	Perich and Partners Ltd—*Ernest Perich*	117 N First St Ste 100, Ann Arbor MI 48104	734-323-0413	R	19*	<.1
372	Peterson Milla Hooks—*Thomas Nowak*	1315 Harmon Pl, Minneapolis MN 55403	612-349-9116	R	19*	<.1
373	Red7e Inc—*Dan Barbercheck*	637 W Main St, Louisville KY 40202	502-585-3403	R	19*	<.1
374	Toth Inc—*Mike Toth*	215 1st St, Cambridge MA 02142	617-252-0787	R	19*	<.1
375	Tri -Auto Enterprises Inc—*Scott Hill*	7225 Georgetown Rd, Indianapolis IN 46268	317-644-5700	R	19*	<.1
376	WKP-Spier LLC—*Tom McCartin*	460 Park Ave S, New York NY 10016	212-679-4441	R	19*	<.1
377	Latorra Paul and McCann Inc—*Mike Ancillotti*	120 E Washington St 10, Syracuse NY 13202	315-476-1646	R	19*	<.1
378	Lisa Adelle Design Inc—*Lisa-Adelle Wright*	2828 Routh St Ste 650, Dallas TX 75201	214-969-0141	R	19*	<.1
379	Chemistry Communications Inc—*Edward Show*	3030 Penn Ave Fl 2, Pittsburgh PA 15201	412-642-0642	R	19*	<.1
380	Stone and Ward Inc—*Millie Ward*	225 E Markham St Ste 4, Little Rock AR 72201	501-375-3003	R	18*	<.1
381	Mpell Solutions LLC—*Oran Thomas*	1330 Specialty Dr Ste, Vista CA 92081	760-727-9600	R	18*	<.1
382	Freed Advertising—*Gerald Freed*	1650 Hwy 6 Ste 400, Sugar Land TX 77478	281-240-4949	R	18*	<.1
383	Allied Advertising—*Jerry Feldman* Allied Advertising Agency	1100 17th St NW Ste 40, Washington DC 20036	202-223-3660	S	18*	<.1
384	Combs and Co—*Ben Combs*	3426 Old Cantrell Rd, Little Rock AR 72202	501-664-3000	R	18*	<.1
385	Marketing Art Science—*Cheryl Guzofsky*	PO Box 371767, Denver CO 80237	303-337-7770	R	18*	<.1
386	Heathcott Associates Inc—*Gary Heathcott*	17300 Chenal Pkwy, Little Rock AR 72223	501-821-9900	R	18*	<.1
387	Shirlee Wenzel and Company Inc—*Shirlee Wenzel*	230 W Delaware Ave, Pennington NJ 08534	609-737-9200	R	18*	<.1
388	Henry Gill Communications—*David Henry*	900 S Browadway Ste 30, Denver CO 80209	303-296-4100	R	18*	<.1
389	Rankin Group Ltd—*Ernest Rankin*	17821 E 17th St Ste 16, Tustin CA 92780	714-832-4100	R	18	<.1
390	Sicola Martin—*Cherie Cox*	206 E 9th Street Ste 1, Austin TX 78701	512-343-0264	R	17*	.1
391	Dana Communications Inc—*Robert Prewitt*	2 E Broad St, Hopewell NJ 08525	609-466-9187	R	17*	<.1
392	Structure Interactive—*Michael Brown*	146 Monroe Cntr NW Ste, Grand Rapids MI 49503	616-364-7423	R	17*	<.1
393	Footsteps LLC—*Verdia E Johnson*	200 Varick St, New York NY 10014	212-924-6432	R	17*	<.1
394	Winstanley Associates—*Nathan Winstanley*	114 Main St, Lenox MA 01240	413-637-9887	R	17*	<.1
395	Yaffe and Co—*Fred Yaffe*	26100 American Dr 4th, Southfield MI 48034	248-262-1700	R	17*	<.1
396	David K Burnap Advertising Inc—*DK Burnap Jr*	36 S Main St, Dayton OH 45402	937-439-4800	R	17*	<.1
397	Martin Interactive—*John B Adams*	71 5th Ave 4th Fl, New York NY 10003	212-405-4800	R	17*	<.1
398	AMPM Inc—*David Well*	PO Box 1887, Midland MI 48641	989-837-8800	R	17*	<.1
399	Felder Communications Group Inc—*Stan Felder*	50 Louis NW Ste 600, Grand Rapids MI 49503	616-459-1200	R	17*	<.1
400	Lenac Warford Stone Inc—*Ralph Lenac*	30012 Ivy Glenn Dr Ste, Laguna Niguel CA 92677	949-363-1158	R	17*	<.1
401	Oliver Russell and Associates Inc—*Russ Stoddard*	PO Box 1930, Boise ID 83702	208-344-1734	R	17*	<.1
402	Three Marketeers Advertising Inc—*Jeffrey A Holmes*	785 The Alameda, San Jose CA 95126	408-293-3233	R	17*	<.1
403	Sigma Marketing Group LLC—*Catherine Mazzotta*	1850 Winton Rd S Ste 1, Rochester NY 14618	585-473-7300	R	17*	.1
404	Brighton Agency Inc—*Roger Yount*	231 S Bemiston Ave Ste, Saint Louis MO 63105	314-726-0700	R	16*	.1
405	Mr Youth—*Matt Britton*	75 9th Ave 4th Fl, New York NY 10011	212-779-8700	R	16*	<.1
406	Callahan Creek—*Cindy Maude*	805 New Hampshire, Lawrence KS 66044	785-838-4774	R	16*	<.1
407	Bigelow Advertising—*Thomas G Bigelow*	3379 Peachtree Rd NE S, Atlanta GA 30326	770-216-2162	R	16*	<.1
408	Broadus Advertising and Public Relations—*Robert F Broadus*	1008 Sea Palms West Dr, Saint Simons Island GA 31522	912-638-0897	R	16*	<.1
409	Graphic Concepts Group Inc—*Scott Turner*	1612 Summit Ave Ste 41, Fort Worth TX 76102		R	16*	<.1
410	Young Co—*Barton E Young*	361 Forest Ave Rm 105, Laguna Beach CA 92651	949-376-8404	R	16*	<.1
411	Love Advertising Inc—*Brenda Love*	770 S Post Oak Ln Ste1, Houston TX 77056	713-552-1055	R	16*	<.1
412	Bonneville Communications—*Greg Garber*	5 Triad Ctr Ste 700, Salt Lake City UT 84180	801-237-2600	D	16*	<.1
413	Graham Group (Lafayette Louisiana)—*George Graham*	PO Box 51145, Lafayette LA 70505	337-232-8214	R	16*	<.1
414	Stream Cos—*Jason Brennan*	255 Great Valley Pky S, Malvern PA 19355		R	16*	<.1
415	Prom Krog Altstiel Inc—*Tom Altstiel*	1009 W Glen Oaks Lane, Mequon WI 53092	262-241-9414	R	16*	<.1
416	Thompson Marketing—*Ken W Thompson*	70 NE Loop 410 Ste 750, San Antonio TX 78216	210-349-9925	R	16*	<.1
417	Flaherty Sabol Carroll—*Edward Flaherty*	707 Grant St Ste 2900, Pittsburgh PA 15219	412-471-3700	R	16*	<.1
418	Kleier Communications Inc	9700 Ormsby Station Rd, Louisville KY 40223	502-339-2020	R	16*	<.1
419	Sillery and Partners—*Russell Sillery*	10 Signal Rd, Stamford CT 06902	203-961-9993	R	16*	<.1
420	Saatchi and Saatchi X Inc—*Dina Howell*	605 W Lakeview Dr, Springdale AR 72764	479-575-0200	R	16*	.2
421	Sawtooth Group Inc—*William Schmermund*	100 Woodbrdge Ctr Dr 1, Woodbridge NJ 07095	732-636-6600	R	16*	.1
422	Kane and Finkel LLC—*Lisa Mcmillan*	534 4th St, San Francisco CA 94107	415-777-4990	R	16*	.1
423	Love Communications LLC—*Peggy Conway*	546 S 200 W, Salt Lake City UT 84101	801-519-8880	R	16*	<.1
424	Affiliate Media Inc—*Warren Jolly*	32 Discovery Ste 270, Irvine CA 92618	714-596-9000	R	15*	<.1
425	Daniels and Roberts Latin America Inc—*Daniel Muggeo*	6420 Congress Ave Ste, Boca Raton FL 33487	561-241-0066	R	15*	<.1
426	Kaiser Marketing—*Michael Kaiser*	11400 West Olympic Blv, Los Angeles CA 90015	310-479-8999	R	15*	<.1
427	Walker and Associates Inc (Memphis Tennessee)—*Ceil Walker*	5100 Poplar Ave, Memphis TN 38137	901-522-1100	R	15*	<.1
428	Blue Horse Inc—*Tom Thiede*	309 N Water St Ste 315, Milwaukee WI 53202	414-291-7620	R	15*	<.1
429	Cintara—*Lisa Tollner*	25 Post St, San Jose CA 95113	408-293-5300	R	15*	<.1
430	Communications Group Inc (Little Rock Arkansas)—*Dan Cowling*	400 W Capitol Ave Ste, Little Rock AR 72201	501-376-8722	R	15*	<.1
431	Conrad Phillips and Vutech—*Kirk Phillips*	1398 Goodale Blvd, Columbus OH 43212	614-224-3887	R	15*	<.1
432	Di Zinno Thompson Integrated Marketing Solutions Inc—*Tom DiZinno*	1830 Columbia St, San Diego CA 92101	619-237-5011	R	15*	<.1
433	Hunt Adkins—*Patrick Hunt*	15 S 5th St 3rd Fl, Minneapolis MN 55402	612-339-8003	R	15*	<.1
434	Joseph Pedott Advertising Inc—*Joseph Pedott*	425 California St Ste, San Francisco CA 94104	415-397-6992	R	15*	<.1
435	Leffler Agency—*Robert Leffler*	2607 N Charles St, Baltimore MD 21218	410-235-5661	R	15*	<.1
436	Mandala Communications Inc—*Matthew Bowler*	2855 NW Crossing Dr St, Bend OR 97701	541-389-6344	R	15*	<.1
437	Milton Samuels Advertising Agency Inc—*Jane Stark*	475 Park Ave S, New York NY 10016	212-532-5151	R	15*	<.1
438	Munn Rabot LLC—*Orson Munn*	33 W 17th St 3rd Fl, New York NY 10011	212-727-3900	R	15*	<.1
439	Red Moon Marketing LLC—*Jim Bailey*	4100 Coca-Cola Plz Ste, Charlotte NC 28211	704-366-1147	R	15*	<.1
440	RMR and Associates Inc—*Robyn M Sachs*	5870 Hubbard Dr, Rockville MD 20852	301-230-0045	R	15*	<.1
441	Turkel—*Bruce Turkel*	2871 Oak Ave, Coconut Grove FL 33133	305-476-3500	R	15*	<.1
442	Weintraub and Associates Advertising—*Rob Weintraub*	7745 Carondelet Ave St, Saint Louis MO 63105	314-721-5050	R	15*	<.1
443	Williams Whittle Associates Inc—*Rob Whittle*	711 Princess St, Alexandria VA 22314	703-836-9222	R	15*	<.1
444	Formedic Communication Ltd—*Dr Joseph Trager*	12D Worlds Fair Dr, Somerset NJ 08873	732-469-7031	R	15*	<.1
445	Richard Desberg and Associates Inc—*Richard Desberg*	15321 Russell Rd, Chagrin Falls OH 44023	440-247-9500	R	15*	<.1
446	Ron Sherman Advertising Inc—*Steve Jumper*	8215 Interstate 30, Little Rock AR 72209	501-568-8100	R	15*	<.1
447	Proof Advertising LLC—*Brian Christian*	114 W 7th St Ste 500, Austin TX 78701	512-345-6658	R	15*	.1
448	Dixon Schwabl Advertising Inc—*Lauren Dixon*	1595 Moseley Rd, Victor NY 14564	585-383-0380	R	15*	.1
449	Member Services Inc—*Jesse Hopkins*	PO Box 1760, Bentonville AR 72712	479-273-1333	R	14*	.1
450	Siegelgale—*Alan Siegel* Omnicom Group Inc	625 Ave of the America, New York NY 10011	212-453-0400	S	14*	.1
451	Ignite Media Solutions—*Michael Ferzacca*	1001 St Petersburg Dr, Oldsmar FL 34677	813-855-5800	R	14*	.1

Note: An asterisk (*) indicates an estimated financial figure. The company type code used is as follows: R = Private, P = Public, S = Private Subsidiary, B = Public Subsidiary, D = Division, J = Joint Venture, I = Investment Fund.

COMPANY RANKINGS BY SALES WITHIN 4-DIGIT SIC

Rank	Company Name—*Executive Officer*	Address, City, State, Zip	Phone	Type	Fin	Empls
452	Mangan Holcomb Rainwater Culpepper Inc—*Chip Culpepper*	2300 Cottondale Ln Ste, Little Rock AR 72202	501-376-0321	R	14*	<.1
453	Weinstein Otterman and Associates Inc—*Ileen Otterman*	137 5th Ave 9th Fl, New York NY 10010	212-505-5650	R	14*	<.1
454	Backe Digital Brand Marketing Inc—*John E Backe*	35 Cricket Terrace Ctr, Ardmore PA 19003	610-896-9260	R	14*	<.1
455	Sanna Mattson MacLeod Inc—*Charlie MacLeod*	811 W Jericho Tpke, Smithtown NY 11787	631-265-5160	R	14*	<.1
456	Coates Kokes—*Jeanie Coates*	421 SW 6th Ave Ste 130, Portland OR 97204	503-241-1124	R	14*	<.1
457	Siddall Inc—*John Siddall*	830 E Main St 24th Fl, Richmond VA 23219	804-788-8011	R	14*	<.1
458	Tiziani Whitmyre Inc—*Robert Tiziani*	2 Commercial St, Sharon MA 02067	781-793-9380	R	14*	<.1
459	Dae Advertising Inc—*Vicky M Wong*	71 Stevenson St Ste 75, San Francisco CA 94105	415-341-1280	R	14*	<.1
460	Rector-Duncan and Associates—*Kyle Montgomery*	PO Box 3879, Cedar Park TX 78630	512-454-5262	R	14*	<.1
461	RMI Advertising—*Ron Morgan*	436 Old Hook Rd, Emerson NJ 07630	201-261-7000	R	14*	<.1
462	Circulation Experti Ltd—*W Garrison Jackson*	445 Hamilton Ave Ste 1, White Plains NY 10601	914-948-8144	R	14*	<.1
463	Holland Communications Inc—*Bill Holland*	8910 Quartz Ave, Northridge CA 91324	818-341-4777	R	14*	<.1
464	Krome Communications Inc—*Bob Neville*	307 4th Ave, Pittsburgh PA 15222	412-471-0840	R	14*	<.1
465	McKinley Communications Inc—*Steve McKinley*	3675 S Noland Rd Ste 1, Independence MO 64055	334-501-8181	R	14*	<.1
466	King Group Inc (Dallas Texas)—*Johnnie King Jr*	1801 N Hampton Ste 410, DeSoto TX 75115	214-720-9046	R	14*	<.1
467	Domain Group Inc—*Richard Perry*	701 Pke St Ste 700, Seattle WA 98101	206-682-3035	R	13*	.1
468	Tuerff-Davis Enviromedia Inc—*Valerie Davis*	1717 W 6th St Ste 400, Austin TX 78703	512-476-4368	R	13*	<.1
469	Simons-Michelson-Zieve Inc—*James Michelson*	900 Wilshire Dr Ste 10, Troy MI 48084	248-362-4242	R	13*	.1
470	Tradeone Marketing Inc—*John Winslow*	11149 Res Blvd Ste 400, Austin TX 78759	512-719-3991	R	13*	.1
471	Middlebrook Group Inc—*William R Roy*	2801 Lucerne Ave, Miami Beach FL 33140	305-447-3888	R	13*	<.1
472	Young Isaac Inc—*Mary Kall*	735 Taylor Rd Ste 200, Gahanna OH 43230	614-552-2871	R	13*	<.1
473	Miller Agency Inc—*Dorthy Miller*	2711 Valley View Ln St, Dallas TX 75234	972-243-2211	R	13*	<.1
474	JW Messner Inc—*Kline Kauramaki*	161 Ottawa NW, Grand Rapids MI 49503	616-458-8384	R	13*	<.1
475	Herrmann Advertising Design—*Paul Hermann*	30 West St, Annapolis MD 21401	410-267-6522	R	13*	<.1
476	CDHM Advertising Inc—*Joseph DelGaldo*	1100 Summer St 1st Fl, Stamford CT 06905	203-967-7200	R	13*	<.1
477	Engagement Marketing Experts LLC—*Andy Arnold*	15851 Dallas Pkwy Ste, Addison TX 75001	972-663-1100	R	13*	.2
478	Price Weber Marketing Communications Inc—*Shanna Columbus*	PO Box 99337, Louisville KY 40269	502-499-9220	R	12*	.1
479	Irama Corp—*Bill Souder*	PO Box 22313, Portland OR 97269	503-653-9025	R	12*	.1
480	Powerpact LLC—*Tim Donnell*	2909 Polo Pkwy, Midlothian VA 23113	804-794-6100	R	12*	.1
481	Redpeg Marketing—*Brad Nierenberg*	727 N Washington St, Alexandria VA 22314	703-519-9000	R	12*	.1
482	Travel Ad Network—*Brian Silver*	55 Broad St 24th Fl, New York NY 10004	212-267-0747	R	12*	<.1
483	al Punto Advertising Inc—*Peggy Goff*	730 El Camino Way, Tustin CA 92780	714-544-0888	R	12*	<.1
484	Lawler Ballard Van Durand—*Tinsley Van Durand*	31 Inverness Center Pk, Birmingham AL 35242	205-995-1775	R	12*	<.1
485	Shaw and Todd Inc—*Mary Melia*	205 Rockingham Rd, Princeton NJ 08540	609-436-0251	R	12*	<.1
486	Weidert Group Inc—*Greg Linnemanstons*	PO Box 387, Appleton WI 54911	920-731-2771	R	12*	<.1
487	Amies Communications—*Grif Amies*	65 Enterprise 3rd Fl, Aliso Viejo CA 92656	949-330-7560	R	12*	<.1
488	Kanet Chambless and Baker—*Ron Chambless*	895 Central Ave 3rd Fl, Cincinnati OH 45202	513-681-9800	R	12*	<.1
489	Marketing Design Group—*Denise Paccione*	420 Walnut Ave, San Diego CA 92103	619-298-1445	R	12*	<.1
490	Olson Communications Inc—*Michelle Olson*	445 W Erle St Ste 109, Chicago IL 60610	312-280-4573	R	12*	<.1
491	Francis Marketing—*Heather Francis*	3615 29th St SE, Grand Rapids MI 49512	616-235-1122	R	12*	<.1
492	Working Media Group—*Kerry P Tracy*	21 W 38th St, New York NY 10018	212-251-0021	R	12*	<.1
493	McNally Temple Associates Inc—*Ray McNally*	1817 Capitol Ave, Sacramento CA 95814	916-447-8186	R	12*	<.1
494	Pete Mathieu and Associates Inc—*Pete Mathieu*	77 Ward St, Montgomery NY 12549	914-457-5100	R	12*	<.1
495	Good Advertising Inc—*Dale Cox*	5100 Poplar Ave Ste 17, Memphis TN 38137	901-761-0741	R	12*	<.1
496	Stone and Simons Advertising Inc—*Doug Stone*	24245 Northwestern Hwy, Southfield MI 48075	248-562-7276	R	12*	<.1
497	GRW Advertising Inc—*Edward C Ronk*	28 W 25th St, New York NY 10010	212-620-0519	R	12*	<.1
498	US Media Consulting—*Bruno Almeida*	1801 SW 3rd Ave 3rd Fl, Miami FL 33129	305-722-5500	R	12	<.1
499	Ypartnership LLC—*Rolf Skala*	423 S Keller Rd Ste 10, Orlando FL 32810	407-875-1111	R	12*	<.1
500	Horich Parks Lebow Advertising and Marketing Inc—*Charles Horich*	101 Schilling Rd Ste 3, Hunt Valley MD 21031	410-329-1950	R	12*	<.1
501	Design 446 Inc—*Tom Villane*	2411 Atlantic Ave Ste, Manasquan NJ 08736	732-292-2400	R	12*	.1
502	Swirl Inc—*Martin Lauber*	1620 Montgomery St Ste, San Francisco CA 94111	415-276-8300	R	12*	.1
503	Dean Media Group—*Jon Dean*	560 W Washington St 4t, Chicago IL 60661	312-386-1130	R	12*	<.1
504	Two Rivers Marketing Group—*Nancy Caylor*	106 E 6th St, Des Moines IA 50309	515-557-2000	R	11*	.1
505	Bkv Inc—*Richard Skaggs*	10561 Barkley St Ste 2, Overland Park KS 66212	404-233-0332	R	11*	.2
506	Hobbs/Herder Advertising—*Greg Herder*	2240 University Dr Ste, Newport Beach CA 92660	949-515-5000	R	11*	.1
507	Point Group Inc—*David Kniffen*	5949 Sherry Ln Ste 180, Dallas TX 75225	214-378-7970	R	11*	.1
508	5 Metacom—*Chris Wirthwein*	630 W Carmel Dr Ste 18, Carmel IN 46032	317-580-7540	R	11*	<.1
509	August Lang and Husak—*Michael August*	4630 Montgomery Ave St, Bethesda MD 20814	301-657-2772	R	11*	<.1
510	Big Bang Idea Engineering Inc—*Mark Drozda*	5571 Lajolla Blvd Ste, La Jolla CA 92037	858-259-2000	R	11*	<.1
511	Geo Advertising and Marketing Inc—*Georgia Lacy*	4251 E 5th St, Tucson AZ 85711	520-323-3221	R	11*	<.1
512	Cappelli Miles spring—*Rod Miles*	101 SW Main St, Portland OR 97204	503-241-1515	R	11*	<.1
513	Ad Methods Inc—*Hesso Bellem*	811 W Jericho Turnpike, Smithtown NY 11787	631-434-3330	R	11*	<.1
514	Killian Branding—*Bob Killian*	322 S Green St, Chicago IL 60607	312-836-0050	R	11*	<.1
515	Roxburgh Agency Inc—*Claudia Roxburgh*	245 Fischer Ave Ste B-, Costa Mesa CA 92626	714-556-4365	R	11*	<.1
516	Sonnhalter—*C John Sonnhalter*	633 W Bagley Rd Ste 4, Berea OH 44017	440-234-1812	R	11*	<.1
517	Taylor/West Advertising Inc—*William West*	4040 Broadway Ste 302, San Antonio TX 78209	210-805-0320	R	11*	<.1
518	Broderick Advertising—*John Broderick*	735 Riverside Dr Ste 2, Jackson MS 39202	601-355-8585	R	11*	<.1
519	Denmark Advertising and Public Relations—*Priscilla Jessup*	6000 Lake Forrest Dr S, Atlanta GA 30328	404-256-3681	R	11*	<.1
520	Harris Marketing Group Inc—*Janice Rosenhaus*	102 Pierce St, Birmingham MI 48009	248-723-6300	R	11*	<.1
521	Moret Advertising Inc—*Richard Moret*	7650 E Broadway Blvd B, Tucson AZ 85710	520-546-8118	R	11*	<.1
522	Pratt and Buehl—*Dan Buehl*	3390 Peachtree Rd NE S, Atlanta GA 30326	404-231-2311	R	11*	<.1
523	Silverstone Adkins and Breit Inc—*Bruce T Silverstone*	1128 Stratford Ave, Stratford CT 06615	203-375-2887	R	11*	<.1
524	Spear/Hall and Associates Inc—*Shelly Hall*	2150 W Washington St, San Diego CA 92110	619-683-3700	R	11*	<.1
525	National Positions USA—*Bernard May*	5012 Chesebro Rd Ste 2, Agoura Hills CA 91301	818-676-9819	R	11	.5
526	Lead Research Group—*Matthew Marsh*	17011 Beach Blvd Ste 8, Huntington Beach CA 92647		R	11	<.1
527	Sharon Brooks and Associates Inc—*Sharon Brooks*	207 W Franklin St, Richmond VA 23220	804-649-3704	R	11*	.1
528	Verdi Devito Inc—*Ellis Verdi*	100 5th Ave Fl 16, New York NY 10011	212-431-4694	R	10*	.1
529	Neiman Group Inc—*Steven Neiman*	614 N Front St Ste B, Harrisburg PA 17101	717-232-5554	R	10*	.1
530	Source Communications Inc—*Lawrence Rothstein*	433 Hackensack Ave Fl, Hackensack NJ 07601	201-343-5222	R	10*	.1
531	Advantage Media Group—*Steven Anderson*	10 Speirs St, Westbrook ME 04092	207-856-5600	R	10*	.1
532	Crosby Marketing Communications Inc—*Raymond Crosby*	705 Melvin Ave Ste 200, Annapolis MD 21401	410-626-0805	R	10*	<.1
533	Miller Brooks Inc—*Thomas Miller*	11712 N Michigan Rd, Zionsville IN 46077	317-873-8100	R	10*	<.1
534	JP Hogan and Company Inc—*Douglas W Hogan*	107 W 5th Ave, Knoxville TN 37917	865-951-1517	R	10*	<.1
535	AMR Advertising and Marketing—*Robert J Ford*	1007 E Chapman Ave, Fullerton CA 92831	714-992-2900	R	10*	<.1
536	Bill Hudson and Associates Inc—*Bill Hudson*	1701 West End Ave, Nashville TN 37203	615-259-9002	R	10*	<.1
537	Pure Octane Inc—*Elizabeth Hargreaves*	3857 Birch St Ste 840, Newport Beach CA 92660	714-799-2728	R	10*	<.1
538	Goldberg Fossa Seid Advertising—*Ira Goldberg*	16 W 22nd St 4th Fl, New York NY 10010	212-727-7110	R	10*	<.1
539	Market First Inc—*Julie Henry*	975 Cobb Pl Blvd Ste 3, Kennesaw GA 30144	770-425-9911	R	10*	<.1

Rank	Company Name—Executive Officer	Address, City, State, Zip	Phone	Type	Fin	Empls
540	Paragon Advertising Inc—James Gillian	43 Court St Ste 1111, Buffalo NY 14202	716-854-7161	R	10*	<.1
541	Magee Marketing Group Inc—Brian R Magee	150 Hartford Ave, Wethersfield CT 06109	860-257-7412	R	10*	<.1
542	Martin-Schaffer Inc	7758 Wisconsin Ave Ste, Bethesda MD 20814	301-951-3388	R	10*	<.1
543	Sloan Advertising Inc—John Sloan	1680 Akron Peninsula R, Akron OH 44313	330-864-4798	R	10	<.1
544	Coyne Advertising and Public Relations Inc—Jack Coyne	3030 Annandale Dr, Presto PA 15142	412-429-8408	R	10*	<.1
545	Edelmann Scott Inc—Richard J Scott	3751 Westerre Pwy Ste, Richmond VA 23233	804-643-1931	R	10*	<.1
546	Bronson Leigh Weeks—Loren Weeks	4710 SW Kelly, Portland OR 97239	503-720-0083	R	10*	<.1
547	Buzzsaw Advertising and Design	19600 Fairchild Rd Ste, Irvine CA 92612	949-453-1393	R	10*	<.1
548	Phoenix Marketing Group Inc—Jean D Radtke	6750 Maple Ter, Milwaukee WI 53213	414-771-1044	R	10*	<.1
549	Spangler and Associates—Jean Spangler	725 Providence Rd, Charlotte NC 28207	704-375-0728	R	10*	<.1
550	Genova Partners—Joseph Genova	487 E Main St Rm 324, Mount Kisco NY 10549	914-666-3982	R	10*	<.1
551	Bbfm Inc—Raymond Araujo	2607 2nd Ave, Seattle WA 98121	206-441-6657	R	10*	<.1
552	B and E Industries LLC—Patrick Reeves	PO Box 200548, Arlington TX 76006	817-807-4700	R	10*	.1
553	Dotomi Inc—John Guiliani	168 N Clinton St Fl 4, Chicago IL 60661	312-588-3600	R	10*	.1
554	Mgh Advertising Inc—Andy Malis	100 Painters Mill Rd S, Owings Mills MD 21117	410-902-5000	R	10*	.1
555	Signature Advertising LLC—David Houston	1755 Kirby Pkwy Ste 20, Memphis TN 38120	901-754-2200	R	10*	.1
556	Korey Kay and Partners Inc—Allen Kay	130 5th Ave Fl 8, New York NY 10011	212-620-4300	R	10*	.1
557	Coams Inc—Nick James	175 W Jackson Blvd Ste, Chicago IL 60604	312-243-2667	R	9*	.1
558	Fleming Hitchcock and Associates Inc—Jack Deleo	500 Wolf Ledges Pkwy, Akron OH 44311	330-376-2111	R	9*	.1
559	Mccaffery and Ratner Inc—William Mc Caffery	PO Box 1376, New York NY 10159	212-661-8940	R	9*	<.1
560	Starmark International Inc—Peggy Nordeen	1815 Griffin Rd, Dania Beach FL 33004	954-874-9000	R	9*	<.1
561	JHG-Townsend—Mary Fechtig	9707 Waples St Ste 102, San Diego CA 92121	858-952-7840	R	9*	<.1
562	M2 Media Group LLC—Michael Borchetta	1127 High Ridge Rd Ste, Stamford CT 06905	203-542-0101	R	9*	<.1
563	J H Benedict-Volusia Inc—James H Benedict	640 N Peninsula Dr, Daytona Beach FL 32118	386-255-1222	R	9*	<.1
564	Estey-Hoover Inc—Daniel Hoover	20201 SW Birch St Ste, Newport Beach CA 92660	949-756-8501	R	9*	<.1
565	Morris Advertising and Design Inc—Anne Morris	229 E Memory Ln, Santa Ana CA 92705	949-833-2142	R	9*	<.1
566	Roberts Group (San Antonio Texas)—Claude Roberts	19206 Huebner Rd, San Antonio TX 78258	210-495-4332	R	9*	<.1
567	Sass and Associates—George Sass Sr	PO Box 1710, Annapolis MD 21404	410-263-8448	R	9*	<.1
568	Sutton Reid Advertising Inc—Steven Reid	266 S Front St, Memphis TN 38103	901-522-8640	R	9	<.1
569	Auritt Communications Group—Joan Reisner Auritt	555 8th Ave Ste 709, New York NY 10018	212-302-6230	R	9*	<.1
570	BFI Marketing Communication Inc—Dennis Pavan	2000 Sycamore St, Cleveland OH 44113	216-875-8860	R	9*	<.1
571	BOC Advertising Inc	422 NW 8th Ave Ste C, Portland OR 97209	503-222-2566	R	9*	<.1
572	Hurley Chandler and Chaffer Advertising Inc—Bob Hurley	2757 Pawtucket Ave Ste, East Providence RI 02914	401-273-5530	R	9*	<.1
573	JayRay—Kathleen Deakins	535 E Dock St Ste 205, Tacoma WA 98402	253-627-9128	R	9*	<.1
574	Ward Media Inc—Philip Friedman	185 Madison Ave 5th Fl, New York NY 10016	212-967-5055	R	9*	<.1
575	Alm Enterprises Inc—Thomas Weston	3130 Wilshire Blvd Fl, Santa Monica CA 90403	310-207-6507	R	9*	<.1
576	Khj Integrated Marketing Inc—Judy Habib	1 Constitution Plz Ste, Charlestown MA 02129	617-241-8000	R	9*	<.1
577	Company C Communications Inc—Nick Nocca	160 Varick St, New York NY 10013	212-561-6000	R	9*	<.1
578	Hart Associates Inc—Michael Hart	1915 Indian Wood Cir, Maumee OH 43537	419-893-9600	R	9*	<.1
579	Woodbine Agency Inc—Maureen Hall	210 S Cherry St, Winston Salem NC 27101	336-724-0450	R	9*	<.1
580	D and S Creative Communications Inc—Terry Neff	PO Box 876, Mansfield OH 44901	419-524-4312	R	8*	.1
581	American Exhibition Services LLC—Charles Allen	2700 2nd Ave S, Birmingham AL 35233	205-323-2211	R	8*	.1
582	Ad Results Inc—Marshall Williams	6110 Clarkson Ln, Houston TX 77055	713-783-1800	R	8*	.1
583	Sterling-Rice Group Inc—Richard Sterling	1801 13th St Ste 400, Boulder CO 80302	303-381-6400	R	8*	.1
584	Leap Partnership Inc—R Steven Lutterbach	350 West Ontario, Chicago IL 60610	312-475-1247	S	8	.1
585	Laughlin Marinaccio and Owens Inc—Cynthia Epley	2000 14th St N Ste 800, Arlington VA 22201	703-875-2193	R	8*	.1
586	Chernoff Newman LLC—George Fletcher	1411 Gervais St Ste 50, Columbia SC 29201	803-254-8158	R	8*	.1
587	Heinrich Marketing Inc—George Eddy	1350 Independence St, Lakewood CO 80215	303-233-8660	R	8*	<.1
588	CJ Advertising LLC—Mike Harris	300 10th Ave S, Nashville TN 37203	615-254-6634	R	8*	<.1
589	Show Media—Laurence Hallier	383 5th Ave 2nd Fl, New York NY 10016	212-883-8783	R	8*	<.1
590	MeringCarson—Dave Mering	1700 I St Ste 210, Sacramento CA 95811	916-441-0571	R	8*	<.1
591	Mercury Mambo—Becky Arreaga	1107 S 8th St, Austin TX 78704	512-447-4440	R	8*	<.1
592	eZangacom Inc—Richard K Kahn	222 Carter Dr Ste 201, Middletown DE 19709	302-279-1020	R	8*	<.1
593	Associated Advertising Agency Inc—Bill Fialka	330 N Mead, Wichita KS 67202	316-683-4691	R	8*	<.1
594	CurrentMarketing Inc—Rick Schardein	1324 E Washington St, Louisville KY 40206	502-589-3567	R	8*	<.1
595	Leonard and Mayer Advertising Inc—Peter Leonard	187 S Old Woodward Ave, Birmingham MI 48009	248-646-2730	R	8*	<.1
596	Maximum Media—Nick DeAngelo	100 Corporate Pl Ste 1, Peabody MA 01960	978-536-9600	R	8*	<.1
597	Seraphein Beyn Inc—Bob Beyn	2319 J St, Sacramento CA 95816	916-441-7911	R	8*	<.1
598	Ad-Ease Communications Inc—Jack D'Amico	PO Box 400, Penn PA 15675	412-678-6266	R	8*	<.1
599	Ashby Dillon Inc—Lowell R Dillon	21690 River Oaks Dr, Rocky River OH 44116	440-331-5252	R	8*	<.1
600	Bradshaw Advertising—Barbara Bradshaw	811 NW 19th Ave, Portland OR 97209	503-221-5000	R	8*	<.1
601	Broadford and Maloney Inc	2 Soundview Dr, Greenwich CT 06831	203-661-2910	R	8*	<.1
602	Cohen and Company Creative Inc—Michael Cohen	12002 Miramar Pkwy Ste, Miramar FL 33025	954-835-1352	R	8*	<.1
603	Corporate Communications Inc—Terrence Palis	108 S Union St, Rochester NY 14607	585-262-3430	R	8*	<.1
604	Feature Advertising and Creative Services—Fred Thal	1415 Elbridge Payne Rd, Chesterfield MO 63017	636-537-3800	R	8*	<.1
605	Flair Communications Agency Inc—Lee Flaherty	214 W Erie St, Chicago IL 60654	312-943-5959	R	8*	<.1
606	Flynn and Friends Advertising—Mitch Flynn	437 Franklin St, Buffalo NY 14202	716-881-2697	R	8*	<.1
607	Geile/Leon Marketing Communications—Timothy Leon	130 S Bemiston Ste 800, Saint Louis MO 63105	314-727-5850	R	8*	<.1
608	GSS Communiqations Inc	5042 Wilshire Blvd Ste, Los Angeles CA 90036	323-939-1181	R	8*	<.1
609	Hercky-Pasqua-Herman Inc—Peter Hercky	324 Chestnut St, Roselle Park NJ 07204	908-241-9474	R	8*	<.1
610	Johnson Clark Associates Inc—Wayne Johnson	2150 River Plz Dr Ste, Sacramento CA 95833	916-473-8866	R	8*	<.1
611	Morey Evans Advertising Inc—Glenn Morey	620 16th St Ste 200, Denver CO 80202	303-296-8011	R	8*	<.1
612	MRW Communications LLC—Tom Matzell	6 Barker Sq Dr, Pembroke MA 02359	781-924-5282	R	8*	<.1
613	Noise Inc—Mary Parodo	1863 N Farwell Ave, Milwaukee WI 53202	414-226-4900	R	8*	<.1
614	Quiller and Blake Advertising—Emily Spensieri	737 Main St, Buffalo NY 14203	716-842-1900	R	8*	<.1
615	RH Blake Inc—Bruce Blake	26600 Renaissance Pky, Cleveland OH 44128	216-595-2400	R	8*	<.1
616	SA Communications Services—Jim Shangle	10801 Electron Dr Ste, Louisville KY 40299	502-267-0999	R	8*	<.1
617	Turec Advertising Associates Inc—Ben Turec	9272 Olive Blvd, St Louis MO 63132	314-993-1190	R	8*	<.1
618	WestRogers Advertising—Becky West	6075 Poplar Ave Ste 12, Memphis TN 38119	901-682-3839	R	8*	<.1
619	Allan R Hackel Organization Inc—Allan Hackel	1330 Centre St Ste 69, Newton Centre MA 02459	617-965-4400	R	8*	<.1
620	Kopf Zimmermann Schultheis Advertising Inc	811 W Jericho Tpke Ste, Smithtown NY 11787	631-348-1440	R	8*	<.1
621	Addison Olian Inc—Addison H Olian II	2024 Broadway St, Redwood City CA 94063	650-369-5566	R	8*	<.1
622	Jackson - Terral Inc—Scott V Jackson	912 Highland Ave, Orlando FL 32801	407-849-9995	R	8*	<.1
623	PostScript Inc—Sara Blum	444 S Union St, Burlington VT 05401	802-863-2568	R	8*	<.1
624	Hazeltine Advertising and Design—Bobbie Hazeltine	6207 Longmont, Houston TX 77057	713-622-9593	R	8*	<.1
625	Maddox Marketing Group Inc—Robert M Maddox	2241 Front St Ste B, Cuyahoga Falls OH 44221	330-945-6232	R	8*	<.1
626	Allen Roche Group Inc—James Roche	5 Middlesex Ave Ste 40, Somerville MA 02145	617-623-0043	R	8*	<.1
627	Alling Henning Associates Inc—Betsy Henning	415 W 6th St Ste 605, Vancouver WA 98660	360-750-1680	R	8*	<.1
628	Bon Advertising Inc—Tim Hellige	307 W Muhammad Ali Blv, Louisville KY 40202	502-589-7711	R	8*	<.1
629	Foti Lazo Inc—Franco Foti	39 Broadway Rm 540, New York NY 10006	212-965-0442	R	8*	<.1

Note: An asterisk (*) indicates an estimated financial figure. The company type code used is as follows: R = Private, P = Public, S = Private Subsidiary, B = Public Subsidiary, D = Division, J = Joint Venture, I = Investment Fund.

COMPANY RANKINGS BY SALES WITHIN 4-DIGIT SIC

Rank	Company Name—Executive Officer	Address, City, State, Zip	Phone	Type	Fin	Empls
630	Thelab LLC—Jim Kiley	637 W 27th St Fl 8, New York NY 10001	212-209-1333	R	8*	.1
631	Collins Travers and Company Inc—Michael Barone	726 Exchange St Ste 50, Buffalo NY 14210	716-842-2222	R	7*	<.1
632	Harris Baio and Mccullough Inc—George Harris	520 S Front St, Philadelphia PA 19147	215-440-9800	R	7*	<.1
633	Camelot Communications Ltd—Brenda Dimaano	8140 Walnut Hill Ln St, Dallas TX 75231	214-373-6999	R	7*	<.1
634	Buntin Group Inc—Jeffrey Buntin	1001 Hawkins St, Nashville TN 37203	615-244-5720	R	7*	.1
635	Harriet Walley Associates—Peter Posner	300 E 42nd St Fl 2, New York NY 10017	212-867-3900	R	7*	.1
636	Advertising Strategies Inc—Karen Wyckoff	37 Rabbit Ridge Dr, Weaverville NC 28787	828-658-4230	R	7*	.1
637	Studeo Inc—David Allen	6405 S 3000 E Frnt, Salt Lake City UT 84121	801-993-2300	R	7*	<.1
638	Flint Communications Inc—Roger Reierson	PO Box 2012, Fargo ND 58107	701-237-4850	R	7*	.1
639	Compas Inc—Stanley R Woodland	4300 Haddonfield Rd, Pennsauken NJ 08109	856-667-8577	R	7*	.1
640	TSE Sports and Entertainment—Robert Tuchman	14 Penn Plz Ste 925, New York NY 10122	212-695-9480	R	7*	<.1
641	Versant Inc—William Ruch	11414 W Park Pl Ste 20, Milwaukee WI 53224	414-410-0500	R	7*	<.1
642	Planit Advertising Inc—Matthew Doud	500 E Pratt St Ste 100, Baltimore MD 21202	410-962-8501	R	7*	<.1
643	Rick Johnson and Company Inc—Erik Lohmeier	1120 Pennsylvania St N, Albuquerque NM 87110	505-266-1100	R	7*	<.1
644	Kuhn and Wittenborn Inc—Whitey Kuhn	2405 Grand Blvd Ste 60, Kansas City MO 64108	816-471-7888	R	7*	<.1
645	ClickSpeed—Dmitry Shcherbinin	6709 W 119th St Ste 39, Leawood KS 66209		R	7*	<.1
646	Perry Ballard Inc—Gary Tipton	526 Upton Dr E, Saint Joseph MI 49085	269-983-0611	R	7*	<.1
647	Witherspoon and Associates—Mike Wilie	PO Box 2137, Fort Worth TX 76113	817-335-1373	R	7	<.1
648	Austin/Lawrence Group—Ken Lempit	1266 E Main St, Stamford CT 06902	203-391-3006	R	7*	<.1
649	Emerson Hayes Advertising and Design—Allan Hayes	125 Hawthorne Ave, Palo Alto CA 94301	650-322-8233	R	7*	<.1
650	Orange Label Art Advertising—Wes Phillips	2043 Westcliff Dr Ste, Newport Beach CA 92660	949-631-9900	R	7*	<.1
651	R and R Advertising—Alex Stinson	3409 Executive Ctr Dr, Austin TX 78731	512-761-3731	R	7*	<.1
652	Beaird Agency Inc—Brice Beaird	3102 Maple Ave, Dallas TX 75201	214-954-1750	R	7*	<.1
653	Brown and Miller Advertising Inc—Craig Brown	24100 Chagrin Blvd Ste, Beachwood OH 44122	216-831-0440	R	8*	<.1
654	Direct Advertising Inc—Angelo A Stamoulis	27 Charles St, Holliston MA 01746	508-429-7488	R	7*	<.1
655	Don Wise and Co—Don Wise	219 E 49th St Fl 1, New York NY 10017	212-371-3333	R	7*	<.1
656	G Williams and Associates Inc—George A Williams	755 Avignon Dr, Ridgeland MS 39157	601-605-8000	R	7*	<.1
657	JCarrington Group—Susan Carrington	655 Craig Rd Ste 252, Saint Louis MO 63141	314-918-9119	R	7*	<.1
658	Montalbano Group—Herb Montalbano	4040 McEwen Rd Ste 300, Dallas TX 75244		R	7*	<.1
659	Rick Warner and Associates Inc—Rick Warner	19 N Fort Thomas Ave, Fort Thomas KY 41075	859-781-7700	R	7*	<.1
660	Creative Communication of America Inc—Ed Sirianno	16 Sage Estate, Albany NY 12204	518-427-6600	R	7*	<.1
661	FRIX Group—John Fricks	393 Caruso Ct Ste 200, Atlanta GA 30350	678-528-1323	R	7*	<.1
662	Miller Group Advertising—Renee Miller	1516 S Bundy Ste 200, Los Angeles CA 90025	310-442-0101	R	7*	<.1
663	Montgomery Stire and Partners—Frank Stire	PO Box 1213, Mandeville LA 70470	504-525-6789	R	7*	<.1
664	Mosaic Advertising and Marketing—Robert Charney	15260 Ventura Blvd Ste, Sherman Oaks CA 91403	818-597-0080	R	7*	<.1
665	Turtledove Clemens Inc—Jay Clemens	1230 SW 1st Ave Ste 20, Portland OR 97204	503-226-3581	R	7*	<.1
666	Wimbley Group Inc—Charles L Wimbley Jr	1100 N Arlington Heigh, Itasca IL 60143		R	7*	<.1
667	Fultz and Associates Inc—Barbara Fultz	1317 E Main St, Richmond VA 23219	804-648-8750	R	7*	<.1
668	Hess Marketing—Eric Hess	650 Poydras St Ste 155, New Orleans LA 70130	504-522-4377	R	7*	<.1
669	Forsythe and Butler Advertising/Marketing—Brad Forysthe	10777 Westheimer Ste 1, Houston TX 77042	713-783-0775	R	7*	<.1
670	Oldfield Davis Inc—Rachel M Davis	2910 N Hall St, Dallas TX 75204	214-745-4545	R	7*	<.1
671	Catapult Communications Inc—Bill Parmer	3276 Old Haleakala Hwy, Makawao HI 96768	808-572-5151	R	7*	<.1
672	Compro International—Greg Smith	PO Box 1971, Eagle ID 83616	280-914-1150	R	7*	<.1
673	Faltis Marketing Communications Inc—Dennis J Faltis	W5433 Lost Nation Rd, Elkhorn WI 53121	262-742-3400	R	7*	<.1
674	Hall Agency—John Hall	3625 N Hall St Ste 530, Dallas TX 75219	214-559-4255	R	7*	<.1
675	B Creative Services Inc—John T Barfuss	6504 28th St SE Ste S2, Grand Rapids MI 49546	616-949-3100	R	7*	<.1
676	Arnold Integrated Solutions—Ed Eskandarian	101 Huntington Ave Ste, Boston MA 02199	617-587-8023	R	7*	<.1
677	Harrison Leifer Dimarco Inc—Roy Dimarco	100 Merrick Rd Ste 516, Rockville Centre NY 11570	516-536-2020	R	7*	<.1
678	Scott Incorporated Of Milwaukee—Charles Reynolds	1031 N Astor St, Milwaukee WI 53202	414-276-1080	R	7*	<.1
679	Zeon Solutions Inc—Rupesh Agrawal	311 E Chicago Ste 520, Milwaukee WI 53202	414-475-6472	R	7	.2
680	Stiegler Wells Brunswick and Roth Inc—Ernie Stiegler	3865 Adler Pl, Bethlehem PA 18017	610-866-0611	R	7*	.1
681	Infospider Inc—Sheffield Nolan	1603 S Main St A, Milpitas CA 95035	408-719-1478	R	7*	.1
682	Intertrend Communications Inc—Julia Huang	555 E Ocean Blvd Ste 9, Long Beach CA 90802	562-733-1888	R	7*	<.1
683	Nova Marketing Inc—Kenneth Vilanova	300 Crown Colony Dr, Quincy MA 02169	617-770-0304	R	7*	<.1
684	Red Bricks Media—Scott Neslund	1062 Folsom St Ste 300, San Francisco CA 94103	415-255-0650	R	7	<.1
685	Brokaw Inc—Bill Brokaw	425 W Lakeside Ave Fl, Cleveland OH 44113	216-241-8003	R	7*	<.1
686	Prime Market Targeting Inc—Scott Duff	7777 W Lincoln Hwy Ste, Frankfort IL 60423	815-469-4555	R	7*	<.1
687	Schifino/Lee Inc—Paola Schifino	511 W Bay St Ste 400, Tampa FL 33606	813-258-5858	R	7*	<.1
688	Hanon-Mckendry Inc—Robert Blanchard	25 Ottawa Ave Sw Ste 6, Grand Rapids MI 49503	616-776-1111	R	6*	<.1
689	East Meets West Production Inc—Darlene Gregory	1024 Leopard St, Corpus Christi TX 78401	361-904-0044	R	6*	.1
690	Studio 13—Dale Bowman	800 S Pacific Coast Hw, Redondo Beach CA 90277	310-837-8107	R	6*	<.1
691	Kensib Inc—Patricia Sibley	3715 Northsid Pkwy Nw, Atlanta GA 30327	404-264-1005	R	6*	<.1
692	Ambassador Advertising Agency—John Campbell	1641 Langley Ave, Irvine CA 92614	714-738-1501	R	6*	<.1
693	Mering and Associates Inc—Debbie Houston	PO Box 19729, Sacramento CA 95819	916-441-0571	R	6*	<.1
694	Roddan Co—Brooks Roddan	2516 Via Tejon Ste 114, Palos Verdes Estates CA 90274	310-791-2755	R	6*	<.1
695	Stevens and Tate Inc—Daniel Gartlan	1900 S Highland Ave St, Lombard IL 60148	630-627-5200	R	6*	<.1
696	Advertising Holding Inc—Steve Thanhauser	PO Box 110186, Durham NC 27709	919-782-2360	R	6*	<.1
697	Angelvision Technologies Inc—Michael Jingozian	7320 SW Hunziker St St, Portland OR 97223	503-620-3377	R	6*	<.1
698	Trisect Inc—Dick Thomas	300 N Elizabeth St Ste, Chicago IL 60607	312-733-1303	R	6*	.1
699	Ott Communications Inc—Jerry Ott	752 Barret Ave, Louisville KY 40204	502-267-6999	R	6*	<.1
700	Ted Chin and Company Inc—Theodore Chin	39 Lewis St Fl 4, Greenwich CT 06830	203-661-0300	R	6*	<.1
701	Digital Pulp Inc—Lee Nadler	220 E 23rd St Ste 900, New York NY 10010	212-679-0676	R	6*	<.1
702	Natrel Communications Inc—Allan Trent	119 Cherry Hill Rd Ste, Parsippany NJ 07054	973-292-8400	R	6*	<.1
703	Sensis—Jose Villa	811 W 7th St Ste 300, Los Angeles CA 90017	213-341-0171	R	6*	<.1
704	Huber Marketing Group Inc—Ursula Huber-Rea	5976 W Las Positas Blv, Pleasanton CA 94588	925-227-9001	R	6*	<.1
705	Portfolio Associates Inc—Beverly A Harper	510 Walnut St Ste 1411, Philadelphia PA 19106	215-627-3660	R	6*	<.1
706	Boscobel Marketing Communications Inc—Joyce Bosc	8606 2nd Ave, Silver Spring MD 20910	301-588-2900	R	6*	<.1
707	Cummings Group—Rick Belinson	5301 E State St Ste 30, Rockford IL 61108	815-398-4289	R	6*	<.1
708	HPN Inc—Beth Miller	4600 W Jefferson Blvd, Fort Wayne IN 46804	260-459-2525	R	6*	<.1
709	Peak Biety Inc—Glen C Peak	501 E Jackson St Ste 2, Tampa FL 33602	813-227-8006	R	6*	<.1
710	Pisarkiewicz Mazur Co—Mary Pisarkiewicz	307 W 38th St, New York NY 10018	212-714-1700	R	6*	<.1
711	Sprowl and Associates Inc—Charles Sprowl	303 Linwood Ave, Fairfield CT 06824	203-255-5958	R	6*	<.1
712	TLW Productions—Tim Weston	401 Whitney Ave Ste 11, Gretna LA 70056	504-393-9002	R	6*	<.1
713	VAMCOM Advertising	PO Box 729, Chester NJ 07930	908-879-0888	R	6*	<.1
714	Garber and Goodman Advertising Inc—Robert Goodman	300 41st St Ste 214, Miami Beach FL 33140	305-673-5177	R	6*	<.1
715	Iris Creative Group LLC—Beth Brodovsky	525 Plymouth Rd Ste 31, Plymouth Meeting PA 19462	610-567-2799	R	6*	<.1
716	Masar-Johnston Advertising and Design Inc—John Masar	8885 Rio San Diego Dr, San Diego CA 92108	619-281-3484	R	6*	<.1
717	McGlinchey and Associates Inc—Melissa McGlinchey	250 N Sunny Slope Ste, Brookfield WI 53005		R	6*	<.1
718	Pell Communications Inc—Gary Pell	21 Main St Ste G, Reisterstown MD 21136	410-667-6443	R	6*	<.1
719	Redhead Cos—Edward Stern	6011 University Blvd S, Ellicott City MD 21043	410-465-1282	R	6*	<.1

Rank	Company Name—*Executive Officer*	Address, City, State, Zip	Phone	Type	Fin	Em
720	Richard Heiman Advertising Inc—*Richard Heiman*	700 Park Regency Pl NE, Atlanta GA 30326	404-261-7777	R	6*	<.
721	Ross and Associates Inc—*Jane M Ross*	1685 Viewpond Dr SE, Grand Rapids MI 49508	616-455-2424	R	6*	<.1
722	Creative Marketing Sales Inc—*Silvio Fernandez*	PO Box 8285, Metairie LA 70011	504-837-5600	R	6*	<.1
723	Hood Marketing Solutions—*Wayne L Hood*	730 Peachtree St Ste 6, Atlanta GA 30308	404-872-2299	R	6*	<.1
724	iDirect Marketing Inc—*Dennis J Hastings*	9880 Research Dr Ste 1, Irvine CA 92618	949-753-7300	R	6*	<.1
725	RJ Gibson Advertising Inc—*Robert J Gibson*	658 W Indiantown Rd, Jupiter FL 33458	561-741-1441	R	6*	<.1
726	Rueckert Advertising and Public Relations LLC—*Dean Rueckert*	638 Albany Shaker Rd, Loudonville NY 12211	518-446-1091	R	6*	<.1
727	Straightline International Inc—*Michael Watras*	107 Grand St 6th Fl, New York NY 10013	212-941-0700	R	6*	<.1
728	Buzzy's Recording—*Andrew Morris*	6900 Melrose Ave, Los Angeles CA 90038	323-931-1867	R	6*	<.1
729	Exposure International Direct Marketing Systems Inc—*Barb Winston*	13179 Clermont Ct, Denver CO 80241	303-255-1022	R	6*	<.1
730	AD1 Agency—*Mariellen Ramsdell*	700 River Ave, Pittsburgh PA 15212	412-322-5535	R	6*	<.1
731	Dimmick and Fornari—*David Dimmick*	1545 River Park Dr Ste, Sacramento CA 95815	916-717-0550	R	6	<.1
732	L Lavery and Co—*Lynn Lavery*	560 Arlington Pl, Macon GA 31201	478-741-8888	R	6*	<.1
733	Papagalos and Associates Inc—*Nicholas Papagalos*	7330 N 16th St Ste B10, Phoenix AZ 85020	602-279-2933	R	6*	<.1
734	Parker and James Communications—*Elenore Parker*	75 McNeil Way, Dedham MA 02026	781-320-0061	R	6*	<.1
735	Steve Schollnick Advertising—*Steve Schollnick*	2828 Metairie Ct, Metairie LA 70002	504-838-9615	R	6*	<.1
736	First Marketing Group Int'l Inc—*Drew Cherner*	2170 W State Rd 434 St, Longwood FL 32779	407-788-7070	R	6*	<.1
737	Spalding Group Inc—*Ted Jackson*	2306 Frankfort Ave, Louisville KY 40206	502-495-1740	R	6*	<.1
738	Buy Owner Inc—*Scott Eckert*	1192 E Newport Center, Deerfield Beach FL 33442	954-202-7777	R	6*	<.1
739	Media Crew—*Ed Kim*	1803 Park Center Dr St, Orlando FL 32835	407-839-0390	R	6	<.1
740	Garrand and Company Inc—*Brenda Garrand*	75 Washington Ave Ste, Portland ME 04101	207-772-3119	R	6*	<.1
741	Domus Inc—*Elizabeth Tuppeny*	123 S Broad St Ste 198, Philadelphia PA 19109	215-772-2800	R	6*	<.1
742	Advertising Company Of America Inc—*Bruce Fletcher*	PO Box 980, East Lansing MI 48826	517-336-7639	R	6*	.1
743	Bulldog Drummond Inc—*Shawn Parr*	2741 4th Ave, San Diego CA 92103	619-528-8404	R	6*	<.1
744	Dedicated Media Inc—*Scott Yamano*	909 N Sepulveda Blvd S, El Segundo CA 90245	310-524-9400	R	6*	<.1
745	John Muller and Company Inc—*Kathleen Muller*	4739 Belleview Ave Ste, Kansas City MO 64112	816-531-1992	R	6*	<.1
746	Rethink Group Inc—*James Offenhartz*	700 Canal St Ste 5, Stamford CT 06902	203-357-9004	R	5*	<.1
747	North County Advertising—*Craig Bryer*	29662 Kingswinn Dr, Laguna Beach CA 92677	949-249-3141	R	5*	.1
748	Kgb Texas Marketing / Public Relations Inc—*Katie Harvey*	1919 Oakwell Farms Pkw, San Antonio TX 78218	210-826-8899	R	5*	<.1
749	Sky Blue Agency Inc—*Robert Farinella*	950 Lowery Blvd Nw Ste, Atlanta GA 30318	404-876-0202	R	5*	<.1
750	Triad Creative Group Inc—*Roger Lex*	3130 Intertech Dr, Brookfield WI 53045	262-781-3100	R	5*	<.1
751	Mediacross Inc—*Mark Travers*	2001 S Hanley Rd Ste 5, Saint Louis MO 63144	314-646-1101	R	5*	<.1
752	Terry Hines and Assoc—*Renee Rascoe*	440 Park Ave S Fl 12, New York NY 10016	212-929-9257	R	5*	<.1
753	Milesbrand Inc—*David Miles*	1101 Bannock St, Denver CO 80204	303-293-9191	R	5*	<.1
754	Image Display Group Inc—*Victor Lanfranco*	1743 S Douglass Rd Ste, Anaheim CA 92806	714-221-4377	R	5*	<.1
755	ADD Marketing Inc—*Scott Leonard*	6600 Lexington Ave, Los Angeles CA 90038	323-790-0500	R	5*	<.1
756	Buzzlogic Inc—*Dave Hills*	425 Brannan St Fl 2, San Francisco CA 94107	415-913-2603	R	5*	<.1
757	Anderson Partners—*Mark Hughes*	6919 Dodge St, Omaha NE 68132	402-341-4807	R	5*	<.1
758	Axiom Marketing Inc—*Michael Keegan*	PO Box 7122, Libertyville IL 60048	847-362-5656	R	5*	<.1
759	Wexley School for Girls LLC—*Brian Marr*	2218 5th Ave, Seattle WA 98121	206-438-8900	R	5	<.1
760	Emma Inc—*Will Weaver*	2120 8th Ave S, Nashville TN 37204	615-292-5888	R	5*	.1
761	Pop Labs Inc—*Gene McCubbin*	7850 Parkwood Cir Ste, Houston TX 77036	713-243-4500	R	5*	<.1
762	Rec World Advertising—*Robert Brady*	10400 Recreational Dr, Summerset SD 57718	605-787-7453	R	5*	<.1
763	Group Loria LLC Joester—*Debra Joester*	860 Broadway Fl 3, New York NY 10003	212-683-5150	R	5*	<.1
764	Visionaire Group—*Dimitry Ioffe*	4221 Redwood Ave, Los Angeles CA 90066	310-823-1800	R	5	<.1
765	Visual Image Media Consultants Inc—*Tim Berney*	125 Park Ave Ste 200, Oklahoma City OK 73102	405-525-0055	R	5*	<.1
766	Sid Paterson Advertising Inc—*Sidney Paterson*	99 Madison Ave Fl 9, New York NY 10016	212-725-9600	R	5*	<.1
767	Unicorn Marketing Group Inc—*Joey Iazzetto*	2875 S 25th Ave, Broadview IL 60155	708-345-4900	R	5*	<.1
768	Kerwin Communications—*Jim Kerwin*	1120 Bloomfield Ave St, West Caldwell NJ 07006	973-244-0301	R	5*	<.1
769	Grant Harrison Advertising LLC—*Mina Mann*	701 Richmond Ave Rm 22, Houston TX 77006	713-627-3210	R	5*	<.1
770	Graphics 55 Inc—*Catherine Lapico*	3011 W Grand Blvd Ste, Detroit MI 48202	313-875-1155	R	5*	<.1
771	P and R Associates International—*Paul Schmitz*	1799 Akron Penninsula, Akron OH 44313	330-928-8000	R	5*	<.1
772	StoreBoard Media LLC—*Rick Sirvaitis*	441 Lexington Ave 14th, New York NY 10017	212-682-3300	R	5*	<.1
773	Acadian Advertising Inc—*Betty Pope*	12030 Lakeland Park Bl, Baton Rouge LA 70809	225-755-1111	D	5*	<.1
774	Arvo Communications Inc—*Thomas Arvo*	1908 Howell Branch Rd, Winter Park FL 32792	407-671-0185	R	5*	<.1
775	Bright Moments Inc—*William Rouselle*	615 Baronne St Ste 304, New Orleans LA 70113	504-592-1800	R	5*	<.1
776	Burton Livingstone and Kirk—*Walter L Hagstrom Jr*	4665 MacArthur Ct Ste, Newport Beach CA 92660	949-250-6363	R	5*	<.1
777	Elisco Advertising—*John Elisco*	3711 Butler St, Pittsburgh PA 15201	412-621-7494	R	5*	<.1
778	GHR Advertising Inc—*Sandy Romaner*	1761 W Hillsboro Blvd, Deerfield Beach FL 33442	954-785-4444	R	5*	<.1
779	L3 Advertising Inc—*Joe Lam*	115 Bowery St 3rd Fl, New York NY 10002	212-966-7050	R	5*	<.1
780	Macrovision Inc (Doylestown Pennsylvania)—*Charles Birkhead*	301 S Main St Ste 3-W, Doylestown PA 18901	215-348-1010	R	5*	<.1
781	Marcus and Associates Inc—*Melinda Marcus*	6022 Meadow Crest Dr, Dallas TX 75230	214-987-2400	R	5*	<.1
782	Morbelli Russo and Partners Advertising—*Mario Marbelli Jr*	2 Sylvan Way Ste 302, Parsippany NJ 07054	973-644-9663	R	5*	<.1
783	Nehmen-Kodner Inc—*Peggy Nehmen*	431 N Polo Dr Unit A, Saint Louis MO 63105	314-721-1404	R	5*	<.1
784	Newton Associates Inc—*Dan Ditzler*	527 Plymouth Rd Ste 41, Plymouth Meeting PA 19462		R	5*	<.1
785	Philips Healthcare Communications Inc—*Dorothy M Philips*	30 Irving Pl 2nd Fl, New York NY 10003	212-614-2847	R	5*	<.1
786	Rabuck Stranger—*Rick Rabuck*	3221 Hutchison Ave Ste, Los Angeles CA 90034	310-815-8225	R	5*	<.1
787	RH Power and Associates Inc—*Roger L Vergara*	9621 4th St NW, Albuquerque NM 87114	505-761-3150	R	5*	<.1
788	Schenk Hampton Advertising—*Larry Hampton*	601 NW Riverside Dr, Evansville IN 47708	812-424-8701	R	5*	<.1
789	Stephens and Associates Advertising Inc—*Chuck Stephens*	7400 W 132nd St Ste 10, Overland Park KS 66213	913-661-0910	R	5*	<.1
790	Verti-Mark Group Inc—*Tom Wiersma*	1324 Lake Dr SE Ste 4, Grand Rapids MI 49506	616-456-9676	R	5*	<.1
791	Artagrafik—*Chris Artabasy*	1123 Zonolite Rd Ste 2, Atlanta GA 30306	678-999-2189	R	5*	<.1
792	Big—*Ed Lacy*	One E Cary St, Richmond VA 23219	804-355-9151	R	5*	<.1
793	Bill Bosse and Associates—*William R Bosse*	6 Gage Ct, Houston TX 77024	832-358-2888	R	5*	<.1
794	Blue Chair Advertising—*Kathy Venaglia*	218 N Lee St 3rd Fl, Alexandria VA 22314	703-556-3990	R	5*	<.1
795	COMMUNIQUE Inc (Jefferson City Missouri)—*Steve Veile*	PO Box 237, Jefferson City MO 65102	573-635-3265	R	5*	<.1
796	Holmes and Company Advertising—*Lisa Holmes*	34 S 600 E, Salt Lake City UT 84102	801-355-2211	R	5*	<.1
797	LMI Advertising—*Gary J Bellanca*	24E E Roseville Rd, Lancaster PA 17601	717-569-8826	R	5*	<.1
798	Pierce Communications Inc—*Gene Pierce*	208 E State St, Columbus OH 43215	614-365-9494	R	5*	<.1
799	Poller and Jordan Advertising Agency—*Robert Poller*	PO Box 166249, Miami FL 33116	305-470-8005	R	5*	<.1
800	Alford Advertising Inc—*Robert Alford*	1055 St Charles Ave St, New Orleans LA 70130	504-581-7500	R	5*	<.1
801	Brashe Advertising Inc—*Harvey Cherkis*	420 Jericho Tpk, Jericho NY 11753	516-935-5544	R	5*	<.1
802	Brightwork Advertising and Training Inc—*Snowden McFall*	2220 County Rd 210 W S, Jacksonville FL 32259	904-940-7355	R	5*	<.1
803	JPM Marketing Communications—*James P Moore*	PO Box 20697, Bloomington MN 55420	952-881-4464	R	5*	<.1
804	Knudsen Gardner and Howe Advertising Inc—*Tim Knudsen*	2103 St Clair Ave, Cleveland OH 44114	216-781-5000	R	5*	<.1
805	Marketing Management Services LLC—*Philip J Cok*	PO Box 273, Coopersville MI 49404	616-997-7387	R	5*	<.1
806	Nolen and Associates Inc—*Pam Nolen*	PO Box 53097, Atlanta GA 30355	404-365-8340	R	5*	<.1
807	Response Advertising and Marketing Corp—*Richard Maloney*	3104 Creekside Village, Kennesaw GA 30144	770-424-5770	R	5*	<.1

Note: An asterisk (*) indicates an estimated financial figure. The company type code used is as follows: R = Private, P = Public, S = Private Subsidiary, B = Public Subsidiary, D = Division, J = Joint Venture, I = Investment Fund.

	Executive Officer	Address, City, State, Zip	Phone	Type	Fin	Empls
	...a and Company Inc—*Daniel P Mecca*	17 Grove St, Williamsville NY 14221	716-633-1218	R	5*	<.1
	...Search—*William R Leake*	6207 Sheridan Ave Ste2, Austin TX 78723	512-583-4200	R	5	.1
	...roductions Inc—*Randy Crow*	1756 Lakeshore Dr, Muskegon MI 49441	231-759-3160	R	5*	<.1
	...ublicidad Siboney Corp—*Jose Cubas*	729 7th Ave Fl 9, New York NY 10019	212-337-8900	R	5*	<.1
	Inferno LLC—*Kathy Long*	505 Tennessee St Ste 1, Memphis TN 38103	901-278-3773	R	5*	<.1
13	Locke Wern-Rausch Advertising Inc—*Todd Locke*	4470 Dressler Rd Nw, Canton OH 44718	330-493-8866	R	5*	<.1
814	Brains On Fire Inc—*Robbin Phillips*	148 River St Ste 100, Greenville SC 29601	864-676-9663	R	5*	<.1
815	John and Low And Company Inc—*John Salzinski*	372 W Ontario St Fl 6, Chicago IL 60654	312-397-2257	R	5*	<.1
816	Psb—*William Berndt*	26012 Atlantic Ocean D, Lake Forest CA 92630	949-465-0772	R	5*	<.1
817	Legal Rights Defenders—*Mary Walker*	1010 S Cabrillo Ave, San Pedro CA 90731	310-519-4050	R	5*	<.1
818	Sms Productions Inc—*Steven Slovon*	10555 Guilford Rd Ste, Jessup MD 20794	301-953-0011	R	5*	<.1
819	Kanter International LLC—*Vinay Bansal*	325 Chestnut St Ste 13, Philadelphia PA 19106	215-413-2686	R	5*	<.1
820	Full Circle Productions LLC	PO Box 191611, Atlanta GA 31119	404-256-4083	R	5*	<.1
821	Gaston LLC—*Jack Gniadecki*	730 W Randolph St Fl 4, Chicago IL 60661	312-379-5454	R	5*	<.1
822	Stephenz Group Inc—*Barbara Zenz*	75 E Santa Clara St, San Jose CA 95113	408-286-9899	R	5*	<.1
823	Franklyn Ideas LLC	1719 State Rt 10 Ste 2, Parsippany NJ 07054	973-644-9009	R	5*	<.1
824	Insight Media Advertising—*Donna Michlak*	2105 W Park Ct, Champaign IL 61821	217-373-7877	R	4*	<.1
825	Level Brand Inc—*John Foley*	724 N 1st St Ste 500, Minneapolis MN 55401	612-338-8000	R	4*	<.1
826	Esrock Partners Advertising Inc—*John Coughlin*	14550 S 94th Ave, Orland Park IL 60462	708-349-8400	R	4*	<.1
827	Walker 360 Inc—*Taylor Blackwell*	2501 E 5th St, Montgomery AL 36107	334-832-4975	R	4*	.1
828	FBRD Company Inc—*Mike Drake*	143 S Kings Rd, Los Angeles CA 90048	323-852-1301	R	4*	<.1
829	Walz Tetrick Advertising Inc—*Charles Tetrick*	6299 Nall Ave Ste 300, Shawnee Mission KS 66202	913-789-8778	R	4*	<.1
830	United Resources Information Inc—*Xochitl Hwang*	3635 Hayden Ave, Culver City CA 90232	310-842-3949	R	4*	<.1
831	VrboCom LLC—*Marvin Floyd*	4255 S Buckley Rd Pmb, Aurora CO 80013	303-680-9280	R	4*	<.1
832	Your Home Town USA Inc—*Sharon Jones*	PO Box 335, Clarklake MI 49234	517-529-9421	R	4*	<.1
833	Phenix Solutions Inc—*James Moore*	8435 Helgerman Ct, Gaithersburg MD 20877	301-230-2023	R	4*	<.1
834	Cirlot Agency Inc—*Liza Looser*	PO Box 16087, Jackson MS 39236	601-664-2010	R	4*	<.1
835	Catalyst Inc—*Brian Odell*	275 Promenade St Ste 2, Providence RI 02908	401-732-1886	R	4*	<.1
836	Jordan Associates (Oklahoma City Oklahoma)—*Rhonda Hooper*	3201 Quail Springs Pky, Oklahoma City OK 73134	405-840-3201	R	4*	.1
837	Norm Marshall and Associates Inc—*Norman Marshall*	11059 Sherman Way, Sun Valley CA 91352	818-982-3505	R	4*	<.1
838	Grant H Rockley—*Grant Rockley*	PO Box 1963, Johnson City TN 37605	423-283-4140	R	4*	<.1
839	Bayer Bauserman and Co—*Carla Acree*	PO Box 2916, Reno NV 89505	775-323-2181	R	4*	<.1
840	Chambers Group—*Keith Chambers*	1537 Pontius Ave 1st F, Los Angeles CA 90025	310-473-0010	R	4*	<.1
841	Adlucent—*Jon Armstrong*	508 E 53rd St Ste 101, Austin TX 78751		R	4*	<.1
842	Strategic Marketing and Media—*Louis F Vargas*	1800 E Lambert Ste 160, Brea CA 92821	714-671-4999	R	4*	<.1
843	DiBona Bornstein and Random Inc—*Stan Bornstein*	46 Waltham St 6th Fl, Boston MA 02118	617-267-6262	R	4*	<.1
844	Creating Results LLC—*Judy Harff*	1400 Crown Crt Ste 211, Woodbridge VA 22193	703-494-7888	R	4*	<.1
845	Groop—*Kristen Hudson*	125 W 4th St Ste 103, Los Angeles CA 90013	213-613-0066	R	4*	<.1
846	Stevens Inc—*Allen Prater*	190 Monroe Ave NW Ste, Grand Rapids MI 49503	616-942-2801	R	4*	<.1
847	Marketing Assistance Inc—*Dick Hersum*	436 Boston Post Rd, Weston MA 02493	781-891-1227	R	4*	<.1
848	FMG Design Inc—*Ferdinand Meyer V*	101 Crawford St Ste 1A, Houston TX 77002	713-222-7979	R	4*	<.1
849	AdMasters Inc—*Tom Dodson*	16901 Dallas Pky Ste 2, Addison TX 75001	972-866-9300	R	4*	<.1
850	Allyn Partners Inc—*Mari Woodlief*	3232 McKinney Ave Ste, Dallas TX 75204	214-871-7723	R	4*	<.1
851	Rockett Interactive Inc— *Mark Rockett*	111 Centrewest Ct, Cary NC 27513	919-678-8994	R	4*	<.1
852	Rumbletree—*Charles Yeaton*	216 Lafayette Rd, North Hampton NH 03862	603-433-6214	R	4*	<.1
853	Slaughter Hanson and Associates Inc—*Terry Slaughter*	2336 20th Ave S, Birmingham AL 35223	205-871-9020	R	4*	<.1
854	West Creative Inc—*Stan Chrzanowski*	10789 S Cedar Niles Ci, Overland Park KS 66210	913-839-2181	R	4*	<.1
855	Burk Advertising and Marketing Inc—*B Bailey Burk*	302 N Market St Ste 40, Dallas TX 75202	214-953-0494	R	4*	<.1
856	Dreamray—*Paul Jerome*	1205 West Loop N Ste A, Houston TX 77055	832-659-0916	R	4*	<.1
857	Frank Freeman and Mathai—*Randy Mathai*	522 S Kenwood Ave, Baltimore MD 21224	410-563-7700	R	4*	<.1
858	KBG Advertising—*Robbie Kemper*	1217 Elm St, Cincinnati OH 45201	513-352-0991	R	4*	<.1
859	Lippi and Company Advertising—*Lawrence R Lippi*	929 W Hill St, Charlotte NC 28208	704-376-2001	R	4*	<.1
860	Selective Marketing Communications Inc—*Jeff Rothe*	PO Box 11030, Charlotte NC 28220	704-342-3400	R	4*	<.1
861	Castells and Asociados Advertising—*Maria (Liz) Castells-Heard*	865 S Figueroa St 11th, Los Angeles CA 90017	213-688-7217	R	4*	<.1
862	Chaffee and Partners—*David S Chaffee*	310 Maple St Ste 102, Barrington RI 02806	401-247-2300	R	4*	<.1
863	D C Tintle and Associates Inc—*David C Tintle*	99 Murray Hill Pky Ste, East Rutherford NJ 07073	201-896-2250	R	4*	<.1
864	Digital VooDoo—*Lisa Dee*	2153 Pleasant Grove Rd, Encinitas CA 92024	760-753-8293	R	4*	<.1
865	Geisz Agency—*John Geisz*	2812 S Brentwood Blvd, St Louis MO 63144	314-968-0575	R	4*	<.1
866	GK and A Advertising Inc—*George Koontz*	1720 Regal Row Ste 235, Dallas TX 75235	214-634-9486	R	4*	<.1
867	Greenfield Advertising Group Inc—*Jerold A Greenfield*	12551 New Brittany Blv, Fort Myers FL 33907	239-437-0000	R	4*	<.1
868	Group Nine Marketing—*Shirley Rivoli*	952 S 3rd St Ste 201, Louisville KY 40203	502-589-5785	R	4*	<.1
869	Kartagener Associates—*Henry Kartagener*	631 Commack Rd Ste 1A, Commack NY 11725	631-858-1270	R	4*	<.1
870	Professional Image Inc (Newport Beach California)—*Angela OMara*	359 San Miguel Dr Ste, Newport Beach CA 92660	949-760-1522	R	4*	<.1
871	Rhycom Advertising Inc—*Rick Rhyner*	10975 Grandview Suite, Overland Park KS 66210	913-451-9102	R	4*	<.1
872	Weitzman Inc—*Allan Weitzman*	3 Church Cir, Annapolis MD 21401	410-263-7771	R	4*	<.1
873	City Beach Films—*David Gottlieb*	12920 Hibiscus Ave Ste, Seminole FL 33776	727-399-2217	R	4*	<.1
874	Larry Smith and Associates Inc—*Larry Smith*	3372 Pigeon Hawk Court, Norcross GA 30092	440-314-3669	R	4*	<.1
875	Time Advertising Inc—*Baron Suen*	50 Victoria Ave Ste 20, Millbrae CA 94030	650-259-9388	R	4*	<.1
876	Weston-Mason And Associates Inc—*Thomas Weston*	3130 Wilshire Blvd Fl, Santa Monica CA 90403	310-207-6507	R	4*	<.1
877	Directory Advertising Specialists Inc—*Karen Korner*	6565 Taft St Ste 201, Hollywood FL 33024	954-893-8112	R	4*	<.1
878	Henkin Schultz Inc—*Joe Henkin*	6201 S Pinnacle Pl, Sioux Falls SD 57108	605-331-2155	R	4*	<.1
879	Simantel Group—*Susan Ketterer*	321 Sw Water St, Peoria IL 61602	309-674-7747	R	4*	<.1
880	Harris D Mckinney Inc—*Daniel Hoexter*	55 W Wacker Dr Ste 702, Chicago IL 60601	312-506-5200	R	4*	<.1
881	Penna Powers Brian And Haynes Inc—*John Haynes*	1706 Major St, Salt Lake City UT 84115	801-487-4800	R	4*	<.1
882	Telemet America Inc—*Frederick Parsons*	325 First St, Alexandria VA 22314	703-548-2042	R	4*	<.1
883	Avalon Digital Marketing Systems Inc—*Daniel D Walter*	5255 N Edgewood Dr Ste, Provo UT 84604	801-225-7073	R	4	.1
884	More Media Direct Inc—*Martin Silverman*	PO Box 190756, Miami Beach FL 33119	305-672-9793	R	4*	<.1
885	Danforth Wallace and Kupersmith Ltd—*Fraser Wallace*	45195 Business Ct Ste, Dulles VA 20166	703-264-6400	R	4*	<.1
886	Lee Tilford Agency Inc—*Anthony Tilford*	5725 W Hwy 290 Ste 201, Austin TX 78735	512-899-1100	R	4*	<.1
887	Moco Inc—*Nathan Morris*	3433 Broadway St Ne St, Minneapolis MN 55413	612-379-8100	R	4*	<.1
888	Mullen Advertising and Public Relations Inc—*Carter Mullen*	3636 N Central Ave Ste, Phoenix AZ 85012	602-222-4300	R	4*	<.1
889	Active Media Corp—*Thomas Lapcevic*	100 Business Ctr Dr St, Pittsburgh PA 15205	412-787-0366	R	3*	<.1
890	Concept Group Inc—*John Ruddy*	190 5th St E Ste 300, Saint Paul MN 55101	651-221-9710	R	3*	<.1
891	Malenke Barnhart LLC	1614 15th St, Denver CO 80202	303-433-4200	R	3*	<.1
892	Leslie Davis—*Leslie Davis*	2720 5th Ave, San Diego CA 92103	619-299-5958	R	3*	<.1
893	Hightower Agency Inc—*Edward Hightower*	PO Box 622, Madison MS 39130	601-853-1822	R	3*	<.1
894	Brigandi And Associates Inc—*George Brigandi*	1918 N Mendell St Ste, Chicago IL 60642	773-278-9911	R	3*	<.1
895	Communication Corporation Of Connecticut—*Irene Makiaris*	306 Industrial Park Rd, Middletown CT 06457	860-854-6380	R	3*	<.1

Rank	Company Name—*Executive Officer*	Address, City, State, Zip	Phone	Type	Fin	Empls
896	Flaherty Sabol Carroll Marketing Communications Inc—*Ed Flaherty*	11 Stanwix St Ste 202, Pittsburgh PA 15222	412-471-3700	R	3*	<.1
897	Johnson and Murphy Advertising LLC—*Sean Bishop*	16122 Sherman Way, Van Nuys CA 91406	818-787-2170	R	3*	<.1
898	Kay Forbes-Smith and Associates Inc—*Kay Forbes-Smith*	421 N Main St, Evansville IN 47711	812-424-3333	R	3*	<.1
899	Plus1 Media LLC—*John Meyer*	2101 Chapel Plaza Ct S, Columbia MO 65203	573-445-3427	R	3	<.1
900	Amos Townsend and Associates Inc—*Edward King*	PO Box 460, Summersville WV 26651	304-872-3000	R	3*	<.1
901	Jordan Azzam Inc—*Gary Jordan*	305 Wshington Ave Ste, Baltimore MD 21204	410-825-1800	R	3*	<.1
902	ACE Marketing and Promotions Inc—*Dean L Julia*	457 Rockaway Ave, Valley Stream NY 11581	516-256-7766	P	3	<.1
903	Superior Internet Solutions—*Scott Kirkpatrick*	8572 Spectrum Ln, San Diego CA 92121	858-436-1180	R	3*	<.1
904	Scott Pipitone Design Ltd—*Scott Pipitone*	3933 Perrysville Ave, Pittsburgh PA 15214	412-321-0879	R	3*	<.1
905	Bradley Reid Communications Inc—*John Tracy*	900 W 5th Ave Ste 100, Anchorage AK 99501	907-276-6353	R	3*	<.1
906	Robinson Radio Inc—*Buck Robinson*	4050 Innslake Dr Ste 3, Glen Allen VA 23060	804-726-6400	R	3*	<.1
907	Bramson and Associates—*Gene Bramson*	7400 Beverly Blvd, Los Angeles CA 90036	323-938-3595	R	3*	<.1
908	Marca Hispanic LLC—*Armando Hernandez*	3390 Mary St Ste 254, Miami FL 33133	305-665-5410	R	3*	<.1
909	Mad*Pow—*Amy Cueva*	27 Congress St, Portsmouth NH 03801	603-436-7177	R	3*	<.1
910	Bedford Granite Group Inc—*Susan Walsh*	707 Chestnut St, Manchester NH 03104	603-627-9600	R	3*	<.1
911	Intellix Media—*Kevin J Bartanian*	11400 W Olympic Blvd S, Los Angeles CA 90064	310-914-0178	R	3*	<.1
912	WelComm Inc—*Greg Evans*	7975 Raytheon Rd, San Diego CA 92111	858-279-2100	R	3*	<.1
913	CS and A Advertising Inc—*Wilson Burge*	PO Box 1643, Bloomington IL 61702	309-664-0707	R	3*	<.1
914	Signal Advertising—*David Zahn*	535 Stone Cutters Way, Montpelier VT 05602	802-229-4149	R	3*	<.1
915	Christopherson and Co—*Anne Christopherson*	5613 DTC Pkwy Ste 590, Greenwood Village CO 80111	303-779-4920	R	3*	<.1
916	Advertising Associates International—*Richard Hersum* Marketing Assistance Inc	63 South St, Hopkinton MA 01748	781-891-1227	D	3*	<.1
917	Anthony Group Inc—*Tony Talbott*	4115 Blackhawk Plaza C, Danville CA 94506	925-736-2222	R	3*	<.1
918	Charles Dolce Inc—*Perry Dolce*	421 Frenchmen St, New Orleans LA 70116	504-949-9052	R	3*	<.1
919	CTSMarketing Inc—*Tom Scholl*	PO Box 1223, Dearborn MI 48121	313-240-9350	R	3*	<.1
920	Ken Slauf and Associates Inc—*Ken Slauf*	1 N Main St, Lombard IL 60148	630-629-7531	R	3*	<.1
921	Lida Advertising Co—*Robert Lida*	222 Commerce St, Wichita KS 67202	316-263-1029	R	3*	<.1
922	Marcy Design Group Inc—*Greg Krivicich*	2461 E Main St, Columbus OH 43209	614-224-6226	R	3*	<.1
923	Oster and Associates Inc—*Beverly Oster*	3525 5th Ave 2nd Fl, San Diego CA 92103	619-906-5540	R	3*	<.1
924	Product Marketing Group Inc—*Beverly B Winesburgh*	978 Douglas Ave Ste 10, Altamonte Springs FL 32714	407-774-6363	R	3	<.1
925	Schultz Communications—*Randall D Schultz*	8205 Spain Rd NE Ste 2, Albuquerque NM 87109	505-822-8222	R	3*	<.1
926	DeBow Communications Ltd—*Thomas DeBow*	P O Box 5432, New York NY 10185	212-977-8815	R	3*	<.1
927	Evergreen Advertising and Marketing Inc—*Bob Kesner*	2 Maple St, Middlebury VT 05753	802-877-3316	R	3*	<.1
928	French/Blitzer/Scott LLC—*Robert Scott*	275 Madison Ave 4th Fl, New York NY 10016	212-255-2650	R	3*	<.1
929	FuseboxWest—*Serafin Canchola*	6101 Del Valle Dr, Los Angeles CA 90048	310-993-7073	R	3*	<.1
930	KCS International Inc (Leola Pennsylvania)—*Karen C Smith-Kerne*	247 N Shippen St Ste 1, Lancaster PA 17602	717-397-7100	R	3*	<.1
931	Norris and Cotes—*Diana Cotes*	316 W 4th St, Cincinnati OH 45202	513-521-5434	R	3*	<.1
932	Shable and Associates—*Jim Shable*	10077 Grogan's Mill Rd, Spring TX 77380	281-363-9000	R	3*	<.1
933	The Fletcher Group—*Lee Fletcher*	321 N 2nd St, Monroe LA 71201	318-323-2700	R	3*	<.1
934	Todd Co—*Britt Todd*	4110 W Interstate 20 S, Arlington TX 76017	817-516-9331	R	3*	<.1
935	Carstens Amaral—*Donn Carstens*	425 Algonquin Pl, Saint Louis MO 63119	314-517-4386	R	3*	<.1
936	Merritt Mosby Advertising Inc—*Merritt Mosby Jr*	5705 Stage Rd Ste190, Bartlett TN 38134	901-386-2117	R	3	<.1
937	Nunn and Associates—*Sally Nunn*	6540 Lusk Blvd, San Diego CA 92121	858-455-5653	R	3*	<.1
938	Richard Lewic Communications Inc—*Gregory Tiberend*	35 West 35th St Ste 50, New York NY 10001	212-827-0020	R	3*	<.1
939	Thelen Plus—*Larry Thelen*	224 N 5th Ave, Phoenix AZ 85003	602-271-4002	R	3	<.1
940	Next Communications Inc—*Dennis Gallaher*	10249 Yellow Cir Dr St, Minnetonka MN 55343	952-934-8220	R	3*	<.1
941	Zeis Group Inc—*Jeffrey Zeis*	12801 Flushing Ste 2, Saint Louis MO 63131	314-966-3113	R	3*	<.1
942	Wolff Associates Inc—*Raymond Monte*	1641 Commons Pkwy, Macedon NY 14502	585-461-8300	R	3*	<.1
943	Black and Tan Corp—*James Flemming*	PO Box 425, Kinderhook NY 12106	518-758-9020	R	3*	<.1
944	Br Direct Marketing—*David Francis*	4600 Madison Ave Ste 1, Kansas City MO 64112	816-960-5115	R	3*	<.1
945	Renaissance Creative Services Inc—*Timothy Hamby*	13901 Sutton Park Dr S, Jacksonville FL 32224	904-332-6536	R	3*	<.1
946	Raindrop Advertising and Specialties Inc—*Jim Lyons*	PO Box 89, Loudonville OH 44842	419-994-4313	R	3*	<.1
947	AMCWE Advertising Sales—*Kim Woods*	2425 Olympic Blvd, Santa Monica CA 90404	310-998-9350	R	3*	<.1
948	R and A Associates—*Gabriella Keith*	17401 Irvine Blvd Ste, Tustin CA 92780	714-838-1230	R	3*	<.1
949	Ron Thomas Advertising Inc—*Ronald Thomas*	2837 N Creek Rd, Hamburg NY 14075	716-648-0874	R	3*	<.1
950	American Printing and Advertising Inc—*Carla Yerga*	5324 Hohman Ave, Hammond IN 46320	219-937-1844	R	3*	<.1
951	Affiliated Business Consultants Inc—*Harold Anderson*	2864 S Cir Dr Ste 540, Colorado Springs CO 80906	719-540-2200	R	3*	<.1
952	Rhina International Direct Inc—*Jan Stumacher*	777 Sunrise Hwy Ste 30, Lynbrook NY 11563	516-593-8787	R	3*	<.1
953	Reid-O'donahue and Associates—*Bruce Reid*	PO Box 1269, Montgomery AL 36102	334-263-7812	R	3*	<.1
954	Bobo's Marketing Services LLC	504 Treehouse Ct, Fort Washington MD 20744	240-291-0500	R	2*	.3
955	WW Promotions Inc—*J Field*	4910 Firth Ln, Atlanta GA 30360	404-256-2247	R	2*	<.1
956	R West—*Sean Blixseth*	1430 Se 3rd Ave Fl 3, Portland OR 97214	503-223-5443	R	2*	<.1
957	Vpp Technologies Inc—*Michael Lyons*	55 Shuman Blvd Ste 250, Naperville IL 60563	630-904-7150	R	2*	<.1
958	Doolim Corp—*Jason Chi*	676 S La Fayette Park, Los Angeles CA 90057	213-381-1212	R	2*	<.1
959	Surabian Advertising—*Arthur Surabian*	42 Lake Ave, Worcester MA 01604	508-792-0650	R	2*	<.1
960	WLTZ NBC 38—*Holly Sutherland*	6140 Buena Vista Rd, Columbus GA 31907	706-563-1569	R	2*	<.1
961	Anderson Advertising—*Sita Anderson*	4716 Bloomingdale Ave, Valrico FL 33596	813-685-9514	R	2*	<.1
962	McLaughlin Delvecchio and Casey Inc—*Pascual Delvecchio*	1 Church St Fl 3, New Haven CT 06510	203-624-4151	R	2*	<.1
963	Advertising Pam Jacobs—*Pam Jacobs*	2810 Cheswick Rd, Quincy IL 62301	217-223-7687	R	2*	<.1
964	Equity Marketing Services Inc—*Herbert Emmerman*	303 W Madison St Ste 1, Chicago IL 60606	312-252-4300	R	2*	<.1
965	Clickfuel Inc—*Steve Pogorzelski*	580 Harrison Ave, Boston MA 02118		R	2*	<.1
966	I Trust Motors—*Damon Williams*	1700 E Desert Inn Rd, Las Vegas NV 89169	702-369-3673	R	2*	<.1
967	Addventures Inc—*Stephen Rosa*	117 Chapman St, Providence RI 02905	401-453-4748	R	2*	<.1
968	Remer Inc—*Dave Remer*	205 Marion St, Seattle WA 98104	206-624-1010	R	2*	<.1
969	World Wide Wadio Inc—*Paul Fey*	6464 Sunset Blvd Ste 1, Hollywood CA 90028	323-957-3399	R	2*	<.1
970	Harold Warner Advertising Inc—*Paul V Offermann*	232 Delaware Ave, Buffalo NY 14202	716-852-4410	R	2*	<.1
971	Michael Bolchalk Marketing Inc—*Michael Bolchalk*	326 S Wilmot Rd Ste C2, Tucson AZ 85711	520-745-8221	R	2*	<.1
972	Spiker Communications Inc—*Wes Spiker*	PO Box 8567, Missoula MT 59807	406-721-0785	R	2*	<.1
973	Idex Inc—*Larry Pardue*	1655 Wynne Rd Ste 101, Cordova TN 38016	901-373-7500	R	2*	<.1
974	Creative Marketing Resource Inc—*Jacqueline Wagner*	325 W Huron St, Chicago IL 60610	312-943-6266	R	2*	<.1
975	HMC Advertising LLC—*Veronica Williams*	65 Millet St Ste 301, Richmond VT 05477	802-253-7141	R	2*	<.1
976	Lubicom Marketing Consulting—*Menachem Lubinsky*	1428 36th St Ste 219, Brooklyn NY 11218	718-854-4450	R	2*	<.1
977	Smith/Junger/Wellman Inc—*Andrew R Wellman*	920 Abbot Kinney Blvd, Venice CA 90291	310-392-8625	R	2*	<.1
978	Badertscher Communications Inc—*Steve Badertscher*	137 S Prospect St, Marion OH 43302	740-383-2633	R	2*	<.1
979	Willis Case Harwood Inc—*Debby Sibert*	4090 Marshall Rd Ste 2, Dayton OH 45429	937-299-7394	R	2*	<.1
980	Mallen and Friends Advertising Arts—*Gary P Mallen*	8522 Cherokee Ln, Leawood KS 66206	913-341-7300	R	2*	<.1
981	Ballard Bratsberg Inc—*Barbara Bratsberg*	506 2nd Ave W, Seattle WA 98119	206-284-8800	R	2*	<.1
982	Energy Energy Design—*Leslie Guidice*	303 Potrero St, Santa Cruz CA 95060	408-395-5911	R	2*	<.1

Note: An asterisk (*) indicates an estimated financial figure. The company type code used is as follows: R = Private, P = Public, S = Private Subsidiary, B = Public Subsidiary, D = Division, J = Joint Venture, I = Investment Fund.

COMPANY RANKINGS BY SALES WITHIN 4-DIGIT SIC

Rank	Company Name—Executive Officer	Address, City, State, Zip	Phone	Type	Fin	Empls
983	Regberg and Associates Inc—Scott L Regberg	10877 Wilshire Blvd, Los Angeles CA 90024	310-475-5735	R	2	<.1
984	Dark Hollow Farm—David Hayden	PO Box 68, Upperco MD 21155	410-239-7075	R	2*	<.1
985	Deady Advertising—James E Deady	7301 Boulder View Ln, Richmond VA 23225		R	2*	<.1
986	Elliott Curson Advertising—Elliot Curson	1900 Rittenhouse Sq, Philadelphia PA 19103	215-732-7111	R	2*	<.1
987	Hank Brandt Associates Inc—Regina M Brandt	6675 E 22nd St, Tucson AZ 85710	520-745-9905	R	2*	<.1
988	Kell Communications—Richard Kell	535 Main St, Laurel MD 20707	301-953-8700	R	2*	<.1
989	MgM Gold Communications Ltd—Mario G Messina	79 5th Ave 16th Fl, New York NY 10003	212-869-7323	R	2*	<.1
990	Montzingo and Associates—John Montzingo	5122 Sunrise Ridge Tr, Middleton WI 53562	608-798-5099	R	2*	<.1
991	Redman Communications Inc—Brian Redman	6110 Executive Blvd, Rockville MD 20852	301-468-6701	R	2*	<.1
992	Tiger Communications—Ty Gurler	PO Box 2939, Southampton NY 11969		R	2*	<.1
993	Waverly Group—Kim Cerny	2301 Hickory St, Saint Louis MO 63104	314-773-8300	R	2*	<.1
994	Working Class Inc—David Metcalf	168 Duane St, New York NY 10013	212-941-1199	R	2*	<.1
995	Augustus Barnett Advertising/Design—Augustus C Barnett IV	PO Box 197, Fox Island WA 98333	253-549-2396	R	2*	<.1
996	Biz-comm Inc—Stephen Wilson	1483 Old Fort Rd, Fairview NC 28730	828-628-0500	R	2*	<.1
997	Corecare Associates—Ian L Cordes	200 Butler St Ste 305, West Palm Beach FL 33407	561-659-5581	R	2*	<.1
998	Frankel and Anderson Inc—Robert Frankel	17645 Royce Dr, Encino CA 91316	818-990-8623	R	2*	<.1
999	Gaffney and Associates Inc—Tom Gaffney	2410 SE 121st Ste 106, Portland OR 97216	503-760-0791	R	2*	<.1
1000	GVA Productions—George Van Allen	827 East Blvd, Charlotte NC 28203	704-375-3775	R	2*	<.1
1001	Hayes Marketing Communication Inc—Allen Hayes	33 Spencer Ave, Sausalito CA 94965	415-332-2599	R	2*	<.1
1002	Heeley Creative Inc—Shelley Heeley	567 North and South Rd, Saint Louis MO 63130	314-727-6737	R	2*	<.1
1003	Intermedia Print Communications—Elizabeth Adams	PO Box 247, Hartford VT 05047	802-295-5327	R	2*	<.1
1004	James Group—James Steidl	710 13th St, San Diego CA 92101	619-393-1930	R	2*	<.1
1005	Main Station Advertising Inc—Robert Walter	901 S Main St, Ft Worth TX 76104	817-332-1040	R	2*	<.1
1006	Pure Advertising LLC—Sidney Shelton	5901 Montrose Rd Ste 1, North Bethesda MD 20852	301-646-4392	R	2*	<.1
1007	Results Marketing Communications LLC—Kristen Gehlbach	PO Box 770, Norwich VT 05055	802-649-8844	R	2*	<.1
1008	Stansfeld and Fairbrother Inc—Elizabeth F Stansfeld	6913 Poncha Pass, Austin TX 78749	512-301-2744	R	2*	<.1
1009	Wise Incentives	2828 4th Ave, San Diego CA 92103	619-291-8585	R	2*	<.1
1010	Worldwide Partners Inc—Al Moffatt	100 Spruce st Sut 203, Denver CO 80230	303-577-9760	R	2*	<.1
1011	Redpepper LLC—Mary Coskery	113 S Perry St, Lawrenceville GA 30046	678-749-7483	R	2*	<.1
1012	Elahi Enterprises Inc—Claudia Mirza	4100 Spring Valley Ste, Dallas TX 75244	214-256-9222	R	1*	<.1
1013	Graham Advertising Of Colorado Inc—Grace Ohl	525 Communication Cir, Colorado Springs CO 80905	719-635-7335	R	1*	<.1
1014	Heckler Associates—Terry Heckler	2701 First Ave Ste 400, Seattle WA 98121	206-352-1010	R	1*	<.1
1015	Hadfield Communications Inc—Linda Hadfield	12715 Telge Rd, Cypress TX 77429	281-304-6464	R	1*	<.1
1016	Vault Communications Inc—Maribeth Roman Schmidt	610 W Germantown Pke S, Plymouth Meeting PA 19462	610-455-2755	R	1*	<.1
1017	Artime Group—Henry Artime	65 N Raymond Ave Ste 2, Pasadena CA 91103	626-583-1855	R	1*	<.1
1018	Cosec International Inc—Scott Hood	3803 S 79th East Ave, Tulsa OK 74145	918-622-3903	R	1*	<.1
1019	Otey White and Associates—Otey L White III	PO Box 3397, Baton Rouge LA 70821	225-201-0032	R	1*	<.1
1020	Diversity Corp—Gary Holstrom	28450 SW Herd Ln, Hillsboro OR 97123	503-628-6358	R	1*	<.1
1021	Epiphany Media LLC—Ashley Mitchell	75 Varick St Fl 6, New York NY 10013	212-601-8370	R	1*	<.1
1022	Hill and Co (Bedford Texas)—Robert Hill	4113 Gateway Dr Ste 10, Colleyville TX 76034	817-571-9665	R	1*	<.1
1023	Advantage Marketing Group Inc—Werner Scott	PO Box 167904, Irving TX 75016	214-929-0639	R	1*	<.1
1024	RadioFilms Inc—Paul Kinney	632 Brickyard Dr, Sacramento CA 95831	916-391-6364	R	1*	<.1
1025	Swearingen Advertising Agency Inc—Tom Swearingen	20917 SW Martinazzi Av, Tualatin OR 97062	503-885-1415	R	1*	<.1
1026	DMMI World Communications—David Milliner	17119 South Bennett Av, South Holland IL 60473	708-339-6312	R	1*	<.1
1027	King and Associates—Timothy G King	8465 Holcomb Bridge Rd, Alpharetta GA 30022	770-992-8969	R	1*	<.1
1028	IdeaWorks—Claudia Ponder	2201 Dupont Dr Ste 150, Irvine CA 92612	949-955-9200	R	1	<.1
1029	Inlandesign Group Inc—John Celuch	222-A N Main St, Edwardsville IL 62025	618-656-8836	R	1*	<.1
1030	LW Ramsey Advertising Agency—David A Pautsch	111 E 3rd St, Davenport IA 52801	563-326-3333	R	1*	<.1
1031	Technell Inc—Marvin Gold	81 Nutmeg Ln, Stamford CT 06905	203-609-9065	R	1*	<.1
1032	Thompson Agency—Joseph F Thompson	115 E Park Ave Ste 114, Charlotte NC 28203	704-333-8821	R	1*	<.1
1033	World's Smallest Ad Agency Inc—Renee Mandis	49 Richmondville Ave S, Westport CT 06880	203-222-9224	R	1*	<.1
1034	Zimmerman and Markman Inc—Bill Zimmerman	212 26th St Rm 145, Santa Monica CA 90402	310-451-2522	R	1*	<.1
1035	Innovative Direct Response LLC—Kelly Burke	2102 Business Ctr Dr S, Irvine CA 92612	949-253-4190	R	1*	<.1
1036	Logan Marketing and Communications Inc—G King Logan II	170 Broadway St, New Orleans LA 70118	504-522-3911	R	1*	<.1
1037	Safian Communications Services Inc—Shelley C Safian	PO Box 1016, Winter Park FL 32790	407-644-6996	R	1	<.1
1038	Vogel Group—Kay Vogel	5228 Blossom, Houston TX 77007	281-960-0235	R	1	<.1
1039	BP Design—Brad Pettengill	One Main St Ste 203, Burlington VT 05401	802-865-3343	R	1*	N/A
1040	Varieties Inc—Lorena Serna	8630 Guilford Rd Ste M, Columbia MD 21046	410-884-1922	R	<1*	<.1
1041	Stauch Vetromile and Mitchell Advertising Inc—Robert Betromile	2 Charles St Unit 3, Providence RI 02904	401-438-0614	R	<1*	<.1
1042	US Media Inc—Theresa Petruzzelli	1 S Ocean Blvd Ste 210, Boca Raton FL 33432	561-393-6005	R	<1*	<.1
1043	Zapcom Corp—Philip Falcone	450 Park Ave 27th Fl, New York NY 10022	212-906-8555	B	<1	<.1
1044	Midwest Energy Emissions Corp—John F Norris Jr	500 W Wilson Bridge Rd, Worthington OH 43085	614-505-6115	P	<1	<.1
1045	Mediacom USA—Stephen Allan MediaCom Worldwide	498 7th Ave, New York NY 10018	212-912-4200	S	N/A	.4
1046	HY Connect—Troy Peterson	1000 N Water St Ste 16, Milwaukee WI 53202	414-289-9700	R	N/A	<.1
1047	Marketing Developments Inc—Stanley Eichelbaum	411 N New River Dr E S, Fort Lauderdale FL 33301	954-467-1780	R	N/A	<.1

TOTALS: SIC 7311 Advertising Agencies

Companies: 1,047					193,462	332.6

7312 Outdoor Advertising Services

Rank	Company Name—Executive Officer	Address, City, State, Zip	Phone	Type	Fin	Empls
1	Clear Channel Outdoor Holdings Inc—William Eccleshare	2201 E Camelback Rd St, Phoenix AZ 85016	602-381-5700	B	3,004	7.8
2	Adams Outdoor Advertising Inc—J Gleason	2802 Paces Ferry Rd SE, Atlanta GA 30339	770-333-0399	R	874*	.4
3	Lamar Texas LP—Bob Buick	PO Box 66336, Baton Rouge LA 70896	804-794-7000	R	145*	3.0
4	Lamar Advertising of Colorado Springs Inc—Kevin Reilly	PO Box 6010, Colorado Springs CO 80904	719-473-4747	S	122*	.2
5	Zoom Media—Dennis Roche	112 Madison Ave, New York NY 10016	212-685-7981	R	102*	.2
6	Cbs Outdoor Inc—Wally Kelly	185 Hwy 46, Fairfield NJ 07004	212-297-6400	R	102*	2.1
7	Brand Connections LLC—Sherry Orel	1540 Broadway Ste 1630, New York NY 10036	212-302-4141	R	68*	.1
8	Coast United Bench Ad Co—Arlan Renfro	8116 Dering Ave, Canoga Park CA 91304	818-313-8644	R	67*	<.1
9	Obie Media Corp—Brian B Obie	4211 W 11th Ave, Eugene OR 97402	541-686-8400	R	43	.2
10	SwarmBuilder Inc—Tom Stockham	224 S 200W Ste 230, Salt Lake City UT 84101		R	37*	.1
11	Transit America Las Vegas LLC—Everett Stewart	1863 Helm Dr, Las Vegas NV 89119	702-873-4600	S	33*	.1
12	Lamar Advertising of Oklahoma Inc—Bill Condon Lamar Oklahoma Holding Company Inc	5205 N Sante Fe, Oklahoma City OK 73118	405-528-2683	S	23*	<.1
13	Lamar Oklahoma Holding Company Inc—Bill Condon	5205 N Sante Fe, Oklahoma City OK 73118	405-528-2683	S	23*	<.1
14	C2C Outdoor—Michael Palatnek	353 Lexington Ave Ste, New York NY 10016	212-209-1519	R	21	<.1
15	Lamar of Birmingham	920 6th St S, Birmingham AL 35205	205-599-2700	D	17*	.1
16	Lamar Advertising of Youngstown Inc—Kevin Reilly	PO Box 468, Girard OH 44420	330-759-8200	S	16*	<.1
17	Trioumph Outdoor Rhode Island LLC—Everett Stewart	PO Box 14069, East Providence RI 02914	401-421-4504	S	16*	<.1
18	Lamar Advertising of Michigan Inc	6405 N Hix Rd, Westland MI 48185	734-729-6430	S	10*	<.1

Rank	Company Name—*Executive Officer*	Address, City, State, Zip	Phone	Type	Fin	Empls
19	Brimad Enterprises Inc—*Eric Glaub*	2900 Adams St Ste B16, Riverside CA 92504	951-354-8187	R	10*	.1
20	Metropolitan Transit Authority—*Paul Ballard*	130 Nestor St, Nashville TN 37210	615-862-5969	R	9*	.2
21	Business Broadcast Systems—*Andrew Milder*	10544 W Pico Blvd, Los Angeles CA 90064		R	8*	<.1
22	National Out Of Home Message Inc—*Terry Steen*	3201 S 26th St, Philadelphia PA 19145	215-551-4883	R	8*	.1
23	Heard Communications Inc—*Craig P Heard*	433 Sand Shore Rd, Hackettstown NJ 07840	908-684-8122	R	6*	<.1
24	Newman Signs Inc—*Harold Newman*	PO Box 1728, Jamestown ND 58402	701-252-1970	R	6*	.1
25	Decaux J L USA—*Jean-Luc Deaux*	200 Crprate Pinte Ste, Culver City CA 90230	310-242-2032	R	5*	.1
26	Trinity Outdoor LLC	420 S Hill St, Buford GA 30518	770-831-5945	R	5*	.1
27	Metropolitan Advertising Company Inc—*Charles Rocker*	3014 W Horatio St, Tampa FL 33609	813-872-8502	R	4*	<.1
28	Billboard Live—*Patrick Lowrdy*	1500 Ocean Dr, Miami Beach FL 33139	305-538-2251	R	4*	<.1
29	HA Steen Industries Inc—*Terry Steen*	3201 S 26th St, Philadelphia PA 19145	215-334-1700	R	3*	<.1
30	Adams Outdoor Advertising Of Kalamazoo LP—*Kathy Wharton*	407 E Ransom St, Kalamazoo MI 49007	269-342-9831	R	3*	<.1
31	Jcdecaux San Francisco LLC—*Bernard Parisot*	1000 Quesada Ave, San Francisco CA 94124	415-487-2300	R	2*	<.1
32	Blue Light Images Company Inc—*Danny Hoots*	PO Box 2409, King NC 27021	336-983-4986	R	2*	<.1
33	Creative Sign Services Inc—*Max Butler*	PO Box 248, Shelby NC 28151	704-487-5971	R	2*	<.1
34	Automotive Services Inc—*Kent Stevinson*	1546 Cole Blvd Ste 100, Lakewood CO 80401	303-232-2006	R	2*	<.1
35	Delta Media Inc—*Jeff Brown*	1317 S Joshua Ave Ste, Parker AZ 85344	928-669-1020	R	2*	<.1
36	Sweetspot Media Group Inc—*Greg Cook*	254 Essex St Ste 208, Salem MA 01970	978-741-4390	R	2*	<.1
37	VJ Smith—*Christina Remirez*	2305 Sparkman St, El Paso TX 79903	915-566-9380	R	1*	<.1
38	Carlson Sign Co—*Peter Carlson*	1605 Ne Forbes Rd, Bend OR 97701	541-382-2182	R	1*	<.1
39	Lamar Advertising of Kentucky Inc—*Brain Ridgway*	PO Box 54786, Lexington KY 40555	859-255-5592	S	1*	<.1

TOTALS: SIC 7312 Outdoor Advertising Services
Companies: 39   **4,807   15.3**

7313 Radio, T.V. & Publisher Representatives

Rank	Company Name—*Executive Officer*	Address, City, State, Zip	Phone	Type	Fin	Empls
1	HAM Media Group—*John T Healy*	305 Madison Ave Ste 30, New York NY 10165	212-297-2575	R	2,782*	3.9
2	Daniel J Edelman Inc—*Richard Edelman*	200 E Randolph St Fl 6, Chicago IL 60601	312-240-3000	R	168*	3.2
3	Hydra LLC—*Selena Treister*	10940 Wilshire Blvd St, Los Angeles CA 90024	310-659-5755	R	69*	.1
4	Charter Advertising Saint Louis LLC—*Mike Szczechura*	1650 Des Peres Road, Saint Louis MO 63131	314-394-2500	S	50*	.1
5	Regent Broadcasting of El Paso Inc—*Brad Dubow*	4180 N Mesa St, El Paso TX 79902	915-544-8864	S	40*	.1
6	Regent Broadcasting of Evansville/Owensboro Inc—*William Stakelin*	117 SE 5th St, Evansville IN 47705	812-425-4226	S	36*	.1
7	Regent Broadcasting of Flint Inc—*William Stakelin*	G-338 E BriStol Rd, Burton MI 48529	810-743-1080	S	36*	.1
8	Times Of Trenton Publishing Corp—*Richard Bilotti*	PO Box 847, Trenton NJ 08605	609-989-5454	R	35*	.7
9	Regent Broadcasting of Ft Collins Inc—*Steven Price*	600 Main St, Windsor CO 80550	970-674-2700	S	32*	<.1
10	Metro Newspaper Advertising Services Inc—*Phyllis Cavaliere*	8 W 38th St 4th Fl, New York NY 10018	212-576-9504	R	27*	<.1
11	Starcom Mediavest Group Inc—*Dennis Donlin*	150 W Jefferson Ave St, Detroit MI 48226	313-237-8100	R	22*	.5
12	Regent Broadcasting of Lexington Inc—*William Stakelin*	100 E RiverCenter Blvd, Covington KY 41011	859-292-0030	S	16*	<.1
13	Oregon Newspaper Publishers Association Inc—*V Gary Husman*	7150 SW Hampton St Ste, Portland OR 97223	503-624-6397	R	11*	<.1
14	Hydra Group LLC—*Zack Brandenberg*	8800 Wilshire Blvd Fl, Beverly Hills CA 90211	310-659-5755	S	10*	.1
15	Village ProfileCom Inc—*Daniel Nugara*	33 N Geneva St, Elgin IL 60120	847-468-6800	R	8*	.1
16	Viamedia LLC—*Annmarie Barndt*	3910 Adler Pl Ste 100, Bethlehem PA 18017	610-398-3800	R	7*	.1
17	Burst Media Corp—*Suranga Chandratillake*	8 New England Exec Par, Burlington MA 01803	781-272-5544	R	7*	.1
18	Horne Tipps Holding Company Inc—*James Tipps*	8198 Woodland Ctr Blvd, Tampa FL 33614	813-635-9100	R	7*	.1
19	Panasonic Avc American Laboratories Inc—*Sai Nalmpally*	5000 Doarborn Cir Ste, Mount Laurel NJ 08054	856-222-2290	R	6*	.1
20	Hydramedia LLC—*Zac Brandenberg*	8800 Wilshire Blvd Fl, Beverly Hills CA 90211	310-659-5755	S	5*	<.1
21	Webworx International Inc—*Ronald Howell*	12400 Ventura Blvd, Studio City CA 91604	818-731-4567	R	4*	<.1
22	Daily Union Inc—*John Montgomery*	PO Box 129, Junction City KS 66441	785-537-9515	R	4*	.1
23	Rivendell Media Inc—*Todd Evans*	1248 Rte 22 West, Mountainside NJ 07092	908-232-2021	R	4*	<.1
24	Jobdango Inc—*Susan King*	PO Box 33710, Portland OR 97292	503-258-1198	R	4*	<.1
25	Silvercarrot Inc—*Philip Schechter*	132 W 36th St Ste 9, New York NY 10018	212-630-0234	R	4*	<.1
26	Fata Inc—*Philip Maher*	3701 Malden Ave Ste A, Baltimore MD 21211	410-578-3600	R	3*	<.1
27	Twentieth Century Fox Licensing and Merchandising Corp—*Peter Byrne*	PO Box 900, Beverly Hills CA 90209	310-369-1000	D	3*	<.1
28	Russell Johns Associates LLC	1001 S Myrtle Ave Ste, Clearwater FL 33756	727-443-7667	R	3*	<.1
29	Comstock Records Ltd—*Frank Fara*	PO Box 19720, Fountain Hills AZ 85269	480-951-3115	R	3*	<.1
30	Network Media Partners Inc—*Charles Boyce*	11350 Mccormick Rd Ste, Hunt Valley MD 21031	410-584-1900	R	3*	<.1
31	Intermdia Cable Advertising Dept—*Terry Kelly*	1102 Thompsn Brg Rd, Gainesville GA 30501	770-536-0803	R	3*	.1
32	My 1063 Fm Klmy—*Julie Gade*	4630 Antelope Creek Rd, Lincoln NE 68506	402-486-1063	R	2*	<.1
33	Senior Life—*Ron Baumgartner*	166 Mallard Pointe Dr, Valparaiso IN 46385	219-476-7020	R	2*	<.1
34	Axcess Broadcast Services Inc—*Otis Conner*	4801 Spring Valley Rd, Dallas TX 75244	972-386-6847	R	2*	<.1
35	KBJX Hot 106—*Bill Fuerst*	1327 E 17th St, Idaho Falls ID 83404	208-528-6813	R	2*	<.1
36	Space Sales Inc—*Bob Probst*	PO Box 209, Mendham NJ 07945	973-543-4994	R	2*	<.1
37	Crystal Media Networks—*Ryan Beck*	7201 Wisconsin Ave Ste, Bethesda MD 20814	240-223-0846	R	2*	<.1
38	Red Truck Films—*Tom Harring*	1610 Midtown Pl, Raleigh NC 27609	919-875-0702	R	2*	<.1
39	Malibu News Enterprises Inc—*Anne Sobel*	PO Box 903, Malibu CA 90265	310-457-6397	R	2*	<.1
40	Netscope Inc—*Michael Beresford*	1100 S Coast Hwy St 3, Laguna Beach CA 92651	949-450-1122	R	2*	<.1
41	Evolution Media Printing Inc—*Juan Gutierrez*	7349 Nw 34th St, Miami FL 33122	305-282-4455	R	2*	<.1
42	Media Spree Marketing—*John Snyder*	636 Montgomery Ln, Port Ludlow WA 98365	360-643-0506	R	<1	<.1

TOTALS: SIC 7313 Radio, T.V. & Publisher Representatives
Companies: 42   **3,432   9.9**

7319 Advertising Nec

Rank	Company Name—*Executive Officer*	Address, City, State, Zip	Phone	Type	Fin	Empls
1	Clear Channel Communications Inc—*Robert Pittman*	200 E Basse Rd, San Antonio TX 78209	210-822-2828	S	4,147*	15.4
2	Media Planning Group—*Charlie Rutman*	195 Broadway, New York NY 10007	646-587-5000	S	4,013*	4.0
3	Initiative Media North America—*Richard Beaven*	885 2nd Ave, New York NY 10017	212-605-7000	S	2,600*	2.5
4	News America Marketing Interactive Inc—*Chris Mixson*	1211 6th Ave, New York NY 10036	212-782-8000	S	1,914*	1.2
5	Novus Print Media Inc—*David Murphy*	2 Carlson Pkwy Ste 410, Plymouth MN 55447		R	1,511*	1.4
6	Katz Media Corp—*Stu O Olds* Clear Channel Communications Inc	125 W 55th St, New York NY 10019	212-424-6000	S	1,439*	1.4
7	Experian Marketing Services—*Rick Erwin*	475 Anton Blvd, Costa Mesa CA 92626	714-830-7000	R	1,355*	1.4
8	Berry Co—*Greg Meineke*	188 Inverness Dr West, Englewood CO 80112	937-296-2121	S	1,023*	2.3
9	Berry Network Inc—*Steve Dimmitt* Berry Co	3100 Kettering Blvd, Dayton OH 45439		S	549*	.3
10	Campaigners Inc—*Melissa Orr*	909 N Sepulveda Blvd S, El Segundo CA 90245	310-643-7500	R	469*	3.0
11	National CineMedia Inc—*Kurt C Hall*	9110 E Nichols Ave Ste, Centennial CO 80112	303-792-3600	P	435	.6
12	QuinStreet Inc—*Douglas Valenti*	950 Tower Ln 6th Fl, Foster City CA 94404	650-578-7700	P	403	.7
13	Welcome Wagon International Inc—*Craig Swill*	5830 Coral Ridge Dr St, Coral Springs FL 33076		R	390*	2.5

Note: An asterisk (*) indicates an estimated financial figure. The company type code used is as follows: R = Private, P = Public, S = Private Subsidiary, B = Public Subsidiary, D = Division, J = Joint Venture, I = Investment Fund.

COMPANY RANKINGS BY SALES WITHIN 4-DIGIT SIC

Rank	Company Name—Executive Officer	Address, City, State, Zip	Phone	Type	Fin	Empls
14	George P Johnson Co—Robert G Vallee Jr	3600 Giddings Rd, Auburn Hills MI 48326	248-475-2500	R	300*	1.0
15	Encore Marketing International Inc—Stanley D Plotnick	4501 Forbes Blvd, Lanham MD 20706	301-459-8020	R	215*	.2
16	MRM Worldwide—Marc Landsberg	622 3rd Ave, New York NY 10017	646-865-6230	R	202*	.2
17	Cable Advertising of Metro Atlanta—Jeff Stone	2975 Courtyards Dr, Norcross GA 30071	770-559-2282	R	197*	.1
18	Independent Television Network Inc—Mike Kammerer	747 3rd Ave 5th Fl, New York NY 10017	212-572-9200	R	188*	.1
19	Horizon Media Inc—William A Koenigsberg	75 Varick St, New York NY 10013	212-220-5000	R	175*	.5
20	ALJ Regional Holdings Inc—John Scheel	244 Madison Ave PMB 35, New York NY 10016	212-883-0083	P	162	<.1
21	Marketing Drive Worldwide Inc—Michael Harris	800 Connecticut Ave 3r, Norwalk CT 06854	203-857-6100	S	159*	.1
22	Success Communications Group—Kurt Schwartz	26 Eastmens Rd, Parsippany NJ 07054	973-992-7800	R	158*	.2
23	Cbs Interactive Inc—Neil Ashe	235 2nd St, San Francisco CA 94105	415-344-2000	S	158*	2.7
24	Stratapult Studios—L David Mounts	2650 Pilgrim Ct, Winston-Salem NC 27106		S	146*	.1
25	e-Dialog—John Rizzi	65 Network Dr Ste 400, Burlington MA 01803	781-863-8117	R	142*	.1
26	Advertisingcom Inc—Lynda Clarizio	1020 Hull Ste Ivory Bl, Baltimore MD 21230	410-244-1370	S	137*	.3
27	MKTG Inc—Charles W Horsey	75 9th Ave 3rd Fl, New York NY 10011	212-660-3800	P	118	6.3
28	Ketchum Directory Advertising Inc—John D Wren	7015 College Blvd Ste, Overland Park KS 66211	913-344-1900	S	115*	.1
29	iMC2—Doug Levy	12404 Park Central Ste, Dallas TX 75251	214-224-1000	R	105*	.1
30	Toyota Motor North America Inc—Yoshimi Inaba	9 W 57th St Ste 4900, New York NY 10019	212-223-0303	S	103*	.1
31	Smiley Media Inc—Stephen Oskoui	701 Brazos St Ste 1600, Austin TX 78701	512-480-9990	R	98*	.1
32	EWI Worldwide—Dominic Silvio	13211 Merriman Rd, Livonia MI 48150		R	97*	.1
33	Biggs and Gilmore Communications—Jane Tamraz	261 E Kalamazoo Ave St, Kalamazoo MI 49007	269-349-7711	R	87*	.1
34	Camelot Communications Inc—Tom Kalahar	8140 Walnut Hill Ste 7, Dallas TX 75231	214-373-6999	R	83*	.1
35	hawthorne direct Inc—Thomas Kelly	300 N 16th St, Fairfield IA 52556	641-472-3800	R	79*	.1
36	Slack and Co—Gary Slack	233 N Michigan Ave Ste, Chicago IL 60601	312-970-5800	R	79*	.1
37	MyPointscom Inc—Mark R Goldston	50 California St 3rd F, San Francisco CA 94111	415-615-1100	S	64*	.3
38	Shumsky Enterprises Inc—Michael Emoff	811 E 4th St, Dayton OH 45402		R	60*	.1
39	Inuvo Inc—Richard K Howe	15550 Lightwave Dr Ste, Clearwater FL 33760	727-324-0211	P	49	<.1
40	SellPoint Inc—Rick Martin	3000 Executive Pky Ste, San Ramon CA 94583		R	48*	.1
41	CTM Media Holdings Inc—Marc E Knoller	11 Largo Dr S, Stamford CT 06907	203-323-5161	R	45*	<.1
42	Ernst Van Praag Inc—Matthew Van Praag	4800 N Federal Hwy Ste, Boca Raton FL 33431	561-447-0557	R	42*	<.1
43	LifeStreet Corp—Mitchell Weisman	981 Industrial Rd Ste, San Carlos CA 94070		R	41	.1
44	Directory Distributing Associates Inc—Judith A Runk	1602 Park 370 Ct, Hazelwood MO 63042	314-592-8600	R	35*	<.1
45	Omnibus Advertising and Marketing—Robert Brumbaugh	546 W Campus Dr, Arlington Heights IL 60004	847-255-6000	R	31*	<.1
46	Advanced Computer Graphics Inc—Tony Butrum	10895 Indeco Dr, Cincinnati OH 45241	513-936-5060	R	30*	<.1
47	Creative Entertainment Services Inc—Richard P Storrs	7009 Valjean Ave, Van Nuys CA 91406	818-748-4800	R	30*	<.1
48	Aviad Corp—Wayne Mansfield	PO Box 192, West Boxford MA 01885	310-617-3257	R	29*	<.1
49	Robinson and Maites Inc—Alan Maites	35 E Wacker Dr Ste 200, Chicago IL 60601	312-372-9333	R	29*	<.1
50	Knight Images—Michael Hinn	130 S Orange Ave Ste 1, Orlando FL 32801	407-206-1011	R	28*	<.1
51	Epicenter Network Inc—Smokey Burns	3500 188th St SW Ste 4, Lynnwood WA 98037	425-744-1474	R	26	<.1
52	Marketing Technology Concepts Inc—George Kriza	1827 Walden Office Sq, Schaumburg IL 60173	847-303-0022	R	26*	<.1
53	Business to Business Marketing Communications—Chris Burke	900 Ridgefield Dr Ste, Raleigh NC 27609	919-872-8172	R	25*	<.1
54	Trilix Marketing Group—Ron Maahs	9105 Northpark Dr, Johnston IA 50131	515-221-4900	R	23*	<.1
55	MMA Creative—Mike McCloud	705 N Dixie Ave, Cookeville TN 38501	931-528-8852	R	22*	<.1
56	Dennis Garberg And Associates Inc—Dennis Garberg	14001 Marshall Dr, Lenexa KS 66215	913-890-0900	R	20*	.5
57	Gage Marketing Group—Edwin C Gage III	10000 Hwy 55, Minneapolis MN 55441	763-595-3800	R	20*	.1
58	Alternate Marketing Networks Inc—Philip Miller	4675 32nd Ave, Hudsonville MI 49426	616-662-6420	P	20	.1
59	Crushing Enterprises Inc—Joey Levine	19 Union Sq W 8th Fl, New York NY 10003	212-352-8833	R	20*	<.1
60	M/C/C Inc—Mike Crawford	8131 LBJ Fwy Ste 275, Dallas TX 75251	972-980-8383	R	20*	<.1
61	Pennyweb Inc—Benoit Pecqueur	1201 W 5th St Ste T300, Los Angeles CA 90017	213-481-8444	R	20*	<.1
62	Public Communications Worldwide—John van Barneveld	11602 Knott Street Sui, Garden Grove CA 92841	714-891-3660	R	20*	<.1
63	SavingsCom Inc—Loren Bendele	2225 S Carmelina Ave, Los Angeles CA 90064	310-442-9802	R	20*	.1
64	Gotham Direct—Greg Messerle	353 Lexington Ave Fl 1, New York NY 10016	212-279-1474	R	19*	<.1
65	WebloyaltyCom Inc—Rick Fernandes	101 Merritt 7 Ste 37, Norwalk CT 06851	203-846-3300	R	18*	.2
66	WDFA Marketing Inc—Raj Prasad	535 Pacific Ave 4th Fl, San Francisco CA 94133	415-391-6600	R	18*	<.1
67	Roosevelt Capital LLC—Loraine Greenburg	PO Box 087601, Racine WI 53408	262-681-7000	R	17*	.2
68	Quantum Loyalty Systems—Ron Randolph-Wall	926 Incline Way Ste 20, Incline Village NV 89451	775-833-0303	R	17*	<.1
69	KDG InterActive—Pat Kirkwood	PO Box 23, Rosemount MN 55068	651-748-8480	R	17*	<.1
70	BravoSolution US	400 Chester Field Pkwy, Malvern PA 19355	610-240-0600	S	16	.1
71	bigdoughcom Inc—Scott C Ganeles	4833 Rugby Ave, Bethesda MD 20814	301-760-2500	R	16*	.1
72	SproutLoud Media Networks LLC—Jared Shusterman	15431 SW 14th St, Sunrise FL 33326	954-476-6211	R	15	.1
73	America's Media Marketing Inc	13169 Jacqueline Rd, Brooksville FL 34613	352-597-6200	R	15*	.1
74	Coast to Coast Tickets LLC—Jason Randall	2002 Guadalupe St Ste, Austin TX 78705	512-419-9888	R	15*	.1
75	Adventure Web Productions—Craig Kahl	612 1/2 Frederick Rd, Baltimore MD 21228	410-788-7007	R	15*	<.1
76	Rockfish Interactive—Kenny Tomlin	3100 Market St, Rogers AR 72758	479-464-0622	R	14	.1
77	Limerick Studios-DVD—Mike Kelley	1512 Camden Rd, Charlotte NC 28203	704-371-4991	R	14*	.1
78	Empower Mediamarketing Inc—Brian Mchale	1111 Saint Gregory St, Cincinnati OH 45202	513-871-9454	R	14*	.2
79	AdMax Media Inc	345 Chapala St, Santa Barbara CA 93101	805-308-9199	S	13*	.3
80	Yesmailcom—Mike Hilts	309 SW 6th Ave Ste 700, Portland OR 97204	503-241-4185	S	13*	.1
81	Words and Images—J Lawrence	343 Soquel Ave PMB 326, Santa Cruz CA 95062	831-818-2766	R	13*	<.1
82	Alpha Scrip Inc—Richard Kennedy	4647 N 32nd St Ste 240, Phoenix AZ 85018	602-840-9506	R	12*	<.1
83	DMX Music—John D Cullen	600 Congress Ave Ste 1, Austin TX 78701	512-380-8500	R	11*	.1
84	Targetcast Tcm—Steven J Farella	909 3rd Ave Fl 31, New York NY 10022	212-500-6900	R	11*	.1
85	Trancos Inc—Brian Nelson	1450 Veterans Blvd Ste, Oakland CA 94603	650-364-3110	R	11*	<.1
86	Promotionscom Inc—Steven Krein	401 W Saint Charles Rd, Lombard IL 60148	773-444-4040	S	11*	<.1
87	RideSafelycom—Max Repik	2 Greenwood Sq Ste 151, Bensalem PA 19020	215-525-3885	R	11*	<.1
88	Bean Creative—Layla Masri	2213 Mt Vernon Ave, Alexandria VA 22301	703-684-5945	R	11*	<.1
89	Dispatch Consumer Services Inc—John Curtain	7801 N Central Dr, Lewis Center OH 43035	740-548-5555	R	10*	.2
90	Gratis Internet LLC—Robert Jewell	700 12th St NW Ste 105, Washington DC 20005	202-299-0761	R	10*	<.1
91	E Group Inc (Minneapolis Minnesota)—Paul Estenson	901 N 3rd St Ste 195, Minneapolis MN 55401		R	10*	<.1
92	HyperDisk Marketing—Nick Singer	18251 McDurmott Ste A, Irvine CA 92614	949-442-9850	R	10*	<.1
93	Pat Meier Associates PR—Pat Meier	120 Broadway St, San Francisco CA 94111	415-389-1700	R	10*	<.1
94	VIPdeskcom Inc—Mary Naylor	324 N Fairfax St, Alexandria VA 22314	703-299-4422	R	9*	.1
95	Lightship Group—Chuck Ehrler	5728 Major Blvd Ste 31, Orlando FL 32819	407-363-7777	S	9*	<.1
96	Fusionary Media—Steve Lewis	220 Grandville SW, Grand Rapids MI 49503	616-454-2357	R	9*	<.1
97	Aldea Communications Inc—Susan Estrada	7668 El Camino Real St, Carlsbad CA 92009	760-510-8407	R	9*	<.1
98	Fulfillment America Inc—John Barry	17 Progress Rd, Billerica MA 01821	978-988-7576	R	9*	<.1
99	M and M Displays Inc—Michael Fell	7700 Brewster Ave, Philadelphia PA 19153	215-365-5200	R	9*	<.1
100	Diversified Mercury Communications LLC—Eitan Cohen	520 Broadway Ste 400, Santa Monica CA 90401	310-451-2900	R	8*	.1
101	2020 Exhibits Inc—Bob Babine	10550 S Sam Huston Pkw, Houston TX 77071	713-354-0900	R	8*	.1
102	Icon Media Direct Inc—Nancy Lazkani	5910 Lemona Ave, Van Nuys CA 91411	818-995-6400	R	8*	.1
103	Twin Associates LC—Laurie Skinner	51260 Danview Tech Ct, Utica MI 48315	586-731-6101	R	8*	<.1

Rank	Company Name—*Executive Officer*	Address, City, State, Zip	Phone	Type	Fin	Empls
104	Panthera Interactive LLC—*Matthew R Sandin*	2831 St Rose Pky Ste 2, Henderson NV 89052	702-202-4740	R	8	<.1
105	MeterNet Corp—*Greg Wible*	723 S Casino Center Bl, Las Vegas NV 89101	562-989-8976	R	8*	<.1
106	Digital Advertising LLC—*Amit Raut*	402 Main St Ste 100-22, Metuchen NJ 08840	732-906-1515	R	8*	<.1
107	Wpromote Inc—*Michael Mothner*	1700 E Walnut Ave 5th, El Segundo CA 90245	310-421-4844	R	7*	.1
108	Bulldog Solutions Inc—*Rob Solomon*	5608 Parkcrest Dr Ste, Austin TX 78731	512-652-2546	R	7*	<.1
109	Karner Blue Marketing—*Rebecca Murtagh*	Box 12754, Albany NY 12203	518-935-4101	R	7*	<.1
110	NetSuccess Inc—*Lori Barber*	17000 Dallas Pky Ste 1, Dallas TX 75248	972-818-9200	R	7*	<.1
111	Richard J Wolk and Associates—*Richard J Wolk*	5830 Ellsworth Ave Ste, Pittsburgh PA 15232	412-361-6833	R	7*	<.1
112	Sea-Net Holdings Inc—*Donald Greenspan*	13200 Danielson St Ste, Poway CA 92064	858-560-2055	R	7*	.1
113	Gil's Distributing Service Inc—*Feleciano Gil*	718 E 8th St, Los Angeles CA 90021	213-627-0539	R	6*	.1
114	Barclay Communications Inc—*Ray Artigue*	2999 N 44th St Ste 300, Phoenix AZ 85018	602-277-3550	R	6*	<.1
115	Jeffrey Alec Communications—*Jeff Levine*	149 S Barrington Ave S, Los Angeles CA 90049	310-476-6700	R	6*	<.1
116	Kaplan Thaler Group Ltd—*Lindal Kaplan Thaler*	825 8th Ave 34th Fl, New York NY 10019	212-474-5000	R	6*	<.1
117	Corinthian Communications Inc—*Larry Miller*	500 8th Ave Fl 5, New York NY 10018	212-279-5700	R	6*	.1
118	Blitz Media Inc—*Chris Perkins*	254 2nd Ave, Needham MA 02494	781-247-7100	R	5*	.1
119	Want Ads Of Pensacola Inc—*Steve Root*	PO Box 16190, Pensacola FL 32507	850-469-9712	R	5*	.1
120	Rise Interactive—*Jon Morris*	325 W Huron St Ste 200, Chicago IL 60654	312-281-9933	R	5*	<.1
121	Commotion Promotions Ltd—*Karen Kravitz*	2999 N 44th St Ste 340, Phoenix AZ 85018	602-996-0006	R	5*	<.1
122	Midnet Media (Columbus Ohio)—*Darrin Caywood*	3400 N High St Ste200, Columbus OH 43202	614-836-1800	S	5*	<.1
123	ARS eCommerce LLC—*Scott Norman*	1001 Reads Lake Rd, Chattanooga TN 37415	423-875-3743	R	5*	<.1
124	Kizmet Interactive—*Lisa Sciortino*	337 East Meadow Ave, East Meadow NY 11554	516-357-2500	R	5*	<.1
125	Burgess Communications—*Donna Weidel*	1450 E Boot Rd Ste 300, West Chester PA 19380	610-647-7900	R	5*	<.1
126	Palazzo Creative—*Richard Roberts*	1525 4th Ave Ste 500, Seattle WA 98101	206-328-5555	R	5*	<.1
127	Wilson Media Group Inc—*H Thomas Wilson*	719R Windsor Ln, Key West FL 33040	305-925-3655	R	5*	<.1
128	Triangle Direct Media—*Anthony Feriozzi*	8420 Chapel Hill Rd St, Cary NC 27513	919-386-5329	R	5	<.1
129	Salon Media Group Inc—*David Talbot*	101 Spear St Ste 203, San Francisco CA 94105	415-645-9200	P	5	<.1
130	LA Prep Inc—*James Kirby*	2700 Signal Pkwy, Signal Hill CA 90755	562-595-8886	R	5*	<.1
131	Ace Designs Inc—*Joseph Hurwitz*	320 George Patterson D, Bristol PA 19007	215-945-0400	R	4*	<.1
132	Phd Michigan LLC—*Lou Bravo*	900 Tower Dr, Troy MI 48098	248-925-5000	R	4*	.1
133	Pro Media Inc—*Nancy Ryan*	31 Home Depot Dr, Plymouth MA 02360	508-651-5200	R	4*	<.1
134	Massini Group Inc—*Joe Krisky*	1323 NE Orenco Station, Hillsboro OR 97124	503-640-9800	R	4*	<.1
135	Recom Group Inc—*Robert Norden*	449 Borrego Ct, San Dimas CA 91773	909-599-1370	R	4*	<.1
136	Noble Marketing Group—*Jeff Baker*	100 E Pine St Ste 305, Orlando FL 32801	317-984-8727	R	4*	<.1
137	Harp Advertising Interactive—*Lisa Harp*	1901S Meyer Rd Ste 130, Oakbrook Terrace IL 60181	630-691-9500	R	4*	<.1
138	Hawk Media Inc—*Kenneth Slater*	PO Box 623, Diablo CA 94528	415-860-2500	R	4*	<.1
139	Artisans Public Relations—*Linda Rosner*	2242 Guthrie Cir, Los Angeles CA 90034	310-837-6008	R	4*	<.1
140	Sports Display Inc—*Terry Parkin*	30051 Comercio, Rcho Sta Marg CA 92688	949-858-5039	R	4*	<.1
141	Reach Sports Marketing Group Inc—*Darren Wercinski*	6440 Flying Cloud Dr S, Eden Prairie MN 55344	952-944-7727	R	3	<.1
142	Cips Marketing Group Inc—*Michael Lynch*	13110 Avalon Blvd, Los Angeles CA 90061	310-970-9000	R	3*	<.1
143	3D Joe Corp—*Brian Almashie*	831 S 19th St, Richmond CA 94804	510-233-2202	R	3*	<.1
144	HoldCube—*Wesley Valverde*	105 NW Railroad Ave, Hammond LA 70401		R	3	<.1
145	Specs Liquor Warehouse	2727 Summer Rd, Spring TX 77373	281-657-1213	R	3*	.1
146	Billmyr Enterprises Inc—*William Squiric*	1705 K Ave Ste A, Plano TX 75074	972-424-1980	R	3*	<.1
147	Progressive Travel Promotions Inc—*Douglas Todd*	933 Motor Pkwy Ste 100, Hauppauge NY 11788	631-689-2980	R	3*	<.1
148	Wyngate International Inc—*Dean Austin*	2000 E Oakland Park Bl, Oakland Park FL 33306		R	3*	<.1
149	People To My Site—*Todd Swickard*	735 Taylor Rd Ste 200, Gahanna OH 43230	614-452-8179	R	3	<.1
150	The JAR Group—*Steve Swartz*	55 Washington Ste 301, Brooklyn NY 11201	646-290-8659	R	3	<.1
151	Salient Mobility LLC—*Steve Collins*	1230 Peachtree St Fl 1, Atlanta GA 30309	404-942-3310	H	3*	<.1
152	MIG Inc	999 Tech Row, Madison Heights MI 48071		S	3*	<.1
153	Shadow Productions—*Matthew J Dugan*	61 N Willard St, Burlington VT 05401	802-863-2076	R	3*	<.1
154	Worldscan Intelligence Services Ltd—*Steven Webster*	2569 New Found Harbor, Merritt Island FL 32952	321-452-4140	R	3*	<.1
155	Acf General Media Corp—*Daniel Klein*	2639 E Broadway Rd Ste, Mesa AZ 85204	480-844-9669	R	2*	<.1
156	Kearney Publishing Corp—*Clay Kearney*	7901 Kingspointe Pkwy, Orlando FL 32819	407-345-8453	R	2*	<.1
157	Worksmart Promotions Inc—*Joan Edwards*	6839 Convoy Ct, San Diego CA 92111	858-552-9280	R	2*	<.1
158	The1stMovement—*Ming Chan*	1010 E Union St Ste 12, Pasadena CA 91106	626-689-4993	R	2	<.1
159	Nikles Design Corp—*Walter Nikles*	2365 Milburn Ave Bldg, Baldwin NY 11510	516-771-9749	R	2*	<.1
160	Ad Tracker—*Noel Umfleet*	PO Box 37, Crocker MO 65452	573-736-2226	R	2*	<.1
161	Opportunity Connection Publishing Co—*Carl Hunt*	17319 Crystal Valley R, Little Rock AR 72210	501-455-5888	R	2*	<.1
162	John Ryan Performance Inc—*John Ryan*	PO Box 27740, Las Vegas NV 89126	702-579-4077	R	2*	<.1
163	Dicom Inc—*Jim Steward*	1650 Des Peres Rd Ste, Saint Louis MO 63131	314-909-0900	R	2*	<.1
164	J and D Enterprises—*John Beresh*	PO Box 1118, Uniontown OH 44685	330-699-0203	R	2*	<.1
165	Nostalgic Whimsy—*Mike Romatowski*	PO Box 2587, Ann Arbor MI 48106	734-930-0003	R	2*	<.1
166	Successfulcom—*Craig Settle*	2869 Vallecito Pl, Oakland CA 94606	510-536-4522	R	2*	<.1
167	Smy Media Inc—*Karen Sheridan*	211 E Ontario St Ste 9, Chicago IL 60611	312-621-9600	R	2*	<.1
168	Montajz Magazine Inc—*Alexjandro Noralez*	468 N Camden Dr Ste 20, Beverly Hills CA 90210	310-601-3171	R	2*	<.1
169	New Jersey Community Publishing Inc—*Jerry Mallach*	11 Melanie Ln Ste 4, East Hanover NJ 07936	973-994-4567	R	2*	<.1
170	Global Intellisystems LLC	1153 Bergen Pkwy No 45, Evergreen CO 80439		R	2*	<.1
171	Department Of Media Studies—*Richard Maxwell*	6530 Kissena Blvd Rm 1, Flushing NY 11367	718-997-2950	R	2*	<.1
172	DJM Sales and Marketing Inc—*Deborah J Marlor*	129 E 50th St, Boise ID 83714	208-853-0693	R	1*	<.1
173	Propel Marketing LLC—*Edward Levens*	624 Holly Springs Rd S, Holly Springs NC 27540	919-346-5530	R	1*	<.1
174	Beach Banners Inc—*Joel Weaner*	3545-1 St John's Bluff, Jacksonville FL 32224	904-642-0721	R	1*	<.1
175	CoBuilder Inc—*Douglas L Davis*	1601 Sepulveda Blvd, Manhattan Beach CA 90266	310-374-0900	R	1*	<.1
176	Online Marketing and Public Relations—*Doug Mealy*	32 N Ferry St, Schenectady NY 12305	518-393-5872	R	1*	<.1
177	Silver Platter Productions Inc—*Bernie Mitchell*	11130 Kingston Pike St, Knoxville TN 37934	865-599-6343	R	1*	<.1
178	AMHN Inc—*Robert Cambridge*	100 N 1st St Ste 104, Burbank CA 91502	310-861-0825	P	1	<.1
179	Aero-Tag Inc	PO Box 234055, Great Neck NY 11023		R	<1	<.1
180	theglobecom Inc—*Michael S Egan*	110 E Broward Blvd Ste, Fort Lauderdale FL 33301	954-769-5900	P	<1	N/A

TOTALS: SIC 7319 Advertising Nec
Companies: 180   25,171   55.2

7322 Adjustment & Collection Services

Rank	Company Name—*Executive Officer*	Address, City, State, Zip	Phone	Type	Fin	Empls
1	NCO Financial Systems Inc—*Michael J Barrist* NCO Group Inc	507 Prudential Rd, Horsham PA 19044	215-441-3000	S	4,322*	9.0
2	Van Ru Credit Corp—*Daniel Calderon*	PO Box 270, Park Ridge IL 60068	847-824-2414	R	3,214*	.9
3	NCO Group Inc—*Ronald A Rittenmeyer*	507 Prudential Rd, Horsham PA 19044	215-441-3000	R	1,467*	30.0
4	BilAmerica Inc—*Scott Risely*	PO Box 144333, Orlando FL 32814	407-422-9831	R	920*	.1
5	JDR Holdings Corp—*Michael Barrist* NCO Group Inc	500 N Franklin Tpke, Ramsey NJ 07446	201-512-2500	S	526*	1.4
6	Portfolio Recovery Associates Inc—*Steven D Fredrickson*	120 Corporate Blvd, Norfolk VA 23502	757-519-9300	P	459	2.8

Note: An asterisk (*) indicates an estimated financial figure. The company type code used is as follows: R = Private, P = Public, S = Private Subsidiary, B = Public Subsidiary, D = Division, J = Joint Venture, I = Investment Fund.

COMPANY RANKINGS BY SALES WITHIN 4-DIGIT SIC

Rank	Company Name—*Executive Officer*	Address, City, State, Zip	Phone	Type	Fin	Empls
7	Pioneer Credit Recovery Inc—*Jack frazier*	PO Box 100, Arcade NY 14009	585-492-1234	S	417*	1.4
8	Asset Acceptance Capital Corp—*Rion B Needs*	PO Box 2036, Warren MI 48090	586-939-9600	P	364	1.2
9	Client Services Inc—*Scott Lindley*	PO Box 1586, Saint Peters MO 63376	636-947-2321	R	266*	.7
10	Asset Management Outsourcing Inc—*Mike Chamberlain*	5655 Peachtree Pky Ste, Norcross GA 30092	678-259-9600	R	237*	1.0
11	OSI Collection Services Inc—*Kevin T Keleghan*	390 S Woods Mill Rd St, Chesterfield MO 63017	314-576-0822	R	211*	4.3
12	Arrow Financial Services LLC—*Michael Walter*	5996 W Touhy Ave, Niles IL 60714	847-557-1100	R	170*	1.5
13	Security Credit Services LLC—*William A Alias Jr*	2653 W Oxford Loop Ste, Oxford MS 38655	662-281-7220	R	168*	.1
14	Tfc Associates LLC	266 Summit Ave, Hackensack NJ 07601	201-678-1144	R	155*	<.1
15	ARS National Services Inc—*Jason Howerton*	201 W Grand Ave, Escondido CA 92025	760-735-2700	R	138*	.4
16	National Educational Acceptance Corp	PO Box 419118, Saint Louis MO 63141		R	131*	.4
17	Consumer Adjustment Company Inc—*Shawn Farris*	PO Box 270480, Saint Louis MO 63127	314-729-1133	R	97*	.4
18	FMA Enterprises Inc—*Alan Spiegelhauer*	12339 Cutten Rd, Houston TX 77066	281-931-5050	R	75*	.4
19	Pinnacle Financial Group Inc—*Tony Michel*	7825 Washingtn Ave S S, Minneapolis MN 55439	952-996-0559	S	74*	.5
20	Trover Solutions Inc—*Robert Bader*	9390 Bunsen Pkwy, Louisville KY 40220	502-214-1340	R	66*	.6
21	Vengroff Williams and Associates Inc—*Mark Vengroff*	2211 Fruitville Rd, Sarasota FL 34237	941-363-5200	R	66*	.3
22	United Recovery Systems Inc—*Douglas Schultz*	5800 N Course Dr, Houston TX 77072	713-977-1234	R	63*	1.4
23	Td Service Financial Corp—*Dale Dykema*	1820 E 1st St Ste 300, Santa Ana CA 92705	714-543-8372	R	60*	.1
24	Portfolio Recovery Associates LLC Portfolio Recovery Associates Inc	120 Corporate Blvd, Norfolk VA 23502	757-519-9300	S	45*	.1
25	First Revenue Assurance LLC—*Judith A LaSpada*	3033 S Parker Rd, Aurora CO 80014	303-595-4400	S	43*	.1
26	Atlantic Credit and Finance Inc—*Richard Woolwine*	2727 Franklin Rd SW, Roanoke VA 24014	540-772-7800	R	42*	.4
27	Enhanced Recovery Company LLC—*Mark Thompson*	8014 Bayberry Rd, Jacksonville FL 32256	904-645-0049	R	36*	.8
28	Bureau of Collection Recovery Inc—*Marty Sarim*	7575 Corporate Way, Eden Prairie MN 55344		R	36*	.1
29	Creditors Interchange Inc—*Gary Holter*	80 Holtz Dr, Cheektowaga NY 14225	716-614-7500	R	31*	.6
30	Premiere Credit of North America LLC—*Rob Meck*	PO Box 19309, Indianapolis IN 46219		R	29*	.4
31	Retrieval-Masters Creditors Bureau Inc—*Russell Fuchs*	PO Box 160, Elmsford NY 10523	914-592-0055	R	28*	.1
32	Hospital Billing and Collection Service—*Brian J Wasilewski*	118 Lukens Dr, New Castle DE 19720	302-552-8000	R	27*	.3
33	Sequoia Concepts Inc—*Roy C du Plessis*	500 N Brand Blvd Ste 1, Glendale CA 91203	818-409-6000	R	25*	.1
34	Regions Interstate Billing Services Inc—*Paul Crawford III*	PO Box 2250, Decatur AL 35609	256-355-1750	S	23*	.2
35	Accounts Receivable Management Inc—*William Cosenza*	PO Box 129, Thorofare NJ 08086	856-931-4500	R	20*	.3
36	House of Adjustments Inc	715 Mamaroneck Ave Ste, Mamaroneck NY 10543	914-381-6000	R	19*	<.1
37	Franklin Collection Service Inc—*Dan Franklin*	PO Box 3910, Tupelo MS 38803	662-844-7776	R	18*	.3
38	Regional Adjustment Bureau Inc—*James Smith*	PO Box 34111, Memphis TN 38184	901-382-0250	R	18*	.3
39	Tate and Kirlin Associates Inc—*Harold Tate*	2810 Southampton Rd, Philadelphia PA 19154	215-464-4500	R	18*	.2
40	Financial Recovery Services Inc—*Brian Bowers*	4900 Viking Dr, Edina MN 55435	952-831-4800	R	18*	.2
41	Network Recovery Services Inc—*Jerry Fields*	3 Expy Plz Ste 200, Roslyn Heights NY 11577	516-622-6730	R	17*	.1
42	Receivables Outsourcing Inc—*Chris Wunder*	PO Box 549, Lutherville Timonium MD 21094	410-616-2500	R	16*	.2
43	Merchant Processing Services Inc—*Vlad Sadovsky*	132 W 36th St Fl 3, New York NY 10018	212-931-5180	R	15	.1
44	Ccb Credit Services Incorporated—*Ron Krech*	PO Box 272, Springfield IL 62705	217-786-4800	R	15*	.4
45	Cmi Group—*Thomas Stockton*	4200 International Pkw, Carrollton TX 75007	972-862-4200	R	14*	.2
46	DataMax Corp (Winston-Salem North Carolina)—*Robert Egleston*	PO Box 3136, Winston Salem NC 27106	336-777-3555	R	14*	.1
47	Associated Creditors Exchange Inc—*Joseph Berardi*	PO Box 33130, Phoenix AZ 85067	602-954-6554	R	14*	.2
48	Cmre Financial Services Inc—*Jack Nixon*	3075 E Imperial Hwy St, Brea CA 92821	714-528-3200	R	13*	.3
49	International Computer Systems Inc—*William Dunkum*	PO Box 3564, Little Rock AR 72203	501-455-1658	R	13*	.2
50	Amcol Systems Inc—*Jay Rickman*	PO Box 21625, Columbia SC 29221	803-798-6370	R	12*	.2
51	Federal Bond And Collection Service Inc—*Joseph Neary*	2200 Byberry Rd Ste 12, Hatboro PA 19040	215-320-5789	R	12*	.1
52	Money Management International	1215 Prytania Ave Ste, New Orleans LA 70130	504-529-2396	S	11*	<.1
53	Argent - A A A Credit Servicing Inc—*William Bull*	7650 Magna Dr, Belleville IL 62223	618-235-4700	R	11*	.2
54	Brown and Joseph Ltd—*Chris Cappuccilli*	1701 Golf Rd Ste 2-100, Rolling Meadows IL 60008	847-758-3000	R	10*	.1
55	Williams Cohen and Gray Inc—*Robert Williams*	6201 Bonhomme Rd Ste 4, Houston TX 77036	713-457-0830	R	10*	.1
56	Betz/Mitchell Associates Inc—*Eric Salmeron*	265 Post Ave, Westbury NY 11590	516-745-0161	R	10*	<.1
57	Commercial Recovery Systems Inc—*Tim Ford*	PO Box 570909, Dallas TX 75357	214-324-9575	R	9*	.2
58	CreditRiskMonitorcom Inc—*Jerome S Flum*	704 Executive Blvd Ste, Valley Cottage NY 10989	845-230-3000	P	9	.1
59	Kca Financial Services Inc—*David Widrick*	PO Box 53, Geneva IL 60134	630-232-2545	R	9*	.1
60	Greenberg Grant and Richards Inc—*Garrick Glascock*	PO Box 571811, Houston TX 77257	713-789-5893	R	8*	.1
61	Northland Group Inc—*John Johnson*	7831 Glenroy Rd Ste 35, Minneapolis MN 55439	952-831-4005	R	8*	.1
62	Credit Watch Services Ltd—*Joseph Tempesta*	4690 Diplomacy Rd Ste, Fort Worth TX 76155	817-864-3300	R	8*	.1
63	Amsher Collection Services Inc—*Martin Sher*	600 Beacon Pky W, Birmingham AL 35209	205-322-4110	R	8*	.1
64	NCO Financial Systems Inc Health Services Div—*Micheal Barrist* NCO Financial Systems Inc	126 S Main St, Saint Charles MO 63301	314-946-6700	S	8*	.1
65	Stephens and Michaels Associates Inc—*Judy Bucciarelli*	PO Box 109, Salem NH 03079	603-328-2800	R	8*	.1
66	R And B Collections Inc—*Ross Gelfand*	PO Box 1870, Roswell GA 30077	770-840-8482	R	8*	.1
67	Security Credit Systems Inc—*Angelo Travale*	622 Main St Ste 301, Buffalo NY 14202	716-882-4515	R	7*	.1
68	Cbsj Financial Corp—*Bertha Martin*	99 W Tasman Dr Ste 205, San Jose CA 95134	408-457-2900	R	7*	.1
69	Seattle Service Bureau Inc—*David Conyers*	PO Box 55789, Seattle WA 98155	206-533-0877	R	7*	.1
70	Receivables Incorporated Corporate—*B Davis*	PO Box 56245, Atlanta GA 30343	602-749-1200	R	7*	.1
71	Rmb Inc—*Neil Koonce*	PO Box 10023, Knoxville TN 37939	865-694-1140	R	7*	.1
72	Bonded Credit Bureau Inc—*Donald Wood*	PO Box 498609, Cincinnati OH 45249	513-793-7900	R	7*	.1
73	Northern California Collection Service Inc—*Larry Cassidy*	PO Box 13765, Sacramento CA 95853	916-929-7811	R	7*	<.1
74	Protocol Recovery Service Inc—*Rick Cerny*	655 Molly Ln Ste 120, Woodstock GA 30189	770-425-8862	R	7*	.1
75	L A Commercial Group Inc—*Robert Merette*	317 S Brand Blvd, Glendale CA 91204	818-551-6800	R	7*	.1
76	Merchants' Credit Guide Co—*Daniel Burtis*	223 W Jackson Blvd Ste, Chicago IL 60606	312-360-3000	R	7*	.1
77	Divine and Service Ltd—*Jo Handsel*	13809 N Hwy 183 Ste 80, Austin TX 78750	512-255-1636	R	7*	.1
78	P and B Capital Group LLC—*Frank Torres*	PO Box 25197, Tampa FL 33622	716-891-5800	R	6*	.1
79	Merchants Credit Corp—*David Quigley*	PO Box 7416, Bellevue WA 98008	425-643-2613	R	6*	.1
80	RMCN Credit Services Inc—*Doug Parker*	1611 Wilmeth Rd Ste B, McKinney TX 75069	972-529-0900	R	6*	.1
81	ARM Solutions—*Brad Jadwin*	PO Box 2929, Camarillo CA 93011		R	6*	<.1
82	Trac-A-Chec Inc—*Rick Berg*	PO Box 2764, Davenport IA 52809	563-355-3400	R	6*	<.1
83	Synergetic Communications Inc—*Michael Orlando*	5450 Nw Central Dr Ste, Houston TX 77092	713-460-3114	R	6*	.1
84	Hanley Lamont and Associates Inc—*John Hanley*	1138 Elm St Ste 2, Manchester NH 03101	603-625-5547	R	6*	.1
85	Viking Collection Service Southwest Inc—*Cory Kloeckner*	2075 W Pinnacle Peak R, Phoenix AZ 85027	623-434-7504	R	6*	.1
86	Harvard Collection Services Inc—*Gloria Kaiser*	4839 N Elston Ave, Chicago IL 60630	773-283-7500	R	5*	.1
87	Doctors and Merchants Credit Bureau Inc—*Leon Gentry*	955 Greene St, Augusta GA 30901	706-823-6200	R	5*	.1
88	Illinois Collection Service Inc—*Daniel Cronin*	8231 185th St Ste 100, Tinley Park IL 60487	708-857-7600	R	5*	.1
89	Automated Collection Services Inc—*Wanda Morris*	PO Box 17423, Nashville TN 37217	615-361-6997	R	5*	.1
90	Roi Eligibility Services Corp—*Gary Hickman*	1920 Greenspring Dr St, Lutherville Timonium MD 21093	410-616-2500	R	5*	.1
91	Max Revenue Solutions Ltd—*Alan Spiegelhauer*	7676 Hillmont St Ste 2, Houston TX 77040	713-329-6166	R	5*	.1
92	Asset Recovery Group Inc—*Michael Schindler*	PO Box 14949, Portland OR 97293	503-230-9522	R	5*	<.1

Rank	Company Name—Executive Officer	Address, City, State, Zip	Phone	Type	Fin	Empls
93	Mutual Assignment and Indemnification Co—Marcus Antone	500 Lincoln Hwy, North Versailles PA 15137	412-823-0733	R	4*	.1
94	Unique Management Services Inc—Lyle Stucki	119 E Maple St, Jeffersonville IN 47130	812-285-0886	R	4*	.1
95	Receivables Control Corp—Luke Vidor	PO Box 9658, Minneapolis MN 55440	763-315-9600	R	4*	.1
96	Suburban Credit Corporation Of Va Inc—Neil Bingaman	PO Box 30640, Alexandria VA 22310	703-924-3000	R	4*	.1
97	Loan Management Services Inc—Randall Mcphillips	PO Box 10595, Newport Beach CA 92658	949-250-5700	R	4*	.1
98	B and B Collections Inc—Jerilyn Brown	PO Box 2137, Toms River NJ 08754	732-349-9200	R	4*	<.1
99	Commercial Collection Corporation Of New York—Robert In-gold	PO Box 288, Tonawanda NY 14151		R	4*	.1
100	Claims Resource Services Inc—Peter Casoni	603 Campbell Tech Pkwy, Campbell CA 95008		R	4*	<.1
101	Credit Adjustments Inc—Gene Osborne	330 Florence St, Defiance OH 43512	419-782-3709	R	4*	.1
102	Broward Adjustment Services Inc—John France	PO Box 11879, Fort Lauderdale FL 33339	954-565-6682	R	4*	.1
103	Lake County Business Bureau Inc—Joseph Zacharias	541 Otis Bowen Dr, Munster IN 46321	219-934-5300	R	4*	.1
104	Universal Collection Systems—Jim Moton	PO Box 751090, Memphis TN 38175	901-452-8900	R	4*	.1
105	Clovis and Roche' Inc—Owen Seiler	PO Box 2309, Hammond LA 70404	985-318-1300	R	4*	.1
106	Metro-Republic Commercial Service Inc—Bruce Christian	PO Box 1357, Corona CA 92878	951-273-7700	R	4*	<.1
107	Jonathan Neil and Associates Inc—John Student	18321 Ventura Blvd Ste, Tarzana CA 91356	818-708-6088	R	4*	<.1
108	Commercial Services Group Inc—Charles Neumann	11603 Shelbyville Rd S, Louisville KY 40243	502-244-6900	R	4*	<.1
109	Evergreen Professional Recoveries Inc—Ken Ross	12100 Ne 195th St Ste, Bothell WA 98011	425-402-6646	R	4*	<.1
110	King's Credit Services—Randall Burchfield	96 Shaw Ave Ste 221, Clovis CA 93612	559-322-2550	R	4*	.1
111	Gcfs Inc—John Graves	PO Box 3470, Paso Robles CA 93447	805-237-2040	R	4*	<.1
112	International Recovery Associates Inc—Paul Zucker	PO Box 651, Nesconset NY 11767	631-361-3500	R	4*	<.1
113	Creditors Collection Service Of Los Angeles—Alfred Shain	1521 W 3rd St, Los Angeles CA 90017	213-484-6279	R	3*	.1
114	Ncsplus Inc—Christopher Rehkow	117 E 24th St Fl 5, New York NY 10010	212-213-3000	R	3*	<.1
115	Credit Service Inc—Ron Brown	PO Box 60566, Oklahoma City OK 73146	405-943-9608	R	3*	<.1
116	Glenn Associates Inc—Edwin Misiph	PO Box 2407, Woburn MA 01888	978-988-1370	R	3*	<.1
117	Ecco Inc—Norman Jerke	706 SW 7th St, Madison SD 57042	605-256-6628	R	3*	.1
118	Asset Management Services Inc—Mark Hablenko	6851 Jericho Tpke Ste, Syosset NY 11791	631-293-7446	R	3*	<.1
119	Berlin-Wheeler Inc—Harold Leydens	PO Box 463, Jefferson City MO 65102	573-634-3030	R	3*	<.1
120	Nationwide Collection Agencies Inc—Alan Jacoby	PO Box 13129, Lansing MI 48901	517-622-2660	R	3*	<.1
121	Puroo Fleet Services Inc—David Purinton	136 S Main St, Spanish Fork UT 84660	801-798-2400	R	3*	<.1
122	Healthcare Claims Management—William Borneman	PO Box 55707, Indianapolis IN 46205	317-257-5500	R	3*	.1
123	United States Credit Bureau—Kim Aqino	90 Locust Ave Ste 1, Danbury CT 06810	203-791-9899	R	3*	.1
124	Audit Systems Inc—William Horwitz	3696 Ulmerton Rd Ste 2, Clearwater FL 33762	727-571-1945	R	3*	<.1
125	Mcb Collection Services Inc—John Rockhill	PO Box 9, Vero Beach FL 32961	772-567-7300	R	3*	<.1
126	Nationwide Credit Service LLC—Dave Spurgeon	PO Box 1787, Longview WA 98632	360-425-6930	R	3*	<.1
127	Fidelity Properties Inc—Paul Boggs	PO Box 2055, Alliance OH 44601	330-821-9700	R	3*	<.1
128	Auvi Coll Inc—Rafael Mederos	4114 Nw 4th Ter, Miami FL 33126	305-642-3231	R	3*	.1
129	Noremac Enterprises LLC	5100 Prkcnter Ave Ste, Dublin OH 43017	440-336-4207	R	3*	<.1
130	Far West Collection Services Inc—Robert Smith	3018 Willow Pass Rd St, Concord CA 94519	925-827-8200	R	3*	<.1
131	Community Cash Management Corp—Paul Finnegan	PO Box 730, Somersworth NH 03878	781-933-8778	R	3*	<.1
132	Green And Son's Agency Inc—Chris Green	PO Box 166, Ogden UT 84402	801-399-3743	R	3*	<.1
133	DBM E Inc—Martin Gross	PO Box 550, Poughkeepsie NY 12602	845-452-4902	R	3*	<.1
134	DBG Collection Inc—Walter Bednarchik	229 Plz Blvd Ste 112, Morrisville PA 19067	215-428-0666	R	3*	<.1
135	Vericore LLC—Timothy Sanderson	10115 Kincey Ave Ste 1, Huntersville NC 28078		R	3*	<.1
136	Apelles LLC—Carl Bloecher	195 W Schrock Rd, Westerville OH 43081	614-899-7322	R	3*	<.1
137	Pacific Credit Exchange—Bud Schaffer	15760 Ventura Blvd A11, Encino CA 91436	818-995-8424	R	3*	<.1
138	Partners Financial Services Inc—Wally Overstreet	PO Box 728, Fenton MO 63026	636-305-9877	R	3*	<.1
139	Custom Medical Services Inc—Byron Turnoff	406 Sw 12th Ave, Deerfield Beach FL 33442	954-426-8840	R	3*	<.1
140	United Collection Service Company Inc—Benjamin Daniels	16040 Christensen Rd S, Tukwila WA 98188	206-682-0432	R	3*	<.1
141	Collection Consultants Of California Inc—Ewing Bartgis	PO Box 29050, Glendale CA 91209	818-551-5600	R	3*	<.1
142	Fidelity Creditor Services Inc—Walter Carleton	PO Box 3963, Glendale CA 91221	818-502-1981	R	3*	<.1
143	Man Data Inc—Stan Dodd	PO Box 40580, Eugene OR 97404	541-688-9445	R	3*	<.1
144	National Creditors Connection Inc—Richard Rodriguez	14 Orchard Ste 200, Lake Forest CA 92630	949-461-7540	R	3*	<.1
145	Universal Fidelity LP—Adriana Block	PO Box 941911, Houston TX 77094	281-647-4100	R	3*	.3
146	Grimley Financial Corp—Charles Grimley	30 Washington Ave Ste, Haddonfield NJ 08033	856-669-2420	R	3*	<.1
147	Receivable Management Inc—John Marcum	107 W Randol Mill Rd S, Arlington TX 76011	817-261-7534	R	3*	<.1
148	Statewide Tax Recovery Inc—David Woodring	PO Box 752, Sunbury PA 17801	570-286-8538	R	2*	<.1
149	Regency Credit LLC—Rini Westfall-Early	1403 W 10th Pl Ste B11, Tempe AZ 85281	480-921-3917	R	2*	<.1
150	Burnstein and Burnstein Inc—Sid Burnstein	PO Box 1234, Indian Rocks Beach FL 33785	727-517-7601	R	2*	<.1
151	Marauder Corp—Ryon Gambill	74923 Us Hwy 111, Indian Wells CA 92210	760-423-1111	R	2*	<.1
152	Federal Check Recovery Inc—Billing Chapman	108 Corporate Lake Dr, Columbia MO 65203	573-256-6540	R	2*	<.1
153	Diversified Account Systems Of Georgia Inc—Jon Dunn	PO Box 870547, Morrow GA 30287	770-961-5400	R	2*	<.1
154	Allied Collection Service Inc—Kevin Hastings	4230 Lbj Fwy Ste 407, Dallas TX 75244	972-404-0808	R	2*	<.1
155	Diversified Creditors Service—Bill Pratt	PO Box 1179, Vancouver WA 98666	360-992-4100	R	2*	<.1
156	Medical Administrators Inc—Tom Spooner	28301 Ranney Pkwy, Westlake OH 44145	440-899-2400	R	2*	<.1
157	Reliant Recovery Services Inc—Virginia Chiappone	PO Box 2449, Monrovia CA 91017	626-303-1903	R	2*	<.1
158	Mutual Collection Company Inc—James Markham	PO Box 11629, Memphis TN 38111	901-324-1441	R	2*	<.1
159	Ccs Labs Inc—Scott Murray	758 S 5th Ave, Mount Vernon NY 10550	914-667-7285	R	2*	<.1
160	Midway Collections Inc—Jerry Curtis	PO Box 702257, Dallas TX 75370	972-798-1000	R	2*	<.1
161	Troon Company LLC	PO Box 26579, Macon GA 31221	478-471-7930	R	2*	<.1
162	Rauch Milliken International Inc—Steve Rauch	PO Box 8390, Metairie LA 70011	504-837-6995	R	2*	<.1
163	Credit Data Resources Inc—Amy Lewis	PO Box 637, Stillwater OK 74076	405-377-2769	R	2*	<.1
164	Dover Holding/Trust—Ronald Pellegrino	301 W Blackwell St, Dover NJ 07801	973-328-3458	R	2*	<.1
165	Sentry Recovery Company Inc—James Gravett	3080 S Durango Dr Ste, Las Vegas NV 89117	702-946-1140	R	2*	<.1
166	Kelkris Associates Inc—Kathryn Parsons	PO Box 150, Fairfield CA 94533	707-429-3211	R	2*	<.1
167	Mbi Associates Inc—Norman Alpren	PO Box 794, Rockville Centre NY 11571	516-678-9705	R	2*	<.1
168	Medical Credit Bureau Inc—Steven Block	234 E Gray St Ste B66, Louisville KY 40202	502-583-0957	R	2*	<.1
169	Commtrak Corp	17493 Nassau Commons B, Lewes DE 19958	302-644-1600	R	2*	<.1
170	Financial Management Control Inc—John Thomas	1909 Tyler St Ste 605, Hollywood FL 33020	954-923-3822	R	2*	<.1
171	Mutual Management Services Inc—David Widrick	PO Box 4777, Rockford IL 61110	815-963-1220	R	2*	<.1
172	Ditore Ruibal and Associates Inc—Alex Ruibal	135 2nd Ave N Ste 3, Jacksonville Beach FL 32250	904-249-2411	R	2*	<.1
173	IRM Inc—William Rock	PO Box 11848, Lexington KY 40578	859-254-6969	R	2*	<.1
174	Mcot Inc—Tom Cole	2004 American Way Ste, Kingsport TN 37660	423-230-4100	R	2*	<.1
175	Oregon Credit Systems Inc—David Halseth	27600 Sw 95th Ave Ste, Wilsonville OR 97070	503-639-6000	R	2*	<.1
176	Synerprise Consulting Services—Richard Mccoy	5068 W Plano Pkwy Ste, Plano TX 75093	972-407-0200	R	2*	<.1
177	Watsonville Bureau Of Collection Inc—David Hemrick	PO Box 339, Watsonville CA 95077	831-724-6328	R	2*	<.1
178	Pro Collect Inc—Larry Gingold	PO Box 550369, Dallas TX 75355	214-341-7788	R	2*	<.1
179	Allied Business Accounts Inc—James Hurlburt	300 One Half S 2nd St, Clinton IA 52732	563-242-2586	R	2*	<.1
180	Equitable Financial Services LLC	2210 Greene Way, Louisville KY 40220	502-495-0064	R	2*	<.1
181	Bibb Collection Service Inc—Mildred Smith	PO Box 978, Macon GA 31202	478-745-3934	R	2*	<.1

Note: An asterisk (*) indicates an estimated financial figure. The company type code used is as follows: R = Private, P = Public, S = Private Subsidiary, B = Public Subsidiary, D = Division, J = Joint Venture, I = Investment Fund.

COMPANY RANKINGS BY SALES WITHIN 4-DIGIT SIC

Rank	Company Name—*Executive Officer*	Address, City, State, Zip	Phone	Type	Fin	Empls
182	Delmarva Collections Inc—*Joanne Grant*	PO Box 37, Salisbury MD 21803	410-546-3742	R	2*	<.1
183	Credit Adjustment Board Inc—*Nicholas Roupas*	306 E Grace St, Richmond VA 23219	804-649-0761	R	2*	<.1
184	Goldsmith and Hull A PC—*William Goldsmith*	16000 Ventura Blvd Ste, Encino CA 91436	818-990-6600	R	1*	<.1
185	Advantage Recovery System Inc—*Jerry Brown*	513 Garrison Ave, Fort Smith AR 72901	479-782-9230	R	1*	<.1
186	Ameracash Solutions Inc—*Chuck Gardner*	7616 City Ave Ste 222, Philadelphia PA 19151	215-877-8974	R	1*	<.1
187	Credit Clearing House Of America Inc—*Mike Gardner*	305 W Market St, Louisville KY 40202	502-583-1666	R	1*	<.1
188	Summit Credit Services Inc—*Jase Bolger*	5320 Holiday Ter Ste 1, Kalamazoo MI 49009	269-372-2800	R	1*	<.1
189	Home Integrity Service Financial Ltd—*Chris Morgan*	501 Shelley Dr Ste 301, Tyler TX 75701	903-593-0063	R	1*	<.1
190	Federal Pacific Credit—*William Stratton*	1795 W 2320 S, Salt Lake City UT 84119	801-972-4550	R	1*	<.1
191	Atlantic Advisors Inc—*Jerald Wagenheim*	PO Box 841, Asbury NJ 07712	732-774-7722	R	1*	<.1
192	Tend Business Services Inc—*Hy Diamond*	PO Box 20402, Floral Park NY 11002	516-775-2010	R	1*	<.1
193	Excel Healthcare Receivable Management and Consulting Corp—*Daisy Martinez*	15476 Nw 77th Ct Ste 4, Hialeah FL 33016	305-821-4137	R	1*	<.1
194	Receivables Recovery—*H Dimsdell*	408 Jenks Ave, Panama City FL 32401	850-785-8249	R	1*	<.1
195	Royal Mercantile Trust Corporation Of America Inc—*Kenneth Kuchler*	10 Se Central Pkwy Ste, Stuart FL 34994	772-220-1300	R	1*	<.1
196	Revenue Group—*John Sheehan*	PO Box 221278, Cleveland OH 44122	216-763-2100	R	1*	.1
197	Biehl and Biehl Inc—*William Biehl*	325 Fullerton Ave, Carol Stream IL 60188	630-653-5400	R	1*	<.1
198	Allied Collections and Credit Bureau Inc—*Rex Gallogly*	8600 Pendergrass Rd, Hoschton GA 30548	706-654-1970	R	1*	<.1
199	Affiliated Management Services Inc—*Rich McCoy*	5651 Broadmoor, Mission KS 66202	913-677-9470	R	1*	<.1
200	Diversified Credit Systems—*Cherese Mcgaughey*	PO Box 3424, Longview TX 75606	903-297-0600	R	1*	<.1
201	Procor Inc—*Geoffrey Norwood*	PO Box 427, Sylva NC 28779	828-631-1700	R	1*	<.1
202	Warman-Lowe and Associates Inc—*James Warman*	1010 N University Blvd, Middletown OH 45042	513-424-1001	R	1*	<.1
203	Friedman and Associates (Reisterstown Maryland)—*Jeffrey L Friedman*	100 Owings Ct Ste 13, Reisterstown MD 21136	410-526-4500	R	1*	<.1
204	Remit Corp—*Harry Strausser*	PO Box 7, Bloomsburg PA 17815	570-387-6470	R	1*	<.1
205	Valley Collection Service—*Dale Lind*	PO Box 520, Glendale AZ 85311	623-931-4325	R	1*	<.1
206	ISA Internationale Inc—*Bernard L Brodkorb*	2564 Rice St, Saint Paul MN 55113	651-484-9850	P	<1	<.1

TOTALS: SIC 7322 Adjustment & Collection Services
Companies: 206 .... 14,871 ... 72.9

7323 Credit Reporting Services

Rank	Company Name—*Executive Officer*	Address, City, State, Zip	Phone	Type	Fin	Empls
1	Experian Information Solutions Inc—*John Saunders*	475 Anton Blvd, Costa Mesa CA 92626	714-830-7000	R	2,300*	13.0
2	Moody's Corp—*Raymond W McDaniel Jr*	7 World Trade Ctr 250, New York NY 10007	212-553-1653	P	2,032	4.5
3	Equifax Inc—*Richard F Smith*	PO Box 4081, Atlanta GA 30302	404-885-8000	P	1,960	6.5
4	Dun and Bradstreet Corp—*Sara Mathew*	103 JFK Pkwy, Short Hills NJ 07078	973-921-5500	P	1,759	5.1
5	Equifax Credit Information Services Inc Equifax Inc	PO Box 740241, Atlanta GA 30374	404-885-8000	S	1,540*	7.0
6	TransUnion LLC—*Siddarth Mehta*	555 W Adams St 6th Fl, Chicago IL 60661	312-258-1717	S	1,112*	4.0
7	CBCInnovis—*Kevin Tyrecl*	250 E Town St, Columbus OH 43215	614-222-4343	R	406*	2.0
8	CSC Credit Services Inc—*Mike Laphen*	652 N Sam Houston Pkwy, Houston TX 77060	281-878-1900	S	185*	.5
9	Transunion Corp—*Andrew Knight*	555 W Adams St Fl 2-9, Chicago IL 60661	312-258-1717	R	167*	3.9
10	Standard and Poor's Securities Evaluations Inc—*James Mitos*	55 Water St Fl 44, New York NY 10041	212-438-3388	R	163*	5.0
11	Moody's Analytics Inc—*Mark Almeida*	405 Howard St Ste 300, San Francisco CA 94105	415-874-6000	R	143*	.9
12	AM Best Company Inc	1 Ambest Rd, Oldwick NJ 08858	908-439-2200	R	106*	.5
13	US Credit-Service Corp—*R Brooks Reed*	12400 Coit Rd Ste 950, Dallas TX 75251	214-630-6655	S	60*	.3
14	LaSalle Business Credit Inc—*Michael D Sharkey*	135 S LaSalle St Ste 4, Chicago IL 60603	312-904-8490	S	35*	.2
15	Harris Infosource International Inc Dun and Bradstreet Corp	2057 E Aurora Rd, Twinsburg OH 44087	330-425-9000	D	26*	.1
16	Advantus—*Tim Handley*	15 W Strong St Ste 20A, Pensacola FL 32501	850-470-9336	R	25*	.1
17	Precheck Inc—*Robert Sartain*	1287 N Post Oak Rd Ste, Houston TX 77055	713-861-5959	R	11*	.2
18	First Stone Credit Consulting—*Bruce Danielson*	4372 Spring Valley Rd, Farmers Branch TX 75244	972-235-1188	R	11*	<.1
19	Aargon Agency Inc—*Duane Christy*	3025 W Sahara Ave, Las Vegas NV 89102	702-220-7037	R	9*	.1
20	Montrenes Financial Services Inc—*Dan Montrenes*	5665 Plz Dr, Cypress CA 90630	714-827-7000	R	6*	.1
21	Blue Book Services Inc—*C Carr*	845 E Geneva Rd, Carol Stream IL 60188	630-668-3500	R	6*	.1
22	National Credit Center Inc—*Grayson Sackett*	2605 Camino Del Rio S, San Diego CA 92108	619-209-3610	R	5*	.1
23	Mortgage Fax Inc—*Joanne Ahmadi*	18685 101 Main St Pmb, Huntington Beach CA 92648	714-899-2656	R	5*	.1
24	National Tenant Network Inc—*Dennis J Harrington*	PO Box 1664, Lake Oswego OR 97035	503-635-1118	R	5*	.1
25	Ann Arbor Credit Bureau Inc—*Robert Barden*	PO Box 7820, Ann Arbor MI 48107	734-665-3611	R	5*	.1
26	Credit Bureau Systems Inc—*Wayne Musselwhite*	550 Greensboro Ave Ste, Tuscaloosa AL 35401	205-345-3030	R	5*	.1
27	Nacm Tampa Inc—*William Meeker*	PO Box 22827, Tampa FL 33622	813-289-8894	R	4*	<.1
28	Credit Information Bureau Inc—*Richard Capobianco*	70 Jefferson Blvd Fl 4, Warwick RI 02888	401-781-7770	R	4*	<.1
29	Kreller Business Information Group Inc—*Joseph Davidoski*	817 Main St Ste 700, Cincinnati OH 45202	513-723-8900	R	4*	<.1
30	Credit Data Idaho Inc—*Michael Macbutch*	1451 N Hartman St, Boise ID 83704	208-322-3000	R	3*	<.1
31	Debtication Incorporated Corporate—*Robert Cooper*	6800 Broken Sound Pkwy, Boca Raton FL 33487	561-241-2500	R	3*	<.1
32	Cic Mortgage Credit Inc	2206 21st Ave S Ste 30, Nashville TN 37212	615-386-2285	R	3*	<.1
33	Credit Bureau Of Placer County Inc—*Steve Kenny*	209 Harding Blvd Ste 2, Roseville CA 95678	916-783-7126	R	3*	<.1
34	Certified Credit Reporting Inc—*Lucy Kereta*	1180 Olympic Dr Ste 20, Corona CA 92881	951-371-3911	R	2*	<.1
35	Credit Bureau USA Inc—*Robert Schumann*	PO Box 663, Hammond IN 46325	219-932-1000	R	2*	<.1
36	Riemer Reporting Service Inc—*Dan Riemer*	PO Box 40120, Cleveland OH 44140	440-835-2477	R	2*	<.1
37	NACM Credit Services Inc—*Patrick Tolle*	PO Box 12370, Shawnee Mission KS 66282	913-383-9300	R	2*	<.1
38	Realty and Relocation Services of GA—*Shundreka Mims*	PO Box 3551, Decatur GA 30031	404-519-0753	R	2*	<.1
39	Color-Ons Ltd—*Mike Deets*	1700 S Eisenhower Ave, Mason City IA 50401	641-424-1511	R	1*	<.1
40	Libscorp LLC	2725 Thatcher Ave Ste, River Grove IL 60171	708-452-2800	R	1*	<.1
41	Integrity Credit Services—*Carl Book*	PO Box 1804, Antioch CA 94509	925-757-2480	R	1*	<.1
42	Credit Central Inc—*Robert Knuth*	PO Box 321, Egg Harbor City NJ 08215	609-965-6660	R	1*	<.1
43	American Tenant Screen Inc—*Jim Scherzer*	525 W Chester Pke Ste, Havertown PA 19083	610-924-0801	R	1*	<.1
44	Health Care Resources Inc—*Lee Stickney*	2310 Paseo Del Prado S, Las Vegas NV 89102	702-735-5525	R	1*	<.1
45	Intego—*Laurent Marteau*	500 N Capital of Texas, Austin TX 78746	512-637-0700	R	1*	<.1
46	Service Bureau LLC—*Mark Taylor*	422 E 39th St, Ogden UT 84403	801-334-0051	R	1*	<.1
47	Creditlink Corp—*David Moffitt*	9320 Chesapeake Dr Ste, San Diego CA 92123	858-496-1010	R	1*	<.1

TOTALS: SIC 7323 Credit Reporting Services
Companies: 47 .... 12,129 ... 54.8

7331 Direct Mail Advertising Services

Rank	Company Name—*Executive Officer*	Address, City, State, Zip	Phone	Type	Fin	Empls
1	Source Interlink Companies Inc—*Michael L Sullivan*	27500 Riverview Center, Bonita Springs FL 34134	239-949-4450	R	2,124*	8.0
2	OgilvyOne Worldwide—*Brian Fetherstonhaugh*	636 11th Ave, New York NY 10036	212-237-4000	S	1,000*	1.9
3	Rapp Collins Worldwide—*Rob Horvath*	437 Madison Ave 3rd Fl, New York NY 10022	212-817-6800	S	759*	3.0
4	InfoGroup Inc—*Michael Iaccarino*	PO Box 27347, Omaha NE 68127	402-593-4500	S	479*	3.1
5	Constant Contact Inc—*Gail Goodman*	1601 Trapelo Rd 3rd Fl, Waltham MA 02451	781-472-8100	P	214	.9

Rank	Company Name—*Executive Officer*	Address, City, State, Zip	Phone	Type	Fin	Empls
6	Paradysz Matera Company Inc—*Chris Paradysz*	5 Hanover Sq, New York NY 10004	212-387-0300	R	150*	.2
7	United Mailing Inc—*James Andersen*	1001 Park Rd, Chanhassen MN 55317	952-474-4182	S	140*	1.0
8	Val-Pak Direct Marketing Systems Inc—*Jimmy W Hayes*	8605 Largo Lakes Dr, Largo FL 33773	727-399-3000	S	134*	1.2
9	Grey Direct Inc	200 5th Ave, New York NY 10010	212-537-3700	S	122*	.4
10	Ryan Direct—*Anne Ryan*	304 W 10th St, Kansas City MO 64105	816-221-9923	R	120*	.3
11	Global Document Solutions Inc—*Mark Goodstadt*	435 Hudson St, New York NY 10014	212-924-5400	R	115*	.4
12	Direct Mail Express Inc—*Michael Panaggio*	2441 Bellevue Ave, Daytona Beach FL 32114	386-257-2500	R	97*	.7
13	Bronner Slosberg Humphrey Inc—*Colin Kinsella*	33 Arch St, Boston MA 02110	617-867-1000	S	96*	.7
14	American List Counsel Inc—*Donn Rappaport*	4300 US Hwy 1 CN 5219, Princeton NJ 08540	609-580-2800	R	80*	.2
15	Hibbert Co—*Timothy Moonan*	PO Box 8116, Trenton NJ 08650	609-394-7500	R	79*	.7
16	Rauxa Direct LLC—*Jill Gwaltney*	275 Mccormick Ave A200, Costa Mesa CA 92626	714-427-1271	R	75*	.1
17	Grizzard Communications Group Inc—*Chip Grizzard*	229 Peachtree St NE St, Atlanta GA 30303	404-522-8330	S	63*	.2
18	International Masters Publishers Inc—*Anders Dahl*	225 Park Ave South, New York NY 10003	212-353-6400	R	62*	.3
19	Modern Solution Inc—*Stephen Hoffman*	1675 Faraday, Carlsbad CA 92008		R	61*	.2
20	Access Plans Inc—*Danny Wright*	900 36th Ave NW Ste 19, Norman OK 73072	405-579-8525	P	53	.1
21	Money Mailer LLC—*Gary Mulloy*	12131 Western Ave, Garden Grove CA 92841	714-265-4100	R	50*	.5
22	Calmark Inc—*Jim Fitzgerald*	1400 W 44th St, Chicago IL 60609	773-247-7200	R	46*	.4
23	A Plus Letter Service Inc—*Kathy Finnegan*	200 Syracuse Ct, Lakewood NJ 08701	732-905-2010	R	41*	.1
24	Database Marketing Group Inc—*John A Engstrom*	5 Peters Canyon Dr Ste, Irvine CA 92606	714-727-0800	R	38*	.1
25	Mail Marketing Systems Inc—*C Schultz*	9420 Gerwig Ln, Columbia MD 21046		R	35*	.1
26	Americomm Direct Marketing Co—*David Craig*	4700 Oakland St Ste 12, Denver CO 80239	303-371-4400	S	35*	.1
27	Communications Corporation Of America—*John Fisher*	13195 Freedom Way, Boston VA 22713	540-547-1700	R	35*	.3
28	Worldata Inc—*Jay Schwedelson*	3000 N Military Trl, Boca Raton FL 33431	561-393-8200	R	34*	.1
29	Russell and Miller Inc—*Bernard Findley*	PO Box 2152, Santa Fe Springs CA 90670	562-946-6900	S	33*	.1
30	Access Direct Systems Inc—*John DiNozzi*	91 Executive Blvd, Farmingdale NY 11735	631-420-0770	R	31*	.5
31	Spectrum Monthly Inc—*Richard Pease*	95 Eddy Rd Ste 101, Manchester NH 03102	603-627-0042	R	30*	.1
32	Quantumdirect—*Steve Damman*	8702 Cross Park Dr Ste, Austin TX 78754	512-837-2300	R	28*	.1
33	Direct Response Consulting Service—*Jerry C Watson*	6849 Old Dominion Dr S, Mc Lean VA 22101	703-749-3100	R	27*	<.1
34	Management by Innovation Inc—*Jim Grogan*	710 W New Hampshire Av, Deland FL 32720	386-736-9998	R	25*	.1
35	Admail West—*Kathy Pescetti*	521 N 10th St, Sacramento CA 95811	916-442-3613	R	24*	.1
36	Media Breakaway LLC—*Scott Richter*	1490 W 121st Ave Ste 2, Westminster CO 80234	303-464-8164	R	24*	.1
37	Alaniz LLC—*Randy Seberg*	PO Box 799, Mount Pleasant IA 52641	319-385-7259	R	24*	.2
38	Ionic Marketing—*Miguel Kubin*	15250 Ventura Blvd Ste, Sherman Oaks CA 91403	818-380-3011	R	23*	<.1
39	Scicom Data Services Ltd—*Timothy Johnson*	10101 Bren Rd E, Minnetonka MN 55343	952-933-4200	R	22*	.1
40	Response Media Products Inc—*Betty Abion*	3155 Medlock Bridge Rd, Norcross GA 30071	770-451-5478	R	21*	.1
41	TABS Direct—*Jim Badum*	1921 Gateway Dr, Irving TX 75038	972-582-2600	S	21*	.1
42	Service Center Ltd—*Randy Musgrove*	6450 Clara Rd Ste 100, Houston TX 77041	713-690-8175	R	20	.1
43	American Student List LLC—*Don Damore*	330 Old Country Rd, Mineola NY 11501	516-248-6100	R	19	<.1
44	Hkm Direct Market Communications Inc—*Robert Durham*	5501 Cass Ave, Cleveland OH 44102	216-651-9500	R	19*	.2
45	Streamlite Inc—*Randall Clark*	3000 Centre Pkwy Ste 1, Atlanta GA 30344	404-836-4000	R	19*	.2
46	Acumark Inc—*Tom Joseph*	702 Exeter Ave Ste 700, West Pittston PA 18643	570-883-1800	R	17*	.1
47	Interstate Edp and Direct Mail Center Inc—*Max Houss*	754 4th Ave, Brooklyn NY 11232	718-965-2500	R	17*	.1
48	Unique Mailing Services Inc—*Dan Kouri*	PO Box 621, Downers Grove IL 60515	630-739-4848	R	16*	.4
49	Advertising Distributors Of America Inc—*Dominick Iannaccone*	80 Orville Dr Ste 102, Bohemia NY 11716	631-231-5700	R	16*	.3
50	Graphic Trade Bindery Inc—*Anthony D'agrosa*	2300 Craftsman Cir, Hyattsville MD 20781	301-773-9400	R	16*	.3
51	American Mailers - Illinois Inc—*Shane Randall*	820 Frontenac Rd, Naperville IL 60563	630-579-8800	R	15*	.2
52	AdSell Marketing and Communications Group—*Mark Shocker*	5001 Southwest Ave, Saint Louis MO 63110	314-773-0500	R	15*	.1
53	Newport Creative Communications Inc—*Mike Walsh*	33 Railroad Ave Ste 1, Duxbury MA 02332	781-934-0586	R	15*	<.1
54	Directconnectgroup Ltd—*Brad Clarke*	5501 Cass Ave, Cleveland OH 44102	216-281-2866	R	14*	.5
55	Premier Ims Inc—*Norman Pegram*	PO Box 230229, Houston TX 77223	713-222-8871	R	14*	.2
56	Questmark Information Management Inc—*Larry Ludeke*	9440 Kirby, Houston TX 77054	713-662-9022	R	14*	<.1
57	Venture Direct Worldwide Inc—*Richard Baumer*	708 3rd Ave Fl 12, New York NY 10017	913-254-6000	R	14*	.1
58	Immediate Mailing Services Inc—*James Tom*	PO Box 399, Syracuse NY 13206	315-437-4883	R	13*	.2
59	Log On Computer and Mailing Services Inc—*Daniel Arnowitz*	520 8th Ave Fl 14, New York NY 10018	212-279-4567	R	12*	.1
60	CognitiveDATA Inc—*Rod Ford*	500 President Clinton, Little Rock AR 72201	501-975-7580	S	12*	<.1
61	Demar Direct Inc—*Thomas Deflorio*	1133 N Ridge Ave, Lombard IL 60148	630-873-1000	R	12*	.2
62	Foley Mailing Services Inc—*Ron Menconi*	321 Manley St, West Bridgewater MA 02379	508-897-0030	R	12*	.2
63	Direct Marketing Solutions Inc—*Michael Sherman*	8534 Ne Alderwood Rd, Portland OR 97220	503-281-1400	R	11*	.1
64	Trahan Burden and Charles Inc—*Thomas Burden*	900 S Wolfe St, Baltimore MD 21231	410-347-7500	R	11*	.1
65	Typed Letters Corp—*Shirley Johnson*	7601 W University St, Wichita KS 67209	316-729-9093	R	11*	.1
66	Bruce W Eberle and Associates Inc—*Bruce W Eberle*	1420 Spring Hill Rd St, Mc Lean VA 22102	703-821-1550	R	11*	<.1
67	Sourcelink Carolina LLC—*Dan Jackson*	PO Box 3628, Greenville SC 29608	864-233-2519	R	11*	.1
68	Dmw Worldwide LLC—*Len Zappolo*	701 Lee Rd Ste 103, Chesterbrook PA 19087	610-407-0407	R	10*	.1
69	Mail Computer Services Inc—*Ron Menconi*	321 Manley St, West Bridgewater MA 02379	508-584-6490	R	10*	.1
70	AccuData America—*Stephen Webster*	5220 Summerlin Commons, Fort Myers FL 33907	239-425-4400	R	10*	.1
71	National Mail Advertising Inc—*Ronald Garrow*	2299 White St, Houston TX 77216	713-869-8551	R	10*	.1
72	Programmers Investment Corp—*Gary Scherer*	PO Box 5010, Des Plaines IL 60017	847-227-4500	R	9*	.2
73	Mb-F Inc—*Bobby Christiansen*	PO Box 22107, Greensboro NC 27420	336-379-9352	R	9*	.1
74	Bluegrass Business Services Inc—*Thomas Nichols*	PO Box 11816, Lexington KY 40578	859-231-7272	R	9*	.1
75	Commercial Letter Inc—*Ken Wartman*	725 N 23rd St, Saint Louis MO 63103	314-231-6006	R	9*	.1
76	Cheap Escape Company Inc—*Robert J Minchak Jr*	3105 Farnham Rd, Richfield OH 44286	330-659-3590	R	9*	.1
77	Door Store (Florence Kentucky)	2950 Robertson Ave Ste, Cincinnati OH 45209	513-731-1200	R	9*	<.1
78	Mail Bag Inc—*Kenneth Rubin*	201 Commerce Dr, Upper Marlboro MD 20774	301-249-7800	R	9*	.1
79	Sms Direct Inc—*Andrew Kuniholm*	8461 Virginia Meadows, Manassas VA 20109	703-392-0123	R	9*	.1
80	Meredith - Webb Printing Company Inc—*Travers Webb*	PO Box 2196, Burlington NC 27216	336-228-8378	R	9*	.1
81	Ace Mailing Service Inc—*Charles Thompson*	1961 S Cobb Industrial, Smyrna GA 30082	770-431-2500	R	9*	.1
82	Northwest Mailing Service Inc—*David Joss*	5501 W Grand Ave, Chicago IL 60639	773-237-2264	R	9*	.1
83	Dms Mail Management Inc—*Robert Prevost*	8282 Siegen Ln Ste B, Baton Rouge LA 70810	225-763-6245	R	9*	.1
84	Ad-Mail Inc—*Bill Stevens*	PO Box 3414, Portland OR 97208	503-223-1101	R	8*	.1
85	Bleuchip International Inc—*Rosemary Aulds*	1025 Hilltop Dr, Itasca IL 60143		R	8*	.1
86	Prompt Mailers Inc—*Andrew Masucci*	66 Willow Ave Ste 4, Staten Island NY 10305	718-447-6206	R	8*	.1
87	Direct Mail Of Maine Inc—*John Cloutier*	PO Box 10, Scarborough ME 04070	207-883-6930	R	8*	.1
88	Business Services Network—*Harry Yue*	1275 Fairfax Ave Ste 1, San Francisco CA 94124	415-282-8161	R	8*	.1
89	Msb Inc—*Lisa Thompson*	5330 Technology Ln, Birmingham AL 35217	205-841-7678	R	8*	.1
90	Advanced Business Fulfillment LLC—*Eric Schaefer*	3183 Rider Trl S, Earth City MO 63045	314-770-2986	R	7*	.1
91	AKA Direct Inc—*Wayne Modica*	PO Box 5217, Portland OR 97208	503-454-2200	R	7*	<.1
92	Market Logic Inc	19975 Victor Pkwy, Livonia MI 48152	734-591-3000	S	7*	<.1
93	Faris Mailing Inc—*Robert Faris*	5517 W Minnesota St, Indianapolis IN 46241	317-246 3315	R	7*	<.1
94	Tenco Assemblies Inc—*Joseph Tentilucci*	620 Nolan Ave, Morrisville PA 19067	215-736-2746	R	7*	.1
95	G A Wright Marketing Inc—*Gary Wright*	10325 E 47th Ave, Denver CO 80238	303-333-4453	R	7*	<.1

Note: An asterisk (*) indicates an estimated financial figure. The company type code used is as follows: R = Private, P = Public, S = Private Subsidiary, B = Public Subsidiary, D = Division, J = Joint Venture, I = Investment Fund.

COMPANY RANKINGS BY SALES WITHIN 4-DIGIT SIC

Rank	Company Name—*Executive Officer*	Address, City, State, Zip	Phone	Type	Fin	Empls
96	Mail Tech Enterprises Inc—*Maryann Peterson*	7917 N Kckapoo Edwards, Edwards IL 61528	309-691-6600	R	7*	.1
97	Word Handlers—*Arthur Kerckhoff*	3190 Rider Trl S, Earth City MO 63045	314-576-6686	R	7*	.1
98	New Pros Communications Inc—*J Dyer*	155 Hidden Ravines Dr, Powell OH 43065	740-201-0410	R	7*	.1
99	Kane And Associates Incorporated Anthony—*Hugh Brown*	44 Joseph Mills Dr, Fredericksburg VA 22408	540-373-1111	R	7*	.1
100	Circular Advertising Company Inc—*Joseph Fetcho*	99 Ray Rd, Baltimore MD 21227	410-737-6770	R	7*	.1
101	Postal Presort Inc—*Bryan Pulliam*	820 W 2nd St N, Wichita KS 67203	316-262-3333	R	7*	.1
102	Communication Logistics Inc—*Darla Hageborn*	PO Box 27, Ferdinand IN 47532	812-357-2545	R	6*	.1
103	Pronto Post Inc—*Joshua Blank*	7885 W 20th Ave, Hialeah FL 33014	305-621-7900	R	6*	.1
104	Creative Communications LLC—*Sheila Mccoy*	89 Bridge St Plz, Wheeling WV 26003	304-242-8081	R	6*	.1
105	Publications Expediting Inc—*Stanley Zielony*	200 Meacham Ave, Elmont NY 11003	516-352-7300	R	6*	.1
106	Novus Marketing Inc—*Joanne Capria*	931 Nicollet Mall, Minneapolis MN 55402	612-252-1618	R	6*	<.1
107	Direct Marketing Alliance Inc—*Pauline Gramiak*	PO Box 687, Ambler PA 19002		R	6*	<.1
108	DDM Direct—*Charles Fallett*	1223 William St, Buffalo NY 14206	716-893-8671	R	6*	<.1
109	Lautman Maska Neill and Co—*Kay Partny-Lautman*	1730 Rhode Island Ave, Washington DC 20036	202-296-9660	R	6*	<.1
110	Innovative Computer Services Inc—*Martin Jerick*	PO Box 24192, Lansing MI 48909	517-394-1890	R	6*	<.1
111	Ces Mail Communications Inc—*Jan Reaves*	PO Box 28151, Raleigh NC 27611	919-833-5785	R	6*	.1
112	Creative Marketing Solutions LLC—*Carmen Neal*	13451 S Point Blvd, Charlotte NC 28273	704-583-9717	R	6*	.1
113	Fms/Magnacraft Inc—*Charles Bucolt*	PO Box 11509, Milwaukee WI 53211	414-332-8466	R	6*	.1
114	Lake Michigan Mailers Inc—*Robert Rhoa*	PO Box 19157, Kalamazoo MI 49019	269-383-9333	R	6*	.1
115	Publisher's Renewal Service Co—*Russell Rahm*	10406 Shwnee Mission P, Shawnee Mission KS 66203	913-248-1800	R	6*	.1
116	Corporate Fulfillment Systems Inc—*Tim Flattery*	PO Box 1204, Norton MA 02766	508-285-2800	R	6*	.1
117	Vincent Graphics LLC—*Mike Cornett*	3560 Millikin Ct, Columbus OH 43228	614-771-5440	R	5*	.1
118	Industrial Services Inc—*Bill Duff*	114 Goldstar Dr Sw, Cleveland TN 37311	423-339-3294	R	5*	.1
119	Contest America Publishers Inc—*Gary Downey*	PO Box 169001, Kansas City MO 64116	816-842-4130	R	5*	.1
120	Patton Kiehl Group Inc—*James Patton*	PO Box 590, Thornburg VA 22565	804-448-8900	R	5*	.1
121	Buderic Inc—*R Strand*	1450 Heggen St, Hudson WI 54016	715-386-8832	R	5*	.1
122	Joseph J Sheeran Inc—*Peggy Sheeran*	71 Southgate Blvd, New Castle DE 19720	302-324-0200	R	5*	.1
123	Proven Direct Inc—*Mike Erwin*	1301 W Canal St, Milwaukee WI 53233	414-383-6610	R	5*	.1
124	G and C Direct Mail Marketing Inc—*Fernando Guzman*	1275 Profit Dr, Dallas TX 75247	214-267-8200	R	5*	.1
125	Ami Acquisition Corp—*Milton Olekson*	4407 Wheeler Ave, Alexandria VA 22304	703-370-4606	R	5*	.1
126	Accurate Mailings Inc—*Joseph Vitangeli*	PO Box 5105, Belmont CA 94002	650-508-8885	R	5*	<.1
127	Salt Lake Mailing and Printing Inc—*Gary McCarver*	1841 S Pioneer Rd, Salt Lake City UT 84104	801-923-4800	R	5*	<.1
128	USADATA Inc—*Ric Murphy*	292 Madison Ave Fl 3, New York NY 10017	212-679-1411	R	5*	<.1
129	Cardinal Mailing Services Ltd—*Malia Lageman*	197 Sand Island Access, Honolulu HI 96819	808-538-3884	R	5	<.1
130	Atlantic List Marketing Div—*Paul Martin*	2425 Wilson Blvd Ste 5, Arlington VA 22201	703-528-7482	R	5*	<.1
131	Odell Simms and Associates—*John Simms*	7704 Leesburg Pke, Falls Church VA 22043	703-903-9797	R	5*	<.1
132	Signature Envelope Inc—*Dennis Ready*	6231 Keyko Ste B, Houston TX 77041	713-868-5055	R	5*	<.1
133	Commercial Mail Service Inc—*Louis Gladfelter*	200 N Cross St, Little Rock AR 72201	501-376-2344	R	5*	.1
134	Solo Values—*Don Duncan*	28180 Schoolcraft Rd, Livonia MI 48150	734-458-5380	R	5*	.1
135	Fps Inc—*Frank Sargent*	3390 Enterprise Ave, Hayward CA 94545	510-293-2200	R	5*	.1
136	Tri-Win Outsourcing Inc—*Scott Fish*	14335 Inwood Rd Ste 10, Dallas TX 75244	214-826-2244	R	5*	<.1
137	M and M Associates Inc—*Mary Edwards*	301 Oxford Valley Rd 1, Yardley PA 19067	215-321-3099	R	5*	<.1
138	Promotions On Campus Inc—*Lita Thorne*	314 Harriman Heights R, Harriman NY 10926	845-783-4569	R	5*	<.1
139	Lynchburg Presort Service—*Richard Tucker*	PO Box 10806, Lynchburg VA 24506	434-237-7080	R	5*	<.1
140	Amity Unlimited Inc—*Robert Jansen*	531 N Wayne Ave, Cincinnati OH 45215	513-554-4500	R	5*	.1
141	California Mailing Service Inc—*Raymond Buckner*	2375 Paragon Dr, San Jose CA 95131	408-435-0990	R	5*	<.1
142	Mailrite Inc—*Whitman Wheeler*	78 River Rd S Ste 1, Putney VT 05346	802-387-5157	R	5*	<.1
143	Zip Mailing Services Inc—*Charlain Bland*	3118 Hubbard Rd, Landover MD 20785	301-386-3633	R	4*	<.1
144	Datadirect Inc—*John Coggin*	2707 Peachtree Sq, Atlanta GA 30340	678-530-0034	R	4*	<.1
145	A M Mailing Services Inc—*Marty Ochs*	100 Interstate Blvd, Edgerton WI 53534	608-884-3452	R	4*	<.1
146	Western American Mailers Inc—*Timothy Higgins*	5510 33rd St Se, Grand Rapids MI 49512	616-957-6245	R	4*	<.1
147	Marketplace Direct Inc—*Theodore Swoger*	1 Sexton Rd, Mc Kees Rocks PA 15136	412-771-6650	R	4*	<.1
148	Commonwealth Mailing Systems Inc—*David Campbell*	1700 Venable St, Richmond VA 23223	804-780-1700	R	4*	<.1
149	Communication Mailing Services Inc—*Ronald Weislow*	429 Prior Ave N, Saint Paul MN 55104	651-645-5280	R	4*	<.1
150	Select Publishing Inc—*Chris Houden*	6417 Normandy Ln Ste 2, Madison WI 53719	608-277-5787	R	4*	<.1
151	Last Word—*Jeff Goodson*	1601 Burlington St, Kansas City MO 64116	816-474-5330	R	4*	<.1
152	A Sort Inc—*James Scott*	5521 Cleveland Rd Ext, South Bend IN 46628	574-237-0087	R	4*	.1
153	United Letter Service Inc—*Erin Grogan*	2200 Estes Ave, Elk Grove Village IL 60007	847-588-7600	R	4*	<.1
154	Clark Mailing Service Inc—*Robert Clark*	41 Jackson St, Worcester MA 01608	508-752-1953	R	4*	<.1
155	Adserts Inc—*Michael Guest*	1675 N Barker Rd Ste 1, Brookfield WI 53045	262-794-9010	R	4*	<.1
156	Fredrick Enterprises Inc—*Stanley Fredrick*	6104 Brown Station Rd, Columbia MO 65202	573-474-8877	R	4*	<.1
157	Woodlands Mailing and Fulfillment—*Beth Andreas*	2319 Timberloch Pl Ste, The Woodlands TX 77380	281-363-9261	R	4*	<.1
158	Creative Strategy Inc—*Sally A Roffman*	5454 Wisconsin Ave Ste, Chevy Chase MD 20815	301-718-4550	R	4*	<.1
159	Corporate Communications Center Inc—*Ben Soderquist*	4030 Harry Hines Blvd, Dallas TX 75219	214-871-2941	R	4*	<.1
160	Datamasters Inc—*David Richenbacher*	6101 Long Praire Rd 74, Flower Mound TX 75028	972-625-2400	R	4*	<.1
161	Intrepid Group Inc—*Erin Maranjian*	1331 Red Cedar Cir, Fort Collins CO 80524	970-493-3793	R	4*	.1
162	Healthways Communications Inc—*Thomas Whelan*	600 Mdwlands Pkwy Ste, Secaucus NJ 07094	201-864-1500	R	4*	<.1
163	Capital Mailing Services Inc—*Julian Kasten*	12051 Indian Creek Ct, Beltsville MD 20705	301-210-4600	R	4*	<.1
164	Source D/M Inc—*Lorraine Noah*	PO Box 10033, Fairfield NJ 07004	973-276-1930	R	4*	<.1
165	Corporate Mailing And Fulfillment Solutions Corp—*Georgia Barsa*	31 Styertowne Rd, Clifton NJ 07012	973-777-3484	R	4*	<.1
166	Blue Chip Mailing Services Inc—*Peter Ruttenberg*	6665 Creek Rd, Blue Ash OH 45242	513-541-4800	R	4*	<.1
167	Aka Printing and Mailing—*Paul Brown*	44 Joseph Mills Dr, Fredericksburg VA 22408	540-373-1111	R	4*	.1
168	On Target Marketing LLC	11611 E 51st Ave, Denver CO 80239	303-307-4203	R	4*	<.1
169	A and E Mailers Inc—*Alan Strober*	126 W 4th St, Plainfield NJ 07060	908-756-3666	R	4*	<.1
170	Hicks and Whittier Inc—*Gregory Wells*	PO Box 5405, Charlottesville VA 22905	434-984-0006	R	4*	<.1
171	JHL Mail Marketing Inc—*Joseph Leek*	3100 Borham Ave, Stevens Point WI 54481	715-341-0581	R	4*	<.1
172	Fulfillment Partners Inc—*Frank Craig*	1978 Stanhome Way, Orlando FL 32804	407-660-8606	R	4*	<.1
173	Ray Flaig—*Ray Flaig*	2594 Leghorn St, Mountain View CA 94043	650-919-1999	R	4*	<.1
174	Suburban Mailing Services Inc—*Margaret Euwema*	2020 Swift Dr, Oak Brook IL 60523	630-368-9800	R	4*	<.1
175	Dayton Mailing Services Inc—*Christine Soward*	PO Box 2436, Dayton OH 45401	937-222-5056	R	4*	<.1
176	G-Plex Inc—*James Craig*	194 Morris Ave Ste 7, Holtsville NY 11742	631-447-9500	R	4*	<.1
177	Corporate Marketing Inc—*Kevin Taylor*	12200 Ford Rd Ste 180, Dallas TX 75234	972-620-2136	R	3*	<.1
178	Yeck Brothers Co—*Robert Yeck*	PO Box 225, Dayton OH 45401	937-294-4000	R	3*	<.1
179	Promotion Execution Partners LLC—*Gustavo Bermudo*	151 W 4th St Ste 700, Cincinnati OH 45202	513-826-0101	R	3*	<.1
180	Direct Mail Services Ltd—*Dan Shaver*	999 S Jason St, Denver CO 80223	303-778-5959	R	3*	<.1
181	Douglas Durand Inc—*Douglas Waldron*	12720 Wentworth St, Arleta CA 91331	818-768-2777	R	3*	<.1
182	GS and W Services Inc—*Lourette Grizzle*	PO Box 703, Walnut CA 91788	909-595-7487	R	3*	<.1
183	Cardinal Services Ltd—*Malia Lageman*	552 N Nimitz Hwy, Honolulu HI 96817	808-538-3884	R	3*	<.1
184	ADS Media Group Inc—*Clark R Doyal*	12758 Cimarron Path St, San Antonio TX 78249	210-655-6613	P	3	<.1

Rank	Company Name—*Executive Officer*	Address, City, State, Zip	Phone	Type	Fin	Empls
185	S and L Mailing Service Inc—*Michael Lynch*	9 Gallen Rd, Kingston MA 02364	781-585-8220	R	3*	<.1
186	Spectrum Business Solutions—*Robert Ruiz*	27 Musick, Irvine CA 92618	949-472-5900	R	3*	<.1
187	Accurate Business Mailers Inc—*John Lovshe*	2321 Locust St, Saint Louis MO 63103	314-231-8220	R	3*	<.1
188	Columbus Capital Partners LLC	7700 Bonhomme Ave Ste, Saint Louis MO 63105	314-692-8060	R	3*	<.1
189	Personal Marketing Company Inc—*John Wendorff*	PO Box 656, Shawnee Mission KS 66201	913-492-0377	R	3*	<.1
190	Direct Response Holdings LLC—*Eric Ziman*	45 W 45th St Ste 16l, New York NY 10036	212-201-0600	R	3*	<.1
191	Best Rate Referrals LLC—*Raymond Bartreau*	6785 W Russell Rd Ste, Las Vegas NV 89118	702-262-1690	R	3	<.1
192	Duffy and Shanley Inc—*Jon Duffy*	10 Charles St, Providence RI 02904	401-274-0001	R	3*	<.1
,193	Postal Mail Sort Inc—*Jeff Hill*	PO Box 6542, Youngstown OH 44501	330-747-1515	R	3*	<.1
194	Crell Advertising Co—*Leonard Castaldi*	410 8th St, Gloucester City NJ 08030	856-456-9396	R	3*	<.1
195	Ozark Mailing Service Inc—*Thomas Barr*	2804 N Oak Grove Ave, Springfield MO 65803	417-866-6100	R	3*	<.1
196	Trevett's Mailing Service LLC	6065 Saint Andrews Rd, Columbia SC 29212	803-781-3150	R	3*	<.1
197	Bus-Let Inc—*Myron Crespin*	2770 Vail Ave, Commerce CA 90040	323-778-6245	R	3*	<.1
198	Expert Communications Inc—*Bara Oscodar*	394 Pacific Ave Fl 1, San Francisco CA 94111	415-981-9900	R	3*	<.1
199	Haynes and Partners Communications Inc—*Charles Krupa*	5745 Lee Rd, Indianapolis IN 46216	317-860-3000	R	3*	<.1
200	MailCoups Inc—*Bill Matthews*	350 Revolutionary Dr, East Taunton MA 02718		S	3*	<.1
201	Hauser List Services Inc—*David Hauser*	91 New York Ave Unit 2, Westbury NY 11590	516-935-8603	R	3*	<.1
202	Mailing Advantages Inc—*John Davies*	14 Lafayette Sq Ste 17, Buffalo NY 14203	716-852-8000	R	3*	<.1
203	Aldinger Inc—*Alan Godfrey*	1669 E Jolly Rd, Lansing MI 48910	517-394-2424	R	3*	<.1
204	Sale Line Inc—*Mark Schlau*	17 W John St Unit 1, Hicksville NY 11801	516-496-4300	R	3*	<.1
205	Automated Direct Mail Service Center Inc—*Max Houss*	3892 Prospect Ave Ste, West Palm Beach FL 33404	561-842-5427	R	3*	<.1
206	DG Printing Inc—*Mark Gagliano*	2401 Palmer Dr Ste B, Schaumburg IL 60173	847-397-7779	R	3*	<.1
207	Automatic Mail Services Inc—*Michael Waskover*	4501 34th St, Long Island City NY 11101	718-361-3091	R	3*	<.1
208	Baker Street Partners Advertising Inc—*Terry Pickett*	15 Lombard St, San Francisco CA 94111	415-659-3900	R	3*	<.1
209	Direct Mail Expertise Inc—*William Lenis*	4915 Nw 159th St, Hialeah FL 33014	305-621-6245	R	3*	<.1
210	Mailings Unlimited—*Paul Rogers*	116 Riverside Industri, Portland ME 04103	207-347-5000	R	3*	<.1
211	Automated Direct Mail Inc—*Jeff Sparks*	1410 N 12th St Ste G, Murray UT 84102	270-753-8887	R	3*	<.1
212	G Amber Corp—*Wes Powell*	2110 Busch Ave, Colorado Springs CO 80904	719-636-1303	R	3*	<.1
213	CJ Mailing and Fulfillment Inc—*Leonard Cerisano*	99 S William St Ste 1, Newburgh NY 12550	845-778-2755	R	3*	<.1
214	Commonwealth Mailing Services Inc—*Michael Stief*	1842 Colonial Village, Lancaster PA 17601	717-560-9107	R	3*	<.1
215	Hathorne Enterprises—*Marilyn Norden*	450 Maple St, Hathorne MA 01937	978-774-2104	R	3*	<.1
216	Creative Mailing Services Inc—*Kevin Kuligowski*	490 Pepper St, Monroe CT 06468	203-459-4007	R	3*	<.1
217	San Jose Mailing Inc—*William Wilson*	1445 S 1st St, San Jose CA 95110	408-971-1911	R	3*	<.1
218	Whittier Mailing Service Inc—*Richard Casford*	12435 Mar Vista St, Whittier CA 90602	562-698-7795	R	3*	<.1
219	Walter Garson Jr and Associates Inc—*Walter Garson*	1370 Adams Rd, Bensalem PA 19020	215-245-6610	R	3*	<.1
220	J and L Marketing Inc—*Scott Joseph*	2100 Nelson Miller Pkw, Louisville KY 40223	502-261-9292	R	3*	<.1
221	Acquire Direct Marketing Inc—*James Hug*	12620 Race Track Rd, Tampa FL 33626	813-854-5700	R	3*	<.1
222	Eye/Communication Inc—*Gregory Gould*	10960 Whtlnds Ave Ste, Santee CA 92071	619-448-6111	R	3*	<.1
223	Cox 1 Inc—*Harry Cox*	593 Berkeley Rd, Columbus OH 43205	614-253-5402	R	2*	<.1
224	Drum Mailing Inc—*George Drum*	1546 E McKinley St, Phoenix AZ 85006	602-252-7142	R	2*	<.1
225	Mass Mailing Inc—*Saul Reichbach*	818 Queens Plz S, Long Island City NY 11101	718-361-9339	R	2*	<.1
226	Red Rose Mailing Services Inc—*Rosy Jedlicka*	6122 Benjamin Rd, Tampa FL 33634	813-676-7673	R	2*	<.1
227	Unit Packaging Corp—*Lynn Voegeding*	119 Enterprise Dr, Ann Arbor MI 48103	734-663-0533	R	2*	<.1
228	Moore Companies Inc—*Christopher Moore*	2001 Dabney Rd, Richmond VA 23230	804-254-8300	R	2*	<.1
229	Direct Resources For Print Inc—*Andrew Constantinou*	PO Box 3992, Houston TX 77253	713-939-9390	R	2*	<.1
230	Computer Assistance Company Inc—*Aileen Sellis*	7650 E Redfield Rd Ste, Scottsdale AZ 85260	480-483-7677	R	2*	<.1
231	American Mailing Service Inc—*Michael Spero*	908 N Hollywood Way, Burbank CA 01505	818-843-6378	R	2*	<.1
232	Ammark Corp—*Jack Hartley*	PO Box 382406, Birmingham AL 35238	205-956-2800	R	2*	<.1
233	Communication Service Center Inc—*Mely Leung*	1099 Mariposa St, San Francisco CA 94107	415-252-1600	R	2*	<.1
234	Quality Mail Marketing Inc—*Jan Hermes*	1651 Badger Rd, Kaukauna WI 54130	920-766-0099	R	2*	<.1
235	Delp Printing and Mailing Inc—*William Delp*	7750 Zionsville Rd Ste, Indianapolis IN 46268	317-872-9744	R	2*	<.1
236	UGM Mailing Service Inc—*William Thompson*	3211 Irving Blvd Ste 1, Dallas TX 75247	214-630-7960	R	2*	<.1
237	Jrc Inc—*Jerry Clark*	PO Box 494155, Redding CA 96049	530-221-6895	R	2*	<.1
238	Greater Data and Mailing Inc—*Steven Loehr*	551 Acorn St, Deer Park NY 11729	631-667-1450	R	2*	<.1
239	Quality Mailing Services Inc—*William Mcandrews*	PO Box 26901, Philadelphia PA 19134	215-291-9552	R	2*	<.1
240	United Forms Finishing Corp—*Elizabeth Demkin*	1413 Chestnut Ave Ste, Hillside NJ 07205	908-687-0494	R	2*	<.1
241	Guaranteed Express Inc—*Mark Whitcomb*	PO Box 62377, Sunnyvale CA 94088	408-729-9200	R	2*	<.1
242	Strategic Market Solutions Inc—*Elaine Ralls*	3419 East University D, Phoenix AZ 85034	480-921-3220	R	2*	<.1
243	Hummel Distributing Corp—*Herbert Hummel*	PO Box 3199, Union NJ 07083	908-688-5300	R	2*	<.1
244	Keary Advertising Company Inc—*Wayne Keary*	PO Box 25966, Baltimore MD 21224	410-285-3700	R	2*	<.1
245	Consolidated Mail Service Inc—*Judy Franco*	98 Reservoir Park Dr, Rockland MA 02370	781-878-4727	R	2*	<.1
246	Gallahers Inc—*John Gallaher*	PO Box 910, Ashland KY 41105	606-329-8383	R	2*	<.1
247	Publisher's Mail Service Inc—*Ronald Fridle*	10545 W Donges Ct, Milwaukee WI 53224	414-354-1423	R	2*	<.1
248	Pacific Rim Printers/Mailers—*Robert Brothers*	5760 Hannum Ave, Culver City CA 90230		R	2*	<.1
249	Turner Marketing Inc—*Hollis Turner*	160 Meister Ave Ste 21, Branchburg NJ 08876	908-595-1400	R	2*	<.1
250	Names In The News California Inc—*Susan Anstrand*	1300 Clay St Fl 11th, Oakland CA 94612	415-989-3350	R	2*	<.1
251	Amerimail Corp—*Edith Duffy*	PO Box 586, North Reading MA 01864	978-664-8222	R	2*	<.1
252	Marketry Inc—*Norm Swent*	11400 SE 8th St Ste 30, Bellevue WA 98004	425-451-1262	R	2*	<.1
253	First Class Direct Inc—*Patty Taylor*	5610 Boeing Dr, Loveland CO 80538	970-224-5066	R	2*	<.1
254	Corsica Enterprises Ltd—*Jay Siff*	812 W Chestnut St, Perkasie PA 18944	215-257-0880	R	2*	<.1
255	Postmark Ink Inc—*Doris Lam*	918 Nichols Ave, Fairhope AL 36532	251-928-1095	R	2*	<.1
256	Allied Mailing and Printing Inc—*Kelli Fonger*	240 N Fenway Dr, Fenton MI 48430	810-750-8291	R	2*	<.1
257	LA Communications Inc—*Blair Talbert*	3110 Odd Fellows Rd, Lynchburg VA 24501	434-847-0620	R	2*	<.1
258	University Of Florida Mail Document Services—*Janet Kiss*	PO Box 112540, Gainesville FL 32611	352-392-0629	R	2*	<.1
259	T and T Transport Inc—*Tyrone Ayers*	4008 Capital Blvd Ste, Raleigh NC 27604	919-790-6822	R	2*	<.1
260	G and H Mail Service LLC	PO Box 901, Columbia SC 29202	803-926-1060	R	2*	<.1
261	Midpoint National Inc—*Ron Freund*	PO Box 411037, Kansas City MO 64141	913-362-7400	R	2*	<.1
262	Western Mailing Lists—*Robert Meyer*	PO Box 220703, Newhall CA 91322	818-781-6216	R	2*	<.1
263	Allied Printing and Mailing Inc—*Jay Berman*	PO Box 142708, Austin TX 78714	512-821-0055	R	2*	<.1
264	Ridgway Mailing And Fulfilment Company Inc—*Alan Linnard*	PO Box 225265, Dallas TX 75222	214-565-0077	R	2*	<.1
265	Alberta Crowe Letter Service Inc—*William Rapp*	108 Metropolitan Park, Liverpool NY 13088	315-457-9333	R	2*	<.1
266	American Mailing and Printing Service Inc—*George Havriluk*	1164 N Kraemer Pl, Anaheim CA 92806	714-630-1361	R	2*	<.1
267	Dunn Dataco Inc—*Stephen Dunn*	2022 Rte 22, Brewster NY 10509	845-278-1200	R	2*	<.1
268	Ars Direct Mail—*Martha Briges*	7480 Bartlett Corp Cv, Memphis TN 38133	901-382-9595	R	2*	<.1
269	Public Service Audience Planners—*M Rafik*	5341 Derry Ave Ste Q, Agoura Hills CA 91301	818-865-1233	R	2*	<.1
270	Full Service Mailers Inc—*Evelio Velez*	PO Box 680, Garfield NJ 07026	973-478-8813	R	2*	<.1
271	Nancy A Palermo—*Nancy Palermo*	91 1 Colin Dr, Holbrook NY 11741	631-926-2630	R	2*	<.1
272	El Paso Mailing Service Inc—*Lorena Armendariz*	PO Box 370943, El Paso TX 79937	915-591-1135	R	1*	<.1
273	Florida Direct Marketing Systems Inc—*Steve Hoffman*	398 S Shell Rd, Debary FL 32713	407-831-0400	R	1*	<.1
274	Streamline Inc—*Roger Palm*	1755 Kirby Pkwy Ste 20, Memphis TN 38120	901-373-2491	R	1*	<.1

Note: An asterisk (*) indicates an estimated financial figure. The company type code used is as follows: R = Private, P = Public, S = Private Subsidiary, B = Public Subsidiary, D = Division, J = Joint Venture, I = Investment Fund.

COMPANY RANKINGS BY SALES WITHIN 4-DIGIT SIC

Rank	Company Name—*Executive Officer*	Address, City, State, Zip	Phone	Type	Fin	Empls
275	Madison Direct Marketing Ltd—*Henry Vega*	60 Long Ridge Rd Ste 2, Stamford CT 06902	203-653-3200	R	1*	<.1
276	Barton and Cooney LLC—*Steve Angel*	300 Richards Run, Burlington NJ 08016	609-747-9300	R	1*	.1
277	JR Mailing Services Inc—*Shelley Romack*	2120 116th Ave Ne Bldg, Bellevue WA 98004	425-454-7443	R	1*	<.1
278	Gilmore Associates LLC—*Sandra Gilmore*	6851 Sw 21st Ct Ste 6, Davie FL 33317	954-474-6851	R	1*	<.1
279	Better Lists Inc—*George Rath*	64 Sunnyside Ave, Stamford CT 06902	203-324-4171	R	1*	<.1
280	Leon Henry Inc—*Leon Henry Jr*	200 N Central Ave Ste, Hartsdale NY 10530	914-285-3456	R	1*	<.1
281	Atlantic List Company Inc—*Ingrid Louikota*	2425 Wilson Blvd Ste 5, Arlington VA 22201	703-528-7482	R	1*	<.1
282	Cleveland Letter Service Inc—*Charles Janes*	2150 Saint Clair Ave N, Cleveland OH 44114	216-781-8300	R	1*	<.1
283	Gnames Media Group Inc—*Holly Z Hammond*	1452 Hughes Rd Rm 320, Grapevine TX 76051	972-871-2828	R	1*	<.1
284	Mailpro Inc—*Ann Makowiecki*	1071 Mill Rd, Duncansville PA 16635	814-695-8822	R	1*	<.1
285	Marketing Company Inc—*Pope Hoffman*	42 South Ave Ste 1, Natick MA 01760	508-655-4300	R	1*	<.1
286	MGP Direct Inc—*Roberta Rosenburg*	PO Box 292, Clarksville MD 21029	410-531-0383	R	1*	<.1
287	World Wide Mailing LLC—*Robert Davis*	1827 Fremont Dr Ste B, Salt Lake City UT 84104	801-973-4057	R	1*	<.1
288	David J Thompson Mailing Corp—*David Thompson*	PO Box 150, Bloomsburg PA 17815	570-759-6690	R	1*	.4
289	Next Generation Energy Corp—*Darryl Reed*	7351 Unit N Lockport P, Lorton VA 22079	703-372-1282	P	<1	<.1
290	Arena Communications LLC—*Peter Valcarce*	1142 W 2320 S, Salt Lake City UT 84119	801-595-8339	R	N/A	<.1

TOTALS: SIC 7331 Direct Mail Advertising Services
Companies: 290   7,922   39.8

7334 Photocopying & Duplicating Services

Rank	Company Name—*Executive Officer*	Address, City, State, Zip	Phone	Type	Fin	Empls
1	FedEx Office and Print Services Inc—*Brian Philips*	13155 Noel Rd Ste 1600, Dallas TX 75240	214-550-7000	S	2,334*	25.0
2	CreoScitex America Inc—*Antonio Perez*	343 State St, Rochester NY 14650		D	113	.6
3	Access to Money Inc—*Richard B Stern*	1101 Kings Highway N S, Cherry Hill NJ 08034		P	78	.1
4	Thomas Reprographics Inc—*Bryan Thomas*	600 N Central Expy, Richardson TX 75080	972-231-7227	R	58*	.5
5	On-Site Sourcing Inc—*Robert Ballou*	832 N Henry St, Alexandria VA 22314	703-276-1123	S	47*	.9
6	Polaris Direct LLC—*Joseph Maloy*	300 Technology Dr, Hooksett NH 03106	603-626-5800	R	42*	.1
7	National Reprographics Inc—*Nan Magid*	44 W 18th St Fl 3, New York NY 10011	212-366-7000	R	18*	.3
8	Mimeo Inc—*Adam Slutsky*	460 Park Ave S Fl 8, New York NY 10016	212-847-3000	R	17*	.1
9	Reliable Copy Service Inc—*Mike Trudgeon*	1801 Market St Ste 660, Philadelphia PA 19103	215-563-3363	R	15*	.3
10	Hon Blue Inc—*Lawrence Heim*	501 Sumner St Ste 3b1, Honolulu HI 96817	808-531-4611	R	12*	.1
11	Quality Associates Inc (Columbia Maryland)—*Paul Swidersky*	8161 Maple Lawn Blvd 2, Fulton MD 20759	410-884-9100	R	11*	.1
12	Crisp Enterprises Inc—*Gary Crisp*	3180 Pullman St, Costa Mesa CA 92626	714-545-2743	R	10*	.1
13	Cushing And Co—*Cathleen Duff*	420 W Huron St, Chicago IL 60654	312-266-8228	R	9*	.1
14	Trace Communications LLC—*Andy Medley*	7225 Georgetown Rd, Indianapolis IN 46268	317-715-5700	R	9	<.1
15	Winter Park Blueprint Company Inc—*Robert Niemi*	PO Box 940959, Maitland FL 32794	407-647-3034	R	9*	.1
16	Structural Research and Analysis Corp—*Charles Edelstenne*	3000 Ocean Park Blvd S, Santa Monica CA 90405	310-309-2800	D	8*	.1
17	Bfs Business Printing Inc—*Benjamin Smith*	320 Stuart St, Boston MA 02116	617-426-1160	R	8*	.1
18	H and H Graphics Inc—*Mary Kohler*	854 N Prince St, Lancaster PA 17603	717-393-3941	R	7*	.1
19	Information On Demand—*Dianne Vollgraff*	4622 E St Rd, Feasterville Trevose PA 19053	215-364-5900	R	7*	.1
20	Reproductions Inc—*Jeff Prideaux*	PO Box 731, Tucson AZ 85702	520-622-7747	R	7*	.1
21	Vci Group Inc—*Paul Magaziner*	PO Box 56264, Houston TX 77256	713-626-4045	R	7*	.1
22	Bennett's Business Systems Inc—*Mike Abney*	4737 Dellwood Ave, Jacksonville FL 32205	904-384-7800	S	7*	.1
23	American Blueprinting and Supply Inc—*Troy Smith*	750 Clay St, Winter Park FL 32789	407-644-5366	R	6*	.1
24	Unlimited Reprographics—*Jeffery Scholz*	PO Box 71467, Los Angeles CA 90071	213-892-9000	R	6*	.1
25	Dsi Document Solutions Inc—*Tom Turner*	414 Union St Ste 1210, Nashville TN 37219	615-255-5343	R	6*	.1
26	Best Imaging Solutions Inc—*Constance Luncsford*	20 E Randolph St Fl Me, Chicago IL 60601	312-357-9050	R	6*	.1
27	Bay Reprographics Inc—*Martha Korman*	5005 W Laurel St Ste 2, Tampa FL 33607	813-286-8520	R	6*	.1
28	Alabama Graphics and Engineering Supply Inc—*John Davis*	2801 5th Ave S, Birmingham AL 35233	205-252-8505	R	5*	.1
29	Litigation Solution Inc—*Terry Vaughan*	901 Main St Ste C121, Dallas TX 75202	214-939-9700	R	5*	<.1
30	GSO Graphics Inc—*Christine Diiorio*	440 9th Ave Fl 14, New York NY 10001	212-695-8300	R	5*	<.1
31	Associated Creditors Inc—*Ramon Trevino*	PO Box 171170, San Antonio TX 78217	210-822-1908	R	5*	<.1
32	Barker Blue Digital Imaging Inc—*Eugene Klein*	363 N Amphlett Blvd, San Mateo CA 94401	650-696-2100	R	4*	<.1
33	Ace Reprographic Service Inc—*Arthur Scialla*	74 E 30th St, Paterson NJ 07514	973-684-5945	R	4*	<.1
34	Campus Copy Partners Inc—*Craig Fairbanks*	2560 Bancroft Way, Berkeley CA 94704	510-655-1906	R	4*	<.1
35	Goodcopy Printing Center Inc—*Louis Goldberg*	PO Box 8088, New Haven CT 06530	203-624-0194	R	4*	<.1
36	Pdq Printing Of Las Vegas Inc—*Charles Lawson*	3820 S Valley View Blv, Las Vegas NV 89103	702-876-3235	R	4*	<.1
37	Copy General Corp—*Kenneth Chaletzky*	102 Executive Dr Ste G, Sterling VA 20166	703-478-5252	R	4*	<.1
38	Savannah Blueprint Co—*George Martin*	PO Box 16417, Savannah GA 31416	912-232-2162	R	4*	<.1
39	All-American Printing Services Corp—*Darren Keffury*	1324 Rand St, Petaluma CA 94954	415-899-1000	R	4*	<.1
40	Tree Towns Reprographics Inc—*Lawrence Hageland*	542 S Spring Rd, Elmhurst IL 60126	630-832-0209	R	4*	<.1
41	Universal Reproductions Inc—*Rikki Parry*	2706 Wilshire Blvd, Los Angeles CA 90057	213-365-7750	R	4*	<.1
42	National Color Corp—*Michael Labadie*	12 Channel St Ste 802, Boston MA 02210	617-330-1200	R	4*	<.1
43	Eastern Engineering Supply Inc—*Mary Langdon*	2810 N Wheeling Ave, Muncie IN 47303	765-284-3119	R	3*	<.1
44	Copy Zone Ltd—*James Collins*	4131 N 10th St, Mcallen TX 78504	956-668-9600	R	3*	<.1
45	Pro-Copy Inc—*Jon Statham*	5219 E Fowler Ave, Temple Terrace FL 33617	813-988-5900	R	3*	<.1
46	University Reader Co—*Bassin Hamadeh*	3970 Sorrento Valley B, San Diego CA 92121	858-552-1120	R	3*	<.1
47	Met Photo Inc—*Jim Fishbach*	1500 Broadway Bsmt C2, New York NY 10036	212-869-6960	R	3*	<.1
48	Art Bookbinders Of America Inc—*Mario Poulet*	451 N Claremont Ave, Chicago IL 60612	312-226-4100	R	3*	<.1
49	Quality Litigation Services Inc—*Angelo Salandra*	1628 Jfk Blvd Ste 1810, Philadelphia PA 19103	215-564-2679	R	3*	<.1
50	Professional Reproductions Inc—*Patrick Maloney*	7415 Cahill Rd, Edina MN 55439	952-946-1200	R	3*	<.1
51	Delmar Office Products—*Bruce Howe*	13465 Gregg St, Poway CA 92064	858-481-8488	R	3*	<.1
52	T Sammi Inc—*Craig Fairbanks*	5901 Christie Ave Ste, Emeryville CA 94608	510-655-1906	R	3*	<.1
53	Abbott's Custom Printing—*Lorri Abbott*	6275 Harrison Dr Ste 5, Las Vegas NV 89120	702-456-8099	R	3*	<.1
54	California On-Site Copying—*Mark Holman*	PO Box 18116, Anaheim CA 92817	714-632-3480	R	3*	<.1
55	Xerographic Reproduction Center Inc—*Roger Gimbel*	350 Hudson St Frnt 3, New York NY 10014	212-929-9100	R	3*	<.1
56	Gurrola Reprographics Inc—*Charles Gurrola*	6161 Washington Ave, Houston TX 77007	713-861-4277	R	3*	<.1
57	Reynolds Brothers Ltd—*James Franklin*	315 N Colorado St, Midland TX 79701	432-682-7393	R	3*	<.1
58	Atlas Blue Print and Supply Co—*Gerald Schueller*	PO Box 305, Columbus OH 43216	614-224-5149	S	3*	<.1
59	Foley's Graphic Center Inc—*Joseph Foley*	1661 Front St Ste 3, Yorktown Heights NY 10598	914-245-3625	R	3*	<.1
60	Profile Digital Printing LLC—*Terry Harmeyer*	5449 Marina Dr, Dayton OH 45449	937-866-4241	R	3*	<.1
61	United Reprographic Services Inc—*Vincent Carbonell*	40 W 25th St Fl 5, New York NY 10010	212-645-6918	R	3*	<.1
62	Copy King Inc—*Margaret Walsh*	3333 Chester Ave, Cleveland OH 44114	216-861-3377	R	3*	<.1
63	Target Copy Inc—*Mayda Williams*	635 W Tennessee St, Tallahassee FL 32304	850-224-3007	R	3*	<.1
64	City Blue Imaging Services Inc—*Mark Cleary*	68 Scio St, Rochester NY 14604	585-454-1695	R	3*	<.1
65	Summit Document Services Of Atlanta LLC—*Chris Despot*	230 Peachtree St Ste 9, Atlanta GA 30303	404-659-6800	R	2*	<.1
66	Zebra Print Solutions Inc—*Charlotte Dileonardo*	9401 Globe Ctr Dr Ste, Morrisville NC 27560	919-981-0517	R	2*	<.1
67	Plan and Print Systems Inc—*John Lipari*	PO Box 218, East Syracuse NY 13057	315-437-3907	R	2*	<.1
68	D Litigation Support Services Inc—*Christopher Egan*	219 E 44th St Fl 5, New York NY 10017	212-697-1101	R	2*	<.1
69	Ashby and Ashby Inc—*William Ashby*	6103 Johns Rd Ste 5, Tampa FL 33634	813-886-0065	R	2*	<.1
70	SE Blueprint Copying—*John Essi*	2035 Hamilton Ave, Cleveland OH 44114	216-274-0584	R	2*	<.1

Rank	Company Name—*Executive Officer*	Address, City, State, Zip	Phone	Type	Fin	Empls
71	Ink Spot Inc—*Cathie Laufketter*	5755 Chippewa St, Saint Louis MO 63109	314-353-0938	R	2*	<.1
72	Taylor Morse Ltd—*Mace Morse*	23422 Mill Creek Dr St, Laguna Hills CA 92653	949-707-5031	R	2*	<.1
73	Business Records Management Services Inc—*Bruce Berkely*	PO Box 953, Harrisburg PA 17108	717-233-2250	R	2*	<.1
74	Paper Mill Graphix Inc—*Sonny Mehta*	2 Armonk St, Greenwich CT 06830	203-661-0020	R	2*	<.1
75	Andrew T Johnson Company Inc—*Robert Leslie*	15 Tremont Pl, Boston MA 02108	617-742-1610	R	2*	<.1
76	Colortech Graphics and Printing Inc—*C Booker*	4000 Business Park Dr, Columbus OH 43204	614-766-2400	R	2*	<.1
77	Morris Mailing Inc—*Michael Morris*	1098 Brown St, Wauconda IL 60084	847-487-5447	R	2*	.1
78	Landmark Document Services-Chicago LLC	200 W Adams St Ste 170, Chicago IL 60606	312-845-1000	R	2*	<.1
79	Reprographics Specialists Inc—*Peter Kennedy*	1620 Eye St Nw, Washington DC 20006	202-467-4444	R	2*	<.1
80	Technigraphics Inc—*John Gross*	PO Box 1846, Iowa City IA 52244	319-354-5950	R	2*	<.1
81	On-Line Copy Corp—*Loren Smuzinich*	48815 Kato Rd, Fremont CA 94539	510-226-6810	S	2*	<.1
82	Snap Print Of Hopkins Inc—*Dan Dorholt*	26 Shady Oak Rd S, Hopkins MN 55343	952-935-0506	R	2*	<.1
83	Consolidated Software Services Inc—*Michael S Brown*	2365 Paragon Dr Ste B, San Jose CA 95131	408-451-0620	R	2*	<.1
84	Service Photo Copy Inc—*Judy Baiamonte*	815 Walker St Ste 101, Houston TX 77002	713-225-1988	R	2*	<.1
85	Copies Plus Printing Inc—*Michael Ewing*	717 N Main St Ste 102, Springville UT 84663	801-489-3456	R	2*	<.1
86	Baker Graphics Corp—*Richard Baker*	1032 Post Rd E, Westport CT 06880	203-226-6928	R	2*	<.1
87	Easy Print Inc—*Ervin Bergen*	501 S Jackson St, Amarillo TX 79101	806-374-8270	R	2*	<.1
88	AB Athens Inc—*Julie Mcleod*	163 E Broad St, Athens GA 30601	706-548-3648	R	2*	<.1
89	Hiatt Enterprises Inc—*Chris Hiatt*	1716 N Wheeling Ave St, Muncie IN 47303	765-289-7756	R	2*	<.1
90	Advanced Photo Copy Services—*Micheal Brown*	3500 5th Ave Ste 202, San Diego CA 92103	619-299-4772	R	1*	<.1
91	La Salle Copy Service—*Ray Kontof*	300 S Wacker Dr Ste 60, Chicago IL 60606	312-341-1443	R	1*	<.1
92	Ssttech Inc—*F Phifer*	788 E Brookhaven Cir, Memphis TN 38117	901-681-9909	R	1*	<.1
93	Transfer Graphics Inc—*Michael Cooper*	1024 Dallas Dr, Denton TX 76205	940-566-2679	R	1*	<.1
94	Gorilla Graphics Inc—*Craig Murphy*	21 Mcgrath Hwy Ste 4, Somerville MA 02143	617-623-2838	R	1*	<.1
95	Unitech Copy Center Inc—*Howard Kopel*	2344 Hempstead Tpke, East Meadow NY 11554	516-735-1500	R	1*	<.1
96	General Operating Corp—*Charles Fraser*	575 Cooke St Ste C, Honolulu HI 96813	808-941-6602	R	1*	<.1
97	Dynamic Reprographics Inc—*Lisa Tipps*	817 W 12 St, Austin TX 78701	512-474-8842	R	1*	<.1
98	Laser Printer Services Co—*Mohammed Mukhtar*	959 S Kingsley Dr, Los Angeles CA 90006	213-739-1551	R	1*	<.1
99	Play-it Productions Inc—*Tony Tyler*	259 W 30th St 3rd Fl, New York NY 10001	212-695-6530	R	1*	<.1
100	Lion Recording Services Inc—*Richard Lion*	7532 Fullerton Ct, Springfield VA 22153	703-569-3200	R	1*	<.1
101	Dataworld Service Inc—*Patricia Yioh*	262 Atlantic St, Stamford CT 06901	203-329-8926	R	<1*	<.1
102	Ridgeleys—*Herbert Mathias*	950 Penn Ave Ste 1, Pittsburgh PA 15222	412-281-1800	H	<1*	<.1

TOTALS: SIC 7334 Photocopying & Duplicating Services
Companies: 102   **3,052**   **31.1**

7335 Commercial Photography

Rank	Company Name—*Executive Officer*	Address, City, State, Zip	Phone	Type	Fin	Empls
1	OnRequest Images Inc—*Carla Stratfold*	1415 Western Ave, Seattle WA 98101	206-774-1555	R	10*	.1
2	Fraternal Composite Service Inc—*Carol Rooney*	169 Campbell Ave, Utica NY 13502	315-733-0593	R	8*	.1
3	Visual Image Photography Inc—*Thomas Hayes*	W63n582 Hanover Ave, Cedarburg WI 53012	262-375-4457	R	7*	.1
4	Image Craft LLC—*Linda Collman*	3401 E Brdwy Rd Ste 15, Phoenix AZ 85040	602-276-2082	R	7*	.1
5	Tribuzio Hilliard Studio Inc—*Charles Hilliard*	PO Box 35307, Greensboro NC 27425	336-855-8220	R	6*	.1
6	Pixxures Inc	15000 W 64th Ave, Arvada CO 80007	303-302-8600	S	5*	<.1
7	Professional Litho-Art Company Inc—*Craig Hanson*	807 13th Ave S, Minneapolis MN 55404	612-338-0400	R	5*	.1
8	Graphics Universal Inc—*A Calvert*	12437 E 60th St, Tulsa OK 74146	918-461-0609	R	5*	.1
9	Neuhaus Investment Company Inc—*Laurence B Neuhaus*	10500 Northwest Fwy St, Houston TX 77092	713-681-2000	R	4*	<.1
10	Colorfast Of New York Inc—*John Arbucci*	121 Varick St Fl 10, New York NY 10013	212-929-2440	R	4*	<.1
11	Fotel Inc—*John Nachtrieb*	1125 E Saint Charles H, Lombard IL 60148	630-932-7520	R	3*	<.1
12	Premium Color Graphics Inc—*John Watson*	95b Industrial St E, Clifton NJ 07012	973-472-7007	R	3*	<.1
13	Sanford Studios Inc—*Donald Sanford*	14108 Whittier Blvd, Whittier CA 90605	562-698-0071	R	3*	<.1
14	Colorvision International Inc—*Mark Simmons*	8250 Exchange Dr Ste 1, Orlando FL 32809	407-851-0103	R	3*	<.1
15	Image Photo Services Inc—*Brynley Davies*	2085 Nw 87th Ave Ste A, Doral FL 33172	305-476-3666	R	3*	<.1
16	Sky Portraits Inc—*Ronald Lemmer*	PO Box 50, Marshfield WI 54449	715-387-0076	R	3*	<.1
17	Bassetti Photo Inc—*Bruce Bassetti*	PO Box 695, Minotola NJ 08341	856-697-0770	R	3*	<.1
18	Aliceblue—*Mary Gibson*	1329 E Cary St Ste 300, Richmond VA 23219	804-545-7260	R	2*	<.1
19	Aero Graphics Inc—*Stan Francis*	40 W Oakland Ave, Salt Lake City UT 84115	801-487-3273	R	2*	<.1
20	Scantech Color Systems Inc—*Robert Venable*	2902 Farber Dr, Champaign IL 61822	217-355-8600	R	2*	<.1
21	Digital Impressions Of Central Florida Inc—*Richard Darden*	5801 Benjamin Ctr Dr S, Tampa FL 33634	813-901-5454	R	2*	<.1
22	Image Studios Inc—*Donna Gehl*	1100 S Lyndale Dr, Appleton WI 54914		R	2*	<.1
23	Brenner Photo Productions—*Jay Brenner*	125 Newton Rd Ste 100, Plainview NY 11803	516-586-5959	R	2*	<.1
24	Grins Sportspage Inc—*Martin Finn*	1807 Cottontail Dr, Oshkosh WI 54904	920-589-1132	R	2*	<.1
25	Propix—*Todd Cherry*	354 Mountain Way Dr, Orem UT 84058	801-224-9696	R	2*	<.1
26	Civil Solutions Inc—*Chris Raymond*	PO Box 579, Hammonton NJ 08037	609-561-7400	R	1*	<.1
27	North Coast Consultants Inc—*Jeannette Kravitz*	411 W Ontario St Apt 7, Chicago IL 60654	312-573-1113	R	1*	<.1
28	Candid Color Photography Ltd—*Stephen Araujo*	PO Box 124, Occoquan VA 22125	703-590-0187	R	1*	<.1
29	Sonneys Photography—*Miles Sonney*	9039 Wattsburg Rd, Erie PA 16509	814-825-1800	R	1*	<.1
30	American Colorscans Inc—*Bruce Westfall*	5174 Sinclair Rd, Columbus OH 43229	614-895-0233	R	1*	<.1
31	Black Star Publishing Company Inc—*Benjamin Chapnick*	116 E 27th St, New York NY 10016	212-679-3288	R	1*	<.1
32	Terry Heffernan Films—*Terry Heffernan*	991 Tennessee St, San Francisco CA 94107	415-641-3000	R	1	<.1
33	Kroll Photography—*Geoffrey Kroll*	3005 S Lamar Blvd, Austin TX 78704	512-913-8700	R	N/A	<.1

TOTALS: SIC 7335 Commercial Photography
Companies: 33   **105**   **1.1**

7336 Commercial Art & Graphic Design

Rank	Company Name—*Executive Officer*	Address, City, State, Zip	Phone	Type	Fin	Empls
1	Continental Graphics Corp—*David Malmo*	6141 Katella Ave, Cypress CA 90630	714-503-4200	S	633*	1.2
2	Advanced Green Technologies Inc—*Fred Drasner*	2100 NW 21st Ave, Fort Lauderdale FL 33311	954-735-2641	R	424	3.2
3	Color By Deluxe—*Cyril Drabinsky*	1377 N Serrano Ave, Hollywood CA 90027	323-960-3600	R	290*	.6
4	Laika—*Dale Wahl*	1400 NW 22nd Ave, Portland OR 97210	503-225-1130	R	221*	.5
5	Image Bank Getty Images—*Johnathan Klein*	75 Varick St, New York NY 10013	646-613-4000	R	143*	.3
6	Concept One Accessories—*Sam Hafif*	119 W 40th St, New York NY 10018	212-868-2590	R	72*	.2
7	VSA Partners Inc—*Dana Arnett*	600 W Chicago Ave Ste, Chicago IL 60654	312-427-6413	R	57*	.1
8	DogHouse Technologies—*Robert Parrack*	1932 Drew St Ste 3, Clearwater FL 33765	727-442-8869	R	49*	.1
9	Moosylvania Marketing—*Norty Cohen*	7303 Marietta, Saint Louis MO 63143	314-644-7900	R	44*	.1
10	Molecular—*Howard Kogan*	343 Arsenal St, Watertown MA 02472	617-218-6500	S	42*	.1
11	Schawk Retail Marketing—*Michael Komasinki*	1 N Dearborn St 7th Fl, Chicago IL 60602	312-666-9200	S	41*	.4
12	Convey Compliance Systems Inc—*Brian Provost*	3650 Annapolis Ln Ste, Plymouth MN 55447		R	37*	.1
13	Curran and Connors Inc—*Scott L Greenberg*	140 Adams Ave Ste 20C, Hauppauge NY 11788	631-435-0400	R	33*	.1
14	Moxie Interactive Inc—*Scott Neslund*	384 Northyards Blvd NW, Atlanta GA 30313	678-916-4500	S	33*	.1
15	Affinity Express Inc—*Kenneth Swanson*	2200 Point Blvd Ste 13, Elgin IL 60123	847-930-3200	R	32*	.8
16	Larsen Design and Interactive—*Tim Larsen*	7101 York Ave S Ste 12, Minneapolis MN 55435	952-835-2271	R	32*	.1

Note: An asterisk (*) indicates an estimated financial figure. The company type code used is as follows: R = Private, P = Public, S = Private Subsidiary, B = Public Subsidiary, D = Division, J = Joint Venture, I = Investment Fund.

COMPANY RANKINGS BY SALES WITHIN 4-DIGIT SIC

Rank	Company Name—*Executive Officer*	Address, City, State, Zip	Phone	Type	Fin	Empls
17	Air Hollywood—*Talaat Captan*	13240 Weidner St, Pacoima CA 91331	818-890-6801	R	29*	.1
18	frog design inc—*Doreen Lorenzo*	660 3rd St 4th Fl, San Francisco CA 94107	415-442-4804	S	29*	.1
19	Cannery—*Doug Textor*	727 S Main St, Burbank CA 91506	818-237-5900	R	27*	.1
20	National Geographic Film Library—*Matthew White*	1145 17th St NW, Washington DC 20036	202-857-7659	R	27*	.1
21	onShore Inc—*Stelios Valavanis*	1407 W Chicago Ave, Chicago IL 60642	312-850-5200	R	26*	.1
22	RDA International LLC—*Michael Racz*	100 Vamdam St1st Fl, New York NY 10013	212-255-7700	R	26*	.1
23	Bright Ideas in Broad Ripple Inc—*Beverly Middaugh*	7425 Westfield Blvd, Indianapolis IN 46240	317-257-4111	R	26*	<.1
24	Believe Media—*Luke Thornton*	1040 N Las Palmas Bldg, Los Angeles CA 90038	323-645-1000	R	25*	.1
25	Idea Bank—*Larry Sivitz*	11022 Wing Point Way N, Seattle WA 98110	206-842-5420	R	25*	.1
26	Bluemedia—*Jared Smith*	1725 W 3rd St, Tempe AZ 85281	480-317-1333	R	24*	.1
27	Lipman Hearne Inc—*Robert Moore*	200 S Michigan Ave Ste, Chicago IL 60604	312-356-8000	R	21*	.1
28	Broad St Productions—*Mark Baltazar*	20 W 22 12th Fl, New York NY 10010	212-780-5700	R	21*	<.1
29	Presentation Strategies Inc—*Robert Befus*	PO Box 13873, Durham NC 27709	919-767-9400	R	21*	<.1
30	Gsp Marketing Technologies Inc—*Geoff Neuhoff*	5400 140th Ave N, Clearwater FL 33760	727-532-0647	R	20*	.2
31	Metro Creative Graphics Inc—*Robert Zimmerman*	519 8th Ave, New York NY 10018	212-947-5100	R	19*	.1
32	Photo Researchers Inc—*Robert Zentmaier*	307 5th Avenue, New York NY 10016	212-758-3420	R	19*	<.1
33	Graphic Design Services Inc—*Jan Noller*	13730 Rose Crans Ave, Santa Fe Springs CA 90670	562-282-8000	R	18*	<.1
34	Gfx International Inc—*Charles Huttinger*	333 Barron Blvd, Grayslake IL 60030	847-543-4600	R	18*	.2
35	Borenstein Group—*Gal Borenstein*	11320 Random Hills Rd, Fairfax VA 22030	703-385-8178	R	16*	<.1
36	Napoleon Videographics—*Marty Napoleon*	420 Lexington Ave Ste, New York NY 10170	212-692-9200	R	16*	<.1
37	Coe-Truman Technologies Inc—*Mark Coe*	500 N Michigan Ave Ste, Chicago IL 60611	312-644-7660	R	14*	<.1
38	Mobium Corp—*Gordon Hochhalter*	360 N Michigan Ave 12t, Chicago IL 60601	312-422-5990	S	14*	<.1
39	National Boston Video Center—*Kathy O'Toole*	115 Dummer St, Brookline MA 02446	617-734-4800	R	14*	<.1
40	Concrete—*Jilly Simmons*	547 S Clark St Ste 130, Chicago IL 60605	312-427-3733	R	13*	<.1
41	Savage Design Group Inc—*Paula S Hansen*	4203 Yoakum Blvd 4th F, Houston TX 77006	713-522-1555	R	13*	<.1
42	Signature Graphics Inc—*Paul Godfrey*	1000 Signature Dr, Porter IN 46304	219-926-4994	R	13*	.1
43	Sport Graphics Inc—*Frank Hancock*	3423 Park Davis Cir, Indianapolis IN 46235	317-899-7000	R	12*	.1
44	HighPoint Solutions—*Steve Brock*	2209 Pacific Ave, Tacoma WA 98402	253-272-8710	R	12*	<.1
45	Larsen Design Office Inc—*Tim Larsen*	3500 Alameda de las Pu, Menlo Park CA 94025	650-233-7777	R	12*	<.1
46	Wasatch Computer Technology Inc—*Mike Ware*	333 S 300 E, Salt Lake City UT 84111	801-575-8043	R	12*	<.1
47	Oscar and Associates Inc—*Mark Bailey*	325 N LaSalle St Ste 4, Chicago IL 60654	312-922-0056	R	11*	<.1
48	Adlife Marketing and Communications Company Inc—*John Puccio*	555 University Ave, Norwood MA 02062	781-762-7317	R	10*	.1
49	Hornall Anderson Design Works LLC—*Ashley Arhart*	710 2nd Ave Ste 1300, Seattle WA 98104	206-467-5800	R	10*	.1
50	ADM Productions Inc—*Anthony Demartino*	40 Seaview Blvd, Port Washington NY 11050	516-484-6900	R	10*	<.1
51	Interface Multimedia Inc—*Jeff Pulford*	8505 Fenton St, Silver Spring MD 20910	301-585-0068	R	10*	<.1
52	Off The Wall Company Inc—*John Chittick*	4814 Bethlehem Pke, Telford PA 18969	215-453-9400	R	10*	<.1
53	Net Dot Stuff—*Keith Thomas*	1137 Dawn View Terr, Mt Pleasant SC 29464	843-388-7485	R	9*	<.1
54	Anderson Perlstein Ltd—*Sheldon Anderson*	1590 S Milwaukee Ave S, Libertyville IL 60048	847-816-3444	R	9*	<.1
55	Phinney/Bischoff Design House—*Lesley Phinney*	614 Boylston Ave E, Seattle WA 98102	206-322-3484	R	9*	<.1
56	Magic Logix—*Hassan Bawab*	16610 Dallas Pky Ste 2, Dallas TX 75248	214-694-2162	R	9*	<.1
57	Moore Partners Inc—*Denise Roath*	3000 Northwoods Pkwy S, Norcross GA 30071	770-225-0321	R	9*	.1
58	Highland Graphics Inc—*Ron Wall*	210 Evergreen Dr, Springfield TN 37172	615-382-7299	R	8*	.1
59	Applied Art and Technology—*Mark Wilke*	2430 106th St, Des Moines IA 50322	515-331-7400	R	8*	<.1
60	Everett Collection Inc—*Ron Harvey*	104 W 27th St 3rd Fl, New York NY 10001	212-255-8610	R	8*	<.1
61	Chicago Art Production Services Inc—*Robin Steele*	329 W 18th St Ste 800, Chicago IL 60616	312-279-5200	R	8*	.1
62	Douglas Maddock Inc—*G Maddock*	111 S Adell Pl, Elmhurst IL 60126	630-279-3939	R	8*	.1
63	Pars Publishing Corp—*Mike Kian*	20850 Plummer St, Chatsworth CA 91311	818-280-0540	R	7*	.1
64	Paramax Productions—*Bill Wicklem*	208 Maple Ave, Red Bank NJ 07701	732-224-1048	R	7*	<.1
65	Internet Concepts Inc—*Neely Loring*	1001 Pinnacle Point Dr, Columbia SC 29223	803-254-4221	R	7	<.1
66	John Hamm and Associates—*John Hamm*	2312 Western Trails St, Austin TX 78745	512-444-0716	R	7*	<.1
67	O Design Group—*J Orit*	259 W 30th St, New York NY 10001	212-398-0100	R	7*	<.1
68	Erica Garment Printing—*Val Jacobo*	1155 S Bonnie Beach Pl, Los Angeles CA 90023	323-268-1771	R	7*	.1
69	CottonimagesCom Inc—*Sandra Hertzbach*	10481 Nw 28th St, Doral FL 33172	305-251-2560	R	7*	.1
70	Service Pak Inc—*Mary Wilkerson*	14740 W 101st Ter, Shawnee Mission KS 66215	913-438-3500	R	7*	.1
71	Studio North Inc—*Mark Mohr*	1616 Green Bay Rd, North Chicago IL 60064	847-473-4545	R	7*	<.1
72	Canyon Graphics Inc—*Scott Moncrieff*	6680 Cobra Way, San Diego CA 92121	858-646-0444	R	7*	.1
73	Image Processing—*Hervey Townshend*	746 E Main St, Branford CT 06405	203-488-3252	R	6*	.1
74	Jpm Inc—*Abel Mallo*	5760 Powerline Rd, Fort Lauderdale FL 33309	954-491-7575	R	6*	.1
75	Atlanta Beck Inc—*Kent Hatterick*	1425 Ellsworth Industr, Atlanta GA 30318	404-351-4340	R	6*	<.1
76	Mad 4 Marketing Inc—*Christine Madsen*	5203 Nw 33rd Ave, Fort Lauderdale FL 33309	954-485-5448	R	6*	<.1
77	Mentus Inc—*Guy Iannuzzi*	6755 Mira Mesa Blvd St, San Diego CA 92121	858-455-5500	R	6*	<.1
78	GravityFree—*Scott Heaps*	1960 Stickney Point Rd, Sarasota FL 34231	941-927-7674	R	6*	<.1
79	Infographics Inc—*Jeff Isler*	370 Lexington Ave, New York NY 10017	212-286-8888	R	6*	.1
80	MacGraphics Services—*Karen Saunders*	3454 S Cimarron Way, Aurora CO 80014		R	6*	<.1
81	Cathey Associates—*Gordon Cathey*	14900 Landmark Blvd St, Dallas TX 75254	214-300-8430	R	6	<.1
82	Identicomm LLC—*Bonnie Zielinski*	4165 Bold Meadows, Rochester MI 48306	248-340-6040	R	6*	.1
83	US Interactive Corp—*Sunil Mathur*	2700 Augustine Dr Ste, Santa Clara CA 95054	408-863-7500	R	6*	<.1
84	Continental Film and Video—*Vicki Amorosi*	1998 NE 150th St, North Miami FL 33181	305-949-4252	R	6*	<.1
85	Imagistic—*Chris McGinness*	4333 Park Terrace Dr S, Westlake Village CA 91361	818-706-9100	R	6*	<.1
86	Modea Corp—*David Catalano*	902 Prices Fork Rd Ste, Blacksburg VA 24060	540-552-3210	R	6*	.1
87	Silkworm Inc—*Robert Chambers*	PO Box 340, Murphysboro IL 62966	618-687-4077	R	6*	.1
88	Wechsler Ross and Partners Inc—*Dan Ross*	11 Madison Ave Ste 14, New York NY 10010	212-675-2810	R	6*	.1
89	Graphic Visions Group Inc—*Anthony Deluca*	159 W 25th St Fl 8, New York NY 10001	212-414-2900	R	6*	.1
90	Cosgrove Associates Inc—*Jerry Cosgrove*	747 3rd Ave Fl 16, New York NY 10017	212-888-7202	R	6*	<.1
91	Leonhardt Group Inc—*Sue Nixon*	1218 3rd Ave Ste 620, Seattle WA 98101	206-624-0551	R	6*	.1
92	Fuller Dyal and Stamper Inc—*Steven Stamper*	500 Chicon St, Austin TX 78702	512-476-7733	R	5*	.1
93	Threespot Media LLC—*Tony Kopetchny*	3333 14th St Nw Ste 30, Washington DC 20010	202-518-0425	R	5*	.1
94	Digital Minute—*Thomas Van Hare*	PO Box 670446, CORAL SPRINGS FL 33067	703-357-0701	R	5*	<.1
95	Creative Graphics Inc—*Joseph Cunningham*	6620 Grant Way, Allentown PA 18106	610-706-0536	R	5*	<.1
96	Design Partners Inc—*Gary Groenke*	338 Main St, Racine WI 53403	262-637-2233	R	5*	<.1
97	Advanced Business Group Inc—*Michael J Mulligan*	266 W 37th St, New York NY 10018	212-398-1010	R	5*	<.1
98	4 Guys Web Design Group—*Dave Nienberg*	8203 Willow Pl S Ste 2, Houston TX 77070	281-807-4344	R	5*	<.1
99	Amadeus Multimedia Technologies Ltd—*Anthony D Mercando*	3 Roland Rd, Irvington NY 10533	914-729-0065	R	5*	<.1
100	Avela Corp—*Gary Young*	4500 Caroline St, Houston TX 77004	713-807-7900	F	5*	<.1
101	Datacore Web Publishing—*Ted Baldanzi*	25 Hanover Rd Bldg B, Florham Park NJ 07932	973-822-1551	R	5*	<.1
102	Direct Images Interactive Inc—*Bill Knowland*	1933 Davis St Ste 314, San Leandro CA 94577	510-613-8299	R	5*	<.1
103	DXM Productions—*Catherine Clarke*	472 S Shoreline Blvd, Mountain View CA 94041	650-969-6580	R	5*	<.1
104	FarnumMorales Inc—*Michelle Farnum*	9 Arch St, Pawling NY 12564	845-855-5642	R	5*	<.1
105	Multimedia Production Services—*Terrace Erend*	5714 Grace Ave, Cincinnati OH 45227	513-561-6568	R	5*	<.1

Rank	Company Name—*Executive Officer*	Address, City, State, Zip	Phone	Type	Fin	Empls
106	Panoramic Images—*Douglas Segal*	2302 Main St, Evanston IL 60202	847-324-7000	R	5*	<.1
107	Riverside Imagesetters—*Howard Kirschner*	2124 Rte 35, Holmdel NJ 07733	732-671-8222	R	5*	<.1
108	Spencer Group—*Sandra Roeder*	PO Box 541158, Houston TX 77254	713-529-4111	R	5	<.1
109	Webteam Inc—*Curt Cvikota*	2031 S 32nd St, La Crosse WI 54601	608-788-8100	R	5*	<.1
110	Whiteboard Labs LLC—*Rodrigo Jimenez*	3100 Richmond Ave Ste, Houston TX 77098	713-333-9944	R	5*	<.1
111	NBC News Archives—*Nancy Cole*	30 Rockefeller Plaza R, New York NY 10112	212-664-3797	D	5*	<.1
112	Harvest Graphics LLC—*Liz Black*	14625 W 100th St, Shawnee Mission KS 66215	913-438-5556	R	5*	<.1
113	Superior Slides Inc—*William Ehrenberger*	10440 Brockwood Rd, Dallas TX 75238	972-437-0542	R	5*	<.1
114	Baron and Baron Inc—*Fabien Baron*	435 Hudson St Fl 5, New York NY 10014	212-397-8000	R	5*	<.1
115	Fashion Graphics—*Steve Demko*	10870 Talbert Ave, Fountain Valley CA 92708	714-545-6997	R	5*	<.1
116	Bethany Lowe Designs Inc—*Bethany Lowe*	16655 County Hwy 16, Osco IL 61274	309-944-6214	R	5*	<.1
117	UREP Inc—*Stephen Ashkinos*	216 E 45th St Fl 15, New York NY 10017	212-213-2200	R	5*	<.1
118	Art Finished Inc—*Donna Johnston*	708 Antone St Nw, Atlanta GA 30318	404-355-7902	R	4*	<.1
119	Silver Fox Productions Inc—*Ellen Moos*	911 E Pke St Ste 310, Seattle WA 98122	206-329-6805	R	4*	<.1
120	Symmetry Creative Production Inc—*Mary B Gasiorowski*	1300 S Grove Ave Ste 1, Barrington IL 60010	847-382-8750	R	4*	<.1
121	Tocco Designs Inc—*James Tocco*	187 S Old Woodward Ste, Birmingham MI 48009	248-646-2730	R	4*	<.1
122	Imagine IT!—*Jared D Gerber*	PO Box 4046, Chatsworth CA 91313	818-368-2604	R	4*	<.1
123	CF Napa Design Inc—*David Schuemann*	2787 Napa Valley Corp, Napa CA 94558	707-265-1891	R	4*	<.1
124	Ocean - 7 Development Inc—*Mark Alhadeff*	520 E 11th St, New York NY 10009	212-533-8460	R	4*	<.1
125	Singlebrook Technology Inc—*Elisa Miller-Out*	119 S Cayuga St Ste 20, Ithaca NY 14850	607-330-1493	R	4*	<.1
126	Waymark Internet Services Inc—*Mark Jones*	5800 Granite Pky Ste 3, Plano TX 75024	972-503-1100	R	4*	<.1
127	Custom Medical Stock Photo/Media MDcom—*Henry Schleich-korn*	3660 W Irving Park Rd, Chicago IL 60618	773-267-3100	R	4*	<.1
128	FILM Archives Inc—*Mark Trost*	35 W 35th St Ste 504, New York NY 10001	212-696-2616	R	4*	<.1
129	Jones Worley Design Inc—*Cynthia Jones*	723 Piedmont Ave NE, Atlanta GA 30308	404-876-9272	R	4*	<.1
130	Kobal Collection—*Martin Dives*	27 W 20th St Ste 1004, New York NY 10003	212-673-5600	R	4*	<.1
131	Langton Cherubino Group Ltd—*David Langton*	119 W 23rd St Ste 700, New York NY 10011	212-533-2585	R	4*	<.1
132	Rayogram—*Jane Beck*	305 W Broadway Ste 275, New York NY 10013	212-627-4088	R	4*	<.1
133	al Design Group Inc—*Rita Montorsi*	3041 Nationwide Pkwy, Brunswick OH 44212	330-220-1147	R	4*	<.1
134	Open Book Systems—*Laura Fillmore*	37-J Whistlestop Mall, Rockport MA 01966	978-546-7346	R	4*	<.1
135	Design 5 Creatives Inc—*Jeannie Friedman*	180 Varick St Fl 15, New York NY 10014	212-727-8899	R	4*	<.1
136	Eyemaginations Inc—*Jeff Peres*	600 Wshington Ave Ste, Towson MD 21204	410-321-5481	R	4*	<.1
137	Bw Reprographics LLC—*Chaneooe Blakely*	34 W 32nd St Fl 11, New York NY 10001	212-643-0600	R	4*	<.1
138	Oden and Associates Inc—*Bill Carkeet*	PO Box 3283, Memphis TN 38173	901-578-8055	R	4*	<.1
139	Silver Quick Associates Inc—*Diane Macwilliams*	18 W Ontario St, Chicago IL 60654	312-943-7622	R	4*	<.1
140	Blue Dog Printing and Design—*Bill Friedman*	1039 Andrew Dr, West Chester PA 19380	610-430-7992	R	4*	<.1
141	Digitaria Interactivo Inc—*Dan Khabie*	350 10th Ave Ste 1200, San Diego CA 92101	619-237-5552	R	4*	<.1
142	Millennium Films Inc—*Denny Dinbort*	6423 Wilchire Blvd, Los Angeles CA 90048	310-388-6900	R	4*	<.1
143	Mw Studios Inc—*Robert Muir*	49 W 38th St Fl 2, New York NY 10018	212-398-3420	R	4*	<.1
144	Pace Deic Corp—*Richard Pace*	403 Hayward Ave N, Saint Paul MN 55128	651-702-2900	R	4*	<.1
145	William G Berlin—*William Berlin*	222 Central Ct, Stockton CA 95204	209-948-2746	R	4*	<.1
146	Universal Concept—*Hasan Shaheed*	6423 Market St, Upper Darby PA 19082	215-539-2711	R	4*	.1
147	M Schwam Inc—*Matthew Schwam*	2211 38th Ave, Long Island City NY 11101	718-369-3212	R	4*	<.1
148	Graphica LLC—*Jerry Taylor*	4501 Lyons Rd, Miamisburg OH 45342	937-866-4013	R	4*	<.1
149	Hockfield Painting And Graphic—*Randy Deli*	736 Rockville Pke, Rockville MD 20852	301-309-3500	R	3*	.1
150	Midtown Printing Inc—*Fred Voncolln*	PO Dox 120188, Nashville TN 37212	615-327-1758	R	3*	<.1
151	Identigraphix Inc—*A Mendoza*	19866 Quiroz Ct, Walnut CA 91789	000-468-4741	R	3*	<.1
152	Sequel Studio LLC—*David Konigsberg*	12 W 27th St Fl 15, New York NY 10001	212-994-4320	R	3*	<.1
153	Scanner Graphics Inc—*Dave Triola*	405 Fairview Ave N, Seattle WA 98109	206-624-4469	R	3*	<.1
154	M Little and Company Inc—*Monica Little*	920 2nd Ave S Ste 1400, Minneapolis MN 55402	612-375-0077	R	3*	<.1
155	Ad Graphics Inc—*Richard Thompson*	3101 W McNab Rd, Pompano Beach FL 33069	954-974-9900	R	3*	<.1
156	Chicago Laminating Inc—*Allen Niemiec*	125 S Weiler Rd, Arlington Heights IL 60005	847-437-6850	R	3*	<.1
157	Blue Water Graphics Inc—*Donald Mader*	3601 Se Dixie Hwy, Stuart FL 34997	772-286-2249	R	3*	<.1
158	Kiku Obata and Co—*Mike Alsup*	6161 Delmar Blvd Ste 2, Saint Louis MO 63112	314-361-3110	R	3*	<.1
159	Brown and Company Graphic Design Inc—*Mary Brown*	801 Islington St Ste 3, Portsmouth NH 03801	603-436-5239	R	3*	<.1
160	Cgi Interactive Communication Inc—*David Kelleher*	76 Otis St Ste 2, Westborough MA 01581	508-898-2595	R	3*	<.1
161	Edwards Creative Services LLC	540 1st St W, Milan IL 61264	309-756-0199	R	3*	<.1
162	Park Industrial Foams Inc—*Andrew Gomes*	26554 Danti Ct, Hayward CA 94545	510-887-7711	R	3*	<.1
163	Digital Signage Inc—*Andy Lotia*	280 Martin Ave Ste 7, Santa Clara CA 95050	408-257-9766	R	3*	<.1
164	Gorilla Polymedia—*Chris Walter*	1015 W Lake St Ste 200, Chicago IL 60607	312-243-8777	R	3*	<.1
165	David K Burnap—*Steve McCann*	36 S Main St, Dayton OH 45458	937-439-4800	R	3*	<.1
166	BKR Studio Inc—*Brian Rideout*	110 E Madison St, South Bend IN 46601	574-245-9576	R	3*	<.1
167	International Color Stock Inc—*Randy Taylor*	1123 Broadway Ste 1006, New York NY 10010	212-463-8300	R	3*	<.1
168	Gateway Design Inc—*Connie Senter*	4299 San Felipe Ste 11, Houston TX 77027	713-572-9600	R	3*	<.1
169	Megamedia Inc—*Stan Coplin*	3 Rose Terrace, Lafayette Hill PA 19444	215-576-7050	R	3*	<.1
170	MR Danielson Advertising—*Michael Danielson*	1464 Summit Ave, Saint Paul MN 55105	651-698-1512	R	3*	<.1
171	Pixel Creative	2801 Post Oak Blvd Ste, Houston TX 77056	713-622-9293	R	3*	<.1
172	Producers Library Service—*Jeff Goodman*	10832 Chandler Blvd, North Hollywood CA 91601	818-752-9097	R	3*	<.1
173	SG and D Communications and Design—*Donna Barger*	900 Commerce Ct Ste 91, Moon Township PA 15108	412-375-7601	R	3*	<.1
174	Speared Peanut Design Studio—*Paul Kremer*	807 W Gray, Houston TX 77019	713-869-4509	R	3*	<.1
175	Bixler Inc—*Josh Bixler*	1600 Tysons Blvd Ste 8, McLean VA 22102	703-894-3000	R	3*	<.1
176	Chan SmartWare Inc—*Jerry Chan*	278 Prospect, Shrewsbury MA 01545	508-842-9888	R	3*	<.1
177	Netwood Design Centre—*Jonus Fornander*	10736 Jefferson Blvd #, Culver City CA 90230	310-442-1530	R	3*	<.1
178	Photoshot—*Marvin Woodyatt*	30 W 63rd St Ste 14J, New York NY 10023	646-329-6242	R	3*	<.1
179	Pig Pen Studios Inc—*Bill Heapps*	30 Manorhaven Blvd, Port Washington NY 11050	516-883-2500	R	3*	<.1
180	Video Tape Library Ltd—*Melody St John*	1525 N Crescent Height, Los Angeles CA 90046	323-656-4330	R	3*	<.1
181	Chimera Design LLC	15490 Ventura Blvd Ste, Sherman Oaks CA 91403	818-815-2800	R	3*	<.1
182	Peak Creative Media—*Michael Davison*	1800 Boulder St Ste 20, Denver CO 80211	303-295-3373	R	3*	<.1
183	Crescent Decal Specialist Inc—*Hal Simeon*	PO Box 160, Kenner LA 70063	504-467-7000	R	3*	<.1
184	RJ Graphics Inc—*Rita Iannelli*	PO Box 293, Thorofare NJ 08086	856-848-1986	R	3*	<.1
185	Graphic Communication Specialists Inc—*Jeff Schroeder*	PO Box 922, West Bend WI 53095	262-338-3998	R	3*	<.1
186	Precision Graphic Services Inc—*Jeffrey Mellander*	106 S Neil St, Champaign IL 61820	217-359-6655	R	3*	<.1
187	Mehigan Bellone and Associates Inc—*Dennis Bellone*	249 Green St Ste 2, Schenectady NY 12305	518-370-0108	R	3*	<.1
188	Art Machine LLC	9724 Washington Blvd S, Culver City CA 90232	310-845-1626	R	3*	<.1
189	Fusebox Inc—*Bryan Thatcher*	36 W 20th St Fl 11, New York NY 10011	212-929-7644	R	3*	<.1
190	Huerta Design Associates—*Barbara Cocks*	801 N Brand Blvd Ste 2, Glendale CA 91203	818-243-6800	R	3*	<.1
191	Crew Cuts Productions Inc—*Clayton Hemmert*	19 Union Sq W Fl 8, New York NY 10003	212-302-2828	R	3*	<.1
192	Snyder Printing And Design—*Richard Snyder*	2536 Verda Ct, Simi Valley CA 93065	805-583-0831	R	3*	<.1
193	Post-Up Stand Inc—*Ram Tamir*	5461 Dunham Rd, Maple Heights OH 44137	212	R	3*	<.1
194	Robinson Graphics Inc—*William Robinson*	1208 Northgte Business, Madison TN 37115	615-612-6440	R	3*	<.1

Note: An asterisk (*) indicates an estimated financial figure. The company type code used is as follows: R = Private, P = Public, S = Private Subsidiary, B = Public Subsidiary, D = Division, J = Joint Venture, I = Investment Fund.

COMPANY RANKINGS BY SALES WITHIN 4-DIGIT SIC

Rank	Company Name—Executive Officer	Address, City, State, Zip	Phone	Type	Fin	Empls
195	Catalina Communications Inc—Jim Loughlin	2261 Cosmos Ct, Carlsbad CA 92011	760-476-3600	R	3*	<.1
196	Penn Street Inc—Tim Burtner	PO Box 3237, Saint Joseph MO 64503	816-233-2394	R	3*	<.1
197	Inventure Group Inc—Howard Schapiro	650 Washington Rd Ste, Pittsburgh PA 15228	412-343-4000	R	3*	<.1
198	Graphics Etc La—Peter Paul	6020 Washington Blvd, Culver City CA 90232	310-826-5305	R	3*	<.1
199	Raincastle Communications Inc—Paul Regensburg	288 Walnut St Ste 310, Newton MA 02460	617-965-2681	R	3*	<.1
200	Pro Graphics LLC—Barbara Osberg	W222n600 Cheaney Rd, Waukesha WI 53186	262-547-0300	R	3*	<.1
201	Promotional Graphics Inc—Ernie Gonzalez	1730 Cordova St, Los Angeles CA 90007	323-737-4277	R	3*	<.1
202	Computer Chrome Inc—Peter Hager	400 1st Ave N Ste 100, Minneapolis MN 55401	651-646-2442	R	3*	<.1
203	Customer First Incorporated Of Naples—Robert Weidenmiller	10940 Harmony Park Dr, Bonita Springs FL 34135	239-949-8518	R	3*	<.1
204	Graphics Arts Production Inc—Steven Williams	12953 Foothill Blvd, Sylmar CA 91342	818-365-9899	R	3*	<.1
205	Newmast Marketing and Communications—Terry Wike	2060 Integrity Dr N, Columbus OH 43209	614-837-1200	R	3*	<.1
206	Nomad Designs and Services LLC	363 Clementina St, San Francisco CA 94103	415-357-1509	R	3*	<.1
207	Alan Jeffrey Corporation Communications—Jeffrey Weissman	54 W 21st St Fl 12, New York NY 10010	212-463-0545	R	3*	<.1
208	Florida Reprographics Inc—Christopher Charles	633 N Franklin St Ste, Tampa FL 33602	813-221-2094	R	3*	<.1
209	Allied Advertising Agency Inc—John Herbots	3700 Blanco Rd, San Antonio TX 78212	210-732-7874	R	2*	<.1
210	CL Graphics Inc—Richard Schildgen	134 Virginia Rd Ste A, Crystal Lake IL 60014	815-455-0900	R	2*	<.1
211	Deutsch Design Works Inc—Barry Deutsch	10 Arkansas St Ste K, San Francisco CA 94107	415-487-8520	R	2*	<.1
212	Nichols Graphics Inc—Raymond Nichols	PO Box 1027, Spencer WV 25276	304-927-5733	R	2*	<.1
213	Scanart—Frederic Lompa	1259 Park Ave, Emeryville CA 94608	510-595-2222	R	2*	<.1
214	Aibus Corp—George Subia	6612 Gulton Ct Ne, Albuquerque NM 87109	505-345-2636	R	2*	<.1
215	Graphic Connections Group LLC	174 Chesterfield Indus, Chesterfield MO 63005	636-519-8320	R	2*	<.1
216	Infinity Interactive Inc	565 Plandome Rd Rm 307, Manhasset NY 11030	212-388-9100	R	2*	<.1
217	Apex Graphics LLC—Todd Barker	3722 Lexington Park Dr, Elkhart IN 46514	574-389-9700	R	2*	<.1
218	Graphic Process Inc—Dave Pomeroy	915 5th Ave S, Nashville TN 37203	615-254-5858	R	2*	<.1
219	Riegner and Associates Inc—Brian Riegner	18481 W 10 Mile Rd, Southfield MI 48075	248-569-4242	R	2*	<.1
220	Etm Studios Inc—Edward Seifert	9201 King St, Franklin Park IL 60131	847-671-5150	R	2*	<.1
221	Supergroup Creative Omnimedia Inc—Gabe Aldridge	154 Krog St Ne Ste 185, Atlanta GA 30307	404-877-1711	R	2*	<.1
222	Clover Graphics Inc—Kenneth Granville	2050 Ocean Ave, Ronkonkoma NY 11779	631-471-2323	R	2*	<.1
223	Wayne Allen Ltd—Daniel Kilcup	14121 Parke Long Ct St, Chantilly VA 20151	703-321-7414	R	2*	<.1
224	Emerging Image Inc—Michael Shields	3530 61st St, Woodside NY 11377	718-424-1110	R	2*	<.1
225	Stellar Concepts Inc—Tony Giudice	6600 Nw 12th Ave Ste 2, Fort Lauderdale FL 33309	954-489-2250	R	2*	<.1
226	24 Hour Co—Dennis Fitzgerald	6521 Arlington Blvd St, Falls Church VA 22042	703-533-7209	R	2*	<.1
227	Nicosia Creative Expresso Ltd—Davide Nicosia	355 W 52nd St 8th Fl, New York NY 10019	212-515-6600	R	2*	<.1
228	Meteor Graphics LLC—Amy Deckerson	11551h Nuckols Rd Ste, Glen Allen VA 23059	804-270-5300	R	2*	<.1
229	Creamer Associates Inc—Ronald Creamer	501 Cambridge St, Cambridge MA 02141	617-374-6000	R	2*	<.1
230	HK Graphics Inc—Christopher Keshishian	82 Spring St, Everett MA 02149	617-387-3301	R	2*	<.1
231	Big Film Design—Randy Balsmeyer	594 Broadway Ste 1001, New York NY 10012	212-627-3430	R	2*	<.1
232	HB Digital Arts and HB Blueprint—Kristy Selleck	1615 Alabama St, Huntington Beach CA 92648	714-536-3939	R	2*	<.1
233	Aplin Uno Creative—Paul Aplin	2685 Marine Way Ste 14, Mountain View CA 94043	650-966-8000	R	2*	<.1
234	Charles M Shultz Creative Associates Inc—Charles Schulz	1 Snoopy Pl, Santa Rosa CA 95403	707-546-7121	R	2*	<.1
235	Historic Films Archive—Joe Lauro	211 3rd St, Greenport NY 11944	631-477-9700	R	2*	<.1
236	Iron Design—Todd Edmonds	120 N Aurora St Ste 5a, Ithaca NY 14850	607-275-9544	R	2*	<.1
237	Alpha Lex—Allen Glazer	21604 Tribune St, Chatsworth CA 91311	818-407-9200	R	2*	<.1
238	Before and After—John McWade	323 Lincoln St, Roseville CA 95678	916-784-3880	R	2*	<.1
239	Cameo Film Library Inc—Janet Meyer	10620 Burbank Blvd N, North Hollywood CA 91601	818-980-8700	R	2*	<.1
240	Carl Waltzer Digital Services Inc—Bill Waltzer	873 Broadway Ste 412, New York NY 10003	212-475-8748	R	2*	<.1
241	Deneen Powell Atelier Inc—Jeri Deneen	2305 El Cajon Blvd, San Diego CA 92104	619-294-9042	R	2*	<.1
242	EYEMG- Interactive Media Group—Andrew Holland	190 N Union St Ste 300, Akron OH 44304	330-434-7873	R	2*	<.1
243	Film and Video Stock Shots—Stephanie Siebert	10442 Burbank Blvd, North Hollywood CA 91602	818-760-2098	R	2*	<.1
244	Gregory Richard Media Group—Richard Sohanchyk	331 Fifth Ave, Pelham NY 10803	914-738-6066	R	2*	<.1
245	Mauk Design—Mitchell Mauk	330 Fell St, San Francisco CA 94102	415-243-9277	R	2*	<.1
246	NeTV Networks LLC—John D Boswell	6666 Santa Monica Blvd, Hollywood CA 90038	323-230-9429	R	2*	<.1
247	Panoptic Communications Inc—Richard Kauffman	2025 Wallace St, Philadelphia PA 19130	215-232-8722	R	2*	<.1
248	Paula Black and Associates—Paula Black	3006 Aviation Ave Ste, Coconut Grove FL 33133	305-859-9554	R	2*	<.1
249	Random Access Inc—Lauren Singer	13 W Las Olas Blvd, Fort Lauderdale FL 33301	954-462-1107	R	2*	<.1
250	Altercom Website Design and Host Inc—Sue Wurfel	22609 Raymond Ct, Saint Clair Shores MI 48082	586-415-0300	R	2*	<.1
251	Clients First Inc—Jeffrey Becker	84 Elm St, Westfield NJ 07090	908-232-1200	R	2*	<.1
252	Fish Films Footage World—David Fishbein	4548 Van Noord Ave, Studio City CA 91604	818-905-1071	R	2*	<.1
253	Forward Design Inc	3638 Kenosha Dr NW, Rochester MN 55901	507-206-3919	R	2*	<.1
254	Hollywood Vaults—David Wexler	742 N Seward St, Hollywood CA 90038	323-461-6464	R	2*	<.1
255	Leonardo Studio Inc—Anthony Leonardo	377 E 33rd Ste 9a, New York NY 10016	212-645-7844	R	2*	<.1
256	Site Specific Inc—Robert Blaylock	1402 3rd Ave Ste 1230, Seattle WA 98101	206-652-0677	R	2*	<.1
257	Stock Media Corp—Randy Taylor	10 E 23rd St Ste 500, New York NY 10010	212-463-8300	R	2*	<.1
258	Web Media Ltd—Hal Josephson	314 11th St, San Francisco CA 94103	415-860-5177	R	2*	<.1
259	Aztec Systems Corp—Paul R Payne	11100 5th St E, Treasure Island FL 33706	727-562-5160	R	2*	<.1
260	iOR Consulting and Design—Kerri Mallory	288 S Pacific Hwy, Talent OR 97540	541-951-6995	R	2*	<.1
261	Wizults LLC—Heather Webster	PO Box 724, Marietta GA 30061	770-366-6283	R	2*	<.1
262	Taylor Made Graphics—James Keserich	7921 Hollenbeck Cir, Cleveland OH 44129	440-885-9644	R	2*	<.1
263	Marilyn Magder—Marilyn Magder	PO Box B, Trenton NJ 08690	609-896-1624	R	2*	<.1
264	Harrison Falk Inc—Stephen Harrison	1300 Baur Blvd, Saint Louis MO 63132	314-531-1410	R	2*	<.1
265	Innova Ideas and Services—Beth Cross	304 Main St, Ames IA 50010	515-232-5373	S	2*	<.1
266	Mccullough Creative Inc—Jack Mccullough	10446 Ironwood Dr, Dubuque IA 52003	563-556-2392	R	2*	<.1
267	Prezenta Presentation Products—Wallace Carter	1502 N 23rd St, Wilmington NC 28405	910-452-3210	R	2*	<.1
268	Graham Critt Graphic Design Ltd—Diane Graham	2970 Clairmont Rd Ne S, Atlanta GA 30329	404-320-1737	R	2*	<.1
269	Custom Graphics And Plates Inc—Robert Spering	1255 Belle Ave Unit 16, Casselberry FL 32708	407-696-5448	R	2*	<.1
270	Graziano Krafft and Zale Inc—Eric Krafft	333 N Michigan Ave Ste, Chicago IL 60601	312-368-4355	R	2*	<.1
271	Parker Group Inc—Charles Ambrogio	PO Box 1444, Clifton NJ 07015	973-340-3030	R	2*	<.1
272	Theme Creations LLC	PO Box 470636, Kissimmee FL 34747	407-688-2900	R	2*	<.1
273	Graphic Globe—David Peters	11100 Astronaut Blvd, Orlando FL 32837	407-856-4173	R	2*	<.1
274	Iconologic LLC—Jamie Horowitz	40 Inwood Cir Ne, Atlanta GA 30309	404-260-4500	R	2*	<.1
275	Crestec Digital Inc—Yoshiki Iwata	1010 Knox St, Torrance CA 90502	310-327-9000	R	2*	<.1
276	Graphic Applications Inc—Felix Piccirilli	977 Mount Read Blvd, Rochester NY 14606	585-254-3988	R	2*	<.1
277	Osborn Jim Reproductions Inc—Susan Osborn	101 Ridgecrest Dr, Lawrenceville GA 30046	770-962-7556	R	2*	<.1
278	N Stuart Design—Cathrine Stuart	66 Scout Hill Rd, Mahopac NY 10541	845-628-7140	R	2*	<.1
279	Santal Corp—Sanford Talley	96 Aberdeen Pl, Saint Louis MO 63105	314-862-2106	R	2*	<.1
280	Hilferty Gerard And Accociates Inc—Dean Clouse	14240 State Rte 550, Athens OH 45701	740-448-3821	R	2*	<.1
281	Rolin Graphics Inc—Donald Rodi	4080 83rd Ave N Ste Ll, Minneapolis MN 55443	763-550-1334	R	2*	<.1
282	Robert Saylers Artiststry—Robert Salyers	1373 Byron Dr, Clearwater FL 33756	727-447-8324	R	1*	<.1
283	Schmidt N Graphic Design Group—Nancy Schmidt	1533 Williamstown Eria, Sicklerville NJ 08081	856-309-3922	R	1*	<.1
284	G 3 Technology Group LLC—Anita Shot	832 Oregon Ave Ste L, Linthicum Heights MD 21090	410-789-6623	R	1*	<.1

Rank	Company Name—*Executive Officer*	Address, City, State, Zip	Phone	Type	Fin	Empls
285	JL Enterprises Inc—*Susan Kelley*	875 Washington St, Canton MA 02021	781-821-6300	R	1*	<.1
286	Burmar Technical Corp—*Norma Novotny*	106 Ransom Ave, Sea Cliff NY 11579	516-484-6000	R	1*	<.1
287	L and J Sharp Graphics—*Bill Biggins*	4231 Clary Blvd, Kansas City MO 64130	816-756-1193	R	1*	<.1
288	Klundt Hosmer Design Assoc Inc—*Darin Klundt*	216 W Pacific Ave Ste, Spokane WA 99201	509-456-5576	R	1*	<.1
289	Executive Arts Inc—*Tod Martin*	384 Northyards Blvd Nw, Atlanta GA 30313	404-614-4299	R	1*	<.1
290	Dearinger Printing and Trophy Inc—*Rick Dearinger*	605 S Lewis St, Stillwater OK 74074	405-377-2800	R	1*	<.1
291	Pangborn Design Ltd—*Dominic Pangborn*	275 Iron St, Detroit MI 48207	313-259-3400	R	1*	<.1
292	Fusion Media Inc—*Kary Smith*	99 N Main St Ste 7, Cedar City UT 84720	435-867-0077	R	1*	<.1
293	Glyphix Studio Inc—*Larry Cohen*	6964 Shoup Ave, West Hills CA 91307	818-704-3994	R	1*	<.1
294	Magic Design/Visual Dynamics Inc—*Cy Furman*	155 Connecticut St, San Francisco CA 94107	415-861-6244	R	1*	<.1
295	AspenMedia—*Rick Romano*	13885 Alton Pky Ste A, Irvine CA 92618	949-454-0124	R	1*	<.1
296	Blimp Photo and Video Co—*Gary Lockhart*	PO Box 26519, Austin TX 78755	512-794-8401	R	1*	<.1
297	Envisioning Business Inc—*Andrzej Olejniczak*	41 W 25th St, New York NY 10010	212-242-1080	R	1*	<.1
298	CommuniCreations Inc—*Alan Feinberg*	3905 Fair Point Ln, Melbourne FL 32934	321-266-6904	R	1*	<.1
299	E-Znet—*Suzanne Smolka*	PO Box 1589, Vancouver WA 98668		R	1*	<.1
300	Ideascape Inc—*Ralph Lucier*	57 Newcomb Rd, Stoneham MA 02180	781-665-3700	R	1*	<.1
301	NavalTees LLC—*Jeff Hobrath*	41665 Fenwick St Ste 1, Leonardtown MD 20650	301-475-0437	R	1*	<.1
302	Patrick Redmond Design—*Patrick Redmond MA*	PO Box 75430, Saint Paul MN 55175	651-646-4254	R	1*	<.1
303	Roger H Silverberg Advertising—*Roger H Silverburg*	9 Emil Ct, Huntington NY 11743	631-424-6911	R	1*	<.1
304	Type and Design—*Luanne Zemanek*	1422 Euclid Ave Ste 43, Cleveland OH 44115	216-479-7775	R	1*	<.1
305	Your Plan B Co—*Jamey Brumfield*	4024 N Sheridan Rd Ste, Chicago IL 60613	773-665-2552	R	1*	<.1
306	Airboss Stock Footage—*Edward Feuerherd*	7 Theater Sq Ste 210, Louisville KY 40202	502-581-8162	R	1*	<.1
307	Cummings 'N' Good—*Peter Good*	PO Box 570, Chester CT 06412	860-526-9597	R	1*	<.1
308	Depthography Inc—*R Anthony Munn*	632 E 11th St, New York NY 10009		R	1*	<.1
309	Dream Entertainment—*Yitzach Ginsberg*	8489 W 3rd St Ste 1096, Los Angeles CA 90048	323-655-5501	R	1*	<.1
310	G-Biz Unlimited—*George Alberts*	6758 Limpkin Dr, Orlando FL 32810	407-758-9458	R	1*	<.1
311	Glowing Designs—*Amy Edwards*	PO Box 1, Newark Valley NY 13811	607-642-5391	R	1*	<.1
312	Hargrove Design Group—*Mark Hargrove*	PO Box 770067, Houston TX 77215	713-789-9815	R	1*	<.1
313	Inspiromedia Corp—*Tom Dean*	1138 Reece Hill Rd, Mountain City TN 37683	678-925-1345	R	1*	<.1
314	Leonard Rue Video Productions Inc—*Leonard Lee Rue III*	138 Millbrook Rd, Hardwick NJ 07825	908-362-8202	R	1*	<.1
315	Panoptic Media—*Jim Prues*	2303 Gilbert Ave, Cincinnati OH 45206	513-281-6500	R	1*	<.1
316	Webicity Web Designs—*Tim Tortt*	3628 Seminole Ln, Marianna FL 32448	850-579-0795	R	1*	<.1
317	Zelacom Electronic Publishing—*Alex Shiffer*	PO Box 669, Ellenville NY 12428	845-647-8711	R	1*	<.1
318	Barnet Levinson Design—*Barnet Levinson*	2217 Sul Ross St, Houston TX 77098	713-528-3330	R	1*	<.1
319	Business Design Studio—*Eileen Parzek*	27 Irving St Ste 1, Albany NY 12202	518-505-6617	R	1*	<.1
320	Diamond Images Inc (Miami Florida)—*Mark Diamond*	29 NE 90th St, Miami FL 33138	305-758-4656	R	1*	<.1
321	Carson Tredgett Serigraphics Inc—*Carson Tredgett*	3530 Dewitt Ln, Charlotte NC 28217	704-525-4884	R	1*	<.1
322	Fuego World Wide Inc—*Joaquin Lira*	100 Parkhouse St Ste 2, Dallas TX 75207	214-749-0900	R	1*	.1
323	Mcduff Designs Inc—*Jo Orr*	2368 Ridgefield Dr Ne, Grand Rapids MI 49505	616-774-0050	R	<1*	<.1
324	Advertising Services International LLC—*Anna Hawthorn*	10000 Lake City Way Ne, Seattle WA 98125	206-623-6963	R	<1*	<.1
325	Bulldog Multimedia—*Carlos Orozco*	3751 N Western Ave, Chicago IL 60618	773-866-1579	R	<1*	<.1
326	General Graphics—*Carlene Gregowich*	PO Box 3192, New Kensington PA 15068	724-337-1470	R	<1*	<.1
327	Ashland Graphic Arts Inc—*Steven Gardner*	1102 Myers Pkwy, Ashland OH 44805	419-289-6816	R	<1*	<.1
328	How It Works—*Chris Terrell*	PO Box 1386, Anacortes WA 98221	360-293-3515	R	<1	<.1
329	Miriello Grafico—*Ron Miriello*	1660 Logan Ave, San Diego CA 92113	619-234-1124	R	<1	<.1
330	Peter Arnold Inc—*Peter Arnold*	1181 Broadway, New York NY 10001		R	<1	<.1
331	Intervideo Duplication Services	3533 S Archer Ave, Chicago IL 60609	773-927-9091	R	<1	<.1
332	QuirkWorks—*Tricia Quirk*	245 Morsetown Rd, West Milford NJ 07480	973-728-7299	R	N/A	<.1
333	PXL8R—*Craig Molenhouse*	PO Box 5400, La Quinta CA 92248	818-901-9306	R	N/A	<.1
334	Telenaut Communications—*David Newman*	PO Box 423174, San Francisco CA 94142	415-437-0112	R	N/A	<.1
335	Wilson Graphics Inc—*Paul David Wilson*	10211 SW 64th Ct, Ocala FL 34476		R	N/A	<.1

TOTALS: SIC 7336 Commercial Art & Graphic Design
Companies: 335   3,702   15.2

7338 Secretarial & Court Reporting

Rank	Company Name—*Executive Officer*	Address, City, State, Zip	Phone	Type	Fin	Empls
1	Esquire Deposition Services LLC	101 Marietta St, Marietta GA 30064	973-377-7750	S	149*	.6
2	Webmedx Inc—*Sean Carroll*	3350 Riverwood Pkwy Se, Atlanta GA 30339	770-522-4881	R	109*	.8
3	Spi Healthcare—*Robert Lynch*	2807 N Parham Rd Ste 3, Richmond VA 23294	804-968-2620	R	25*	.7
4	JLG Medical Inc—*Giselle Gay*	141 Stevens Ave Ste 15, Oldsmar FL 34677	813-286-1977	R	20*	.3
5	Transhealth LLC Webmedx Inc	5410 Maryland Way Ste, Brentwood TN 37027	615-846-1200	S	11*	.1
6	Lee-Perfect Transcribing Company Inc—*Linda L Manderfeld*	680 N Lake Shore Dr St, Chicago IL 60611	312-664-1877	R	6*	<.1
7	Veritext/Florida Reporting Company LLC	19 W Flagler St Ste 10, Miami FL 33130	305-371-1884	R	5*	.1
8	Knipes-Cohen Associates Inc—*Robert Cohen*	400 Market St Fl 11, Philadelphia PA 19106	215-928-9300	R	4*	.1
9	Jmm Type Inc—*Janet Miranda*	161 Main St, Kings Park NY 11754	631-544-0837	R	4*	.1
10	York Stenographic Services Inc—*Janie Busch*	34 N George St, York PA 17401	717-854-0077	R	3*	.1
11	Rta Inc—*Susan Balcerzak*	121 Executive Ctr Dr S, Columbia SC 29210	803-798-1919	R	3*	.1
12	Northern Counties Secretarial Service Inc—*Carol Lublin*	6139 157th Ln Nw, Anoka MN 55303	763-427-0166	R	3*	.1
13	SPI Healthcare Documentation LLC—*David Woodrow*	417 Welshwood Dr Ste 2, Nashville TN 37211	615-301-8420	S	3*	<.1
14	Bureau Of Office Services Inc—*Richard Piasecki*	11s270 S Jackson St St, Burr Ridge IL 60527	630-323-2600	R	3*	<.1
15	Diacritech Inc—*Michael Hodges*	670 N Commercial St St, Manchester NH 03101	603-606-5800	R	3*	<.1
16	Transcription Express Inc—*Terry Hurst*	925 N Mcqueen Rd Ste 1, Gilbert AZ 85233	480-497-1569	R	3*	<.1
17	Matz-Traktman Inc—*Gerald Traktman*	19 W Flagler St Ste 10, Miami FL 33130	305-377-1514	R	2*	.1
18	Kwatros Corp—*Glen Larsen*	175 W 200 S Ste 4004, Salt Lake City UT 84101	801-359-1621	R	2*	<.1
19	Gore Reporting Company Inc—*Ronald Gore*	515 Olive St Ste 700, Saint Louis MO 63101	314-241-6750	R	2*	<.1
20	Documentation Services Group Inc—*Noel Bambrough*	990 Hammond Dr Ne Ste, Atlanta GA 30328	404-591-1270	R	2*	<.1
21	Keystrokes Transcription Inc—*Lee Tkachuk*	220 Garden St, Yorkville IL 60560	630-553-3680	R	2*	.1
22	Mehler And Hagestrom Inc—*Edward Mehler*	101 W Prospect Ave Ste, Cleveland OH 44115	216-621-4980	R	2*	<.1
23	Century Court Reporters Inc—*Stephen Reymer*	2049 Century Park E St, Los Angeles CA 90067	310-284-9000	R	2*	<.1
24	ExecuScribe Inc—*Linda Yaniszewski*	1320 University Ave, Rochester NY 14607	585-256-6220	R	2*	<.1
25	Doerner Goldberg M Frannicola Inc—*Marshall Goldberg*	Vreeland Rd Ste 301b, Florham Park NJ 07932	973-740-1100	R	2*	<.1
26	Soap Transcription Services—*Faye Thayer*	2855 Anthony Ln S Ste, Minneapolis MN 55418	612-706-1588	R	2*	<.1
27	Agren Blando Court Reporting and Video Inc—*Michael Pace*	216 16th St Ste 650, Denver CO 80202	303-296-0017	R	2*	<.1
28	Guy J Renzi and Associates—*Mark Renzi*	2277 Hwy 33 Ste 410, Trenton NJ 08690	609-989-9199	R	2*	<.1
29	Ross Reporting Service Inc—*David Ross*	11706 Playa Ct, Houston TX 77034	281-484-0770	R	2*	<.1
30	Spryance Inc—*Vincent Estrada*	3101 Executive Pkwy St, Toledo OH 43606	419-578-6300	R	2*	<.1
31	Tom Crites and Associates International Inc—*Tommy Crites*	PO Box 9438, Savannah GA 31412	912-233-1883	R	2*	<.1
32	Mccorkle Reporting Co—*Katherine Mccorkle*	200 N Lasalle St Ste 3, Chicago IL 60601	312-263-0052	R	1*	<.1
33	Transcribing Unlimited 2000 Inc—*Gina Hutchings*	8283 E Sanders Ct, Fresno CA 93737	559-256-8700	R	1*	<.1

Note: An asterisk (*) indicates an estimated financial figure. The company type code used is as follows: R = Private, P = Public, S = Private Subsidiary, B = Public Subsidiary, D = Division, J = Joint Venture, I = Investment Fund.

COMPANY RANKINGS BY SALES WITHIN 4-DIGIT SIC

Rank	Company Name—*Executive Officer*	Address, City, State, Zip	Phone	Type	Fin	Empls
34	Benjamin Reporting Service—*Irwin Benjamin*	1350 Broadway Rm 1407, New York NY 10018	212-374-1138	R	1*	<.1
35	Answer-All Secretarial Service Inc—*Gwen Corbett*	PO Box 1129, Westminster CO 80036	303-428-7521	R	1*	<.1
36	M and M Reporting Inc—*Mary D'andrea*	1 Pierce Pl Ste 295e, Itasca IL 60143	630-775-1503	R	1*	<.1
37	Integrity First Inc—*Gerald Denson*	6051d Arlington Blvd S, Falls Church VA 22044	703-521-1260	R	1*	<.1
38	M and F Reporting—*Hilda Finer*	3 Shuart Dr, Spring Valley NY 10977	845-425-7731	R	1*	<.1
39	Gillespie Shorthand Reporting Corp—*Judy Gillespie*	3333 Central Ave Ste D, Riverside CA 92506	951-682-5686	R	1*	<.1
40	Preferred Legal Services Inc—*Joann Norton*	PO Box 551387, Dallas TX 75355	214-750-0047	R	1*	<.1
41	Shelburne Sherr Court Reporters Inc—*Kathleen Shelburne*	501 W Broadway Ste 133, San Diego CA 92101	619-234-9100	R	1*	<.1
42	Valentine Transcribing Service—*Penny Valentine*	2965 S Newark Pl, Aurora CO 80014	303-745-6678	R	1*	<.1
43	Brooks Reporting Inc—*Dana Brooks*	PO Box 2025, Dacula GA 30019	770-237-8990	R	1*	<.1
44	Court Reporters International Inc—*Marsha Naegeli*	111 Sw 5th Ave Ste 202, Portland OR 97204	503-227-1544	R	1*	<.1
45	Doris O Wong Associates Inc—*Doris Wong*	50 Franklin St Side, Boston MA 02110	617-426-2432	R	1*	<.1
46	Jan Britton and Associates Inc—*Paula Blosser*	124 E 3rd St Ste 400, Dayton OH 45402	937-228-3370	R	1*	<.1
47	Keith and Miller PC—*Roger Miller*	100 N Stanton St Ste 1, El Paso TX 79901	915-533-7108	R	1*	<.1
48	Med-Scribe Transcription Service Inc—*Louise Wolkis*	121 Cedar Ln Ste 3, Teaneck NJ 07666	201-836-0808	R	1*	<.1
49	Precise Medical Transcription—*Thomas Mccarthy*	5830 Montana Ave, New Port Richey FL 34652	727-846-0077	R	1*	<.1
50	Thacker and Company LLC—*Kelly Thacker*	50 W Broadway Ste 900, Salt Lake City UT 84101	801-983-2180	R	1*	<.1
51	Anthrobytes Consulting—*Sharon Burton*	3055 Priscilla St, Riverside CA 92506	951-369-8590	R	1*	<.1
52	Winkler And Chimniak Ltd—*Robin Chimniak*	200 N Dearborn St Ste, Chicago IL 60601	312-236-1661	R	1*	<.1
53	A American High Tech Transcription And Reporting Inc—*Susan Segal*	4175 E Bay Dr Ste 103, Clearwater FL 33764	727-535-1066	R	1*	<.1
54	New England Transcription Inc—*Jeff Myers*	276 Main St Ste 2, Portland CT 06480	860-342-3406	R	1*	<.1
55	Itmedica Inc—*David Rosen*	411 Sette Dr Ste N3, Paramus NJ 07652	201-262-9000	R	1*	<.1
56	Albany Word Processing Services and One Plus Mail Inc—*Hugh Waters*	105 Baldwin Dr, Albany GA 31707	229-883-5291	R	1*	<.1
57	EM Transcriptions Inc—*Ellen Mcintee*	3472 3 Mile Rd Ne, Grand Rapids MI 49525	616-361-8150	R	1*	<.1
58	Mccallum and Associates Inc—*Amy Morris*	5300 Memorial Dr Ste 6, Houston TX 77007	713-861-0203	R	1*	<.1

TOTALS: SIC 7338 Secretarial & Court Reporting
Companies: 58

					411	4.3

7342 Disinfecting & Pest Control Services

Rank	Company Name—*Executive Officer*	Address, City, State, Zip	Phone	Type	Fin	Empls
1	ServiceMaster Consumer Services LP—*Patrick Spainhour*	860 Ridge Lake Blvd, Memphis TN 38120	901-766-1400	S	910*	15.0
2	Orkin Inc—*Gary W Rollins*	2170 Piedmont Rd NE, Atlanta GA 30324	404-888-2000	S	660*	7.0
3	Swisher Hygiene Inc—*Steven Berrard*	4725 Piedmont Row Dr S, Charlotte NC 28210	704-602-7116	P	64	1.1
4	Western Exterminator Co—*Michael Katz*	305 N Crescent Way, Anaheim CA 92801	714-517-9000	R	61*	1.0
5	Terminix Service Inc—*Thomas N Fortson*	PO Box 2627, Columbia SC 29202	803-772-1783	R	56*	.6
6	Cook's Pest Control Inc—*Jim Aycock*	PO Box 2065, Decatur AL 35602	256-353-6461	R	50*	.9
7	Truly Nolen of America Inc—*Scott Nolen*	3636 E Speedway, Tucson AZ 85716	520-327-3447	R	47*	1.0
8	Dodson Brothers Exterminating Company Inc—*Bertram F Dodson Jr*	3714 Campbell Ave, Lynchburg VA 24501	434-846-2747	R	29*	.5
9	Massey Services Inc—*Harvey L Massey*	315 Groveland St, Orlando FL 32804	407-645-2500	R	23*	.4
10	Allgood Services Of Georgia Inc—*Rufus Tindol*	PO Box 465598, Lawrenceville GA 30042	770-339-4500	R	18*	.2
11	Wrenn Enterprises Inc—*Edward Wrenn*	PO Box 4388, Gadsden AL 35904	256-547-9868	R	9*	.1
12	A-Able Inc—*Michael Herson*	17801 Ventura Blvd, Encino CA 91316	323-658-5779	R	8*	.1
13	JP Mchale Pest Management Inc—*James Mchale*	PO Box 98, Montrose NY 10548	914-734-7413	R	8*	.1
14	Sexton Pest Control Inc—*Paul Sexton*	1401 N 29th Ave, Phoenix AZ 85009	602-331-0611	R	7*	.1
15	Smithereen Company Del—*Richard Jennings*	7400 N Melvina Ave, Niles IL 60714	847-675-0010	R	7*	.1
16	Griffin Pest Control Inc—*Linden Griffin*	2700 Stadium Dr, Kalamazoo MI 49008	269-353-0934	R	7*	.1
17	Scherzinger Corp—*Steven Scherzinger*	5164 Kennedy Ave, Cincinnati OH 45213	513-531-7848	R	7*	.1
18	Wilson Pest Control Company Inc—*Bob Wanzer*	PO Box 1265, Winston Salem NC 27102	336-722-1193	R	6*	.1
19	Sandwich Isles Termite and Pest Control—*Michael Botha*	96-1368 Waihona St Ste, Pearl City HI 96782	808-456-7716	R	5*	<.1
20	Demco Enterprises Inc—*Diane Colton*	PO Box 261127, San Diego CA 92196	858-695-0455	R	5*	.1
21	Cooper Pest Solution Inc—*Phillip Cooper*	351 Lawrence Station R, Lawrenceville NJ 08648	609-799-1300	R	5*	.1
22	New England Pest Control Company Inc—*Stephen Goldman*	161 Oconnell St, Providence RI 02905	401-941-5700	R	5*	.1
23	Pestmaster Services Inc—*Jeffrey Van Diepen*	137 E S St, Bishop CA 93514	760-873-8100	R	5*	.1
24	Baco Exterminating Services LLC	6120 Northbelt Pkwy St, Norcross GA 30071	770-409-8882	R	5*	.1
25	Arrow Exterminating Company Inc—*Bernard Stegman*	PO Box 864, Lynbrook NY 11563	631-744-5995	R	5*	.1
26	Phoenix Pest Control Inc—*Donald Vanasse*	PO Box 11067, Phoenix AZ 85061	602-252-4212	R	5*	.1
27	Arrow Services Inc—*Everett Colvin*	PO Box 515, Plymouth IN 46563	574-936-9955	R	4*	.1
28	Allstate Services Inc—*Jim Humphries*	PO Box 3067, Fort Myers FL 33918	239-656-1711	R	4*	.1
29	Able Exterminators Inc—*Helene Mcdonald*	PO Box 5339, San Jose CA 95150	408-251-6500	R	4*	.1
30	Aa Southern Pest Control Inc—*Robert Mcmichael*	2697 International Pkw, Virginia Beach VA 23452	757-468-8818	R	4*	.1
31	Ameri-Tech Termite and Pest Control Inc—*Craig Martin*	6400 Boat Club Rd Ste, Fort Worth TX 76179	817-745-2844	R	4*	<.1
32	Morgan Brothers Inc—*Calvin Morgan*	2343 N Larkin Ave, Fresno CA 93727	559-291-2200	R	4*	<.1
33	Chem Free Organic Pest Control Inc—*Robert Jenkins*	9475 E Hwy 290, Austin TX 78724	512-837-9681	R	4*	<.1
34	Green Magic LLC—*Mohinder Maan*	267 Puuhale Rd, Honolulu HI 96819	808-841-5855	R	4*	.1
35	JP McHale Management Co—*James McHale*	PO Box 98, Montrose NY 10548	914-739-4472	R	4*	<.1
36	Animal Pest Management Services Inc—*Dan Fox*	13655 Redwood Ct, Chino CA 91710	909-591-9551	R	4*	<.1
37	Northstar Exterminators Inc—*Matthew Evans*	PO Box 11, Bloomington CA 92316	909-877-1810	R	3*	<.1
38	Wickenburg Pest Control—*Dallas Gant*	PO Box 20064, Wickenburg AZ 85358	928-684-2728	R	3*	.1
39	Magic Exterminating Company Inc—*Harold Byer*	59 01 Kissena Blvd, Flushing NY 11355	718-961-9000	R	3*	.1
40	Dallas Pest and Termite Services—*Jeffrey Smith*	3033 Kellway Dr Ste 10, Carrollton TX 75006	972-416-9999	R	3*	.1
41	Suburban Exterminating Service Inc—*Martin Byer*	879 Jericho Tpke, Smithtown NY 11787	516-541-7214	R	3*	.1
42	Kingsway Exterminating Company Inc—*Richard Kourbage*	2216 Flatbush Ave Fl 2, Brooklyn NY 11234	718-859-8448	R	3*	.1
43	Bugs Burger Bug Killers Inc—*Andrew Burger*	1666 J F Kennedy Cause, North Bay Village FL 33141	305-865-3611	R	3*	<.1
44	Jlh Coastal Fumigators Inc—*Leo Holder*	1119 W 34th St, Houston TX 77018	713-863-7378	R	3*	<.1
45	Tri State Pest Control Inc—*Sam Halgopian*	84 Grand Ave, River Edge NJ 07661	201-996-9444	R	3*	<.1
46	Sunrise Pest Control Inc—*Bob Richardson*	4032 Leos Ln, Carmichael CA 95608	916-944-7378	R	3*	<.1
47	Doctor Fume Inc—*Victor Tinoco*	624 N Eckhoff St, Orange CA 92868	714-938-1243	R	3*	<.1
48	Modern Exterminating and Termite Control Inc—*James Kerr*	2200 Macdade Blvd, Holmes PA 19043	610-586-5525	R	3*	<.1
49	Bliss Termite Control Div	20 Jerusalem Ave, Hempstead NY 11550	516-489-3707	R	3*	<.1
50	Okolona Pest Control Inc—*Donnie Blake*	PO Box 19201, Louisville KY 40259	502-969-9635	R	3*	<.1
51	Wayne's Pest Control—*Steven Splawn*	2195 Pky Lake Dr, Birmingham AL 35244	205-985-7009	R	3*	<.1
52	Tomasello Inc—*Charles Doll*	PO Box 6697, West Palm Beach FL 33405	561-585-2551	S	3*	<.1
53	Killingsworth Enviromental Inc—*Clifford Killingsworth*	PO Box 7558, Pensacola FL 32534	850-474-4000	R	3*	<.1
54	Griggs and Browne Company Inc—*George Ford*	549 Grove St Ste 1, Worcester MA 01605	508-852-4066	R	3*	<.1
55	Killingsworth Pest Control—*Billy Killingsworth*	PO Box 7558, Pensacola FL 32534	850-474-0365	R	2*	<.1
56	Class Termite and Pest Control Inc—*Roger Class*	1640 Cabrillo Ave, Torrance CA 90501	310-328-7781	R	2*	<.1
57	Able Torco Pest Control	254 S Main St, Franklin OH 45005	937-743-5919	R	2*	<.1
58	Houston CPC Inc—*David Young*	10696 Haddington Dr St, Houston TX 77043	713-461-2333	R	2*	<.1

Rank	Company Name—*Executive Officer*	Address, City, State, Zip	Phone	Type	Fin	Empls
59	Catseye Pest Control Inc—*John Gagne*	31 Commercial Dr, Castleton On Hudson NY 12033	518-869-5042	R	2*	<.1
60	Geese Police Inc—*David Marcks*	PO Box 656, Howell NJ 07731	732-938-9093	R	2*	<.1
61	Hilton Head Exterminators Inc—*A Culbreth*	37 Hunter Rd, Hilton Head Island SC 29926	843-681-2590	R	2*	<.1
62	Business Industry and Environment Inc—*David Lovenvirth*	4617 Auburn Blvd, Sacramento CA 95841	916-481-0268	R	2*	<.1
63	Berrett Talega Corp—*Jon Berrett*	PO Box 8745, Brea CA 92822	714-257-9277	R	2*	<.1
64	Leo's Exterminating Company Inc—*Perry Carrier*	PO Box 3110, Bristol TN 37625	423-968-3442	R	2*	.1
65	J and J Exterminating Company Of Lake Charles Inc—*Tim Broussard*	1717 W Prien Lake Rd, Lake Charles LA 70601	337-474-7377	R	2*	<.1
66	Russell's Exterminating Company Inc—*Vicki Bull-Nadolski*	PO Box 11789, Knoxville TN 37939	865-584-8549	R	2*	<.1
67	All-American Services Inc—*Bliss Foster*	PO Box 310044, Atlanta GA 31131	404-344-5985	R	2*	<.1
68	Discount Fumigation Inc—*Kristopher Nybackken*	260 Cimino St, San Jose CA 95125	408-279-2040	R	2*	<.1
69	May Exterminating Co—*David Dillingham*	PO Box 116, Jacksonville NC 28541	910-455-5888	R	2*	<.1
70	Aaa Exterminating Inc—*Scott Intyre*	4412 Conner St, Noblesville IN 46060	317-773-3797	R	2*	<.1
71	Bug Off Exterminators Inc—*John Jacobsen*	1064 Nw 54th St, Fort Lauderdale FL 33309	954-772-8338	R	2*	<.1
72	Craig and Sons Termite and Pest Control Inc—*Christine Likins*	PO Box 8430, Redlands CA 92375	909-335-1486	R	2*	<.1
73	Travis Pest Management Inc—*Gerald Travis*	1976 16th Ave, Vero Beach FL 32960	772-563-2669	R	2*	<.1
74	Hunley Exterminating Co—*Homer Hunley*	PO Box 488, Joelton TN 37080	615-876-0603	R	2*	<.1
75	Jc Brown Inc—*James Brown*	705 E Milana Rd, San Juan TX 78589	956-787-3206	R	2*	<.1
76	Andrews Termite and Pest Control—*Andrew Davis*	2580 Hwy 78, Loganville GA 30052	770-267-7977	R	2*	<.1
77	Thrasher Termite and Pest Control—*Janet Thrasher*	17427 Farley Rd W, Los Gatos CA 95030	408-354-9944	R	2*	<.1
78	Canadys Services Inc—*Terry Canady*	PO Box 440, Lumber Bridge NC 28357	910-843-3118	R	2*	<.1
79	Springfield Public Works—*Allen Ellis*	2809 Clinard Dr, Springfield TN 37172	615-384-2746	R	2*	<.1
80	Mc Gee Pest Control Inc—*Mark Gee*	PO Box 674, Hopkinsville KY 42241	270-885-5623	R	2*	<.1
81	Gima Pest Control Inc—*David Gima*	96 1225 Waihona St Ste, Pearl City HI 96782	808-454-0845	R	2*	<.1
82	Bugmobile Pest and Termite Control—*Bernhard Muller*	2305 N Laurent St, Victoria TX 77901	979-245-8071	R	1*	<.1
83	First Service Pest Control—*Emma Fielder*	9503 E 63rd St Ste 113, Raytown MO 64133	816-356-2849	R	1*	<.1
84	Paramount Termite Control Of Fresno Inc—*Jan Hallburton*	5250 N Cornelia Ave, Fresno CA 93722	559-277-4333	R	1*	<.1
85	Wood Termite and Pest Control Inc—*Mack Lingdon*	PO Box 1831, Smithfield NC 27577	919-934-7961	R	1*	<.1
86	Whitman Exterminating Co—*Richard Whitman*	601 S Oakwood Ave, Beckley WV 25801	304-253-3331	R	1*	<.1
87	Anti-Pest Company Inc—*J May*	PO Box 4266, Shreveport LA 71134	318-221-6181	R	1*	<.1
88	H And H Pets And Waterproofing—*Alan Langley*	520 E Dixon Blvd, Shelby NC 28152	828-287-2847	R	1*	<.1
89	De Sousa Inc—*Stephen Goff*	PO Box 560677, Rockledge FL 32956	321-632-9262	R	1*	<.1
90	A Pest Control Inc—*Randall Blixt*	2640 E 84th Pl, Merrillville IN 46410	219-769-2228	R	1*	<.1
91	Scientific Exterminating Services—*Mark Giordano*	599 Lake Ave, Saint James NY 11780	631-265-5252	R	1*	<.1
92	Womack Industries Inc—*John Burkinshaw*	131 Congressional Ln, Rockville MD 20852	301-881-5181	R	1*	<.1
93	Parker Pest Control Inc—*Brad Parker*	3616 Lake Rd, Ponca City OK 74604	580-762-6614	R	1*	<.1
94	JC Ehrlich Company Inc—*Sean Hunter*	PO Box 13848, Reading PA 19612	610-372-4500	S	1*	.1
95	Brasure's Pest Control Inc—*Carroll Brasure*	PO Box 1100, Selbyville DE 19975	302-436-8140	R	1*	<.1
96	Bales Services Inc—*Keith Bales*	609 Briarfield Rd, Newport News VA 23605	757-244-7881	R	1*	<.1
97	Jones and Son Pest Control—*James Bows*	1520 63rd Ave E, Bradenton FL 34203	941-758-7723	R	1*	<.1
98	Connecticut Pest Elimination Inc—*Michael Lipsett*	PO Box 422, West Haven CT 06516	203-931-7378	R	1*	<.1
99	Express Pest Control Company Inc—*Shawn Felts*	323 Industrial Blvd St, Mckinney TX 75069	972-562-9999	R	<1*	<.1
100	TOMI Environmental Solutions Inc—*Halden Shane*	9454 Wilshire Blvd PH/, Beverly Hills CA 90212	310-275-2255	P	<1	<.1

TOTALS: SIC 7342 Disinfecting & Pest Control Services
    Companies: 100   2,180   31.2

7349 Building Maintenance Services Nec

Rank	Company Name—*Executive Officer*	Address, City, State, Zip	Phone	Type	Fin	Empls
1	One Source Management Inc—*Henrik C Slipsager* ABM Industries Inc	1600 Parkwood Cir SE S, Atlanta GA 30339	770-436-9900	S	64,730*	31.0
2	Somers Building Maintenance Inc—*Charles Somers*	5241 Arnold Ave, McClellan CA 95652	916-922-7600	R	13,110*	6.0
3	ABM Industries Inc—*Henrik C Slipsager*	551 5th Ave Ste 300, New York NY 10176	212-297-0200	P	3,496	96.0
4	GSF Safeway Inc—*Troy L Bargmann*	107 S Pennsylvania St, Indianapolis IN 46204	317-262-1133	R	2,317*	13.0
5	Management Cleaning Controls, LLC—*Ruth Broom*	10101 Linn Station Rd, Louisville KY 40223	502-426-5327	R	1,920*	2.0
6	Pride Industries—*Michael Ziegler*	PO Box 1200, Rocklin CA 95677	916-788-2100	R	1,822*	4.3
7	Mason and Hanger Corp—*Richard Loghry*	300 W Vine St Ste 1300, Lexington KY 40507	859-252-9980	R	1,300*	<.1
8	Rollins Inc—*Gary W Rollins*	PO Box 647, Atlanta GA 30301	404-888-2000	P	1,137	10.3
9	Healthcare Services Group Inc—*Daniel P McCartney*	3220 Tillman Dr Ste 30, Bensalem PA 19020		P	889	6.9
10	Initial Contract Services USA	4067 Industrial Park D, Norcross GA 30071	770-476-2580	D	807*	5.0
11	ABM Janitorial Services—*Henrik Slipsager* ABM Industries Inc	420 Taylor St Ste 200, San Francisco CA 94102	415-351-4500	D	614*	35.0
12	Unicco Service Co—*George Keches*	275 Grove St, Newton MA 02466	617-527-5222	S	508*	18.5
13	Mitch Murch's Maintenance Management Co—*Tim M Murch*	2827 Clark Ave, Saint Louis MO 63103	314-535-2100	R	450*	3.0
14	American Reprographics Co—*K Suriyakumar*	1981 N Broadway Ste 38, Walnut Creek CA 94596	925-949-5100	P	442	3.2
15	McLemore Building and Maintenance Inc—*Don E McLemore*	110 Fargo, Houston TX 77006	713-528-7775	R	422*	.9
16	Rayben Enterprises Inc—*Raymond Walker*	31 Railroad Ave, Albany NY 12205	518-426-7643	R	391*	.2
17	Temco Service Industries Inc—*Henrik Thomassian*	1 Park Ave, New York NY 10016	212-889-6353	R	365*	10.0
18	Harvard Maintenance Inc—*Stanley Doobin*	570 7th Ave Fl 15, New York NY 10018	212-730-0001	R	215*	3.0
19	Paro Services Co—*Daniel Zelman*	1755 Enterprise Pkwy S, Twinsburg OH 44087	330-467-1300	R	200*	.2
20	Pelco Industries Inc—*William Pelloni*	1220 Yeamans Hall Rd, Hanahan SC 29410	843-529-1169	R	180*	<.1
21	Pritchard Industries Inc—*Peter Pritchard*	1120 Ave Of The Amrcs, New York NY 10036	212-382-2295	R	164*	4.1
22	Superior Services Inc—*Sheila Guarderas*	1505 N Chestnut Ave, Fresno CA 93703	559-458-0507	R	152*	.7
23	MPW Industrial Services Group Inc—*Monte Black*	PO Box 10, Hebron OH 43025	740-927-8790	R	145*	2.0
24	Amtech Lighting Services—*Ronald Gilcrease* ABM Industries Inc	2390 E Orangewood Ave, Anaheim CA 92806	714-940-4000	S	124*	.8
25	Servpro Intellectual Property Inc—*Sue Steen*	PO Box 1978, Gallatin TN 37066	615-451-0200	R	123*	.1
26	Diversified Maintenance Systems Inc—*Alan Butcher*	5110 Eisenhower Blvd S, Tampa FL 33634	813-383-0238	R	117*	4.5
27	FM Facility Maintenance LLC—*Jim Reavey*	10 Columbus Blvd 4th F, Hartford CT 06106	860-466-7400	R	115*	.4
28	Impace Building Services Inc—*John Yates Jr*	1409 Brittmoore Rd, Houston TX 77043	713-461-8925	R	104*	.2
29	Royal Services Inc—*Percy Rosenbloom Jr*	4526 Lenox Ave, Jacksonville FL 32205		R	99*	.7
30	Professional Janitorial Service of Houston Inc—*Floyd Mahanay*	2303 Nance St, Houston TX 77020	713-850-0287	R	62*	.3
31	Lacosta Facility Support Services—*Karla Johnson*	PO Box 6065, Wauconda IL 60084	847-526-9556	R	55*	2.8
32	Sunair Services Corp—*Jack I Ruff*	595 S Federal Hwy Ste, Boca Raton FL 33432	561-208-7400	S	51	.5
33	Wyatt Field Service Co—*Roy Cuny*	PO Box 3052, Houston TX 77253	713-570-2000	S	49*	.2
34	BMS Enterprises Inc—*Kirk Blackmon*	308 Arthur St, Fort Worth TX 76107	817-810-9200	R	41*	.3
35	Faulk Co—*Tim Faulk*	8855 West Fwy, Fort Worth TX 76116	817-332-9157	R	41*	.3
36	Cloaning Service Group Inc—*Rochelle O'brien*	230 N St, Danvers MA 01923		R	40*	3.0
37	Molly Maid Inc—*David McKinnon*	3948 Ranchero Dr, Ann Arbor MI 48108	734-665-7575	R	35*	<.1
38	Cavalier Maintenance Services Inc—*Kevin Rohan*	2722 Merrilee Dr Ste 3, Fairfax VA 22031	703-849-1100	R	33*	1.8
39	G and R Mineral Services Inc—*Bobby Rushen*	PO Box 100939, Birmingham AL 35210	205-956-7300	R	31*	1.5

Note: An asterisk (*) indicates an estimated financial figure. The company type code used is as follows: R = Private, P = Public, S = Private Subsidiary, B = Public Subsidiary, D = Division, J = Joint Venture, I = Investment Fund.

COMPANY RANKINGS BY SALES WITHIN 4-DIGIT SIC

Rank	Company Name—Executive Officer	Address, City, State, Zip	Phone	Type	Fin	Empls
40	Eastco Building Services Inc—Steven Brown	130 Brook Ave Ste A, Deer Park NY 11729	631-243-4444	R	30*	.3
41	Texas Maintenance Systems Inc—Il Kwon	9106 Bellflower, Houston TX 77063	713-782-7066	R	29*	.2
42	Enviro-Clean Services Inc—Dan Koster	PO Box 2818, Holland MI 49422	616-392-3775	R	29*	.9
43	J and J - Bmar Joint Venture LLP—Johnny Voudouris	3755 S Capital Of Texa, Austin TX 78704	512-444-7271	R	28*	.1
44	Potomac Services LLC—Patricia Cooney	4401 E W Hwy Ste 500, Bethesda MD 20814	301-654-4360	R	27*	2.0
45	St Moritz Building Services Inc—Philip Moritz	4616 Clairton Blvd, Pittsburgh PA 15236	412-885-2100	R	27*	1.3
46	Interstate Cleaning Corp—John Brauch	PO Box 21584, Saint Louis MO 63132	314-428-0566	R	26*	1.3
47	General Building Maintenance Inc—Sunny Park	3835 Presidential Pkwy, Atlanta GA 30340	770-457-5678	R	26*	.5
48	J and E Associates—James W Harris	6031 S Loop E, Houston TX 77033	713-640-1177	R	26*	.1
49	American Industrial Cleaning Company Inc—Myron Stempa	10 Chelsea Pl, Great Neck NY 11021	516-482-8424	R	25*	1.2
50	UNIBAR Maintenance Services Inc—G Jean Davis	4325 Concourse Dr, Ann Arbor MI 48108	734-769-2600	R	25*	1.2
51	Accredited Building Services Inc—Roy Felder	17320 Groeschke Rd, Houston TX 77084	281-578-2296	R	25*	.2
52	Redlee Inc—Charles L Redfearn Jr	10425 Olympic Dr, Dallas TX 75220	214-357-4753	R	25*	.1
53	Suburban Contract Cleaning Inc—Glenn Pratt	PO Box 850914, Braintree MA 02185	781-356-4400	R	25*	1.1
54	SRS Inc (Gallatin Tennessee)—T Dewayne Scott	PO Box 626, Gallatin TN 37066	615-230-2966	R	24*	.1
55	All Star Maintenance Inc—Michael D Ebert	12250 El Camino Real S, San Diego CA 92130	858-259-0900	S	23*	1.0
56	Centaur Building Services Inc—Frank Joubert	4401 Ridgewood Ave, Saint Louis MO 63116	314-752-7770	R	23*	1.0
57	Jani-King of Fort Worth—Jerry Crawford Jani-King International Inc	235 NE Loop 820 Ste 10, Hurst TX 76053	817-284-5600	S	23*	.1
58	Vador Ventures Inc—Victor Moran	3619 14th St Nw, Washington DC 20010	202-722-2240	R	23*	.6
59	TUCS Cleaning Service Inc—Sergio Artazu	166 Central Ave, Orange NJ 07050	973-673-0700	R	21*	.4
60	Corporate Cleaning Systems Inc—Benjamin Alper	PO Box 75026, Cincinnati OH 45275		R	21*	1.2
61	Universal Building Services And Supply Co—Grace Brusseau	3120 Pierce St, Richmond CA 94804	510-527-1078	R	20*	.9
62	Sightline Health LLC—TJ Farnsworth	1415 N Loop W Ste 1200, Houston TX 77008	713-589-6879	R	18	.1
63	Clean-Tech Co—James M Fiala	211 S Jefferson Ave, Saint Louis MO 63103	314-652-2388	R	18*	1.4
64	Acme Building Maintenance Company Inc—Rick Sanchez	PO Box 158, San Jose CA 95126	408-263-5911	R	18*	.1
65	Capital Cleaning Contractors Inc—Linda Kaplan	88 Duryea Rd, Melville NY 11747		R	18*	.1
66	Commercial Building Maintenance Corp—David Parsons	200 Oak Dr Unit 201, Syosset NY 11791	516-364-0957	R	17*	.8
67	Service Force USA LLC—Jim Galliera	45662 Terminal Dr 210, Dulles VA 20166	703-481-0222	R	17*	1.0
68	US Metro Group Inc—Charles Kim	3171 W Olympic Blvd 55, Los Angeles CA 90006	213-382-6435	R	16*	.8
69	Intensive Maintenance Care Inc—Chris Walters	PO Box 489, Chesterfield MO 63006	314-524-6615	R	16*	1.0
70	Southern Cleaning Service Inc—Harry Goforth	106 S Chalkville Rd, Trussville AL 35173	205-655-8326	R	15*	.8
71	City Wide Maintenance Company Inc—Jeff Oddo	8454 Nieman Rd, Shawnee Mission KS 66214	913-888-5700	R	15*	.1
72	Nesbitt Services Inc—Rodney Nesbitt	7348 Grapevine Hwy, Fort Worth TX 76180	817-284-1213	R	15*	.1
73	Sanitors Southwest Of San Antonio Inc—Darrell Glover	8506 Speedway Dr, San Antonio TX 78230	210-349-4647	S	15*	.8
74	Pacific Maintenance Co—Larry Wishart	2175 Martin Ave, Santa Clara CA 95050	408-727-9393	R	14*	.8
75	Master Klean Janitorial Inc—Steven Jetter	PO Box 22044, Denver CO 80222	303-753-6084	R	14*	.8
76	ACA Industries Inc—A Alex	385 W Main St, Babylon NY 11702	631-587-2485	R	13*	.6
77	Centurion Group Inc—Oscar Valdez	PO Box 62358, Colorado Springs CO 80962	719-268-2953	R	13*	.1
78	Powerlink Environmental Services LLC—Kathleen Howard	3031 W Grand Blvd Ste, Detroit MI 48202	313-309-2020	R	12*	.3
79	JESCO Industrial Services Inc—Bruce Roberson	5526 Industrial Pky, Calvert City KY 42029	270-395-7226	S	12*	.1
80	Allegiance Industries Inc—Gary Mc Laurin	PO Box 12251, Columbia SC 29211	803-779-1961	R	12*	.6
81	V-Tech Services Inc—Thanh Nguyen	1505 Chester Pke Ste 1, Folcroft PA 19032	610-237-0447	R	12*	.6
82	Sj Services Inc—Shawn Shea	20 Locust St Ste 202, Danvers MA 01923	978-750-1033	R	12*	.5
83	Scrub Inc—Roman Chmiel	6033 N Milwaukee Ave, Chicago IL 60646	773-631-0400	R	12*	.7
84	Cristi Cleaning Service Corp—Cristina Lopez	77 Trinity Pl, Hackensack NJ 07601	201-883-1717	R	11*	.4
85	Corporate Building Systems Inc—Randy Sanders	1351 Abbott Ct, Buffalo Grove IL 60089	847-913-0085	R	11*	.6
86	Ameritac Inc—Isiah Harris	2280 Diamond Blvd Ste, Concord CA 94520	925-691-8360	R	11*	.1
87	Continental Building Maintenance Company Inc—Mike Martins	14310 Sullyfield Cir S, Chantilly VA 20151	703-631-7300	R	11*	.8
88	Midwest Maintenance Company Inc—Jamie Gutierrez	2901 Q St, Omaha NE 68107	402-733-1114	R	10*	.5
89	Associated Building Maintenance Company Inc—Deborah Zagami	2140 Priest Bridge Ct, Crofton MD 21114	410-721-1818	R	10*	.6
90	New Image Building Services Inc—John Ezzo	320 Church St, Mount Clemens MI 48043	586-465-4420	R	10*	.5
91	Trinity Building Services—Mike Boschetto	430 N Canal St Ste 2, South San Francisco CA 94080	650-873-2121	R	10*	.3
92	Kleenmark Services Corp—Scott Stevenson	1210 Ann St, Madison WI 53713	608-258-3131	R	10*	.6
93	Entrust One Facility Services Inc—Aaron Liverpool	11142 Shady Trl, Dallas TX 75229	972-669-8485	R	10*	.5
94	Aimm Technologies Inc—Brooks Bradford	PO Box 369, La Marque TX 77568	409-945-5414	R	10*	.1
95	One Stop Facilities Maintenance Corp—Brett Finkelstein	267 5th Ave Rm B-103, New York NY 10016	212-217-9938	R	9*	.7
96	Golden Gate Service Inc—Ki Hong	2812 Old Lee Hwy Ste 3, Fairfax VA 22031	703-425-6200	R	9*	.5
97	Richco Janitor Service Inc—Charles Magriel	PO Box 1250, Springfield MA 01101	413-781-5686	R	9*	.3
98	Performance Clean LLC	1 Brewers Way, Milwaukee WI 53214	414-902-4780	R	9*	.5
99	Mardone Inc—William Pidone	9411 Lee Hwy Ste O, Fairfax VA 22031	703-273-6464	R	9*	.5
100	BuildingStars St Louis Inc—Chris Blase	11489 Page Service Dr, Saint Louis MO 63146	314-991-3356	R	9*	<.1
101	Integratas Maintenance Corp—Michael O'neill	1785 Lakeland Ave, Ronkonkoma NY 11779	631-737-7655	R	8*	.8
102	GSF Safeway LLC—Tim Rupard GSF Safeway Inc	107 S Pennsylvania St, Indianapolis IN 46204	317-262-1133	S	8*	.6
103	Gmi Building Services Inc—Larry Abrams	8001 Vickers St, San Diego CA 92111	858-279-6262	R	8*	.2
104	Advanced Facilities Services International Inc—Brian Brault	805 Rein Rd, Cheektowaga NY 14225	716-633-2331	R	8*	.2
105	Duo Building Maintenance Inc—Burt Jacobson	PO Box 1167, Hightstown NJ 08520	609-448-8355	R	8*	.2
106	Tuttle Family Enterprises Inc—Tim Tuttle	21020 Superior St, Chatsworth CA 91311	818-834-0297	R	8*	.4
107	Syntecos Inc—Guido Costantini	9000 Southwest Fwy Ste, Houston TX 77074	713-660-6271	R	8*	.3
108	Unity Building Services Inc—Ernest Cerone	379 5th Ave Fl 2, New York NY 10016	212-685-2211	R	8*	.2
109	Held's Janitorial Service Inc—William Held	1 Hsbc Ctr Ste 1, Buffalo NY 14203	716-854-1408	R	7*	.4
110	Ameriklean Inc—Barbara Brawn	PO Box 5264, Anderson SC 29623	864-231-8903	R	7*	.3
111	JAN Services Inc—Ellen Freemo	824 W Streetsboro St, Hudson OH 44236	330-650-4611	R	7*	.3
112	PIC Maintenance Inc—Eric Raykinstinste	27734 Franklin Rd, Southfield MI 48034	248-799-7720	R	7*	.3
113	Pjs Of Texas Inc—Don Dyer	1304 W Oltorf St, Austin TX 78704	512-447-0477	R	7*	.3
114	Scioto Services LLC—Thomas Kruse	405 S Oak St, Marysville OH 43040	937-644-0888	R	7*	.3
115	Campbells Janitorial and Lawn Maintenance—Matthew Campbell	2212 Primrose Ave Ste, Mcallen TX 78504	956-687-6243	R	7*	.3
116	Zapata Janitorial Building and General Services Inc—Alfonzo Zapata	PO Box 266515, Houston TX 77207	713-827-0205	R	7*	.3
117	Top Quality Maintenance Inc—Luis Maldonado	2728 Parsons Run Ct, Henderson NV 89074	702-263-9495	R	7*	.3
118	Prestige Maintenance Inc—Lorenzo Henderson	2350 S Midwest Blvd St, Midwest City OK 73110	405-732-4330	R	7*	.2
119	Alban Service Industries LLC—Tim Zerka	130 Market St, Kenilworth NJ 07033	908-298-6888	R	7*	.1
120	Melton Franchise Systems Inc—Mark Melton	6430 Via Real Ste 5, Carpinteria CA 93013	805-684-8850	R	7*	<.1
121	At Once Cleaning Services Inc—Lenny Robinson	3811 Fear Ave, Baltimore MD 21215	410-367-1700	R	7*	.3
122	Tcb Systems Inc—Robert Orue	PO Box 960786, Miami FL 33296	305-385-2229	R	7*	.2
123	Kleenco Corp—Danny Perry	3015 Koapaka St Ste A, Honolulu HI 96819	808-831-7600	R	7*	.4
124	Rnr Enterprises Inc—Robin Navert	5808 Franklin St, Denver CO 80216	303-988-4166	R	7*	.1

Rank	Company Name—*Executive Officer*	Address, City, State, Zip	Phone	Type	Fin	Empls
125	Master Maintenance Inc—*Jason Hodge*	PO Box 272758, Tampa FL 33688	813-931-7177	R	6*	.2
126	Pegasus Cleaning Corp—*Violet Lewis*	1412 Main St Fl 2, Buffalo NY 14209	716-886-3407	R	6*	.2
127	Spencer Building Maintenance Inc—*Aaron Spencer*	1336 Dixieanne Ave, Sacramento CA 95815	916-922-1900	R	6*	.3
128	Brite Cleaning Service Inc—*Arnold Yarger*	PO Box 341264, Memphis TN 38184	901-266-5055	R	6*	.2
129	Haynes Building Service Inc—*John Scharler*	125 W Maple Ave, Monrovia CA 91016	626-359-6100	R	6*	.2
130	Janitorial Services Inc—*Ronald Martinez*	5795 Canal Rd, Cleveland OH 44125	216-341-8601	R	6*	.3
131	Jani-King International Inc—*Jerry Crawford*	16885 Dallas Pkwy, Addison TX 75001	972-991-0900	R	6*	.3
132	Cadence Mtc LLC—*Judy Boyer*	2535 Reavest Dr S, Indianapolis IN 46203	317-782-1800	R	6*	.2
133	77 Deerhurst Corp—*Charles Cestaro*	1315 Blondell Ave, Bronx NY 10461	718-409-2310	R	6*	.2
134	Signature Cleaning Services Inc—*Andrew Weisbach*	231 W 29th St Rm 402, New York NY 10001	212-502-4700	R	6*	.2
135	Jack's Maintenance Service Inc—*Lauri Struck*	PO Box 664, Neenah WI 54957	920-722-5136	R	6*	.1
136	Support Services of America Inc—*Alex E Fortunati*	12440 Firestone Blvd S, Norwalk CA 90650	562-868-3550	R	6*	.1
137	Fidelity Building Services Industries LLC	29 Flanders Rd, Budd Lake NJ 07828	973-347-8246	R	6*	<.1
138	Pci Services Inc—*Mark Wild*	843 N Madison St, Rockford IL 61107	815-961-1300	R	6*	.3
139	Extra Clean Inc—*Stanley Gittleson*	11777 Parklawn Dr Ste, Rockville MD 20852	301-770-3000	R	6*	.2
140	Clean Innovation Corp—*Raffy Espiritu*	3350 Scott Blvd Bldg 8, Santa Clara CA 95054	408-330-9350	R	6*	.2
141	Quarles Building Maintenance Inc—*David Quarles*	PO Box 3451, Memphis TN 38173	901-345-3015	R	6*	.2
142	Giant Janitorial Service Inc—*Laura Huthwaite*	18485 Mack Ave, Detroit MI 48236	313-886-7797	R	6*	.3
143	Allied Reliability Inc—*John Schultz*	4200 Faber Pl Dr, North Charleston SC 29405	843-414-5760	R	6*	.2
144	Pacific Building Services Inc—*John Howgate*	PO Box 1476, Bellevue WA 98009	425-889-8888	R	6*	.2
145	RS Felder Enterprises Inc—*Suzanne Felder*	PO Box 218707, Houston TX 77218	281-578-2296	R	6*	.2
146	Sunbright Services Building Maintenance Specialists Corp—*Frank Baran*	PO Box 5273, Parsippany NJ 07054	973-428-0800	R		.3
147	Sbm Site Services—*Charles Somers*	15400 Sw Millikan Way, Beaverton OR 97006	503-693-2927	R	5*	.3
148	Designmark Building Services Inc—*Patrick Rae*	1331 H St NW Ste 1100, Washington DC 20005	202-783-1401	R	5*	.2
149	Ceiling Pro Of San Antonio LLC—*Lisa Beath*	2300 W Commerce St Ste, San Antonio TX 78207	210-224-9588	R	5*	.2
150	Dycos Services Inc—*Jimmy Saxon*	PO Box 4243, Greenville SC 29608	864-295-1971	R	5*	.3
151	Servi-Tek LLC	3970 Sorrento Valley B, San Diego CA 92121	858-638-7735	R	5*	.3
152	Prime Cleaning Services Inc—*Pinchas Rottenberg*	199 Lee Ave 182, Brooklyn NY 11211	718-504-1443	R	5*	.2
153	Basol Maintenance Service Inc—*William Mc Mahon*	PO Box 613, Findlay OH 45839	419-422-0946	R	5*	.2
154	Mckowski's Maintnce Systems Inc—*James Mcelwee*	12125 Paine St, Poway CA 92064	858-679-4700	R	5*	.1
155	Abstract Janitorial Services Inc—*Carol Hayes*	403 Glenn Dr Ste 12, Sterling VA 20164	703-406-4401	R	5*	.3
156	Thoreau Janitorial Services Inc—*Nicki Frank*	5301 Beethoven St Ste, Los Angeles CA 90066	310-822-8017	R	5*	.2
157	W and J Schafer Enterprises Inc—*Wallace Schafer*	15 W 8th Ave, Mesa AZ 85210	480-649-9603	R	5*	.6
158	N and K Enterprises Inc—*Neville Jennings*	1971 Ne 149th St, North Miami FL 33181	305-947-4524	R	5*	.2
159	Task Masters Inc—*Gerald Boarman*	PO Box 188, Camp Hill PA 17001	717-737-7311	R	5*	.2
160	New England Health And Maintenance Corp—*Thomas Keenan*	1565 Main St Ste 201, Tewksbury MA 01876	978-851-8974	R	5*	.2
161	Whayne And Sons Enterprises Inc—*Richard Whayne*	10515 E 40th Ave Ste 1, Denver CO 80239	303-375-8000	R	5*	.1
162	Dawson Welding Co—*Don Dawson*	615 E Sawyer St, Blytheville AR 72315	870-763-4709	R	5*	.1
163	Automated Teller Accessories Inc—*Michael L Robson*	2796 S Redwood Rd, Salt Lake City UT 84119	801-975-8860	R	5*	<.1
164	Aja Landscaping And Maintenance Inc—*Jennifer Regateiro*	55 Villanova Ln, Dix Hills NY 11746	631-486-8253	R	5*	<.1
165	Regency Janitorial Service—*Patrick Kusch*	2330 S Commerce Dr, New Berlin WI 53151	262-641-9090	R	5*	.2
166	Kleenco Maintenance and Construction Inc—*Kurt Tatman*	PO Box 461, Alexandria IN 46001	765-724-3554	R	5*	.2
167	Alexander Wall Corp—*Gary Alexander*	60 Raynor Ave, Ronkonkoma NY 11779	631-471-3131	R	5*	<.1
168	Tscm Corp—*Margaret Pappano*	17791 Jamestown Ln, Huntington Beach CA 92647	714-841-1988	R	5*	.1
169	Professional Maintenance Of New Orleans La Inc—*Joseph Oshea*	4809 Alexander Dr, Metairie LA 70003	504-486-2113	R	5*	.3
170	Multipurpose Cleaning Services Inc—*Mary Coffey*	PO Box 12117, Pittsburgh PA 15231	412-922-6970	R	5*	.2
171	Shepard Industries Inc—*Michael Florentino*	45 Horsehill Rd Ste 10, Cedar Knolls NJ 07927	973-695-0410	R	5*	.1
172	Mccullers Investments Inc—*C Kenneth Mc Cull*	715 Iredell St, Durham NC 27705	919-286-4449	R	5*	.3
173	Cj Model Home Maintenance Inc—*Carrie Wevill*	PO Box 5547, Pleasanton CA 94566	925-485-3280	R	5*	.2
174	Combined National Systems Inc—*David Kwak*	7700 Little River Tpke, Annandale VA 22003	703-658-5154	R	5*	.2
175	Done Right Building Services Inc—*Anthony Samuels*	4 Copley Pl Ste 125, Boston MA 02116	617-236-0155	R	5*	.1
176	Capitol Hill Building Maintenance Inc—*Sarian Bouma*	834 Coachway, Annapolis MD 21401	301-261-8585	R	5*	.1
177	Bell Building Maintenance Co—*Chan Yang*	5170 Sepulveda Blvd St, Sherman Oaks CA 91403	818-385-0790	R	5*	.1
178	International Building Services—*Charles Solem*	PO Box 8095, Falls Church VA 22041	703-931-1000	R	4*	.2
179	Professional Maintenance Of Michigan Inc—*Clair Phillips*	1640 Elizabeth Ave Nw, Grand Rapids MI 49504	616-774-0682	R	4*	.2
180	K and S Management Supply Inc—*Sang Park*	2110 Gallows Rd Ste B1, Vienna VA 22182	703-442-8136	R	4*	.2
181	Reliable Cleaning Service Inc—*Karen Stephenson*	1015 Production Rd, Fort Wayne IN 46808	260-483-3478	R	4*	.2
182	Asi Of Miami Inc—*Lewis Rossi*	14054 Nw 82nd Ave, Hialeah FL 33016	305-821-3169	R	4*	.2
183	Rogan Building Services Inc—*Byron Rogan*	1531 7th St, Riverside CA 92507	951-248-1261	R	4*	.1
184	Charmay Inc—*Jane Gandee*	7551 Fordson Rd, Alexandria VA 22306	703-212-7000	R	4*	<.1
185	Clean Management Inc—*Carlos Valencia*	PO Box 519, Pawtucket RI 02862	401-722-7858	R	4*	.1
186	Superior Building Maintenance Inc—*Dan Thibault*	2007 S W St, Wichita KS 67213	316-943-2347	R	4*	.3
187	Rubicon Enterprises Inc—*Richard Aubry*	2500 Bissell Ave, Richmond CA 94804	510-235-1516	R	4*	.2
188	One Source Facility Services Inc—*Patrick Mcginley*	50 Federal Rd, Danbury CT 06810	203-744-3488	R	4*	.2
189	Hunter Easterday Corp—*Sam Easterday*	1475 N Hundley St, Anaheim CA 92806	714-238-3400	R	4*	.1
190	Rhino Building Services Inc—*Cody Sears*	6650 Flanders Dr Ste K, San Diego CA 92121	858-455-1440	R	4*	.1
191	American Building Maintenance Of Louisiana Inc—*William Edwards*	910 S Acadian Thruway, Baton Rouge LA 70806	225-387-0028	R	4*	.4
192	Carolina Kneece's Cleaning Service Inc—*Charles Kneece*	602 Railroad Ave, Johnston SC 29832	803-254-2174	R	4*	.3
193	Rock Solid Janitorial Inc—*Arvella Gardner*	2705 W Mercury Blvd, Hampton VA 23666	757-766-7223	R	4*	.2
194	One Source Internationl Maintenance Inc—*Olive Socosoki*	4410 Dillon Ln Ste 50, Corpus Christi TX 78415	361-855-1831	R	4*	.2
195	Protec Association Services—*J Rauch*	5555 Kearny Villa Rd, San Diego CA 92123	858-569-1080	R	4*	.2
196	Cardinal Building Maintenance—*James Grado*	4952 W 128th Pl, Alsip IL 60803	708-430-3340	R	4*	.1
197	Cardinal Maintenance and Service Company Inc—*Dan Pohl*	180 E Miller Ave, Akron OH 44301	330-252-0282	R	4*	.1
198	Penn and Sons Inc—*Willie Penn*	4252 Carmichael Rd Ste, Montgomery AL 36106	334-272-0411	R	4*	.1
199	A Bee C Service Inc—*Alan Sutton*	7589 First Pl, Cleveland OH 44146	440-735-1505	R	4*	.1
200	Munters Moisture Control Services	2008 Bloomingdale Rd, Glendale Heights IL 60139		S	4*	.3
201	Burns Janitor Service Inc—*Shea Burns*	1631 W Hill St, Louisville KY 40210	502-585-4548	R	4*	.1
202	Environmental Control Building Maintenance Co—*William Sanders*	17231 Railroad St Ste, City of Industry CA 91748	626-839-8138	R	4*	.1
203	Jhn Inc—*Maryanne Newby*	950 Enchanted Way Ste, Simi Valley CA 93065	805-306-8000	R	4*	<.1
204	Fernic Inc—*Luis Pardo*	7505 Glenview Dr Ste 1, Richland Hills TX 76180	817-640-4183	R	4*	.2
205	Maintenance Mart Inc—*Christine Manville*	PO Box 5155, Old Bridge NJ 08857	732-335-4900	R	4*	.2
206	Complete Property Maintenance Inc—*Keith Carracher*	4101 Vinkemulder Rd, Coconut Creek FL 33073	954-973-3333	R	4*	.1
207	Quality Wholesale and Supply Inc—*Robert Monti*	PO Box 677, Luling LA 70070	985-785-2652	R	4*	.1
208	Chores Unlimited Inc—*Jane Byrne*	26285 Broadway Ave Uni, Bedford OH 44146	440-439 5455	R	4*	.1
209	Cleanserv Inc—*James Daugherty*	7213 Manchester Rd, Saint Louis MO 63143	314-644-5715	R	4*	.1
210	American Cleaning Service Company Inc—*Charles Schmoeger*	616 W Front St, Boise ID 83702	208-344-8464	R	4*	.2

Note: An asterisk (*) indicates an estimated financial figure. The company type code used is as follows: R = Private, P = Public, S = Private Subsidiary, B = Public Subsidiary, D = Division, J = Joint Venture, I = Investment Fund.

COMPANY RANKINGS BY SALES WITHIN 4-DIGIT SIC

Rank	Company Name—Executive Officer	Address, City, State, Zip	Phone	Type	Fin	Empls
211	Platinum Maintenance Services Corp—Selim Rusi	120 Broadway Fl 36, New York NY 10271	212-535-9700	R	4*	.1
212	Heits Building Services Inc—David Heitner	777 Ter Ave Ste 301, Hasbrouck Heights NJ 07604	201-288-7708	R	4*	<.1
213	ACT Janitorial Services Company Inc—Robert Marks	1570 N Powerline Rd, Pompano Beach FL 33069	954-960-1000	R	4*	.2
214	York Building Maintenance Inc—Albert Tharp	4748 Broadview Rd, Cleveland OH 44109	216-398-8100	R	4*	.1
215	Rainbow Maintenance and Cleaning Corp—Fred Fuentes	599 Albany Ave Ste A, Amityville NY 11701	631-842-6044	R	4*	.1
216	Roth Property Maintenance LLC—Dan Mischel	7808 Cherry Creek Sotu, Denver CO 80231	303-694-0300	R	4*	.2
217	Com-Jan Inc—Mercedes Lewis	6603 Mcgrew St, Houston TX 77087	713-640-1134	R	4*	.2
218	Youngstown Window Cleaning Company Inc—Steven Altman	1057 Trumbull Ave Ste, Girard OH 44420	330-743-3880	R	4*	.2
219	Wilson Building Maintenance—Anita Oberwortmann	PO Box 2041, Wichita KS 67201	316-264-0699	R	4*	.1
220	Atlantic Maintenance Corp—David Goldberg	154 Conover St, Brooklyn NY 11231	718-222-4549	R	4*	.1
221	Personal Touch Cleaning and Maintenance Inc—Patrick Obrien	340 Goddard, Irvine CA 92618	949-727-4135	R	4*	.1
222	Etna Prestige Technology Inc—Nelson Martayan	68 Whitehall St, Lynbrook NY 11563	516-593-2111	R	4*	<.1
223	Industrial Janitor Service Inc—Darla Artura	7124 De Celis Pl Ste A, Van Nuys CA 91406	818-782-5658	R	3*	.1
224	Mrr Dr Inc—Todd Russell	1593 Palma Dr, Ventura CA 93003	805-642-8779	R	3*	<.1
225	Advant Services Inc—William Ronay	3135 Commerce Ctr Pl, Louisville KY 40211	502-581-1021	R	3*	.1
226	Nelson Services Systems Inc—Nelson Gisbert	199 Nepperhan Ave, Yonkers NY 10701	914-963-1343	R	3*	.1
227	Tricounty Maintenance Inc—Troy Rice	PO Box 6038, Lynchburg VA 24505	434-528-1208	R	3*	.1
228	Duncan and Sons Building Maintenance Inc—Gary Duncan	1401 N Central St, Knoxville TN 37917	865-524-3225	R	3*	.1
229	R C Williams Enterprises Inc—Emery Williams	PO Box 2272, Texas City TX 77592	409-945-5539	R	3*	.1
230	Eagle Maintenance and Janitorial Services Inc—Richard Tynes	611 L St Nw, Washington DC 20001	202-291-0200	R	3*	.1
231	Linn Building Maintenance Inc—Steve Kissell	1899 Rice St, Saint Paul MN 55113	651-778-1322	R	3*	.1
232	Nix and Company Inc—Edward Nix	PO Box 6549, Lincoln NE 68506	402-476-2194	R	3*	.1
233	Infinity Service Management LLC—David Zun	1550 S Indiana Ave Sto, Chicago IL 60605	312-583-0777	R	3*	.1
234	Complete Maintenance and Janitorial Inc—Peter Zayas	PO Box 2490, Lutz FL 33548	813-949-3365	R	3*	.1
235	Clean Tech Systems Inc—David Mcginn	153 Andover St Ste 115, Danvers MA 01923	978-762-0110	R	3*	.2
236	General Services Inc—Bruce Weintraub	PO Box 357, Manchester CT 06045	860-649-5334	R	3*	.2
237	Servicemaster Of Central North Dakota Inc—Mike Nygaard	1967 Frontier Dr, Bismarck ND 58504	701-258-2246	R	3*	.1
238	T and M Services Inc—Thomas Mc Mahon	31 Ne 1st St, Pompano Beach FL 33060	954-942-8768	R	3*	.1
239	Tenacious Cleaning Services Inc—Theresa Smith	481 S Irmen Dr Ste A, Addison IL 60101	630-458-9064	R	3*	.1
240	Buttweiler Environmental Inc—Tim Buttweiler	PO Box 931, Saint Cloud MN 56302	320-251-4385	R	3*	.1
241	Gene Rhodes Enterprises Inc—Gene Rhodes	PO Box 766, Houma LA 70361	985-872-1029	R	3*	.1
242	Pacific Facility Service Inc—Peter Gomez	PO Box 26222, Honolulu HI 96825	808-478-9866	R	3*	.1
243	Union Building Services Inc—Bruce Yi	PO Box 395, Palisades Park NJ 07650	201-944-1577	R	3*	.1
244	LT Services Inc—Michael Nguyen	2815 Hartland Rd Ste 3, Falls Church VA 22043	703-698-8838	R	3*	.1
245	New York's Little Elves Inc—Barbara Fierman	151 1st Ave Ste 204, New York NY 10003	212-674-2629	R	3*	.1
246	ABCO Maintenance Inc—Dolores Virga	834 Morrow St, Staten Island NY 10303	718-816-7575	R	3*	<.1
247	Amf Facility Services Inc—A Fowler	844 Oakleaf Dr, Dayton OH 45417		R	3*	<.1
248	Chimney Solutions Inc—John Susong	1155 Mcfarland 400 Dr, Alpharetta GA 30004	770-255-1300	R	3*	<.1
249	Dunnwell LLC—Crystal Dees	4601 Creekstone Dr Ste, Durham NC 27703	919-661-5744	R	3*	<.1
250	CSI International Inc	6700 N Andrews Blvd, Fort Lauderdale FL 33309	954-308-4300	R	3*	<.1
251	Lisbon Cleaning Inc—Jan Alderson	PO Box 5040, Newark NJ 07105	973-589-0028	R	3*	<.1
252	Whittington Service Group Inc—Jennifer Whittington	3999 Whispering Meadow, Randallstown MD 21133	410-521-0457	R	3*	.1
253	Commercial Building Services Inc—Alex Ward	PO Box 4165, Cleveland TN 37320	423-472-9344	R	3*	.1
254	NJS Systems Inc—Daniel Draper	3002 N Holmes St, Mishawaka IN 46545	574-288-0404	R	3*	.1
255	Darrco Building Maintenance Inc—Celia Rock	PO Box 600876, San Diego CA 92160	619-287-2200	R	3*	.1
256	Signature Building Maintenance Inc—Anna Murphy	PO Box 110340, Campbell CA 95011	408-377-8066	R	3*	.1
257	Rockefeller's Cleaning And Restoration Co—Larry Borgeson	5514 Coal Ave Se, Albuquerque NM 87108	505-268-5585	R	3*	.1
258	Ibs-Building Service Contractors Inc—Patrick Comaskey	3606 43rd Ave Fl 2, Long Island City NY 11101	212-571-6832	R	3*	.1
259	Mi-Jenn Ventures Inc—Harold Cumbie	2197 Canton Rd Ste 207, Marietta GA 30066	678-594-0095	R	3*	<.1
260	Tim Hofer Inc—Timothy Hofer	PO Box 6445, Visalia CA 93290	559-732-6676	R	3*	.1
261	Building Services Inc—Thomas Harris	921 E Main St, Chattanooga TN 37408	423-622-7770	R	3*	.1
262	Rembrandt Commercial Cleaning Inc—James Grunewald	20900 Swenson Dr Ste 2, Waukesha WI 53186	262-754-9106	R	3*	.1
263	Any Domest Work Inc—Joseph Sokolowski	PO Box 107, Hinckley OH 44233	440-845-9911	R	3*	.1
264	Pro-Sweep LLC—Kim Sandra	PO Box 41901, Mesa AZ 85274	480-464-8050	R	3*	.1
265	Service First Inc—Susan Basile	26 Cook St, West Springfield MA 01089	413-734-0005	R	3*	.1
266	Reed's Cleaning Service Inc—Dana Reed	PO Box 1245, Hickory NC 28603	828-324-8448	R	3*	.1
267	Lakeman Inc—Paul Cooper	501 Ridgelawn Ave I, Hamilton OH 45013	513-863-5505	R	3*	.1
268	Willamette Valley Rehabilitation Center Inc—Martin Baughman	1853 W Airway Rd, Lebanon OR 97355	541-258-8121	R	3*	.1
269	Maintenance Management Company Inc—Gregory Petras	5425 Industrial Rd, Fort Wayne IN 46825	260-483-3123	R	3*	.1
270	Skyline Building Maintenance Inc—James Lee	17446 Boones Ferry Rd, Lake Oswego OR 97035	503-635-1940	R	3*	.1
271	Sweeney Industries Inc—Rory Sweeney	18931 Premiere Ct, Gaithersburg MD 20879	301-977-1144	R	3*	.1
272	Custom Care Building Services Inc—Charles Troccolo	59-67 Federal Rd, Danbury CT 06810	203-744-0106	R	3*	.1
273	Detail Services Inc—Christine Deleo	42 S Prince St, Lancaster PA 17603	717-392-7501	R	3*	.1
274	Eastek Services LLC—Jea Kim	9015 Rhode Island Ave, College Park MD 20740	301-220-1818	R	3*	.1
275	Gylan Building Services Inc—Tae Kim	2205 Royal Ln, Dallas TX 75229	972-620-7338	R	3*	.1
276	Makro Janitorial Services—Miguel Valladares	PO Box 1536, Rockville MD 20849	301-948-3395	R	3*	.1
277	Valley Enterprises Building Maintenance Inc—Dena Zundel	PO Box 28288, Las Vegas NV 89126	702-658-8854	R	3*	.1
278	Facilities Consulting Group—Edwin Mendenhall	PO Box 35526, Dallas TX 75235	214-631-4453	R	3*	.1
279	Major Commercial Cleaning Inc—Robert Stewart	105 Haywood Ln, Antioch TN 37013	615-983-8700	R	3*	.1
280	Bahen Inc—Andy Bahen	12001 Deerhill Rd, Midlothian VA 23112	804-378-2323	R	3*	.1
281	Bechtel Building Maintenance Corporation Of Columbus Inc—John Bechtel	3734 Logan Gate Rd, Youngstown OH 44505	330-759-2797	R	3*	.1
282	Hunter Service Group Inc—Debrina Handler	1 Old Country Rd Ste 4, Carle Place NY 11514	516-551-4797	R	3*	.1
283	Kc Cleaning Solutions—Tim Roccia	7451 Switzer St Ste 10, Shawnee Mission KS 66203	913-236-0040	R	2*	.1
284	Mhrh Facilities—Ed Rudegeair	PO Box 8268, Cranston RI 02920	401-462-3045	R	2*	.1
285	A-Ceptional Inc—Roy Musselman	434 Lower Rd, Souderton PA 18964	215-723-8222	R	2*	.1
286	Millennium Commercial Cleaning Services Inc—Fabricio Montesdeoca	PO Box 1733, Oldsmar FL 34677	813-925-3565	R	2*	.1
287	Allstate Building Maintenance—Mike Ko	4890 Saint Andrews Ave, Buena Park CA 90621	714-739-8080	R	2*	.1
288	Eagle Enterprises Ltd—Richard Gottheardt	12247 W Fairview Ave, Milwaukee WI 53226	414-431-9600	R	2*	.1
289	Servico Building Maintenance Company Inc—Gary Acquisto	PO Box 25, Glen Ellen CA 95442	707-935-1224	R	2*	.1
290	Aerostar Services—Maria Garcia	101 Q St Ne Ste 2, Washington DC 20002	202-269-0599	R	2*	.1
291	Pioneer Janitorial Services Inc—John Deluca	6 Lakeside Office Park, Wakefield MA 01880	781-245-1552	R	2*	.1
292	Professional Systems Maintenance Corp—Andy Kim	1960 Gallows Rd Ste 12, Vienna VA 22182	703-356-7244	R	2*	.1
293	SBS—Un Kim	13400 Ne 20th St Ste 7, Bellevue WA 98005	425-746-8709	R	2*	.1
294	Executive Janitorial Service Inc—Terry Ercanbrack	3007 S W Temple Ste I, Salt Lake City UT 84115	801-484-3961	R	2*	.1
295	Office and Commercial Cleaning-Wv LLC	PO Box 1002, Dunbar WV 25064	304-768-6309	R	2*	.1
296	Annie Maid Inc—Anne Sutorius	PO Box 50618, Henderson NV 89016	702-739-8888	R	2*	.1
297	Harper's Model Home Maintenance Inc—Karen Harper	PO Box 4590, El Dorado Hills CA 95762	707-685-3118	R	2*	.1
298	Express Maintenance Company Inc—Gregory Choo	PO Box 250147, San Francisco CA 94125	650-697-7735	R	2*	.1

Rank	Company Name—*Executive Officer*	Address, City, State, Zip	Phone	Type	Fin	Empls
299	Four Star General Cleaning Corp—*Fredrick Ross*	19 W 21st St Rm 601a, New York NY 10010	212-741-9400	R	2*	.1
300	TSS Facility Services—*Kenneth Battiato*	PO Box 3612, Union NJ 07083	908-964-3773	R	2*	.1
301	Pinnacle Building Services Inc—*Michael Meade*	105 S Paint St, Chillicothe OH 45601	740-851-4811	R	2*	.1
302	Majesty Maintenance Company Inc—*Steven Jamrozik*	390 E Irving Park Rd, Wood Dale IL 60191	630-860-0997	R	2*	.1
303	Royal Enterprise Cleaning System—*Mario Pereira*	90 Marshall St, Somerville MA 02145	617-623-6799	R	2*	.1
304	South Central Maintenance—*Robert Goldberg*	2925 Nw 41st St, Miami FL 33142	305-995-4310	R	2*	.1
305	Houston Independent Maintenance—*Al Ramos*	9229 Bowman St, Houston TX 77022	713-696-6100	R	2*	.1
306	Continental Building Services Inc—*Stanley Rosenbloom*	PO Box 348, Kenilworth IL 60043	773-561-7300	R	2*	.1
307	Intercity Maintenance Inc—*Michael Bouthillette*	15 Clarkson St, Providence RI 02908	401-351-0117	R	2*	.1
308	Dependable Cleaning Contractors Inc—*Wayne Trubiano*	38230 Glenn Ave, Willoughby OH 44094	440-953-9191	R	2*	.1
309	Opportunity Industries Inc—*Paula Kopczynski*	PO Box 259, Rockford WA 99030	509-291-5016	R	2*	<.1
310	Eli Diamant—*Eli Diamant*	2165 S Platte River Dr, Denver CO 80223	303-727-8656	R	2*	.1
311	Executive Cleaning Services Of Albany Inc—*Melvin Welcoth*	PO Box 5, Guilderland NY 12084	518-765-5700	R	2*	.1
312	Rbm Services Inc—*Chuck Greenberg*	1107 Hazeltine Blvd St, Chaska MN 55318	952-361-0897	R	2*	.1
313	Contract Services Inc—*Clemens Boltz*	1350 Louis Ave, Elk Grove Village IL 60007	847-981-1210	R	2*	.1
314	Superior Cleaning Inc—*Rachel Baldwin*	PO Box 14533, Bradenton FL 34280	941-795-0983	R	2*	.1
315	Dove Building Services Inc—*Vernon Gibson*	1691 Cleveland Ave, Columbus OH 43211	614-299-4700	R	2*	.1
316	Gse Facility Services LLC—*Ricky Byrd*	230 Peachtree St Ste 1, Atlanta GA 30303	404-230-2900	R	2*	<.1
317	Certified Maintenance Services Inc—*Mark Shearholdt*	660 Harvey Rd, Manchester NH 03103	603-626-0505	R	2*	<.1
318	Janitorialex Building Services Inc—*Dan Calello*	1830 Sw W 2nd St, Pompano Beach FL 33069	561-994-5627	R	2*	.4
319	State Cleaning Service Inc—*Jennifer Friedman*	214 Lincoln St, Boston MA 02134	617-789-3500	R	2*	.3
320	Federal Cleaning Contractors Inc—*Steve Kault*	1415 Louisiana St, Houston TX 77002	713-400-5632	R	2*	.1
321	Spain Agility First Support LLC—*Edward Hoffman*	480 Production Ave, Madison AL 35758	256-772-7743	R	2*	.1
322	Byles Janitorial Services—*William Byles*	1413 Jefferson St Uppr, Nashville TN 37208	615-342-0004	R	2*	.1
323	Almac Building Maintenance Inc—*Alan Tokarz*	920 Portland Ave, Rochester NY 14621	585-544-8940	R	2*	.1
324	Shepherd's Co—*Thomas Mahaney*	777 Shepherdsfield Rd, Fulton MO 65251	573-642-1439	R	2*	.1
325	Amko Building Services Inc—*Paul Pak*	517 Blairhill Rd, Charlotte NC 28217	704-527-4850	R	2*	.1
326	A One Cleaning Services Inc—*Donald Walker*	PO Box 22233, Huntsville AL 35814	256-722-7951	R	2*	.1
327	Midwest Maintenance Inc—*David Lashley*	PO Box 12944, Oklahoma City OK 73157	405-946-0656	R	2*	.1
328	Swayzer's Inc—*Samuel Swayzer*	PO Box 4365, Carson CA 90749	323-979-7223	R	2*	.1
329	Gmi Group Inc—*Joseph Woodson*	470 Satellit Blvd Ne R, Suwanee GA 30024	678-482-5288	R	2*	<.1
330	First Quality Cleaning Service Inc—*Bryant Sanders*	PO Box 10467, Rock Hill SC 29731	803-329-1917	R	2*	<.1
331	Ww Painting And Construction Solutions Inc—*Ray Wiest*	5833 Fremont St, Riverside CA 92504	951-354-2262	R	2*	<.1
332	VIP Holdings Inc—*Curt Betz*	PO Box 503477, San Diego CA 92150	858-693-9115	R	2*	<.1
333	Nam LLC—*Har Khalsa*	PO Box 32551, Santa Fe NM 87594	505-988-7991	R	2*	.2
334	Campbells Floorcare Service—*Matthew Campbells*	PO Box 720814, Mcallen TX 78504	956-687-7540	R	2*	.1
335	HUSD Maintenance Operation—*Joseph Zanini*	24400 Amador St, Hayward CA 94544	510-784-2666	R	2*	.1
336	Peninsula Mobil Wash—*Angel Velasco*	891 Barron Ave Ste 1, Redwood City CA 94063	650-556-0602	R	2*	.1
337	KIC Enterprises—*Alfonse Leal*	PO Box 32237, San Jose CA 95152	408-453-0394	R	2*	.1
338	Advanced Cleaning Systems Inc—*Kenneth Brauer*	10 Mcglashen Dr, South Barrington IL 60010	847-304-0100	R	2*	.1
339	Road Runr Maintenance Inc—*Vincent Hebel*	747 Orchard Lake Rd, Pontiac MI 48341	248-332-4242	R	2*	.1
340	Squeaky Clean LLC	146 Wedgewood Dr, Naugatuck CT 06770	203-729-1381	R	2*	.1
341	Crest Building Royal Maintenance—*Robert Young*	PO Box 391, Buena Park CA 90621	714-562-5034	R	2*	.1
342	Pacific Cleaning Service Inc—*Jeff Murray*	3334 E Pcf Coast Hwy 2, Corona Del Mar CA 92625	949-829-8790	R	2*	.1
343	Mks Services Inc—*Lynn Katofsky*	1951 Lincoln Hwy, North Versailles PA 15137	412-825-5480	R	2*	<.1
344	Crystal Blue Cleaning Service Inc—*Thomas Olin*	578 Nepperhan Ave Ste, Yonkers NY 10701	914-963-5883	R	2*	.1
345	Ram Custom Services Inc—*Jean Reid*	PO Box 608, Churchton MD 20733	301 261-5588	R	2*	.1
346	Dun-Well Maintenance Inc—*Victoria Williams*	2621 Lincoln Blvd, Merrick NY 11566	516-868-4106	R	2*	.1
347	Alabama Janitorial Services Inc—*Early Rogers*	PO Box 39463, Birmingham AL 35208	205-785-5271	R	2*	.1
348	Sparkle Performance Joint Venture Ii—*Celina Quintana*	5827 4th St Nw, Albuquerque NM 87107	505-345-5501	R	2*	.1
349	Danish Environment Inc—*Jens Grau*	9424 Eton Ave Ste G, Chatsworth CA 91311	818-992-6722	R	2*	.1
350	Facilities Services Group Inc—*Edward Gales*	PO Box 20, Farmington CT 06034	860-677-9100	R	2*	.1
351	Venango Training and Development Center—*Colleen Stuart*	239 Quaker Dr, Seneca PA 16346	814-676-5755	R	2*	.1
352	EPS Evans Co—*Wilbert Evans*	3460 E Ellsworth Rd, Ann Arbor MI 48108	734-971-5190	R	2*	.1
353	JB Clark Services Inc—*Jeffrey Clark*	PO Box 12125, Alexandria LA 71315	318-442-7378	R	2*	.1
354	D Box Inc—*Dennis Box*	PO Box 667, Euless TX 76039	817-858-6920	R	2*	.1
355	Abc Building Service Corp—*Horacio Tijman*	12220 Wilkins Ave, Rockville MD 20852	301-881-6337	R	2*	.1
356	Crosby Inc—*Randall Crosby*	1801 130th Ave Ne Ste, Bellevue WA 98005	425-885-5557	R	2*	.1
357	Palm Beach Maintenance Inc—*Leonard Schultz*	9337 Howell Ln Unit B, Palm Beach Gardens FL 33418	561-776-0910	R	2*	.1
358	Aim Industrial Maintenance Inc—*Vincent Pacella*	PO Box 1299, West Babylon NY 11704	631-321-6900	R	2*	<.1
359	Machado Environmental Corp—*George Machado*	2219 Broadview Dr, Glendale CA 91208	818-249-3620	R	2*	<.1
360	Larry's Window Service Inc—*Carl O'connor*	PO Box 1471, Des Moines IA 50305	515-244-0560	R	2*	<.1
361	A and A Facility Services Inc—*Albert Mitchell*	503 Cornelius Harnett, Wilmington NC 28401	910-763-5447	R	2*	.2
362	Central Maine Cleaning Inc—*Allison Reed*	987 Finson Rd, Bangor ME 04401	207-990-3811	R	2*	.1
363	Am Cleaning Inc—*Andrius Doniela*	PO Box 40322, Indianapolis IN 46240	317-578-2290	R	2*	.1
364	All 1 Service Inc—*Debra Dumitras*	PO Box 1981, Douglasville GA 30133	770-920-2140	R	2*	.1
365	Taplin Environmental Contracting Corp—*Michael Taplin*	5100 W Michigan Ave, Kalamazoo MI 49006	269-375-9595	R	2*	.1
366	Tujays Janitorial Service Inc—*James Obrien*	PO Box 403, Harvey LA 70059	504-368-2878	R	2*	.1
367	Acme Service Group LLC—*Mark Vasil*	400 Middle St, Bristol CT 06010	860-589-7711	R	2*	.1
368	D Lariat D Enterprises Inc—*Seann Slosson*	1113 Ironwood Ct, Fort Worth TX 76140	817-355-0044	R	2*	.1
369	Kelly's Professional Cleaning Service Inc—*Kelly Gilreath*	PO Box 1009, Mauldin SC 29662	864-299-8900	R	2*	.1
370	Topco Inc—*James Kim*	6295 Edsall Rd Ste 640, Alexandria VA 22312	703-212-0889	R	2*	.1
371	Freitec Services—*Michael Turula*	PO Box 14178, Fremont CA 94539	408-246-9083	R	2*	.1
372	Perry Contract Services Inc—*Anthony Perry*	2407 Scioto Harper Dr, Columbus OH 43204	614-274-4350	R	2*	.1
373	Threefold Janitorial Services Inc—*Scott Stiffler*	2490 Catherine St, York PA 17408	717-792-3441	R	2*	.1
374	Aaa Building Services Corp—*John Kiely*	280 Madison Ave Rm 710, New York NY 10016	212-545-8312	R	2*	.1
375	Afford Building Maintenance Company Inc—*Fernando Rivero*	4010 Blackburn Ln, Burtonsville MD 20866	301-476-9581	R	2*	.1
376	Building Service Company Inc—*Millard Barnes*	PO Box 2214, Birmingham AL 35201	205-252-5040	R	2*	.1
377	KK Custom Improvements Inc—*Karen Adams*	PO Box 14072, Kansas City MO 64152	816-472-8181	R	2*	.1
378	Merry Maids Of Oklahoma Inc—*Marshall Kittelson*	5656 S Mingo Rd, Tulsa OK 74146	918-250-7318	R	2*	.1
379	White Glove Janitorial and Building Maintenance Inc—*Brian Quigley*	PO Box 3643, Joliet IL 60434	815-722-5963	R	2*	.1
380	City Wide General Cleaning and Maintenance Service Inc—*Brian Rutter*	PO Box 541503, Flushing NY 11354	718-278-6800	R	2*	.2
381	Water and Sewer Maintenance—*Ken Mosley*	313 Cree Meadows Dr, Ruidoso NM 88345	575-257-2386	R	2*	.1
382	Gemini Building Systems LLC—*Wendy Meehan*	PO Box 9309, Wilmington DE 19809	302-654-5310	R	2*	.1
383	Sentinel Service Inc—*William Slingluff*	15404 Wentbridge Ct, Silver Spring MD 20906	301-438-7720	R	2*	.1
384	Finishing Touch Janitorial Service Inc—*Glenda Robinson*	PO Box 165, Longmont CO 80502	303-651-2464	R	2*	.1
385	Progressive Maintenance—*Dennis Delzer*	1707 E Broadway Ave St, Bismarck ND 58501	701-255-3194	R	2*	.1
386	John T Wilson—*John Wilson*	PO Box 24092, Tempe AZ 85285	480-507-3497	R	2*	.1

Note: An asterisk (*) indicates an estimated financial figure. The company type code used is as follows: R = Private, P = Public, S = Private Subsidiary, B = Public Subsidiary, D = Division, J = Joint Venture, I = Investment Fund.

COMPANY RANKINGS BY SALES WITHIN 4-DIGIT SIC

Rank	Company Name—Executive Officer	Address, City, State, Zip	Phone	Type	Fin	Empls
387	A and O Inc—Herbert Houston	2848 Queen City Dr Ste, Charlotte NC 28208	704-393-2470	R	2*	.1
388	Busy Bee Janitorial Services LLC	17 Malcolm Hoyt Dr, Newburyport MA 01950	978-465-5335	R	2*	.1
389	Alpine Building Maintence Inc—Perry Hoover	PO Box 120451, Arlington TX 76012	817-795-6470	R	2*	.1
390	Earl Horne Inc—W Horne	PO Box 2608, Jacksonville FL 32203	904-358-2500	R	2*	.1
391	HT And Associates Inc—Yvette Bing	17251 W 12 Mile Rd Ste, Southfield MI 48076	248-443-4949	R	2*	.1
392	Majestic Cleaning Service Inc—Peter Salonikidis	4510 Bryan St, Dallas TX 75204	214-750-1960	R	2*	.1
393	Sunnyside Janitorial Service—Louis Ferdinando	PO Box 68, West Orange NJ 07052	973-675-1111	R	2*	.1
394	Wilkes Barre Window Cleaning Inc—Glenn Kornblau	140 142 Lehigh St, Wilkes Barre PA 18702	570-823-7018	R	2*	<.1
395	Collins Building Services Corp—Joseph Collins	1775 Broadway Ste 1420, New York NY 10019	212-896-5100	R	2*	<.1
396	D and D Roland Enterprises LLC—Darrel Roland	1120 S Florence St, Wichita KS 67209	316-942-6474	R	2*	<.1
397	C and R Anderson Inc—Ronald Anderson	3231 Ruckriegel Pkwy S, Louisville KY 40299	502-261-1755	R	2*	<.1
398	Wurm's Janitorial Service Inc—Larry Stewart	544 Bateman Cir, Corona CA 92880	951-582-0003	R	1*	.1
399	Hoffman Management Co—Chris Hoffman	4618 N Classen Blvd, Oklahoma City OK 73118	405-946-6735	R	1*	.1
400	Premier Cleaning Service Inc—Michael Winters	2236 Nw 10th St Ste 11, Oklahoma City OK 73107	405-702-8071	R	1*	.1
401	Badger Building Maintenance—Debra George	4601 W Greenfield Ave, Milwaukee WI 53214	414-643-3570	R	1*	.1
402	LET Corp—Lynn Tucker	1117 Fuller St, Raleigh NC 27603	919-755-1555	R	1*	.1
403	Angel's Cleaning Service Inc—Samuel Fidell	PO Box 272, Ellwood City PA 16117	724-758-3055	R	1*	.1
404	Regal Office Services Inc—Dale Shallbetter	PO Box 373, Boca Raton FL 33429	561-362-0081	R	1*	.1
405	Absolute Maintenace Inc—Marisol Vasquez	PO Box 9337, Silver Spring MD 20916	301-933-7005	R	1*	.1
406	Building Services Co—Melinda Herzberg	1880 Haslett Rd Ste C, East Lansing MI 48823	517-337-1012	R	1*	.1
407	Qsc Of Northfield Inc—Danny Ayotte	PO Box 171, Northfield MN 55057	507-366-7149	R	1*	.1
408	Service Master Of Springfield Inc—Brian Wilkins	PO Box 51011, Springfield MA 01151	413-543-8282	R	1*	.1
409	Sunset Building Maintance Inc—Marisela Rio	1920 Lafayette St Ste, Santa Clara CA 95050	408-727-3408	R	1*	.1
410	Williams Maintenance Inc—Donna Williams	11001 Pierson Dr Ste A, Fredericksburg VA 22408	540-371-6695	R	1*	<.1
411	Dahlinger Enterprises Inc—David Dahlinger	2411 Industrial St, Wisconsin Rapids WI 54495	715-384-8771	R	1*	<.1
412	John A Hilt Enterprises Inc—John Hilt	9205 Kneupper Ln, Converse TX 78109	210-659-6877	R	1*	<.1
413	California Office Maintenance—Joe Johnson	13100 Kirkham Way Ste, Poway CA 92064	858-513-2767	R	1*	<.1
414	Mid-America Services Inc—Robert Austin	4928 Beeman Ave, Dallas TX 75223	214-821-9000	R	1*	<.1
415	Capital Building Maintenance Services Inc—Dennis Debattista	183 Beacon St, South San Francisco CA 94080	650-588-9808	R	1*	<.1
416	Genett Group Inc—Shirley Basso	76 Mamaroneck Ave Ste, White Plains NY 10601	914-761-3070	R	1*	<.1
417	1776 Housekeeping Associates LLC—April Corswell	201 Kings Gate Pkwy, Williamsburg VA 23185	757-564-5714	R	1*	.1
418	Westbrook Jr Howard Wayne—Howard Westbrook	10337 E Lakeshore Dr, Tyler TX 75709	903-561-7989	R	1*	.1
419	Alianza Building Services Inc—Erika Cabezas	PO Box 10541, Gaithersburg MD 20898	301-519-7500	R	1*	.1
420	Berea College Facilities Management—Larry Shinn	310 Main St N, Berea KY 40403	859-985-3828	R	1*	.1
421	Hartco Facilities Support Services Inc—Mary Hart	12304 Arrow Park Dr, Fort Washington MD 20744	301-316-0585	R	1*	.1
422	Total Quality Maintenance Systems Inc—Ellen Glood	PO Box 7604, Rapid City SD 57709	763-377-6530	R	1*	.1
423	Joyce Janitorial Services—Peter Morrissette	PO Box 6245, Laconia NH 03247	603-223-0943	R	1*	.1
424	Kettler Janitorial Services Inc—David Kettler	1973 Telford Dr, Saint Louis MO 63125	314-544-3233	R	1*	.1
425	Eugene Carter Enterprises Inc—Eugene Carter	6161 El Cajon Blvd Ste, San Diego CA 92115	619-287-5551	R	1*	.1
426	Aaa Quality Maintenace Corp—Kevin Chambres	3792 Rte 27 Bldg 1, Princeton NJ 08540	732-951-1006	R	1*	.1
427	Commercial Janitor Service Corp—John Leckrone	119 Mifflin Ave, Lansing MI 48912	517-485-3130	R	1*	.1
428	G and C Building Maintenance Services Inc—Ray Porras	13309 Reeveston Rd 1, Houston TX 77039	281-227-7552	R	1*	.1
429	M J Hoffmann Services LLC—Nancy Lasseck	2156 S 4th St, Milwaukee WI 53207	414-384-4620	R	1*	<.1
430	MGM Service Co—Mathieu Poulard	8001 Branch Ave, Clinton MD 20735	301-868-0080	R	1*	<.1
431	Bay Contract Maintenance—Pedro Rivera	1129 Airport Blvd, South San Francisco CA 94080	650-737-0979	R	1*	<.1
432	Kilgore Pavement and Maintenance—Jason Kilgore	PO Box 869, Magna UT 84044	801-382-6575	R	1*	<.1
433	Mira Lighting and Electrical Service Inc—Rheba Golub	PO Box 2697, Clifton NJ 07015	973-478-4909	R	1*	<.1
434	Summit Building Services—Matt Colchico	1128 Willow Pass Ct, Concord CA 94520	925-827-9500	R	1*	<.1
435	Rory Properties Inc—Esther Brown	3030 W Chicago Ave, Chicago IL 60622	773-533-3030	R	1*	<.1
436	Republic Enterprise Systems—Candace Westlake	1422 E Fletcher Ave, Tampa FL 33612	813-903-8000	R	1*	<.1
437	Presidential Service Industries Inc—Brice Alexander	1320 Fenwick Ln Ste Ll, Silver Spring MD 20910	301-589-3900	R	1*	.1
438	Landstar Inc—Shannon Mcginn	21523 Cubbage Pond Rd, Lincoln DE 19960	302-422-7370	R	1*	.1
439	De La Cantera Ernesto—Ernesto De La Cantera	4504 Parkwood Sq, Niceville FL 32578	850-897-0191	R	1*	.1
440	Gator Building Maintenance Inc—John Dooley	283 Cranes Roost Blvd, Altamonte Springs FL 32701	407-379-0041	R	1*	.1
441	Hausmeister Inc—Phyllis Jones	27558 Harness Ln, Salisbury MD 21801	410-749-8966	R	1*	.1
442	Mac Fawn Enterprises Inc—Joseph Macfawn	PO Box 13205, Albany NY 12212	518-785-6719	R	1*	.1
443	Leandro M and E Inc—Marcello Leandro	PO Box 911, Provo UT 84603	801-356-1905	R	1*	<.1
444	Select Janitorial Services Inc—Bruce Anderson	312 Otterson Dr Ste O, Chico CA 95928	530-898-0100	R	1*	<.1
445	Beck Building Services Inc—Danny Beck	PO Box 993, Newnan GA 30264	770-304-1763	R	1*	<.1
446	Champion Cleaning Systems Inc—Joel Reets	3010 Poplar Rd, Sharpsburg GA 30277	770-253-6070	R	1*	<.1
447	Natural Stone Care Inc—Jerry Collins	2131 W 7th St, Tempe AZ 85281	480-921-9799	R	1*	<.1
448	Brydon Cleaning Co—Al Miraballes	8522 Agusta St, Philadelphia PA 19152	215-725-0281	R	1*	<.1
449	Restoration Resources Inc—Bruce Johnson	1546 Georgetown Rd, Hudson OH 44236	330-650-4486	R	1*	<.1
450	Powells Inhome Services Inc—Dallas Powell	1417 Peters Creek Rd N, Roanoke VA 24017	540-562-4279	R	1*	<.1
451	Masino Maintenance Corp—Charles Masino	PO Box 431, Wharton NJ 07885	973-361-1658	R	1*	<.1
452	Facility Services Partners LLC—Ron Harris	52 Main St Ste 2, South River NJ 08882	732-967-8500	R	1*	<.1
453	E Wynn—Lynn Elliott	PO Box 2201, Columbus OH 43216	614-444-5288	R	1*	<.1
454	Commercial Cleaning Corp—Michael Rosen	1602 Pennington Rd, Ewing NJ 08618	609-882-7400	R	1*	.1
455	White Glove Janitorial Services and Supply Inc—Roger Dickens	356 E Irving Park Rd, Wood Dale IL 60191	630-766-7466	R	1*	.1
456	Choice Cleaning Contractors—Kurt Maddocks	PO Box 1808, Rogers AR 72757	479-621-6555	R	1*	.1
457	Front Range Custodial And Maintenance Inc—Bruce Kelp	PO Box 17842, Colorado Springs CO 80935	719-392-5020	R	1*	.1
458	American Custodial Inc—James Jacobs	3917 Yakima Ave Ste 3, Tacoma WA 98418	253-475-3338	R	1*	.1
459	Jackson's Cleaning Service Inc—George Jackson	2929 202nd St, Lynwood IL 60411	708-418-1070	R	1*	<.1
460	Quality Facility Specialists Inc—Michael Cavanaugh	4106 Duval St, Houston TX 77087	713-522-8429	R	1*	<.1
461	Armor Property Maintenance Inc—Ben Sutton	1320 Irwin Dr Unit F, Erie PA 16505	814-452-4099	R	1*	<.1
462	Avalon Home Cleaning Inc—Norine Tiz	PO Box 402, Avalon NJ 08202	609-967-5446	R	1*	<.1
463	Brittany Maids Ltd—Richard Wilson	50 Executv Prk S Ne 50, Atlanta GA 30329	404-633-5152	R	1*	<.1
464	Ga Janitorial Cleaning Services Inc—Glenda Allen	PO Box 61745, Jacksonville FL 32236	904-768-9740	R	1*	<.1
465	Puritan Maintenance Company Inc—Paul Daniele	PO Box 819, Needham MA 02494	781-449-5552	R	1*	<.1
466	American Land and Leisure Inc—Richard Kemp	747 E 1000 S, Orem UT 84097	801-226-3564	R	1*	<.1
467	Courtesy Cleaning Service Inc—John Cardillo	1551 Roosevelt Ave, Bohemia NY 11716	631-563-8642	R	1*	<.1
468	Detail Dynamics SC Inc—Pamela Olson	PO Box 470249, Lake Monroe FL 32747	407-322-7911	R	1*	<.1
469	Kate's Klean Company Inc—Kate Sweeney	1408 Lake St Ste 3, Elmira NY 14901	607-734-1815	R	1*	<.1
470	Maicon LLC	1840 Delaware Pl Unit, Longmont CO 80501	720-494-9544	R	1*	<.1
471	Luminaire Service Inc—Charles Ryerson	2828 N Webster, Indianapolis IN 46219	317-808-7010	R	1*	<.1
472	Al Mar Building Maintenance Inc—Neyra Aceveto	200 S Fielder Dr, Arlington TX 76013	817-261-3824	R	1*	<.1
473	IceSolv Inc—Paul LeBlanc	160 N Forge Rd, Palmyra PA 17078	717-838-0400	R	1*	<.1
474	Anderson Cleaning Systems—Tony Gruber	435 Algoma Blvd Ste 2, Oshkosh WI 54901	920-231-8060	R	1*	.1
475	Ops Inc	10052 Astoria Ct, Littleton CO 80124	303-708-8056	R	1*	.1

Rank	Company Name—*Executive Officer*	Address, City, State, Zip	Phone	Type	Fin	Empls
476	Leisure Deck Inc—*Alan Robbins*	540 S Main St, Akron OH 44311	330-252-1904	R	1*	<.1
477	Colonial Maintenance Contractors Inc—*George Davey*	PO Box 621, Avon MA 02322	508-587-6307	R	1*	<.1
478	Maverick Services Inc—*George Ratliff*	PO Box 1038, Calistoga CA 94515	707-942-4355	R	1*	<.1
479	Scottsdale House Inc—*William Classen*	4800 N 68th St Unit 28, Scottsdale AZ 85251	480-947-2292	R	1*	<.1
480	Alpha Technical Services Corporaton—*Mike Howerton*	5100 Underwood Rd, Pasadena TX 77507	281-291-7453	R	1*	<.1
481	Magic Maintenance Inc—*Ronald Murphy*	24840 Ave Rockefeller, Valencia CA 91355	661-259-3373	R	1*	<.1
482	American Building Janitorial Inc—*Mike Alvidrez*	2675 Junipero Ave Ste, Signal Hill CA 90755	562-986-4474	R	1	N/A
483	Excell Management Corp—*Brian Brinson*	PO Box B338, Highland MD 20777	301-854-0300	R	1*	.1
484	Shallis' Services Inc—*Glenn Shallis*	1 N Bacton Hill Rd Ste, Malvern PA 19355	610-296-6343	R	1*	<.1
485	Baysouth Maintenance Service Inc—*Clara Orazio*	PO Box 3484, Pasadena TX 77501	713-477-2339	R	1*	<.1
486	Jani Serv Inc—*Robert Twilley*	1832 S Macdonald, Mesa AZ 85210	480-921-3566	R	1*	<.1
487	Servpro Of Hanover Inc—*David Butler*	306 Ashcake Rd Ste H, Ashland VA 23005	804-730-6788	R	1*	<.1
488	Sms Cleaning Inc—*Sang So*	1401 S Sprague Ave Ste, Tacoma WA 98405	253-582-0777	R	1*	<.1
489	Advanced Chimney Inc—*Michael Steeneck*	710 Union Pkwy Ste 1, Ronkonkoma NY 11779	631-981-0214	R	1*	<.1
490	Project-One-Services Inc—*Robert Cutrona*	899 Manor Rd, Staten Island NY 10314	718-761-8390	R	1*	<.1
491	National Telecoin Corp—*Paul Rosenberg*	PO Box 37017, Philadelphia PA 19122	215-928-9875	R	1*	<.1
492	Smith Janitorial Service Inc—*Jeff Smith*	PO Box 25145, Charlotte NC 28229	704-537-9644	R	1*	.1
493	Southwestern Building Maintenance—*Eriskia Smith*	3933 E 29th St Ste 501, Tucson AZ 85711	520-790-6200	R	1*	.1
494	Jubilee Enterprises Inc—*George Falconer*	PO Box 615, Marshall MN 56258	507-532-2332	R	1*	<.1
495	High Rise Windows Inc—*Marie Amodeo*	425 W Mockingbird Ln, Dallas TX 75247	214-630-3999	R	1*	<.1
496	20/20 Window Care Inc—*Ruben Chavez*	2533 Connie Dr, Sacramento CA 95815	916-484-2020	R	1*	<.1
497	Bti Environmental Services—*Bruce Irion*	6084 Sorrento Ave Nw, Canton OH 44718	330-854-2897	R	1*	<.1
498	Master Clean Inc—*Matthew Brown*	415 Dixon Ave, Elgin IL 60120	847-741-3090	R	1*	<.1
499	Pro Clean Janitorial Service Inc—*Patrick Smith*	PO Box 1501, Fort Smith AR 72902	479-646-0767	R	1*	.1
500	Integrity Building Services—*Latonya Ordaz*	PO Box 182912, Arlington TX 76096	214-333-6489	R	1*	<.1
501	Stewart's Cleaning Service LLC—*B Blow*	2828 Georgia Ave NW, Washington DC 20001	202-232-0661	R	1*	<.1
502	Billeting Fund—*Ray Ripple*	Nimtz Rd Bldg 503, Kaneohe HI 96744	808-257-2409	R	1*	<.1
503	Metro Cleaners Of Knoxville Inc—*Jim Klonaris*	11130 Kingston Pke Ste, Knoxville TN 37934	865-679-8198	R	1*	<.1
504	Olympic Janitorial—*Mike Davey*	PO Box 1050, Linden CA 95236	209-609-1127	R	1*	.1
505	Central Building Maintenance Inc—*Roman Gembarowicz*	7324 Burke Meadow Dr, Fairfax Station VA 22039	703-425-1177	R	1*	<.1
506	Industrial Silosource Inc—*Larry Curry*	PO Box 276, Williamstown WV 26187	304-375-2866	R	1*	<.1
507	Sweeney Cleaning And Restoration Inc—*Mark Sawher*	2514 Chestnut St, Port Huron MI 48060	810-987-4709	R	1*	<.1
508	Tom and Zee Hunt Inc—*Tiffany Mitchell*	3201 Ohio St, Michigan City IN 46360	219-929-4174	R	1*	<.1
509	Well-Don Inc—*Ann Disaia*	805 S Union Ave, Los Angeles CA 90017	213-388-9395	R	1*	<.1
510	FBG Corp—*Terri Gogetap*	1615 Ne 58th Ave, Des Moines IA 50313	515-299-4683	R	1*	.1
511	Notlob Inc—*Brian Bolton*	PO Box 1921, Manteca CA 95336		R	1*	<.1
512	A1 Contract Cleaning Inc—*Bob Todman*	7600 Boone Ave N Ste 7, Minneapolis MN 55428	763-544-3847	R	1*	<.1
513	Donnar Inc—*Michele Donnley*	4416 Garden Club St, High Point NC 27265	336-854-0639	R	1*	<.1
514	Residential Cleaning Co—*Glenda Snyder*	7275 Padova Dr, Goleta CA 93117	805-685-6766	R	1*	<.1
515	Young's Cleaning International Inc—*Michael Young*	PO Box 11189, Atlanta GA 30310	770-938-5502	R	1*	<.1
516	Hardy Corp—*William Hardy*	711 W 103rd St, Chicago IL 60628	773-779-6600	R	1*	<.1
517	Kleen-Rite Building Maintenance Inc—*Lonnie Simmons*	5821 N 160th Ave, Omaha NE 68116	402-934-5292	R	<1*	<.1
518	Mjs Cleaning Services Inc—*Mike Godfrey*	619 S Kansas Ave, Topeka KS 66603	785-640-2690	R	<1*	<.1
519	Rtw Janitorial LLC—*Robert Wolflick*	2737 S Joslin Ct, Denver CO 80227	303-984-2240	R	<1*	<.1
520	Amazing Maid Services—*Unam Stein*	1625 Rayford Rd Ste B, Spring TX 77386	281-298-6345	R	<1*	<.1
521	Angel Touch Commercial Cleaning *Emily Wedel*	11821 E 33rd Ave Unit, Aurora CO 80010	303-340-0284	R	<1*	<.1
522	Arms Etc Inc—*Edward Colgan*	PO Box 696, Lumberton NJ 08048	609-265-2200	R	<1*	<.1
523	Hjs Inc—*John Stiles*	PO Box 1653, Titusville FL 32781	321-631-7976	R	<1*	<.1
524	A and C Maintenance—*Carlos Yanneo*	4042 Isola Dr, Fremont CA 94555	510-489-4570	R	<1*	<.1
525	Milestone Cleaning LLC	5203 Alta Loma Rd, Colorado Springs CO 80918	719-272-3846	R	<1*	<.1
526	Algon Services Inc—*Aldo Gonzalez*	12181 Queens Brigade D, Fairfax VA 22030	703-818-0954	R	<1*	<.1
527	Little Cleaning Services Inc—*Lacornes Little*	1513 Cleveland Ave 108, Atlanta GA 30344	404-768-0400	R	<1*	<.1
528	Brighton Brave Enterprises Inc—*Christopher Mcmillan*	2602 Ne 130th St, Seattle WA 98125	425-489-0776	R	<1*	<.1
529	Peck Sosa Inc—*Judy Peck*	20 Pimentel Ct, Novato CA 94949	415-884-4484	R	<1*	<.1
530	Sfm Services Inc—*Jose Infante*	9700 Nw 79th Ave, Hialeah FL 33016	305-818-2424	R	N/A	.3
531	United Services Associates Inc—*John W Nixon Jr*	1728 20th St N, Birmingham AL 35211	205-785-3154	R	N/A	<.1
532	Professional Polish Inc—*Carren Cavanaugh*	5450 E Loop 820 S, Fort Worth TX 76119	817-572-7353	R	N/A	<.1

TOTALS: SIC 7349 Building Maintenance Services Nec

Companies: 532					99,092	350.7

7352 Medical Equipment Rental

Rank	Company Name—*Executive Officer*	Address, City, State, Zip	Phone	Type	Fin	Empls
1	Apria Healthcare Group Inc—*Norman C Payson*	26220 Enterprise Ct, Lake Forest CA 92630	949-639-2000	S	1,632*	13.3
2	Universal Hospital Services Inc—*Gary Blackford*	7700 France Ave S Ste, Edina MN 55435	952-893-3200	R	379*	2.0
3	Orthofix Inc—*Alan W Milinazzo*	3451 Plano Pky, Lewisville TX 75056	214-937-2000	S	118*	.4
4	Progressive Medical Inc—*David Bianconi*	250 Progressive Way, Westerville OH 43082	614-794-3300	R	91*	.3
5	King's Medical Group—*Albert Van Kirk*	1894 Georgetown Rd, Hudson OH 44236	330-653-3968	R	52*	.2
6	InfuSystem Holdings Inc—*Sean McDevitt*	31700 Research Park Dr, Madison Heights MI 48071		P	47	.2
7	Parata Systems APS—*Dan Pantano*	2600 Meridian Parkway, Durham NC 27713	919-433-4300	R	27*	.4
8	Timberlake Corp—*Steve Vinci*	8400 Carbide Ct, Sacramento CA 95828	916-423-2198	S	21*	.1
9	United Medical Equipment Co—*Abraham Landa*	5744 W Irving Park Rd, Chicago IL 60634	773-777-4500	R	21*	.2
10	TMC Orthopedic LP—*Joe Sansone*	1000 S Loop W Ste 150, Houston TX 77054	713-669-1800	R	15*	.1
11	United Health Care Services Inc—*Michael Bronfien*	9 Creek Pkwy, Upper Chichester PA 19061	610-364-2700	R	14*	.1
12	Recover Care—*Andrew Stenberg*	PO Box 436509, Louisville KY 40253	813-854-2555	R	13*	.1
13	Ziegler Leasing Corp—*Tom Paprocki*	1700 South silverbrook, West Bend WI 53095	262-334-2882	S	13*	<.1
14	Home Care Specialists Inc—*Gary Rudis*	PO Box 8237, Haverhill MA 01835	978-373-7771	R	12*	.1
15	Fletcher's Medical Supplies Inc—*David Fletcher*	6851 Distribution Ave, Jacksonville FL 32256	904-387-4481	R	11*	.1
16	R and A Equipment Corp—*Rajan Gulati*	111 Maltese Dr, Middletown NY 10940	845-342-4774	R	10*	.1
17	Strada Capital Corp—*Bradley Kissler*	23046 Avenida de la Ca, Laguna Hills CA 92653	949-789-8850	R	10*	<.1
18	Medi-Rents and Sales Inc—*Thomas Petr*	743 S Conkling St, Baltimore MD 21224	410-327-7252	R	9*	.1
19	Home Care Supply—*Kevin Heffernan*	103 4th Ave, Waltham MA 02451	781-902-1800	R	8*	.1
20	Monitor Medical Inc—*Richard Webb*	PO Box 2527, Sugar Land TX 77487	281-240-7222	R	8*	.1
21	Mediserve Medical Equipment Of Kingsport Inc—*J Higgins*	PO Box 8839, Gray TN 37615	423-477-9806	R	8*	.1
22	San Antonio Extended Medical Care Inc—*Richard Hernandez*	21195 W Ih 10 Ste 1101, San Antonio TX 78257	210-697-9933	R	8*	.1
23	Home Care Equipment Inc—*Robert Mathews*	1135 Lester St, Poplar Bluff MO 63901	573-686-3720	R	7*	.1
24	Carolina Home Care Medical Equipment Center Inc—*Jackie Bolt*	1136 Grove Rd, Greenville SC 29605	864-271-8258	R	6*	<.1
25	Ed - Medical Inc—*James Johnston*	PO Box 2115, Hendersonville TN 37077	615-822-8888	R	6*	.1
26	New Hartford Medical Supply—*Steven Edline*	1729 Burrstone Rd, New Hartford NY 13413	315-798-1694	R	6*	.1
27	Care Medical Of Athens Inc—*William Childers*	1242 Prince Ave, Athens GA 30606	706-354-4136	R	5*	<.1

Note: An asterisk (*) indicates an estimated financial figure. The company type code used is as follows: R = Private, P = Public, S = Private Subsidiary, B = Public Subsidiary, D = Division, J = Joint Venture, I = Investment Fund.

COMPANY RANKINGS BY SALES WITHIN 4-DIGIT SIC

Rank	Company Name—Executive Officer	Address, City, State, Zip	Phone	Type	Fin	Empls
28	Delta Land Developers—Edward Cahill	333 E Alpine Ave, Stockton CA 95204	209-948-3333	R	5*	<.1
29	Alternative Care Providers Inc—Catherine Schleipfer	51 Middlesex St Unit 1, North Chelmsford MA 01863	978-251-7077	R	5*	<.1
30	Central Medical Equipment Co—Terry Luft	35 Sarhelm Rd, Harrisburg PA 17112	717-657-2100	R	5*	<.1
31	Ocean Breeze Respiratory Service—Andrew Passeri	PO Box 5348, Toms River NJ 08754	718-979-6283	R	4*	.1
32	Suncoast Medicare Supply Co—Barry Baldwin	656 Central Ave, Saint Petersburg FL 33701	727-821-7015	R	4*	<.1
33	Suffield Oxygen Sales Inc—Christine Dumala	31 Main St, Chicopee MA 01020	413-594-2121	R	4*	<.1
34	Homedeq Inc—A Kennedy	PO Box 25242, Houston TX 77265	713-748-6225	R	4*	<.1
35	SA Extended Medical Inc—Doyle Walsh	21195 Ih 10 W Ste 1101, San Antonio TX 78257	210-697-9933	R	4*	<.1
36	American Home Health Care Inc—Brad Yakam	691 Green Crest Dr, Westerville OH 43081	614-868-9751	R	4*	<.1
37	Access Center Soke Shop—Louis Frick	1295 University Ave St, San Diego CA 92103	619-296-8012	R	4*	<.1
38	Cornerstone Medical Services - Midwest LLC	453 S High St Ste 201, Akron OH 44311	330-374-0229	R	3*	<.1
39	C and C Laboratory Leasing Corp—Howard Pickett	12911 18th Ave, College Point NY 11356	718-961-8705	R	3*	<.1
40	Linde Rss LLC	104b W Ct Sq, Livingston TN 38570	931-823-3702	R	3*	<.1
41	Pioneer Medical Inc—David Smith	PO Box 92545, Nashville TN 37209	615-242-7832	R	3*	<.1
42	Total Care Health Industries Inc—Tony Strilcic	40 Nassau Terminal Rd, New Hyde Park NY 11040	516-326-4999	R	3*	<.1
43	Apache Oxy-Med Inc—Tarik Shirif	105 N Pasadena St, Gilbert AZ 85233	480-926-0133	R	3*	<.1
44	Cardiomedix Inc—David Zipora	1840 Oak Ave, Evanston IL 60201	847-869-0230	R	3*	<.1
45	Alpha Medical Resources Inc—Frank Uchalak	7990 San Fernando Rd, Sun Valley CA 91352	818-504-9090	R	3*	<.1
46	Mcnamed Inc—David Mcnamara	PO Box 4369, Brandon MS 39047	601-932-8880	R	3*	<.1
47	Tgz Acquisition Company LLC	5 Rockhill Rd Ste 2, Cherry Hill NJ 08003	856-669-6600	R	3*	<.1
48	Abf Health Services Inc—Jerome Bogowith	12984 Mrer IndustrialD, Saint Louis MO 63127	314-842-6750	R	2*	<.1
49	Medical Laser Rental and Service Co—Scott Piper	4740 Interstate Dr Ste, Cincinnati OH 45246	513-489-5595	R	2*	<.1
50	Medi-Quip Inc—Thomas Beuerlein	111 N Columbia Ave, Lawrenceburg TN 38464	931-762-5112	R	2*	<.1
51	Methodist Home Medical Equipment LLC—Bob Gestrine	PO Box 87, Peoria IL 61650	309-691-2800	R	2*	<.1
52	Oklahoma Respiratory Care Inc—Aaron Barnes	623 N Porter Ste 100, Norman OK 73071	405-360-4405	R	1*	<.1
53	Integrative Health Technologies Inc—Gilbert R Kaats	4940 Broadway Ste 202, San Antonio TX 78209	210-824-4200	P	<1	N/A

TOTALS: SIC 7352 Medical Equipment Rental
Companies: 53   2,638   19.0

7353 Heavy Construction Equipment Rental

Rank	Company Name—Executive Officer	Address, City, State, Zip	Phone	Type	Fin	Empls
1	GE Transportation Finance—Lorenzo Simonelli	2901 E Lake Rd Bldg 9-, Erie PA 16531	814-875-3175	S	3,500*	8.0
2	Maxim Crane Works—Art Innamorato	1225 Washington Pike, Bridgeville PA 15017	412-504-0200	R	1,978*	2.9
3	RSC Equipment Rental—Erik Olsson	6929 E Greenway Pkwy S, Scottsdale AZ 85254	480-905-3300	S	1,461*	4.9
4	Sunbelt Rentals Inc—Joseph James Phelan	2341 Deerfield Dr, Ft Mill SC 29715		S	545*	1.0
5	All Erection and Crane Co—Michael Liptak Jr	4700 Acorn Dr, Independence OH 44131	216-524-6550	R	386*	.2
6	Kirby - Smith Machinery Inc—Ed Kirby	PO Box 270300, Oklahoma City OK 73137	405-495-7820	R	149*	.3
7	Cecil I Walker Machinery Co—Richard Walker	PO Box 2427, Charleston WV 25329	304-949-6400	R	94*	.6
8	Essex Crane Rental Corp—Devin Sullivan Essex Rental Corp	1110 Lake Cook Rd Ste, Buffalo Grove IL 60089	847-215-6500	S	85*	<.1
9	Morrow Equipment Company LLC—Richard Morrow	PO Box 3306, Salem OR 97302	503-585-5721	R	79*	.2
10	Handy Rents—Mike Miller	35571 Vine St, Eastlake OH 44095	440-946-2194	R	62*	.1
11	G and C Equipment Corp—Gene Hale	1875 W Redondo Beach B, Gardena CA 90247	310-515-6715	R	55*	<.1
12	Bakercorp—Bryan Livingston	3020 Old Ranch Pkwy St, Seal Beach CA 90740	562-430-6262	R	48*	.1
13	Essex Rental Corp—Ronald Schad	1110 Lake Cook Rd Ste, Buffalo Grove IL 60089	847-215-6500	P	42	.3
14	Beco Construction Power Co—Ken Wilhelm	5555 Dahlia St, Commerce City CO 80022	303-288-2613	R	41*	.1
15	Scott Powerline Utility and Equipment LLC	PO Box 4008, Monroe LA 71211	318-388-9269	R	38*	<.1
16	Nationwide Equipment Company Inc—Edward Kostenski	11950 New Kings Rd, Jacksonville FL 32219	904-924-2500	R	33*	<.1
17	Frank's International Inc—Keith Mosing	10260 Westheimer Rd St, Houston TX 77042	281-966-7300	R	31*	.6
18	Wales Industrial Service Inc—Greg Schroeder	22006 Bush Dr, Woodway TX 76712	254-772-3310	R	27*	<.1
19	Keystone Leasing Services LLC—Robert Gunther	105 Fairway Ter, Mount Laurel NJ 08054	856-642-0200	R	25*	<.1
20	TNT Crane and Rigging Inc—John Heck	PO Box 10304, Corpus Christi TX 78460	361-289-5438	S	19*	.1
21	Schooner Petroleum Services Inc—R McGee	1600 E Hwy 6 Ste 418, Alvin TX 77511	281-894-1770	R	18*	.1
22	Neil F Lampson Inc—William Lampson	PO Box 6510, Kennewick WA 99336	509-586-0411	R	17*	.2
23	Kt-Grant Inc—Ruth Grant	3073 Rte 66, Export PA 15632	724-468-4700	R	15*	.2
24	Craneworks Inc—David Upton	PO Box 336, Birmingham AL 35201	205-278-5438	R	13*	.1
25	D and R Crane Inc—Jody Regan	1324 N Magnolia Ave, El Cajon CA 92020	619-444-1919	R	13*	<.1
26	Marr Scaffolding Co—Robert Marr	1 D St, Boston MA 02127	617-269-7200	R	13*	.1
27	Downs Equipment Rentals Inc—Gordon Downs	PO Box 80536, Bakersfield CA 93380	661-834-5526	R	12*	.1
28	Maha USA LLC—Wolfgang Raffler	PO Box 194, Pinckard AL 36371	334-984-0153	R	12*	.1
29	International Machine and Welding Inc—Don Harrison	1400 Chamber Dr, Bartow FL 33830	863-533-5670	S	12*	<.1
30	Superior Scaffold Services Inc—Albert Bianchini	520 E Luzerne St, Philadelphia PA 19124	215-423-0100	R	11*	.1
31	Abel Enterprises Inc—Troy Abel	PO Box 476, Mountville PA 17554	717-285-2020	R	11*	.2
32	Interstate Treating Inc—Ronald Rains	PO Box 1386, Odessa TX 79760	432-362-9291	R	10*	.1
33	Ja Oilfield Manufacturing Inc—James Acquaye	PO Box 95545, Oklahoma City OK 73143	405-672-2299	R	10*	.1
34	Mega International Inc—Christian Wadleigh	101 Galbert Rd, Lafayette LA 70506	337-266-5121	R	10*	.1
35	LJ Cos—Stacey Izzo	522 Jefferson Blvd, Warwick RI 02886	401-681-4500	R	10*	<.1
36	Anthony Ray International Inc—Ray Anthony	280 Nw 12th Ave, Pompano Beach FL 33069	954-725-1404	R	10*	.1
37	M and N Equipment LLC—Tom Blevins	PO Box 2490, Casper WY 82602	307-234-0583	R	9*	.1
38	L W Connelly and Son Inc—Michael Connelly	12635 Marion, Redford MI 48239	313-531-2700	R	9*	.1
39	Savala Equipment Company Inc—Sean Savala	16402 Construction Cir, Irvine CA 92606	949-552-1859	R	9*	.1
40	Aztec Rental Center No 2 Inc—Richard Sorsby	5702 Bissonnet St, Houston TX 77081	713-667-5651	R	9*	.1
41	Jensen and Koerner Crane Service Inc—Edward Shinn	400 Franklin Ave, Rockaway NJ 07866	973-267-9300	R	9*	.1
42	Kropp Equipment Inc—Albert Kropp	1020 Kennedy Ave Ste 4, Schererville IN 46375	219-865-3333	R	8*	.1
43	Twin Tower Erection And Maintenance Inc—William West	PO Box 429, Kernersville NC 27285	336-996-8499	R	8*	<.1
44	D and D Equipment Rental LLC—Gary Darnell	10936 Shoemaker Ave, Santa Fe Springs CA 90670	562-595-4555	R	8*	<.1
45	Tony R Crisalli Inc—Tony Crisalli	3468 Campbell St, Riverside CA 92509	951-727-0110	R	8*	.1
46	Brewer Corp—Brent Brewer	10125 Channel Rd, Lakeside CA 92040	619-390-8252	R	8*	.1
47	Marentco Inc—Matt Musgrove	1212 N 23rd St, Mcallen TX 78501	956-682-1312	R	8*	.1
48	United Crane Rentals Inc—Timothy Shinn	PO Box 8, Kenilworth NJ 07033	908-245-6260	R	7*	.1
49	RJ Allen Inc—Andrew Allen	10392 Stanford Ave, Garden Grove CA 92840	714-539-1022	R	7*	.1
50	High Plains Services Inc—L Price	PO Box 1865, Elk City OK 73648	580-225-7388	R	7*	.1
51	Crane Rental Service Inc—Edward Hass	1115 W Ranch Rd, Tempe AZ 85284	480-893-0081	R	7*	<.1
52	Consolidated Crane And Rigging Ltd—George Turner	6370 Long Dr, Houston TX 77087	713-641-3330	R	7*	.1
53	William E Baldwin—William Baldwin	232 Andover St, Wilmington MA 01887	978-657-7555	R	7*	<.1
54	International Construction Equipment Inc—T Morris	301 Warehouse Dr, Matthews NC 28104	704-821-8200	R	7*	.1
55	Marr Equipment Corp—Robert Marr	1 D St, Boston MA 02127	617-269-7200	R	7*	<.1
56	R and M Equipment Rentals Inc—Don Rydberg	2329 29th Ave N, Birmingham AL 35207	205-326-1111	R	6*	<.1
57	Central Leasing Inc—Pamp Maiers	PO Box 850, Moses Lake WA 98837	509-765-5885	R	6*	.1
58	IB Dickinson and Sons Inc—Donald Dickinson	1089 Van Reed Rd, Reading PA 19605	610-376-6367	R	6*	<.1
59	Bobcat Of New York Inc—Elliot Prigozen	5864 Maurice Ave Ste A, Maspeth NY 11378	718-366-7930	R	6*	<.1

Rank	Company Name—*Executive Officer*	Address, City, State, Zip	Phone	Type	Fin	Empls
60	Heaton Erecting Inc—*Jacob Heaton*	PO Box 1005, Forest Park GA 30298	404-363-3130	R	6*	<.1
61	Miken Specialties—*Russell Klinegardner*	13491 Hwy 90 Ste 2, Boutte LA 70039	985-331-2289	R	5*	.1
62	Danella Equipment Rentals Inc—*James Danella*	2290 Butler Pke, Plymouth Meeting PA 19462	610-828-6200	R	5*	.1
63	Nessinger Inc—*Edward Nessinger*	244 Colgan Ave, Santa Rosa CA 95404	707-541-0107	R	5*	<.1
64	Bob Turner's Crane Service Inc—*Robert Turner*	12101 Hwy 67, Lakeside CA 92040	619-272-4238	R	5*	<.1
65	Time Savers Inc—*Larry Kozlicki*	725 Kimberly Dr, Carol Stream IL 60188	630-782-7666	R	5*	<.1
66	Parreco Equipment Company Inc—*Arnold Parreco*	2911 52nd Ave Ste C, Hyattsville MD 20781	301-277-8220	R	5*	.1
67	Allingham Corp—*Lawrence Allingham*	21250 W 8 Mile Rd, Southfield MI 48075	248-357-5400	R	5*	<.1
68	Grand Equipment Company LLC—*Emily King*	3310 Hudson Trl Dr, Hudsonville MI 49426	616-896-7700	R	5*	<.1
69	U'ren Sound and Power Systems Inc—*Richard U'ren*	1120 Connecting Rd, Niagara Falls NY 14304	716-773-4104	R	4*	<.1
70	Magnum Mud Equipment Company Inc—*Chapman Burguieres*	PO Box 4258, Houma LA 70361	985-872-1755	R	4*	<.1
71	Turner Pump—*Roy Turner*	PO Box 174, Hartline WA 99135	509-639-0108	R	4*	.1
72	Lowe Leasing Co—*Richard Lowe*	2535 Bader Rd, Horton MI 49246	517-529-9406	R	4*	<.1
73	Champion Crane Rental Inc—*Mike Konle*	12521 Branford St, Pacoima CA 91331	818-781-3497	R	4*	<.1
74	Lewis Barricade Inc—*John Lewis*	PO Box 70338, Bakersfield CA 93387	661-363-0912	R	4*	<.1
75	J Ray Patterson Inc—*Sam Ganow*	3201 W 2nd St, Chester PA 19013	610-494-6620	R	4*	<.1
76	Chellino Crane Inc—*Gregory Chellino*	915 Rowell Ave, Joliet IL 60433	815-723-2829	R	4*	<.1
77	American Platform and Scaffolding Inc—*James Goode*	823 Fairview Ave, Linthicum Heights MD 21090	410-636-5500	R	4*	<.1
78	Clifton Equipment Rental Company Inc—*Alex Clifton*	PO Box 7003, Garden City GA 31418	912-964-0345	R	4*	<.1
79	David L Addison Inc—*Corey Addison*	10206 Elm Ave, Fontana CA 92335	909-822-8282	R	4*	<.1
80	Two College Guys—*Greg Blacke*	599 Nugget Ave, Sparks NV 89431	775-356-5536	R	4*	<.1
81	Coonrod Wrecker and Crane Service—*Diane Spicer*	4000 E Ave Nw, Cedar Rapids IA 52405	319-396-7600	R	4*	<.1
82	Spike Enterprise Inc—*Dan Spicer*	200 Jernigan Rd, Oklahoma City OK 73128	405-324-1100	R	3*	<.1
83	Royall-Matthiessen Equipment And Supply Co—*Mark Royall*	PO Box 7307, San Antonio TX 78207	210-734-4363	R	3*	<.1
84	Taylor Made Oil Tools Inc—*Billy Mcdonald*	PO Box 3404, Houma LA 70361	985-851-5081	R	3*	<.1
85	Eastland Crane Service Inc—*Robert Marshall*	2190 S Hamilton Rd, Columbus OH 43232	614-751-0636	R	3*	<.1
86	Mud Control Equipment Corp—*Shelby Roussell*	100 W Angus Dr, Youngsville LA 70592	337-856-6034	R	3*	<.1
87	Five JAB Rig Services LLC	PO Box 1063, Tomball TX 77377	281-356-7767	R	3*	<.1
88	Johnson Crane Service Inc—*Robert Johnson*	11708 Old Baltimore Pk, Beltsville MD 20705	301-937-5888	R	3*.	<.1
89	Action Rental Center Inc—*Andrew Budick*	4535 Broadway, Allentown PA 18104	610-395-3500	R	3*	<.1
90	All Road Barricades Inc—*Peggy Shalla*	PO Box 29196, Lincoln NE 68529	402-467-2553	R	3*	<.1
91	Crocker Crane Rentals LP—*Joyce Crocker*	PO Box 1469, Leander TX 78646	512-258-1323	R	3*	<.1
92	Rooney Contracting Company Inc—*Patrick Rooney*	PO Box 271, Bad Axe MI 48413	989-269-6213	R	3*	<.1
93	Equipment Rental Co—*Bill Raymond*	4788 1st Ave N, Duluth MN 55803	218-728-4441	R	3*	<.1
94	Russells Crane Service Inc—*Phil Russell*	1645 W Orangewood Ave, Orange CA 92868	714-771-8522	R	3*	<.1
95	Crane Rental Division Inc—*Peggy Ferrugia*	5902 Allison Rd, Houston TX 77048	713-991-6180	R	3*	<.1
96	Big West Oilfield Services—*Koleen Deleon*	PO Box 111, Riverton WY 82501	307-857-3821	R	3*	<.1
97	Mc Cord Crane Service Inc—*Paula Cord*	PO Box 100862, Nashville TN 37224	615-256-3606	R	3*	<.1
98	Y and B Equipment Corp—*Charles Yow*	PO Box 543, Mechanicsville MD 20659	301-423-8393	R	3*	<.1
99	Skelly Oil and Land Co—*David Roberts*	PO Box 415, Midland TX 79702	432-520-0012	R	3*	<.1
100	American Equipment and Fabricating Corp—*Carlton Aldrich*	100 Water St, East Providence RI 02914	401-438-2626	R	3*	<.1
101	Jade Restoration Corp—*John O'rielly*	2306 31st Ave, Astoria NY 11106	718-937-2135	R	2*	<.1
102	Mdp Contracting Inc—*Mario Quintero*	6531 Mid Cities Ave 12, Beltsville MD 20705	301-595-5925	R	2*	<.1
103	Try Green Equipment—*James Jewell*	340 9th Ave N, Franklin TN 37064	615-794-8187	R	2*	<.1
104	Dotlich Inc—*Doreen Devitt*	1111 Polco St, Indianapolis IN 46222	317-247-6611	R	2*	<.1
105	Pioneer Oilfield Services Inc—*Brian Merz*	2020 N Randall Ave, Elk City OK 73644	580-243-4004	R	2*	<.1
106	Premier Rental Center—*Ron Dorn*	1009 E Wisconsin St, Portago WI 53901	608-745-0426	R	2*	<.1
107	Don D Corp—*Don Deaven*	1615 E Ayre St, Wilmington DE 19804	302-994-5793	R	2*	<.1
108	Bragg Crane Service LLC—*Bret Smith*	PO Box 56547, Phoenix AZ 85079	602-233-0205	R	2*	<.1
109	Duane Equipment Corp—*Toby Duane*	51 Park St, Dorchester MA 02122	617-282-4885	R	2*	<.1
110	Conveyor Sales Co—*Paul Helmick*	PO Box 60128, Phoenix AZ 85082	602-273-1455	R	1*	<.1
111	Mcguire Industries Inc—*Loraine Mcguire*	6776 Leopard St, Corpus Christi TX 78409	361-289-9446	R	<1*	<.1

TOTALS: SIC 7353 Heavy Construction Equipment Rental
    Companies: 111   9,242   23.5

7359 Equipment Rental & Leasing Nec

Rank	Company Name—*Executive Officer*	Address, City, State, Zip	Phone	Type	Fin	Empls
1	Rent-A-Center Inc—*Mark E Speese*	5501 Headquarters Dr, Plano TX 75024	972-801-1100	P	2,882	19.7
2	Exterran Holdings Inc—*D Bradley Childers*	16666 Northchase Dr, Houston TX 77060	281-836-7000	P	2,683	10.4
3	GES Exposition Services Inc—*Paul B Dykstra*	950 Grier Dr, Las Vegas NV 89119	702-263-1500	S	2,538*	1.8
4	RSC Holdings Inc—*Kevin Groman*	6929 E Greenway Pky St, Scottsdale AZ 85254	480-905-3300	P	1,522	4.7
5	United Coin Machine Co—*Grant Lincoln*	600 Pilot Rd Ste E, Las Vegas NV 89119	702-270-7500	S	1,070*	.7
6	Equipment Depot—*Don Moes*	4100 S Interstate 35, Waco TX 76705	254-662-4322	S	975*	.7
7	Hertz Claim Management—*Mark P Frissora*	225 Brae Blvd, Park Ridge NJ 07656	201-307-2000	S	934*	.7
8	Hertz Truck and Van Rental—*Mark P Frissora*	225 Brae Blvd, Park Ridge NJ 07656	201-307-2000	S	934*	.7
9	Brambles USA Inc—*Al Trujillo*	180 Technology Pkwy, Norcross GA 30092	770-451-7520	R	760*	4.0
10	H and E Equipment Services Inc—*John M Engquist*	11100 Mead Rd Ste 200, Baton Rouge LA 70816	225-298-5200	P	721	1.6
11	Williams Scotsman International Inc—*Gerald E Holthaus*	8211 Town Center Dr, Baltimore MD 21236	410-931-6000	R	681	1.9
12	Chep USA—*Jim Ritchie*	8517 S Park Cir, Orlando FL 32819	407-370-2437	R	679*	.5
13	International Lease Finance Corp—*John Plueger*	10250 Constellation Bl, Los Angeles CA 90067	310-788-1999	S	618*	.1
14	LeasePlan USA—*Mike Pitcher*	1165 Sanctuary Pky, Alpharetta GA 30009	770-933-9090	S	604*	.5
15	NES Rentals Holdings Inc—*Andrew P Studdert*	5440 N Cumberland Ave, Chicago IL 60656	773-695-3999	S	582	2.8
16	Williams Scotsman Inc Williams Scotsman International Inc	8211 Town Center Dr, Baltimore MD 21236		S	526*	1.3
17	Brook Furniture Rental Inc—*Robert W Crawford Jr*	100 N Field Dr Ste 220, Lake Forest IL 60045	847-810-4000	R	518*	.4
18	TAL International Group Inc—*Brian M Sondey*	100 Manhattanville Rd, Purchase NY 10577	914-251-9000	P	517	.2
19	Rotech Healthcare Inc—*Philip L Carter*	2600 Technology Dr Ste, Orlando FL 32804	407-822-4600	P	496	3.8
20	Marlin Business Services Corp—*Daniel P Dyer*	300 Fellowship Rd, Mount Laurel NJ 08054	856-359-9111	P	468	.2
21	Bestway Rental Inc—*R Brooks Reed* Bestway Inc	7800 Stemmons Fwy Ste, Dallas TX 75247	214-630-6655	S	427*	.3
22	Aaron's Rental Purchase Div	309 E Paces Ferry Rd N, Atlanta GA 30305	404-231-0011	D	408*	5.0
23	Telerent Leasing Corp—*George H Fleming*	PO Box 26627, Raleigh NC 27611	919-772-8604	S	397*	.3
24	Ecologic Transportation Inc—*William N Plamondon III*	1327 Ocean Ave Ste B, Santa Monica CA 90401	310-899-3900	P	387	<.1
25	Interpool Inc—*Martin Tuchman*	211 College Rd E, Princeton NJ 08540	609-452-8900	R	374*	.3
26	McGrath Rentcorp—*Dennis C Kakures*	5700 Las Positas Rd, Livermore CA 94551	925-606-9200	P	343	.7
27	SEI Aaron's Inc—*Charles Smithgall*	3108 Piedmont Rd NE St, Atlanta GA 30305	404-495-9707	R	315*	.2
28	CORT Furniture Rental Corp—*Paul N Arnold*	11250 Waples Mill Ln S, Fairfax VA 22030	703-968-8500	S	312*	2.5
29	Neff Corp—*Graham Hood*	6501 NW 87th Ave, Miami FL 33178		S	286*	1.1
30	Electro Rent Corp—*Daniel Greenberg*	6060 Sepulveda Blvd, Van Nuys CA 91411	818-787-2100	P	229	.4
31	TRS-RenTelco McGrath Rentcorp	PO Box 619260, Dallas TX 75261	972-456-4000	S	221*	.1
32	Andy Gump Inc—*Barry Gump*	26410 Summit Cir, Santa Clarita CA 91350	661-251-7721	R	165*	.1

Note: An asterisk (*) indicates an estimated financial figure. The company type code used is as follows: R = Private, P = Public, S = Private Subsidiary, B = Public Subsidiary, D = Division, J = Joint Venture, I = Investment Fund.

COMPANY RANKINGS BY SALES WITHIN 4-DIGIT SIC

Rank	Company Name—Executive Officer	Address, City, State, Zip	Phone	Type	Fin	Empls
33	Aircraft Finance Trust	2401 Kerner Blvd, San Rafael CA 94901	415-485-4500	R	142*	N/A
34	Event Rentals Inc—John Campanelli	11766 Wilshire Blvd St, Los Angeles CA 90025	310-966-4900	R	117*	2.5
35	CAI International Inc—Victor Garcia	1 Market Plza Ctr Ste, San Francisco CA 94105	415-788-0100	P	78	.1
36	Mitcham Industries Inc—Billy F Mitcham Jr	PO Box 1175, Huntsville TX 77342	936-291-2277	P	71	.1
37	Royal Audio Video Supply Inc—Randy Gervais	235 N Causeway Blvd, Metairie LA 70001	504-831-9779	R	68*	.1
38	Flexi-Van Leasing Inc—George Elkas	251 Monroe Ave, Kenilworth NJ 07033	908-276-8000	R	66*	.2
39	T and V Rental Company Inc—Ed Koch	6069 Woodhaven Blvd, Elmhurst NY 11373	718-458-2211	R	65*	.6
40	Sound Chek Music—Chris Brown	PO Box 23831, New Orleans LA 70183	504-734-7529	R	64*	<.1
41	VLPS Lighting Services International Inc—Steve Washington	8617 Ambassador Row St, Dallas TX 75247	214-630-1963	S	60*	.3
42	Pacific Rim Capital Inc—Marc C Mills	15 Enterprise Ste 400, Aliso Viejo CA 92656	949-389-0800	R	54*	<.1
43	Bestway Inc—David A Kraemer	12400 Coit Rd Ste 950, Dallas TX 75251	214-630-6655	P	52	N/A
44	HPS Office Systems—Leon Mordon	5561 W 74th St, Indianapolis IN 46268	317-875-6000	R	51*	.1
45	Traffic Control Service Inc—Scott Westphal	1818 E Orangethorpe Av, Fullerton CA 92831	714-526-9500	R	50*	.2
46	Western Precooling Systems—Craig Miller	PO Box 1338, Fremont CA 94538	510-656-2220	R	42*	.1
47	General Furniture Leasing Co—Paul Arnold CORT Furniture Rental Corp	1641 Cobb Pkwy, Marietta GA 30060	770-729-8773	D	38*	.4
48	Tiger Equipment Inc—Forest Nabors	PO Box 490, Belden MS 38826	901-458-8977	R	38*	<.1
49	Buck's Sanitary Service Inc—Scott Weld	PO Box 21527, Eugene OR 97402	541-342-3905	R	34*	<.1
50	Lifting Gear Hire Corp—Tony Fiscelli	9925 Industrial Dr, Bridgeview IL 60455	708-598-4727	R	33*	.1
51	Lawrence Leasing Ii LLC—Eric Lawrence	860 Bench St, Red Wing MN 55066	651-388-7067	R	30*	.1
52	Display Group—Richard Portwood	1700 W Fort St, Detroit MI 48216	313-965-3344	R	27*	<.1
53	Womack Material Handling Systems Inc—John Croce	40 Carpenter Ln, Wallingford CT 06492	203-265-2887	R	25*	.1
54	Compressor Systems Inc—David Murdock	PO Box 60760, Midland TX 79711	432-563-1170	R	25*	.5
55	Musco Corp—Joe Crookham	100 1st Ave W, Oskaloosa IA 52577	641-673-0411	R	23*	.7
56	AeroCentury Corp—Neal D Crispin	1440 Chapin Ave Ste 31, Burlingame CA 94010	650-340-1888	P	23	N/A
57	T And B Equipment Company Inc—Thomas Ellis	11065 Leadbetter Rd, Ashland VA 23005	804-798-2000	R	22*	.2
58	Franks Supply Company Inc—Melissa Deaver-Rivera	3311 Stanford NE, Albuquerque NM 87107	505-884-0000	R	20*	.1
59	Kenmore Air Harbor Inc	6321 NE 175th St, Kenmore WA 98028	425-486-1257	R	18*	.2
60	Feature Marketing Inc—Tom Packouz YouChange Holdings Corp	16000 N 80th St Ste D, Scottsdale AZ 85260	480-947-9912	S	17*	<.1
61	Rdss and Company LLC—Shu Chiu	134 Morgan Ave, Brooklyn NY 11237	718-821-4000	R	16*	.2
62	Marr Scaffolding Company Inc—Robert Marr	1 D St, South Boston MA 02127	617-269-7200	R	15*	.1
63	Creative Presentations Inc—Barry Edwards	4500 York St Ste 200, Metairie LA 70001	504-454-2749	R	14*	.1
64	Dutel Telecommunications Inc—Melvena Kaye	7041 Vineland Ave, North Hollywood CA 91605	818-765-2799	R	14*	<.1
65	Project Horizon Inc—Michael Freedman	4801 Executive Park Ct, Jacksonville FL 32216	904-332-0450	R	13*	.2
66	North Jersey Bobcat Inc—Vincent Ryan	201 Maltese Dr, Totowa NJ 07512	973-774-9500	R	13*	<.1
67	Audio Visual Mart Inc—Rick Peyton	603 Williams Blvd, Kenner LA 70062	504-712-0400	R	13*	<.1
68	P L Custom Body And Equipment Company Inc—Robert Stevenson	2201 Atlantic Ave, Manasquan NJ 08736	732-223-1411	R	12*	.1
69	Be Our Guest Inc—Albert Lovata	24 Blue Hill Ave, Roxbury MA 02119	617-427-2700	R	12*	.1
70	Southern Audio Visual Inc—Paul Lowenthal	11700 Nw 102nd Rd Ste, Medley FL 33178	305-591-3888	R	11*	.2
71	Collins Entertainment Co—Felicia Robins	1341 Rutherford Rd, Greenville SC 29609	864-268-1111	R	11*	<.1
72	Renaissance Capital Alliance—Ronald Hall Sr	2005 W Hamlin Rd Ste 2, Rochester Hills MI 48309	248-299-7800	R	11*	<.1
73	Academy Tent And Canvas Inc—Tom Shapiro	5035 Gifford Ave, Vernon CA 90058	323-277-8368	R	10*	.2
74	Ez Acceptance Inc—Ronald Zagami	7651 Ronson Rd, San Diego CA 92111	858-278-8351	R	10*	.1
75	Scharff Weisberg Inc—Josh Weisberg	3636 33rd St Ste 204, Long Island City NY 11106	718-610-1660	R	10*	.1
76	WH Paige and Company Inc—Mark Goff	5282 E 65th St Ste A, Indianapolis IN 46220	317-842-2102	R	10*	.1
77	Crescent Sound and Light Inc—Mike Smith	25 Veterans Blvd, Kenner LA 70062		R	10*	<.1
78	Cartwright and Daughters Party Rentals—Jerry Cartwright	1707 Rte 6, Carmel NY 10512	845-225-9200	R	10*	<.1
79	NLB Leasing LLC—Forrest Shook	29830 Beck Rd, Wixom MI 48393	248-624-5555	R	10*	.3
80	Leonard Fountain Specialties Inc—Leonard Bugajewski	4225 Nancy St, Detroit MI 48212	313-891-4141	R	10*	.1
81	National Lift Truck Inc—Perry Du Bose	3333 Mount Prospect Rd, Franklin Park IL 60131	630-782-1000	R	10*	.1
82	Massachusetts Audio Visual Equipment Corp—Patricia Basteri	755 Middlesex Tpke, Billerica MA 01821	978-670-0027	R	10*	.1
83	Aero Contractors Ltd—Dolphin Overton	PO Box 1139, Smithfield NC 27577	919-934-0978	R	9*	.1
84	Magic Industries Inc—Woodward Thomas	3024 Bells Rd, Richmond VA 23234	804-230-1500	R	9*	.1
85	Hall's Rental Service Inc—John Luft	6130 W Howard St, Niles IL 60714	847-929-2222	R	9*	.1
86	Durden Outdoor Displays Inc—W Durden	PO Box 2146, Dothan AL 36302	334-792-5056	R	9*	<.1
87	Orlando Waste Paper Company Inc—Jerry Vestal	PO Box 547874, Orlando FL 32854	407-299-1380	R	8*	.1
88	Mrs Homecare Inc—E Riddle	PO Box 568, Albany GA 31702	229-439-2403	R	8*	.1
89	Dnm Enterprises—Dee Deefioretti	3000 N Grfield St Ste, Midland TX 79705	432-684-5829	R	8*	<.1
90	Access National Leasing Corp	1800 Robert Fulton Dr, Reston VA 20191	703-871-2100	S	8*	<.1
91	Clairmont Camera Inc—Denny Clairmont	4343 Lankershim Blvd, North Hollywood CA 91602	818-761-4440	R	8*	.1
92	Hughes Rental And Sales Inc—James Hughes	1611 S Gregg St, Big Spring TX 79720	432-263-0234	R	8*	.1
93	Laitram Machinery Inc—Barry Lacour	PO Box 50699, New Orleans LA 70150	504-733-6000	R	8*	.1
94	New Avenues Lease Ownership LLC—Margaret Keiser	3440 Preston Ridge Rd, Alpharetta GA 30005	678-823-4700	R	8*	.1
95	Burkhalter Rigging Inc—Delynn Burkhalter	PO Box 9360, Columbus MS 39705	662-327-7711	R	8*	.1
96	South East Industrial Sales And Service Inc—Louis Laurito	PO Box 8247, Tampa FL 33674	813-247-2780	R	8*	.1
97	Elliott Tool Technologies Ltd—Joseph Smith	PO Box 1165, Dayton OH 45401	937-253-6133	R	8*	.1
98	Excalibur Energy Services Inc—James Lewis	PO Box 217, Ratliff City OK 73481	580-856-3580	R	7*	.1
99	Scaffolding Solutions LLC—Johnny Laws	PO Box 24623, Richmond VA 23224	804-232-9080	R	7*	.1
100	Lookout Leasing Co—R Morrison	410 Spring St, Chattanooga TN 37405	423-756-2940	R	7*	.1
101	Art's Rental Equipment Inc—Kenneth Arlinghaus	215 E 6th St, Newport KY 41071	859-431-4519	R	7*	.1
102	Business Aircraft Leasing Inc—Charles Mulle	PO Box 17056, Nashville TN 37217	615-361-3781	R	7*	<.1
103	Clair Brothers Audio Enterprises Inc—Roy Clair	PO Box 396, Lititz PA 17543	717-626-4000	R	7*	.1
104	Prestige Audio Visual Inc—Tony Ramstetter	4835 Para Dr, Cincinnati OH 45237	513-641-1600	R	7*	.1
105	Golden Business Machines Inc—Carol Douds	PO Box 1700, Kingston PA 18704	570-288-7554	R	7*	.1
106	RSVP Party Rentals Inc—John Smithers	4445 S Valley View Blv, Las Vegas NV 89103	702-878-0144	R	6*	.1
107	Landmark Financial Corp (Englewood Colorado)—Peter H Suthurland	5600 Greenwood Plz Blv, Greenwood Village CO 80111		S	6*	.1
108	Miller Equipment Company Inc—Geary Byrd	PO Box J, Hugo OK 74743	580-326-3173	R	6*	.1
109	Express Business Resources LLC	55 Hitchcock Way Ste 1, Santa Barbara CA 93105	805-898-3855	R	6*	.1
110	Advantage Leasing Corp—Lawrence Elton	324 E Wscnsin Ave Ste, Milwaukee WI 53202	414-291-3400	R	6*	<.1
111	Pinamar LLC—Judy Mcquade	295 S Vasco Rd, Livermore CA 94551	925-243-8979	R	6*	.1
112	Basha Equipment Leasing Co—Yahya Mossa-Basha	30701 Woodward Ave Ste, Royal Oak MI 48073	248-288-1600	R	6*	.1
113	Riverview Systems Group Inc—Christopher Thorne	1565 Mabury Rd Ste C, San Jose CA 95133	408-347-3700	R	6*	.1
114	Phoenix Aerial Tow Operations—Mark Thompson	177 Hwy 61 Se, Cartersville GA 30120	770-383-3545	R	6*	.1
115	Digital Office Systems Inc—Kimberly Bayes	530 S Hydraulic St, Wichita KS 67211	316-262-7700	R	6*	<.1
116	Adams Tv Rental Of New Hampshire—Paul Berube	102 Elm St, Claremont NH 03743	603-298-8717	R	6*	.1
117	Centex Pipe and Equipment Inc—Tom Wright	PO Box 1145, Luling TX 78648	830-875-3950	R	5*	.1
118	Play Time Toys Inc—George Asbate	6235 Edgewater Dr, Orlando FL 32810	407-296-9898	R	5*	.1

Rank	Company Name—*Executive Officer*	Address, City, State, Zip	Phone	Type	Fin	Empls
119	Coe Press Sales Corp—*John Coe*	40549 Brentwood Dr, Sterling Heights MI 48310	586-979-4400	R	5*	.1
120	River Hawk Aviation Inc—*Calvin Humphrey*	3103 9th Ave Dr NW, Hickory NC 28601	828-322-6044	R	5	<.1
121	Wyatt Compressor Service Inc—*William Wyatt*	PO Box 1620, Broussard LA 70518	337-837-1142	R	5*	<.1
122	O'neil Awning And Tent Inc—*Dennis Ritchey*	895 W Walnut St, Canal Winchester OH 43110	614-837-6352	R	5*	.1
123	Canopies LLC	7234 N 60th St, Milwaukee WI 53223	414-760-0770	R	5*	.1
124	A-1 Coast Rentals Inc	24000 Crenshaw Blvd, Torrance CA 90505	310-326-1910	R	5*	.1
125	C Johnnie-On-The-Spot Portable Toilets Inc—*Wayne Colicher*	PO Box 1583, Nederland TX 77627	409-724-6647	R	5*	<.1
126	Canyon Ridge Contractors Inc—*Mark Moss*	PO Box 271, Colton CA 92324	909-824-1991	R	5*	<.1
127	Complete Dewatering Pumps and Wellpoints Inc—*Howard Brunet*	PO Box 36, Edgewater FL 32132	386-426-1345	R	5*	<.1
128	LB Industries Inc—*Lawrence B Barnes*	5983 W State St Ste D, Boise ID 83703	208-424-2022	R	5*	<.1
129	Barrett Capital Corp—*Barry P Korn*	27 Horton Ave 2nd Fl, New Rochelle NY 10801		R	5*	<.1
130	Warwick Communications Inc—*Ryan Shorts*	2806 Payne Ave, Cleveland OH 44114	216-787-0300	R	5*	<.1
131	US Surf Company Inc—*D Nachnani*	316 21st St, Virginia Beach VA 23451	757-491-9011	R	5*	.1
132	Digital Music Systems Inc—*David Ruthruff*	21009 108th Ave Se, Kent WA 98031	253-852-9692	R	5*	<.1
133	Macquarie Airfinance Ltd—*John Willingham*	2 Embarcadero Ctr Ste, San Francisco CA 94111	415-829-6600	R	5*	.1
134	Imperial Leasing Inc—*Allen Schefers*	1771 Yankee Doodle Rd, Saint Paul MN 55121	651-454-3330	R	5*	.1
135	Tradeshow Equipment Rentals Inc—*Liem Huynh*	2043 Lawrence St, Atlanta GA 30344	770-294-1110	R	4*	.1
136	Statewide Safety and Signs Inc—*Don Nicholas*	PO Box 1440, Pismo Beach CA 93448	805-929-5070	R	4*	<.1
137	Aztech Rentals Of San Antonio Inc—*Douglas Raney*	3439 Roosevelt Ave, San Antonio TX 78214	210-924-5505	R	4*	<.1
138	Architects Leasing Inc—*Cameron Hyde*	1200 Nw Naito Pkwy Ste, Portland OR 97209	503-228-5617	R	4*	<.1
139	Avalon Equipment Corp—*Steve Mcilhon*	2453 Cades Way Bldg B, Vista CA 92081	760-536-0191	R	4*	<.1
140	ZGC Inc—*Les Zellan*	264 Morris Ave, Mountain Lakes NJ 07046	973-335-4460	R	4*	<.1
141	East Tennessee Rent-Alls Inc—*James Baxter*	PO Box 3856, Johnson City TN 37602	423-282-3221	R	4*	<.1
142	National Barricade Company LLC—*Jim Humphrey*	6518 Ravenna Ave Ne, Seattle WA 98115	206-523-4045	R	4*	<.1
143	Carbonator Rental Service Inc—*Andrew Pincus*	PO Box 33327, Philadelphia PA 19142	215-726-9100	R	4*	<.1
144	Field Environmental Instruments Inc—*Mitchell Brourman*	301a Brushton Ave, Pittsburgh PA 15221	412-436-2600	R	4*	<.1
145	Lasting Impressions Event and Party Rentals Inc—*J Fritz*	1890 E Main St, Columbus OH 43205	614-252-5400	R	4*	.1
146	Abbey Party Rents Of San Diego And Riverside Counties Inc—*Richard Cutting*	8860 Production Ave, San Diego CA 92121	858-597-0201	R	4*	<.1
147	Automatic Laundry Services Company Inc—*Salvatore Scarpato*	45 Border St, Newton MA 02465	617-969-4340	R	4*	<.1
148	Prolease Of America Inc—*Nelson Saavedra*	PO Box 315, Morganville NJ 07751	732-617-2100	R	4*	<.1
149	Foley Supply LLC—*Diane Rogers*	1210 S W St, Wichita KS 67213	316-944-7368	R	4*	<.1
150	Charter Services Inc—*Robert Marks*	PO Box 88043, Mobile AL 36608	251-633-6090	R	4*	<.1
151	Anthony Wayne Vending Company Inc—*Larry Yarnell*	530 Wolfe Dr, Fort Wayne IN 46825	260-482-7475	R	4*	<.1
152	Mac Productions Inc—*Michael Claypool*	242 Pke St, Covington KY 41011	859-655-3080	R	3*	<.1
153	Hill Aircraft And Leasing Corp—*Guy Hill*	3948 Aviation Cir Nw, Atlanta GA 30336	404-691-3330	R	3*	<.1
154	Color Methods Inc—*Eric Smith*	400 Mile Crossing Blvd, Rochester NY 14624	585-424-1900	R	3*	<.1
155	LLC Whitaker Brothers—*Michael Whitaker*	97 Wood St, Bristol PA 19007	215 785-1595	R	3*	<.1
156	Lasalle Systems Leasing I—*David Hackman*	350 N Old Woodward Ave, Birmingham MI 48009	248-646-5565	R	3*	<.1
157	Boone Rentals Inc—*J Campbell*	PO Box 1816, Boone NC 28607	828-264-5000	R	3*	<.1
158	Monaco Air Duluth LLC—*Scott Paulin*	4535 Airport Approach, Duluth MN 55811	218-727-2911	R	3*	<.1
159	Atlantic Rentals and Sales Corp—*John Colvin*	830b Old Corlies Ave, Neptune NJ 07753	732-922-8958	R	3*	<.1
160	Advance Laundry Systems Inc—*Donald Leach*	1177 Industrial Dr, Bensenville IL 60106	630-766-2000	R	3*	.1
161	Hawaii Stage And Lighting Rentals Inc—*Craig Maddocks*	822 Mapunapuna St, Honolulu HI 96819	808-831-0333	R	3*	<.1
162	Schulz Clearwater Sanitation Inc—*Michael Lumber*	PO Box 1404, Tualatin OR 97062	503-253-7586	R	3*	<.1
163	Dx Service Co—*S Morian*	PO Box 130410, Houston TX 77219	713 863 1947	R	3*	<.1
164	Baker Equipment And Materials Ltd—*Daniel Baker*	PO Box 526, Monroe OH 45050	513-422-0680	R	3*	<.1
165	Casino Party Masters—*Anna Coplen*	7770 E Iliff Ave Ste E, Denver CO 80231	720-747-1800	R	3*	.1
166	United Reynolds—*D Carter*	1824 S Patterson St, Valdosta GA 31601	229-242-1774	R	3*	<.1
167	Durant's Tents And Events LLC—*Susan Kennedy*	1155 Rte 9, Wappingers Falls NY 12590	845-298-0011	R	3*	<.1
168	Dust Catchers Inc—*Michael Normandie*	8801 S S Chicago Ave, Chicago IL 60617	773-768-1440	R	3*	<.1
169	Florida Rental Solutions LLC	4771 Bayou Blvd Ste 32, Pensacola FL 32503	850-475-4105	R	3*	<.1
170	Desktop Visual Products Inc—*Rick Frandsen*	411 W 400 S, Salt Lake City UT 84101	801-359-5808	R	3*	<.1
171	MB Productions Inc—*Brian Brooks*	4 Edison Pl Ste 5, Fairfield NJ 07004	973-439-0044	R	3*	<.1
172	Energy Equipment Resources Inc—*Mike Mullen*	8411 Preston Rd Ste 73, Dallas TX 75225	214-692-6690	R	3*	<.1
173	Technology Project Finance LLC—*Sam Khanna*	PO Box 673, Wilton CT 06897	203-529-3088	R	3*	<.1
174	Distinctive Event Rentals Inc—*William Cabell*	1111 International Plz, Chesapeake VA 23323	757-420-7000	R	3*	.1
175	Beach Sound Inc—*Andres Serafini*	1001 Park Centre Blvd, Miami FL 33169	305-623-3339	R	3*	<.1
176	Miller And Company Portable Toilet Services Inc—*Ronald Miller*	2400 Shepler Ch Ave Sw, Canton OH 44706	330-453-9472	R	3*	<.1
177	Prestige Party Rental Inc—*Thomas Hazen*	241 N 10th St, Prospect Park NJ 07508	973-942-5300	R	3*	<.1
178	Blinker-Lite Safety Inc—*Charles Potter*	PO Box 90421, Nashville TN 37209	615-783-0700	R	3*	<.1
179	Pajukale Inc—*Patricia Zygmun*	6700 W Touhy Ave, Niles IL 60714	847-647-5000	R	3*	<.1
180	Serb Systems Inc—*Andrew Serb*	800 Alfred Nobel Dr, Hercules CA 94547	510-741-2925	R	3*	<.1
181	Bloomfield Party Rental Corp—*Sara Reizen*	2390 Franklin Rd, Bloomfield Hills MI 48302	248-332-4700	R	3*	<.1
182	Action Rental And Sales Inc—*Paul Nottingham*	1861 N Eastman Rd, Kingsport TN 37664	423-246-5181	R	3*	<.1
183	Instrumentation Northwest Inc—*Gregg Gustafson*	8902 122nd Ave Ne, Kirkland WA 98033	425-822-4434	R	3*	<.1
184	Atel Cash Distribution Fund Vi LP—*Dean Cash*	600 California St Fl 6, San Francisco CA 94108	415-989-8800	R	3*	.1
185	Aqua Spas—*Rich Strick*	4731 W 10th St Unit D, Greeley CO 80634	970-352-7140	R	3*	<.1
186	DVL—*Jerry Southwood*	209 7th Ave N, Nashville TN 37219	615-244-1818	R	3*	<.1
187	Aries Party Rental Company Inc—*Fred Barrera*	4940 Northrup Ave, Saint Louis MO 63110	314-664-6610	R	3*	<.1
188	Silsam Inc—*Sam Emerson*	4215 Bertsos Dr Ste A, Las Vegas NV 89103	702-252-0152	R	3*	<.1
189	Bill Veazey's Party Store Inc—*Mary-Jane Veazey*	1640 W Main St, Oklahoma City OK 73106	405-236-4567	R	3*	<.1
190	American Tent and Awning Company Inc—*Terry Simpson*	205 E Palmer St, Indianapolis IN 46225	317-632-7226	R	3*	<.1
191	Hays Rental and Sales Company Inc—*John Hays*	PO Box 230, El Dorado AR 71730	870-862-4935	R	3*	<.1
192	Stevens Enterprises Inc—*Perry Stevens*	1500 Main St, Newberry SC 29108	803-276-5535	R	3*	<.1
193	A J Inc—*Bruce Ibach*	2470 S 11th St, Beaumont TX 77701	409-835-1859	R	3*	<.1
194	Joelle's Salon Day SpA—*Joe Roccosorte*	11740 Carmel Mountain, San Diego CA 92128	858-946-0178	R	3*	<.1
195	Cmc Scaffolding Contractors Inc—*Gloria Gilbreath*	PO Box 16298, Houston TX 77222	713-692-8591	R	3*	<.1
196	Kent Investment Corp—*Steve Kent*	PO Box 279, Ash Flat AR 72513	870-994-3535	R	3*	<.1
197	Maxam Vending Services Inc—*Scott Salonya*	5600 Greenwood Plz Blv, Greenwood Village CO 80111	303-298-8363	R	3*	<.1
198	Necco Coffee Company Inc—*Anthony Simone*	1001 E 11th St, Kansas City MO 64106	816-842-1684	R	3*	<.1
199	Twin Otter International Ltd—*Alan Stephen*	2806 Perimeter Rd, North Las Vegas NV 89032	702-646-8837	R	3*	<.1
200	Bbi Engineering Inc—*Philip Bailey*	241 Quint St, San Francisco CA 94124	415-695-9555	R	3*	<.1
201	Greenery Unlimited—*George Aiello*	6691 33rd St E Ste B3, Sarasota FL 34243	941-752-1039	R	2*	<.1
202	Parties Plus Tucson LLC	3510 S Campbell Ave, Tucson AZ 85713	520-792-8368	R	2*	<.1
203	Sbs Investments Of Dade County Inc—*Jose Segarra*	9740 E Evergreen St, Cutler Bay FL 33157	305-969-1025	R	2*	<.1
204	Heberts Trucking and Equipment Service LLC	5110 Carmelite St, Marrero LA 70072	504-689-2420	R	2*	<.1

Note: An asterisk (*) indicates an estimated financial figure. The company type code used is as follows: R = Private, P = Public, S = Private Subsidiary, R = Public Subsidiary, D = Division, J = Joint Venture, I = Investment Fund.

COMPANY RANKINGS BY SALES WITHIN 4-DIGIT SIC

Rank	Company Name—*Executive Officer*	Address, City, State, Zip	Phone	Type	Fin	Empls
205	Universal Dove Corp—*Ernest Marciel*	91-316 Komohana St, Kapolei HI 96707	808-682-2466	R	2*	<.1
206	Camera House Inc—*Rufus Burnham*	7351 Fulton Ave, North Hollywood CA 91605	818-997-3802	R	2*	<.1
207	Hotubs Inc—*Sandy Perkins*	1777 Camper View Rd, San Dimas CA 91773	909-592-2222	R	2*	<.1
208	Party Rentals—*Ross Condit*	4623 Mchenry Ave, Modesto CA 95356	209-524-1966	R	2*	<.1
209	Frontier Leasing Corp—*Dave Lyon*	1200 Valley W Dr Ste 4, West Des Moines IA 50266	515-251-6920	R	2*	<.1
210	Baldwin Portable Toilets And Septic Tanks Inc—*Brenda Boyett*	31378 Us Hwy 90, Seminole AL 36574	251-946-3250	R	2*	<.1
211	Comfort House Inc—*John Sharp*	2450 Titan Row, Orlando FL 32809	407-647-2002	R	2*	<.1
212	Communications USA Inc—*Roger Schuknecht*	2229 Enterprise St, Escondido CA 92029	858-674-1370	R	2*	<.1
213	Aaron's Rental Purchase—*William Kemp*	1128 E March Ln, Stockton CA 95210	209-954-9668	R	2*	<.1
214	Lease Midwest Inc—*Reed Taylor*	7015 Scott Hamilton Dr, Little Rock AR 72209	501-565-4800	R	2*	<.1
215	Florida Medical Development Inc—*H Kresge*	670 N Orlando Ave Ste, Winter Park FL 32789	407-629-9277	R	2*	<.1
216	Perrier Party Rentals Inc—*Jim Perrier*	109 Industrial Ave, Jefferson LA 70121	504-834-8570	R	2*	<.1
217	Sure Sound and Lighting Inc—*Larry Suhr*	331 N Jefferson St, Grand Island NE 68801	308-382-2961	R	2*	<.1
218	Michigan Carbonic Of Saginaw Inc—*Paul Marshall*	PO Box 376, Bridgeport MI 48722	989-777-5170	R	2*	<.1
219	Haynes Scaffolding and Supply Inc—*Eugene Haynes*	1210 Ortega Rd, West Palm Beach FL 33405	561-833-8689	R	2*	<.1
220	Etching Industries Corp—*Richard Firkser*	4530 N Keystone Ave, Indianapolis IN 46205	317-591-3500	R	2*	<.1
221	Ste-Del Services Inc—*Steven Delonga*	5505 Vine St, Alexandria VA 22310	703-971-1660	R	2*	<.1
222	Austin's Tropical Plant Leasing Inc—*Jeff Arbogust*	10211 FM 969, Austin TX 78724	512-928-1974	R	2*	<.1
223	Make It Or Break It Videos—*Ira Cohen*	3053 W Craig Rd Ste E, North Las Vegas NV 89032	702-399-7254	R	2*	<.1
224	Grant Leasing Inc—*Harry Bauge*	1701 Capital Ave, Plano TX 75074	972-424-3531	R	2*	<.1
225	A C Company Of South Lousiana Inc—*Jonathan Gibson*	PO Box 9805, New Iberia LA 70562	337-365-7216	R	2*	<.1
226	Chep International Inc—*Victor Mendes*	8517 Southpark Cir Ste, Orlando FL 32819	407-370-2437	R	2*	<.1
227	Irmo Equipment Rental Inc—*Jimmy Gist*	1839 Chapin Rd, Chapin SC 29036	803-345-0039	R	2*	<.1
228	Purewater Dynamics Inc—*Marty Josephs*	30 Kalamath St, Denver CO 80223	303-922-4383	R	2*	<.1
229	Sani-Hut Company Inc—*Fred Cutler*	PO Box 7455, Reno NV 89510	775-358-6720	R	2*	<.1
230	Scherr Furniture Rentals Inc—*Stanley Scherr*	12340 Parklawn Dr, Rockville MD 20852	301-881-8960	R	2*	<.1
231	Nichelson Rentals—*Charels Nichelson*	592 W Lakeshore Dr, Lincoln NE 68528	402-435-5657	R	2*	<.1
232	Eagle Rentals and Sales—*Michael Stokes*	155 E 1400 N Ste 101, Logan UT 84341	435-752-2002	R	2*	<.1
233	Logico Response Corp—*Belkys Perez*	8150b Nw 90th St, Medley FL 33166	786-367-0028	R	2*	<.1
234	Party Maxx Inc—*Cathy Roda*	3510 S Campbell Ave, Tucson AZ 85713	520-792-8368	R	2*	<.1
235	Hogue Enterprises Inc—*Robyn Hogue*	8251 Telegraph Rd Ste, Odenton MD 21113	410-674-7500	R	2*	<.1
236	Cromers Inc—*Burns Corley*	1700 Huger St, Columbia SC 29201	803-779-2290	R	2*	<.1
237	Rent and Rave Inc—*Royce Lawrence*	1210 Truman Park Dr, Louisville KY 40245	502-245-9966	R	2*	<.1
238	Rent Rite Equipment Co—*Albert Weiss*	1260 E Higgins Rd, Elk Grove Village IL 60007	847-640-8860	R	2*	<.1
239	Rox Trucking Inc—*Edward Buick*	100 River Rd, Mc Kees Rocks PA 15136	412-331-0988	R	2*	<.1
240	Abc Sanitation and Septic Inc—*Steve Youngblood*	PO Box 1700, Nampa ID 83653	208-888-2450	R	2*	<.1
241	America Tent Rentals Inc—*Salvador Castillo*	2110 Coors Blvd Sw, Albuquerque NM 87121	505-888-5821	R	2*	<.1
242	Stevens Desposole—*Kathy Chlegel*	16929 Industriale W Rd, Petersburg MI 49270	734-856-4113	R	2*	<.1
243	Alar Leasing Co—*Vickey Hansen*	9651 196th St, Mokena IL 60448	708-479-6100	R	2*	<.1
244	Keinath Leasing Co—*Keith Bevzriege*	12800 Hwy 13 S Ste 500, Savage MN 55378	952-944-8000	R	2*	<.1
245	A-Nuh-Tha Level Of Louisiana Inc—*Lamont Roach*	14241 Coursey Blvd A-1, Baton Rouge LA 70817	225-279-3685	R	2*	<.1
246	Vidtech Audio Visual Inc—*Scott Henderson*	1974b Ohio St, Lisle IL 60532	630-241-0292	R	2*	<.1
247	Valley Services Inc—*Howard Cayton*	401 Highland Ave Se, Roanoke VA 24013	540-342-6015	R	2*	<.1
248	A Give-Em Brake Safety Inc—*Dan Babcock*	2610 Sanford Ave Sw, Grandville MI 49418	616-531-8705	R	2*	<.1
249	Connecticut Rental Centers Inc—*Robert Byrne*	30 Dekoven Dr, Middletown CT 06457	860-347-4688	R	2*	<.1
250	Hooker Creek Equipment and Supply—*Mat Day*	63101 Nels Anderson Rd, Bend OR 97701	541-389-4677	R	2*	<.1
251	NY One Corporate Car Inc—*Joseph Acierno*	1440 39th St, Brooklyn NY 11218	718-438-1100	R	2*	<.1
252	Save-U-Rental Center Inc—*Don Larson*	2221 N 24th St, Quincy IL 62301	217-223-8126	R	2*	<.1
253	J And C Water Inc—*Greg Chapman*	220 W Saint Charles Rd, Villa Park IL 60181	630-832-9393	R	2*	<.1
254	Cartwright and Daughters Tent and Party Rentals Inc—*Gerard Cartwright*	1707 Rte Ste 6, Carmel NY 10512	845-225-9200	R	2*	<.1
255	Festive Occasions—*John Patterson*	2507 Duss Ave, Ambridge PA 15003	724-266-6515	R	2*	<.1
256	Trailer Space Inc—*Jim Parker*	2044 S College St, Auburn AL 36832	334-826-0444	R	2*	<.1
257	Tropical Tents Inc—*Lawrence Keller*	10530 SW 184th Ter, Miami FL 33157	305-253-3984	R	2*	<.1
258	Rental World Of Osceola County Inc—*Richard Burson*	1717 N Main St, Kissimmee FL 34744	407-847-7777	R	2*	<.1
259	Asb Properties LLC—*Andy Barry*	2514 E 3707 N, Twin Falls ID 83301	208-733-5577	R	1*	<.1
260	Party Planning By Stephanie LLC	100 Beaman Blvd Unit 4, Atlantic Highlands NJ 07716	732-957-0213	R	1*	<.1
261	Premiere Copier Inc—*Todd North*	7442 S Tucson Way Ste, Englewood CO 80112	303-751-7307	R	1*	<.1
262	Anderson Rentals Inc—*Bill Anderson*	1312 W 6th St, Lawrence KS 66044	785-843-2044	R	1*	<.1
263	Arizona Domestic and Banquet Rentals and Sales Inc—*Julius Kaprinyak*	7104 N 7th St, Phoenix AZ 85020	602-944-5561	R	1*	<.1
264	S R Holding Company Inc—*Jamie Gumm*	1385 Pridemore Ct, Lexington KY 40505	859-255-0717	R	1*	<.1
265	Celebration Rentals Inc—*Megan Jones*	17 Georges Pl, Clinton NJ 08809	908-730-7180	R	1*	<.1
266	Vtr Inc—*Stephen Sawin*	PO Box 98, Buellton CA 93427	949-333-6500	R	1*	<.1
267	United Manufacturing Corp—*Wendy Ong*	23 Commerce Rd Ste H, Fairfield NJ 07004	973-575-5070	R	1*	<.1
268	A-Packaged Parties—*Sylvia Siebert-Lowry*	PO Box 570553, Tarzana CA 91357	818-710-1222	R	1*	<.1
269	North Shore Rental Inc—*Christopher Leblanc*	464 Lowell St, Peabody MA 01960	978-535-5035	R	1*	<.1
270	MG Digital Rentals	8549 Higuera St Ste 10, Culver City CA 90232	310-558-3907	R	1	<.1
271	Tinker and Rasor—*Mark Byerley*	PO Box 3456, Shreveport LA 71133	318-635-5351	R	1*	<.1
272	Party Rentals By Lisa Inc—*Lisa Hare*	2643 Randleman Rd, Greensboro NC 27406	336-273-3814	R	1*.	.1
273	Plant Sitters Inc—*Joann Hilton*	1401 W River Rd Ste 1, Minneapolis MN 55411	612-340-9157	R	1*	<.1
274	Fort Bragg Rent-All Inc—*Holly Kuchar*	PO Box 911, Fort Bragg CA 95437	707-964-6661	R	1*	<.1
275	Agricultural Installations Inc—*Gerald Shelton*	PO Box 461059, Escondido CA 92046	760-489-2689	R	1*	<.1
276	Sir Bounce A Lot Inc—*Timothy Nedin*	4012 E Broadway Rd Ste, Phoenix AZ 85040	602-438-1313	R	<1*	<.1
277	O-Sun Company Inc—*Richard O'malley*	PO Box 334, Thiensville WI 53092	262-242-6200	R	<1*	<.1
278	Sabre International Inc—*Ben Kemendo*	12242 E 60th St, Tulsa OK 74146	918-437-0770	R	<1*	<.1
279	Snyder Manufacturing Company Ltd—*Kenneth Garman*	PO Box 188, Dover OH 44622	330-343-4456	R	<1*	<.1
280	YouChange Holdings Corp—*Jeffrey Rassas*	7154 E Stetson Dr Ste, Scottsdale AZ 85251		P	<1	<.1
281	Protocol Telecommunications Inc—*Susan Turner*	16844 Saticoy St, Van Nuys CA 91406	818-782-5705	R	<1	<.1
282	Mako Rentals Inc—*Kip Robichaux*	PO Box 220, Bourg LA 70343	985-851-7072	R	<1*	<.1

TOTALS: SIC 7359 Equipment Rental & Leasing Nec
Companies: 282 — 26,856 — 83.6

7361 Employment Agencies

Rank	Company Name—*Executive Officer*	Address, City, State, Zip	Phone	Type	Fin	Empls
1	Sutherland Global Services—*Dilip R Vellodi*	1160 Pittsford-Victor, Pittsford NY 14534	585-586-5757	R	187,500*	30.0
2	Allegis Group Inc—*Michael Salandra*	7301 Parkway Dr, Hanover MD 21076		R	9,318*	8.0
3	Adecco Inc—*Dieter Scheiff*	175 Broadhollow Rd, Melville NY 11747	631-844-7800	S	8,800*	3.3
4	AECOM Technology Corp—*John M Dionisio*	555 S Flower St Ste 37, Los Angeles CA 90071	213-593-8000	P	8,037	45.0
5	TAC Worldwide Cos—*Robert P Badavas*	PO Box 9100, Dedham MA 02027	781-251-8000	R	1,100	1.3
6	Korn/Ferry International—*Gary D Burnison*	1900 Ave of the Stars, Los Angeles CA 90067	310-552-1834	P	776	2.5

Rank	Company Name—*Executive Officer*	Address, City, State, Zip	Phone	Type	Fin	Empls
7	Q and A Recruitting LLP—*Michelle Crespin*	14241 Dallas Pkwy Ste, Dallas TX 75254	972-720-1020	R	732*	<.1
8	Express Employment Professionals—*Robert Funk*	8516 NW Expy, Oklahoma City OK 73162	405-840-5000	R	727*	.2
9	AppleOne Inc—*Bernard Howroyd*	PO Box 29048, Glendale CA 91209	818-240-8688	R	721*	1.9
10	OnStaff—*David L Dunkel*	75 Rowland Way Ste 200, Novato CA 94945	415-895-2200	D	665*	1.8
11	Mission Essential Personnel LLC—*Chris Taylor*	4343 Easton Commons St, Columbus OH 43219	614-416-2345	R	629	7.4
12	Act-1 Personnel Service—*Janice Bryant Howroyd*	1999 W 190th St, Torrance CA 90504	310-750-3400	R	627	.4
13	Management Recruiters International Inc—*William Olson*	1717 Arch St Fl 36, Philadelphia PA 19103		S	570*	5.0
14	Nesco Inc (Mayfield Heights Ohio)—*Robert J Tomsich*	6140 Parkland Blvd Ste, Mayfield Heights OH 44124	440-461-6000	R	553*	5.0
15	CORESTAFF Services—*James Boone*	1775 St James Pl Ste 3, Houston TX 77056	713-438-1400	S	552*	30.0
16	Insight Global—*Glenn Johnson*	4170 Ashford Dunwoody, Atlanta GA 30319	404-257-7900	R	549*	.5
17	Heidrick and Struggles International Inc—*L Kevin Kelly*	233 S Wacker Dr Ste 42, Chicago IL 60606	312-496-1200	P	513	1.5
18	Altos Federal Group Inc—*Paula Shaw*	962 Wayne Ave Ste 900, Silver Spring MD 20910	202-726-7700	R	418*	.4
19	Cross Country Travcorps Inc—*Bruce Cerullo*	6551 Park of Commerce, Boca Raton FL 33487		S	400	N/A
20	Apex Systems Inc—*Brian J Callaghan*	4400 Cox Rd Ste 100, Glen Allen VA 23060	804-342-9090	R	384	.7
21	Terrahealth Inc—*Ted Terrazas*	5710 W Hausman Ste 108, San Antonio TX 78249	210-475-9881	R	331*	.3
22	LSI Staffing Solutions—*Ron King*	250 N Kansas St, Wichita KS 67214	316-262-0162	R	327*	.9
23	Russell Reynolds Associates Inc—*Matthew Wright*	200 Park Ave Ste 2300, New York NY 10166	212-351-2000	R	311*	1.0
24	DHR International Inc—*David H Hoffmann*	10 S Riverside Plz Ste, Chicago IL 60606	312-782-1581	R	294*	.3
25	Spencer Stuart and Associates Inc—*David Daniel*	401 N Michigan Ave Ste, Chicago IL 60611	312-822-0080	R	287*	1.0
26	Fusion Solutions—*Tahir Hussain*	16901 N Dallas Pkwy St, Addison TX 75001	972-764-1708	R	276*	.3
27	Spectra Enterprises Corp—*Sybil Goldberg*	3200 N Hayden Rd Ste 2, Scottsdale AZ 85251	480-481-0411	R	250*	<.1
28	Quest Group—*Ty Richardson*	9300 Wade Blvd Ste 315, Frisco TX 75035	972-731-0021	R	248*	.2
29	Jobingcom LLC—*Aaron Matos*	1010 N Finance Ctr Dr, Tucson AZ 85710	520-434-2000	R	213*	.3
30	Ajilon Finance—*Neil S Lebovits*	Park 80 W Plz II 9th F, Saddle Brook NJ 07663	201-843-0006	R	203*	<.1
31	CLP Resources Inc—*Frank Troppe*	10539 Professional Cir, Reno NV 89521	775-321-8000	S	199*	.2
32	Alpha Rae Personnel Inc—*Rae Pearson*	347 W Berry St 7th Fl, Fort Wayne IN 46802	260-426-8227	R	174*	.2
33	Lucas Associates Inc—*Andrea Jennings*	3384 Peachtree Rd Ste, Atlanta GA 30326	404-239-5630	R	160*	.4
34	Atc Staffing Services Inc—*David Savitsky*	1983 Marcus Ave Ste E1, New Hyde Park NY 11042	516-750-1600	R	153*	5.6
35	Ablest Inc—*Kurt R Moore*	1511 N Westshore Blvd, Tampa FL 33607	813-830-7680	R	141	.2
36	Cherokee Staffing LLC—*Francis J Welch*	14181 Northwest Fwy, Houston TX 77040	713-462-5627	R	137*	.4
37	Vaco (Brentwood Tennessee)—*Brian Waller*	5410 Maryland Way Ste, Brentwood TN 37027	615-324-9817	R	120*	.3
38	Mitchell/Martin Inc—*Eugene Holtzman*	307 W 38th St Rm 1305, New York NY 10018	212-943-1404	R	115*	.2
39	Personnel One (Dallas Texas)	5400 LBJ Fwy Ste 120, Dallas TX 75240	972-982-8500	S	114*	1.2
40	Employer Flexible—*Mike Greathouse*	7850 N Sam Houston Pky, Houston TX 77064	281-444-0900	R	112*	.1
41	Burnett Companies Consolidated Inc—*Sue Burnett*	9800 Richmond Ave Ste, Houston TX 77042	713-977-4777	R	106*	.1
42	Recruitment Group—*Robin Connata*	PO Box 410, Williamsville NY 14231	716-631-9282	R	101*	<.1
43	Lee Hecht Harrison Inc—*Peter Alcide* Adecco Inc	50 Tice Blvd, Woodcliff Lake NJ 07677	201-930-9333	S	100*	.6
44	Dinte Resources Inc—*Paul Dinte*	8300 Greensboro Dr Ste, Mc Lean VA 22102	703-448-3300	R	91*	<.1
45	HotJobscom Ltd—*Jeff Kinder*	45 West 18th St 6th Fl, New York NY 10001	646-351-5300	S	86*	.1
46	Cascade Health Services—*Jonna Weissenbach*	510 W 5th St 1st Fl, Kansas City MO 64105	816-229-5800	R	85*	<.1
47	Connecticut Staffing Works Corp—*Kimberly Nystrom*	PO Box 1092, Cromwell CT 06416	860-632-3945	S	81*	.2
48	Spencer Reed Group Inc—*William Solon*	6900 College Blvd Ste, Overland Park KS 66211	913-663-4400	R	77*	.5
49	Natural Data Inc—*Patrick Smith*	16585 92nd St Rm 111, Scottsdale AZ 85260	602-242-8222	R	75*	.2
50	HVS Executive Search—*Steve Rushmore*	369 Willis Ave, Mineola NY 11501	516-248-8828	R	74*	.2
51	Winston Resources Inc—*Seymour Kugler*	535 5th Ave Ste701, New York NY 10017	212-557-5000	R	74*	.2
52	BluWater Consulting Inc—*Terry Dehrkoop*	14335 NE 24th St Ste 2, Bellevue WA 98007	425-283-1440	R	74*	.1
53	Peoplelink Staffing Solutions—*Jay Wilkinson*	5401 S Sheridan Ave St, Tulsa OK 74145	918-745-6500	R	64*	.2
54	Isaacson Miller Inc—*John Isaacson*	334 Boylston St Ste 50, Boston MA 02116	617-262-6500	R	63*	.1
55	Transportation Financial Systems Inc—*Michael Boudreaux*	101 Pailet Dr, Harvey LA 70058	504-366-8116	R	61*	<.1
56	Triad Personnel Services Inc General Employment Enterprises Inc	1 Tower Ln Ste 2200, Oakbrook Terrace IL 60181	630-954-0400	S	60*	.2
57	Roytman Information Services Inc—*Mikhail Roytman*	504 Old Harbor Ct, Dayton OH 45458	937-885-0821	R	60*	.1
58	Solomon-Page Group Ltd—*Lloyd Solomon*	1140 Ave of the Americ, New York NY 10036	212-403-6100	R	56	.2
59	Management Recruiters of Portland Inc—*Steve Ross*	2020 Lloyd Center, Portland OR 97232	503-287-8701	R	56*	.1
60	Advanced Software Talent LLC—*Dominique S Black*	1325 Howard Ave Ste 80, Burlingame CA 94010	650-596-2800	R	54*	.1
61	Richard Wayne and Roberts—*Neal Hirsch*	24 Greenway Plz Ste 13, Houston TX 77046	713-629-6681	R	53*	.1
62	Ahac Inc—*Joe Wardy*	1414 Ability Dr, El Paso TX 79936	915-833-1145	R	52*	2.5
63	G and A StaffSourcing Inc—*Antonio R Grijalva*	4801 Woodway Ste 210, Houston TX 77056	713-784-1181	S	51*	.1
64	Professional Placement Inc—*Wayne Calhoun*	4040 E Camelback Rd St, Phoenix AZ 85018	602-955-0870	R	50*	<.1
65	Beacon Hill Staffing Group LLC—*Andrew Wang*	152 Bowdoin St, Boston MA 02108	617-326-4000	R	46*	.1
66	Angel Staffing Inc—*Shannon Ralston*	1202 E Sonterra Ste St, San Antonio TX 78258	210-616-9526	R	42*	.7
67	Dice Career Solutions Inc	4101 NW Urbandale Dr, Urbandale IA 50322	515-280-1144	S	42*	.1
68	Kimco Staffing Services Inc—*Kim I Megonigal*	17872 Cowan Ave, Irvine CA 92614	949-752-6996	R	41*	.2
69	Meador Staffing Services Inc—*Ben Meador*	722A Fairmont Pkwy, Pasadena TX 77504	713-941-0616	R	40*	.1
70	Carlyle Group Ltd—*Max DeZara*	625 N Michigan Ave Ste, Chicago IL 60611	312-587-3030	R	40*	<.1
71	Rhodes Associates Executive Search Inc—*Steven Littman*	555 5th Ave Fl 6, New York NY 10017	212-983-2000	R	40*	<.1
72	Sigma Temps Inc—*Thea Linker*	535 Broadhollow Rd Ste, Melville NY 11747	631-694-7707	R	39*	1.5
73	General Employment Enterprises Inc—*Salvatore J Zizza*	1 Tower Ln Ste 2200, Oakbrook Terrace IL 60181	630-954-0400	P	37	.1
74	DatamanUSA LLC—*Nidhi Saxena*	6890 S Tucson Way Ste, Centennial CO 80112	720-248-3100	R	37*	<.1
75	Penmac Personnel Services Inc—*Paula Adams*	447 South Ave, Springfield MO 65806	417-831-9100	R	37*	<.1
76	White Glove Placement Inc—*Meir Lefkowitz*	85 Bartlett St, Brooklyn NY 11206	718-387-8163	R	37*	3.1
77	Accountemps—*Harold Messmer*	2884 Sand Hill Rd, Menlo Park CA 94025	650-234-6000	D	34*	.1
78	Data Systems Search Consultants—*John R Martinez*	1615 Bonanza St Ste 40, Walnut Creek CA 94596	925-256-0635	R	34*	<.1
79	PeopleServe Inc—*Linda Moraski*	643 VFW Pkwy, Chestnut Hill MA 02467	617-469-9779	S	32*	<.1
80	Professional Placement Resources Inc—*Randy Watts*	333 1st St N Ste 200, Jacksonville Beach FL 32250		R	31*	.4
81	HumCap	16301 Quorum Dr Ste 10, Addison TX 75001	214-520-0760	R	30*	<.1
82	Medical Solutions—*Scott Anderson*	909 N 96th St Ste 201, Omaha NE 68114		R	29*	.5
83	First Pro Inc—*April F Nagel*	5607 Glenridge Dr NE S, Atlanta GA 30342	404-252-9422	R	29	.1
84	Hastings and Hastings Inc—*Lois Kleinman*	1201 Brickell Ave Ste, Miami FL 33131	305-374-2255	R	28*	<.1
85	Emerald Resource Group Inc—*Mark Krusinski*	40 Eagle Valley Ct, Broadview Heights OH 44147	440-922-9000	R	28*	<.1
86	Future Presence Inc—*Rose Hsu*	454 Las Gallinas Ave S, San Rafael CA 94903	707-585-0282	R	28*	<.1
87	Liberty Group (Houston Texas)—*Kenneth J Bohan*	7500 San Felipe Ste 95, Houston TX 77063	713-961-7666	R	28*	<.1
88	Solutions Staffing—*Peggy Mativi*	1237 Dublin Rd, Columbus OH 43215	614-732-5800	R	28*	<.1
89	Diverse Staffing Inc—*Fred Flores*	1800 E Lambert Rd Ste, Brea CA 92821	714-482-0499	R	27*	1.2
90	Mid-Valley Labor Services Inc—*Samuel Mascarenas*	PO Box 899, Madera CA 93639	559-661-6390	R	27*	.5
91	Rose International Inc—*Himanshu Bhatia*	16401 Swingley Ridge R, Chesterfield MO 63017	636-812-4000	R	27*	<.1
92	Baseline Engineering Inc	1046 W Taylor St Ste 2, San Jose CA 95126	408-243-7700	R	27*	<.1
93	J J and H Ltd—*Richard Jacobson*	120 S Lasalle St Ste 1, Chicago IL 60603	312-726-1578	R	25*	.8
94	Allstaff Services Inc—*Paul Smith*	432 N 44th St Ste 150, Phoenix AZ 85008	602-277-3381	R	25*	<.1

Note: An asterisk (*) indicates an estimated financial figure. The company type code used is as follows: R = Private, P = Public, S = Private Subsidiary, B = Public Subsidiary, D = Division, J = Joint Venture, I = Investment Fund.

COMPANY RANKINGS BY SALES WITHIN 4-DIGIT SIC

Rank	Company Name—*Executive Officer*	Address, City, State, Zip	Phone	Type	Fin	Empls
95	Miss Paige Ltd—*Karen Horwitz*	8430 W Berwyn Ave Ste, Chicago IL 60656	773-693-0480	R	24*	.1
96	APN Consulting Inc—*Vedant Pathak*	1100 Cornwall Rd Ste 2, Monmouth Junction NJ 08852	609-924-3400	R	24*	<.1
97	SEEK Inc—*Joel Schneider*	PO Box 148, Grafton WI 53024	262-377-8888	R	23*	.1
98	Techlink Northwest Inc—*Donn Harvey*	16650 NE 79th St Ste 2, Redmond WA 98052	425-284-7777	R	22*	<.1
99	JC Malone Associates—*Joe Malone*	1941 Bishop Ln Ste 100, Louisville KY 40218	502-456-2380	R	21*	<.1
100	Temporary Solutions Inc—*Jana W Yeates*	10550 Linden lake Plz, Manassas VA 20109	703-361-2220	S	21*	<.1
101	Pemer Packing Company Inc—*Pedro Mercado*	PO Box 4783, Salinas CA 93912	831-758-8586	R	20*	.8
102	Cue Data Services Inc	45 Accord Park Dr, Norwell MA 02061	781-749-3675	R	20	.1
103	Robert Shields and Associates—*George F Black*	PO Box 890646, Houston TX 77289	281-488-7961	R	20*	<.1
104	Chipton-Ross Inc—*Sharon King*	343 Main St, El Segundo CA 90245	310-414-7800	R	19*	.4
105	Quick Solutions Inc—*Tom Campbell*	440 Polaris Pkwy Ste 5, Westerville OH 43082	614-825-8000	R	19*	.2
106	Miller Isaacson Inc—*John Isaacson*	263 Summer St Fl 7, Boston MA 02210	617-262-6500	R	19*	.1
107	Lakeshore Staffing Group Inc—*John Paller*	1 N Franklin St Ste 60, Chicago IL 60606	312-251-7575	R	18*	<.1
108	Experiencecom Inc—*Jenny Floren*	2 Faneuil Hall Marketp, Boston MA 02109	617-305-7400	R	18*	<.1
109	Entelligence LLC—*Stephen R Satterwhite*	2800 Post Oak Blvd Ste, Houston TX 77056	713-355-4450	R	17*	<.1
110	Icon Information Consultants LP—*Pamela Orouke*	100 Waugh Dr Ste 300, Houston TX 77007	713-438-0930	R	17*	.7
111	ENTEGEE Inc—*Robert Cecchini*	70 Blanchard Rd Ste 10, Burlington MA 01803		R	16	.1
112	All About People Inc—*Sherri Mitchell*	2141 E Camelbck Rd Ste, Phoenix AZ 85016	602-955-1212	R	16*	<.1
113	Healing Staff Inc—*David Eppling*	10100 Reunion Pl Ste 7, San Antonio TX 78216	210-299-7623	R	15*	.2
114	Hirestrategy Inc—*Paul Villella*	1875 Explorer St Ste 5, Reston VA 20190	703-547-6700	R	15*	.2
115	PeopleShare—*Vicki Sack*	1601 Market St, Philadelphia PA 19103	215-988-0700	R	15*	<.1
116	Albin Engineering Services Inc—*Marc G Albin*	3350 Scott Blvd Ste 27, Santa Clara CA 95054	408-733-2374	R	15*	<.1
117	Ken Leiner Associates—*Ken Leiner*	11510 Georgia Ave Ste, Wheaton MD 20902	301-933-8800	R	15*	<.1
118	Whitney Partners LLC—*Gary Goldstein*	555 5th Ave 6th Fl, New York NY 10017	212-508-3500	R	15*	<.1
119	Softworld Inc—*David S Teitelman*	281 Winter St Ste 301, Waltham MA 02451	781-466-8882	R	14*	.2
120	Accentuate Staffing—*Susan Waldo*	3200 Fairhill Dr Ste 1, Raleigh NC 27612	919-844-2900	R	14*	<.1
121	Michigan State Afl-Cio Human Resources Development Inc—*Fran Sibley*	419 S Wash Sq Ste 300, Lansing MI 48933	517-372-0784	R	14*	.1
122	Equity Staffing Group Inc—*Travis Hunt*	8310 S Valley Hwy Fl 3, Englewood CO 80112	303-524-1300	R	14*	.2
123	English Language Institute/China—*Tim Davis*	PO Box 3000, Fort Collins CO 80522	970-530-8300	R	14*	.1
124	Brian Cork Human Capital—*Brian Cork*	1100 Old Ellis Rd The, Roswell GA 30076		R	13	<.1
125	Thompson Technologies Inc—*David Thompson*	114 TownPark Dr Ste 10, Kennesaw GA 30144	770-794-8380	R	13*	.2
126	Hornberger Management Co—*Frederick Hornberger*	1 Commerce Center 7th, Wilmington DE 19801	302-573-2541	R	13	<.1
127	HP Service Inc—*Gary Pitts*	PO Box 1412, Alvin TX 77512	281-331-0669	R	12*	.6
128	Heitmeyer Group LLC—*Norm Heitmeyer*	283 S State St Ste 102, Westerville OH 43081	614-573-5571	R	12*	.3
129	Providus—*Joe Tarano*	1177 W Loop S Ste 1550, Houston TX 77027	713-586-6586	R	12*	.2
130	Virpie Inc—*Shre Thammana*	1449 Old Waterbury Rd, Southbury CT 06488	203-264-0999	R	12*	.1
131	Professional Staffing Group Inc—*Aaron Green*	89 Devonshire St, Boston MA 02109	617-250-1000	R	12*	.1
132	Select Group—*Sheldon Wolitski*	5420 Wade Park Blvd St, Raleigh NC 27607	919-459-1400	R	12*	<.1
133	JWS Health Consultants Inc—*Jolyn West Scheirman*	1818 Memorial Dr Ste 2, Houston TX 77007	713-522-7100	R	12*	<.1
134	Sedona Group—*Guy Nicholson*	612 Valley View Dr, Moline IL 61265	309-797-8367	R	12*	<.1
135	Bowdoin Group Inc—*David Melville*	40 William St, Wellesley MA 02481	781-239-9933	R	11*	<.1
136	Medstaff Contract Nursing Inc—*Richard C Davis*	4801 E Independence Bl, Charlotte NC 28212	704-537-1831	R	10*	.5
137	Worldwide Travel Staffing—*Leo Blatz*	2829 Sheridan Dr, Tonawanda NY 14150	716-821-9001	R	10*	.2
138	Trinity Healthcare Staffing Group Inc—*Matt Floyd*	PO Box 5955, Florence SC 29502	843-665-0343	R	10*	.1
139	MurTech Consulting LLC—*Ailish Murphy*	4807 Rockside Rd Ste 3, Independence OH 44131	216-328-8580	R	10	.1
140	Woodward Sharf and Associates Inc—*Bernard Sharf*	5900 Sepulvda Blvd Ste, Van Nuys CA 91411	818-989-2200	R	10*	.1
141	Whitridge Associates Inc—*Kevin Grassa*	744 E Squantum St, Quincy MA 02171	617-472-2292	R	10*	.1
142	Resource Options Inc (Needham Massachusetts)—*Matthew Carlin*	200 Highland Ave, Needham MA 02494	781-455-0224	R	10*	<.1
143	CoreMedical Group—*Armand L Circharo*	2 Keewaydin Dr, Salem NH 03079	603-893-4515	R	10*	<.1
144	Forty Plus of New York Inc—*Stanley Moore*	470 7th Ave Ste 403, New York NY 10018	212-947-4230	R	10*	<.1
145	Hire Priority—*James Lenhardt*	1800 St James Pl Ste 1, Houston TX 77056	713-960-9906	R	10*	<.1
146	Personnel Resource Corp—*Steven S Swartz*	1110 E Missouri Ave St, Phoenix AZ 85014	602-248-0010	R	10*	<.1
147	Rusher Loscavio and LoPresto—*William H Rusher Jr*	369 Pine St Ste 221, San Francisco CA 94104	415-765-6600	R	10*	<.1
148	College Nannies and Tutors Inc—*Joseph Keeley*	PO Box 213, Wayzata MN 55391	952-476-0613	R	10*	<.1
149	Incendia Partners—*Robert Recchia*	161 Worcester Rd Ste 4, Framingham MA 01701	508-507-3555	R	10*	<.1
150	Corporate Brokers LLC—*Quinn Salamandra*	170 Jennifer Rd Ste 23, Annapolis MD 21401	410-573-0003	R	10	<.1
151	Linda Weston Personnel Inc—*Linda Weston*	1700 W Big Beaver Rd S, Troy MI 48084	248-643-0076	R	9*	.1
152	Jacor LLC	5076 Park Ave W, Seville OH 44273	330-722-0010	R	9*	.6
153	Stat Nursing Services Inc—*Charles Duck*	2740 Van Ness Ave Ste, San Francisco CA 94109	415-673-9791	R	9*	.4
154	Eclaro International Inc—*Daniel Park*	450 7th Ave Ste 506, New York NY 10123	212-258-2626	R	9*	.2
155	Human Resource Staffing LLC—*Brian Green*	1456-A Triad Center Dr, Saint Peters MO 63376	636-477-8889	R	9*	<.1
156	Independent Nursing Services-New Inc—*Laura Burch*	7166 Baker Blvd Ste B, Richland Hills TX 76118	817-595-3291	R	9*	.3
157	Alpha Consulting Corp—*Marie Donzella*	PO Box 6969, East Brunswick NJ 08816	732-257-3003	R	9*	.2
158	Healthcare Resource Network LLC—*Laura Bankeroff*	12154 Darnestown Rd St, Gaithersburg MD 20878	301-926-9690	R	9	.1
159	American Driver Leasing Inc—*Douglas Williams*	1925 E Vernon Ave Ste, Vernon CA 90058	323-235-7600	R	9*	.4
160	Sirsai Multisourcing—*Vijay Gunturu*	9 Lake Bellevue Dr Ste, Bellevue WA 98005	425-533-2158	R	8	.2
161	Jc Bowling and Company LLC—*Jenifer Mindozas*	1755 Wittington Pl Ste, Dallas TX 75234	214-442-4000	R	8*	.2
162	Crystal Employment Services LLC—*Leeanne Kizy*	32355 Howard Ave, Madison Heights MI 48071	248-588-9540	R	8*	.2
163	Technology Resources Inc—*Robert Marchetti*	416 New London Tpke, Glastonbury CT 06033	860-659-9960	R	8*	.1
164	Custom Staffing Incorporated (Jacksonville Florida)—*Chris Flakus*	9995 Gate Parkway Nort, Jacksonville FL 32246	904-338-9515	R	8*	.1
165	Healthcare Partners Inc—*Ruddy Polhill*	1735 N Brown Rd Ste 10, Lawrenceville GA 30043	678-218-4040	R	8*	<.1
166	Vivo Inc (Pleasanton California)—*Marilyn Weinstein*	7901 Stoneridge Dr Ste, Pleasanton CA 94588	925-271-6800	R	8*	<.1
167	Hcap International LLC—*Gary Abram*	6811 W 63rd St Ste 204, Overland Park KS 66202	913-384-1020	R	8*	<.1
168	Golden Key Group LLC—*Bruce Tarpinian*	6728 Cedar Spring Rd, Centreville VA 20121	703-815-0290	R	8	.1
169	America's Staffing Associates Inc—*Antonio Escobar*	4195 Chino Hills Pkwy, Chino Hills CA 91709	909-464-0220	R	8*	.3
170	Sourcewave Inc—*Richard Lambert*	421 Adley Rd, Fairfield CT 06825	203-373-6831	R	8*	<.1
171	Ayala Corp—*Piedad Ayala*	PO Box 187, Riverdale CA 93656	559-867-5700	R	7*	.2
172	H Roslin Staffing Group LLC	1140 Empire Central Dr, Dallas TX 75247	214-267-8882	R	7*	.2
173	Construction Force Services Inc—*Hillary Terline*	3064 Whitestone Expy, Flushing NY 11354	718-762-6333	R	7*	.4
174	Keepers Inc—*Joseph Mcdermott*	2625 Housley Rd, Annapolis MD 21401	410-224-8833	R	7*	.2
175	Relief Enterprise Inc—*Clarence Williams*	PO Box 15088, Austin TX 78761	512-467-0115	R	7*	.2
176	Dial A Nurse Of Fort Myers Inc—*Lynette Wolfendale*	3949 Evans Ave Ste 303, Fort Myers FL 33901	239-939-1228	R	7*	.2
177	Psinapse Technology Ltd—*Sylvia Luneau*	5700 Stoneridge Mall R, Pleasanton CA 94588	925-225-0400	R	7*	.2
178	HR Staffing Solutions Inc—*Graham Atkinson*	PO Box 663, Fayetteville NY 13066	315-449-0500	R	7*	.1
179	Aequor Healthcare Services LLC—*Manmeet Virdi*	33 Wood Ave S Ste 500, Iselin NJ 08830	732-494-4999	R	7*	.1
180	e-IT Professionals Corp—*Rao P Nalamothu*	44968 Ford Rd Ste L, Canton MI 48187	734-416-0059	R	7*	.1
181	Milwaukee Job Center North—*Barbara Sibley*	4030 N 29th St, Milwaukee WI 53216	414-486-5200	R	7*	<.1

Rank	Company Name—*Executive Officer*	Address, City, State, Zip	Phone	Type	Fin	Empls
182	Elwood Staffing Services Inc—*Mark Elwood*	PO Box 1024, Columbus IN 47202	812-372-6200	R	7*	.2
183	Britstan Technology Inc—*Debbie Reames*	451 W Lambert Rd Ste 2, Brea CA 92821	714-255-9111	R	7	<.1
184	Dds Staffing Resources Inc—*Katherine Simons*	9755 Dogwood Rd Ste 20, Roswell GA 30075	770-998-7770	R	7*	<.1
185	Associated Marine and Industrial Staffing Inc—*Richard Tatum*	PO Box 6923, Kingwood TX 77325	713-450-1664	R	6*	.2
186	Workforce 2000 Staffing Inc—*Walter Ghosten*	1545 Western Ave, Knoxville TN 37921	865-522-7581	R	6*	.2
187	Balance Staffing—*John Moss*	6261 NW 6th Way Ste 20, Ft Lauderdale FL 33309	954-772-4888	R	6*	.1
188	Synergis—*Cindy Ross*	11675 Rainwater Dr Ste, Alpharetta GA 30004	770-346-7200	R	6*	.1
189	Myers Group Inc—*Tom Myers*	7 Heritage Plz, Bourbonnais IL 60914	815-929-1900	R	6*	.1
190	nGroup Inc—*David Hair*	1974 Carolina Pl Dr St, Fort Mill SC 29708	803-367-2469	R	6*	<.1
191	Lumen Legal LLC—*David Galbenski*	1025 N Campbell Rd, Royal Oak MI 48067	248-597-0400	R	6*	<.1
192	SunRay Enterprise Inc—*Ravi Srinivasan*	3621 Vinings Slope SE, Atlanta GA 30339	678-584-1312	R	6*	<.1
193	Advanced Resources LLC—*Leo Sheridan*	1300 E Woodfield Rd St, Schaumburg IL 60173	847-995-9111	S	6*	<.1
194	Reliable Review Services—*Jim Franklin*	621 NW 53rd St Ste 250, Boca Raton FL 33487	561-893-0123	R	6*	<.1
195	CPI Group—*Mark Smith*	PO Box 828, Columbus MS 39703	662-328-1042	R	6*	<.1
196	Pederson Kolb and Associates Inc—*Richard Pederson*	2504 Niagara Falls Blv, Tonawanda NY 14150	716-695-6300	R	6*	<.1
197	Excel Business Partners—*Melissa Carmen*	165 E Union St Ste 321, Newark NY 14513	315-331-5435	R	6*	.3
198	Winter Wyman and Company Inc—*Robert Boudreau*	950 Winter St Ste 3100, Waltham MA 02451	781-890-7000	R	6*	.1
199	Resumes On-Line Inc—*Bob Bidwell*	333 W Hampden Ave Ste, Englewood CO 80110	303-781-0055	R	6*	.2
200	American Nuclear Resources Inc—*Lydia Demski*	2095 Niles Rd Ste 1, Saint Joseph MI 49085	269-983-4835	R	6*	.3
201	Tempmate Inc—*Jerry Spikes*	3905 Bowens Mill Rd, Douglas GA 31533	912-389-0990	R	6*	.3
202	A Caring Experience Nursing Services Inc—*Dean Denuccio*	21 Douglas Ave, Providence RI 02908	401-453-4545	R	6*	.2
203	Nurstat—*Linda Kester*	4a Gateway Shopping Ct, Kingston PA 18704	570-287-4650	R	5*	.2
204	Chester Lancaster Disabilities Inc—*Jay Altman*	PO Box 577, Lancaster SC 29721	803-285-4368	R	5*	.1
205	Autumn Enterprises Inc—*Eric Broder*	3025 S Parker Rd Ste 8, Aurora CO 80014		R	5*	<.1
206	Pacific Rim Resources Search Agency—*Trang Tran*	14148 Brookhurst St, Garden Grove CA 92843	714-638-0307	R	5*	.2
207	New York Staffing Services Inc—*Michael S Robinson*	40 Exchange Pl, New York NY 10005	212-425-2979	R	5*	.3
208	Americare Staffing Service Inc—*Amare Berhie*	2233 University Ave W, Saint Paul MN 55114	651-917-1995	R	5*	.1
209	Hollister Associates Inc—*Kip Hollister*	75 State St Fl 9, Boston MA 02109	617-654-0200	R	5*	.1
210	Personnel Inc—*Gail Toler*	621 4 Mile Rd, Racine WI 53402	262-639-5666	R	5*	.1
211	PANGEATWO—*Jody Jones*	3595 Grandview Pky Ste, Birmingham AL 35243	205-444-0080	R	5*	<.1
212	Phillips Oppenheim Group Inc—*Debra Oppenheim*	521 5th Ave Rm 2900, New York NY 10175	212-953-1770	R	5*	<.1
213	iplacement Inc—*Randy Davis*	1516 E Colonial Dr Ste, Orlando FL 32803	407-893-3711	R	5*	<.1
214	Berks and Beyond Employment Services Inc—*Chris Garner*	926 Penn Ave, Wyomissing PA 19610	610-376-9675	R	5*	<.1
215	Hunter Placement Inc—*Gina Collora*	897 Delaware Ave, Buffalo NY 14209	716-362-0964	R	5*	<.1
216	Windsor Consultants Inc—*Daniel Narsh*	13201 Northwest Fwy St, Houston TX 77040	713-460-0586	R	5*	<.1
217	Blue Streak Partners Inc—*Dominique Jodoin*	825 Third Ave 2nd Fl, New York NY 10022	212-380-1633	R	5	<.1
218	Accent Human Resource Specialists—*Kathy Staudohar*	7150 E Camelback Rd St, Scottsdale AZ 85251	602-955-2222	R	5*	<.1
219	Kozlin Associates Inc—*Jeff M Kozlin*	9280 Transit Rd, East Amherst NY 14051	716-634-5955	R	5*	<.1
220	OnDemand Resources LLC—*Jan Malasek*	PO Box 823, Great Falls VA 22066		R	5*	<.1
221	TLC Staffing—*Abe Ajarmi*	101 Palmwood Dr Ste 5, Victoria TX 77901	361-578-8588	R	5*	.2
222	A 1 Tremendous Temporaries LLC	6100 Dutchmans Ln Ste, Louisville KY 40205	502-473-0310	R	5*	.2
223	Bradley-Morris Inc—*Sandra Morris*	1825 Barrett Lakes Blv, Kennesaw GA 30144	770-794-8318	R	5*	.1
224	Jmpb Inc—*Johnna Bowen*	1604 Benton Ave, Benton ME 04901	207-453-4708	R	5*	.2
225	Nurse Bank Inc—*Laura Hendelberg*	3701 Old Ct Rd Ste 15, Pikesville MD 21208	410-486-3350	R	5*	.2
226	Kenney and Company Staffing Inc—*William Burt*	99 Smallwood Dr Ste 10, Waldorf MD 20602	301-638-0606	R	5*	.2
227	Staffing Plus Inc—*Lisa Spector*	551 W Lancaster Ave St, Haverford PA 19041	610-525-4000	R	5*	.1
228	LA Hair Inc—*Linda Worthington*	733 Biroh Ave, Langhorne PA 19047	215-757-6360	R	5*	.1
229	Tuttle Agency LLC—*Teodore Angelus*	295 Madison Ave Fl 14, New York NY 10017	212-499-0759	R	5*	.1
230	Employment and Employer Services Inc—*Jack Fitzpatrick*	208 S Lasalle St Ste 1, Chicago IL 60604	312-629-5627	R	5*	.1
231	T and T Staff Management Inc—*Thad Steele*	511 Executive, El Paso TX 79902	915-771-0393	R	5*	.1
232	S B Phillips Company Inc—*Samuel Phillips*	PO Box 5664, Greenville SC 29606	864-242-4144	R	5*	.1
233	Stratus Technology Services LLC—*Donald Feidt*	149 Ave At The Cmn Ste, Shrewsbury NJ 07702	732-380-0323	R	5*	.1
234	Execu-Search Inc—*Edward Fleischman*	675 3rd Ave Fl 5, New York NY 10017	212-922-1001	R	5*	.1
235	C2p Group LLC	530 E Corp Dr Ste 100, Lewisville TX 75057	214-260-3200	R	5*	.1
236	Emerald Produce Company Inc—*Golinda Chavez*	PO Box 295, Chualar CA 93925	831-455-0448	R	4*	.1
237	First Call Medical Staffing Inc—*Shelly Vento*	2525 N Mayfair Rd Ste, Milwaukee WI 53226	414-774-5600	R	4*	.1
238	Diversified Executive Systems Inc—*Walter Decastro*	2649 Valleydale Rd Ste, Birmingham AL 35244	205-408-0922	R	4*	.1
239	Clinical Resources LLC—*Jennifer L Scully*	5775 Glenridge Dr Bldg, Atlanta GA 30328	404-343-7227	R	4*	<.1
240	Penn Staffing Services LLC	1218 Chestnut St Ste 3, Philadelphia PA 19107	215-925-3980	R	4*	.1
241	Allstar Staffing Inc—*Rita King*	7040 Avenida Encinas S, Carlsbad CA 92011	760-929-2310	R	4*	.3
242	C and A Industries Inc—*Larry Courtnage*	13609 California St St, Omaha NE 68154	402-891-0009	R	4*	.3
243	Center For International Education Inc—*David Young*	PO Box 3566, Chapel Hill NC 27515	919-967-5144	R	4*	.1
244	Smartit Staffing Inc—*Karen Cooper*	1 Indiana Sq Ste 2350, Indianapolis IN 46204	317-634-0211	R	4*	.1
245	Account Abilities Inc—*Jay Schecter*	195 Rte 9 S, Manalapan NJ 07726	732-333-3622	R	4*	.1
246	Kroll Becker and Wing LLC—*Jason Kroll*	17 Commerce Dr Ste 7, Bedford NH 03110	603-792-2345	R	4	<.1
247	CareerStaff Inc—*Larry Castro*	18952 MacArthur Blvd S, Irvine CA 92612	949-250-4414	R	4*	<.1
248	CGR/seven—*Adrienne Plotch*	237 Park Avenue, New York NY 10017	212-254-8600	R	4*	<.1
249	Burlington Healthcare Providers—*Randall J Vodnik*	9875 S Franklin Dr Ste, Franklin WI 53132	414-858-2401	R	4*	<.1
250	Portfolio Creative Inc—*Catherine Lang-Cline*	3763 N High St Ste A, Columbus OH 43214	614-839-4897	R	4*	<.1
251	Accounting and Finance Personnel Inc—*Mike Nolan*	1702 E Highland Ave St, Phoenix AZ 85016	602-277-3700	R	4*	<.1
252	Allerton Heneghan and O'Neill—*Donald Heneghan*	1Tower Ln Ste 1700, Oakbrook Terrace IL 60181	630-645-2294	R	4*	<.1
253	Betatech Inc—*Peter J Kennedy*	10401 Connecticut Ave, Kensington MD 20895	301-942-7840	R	4*	<.1
254	JA Snyder and Associates Inc—*Jeff Snyder*	PO Box 398, Woodland Park CO 80866	719-686-8810	S	4*	<.1
255	AAA Employment Agency Inc—*John Menzel*	1501 Edgemore Ave Ste, Salisbury MD 21801	410-546-5955	R	4*	.3
256	Swds Inc—*Deborah Jones*	11767 Katy Fwy Ste 210, Houston TX 77079	281-584-9596	R	4*	.1
257	Cobi Digital—*Patsy Smullin*	PO Box 1489, Medford OR 97501	541-779-5417	R	4*	.1
258	Mega Solutions Of Massachusetts—*Ian Perlman*	PO Box 70, Seekonk MA 02771	508-336-7801	R	4*	.1
259	ISIS Banner Personnel Service—*Karen Blazich*	1701 E Wdfield Rd Ste, Schaumburg IL 60173	847-706-9180	R	4*	.1
260	Step Industries Inc—*Hugh Holly*	1010 Strohmeyer Dr, Neenah WI 54956	920-722-2345	R	4*	.1
261	Abbott and Associates Professional Placement Inc—*Joan Wiederspiel*	2933 Ne Broadway St, Portland OR 97232	503-243-4630	R	4*	.1
262	Zi Solutions LLC—*Brian Zecher*	4300 Rte 1, Princeton NJ 08540	609-580-2660	R	4*	<.1
263	Northwest Arkansas Certified Development Co—*Susan Sangren*	PO Box 1613, Harrison AR 72602	870-741-9434	R	4*	<.1
264	Clovis Group LLC—*Richard Mazelsky*	10411 Motor City Dr St, Bethesda MD 20817	301-841-4111	R	4*	.1
265	Sandoval Brothers Inc—*Valdemar Sandoval*	PO Box 1183, Soledad CA 93960	831-678-1465	R	4*	.1
266	World Information Technology Solutions LLC—*James Stark*	1101 Mchantile Ln Ste, Largo MD 20774	301-333-6130	R	4*	.1
267	Professional Management Recruiters Inc—*Paul Gartlan*	7270 NW 12th St Ste 50, Miami FL 33126	305-593-5050	R	4*	.1
268	Tempus It Staffing LLC	1117 Perimetr Ctr W E1, Atlanta GA 30338	404-832-2200	R	4*	.1
269	P and P Agrilabor—*P Baclig*	Hwy 101 Floretta Rd, Chualar CA 93925	831-679-2307	R	4*	.1

Note: An asterisk (*) indicates an estimated financial figure. The company type code used is as follows: R = Private, P = Public, S = Private Subsidiary, B = Public Subsidiary, D = Division, J = Joint Venture, I = Investment Fund.

COMPANY RANKINGS BY SALES WITHIN 4-DIGIT SIC

Rank	Company Name—*Executive Officer*	Address, City, State, Zip	Phone	Type	Fin	Empls
270	Allstaff LLC—*Kellie Paisley*	611 N Garden St, Columbia TN 38401	931-381-5193	R	4*	.1
271	Kardon Communications Inc—*Karinne Gordon*	612 W 11th St Ste 101, Tracy CA 95376	209-609-9393	R	4*	<.1
272	Mega Staffing Services—*Alexis Lewis*	230 Park Ave Fl 10, New York NY 10169	212-631-1077	R	3*	.1
273	Peopleware Technical Resources Inc—*Sheryl Rooker*	302 W Grand Ave Ste 4, El Segundo CA 90245	310-640-2406	R	3*	.1
274	Dental Solutions Inc—*Kathy Richards*	1028 Cresthaven Rd Ste, Memphis TN 38119	901-763-1028	R	3*	.2
275	Fozzard Services Inc—*Jerry Fozzard*	425 Joliet St Ste 312, Dyer IN 46311		R	3*	.2
276	Indiana Home Health Care Corp—*Lee Marchant*	3800 W Gifford Rd, Bloomington IN 47403	812-334-1857	R	3*	.1
277	Valley Labor Service Inc—*Jane Hobbs*	PO Box 775, Dinuba CA 93618	559-591-5591	R	3*	.1
278	Direct Way Personnel—*Felipe Rivas*	7300 Alondra Blvd Ste, Paramount CA 90723	562-531-8808	R	3*	.1
279	Landmark Staffing Resources Inc—*Monica Vomastic*	PO Box 1755, Appleton WI 54912	920-257-2300	R	3*	.1
280	Tiger Personnel Services Inc—*Sylvia Dixon-Devoe*	1320 Fenwick Ln Ste 50, Silver Spring MD 20910	301-578-8585	R	3*	.1
281	Acsys Inc—*Louis Boohaer*	5 Concourse Pkwy Ne, Atlanta GA 30328	770-395-0014	R	3*	.1
282	Job Finders Employment Service Co—*Ann Williams*	1729 W Broadway Ste 4, Columbia MO 65203	573-446-4250	R	3*	.1
283	Trinity Health Care Services Inc—*Gabriel Smith*	6151 Miramar Pkwy Ste, Miramar FL 33023	954-986-1754	R	3*	.1
284	Business Connections—*Lynne Moule*	332 Pine St, Red Bluff CA 96080	530-527-6229	R	3*	.1
285	MM Temps Inc—*Maria Mongillo*	PO Box 617, Bradford PA 16701	814-362-4650	R	3*	.1
286	TWR Framing—*Tom Rhodes*	1661 Railroad St, Corona CA 92880	951-279-2000	R	3*	.1
287	Unique Personnel Consultants—*Gary Hunsche*	1111 W Morton Ave Ste, Jacksonville IL 62650	217-245-6200	R	3*	.1
288	Babich and Associates Inc—*Anthony Beshara*	6030 E Mockingbird Ln, Dallas TX 75206	214-823-9999	R	3*	.1
289	Boston Networking Group Inc—*Tammy Petrocelli*	265 Franklin St Bsmt 2, Boston MA 02110	617-720-7151	R	3*	<.1
290	Hq Group LLC	2023 S Pacific St, Oceanside CA 92054	760-438-5859	R	3*	.1
291	Liberty Personnel Services Inc—*Daniel Gallagher*	410 Feheley Dr, King Of Prussia PA 19406	610-941-6300	R	3*	.1
292	Mark/Ryan Associates Ltd—*Ryan Paquette*	1375 E Woodfield Rd St, Schaumburg IL 60173	847-240-9100	R	3*	<.1
293	Employment and Training Association Inc—*James Erlenborn*	1819 Aberg Ave Ste D, Madison WI 53704	608-242-7402	R	3*	<.1
294	Westchester Employment Agency Inc—*Alan Gordon*	109 Croton Ave Ste 2, Ossining NY 10562	914-941-6107	R	3*	<.1
295	Protis Executive Innovations Inc—*Bert Miller*	6640 Intech Blvd Rm 29, Indianapolis IN 46278	317-272-5400	R	3*	<.1
296	Igenti—*James McArdle*	12200 W Colonial Dr St, Winter Garden FL 34787	407-877-5992	S	3*	<.1
297	Roys and Associates LLC—*Deam Roys*	1603 Aviation Blvd Ste, Redondo Beach CA 90278	310-318-8085	R	3*	<.1
298	Xsell Resources Inc—*Colleen Haviland*	630 Fitzwatertown Rd B, Willow Grove PA 19090	215-706-4500	R	3*	<.1
299	Creative Employment Opportunities Inc—*Laura Owens-Johnson*	1421 N Water St, Milwaukee WI 53202	414-277-8506	R	3*	<.1
300	Alpine Staffing Inc—*Richard Donnelly*	13570 Grove Dr Ste 126, Osseo MN 55311	763-545-9000	R	3*	<.1
301	Hopkins and Company Inc—*Nancy H Kramer*	492B Main St, Acton MA 01720	978-263-7899	R	3*	<.1
302	Kestrel Consulting Ltd—*Christine Wisch*	7601 Stonewood Ct, Edina MN 55439	952-903-0676	R	3*	<.1
303	ComQuest International—*Joe Pagan*	1425 Brook Dr, Melbourne FL 32935	321-984-9897	R	3*	<.1
304	Employment Atlanta—*Ed Freeman*	3301 Buckeye Rd Ste 10, Atlanta GA 30341	404-255-4201	R	3*	<.1
305	Pathfinders Inc—*Keenan Goggin*	308 W Lancaster Ave St, Wayne PA 19087	610-407-7000	R	3*	.1
306	Tlc Nursing Services Inc—*George Gibbs*	PO Box 2530, Blue Ridge GA 30513	706-632-6295	R	3*	.8
307	Loyalty Nursing Service—*Robin Henderson*	2 Post Office Rd, Waldorf MD 20602	301-645-0064	R	3*	.1
308	Options Group Inc—*Michael Karp*	121 E 18th St Lbby L, New York NY 10003	212-982-2800	R	3*	<.1
309	Profile Of Santa Cruz—*Milt Gold*	2045 40th Ave Ste B, Capitola CA 95010	831-479-0393	R	3*	.1
310	Ajettix Inc—*Sue Newhouse*	100 Town Centre Dr Ste, Rochester NY 14623	585-784-7700	R	3*	.1
311	Unistaff Inc—*Earle Vandyke*	671 E Big Beaver Rd, Troy MI 48083	248-680-0900	R	3*	.1
312	Workforce Solutions Group Of Montgomery County Inc—*Douglas Propheter*	11002 Veirs Mill Rd, Silver Spring MD 20902	301-929-6880	R	3*	<.1
313	Sunwest Peo Of Florida Vi Inc—*D Arfons*	6407 Parkland Dr, Sarasota FL 34243	941-925-2990	R	3*	.1
314	Computer Management Services Inc—*Albert Magnus*	5457 Twin Knolls Rd, Columbia MD 21045	301-236-4900	R	3*	.1
315	Rph Recruiter Inc—*Rich Barnhart*	2601 Blake St Ste 400, Denver CO 80205	720-941-7199	R	3*	.1
316	Software Methods Inc—*Stuart Laderman*	770 E Market St Ste 21, West Chester PA 19382	610-430-8956	R	3	<.1
317	Crickett Staffing Services Inc—*Gayle Fitch*	159 Main St, Ossining NY 10562	914-941-6000	R	3*	<.1
318	Progressive Nursing Staffers—*Gary Hughes*	4917 Waters Edge Dr St, Raleigh NC 27606	919-233-9669	R	3*	.1
319	Women's Center Of Tarrant County Inc—*Laura Hilgart*	1723 Hemphill St, Fort Worth TX 76110	817-927-4006	R	3*	.1
320	Construction Labor Services Inc—*Marie Stech*	PO Box 460, Richland MI 49083	269-629-9708	R	3*	.1
321	Firstcare Nursing Services Inc—*Matthew Massaquoi*	7676 NH Ave Ste 230, Takoma Park MD 20912	301-408-2900	R	3*	.1
322	Marc Nichols Associates Inc—*Marc Nichols*	220 E 23rd St Ste 400, New York NY 10010	212-725-1750	R	3*	<.1
323	Excel Services—*Jennifer Beal*	2021 Broadway St Ste 1, Paducah KY 42001	270-444-0064	R	2*	.1
324	Chapman Williams International Inc—*Judith Chapman*	428b Marin Ave, Mill Valley CA 94941	415-392-1835	R	2*	.1
325	Julien LLC—*Robert Curtis*	1833 Magnavox Way, Fort Wayne IN 46804	260-434-1981	R	2*	.1
326	Enterprise Staffing Agency LLC	1349 Empire Central Dr, Dallas TX 75247	214-637-1128	R	2*	<.1
327	Nurses Prn Staffing Inc—*Jane Hooker*	615 N Commerce St Ste, Ardmore OK 73401	580-226-9776	R	2*	.1
328	Davis Staffing Inc—*Robbin Davis*	475 Century Park Dr St, Yuba City CA 95991	530-673-3126	R	2*	<.1
329	Morley Group Inc—*Michael Morley*	6201 Corporate Dr Ste, Indianapolis IN 46278	317-879-4770	R	2*	.1
330	Private Duty Registry Services Inc—*Linda Walden*	PO Box 11010, Montgomery AL 36111	334-396-5574	R	2*	.1
331	Professional Medical Staffing Corp—*Thomas Michalsen*	1848 Daimler Rd Ste 1, Rockford IL 61112	815-654-8530	R	2*	.1
332	Superior Search Group Inc—*Steve Maestre*	2314 Rte 59, Plainfield IL 60586	815-254-8930	R	2*	.1
333	Ultimate Medical Services Inc—*Eva Thornton*	10 Valley Ln, Annville PA 17003	717-269-5653	R	2*	<.1
334	Travis Associates Inc—*Diane Stack*	203 Middlesex Tpke Ste, Burlington MA 01803	781-272-6750	R	2*	.1
335	Contech Systems—*Joseph Contino*	239 Connecticut St, Staten Island NY 10307	732-632-8818	R	2*	.1
336	Future Unlimited Inc—*Geraldine Moner*	1407 Jefferson Ave, Brunswick OH 44212	330-273-6677	R	2*	.1
337	Illinois Educational and Training Center—*Anne Schneider*	1300 S 9th St, Springfield IL 62703	217-782-3846	R	2*	.1
338	International Consulting Resources Group—*Allen Miller*	1400 Fashion Island Bl, San Mateo CA 94404	650-377-0990	R	2*	<.1
339	Professional Employment Group Inc—*Andy Spann*	999 Executive Pky Dr S, Saint Louis MO 63141	314-275-2000	R	2*	<.1
340	Universal Work Force Development Center—*Abdul-Rahim Islam*	1427 Catharine St, Philadelphia PA 19146	215-546-1880	R	2*	<.1
341	Associated Home Health Nurses Of America Inc—*Marie Temmink*	3293 Pacific Ave, Long Beach CA 90807	562-981-3100	R	2*	.2
342	Saicon Consultants Inc—*Ramesh S Lokre*	9300 W 110th St Ste 65, Overland Park KS 66210	913-451-1178	R	2*	.1
343	Staff One Ltd—*Sandy Grady*	6737 W Washington St S, Milwaukee WI 53214	414-302-9170	R	2*	.1
344	Colliers Reserve Gatehouse—*Sal Hinkes*	11300 Colliers Reserve, Naples FL 34110	239-566-2211	R	2*	.1
345	Patriot Services Inc—*Stephanie Blackmon*	824 S Hill St Pmb 372, Griffin GA 30224	770-229-5963	R	2*	.1
346	Per Diem Inc—*Ernie Wates*	1292 Paddock Hills Ave, Cincinnati OH 45229	513-242-5055	R	2*	.1
347	Louisiana Staffing Unlimited Inc—*Jill Poirrier*	PO Box 1728, Gonzales LA 70707	225-621-3212	R	2*	.1
348	Marcom LLC	PO Box 50077, Idaho Falls ID 83405	208-522-7929	R	2*	.1
349	Relief Nursing Services Inc—*David Neiman*	876 Haddon Ave, Collingswood NJ 08108	856-854-7577	R	2*	<.1
350	Veteran Solutions Inc—*John Chenery*	32 Defense St, Annapolis MD 21401	301-599-5511	R	2*	<.1
351	Audrey Golden Associates Ltd—*Audrey Golden*	633 3rd Ave Fl 8, New York NY 10017	212-661-5123	R	2*	<.1
352	Empire Staffing Solutions Inc—*Edwin Nieves*	632 Broadway, Newark NJ 07104	973-481-0088	R	2*	<.1
353	Executive Direction Inc—*Fred Naderi*	847 Sansome St Ste 400, San Francisco CA 94111	415-394-5500	R	2*	<.1
354	Missoula Area Education Coop—*Linda Maass*	438 W Spruce St, Missoula MT 59802	406-523-4861	R	2*	<.1
355	SoftNice Inc—*Mahrookh Shaikh*	5050 Tilghman St Ste 1, Allentown PA 18104	610-871-2944	R	2*	<.1

Rank	Company Name—*Executive Officer*	Address, City, State, Zip	Phone	Type	Fin	Empls
356	American Legal Search LLC—*Richard Brock*	2901 2nd Ave S Ste 130, Birmingham AL 35233	205-397-9500	R	2*	<.1
357	Management Recruiters Of North Oakland County Inc—*Mark Angott*	101 S Main St Ste 400, Rochester MI 48307	248-650-4800	R	2*	<.1
358	Slone Partners—*Adam Slone*	400 Alton Rd Ste 2103, Miami Beach FL 33139	305-531-4733	R	2*	<.1
359	David Gomez and Associates Inc—*David Gomez*	65 E Wacker Pl, Chicago IL 60601	312-346-5525	R	2*	<.1
360	F Gloss International—*Fred Gloss*	1309 Vincent Pl, Mc Lean VA 22101	703-847-0010	R	2*	<.1
361	Daubenspeck and Associates Ltd—*Kenneth Daubenspeck*	Two Prudential Plz 180, Chicago IL 60601	312-297-4100	R	2	<.1
362	'jm' Temporary Services and Affiliates Inc—*Chiquita Bell*	554 E Fthill Blvd Ste, San Dimas CA 91773	909-599-1494	R	2*	<.1
363	Rurak and Associates Inc—*Zbigniew T Rurak*	1875 Ash St Ste 500, Washington DC 20006	202-293-7603	R	2*	<.1
364	Crouch Business Solutions Inc—*Karen Crouch*	1617 Tanglewood Dr, Harker Heights TX 76548	254-690-5627	R	2*	.1
365	Technical Connection Inc—*Carol Boyd*	PO Box 1402, Burlington VT 05402	802-658-8324	R	2*	.1
366	Tri-Worth Solutions LLC—*Bob Aylsworth*	2220 Village Walk Dr S, Henderson NV 89052	312-458-9808	R	2*	.1
367	Medical Professionals On Call Inc—*Hagar Wiafe*	10875 Main St Ste 112, Fairfax VA 22030	703-273-8818	R	2*	<.1
368	Noll Inc—*William Noll*	12905 W Dodge Rd, Omaha NE 68154	402-391-7736	R	2*	<.1
369	Dominion Care Home Health—*Elsie Cortez*	8207 Callaghan Rd Ste, San Antonio TX 78230	210-342-9922	R	2*	<.1
370	Quality Staffing Services—*Joe Anthony*	1386 Stuyvesant Ave, Union NJ 07083	908-964-4333	R	2*	<.1
371	Ronnie Gale Personnel Corp—*Gail Landres*	11821 Queens Blvd Ste, Flushing NY 11375	718-261-1111	R	2*	<.1
372	Staffing Resources Of Miami Inc—*Cindy Perozo*	7750 Sw 117th Ave Ste, Miami FL 33183	305-275-6015	R	2*	<.1
373	Medliant—*Al Miller*	1400 Fashion Island Bl, San Mateo CA 94404	650-377-0333	R	2*	<.1
374	Resources For You Inc—*Rhonda Vandesteeg*	1218 Greeley Ave N, Glencoe MN 55336	320-864-5871	R	2*	.1
375	Acetech Communication Inc—*Tom Carper*	700 Cw Stevens Blvd, Grayson KY 41143	606-475-3739	R	2*	.1
376	T and L Companions Inc—*Tamara Arnold*	105 Crofton Pl Ste 5, Palmyra VA 22963	434-589-2700	R	2*	.1
377	Urgent Nursing Resource Inc—*Rod Santa-Ines*	14752 Beach Blvd Ste 1, La Mirada CA 90638	714-523-4178	R	2*	<.1
378	Corporate Source Group Inc—*Dana Willis*	280 S Main St, Andover MA 01810	978-475-6400	R	2*	<.1
379	Genesis Consolidated Services Inc—*Robert Burbidge*	76 Blanchard Rd, Burlington MA 01803	781-272-4900	R	2*	<.1
380	Conolog Corp—*Robert S Benou*	5 Columbia Rd, Somerville NJ 08876	908-722-8081	P	2	<.1
381	Computer Staffing Services LLC—*Tom Clarke*	263 E Main St Ste A, Newark DE 19711	302-737-4920	R	2*	<.1
382	Hope Resource Center Inc—*Sheryl Taylor*	2700 Painter Ave, Knoxville TN 37919	865-525-4673	R	2*	<.1
383	Urpan Technologies—*Padmanabhan Swami*	341 Cobalt Way Ste 208, Sunnyvale CA 94085	408-245-0006	R	2*	<.1
384	Nursestat LLC—*Dinah Giefer*	PO Box 5, Saint Paul KS 66771	620-449-2525	R	2*	.3
385	Quality Coast Inc—*Consuelo Rosengreen*	2520 Main St Ste E, Chula Vista CA 91911	619-443-9192	R	2*	.1
386	Harbor Work Source Center—*Carl Frerson*	1851 N Gaffey St Ste F, San Pedro CA 90731	310-732-5700	R	2*	<.1
387	Casual Driver Leasing Services Inc—*Layne Morrison*	440 Benmar Dr Ste 1400, Houston TX 77060	281-447-0885	R	2*	<.1
388	Howard Fischer Associates Inc—*Howard Fischer*	1800 Jf Kennedy Blvd S, Philadelphia PA 19103	215-568-8363	R	2*	<.1
389	Bartunek Group Inc—*Jeri Bartunek*	7500 College Blvd Ste, Overland Park KS 66210	913-327-8800	R	2*	<.1
390	Cyberforce Inc—*Vito Abbruscato*	25 Church St 2, Keyport NJ 07735	732-203-1007	R	2*	<.1
391	Amp Information Services Inc—*Armand Posner*	PO Box 15214, Arlington VA 22215	703-413-0267	R	2*	<.1
392	Corporate Information Systems Inc—*Carmine Marinaro*	71 Union Ave Ste 101, Rutherford NJ 07070	201-896-0600	R	2*	<.1
393	Creative Circle—*Kelly Connor*	599 Broadway Fl 9, New York NY 10012	212-777-8001	R	1*	<.1
394	Nursing Corporation Of America Inc—*Dwane Hargroder*	105 N Main St Ste 301, Opelousas LA 70570	337-942-4622	R	1*	<.1
395	National Tech Design Inc—*Michael Lemmen*	PO Box 8064, Holland MI 49422	616-395-9600	R	1*	<.1
396	Scaffold Erections Inc—*Robert Gilbreath*	PO Box 16298, Houston TX 77222	713-692-7907	R	1*	<.1
397	Vantro Systems LLC	11401 Rupp Dr, Burnsville MN 55337	952-890-2080	R	1*	<.1
398	Med-Stat Health Care Inc—*Jose Joy*	150 Orange St, Bloomfield NJ 07003	973-429-4994	R	1*	<.1
399	Objective Solutions Inc—*Steven Wolfe*	500 5th Ave Ste 1820, New York NY 10110	212-885-0700	R	1*	<.1
400	Pro Tech Search Inc—*John Dickinson*	160 Kings Way, Royal Palm Beach FL 33411	561-795-7440	R	1*	<.1
401	M Logic Inc—*Marvin Hecht*	1350 Broadway Rm 408, New York NY 10018	212-590-5955	R	1*	<.1
402	Clark Business Services Inc—*Charles Clark*	1735 Guess Rd Ste 100, Durham NC 27701	919-416-9693	R	1*	.3
403	Asap Consultants Inc—*Richard Mumme*	704 Hunters Row Ct, Mansfield TX 76063	817-453-0077	R	1*	<.1
404	Adams Inc—*Jay Adams*	17330 Wright St Ste 10, Omaha NE 68130	402-333-3009	R	1*	<.1
405	Employment Trust Inc—*Robert Franciose*	2301 Congress St, Portland ME 04102	207-775-1924	R	1*	<.1
406	Sporn Group Inc—*David Sporn*	11 Broadway Ste 521, New York NY 10004	212-344-5050	R	1*	<.1
407	Telequest Communications Inc—*Tom Bartchak*	PO Box 94, Mahwah NJ 07430	845-371-3500	R	1*	<.1
408	Adkins and Associates Ltd—*R Adkins*	PO Box 16062, Greensboro NC 27416	336-378-1261	R	1*	<.1
409	Prince Perelson and Associates LLC—*Joann Seguin*	2180 S 1300 E, Salt Lake City UT 84106	801-532-1000	R	1*	<.1
410	Home Aide Home Care Inc—*Mellisa Neylan*	1544 B St Ste 7, Hayward CA 94541	510-247-1200	R	1*	<.1
411	Boly-Welch Inc—*Patricia Welch*	625 Sw Broadway Ste 50, Portland OR 97205	503-242-1300	R	1*	<.1
412	Jefferson Associates Inc—*Limas Jefferson*	17045 El Camino Real S, Houston TX 77058	281-286-4000	R	1*	<.1
413	Regal Employment Inc—*Julie Murphy*	PO Box 887, Hartselle AL 35640	256-773-8522	R	1*	.5
414	Ascend HR Solutions—*Mark Holland*	450 East 1000 N, North Salt Lake UT 84054	801-299-6400	R	1*	<.1
415	Douglas Patrick Inc—*Robert Maher*	4807 Rockside Rd Ste 2, Cleveland OH 44131	216-642-8600	R	1*	<.1
416	Software Folks Inc—*Rohit Mahajan*	50 Bridge St, Metuchen NJ 08840	609-448-7095	R	1*	<.1
417	Precision Personnel Inc—*Stephen Ferguson*	600 Cleveland St Ste 7, Clearwater FL 33755	727-449-0600	R	1*	<.1
418	Arjay Search Inc—*Patrick Jones*	598 S Milledge Ave Ste, Athens GA 30605	706-548-6799	R	1*	<.1
419	Urooj LLC—*Naela Urooj*	301 Rte 17 N Ste 800, Rutherford NJ 07070	201-933-7861	R	1*	<.1
420	Techlink Systems Inc—*Jane Kim*	51 E 42nd St Ste 1600, New York NY 10017	212-661-2707	R	1*	<.1
421	Loan Administration Network Inc—*Charlene Nichols*	18952 MacArthur Blvd S, Irvine CA 92612	949-752-5246	R	1*	<.1
422	Prn Resources Inc—*Frank Milano*	2417 Colt Ln, Crowley TX 76036	817-361-9776	R	1*	<.1
423	Institech Inc—*Liz Fuller*	PO Box 364, Butler WI 53007	262-252-8484	R	1*	<.1
424	Dick Williams and Associates—*Dick Williams*	7901 Stoneridge Dr Ste, Pleasanton CA 94588	925-468-0304	R	1*	<.1
425	Talent Retriever LLC—*David Barbato*	54 Mall Rd Ste G01, Burlington MA 01803	781-425-5550	R	1*	<.1
426	Executive Recruiting Solutions—*Tom Kelly*	2500 Towering Ridge Ln, Florence KY 41042	513-564-8885	R	1	<.1
427	Corporate Solutions Group Inc—*Justin Bryant*	PO Box 1797, Stockbridge GA 30281	678-289-2310	R	1*	<.1
428	M and F Development LLC—*Tony Mayer*	111 Filer Ave, Twin Falls ID 83301	208-733-7300	R	1*	<.1
429	D and A Professional Resources Ltd—*Derrick Jeziorowski*	610 Iris Ct, Crystal Lake IL 60014	815-356-7926	R	1*	<.1
430	Hired Hands And Associates Inc—*Anna Burns*	1035 Whippingham Pkwy, Carrollton VA 23314	757-238-9400	R	1*	<.1
431	Bsp Solutions Inc—*Paul Chakoian*	5 Lisa Ln, North Reading MA 01864	978-664-1310	R	1*	<.1
432	First Call Personnel Services Inc—*Lisa Vise*	2400 Augusta Dr Ste 35, Houston TX 77057	713-974-4479	R	1*	<.1
433	Procore Solutions LLC—*Greg Steel*	PO Box 4610, Marietta GA 30061	678-355-3550	R	1*	<.1
434	Dna Search Inc—*Daniel Levy*	6934 Canby Ave Ste 103, Reseda CA 91335	818-986-6300	R	<1*	<.1
435	Assurance Group	25 E Spring Valley Ave, Maywood NJ 07607	201-845-6444	R	N/A	<.1

TOTALS: SIC 7361 Employment Agencies
Companies: 435   232,250   201.1

7363 Help Supply Services

1	Manpower Inc—*Jeffrey A Joerres*	100 Manpower Pl, Milwaukee WI 53212	414-961-1000	P	18,867	30.0
2	Volt Services Group Div—*Steven Shaw* Volt Information Sciences Inc	2401 N Glassell St, Orange CA 92865	714-921-8800	D	11,056*	31.0
3	Altres Inc—*Barron Guss*	967 Kapiolani Blvd, Honolulu HI 96814	808-591-4940	R	7,792*	22.0

Note: An asterisk (*) indicates an estimated financial figure. The company type code used is as follows: R = Private, P = Public, S = Private Subsidiary, B = Public Subsidiary, D = Division, J = Joint Venture, I = Investment Fund.

COMPANY RANKINGS BY SALES WITHIN 4-DIGIT SIC

Rank	Company Name—Executive Officer	Address, City, State, Zip	Phone	Type	Fin	Empls
4	Kelly Services Inc—Carl T Camden	999 W Big Beaver Rd, Troy MI 48084	248-362-4444	P	5,551	563.2
5	Robert Half International Inc—Harold M Messmer Jr	2884 Sand Hill Rd, Menlo Park CA 94025	650-234-6000	P	3,777	11.3
6	Olsten Staffing Services—Edward Blechschmidt	175 Broad Hollow Rd, Melville NY 11747	631-844-7800	S	3,283*	11.7
7	Nursefinders Inc—Robert Livonius	524 E Lamar Blvd Ste 3, Arlington TX 76011	817-460-1181	S	3,145*	8.5
8	Volt Information Sciences Inc—Steven A Shaw	1065 Ave of the Americ, New York NY 10018	212-704-2400	P	2,427	42.0
9	SFN Group Inc—Roy G Krause	2050 Spectrum Blvd, Fort Lauderdale FL 33309	954-308-7600	P	2,053	171.0
10	Group Management Services Inc—Mike Kahoe	3296 Columbia Rd Ste10, Richfield OH 44286	330-659-0100	R	1,624*	5.0
11	CareerStaff Unlimited Inc—Rick Peranton	6191 N State Hwy 161 S, Irving TX 75038	972-812-3200	R	1,598*	6.0
12	TrueBlue Inc—Steven C Cooper	PO Box 2910, Tacoma WA 98402	253-383-9101	P	1,316	2.7
13	Randstad USA—Linda Galipeau	2015 S Park Pl SE, Atlanta GA 30339	770-937-7000	S	1,304*	2.1
14	MATRIX Resources Inc—Tom Kapish	115 Perimeter Center P, Atlanta GA 30346	770-677-2400	R	1,267*	1.4
15	Kforce Inc—David L Dunkel	1001 E Palm Ave, Tampa FL 33605	813-552-5000	P	1,111	12.4
16	TeleTech Holdings Inc—Kenneth Tuchman	9197 S Peoria St, Englewood CO 80112	303-397-8100	P	1,095	45.5
17	Monster Worldwide Inc—Sal Iannuzzi	622 3rd Ave 39th Fl, New York NY 10017	212-351-7000	P	1,040	6.0
18	Compass Diversified Holdings—Alan Offenberg	61 Wilton Rd 2nd Fl, Westport CT 06880	203-221-1703	P	984	.4
19	Hudson Highland Group Inc—Manuel Marquez	560 Lexington Ave 5th, New York NY 10022	212-351-7400	P	934	2.2
20	Comprehensive Designers Inc—Paulett Eberhart	1717 Arch St 35th Fl, Philadelphia PA 19103	215-282-8050	P	926	10.0
21	Stream Global Services Inc—Kathryn V Marinello	20 William St Ste 310, Wellesley MA 02481	781-340-1800	P	847	31.0
22	MSX International Inc—Frederick Minturn	1950 Concept Dr, Warren MI 48091	248-299-1000	R	803*	7.0
23	ADP TotalSource Group Inc—Arthur Weinbach	1 ADP Blvd, Roseland NJ 07068	973-974-5000	S	775*	44.0
24	ZeroChaos—Harold Mills	420 S Orange Ave Ste 6, Orlando FL 32801	407-770-6161	R	727*	11.9
25	Spectrum Healthcare Resources—George Tracy	12647 Olive Blvd Ste 6, Creve Coeur MO 63141		R	727*	2.5
26	Comsys IT Partners Inc—Larry Enterline Manpower Inc	4400 Post Oak Pkwy Ste, Houston TX 77027	713-386-1400	S	649	4.6
27	Tandem Staffing Solutions Inc—Charles Abadei	5901 Broken Sound Pky, Boca Raton FL 33487	561-226-8110	R	594	35.0
28	StaffMark Inc—Lesa Francis	111 Center St, Little Rock AR 72201	501-954-8484	R	586*	2.0
29	COMFORCE Corp—Harry Maccarrone	999 Stewart Ave Ste 10, Bethpage NY 11714	516-437-3300	R	564	.6
30	Outsource Partners International Inc—Kishore Mirchandani	444 Madison Ave 15th, New York NY 10022	212-768-9393	R	555*	1.1
31	Remedy Intelligent Staffing—D Stephen Sorenson	3820 State St, Santa Barbara CA 93105	805-882-2200	R	514*	.6
32	Cross Country Healthcare Inc—Joseph Boshart	6551 Park of Commerce, Boca Raton FL 33487	561-998-2232	P	469	1.1
33	On Assignment Inc—Peter T Dameris	26745 Malibu Hills Rd, Calabasas CA 91302	818-878-7900	P	438	1.1
34	Employmentgroup Holdings Corp—Mark Lancaster	4625 Beckley Rd Bldg 2, Battle Creek MI 49015	269-979-9778	R	434*	.1
35	Landrum Professional Employer Services Inc—H Landrum	PO Box 15698, Pensacola FL 32514	850-476-5100	R	366*	11.0
36	Cross Country Local Inc Cross Country Healthcare Inc	6551 Park of Commerce, Boca Raton FL 33487	561-998-2232	S	350*	1.0
37	Medical Staffing Network Holdings Inc—Robert J Adamson	901 Yamato Rd Ste 110, Boca Raton FL 33431	561-322-1300	P	341	1.0
38	Pinnacle Staffing Inc—Ryan D Hendley	PO Box 17589, Greenville SC 29606		R	325*	1.0
39	Accord Human Resources Inc—Dale Hageman	210 Park Ave Ste 1200, Oklahoma City OK 73102	405-232-9888	R	320*	11.0
40	CHG Healthcare Services Inc—Michael R Weinholtz	6440 S Millrock Dr Ste, Salt Lake City UT 84121		S	312*	1.1
41	Accretive Solutions Inc—David J Weinfuter	105 Maxess Rd Ste 107, Melville NY 11747	631-348-9100	R	297*	.9
42	Barrett Business Services Inc—Michael Elich	8100 NE Pkwy Dr Ste 20, Vancouver WA 98662	360-828-0700	P	273	32.8
43	Employers Resource Management Company Inc—George Gersema	1301 S Vista Ave Ste 2, Boise ID 83705	208-376-3000	R	264*	.1
44	COMFORCE Telecom Inc—Elizabeth DiSalvo COMFORCE Corp	PO Box 969, Bethpage NY 11714	516-470-6996	S	229*	.8
45	Source One Staffing LLC—Michael Rodriguez	5312 Irwindale Ave Ste, Baldwin Park CA 91706	626-337-0560	R	226*	9.5
46	Select StaffingSM—D Stephen Sorensen	3820 State St, Santa Barbara CA 93105	805-882-2200	R	212*	.5
47	Stefanini TechTeam Inc—Gary J Cotshott	27335 W 11 Mile Rd, Southfield MI 48034	248-357-2866	S	211	2.3
48	Bartech Group Inc—Jon E Barfield	17199 N Laural Park Dr, Livonia MI 48152	734-953-5050	R	185*	3.7
49	SOS Staffing Services Inc—JoAnn W Wagner	2650 S Decker Lake Blv, Salt Lake City UT 84119	801-484-4400	R	181*	.3
50	Shg Services Inc—William Mathies	101 Sun Ave Ne, Albuquerque NM 87109	505-821-3355	R	176*	4.0
51	The Aspire Group—Len McCormack	2151 Michelson Dr Ste, Irvine CA 92612		R	170*	.6
52	NJ Protocall Inc—Janis Bude	1 Mall Dr Ste 100, Cherry Hill NJ 08002	856-667-9003	R	160*	7.0
53	Jackson Healthcare Solutions—Richard L Jackson	2655 Northwinds Pkwy, Alpharetta GA 30009	770-643-5500	R	160*	.6
54	Northwest Staffing Resources Inc—Molly Kalomiris	700 Sw Taylor St Ste 2, Portland OR 97205	503-219-6735	R	159*	6.7
55	Area Temps Inc—Raymond Castelluccio	1228 Euclid Ave Ste 11, Cleveland OH 44115	216-781-5350	R	156*	7.0
56	Transportation Unlimited Inc—Samuel Lucarelli	3740 Carnegie Ave Ste, Cleveland OH 44115	216-426-0088	R	156*	8.0
57	Certified Temporary Services Inc—Bill Taylor	16951 Feather Craft Ln, Houston TX 77058	281-280-9500	R	152*	.3
58	CORESTAFF (Washington DC)	815 Connecticut Ave NW, Washington DC 20006	202-223-4900	D	150*	1.5
59	Delta-T Group Inc—Joanne Mcandrews	950 E Haverford Rd Ste, Bryn Mawr PA 19010	610-527-0830	R	149*	6.0
60	RCM Technologies Inc—Leon Kopyt	2500 McClellan Ave Ste, Pennsauken NJ 08109	856-356-4500	P	144	1.3
61	Contract Professionals Inc—Steve York	4141 W Walton Blvd, Waterford MI 48329	248-673-3800	R	142*	.5
62	McClendon Corp	14900 Bogle Dr Ste 300, Chantilly VA 20151	703-263-0490	S	138*	.5
63	Larkin Enterprises Inc—Richard Larkin	PO Box 405, Lincoln ME 04457	207-794-8700	R	133*	.4
64	Roth Staffing Companies LP—Ben Roth	333 City Blvd W Ste 10, Orange CA 92868		R	132*	.3
65	Corporate Resource Services Inc—Jay H Schecter	160 Broadway 11th Fl, New York NY 10038	646-443-2380	P	128	.4
66	Hawkins Associates Inc—Sally Hawkins	909 Ne Loop 410 Ste 10, San Antonio TX 78209	210-349-9911	R	123*	5.6
67	VisionIT—David Segura	3031 W Grand Blvd Ste, Detroit MI 48202	313-420-2000	R	123*	1.0
68	Kelly Staff Leasing Inc—Carl T Camden Kelly Services Inc	999 W Big Beaver Rd, Troy MI 48084	248-362-4444	S	120*	3.0
69	LJ Gonzer Associates—Marc Gonzer	14 Commerce Dr, Cranford NJ 07016	908-709-9494	R	111*	.4
70	Signature Consultants LLC—Amy Bomes	2200 W Commercial Blvd, Fort Lauderdale FL 33309	954-677-1020	R	107*	.5
71	Uniforce Services Inc—John Fanning COMFORCE Corp	PO Box 9006, Woodbury NY 11797	516-437-3300	S	106*	.2
72	Alcott Group Inc—Louis Basso	PO Box 160, Farmingdale NY 11735	631-420-0100	R	105*	4.4
73	Sai People Solutions Inc—Siva P Tayi	2313 Timber Shadows Dr, Kingwood TX 77339	281-358-1858	R	102*	.4
74	MedTeams—Judy Haeberle	725 American Ave, Waukesha WI 53188	262-928-1000	R	96*	.4
75	Human Capital LLC—Seth Seidell	2055 Crooks Rd Lower L, Rochester Hills MI 48309		R	95*	<.1
76	Better Business Systems Inc—Arthur Geiger	PO Box 81590, Billings MT 59108	406-255-7470	R	92*	.1
77	Tilson HR Inc—Brent R Tilson	1530 American Way Ste, Greenwood IN 46143	317-885-3838	R	88*	<.1
78	Eastridge Group—Robert Svet	2355 Northside Dr, San Diego CA 92108	619-260-2000	R	84*	.3
79	Allstaff Management Inc—Jeffrey Reichel	PO Box 957869, Duluth GA 30095	770-339-0000	R	72*	1.5
80	Command Center Inc—Glenn Welstad	3773 W 5th Ave, Post Falls ID 83854	208-773-7450	P	69	29.2
81	Starpoint Solutions—Jeffrey Najarian	22 Cortlandt St Fl 14, New York NY 10007	212-962-1550	S	65*	.7
82	NextRidge Inc—Shaun P Mahoney	12 Elmwood Rd, Albany NY 12204	518-292-6505	R	65*	.2
83	Alliance of Professionals and Consultants Inc—Roy Roberts	8200 Brownleigh Dr, Raleigh NC 27617	919-510-9696	R	63*	.6
84	Leed Corporate Services Inc—Sanford Bennett	828 Federal Rd, Brookfield CT 06804	203-775-6840	R	63*	.2
85	Hospital Shared Services—Wayne Schell	900 S Broadway Ste 100, Denver CO 80209	303-603-3000	R	61*	2.4
86	Spartan Staffing—John Demarest TrueBlue Inc	7001 Pelham Rd Ste K, Greenville SC 29615		S	61*	.3

Rank	Company Name—*Executive Officer*	Address, City, State, Zip	Phone	Type	Fin	Empls
87	MSI International Inc—*Eric Lindberg*	245 Peachtree Ctr Ave, Atlanta GA 30303	404-659-5050	R	61*	.2
88	Energy Services Group International Inc—*Tom Gillman*	3601 La Grange Pky, Toano VA 23168	757-741-4040	R	57*	.2
89	Westaff Support Inc	3820 State St, Santa Barbara CA 93105	805-882-2200	S	56*	.2
90	Westaff USA Inc	3820 State St, Santa Barbara CA 93105	805-882-2200	S	56*	.2
91	Datrose Inc—*William W Rose*	660 Basket Rd, Webster NY 14580	585-265-1780	R	54*	.8
92	Interim Healthcare Inc—*Kathleen Gilmartin* SFN Group Inc	1601 Sawgrass Corporat, Sunrise FL 33323		S	50*	.2
93	Integrity Staffing Solutions Inc—*Todd B Bavol*	750 Shipyard Dr Rm 300, Wilmington DE 19801	302-661-8776	R	50*	.2
94	Management Decisions Inc—*Ella Koscik*	35 Technology Pkwy S S, Norcross GA 30092	770-416-7949	R	47*	.5
95	Consultis Inc—*Barbara Fleming*	4401 N Federal Hwy Ste, Boca Raton FL 33431	561-750-8745	R	46*	3.2
96	Cherokee Nation Industries LLC—*James Brown*	Rr 3 Box 498, Stilwell OK 74960	918-696-3151	R	44*	.4
97	Clear Staff—*Richard Simmons*	718 Irving Park Rd, Bensenville IL 60106	630-521-1400	R	43*	.1
98	Peak Technical Services Inc—*Joseph Salvucci*	583 Epsilon Dr, Pittsburgh PA 15238	412-696-1080	R	42*	.1
99	TeamStaff Inc—*Zachary Parker*	1 Executive Dr Ste 130, Somerset NJ 08873		P	42	.9
100	All-Star Group Companies Inc—*Curtis McCrary*	3710 Commerce Dr Ste 1, Halethorpe MD 21227	443-543-7800	R	42*	.3
101	People Care Inc—*Bruce Jacobson*	116 W 32nd St Fl 15, New York NY 10001	212-631-7300	R	38*	1.7
102	Ford Models Inc—*Katie Ford*	111 5th Ave, New York NY 10003	212-219-6500	R	38*	.1
103	Security Personnel Inc—*Nancy Hyndman*	PO Box 623, Butler WI 53007	262-252-2500	R	37*	.1
104	Transportation Personnel Services Inc—*William Carpenter*	1000 Jorie Blvd Ste 22, Oak Brook IL 60523	630-990-2550	R	36*	.5
105	Lab Support Inc—*Emmett McGrath* On Assignment Inc	26651 W Agoura Rd, Calabasas CA 91302	818-878-7900	D	35*	.1
106	TR Bryant Associates Inc—*Jean Bryant*	377 Hoes Ln, Piscataway NJ 08854	732-981-0440	R	33*	1.5
107	Hi-Tek Professionals Inc—*Joseph Parcell*	PO Box 233, Glenolden PA 19036	610-534-8701	R	33*	.2
108	Show Pros Entertainment Services Inc—*Paul Manley*	PO Box 12599, Charlotte NC 28220	704-525-3784	R	31*	1.5
109	Imprimis Group Inc—*Valerie Freeman*	4835 LBJ Fwy Ste 1000, Dallas TX 75244	972-419-1700	R	31*	.1
110	United Staffing Systems Inc—*Barry Saide*	261 Madison Ave Fl 2, New York NY 10016	212-743-0200	R	31*	.1
111	Staff Force Inc—*David Howard*	15915 Katy Fwy Ste160, Houston TX 77094	281-492-6044	R	31*	.1
112	Tri-Com Technical Services—*Matt Sharples*	9240 Glenwood, Overland Park KS 66212	913-652-0600	R	30*	.1
113	NRI Staffing Resources—*Robb Mulberger*	1015 18th St NW Ste 71, Washington DC 20036	202-466-2160	R	29*	.1
114	Northwest Administrators Inc—*Chris R Hughes*	2323 Eastlake Ave E St, Seattle WA 98102	206-329-4900	R	27*	.4
115	Dependable Personnel Inc—*Judy Warren*	700 N Country Club Ste, Tucson AZ 85716	520-325-1131	R	27*	.1
116	Talagy—*Amy McGeorge*	245 Riverside Ave Ste, Jacksonville FL 32202		R	27*	.1
117	Entech Personnel Services Inc—*Pam Barney*	363 W Big Beaver Rd St, Troy MI 48084	248-528-1474	R	26*	.1
118	Soliant Health Inc—*David Alexander*	1979 Lakeside Pkwy Ste, Tucker GA 30084		S	26*	.1
119	Vanguard Temporaries Inc—*John Mcgrath*	633 3rd Ave Fl 12, New York NY 10017	212-682-6400	R	25*	.1
120	Advantis Global Inc—*Bryan Barber*	301 Howard St Ste 1400, San Francisco CA 94105	415-395-4444	R	24	.4
121	Technology and Management Services Inc—*Richard Paoticelli*	9210 Corporate Blvd St, Rockville MD 20850	301-740-2100	S	24*	.3
122	Sequent Inc—*Bill Hutter*	4700 Lakehurst Ct Ste, Dublin OH 43016	614-436-5880	R	24*	.1
123	Professional Project Services Inc—*L Barry Goss*	1100 Bethel Valley Rd, Oak Ridge TN 37830	865-220-4300	R	23*	.3
124	Los Angeles Conservation Corps—*Janet Karatz*	PO Box 15868, Los Angeles CA 90015	213-749-3601	R	23*	.1
125	Trialon Corp—*Patricia Crowder*	1477 Walli Strasse Blv, Burton MI 48509	810-742-8500	R	22*	.3
126	Global Employment Solutions Inc—*Howard Brill*	10375 Park Meadows Dr, Littleton CO 80124	303-216-9500	R	21*	1.9
127	Counter Technology Inc—*San F Garza*	20410 Observation Dr, Germantown MD 20876	301-907-0127	R	21*	.1
128	Veritude Inc—*Douglas Orci Ani*	155 Seaport Blvd, Boston MA 02210	617-563-4915	R	21*	.1
129	Personnel One Inc	2510 NW 97th Ave Ste 1, Doral FL 33172	305-477-6944	S	20*	.2
130	Hallmark Aviation Services LP—*Betsey Duffes*	5757 W Century Blvd St, Los Angeles CA 90045	310-215-0701	R	20*	.8
131	Partners Human Resources Co—*Roger D Rook*	3420 N Santa Fe, Oklahoma City OK 73118	405-917-1020	R	19*	1.9
132	Global Technology Associates Ltd—*Leo Hagan*	1 Parklane Blvd Ste 20, Dearborn MI 48126	313-593-0600	R	19*	.3
133	Select Staffing Services—*D Stephen Sorensen*	3820 State St, Santa Barbara CA 93105	805-882-2200	R	18*	.1
134	Link Staffing Services—*William T Pitts*	1800 Bering Dr Ste 800, Houston TX 77057	713-784-4400	R	18*	.1
135	ATR International Inc—*Jerry Brenholz*	1230 Oakmead Pkwy Ste, Sunnyvale CA 94086	408-328-8000	R	18*	.1
136	Davis Cos—*Bob Davis*	325 Donald J Lynch Blv, Marlborough MA 01752	508-481-9500	R	18*	.1
137	Productive Data Commercial Solutions Inc—*Joseph Martinez*	6160 S Syracuse Way St, Greenwood Village CO 80111	303-220-7165	R	18*	.5
138	Southern Healthcare Agency Inc—*Jackie Mcmillan*	PO Box 320999, Jackson MS 39232	601-933-0037	R	17*	.9
139	G and G Organization Ltd—*Jeff Gorski*	7670 Woodway Dr Ste 25, Houston TX 77063	713-784-4499	R	17*	.3
140	Axios Inc (Grand Rapids Michigan)—*Dan Barcheski*	801 Broadway NW Rm 200, Grand Rapids MI 49504	616-949-2525	R	17*	.1
141	Silicon Valley Staffing Group Inc—*Eugene Lupario*	2200 Powell Ste 510, Emeryville CA 94608	510-923-9898	R	17*	<.1
142	Eagle Support Services Corp—*James Spencer*	2705 Artie St Sw Ste 3, Huntsville AL 35805	256-534-2274	R	17*	.8
143	Mercy Special Care Hospital—*John Starcher*	128 W Washington St, Nanticoke PA 18634	570-735-5000	R	16*	.2
144	Goodwill Of Silicon Valley—*Frank Kent*	1080 N 7th St, San Jose CA 95112	408-998-5774	R	15*	.5
145	Chrislex Staffing Ltd—*Kathy Rudolph*	140 Huguenot St Ste L, New Rochelle NY 10801	914-633-7810	R	14*	.6
146	Quantum Resources—*Chris Gossard*	300 Arboretum Pl Ste 5, Richmond VA 23236	804-320-4800	S	14*	<.1
147	Bridgemark LLC	11970 Borman Dr Ste 10, Saint Louis MO 63146	314-431-0511	R	14*	.8
148	Commercial Drywall Inc—*R Marek*	3539 Oak Forest Dr, Houston TX 77018	713-681-9287	R	14*	.8
149	EuroSoft Inc—*Nancy Miller*	1705 S Capital of Texa, Austin TX 78746	512-329-8100	R	13*	.6
150	Power Advocate Inc—*Daniel Sullivan*	179 Lincoln St, Boston MA 02111	857-453-5700	R	13*	.1
151	BAL Associates Inc—*Larry Enterline*	245 5th Ave Fl 3, New York NY 10016	212-763-6999	S	13*	.1
152	America's Career Opportunities Inc—*William Layfield*	PO Box 848, Mobile AL 36601	251-433-7788	R	13*	<.1
153	Rockmor Group Inc—*Michael Moran*	13412 W Star Dr, Shelby Township MI 48315	586-997-3235	R	12*	.3
154	Sarach Systems Inc—*Thomas Sarach*	1215 Volvo Pkwy Ste 20, Chesapeake VA 23320	757-382-7222	R	12*	.8
155	Accuforce Staffing Services LLC—*Larry Nunley*	2003 Eastman Rd Ste 19, Kingsport TN 37660	423-247-1835	R	12*	<.1
156	Search Wizards Inc—*Leslie O Connor*	1427 Cartecay Dr NE, Atlanta GA 30319	404-846-9500	R	12*	<.1
157	Professional Resources In Information Systems Management Inc—*Mark Johnson*	1801 Old Reston Ave St, Reston VA 20190	703-264-1200	R	12*	.1
158	Total Employment Company Inc—*Brian Henderson*	5050 W Lemon St, Tampa FL 33609	813-289-5566	R	11*	<.1
159	Radiation Management Associates LLC—*Betty Cameron*	10210 Greenbelt Rd Ste, Lanham MD 20706	301-220-3515	R	11*	.1
160	Black Tie Hospitality Inc—*Mark Blandford*	301 Burgundy St Ste E, New Orleans LA 70112	504-586-9313	R	11*	.6
161	Meridian Healthcare Group Inc—*Tom Futch*	3500 Financial Plz Ste, Tallahassee FL 32312	850-325-7777	R	10*	.5
162	Peopletree Staffing Solutions—*Laura Oakley*	3215 Guess Rd Ste 102, Durham NC 27705	919-620-1889	R	10*	.5
163	Medfone Nationwide Inc—*Jay Moses*	3305 Jerusalem Ave Ste, Wantagh NY 11793	516-679-7629	R	10*	.3
164	Titan Medical Group LLC—*Brian Wilke*	4526 S 143rd St Ste 10, Omaha NE 68137	402-332-5200	R	10*	.2
165	Quick Lease Inc—*Victoria Guerriero*	773 S Indiana Ave Unit, Englewood FL 34223	941-473-2702	R	10*	.1
166	ICONMA LLC—*Claudine George*	850 Stephenson Hwy Ste, Troy MI 48083		R	10*	<.1
167	KNF and T Staffing Resources—*Jeanne Fiol*	3 Post Office Sq, Boston MA 02109	617-574-8200	R	10*	<.1
168	Tango Air Inc—*Henry Schubach*	2100 Palomar Airpt Rd, Carlsbad CA 92011	760-929-0307	R	10*	<.1
169	Flexible Resources Inc—*Nadine Mockler*	78 Harvard Ave Ste 200, Stamford CT 06902	203-351-1180	R	10*	<.1
170	L and D Drivers Service Inc—*John Ryan*	111 S 7th Ave, Maywood IL 60153	708-345-0900	R	10*	.3
171	Technical Solutions Inc—*Thomas Campbell*	1817 Golden Mile Hwy, Pittsburgh PA 15239	724-733-2100	R	9*	.2
172	Employer's Relief Inc—*Trudy Bullard*	108 Hedrick Dr, Kernersville NC 27284	336-996-1627	R	9*	.3
173	Companies Of Jj Young LLC—*Brian Champagne*	1500 Central Ave Ste 2, Albany NY 12205	518-452-7090	R	9*	.3

Note: An asterisk (*) indicates an estimated financial figure. The company type code used is as follows: R = Private, P = Public, S = Private Subsidiary, B = Public Subsidiary, D = Division, J = Joint Venture, I = Investment Fund.

COMPANY RANKINGS BY SALES WITHIN 4-DIGIT SIC

Rank	Company Name—Executive Officer	Address, City, State, Zip	Phone	Type	Fin	Empls
174	D and S Leasing Inc—Chad Dust	PO Box 245, Effingham IL 62401	217-342-3011	R	9*	.1
175	Trasys LLC—Mary Lou Rimsky	10250 Alliance Rd Ste, Cincinnati OH 45242	513-793-4414	R	9*	.1
176	Primary Services LP—Regina Mellinger	520 Post Oak Blvd Ste, Houston TX 77027	713-850-7010	R	9*	<.1
177	Richard L Aronson Inc—Richard Aronson	175 Main St Ste Ll1, White Plains NY 10601	914-428-1515	R	9*	.6
178	Alphastaff Inc—Jay Starkman	800 Corporate Dr Ste 6, Fort Lauderdale FL 33334	954-267-1802	R	9*	.3
179	South East Personnel Leasing Inc—John Porreca	2739 Us Hwy 19 Ste 100, Holiday FL 34691	727-938-5562	R	8*	.2
180	Health Care Innovations Inc—Rick Creyts	7701 Grand River Rd St, Brighton MI 48114	810-227-7544	R	8*	.4
181	Action Temporary Service Inc—Kim Devine	PO Box 15398, Evansville IN 47716	812-479-8373	R	8*	<.1
182	Houston City Temporaries—Linda Karcher	2401 Fountainview Ste, Houston TX 77057	713-784-0656	R	8*	<.1
183	Life Style Staffing—John Rupcich	PO Box 2508, Madison WI 53701	608-257-0511	R	8*	<.1
184	Steverson and Company Inc—Tommie Steverson	1155 Dairy Ashford Ste, Houston TX 77079	281-496-5313	R	8*	<.1
185	Turner Staffing Ltd—Roland M Toups	PO Box 2750, Baton Rouge LA 70821	225-922-5050	S	8*	<.1
186	Job Store Inc—Dorothy Grandbois	7100 E Hampden Ave, Denver CO 80224	303-757-7686	R	8*	<.1
187	American Critical Care Services Inc—Carolyn Mc Crocklin	PO Box 35717, Richmond VA 23235	804-320-1113	R	8*	.4
188	Laury Group Agency Inc—Laury Jeambon	630 3rd Ave Rm 1500, New York NY 10017	212-688-8875	R	8*	.3
189	Temps Today Inc—Sheila Navarre	PO Box 231022, New Orleans LA 70183	504-523-2275	R	8*	.4
190	Virtual Resource Management Corp—Glenn Mc Clain	PO Box 598, Clarksburg NJ 08510	609-208-2400	R	7*	.1
191	Temps Inc—Todd Kane	12158 Ntrl Brdg Rd 101, Bridgeton MO 63044	314-427-4440	R	7*	.2
192	Reimbursement Concepts LLC	3236 Main St, Weirton WV 26062	304-723-0091	R	7*	<.1
193	Smith Temps Inc—Joe Roberts	501 Hemphill St, Fort Worth TX 76104	817-332-7903	R	7*	.3
194	Grid One Solutions Inc	700 Turner Way Ste 205, Aston PA 19014		S	7*	.3
195	Working World Inc—Nancy Wenzel	PO Box 1768, Crystal Lake IL 60039	815-455-4490	R	7*	.3
196	Radiology Resource Inc—Mathew Broderick	14275 Midway Rd Ste 22, Addison TX 75001	972-934-3674	R	7*	.1
197	TemPositions Group of Cos—James A Essey	420 Lexington Ave 21st, New York NY 10170	212-490-7400	R	7*	<.1
198	AllBusiness—Fredric Paul	650 Townsend St Ste 45, San Francisco CA 94103	415-694-5000	R	7*	<.1
199	Thinknicity LLC—Dyana King	5 Third St Ste 500, San Francisco CA 94103	415-247-7700	R	7*	<.1
200	Quality Staffing Solutions Inc—Phyllis Moffett	PO Box 5005, Cary NC 27512	919-481-4114	R	7*	<.1
201	St Vincent Depaul Rehabilitation Services Of Texas Inc—Charlie Graham	314 E Highland Mall Bl, Austin TX 78752	512-453-8833	R	7*	.3
202	Employment Contractor Services Inc—Edward Kelly	1 Kattelville Rd Ste 4, Binghamton NY 13901		R	7*	.2
203	Gary Halgran—Gary Halgran	2200 University Ave W, Saint Paul MN 55114	651-917-3634	R	7*	.4
204	Value Leasing Corp—Peter Pastorelli	52 Elm St Ste 7, Huntington NY 11743	631-271-6663	R	7*	.2
205	First Team Staffing Inc—Richard Savaro	5517 Selma Ave 19, Baltimore MD 21227	410-242-2810	R	7*	.3
206	Sonic Systems International Inc—Bill Aston	1880 S Dairy Ashford S, Houston TX 77077	281-531-7611	R	6*	.3
207	Seville Temporary Services Inc—Alisa Winston	180 N Michigan Ave Ste, Chicago IL 60601	312-368-1144	R	6*	.2
208	Teamworks USA Inc—Martin Herman	10612 Beaver Dam Rd, Hunt Valley MD 21030	410-785-1212	R	6*	.4
209	Pvp Contracting Company Inc—Visa Lay	229 McClellan St A, Philadelphia PA 19148	215-327-5157	R	6*	.1
210	Advantage Federal Resourcing Inc—Richard Koenig	25 Braintree Hill Park, Braintree MA 02184	781-930-3175	R	6*	<.1
211	Arvon Staffing LLC—Robert Walker	196 Bsineva Pk Dr Ste, Virginia Beach VA 23462	757-499-9900	R	6*	.4
212	Stanton's Inc—Bonnie Stanton	PO Box 186, Palm Harbor FL 34682	727-785-1549	R	6*	.3
213	A Better Industrial Temporary Inc—Les Kepley	6100 Dutchmans Ln Ste, Louisville KY 40205	502-452-1306	R	6*	.2
214	Spherion of Central Kentucky Inc—David Jacobs	2343 Alexandria Dr Ste, Lexington KY 40504	859-223-5200	R	6*	.3
215	Kokua Nurses—Cheryl Burnette	1210 Artesian St Ste 2, Honolulu HI 96826	808-594-2326	R	6*	.2
216	Phoenix Engineering Company Inc—Silvia Lugo	PO Box 66395, Los Angeles CA 90066	310-532-1134	R	6*	.1
217	Kaye Personnel Inc—Stephen Kaye	1868 Rte 70 E, Cherry Hill NJ 08003	856-489-1200	R	6*	<.1
218	Medforce Inc—Jon Bucklaw	3615 Chain Bridge Rd C, Fairfax VA 22030	703-691-7500	R	5*	.2
219	Blass Employment Corp—Paul Ruina	334 W 37th St Frnt 2, New York NY 10018	212-563-6320	R	5*	.2
220	Cpe Peo Incorporated—Lee Samson	9200 W Snset Blvd Ste, West Hollywood CA 90069	310-385-1000	R	5*	.1
221	Staffing Tree LLC	1877 Orchard Lake Rd S, Sylvan Lake MI 48320	248-858-9706	R	5*	.1
222	Ashley's Quality Care Inc—Frankie Redditt	1727 S Industry Ave St, Chicago IL 60616	312-786-9297	R	5*	.3
223	Driving Momentum Inc—William Graham	PO Box 73681, Houston TX 77273	281-893-0097	R	5*	.2
224	Protemps Health Services Inc—Andrew Simpson	107 Willamette Dr, Bear DE 19701	302-836-5502	R	5*	.2
225	Supplemental Medical Services Inc—Gretchen Curry	2258 Schuetz Rd Ste 10, Saint Louis MO 63146	314-997-8833	R	5*	.2
226	MK Technical Services Inc—Margie King	4349 San Felipe Rd, San Jose CA 95135	408-528-0401	R	5*	.1
227	Rn Specialties Inc—Elizabeth Dillon	409 Mnchusetts Ave Fl, Indianapolis IN 46204	317-254-1132	R	5*	.2
228	Barr Air Patrol LLC	1442 Airport Blvd Ste, Mesquite TX 75181	972-222-0229	R	5*	<.1
229	Professional Respiratory Care Service Inc—Jean Mathews	3801 N 24th St, Phoenix AZ 85016	602-508-0100	R	5*	.1
230	Doherty Employment Group Inc—Timothy Doherty	7625 Parklawn Ave, Minneapolis MN 55435	952-832-8383	R	5*	.1
231	Home and Hospital Medical Personnel Inc—Sheila O'connell	799 Bloomfield Ave Ste, Verona NJ 07044	973-857-9200	R	5*	.1
232	Xemplar Models LLC—Cherly Saunders	110 Saint Paul St, Baltimore MD 21202	410-945-0793	R	5*	.1
233	Callos Management Succession Team Inc—Thomas Walsh	5083 Market St, Youngstown OH 44512	330-788-4001	R	5*	.1
234	Horizon Personnel Resources—Daniel Schivitz	1516 Lincoln Rd, Wickliffe OH 44092	440-585-0031	R	5*	.2
235	National Staffing Associates Inc—Vincent Huggins	134 Evergreen Pl Fl 4-, East Orange NJ 07018	973-675-1163	R	5*	.2
236	Aspen Diversified Industries Inc—Kenneth Barela	220 Ruskin Dr, Colorado Springs CO 80910	719-391-2550	R	5*	.1
237	Ams Temporaries Inc—Sharon Goodlet	519 Barret Ave, Louisville KY 40204	502-581-1725	R	5*	.1
238	Neo-Pet LLC—Audry Schmidt	34555 Chagrin Blvd Ste, Moreland Hills OH 44022	440-893-9949	R	5*	<.1
239	Stl Office Solutions Inc—Timothy Norman	PO Box 1899, Bloomington IL 61702	309-661-7851	R	4*	.1
240	Expeditors and Production Services Co—Scott Belanger	PO Box 80644, Lafayette LA 70598	337-839-2735	R	4*	.1
241	G R Helm Inc—Gordon Helm	5050 Rbert J Mathews P, El Dorado Hills CA 95762	916-933-9669	R	4*	.1
242	Staffing Source Personnel Inc—Jinan Dalloo	15340 Michigan Ave, Dearborn MI 48126	313-624-9500	R	4*	.1
243	Southern Industrial Constructors Inc—John Fife	1048 Florida Blvd, Baton Rouge LA 70802	225-383-1256	R	4*	.1
244	P and A Administrative Services—Joseph Priselac	17 Ct St Ste 500, Buffalo NY 14202	716-852-2611	R	4*	.1
245	Evinco Professional Services Inc—Brad Smith	PO Box 1006, Alcoa TN 37701	865-977-9326	R	4*	.2
246	PDS Services—Mary Ann Pompea	37633 Pembroke Ave, Livonia MI 48152	734-953-9700	R	4*	.2
247	InSource Inc—Scot Keefer	900 W Valley Rd Ste 70, Wayne PA 19087	610-592-0800	R	4*	.1
248	Pro-Touch Nurses Inc—Kim Sharma	17822 Davenport Rd Ste, Dallas TX 75252	972-713-1700	R	4*	<.1
249	Immediate Connections Inc—Patricia McGoldrick	50 Terminal St Bldg 2, Charlestown MA 02129	617-242-2555	R	4*	<.1
250	Martin Francis International Associates Inc—F Siegel	150 Broadway Rm 1717, New York NY 10038	212-267-6152	R	4*	.1
251	A-Com Enterprises Inc—Ron Beck	PO Box 700, Fortson GA 31808	706-322-1870	R	4*	.1
252	Life Quest Inc—Evangeline Zamora	907 N Pope St, Silver City NM 88061	575-388-1976	R	4*	.1
253	Csr Medical Inc—James Dramby	PO Box 33353, Charlotte NC 28233	704-373-5991	R	4*	.1
254	Progressive Information Technology—Scott Miller	5220 Spring Valley Rd, Dallas TX 75254	972-239-6055	R	4*	.1
255	Personnel Preference Inc—Jill Tillinghast	150 Boles St Ste A, Weed CA 96094	530-938-3909	R	4*	.2
256	Primestaff Inc—Kathleen Carlsen	3434 Lexington Ave N S, Saint Paul MN 55126	651-697-2120	R	4*	.1
257	Interstaff Inc—Randy Richards	16107 Kensington Dr St, Sugar Land TX 77479	713-980-2500	R	4*	.1
258	Wisne Automation And Engineering Co—Lawrence Wisne	42445 W 10 Mile Rd, Novi MI 48375	248-348-7070	R	4*	.1
259	George Konik Associates Inc—George Konik	7242 Metro Blvd, Minneapolis MN 55439	952-835-5550	R	4*	.1
260	Conexx Staffing Services LLC	3319 Kirby Pkwy, Memphis TN 38115	901-363-7474	R	3*	.1
261	Drug Consultants Inc—Carl Rowe	11751 Davis St, Moreno Valley CA 92557	951-485-2640	R	3*	.1
262	Smith Temporary Office Service Inc—Ella Smith	35 Marie Dr, Gretna LA 70053	504-366-3200	R	3*	.1

Rank	Company Name—Executive Officer	Address, City, State, Zip	Phone	Type	Fin	Empls
263	Preferred Labor Corp—David Booth	305 W Lorenz Blvd, Jackson MS 39213	601-362-3627	R	3*	.1
264	Minnesota Professional Nursing Services—Benjamin Narh	2021 E Hennepin Ave St, Minneapolis MN 55413	612-627-9524	R	3*	.1
265	Home Healthcare Inc—Arthur Schwabe	360 Hamilton Ave Ste 1, White Plains NY 10601	914-428-7722	R	3*	.1
266	Ashland Services LLC—Cheryl Morgan	3260 Barataria Blvd, Marrero LA 70072	504-340-2792	R	3*	.1
267	CPR Inc—John Wills	1921 Wright Blvd, Schaumburg IL 60193	847-895-7700	R	3*	.1
268	Ambrose Employer Group LLC—Sean Campbell	199 Water St Rm 2800, New York NY 10038	212-660-3500	R	3*	<.1
269	Engstrom Inc—Cherie Campion	PO Box 40, Two Rivers WI 54241	920-755-3277	R	3*	.2
270	Kelly It Engineering Resources—Tim Halloran	237 Park Ave, New York NY 10017	212-949-5308	R	3*	.1
271	Home Care Services Of H R M C—Beverley Murray	560 Leroy George Dr, Clyde NC 28721	828-452-8292	R	3*	.1
272	Mindsource Inc—David Clark	555 Clyde Ave Ste 100, Mountain View CA 94043	650-254-8909	R	3*	.1
273	Staff Tech Inc—Dan Kohnke	193 Blue Ravine Rd Ste, Folsom CA 95630	916-932-1234	R	3*	<.1
274	Add Staff Inc—Cari Shaffer	2118 Hollow Brook Dr, Colorado Springs CO 80918	719-528-8888	R	3*	<.1
275	Action Labor—Karen Hoover	900 Osceola Dr Ste 222, West Palm Beach FL 33409	561-683-1211	R	3*	<.1
276	Quest Personnel Resources Inc—Terri Martinez	50 Briar Hollow Ste 51, Houston TX 77027	713-961-0605	R	3*	<.1
277	Riverway Personnel	5213 Spruce St Ste 100, Bellaire TX 77401	713-664-5900	R	3*	<.1
278	BOLT Staffing Service Inc—Joanne Sanders	3427 Broadway Ste F4, American Canyon CA 94503	707-552-7800	R	3*	<.1
279	Royal Personnel Services—Joe Cummings	14011 Ventura Blvd Ste, Sherman Oaks CA 91423	818-981-1080	R	3*	<.1
280	Charter Oak Service Corp—Demerise Grane	PO Box 1005, Torrington CT 06790	860-489-4151	R	3*	.1
281	Insurance Temporary Services Inc—Susan Lowry	PO Box 565584, Dallas TX 75356	214-638-7000	R	3*	.1
282	Acloche LLC—Tom Blanchard	1800 Watermark Dr Ste, Columbus OH 43215	614-824-3700	R	3*	.1
283	Nextech Solutions LLC	9054 Valley Crest Ln S, Germantown TN 38138	901-755-0158	R	3*	.1
284	Attentive Personnel Inc—Brian Botshon	5 Computer Dr W Ste 10, Albany NY 12205	518-438-6021	R	3*	.1
285	South Bay Alcoholism Services—Michael Ballue	1334 Post Ave, Torrance CA 90501	310-328-1460	R	3*	.1
286	Jenesse Center Inc—Karen Earl	PO Box 8476, Los Angeles CA 90008	323-731-6500	R	3*	<.1
287	Mitchell Temporary Services Inc—Kimberly Mccullers	PO Box 1027, Smithfield NC 27577	919-934-0909	R	3*	.1
288	Avalon Place Trinity—William Macale	PO Box 631, Trinity TX 75862	936-594-7521	R	3*	.1
289	American Telecare Inc—Randall Moore	15159 Technology Dr, Eden Prairie MN 55344	952-897-0000	R	3*	<.1
290	Adtec Staffing Services—Robert Curtis	3330 University Ave St, Madison WI 53705	608-231-3210	R	3*	.1
291	Delivery Management Services Corp—Marcus Felix	24 W 40th St Fl 17, New York NY 10018	646-251-6431	R	3*	.1
292	Arcservices Inc—Elaine Redfearn	PO Box 597, Chesterfield SC 29709	843-623-3200	R	3*	.1
293	Computerized Management—Dale Fazvale	PO Box 190, Simi Valley CA 93062	805-522-5999	R	3*	.1
294	Airetel Staffing Inc—Rita Tomaso	PO Box 915864, Longwood FL 32791	407-788-2015	R	3*	<.1
295	Employee Leasing Systems Inc—Andrew Kluger	70 Mitchell Blvd Ste 2, San Rafael CA 94903	415-479-6000	D	3	<.1
296	Technical Group Inc—Steve Howeth	PO Box 1476, Shepherd TX 77371	936-628-6972	R	3*	<.1
297	Tempcare Homehealth Services Inc—Conrado Bali	950 E Alton Gloor Blvd, Brownsville TX 78526	956-541-4410	R	2*	.1
298	Ivedha Inc—Kumar Ratnam	244 5th Ave Ste 2561, New York NY 10001	347-534-1429	R	2*	.1
299	Medifax Inc—Len Gaudio	240 N W Ave, Elmhurst IL 60126	630-516-4270	R	2*	.1
300	Sterling Culturally Diversified Services Inc—Robert Macdonald	2415 E Camelback Rd St, Phoenix AZ 85016	602-470-8012	R	2*	.1
301	Wightman Enterprises Inc—Michelle Wightman	8017 Sacramento St, Fair Oaks CA 95628	916-961-1166	R	2*	.1
302	National Temporary Personnel Service—Oscar Torres	778 Centre St, Trenton NJ 08611	609-989-0076	R	2*	.1
303	LSEC—Akram Isimial	8100 County Rd 44 Leg, Leesburg FL 34788	352-323-1995	R	2*	.1
304	Support Technology Inc—Kenneth Haase	PO Box 38425, Pittsburgh PA 15238	412-630-9404	R	2*	<.1
305	John Leonard Employment Services Inc—Linda Poldoian	75 Federal St Ste 1120, Boston MA 02110	617-423-6800	R	2*	<.1
306	Locke Technical Services Inc—John Debowski	25700 Interstate 45 St, Spring TX 77386	281-367-3390	R	2*	.1
307	Sundance Staffing Minnesota LLC	12805 Hwy 55 Ste 106, Minneapolis MN 55441	763-559-7700	R	2*	.1
308	Strategic Logistics Staffing LLC (Jenkintown Pennsylvania)	930 Pine Valley Cir, Jenkintown PA 19046	215-885-4306	R	2*	.1
309	R and D Medical Staffing Inc—Rodney Priest	1425 S University Ave, Little Rock AR 72204	501-661-9995	R	2*	.1
310	Masterstaff Ii Inc—Robert Carie	3181 Packard St, Ann Arbor MI 48108	734-973-0420	H	2*	.2
311	Mbl Associates Inc—Munjanja Litell	PO Box 258, Boyds MD 20841	301-528-8337	R	2*	.1
312	C and S Associates LLC—Christine Sanchez	2105 Leeds Dr, Plano TX 75025	972-527-2623	R	2*	.1
313	Tri-Serv Inc—Walter Braczynski	PO Box 644, Cockeysville MD 21030	410-561-1740	R	2*	.1
314	New Age Software Services Corp—Tim O'donohue	20 Mary E Clark Dr Ste, Hampstead NH 03841	603-329-9327	R	2*	<.1
315	Heritage Homecare Inc—Linda Clark	PO Box 783, Sharon CT 06069	860-364-5799	R	2*	.1
316	United Industrial Engineering Corp—Jamie Griffin	770 W Maple Rd Frnt Fr, Troy MI 48084	248-362-1533	R	2*	<.1
317	Custom Staffing Inc—Diane McGaw	228 E 45th St 12th Fl, New York NY 10017	212-818-0300	R	2*	<.1
318	Human Resources Alternatives Inc—Sandra J Botson	PO Box 152, Havertown PA 19083	610-407-9010	R	2*	<.1
319	International Millennium Consultants Inc—Rosalyn Berns	550 Frontage Rd Ste 25, Northfield IL 60093	847-446-0300	R	2*	<.1
320	Opportunity Search—H Bradley Lucarell	1545 Bethel Rd, Columbus OH 43220	614-457-9500	R	2*	<.1
321	Spectrum Staffing and Software Solutions Inc—Lisa Guard	6562 Ridings Rd, Syracuse NY 13206	315-362-8500	R	2*	<.1
322	Accounting Connections—Pamela Ake	PO Box 10823, Portland OR 97296	503-228-2335	R	2*	<.1
323	Mclellan Temporaries Inc—Kevin Mclellan	PO Box 901, Corvallis OR 97339	541-754-9616	R	2*	.1
324	Consolidated Personnel Services Inc—Jerry Persson	PO Box 44030, Phoenix AZ 85064	602-230-8940	R	2*	.1
325	Nice People Home Care and Staffing—Molly Miceli	540 W Briar Pl Ste B, Chicago IL 60657	773-388-0300	R	2*	<.1
326	Gemini Employee Leasing Inc—Debbie Helgeson	107 N Eau Claire St, Mondovi WI 54755	715-926-5966	R	2*	.1
327	Imtc—Kelsie Giles	15210 Mcdam Rd S Apt D, Tukwila WA 98188	206-243-5625	R	2*	.1
328	On-Board Services Inc—Robert Wilson	50 Millstone Rd Ste 30, East Windsor NJ 08520	609-945-8003	R	2*	.1
329	Superior Home Services—Boris Weiss	330 Granfield Ave, Bridgeport CT 06610	203-362-2024	R	2*	.1
330	Quality Home Staffing Inc—Beverly Mino	PO Box 490, Windsor NC 27983	252-794-4227	R	2*	<.1
331	People's Express Inc—Jan Roers	15578 Shady Acres Dr, Wadena MN 56482	218-631-2909	R	2*	<.1
332	Kelco Inc—Steven Kellenaers	PO Box 1952, Farmington NM 87499	505-325-6372	R	2*	<.1
333	Backup Communications—Sandra Keeney	PO Box 99, Lake Villa IL 60046	847-356-8658	R	2*	<.1
334	Contemporary Personnel Staffing Inc—Laura Liechty	904 7th N St, Liverpool NY 13088	315-457-2500	R	2*	<.1
335	S Dulek Enterprises Inc—Tom Ducey	934 S Andreasen Dr Ste, Escondido CA 92029	760-735-9068	R	2*	<.1
336	Perris Valley Aviation Services Inc—Patrick Conatser	PO Box 1823, Perris CA 92572	951-657-3904	R	2*	<.1
337	Prostar Staffing Services Inc—Michael Williams	1185 Bordeaux Dr Ste D, Sunnyvale CA 94089	408-735-0180	R	2*	<.1
338	Bontempo Group Inc—Mary Bontempo	PO Box 595, Feasterville Trevose PA 19053	215-357-6590	R	2*	.1
339	Cavanaugh and Associates Inc—Mike Lane	8111 Lydn B Jhsn Fry 1, Dallas TX 75251		R	2*	<.1
340	Payplus Inc—Jay Ryan	8631 W Foothill Dr, Peoria AZ 85383	623-572-9245	R	2*	<.1
341	Fladger and Associates Inc—Michael Fladger	204 Stewards Ct, Bear DE 19701	302-836-3100	R	2*	<.1
342	Alternative Staffing Inc—Karen Howard	3001 Metro Dr Ste 480, Minneapolis MN 55425	952-888-6077	R	2*	<.1
343	Labor Remedy Inc—Demi Loeser	PO Box 8062, Toledo OH 43605	419-243-0200	R	2*	<.1
344	Toss Inc—Sharon Girod	1525 N Norma St Ste A, Ridgecrest CA 93555	760-446-8677	R	2*	.1
345	Cal-Temperature Services Inc—Jerry Palmer	2464 S Union Ave, Bakersfield CA 93307	661-397-4566	R	2*	<.1
346	Frontline Medical Associates Inc—Paul Turley	PO Box 261610, Encino CA 91426	818-408-2500	R	2*	<.1
347	Amp Residential Services LLC—William Ziff	2000 S Ocean Blvd, Lantana FL 33462	561-533-0805	R	1*	.1
348	Southwest Fab Inc—Breck Colquett	3913 75th St, Lubbock TX 79423	806-793-9826	R	1*	.1
349	Caring Hrts Homecare Southeast Mo LLC	PO Box 211, Dexter MO 63841	573-624-9100	R	1*	<.1
350	Professional Transcriptions Of Northwest Florida—Jeannette Nelson	1310 Dunmire St Ste B, Pensacola FL 32504	850-478-5969	R	1*	<.1
351	New York Brite Inc—Dorit Galante	175 5th Ave Ste 2353, New York NY 10010	212-473-9838	R	1*	<.1

Note: An asterisk (*) indicates an estimated financial figure. The company type code used is as follows: R = Private, P = Public, S = Private Subsidiary, B = Public Subsidiary, D = Division, J = Joint Venture, I = Investment Fund.

COMPANY RANKINGS BY SALES WITHIN 4-DIGIT SIC

Rank	Company Name—*Executive Officer*	Address, City, State, Zip	Phone	Type	Fin	Empls
352	Payroll Consulting Services Inc—*Andrew Beavais*	10124 Royce Dr, South Lyon MI 48178	248-390-6972	R	1*	<.1
353	Speed Industrial Service Of Texas LLC	11460 I 10 E, Baytown TX 77520	251-599-4230	R	1*	<.1
354	Os Employee Leasing Services Inc—*Ronald Heineman*	3235 Omni Dr, Cincinnati OH 45245	513-943-4243	R	1*	<.1
355	Stride Contractors Inc—*Maria Arellano*	7051 Sw 12th St, Miami FL 33144	305-994-9901	R	1*	<.1
356	Bret Robinson Inc—*Margaret Buchannon*	24837 Canal Rd, Orange Beach AL 36561	251-974-5647	R	1*	<.1
357	NAADM Inc—*Mark Nihan*	8 Gloria Way, Wilmington MA 01887	978-658-7850	R	1*	<.1
358	E Practical Solutions Inc—*Jim Mendenhall*	4000 W 106th St Ste 1, Carmel IN 46032	317-286-4000	R	1*	<.1
359	High Tech Resources Inc—*Marylee Robison*	6120 S Yale Ave Ste 10, Tulsa OK 74136	918-481-8822	R	1*	<.1
360	Resource Management Systems Inc—*Ronald Hamann*	6465 Grnwood Plz Blvd, Englewood CO 80111	303-488-2220	R	1*	<.1
361	American Green Cross Inc—*Fidel Ferreiro*	2500 Nw 79th Ave Ste 2, Doral FL 33122	305-470-0033	R	1*	<.1
362	Axiom Hr Solutions Inc—*Gerald Diddle*	8345 Lenexa Dr Ste 100, Shawnee Mission KS 66214	913-383-2999	R	1*	<.1
363	Holiday Statistics Inc—*Charles Efros*	535 5th Ave Fl 20, New York NY 10017	212-986-2541	R	1*	<.1
364	Add-A-Tech Inc—*Daisy McCann*	3139 S Wayne Rd, Wayne MI 48184	734-722-2722	R	1*	<.1
365	Datalis Solutions Corp—*Scott Peters*	136 Summit Ave Ste 103, Montvale NJ 07645	201-505-0833	R	1*	<.1
366	Barrettemps Inc—*Joseph Thielman*	100 N La Salle St Ste, Chicago IL 60602	312-443-8877	R	1*	<.1
367	Brookmeade Inc—*Michael Peterson*	1925 Vaughn Rd Nw Ste, Kennesaw GA 30144	770-590-9560	R	1*	<.1
368	Futurelink Consulting Inc—*Nagi Mysore*	210 Brighton Path, Peachtree City GA 30269	770-734-9797	R	1*	<.1
369	Guthrie Center Assembly LLC—*Frankie Railsback*	2221 215th St, Guthrie Center IA 50115	641-747-8710	R	1*	<.1
370	3d Medical Staffing LLC—*Susie Young*	4700 S 900 E Ste 13, Salt Lake City UT 84117	801-268-8822	R	1*	<.1
371	Greysmith Cos—*Cheryl Dewolf*	321 S Main St Ste 502, Providence RI 02903	401-272-7200	R	1*	<.1
372	Carlton Staffing	24 E Greenway Plz Ste, Houston TX 77046	713-629-0116	R	1*	<.1
373	SkillSource Staffing LLC—*Peter Green*	3510 Scotts Ln Ste 291, Philadelphia PA 19129	484-368-3065	R	1*	<.1
374	Diversified Personnel—*Vicki Unger*	505 14th St Ste 850, Oakland CA 94612	510-451-4175	R	1	<.1
375	Mental Health Assoc—*Nancy Kreisher*	4814 River Rd, Washington NC 27889	252-946-9538	R	1*	<.1
376	Facility Healthcare Services Inc—*Sheila Geesa*	736 S Poplar St, Denver CO 80224	303-424-9224	R	1*	<.1
377	Atrium Hr Boston LLC—*Jill Ikens*	143 Newbury St Fl 4, Boston MA 02116	617-447-2000	R	1*	<.1
378	FJM Of Louisianna Inc—*Fred Mancheski*	909 W Esplanade Ave St, Kenner LA 70065	504-464-1931	R	1*	<.1
379	Surgimed Inc—*John Hoffman*	1301 Dove St Ste 800, Newport Beach CA 92660	949-757-0250	R	1*	<.1
380	New Office Temps Ltd—*Chuck Smith*	105 W Madison St Ste 7, Chicago IL 60602	312-923-0054	R	1*	<.1
381	Storm Ridge South LLC—*Darren Swalberg*	9350 S 900 E, Marysvale UT 84750	435-326-4300	R	1*	<.1
382	Contract People Corp—*Terry Wallace*	PO Box 3112, Southfield MI 48037	248-304-9900	R	1*	<.1
383	Nightingale Services Inc—*Phillip Chung*	6220 Westpark Dr Ste 2, Houston TX 77057	713-780-0695	R	1*	<.1
384	Sharestaff Inc—*James Lott*	1660 S Albion St Ste 3, Denver CO 80222	303-300-1100	R	1*	.1
385	Unlimited Services Available—*Shaun Merrell*	PO Box 768, Owings Mills MD 21117	410-526-3520	R	1*	<.1
386	Selectleaders LLC	909 3rd Ave Fl 5, New York NY 10022	212-661-3232	R	1*	<.1
387	Rudy Salem Staffing Services—*Chris Ferry*	3205 S Meadow Ave, Sioux Falls SD 57106	605-221-0773	R	<1*	.1
388	Advance Personnel—*Sandra Quiggins*	3313 Free Zion Rd, Caneyville KY 42721	270-879-9260	R	<1*	<.1
389	Spotless Cleaning Co—*Ivan Almida*	PO Box 457, Natick MA 01760	508-650-5305	R	<1*	<.1

TOTALS: SIC 7363 Help Supply Services
Companies: 389

					91,039	1,350.6

7371 Computer Programming Services

Rank	Company Name—*Executive Officer*	Address, City, State, Zip	Phone	Type	Fin	Empls
1	Keane Inc Healthcare Solutions Div	100 City Sq, Boston MA 02129		D	4,949*	10.0
2	Cognizant Technology Solutions Corp—*Francisco D'Souza*	500 Frank W Burr Blvd, Teaneck NJ 07666	201-801-0233	P	4,592	104.0
3	Leadstream—*Chris Scotton*	8150 Leesburg Pike Ste, Vienna VA 22182		S	4,078*	9.0
4	CACI Technologies Inc—*Paul Cofoni*	1100 N Glebe Rd, Arlington VA 22201	703-841-7800	S	4,017*	5.0
5	NetVersant Solutions Inc—*Scott L Fordham*	777 Post Oak Ste 400, Houston TX 77056	713-403-3800	R	2,728*	2.8
6	GTECH Corp—*Jaymin B Patel*	10 Memorial Blvd, Providence RI 02903	401-392-1000	S	2,259*	7.7
7	Citrix—*Mark B Templeton*	851 W Cypress Creek Rd, Fort Lauderdale FL 33309	954-267-3000	R	2,107*	4.6
8	IFS North America Inc—*Cindy Jaudon*	300 Park Blvd Ste 555, Itasca IL 60143		S	1,589*	3.4
9	EarthLink Inc—*Rolla P Huff*	1375 Peachtree St, Atlanta GA 30309	404-815-0770	P	1,216	3.2
10	Medcomsoft—*Robert G Wilson III*	378 Industrial Park Rd, Ebensburg PA 15931		R	1,122	N/A
11	Siemens PLM Software—*Tony Affuso*	5800 Granite Pky Ste 6, Plano TX 75024	972-987-3000	R	1,115*	7.2
12	CIBER Inc—*David Peterschmidt*	6363 S Fiddler's Green, Greenwood Village CO 80111	303-220-0100	P	1,071	7.5
13	SpectraCom Inc (Milwaukee Wisconsin)—*Jorian Clarke*	131 W Seeboth St, Milwaukee WI 53204	414-272-7742	R	998*	<.1
14	Epam Systems Inc—*Arkadiv Dobkin*	41 University Dr Rm 20, Newtown PA 18940	267-759-9000	R	903*	2.5
15	Aspect Software Inc—*Jim Foy*	300 Apollo Dr, Chelmsford MA 01824		R	833*	1.7
16	Commercial Legal Software Inc—*Steven H Goldman*	170 Changebridge Rd St, Montville NJ 07045	973-575-5646	R	701*	<.1
17	CT Corp	3 Winners Cir 3rd Fl, Albany NY 12205	855-316-8944	S	691*	1.5
18	VeriSign Inc—*Mark McLaughlin*	487 E Middlefield Rd, Mountain View CA 94043	650-961-7500	P	681	1.0
19	TYBRIN Corp—*Bill A Pennington*	1030 Titan Ct, Fort Walton Beach FL 32547	850-337-2500	R	678*	1.5
20	Syntel Inc—*Prashant Ranade*	525 E Big Beaver 3rd F, Troy MI 48083	248-619-2800	P	642	13.8
21	ITG Software Inc	400 Corporate Pt Ste 6, Culver City CA 90230		S	599*	1.3
22	Storage Inc—*Simon S Lee*	11710 Plz America Dr S, Reston VA 20190	703-691-2480	R	591*	1.2
23	Stratus Technologies Inc—*David J Laurello*	111 Powdermill Rd, Maynard MA 01754	978-461-7000	R	569*	2.3
24	Zinc Software Inc Wind River Systems Inc	500 Wind River Way, Alameda CA 94501	510-748-4100	S	462*	1.0
25	Covansys Corp—*Ravindran Ganapathy*	32605 W 12 Mile Rd Ste, Farmington Hills MI 48334	248-488-2068	S	456	8.4
26	Southwest Research Institute—*Dan Bates*	PO Drawer 28510, San Antonio TX 78228	210-684-5111	R	455*	3.0
27	Technosoft Corp—*Rajiv Tandon*	28411 Northwestern Hwy, Southfield MI 48034	248-603-2600	R	450*	<.1
28	Computer Task Group Inc—*James R Boldt*	800 Delaware Ave, Buffalo NY 14209	716-882-8000	P	396	3.7
29	Attachmate Corp—*Bob Flynn*	1500 Dexter Ave N, Seattle WA 98109	206-217-7100	R	396*	.8
30	Software AG USA Inc—*Karl H Streibich*	11700 Plaza America Dr, Reston VA 20190	703-860-5050	S	371*	.8
31	Wyle Information System Group—*Rodney P Hunt*	1000 Wilson Dr, McLean VA 22102	703-734-7800	S	363*	1.8
32	Wind River Systems Inc—*Ken Klein*	500 Wind River Way, Alameda CA 94501	510-748-4100	R	344*	1.6
33	DigitalNet Holdings Inc—*William Shernit*	2525 Network Pl, Herndon VA 20171	703-563-7500	S	336*	1.7
34	RealNetworks Inc—*Mike Lunsford*	PO Box 91123, Seattle WA 98111	206-674-2700	P	336	1.2
35	Advent Software Inc—*Stephanie DiMarco*	600 Townsend St 5th Fl, San Francisco CA 94103	415-543-7696	P	326	1.2
36	PlumChoice Inc—*Ted Werth*	5 Federal St, Billerica MA 01821		R	321*	.7
37	Harris Information Technology Services—*Howard L Lance*	21000 Atlantic Blvd St, Dulles VA 20166	703-483-8000	S	312*	.7
38	Dassault Systemes Simulia Corp—*Mark Goldstein*	166 Valley St Bldg 3, Providence RI 02909	401-276-4400	R	311*	.2
39	R Systems Inc—*Rekhi Singh*	5000 Windplay Dr, El Dorado Hills CA 95762		R	310*	2.7
40	NAL Worldwide Inc—*Doug Witt*	1200 N Greenbriar Dr, Addison IL 60101	630-261-3100	R	288*	.6
41	EPIQ Systems Inc—*Tom W Olofson*	501 Kansas Ave, Kansas City KS 66105	913-621-9500	P	283	1.0
42	Yellow Roadway Technologies Inc—*William D Zollars*	PO Box 7270, Shawnee Mission KS 66207	913-344-3000	S	283*	.3
43	iGate Corp—*Phaneesh Murthy*	2000 Cliff Mine Rd Ste, Pittsburgh PA 15275	412-490-9620	P	281	8.3
44	DELTEK Inc—*Namita Dhailian*	13880 Dulles Corner Ln, Herndon VA 20171	703-734-8606	P	280	1.6
45	Fiserv	600 Colonial Center Pk, Lake Mary FL 32746	407-513-5200	R	275*	.6
46	Data Domain Inc (Santa Clara California)—*Frank Slootman*	2421 Mission College B, Santa Clara CA 95054	408-980-4800	S	274	.8
47	Artech Information Systems LLC—*Alexis Adubato*	240 Cedar Knolls Rd St, Cedar Knolls NJ 07927	973-998-2500	R	270*	4.0

Rank	Company Name—*Executive Officer*	Address, City, State, Zip	Phone	Type	Fin	Empls
48	Valocity LLC	222 Little Canada Rd, St Paul MN 55117	612-235-5600	R	262*	.5
49	Sorenson Media Inc—*Pat Nola*	4192 S Riverboat Rd, Salt Lake City UT 84123	801-287-9400	R	247*	.5
50	Mission Solutions Engineering LLC—*Tim Caswell*	1550 Crystal Dr Ste 50, Arlington VA 22202	856-252-2000	R	239*	.5
51	Wind River Sales Company Inc Wind River Systems Inc	500 Wind River Way, Alameda CA 94501	510-748-4100	S	236*	1.1
52	Wind River Services Inc Wind River Systems Inc	500 Wind River Way, Alameda CA 94501	510-748-4100	S	236	1.1
53	QSS Group Inc—*Frank Islam*	4500 Forbes Blvd Ste 2, Lanham MD 20706		S	235*	1.2
54	Exact Software North America Inc—*Mitchell Alcon*	35 Village Rd, Middleton MA 01949	978-560-6900	R	231*	2.4
55	TechniSource Inc—*Michael Winwood*	2050 Spectrum Blvd, Fort Lauderdale FL 33309	954-308-7600	R	229*	2.0
56	Virtusa Corp—*Kris Canekeratne*	2000 W Park Dr, Westborough MA 01581	508-389-7300	P	218	5.1
57	General Data Company Inc—*Peter Wenzel*	4354 Ferguson Dr, Cincinnati OH 45245	513-752-7978	R	216*	.9
58	Perficient Inc—*Jeffrey S Davis*	520 Maryville Centre D, St Louis MO 63141	314-529-3600	P	215	1.1
59	Aspen Technology Inc—*Mark E Fusco*	200 Wheeler Rd, Burlington MA 01803	781-221-6400	P	198	1.3
60	Huawei Technologies USA—*Zhengfei Ren*	1700 Alma Ste 500, Plano TX 75075	972-509-5599	S	194*	.4
61	PSI International Inc—*Nazim Dhanani*	4000 Legato Rd Ste 850, Fairfax VA 22033	703-621-5825	R	194*	.2
62	Applied Underwriters Inc—*Sidney R Ferenc*	PO Box 281900, San Francisco CA 94128		R	192*	.4
63	Technology Integration Group Inc—*Bruce Geier*	7810 Trade St, San Diego CA 92121	858-566-1900	R	191*	.4
64	Overwatch Systems Ltd—*Randy Averitte*	PO Box 91269, Austin TX 78709	512-358-2600	S	185*	.4
65	Provider HealthNet Services Inc—*Richard Garnick*	5400 LBJ Fwy Ste 200, Dallas TX 75240	214-257-7000	R	180*	1.5
66	Symphony Service Corp—*Sanjay Dhawan*	2475 Hanover St, Palo Alto CA 94304	650-935-9500	R	180*	3.0
67	Iris Software Inc—*Sanjiv Khanna*	200 Metroplex Dr Ste 3, Edison NJ 08817	732-393-0034	R	176*	.5
68	Marlabs Inc—*Siby Vadakekkara*	1 Corporate Pl S, Piscataway NJ 08854	732-694-1000	R	172*	1.8
69	Yardi Systems Inc—*Anant Yardi*	430 S Fairview Ave, Santa Barbara CA 93117	805-699-2040	R	170*	1.8
70	Care Management International Inc—*Minalkumar Patel*	50 Harrison St Ste 119, Hoboken NJ 07030	201-420-6686	R	168*	.4
71	KRA Corp—*Knowlton R Atterbeary*	8757 Georgia Ave Ste 1, Silver Spring MD 20910	301-562-2300	R	161*	.4
72	InDyne Inc—*C Donald Bishop*	11800 Sunrise Valley D, Reston VA 20191	703-903-6900	R	160	1.9
73	Computer Programs and Systems Inc—*J Boyd Douglas*	6600 Wall St, Mobile AL 36695		P	153	1.2
74	QuadraMed Corp—*Duncan W James*	12110 Sunset Hills Rd, Reston VA 20190	703-709-2300	P	150	.6
75	Global Market Insite Inc—*Michael A Brochu*	1100 112th Ave NE Ste, Bellevue WA 98004	206-315-9300	R	148*	.3
76	SmartForce Ireland Ltd—*Chuck Moran*	107 Northeastern Blvd, Nashua NH 03062	603-324-3000	D	147*	.5
77	Isaac Fair Corp—*Chris Anderson*	3550 Engineering Dr St, Norcross GA 30092	770-810-8000	R	145*	3.0
78	SummitWorks Technologies Inc—*Sanjay Shahani*	50 Cragwood Rd Ste 106, South Plainfield NJ 07080	732-548-9300	R	143*	.3
79	Eclinicalworks LLC—*Pamela Hanner*	2 Technology Dr, Westborough MA 01581		R	140*	.8
80	GX Technology Corp—*Robert P Peebler*	2105 CityWest Blvd Ste, Houston TX 77042	713-789-7250	S	136*	.3
81	Napster Inc—*Christopher Allen*	9044 Melrose Ave, Los Angeles CA 90069	310-281-5000	S	130*	.1
82	ITA Software Inc—*Jeremy Wertheimer*	141 Portland St 7th Fl, Cambridge MA 02139	617-714-2100	R	127*	.3
83	21st Century Systems Inc—*Jeffrey Hicks*	2611 Jefferson Davis H, Arlington VA 22202	703-418-9333	R	127*	.2
84	Silverpop Systems Inc—*Bill Nussey*	200 Galleria Pkwy Ste, Atlanta GA 30339	678-247-0500	R	126*	.3
85	Core Education And Consulting Solutions Inc—*Shekhar Iyer*	3 Ravinia Dr Ste 1900, Atlanta GA 30346	678-578-7711	R	126*	.4
86	Vangent Inc—*Allen Shay*	4250 N Fairfax Dr Ste, Arlington VA 22203	703-526-7000	S	122*	.3
87	MTCSC Inc—*David Camarata*	678 Third Ave Ste 305, Chula Vista CA 91910	619-585-2100	S	120*	.3
88	Infragistics Corp—*Dean Guida*	2 Commerce Dr, Cranbury NJ 08512	609-448-2000	R	120*	.2
89	Eze Castle Integration—*John Cahaly*	200 Franklin St 12th F, Boston MA 02110	617-217-3000	R	118*	.3
90	Inforeliance Corp—*William Williams*	4050 Legato Rd Ste 700, Fairfax VA 22033	703-246-9360	R	114*	.3
91	Strategic Staffing Solutions LLC—*Cynthia Pasky*	645 Griswold St Ste290, Detroit MI 48226		R	113*	1.7
92	Blast Radius—*Gurval Caer*	594 Broadway Ste 206, New York NY 10012	212-925-4900	R	110*	.2
93	Sapient Securities Corp—*Alan Herrick*	131 Dartmouth St 3rd F, Boston MA 02116	617-621-0200	S	110*	.2
94	eClinicalWorks—*Girish Kumar Navani*	112 Turnpike Rd Westbo, Westborough MA 01581	508-836-2700	R	109*	.8
95	Lansa Inc—*Peter Draney*	3010 Highland Pkwy Ste, Downers Grove IL 60515	630-874-7000	R	108*	.2
96	Analysts International Corp—*Brittany McKinney*	7700 France Ave S Ste, Minneapolis MN 55435	952-835-5900	P	107	.9
97	Tangoe Inc—*Al Subbloie*	35 Executive Blvd, Orange CT 06477	203-859-9300	P	105*	.4
98	Synova Inc—*Raj Vattikutl*	1000 Town Ctr Ste 700, Southfield MI 48075	248-281-2500	R	103*	1.8
99	Opsware Inc	3000 Hanover St, Palo Alto CA 94304	650-857-1501	S	102	.5
100	Actimize Inc—*Amir Orad*	1359 Broadway Fl 5, New York NY 10018	212-643-4600	R	100*	.4
101	Bowne Management Systems Inc—*George L Fagan*	PO Box 109, Mineola NY 11501	516-746-2350	S	100*	.1
102	Entrust Inc—*F William Conner*	5400 LBJ Fwy Ste 1340, Dallas TX 75240	972-728-0447	R	100	.4
103	InfoTech Inc—*James T McClave*	5700 SW 34th St Ste 12, Gainesville FL 32608	352-381-4400	R	99*	.2
104	Beiswenger Hoch and Associates Inc—*Francisco A Norona*	510 Shotgun Rd Ste 400, Sunrise FL 33326	954-334-9000	R	99*	.1
105	Pragmatics Inc—*Long Nguyen*	7926 Jones Branch Dr S, McLean VA 22102	703-761-4033	R	97*	.2
106	Actional Corp—*Joseph Alsop*	800 W El Camino Real S, Mountain View CA 94040		S	97*	.1
107	Datacenterinccom—*John Jones*	20 W 2nd Ste 300, Hutchinson KS 67501	620-694-6800	R	96*	.2
108	InterSystems Corp—*Phillip T (Terry) Ragon*	One Memorial Dr, Cambridge MA 02142		R	96*	.2
109	Acronis Inc—*Jason Donahue*	23 3rd Ave, Burlington MA 01803	781-222-0920	R	96*	.1
110	Fujitsu America Inc—*Hiroshi Haruki*	1250 E Arques Ave, Sunnyvale CA 94085	408-746-6200	S	95*	3.0
111	Enterpulse Inc—*Jerry Eickhoff*	125 Clairemont Ave, Decatur GA 30030	404-377-1489	R	95*	.1
112	Quality Business Solutions Inc—*Martin Buekhof*	12701 Whitewater Dr St, Minnetonka MN 55343	952-564-3088	R	93*	<.1
113	Professional Software Engineering Inc—*Paul K Wong*	780 Lynnhaven Pky Ste, Virginia Beach VA 23452	757-431-2400	R	92*	.2
114	Web Spiders Inc—*Siddharth Jhunjhunwala*	1 Valley View Rd, Wayland MA 01778		S	92*	.2
115	3-i Infotech Inc—*Kathleen Hamburger*	450 Rariton Center Pky, Edison NJ 08837	732-225-4242	R	91*	.2
116	NDS Americas Inc—*Jesper Knuttson*	3500 Hyland Ave, Costa Mesa CA 92626	714-434-2100	S	91*	.2
117	Nemetschek North America Inc—*Sean Flaherty*	7150 Riverwood Dr, Columbia MD 21046	410-290-5114	R	91*	.1
118	Neat Co—*Jim Foster*	3401 Market St Ste 120, Philadelphia PA 19104	215-382-3300	R	90*	1.6
119	Healthcare Management Systems Inc—*Tom Stephenson*	3102 W End Ave Ste 400, Nashville TN 37203	615-383-7300	R	90*	.4
120	Daugherty Systems—*Ron Daugherty*	3 CityPlace Dr Ste 400, Saint Louis MO 63141	314-432-8200	R	89*	.5
121	YASH Technologies Inc—*Manoj Baheti*	605 17th Ave, East Moline IL 61244	309-755-0433	R	87*	.2
122	FGM Inc—*Scott Gessay*	12021 Sunset Hills Rd, Reston VA 20190	703-885-1000	R	86*	.2
123	Sage Accpac—*David M Hood*	6700 Koll Center Pkwy, Pleasanton CA 94566	925-461-2625	S	85	.6
124	Ticket Software LLC—*Donald Vaccaro*	137 Bolton Rd, Vernon CT 06066	860-870-3400	R	84	.2
125	Ames Safety Envelope Co—*Kirk Ramsauer*	PO Box 120, Somerville MA 02143	617-684-1000	R	82*	.2
126	Potomac Management Group Inc—*Dennis Garcia*	510 King St Ste 200, Alexandria VA 22314	703-836-1037	R	82*	.2
127	Quorum Business Solutions Inc—*Paul Weidman*	3010 Briarpark Dr Ste, Houston TX 77042	713-430-8600	R	81*	.3
128	Agentrics LLC—*Wellington Machado*	625 N Washington St, Alexandria VA 22314	703-234-5100	R	81*	.2
129	Netsmart New York Inc—*Jerry Koop*	3500 Sunrise Hwy, Great River NY 11739	631-968-2011	R	80*	.3
130	Mindshift Technologies Inc—*Paul W Chisholm*	309 Waverley Oaks Rd S, Waltham MA 02452	617-243-2700	R	78*	.2
131	Blue Atlas Interactive LLC	12 S Summit Ave Ste 31, Gaithersburg MD 20877	301-540-5950	R	76*	.2
132	System Automation Corp *Charles Rubin*	7110 Samuel Morse Dr F, Columbia MD 21046	301-837-8000	R	76*	.1
133	Labware Holdings Inc—*Vance Kershner*	3 Mill Rd Ste 102, Wilmington DE 19806	302-658-8444	R	75*	.2
134	Atex Media Solutions Inc—*Scott Roessler*	5 Burlington Woods Ste, Burlington MA 01803	781-685-3240	R	75*	.5
135	Haestad Methods Inc—*John Haestad*	37 Brookside Rd, Waterbury CT 06708	203-755-1666	S	75*	.5

Note: An asterisk (*) indicates an estimated financial figure. The company type code used is as follows: R = Private, P = Public, S = Private Subsidiary, B = Public Subsidiary, D = Division, J = Joint Venture, I = Investment Fund.

COMPANY RANKINGS BY SALES WITHIN 4-DIGIT SIC

Rank	Company Name—Executive Officer	Address, City, State, Zip	Phone	Type	Fin	Empls
136	Thomas Technology Solutions Inc—Darryl J Fisher	1 Progress Dr, Horsham PA 19044	215-682-5000	S	75*	.3
137	Nimsoft—Gary Read	1919 S Bascom Ave Ste, Campbell CA 95008	408-796-3400	R	75*	.2
138	Bluewolf Inc—Eric Berridge	11 E 26th St 21st Fl, New York NY 10010	646-336-6400	R	72*	.2
139	Pro Unlimited Inc—Andrew Schultz	301 Yamato Rd Ste 3199, Boca Raton FL 33431		R	72*	.2
140	i365—Phil Gilmour	6121 Hollis St, Emeryville CA 94608	925-944-2422	S	71*	.2
141	Tape to Film—William Fitzgerald	2820 W Olive Ave, Burbank CA 91505	818-840-7141	R	71*	.1
142	DivX Inc—Kevin Hell	4780 Eastgate Mall, San Diego CA 92121	858-882-0600	S	71	.3
143	Agnity Inc—Sanjeev Chawla	42808 Christy St Ste 2, Fremont CA 94538	510-270-2669	R	70*	.2
144	Database Solutions Inc (Cherry Hill New Jersey)—George Brown	555 Croton Rd Ste 201, King of Prussia PA 19406		R	70*	.1
145	Pratham Software Inc—Puneet Mittal	21860 Via Regina, Saratoga CA 95070	408-877-2424	S	69*	.2
146	Primus Software Corp—Veena Kalale	3061 Peachtree Industr, Duluth GA 30097	770-300-0004	R	69*	.2
147	Syscom Inc (Baltimore Maryland)—Theodore F Bayer	400 E Pratt St Ste 200, Baltimore MD 21202	410-539-3737	R	69*	.2
148	Avista Inc—R Brad Lawrence	PO Box 636, Platteville WI 53818	608-348-8815	S	68*	.2
149	SightLine Systems Corp—Brandon Witte	11130 Fairfax Blvd Ste, Fairfax VA 22030	703-563-3000	R	68*	.2
150	Bindview Corp	5151 San Felipe Ste 24, Houston TX 77056	713-561-4000	S	68	N/A
151	XYEnterprise Inc—Kevin Duffy	101 Edgewater Dr, Wakefield MA 01880	781-756-4400	R	66*	.1
152	AppaNeta—Jack Sweeney	110 Cedar St, Wellesley Hills MA 02481	604-433-2333	R	64*	.1
153	Service-Nowçom Inc—Frank Slootman	2225 El Camino Real St, San Diego CA 92130	858-720-0477	R	62	.3
154	EMS Consulting—Elaine Myrbach	5550 W Executive Dr ST, Tampa FL 33609	813-287-2486	R	62*	.1
155	Systems Group Inc (Galstonbury Connecticut)—Charles A Abadie	100 Western Blvd, Glastonbury CT 06033	860-633-0359	S	62*	.1
156	PDF Solutions Inc—John K Kibarian	333 W San Carlos St St, San Jose CA 95110	408-280-7900	P	62	.3
157	Ortec International USA Inc—Corne Aantjes	3630 Peachtree Rd Ne, Atlanta GA 30326	404-736-9800	R	60*	.6
158	BackOffice Associates LLC—David Booth	PO Box 808, South Harwich MA 02661	508-430-7100	R	60*	.4
159	AdvizeX Technologies LLC—Alfred Traversi	6480 Rockside Woods Bl, Independence OH 44131	216-901-1818	R	60*	.1
160	Symitar Systems Inc—Kathy Burress	8985 Balboa Ave, San Diego CA 92123	619-542-6700	S	59*	.5
161	Prime Technology Group Inc—Sudhakar Goverdhanam	1006 West Ninth Ave St, King of Prussia PA 19406	610-205-8740	R	58*	.3
162	Resolute Solutions Corp—Michael Fawcett	10900 NE 4th St Ste 21, Bellevue WA 98004	425-467-9191	R	58*	.1
163	Bancvue Ltd—Gabriel Krajicek	4516 Seton Ctr Pky Ste, Austin TX 78759		R	57	.3
164	Pro-Telligent LLC—Bobbie Boykin	1225 S Clark St Ste 14, Arlington VA 22202	703-414-5520	S	57*	.5
165	FAAC Inc—Dean Krutty	1229 Oak Valley Dr, Ann Arbor MI 48108	734-761-5836	S	57*	.1
166	Solutionary Inc—Steve Idelman	9420 Underwood Ave 3rd, Omaha NE 68114	402-361-3000	R	56*	.1
167	NetReach Inc—William Bast	124 S Maple St 2nd FL, Ambler PA 19002	215-283-2300	R	56*	.1
168	Radiance Technologies Inc—George M Clark	350 Wynn Dr, Huntsville AL 35805	256-704-3400	R	55*	.3
169	Systems Group Inc—Sidney Sakamaki	50 So Beretania St Ste, Honolulu HI 96813	808-526-1551	R	55*	<.1
170	Organic Inc—Jonathan Nelson	555 Market St 4th Fl, San Francisco CA 94105	415-581-5300	S	54*	.4
171	Vitec Solutions—Tom Alfonso	455 Commerce Dr Ste 3, Amherst NY 14228	716-204-9200	S	54*	.1
172	Teklinks Inc—Stuart Raburn	201 Summit Pkwy, Birmingham AL 35209	205-314-6600	R	54*	.1
173	Vovici Corp—Greg Stock	196 Van Buren St Ste 4, Herndon VA 20170	703-481-9326	S	52*	.1
174	Trigyn Technologies Inc—Homiyar Panday	100 Metroplex Dr Ste 1, Edison NJ 08817	732-777-0050	R	51*	.8
175	Laird Telemedia—Mark S Braunstein	PO Box 720, Mount Marion NY 12456	845-339-9555	R	51*	.1
176	Thomson Professional and Regulatory Inc—John Baron	7322 Newman Blvd, Dexter MI 48130	734-426-5860	R	50*	.9
177	ERT Inc—Jingli Lang	6100 Frost Pl Ste A, Laurel MD 20707	240-554-0161	R	50*	.3
178	Synthetic Aperture—Robert Currier	31351 Rancho Viejo Rd, San Juan Capistrano CA 92675	949-493-3444	R	50*	.1
179	Communications and Power Engineering Inc—Andy Trayler	1040 Flynn Rd, Camarillo CA 93012	805-389-7414	R	50*	.1
180	DataSource Inc—Pamela Hopkins	8200 Greensboro Dr Ste, McLean VA 22102	703-748-7180	R	49*	.1
181	Maden Tech Consulting Inc—Omar Maden	2110 Washington Blvd S, Arlington VA 22204	703-769-4440	R	49*	.1
182	Unicast Communications Corp—Adam Moore	200 W Cesar Chavez Ste, Austin TX 78701	512-469-5900	S	49*	.1
183	VSoft Corp—Murthy Veeraghanta	6455 E Johns Crossing, Duluth GA 30097	770-840-0097	R	49*	.1
184	Henggeler Computer Consultants Inc—Richard Henggeler	6760 Alexander Bell Dr, Columbia MD 21046	301-317-8995	R	48*	.1
185	Computer Generated Solutions Inc—Phil Friedman	200 Vesey St 27th Fl 3, New York NY 10281	212-408-3800	R	48*	1.5
186	Clear Technology Inc—Randall Jacops	10955 Westmoor Dr Fl 4, Broomfield CO 80021	303-500-8030	R	48*	.1
187	E5 Systems Inc—Ric Stroup	22375 Broderick Dr Ste, Sterling VA 20166	703-674-5060	R	48*	.1
188	HOPS International Inc—Simeon Kohl	15105 NW 77th Ave, Miami Lakes FL 33014	305-827-8600	R	48*	.1
189	Mortgage Cadence Inc—Michael Detwiler	999 18th St Ste 2300, Denver CO 80202	303-991-8200	S	48*	.1
190	Pipeline Software Inc—Charlie Sundling	2850 Red Hill Ave, Santa Ana CA 92705	949-296-8375	R	48*	.1
191	Vidsys Inc—Chuck Teubner	8219 Leesburg Pke Ste, Vienna VA 22182	703-883-3730	R	48*	.1
192	cyberThink Inc—Ravinder S Thind	1125 US Hwy 22 Ste 1, Bridgewater NJ 08807	908-429-8008	R	47*	.1
193	Portellus Inc—John N Le	2010 Main St Ste 450, Irvine CA 92614	949-250-9600	R	47*	.1
194	Dextrys—Brian Kene	201 Edgewater Dr, Wakefield MA 01880	781-246-8234	R	46*	.1
195	Dynaxys LLC—Lisa Miller	11911 Tech Rd, Silver Spring MD 20904	301-622-0950	R	46*	.1
196	eBizAutos—Parker Dunn	5584 S Fort Apache Rd, Las Vegas NV 89148		R	46*	.1
197	Intersoft Inc—Rahul Reddy	15110 SW Boones Ferry, Lake Oswego OR 97035	503-675-6700	R	46*	.1
198	Rocket Software Inc—Donald P Addington	3340 Peachtree Rd NE S, Atlanta GA 30326	404-760-1560	R	46*	.1
199	Speech Design International Inc—Jonathan Guss	50 Spring St, Ramsey NJ 07446	201-934-8500	S	46*	.1
200	Thor USA—Jonathan Guss	50 Spring St, Ramsey NJ 07446	201-934-8500	S	46*	.1
201	Palo Alto Networks Inc—Lane Bess	232 E Java Dr, Sunnyvale CA 94089	408-738-7700	R	45*	.2
202	Sensor Technologies Inc—Michael Gualario	200 Schultz Dr Ste 6, Red Bank NJ 07701	732-936-9600	S	45*	.1
203	Beatnik Inc—Don Millers	60 E 3rd Ave Ste 302, San Mateo CA 94401	650-295-2300	R	45*	.1
204	Covario Inc—Russ Mann	3611 Valley Centre Dr, San Diego CA 92130	858-397-1500	R	45*	.1
205	July Systems Inc—Kelvin Rowlette	2029 Century Park E St, Los Angeles CA 90067		R	44*	.1
206	Interface and Control Systems Inc—Jay Offutt	122 Fourth Ave, Indialantic FL 32903	321-723-0399	R	42*	<.1
207	Mirror Image Internet Inc—Gustov Vik	2 Highwood Dr, Tewksbury MA 01876	781-376-1100	S	41*	.1
208	Systalex Corp—Weipo Liao	555 Quince Orchard Rd, Gaithersburg MD 20878	301-251-8889	R	41*	.1
209	Teledata Technology Solutions Inc—David Price	1255 Treat Blvd Ste 14, Walnut Creek CA 94597	925-952-6500	R	40*	.3
210	Logix Development Corp—D Keith Howington	473 Post St, Camarillo CA 93010	805-384-1460	R	40*	.1
211	Mitsubishi Electric Research Laboratories—Richard C Waters	Cambridge Research Ctr, Cambridge MA 02139	617-621-7500	R	40*	.1
212	Time Sharing Resources Inc (Hauppauge New York)—Joseph F Hughes	400 Oser Ave Ste 150, Hauppauge NY 11788	631-231-0333	P	39	.2
213	Auxis Inc—Raul Vega	7901 SW 6th Ct Ste 130, Plantation FL 33324	954-236-6682	R	39*	.1
214	Data Access Corp—Charles Casanave	14000 SW 119 Ave, Miami FL 33186	305-238-0012	R	39*	.1
215	Enerjy Software—Nigel Cheshire	900 Cummings Ctr Ste 3, Beverly MA 01915		S	39*	.1
216	Amtex Systems Inc—Sainath Pokala	50 Broad St Ste 801, New York NY 10004	212-269-6448	R	38*	.4
217	Integrated Mobile Inc—Alan Morse	8889 Commerce Loop Dr, Columbus OH 43240	614-839-9922	R	38*	.1
218	Medical Present Value Inc—Tom Stampiglia	5000 Plaza on the Lake, Austin TX 78746	512-795-0015	R	38*	.1
219	Evolving Systems Inc—Thad Dupper	9777 Pyramid Ct Ste 10, Englewood CO 80112	303-802-1000	P	37	.2
220	GHR Systems Inc—Allan J Redstone	640 Lee Rd, Wayne PA 19087	610-540-0011	R	37*	.2
221	AnviCom Inc—Quan Hoang	1934 Old Gallows Rd St, Vienna VA 22182	703-970-7300	R	37*	.2
222	Configuration Solutions Inc—Dale Colosky	4280 Commercial Ave St, Portage MI 49002	269-329-2500	R	37*	.1

Rank	Company Name—*Executive Officer*	Address, City, State, Zip	Phone	Type	Fin	Empls
223	Kanoodlecom Inc	2390 N Forest Rd Ste 1, Getzville NY 14068	716-817-5000	R	37*	.1
224	ISI Telemanagement Systems—*Irwin Friedman*	1051 Perimeter Dr Ste, Schaumburg IL 60173	847-995-0002	R	36*	.2
225	Skyscape Inc—*Sandeep Shah*	293 Boston Post Rd W S, Marlborough MA 01752	508-460-6500	S	36*	.1
226	Beyondcom Inc—*Richard P Milgram*	1060 1st Ave Ste 100, King of Prussia PA 19406	610-878-2800	R	36*	.1
227	Earnest and Associates Inc—*Rob Mills*	808 Landmark Dr Ste 11, Glen Burnie MD 21061		R	36*	.1
228	Powersports Network Inc—*Kevin Brandenberg*	N56 W 24660 N Corporat, Sussex WI 53089	262-246-7900	R	36*	.1
229	Paradigm Holdings Inc—*Peter B LaMontagne*	9715 Key West Ave 3rd, Rockville MD 20850	301-468-1200	S	35	.2
230	Trandes Corp—*Doug Halo*	4601 Presidents Dr Ste, Lanham MD 20706	301-459-0200	R	34*	.3
231	ISH Industries Inc—*Jeffrey J Uliano*	30 Two Bridges Rd Ste, Fairfield NJ 07004	973-669-1756	R	34*	.2
232	Protech Solutions Inc—*Satish Garimalla*	303 W Capitol Ave Ste, Little Rock AR 72201	501-687-2400	R	34*	.1
233	Automated Media Inc—*Mark Gentile*	12171 Beech Daly Rd, Redford MI 48239	313-937-5000	R	34*	.1
234	TeleSynthesis Inc—*David Taylor*	PO Box 1223, Castle Rock CO 80104	303-814-0825	R	34*	.1
235	Systems Made Simple Inc—*Ron Fishbeck*	149 Northern Concourse, Syracuse NY 13212	315-455-3200	R	34*	.1
236	Rescot Systems Group Inc	1 Neshaminy Interplex, Trevose PA 19053	215-638-8000	R	34*	<.1
237	Skywire Software—*Patrick Brandt*	2401 Internet Blvd Ste, Frisco TX 75034	972-377-1110	S	33	.5
238	Zix Corp—*Richard D Spurr*	2711 N Haskell Ave Ste, Dallas TX 75204	214-370-2000	P	33	.1
239	Cittio Inc—*Jamie Lerner*	667 Mission St 4th Fl, San Francisco CA 94105	415-896-2519	R	33*	.1
240	True Commerce Inc—*Nicholas W Manolis*	800 Cranberry Woods Dr, Cranberry Twp PA 16066		R	33*	.1
241	Integrated Software Specialists Inc—*Michael Locascio*	1901 N Roselle Rd Ste, Schaumburg IL 60195	847-240-5070	R	33*	<.1
242	Maricom Systems Inc—*Maria Beckett*	PO Box 47399, Baltimore MD 21244	410-298-2770	R	32*	.2
243	DefenseWeb Technologies Inc—*Robert Nascenzi*	10182 Telesis Ct, San Diego CA 92121	858-272-8505	R	32*	.1
244	Profit Technologies Corp—*Patrick Fox*	PO Box 4479, Davidson NC 28036	704-896-5230	R	32*	.1
245	Dahl Consulting Inc—*Kenneth Olsen*	418 County Rd D E, Saint Paul MN 55117	651-772-9225	R	31*	.6
246	Acorn Energy Inc—*John A Moore*	PO Box 9, Montchanin DE 19710	302-656-1707	P	31	.2
247	Arcadian Networks Inc—*Ed Solar*	400 Columbus Ave Ste 2, Valhalla NY 10595	914-579-6300	R	31*	.1
248	Broadspire Inc—*Steven Huot*	617 W 7th St Ste 601, Los Angeles CA 90017	213-986-1050	R	31*	.1
249	Medallia Inc—*Borge Hald*	395 Page Mill Rd Ste 1, Palo Alto CA 94306	650-321-3000	R	31*	.1
250	Amdex Corp—*Devinder Singh*	8403 Colesville Rd Ste, Silver Spring MD 20910	301-588-4000	R	30*	.2
251	Compugain Corp—*Debasish Hota*	13241 Woodland Pk Rd S, Herndon VA 20171	703-956-7500	R	30*	.3
252	IEX Corp—*Debbie May*	2425 N Central Expy, Richardson TX 75080	972-301-1300	S	30*	.3
253	Integris (Billerica Massachusetts)—*Jonathan Burbank*	285 Billerica Rd, Chelmsford MA 01824	978-294-6000	S	30*	.2
254	Moai Technologies Inc—*Ramesh Mehta*	100 1st Ave 9th Fl, Pittsburgh PA 15222	412-454-5550	R	30*	.1
255	iET Solutions LLC—*Walter Elliot*	959 Concord St, Framingham MA 01701		S	30*	.1
256	MedioStream Inc—*Cheng C Kao*	4962 El Camino Real St, Los Altos CA 94022	650-625-8900	R	30*	.1
257	Innovation First Notice—*Eric Wadsworth*	95 Wells Ave Ste 320, Newton Center MA 02459	617-886-2000	R	30	.4
258	Pinnacle Data Systems Inc—*John D Bair*	6600 Port Rd, Groveport OH 43125	614-748-1150	P	29	.1
259	LTM Inc (Havelock North Carolina)	925 E Main St Ste 66, Havelock NC 28532	252-444-6880	R	29*	.3
260	Kingland Companies Ltd—*David J Kingland*	1401 6th Ave S, Clear Lake IA 50428	641-355-1000	R	29*	.1
261	Halfcom—*Meg Whitman*	1100 E Hector St Ste 4, Conshohocken PA 19428	610-567-1090	S	29*	.1
262	Iovation Inc—*Greg Pierson*	111 SW 5th Ave Ste 320, Portland OR 97204	503-224-6010	R	29*	.1
263	Nu Info Systems Inc—*Niraj Kumar*	9218 Cypress Green Dr, Jacksonville FL 32256	904-448-8885	R	29*	.1
264	BPO Management Services Inc—*Patrick Dolan*	1290 N Hancock St Ste2, Anaheim CA 92807	714-974-2670	P	28	.3
265	Sentinel Technologies Inc—*Dennis Hoelzer*	2550 Warrenville Rd, Downers Grove IL 60515	630-769-4343	R	28*	.4
266	C3D/Strata Software—*Gary Bringhurst*	3013 Santa Clara Dr, Santa Clara UT 84765	435-628-5218	R	28*	.1
267	Automated Systems Inc (Lincoln Nebraska)—*Richard C Perry*	1201 Libra Dr, Lincoln NE 68512	402-420-6000	R	28*	.1
268	Information Concepts Inc (Washington DC)—*Cary Toor*	503 Carlisle Dr, Herndon VA 20170	703-796-0005	R	28*	.1
269	Integrien Corp—*Dale Quayle*	114 Pacifica Ste 290, Irvine CA 92618	949-788-0555	R	28*	.1
270	Systems/Software Engineering—*Tom Dinnella*	940 W Valley Rd Ste 16, Wayne PA 19087	610-341-9017	R	28*	<.1
271	Horizon Payroll Services Inc—*Marilynne Saliwanchik*	2700 Miamisburg Center, Dayton OH 45459	937-434-8244	R	28*	<.1
272	Paramount Software Associations Inc	PO Box 19096, Amarillo TX 79114	806-358-8928	R	28*	<.1
273	Open Systems International Inc—*Bahman Hoveida*	4101 Arrowhead Dr, Medina MN 55340	763-551-0559	R	28*	.2
274	Total Attorneys Inc—*Edmund Scanlan*	25 E Washington Ste 40, Chicago IL 60602		R	27*	.2
275	Gray Research Inc—*Cynthia Gray*	655 Discovery Dr Ste 3, Huntsville AL 35806	256-922-9952	R	27*	.1
276	Collexis Holdings Inc	1201 Main St Ste 980, Columbia SC 29201	770-301-3126	S	27*	.1
277	Charles River Analytics Inc—*Greg Zacharias*	625 Mt Auburn St, Cambridge MA 02138	617-491-3474	R	27*	.1
278	Choicestream Inc—*Steve Johnson*	210 Broadway 4th Fl, Cambridge MA 02139	617-498-7800	R	27*	.1
279	OpenService Inc—*Jeff Lavin*	4 Mount Royal Ave Ste, Marlborough MA 01752	508-597-5300	R	27*	.1
280	Vistronix Inc—*Deepak Hathiramani*	1851 Alexander Belle D, Reston VA 20191	703-463-2059	R	26	.5
281	Bridgeline Digital Inc—*Thomas L Massie*	10 Sixth Rd, Woburn MA 01801	781-376-5555	P	26	.1
282	Data Systems Analysts Inc—*Fran Pierce*	8 Neshaminy Interplex, Trevose PA 19053	215-245-4800	R	26*	.2
283	Advanced Programs Group LLC—*Bekim Veseli*	11990 Market St Ste 20, Reston VA 20190		R	26*	.1
284	Groundwork Open Source Solutions Inc—*Peter Jackson*	139 Townsend St Ste 10, San Francisco CA 94107		R	26*	.1
285	Ping Identity Corp—*Andre Durand*	1099 18th St Ste 2950, Denver CO 80202	303-468-2900	R	26*	.1
286	UBICS Inc—*Vijay Mallya*	333 Technology Dr Ste, Canonsburg PA 15317	724-746-6001	P	26	.3
287	Innovative Solutions and Support Inc—*Geoffrey SM Hedrick*	720 Pennsylvania Dr, Exton PA 19341	610-646-9800	P	26	.1
288	Computershare Technolgy Sources Inc—*Steve Rotheloon*	2 Enterprise Dr Ste 40, Shelton CT 06484	203-944-7300	R	26*	.2
289	Systems Technology Group Inc—*Anup Popat*	3155 W Big Beaver Rd, Troy MI 48084	248-643-9010	R	25*	.4
290	Dha Group Inc—*David Hale*	1101 Penn Ave Nw Ste 5, Washington DC 20004	202-669-5974	R	25*	.2
291	Ascent Logic Corp—*Susan Rice Rappaport*	4300 Rte 1, Princeton NJ 08543	609-580-2800	R	25*	.1
292	MCA Solutions Inc—*Robert M Salvucci*	1500 John FKennedy Blv, Philadelphia PA 19102	215-717-2180	R	25*	.1
293	Techflow Inc—*Larry M Trammell*	6405 Mire Mesa Blvd St, San Diego CA 92121	858-412-8000	R	25*	.1
294	YellowPepper Wireless LLC—*Rafael Russ*	20900 NE 30th Ave 8th, Aventura FL 33180	786-924-3814	R	25*	.1
295	Positive Networks Inc—*Timothy Sutton*	2000 Town Center Ste 2, Southfield MI 48075		R	25*	.1
296	Rochester Software Associates Inc—*Robert Bader*	69 Cascade Dr, Rochester NY 14614		R	25*	.1
297	Vigilant LLC—*Alison Andrews*	66 York St, Jersey City NJ 07302		R	25*	.1
298	ITCN Inc—*Roy Penwell*	591 Congress Park Dr, Dayton OH 45459		R	25*	<.1
299	Ost Inc—*Vijay Narula*	2001 M St Nw Ste 3000, Washington DC 20036	202-467-7670	R	25*	.2
300	Vision Systems Group Inc—*Viswa Mandalapu*	1001 Durham Ave Ste 30, South Plainfield NJ 07080	732-537-9000	R	24*	.3
301	Consulting Services Inc (Oklahoma City Oklahoma)—*Ken Novotny*	4420 E I-240 Service R, Oklahoma City OK 73135	405-526-1030	R	24	.2
302	Applied Information Sciences Inc—*Fred Elleman*	11400 Commerce Park Dr, Reston VA 20191	703-860-7800	R	24*	.2
303	JYACC Inc—*Satya Bolli*	114 W 47th St 20th Fl, New York NY 10036	212-267-7722	R	24*	.2
304	Aculis Inc—*Michele Stone*	852 East 1910 S Ste 3, Provo UT 84606	801-377-5360	R	24*	.1
305	Armedia LLC—*Jim Nasr*	200 Galleria Pkwy Ste, Atlanta GA 30339	678-945-4417	R	24*	.1
306	Identrust Inc—*Karen J Wendel*	55 Hawthorne St Ste 40, San Francisco CA 94105	415-486-2900	R	24*	.1
307	ITAAS Inc—*Vibha Rustagi*	11695 E Johns Creek Pk, Duluth GA 30097	770-368-4024	R	24*	.1
308	McdVontive LLC—*Nancy J Ham*	400 5th Ave Ste 200, Waltham MA 02451		R	24*	.1
309	Mountain Network Systems Inc—*Jason Ciment*	1800 S Robertson Blvd, Los Angeles CA 90035		R	24*	.1
310	MuleSoft Inc—*Greg Schott*	30 Maiden Ln Ste 500, San Francisco CA 94108	415-229-2009	R	24*	.1
311	MyPRGenie Inc—*Miranda Tan*	1501 Broadway 25th Fl, New York NY 10036	212-807-8300	R	24*	.1

Note: An asterisk (*) indicates an estimated financial figure. The company type code used is as follows: R = Private, P = Public, S = Private Subsidiary, B = Public Subsidiary, D = Division, J = Joint Venture, I = Investment Fund.

COMPANY RANKINGS BY SALES WITHIN 4-DIGIT SIC

Rank	Company Name—Executive Officer	Address, City, State, Zip	Phone	Type	Fin	Empls
312	Quantum Retail Technology Inc—Vicki Raport	100 S 5th St Ste 1700, Minneapolis MN 55402		R	24*	.1
313	Secnap Network Security Corp—Michael Scheidell	6421 Congress Ave Ste, Boca Raton FL 33487	561-999-5000	R	24*	.1
314	TheNextRound Inc—Vipul Minocha	1881 Worcester Rd, Framingham MA 01701	508-665-5200	S	24*	.1
315	OPTIMUS Corp (Fort Collins Colorado)—Roland Straub	605 S College Ave, Fort Collins CO 80524	970-226-3466	R	24*	<.1
316	DOBBS RAM and Co—Ronald McCrae	1349 W Peachtree St NE, Atlanta GA 30308	404-897-1033	R	24*	<.1
317	Horizon Companies Inc—Shirish Nadkarni	3830 Park Ave Ste 201, Edison NJ 08820	732-650-0052	R	23*	.2
318	Bitstream Inc—Amos Kiminski	500 Nickerson Rd, Marlborough MA 01752	617-497-6222	P	23	.1
319	Adaptive Planning Inc—John Herr	2041 Landings Dr Bldg, Mountain View CA 94043	650-528-7500	R	23*	.1
320	OrderMotion Inc—Marty Fahey	5 Burlington Woods Dr, Burlington MA 01803		R	23*	.1
321	Software Quality Leaders Inc—Sareena Awla	860 Hebron Pky 301, Lewisville TX 75057	972-539-4100	R	23*	.1
322	SQN Banking Systems Inc—Joe Uhland Jr	PO Box 423, Rancocas NJ 08073		R	23*	.1
323	TimeCentre Inc—Frank Hightower	7094 Peachtree Industr, Norcross GA 30071	303-444-8771	R	23*	.1
324	Zenoss Inc—Bill Karpovich	275 W St Ste 204, Annapolis MD 21401	410-990-0274	R	23*	.1
325	Pantheon Inc—Sujatha Panavally	1801 Robert Fulton Dr, Reston VA 20191	703-391-5633	R	23*	.5
326	Proofpoint Inc—Gary Steele	892 Ross Dr, Sunnyvale CA 94089	408-517-4710	R	23*	.2
327	Wisdom Infotech Ltd—Atanu Banerji	18650 W Corporate Dr S, Brookfield WI 53045	262-792-0200	R	22*	.3
328	Credant Technologies—Bob Heard	15303 Dallas Pky Ste 1, Addison TX 75001	972-458-5408	R	22*	.1
329	Akorri Networks—Allan Wallack	305 Foster St, Littleton MA 01460	781-768-5300	R	22*	.1
330	Vpisystems Corp—Kay Iverson	943 Holmdel Rd, Holmdel NJ 07733	732-332-0233	R	22*	.2
331	Vm Services Inc—Chin Wong	6701 Mowry Ave, Newark CA 94560	510-744-3720	R	22*	.2
332	Ensynch Inc—Gene Holmquist	125 S 52nd St, Tempe AZ 85281	480-894-3500	R	22	.1
333	Stonebranch Inc—Wolfgang Bothe	950 N Point Pkwy Ste 2, Alpharetta GA 30005	678-366-7887	R	21*	.1
334	Client/Server Software Solutions Inc—Lisa Wolford	3906 Raynor Pkwy Ste 2, Bellevue NE 68123	402-393-8059	R	21*	.1
335	DataViews Corp—Andrew Copeland	1 Columbia Circle Dr, Albany NY 12203	518-464-4500	D	21*	.1
336	Melodeo Inc—Jim Billmaier	701 Pike St Ste 1100, Seattle WA 98101	206-812-4300	R	21*	<.1
337	PerformTech Inc—Katie Moran	810 King St, Alexandria VA 22314	703-548-0320	S	21*	<.1
338	Trapeze Software Group Inc—Rick Bacchus	5265 Rockwell Dr Ne, Cedar Rapids IA 52402	319-363-2700	R	21*	.2
339	Gnuco LLC—Tim Moriarty	20 N Wacker Dr Ste 187, Chicago IL 60606	312-669-9600	R	21*	.1
340	Sadaka Technology Consultants LLC	7701 France Ave S 203, Minneapolis MN 55435	952-841-6363	R	20*	.7
341	Elite Computer Consultants LP—Paula Malorie	10333 N W Fwy Ste 414, Houston TX 77092	713-686-9740	R	20*	.3
342	Patientkeeper Inc—Paul Brient	880 Winter St Ste 300, Waltham MA 02451	781-373-6300	R	20*	.2
343	Intrinsix Corp—James Gobes	100 Campus Dr, Marlborough MA 01752	508-658-7600	R	20*	.1
344	Qorval Integrated Solutions Inc—William Muns	8445 Freport Pkwy Ste, Irving TX 75063	972-915-0030	R	20*	.1
345	Pentagon 2000 Software Inc—Gabriel Mofaz	15 W 34th St Fl 5, New York NY 10001	212-629-7521	R	20*	.1
346	Imagitek Ltd—Fabrice Buron	2951 Marina Bay Dr Ste, League City TX 77573	281-334-6970	R	20*	<.1
347	Netline Corp—Robert S Alvin	750 University Ave Ste, Los Gatos CA 95032	408-340-2200	R	20*	<.1
348	projekt202 LP—Peter Eckert	1300 Guadalupe St Ste, Austin TX 78701	512-485-3070	R	20*	<.1
349	Abaris Inc—Sean M Chawla	PO Box 1210, Lake Forest CA 92609	949-333-3500	R	20*	<.1
350	Imperva Inc—Shlomo Kramer	3400 Bridge Pkwy Ste 2, Redwood Shores CA 94065	650-345-9000	P	20*	<.1
351	Actix Inc—Bill McHale	12012 Sunset Hills Rd, Reston VA 20190	703-707-4777	S	20*	<.1
352	RSA Netwitness—Amit Yoran	10700 Parkridge Blvd 6, Reston VA 20191	703-889-8950	D	20*	<.1
353	Advanced Acoustic Concepts LLC—Michael Carnovale	425 Oser Ave Unit 1, Hauppauge NY 11788	631-273-5700	R	20*	.2
354	Globalcynex Inc—Kishore Putta	21155 Whitfield Pl Ste, Sterling VA 20165	703-433-2586	R	19*	.4
355	Noteworthy Medical Systems Inc—Rick Mullins	3300 N Central Ave Ste, Phoenix AZ 85012	602-277-6277	R	19*	.2
356	Volt Delta Resources Inc—Joe Diangelo	560 Lexington Ave 14th, New York NY 10022	212-827-2600	S	19*	.2
357	John Tyler Enterprises Inc—Robert Almond	550 Crescent Blvd, Brooklawn NJ 08030	856-456-5668	R	19*	.1
358	IntelliNet Technologies Inc—Anjan Ghosal	1990 W New Haven Ave S, Melbourne FL 32904	321-726-0686	R	19*	<.1
359	Scientific Monitoring Inc—Link Jaw	8777 E Via De Ventura, Scottsdale AZ 85258	480-752-7909	R	19*	<.1
360	twentysix New York—Jay Harris Rabin	62 W 45th St, New York NY 10036	212-840-0008	S	19*	<.1
361	instaCare Corp—Keith Berman	2660 Townsgate Rd Ste, Westlake Village CA 91361	805-446-1973	P	19	<.1
362	Talent Technical Services Inc—David Iacarella	5353 Wayzata Blvd Ste, Minneapolis MN 55416	952-417-3600	R	19*	.1
363	Planit Solutions Inc—George Daum	PO Box 71146, Tuscaloosa AL 35407	205-556-9199	R	19*	.1
364	Zoot Enterprises Inc—Chris Nelson	555 Zoot Enterprise Ln, Bozeman MT 59718	406-586-5050	R	18*	.2
365	Alta It Services LLC—Tonya Avent	9210 Corp Blvd Ste 200, Rockville MD 20850	301-740-2100	R	18*	.2
366	Meridian Technology Group Inc—Richard Creson	12909 SW 68th Pky Ste, Portland OR 97223	503-697-1600	R	18*	.1
367	SmartSynch Inc—Stephen D Johnston	PO Box 12250, Jackson MS 39236	601-362-1780	R	18*	.1
368	Brandt Information Services Inc—Richard Wise	1377 Cross Creek Cir, Tallahassee FL 32301	850-877-7713	R	18*	.1
369	Gcom Software Inc—Girish Bhatia	24 Madison Ave Ext Ste, Albany NY 12203	518-869-1671	R	18*	.1
370	Emagia Corp—Veena Gundavelli	4500 Great America Pkw, Santa Clara CA 95054	408-654-6575	R	18*	<.1
371	LawLogix Group—Dan Siciliano	2828 N Central Ave Ste, Phoenix AZ 85004	602-357-4240	R	18*	<.1
372	BuilderFusion Inc—Mitchell C Merrifield	532 E 800 N, Orem UT 84057	801-765-0191	R	18*	<.1
373	Certus Software Inc—Terry Allen	2665 N First St Ste 20, San Jose CA 95134	408-380-8900	R	18*	<.1
374	ESP Technologies LLC—David Sher	140 Broadway 21st FL, New York NY 10005	212-485-5120	R	18*	<.1
375	Information Technology Services Inc—David C Munn	420 Bedford St Ste 110, Lexington MA 02420	781-862-8500	R	18*	<.1
376	PNT Marketing Services Inc—Tony Coretto	24-20 Jackson Ave, Long Island City NY 11101		R	18*	<.1
377	Hughes Systique Corp—Pradeep Kaul	15245 Shady Grove Rd, Rockville MD 20850	301-527-1629	R	18*	<.1
378	Application Design Group Inc—Jay Rowan	4227 Earth City Expy S, Earth City MO 63045	314-223-8580	R	18*	<.1
379	Surgical Information Systems LLC—Kathleen Brooks	11605 Haynes Bridge Rd, Alpharetta GA 30009	678-507-1610	R	18*	.2
380	Recommind Inc—Robert Tennant	650 Clfornia St Fl 12, San Francisco CA 94108	415-394-7899	R	17*	.2
381	Compusearch Software Systems Inc—Peter DiGiammarino	21251 Ridgetop Cir Ste, Dulles VA 20166	703-481-3699	S	17*	.2
382	Enterprise Data Management—Carl Hall	4380 Malsbary Rd Rm 25, Cincinnati OH 45242	513-791-7272	R	17*	<.1
383	IBM Support Systems—Deidre Paknad	4100 N First Street, San Jose CA 95134		R	17*	<.1
384	Imperia Software Solutions (USA) GmbH—Sebastian Bottger	858 35th Ave, San Francisco CA 94121	415-269-6621	R	17*	<.1
385	Infinite Software Inc—Bruce Acacio	28202 Cabot Rd Ste 300, Laguna Niguel CA 92677	949-498-9300	R	17*	<.1
386	Tizor Systems Inc—Prat Moghe	26 Forest St, Marlboro MA 01752	508-382-8200	S	17*	<.1
387	United Systems and Software Inc	PO Box 958444, Lake Mary FL 32795	407-875-2120	R	17*	<.1
388	OmniTI Computer Consulting Inc—Theo Schlossnagle	7070 Samuel Morse Dr S, Columbia MD 21046	443-325-1357	R	17*	<.1
389	Micro Focus Group PLC—Stephen Kelly	700 King Farm Blvd Fl, Rockville MD 20850	301-838-5000	R	17*	.2
390	Emeter Corp—Gary Bloom	2215 Bridgepointe Pkwy, Foster City CA 94404	650-227-7770	R	17*	.1
391	Lake Superior Software Inc—Howard Messing	6423 City W Pkwy, Eden Prairie MN 55344	952-941-1000	R	17*	.1
392	Macrosoft Inc—Ronald Mueller	2 Sylvan Way Ste 300, Parsippany NJ 07054	973-889-0500	R	16*	.2
393	Crystal Clear Technologies LLC—Loretta Rinaldi	5534 Galeria Dr Ste D, Baton Rouge LA 70816	225-291-9001	R	16*	<.1
394	Aditi Technologies Private Ltd—Pradeep Singh	2002 156th Ave Ne Ste, Bellevue WA 98007	425-378-6500	R	16*	.4
395	ACS-MIDAS—Jim Deweese	4801 E Broadway Blvd S, Tucson AZ 85711	520-296-7398	S	16*	.2
396	Schoolnet Inc—Jonathan D Harber	525 7th Ave 4th Fl, New York NY 10018	646-496-9000	R	16*	.1
397	Thaumaturgix Inc—Peter Dolch	19 W 44th St Ste 810, New York NY 10036	212-918-5000	R	16*	.1
398	Enerdyne Technologies Inc—Steve Gardner	1935 Cordell Ct, El Cajon CA 92020	619-438-6000	S	16*	.1
399	Innovate E-Commerce Inc—Karen F Puchalsky	1000 Brooktree Rd Rm 1, Wexford PA 15090	412-681-7090	R	16*	<.1
400	Reaction Design Inc—Bernie Rosenthal	6440 Lusk Blvd Ste D20, San Diego CA 92121	858-550-1920	R	16*	<.1
401	Tek-Tools Inc—Ken Barth	4040 McEwen Rd Ste 240, Dallas TX 75244	972-980-2890	R	16*	<.1

Rank	Company Name—*Executive Officer*	Address, City, State, Zip	Phone	Type	Fin	Empls
402	TERA Technologies Inc—*Nirmal Agarwal*	3859 SW Hall Blvd, Beaverton OR 97005	503-643-4835	R	16*	<.1
403	StrataVia Corp—*Thor Culverhouse*	707 17th St Ste 2100, Denver CO 80202	303-991-4850	S	16*	<.1
404	Pikewerks Corp—*Sandra Ring*	105 A Church St, Madison AL 35758	256-325-0010	R	16*	<.1
405	Integrated Decision Support Corp—*Richard Murphy*	899 Presidential Dr St, Richardson TX 75081	972-671-0045	R	16*	<.1
406	Metasys Technologies Inc—*Sandeep Gauba*	3460 Summit Ridge Pkwy, Duluth GA 30096	678-218-1600	R	16*	.1
407	I/NET Inc	PO Box 3338, Kalamazoo MI 49003	269-978-6816	R	16	N/A
408	Safenet Consulting Inc—*Martin Miller*	5810 Baker Rd Ste 100, Minnetonka MN 55345	952-930-3636	R	15*	.1
409	Autobase Inc—*Bryan Anderson*	201 W 103 St Ste 600, Indianapolis IN 46290	317-842-4242	R	15*	.1
410	AtTask Inc—*Eric Morgan*	1313 N Research Way, Orem UT 84097	801-373-3266	R	15*	.1
411	NCE Computer Group—*Jim Raven*	1866 Friendship Dr, El Cajon CA 92020	619-212-3000	R	15*	.1
412	SofTechnics Inc—*Mike Mayoras*	308 N Cleveland Massil, Akron OH 44333	330-665-1698	S	15*	.1
413	Westbrook Technologies Inc—*Einar Haukeland*	22 Summit Pl, Branford CT 06405	203-483-6666	R	15*	.1
414	DAKSOFT Inc—*David R Emery*	1140 Plant St, Rapid City SD 57702	605-721-2100	S	15*	.1
415	Athoc Inc—*Guy Miasnik*	2215 Bridgepointe Pkwy, Foster City CA 94404	650-685-3000	R	15*	<.1
416	Carbonetworks Corp—*Michael Meehan*	1700 Montgomery St Ste, San Francisco CA 94111	415-217-7021	R	15*	<.1
417	Handysoft Global Corp—*Harry Clarke*	3141 Fairview Park Dr, Falls Church VA 22042	703-645-4500	R	15*	<.1
418	Internet Advertising Group Inc—*Michael Weinsoff*	3111 N University Dr S, Coral Springs FL 33065	954-933-0199	R	15*	<.1
419	NE Technologies Inc—*Dilip Naik*	520 Guthridge Ct Ste 2, Norcross GA 30092	770-453-9190	R	15*	<.1
420	JaRay Software Inc—*Jane Jantz*	2030 S Mead St, Wichita KS 67211	316-262-4678	R	15*	<.1
421	One Source Networks—*Ernest Cunningham*	14402 Blanco Rd Ste 30, San Antonio TX 78216	610-679-4600	R	15	<.1
422	DrfirstCom Inc—*James Chen*	9420 Key W Ave, Rockville MD 20850	301-231-9510	R	15*	.2
423	Rtp LLC—*Robert Savage*	PO Box 8890, Avon CO 81620	970-477-4800	S	15*	N/A
424	Dataart Solutions Inc—*Eugene Goland*	475 Park Ave S Fl 9, New York NY 10016	212-378-4108	R	15*	.6
425	Cook Systems International Inc—*Wayne Cook*	6799 Great Oaks Rd Ste, Memphis TN 38138	901-757-8877	R	15*	.2
426	Sudhko Inc—*Suseela Kodali*	13911 Ridgedale Dr Ste, Hopkins MN 55305	952-595-8500	R	15*	<.1
427	Orchard Software Corp—*Robert Bush*	701 Congressional Blvd, Carmel IN 46032		R	14*	.1
428	Vital Records Inc—*Ron Riemann*	PO Box 688, Flagtown NJ 08821	908-369-6900	R	14*	.1
429	Reciprocal Inc—*Steve Potash*	620 Main St, Buffalo NY 14202	716-845-7880	R	14*	.1
430	Get Well Network Inc—*Micheal Neal*	7920 Norfolk Ave Ste 1, Bethesda MD 20814	240-482-3200	R	14*	.1
431	Digineer Inc *Michael Lacey*	505 N Hwy 169 Rm 750, Plymouth MN 55441	763-210-2300	R	14*	.1
432	SunGard Trading and Risk Systems (Boston Massachusetts)—*James Ashton*	100 High St 19th Fl, Boston MA 02110	617-542-2800	S	14*	.1
433	Diamond Technologies Inc (New Castle Delaware)—*Greg Ballance*	551 Mews Dr Ste A, New Castle DE 19720	302-656-6050	R	14*	<.1
434	Pioneer Data Systems Inc—*Naushad Mulji*	379 Thornall St, Edison NJ 08837	732-603-0001	R	14*	<.1
435	Ivory Systems Inc—*Michael Elfenbein*	1 Gatehall Dr, Parsippany NJ 07054	973-993-1300	R	14*	<.1
436	Allied Solutions Group Inc—*Craig Robinson*	PO Box 41178, Brecksville OH 44141	440-717-9443	R	14	<.1
437	Add-On Data—*Stephen Shaheen*	323 Andover St, Wilmington MA 01887	978-988-1900	R	14*	<.1
438	Adhost—*Will Riffle*	140 4th Ave N Ste 360, Seattle WA 98109	206-404-9000	R	14*	<.1
439	Apollo Enterprise Solutions LLC—*Christopher Imrey*	111 W Ocean Blvd Ste 1, Long Beach CA 90802	562-513-3700	R	14*	<.1
440	Ashlar-Vellum—*Robert Bou*	9600 Great Hills Trl S, Austin TX 78759	512-250-2186	R	14*	<.1
441	AVG Technologies USA Inc—*JR Smith*	1 Executive Dr 3rd Fl, Chelmsford MA 01824	828-459-5422	R	14*	<.1
442	Global Relief Technologies LLC—*Michael Gray*	30 New Hampshire Ave, Portsmouth NH 03801	603-422-7333	R	14*	<.1
443	Habanero Computing Solutions Inc—*Victor Mattison*	712 N 2nd St Ste 300, Saint Louis MO 63102	314-771-5522	R	14*	<.1
444	iSoft Integration Systems Inc—*John Moriarty*	1 Central St Ste 203, Middleton MA 01949	978-774-4100	R	14*	<.1
445	Materials Software System Inc *Venu Madhav*	11513 Allecingie Pky, Richmond VA 23235	804-272-0081	R	14*	<.1
446	Merry Mechanization Inc—*Ted Merry*	333 S Indiana Ave, Englewood FL 34223	941-475-1788	R	14*	<.1
447	Principia Partners LLC—*Jim Morton*	604 Gordon Dr, Exton PA 19341	610-363-7815	R	14*	<.1
448	Signacert Inc—*Wyatt Starnes*	707 SW Washington St 7, Portland OR 97205	503-227-2207	R	14*	<.1
449	SimpleTuition Inc—*Kevin Walker*	268 Summer St Ste 502, Boston MA 02210		R	14*	<.1
450	TiER1 Performance Solutions—*Greg Harmeyer*	6 E 5th St, Covington KY 41011	859-663-2114	R	14*	<.1
451	TV Specialists Inc—*Jerry Bollinger*	180 E 2100 S, Salt Lake City UT 84115	801-486-5757	R	14*	<.1
452	UBMatrix—*Sunir Kapoor*	11808 Northup Way Ste, Bellevue WA 98005	425-285-0200	R	14*	<.1
453	Industrybrains Inc—*John Keister*	450 Park Ave S 6th Fl, New York NY 10016	212-209-3300	S	14*	<.1
454	NewEra Software Inc—*Robert Tapia*	155 East Main Ave Ste, Morgan Hill CA 95037	408-201-7000	R	14*	<.1
455	B Jacqueline And Associates Inc—*Jacqueline Buickians*	PO Box 40340, Pasadena CA 91114	626-844-1400	R	14*	.3
456	Varolii Corp—*Dan Dawson*	821 2nd Ave Ste 1000, Seattle WA 98104	206-902-3900	R	14*	.1
457	Stenograph LLC—*Lisa Balderstone*	596 W Lamont Rd, Elmhurst IL 60126	630-532-5100	R	14*	.2
458	Infinite Campus Inc—*Charles Kratsch*	4321 109th Ave Ne, Minneapolis MN 55449	651-631-0000	R	13*	.1
459	Software International Inc—*Suneel Sawant*	2 Executive Dr Ste 460, Somerset NJ 08873	732-302-1900	R	13*	.2
460	Cri Advantage Inc—*Gary Brookshier*	12754 W Lasalle St, Boise ID 83713	208-343-9192	R	13*	.2
461	Acceller Inc—*Steven McKean*	815 NW 57th Ave Ste 40, Miami FL 33126	305-265-0136	R	13*	.1
462	In-Style Software Inc—*Stephen Smith*	315 Lemay Ferry Rd Ste, Saint Louis MO 63125	314-631-6982	R	13*	<.1
463	DFA Capital Management Inc	100 Manhattanville Rd, Purchase NY 10577	914-701-7200	S	13*	<.1
464	ELC Technologies—*Lex Sisney*	PO Box 247, Santa Barbara CA 93102		R	13*	<.1
465	Longboard Inc—*Hari Haran*	3121 Jay St, Santa Clara CA 95054	408-571-3310	R	13*	<.1
466	Language Weaver Inc—*Mark Tapling*	6060 Center Dr Ste 150, Los Angeles CA 90045	310-437-3700	R	13*	<.1
467	Soft Solutions Inc	2900 Chamblee Tucker R, Atlanta GA 30341	770-457-9400	R	13*	<.1
468	Micro Strategies Inc—*Anthony Bongiovanni*	PO Box 1139, Denville NJ 07834	973-625-7721	R	13*	.1
469	Vertiglo—*Luke Roopra*	121 S Orange Ave Plaza, Orlando FL 32801		R	13	.1
470	Three Pillar Global Inc—*David Dewolf*	3975 Fair Ridge Dr Ste, Fairfax VA 22033	703-435-6365	R	13	.2
471	Pillar Technology Group LLC—*Jay Aho*	5180 Washakie Trl, Brighton MI 48116	248-321-9723	R	13*	.1
472	Data Inc—*Arun Verma*	72 Summit Ave Ste 1, Montvale NJ 07645	201-802-9800	R	12*	.1
473	INDUSA Technical Corp—*Kamlesh Shah*	1 TransAm Plz Dr Ste 3, Villa Park IL 60181		R	12	.1
474	Prodege LLC—*Josef Gorowitz*	3830 Del Amo Blvd, Torrance CA 90503	347-314-9882	R	12	.1
475	Unicon International Inc—*Peichen Lee*	241 Outerbelt St, Columbus OH 43213	614-861-7070	R	12*	.1
476	Wideorbit Inc—*Eric Mathewson*	2 Harrison St Fl 6, San Francisco CA 94105	415-675-6700	R	12*	.1
477	Smart Bear Software Inc—*Joseph Krivikas*	100 Cummings Ctr Ste 2, Beverly MA 01915	978-236-7900	R	12*	.2
478	Blue Ally—*GV Kumar*	13461 Sunrise Valley D, Herndon VA 20171	703-793-0101	S	12*	.1
479	Internet Corporation for Assigned Names and Numbers—*Rod Beckstrom*	4676 Admiralty Way Ste, Marina del Rey CA 90292	310-823-9358	R	12*	.1
480	V2soft Inc—*Varchasvi Shankar*	300 Enterprise Ct Ste, Bloomfield Hills MI 48302	248-904-1705	R	12*	.1
481	Riptide Software Inc—*Philip Loeffel*	200 E Palm Valley Dr, Oviedo FL 32765	321-296-7724	R	12*	.1
482	Stromberg LLC—*Seth Bernstein*	255 Primera Blvd Ste 5, Lake Mary FL 32746	407-333-3282	S	12*	.1
483	Vacava Inc—*Charlie Harter*	3131 Superior Dr Nw St, Rochester MN 55901	507-252-9076	R	12*	<.1
484	Jadtec Computer Group—*John W Lusty*	1520 W Yale Ave, Orange CA 92867	714-637-2900	R	12*	<.1
485	Tri-Cord Healthcare Information Systems Inc—*Florian Wieland*	22912 Mill Creek Dr St, Laguna Hills CA 92653	949-581-6734	R	12*	<.1
486	Concurrent Controls Inc—*Ray Novarina*	PO Box 371540, Montara CA 94037	650-728-9148	R	12*	<.1
487	Forte Systems Inc—*Dion Nugent*	5137 Golden Foothill P, El Dorado Hills CA 95762	916-673-4850	R	12*	<.1
488	Fugent Inc—*John Detwiler*	5131 Post Rd Ste 210, Dublin OH 43017		R	12*	<.1

Note: An asterisk (*) indicates an estimated financial figure. The company type code used is as follows: R = Private, P = Public, S = Private Subsidiary, B = Public Subsidiary, D = Division, J = Joint Venture, I = Investment Fund.

COMPANY RANKINGS BY SALES WITHIN 4-DIGIT SIC

Rank	Company Name—*Executive Officer*	Address, City, State, Zip	Phone	Type	Fin	Empls
489	Heartland ITS—*Monte Washburn*	3206 Mountainview Dr S, Decatur AL 35603	256-301-5457	R	12*	<.1
490	Nichols and Company Inc—*John F Nichols*	804 Venice Blvd, Venice CA 90291	310-670-7447	R	12*	<.1
491	Parlano Inc—*Nick Fera*	120 S Riverside Pl Ste, Chicago IL 60606	312-655-8330	R	12*	<.1
492	Pinneastcom Inc—*Brian Popken*	5 Lake Carolina Way St, Columbia SC 29229	803-926-9511	S	12*	<.1
493	PixelTools Corp—*Richard Kors*	10721 Wunderlich Dr, Cupertino CA 95014	408-374-5327	R	12*	<.1
494	PRC Digital Media—*Ray Hayes*	476 Riverside Ave, Jacksonville FL 32202	904-354-1500	R	12*	<.1
495	Protonmedia Inc—*Ronald J Burns*	1690 Sumneytown Pke St, Lansdale PA 19446	215-631-1401	R	12*	<.1
496	Synergy Software Technologies Inc—*Joseph Sander*	25 New England Dr, Essex Junction VT 05452	802-878-8514	S	12*	<.1
497	Timecruiser Computing Corp—*Allen Wang*	9 Law Dr, Fairfield NJ 07004	973-244-7856	R	12*	<.1
498	Incuity Software Inc	20532 El Toro Rd Ste 3, Mission Viejo CA 92692	949-465-0390	D	12*	<.1
499	Think Subscription Inc—*Paul Russell*	250 W Center St 2nd Fl, Provo UT 84601	801-373-2246	R	12*	<.1
500	Advanced Access—*John Morris*	8101 E Kaiser Blvd Ste, Anaheim CA 92808	714-701-3910	R	12*	.1
501	Scimage Inc—*Sai Raya*	4916 El Camino Real St, Los Altos CA 94022	650-694-4858	R	12*	<.1
502	Aries Technology Inc—*Nguyen Quach*	1445 W 12th Pl, Tempe AZ 85281	480-784-4818	R	12*	.2
503	Vermont Information Processing Inc—*Daniel Byrnes*	402 Watertower Cir, Colchester VT 05446	802-655-9400	R	12*	.1
504	Storis Inc—*Donald Surdoval*	400 Valley Rd Ste 302, Mount Arlington NJ 07856	973-601-8200	R	11*	.1
505	Creative Infocity Ltd—*Dilip Barot*	4243 Northlake Blvd St, Palm Beach Gardens FL 33410	561-627-7988	R	11*	.2
506	Flashpoint Technology Inc—*David Pratt*	20 Depot St Unit 210, Peterborough NH 03458	603-924-9333	R	11*	.1
507	Atac—*Scott Simcox*	755 N Mathilda Ave Ste, Sunnyvale CA 94085	408-736-2822	R	11*	.1
508	Nextlinx Corp—*Rajiv Uppal*	400b E Gude Dr, Rockville MD 20850	301-315-4700	R	11*	.2
509	Systems And Software Enterprises Inc—*Joseph Renton*	2929 E Imperial Hwy St, Brea CA 92821	714-854-8600	R	11*	.1
510	Rothe Development Inc—*Susan Patenoude*	4614 Sinclair Rd, San Antonio TX 78222	210-648-3131	R	11*	.3
511	Telesis Corp—*Payal Tak*	4700 Corridor Pl Ste D, Beltsville MD 20705	240-241-5600	R	11*	.2
512	GDI Infotech Inc—*Madhuri Deshpande*	3775 Varsity Dr, Ann Arbor MI 48108	734-477-6900	R	11*	.1
513	Tlm Inc—*Robert Mcneel*	3670 Woodland Park Ave, Seattle WA 98103	206-545-7000	R	11*	<.1
514	Ayoka—*Eknauth Persaud*	202 E Border St Ste 33, Arlington TX 76010	817-210-4042	R	11*	<.1
515	Dawning Technologies Inc—*John Selmyer*	8140 College Pkwy Ste, Fort Myers FL 33919	239-931-6004	R	11*	<.1
516	VEIL Interactive Technologies—*Edward J Koplar*	50 Maryland Plaza Ste, Saint Louis MO 63108	314-345-1079	R	11*	<.1
517	Vidipax LLC—*Jim Lindner*	30-00 47th Ave 6th Fl, Long Island City NY 11101	718-482-7111	R	11*	<.1
518	Cellit LLC—*David Wachs*	213 W Institute Pl St, Chicago IL 60610	312-985-.080	R	11*	<.1
519	CompuLink Electronic Inc—*Rafael Arboleda*	214 W 29th St Ste 201, New York NY 10001	212-695-5465	R	11*	<.1
520	Bitwise Software International Inc—*Jay Falconer*	14225 N 17 Pl, Phoenix AZ 85022	602-569-4993	R	11*	<.1
521	Kinetic Software Inc—*Bill Ashton*	12672 Skyline Blvd, Woodside CA 94062	650-851-4484	R	11*	<.1
522	Neteffects Inc—*Jack Bader*	500 Chstrfeld Ctr Ste, Chesterfield MO 63017	636-237-1000	R	11*	.2
523	Incredible Technologies Inc—*Elaine Hodgson*	3333 N Kennicott Ave, Arlington Heights IL 60004	847-870-7027	R	11*	.1
524	enherent Corp—*Pamela Fredette*	100 Wood Ave S Ste 116, Iselin NJ 08830	732-321-1004	P	11	.1
525	Intelligent Security Systems International Inc—*Roman Jarkoi*	1480 Rte 9 N Ste 203, Woodbridge NJ 07095	732-855-1111	R	11*	.2
526	Resourcesoft Inc—*Anita Rana*	PO Box 42, Marlborough MA 01752	508-787-0882	R	11*	.1
527	Redwood Software Inc—*Dennis Walsh*	3000 Aerial Ctr Pkwy S, Morrisville NC 27560	919-460-5400	R	11*	.2
528	Avanquest North America Inc—*Roger Bloxberg*	23801 Calabasas Rd Ste, Calabasas CA 91302	818-591-9600	R	11*	.1
529	Netforensics Inc—*Dale Cline*	200 Metroplex Dr Ste 3, Edison NJ 08817	732-393-6000	R	11*	.1
530	Kryptiq Corp—*Luis Machuca*	1920 Nw Amberglen Pkwy, Beaverton OR 97006	503-906-6300	R	10*	.1
531	Syllogisteks Co—*Marilyn Smith*	PO Box 189, Chesterfield MO 63006	636-736-2100	R	10*	.1
532	Ferguson Consulting Inc—*Susan Ferguson*	1350 Timberlake Manor, Chesterfield MO 63017	636-728-4400	R	10*	.1
533	Webpower Inc—*Allan Hadhazy*	7765 Lake Worth Rd Ste, Lake Worth FL 33467	561-963-9005	R	10*	.1
534	Shop Systems Inc—*Swami Reddy*	7500 Grnwy Ctr Dr Ste, Greenbelt MD 20770	301-614-1322	R	10*	.1
535	Resource International Inc—*Farah Majidzadeh*	6350 Presidential Gate, Columbus OH 43231	614-823-4949	R	10*	.2
536	Diversified International Sciences Corp—*George Hill*	4550 Forbes Blvd Ste 3, Lanham MD 20706	301-731-9070	R	10*	.1
537	Camp Systems International LLC—*Ken Gray*	999 Marconi Ave, Ronkonkoma NY 11779	631-588-3200	R	10*	.1
538	Iconixx Corp	901 S Mopac Ste 100, Austin TX 78746	512-904-3400	S	10	.1
539	Visible Technologies Inc—*Kelly A Pennock*	3535 Factoria Blvd SE, Bellevue WA 98006	425-957-6100	R	10*	.1
540	Premium Technology Inc—*Kenny Leung*	32 Broadway Ste 1201, New York NY 10004	212-855-5511	R	10*	.1
541	Dynamic Animation Systems Inc—*Susana Slayton*	12015 Lee Jackson Memo, Fairfax VA 22033	703-503-0500	R	10*	.1
542	Siteworx Inc—*Tim McLaughlin*	11480 Commerce Park Dr, Reston VA 20191	703-964-1700	R	10*	.1
543	Intelligent Information Systems Inc—*Shailendra Jain*	2775 Meridian Pkwy, Durham NC 27713	919-572-0901	R	10*	.1
544	Adonix—*Alex Attal*	2200 Georgetowne Dr, Sewickley PA 15143	724-933-1377	R	10*	.1
545	Concerro Inc—*Graham Barnes*	9276 Scranton RdSte 40, San Diego CA 92121		R	10*	<.1
546	Global Technology Systems Consortium Inc—*James Rhee*	205 S Whiting St Ste 2, Alexandria VA 22304	703-461-8595	R	10*	<.1
547	Spiceworks Inc—*Scott Abel*	9005 Mountain Ridge Dr, Austin TX 78759	512-346-7743	R	10*	<.1
548	Advicon Inc—*Alan W Kennebeck*	809 W 1st St Ste F, Cedar Falls IA 50613	319-266-7906	S	10*	<.1
549	Altnet Inc—*Kevin Bermeister*	12711 Ventura Blvd Ste, Studio City CA 91604	818-386-2180	J	10*	<.1
550	Avenue Code LLC	300 Beale St, San Francisco CA 94105	415-300-6652	R	10*	<.1
551	Compiled Logic Corp—*Larry Estes*	PO Box 235, Bellaire TX 77402		R	10*	<.1
552	Medisyn Technologies Inc—*David Land*	6109 Blue Circle Dr St, Minnetonka MN 55343	952-475-8084	R	10*	<.1
553	Mentat Inc—*Brian NeSmith*	1145 Gayley Ave, Los Angeles CA 90024	310-208-2680	R	10*	<.1
554	Triticom—*Barry Trent*	9971 Valley View Rd St, Eden Prairie MN 55344	952-829-8019	R	10*	<.1
555	Videotex Systems Inc—*Bob Gilman*	10255 Miller Rd, Dallas TX 75238	972-231-9200	R	10*	<.1
556	WaveTwo LLC—*John Arnott Sr*	1431 Greenway Dr Ste 2, Irving TX 75038	214-271-0033	R	10*	<.1
557	MC2 Studios Inc—*Malcom Coon*	4242 Medical Dr Ste 12, San Antonio TX 78229	210-824-4106	R	10*	<.1
558	HSR Interactive—*Howard Schwartz*	420 Lexington Ave Ste, New York NY 10170	212-687-4180	D	10	<.1
559	Premier Software Ventures Inc—*Thomas Dayton*	12202 Wanderer Rd, Auburn CA 95602	530-268-1461	R	10*	<.1
560	DSET Corp—*Dilip Naik* NE Technologies Inc	520 Guthridge Ct Ste 2, Norcross GA 30092	770-453-9190	S	10	<.1
561	Interpro Inc—*Manu Gehani*	3265 Orchard Lake Rd E, Keego Harbor MI 48320	248-738-1590	R	10*	.1
562	Sampoerna Holdings USA Inc—*James Barnes*	601 Montgomery St Ste, San Francisco CA 94111	415-956-3999	R	10*	.1
563	Geneca LLC—*Eric Daugherty*	1815 S Meyers Rd Ste 9, Oakbrook Terrace IL 60181	630-599-0900	R	10*	.1
564	Xactly Corp—*Christopher Cabrera*	35 S Market St, San Jose CA 95113	408-977-3132	R	10*	.1
565	Qumas Inc—*Kevin O'leary*	66 York St Ste 1, Jersey City NJ 07302	973-377-8750	R	10*	.1
566	Impaqt LLC—*Richard Hagerty*	680 Andersen Dr, Pittsburgh PA 15220	412-733-7100	R	10*	.1
567	Collegenet Inc—*James Wolfston*	805 Sw Broadway Ste 16, Portland OR 97205	503-973-5200	R	10*	.1
568	Synapsis Technology Inc—*Lonnie Gillihan*	PO Box 747, Spring House PA 19477	215-793-0200	R	9*	.1
569	Trisept Corp—*Robert Spicer*	14425 Penrose Pl Ste 2, Chantilly VA 20151	703-297-4622	R	9*	<.1
570	Genome International Corp—*Roopa Senapathy*	8000 Excelsior Dr Ste, Madison WI 53717	608-833-5855	R	9*	.1
571	Intermedia Interactive Software Inc—*Sanjay Deshpande*	20 Ash St, Conshohocken PA 19428	484-530-0800	R	9*	.1
572	Rothtec Engraving Corp—*Frederick Roth*	PO Box 50060, New Bedford MA 02745	508-995-4601	R	9*	.1
573	Datum Software Inc—*Latha Ganeshan*	12000 Findley Rd Ste 3, Johns Creek GA 30097	678-894-7672	R	9*	.1
574	Tdk Technologies LLC—*Ilene Brian*	12977 N 40 Dr Ste 108, Saint Louis MO 63141	314-878-1005	R	9*	.1
575	Catapult Systems Corp—*Sam Goodner*	1221 S Mopac Expy Ste, Austin TX 78746	512-328-8181	R	9*	.1
576	Data Management Associates Of Brevard Inc—*D Larson*	3225 Jordan Blvd, Malabar FL 32950	321-725-8081	R	9*	.1
577	Exec Search Inc—*Upendra Rachupally*	2325 Parklawn Dr Ste G, Waukesha WI 53186	262-782-7533	R	9*	.1

Rank	Company Name—Executive Officer	Address, City, State, Zip	Phone	Type	Fin	Empls
578	Automation Technologies Inc—Sheila Corbett	8219 Leesburg Pike Ste, Vienna VA 22182	703-883-1410	R	9*	.1
579	Tidal Software Inc	170 W Tasman Dr, San Jose CA 95134		S	9*	.1
580	Incisent Technologies—Pat Ryan Jr	833 W Jackson Blvd Ste, Chicago IL 60607		R	9*	.1
581	Sal Johnson and Associates Inc—Henry Sal	791 Piedmont Wekiwa Rd, Apopka FL 32703	407-598-1800	R	9*	.1
582	Wellsource Inc—Don Hall	PO Box 569, Clackamas OR 97015	503-656-7446	R	9*	<.1
583	Azuro Inc—Paul Cunningham	5201 Great America Pkw, Santa Clara CA 95054	408-970-8200	R	9*	<.1
584	Computility Inc—Mike Stuart	10641 Justin Dr, Des Moines IA 50322	515-331-3003	S	9*	<.1
585	Instrumental Inc—Kim Schumann	2748 E 82nd St, Bloomington MN 55425	952-345-2820	R	9*	<.1
586	Skyler Technology Inc—Mark Ford	201 Spear St Ste 1100, San Francisco CA 94105	925-689-9814	R	9*	<.1
587	Valtira LLC—David Bagley	1201 Marquette Ave Ste, Minneapolis MN 55403	612-338-3794	R	9*	<.1
588	Volchok Consulting Inc—Michael Volchok	120 W 20th St, New York NY 10011	212-777-7433	R	9*	<.1
589	WaveMaker Software Inc—Christopher Keene	1000 Sansome St Ste 25, San Francisco CA 94111	415-357-0210	R	9*	<.1
590	Citizenhawk Inc—Dave Duckwitz	27068 La Paz Rd Ste 10, Aliso Viejo CA 92656		R	9*	<.1
591	Siderean Software Inc—Michael A Schmitt	909 N Sepulevda Blvd S, El Segundo CA 90245	310-647-4266	R	9*	<.1
592	Software Technology Group Inc—Yogesh Vaidya	2975 Bowers Ave Ste 30, Santa Clara CA 95051	408-970-9100	R	9*	<.1
593	Integrated Systems and Contraols of NY Inc—John Maute	520 Stokes Rd Ste C1, Medford NJ 08055	609-714-8441	R	9*	<.1
594	Automation Resources Inc—Allen Carty	P O Box 44759, Eden Prairie MN 55344	952-563-5440	R	9*	<.1
595	Pyramid Solutions Inc—Daniel Kosmalski	30150 Telg Rd Ste 200, Franklin MI 48025	248-549-1200	R	9*	<.1
596	Progressive Computing LLC—Glen Kelly	3615 Krny Vlla Rd Ste, San Diego CA 92123	858-707-0707	R	9*	.1
597	IPKeys Technologies LLC—Lanfen C Nawy	1 Industrial Way W Bld, Eatontown NJ 07724	732-389-8112	R	9	.1
598	Arena Solutions Inc—Craig Livingston	4100 E 3rd Ave Ste 300, Foster City CA 94404	650-513-3500	R	9*	.1
599	Core2 Business Consulting Inc—David Roberts	33 Broad St 10, Boston MA 02109	617-439-7070	R	9*	.1
600	IT Source Corp—Ed Bowman	3701 Wilshire Blvd Ste, Los Angeles CA 90010	213-550-4482	R	9	.1
601	Sierra Bravo Corp—Luke Bucklin	9555 James Ave S Ste 2, Bloomington MN 55431	952-948-1211	R	9*	.1
602	Plcs Plus International Inc—Lee Britt	PO Box 20238, Bakersfield CA 93390	661-322-4470	R	9*	.1
603	Heritage Makers Inc—Doug Cloward	1837 S East Bay Blvd S, Provo UT 84606	801-437-8000	R	9	.1
604	Strata Marketing Inc—Bruce Johnson	30 W Monroe St Ste 190, Chicago IL 60603	312-346-2852	R	8*	.1
605	Tandel Systems Inc—Mike Varga	3982 Tampa Rd, Oldsmar FL 34677	813-852-6751	R	8*	.1
606	Airversent Inc—Michael Lee	11460 Cronridge Dr Ste, Owings Mills MD 21117	443-394-5180	R	8*	.1
607	Trust Ownership Group Inc—Kathy Jackson	5804 Churchman By Pass, Indianapolis IN 46203	317-791-1414	R	8*	.1
608	Ultimo Software Solutions Inc—Subhash Pasumarthy	2860 Zanker Rd Ste 203, San Jose CA 95134	408-943-1490	R	8*	.1
609	Techdemocracy LLC—Srikiran Patibandla	499 Thornall St Ste 30, Edison NJ 08837	732-404-8350	R	8*	.1
610	Animax Interactive LLC—Michael Bellavia	6627 Valjean Ave, Van Nuys CA 91406	818-787-4444	R	8*	.1
611	BlackLine Systems—Therese Tucker	23586 Calabasas Rd, Calabasas CA 91302	818-223-9008	R	8*	.1
612	Ceon Corp—Jeff Fox	1600 Seaport Blvd Ste, Redwood City CA 94063	650-817-6300	S	8*	.1
613	Performance Software Corp—Timothy A Bigelow	2095 W Pinnacle Peak R, Phoenix AZ 85027	623-337-8003	R	8*	<.1
614	Involta Inc—Bruce Lehrman	PO Box 1986, Cedar Rapids IA 52406	319-364-3061	R	8*	<.1
615	Software Architects Inc—Robert Zollo	610 Market St Ste 200, Kirkland WA 98033		R	8*	<.1
616	Meridian Partners—Wil Martinez	420 Lincoln Rd Ste 324, Miami Beach FL 33139	305-444-1811	R	8*	<.1
617	James River Technical Inc—Leo Iantosca	4439 Cox Rd, Glen Allen VA 23060	804-935-0150	R	8*	<.1
618	NewVision Systems Corp—Ronald R Watkins	50 Locust Ave, New Canaan CT 06840		R	8*	<.1
619	Cat's Pajamas LLC—Wayne Olson	12559 Pulver Rd, Burlington WA 98233	360-707-5300	D	8*	<.1
620	Netmagic Systems Inc—Sandip Gupta	245 W 104th St Ste 10E, New York NY 10025		R	8*	<.1
621	Verinform Systems Inc—Dina Dickerson	1275 First Ave Ste 234, New York NY 10065	503-231-8912	R	8*	<.1
622	Avexxis Corp—Frank Hanshaw	30 Avon Meadow Ln, Avon CT 06001	860-676-9006	R	8*	<.1
623	MDG Computer Services Inc	641 Industrial Dr, Cary IL 60013	847-462-4004	R	8*	<.1
624	EOL Inc—Dennis G Wadsworth	PO Box 553, Westborough MA 01581	508-898-3600	R	8*	<.1
625	ePolk—Michael Kingham	25 5th St NW, Winter Haven FL 33881	863-291-4268	R	8*	<.1
626	JO'B Consultants—John OBrien	866 Woodfield Rd, Franklin Lakes NJ 07417	201-337-0316	R	8*	<.1
627	Vinculum Solutions Inc—Bruce Pitt	3945 Island Landing Ct, Broomes Island MD 20615	540-538-5851	R	8*	<.1
628	Futurenet Technologies Corp—Tom Liu	222 E Huntington Dr St, Monrovia CA 91016	626-358-7912	R	8*	.1
629	3tier Environmental Forecast Group Inc—Pascal Storck	2001 6th Ave Ste 2100, Seattle WA 98121	206-325-1573	R	8*	.1
630	Qatalys Inc—Rao Telidevara	222 Las Colinas Blvd W, Irving TX 75039	214-630-1480	R	8*	.1
631	Integrated Systems Management Inc—Divan Dave	303 S Broadway Ste 101, Tarrytown NY 10591	914-332-5590	R	8*	.1
632	ARK Solutions Inc—Bhavna Vasisht	14161 Robert Paris Ct, Chantilly VA 20151	703-502-6999	R	8	.1
633	Seh Enterprises Inc—Sam Hodges	PO Box 490655, Leesburg FL 34749	352-326-5407	R	8*	.1
634	Entirenet LLC—Mike Bryan	14450 Ne 29th Pl Ste 2, Bellevue WA 98007	425-558-1000	R	8*	.1
635	Sportsmedia Technology Corp—Gerard Hall	3511 University Dr, Durham NC 27707	919-493-9390	R	8*	.1
636	Aquitec Inc—Frank Arico	547 W Jackson Blvd Ste, Chicago IL 60661	312-264-1900	R	8*	.1
637	Steelhead Data LLC—Christian Coulter	1532 Eureka Rd Ste 101, Roseville CA 95661	916-784-1004	R	8*	<.1
638	Itcube LLC—Nitin Mehta	10999 Reed Hartman Hwy, Blue Ash OH 45242	513-891-7300	R	7*	.1
639	Winware Inc—Larry Harper	1955 W Oak Cir, Marietta GA 30062	770-419-1399	R	7*	.1
640	Digital Solutions Inc—Anthony Bambocci	PO Box 2868, Mobile AL 36652	814-944-0405	R	7*	.1
641	Three Stage Media Inc—William Geritz	5523 Research Park Dr, Baltimore MD 21228	410-402-1028	R	7*	.1
642	Digital IMS Inc—Jay Wilkinson	1200 N St Ste 100, Lincoln NE 68508	402-437-0133	R	7*	.1
643	Digital Chocolate Inc—Trip Hawkins	1855 S Grant St Ste 20, San Mateo CA 94402	650-372-1600	R	7*	.1
644	Health Systems Solutions Inc—Stanley Vashovsky	405 N Reo St Ste 300, Tampa FL 33609	813-282-3303	R	7	.1
645	Lewis Computer Services Inc—Jeffrey Lewis	8549 United Plz Blvd, Baton Rouge LA 70809	225-709-2000	R	7*	.1
646	Firstborn Multimedia Corp—Michael Ferdman	630 9th Ave Ste 910, New York NY 10036	212-581-1100	R	7*	.1
647	I-Prospect Inc—Amit Maheshwari	400 Talcott Ave Ste 1, Watertown MA 02472	617-393-2338	R	7*	.1
648	Ventech Solutions Inc—Herb Jones	8760 Orion Pl Ste 204, Columbus OH 43240	614-751-1167	R	7	.1
649	NorthStar Systems International Inc—Bob Skea	575 Market St Fl 14, San Francisco CA 94105	415-344-6100	R	7*	.1
650	Advanced Technologies Group Inc—Atul Gupta	1601 48th St Ste 220, West Des Moines IA 50266	515-221-9344	R	7*	<.1
651	Sentek Consulting Inc—Eric Basu	651 Arroyo Dr, San Diego CA 92103	619-543-9550	R	7*	<.1
652	Image Metrics Inc—Robert Gehorsam	1918 Main St 2nd Fl, Santa Monica CA 90405	310-656-6565	P	7	<.1
653	KeyMark Inc—Jim Wanner	105 Tech Ln, Liberty SC 29657	864-343-0500	R	7*	<.1
654	Ideal Financial Solutions Inc—Steven L Sunyich	5940 S Rainbow Blvd, Las Vegas NV 89118		P	7	<.1
655	Broadness LLC—Randolph A Hudson III	524 Broadway, New York NY 10012	212-818-1313	R	7*	<.1
656	CompanionLink Software Inc—Wayland Bruns	811 SW Naito Pkwy Ste, Portland OR 97204	503-243-3400	R	7*	<.1
657	Dafca Inc—Dennis Shepard	10 Speen St 2nd Fl, Framingham MA 01701	774-204-0200	R	7*	<.1
658	ECD Systems Inc—Jack Hart	3821 Falmouth Rd, Marstons Mills MA 02648	508-420-6950	R	7*	<.1
659	Intesource Inc—Ronald S Southard	2111 E Highland Ave St, Phoenix AZ 85016	602-445-2200	R	7*	<.1
660	Market Line Associates Inc—Scott Storbeck	1605 Chantilly Dr, Atlanta GA 30324	404-248-1100	R	7*	<.1
661	Minnetonka Audio Software—John Schur	17113 Minnetonka Blvd, Minnetonka MN 55345	952-449-6481	R	7*	<.1
662	TMC Software Inc	575 Market St Ste 2028, San Francisco CA 94105	415-956-3611	R	7*	<.1
663	Lambda Research Corp—Edward Freniere	25 Porter Rd, Littleton MA 01460	978-486-0766	R	7*	<.1
664	Entreprencur Consulting Group Inc—Greg Boyd	PO Box 112369, Carrollton TX 75011	972-818-9600	R	7*	<.1
665	ChannelinxCom Inc—Daniel Schmidt	150 Executive Ctr Dr B, Greenville SC 29615	864-527-3500	R	7*	<.1
666	Data Systems Group Of California—John Baird	2331 Alhambra Blvd, Sacramento CA 95817	916-443-4944	R	7*	<.1
667	Walklett Group Inc—Thomas Walklett	20 Valley Stream Pkwy, Malvern PA 19355	610-722-9600	R	7*	.1

Note: An asterisk (*) indicates an estimated financial figure. The company type code used is as follows: R = Private, P = Public, S = Private Subsidiary, B = Public Subsidiary, D = Division, J = Joint Venture, I = Investment Fund.

COMPANY RANKINGS BY SALES WITHIN 4-DIGIT SIC

Rank	Company Name—Executive Officer	Address, City, State, Zip	Phone	Type	Fin	Empls
668	Tax Compliance Inc—Scott Strauss	10200 Willow Creek Rd, San Diego CA 92131	858-547-4100	R	7*	.1
669	Liaison International Inc—George Haddad	311 Arsenal St Ste 15, Watertown MA 02472	617-926-0504	R	7*	.1
670	Vigilant Services Corp—George Arnold	PO Box 986, Lorton VA 22199	703-339-4272	R	7*	<.1
671	Innovative Alternatives Inc—Zorica Prodanov	999 N Plz Dr Ste 670, Schaumburg IL 60173	847-995-8100	R	7*	.1
672	Continuum Performance Systems Inc—Brad Turley	634 Boston Post Rd, Madison CT 06443	203-245-5000	R	7*	<.1
673	Albano Systems Inc—Keith Albano	360 Bloomfield Ave Ste, Windsor CT 06095	860-688-9555	R	7*	<.1
674	Packet Design Inc—Jack Bradley	2455 Augustine Dr Ste, Santa Clara CA 95054	408-490-1000	R	6*	.1
675	Webcollage Inc—Eli Singer	462 7th Ave Fl 9, New York NY 10018	212-563-2112	R	6*	.1
676	Rapture Technologies Inc—Casey Fronczek	701 Palomar Airpt Rd S, Carlsbad CA 92009	760-931-4756	R	6*	.2
677	American Computer And Telephone Inc—Michael Rohleder	300 Johnny Bench Dr St, Oklahoma City OK 73104	405-216-8080	R	6*	.1
678	Transzap Inc—Peter Flanagan	1999 Broadway Ste 1900, Denver CO 80202	303-863-8600	R	6*	.1
679	Agiliance Inc—Joe Fantuzzi	2001 Gateway Pl Ste 31, San Jose CA 95110	408-200-0400	R	6*	.1
680	Public Systems Associates Inc—Lawrence Leftoff	2431 S Acadian Twy Ste, Baton Rouge LA 70808	225-346-0618	R	6*	.1
681	Sadler-Necamp Financial Services Inc—Randal Sadler	7621 E Kemper Rd, Cincinnati OH 45249	513-489-5477	R	6*	<.1
682	Ariadne Genomics Inc—Ilya Mazo	9430 Key W Ave Ste 113, Rockville MD 20850	240-453-6296	R	6*	<.1
683	Tessolvedts Inc—Jill Johnston	4360 W Chandler Blvd S, Chandler AZ 85226	480-632-0312	R	6*	<.1
684	ARCLITE Lab - Brigham Young University—Daniel Standage	A-41 ASB Brgham young, Provo UT 84602	801-422-1976	R	6*	<.1
685	Ants Software Inc—Joseph Kozak	1031-F Cambridge Sq, Alpharetta GA 30009	650-931-0500	P	6	.1
686	Cardiopulmonary Corp—James Biondi	200 Cascade Blvd Ste B, Milford CT 06460	203-877-1999	R	6*	<.1
687	Vanguard Appraisals Inc—Robert Kocer	1500 2nd Ave SE Ste 30, Cedar Rapids IA 52403	319-365-8625	R	6*	.1
688	Clarus Systems Inc—Brendan Reidy	2200 Bridge Pkwy Ste 1, Redwood City CA 94065	650-632-2800	R	6*	.1
689	Voice Systems Engineering Inc—Gary Baron	900 Wheeler Way A, Langhorne PA 19047	215-953-8568	R	6*	.1
690	Intertech Inc—Thomas Salonek	1020 Discovery Rd Ste, Saint Paul MN 55121	651-994-8558	R	6*	<.1
691	Enhanced Telecommunications Inc—Pete Pifer	6065 Atlantic Blvd, Norcross GA 30071	770-242-3620	R	6*	<.1
692	Trawick and Associates—Mark Kleckner	8270 Greensboro Dr Ste, McLean VA 22102	703-584-8600	R	6*	.1
693	Servient Inc—Ian Wilson	9990 Richmond Ave Ste, Houston TX 77042	713-980-1992	R	6*	.1
694	Paladin Data Systems Corp—Jim Nall	19362 Powder Hill Pl N, Poulsbo WA 98370	360-779-2400	R	6*	.1
695	Service Power Inc—Mark Duffin	222 Severn Ave Ste 31, Annapolis MD 21403	410-571-6333	R	6*	.1
696	Appareo Systems LLC—Barry Batcheller	1810 NDSU Research Cir, Fargo ND 58102	701-356-2200	R	6*	.1
697	IQ Stored Inc—James Schellhase	4401 W Gate Blvd Ste 3, Austin TX 78745	512-334-3100	R	6*	.1
698	FinTrack Systems Corp—Murugan Manivannan	11 Broadway Ste 702, New York NY 10004	212-742-1800	R	6*	.1
699	International Software Systems Inc (Greenbelt Maryland)—Bhaskar U Ganti	7337 Hanover Pky Ste A, Greenbelt MD 20770	301-982-9700	R	6*	.1
700	Starlight Networks Inc—Stephen Lorentzen	205 Ravendale Dr, Mountain View CA 94043	650-967-2774	S	6	.1
701	XCEL Solutions Corp—Jit Kumar	254 Rte 34 Ste 3, Matawan NJ 07747	732-765-9235	R	6*	<.1
702	Mayer Cherbonnier and Associates Inc—Ben Cherbonnier	8180 Ymca Plz Dr Ste A, Baton Rouge LA 70810	225-927-9200	R	6*	<.1
703	Soft Pros Inc—Chand Akkineni	4470 Chamblee Dunwoody, Atlanta GA 30338	770-234-0222	R	6*	<.1
704	ABS Associates Inc—Rosemarie Mitchell	2100 Golf Rd Ste 110, Rolling Meadows IL 60008	847-437-8700	R	6*	<.1
705	InterTech Information Management Inc—Tom Salonek	1020 Discovery Rd Ste, Saint Paul MN 55121	651-994-8558	R	6*	<.1
706	Systems Conversion Ltd—Jeff Culverhouse	202 S Erwin St, Cartersville GA 30120	770-606-9615	R	6	<.1
707	SalesPage Technologies Inc—Greg Ozuzu	PO Box 2707, Kalamazoo MI 49003	269-567-7400	R	6*	<.1
708	Teccon Inc—Robert Darling	2540 Bengal Blvd Ste 1, Salt Lake City UT 84121	801-993-1460	R	6*	<.1
709	Providge Consulting LLC—Michael Carr	2207 Concord Pike Ste, Wilmington DE 19803		R	6*	<.1
710	Interlink Technologies—Jessie Miller	PO Box 970, Perrysburg OH 43551	419-893-9011	R	6*	<.1
711	Logosol Inc—Lubomir Kostov	1155 Tasman Dr, Sunnyvale CA 94089	408-744-0974	R	6*	<.1
712	Contemporary Software Concepts Inc—John P Scott	455 Pennsylvania Ave S, Fort Washington PA 19034	610-687-6000	R	6*	<.1
713	Embedded Planet Inc—Mark Lowdermilk	4760 Richmond Rd Ste 4, Warrensville Heights OH 44128	216-245-4180	R	6*	<.1
714	Technicolor Creative Services—Lanny Raimondo	110 Leroy St 3rd Fl, New York NY 10014	212-609-9400	S	6*	<.1
715	heskethcom Inc—Heather Hesketh	1101 Haynes St Ste 109, Raleigh NC 27604	919-834-2552	R	6*	<.1
716	Bada Networks—Anson Chen	4701 Patrick Henry Dr, Santa Clara CA 95054	408-987-9900	R	6*	<.1
717	Entiera LLC—Ted Ansusinha	3515 Plymouth Blvd Ste, Minneapolis MN 55447	763-559-0902	R	6*	<.1
718	Global Internet Management Corp—Eli Avershal	150 Monument Rd Ste 21, Bala Cynwyd PA 19004	610-617-4515	R	6*	<.1
719	Plus Three LP—Juan Proano	PO Box 971, New York NY 10274	212-206-7819	R	6*	<.1
720	Adometry Inc—Paul Pellman	4301 Westbank Dr Bldg, Austin TX 78746	512-852-7100	R	6*	<.1
721	Conducive Corp—James Hill	55 Broad St 23rd Fl, New York NY 10004	212-925-2022	R	6*	<.1
722	CyberLink USA—Alice H Chang	4800 Great American Pk, Santa Clara CA 95054		R	6*	<.1
723	Findology Interactive Media Inc—Jon Waterman	1158 26th St Ste 464, Santa Monica CA 90403	310-556-4440	R	6*	<.1
724	Global Technologies Inc (Atlanta Georgia)—Mary O'Malley	PO Box 18738, Atlanta GA 31126	404-995-9840	R	6*	<.1
725	IGA Worldwide—Peter Bilotta	111 Broadway, New York NY 10006	212-381-0950	R	6*	<.1
726	Orsus Solutions—Zeevi Bregman	1 Penn Plz Ste 6210, New York NY 10119	212-594-5288	S	6*	<.1
727	Digital Media Performance Labs Inc—Christopher Hipp	1950 N Stemmons Fwy, Dallas TX 75207	214-800-8400	R	6*	<.1
728	Ackermans Icu Software—Jerry Ackerman	12253 23rd Ave S, Burnsville MN 55337	952-894-6800	R	6*	<.1
729	Larimore Associates Inc—Joe Larimore	PO Box 8, Chesterfield MO 63006	636-537-3112	R	6*	<.1
730	Fishbowl Inventory—David Williams	580 E Technology Ave S, Orem UT 84097	801-932-1100	R	6	.1
731	Wishbone Systems Inc—Ashok Samuel	619 E Palisade Ave, Englewood Cliffs NJ 07632	201-541-7000	R	6*	.1
732	Dancik International Ltd—Mitchell Dancik	2000 Centre Green Way, Cary NC 27513	919-379-3800	R	6*	.1
733	Okaya Infocom Private Ltd—Sanjiv Gupta	33 Peachtree Ct, Holtsville NY 11742	631-675-6674	R	6*	.1
734	Riot Games Inc—Brandon Beck	100 Crprate Pinte Ste, Culver City CA 90230	424-231-1111	R	6*	<.1
735	Tobii Assistive Technology Inc—Tara Rudnicki	333 Elm St Ste 115, Dedham MA 02026	781-461-8200	R	6*	<.1
736	Pkmm Inc—Ralph Pallotta	PO Box 70, Oceanport NJ 07757	732-935-1927	R	6*	<.1
737	Inscribe Inc—Joseph Sieber	35 Olympia Ave Ste 2, Woburn MA 01801	781-933-3331	R	6*	<.1
738	Laxmi Group Inc	4699 Old Ironsides DrS, Santa Clara CA 95054	408-329-7733	S	6	.1
739	Enterprise Infra Corp—Christopher Wade	5000 E Spring St Ste 7, Long Beach CA 90815	562-733-7500	R	6*	.1
740	3s Realserv—Scott Steele	5700 Executive Dr, Baltimore MD 21228	410-719-2300	R	6*	.1
741	Idbs Inc—David Morgan	1301 Marina Village Pk, Alameda CA 94501	510-814-4900	R	6*	.1
742	Independent Technology Systems America Inc—Fred Brott	2711 Lbj Fwy Ste 512, Dallas TX 75234	972-850-1937	R	6*	.1
743	Apptricity Corp—Timothy Garcia	5605 N Macarthur Blvd, Irving TX 75038	214-596-0601	R	6*	<.1
744	Collins Computing Inc—Steven Collins	26050 Acero, Mission Viejo CA 92691	949-457-0500	R	6*	<.1
745	Confirmit Inc—Henning Hansen	424 W 33rd St Rm 410, New York NY 10001	212-660-1800	R	6*	<.1
746	Lifecare Technologies Inc—Bruce Wilson	PO Box 236, Tilton NH 03276	813-886-7500	R	6*	.1
747	Datahouse Holdings Corp—Creighton Arita	1585 Kplani Blvd Ste 1, Honolulu HI 96814	808-942-8108	R	6*	.1
748	1010data Inc—Joel Kaplan	230 Park Ave Fl 27, New York NY 10169	212-405-1010	R	6*	.1
749	Xyant Technology Inc—Sreenivasan Rajappa	1218 W Rock Creek Rd, Norman OK 73069	405-447-8337	R	6*	.1
750	Adil Business Systems Inc—Sushil Chachra	167 Madison Ave Rm 305, New York NY 10016	212-683-5096	R	6*	.1
751	Adaptive Computing—Robert Clyde	1656 Se Bay Blvd Ste 3, Provo UT 84606	801-717-3700	R	6*	.1
752	B2b Technologies LLC—Frank Fuerst	1776 Peachtree St Nw S, Atlanta GA 30309	404-892-1500	R	6*	<.1
753	Enterprise Technology Servs LLC—Kurt Bohman	730 N 52nd St Ste 100, Phoenix AZ 85008	602-426-8600	R	6*	.1
754	Instructional Technology Inc—Ruchi Kumar	777 E Eisenhower Pkwy, Ann Arbor MI 48108	734-717-3862	R	5*	.1
755	Eloquent Inc—Clifford A Reid	1730 S El Camino Real, San Mateo CA 94402	650-294-6500	S	5	.1
756	Medflow Inc—Dominic Riggi	6739 Fairview Rd Ste A, Charlotte NC 28210	704-927-9800	R	5*	.1

Rank	Company Name—*Executive Officer*	Address, City, State, Zip	Phone	Type	Fin	Empls
757	4 Consulting Inc—*Vivek Anand*	1221 Abrams Rd Ste 326, Richardson TX 75081	214-698-8633	R	5*	.1
758	Masque Publishing—*Jim Wisler*	8400 Park Meadows Dr, Littleton CO 80124	303-290-9853	R	5*	<.1
759	Coyotedata Security Limited Inc—*Lewis Sckolnick*	130 Rattlesnake Gutter, Leverett MA 01054	413-367-0303	R	5*	.1
760	Uni/Care Systems Inc—*May Ahdab*	PO Box 3618, Sarasota FL 34230	941-954-3403	R	5*	.1
761	Share One Inc—*Daryl Tanner*	2650 Thousand Oks Blvd, Memphis TN 38118	901-795-3512	R	5*	.1
762	Oil and Gas Consultants International Inc—*James Brett*	PO Box 35448, Tulsa OK 74153	918-828-2500	R	5*	<.1
763	Earthcam Inc—*Brian Cury*	84 Kennedy St, Hackensack NJ 07601	201-488-1111	R	5*	<.1
764	Mindpix Corp—*Thomas Aliprandi*	138 E 12300 S, Draper UT 84020	801-755-6859	R	5*	.1
765	Intelligraphics Inc—*Scott Lawson*	1401 N Central Expy St, Richardson TX 75080	972-479-1770	R	5*	.1
766	Rolloversystems LLC—*Ted Benna*	4135 Southstream Blvd, Charlotte NC 28217	704-295-1234	R	5*	.1
767	Shark Technology Inc—*T Watkins*	PO Box 99336, Raleigh NC 27624	919-696-6812	R	5*	<.1
768	Optier Inc—*Ronen Fischler*	130 W 42nd St Ste 1804, New York NY 10036	212-679-2700	R	5*	<.1
769	Intellione Technologies Corp—*Ronald Herman*	3100 Interstate Ste 10, Atlanta GA 30339	404-969-3700	R	5*	<.1
770	I-Solutions Global Ltd—*Paul Docherty*	581 Boylston St Ste 32, Boston MA 02116	617-267-9595	R	5*	.1
771	Legal Applications Holding Corp—*Matthew Mcisacc*	1215 Hightower Trl A20, Atlanta GA 30350	770-640-0300	R	5*	.1
772	Trondent Development Corp—*David Wood*	1300 S Grove Ave Ste 2, Barrington IL 60010	847-277-0800	R	5*	.1
773	Konami Computer Entertainment Of America Inc—*Akira Ki-nebuchi*	2222 Kalakaua Ave Ste, Honolulu HI 96815	808-923-0573	R	5*	<.1
774	Cerylion Inc—*Ilan Rozenblat*	8 New England Exec Par, Burlington MA 01803	781-494-0871	R	5*	<.1
775	Experience Inc—*Jennifer Floren*	1 Faneuil Hall Market, Boston MA 02109	617-305-7400	R	5*	<.1
776	IONA Technologies—*Christopher J Horn Ph D*	200 West St Ste 4, Waltham MA 02451	781-902-8000	S	5*	.2
777	Cyberwerx Inc—*John Murphy*	PO Box 4726, Cary NC 27519	919-424-5089	R	5*	.1
778	Terasoft International Inc—*Venkat Akkina*	2025 S Arlington Hts, Arlington Heights IL 60005	847-427-1717	R	5*	.1
779	Segue Technologies Inc—*Brian Callahan*	2300 Wilson Blvd Ste 4, Arlington VA 22201	703-549-8033	R	5*	.1
780	Sigmatech Inc—*Gurmej Sandhu*	4901 Corporate Dr NW S, Huntsville AL 35805	256-382-1188	R	5*	.1
781	Syncro Technologies Inc—*Sonny Mujumdar*	PO Box 632, South Plainfield NJ 07080	908-668-7962	R	5*	.1
782	Four Rivers Software Systems Inc—*Henry Wilde*	1501 Ardmore Blvd 2nd, Pittsburgh PA 15221	412-256-9020	R	5*	.1
783	Intersoft Corp—*Monishi Sanyal*	2001 Gateway Pl Ste 50, San Jose CA 95110	408-987-5300	R	5*	.1
784	Systems Resource Management Inc—*Otis Sampsan*	42 Valley Rd, Middletown RI 02842	401-849-2913	R	5*	.1
785	Terocelo Inc—*Antonio E Turgeon*	30651-A1 Thousand Oaks, Agoura Hills CA 91301		R	5*	.1
786	Vpg Integrated Media Inc—*Robert Price*	200 Portland St Ste 20, Boston MA 02114	617-523-1770	R	5*	.1
787	Catalis Inc—*Frank Taylor*	916 S Capital Of Texas, West Lake Hills TX 78746	512-874-7600	R	5*	.1
788	Dhap Digital Inc—*Philip Dzilvelis*	235 Montgomery St Ste, San Francisco CA 94104	415-962-4900	R	5*	.1
789	Global Solutions Network Inc—*Ron Newlan*	121 Congressional Ln S, Rockville MD 20852	703-768-5200	R	5*	.1
790	Redmond Technology Partners LLC—*Brett Stallman*	1975 112th Ave Ne Ste, Bellevue WA 98004	425-451-9855	R	5*	.1
791	Source of Future Technology Inc—*Cathy Grubiak*	161 Ave of the America, New York NY 10013	212-633-1515	R	5*	.1
792	STF Technologies Inc	51 Columbia, Aliso Viejo CA 92656	949-362-5800	S	5*	.1
793	Way Forward Technology Inc—*Voldi Way*	27931 Smyth Dr, Valencia CA 91355	661-286-2769	R	5*	.1
794	Evisions Inc—*Kevin Jones*	410 Exchange Ste 250, Irvine CA 92602	714-824-5252	R	5*	<.1
795	Excent Corp—*Scott Shickler*	60 King St, Roswell GA 30075	678-735-4210	R	5*	<.1
796	Autologue Computer Systems Inc—*James Franco*	8452 Commonwealth Ave, Buena Park CA 90621	714-522-3551	R	5*	<.1
797	Eye Street Software Corp	1602 Village Market Bl, Leesburg VA 20175		R	5*	<.1
798	InherentCom Inc—*Debra Kamys*	1 Embarcadero Center S, San Francisco CA 94111	415-399-9733	R	5*	<.1
799	Visual Analytics Inc—*Christopher Westphal*	50 Citizens Way Ste 20, Frederick MD 21701	240-215-6600	R	5*	<.1
800	Daniel H Wagner Associates Inc—*C Butler*	559 W Uwchlan Ave Ste, Exton PA 19341	610-280-3830	R	5*	<.1
801	Kelar Corp—*Adriana Vernon*	PO Box 4278, Jackson Hole WY 83001	307-733-3458	R	5*	<.1
802	Markov Processes International LLC	37 Landsdowne Rd, East Brunswick NJ 08816	732-390-8986	R	5*	<.1
803	Atalasoft Inc—*William Bither*	116 Pleasant St Ste 32, Easthampton MA 01027	413-572-4443	R	5*	<.1
804	Weiland Financial Group Inc—*Patricia D Weiland*	2275 Half Day Rd Ste 1, Bannockburn IL 60015	847-735-0577	S	5*	<.1
805	Meridianlink Inc—*Binh Dang*	1124 Bristol St, Costa Mesa CA 92626	714-708-6950	R	5*	<.1
806	Atlas Development Corp—*Robert Atlas*	26679 W Agoura Rd Ste, Calabasas CA 91302	818-340-7080	R	5*	<.1
807	Kirkey Products Group—*Stan Ruggiero*	931 N State Rd 434 Ste, Altamonte Springs FL 32714	407-331-5151	R	5*	<.1
808	Krozak Information Technologies Inc—*Jennifer Krozak*	201 Linton Knoll Ct, Silver Spring MD 20904	301-384-4340	R	5*	<.1
809	TS Traker Systems—*Larry Kudray*	43460 Ridge Park Dr St, Temecula CA 92590	951-693-1376	R	5*	<.1
810	Community Techknowledge Inc—*Kathryn Engelhardt-Cron*	701 Brazos St Ste 1425, Austin TX 78701	512-345-9090	R	5*	<.1
811	Greenview Data Inc—*Ted Green*	PO Box 1586, Ann Arbor MI 48106	734-426-7500	R	5*	<.1
812	Visual Solutions Inc—*Peter Darnell*	487 Groton Rd, Westford MA 01886	978-392-0100	R	5*	<.1
813	Halter Capital Corp—*Kevin Halter Jr*	2591 Dallas Pkwy Ste 1, Frisco TX 75034	469-633-0100	R	5*	<.1
814	Accurate Bit Copy Inc—*Stephan Waite*	6 Otis Park Dr, Bourne MA 02532	508-759-2129	R	5*	<.1
815	DataCal Enterprises LLC—*Randall Clark*	1345 N Mondel Dr, Gilbert AZ 85233	480-813-3100	R	5*	<.1
816	Information Technology Resources Inc—*Jim Cisneros*	7001 Village Dr Ste 15, Buena Park CA 90621	714-573-7450	R	5*	<.1
817	Software Data Design Inc—*Ron Parham*	306 W Katella Ave Ste, Orange CA 92867	714-633-3077	R	5*	<.1
818	TOLIS Group Inc—*Tim Jones*	8687 E Via de Ventura, Scottsdale AZ 85258	480-505-0488	R	5*	<.1
819	Advanced Media Post—*Adam Lesh*	4001 W Magnolia Blvd, Burbank CA 91505	818-973-1660	R	5*	<.1
820	Ambient Digital Media Inc—*Lee Evans*	4551 Glencoe Ave Ste 2, Marina Del Rey CA 90292	310-396-7375	R	5*	<.1
821	ASEC International Inc—*Norman E Green*	11400 W Olympic Blvd S, Los Angeles CA 90064	310-478-7755	R	5*	<.1
822	Boomerang Software Inc—*Richard Bezjian*	90 Concord Ave Ste 1, Belmont MA 02478	617-489-3000	R	5*	<.1
823	Cleanscape Software International—*Chris Niggeler*	172 College St Ste A, Spencer TN 38585	931-946-1015	R	5*	<.1
824	Computer Marketplace Inc (Tewksbury Massasschusetts)—*Dave Burke*	885 Main St, Tewksbury MA 01876	978-851-5317	R	5*	<.1
825	Cullimore and Ring Technologies Inc—*Brent Cullimore*	2501 Briarwood Dr, Boulder CO 80305	303-971-0292	R	5*	<.1
826	Express Technologies Corp—*Bernard Reznicek*	400 Reid St Ste O, De Pere WI 54115	920-337-1640	R	5*	<.1
827	Imerge Consulting Group LLC—*Ron Tussy*	2616 Carlmont Dr, Belmont CA 94002	650-631-5737	R	5*	<.1
828	ISE Inc—*Bengt Mossberg*	PO Box 836, Hawthorne CA 90251	310-643-7310	R	5*	<.1
829	Los Altos Technologies Inc—*Richard Mahn*	111 Corning Rd Ste 160, Cary NC 27518	919-233-9889	R	5*	<.1
830	Murano Software Inc—*Dimitri Nikouline*	28348 Roadside Dr Ste, Agoura Hills CA 91301	818-597-9470	R	5*	<.1
831	OpenWater Software Inc—*Michael Rocha*	1825 S Grant St, San Mateo CA 94402	650-432-6100	R	5*	<.1
832	Planetweb Inc—*Ken Soohoo*	303 Twin Dolphin Dr St, Redwood City CA 94065	650-632-4356	R	5*	<.1
833	Prestige Software Inc—*Paul Simmons*	22885-G Savi Ranch Pkw, Yorba Linda CA 92887	714-283-2323	R	5*	<.1
834	Rolling Thunder Software Inc—*Jeff Hill*	122 Escondido Ave Ste, Vista CA 92084	760-407-0191	R	5*	<.1
835	Saltec Systems—*Salmon Maqsood*	116 Kellogg Ave Ste 3, Ames IA 50010	515-598-4347	R	5*	<.1
836	SARS Software Products Inc—*James A Doty*	2175 E Francisco Blvd, San Rafael CA 94901	415-226-0040	R	5*	<.1
837	SeeSaw Networks Inc—*Peter Bowen*	100 Bush St Ste 950, San Francisco CA 94104		R	5*	<.1
838	Small Business Computers of New England Inc—*Gene Calvano*	25 Lowell St Ste 401, Manchester NH 03101		R	5*	<.1
839	Software Business Systems Inc—*Curtis Cerf*	7300 Metro Blvd Ste 62, Minneapolis MN 55439	952-835-0100	R	5*	<.1
840	Streambox Inc—*Robert Hildeman*	1848 Westlake Ave N, Seattle WA 98109	206-956-0544	R	5*	<.1
841	Weber Systems Inc—*Robert Fischer*	4700 Keeley Drive, Slinger WI 53086	262-782 0181	R	5*	<.1
842	Onyx Computing Inc—*Dr Bojana Bosanac*	10 Avon St, Cambridge MA 02138	617-876-3876	R	5*	<.1
843	MacUpdate LLC—*Joel Mueller*	526 W 14th St Ste 100, Traverse City MI 49684	269-873-1357	R	5*	<.1

Note: An asterisk (*) indicates an estimated financial figure. The company type code used is as follows: R = Private, P = Public, S = Private Subsidiary, B = Public Subsidiary, D = Division, J = Joint Venture, I = Investment Fund.

COMPANY RANKINGS BY SALES WITHIN 4-DIGIT SIC

Rank	Company Name—Executive Officer	Address, City, State, Zip	Phone	Type	Fin	Empls
844	Creative Research Systems Inc	411 B St Ste 2, Petaluma CA 94952	707-765-1001	R	5*	<.1
845	Seamless Peer To Peer LLC—Lucanus Rippy	2101 E Coast Hwy 102, Newport Beach CA 92660	949-235-7178	R	5*	<.1
846	Still Current Development Inc—Marek Neyman	10705 Cauley Creek Dr, Duluth GA 30097		R	5*	<.1
847	Saratogo On Line Systems Inc—James Ball	12 Cornell Rd Ste 3, Latham NY 12110	518-786-8030	R	5*	.1
848	Interimage Inc—Leslie Steele	4301 Fairfax Dr Ste 20, Arlington VA 22203	703-522-7400	R	5*	.1
849	Leading Edge Systems Richmond Inc—Adish Jain	3711 Westerre Pkwy Ste, Richmond VA 23233	804-673-5100	R	5*	<.1
850	Troll Systems Corp—Michele Scott	24950 Anza Dr, Valencia CA 91355	661-702-8900	R	5*	<.1
851	Earnware Corp—John Valenty	6451 El Camino Real St, Carlsbad CA 92009	760-804-2600	R	5*	<.1
852	KSM Associates Inc—Jason Kim	106 Beech Dr, Hatboro PA 19040	215-860-1200	R	5*	<.1
853	Structured Programming Services Inc—Gerald Feickert	7 Mount Lassen Dr D256, San Rafael CA 94903	415-472-5288	R	5*	<.1
854	2m Associates Inc—Madhavan Chakravarthi	1804 Vernon St Nw Ste, Washington DC 20009	202-387-5622	R	5*	.1
855	Strands Incorporated A Delaware Corp—Francisco Martin	760 Sw Madison Ave Ste, Corvallis OR 97333	541-753-4426	R	5*	.1
856	Data Financial Inc—James Holtz	1100 W Glen Oaks Ln 12, Mequon WI 53092	262-243-5511	R	5*	<.1
857	Litescape Technologies Inc—Gary Griffiths	PO Box 98, Belmont CA 94002	650-227-0220	R	5*	<.1
858	Visionary Medical Systems Inc—Jason Patchen	5600 Mariner St Ste 22, Tampa FL 33609	813-594-1026	R	5*	<.1
859	Sunup Design Systems Inc—Dinesh Mehta	2903 Bunker Hill Ln St, Santa Clara CA 95054	408-437-4500	R	5*	<.1
860	Agtek Development Company Inc—John Fletcher	396 Earhart Way, Livermore CA 94551	925-606-8197	R	5*	<.1
861	Lavastorm Inc—Andrew Rockwell	321 Summer St Fl 5, Boston MA 02210	617-345-5422	R	5*	<.1
862	Vinitech—Nick Grivas	11710 Plaza America St, Reston VA 20190	703-871-5353	R	5	<.1
863	Nextlabs Inc—Keng Lim	2 Waters Park Dr Ste 2, San Mateo CA 94403	650-577-9101	R	5*	.1
864	HEURIS—Brian Quandt	1136 Washington Ave7th, Saint Louis MO 63101	323-201-2705	R	5*	<.1
865	SurphoriaCom Inc—Chris Akin	934 Broadway Ste Ll, Tacoma WA 98402	253-573-1095	R	5*	<.1
866	3K Technologies LLC—Sireesha Chittabathini	161 Mission Falls Ln S, Fremont CA 94539	408-716-5900	R	5	<.1
867	Attero Tech LLC	1315 Dirs Row Ste 107, Fort Wayne IN 46808	260-496-9668	R	5*	<.1
868	Selectron Technologies Inc—Todd Johnston	7405 Sw Tech Ctr Dr St, Portland OR 97223	503-443-1400	R	5*	<.1
869	Softshare Inc—Frank Gott	9011 Olive St, Santa Barbara CA 93101	805-899-2366	R	5*	<.1
870	Tenex Systems Inc—Donald Roskos	2011 Renaissance Blvd, King Of Prussia PA 19406	610-239-9988	R	5*	<.1
871	Cello Development Corp—Karl A Simmons	PO Box 1439, Bethel Island CA 94511	925-684-0808	R	5	<.1
872	Data Tree Incorporated Of Virginia—C Tseronis	13 Firstfield Rd Ste 1, Gaithersburg MD 20878	301-869-6662	R	5*	<.1
873	Information Technologies International Inc—Billy Mccoy	4885 S 900 E Ste 100, Salt Lake City UT 84117	801-268-8600	R	5*	<.1
874	Infovista Technology LLC	5976 W Las Positas Blv, Pleasanton CA 94588	408-739-2870	R	5*	.1
875	Micro Design Services LLC—T Botell	2001 US Hwy 46 Ste 502, Parsippany NJ 07054	973-402-4334	R	5*	<.1
876	Farsight Technologies Inc—Jay Obernolte	611 Spruce Rd, Big Bear Lake CA 92315	909-866-0501	R	5*	<.1
877	Qflow Systems LLC—Tim Koehler	9317 Manchester Rd, Saint Louis MO 63119	314-968-1428	R	5*	<.1
878	Megasoft Ltd—Vijay K Tanamala	13461 Sunrise Valley D, Herndon VA 20171	703-793-0101	R	5	N/A
879	Dw Practice LLC	1853 Peeler Rd Ste C, Atlanta GA 30338	678-999-8197	R	4*	<.1
880	C-Systems Software Inc—Steve Stinson	2201 Arlington Downs R, Arlington TX 76011	817-649-3100	R	4*	<.1
881	PSI Software Inc—P Smith	PO Box 221560, El Paso TX 79913	915-584-4100	S	4	<.1
882	Worklogix Management Inc—Prasad Challa	195 Sarasota Cir S, Montgomery TX 77356	832-725-6391	R	4*	<.1
883	Christopherson John—Jim Bradley	8009 34th Ave S, Minneapolis MN 55425	952-814-7185	R	4*	.1
884	Nasoft USA Inc—Guillermo Gower	417 E Carmel St Ste 20, San Marcos CA 92078	760-410-1210	R	4*	<.1
885	Melange Computer Services Inc—Rick White	808 Century Blvd Ste 1, Lansing MI 48917	517-321-8434	R	4*	<.1
886	Total Quality Systems Inc—Tony Pombo	4066 S 1900 W Ste A, Roy UT 84067	801-731-2150	R	4*	<.1
887	Rolands and Associates Corp—Ronald Roland	120 Del Rey Gardens Dr, Monterey CA 93940	831-373-2025	R	4*	<.1
888	Executive Business Services Inc—Steve Williams	43398 Business Park Dr, Temecula CA 92590	951-693-0440	R	4	<.1
889	Mangrove Employer Services Inc—Tom Wood	1501 S Church Ave, Tampa FL 33629	813-387-3110	R	4*	<.1
890	Quardev Inc—Joseph Dillon	2707 Ne Blakeley St, Seattle WA 98105	206-547-7771	R	4*	<.1
891	Nts Data Service Inc—Charles Dewald	1342 Military Rd, Niagara Falls NY 14304	716-692-2274	R	4*	<.1
892	Nvoq Inc—Charles Corefield	1715 38th St, Boulder CO 80301	720-562-4500	R	4*	<.1
893	Cad-Tel Systems Inc—Linda Simmons	16435 N Scottsdale Rd, Scottsdale AZ 85254	602-953-4888	R	4*	<.1
894	Maya Design Inc—Michael Mcmanus	2730 Sidney St Ste 300, Pittsburgh PA 15203	412-488-2900	R	4*	<.1
895	Iic Technologies Inc—Frederick Ganjon	5550 Sterrett Pl Ste 2, Columbia MD 21044	410-997-7631	R	4*	<.1
896	Profileright Inc—Rishav Gupta	55 Linwood Ave, Cresskill NJ 07626	617-290-4404	R	4*	.1
897	80-20 Software Inc—Mark Ross	PO Box 40185, Bellevue WA 98015	425-739-6767	R	4*	<.1
898	Psi Fire—Thomas Strickland	820 Eschenburg Dr, Gilroy CA 95020	408-219-1538	R	4*	<.1
899	Syncro Technology Corp—Dale Aken	886 Town Ctr Dr, Langhorne PA 19047	215-741-0300	R	4*	<.1
900	Center Of Financial Technologies Inc—Ina Smirnova	601 Skokie Blvd Ste 10, Northbrook IL 60062	847-272-4740	R	4*	.1
901	Remco Software Inc—Robert Mcneill	528 21st St W Ste B, Dickinson ND 58601	701-456-5710	R	4*	.1
902	Simplicity Group LLC—Adam K Wilkinson	2250 W Center St, Springville UT 84663	801-623-6974	R	4*	.1
903	LC I-Connect—Helen Miltenberger	11465 Sunset Hills Rd, Reston VA 20190	703-471-3964	R	4*	.1
904	Balihoo Inc—Peter Gombert	404 S 8th St Ste 300, Boise ID 83702	208-286-2159	R	4*	.1
905	Datahouse Inc—Clyde Shiigi	1585 Kapiolani Blvd St, Honolulu HI 96814	808-942-8108	R	4*	.1
906	Eclipse Consulting Inc—Joseph Lamberger	PO Box 1451, Noblesville IN 46061	317-776-1406	R	4*	.1
907	Etest It Inc—Slava Kreynin	200 S Wacker Dr Fl 15, Chicago IL 60606	312-924-1042	R	4*	<.1
908	Nitro Pdf Inc—Sam Chandler	575 Market St Ste 3625, San Francisco CA 94105	415-369-9296	R	4*	<.1
909	Policy Administration Solutions Inc—Peter Pantelides	PO Box 540869, Flushing NY 11354	718-357-0771	R	4*	<.1
910	Economic Modeling Specialists Inc—Andrew Crapuchettes	PO Box 9008, Moscow ID 83843	208-883-3500	R	4*	.1
911	Innomedia Inc—Kai Ng	1901 Mccarthy Blvd, Milpitas CA 95035	408-943-8604	R	4*	<.1
912	ExpressoCom Corp—George Langan	2225 E Byshore Rd Ste, Palo Alto CA 94303	650-320-1730	R	4*	<.1
913	Jacer International Inc—Edgar Caburian	11304 Chapel Rd, Fairfax Station VA 22039	703-425-5167	R	4*	<.1
914	Collaborative Fusion Inc—Atila Omer	5849 Forbes Ave, Pittsburgh PA 15217	412-422-3463	R	4*	<.1
915	Datalight Inc—Roy Sherrill	21520 30th Dr SE Ste 1, Bothell WA 98021	425-951-8086	R	4*	<.1
916	Datanational Inc—Jerry DiPippo	23382 Commerce Dr, Farmington Hills MI 48335	248-426-0200	R	4*	<.1
917	Innovative Decisions Inc—Barry Lynch	600 Braddock Ave Ste A, Turtle Creek PA 15145	412-829-3010	R	4*	<.1
918	Software System and Solutions Inc—Kannan Venkataraman	2500 W Higgins Rd Ste, Hoffman Estates IL 60169	847-882-7971	R	4*	<.1
919	Nebraska Electronic Transfer Systems Inc—Phil Jossi	6130 S 58th St Ste D, Lincoln NE 68516	402-434-8200	R	4*	<.1
920	Orion Group Software Engineers Inc—William Street	5770 Nimtz Pky, South Bend IN 46628	574-233-3401	R	4*	<.1
921	Paraben Corp—Amber Schroader	PO Box 970483, Orem UT 84097	801-796-0944	R	4*	<.1
922	Viva Vision—Nicholas Montes	10171 Pacific Mesa Blv, San Diego CA 92121	858-558-7200	R	4*	<.1
923	Archway Technology Partners Inc—Jason Brown	9100 Keystone Crossing, Indianapolis IN 46240	317-819-5500	R	4*	<.1
924	InnoSys Inc—Mike Ridenhour	4118 Lakeside Dr, Richmond CA 94806	510-222-7717	R	4*	<.1
925	Saferock Retail—Shah Karim	25 E Spring Valley Ave, Maywood NJ 07607		R	4*	<.1
926	FORTH Inc—Mike Forino	5959 W Century Blvd St, Los Angeles CA 90045	310-491-3356	R	4*	<.1
927	AS Software Inc—Ari Sandman	560 Sylvan Ave Ste 55, Englewood Cliffs NJ 07632	201-541-1900	R	4*	<.1
928	First Lenders Data Inc—Tedd R Smith	6618 Sitio Del Rio Blv, Austin TX 78730	512-418-8989	R	4*	<.1
929	Ascend Intelligence LLC	3803 Fairfax Dr Ste 40, Arlington VA 22203	301-542-3579	R	4*	<.1
930	Co-Ordinated Management Systems—John Lewis	PO Box 418, Cloverdale CA 95425	707-778-6800	R	4*	<.1
931	hereUare Inc—Benedict Van	2900 Gordon Ave Ste 10, Santa Clara CA 95051	408-735-1288	R	4*	<.1
932	Forest Post Productions Ltd—Marty Johnson	31400 Northwestern Hwy, Farmington Hills MI 48334	248-855-4333	R	4*	<.1
933	IPS of Boston—Gary McNamee	PO Box 768, Middleboro MA 02346	508-923-3500	R	4*	<.1

Rank	Company Name—*Executive Officer*	Address, City, State, Zip	Phone	Type	Fin	Empls
934	LiveDeal Inc—*Jon Isaac*	2490 E Sunset Rd Ste 1, Las Vegas NV 89120	408-855-9988	P	4	<.1
935	Combined Computer Technology Inc—*Stuart McColl*	1038 Hooker Rd, Sequim WA 98382	360-582-0202	R	4*	<.1
936	Dreamsite Productions—*Jenna Shaunessy*	3619 W Magnolia Blvd, Burbank CA 91505	818-566-1818	R	4*	<.1
937	Hegemony Inc—*William Edgar*	2 East 22nd St Ste 307, Lombard IL 60148	630-690-5200	R	4*	<.1
938	Frontline Communications—*Rollyne Deallie*	PO Box 98, Orangeburg NY 10962		R	4*	<.1
939	Thought Convergence Inc—*Kevin Vo*	11300 W Olympic Blvd S, Los Angeles CA 90064	310-909-7891	R	4*	<.1
940	Architext Inc	121 Interpark Blvd Ste, San Antonio TX 78216	210-490-2240	R	4*	<.1
941	Computer Programmers Unlimited Inc—*Phillip Wagner*	500 Valence St, New Orleans LA 70115	504-269-4492	R	4*	<.1
942	Evans Data Corp—*Janel Garvin*	312 Lincoln St, Santa Cruz CA 95060	831-425-8451	R	4*	<.1
943	Modena Software Inc—*Atul Saini*	718 University Ave, Los Gatos CA 95032	408-354-3210	R	4*	<.1
944	NELiX Inc—*Jaeme Adams*	1340 Remington Rd Ste, Schaumburg IL 60173	847-407-9400	R	4*	<.1
945	New Target Inc—*Laura Machanic*	815 N Royal St Ste 100, Alexandria VA 22314	703-548-3433	R	4*	<.1
946	Systems Implementation Inc—*Taber Alder*	105 Jordan Rd, Troy NY 12180	518-283-3290	R	4*	<.1
947	WebSine Inc—*Robert Gould*	3 Hanover Sq Ste 23 B, New York NY 10004	212-809-4343	R	4*	<.1
948	FlexSoft Inc—*Marco A Brown*	369 Pine St Ste 516, San Francisco CA 94104	415-362-1014	R	4*	<.1
949	Tek-Star Computer Service Inc—*Charlie Collera*	5756 W Park Rd, Hollywood FL 33021	954-964-1800	R	4*	<.1
950	Aim Services Inc—*Don Harmeier*	PO Box 293730, Kerrville TX 78029	830-896-3025	R	4*	.1
951	Axiom Systems Inc—*Vijay Vasandani*	11575 Great Oaks Way S, Alpharetta GA 30022	770-645-0770	R	4*	<.1
952	Phoenix Vanguard Inc—*Patricia Lennon*	450 7th Ave Ste 506, New York NY 10123	212-258-2626	R	4*	<.1
953	Promptu Systems Corp—*Giuseppe Staffaroni*	333 Ravenswood Ave, Menlo Park CA 94025	650-859-5800	R	4*	<.1
954	Promark Research Corp—*Steven Werner*	10200 Grogans Mill Rd, Spring TX 77380	281-587-7601	R	4*	<.1
955	Simultaneous Solutions Inc—*Frank Postava*	PO Box 4701, Winter Park FL 32793	407-384-8818	R	4*	<.1
956	Aerocomputers Inc—*Mark Gassawy*	2889 W 5th St Ste 111, Oxnard CA 93030	805-985-3390	R	4*	<.1
957	Lyons Direct Inc—*Henry Schuyler*	1166 W Newport Ctr Dr, Deerfield Beach FL 33442	954-596-4134	R	4*	.1
958	Interactive Technologies Group Inc—*Mark Newsome*	1601 River Dr Ste 210, Moline IL 61265	309-757-7172	R	4*	<.1
959	Anark Corp—*Stephen Collins*	1434 Spruce St Ste 200, Boulder CO 80302	303-545-2592	R	4*	<.1
960	Cyberarts Licensing LLC	51 Arbor St, San Francisco CA 94131	415-584-2100	R	4*	<.1
961	Mckinney and Mckinney Technical Services Inc—*Michelle Mckinney*	3122 Glansky Blvd Ste, Woodbridge VA 22192	703-580-1995	R	4*	<.1
962	Norton-Lambert Corp—*Bob Lambert*	PO Box 4085, Santa Barbara CA 93140	805-964-6767	R	4	<.1
963	Global Bridge Infotech Inc—*Hari Naginoni*	5525 N Macarthur Blvd, Irving TX 75038	972-550-9400	R	4*	<.1
964	Citytech Inc—*Janet Bergen*	211 W Wacker Dr Ste 13, Chicago IL 60606	312-673-6433	R	4*	<.1
965	Technology Solutions Inc—*Cathy Lanier*	PO Box 212098, Columbia SC 29221	803-359-6079	R	4*	<.1
966	Blum Investment Group Inc—*Jeffrey Blum*	3581 Excel Dr, Medford OR 97504	541-858-3399	R	4*	<.1
967	Crop Data Management Systems Inc—*Vincent Naso*	423 4th St Fl 7, Marysville CA 95901	530-743-7605	R	4*	<.1
968	Vertigo Software Inc—*Scott Stanfield*	503 Canal Blvd Ste A, Richmond CA 94804	510-307-8200	R	4*	<.1
969	Bid2win Software Inc—*Paul McKeon*	1 NH Ave Ste 209, Portsmouth NH 03801	603-427-0440	R	4*	<.1
970	Dsoft Technology Co—*David Hollenbach*	7222 Communication Cnt, Colorado Springs CO 80919	719-598-7107	R	4*	<.1
971	Advanced Business Computers Of America Incorpor—*Shad Hedy*	PO Box 54221, Jacksonville FL 32245	904-354-2073	R	4*	<.1
972	Think Development Systems Inc—*Pulukottil Joy*	6292 Lawrenceville Hwy, Tucker GA 30084	770-723-7777	R	4*	.1
973	Active Web Services LLC	1646 Braeside Ln, Northbrook IL 60062	847-559-0858	R	4*	.1
974	Corepoint Health LLC	3010 Gaylord Pkwy Ste, Frisco TX 75034	214-618-7000	R	4*	<.1
975	Visioncor Inc—*Sherry Barretta*	1901 Roxborough Rd Ste, Charlotte NC 28211	704-366-7979	R	4*	<.1
976	Exodus Integrity Service—*Jim Ciricola*	37111 Euclid Ave Ste F, Willoughby OH 44094	440-918-0140	R	4*	<.1
977	Metron-Athene Inc—*Paul Malton*	6320 Canoga Ave Ste 15, Woodland Hills CA 91367	818-227-5019	R	4*	<.1
978	Us Netcom Corp—*J Kelly*	1531 W 32nd St Ste 209, Joplin MO 64804	417-659-8040	R	4*	<.1
979	Itx Corp—*Ralph Dandrea*	1169 Pittsford Victor, Pittsford NY 14534	585-899-4800	R	4*	<.1
980	Knoa Software Inc—*Thad Eidman*	5 Union Sq W Fl 4, New York NY 10003	212-807-9608	R	4*	<.1
981	Riconda Data Systems LLC—*Ann Savino*	200 Knickerbocker Ave, Bohemia NY 11716	631-218-5280	R	4*	<.1
982	Computer Arts Inc—*Shane Harris*	320 Sw 5th Ave, Meridian ID 83642	208-385-9335	R	4*	<.1
983	TeamSoft Inc (Middleton Wisconsin)—*Richard Bird*	1350 Deming Way Ste 25, Middleton WI 53562	608-827-7772	R	4	<.1
984	Technical Solutions And Maintenance Inc—*Kiralfy Forte*	205 S Whiting St Ste 4, Alexandria VA 22304	703-370-1104	R	4*	<.1
985	Comsoft Corp—*Kelly Gdovic*	100 N Constitution Dr, Grafton VA 23692	757-890-2801	R	4*	<.1
986	Digital Cheetah Solutions Inc—*Aj Tidwell*	510 S Cngretx Ave Ste, Austin TX 78704	512-539-5500	R	4*	<.1
987	Gurus Information Technology Services LLC—*Mahalingam Mali*	517 Georges Rd, North Brunswick NJ 08902	732-247-7747	R	4*	<.1
988	Information Sciences Corp—*Gregory Portnoy*	3720 Frrget Ave Ste 30, Kensington MD 20895	301-962-5837	R	4*	<.1
989	Jbi Technologies Inc—*Jo Bell*	312 Third St Ste 2, Annapolis MD 21403	410-263-9484	R	4*	<.1
990	Petrotechnics USA Inc—*Phil Murray*	11210 Equity Dr Ste 25, Houston TX 77041	713-856-3300	S	4*	<.1
991	Boundless Flight Inc—*Gary Baney*	PO Box 360109, Strongsville OH 44136	440-610-3683	R	4*	<.1
992	On Center Software Inc—*Leonard Buzz*	1400 Woodloch Forest D, The Woodlands TX 77380	281-297-9000	R	4*	<.1
993	Paradigm Services Inc—*Richard Clark*	311 California St Ste, San Francisco CA 94104	415-616-0920	R	4*	<.1
994	Hubspan Inc—*Trisha Gross*	505 5th Ave S Ste 350, Seattle WA 98104	206-838-5400	R	4*	<.1
995	Emac Inc—*Eric Rossi*	PO Box 2042, Carbondale IL 62902	618-529-4525	R	4*	<.1
996	Scadaware Inc—*Rick Caldwell*	1602 Rhodes Ln, Bloomington IL 61704	309-665-0135	R	4*	<.1
997	Archonix Systems LLC—*Stephanie Dewyfockie*	17000 Commerce Pkwy St, Mount Laurel NJ 08054	856-787-0020	R	4*	<.1
998	Data Directions—*Steve O'Brien*	PO Box 3210, Beaumont CA 92223	951-845-7574	R	4	<.1
999	Care Is 1 A California Corp—*Richard Yonis*	17780 Fitch Ste 185, Irvine CA 92614	949-753-1900	R	4*	<.1
1000	Ethostream—*Jason Tienor*	10200 Innovation Dr St, Milwaukee WI 53226	414-223-0473	S	4	N/A
1001	Advanced Delphi Systems—*Richard Maley*	12613 Maidens Bower Dr, Potomac MD 20854	240-604-1702	R	3*	.1
1002	Crisnet Inc—*Mark Stiegemeier*	756 E Winchester St St, Salt Lake City UT 84107	801-486-9939	R	3*	<.1
1003	Fischer Solutions Inc—*Clifford Fischer*	13455 Noel Rd Ste 1900, Dallas TX 75240	972-980-7115	R	3*	<.1
1004	Ddi System LLC	75 Glen Rd, Newtown CT 06470	203-364-1200	R	3*	<.1
1005	Truefit Solutions Inc—*Darrin Grove*	800 Cranberry Woods Dr, Cranberry Township PA 16066	724-772-5959	R	3*	<.1
1006	Createhope Inc—*Robert Meagher*	2201 Wisconsin Ave Nw, Washington DC 20007	202-903-2585	R	3*	<.1
1007	Packetmotion Inc—*Paul Smith*	110 Baytech Dr Fl 2, San Jose CA 95134	408-449-4300	R	3*	<.1
1008	Revention Inc—*Jeff Doyle*	12000 Westheimer Rd St, Houston TX 77077	281-589-2500	R	3*	<.1
1009	Elcom International Inc—*William Lock*	10 Oceana Way, Norwood MA 02062	781-501-4000	P	3	<.1
1010	Industrial Network Systems Corp—*Harry Mccollum*	479 E Bus Ctr Dr Ste 1, Mount Prospect IL 60056	847-298-4777	R	3*	<.1
1011	Openlogix Corpration—*Sreedhar Lokam*	28345 Beck Rd Ste 308, Wixom MI 48393	248-869-0080	R	3*	<.1
1012	Objects Worldwide Inc—*Tamilmaran Arulmozhidurai*	PO Box 642, Merrifield VA 22116	703-623-7861	R	3*	<.1
1013	Mlogica Inc—*Amitabh Okhandiar*	2100 W Orangewood Ave, Orange CA 92868	714-630-2500	R	3*	<.1
1014	Veda System Solutions Corp—*Sundar Balasuryan*	23 Crosby Dr Ste 5, Bedford MA 01730	781-275-9191	R	3*	.1
1015	ASCI Corp—*Rehan Haque*	6725 Curran St Ste 2, Mc Lean VA 22101	703-847-0000	R	3*	<.1
1016	Clairsol Inc—*Shaleen Vajpayee*	16 Wernik Pl Ste C, Metuchen NJ 08840	732-321-1155	R	3*	<.1
1017	Accent Technologies Inc—*Peter Mcchrystal*	1270 Lake Washington R, Melbourne FL 32935	321-242-7438	R	3*	<.1
1018	Streambase Systems Inc—*Mark Palmer*	181 Spring St, Lexington MA 02421	781-761-0800	R	3*	<.1
1019	Mza Associates Corp—*Robert Praus*	2021 Girard Blvd Se St, Albuquerque NM 87106	505-245-9970	R	3*	<.1
1020	Miningham and Oellerich Inc—*Robert Miningham*	40 Fulton St Fl 9, New York NY 10038	212-349-4410	R	3*	<.1
1021	Oden Industries Inc—*Michael Oden*	268 W Hospitality Ln S, San Bernardino CA 92408	909-386-0310	R	3*	<.1

Note: An asterisk (*) indicates an estimated financial figure. The company type code used is as follows: R = Private, P = Public, S = Private Subsidiary, B = Public Subsidiary, D = Division, J = Joint Venture, I = Investment Fund.

COMPANY RANKINGS BY SALES WITHIN 4-DIGIT SIC

Rank	Company Name—*Executive Officer*	Address, City, State, Zip	Phone	Type	Fin	Empls
1022	Business Logic Holding Corp—*John Patterson*	440 N Wells St Ste 320, Chicago IL 60654	312-264-7000	R	3*	<.1
1023	Interactive Telesis Inc—*Al Staerkel*	2292 Faraday Ave Ste 1, Carlsbad CA 92008	760-496-7700	R	3	<.1
1024	Ibridge Group Inc—*Tim Lindstrom*	7000 N Mopac Ste 490, Austin TX 78731	512-345-8000	R	3*	<.1
1025	Intellica Corp—*Jose Lago*	209 W Poplar St, San Antonio TX 78212	210-341-3101	R	3*	<.1
1026	Computer Visionaries—*Mark Aurling*	2316 Pine Hollow Dr, Florence SC 29501	843-615-0389	R	3*	<.1
1027	Saturn Systems Inc—*Keith Erickson*	314 W Superior St Ste, Duluth MN 55802	218-727-5343	R	3*	<.1
1028	Centerprise Information Solutions Inc—*Doug Weintiob*	2857 Riviera Dr Ste 10, Fairlawn OH 44333	330-873-2400	R	3*	<.1
1029	Five Star Development Inc—*David Colaizzi*	1501 Preble Ave Ste 1, Pittsburgh PA 15233	412-802-2500	R	3*	<.1
1030	Amtex Enterprises Inc—*Asker Junaid*	520 E Weddell Dr Ste 1, Sunnyvale CA 94089	408-734-4050	R	3*	<.1
1031	Artis And Associates Inc—*Gary Artis*	8100 Tower Point Dr, Charlotte NC 28227	704-846-6750	R	3*	<.1
1032	Parity Computing Inc—*Mohan Paturi*	6160 Lusk Blvd Ste 205, San Diego CA 92121	858-535-0516	R	3*	<.1
1033	Agate Software Inc—*Timothy Pearl*	2214 University Park D, Okemos MI 48864	517-336-2500	R	3*	<.1
1034	International Technology Concepts Inc—*Naum Pinkhasik*	1244 Quarry Ln Ste B, Pleasanton CA 94566	925-401-0010	R	3*	<.1
1035	IEPC Corp—*Ron Flores*	PO Box 2180, Huntington Beach CA 92647	714-892-4443	R	3*	<.1
1036	Mbms Inc—*James Kunert*	11 Pinchot Ct Ste 1, Buffalo NY 14228	716-689-2594	R	3*	<.1
1037	Optimal Synthesis Inc—*P Menon*	95 1st St Ste 240, Los Altos CA 94022	650-559-8585	R	3*	<.1
1038	Impression Technology—*Michael Tokuyama*	1777 N Calif Blvd Ste, Walnut Creek CA 94596	925-280-0010	R	3*	<.1
1039	Velocity Group LLC	650 Castro St Ste 1203, Mountain View CA 94041	650-327-8863	R	3*	<.1
1040	Ionidea Inc—*Kishan Ananthram*	3913 Old Lee Hwy Ste 3, Fairfax VA 22030	703-691-0400	R	3*	<.1
1041	Denim Group Ltd—*Timothy Brosseau*	3463 Magic Dr Ste 315, San Antonio TX 78229	210-572-4400	R	3*	<.1
1042	Airspeed LLC—*Simon Gray*	980 Corporate Dr Ste 2, Hillsborough NC 27278	919-644-1222	R	3*	<.1
1043	5280 Solutions—*Mark Voegele*	709 E Riverpark Ln Ste, Boise ID 83706	208-344-3776	R	3*	<.1
1044	Integral 7 Inc—*E Porter*	100 S 5th St Ste 1725, Minneapolis MN 55402	612-436-0701	R	3*	<.1
1045	Txvia Inc—*Anit Aggarwal*	340 Madison Ave Fl 3, New York NY 10173	212-937-4108	R	3*	<.1
1046	Electrical Manufacturing and Distributors Inc—*Bruce Parker*	1411 Twin Oaks St, Wichita Falls TX 76302	940-322-2206	R	3*	<.1
1047	Corvin Inc—*George Mismas*	925 Sherman Ave, Hamden CT 06514	203-288-3523	R	3*	<.1
1048	Officemate Software Solutions Inc—*Ed Buffington*	15375 Barranca Pkwy L, Irvine CA 92618	949-754-5000	R	3*	<.1
1049	Open Systems Integrators Inc—*Bill Baroska*	207d Woodward Rd, Manalapan NJ 07726	732-792-2112	R	3*	<.1
1050	Hdf Group—*Michael Folk*	1800 S Oak St Ste 203, Champaign IL 61820	217-531-6100	R	3*	<.1
1051	E-Resources LLC—*Carrie Gress*	1423 Powhatan St Ste 1, Alexandria VA 22314	202-216-0124	R	3*	<.1
1052	Professional Systems Associates Inc—*S Parker*	1308 Florida Ave, Panama City FL 32401	850-763-2192	R	3*	<.1
1053	Secured Services Inc—*Dale Quick*	11490 Commerce Park Dr, Reston VA 20191		R	3*	.1
1054	Inspira Inc—*Ravindra Gudapati*	4125 Blackford Ave Ste, San Jose CA 95117	408-247-9500	R	3*	.1
1055	Target Labs Inc—*Larry Poltavtsev*	PO Box 3051, West Mclean VA 22103	703-891-5000	R	3*	.1
1056	iMove Inc—*John Herring*	1732 NW Quimby St Ste, Portland OR 97209	503-221-2449	R	3*	<.1
1057	Moderntech SL—*Joe Kriby*	404 Bna Dr Ste 302, Nashville TN 37217	615-365-4223	R	3*	<.1
1058	Xinet Inc—*Scott Seabass*	2560 9th St Ste 312, Berkeley CA 94710	510-845-0555	R	3*	<.1
1059	Gresham Enterprise Storage—*Chris Errington*	505 E Huntland Dr Ste, Austin TX 78752	512-450-0900	D	3*	<.1
1060	Optimal Blue LLC—*Ron Harrison*	5601 Democracy Dr Ste, Plano TX 75024	972-781-0200	R	3*	<.1
1061	Computer Automation Systems Inc—*Harvey Hughes*	PO Box 590, Mountain Home AR 72654	870-425-6933	R	3*	<.1
1062	Cicero Inc—*John Broderick*	8000 Regency Pky Ste 5, Cary NC 27518	919-380-5000	P	3	<.1
1063	Knowledge Factor Inc—*Larry Gray*	4775 Walnut St Ste 210, Boulder CO 80301	720-214-4874	R	3*	<.1
1064	Redwood Health Services—*John Nacol*	3033 Cleveland Ave Ste, Santa Rosa CA 95403	707-544-2010	R	3*	<.1
1065	Trans Cosmos America Inc—*Yasuki Matsumoto*	879 W 190th St Ste 105, Gardena CA 90248	310-630-0072	R	3*	<.1
1066	AgileThought Inc—*David Romine*	2502 North Rocky Point, Tampa FL 33607		R	3*	<.1
1067	Aware Systems Inc—*Jeremy Ziegler*	1660 Hwy 100 S Ste 500, Minneapolis MN 55416		R	3*	<.1
1068	Fyx Inc—*Dale Burley*	PO Box 511, Leslie MI 49251	517-589-5903	R	3*	<.1
1069	Genomic Solutions Inc	84 October Hill Rd, Holliston MA 01746	508-893-3130	S	3*	<.1
1070	Master Solutions LLC—*Don Turner*	1880 Office Club Pt, Colorado Springs CO 80920	719-272-8018	R	3*	<.1
1071	Remanage Inc—*Dan Hooper*	3500 Oak Lawn Ave Ste, Dallas TX 75219	214-523-9668	R	3*	<.1
1072	Retail Technologies Corp—*Bruce Hicks*	975 Cobb Pl Blvd NW St, Kennesaw GA 30144	770-425-0401	R	3*	<.1
1073	Systems Alternatives International Inc—*John Underwood*	1705 Indian Wood Cir S, Maumee OH 43537	419-891-1100	R	3*	<.1
1074	System Design Group Inc—*Steven Bousamra*	8739 Castle Park Dr, Indianapolis IN 46256	317-598-8556	R	3*	<.1
1075	Cothern Computer Systems Inc—*Allen Cothern*	1640 Lelia Dr Ste 200, Jackson MS 39216	601-969-1155	R	3*	<.1
1076	Bcl Technologies—*Hassan Alam*	990 Linden Dr Ste 203, Santa Clara CA 95050	408-557-2080	R	3*	<.1
1077	Computer Mail Services Inc	44648 Mound Rd Ste 812, Sterling Heights MI 48314	248-352-6700	R	3*	<.1
1078	EDI Support Inc—*Faith Lamprey*	5 Old Nasonville RD, Harrisville RI 02830	775-786-5522	R	3*	<.1
1079	GenSource Corp—*Nora Kenner*	25572 Ave Stanford, Valencia CA 91355		S	3*	<.1
1080	Laureate Learning Systems Inc—*Mary Sweig Wilson*	110 E Spring St, Winooski VT 05404	802-655-4755	R	3*	<.1
1081	Northwrite Inc—*Patrick O-Neill*	1300 Godward St Ne Ste, Minneapolis MN 55413		R	3*	<.1
1082	Salamander Technologies Inc—*Russell Miller*	122 W State St, Traverse City MI 49684	231-932-4397	R	3*	<.1
1083	Miicor Inc—*Richard Miller*	409 S 8th St Ste 102, Boise ID 83702	208-344-4437	R	3*	<.1
1084	Packaged Business Solutions Inc—*Natalie Kilner*	2151 Salvio St Ste 310, Concord CA 94520	925-671-7071	R	3*	<.1
1085	Root Consulting Inc—*Scott Taylor*	PO Box 1275, Perry FL 32348	713-523-8976	R	3*	<.1
1086	Advanced Rotocraft Technology Inc—*Ronald DuVal*	635 Vaqueros Ave, Sunnyvale CA 94085	408-523-5100	R	3	<.1
1087	Alto Consulting and Training—*Brian Allar*	7210 Metro Blvd, Minneapolis MN 55439	952-831-6604	R	3*	<.1
1088	Cyberscience Corp—*Nigel Brownjohn*	6334 South Racine Circ, Centennial CO 80111	303-745-3900	R	3*	<.1
1089	FMR Systems Inc—*Jack Leiss*	37 Plum Grove Rd, Palatine IL 60067	847-934-5566	R	3*	<.1
1090	MicroUnity Systems Engineering Inc—*Tom Buckmaster*	4 Main St Ste 100, Los Altos CA 94022	408-734-8100	R	3*	<.1
1091	Noran-Land Engineering Corp—*David Weinberg*	5555 Garden Grove Blvd, Westminster CA 92683	714-899-1220	R	3*	<.1
1092	Regional Economic Models Inc—*Frederick Treyz*	433 West St Ste 4, Amherst MA 01002	413-549-1169	R	3*	<.1
1093	Advanced Business Information Systems Inc—*Russell Schulte*	2190 N Loop W Ste 400, Houston TX 77018	713-680-2247	R	3*	<.1
1094	Technology Systems Inc—*Charles Benton*	14 Maine St Ste 306, Brunswick ME 04011	207-798-4646	R	3*	<.1
1095	TimeTrak Systems Inc—*Michael D Bonner*	933 Pine Grove Ave, Port Huron MI 48060	810-984-1313	R	3*	<.1
1096	Casco Development Inc—*Richard Deeran*	2 Portland Fish Pier S, Portland ME 04101	207-773-0944	R	3*	<.1
1097	Spokane Computer Inc—*Daniel L Olson*	915 W 2nd Ave Rm 10, Spokane WA 99201	509-624-4248	R	3*	<.1
1098	Virtual Information Systems—*Chris Huber*	9 Lake Bellevue Dr Ste, Bellevue WA 98005	425-828-9495	R	3*	<.1
1099	Aliroo America Inc—*Meir Zorea*	16 E Main St Ste 420, Rochester NY 14614	585-262-8020	R	3*	<.1
1100	Asset Management Concepts Inc—*Tommy Thompson*	4654 Kenmore St Ste 26, Chicago IL 60640	773-878-5150	R	3*	<.1
1101	Software In Vision Inc—*Joseph Spiteri*	110 Lake Ave S Ste 35, Nesconset NY 11767	631-360-3400	R	3*	<.1
1102	Agistix Inc—*Trevor Read*	643 Bair Island Rd Ste, Redwood City CA 94063	650-362-2000	R	3*	<.1
1103	Cdg Holding Co—*Deborah Driskill*	PO Box 702527, Dallas TX 75370	972-250-4104	R	3*	<.1
1104	Cosmotech Inc—*Tarun Maini*	4728 Walden Dr, Troy MI 48098	248-526-9700	R	3*	<.1
1105	GTC Group Inc—*Doug Morgan*	6915 La Granada Dr, Houston TX 77083	281-530-1195	R	3*	<.1
1106	MShift—*Scott Moeller*	40460 Encyclopedia Cir, Fremont CA 94538	408-437-2740	R	3*	<.1
1107	FLEXquarterscom Ltd—*Brad Waddell*	2620 S Maryland Pky St, Las Vegas NV 89109	248-886-1662	R	3*	<.1
1108	ScreamDVD—*Mark Ashkinos*	247 W 35th St 7th Fl, New York NY 10001	212-951-7171	R	3*	<.1
1109	ARS Nova Software—*Dennis J Evans*	PO Box 3370, Redmond WA 98073	425-869-0625	R	3*	<.1
1110	CodeLab Technology Group—*David Ritchie*	26 Princess St 2nd Fl, Wakefield MA 01880	781-213-6917	S	3*	<.1
1111	Nixon Software Solutions Inc—*John Nixon IV*	2099 Brown Ave, Santa Clara CA 95051	408-261-0443	R	3*	<.1

Rank	Company Name—*Executive Officer*	Address, City, State, Zip	Phone	Type	Fin	Empls
1112	Prime Recognition Corp—*Kenn Dahl*	21827 Ne 137th St, Woodinville WA 98077	425-895-0550	R	3*	<.1
1113	Dignus LLC—*Dave Rivers*	8378 Six Forks Rd Ste, Raleigh NC 27615	919-676-0847	R	3*	<.1
1114	Eurekster Inc—*Steven E Marder*	433 California St Ste, San Francisco CA 94104	415-986-2826	R	3*	<.1
1115	Patotech Software Inc—*Sonya Shaw*	PO Box 206, Danville CA 94526	925-837-2327	R	3*	<.1
1116	VMLogix Inc—*Sameer Dholakia*	2350 Mission College B, Santa Clara CA 95054	650-451-5555	R	3*	<.1
1117	ZH Computer Inc—*Frederic H Sweeny*	7400 Metro Blvd Ste 35, Minneapolis MN 55439	952-844-0915	R	3*	<.1
1118	Ekk Inc—*Chung-Whee Kim*	37682 Enterprise Ct, Farmington Hills MI 48331	248-624-9957	R	3*	<.1
1119	PC Accountant Inc—*Bob Arcese*	PO Box 2278, Kirkland WA 98083	425-405-5640	R	3*	<.1
1120	Andhus Technologies Inc—*Krishna Atluri*	650 E Devon Ave Ste 13, Itasca IL 60143	630-438-5116	R	3*	.1
1121	Mayfare Software Solutions LLC—*Martin Lippiett*	33 Newark St 41, Hoboken NJ 07030	201-792-7743	R	3*	<.1
1122	Softplan Systems Inc—*Ken Montag*	8118 Isabella Ln, Brentwood TN 37027	615-370-1121	R	3*	<.1
1123	Dynalog Inc—*Dan Hasley*	6001 N Adams Rd Ste 20, Bloomfield Hills MI 48304	248-203-9602	R	3*	<.1
1124	Mammography Reporting System Inc—*Mark Morris*	9709 3rd Ave Ne Ste 20, Seattle WA 98115	206-633-6145	R	3*	<.1
1125	Untangle Inc—*Bob Walters*	2800 Campus Dr Ste 100, San Mateo CA 94403	650-345-5120	R	3*	<.1
1126	Triad Governmental Systems Inc—*Tod Rapp*	358 S Monroe St, Xenia OH 45385	937-376-5446	R	3*	<.1
1127	Arsenault Associates Inc—*Charles Arsenault*	6 Terri Ln Ste 700, Burlington NJ 08016	609-747-8800	R	3*	<.1
1128	Eoir Technologies Inc—*Mary Carroll*	150 River Rd Ste B3, Montville NJ 07045	973-331-7974	R	3*	<.1
1129	Kamakura Corporation Dba Delaware Kamakura—*Warren Sherman*	2222 Kalakaua Ave Ste, Honolulu HI 96815	808-791-9888	R	3*	<.1
1130	Syntonic Systems Inc—*Robert Lichterman*	80 8th Ave Ste 901, New York NY 10011	212-989-8787	R	3*	<.1
1131	Chain System Corparation—*Rathinam Ganesan*	325 S Clinton St Ste 2, Grand Ledge MI 48837	517-627-1173	R	3*	<.1
1132	Datatech Software Corp—*Robert Glass*	1355 15th St Ste 240, Fort Lee NJ 07024	201-592-1412	R	3*	<.1
1133	Component ControlCom Inc—*Zvi Baron*	1731 Kettner Blvd, San Diego CA 92101	619-702-3112	R	3*	<.1
1134	Universal System Technologies Inc—*Sanjay Prasad*	1307 S International P, Lake Mary FL 32746	407-688-0065	R	3*	.1
1135	Augme Technologies Inc—*Paul R Arena*	43 W 24th St Ste 11B, New York NY 10010	855-423-5433	P	3	.1
1136	Alterian Inc—*David Eldridge*	35 E Wacker Dr Ste 200, Chicago IL 60601	312-704-1700	R	3*	<.1
1137	Genova Technologies Inc—*Dawn Ainger*	5270 N River Blvd Ne, Cedar Rapids IA 52411	319-378-8455	R	3*	<.1
1138	Premier It Solutions—*Ram Bobba*	801 E Campbell Rd Ste, Richardson TX 75081	972-231-4747	R	3*	<.1
1139	Fusionsoft LLC	7602 Woodland Dr Ste 1, Indianapolis IN 46278	317-955-1300	R	3*	<.1
1140	SRI Systems Inc—*Ravi Sadasivuni*	2 Austin Ave Ste 2a, Iselin NJ 08830	732-326-5888	R	3*	<.1
1141	Donnell Systems Inc—*Lynn Donnell*	300 S Saint Louis Bvl, South Bend IN 46617	574-232-3784	R	3*	<.1
1142	Quicksilver Software Inc—*William Fisher*	18261 Mcdurmott W, Irvine CA 92614	949-474-2150	R	3*	<.1
1143	Teksync Inc—*Jose Chavez*	2260 W Holcombe Blvd, Houston TX 77030	832-731-0720	R	3*	<.1
1144	Systex Inc—*Kris Koshy*	15245 Shady Grove Rd, Rockville MD 20850	301-330-9600	R	3*	<.1
1145	Synapsis Enterprise LLC	PO Box 747, Spring House PA 19477	215-793-0200	R	3*	<.1
1146	Lvm Systems Inc—*Les Mortensen*	4262 E Florian Ave, Mesa AZ 85206	480-633-8200	R	3*	<.1
1147	Codestreet LLC—*Lara Zardze*	317 Madison Ave Rm 718, New York NY 10017	646-442-2800	R	3*	<.1
1148	Fiserv Imagesoft—*Ron Thompson*	901 International Pkwy, Lake Mary FL 32746	407-833-4800	R	3*	<.1
1149	Eon Systems Inc—*Rose Greenwood*	620 Lakeview Rd, Clearwater FL 33756	727-298-5502	R	3*	<.1
1150	Houston Area Services—*Kamron Kirkconnel*	PO Box 630309, Houston TX 77263	713-975-6000	R	3*	<.1
1151	Subuthi Overseas Inc—*Manoharan Kutti*	3723 Haven Ave Ste 103, Menlo Park CA 94025	650-980-3320	R	3*	<.1
1152	Liberty Communication Software Solutions Inc—*Padmanbhan Sathyanarayana*	1050 Kingsmill Pkwy, Columbus OH 43229	614-318-5000	R	3*	<.1
1153	Blackhawk Color—*Stuart Sanderson*	14540 58th St N, Clearwater FL 33760	727-535-4641	R	3*	<.1
1154	Advanced Workstations In Education Inc—*Karl Thornton*	2501 Saport Dr Ste 410, Chester PA 19013	610-833-6400	R	3*	<.1
1155	Triad Interactive Inc—*Cheryl Manning*	1101 Connecticut Ave N, Washington DC 20036	202-347-0900	R	3*	<.1
1156	Micron Systems Inc—*Mohan Rao*	3240 E State St Ext, Hamilton NJ 08619	973-751-3225	R	3*	<.1
1157	Require LLC—*Kelly Doley*	5029 Corp Woods Dr Ste, Virginia Beach VA 23462	757-552-0300	R	3*	<.1
1158	Global Solutions Systems Inc—*Sam Balog*	5401 S Kirkman Rd Ste, Orlando FL 32819	407-299-9612	R	3*	<.1
1159	Real Vision Software Inc—*Monty Chicola*	PO Box 12958, Alexandria LA 71315	318-449-4579	R	3*	<.1
1160	Financial Software Systems Inc—*Larry Eggleston*	1605 Tower Dr, Moore OK 73160	405-794-4900	R	3*	<.1
1161	Implement Dot Com LLC	701 N 36th St Ste 310, Seattle WA 98103	206-547-8100	R	3*	<.1
1162	Interactive Sites Inc—*Michael Waltman*	14988 N 78th Way Ste 2, Scottsdale AZ 85260	480-707-1600	R	3*	<.1
1163	Object Innovation Inc—*John Grow*	8130 Baymeadows Way W, Jacksonville FL 32256	904-739-0300	R	3*	<.1
1164	Alpha Star Corp—*Kay Matin*	5150 E Pacific Coast H, Long Beach CA 90804	562-961-7827	R	3*	<.1
1165	Pka Technologies Inc—*Felise Katz*	1 Executive Blvd Ste 1, Suffern NY 10901	845-357-0170	R	3*	<.1
1166	Gps Information Guidance LLC	4835 University Sq Ste, Huntsville AL 35816		R	3*	<.1
1167	Tightrope Media Systems Inc—*John Parker*	800 Transfer Rd Ste 1b, Saint Paul MN 55114	612-866-4118	R	3*	<.1
1168	Application Development Consultants Inc—*Steve Loveridge*	13528 Prestige Pl Ste, Tampa FL 33635	813-814-2863	R	3*	<.1
1169	Cisys Inc—*James Saunders*	8386 Six Forks Rd Ste, Raleigh NC 27615	919-870-1436	R	3*	<.1
1170	Media Fx Technologies Inc—*William Huang*	950 Fee Ana St Ste A, Placentia CA 92870	714-993-9988	R	3*	<.1
1171	Gyrocon Inc—*Karan Sridher*	1254 Beaver Ruin Rd St, Norcross GA 30093	770-279-2992	R	3*	<.1
1172	Reba Software and Services Inc—*Mohinder Lamba*	1612 Locust Ave Ste B, Bohemia NY 11716	631-218-8580	R	3*	<.1
1173	Softvu LLC—*Steve Garver*	12920 Metcalf Ave Ste, Overland Park KS 66213	913-696-9700	R	3*	<.1
1174	Aurora Software Inc—*Neil Arora*	375 Park Ave Ste 3501, New York NY 10152	212-906-0050	R	3*	<.1
1175	Syn-Apps LLC	2812 N Norwalk Ste 112, Mesa AZ 85215	480-664-6071	R	3*	<.1
1176	Abacus 21 Inc—*Butch Lesniak*	2746 Delaware Ave, Buffalo NY 14217	716-873-2155	R	3*	<.1
1177	Client Marketing Systems Inc—*Patrick Dempsey*	880 Price St, Pismo Beach CA 93449	805-773-7981	R	3*	<.1
1178	Endai Corp—*Michael Ferranti*	217 Water St Fl 3, New York NY 10038	212-430-0808	R	3*	<.1
1179	Hadron Systems Inc—*Lee Silverman*	PO Box 6, Belmont MA 02478	508-847-7353	R	3*	<.1
1180	Cyberwolf Inc—*Larry Wolf*	1596 Pacheco St Ste 20, Santa Fe NM 87505	505-983-6463	R	3*	<.1
1181	ALH Group Inc—*Allan Hernandez*	880 Industrial Way, San Luis Obispo CA 93401	805-541-8739	R	3*	<.1
1182	Strategic Business Solutions Inc—*Patricia Guzinsky*	17011 Beach Blvd Ste 9, Huntington Beach CA 92647	714-375-6616	R	3*	<.1
1183	Hypercomp Inc—*Devika Shankar*	2629 Townsgate Rd Ste, Westlake Village CA 91361	805-371-7556	R	3*	<.1
1184	Techstructures LLC—*Robert Birch*	1950 Abbott St Ste 601, Charlotte NC 28203	704-973-5640	R	3*	<.1
1185	Userthink Inc—*Jeffrey Millians*	1029 N Peachtree Pkwy, Peachtree City GA 30269	770-487-1097	R	3*	<.1
1186	Vektrex Electronic Systems Inc—*Melissa Ford*	10225 Barnes Cnyon Rd, San Diego CA 92121	858-558-8282	R	3*	<.1
1187	Flight One Software Inc—*Steve Halpern*	3355 Lenox Rd Ne Ste 7, Atlanta GA 30326	404-504-7010	R	3*	<.1
1188	Mann Group—*Alan Mann*	1000 18th St 200, Plano TX 75074	972-516-0953	R	3*	<.1
1189	Energy Efficiency Systems Corp—*W Hougland*	2311 G St, Washougal WA 98671	360-835-7838	R	2*	<.1
1190	Dai Systems LLC—*Sonya Fruendt*	2701 N Dallas Pkwy Ste, Plano TX 75093	214-556-8040	R	2*	<.1
1191	Grace Technology Solutions—*Julius King*	33 Flower Valley Shopp, Florissant MO 63033	314-838-0088	R	2*	<.1
1192	Conover John—*John Conover*	631 Lamont Ct, Campbell CA 95008	408-370-2688	R	2*	<.1
1193	Institute For Independent Information Technology Professionals LLC	1325 Howard Ave Ste 80, Burlingame CA 94010	650-596-2800	R	2*	<.1
1194	Seeburger Inc—*Albert Weessies*	1230 Peachtree St Se 1, Atlanta GA 30309	678-904-3300	R	2*	<.1
1195	Transcendent LLC—*Brandon Lundt*	1040 Cottonwood Ave St, Hartland WI 53029	262-953-2750	R	2*	<.1
1196	Prime Factors Inc—*FW Hulse IV*	4725 Village Plaza Loo, Eugene OR 97401	541-345-4334	R	2	<.1
1197	Critical Path Software Inc—*Steve Romero*	621 SW Alder St Ste 20, Portland OR 97205	503-222-2922	R	2*	<.1
1198	Know-Ware Consulting Inc—*Peter Jastreboff*	75 Maiden Ln 1001, New York NY 10038	212-376-4789	R	2*	<.1

Note: An asterisk (*) indicates an estimated financial figure. The company type code used is as follows: R = Private, P = Public, S = Private Subsidiary, B = Public Subsidiary, D = Division, J = Joint Venture, I = Investment Fund.

COMPANY RANKINGS BY SALES WITHIN 4-DIGIT SIC

Rank	Company Name—*Executive Officer*	Address, City, State, Zip	Phone	Type	Fin	Empls
1199	Transact Communications Inc—*Richard Passovoy*	5105 200th St Sw Ste 2, Lynnwood WA 98036	425-977-2100	R	2*	<.1
1200	Bay Technologies Consulting Group Inc—*Catherine Rice*	1 Research Ct Ste 450, Rockville MD 20850	410-224-2595	R	2*	<.1
1201	Linton Shafer Computer Services Inc—*Barbara Richards*	333 W Patrick St, Frederick MD 21701	301-695-5333	R	2*	<.1
1202	Actant Inc—*Joshua Hodge*	412 S Wells St Fl 10, Chicago IL 60607	312-577-0300	R	2*	<.1
1203	Data Point Systems Inc—*Paddy Sharma*	50 Executv Park S Ne 5, Atlanta GA 30329	404-633-9771	R	2*	<.1
1204	Horizon Educational Systems Inc—*Kenneth Bouldin*	PO Box 158719, Nashville TN 37215	615-850-2643	R	2*	<.1
1205	Mindmatters Technologies Inc—*John Gabrick*	333 Technology Dr Ste, Canonsburg PA 15317	724-743-4242	R	2*	<.1
1206	Technology Planning Inc—*Robert Mallet*	14358 Chesterfield Rd, Rockville MD 20853	301-340-9310	R	2*	<.1
1207	Apacheta Corp—*John Major*	75 W Baltimore Pke, Media PA 19063	610-558-5852	R	2*	<.1
1208	Envisage Technologies Corp—*Ari Vidali*	101 W Kirkwood Ave Ste, Bloomington IN 47404	812-330-7101	R	2*	<.1
1209	Family Information Systems Inc—*Joyce Ramaay*	16475 Dallas Pkwy Ste, Addison TX 75001	972-381-4690	R	2*	<.1
1210	Invidi Technologies Corp—*David Downey*	420 Lexington Ave Rm 8, New York NY 10170	212-867-6881	R	2*	<.1
1211	Cql Inc—*Mark Carpenter*	3344 Grand Ridge Dr Ne, Grand Rapids MI 49525	616-365-1000	R	2*	<.1
1212	Add On Systems Inc—*Hugh Fish*	100 Nw 63rd St Ste 215, Oklahoma City OK 73116	405-843-8142	R	2*	<.1
1213	Oncall Interactive Inc—*Christina Pascente*	216 S Jefferson St Ste, Chicago IL 60661	312-226-1259	R	2*	<.1
1214	Twin Oaks Software Development Inc—*Eric Shuler*	1463 Berlin Tpke Ste D, Berlin CT 06037	860-829-6000	R	2*	<.1
1215	Millennium Business Solutions Group Inc—*Kevin Bowe*	31255 Cedar Valley Dr, Westlake Village CA 91362	818-865-1373	R	2*	<.1
1216	Software Solutions Group Inc—*Ganesh Murthy*	11099 S La Cienega Blv, Los Angeles CA 90045	972-714-9919	R	2*	<.1
1217	Splyce Inc—*Michael Ditter*	5775 Soundview Dr E103, Gig Harbor WA 98335	253-857-6411	R	2*	<.1
1218	Castle Rock Innovations LLC—*Michael Marr*	225 N Michigan Ave Ste, Chicago IL 60601	312-239-6090	R	2	<.1
1219	Science Horizons Inc—*J Cherry*	PO Box 758, Licking MO 65542	573-674-3036	R	2*	<.1
1220	Cognitive Enterprises	9 El Camino Dr, Corte Madera CA 94925	415-992-7800	R	2*	<.1
1221	Infused Solutions LLC	22636 Davis Dr Ste 100, Sterling VA 20164	703-349-0628	R	2*	.3
1222	Csi International—*John Rankin*	615 E 132nd St, Burnsville MN 55337	952-882-9115	R	2*	<.1
1223	Infinitec—*Doug Rozean*	410 W 5th St, Colby KS 67701	785-462-3063	R	2*	<.1
1224	Goodsx Ltd—*John Farrier*	700 Central Expy S Ste, Allen TX 75013	972-612-7121	R	2*	<.1
1225	Excelstor Technology Inc—*Eddie Lui*	PO Box 2309, Longmont CO 80502	303-684-7260	R	2*	<.1
1226	Advantage Technology Group Inc—*Douglas Lantz*	7723 Tylers Pl Blvd St, West Chester OH 45069	513-563-3560	R	2*	<.1
1227	Ram Information System Inc—*Richard Matist*	407 Park Ave S Apt 9c, New York NY 10016	212-481-0929	R	2*	<.1
1228	Aerosystems International Inc—*Andrew Keefe*	5850 T G Lee Blvd Ste, Orlando FL 32822	407-381-0329	R	2*	<.1
1229	Automation Services Company Inc—*Michael Buchanan*	PO Box 940, Cape Girardeau MO 63702	573-335-5157	R	2*	<.1
1230	Competenet Inc—*J Radcliff*	PO Box 767333, Roswell GA 30076	678-461-4820	R	2*	<.1
1231	Eoriginal Inc—*Stephen Bisbee*	351 W Camden St Ste 80, Baltimore MD 21201	410-659-9796	R	2*	<.1
1232	Bluetech LLC—*Abby Johnson*	2828 Sw Corbett Ave St, Portland OR 97201	503-223-2583	R	2*	<.1
1233	Interactive Management Systems Corp—*Robert Ross*	555 E Pikes Peak Ave, Colorado Springs CO 80903	719-634-7755	R	2*	<.1
1234	Votara Corp—*Rakesh Thakur*	9250 Bendix Rd, Columbia MD 21045	410-480-7280	R	2*	<.1
1235	21st Century Software Inc—*Peter Wilson*	940 W Valley Rd Ste 16, Wayne PA 19087	610-971-9946	R	2*	<.1
1236	Immediatek Inc—*Timothy Rice*	3301 Airport Fwy Ste 2, Bedford TX 76021	972-893-3301	R	2*	<.1
1237	Pen-Link Ltd—*Mike Murman*	5936 Vandervoort Dr, Lincoln NE 68516	402-421-8857	R	2*	<.1
1238	OnediscCom Inc—*Tom Vanderpool*	4668 Murray Ave, Saint Paul MN 55110	651-407-1805	R	2*	<.1
1239	Sales Graphics Corp—*George Chevalier*	138 W 25th St Ste 1201, New York NY 10001	212-255-5300	R	2*	<.1
1240	Pri Systems Inc—*Shilpa Kumar*	1 Herder Dr, Hillsborough NJ 08844	908-369-8024	R	2*	<.1
1241	Rainbow Technology Inc	17106 Thatcher Ct, Olney MD 20832	301-570-5025	R	2*	<.1
1242	Transvirtual Systems LLC	31 Puritan Ave, Flushing NY 11375	718-874-6093	R	2*	<.1
1243	Lexitech Inc—*Alex Richardson*	2 Henry Adams St Ste 3, San Francisco CA 94103	415-490-8600	R	2*	<.1
1244	Breze Inc—*Rita Patel*	PO Box 570, Plainsboro NJ 08536	609-936-9008	R	2*	<.1
1245	Csc Technologies Group Inc—*Corye Clarke*	10406 Jib Ct, Cheltenham MD 20623	301-372-8470	R	2*	<.1
1246	Digitiliti Inc—*Jack Scheetz*	266 E 7th St, Saint Paul MN 55101	651-925-3200	P	2	<.1
1247	Lm Technologies Corp—*Kent Meyer*	7031 Corp Way Ste 200, Dayton OH 45459	937-439-9384	R	2*	<.1
1248	Mojo Interactive Corp—*Glen Lubbert*	1060 Woodcock Rd, Orlando FL 32803	407-206-0700	R	2*	<.1
1249	Practical Software Solutions Inc—*Vince Stamey*	452 Penny Ln, Concord NC 28025	704-721-6800	R	2*	<.1
1250	Wheatland Systems Inc—*David Miles*	2110 Delaware St Ste A, Lawrence KS 66046	785-841-2974	R	2*	<.1
1251	Premier Software Associates Inc—*John Smith*	997 W 950 N Ste 200, Centerville UT 84014	801-299-8772	R	2*	<.1
1252	Multimedia Abacus Corp—*Farzad Yadidian*	9800 S La Cienega Blvd, Inglewood CA 90301	310-645-0598	R	2*	<.1
1253	Systems Design Simplified Inc—*Sam Jiwani*	13700 Marina Pointe Dr, Marina Del Rey CA 90292	310-837-9464	R	2*	<.1
1254	Jiva Infotech Inc—*Vanit Kumar*	155 Gibbs St Unit 512, Rockville MD 20850	301-760-7199	R	2*	.1
1255	Equiom Inc—*Saed Nashef*	3181 156th Ave Se Ste, Bellevue WA 98007	425-818-3043	R	2*	.1
1256	Object Frontier Inc—*James Walters*	1000 Windward Concours, Alpharetta GA 30005	678-218-5210	R	2*	.1
1257	Hb Software Solutions—*Himanshu Bhatnagar*	1600 Osgood St Ste 2-5, North Andover MA 01845	978-379-0010	R	2*	<.1
1258	Infiniedge Software Inc—*Czarina Walker*	14320 Infiniedge Way, Prairieville LA 70769	225-677-8902	R	2*	<.1
1259	Lightmaker USA Inc—*Ian Hilton*	6881 Kingspointe Pkwy, Orlando FL 32819	321-293-0500	R	2*	<.1
1260	MindVision Software Inc—*Steve West*	826 P St Ste 300, Lincoln NE 68508	402-323-6600	R	2*	<.1
1261	Altus Technologies Inc—*Vishnu Katikirebdy*	46179 Westlake Dr Ste, Sterling VA 20165	703-310-7053	R	2*	<.1
1262	Proex Inc—*Randy Henderson*	7842 S 1300 W, West Jordan UT 84088	801-569-8500	R	2*	<.1
1263	Alliance Systems and Programming Inc—*Robert A Howard*	900 S Hwy Dr, Fenton MO 63026	636-349-4434	R	2*	<.1
1264	Byallaccounts Inc—*James Carney*	10 State St Ste 2a, Woburn MA 01801	781-376-0801	R	2*	<.1
1265	Innovative Security Systems Inc—*Andrew Jones*	1809 Woodfield Dr, Savoy IL 61874	217-355-6308	R	2*	<.1
1266	Nc4 Public Sector LLC—*Randy Smith*	PO Box 919, El Segundo CA 90245	310-606-4444	R	2*	<.1
1267	Retail Information Systems—*Sylvia Arreola*	2555 Westhollow Dr, Houston TX 77082	281-558-5910	R	2*	<.1
1268	Visionia Ltd—*Shijing Zhang*	5657 Prospect Pl, Mason OH 45040	513-234-0946	R	2*	<.1
1269	Secure64 Software Corp—*Steve Goodbarn*	5600 S Quebec St Ste 3, Greenwood Village CO 80111	303-242-5890	R	2*	<.1
1270	Turner Consulting Group Inc—*Daniel A Turner*	306 Florida Ave NW, Washington DC 20001	202-986-5533	R	2*	<.1
1271	Indigo Office Inc—*Peter Frost*	212 Sutter St, San Francisco CA 94108	415-616-6820	R	2*	<.1
1272	Bp Logix Inc—*Edward Skiko*	410 S Melrose Dr Ste 1, Vista CA 92081	760-643-4121	R	2*	<.1
1273	Electronic Registry Systems Inc—*Ashok Ramaswamy*	270 Northland Blvd Ste, Cincinnati OH 45246	513-771-7330	R	2*	<.1
1274	Innovative Routines International—*Paul Friedland*	2194 Hwy A1a Ste 303, Indian Harbour Beach FL 32937	321-777-8889	R	2*	<.1
1275	Kildrummy Inc—*Kenneth Beer*	9801 Westheimer Rd Ste, Houston TX 77042	713-339-2678	R	2*	<.1
1276	Zortec International Inc—*Jennie W Harrell*	25 Century Blvd Ste 10, Nashville TN 37214	615-361-7000	R	2*	<.1
1277	Ferrell Companies Inc—*Jerry Ferrell*	7456 W 5th Ave, Lakewood CO 80226	303-233-2400	R	2*	<.1
1278	Quantum Leap Innovations Inc—*Joseph Elad*	3 Innovation Way Ste 1, Newark DE 19711	302-894-8000	R	2*	<.1
1279	Axis Clinical Software Inc—*Scott Page*	6443 SW Beaverton-Hill, Portland OR 97221	503-292-3022	R	2*	<.1
1280	Inman Associates Inc—*William Inman*	3807 Charlotte Ave, Nashville TN 37209	615-321-5591	R	2*	<.1
1281	Omni Consulting Group Inc—*Joseph Phillips-Bella*	225 Delaware Ave Ste 1, Buffalo NY 14202	716-853-2100	R	2*	<.1
1282	Commercial Timesharing Inc—*Ronald Symens*	2740 Cory Ave, Akron OH 44314	330-644-3059	R	2*	<.1
1283	Dimension Technology Solutions Inc—*Curt Morgan*	9800 Mt Pyramid Ct Ste, Englewood CO 80112	303-406-2400	R	2*	<.1
1284	Nisus Software Inc—*Jerzy Lewak*	PO Box 1302, Solana Beach CA 92075	858-481-1477	R	2*	<.1
1285	Breuer and Co—*Tom E Breuer*	701 Edgewater Dr, Wakefield MA 01880	781-246-0010	R	2*	<.1
1286	Documentation Strategies Inc—*Ann Moynihan*	15 2nd Ave, Rensselaer NY 12144	518-432-1233	R	2*	<.1
1287	Dynatrace Software Inc—*John Van Siclen*	400 Totten Pond RdSte, Waltham MA 02451	781-768-4900	S	2*	<.1
1288	EGB Systems and Solutions Inc—*Ganesh Ekambaram*	1234 Summer St 6th Fl, Stamford CT 06905	203-653-2741	R	2*	<.1

Rank	Company Name—*Executive Officer*	Address, City, State, Zip	Phone	Type	Fin	Empls
1289	Gunther Douglas Inc—*Lisa Gunther*	3400 Mariposa St, Denver CO 80211	303-534-4441	R	2*	<.1
1290	Peninsula Software Of Virginia Inc—*Leroy Newman*	151 Enterprise Dr, Newport News VA 23603	757-873-2976	R	2*	<.1
1291	RB Zack and Associates Inc—*Tim Nolan*	23844 Hawthorne Blvd S, Torrance CA 90505	310-303-3320	R	2*	<.1
1292	Urbancode Inc—*Maciej Zawadzki*	2044 Euclid Ave Ste 60, Cleveland OH 44115	216-858-9000	R	2*	<.1
1293	XYPRO Technology Corp—*Dale Blommendahl*	3325 Cochran St Ste 20, Simi Valley CA 93063	805-583-2874	R	2*	<.1
1294	Healthware Solutions LLC—*Marc Chaton*	901 O St Ste C, Arcata CA 95521	707-825-1940	R	2*	<.1
1295	LH Network Inc—*Mani Ganesh*	2 Sycamore Dr, Roslyn NY 11576	516-446-1356	R	2*	<.1
1296	Amalgamated Software of North America Inc—*Carlos Valero*	14210 Northbrook Dr, San Antonio TX 78232	210-408-0212	S	2*	<.1
1297	Burns Data Control Inc—*Michael Burns*	PO Box 701133, Tulsa OK 74170	918-877-4241	R	2*	<.1
1298	Charismac Engineering Inc—*Wyler Furgeson*	9410 Crater Hill Rd St, Auburn CA 95603	530-885-4420	R	2*	<.1
1299	Cycle Computer Consultants Inc—*Anthony J Manzolillo*	95 Jerusalem Ave, Hicksville NY 11801	516-733-1892	R	2*	<.1
1300	RATA Associates LLC—*John R Woloshen*	1916 Boothe Cir, Longwood FL 32750	407-831-7282	R	2*	<.1
1301	Turn-Key Business Systems Inc—*Ken Golden*	PO Box 1086, Russellville AR 72811	479-968-7280	R	2*	<.1
1302	Allgress Inc—*Jeff Bennett*	2600 Kitty Hawk Rd Ste, Livermore CA 94551		R	2*	<.1
1303	Dls Solutions Inc—*Jeff Levi*	PO Box 128, Trumbull CT 06611	203-459-8277	R	2*	<.1
1304	Ivs 3d Inc—*Lindsay Gee*	PO Box 4639, Portsmouth NH 03802	603-766-6000	R	2*	<.1
1305	Solutions Software Corp	800 W 4th St, Williamsport PA 17701	570-323-1010	S	2*	<.1
1306	Creative Media Group—*Ralph Stoeber*	1 Mill Ridge Ln Ste 20, Chester NJ 07930	908-879-9565	R	2*	<.1
1307	Alligator Technologies Inc	2183 Fairview Rd Ste 2, Costa Mesa CA 92627	949-515-1400	R	2*	<.1
1308	BusinessWare Inc—*Peter Shikli*	940 Calle Amanecer Ste, San Clemente CA 92673	949-369-1638	R	2*	<.1
1309	Computermart Medical Services Inc—*Charles Shelton*	356 Corporate Ctr Ct, Stockbridge GA 30281	770-474-1498	R	2*	<.1
1310	Corder Associates Inc—*Kelly D Corder*	PO Box 40518, Mesa AZ 85274	480-752-8533	R	2*	<.1
1311	DRD Technology Corp	5506 S Lewis Ave, Tulsa OK 74105	918-743-3013	R	2*	<.1
1312	Eidogen and Sertanty Inc—*Steven Muskal*	3460 Mrron Rd Ste 103-, Oceanside CA 92056	760-729-0211	R	2*	<.1
1313	Electronic Data Collection Corp—*C Genung*	13 Dwight Park Dr Stop, Syracuse NY 13209	315-706-0310	R	2*	<.1
1314	Government Systems Inc	1800 Diagonal Rd Ste 6, Alexandria VA 22314	703-860-0263	R	2*	<.1
1315	Lackner Group Inc—*Vincent Lackner*	800 N Bell Ave Ste 290, Carnegie PA 15106	412-279-2121	R	2*	<.1
1316	On Time Systems Inc—*Matthew Ginsberg*	355 Goodpasture Island, Eugene OR 97401	541-654-5800	R	2*	<.1
1317	Software Engineering Associates Inc—*Robert Engelmann*	3609 Pacific Ave, Manhattan Beach CA 90266	310-963-8901	R	2*	<.1
1318	Transcend Business Solutions LLC	30 Grassy Plain St Ste, Bethel CT 06801	203-790-5222	R	2*	<.1
1319	Coastal Technologies	615 Valley Rd, Montclair NJ 07043	973-744-2900	R	2*	<.1
1320	Datamate Inc—*Charles Talbert*	7501 Westview Dr, Houston TX 77055	713-464-8881	R	2*	<.1
1321	Lexnet Consulting Group Inc—*Stephen Chipman*	PO Box 29129, San Francisco CA 94129	415-472-3100	R	2*	<.1
1322	TechArts—*Steve Diederich*	5701 E Circle Dr Ste 3, Cicero NY 13039	315-350-3755	R	2*	<.1
1323	Tierra Innovation Inc—*James Trowbridge*	400 Lafayette St Ste 4, New York NY 10003	347-410-5901	R	2*	<.1
1324	Coolware Company Inc—*Mark Armenda*	5801 Coyote Pass Rd, Shingle Springs CA 95682	916-369-8400	R	2*	<.1
1325	Knowledge Ag Inc—*Spencer Brown*	4500 Weldon Dr, Temple Hills MD 20748	301-423-7187	R	2*	<.1
1326	Astonish SEO—*Brian Mcgee*	14 Westford St Fl 2, Haverhill MA 01832	978-374-1689	R	2*	<.1
1327	Chuckwalla Inc—*Brian Aspland*	4699 Old Ironsides Dr, Santa Clara CA 95054	408-330-8700	R	2*	<.1
1328	Diffraction International Inc—*Steven Arnold*	5810 Baker Rd Ste 225, Minnetonka MN 55345	952-945-9912	R	2*	<.1
1329	Ironsoft Ltd—*Barbara Barczuk*	11743 Frankstown Rd St, Pittsburgh PA 15235	412-247-3560	R	2*	<.1
1330	Live Oak Multimedia Inc—*David Antoniuk*	255 3rd St Ste 305, Oakland CA 94607	510-834-9667	R	2*	<.1
1331	NuZoo Media Inc—*Dan Pulik*	606 W 18th St, Chicago IL 60616	312-421-2129	R	2*	<.1
1332	Octave Software Group Inc—*David Simon*	1855 Hamilton Ave Ste, Los Altos CA 94022	408-371-3060	R	2*	<.1
1333	Pacific Data Management Inc—*Dave Terry*	111 W St John Rm 404, San Jose CA 95113	408-283-5900	R	2*	<.1
1334	Paragon Software Inc—*Lynn Graybiel*	4949 E Spruce Dr, Dunnellon FL 34434	352-816-7603	R	2*	<.1
1335	ProHelp Systems Inc	418 E Waterside Dr, Seneca SC 29672	864-885-0094	R	2*	<.1
1336	Software Made Easy LLC—*Kim Lanners*	8626 Mustang Dr, Naples FL 34113	239-732-5300	R	2*	<.1
1337	Software Systems and Services International Inc—*Donald W Addiss*	5252 Balboa Ave Ste 80, San Diego CA 92117	858-278-3742	R	2*	<.1
1338	Synthetik Software Inc—*John Dalton*	500 Ala Moana Blvd Ste, Honolulu HI 96813		R	2*	<.1
1339	TDC Group Inc—*Matthew Reddington*	3055 Kettering Blvd St, Dayton OH 45439	937-461-2000	R	2*	<.1
1340	Teknowledge Corp—*Neil A Jacobstein*	2225 E Bayshore Rd Ste, Palo Alto CA 94303	650-424-0500	P	2*	<.1
1341	Tilden Park Software Inc—*Lance Batten*	2269 Chestnut St Ste 5, Lafayette CA 94549	925-283-5139	R	2*	<.1
1342	Command X—*Mark Cretcher*	1018 Delta Ave Ste 201, Cincinnati OH 45208	513-281-6585	R	2*	<.1
1343	Computel Systems Inc—*Deepak Jain*	7400 Carmel Exec Park, Charlotte NC 28226	704-541-8950	R	2*	<.1
1344	New Aspects of Software Inc—*Ronald J Bodkin*	134 Lockhart Ln, Los Altos CA 94022	650-941-8344	R	2*	<.1
1345	onProject Inc—*Joe Murgio*	PO Box 104, Franklin Lakes NJ 07417	973-971-9970	R	2*	<.1
1346	Qualution Systems Inc—*Pedram Toussi*	28720 Roadside Dr Ste, Agoura Hills CA 91301	818-889-4488	R	2*	<.1
1347	Universal Productions International Inc—*Bob Canes Jr*	4415 W Forest Home Ave, Milwaukee WI 53219	414-321-0874	R	2*	<.1
1348	Visual Database Systems—*John Blakney*	PO Box 24267, Little Rock AR 72221	501-376-2091	R	2*	<.1
1349	Alloso Technologies LLC	3701 National Dr Ste 1, Raleigh NC 27612	919-792-1600	R	2*	<.1
1350	Peirce Software Inc	649 Spinnaker Dr, Lewis Center OH 43035		R	2*	<.1
1351	RaceCom Inc	PO Box 730955, Ormond Beach FL 32173	386-575-0088	R	2*	<.1
1352	Wachusett Programming—*William F Banks III*	9 Oakcrest Rd, Holden MA 01520		R	2*	<.1
1353	Amazon Technologies Co—*Alvaro Karam*	150 Alhambra Cir Ste 1, Coral Gables FL 33134	305-921-9562	R	2*	<.1
1354	Voip Group Inc—*Edward Perry*	290 Nw 165th St, Miami FL 33169	305-424-3616	R	2*	<.1
1355	Vsecure Technoliges—*Izhar Shay*	1 Park 80 Plz W, Saddle Brook NJ 07663	201-291-2845	R	2*	<.1
1356	Labwerks Inc—*John Kuntz*	3618 Penn Ave, Pittsburgh PA 15201	412-621-9375	R	2*	<.1
1357	Wisdomtools Enterprises Inc	501 N Morton St Ste 20, Bloomington IN 47404	812-856-4202	R	2*	<.1
1358	Enterprise Technology System Inc—*Peter Chan*	4221 Technology Dr, Fremont CA 94538	510-683-0899	R	2*	<.1
1359	Equal-Plus Inc—*Henri Eberhardt*	PO Box 500129, Atlanta GA 31150	678-467-3047	R	2*	<.1
1360	Gambit Communications Inc—*Pankaj Shah*	76 Northeastern Blvd 2, Nashua NH 03062	603-881-3500	R	2*	<.1
1361	Vvm Inc—*Andrew Higgins*	PO Box 1391, Temple TX 76503	254-778-8028	R	2*	<.1
1362	Prometheus Research LLC—*Peter Harker*	55 Church St Fl 7, New Haven CT 06510	203-752-9410	R	2*	<.1
1363	Casamba Inc—*Aharon Amrany*	5210 Lewis Rd Ste 10, Agoura Hills CA 91301	818-991-9111	R	2*	<.1
1364	Software Consulting Network Inc—*William Schmidt*	31 Marjac Rd, Mansfield MA 02048	508-339-7504	R	2*	<.1
1365	Quadrant Software Inc—*Gary Langton*	PO Box 200, Mansfield MA 02048	508-594-2700	R	2*	<.1
1366	Mainstream Software Inc—*Peter Wallace*	2198 E Enterprise Pkwy, Twinsburg OH 44087	330-963-0103	R	2*	<.1
1367	Liquid 8 Technologies Inc—*Richard Greene*	6700 Lee Hwy, Arlington VA 22205	703-533-3100	R	2*	<.1
1368	Analytiks International Inc—*Rafi Sheikh*	10 S 5th St Ste 720, Minneapolis MN 55402	612-305-4312	R	2*	<.1
1369	Chartscape LLC	12424 Wilshire Blvd St, Los Angeles CA 90025	310-392-2120	R	2*	<.1
1370	Mountain Creek Entertainment LLC—*Russell Clophus*	2747 Excalibur Dr, Grand Prairie TX 75052	214-850-3263	R	2*	<.1
1371	Tensor Systems Corp—*Dary Wilson*	5442 Nw 42nd Way, Coconut Creek FL 33073	954-725-6194	R	2*	<.1
1372	Avidian Technologies Inc—*James Huang*	2053 152nd Ave Ne, Redmond WA 98052	206-686-3001	R	2*	<.1
1373	Rina Systems Inc—*Leo Zamansky*	8180 Corporate Park Dr, Cincinnati OH 45242	513-469-7462	R	2*	<.1
1374	Tbd Networks Inc—*Thomas Ludwig*	2 N 1st St Fl 2, San Jose CA 95113	408-278-1590	R	2*	<.1
1375	Logical Resources Inc—*Richard Jenkins*	4004 Belt Line Rd Ste, Addison TX 75001	972-385-3422	R	2*	<.1
1376	American International Management Inc—*Rom Cheruquri*	162 Port Richmond Ave, Staten Island NY 10302	718-727-9744	R	2*	<.1
1377	Engenium Corp—*David Chaplin*	14901 Quorum Dr Ste 81, Dallas TX 75254	469-374-9464	R	2*	<.1

Note: An asterisk (*) indicates an estimated financial figure. The company type code used is as follows: R = Private, P = Public, S = Private Subsidiary, B = Public Subsidiary, D = Division, J = Joint Venture, I = Investment Fund.

COMPANY RANKINGS BY SALES WITHIN 4-DIGIT SIC

Rank	Company Name—*Executive Officer*	Address, City, State, Zip	Phone	Type	Fin	Empls
1378	Probaris Technologies Inc—*Charles Durkin*	718 Arch St Ste 200s, Philadelphia PA 19106	215-238-0510	R	2*	<.1
1379	Psd Solutions Inc—*Howard Simon*	350 W Hubbard St Ste 2, Chicago IL 60654	312-828-9260	R	2*	<.1
1380	Vertex Systems Corp—*Sanford Chandler*	440 Polaris Pkwy Ste 1, Westerville OH 43082	614-318-7100	R	2*	<.1
1381	PG Calc Inc—*Gary Pforzheimer*	129 Mount Auburn St St, Cambridge MA 02138	617-497-4970	R	2*	<.1
1382	Retrieval Systems Corp—*B Basheer*	2071 Chain Bridge Rd S, Vienna VA 22182	703-749-0012	R	2*	<.1
1383	Microvisions Computer Systems Inc—*Barbara Laws*	207 Townepark Cir Ste, Louisville KY 40243	502-254-1789	R	2*	<.1
1384	Jano Justice Systems Inc—*Vasco Bridges*	4798 Mcwillie Dr Ste C, Jackson MS 39206	601-362-7601	R	2*	<.1
1385	Pro Logic Computer Systems Inc—*Jose Kudja*	14411 Commerce Way Ste, Hialeah FL 33016	305-824-8648	R	2*	<.1
1386	Teamf1 Inc—*Mukesh Lulla*	39270 Paseo Padre Pkwy, Fremont CA 94538	510-505-9931	R	2*	<.1
1387	Artwork Conversion Software Inc—*Steve Dibartolomeo*	417 Ingalls St, Santa Cruz CA 95060	831-426-6163	R	2*	<.1
1388	Synergis Group LLC	11469 Olive Blvd Ste 2, Saint Louis MO 63141	314-941-4234	R	2*	<.1
1389	Capital Computer Associates Inc—*Larry Steinhart*	1 Winners Cir Ste 99, Albany NY 12205	518-435-0500	R	2*	<.1
1390	Quandis Inc—*Scott Stoddard*	23272 Mill Creek Dr St, Laguna Hills CA 92653	949-206-0008	R	2*	<.1
1391	3rd Angle Technologies Inc—*Laura Spadafino*	800 Westchester Ave N6, Rye Brook NY 10573	914-328-6183	R	2*	<.1
1392	Alto Palo Broadcasting Co—*John Schad*	PO Box 284, Emmetsburg IA 50536	712-852-4047	R	2*	<.1
1393	Information Access Solutions Inc—*Timothy Corley*	PO Box 7621, Woodbridge VA 22195	703-680-7178	R	2*	<.1
1394	Management Data Inc—*Patrick Michael*	2060 Oak Mountain Dr, Pelham AL 35124	205-378-1380	R	2*	<.1
1395	Megasys Hospitality Systems Inc—*Mark Jewart*	5800 E Skelly Dr Ste 6, Tulsa OK 74135	918-743-0100	R	2*	<.1
1396	Millenium Technologies—*Stephen Pursley*	597 Stringer Rd, Burke TX 75941	936-632-3860	R	2*	<.1
1397	Contextual Inc—*Robin Green*	6504 Bridge Point Pkwy, Austin TX 78730	512-225-6400	R	2*	<.1
1398	Centrifuge Systems Inc—*Renee Lorton*	7926 Jones Branch Dr S, Mc Lean VA 22102	571-830-1300	R	2*	<.1
1399	Global It Solutions Usi Inc—*Venkata Suryadevara*	1133 E 35th St Apt 2d, Brooklyn NY 11210	718-377-4525	R	2*	<.1
1400	Latenzero Inc—*Dan Watkins*	160 Federal St, Boston MA 02110	617-204-1102	R	2*	<.1
1401	Fenetech Inc—*Ron Crowl*	1455 Danner Dr, Aurora OH 44202	330-995-2830	R	2*	<.1
1402	Florida Software and Data Systems Inc—*David Chapnick*	2030 Nw Boca Raton Blv, Boca Raton FL 33431	561-394-4222	R	2*	<.1
1403	Asa Solutions Inc—*David Atkins*	8040 E Morgan Trl Ste, Scottsdale AZ 85258	480-922-9532	R	2*	<.1
1404	Mekorma Enterprises Inc—*Ora Goldman*	8265 W Sunset Blvd Ste, West Hollywood CA 90046		R	2*	<.1
1405	Red Canyon Software Inc—*Barry Hamilton*	1200 Penn St Apt 100, Denver CO 80203	303-503-1990	R	2*	<.1
1406	Viatronix Inc—*Zaffar Hayat*	25 E Loop Rd Ste 204, Stony Brook NY 11790	631-444-9700	R	2*	<.1
1407	Telebright Software Corp—*Chet Thaker*	40 W Gude Dr, Rockville MD 20850	301-296-3800	R	2*	<.1
1408	Vostrom Holdings Inc—*Victor Oppleman*	576 N Birdneck Rd 710, Virginia Beach VA 23451		R	2*	<.1
1409	Sar Inc—*Susan Reuter*	2965 Colonnade Dr Ste, Roanoke VA 24018	540-777-5621	R	2*	<.1
1410	Frontline Data Solutions Inc—*Mahendra Bathia*	10701 Corp Dr Ste 370, Stafford TX 77477	281-313-8200	R	2*	<.1
1411	Computer Simulation and Analysis Inc—*Craig Peterson*	PO Box 51596, Idaho Falls ID 83405	208-529-1700	R	2*	<.1
1412	Latis Technologies LLC—*Ilango Marag*	1100 N Glebe Rd Ste 10, Arlington VA 22201	703-224-8042	R	2*	<.1
1413	Informa Systems Inc—*Greg Seally*	624 N Main St Ste 204, Boerne TX 78006	830-815-1600	R	2*	<.1
1414	Vectorsite—*Tim Christensen*	1709 Perkins Rd, Belle Isle FL 32809	407-855-4465	R	2*	<.1
1415	IT Staff Inc—*Jim Ivon*	485 Fashion Ave Rm 100, New York NY 10018	212-338-9595	R	2*	<.1
1416	Birmingham Data Systems Inc—*Alexander Begin*	1950 Livernois Rd, Troy MI 48083	248-528-0250	R	2*	<.1
1417	Ticketreturn LLC—*Aron Clark*	PO Box 241632, Charlotte NC 28224	704-536-0042	R	2*	<.1
1418	Connexxia LLC—*Peter Flur*	400 Interstate N Pkwy, Atlanta GA 30339	678-627-8600	R	2*	<.1
1419	Facility Wizard Software Inc—*Dave Johnson*	4147 N Ravenswood Ave, Chicago IL 60613	773-832-0200	R	2*	<.1
1420	Nuparadigm Government Systems Inc—*Harry Haury*	12977 N 40 Dr Ste 200, Saint Louis MO 63141	636-537-5558	R	2*	<.1
1421	United Developers LLC—*Ron Dimant*	2019 N Lamar St Ste 30, Dallas TX 75202	214-855-5955	R	2*	<.1
1422	Accelerated Computer Technologies—*Mark Levey*	1000 W Mcnab Rd Ste 32, Pompano Beach FL 33069	954-786-0883	R	2*	<.1
1423	Aligned Development Strategies Inc—*Dale James*	1900 L St Nw Ste 600, Washington DC 20036	202-659-2807	R	2*	<.1
1424	Ensyte Energy Software International—*Michael Smith*	770 S Post Oak Ln Ste, Houston TX 77056	713-622-2875	R	2*	<.1
1425	Ideation International Inc—*Zion Bar-El*	32000 Northwestern Hwy, Farmington Hills MI 48334	248-737-8854	R	2*	<.1
1426	Seanet Technologies Inc—*Bernie Davidovics*	125 10 Queens Blvd, Kew Gardens NY 11415	718-544-1778	R	2*	<.1
1427	Infoware Systems Inc—*Barbara Linton*	600 Jackson Ct, Satellite Beach FL 32937	321-773-5881	R	2*	<.1
1428	Cyber Group Inc—*Bhopi Dhall*	12900 Preston Rd Ste 1, Dallas TX 75230	469-916-7730	R	2*	<.1
1429	Inland Productivity Solutions Inc—*Eric Hanson*	PO Box 1448, Upland CA 91785	909-981-4500	R	2*	<.1
1430	Facts Inc—*Albert Curry*	2737 Front St, Cuyahoga Falls OH 44221	330-928-2332	R	2*	<.1
1431	Universal Automation Labs Solutions Group—*Terri Thrash*	1010 Wayne Ave Ste 110, Silver Spring MD 20910	301-565-0032	R	2*	<.1
1432	Scorelogix LLC—*Tim Gorla*	2 Reads Way Ste 226, New Castle DE 19720	302-328-1210	R	2*	<.1
1433	Phone Acce Enterprise Inc—*Donald Millhofer*	PO Box 37, Dublin OH 43017	614-889-0697	R	2*	<.1
1434	Best Computer Consulting Inc—*Josey Ozdil*	26400 Lahser Rd Ste 41, Southfield MI 48033	248-355-5580	R	2*	<.1
1435	Bm Associates Inc—*Senthil Muniappan*	9783 Swan Lake Dr, Granite Bay CA 95746	810-423-4279	R	2*	<.1
1436	Floor Covering Exchange Inc—*Dev O'reilly*	201 Saint Charles Ave, New Orleans LA 70170	504-599-5949	R	2*	<.1
1437	Healex Systems Ltd—*Nicolas Place*	11 Middleton Dr, Wilmington DE 19808	302-235-5750	R	2*	<.1
1438	Nuvek LLC—*Donald Aslett*	315 S 5th Ave, Pocatello ID 83201	208-232-8598	R	2*	<.1
1439	Syslogic Inc—*Tina Chang*	375 Bishops Way Ste 10, Brookfield WI 53005	262-780-0380	R	2*	<.1
1440	Automanager Inc—*Reinv Tfrechi*	12340 Santa Monica Blv, Los Angeles CA 90025	310-207-2202	R	2*	<.1
1441	Kyran Research Associates Inc—*Nancy Whitehead*	PO Box 3780, Newport RI 02840	401-849-7734	RI	2*	<.1
1442	Stepone Systems LLC—*Craig Reeder*	555 N Bell Ave Ste 203, Carnegie PA 15106	412-894-8545	R	2*	<.1
1443	Ulysses Group Associates Inc—*Timothy Smelyansky*	334 Main St, Matawan NJ 07747	732-208-5040	R	2*	<.1
1444	Academic Performance Institute Inc—*Robert Mcintyre*	167 W Main St Ste 210, Lexington KY 40507	859-233-2006	R	2*	<.1
1445	Codefab Inc—*Alex Cone*	320 W 37th St 8b, New York NY 10018	212-465-8484	R	2*	<.1
1446	B Drive Inc—*Mike Salari*	39555 Orchard Hill Pl, Novi MI 48375	248-380-0815	R	2*	<.1
1447	Computational Applications and Systems Integrations Inc—*Pravin Vaidya*	2001 S 1st St, Champaign IL 61820	217-244-7875	R	2*	<.1
1448	Edmund Jung and Associates Inc—*Edmund Jung*	10815 Canoga Ave, Chatsworth CA 91311	818-709-6055	R	2*	<.1
1449	Firm58 Inc—*Nick Fera*	130 S Jefferson St Ste, Chicago IL 60661	312-863-2390	R	2*	<.1
1450	Laserplus Inc—*Jeff Hill*	6255 Corporate Dr, Houston TX 77036	713-774-1222	R	2*	<.1
1451	Mica Information Systems—*James Price*	PO Box 25406, Winston Salem NC 27114	336-768-5348	R	2*	<.1
1452	Aeon Nexus Corp—*Omar Usmani*	PO Box 4595, Glens Falls NY 12804	518-338-1551	R	2*	<.1
1453	Automated Tech Tools Inc—*Thomas Abel*	3401 Enterprise Pkwy S, Cleveland OH 44122	440-717-6000	R	2*	<.1
1454	Data Management Solutions Corp—*Frank Pena*	707 Hunters Creek Way, Hockley TX 77447	713-408-7835	R	2*	<.1
1455	Sharp Bancsystems Inc—*Joe Sharp*	4009 Airport Fwy, Bedford TX 76021	817-553-2550	R	2*	<.1
1456	Chaash Inc—*Asha Motwani*	13564 Plumbago Dr, Centreville VA 20120	703-830-4952	R	2*	<.1
1457	Larson Automation Inc—*Wayne Larson*	960 Rincon Cir, San Jose CA 95131	408-432-4800	R	2*	<.1
1458	Quality Team Associates Inc—*Mitchell Proyect*	13535 Sw 72nd Ave Ste, Portland OR 97223	503-443-2102	R	2*	<.1
1459	Practical Engineering Inc—*Edwin Luff*	2 Central St, Framingham MA 01701	508-877-5225	R	2*	<.1
1460	LC Radise International—*Rekha Jadala*	4152 Blue Heron Blvd W, Riviera Beach FL 33404	561-841-0103	R	2*	<.1
1461	Longwood Systems Inc—*Peter Keppelman*	200 Reservoir St Ste 1, Needham MA 02494	781-455-6846	R	2*	<.1
1462	Imaginary Universes—*Stephen Dukes*	PO Box 250, Stanwood WA 98292	360-387-8667	R	2*	<.1
1463	Innovision Design Inc—*Jose Carrasquillo*	3638 Waynoka Dr, Carrollton TX 75007	972-394-1056	R	2*	<.1
1464	Srisys Inc—*Vijaya Sabbineni*	7908 Cincinnati Dayton, West Chester OH 45069	513-298-1151	R	2*	<.1
1465	Castello Cities Internet Network—*Michael Castello*	500 E Amado Rd Unit 51, Palm Springs CA 92262	760-416-2526	R	2*	<.1
1466	Interactive Data Visualization Inc—*Chris King*	5446 Sunset Blvd Ste 2, Lexington SC 29072	803-356-1999	R	2*	<.1

Rank	Company Name—*Executive Officer*	Address, City, State, Zip	Phone	Type	Fin	Empls
1467	Process Networks Plus Inc—*Jack Krohner*	651 N Us Hwy 183, Leander TX 78641	512-260-1699	R	2*	<.1
1468	Banzai Research Institute Inc—*John Choi*	2030 Main St Ste 1300, Irvine CA 92614	949-215-2035	R	2*	<.1
1469	Caseintel Corp—*Trevor Hayward*	PO Box 212, Bellevue WA 98009	206-774-6712	R	2*	<.1
1470	Nisus Technology Corp—*Joe Sperber*	7120 Minstrel Way Ste, Columbia MD 21045	443-259-0156	R	1*	<.1
1471	Ampex Co—*Afaok Mittal*	20 Broad St, Eatontown NJ 07724	732-389-1113	R	1*	<.1
1472	Infiniti Information Solutions—*Gus Bell*	5568 General Washingto, Alexandria VA 22312	703-941-5700	R	1*	<.1
1473	Iviz Group Inc—*Dave Ferguson*	700 Tower Dr Ste 400, Troy MI 48098	248-528-7160	R	1*	<.1
1474	Kgf Associates Inc—*Niaz Sariz*	777 Washington Rd Ste, Sayreville NJ 08871	732-698-2100	R	1*	<.1
1475	Spinks Technologies—*Gerard Spinks*	PO Box 922, Atlanta GA 30301		R	1*	<.1
1476	Colorado PC Doctors Inc—*Amie Paxton*	111 W Fillmore St, Colorado Springs CO 80907	719-632-1024	R	1*	<.1
1477	Vidisolutions Inc—*Fred Mueller*	2 Penn Plz Ste 15000, New York NY 10121	212-465-2337	R	1*	<.1
1478	Data Star Inc—*Addie Ramsay*	PO Box 1200, Picayune MS 39466	601-799-2439	R	1*	<.1
1479	East End Resources Inc—*Kathleen Hugh*	530 E 90th St, New York NY 10128	212-996-4700	R	1*	<.1
1480	Fish Software Inc—*Michael Gilvar*	1434 Patton Pl Ste 190, Carrollton TX 75007	214-764-7145	R	1*	<.1
1481	Infosurv Inc—*Leroy Caudle*	555 Sparkman Dr Nw Ste, Huntsville AL 35816	256-721-1622	R	1*	<.1
1482	Intertech USA Inc—*William Gillespie*	6070 Industrial Rd, Missoula MT 59808	406-549-8998	R	1*	<.1
1483	Klt Associates Inc—*Kenneth Thompson*	100 Corporate Pl Ste 2, Peabody MA 01960	978-536-9100	R	1*	<.1
1484	Novodynamics Inc—*David Rock*	123 N Ashley St Ste 21, Ann Arbor MI 48104	734-205-9100	R	1*	<.1
1485	OSS Corp—*Suresh Pillai*	PO Box 2092, Shelton CT 06484	203-925-1083	R	1*	<.1
1486	Web Teks Inc—*Dyanne Walker*	676 Independence Pkwy, Chesapeake VA 23320	757-578-4923	R	1*	<.1
1487	Indianer Computer Corp—*Evan Indianer*	3127 Penn Ave, Pittsburgh PA 15201	412-697-7000	R	1*	<.1
1488	Mcalister Design Inc—*Troy Alister*	510 Pickett St, Greenville SC 29609	864-232-8325	R	1*	<.1
1489	Netsource One Inc—*Norbert Hages*	5410 Hampton Pl, Saginaw MI 48604	989-498-4534	R	1*	<.1
1490	Orena Development Corp—*Robert Rickal*	PO Box 31712, San Francisco CA 94131	415-710-7125	R	1*	<.1
1491	B To B Vision LLC—*Robert Deluca*	41 Orchard St, Ramsey NJ 07446	201-995-9666	R	1*	<.1
1492	Crw Systems Inc—*Chris Wuerz*	16980 Via Tazon Ste 32, San Diego CA 92127	858-451-3030	R	1*	<.1
1493	Electric Vine Inc—*Joshua Rich*	3 Executive Dr Ste 325, Somerset NJ 08873	732-868-8463	R	1*	<.1
1494	Systems and System Software Solutions LLC—*Andres Sandin*	PO Box 2686, Laurel MD 20709	301-805-0620	R	1*	<.1
1495	Micro Performance Inc—*Ron Shurie*	2569 Housley Rd, Annapolis MD 21401	410-224-3100	R	1*	<.1
1496	Systems and Communications Sciences Inc—*Craig Dudley*	244 Poor Farm Rd, New Ipswich NH 03071	603-878-1148	R	1*	<.1
1497	Leadsoft Inc—*Swapan Shah*	19727 Executive Park C, Germantown MD 20874	301-515-7083	R	1*	<.1
1498	4mf LLC—*Richard Conner*	17 W Mercer St Apt 304, Seattle WA 98119	253-229-8040	R	1*	<.1
1499	BTE Consulting Inc—*John Sinkus*	750 W Lake Cook Rd Ste, Buffalo Grove IL 60089	847-541-1400	R	1*	<.1
1500	Online Expansions—*Denise Gee*	6503 Highland Grass, Converse TX 78109	210-833-6673	R	1*	<.1
1501	Tag Easy Corp—*Sergio Mastronardi*	334 Cornelia St Ste 2, Plattsburgh NY 12901		R	1*	<.1
1502	Luxology LLC—*Robin Hastings*	2525 Charleston Rd Ste, Mountain View CA 94043	650-336-1380	R	1*	<.1
1503	Oak Enterprises Data Services Inc—*Timothy Waterloo*	800 Roosevelt Rd Bldg, Glen Ellyn IL 60137	630-858-4443	R	1*	<.1
1504	High Tech Research Inc—*Steven Birman*	1020 Milwaukee Ave Ste, Deerfield IL 60015	847-215-9797	R	1*	<.1
1505	It Works Inc—*Damien Agostinelli*	3416 9th St Ne, Washington DC 20017	202-455-4781	R	1*	<.1
1506	Tangent Systems Inc—*Steve Mack*	2155 Stnngton Ave Ste, Hoffman Estates IL 60195	847-882-3833	R	1*	<.1
1507	Xtron Software Services Inc—*Jag Puttanna*	3080 Olcott St Ste 220, Santa Clara CA 95054	408-855-9800	R	1*	<.1
1508	Compu-Tech Inc—*James Seal*	PO Box 503, Wenatchee WA 98807	509-884-1542	R	1*	<.1
1509	Datascape Inc—*Richard Wagner*	7840 Roswell Rd Ste 32, Atlanta GA 30350	770-804-0924	R	1*	<.1
1510	Eagle Technology Management Inc—*Larry Kane*	1425 60th St Ne Ste 20, Cedar Rapids IA 52402	515-237-5555	R	1*	<.1
1511	Firestar Software Inc—*Kenneth Lord*	59 Lowes Way, Lowell MA 01851	978-635-9320	R	1*	<.1
1512	Galatea Associates LLC—*Mike Higgins*	20 Holland St Ste 405, Somerville MA 02144	617-623-5466	R	1*	<.1
1513	Geckobytecom Inc—*Kris Hocevar*	207 1/2 E Superior St, Duluth MN 55802	218-722-3419	R	1*	<.1
1514	Systems Design Northwest Inc—*Roger Zegers*	PO Box 3510, Silverdale WA 98383	360-692-5242	R	1*	<.1
1515	Trade Quotes Inc—*Leonard Phillips*	675 Msschsetts Ave Ste, Cambridge MA 02139	617-492-0600	R	1*	<.1
1516	Ulink Technology Inc—*Gracie Chen*	3120 De La Cruz Blvd, Santa Clara CA 95054	408-446-8455	R	1*	<.1
1517	Computer Systems And Services Inc—*James Oliverio*	12411 Telecom Dr, Temple Terrace FL 33637	813-972-2441	R	1*	<.1
1518	Cube Six Inc—*Robert Webster*	PO Box 3049, Matthews NC 28106	704-821-4141	R	1*	<.1
1519	Paramount Software Associates Inc—*William Simpson*	PO Box 19096, Amarillo TX 79114	806-358-8928	R	1*	<.1
1520	Applied Logic Inc—*William Terry*	1432 Strassner Dr, Saint Louis MO 63144	314-918-8877	R	1*	<.1
1521	Eml Inc—*Vijay Rengan*	8500 N Mo Pac Expy Ste, Austin TX 78759	512-431-1853	R	1*	<.1
1522	Ifworld Inc—*Jeremy Webb*	4058 N College Ave Ste, Fayetteville AR 72703	479-582-5100	R	1*	<.1
1523	Regional Data Services Inc—*Rosalind Henderson*	1260 Arrowhead Ct, Crown Point IN 46307	219-661-3200	R	1*	<.1
1524	AJ Rhem and Associates Inc—*Anthony Rhem*	500 N Michigan Ave Ste, Chicago IL 60611	312-396-4024	R	1*	<.1
1525	Bit Computers Inc—*Leo Loo*	80 Smith St Ste 3, Farmingdale NY 11735	631-293-7700	R	1*	<.1
1526	Equus Software LLC—*Tyler Reynolds*	1331 17th St Ste 515, Denver CO 80202	303-292-4200	R	1*	<.1
1527	Intellipro Inc—*Ricky Clinton*	255 Old New Brnswk Rd, Piscataway NJ 08854	732-981-0445	R	1*	<.1
1528	Leading Edge Design and Systems Inc—*Joseph Gordon*	510 Mccormick Dr Ste A, Glen Burnie MD 21061	410-787-7036	R	1*	<.1
1529	Mirac Inc—*Ralph Captain*	PO Box 517, Lynchburg OH 45142	937-364-2920	R	1*	<.1
1530	Pattern Associates Inc—*Stewart Cornew*	66 Abbottsford Rd, Winnetka IL 60093	847-501-4264	R	1*	<.1
1531	Precision Computer Solutions Inc—*Ronda Ryan*	1411 3rd St Ste C, Port Huron MI 48060	810-987-8748	R	1*	<.1
1532	Mediatechnics Corp—*Ari Bass*	22 W Bryan St Ste 240, Savannah GA 31401	912-236-1139	R	1*	<.1
1533	Crescent Design Inc—*Steve Royce*	9932 Mesa Rim Rd Ste B, San Diego CA 92121	858-452-3240	R	1*	<.1
1534	Csoft Inc—*Sunil Sunkara*	221 E Main St Ste 203, Milford MA 01757	508-478-6680	R	1*	<.1
1535	Dynamics Direct Inc—*Jason McNamara*	28494 Westinghouse Pl, Valencia CA 91355	661-600-2059	R	1*	<.1
1536	Pinnacom Solutions Inc—*Steven Kania*	2039 W Wabansia Ave St, Chicago IL 60647	773-342-6331	R	1*	<.1
1537	Launch Technologies Of Georgia LLC	12540 Broadwell Rd, Alpharetta GA 30004	678-218-4020	R	1*	<.1
1538	Edj Enterprises Inc—*David Courtney*	3125 Pplrwood Ct Ste G, Raleigh NC 27604	919-790-7711	R	1*	<.1
1539	Quadratic Systems Inc—*Anil Koripelly*	1082 Savoy Ct, Elk Grove Village IL 60007	847-275-8059	R	1*	<.1
1540	Applied Maths Inc—*Luc Vauterin*	13809 Res Blvd Ste 645, Austin TX 78750	512-482-9700	R	1*	<.1
1541	Dragonpoint Inc—*Suzie Debusk*	365 Gus Hipp Blvd, Rockledge FL 32955	321-636-9747	R	1*	<.1
1542	Omni-Tech Corp—*Pete ARA*	1490 Torrey Rd Ste A, Fenton MI 48430	810-750-6474	R	1*	<.1
1543	Strategic Support Systems Inc—*Nathan Gantt*	1139 Ascott Valley Dr, Duluth GA 30097	678-248-4060	R	1*	<.1
1544	Blu Consulting Inc—*Randy Rucker*	10503 Great Plains Ln, Houston TX 77064	713-503-3528	R	1*	<.1
1545	C-Lutions Inc—*John Mccann*	39379 Mechling Farm Ln, Leesburg VA 20175	703-777-1890	R	1*	<.1
1546	Letsgolearn Inc—*Richard Capone*	705 Wellesley Ave, Kensington CA 94708	510-558-8844	R	1*	<.1
1547	Synchronicity Systems Solutions—*Aatreyee Eitland*	33 Cider Mill Rd, Andover CT 06232	860-428-6230	R	1*	<.1
1548	Cybersoft North America Inc—*Glenn Outerbridge*	1500 S Dairy Ashford S, Houston TX 77077	281-752-0600	R	1*	<.1
1549	Ant USA Inc—*Dmitry Goykhman*	132 Main St, Acton MA 01720	978-635-0877	R	1*	<.1
1550	Business Transactions Technologies Inc—*Robert Bell*	PO Box 2227, Bonita Springs FL 34133	239-992-5115	R	1*	<.1
1551	Equisys Inc—*Chris Oswold*	30000 Mill Creek Ave S, Alpharetta GA 30022	770-772-7201	R	1*	<.1
1552	Euclid Discoveries LLC—*Richard Wingard*	30 Monument Sq Ste 212, Concord MA 01742	978-369-8303	R	1*	<.1
1553	Kompany Com—*Shawn Gordon*	PO Box 80265, Rcho STA Marg CA 92688	949-713-3276	R	1*	<.1
1554	Linkpro Technologies Inc—*Frank Reinhart*	4199 Campus Dr Sto 550, Irvine CA 92612	949-854-3322	R	1*	<.1
1555	Omnicia Inc—*Reuben Jenkins*	400 Oyster Point Blvd, South San Francisco CA 94080	650-588-2188	H	1*	<.1
1556	Redix International Inc—*Pen Chiang*	4 Harvest Ln, Freehold NJ 07728	732-462-6887	R	1*	<.1

Note: An asterisk (*) indicates an estimated financial figure. The company type code used is as follows: R = Private, P = Public, S = Private Subsidiary, B = Public Subsidiary, D = Division, J = Joint Venture, I = Investment Fund.

COMPANY RANKINGS BY SALES WITHIN 4-DIGIT SIC

Rank	Company Name—*Executive Officer*	Address, City, State, Zip	Phone	Type	Fin	Empls
1557	Smd Software Inc—*Ross Lampe*	PO Box 19744, Raleigh NC 27619	919-865-0789	R	1*	<.1
1558	BrainxCom Inc—*Bruce Lewolt*	45 Rincon Dr Unit 103-, Camarillo CA 93012	805-384-1001	R	1*	<.1
1559	Appolis Inc—*Jim Willems*	333 Washington Ave N S, Minneapolis MN 55401	612-373-7010	R	1*	<.1
1560	Leepfrog Technologies Inc—*Lee Brintle*	2105 Act Cir, Iowa City IA 52245	319-337-3877	R	1*	<.1
1561	Voice Poll Communications Inc—*Roger Pawley*	PO Box 65, Everett WA 98206	425-259-4205	R	1*	<.1
1562	Xvd Corp—*Sam Takagi*	111 Pine St Ste 1410, San Francisco CA 94111		R	1*	<.1
1563	Aspen Test Engineering Inc—*Walter Oshetski*	1200 Diamond Cir Ste C, Lafayette CO 80026	303-665-2324	R	1*	<.1
1564	Chelsea Technologies Inc—*Meyer Ben-Reuven*	22 Cortlandt St Fl 14, New York NY 10007	212-966-3355	R	1*	<.1
1565	Genexus USA Inc—*Dane Drotts*	1143 W Rundell Pl Ste, Chicago IL 60607	312-836-9152	R	1*	<.1
1566	Integration Services Inc—*Kathy Rinna*	24681 Nrthwstrn Hwy 31, Southfield MI 48075	248-355-2290	R	1*	<.1
1567	Language Computer Corp—*Andrew Hickl*	1701 N Collins Blvd St, Richardson TX 75080	972-231-0052	R	1*	<.1
1568	Proactive Technology LLC—*Arthur Hopkins*	631 S Main St Ste 401, Greenville SC 29601	864-421-9247	R	1*	<.1
1569	Series 1 Support Services Inc—*Al Horton*	14 Stockton Bridge Rd, Pemberton NJ 08068	609-894-2240	R	1*	<.1
1570	Smart Solutions and Services Inc—*Patrick Saliba*	13005 SW 122nd Ave, Miami FL 33186	786-430-4330	R	1*	<.1
1571	Healthware Corp—*Walter Voytek*	6266 N W St, Pensacola FL 32505	850-479-9035	R	1*	<.1
1572	Landeck Group LLC	PO Box 1748, Midlothian VA 23113	804-521-4363	R	1*	<.1
1573	Performance Oriented Solutions Inc—*James Cagle*	4280 Piedmont Pkwy Ste, Greensboro NC 27410	336-510-7854	R	1*	<.1
1574	Ts Tech Enterprises Inc—*Todd Schorle*	3 Park Plz Ste 306, Reading PA 19610	610-288-0780	R	1*	<.1
1575	Progressive Resources LLC—*Sarah Cox*	8645 Guion Rd Ste A, Indianapolis IN 46268	317-471-1577	R	1*	<.1
1576	Infotility Inc—*David Cohen*	2060 Broadway St Ste 3, Boulder CO 80302	720-210-1984	R	1*	<.1
1577	Space Projects Ltd—*Donald Bass*	3494 Bass Springs Rd, Midland VA 22728	540-788-9090	R	1*	<.1
1578	Executive Consultants—*Will Loftin*	6007 Financial Plz Ste, Shreveport LA 71129	318-868-8000	R	1*	<.1
1579	Infinite Software Solutions Inc—*Ed Knowling*	9108 Linksvue Dr, Knoxville TN 37922	865-588-1780	R	1*	<.1
1580	Genusys Inc—*Mohammed Rahman*	17106 Preston Bend Dr, Dallas TX 75248	214-493-3499	R	1*	<.1
1581	Indigo Systems and Technology Inc—*Rajeev Parekh*	127 E Main St, Barrington IL 60010	847-304-7800	R	1*	<.1
1582	Microtelecom Systems LLC	3601 36th Ave, Long Island City NY 11106	718-707-0012	R	1*	<.1
1583	Proxy Networks Inc—*Andy Kim*	320 Congress St Fl 3, Boston MA 02210	617-453-2700	R	1*	<.1
1584	Em Microelectronic Us Inc—*James Lauffenburger*	5475 Mark Dabling Blvd, Colorado Springs CO 80918	719-598-9224	R	1*	<.1
1585	Intern Inc—*Ajay Surena*	2049 Rte 520, Englishtown NJ 07726	732-316-9305	R	1*	<.1
1586	Soph-Ware Associates Inc—*Ronald Turner*	624 W Hastings Rd Ste, Spokane WA 99218	509-468-8264	R	1*	<.1
1587	Sponsor Direct LLC—*James Cooper*	580 White Plains Rd St, Tarrytown NY 10591	914-729-7200	R	1*	<.1
1588	Syntrio Inc—*Clair Kerner*	33 New Montgomery St S, San Francisco CA 94105	415-951-7913	R	1*	<.1
1589	Technology Management Resources Inc—*Timothy Clifford*	766 N State Rd 434, Altamonte Springs FL 32714	407-830-4222	R	1*	<.1
1590	Cardea Technology Inc—*Michael Dichiappari*	PO Box 162, Somerville MA 02143	617-627-9399	R	1*	<.1
1591	Coolearth Technologies Inc—*Carsten Erickson*	226 S Orcas St Ste A, Seattle WA 98108	206-770-9061	R	1*	<.1
1592	Exigen Services (USA) Inc—*Nick Puntikov*	345 California St Fl 1, San Francisco CA 94104	415-402-2677	R	1*	<.1
1593	Omnesys Technologies Inc—*Anant Pandit*	1 Blue Hill Plz Fl 10, Pearl River NY 10965	845-735-5000	R	1*	<.1
1594	Prescription Software Inc—*Jeffrey Taubman*	201 E Broad St, Columbus OH 43215	614-228-6620	R	1*	<.1
1595	Profiling Solutions Inc—*Ron Fisher*	174 Carroll St Se, Atlanta GA 30312	404-525-8003	R	1*	<.1
1596	Threshold Data Technology Inc—*Michael Rosenberg*	23900 Commerce Park, Cleveland OH 44122	216-292-1030	R	1*	<.1
1597	Pinzar Technology Inc—*Irene Shen*	297 Kinderkamack Rd, Oradell NJ 07649	201-291-2635	R	1*	<.1
1598	Ip Fabrics Inc—*Glenford Myers*	14976 Nw Greenbrier Pk, Beaverton OR 97006	503-444-2400	R	1*	<.1
1599	Ovo Studios LLC	236 High St, Chagrin Falls OH 44022	440-247-2501	R	1*	<.1
1600	Grapecity Inc—*Naoyuki Baba*	720 4th Ave Ste 220, Kirkland WA 98033	425-828-4440	R	1*	.7
1601	Plattform Holdings Inc—*David Admire*	15500 W 113th St Ste 2, Lenexa KS 66219	913-254-6000	R	1*	.3
1602	Nextconstruct Inc—*Ujjual Bhatnagar*	14361 Howard Rd, Dayton MD 21036	301-206-9111	R	1*	.2
1603	Poseidon Design Systems Inc—*Ravi A K Janak*	4501 Circle 75 Pky Ste, Atlanta GA 30339	408-256-8828	R	1*	.1
1604	ParAccel Inc—*Chuck Berger*	9920 Pacific Heights B, San Diego CA 92121		R	1*	.1
1605	Dot VN Inc—*Thomas M Johnson*	9449 Balboa Ave Ste 11, San Diego CA 92123	858-571-2007	P	1	<.1
1606	Resource International Publishing Inc—*Jan Schwenk*	PO Box 2016, Frisco TX 75034	972-712-8788	R	1*	<.1
1607	Information Products Inc—*Roger Hernsdorf*	PO Box 558, East Granby CT 06026	860-653-7822	R	1*	<.1
1608	Van der Roest Group Inc—*Martin van der Roest*	1592 N Batavia St Bldg, Orange CA 92867	714-921-9300	R	1*	<.1
1609	Harvey Software Inc—*Bert Hamilton*	PO Box 60596, Fort Myers FL 33906		R	1*	<.1
1610	Nogginlabs Inc—*Brian Knudson*	4619 N Ravenswood Ave, Chicago IL 60640	773-878-9011	R	1*	<.1
1611	Trivision Group Inc—*Andy Shenoy*	25 W 45th St Ste 1203, New York NY 10036	212-869-5455	R	1*	<.1
1612	Comet Solutions Inc—*Daniel Meyer*	11811 Menaul Blvd Ne S, Albuquerque NM 87112	505-323-2525	R	1*	<.1
1613	Gravic Remark Products Group—*Bruce Holenstein*	301 Lindenwood Dr Ste, Malvern PA 19355	610-647-7850	R	1*	<.1
1614	Solutionersnet Inc—*Horace Gaynor*	506 Jones Fall Ct, Bowie MD 20721	301-262-3544	R	1*	<.1
1615	Tdi Technologies Inc—*William Johnson*	1600 10th St Ste B, Plano TX 75074	972-881-1553	R	1*	<.1
1616	Sun Sierra Software Inc—*William L Hedges*	PO Box 2883, Carmichael CA 95609	916-944-8281	R	1*	<.1
1617	Amgraf Inc—*Franklin J Garner III*	1501 Oak St, Kansas City MO 64108	816-474-4797	R	1*	<.1
1618	Computer Workstations Inc—*Clark Musgrove*	11273 W 28th Ave, Lakewood CO 80215	303-987-2376	R	1*	<.1
1619	East Shore Technologies Inc—*Terry Lindh*	80 Campbell Ave, Troy NY 12180	518-274-6510	R	1*	<.1
1620	Innovative Software Products Inc—*Daniel Weimer*	2052 Poplar Ridge Rd, Pasadena MD 21122	410-271-2881	R	1*	<.1
1621	Linux Labs International Inc—*Sparrow Marcioni*	3276 Bford Dr Ste 104-, Atlanta GA 30329		R	1*	<.1
1622	Metier—*Matthew Bennett*	16097 Red Fox Ln, Colorado Springs CO 80921	719-488-1736	R	1*	<.1
1623	Radio Data Group Inc—*Michael Rau*	15303 Ventura Blvd Ste, Sherman Oaks CA 91403	818-528-8860	S	1	<.1
1624	UTSI International Corp—*Daniel Nagala*	1560 W Bay Area Blvd S, Friendswood TX 77546	281-480-8786	R	1*	<.1
1625	Exact Software Co—*Michael Juliano*	126 Commons Ct, Chadds Ford PA 19317	610-358-9295	R	1*	<.1
1626	Envisage Information Systems—*Stefan Mcgonagle*	1582 Mcallister Rd, Genoa NY 13071	315-497-9202	R	1*	<.1
1627	Kinetik Information Technology—*Josette van Stiphout*	7878 N 16th St Ste 200, Phoenix AZ 85020	602-957-0058	R	1*	<.1
1628	Proplanner Inc—*David Sly*	2321 N Loop Dr Ste 134, Ames IA 50010	515-296-9914	R	1*	<.1
1629	Applied Knowledge Systems Int'l Ltd—*Gerald Fingerhut*	140 Cabrini Blvd Ste 1, New York NY 10033	212-795-5503	R	1*	<.1
1630	Cyber Tv LLC	PO Box 2184, Windermere FL 34786	407-909-9718	R	1*	<.1
1631	Db Marketing Technologies LLC	420 Lexington Ave Rm 3, New York NY 10170	212-717-6000	R	1*	<.1
1632	FreeTripcom Inc—*Ann Shack*	PO Box 1271, Alexandria VA 22313	703-837-1120	R	1	<.1
1633	Information Processing Corp—*Doyle Kitchen*	13747 Montfort Dr Ste, Dallas TX 75240	972-404-9244	R	1*	<.1
1634	Megadyne Information Systems	5250 W Century Blvd St, Los Angeles CA 90045	310-474-5373	R	1*	<.1
1635	Natural Selection Inc—*David B Fogel*	9330 Scranton Rd Ste 1, San Diego CA 92121	858-455-6449	R	1*	<.1
1636	Pathfinder Systems Inc—*Sheila Jaszlics*	200 Union Blvd Ste 300, Lakewood CO 80228	303-763-8660	R	1*	<.1
1637	WaveFrame Corp—*Micheal Bard*	5818 Vallejo St, Emeryville CA 94608	503-419-3911	R	1*	<.1
1638	Auction Software Inc—*Ronald Ball*	518 Signal Hill Dr Ext, Statesville NC 28625	704-872-2458	R	1*	<.1
1639	M Systems International Inc—*Hal Maner*	PO Box 51125, Durham NC 27717	919-493-6012	R	1*	<.1
1640	Piedmont Triad Computer Consulting Inc—*Hal Willis*	PO Box 450, Clemmons NC 27012	336-766-5555	R	1*	<.1
1641	Provista Software International—*Joanne Taylor*	PO Box 3011, Fremont CA 94539	510-794-1884	R	1*	<.1
1642	Torrential Data Solutions Inc—*Bradford Bimson*	5604 Virginia Beach Bl, Virginia Beach VA 23462	757-222-2000	R	1*	<.1
1643	Arts and Letters Corp—*Nina Schoeler*	2201 Midway Rd Ste106, Carrollton TX 75006	972-661-8960	R	1*	<.1
1644	Baseline Data Systems Inc—*Ralph Brackert*	3655 Torrance Blvd Ste, Torrance CA 90503	310-214-8528	R	1*	<.1
1645	Data 21	3820 Del Amo Blvd Ste, Torrance CA 90503	310-921-9200	R	1*	<.1
1646	ICG Link Inc—*Jack Massari*	7003 Chadwick Dr Ste 1, Brentwood TN 37027	615-370-1530	R	1*	<.1

Rank	Company Name—*Executive Officer*	Address, City, State, Zip	Phone	Type	Fin	Empls
1647	Iifotech International LLC	3401 Phillips Hwy, Jacksonville FL 32207	904-338-9234	R	1*	<.1
1648	InfoAmerica Inc—*Paul Knight*	2600 Canton Ct Ste G, Fort Collins CO 80525	970-221-5599	S	1*	<.1
1649	Intelligent Micro Systems Inc—*Joseph Scandura*	1249 Greentree Ste 100, Narberth PA 19072	610-664-1207	R	1*	<.1
1650	Leader Technologies Inc—*Dana Wood*	8809 Washington St NE, Albuquerque NM 87113	505-856-6400	R	1*	<.1
1651	Lincoln and Co	321 Billerica Rd, Chelmsford MA 01824	978-244-0250	D	1*	<.1
1652	LiveOnTheNet—*Roger Schneider*	200 Clinton Ave Ste 80, Huntsville AL 35801	256-705-7000	R	1*	<.1
1653	Perfect Software (Arcadia California)—*Rick Guerrero*	41 E Foothill Blvd Ste, Arcadia CA 91006	626-445-9700	R	1*	<.1
1654	Ram Software Systems Inc—*Michael Mcintyre*	892 New Castle Rd, Slippery Rock PA 16057	724-794-1222	R	1*	<.1
1655	Rocket Software OSS Unit	5915 Hollis St Bldg A, Emeryville CA 94608	510-740-7400	D	1*	<.1
1656	Signature Software Inc—*Rhonda Anderson*	509 Cascade Ste H, Hood River OR 97031	541-387-2800	R	1*	<.1
1657	Soflex Corp—*Angelo Sifakes*	PO Box 540, Tallevast FL 34270	941-355-3227	R	1*	<.1
1658	SurveyConnect Inc	2960 Diagonal Hwy Ste, Boulder CO 80301	303-449-2969	R	1*	<.1
1659	Teq Solutions Inc—*William Derrer*	1811 Executive Dr Ste, Indianapolis IN 46241	317-227-2610	R	1*	<.1
1660	Fike and Fike Inc—*Rod Fike*	1701 Clearwater Ave St, Bloomington IL 61704	309-663-5254	R	1*	<.1
1661	Midrange Support and Service Inc—*Steve Marinak*	1122 E Atlantic Ave St, Delray Beach FL 33483	561-272-5883	R	1*	<.1
1662	Streams Online Media Development Corp—*Dave Skwarczek*	5550 Touhy Ave, Skokie IL 60077	847-673-0900	R	1	<.1
1663	Bbsi Inc—*Norton Lovold*	PO Box 2697, Bismarck ND 58502	701-323-9200	R	1*	<.1
1664	Camcad Technologies Inc—*Donald Mckillop*	5840 Red Bug Lake Rd S, Winter Springs FL 32708	407-327-4975	R	1*	<.1
1665	ChemShare Corp—*Robin Mulloy*	PO Box 1885, Houston TX 77251	281-565-6700	R	1*	<.1
1666	Eccounting Solutions LLC	PO Box 492, Mansfield MA 02048	508-337-4204	R	1*	<.1
1667	Montgomery Investment Technology Inc—*George Montgomery*	200 Federal St Ste 200, Camden NJ 08103	610-688-8111	R	1*	<.1
1668	Programmable Devices Inc—*John Puchniak*	153 Andover St Ste 107, Danvers MA 01923	978-750-9800	R	1*	<.1
1669	Software And Engineering Associates Inc—*Douglas Coats*	1802 N Carson St Ste 2, Carson City NV 89701	775-882-1966	R	1*	<.1
1670	Technotel Inc—*Juan Chavez*	4995 Nw 72nd Ave Ste 2, Miami FL 33166	305-599-7058	R	1*	<.1
1671	DataWave Technologies Corp	1435 West 29th, Loveland CO 80538	970-669-6350	R	1*	<.1
1672	Droege Computing Services Inc—*Thomas Droege*	20 W Colony Pl Ste 120, Durham NC 27705	919-403-9459	R	1*	<.1
1673	KD Consulting Group Inc—*Kurt Johnson*	5768 Fairridge Ln, Hamilton OH 45011	513-795-0901	R	1*	<.1
1674	NBS Systems Inc—*Bill Gascon*	1000 S Old Rte 66, Mount Olive IL 62069		R	1*	<.1
1675	Pick Professionals Inc—*David Wasylenko*	PO Box 4214, Hazelwood MO 63042	314-522-4949	R	1*	<.1
1676	Sonoma Software Solutions Inc—*Edward Joseph Kirk*	6585-H Commerce Blvd, Rohnert Park CA 94928	707-583-6336	R	1*	<.1
1677	Terra-Mar Resource Information Services Inc—*Donn Walklet*	918 Oak St, Hood River OR 97031	541-387-2485	R	1*	<.1
1678	Abelson Communications Inc—*Glen Abelson*	15 Bramshott Ct Ste 20, Rockville Centre NY 11570	516-596-9610	R	1*	<.1
1679	Commitment Software Inc—*John Sauvigne*	7700 N Kendall Dr Ste, Miami FL 33156	305-662-9665	R	1*	<.1
1680	Ect Technologies LLC—*Jeffrey Olsson*	100 W Shore Dr, Pennington NJ 08534		R	1*	<.1
1681	Engagent Inc—*Fred Felker*	17455 68th Ave Ne Ste, Kenmore WA 98028	425-485-8754	R	1*	<.1
1682	Exploration Resources Inc—*Michael Rainer*	824 S Milledge Ave, Athens GA 30605	706-353-7983	R	1*	<.1
1683	Integrated Business Group Inc—*Brian Caslow*	165 Montgomery Rd, Altamonte Springs FL 32714	407-677-0370	R	1*	<.1
1684	Labsoft Inc—*Gary Yancich*	9104 Shenandoah Run, Wesley Chapel FL 33544	813-929-7931	R	1*	<.1
1685	Measurement and Control Systems Inc—*Neil Douglas*	13004 Murphy Rd Ste 21, Stafford TX 77477	281-240-4403	R	1*	<.1
1686	Metadata Co—*Steve Peacock*	5409 Maryland Way Ste, Brentwood TN 37027	615-301-5300	R	1*	<.1
1687	Michigan Software Services Inc—*Joe LeBlanc*	5820 N Canton Ctr Rd S, Canton MI 48187	734-453-4474	R	1*	<.1
1688	Mogility Technology Inc—*Angle Group*	11 Seton Hill Rd, Auburndale MA 02466	617-202-9299	R	1*	<.1
1689	Phantom Reality Inc—*John Hewitt*	1200 35th St Rm 304-2, West Des Moines IA 50266	515-224-4045	R	1*	<.1
1690	Primero Systems Inc—*Gary Saner*	PO Box 720490, San Diego CA 92172	858-433-1478	R	1*	<.1
1691	Advanced Communications Systems Inc (North Olmsted Ohio)—*Bob Stone*	23201 Lorain Rd Ste 6, North Olmsted OH 44070	440-779-5424	R	1*	<.1
1692	Answer Software Corp	PO Box 3155, Los Altos CA 94024	650-948-9584	R	1*	<.1
1693	Cheshire Engineering Corp—*Shal Farley*	120 W Olive Ave, Monrovia CA 91016	626-303-1602	R	1*	<.1
1694	Competition Data Systems Inc—*Peter Kelly*	8050 Wehrle Dr, Williamsville NY 14221	716-631-2880	R	1*	<.1
1695	Kidder and Associates Inc—*Aaron Kidder*	17266 Hillside Dr Ste, Lodi CA 95240	209-727-3617	R	1*	<.1
1696	Level One Consulting Inc—*Theresa Smith*	1616 Anderson Rd Ste 3, Mc Lean VA 22102	703-725-5570	R	1*	<.1
1697	Multix Inc—*Judy Yen*	13618 Neutron Rd, Farmers Branch TX 75244	972-239-4989	R	1*	<.1
1698	Netwest Inc—*Tommy Franklin*	80845 Us Hwy 231, Blountsville AL 35031	256-586-2483	R	1*	<.1
1699	Networkers Inc—*Michael Hennessy*	32 Brandy St, Bolton CT 06043	860-643-1547	R	1*	<.1
1700	Pinpoint Systems Inc—*Paul Becker*	8605 Trethorne Ct, Waxhaw NC 28173		R	1*	<.1
1701	Polytechs Software Development Group Inc—*Frank Feinland*	4849 Ronson Ct, San Diego CA 92111	858-268-9300	R	1*	<.1
1702	Smart Engineering Tools Inc—*Sigmund Shvimer*	55 N Pond Dr Ste 1, Walled Lake MI 48390	248-669-7262	R	1*	<.1
1703	Beige Bag Software Inc—*Jon Engelbert*	623 W Huron Ste 2, Ann Arbor MI 48103	734-332-0487	R	1*	<.1
1704	Business Modeling Techniques Inc—*Shirley Harty*	7306 Golden Iris Ct, Springfield VA 22153	703-913-5311	R	1*	<.1
1705	Creative Courseware Inc—*Connie Swartz*	PO Box 8689, Prairie Village KS 66208	816-363-6733	R	1*	<.1
1706	Intracellular Imaging Inc—*Eric Gruenstein*	118 William Howard Taf, Cincinnati OH 45219	513-351-4260	R	1*	<.1
1707	Processmodel Inc—*Scott Baird*	10602 S Cvered Bridge, Spanish Fork UT 84660	801-356-7165	R	1*	<.1
1708	Routercad Inc—*Tony Shaw*	6311 Malcolm Dr, Dallas TX 75214	214-828-9595	R	1*	<.1
1709	Ars International Consulting—*Sanjeez Bhai*	4 Pke, Irvine CA 92620	714-505-5620	R	1*	<.1
1710	Data Sciences Inc (Silver Spring Maryland)—*Mark Ganslaw*	14900 Sweitzer Ln Ste, Laurel MD 20707	301-957-0100	R	1*	<.1
1711	DaVinci Technology Corp—*Anthony T Curlo*	89 Headquarters Plz 14, Morristown NJ 07960	973-993-4860	R	1*	<.1
1712	Great Migrations LLC—*Mark E Juras*	7453 Katesbridge Ct, Dublin OH 43017		R	1*	<.1
1713	Inductive Solutions Inc—*Roy Freedman*	380 Rector Pl Ste 4A, New York NY 10280	212-945-0630	R	1*	<.1
1714	Media Tech Inc—*Blake Pilgreen*	12999 E Adam Aircraft, Englewood CO 80112	303-741-6878	R	1*	<.1
1715	Sy-Con Systems Inc—*Mike Assia*	1700 Northampton St, Easton PA 18042	610-253-0900	R	1*	<.1
1716	Talisman Technologies Inc—*Darlene Hejnas*	PO Box 262, Central Valley NY 10917	845-928-2115	R	1*	<.1
1717	TradeWinds Software Corp	402 Locust St, Shreveport LA 71105	318-868-0160	R	1*	<.1
1718	Vermont Creative Software Inc—*Richard Douglas*	PO Box 250, Richford VT 05476		R	1*	<.1
1719	3rd Coast Technologies LLC—*Steven Fortman*	12261 Cleveland Ave St, Nunica MI 49448	616-837-0899	R	1*	<.1
1720	Amzil Inc—*Dennis C Merritt*	1 Galax Ave, Asheville NC 28806	828-350-0350	R	1*	<.1
1721	Analytic Concepts Inc	2548 Butch Dr, Gilroy CA 95020	408-371-3962	R	1*	<.1
1722	Association Computer Services Inc—*Frank Cook*	445 N Pennsylvania St, Indianapolis IN 46244	317-974-3000	R	1*	<.1
1723	Butler Computer Systems—*Barry A Butler*	PO Box 5306, Walnut Creek CA 94596	925-256-8401	R	1*	<.1
1724	Captured Live Productions LLC—*Matthew Levin*	3431 Wesley St Ste D, Culver City CA 90232	310-559-5483	R	1*	<.1
1725	CyberCrow Inc—*Vikas Kamat*	722 37th St S, Birmingham AL 35222	205-251-5977	R	1*	<.1
1726	Graphic Detail Inc—*Bruce Sauls*	7824 Harbor Dr, Raleigh NC 27615	919-847-8490	R	1*	<.1
1727	Interactive Technology Inc—*Roger A Brown*	4400 SW 110th Ave Ste, Beaverton OR 97005	503-644-0111	R	1*	<.1
1728	Leaning Post Productions—*Laurie Greenly*	487 Hulsetown Rd, Campbell Hall NY 10916	845-496-4709	R	1*	<.1
1729	Primax Software Corp—*Malay Jalundhwala*	1010 Capitol Ave, San Francisco CA 94112	415-587-1584	R	1*	<.1
1730	Qdea Inc—*Hugh Sontag*	2501 Skyblue Ct, Saint Paul MN 55110	651-779-0955	R	1*	<.1
1731	Ray Sauers Associates Inc—*Ray Sauers*	46 Englewood Rd, Clifton NJ 07012	973-955-2782	R	1*	<.1
1732	SIGNERA—*David Fields*	11804 Greencastle Pike, Hagerstown MD 21740	301-714-0110	R	1*	<.1
1733	WebGecko Software—*Jim Vanderslice*	201 Galer St Ste 369, Seattle WA 98109	206-285-8391	R	1*	<.1
1734	HBS Consulting—*Thomas Sutton*	PO Box 9004, San Rafael CA 94912	415-453-4268	R	1*	<.1
1735	NetEffects Inc—*James S Hunter*	6475 Dwyer Ct, San Jose CA 95120	408-324-1200	R	1*	<.1

Note: An asterisk (*) indicates an estimated financial figure. The company type code used is as follows: R = Private, P = Public, S = Private Subsidiary, B = Public Subsidiary, D = Division, J = Joint Venture, I = Investment Fund.

COMPANY RANKINGS BY SALES WITHIN 4-DIGIT SIC

Rank	Company Name—Executive Officer	Address, City, State, Zip	Phone	Type	Fin	Empls
1736	Software Juice Inc—Jeffrey W Smith	318 N Carson St, Carson City NV 89701	619-261-4824	R	1*	<.1
1737	Software Pronto Inc—Jamila Mangondato	929 E El Camino Real S, Sunnyvale CA 94087	408-393-0808	R	1*	<.1
1738	Boxer Software—David Hamel	PO Box 14545, Scottsdale AZ 85267		R	1*	N/A
1739	Elefunt Software—Stephen Cleveland	724 Allston Way, Berkeley CA 94710	510-558-9400	R	1*	N/A
1740	Information Advantage—Kate Cook	713 W Harrison St, Kent WA 98032	253-852-1638	R	1*	N/A
1741	ACI Media—John Newman	2485 S Marion Ave, Lake City FL 32025	386-758-2266	R	1*	<.1
1742	Convina LLC—Jake Seethaler	5084 Cedar Point Peak, Riverton UT 84096	801-269-0211	R	1*	<.1
1743	Lextek International Inc—Art Pollard	1051 Fir Ave, Provo UT 84604	801-375-8332	R	1*	<.1
1744	Adiva Corp—John Milks	21351 Gentry Dr Ste 25, Sterling VA 20166	703-547-9400	R	1*	<.1
1745	Alta Computer Services LLC—Willie Klebmoen	1887 S 700 W, Salt Lake City UT 84104	801-972-8160	S	1*	<.1
1746	Clemons Inc—Kevin Clemons	714 E Monument Ave, Dayton OH 45402	937-531-6645	R	1*	<.1
1747	Proposal Technologies Network Inc—Jeffrey Spencer	4000 Barranca Pkwy Ste, Irvine CA 92604	310-826-1885	R	1*	<.1
1748	Avow Systems Inc—Mark Johnston	8055 E Tufts Ave Ste 2, Denver CO 80237	303-350-3700	R	1*	<.1
1749	Bright Computer Inc—David Lee	10 Meadowlark Ln, Oyster Bay NY 11771	516-628-1010	R	1*	<.1
1750	Bristol Capital Inc—Walter Karpoczyc	160 Summit Ave, Montvale NJ 07645	201-476-0600	R	1*	<.1
1751	Data Specialists Inc—James Jones	715 Florida Ave S Ste, Minneapolis MN 55426	763-541-0440	R	1*	<.1
1752	Dsi Of Hawaii Inc—Malcolm Chong	738 Kaheka St Ste 202, Honolulu HI 96814	808-955-6319	R	1*	<.1
1753	Elan Gmk Inc—Zoltan Soos	4514 Ish Dr Ste 107, Simi Valley CA 93063	805-577-0288	R	1*	<.1
1754	Linear Logic Computers Inc—Vinita Gandhi	51650 Oro Dr, Shelby Township MI 48315		R	1*	<.1
1755	Peripheral Sciences Inc—Turin Leung	10 John St, Newton MA 02459	617-332-9574	R	1*	<.1
1756	Production Ready Programming Inc—Zia Rab	4200 E La Palma Ave, Anaheim CA 92807	714-528-5001	R	1*	<.1
1757	Ec Sourcing Group Inc—Andrew Caetta	18 Cattano Ave Ste 2, Morristown NJ 07960	973-327-4610	R	1*	<.1
1758	Computer Resources and Technology International Inc—Ronald Pierner	PO Box 160, Eagle WI 53119	715-763-3400	R	1	<.1
1759	System/Technology Development Corp—Christine Robinson	11125 Glade Dr, Reston VA 20191	703-620-3807	R	1*	<.1
1760	Lucero Research Corp—Howard Jones	3191 S White Mountain, Show Low AZ 85901	928-537-1300	R	1*	<.1
1761	Gecko Systems of Georgia Inc—R Spencer	1640 Hwy 212 SW, Conyers GA 30094	678-413-9236	R	1*	<.1
1762	Industry Avenue LLC	2300 Old Spanish Trl S, Houston TX 77054	281-556-0399	R	1*	<.1
1763	JC Doyle Inc—Doyle Henke	PO Box 2303, Grand Island NE 68802	308-384-5380	R	1*	<.1
1764	Provect Technologies Inc—Jeffrey Coyne	25300 Telegraph Rd, Southfield MI 48033	248-263-0000	R	1*	<.1
1765	Talos Technology Consulting Inc—Robert Smith	3336 Fern Hollow Pl 10, Herndon VA 20171	703-715-3500	R	1*	<.1
1766	Dynamic Healthcare Systems Inc—Kenneth Stockman	16775 Von Karman Ave S, Irvine CA 92606	949-333-4565	R	1*	<.1
1767	Tree-D Inc—Harry Qualls	2012 N Point Blvd Ste, Tallahassee FL 32308	850-906-9335	R	1*	<.1
1768	Lightspeed Data Solutions Inc—Marvin Sauer	6330 San Vicente Blvd, Los Angeles CA 90048	323-954-3000	R	1*	<.1
1769	SynApps Software Inc—Kristian Harness	2208 NW Market St Ste, Seattle WA 98107	206-784-7085	R	1	<.1
1770	Global Electro-Communication International Inc—David Mureeba	5720 Lbj Fwy Ste 420, Dallas TX 75240	972-387-7860	R	1*	<.1
1771	Homes Factory Dot Com—Patrick Wilson	19312 60th Ave W Ste B, Lynnwood WA 98036	425-744-5544	R	1*	<.1
1772	K Tek Systems Inc—Kimberly During	2536 Countryside Blvd, Clearwater FL 33763	727-726-1700	R	1*	<.1
1773	3d Incorporated Of Federal Way—Kip Descombes	5380 E Seltice Way Ste, Post Falls ID 83854	208-773-3900	R	1*	<.1
1774	Keystone Consulting—Carlos Lage	38 Hawkins Cir, Wheaton IL 60189	630-871-7675	R	1*	<.1
1775	Netvigilance Inc—Jesper Jursenocks	14525 SW Ml Ste 34, Beaverton OR 97005	503-524-5758	R	1*	<.1
1776	Bearware Inc—Jeff Berichon	7160 Chagrin Rd Ste 21, Chagrin Falls OH 44023	440-893-2327	R	1*	<.1
1777	First Link Technology Inc—Jeff Luinstra	4260 E Evans Ave, Denver CO 80222	303-691-8200	R	1*	<.1
1778	Inventrix Inc—Richard Pickard	201 S College St Ste 1, Charlotte NC 28244	704-334-8356	R	1*	<.1
1779	Data Control And Research Ltd—Erin Hoarstman	8161 S Cass Ave, Darien IL 60561	630-241-2202	R	1*	<.1
1780	Software 21 Inc—Rob Foulkes	906 Market St, Kirkland WA 98033	425-822-4941	R	1*	<.1
1781	Data Builders Inc—Robert Wilmer	41640 Corning Pl Ste 1, Murrieta CA 92562	951-696-7568	R	1*	<.1
1782	Kanecal Inc—Jeffrey Kane	4312 Shetland Ln, Riverside CA 92509	951-681-9495	R	1*	<.1
1783	Terminus Design Inc—Sally Barr	1955 Panola Rd Ste 200, Ellenwood GA 30294	770-474-4866	R	1*	<.1
1784	Digital Graphiti Inc—Tim Knox	1277 Douglass Rd Nw, Huntsville AL 35806	256-489-2557	R	1*	<.1
1785	Teratron Inc—Edward Lipartito	716 N Bethlehem Pke St, Ambler PA 19002	215-461-2400	R	1*	<.1
1786	Poynting Products Inc—Michael Belanger	PO Box 1564, Oak Park IL 60304	708-386-2139	R	1*	<.1
1787	Bts Consulting Group Ltd—Karen Treat	355 Glen Arms Dr, Danville CA 94526	925-837-1730	R	1*	<.1
1788	Centraliant Inc—Barry Battista	4551 Cox Rd Ste 400, Glen Allen VA 23060	804-915-1449	R	1*	<.1
1789	RPR Wyatt Inc—Ronald Gilbert	2200 N Central Ave Ste, Phoenix AZ 85004	602-263-7779	R	1*	<.1
1790	Relativity Inc—Dillon Watkins	PO Box 28, Jonesboro AR 72403	870-802-3622	R	1*	<.1
1791	Amogha Solutions LLC—Usharani Tangella	1802 N Carson St Ste 2, Carson City NV 89701	702-425-2335	R	1*	<.1
1792	Micro Innovations Inc—Harold Brown	910 Belle Ave Ste 1046, Winter Springs FL 32708	407-696-9800	R	1*	<.1
1793	Realtime Solutions Group LLC—Kim Sullivan	900 S Frontage Rd Ste, Woodridge IL 60517	312-528-3960	R	1*	<.1
1794	Pass Consulting Corp—Michael Strauss	420 Lincoln Rd Ste 219, Miami Beach FL 33139	305-269-6975	R	1*	<.1
1795	Stellar Systems Inc—William Spetz	1944 Harrison Ave, Cincinnati OH 45214	513-921-8748	R	1*	<.1
1796	Webroomz Inc—Lee Sessions	3445 Peachtree Rd Ne S, Atlanta GA 30326	404-495-7557	R	1*	<.1
1797	Welis LLC	725 Canton St Ste 6, Norwood MA 02062	781-255-6990	R	1*	<.1
1798	Intellilink Services Inc—David Thomas	7738 Governors Dr W, Huntsville AL 35806	256-430-0077	R	1*	<.1
1799	Parallel Quantum Solutions LLC—Peter Pulay	2013 N Green Acres Rd, Fayetteville AR 72703	479-521-5118	R	1*	<.1
1800	A and M Data Systems Inc—Alan Agdern	100 Crossways Park Dr, Woodbury NY 11797	516-496-3520	R	1*	<.1
1801	Bascom Global Internet Services Inc—Peter Cirasole	601 Veterans Hwy Ste 2, Hauppauge NY 11788	631-434-6600	R	1*	<.1
1802	Intellectual Property Enterprises LLC—Jane Klimasauskas	409 Elk St Ste 200, Carnegie PA 15106	412-278-6280	R	1*	<.1
1803	Uptime Technology Inc—Donald Lewis	9811 Ne Hendricks Rd, Carlton OR 97111	503-537-0340	R	1*	<.1
1804	Xerex Inc—Tom Magami	567 San Nicolas Dr Ste, Newport Beach CA 92660	949-719-6767	R	1*	<.1
1805	Seattle Sound and Vibration Inc—David Forrest	14158 177th Ave Ne, Redmond WA 98052	425-885-4076	R	1*	<.1
1806	Dot C Software Inc—Cheryl Lamont	182 Kuuhale St, Kailua HI 96734	808-262-6715	R	1*	<.1
1807	Speedus Corp—Shant S Hovnanian	1 Dag Hammarskjold Blv, Freehold NJ 07728		P	1	<.1
1808	Medical Documenting Systems Inc	3518 W Liberty Rd, Ann Arbor MI 48103	734-930-9053	R	1*	<.1
1809	Programming Resources Inc—Fred Evans	4711 Trousdale Dr Ste, Nashville TN 37220	615-331-9774	R	1*	<.1
1810	Nexic Inc—Marshall Morrise	635 Technology Ave, Orem UT 84097	801-434-4717	R	1*	<.1
1811	Avtec Corp—Charles Mc Cullough	818 Brentwood St, Austin TX 78757	512-454-1481	R	1*	<.1
1812	Absolute Technologies—Frank Fisher	2350 Fowlerville Rd, Fowlerville MI 48836	517-223-9113	R	1*	<.1
1813	Adwire Inc—Wendy Nield	1100 Glendon Ave Fl 17, Los Angeles CA 90024	310-689-7470	R	1*	<.1
1814	Graph-X Inc—Douglas Turner	290 Sky Line Dr, Easton PA 18042	610-797-5515	R	1*	<.1
1815	IV S LLC—Mike Mountjoy	10001 Linn Station Rd, Louisville KY 40223	502-426-7905	R	1*	<.1
1816	Pentana Inc—Ken Ebbage	113 Molesey Hurst, Williamsburg VA 23188	757-565-7988	R	1*	<.1
1817	Rto Software Inc—Kevin Goodman	6120 Windward Pkwy Ste, Alpharetta GA 30005	678-987-4300	R	1*	<.1
1818	Amtec Systems Corp—Nino Posella	3385 Overland Ave, Los Angeles CA 90034	310-204-3636	R	1*	<.1
1819	Base 2 Corp—Paul Gutelius	1525 Wisconsin Ave Ste, Grafton WI 53024	262-387-1140	R	1*	<.1
1820	Computer Systems Approach Inc—Larry Canter	1807 N Raymond Ave, Anaheim CA 92801	714-738-3414	R	1*	<.1
1821	ESolve Technologies Inc—Prakash Teli	71 Furnace St, Sharon MA 02067	781-793-0450	R	1*	<.1
1822	Imaging 101 Inc—Jacob Russo	7850 Nw 146th St Ste 5, Hialeah FL 33016	954-659-3101	R	1*	<.1
1823	Aureus Solutions Inc—Carol Parks	4929 Green Valley Rd, Monrovia MD 21770	301-607-6856	R	1*	<.1

Rank	Company Name—*Executive Officer*	Address, City, State, Zip	Phone	Type	Fin	Empls
1824	Better Programs Inc—*Charles Oleson*	5852 W Pacific Cir, Lakewood CO 80227	303-986-1969	R	1*	<.1
1825	Crane Cost and Care Inc—*Lawrence Curran*	865 S Fort St, Detroit MI 48217	313-841-2900	R	1*	<.1
1826	Eye On Technology Inc—*Justin Harris*	6463 W 77th St, Los Angeles CA 90045	310-417-8772	R	1*	<.1
1827	G and G Instrument Corp—*Hal Levy*	PO Box 604, Ardsley NY 10502	914-693-6000	R	1*	<.1
1828	Software Packaging Inc—*Edward Streit*	1001 4th Ave Ste 3200, Seattle WA 98154	206-389-9919	R	1*	<.1
1829	TLC Communications Inc—*G Liebscher*	1045 Wildwood Blvd Sw, Issaquah WA 98027	425-392-9592	R	1*	<.1
1830	Union International Systems Inc—*Michael Roberts*	1372 Hancock St Ste 30, Quincy MA 02169	617-770-3800	R	1*	<.1
1831	BB Computer Concepts Inc—*Boris Prodsky*	222 W 37th St Rm 501, New York NY 10018	212-239-8055	R	1*	<.1
1832	Twinstar Inc—*Steve Gaumond*	8703 Yates Dr Ste 115, Westminster CO 80031	303-430-7101	R	1*	<.1
1833	LP Systems—*Leroy Parker*	456 Eastview Dr, Alpine UT 84004	801-362-7278	R	1*	<.1
1834	Cognitronix (Poway California)—*Robert Frantz*	13446 Poway Rd Ste 120, Poway CA 92064		R	1	N/A
1835	Ipso Facto Consulting Inc—*Gretchen Singh*	PO Box 160547, Austin TX 78716	512-372-9880	R	<1*	<.1
1836	Virtual Impact Productions Inc—*Michelle Robinson*	607 Saint Andrews Dr, Longwood FL 32779	321-206-0372	R	<1*	<.1
1837	Global Software Technologies Inc—*Vasanthi Aharam*	13407 Trey Ln, Clifton VA 20124	703-830-1059	R	<1*	<.1
1838	Champion Systems—*Saul Hernadez*	5411 Dishner Valley Rd, Bristol VA 24202	276-466-8060	R	<1*	<.1
1839	Buzzword Inc—*James Gleason*	633 W Short St, Lexington KY 40508	859-367-7536	R	<1*	<.1
1840	Caliper Designs Inc—*Stephen Curtis*	99 Factory St Ste 4, Nashua NH 03060	603-881-8388	R	<1*	<.1
1841	A Business Computer Consulting Firm—*Kenneth Wrtenberg*	16969 Nw 67th Ave Ste, Hialeah FL 33015	305-827-3118	R	<1*	<.1
1842	Advancecom Technologies Inc—*Jeet Basu*	230 N Hayden Pkwy, Hudson OH 44236	330-342-9106	R	<1*	<.1
1843	Customer Directory Inc—*Thomas Fass*	PO Box 6292, Newport News VA 23606	757-599-4644	R	<1*	<.1
1844	Expertez Inc—*Daniel Weinberg*	PO Box 6435, Reno NV 89513	775-324-0991	R	<1*	<.1
1845	Jones Professional Services Corp—*Robert Jones*	3564 Avalon Park E Blv, Orlando FL 32828	407-256-2332	R	<1*	<.1
1846	Productivity Innovations Inc—*Timothy Snyder*	809 S 7th Ave, Bozeman MT 59715	406-587-2101	R	<1*	<.1
1847	Sequoyah Software And Consulting Inc—*Michael Brown*	PO Box 2726, Claremore OK 74018	918-342-2121	R	<1*	<.1
1848	Computer Organization System Inc—*Bill Michaelson*	9 Huron Way, Lawrenceville NJ 08648	646-506-9966	R	<1	<.1
1849	Dominion Technical Group Inc—*Dawn Chernoff*	5990 Baltusrol Dr, Gilroy CA 95020	408-710-1661	R	<1*	<.1
1850	North Coast Web Design—*Kevin Gumina*	7301 Brecksville Rd, Independence OH 44131	216-280-4755	R	<1	<.1
1851	Avantcom Corp—*Lawrence Simmons*	952 Gypsy Bay Rd, Sagle ID 83860	208-265-7878	R	<1*	<.1
1852	Bee Zee Systems—*Ben Weingarten*	15 Beekman St 725, New York NY 10038	212-962-1163	R	<1*	<.1
1853	Orionsoft—*Derek Barbosa*	1001 Durham Ave Ste 30, South Plainfield NJ 07080	732-537-9000	R	<1*	<.1
1854	WJ Kinney and Company Inc—*Linda Kinney*	112 Conger Rd 1, Madison AL 35758	256-461-0230	R	<1*	<.1
1855	Expert Computer Technologies Inc—*Michael Painter*	1600 S Gold St Ste 4, Centralia WA 98531	360-736-7000	R	<1*	<.1
1856	Steven E Douglas—*Steven Douglas*	10542 Birch St, Thornton CO 80233	303-457-6876	R	<1*	<.1
1857	Enternet Solutions Inc—*William Deweese*	PO Box 650577, Sterling VA 20165	703-380-5999	R	<1*	<.1
1858	Multicase Inc—*Gilles Klopman*	23811 Chagrin Blvd Ste, Cleveland OH 44122	216-831-3740	R	<1*	<.1
1859	Software North LLC—*Donald Anderson*	2230 E 52nd Ave Apt 2, Anchorage AK 99507	907-561-4412	R	<1*	<.1
1860	Therapeias Health Management—*William Work*	140 W Foothill Blvd St, Claremont CA 91711	909-626-6380	R	<1*	<.1
1861	America's Business Software—*John Vranich*	PO Box 585, Carmichael CA 95609	916-483-7266	R	<1*	<.1
1862	Centermark Technologies Inc—*Brett Hofer*	6 Way Rd Ste 105, Middlefield CT 06455	860-349-7038	R	<1*	<.1
1863	ConnectU—*Eric Wichhart*	2880 David Walker Dr S, Eustis FL 32726	352-702-0354	R	<1	<.1
1864	Cybernetic Learning Systems Inc—*Oliver Mcclellane*	3510 Lester Ct Sw, Lilburn GA 30047	770-982-5517	R	<1*	<.1
1865	Greenware Systems Inc—*John Green*	7350 Airport Hwy Ste 9, Holland OH 43528	419-865-8535	R	<1*	<.1
1866	Ironwood Software Inc—*William Becker*	111 N 50th St, Seattle WA 98103	206-789-3695	R	<1*	<.1
1867	Sales Record Publishing Company Inc—*Brian Jessurun*	PO Box 206, Pomfret CT 06258	860-928-7258	R	<1*	<.1
1868	Turnkey Technology Corp—*Richard Doyle*	1122 Village Gate Dr, Mount Airy MD 21771	301-831-5974	R	<1*	<.1
1869	Welcome Driver Inc—*Edward Seidman*	16400 Ventura Blvd Ste, Encino CA 91436	818-905-0015	R	<1*	<.1
1870	Sys-10 Inc—*Linda Scherzer*	660 Dean Dr, South Elgin IL 60177	847-741-7113	R	<1*	<.1
1871	Knova Software Inc—*Pete Strom*	10201 Torre Ave Ste 35, Cupertino CA 95014	408-863-5900	R	<1	.1
1872	Virnetx Holding Corp—*Kendall Larsen*	5615 Scotts Valley Dr, Scotts Valley CA 95066	831-438-8200	P	<1	<.1
1873	Linguatech International Inc—*John Snideman*	1113 S Orem Blvd, Orem UT 84058	801-226-2525	R	<1*	<.1
1874	Aggregate Innovations LC—*Louis Derwilt*	2414 SE 7th St, Des Moines IA 50315	515-242-0222	R	<1*	<.1
1875	Perfect Web Technologies Inc—*Thomas L DiStefano III*	21218 St Andrews Blvd, Boca Raton FL 33433	561-705-4386	P	<1	<.1
1876	Nis Inc—*Arden Scott*	12995 Thomas Creek Rd, Reno NV 89511	775-852-0640	R	<1*	<.1
1877	Starsoft Technologies Inc—*Scott Meredith*	3508 N Calispel St, Spokane WA 99205	509-327-1476	R	<1*	<.1
1878	Downhome Solutions—*Erik Wogstad*	3971 Evanston Ave N, Seattle WA 98103	206-634-0884	R	<1*	<.1
1879	Blueteam Software Inc—*Richard Blanchard*	1001 George Town Dr, Elon NC 27244	336-263-8806	R	<1*	<.1
1880	Grt Consulting Inc—*Joseph Hodge*	2261 Blake St Apt 3a, Denver CO 80205	303-244-9999	R	<1*	<.1
1881	Netinfo Inc—*Ketan Parekh*	1823 Loma Roja, Santa Ana CA 92705	714-544-1545	R	<1*	<.1
1882	Z Infinite—*Michael Vesely*	617 41st Ave, Santa Cruz CA 95062	831-465-6575	R	<1*	<.1
1883	Castle Solutions Inc—*Rick Glessman*	114 Sandhurst Dr, Simpsonville SC 29680	864-963-9477	R	<1*	<.1
1884	EMS Professional Software—*Eric Engelmann*	6829 Needwood Rd, Derwood MD 20855	240-683-5949	R	<1	<.1
1885	Finn Enterprises Inc—*Shawn Finn*	7 Teamquest Way, Clear Lake IA 50428	641-355-2700	R	<1*	<.1
1886	Grw Systems—*George Wilde*	24402 Broadwell Ave, Harbor City CA 90710	310-325-4456	R	<1*	<.1
1887	Information Analysis Corp—*Ronald Code*	PO Box 366, Crystal Bay NV 89402	775-832-4442	R	<1*	<.1
1888	Momentum India Private Ltd—*Pankaj Agarwal*	14040 Ne 8th St Ste 21, Bellevue WA 98007	425-641-2644	R	<1*	<.1
1889	Philip Morse—*Philip Morse*	305 E Locust St, Bloomington IL 61701	309-829-9257	R	<1*	<.1
1890	Revelation Design Inc—*Joel Ruths*	207 S Forney Ave, Hanover PA 17331	717-630-2121	R	<1*	<.1
1891	Silver Software Inc—*Mitchell Silver*	404 Pulehuiki Rd, Kula HI 96790	808-878-2714	R	<1*	<.1
1892	Thomas Ho Co—*Thomas Ho*	55 Liberty St Apt 4b, New York NY 10005	212-732-2878	R	<1*	<.1
1893	Wcc Services Us Inc—*Peter Went*	228 Hamilton Ave Ste 3, Palo Alto CA 94301	650-798-5117	R	<1*	<.1
1894	Micro Map and CAD—*Randy George*	12210 Jones Park Ct, Colorado Springs CO 80921	719-487-1031	R	<1	<.1
1895	Middle Bay Consulting Inc—*Douglas Greene*	59 Saint Joseph St, Mobile AL 36602	251-895-8908	R	<1*	<.1
1896	Value Added Software—*Peter Helgren*	1511 Harvard Ave, Salt Lake City UT 84105	801-581-1154	R	<1*	<.1
1897	Linden Lab—*Philip Rosedale*	945 Battery St, San Francisco CA 94111	415-243-9000	R	<1	.2
1898	Etelos Inc—*H Tate Holt*	1100 Larkspur Landing, Larkspur CA 94939	415-464-4849	P	<1	<.1
1899	Planet Studio LLC—*Larnie Higgins*	7820 Roswell Rd, Atlanta GA 30350	770-392-1000	R	<1	<.1
1900	International Software Products—*John Abell*	7128 Parkside Ln Unit, Racine WI 53406		R	<1	<.1
1901	Maintain Systems Inc—*Fred Marshall*	12200 N Stemmons Fwy, Dallas TX 75234	972-409-7202	R	<1*	<.1
1902	En2go International Inc—*Robert Rosner*	644-1812 W Burbank Blv, Burbank CA 91506	818-433-7191	P	<1	<.1
1903	Rapidware Inc—*Lance Smith*	108 E Main St Ste 2, Milan MI 48160	734-439-3990	R	<1*	<.1
1904	ICUS Software Systems—*Lenny Tropiano*	PO Box 867, Cedar Park TX 78630	512-249-1582	R	<1*	<.1
1905	Ionglyph Inc—*Hartwig Kelley*	1306 Reed Ranch Rd, Boulder CO 80302	303-482-1479	R	<1*	<.1
1906	Lone Eagle Systems Inc—*Steve Gaede*	3023 4th St, Boulder CO 80304	303-444-9114	R	<1*	<.1
1907	Simpla Fax Inc—*Gary Kleinerman*	195 Mandalay Rd, Lee MA 01238	413-243-6718	R	<1*	<.1
1908	Synful LLC—*Bonnie Mettler*	2975 18th St, Boulder CO 80304	303-786-7619	R	<1*	<.1
1909	Tree Top Industries Inc—*David Reichman*	511 6th Ave Ste 800, New York NY 10011	775-261-3728	P	<1	<.1
1910	Carpenter Melisa—*Melisa Carpenter*	1311 S Idalia Ct, Superior CO 80027	303-494-5530	R	<1*	<.1
1911	Cephas Holding Corp—*Peter C Klamka*	2942 N 24th St Ste 114, Phoenix AZ 85016	480-639-6404	P	<1	<.1
1912	Gizmolab Inc—*Jonathan Sand*	175 S St, Boulder Creek CA 95006	831-338-4885	R	<1*	<.1
1913	Lns Software Solutions LLC	10216 Se 256th St 321, Kent WA 98030	253-850-2457	R	<1*	<.1

Note: An asterisk (*) indicates an estimated financial figure. The company type code used is as follows: R = Private, P = Public, S = Private Subsidiary, B = Public Subsidiary, D = Division, J = Joint Venture, I = Investment Fund.

COMPANY RANKINGS BY SALES WITHIN 4-DIGIT SIC

Rank	Company Name—*Executive Officer*	Address, City, State, Zip	Phone	Type	Fin	Empls
1914	ML Pace Computer Consulting—*Michael Pace*	169 Hannon Ave, Mobile AL 36604	251-473-6033	R	<1*	<.1
1915	Oxymoron Unlimited—*Alex Howard*	233 79th St, North Bergen NJ 07047	201-868-7681	R	<1*	<.1
1916	Parameter Developments Inc—*William Andrews*	99982 Winchuck River R, Brookings OR 97415	541-412-0321	R	<1*	<.1
1917	Phased Logic Microsystems—*Don Culbertson*	PO Box 90459, Houston TX 77290	281-440-9788	R	<1*	<.1
1918	Veterans Tech LLC	3610 N 31st St, Phoenix AZ 85016	602-667-3777	R	<1*	<.1
1919	Technology for Productivity—*Richard Giles*	1250 N Tustin Ave, Anaheim CA 92807	714-238-2000	S	N/A	.5
1920	SirsiDynix—*Gary M Rautenstrauch*	101 Washington St SE, Huntsville AL 35801	256-704-7000	R	N/A	.2
1921	HBMG Inc—*Manuel Zarate*	1033 La Posada, Austin TX 78752	512-459-2600	R	N/A	.1
1922	Microfinish International Technologies—*Camilo Correa*	1616 Anderson Rd, Mc Lean VA 22102	703-861-4067	R	N/A	<.1
1923	Strafford Technology Inc—*Steven R Berry*	1D Commons Dr Unit 21, Londonderry NH 03053	603-434-2550	R	N/A	<.1
1924	Network Cybernetics Corp—*R Steven Rainwater*	3720 Canton St Ste 202, Dallas TX 75226	972-404-0248	R	N/A	<.1
1925	Snow International Corp (Clearwater Florida)—*Scott Snow*	3330 Fisher Rd, Clearwater FL 33763	727-784-6699	R	N/A	<.1
1926	Stevens Creek Software LLC	PO Box 2126, Cupertino CA 95015	408-725-0424	R	N/A	<.1
1927	Unisoft Corp—*Guy Hadland*	10 Rollins Rd Ste 118, Millbrae CA 94030	650-259-1290	R	N/A	<.1
1928	Charles Kessler and Associates—*Charles Kessler*	5767 Uplander Way Ste, Culver City CA 90230	310-215-0005	R	N/A	<.1
1929	Genesis Total Solutions Inc—*Bill Miller*	3524 Decatur Hwy Suite, Fultondale AL 35068	205-877-3228	R	N/A	<.1
1930	Integrated Software Systems—*Larry Ridenour*	PO Box 4727, San Luis Obispo CA 93403	805-773-5438	R	N/A	<.1
1931	LinuxForce Inc—*Chris J Fearnley*	240 Copley Rd, Upper Darby PA 19082	610-734-1900	R	N/A	<.1
1932	Lone Star Software Engineering Services Inc—*Tony Payne*	29236 N Discovery Ridg, Saugus CA 91390	818-723-8527	R	N/A	<.1
1933	MRG Software Inc—*Mark Gilligan*	1850 Woodhaven Way, Oakland CA 94611	415-350-6681	R	N/A	<.1
1934	Porcini Software Inc—*Michael R Rizzi*	5548 Carlton St, Oakland CA 94618	510-652-2441	R	N/A	<.1
1935	WynnComm (Statesville North Carolina)—*Phil Whitesell*	3440 E Broad St, Statesville NC 28677	704-873-1000	D	N/A	N/A

TOTALS: SIC 7371 Computer Programming Services
Companies: 1,935

					73,372	380.4

7372 Prepackaged Software

Rank	Company Name—*Executive Officer*	Address, City, State, Zip	Phone	Type	Fin	Empls
1	Microsoft Corp—*Steven A Ballmer*	1 Microsoft Way, Redmond WA 98052	425-882-8080	P	69,943	90.0
2	GlobalLogic—*Peter Harrison*	1420 Spring Hill Rd St, McLean VA 22102	703-847-5900	R	50,000	6.0
3	Oracle Corp—*Lawrence J Ellison*	500 Oracle Pkwy, Redwood City CA 94065	650-506-7000	P	35,622	108.0
4	Siemens Medical Solutions USA Inc (Malvern Pennsylvania)—*Thomas McCausland*	51 Valley Stream Pky, Malvern PA 19355	610-219-6300	S	9,135*	13.0
5	CDW LLC—*John A Edwardson*	200 N Milwaukee Ave, Vernon Hills IL 60061	847-465-6000	R	8,100	6.2
6	Symantec Corp—*Steve Bennett*	350 Ellis St, Mountain View CA 94043	650-527-8000	P	6,190	18.6
7	Activision Blizzard Inc—*Robert A Kotick*	3100 Ocean Park Blvd, Santa Monica CA 90405	310-255-2000	B	4,447	7.6
8	CA Technologies—*William McCracken*	1 CA Plaza, Islandia NY 11749		P	4,429	13.4
9	SAP Americas Inc—*Bill McDermitt*	3999 West Chester Pike, Newtown Square PA 19073	610-661-1000	S	4,350	5.2
10	Intuit Inc—*Brad Smith*	2632 Marine Way, Mountain View CA 94043	650-944-6000	P	3,851	8.0
11	Adobe Systems Inc—*Shantanu Narayen*	PO Box 2704, San Jose CA 95110	408-536-6000	P	3,800	9.1
12	Aricent Inc—*Sudip Nandy*	700 Hansen Way, Palo Alto CA 94304	650-391-1088	S	3,715*	9.5
13	Electronic Arts Inc—*John Riccitiello*	209 Redwood Shores Pky, Redwood City CA 94065		P	3,589	7.6
14	ADC Software Systems USA Inc—*Dilip Singh*	1 Van de Graaff Dr, Burlington MA 01803	781-270-8500	S	3,287	.1
15	Amdocs Inc—*Eli Gelman*	1390 Timberlake Manor, Chesterfield MO 63017	314-212-7000	S	2,984	4.2
16	VMware Inc—*Paul Maritz*	3401 Hillview Dr, Palo Alto CA 94304		B	2,857	9.0
17	Packet Video Technologies—*James C Brailean PhD*	10350 Science Center D, San Diego CA 92121	858-731-5300	S	2,624*	.4
18	SYColeman Corp—*Jared Bates*	241 18th St S, Arlington VA 22202	703-769-1418	S	2,459*	1.0
19	PROIV Technology Inc	100 Pacifica Ste 200, Irvine CA 92618	949-748-7309	S	2,363*	6.0
20	SAS Institute Inc—*James H Goodnight*	100 SAS Campus Dr, Cary NC 27513	919-677-8000	R	2,358*	11.0
21	BMC Software Inc—*Robert E Beauchamp*	PO Box 201040, Houston TX 77216	713-918-1371	P	2,065	6.2
22	L-3 Communications Titan Corp—*A Anton Frederickson*	3033 Science Park Rd, San Diego CA 92121	858-552-9500	S	2,047	12.0
23	McAfee Inc—*David DeWalt*	2821 Mission College B, Santa Clara CA 95054	408-963-8000	S	2,015*	6.2
24	Baker Atlas—*William Fankel*	PO Box 1407, Houston TX 77251	713-625-4200	D	2,000*	<.1
25	Fiserv (Stafford Texas)—*Jorge Diaz*	13100 N Promenade Blvd, Stafford TX 77477	281-240-3636	D	1,979*	.3
26	Infor Enterprise Solutions Holdings Inc—*Jim Schaper*	13560 Morris Rd Ste 41, Alpharetta GA 30004	678-319-8000	R	1,975*	8.0
27	Cybernet Software Systems Inc—*Madan S Kumar*	3031 Tisch Way Ste 100, San Jose CA 95128	650-385-3421	R	1,958*	5.0
28	Autodesk Inc—*Carl Bass*	111 McInnis Pkwy, San Rafael CA 94903	415-507-5000	P	1,952	6.8
29	3M Health Information Systems—*George W Buckley*	575 W Murray Blvd, Murray UT 84123	801-265-4400	D	1,950*	.7
30	ZOHO Corp—*Sridhar Vembu*	4900 Hopyard Ste 310, Pleasanton CA 94588	925-924-9500	R	1,920*	.8
31	Citrix Systems Inc—*Mark B Templeton*	851 W Cypress Creek Rd, Fort Lauderdale FL 33309	954-267-3000	P	1,875	5.6
32	Telwares—*Charlotte Yates*	7901 Stoneridge Dr, Pleasanton CA 94588	925-224-7800	R	1,768*	.5
33	DST Systems Inc—*Thomas A McDonnell*	333 W 11th St, Kansas City MO 64105	816-435-1000	P	1,744	12.3
34	Trading Technologies International Inc—*Harris Brumfield*	222 S Riverside Plz St, Chicago IL 60606	312-476-1000	R	1,689*	.6
35	Advanced Interactive Systems Inc—*Steven Kalman*	665 Andover Park W, Seattle WA 98188	206-575-9797	R	1,683*	.7
36	InfoTel Corp—*Bernard Connes-Lafforet*	PO Box 5158, Saint Petersburg FL 33737	727-343-5958	R	1,680*	.7
37	SRA International Inc—*William C Ballhaus*	4300 Fair Lakes Ct, Fairfax VA 22033	703-803-1500	P	1,667	7.1
38	Telcordia Technologies Inc—*Mark Greenquist*	1 Telcordia Dr, Piscataway NJ 08854	732-699-2000	S	1,604*	7.0
39	Synopsys Inc—*Manoj Gandhi*	700 E Middlefield Rd, Mountain View CA 94043	650-584-5000	P	1,536	6.8
40	SyCom Services Inc—*Sterling Phillips*	10480 Little Patuxent, Columbia MD 21044	410-740-3206	S	1,438*	.5
41	P2 Energy Solutions Inc—*Bret Bolin*	1221 Lamar Ste 1400, Houston TX 77010	713-481-2000	R	1,389*	.6
42	Waterford Institute Inc—*Dustin Heuston*	55 W 900 S, Salt Lake City UT 84101	801-349-2200	R	1,350*	.2
43	Oracle USA Inc—*George Shaheen* Oracle Corp	2207 Bridgepointe Pkwy, San Mateo CA 94404	650-295-5000	S	1,340	5.0
44	Nuance Communications Inc—*Paul Ricci*	1 Wayside Rd, Burlington MA 01803	781-565-5000	P	1,319	7.3
45	VeriFone Systems Inc—*Douglas G Bergeron*	2099 Gateway Pl Ste 60, San Jose CA 95110	408-232-7800	B	1,304	3.8
46	National Information Solutions Cooperative Inc—*Vern Dosch*	One Innovation Circle, Lake Saint Louis MO 63367		R	1,279*	.5
47	Capco—*Rob Heyvaert* Fidelity Information Services Inc	120 Broadway 29th FL, New York NY 10271	212-284-8600	S	1,231*	.5
48	Harris MyCFO Inc—*Mark K Castelin*	1700 Seaport Blvd, Redwood City CA 94063	650-210-5000	S	1,204*	.3
49	Rocket Software Inc—*Andy Youniss*	275 Grove St Ste 3-410, Newton MA 02466	617-614-4321	R	1,197*	.5
50	DST Output—*Steve Towle* DST Systems Inc	125 Ellington Rd, South Windsor CT 06074	860-290-7000	S	1,176*	3.3
51	Sybase Inc—*John S Chen* SAP Americas Inc	1 Sybase Dr, Dublin CA 94568	925-236-5000	S	1,171	3.8
52	Parametric Technology Corp—*James E Heppelmann*	140 Kendrick St, Needham MA 02494	781-370-5000	P	1,167	6.1
53	Cadence Design Systems Inc—*Lip-Bu Tan*	2655 Seely Ave, San Jose CA 95134	408-943-1234	P	1,150	4.7
54	Take-Two Interactive Software Inc—*Strauss Zelnick*	622 Broadway, New York NY 10012	646-536-2842	P	1,137	2.1
55	National Instruments Corp—*James J Truchard*	11500 N MoPac Expwy, Austin TX 78759	512-338-9119	P	1,024	6.2
56	Xiotech Corp—*George Symons*	9950 Federal Dr Ste 10, Colorado Springs CO 80921	719-388-5500	S	974*	.4
57	Command Alkon Inc—*Phil Ramsey*	1800 International Par, Birmingham AL 35243	205-879-3282	R	969*	.4
58	ATEN Technology Inc—*Jennifer Tynes*	19641 Da Vinci, Foothill Ranch CA 92610	949-428-1111	R	961*	.4
59	iAnywhere Inc—*Terry Stepien* Sybase Inc	1 Sybase Dr, Dublin CA 94568	519-883-6898	S	956*	.4
60	Equitrac Corp—*Michael Rich*	1000 S Pine Island Rd, Plantation FL 33324	954-888-7800	S	954*	.4

Rank	Company Name—*Executive Officer*	Address, City, State, Zip	Phone	Type	Fin	Empls
	Nuance Communications Inc					
61	AT and T Software Solutions—*Randal L Stevenson*	32 Ave of the Americas, New York NY 10013	212-387-5400	R	950*	2.5
62	Savvis Inc—*Jim Ousley*	1 Savvis Pky, Town and Country MO 63017	314-628-7000	B	933	2.4
63	Compuware Corp—*Bob Paul*	1 Campus Martius, Detroit MI 48226	313-227-7300	P	929	4.4
64	TIBCO Software Inc—*Vivek Y Ranadive*	3303 Hillview Ave, Palo Alto CA 94304	650-846-1000	P	920	3.0
65	CDS Global Inc—*Chris Holt*	1901 Bell Ave, Des Moines IA 50315	515-246-6837	S	917*	3.0
66	Red Hat Inc—*James M Whitehurst*	1801 Varsity Dr, Raleigh NC 27606	919-754-3700	P	909	3.7
67	MedAssurant Inc—*Keith R Dunleavy*	4321 Collington Rd, Bowie MD 20716	301-809-4000	R	881*	2.1
68	SegaSoft Networks Inc—*Naoya Tsurumi*	350 Rhode Island St St, San Francisco CA 94103	415-701-6000	R	873*	.2
69	OHM Systems Inc—*Joseph Kopetsky*	10250 Chester Rd, Cincinnati OH 45215	513-771-0008	R	868*	.1
70	Quest Software Inc—*Steve Dickson*	5 Polaris Way, Aliso Viejo CA 92656	949-754-8000	P	857	3.9
71	Vertis Inc—*Gerald Sokol Jr*	250 W Pratt St Ste 180, Baltimore MD 21201	410-528-9800	R	853*	5.0
72	ScriptLogic Corp—*Andy Langsam*	6000 Broken Sound Pkwy, Boca Raton FL 33487	561-886-2400	R	842*	.1
73	Intellinex—*Roy Brown*	925 Euclid Ave, Cleveland OH 44115	216-685-6000	S	840*	.3
74	VIPS Inc—*Arthur Lehrer*	1 W Pennsylvania Ave S, Baltimore MD 21204	410-832-8300	R	825*	.3
75	CDC Software—*Bruce Cameron*	2002 Summit Blvd Ste 7, Atlanta GA 30319	770-351-9600	S	813*	2.1
76	Novell Inc—*Ronald Hovsepian*	404 Wyman St Ste 500, Waltham MA 02451		R	812	3.4
77	Evans and Sutherland Graphics Corp	770 Komas Dr, Salt Lake City UT 84108	801-588-1000	S	808*	.3
78	Pivot Inc—*John H Eley*	215 1st St, Cambridge MA 02142	617-654-1500	R	802*	2.0
79	OSI Financial Technologies—*Louis Hernandez Jr*	455 Winding Brook Dr, Glastonbury CT 06033	860-652-3155	S	801*	.3
	Open Solutions Inc					
80	Nexidia Inc—*John Willcutts*	3565 Piedmont Rd NE Bl, Atlanta GA 30305	404-495-7220	R	794*	2.0
81	Advent Business Systems	901 Mariners Island Bl, San Mateo CA 94404	650-572-8866	S	792*	2.0
82	Lotus Development Corp—*Al Zollar*	55 Cambridge Pky Ste 5, Cambridge MA 02142	617-577-8500	S	790*	7.9
83	Informatica Corp—*Sohaib Abbasi*	100 Cardinal Way, Redwood City CA 94063	650-385-5000	P	784	2.6
84	TradeStation Securities Inc—*Salomon Sredni*	8050 SW 10th St Ste 20, Plantation FL 33324	954-652-7000	S	743*	.3
	TradeStation Group Inc					
85	Lawson Software Inc—*Harry Debes*	380 St Peter St, Saint Paul MN 55102	651-767-7000	R	736	3.9
86	Moody's KMV Co (Walnut Creek California)—*Geoff Fite*	405 Howard St Ste 300, San Francisco CA 94105	415-874-6000	S	736*	.3
87	Tellme Networks Inc—*Mike McCue*	1310 Villa St, Mountain View CA 94041	650-930-9000	S	735*	.3
	Microsoft Corp					
88	Actuate International Corp—*Peter I Cittadini*	2207 Bridgepointe Pkwy, San Mateo CA 94404	650-645-3000	S	732*	.3
	Actuate Corp					
89	Sterling Commerce Inc—*Bob Irwin*	PO Box 8000, Dublin OH 43016	614-793-7000	S	723*	2.7
90	DRS Infrared Technologies LP—*James Baird*	PO Box 740188, Dallas TX 75374	972-560-6000	S	700*	.3
91	ANSYS Inc—*James E Cashman III*	275 Technology Dr, Canonsburg PA 15317	724-746-3304	P	691	2.1
92	Solera Holdings Inc—*Tony Aquila*	7 Village Cir Ste 350, Westlake TX 76262		P	685	2.3
93	THQ Inc—*Brian J Farrell*	29903 Agoura Rd, Agoura Hills CA 91301	818-871-5000	P	665	1.8
94	MSCI Barra Inc—*Henry Fernandez*	2100 Milvia St, Berkeley CA 94704	510-548-5442	R	663*	2.1
95	Denali Advanced Integration Inc—*Mike Daher*	17735 NE 65th St Ste 1, Redmond WA 98052	425-885-4000	R	656*	.3
96	Epicor Software Corp—*Pervez A Qureshi*	7683 Southfront Rd, Livermore CA 94551	949-585-4000	S	646*	4.0
97	Marketron Broadcast Solutions—*Steve Minisini*	101 Empty Saddle Trl, Hailey ID 83333	208-788-6800	S	644*	.3
98	Kronos Inc—*Aron J Ain*	297 Billerica Rd, Chelmsford MA 01824	978-250-9800	R	631*	3.0
99	JDA Software Group Inc—*Hamish Brewer*	14400 N 87th St, Scottsdale AZ 85260	480-308-3000	P	617	3.0
100	Lectra North America—*Daniel Harari*	889 Franklin Rd SE, Marietta GA 30067	770-422-8050	S	614*	1.4
101	Quark Inc—*Raymond Schiavone*	1225 17th St Ste 1200, Denver CO 80202	303-894-8888	R	598*	1.0
102	Ligature Software Inc—*Raz Itzhaki*	234 Littleton Rd, Westford MA 01886	978-727-0026	S	594*	.1
103	Pyramid Consulting Inc—*Sanjeev Tirath*	11100 Atlantis Pl, Alpharetta GA 30022	678-514-3500	R	580*	1.6
104	Lumension Security Inc—*Patrick Clawson*	8660 E Hartford Dr, Scottsdale AZ 85255		R	588*	.3
105	MicroStrategy Inc—*Michael J Saylor*	1850 Towers Crescent P, Vienna VA 22182	703-848-8600	P	562	3.1
106	GXS Inc—*Bob Segert*	9711 Washington Blvd, Gaithersburg MD 20878	301-340-4000	R	538*	2.0
107	SAP Labs Inc—*Robert Enslin*	3410 Hillview Ave, Palo Alto CA 94304	650-849-4000	S	537*	1.5
	SAP Americas Inc					
108	Progress Software Corp—*Jay Bhatt*	14 Oak Park Dr, Bedford MA 01730	781-280-4000	P	534	1.7
109	Direct Affect Marketing—*Roland Varesko*	12007 Sunrise Valley D, Reston VA 20191	703-264-7437	R	528*	.2
110	Mirapoint Inc—*Barry M Ariko*	909 Hermosa Ct, Sunnyvale CA 94085	408-720-3700	R	519*	.2
111	SunGard Corbel Inc—*Don Mackanos*	PO Box 47470, Jacksonville FL 32247	904-399-5888	S	505*	.2
112	MathWorks Inc—*Jack Little*	3 Apple Hill Dr, Natick MA 01760	508-647-7000	R	500*	2.2
113	Quantum Compliance Systems Inc—*Patricia Brooks*	2111 Golfside Ste 1, Ypsilanti MI 48197	734-572-1000	R	492*	.1
114	Apex Analytix—*Steve Yurko*	1501 Highwoods Blvd St, Greensboro NC 27410	336-422-7371	R	491*	.2
115	Central Command Inc—*Keith Peer*	PO Box 468, Medina OH 44258	330-723-2062	R	472*	.2
116	NetCracker Technology Corp—*Andrew Feinberg*	95 Sawyer Rd, Waltham MA 02453	781-419-3300	S	471*	.2
117	ACI Worldwide Inc—*Philip G Heasley*	120 Broadway Ste 3350, New York NY 10271	646-348-6700	P	465	2.1
118	iTalk LLC—*John Cunningham*	2 N Cascade Ave, Colorado Springs CO 80903	303-926-0111	R	461*	.1
119	Ventyx—*Vince Burkett*	3301 Windy Ridge Pkwy, Atlanta GA 30339	770-952-8444	R	457*	1.2
120	QAD Eastern United States—*Pamela Lopker*	10000 Midlantic Dr Ste, Mount Laurel NJ 08054	856-273-1717	D	453*	1.3
	QAD Inc					
121	Blackboard Inc—*Michael L Chasen*	650 Massachusetts Ave, Washington DC 20001	202-463-4860	S	447	1.8
122	MediaSpan Media Software—*Frank Campagnoni*	300 North Dr Rm 100, Melbourne FL 32934	321-242-5000	S	447*	.2
	MediaSpan Group Inc					
123	Ifinix Corp—*Isaiah Israel*	255 Executive Dr Ste 4, Plainview NY 11803	516-504-3981	P	447	<.1
124	Ariba Inc—*Robert M Calderoni*	910 Hermosa Ct, Sunnyvale CA 94085	650-390-1000	P	444	2.4
125	Management Dynamics Inc—*James Preuninger*	1 Meadowlands Plz, East Rutherford NJ 07073	201-935-8588	R	434*	.2
126	Fortinet Inc—*Ken Xie*	1090 Kifer Rd, Sunnyvale CA 94086	408-235-7700	P	434	1.6
127	Consist International Inc—*Dany Segev*	535 5th Ave Ste 201, New York NY 10017	212-759-2100	R	428*	1.1
128	Double Helix Games—*Michael Saxs Persson*	17600 Gillette Ave Ste, Irvine CA 92614	949-698-1500	R	427*	.2
129	Epic Systems Corp—*Judith R Faulkner*	1979 Milky Way, Verona WI 53593	608-271-9000	R	424*	3.0
130	Dendrite International Inc—*Joseph Ripp*	1425 Rte 206 S, Bedminster NJ 07921	908-443-2000	S	424*	2.5
131	Kabira Technologies Inc—*Paul Sutton*	1850 Gateway Dr 5th Fl, San Mateo CA 94404	650-931-3700	R	423*	.2
132	MediaSpan Group Inc—*Dan Roberts*	2725 S Industrial Hwy, Ann Arbor MI 48104		R	421*	.2
133	Computer Aid Inc—*Anthony Salvaggio*	1390 Ridgeview Dr, Allentown PA 18104	610-530-5000	R	420*	1.4
134	Neversoft Entertainment Inc—*Ron Doornick*	6041 Variel Ave, Woodland Hills CA 91367	818-610-4100	S	420*	.2
	Activision Blizzard Inc					
135	Treyarch Corp—*Don Likeness*	3420 Ocean Park Blvd S, Santa Monica CA 90405		S	419*	.2
	Activision Blizzard Inc					
136	RedPrairie Holding Inc—*R Michael Mayoras*	3905 Brookside Pky, Alpharetta GA 30022	678-639-5000	S	418*	1.6
137	Kronos Inc (Beaverton Oregon)	9525 SW Gemini Dr, Beaverton OR 97008	503-596-3100	D	415*	.2
	Kronos Inc					
138	Automated License Systems Inc—*Sarah Wilson*	3055 Lebanon Pke Bldg, Nashville TN 37214	615-263-4257	R	410*	.2
139	MedAssets Inc—*John A Bardis*	100 N Point Center E S, Alpharetta GA 30022	678-323-2500	P	391	3.1

Note: An asterisk (*) indicates an estimated financial figure. The company type code used is as follows: R = Private, P = Public, S = Private Subsidiary, B = Public Subsidiary, D = Division, J = Joint Venture, I = Investment Fund.

COMPANY RANKINGS BY SALES WITHIN 4-DIGIT SIC

Rank	Company Name—*Executive Officer*	Address, City, State, Zip	Phone	Type	Fin	Empls
140	Chesapeake System Solutions Inc—*Peter Vogelberger*	10461 Mill Run CirSte, Owings Mills MD 21117	410-356-6805	R	390*	.1
141	TeleCommunication Systems Inc—*Maurice B Tose*	275 West St, Annapolis MD 21401	410-263-7616	P	389	1.2
142	Invention Machine Corp—*Mark Atkins*	28 State St Ste 3600, Boston MA 02109	617-305-9250	R	379*	.2
143	Translationscom Inc—*Phil Shawe*	3 Park Ave 40th Fl, New York NY 10016	212-689-1616	R	379*	.2
144	Avectra Inc—*Richard Davis*	7901 Jones Branch Dr S, McLean VA 22102	703-506-7000	R	378*	.2
145	CCC Information Services Inc—*Githesh Ramamurthy* CCC Information Services Group Inc	222 Merchandise Mart P, Chicago IL 60654	312-222-4636	S	376*	.9
146	Blackbaud Inc—*Marc E Chardon*	2000 Daniel Island Dr, Charleston SC 29492	843-216-6200	P	371	2.3
147	NaviMedix Inc—*Bradley Waugh*	179 Lincoln St, Boston MA 02111		R	368*	.1
148	Morneau Sobeco—*Alan Torrie*	875 Greentree Rd, Pittsburgh PA 15220	412-919-4800	S	359*	2.4
149	Dassault Systemes of America—*Bernard Charles*	175 Wyman St, Waltham MA 02451	781-810-3000	S	358*	.8
150	Concur Technologies Inc—*S Steven Singh*	18400 NE Union Hill Rd, Redmond WA 98052	425-702-8808	P	350	1.6
151	Systech Solutions Inc—*Arun Gollapudi*	700 N Brand Blvd Ste 8, Glendale CA 91203	818-550-9690	R	349*	.1
152	IQor Inc—*Vikas Kapoor*	3000 Corporate Exchang, Columbus OH 43231	646-274-3019	R	348*	10.5
153	IBM Software Support	6303 Barfield Rd, Atlanta GA 30328	404-236-2700	D	345*	1.2
154	Onyx Graphics Inc—*Jeb Hurley*	6915 S High Tech Dr, Midvale UT 84047	801-568-9900	R	341*	.1
155	Integrated Decisions and Systems Inc—*Ravi Mehrotra*	8500 Normandale Lake B, Minneapolis MN 55437	952-698-4200	R	340*	.1
156	Active Network Inc—*Dave Alberga*	10182 Telesis Ct Ste 3, San Diego CA 92121	858-964-3800	P	337	3.0
157	Pegasystems Inc—*Alan Trefler*	101 Main St, Cambridge MA 02142	617-374-9600	P	337	1.5
158	Retek Retail Systems—*Larry Ellison* Oracle Corp	950 Nicollet Mall, Minneapolis MN 55403		D	336*	1.0
159	Outstart Inc—*Christine Chiang*	745 Atlantic Ave 4th F, Boston MA 02111	617-897-6800	R	336*	.1
160	FileMaker Inc—*Dominique Goupil*	5201 Patrick Henry Dr, Santa Clara CA 95054	408-987-7000	S	331*	.3
161	Manhattan Associates Inc—*Peter F Sinisgalli*	2300 Windy Ridge Pky S, Atlanta GA 30339	770-955-7070	P	329	2.1
162	SS and C Technologies Inc—*William C Stone*	80 Lamberton Rd, Windsor CT 06095	860-298-4500	B	329*	1.4
163	Travidia Inc—*Rand Hutchison*	265 Airpark Blvd Ste 5, Chico CA 95973	530-343-6400	R	328*	.1
164	Fiserv (Lincoln Nebraska)—*Michael Young*	1345 Old Cheney Rd, Lincoln NE 68512	402-423-2682	S	325*	.7
165	Qlik Technologies Inc—*Lars Bjork*	150 N Radnor Chester R, Radnor PA 19087		P	321	1.1
166	Ecova Inc (Spokane Washington)—*Jeff D Heggedahl*	1313 N Atlantic St Ste, Spokane WA 99201		S	320*	.9
167	Centive Inc—*Christopher W Cabrera*	900 Chelmsford St7th F, Lowell MA 01851	781-852-3500	S	319*	.1
168	GlobalTec Solutions LLP—*George Thompson*	6900 N Dallas Pkwy Ste, Plano TX 75024	972-387-4728	S	316*	.1
169	CommVault Systems Inc—*Robert Hammer*	PO Box 900, Oceanport NJ 07757		P	315	1.3
170	PHT Corp—*Philip Lee*	500 Rutherford Ave, Boston MA 02129	617-973-1600	R	312*	.1
171	Medical Information Technology Inc—*Neil Pappalardo*	1 Meditech Cir, Westwood MA 02090	781-821-3000	R	310*	2.5
172	Tyler Technologies Inc—*John S Marr Jr*	5949 Sherry Ln Ste 140, Dallas TX 75225	972-713-3700	P	309	2.1
173	Kanbay International Inc—*Kenneth M Harvey*	6400 Shafer Ct Ste 100, Rosemont IL 60018	847-384-6100	S	303*	6.9
174	SPSS Inc—*Deepak Advani*	233 S Wacker Dr 11th F, Chicago IL 60606	312-651-3000	S	303	1.2
175	DoubleClick Inc—*David Rosenblatt*	111 8th Ave 10th Fl, New York NY 10011	212-271-2542	S	302	1.5
176	Lockheed Martin Management	PO Box 8048, Philadelphia PA 19101	610-531-7400	S	301	2.1
177	Paradigm Infotech Inc—*Sridhar Gadhi*	8830 Stanford Blvd Rm, Columbia MD 21045	410-872-1008	R	301*	.8
178	ARM Inc	150 Rose Orchard Way, San Jose CA 95134	408-576-1501	S	298*	1.7
179	E-Z Data Inc—*Dale Okuno* Ebix Inc	918 E Green St, Pasadena CA 91106		S	295*	.1
180	MediQual Systems Inc—*Ron Labrum*	293 Boston Post Rd W, Marlborough MA 01752	508-571-5100	S	295*	.1
181	Inovis Inc (Alpharetta Georgia)—*Sean Feeney*	11720 AmberPark Dr Ste, Alpharetta GA 30009	404-467-3000	R	288*	.8
182	Epsilon Data Management Inc—*Bryan Kennedy*	601 Edgewater Dr, Wakefield MA 01880	781-685-6000	S	287*	2.2
183	CoreHarbor Inc—*Jay Chaudhry*	One USi Plz, Annapolis MD 21401	410-897-4440	R	286*	.7
184	Consona Corp—*Jeff Tognoni*	450 E 96th St Ste 300, Indianapolis IN 46240	317-249-1700	R	281*	.7
185	Initiate Systems Inc—*William Conroy*	200 W Madison Ste 2300, Chicago IL 60606	312-759-5030	R	279*	.1
186	DTN Energy Services LLC—*John Leiferman*	9110 W Dodge Rd Ste 20, Omaha NE 68114		S	278*	.7
187	Network Engines Inc—*Gregory A Shortell*	25 Dan Rd, Canton MA 02021	781-332-1000	P	273	.2
188	Ultimate Software Group Inc—*Scott Scherr*	2000 Ultimate Way, Weston FL 33326	954-331-7000	P	269	1.3
189	Centerstone Software—*Craig Gillespie*	235 South St, Hopkinton MA 01748	508-435-1510	R	269*	.1
190	Meditech Solutions Group—*Carrick Carpenter*	120 Royall St, Canton MA 02021	781-575-1100	R	268*	.1
191	Physmark Inc—*Jacob Kuriyan*	101 E Park Blvd Rm 600, Plano TX 75074	972-231-8000	R	268*	.1
192	ProactiveNet Inc—*Ajay Singh* BMC Software Inc	2055 Laurelwood Rd Ste, Santa Clara CA 95054	408-454-4500	S	266*	.1
193	Cogent Communications Group Inc—*David Schaeffer*	1015 31st St NW, Washington DC 20007	202-295-4200	P	263	.6
194	Unitime Systems Inc—*Doug Peterman*	4900 Pearl E Cir Ste11, Boulder CO 80301	303-473-0330	R	263*	<.1
195	Autonomy Interwoven Inc—*Mike Lynch*	160 E Tasman Dr, San Jose CA 95134	408-774-2000	S	260	1.0
196	Overseenet—*Jeff Kupietzky*	515 S Flower St Ste 44, Los Angeles CA 90071	213-408-0080	R	260*	.2
197	RealPage Inc—*Steve T Winn*	4000 International Pky, Carrollton TX 75007	972-820-3000	P	258	2.3
198	Information Builders Inc—*Gerald D Cohen*	2 Penn Plz, New York NY 10121	212-736-4433	R	258*	1.4
199	Apogee Interactive Inc—*Susan Gilbert*	100 Crescent Centre Pk, Tucker GA 30084	678-684-6800	R	258*	.6
200	Combinenet Inc—*Rich Wilson*	15 27th St, Pittsburgh PA 15222	412-471-8200	R	257*	.1
201	Versata Software Inc—*Randall Jacobs*	6011 W Courtyard Dr, Austin TX 78730	512-377-9700	S	256*	.7
202	i2 Technologies Inc—*Jackson L Wilson Jr* JDA Software Group Inc	11701 Luna Rd, Dallas TX 75234	469-357-1000	S	256	1.3
203	MSC Software Corp—*Dominic Gallello*	2 MacArthur Pl, Santa Ana CA 92707	714-540-8900	S	254*	1.0
204	Activant Solutions Holdings Inc—*Pervez Qureshi*	804 Las Cimas Pkwy Ste, Austin TX 78746	512-328-2300	R	253*	2.0
205	WildTangent Inc—*Alex St John*	18578 NE 67th Ct Bldg, Redmond WA 98052	425-497-4500	R	246*	.1
206	Business Software Inc (Norcross Georgia)—*Ralph Rindik*	155 Technology Pkwy St, Norcross GA 30092	770-449-3200	R	246*	.1
207	Acsis Inc—*Gene Eubanks*	9 E Stow Rd, Marlton NJ 08053	856-673-3000	S	245*	.1
208	DataViz Inc—*Dick Fontana*	612 Wheelers Farms Rd, Milford CT 06460	203-874-0085	R	241*	.1
209	Open Solutions Inc—*Louis Hernandez Jr*	455 Winding Brook Dr, Glastonbury CT 06033	860-652-3155	S	240*	2.1
210	Avanquest Global Software Publishing	7031 Koll Center Pkwy, Pleasanton CA 94566	925-474-1700	S	238*	.6
211	National Transportation Exchange Inc—*Robert Rocque*	200 W 22nd St Ste 20, Lombard IL 60148		R	238*	.1
212	Taleo Corp—*Michael Gregoire*	4140 Dublin Blvd Ste 4, Dublin CA 94568	925-452-3000	P	237	1.2
213	NetSuite Inc—*Zachary A Nelson*	2955 Campus Dr Ste 100, San Mateo CA 94403	650-627-1000	P	236	1.3
214	Vivendi Universal Interactive Publishing—*Bruce Hack*	6060 Center Dr 5th FL, Los Angeles CA 90045	310-649-8033	S	236*	.6
215	Avalara Inc—*Scott McFarlane*	100 Ravine Lane NE Ste, Bainbridge Island WA 98110	206-826-4900	R	236*	.1
216	Managed Objects Solutions Inc	404 Wyman St, Waltham MA 02451		R	236*	.1
217	Pencom Systems Inc—*Wade Saadi*	152 Remsen St, Brooklyn NY 11201	718-923-1111	S	235*	.6
218	Midway Interactive Inc—*Mathew Booty*	2704 W Roscoe St, Chicago IL 60618	773-961-2222	S	233*	.6
219	ICS Inc (Jacksonville Florida)—*Adrain Thomas*	1650 Prudential Dr Ste, Jacksonville FL 32207	904-399-8500	R	233*	.1
220	Merge Healthcare Inc—*Jeffery A Surges*	200 E Randolph St Ste, Chicago IL 60601	312-565-6868	P	232	.9
221	3D Systems Corp—*Abe N Reichental*	333 Three D Systems Ci, Rock Hill SC 29730	803-326-3900	P	230	.7
222	Feed Management Systems Inc—*Richard Reynertson*	PO Box 767, Fairmont MN 56031	763-560-8139	R	230*	<.1
223	Synchronoss Technologies Inc—*Stephen G Waldis*	750 Rte 202 S Ste 600, Bridgewater NJ 08807		P	229	1.0
224	NextGen Healthcare Information Systems Inc—*Patrick Cline*	795 Horsham Rd, Horsham PA 19044	215-657-7010	S	228*	.6

Rank	Company Name—Executive Officer	Address, City, State, Zip	Phone	Type	Fin	Empls
225	Perceptive Software Inc—Scott Coons	22701 W 68th Ter, Shawnee KS 66226	913-422-7525	R	227*	.6
226	Kalido—Bill Hewitt	1 Wall St, Burlington MA 01803	781-202-3200	R	224*	.1
227	Wonderware Corp—Sudipta Bhattacharya	26561 Rancho Pky S, Lake Forest CA 92630	949-727-3200	S	223*	1.1
228	QAD Inc—Karl Lopker	100 Innovation Pl, Santa Barbara CA 93108	805-684-6614	P	220	1.4
229	Cognos Corp—Rob Ashe	15 Wayside Rd, Burlington MA 01803	781-229-6600	S	216*	.5
230	AAC Associates Inc—James Francis	8470 Tyco Rd, Vienna VA 22182	703-918-6300	R	216*	.1
231	CYA Technologies Inc—Wayne Crandall	4 Research Dr 2nd Fl, Shelton CT 06484	203-513-3111	R	214*	.1
232	Black Diamond Inc—Peter Metcalf	2084 E 3900 S, Salt Lake City UT 84124	801-278-5552	P	213	.5
233	Viewlocity Inc—Jim Wilson	3475 Piedmont Rd Ste 1, Atlanta GA 30305	404-267-6400	R	212*	.5
234	Protegrity Inc—Suni Munshani	5 High Ridge Park, Stamford CT 06905	203-326-7200	R	211*	.1
235	United BioSource Corp—Ethan D Leder	7501 Wisconsin Ave Ste, Bethesda MD 20814	240-644-0420	S	210*	1.4
236	S1 Corp—Johann J Dreyer	705 Westech Dr, Norcross GA 30092	404-923-3500	P	209	1.7
237	BlueTie Inc—David Koretz	220 Kenneth Dr, Rochester NY 14623	585-586-2000	R	209*	.1
238	Synygy Inc—Mark A Stiffler	2501 Seaport Dr Ste 10, Chester PA 19013	610-494-3300	R	208*	.5
239	Risk Management Association—William F Githens	1801 Market St Ste 300, Philadelphia PA 19103	215-446-4000	R	207*	.1
240	SuccessFactors Inc—Lars Dalgaard	1500 Fashion Island Bl, San Mateo CA 94404	650-645-2000	P	206	1.0
241	MRO Software Inc—Chip Drapeau	100 Crosby Dr, Bedford MA 01730	781-280-2000	S	199	.9
242	Zomax US Inc—Anthony Angelini	5353 Nathan Ln, Plymouth MN 55442	763-553-9320	R	199*	1.3
243	CCC Information Services Group Inc	222 Merchandise Mart P, Chicago IL 60654	312-222-4636	S	199	1.1
244	Solarwinds Inc—Kevin B Thompson	3711 S MoPac Expy Bldg, Austin TX 78746	512-682-9300	P	198	.6
245	Schema Inc—Menahem Tirosh	218 Rte 17 N, Rochelle Park NJ 07662	201-556-3100	R	197*	.1
246	TSC Solutions LLC—Gary Liggett	2430 Camino Ramon Ste, San Ramon CA 94583	925-790-1000	R	197*	.1
247	Kenexa Corp—Nooruddin Karsan	650 E Swedesford Rd 2n, Wayne PA 19087		P	196	2.0
248	Yurcor—Richard McCann	150 E Palmetto Park Rd, Boca Raton FL 33432	561-278-1351	R	196*	.5
249	Don Johnston Inc—Don Johnston	26799 W Commerce Dr, Volo IL 60073	847-740-0749	R	195*	.1
250	Marketing Management Analytics Inc—Randolph Stone	15 River Rd, Wilton CT 06897	203-834-3300	S	194*	.5
251	Yodleecom—Anil Arora	3600 Bridge Pkwy Ste 2, Redwood City CA 94065	650-980-3600	R	191*	.1
252	Bottomline Technologies Inc—Robert A Eberle	325 Corporate Dr, Portsmouth NH 03801	603-436-0700	P	189	.9
253	Global 360 Inc—David Mitchell	5400 LBJ Frw Ste 300, Dallas TX 75240	214-520-1660	S	189	.5
254	Iron Data LLC—Jeff Smock	3033 Maple Dr NE, Atlanta GA 30305	404-817-0033	R	189*	.4
255	Multi-Health Systems Inc—Steven J Stein PhD	PO Box 950, North Tonawanda NY 14120	416-492-2627	R	189*	.1
256	Zilliant Inc (Austin Texas)—Greg Peters	3815 S Capital of Texa, Austin TX 78704	512-531-8500	R	189*	.1
257	New Era of Networks Inc—John Chen Sybase Inc	6399 S Fiddler's Green, Greenwood Village CO 80111	303-694-3933	S	188*	1.1
258	AssetWorks Inc—John Hines Trapeze Software Inc	998 Old Eagle School R, Wayne PA 19087	610-687-9202	S	186*	.1
259	MERANT Inc Serena Software Inc	1900 Seaport Blvd 2nd, Redwood City CA 94063	650-481-3400	S	186	1.9
260	RightNow Technologies Inc—Greg R Gianforte	PO Box 9300, Bozeman MT 59719	406-522-4200	P	186	.9
261	PharMetrics Inc—Michael Weintraub	311 Arsenal St, Watertown MA 02472	617-972-8590	R	185*	.1
262	Applied Wave Research Inc—Dan Collins	1960 E Grand Ave Ste 4, El Segundo CA 90245	310-726-3000	R	185	.1
263	IntraLinks Holdings Inc—J Andrew Damico	150 E 42nd St 8th Fl, New York NY 10017	212-543-7700	P	184	.5
264	Arel Communications and Software (USA) Ltd—Philippe Szwarc	1200 Ashwood Pkwy Ste, Atlanta GA 30338	770-396-8105	S	183*	.1
265	ArcSight LLC—Joni Kahn	5 Results Way, Cupertino CA 95014	408-864-2600	S	181	.5
266	OpenLink Software Inc—Kingsley Idehen	10 Burlington Mall Rd, Burlington MA 01803	781-273-0900	R	180*	.1
267	ACI Worldwide Inc (Riverside Rhode Island)—Phillip Heasley	100 Amaral St, Riverside RI 02915	401-438-0700	S	179*	1.1
268	Art Technology Group Inc (Cambridge Massachusetts)—Dorian Daley Oracle Corp	1 Main St, Cambridge MA 02142	617-386-1000	S	179*	.5
269	Headstrong Corp—Sandeep Sahai	11911 Freedom Dr Ste 9, Reston VA 20190	703-272-6700	R	178*	2.0
270	Digital Envoy—Bill Calpin	250 Scientific Dr, Norcross GA 30092	678-258-6300	S	178*	.1
271	Bentley Systems Inc—Gregory S Bentley	685 Stockton Dr, Exton PA 19341	610-458-5000	R	177*	1.0
272	Hyphen Solutions Ltd—David B Deniger	16301 Quorum Dr, Addison TX 75001	972-728-8100	S	177*	.1
273	Charles River Systems Inc—Peter Lambertus	7 New England Executiv, Burlington MA 01803	781-238-0099	S	176*	.5
274	Business and Decision North America Inc (Wayne PA)—Robin Kearon	900 W Valley Rd Ste 10, Wayne PA 19087	610-230-2500	R	175*	2.8
275	Go Daddy Group Inc—Robert R Parsons	14455 N Hayden Rd Ste, Scottsdale AZ 85260	480-505-8899	R	175*	1.4
276	Enterprise Software Solutions Inc—Raj Talafine	200 Metroplex Dr, Edison NJ 08817	732-572-7400	R	175*	.1
277	Applied Information Group—Mitchell Rubin	100 Market St, Kenilworth NJ 07033	908-241-7007	R	174*	<.1
278	SunGard Recovery Services LP—Mike Beck	680 E Swedesford Rd, Wayne PA 19087	618-878-2644	S	173*	.5
279	Contera Inc—Jeff Swift	20 CareMatrix Dr, Dedham MA 02026	781-752-1200	R	173*	.3
280	Informative Graphics Corp—Gary Heath	4835 E Cactus Rd Ste 4, Scottsdale AZ 85254	602-971-6061	R	173*	.1
281	Life Cycle Engineering Inc—James R Fei	4360 Corporate Rd, Charleston SC 29405	843-744-7110	R	172*	.4
282	Workday Inc—Dave Duffield	6230 Stoneridge Mall R, Pleasanton CA 94588	925-951-9000	R	169*	.4
283	Visual One Systems—Martin Ellis	5310 Spectrum Pl Rm A, Frederick MD 21703	301-698-9868	R	169*	.1
284	Software Engineering of America Inc—Salvatore Simeone	1230 Hempstead Tpke, Franklin Square NY 11010	516-328-7000	R	167*	.4
285	Medidata Solutions Inc—Tarek Sherif	79 5th Ave 8th Fl, New York NY 10003	212-918-1800	P	166	.6
286	Interactive Intelligence Inc—Donald E Brown	7601 Interactive Way, Indianapolis IN 46278	317-872-3000	P	166	.8
287	Sourcefire Inc—John Burris	9770 Patuxent Woods Dr, Columbia MD 21046	410-290-1616	P	166	.4
288	Easylink Services International Corp—Thomas J Stallings	6025 The Corners Pky S, Norcross GA 30092	678-533-8000	R	165	.5
289	Foundation Software Inc—Fred Ode	150 Pearl Rd, Brunswick OH 44212	330-220-8383	R	164*	.1
290	Mindspeed Technologies Inc—Raouf Y Halim	4000 MacArthur Blvd Ea, Newport Beach CA 92660	949-579-3000	P	162	.5
291	Cover-All Systems Inc Cover-All Technologies Inc	18-01 Pollitt Dr, Fair Lawn NJ 07410	973-461-5190	S	162*	.1
292	Workscape Inc—Timothy T Clifford	123 Felton St, Marlborough MA 01752	508-573-9000	S	160*	.4
293	GIS Information Systems Inc—Bill Schickling	PO Box 4903, Syracuse NY 13221		R	159*	.1
294	PML Exploration Services LLC—Bill Faulkner	5208 W Reno Ave Ste 32, Oklahoma City OK 73127	405-606-2701	R	159*	.5
295	TechSkills LLC—Kevin Paulsen	108 Wild Basin Rd Ste, Austin TX 78746	512-328-4235	R	158*	.4
296	CAPE Systems Inc—Nicholas Toms Cape Systems Group Inc	100 Allentown Pkwy Ste, Allen TX 75002	972-359-1100	S	158*	<.1
297	StayinFront Inc—Thomas R Buckley	107 Little Falls Rd, Fairfield NJ 07004	973-461-4800	S	157*	.5
298	Analytical Services Inc—Cynthia Achorn	350 Voyager Way, Huntsville AL 35806	256-562-2100	R	157*	.4
299	Dexterra Inc—Rob Loughan	21540 30TH Dr SE, Bothell WA 98021	425-939-3100	S	156*	.1
300	Openwave Systems Inc—Mike Mulica	2100 Seaport Blvd, Redwood City CA 94063	650-480-8000	P	156	.5
301	PowerQuest Corp Symantec Corp	PO Box 1911, Orem UT 84059	801-437-8900	S	155*	.4
302	Pageflex Inc—Amos Kaminski	500 Nickerson Rd, Marlborough MA 01752	617-520-8600	D	155*	.1
303	InfoPro Corp—JoAnn P Longshore	PO Box 2886, Huntsville AL 35804	256-382-9700	R	152*	.4
304	Schrodinger LLC—Rami Farid	101 SW Main St Ste 130, Portland OR 97204	503-299-1150	R	152*	.1

Note: An asterisk (*) indicates an estimated financial figure. The company type code used is as follows: R = Private, P = Public, S = Private Subsidiary, B = Public Subsidiary, D = Division, J = Joint Venture, I = Investment Fund.

COMPANY RANKINGS BY SALES WITHIN 4-DIGIT SIC

Rank	Company Name—*Executive Officer*	Address, City, State, Zip	Phone	Type	Fin	Empls
305	Real-Time Innovations Inc—*Stan Schneider*	385 Moffett Park Dr, Sunnyvale CA 94089	408-990-7400	R	151*	.1
306	Cornerstone Information Systems Inc (Bloomington Indiana)—*Mat Orrego*	304 W Kirkwood Ave, Bloomington IN 47404	812-330-4361	R	151*	<.1
307	Advanced Concept Technologies	8910 N Dale Mabry Hwy, Tampa FL 33614	813-936-2331	R	151*	<.1
308	Risk Management Solutions Inc—*Hemant Shah*	7575 Gateway Blvd, Newark CA 94560	510-505-2500	R	150*	1.5
309	BNA Software	1801 S Bell St, Arlington VA 22202		D	150	1.0
310	CAD Consulting USA	1777 Saratoga Ave Ste, San Jose CA 95129	408-873-9979	D	149*	<.1
311	Forex International Trading Corp—*Liat Franco*	44 Wall St 7th Fl, New York NY 10005	908-731-0750	B	148	<.1
312	OPNET Technologies Inc—*Marc A Cohen*	7255 Woodmont Ave, Bethesda MD 20814	240-497-3000	P	148	.6
313	Wolters Kluwer Health Inc—*Jeffery Mccaulley*	530 Walnut St Fl 7, Philadelphia PA 19106	215-646-8700	R	147*	2.6
314	Blizzard Entertainment Inc—*Michael Morhaime* Activision Blizzard Inc	PO Box 18979, Irvine CA 92623	949-955-0283	S	146*	.2
315	Newmerix Inc—*Dan Gannon*	1100 South McCaslin Bl, Superior CO 80027	303-350-3075	R	146*	.1
316	SECURUS Technologies Inc—*Richard A Smith*	PO Box 1109, Addison TX 75001	972-277-0300	S	145*	.6
317	Patriot Technologies Inc—*Bruce Tucker*	5108 Pegasus Ct Ste F, Frederick MD 21704	301-695-7500	R	145*	.1
318	Financial Engines Inc—*Jeff Maggioncalda*	1804 Embarcadero Rd, Palo Alto CA 94303	650-565-4900	P	144	.4
319	Healthland—*Angela Franks*	625 S Lakeshore Dr, Glenwood MN 56334	320-634-5331	S	144*	.4
320	PLATO Inc—*Vin Riera*	5600 W 83rd St Ste 300, Bloomington MN 55437	952-832-1000	S	142*	.8
321	Cincom Systems Inc—*Thomas Nies*	55 Merchant St, Cincinnati OH 45246	513-612-2300	R	141*	.9
322	Magma Design Automation Inc—*Rajeev Madhavan*	1650 Technology Dr, San Jose CA 95110	408-565-7500	P	139	.7
323	Open Link Financial Inc—*Kevin Hesselbirg*	1502 RXR Pl 15th Fl, Uniondale NY 11556	516-227-6600	R	139*	.6
324	Shift4 Corp—*J David Oder*	1491 Center Crossing R, Las Vegas NV 89144	702-597-2480	R	139*	.1
325	Broadsoft Inc—*Michael Tessler*	9737 Washingtonian Blv, Gaithersburg MD 20878	301-977-9440	P	138	.5
326	Operation Technology Inc—*Farrokh Shokooh*	17 Goodyear Ste 100, Irvine CA 92618	949-462-0100	R	138*	.1
327	Datatel Inc (Fairfax Virginia)—*John Speer III*	4375 Fair Lakes Ct, Fairfax VA 22033	703-968-9000	R	137*	.6
328	MDI Achieve Inc—*Marc P Brunet*	940 W Port Plaza Dr St, St Louis MO 63146	314-439-6400	S	137*	.5
329	Fair Isaac - San Diego—*Mark Greene*	3661 Valley Centre Dr, San Diego CA 92130	858-369-8000	S	136*	.4
330	Global Factory Inc—*Sharone Zehavi*	100 Saratoga Ave Ste 2, Santa Clara CA 95051	408-551-6450	R	135*	.1
331	TAMP Computer Systems Inc—*Tom Abruzzo*	1732 Remson Ave, Merrick NY 11566	516-623-2038	R	135*	.1
332	Enigma Software Group Inc—*Colorado Stark*	2643 Gulf to Bay Blvd, Clearwater FL 33759		R	135*	<.1
333	TradeStation Group Inc—*Salomon Sredni*	8050 SW 10th St Ste 20, Plantation FL 33324	954-652-7000	S	135	.4
334	iCentera Corp—*Craig Nelson* Callidus Software Inc	14551 Judicial Rd Ste, Burnsville MN 55306	952-898-0888	S	134*	.3
335	Motricity Inc—*Jim Smith*	601 108 Ave NE Ste900, Bellevue WA 98004	425-957-6200	P	133	.3
336	WOW Global Corporation LLC—*Sarita Khatri*	5168 Campbells Run Rd, Pittsburgh PA 15205	412-747-7744	R	133*	.4
337	Drake Enterprises Ltd—*Tim Hubbs*	235 E Palmer St, Franklin NC 28734	828-524-8020	R	132*	.3
338	Renaissance Corporate Services—*Bonnie Dunn* Renaissance Learning Inc	12115 NE 99th St Ste 1, Vancouver WA 98682	360-944-8996	S	132*	.1
339	Generation21 Learning Systems Inc—*John Stearns* Renaissance Learning Inc	575 Union Blvd Ste 107, Lakewood CO 80228	303-233-2100	S	132*	.1
340	Jetstream Software Inc—*Mike Moskowitz*	290 Central Way, Kirkland WA 98033	425-827-9273	R	132*	.1
341	Actuate Corp—*Peter I Cittadini*	2207 Bridgepointe Pky, San Mateo CA 94404	650-645-3000	P	132	.6
342	SSI Group Inc—*Bobby Smith*	4721 Morrison Dr, Mobile AL 36609	251-345-0000	R	131*	.4
343	Operative Inc—*R Michael Leo*	40 W 25th St 10th Fl, New York NY 10010	212-994-8930	R	131*	.3
344	MacSolutions Inc	12437 Wilshire Blvd, Los Angeles CA 90025	310-394-0001	R	131*	<.1
345	MATISSE Software Inc—*Didier Cabannes*	930 San Marcos Circle, Mountain View CA 94043	650-861-9895	R	131*	<.1
346	Triweb Solutions LLC—*Greg Jones*	10940 SW Barnes Rd Rm, Portland OR 97225	503-643-7900	R	131*	<.1
347	Renaissance Learning Inc—*Glen R James*	PO Box 8036, Wisconsin Rapids WI 54495	715-424-3636	P	130	.9
348	SDL Waltham—*Mark Lancaster*	69 Hickory Dr 3rd Fl, Waltham MA 02451	781-464-6000	S	130*	.1
349	RegScan Inc—*Ned Ertel*	800 W 4th St Ste 202, Williamsport PA 17701	570-323-1010	R	130*	.1
350	Security Source Inc—*Bruce Rogoff*	439 S Union St Ste 401, Lawrence MA 01843	978-983-8000	R	128*	.1
351	Multimedia Games Holding Company Inc—*Patrick Ramsey*	206 Wild Basin Rd Bldg, Austin TX 78746	512-334-7500	P	128	.4
352	FrontRange Solutions Inc—*Michael McCloskey*	5675 Gibraltar Dr, Pleasanton CA 94588	925-398-1800	S	127*	.7
353	GS1 US Inc—*Robert Carpenter*	1009 Lenox Dr Ste 202, Lawrenceville NJ 08648	609-620-0200	R	127*	.3
354	Gold Systems Inc—*Terry Gold*	4840 Pearl E Cir Ste 1, Boulder CO 80301	303-447-2774	R	126*	.1
355	Majesco Entertainment Co—*Jesse Sutton*	160 Raritan Center Pkw, Edison NJ 08837	732-225-8910	P	125	.1
356	Dell Compellent—*Philip E Soran*	7625 Smetana Ln, Eden Prairie MN 55344	952-294-3300	D	125	.4
357	HealthTrans LLC—*Jack McClurg*	8300 E Maplewood Ave S, Greenwood Village CO 80111		R	125*	.1
358	TRAMS Inc—*Rajiv Rajian*	5777 W Century Blvd St, Los Angeles CA 90045	310-641-8726	S	125*	.1
359	Ligos Corp—*Ricky Cowart*	6001 Chatham Center Dr, Savannah GA 31405	912-236-8993	R	125*	<.1
360	Eidos Interactive Inc—*Michael McGarvey*	1300 Seaport Blvd Ste, Redwood City CA 94063	650-421-7600	S	124*	.1
361	AnchorPoint—*Eytan Bar*	46 Park St, Framingham MA 01702	508-628-4500	R	124*	.1
362	Clear Technologies Inc—*James W Hargis*	1199 S Beltline Rd Ste, Coppell TX 75019	972-906-6500	R	124*	<.1
363	Stellent Inc—*Lawrence J Ellison* Oracle Corp	7500 Flying Cloud Dr S, Eden Prairie MN 55344	952-903-2000	S	123	.5
364	Hyland Software Inc—*AJ Hyland*	28500 Clemens Rd, Westlake OH 44145	440-788-5000	R	123*	.9
365	Stay In Front—*Thomas R Buckley*	107 Little Falls Rd, Fairfield NJ 07004	973-461-4800	D	123*	.3
366	Koyosha Graphics of America Inc	465 California St Ste, San Francisco CA 94104	415-283-1800	R	123*	<.1
367	SCI Solutions—*John Holton*	655 Campbell Technolog, Campbell CA 95008	408-378-0262	R	122*	.1
368	Amerinex Applied Imaging Inc—*Andy Lipman*	PO Box 6473, Monroe Township NJ 08831		R	121*	.1
369	Webcom Group Inc—*David L Brown*	12808 Gran Bay Pkwy W, Jacksonville FL 32258	904-680-6600	P	120	.4
370	OpenTV Corp—*Nigel W Bennett*	275 Sacramento St, San Francisco CA 94111	415-962-5000	S	120	.6
371	Chrome Systems Corp—*David Mingle*	700 NE Multnomah, Portland OR 97232	503-963-6300	S	120*	.5
372	Axis Computer Systems Inc—*Janna Hoiberg* Consona Corp	293 Boston Post Rd W, Marlborough MA 01752	508-481-9600	S	120*	.1
373	Barracudaware	3175 Winchester Blvd, Campbell CA 95008	408-342-5400	S	120*	.1
374	BeyondTrust—*John Mutch*	30401 Agoura Rd Ste 20, Agoura Hills CA 91301	818-575-4000	R	120*	.1
375	Gearworks Inc	2770 Blue Water Rd Ste, Saint Paul MN 55121	651-209-0350	S	120*	.1
376	Axiom Software Laboratories Inc—*Alex Tsigutkin*	67 Wall St, New York NY 10005	212-248-4188	R	120*	<.1
377	NetMedia Inc—*Jack Schoof*	10940 N Stallard Pl, Tucson AZ 85737	520-544-4567	R	120*	<.1
378	US Travel Northwest Inc—*Mark Eliason*	2003 Western Ave, Seattle WA 98121	206-674-4400	R	120*	<.1
379	LogMeIn Inc—*Michael K Simon*	500 Unicorn Park Dr, Woburn MA 01801	781-638-9050	P	120	.5
380	Geeknet Inc—*Kenneth L Langone*	11216 Waples Mills Rd, Fairfax VA 22030	703-673-0075	P	120	.1
381	Pitney Bowes Business Insight—*Alan Slater*	4200 Parliament Pl Ste, Lanham MD 20706	301-731-2300	S	119*	.6
382	Construction Systems Associates Inc—*Richard Spencer*	280 Interstate North C, Atlanta GA 30339	770-955-3518	R	119*	.1
383	Nagarro Inc—*Vikas Sehgal*	226 Airport Pky, San Jose CA 95110	408-436-6170	R	118*	.3
384	Cashedge Inc—*Sanjeev Dheer*	215 Park Ave S Ste 130, New York NY 10003	212-478-6023	S	118*	.3
385	Arete Associates—*David Kier*	1550 Crystal Dr Ste 70, Arlington VA 22202	703-413-0290	R	118*	.3
386	Dentrix Dental Systems Inc—*Kimball Wirig*	727 E Utah Valley Dr S, American Fork UT 84003	801-763-9300	S	118*	.3

Rank	Company Name—*Executive Officer*	Address, City, State, Zip	Phone	Type	Fin	Empls
387	Commerce Velocity Inc	300 Commerce Dr Ste 10, Irvine CA 92602	714-338-7140	R	118*	.1
388	Saba Software Inc—*Bobby Yazdani*	2400 Bridge Pky, Redwood City CA 94065	650-581-2500	P	117	.7
389	Responsys Inc—*Dan Springer*	900 Cherry Ave 5th Fl, San Bruno CA 94066	650-745-1700	R	116	.2
390	Everest Software Inc—*Edwin A Miller*	21631 Ridgetop Circle, Dulles VA 20166	703-234-6600	R	116*	.4
391	IHS Engineering—*Jerry Stead*	15 Inverness Way E, Englewood CO 80112	303-730-0600	D	115*	1.2
392	Empirix Inc—*John D'Anna*	20 Crosby Dr, Bedford MA 01730	781-266-3200	R	115*	.4
393	Vocus Inc—*Rick Rudman*	12051 Indian Creek Ct, Beltsville MD 20705	301-459-2590	P	115	.7
394	Zuken USA Inc—*Makato Kaneko*	238 Littleton Rd Ste 1, Westford MA 01886	978-692-4900	R	114*	1.3
395	Kelly Mitchell Group Inc—*Cassandra R Sanford*	8229 Maryland Ave, St Louis MO 63105	314-727-1700	R	114*	.3
396	Omnipod Inc	205 Hudson St Fl 7, New York NY 10013	212-620-2845	S	114*	<.1
397	Indus Corp—*Shiv Krishnan*	1951 Kidwell Dr, Vienna VA 22182	703-506-6700	R	112	.5
398	Talisma Corp—*Timothy B Loomer*	777 Yamato Rd, Boca Raton FL 33431	561-923-2500	R	111*	.3
399	Mega International Corp—*Lucio de Risi*	175 Paramount Dr Ste 3, Raynham MA 02767	781-784-7684	R	111*	.3
400	Market Scan Information Systems Inc—*Ronald H Means*	811 Camarillo Springs, Camarillo CA 93012		R	110*	.3
401	Foliage Software Systems—*Tim Bowe*	168 Middlesex Tpke, Burlington MA 01803	781-993-5500	R	110*	.1
402	CustomerLink Systems Inc—*Mark Hockridge*	1376 Lead Hill Blvd St, Roseville CA 95661	916-781-4344	R	110*	<.1
403	DynaVox Inc—*Ed Donnelly Jr*	2100 Wharton St Ste 40, Pittsburgh PA 15203	412-381-4883	P	108	.4
404	Franz Inc—*Jans Aasman*	2201 Broadway Ste 715, Oakland CA 94612	510-452-2000	R	108*	<.1
405	Q-Matic Corp—*Micheal Hallahn*	2400 Commerce Ave Bldg, Duluth GA 30096	770-817-4250	S	107*	.5
406	Industrial Peer-To-Peer LLC—*John B Kalanik Jr* InStep Software LLC	55 E Monroe St Ste 271, Chicago IL 60603	312-894-7837	S	107*	<.1
407	Accelrys Inc—*Max Carnecchia*	10188 Telesis Ct Ste 1, San Diego CA 92121	858-799-5000	P	107	.6
408	Monotype Imaging Holdings Inc—*Douglas J Shaw*	500 Unicorn Park Dr, Woburn MA 01801	781-970-6000	P	107	.3
409	Cobalt Group Inc—*John WP Holt*	605 5th Ave S Ste 800, Seattle WA 98104	206-269-6363	S	106*	1.0
410	Book Systems Inc—*William D Jones*	4901 University Sq Ste, Huntsville AL 35816	256-533-9746	R	106*	<.1
411	Deerfield Communications Inc—*Mike Courterier*	PO Box 851, Gaylord MI 49735	989-732-8856	R	106*	<.1
412	Supplyworks Inc Consona Corp	450 E 96th St, Indianapolis IN 46240		S	105*	<.1
413	Guidance Software Inc—*Victor Limongelli*	215 N Marengo Ave Ste, Pasadena CA 91101	626-229-9191	P	105	.4
414	Levi Ray and Shoup Inc	2401 W Monroe St, Springfield IL 62704	217-793-3800	R	104*	.6
415	EPLAN Software and Services LLC—*Hans Hassig*	37000 Grand River Ave, Farmington Hills MI 48335	248-945-9204	S	104*	.3
416	Entrust Technologies LLC	1 Hanover Park 16633 D, Addison TX 75001	972-713-5800	S	103	.7
417	Datastream Systems Inc—*Larry G Blackwell*	50 Datastream Plz, Greenville SC 29605	864-422-5001	S	103*	.6
418	Globalware Solutions—*David Beatson*	200 Ward Hill, Haverhill MA 01835	978-469-7500	R	103*	.4
419	ACS International Resources Inc—*Milan Patel*	1290 Baltimore Pke Ste, Chadds Ford PA 19317	610-387-6005	R	103*	.3
420	Global Turnkey Systems Inc	2001 Rte 46 Ste 203, Parsippany NJ 07054	973-331-1010	S	103*	<.1
421	Parish Data Systems Inc—*Mike Boyle*	10210 N 25th Ave Ste23, Phoenix AZ 85021		R	102*	<.1
422	Parsoft International—*Elizabeth Kolawa*	101 E Huntington Dr, Monrovia CA 91016	626-256-3680	R	101*	.3
423	Ingenix—*Andy Slavitt*	12125 Technology Dr, Eden Prairie MN 55344	952-833-7100	S	100*	.5
424	Network Instruments LLC—*Roman Oliynyk*	10701 Red Circle Dr, Minnetonka MN 55343	952-358-3800	H	100*	.3
425	Pointandship Software Inc—*Ted C Mesa*	500 Ygnacio Valley Rd, Walnut Creek CA 94596	925-934-8300	R	100*	<.1
426	Ebix Inc—*Robin Raina*	5 Concourse Pkwy Ste 3, Atlanta GA 30328	678-281-2020	P	98*	1.0
427	Serena Software Inc—*John Nugent*	1900 Seaport Blvd 2nd, Redwood City CA 94063	650-481-3400	S	98*	.7
428	Unica Corp—*Yuchun Lee*	170 Tracer Ln, Waltham MA 02451	781-839-8000	S	98	.4
429	Millennium Pharmacy Systems Inc—*Richard Scardina*	1515 W 22nd St Ste 910, Oak Brook IL 60523	630-928-1650	R	98*	.3
430	Innovative Interfaces Inc—*Jerry Kline*	5850 Shellmound Way, Emeryville CA 94608	510-655-6200	R	98*	.3
431	Electronic Transaction Consultants Corp—*Tim Gallagher*	1705 N Plano Rd, Richardson TX 75081	214-615-2302	R	98*	.3
432	Innominds Software Inc—*Rao Vemula*	2055 Junction Ave Ste, San Jose CA 95131	408-434-6463	R	98*	.3
433	Syncsort Inc—*Flavio Santoni*	50 Tice Blvd, Woodcliff Lake NJ 07677	201-930-8200	R	98*	.3
434	SilkRoad Technology Inc—*Andrew J Filipowski*	102 W 3rd St Ste 250, Winston-Salem NC 27101	336-201-5100	S	98*	<.1
435	Figtree Consulting Inc—*Steve Rosenstein*	101 Gibraltar Dr, Morris Plains NJ 07950		R	98*	<.1
436	Digital Domain Productions Inc—*Cliff Plumer*	300 Rose Ave, Venice CA 90291	310-314-2800	R	97*	.4
437	DHI Computing Service Inc—*Earl Jorgensen*	PO Box 51427, Provo UT 84605		R	97*	.3
438	FRS—*Steve Husk* S1 Corp	415 Madison Ave 14th F, New York NY 10017	646-673-8429	S	97*	.3
439	ESET LLC—*Andrew Lee*	610 W Ash St Ste 1900, San Diego CA 92101	619-876-5400	R	97	.2
440	PROS Holdings Inc—*Andres Reiner*	3100 Main St Ste 900, Houston TX 77002	713-335-5151	P	97	.5
441	Primavera Systems Inc—*Joel Koppelman*	3 Bala Plz W Ste 700, Bala Cynwyd PA 19004	610-667-8600	R	96*	.5
442	ExLibris Inc USA—*Matti Shem Tov*	1350 E Touhy Ave Ste 2, Des Plaines IL 60018	847-296-2200	S	96*	.3
443	AcAe—*William J Basten*	1057 Maitland Center C, Maitland FL 32751	407-660-3140	R	96*	<.1
444	Comtronic Systems Inc—*Jeff Dantzler*	205 N Harris Ave, Cle Elum WA 98922	509-573-4300	R	96*	<.1
445	Mediaplatform Inc—*Jim McGovern*	8484 Wilshire Blvd Ste, Beverly Hills CA 90211	310-909-8410	R	96*	<.1
446	NovaStor Corp—*Stefan Utzinger*	29209 Canwood St, Agoura Hills CA 91301	805-579-6700	R	96*	<.1
447	Tradepaq Corp—*Gad Janay*	1 Exchange Pl 8th Fl, Jersey City NJ 07302	212-482-8080	R	95*	.2
448	CUSA Technologies Inc—*Dennis Connick*	4897 Lake Park Blvd, Salt Lake City UT 84120	801-902-7760	D	94*	.4
449	Macro 4 Inc—*Ronnie Wilson*	300 Lanidex Plz, Parsippany NJ 07054	973-526-3900	D	94*	.2
450	BETA Systems Software of North America Inc—*Jurgen Herbott*	2201 Cooperative Way, Herndon VA 20171	703-889-1240	S	94*	.2
451	iPay Technologies LLC—*Bill Ready*	801 N Black Branch Rd, Elizabethtown KY 42701	270-737-0590	R	94*	.2
452	E Team Inc—*Jim Montagnino*	100 N Sepulveda Blvd, El Segundo CA 90245	310-606-6444	R	94*	<.1
453	PurchasingNet Inc—*Scott Buoy* Versata Inc	125 Half Mile Rd, Red Bank NJ 07701	732-212-1500	S	93*	1.4
454	Byers Engineering Co—*Kenneth Byers Jr*	6285 Barfield Rd, Atlanta GA 30328	404-843-1000	R	93*	1.0
455	Mediaplex Inc—*David A Yovanno*	160 Spear St 15 Fl, San Francisco CA 94105	415-644-1400	S	93*	.2
456	Homescom Inc	150 Granby St, Norfolk VA 23510	754-351-7000	S	93*	.2
457	Micro Methods—*David Edwards*	PO Box 2027, Evansville IN 47728	812-476-0999	R	93*	<.1
458	Sapiens Americas Inc—*Roni Al-Dor*	4000 CentreGreen Way S, Cary NC 27513	919-405-1500	S	92	.8
459	Innoveda Inc—*Gregory Hickle*	300 Nickerson Rd Ste 2, Marlboro MA 01752	508-480-0881	S	91	.4
460	Data Exchange Corp—*Sheldon Malchicoff*	3600 Via Pescador, Camarillo CA 93012	805-388-1711	R	91*	.3
461	Digital DataVoice Corp—*Marty Gliva*	1210 Northland Dr Ste, Mendota Heights MN 55120	651-452-0300	R	91*	<.1
462	Linedata Services Inc	260 Franklin St, Boston MA 02110	617-912-4700	S	90*	.6
463	MicahTek Inc—*Michael T Conners*	8215 S Elm Pl, Broken Arrow OK 74011	918-449-3300	R	90*	.5
464	CentrePath Network Inc	265 Winter St, Waltham MA 02451	781-902-5100	S	90*	.3
465	Sigma Systems Inc (Marlborough Massachusetts)—*Mohan Nannapaneni*	201 Boston Post Rd W S, Marlborough MA 01752	508-357-6300	R	90*	.2
466	Columbia Ultimate Business Systems Inc—*R Fred Houston*	4400 NE 77th Ave Ste 1, Vancouver WA 98662	360-256-7358	R	90*	.2
467	Ansoft Corp—*Nicholas Csendes* ANSYS Inc	225 W Station Sq Dr St, Pittsburgh PA 15219	412-261-3200	S	89	.3
468	Emptoris—*Patrick D Quirk*	200 Wheeler Rd, Burlington MA 01803	781-993-9212	R	89*	.2
469	Technalysis Inc—*Akin Ecer*	7172 Waldemar Dr, Indianapolis IN 46268	317-291-1985	R	89*	<.1
470	Village Software Inc (Boston Massachusetts)—*Ford D Cavallari*	76 Summer St, Boston MA 02110	617-695-9332	R	88*	.4

Note: An asterisk (*) indicates an estimated financial figure. The company type code used is as follows: R = Private, P = Public, S = Private Subsidiary, B = Public Subsidiary, D = Division, J = Joint Venture, I = Investment Fund.

COMPANY RANKINGS BY SALES WITHIN 4-DIGIT SIC

Rank	Company Name—*Executive Officer*	Address, City, State, Zip	Phone	Type	Fin	Empls
471	Groove Networks Inc—*Ray Ozzie* Microsoft Corp	1 Memorial Dr, Cambridge MA 02142	857-453-6000	S	88*	.3
472	Wintronix Inc	9625 W 76th St, Eden Prairie MN 55344	719-576-0123	S	87*	.2
473	Harte-Hanks Data Technologies LLC—*Gary Skidmore*	25 Linnell Cir, Billerica MA 01821	978-663-9955	S	86*	.6
474	WatchGuard Technologies Inc—*Joe Wang*	505 5th Ave S Ste 500, Seattle WA 98104	206-613-6600	R	86*	.4
475	Knowledge Adventure Inc—*David Lord* Vivendi Universal Interactive Publishing	2377 Crenshaw Blvd Ste, Torrance CA 90501	310-533-3400	D	86*	.2
476	Par Springer Miller Systems Inc—*Lawrence W Hall*	PO Box 1547, Stowe VT 05672	802-253-7377	S	86*	.2
477	Continuent Inc—*Robert Hodges*	560 S Winchester Blvd, San Jose CA 95128	510-903-9600	R	86*	<.1
478	American Software Inc—*James C Edenfield*	470 E Paces Ferry Rd, Atlanta GA 30305	404-264-5296	P	86	.3
479	ACI Worldwide—*Philip Heasley* ACI Worldwide Inc (Riverside Rhode Island)	4965 Preston Park Blvd, Plano TX 75093	972-599-5600	S	85*	.2
480	Accela Inc—*Maury Blackman*	2633 Camino Ramon Ste, San Ramon CA 94583	925-659-3200	R	85*	<.1
481	DeepNines Inc—*Daniel Jackson*	14800 Quorom Dr Ste 48, Dallas TX 75254	972-590-9690	R	85*	<.1
482	SAT Corp Wonderware Corp	10111 Richmond Ave Ste, Houston TX 77042	713-344-2600	S	85*	<.1
483	Hobsons—*Craig Heldman*	50 E-Business Way Ste, Cincinnati OH 45241	513-891-5444	D	84*	.3
484	CCE—*Kumar Rajan*	28800 Orchard Lake Rd, Farmington Hills MI 48334	248-932-5295	R	84*	.2
485	Open Text Digital Media Group—*Scott Bowen*	700 King Farm Blvd Ste, Rockville MD 20850	301-548-4000	S	84*	.2
486	ePlus Government Inc—*Phillip Norton*	13595 Dulles Technolog, Herndon VA 20171	703-984-8400	S	84	.2
487	COMPanion Corp—*Bill Schjelderup*	1831 Fort Union Blvd, Salt Lake City UT 84121	801-943-7277	R	84*	.1
488	Cuadra Associates Inc—*Carlos Cuadra*	3415 S Sepulveda Blvd, Los Angeles CA 90034	310-591-2490	R	84*	<.1
489	Lightspeed Systems—*Joel Heinrichs*	1800 19th St, Bakersfield CA 93301	661-716-7600	R	84*	<.1
490	Shopsite—*David Hill*	384 A Commerce Loop, Orem UT 84058	801-705-4100	R	83	.4
491	Double-Take Software Inc—*Dean Goodermote* Vision Solutions Inc (Irvine California)	257 Turnpike Rd, Southboro MA 01772	508-229-8483	S	83*	.4
492	GHG Corp—*Israel Galvan*	960 Clear Lake City Bl, Webster TX 77598	281-488-8806	R	83*	.3
493	Homesphere Inc—*James Waldrop*	14142 Denver West Pkwy, Lakewood CO 80401		R	83*	<.1
494	Wynne Systems—*Terrence Wynne*	2603 Main St Ste 710, Irvine CA 92614	949-224-6300	S	83*	<.1
495	FalconStor Software Inc—*James P McNiel*	2 Huntington Quadrangl, Melville NY 11747	631-777-5188	P	83	.5
496	DemandTec Inc—*Daniel R Fishback*	1 Franklin Pky Bldg 91, San Mateo CA 94403	650-645-7100	P	82	.1
497	Software AG Inc—*Mark Edwards*	11700 Plaza America Dr, Reston VA 20190	703-860-5050	S	82*	.4
498	Postini Inc—*Eric E Schmidt*	1600 Amphitheatre Pkwy, Mountain View CA 94043	650-486-8100	S	82*	.3
499	AgriLogic Inc—*Joe K Davis*	PO Box 2012, Mansfield TX 76063	817-473-8771	R	82*	<.1
500	Digidesign—*Gerard Tex Schenkkar*	2001 Junipero Serra Bl, Daly City CA 94014	650-731-6300	D	81*	.3
501	StrataCare Inc—*Scott R Green*	17838 Gillette Ave, Irvine CA 92614		R	81*	.2
502	PostMaster Software Inc—*Josh Fabel*	6251 Park of Commerce, Boca Raton FL 33487	561-995-8800	R	81*	<.1
503	MediaMind Technologies Inc—*Gal Trifon*	135 W 18th St 5th Fl, New York NY 10011	646-202-1320	D	81	.4
504	Alliance Consulting Group Associates Inc—*John Castleman*	181 Washington St Ste, Conshohocken PA 19428	610-234-4301	R	80*	.5
505	Ontario Systems Corp—*Tony Reisz*	1150 W Kilgore Ave, Muncie IN 47305	765-751-7000	S	80*	.5
506	MDSS Inc—*John Leibert*	23400 Mercantile Ste 1, Cleveland OH 44122	216-514-5141	R	80*	.2
507	Atari Inc—*Jim Wilson*	417 5th Ave, New York NY 10016	212-726-6500	S	80*	.1
508	Inmedius Inc—*Gary L Schaffer*	4900 Perry Hwy 2nd Fl, Pittsburgh PA 15229	412-459-0310	R	80*	<.1
509	MAK Technologies Inc—*Warren Katz*	68 Moulton St, Cambridge MA 02138	617-876-8085	R	80*	<.1
510	Ramapo Information Systems Inc—*Bill Scura*	510 Hamburg Tpke Ste 1, Wayne NJ 07470	973-389-1904	R	80*	<.1
511	MyWeather LLC—*Terry Kelly*	401 Charmany Dr Ste 20, Madison WI 53719	608-441-0400	R	80*	<.1
512	Synamco LLC Integrated Business Systems and Services Inc	1601 Shop Rd Ste E, Columbia SC 29201	803-736-5595	S	80*	<.1
513	Cinedigm Digital Cinema Corp—*Chris McGurk*	55 Madison Ave Ste300, Morristown NJ 07960	973-290-0080	P	80	.2
514	Value Line Publishing LLC—*Howard Brecher*	220 E 42nd St, New York NY 10017	212-907-1500	S	79*	.2
515	Innovative Managed Care Systems Ltd—*Gary A Cohen*	14241 Dallas Parkway S, Dallas TX 75244	972-960-2726	R	79*	.2
516	Numara Software Inc—*Dave Hansen* Intuit Inc	2202 N West Shore Blvd, Tampa FL 33607	813-227-4500	S	79*	.2
517	Parago Inc—*Juli Spottiswood*	700 State Hwy 121 Bypa, Lewisville TX 75067	972-538-3900	S	79*	.2
518	Magento Inc (Culver City California)—*Roy Rubin*	10441 Jefferson Blvd S, Culver City CA 90232		S	79*	.2
519	Emprise Technologies LLC—*Neal M Pollon*	S Pittsburgh Technolog, Bridgeville PA 15017	412-257-9060	R	79*	<.1
520	Mastery Technologies Inc—*Bill Marker*	41216 Bridge St, Novi MI 48375		R	79*	<.1
521	Smallworld Systems Inc	5600 Greenwood Plaza B, Greenwood Village CO 80111	303-779-6980	S	79	.4
522	Infor CRM Epiphany—*Charles Phillips*	475 Concar Dr, San Mateo CA 94402	650-356-3800	S	78*	.4
523	Informatix Inc—*Raul Ocazionez*	1740 Creekside Oaks Dr, Sacramento CA 95833	415-365-1515	R	78*	.2
524	Chordiant Software Inc Pegasystems Inc	20400 Stevens Creek Bl, Cupertino CA 95014	408-517-6100	S	78	.2
525	Jive Software—*Tony Zingale*	325 Lytton Ave Ste 200, Palo Alto CA 94301	503-295-3700	P	77*	.2
526	Perry Johnson Inc—*Perry Johnson*	755 W Big Beaver Rd St, Troy MI 48084	248-356-4410	R	76*	.4
527	Infor (Alpharetta Georgia)—*Jim Schaper*	13560 Morris Rd Ste 41, Alpharetta GA 30004	678-319-8000	R	76*	.3
528	Data Integrity Inc (Newton Massachusetts)—*Allen G Burgess*	228 Highland Ave, West Newton MA 02465	617-224-2324	R	76*	<.1
529	International Decision Systems—*Michael Campbell*	1500 IDS Center 80 S 8, Minneapolis MN 55402	612-851-3200	S	75*	.2
530	Platinum Solutions Inc—*Laila Rossi* SRA International Inc	PO Box 3527, Reston VA 20195	703-471-9793	S	75*	.2
531	e-MDs Inc—*Michael Stearns*	9900 Spectrum Dr, Austin TX 78717	512-257-5200	R	75*	.2
532	Cigital Inc—*John Wyatt*	21351 Ridgetop Cir Ste, Dulles VA 20166	703-404-9293	R	75*	<.1
533	New Century Education Corp—*Jim Griffin*	220 Old New Brunswick, Piscataway NJ 08854		R	75*	<.1
534	Saltmine Inc—*PK Samal*	1951 152nd PL NE Ste 1, Bellevue WA 98007	425-748-5141	R	75*	<.1
535	Tripwire Inc—*Jim B Johnson*	101 SW Main St Ste 150, Portland OR 97204	503-276-7500	R	74*	.3
536	Dymo CardScan—*Bob Kibbe*	383 Main Ave 4th Fl, Norwalk CT 06851	617-492-4200	R	74*	<.1
537	Futuremark Corp (Saratoga California)—*Tero Sarkkinen*	12930 Saratoga Ave, Saratoga CA 95070	408-517-9020	R	74*	<.1
538	Infoglide Corp—*Michael Shultz*	6500 River Pl Blvd Bld, Austin TX 78730	512-532-3500	R	74*	<.1
539	FleetBoss Global Positioning Solutions Inc—*Brian C Carroll*	241 OBrien Rd, Fern Park FL 32730	407-265-9559	R	73*	<.1
540	FutureSoft Inc—*Tim Farrell*	12012 Wickchester Ln S, Houston TX 77079	281-496-9400	R	73*	<.1
541	Vertical Communications Inc—*Peter Bailey*	3940 Freedom Cir, Santa Clara CA 95054	408-404-1600	R	73	.2
542	Serif Inc—*Ryan Papillo*	17 Hampshire Dr Ste 1, Hudson NH 03051	603-889-8650	R	72*	.3
543	ProcureStaff Technologies Ltd—*John Campellone*	1065 Avenue of the Ame, New York NY 10018	212-901-2828	S	72*	.2
544	Viewpoint Construction Software—*JayS Haladay* Coaxis Inc	1515 SE Water Ave Ste, Portland OR 97214	971-255-4800	D	72*	.2
545	Stonebridge Technologies Inc—*James Ivy*	15301 Spectrum Dr Ste, Addison TX 75001	972-404-9755	R	72*	.2
546	Green Hills Software Inc—*Dan O'Dowd*	30 W Sola St, Santa Barbara CA 93101	805-965-6044	R	72*	.2
547	Apparel Business Systems Inc—*George Graham*	2 W Lafayette St Ste 3, Norristown PA 19401	610-592-0880	R	72*	<.1
548	Computers for Marketing—*Richard Rands*	547 Howard St, San Francisco CA 94105	415-777-0470	R	72*	<.1
549	Olympia Computing Company Inc—*Kurt Miyatake* Tyler Technologies Inc	7249 Old Hwy 99 SW, Tumwater WA 98501	360-352-0922	S	72*	<.1

Rank	Company Name—*Executive Officer*	Address, City, State, Zip	Phone	Type	Fin	Empls
550	Salford Systems—*Dan Steinberg*	9685 Via Excelencia St, San Diego CA 92123	619-543-8880	R	72*	<.1
551	ServiceBenchcom Inc—*Tony Nader*	22894 Pacific Blvd, Sterling VA 20166	571-323-7146	S	72*	<.1
552	Versata Inc—*Randall Jacops*	6011 W Courtyard Dr, Austin TX 78730	512-377-9700	R	71*	.4
553	GFI Software USA Inc—*Walter Scott*	15300 Weston Pky Ste 1, Cary NC 27513	919-379-3397	R	71*	.2
554	Xpitax LLC—*Mark Albrecht*	639 Granite St, Braintree MA 02184	781-303-0136	R	71*	.2
555	Astaro Corp—*Jan Hichert*	260A Fordham Rd, Wilmington MA 01887	978-974-2600	R	71*	.2
556	Global Trade Information Services Inc—*C Donald Brasher*	2218 Devine St, Columbia SC 29205	803-765-1860	R	71*	<.1
557	Callidus Software Inc—*Leslie J Stretch*	6200 Stoneridge Mall R, Pleasanton CA 94588	925-251-2200	P	71	.3
558	Lacerte Software Corp—*Brad Smith* Intuit Inc	5601 Headquarters Dr, Plano TX 75024	214-387-2000	S	70*	.5
559	Island Computer Products Inc—*Michelle Fabozzi*	20 Clifton Ave, Staten Island NY 10305	718-556-6700	R	70*	.2
560	Griptonite Games Glu Mobile Inc	12421 Willows Rd NE St, Kirkland WA 98034	425-825-6800	S	70*	.2
561	Perfect Commerce Inc—*Hampton Wall*	PO Box 12079, Newport News VA 23612	757-766-8211	R	70*	.1
562	Bantu Inc—*Lawrence D Schlang*	8133 Leesburg Pike Ste, Vienna VA 22182	703-766-4577	R	70*	<.1
563	MCBA Inc—*Mike Gunnells*	6767 Old Madison Pke S, Huntsville AL 35806	256-890-2026	R	70*	<.1
564	Vertex Inc—*Jeffrey R Westphal*	1041 Old Cassatt Rd, Berwyn PA 19312	610-640-4200	R	69*	.6
565	Rosetta Stone Ltd—*Tom Adams*	1919 N Lynn St 7th Fl, Arlington VA 22209	540-432-6166	R	69*	.5
566	Planned Systems International Inc—*Terry Lin*	10632 Little Patuxent, Columbia MD 21044	410-964-8000	R	69*	.2
567	Captiva Software Corp—*Joseph M Tucci*	10145 Pacific Heights, San Diego CA 92121	858-320-1000	S	68*	.3
568	Omneon Video Networks Inc—*Suresh Vasudevan*	4300 N First Street, San Jose CA 95134	408-542-2500	R	68*	.3
569	Navitaire Inc—*John Dabkowski*	333 S Seventh St Ste 5, Minneapolis MN 55402	612-317-7000	S	68*	.2
570	Maconomy Inc—*Kevin Parker*	2291 Wood Oak Dr, Herndon VA 20171		S	68*	.2
571	Escape Technology Inc—*Bob Towery*	3721 Douglas Blvd Ste, Roseville CA 95661	916-773-6363	R	68*	<.1
572	Asset Management Technologies Inc—*Scott Schubert*	17039 Kenton Dr Ste 20, Cornelius NC 28031	704-896-3118	R	68*	<.1
573	Core Software Inc	29508 Lazy Ln, Spring TX 77386		R	68*	<.1
574	Softlink America Inc—*Kim Duffey*	720 Third Ave Ste 2220, Seattle WA 98104		S	68	N/A
575	Phoenix Technologies Ltd—*Rich Geruson*	915 Murphy Ranch Rd, Milpitas CA 95035	408-570-1000	R	68	.5
576	Objective Systems Integrators Inc—*Hamish Butler*	1101 Creekside Ridge S, Roseville CA 95678	916-872-6200	S	67	.4
577	EPSIIA Corp—*John C Peterson*	1101 Capital of Texas, Austin TX 78746	512-329-0081	S	67*	.2
578	Capital Legal Solutions—*Gita Shingala*	150 S Washington St St, Falls Church VA 22046	703-226-1500	R	67*	.2
579	ZeOmega LLC—*Sathya Hangaswamy*	3010 Gaylord Pky Ste 2, Frisco TX 75034	214-618-9880	R	67*	.2
580	Advanced Technologies—*Ron Johnson*	2001 Columbus St, Bakersfield CA 93305	661-872-4807	R	67*	<.1
581	Altoros Systems—*Andrei Yurkevich*	830 Stewart Dr Ste 227, Sunnyvale CA 94085	650-395-7002	R	66*	.2
582	Benchmark Technologies	7 Kimball Ln Bldg E, Lynnfield MA 01940	781-246-3303	R	66*	<.1
583	NotePage Inc	PO Box 296, Hanover MA 02339	781-829-0500	R	66*	<.1
584	Madison Research Corp—*Richard Selvaggio*	401 Wynn Dr, Huntsville AL 35805	256-864-7200	R	66*	.7
585	eXcelon Corp—*Richard Reidy* Progress Software Corp	14 Oak Park Dr, Bedford MA 01730	781-280-4000	S	65*	.6
586	Lombardi Software Inc—*Rod Favaron*	4516 Seton Center Pkwy, Austin TX 78759	512-382-8200	R	65*	.2
587	Miles 33 International Ltd—*Michael Moore*	40 Richards Ave Ste 30, Norwalk CT 06854	203-838-2333	R	65*	.2
588	AdvancedMD Software Inc—*Raul Villar*	10876 S River Front Pk, South Jordan UT 84095	801-984-9500	R	65*	.2
589	Globoforce Ltd—*Eric Mosley*	144 Turnpike Rd Ste 31, Southborough MA 01772		R	65*	.2
590	Affinnova Inc—*Waleed Al-Atraqchi*	265 Winter St 4th Fl, Waltham MA 02451	781-464-4700	R	65*	.1
591	Glu Mobile Inc—*Niccolo de Masi*	45 Fremont St Ste 2800, San Francisco CA 94105	415-800-6100	P	64	.4
592	Triple Point Technology Inc—*Peter F Armstrong*	301 Riverside Ave, Westport CT 06880	203-291-7979	R	64*	.4
593	Medical Communication Systems Inc—*Udayan Mandavia*	1 Woodbridge Ctr Ste 8, Woodbridge NJ 07095	732-607-2400	R	64*	.2
594	MedVantx Inc—*Robert Feeney*	5810 Nancy Ridge Dr St, San Diego CA 92121	858-625-2990	R	64*	.1
595	Wavefunction Inc—*Warren Hehre*	18401 Von Karman Ave S, Irvine CA 92612	949-955-2120	R	64*	<.1
596	Bladelogic Inc—*Dev Ittycheria* BMC Software Inc	10 Maguire Rd Bldg 3, Lexington MA 02421	781-907-6500	S	63*	.3
597	Paladyne Systems Inc—*Sameer Shalaby*	420 Lexington Ave Ste, New York NY 10170	646-214-3700	R	63*	.2
598	Domin-8 Enterprise Solutions—*Greg McGrath*	4660 Duke Dr, Mason OH 45040	513-492-5800	R	63*	.2
599	Integral Development Corp—*Harpal Sandhu*	2023 Stierlin Ct, Mountain View CA 94043	650-919-1000	R	63*	.2
600	Solid Oak Software Inc—*Brian Milburn*	PO Box 6826, Santa Barbara CA 93160	805-967-9853	R	63*	<.1
601	ViaLogy Corp—*Robert Dean*	283 S Lake Ave Ste 205, Pasadena CA 91101		R	63*	<.1
602	Environmental Resource Center Inc—*Brian Karnofsky*	101 Center Pointe Dr, Cary NC 27513	919-469-1585	R	63*	<.1
603	Hash Inc—*Martin Hash*	10411 NE 110th Cir, Vancouver WA 98662	360-750-0042	R	63*	<.1
604	Soft Computer Consultants Inc—*Gilbert Hakim*	5400 Tech Data Dr, Clearwater FL 33760	727-789-0100	R	62*	.7
605	Rockwell Software Inc—*Keith Nosbusch*	1201 S 2nd St, Milwaukee WI 53204	414-382-2000	S	62*	.4
606	Players Computer Inc—*Christian Kropac Jr*	11632 Harrisburg Rd, Fort Mill SC 29715	803-578-7700	R	62*	.2
607	Dorado Corp—*Dain Ehring*	1200 Park Pl, San Mateo CA 94403	650-227-7300	R	62*	.2
608	Applied Systems Inc (University Park Illinois)—*Jim Kellner*	200 Applied Pky, University Park IL 60466	708-534-5575	S	61*	.7
609	DataDirect Technologies Ltd—*John Goodson* Progress Software Corp	14 Oak Park, Bedford MA 01730	919-461-4200	S	61*	.2
610	CyberShift Inc—*John Borgerding*	600 Parsippany Rd 2nd, Parsippany NJ 07054	973-364-0480	R	61*	.2
611	Newscale Inc—*Scott Hammond*	170 West Tasman Dr, San Jose CA 95134	650-403-7700	R	61*	.2
612	Brainworks Software Inc—*John Barry*	100 S Main St, Sayville NY 11782	631-563-5000	R	61*	<.1
613	Chesapeake Interlink Ltd—*Burton L Bank*	8 Music Fair Rd, Owings Mills MD 21117	410-363-1976	R	61*	<.1
614	BakBone Software Inc—*Douglas F Garn* Quest Software Inc	9540 Towne Centre Dr S, San Diego CA 92121	858-450-9009	S	61	.2
615	Metastorm Inc—*Mark Barrenchea*	500 E Pratt St Ste 125, Baltimore MD 21202	443-874-1300	R	60*	.3
616	Valassis 1 to 1 Solutions—*Alan F Schultz*	19975 Victor Pkwy, Livonia MI 48152	734-591-3000	S	60*	.2
617	RABA Technologies LLC—*Stanton D Sloane* SRA International Inc	8830 Stanford Blvd Ste, Columbia MD 21045		S	60*	.2
618	Roxio Inc	455 El Camino Real, Santa Clara CA 95050	408-367-3100	D	60*	.2
619	SoftPress Systems Inc—*Richard E Logan*	3020 Bridgeway Ste 408, Sausalito CA 94965	415-331-4820	S	60*	.2
620	Sypro Impact Software Inc—*Jeffery Stein*	959 S Coast Dr Ste 100, Costa Mesa CA 92626	714-437-1000	R	60	.2
621	Anjana Software Solutions Inc—*Saravana Kumarasamy*	5455 Wilshire Blvd Ste, Los Angeles CA 90036	323-525-1766	R	60*	.2
622	Alas Inc—*Erik Digiacomo*	7 Times Sq Ste 4305, New York NY 10036	212-944-1199	R	60*	.2
623	Primus Knowledge Solutions Inc Art Technology Group Inc (Cambridge Massachusetts)	1601 5th Ave Ste 1900, Seattle WA 98101	206-834-8100	S	60*	.2
624	MediaTrust—*Keith Cohn*	404 Park Ave S 2nd Fl, New York NY 10016	212-802-1160	R	60*	.1
625	Helius Inc—*Mike Tippets*	333 S 520 W Ste 330, Lindon UT 84042	801-764-9020	R	60*	<.1
626	O'PIN Systems Inc—*Ray Pinson*	7900 International Dr, Bloomington MN 55425		R	60*	<.1
627	Counterpoint Systems Ltd—*Amos Biegun*	11835 W Olympic Blvd S, Los Angeles CA 90064	310-473-0200	R	60*	<.1
628	Menusoft Systems Corp	7370 Steel Mill Dr, Springfield VA 22150	703-912-3000	R	60*	<.1
629	Best Case Solutions Inc—*Susan Berry*	PO Box 32, Evanston IL 60204	847-492-8037	S	60*	<.1
630	Caine Farber and Gordon Inc—*Im Caine*	1010 E Union St Ste 20, Pasadena CA 91106		R	60*	<.1

Note: An asterisk (*) indicates an estimated financial figure. The company type code used is as follows: R = Private, P = Public, S = Private Subsidiary, B = Public Subsidiary, D = Division, J = Joint Venture, I = Investment Fund.

COMPANY RANKINGS BY SALES WITHIN 4-DIGIT SIC

Rank	Company Name—*Executive Officer*	Address, City, State, Zip	Phone	Type	Fin	Empls
631	Circadence Corp—*Michael J Moniz*	1011 Walnut St Ste 400, Boulder CO 80302	303-413-8800	R	60*	<.1
632	Vital Images Inc—*Michael H Carrel*	5850 Opus Pkwy Ste 300, Minnetonka MN 55343	952-487-9500	P	60	.2
633	Netiq Corp—*Jeff Hawn*	1233 W Loop S Ste 810, Houston TX 77027	713-418-5000	S	60*	.9
634	Dorado Software—*James Hsieh*	110 Woodmere Rd Ste 20, Folsom CA 95630	916-673-1100	R	59*	.2
635	Accuity Inc—*Hugh M Jones IV*	4709 W Golf Rd, Skokie IL 60076	847-676-9600	D	59*	.2
636	Concentrix Corp—*Stephen Hodownes*	3750 Monroe Ave, Pittsford NY 14534	585-218-5300	S	59*	.2
637	DataScan Technologies LLC	5925 Cabot Pky, Alpharetta GA 30005	770-521-6500	D	59*	.2
638	InQuira—*Michael Murphy*	900 Cherry Ave, San Bruno CA 94066	650-246-5000	R	59*	.2
639	Optimum Solutions Corp—*Michael Kerr*	266 Merrick Rd Rm 300, Lynbrook NY 11563	516-247-5300	R	59*	.2
640	ProCard Inc—*Ian Hill*	1819 Denver W Dr Bldg, Lakewood CO 80401	303-279-2255	S	59*	.2
641	Roundarch Inc—*Jeff Maling*	350 N LaSalle St 12th, Chicago IL 60654		R	59*	.2
642	Ellie Mae Inc—*Sig Anderman*	4155 Hopyard Road Ste, Pleasanton CA 94588	925-227-7000	P	58*	.2
643	Adexa Inc—*Cyrus Hadavi*	5933 W Century Blvd 12t, Los Angeles CA 90045	310-642-2100	R	58*	.2
644	ArrayComm Inc—*Martin Cooper*	2480 N 1st St Ste 200, San Jose CA 95131	408-428-9080	R	58*	.2
645	Intellitax—*Andrew Priest*	15395 SE 30th Pl Ste 3, Bellevue WA 98007	425-649-8291	R	58*	.2
646	Holstein Association USA Inc—*John Meyer*	PO Box 808, Brattleboro VT 05302	802-254-4551	R	58*	.1
647	Advanced Software Development Corp—*Dean Shoultz*	723 Point St, Houma LA 70360	985-851-6600	R	58*	<.1
648	Cadalog Inc—*David Wayne*	1448 King St, Bellingham WA 98229	360-647-2426	R	58*	<.1
649	JL Systems Inc—*Jacqueline Danforth*	4312 Evergreen Ln Ste, Annandale VA 22003	703-941-0077	R	58*	<.1
650	Smith Micro Software Inc—*William W Smith Jr*	51 Columbia Ste 200, Aliso Viejo CA 92656	949-362-5800	P	58	.4
651	Actividentity Corp—*Jerome Becquart*	6623 Dumbarton Cir, Fremont CA 94555	510-574-0100	S	58	.2
652	Paradigm Solutions Corp—*Peter LaMontagne*	9715 Key West Ave 3rd, Rockville MD 20850	301-468-1200	D	57*	.3
653	SunGard Bi-Tech Inc—*Russ Fradin*	680 E Swedesford Rd, Wayne PA 19087	530-879-2731	S	57*	.2
654	IntelliCorp Inc—*Jerome Klajbor*	2900 Lakeside Dr Ste 2, Santa Clara CA 95054	408-454-3500	R	57*	.2
655	Monolith Productions Inc—*Samantha Ryan*	10516 NE 37th Cir, Kirkland WA 98033	425-739-1500	S	57*	.1
656	Nicholas Data Services Inc—*Peter L Vosotas*	2454 McMullen-Booth Rd, Clearwater FL 33759	727-726-0763	S	57*	.1
657	ATX/Kleinrock—*Jeff Gramlich* Universal Tax Systems Inc	PO Box 1040, Caribou ME 04736		S	56*	.6
658	Quorum Business Solutions (USA) Inc—*Paul Weidman*	1420 W Mockingbird Ln, Dallas TX 75247	214-630-6442	R	56*	.4
659	VED Software Services Inc—*Sampath Seshadri*	37811 W 12 Mile Rd Ste, Farmington Hills MI 48331	248-851-7400	R	56*	.2
660	Proven Method Inc—*Jack Nail* American Software Inc	470 E Paces Ferry Rd, Atlanta GA 30305	404-238-8480	S	56*	.2
661	Solid Concepts Inc—*Joe Allison*	28309 Ave Crocker, Valencia CA 91355	661-295-4400	R	56*	.2
662	eScreen Inc—*Robert D Thompson*	PO Box 25902, Overland Park KS 66225	913-327-5915	R	56*	.1
663	GridPoint Inc—*John B Spirtos*	2801 Clarendon Blvd St, Arlington VA 22201	703-667-7000	R	56*	.1
664	Apexon Inc—*Alan Harlan*	2460 N 1st St Ste 220, San Jose CA 95131	408-324-2500	R	56*	<.1
665	Casahl Technology Inc—*Harry Wong*	12647 Alcosta Blvd Ste, San Ramon CA 94583	925-328-2828	R	56*	<.1
666	Connect3 Systems Inc—*Dale Byrne*	11100 E Artesia Blvd S, Cerritos CA 90703	562-741-0380	R	56*	<.1
667	Glenn Computer—*Glenn Liebowitz*	24370 Northwestern Hwy, Southfield MI 48075		R	56*	<.1
668	Knorr Associates Inc—*Norm Dotti*	PO Box 400, Butler NJ 07405	973-492-8500	R	56*	<.1
669	Urban Science Applications Inc—*Jim Anderson*	200 Renaissance Ctr St, Detroit MI 48243	313-259-9900	R	55*	.4
670	Scrollmotion Inc—*Josh Koppel*	7 Penn Plz Ste 1112, New York NY 10001	212-608-9146	R	55*	.1
671	Meta Health Technology Inc—*Eli Nahmias*	330 Seventh Ave, New York NY 10001	212-695-5870	R	55*	<.1
672	Leading Market Technologies Inc—*Jay Kemp Smith*	1 Kendall Sq Bldg 100, Cambridge MA 02139	617-494-4747	R	55*	<.1
673	Follett Software Co—*Simona Rollinson*	1391 Corporate Dr, McHenry IL 60050	815-344-8700	S	54*	.5
674	Turning Technologies LLC—*Mike Broderick*	265 W Federal St, Youngstown OH 44503	330-746-3015	R	54*	.1
675	QuestSoft—*Leonard Ryan*	23441 S Pointe Dr, Laguna Hills CA 92653	949-837-9506	R	54*	<.1
676	Quiksoft Corp—*John Alessi*	501 Abbott Dr, Broomall PA 19008	484-418-1281	R	54*	<.1
677	RiskWatch International—*Caroline Hamilton*	1421 5th St Ste A, Sarasota FL 34236		R	54*	<.1
678	Vitria Technology Inc—*JoMei Chang PhD*	945 Stewart Dr, Sunnyvale CA 94085	408-212-2700	R	54	.2
679	SciQuest Inc—*Stephen Wiehe*	6501 Weston Pky Ste 20, Cary NC 27513	919-659-2100	B	53	.3
680	Automated Financial Systems Inc—*James Greenwood*	123 Summit Dr, Exton PA 19341	610-524-9300	R	53*	.4
681	CP Software Group Inc—*David Saykally*	716 Figueroa St, Folsom CA 95630	916-985-4445	R	53*	.2
682	Telestream Inc—*Dan Castles*	848 Gold Flat Rd Ste 1, Nevada City CA 95959	530-470-1300	S	53*	.2
683	TradeBeam Inc—*Ed Flaherty*	2 Waters Park Dr Ste 1, San Mateo CA 94403	650-653-4800	R	53*	.1
684	E Commerce Group Inc—*Hikmet Ersek*	17 Dey St, New York NY 10007	212-791-9700	S	53*	.1
685	Flipside Inc—*Keith Cohn*	335 Madison Ave Ste 84, New York NY 10007	646-307-8600	R	53*	.1
686	Blue Lance Inc—*Umesh Verma*	410 Pierce Street Ste, Houston TX 77002	713-255-4800	R	53*	.1
687	Envoy Technologies Inc—*Shashi Prasad*	555 Rte 1 S, Iselin NJ 08830	732-636-4700	R	53*	<.1
688	Lightning Phase II Inc	10700 76th Ct, Largo FL 33777	727-431-4400	R	53*	<.1
689	MAXON Computer Inc—*Harald Egel*	2640 Lavery Ct Ste A, Newbury Park CA 91320	805-376-3333	D	53*	<.1
690	Visual Networks Systems—*Lawrence S Barker*	2075 Research Pkwy Ste, Colorado Springs CO 80920	425-446-6400	S	53	.2
691	Aprimo Inc—*William M Godfrey*	900 E 96th St Ste 400, Indianapolis IN 46240	317-803-4300	R	52*	.4
692	Adams Media Corp—*David B Nussbaum*	57 Littlefield St, Avon MA 02322	508-427-7100	R	52*	<.1
693	Sure Solutions Inc—*Brian Johnson*	36 Broad St, Manasquan NJ 08736	732-528-7635	R	52*	<.1
694	CAD/CAM Consulting Services Inc—*Tom Shelar*	996 Lawrence Dr Ste 10, Newbury Park CA 91320		R	52*	<.1
695	Cyber-SIGN Inc—*John Golden*	600 Anton 11th Fl, Costa Mesa CA 92626	714-371-4044	S	52*	<.1
696	PipingSolutions Inc—*Reid McNally*	6219 Brittmoore Rd, Houston TX 77041	713-849-3366	R	52*	<.1
697	Ex Libris Group—*Matti Shem Tov*	1350 E Touhy Ave Ste 2, Des Plaines IL 60018	847-296-2200	S	51*	.4
698	Savvion Inc—*Ma Ketabahn*	5104 Old Ironsides Dr, Santa Clara CA 95054	408-330-3400	R	51*	.1
699	Virtual Services Inc—*Michael Watson*	4321 Sahara Ln Ste 100, Plano TX 75093	972-596-7016	R	51*	.1
700	JMT Consulting Group Inc—*Jacqueline M Tiso*	2200-2202 Rte 22, Patterson NY 12563	845-278-9262	R	51*	<.1
701	PRN Medical Software—*Barbara Feinstein* Right On Programs	778 New York Ave Ste21, Huntington NY 11743	631-424-7777	D	51*	<.1
702	Interplay Productions Interplay Entertainment Corp	16815 Von Karman Ave, Irvine CA 92606	949-553-6655	D	50*	.3
703	eCopy Inc—*Edward Schmid*	1 Oracle Dr, Nashua NH 03062	603-881-4450	R	50*	.3
704	RSA Data Security Inc—*Arthur W Coviello Jr*	177 Bovet Rd Ste 200, San Mateo CA 94402	650-295-7600	D	50*	.1
705	TradeCard Inc—*Kurt Cavano*	75 Maiden Ln 12th Fl, New York NY 10038	212-405-1800	R	50*	.1
706	Global Graphics Software Inc	31 Nagog Park Ste 315, Acton MA 01720	978-849-0011	S	50*	.1
707	geoVue—*Jim Stone*	500 W Cummings Park St, Woburn MA 01801	781-938-3800	R	50*	<.1
708	Lieberman and Associates—*Philip Lieberman*	1900 Aveof the Stars S, Los Angeles CA 90067	310-550-8575	R	50*	<.1
709	Secured Data Inc—*David Greene*	612 Pierce Blvd, O Fallon IL 62269	618-726-5200	R	50*	<.1
710	GeoLearning Inc—*Frank Russell*	4600 Westown Pkwy Ste, West Des Moines IA 50266	515-222-9903	S	49*	.2
711	Daptiv Inc—*Chase Franklin*	1008 Western Ave Ste 5, Seattle WA 98104	206-341-9117	R	49*	.1
712	Miller Systems Inc (Boston Massachusetts)—*Seth A Miller*	31 St James Ave Ste 94, Boston MA 02116	617-266-4200	R	49*	<.1
713	Pervasive Software Inc—*John Farr*	12365 Riata Trace Pky, Austin TX 78727	512-231-6000	P	48	.3
714	Internet Pipeline Inc—*Timothy Wallace*	750 Springdale Dr, Exton PA 19341	484-348-6555	R	48*	.2
715	Exigen Inc—*Greg Shenkman*	345 California St 22nd, San Francisco CA 94104	415-402-2600	R	48	.6
716	Friendfinder Networks Inc—*Marc H Bell*	6800 Broken Sound Pky, Boca Raton FL 33487	561-912-7000	P	48*	.4

Rank	Company Name—*Executive Officer*	Address, City, State, Zip	Phone	Type	Fin	Empls
717	Automated Logic Design Company Inc—*David Rinehart*	2260 Corporate Cir, Henderson NV 89074	702-990-4400	R	48*	.2
718	A and T Systems Inc—*Ashok K Thareja*	12200 Tech Rd, Silver Spring MD 20904	301-384-1425	R	48*	.1
719	Axiom International Services Inc—*David Greenbaum*	1805 Drew St, Clearwater FL 33765	727-442-7774	R	48*	<.1
720	Business Systems of America Inc	8701 Mallard Creek Rd, Charlotte NC 28262		R	48*	<.1
721	Derby Associates International—*Errol Lafayette*	1 Old Town Sq Ste 300, Fort Collins CO 80524	970-221-0111	R	48*	<.1
722	DSP Development Corp—*Jim Pierson*	1 Bridge St, Newton MA 02458	617-969-0185	R	48*	<.1
723	Fairhaven Software Products Inc—*Candie Mendes*	PO Box 40087, New Bedford MA 02744	508-994-6400	R	48*	<.1
724	JustConnect Corp—*David Schlup*	7670 S Vaughn Ct Ste 1, Englewood CO 80112	303-706-0990	R	48*	<.1
725	Agency Software Inc—*Mitch McInelly*	215 W Commerce Dr, Hayden Lake ID 83835	208-762-7188	R	48*	<.1
726	Process Control Technology Inc—*Don W Haynes*	4335 Piedras Dr W Ste, San Antonio TX 78228		R	48*	<.1
727	GVI Security Solutions Inc—*Steven E Walin*	2801 Trade Center Dr S, Carrollton TX 75007	972-245-7353	R	47	.1
728	DataVantage Corp—*Chaz Napoli*	30500 Bruce Industrial, Solon OH 44139	440-498-4414	S	47*	.4
729	Nexvisionix Inc	2 Peters Canyon Ste 20, Irvine CA 92606	714-665-6240	R	47*	.3
730	Daegis Inc—*Todd E Wille*	1420 Rocky Ridge Dr St, Roseville CA 95661	916-865-3300	P	47	.2
731	Cellomics Inc	100 Technology Dr, Pittsburgh PA 15219	412-770-2200	S	47*	.1
732	CFD Research Corp—*Ashok Singhal*	215 Wynn Dr, Huntsville AL 35805	256-726-4800	R	47*	.1
733	Informa Investment Solutions Inc—*Barry J Effron*	4 Gannett Dr, White Plains NY 10604	914-640-0200	S	47*	.1
734	MetaCommunications Inc—*Robert T Long*	1210 S Gilbert St, Iowa City IA 52240	319-337-8599	R	47*	.1
735	Strongmail Systems Inc—*Sam Cece*	1300 Island Dr Ste 200, Redwood City CA 94065	650-421-4200	R	47*	.1
736	Psychological Software Solutions Inc—*Stewart Pisecco*	4119 Montrose Blvd 5th, Houston TX 77006	713-965-6941	R	47*	<.1
737	Color Savvy Systems Ltd—*Steven Mace*	3090 S TECH BLVD, Miamisburg OH 45342	937-885-9000	R	47*	<.1
738	Salarycom Inc—*Paul Daoust* Kenexa Corp	160 Gould St, Needham MA 02494	781-464-7300	S	46*	.5
739	EchoMail Inc—*Haribaran Subramanian*	701 Concord Ave, Cambridge MA 02138	617-354-8585	R	46*	.2
740	MarketMAX Inc—*Jim Goodnight* SAS Institute Inc	35 Village Rd, Middleton MA 01949	978-646-8100	S	46*	.2
741	Mindjet Corp—*Scott Raskin*	1160 Battery St 4th Fl, San Francisco CA 94111	415-229-4200	R	46*	.1
742	MetricStream Inc—*Shellye Archambeau*	2600 E Bayshore Rd, Palo Alto CA 94303	650-620-2900	R	46*	.1
743	Extensis Products Group—*Osamu Ikeda*	1800 SW First Ave Ste, Portland OR 97201	503-274-2020	S	46*	.1
744	Brentmark Software—*Gregory Kolojeski*	3505 Lake Lynda Dr Ste, Orlando FL 32817	407-306-6160	R	46*	<.1
745	GenesisFour Corp—*Fred Vibert*	PO Box 773, Andrews SC 29510	843-461-4177	R	46*	<.1
746	CyberDefender Corp—*Gary Guseinov*	617 W 7th St, Los Angeles CA 90017	213-689-8631	P	46	.4
747	Mercury Insurance Services LLC—*Gabe Tridor*	4484 Wilshire Blvd, Los Angeles CA 90010	323-937-1060	S	46*	.1
748	C3i Inc—*Joel H Morse*	25 Lindsley Dr, Morristown NJ 07960	973-401-6000	R	45*	.5
749	InstallShield Software Corp—*Mark Bishof*	1000 E Woodfield Rd St, Schaumburg IL 60173	847-466-4000	S	45*	.3
750	MEDecision Inc—*Deborah M Gage*	601 Lee Rd Chesterbroo, Wayne PA 19087	610-540-0202	R	45*	.3
751	Diskeeper Corp—*Jerry Baldwin*	7590 N Glenoaks Blvd, Burbank CA 91504	818-771-1600	R	45*	.2
752	Curl Corp—*Nobuhide Nakaido*	201 Broadway 2nd Fl, Cambridge MA 02139	617-761-1200	R	45*	.2
753	HTE/UCS Inc	1000 Business Center D, Lake Mary FL 32746	407-304-3235	S	45*	.2
754	Junction Solutions—*Jeff Grell*	9781 S Meridian Blvd S, Englewood CO 80112	303-327-8800	R	45*	.1
755	Manatron ProVal Corp—*Paul Sylvester*	510 E Milham Ave, Portage MI 49002		S	45	.1
756	Intetics Co—*Boris Kontsevoi*	809 Ridge Hd Ste 205, Wilmette IL 60091	847-512-4272	R	45*	.1
757	Daz Systems—*Walt Zipperman*	880 Apollo St Ste 201, El Segundo CA 90245	310-640-1300	R	45*	.1
758	Innovation Data Processing Inc—*Anthony Mazzone*	275 Paterson Ave Ste 3, Little Falls NJ 07424	973-890-7300	R	45*	.1
759	SafeStone Technologies Ltd—*John Todd*	1364 Welsh Rd Ste B1, North Wales PA 19454	215-540-8517	R	45*	.1
760	Visibility Inc—*John Nugent*	100 Fordham Rd, Wilmington MA 01887	978-694-8000	R	45*	<.1
761	eGAIN Communications Corp—*Ashutosh Roy*	345 E Middlefield Rd, Mountain View CA 94043	650-230-7500	P	44	.3
762	AvePoint Inc—*Kai Gong*	3 Second St 9th Fl, Jersey City NJ 07302	201-793-1111	R	44*	1.0
763	Sciforma Corp—*Gary Hudson*	985 University Ave Ste, Los Gatos CA 95032	408-354-0144	R	44*	.8
764	Universal Tax Systems Inc—*Bill Anderson*	6 Mathis Dr NW, Rome GA 30165	706-290-7200	S	44*	.6
765	Hospitality Solutions International Inc—*Cyndi Shepley*	9977 North 90th St Ste, Scottsdale AZ 85258	480-596-5156	D	44*	.4
766	Princeton Financial Systems Inc—*James Russo*	600 College Rd E, Princeton NJ 08540	609-987-2400	S	44*	.3
767	Benefit Concepts Incorporated of Rhode Island—*John Hoder*	20 Risho Ave, East Providence RI 02914	401-438-7100	R	44*	.3
768	Relativity Technologies Inc	2300 Rexwoods Dr Ste 1, Raleigh NC 27607	919-786-2800	S	44*	.2
769	OverDrive Inc—*Steve Potash*	8555 Sweet Valley Dr S, Cleveland OH 44125	216-573-6886	R	44*	.1
770	Fatwire Corp—*Yogesh Gupta*	330 Old Country Rd Ste, Mineola NY 11501	516-328-9473	R	44*	.1
771	Melillo Consulting Inc—*Mark Melillo*	285 Davidson Ave Ste 2, Somerset NJ 08873	732-563-8400	R	44*	.1
772	Pacific Timesheet—*Jason Trend*	5348 Vegas Dr, Las Vegas NV 89108		R	44*	.1
773	Mesonic America Inc—*Doron Amiran*	628 Levering Ave Ste B, Los Angeles CA 90024	818-470-7929	S	44*	.1
774	ERisk Holdings Inc—*Mark Trachy*	825 3rd Ave 27th Fl, New York NY 10022	212-819-0170	S	44*	<.1
775	Artemis International Solutions Corp—*Randall Jacobs* Versata Software Inc	6011 W Courtyard Drive, Austin TX 78730	512-377-9700	S	43*	.3
776	TradeStation Technologies Inc—*Salomon Sredni* TradeStation Group Inc	8050 SW 10th St Ste 20, Plantation FL 33324	954-652-7000	S	43*	.3
777	AMCOM Software Inc—*Chris Heim*	10400 Yellow Circle Dr, Eden Prairie MN 55343	952-230-5200	S	43*	.3
778	JS Paluch Company Inc—*William Rafferty*	3708 River Rd Ste 400, Franklin Park IL 60131	847-678-9300	R	43*	.2
779	Rogue Wave Software Inc—*Brian Pierce*	5500 Flatiron Pky, Boulder CO 80301	303-473-9118	R	43*	.2
780	Transamerica Life and Protection	400 Galleria Pkwy SE S, Atlanta GA 30339		S	43	.2
781	Ascentis Sofware Corp—*Les Goldstein*	PO Box 53330, Bellevue WA 98015	425-462-7171	R	43*	.1
782	Telogy Networks Inc—*Joseph A Crupi*	20450 Century Blvd, Germantown MD 20874	301-515-8762	S	43*	.1
783	Gigatron Software Corp—*Bill Holmes*	7 Corporate Park Ste15, Irvine CA 92606	949-475-0320	R	43*	.1
784	Mad Catz Inc—*Darren Richardson*	7480 Mission Valley Rd, San Diego CA 92108	619-683-9830	S	43*	.1
785	Clearspring Technologies—*Ramsey McGrory*	8000 Westpark Dr Ste 6, McLean VA 20598	703-677-3999	R	43*	.1
786	AdKnowledge Inc—*Scott L Kauffman*	4600 Madison Ave FL 10, Kansas City MO 64112	816-931-1771	R	43*	.1
787	Peak 10 (Richmond Virginia)—*David Jones*	8801 Park Central Dr S, Richmond VA 23227	804-264-8621	S	43*	<.1
788	Newmarket International Inc—*Jeff Hiscox*	75 New Hampshire Ave, Portsmouth NH 03801	603-436-7500	R	42*	.4
789	CompassLearning—*Eric Loeffel*	203 Colorado St, Austin TX 78701	512-478-9600	R	42*	.3
790	Transentric—*Mark Davis*	1400 Douglas St Ste 08, Omaha NE 68179	402-544-6000	R	42*	.3
791	Opto 22 Inc—*Mark Engman*	43044 Business Park Dr, Temecula CA 92590	951-695-3000	R	42*	.2
792	Logility Inc—*J Michael Edenfield* American Software Inc	470 E Paces Ferry Rd, Atlanta GA 30305	404-261-9777	S	42*	.1
793	Orsus Solutions Ltd—*Zeevi Bregman*	1 Penn Plz Ste 6210, New York NY 10119	212-594-8255	R	42*	.1
794	Applied Insurance Research Inc—*Karen Clark*	131 Dartmouth St, Boston MA 02116	617-267-6645	R	42*	.1
795	Rivermine Software Inc—*Mark Logan*	3975 Fair Ridge Dr Ste, Fairfax VA 22033	703-995-6000	R	42*	.1
796	Pano Logic Inc—*John Kish*	2000 Seaport Blvd Ste, Redwood City CA 94063	650-454-8940	R	42*	.1
797	Velos Inc—*John McIlwain*	2201 Walnut Ave Ste 20, Fremont CA 94538	510-739-4010	R	42*	.1
798	Magee Enterprises Inc—*Marshall Magee*	PO Box 979, Skaneateles NY 13152		R	42*	<.1
799	Rand Worldwide Inc—*Marc L Delude*	5000 Birch St Ste 4500, Newport Beach CA 92660		P	42	.2
800	MKS Software Inc—*Michael Harris*	12701 Fair Lakes Cir S, Fairfax VA 22033	703-803-3343	S	41*	.3
801	I-Many Inc—*Al Smith*	1735 Market St 37th Fl, Philadelphia PA 19103	215-344-1900	R	41*	.2

Note: An asterisk (*) indicates an estimated financial figure. The company type code used is as follows: R = Private, P = Public, S = Private Subsidiary, B = Public Subsidiary, D = Division, J = Joint Venture, I = Investment Fund.

COMPANY RANKINGS BY SALES WITHIN 4-DIGIT SIC

Rank	Company Name—Executive Officer	Address, City, State, Zip	Phone	Type	Fin	Empls
802	StorePerform Technologies Inc—Srikant Vason RedPrairie Holding Inc	1700 Broadway, Denver CO 80290	303-385-5300	S	41*	.1
803	Coveo Software Inc—Louis Tetu	945 Lakesview Pkwy, Vernon Hills IL 60061		R	41*	.1
804	Vernier Software and Technology—David Vernier	13979 SW Millikan Way, Beaverton OR 97005	503-277-2299	R	41*	.1
805	Intek Integration Technologies Inc—Mac Cutchins	35328 SE Center St, Snoqualmie WA 98065	425-455-9935	R	41*	<.1
806	Interactive Effects Inc	2133 S Bundy Dr, Los Angeles CA 90064	310-998-8364	R	41*	<.1
807	Rockliffe Inc—John Davies	1901 S Bascom Ave Ste, Campbell CA 95008	408-879-5600	R	41*	.1
808	Apptix ASA—David Ehrhardt	13461 Sunrise Valley D, Herndon VA 20171	703-890-2800	P	41	N/A
809	SouthPeak Interactive Corp—Melanie Mroz	2900 Polo Pky Ste 104, Midlothian VA 23113	804-378-5100	P	40	.1
810	Lyris Inc—Wolfgang Maasberg	6401 Hollis St Suite 1, Emeryville CA 94608	510-844-1600	P	40	.2
811	DATAIR Employee Benefit Systems Inc—Aaron Venouziou	735 N Cass Ave, Westmont IL 60559	630-325-2600	R	40*	.4
812	J and B Software Inc—Kathy Hamburger	510 E Township Line Rd, Blue Bell PA 19422	215-641-1500	S	40*	.3
813	ReadSoft North America—Jan Andersson	3838 N Causeway Blvd S, Metairie LA 70002	504-841-0100	S	40*	.2
814	Coradiant Inc—Brett Helm BMC Software Inc	16875 W Bernardo Dr St, San Diego CA 92127	858-386-5601	S	40*	.1
815	DeCarta Inc—J Kim Fennell	4 N 2nd St Ste 950, San Jose CA 95113	408-294-8400	R	40*	.1
816	Diamond Phoenix Corp—Tom Coyne	PO Box 1608, Lewiston ME 04241	207-784-1381	R	40*	.1
817	Seapine Software Inc—Richard Riccetti	5412 Courseview Dr Ste, Mason OH 45040	513-754-1655	R	40*	.1
818	Tranzact Technologies Inc—Jean Regan	360 W Butterfield Rd 4, Elmhurst IL 60126	630-833-0890	R	40*	.1
819	Cloudmark Inc—Hugh McCartney	128 King St 2nd Fl, San Francisco CA 94107	415-946-3800	R	40*	.1
820	NitroSecurity Inc—Ken Levine	230 Commerce Way, Portsmouth NH 03801	603-766-8160	S	40*	.1
821	Cerasis Inc	3200 Courthouse Ln, Eagan MN 55121	651-686-4725	R	40*	<.1
822	Case Consult Corp	18 Lyman St Ste O, Westborough MA 01581	508-651-9898	S	40*	<.1
823	Premier Design Systems Inc—Tim Gotham	12527 Central Ave NE S, Minneapolis MN 55434	612-305-1310	R	40*	<.1
824	Kaidara Software Inc—Eric Hinkle	5150 El Camino Real St, Los Altos CA 94022	650-417-2350	S	40*	<.1
825	Lone Star Software Corp—Jeffrey Hyman	509 E Ridgeville Blvd, Mount Airy MD 21771	301-829-1622	R	40*	<.1
826	ShowCase Corp—Jack Noonan SPSS Inc	233 S Wacker Dr 11th F, Chicago IL 60606	312-261-6565	D	40	.3
827	DP Technology Corp	1150 Avenida Acaso, Camarillo CA 93012	805-388-6000	R	39*	.2
828	Smarthome Inc—Joe Dada	16542 Millikan Ave, Irvine CA 92606	949-477-5505	R	39*	.1
829	D and B Sales and Marketing Solutions—Steven Alesio	460 Totten Pond Rd, Waltham MA 02451	781-672-9200	S	39*	.1
830	DocuTech Corp (Idaho Falls Idaho)—Ty Jenkins	PO Box 1835, Idaho Falls ID 83403	208-523-5531	R	39*	.1
831	HDI Solutions Inc—Jim Wilkerson	1510 Pumphrey Ave, Auburn AL 36832	334-821-0947	R	39*	.1
832	Medsphere Systems Corp—Michael J Doyle	1917 Palomar Oaks Way, Carlsbad CA 92008	760-692-3700	R	39*	.1
833	MortgageFlex Systems Inc—Lester Dominick	10151 Deerwood Park Bl, Jacksonville FL 32256	904-356-2490	R	39*	.1
834	PenFact Inc—Matt Keith	500 Harrison Ave Rm 3, Boston MA 02118	617-482-6900	R	39*	.1
835	Rosetta Inpharmatics LLC—SJ Rupert Vessey	401 Terry Ave N, Seattle WA 98104	206-802-7000	S	39*	.1
836	Solutions-II Inc—W Todd Bowling	8822 S Ridgeline Blvd, Littleton CO 80129	303-796-8393	R	39*	<.1
837	Insurance Technology Consultants Inc—Peter Whalen	681 S Parker St Ste 26, Orange CA 92868	714-836-0671	R	39*	<.1
838	Capterra Inc—Michael Ortner	901 N Glebe Rd, Arlington VA 22203	703-994-4500	R	39*	<.1
839	Analytical Graphics Inc—Paul Graziani	220 Valley Creek Blvd, Exton PA 19341	610-981-8000	R	38*	.3
840	Accu-Med Services LLC—Thomas W Ludeke	300 Technecenter Dr St, Milford OH 45150	513-831-1207	S	38*	.3
841	Advantageware Inc—Antoinette Molodowitz	PO Box 230308, New York NY 10023	212-319-1903	R	38*	.1
842	Loan Protector Insurance Services—Ron Wiser	6001 Cochran Rd Ste 40, Solon OH 44139		R	38*	.1
843	Loftware Inc—Eric Anderson	166 Corporate Dr, Portsmouth NH 03801	603-766-3630	R	38*	.1
844	Precision Systems Concepts Inc—Andrew Lauter	1051 Perimeter Dr Ste, Schaumburg IL 60173	847-517-7200	R	38*	.1
845	Tritech Software Systems—Chris Maloney	9860 Mesa Rim Rd, San Diego CA 92121	858-799-7000	R	38*	.1
846	Tenable Network Security Inc—Ron Gula	7063 Columbia Gateway, Columbia MD 21046	410-872-0555	R	38*	.1
847	BQE Software Inc—Shafat Qazi	2601 Airport Dr Ste 38, Torrance CA 90505	310-602-4010	R	38*	.1
848	KPA LLC—Vane Clayton	1380 Forest Park Cir S, Lafayette CO 80026		R	38*	.1
849	Kewill Electronic Commerce—Paul Nichols	1 Executive Dr, Chelmsford MA 01824	978-482-2500	S	38*	.1
850	LearningWare Inc—Dan Yaman	700 Raymond Ave, St Paul MN 55114	612-904-6878	R	38*	<.1
851	Magnify Inc—Derek Smith	100 S Wacker Dr Ste 11, Chicago IL 60606	312-214-1420	R	38*	<.1
852	Optimation Inc—Michael D Lundy	18600 E 37th Terrace S, Independence MO 64057	816-228-2100	R	38*	<.1
853	Ringgold Management Systems Inc—Donald Chvatal	PO Box 368, Beaverton OR 97075	503-977-1313	R	38*	<.1
854	Thinkstream Inc—Barry Bellue Sr	7150 SW Hampton St Ste, Tigard OR 97223	503-968-1656	R	38*	<.1
855	Caremedic Systems Inc—Sheila Schweitzer	800 Carillon Pky Ste 2, Saint Petersburg FL 33716	727-896-2731	R	37*	.1
856	Demand Management Inc—Bill Harrison Logility Inc	165 North Meramec Ste, Clayton MO 63105	314-727-4448	S	37*	.1
857	Apptio—Sunny Gupta	225 108th Ave NE 2nd F, Bellevue WA 98004	425-453-5861	R	37*	.1
858	Blackball Inc—Bob Brown	12625 High Bluff Dr, San Diego CA 92130	858-523-9944	R	37*	<.1
859	Polygon Industries Inc—Barrett Leibe	PO Box 24096, New Orleans LA 70184	504-451-5721	R	37*	<.1
860	Recursion Software Inc—Paul Lipari	2591 N Dallas Pkwy Ste, Frisco TX 75034	972-731-8800	R	37*	<.1
861	Tracer Technologies—Curtis Crow	PO Box 189, Windsor PA 17366		R	37*	<.1
862	Keystone Systems Inc—Keiko Kay Holloman	8016 Glenwood Ave Ste, Raleigh NC 27612	919-782-1143	R	37*	<.1
863	Netsol Technologies Inc—Najeeb Ghauri	23901 Calabasas Rd Ste, Calabasas CA 91302	818-222-9195	P	37	.9
864	Mediconnect Global Inc—Amy Rees Anderson	10897 S River Front Pk, South Jordan UT 84095	801-545-3700	R	36*	1.2
865	FDI Consulting Inc—Chris Hodge	9750 Goethe Rd, Sacramento CA 95827		R	36*	.5
866	Peopleclick Authoria Inc—Charles S Jones	2 Hannover Sq 7th Fl, Raleigh NC 27601	919-645-2800	R	36*	.3
867	Waypoint Global LLC—Dave Chambliss	6910 N Shadeland Ave, Indianapolis IN 46220	317-624-4000	R	36*	.3
868	AR Group Inc	2925 Briarpark Dr 7th, Houston TX 77042	713-430-7200	S	36*	.2
869	SofterWare Inc—Douglas Schoenberg	132 Welsh Road Ste 140, Horsham PA 19044	215-628-0400	R	36*	.1
870	aeonware Inc—Michael Mildenberger	290 S Main St Ste 1000, Alpharetta GA 30004	678-624-9792	S	36*	.1
871	Distinct Corp—Tarcisio Pedrotti	3315 Almaden Expy Ste, San Jose CA 95118	408-445-3270	R	36*	.1
872	Taj Technologies Inc—KC Sukumar	1168 Northland Dr, Mendota Heights MN 55120	651-688-2801	R	36*	.1
873	Coupons Inc—Steven Boal	400 Logue Ave, Mountain View CA 94043	650-605-4600	R	36*	.1
874	Distribution Management Systems Inc (Omaha Nebraska)—James P Hassenstab	17002 Marcy St, Omaha NE 68118	402-330-6620	R	36*	.1
875	IPRO Tech—Jim King	6811 E Mayo Blvd Ste 3, Phoenix AZ 85054	602-324-4776	R	36*	.1
876	Chicago-Soft Ltd—Robert Rich	1 Maple St, Hanover NH 03755	603-643-4002	R	36*	<.1
877	Concept Software Inc—Michael Wozniak	PO Box 770459, Winter Garden FL 34777	321-221-1497	R	36*	<.1
878	Education Systems Inc—Andrew Nassir	1111 Torrey Pines Rd, La Jolla CA 92037		R	36*	<.1
879	MainStreet Software Corp—Jerry Canada Jr	2429 Military Rd Ste 3, Niagara Falls NY 14304	716-297-8005	S	36*	<.1
880	Preferred Data Systems LLC—Chad Muncy	39100 Country Club Dr, Farmington Hills MI 48331	248-553-6410	R	36*	<.1
881	Rockware Inc	2221 E St Ste 1, Golden CO 80401	303-278-3534	R	36*	<.1
882	Saltire Software Inc—Robin McLeod	PO Box 230755, Tigard OR 97281	503-968-6251	R	36*	<.1
883	SAT Corp (Sunnyvale California)—Robert Potter	321 Soquel Way, Sunnyvale CA 94085	408-530-1020	S	36*	<.1
884	Systems Consulting Services Inc—Kenneth L Wayman	5058 Dorsey Hall Dr, Ellicott City MD 21042	410-730-4040	R	36*	<.1
885	Information Management Consultants Inc (McLean Virginia)—Sudhakar V Shenoy	11480 Commerce Park Dr, Reston VA 20191	703-871-8700	R	35*	.4

Rank	Company Name—*Executive Officer*	Address, City, State, Zip	Phone	Type	Fin	Empls
886	Ultimus Inc (Carey North Carolina)—*Leigh Michl*	15000 Weston Pkwy, Cary NC 27513	919-678-0900	R	35*	.3
887	ON Technology Corp—*Enrique Salem* Symantec Corp	266 2nd Ave, Waltham MA 02451	781-530-2200	S	35*	.2
888	CNC Software Inc	671 Old Post Rd, Tolland CT 06084	860-875-5006	R	35*	.1
889	LiveOffice LLC—*Nick Mehta*	2780 Skypark Dr Ste 30, Torrance CA 90505	310-539-6980	R	35*	.1
890	Computer Guidance Corp—*Roger D Kirk*	15035 N 75th St, Scottsdale AZ 85260	480-444-7000	R	35*	.1
891	Able Software Inc—*Ming Li*	30 Corporate Park Suit, Irvine CA 92606	949-252-3100	R	35*	.1
892	Intex Solutions Inc—*Tonya Hatoon*	110 A St, Needham MA 02494	781-449-6222	R	35*	.1
893	ePlus Technology of NC Inc—*Phillip Norton*	13595 Dulles Technolog, Herndon VA 20171	703-984-8400	S	35*	.1
894	Fortress Technologies Inc—*Richard Condon*	4023 Tampa Rd Ste 2000, Oldsmar FL 34677	813-288-7388	R	35*	.1
895	Netcube Systems Inc—*Mallikarjuna Reddy*	1275 Arbor Ave, Los Altos CA 94024	650-862-7858	R	35*	.1
896	Bowstreet Inc	1 New Orchard Rd, Armonk NY 10504		S	35*	.1
897	About Learning Inc—*Michael McCarthy*	1150 Brown St, Wauconda IL 60084	847-487-1800	R	35*	<.1
898	Certain Software Inc—*Peter Micciche*	75 Hawthorne St Ste300, San Francisco CA 94105	415-353-5330	R	35*	<.1
899	Raosoft Inc—*Catherine Rao*	6645 NE Windermere Rd, Seattle WA 98115	206-525-4025	S	35*	<.1
900	Jenark Business Systems Inc—*Mark Jennings*	7300 Westmore Rd Ste 3, Rockville MD 20850	301-840-6292	R	35*	<.1
901	Phytel Inc—*Neil Smiley*	11511 Luna Rd Ste 600, Dallas TX 75234	214-750-9922	R	35*	.1
902	E Commerce Group Products Inc—*Darren Manelski*	199 Water St 29th Fl, New York NY 10038		S	34	.1
903	QS/1 Data Systems—*William Cobb*	201 W Saint John St, Spartanburg SC 29306	864-253-8600	D	34*	.4
904	Trinity Consultants Inc—*Jay Hofmann*	12770 Merit Dr Ste 900, Dallas TX 75251	972-661-8100	R	34*	.2
905	MultiAd Inc—*James Douglas*	1720 W Detweiller Dr, Peoria IL 61615	309-692-1530	R	34*	.2
906	Unicorn HRO—*Frank Diassi*	25B Hanover Rd, Florham Park NJ 07932	973-360-0688	R	34*	.2
907	Mythic Entertainment Inc—*Mark B Jacobs*	4035 Ridge Top Rd 8th, Fairfax VA 22030	703-934-0169	R	34*	.2
908	SecureInfo Corp—*Christopher Fountain*	211 N Loop 1604 E Ste, San Antonio TX 78232	210-403-5600	R	34*	.2
909	GT Nexus Inc—*Aaron Sasson*	300 Lakeside Dr Ste 40, Oakland CA 94612	510-808-2222	R	34*	.1
910	Lumedx Corp—*Allyn McAuley*	555 Twelfth St Ste 206, Oakland CA 94607		R	34*	.1
911	Infor Library and Information Solutions	550 Cochituate Rd, Framingham MA 01701		D	34*	.1
912	Ergonomic Solutions—*Morten Winston Bligaard*	PO Box 7052, Plainville CT 06062		R	34*	.1
913	Kurtosys Systems Inc—*Mash Patel*	750 Third Ave 9th Fl, New York NY 10017	212-783-6550	R	34*	.1
914	Mediaspectrum Inc—*Scott W Killoh*	15 New England Executi, Burlington MA 01803	781-685-4648	R	34*	.1
915	Reddwerks Corp—*Jean Belanger*	1122 S Capital of Texa, Austin TX 78746	512-257-3031	R	34*	.1
916	Analytical Group Inc—*Jack Pollack*	16638 N 90th St, Scottsdale AZ 85260	480-483-2700	R	34*	.1
917	GivenHansco Inc—*Michael Sanders*	2400 Corporate Exchang, Columbus OH 43231	614-310-0060	R	34*	<.1
918	Computerised Business Systems Inc—*Charlie Hinders*	115 S Walnut, La Crescent MN 55947	507-895-8600	R	34*	<.1
919	OCO Inc—*William C Copacino*	100 5th Ave, Waltham MA 02451	781-810-2100	R	34*	<.1
920	iAnywhere Solutions Inc Sybase Inc	1 Sybase Dr, Dublin CA 94568		S	33	N/A
921	Gomez Inc—*Peter Karmanos*	10 Maguire Rd Ste 330, Lexington MA 02421	781-778-2700	R	33*	.2
922	Ratheon Solipsys—*Mark Trenor*	8170 Maple Lawn Blvd R, Fulton MD 20759	240-554-8100	S	33*	.2
923	Open Software Technologies Inc	PO Box 162652, Altamonte Springs FL 32716	407-788-7173	R	33*	.1
924	ETI—*Andrew Hall*	440 N Federal Hwy Ste, Boca Raton FL 33432	561-395-2278	R	33*	.1
925	Shaw Systems Associates Inc—*Roy Shaw Jr*	6200 Savoy Dr Ste 600, Houston TX 77036	713-782-7730	R	33*	.1
926	Allen Interactions Inc—*Michael W Allen*	1120 Centre Pointe Dr, Mendota Heights MN 55120		R	33*	.1
927	Net Nanny Software Inc—*Russ Warner*	2369 W Orton Cir, Salt Lake City UT 84119	801-977-7777	S	33*	<.1
928	Voice Documentation Systems LLC—*Dennis Howley*	PO Box 1232, Belvedere Tiburon CA 94920		R	33*	<.1
929	PFR Engineering Systems Inc—*Joseph M Pundyk*	6151 W Century Blvd St, Los Angeles CA 90045	310-410-1612	S	33*	<.1
930	Network-1 Security Solutions Inc—*Corey M Horowitz*	PO Box 909, Framingham MA 01701	212-829-5770	P	33	<.1
931	MedPlus Inc—*Richard A Mahoney*	4690 Parkway Dr, Mason OH 45040	513-229-5500	S	32*	.4
932	Library Corp—*Annette Harwood Murphy*	Research Park, Inwood WV 25428	304-229-0100	R	32*	.2
933	Advanced Digital Data Inc—*Bruce C Bott*	6 Laurel Dr, Flanders NJ 07836	973-584-4026	R	32*	.2
934	Altium Inc—*Nick Martin*	3207 Grey Hawk Ct, Carlsbad CA 92010	858-485-4639	S	32*	.2
935	Capcom USA Inc—*Kenzo Tsujimoto*	800 Concar Dr Ste 300, San Mateo CA 94402	650-350-6500	S	32*	.2
936	Computer Packages Inc—*Valerie Flagg*	414 Hungerford Dr 3rd, Rockville MD 20850	301-424-8890	R	32*	.1
937	Courion Corp—*Christopher Zannetos*	1881 Worcester Rd, Framingham MA 01701	508-879-8400	R	32*	.1
938	Honeywell Access—*John Lorenty*	135 W Forest Hills Ave, Oak Creek WI 53154	414-766-1700	S	32*	.1
939	Lenel Systems International Inc—*Luis Orbegoso*	1212 Pittsford-Victor, Pittsford NY 14534	585-248-9720	R	32*	.1
940	MedeFinance Inc—*Michael E Gallagher*	5858 Horton St Ste 475, Emeryville CA 94608	510-647-1300	R	32*	.1
941	Novologix—*David McLean*	10400 Viking Dr Ste 20, Eden Prairie MN 55344	952-826-2500	R	32*	.1
942	Vibes Media—*Alex Campbell*	300 W Adams St 7th Fl, Chicago IL 60606	312-753-6330	R	32*	.1
943	Exact—*Mitchell Alcon*	3600 American Blvd W S, Bloomington MN 55431		R	32*	.1
944	Mainconcept LLC—*Markus Moening*	5201 Great America Pky, Santa Clara CA 95054	408-524-2910	R	32*	.1
945	NeoAccel Inc—*Michel Susai*	3401 Hillview Ave, Palo Alto CA 94304		R	32*	.1
946	TIES—*Betty Schweizer*	1667 Snelling Ave N, Saint Paul MN 55108	651-999-6000	R	32*	.1
947	Topics Entertainment Inc—*Greg James*	3401 Lind Ave SW, Renton WA 98055	425-656-3621	R	32*	<.1
948	Lincoln Data—*Cliff Hackney*	10003 N Division St St, Spokane WA 99218	509-466-1744	R	32*	<.1
949	Wolfram Research Inc—*Stephen Wolfram*	100 Trade Ctr Dr, Champaign IL 61820	217-398-0700	R	31*	.2
950	Advanced Internet Technologies Inc—*Clarence Briggs III*	PO Box 404798, Atlanta GA 30384	910-321-1300	R	31*	.2
951	Cardiff Software Inc—*Dennis Clerke*	3220 Executive Ridge D, Vista CA 92081	760-936-4500	S	31*	.2
952	ASA International Ltd Business Systems Div—*Alfred Angelone*	10 Speen St, Framingham MA 01701	508-626-2727	D	31*	.1
953	NetMotion Wireless Inc—*Bob Hunsberger*	701 N 34th St Ste 250, Seattle WA 98103	206-691-5500	R	31*	.1
954	Reuters Information Technology LLC—*John Stingelin*	1111 W 22nd St Ste 500, Oak Brook IL 60523	630-574-7424	S	31*	.1
955	Teklynx International—*Kevin Hayes*	PO Box 1786, Milwaukee WI 53201	414-228-3335	R	31*	.1
956	BCC Software Inc—*Chris Lien*	75 Josons Dr, Rochester NY 14623	585-272-9130	S	31*	.1
957	Financial Neural Computing—*William B Rayburn*	1214 Office Park Dr, Oxford MS 38655	662-236-2020	R	31*	.1
958	Medio Systems Inc—*Robert P Lilleness*	701 Pike St 15th Fl, Seattle WA 98101	206-262-3700	R	31*	.1
959	Mercury Media Holdings—*John Barnes*	520 Broadway Ste 400, Santa Monica CA 90401	310-451-2900	R	31*	.1
960	ScheduAll Software—*Joel Ledlow*	2719 Hollywood Blvd, Hollywood FL 33020	954-334-5400	R	31*	.1
961	SeaSolve Software Incorporated—*Mehraj Lanker*	1798 Technology Dr Ste, San Jose CA 95110	408-437-9306	R	31*	.1
962	System Dynamics International Inc—*Lisa Williams*	560 Discovery Dr, Huntsville AL 35806	256-895-9000	R	31*	.1
963	Tri-Pacific Software Inc—*Peter Kortmann*	909 Marina Village Pky, Alameda CA 94501	510-814-1770	R	31*	.1
964	Autonomy Inc—*Michael Lynch*	1 Market Plz Ste 1900, San Francisco CA 94105	415-243-9955	S	31*	.1
965	Health Language Inc—*George T Schwend*	4600 S Syracuse St Ste, Denver CO 80237	720-940-2900	R	31*	.1
966	EMC Documentum Inc—*Joseph M Tucci*	6801 Koll Center Pky, Pleasanton CA 94566	925-600-6800	D	31	.1
967	IronPort—*John Chamberlin*	950 Elm Ave, San Bruno CA 94066	650-989-6500	R	30*	.5
968	First DataBank Inc—*Gregory Dorn*	701 Gateway Blvd Ste 6, South San Francisco CA 94080	650-588-5454	S	30*	.2
969	Advanced Solutions International Inc—*Bob Alves*	901 N Pitt St Ste 200, Alexandria VA 22314	703-739-3100	R	30*	.2
970	eRoom Technology Inc—*Joseph M Tucci* EMC Documentum Inc	176 South St, Hopkinton MA 01748	508-435-1000	S	30	.1
971	Spotfire Inc—*Rock Gnatovich* TIBCO Software Inc	212 Elm St, Somerville MA 02144	617-702-1600	S	30*	.2

Note: An asterisk (*) indicates an estimated financial figure. The company type code used is as follows: R = Private, P = Public, S = Private Subsidiary, B = Public Subsidiary, D = Division, J = Joint Venture, I = Investment Fund.

COMPANY RANKINGS BY SALES WITHIN 4-DIGIT SIC

Rank	Company Name—*Executive Officer*	Address, City, State, Zip	Phone	Type	Fin	Empls
972	Synacor Inc—*Ron Frankel*	40 La Riviere Dr Ste 3, Buffalo NY 14202	716-853-1362	R	30*	.2
973	Delmia Corp—*Phillippe Charles*	900 N Squirrel Rd, Auburn Hills MI 48326	248-267-9696	S	30*	.2
974	MODCOMP Inc—*Victor Dellovo*	1500 S Powerline Rd, Hernando FL 34442	954-571-4600	S	30*	.2
975	Aonix Corp—*Nicolas Hadjidakis*	5930 Cornerstone Crt W, San Diego CA 92121	858-457-2700	S	30*	.1
976	Arcot Systems Inc—*Ram Varadarajan*	455 W Maude Ave, Sunnyvale CA 94085	408-969-6100	R	30*	.1
977	Conversational Computing Corp—*Stephen A Rondel*	15375 NE 90th St, Redmond WA 98052	425-895-1800	R	30*	.1
978	Magix Entertainment Corp—*Juergen Jaron*	1105 Terminal Way #202, Reno NV 89502	905-470-0400	R	30*	.1
979	Mitratech Holdings Inc—*Afshin Behnia*	5900 Wilshire Blvd Ste, Los Angeles CA 90036	323-900-1700	R	30*	.1
980	Centric Software Inc—*Chris Groves*	655 Campbell Technolog, Campbell CA 95008	408-574-7802	R	30*	.1
981	George Davidson and Son	55 Broad St 26th Fl, New York NY 10004	212-208-0100	R	30*	.1
982	Kickapps Corp—*Alex Blum*	26 W 17th St 2nd Fl, New York NY 10011	212-730-4558	R	30*	.1
983	Software Technology Inc (Mobile Alabama)—*Ruby McCullough*	307 University Blvd N, Mobile AL 36688	251-639-1851	R	30*	.1
984	Automated Trading Desk LLC—*Jeff Martin*	11 eWall St, Mount Pleasant SC 29464	843-789-2000	S	30*	.1
985	Celerant Technology Corp—*Ian Goldman*	4830 Arthur Kill Rd, Staten Island NY 10309	718-605-7733	R	30*	.1
986	Contactual Inc—*Chris Brennan*	1000 Bridge Pkwy Ste 2, Redwood City CA 94065		R	30*	.1
987	IMN Inc—*David A Fish*	200 5th Ave, Waltham MA 02451	781-672-7000	R	30*	.1
988	Tideworks Technology Inc—*Mike Schwank*	PO Box 24205, Seattle WA 98124	206-382-4470	S	30*	.1
989	Cymfony Inc—*Richard Pasewark*	501 Boylston St, Boston MA 02116	617-912-2828	D	30*	.1
990	TempWorks Software Inc—*Gregg Dourgarian*	3140 Neil Armstrong Bl, Eagan MN 55121	651-452-0366	R	30*	.1
991	Optiant Inc—*J Micheal Edenfield*	8 New England Executiv, Burlington MA 01803	781-238-8855	R	30*	<.1
992	Activeworlds Inc—*Rick Noll*	95 Parker St, Newburyport MA 01950	978-499-0222	R	30*	<.1
993	Auralog SA—*Nagi Sioufi*	3710 E University Dr S, Phoenix AZ 85034	602-470-0311	R	30*	<.1
994	Edge Technologies Inc—*Gary Hughes*	7350 Cirque Dr W Ste 1, University Place WA 98467		R	30*	<.1
995	OneSource Software Solutions—*Steve Childs*	10150 S Centennial Pky, Sandy UT 84070	801-748-4804	R	30*	<.1
996	Ellis Enterprises Inc—*John W Ellis*	5100 N Brookline Ave S, Oklahoma City OK 73112	405-948-1766	R	30*	<.1
997	TEdec System Inc—*Teddar Brooks*	207 Court St, Little Valley NY 14755	716-938-9133	R	30*	<.1
998	Wayne McCall and Associates—*Michael R McCall*	281 Oak Rd, Santa Barbara CA 93108	805-969-3153	R	30*	<.1
999	Vision Solutions Inc (Irvine California)—*Nicolaas Vlok*	17911 Von Karman Ave 5, Irvine CA 92614		R	30	.2
1000	Keyware Technologies Inc—*Stephane Vandervelde*	500 W Cummings Park St, Woburn MA 01801	781-933-1311	R	29*	.3
1001	ExperExchange Inc—*QR Wang*	46751 Fremont Blvd, Fremont CA 94538	510-623-7071	R	29*	.2
1002	Appian Corp (Vienna Virginia)—*Matthew W Calkins*	1875 Explorer St 4th F, Reston VA 20190	703-442-8844	R	29*	.2
1003	A La Mode Inc—*Brenda Huffman*	3705 W Memorial Bldg 4, Oklahoma City OK 73134		R	29*	.1
1004	Meridium Inc—*Bonz Hart*	10 S Jefferson St 11th, Roanoke VA 24011	540-344-9205	R	29*	.1
1005	fusionOne Inc—*Mike Mulica*	55 Almaden Blvd Fl 5, San Jose CA 95113	408-282-1200	R	29*	.1
1006	Guidewire Software Inc—*John Raguin*	2211 Bridgepointe Pkwy, San Mateo CA 94404	650-357-9100	R	29*	.1
1007	Syclo LLC—*Richard Padula*	1721 Moon Lake Blvd St, Hoffman Estates IL 60169	847-230-3800	R	29*	.1
1008	Avatier Corp—*Nelson Cicchitto*	PO Box 719, San Ramon CA 94583	925-217-5170	R	29*	.1
1009	Peer Media Technologies—*Dimitri Villard*	9046 Lindblade St, Culver City CA 90232	310-956-3300	S	29*	.1
1010	ACE Software Solutions Inc—*Parth Desai*	33 Wood Ave S Ste 600, Iselin NJ 08830	732-603-4997	R	29*	.1
1011	Creaxion Corp—*Mark Pettit*	619 Edgewood Ave SE St, Atlanta GA 30312	404-321-4322	R	29*	<.1
1012	Rocksteady Networks LLC—*Robert Hughes*	PO Box 66068, Austin TX 78766	512-427-1300	R	29*	<.1
1013	Simunet Corp—*Kevin O'Rourke*	PO Box 7289, Alhambra CA 91802	626-688-4565	R	29*	<.1
1014	SIMS Software—*Jim Conrad*	PO Box 607, Solana Beach CA 92075	858-481-9292	R	29*	<.1
1015	Cast Software Inc—*Vincent Delaroche*	373 Park Ave S 5th Fl, New York NY 10016	212-871-8330	R	29*	.2
1016	VASCO Data Security Inc—*T Kendall Hunt*	1901 S Meyers Rd Ste 2, Oakbrook Terrace IL 60181	630-932-8844	S	28	.2
1017	Research Design Resources Inc—*Cal Sasai*	5900 Trinity Pky Ste 3, Centreville VA 20120	703-266-4000	R	28*	.2
1018	Vexcel Corp Microsoft Corp	5775 Flatirons Pky Ste, Boulder CO 80301	303-415-6000	S	28*	.2
1019	Help/Systems Inc—*Janet Dryer*	6533 Flying Cloud Dr S, Eden Prairie MN 55344	952-933-0609	S	28*	.1
1020	ADAM Inc—*Robin Raina* Ebix Inc	10 10th St NE Ste 500, Atlanta GA 30309	404-604-2757	S	28*	.1
1021	Sanctum Inc—*Peggy Weigle*	2901 Tasman Dr Ste 205, Santa Clara CA 95054	408-855-9500	S	28*	.1
1022	Wily Technology Inc—*Dick Williams*	6000 Shoreline Ct, South San Francisco CA 94080	650-534-9400	D	28*	.1
1023	EDI-Health Group Inc—*Ali H Zadeh*	17701 Cowan Ste 250, Irvine CA 92614		R	28*	.1
1024	Powered Inc—*Ken Nicolson*	206 E 9th St 14th Fl, Austin TX 78701	512-682-3200	R	28*	.1
1025	C Management Solutions for Government—*Craig Ross*	424 S Woods Mill Rd St, Chesterfield MO 63017	314-275-8877	D	28*	.1
1026	Townsend Analytics Ltd—*Stuart Breslow*	100 S Wacker Dr 20th F, Chicago IL 60606	312-621-0141	R	28*	.1
1027	Zenimax Media Inc—*Robert A Altman*	1370 Piccard Dr Ste 12, Rockville MD 20850	301-926-8300	R	28*	.1
1028	Aquire—*Lois Melbourne*	400 E Las Colinas Blvd, Irving TX 75039	214-574-5020	R	28*	.1
1029	Neverfail Inc—*Peter Parker*	3839 Bee Caves Rd Ste, Austin TX 78746	512-327-5777	R	28*	.1
1030	Jim Sloan Inc—*Jim Sloan*	2900 Westchester Ave, Purchase NY 10577	914-251-9494	R	28*	<.1
1031	Fleet-Net Corp—*Clive Newell*	9183 W Flamingo Rd Ste, Las Vegas NV 89147	702-873-2228	R	28*	<.1
1032	Mortgage Builder Software Inc—*Keven Smith*	24370 Northwestern Hwy, Southfield MI 48075	248-208-3223	R	28*	<.1
1033	PrintPoint Inc—*Morrie Brown*	57 Ludlow Ln, Palisades NY 10964	845-359-0298	R	28*	<.1
1034	OneCommand—*Al Babbington*	11500 Northlake Dr Ste, Cincinnati OH 45249		R	28	.2
1035	Gentia Software Inc—*Andy Youniss* Rocket Software Inc	275 Grove St Ste 3-410, Newton MA 02466	617-614-4321	S	27	.1
1036	SolutionsIQ Inc—*Charlie Rudd*	10785 Willows Rd NE St, Redmond WA 98052	425-451-2727	R	27*	.3
1037	Tom Snyder Productions Inc—*Richard Abrams*	100 Talcott Ave, Watertown MA 02472		S	27*	.2
1038	Applied Global Technologies—*Ben Atha*	5575 South US 1, Rockledge FL 32955	321-638-2007	R	27*	.1
1039	VFA Inc—*Jerry Kokos*	266 Summer St, Boston MA 02210	617-451-5100	R	27*	.1
1040	Digital Harbor—*Rohit Agarwal*	1851 Alexander Bell Dr, Reston VA 20191	703-476-7378	S	27*	.1
1041	Orchestria Corp—*Bo Manning*	437 Madison Ave, New York NY 10022	212-364-5300	R	27*	.1
1042	Provenir—*Larry Smith*	300 Interpace Pky Bldg, Parsippany NJ 07054	973-316-8680	R	27*	.1
1043	Black Duck Software Inc—*Tim Yeaton*	265 Winter St, Waltham MA 02451	781-891-5100	R	27*	.1
1044	Firaxis Games Inc—*Steve Martin* Take-Two Interactive Software Inc	11350 McCormick Rd Exe, Hunt Valley MD 21031		S	27*	.1
1045	Marshall and Swift/Boeckh—*Salil Donde*	350 S Grand Ave, Los Angeles CA 90071	213-683-9000	S	27*	.1
1046	Saratoga Systems Inc—*Peter Yip* CDC Software	910 Campisi Way Ste 2, Campbell CA 95008		S	27*	.1
1047	Myprint Corp—*Tom Baird*	2850 Red Hill Ave Ste, Santa Ana CA 92705	949-261-0333	S	27*	.1
1048	Scalable Software Inc—*Mark Cresswell*	14100 Southwest Frwy, Sugar Land TX 77478	713-316-4900	R	27*	.1
1049	Naverus Inc—*Steve Forte*	20415 72nd Ave S Ste 3, Kent WA 98032	253-867-3900	S	27*	.1
1050	nth Generation Computing Inc—*Jan Baldwin*	17055 Camino San Berna, San Diego CA 92127	858-451-2383	R	27*	.1
1051	Solutions by Computer Inc—*Jack Shea*	191 Chestnut St, Springfield MA 01103	413-737-0499	S	27*	.1
1052	Encore Software Inc—*Cal Morrell*	999 N Sepulveda Blvd S, El Segundo CA 90245	310-768-1800	S	27*	.1
1053	Mayflower Software Inc—*Frank Paolino*	44 Stoneymeade Way, Acton MA 01720	978-635-1700	R	27*	<.1
1054	Life Science Associates—*Jo Ann Mandriota*	1 Fenimore Rd, Bayport NY 11705	631-472-2111	R	27*	<.1
1055	i-Logix Inc—*Gene Robinson*	9401 Jeronimo Rd, Irvine CA 92618	949-830-8022	S	27	.1
1056	Eze Castle Software Inc—*Thomas P Gavin*	12 Farnsworth St 6th F, Boston MA 02210	617-316-1100	S	26*	.2

Rank	Company Name—*Executive Officer*	Address, City, State, Zip	Phone	Type	Fin	Empls
1057	Films Media Group of Cos—*Betsy Sherer*	132 W 31st St 17th Fl, New York NY 10001	609-671-1000	R	26*	.1
1058	Plex Systems Inc—*Mark Symonds*	1731 Harmon Rd, Auburn Hills MI 48326	248-391-8001	S	26	.1
1059	FieldCentrix Inc—*Zack B Bergreen* Astea International Inc	8 Hughes, Irvine CA 92618	949-784-5000	D	26*	.1
1060	MetraTech Corp—*Scott Swartz*	200 West St, Waltham MA 02451	781-839-8300	R	26*	.1
1061	Rocket Aldon—*Matt Scholl* Rocket Software Inc	6001 Shellmound St Ste, Emeryville CA 94608	510-839-3535	S	26*	.1
1062	Cedar Document Technologies Inc—*Pete Kenning*	1 Ravinia Dr Ste 200, Atlanta GA 30346	770-395-5000	R	26*	.1
1063	Ektron Inc—*William Rogers*	542 Amherst St, Nashua NH 03063	603-594-0249	R	26*	.1
1064	Media Shoppe Sdn Bhd—*Christopher Chan*	1310 Valley Reserve Dr, Kennesaw GA 30152	770-419-9321	S	26*	.1
1065	TestQuest Inc	18976 Lake Dr E, Chanhassen MN 55317	952-988-8285	S	26*	.1
1066	ForeScout Technologies Inc—*Gord Boyce*	10001 N De Anza Blvd, Cupertino CA 95014	408-213-3191	R	26*	.1
1067	Humedica—*Michael Weintraub*	1380 Soliders Field Rd, Boston MA 02135	617-475-3800	R	26*	.1
1068	Demandware Inc—*Thomas Ebling*	5 Wall St, Burlington MA 01803	781-425-1222	R	26*	.1
1069	Chronicle Guidance Publications Inc—*Cheryl Fickeisen*	66 Aurora St, Moravia NY 13118		R	26*	<.1
1070	Matrix Logic Corp—*Dan Graber*	1354 East Ave Ste R-24, Chico CA 95926	415-893-9897	R	26*	<.1
1071	Amicus Inc—*Marshall Huwe*	8500 Shoal Creek Blvd, Austin TX 78757	512-531-3480	R	26*	<.1
1072	House Industries Inc—*Rich Roat*	PO Box 166, Yorklyn DE 19736	302-234-2356	R	26*	<.1
1073	InterSearch Group Inc—*Dan ODonnell*	222 Kearny St Ste 550, San Francisco CA 94108	415-962-9795	D	26	<.1
1074	Halo Technology Holdings Inc—*Rodney Bienvenu Jr*	1 Landmark Sq Fl 5, Stamford CT 06901	203-391-7985	P	25	.2
1075	Sonic Foundry Inc—*Gary R Weis*	222 W Washington Ave, Madison WI 53703	608-443-1600	P	25	.1
1076	SunGard Employee Benefit Systems—*Russ Fradin*	600 E Swedesford Rd, Wayne PA 19087	205-437-7500	S	25*	.4
1077	3E Co—*Robert S Christie*	1905 Aston AveSte 100, Carlsbad CA 92008	760-602-8700	R	25*	.3
1078	CBORD Group Inc—*Tim Tighe*	61 Brown Rd, Ithaca NY 14850	607-257-2410	R	25*	.3
1079	Acta Technology Inc SAP Americas Inc	3999 W Chester Pike, Newtown Square PA 19073	610-661-1000	S	25	.2
1080	IPS-Sendero—*Dave Ulrich*	107 Technology Pkwy, Norcross GA 30092		S	25*	.2
1081	Unicru Inc—*Chris Marsh* Kronos Inc	9525 SW Gemini Dr, Beaverton OR 97008	503-596-3100	S	25*	.2
1082	Picis Inc (Wakefield Massachusetts)—*Todd Cozzens*	100 Quannapowitt Pkwy, Wakefield MA 01880	781-557-3000	R	25*	.2
1083	TMA Resources Inc—*Edi Dor*	1919 Gallows Rd Ste 40, Vienna VA 22182	703-564-5200	R	25*	.2
1084	PlanView Inc—*Patrick Durbin*	8300 N Mopac Ste 300, Austin TX 78759	512-346-8600	R	25	.1
1085	IMS System Company Ltd (New York New York)—*Wha Rim*	213 W 35th St Ste 903, New York NY 10001	212-568-5225	R	25	.1
1086	NextPage Inc—*Darren Lee*	13997 S Minuteman Dr, Draper UT 84020	801-748-4400	R	25*	.1
1087	Valve LLC—*Gabe Newell*	PO Box 1688, Bellevue WA 98009	425-889-9642	R	25*	.1
1088	D2K Inc—*Andrew Gonczi*	25 Ave at Port Imperia, West New York NJ 07093	732-476-5403	R	25*	.1
1089	FieldGlass Inc—*Jai Shekhawat*	125 S Wacker Dr Ste 24, Chicago IL 60606	312-279-8700	R	25*	.1
1090	Image Process Design—*Steven M Racine*	36800 Woodward Ave Ste, Bloomfield Hills MI 48304	248-723-9733	R	25*	.1
1091	InterCare DX Inc—*Anthony C Dike*	4477 W 118th St Ste 30, Hawthorne CA 90250		P	25*	.1
1092	IDP Companies Inc	490 Boston Post Rd, Sudbury MA 01776	978-218-5900	R	25*	.1
1093	BinaryTreecom—*Henry Bestritsky*	250 W 34th St 33rd Fl, New York NY 10119	212-244-3635	R	25*	.1
1094	Cogency Software Inc—*Jeffrey Axelrod*	500 Airport Blvd Ste 1, Burlingame CA 94010	650-685-2500	R	25*	.1
1095	ServerLogic Corp—*Terry Lelievre*	2800 Northup Way Ste 1, Bellevue WA 98004	425-803-0378	R	25*	.1
1096	LabWare Inc—*Vance Kershner*	3 Mill Rd Ste 102, Wilmington DE 19806	302-658-8444	R	25*	<.1
1097	Acess411—*William Morrison*	52 Grumbacher Rd, York PA 17406		R	25*	<.1
1098	Attention Software Inc—*Robert Luth*	2175 N Academy Cir Ste, Colorado Springs CO 80909	719-591-9110	R	25*	<.1
1099	Basic Software Systems—*Mike Holland*	905 N Kings Hwy, Texarkana TX 75501	903-792-4421	R	25*	<.1
1100	Data West Corp—*Richard Brown*	72 Suttle St Ste M, Durango CO 81303	970-259-2030	R	25*	<.1
1101	End2End Inc—*Allen Shumway*	6366 Commerce Blvd Ste, Rohnert Park CA 94928	662-513-0999	R	25*	<.1
1102	Engineering DataXpress Inc	5255 Stevens Creek Blv, Santa Clara CA 95051	408-243-8786	R	25*	<.1
1103	Facilities Technology Group—*Don Cooper*	1110 E 32nd St Bldg 2, Austin TX 78722	512-480-0883	R	25*	<.1
1104	IES Interactive Training Inc	1229 Oak Valley Dr, Ann Arbor MI 48108	303-956-7510	S	25*	<.1
1105	Mediafour Corp—*Brian Landwehr*	1854 Fuller Rd, West Des Moines IA 50265	515-225-7409	R	25*	<.1
1106	NETEC International Inc—*Gary W Goodwin*	PO Box 180549, Dallas TX 75218	214-343-9744	R	25*	<.1
1107	Scan/US Inc—*Ken Needham*	120 Stagecoach Rd, West Hills CA 91307	310-828-1450	R	25*	<.1
1108	SecureNet Technologies Inc—*John Fuller*	19105 36th Ave W Ste 2, Lynnwood WA 98036	425-776-2891	R	25*	<.1
1109	Superior Software Inc—*Neal Rimer*	16055 Ventura Blvd Ste, Encino CA 91436	818-990-1135	R	25*	<.1
1110	WizSoft Inc—*Abraham Meidan*	6800 Jericho Tpke Ste, Syosset NY 11791	516-393-5841	R	25*	<.1
1111	Zontec Inc—*Warren T Ha*	1389 Kemper Meadow Dr, Cincinnati OH 45240	513-648-9695	R	25*	<.1
1112	SXC Health Solutions Corp (Lisle Illinois)—*Mark Thierer*	2441 Warrenville Rd St, Lisle IL 60532	630-577-3100	S	24*	.2
1113	Liquent Inc—*Rick Riegel*	101 Gibralter Rd Ste 2, Horsham PA 19044	215-328-4444	S	24	.2
1114	Strohl Systems Group Inc—*Andrew A Stern*	631 Park Ave, King of Prussia PA 19406	610-768-4120	S	24*	.2
1115	MediaRingcom Inc—*Khaw Joo*	42840 Christy St Ste 1, Fremont CA 94538	510-683-9636	R	24	.1
1116	MICROS-Retail—*John E Gularson*	1800 West Park Dr, Westboro MA 01581	508-655-7500	R	24*	.1
1117	Open Systems Inc (Shakopee Minnesota)—*Michael Bertini*	4301 Dean Lakes Blvd, Shakopee MN 55379	952-403-5700	R	24*	.1
1118	Asynchrony Solutions Inc—*Bob Elfanbaum*	1701 Washington Ave St, Saint Louis MO 63103	314-678-2200	R	24*	.1
1119	Tavve Software Co—*Ken O Herron*	1 Copley Pky Ste 480, Morrisville NC 27560	919-460-1789	R	24*	.1
1120	Art and Logic Inc—*Paul Hershenson*	2 N Lake Ave Ste 1050, Pasadena CA 91101	815-500-1933	R	24	.1
1121	Baldwin Hackett and Meeks Inc—*Lynne J Baldwin*	11602 W Center Rd, Omaha NE 68144	402-333-3300	R	24*	.1
1122	Cyber-Ark Software Inc—*Udi Mokady*	57 Wells Ave Ste 20A, Newton MA 02459	617-965-1544	R	24	.1
1123	Eventra Inc	35 Nutmeg Dr Trumbull, Trumbull CT 06611		S	24*	.1
1124	IQ Software Services	137 N Larchmont Blvd S, Los Angeles CA 90004	323-735-7272	S	24*	.1
1125	SupplyPro Inc—*David J Simbari*	8572 Spectrum Ln, San Diego CA 92121	858-587-6400	R	24*	.1
1126	Truelink—*John Danaher*	100 Cross St Ste 202, San Luis Obispo CA 93401	805-782-8282	R	24*	.1
1127	AZMY Thinkware Inc—*Ashraf Azmy*	7000 E Guttenberg Blvd, Guttenberg NJ 07093	201-388-6550	R	24*	<.1
1128	BMT Micro Inc—*Thomas Bradford*	PO Box 15016, Wilmington NC 28408	910-792-9100	R	24*	<.1
1129	Coconut Info—*Simon Linford*	PO Box 75460, Honolulu HI 96836	808-947-6543	R	24*	<.1
1130	Compu-Teach Corp—*David Urban*	16541 Redmond Way Ste, Redmond WA 98052	425-885-0517	R	24*	<.1
1131	Computers and Structures Inc—*Ashraf Habibullah*	1995 University Ave St, Berkeley CA 94704	510-649-2200	R	24*	<.1
1132	Datacom International Inc—*Don Roepke*	5001 American BlvdW St, Bloomington MN 55437	952-835-1041	R	24*	<.1
1133	InSight Medical Management Systems Inc—*Eran Peery*	17337 Ventura Blvd Ste, Encino CA 91436		R	24*	<.1
1134	Lapcad Engineering	8305 Vickers Ste Ste 2, San Diego CA 92111	858-467-1947	R	24*	<.1
1135	MasterPlan Financial Software—*Mark Robinson*	476 Deodara St, Vacaville CA 95688	707-451-8985	R	24*	<.1
1136	MicroSECONDS International Inc—*J Larry Nederlof*	PO Box 980, Escondido CA 92033	760-294-1926	R	24*	<.1
1137	Money Tree Software—*Mark Vitkauskas*	2430 NW Professional W, Corvallis OR 97330		R	24*	<.1
1138	MTI Systems Inc—*Thomas Tharkiewicz*	59 Interstate Dr Ste 5, West Springfield MA 01089	413-733-1972	R	24*	<.1
1139	Optimum Resource Inc—*Richard Hefter*	1 Mathews Dr Ste 107, Hilton Head Island SC 29926	843-689-8000	R	24*	<.1
1140	printLEADER Software—*John Fleming*	4237 SW High Meadow Av, Palm City FL 34990		R	24*	<.1
1141	Stoltz Enterprises Inc—*James Stoltz*	PO Box 6118, Slidell LA 70469	985-781-1015	R	24*	<.1
1142	Future Systems Solutions Inc—*James Streater*	8888 Keystone Crossing, Indianapolis IN 46240	317-579-3100	R	24*	<.1

Note: An asterisk (*) indicates an estimated financial figure. The company type code used is as follows: R = Private, P = Public, S = Private Subsidiary, B = Public Subsidiary, D = Division, J = Joint Venture, I = Investment Fund.

COMPANY RANKINGS BY SALES WITHIN 4-DIGIT SIC

Rank	Company Name—Executive Officer	Address, City, State, Zip	Phone	Type	Fin	Empls
1143	Trilobyte Software Systems—Jerry Draper	11 Sacramento Ave, San Anselmo CA 94960	415-457-3431	R	24*	<.1
1144	Sendmail Inc—Donald J Massaro	6475 Christie Ave Ste, Emeryville CA 94608	510-594-5400	R	23*	.2
1145	Sonic Software Corp Progress Software Corp	14 Oak Park, Bedford MA 01730	781-999-7000	S	23*	.2
1146	Authoria Inc—James J McDevitt	300 Fifth Ave, Waltham MA 02451	781-530-2000	R	23*	.1
1147	PI Technology—Malcolm P Burke	47023 W Five Mile Rd, Plymouth MI 48170	734-656-0140	R	23*	.1
1148	DRB Systems Inc—Dale Brott	PO Box 550, Uniontown OH 44685		R	23*	.1
1149	FarStone Technology Inc—Thomas Lin	350 S Hope Ave Rm A, Santa Barbara CA 93105		R	23*	.1
1150	Trapeze Networks—Kevin Johnson	1194 N Mathilda Ave, Sunnyvale CA 94089	925-474-2200	R	23*	.1
1151	Financial Software Systems—Gerald H Thurston	240 Gibralter Rd Ste 2, Horsham PA 19044	215-784-1100	R	23*	.1
1152	Max Group Corp—Johnny Tsai	17011 Green Dr, City of Industry CA 91745	626-935-0050	R	23*	.1
1153	Epic Games Inc—Michael Capps	620 Crossroads Blvd, Cary NC 27511	919-854-0070	R	23*	.1
1154	HOMISCO/VoiceNet—Ronald Contrado	99 Washington St, Melrose MA 02176	781-665-1997	R	23*	.1
1155	TaxStream—Roy M Martin	121 River St, Hoboken NJ 07030	201-610-1211	S	23*	.1
1156	Lightspeed Trading LLC—Stephen Ehrlich	148 Madison Ave 9th Fl, New York NY 10016	646-393-4800	R	23*	.1
1157	Medical Artificial Intelligence—Steve Epstein	4901 Vineland Rd Ste 4, Orlando FL 32811	321-281-4480	R	23*	.1
1158	Oatsystems Inc—Michael G George	309 Waverley Oaks Rd S, Waltham MA 02452	781-907-6100	R	23*	.1
1159	Visto Corp—King R Lee	101 Redwood Shores Pky, Redwood City CA 94065	650-486-6000	R	23*	.1
1160	Nihilistic Software Inc—Robert Huebner	5 Hamilton Landing Han, Novato CA 94949	415-883-8690	R	23*	.1
1161	QPR Software Inc (Alameda California)—Jari Jaakkola	1150 Ballena Blvd Ste, Alameda CA 94501	510-931-6477	S	23*	.1
1162	Potomac Fusion Inc—Russ Richardson	14130 Sullyfield Cir S, Chantilly VA 20151	703-378-6031	R	23*	.1
1163	Radixx Solutions International Inc—Ronald Peri	6310 Hazeltine Nationa, Orlando FL 32822	407-856-9009	R	23*	.1
1164	ComAxis Technology—Fred Krefetz	2318 Second Ave, Seattle WA 98121	206-842-4869	R	23*	<.1
1165	RockySoft Corp—Larry Watson	736 Whalers Way Ste F-, Fort Collins CO 80525	970-493-0868	R	23*	<.1
1166	Jagged Peak Inc—Paul Demirdjian	3000 Bayport Dr Ste 25, Tampa FL 33607	813-637-6900	P	22	.1
1167	Inova Technology Inc—Adam Radly	2300 W Sahara Ave Ste, Las Vegas NV 89102		P	22	N/A
1168	ArborText Inc—Ray Schiavone Parametric Technology Corp	1000 Victors Way, Ann Arbor MI 48108	734-997-0200	S	22*	1.8
1169	Ramco Systems Corp—P R Venketrama Raja	3150 Brunswick Pike St, Lawrenceville NJ 08648	609-620-4800	S	22*	1.3
1170	ArcSoft Inc—Michael Deng	46601 Fremont Blvd, Fremont CA 94538	510-440-9901	R	22*	.4
1171	HighJump Software Inc—Russell Fleischer	6455 City W Pkwy, Eden Prairie MN 55344	952-947-4088	S	22*	.2
1172	Compulink Management Center Inc—Nien-Lieng Wacker	1205 Gandy Blvd N, St Petersburg FL 33702	727-579-1500	R	22*	.2
1173	CambridgeSoft Corp—Michael G Tomasic	100 CambridgePark Dr, Cambridge MA 02140	617-588-9100	R	22*	.2
1174	Collaborative Consulting—William C Robichaud Sr	70 Blanchard Road Ste, Burlington MA 01803	781-565-2600	R	22*	.2
1175	Formtek Inc—Gary P Mann	1855 Gateway Blvd Ste, Concord CA 94520	925-459-0482	R	22*	.2
1176	EMC Captiva—Joseph M Tucci Captiva Software Corp	25 Metro Dr Ste 400, San Jose CA 95110	408-441-2200	D	22*	.1
1177	Miner and Miner Consulting Engineers—Jeff Meyers	4701 Royal Vista Cir, Fort Collins CO 80528	970-223-1888	S	22*	.1
1178	Advanced Data Exchange—Dave Parker	2201 Walnut Ave Ste 11, Fremont CA 94538	510-896-2200	S	22*	.1
1179	Air2Web Inc—Tom Cotney	1230 Peachtree St NE F, Atlanta GA 30309	404-942-5300	R	22*	.1
1180	WorkDynamics Technologies Inc—Grant Bifolchi	620 Herndon Pkwy Ste 2, Herndon VA 20170	703-481-9874	R	22*	.1
1181	Stratify Inc—Ramana Venkata	501 Ellis St, Mountain View CA 94043	650-988-2000	S	22*	.1
1182	Backsoft Corp—Berthold Kastel	2850 Red Hill Ave Ste, Santa Ana CA 92705	949-296-8375	S	22*	.1
1183	Manufacturing and Consulting Services Inc—Patrick Hanratty	PO Box 250, Cave Creek AZ 85327	480-991-8700	R	22*	.1
1184	Aptima Inc—Daniel Serfaty	12 Gill St Ste 1400, Woburn MA 01801	781-935-3966	R	22*	.1
1185	BlueRoads Corp	1825 S Grant St, San Mateo CA 94402	650-349-8500	S	22*	.1
1186	Doozer Software Inc—Sandy Syx	2 Chase Corporate Dr S, Birmingham AL 35244	205-413-8302	R	22*	.1
1187	Green Beacon Solutions LLC—Benjamin Holtz	255 Washington St Ste, Newton MA 02458	617-485-5000	R	22*	.1
1188	Naviant—Dan Nordloh	201 Prairie Heights Dr, Verona WI 53593	608-848-0900	R	22*	.1
1189	Software Solutions Inc (Lebanon Ohio)—Terry Moore	420 E Main St, Lebanon OH 45036		R	22*	.1
1190	Zendesk Inc—Mikkel Svane	410 Townsend St, San Francisco CA 94107	415-418-7506	R	22*	.1
1191	Dynamic Information Systems Corp—Jeff McGlynn	2585 Central Ave, Boulder CO 80301	303-444-4000	R	22*	.1
1192	Grossman and Associates Inc—Robert M Grossman	710 N Neil St, Champaign IL 61820	217-398-1978	R	22*	.1
1193	Progeni Corp—Norman Praed	3237 Satellite Blvd Bl, Duluth GA 30096	770-840-7550	R	22*	.1
1194	Suzy Systems Inc	477 Main St, Hackensack NJ 07601	201-489-5888	R	22*	.1
1195	Agri-Data Systems Inc—William Holder	1831 Forest Dr Ste H, Annapolis MD 21401	410-267-5540	R	22*	<.1
1196	Astea International Inc—Zack B Bergreen	240 Gibraltar Rd, Horsham PA 19044	215-682-2500	P	21	.2
1197	Merced Systems Inc—Matthew Glickman	333 Twin Dolphin Dr St, Redwood City CA 94065	650-486-4000	R	21*	.2
1198	Creative Socio-Medics Corp	3500 Sunrise Hwy Ste D, Great River NY 11739	631-968-2000	S	21	N/A
1199	Touchpaper—Graham Ridgway	440 9th Ave 8th Fl, New York NY 10001	646-205-3400	R	21*	.2
1200	ACS Government Systems Inc—Will Saunders	1733 Harrodsburg Rd, Lexington KY 40504	859-277-1500	S	21*	.2
1201	SolidWorks Corp—Jeff Ray	300 Baker Ave, Concord MA 01742		S	21	.2
1202	Computers Unlimited Inc (Billings Montana)—David Schaer	2407 Montana Ave, Billings MT 59101	406-255-9500	R	21*	.2
1203	Open Solutions FiTECH Systems—Michael Evans Open Solutions Inc	3098 Piedmont Rd Ste 2, Atlanta GA 30305	404-262-2298	S	21*	.2
1204	CORPTAX LLC—Dave Shea	1751 Lake Cook Rd Ste, Deerfield IL 60015		S	21*	.2
1205	CSC Group Holding Co—William F Zimmerman	17999 Foltz Pky, Strongsville OH 44149	440-546-4272	R	21*	.2
1206	TECSYS US Inc—Peter Brereton	1515 E Woodfield Rd St, Schaumburg IL 60173	847-969-8800	S	21*	.2
1207	Data Pro Accounting Software Inc	111 2nd Ave NE Rm 1200, Saint Petersburg FL 33701	727-803-1500	R	21*	.1
1208	FileTek Inc—William P Loomis	9400 Key West Ave, Rockville MD 20850	301-251-0600	R	21	.1
1209	Camstar Systems Inc—Scott Toney	2815 Coliseum Centre D, Charlotte NC 28217	704-227-6600	R	21*	.1
1210	McCabe and Associates Inc—David Belhumeur	41 Sharpe Dr, Cranston RI 02920	401-572-3100	R	21*	.1
1211	SOFTRAX Corp—Robert O'Connor	45 Shawmut Rd 3rd Fl, Canton MA 02021	972-715-4040	R	21	.1
1212	Systems and Software Consortium—Mark Schuler	11480 Commerce Park Dr, Reston VA 20191	703-896-4360	R	21*	.1
1213	Ecora Corp—Atanas Popov	6011 W Courtyard Dr St, Austin TX 78730	603-287-4130	R	21*	.1
1214	iPhrase Technologies Inc—Dan Keshian	36 Crosby Dr, Bedford MA 01730	781-533-7300	S	21*	.1
1215	Lumigent Technologies Inc—John Capobianco	289 Great Rd, Acton MA 01720	978-206-3700	R	21*	.1
1216	Audience Science—Jeff Pullen	420 Lexington Ave Ste, New York NY 10170	646-443-2310	R	21*	.1
1217	Real D Scientifics—Michael Lewis	100 N Crescent Dr Ste, Beverly Hills CA 90210	310-385-4000	R	21*	.1
1218	Ecast Inc—John Taylor	49 Geary St Mezzanine, San Francisco CA 94108	415-277-3500	R	21*	.1
1219	Solbright Inc—Michael Leo Operative Inc	40 W 25th St10th Fl, New York NY 10010	212-994-8930	S	21*	.1
1220	QuickArrow Inc—Kevin Bury NetSuite Inc	11675 Jollyville Rd St, Austin TX 78759	512-381-0600	S	21*	.1
1221	RainMaker Software Inc—James Hammond	1777 Sentry Pkwy W, Blue Bell PA 19422		D	21*	.1
1222	GovDelivery Inc—Scott Burns	408 St Peter St Ste 60, Saint Paul MN 55102		R	21*	.1
1223	Click4Care Inc—Rob Gillette	50 S Liberty St Ste 20, Powell OH 43065	614-431-3700	R	21*	.1
1224	Dekker Ltd—Simon Dekker	3633 E Inland Empire B, Ontario CA 91764	909-384-9000	R	21*	.1
1225	iTok LLC—Seth Bailey	3400 N Ashton Blvd Ste, Lehi UT 84043		S	21*	.1
1226	J River Inc—James Hillegass	125 N First St, Minneapolis MN 55401	612-677-8200	R	21*	.1

Rank	Company Name—*Executive Officer*	Address, City, State, Zip	Phone	Type	Fin	Empls
1227	Lsoft International Inc—*Eric Thomas*	8100 Corporate Dr Ste, Landover MD 20785	301-731-0440	R	21*	.1
1228	Mercom Systems Inc—*Avi Margolin*	9 Polito Ave, Lyndhurst NJ 07071	201-507-8800	S	21*	.1
1229	NexTec Group Inc—*Eric Frank*	1111 N Loop West Rm 81, Houston TX 77008	713-957-8350	R	21*	.1
1230	Viaserv Inc—*Kim Manchak*	550 NW Franklin Ave St, Bend OR 97701	303-482-1837	R	21*	.1
1231	CWC Software Inc—*Jeffrey Bean*	150 Grossman Dr, Braintree MA 02184	781-843-2010	R	21*	<.1
1232	Against All Odds Productions—*Rick Smolan*	PO Box 1189, Sausalito CA 94966	415-331-6300	R	21*	<.1
1233	Axiom Technology Inc (Madison Alabama)—*Michael Mayer*	115 Murry Dr, Madison AL 35758	256-722-0015	R	21*	<.1
1234	Inbit Inc—*Jin Wang*	1340 S De Anza Blvd, San Jose CA 95129	408-777-9700	R	21*	<.1
1235	ACS Technologies—*Tom Rogers*	180 Dunbarton Dr, Florence SC 29501	843-679-4900	R	20*	.3
1236	ECRI Institute—*Jeffrey C Lerner*	5200 Butler Pke, Plymouth Meeting PA 19462	610-825-6000	R	20*	.3
1237	SunGard iWorks LLC—*Harold Finders*	11560 Great Oaks Way S, Alpharetta GA 30022	770-587-6800	S	20*	.3
1238	E*Trade Business Solutions Group Inc—*Mitchell Caplan*	135 E 57th St, New York NY 10022	646-521-4300	S	20*	.2
1239	PB Farradyne Inc—*Manuel Ortega*	3206 Tower Oaks Blvd, Rockville MD 20852	301-468-5568	S	20*	.2
1240	TRISYS TELECOM Inc—*Michael Shevelev*	215 Ridgedale Ave, Florham Park NJ 07932	973-360-2300	R	20*	.2
1241	Gauss Interprise USA—*Tom Jenkins*	8717 Research Dr, Irvine CA 92618	949-784-8000	S	20*	.2
1242	Tallan Inc—*Craig Branning*	175 Capital Blvd Ste 4, Rocky Hill CT 06067	860-677-3693	R	20*	.2
1243	Metrix Inc—*Larry Laux*	20975 Swenson Dr, Waukesha WI 53186	262-717-6500	R	20*	.2
1244	Financial Profiles Inc—*Mark Evans*	5421 Avenida Encinas, Carlsbad CA 92008	760-431-9400	R	20*	.1
1245	Ipswitch Inc—*Roger Greene*	83 Hartwell Ave, Lexington MA 02421	781-676-5700	R	20*	.1
1246	CSSC Inc—*Wayne Bordone*	30 Mayfield Ave, Edison NJ 08837	732-225-5555	R	20*	.1
1247	Maxis Electronic Arts Inc	5980 Horton St, Emeryville CA 94608	510-428-4600	D	20	.1
1248	St Bernard Software Inc—*Vince Rossi*	15015 Ave of Science, San Diego CA 92128	858-676-2277	R	20*	.1
1249	Artwork Systems—*Mark Quinlan*	219A Rittenhouse Cir, Bristol PA 19007	215-826-4500	S	20*	.1
1250	HelpSTARcom Inc—*Igal Hauer*	1328 N Ferdon Blvd Ste, Crestview FL 32536	905-829-3405	R	20*	.1
1251	Satmetrix Systems Inc—*Richard Owen*	2755 Campus Dr Ste 300, San Mateo CA 94403	650-227-8300	R	20*	.1
1252	Cape Clear Software Inc—*Dave Duffield* Workday Inc	880 Winter St Ste 300, Waltham MA 02451	781-622-2258	S	20*	.1
1253	Vaultus Mobile Technologies Inc—*James Hemmer* Antenna Software Inc	263 Summer St, Boston MA 02210	617-338-9849	S	20*	.1
1254	Vindigo Inc—*Scott Jensen*	500 7th Ave, New York NY 10018	212-590-0500	R	20*	.1
1255	IP Commerce Inc—*Alfred Kahn IV*	1400 16th St Ste 220, Denver CO 80202	720-377-3700	R	20*	.1
1256	Arxan Technologies Inc—*Michael Dager*	6903 Rockledge Dr Ste, Bethesda MD 20817	301-968-4290	R	20*	.1
1257	Avilar Technologies Inc—*Thomas Grobicki*	6760 Alexander Bell Dr, Columbia MD 21046	410-290-0008	R	20*	.1
1258	CBT Direct	905 E Martin Luther Ki, Tarpon Springs FL 34689		D	20*	.1
1259	Convergent Software Systems Inc—*Trevor X Pereira*	2341 Jeffers, Carlsbad CA 92008	760-602-9414	R	20*	.1
1260	CORESense Inc—*Chris Martin*	125 High Rock Ave, Saratoga Springs NY 12866	518-306-3043	R	20*	.1
1261	CSI Software Inc—*Jonathan Ross*	3333 Richmond 2nd Fl, Houston TX 77098	713-942-7779	R	20*	.1
1262	CygnaCom Solutions Inc—*Santosh Chokhani*	7925 Jones Branch Dr, McLean VA 22102	703-848-0883	S	20*	.1
1263	Global Software Resources Inc—*Prem Hinduja*	4447 Stoneridge Dr, Pleasanton CA 94588	925-249-2200	R	20*	.1
1264	Intelliworks Inc—*Todd Gibby*	7315 Wisconsin Ave Ste, Bethesda MD 20814	240-238-3210	R	20*	.1
1265	IQMS—*Randy Flamm*	2231 Wisteria Ln, Paso Robles CA 93446	805-227-1122	R	20*	.1
1266	Laszlo Systems Inc—*George Shahid*	2600 Campus Dr Ste 200, San Mateo CA 94403	650-358-2700	R	20*	.1
1267	Legrand Software Inc—*Alain Legrand*	242 E Airport Dr, San Bernardino CA 92408		S	20*	.1
1268	Managing Editor Inc—*Dennis McGuire*	610 Old York Rd Ste 25, Jenkintown PA 19046	215-886-5662	R	20*	.1
1269	MAQ Software—*Rajeev Agarwal*	15446 Bel-Red Rd Ste 1, Redmond WA 98052	425-526-5399	R	20*	.1
1270	NDS Systems LC—*Don Voeikert*	4700 140th Ave N Ste 1, Clearwater FL 33762	727-538-2250	R	20*	.1
1271	NEC Sphere Communications Inc—*Graeme Robinson*	300 Tri-State Internat, Lincolnshire IL 60069	847-793-9600	R	20*	.1
1272	Net Optics Inc—*Bob Shaw*	5303 Betsy Ross Dr, Santa Clara CA 95054	408-737-7777	R	20*	.1
1273	PanGo Networks Inc—*Ed Cantwell*	959 Concord St Ste 100, Framingham MA 01701	508-626-8900	S	20*	.1
1274	TelStar Associates Inc—*Jose M Tellaria Jr*	901 Pier View Dr Ste 2, Idaho Falls ID 83402	208-343-3894	R	20*	.1
1275	Tradition Software Inc—*Craig Altman*	8860 Industrial Ave, Roseville CA 95678	916-724-5990	R	20*	.1
1276	Trubiquity—*Stephen Koons*	5480 Corp Drive, Troy MI 48098	248-833-9000	S	20*	.1
1277	Vikmere Software Inc—*Varun Bamba*	3723 Watseka Ave Ste 7, Los Angeles CA 90034	310-836-2802	R	20*	.1
1278	Worden Brothers Inc—*Chris Worden*	Five Oaks Office Pk 49, Durham NC 27707	919-408-0542	R	20*	.1
1279	zipLogix—*Joel Singer*	PO BOX 130, Fraser MI 48026		S	20*	.1
1280	Cernium Corp—*Craig Chambers*	1925 Isaac Newton Sq 3, Reston VA 20190		R	20*	<.1
1281	Aatrix Software Inc—*Steve Lunseth*	2100 Library Cir, Grand Forks ND 58201	701-746-6017	R	20*	<.1
1282	Digital Matrix Systems Inc—*David McGough*	15301 Spectrum Dr 2nd, Addison TX 75001	972-341-0000	R	20*	<.1
1283	MSDSpro LLC—*Ali Zaarour*	1300 E 68th Ave Ste 20, Anchorage AK 99518	907-272-6635	R	20*	<.1
1284	Midrange Software Inc—*Jacques Ohana*	12716 Riverside Dr, Studio City CA 91607	818-762-8539	R	20*	<.1
1285	Cybersoft Co—*Peter V Radatti*	1958 Butler Pike Rm 10, Conshohocken PA 19428	610-825-4748	R	20*	<.1
1286	Disaster Recovery Services Inc—*Steven King*	10336 Southern Loop Bl, Pineville NC 28134	704-525-0096	R	20*	<.1
1287	Tally Systems Corp—*Ted Jastrzembski* Novell Inc	404 Wyman St, Waltham MA 02451	603-643-1300	S	19*	.2
1288	Apriso Corp—*Jim Henderson*	301 E Ocean Blvd Ste 1, Long Beach CA 90802	562-951-8000	R	19*	.2
1289	Dealer Information Systems Corp—*Bob Brim*	1315 Cornwall Ave, Bellingham WA 98225	360-733-7610	R	19*	.2
1290	TMW Systems Inc—*David W Wangler*	21111 Chagrin Blvd, Beachwood OH 44122	216-831-6606	R	19*	.2
1291	ICIMS Inc—*Colin Day*	Concord Ctr Bldg 1 130, Hazlet NJ 07730	732-847-1941	R	19*	.1
1292	Universal Software Corp—*Kishore Deshpande*	20 Industrial Park Dr, Nashua NH 03062	603-689-2600	R	19*	.1
1293	CD Group Inc—*Larry Campbell*	5550 Triangle Pky Ste, Norcross GA 30092	678-225-2600	R	19*	.1
1294	Noetix Corp—*Morris Beton*	5010 148th Ave NE Ste, Redmond WA 98052	425-372-2699	R	19*	.1
1295	Multisystems Inc—*Brian Larson*	10 Fawcett, Cambridge MA 02138	787-751-2720	R	19*	.1
1296	Link Computer Corp—*Tim Link*	PO Box 250, Bellwood PA 16617	814-742-7700	R	19*	.1
1297	Rapt Inc—*Tom Chavez*	625 2nd St 2nd Fl, San Francisco CA 94107	415-932-2700	R	19*	.1
1298	Lancope Inc—*Mike Potts*	3650 Brookside Pkwy St, Alpharetta GA 30022	770-225-6500	R	19*	.1
1299	DB Consultants Inc—*Don Biresch*	1642 N West End Blvd, Quakertown PA 18951	215-536-6066	R	19*	.1
1300	HumanConcepts—*Martin Sacks*	3 Harbor Dr Ste 200, Sausalito CA 94965	415-332-3030	R	19*	.1
1301	Jones Digital Century Inc—*Glen Jones*	9697 E Mineral Ave, Centennial CO 80112	303-792-3111	S	19*	.1
1302	Leanlogistics—*Dan Dershem*	1351 S Waverly Rd, Holland MI 49423	616-738-6400	S	19*	.1
1303	Misys International Banking Systems—*Mike Lawrie*	1180 6th Ave, New York NY 10036	212-898-9500	S	19*	.1
1304	Optical Research Associates—*George Bayz*	3280 E Foothill Blvd S, Pasadena CA 91107	626-795-9101	R	19*	.1
1305	SearchWare Inc—*Norman Mazer*	PO Box 9182, Calabasas CA 91372		D	19*	.1
1306	Tec-Masters Inc—*Marvin Carroll*	1500 Perimeter Pky Ste, Huntsville AL 35806	256-830-4000	R	19*	.1
1307	TMA Systems LLC—*John C Smith*	5100 E Skelly Dr Ste 9, Tulsa OK 74135	918-858-6600	R	19*	.1
1308	Vcommerce Corp—*Rob Wright*	1375 N Scottsdale Rd S, Scottsdale AZ 85257	321-939-5600	R	19*	.1
1309	X-10 Wireless Technology Inc—*Peter A Lesser*	620 Naches Ave SW, Renton WA 98057	425-203-3900	R	19*	.1
1310	CADENCE Management Corp—*John R Patton*	1515 SW 5th Ave Ste 92, Portland OR 97201	503-223-3623	R	19*	<.1
1311	Cybernet Systems Corp—*Heidi Jacobus*	3885 Research Park Dr, Ann Arbor MI 48108	734-668-2567	R	19*	<.1
1312	ParishSOFT—*William Pressprich*	825 Victors Way Ste 20, Ann Arbor MI 48108	734-205-1000	R	19*	<.1

Note: An asterisk (*) indicates an estimated financial figure. The company type code used is as follows: R = Private, P = Public, S = Private Subsidiary, B = Public Subsidiary, D = Division, J = Joint Venture, I = Investment Fund.

COMPANY RANKINGS BY SALES WITHIN 4-DIGIT SIC

Rank	Company Name—*Executive Officer*	Address, City, State, Zip	Phone	Type	Fin	Empls
1313	PCLendercom—*Lionel Urban*	PO Box 1580, Hockessin DE 19707		R	19*	<.1
1314	Seapass Solutions Inc—*Eric Gewirtzman*	90 Park Ave Ste 1720, New York NY 10016	212-608-4646	R	19*	<.1
1315	Blue Tech Inc—*Susan Stone*	2251 San Diego Ave Ste, San Diego CA 92110	619-497-6060	R	19*	<.1
1316	Systems Integration Specialists Company Inc—*John Martin*	6605 19 1/2 Mile Rd, Sterling Heights MI 48314	586-254-0020	R	19*	<.1
1317	Griffin Technologies LLC—*Bennett Griffin*	916 Massachusetts St S, Lawrence KS 66044	785-832-2070	R	19*	<.1
1318	Interlink Networks Inc—*Mike Klein*	2531 Jackson Rd Ste 30, Ann Arbor MI 48103	734-821-1200	R	19*	<.1
1319	SoftVelocity Corp—*Yong Kim*	2335 E Atlantic Blvd S, Pompano Beach FL 33062	954-785-4555	R	19*	<.1
1320	Viewpoint Corp—*Patrick Vogt*	498 7th Ave Ste 1810, New York NY 10018	212-201-0800	D	19	.1
1321	Globalscape Inc—*James R Morris*	4500 Lockhill-Selma St, San Antonio TX 78249	210-308-8267	P	19	.1
1322	GTESS Corp—*Donna Taylor*	2435 N Central Expy St, Richardson TX 75080	972-792-5500	R	18*	.2
1323	Ubi Soft Entertainment Inc—*Yves Guillemot*	4335 Directors Row, Houston TX 77092	713-681-2100	R	18*	.2
1324	Enigma Inc—*Jonathan Yaron*	200 Wheeler Rd, Burlington MA 01803	781-273-3600	R	18*	.2
1325	Appriss Inc—*Doug Cobb*	10401 Linn Station Rd, Louisville KY 40223	502-561-8463	R	18*	.1
1326	Infogix Inc—*Madhavan Nayar*	1240 E Diehl Rd Ste 40, Naperville IL 60563	630-505-1800	R	18*	.1
1327	ERDAS Inc—*Andy Gutman*	5051 Peachtree Corners, Norcross GA 30092	770-776-3400	S	18*	.1
1328	Davidsohn Group—*Joseph Davidsohn* George Davidson and Son	88 Pine St Ste 2601, New York NY 10005	212-208-0100	S	18*	.1
1329	Envision Telephony Inc—*Rodney Kuhn*	520 Pike St Ste 1600, Seattle WA 98101	206-225-0800	R	18*	.1
1330	Argo Data Resources Inc—*Max Martin*	1500 N Greenville Ave, Richardson TX 75081	972-866-3300	R	18*	.1
1331	CaseCentral Inc—*Tom Thimot*	50 California St Ste 2, San Francisco CA 94111	415-989-2300	R	18*	.1
1332	Heroix Corp—*Howard Reisman*	165 Bay State Dr, Braintree MA 02184	781-848-1701	R	18*	.1
1333	MicroMass Communications Inc—*Jay Bigelow*	11000 Regency Pkwy Ste, Cary NC 27511	919-851-3182	R	18*	.1
1334	NetPro Computing Inc—*Kevin Hickey* Quest Software Inc	4747 N 22nd St, Phoenix AZ 85016	602-346-3600	S	18*	.1
1335	Sungard EXP—*Cristobal Conde*	104 Inverness Ctr Pl, Birmingham AL 35242	205-437-7500	S	18*	.1
1336	Global Software Inc—*Matthew Kupferman*	3201 Beechleaf Court S, Raleigh NC 27604	919-872-7800	R	18*	.1
1337	Data Processing Services Inc (Indianapolis Indiana)—*Daniel Barrow*	3685 Priority Way S Dr, Indianapolis IN 46240	317-574-4300	R	18*	.1
1338	Xenos Group—*George Fowlie*	1909 Woodall Rodgers F, Dallas TX 75201	905-709-1020	S	18*	.1
1339	ObjectFX Corp—*Bill Pardue*	1200 S Washington Ave, Minneapolis MN 55415	612-312-2002	R	18*	.1
1340	Ortho Computer Systems Inc—*Dan Sargent*	1107 Buckeye Ave, Ames IA 50010	515-233-1026	R	18*	.1
1341	Bentley Yorba Linda—*Greg Bentley* Bentley Systems Inc	22700 Savi Ranch Pkwy, Yorba Linda CA 92887	714-974-2500	D	18*	.1
1342	ClassroomDirectcom—*Roger Smith*	PO Box 830677, Birmingham AL 35283	205-251-9171	S	18*	.1
1343	CorrectNet Global Information Solutions Inc—*Robert J Miller*	102 Motor Pkwy Ste 250, Hauppauge NY 11788	631-574-6100	R	18*	.1
1344	InfoSource Inc—*Michael Werner*	1300 City View Ctr, Oviedo FL 32765	407-796-5200	R	18*	.1
1345	FutureTrade Technologies—*Thomas Peterfly*	1 Pickwick Plz, Greenwich CT 06830	203-618-5800	S	18*	.1
1346	PeopleMedCom Inc	4925 Robert J Mathews, El Dorado Hills CA 95762		S	18*	.1
1347	Quality Systems Laboratories Inc—*Eric Sun*	5 Park Plz Ste 1550, Irvine CA 92614	949-862-5000	R	18*	.1
1348	Solution Systems Inc—*Stuart Zirin*	3201 Tollview Dr, Rolling Meadows IL 60008	847-590-3000	R	18*	.1
1349	Vermont Systems Inc—*Giles Willey*	12 Market Pl, Essex Junction VT 05452	802-879-6993	R	18*	.1
1350	Waves Inc—*Gilad Keren*	2800 Merchants Dr, Knoxville TN 37912	865-909-9200	S	18*	.1
1351	Carnegie Learning Inc—*Dennis Ciccone*	Frick Bldg 20th Fl 437, Pittsburgh PA 15219	412-690-6284	R	18*	<.1
1352	Ensure Technologies—*Dennis Blanchetter*	135 South Prospect, Ypsilanti MI 48198	734-668-8800	R	18*	<.1
1353	Group Logic Inc—*T Reid Lewis*	PO Box 100310, Arlington VA 22201	703-528-1555	R	18*	<.1
1354	NeuCo Inc—*Peter J Kirk*	33 Union St 4th Fl, Boston MA 02108	617-587-3100	S	18*	<.1
1355	Oncontact Software Corp—*George Kauffman*	W67N222 Evergreen Blvd, Cedarburg WI 53012	262-375-6555	R	18*	<.1
1356	Perforce Software Inc—*Christopher Seiwald*	2320 Blanding Ave, Alameda CA 94501	510-864-7400	R	18*	<.1
1357	Rainbow Studios—*Brian J Farrell*	4277 N 24th St, Phoenix AZ 85016	602-230-1300	R	18*	<.1
1358	Ross Computer Systems Inc AFS Technologies Inc (Phoenix Arizona)	19 W 44th St Ste 715, New York NY 10036	212-221-7677	S	18*	<.1
1359	Tradestone Software Inc—*Sue Welch*	17 Rogers St, Gloucester MA 01930	978-281-3723	R	18*	<.1
1360	TriMin Systems Inc—*Bill Metzger*	2277 Hwy 36 W Ste 101E, Roseville MN 55113	651-636-7667	R	18*	<.1
1361	Specialists In Custom Software Inc—*Helen Russell*	2120 Colorado Ave Ste, Santa Monica CA 90404	310-315-9660	R	18*	<.1
1362	Curriculum Advantage Inc—*Lindsey Cook*	1735 N Brown Rd Ste400, Lawrenceville GA 30043		R	18*	<.1
1363	Wetpaintcom Inc—*Ben Elowitz*	710 2nd Ave Ste 1100, Seattle WA 98104	206-859-6300	R	18*	<.1
1364	DataSoft Corp—*Vik Patel*	1475 N Scottsdale Rd S, Scottsdale AZ 85257	480-763-5777	R	18*	<.1
1365	TigerPAW Inc—*James Foxall*	2201 Thurston Cir, Bellevue NE 68005	402-592-4544	R	18*	<.1
1366	Unidesk Corp—*Don Bulens*	313 Boston Post Rd W, Marlborough MA 01752	508-573-7800	R	18*	<.1
1367	Speech Cycle Inc—*Zor Gorelov*	26 Broadway 11th Fl, New York NY 10004	646-826-2300	R	18*	<.1
1368	CGTech Inc—*Jae-Young Lim*	9000 Research Dr, Irvine CA 92618	949-753-1050	R	18*	<.1
1369	System Essentials Inc	14858 Grassmere Ct, Chesterfield MO 63017	636-537-9537	R	18*	<.1
1370	Datawatch Corp—*Michael Morrison*	271 Mill Rd, Chelmsford MA 01824	978-441-2200	P	18	.1
1371	Dorado Network Systems Corp—*Dain Ehring*	1200 Park Pl Ste 330, San Mateo CA 94403	650-227-7300	R	18*	.1
1372	Vendormate Inc—*Andy Monin*	3445 Peachtree Rd NE S, Atlanta GA 30326		R	18	.1
1373	Cover-All Technologies Inc—*John W Roblin*	55 Lane Rd Ste 300, Fairfield NJ 07004	973-461-5200	P	18	.1
1374	VinSolutions LLC—*Mike Dullea*	6405 Metcalf Ave Clove, Overland Park KS 66202	913-825-6124	R	17	.2
1375	MakeMusic Inc—*Karen van Lith*	7615 Golden Triangle D, Eden Prairie MN 55344	952-937-9611	P	17	.1
1376	Attunity Inc—*Shimon Alon*	70 Blanchard Rd, Burlington MA 01803		R	17*	.2
1377	HRsmart Inc—*Mark Hamdan*	2929 N Central Expy St, Richardson TX 75080		R	17*	.2
1378	Mintec Inc—*John C Davies*	3544 E Fort Lowell Rd, Tucson AZ 85716	520-795-3891	R	17*	.2
1379	Springer-Miller Systems Inc—*John Springer-Miller*	PO Box 1547, Stowe VT 05672	802-253-7377	S	17*	.2
1380	Spillman Technologies Inc—*Lance Clark*	4625 West Lake Park Bl, Salt Lake City UT 84120	801-902-1200	R	17*	.2
1381	Securities Industry Software—*Ted Carl*	4725 Independence St, Wheat Ridge CO 80033	303-590-6000	D	17*	.2
1382	ILOG Inc—*Michel Alard*	1195 W Fremont Ave, Richmond CA 94807	408-991-7000	S	17*	.1
1383	Emphasys Software—*Mike Byrne*	3890 Charlevoix Ave S, Petoskey MI 49770		S	17*	.1
1384	WildPackets Inc—*Timothy D McCreery*	1340 Treat Blvd Ste 50, Walnut Creek CA 94597	925-937-3200	R	17*	.1
1385	Alogent Corp—*Charles E Potts*	350 Technology Pky Ste, Norcross GA 30092	770-752-6400	S	17*	.1
1386	MRE Consulting Ltd—*K Michael Short*	3333 Richmond Ave Ste3, Houston TX 77098	713-844-6401	R	17*	.1
1387	Carrera Systems and Service LLC—*Ray McIntyre*	PO Box 79, Kingston MA 02364	508-746-7341	R	17*	.1
1388	Logical Information Machines Inc—*Tony Kolton*	22 W Washington St, Chicago IL 60602	312-456-3000	R	17*	.1
1389	ESQ Business Services Inc (Pleasanton California)—*Joe Haggarty*	20660 Stevens Creek Bl, Cupertino CA 95014	925-734-9800	R	17*	<.1
1390	Customer Potential Management Corp—*John Hallick*	8310 Excelsior Dr, Madison WI 53717	608-831-7880	R	17*	<.1
1391	Tatara Systems Inc—*EY Snowden*	35 Nagog Park, Acton MA 01720	978-206-0800	R	17*	<.1
1392	Black Diamond Performance Reporting LLC—*Reed Colley*	13901 Sutton Park Dr S, Jacksonville FL 32224	904-241-2444	R	17*	<.1
1393	Exaktime Inc—*Tony Pappas*	27001 Agoura Rd Ste 28, Calabasas CA 91301	818-222-1836	R	17*	<.1
1394	UnboundID Corp—*Stephan Shoaff*	13809 Research Blvd St, Austin TX 78717	512-600-7700	R	17*	<.1
1395	CMS Associates Inc (Naperville Illinois)—*Doug Dallmer*	8500 W 185th StUnit A, Tinley Park IL 60487	708-633-1166	R	17*	<.1
1396	Delta Tao Software Inc—*Joe Williams*	8032 Twin Oaks Ave, Citrus Heights CA 95610	408-730-9336	R	17*	<.1

Rank	Company Name—*Executive Officer*	Address, City, State, Zip	Phone	Type	Fin	Empls
1397	InvisibleHand Networks Inc—*Nemo Semret*	670 Broadway Ste 302, New York NY 10012	212-400-7416	R	17*	<.1
1398	Lamar Software Inc—*Gary Halvorsen*	897 Oak Park Blvd Ste, Pismo Beach CA 93449	805-929-1482	R	17*	<.1
1399	Market Dimensions Inc—*John J Morissey*	703 Grove St, Rockford IL 61104	815-963-2435	R	17*	<.1
1400	Mindbridge Systems Inc Realtrac Div—*Tom Ingraham*	PO Box 51476, Irvine CA 92614	949-852-8818	R	17*	<.1
1401	TRIUS Inc—*Paris Karahalios*	PO Box 249, North Andover MA 01845	978-794-9377	R	17*	<.1
1402	Sunbelt Computer Systems Inc—*Steve White*	13090 Swan Lake Rd CR-, Tyler TX 75704	903-881-0400	R	17*	<.1
1403	Qqest Software Systems Inc—*Burke Plummer*	9350 S 150 E Ste 300, Sandy UT 84070	801-262-1611	R	17*	.2
1404	CGAP Software Inc—*Elizabeth L Littlefield*	1818 H St NW, Washington DC 20433	202-473-9594	R	17	N/A
1405	Omtool Ltd—*Robert L Voelk*	6 Riverside Dr, Andover MA 01810		P	17	.1
1406	MAI Systems Corp—*Stephen VanTassel*	26110 Enterprise Way S, Lake Forest CA 92630	949-598-6000	S	16	.2
1407	Versant Corp—*Bernhard Woebker*	255 Shoreline Dr Ste 4, Redwood City CA 94065	650-232-2400	P	16	.1
1408	Merge eClinical—*M Denis Connaghan* Merge Healthcare Inc	4000 Aerial Center Pkw, Morrisville NC 27560	919-653-3400	S	16	.1
1409	Openpages Inc—*Michael Duffy*	201 Jones Rd, Waltham MA 02451	781-647-3800	R	16*	.2
1410	Baker Hill Corp—*Joe Kuntz*	12900 N Meridian Ste 2, Carmel IN 46032	317-571-2000	R	16*	.2
1411	MicroEdge LLC (New York New York)—*Preston McKenzie*	619 W 54th St 10th Fl, New York NY 10019	212-757-1522	S	16*	.1
1412	DataCore Software Corp—*George S Teixeira*	6300 NW 5th Way, Fort Lauderdale FL 33309	954-377-6000	R	16*	.1
1413	Lexis Nexis InterAction—*Nathan Fineberg*	2000 Clearwater Dr#100, Oak Brook IL 60523	630-572-1400	S	16*	.1
1414	NovaLogic Inc—*John Garcia*	27489 Agoura Rd, Agoura Hills CA 91301	818-880-1997	R	16*	.1
1415	StatSoft Inc—*Paul Lewicki*	2300 E 14th St, Tulsa OK 74104	918-749-1119	R	16*	.1
1416	AnyDoc Software Inc—*Charles Jackson*	201 N Franklin St Ste, Tampa FL 33602	813-222-0414	R	16*	.1
1417	Electronics Workbench—*William Wignall* National Instruments Corp	60 Industrial Park Ste, Cheektowaga NY 14227		S	16*	.1
1418	Gensym Corp—*Danielle Royston* Versata Software Inc	6011 W Courtyard Dr, Austin TX 78730	512-377-9700	S	16*	.1
1419	Liberty Information Management Systems—*AJ Hyland*	The Liberty Bldg 3158, Costa Mesa CA 92626	714-751-6900	R	16*	.1
1420	Software Earnings Inc—*Larry C Thornton*	8700 Trail Lake Dr W S, Memphis TN 38125	901-756-4555	R	16*	.1
1421	D2Hawkeye—*J Christian Kryder*	201 Jones Rd Fl 4, Waltham MA 02451		R	16*	<.1
1422	Tenebril Inc—*Christian Carrillo* Process Software Corp	959 Concord St, Framingham MA 01701	617-912-6600	S	16*	<.1
1423	Serus Corp—*Indu Navar*	785 N Mary Ave Ste 100, Sunnyvale CA 94085	408-716-6200	R	16*	<.1
1424	Teleran Technologies Inc—*Nathan Roseman*	333A Rt 46 W, Fairfield NJ 07004	973-439 1820	R	16*	<.1
1425	Atlas Software Technologies Inc—*Susan Davitt*	10 Duff Rd Ste 207, Pittsburgh PA 15235	412-247-1132	R	16*	<.1
1426	Cornerstone Software Inc—*John Rindone*	15 N Southwood Dr, Nashua NH 03063	603-595-7480	R	16*	<.1
1427	eEmpACT—*Tim Giehll*	2051 Killebrew Dr Ste, Bloomington MN 55425		S	16*	<.1
1428	NetBotz Inc—*Rodger B Dowdelll Jr*	11044 Research Blvd Bl, Austin TX 78759		S	16*	<.1
1429	Numerical Control Computer Sciences Inc	2600 Michelson Dr Ste, Irvine CA 92612	949-852-3664	R	16*	<.1
1430	Reaxion Corp—*Colin Prior*	1408 4th Ave Ste 500, Seattle WA 98101	206-344-8200	S	16*	<.1
1431	Skybox Security Inc—*Gidi Cohen*	2077 Gateway Pl Ste 55, San Jose CA 95110	650-565-8060	R	16*	<.1
1432	Stardock Systems Inc—*Brad Wardell*	15090 N Beck Road Ste, Plymouth MI 48170	734-927-0677	R	16*	<.1
1433	Sys-Com Inc—*Matt Moore*	PO Box 11, Oshkosh WI 54902	920-426-1411	R	16*	<.1
1434	UniPrise—*Michael Matteo*	450 Columbus Blvd, Hartford CT 06103		D	16*	<.1
1435	elcom Inc—*William Lock*	10 Oceana Way, Norwood MA 02062		S	16*	<.1
1436	United Sample Inc—*Matt Dusig*	16501 Ventura Blvd Ste, Encino CA 91436	818-524-1218	R	16*	<.1
1437	Invodo Inc—*Craig Wax*	211 E 7th St 10th Fl S, Austin TX 78701		R	16*	<.1
1438	SQN Signature Systems—*Joe Uhland*	PO Box 423, Rancocas NJ 08073		R	16*	<.1
1439	DEPCO Inc—*Terry Graham*	PO Box 178, Pittsburg KS 66762	620-231-0019	R	16*	<.1
1440	Wellsoft Corp—*John Santmann*	27 Worlds Fair Dr, Somerset NJ 08873	732-507-7200	R	16*	<.1
1441	HWA International Inc—*Harry Sullivan*	8363 Wolf Lake Dr Ste, Memphis TN 38133	901-388-6120	R	16*	<.1
1442	ID Software Inc—*Todd Hollenshead* Zenimax Media Inc	3819 Towne Crossing Bl, Mesquite TX 75150	972-613-3589	S	16*	<.1
1443	CRC Design Inc—*James Cosgrove*	2521 3rd Ave, Seattle WA 98121	206-441-5042	R	16*	<.1
1444	Stone Timber River LLC—*Derek DeBree*	PO Box 6307, Fair Haven NJ 07704	732-383-6500	R	16*	<.1
1445	HubSpot Inc—*Brian Halligan*	25 First St 2nd Fl, Cambridge MA 02142		R	16*	.2
1446	Intelligent Systems Corp—*J Leland Strange*	4355 Shackleford Rd, Norcross GA 30093	770-381-2900	P	15	.2
1447	CorVu Corp—*Andy Youniss* Rocket Software Inc	275 Grove St Ste 3-410, Newton MA 02466	617-614-4321	S	15	.1
1448	Demandforce Inc—*Rick Berry*	22 4th St 12th Fl, San Francisco CA 94103		R	15	.1
1449	CTI Group Holdings Inc—*John Birbeck*	333 N Alabama St Ste 2, Indianapolis IN 46204	317-262-4666	P	15	.1
1450	Compunnel Software Group Inc—*Andy Gaur*	103 Morgan Ln Ste 102, Plainsboro NJ 08536	609-606-9010	R	15*	.3
1451	Karmak Inc—*J Richard Schien*	PO Box 680, Carlinville IL 62626	217-854-4420	R	15*	.2
1452	ClickSoftware Inc	35 Corporate Dr Ste 14, Burlington MA 01803	781-272-5903	S	15*	.2
1453	MX Logic Inc—*John Street* McAfee Inc	9781 S Meridian Blvd S, Englewood CO 80112	720-895-5700	S	15*	.2
1454	CodeSoft International Inc—*Dwight A Mendes*	6 Concourse Pkwy 5th F, Sandy Springs GA 30328	770-913-0101	R	15*	.2
1455	Infinity Software Development Inc—*Jon Taylor*	1901 Commonwealth Ln, Tallahassee FL 32303	850-383-1011	R	15*	.2
1456	Infusionsoft—*Clate Mask*	2065 W Obispo Ave Ste, Gilbert AZ 85233		R	15*	.1
1457	Percussion Software Inc—*Joseph Wykes*	600 Unicorn Park Dr, Woburn MA 01801	781-438-9900	R	15*	.1
1458	Viacore Inc—*Fadi Chehade*	University Research Pa, Irvine CA 92617	949-725-1200	S	15*	.1
1459	O'Neil Software Inc—*Darryl Heinly*	8 Mason, Irvine CA 92618	949-458-0500	R	15*	.1
1460	Oblicore Inc—*Eric Converse*	460 Totten Pond Rd Ste, Waltham MA 02451	781-466-7700	R	15*	.1
1461	Symphony Services—*Pallab Chatterjee*	14881 Quorum Dr Ste 80, Dallas TX 75254	972-581-7300	S	15*	.1
1462	Isys Search Software (Englewood Colorado)—*Scot Coles*	8765 E Orchard Rd, Greenwood Village CO 80111	303-689-9998	D	15*	.1
1463	Pavilion Technologies Inc—*Ralph Carter*	10415 Morado Cir Bldg3, Austin TX 78759		R	15*	.1
1464	Rand McNally-TDM Inc—*Andrzej Wrobel*	PO Box 7600, Chicago IL 60680	847-329-8100	S	15*	.1
1465	Dantz Development Corp—*Khalid Arif*	3003 Oak Rd 3rd Fl, Walnut Creek CA 94597	925-948-9000	S	15	.1
1466	RSD America Inc—*Pierre Van Beneden*	300 Frank W Burr Blvd, Teaneck NJ 07666	201-996-1000	R	15*	.1
1467	Connect Inc (Lisle Illinois)—*James Christofferson*	931 W 75th St Ste 137-, Naperville IL 60565	630-717-7200	R	15*	.1
1468	CACI Products Co—*JP Jack*	1455 Frazee Rd Rm 700, San Diego CA 92108	858-824-5200	S	15*	.1
1469	Digital Cyclone Inc—*Craig Burfiend*	18791 Lake Dr E, Chanhassen MN 55317	952-974-3300	S	15*	.1
1470	Multiview Corp—*John Leslie*	220 Lowell St Ste A, Peabody MA 01960		R	15*	.1
1471	Circle Noetic Services Inc—*Alexander Nizhnikov*	5 Pine Knoll Dr, Mont Vernon NH 03057	603-283-6462	R	15*	.1
1472	Expandable Software Inc—*Bob Swedroe*	900 Lafayette St Ste 4, Santa Clara CA 95050	408-261-7880	R	15*	.1
1473	Galaxy Hotel Systems LLC—*Dan Hogan*	15621 Red Hill Ave Ste, Tustin CA 92780	714-258-5800	S	15*	.1
1474	National Healing Corp—*James E Patrick*	4850 T Rex Ave Ste 300, Boca Raton FL 33431	561-994-1174	R	15*	.1
1475	Trans International Company Inc—*Tom Schmitt*	N93 W16288 Megal Dr, Menomonee Falls WI 53051	262-253-3500	R	15*	.1
1476	Automotive Business Management Consulting Inc—*Dan Hamilton*	30500 State Hwy 181 St, Spanish Fort AL 36527		R	15*	.1
1477	Access International Group Inc—*John P Foss*	PO Box 245, East Hanover NJ 07936	973-360-0750	R	15*	.1
1478	Benelogic LLC—*Matthew Oros*	2118 Greenspring Dr, Timonium MD 21093	443-322-2494	R	15*	.1

Note: An asterisk (*) indicates an estimated financial figure. The company type code used is as follows: R = Private, P = Public, S = Private Subsidiary, B = Public Subsidiary, D = Division, J = Joint Venture, I = Investment Fund.

COMPANY RANKINGS BY SALES WITHIN 4-DIGIT SIC

Rank	Company Name—*Executive Officer*	Address, City, State, Zip	Phone	Type	Fin	Empls
1479	Calyx Software—*Douglas Chang*	6475 Camden Ave Ste 20, San Jose CA 95120	408-997-5525	R	15*	.1
1480	DigitalPersona Inc—*Fabio Righi*	720 Bay Rd, Redwood City CA 94063	650-474-4000	R	15*	.1
1481	Financial Publishing Co	PO Box 570, South Bend IN 46628		R	15*	.1
1482	Healthworks Alliance Inc—*Dave Tribbett*	500 N Gulph Rd Ste 400, King of Prussia PA 19406		S	15*	.1
1483	Iameter Inc—*William Mohlenbrock*	248 B Harbor Blvd Rm B, Belmont CA 94002	650-802-1014	R	15*	.1
1484	Inspiration Software Inc—*Donald Helfgott*	9400 SW Beaverton Hill, Beaverton OR 97005	503-297-3004	R	15*	.1
1485	Journyx Inc—*Curt Finch*	9011 Mountain Ridge Dr, Austin TX 78759	512-834-8888	R	15*	.1
1486	Megaputer Intelligence Inc—*Sergei Ananyan*	120 W 7th St Ste 314, Bloomington IN 47404	812-330-0110	R	15*	.1
1487	Navagate Inc—*Greg Rorke*	130 W 42nd St Ste 1100, New York NY 10036	646-918-5280	R	15*	.1
1488	One Touch Systems Inc—*Larry Speckels*	40 Airport Pky, San Jose CA 95110	408-436-4600	S	15*	.1
1489	Scientific Systems Company Inc—*Raman Mehra*	500 W Cummings Parkk S, Woburn MA 01801	781-933-5355	R	15*	.1
1490	Snowbound Software Corp—*Simon Wieczner*	309 Waverly Oaks Rd St, Waltham MA 02452	617-607-2000	R	15*	.1
1491	Visioneer Inc—*J Larry Smart*	5673 Gibraltar Dr Ste, Pleasanton CA 94588	925-251-6398	R	15*	.1
1492	DAKCS Software Systems—*Lex Patterson*	3017 Taylor Ave, Ogden UT 84403	801-394-5791	R	15*	<.1
1493	Entuity Inc—*Michael Jannery*	4 Mount Royal Ave Ste, Marlborough MA 01752		R	15*	<.1
1494	Exit41 Inc—*Chet Barnard*	3 Dundee Pk, Andover MA 01810	978-749-9000	R	15*	<.1
1495	H and W Computer Systems Inc—*Mary Chaffin*	6154 N Meeker Pl Ste 1, Boise ID 83713	208-377-0336	R	15*	<.1
1496	Permabit Inc—*Tom Cook*	Ten Canal Park 3rd Fl, Cambridge MA 02141	617-252-9600	R	15*	<.1
1497	QStar Technologies Inc—*Riccardo Finotti*	2175 W Hwy 98, Mary Esther FL 32569	850-243-0900	R	15*	<.1
1498	RhinoCorps Limited Co—*Fred Jonas*	1128 Pennsylvania NE S, Albuquerque NM 87110	505-323-9836	R	15*	<.1
1499	Zombie Inc—*Mark Long*	420 4th Ave, Seattle WA 98104	206-623-9655	R	15*	<.1
1500	Kenexa (Philadelphia Pennsylvania)—*Rudy Karsan* Kenexa Corp	650 E Swedesford Rd 2n, Wayne PA 19087		D	15*	<.1
1501	eVestment Alliance—*Jim Minnick*	5000 Olde Towne Pkwy S, Marietta GA 30068		R	15*	<.1
1502	Phoenix Software International Inc—*Fred Hoschett*	831 Parkview Dr North, El Segundo CA 90245	310-338-0400	R	15*	<.1
1503	MindFire Inc—*Moe Farsheed*	30 Corporate Park Ste, Irvine CA 92606		R	15*	<.1
1504	Mobi—*Benjamin Bromberg*	110 Wild Basin Rd S St, Austin TX 78746	512-617-5300	R	15*	<.1
1505	Computhink Inc—*Joe Wharram*	860 Parkview Blvd, Lombard IL 60148	630-705-9050	R	15*	<.1
1506	Idea Sciences Inc—*Mary E Crannell*	205 The Strand, Alexandria VA 22314	703-299-3480	R	15*	<.1
1507	Mikon Systems—*Rick Curtis*	6 Concourse Pkwy Ste 1, Atlanta GA 30328	770-804-5885	R	15*	<.1
1508	Roadmap Technologies Inc—*Rudolph Pizzano*	100 Cummings Ctr, Beverly MA 01915	978-232-8901	R	15*	<.1
1509	Touch N Go Systems Inc—*Jim Gottstein*	PO Box 211032, Anchorage AK 99521	907-338-8188	R	15*	<.1
1510	Aldec Inc—*Stanley Hyduke*	2260 Corp Cir Ste 490, Henderson NV 89074	702-990-4400	R	15*	.1
1511	eMASON Inc—*Jane Mason*	4592 Ulmerton Rd Ste 1, Clearwater FL 33762	727-507-3440	R	15	.1
1512	Document Capture Technologies Inc—*David P Clark*	4255 Burton Dr, Santa Clara CA 95054	408-436-9888	P	15	<.1
1513	Viyya Technologies Inc—*John Bay*	87 Fairfield Rd, Fairfield NJ 07004	973-276-0555	P	15	<.1
1514	MCK Communications Inc—*Steve Odom*	400 Galleria Pkwy Ste, Atlanta GA 30339	678-589-3500	S	15	.1
1515	Radiant Systems Inc (South Plainfield New Jersey)—*Venu My-neni*	107 B Corporate Blvd, South Plainfield NJ 07080	908-668-1080	R	15	.2
1516	LynuxWorks Inc—*Gurjot Singh*	855 Embedded Way, San Jose CA 95138	408-979-3900	R	14*	.2
1517	Minitab Inc—*Barbara Ryan*	1829 Pine Hall Rd, State College PA 16801	814-238-3280	R	14*	.2
1518	Tomax Corp—*Eric Olafson*	224 S 200 W, Salt Lake City UT 84101	801-990-0909	R	14*	.2
1519	Image Recognition Integrated Systems Inc—*Jean-Marc Fontaine*	4731 W Atlantic Ave St, Delray Beach FL 33445	561-921-0847	D	14	.2
1520	Hansen Information Technologies Inc—*Mark Watts*	11092 Sun Center Dr, Rancho Cordova CA 95670	916-921-0883	R	14*	.2
1521	Spanlink Communications Inc—*Brett A Shockley*	605 Hwy 169 N Ste 900, Minneapolis MN 55441	763-971-2000	R	14*	.1
1522	PacketVideo Corp—*James C Brailean*	10350 Science Center D, San Diego CA 92121	858-731-5300	S	14*	.1
1523	AlphaSoft Services Corp—*Sachin Aggarwal*	2035 Lincoln Hwy Ste 1, Edison NJ 08817	925-952-6300	R	14*	.1
1524	Acucorp Inc—*Stephane Croce*	8515 Miralani Dr, San Diego CA 92126		S	14*	.1
1525	Edward Speir Enterprises Inc—*Jason E (Eddie) Speir*	5970 Greenwood Plaza B, Greenwood Village CO 80111†	303-858-8800	R	14*	.1
1526	SunGard Securities Processing—*Cristobal Conde*	601 Second Ave S, Hopkins MN 55343	952-935-3300	S	14	.1
1527	Application Security Inc—*John B Ottman*	350 Madison Ave 6th Fl, New York NY 10017	212-912-4100	R	14*	.1
1528	Basys Inc—*Mike Davis*	7th Fl 857 Elkridge La, Linthicum MD 21090	410-850-4900	R	14*	.1
1529	CMA Consulting Services Inc—*Kay Stafford*	700 Troy-Schenectady R, Latham NY 12110	518-783-9003	R	14*	.1
1530	Elixir Technologies Corp—*Basit Hamid*	721 E Main St, Ventura CA 93001	805-641-5900	R	14*	.1
1531	Exa Corp—*Stephen Remondi*	55 Network Dr, Burlington MA 01803	781-564-0200	R	14*	.1
1532	Health Care Software Inc—*Joseph J Fahey*	PO Box 2430, Farmingdale NJ 07727		R	14*	.1
1533	Software House—*John Rzewnicki*	6 Technology Park, Westford MA 01886	978-577-4145	R	14*	.1
1534	Spectrum Human Resource Systems Corp—*Sybll K Romley*	707 Seventeenth St Ste, Denver CO 80202	303-592-3200	R	14*	.1
1535	CTR Systems Inc—*Dru Duffy*	555 Keystone Dr, Warrendale PA 15086	724-772-2400	R	14*	.1
1536	iNOVA Corp—*Tom Hubbard*	110 Avon St, Charlottesville VA 22902	434-817-8000	R	14*	.1
1537	Digital Controls Corp—*Mike Denny*	444 Alexandersville Rd, Miamisburg OH 45342	937-384-0444	R	14*	.1
1538	Iconics Inc—*Russell Agrusa*	100 Foxborough Blvd, Foxborough MA 02035	508-543-8600	R	14*	.1
1539	Scanvec Amiable Ltd—*Mark Blundell*	PO Box 16109, Salt Lake City UT 84116	801-478-1900	R	14*	.1
1540	AuctionPay—*Steve Sterba*	13221 SW 68th Pkwy Ste, Portland OR 97223		R	14*	.1
1541	Aegistech Inc—*Stanley Adelman*	7 Penn PlzSte 806, New York NY 10001	212-268-3100	R	14*	.1
1542	Clickability Inc—*Jeff Freund*	580 California St 7th, San Francisco CA 94104	415-200-0410	R	14*	.1
1543	Economic Research Institute Inc—*David Thompson*	8575 164th Ave NE Ste, Redmond WA 98052	425-556-0205	R	14*	.1
1544	FourthWall Media—*Timothy Peters*	5800 Granite Pky Ste 4, Plano TX 75024	972-464-5880	R	14*	.1
1545	InfoTouch Corp—*Keith Neerman*	1201 Peachtree St NE 4, Atlanta GA 30361		S	14*	.1
1546	Kiwiplan Inc—*Rodney McGee*	8650 Governors Hill Dr, Cincinnati OH 45249	513-554-1500	R	14*	.1
1547	SL Corp—*Tom Lubinski*	240 Tamal Vista Blvd, Corte Madera CA 94925	415-927-8400	R	14*	<.1
1548	Automated Training Systems Inc—*Ray Bahae*	4545 E Industrial St S, Simi Valley CA 93063	805-520-1509	R	14*	<.1
1549	Financial Computer Support Inc—*David Huxford Jr*	14 Commerce Dr, Oakland MD 21550	301-334-1800	R	14*	<.1
1550	Financial Information Network Inc—*Stephen Seig*	PO Box 7954, Van Nuys CA 91409	818-782-0331	R	14*	<.1
1551	ARCHIBUS Inc—*Bruce Forbes*	18 Tremont St, Boston MA 02108	617-227-2508	R	14*	<.1
1552	Mapframe Corp—*Paul Wilson*	5420 LBJ Fwy Ste 1250, Dallas TX 75240	214-741-2264	S	14*	<.1
1553	IssueTrak—*Hank Luhring*	249 Central Park Ave S, Virginia Beach VA 23462		R	14*	<.1
1554	Olive Software Inc—*Yoni Stern*	13900 E Harvard Ave, Aurora CO 80014	720-747-1220	R	14*	<.1
1555	FarPoint Technologies Inc—*Rick Williamson*	808 Aviation Pkwy Ste, Morrisville NC 27560	919-460-4551	R	14*	<.1
1556	Maintenance Connection Inc—*Brad Squires*	1477 Drew Ave Ste 103, Davis CA 95618		R	14*	<.1
1557	Preferred Medical Marketing Corp—*Roger L Shaul*	15720 John J Delaney D, Charlotte NC 28277	704-543-8103	R	14*	<.1
1558	ABACAB Software Inc—*Srinath Murthy*	3000 Scott Blvd Ste 10, Santa Clara CA 95054	408-988-4466	R	14*	<.1
1559	ABBYY USA Software House Inc—*Sergey Andreyev*	880 N McCarthy Blvd #, Milpitas CA 95035	408-457-9777	S	14*	<.1
1560	Aegis Software Corp—*Jason Spera*	5 Walnut Grove Dr, Horsham PA 19044	215-773-3571	R	14*	<.1
1561	Continental Computer Corp—*Nadine Smith*	3615 S Stadium Blvd, Jonesboro AR 72404	870-932-0081	R	14*	<.1
1562	CRC Information Systems Inc—*Michael Bihlmeier*	16100 N Greenway Hayde, Scottsdale AZ 85260	480-443-9494	R	14*	<.1
1563	Datalogics Inc—*Kevin McNeil*	101 N Wacker Dr Ste 18, Chicago IL 60606	312-853-8200	R	14*	<.1
1564	EnvironMax Inc	2875 S Decker Lake Dr, Salt Lake City UT 84119		S	14*	<.1
1565	Gravic Inc—*Bruce D Holenstein*	301 Lindenwood Dr Ste, Malvern PA 19355	610-647-6250	R	14*	<.1

Rank	Company Name—Executive Officer	Address, City, State, Zip	Phone	Type	Fin	Empls
1566	MedInformatix Inc—Thomas McGonigle	5777 W Century Blvd St, Los Angeles CA 90045	310-348-7367	R	14*	<.1
1567	Metreo Inc—Dafney Carmeli	3500 W Bayshore Rd, Palo Alto CA 94303	650-855-0550	S	14*	<.1
1568	OSS Nokalva Inc—Bancroft Scott	1 Executive Dr Ste 450, Somerset NJ 08873	732-302-0750	R	14*	<.1
1569	Patient Care Technology Systems—Tony Marsico Consulier Engineering Inc	27261 Las Ramblas Rm 2, Mission Viejo CA 92691		S	14*	<.1
1570	RF Code Inc—Mitch Medford	9229 Waterford Ctr Blv, Austin TX 78758	512-439-2200	R	14*	<.1
1571	RW3 Technologies Inc—Bruce Nagle	3201 Danville Blvd Ste, Alamo CA 94507		R	14*	<.1
1572	Xpel Technologies Corp	618 W Sunset Rd, San Antonio TX 78216	210-678-3700	R	14*	<.1
1573	Datacor Inc—Sean O'Donnell	25 Hanover Rd Bldg B, Florham Park NJ 07932	973-822-1551	R	14*	<.1
1574	Landslide Technologies Inc—Rick Faulk	2000 Cliff Mine Rd Ste, Pittsburgh PA 15275	412-489-1700	R	14*	<.1
1575	MainSoft Corp—Yaacov Cohen	314 E State St Ste A, Geneva IL 60134	408-200-4000	R	14*	<.1
1576	Qube Software Inc—Kent D Greene	7210 Estrella de Mar R, Carlsbad CA 92009	760-804-3721	R	14*	<.1
1577	TECMO KOEI AMERICA CORP—Keiko Erikawa	1818 Gilbreth Rd Ste 2, Burlingame CA 94010	650-692-9080	S	14*	<.1
1578	Dataworks Development Inc—Adekunle Raji	PO Box 174, Mountlake Terrace WA 98043	425-673-1974	R	14*	<.1
1579	Davidson Software Systems Inc—Jim Dyke	860 F Ave Ste 104, Plano TX 75074	972-398-7998	S	14*	<.1
1580	HealthTrio Inc—Malik M Hasan	400 S Colorado Blvd St, Denver CO 80246	303-397-3000	R	14*	<.1
1581	TCS Consultants Inc—Robert Simmons	PO Box 884, Montgomery TX 77356	936-588-3200	R	14*	<.1
1582	AICO Arena International Corp	PO Box 365, Fair Oaks CA 95628		R	14*	<.1
1583	Camera Bits—Dennis Walker	472 S 1st Ave, Hillsboro OR 97123	503-547-8888	R	14*	<.1
1584	CC Software Inc—Fredric Hansen	3505 W California Ave, Salt Lake City UT 84104	801-887-7998	R	14*	<.1
1585	ChipChat Technology Group—Marty Cowthon	24224 Michigan Ave, Dearborn MI 48124	313-565-4000	R	14*	<.1
1586	Infinite Options Inc—Dorothy Tutt	2019 Lovell Rd, Knoxville TN 37932	865-539-9977	R	14*	<.1
1587	Palmer Computer Services Inc—Jason M Palmer	230 New York Ave, Huntington NY 11743	631-300-1710	R	14*	<.1
1588	UA Systems Inc	9087 Arrow Route Ste 2, Rancho Cucamonga CA 91730	909-941-1577	R	14*	<.1
1589	Valid Data Inc—Frank Kavanagh	One Dupont St Ste 111, Plainview NY 11803	516-349-1021	R	14*	<.1
1590	VS Software—L Elizabeth Bowles	401 W Capitol Ave Ste, Little Rock AR 72201	501-376-2083	R	14*	<.1
1591	Z-Law Software Inc—Gary L Sherman	PO Box 40602, Providence RI 02940	401-331-3002	R	14*	<.1
1592	TigerLogic Corp—Richard W Koe	25A Technology Dr Ste, Irvine CA 92618	949-442-4400	P	14	.1
1593	AXS-One Inc—William P Lyons Daegis Inc	301 Rte 17 N, Rutherford NJ 07070	201-935-3400	S	13	.1
1594	TelemateNet Software Inc—Monty Bannerman	5555 Triangle Pkwy NW, Norcross GA 30092	678-589-3500	S	13*	.2
1595	Plateau Systems Ltd—Paul Sparta	4401 Wilson Blvd Ste 4, Arlington VA 22203	703-678-0000	R	13*	.2
1596	Zone Labs Inc—Gregor Freund	800 Bridge Parkway, Redwood City CA 94065	415-633-4500	S	13*	.2
1597	Aperture Technologies Inc—Tom Waun	9 Riverbend Dr S, Stamford CT 06907	203-357-0800	R	13*	.1
1598	Acroprint Time Recorder Co—Glenn Robbins	5640 Departure Dr, Raleigh NC 27616	919-872-5800	R	13*	.1
1599	Aptify—Amith Nagarajan	1850 K St NW 3rd Fl, Washington DC 20006	202-223-2600	R	13*	.1
1600	QuickStart Intelligence Inc—Monica Banguelos	16815 Von Karman Ave S, Irvine CA 92618	949-486-1351	R	13*	.1
1601	TechSmith Corp—William Hamilton	2405 Woodlake Dr, Okemos MI 48864	517-381-2300	R	13*	.1
1602	Teoco Corp—Atul Jain	12150 Monument Dr Ste, Fairfax VA 22033	703-322-9200	R	13*	.1
1603	Travel Agency Management Systems Inc—Lee Rosen	5777 W Century Blvd, Los Angeles CA 90045	310-641-8726	R	13*	.1
1604	Shelby Systems Inc—Frank Canady	7345 Goodlett Farms Pk, Cordova TN 38016	901-757-2372	R	13*	.1
1605	Sage Timeslips	1715 N Brown Rd NW, Lawrenceville GA 30043		D	13*	.1
1606	Shams Group Inc—Kam Shams	1304 W Walnut Hill Ln, Irving TX 75038	469-586-3317	R	13*	.1
1607	Accusoft Pegasus—Jack Berlin	4001 N Riverside Dr, Tampa FL 33603	813-875-7575	R	13*	.1
1608	Thomson Scientific IP Management Services—Thomas H Glocer	29100 Northwestern Hwy, Southfield MI 48034	248-352-5810	D	13*	.1
1609	SDCR Business Systems—Matt Richardson	7940 Arjons Dr, San Diego CA 92126		R	13*	.1
1610	Apex Voice Communications Inc—Ben Levy	21001 Ventura Blvd 2nd, Woodland Hills CA 91364	818 370 8400	R	13	.1
1611	SWC Technology Partners—Bob Knott	1420 Kensington Rd Ste, Oak Brook IL 60523	630-572-0240	R	13*	.1
1612	Synergex International Corp—Michele Wong	2330 Gold Meadow Way, Gold River CA 95670	916-635-7300	R	13*	.1
1613	Objectivity Inc—John Jarrell	640 W California Ave S, Sunnyvale CA 94086	408-992-7100	R	13*	.1
1614	Springbrook Software Inc—Cathy Brucker	111 SW 5th Ave Ste 185, Portland OR 97204	503-820-2200	R	13*	.1
1615	InStep Software LLC—John P Kalanik Jr	200 W Jackson Blvd 28t, Chicago IL 60606	312-894-7837	R	13*	<.1
1616	ACR Systems Inc—John Huffman	122 N Jefferson St, Jacksonville FL 32204	904-296-8554	R	13*	<.1
1617	A-1 Technology Inc—Ishwari Singh	115 Broadway Fl 13, New York NY 10006		R	13*	<.1
1618	Anderson Imaging Group Inc—Miguel Champalanne	2046 Treasure Coast Pl, Vero Beach FL 32960	949-215-0638	R	13*	<.1
1619	Hypercube Inc—Neil S Ostlund	1115 NW 4th St, Gainesville FL 32608	352-371-7744	R	13*	<.1
1620	Orion Mobility Solutions LLC—Peter Foncesca	88 Danbury Rd, Wilton CT 06897	203-762-0365	S	13*	<.1
1621	ProSolutions Inc—Valerie Oberle	22255 Larkspur Trl, Boca Raton FL 33433	561-487-9692	R	13*	<.1
1622	Tom Sawyer Software Corp—Brendan Madden	181 Montecito Ave, Oakland CA 94610	510-208-4370	R	13*	<.1
1623	YellowZone Inc—Paul Cohen	16055 Ventura Blvd Ste, Encino CA 91436	818-788-7810	R	13*	<.1
1624	Anvita Health—Christina Weaver	7090 Miratech Dr, San Diego CA 92121	858-554-1886	S	13*	<.1
1625	MediData Solutions Worldwide (Conshohocken Pennsylvaina) Medidata Solutions Inc	20 Ash St Millennium 1, Conshohocken PA 19428	215-358-1400	D	13*	<.1
1626	SoftPLC Corp—Richard Hollenbeck	25603 Red Brangus Dr, Spicewood TX 78669	512-264-8390	R	13*	<.1
1627	Performix (Houston Texas)—Sham Afzalpurkar	9800 Richmond Ave Ste, Houston TX 77042		R	13*	<.1
1628	Accessible Archives Inc—Tom Nagy	697 Sugartown Rd, Malvern PA 19355		R	13*	<.1
1629	Business Software Solutions	334 N Marshall Way Ste, North Salt Lake UT 84054	801-336-3303	R	13*	<.1
1630	Index Engines Inc—Tim Williams	960 Holmdel Rd Ste 1, Holmdel NJ 07733	732-817-1060	R	13*	<.1
1631	Insideview Inc—Umberto Milletti	444 De Haro St Ste 210, San Francisco CA 94107	415-728-9300	R	13*	<.1
1632	Jaguar Consulting Inc—Randolph Johnson	117 E Colorado Blvd St, Pasadena CA 91105	626-796-1955	R	13*	<.1
1633	PrimeQ Solutions Inc—Jason McClain	26035 Acero, Mission Viejo CA 92691	949-707-8500	R	13*	<.1
1634	Royal 4 Systems Inc—Sam Elasmar	5000 E Spring St Ste 4, Long Beach CA 90815	562-420-9594	R	13*	<.1
1635	Xpient Solutions LLC—Christopher Sebes	11525 Carmel Commons B, Charlotte NC 28226	704-295-7000	R	13*	<.1
1636	Grocery Shopping Network Inc—Scott Lutz	900 Lumber Exchange Bl, Minneapolis MN 55402	612-238-4940	R	13*	<.1
1637	Phoenix Data Systems Inc—Bernard Mannisto	24293 Telegraph Rd Ste, Southfield MI 48033	248-358-3366	R	13*	<.1
1638	Cimulus Inc—Dennis Carmichael	801 W Ellsworth Ste 20, Ann Arbor MI 48108	734-327-9532	R	13*	<.1
1639	Applied Communication Services Inc—Jeffrey C Dillow ACI Worldwide Inc (Riverside Rhode Island)	15 Natures Way, Sparta NJ 07871	973-729-1897	S	13*	<.1
1640	Extend Inc—Lorraine Ling	4847 Hopyard Rd Ste 4P, Pleasanton CA 94588	925-484-0395	R	13*	<.1
1641	G and E Systems Inc—Bryan Kocher	250 Edge Hill Rd, Sharon MA 02067	781-784-1007	R	13*	<.1
1642	Gold-Data—Rick B Goldstein	26 Sage Hill Ct, Danville CA 94526	925-866-6652	R	13*	<.1
1643	Hero Inc—Carl Pearson	PO Box 70525, Seattle WA 98107	206-632-2005	R	13*	<.1
1644	Infopro Inc—John E Michelsen	2920 Norwalk Ct, Aurora IL 60504	630-978-9231	R	13*	<.1
1645	Infotech Systems Inc—Bob Gomez	4780 Dairy Rd Ste 101, Melbourne FL 32904	321-726-9587	R	13*	<.1
1646	Mainstreet Systems and Software Inc—Ellen Whelan	656 Harleysville Pke S, Harleysville PA 19438	215-256-4535	R	13*	<.1
1647	Niwot Networks Inc—William Gibson	721 9th Ave, Longmont CO 80501	303-772-8664	R	13*	<.1
1648	QQQ Software Inc—Pamela Weeks	302 N Irving St, Arlington VA 22201	703-528-1288	R	13*	<.1
1649	Senecio Software Inc—Jerry W Wicks	125 N Main St, Bowling Green OH 43402	419-352-4371	R	13*	<.1
1650	Software Labs Inc	PO Box 6064, Bellevue WA 98008	425-653-2432	R	13*	<.1

Note: An asterisk (*) indicates an estimated financial figure. The company type code used is as follows: R = Private, P = Public, S = Private Subsidiary, B = Public Subsidiary, D = Division, J = Joint Venture, I = Investment Fund.

COMPANY RANKINGS BY SALES WITHIN 4-DIGIT SIC

Rank	Company Name—*Executive Officer*	Address, City, State, Zip	Phone	Type	Fin	Empls
1651	Software Options Inc—*Cathy Cullen*	4860 N Paulina Ave, Chicago IL 60640	773-784-4339	R	13*	<.1
1652	Cybersoft Solutions Inc—*Paul McLennan*	9709 Hillshire Dr, Richmond IL 60071	815-307-8164	R	13*	<.1
1653	Axeda Corp—*Jack Sweeney*	25 Forbes Blvd Ste 3, Foxboro MA 02035	508-337-9200	R	13	.1
1654	Enablence Systems Inc—*Gary Davis*	230 Commerce Way Ste 2, Portsmouth NH 03801	603-766-5100	R	13*	.1
1655	Intelli-Check Mobilisa Inc—*Steve Williams*	191 Otto St, Port Townsend WA 98368	360-344-3233	P	12	<.1
1656	Software Professionals Inc (Irving Texas)—*Reena Batra*	1200 W Walnut Hill Ln, Irving TX 75038	972-518-0198	R	12*	.2
1657	MQSoftware Inc BMC Software Inc	3800 American Blvd W S, Bloomington MN 55431	952-563-1340	S	12*	.1
1658	T2 Systems Inc—*Mike Simmons*	7835 Woodland Dr Ste 2, Indianapolis IN 46278	317-524-5500	R	12*	.1
1659	Smarterkidscom Inc—*Al Noyes*	2 Lower Ragsdale Dr St, Monterey CA 93940	831-333-2000	S	12*	.1
1660	Digital Wizards Inc—*Stephen Stamper*	2727 Camino del Rio S, San Diego CA 92108	619-260-1180	R	12*	.1
1661	Genesys Software Systems Inc—*Barry Nadell*	5 Branch St, Methuen MA 01844	978-685-5400	R	12*	.1
1662	Infosys International Inc—*Raj Mehta*	110 Terminal Dr, Plainview NY 11803	516-576-9494	R	12*	.1
1663	TransEra Corp—*Daniel Radcliffe*	12896 Pony Express Rd, Draper UT 84020	801-572-2074	R	12*	.1
1664	Digital Fuel Technologies Inc—*Yisrael Dancziger*	951 Mariners Island Bl, San Mateo CA 94404	650-524-2520	R	12*	.1
1665	Health Business Systems Inc—*Gordon Glenn*	738 Louis Dr, Warminster PA 18974	267-280-5100	S	12*	.1
1666	Flow Management Technologies Inc—*Craig Skevington*	125 High Rock Ave, Saratoga Springs NY 12866	518-580-9844	R	12*	.1
1667	ManageSoft Corporation Inc—*Steve B Butler*	100 N Washington St 4t, Boston MA 02114	617-532-1600	S	12*	.1
1668	Mergent International Inc—*Jonathan Worrall*	5250 77 Ctr Dr Ste 150, Charlotte NC 28217		R	12*	.1
1669	Friedman Corp—*Mark Thompson*	1 Parkway N Ste 400S, Deerfield IL 60015	847-948-7180	S	12*	.1
1670	Heavy Construction Systems Specialists Inc—*Mike Rydin*	13151 W Airport Blvd, Sugar Land TX 77478	713-270-4000	R	12*	.1
1671	Mincron SBC Corp—*James Iversen*	333 N Sam Houston Pky, Houston TX 77060		R	12*	.1
1672	Professional Control Corp—*Robert Dumke*	PO Box 130, Germantown WI 53022	262-251-3000	R	12*	.1
1673	Omnikron Systems Inc—*Sudipta Ghosh*	6301 Owensmouth Ave St, Woodland Hills CA 91367	818-591-7890	R	12*	.1
1674	Pyramid Digital Solutions LLC—*Dharmesh Shah*	3000 Riverchase Galler, Birmingham AL 35244	205-271-6100	R	12*	.1
1675	Cipher Systems—*Peter McKenney*	2661 Riva Rd 5th Fl Bl, Annapolis MD 21401	410-412-3326	R	12*	.1
1676	Gallium Visual Systems—*Brian Vernon*	10224 Crosscut Wy, Damascus MD 20872	858-456-3562	R	12*	.1
1677	Market Technologies LLC—*Louis B Mendelsohn*	5807 Old Pasco Rd, Wesley Chapel FL 33544	813-973-0496	R	12	.1
1678	Raven Software Corp—*Brain Raffel* Activision Blizzard Inc	8496 Greenway Blvd, Middleton WI 53562	310-255-2000	S	12*	.1
1679	RealLegal—*Jason Primuth* West LiveNote (San Francisco California)	425 Market St 4th Fl, San Francisco CA 94105		D	12*	.1
1680	SafeSurf—*Clinton Signs*	1300-G El Paseo Ste 10, Las Cruces NM 88001		R	12*	.1
1681	Pro-Am Software (Warrendale Pennsylvania)—*Jim DiNardo*	551 Keystone Dr, Warrendale PA 15086	724-776-1818	D	12*	<.1
1682	ADB Systems International ASA—*Jeff Lymburner*	3001 N Rocky Point Dr, Tampa FL 33607		S	12*	<.1
1683	BINOMIAL International Inc—*Jeffrey Williams*	812 Proctor Ave, Ogdensburg NY 13669		R	12*	<.1
1684	Bradley Co—*Terry Light*	4829 Galaxy Pkwy, Cleveland OH 44128	216-292-7220	S	12*	<.1
1685	Broughton International—*Jim Bobbit* SARS Corp	1077 Celestial St, Cincinnati OH 45202	513-977-4561	D	12*	<.1
1686	Citect Inc—*John Ross*	30000 Mill Creek Ave S, Alpharetta GA 30022	770-521-7511	R	12*	<.1
1687	CSG Interactive Messaging—*Mr Kalan*	2525 N 117th Ave, Omaha NE 68164	402-431-7000	S	12*	<.1
1688	IMS Inc (Sherman Oaks California)—*Juan G Ledo*	14148 Magnolia Blvd, Sherman Oaks CA 91423	818-206-8694	R	12*	<.1
1689	Kovair Inc—*Bipin Shah*	1533 California Cir, Milpitas CA 95035	408-262-0200	R	12*	<.1
1690	Lyris Technologies Inc—*Wolfgang Maasberg* Lyris Inc	6401 Hillis St Ste 125, Emeryville CA 94608	510-844-1600	S	12*	<.1
1691	OASIS Technology Inc—*George Baldonado*	601 E Daily Dr Ste 226, Camarillo CA 93010	805-445-4833	R	12*	<.1
1692	Varolii Corp—*Nicholas Tiliacos*	1 Wall St, Burlington MA 01803	781-482-2100	R	12*	<.1
1693	Xpriori LLC—*Tim Dix*	2864 S Circle Dr Ste 4, Colorado Springs CO 80906	719-210-5318	R	12*	<.1
1694	ZEH Software Inc—*David Zeh*	1900 St James Place Rm, Houston TX 77056	713-956-2165	R	12*	<.1
1695	Final Draft Inc—*Marc Madnick*	26707 W Agoura Rd Ste, Calabasas CA 91302	818-995-8995	R	12*	<.1
1696	Epylon Corp—*Tim Blanton*	3675 Mt Diablo Blvd St, Lafayette CA 94549	925-407-1020	R	12*	<.1
1697	OriginLab Corp—*CP Yang*	One Roundhouse Plz Ste, Northampton MA 01060	413-586-2013	S	12*	<.1
1698	Attensity Corp—*Craig Norris*	2483 E Bayshore Rd Ste, Palo Alto CA 94303	650-433-1700	R	12*	<.1
1699	AERIES Software Inc—*Jerry D Lloyd*	1065 N PacifiCenter Dr, Anaheim CA 92805	714-571-1899	R	12*	<.1
1700	CrossTec Corp—*John Chambers*	500 NE Spanish River B, Boca Raton FL 33431	561-391-6560	R	12*	<.1
1701	Megabyte International Corp	5318 W Crenshaw St, Tampa FL 33634	813-884-8780	R	12*	<.1
1702	ADC Legal Systems Inc—*Monty Helin*	PO BOX 540086, Orlando FL 32854	407-843-8992	R	12*	<.1
1703	ApplianceWare Inc—*Stacy Kenworthy*	3636 Habersham Rd Ste, Atlanta GA 30305	404-543-3270	R	12*	<.1
1704	Application Consulting Group—*Peter Edwards*	1639 Rt 10 E, Parsippany NJ 07054	973-898-0012	R	12*	<.1
1705	Applied Educational Systems Inc—*James Schultz*	208 Bucky Dr, Lititz PA 17543	717-627-7710	R	12*	<.1
1706	Bricsnet America Inc—*Hector Rodriquesz*	260 California St Ste, San Francisco CA 94111	415-321-2650	R	12*	<.1
1707	Coupa Software Inc—*Rob Bernshteyn*	2 W 5th Ave Ste 300, San Mateo CA 94402	650-931-3200	R	12*	<.1
1708	Electronic Online Systems International—*Scot Cheatham*	2292 Faraday Ave, Carlsbad CA 92008	760-431-8400	R	12*	<.1
1709	Global Management Technologies Corp—*Simon Angove*	2831 Peterson Pl, Norcross GA 30071	770-416-6000	R	12*	<.1
1710	Global Weather Dynamics Inc—*Duncan Macdonald*	201 Calle Del Oaks Ste, Monterey CA 93940	831-392-0430	R	12*	<.1
1711	Hilgraeve Inc—*John Zarb*	115 E Elm Ave, Monroe MI 48162	734-243-0576	R	12*	<.1
1712	Integra Business Systems Inc—*Alan Wiessner*	701 Enterprise Rd E Bl, Safety Harbor FL 34695	727-725-4507	R	12*	<.1
1713	Morse Data Corp—*James L Morse*	16 Pierce St, Dover NH 03820	603-742-2500	R	12*	<.1
1714	Optus Software Inc—*Frank Kaufman*	100 Davidson Ave, Somerset NJ 08873	732-271-9568	R	12*	<.1
1715	Power Analytics Inc—*Mark A Ascolese*	16870 W Bernardo Ct St, San Diego CA 92127	858-675-9211	R	12*	<.1
1716	QuestaWeb Inc—*Leon Turetsky*	649 Central Ave, Westfield NJ 07090	908-233-2300	R	12*	<.1
1717	Research Triangle Software—*Jeff LeRose*	1140 Kildaire Farm Rd, Cary NC 27511	919-657-0505	R	12*	<.1
1718	Transparent Language Inc—*Michael Quinlan*	1 Murphy Dr, Nashua NH 03062	603-262-6300	R	12*	<.1
1719	Unibased Systems Architecture Inc—*Lawrence Covington*	14323 S Outer 40 Rd St, Chesterfield MO 63017	314-878-6050	R	12*	<.1
1720	Valley Agricultural Software Inc—*Connor M Jameson*	3950 South K St, Tulare CA 93274	559-686-9496	R	12*	<.1
1721	Vector Fields Inc—*Kevin Ward*	1700 N Farnsworth Ave, Aurora IL 60505	630-851-1734	S	12*	<.1
1722	XPRESSCHEX Inc—*Joel M Barry*	215 Central NW Fl 3, Albuquerque NM 87102	505-998-3141	R	12*	<.1
1723	HiT Software Inc—*Giancomo Lorenzin*	4040 Moorpark Ave Ste, San Jose CA 95117	408-345-4001	R	12*	<.1
1724	NETcellent System Inc—*Edward Kwang*	4030 W Valley Blvd Ste, Walnut CA 91789	909-598-9019	R	12*	<.1
1725	Tree Star Inc—*Adam Treister*	340 A St Ste 206, Ashland OR 97520	541-201-0022	R	12*	<.1
1726	Advanced Micro Solutions Inc	1709 S State St, Edmond OK 73013		R	12*	<.1
1727	Application Link Inc—*Michael Reed*	4449 EastonWay Blvd 2n, Columbus OH 43219	614-469-1981	R	12	<.1
1728	Add on Software Inc—*Nico Spence* Open Systems Inc (Shakopee Minnesota)	5901 Jefferson St NE, Albuquerque NM 87109	505-345-5232	S	12*	<.1
1729	Cayman Graphics—*Jeff McOmie*	3049 W 10755 S, South Jordan UT 84095	801-254-6979	R	12*	<.1
1730	CompuBridge Inc—*Harald Nagel*	12651 S Dixie Hwy Ste, Miami FL 33156	305-253-1212	R	12*	<.1
1731	CyberTools Inc—*Mark V Roux*	Blanchard House 249 Ay, Harvard MA 01451	978-772-9200	R	12*	<.1
1732	DDI Inc—*Judith Mack*	1939 Waukegan Rd Ste 2, Glenview IL 60025	847-486-0003	R	12*	<.1
1733	Elfring Soft Fonts Inc—*Gary Elfring*	2020 Dean St Unit N, Saint Charles IL 60174	630-377-3520	R	12*	<.1
1734	Eurosoft Inc (Cary North Carolina)—*John Liedl*	1628 Old Apex Rd, Cary NC 27513	919-468-3003	R	12*	<.1

Rank	Company Name—*Executive Officer*	Address, City, State, Zip	Phone	Type	Fin	Empls
1735	Hex Laboratory Systems—*Phillip Royce*	1042B El Camino Real S, Encinitas CA 92024	336-584-4010	R	12*	<.1
1736	Hitec Integration Inc—*Jim Scavio*	1502 E Cliff Rd, Burnsville MN 55337	952-808-3250	R	12*	<.1
1737	Munimetrix System Corp—*Bruce Rector*	1575 Delucchi Ln Ste 2, Reno NV 89502	775-334-4777	R	12*	<.1
1738	Oakdale Engineering—*John Gillmore*	23 Tomey Rd, Oakdale PA 15071	724-693-0320	R	12	<.1
1739	Perfect Circle Solutions Inc—*Fred Young*	3915 Mission Ave Ste D, Oceanside CA 92058	310-395-5127	R	12*	<.1
1740	Plotworks Inc—*Michael L Van Woert*	16440 Eagles Crest Rd, Ramona CA 92065	858-457-5090	R	12*	<.1
1741	Precision Computer Service Inc—*Jarrett Volver*	517 Oothcalooga St Ste, Calhoun GA 30701	706-625-5399	R	12*	<.1
1742	RTG Data Systems—*Robert Hallem*	2118 Wilshire Blvd Ste, Santa Monica CA 90403		R	12*	<.1
1743	Software FX Inc—*Rene Garcia*	951 Yamato Rd Ste 101, Boca Raton FL 33431	561-999-8888	R	12*	<.1
1744	THEOS Software Corp—*Robert Fritz*	1280 Boulevard Way Ste, Walnut Creek CA 94595	925-935-1118	R	12	<.1
1745	Toledo and Associates Inc—*Joe Toledo*	PO Box 2437, Chino CA 91708	909-591-2798	R	12*	<.1
1746	United Data Inc—*James Falcon*	312 Wickenden St, Providence RI 02903	401-351-3800	R	12*	<.1
1747	Valencia Systems Inc—*Steve Christle*	3165 McCrory Pl Ste 10, Orlando FL 32803	407-228-4417	R	12*	<.1
1748	American Bible Sales—*Pike Lambeth*	PO Box 2935, La Habra CA 90632	714-879-2283	R	12*	<.1
1749	Breakthrough Productions—*Gregg Sanderson*	410 Lorna Dr, Nashville TN 37214	615-884-1307	R	12*	<.1
1750	Xyquad Inc	2921 S Brentwood Blvd, Saint Louis MO 63144	314-961-5995	R	12	.1
1751	AcademixDirect Inc—*Karen Francis*	1901 Landings Dr, Mountain View CA 94043	650-265-1500	R	12	<.1
1752	Squarespace Inc—*Anthony Casalena*	459 Broadway 5th Fl, New York NY 10013	347-758-4644	R	12	.1
1753	Homeportfolio Inc—*Dale Williams*	288 Walnut St Ste 500, Newton MA 02460	617-965-0565	R	12*	.1
1754	Visionair Inc—*Mike Lyons*	5601 Barbados Blvd, Castle Hayne NC 28429	910-675-9117	R	12*	.1
1755	Atypon Systems Inc—*Georgios Papadapoulos*	5201 Great America Pkw, Santa Clara CA 95054	408-988-1240	R	12*	.1
1756	Slingshot Software Inc—*Paul Carr*	990 Washington St Ste, Dedham MA 02026	781-329-1900	R	12	.1
1757	Q2 Software Inc—*RH Seale III*	9430 Research Blvd Ste, Austin TX 78759	512-275-0072	R	11	.2
1758	HelloSoft Inc—*Krishna Yarlagadda*	640 W California Ave, Sunnyvale CA 94086	408-441-7110	R	11	.1
1759	Eq Technologic Inc—*Dinesh Khaladkar*	500 Office Ctr Dr Ste, Fort Washington PA 19034	215-891-9010	R	11*	.2
1760	ViryaNet Ltd—*Memy Ish-Shalom*	112 Turnpike Rd, Westborough MA 01581	508-490-5900	P	11	.1
1761	MarketLive Inc—*Mark Pierce*	617B 2nd St, Petaluma CA 94952	707-773-3434	R	11*	.2
1762	CoWare Inc Synopsys Inc	700 E Middlefield Rd, Mountain View CA 94043	650-584-5000	S	11*	.1
1763	Pitney Bowes Software Systems—*Murray D Martin*	750 Warrenville Rd, Lisle IL 60532	630-435-7500	D	11*	.1
1764	Symon Communications Inc—*Charles Ansley*	500 N Central Expy Ste, Plano TX 75074	972-578-8484	R	11*	.1
1765	TAKE Supply Chain—*Kishore Rachapudi*	6805 N Capital of Texa, Austin TX 78731	512-231-8191	D	11*	.1
1766	Unique Business Systems Corp—*Pradeep Batra*	1100 Colorado Ave, Santa Monica CA 90401	310-396-3929	R	11*	.1
1767	KBC Advanced Technologies Inc—*W George Bright*	15021 Katy Fwy Ste 600, Houston TX 77094	281-293-8200	S	11*	.1
1768	CARDtools Systems Corp	101 Metro Dr Ste 250, San Jose CA 95110	408-559-4240	R	11*	.1
1769	Revere Inc—*Aivars Lode*	2125 Data Office Dr St, Birmingham AL 35244	205-967-4905	S	11	.1
1770	Vormittag Associates Inc—*Bob Vormittag*	120 Comac St, Ronkonkoma NY 11779		R	11*	.1
1771	Maxwell Systems Inc—*Jim Flynn*	1000 1st Ave Ste 200, King of Prussia PA 19406	610-277-3515	R	11*	.1
1772	Juris Inc—*Andrew Prozes*	5106 Maryland Way, Brentwood TN 37027	615-377-3740	R	11*	.1
1773	McCallie Associates Inc—*Jennifer Maassen*	3906 Raynor Pkwy Ste 2, Bellevue NE 68123	402-291-2203	R	11*	.1
1774	REAL Software Systems LLC	21255 Burbank Blvd Ste, Woodland Hills CA 91367	818-313-8000	R	11*	.1
1775	SBI Razorfish—*Charley White*	1914 Main St, Santa Monica CA 90405	310-566-1300	R	11*	<.1
1776	Integrys Consults LLC—*Bill Cox*	770 Pelham Rd Ste 200, Greenville SC 29615	864-297-9290	R	11*	<.1
1777	Pharmacy Computer Services Inc—*Tim Evans*	129 NW E St, Grants Pass OR 97526	541-476-3139	R	11*	<.1
1778	PKWARE Inc—*V Miller Newton*	648 N Plankinton Ave S, Milwaukee WI 53203	414-289-9788	R	11*	<.1
1779	Reasoning LLC—*John Shangler*	PO Box 61333, Raleigh NC 27661		R	11*	<.1
1780	Aladdin Knowledge Systems Inc—*Chris Fedde*	601 Campus Dr, Arlington Heights IL 60004	847-818-3800	S	11*	<.1
1781	Applied Visions Inc—*Frank J Zinghini Jr*	6 Bayview Ave, Northport NY 11768	631-754-4920	R	11*	<.1
1782	CaseWare International Inc—*Dwight Wainman*	2425B Channing Way Ste, Berkeley CA 94704		R	11*	<.1
1783	CDB Software Inc—*Richard Barry*	PO Box 420789, Houston TX 77242	713-588-1778	R	11*	<.1
1784	Individual Software Inc—*Jo-L Hendrickson*	4255 Hopyard Rd Ste2, Pleasanton CA 94588	925-734-6767	R	11*	<.1
1785	Infotree Web Services—*Janaura S Bishop*	8 Griffin Rd N Ste 105, Windsor CT 06095	860-925-6891	R	11*	<.1
1786	Line4 Inc—*Laurence Fitzsimon*	1320 Harbor Bay Pky St, Alameda CA 94502	510-748-1500	R	11*	<.1
1787	NetVision Inc—*David Rowe*	752 E 1180 S Ste 120, American Fork UT 84003	801-770-3700	R	11*	<.1
1788	New BoundaryTechnologies Inc—*Kim Pearson*	1300 Godward St NE Ste, Minneapolis MN 55413	612-379-3805	R	11*	<.1
1789	Pipkins Inc—*James Pipkins*	16690 Swingley Ridge R, Chesterfield MO 63017	314-469-6106	R	11*	<.1
1790	Thomson Grass Valley (San Jose California)—*Hiro Yamada*	711 Charcot Ave, San Jose CA 95131	408-954-4500	S	11*	<.1
1791	AgVantage Software Inc—*Michelle Blomberg*	107 Woodlake Dr SE, Rochester MN 55904	507-282-6353	R	11*	<.1
1792	Accelera Romar Corp—*Royce Leavelle*	300 E Lombard St, Baltimore MD 21202	443-451-3800	R	11*	<.1
1793	Black Mountain Software Inc—*Wayne Carrier*	1680 Aspen St, Helena MT 59601		R	11*	<.1
1794	Surado Solutions Inc—*Sundip Doshi*	588 Technology Crt Ste, Riverside CA 92507	951-682-4895	R	11*	<.1
1795	Thursby Software Systems Inc—*William Thursby*	4901 S Collins St, Arlington TX 76018	817-478-5070	R	11*	<.1
1796	Networks in Motion Inc—*Doug Antone*	6A Liberty Ste 200, Aliso Viejo CA 92656	949-453-1646	R	11*	<.1
1797	Payroll Associates Inc—*Robert Digby*	840 Lenola Rd -, Unit 6, Moorestown NJ 08057	856-231-4667	R	11*	<.1
1798	Computer Power Solutions of Illinois Inc—*Michelle Elia*	235 Southwoods Center, Columbia IL 62236		R	11*	<.1
1799	Smart Communications Inc—*John M Smart*	115 E 57th St 11th Fl, New York NY 10022	212-486-1894	R	11*	<.1
1800	Advanced Software Products Group Inc—*Cathryn Thompson*	3185 Horseshoe Dr, Naples FL 34104	239-649-1548	R	11*	<.1
1801	AVTECH Software Inc—*Michael Sigourney*	16 Cutler St Cutler Mi, Warren RI 02885	401-628-1600	R	11*	<.1
1802	Boothroyd Dewhurst Inc—*John Gilligan*	138 Main St, Wakefield RI 02879	401-783-5840	R	11*	<.1
1803	Jove LLC—*John Volatile*	855 Waterman Ave, East Providence RI 02914	401-438-5500	R	11*	<.1
1804	AMC Technology LLC—*Anthony X Uliano*	15521 Midlothian Turnp, Midlothian VA 23113	804-419-8600	R	11*	<.1
1805	Actioneer Inc—*Thomas G Hagen*	56 John F Kennedy St, Cambridge MA 02138	617-864-1400	R	11*	<.1
1806	Envyr Corp—*Ralph Jordan*	4915 Waters Edge Dr St, Raleigh NC 27606	919-851-2239	R	11*	<.1
1807	InfoTech Marketing—*Tim Walters*	8601 W Cross Dr Unit F, Littleton CO 80123	720-732-4588	R	11*	<.1
1808	International Typeface Corp Monotype Imaging Holdings Inc	500 Unicorn Park Dr, Woburn MA 01801	781-970-6020	S	11*	<.1
1809	Mental Automation Inc—*Laurence Johnson*	6603 84th St Ct NW, Gig Harbor WA 98332	253-858-8104	R	11*	<.1
1810	Mesquite Software Inc—*Nan Schwetman*	PO Box 63206, Austin TX 78755	512-338-9153	R	11*	<.1
1811	Pallas International Corp	PO Box 612525, San Jose CA 95161	408-923-5509	R	11*	<.1
1812	Petrospec Technologies—*Mark Herkommer*	409 N Loop 336 W Ste 6, Conroe TX 77301	936-788-7778	R	11*	<.1
1813	PTV America Inc—*Thomas Bauer*	9755 SW Barnes Rd Ste, Portland OR 97225	503-297-2556	R	11*	<.1
1814	Qsoft Solutions Corp—*Masayoshi Matsumoto*	725 S Adams Rd Ste L-7, Birmingham MI 48009		R	11*	<.1
1815	SYSTEK Technologies Inc—*Shashi Menon*	PO Box 2550, Lake Havasu City AZ 86405	928-453-9587	R	11*	<.1
1816	CardSystems Inc—*John M Perry*	1721 SE 47th Ter, Cape Coral FL 33904	239-549-5055	R	11	.2
1817	Clickfox Inc—*Marco Pacelli*	3445 Peachtree Rd Ne S, Atlanta GA 30326	404-351-8020	R	11*	.1
1818	Doculynx Inc—*Farhad Khalafi*	6916 N 97th Cir Ste C-, Omaha NE 68122	402-339-9972	R	11	.1
1819	Long Wave Inc—*Phil Miller*	115 E California Ste 4, Oklahoma City OK 73104	405-235-2217	R	10	.1
1820	Allume Systems Inc—*William W Smith Jr* Smith Micro Software Inc	185 Westridge Dr, Watsonville CA 95076	831-761-6200	S	10	.1
1821	Gitano Software—*Jesus Moreno*	2305 E 1050 S, Springville UT 84663	801-489-7883	R	10*	2.0

Note: An asterisk (*) indicates an estimated financial figure. The company type code used is as follows: R = Private, P = Public, S = Private Subsidiary, B = Public Subsidiary, D = Division, J = Joint Venture, I = Investment Fund.

COMPANY RANKINGS BY SALES WITHIN 4-DIGIT SIC

Rank	Company Name—Executive Officer	Address, City, State, Zip	Phone	Type	Fin	Empls
1822	Resonate Inc—Peter R Watkins	90 Great Oaks Blvd Ste, San Jose CA 95119	408-545-5501	S	10*	.2
1823	Seismic Micro-Technology Inc—Arshad Matin	8584 Katy Fwy Ste 400, Houston TX 77024	713-464-6188	S	10*	.1
1824	Meridian Systems—John Bodrozic	1720 Prairie City Rd S, Folsom CA 95630	916-294-2000	R	10*	.1
1825	TYX Corp—Narayanan Ramachandran	1861 Wiehle Ave Ste 31, Reston VA 20190	703-264-1080	R	10*	.1
1826	LaserFiche Document Imaging—Nien-Ling Wacker Compulink Management Center Inc	3545 Long Beach Blvd, Long Beach CA 90807	562-988-1688	D	10*	.1
1827	Micro Analysis and Design Inc—K Ronald Laughery	4949 Pearl E Cir Ste 3, Boulder CO 80301	303-442-6947	S	10*	.1
1828	ChartLogic Inc—Zubin Emsley	3995 S 700 East Ste 20, Salt Lake City UT 84107	801-365-1800	R	10*	.1
1829	Blackwell Global Consulting LLC—Rod Beeler	100 S Wacker Dr Ste 80, Chicago IL 60606	312-553-0730	S	10*	.1
1830	Nemetschek Vectorworks Inc—Sean Flaherty	7150 Riverwood Dr, Columbia MD 21046	410-290-5114	S	10*	.1
1831	AMTECH Inc (Bensalem Pennsylvania)—Cosmo DeNicola	515 Pennsylvania Ave S, Fort Washington PA 19034	215-639-9540	R	10*	.1
1832	International Business Systems-United States Inc—Christian Paulsson	90 Blue Ravine Rd, Folsom CA 95630		S	10*	.1
1833	Paciolan Systems Inc—Dave Butler	5171 California Ave St, Irvine CA 92617		R	10*	.1
1834	Tone Software Corp—John Hutchison	1735 S Brookhurst St, Anaheim CA 92804	714-991-9460	R	10*	.1
1835	ComFrame Software Corp—Marc Guthrie	100 Corporate Pkwy Ste, Birmingham AL 35242	205-329-7300	R	10*	.1
1836	Compris Technologies Inc—Alaa Pasha	2651 Satellite Blvd, Duluth GA 30096	770-418-4616	S	10*	.1
1837	Diamond Data Systems Inc	2561 Citiplace Ct Ste, Baton Rouge LA 70808	228-688-3145	S	10*	.1
1838	National Law Library Inc—David Harriman	4301 Windfern Rd Ste 2, Houston TX 77041		R	10*	.1
1839	TREEV—David E MacWhorter	13454 Sunrise Valley D, Herndon VA 20171	703-478-2260	R	10*	.1
1840	Brodart Co- Books and Automation Div	500 Arch St, Williamsport PA 17701	570-326-2461	D	10*	.1
1841	Bristol Technology Inc—Keith Blackwell	39 Old Ridgebury Rd, Danbury CT 06810	203-798-1017	R	10*	.1
1842	Codman and Shurtleff Inc—P Laxmin Laxminarain	325 Paramount Dr, Raynham MA 02767	508-880-8100	S	10*	.1
1843	ESI Systems Inc—Sean Murphy	PO Box 15888, Tallahassee FL 32303	850-575-0179	R	10*	.1
1844	eSoft Inc—Jeffery J Finn	295 Interlocken Blvd, Broomfield CO 80021	303-444-1600	R	10*	.1
1845	PC-Doctor Inc—Aki Mak	10345 Professional Cir, Reno NV 89521	775-336-4000	R	10*	.1
1846	FACTOR—Jerry Hess	3030 NW Expy Ste 1500, Oklahoma City OK 73112		R	10*	.1
1847	Khameleon Software—Douglas Angelone	400 N Ashley Dr Ste 22, Tampa FL 33602	813-223-4148	D	10*	.1
1848	Dexter and Chaney Inc—John Chaney	9700 Lake City Way NE, Seattle WA 98115	206-364-1400	R	10*	.1
1849	Dimensional Insight Inc—Frederick Powers	60 Mall Rd, Burlington MA 01803	781-229-9111	R	10*	.1
1850	FutureSoft Engineering Inc—Tim Farrell	12012 Wickchester Ln S, Houston TX 77079	281-496-9400	R	10	.1
1851	SoftLanding Systems Inc—Paul Schlieben	84 Elm St, Peterborough NH 03458	818-838-0606	D	10*	.1
1852	American Education Corp—Thomas A Shively	7506 N Broadway Ext St, Oklahoma City OK 73116	405-840-6031	R	10*	.1
1853	Astute Inc—Joseph M Sanda	2400 Corporate Exchang, Columbus OH 43231	614-508-6100	R	10*	.1
1854	Optical Image Technology Inc—Ron Prichardt	100 Oakwood Ave Ste 70, State College PA 16803	814-238-0038	R	10*	.1
1855	Intrix Systems Group Inc—Jeff Connors	2260 Douglas Blvd Ste, Roseville CA 95661	916-577-1315	R	10*	.1
1856	Mitem Corp—Aurel Kleinerman	640 Menlo Ave, Menlo Park CA 94025	650-323-1500	R	10*	.1
1857	ESI/Technologies Inc—John Davies	14 Lafayette Sq Ste172, Buffalo NY 14203	716-852-8000	R	10*	<.1
1858	Feith Systems and Software Inc—Don Feith	425 Maryland Dr, Fort Washington PA 19034	215-646-8000	R	10*	<.1
1859	GoAhead Software Inc—John Hansen	10900 NE 8th St Ste 12, Bellevue WA 98004	425-453-1900	R	10*	<.1
1860	InterTrade Systems Corp—Sia Hashemi	1501 Broadway 12th Fl, New York NY 10036	450-786-1666	R	10*	<.1
1861	Professional Computer Systems Co—Kim Ingerslev	PO Box 116, Denison IA 51442	712-263-3106	R	10*	<.1
1862	Allen Communication Inc—Ron Zamir	175 W 200 S Ste 100 Ga, Salt Lake City UT 84101	801-537-7800	R	10*	<.1
1863	Aristotle International Inc—John Aristotle Phillips	205 Pennsylvania Ave S, Washington DC 20003	202-543-8345	R	10*	<.1
1864	Schoolhouse Software Inc—Robert Levine	2540 Warren Dr Ste A, Rocklin CA 95677	916-577-2900	R	10*	<.1
1865	TechExcel Inc—Tieren Zhou	3675 Mt Diablo Blvd St, Lafayette CA 94549	925-871-3900	R	10*	<.1
1866	Equilibrium—Sean Barger	3 Harbor Ste 100, Sausalito CA 94965	415-332-4343	R	10*	<.1
1867	Knight BondPoint Inc—Thomas Joyce	2859 Paces Ferry Rd, Atlanta GA 30339		S	10*	<.1
1868	Visual Network Design Inc—Emmett Demoss	101 California St Ste, San Francisco CA 94111	415-946-8949	R	10*	<.1
1869	Advisor Software Inc—Andrew Rudd PhD	2175 N California Blvd, Walnut Creek CA 94596	925-299-7782	R	10*	<.1
1870	Chip Estimate Cadence Design Systems Inc	2655 Seely Ave, San Jose CA 95134	408-943-1234	S	10*	<.1
1871	Investment Support Systems Inc—Peter F Armstrong	222 New Rd, Parsippany NJ 07054	973-244-1661	R	10*	<.1
1872	Xtiva Financial Systems Inc—William Lieberman	100 Bush St Ste 700, San Francisco CA 94104	415-229-9700	R	10*	<.1
1873	2nd Sight Software Inc—Gary Angel	7430 Redwood Blvd Ste, Novato CA 94945	415-493-2580	R	10*	<.1
1874	Global Business Dimensions Inc—Sanjay Prasad	220 West Pkwy Ste 8, Pompton Plains NJ 07444	973-831-5866	R	10*	<.1
1875	Napersoft Inc—Bartley J Carlson	40 Shuman Blvd, Naperville IL 60563	630-420-1515	R	10*	<.1
1876	Advanced Information Services Inc—Stephen Shook	5407 N University St S, Peoria IL 61614	309-690-7500	R	10*	<.1
1877	AgriSoft CMC—Anthony Barton	9130 Anaheim Pl, Rancho Cucamonga CA 91730	909-980-5338	R	10*	<.1
1878	AlarmSoft Inc—Joe Agreste	800 Seahawk Cir Ste 13, Virginia Beach VA 23452	757-226-7226	R	10*	<.1
1879	Apunix Computer Services Inc—Peter Berens	11610 Iberia Pl Ste 10, San Diego CA 92128	858-673-8649	R	10*	<.1
1880	BulletProof Corp	2400 E Las Olas Blvd S, Fort Lauderdale FL 33301		R	10*	<.1
1881	Cirius Group Inc—Paul Bartlett	140 Gregory Ln Ste240, Pleasant Hill CA 94523	925-685-9300	R	10*	<.1
1882	Cogility Software Inc—Matthew Ghourdjian	111 N Market St, San Jose CA 95113	949-752-4694	R	10*	<.1
1883	Cogix Corp—Camilo Wilson	135 W Franklin St, Monterey CA 93940	831-657-9541	R	10*	<.1
1884	Core Logic Software Inc—Francisco Caceres	2300 Elliott Ave Ste 5, Seattle WA 98121	206-801-1717	R	10*	<.1
1885	Dew Software Inc—Surefh Deopura	983 Corporate Way, Fremont CA 94539	510-490-9995	R	10*	<.1
1886	Digital Fountain Inc—Charlie Oppenheimer	39141 Civic Center Dr, Fremont CA 94538	510-284-1400	R	10*	<.1
1887	dt Search Corp	6852 Tulip Hill Ter, Bethesda MD 20816	301-263-0731	R	10*	<.1
1888	e-Agency Inc—David Dunn	291 3rd St, Oakland CA 94607	510-496-2300	R	10*	<.1
1889	e-Builder Inc—Jonathan Antevy	1800 NW 69th Ave Ste 2, Plantation FL 33313	954-938-6288	R	10*	<.1
1890	EDGE Software Services Inc—Kevin Clark	4196 Merchant Plz Ste, Woodbridge VA 22192	703-492-4955	R	10*	<.1
1891	GMC Software Technology Inc—Rene Muller	529 Main St Ste 223, Charlestown MA 02129	617-712-1200	R	10*	<.1
1892	InfoPro Inc (McLean Virginia)—Suteera Graham	8200 Greensboro Dr Ste, McLean VA 22102	703-226-2520	R	10*	<.1
1893	Innovative Routines International Inc—Paul Friedland	2194 Hwy A1A 3rd Fl, Melbourne FL 32937	321-777-8889	R	10*	<.1
1894	InSync Software Inc (San Jose California)—Ashish Chona	224 Airport Pkwy Ste S, San Jose CA 95110	408-352-0600	R	10*	<.1
1895	Integrated Management Concepts—Mark Tillema	299 W Hillcrest Dr Ste, Thousand Oaks CA 91360	805-778-1629	R	10*	<.1
1896	Jefferies and Company Inc—Richard B Handler	11100 Santa Monica Blv, Los Angeles CA 90025	310-445-1199	S	10*	<.1
1897	Linographics Inc	1116 W Collins Ave, Orange CA 92867	714-639-0511	R	10*	<.1
1898	LOGICARE Corp—David Elvig	2620 Stein Blvd, Eau Claire WI 54701	715-839-0700	R	10*	<.1
1899	MachroTech LLC—Manish Chowdhary	10 Middle St Park City, Bridgeport CT 06604	203-336-2284	R	10*	<.1
1900	Micro J Systems Inc—Mimi Slater	200 E Del Mar Blvd Ste, Pasadena CA 91105	310-458-1997	R	10*	<.1
1901	NetAcquire Corp—Preston Hauck	12000 115th Ave NE, Kirkland WA 98034	425-821-3100	R	10*	<.1
1902	Oil and Gas Information Systems Inc—Charles E Blanton	6500 W Fwy Ste 1020, Fort Worth TX 76116	817-877-5341	R	10*	<.1
1903	Persystent Software—Joseph M Loughry III	3930 Premier North Dr, Tampa FL 33618	813-264-2999	R	10*	<.1
1904	Property Automation Software Corp Domin-8 Enterprise Solutions	4000 International Pky, Carrollton TX 75007	972-820-3000	S	10*	<.1
1905	R Michael Donovan and Company Inc—R Michael Donovan	945 Concord St, Framingham MA 01701	508-788-1100	R	10*	<.1
1906	Rampage Systems Inc—Thomas Genova	411 Waverley Oaks Rd S, Waltham MA 02452	781-891-9400	R	10*	<.1
1907	Rental Management Inc—Paul Chapdelaine	40 Darling Dr, Avon CT 06001	860-677-1005	R	10*	<.1

Rank	Company Name—*Executive Officer*	Address, City, State, Zip	Phone	Type	Fin	Empls
1908	Saqqara Systems Inc—*Horacio R Woolcott*	3155 Kearney St Ste 22, Fremont CA 94538	510-360-5361	R	10*	<.1
1909	Sendside Networks Inc—*William Borghetti*	6440 S Millrock Dr Ste, Salt Lake City UT 84121	801-747-6320	R	10*	<.1
1910	Slickedit Inc—*J Clark Maurer*	3000 Aerial Ctr Pky St, Morrisville NC 27560	919-473-0070	R	10*	<.1
1911	Software Diversified Services Inc—*John Lampi*	1322 81st Ave NE, Spring Lake Park MN 55432	763-571-9000	R	10*	<.1
1912	Strategic Insurance Software LLC—*Alex Deak*	4181 Arlingate Plaza, Columbus OH 43228		S	10*	<.1
1913	TrueDemand Software Inc—*Robert E Hill*	485 Alberto Way Ste 20, Los Gatos CA 95032	408-399-1924	R	10*	<.1
1914	Univa UD—*Gary Tyreman*	1001 Warrenville Rd St, Lisle IL 60532	630-563-8600	R	10*	<.1
1915	UpNet Technologies Inc—*Jennifer Amys*	7825 Washington Ave St, Minneapolis MN 55439	952-944-2345	R	10*	<.1
1916	Upstream Technologies LLC—*Dave Locke*	114 Eagle Ct, Golden CO 80403	303-215-0007	R	10*	<.1
1917	VanDyke Software Inc—*Jeff P Van Dyke*	4848 Tramway Ridge Dr, Albuquerque NM 87111	505-332-5700	R	10*	<.1
1918	Sentrigo Inc—*Nathan Shuchami* McAfee Inc	2821 Mission College B, Santa Clara CA 95054	408-346-3016	S	10*	<.1
1919	DataMotion—*Bob Bales*	35 Airport Rd Ste 120, Morristown NJ 07960	973-455-1245	R	10*	<.1
1920	SourceGear LLC—*Eric Sink*	115 N Neil St Ste 408, Champaign IL 61820	217-356-0105	R	10*	<.1
1921	Serenity Information Tech Inc—*Kakarlapudi Varma*	2750 Peachtree Industr, Duluth GA 30097	770-242-9966	R	10*	<.1
1922	Quickoffice Inc—*Alan Masarek*	4965 Preston Park Blvd, Plano TX 75093	972-931-8181	R	10*	<.1
1923	CIMS Lab Inc—*Samuel Palmisano*	3013 Douglas Blvd Ste, Roseville CA 95661	916-783-8525	R	10*	<.1
1924	Datasurge—*Nadim Ash*	70 Autran Ave, North Andover MA 01845	978-974-0857	R	10*	<.1
1925	North Atlantic Publishing Systems Inc	66 Commonwealth Ave, Concord MA 01742	978-371-8989	R	10*	<.1
1926	Open Systems Management Inc—*Neil Chaney*	1511 3rd Ave Ste 905, Seattle WA 98101	206-583-8373	R	10*	<.1
1927	Fog City Software Inc—*Will Mayall*	1840 41st Ave Ste 710, Capitola CA 95010	831-475-5258	R	10*	<.1
1928	King Computer Services Inc—*Morrison Budlong*	3115 Foothill Blvd Ste, La Crescenta CA 91214	818-951-5240	R	10*	<.1
1929	MediaNet Inc—*Tom Mucciolo*	305 Madison Ave, New York NY 10165	212-682-2250	R	10*	<.1
1930	Sierra Solutions—*Jeffrey Soloman*	637 Lucerne Rd, Cayucos CA 93430		R	10*	<.1
1931	StatPac Inc—*David Walonick*	8609 Lyndale Ave S Ste, Minneapolis MN 55420	715-442-2261	R	10*	<.1
1932	Technical Advisors Group Inc—*Suinder Sud*	5918 Lilley Rd Ste 1, Canton MI 48187	734-981-3430	R	10*	<.1
1933	Trident Software Inc (Hamden Connecticut)—*Andrew Abate*	PO Box 5608, Hamden CT 06518	203-877-4331	R	10*	<.1
1934	GameHouse—*Garr Godfrey*	PO Box 91123, Seattle WA 98111	206-442-5881	S	10	N/A
1935	Retirement Plan Company LLC—*John Kopra*	PO Box 1429, Brentwood TN 37024	615-986-5500	S	10*	N/A
1936	Practice Manager Group LLC—*Jason Primuth*	3025 S Parker Rd Ste 1, Aurora CO 80014	303-302-7600	R	10*	.1
1937	Serenic Corp—*Randy Keith*	7175 W Jefferson Ave S, Lakewood CO 80235	303-980-6007	P	9	N/A
1938	Industrial and Financial Systems Inc—*Alastair Sorbie*	250 S Craycroft Rd Ste, Tucson AZ 85711	520-512-2000	S	9*	.5
1939	SE Technologies Inc (Stamford Connecticut)—*Phil Pead*	2777 Summer St 6th Fl, Stamford CT 06905	203-357-1772	R	9*	.2
1940	Valve Corp—*Gabe Newell*	PO Box 1688, Bellevue WA 98009	425-889-9642	R	9*	.2
1941	SPS Commerce Inc—*Archie Black*	333 S 7th St Ste 1000, Minneapolis MN 55402	612-435-9400	R	9*	.1
1942	Propel Software Corp—*Steve Kirsch*	1010 Rincon Cir, San Jose CA 95131	408-571-6300	R	9*	.1
1943	Century Distribution Systems Inc—*Toshio Suzuki*	8730 Stony Point Pky S, Richmond VA 23235	804-327-4401	S	9*	.1
1944	Heartbeat Digital Inc—*Bill Drummy*	200 Husdon St 9th Fl, New York NY 10013	212-343-2064	R	9*	.1
1945	Numerical Algorithms Group—*Rob Meyer*	1431 Opus Pl Ste 220, Downers Grove IL 60515	630-971-2337	R	9*	.1
1946	Sageworks Inc—*Brian Hamilton*	5565 Centerview Dr Ste, Raleigh NC 27606	919-851-7474	R	9*	.1
1947	iBASEt—*Ladeira Poonian*	27442 Portola Pky Ste, Foothill Ranch CA 92610	949-598-5200	R	9*	.1
1948	Jobscope Corp—*Hank Sanders*	PO Box 6767, Greenville SC 29606	864-458-3143	R	9*	.1
1949	ProSight Inc—*John Cimral* Primavera Systems Inc	9600 SW Barnes Rd Ste, Portland OR 97225	503-889-4800	D	9*	.1
1950	Algor Inc—*Michael Bussler*	150 Beta Dr, Pittsburgh PA 15238	412-967-2700	R	9*	.1
1951	Intuit Construction Business Solutions—*Brad Smith* Intuit Inc	2632 Marine Way, Mountain View CA 94043	650-944-6000	D	9*	.1
1952	Baudville Inc—*Debara Sikanas*	5380 52nd St SE, Grand Rapids MI 49512	616-698-0889	R	9*	.1
1953	Melissa Data Corp—*Raymond F Melissa*	22382 Avenida Empresa, Rancho Santa Margarita CA 92688	949-858-3000	R	9*	.1
1954	Telecorp Products Inc	2000 E Oakley Park Rd, Walled Lake MI 48390	248-960-1000	R	9*	.1
1955	Luminex Software Inc—*Arthur Tolsma*	871 Marlborough Ave, Riverside CA 92507	951-781-4100	R	9*	<.1
1956	D-TECH Inc—*Harvey Diez*	PO BOX 480942, Tulsa OK 74148		R	9*	<.1
1957	Dydacomp Development Corp—*Fred Lizza*	11-D Commerce Way, Totowa NJ 07512	973-237-9415	R	9*	<.1
1958	PSG International Inc—*Steve Toth Jr*	PO Box 498, Cornwall NY 12518	201-784-9003	R	9*	<.1
1959	UAI Technology Inc—*Steven Maier*	PO Box 13628, Research Triangle Park NC 27709	919-541-9339	R	9*	<.1
1960	Ricomm Systems Inc—*C Anthony Lawry*	20000 Horizon Way Ste, Mount Laurel NJ 08054	856-359-9090	R	9*	<.1
1961	Human Software Company Inc	PO Box 16, Wrightsville Beach NC 28480	408-399-0057	R	9*	<.1
1962	Interactive Solutions Inc (Hasbrouck Heights New Jersey)—*James Ning*	377 Rte 17 S Ste 618, Hasbrouck Heights NJ 07604	908-322-5991	R	9*	<.1
1963	Idea Art Inc—*Steve Chamberlain*	825 N Cascade Ave, Colorado Springs CO 80903		R	9*	<.1
1964	Stampede Technologies Inc—*Gordon Dorworth*	80 Rhoads Ctr Dr, Dayton OH 45458	937-291-5035	R	9*	<.1
1965	EnFocus Software Inc—*David van Driessche*	16000 Ventura Blvd Ste, Encino CA 91436	818-501-2380	R	9*	<.1
1966	AL Systems Inc—*Jim Iversen*	385 Franklin Ave Ste C, Rockaway NJ 07866	973-586-8500	R	9*	<.1
1967	AssurX—*Eric June*	18525 Sutter Blvd Ste, Morgan Hill CA 95037	408-778-1376	R	9*	<.1
1968	DSI (Englewood Colorado)—*Steve Suttman*	1 Inverness Dr E, Englewood CO 80112	303-754-2000	R	9*	<.1
1969	Pedagogue Solutions—*Steve Just*	1060 State Rd Ste 101, Princeton NJ 08540	609-921-7585	R	9*	<.1
1970	The Allegiant Group Inc—*Steven Drees*	7577 Central Park Blvd, Mason OH 45040	513-984-1822	R	9*	<.1
1971	Vector Networks Inc—*Ester Weaver*	541 10th St Unit 123, Atlanta GA 30318	770-622-2850	R	9*	<.1
1972	Computer Helper Publishing Inc—*Mel Wygant*	PO Box 30191, Gahanna OH 43230		R	9*	<.1
1973	AccuRev Inc—*Lorne Cooper*	10 Maguire Rd Bldg 1, Lexington MA 02421	781-861-8700	R	9*	<.1
1974	Senior Systems Inc—*R Russell Alfieri*	201 Boston Post Rd W, Marlborough MA 01752	508-480-0101	R	9*	<.1
1975	Upstanding LLC—*Ed Cisek*	70 Discovery, Irvine CA 92618	949-453-2000	R	9*	<.1
1976	Astera Software Inc—*Ibrahim Surani*	16530 Ventura Blvd, Encino CA 91436	805-579-0004	R	9*	<.1
1977	Global Technology Associates Inc—*Nick Squire*	3505 Lake Lynda Dr Ste, Orlando FL 32817	407-380-0220	R	9*	<.1
1978	ORSYP Software Inc—*Mark Shotwell*	300 Trade Center Ste 5, Woburn MA 01801	781-782-5715	S	9*	<.1
1979	Cirqit Inc—*Carlos Mena*	100 S Jefferson Rd 1st, Whippany NJ 07981	973-319-8205	R	9*	<.1
1980	Crossbeam Systems Inc—*Mike Ruffolo*	80 Central St, Boxborough MA 01719	978-318-7500	R	9*	<.1
1981	Akshay Software International Inc—*Asant Viswanath*	103 Carnegie Ctr Ste 3, Princeton NJ 08540	609-750-1995	R	9*	<.1
1982	Ascend Software Inc—*Lee Blattner*	500 S Kraemer Blvd Ste, Brea CA 92821		R	9*	<.1
1983	MiniSoft Inc—*Bob Taylor*	1024 1st St, Snohomish WA 98290	360-568-6602	R	9*	<.1
1984	Sea Change Systems Inc—*Philip T Adams*	83 Pine St, Peabody MA 01960		R	9*	<.1
1985	Softbase Systems Inc—*Stephen Woodward*	20 Fall Pippln Ln Ste, Asheville NC 28803		R	9*	<.1
1986	Trans-Micro Inc	PO Box 898, Fairfield FL 32634		R	9*	<.1
1987	WireSpring Technologies Inc—*Bill Gerba*	1901 W Cypress Creek R, Fort Lauderdale FL 33309	954-548-3300	R	9*	<.1
1988	Zuberance Inc—*Rob Fuggetta*	628 El Camino Real, San Carlos CA 94070		R	9*	<.1
1989	Altima Technologies Inc—*Sara Clark*	2300 Cabot Dr Ste 535, Lisle IL 60532	630-281-6464	R	9*	<.1
1990	APTE Ino—*Sally deVincentis*	820 Davis St Ste 300, Evanston IL 60201	847-866-1872	R	9*	<.1
1991	BBI Computer Systems Inc	14105 Heritage Ln, Silvor Spring MD 20906	301-871-1094	R	9*	<.1
1992	Datatex Textile Information Systems Inc—*Ronen Hagin*	11810 Northfall Ln, Alpharetta GA 30009	770-667-8656	S	9*	<.1
1993	Havok Inc—*David O'Meara*	49 Stevenson St Fl 11, San Francisco CA 94105	415-543-4620	R	9*	<.1

Note: An asterisk (*) indicates an estimated financial figure. The company type code used is as follows: R = Private, P = Public, S = Private Subsidiary, B = Public Subsidiary, D = Division, J = Joint Venture, I = Investment Fund.

COMPANY RANKINGS BY SALES WITHIN 4-DIGIT SIC

Rank	Company Name—*Executive Officer*	Address, City, State, Zip	Phone	Type	Fin	Empls
1994	HowardSoft—*JE Howard*	7852 Ivanhoe Ave, La Jolla CA 92037	858-454-0121	R	9*	<.1
1995	Meeting Maker Inc—*John T Anderson*	111 Speen St, Framingham MA 01701	508-416-3600	R	9*	<.1
1996	NaturalInsight—*Stefan T Midford*	21240 Ridgetop Cir Ste, Sterling VA 20166		R	9*	<.1
1997	NedGraphics Inc—*Pieter Aarts*	104 W 40th St 12th Fl, New York NY 10018	212-921-2727	S	9*	<.1
1998	Network Automation Inc—*Gary Bishop*	3530 Wilshire Blvd Ste, Los Angeles CA 90010	213-738-1700	R	9*	<.1
1999	Panda Software—*Mikel Urizarbarrena*	PO Box 10578, Glendale CA 91209	818-543-6901	R	9*	<.1
2000	Prospx Inc—*Todd L Young*	7600B N Capital of Tex, Austin TX 78731	512-419-9970	R	9*	<.1
2001	Revelwood Inc—*Kenneth M Wolf*	14 Walsh Dr Ste 303, Parsippany NJ 07054	201-984-3030	R	9*	<.1
2002	TV One Multimedia Solutions Inc—*Dave Barnes*	2791 Circleport Dr, Erlanger KY 41018	859-282-7303	R	9*	<.1
2003	Quality Systems International Corp—*Wayne Verost*	445 Godwin Ave, Midland Park NJ 07432	201-251-2101	R	9*	<.1
2004	Waterloo Manufacturing Software—*Andrew Gilman*	PO Box 81264, Wellesley MA 02481	781-237-2678	R	9*	<.1
2005	FreedomWare Software Products Inc—*Doug Griffith*	PO Box 2604, Joplin MO 64803	417-623-8761	R	9*	<.1
2006	Phoenix Phive Software Corp—*Murray Whipps*	7802 E Gray Road Ste 1, Scottsdale AZ 85260	480-483-0991	R	9*	<.1
2007	Simul8 Corp—*Mark Elder*	225 Franklin St 26th F, Boston MA 02110		S	9*	<.1
2008	Pradeep K Gupta Inc—*Pradeep Gupta*	117 Southbury Rd, Clifton Park NY 12065	518-383-1167	R	9*	<.1
2009	Zen Software Inc—*Harlan Cooper*	136 Old Dike Rd, Trumbull CT 06611	203-380-9047	R	9*	<.1
2010	Alberg Software Inc—*Uma Marupudi*	800 W 5th Ave Ste 201a, Naperville IL 60563	630-470-6244	R	9*	.1
2011	Rm Educational Software Inc—*Kevin Pawsey*	310 Varstable Rd Ste 1, Hyannis MA 02601	508-862-0700	S	9*	.1
2012	Corrugated Services Corp—*Cosmo Denicola*	515 Pennsylvania Ave S, Fort Washington PA 19034	215-639-9540	R	9*	.1
2013	Knowland Group Inc—*Michael K McKean*	2424 Northgate Dr, Salisbury MD 21801	410-860-2270	R	9	.1
2014	TechRadium Inc—*Ryan Rodkey*	1 Sugar Creek Center B, Sugar Land TX 77478	281-207-4893	R	9	<.1
2015	CPA Global North America LLC—*Jeffrey Maddox*	2318 Mill Rd Fl 12, Alexandria VA 22314	703-739-2234	R	9*	<.1
2016	Swce Inc—*Terrence Schroeder*	360 Mount Harmony Rd, Bernardsville NJ 07924	908-766-5695	R	9*	<.1
2017	Dainippon Screen Engineering of America Inc	17942 Cowan Ave, Irvine CA 92614	949-477-4810	R	9	<.1
2018	Nucleus LLC	570 Lake Cook Rd Ste 1, Deerfield IL 60015	847-948-7585	R	9*	<.1
2019	Pacific WebWorks Inc—*Kenneth W Bell*	230 W 400 S 1st Fl, Salt Lake City UT 84101	801-518-9020	P	9	<.1
2020	Rivet Software—*Mike Rohan*	4340 S Monaco St Ste 1, Denver CO 80237	720-249-2100	R	8	.4
2021	Possiblenow Inc—*Scott Frey*	4400 River Green Pkwy, Duluth GA 30096	770-255-1020	R	8*	.1
2022	Local Matters Inc—*Mat Stover*	1221 Auraria Pky, Denver CO 80204	303-572-1122	R	8*	.2
2023	Auto-trol Technology Corp—*Howard B Hillman*	11030 CirclePoint Rd S, Westminster CO 80020	303-452-4919	R	8*	.2
2024	1SYNC Inc—*Robert Noe* GS1 US Inc	1009 Lenox Dr Ste 202, Lawrenceville NJ 08648	609-620-0200	S	8*	.2
2025	Mindbody Inc—*Rick Stollmeyer*	4051 Broad St Ste 220, San Luis Obispo CA 93401	805-546-2000	R	8*	.1
2026	Tenrox Inc—*Rudolf Melik*	1010 N Central Ave, Glendale CA 91202	626-796-6640	R	8*	.1
2027	WordSmart Corp—*DavidA Kay*	10025 Mesa Rim Rd, San Diego CA 92121	858-565-8068	R	8*	.1
2028	Wenn/Soft Inc—*Jim Wenninger*	1970 S Calhoun Rd, New Berlin WI 53151	262-821-4100	R	8*	.1
2029	Campus Management Corp—*Timothy B Loomer*	777 Yamato Rd, Boca Raton FL 33431	561-923-2500	R	8*	.1
2030	DP Solutions Inc—*Frederick Riek*	1801 Stanley Rd Ste 30, Greensboro NC 27407	336-854-7700	R	8*	.1
2031	Kingland Systems Corp—*David J Kingland*	1401 6th Ave S, Clear Lake IA 50428	641-355-1000	S	8*	.1
2032	Parasoft Corp—*Wayne Ariola*	101 E Huntington Dr, Monrovia CA 91016	626-256-3680	R	8*	.1
2033	StataCorp LP—*William Gould*	4905 Lakeway Dr, College Station TX 77845	979-696-4600	R	8*	.1
2034	Systemware Inc (Dallas Texas)—*Dan Basso*	15301 Dallas Pky Ste 1, Addison TX 75001	972-239-0200	R	8*	.1
2035	VergeTech Inc—*Philip Verges*	14860 Montfort Dr, Dallas TX 75240	972-386-3372	R	8*	.1
2036	Transnational Computer Technology—*Ravi Kumar*	100 N Sepulveda Blvd 1, El Segundo CA 90245	310-615-0881	R	8*	.1
2037	Insurance Information Technologies Inc—*Ray Simon*	1811 Centre Point Cir, Naperville IL 60563		R	8*	.1
2038	Softsol Resources Inc—*Srini Madala*	48383 Fremont Blvd Ste, Fremont CA 94538	510-824-2000	R	8*	.1
2039	Sigma Micro Corp—*Matthew Konkle*	6720 Parkdale Pl, Indianapolis IN 46254	317-631-0907	R	8*	.1
2040	AFS Technologies Inc (Phoenix Arizona)—*Kurien Jacob*	2141 E Highland Ave St, Phoenix AZ 85016	602-522-8282	R	8*	.1
2041	Dunn Solutions Group—*William Dunn*	5550 W Touhy Ave Ste 4, Skokie IL 60077	847-673-0900	R	8*	.1
2042	Silvon Software Inc—*Mike Hennel*	900 Oakmont Ln Ste 400, Westmont IL 60559	630-655-3313	R	8*	.1
2043	Global Shop Solutions Inc—*Dustin Alexander*	975 Evergreen Cir, The Woodlands TX 77380	281-681-1959	R	8*	.1
2044	Innovative Computing Corp—*Ernest Betancourt*	5924 NW 2nd Ste 100, Oklahoma City OK 73127	405-495-8788	S	8*	.1
2045	Cerner BeyondNow Inc	2800 Rockcreek Pkwy, Kansas City MO 64117	816-201-1024	S	8*	.1
2046	CosmoCom Inc—*Ari Sonesh*	121 Broad Hollow Rd, Melville NY 11747	631-940-4200	R	8*	.1
2047	Gomembers Inc CDC Software	PO Box 747, Herndon VA 20172	571-262-5171	S	8*	.1
2048	Gasper Corp—*Richard Leone*	1700 S Patterson Blvd, Dayton OH 45479	937-445-4201	S	8*	.1
2049	Rediker Software Inc—*Richard Rediker*	2 Wilbraham Rd, Hampden MA 01036	413-566-3463	R	8*	.1
2050	Kaba Benzing America Inc—*Richard Souders*	3015 N Commerce Pkwy, Miramar FL 33025	954-416-1720	S	8*	.1
2051	Software Technology Inc (Lincoln Nebraska)—*Brad Berlin*	1621 Cushman Dr, Lincoln NE 68512	402-423-1440	R	8*	.1
2052	Metier Ltd—*Douglas D Clark*	2611 Jefferson Davis H, Arlington VA 22202	703-465-9500	R	8*	.1
2053	QualityLogic Inc—*Dave Jollata*	5401 Tech Cir, Moorpark CA 93021	805-531-9030	R	8*	.1
2054	Spatial Technologies—*Jean Marc Guillard*	310 Interlocken Pky St, Broomfield CO 80021	303-544-2900	R	8*	.1
2055	Magnum Communications Ltd—*Carl E Eikhoff*	280 Interstate N Cir S, Atlanta GA 30339	770-952-4940	S	8*	.1
2056	Triple Point Technology—*Peter ArmStrong*	222 New Rd, Parsippany NJ 07054	973-244-1661	R	8*	.1
2057	Market Planning Solutions Inc—*James C Auten*	4343 S 118th E Ave Ste, Tulsa OK 74146	918-877-6774	R	8*	.1
2058	CommuniGate Systems Inc—*Vladimir Butenko*	655 Redwood Hwy Ste 27, Mill Valley CA 94941	415-383-7164	R	8	.1
2059	Dharma Systems Inc—*Ken Irinaga*	55 Rte 13, Brookline NH 03033	603-732-4001	R	8*	.1
2060	Digite Inc—*A V Sridhar*	82 Pioneer Way Ste 102, Mountain View CA 94041	650-210-3900	R	8*	.1
2061	Financial Engineering Associates Inc—*Mark Garman*	2100 Milvia St, Berkeley CA 94704	510-548-6200	S	8*	.1
2062	Palo Alto Software Inc—*Sabrina Parsons*	488 E 11th Ave Ste 220, Eugene OR 97401	541-683-6162	R	8*	.1
2063	Penta Technologies Inc—*Karl Koenig*	250 S Executive Dr Ste, Brookfield WI 53005	262-782-7700	R	8*	.1
2064	Sigma Design	5521 Jackson St, Alexandria LA 71303	318-449-9900	R	8*	<.1
2065	Hitachi Software Engineering America Ltd—*Ted Wakabayashi*	601 Gateway Blvd Ste 1, South San Francisco CA 94080	650-615-7600	S	8*	<.1
2066	Wercs Ltd—*Louis Desorbo*	23 British American Bl, Latham NY 12110	518-640-9200	R	8*	<.1
2067	On Demand Technologies Inc—*Tom VanGoethem*	9291 Cody St, Overland Park KS 66214	913-438-1800	R	8*	<.1
2068	OnSet Technology Inc—*Rafi Kaminer*	460 Totten Pond Rd, Waltham MA 02451	781-916-0040	R	8*	<.1
2069	Perimeter Technology Inc—*Donald Brown*	540 N Commercial St, Manchester NH 03101	603-645-1616	R	8*	<.1
2070	V Communications Inc—*Frank van Gilluwe*	2290 N First St Ste 10, San Jose CA 95131	925-474-1801	S	8*	<.1
2071	Architectural Computer Services Inc—*Christopher G Bushnell*	332 E 500 S, Salt Lake City UT 84111	801-521-9162	R	8*	<.1
2072	BatchMaster Software Inc—*Sahib A Dudani*	24461 Ridge Rte DrSte, Laguna Hills CA 92653	949-583-1646	D	8	<.1
2073	CompuLaw LLC—*David Kalmick*	PO Box 67720, Los Angeles CA 90067	310-553-3355	S	8*	<.1
2074	Digital Foundry Inc—*Brad Stauffer*	1707 Tiburon Blvd, Tiburon CA 94920	415-789-1600	R	8*	<.1
2075	HEC Reading Horizons—*Tyson J Smith*	PO Box 849, Bountiful UT 84011	801-295-7054	R	8*	<.1
2076	Lattice Engines—*Shashi Upadhyay*	1825 S Grant Ave Ste 5, San Mateo CA 94402		R	8*	<.1
2077	Micronetics Incorporated Information Management Systems—*David Robbins*	14148 Magnolia Blvd, Sherman Oaks CA 91423	818-784-6890	D	8*	<.1
2078	Strategic Management Group Inc—*Rommin Adl*	6 Tower Bridge Ste 540, Conshohocken PA 19428	484-391-2900	R	8*	<.1
2079	TriVium Systems Inc—*Mathews Manaloor*	1865 NW 169th Place St, Beaverton OR 97006	503-439-9338	R	8*	<.1
2080	Optimum Solutions Inc—*Nabil Hijazi*	210 25th Ave N Ste 700, Nashville TN 37203	615-329-2313	R	8*	<.1

Rank	Company Name—*Executive Officer*	Address, City, State, Zip	Phone	Type	Fin	Empls
2081	Dynamic Interface Systems Corp—*Eric Christeson*	5959 W Century Blvd St, Los Angeles CA 90045	310-568-4567	R	8*	<.1
2082	IQue Inc	101 Larkspur Landing C, Larkspur CA 94939	415-461-7697	S	8*	<.1
	Digital Matrix Systems Inc					
2083	Spectorsoft Corp—*Doug Fowler*	1555 Indian River Blvd, Vero Beach FL 32960	772-770-5670	R	8*	<.1
2084	McCormick Systems Inc—*Todd McCormick*	149 W Boston St, Chandler AZ 85225	480-831-8914	R	8*	<.1
2085	BridgeHead Software—*Tony Cottrill*	400 W Cummings Park St, Woburn MA 01801	781-939-0780	R	8	<.1
2086	CIRCA Information Technologies Inc—*Todd Gilman*	12001 Woodruff Ave Ste, Downey CA 90241	562-803-1594	R	8*	<.1
2087	ComponentOne LLC—*Gustavo Eydelsteyn*	201 S Highland Ave 3rd, Pittsburgh PA 15206	412-681-4343	R	8*	<.1
2088	Perfect Software Inc—*Michael Gabriele*	200 Connecticut Ave, Norwalk CT 06854	203-852-9100	R	8*	<.1
2089	Quality Software Systems Inc	80 Cottontail Ln Ste 1, Somerset NJ 08873	732-805-0400	R	8*	<.1
2090	SystemSoft Corp—*Andy Youniss*	275 Grove St Ste 1-300, Newton MA 02466	617-614-4315	S	8*	<.1
	Rocket Software Inc					
2091	Orchard Learning Inc—*Timothy J Tegeler*	301 Meadow Brook Estat, Wentzville MO 63385		S	8*	<.1
2092	Option Technologies Interactive LLC—*Mark Fite*	3301 Bartlett Boulevar, Orlando FL 32811	407-872-3333	S	8*	<.1
2093	Insite Group Inc	12810 Willow Centre Dr, Houston TX 77066	713-952-9822	R	8*	<.1
2094	Syncronex Inc—*Bruce Leader*	22525 SE 64th Pl Ste 2, Issaquah WA 98027	425-557-3685	R	8*	<.1
2095	ASA Tire Systems—*Wayne Croswell*	25 Manchester St Ste 1, Nashua NH 03063	603-889-8700	D	8*	<.1
2096	Burgiss Group Inc—*James Kocis*	111 River St FL10, Hoboken NJ 07030	201-427-9600	R	8*	<.1
2097	Datamann Inc—*John Mann*	PO Box 1930, Wilder VT 05088	802-295-6600	R	8*	<.1
2098	Edge Systems LLC—*Sam Bishop*	3S721 West Ave Ste 200, Warrenville IL 60555	630-810-9669	R	8*	<.1
2099	Horizon Technology Inc (Lake Forest California)—*Kurt Johnson*	1 Rancho Cir, Lake Forest CA 92630	949-595-8244	R	8*	<.1
2100	Interactive Design and Development Inc—*Mary Miller*	2608 Sheffield Dr, Blacksburg VA 24060	540-953-2627	R	8*	<.1
2101	Iris Medical Inc—*Marsha Black*	563 W 500 S Ste 120, Bountiful UT 84010	801-295-9811	R	8*	<.1
2102	JAMIS Software Corp—*Jeffrey Noolas*	5473 Kearny Villa Rd, San Diego CA 92123		R	8*	<.1
2103	LegalEdge Software—*David Kedson*	175 Strafford Ave Ste, Wayne PA 19087	610-975-5888	R	8*	<.1
2104	MyBizOffice Inc—*Gene Zaino*	13454 Sunrise Valley D, Herndon VA 20171	703-793-6000	R	8	<.1
2105	NewView Technologies Inc—*Scott F Prince*	2124 Mistletoe Blvd, Fort Worth TX 76110	817-335-0300	R	8*	<.1
2106	Software North—*Don Anderson*	2230 E 52nd Ave, Anchorage AK 99507	907-561-4412	R	8*	<.1
2107	CoffeeCup Software Inc—*Nicholas Longo*	165 Courtland St Ste A, Atlanta GA 30303	678-495-3480	R	8*	<.1
2108	ISYS/Biovation—*Robert Liebeskind*	208 E 2nd St, Mineola NY 11501	516-877-7405	R	8*	<.1
2109	DreamFactory Software Inc—*Eric Rubin*	1999 Bascom Ave Ste 92, Campbell CA 95008	650-641-1800	R	8*	<.1
2110	AMTSystems Inc—*Dave Stewart*	220 Reality Dr, Cheshire CT 00410	203 260-7226	R	8*	<.1
2111	Glenn Welt Studios Inc—*Ira Bostic*	342 Island Reef Ave, Henderson NV 89012	702-568-6207	R	8*	<.1
2112	4D Vision LLC	9674 E Arapahoe Rd PMB, Englewood CO 80112	303-843-8321	R	8*	<.1
2113	Able Software Corp—*Ted Wu*	5 Appletree Ln, Lexington MA 02420	781-862-2804	R	8*	<.1
2114	Acumen International	2200 Powell St Ste 102, Emeryville CA 94608	510-899-7404	S	8*	<.1
2115	AdWriter Inc—*Harold Douthit*	PO Box 760, Sandusky OH 44870	419-621-2127	S	8*	<.1
2116	Airframe Business Software Inc—*Robert Gryphon*	800 Southwood Blvd Ste, Incline Village NV 89451	775-832-9118	R	8*	<.1
2117	Aras Corp—*Peter Schroer*	300 Brickstone Sq Ste, Andover MA 01810	978-691-8900	R	8*	<.1
2118	Brightdoor Systems Inc—*Deven K Spear*	6501 Weston Pkwy Ste 3, Cary NC 27513	919-678-9940	R	8*	<.1
2119	BroadCast Software International—*Chris Kehoe*	503 E 11th Ave, Eugene OR 97401	541-338-8588	S	8*	<.1
2120	Buildtopia Inc—*Matt McShane*	2031 Clipper Pk Rd Ste, Baltimore MD 21211	240-399-0110	R	8*	<.1
2121	Centerfield Technology Corp—*Curt Sippel*	3131 Superior Dr NW St, Rochester MN 55901	507-287-8119	R	8*	<.1
2122	Cognitech Inc—*Lenny Rudin*	225 S Lake Ave Ste 601, Pasadena CA 91101	626-796-0326	R	8*	<.1
2123	Columbia Data Products Inc—*Alan Welsh*	925 Sunshine Ln Ste 10, Altamonte Springs FL 32714	407-869-6700	R	8*	<.1
2124	Common Sense Solutions Inc—*Terry O'Rourke*	7650 S County Line Rd, Burr Ridge IL 60527	630-379-0330	R	8*	<.1
2125	Computer Management and Marketing Associates Inc—*Colby Kent*	7599 Beth-Bath Pike, Bath PA 18014	610-837-8262	R	8*	<.1
2126	CONNX Solutions Inc—*Douglas D Wright*	2039 152nd Ave NE, Redmond WA 98052	425-519-6600	R	8*	<.1
2127	Continuex Corp—*Rick Kerns*	11747 NE 1st St Ste 31, Bellevue WA 98005	425-453-9450	R	8*	<.1
2128	ContrAcct Systems Corp—*Jay Albrecht*	208 N Washington St, Naperville IL 60540	630-355-8188	R	8*	<.1
2129	Cougaar Software Inc—*Todd Carrico*	7600 Leesburg Pike Eas, Falls Church VA 22043	703-506-1700	R	8*	<.1
2130	Crowell Systems—*Edward Crowell*	One LakePointe Plz 423, Charlotte NC 28217	704-665-2000	R	8*	<.1
2131	CyberAngel Security Solutions Inc—*Bradley Lide*	475 Metroplex Dr Ste 1, Nashville TN 37211		R	8*	<.1
2132	Dakota Software Corp	95 Allens Creek Rd Bld, Rochester NY 14618	585-244-3300	R	8*	<.1
2133	DataHouse Inc (Birmingham Alabama)	1 Perimeter Park S Ste, Birmingham AL 35243	205-972-9292	R	8*	<.1
2134	DataLink Technologies Group Inc—*Morgan Jack*	1465 Slater Rd, Ferndale WA 98248	360-306-5878	R	8*	<.1
2135	Datasystem Solutions Inc—*Gay H Manning*	6310 Lamar Ave Ste 200, Overland Park KS 66202	913-362-6969	R	8*	<.1
2136	Daystar Computer Systems Inc—*Ron Cichon*	600 W Jackson Ste 580, Chicago IL 60661	312-559-0900	R	8*	<.1
2137	Decision Technology Inc—*Mark Berkowitz*	4390 US Rte 1 N, Princeton NJ 08540	609-987-8950	R	8*	<.1
2138	Digital Dynamics Software Inc—*Tony Antonucci*	1450 E American Ln Ste, Schaumburg IL 60173	847-330-3830	R	8*	<.1
2139	En Technology Corp—*Matthew Cookson*	PO Box 505, Marlow NH 03456	603-446-3700	R	8*	<.1
2140	Engineered Software Inc—*Ray Hardee*	4529 Intelco Loop SE, Lacey WA 98503	360-412-0702	R	8*	<.1
2141	Express Matrix LLC—*Kris Barker*	200 W Mercer St, Seattle WA 98119	206-691-7900	R	8*	<.1
2142	Finjan Software Inc—*John Vigouroux*	2025 Gateway Pl Ste 18, San Jose CA 95110	408-452-9700	S	8*	<.1
2143	Firebrand Technologies—*Fran Toolan*	44 Merrimac St, Newburyport MA 01950	978-465-7755	R	8*	<.1
2144	Fundamental Software Inc—*Peter Ward*	5865 Sills Rd, Arbuckle CA 95912	530-476-2459	R	8*	<.1
2145	Gehry Technologies LLC—*Frank Gehry*	12541-A Beatrice St, Los Angeles CA 90066	310-862-1200	R	8*	<.1
2146	Gillani Inc—*Syed Kamal*	833 E Arapaho Rd Ste 1, Richardson TX 75081	972-918-0400	R	8*	<.1
2147	gINT Software Inc—*Salvatore Caronna*	1160 N Dutton Ave Ste1, Santa Rosa CA 95401	707-284-2200	R	8*	<.1
2148	GRMS Inc—*Alan Rosenbloom*	218 Main St Ste 33, East Setauket NY 11733	631-218-7600	R	8	<.1
2149	Gyrus Systems Inc—*Viren Kapadia*	5400 Glenside Dr Ste B, Henrico VA 23228	804-320-1414	R	8*	<.1
2150	HyperLogic Corp	PO Box 300010, Escondido CA 92030	760-746-2765	R	8*	<.1
2151	IDAutomationcom Inc—*Brant Anderson*	550 N Reo St Ste 230, Tampa FL 33609	813-514-2564	R	8*	<.1
2152	Imecom Group Inc—*David Horton*	8 Governor Wentworth H, Wolfeboro NH 03894	603-569-0600	S	8*	<.1
2153	Infinata Inc—*Ruth Henry*	100 River Ridge Dr Ste, Norwood MA 02062	781-762-8920	R	8*	<.1
2154	InfinityQS International Inc—*Michael A Lyle*	14900 Conference Cente, Chantilly VA 20151	703-961-0200	R	8*	<.1
2155	Information Development Consultants Inc—*Carolyne Turner*	1 E Erie St Ste 630, Chicago IL 60611	312-464-1020	S	8*	<.1
2156	Integrated Systems Technology Inc—*Mike Kolker*	1925 W John Carpenter, Irving TX 75063	214-630-4379	R	8*	<.1
2157	Intersystem Concepts Inc—*Steven Okonski*	PO Box 477, Fulton MD 20759	410-531-9000	R	8*	<.1
2158	KnowledgeSum Inc—*Rachel Lyubovitzky*	726 Rte 202 S Ste 320-, Bridgewater NJ 08807		R	8*	<.1
2159	Manufacturing Action Group Inc	4695 44th St SE Rm B-1, Grand Rapids MI 49512	616-956-5345	R	8*	<.1
2160	Marsoft Inc—*Paul L Eckbo*	155 Federal St Ste 901, Boston MA 02110	617-369-7800	R	8*	<.1
2161	Medical Systems Support Inc—*Harold Poe*	4000 Eagle Point Corpo, Birmingham AL 35242	205-314-5775	R	8*	<.1
2162	MicroWorks Inc—*Joel Gyllenskog*	2808 N Cole Rd, Boise ID 83704	208-375-1234	R	8*	<.1
2163	Mortgage Computer Applications Inc—*Gordon L Belnap*	2650 Washington Blvd S, Ogden UT 84401	801-621-3900	R	8*	<.1
2164	Multicitycom Inc—*Alain Hanash*	PO Box 9007, Vienna VA 22182	703-790-0063	R	8*	<.1
2165	NFATOCOM	250 Dodge Ave, East Haven CT 06512	203-466-5170	D	8*	<.1
2166	Odyssey Computing Inc—*Steven Churchill*	5820 Oberlin Dr Ste 20, San Diego CA 92121	858-623-3310	R	8*	<.1
2167	Port80 Software Inc—*Joseph Lima*	2105 Garnet Ave, San Diego CA 92109	858-274-4497	R	8*	<.1

Note: An asterisk (*) indicates an estimated financial figure. The company type code used is as follows: R = Private, P = Public, S = Private Subsidiary, B = Public Subsidiary, D = Division, J = Joint Venture, I = Investment Fund.

COMPANY RANKINGS BY SALES WITHIN 4-DIGIT SIC

Rank	Company Name—*Executive Officer*	Address, City, State, Zip	Phone	Type	Fin	Empls
2168	ppoONE Inc—*Joe Hensley*	1311 W President Georg, Richardson TX 75080	214-273-8917	S	8*	<.1
2169	Proximex Corp—*Jack Smith*	440 N Wolfe Rd, Sunnyvale CA 94085	408-216-5190	S	8*	<.1
2170	RemedyMD Inc—*Gary Kennedy*	9350 S 150th E Ste 850, Sandy UT 84070	801-733-3300	R	8*	<.1
2171	RES-Q Healthcare Systems Inc—*Michael Meisel*	26500 W Agoura Rd Ste, Calabasas CA 91302	818-878-9747	R	8*	<.1
2172	SamePage Solutions LLC—*Andrew Vaeth*	1099 Akron Rd, Wooster OH 44691	330-264-9892	R	8*	<.1
2173	SDD Inc—*Ron Tarro*	800 NW 17th Ave, Delray Beach FL 33445	561-276-7004	R	8*	<.1
2174	Seewhy Inc—*Scott G Silk*	300 Brickstone Sq Ste, Andover MA 01810	617-502-2077	R	8*	<.1
2175	SharpeSoft Inc	925 Market St, Yuba City CA 95991	530-671-6499	R	8*	<.1
2176	Silicor Technologies Inc—*John Sires*	16654 Soledad Canyon R, Canyon Country CA 91387	661-295-4951	R	8*	<.1
2177	Silverlink Communications Inc—*Stan Nowak*	67 S Bedford St Ste 30, Burlington MA 01803	781-425-5700	R	8*	<.1
2178	Software Development Inc (Roseville California)	3825 Hopyard Rd Ste 10, Pleasanton CA 94588	925-847-8823	S	8*	<.1
2179	Specialty Software Inc	PO Box 110277, Palm Bay FL 32911	321-821-9422	R	8*	<.1
2180	Stratacache—*Chris Riegel*	1031 E Third St, Dayton OH 45402	937-224-0485	S	8*	<.1
2181	Stratasoft Inc—*Asim Saber*	519 N Sam Houston Pkwy, Houston TX 77060	832-446-4499	S	8*	<.1
2182	Verticent Inc—*Omar Peraza*	400 N Ashley Dr Ste 26, Tampa FL 33602	813-226-2600	D	8*	<.1
2183	Infinity Box Inc—*Chris Campbell*	12157 W Linebaugh Ave, Tampa FL 33626		S	8*	<.1
2184	IPExtreme Inc—*Warren Savage*	54 N Central Ave Ste 2, Campbell CA 95008	408-540-0095	R	8*	<.1
2185	Direct Tech Inc—*Craig Harding*	13259 Millard Ave Ste, Omaha NE 68137	402-895-2100	R	8*	<.1
2186	Ebeling Associates Inc—*Allan D Robison*	9 Corporate Dr, Clifton Park NY 12065	518-688-8700	R	8*	<.1
2187	On-Line Instrument Systems Inc—*Richard J DeSa*	130 Conway Dr Ste A B, Bogart GA 30622	706-353-6547	R	8*	<.1
2188	Shortcuts Software Inc—*Paul Tate*	7777 Center Ave Ste 10, Huntington Beach CA 92647	714-622-6600	S	8*	<.1
2189	FastSpring—*Daniel Engel*	11 W Victoria St Ste 2, Santa Barbara CA 93101		R	8*	<.1
2190	Vision's Edge Inc—*Dacques Viker*	3502 Limerick Dr, Tallahassee FL 32309	850-386-4573	R	8*	<.1
2191	Air Academy Associates LLC—*Richard C Murrow*	1650 Telstar Dr Rm 110, Colorado Springs CO 80920	719-531-0777	R	8*	<.1
2192	Advanced Teaching Resources Inc—*Craig Lehman*	3889 N Van Ness Blvd, Fresno CA 93704	559-222-7879	R	8*	<.1
2193	Beach Media	221 Arbor Dr, San Diego CA 92103	619-299-6656	R	8*	<.1
2194	Catspaw Inc—*Mark B Emmer*	PO Box 1123, Salida CO 81201	719-539-3884	R	8*	<.1
2195	CleoSci—*Garrett Krueger*	PO Box 17037, Saint Paul MN 55117	651-771-9209	R	8*	<.1
2196	DesAcc Inc—*Hugh Lyshkow*	0844 SW Curry St, Portland OR 97239		R	8*	<.1
2197	Howard Way and Associates—*Arthur S Liebeskind*	5905 Bonnie View Dr, Baltimore MD 21209		R	8*	<.1
2198	Major Micro Systems Inc—*John Crombe*	23710 Samoset Trl, Southfield MI 48033		R	8*	<.1
2199	MurkWorks Inc—*Brad Clements*	PO Box 610, Potsdam NY 13676	315-268-1000	R	8*	<.1
2200	Ozone Inc—*Orrin Zucker*	PO Box 743, Needham MA 02494	781-449-6282	R	8*	<.1
2201	Paul Guggenheim and Associates Inc—*Paul Guggenheim*	1788 2nd St Ste 200, Highland Park IL 60035	847-926-9800	R	8*	<.1
2202	Peng Engineering—*LC Peng*	PO Box 801167, Houston TX 77280	713-462-7390	R	8*	<.1
2203	RFX Inc—*Ray Feeney*	748 Seward St, Hollywood CA 90038	323-962-7400	R	8*	<.1
2204	RPV Business Systems—*Rodger L Verdieck*	4298 Gravenstein Hwy S, Sebastopol CA 95472	707-829-3932	R	8*	<.1
2205	ShopKeeper Software—*Eileen Nudd*	1005 Lakewood Ln, Round Rock TX 78681	512-388-3290	R	8*	<.1
2206	Spiral Software—*Stuart Karon*	113 Upper Pasture Rd, Norwich VT 05055	802-649-1911	R	8*	<.1
2207	Trilogy Design	PO Box 2270, Grass Valley CA 95945	530-273-1985	R	8*	<.1
2208	Wall Street Software—*Cynthia Kase*	6212 Samuell Blvd Ste, Dallas TX 75228	903-455-9860	R	8*	<.1
2209	Palisades Research—*John Vitale*	869 Via De La Paz, Pacific Palisades CA 90272	310-459-7528	R	8*	<.1
2210	SigmaTech Software—*Fred Clabuesch*	9451 Crescent Beach Rd, Sand Point MI 48755	989-856-2653	R	8*	<.1
2211	Kaspersky Lab Inc—*Steven Orenberg*	500 Unicorn Park Dr St, Woburn MA 01801	781-503-1800	R	8*	.1
2212	Smartops Corp—*Martin Barkman*	1 N Shore Ctr Ste 400, Pittsburgh PA 15212	412-231-0115	R	8*	.1
2213	Alom Technologies Corp—*Hannah Kain*	48105 Warm Springs Blv, Fremont CA 94539	510-630-3600	R	8*	.1
2214	Rhythm Engineering—*Regie Chandra*	12351 W 96th Terrace S, Lenexa KS 66215	913-227-0603	R	8	<.1
2215	Fastrack Healthcare Systems Inc—*Spencer Kay*	255 Executive Dr Ste 2, Plainview NY 11803	516-349-9136	R	8	<.1
2216	Jenzbar Inc—*Robert A Maginn*	101 Huntington Ave, Boston MA 02199	617-492-9099	R	8*	<.1
2217	Superbase Developers Inc—*Richard Tannenbaum*	4 Rockne St, Huntington NY 11743	631-757-3110	R	8*	<.1
2218	GraphOn Corp—*Robert P Dilworth*	5400 Soquel Ave Ste A2, Santa Cruz CA 95062	603-225-3525	P	8	<.1
2219	Virtual Boardwalk—*Debra Chong*	180 Howard St Ste 340, San Francisco CA 94105	415-281-8828	R	8*	<.1
2220	Intuitive Manufacturing Systems Inc—*Chuck Gillam* Consona Corp	12131 113th Ave NE Ste, Kirkland WA 98034	425-250-5900	S	7	.1
2221	Cougar Mountain Software Inc—*Robert Gossett*	7180 W Potomac Dr, Boise ID 83704	208-375-4455	R	7*	.1
2222	Andera Inc—*Charles Kroll*	204 Westminster St Ste, Providence RI 02903	401-621-7900	R	7*	.1
2223	Ketera Technologies Inc—*Stephen Savignano*	3055 Olin Ave Ste 2200, San Jose CA 95128	408-572-9500	S	7*	.1
2224	Enterworks Inc—*Robert W Lewis*	45940 Horseshoe Dr Ste, Sterling VA 20166		R	7*	.1
2225	SoftPro Corp—*Joyce Weiland*	4800 Falls of Neuse Rd, Raleigh NC 27609	919-829-1122	R	7*	.1
2226	Trimble (Corvallis Oregon)—*Bill Martin*	345 SW Avery Ave, Corvallis OR 97333	541-753-9322	S	7*	.1
2227	Cintech LLC—*Dennis Carrol*	4600 Montgomery Rd, Cincinnati OH 45212	513-731-6000	R	7*	.1
2228	Eagle Point Software Corp—*John F Biver*	4131 Westmark Dr, Dubuque IA 52002	563-556-8392	R	7*	.1
2229	Wonderlic Inc—*Charles F Wonderlic Jr*	400 Lakeview Pkwy Ste, Vernon Hills IL 60061		R	7*	.1
2230	Seven Networks Inc—*Ross Bott*	2100 Seaport Blvd Ste, Redwood City CA 94063	650-381-2500	R	7*	.1
2231	Vedicsoft Solutions Inc—*Venka Yerubandi*	100 Wood Ave Ste 200, Iselin NJ 08830	732-906-3200	R	7*	.1
2232	Welcom—*Kevin Parker*	15990 N Barkers Landin, Houston TX 77079	281-558-0514	S	7*	.1
2233	Master Control Inc—*Jonathan Beckstrand*	6322 S 3000 E Ste 110, Salt Lake City UT 84121	801-942-4000	R	7*	.1
2234	Logical Design Solutions Inc—*Mimi Brooks*	200 Park Ave Ste 210, Florham Park NJ 07932	973-210-6300	R	7*	.1
2235	Healthcare Automation Inc—*Ken Pereira*	41 Sharpe Dr, Cranston RI 02920	401-572-3040	S	7*	.1
2236	Engineering Mechanics Research Corp—*Kant Kothawala*	1607 E Big Beaver Rd, Troy MI 48083	248-689-0077	D	7*	.1
2237	Dome Publishing Company Inc—*Nicholas Picchione II*	PO Box 1220, Warwick RI 02887	401-738-7900	R	7*	.1
2238	Groupware Inc—*Daren Nelson*	110 E 17th St, Vancouver WA 98663	360-397-1098	R	7*	.1
2239	Imagine That Inc—*Bob Diamond*	6830 Via Del Oro Ste 2, San Jose CA 95119	408-365-0305	R	7*	.1
2240	Infinite Graphics Inc—*Edwin F Snyder*	4611 E Lake St, Minneapolis MN 55406	612-728-1314	R	7*	.1
2241	Intercim LLC—*John Todd* Industrial and Financial Systems Inc	1915 Plaza Dr, Eagan MN 55122	651-289-5700	D	7*	.1
2242	MSS Technologies Inc—*Mike Hawksworth*	1555 E Orangewood Ave, Phoenix AZ 85020	602-387-2100	R	7*	.1
2243	Nichimen Graphics Inc	4712 Admiralty Way Ste, Marina del Rey CA 90292	310-388-1509	R	7*	.1
2244	Productivity Quality Systems	210B East Spring Valle, Dayton OH 45458	937-885-2255	R	7*	.1
2245	Prosig USA Inc—*Al Brower*	29200 Southfield Rd St, Southfield MI 48076	248-443-2470	R	7*	.1
2246	TeleDirect International Inc—*Kathleen Kelly*	17255 N 82nd St, Scottsdale AZ 85255	404-851-1331	R	7*	.1
2247	White Stone Group Inc—*Guille B Cruze*	2030 Falling Water Rd, Knoxville TN 37922	865-531-4545	R	7*	.1
2248	Accipiter Inc—*Brian Handly*	8601 Six Forks Rd, Raleigh NC 27615	919-872-7755	S	7*	<.1
2249	Surfware Inc—*Stephen Dielh*	100 Camino Ruiz, Camarillo CA 93012	818-991-1960	R	7*	<.1
2250	WebTrends Corp—*Alex Yoder*	851 SW 6th Ave Ste 160, Portland OR 97204	503-294-7025	D	7*	<.1
2251	Winco Identification Corp	237 Main Dunstable Rd, Nashua NH 03062	603-598-1553	R	7*	<.1
2252	TeamStudio Inc—*Nigel Cheshire*	900 Cummings Ctr Ste 3, Beverly MA 01915	978-232-0145	R	7*	<.1
2253	CSS Group Inc—*Steve MacKenzie*	1120 W Blanco Rd, San Antonio TX 78232	210-691-8444	R	7*	<.1
2254	Omni Group Inc—*Ken Case*	3257 16th Ave W, Seattle WA 98119	206-523-4152	R	7*	<.1
2255	Lanner Group Inc—*David Jones*	10777 Westheimer Rd St, Houston TX 77042	713-532-8008	S	7*	<.1

Rank	Company Name—*Executive Officer*	Address, City, State, Zip	Phone	Type	Fin	Empls
2256	Software UNO Ltd—*Jesus Alvarez*	15 Bodwell Ter, Millburn NJ 07041	787-723-5000	R	7*	<.1
2257	Computer Media Technology	2070 S 7th St Bldg E, San Jose CA 95112	408-734-3339	R	7	<.1
2258	Binary Research International Inc—*Annette Dow*	5215 N Ironwood Rd Ste, Glendale WI 53217	414-961-7077	R	7*	<.1
2259	DataFaction—*Brian Kleinman*	5757 W Century Blvd St, Los Angeles CA 90045	323-291-5700	S	7*	<.1
2260	Emrys Technologies Inc—*Carl Gideon*	8150 N Central Expy St, Dallas TX 75206	469-232-9502	R	7*	<.1
2261	RentRight Inc—*Jill Shaffer*	574 N Main St, Springboro OH 45066		S	7*	<.1
2262	Spacetrack Travel Solutions	304 Park Ave 11th Fl, New York NY 10010	212-590-2638	R	7*	<.1
2263	TrustWave Corp—*Robert McCullen*	70 W Madison St Ste 10, Chicago IL 60602	312-873-7500	R	7*	<.1
2264	Robert McNeel and Associates Inc—*Robert McNeel*	3670 Woodland Park Ave, Seattle WA 98103	206-545-7000	R	7*	<.1
2265	Sneakers Software Inc—*Paul Greenman*	519 8th Ave Ste 812, New York NY 10018	646-674-1210	R	7*	<.1
2266	ClearForest Corp—*Barak Pridor*	1601 Trapelord Ste 190, Waltham MA 02451	781-250-4300	S	7*	<.1
2267	e-Quantum Inc—*Ross Barker*	PO Box 11155, Reno NV 89510	775-856-2800	R	7*	<.1
2268	Network Controls International Inc—*Olof Ezelius*	9 Woodlawn Green Ste 1, Charlotte NC 28217	704-527-4357	R	7*	<.1
2269	Nova CTI Inc—*Gregory Borton*	1518 Walnut St, Philadelphia PA 19146	215-772-0562	R	7*	<.1
2270	Automation ONSPEC Software Inc—*Mike McMann*	PO Box 743, Rancho Cordova CA 95741	916-362-5867	R	7*	<.1
2271	COREMedia Systems Inc—*Glenn DeKraker*	695 Rte 46 W, Fairfield NJ 07004	973-276-0882	R	7*	<.1
2272	Intellisense Software Corp—*Sandeep Akkaraju*	600 W Cummings Park St, Woburn MA 01801	781-933-8098	R	7*	<.1
2273	Online Insight Inc—*David Fiacco*	1519 Johnson Ferry Rd, Marietta GA 30062	770-508-1440	R	7*	<.1
2274	STEP Tools Inc—*Martin Hardwick*	14 First St, Troy NY 12180	518-687-2848	R	7*	<.1
2275	TimeValue Software—*Michael Applegate*	22 Mauchly, Irvine CA 92618	949-727-1800	R	7*	<.1
2276	World Software Corp	266 Harristown Rd Ste, Glen Rock NJ 07452	201-444-3228	R	7*	<.1
2277	ERA Software Systems Inc—*Dianne Bozler*	100 W Broadway Ste 360, Long Beach CA 90802	562-983-7510	R	7*	<.1
2278	Evans Griffiths and Hart Inc—*Lauren Crocker*	55 Waltham St, Lexington MA 02421	781-861-0670	R	7*	<.1
2279	DPC Systems Inc—*William Ward*	6321 Southwest Blvd, Fort Worth TX 76132	817-731-4060	R	7*	<.1
2280	Economic Analysis Group Ltd—*Douglas Land*	1828 L St NW Ste 1060, Washington DC 20036	202-367-2950	R	7*	<.1
2281	Fonts and Software USA Inc—*Petra Weitz*	149 9th St Ste 302, San Francisco CA 94103	415-252-1003	R	7*	<.1
2282	FW Davison and Company Inc—*Scott Hastings*	50 Resnik Rd Ste 200, Plymouth MA 02360	508-747-7261	R	7*	<.1
2283	Intelligent Systems Technology Inc—*Azad Madni*	12122 Victoria Ave Los, Los Angeles CA 90066	310-581-5440	R	7*	<.1
2284	Napa Group LLC—*Peter Chatzky*	10 E 40th St 27th Fl, New York NY 10016	212-689-9100	R	7*	<.1
2285	Professional System Associates Inc—*K Smith*	1308 Florida Ave, Panama City FL 32401	850-763-2192	R	7*	<.1
2286	Quintessential School Systems—*Jeff McLaughlin*	867 American St 2nd Fl, San Carlos CA 94070	650-372-0200	R	7*	<.1
2287	Connecticut Data Systems Inc—*Ken Munson*	100 Riverview Ctr Ste, Middletown CT 06457	860-854-6125	R	7*	<.1
2288	DAPCO Software Engineering Inc—*David Partridge*	1800 E Garry Ave Ste 2, Santa Ana CA 92705	714-964-7400	R	7*	<.1
2289	Dataflow Systems Inc—*Larry Messer*	4544 Independence Sq, Indianapolis IN 46203	317-781-1111	R	7*	<.1
2290	Mansell Group Inc—*Allen Nance*	3630 Peachtree Road NE, Atlanta GA 30326	404-995-8600	R	7*	<.1
2291	Manufacturing Information System Inc—*Dave Brown*	PO Box 795, Woodstock VT 05091	802-457-4600	R	7*	<.1
2292	Revelation Technologies Inc—*Mike Ruane* WinWin Solutions Inc	99 Kinderkamack Rd Ste, Westwood NJ 07675	201-594-1422	S	7*	<.1
2293	Blue Mountain Data Systems Inc—*Paul T Vesely*	366 Victory Dr, Herndon VA 20170	703-502-3416	R	7*	<.1
2294	VIEW Micro-Metrology—*Frank Curtin*	1711 W 17th St, Tempe AZ 85281	480-295-3150	S	7*	<.1
2295	1mage Software Inc—*David R DeYoung*	384 Inverness Pkwy Ste, Englewood CO 80112	303-773-1424	R	7*	<.1
2296	Covient Inc—*Moujan Ahouraian*	468 N Camden Dr Ste 20, Beverly Hills CA 90210	310-860-4704	R	7*	<.1
2297	Focus Technology Group Inc—*Charles Thiel*	300 Rosewood Dr, Danvers MA 01923	978-535-9626	R	7*	<.1
2298	Kord Information Systems—*Annette Kord*	7814 La Cresta St, Highland CA 92346	909-816-6230	R	7*	<.1
2299	Medicomp Systems Inc—*Peter S Goltra*	14500 Avion Pky Ste 17, Chantilly VA 20151	703-803-8080	R	7*	<.1
2300	Red Earth Software Inc—*Mike Spykerman*	4845 Pearl E Circle, Boulder CO 80301	720-377-3728	R	7*	<.1
2301	Systat Software Inc—*Rudra Pratap*	225 W Washington St St, Chicago IL 60606	312-220-0060	S	7*	<.1
2302	System Concepts Inc—*Bill Schwartz*	15900 N 78th St, Scottsdale AZ 85260	480-951-8011	R	7*	<.1
2303	Thought Inc—*Richard Lamb*	5 3rd St Ste 815, San Francisco CA 94103	415-836-9199	R	7*	<.1
2304	Trident Services—*Tim Humphreys*	1260 41st Ave Ste K, Capitola CA 95010	831-465-7661	R	7*	<.1
2305	Management Systems Inc (Fort Collins Colorado)—*Mitchell Gross*	2629 Redwing Rd MS: 27, Fort Collins CO 80527	970-223-1530	R	7*	<.1
2306	Digital Destinations—*John Neitzel*	437 Washington Ave 2nd, New York NY 10013	212-989-2236	R	7*	<.1
2307	Altura Ventures LLC—*Lee Lorenzen*	9600 Blue Larkspur Ln, Monterey CA 93940	831-595-7501	R	7*	<.1
2308	BancLease—*Don Burnett*	PO Box 1526, Sikeston MO 63801	573-472-2002	R	7*	<.1
2309	Central Technologies Inc—*Joe Baumgardner*	5005 N Pennsylvania Av, Oklahoma City OK 73112	405-843-9284	R	7*	<.1
2310	F-Chart Software	Box 44042, Madison WI 53744	608-274-4262	R	7*	<.1
2311	Gabel Systems Inc—*Jeff Campbell*	PO Box 2425, Colorado Springs CO 80901		R	7*	<.1
2312	Highland Consulting Group Inc—*Richard Bennett*	PO Box 555, Atlantic Highlands NJ 07716	732-291-2991	R	7*	<.1
2313	Rapp Industries Inc—*Robert W Rapp*	233 Rock Rd Ste 113, Glen Rock NJ 07452	201-670-9084	R	7*	<.1
2314	Ron Callis CPA—*Ron Callis*	318 W Coates St Ste 10, Moberly MO 65270	660-263-7960	R	7*	<.1
2315	DataTRAK International Inc—*Laurence P Birch*	6150 Parkland Blvd Ste, Mayfield Heights OH 44124	440-443-0082	P	7	<.1
2316	Internet America Inc—*William E Ladin Jr*	PO Box 690753, Houston TX 77269	713-968-2500	P	7	<.1
2317	Information Analysis Inc—*Sandor Rosenberg*	11240 Waples Mill Rd S, Fairfax VA 22030	703-383-3000	P	7	<.1
2318	AppAssure Software Inc—*Najaf Husain*	1925 Isaac Newton Squa, Reston VA 20190		R	7	.1
2319	Jka Technologies Inc—*John Kessler*	9881 Broken Land Pkwy, Columbia MD 21046	443-393-2010	R	7*	.1
2320	Alventive Inc—*Dave Conner*	PO Box 584, Cupertino CA 95015	408-969-8000	R	7*	.1
2321	Cimetrix Inc—*Robert H Reback*	6979 S High Tech Dr, Midvale UT 84047	801-256-6500	P	7	<.1
2322	Innuity Inc—*John Wall*	8644 154th Ave NE, Redmond WA 98052	425-497-9909	P	7	.2
2323	Enterprisewizard Inc—*Colin Earl*	460 Seaport Ct Ste 200, Redwood City CA 94063	650-587-8615	R	7*	<.1
2324	SEEC Inc—*Ramaswami SR*	2730 Sidney St Ste 200, Pittsburgh PA 15203	412-297-0050	S	6	.1
2325	Provider Gateway Inc—*Andrew Banks*	3700 Euclid Ave 2nd Fl, Cleveland OH 44115	216-432-6912	R	6	.1
2326	Meetingmatrix International Inc—*J Keller*	195 New Hampshire Ave, Portsmouth NH 03801	603-610-1600	R	6*	<.1
2327	NetSteps Inc—*Kevin Vitale*	2435 W 450 S Ste 201, Pleasant Grove UT 84062	801-642-3777	R	6	<.1
2328	Agile View Software Inc—*Senraj Soundararajan*	2 Keeway Dr, Salem NH 03079	603-685-6902	R	6*	.1
2329	BidSync—*Sabrina Stover*	629 Quality Dr Ste 101, American Fork UT 84003	801-765-9245	R	6	.1
2330	edocs Inc Oracle USA Inc	500 Oracle Pkwy, Redwood City CA 94065	650-506-7000	S	6*	.2
2331	CapTech Ventures Inc—*Sandy Williamson*	1118 W Main St, Richmond VA 23220	804-355-0511	R	6*	.1
2332	InMage Systems Inc—*Kumar Malavalli*	3255-1 Scott Blvd Ste, Santa Clara CA 95054	408-200-3840	R	6*	.1
2333	BST Consultants Inc—*Carlos Baldor*	5925 Benjamin Center D, Tampa FL 33615	813-886-3300	R	6*	.1
2334	eIQnetworks Inc—*Vijay Basani*	31 Nagog Park, Acton MA 01720	978-266-9933	R	6*	.1
2335	PolySystems Inc—*Roger Smith*	30 N LaSalle St Ste 36, Chicago IL 60602	312-332-5670	R	6*	.1
2336	ResCom Mortgage Corp—*Moghees Adil*	9101 Greenwood Ave Ste, Niles IL 60714	847-296-0300	R	6*	.1
2337	PCI Geomatics—*Terry Moloney*	1655 N Fort Myer Dr St, Arlington VA 22209		R	6*	.1
2338	HealthLine Systems Inc—*Dan Littrell*	17085 Camino San Berna, San Diego CA 92127	858-673-1700	R	6*	.1
2339	Pindar Systems Inc—*Andrew Pindar*	414 N Orleans St Ste 6, Chicago IL 60610	312-840-4800	S	6*	.1
2340	Investment Scorecard Inc—*Joe Maxwell*	601 Grassmere Pk Ste 1, Nashville TN 37211	615-665-1234	R	6*	.1
2341	Construction Industry Solutions Corp—*Derek Leaver*	6 Airport Pk Blvd, Latham NY 12110	518-242-7200	R	6*	.1
2342	Neovest Inc—*Bryce Byers*	1145 S 800 East Ste 31, Orem UT 84097		S	6*	.1

Note: An asterisk (*) indicates an estimated financial figure. The company type code used is as follows: R = Private, P = Public, S = Private Subsidiary, B = Public Subsidiary, D = Division, J = Joint Venture, I = Investment Fund.

COMPANY RANKINGS BY SALES WITHIN 4-DIGIT SIC

Rank	Company Name—Executive Officer	Address, City, State, Zip	Phone	Type	Fin	Empls
2343	Recognition Research Inc—Cristobal Conde Sungard EXP	1750 Kraft Dr Ste 200, Blacksburg VA 24060	540-961-6500	S	6*	.1
2344	Daffron and Associates Inc—Carl Daffron	1 Solution Pl, Bowling Green MO 63334	314-569-9600	R	6*	.1
2345	Nestor Inc—William B Danzell	42 Oriental St, Providence RI 02908	401-274-5658	R	6	.1
2346	OMD Corp—Laryssa Alexander	PO Box 6760, Jefferson City MO 65102	573-893-8930	R	6*	.1
2347	GE Continental Controls Inc—Lloyd Trotter	2500 Austin Dr, Charlottesville VA 22911	434-978-5000	R	6*	.1
2348	Capital Stream Inc—Kevin Paul Riegelsberger	1111 3rd Ave E Ste 950, Seattle WA 98101	206-545-8679	R	6*	.1
2349	Famous Software LLC—Curt Tarris	8080 N Palm Ave Ste 21, Fresno CA 93711	559-438-3600	R	6*	.1
2350	Soffront Software Inc—Manu Das	45437 Warm Springs Blv, Fremont CA 94539	510-413-9000	R	6*	.1
2351	Starmine Corp—Joe Gatto	199 Fremont St 4th Fl, San Francisco CA 94105	415-874-8100	S	6*	.1
2352	BobCAD-CAM Inc—Larry Pendleton	28200 US Hwy 19 N Ste, Clearwater FL 33761		R	6*	.1
2353	Relevant Business Systems Inc—Patrick Garrehy Intuitive Manufacturing Systems Inc	450 E 96th St Ste 300, Indianapolis IN 46240	925-867-3830	S	6*	.1
2354	Engineering Planning and Management Inc—Wade Larson	959 Concord St Ste 310, Framingham MA 01701	508-875-2121	R	6*	.1
2355	Jenzabar (Knoxville Tennessee)—Robert Maginn	308 N Peters Rd Ste 12, Knoxville TN 37922	865-523-9506	D	6*	.1
2356	Keystone Information Systems Inc—Judson B Van Dervort Jr	1000 Lenola Rd, Maple Shade NJ 08052	856-722-0700	R	6*	.1
2357	LXI Corp—Nancy Pojatina	391 E Las Colinas Blvd, Irving TX 75039	214-260-9002	R	LXI	.1
2358	System Management Arts Inc—Shaula Yemini	44 S Broadway 7th Fl, White Plains NY 10601	914-948-6200	S	6*	.1
2359	Visible Systems Corp—George Cagliuso	63 Fountain St, Framingham MA 01702	781-778-0200	R	6*	.1
2360	Simutronics Corp—David Whatley	349 Main St, Gaithersburg MD 20878	301-330-0726	R	6*	<.1
2361	Akimbo Systems Inc—Thomas Frank	411 Borel Ave Ste100, San Mateo CA 94402	650-292-3330	R	6*	<.1
2362	Arkeia Corp—William Evans	1808 Aston Ave Ste 220, Carlsbad CA 92008	760-431-1319	R	6*	<.1
2363	Canto Software Inc—Ulrich Knocke	221 Main St Ste 460, San Francisco CA 94105	415-495-6545	S	6*	<.1
2364	Cardinal Engineering Inc—G Stephen Mason	1015 N Broadway Ste 30, Oklahoma City OK 73102	405-842-1066	R	6*	<.1
2365	Financial Database Services Inc—Eddie Hillard	9560 Waples St Ste A, San Diego CA 92121	858-526-8100	R	6*	<.1
2366	Mandex Inc—Randall Scott	12500 Fair Lakes Cir S, Fairfax VA 22033	703-227-0900	S	6*	<.1
2367	Soneticom Inc—Timothy Reynolds	1045 S John Rodes Blvd, West Melbourne FL 32904	321-733-0400	S	6*	<.1
2368	Visionet Systems Inc—Arshad Masood	48 Cedar Brook Dr, Cranbury NJ 08512	609-452-0700	R	6*	<.1
2369	Sage BusinessVision—Carlton Collins	2550 Warren Dr, Rocklin CA 95677		S	6*	<.1
2370	Optas Inc—Stephen Smith Dendrite International Inc	500 Unicorn Park Dr St, Woburn MA 01801	781-937-9400	S	6*	<.1
2371	ADL Data Systems Inc—David Pollack	9 Skyline Dr, Hawthorne NY 10532	914-591-1800	R	6*	<.1
2372	American Arium	14811 Myford Rd, Tustin CA 92780	714-731-1661	R	6*	<.1
2373	CPU Medical Management Systems—Michael Stringer	9235 Activity Rd Ste10, San Diego CA 92126	858-530-0875	R	6*	<.1
2374	Fabtrol Systems Inc—Garry Cochrane	1025 Willamette St Ste, Eugene OR 97401	541-345-1494	R	6*	<.1
2375	MBI International—Bobby Bringi	PO Box 27609, Lansing MI 48909	517-337-3181	R	6*	<.1
2376	MicroPact Engineering Inc—Kris Collo	2250 Corporate Park Dr, Herndon VA 20171	703-709-6110	R	6*	<.1
2377	Relavis Corp—Robert DeMaio	40 Wall St 33rd Fl, New York NY 10005	212-995-2900	R	6*	<.1
2378	Sunburst Technology Corp—Dan Figurski	1550 Executive Dr, Elgin IL 60123		S	6*	<.1
2379	Thoroughbred Software International Inc (Somerset New Jersey)—John L Johnson	285 Davidson Ave Ste 3, Somerset NJ 08873	732-560-1377	R	6*	<.1
2380	AutoData Systems—Brad Slye	6111 Blue Circle Dr, Minneapolis MN 55343	952-938-4710	D	6*	<.1
2381	CIMNET Inc—Mike Caliel Wonderware Corp	925 Berkshire Blvd, Wyomissing PA 19610	610-790-1824	S	6*	<.1
2382	Tactician Corp—Tony Buxton	305 N Main St, Andover MA 01810	978-475-4475	R	6*	<.1
2383	Experior Corp—Richard Presser	5710 Coventry Ln, Fort Wayne IN 46804	260-432-2020	R	6*	<.1
2384	Proforma Corp—Robert Farrell	26261 Evergreen Rd Ste, Southfield MI 48076	248-281-8900	R	6*	<.1
2385	Raxco Software Inc—Robert E Nolan	6 Montgomery Village A, Gaithersburg MD 20879	301-527-0803	R	6*	<.1
2386	SwiftView Inc	9205 SW Gemini Dr Ste, Beaverton OR 97008	971-223-2600	D	6*	<.1
2387	Viking Software Solutions—Fred G Hoschett Phoenix Software International Inc	6804 S Canton Ave Ste, Tulsa OK 74136	918-491-6144	D	6*	<.1
2388	Abacus Data Systems—Judd Kessler	3601 Algonquin Rd, Rolling Meadows IL 60008	847-632-0303	R	6*	<.1
2389	Backbone Entertainment—Nolan Bushnell	6425 Christie Ave Ste, Emeryville CA 94608	510-379-2400	R	6*	<.1
2390	DECISIONMARK Corp—Jack Perry	818 Dows Rd SE, Cedar Rapids IA 52403	319-365-5597	R	6*	<.1
2391	Denmac Systems Inc—Lou Bevento	570 Lake Cook Rd Ste 2, Deerfield IL 60015	847-317-9610	R	6*	<.1
2392	Interactive Network Technologies Inc—Jeffrey Pferd	2901 Wilcrest Dr Ste 1, Houston TX 77042	713-975-7434	R	6*	<.1
2393	Kettley Publishing Co—Richard M Kettley	20271 SW Birch St Ste, Newport Beach CA 92660	949-250-0794	R	6*	<.1
2394	Mantissa Corp—Neil Saunders	1121 Edenton St, Birmingham AL 35242	205-968-3939	R	6*	<.1
2395	Merchant Technologies	5504 Business Dr, Wilmington NC 28405	910-452-9808	R	6*	<.1
2396	Micro-Tel Inc	3700 Holcomb Bridge Rd, Norcross GA 30092	770-447-5408	R	6*	<.1
2397	Neasi-Weber International—Dennis Neasi	25115 Ave Stanford Ste, Valencia CA 91355	818-895-6900	R	6*	<.1
2398	netViz Corp—William E McCracken	One CA Plz, Islandia NY 11749		R	6*	<.1
2399	ONGroup—Tim Spells	200 Summit Blvd Ste 30, Atlanta GA 30342	404-460-5503	R	6*	<.1
2400	Principal Decision Systems International—Greg Ekstrom	50 Corporate Park, Irvine CA 92606		R	6*	<.1
2401	Ruf Strategic Solutions—J Ruf	1533 E Spruce St, Olathe KS 66061	913-782-8544	R	6*	<.1
2402	Visual Mining Inc—Tristan Zeigler	2099 Gaither Rd Ste 22, Rockville MD 20850	301-795-2200	R	6*	<.1
2403	TimeKeeping Systems Inc—Berry Markwitz	30700 Bainbridge Rd, Solon OH 44139	216-595-0890	R	6*	<.1
2404	WorkMovr Corp—Frank Pesek	708 Gravenstein HwyN R, Sebastopol CA 95472	310-721-4050	R	6*	<.1
2405	Advanced Systems Concepts Inc (Hoboken New Jersey)—Ben Rosenburg	1180 Headquarters Plz, Morristown NJ 07960	973-539-2660	R	6*	<.1
2406	Century Software Inc (Salt Lake City Utah)—Gregory Haerr	6465 S 3000 E Ste 104, Holladay UT 84121	801-268-3088	R	6*	<.1
2407	KOM NETWORKS Inc—Taher Shaath	20 Trafalgar Sq Ste 45, Nashua NH 03063		R	6*	<.1
2408	Sescoi USA Inc	2000 Town Ctr Ste 1730, Southfield MI 48075	248-351-9300	S	6*	<.1
2409	Breen Systems Management Inc—James Breen	PO Box 131, Vergennes VT 05491	802-879-4212	R	6*	<.1
2410	Markzware Software—Patrick Marchese	1805 E Dyer Rd Ste, Santa Ana CA 92705		R	6*	<.1
2411	DMI Computer Technologies—Jose Laracuente	1601 N Ankeny Blvd, Ankeny IA 50023	515-964-0708	R	6*	<.1
2412	Pygmy Computer Systems Inc—Mark Geigel	12651 S Dixie Hwy Ste, Miami FL 33156	305-253-1212	R	6*	<.1
2413	ADINA R and D Inc—Zorka Bathe	71 Elton Ave, Watertown MA 02472	617-926-5199	R	6*	<.1
2414	ALR Systems and Software Inc—Larry H Andrews	11707 M Cir, Omaha NE 68137	402-891-1500	R	6*	<.1
2415	Altia Inc—Mike Juran	7222 Commerce Center D, Colorado Springs CO 80919	719-598-4299	R	6*	<.1
2416	American Health Care Software Enterprises Inc—Marcia DeRosia	99 Swift St Ste 300, South Burlington VT 05403	802-872-3484	R	6*	<.1
2417	Apani Networks—Koichi Takazawa	1800 E Imperial Hwy St, Brea CA 92821	714-674-1600	R	6*	<.1
2418	ARCLOGIX Inc—Rick Murphy	20 Saunders Ter, Wellesley MA 02481	781-239-0222	R	6*	<.1
2419	Computer Manager Inc—Gary Grout	PO Box 1961, Poulsbo WA 98370		R	6*	<.1
2420	Dr Schueler's Health Informatics Inc—Stephen Schueler	1129 US Hwy 1 2nd Fl, Rockledge FL 32955	321-637-0321	R	6*	<.1
2421	Fenestrae Inc—Wim de Koning	303 Research Dr Rm 140, Norcross GA 30092	770-622-5445	S	6*	<.1
2422	Generic Systems Inc—James Fletcher	PO Box 153, Perrysburg OH 43552	419-841-8460	R	6*	<.1
2423	Genesis V Systems Ltd	2845 Highview Ter, Eagan MN 55121	651-456-9909	R	6*	<.1
2424	Greentree Systems Inc—Terry Russey	1686 Dell Ave, Campbell CA 95008	408-879-1410	R	6*	<.1

Rank	Company Name—*Executive Officer*	Address, City, State, Zip	Phone	Type	Fin	Empls
2425	GVOX—*Richard Hotchkiss*	199 Rt 18, East Brunswick NJ 08816	732-565-3842	R	6*	<.1
2426	Leadership Companies Inc—*William Badenhoff*	42 Davis Rd, Acton MA 01720	978-264-2900	R	6*	<.1
2427	Mainstay—*Lance Merker*	770 Paseo Camarillo St, Camarillo CA 93010	805-484-9400	R	6*	<.1
2428	Melyx Corp—*Richard Johnston*	21830 Industrial Blvd, Rogers MN 55374		R	6*	<.1
2429	MicroVision Development Inc—*Rick Rutkowski*	5541 Fermi Ct Ste 120, Carlsbad CA 92008	760-438-7781	R	6*	<.1
2430	ORION Law Management Systems Inc—*Paul G Yelton*	1827 Powers Ferry RdBl, Atlanta GA 30339		R	6*	<.1
2431	ReCor Corp—*Jack Kelly*	820 Davis St Ste113, Evanston IL 60201	847-424-8700	R	6*	<.1
2432	Regent Education Inc—*Randy Jones*	112 W Church St, Frederick MD 21701	301-662-5592	R	6*	<.1
2433	Ripple Technologies Inc—*Ken Levine*	555 E North Ln Ste 604, Conshohocken PA 19428	610-862-4000	R	6*	<.1
2434	Syscon Computers Inc—*Bob Wilson*	94 McFarland Blvd, Northport AL 35476	205-758-2000	R	6*	<.1
2435	VLSystems Inc—*Tom White*	9 Corporate Park, Irvine CA 92606	949-660-8855	R	6*	<.1
2436	WebRecruiter LLC—*Tom FitzSimmons*	11 Broadway, New York NY 10004	212-422-1300	R	6*	<.1
2437	BinaryLabs Inc—*Frank Jensen*	960 Grand Ave, San Diego CA 92109	858-274-8520	R	6*	<.1
2438	Bellwether Software Corp—*Sunny Dronawat*	9900 Shelbyville Rd St, Louisville KY 40223	502-426-5463	R	6*	<.1
2439	AllMax Professional Solutions Inc—*Russell Maxwell*	PO Box 40, Kenton OH 43326	419-673-8863	R	6*	<.1
2440	Lanyon Inc—*Todd Tyler*	104 Decker Ct Ste 110, Irving TX 75062	817-226-5656	R	6*	<.1
2441	ABOL Software Inc—*Maik Goettel*	413 Creekstone Ridge, Woodstock GA 30188		R	6*	<.1
2442	Advanced Data Management Inc—*John E Nichols*	2000 Sheridan Dr, Buffalo NY 14223	716-874-5650	R	6*	<.1
2443	Blaze Systems Corp—*Larry E DeHeer*	300 Creek View Rd /ste, Newark DE 19711	302-733-7236	R	6*	<.1
2444	Certified Management Software Inc	807 E S Temple Ste 203, Salt Lake City UT 84102	801-534-1231	R	6*	<.1
2445	Mark III Systems Inc—*Leslie Powell*	3600 S Gessner Rd Ste, Houston TX 77063	713-664-9850	R	6*	<.1
2446	Productive Data Management Inc—*John Boone*	19745 Colima Rd Ste 1-, Rowland Heights CA 91748	323-725-2904	R	6*	<.1
2447	AlignMark—*Cabot Jaffee*	500 Winderley Pl Ste 2, Maitland FL 32751	407-875-1102	R	6*	<.1
2448	Ascar Business Systems	4041 9th St Bldg B, Acton CA 93510	661-269-8800	R	6*	<.1
2449	Attorneys Software Inc—*Deborah Jackson*	11739 W Washington Blv, Los Angeles CA 90066	310-578-9200	R	6*	<.1
2450	Berland Technologies Inc	11242 Playa Ct, Culver City CA 90230	310-398-6000	R	6*	<.1
2451	Business Computer Design International Inc—*Duncan Kenzie*	950 York Rd, Hinsdale IL 60521	630-986-0800	R	6*	<.1
2452	Catharon Software Corp—*Betsy Feinberg*	PO Box 20399, Sedona AZ 86341	928-203-0676	R	6*	<.1
2453	Classic Information Systems Inc—*Philip D Lewis*	15210 97th Rd N, West Palm Beach FL 33412	561-333-2590	R	6*	<.1
2454	Data Code Inc (Bohemia New York)—*Alan Christopherson*	640 Johnson Ave Ste 00, Bohemia NY 11716	631-218-4300	R	6*	<.1
2455	Data Linkage Software Inc	2421 W 205th St Ste D2, Torrance CA 90501	310-781-3057	R	6*	<.1
2456	Datastick Systems Inc—*Penny Melrose*	PO Box 6147, San Jose CA 95150	408-987-3400	R	6*	<.1
2457	Dayton Data Processing Inc	4247 Philadelphia Dr, Dayton OH 45405	937-277-7072	R	6*	<.1
2458	Deneb Inc—*Ken Lykins*	16824 Ave of the Fount, Fountain Hills AZ 85268		R	6*	<.1
2459	Executive Data Systems Inc—*Laura Spann*	1640 Powers Ferry Rd B, Marietta GA 30067	770-955-3374	R	6*	<.1
2460	FlexSim Software Products Inc—*Bill Nordgren*	1577 N Technology Way, Orem UT 84097	801-224-6914	R	6*	<.1
2461	GraphiCode—*Lew Wentworth*	1924 Bickford Ave Ste, Snohomish WA 98290	360-282-4888	R	6*	<.1
2462	Hula Software Inc—*John Smetona*	19201 Cook St, Foothill Ranch CA 92610		R	6*	<.1
2463	Interactive Technologies Inc (Missoula Montana)—*Tim Gillespie*	6070 Industrial Rd, Missoula MT 59808	406-549-8998	R	6*	<.1
2464	Intesel Inc—*Christopher G Moon*	7106 Southgate, Sarasota FL 34243	952-440-2226	R	6*	<.1
2465	Kardia Health Systems Inc	221 1st Ave SW Ste 300, Rochester MN 55902		R	6*	<.1
2466	KCI Computing Inc—*Max Kay*	3625 Del Amo Blvd Ste, Torrance CA 90503	310-921-6222	R	6*	<.1
2467	Lawrence Productions Inc—*Jerald M Brown*	25 Ottawa Ave SW Ste 2, Grand Rapids MI 49503		R	6*	<.1
2468	LTI Optics LLC	10850 Dover St Ste 300, Broomfield CO 80021	720-891-0030	R	6*	<.1
2469	Meta Software Corp—*Robert Seltzer*	150 Cambridge Park Dr, Cambridge MA 02140	781-238-0293	R	6*	<.1
2470	Optical Software Solutions Inc—*Travis Turner*	1031 Rt 32 Ste 2 and 3, Uncasville CT 06382	860-889-7005	R	6*	<.1
2471	PagePath Technologies Inc—*Gregory Wltek*	13 E Main St, Plano Il 60545	630-689-4111	R	6*	<.1
2472	Paul D Sheriff and Associates Inc—*Paul D Sheriff*	17852 E 17th St Ste 20, Tustin CA 92780	714-734-9792	R	6*	<.1
2473	Photodex Corp—*Paul Schmidt*	11100 Metric Blvd Ste, Austin TX 78758	512-419-7000	R	6*	<.1
2474	Proclivity Systems—*Sheldon Gilbert*	22 W 19th St 9th Fl, New York NY 10011	646-237-3737	R	6*	<.1
2475	Reams Computer Corp—*F Gordon Reams*	11838 Canon Blvd Ste 1, Newport News VA 23606	757-873-0233	R	6*	<.1
2476	Renesan Software—*Neeraj Sinha*	400 Continental Blvd F, El Segundo CA 90245	310-598-6223	R	6*	<.1
2477	SBT Business Technologies Inc—*John Holden*	11 Racetrack Rd NE Ste, Fort Walton Beach FL 32547	850-315-4944	R	6*	<.1
2478	Software Illustrated Inc—*Barbara Johnson*	PO Box 884, Tracy CA 95378	209-832-7353	R	6*	<.1
2479	Steele Systems Inc	PO Box 241844, Los Angeles CA 90024		R	6*	<.1
2480	Symmetry Software Corp—*Tom Reahard*	14350 N 87th St Ste 25, Scottsdale AZ 85260	480-998-9106	R	6*	<.1
2481	Taro Systems Inc—*Doug Lee*	6157 28th St SE Ste 7, Grand Rapids MI 49546	616-940-0007	R	6*	<.1
2482	TuVox Inc—*Mark Lazar*	550 S Winchester Blvd, San Jose CA 95128	408-625-1770	S	6*	<.1
2483	Tykon Inc—*Dan Cooley*	PO Box 592, Pewaukee WI 53072	262-347-2999	S	6*	<.1
2484	Zeiler-Pennock Inc—*Paul Pennock*	2727 Bryant St Ste 600, Denver CO 80211	303-455-3322	R	6*	<.1
2485	Accredical Software Inc—*Martin Bakker*	7726 Arjons Dr, San Diego CA 92126	858-621-2630	D	6*	<.1
2486	Amanda Company Inc—*Brian Bonar*	4079 Govenor Dr, San Diego CA 92122	858-866-9944	R	6*	<.1
2487	ComputerEase Construction Software—*John Meibers*	6460 Harrison Ave Ste, Cincinnati OH 45247	513-481-5800	R	6*	<.1
2488	Insmark Inc—*Robert B Ritter Jr*	2400 Camino Ramon, San Ramon CA 94583	925-543-0500	R	6*	<.1
2489	Mersoft International LLC—*Ronald Sloop*	Corporate Woods Bldg 5, Overland Park KS 66210	913-871-6200	R	6*	<.1
2490	Health Financial Systems—*Becky Dolan*	8109 Laguna Blvd, Elk Grove CA 95758	916-686-8152	R	6	<.1
2491	Dicom Solutions—*Chad Hutchison*	548 Wald, Irvine CA 92618	949-606-8631	R	6*	<.1
2492	Commercial Logic Inc—*Peter Coburn*	PO Box 331, Hanover NH 03755	603-643-1900	R	6*	<.1
2493	American Group LLC—*Daniel Krivickas*	75 W Baseline Rd Ste 1, Gilbert AZ 85233	480-406-6102	R	6	<.1
2494	Irides Web Hosting—*Scott Young*	1000 Wilson Blvd Ste 2, Arlington VA 22209	703-236-7900	R	6	<.1
2495	Stratford Software Inc—*Ken McGinnis*	2700 Las Vegas Blvd St, Las Vegas NV 89109		R	6*	<.1
2496	Brilliant Digital Entertainment Inc—*Kevin Bermeister*	12711 Ventura Blvd Ste, Studio City CA 91604		R	6*	<.1
2497	Hyde Company Inc—*John Cuches*	1639 Spalding Drive, Atlanta GA 30350	678-731-9918	R	6*	<.1
2498	Least Cost Formulations Ltd—*Robert Labudde*	824 Timberlake Dr, Virginia Beach VA 23464	757-467-0954	R	6*	<.1
2499	Transpower Corp—*Ronald Satz*	PO Box 7132, Penndel PA 19047	215-355-7011	R	6*	<.1
2500	Activestrategy Inc—*Jack Steele*	620 W Germantown Pke, Plymouth Meeting PA 19462	484-690-0700	R	6*	<.1
2501	Vertical Computer Systems Inc—*Richard Wade*	101 W Renner Rd Ste 30, Richardson TX 75082	972-437-5200	P	6	<.1
2502	Cfs Tax Software—*Ted Sullivan*	PO Box 879, Simi Valley CA 93062	805-522-1157	R	6*	.1
2503	ImageWare Systems Inc—*Jim Miller*	10815 Rancho Bernardo, San Diego CA 92127	858-673-8600	P	6	.1
2504	Now Solutions LLC—*Marianne Franklin* Vertical Computer Systems Inc	101 W Renner Rd Ste 30, Richardson TX 75082	972-437-3339	S	6	<.1
2505	Zyrion Inc—*Vikas Aggarwal*	440 N Wolfe Rd, Sunnyvale CA 94085	408-524-7424	R	6*	.1
2506	ADVIZOR Solutions Inc—*Douglas A Cogswell*	1333 Butterfield Rd St, Downers Grove IL 60515	630-971-5250	R	6*	.1
2507	MicroLeague Multimedia Inc—*Neil B Swartz*	2663 Upper Park Rd, Orlando FL 32814	305-434-8850	R	6*	.1
2508	Auto-Graphics Inc—*Paul R Cope*	3201 Temple Ave Ste 10, Pomona CA 91768	909-595-7004	S	6	<.1
2509	ProdEx Technologies Inc—*Chandra Bodapati*	1340 S De Anza Blvd St, San Jose CA 95129	408-872-3100	R	6	.1
2510	Wizzard Software Corp—*Chris Spencer*	5001 Baum Blvd Ste 770, Pittsburgh PA 15213	412-621-0902	P	6	.1
2511	Listingbook LLC—*Randall Catlin*	PO Box 10768, Greensboro NC 27404	336-722-3456	R	6*	.1
2512	Mind Software Inc—*Monica Eisnger*	12520 Prosperity Dr St, Silver Spring MD 20904	301-572-1100	R	6*	.1
2513	Smartcop Inc—*George Stephenson*	180 N Palafox St, Pensacola FL 32502	850-436-5983	R	6*	.1

Note: An asterisk (*) indicates an estimated financial figure. The company type code used is as follows: R = Private, P = Public, S = Private Subsidiary, B = Public Subsidiary, D = Division, J = Joint Venture, I = Investment Fund.

COMPANY RANKINGS BY SALES WITHIN 4-DIGIT SIC

Rank	Company Name—Executive Officer	Address, City, State, Zip	Phone	Type	Fin	Empls
2514	Craneware Inc—Keith Neilson	6240 E Thomas Rd Ste 3, Scottsdale AZ 85251	480-429-9138	R	5*	.1
2515	Fidelity Information Services Inc—Frank R Martire	601 Riverside Ave, Jacksonville FL 32204	904-854-5000	S	5	33.0
2516	Open Mind Technologies USA Inc—Werner Schwenkert	39111 W Six Mile Rd, Livonia MI 48152	734-779-1625	S	5	<.1
2517	Medlink International Inc—Ray Vuono	1 Roebling Ct, Ronkonkoma NY 11779	631-342-8800	P	5	<.1
2518	Inspiration Technology Inc—Sam Khashman	6000 Fairview Rd Ste 1, Charlotte NC 28210	704-553-0805	R	5*	<.1
2519	Attest Systems Inc—Herbert M Gottlieb	PO Box 2851, Novato CA 94948	415-884-7590	R	5	<.1
2520	Simplicti Software Solutions—Wen-Kai Ho	1255 Crescent Green St, Cary NC 27518	919-858-8898	R	5*	<.1
2521	DataArt Inc—Eugene Goland	475 Park Ave S Fl 9, New York NY 10016	212-378-4108	R	5*	.2
2522	Blazent Inc—Gary Oliver	1820 Gateway Dr, San Mateo CA 94404	650-286-5500	R	5*	.1
2523	Everest Software Corp—Peter Bender-Samuel	13455 Noel Road Ste 21, Dallas TX 75240	214-451-3000	R	5*	.1
2524	Insurance Technologies Corp—John Hartley	1335 Valwood Pkwy Ste, Carrollton TX 75006	972-245-3660	R	5*	.1
2525	Syncrotech Software Corp—Edwin Y Ogata	6405 Mira Mesa Blvd Su, San Diego CA 92121	858-412-8000	R	5*	.1
2526	Visionael Corp—Craig Nichols	201 San Antonio Circle, Mountain View CA 94040	650-470-8920	R	5*	.1
2527	DST International—Tom Abraham DST Systems Inc	27 Melcher St 1st Fl, Boston MA 02210	617-482-8800	S	5*	.1
2528	PKC Corp—Howard Pierce	1 Mill St Box C13 Ste, Burlington VT 05401	802-658-5351	R	5*	.1
2529	Acclivity—Christopher Lee	300 Roundhill Dr Rm 2, Rockaway NJ 07866		S	5*	.1
2530	Communispace Corp—Diane Hessan	100 Talcott Ave, Watertown MA 02472	617-607-1400	R	5*	.1
2531	Netkey Inc—Miller Newton	100 S Shore Dr, East Haven CT 06512	203-285-1420	S	5*	.1
2532	NTP Software Inc—Bruce Backa	20A NW Blvd Ste 136, Nashua NH 03063	603-622-4400	R	5*	.1
2533	Vision Software Technologies Inc—Philip Patterson	116 N Main St, Goodlettsville TN 37072	615-859-6718	R	5*	.1
2534	Antenna Software Inc—James J Hemmer	111 Town Square Pl, Jersey City NJ 07310	201-239-2300	R	5*	.1
2535	Equis International LLC Reuters Information Technology LLC	90 S 400 W Ste 620, Salt Lake City UT 84101	801-265-9996	S	5*	.1
2536	Inforonics Inc—Bruce Mills	25 Porter Rd, Littleton MA 01460		S	5*	.1
2537	Ingenious Inc—Vibhu Sharma	10700 Richmond Ave Ste, Houston TX 77042	832-242-0220	R	5*	.1
2538	Restaurant Technology Inc—Greg Waddell	1325 Williams Dr, Marietta GA 30066	770-590-4300	R	5*	.1
2539	Edashop Inc—Carlos Leao	6601 Lyons Rd Ste E5, Coconut Creek FL 33073	954-429-3433	R	5*	.1
2540	Blacksmith Inc	11654 Plz America Dr S, Reston VA 20190	757-645-0259	R	5*	.1
2541	Bradmark Inc—Bradley Tashenberg	4265 San Felipe St Ste, Houston TX 77027	713-621-2808	R	5*	.1
2542	Cambar Software Inc—Wade R Register Jr	2430 Mall Dr Ste 320, North Charleston SC 29406	843-614-8000	R	5*	.1
2543	Computer Decisions International LLC—Sam Mancuso	23933 Research Dr, Farmington Hills MI 48335	248-347-4600	R	5*	.1
2544	Datatrac Corp—Garland Duvall	4550 North Point Pkwy, Alpharetta GA 30022	770-552-3866	R	5*	.1
2545	ENCOMPIX Software Inc—Chuck Stewart Consona Corp	4010 Executive Park Dr, Cincinnati OH 45241	513-733-0066	S	5*	.1
2546	Financial Industry Computer Systems Inc—Dawn Gibbs	14285 Midway Rd Ste 20, Addison TX 75001	972-458-8583	R	5*	.1
2547	GE Medical Systems Information Technologies—Mark Vachon	3330 Keller Springs Rd, Carrollton TX 75006	972-295-7700	S	5*	.1
2548	GT Software Inc—Eric Nelson	235 Peachtree St NE St, Atlanta GA 30303	404-253-1300	R	5*	.1
2549	LeaseTeam Inc—Russ Hallberg	4139 S 143rd Cir, Omaha NE 68137	402-493-3445	R	5*	.1
2550	Micron Systems Corp—Carole Schiller	266 Harristown Rd Ste, Glen Rock NJ 07452	201-652-2229	R	5*	.1
2551	Occupational Health Research—Michael Keller	28 Research Dr, Skowhegan ME 04976		R	5*	.1
2552	Orange Technologies Inc—Sharad Talk	401 Professional Dr St, Gaithersburg MD 20879	301-840-2220	S	5*	.1
2553	Paisley Consulting Inc—Tim Welu	17400 Medina Rd Ste 85, Minneapolis MN 55447	763-450-4700	R	5*	.1
2554	Scala Inc—Gerard Bucas	350 Eagleview Blvd, Exton PA 19341	610-363-3350	R	5*	.1
2555	Softeq Development Ltd—Chris Howard	1155 Dairy Ashford St, Houston TX 77079	281-552-5000	R	5*	.1
2556	Solarsoft Business Systems (Lombard Illinois)—Shawn McMorran	1 East 22nd St Ste 301, Lombard IL 60148	630-834-0600	R	5*	.1
2557	IBS America Inc—Matthias Grossmann	125 Hartwell Ave, Lexington MA 02421	781-862-9002	S	5*	<.1
2558	McCracken Financial Solutions Corp—Frank McCraken	8 Suburban Park Dr, Billerica MA 01821	978-439-9000	S	5*	<.1
2559	EM-Assist Inc—Jeremy Burr	90 Blue Ravine Rd Rm 1, Folsom CA 95630	916-355-8444	R	5*	<.1
2560	NMT Corp—Daniel Gelatt	PO Box 2287, La Crosse WI 54602	608-781-0850	R	5*	<.1
2561	Northwoods Software Development Inc—Patrick Bieser	4600 W Schroeder Dr, Brown Deer WI 53223	414-434-8200	R	5*	<.1
2562	Petz Enterprises Inc—Leroy E Petz Sr	PO Box 611, Tracy CA 95378	209-835-2720	R	5*	<.1
2563	System Studies Inc—Robert A Simpkins	2-1340 E Cliff Dr, Santa Cruz CA 95062	831-475-5777	R	5*	<.1
2564	Psyche Systems Corp—Bob Sage	321 Fortune Blvd, Milford MA 01757	508-473-1500	R	5*	<.1
2565	CCG Systems Inc—Pamela J Nelson	2730 Ellsmere Ave, Norfolk VA 23507	757-623-1700	R	5*	<.1
2566	ProfitKey International Inc—Joseph DiZazzo Halo Technology Holdings Inc	50 Stiles Rd, Salem NH 03079		S	5*	<.1
2567	PROFITsystems Inc—Jeff Niskern	422 E Vermijo Ste 100, Colorado Springs CO 80903	719-471-3858	R	5*	<.1
2568	Software Consulting Services LLC—Richard Cichelli	630 Selvaggio Dr Ste 4, Nazareth PA 18064	610-746-7700	R	5*	<.1
2569	Red Wing Software Inc—Jim Long	491 Hwy 19 Blvd, Red Wing MN 55066	651-388-1106	R	5*	<.1
2570	Alexander Utility Engineering Inc—Richard Alexander	975 W Bitters Rd, San Antonio TX 78216	210-496-3200	R	5*	<.1
2571	BASIS International Ltd—Nico Spence	5901 Jefferson St NE, Albuquerque NM 87109	505-345-5232	R	5*	<.1
2572	FORESIGHT Corp—Robert Fisher	655 Metro Pl S Ste 900, Dublin OH 43017	614-791-1600	R	5*	<.1
2573	Formula Consultants Inc—R Joseph Dale	PO Box 544, Anaheim CA 92815	714-778-0123	R	5*	<.1
2574	GAINSystems—William C Benton	1415 W 22nd St Ste 950, Oak Brook IL 60523	630-505-3030	R	5*	<.1
2575	Management Computer Controls Inc	5100 Poplar Ave Ste 34, Memphis TN 38137	901-685-6061	R	5*	<.1
2576	Metafile Information Systems Inc—Allan Sprau	2900 43rd St NW, Rochester MN 55901	507-286-9232	R	5*	<.1
2577	NewGeneration Software Inc—Bernard Gough	3835 N Fwy Blvd Ste 20, Sacramento CA 95834	916-920-2200	R	5*	<.1
2578	Omega Legal Systems Inc—Donald A Gall	7272 E Indian School R, Scottsdale AZ 85251	602-952-5240	R	5*	<.1
2579	Perfman—James VanArtsdalen	1 Bethlehem Plz, Bethlehem PA 18018	610-865-0300	R	5*	<.1
2580	Satori Software Inc—Hugh Rogovy	1301 5th Ave Rm 2200, Seattle WA 98101	206-357-2900	R	5*	<.1
2581	Triton Technologies Inc—Jeff Smoke Vertical Communications Inc	4009 Plainfield Ave, Grand Rapids MI 49525	616-980-8761	S	5*	<.1
2582	Trinary Systems Inc—Stephen Koons Trubiquity	5480 Corporate Dr Ste, Troy MI 48098	248-833-9000	S	5*	<.1
2583	Ratchet—Martin Davis	800 Washington Ave N S, Minneapolis MN 55401	612-460-4760	R	5*	<.1
2584	infraWise Inc (Chicago Illinois)—David Collins	225 W Wacker Dr Ste 22, Chicago IL 60606	312-726-7587	R	5*	<.1
2585	Media Cybernetics Inc—Doug Paxton	4340 East-West Hwy Ste, Bethesda MD 20814	301-495-3305	S	5*	<.1
2586	Qantel Technologies Inc—Michael Galvin	3506 Breakwater Ct, Hayward CA 94545	510-731-2080	R	5*	<.1
2587	Systems Design and Development Inc—Ron Tarro	800-A NW 17th Ave, Delray Beach FL 33445	561-276-7004	R	5*	<.1
2588	Viador Inc—Sherry Chen	4677 Old Ironsides Dr, Santa Clara CA 95054	408-567-6000	R	5	<.1
2589	Software Productivity Research Inc—Michael Lester Artemis International Solutions Corp	1734 Brevard Rd Ste 18, Hendersonville NC 28791	973-273-5829	S	5*	<.1
2590	ADAX Inc—Barry Zuckerman	2900 Lakeshore Ave, Oakland CA 94610	510-548-7047	R	5*	<.1
2591	Summit Software Co—William P Fisher	4933 Jamesville Rd, Jamesville NY 13078	315-445-9000	R	5*	<.1
2592	VRC Insurance Systems—Peter R Cooper	32121 W Lindero Canyon, Westlake Village CA 91361	818-707-4295	R	5*	<.1
2593	Apta Software—Stephen Gardner	5151 E Broadway Ste 90, Tucson AZ 85711	520-663-0250	R	5*	<.1
2594	Advanced Medical Systems	820 Bear Tavern Rd, West Trenton NJ 08628	609-882-6889	R	5*	<.1
2595	Commence Corp—Betsy Conco	200 Tornillo Way Ste 2, Tinton Falls NJ 07712	732-380-9100	R	5*	<.1

Rank	Company Name—Executive Officer	Address, City, State, Zip	Phone	Type	Fin	Empls
2596	Computer Security Consultants Inc	590 Danbury Rd, Ridgefield CT 06877	203-431-8730	R	5*	<.1
2597	FDS International Inc—Andreas Z Roubian	18 W Ridgewood Ave, Paramus NJ 07652	201-670-1300	R	5*	<.1
2598	Gordon Haskett and Co—Susan Brewer	12526 High Bluff Dr St, San Diego CA 92130	858-847-3000	R	5*	<.1
2599	Internet Development Inc—Kevin Griffith Solutions X Global	462 E 800 N, Orem UT 84097	801-224-4444	S	5*	<.1
2600	JUMP Technology Services—Denise Brinkmeyer	5801 E 41st St Rm 707, Tulsa OK 74135	405-708-4813	R	5*	<.1
2601	MEI Solutions	1235 N Post Ste 200, Spokane WA 99201	509-232-3177	R	5*	<.1
2602	Nesbit Systems Inc—Irene S Nesbit	243 N Union St Ste 202, Lambertville NJ 08530	609-397-7720	R	5*	<.1
2603	nQativ	PO Box 64610, Lubbock TX 79464	806-687-8500	R	5*	<.1
2604	NSS Corp—Doug Pearson	PO Box 10190, Bedford NH 03110	603-296-2900	R	5*	<.1
2605	Prosoft Engineering Inc—Greg Brewer	1599 Greenville Rd, Livermore CA 94550	925-426-6100	R	5*	<.1
2606	Questys-Solutions	1401 N Tustin Ave Ste, Santa Ana CA 92705	949-855-6885	R	5*	<.1
2607	System Innovators Inc—Roger Nelson	10550 Deerwood Park Bl, Jacksonville FL 32256		R	5*	<.1
2608	Champ Systems Inc—Norm Champ	6060 Freeport Blvd, Sacramento CA 95822		R	5*	<.1
2609	Kaon Interactive Inc—Gavin A Finn	5 Clock Tower Pl Ste 1, Maynard MA 01754	978-823-0111	R	5*	<.1
2610	Advantage Data Inc—Renee Robert	33 Arch St Ste 2103, Boston MA 02110	617-261-9700	R	5*	<.1
2611	Agentek Inc—Jeff Jarvis	5900 Windward Pkwy Ste, Alpharetta GA 30005	678-393-1808	R	5*	<.1
2612	Autopower Corp—Michael J Mallory	525 Technology Pk Ste, Lake Mary FL 32746	407-695-7300	R	5*	<.1
2613	Bear River Associates Inc—Randall Matamoros	436 14th St Ste 300, Oakland CA 94612	510-834-5300	R	5*	<.1
2614	CAPISoftware—Chuck Atkinson	4100 International Plz, Fort Worth TX 76109	817-560-8139	R	5*	<.1
2615	Catalyst Development Corp—Cary Harwin	56925 Yucca Trl PMB 25, Yucca Valley CA 92284	760-228-9653	R	5*	<.1
2616	ecfirstcom Inc—Uday O Ali Pabrai	14225 University Ave S, Waukee IA 50263	515-453-8247	R	5*	<.1
2617	OPTIMUM Software Corp	1100 S Gilpin St, Denver CO 80210	303-698-2873	R	5	<.1
2618	Proficient Computing Solutions Corp—Turner Phil	4635 Trueman Blvd Ste, Hilliard OH 43026	614-272-1035	R	5*	<.1
2619	Vilden Associates Inc—Armando Villavicencio	2525 Cherry Ave Ste 20, Signal Hill CA 90755	562-997-7000	R	5*	<.1
2620	arcplan Inc—Detlef Kamps	1055 Westlakes Dr Ste, Berwyn PA 19312	610-902-0688	S	5	<.1
2621	Computer Engineering Inc—Jim Shearer	509 NW 5th St, Blue Springs MO 64014	816-228-2976	R	5*	<.1
2622	Question Mark Corp—Eric Shepard	535 Connecticut Ave St, Norwalk CT 06854		R	5*	<.1
2623	SLICE Technologies	200 Techne Center Dr S, Milford OH 45150		R	5*	<.1
2624	Associated Computer Systems Ltd—Tony Foth	11201 Aurora Ave, Des Moines IA 50322	515-223-0078	R	5*	<.1
2625	EH SofSolutions Inc—Curtis Palm	5062 S 108th St Ste 16, Omaha NE 68137	402-332-5611	R	5	<.1
2626	Engineering Dynamics Inc (Kenner Louisiana)—David Garland	2113 38th St, Kenner LA 70065	504-443-5481	R	5*	<.1
2627	Progressive Group Inc—Brian Wilton	5177 Richmond Ave Ste, Houston TX 77056	713-626-5678	R	5*	<.1
2628	Semaphore Corp (Seattle Washington)—Roy Simperman	9675 SE 36th St Ste 11, Mercer Island WA 98040	206-905-5000	R	5*	<.1
2629	Travel Computer Systems Inc—Jack Revel	4256 Overland Ave, Culver City CA 90230	310-558-0262	R	5*	<.1
2630	Academic Software Inc—Warren Lacefield	3504 Tates Creek, Lexington KY 40517	859-552-1020	R	5*	<.1
2631	Adpac Corp—Ed Severs	1996 Holmes St, Livermore CA 94550	415-777-5400	R	5*	<.1
2632	Brownstone Research Group—Carol Vallon	512 Riverside Pkwy Ste, Rome GA 30161	706-802-1713	S	5*	<.1
2633	Butler and Curless Associates Inc—Don Curless	3716 National Dr Ste 2, Raleigh NC 27612	919-877-0017	R	5*	<.1
2634	e2value Inc—Todd Rissel	PO Box 3518, Stamford CT 06905	203-975-7990	R	5*	<.1
2635	Encite Inc—Ed Horner	2725 Water Ridge Pky S, Charlotte NC 28217	704-461-1255	R	5*	<.1
2636	Forum Communication Systems Inc—Raj Natarajan	1223 N Glenville Dr, Richardson TX 75081	972-680-0700	R	5*	<.1
2637	Innovation Management Group Inc—Jerry Hussong	179 Niblick Rd #454, Paso Robles CA 93446		R	5*	<.1
2638	Innovative Programming Associates Inc—Kathleen Updike	54 Traditions Way, Lawrenceville NJ 08648	609-924-7272	R	5*	<.1
2639	LandWare Inc—Ken Landau	PO Box 25, Paramus NJ 07652	201-670-0144	R	5*	<.1
2640	New Generation Technologies Inc—Roy Lepik	PO Box 34069 Dept 844, Seattle WA 98124		R	5*	<.1
2641	PIC Business Systems Inc—Richard Schomme	5119 Beckwith Blvd Ste, San Antonio TX 78249	210-690-9106	R	5*	<.1
2642	Square One—Keith Martin	960 Holmdel Rd, Holmdel NJ 07733	732-332-1300	R	5*	<.1
2643	Statistical Graphics Corp—Caroline Chopek	560 Broadview Ave Ste, Warrenton VA 20186	540-428-0084	R	5*	<.1
2644	Bourque Data Systems Inc—Steve Bourque	1610 Woodstead Ct Ste, The Woodlands TX 77380	281-362-1513	R	5*	<.1
2645	interlinkONE Inc—John P Foley Jr	21 Concord St Ste 200, Wilmington MA 01887	978-694-9992	R	5*	<.1
2646	ITM Associates Inc—Ian Altman	1700 Rockville Pke Ste, Rockville MD 20852	301-984-6060	R	5*	<.1
2647	Vanquish Inc—Philip Raymond	201 Boston Post Rd W S, Marlborough MA 01752	508-486-9040	R	5*	<.1
2648	Chronos LLC	PO Box 949, Heber City UT 84032		R	5*	<.1
2649	Computer Pundits Corp—Prashubh Batham	5001 American Blvd W S, Bloomington MN 55437	952-854-2422	R	5*	<.1
2650	DogBreath Software Inc—Gary B Carr	6235 Lusk Blvd, San Diego CA 92121	858-558-3696	R	5*	<.1
2651	Financial Software Innovations Inc—Cecil Patton	3102 Bee Caves Rd Ste, Austin TX 78746	512-328-1584	R	5*	<.1
2652	JNetDirect Inc—Ron Wright	PO Box 404, Herndon VA 20172		S	5*	<.1
2653	JS Technologies Inc—Kurt Baese	804 Moorefield Pk Dr S, Richmond VA 23236	804-288-7850	R	5*	<.1
2654	Media Computing Inc—Michael Rich	PO Box 4169, Phoenix AZ 85030	480-575-7281	R	5*	<.1
2655	SkyLine Tools Imaging—Jan Dekkers	13078 Mindanao Way Uni, Marina Del Rey CA 90292	310-306-8200	S	5*	<.1
2656	Verisurf Software Inc—Ernie Husted	1553 N Harmony Cir, Anaheim CA 92807	714-970-1683	R	5*	<.1
2657	WorkZone LLC—Rick Mosenkis	16 W Township Line Rd, East Norriton PA 19401	610-275-9861	R	5*	<.1
2658	Admins Inc—Dagfinn Saether	1035 Cambridge St, Cambridge MA 02141	617-494-5100	R	5*	<.1
2659	Applied Computer Systems Inc (Knoxville Tennessee)—Rick DeLand	302 Westfield Rd, Knoxville TN 37919	865-584-0535	R	5*	<.1
2660	Applied Testing and Technology Inc—Jennifer Wolcott	9298 Central Ave Ste 3, Minneapolis MN 55434	763-786-8160	R	5*	<.1
2661	Atlas Business Solutions Inc—Fred Anvary	PO Box 9013, Fargo ND 58106	701-235-5226	R	5*	<.1
2662	Bayside Business Solutions Inc—Russ Opper	2 20th St N Ste 1600, Birmingham AL 35203	205-972-8900	R	5*	<.1
2663	BigStage—Jonathan Strietzel	15303 Ventura Blvd Ste, Sherman Oaks CA 91403	818-743-1424	R	5*	<.1
2664	Blue Pearl Software Inc—Ellis Smith	4699 Old Ironsides Dr, Santa Clara CA 95054	408-961-0121	R	5*	<.1
2665	Bonafide Management Systems Inc—Larry Lai	241 Lombard St, Thousand Oaks CA 91360	805-908-2333	R	5*	<.1
2666	CallMe Corp—Darrin J Stock	4300 Brighton Blvd, Denver CO 80216		R	5*	<.1
2667	Cimple Systems Inc—Arthur Ardolino	116 Village Blvd, Princeton NJ 08540		R	5*	<.1
2668	Computer Golf Software Inc—Neil Haynie	1700 SW 12th Ave, Boca Raton FL 33486	561-392-6740	R	5*	<.1
2669	Cosmic Software Inc—Maurcie Fathi	17 Bridge St Ste 101, Billerica MA 01821	978-667-2556	R	5*	<.1
2670	CRT International Inc—Ron Pierner	52260 Old Grade Rd, Mason WI 54856	715-763-3400	R	5*	<.1
2671	Dartware LLC—Rich Brown	PO Box 130, Hanover NH 03755	603-643-9650	R	5*	<.1
2672	Data Management Associates Inc—Randall Nettling	4000 Executive Park Dr, Cincinnati OH 45241	513-563-7300	R	5*	<.1
2673	Davka Corp—Susan Schwartz	2750 W Pratt Blvd, Chicago IL 60645		R	5*	<.1
2674	Eberhard Klemens Company Inc—Eberhard R Klemens	10400 W Higgins Rd Ste, Rosemont IL 60018	847-296-8010	R	5*	<.1
2675	EES Companies Inc—Hank Szretter	PO Box 902, Framingham MA 01701	508-653-6911	R	5*	<.1
2676	Gardenia Software Systems Inc—Frederick H Thomas	5907 Whippoorwill Holl, Milford OH 45150	513-861-3748	R	5*	<.1
2677	ImageXpert Inc	460 Amherst St, Nashua NH 03063	603-598-2500	R	5*	<.1
2678	I-Tech Automation Inc—Dan Candwell	25711 Hillview Ct, Mundelein IL 60060	847-726-9340	R	5*	<.1
2679	KeyResults Solutions—Kenny Manchester	11222 Wind Pine MS-204, Tomball TX 77375	281-376-5378	R	5*	<.1
2680	Medcom Information Systems Inc—John Holub	2117 Stonington Ave, Hoffman Estates IL 60169	847-885-1553	R	5*	<.1
2681	Mercantec Inc—Bill Tait	16355 W Freistadt Rd, Germantown WI 53022	414-604-6372	R	5	<.1
2682	Mr Software of East Coast Inc	135 W 36th St, New York NY 10018	212-947-6272	S	5*	<.1
2683	NECS Inc—Chris Anatra	168 Boston Post Rd Ste, Madison CT 06443	203-245-3999	R	5*	<.1

Note: An asterisk (*) indicates an estimated financial figure. The company type code used is as follows: R = Private, P = Public, S = Private Subsidiary, B = Public Subsidiary, D = Division, J = Joint Venture, I = Investment Fund.

COMPANY RANKINGS BY SALES WITHIN 4-DIGIT SIC

Rank	Company Name—*Executive Officer*	Address, City, State, Zip	Phone	Type	Fin	Empls
2684	Pointwise Inc—*John R Chawner*	213 S Jennings Ave, Fort Worth TX 76104	817-377-2807	R	5*	<.1
2685	PowerProduction Software Inc—*Sally Walsh*	15732 Los Gatos Blvd S, Los Gatos CA 95032	408-559-0800	R	5*	<.1
2686	QwikQuote Development	PO Box 486, Bordentown NJ 08505	609-291-9276	R	5*	<.1
2687	R A Wood Associates	1001 Broad St Ste 450, Utica NY 13501	315-735-4217	R	5*	<.1
2688	Redseal Systems Inc—*Parveen Jain*	2121 S El Camino Real, San Mateo CA 94403		R	5*	<.1
2689	Revelation Software WinWin Solutions Inc	99 Kinderkamack Rd Ste, Westwood NJ 07675	201-594-1422	S	5*	<.1
2690	Sidebar Inc—*Patrick Kennedy*	2890 Colorado Ave, Santa Monica CA 90404	310-382-5262	R	5*	<.1
2691	Turnaround Computing Inc	2912 Mollimar Dr, Plano TX 75075		R	5*	<.1
2692	Unisun Corp—*Terry Hutt*	7790 Mossy Cup St, Boise ID 83709	208-362-3773	R	5*	<.1
2693	Zeesoft Inc—*Jitendra Maheshwari*	4320 Stevens Creek Blv, San Jose CA 95129	408-247-2987	R	5*	<.1
2694	Evident Software Inc—*Scott Barnett*	211 Warren St Ste 209, Newark NJ 07103	973-622-5656	R	5*	<.1
2695	Remitdata Inc—*Dave Ellett*	80 Monroe Ave Ste 300, Memphis TN 38103		R	5*	<.1
2696	REP Profit Management System—*Jim Adam*	11771 W 112th St, Overland Park KS 66210	913-338-0266	R	5*	<.1
2697	VizSeek—*Nainesh Rathod*	3495 Kent Ave Ste A100, West Lafayette IN 47906	765-464-1700	R	5*	<.1
2698	Transend Corp—*Fred Krefetz*	225 Emerson St, Palo Alto CA 94301	650-324-5370	R	5*	<.1
2699	IQS Inc—*Michael Rapaport*	25000 Country Club Blv, North Olmsted OH 44070	440-333-1344	R	5*	<.1
2700	Seaport Software Inc—*Clell Beavers*	315 Main St, Broken Arrow OK 74012	918-258-8611	R	5*	<.1
2701	Aardvark Software Inc—*Walter Sloan*	399 E 72 St Ste 18A, New York NY 10021	212-327-1964	R	5*	<.1
2702	Acclaim Software—*James DeRose*	1907 Chesapeake Trl SW, Decatur AL 35603		R	5*	<.1
2703	Amerifax Services Corp—*David Eid*	572 W Market St Ste 6, Akron OH 44303	330-253-8787	R	5*	<.1
2704	Analytical Software—*Jack Noonan*	PO Box 12185, Tallahassee FL 32317	850-893-9371	R	5*	<.1
2705	Applications Software Inc—*Donald H Sundeen*	7441 Garden Grove Blvd, Garden Grove CA 92841	714-891-2616	R	5*	<.1
2706	Armasi Inc—*Jim Hatchitt*	3966 SW 98th Dr, Gainesville FL 32608	352-333-8393	R	5*	<.1
2707	AS/SURE Software—*Kristine Barnes*	PO Box 886, Cary NC 27512	919-467-2484	R	5*	<.1
2708	Best Impressions Inc—*Dawn Waldrop*	6797 Scenic Woods Dr, Valley City OH 44280	330-483-0411	R	5*	<.1
2709	Braided Matrix Inc—*Lincoln Stoller*	148 Dubois Rds, Shokan NY 12481	845-657-6411	R	5*	<.1
2710	dSoft Development Inc—*Robert Echols*	4334 NW Expy Ste 243, Oklahoma City OK 73116	405-842-8084	R	5*	<.1
2711	Eifrid Systems Development—*James Taylor*	PO Box 1221, Carpinteria CA 93014		R	5*	<.1
2712	Eric Isaacson Software—*Eric Isaacson*	416 E University Ave, Bloomington IN 47401	812-339-1811	R	5*	<.1
2713	Guia International Corp—*Jan Jansen*	1040 Satinleaf St, Hollywood FL 33019	954-889-5830	R	5*	<.1
2714	Home Plan Software Inc—*Chuck Herndon*	8437 W Center St, Mokelumne Hill CA 95245	209-286-1021	R	5*	<.1
2715	IBI Co—*Juan Inchauste*	PO Box 3194, Bellevue WA 98009	425-450-0316	R	5*	<.1
2716	IEP Publishers—*Donald Cahill*	PO Box 546, Fork Union VA 23055		R	5*	<.1
2717	InfoHarvest Inc—*Philip J Murphy*	316 Occidental Ave S, Seattle WA 98104	206-686-2729	R	5*	<.1
2718	J Vilkaitis Consultants—*John Vilkaitis*	PO Box 26, Thomaston CT 06787	408-705-2284	R	5*	<.1
2719	Knowledge Quest—*Mark Dawson*	301 Forest Ave, Laguna Beach CA 92651	949-376-8150	R	5*	<.1
2720	Language Quest Software Co—*Jay Havlice*	309 N Mt Shasta Blvd, Mount Shasta CA 96067	530-918-9540	R	5*	<.1
2721	Linked Software—*Holli Emore*	1857 Stonecrest Blvd S, Tyler TX 75703	903-534-0620	R	5*	<.1
2722	MARBLE Computer Inc—*Marshall Crawford*	PO Box 920692, El Paso TX 79902	915-845-0963	R	5*	<.1
2723	MathTensor Inc—*Steven M Christensen*	PO Box 16175, Chapel Hill NC 27516	919-382-5584	R	5*	<.1
2724	Matrix Plus Inc—*Ileta Rutherford*	PO Box 14549, Monroe LA 71207	318-388-8955	R	5*	<.1
2725	Medina Software Inc—*George Medina*	PO Box 952440, Lake Mary FL 32795	407-227-4112	R	5*	<.1
2726	Northern Lights Software—*Pertti Karjalainen*	112 Bothin Rd, Fairfax CA 94930	415-453-0481	R	5*	<.1
2727	Petroway Inc	926 Bautista Ct, Palo Alto CA 94303	650-494-2037	R	5*	<.1
2728	SKY Software—*Kamm Schreiner*	114 Lariat Ct, Stephens City VA 22655	540-869-6581	R	5*	<.1
2729	Software Exchange LLC—*Howard Berenbon*	PO Box 251682, West Bloomfield MI 48325	248-788-3342	R	5*	<.1
2730	Stewart Technologies Inc—*Warren Stewart*	PO Box 171702, Arlington TX 76003		R	5*	<.1
2731	Vertechs Associates Inc—*Charles E Verner*	PO Box 224, Amherst MA 01004	413-253-7535	R	5*	<.1
2732	Visidaq Solutions Inc—*Vito Bagdonavicon*	1970 Swarthmore Ave, Lakewood NJ 08701		R	5*	<.1
2733	Wheeler Arts—*Stephen Wheeler*	66 Chestnut Ct, Champaign IL 61822	217-359-6816	R	5*	<.1
2734	Wolverine Software Corp—*James O Henriksen*	3131 Mount Vernon Ave, Alexandria VA 22305	703-535-6760	R	5*	<.1
2735	ZPAY Payroll Systems Inc—*Paul Mayer*	10745 Serenity Lane, Savanna IL 61074	815-273-2322	R	5*	<.1
2736	IGC Inc—*Henri Ganancia*	5550 Touhy Ave Ste 300, Skokie IL 60077	847-593-2626	D	5	N/A
2737	Systar Inc—*Guy Kuster*	8618 Westwood Center D, Vienna VA 22182	703-556-8400	S	5	<.1
2738	Answers Corp—*Robert S Rosenschein*	237 W 35th St Ste 1101, New York NY 10001	646-502-4777	S	5	.1
2739	Esker Inc—*Jean-Michel Berard*	1212 Deming Way Ste 35, Madison WI 53717	608-828-6000	S	5	.1
2740	Design Data Corp—*H Dager*	1501 Old Cheney Rd, Lincoln NE 68512	402-441-4000	R	5*	<.1
2741	Forproject Technology Inc—*Glenn Gallop*	4020 N Macarthur Blvd, Irving TX 75038	214-550-8156	R	5*	<.1
2742	Objecuve Inc—*Constantinos Kelleas*	2125 Ctr Ave Ste 411, Fort Lee NJ 07024	201-242-1522	R	5*	<.1
2743	Tekever Corp—*Pedro Sinogas*	5201 Great America Pkw, Santa Clara CA 95054	408-730-2617	R	5*	<.1
2744	E Scan Technologies Corp—*Kelly Herrera*	12140 Severn Way, Riverside CA 92503	951-270-1911	R	5*	.1
2745	Netbrain Technologies Inc—*Lingping Gao*	23 3rd Ave, Burlington MA 01803	781-221-7199	R	5*	.1
2746	Software On Contact Corp—*George Kofman*	W67n222 Evergreen Blvd, Cedarburg WI 53012	262-375-6555	R	5*	.1
2747	Management Controls Inc—*Bob Harrell*	15600 Jfk Blvd Ste 220, Houston TX 77032	281-590-5881	R	5*	<.1
2748	Hammers Co—*Stephan Hammers*	7474 Greenway Ctr Dr S, Greenbelt MD 20770	301-345-5300	R	4*	<.1
2749	Black Mountain Systems LLC—*Andy Horwitz*	12520 High Bluff Dr St, San Diego CA 92130	858-866-8989	R	4	<.1
2750	Detto Technologies Inc—*Larry Mana'o*	207 E 860 S, Orem UT 84058	801-224-8900	P	4	<.1
2751	Korem Corp—*Sebastian Vachon*	7000 E Belleview Ave S, Greenwood Village CO 80111	720-200-4488	R	4*	<.1
2752	Geysers International Inc—*Mani Nallapillai*	4811 Beach Blvd Ste 40, Jacksonville FL 32207	904-356-1100	R	4*	<.1
2753	Cityon Systems Inc—*Preet Kumar*	2000 N Central Expy St, Plano TX 75074	972-424-6668	R	4*	<.1
2754	RE Systems Group Inc—*George Gramlich*	1060 Main St, River Edge NJ 07661	201-883-1572	R	4	<.1
2755	Appro Systems Inc—*Tracy Warren*	7173 Florida Blvd Ste, Baton Rouge LA 70806		S	4*	.1
2756	American Hytech Corp—*Ramesh Mehta*	125 UPark Rd, Pittsburgh PA 15238	412-826-3333	R	4*	.1
2757	SMC3 Atlanta—*Jack Middleton*	PO Box 2040, Peachtree City GA 30269	770-486-5800	R	4*	.1
2758	Access International—*Bill Wood*	1035 Cambridge St, Cambridge MA 02141	617-218-5000	R	4*	.1
2759	Heat Transfer Research Inc—*Claudette D Beyer*	150 Venture Dr, College Station TX 77845	979-690-5050	R	4*	.1
2760	Geocomp Corp—*W Allen Marr*	125 Nagog Park, Acton MA 01720	978-635-0012	R	4*	.1
2761	Media Services Group Ltd—*Jeff Shine*	1 Landmark Sq 8th Fl, Stamford CT 06901	203-921-1771	R	4*	.1
2762	Marlin Blue Systems Inc—*Dan Gupta*	PO Box 241, Succasunna NJ 07876	973-442-6480	R	4*	.1
2763	Uniplus Consultants Inc—*Sharad Gupta*	8140 Ashton Ave Ste 21, Manassas VA 20109	703-365-2227	R	4*	.1
2764	Gateway Ticketing Systems Inc—*Michael Andre*	315 E 2nd St, Boyertown PA 19512		R	4*	.1
2765	Hitcents Inc—*Chris Mills*	2425 Nashville Rd, Bowling Green KY 42101	270-796-5063	S	4*	.1
2766	Aspen Research Group Ltd—*John Praetorius*	PO Box 1370, Glenwood Springs CO 81602	970-945-2921	R	4*	.1
2767	Caselle Inc—*Steven D Hutchings*	1656 S East Bay Blvd S, Provo UT 84606		R	4*	.1
2768	Coventor Inc—*Michael J Jamiolkowski*	4000 Centre Green Way, Cary NC 27513	919-854-7500	R	4*	.1
2769	Cyan Worlds Inc—*Rand Miller*	14617 Newport Hwy, Mead WA 99021	509-468-0807	R	4*	.1
2770	Extol Inc—*Anthony Baran*	795 Franklin Ave, Franklin Lakes NJ 07417	201-847-1200	R	4*	.1
2771	FundBalance—*John S Marr* Tyler Technologies Inc	1194 Oak Valley Dr Ste, Ann Arbor MI 48108	734-677-0550	S	4*	.1

Rank	Company Name—Executive Officer	Address, City, State, Zip	Phone	Type	Fin	Empls
2772	Information Systems and Services Inc	8601 Georgia Ave Ste 7, Silver Spring MD 20910	301-588-3800	R	4*	.1
2773	Inmagic Inc—Paul Puzzanghera	200 Unicorn Park Dr 4t, Woburn MA 01801	781-938-4444	R	4*	.1
2774	Kinetic Presentations Inc—Ray Schuhmann Kinetic Technology Agency	200 Distillery Commons, Louisville KY 40206	502-583-1679	S	4*	.1
2775	Newtek Inc—Dominique Pouliquen	5131 Beckwith Blvd, San Antonio TX 78249	210-370-8000	R	4*	.1
2776	Practice Partner—John Hammergren	2401 4th Ave Ste 700, Seattle WA 98121	206-441-2400	R	4*	.1
2777	Software Solutions Unlimited Inc—Mark McCausland	7500 Jefferson NE Ste, Albuquerque NM 87109	505-828-9000	R	4	.1
2778	Vendavo Inc—Alan Crites	1029 Corporation Way, Palo Alto CA 94303	650-960-4300	R	4*	.1
2779	BeneSoft Inc—John Haley	440 Wheelers Farms Rd, Milford CT 06461		R	4*	<.1
2780	eQuorum Corp—Frank Fortson	6285 Barfield Rd Ste 2, Atlanta GA 30328	404-497-8100	R	4*	<.1
2781	Gravity Payments Inc—Lucas Price	1434 Elliott Ave W Ste, Seattle WA 98119		R	4*	<.1
2782	Phoenix Systems Inc (Atlanta Georgia)—Sandra Perkowitz	2970 Clairmont Rd NE S, Atlanta GA 30329	404-633-2466	R	4*	<.1
2783	Tecplot Inc—Mike Peery	PO Box 52708, Bellevue WA 98015	425-653-1200	R	4*	<.1
2784	Vinzant Inc	904 W Old Ridge Rd Ste, Hobart IN 46342	219-942-9544	R	4*	<.1
2785	Kinnser Software Inc—Christopher Hester	2600 Via Fortuna Dr St, Austin TX 78746	512-879-3135	R	4	<.1
2786	Fourth Dimension Software—Ilya Pavolotsky	255 Shoreline Dr 5th F, Redwood City CA 94065	650-592-4400	R	4*	<.1
2787	Innovative Systems Inc—Robert J Colonna	790 Holiday Dr, Pittsburgh PA 15220	412-937-9300	R	4*	<.1
2788	Orbital Technologies Corp—Eric E Rice	1212 Fourier Dr, Madison WI 53717	608-827-5000	R	4*	<.1
2789	Prophesy Transportation Solutions Inc—Edward J Forman	204C W Newberry Rd, Bloomfield CT 06002	860-243-0533	R	4*	<.1
2790	Solcom Inc—Marv Addink	4510 N Lewis Ave, Sioux Falls SD 57104	605-357-8212	R	4*	<.1
2791	StoneEagle Insurance Systems Inc—Jack Mellon	111 W Spring Valley Rd, Richardson TX 75081	972-934-1751	R	4*	<.1
2792	Warren-Forthought Inc—Carlos Suarez	1212 N Velasco Ste 207, Angleton TX 77515	979-849-1239	S	4*	<.1
2793	Applied Expert Systems Inc—Catherine H Liu	149 Commonwealth Dr, Menlo Park CA 94025	650-617-2400	R	4*	<.1
2794	Kinesix Corp—Russell E Jamerson	5120 Woodway Ste 10012, Houston TX 77056	713-953-8300	R	4*	<.1
2795	Grassroots Enterprise Inc—Arvind Rajan	120 Montgomery St Ste, San Francisco CA 94103	415-633-1100	R	4*	<.1
2796	JWS Corp—James Wilson Command Alkon Inc	10000 W 75th St Ste 10, Shawnee Mission KS 66204	913-384-0880	D	4*	<.1
2797	Lund Performance Solutions—Robert Lund	240 2nd Ave SW, Albany OR 97321	541-812-7600	R	4*	<.1
2798	Micro 2000 Inc—Rob McFarlane	700 N Central Ave 6th, Glendale CA 91203		R	4*	<.1
2799	Mitchell Humphrey and Co—Mitchell Humphrey	11720 Borman Dr Ste 31, Saint Louis MO 63146	314-991-2440	R	4*	<.1
2800	Performance Associates International Inc—Steven Brown	10195 N Oracle Rd, Tucson AZ 85704	520-544-2220	R	4*	<.1
2801	Seattle Lab Inc—Brendan Nolan	19700 Fairchild Ste 30, Irvine CA 92612	949-428-9330	S	4*	<.1
2802	Haverly Systems Inc (Ventura California)—Larry Haverly	PO Box 1110, Denville NJ 07834	973-627-1424	R	4*	<.1
2803	KVS Information Systems Inc—Edward M Warnke	821 Maple Rd, Williamsville NY 14221	716-626-1976	R	4*	<.1
2804	Forecross Corp—Kim O Jones	505 Montgomery St 11th, San Francisco CA 94111	415-543-1515	P	4	<.1
2805	Piracle Inc—John Bechard	556 Confluence Ave, Murray UT 84123	801-322-5222	R	4*	<.1
2806	SIXNET LLC—Hilton Nicholson	PO Box 767, Clifton Park NY 12065	518-877-5173	R	4*	<.1
2807	Access International Inc—Doug Kadish	333 N Michigan Ave Ste, Chicago IL 60601	312-920-9366	R	4*	<.1
2808	Business Automation Inc—Doug Nation	1544 W Yale Ave, Orange CA 92867	714-998-6600	R	4*	<.1
2809	American Business Systems Inc—James Hamilton	315 Littleton Rd, Chelmsford MA 01824		R	4*	<.1
2810	Bradford Technologies Inc—Jeff Bradford	302 Piercy Rd, San Jose CA 95138	408-360-8520	R	4*	<.1
2811	Imperial Software Technology Ltd—Derek Lambert	883 N Shoreline Boulev, Mountain View CA 94043	650-919-0200	R	4*	<.1
2812	Legal Files Software Inc—John Kanoski	801 S Durkin Dr Ste A, Springfield IL 62704	217-726-6000	R	4*	<.1
2813	MetaWare Inc—George Malek	2025 Gateway Pl Ste 14, San Jose CA 95110	408-437-3480	S	4*	<.1
2814	NPO Solutions Inc—Michael Church MicroEdge LLC (New York New York)	89 N State St, Concord NH 03301	603-224-3400	S	4*	<.1
2815	PROMODEL Solutions—Keith Vadas	566 E Technology Ave, Orem UT 84097	801-223-4600	D	4*	<.1
2816	SBC Systems Company Inc—Peggy Horn	115 Perimeter Center P, Atlanta GA 30346	770-399-0321	R	4*	< 1
2817	William Stucky and Associates Inc—William Stucky	2 Embarcadero Ctr Ste, San Francisco CA 94111	415-788-2441	R	4*	<.1
2818	Zyto Corp—Vaughn R Cook	387 S 520 W Ste 200, Lindon UT 84042	801-224-7199	P	4	<.1
2819	Adaptive Research—Kevin O'Rourke Simunet Corp	PO Box 7289, Alhambra CA 91801	626-688-4565	S	4*	<.1
2820	AEC Design Group—Paul Hutchins Orange Technologies Inc	401 Professional Dr St, Gaithersburg MD 20879	301-840-6919	S	4*	<.1
2821	AutoDesSys Inc—Chris Yessios	2011 Riverside Dr, Columbus OH 43221	614-488-8838	R	4*	<.1
2822	Children's Progress Inc—Eugene Galanter	108 W 39th St Ste 1300, New York NY 10018		R	4*	<.1
2823	Cognition Corp—Dale Gallaher	213 Burlington Rd Ste, Bedford MA 01730	781-271-9300	R	4*	<.1
2824	FullArmor Corp—Richard Farrell	399 Boylston St 7th Fl, Boston MA 02116	617-457-8100	R	4*	<.1
2825	Ironware Technologies LLC—Stephanie Dusatko	1900 Grant St Ste 600, Denver CO 80203	303-832-3970	R	4*	<.1
2826	LAWTRAC Development Corp—Frank Orzo	90 Merrick Ave Ste 101, East Meadow NY 11554	516-390-4700	R	4*	<.1
2827	NFS-Radiation Protection Systems Inc—William Rambow	PO Box 890, Groton CT 06340	860-445-0334	R	4*	<.1
2828	Process Software Corp—Brian McDonald Halo Technology Holdings Inc	959 Concord St, Framingham MA 01701	508-879-6994	S	4*	<.1
2829	ROC EasySpooler—Carl Wohletz	3305 Northland Dr Ste, Austin TX 78731	512-336-4200	D	4*	<.1
2830	Studio Visia Inc—Nikolay Arsov	9250 Wilshire Blvd Ste, Beverly Hills CA 90212	310-860-0016	R	4*	<.1
2831	Top Down Systems Corp—Dennis M Birke	9210 Corporate Blvd St, Rockville MD 20850	301-417-9660	R	4*	<.1
2832	Unimax Systems Corp—Phil Moen	50 S 6th St Ste 900, Minneapolis MN 55402	612-341-0946	R	4*	<.1
2833	Relational Architects International Inc—Carl Feinberg	33 Newark St Ste 3A, Hoboken NJ 07030	201-420-0400	R	4*	<.1
2834	System Management Software Inc—James D Thom	1935 County Rd B-2 Ste, Saint Paul MN 55113	651-633-2552	R	4*	<.1
2835	TIE Commerce—Brian Tervo	1360 Energy Park Dr St, Saint Paul MN 55108	651-999-8600	D	4*	<.1
2836	Challenger Corp—Robert E Sweeney	5050 Poplar Ave Ste 43, Memphis TN 38157	901-762-8449	R	4*	<.1
2837	Obsidian Software Inc—Eric T Hennenhoefer	609 Castle Ridge Rd St, Austin TX 78746	512-330-9818	R	4*	<.1
2838	3D Nature LLC—Gary Huber	13195 Chenango Ave, Morrison CO 80465	303-659-4028	R	4*	<.1
2839	AimaSoft Inc—Anand Ayyar	530 Alameda Del Prado, Novato CA 94949	415-453-2063	R	4*	<.1
2840	Amadeus Revenue Integrity Inc—Scott Kimbriel	3530 E Campo Abierto S, Tucson AZ 85718	520-577-6550	R	4*	<.1
2841	CADD Microsystems Inc—Micheal Hoover	6359 Walker Ln Ste 110, Alexandria VA 22310	703-719-0500	R	4*	<.1
2842	Computational Engineering International Inc—Anders Grimsrud	2166 N Salem St Ste 10, Apex NC 27523	919-363-0883	R	4*	<.1
2843	Concord USA Inc—Martin Bradley	2251 Perimeter Park Dr, Atlanta GA 30341	770-200-7465	R	4*	<.1
2844	Delta Data Software Inc—Don W Beck	700 Brookstone Centre, Columbus GA 31904		R	4*	<.1
2845	Diversified Computer Systems Inc	3933 Highplains Dr, Berthoud CO 80513	303-447-9251	R	4*	<.1
2846	Execu/Tech Systems Inc—Allison Hurt	535 Harrison Ave, Panama City FL 32401		R	4*	<.1
2847	Frontline Test Equipment Inc—Eric Kaplin	PO Box 7507, Charlottesville VA 22906	434-984-4500	R	4*	<.1
2848	Geodesic Systems Inc	414 N Orleans St Ste 4, Chicago IL 60610	312-832-1221	R	4*	<.1
2849	Graphisoft US Inc—Dominic Gallello	One Gateway Ctr Ste 30, Newton MA 02458	617-485-4200	S	4*	<.1
2850	Health Systems Resources Inc	4275 Shackleford Rd St, Norcross GA 30093	770-452-6500	R	4*	<.1
2851	Innovative Products and Services of Boston—Kathleen Cotter	PO Box 768, Middleboro MA 02346	508-923-7390	R	4*	<.1
2852	Integrated Computer Solutions Inc—Peter Winston	54 Middlesex Tpke Ste, Bedford MA 01730	617-621-0060	R	4*	<.1
2853	Intercon Associates Inc—Mark Basta	95 Allens Creek Rd, Rochester NY 14618		R	4	<.1
2854	KIDASA Software Inc—Susan Butler	1114 Lost Creek BlvdSt, Austin TX 78746		R	4*	<.1
2855	Lattice Inc (Wheaton Illinois)—Paul Burgess	1751 S Naperville Rd S, Wheaton IL 60189	630-949-3250	R	4*	<.1

Note: An asterisk (*) indicates an estimated financial figure. The company type code used is as follows: R = Private, P = Public, S = Private Subsidiary, B = Public Subsidiary, D = Division, J = Joint Venture, I = Investment Fund.

COMPANY RANKINGS BY SALES WITHIN 4-DIGIT SIC

Rank	Company Name—*Executive Officer*	Address, City, State, Zip	Phone	Type	Fin	Empls
2856	Niakwa Inc—*Alan Green*	500 Park Ave Ste 112, Lake Villa IL 60046	847-265-7400	R	4*	<.1
2857	Noguska Industries—*Norman Gibat*	741 N Countyline St, Fostoria OH 44830	419-435-0404	R	4*	<.1
2858	P-Stat Inc—*Roald Buhler*	230 Lambertville Hopew, Hopewell NJ 08525	609-466-9200	R	4*	<.1
2859	Reliability Center Inc—*Charles J Latino*	501 Westover Ave, Hopewell VA 23860	804-458-0645	R	4*	<.1
2860	Retail Anywhere—*Branden Jenkins*	4450 El Camino Real, Atascadero CA 93422	805-546-2900	R	4*	<.1
2861	ServiceCentral Technologies Inc—*Steve Teel*	5871 Glenridge Dr Ste, Atlanta GA 30328	404-870-7070	R	4*	<.1
2862	Sigma Systems Inc (Denver Colorado)—*Raymond Timmons*	2305 S Colorado Blvd S, Denver CO 80222	303-758-4610	R	4*	<.1
2863	SKM Systems Analysis Inc	1 Pearl St, Redondo Beach CA 90277	310-698-4700	R	4*	<.1
2864	Smart Software Inc—*Charles Smart*	4 Hill Rd, Belmont MA 02478	617-489-2743	R	4*	<.1
2865	Softsystems Inc (Fort Worth Texas)	1007 Mallick Twr 1 Sum, Fort Worth TX 76102	817-877-5070	R	4*	<.1
2866	STAT! Systems Inc—*Fred Dietrich*	2560 Ninth St Ste 317, Berkeley CA 94710	510-705-8700	R	4*	<.1
2867	Touch Technologies Inc—*Mike McCormick*	10650 Scripps Ranch Bl, San Diego CA 92131		R	4*	<.1
2868	Twenty-First Century Computer Systems Inc—*Robert Bullemer*	PO Box 1419, Santa Barbara CA 93102	805-964-6677	R	4*	<.1
2869	Veritools Inc—*Bob Schopmeyer*	95 1st St Ste 138, Los Altos CA 94022	650-949-8665	R	4*	<.1
2870	Brittenford Systems—*Michael A Mahoney*	12359 Sunrise Valley D, Reston VA 20191	703-860-6945	R	4*	<.1
2871	Breveon Inc—*Jane Kundin*	953 Industrial Ave Ste, Palo Alto CA 94303		R	4	<.1
2872	GeoFocus LLC—*Gary Wisgo*	3651 Fau Blvd Ste 215, Boca Raton FL 33431	561-955-1480	S	4*	<.1
2873	Enmark Systems Inc—*Michael Rybicki*	75 Aprill Dr, Ann Arbor MI 48103	734-669-0110	R	4*	<.1
2874	Xi Graphics Inc—*David Methvin*	1580 Logan St Ste 550, Denver CO 80203	303-298-7478	R	4*	<.1
2875	Bristol Group Ltd—*Louis Leger*	3070 Kerner Blvd, San Rafael CA 94901	415-256-2525	R	4*	<.1
2876	Capella Technologies LLC—*Robert Blanchet*	2099 S State College B, Anaheim CA 92806	714-385-4900	R	4*	<.1
2877	Color Dreams Inc—*James Chan*	6820 Orangethorpe Ave, Buena Park CA 90620	714-228-9282	R	4*	<.1
2878	EBS IT Solutions—*Neil Anderson*	3311 Richmond Ave Ste, Houston TX 77098	713-522-3480	R	4*	<.1
2879	Eidelman Associates—*Jim Eidelman*	317 S Division Ste 187, Ann Arbor MI 48104	734-769-1500	R	4*	<.1
2880	Fire Programs—*Gary Ewers*	4473 N Lecanto Hwy, Beverly Hills FL 34465	352-447-5000	R	4*	<.1
2881	Funk Software Inc—*Paul Funk*	222 Third St, Cambridge MA 02142	617-497-6339	S	4*	<.1
2882	Investors FastTrak—*Lance Holmes*	PO Box 77577, Baton Rouge LA 70879	225-612-8632	R	4*	<.1
2883	Medweb Inc—*Peter Killcommons*	667 Folsom St 2nd Fl, San Francisco CA 94107	415-541-9980	R	4*	<.1
2884	Mil-Pac Technology Inc—*Greg Tsiknas*	PO Box 2066, Ramona CA 92065	760-788-3030	R	4*	<.1
2885	P and C Insurance Systems Inc—*Michael Loizou*	55 Broadway 30th Fl, New York NY 10006	212-425-9200	R	4*	<.1
2886	Requirement Experts—*Ivy Hooks*	217 E Bandera Ste 200, Boerne TX 78006	830-249-0308	R	4*	<.1
2887	ROYDAN Enterprises Ltd—*Daniel R Hornung*	602 N 9th St, Manitowoc WI 54220	920-684-3688	R	4*	<.1
2888	Solutionsoft Inc—*Troy Murphy*	370 Altair Way Ste 200, Sunnyvale CA 94086	408-736-1431	R	4*	<.1
2889	WinWin Solutions Inc—*Michael Ruane*	99 Kinderkamack Rd Ste, Westwood NJ 07675	201-722-9814	R	4*	<.1
2890	Dynamic Concepts Inc (Aliso Viejo California)—*Doug Chadwick*	18 B Journey, Aliso Viejo CA 92656	949-215-1200	R	4*	<.1
2891	Headspring Systems—*Dustin Wells*	PO Box 161954, Austin TX 78716	512-459-2260	R	4*	<.1
2892	MindGate Technologies Inc—*Lawrence Beyl*	164 Oliver Smith Rd, Flintville TN 37335	931-937-6800	R	4*	<.1
2893	Vanguard Software Corp—*Rob Suggs*	1100 Crescent Green Dr, Cary NC 27518	919-859-4101	R	4*	<.1
2894	CadSoft Computer Inc—*Edwin Robledo*	19620 Pines Blvd, Pembroke Pines FL 33029	954-237-0932	R	4*	<.1
2895	Data Concepts Inc (San Antonio Texas)—*Philip Beck*	900 Isom Rd Ste 103, San Antonio TX 78216	210-366-3982	R	4*	<.1
2896	InfiNetwork—*Steve Myers*	3401 N Tamiami Trl Ste, Naples FL 34103	239-263-4454	R	4*	<.1
2897	Advanced Systems Consultants Inc—*Pete Gilstrap*	4074 E Patterson Rd, Dayton OH 45430	937-429-1428	R	4*	<.1
2898	Ambrosia Software Inc—*Andrew Welch*	PO Box 23140, Rochester NY 14692	585-325-1910	R	4*	<.1
2899	APPTECH Inc—*Darrel Bowman*	2522 N Proctor Ste 454, Tacoma WA 98406	253-566-9155	R	4*	<.1
2900	Artifex Software Inc—*Miles Jones*	7 Mt Lassen Dr Ste A-1, San Rafael CA 94903	415-492-9861	R	4*	<.1
2901	Busware Inc	260 School House Dr, Linwood NJ 08221	609-601-0400	R	4*	<.1
2902	CASEMaker Inc—*Stephanie Myers*	1680 Civic Ctr Dr, Santa Clara CA 95050	408-261-8265	S	4*	<.1
2903	Computer Employment Applications Inc—*Richard J Phannen-still*	606 W Wisconsin Ave St, Milwaukee WI 53203	414-281-2590	R	4*	<.1
2904	Daprex Inc—*Laura Hallick*	860 Canal St, Stamford CT 06902	203-324-2474	R	4*	<.1
2905	Derek Consulting Group Inc—*Fedor Derek*	43 Sibelius Rd Ste 100, Newtown PA 18940	215-497-9830	R	4*	<.1
2906	Handicomp Inc—*Stewart Healey*	PO Box 87, Jenison MI 49429		R	4*	<.1
2907	Hi-Tec Systems Inc—*Trib Singh*	500 Scarborough Dr Ste, Egg Harbor Township NJ 08234	609-272-1515	R	4*	<.1
2908	InfoTree Inc	289 Great Rd, Acton MA 01720	978-263-8558	R	4*	<.1
2909	Outlook Technologies Inc—*Elias (Lou) Manousos*	7257 W Touhy Ste 201, Chicago IL 60631	773-775-1595	R	4*	<.1
2910	Paradigm Systems Inc—*Rick Naro*	518 Hooper Rd MD 280, Endwell NY 13760	607-748-5966	R	4*	<.1
2911	PennComp Inc—*Paul Pennington*	4660 Beechnut St Ste 2, Houston TX 77096	713-669-0965	R	4*	<.1
2912	Pliner Solutions Inc—*Bradley Pliner*	2300 Computer Ave Ste, Willow Grove PA 19090	215-658-1601	R	4*	<.1
2913	Quinn Communication LLC—*Mark Quinn*	1155 Main St Ste 109, Jupiter FL 33458	561-622-7577	R	4*	<.1
2914	Software Abroad LLC—*Mike Held*	133 Vintage Bay Dr Ste, Marco Island FL 34145	954-376-8463	R	4*	<.1
2915	Synapsis LLC	PO Box 13265, Las Vegas NV 89112	702-365-9755	R	4*	<.1
2916	Systems Associates Inc (Bowling Green Ohio)—*J David Cod-ding*	500 Lehman Ave, Bowling Green OH 43402	419-354-3900	R	4*	<.1
2917	TAG Online Inc—*Amy Gideon*	6 Prospect Village Plz, Clifton NJ 07013	973-783-5583	R	4*	<.1
2918	West LiveNote (San Francisco California)—*Peter Warwick*	221 Main St Ste 1250, San Francisco CA 94105	415-321-2300	S	4*	<.1
2919	WorldView Software—*Jerry Kleinstein*	76 N Broadway Ste 2002, Hicksville NY 11801		R	4*	<.1
2920	Zasio Enterprises Inc—*Kevin Zasio*	12601 W Explorer Dr St, Boise ID 83713	208-375-8000	R	4*	<.1
2921	Acrendo Software Inc—*Casey Guss*	1010 University Ave, San Diego CA 92103	858-268-1150	R	4*	<.1
2922	Advanced Personnel Systems—*Doug Coull*	4167 Avenida de la Pla, Oceanside CA 92056	760-941-2800	R	4*	<.1
2923	BCD Software Services Inc—*Peter Hedrick*	2450 Mission St Ste 6, San Marino CA 91108	626-441-1203	R	4*	<.1
2924	Data Processing Consultants Inc—*David Parker*	PO Box 77954, Greensboro NC 27417	336-856-7091	R	4*	<.1
2925	Hann's On Software Inc—*Phillip Hann*	3510 Unocal Pl Ste 109, Santa Rosa CA 95403	707-547-1711	R	4*	<.1
2926	InVision Software Inc—*Joseph Spiteri*	110 Lake Ave S Ste 35, Nesconset NY 11767	631-360-3400	R	4*	<.1
2927	ITC Integrated Systems Inc—*Marvin Hersher*	2008 Raccoon Run, Clayton NC 27527	919-607-1010	R	4*	<.1
2928	McMurtrey/Whitaker and Associates Inc—*Shannon Whitaker*	300 S Jefferson Ave St, Springfield MO 65806	417-865-1283	R	4*	<.1
2929	Midrange Performance Group Inc—*William Watson*	100 Arapahoe Ave Ste 1, Boulder CO 80302	303-939-9648	R	4*	<.1
2930	Noetic Software Inc—*Michael J Kiernan*	2300 Computer Ave Ste, Willow Grove PA 19090	215-784-9580	R	4*	<.1
2931	Tech Time Inc—*Kim Hanson*	3627 O'Shea Cir, Billings MT 59101	406-256-0627	R	4*	<.1
2932	Wise Software and Computer Products Inc—*Thomas H Wise*	1041 West Ave Ste M-14, Palmdale CA 93551	661-266-9181	R	4*	<.1
2933	3PL Software Inc—*Randy Stephenson*	10316 Feldfarm Ln Ste, Charlotte NC 28210	704-554-1670	D	4*	<.1
2934	Accelerate Software Inc—*Iris Han*	7494 Bellinger Rd, Cupertino CA 95014		R	4*	<.1
2935	Advanced Business Software Inc—*Robert Eldon*	2050 W Chapman Ave Ste, Orange CA 92868	714-634-2677	R	4*	<.1
2936	AGETEC Inc—*Hide Aki Irie*	1070 Stewart Dr Ste 4, Sunnyvale CA 94086	408-736-0800	R	4*	<.1
2937	Analyze Software Inc—*Akash Gaur*	16516 Bernardo Center, San Diego CA 92128	858-676-4321	R	4*	<.1
2938	Apogee Software Inc—*George Malek*	1999 S Bascom Ave Ste, Campbell CA 95008	408-369-9001	R	4*	<.1
2939	Applied Automation Techologies Inc—*Ray Karadayi*	1703 Star Batt Dr, Rochester Hills MI 48309	248-656-4930	R	4*	<.1
2940	Applied Information Systems Inc (Chapel Hill North Carolina)—*Arthur Coston*	121 S Estes Dr, Chapel Hill NC 27514	919-942-7801	R	4*	<.1
2941	Apricot Medical Services Inc—*Louis Maletz*	11777 Bernardo Plz Ct, San Diego CA 92128		R	4*	<.1
2942	Autosig Systems Inc—*Steven Drew*	201 Price Hills Trail, Sugar Hill GA 30518	770-408-0683	R	4*	<.1

Rank	Company Name—*Executive Officer*	Address, City, State, Zip	Phone	Type	Fin	Empls
2943	Axios Products Inc—*David Cook*	353 Veterans Hwy Ste 2, Commack NY 11725	631-864-3666	R	4*	<.1
2944	Aya Associates Inc—*Edgar Aya*	331 N Maitland Ave Ste, Maitland FL 32751	407-539-1800	R	4*	<.1
2945	Benchmark Software Inc—*Charles Carr*	9986 Stonehurst Ave, Sun Valley CA 91352	818-394-9374	R	4*	<.1
2946	BIOQUANT Image Analysis Corp	5611 Ohio Ave, Nashville TN 37209	615-350-7866	R	4*	<.1
2947	Blue Sky Research Inc—*Chris Gladding*	PO Box 80424, Portland OR 97280	503-222-9571	R	4*	<.1
2948	Bug Busters Software Engineering Inc JDA Software Group Inc	2208 NW Market St Ste, Seattle WA 98107	206-633-1187	S	4*	<.1
2949	CHAMP Software Inc—*David Rosebaugh*	100 Memorial View Ct S, Mankato MN 56001	507-388-4141	R	4*	<.1
2950	Charter Software Inc	5951 S Middlefield Rd, Littleton CO 80123	303-932-6875	R	4*	<.1
2951	Clancy Systems International Inc—*Stanley J Wolfson*	2149 S Grape St, Denver CO 80222	303-753-0197	P	4	<.1
2952	ComCom Systems Inc—*Chris Benham*	2420 Enterprise Rd Ste, Clearwater FL 33763	727-725-3200	R	4*	<.1
2953	Comet Way Inc—*Damien Miller*	4800 Liberty Ave, Pittsburgh PA 15224	412-682-5282	R	4*	<.1
2954	Comptron Data Inc—*Gayland Yarbrough*	6164 S Hwy 92, Hereford AZ 85615		R	4*	<.1
2955	Computer Management Enterprises	PO Box 1488, Lebanon PA 17042	717-272-2523	R	4*	<.1
2956	Computer Prompting and Captioning Co—*Dr Dilip K Som*	1010 Rockville Pke Ste, Rockville MD 20852	301-738-8487	R	4*	<.1
2957	ComputerWorks Inc (Albany New York)—*Greg Rosano*	12 Corporate Woods Blv, Albany NY 12211	518-436-7787	R	4*	<.1
2958	Conducive Technology Corp—*Jeff Kennedy*	317 SW Alder St Ste 50, Portland OR 97204	503-274-0938	R	4*	<.1
2959	Coresoft Technologies Inc—*Dave Connelly*	2 S Pointe Dr Ste 140, Lake Forest CA 92630	949-206-0636	R	4*	<.1
2960	Cougar Software Solutions Inc—*Jerry Reynonlds*	2383 Dos Lomas, Fallbrook CA 92028	760-451-0263	R	4*	<.1
2961	CTI Communications	PO Box 964, Sparta NJ 07871	201-563-7800	D	4*	<.1
2962	Cuesta Technologies LLC—*Monty Swiryn*	20 Avenue Portola Ste, El Granada CA 94018	408-376-2001	R	4*	<.1
2963	Cyberspace HQ LLC—*Mark Joyner*	PO Box 410316, Melbourne FL 32941	818-923-1144	R	4*	<.1
2964	Damomics Computer Systems—*Gloria Friedman*	120 W Water St, Elmira NY 14901	607-732-5122	R	4*	<.1
2965	DART Communications—*Michael Baldwin*	421 Broad St Ste 9, Utica NY 13501	315-790-5456	R	4*	<.1
2966	Data Optics International Inc—*Richard Nunez Sr*	750 Main St, Hartford CT 06103	860-246-8844	R	4*	<.1
2967	DataMotion Inc—*Bob Bales*	35 Airport Road Ste 12, Morristown NJ 07960	973-455-1245	R	4*	<.1
2968	DTO Solutions Inc—*Damon Edwards*	1840 Gateway Dr Ste 20, San Mateo CA 94404	650-292-9660	R	4*	<.1
2969	Emerson Process Mangement—*Steve Sonnenberg*	1111 3rd Ave W 2nd Fl, Bradenton FL 34205	941-748-8100	D	4*	<.1
2970	Empagio—*Seth Bernstein* Halo Technology Holdings Inc	225 E Robinson St Ste, Orlando FL 32801	407-488-1500	S	4*	<.1
2971	Encirq Corp—*Debra Goslin*	577 Airport Blvd, Burlingame CA 94010	650-292-3535	R	4*	<.1
2972	Energid Technologies—*James English*	1 Mlfflin Pl Ste 400, Cambridge MA 02138	617-340-7090	R	4*	<.1
2973	Estorian Inc—*Kevin Paul Riegelsberger*	1525 4th Ave Ste 500, Seattle WA 98101	425-709-2900	R	4*	<.1
2974	Excelltech Inc—*Jay Williams*	PO Box 839, Yankton SD 57078	605-665-5811	R	4*	<.1
2975	ExecUtron Development Corp—*Dan Mosier*	3094 Coffey Ln, Santa Rosa CA 95403		R	4*	<.1
2976	File On Q Inc—*Kim Webley*	832 Industry Dr, Seattle WA 98188	206-575-3488	R	4*	<.1
2977	Financial Technology Laboratories Inc—*James Rucker*	1050 W NASA Blvd Ste 1, Melbourne FL 32901	321-248-4248	R	4*	<.1
2978	Flowerfire—*Jo Dee Koller*	125 Water St Ste A1, Santa Cruz CA 95060	831-425-1758	R	4*	<.1
2979	Foresight Software Inc—*Mark Tyndall* Halo Technology Holdings Inc	2180 Satellite Blvd St, Duluth GA 30097	770-206-1000	S	4*	<.1
2980	ForestWorld Inc—*Chris Anderson*	304 A Pomona Dr, Greensboro NC 27407	302-541-4541	R	4*	<.1
2981	Genesis Group Software Developers Inc—*Siraj Rizvi*	4055 E La Palma Ave St, Anaheim CA 92807	714-632-3648	R	4*	<.1
2982	Golden Software Inc—*Patrick Madison*	809 14th St, Golden CO 80401	303-279-1021	R	4*	<.1
2983	Handley Computer Corp—*Bill Bradley*	PO Box 3039, Boulder CO 80307	303-494-5412	R	4*	<.1
2984	Herbert Software Solutions Inc—*Hendrik Bruhns*	1040 Marina Village Pk, Alameda CA 94501	510-814-9065	R	4*	<.1
2985	HPS Simulations—*Scott Hamilton*	PO Box 3245, Santa Clara CA 95055	408-554-8381	R	4*	<.1
2986	HREF Tools Corp—*Ann Lynnworth*	1585 Terrace Way Ste10, Santa Rosa CA 95404	707-206-6195	R	4*	<.1
2987	IAR Systems Software Inc—*Stefan Skarin*	Century Plz 1065 E Hil, Foster City CA 94404	650-287-4250	S	4*	<.1
2988	IEA Software Inc—*Jeff Albrecht*	PO Box 1170, Veradale WA 99037	509-444-2455	R	4*	<.1
2989	Imagine Products Inc—*Dan Montgomery*	1052 Summit Dr, Carmel IN 46032	317-843-0706	R	4*	<.1
2990	Incompass Solutions Inc—*David F Haydon*	821 Corporate Dr, Lexington KY 40503		S	4*	<.1
2991	InfoExpress Inc—*Stacey Lum*	170 S Whisman Rd Ste B, Mountain View CA 94041	650-623-0260	R	4*	<.1
2992	James Halstead and Associates PC—*James Halstead*	1503 Plainfield Rd, Joliet IL 60435	815-729-1900	R	4*	<.1
2993	JRH GoldenState Software Inc—*Jerry Doong*	29011 Golden Meadow Dr, Rancho Palos Verdes CA 90275	310-544-1497	R	4*	<.1
2994	Knozall Software Inc	9386 N Linnet Rd, Casa Grande AZ 85194	520-426-3859	R	4*	<.1
2995	LAN-ACES Inc	6801 Sanger Ave Ste 22, Waco TX 76710	254-230-4247	R	4*	<.1
2996	Lynx Media Inc—*Len Latimer*	12501 Chandler Blvd St, Valley Village CA 91607	818-761-5859	R	4*	<.1
2997	Mad Scientist Software—*Bruce Argyle*	169 W Main St, Lehi UT 84043		R	4*	<.1
2998	Mainstay Software Corp—*Dan Walkovitz*	6860 S Yosemite Ct Ste, Centennial CO 80112	303-220-8780	R	4*	<.1
2999	MaxIT Corp—*Philip Baruch*	2771-29 Monument Rd MS, Jacksonville FL 32225	904-998-9520	R	4*	<.1
3000	Microsearch Corp—*Chuck Kelly*	5 Broadway Ave, Saugus MA 01906	781-231-9991	R	4*	<.1
3001	Monfox LLC—*Stefan King*	3840 Windermere Pkwy S, Cumming GA 30041	678-366-3410	R	4*	<.1
3002	New World Graphics Inc—*Miroslav Straka*	2500 Baynard Blvd, Wilmington DE 19802	610-623-0404	R	4*	<.1
3003	Newport-West Data Services Inc—*John Harker*	2092 Omega Rd Ste J, San Ramon CA 94583	925-855-1131	R	4*	<.1
3004	Oakwood Solutions LLC—*Terry Schmitz*	4 Brookwood Ct, Appleton WI 54914		R	4*	<.1
3005	OpenBase International Ltd—*Scott Keith*	608 Robin Rd, Lakeland FL 33803	863-450-3310	R	4*	<.1
3006	Parijat Controlware Inc—*Rakesh Verma*	9603 Neuens Rd, Houston TX 77080	713-935-0900	R	4*	<.1
3007	PASport Software Programs Inc—*Jon Gornstein*	PO Box 100, Sausalito CA 94966	415-331-2606	R	4*	<.1
3008	Payment Software Corp—*Tom Arnold*	1340 S De Anza Blvd, San Jose CA 95129	408-228-0961	R	4*	<.1
3009	PCG Software Inc—*Michael Lubao*	7065 W Ann Rd #130-549, Las Vegas NV 89130		R	4*	<.1
3010	Plum Hall Inc—*Thomas Plum*	PO Box 44610, Kamuela HI 96743	808-882-1255	R	4*	<.1
3011	Professional Resource Management Inc—*Sean Passley*	309 W Washington St St, Chicago IL 60606	847-359-3990	R	4*	<.1
3012	Progressive Microtechnology Inc—*John Alex*	401 McMillan St, Cincinnati OH 45206	513-782-5050	R	4*	<.1
3013	Quantitative Micro Software—*David Lilien*	4521 Campus Dr Ste336, Irvine CA 92612	949-856-3368	R	4*	<.1
3014	Rabbitsoft—*Harvey Arkawy*	43853 Tranquility Ct, Lancaster CA 93535	661-752-5625	R	4*	<.1
3015	Real Time Data—*Michael Cummings*	1301 E Lincoln Ave Ste, Orange CA 92865	714-279-0411	R	4*	<.1
3016	Rhintek Inc—*Rhiner McCowen*	8835c Columbia 100 Pkw, Columbia MD 21045	410-730-2575	R	4*	<.1
3017	Rigden Inc—*Jim Jobson*	PO Box 17187, Boulder CO 80308	303-442-8190	R	4*	<.1
3018	RTZ Software—*Seth Snyder*	PO Box 610457, Miami FL 33261	305-945-9774	R	4*	<.1
3019	Savingsbondscom Inc—*Jack Quinn Sr*	2022 Rte 71 Ste 200, Spring Lake Heights NJ 07762	732-280-4024	R	4*	<.1
3020	Secure Computing Systems Inc—*Leo Radosta*	822 Camp St, New Orleans LA 70130	504-525-0620	R	4*	<.1
3021	Sesame Software Inc—*Rick Banister*	PO Box 60000, San Francisco CA 94160	831-234-0754	R	4*	<.1
3022	SET Enterprises Inc—*Bob Moog*	16537 E Laser Dr Ste 6, Fountain Hills AZ 85268	480-837-3628	R	4*	<.1
3023	Simplicity Systems Inc	25 Birchwood Ln, Asheville NC 28805	828-712-3386	R	4*	<.1
3024	Software Anywhere Inc—*Jeffrey Scott*	30131 Town Center Dr S, Laguna Niguel CA 92677	949-373-2400	R	4*	<.1
3025	Software Sourcery Systems Inc—*Chendal Coulter*	2741 Lemon Grove Ave S, Lemon Grove CA 91945	619-469-4844	R	4*	<.1
3026	Source Dynamics Inc	22525 SE 64th Pl Ste 2, Issaquah WA 98027	425-557-3630	R	4*	<.1
3027	SpotMagic Inc—*John Armstrong*	44 Montgomery Ste 1900, San Francisco CA 94104		R	4*	<.1
3028	TechniCon Computer Services—*Mark Keenan*	155 Filbert St, Oakland CA 94607	510-653-9163	R	4*	<.1
3029	Technova Group Inc—*Ron Marray*	6804 W 107th Ste 102, Overland Park KS 66212	913-338-2121	R	4*	<.1

Note: An asterisk (*) indicates an estimated financial figure. The company type code used is as follows: R = Private, P = Public, S = Private Subsidiary, B = Public Subsidiary, D = Division, J = Joint Venture, I = Investment Fund.

COMPANY RANKINGS BY SALES WITHIN 4-DIGIT SIC

Rank	Company Name—*Executive Officer*	Address, City, State, Zip	Phone	Type	Fin	Empls
3030	Thomson/Health Care Data—*Leonard Rogers*	PO Box 234010, Encinitas CA 92023	760-795-1200	S	4*	<.1
3031	Tradewind Software Inc—*Herb Siedschlag*	PO Box 36, Glendora CA 91740	626-335-7007	R	4*	<.1
3032	Transportation Systems Consulting Corp—*Paul Andrews*	2451 Mc Mullen Booth R, Clearwater FL 33759	727-457-1267	R	4*	<.1
3033	Tri-Digital Software Inc—*Mark Moneran*	8424 154th Ave NE, Redmond WA 98052	425-284-3888	R	4*	<.1
3034	True BASIC Inc—*John Kemeny*	155 Maple St, White River Junction VT 05001	802-296-2711	R	4*	<.1
3035	Tugboat Software Inc—*Pat Schilling*	20301 Birch St Ste 202, Newport Beach CA 92660	949-794-8915	R	4*	<.1
3036	Tyrell Software Corp—*Anne Murphy*	23 Spectrum Pointe Ste, Lake Forest CA 92630	949-458-1911	R	4*	<.1
3037	Unbeaten Path International Ltd—*Milton Habeck*	132 E Parkfield Ct, Racine WI 53402	262-681-3151	R	4*	<.1
3038	Universal Accounting Software Inc—*Raza Malik*	115 River Rd Ste 820, Edgewater NJ 07020	201-313-0040	R	4*	<.1
3039	Universal Business Computing Co—*Ken Garen*	PO Box 758, Taos NM 87571		R	4*	<.1
3040	Valusource—*David Fein*	4575 Galley Rd Ste 200, Colorado Springs CO 80915	719-548-4900	S	4*	<.1
3041	Vanguard Software Solutions Inc—*Irena Terterov*	229 Polaris Ave Ste 5, Mountain View CA 94043	650-961-3098	R	4*	<.1
3042	VayTek Inc—*Kazuo Yorimitsu*	51 W Washington Ave, Fairfield IA 52556	641-472-2227	R	4*	<.1
3043	VLetter Inc—*Dave Fenwick*	509 Cascade Ste H, Hood River OR 97031	541-387-2800	R	4*	<.1
3044	Zeland Software Inc—*Jain-Xioug Zheng*	48834 Kato Rd Ste 103A, Fremont CA 94538		R	4*	<.1
3045	ADAPT Software Applications Inc—*Brian Stein*	959 S Coast Dr Ste 100, Costa Mesa CA 92626	714-389-1584	R	4*	<.1
3046	AME Software Products Inc—*William Christel*	205 W 5th Ave Ste 101, Escondido CA 92025	760-738-3720	R	4*	<.1
3047	Axure Software Solutions Inc—*Victor Hsu*	311 4th Ave Ste 617, San Diego CA 92101		R	4*	<.1
3048	Centage Corp—*Kamran Sassoon*	24 Prime Pkwy Ste 202, Natick MA 01760	508-948-0088	R	4*	<.1
3049	Digitronics Software Inc—*Ken Burleigh*	Po Box 7, Brea CA 92822	714-255-1312	R	4*	<.1
3050	Hamilton Software Inc	6432 E Mineral Pl, Centennial CO 80112	303-795-5572	R	4*	<.1
3051	iambic Inc—*Barbara Prince*	PO Box 9344, San Jose CA 95157	408-317-0346	R	4*	<.1
3052	Inspironix Inc—*Cary Parkins*	3400 Cottage Way Ste L, Sacramento CA 95825	916-488-3222	R	4*	<.1
3053	Internet Data Technology—*David Subers*	2300 Computer Ave Ste, Willow Grove PA 19090		R	4*	<.1
3054	LPI Information Systems—*David Land*	10020 Fontana, Overland Park KS 66207	913-381-9118	R	4*	<.1
3055	MicroServ Inc—*Carl V Cotroneo*	276 5th Ave Ste 1011, New York NY 10001	212-683-2811	R	4*	<.1
3056	PowerMate Software LLC—*Susan Jaeger*	4932 W Evans Creek, Rogue River OR 97537	541-582-8000	R	4*	<.1
3057	VI Laboratories Inc—*Joe Noonan*	130 Turner St Bldg 3 5, Waltham MA 02453	781-398-3400	R	4*	<.1
3058	Arkansas Data Services Inc—*Lynnon Gadberry*	27 MacArthur Dr, Conway AR 72032	501-327-8000	R	4*	<.1
3059	ILAR Systems Inc—*John F Richardson*	334 Baywood Dr, Newport Beach CA 92660		R	4*	<.1
3060	Ratepoint Inc—*Keith Cooper*	145 Rosemary St Ste D, Needham MA 02494	781-455-1100	R	4*	<.1
3061	Shin Shin America—*Steve Nishishiba*	3655 Torrance Blvd Ste, Torrance CA 90503	310-540-1712	S	4*	<.1
3062	Wavecrest Computing Inc	2006 Vernon Pl, Melbourne FL 32901	321-953-5351	R	4*	<.1
3063	AUCOTEC Inc—*Horst Beran*	2570 Foxfield Rd Ste 1, Saint Charles IL 60174	630-485-5600	R	4*	<.1
3064	EZ-Filing Inc—*David Smith*	600 17th St Ste 510S, Denver CO 80202	720-917-1100	R	4*	<.1
3065	Multiware Inc—*Robert Walraven*	216 F St Ste161, Davis CA 95616	530-756-3291	R	4*	<.1
3066	Stone Design Corp—*Andrew C Stone*	PO Box 6799, Albuquerque NM 87197	505-345-4800	R	4	<.1
3067	Warren Computer Center—*Sandie Warren*	1945 E Mitchell Ave, Waterloo IA 50702	319-232-9504	R	4*	<.1
3068	Sophos Inc—*Stephen Munford*	3 Van de Graaff Dr 2nd, Burlington MA 01803	781-494-5800	S	4*	<.1
3069	Edison Design Group Inc—*Steve Adamczyk*	11 Rocky Way, West Orange NJ 07052	973-325-6840	R	4*	<.1
3070	FitCentric Technologies Inc—*Ken Burres*	9635 Monte Vista Ave S, Montclair CA 91763		R	4*	<.1
3071	M Bryce and Associates—*Tim Bryce*	PO Box 1637, Palm Harbor FL 34682	727-786-4567	D	4*	<.1
3072	Consulier Engineering Inc—*Warren B Mosler*	2391 Old Dixie Hwy, Riviera Beach FL 33404	561-842-2492	P	4	.1
3073	Entomo Inc—*Sanjoy Chatterji*	10940 Ne 33rd Pl Ste 2, Bellevue WA 98004	425-372-0524	R	4*	<.1
3074	Tricerat Inc—*John Byrne*	10320 Little Patuxent, Columbia MD 21044	410-715-4226	R	4*	<.1
3075	4D Inc—*Brendan Coveney*	3031 Tisch Way Ste 900, San Jose CA 95128	408-557-4600	S	4	<.1
3076	Trapeze Software Inc—*Rick Bacchus*	5265 Rockwell Dr NE, Cedar Rapids IA 52402	319-363-2700	S	4*	<.1
3077	NextAce Corp—*Don Cantral*	1100 W Town and Countr, Orange CA 92868	714-953-9300	R	4	.1
3078	Relational Security Corp—*Ivek Shivananda*	700 Plz Dr Ste 205, Secaucus NJ 07094	201-867-1330	R	4*	<.1
3079	Prg Systems—*Uma Pandey*	180 Centennial Ave Ste, Piscataway NJ 08854	732-885-0800	R	4*	<.1
3080	So Cal Soft-Pak Inc—*Brian Porter*	3550 Camino Del Rio N, San Diego CA 92108	619-283-2330	R	4*	<.1
3081	Yahara Software—*Eric Thomas*	1102 Stephenson Ln, Waunakee WI 53597	608-274-9945	R	4	<.1
3082	United Systems Technology Inc—*Thomas E Gibbs*	1430 Valwood Pkwy Ste, Carrollton TX 75006	972-402-8600	R	4	<.1
3083	Corrugated Technologies Inc—*Gordon Hay*	15150 Ave Of Science, San Diego CA 92128	858-578-3550	R	4	<.1
3084	Dairyland Midwest Inc—*Jose Laracuente*	1601 N Ankeny Blvd, Ankeny IA 50023	515-964-0708	R	4	<.1
3085	Cape Systems Group Inc—*Nicolas Toms*	45 Knightsbridge Rd St, Piscataway NJ 08854	908-756-2000	R	4	<.1
3086	Virtualosity Solutions LLC—*Tri Steve Nguyen*	3370 N Baldwin St, Portland OR 97217		R	3	.1
3087	Overnite Software Inc—*Armando Caceres*	1212 N Velasco St Ste, Angleton TX 77515	979-849-2002	R	3*	<.1
3088	Agile Global Solutions Inc—*Raja Krishnan*	12401 Folsom Blvd Ste, Rancho Cordova CA 95742	916-353-1780	R	3*	<.1
3089	BesttransportCom Inc—*Patrick Taylor*	400 W Wilson Bridge Rd, Worthington OH 43085	614-888-2378	R	3*	<.1
3090	Cimx LLC—*Glen Baldrige*	5400 Dupont Cir Ste B, Milford OH 45150	513-248-7700	R	3*	<.1
3091	Knowledge Marketing—*Duane Crandall*	15301 Hwy 55 Ste 3A, Plymouth MN 55447	763-746-2780	R	3	<.1
3092	Workforce ROI Corp—*Ritchie A Kaul*	PO Box 802, West Fargo ND 58078	701-492-7800	R	3	.2
3093	Exari Systems Inc—*Reginald Foster*	745 Boylston St Lbby 6, Boston MA 02116	617-938-3777	R	3*	<.1
3094	Cyberlogic Technologies Inc—*Pawel Mikulski*	5480 Corporate Dr Ste, Troy MI 48098	248-631-2200	R	3*	<.1
3095	Zona Technology Inc—*Danny Liu*	9489 Eironwood Sq Dr 1, Scottsdale AZ 85258	480-945-9988	R	3*	<.1
3096	Navitaire—*Thomas Cook*	9130 Jollyville Rd Ste, Austin TX 78759	512-345-0001	R	3*	.1
3097	Smart Bomb—*Kris Johnson*	105 N 400 W, Salt Lake City UT 84103	801-355-4440	R	3*	<.1
3098	Classroom Inc—*Jane Canner*	245 5th Ave Fl 20, New York NY 10016	212-545-8400	R	3*	.1
3099	eGames Inc—*Gerald W Klein*	2000 Cabot Blvd W Ste, Langhorne PA 19047	215-750-6606	P	3*	<.1
3100	LizardTech Inc—*Carlos Domingo*	1008 Western Ave Ste 2, Seattle WA 98104	206-652-5211	S	3*	.1
3101	NetFormx Ltd—*Ittai Bareket*	400 Race St Ste 201, San Jose CA 95126	408-423-6600	R	3*	.1
3102	E-SoftSys LLC—*Kat Shenoy*	1061 Dekalb Pike Ste 2, Blue Bell PA 19422		S	3*	.1
3103	Resolution Consulting—*Robin Bradbury*	2655 W Midway Blvd Ste, Broomfield CO 80020	303-530-0396	R	3*	.1
3104	Infusion Software Inc—*Clate Mask*	2065 W Obispo Ave Ste, Gilbert AZ 85233		R	3*	.1
3105	SJB Group LLC—*Wilfred Barry*	PO Box 1751, Baton Rouge LA 70821	225-769-3400	R	3*	.1
3106	Target Software Inc—*Lee Gartley* Blackbaud Inc	1030 Massachusetts Ave, Cambridge MA 02138	617-583-8500	S	3*	.1
3107	Framework Technologies Corp—*Chris Groves* Centric Software Inc	50 Las Colinas Ln, San Jose CA 95119		S	3*	.1
3108	Gibbs and Associates—*Don Merfert*	323 Science Dr, Moorpark CA 93021	805-523-0004	R	3*	.1
3109	Gold Standard Inc (Tampa Florida)—*Marianne Messer*	302 Knights Run Ave St, Tampa FL 33602	813-258-4747	R	3*	.1
3110	Kinetic Technology Agency—*G Raymond Schuhmann*	200 Distillery Commons, Louisville KY 40206	502-719-9500	R	3*	.1
3111	MarketTools Inc—*Scott Arnold*	150 Spear St Ste 600, San Francisco CA 94105	415-957-2200	R	3*	.1
3112	Keymark Enterprises LLC—*Keith Deitzen*	6707 Winchester Cir, Boulder CO 80301	303-443-8033	R	3*	<.1
3113	Nielsen BuzzMetrics—*Jonathan Carson*	770 Broadway, New York NY 10003	646-654-7990	S	3*	<.1
3114	PaperWise Inc—*Dan Langhofer*	3171 East Sunshine, Springfield MO 65804	417-886-7505	R	3*	<.1
3115	Bluebird Auto Rental Systems—*Angela Margolit*	200 Mineral Springs Dr, Dover NJ 07801	973-989-2423	R	3*	<.1
3116	Global Scholar—*William Zaggle*	980 37th Ave Crt, Greeley CO 80634	970-353-8311	R	3*	<.1
3117	Lender Support Systems Inc—*Cary G Burch*	13475 Danielson St Ste, Poway CA 92064	858-268-7100	R	3*	<.1

Rank	Company Name—*Executive Officer*	Address, City, State, Zip	Phone	Type	Fin	Empls
3118	Systran Software Inc—*Dennis Gachot*	4445 Eastgate Mall Ste, San Diego CA 92121	858-457-1900	S	3	<.1
3119	Tel Tech International—*Donald Wuerfl*	200 Broadhollow Rd Ste, Melville NY 11747	516-393-5174	R	3*	<.1
3120	Tyler Retail Systems Inc—*Scott Tyler*	4625 E Bay Dr Ste 201, Clearwater FL 33764	727-536-5588	R	3*	<.1
3121	Vision Data Equipment Corp—*Thomas Dempsey*	1377 3rd St, Rensselaer NY 12144	518-434-2193	R	3*	<.1
3122	Write Brothers Inc—*Stephen Greenfield*	348 E Olive Ave Rm H, Burbank CA 91502	818-843-6557	R	3*	<.1
3123	Enterprise Informatics Inc—*Alan Kiraly*	10052 Mesa Ridge Ct St, San Diego CA 92121	858-625-3000	R	3*	<.1
3124	Service Station Computer Systems Inc—*Lee Scott*	650 Work St, Salinas CA 93901	831-755-1800	R	3*	<.1
3125	Barratt Edwards International Corp—*Morgan Edwards*	15015 Main St Ste 200, Bellevue WA 98007	425-644-6000	R	3*	<.1
3126	FlexiInternational Software Inc—*Stefan R Bothe*	2 Enterprise Dr, Shelton CT 06484	203-925-3040	R	3*	<.1
3127	NeuralWare Inc—*Jack Copper*	409 Elk St Ste 200, Carnegie PA 15106	412-278-6280	R	3*	<.1
3128	Numeric Computer Systems Inc—*Robert Hochberg*	275 Oser Ave, Hauppauge NY 11788	631-486-9000	R	3	<.1
3129	ART Plus Technology Inc—*Brad Caudell*	12 Manor Pky, Salem NH 03079	603-314-5800	R	3*	<.1
3130	Nobeltec Inc—*Ronald Moody*	15242 NW Greenbriar Pk, Beaverton OR 97006	503-579-1414	R	3*	<.1
3131	3C Software Inc—*Matthew Smith*	1300 Parkwood Cir Ste, Atlanta GA 30339	770-956-7744	R	3*	<.1
3132	Compco Inc—*Gerald Skinner*	5120 Virginia Way Ste, Brentwood TN 37027	615-373-3636	R	3*	<.1
3133	Data Life Associates Inc—*Simon Jacob*	500 Bloomfield Ave, Verona NJ 07044	973-239-7500	R	3*	<.1
3134	Ensign Systems Inc—*Alan Thurgood*	1330 W Flint Meadow Dr, Kaysville UT 84037	801-546-1616	R	3*	<.1
3135	Harrington Group Inc—*Richard Harrington*	11501 Lake Underhill R, Orlando FL 32825	407-382-7005	R	3*	<.1
3136	Human Resource MicroSystems Inc—*Patrick Dolan*	142 Sansome St 4th Fl, San Francisco CA 94104	415-362-8400	S	3*	<.1
3137	Invision Research Corp—*John Friske Quark Inc*	150 2nd Ave N 5th Fl, Saint Petersburg FL 33701	727-822-7200	S	3*	<.1
3138	LEAD Technologies Inc—*Richard Little*	1927 S Tryon St 200, Charlotte NC 28203	704-332-5532	R	3*	<.1
3139	Lumen Systems Inc—*William Porter*	920 Saratoga Ave Ste 2, San Jose CA 95129	408-984-8134	R	3*	<.1
3140	Mark of the Unicorn Inc—*Jim Cooper*	1280 Massachusetts Ave, Cambridge MA 02138	617-576-2760	R	3*	<.1
3141	Medical Office Software Inc—*Carolyn Longstreet*	6400 N Andrews Ave Ste, Fort Lauderdale FL 33309		S	3*	<.1
3142	Objective Interface Systems Inc—*Bill Beckwith*	220 Spring St Ste 530, Herndon VA 20170	703-295-6500	R	3*	<.1
3143	Passport Corp—*Alan Tonnesen*	85 Chestnut Ridge Rd S, Montvale NJ 07645	201-573-0038	R	3*	<.1
3144	SoftArtisans Inc—*David Wihl*	3 Brook St, Watertown MA 02472	617-607-8800	R	3*	<.1
3145	Trifecta Technologies Inc—*Doug Pelletier*	5012 Medical Ctr Cir, Allentown PA 18106	610-530-7200	R	3*	<.1
3146	Winshuttle Inc—*Lewis Carpenter*	18323 Bothell Everett, Bothell WA 98012	425-368-2708	R	3*	<.1
3147	Palisade Corp—*Sam McLafferty*	798 Cascadilla St, Ithaca NY 14850	607-277-8000	R	3*	<.1
3148	Spruce Computer Systems Inc	9 Cornell Rd, Latham NY 12110		R	3*	<.1
3149	Hitech Systems Inc—*Henry Unger*	16030 Ventura Blvd Ste, Encino CA 91436	310-282-9919	R	3*	<.1
3150	WinEstimator Inc—*Steve Watt*	19450 68th Ave S, Kent WA 98032	253-395-3631	R	3*	<.1
3151	Public Sector Solutions Inc—*Kostas Alexakis*	900 S Washington St, Falls Church VA 22046	703-891-4000	R	3*	<.1
3152	Appgen Business Software Inc	3220 Rosedale St Ste 1, Gig Harbor WA 98335		R	3*	<.1
3153	AR Traffic Consultants Inc—*Arnold Riback*	5 Hanover Sq Ste 1202, New York NY 10004	212-736-8565	R	3*	<.1
3154	Kalinda Software—*Mary Mattingly*	1195 Park Ave, Emeryville CA 94608	510-658-9900	R	3*	<.1
3155	LC Elite Marketing—*Alexis Hickman*	4000 E Hwy 6, Spanish Fork UT 84660	801-375-4945	R	3*	<.1
3156	MD On-Line Inc—*Bill Bartzak*	4 Campus Dr, Parsippany NJ 07054	973-734-9900	R	3*	<.1
3157	Media Lab Inc	2501 Lanyon Dr, Longmont CO 80503	303-546-7929	R	3*	<.1
3158	Para Research Inc	85 Eastern Ave, Gloucester MA 01930	978-282-1100	R	3	<.1
3159	Portrait Displays Inc—*Michael James*	6663 Owens Dr, Pleasanton CA 94588	925-227-2700	R	3*	<.1
3160	RTI Software—*Stan Schneider*	1001 Warrenville Rd St, Lisle IL 60532	630-515-0780	R	3*	<.1
3161	Software Services of Delaware Inc	1024 Justison St, Wilmington DE 19801	302-652-3370	R	3*	<.1
3162	Sonnet Software Inc—*James C Rautio*	100 Elwood Davis Rd, North Syracuse NY 13212	315-453-3096	R	3*	<.1
3163	SouthWare Innovations Inc—*James F Clemens*	PO Box 3040, Auburn AI 36831	334-821-1108	R	3*	<.1
3164	Wilke/Thornton Inc—*Mike Wilke*	545 Metro Pl S Ste 200, Dublin OH 43017	614-792-0900	R	3*	<.1
3165	Accumedic Computer Systems Inc—*Mark Kollenscher*	11 Grace Ave Ste 401, Great Neck NY 11021	516-466-6800	R	3*	<.1
3166	Christensen Computer Company Inc—*Alan Christensen*	12005 N Panorama Dr, Fountain Hills AZ 85268	480-837-7003	R	3*	<.1
3167	jBase Software Inc—*Jason Shatzkamer*	10260 SW Greenburg Rd, Portland OR 97223	503-290-1200	R	3*	<.1
3168	MIRA Digital Publishing—*James McKelvey Jr*	3800 Park Ave, Saint Louis MO 63110	314-776-6666	R	3*	<.1
3169	PACE Applied Technology Inc—*Marcia Palmer*	4192 Aiken Dr, Warrenton VA 20187	703-369-3200	R	3*	<.1
3170	AEC Software Inc—*Dennis Bilowus*	22611 Markey Ct Ste 11, Sterling VA 20166	703-450-1980	R	3*	<.1
3171	Blue Angel Technologies Inc—*James P Restivo*	1000 W 9th Ave Ste B, King of Prussia PA 19406	610-337-1403	R	3*	<.1
3172	GrammaTech Inc—*Tim Teitelbaum*	531 Easy St, Ithaca NY 14850		R	3*	<.1
3173	Dolbey Systems Inc—*Bill Jasper*	7280 Auburn Rd, Painesville OH 44077		R	3*	<.1
3174	Accura Software Inc	1190 Commerce Dr, Richardson TX 75081	214-404-1643	R	3*	<.1
3175	Alpha Software Inc	70 Blanchard Rd, Burlington MA 01803	781-229-4500	R	3*	<.1
3176	Aptech Computer Systems Inc—*Jay Troutman*	135 Delta Dr, Pittsburgh PA 15238	412-963-7440	R	3*	<.1
3177	Blast Internet Services—*Brett Pedigo*	PO Box 818, Pittsboro NC 27312	919-533-0143	R	3*	<.1
3178	CMX Group—*Sidney Finehirsh*	250 W 57th St, New York NY 10107	212-346-7560	R	3*	<.1
3179	Cognetics Corp—*Charles Kreitzberg*	PO Box 386, Princeton Junction NJ 08550	609-799-5005	R	3*	<.1
3180	Core Technology Corp—*David Hadsall*	7435 Westshire Dr, Lansing MI 48917	517-627-1521	R	3*	<.1
3181	CYMA Systems Inc	2330 W University Dr S, Tempe AZ 85281	480-303-2962	R	3*	<.1
3182	Dean Evans and Associates Inc—*Dean Evans*	6465 S Greenwood Plz B, Centennial CO 80111		R	3*	<.1
3183	DonorWare LLC—*Mike Schroeder*	2207 Concord Pike Ste, Wilmington DE 19803		R	3*	<.1
3184	Dynamic Logic Systems Inc—*Tammy Byrum*	15065 Lebanon Rd Ste 2, Old Hickory TN 37138	615-758-5577	R	3*	<.1
3185	eB2B Commerce Inc—*Robert Bacchi*	665 Broadway Ste 301, New York NY 10012	212-477-1700	R	3*	<.1
3186	Elsinore Technologies Inc—*Ray Allen*	4700 Six Forks Rd Ste, Raleigh NC 27609	919-532-0022	R	3*	<.1
3187	Farin and Associates Inc—*Tom Farin*	2924 Marketplace Dr St, Madison WI 53711	608-273-1004	R	3*	<.1
3188	Geometric Technologies Inc—*Vicky Duffy*	15974 N 77th St Ste 10, Scottsdale AZ 85260	480-367-0132	D	3*	<.1
3189	Intellisoft Inc—*Douglas Ibarra*	7735 NW 146 St Ste 306, Miami Lakes FL 33016	305-471-5111	R	3*	<.1
3190	JustSystems Evans Research Inc—*David A Evans*	5001 Baum Blvd Ste 700, Pittsburgh PA 15213	412-621-0570	R	3*	<.1
3191	Level II Inc	555 Andover Park W Ste, Tukwila WA 98188	206-575-7682	R	3*	<.1
3192	Marcive Inc—*Robert L Fleming*	PO Box 47508, San Antonio TX 78265	210-646-6161	R	3*	<.1
3193	Netsmart Public Health Inc	37 Villa Rd Ste 508, Greenville SC 29615	864-232-2666	S	3*	<.1
3194	Oak Group—*Steve Pearl*	340 W Butterfield Rd, Elmhurst IL 60126	630-833-9770	R	3*	<.1
3195	OC Systems Inc—*Oliver E Cole*	10521 Rosehaven Street, Fairfax VA 22030	703-359-8160	R	3*	<.1
3196	Pocket Soft Inc	7676 Hillmont St Ste 1, Houston TX 77040	713-460-5600	R	3*	<.1
3197	Smyth Systems Inc—*Brock Philp*	5 Walnut Grove Dr Ste, Horsham PA 19044		S	3*	<.1
3198	SoftLinx Inc—*Hikyu Lee*	85 Rangeway Rd Bldg 1, North Billerica MA 01862	978-439-0100	R	3*	<.1
3199	Software Pursuits Inc	1900 S Norfolk St Ste, San Mateo CA 94403	650-372-0900	R	3*	<.1
3200	Synergistic Systems Inc (Neptune Beach Florida)—*Lee Wintrode*	442 3rd St, Neptune Beach FL 32266	904-249-0201	S	3*	<.1
3201	Tabernus LLC	11130 Jollyville Rd St, Austin TX 78759		R	3*	<.1
3202	Treehouse Software Inc—*George Szakach*	2605 Nicholson Rd Ste, Sewickley PA 15143	724-759-7070	R	3*	<.1
3203	Versatile Group Inc—*John Stafford*	4410 Spring Valley Rd, Dallas TX 75244	972-991-1368	R	3*	<.1
3204	Windows Support Group—*William Cornfield*	393 5th Ave 8th Fl, New York NY 10016	212-675-2500	R	3*	<.1
3205	Xante California—*Lenny Mizusaka*	7920 Alta Sunrise Dr S, Citrus Heights CA 95610	916-962-7050	S	3*	<.1

Note: An asterisk (*) indicates an estimated financial figure. The company type code used is as follows: R = Private, P = Public, S = Private Subsidiary, B = Public Subsidiary, D = Division, J = Joint Venture, I = Investment Fund.

COMPANY RANKINGS BY SALES WITHIN 4-DIGIT SIC

Rank	Company Name—*Executive Officer*	Address, City, State, Zip	Phone	Type	Fin	Empls
3206	Computer Solutions Inc (Miami Florida) Friedman Corp	13701 N Kendall Dr, Miami FL 33186	305-558-7000	S	3*	<.1
3207	AccountMate Software Corp—*David Dierke*	1445 Technology Ln Ste, Petaluma CA 94954	707-774-7590	R	3*	<.1
3208	Data Harmony Inc—*Marjorie Hlava*	4725 Indian School Rd, Albuquerque NM 87110	505-265-3591	D	3*	<.1
3209	Gold Hill Inc—*Vince McGugan*	36 Arlington Rd, Chestnut Hill MA 02467	617-731-8333	R	3*	<.1
3210	Oakland Corp (Story City Iowa)—*Roger Oakland*	414 Broad St, Story City IA 50248	515-733-5114	R	3*	<.1
3211	Udenberg and Associates Inc—*Michelle Blomberg*	107 Woodlake Dr SE, Rochester MN 55904	507-282-6353	R	3*	<.1
3212	Electronic Storage Corp—*Brad Jensen*	5127 S 95 E Ave, Tulsa OK 74145		R	3*	<.1
3213	Magnatron Inc—*Thomas N Cate*	PO Box 32534, Knoxville TN 37930	865-769-2622	R	3*	<.1
3214	Arete Image Software—*Stanton Rutledge* Arete Associates	5000 Van Nuys Blvd Ste, Sherman Oaks CA 91403	818-501-1045	S	3*	<.1
3215	BitWise Solutions Inc—*Ron Brumbarger*	11495 N Pennsylvania S, Carmel IN 46032	317-805-4376	R	3*	<.1
3216	Nortridge Software Inc—*Kim Stempel*	2 S Point Dr Ste 250, Lake Forest CA 92630	714-573-7988	R	3	<.1
3217	TeraTech Inc—*Michael Smith*	405 E Gude Dr Ste 207, Rockville MD 20850	301-424-3903	R	3*	<.1
3218	Allegro Software Development Corp—*Bob Andel*	1740 Massachusetts Ave, Boxborough MA 01719	978-264-6600	R	3*	<.1
3219	Bar Scan Inc—*Michelle Milazzo*	4607 Lakeview Canyon R, Westlake Village CA 91361	805-777-0079	R	3*	<.1
3220	BYTWARE Inc	6533 Flying Cloud Dr S, Eden Prairie MN 55344	775-851-2900	S	3*	<.1
3221	Computer Analytics Corp—*Dale Jessen*	1011 E Touhy Ave Ste 1, Des Plaines IL 60018	847-297-5290	R	3*	<.1
3222	Eagle Research Inc—*E Allen Gleazer*	2375 Bush St, San Francisco CA 94115	415-495-3131	R	3*	<.1
3223	Fairfax Imaging Inc—*Steve Chahal*	4200-A Lafayette Cente, Chantilly VA 20151	703-802-1220	R	3*	<.1
3224	Kirkbride Bible and Technology Inc—*J Marshall Gage*	PO Box 606, Indianapolis IN 46206	317-633-1900	D	3*	<.1
3225	Leap Software Inc Bentley Systems Inc	685 Stockton Dr, Exton PA 19341	610-458-5000	S	3*	<.1
3226	Lumtron Technologies Inc—*Danie Destoro*	820 E Terra Cotta Ave, Crystal Lake IL 60014	815-788-0088	R	3*	<.1
3227	MicroWest Software Systems Inc	10981 San Diego Missio, San Diego CA 92108	619-280-0440	R	3*	<.1
3228	Software Shelf International Inc—*William Feeley*	601 Cleveland St Ste 7, Clearwater FL 33755	727-445-1920	R	3*	<.1
3229	StarNet Communications Corp—*Steve Schoch*	1270 Oakmead Pkwy Ste, Sunnyvale CA 94085	408-739-0881	R	3*	<.1
3230	Startech Software Systems Inc—*Mark Churella*	39500 High Pointe Blvd, Novi MI 48375	248-348-8200	S	3*	<.1
3231	TAI Inc (Orland Park Illinois)—*John P Carroll*	10727 Winterset Dr, Orland Park IL 60467	708-403-7775	R	3*	<.1
3232	TeleSoft International Inc—*Charles Crow*	11502 Saddle Mtn Trail, Austin TX 78739	512-373-4224	R	3*	<.1
3233	Three D Graphics Inc	11340 W Olympic Blvd S, Los Angeles CA 90064		R	3*	<.1
3234	Valiantica Inc—*Peiwei Mi*	1340 S De Anja Blvd St, San Jose CA 95129	408-694-3803	R	3*	<.1
3235	Cybernetics InfoTech Inc	101 Lake Forest Blvd S, Gaithersburg MD 20877	301-740-9881	R	3*	<.1
3236	Eview Technology Inc—*Ellis Gregory*	4909 Green Rd Ste 133, Raleigh NC 27616	919-878-5199	R	3*	<.1
3237	David L Aldridge Company Inc—*David Aldridge*	PO Box 56506, Houston TX 77256	713-403-9150	R	3*	<.1
3238	fP Technologies Inc—*Terry Calvert*	8383 Craig St Ste 270, Indianapolis IN 46250		R	3*	<.1
3239	Market Line Computers—*Andy Alper*	317 Harrington Ave, Closter NJ 07624	201-768-8887	R	3*	<.1
3240	Numina Group—*Dan Hanrahan*	10331 Werch Dr, Woodridge IL 60517	630-343-2600	R	3*	<.1
3241	RAD Game Tools Inc—*Andre LaMothe*	550 Kirkland Way Ste 4, Kirkland WA 98033	425-893-4300	R	3*	<.1
3242	cfSOFTWARE Inc	2454 E Dempster St Ste, Des Plaines IL 60016	847-824-7180	R	3*	<.1
3243	Encomium Data International Inc—*Frank Tanntra*	5755 Granger Rd Ste 34, Independence OH 44131	216-674-0139	R	3*	<.1
3244	Media Flex Inc—*Harry Chan*	PO Box 1107, Champlain NY 12919	518-298-3330	R	3*	<.1
3245	NexTech Systems Corp—*Ravi Agotti*	3671 Old Yorktown Rd, Shrub Oak NY 10588	914-962-6000	R	3*	<.1
3246	Tek Data Systems Co	1111 W Park Ave, Libertyville IL 60048	847-367-8800	R	3*	<.1
3247	Applied Information Technologies Inc	9891 Broken Land Pkwy, Columbia MD 21046	410-312-7272	R	3*	<.1
3248	Aptek Inc—*Yvonne D Murray*	3750 W Lansing Rd Ste, Perry MI 48872	517-625-4112	R	3*	<.1
3249	Lone Wolf Software Inc—*Fred Schmitthammer*	6097 N 57th Dr, Glendale AZ 85301	623-824-1140	R	3*	<.1
3250	MacKinney Systems Inc—*Mike Marler*	4411 E State Hwy D Ste, Springfield MO 65809	417-882-8012	R	3*	<.1
3251	Northwest Information Systems Inc—*Mark Brady*	11211 Slater Ave NE St, Kirkland WA 98033	425-828-0812	R	3*	<.1
3252	Shunra Software Ltd—*Gary Jackson*	1800 JFK Blvd, Philadelphia PA 19103	215-564-4046	R	3*	<.1
3253	Account Ware Inc—*James L Parker*	PO Box 20502, Carson City NV 89721	775-883-9363	R	3*	<.1
3254	AccuZip Inc—*Steve Belmonte*	3216 El Camino Real, Atascadero CA 93422		R	3*	<.1
3255	AJACOM Corp—*Nancy Nusser*	PO Box 261941, Plano TX 75026	972-889-3880	R	3*	<.1
3256	Carter-Pertaine Inc—*Jeff McLaughlin* Quintessential School Systems	12651 Briar Forest Dr, Houston TX 77077	281-558-1270	S	3*	<.1
3257	Cetec Automation Inc—*Zaki Farhat*	553 Pilgrim Dr Ste A, Foster City CA 94404	650-570-7557	R	3*	<.1
3258	Computer Application Services Inc—*Robert Labayne*	10231 Slater Ave Ste 1, Fountain Valley CA 92708	714-378-1109	R	3*	<.1
3259	Computer Dynamics—*Dale Brooks*	PO Box 490, Grimesland NC 27837	252-758-9948	R	3*	<.1
3260	Dalanco Spry	89 Winslow Ave, Rochester NY 14620	585-473-3610	R	3*	<.1
3261	DATACAD LLC—*Mark Madura*	20 Tower Ln, Avon CT 06001	860-217-0490	R	3*	<.1
3262	DollarLink Software—*Stan Lekach*	1407 Douglass St, San Francisco CA 94131	415-641-0721	R	3*	<.1
3263	Dynasty Technologies Inc—*Larry L Hammond*	2630 Fountain View Ste, Houston TX 77057	832-533-2100	R	3*	<.1
3264	EFAX Corp—*Howard Larson*	616 Burning Tree Lane, Naperville IL 60563	630-279-9292	R	3*	<.1
3265	ESF Computer Services Inc	141-32 72nd Dr, Kew Gardens Hills NY 11367	718-577-5604	R	3*	<.1
3266	FirstBase Software Inc—*John Bolding*	7320 N La Cholla Ste 1, Tucson AZ 85741	520-742-7897	R	3*	<.1
3267	Freehand Graphics Inc	31 Ridgefield Dr, Shoreham NY 11786	631-744-4330	R	3*	<.1
3268	HiSoftware Inc—*Kurt A Mueffelmann*	1 Trafalgar Square Ste, Nashua NH 03063	603-578-1870	R	3*	<.1
3269	Ignite Technologies Inc—*Jim Janicki*	3211 Internet Blvd Ste, Frisco TX 75034	972-348-6400	R	3*	<.1
3270	ILOG CPlex Div—*Pierre Haren* ILOG Inc	889 Alder Ave Ste 200, Incline Village NV 89451	775-881-2800	D	3*	<.1
3271	Interior Systems Design Inc—*Toby Kaufman*	9860 Glenoaks Blvd, Sun Valley CA 91352	818-767-3162	R	3*	<.1
3272	Lotus Consulting Group—*Sidart Deb*	4962 El Camino Real St, Los Altos CA 94022	650-962-9670	R	3*	<.1
3273	Marshall Graphics Systems—*Rick Hite*	1625 Galleria Blvd, Brentwood TN 37027	615-399-8896	R	3*	<.1
3274	MBSIINet LLC—*Timothy Thomas*	PO Box 425, Southbury CT 06488		R	3*	<.1
3275	Micro Logic Corp—*James Lewis*	31 Industrial Ave, Mahwah NJ 07430	201-962-7510	R	3*	<.1
3276	Micrograms Inc—*Richard Shelain*	5615 Jensen Dr, Loves Park IL 61111	815-877-4455	R	3*	<.1
3277	Oak Group Inc—*David Maltz*	321 Commonwealth Rd St, Wayland MA 01778		R	3*	<.1
3278	OGAS—*Clayton Williams Jr*	6 Desta Dr Ste 5400, Midland TX 79705	432-688-3470	D	3*	<.1
3279	PathGuide Technologies Inc—*David Allais*	8221 44th Ave W Ste G, Mukilteo WA 98275	425-438-2899	R	3*	<.1
3280	Priasoft Inc—*Chris Johnson*	2550 N Thunderbird Cir, Mesa AZ 85215	602-801-2400	R	3*	<.1
3281	Productive Systems Inc (Auburn Hills Michigan)—*Ronald W Tarrant*	4141 N Atlantic Blvd S, Auburn Hills MI 48326	248-853-7500	R	3*	<.1
3282	Protronics Computer Systems—*Steve Walker*	PO Box 724833, Atlanta GA 31139	404-272-7001	R	3*	<.1
3283	Reactive Systems Inc—*Steve Sims*	341 Kilmayne DrSte 101, Cary NC 27511	919-324-3507	R	3*	<.1
3284	RTMX Inc	PO Box 1030, Hillsborough NC 27278	919-644-7869	R	3*	<.1
3285	Sector Micro Computer Inc—*Chris G Kanieski*	399 Hoover Ave, Bloomfield NJ 07003	973-429-1113	R	3*	<.1
3286	Software Consulting Associates Inc—*Dod Crane*	54 Elizabeth St Ste 17, Red Hook NY 12571	845-758-0104	R	3*	<.1
3287	Solid Earth Inc—*Madison Fowler*	113 Clinton Ave, Huntsville AL 35801	256-536-0606	R	3*	<.1
3288	Synergy Software (Reading Pennsylvania)—*Howard Maxwell*	2457 Perkiomen Ave, Reading PA 19606	610-779-0522	R	3*	<.1
3289	Touchtone Corp—*Reza Saraf*	3151 Airway Ave Bldg I, Costa Mesa CA 92626	714-755-2810	R	3*	<.1

Rank	Company Name—*Executive Officer*	Address, City, State, Zip	Phone	Type	Fin	Empls
3290	Tridia Corp—*Vince Frese*	1355 Terrell Mill Road, Marietta GA 30067	770-428-5000	R	3*	<.1
3291	Verific Design Automation Inc—*Rob Dekker*	1516 Oak St Ste 115, Alameda CA 94501	510-522-1555	R	3*	<.1
3292	VITAL Soft Inc—*John Overton*	PO Box 501, Stanwood WA 98292	360-654-8160	R	3*	<.1
3293	ABS Software Inc—*Victor Benjamin*	3060 Coronado Dr, Santa Clara CA 95054		R	3*	<.1
3294	Ad Systems Inc (Wake Forest North Carolina)—*Dino Radosta*	PO Box 2066, Wake Forest NC 27588	919-562-4248	R	3*	<.1
3295	Clinical Software Solutions—*Bryan Jones*	20940 E Mewes Rd, Queen Creek AZ 85242	480-888-9447	R	3*	<.1
3296	Eclipse Data Technologies—*Kevin McDonnell*	5139 Johnson Dr, Pleasanton CA 94588	925-224-8880	R	3*	<.1
3297	Forte Internet Software Inc—*Charles Dazler Knuff*	PO Box 131477, Carlsbad CA 92013		R	3*	<.1
3298	Fourth Generation Software Solutions Corp—*James White*	700 Galleria Pky Ste 4, Atlanta GA 30339	770-432-7623	R	3*	<.1
3299	Henning Industrial Software Inc—*Richard G Henning*	102 1st St Ste 211, Hudson OH 44236	330-650-4212	R	3*	<.1
3300	Maximized Software Inc—*Ken Spreitzer*	85 Ashford Ave, Mill Valley CA 94941	415-347-6294	R	3*	<.1
3301	Quality Assurance Institute Inc—*Navyug Mohnot*	2101 Park Center Dr St, Orlando FL 32835	407-363-1111	R	3*	<.1
3302	Resource One Inc (Commerce Georgia)—*Mickey Newbury*	160 State St, Commerce GA 30529	706-335-5684	R	3*	<.1
3303	Rubberball Productions—*Mark Anderson*	102 S Mountain Way Dr, Orem UT 84058	801-224-6886	R	3*	<.1
3304	Software One Inc (Troy Michigan)—*Jeff Dudzinski*	360 E Maple Rd Ste M, Troy MI 48083	248-583-9714	R	3*	<.1
3305	Accountix Inc—*Keith Kelly*	871 S Orem Blvd, Orem UT 84058	801-224-2900	R	3*	<.1
3306	ARBA Retail Systems Corp—*Bill Hochmuth*	2760 Forgue Dr Ste 104, Naperville IL 60564	630-620-8566	D	3*	<.1
3307	Arisen Corp—*Michael C Arizen*	PO Box 969, Milford PA 18337	570-296-8524	R	3*	<.1
3308	Automated Case Management Systems Inc—*Andrae Corrigan*	803 N Wilcox Ave Ste 7, Hollywood CA 90038	323-460-7700	R	3*	<.1
3309	AV Systems Inc—*Andrew Rudnik*	4657 Platt Rd, Ann Arbor MI 48108	734-973-3000	R	3*	<.1
3310	B and C Management Systems Inc—*Fred Corson*	2235 Technical Pkwy St, North Charleston SC 29406	843-572-5900	R	3*	<.1
3311	Cheetah International—*Don Miller*	655 BroadwaySte 600, Denver CO 80203	303-468-7575	R	3*	<.1
3312	Computer Keyes—*John Keyes*	21929 Makah Rd, Woodway WA 98020	425-776-6443	R	3*	<.1
3313	CoreObjects Software Inc—*Fadi Chehade*	5120 W GoldLeaf Cir St, Los Angeles CA 90056	323-389-0100	S	3*	<.1
3314	Dacor Inc (Bowling Green Ohio)—*Michael Joseph*	600 Antone Blvd Ste 10, Costa Mesa CA 92626	626-799-1000	R	3*	<.1
3315	Easton Lakes Software—*Charles Swihart*	15531 Southwest Frwy, Sugar Land TX 77478	281-494-0894	R	3*	<.1
3316	Groupware Technologies Inc—*Bret Ballinger*	10437 Innovation Dr St, Wauwatosa WI 53226	414-454-0161	R	3*	<.1
3317	Industry Specific Software Inc—*Carol Early*	1200 Woodruff Rd C19, Greenville SC 29607	864-297-7086	R	3*	<.1
3318	Information Management Consultants and Associates Inc—*Julius Neumeyer*	3525 N Causeway Blvd S, Metairie LA 70002	504-832-3186	R	3*	<.1
3319	Interpretive Software Inc—*Stuart James*	1421 Sachem Pl Ste 2, Charlottesville VA 22901	434-979-0245	R	3*	<.1
3320	Kamel Software Inc—*Keith Linn*	2822 Forsyth Rd Ste102, Winter Park FL 32792	407-672-0202	R	3*	<.1
3321	Manufacturing System Services Inc—*Bill Crumpecker*	2929 Eskridge Rd Ste 2, Fairfax VA 22031	703-752-2713	R	3*	<.1
3322	Medtuity Inc—*Matthew Chase*	4111 Executive Pkwy St, Westerville OH 43081	614-259-2000	R	3*	<.1
3323	/n software Inc—*Gent Hito*	5007 Southpark Dr Ste, Durham NC 27713	919-544-7070	R	3*	<.1
3324	NeuroDimension Inc—*Gary Geniesse*	3701 NW 40th Ter Ste 1, Gainesville FL 32606	352-377-5144	R	3*	<.1
3325	NewSoft America Inc—*James Li*	47102 Mission Fallas C, Fremont CA 94539	510-770-8900	S	3*	<.1
3326	Opus Educational Software Co—*Arnaldo Ghersi*	3181 NW 125th Ave, Sunrise FL 33323	954-296-0568	R	3*	<.1
3327	Pacware Software Development Inc—*Byron Maynard*	123 Commerce Circle, Sacramento CA 95815		R	3*	<.1
3328	Patrick Townsend and Associates Inc—*Patrick Townsend*	724 Columbia St NW Ste, Olympia WA 98501	360-357-8971	R	3*	<.1
3329	Pinwheel Software Inc—*Jeffrey W Rose*	370 Park Ranch Pl, Escondido CA 92025	760-741-6416	R	3*	<.1
3330	Prism Visual Software Inc—*Lorraine Keating*	1 Sagamore Hill Dr, Port Washington NY 11050	516-944-5920	R	3*	<.1
3331	Radiant Technologies Inc—*Joseph Evans*	2835 Pan American Fwy, Albuquerque NM 87107	505-842-8007	R	3*	<.1
3332	Saicomm Inc—*Lalit Khanna*	1340 Fulton Pl, Fremont CA 94539	510-438-4550	R	3*	<.1
3333	Tenmast Software Inc—*James Mauch*	132 Venture Ct Ste 1, Lexington KY 40511		R	3*	<.1
3334	Thomas V Sobczak Consultants—*Thomas V Sobczak*	PO Box 0433, Baldwin NY 11510	516-623-6295	R	3*	<.1
3335	20-20 Technologies—*Jean Francois Grou*	550 3 Mile Rd NW, Grand Rapids MI 49544		R	3*	<.1
3336	Advanced Relay Corp—*Esther Celis*	1896 Columbia St, Eugene OR 97403	541 345-9178	R	3*	<.1
3337	Attend Software Corp—*Clark Hewitt*	2351 Sunset Blvd Rm 17, Rocklin CA 95765	916-435-5243	R	3*	<.1
3338	Avontus Software Corp—*M Brian Webb*	851 Ramona Ave, Albany CA 94706		R	3*	<.1
3339	Bedford Associates Inc—*Nick Kroot*	211 Greenwood Ave 2-2, Bethel CT 06801	203-846-0230	R	3*	<.1
3340	Binary Star Development Corp—*Lee Bacall*	1640 Riverland Rd, Fort Lauderdale FL 33312	954-791-8575	R	3*	<.1
3341	Comlink Information Systems Inc—*Dave Martin*	7767 Elm Creek Blvd St, Maple Grove MN 55369	763-478-9174	R	3*	<.1
3342	Database Inc—*W Ed Hammond*	3342 Rose of Sharon Rd, Durham NC 27712	919-309-7918	R	3*	<.1
3343	DBMS Inc—*Keith Grill*	PO Box 19647, Shreveport LA 71149	318-635-0757	R	3*	<.1
3344	Disk Software Inc—*Paul F Scheibe*	205 Ridgestone Dr, Plano TX 75094	972-423-7288	R	3*	<.1
3345	Dove Tree Canyon Software Inc—*Bill Woo*	701 B St Ste 175, San Diego CA 92101	619-236-8895	R	3*	<.1
3346	EASE Inc—*Trevor McAlester*	27405 Puerta Real Ste, Mission Viejo CA 92691	949-348-7511	R	3*	<.1
3347	Embedded Software Development Systems Inc—*Duraiappan Rajasekaran*	19925 Stevens Creek Bl, Cupertino CA 95014	408-725-7159	R	3*	<.1
3348	EXCELCARE Inc—*Bill Daugherty*	3501 Rte 711 Ste 2, Ligonier PA 15658	724-238-9599	R	3*	<.1
3349	Gateway Software Corp—*Richard A Brown*	PO Box 1148, Laurel MT 59044	406-628-9879	R	3*	<.1
3350	GFM Consulting Inc—*Gordon Morris*	PO Box 361666, Birmingham AL 35236	205-985-5258	R	3*	<.1
3351	Gregory L Seelenbinder and Associates—*Gregory Seelenbinder*	3482 Trenton Rd, Columbus OH 43232	614-833-6952	R	3*	<.1
3352	Hitech Software Inc	6934 Canby Ave # 108, Reseda CA 91335	818-881-8593	R	3*	<.1
3353	Interactive Sales Solutions Inc	PO Box 1183, Coppell TX 75019	214-352-9575	R	3*	<.1
3354	Laboratory Systems Group Inc—*Tom Mueller*	1718 E Rose Ln, Phoenix AZ 85016		R	3*	<.1
3355	LBM Systems LLC—*David Vesty*	145 Cherry St, New Canaan CT 06840	203-966-0661	R	3*	<.1
3356	Magsoft Corp—*Shep Salon*	1 Fairchild Sq Ste 108, Clifton Park NY 12065	518-884-0505	R	3*	<.1
3357	Micro Estimating Systems Inc	200 S Executive Dr, Brookfield WI 53005	262-860-0560	R	3*	<.1
3358	Mitchell A Fink Associates Inc—*Mitchell A Fink*	350 Albany St, New York NY 10280	212-945-2882	R	3*	<.1
3359	Mount Taylor Programs—*Paul Ziegler*	2777 Yulupa Ave Ste 30, Santa Rosa CA 95405	707-542-1230	R	3*	<.1
3360	Nixon Software Group Inc—*John N Nixon III*	2099 Brown Ave, Santa Clara CA 95051	408-261-0443	R	3*	<.1
3361	Pendulab Ltd—*Jim Capps*	111 N Chestnut St Ste, Winston-Salem NC 27101	336-201-5656	S	3*	<.1
3362	POS International Inc—*Michael Turner*	5079 N Dixie Hwy Rm 28, Oakland Park FL 33334	954-376-4634	R	3*	<.1
3363	Productivity Center Inc—*Claire Keimig*	10850 Richmond Ave Ste, Houston TX 77042	713-939-9777	R	3*	<.1
3364	Research Software Consulting Group Inc—*Harlan Arthur Hurwitz*	9 Irene Ct, River Edge NJ 07661	201-262-3620	R	3*	<.1
3365	Starfire Computer Solutions—*Thomas Staniek*	3070 Berrum Pl Ste 2, Reno NV 89509	775-247-3083	R	3*	<.1
3366	Synergy Development Systems Inc—*Tom Kaufman*	4391 120th Ave N, Royal Palm Beach FL 33411		R	3*	<.1
3367	Techni-Soft—*Patricia Candy*	PO Box 466, Livermore CA 94551	925-915-1946	R	3*	<.1
3368	Think 1 Software—*Bill Hanson*	101 E Main St Ste 1, Bozeman MT 59715	406-586-7020	R	3*	<.1
3369	VisionTree Software Inc—*Martin Pellinat*	8885 Rio San Diego Dr, San Diego CA 92108	619-295-2800	R	3*	<.1
3370	Xvionics Inc—*Adam Cohn*	8300 Bonne Blvd Ste 63, Vienna VA 22182	703-893-5322	R	3*	<.1
3371	Glyph Systems LP	PO Box 134, Andover MA 01810	978-658-6800	R	3*	<.1
3372	Hot Door Inc—*Shari Cleves*	PO Box 5220, Laguna Beach CA 92652		R	3*	<.1
3373	Nucomm Data Inc	7515 Wayzata Blvd Ste, Minneapolis MN 55426	952-591-0820	R	3*	<.1
3374	Pacific Codeworks Inc—*Rob Tarte*	PO Box 29050, San Francisco CA 94129	831-426-7582	R	3*	<.1
3375	Signalogic Inc—*Jeff Brower*	9617 Wendell, Dallas TX 75243	214-349-5551	R	3*	<.1

Note: An asterisk (*) indicates an estimated financial figure. The company type code used is as follows: R = Private, P = Public, S = Private Subsidiary, B = Public Subsidiary, D = Division, J = Joint Venture, I = Investment Fund.

COMPANY RANKINGS BY SALES WITHIN 4-DIGIT SIC

Rank	Company Name—Executive Officer	Address, City, State, Zip	Phone	Type	Fin	Empls
3376	Standard Performance Evaluation Corp—Dianne Rice	7001 Heritage Village, Gainesville VA 20155	703-579-8460	R	3*	<.1
3377	VETECH Software Services Inc—Ron Detjen	150 N Wiget Ln Ste 211, Walnut Creek CA 94598	925-932-5044	S	3*	<.1
3378	Voice Information Systems Inc—Andrew Michalik	2118 Wilshire Blvd Ste, Santa Monica CA 90403	310-392-8780	R	3*	<.1
3379	Data Tracking Systems Inc—Kevin Conley	7401 Round Pond Rd, Syracuse NY 13212	315-432-0883	D	3*	<.1
3380	Eisner Associates Inc—Averell Eisner	516 N Ave E, Westfield NJ 07090	908-233-6585	R	3*	<.1
3381	Portage Communications Inc—Stuart Harris	13827 W Pine St, Sandpoint ID 83864	208-263-6776	R	3*	<.1
3382	Stokes Publishing Co—William Stokes	1292 Reamwood Ave, Sunnyvale CA 94089	408-541-9145	R	3*	<.1
3383	Alki Software Corp—Peter Rinearson	300 Queen Anne Ave N S, Seattle WA 98109		R	3	<.1
3384	Karl Albrecht International—Karl Albrecht	3120 Old Bridgeport Wa, San Diego CA 92111	858-576-3535	R	3*	<.1
3385	Technology Associates Inc—Eric Hobbs	PO Box 4409, Cary NC 27519	919-459-0100	R	3*	<.1
3386	Bowler Petrophysics Inc—Jack Bowler	730 17th St Ste 835, Denver CO 80202	303-860-1641	R	3*	<.1
3387	Brooks Harris Film and Tape Inc—Brooks Harris	14002 Palawan Way Ste, Marina del Rey CA 90292	310-577-0383	R	3*	<.1
3388	DesignWare Inc (Watertown Massachusetts)—Donald Jameson	54 Fieldstone-Bashan D, East Haddam CT 06423	860-873-8938	R	3*	<.1
3389	Digital Hearing Systems Corp—Anthony J Miltich	9679 E High Meadows, Rogers AR 72756	479-925-7700	R	3*	<.1
3390	Model Master LLC	37 Sherwood Terrace St, Lake Bluff IL 60044	847-235-2074	R	3*	<.1
3391	Peperkins Toolworks—Peter Perkins	PO Box 23427, Tigard OR 97281	503-452-1201	R	3*	<.1
3392	Photo Agora—Robert Maust	3711 Hidden Meadow Ln, Keezletown VA 22832	540-269-8283	R	3*	<.1
3393	Structured Software Systems Inc—Richard Bender	213 Irick Rd, Mount Holly NJ 08060	609-267-1616	R	3*	<.1
3394	MedCom USA Inc—Robert H Kite	1930 Village Ctr Cir 3, Las Vegas NV 89134	949-466-1534	P	3	<.1
3395	Ekagra Software Technologies Ltd—Kalpesh Patel	23296 Meadowvale Glen, Sterling VA 20166	703-631-3178	R	3*	<.1
3396	Tecra Systems Inc—Giridhar Gondi	6005 E Executive Dr, Westland MI 48185	248-888-1116	R	3*	<.1
3397	Continuum Technology Corp—Stephen Hafer	220 Continuum Dr, Fletcher NC 28732	828-684-8682	R	3*	<.1
3398	Providenet Communications Corp—Greg Mcnab	20 Great Oaks Blvd, San Jose CA 95119	408-398-6335	R	3*	<.1
3399	ePsolutions Inc—Steve Langerock	317 Ranch Rd 620 S Ste, Austin TX 78734	512-263-8765	R	3	<.1
3400	Structured Healthcare Management Inc—Maurice Reifman	456 Nordhoff Pl, Englewood NJ 07631	201-569-3290	R	3*	<.1
3401	Primepoint LLC	163 Us Hwy 130 Ste 1c, Bordentown NJ 08505	609-298-1970	R	3*	<.1
3402	Adaptive Inc—Jeff Goins	65 Enterprise, Aliso Viejo CA 92656	949-389-5800	R	3*	<.1
3403	Semi Logic Entertainments Inc—Pete Adams	PO Box 923, Palo Cedro CA 96073	530-547-3730	R	3*	<.1
3404	Orion Behavioral Healthcare Services—William Allan	1016 Leavenworth St, Omaha NE 68102	402-341-8880	R	3*	<.1
3405	Ipressroom Inc—Chris Bechtel	13428 Maxella Ave Ste, Marina Del Rey CA 90292	310-499-0544	R	3*	<.1
3406	Veros Software Inc—Darius Bozorgi	2333 N Broadway Ste 35, Santa Ana CA 92706	714-415-6300	R	3*	<.1
3407	MARX Software Security	2900 Chamblee Tucker R, Atlanta GA 30341	770-986-8887	R	3*	<.1
3408	Ascella Technologies Inc—Amith Varghese	1420 Spring Hill Rd St, Mc Lean VA 22102	703-635-3180	R	3*	<.1
3409	Micro Planning International Inc—John Strohl	2356 Cypress Cove Cir, Herndon VA 20171	703-926-4449	R	3	.1
3410	TMT Software Co—Richard Rosenberg	6350 Quadrangle Dr Ste, Chapel Hill NC 27517	919-493-4700	R	3	<.1
3411	Hometelos LP—Nancy Richards	14651 Dallas Pkwy Ste, Dallas TX 75254	972-233-4477	R	3*	<.1
3412	Cimmaron Software Inc—Richard Lidstrom	12396 World Trade Dr, San Diego CA 92128	858-385-1291	R	3*	<.1
3413	Mansai Corp—Aparna Iyer	8001 Craddock Rd, Greenbelt MD 20770	301-552-5372	R	3*	<.1
3414	Software Experts Inc—Rao Mallik	10 Curren Dr, Westford MA 01886	978-692-5343	R	3*	<.1
3415	Furukawa Information Technology Inc—Janise Harmon	760 N Euclid St Ste 10, Anaheim CA 92801	714-956-3171	R	3	<.1
3416	MCS Management Corp—Wayne Barto	5 Keuka Ct, Hawthorn Woods IL 60047	847-680-3707	R	3	<.1
3417	Event Inc—Reggie Aggarwall	200 N Glebe Rd Office, Arlington VA 22203	703-226-3544	R	2*	<.1
3418	Transplant Connect Inc—John Piano	2701 Ocean Park Blvd S, Santa Monica CA 90405	310-392-1400	R	2*	<.1
3419	Jian Tools For Sales Inc—Burke Franklin	104 Estates Dr, Chico CA 95928	530-267-6293	R	2	<.1
3420	Guide Technologies LLC—Julia Linge	250 E 96th St Ste 525, Indianapolis IN 46240	317-844-3162	R	2*	<.1
3421	COPsync Inc—Ronald A Woessner	2010 FM 2673, Canyon Lake TX 78133	830-964-3838	P	2	<.1
3422	Oli Systems Inc—Marshall Rafal	108 American Rd, Morris Plains NJ 07950	973-539-4996	R	2*	<.1
3423	Sharp Electronics Satellite—Richie Ardahji	8373 Kingston Pke Ste, Knoxville TN 37919	865-539-4900	R	2*	<.1
3424	C2C Systems Inc—Dave Hunt	1 Federal St Bldg 103, Springfield MA 01105	413-739-8575	R	2*	<.1
3425	Jakeel Consulting Inc—Jamie Valentine	PO Box 441707, Fort Washington MD 20749	301-567-8680	R	2*	<.1
3426	MTA Systems Inc	4312 W Genesee St, Syracuse NY 13219	315-488-1518	D	2	<.1
3427	Applied Business Services Inc	900 Wind River Ln Ste, Gaithersburg MD 20878	301-417-2999	R	2	<.1
3428	Computer Programming and Systems Inc—Samuel Urda	45 Church St Ste 201, Stamford CT 06906	203-324-9203	R	2*	<.1
3429	Hrd Inc—Vasantha Jandhyala	7827 Somerset Ct, Greenbelt MD 20770	301-345-7872	R	2*	<.1
3430	Ptg International Inc—Eugene Ribeaux	13227 Executive Park T, Germantown MD 20874	301-972-2626	R	2*	<.1
3431	Daniel Lampert Communications—Daniel Lampert	PO Box 151719, Altamonte Springs FL 32715	407-327-7000	R	2*	<.1
3432	CyberAccess Inc—William D Vasu	23 N Franklin St Ste 1, Chagrin Falls OH 44022		R	2	<.1
3433	Fidelis Software Inc—Jerry Knight	2763 Meadow Church Rd, Duluth GA 30097	678-473-6790	R	2*	<.1
3434	Zephyr Associates Inc—Charles Martin	PO Box 12368, Zephyr Cove NV 89448	775-588-0654	R	2*	<.1
3435	RAM Technologies Inc (Fort Washington Pennsylvania)—Robert Tulio	275 Commerce Dr Ste 10, Fort Washington PA 19034	215-654-8810	R	2*	<.1
3436	Objectif Lune LLC—Howard Silverstein	300 Broadacres Dr Ste, Bloomfield NJ 07003	973-780-0100	R	2*	<.1
3437	FSTW Inc—Richard T Brock	7000 Central Pkwy NE S, Atlanta GA 30328	678-672-3100	P	2	<.1
3438	Quinstar Corp—Bill Rose	4020 S Industrial Dr S, Austin TX 78744	512-326-1011	R	2*	<.1
3439	VTLS Inc—Vinod Chachra	1701 Kraft Dr, Blacksburg VA 24060	540-557-1200	R	2*	.2
3440	ExacTax Inc—Kevin Love	2301 W Lincoln Ave Ste, Anaheim CA 92801	714-284-4802	R	2*	.1
3441	TPT Technologies Inc—Jack Daley	3960 Howard Hughes Pkw, Las Vegas NV 89169		R	2*	.1
3442	Electronic Healthcare Systems Inc—Sanders Pitman	One Metroplex Dr Ste 5, Birmingham AL 35209	205-871-1031	R	2*	.1
3443	Keystone Computer Associates Inc—Leon Ellerson	1055 Virginia Dr, Fort Washington PA 19034	215-643-3800	R	2*	.1
3444	Universal Technical Systems Inc—Jack Marathe	202 W State St Ste 700, Rockford IL 61101	815-963-2220	R	2*	.1
3445	EDICT Systems Inc—Jason K Wadzinski	2434 Esquire Rd, Beavercreek OH 45431	937-429-4288	R	2*	.1
3446	CarteGraph Systems Inc—Scott Taylor	3600 Digital Dr, Dubuque IA 52003	563-556-8120	R	2*	<.1
3447	Advanced Relational Technology Inc—Vince Kunasek	6500 N Mineral Dr, Coeur D Alene ID 83815	208-292-3400	R	2*	<.1
3448	NuParadigm Systems Inc—Harry Haury	12977 North Outer Fort, Saint Louis MO 63141	636-537-5558	R	2*	<.1
3449	Visual Systems Inc (San Luis Obispo California)—Chris Smith	994 Mill St 2nd Fl, San Luis Obispo CA 93401	805-781-3580	R	2*	<.1
3450	C and S Research Corp—Paul Macaluso	625 Clark Ave Ste 21B, King of Prussia PA 19406		R	2*	<.1
3451	Computer Resources LLC—Patrick Grace SofterWare Inc	1037 Calef Highway Sui, Barrington NH 03825		S	2*	<.1
3452	ScanData Systems Inc—John Dalton	9701 Brodie Ln Bldg 10, Austin TX 78748	512-358-1585	R	2*	<.1
3453	Adacel Systems Inc—Fred Sheldon	1825 I St NW Ste 400, Washington DC 20006	202-429-7120	R	2*	<.1
3454	Construction Data Control Inc—Johri Geoffrey	3980 Dekalb Technology, Atlanta GA 30340		R	2*	<.1
3455	Data Strategies Inc—Lesley Jacobs	13475 Danielson St Ste, Poway CA 92064	858-514-0300	R	2*	<.1
3456	DNASTAR Inc—Frederick R Blattner	3801 Regent St, Madison WI 53705	608-258-7420	R	2*	<.1
3457	First Step Research Inc—Kevin Owen	PO Box 9587, Moscow ID 83843	208-882-8869	R	2*	<.1
3458	Hertzler Systems Inc—Evan Miller	2312 Eisenhower Dr N, Goshen IN 46526	574-533-0571	R	2*	<.1
3459	Hickman-Kenyon Systems Inc—Mary Cockerill	2323 S 171st St Ste 20, Omaha NE 68130	402-398-2200	R	2*	<.1
3460	InterNoded Inc—Julie Palen	1440 Main St, Waltham MA 02451	781-890-0902	D	2*	<.1
3461	Magic Software Enterprises Inc—Regev Yativ	23046 Avenida de la Ca, Laguna Hills CA 92653	949-250-1718	D	2*	<.1
3462	Miva Corp—Peter Corrao	5060 Shoreham Pl Ste 3, San Diego CA 92122	858-490-2570	D	2*	<.1
3463	People's Computer Company Inc—John Canning	20 Winooski Falls Way, Winooski VT 05404	802-846-8177	R	2*	<.1

Rank	Company Name—*Executive Officer*	Address, City, State, Zip	Phone	Type	Fin	Empls
3464	Professional Computing Resources Inc	4635 N Breton Ct SE, Grand Rapids MI 49508	616-554-0000	S	2*	<.1
3465	Quadralay Corp—*Tony McDow*	9101 Burnet Rd Ste 105, Austin TX 78758	512-719-3399	R	2*	<.1
3466	Software Technologies Group Inc—*Christian G Herzog*	10330 W Roosevelt Rd S, Westchester IL 60154	708-547-0110	R	2*	<.1
3467	Varsity Logistics Inc—*Chris Anderson*	91 Westborough Blvd St, South San Francisco CA 94080	650-392-7979	R	2*	<.1
3468	WLT Software of Florida Inc—*Tom Brooks*	26133 US Hwy 19 N Fl 4, Clearwater FL 33763	727-442-9296	R	2*	<.1
3469	Ascent Technology Inc—*Patrick Winston*	1 Kendall Sq Ste B2402, Cambridge MA 02139	617-395-4800	R	2	<.1
3470	Integrated Business Systems and Services Inc—*George Mendenhall*	1601 Shop Rd Ste E, Columbia SC 29201	803-736-5595	P	2	<.1
3471	Pacific Software Publishing Inc—*Kenichi Uchikura*	1404 140th Pl NE, Bellevue WA 98007	425-957-0808	R	2*	<.1
3472	Kreg Information Systems—*Greg Ferguson*	2 Piedmont Ctr Ste 500, Atlanta GA 30305	404-261-5734	R	2	<.1
3473	Passageways LLC—*William F Connors*	1551 Win Hentschel Blv, West Lafayette IN 47906	765-497-8829	R	2*	<.1
3474	Resort Data Processing Inc—*Barry Biegler*	PO Box 1170, Vail CO 81658	970-845-1140	R	2*	<.1
3475	Abacus Data Systems Inc—*Judd Kessler*	9191 Towne Centre Dr S, San Diego CA 92122	858-452-4245	R	2*	<.1
3476	Advanced Business Technologies Inc	PO Box 218, Slatersville RI 02876	401-766-4447	R	2*	<.1
3477	ANN Automation Inc—*David Griffith*	28720 Roadside Dr Ste, Agoura Hills CA 91301	818-879-0000	R	2*	<.1
3478	BIS Computer Solutions Inc—*Miro Macho*	2428 Foothill Blvd, La Crescenta CA 91214	818-248-5023	R	2*	<.1
3479	Bitek Inc—*Graham Butler*	6 Hutton Centre Dr Ste, Santa Ana CA 92707		R	2*	<.1
3480	BLAZE SSI Corp	PO Box 333, Brielle NJ 08730	732-223-5575	R	2*	<.1
3481	Building Systems Design Inc—*John Witherspoon*	3565 Piedmont Rd NE St, Atlanta GA 30305	404-365-8900	R	2*	<.1
3482	Century Consultants Ltd—*Joseph Shearn*	150 Airport Rd Ste 150, Lakewood NJ 08701	732-363-9300	R	2*	<.1
3483	Codeware Inc—*Les Bildy*	5224 Station Way, Sarasota FL 34233	941-927-2670	R	2*	<.1
3484	COIN Educational Products Inc—*Rod Durgin*	3130 Executive Pky Ste, Toledo OH 43606		R	2*	<.1
3485	Conetic Software Systems Inc—*Andres Garza*	1012 Navarro St, San Antonio TX 78205	210-225-5185	R	2*	<.1
3486	Cybermetrics Corp—*Dave Banerjea*	1523 W Whispering Wind, Phoenix AZ 85085		R	2*	<.1
3487	DAVID Corp—*H Alex Aminian* Halo Technology Holdings Inc	200 Pine St 2nd Fl, San Francisco CA 94104	415-362-4555	S	2*	<.1
3488	DynEd International Inc—*Ian Adam*	1350 Bayshore Hwy Ste, Burlingame CA 94010	650-375-7011	R	2*	<.1
3489	Information Management Corp—*Chris Maloney* Tritech Software Systems	13 Centennial Dr, North Grafton MA 01536	508-839-6445	S	2*	<.1
3490	Integrated Software Design Inc—*Ramin Khoshatefeh*	171 Forbes Blvd, Mansfield MA 02048	617-419-2444	R	2*	<.1
3491	Internodal International Inc—*Rosemary Verrecchio*	PO Box 1173, Southold NY 11971	631-765-0037	R	2*	<.1
3492	Lane Telecommunications Inc—*John P Hughes*	10 Lanidex Plz W Ste 2, Parsippany NJ 07054	973-526-2979	R	2*	<.1
3493	Momentum Systems Ltd—*James P Byrne*	41 Twosome Dr Ste 9, Moorestown NJ 08057	856-727-0777	R	2*	<.1
3494	Privacy Inc—*Kenneth Good*	12720 Hillcrest Rd Ste, Dallas TX 75230	972-354-1300	R	2*	<.1
3495	Quadros Systems Inc—*Andrew Barrett*	10450 Stancliff Rd Ste, Houston TX 77099		R	2*	<.1
3496	Ron Turley Associates Inc—*Larry Turley*	20823 N 19th Ave Ste 4, Phoenix AZ 85027	623-581-2447	R	2*	<.1
3497	Rutherford and Associates Inc—*Michael Rutherford*	1009 Productions Ct, Holland MI 49423	616-392-5000	R	2*	<.1
3498	Seagull Scientific Inc—*Jeremy Seigel*	1616 148th Ave SE, Bellevue WA 98007	425-641-1408	R	2*	<.1
3499	Suite Solutions Inc—*Alan Perlmutter*	100 Corporate Pkwy Ste, Amherst NY 14226	716-929-3050	R	2*	<.1
3500	Travis Software Corp—*Alan Williams*	PO Box 820469, Houston TX 77282	281-496-3737	R	2*	<.1
3501	Micro Analytics Of Virginia Inc—*J Hooban*	2009 14th St N Ste 302, Arlington VA 22201	703-841-0414	R	2*	<.1
3502	MicroAnalytics Inc—*Mike Hooban*	2009 14th St Rm 302, Arlington VA 22201	703-841-0414	R	2*	<.1
3503	TaxSimple Inc—*John Vora*	8 Emery Ave, Randolph NJ 07869		S	2*	<.1
3504	Chapura Inc—*Paul Leeper*	PO Box 16247, Mobile AL 36616	251-470-1963	R	2*	<.1
3505	EasyRun Inc—*Shlomo Shur*	477 Main St Ste 214, Monroe CT 06468	203-445-0006	R	2*	<.1
3506	InfoStreet Inc—*Siamak Farah*	18345 Ventura Blvd 4th, Tarzana CA 91356	818-776-8080	R	2*	<.1
3507	SAE Group Inc—*Lynn Jaeger*	238 Ne 1st Ave, Delray Beach FL 33444	561-279-8200	R	2*	<.1
3508	Software Marketing Associates Inc—*Denise Lunden*	1086 Elm St Ste 200, Rocky Hill CT 06067	860-721-8929	R	2*	<.1
3509	Ace Software Inc	6110 Enterprise Pkwy, Grove City OH 43123		R	2*	<.1
3510	Advanced Software Applications Corp—*Bill Gossman*	3117 Washington Pke, Bridgeville PA 15017	412-220-9300	R	2*	<.1
3511	Alsoft Inc—*Al Dion*	PO Box 5150, Kingwood TX 77325	281-353-4090	R	2*	<.1
3512	Apian Software Inc—*William Ray*	115 N 85th St Ste 204, Seattle WA 98103	206-547-5321	R	2*	<.1
3513	Appian Logistics Software Inc—*Mike Kositzky*	10317 Greenbriar Pl St, Oklahoma City OK 73159	405-692-1683	R	2*	<.1
3514	Applied Information Management Inc—*David A Isacowitz*	98 Cuttermill Rd, Great Neck NY 11021	516-773-3294	R	2*	<.1
3515	Argos Software—*Ron Heffernan*	5737 N Fresno St, Fresno CA 93710	559-227-1000	R	2*	<.1
3516	AST Engineering Services Inc	12200 E Briarwood Ave, Englewood CO 80112	303-478-6822	R	2	<.1
3517	Berkley Integrated Audio Software Inc—*Steve Berkley*	121 H St, Petaluma CA 94952	707-782-1866	R	2*	<.1
3518	Binary Research Inc—*Somers K Butcher*	7100 E Valley Green Rd, Fort Washington PA 19034	215-233-3200	R	2*	<.1
3519	CaterMate—*Tim Tighe* CBORD Group Inc	61 Brown Rd, Ithaca NY 14850	607-257-2410	D	2*	<.1
3520	CGS Technology Associates Co—*Michael Szot*	242 Old New Brunswick, Piscataway NJ 08854	732-750-4141	R	2*	<.1
3521	CHAMPS Software Inc—*Chandra Patel*	1255 N Vantage Point D, Crystal River FL 34429	352-795-2362	R	2*	<.1
3522	Clients and Profits Inc—*Mark Robillard*	4755 Oceanside Blvd St, Oceanside CA 92056	760-945-4334	R	2*	<.1
3523	CQ Computer Communications Inc—*John Thomas*	570 Peachtree Pky, Cumming GA 30041	770-844-0233	R	2*	<.1
3524	CrystalGraphics Inc—*Ron Hood*	3350 Scott Blvd Bldg S, Santa Clara CA 95054	408-496-6175	R	2*	<.1
3525	Datamatics Management Services Inc—*Norman Heinle*	330 New Brunswick Ave, Fords NJ 08863	732-738-9600	R	2*	<.1
3526	DDC-I Inc—*Bob Morris*	4600 E Shea Rd Ste 102, Phoenix AZ 85028	602-275-7172	R	2*	<.1
3527	DPS Software Systems Inc—*Dave Scheidler*	41 E Foothill Blvd Rm, Arcadia CA 91006	626-445-9190	R	2*	<.1
3528	Elan Computer Group Inc	PO Box 4730, Mountain View CA 94040	650-276-0356	R	2*	<.1
3529	Electrosonics Inc—*Dave Barker*	17150 15 Mile Rd, Fraser MI 48026	586-415-5555	R	2*	<.1
3530	Envelope Manager Software—*Harry Whitehouse*	247 High St, Palo Alto CA 94301	650-321-2640	S	2*	<.1
3531	Filemark Corp—*William Zaftrow*	1 Taylor Dr, Spencer MA 01562	774-745-8224	R	2*	<.1
3532	Fiscal Systems Inc—*Philip Moore*	102 Commerce Cir, Madison AL 35758	256-772-8920	R	2*	<.1
3533	Foresight Solutions Inc	431 Crooked Creek Rd, Hendersonville NC 28739	828-692-3301	R	2*	<.1
3534	Fortres Grand Corp—*John Pitsch*	PO Box 888, Plymouth IN 46563	574-935-3868	R	2*	<.1
3535	Gallery Systems Inc—*Jay Hoffman*	261 W 35th St 12th Fl, New York NY 10001	646-733-2239	R	2*	<.1
3536	Hudson Control Group Inc—*Philip Farrelly*	10 Stern Ave, Springfield NJ 07081	973-376-7400	R	2*	<.1
3537	Infosystems Technology Inc—*Greg Barnes*	4 Professional Dr Ste, Gaithersburg MD 20879	202-412-0152	R	2*	<.1
3538	Intersoft Systems Inc (Beaverton Oregon)—*Dan Cotton*	PO Box 1050, Beaverton OR 97005	503-644-3761	R	2*	<.1
3539	Irvine Compiler Corp—*Dan Eilers*	15635 Alton Pky Ste 23, Irvine CA 92618	949-727-3350	R	2*	<.1
3540	Manufacturing Automation Software and Systems Group Inc—*Gamal Balady*	21601 Devonshire St, Chatsworth CA 91311	818-709-1255	R	2*	<.1
3541	Menlo Business Systems Inc—*Victor Mennell*	199 Stanford Ave, Menlo Park CA 94025	650-948-7920	R	2	<.1
3542	MicroAutomation Inc—*Suresh Gursahaney*	5870 Trinity Pkwy Ste, Centreville VA 20121	703-543-2100	R	2*	<.1
3543	MiraLink Corp—*Ron McCabe*	6835 SE 78th Ave, Portland OR 97206	503-208-0076	R	2*	<.1
3544	Nirvana Systems Inc—*Ed Downs*	7000 N Mopac Ste 425, Austin TX 78731		R	2*	<.1
3545	Ohio Distinctive Enterprises Inc—*Stanford Apseloff*	6500 Fiesta Dr, Columbus OH 43235	614-459-0453	R	2*	<.1
3546	Ormandy Inc—*Foad Monajem*	282 Rockbridge Rd NW, Lilburn GA 30047	770-662-5533	R	2*	<.1
3547	PowerBASIC Inc—*Robert Zale*	2061 Englewood Rd, Englewood FL 34223	941-473-7300	R	2*	<.1
3548	PowerSource Online Inc—*Steve Smith*	3901 Coconut Palm Dr S, Tampa FL 33619	813-675-6320	D	2*	<.1

Note: An asterisk (*) indicates an estimated financial figure. The company type code used is as follows: R = Private, P = Public, S = Private Subsidiary, B = Public Subsidiary, D = Division, J = Joint Venture, I = Investment Fund.

COMPANY RANKINGS BY SALES WITHIN 4-DIGIT SIC

Rank	Company Name—*Executive Officer*	Address, City, State, Zip	Phone	Type	Fin	Empls
3549	Profitool Inc—*Keith Lightfield*	6855 S Havana St Ste 6, Centennial CO 80112	303-571-1555	R	2*	<.1
3550	Quantitative Software Management Inc—*Larry Putnam Sr*	2000 Corporate Ridge S, McLean VA 22102	703-790-0055	R	2*	<.1
3551	Reliable Health Systems Inc—*Harry Zelcer*	2610 Nostrand Ave, Brooklyn NY 11210	718-338-2400	R	2*	<.1
3552	Scientific Computing Associates Inc—*Beverly Thalberg*	One Century Twr 265 Ch, New Haven CT 06510	203-777-7442	R	2*	<.1
3553	Software and Management Associates—*Michael Taylor*	3939 Glade Valley Dr S, Kingwood TX 77339	281-446-5000	R	2*	<.1
3554	Stibo Systems Inc—*Mikael Lyngsoe*	1990 Vaughn Rd Ste 210, Kennesaw GA 30144	770-425-3282	S	2*	<.1
3555	TIW Technology Inc—*Rod Hatcher*	769 Youngs Hill Rd, Easton PA 18040	610-258-5161	R	2*	<.1
3556	Trellis Network Services Inc—*Jack Atwell*	20 Sheffield Dr, Columbus NJ 08022		R	2*	<.1
3557	Wizdom Systems Inc—*Rosemary M Wisnosky*	1300 Iroquois Ave, Naperville IL 60563	630-357-3000	R	2*	<.1
3558	Xcel Controls Inc—*John Brickley*	1600 W 6th St, Mishawaka IN 46544	574-259-7804	R	2*	<.1
3559	Xybernaut Solutions Inc—*Perry L Nolan*	5175 Parkstone Dr Ste, Chantilly VA 20151	703-480-0480	S	2*	<.1
3560	Blue Marble Geographics—*Patrick J Cunningham*	397 Water St Ste 100, Gardiner ME 04345	207-582-6747	R	2*	<.1
3561	Providence Software Solutions Inc—*Don Hames*	202 New Edition Ct, Cary NC 27511	919-854-1800	R	2*	<.1
3562	Church Art Works—*Dave Adamson*	890 Promontory Pl SE, Salem OR 97302	503-370-9377	R	2*	<.1
3563	Drawbase Software—*Evan Kontos*	1 Sweetwood Dr, Randolph NJ 07869	973-927-6814	R	2*	<.1
3564	EasyAsk Inc—*Craig Bassin*	200 Wheeler Rd South T, Burlington MA 01803	781-402-5635	R	2*	<.1
3565	JMSI Inc—*Jeanne Mara*	301 State Rte 17 N, Rutherford NJ 07070	201-460-4700	R	2	<.1
3566	MSI Data Systems Inc—*Steve Kraninger*	PO Box 240151, Milwaukee WI 53224	262-241-7800	R	2*	<.1
3567	Muller Media Conversions Inc—*Chris Muller*	21 Locust St, Manhasset NY 11030	516-833-3067	R	2*	<.1
3568	Right On Programs—*Barbara Feinstein*	27 Bowdon Rd Ste B, Greenlawn NY 11740	631-424-7777	R	2	<.1
3569	Spellex Corp—*Ralph Schroeder*	10820 Sheldon Rd, Tampa FL 33626	813-792-7000	R	2	<.1
3570	Artbeats Software Inc—*Phil Bates*	PO Box 709, Myrtle Creek OR 97457	541-863-4429	R	2*	<.1
3571	Creative Thinking Inc—*Bill Watson*	3700 S 14th, Lincoln NE 68502	402-423-7851	R	2*	<.1
3572	hal Systems Corp—*Greg Hahn*	8111 LBJ Freeway Ste 8, Dallas TX 75251	214-691-4700	R	2*	<.1
3573	ABBASOFT Technologies Inc—*James Baskin*	23161 Mill Creek Dr St, Laguna Hills CA 92653	949-830-5113	R	2*	<.1
3574	Anyware Technology Inc—*Roy Han*	1925 N Central Ave, South El Monte CA 91733	626-839-6890	R	2*	<.1
3575	Associated Systems Inc—*Sharon Steele*	200 W Broadway Ste 240, Wichita KS 67202		R	2*	<.1
3576	Cibar Inc—*Loren Shannon*	4575 Hilton Pky Ste 20, Colorado Springs CO 80907	719-260-6700	R	2*	<.1
3577	Combined Computer Resources Inc—*Paul Montgomery*	2777 Stemmons Fwy Ste, Dallas TX 75207	214-267-1010	R	2*	<.1
3578	Comprehensive Microsystems Inc—*Ron Tolman*	PO Box 86, Safford AZ 85548	928-428-7225	R	2*	<.1
3579	Cycle INN Incorporated Engineered Software—*WL Stanley*	PO Box 18344, Greensboro NC 27419	336-299-4843	R	2*	<.1
3580	Data Innovations Inc—*Gregory Vail*	120 Kimball Ave Ste 10, South Burlington VT 05403	802-658-2850	R	2*	<.1
3581	GCOM Inc—*David Grothe*	1800 Woodfield Dr, Savoy IL 61874	217-351-4241	R	2*	<.1
3582	General Data Systems Inc (St Louis Missouri)—*David Whiting*	10801 Indian Head Indu, Saint Louis MO 63132	314-427-1661	R	2*	<.1
3583	Immersive Design Inc—*Gregory Smith*	43 Nagog Park, Acton MA 01720	978-266-1800	R	2*	<.1
3584	Mindwrap Technologies Inc—*James A Small*	PO Box 430, Flint Hill VA 22627	540-675-3015	S	2*	<.1
3585	Zephyr Development Corp—*Gregg Ledford*	3355 W Alabama Ste 122, Houston TX 77098	713-623-0089	R	2*	<.1
3586	ACS Software Inc—*Anthony Stewart*	PO Box 449, Torrance CA 90508	310-755-6040	R	2*	<.1
3587	Adaco Hospitality Solutions—*Sunil Ippagunta*	40 Richards Ave, Norwalk CT 06854	203-838-3700	R	2*	<.1
3588	Advanced Concepts Inc—*Jeff Wohlfahrt*	8875 N 55th St Ste 200, Milwaukee WI 53223	414-362-9640	R	2*	<.1
3589	Advanced Logic Solutions Inc—*Karl H Touset*	1000 Johnson Ferry Rd, Marietta GA 30068	770-578-6771	R	2*	<.1
3590	AIM Software Systems Inc—*DJ Martin*	1747 Veterans Hwy Ste, Islandia NY 11749	631-234-0621	R	2*	<.1
3591	Alexander LAN Inc—*Dirk Smith*	PO Box 1566, Nashua NH 03061	603-880-8800	R	2*	<.1
3592	Alien Skin Software LLC—*Jeff Butterworth*	1111 Haynes St Ste 113, Raleigh NC 27604	919-832-4124	R	2*	<.1
3593	Aspetuck Systems Inc—*Michael Gabriele*	200 Connecticut Ave, Norwalk CT 06854	203-852-9100	R	2*	<.1
3594	AuriQ Systems Inc—*Koichiro Ikudome*	301 N Lake Ave Ste 100, Pasadena CA 91101	626-564-2781	R	2*	<.1
3595	BarControl Systems and Services Inc—*Steven Bardos*	PO Drawer 6339, Greenville SC 29606		R	2*	<.1
3596	Clearview Software International Inc—*Richard Lowney*	PO Box 1370, Amherst NH 03031	603-472-7115	R	2*	<.1
3597	Comeau Computing—*Greg Comeau*	9134 120th St, Richmond Hill NY 11418	718-945-0009	R	2*	<.1
3598	Commetrex Corp—*Mike Coffee*	1225 Northmeadow Pkwy, Roswell GA 30076	770-449-7775	R	2*	<.1
3599	Configuration Data Services Inc—*Mitch Klinman*	18662 MacArthur Blvd S, Irvine CA 92612	714-546-1892	R	2*	<.1
3600	Corbin Willits Systems Inc—*Roland Willits*	3755 Washington Blvd, Fremont CA 94538	510-979-5600	R	2*	<.1
3601	Crystal Point Inc—*Chris Smith*	6619 N Scottsdale Rd, Scottsdale AZ 85250	425-487-3656	R	2*	<.1
3602	Cuffs Planning and Models Ltd	PO Box 1041, Larchmont NY 10538	914-576-1831	R	2*	<.1
3603	Cyco Software Americas—*Martin Jammatt*	2400 Lake Park Dr Ste4, Smyrna GA 30080	404-634-3302	D	2*	<.1
3604	Design Science Inc—*Paul R Topping*	140 Pine Ave 4th Fl, Long Beach CA 90802	562-432-2920	R	2*	<.1
3605	Digital Designs Inc	15800 John J Delaney D, Charlotte NC 28277	704-790-7100	R	2*	<.1
3606	DisplayMate Technologies Corp—*Raymond Soneira*	PO Box 550, Amherst NH 03031	603-672-8500	R	2*	<.1
3607	Entropy Ltd—*Ronald Christensen*	345 S Great Rd, Lincoln MA 01773	781-259-8901	R	2*	<.1
3608	EPL Inc—*Wayne Benson*	22 Inverness Ctr Pkwy, Birmingham AL 35242	205-408-5300	R	2*	<.1
3609	ExperTune Inc—*John Gerry*	1020 James Dr Ste A, Hartland WI 53029	262-369-7711	R	2*	<.1
3610	Frontier Technologies Corp—*Prakash Ambegaonkar*	1105 Waverly Way, McLean VA 22101	703-734-1224	R	2*	<.1
3611	Grafx Systems—*Brian Feldman*	11900 Torreyanna Cir, West Palm Beach FL 33412	561-691-0900	R	2*	<.1
3612	Greystone Solutions Inc—*Bob Shear*	186 Lincoln St, Boston MA 02111	617-832-9200	R	2*	<.1
3613	ICONIX Software Engineering Inc—*Dean Sleeper*	11301 W Olympic Blvd S, Los Angeles CA 90064	310-474-8482	R	2*	<.1
3614	Image Architects Inc—*Peter Nirenberg*	784 Morris Tpke, Short Hills NJ 07078	973-912-9334	R	2*	<.1
3615	Independent Systems and Programming Inc—*John P Osman* Avalara Inc	12 W Wilson St, Batavia IL 60510	630-879-6550	S	2*	<.1
3616	Information Planning Associates Inc—*Jo Ann Byrd*	5203 Leesburg Pke Ste, Falls Church VA 22041	703-820-6100	R	2*	<.1
3617	International Systems Marketing Inc—*Norman Young*	611 Rockville Pike, Rockville MD 20852	301-670-1813	R	2*	<.1
3618	Learning Tools International—*Cathy Zier*	2391 Circadian Way, Santa Rosa CA 95407	707-521-3530	R	2*	<.1
3619	MacKichan Software Inc—*Barry MacKichan*	19307 8th Ave Ste C, Poulsbo WA 98370	360-394-6033	R	2*	<.1
3620	Mentalix Inc—*Brian Gross*	1255 W 15th St Ste 370, Plano TX 75075	972-423-9377	R	2*	<.1
3621	Netrics Inc—*Stefanos Damianakis*	707 State Rd Ste 212, Princeton NJ 08540	609-683-4002	R	2*	<.1
3622	OpenTech Systems Inc—*Steve Sydow*	405 State Hwy 121 Ste, Lewisville TX 75067	469-635-1500	R	2*	<.1
3623	OptionVue Systems International Inc—*Len Yates*	950 Technology Way Ste, Libertyville IL 60048	847-816-6610	R	2*	<.1
3624	Pegasus Software Systems Inc—*Ron West*	PO Box 14514, Fort Worth TX 76117	817-938-1383	R	2*	<.1
3625	Prism Software Solutions Inc—*David Best*	1101 E 78th St, Bloomington MN 55420	651-687-9554	R	2*	<.1
3626	Puzzle Systems Corp	PO Box 1893, Morgan Hill CA 95038	408-779-9809	R	2*	<.1
3627	Qualitech Solutions Inc—*Chris Sewell*	11301 Carmel Commons B, Charlotte NC 28226	704-944-6040	R	2*	<.1
3628	Raritan Valley Technology Group Inc—*Linda McAfee*	1090 King Georges Post, Edison NJ 08837	732-738-6500	R	2*	<.1
3629	RH Positive Computer Systems—*Mike Wessinger*	246 E Campus View Blvd, Columbus OH 43235		R	2*	<.1
3630	Software Research Inc (San Francisco California)—*William Wulf*	1663 Mission St Ste 40, San Francisco CA 94103	415-861-2800	R	2*	<.1
3631	Stevens Group Inc—*Ed Pauley*	23655 Via Del Rio Ste, Yorba Linda CA 92887	714-660-1250	R	2*	<.1
3632	Systems Products International Inc—*Karl Lange*	2600 SW 3rd Ave 5th Fl, Miami FL 33129	305-858-9505	R	2*	<.1
3633	Trax Softworks Inc—*Len Fischer*	1800 S Robertson Blvd, Los Angeles CA 90035	805-649-5800	R	2*	<.1
3634	Universal Software Inc	304 Federal Rd Ste 212, Brookfield CT 06804	203-792-5100	R	2*	<.1
3635	Versys Corp—*Richard Wilke*	22 Battery St Ste 510, San Francisco CA 94111	415-693-1700	R	2*	<.1
3636	W David Scott Inc—*W David Scott*	1180 S State Hwy 157 P, Edwardsville IL 62025		R	2*	<.1

Rank	Company Name—*Executive Officer*	Address, City, State, Zip	Phone	Type	Fin	Empls
3637	Work Technology Corp—*E Jackson Hall*	255 Elm St Ste 300, West Somerville MA 02144	617-625-5888	R	2*	<.1
3638	Wrightsoft Corp—*Bill Wright*	131 Hartwell Ave, Lexington MA 02421	781-862-8719	R	2*	<.1
3639	AIQ Systems Div—*Jay Kaeppel*	PO Box 34764, Reno NV 89533	775-747-8404	S	2*	<.1
3640	Aldebaron Inc—*James Brown*	15839 Crabbs Branch Wa, Rockville MD 20855	301-670-0858	R	2*	<.1
3641	Easy Soft Inc—*William Mayweather III*	212 North Center Dr, North Brunswick NJ 08902	732-398-0136	R	2*	<.1
3642	ESHA Research Inc—*Elizabeth Hands*	PO Box 13028, Salem OR 97309	503-585-6242	R	2*	<.1
3643	FORMation mg Inc—*Daniel G Forster*	30221 Aventura, Rancho Santa Margarita CA 92688	949-598-8890	R	2*	<.1
3644	Metasystems Inc	13700 State Rd Ste 1, North Royalton OH 44133	440-526-1454	R	2*	<.1
3645	PRODATA Computer Services Inc—*Allen Hartley*	2809 S 160th St, Omaha NE 68130	402-697-7575	R	2*	<.1
3646	Sensible Software Inc—*Dave Tucker*	218 W Patrick St, Frederick MD 21701		R	2*	<.1
3647	Acumen Systems Inc—*Meir Plevinski*	1481 47th St, Brooklyn NY 11219	718-438-5100	R	2*	<.1
3648	Ai Squared (Manchester Center Vermont)—*David Wu*	PO Box 669, Manchester Center VT 05255	802-362-3612	R	2*	<.1
3649	CADint Inc—*Mary Leasure*	16012 N 3rd Dr, Phoenix AZ 85023	303-520-0907	R	2*	<.1
3650	Chemstations Inc—*Nathan Massey*	2901 Wilcrest Ste 305, Houston TX 77042	713-978-7700	R	2*	<.1
3651	Comtek Services LLC	99 Ledgewood Hills Dr, Nashua NH 03062		R	2*	<.1
3652	CSF International Inc—*Eric Severino*	1629 Barber Rd, Sarasota FL 34240	941-379-0881	R	2*	<.1
3653	National Distributor Systems Inc—*Jennifer Hillgen*	2336 Main St, Stratford CT 06615	203-378-6010	R	2*	<.1
3654	Advanced Management Solutions Inc	PO Box 9445, Redlands CA 92375	909-790-4680	R	2*	<.1
3655	Advanced Technologies and Services Inc—*Randall B Guthrie*	1501 Hamburg Tpke 4th, Wayne NJ 07470	973-696-0990	R	2*	<.1
3656	Aspect 1—*Paul Emmons*	PO Box 3328, Flagstaff AZ 86003	623-505-0205	R	2*	<.1
3657	Aspen Leaf Software Inc—*Richard Pedersen*	6000 Greenwood Plz Blv, Greenwood Village CO 80111	303-798-5458	R	2*	<.1
3658	Automated Programming Technologies Inc—*Mark F Blumenau*	4251 Timberview Dr, Howell MI 48843	586-268-3846	R	2*	<.1
3659	Collection Data Systems—*Mike Lim*	2225 1st St Ste 102, Simi Valley CA 93065	805-527-9977	R	2*	<.1
3660	Computer Applications Company Inc—*Jim Isabella*	960 Windham Ct Ste 3, Boardman OH 44512	330-757-3711	R	2*	<.1
3661	Computer Trust Corp—*David Liberman*	One State St Ste 700, Boston MA 02109	617-557-9264	R	2*	<.1
3662	Desloge Oxygen and Medical Equipment—*Bryan M Desloge*	PO Box 12385, Tallahassee FL 32308	850-656-8900	R	2*	<.1
3663	Distinctive Solutions Corp—*Bert Goldberg*	555 Chorro St Ste B, San Luis Obispo CA 93405	805-544-8327	R	2*	<.1
3664	Eagle Software Inc—*Dave Hiechel*	124 Indiana Ave, Salina KS 67401	785-823-7257	R	2*	<.1
3665	Edgil Associates Inc—*Daniel Nadeau*	6 Fortune Dr Ste 201, Billerica MA 01821	978-262-9799	D	2*	<.1
3666	Ensemble Business Software Inc—*Jon Walker*	22250 S Marilyns Ave, Beavercreek OR 97004	503-501-2346	R	2	<.1
3667	Foundation Systems Inc—*Marvin Teller*	890 E 700 N, American Fork UT 84003	801-785-7720	R	2*	<.1
3668	Future Tech Systems Inc—*Leon Stucki*	824 E Main St, Auburn WA 98002	253 939-7552	R	2*	<.1
3669	Indisoft LLC—*Sanjeev Dahiwadkar*	5550 Sterrett Pl Ste 3, Columbia MD 21044	410-730-0667	R	2	<.1
3670	Information Services International	1516 N Elmhurst Rd Ste, Mount Prospect IL 60056	847-222-7150	R	2	<.1
3671	Intusoft—*Lawrence G Meares*	One 2500 Via Cabillo M, San Pedro CA 90731	310-952-0657	R	2*	<.1
3672	Management Software Inc—*Victor Siegle*	75 S Main St, Homer NY 13077		R	2*	<.1
3673	Momentum Data Systems Inc—*Jerry Purcell*	17330 Brookhurst St St, Fountain Valley CA 92708	714-378-5805	R	2*	<.1
3674	PerfectSoftware (Norwalk Connecticut)—*Michael Gabriele* Aspetuck Systems Inc	200 Connecticut Ave, Norwalk CT 06854	203-852-9100	D	2*	<.1
3675	Pontem Software—*Sherry Hood*	215 Dexter, Eaton Rapids MI 48827	517-663-7139	R	2*	<.1
3676	SmartSound Software Inc—*Kevin Klingler*	8550 Balboa Blvd Ste 1, Northridge CA 91325		R	2*	<.1
3677	SoftSource LLC	3112 Maple Ridge Ct, Bellingham WA 98229	360-676-0999	R	2*	<.1
3678	SystemsNet Inc—*Paul DeLaurentis*	400 Lakeside Dr Ste 10, Horsham PA 19044	215-340-1951	R	2*	<.1
3679	Teknon Inc—*Vernon Reynolds*	2932 NW 122nd St Ste 2, Oklahoma City OK 73120	405-755-6710	R	2*	<.1
3680	TimeSaver Software—*Les Brewer*	35 Alegria, Irvine CA 92620		R	2*	<.1
3681	TPS Systems Inc—*Barry J Engelbrecht*	14100 San Pedro Ave St, San Antonio TX 78232	210-496-1984	R	2*	<.1
3682	VI Technology Inc—*Alex Backus*	3700 W Parmer Ln Ste 2, Austin TX 78727	512-327-3348	R	2*	<.1
3683	CYRANO Inc	26 Parker St, Newburyport MA 01950	978-402-0737	R	2*	<.1
3684	Drakontas LLC—*Brian Regli*	200 Federal St Ste 300, Camden NJ 08103	856-283-3327	R	2*	<.1
3685	MicroPress Inc—*Michael Vulis*	68-30 Harrow St, Forest Hills NY 11375	718-575-8038	R	2*	<.1
3686	Transportation Costing Group Inc—*Ken Manning*	1355 Piccard Dr Ste 31, Rockville MD 20850	240-399-0730	R	2*	<.1
3687	AeroSoft Inc—*Bob Walters*	2000 Kraft Dr Ste 1400, Blacksburg VA 24060	540-557-1900	R	2*	<.1
3688	Agent Systems Inc—*Brian Waters*	PO Box 906, Addison TX 75001	972-774-0400	R	2*	<.1
3689	Amplexus Corp—*Ken Levin*	7665 Redwood Blvd Ste, Novato CA 94945	415-897-3700	R	2*	<.1
3690	API International Inc—*Mark Watson*	11600 Manchaca Rd Ste, Austin TX 78748	512-280-4391	R	2*	<.1
3691	Artifice Inc—*Kevin Matthews*	PO Box 1588, Eugene OR 97440	541-345-7421	R	2*	<.1
3692	Balboa Software—*Harry Hahne*	PO Box 3751, Scottsdale AZ 85271		R	2*	<.1
3693	Bayern Company Inc—*Greg Bayern*	2730 W Agua Fria Frwy, Phoenix AZ 85027	623-298-5228	R	2*	<.1
3694	Comprose Inc—*Kathy Anton*	9648 Olive Blvd Ste 20, Olivette MO 63132		R	2*	<.1
3695	Computer Detailing Corp	472 Second St Pke 128, Southampton PA 18966	215-938-6860	R	2*	<.1
3696	Computer Software for Professionals Inc	5346 College Ave, Oakland CA 94618	510-547-8159	R	2*	<.1
3697	Computyme	980 Old York Rd, Abington PA 19001	215-886-8520	R	2*	<.1
3698	Comsec LLC—*Bob Taylor*	16 Palmyra Ln, Palm Coast FL 32164	386-585-3572	R	2*	<.1
3699	Convenience Store Automation Inc—*Paul Metko*	2501 S Oneida St, Appleton WI 54915	920-830-9575	R	2*	<.1
3700	Cosmic Patterns—*Fei Cochrane*	6212 NW 43rd St Ste B, Gainesville FL 32653	352-373-1504	R	2*	<.1
3701	Cybra Corp—*Harold Brand*	1 Executive Blvd, Yonkers NY 10701	914-963-6600	R	2*	<.1
3702	Data Plus Inc—*Bruce Bensetler*	55 Middlesex StSte 219, North Chelmsford MA 01863	978-888-6300	R	2*	<.1
3703	Data-Trak Inc	PO Box 2444, Friendswood TX 77546		S	2*	<.1
3704	DV Studio Technologies LLC—*Ash Pahwa*	2740 S Harbor Blvd Ste, Santa Ana CA 92704	714-241-7901	R	2*	<.1
3705	EDGAR Inc—*Peter Caswell*	332 Pine St Ste 202, San Francisco CA 94104	415-986-3456	R	2*	<.1
3706	Electrocon International Inc—*Paul F McGuire*	405 Little Lake Dr Ste, Ann Arbor MI 48103	734-761-8612	R	2*	<.1
3707	Executive Technologies Inc—*Jim Geer*	5346 Stadium Trace Pkw, Birmingham AL 35205	205-985-7686	R	2	<.1
3708	Financial Navigator International—*Edward Van Deman*	883 N Shoreline Blvd R, Mountain View CA 94043	650-962-0300	R	2*	<.1
3709	Fleet Computing International Inc	PO Box 1600, Alamogordo NM 88311	575-434-2323	R	2*	<.1
3710	Flow Science Inc—*Tony Hirt*	683 Harkle Rd Ste A, Santa Fe NM 87505	505-982-0088	R	2*	<.1
3711	Frontline Systems Inc—*Daniel Fylstra*	PO Box 4288, Incline Village NV 89450	775-831-0300	R	2*	<.1
3712	FUND E-Z Development Corp	106 Corporate Park Dr, White Plains NY 10604		R	2*	<.1
3713	GAMS Development Corp—*Alexander Meeraur*	1217 Potomac St NW, Washington DC 20007	202-342-0180	R	2*	<.1
3714	Group 42 Inc CP Software Group Inc	715 Sutter St, Folsom CA 95630		S	2*	<.1
3715	Hawkeye Information Systems—*Richard Burcham*	PO Box 2167, Fort Collins CO 80522	970-498-9000	R	2*	<.1
3716	Hendela Systems Consultants Inc—*Art Hendela*	163 E Main St Ste 314, Little Falls NJ 07424		R	2*	<.1
3717	Icas Computer Systems Inc—*Rudy Ventker*	44 N Morris St, Dover NJ 07801	973-366-1900	R	2*	<.1
3718	Image Advantage—*Michael Lyons*	55 Shuman Blvd Ste 250, Naperville IL 60563	630-904-7150	R	2*	<.1
3719	Infometrix Inc—*Brian Rohrback*	10634 E Riverside Dr S, Bothell WA 98011	425-402-1450	R	2*	<.1
3720	Inner Media Inc—*Inner Medias*	60 Plain Rd, Hollis NH 03049	603-465-3216	R	2*	<.1
3721	ITEDO Software LLC Parametric Technology Corp	140 Kendrick St, Needham MA 02494	781-370-5000	S	2*	<.1
3722	Lexington Technology Inc	18021 Sky Park Cir Ste, Irvine CA 92614	949-428-7888	R	2*	<.1
3723	Logical Solutions Inc—*Richard S Music*	425 Broadhollow Rd, Melville NY 11747	516-731-1314	R	2*	<.1

Note: An asterisk (*) indicates an estimated financial figure. The company type code used is as follows: R = Private, P = Public, S = Private Subsidiary, B = Public Subsidiary, D = Division, J = Joint Venture, I = Investment Fund.

COMPANY RANKINGS BY SALES WITHIN 4-DIGIT SIC

Rank	Company Name—*Executive Officer*	Address, City, State, Zip	Phone	Type	Fin	Empls
3724	Manning NavComp Inc—*Robert W Thompson*	13809 Research Blvd St, Austin TX 78750	512-918-0700	R	2*	<.1
3725	Mark V Systems Ltd—*Chag Sameach*	16400 Ventura Blvd Ste, Encino CA 91436	818-995-7671	R	2*	<.1
3726	Methods and Solutions Inc—*Judith Bliss*	4400 E Broadway Blvd S, Tucson AZ 85711	520-888-1800	R	2*	<.1
3727	Michaels Ross and Cole Ltd—*Joe Stangarone*	555 Waters Edge Ste 12, Lombard IL 60148	630-916-0662	R	2*	<.1
3728	Micro Craft Inc (Huntsville Alabama)—*Eric Vaughan*	123 Fairington Rd, Huntsville AL 35806	256-830-9746	R	2*	<.1
3729	MTW Solutions LLC—*Randy Arnold*	1756 Southridge Dr, Jefferson City MO 65109	573-893-7997	R	2*	<.1
3730	NetResults Corp—*Jack Bates*	PO Box 61957, Sunnyvale CA 94088		R	2*	<.1
3731	Nevrona Designs—*Mack McLendon*	5301 S Superstition Mo, Gold Canyon AZ 85218		R	2*	<.1
3732	OAS Software Corp—*Anthony G Shaneen*	3755 E Main St Ste 100, Saint Charles IL 60174		R	2*	<.1
3733	Online Computers Inc—*Paul Byrne*	181 Notre Dame St, Westfield MA 01085	413-568-2777	R	2*	<.1
3734	Perennial Inc—*Barry Hedquist*	15810 Miradero Ave Ste, San Jose CA 95127	408-347-7800	R	2*	<.1
3735	Prime Label Consultants Inc—*Elizabeth Bechtold*	PO Box 15240, Washington DC 20003	202-546-3333	R	2*	<.1
3736	Queue Inc—*Jonathan Kantrowitz*	One Controls Dr, Shelton CT 06484	203-446-8100	R	2*	<.1
3737	Recital Corporation Inc—*Barry Mavin*	100 Cummings Ctr Ste 3, Beverly MA 01915	978-921-5594	R	2*	<.1
3738	Responsive Systems Co—*Joel Goldstein*	281 Hwy 79, Morganville NJ 07751	732-972-1261	R	2*	<.1
3739	Roughneck Systems Inc	107 E US Hwy 80, Forney TX 75126	972-552-5204	R	2*	<.1
3740	RPD Inc—*Robert Davidson*	PO Box 1189, Cheshire CT 06410	203-271-7991	R	2*	<.1
3741	Sax Software Corp—*Mike Sax*	2852 Willamette St Ste, Eugene OR 97405	541-344-2235	R	2*	<.1
3742	Show-Me Software LLC	3769 E Evergreen, Springfield MO 65803	417-877-9494	R	2*	<.1
3743	Smart Source Corp—*Mike Curtin*	3 New England Executiv, Burlington MA 01803		R	2*	<.1
3744	SoftQuest Corp—*Sam Rifaey*	1 Selleck St Ste 510, Norwalk CT 06855		R	2*	<.1
3745	Strategic Data and Telecom Inc—*Charles Borso*	121 S Webster St, Naperville IL 60540	630-355-7331	R	2*	<.1
3746	Tele Type Co Inc	44 School St 10th Fl, Boston MA 02108	617-542-6220	R	2*	<.1
3747	Testmasters Inc—*Larry Cooke*	5938 Priestly Dr Ste 1, Carlsbad CA 92008	760-579-0887	R	2*	<.1
3748	Tetrad Computer Applications Inc	Po Box 5007, Ferndale WA 98248	360-734-3318	R	2*	<.1
3749	Triumph Learning LLC—*William Zuberbuhler*	7702 Gunston Plz, Lorton VA 22079		S	2*	<.1
3750	VersaForm Systems Corp—*Joe Landau*	591 W Hamilton Ave Ste, Campbell CA 95008	408-370-2662	R	2*	<.1
3751	Wise Software Solutions Inc—*Andy Wise*	2700 E 9th St Ste 100, Newberg OR 97132	503-554-8855	R	2*	<.1
3752	Ziegner Technologies Inc—*Tim Ziegner*	7514 N Mopac Expy Ste, Austin TX 78731	512-372-8000	R	2*	<.1
3753	Zygote Media Group Inc—*Bryan Brandenburg*	1045 S 500 E Ste 200, American Fork UT 84003	801-765-4141	R	2*	<.1
3754	Applied Software Inc	PO Box 566, New Hope PA 18938	215-297-9441	R	2*	<.1
3755	Archway Systems Inc—*Mike Lazear*	2134 Main St Ste 160, Huntington Beach CA 92648	714-374-0440	R	2*	<.1
3756	GeneXus Inc—*Breogan Gonda*	400 N Michigan Ave Ste, Chicago IL 60611	312-836-9152	S	2*	<.1
3757	LANDTECH Data Corp—*Wyatt Bell*	1460 Royal Palm Beach, Royal Palm Beach FL 33411	561-790-1265	R	2*	<.1
3758	Mobile Solutions Inc—*Brian Kovalsky*	14720 Harrisville Rd, Mount Airy MD 21771	909-790-3058	R	2*	<.1
3759	Pulsar Systems Inc—*Carl Dula*	271 Rte 46 W Ste H209, Fairfield NJ 07004	973-227-8440	R	2*	<.1
3760	TOSC International Inc—*Glenn Stancil*	550 Post Oak Blvd Ste, Houston TX 77027	713-961-1201	R	2	<.1
3761	Wilson WindowWare Inc—*Morrie Wilson*	5421 California Ave SW, Seattle WA 98136	206-938-1740	R	2*	<.1
3762	World Information Systems Inc—*Llyod McCall*	624-F Guilford College, Greensboro NC 27409		R	2*	<.1
3763	38 Caliber—*Kenneth Locke*	451 W Bonita Ave Ste 1, San Dimas CA 91773	909-394-1724	R	2*	<.1
3764	Applied Biomathematics Corp—*Richard Belzer*	100 N Country Rd, Setauket NY 11733	631-751-4350	R	2*	<.1
3765	APPX Software Inc—*Steven Frizzell*	11363 San Jose Blvd St, Jacksonville FL 32223	904-880-5560	R	2*	<.1
3766	Arial Software LLC—*Mike Adams*	1501 Stampede Ave Ste, Cody WY 82414	949-218-3852	R	2*	<.1
3767	Bruce Bell and Associates Inc—*Perry Williams*	PO Box 400, Canon City CO 81215	719-275-1661	R	2*	<.1
3768	Business Resource Software Inc—*Kylon Gustin*	1779 Wells Branch Pky, Austin TX 78728	512-251-7541	R	2*	<.1
3769	Celantra Management Solutions—*Hans Kolbe*	3722 21st St, San Francisco CA 94114	415-824-8344	R	2*	<.1
3770	CMX Systems Inc—*Chuck Behrmann*	12276 San Jose Blvd St, Jacksonville FL 32223	904-880-1840	R	2*	<.1
3771	Data Description Inc—*Paul F Velleman*	PO Box 4555, Ithaca NY 14852	607-257-1000	R	2*	<.1
3772	Douloi Automation Inc—*J Randolph Andrews*	3517 Ryder St, Santa Clara CA 95051	408-735-6942	R	2*	<.1
3773	Entisoft—*John Kallie*	149 S Barrington Ct St, Los Angeles CA 90049	310-472-3736	R	2*	<.1
3774	Genesistems Inc—*Eric Muench*	1900 W Bloomfield Rd, Honeoye Falls NY 14472	585-475-9180	R	2*	<.1
3775	ITP Business Communications Inc	PO Box 866, Hickory NC 28603	828-322-6261	R	2*	<.1
3776	Jetsoft Development Co	629 Old State Rt 74 St, Cincinnati OH 45244	513-528-8668	R	2*	<.1
3777	K and R Custom Software Inc—*Thomas Rees*	453 McLaws Cir Ste 2, Williamsburg VA 23185	757-229-5454	R	2*	<.1
3778	Logic eXtension Resources	435 Marina Dr, Georgetown SC 29440	843-520-2992	D	2*	<.1
3779	Media Management Systems Inc—*Cliff Johnson*	PO Box 870027, Stone Mountain GA 30087	770-979-8855	R	2*	<.1
3780	Mystic Management Systems Inc—*Robert Sullivan*	190 West Town St, Norwich CT 06360	860-887-2900	R	2*	<.1
3781	People Sciences Inc	52 Richard J Glattly D, Denville NJ 07834	973-328-4040	R	2*	<.1
3782	Pro-Ware—*John J Fattee*	3909 S 147th St Ste 13, Omaha NE 68144	402-861-8800	R	2*	<.1
3783	Second Nature Software Inc	8626 NW Lakeshore Ave, Vancouver WA 98665	360-737-4170	R	2*	<.1
3784	SH Pierce and Co—*Steve Hollinger*	21 Wormwood St St, Boston MA 02210	617-338-2222	R	2*	<.1
3785	Silvaco Inc—*Ivan Pesic*	4701 Patrick Henry Dr, Santa Clara CA 95054	408-567-1000	R	2*	<.1
3786	Surfside Software Inc—*Robert W Fellows*	PO Box 1505, East Orleans MA 02643	508-255-1120	R	2*	<.1
3787	TTG Inc—*David Pinals*	209 Burlington Rd Ste, Bedford MA 01730	781-272-8900	R	2*	<.1
3788	Yamada Science and Art Corp—*Ted Yamada PhD*	13 Heiwa Dr, Santa Fe NM 87506	505-989-7351	R	2*	<.1
3789	Apago Inc—*Dwight Kelly*	4080 McGinnis Ferry Rd, Alpharetta GA 30005	770-619-1884	R	2*	<.1
3790	Compass Software Solutions—*Dick O'Bryan*	9509 US Hwy 42 Ste 108, Prospect KY 40059	502-228-7805	R	2*	<.1
3791	Corelis Inc—*George B LaFever*	13100 Alondra Blvd, Cerritos CA 90703	562-926-6727	S	2*	<.1
3792	CreativeSoft Inc—*Linda Rose*	21201 Victory Blvd Ste, Woodland Hills CA 91303	818-226-1227	D	2*	<.1
3793	David Groth and Associates Inc—*David Groth*	8700 Schaal Rd, Burlington WI 53105	847-296-9675	R	2*	<.1
3794	European Mikrograph Corp	3031 Branch St, Sacramento CA 95815	916-923-3520	R	2*	<.1
3795	Fitnesoft Inc—*Bruce Bastian*	1455 S 185 W, Orem UT 84058	801-812-8187	R	2*	<.1
3796	Gefen Inc—*Hagai Gefen*	20600 Nordhoff St, Chatsworth CA 91311	818-772-9100	R	2*	<.1
3797	Graphsim Entertainment	5015 Addison Cir Ste 4, Addison TX 75001	972-386-7575	R	2*	<.1
3798	Hi-Tech Advisers	PO Box 129, Ravena NY 12143	518-731-1100	R	2*	<.1
3799	Lakeshore Group Ltd—*Robert Klenke*	5723 Superior Ste A1, Baton Rouge LA 70816	225-292-7422	R	2*	<.1
3800	Manta Technologies Inc	6850 Vista Lodge Loop, Castle Rock CO 80108		R	2*	<.1
3801	Printers Software Inc—*Paul N Greico*	3665 Bee Ridge Rd Ste, Sarasota FL 34233	941-923-9010	R	2*	<.1
3802	Pst Technologies Inc—*John Dewey*	1033 Sterling Rd Ste 1, Herndon VA 20170	703-707-0911	R	2*	<.1
3803	Rinda Technologies Inc—*Edward Rinda*	4563 N Elston Ave, Chicago IL 60630	773-736-6633	R	2*	<.1
3804	Rothschild Strategies Unlimited LLC—*William Rothschild*	PO Box 7568, Wilton CT 06897	203-846-6898	R	2*	<.1
3805	Sirius GT Inc—*Larry Kaufman*	7229 Taylorsville Rd S, Huber Heights OH 45424	937-237-4849	R	2*	<.1
3806	VITAL Inc (Plano Texas)—*Rohit Mehrotra*	PO Box 260674, Plano TX 75026	972-378-3843	R	2*	<.1
3807	Active Ink Software Inc—*Allan Warren*	500 Chaparral Dr, Paradise CA 95969	949-363-6903	R	2*	<.1
3808	Advantage Systems—*Brain Lynch*	2 Executive Cir Ste 15, Irvine CA 92614	949-250-0260	R	2*	<.1
3809	AJS Publishing Inc—*Jack Carter*	PO Box 83220, Los Angeles CA 90083	310-215-9145	R	2*	<.1
3810	Applied Ideas Inc—*Pia Maffei*	30370 Via Brisa, Temecula CA 92592	909-587-8245	R	2*	<.1
3811	Business Software Systems Inc	PO Box 7416, Fairfax Station VA 22039	703-503-5600	R	2*	<.1
3812	CAE-Link Corp (Albuquerque New Mexico)	PO Box 14455, Albuquerque NM 87191	505-717-4178	R	2*	<.1
3813	CaneFire Software	261 Kekuanaoa St, Hilo HI 96720	808-969-1166	R	2*	<.1

Rank	Company Name—*Executive Officer*	Address, City, State, Zip	Phone	Type	Fin	Empls
3814	CASPR Library Systems Inc—*Norman Kline*	100 Park Center Plz Rm, San Jose CA 95113	408-741-2322	R	2*	<.1
3815	Competence Software Inc—*Jack Welch*	PO Box 353, Clearwater FL 33757	727-298-0341	R	2*	<.1
3816	Comprompter Inc—*Ralph King*	1601 Calendona Ste E, La Crosse WI 54603	608-785-7766	R	2*	<.1
3817	Computerized Management of Vehicles Inc	100 S Marion Rd, Sioux Falls SD 57107		R	2*	<.1
3818	Custom Computing Inc—*Gerald Beck*	5172 E 65th St, Indianapolis IN 46220	317-579-2525	R	2*	<.1
3819	Data Tech Communications Inc—*Terry Sams*	1495 Hembree Rd Ste 13, Roswell GA 30076	770-664-1668	R	2*	<.1
3820	Data Workers—*Bill Todd*	Po Box 25808, Santa Ana CA 92799	714-546-5558	R	2*	<.1
3821	Design Simulation Technologies Inc—*Alan Wegienka*	43311 Joy Rd Ste 237, Canton MI 48187	734-446-6935	R	2*	<.1
3822	DVO Enterprises Inc—*Daniel Oaks*	620 E Windsor Ct, Alpine UT 84004	801-492-1290	R	2*	<.1
3823	HydroCad Software Solutions LLC—*Peter Smart*	PO Box 477, Chocorua NH 03817	603-323-8666	R	2*	<.1
3824	ID Insight Inc—*Adam Elliott*	3673 Lexington Ave N, Northfield MN 55057	651-291-3557	R	2*	<.1
3825	Ideaform Inc—*Jeff Bezos*	2197 236th Blvd, Fairfield IA 52556	641-472-7256	R	2*	<.1
3826	InfoUse—*Susan Stoddard*	2560 9th St Ste 320, Berkeley CA 94710	510-549-6520	R	2*	<.1
3827	Innovak International Inc—*David Watson*	119 Boy St, Spartanburg SC 29303		R	2*	<.1
3828	Interaction Research Institute Inc—*Thomas D Affourtit*	4428 Rockcrest Dr, Fairfax VA 22032	703-978-0313	R	2*	<.1
3829	International Expert Systems Inc	6300 Richmond Ave, Houston TX 77057		R	2*	<.1
3830	International Information Services—*Dennis Fleming*	2337 Hemlock Farms, Hawley PA 18428	570-775-7593	R	2*	<.1
3831	JobTime Systems Inc—*Randy Brite*	PO Box 6100, San Mateo CA 94403	650-570-7900	R	2*	<.1
3832	Kisco Information Systems—*Richard C Loeber*	89 Church St, Saranac Lake NY 12983	518-897-5002	R	2*	<.1
3833	Liaison Software Company LLC	2021 E 4th St Ste 218, Santa Ana CA 92705	714-543-9877	R	2*	<.1
3834	Management Information Control Systems Inc—*Cesar Bosio*	2025 9th St, Los Osos CA 93402		R	2*	<.1
3835	Mariner Software Inc—*Michael Wray*	401 N 3rd St Ste 570, Minneapolis MN 55401	612-529-3770	R	2*	<.1
3836	Mercury International Technology Inc—*Ralph Gobeli*	20 E 5th St Ste 1170, Tulsa OK 74137	918-492-1677	R	2*	<.1
3837	New Light Industries Ltd—*Stephen McGrew*	9715 W Sunset Hwy, Spokane WA 99224	509-456-8321	R	2*	<.1
3838	OnLine ToolWorks Corp—*Charles Rice*	16055 SW Walker Rd Ste, Beaverton OR 97006	503-297-0609	R	2*	<.1
3839	ParaComp Inc—*Harry Keller*	13908 Figi Way Ste 163, Marina Del Rey CA 90292	310-802-1600	R	2*	<.1
3840	PC Dynamics Inc—*Peter Avritch*	6104 Bryndale Ave, Oak Park CA 91377	818-889-1741	R	2*	<.1
3841	Pharaoh Information Services Inc—*Mike Kenyon*	15707 Rockfield Blvd S, Irvine CA 92618		R	2*	<.1
3842	Piney Mountain Press Inc—*Cliffe Rice*	PO Box 86, Cleveland GA 30528		R	2*	<.1
3843	Pointcross Inc—*Suresh Madhavan*	1291 E Hillsdale Blvd, Foster City CA 94404	650-350-1900	R	2*	<.1
3844	Poly Software International Inc—*John Wang*	PO Box 60, Pearl River NY 10965	845-735-9301	R	2*	<.1
3845	RICS Software—*Dave Becker*	7602 E 88th Pl, Indianapolis IN 46256		R	2*	<.1
3846	SCS Engineering Inc	23430 Hawthorne Blvd S, Torrance CA 90505	310-373-4243	R	2*	<.1
3847	Tetradyne Software Inc—*JOHN SON*	PO Box 2677, Castro Valley CA 94546	510-581-7639	R	2*	<.1
3848	Trust Service Company Inc—*Joe Whittle*	50 Millstone Rd Bldg 4, East Windsor NJ 08520	302-234-0850	R	2*	<.1
3849	UniTrends Software Corp—*Michael Coney*	7 Technology Cir Ste 1, Columbia SC 29203	803-454-0300	R	2*	<.1
3850	Zero Virtual—*Reynaldo Gil*	530 Lytton Ave Ste 200, Palo Alto CA 94301	650-617-3366	R	2*	<.1
3851	Abacus Business Systems Inc—*Gary Labonte*	4 Plain St E, Berkley MA 02779	508-822-8873	R	2*	<.1
3852	Accidental Software—*Terry Hastlings*	13245 Skiomah Rd, Apple Valley CA 92308	760-247-2804	R	2*	<.1
3853	Advanced Medical Psychiatric Software Inc—*Rudy Chavez*	180 N San Gabriel, Pasadena CA 91107	626-905-5029	R	2*	<.1
3854	Agent Software Corp—*W Allan Goode*	685 Rock Ct, Mountain View CA 94043	650-964-8010	R	2*	<.1
3855	Alba Editorial Inc—*Joseph Roonoy*	19706-B One Norman Blv, Cornelius NC 28031	704-894-0639	R	2*	<.1
3856	Alem Computer Software Inc—*Tesfaldet A Meharenna*	16440 Monterey Rd, Cerritos CA 90703	562-802-8087	R	2*	<.1
3857	Alpha-Omega Software Technologies Inc—*Philip Houghtaling*	7730 Jason Ave, Canoga Park CA 91304	818-399-3653	R	2*	<.1
3858	Analysis and Information Services Inc—*Mark Hambleton*	PO Box 192, Timonium MD 21093	410-561-0778	R	2*	<.1
3859	AppFinity Software Corp—*Dennis Lo*	3450 Sacramento St Ste, San Francisco CA 94118	415-668-1100	R	2*	<.1
3860	Araize Inc—*Joseph Scarano*	130 Iowa Lane Ste 102, Cary NC 27511	919-460-3990	R	2*	<.1
3861	Arehart Consulting—*Patrick Arehart*	8921 Treeland Ln, Dayton OH 45458	937-439-0444	R	2*	<.1
3862	Arity Corp—*Peter Gabel*	200 Friberg Pkwy, Westborough MA 01581	978-897-0004	R	2*	<.1
3863	AstroGraph Software Inc—*Henry Seltzer*	251 Dufour St, Santa Cruz CA 95060	831-425-6548	R	2*	<.1
3864	Azalea Software Inc—*Jerry Whiting*	PO Box 16660, Seattle WA 98116	206-336-9575	R	2*	<.1
3865	Az-Tech Software Inc—*Bill J Lewis*	201 E Franklin St Ste, Richmond MO 64085	816-533-7206	R	2*	<.1
3866	Balenz Software Inc—*Ram Raja*	3335 Kifer Rd, Santa Clara CA 95051	408-737-7758	R	2*	<.1
3867	Benedict Group Inc	900 Small Dr, Elizabeth City NC 27909	252-330-4892	R	2*	<.1
3868	Browntech Inc—*Clifton Brown*	19 Twilight Dr, Foxborough MA 02035	508-543-0211	R	2*	<.1
3869	Bruce Jones Design Inc—*Bruce Jones*	661 Washington St, Norwood MA 02062	781-255-7171	R	2*	<.1
3870	Buell Consulting Inc—*William P Buell*	2324 University Ave W, Saint Paul MN 55114	651-225-0792	R	2*	<.1
3871	Canary Labs Inc—*Gary Stern*	PO Box 208, Martinsburg PA 16662	814-793-3770	R	2*	<.1
3872	Capital Computer Solutions Inc—*Mitchell Nichols*	32985 Hamilton Ct Ste, Farmington Hills MI 48334	248-987-6100	R	2*	<.1
3873	Captools Co	PO Box 9, Issaquah WA 98027	425-391-4250	R	2*	<.1
3874	Carey Systems Inc—*Donald F Brown*	9800 Shelard Pky Ste 2, Plymouth MN 55441	763-593-5131	R	2*	<.1
3875	Cascade Data Solutions—*John Miller*	PO Box 2677, Albany OR 97321	541-924-5714	R	2*	<.1
3876	Champlain Software Inc Para Research Inc	85 Eastern Ave, Gloucester MA 01930	978-282-1114	S	2*	<.1
3877	Chart Software—*Mark Watson*	352 Flanders Dr, Indialantic FL 32903	321-729-0705	R	2*	<.1
3878	Coaxis Inc	PO Box 281, Huntsville AL 35804	256-882-6820	R	2*	<.1
3879	CoLinear Systems Inc—*Scott Weaver*	2650 Holcomb Bridge Rd, Alpharetta GA 30022	770-643-0000	R	2*	<.1
3880	Comm-Pro Associates Inc—*Jim Jacobs*	25852 McBean Pkwy Ste, Santa Clarita CA 91355		R	2*	<.1
3881	Computer Consulting and Software Inc—*Mike O'Brien*	400 China Rose Ct, Lincoln CA 95648	949-855-9020	R	2*	<.1
3882	Conceptual Systems International—*Steve Forrer*	5 Pinebark Ct, Brinklow MD 20862	301-774-9700	R	2*	<.1
3883	Cornucopia Software—*Phil Manfield*	1205 Brighton Ave, Albany CA 94706	510-528-7000	R	2*	<.1
3884	CounterSign Software Inc—*Jonathan Emery*	4183 First St Ste Q, Pleasanton CA 94566	925-462-1913	R	2*	<.1
3885	Crystal Software Inc—*Robert Hansen*	329 Fire Lake Rd, Crystal Falls MI 49920	906-822-7934	R	2*	<.1
3886	Database Creations LLC—*Diana Reid*	44 Scott Dr, Vernon CT 06066	860-644-5891	R	2*	<.1
3887	Database Publishing Software Inc	9 Bartlet St Ste 376, Andover MA 01810	978-686-7615	R	2*	<.1
3888	Datacut Inc—*Hal Levy*	466 Saw Mill River Rd, Ardsley NY 10502	914-693-6000	S	2*	<.1
3889	DC Micro Development Inc—*David Cecil*	1890 Star Shoot PkwySt, Lexington KY 40509	859-317-2352	R	2*	<.1
3890	DeltaOne Software Inc—*Greg Fox*	2841-G Saturn St, Brea CA 92821	714-528-7226	R	2*	<.1
3891	Design 3000 Inc—*Ken Vestal*	1700 E Main St Ste D, Hendersonville TN 37075	615-264-2565	R	2*	<.1
3892	Diakonia Software Co—*Edward Johnson*	PO Box 618, Manchester MO 63011	314-256-9073	R	2*	<.1
3893	Diversified Alliances Inc—*Larry Taylor*	36 Greenwood Hill St, Stamford CT 06902	203-977-1581	R	2*	<.1
3894	DP Software Inc—*Ronald Pearce*	39 Mine St, Flemington NJ 08822	908-806-0447	R	2*	<.1
3895	Dymax Systems Inc—*Ralph Barnhardt*	3455 Rte 66, Neptune NJ 07753	732-918-2424	R	2*	<.1
3896	Dynamic Traders Group Inc—*Robert Miner*	6336 N Oracle Rd Ste 3, Tucson AZ 85704	312-893-5151	R	2*	<.1
3897	Electronic Recordkeeping Services Inc—*Don Hyerman*	13528 Water Crest Dr, Fishers IN 46038	317-713-1000	R	2*	<.1
3898	Engineering Dynamics Corp (Beaverton Oregon)—*Terry D Day*	8625 SW Cascade Ave St, Beaverton OR 97008	503-644-4500	R	2*	<.1
3899	Entegration Inc—*Chennapan Padmanaban*	830 Stewart Dr Ste B7, Sunnyvale CA 94085		R	2*	<.1
3900	Enterprise Solutions Inc—*John R Ruehle*	4746 44th Ave SW Ste 1, Seattle WA 98116		R	2*	<.1
3901	Estima—*Thomas Doan*	1560 Sherman Ave Ste 5, Evanston IL 60201	847-864-8772	R	2*	<.1
3902	Extended Software Solutions LLC—*Paul Lech*	453 S Willard St, Burlington VT 05401	302-200-9800	R	2*	<.1

Note: An asterisk (*) indicates an estimated financial figure. The company type code used is as follows: R = Private, P = Public, S = Private Subsidiary, B = Public Subsidiary, D = Division, J = Joint Venture, I = Investment Fund.

COMPANY RANKINGS BY SALES WITHIN 4-DIGIT SIC

Rank	Company Name—*Executive Officer*	Address, City, State, Zip	Phone	Type	Fin	Empls
3903	Florida Software Inc—*King Woolf*	435 Ericksen Ave NE St, Bainbridge Island WA 98110		S	2*	<.1
3904	Fred's Micro Inc—*Fred Rennpferd*	11144 US Hwy 169 S, Amboy MN 56010	507-674-3068	R	2*	<.1
3905	FutureWare Inc—*Raymond Westwater*	475 Wall St, Princeton NJ 08540	609-924-4269	R	2*	<.1
3906	General Cybernation Group Inc—*George Cheng*	2868 Prospect Park Dr, Rancho Cordova CA 95670	916-631-6313	R	2*	<.1
3907	Halloran Software—*Gary Stiffler*	PO Box 75713, Los Angeles CA 90075	818-901-1221	R	2*	<.1
3908	Handshake Software—*Doug Horton*	1455 Alderman Dr, Alpharetta GA 30005	770-777-0920	R	2*	<.1
3909	Harvard Associates Inc—*William R Glass III*	955 Massachusetts Ave, Cambridge MA 02139	508-487-4141	R	2*	<.1
3910	Hillary Software Inc—*Charles Nickerson*	309 Morris Ave, Spring Lake NJ 07762	732-974-8484	R	2*	<.1
3911	Hunnicutt Software Inc—*Sam Hunnicutt*	155 Granada St Ste R, Camarillo CA 93010	805-987-0325	R	2*	<.1
3912	ImageMind Software Inc—*John F Cruz*	426 S 1000 E Apt 405, Salt Lake City UT 84102	801-397-7570	R	2*	<.1
3913	Infinite Resource—*David Phipps*	140 Dominican Dr, San Rafael CA 94901	415-457-7495	R	2*	<.1
3914	Infoflex Inc—*Gerard Menicucci*	PO Box 1596, Burlingame CA 94011	650-270-1019	R	2*	<.1
3915	Infovision Software Inc—*Bruce Elliot*	8842 Goldeneye Ln, Blaine WA 98230		R	2*	<.1
3916	Integrated Productivity Systems Inc—*Doug Elliott*	PO Box 97, Blue Bell PA 19422	215-654-1871	R	2*	<.1
3917	Interactive Solutions Inc (Pleasanton California)—*Bill LaCommare*	2843 Hopyard Rd Ste159, Pleasanton CA 94588	925-485-0702	R	2*	<.1
3918	Leister Productions Inc—*Frank Leister*	PO Box 289, Mechanicsburg PA 17055	717-697-1378	R	2*	<.1
3919	Linn Software Inc—*William E Linn*	PO Box 1135, Conyers GA 30012	770-761-8551	R	2*	<.1
3920	Lumina Decisions Systems Inc—*Max Henrion*	26010 Highland Way, Los Gatos CA 95033	650-212-1212	R	2*	<.1
3921	Magic Teleprompting Inc—*Japji Khalsa*	1390 Waller St, San Francisco CA 94117	415-626-5283	R	2*	<.1
3922	Marietta Design Group Inc—*Robert Tarabella*	82 Plantation Point St, Fairhope AL 36532	251-990-3568	R	2*	<.1
3923	Mariner Software Inc(Minneapolis Minnesota)—*Michael Wray*	401 N 3rd St Ste 570, Minneapolis MN 55401	612-529-3770	R	2*	<.1
3924	Mark/Space Inc—*Brian Hall*	654 N Santa Cruz Ave S, Los Gatos CA 95030	408-293-7299	R	2*	<.1
3925	Marsh Software Systems Inc—*Donald Marsh*	1020-A Central Dr, Concord NC 28027	704-788-9335	R	2*	<.1
3926	Melco Group International Inc—*Erwin Melzer*	4041 Williams Blvd Ste, Kenner LA 70065		R	2*	<.1
3927	Mitten Software Inc—*James Morgan*	2354 W Wayzata Blvd, Long Lake MN 55356	952-745-4941	R	2*	<.1
3928	Monarch Bay Software Inc—*Sarah Phillips*	PO Box 96126, Houston TX 77213	713-450-2800	R	2*	<.1
3929	National Business Data Systems Inc—*Thomas P Collins*	800 Transfer Rd Ste 25, Saint Paul MN 55114		R	2	<.1
3930	Neusys Inc—*Dave Neuendorf*	PO Box 366, Aurora IN 47001	812-926-1828	R	2*	<.1
3931	Next Step Technologies Inc	PO Box 070097, Milwaukee WI 53207	414-744-8101	R	2*	<.1
3932	North Coast Software Inc (Oswego New York)—*George Van Wert*	335 W First St, Oswego NY 13126	315-342-8470	R	2*	<.1
3933	Now Technology Group—*Steven Stern*	300 E Lombard St Ste 8, Baltimore MD 21202		R	2*	<.1
3934	OEA International Inc—*O Ersed Akcasu*	155 E Main Ave Ste 110, Morgan Hill CA 95037	408-778-6747	R	2*	<.1
3935	One Mile Up Inc—*Jim Stein*	7011 Evergreen Ct, Annandale VA 22003	703-642-1177	R	2*	<.1
3936	PAC Software Inc—*Harry Macintosh*	6510 S Xenon St, Littleton CO 80127	303-904-1920	R	2*	<.1
3937	Panasoft Software—*John Telage*	15611 Ventura Blvd, Encino CA 91436		R	2*	<.1
3938	Pendragon Software Corp—*Ivan Phillips*	PO Box 7350, Buffalo Grove IL 60089	847-816-9660	R	2*	<.1
3939	Performance Software Group—*Nick Demos*	12 Hillview Dr, Baltimore MD 21228	410-788-6777	R	2*	<.1
3940	Porter Valley Software Inc—*Lorne Steiner*	810 N Farrell Dr, Palm Springs CA 92262	760-327-5284	R	2*	<.1
3941	Progressive Solutions Inc (Brea California)—*Mark Sarpa*	PO Box 783, Brea CA 92821	714-671-1597	R	2*	<.1
3942	Quality Industrial Solutions—*Daniel Bernacchi*	4633 W US Hwy 6, Union Mills IN 46382	219-767-2356	R	2*	<.1
3943	Questor Systems Inc—*Richard C Schleicher*	3878 Carson St Ste 218, Torrance CA 90503	310-316-9500	R	2*	<.1
3944	Realtrac—*Tom Ingraham* Mindbridge Systems Inc Realtrac Div	PO Box 51476, Irvine CA 92614	949-852-8818	D	2*	<.1
3945	Redoc Inc—*Gerry Stone*	17497 114 Rd, Hoyt KS 66440	785-422-0296	R	2*	<.1
3946	RL Russ and Associates Inc—*Ron L Russ*	3813 Easy St, Alvarado TX 76009	817-790-8267	R	2*	<.1
3947	Roy N Dailey Inc—*Roy N Dailey*	984 N Broadway Ste 505, Yonkers NY 10701	914-963-4401	R	2*	<.1
3948	Salestream Software Inc—*Jeff Frasier*	9050 Pulsar Ct Ste C, Corona CA 92883	951-277-4225	R	2*	<.1
3949	Serengeti Systems Inc—*David Keenan*	1108 Lavaca St Ste 110, Austin TX 78701	512-345-2211	R	2*	<.1
3950	Source III Inc—*John Cosley*	3941 Park Dr Ste20-342, El Dorado Hills CA 95762	916-941-9403	R	2*	<.1
3951	Stephen Computer Services Inc	1857 W Maple Rd E, Walled Lake MI 48390	248-960-3535	R	2*	<.1
3952	Structural Analysis Inc—*Al Morgan*	1405 Weston Ln, Austin TX 78733	512-328-8198	R	2*	<.1
3953	Systemetrics Inc (Cambridge Massachusetts)	153 Lexington Ave, Cambridge MA 02138	617-868-8308	R	2*	<.1
3954	TCA Reservoir Engineering Services Inc	101 County Rd 202, Durango CO 81301	970-385-4810	R	2*	<.1
3955	Telework Analytics International Inc	21300 Highwood Ct, Potomac Falls VA 20165	571-434-7444	R	2*	<.1
3956	Tennyson Maxwell Information Systems Inc—*Michael Del Monte*	627 Rte 9D, Garrison NY 10524	845-214-0633	R	2*	<.1
3957	Tess Data Systems Inc—*Javed Aslam*	4422 FM 1960 W Ste 405, Houston TX 77068	281-440-6943	R	2*	<.1
3958	Thedra Technologies Inc—*Walter R Siekierski*	PO Box 1912, Troy MI 48099	248-689-1089	R	2*	<.1
3959	Thought Communications Inc	PO Box 988, Morgan Hill CA 95038	408-782-7904	R	2*	<.1
3960	Time Gathering Systems	602 N Roan St, Johnson City TN 37601		R	2*	<.1
3961	Trendsetter Software Inc—*Jeff Borowitz*	3419 E Chapman Ave Ste, Orange CA 92869	714-997-9295	R	2*	<.1
3962	Trier Software Inc—*Barbara Aquino*	35440 Thomas Rd, Agua Dulce CA 91390	661-993-8029	R	2*	<.1
3963	Universal Construction Software Inc—*Greg Kirk*	1250 S US Hwy 17-92 La, Longwood FL 32750	407-834-0700	R	2*	<.1
3964	Urbana Software Inc—*Michael Flahaty*	470 Castro St Ste 200, San Francisco CA 94114	415-934-8378	R	2*	<.1
3965	Venustar Software and Engineering Inc—*Dana L Burket*	PO Box 692188, San Antonio TX 78269	210-748-3737	R	2*	<.1
3966	Warehouse Optimization LLC—*Thomas A Moore*	4650 Everal Ln, Franklin TN 37064	615-791-8000	R	2*	<.1
3967	West Portal Software Corp—*Roger H Hofmann*	55 New Montgomery St S, San Francisco CA 94105	415-677-0320	R	2*	<.1
3968	WindoWare Inc—*Jean Vallee*	219 Windsor Castle Dr, Newport News VA 23608	757-886-0116	R	2*	<.1
3969	WineWare Software Corp—*Jeff Weidler*	630 10th St, Paso Robles CA 93446	805-227-0202	R	2*	<.1
3970	XpertRule Software Ltd—*Ian Templeton*	14 Fruit St, Newburyport MA 01950	978-465-5111	R	2*	<.1
3971	Youm-Tzib Software Solutions Inc	9645 Church St, Rancho Cucamonga CA 91730	909-266-1612	R	2*	<.1
3972	ZaxWerks Inc—*Zax Dow*	5724 Camelia Ave, Temple City CA 91780	626-309-9102	R	2*	<.1
3973	Zee Software Solutions Inc—*Shakar Pasumarthi*	20192 Rodriguez Ave, Cupertino CA 95014	408-482-3470	R	2*	<.1
3974	Zeus Concepts LLC—*Robert Schaudt*	1356 Shermer Rd, Northbrook IL 60062	847-291-0410	R	2*	<.1
3975	Accountant's Edge Software Services Inc—*Kevin Smith*	35436 Panorama Dr, Yucaipa CA 92399		R	2*	<.1
3976	Aircraft Designs Inc—*Martin Hollmann*	5 Harris Ct Bldg S, Monterey CA 93940	831-621-8760	R	2*	<.1
3977	Aspirin Software Inc—*Brad Stone*	1799 Croner Ave, Menlo Park CA 94025	650-678-8378	R	2*	<.1
3978	A-Systems Corp—*Arnold Grundvig*	4141 Highland Dr Ste 2, Salt Lake City UT 84124		R	2*	<.1
3979	Auspex Inc—*Richard Newell*	12475 Gulf Fwy Ste G1, Houston TX 77034	713-524-3100	R	2*	<.1
3980	AutoGraph International Inc—*Lisbeth Andersen*	12 S 1st St Ste 819, San Jose CA 95113	408-282-7880	R	2*	<.1
3981	BeachWare Inc—*Tom Gilleland*	4980 N Campbell Ave, Tucson AZ 85718	520-577-8945	R	2*	<.1
3982	Beshton Software Inc—*Dave Wang*	19925 Stevens Creek Bl, Cupertino CA 95014	408-647-6699	R	2*	<.1
3983	BoutellCom Inc—*Tom Boutell*	PO Box 63767, Philadelphia PA 19147	215-574-7655	R	2*	<.1
3984	CAD Technology Corp—*John Boertjens*	PO Box 1117, Franklin NC 28744	828-369-3979	R	2*	<.1
3985	CD Light LLC—*George Chamberlan*	230 N Tranquil Path Dr, The Woodlands TX 77380	281-292-3270	R	2*	<.1
3986	CEG Technologies—*David Johnson*	5 Reeve Rd, Rockville Centre NY 11570	516-678-0275	R	2*	<.1
3987	CFM Inc—*Ronald Cordes*	PO Box 353, Bedford MA 01730	781-275-5258	R	2*	<.1
3988	Computer Graphics Systems Development Corp—*Roy Latham*	2483 Old Middlefield W, Mountain View CA 94043	650-903-4920	R	2*	<.1

Rank	Company Name—*Executive Officer*	Address, City, State, Zip	Phone	Type	Fin	Empls
3989	Computer Operation Resource Group—*Ralph Bosson*	145 Durham Rd Ste 9, Madison CT 06443	203-318-1712	R	2*	<.1
3990	Computer Services Co—*Tom Garrison*	4106 Ruvsam St, Wichita Falls TX 76308	940-696-3010	R	2*	<.1
3991	Core Software Technology—*Joe Paresi*	133 N Altadena Dr 4th, Pasadena CA 91107	626-796-9155	R	2*	<.1
3992	Crest Software Corp—*Russell J Chatfield*	1414 Gold St, Redding CA 96001	530-241-9317	R	2*	<.1
3993	Data Pro Inc—*Donald Ponozzo*	PO Box 457, Plainwell MI 49080	269-685-9214	R	2*	<.1
3994	Deccan Software Inc—*Asokan Selvaraj*	7950 Silverton Ave Ste, San Diego CA 92126	858-449-4554	R	2*	<.1
3995	EHR3 and Associates Inc—*Ernest Rice*	11 Haas Rd Ste 930, Basking Ridge NJ 07920	908-647-1477	R	2*	<.1
3996	Flash Appointments—*Alison Maddox*	920 Hartford Dr, Boulder CO 80305	303-499-4109	R	2*	<.1
3997	Front Row Systems—*Jason Musgrove*	PO Box 49568, Atlanta GA 30359	404-728-1120	R	2*	<.1
3998	Full Information Software Inc—*James Streets*	6417 Loisdale Rd, Springfield VA 22150	703-971-5122	R	2*	<.1
3999	Kim Evans and Associates—*Kim Evans*	10051 Se County Rd 763, Arcadia FL 34266	863-494-6686	R	2*	<.1
4000	KMJ Commuications Inc—*Kent Johnson*	7380 32nd Ave N Ste 20, Minneapolis MN 55427	763-536-9709	R	2*	<.1
4001	Manual Labour Inc—*Bonni Graham*	4079 Governor Dr Ste 3, San Diego CA 92122	619-768-2389	R	2*	<.1
4002	Maxum Development Corp—*John O'Fallon*	PO Box 315, Crystal Lake IL 60039	815-444-0100	R	2*	<.1
4003	Multivariate Software Inc—*Peter M Bentler*	15720 Ventura Blvd, Encino CA 91436	818-906-0740	R	2*	<.1
4004	New Data Systems Inc	19 Claremont Ln, Suffern NY 10901		R	2*	<.1
4005	Noran Engineering Inc—*Dave Weinberg*	5555 Garden Grove Blvd, Westminster CA 92683	714-899-1220	R	2*	<.1
4006	Nullstone Corp	3336 Medallion Ct, Pleasanton CA 94588	925-461-5990	R	2*	<.1
4007	Paladin Software Inc	17110 Petrolia Ct, Ramona CA 92065	760-789-9530	R	2*	<.1
4008	Patton and Patton Software Corp—*Keith Patton*	1796 W Wimbledon Way, Oro Valley AZ 85737	520-638-8738	R	2*	<.1
4009	Professional Systems Corp	1210 E 223rd St Ste 32, Carson CA 90745	310-233-7370	R	2*	<.1
4010	ProminicNet Inc—*Jon Schultz*	PO Box 7301, Champaign IL 61826	217-356-2888	R	2*	<.1
4011	Sigma Six Corp—*Steve Johnson*	PO Box 1106, Hunt Valley MD 21030	410-472-4769	R	2*	<.1
4012	Simple Simon—*John C Harrison*	6628 Willow View Dr, Watauga TX 76148	817-479-3414	R	2*	<.1
4013	Software Arts Inc—*Doug Spencer*	6830 Via Del Oro Ste 1, San Jose CA 95119	408-226-7321	R	2*	<.1
4014	Software Concepts Inc—*Patrick Salsman*	8095 SW Cirrus Dr Ste, Beaverton OR 97008	503-641-1060	R	2*	<.1
4015	Software Unlimited Corp—*June Getty*	922 Lynn Cir, Tupelo MS 38804		R	2*	<.1
4016	Spectrum Software Technology Inc—*Sid Leung*	Atlantic City Internat, Egg Harbor Township NJ 08234	609-645-6882	R	2*	<.1
4017	STI Tech Inc—*Tom Butler*	13304 NE 74th St, Redmond WA 98052	425-558-0559	R	2*	<.1
4018	Symbolic Sound Corp—*Carla Scaletti*	PO Box 2549, Champaign IL 61825	217-355-6273	R	2*	<.1
4019	Synchris Inc—*William L Schrader*	46030 Manekin Plz Ste, Sterling VA 20166	571-434-2982	R	2*	<.1
4020	Tiger Software—*Michael Eisner*	PO Box 9491, San Diego CA 92169	858-273-5900	R	2*	<.1
4021	UDATAnet—*Tom Utley*	13910 US Hwy 330, Upper Sandusky OH 43351	419-294-4141	R	2*	<.1
4022	UniSolutions Associates—*Haral Tsitsivas*	33586 Via Lagos, Dana Point CA 92629	949-488-3960	R	2*	<.1
4023	Visual Access Technology Inc—*Howie Berger*	24 Bank St Ste A, New Milford CT 06776	860-210-2190	R	2*	<.1
4024	VITEC Multimedia USA—*Phillip Wetzel*	1800 Century Blvd NE S, Atlanta GA 30345	404-320-0110	S	2*	<.1
4025	Whiz Integrated Systems Software Incorporated—*Linda Darnell Wade*	18726 S Western Ave S, Gardena CA 90248	310-532-5052	R	2*	<.1
4026	WISCO Computing—*Terry L Jepson*	PO Box 8, Wisconsin Rapids WI 54495	715-423-8189	R	2*	<.1
4027	WM Software Inc—*Michael Monastario*	3660 Center Road Ste 3, Brunswick OH 44212	330-558-0501	R	2*	<.1
4028	WYSIWYG Corp—*Charles Simonyi*	1900 S Sepulveda Blvd, Los Angeles CA 90025	310-575-1991	R	2*	<.1
4029	Zanden Communications Ltd—*Bill Herrin*	1636 N Wells St Ste 30, Chicago IL 60614	312-266-9680	R	2*	<.1
4030	ZGRAF Software Products—*John Jakob*	27905 N 18th Dr, Phoenix AZ 85085	623-234-8129	R	2*	<.1
4031	Aerio Software Inc	37600 Central Ct Ste 2, Newark CA 94560	510-323-2643	R	2*	<.1
4032	Applied Systems and Technologies Inc—*George Bittner*	7794 Hallenbeck Rd, Cleveland NY 13042	315-675-8584	R	2*	<.1
4033	BMA Software Solutions Inc—*Marc LaVecchia*	1057 E Imperial Hwy St, Placentia CA 92870	714-455-2717	R	2*	<.1
4034	Capstone Technology Inc—*Richard L Drolet*	19090 Lambert Lake Rd, Sonora CA 95370	209-532-4595	R	2*	<.1
4035	EnGarde Systems Inc—*Michael Neuman*	18352 S Crossbill Rd, Couer d'Alene ID 83814		R	2*	<.1
4036	Executive Compumetrics Inc—*Stephen A Gierach*	PO Box 95, Tinley Park IL 60477	708-633-1190	R	2*	<.1
4037	Faast Software—*Russ Greenlaw*	3062 E Ave, Livermore CA 94550	925-381-8057	R	2*	<.1
4038	Facility Innovations—*Daniel Nolte*	19510 Buggy Whip Cir, Walnut CA 91789	626-810-8031	R	2*	<.1
4039	Fine Line International—*Bill Lavallie*	19474 State Hwy 88 Ste, Pine Grove CA 95665	209-296-4450	R	2*	<.1
4040	Investment Technologies—*Brian M Rom*	320 E 72 St Ste 9C, New York NY 10021	212-724-7535	R	2*	<.1
4041	Management Planning Systems—*Edward J Degner*	174 E 16th Ave, Eugene OR 97401	541-484-1004	R	2*	<.1
4042	Mind Design Systems—*Kent Bailey*	2727 N Washington Blvd, North Ogden UT 84414	801-782-5544	R	2*	<.1
4043	Mnemonics Inc (Mount Laurel New Jersey)	102 Gaither Dr Ste 4, Mount Laurel NJ 08054	856-234-0970	R	2*	<.1
4044	Nutrition Co—*Carol Byrd-Bredbeder*	PO Box 477, Long Valley NJ 07853	908-876-5580	R	2*	<.1
4045	Open Door Networks Inc—*Alan Oppenheimer*	110 S Laurel St, Ashland OR 97520	541-488-4127	R	2*	<.1
4046	Serendipity Systems Inc—*Eric Sacher*	PO Box 774507, Steamboat Springs CO 80477	720-246-8925	R	2*	<.1
4047	Soundtrek—*David F Castles*	5453 Royal Jasmine Way, Stone Mtn GA 30518	770-831-8515	R	2*	<.1
4048	Southern Technology Group—*Robert McCoy*	619 Fagan Springs Dr S, Huntsville AL 35805	256-532-1991	R	2*	<.1
4049	TNT Software Inc—*Steve Taylor*	2001 Main St, Vancouver WA 98660	360-546-0878	R	2*	<.1
4050	AlphaSoft Marketing International—*Gary Wicklund*	1805 N Carson St Ste 3, Carson City NV 89701	775-883-4040	R	2*	<.1
4051	LavaTurtle Software Inc—*Susan Hope*	20532 El Toro Rd, Mission Viejo CA 92692	949-713-3570	R	2*	<.1
4052	Professional Software Development Corp—*Doran Eskinazi*	5781 Valerie Ave, Woodland Hills CA 91367	818-610-1520	R	2*	<.1
4053	Ventura Educational Systems—*Fred Ventura*	PO Box 1622, Arroyo Grande CA 93421		R	2*	<.1
4054	Catamount Software—*Hardy Macia*	120 Canterbury Shore D, Canterbury NH 03224	802-372-9512	R	2*	<.1
4055	Cobalt Blue LLC	5020 New Chapel Hill W, Cumming GA 30041	678-521-7335	R	2*	<.1
4056	Computer Solutions of Centerville—*Edward K Merrick*	29884 E Trimmer Spring, Sanger CA 93657	559-787-3199	R	2*	<.1
4057	Ecological Linguistics—*Lloyd B Anderson*	PO Box 15156, Washington DC 20003	202-247-7678	R	2*	<.1
4058	Gary R Olhoeft—*Gary R Olhoeft*	PO Box 10870, Golden CO 80401	303-273-3458	R	2*	<.1
4059	Hufnagel Software—*Hank Hufnagel*	PO Box 747, Clarion PA 16214	814-226-5600	R	2*	<.1
4060	Hyperionics Technology LLC—*Greg Kochaniak*	3146 Chestnut St, Murrysville PA 15668	724-964-4441	R	2*	<.1
4061	John Juliano Computer Services Co—*John Juliano*	2152 Willivee Pl, Decatur GA 30033	404-327-6010	R	2*	<.1
4062	MegageM Digital Media—*Dan Wolfe*	620 W El Camino, Santa Maria CA 93454	805-349-1104	R	2*	<.1
4063	Robert Ramey Software Development—*Robert Ramey*	830 Cathedral Vista Ln, Santa Barbara CA 93110	805-569-3793	R	2*	<.1
4064	Ron Scott Photography Inc—*Ron Scott*	2020 Colquitt St, Houston TX 77098	713-529-5868	R	2*	<.1
4065	SYCS Productions—*Steve Yesconis*	233 E Maple St, Palmyra PA 17078	717-805-9714	R	2*	<.1
4066	Web Broadcasting Corp—*Eric Vickford*	236 Hamilton Ave, Palo Alto CA 94301	650-274-4652	R	2*	<.1
4067	Insync Inc—*Jeff Balaguras*	539 Bryant St Ste 404, San Francisco CA 94107	415-546-7962	R	2*	<.1
4068	Irrc Solutions—*Rajan Singh*	2518 Alvin St, Mountain View CA 94043	404-513-5867	R	2*	<.1
4069	Systech Software Products Inc—*John R Mull*	PO Box 1384, Bolingbrook IL 60440	630-759-4805	R	2	<.1
4070	Macro Enter Corp—*Robert Coulling*	418 S Military Trl, Deerfield Beach FL 33442	561-395-9996	R	2	<.1
4071	National Subscription Fulfillment Service—*Robin Button*	5411 E La Palma Ave, Anaheim CA 92807	714-693-3440	R	2*	<.1
4072	J Paul Horst and Associates Inc—*Horst Paul*	5600 Nw Central Dr, Houston TX 77092	713-460-9386	R	2*	<.1
4073	Verilogix Inc—*Tom Christy*	PO Box 3472, Pls Vrds Pnsl CA 90274	310-527-5100	R	2*	<.1
4074	Stepstone Solutions Inc—*Matthew Parker*	PO Box 1644, Wimberley TX 78676	512-351-7809	R	2*	<.1
4075	EZX Corp	917 Oakgrove Dr, Houston TX 77058		R	2	<.1
4076	FindExcom Inc—*Steven Malone*	4437 S 134th St, Omaha NE 68137	402-333-1900	P	2	<.1
4077	ISI-Biz Inc—*John E Scott*	PO Box 3968, Evergreen CO 80437	303-526-1662	R	2	<.1

Note: An asterisk (*) indicates an estimated financial figure. The company type code used is as follows: R = Private, P = Public, S = Private Subsidiary, B = Public Subsidiary, D = Division, J = Joint Venture, I = Investment Fund.

COMPANY RANKINGS BY SALES WITHIN 4-DIGIT SIC

Rank	Company Name—Executive Officer	Address, City, State, Zip	Phone	Type	Fin	Empls
4078	Abracadata Ltd—Sue Tidswell	PO Box 2440, Eugene OR 97402		R	2	<.1
4079	Bilingual Software Inc	PO Box 3000, Prescott AZ 86302		R	2	<.1
4080	Thunderstone Expansion Programs International Inc—P Barton Richards	11115 Edgewater Dr, Cleveland OH 44102	216-631-8544	R	2	N/A
4081	Zandar Corp—Harry Summerfield	PO Box 445, Essex Junction VT 05453	802-662-0556	R	2	N/A
4082	4skware Technologies Inc—Steven Bobrowski	PO Box 2325, Chapel Hill NC 27515	919-338-0956	R	2*	<.1
4083	LearningstationCom Inc—James Kirchner	8008 Corp Ctr Dr Ste 2, Charlotte NC 28226	704-926-5400	R	2*	<.1
4084	Connect Imaging Inc—Phillip Manly	PO Box 240370, Honolulu HI 96824	808-373-7048	R	2*	<.1
4085	Model Technology Inc—Gregory Hinckley	8005 SW Boeckman Rd, Wilsonville OR 97070	503-685-7000	S	2	<.1
4086	Left Behind Games Inc—Troy A Lyndon	25060 Hancock Ave Ste, Murrieta CA 92562	951-894-6597	P	2	<.1
4087	Infofusion LLC—Don Jewell	9956 W Remington Pl, Littleton CO 80128	303-234-0300	R	2*	<.1
4088	Devington Technologies Corp—Alan Rajlevsky	9610 23rd Ave, New York NY 10018	212-967-0601	R	2*	<.1
4089	Health Data Services Inc—Daniel Brody	504 Old Lynchburg Rd, Charlottesville VA 22903	434-817-9000	R	2*	<.1
4090	American Viking Enterprises of Florida Inc—Varia Vike-Freiberga	3586 Aloma Ave, Winter Park FL 32792	407-657-9358	R	2	<.1
4091	Teq Digital	30161 Avenida Banderas, Rancho Santa Margarita CA 92688	949-709-4040	R	2	<.1
4092	Applied Business Software Inc—Jerry Delgado	2847 Gundry Ave, Signal Hill CA 90755	562-426-2188	R	2*	<.1
4093	Powersim Solutions Inc—Imrana A Umar	500 Grove St Ste 210, Herndon VA 20170	703-467-0910	R	2	<.1
4094	Systems and Synchronous Inc—Andy Austin	489 Taft Ave, Glen Ellyn IL 60137	630-858-0368	R	2	<.1
4095	Bentley Solutions Center Bentley Yorba Linda	22700 Savi Ranch Pkwy, Yorba Linda CA 92887	714-974-2500	S	2	<.1
4096	Computer Management and Integraters Inc—Mark Fortin	PO Box 83, Colchester CT 06415	860-537-6564	R	2*	<.1
4097	Exigo Office Inc—David Thompson	8130 John W Carpenter, Dallas TX 75247	214-905-0919	R	2*	<.1
4098	Questa Corp (New York New York)—Leon Turetsky	59 John St 3rd Fl, New York NY 10038	212-714-0440	R	2	<.1
4099	Corsoft Corp—Chirag Patel	1710 S Amphlett Ste 20, San Mateo CA 94402	650-286-2870	R	2*	<.1
4100	MumboJumbo—Mark Cottam	2019 N Lamar St Ste 30, Dallas TX 75202		R	2	<.1
4101	Health Path Products LLC—Brittny Brimhall	1626 N Country Club Dr, Mesa AZ 85201	480-964-5198	R	2*	<.1
4102	Conarc Inc—Chet Joglekar	30000 Mill Creek Ave S, Alpharetta GA 30022	770-849-0508	R	2*	<.1
4103	Respond 2-U Inc—Charles Beldsoe	10765 Mueller Ct, Tustin CA 92782	714-424-9830	R	2*	<.1
4104	Corprasoft Inc—Jim Bridges	7557 Rambler Rd, Dallas TX 75231	214-580-8500	S	1	<.1
4105	Specialized Business Software Inc—Steven Wiser	6325 Cochran Rd Ste 1, Solon OH 44139	440-519-1597	R	1*	<.1
4106	Surequest Systems Inc—T J (Tim) Sudderth	3330 Keller Springs Rd, Carrollton TX 75006	972-238-7200	P	1	<.1
4107	Computer-Integrated-Manufacturing America LLC—Don Macary	898 Airport Park Rd St, Glen Burnie MD 21061	410-760-8754	R	1	<.1
4108	Quest - Iv Inc—Donald Mccullough	7116 Summerfield Rd, Lambertville MI 48144	734-847-5487	R	1*	<.1
4109	Qualedi Inc—Stephen Morocco	121 W Main St Ste 4, Milford CT 06460	203-874-4334	R	1*	<.1
4110	Simulyze Inc—Kevin Gallagher	12020 Sunrise Valley D, Reston VA 20191	703-391-7001	R	1*	<.1
4111	Interplay Entertainment Corp—Herve Caen	12301 Wilshire Blvd St, Los Angeles CA 90025	310-979-7070	P	1	<.1
4112	Executive Suites—Kim Moore	1115 Elkton Dr Ste 300, Colorado Springs CO 80907	719-528-8198	R	1*	<.1
4113	Maddenco Inc—Gregory Madden	4847 E Virginia St Ste, Evansville IN 47715	812-474-6245	R	1*	<.1
4114	Assurance Systems Inc—William Capps	6037 Financial Dr, Norcross GA 30071	770-242-6832	R	1*	<.1
4115	Desert Sky Software Inc—Luke Holton	103 W Highland Ave Ste, Phoenix AZ 85013	602-279-4600	R	1*	<.1
4116	IsongCom Inc—Stephen Kennedy	2811 Mckinney Ave Ste, Dallas TX 75204	214-855-3727	R	1*	<.1
4117	Teletypesetting Company Inc—Edward Friedman	44 School St Ste 1000, Boston MA 02108	617-542-6220	R	1*	<.1
4118	Xaktsoft Inc—Anthony Lewis	PO Box 1586, Powell OH 43065	614-734-0597	R	1*	<.1
4119	Resource Optimization Inc—T Mayfield	PO Box 2695, Knoxville TN 37901	865-522-2211	R	1*	<.1
4120	Sedona Corp—David R Vey	1003 W 9th Ave 2nd Fl, King of Prussia PA 19406	610-337-8400	P	1	<.1
4121	Eagle Business Solutions LLC—Michael Bond	PO Box 15158, Clearwater FL 33766	727-535-3592	R	1*	<.1
4122	Link2consult Inc—Peter McCree	1 Bridge Plaza, Fort Lee NJ 07024	201-308-9101	S	1*	<.1
4123	Remotescan Corp—Steve Saroff	305 S 4th St E, Missoula MT 59801	406-721-0319	R	1*	<.1
4124	DPC Inc (Paris Tennessee)—Bo Caldwell	1015 Maurice Fields Dr, Paris TN 38242		R	1	<.1
4125	MD Solutions Inc—Jack Woodham	7922 Veterans Pkwy, Columbus GA 31909	706-255-1384	R	1*	<.1
4126	Summit National Inc	PO Box 37, Kenilworth IL 60043	312-373-1505	R	1	<.1
4127	Mission Data LLC—David Armstrong	12910 Shelbyville Rd S, Louisville KY 40243	502-245-6756	R	1*	<.1
4128	Predator Software Inc—James Abbassian	8835 Sw Canyon Ln Ste, Portland OR 97225	503-292-7151	R	1*	<.1
4129	2ab Nc—Carol Burt	PO Box 335, Helena AL 35080	205-621-7455	R	1*	<.1
4130	Davis Crowley Research Inc—Bill Crowley	280 S Academy Ave Ste, Eagle ID 83616	208-939-2976	R	1*	<.1
4131	Itech Retail Inc—Francis Tran	3000 Atrium Way Ste 11, Mount Laurel NJ 08054	856-273-6924	R	1*	<.1
4132	Global Micro Solutions Inc—Mike Uesugi	21250 Hawthorne Blvd S, Torrance CA 90503	310-218-5678	R	1*	<.1
4133	Redstar Inc—William Oleksinski	160 Oak St Ste 104, Glastonbury CT 06033	860-657-3099	R	1*	<.1
4134	PaceWorks Inc—Phac Le Tuan	16780 Lark Ave, Los Gatos CA 95032	408-354-5711	R	1*	<.1
4135	Intuit Inc Personal Finance Div—Brad Smith Intuit Inc	2632 Marine Way, Mountain View CA 94043	650-944-6000	D	1	4.5
4136	Systems Consultants—Don Sefton	PO Box 2040, Fallon NV 89407	775-423-1345	R	1*	.1
4137	LevelfieldCom Inc—Jude Samson	11675 Jllyvlle Rd Ste, Austin TX 78759	512-401-9200	R	1*	<.1
4138	Shoulders Corp—L Love	42 Stoneridge Dr Ste 1, Waynesboro VA 22980	540-949-5422	R	1*	<.1
4139	Ascert LLC	759 Bridgeway, Sausalito CA 94965	415-339-8500	R	1*	<.1
4140	Mbsiinet Inc—Tim Thomas	PO Box 425, Southbury CT 06488	203-262-1306	R	1*	<.1
4141	Corelogic Marketlinx Inc—Ben Graboske	1400 Centerpoint Blvd, Knoxville TN 37932		S	1*	.1
4142	Anchor Computer Inc—Gary M Siegel	1900 New Hwy, Farmingdale NY 11735	631-293-6100	R	1*	.1
4143	Smart Online Inc—Dror Zoreff	4505 Emperor Blvd Ste, Durham NC 27703	919-578-9000	P	1	.1
4144	Argent Software Inc—Andrew Blencowe	2 Bridgewater Rd, Farmington CT 06032	860-674-1700	R	1*	.1
4145	Time Domain Inc—Rachel Reinhardt	4955 Corporate Dr Ste, Huntsville AL 35805	256-922-9229	R	1*	.1
4146	Polaris Software Inc—Arun Jain	38750 Paseo Padre Pky, Fremont CA 94536	510-745-9986	R	1	.1
4147	CyberSoft Technologies Inc—Asfar Manzoor	25 Burlington Mall Rd, Burlington MA 01803	781-238-0229	R	1*	.1
4148	Transoft Networks—Jim Wolffe	532 Santa Barbara St, Santa Barbara CA 93101	805-730-7772	R	1*	.1
4149	Capital Access International—Michael Peace	350 Mount Kemble Ave S, Morristown NJ 07960	973-753-1700	R	1*	.1
4150	Eclipse Computing Inc—Gary Waylett	123 Broadway, Woodcliff Lake NJ 07677	201-746-6255	R	1*	.1
4151	Laser Systems Inc (Kaysville Utah)—Colette Cozean	350 N 400 W, Kaysville UT 84037	801-552-8800	R	1*	.1
4152	Xplore Infosystems—Mark Anderson	501 Silverside Rd Ste, Wilmington DE 19809	302-407-1615	R	1*	.1
4153	RingCentral Inc—Vlad Shmunis	999 Baker Way, San Mateo CA 94404		R	1*	<.1
4154	Scientific Technologies Corp—Michael Popovich	4400 E Broadway Blvd S, Tucson AZ 85711	520-202-3333	R	1*	<.1
4155	Data Consultants Inc (Fresno California)—Bill Pardini	3586 N Hazel Ave, Fresno CA 93722		R	1*	<.1
4156	Infogenic Systems—Mazen Alnafakh	2901 N Prospect Rd, Peoria IL 61603	309-682-0100	R	1*	<.1
4157	InterTrust Technologies Corp—Talal G Shamoon	955 Stewart Dr, Sunnyvale CA 94085	408-616-1600	R	1*	<.1
4158	Jabber Inc	1899 Wynkoop St Ste 60, Denver CO 80202	303-308-3231	S	1*	<.1
4159	Spalding Software Inc	PO Box 921188, Norcross GA 30092	770-449-0594	R	1*	<.1
4160	MEDTRON Software Intelligence Corp—RT McDaniel	120 Innwood Dr, Covington LA 70433	985-893-2550	R	1*	<.1
4161	Northwest Analytical Inc—Bob Ward	111 SW 5th Ave Ste 800, Portland OR 97204	503-224-7727	R	1*	<.1
4162	Linspire Inc (San Diego California)—Andreas Typaldos	5960 Cornerstone Ct W, San Diego CA 92121	858-587-6700	S	1*	<.1

Rank	Company Name—*Executive Officer*	Address, City, State, Zip	Phone	Type	Fin	Empls
4163	ViryaNet Inc—*Memy Ish-Shalom* ViryaNet Ltd	112 Turnpike Rd, Westborough MA 01581	508-490-5900	S	1*	<.1
4164	Ram Enterprises Inc—*Arlo Smith*	PO Box 1270, Aberdeen SD 57402	605-229-0180	R	1*	<.1
4165	Cornerstone Information Systems Inc (Hopkinsville Kentucky)—*David Smith*	800 S Main St, Hopkinsville KY 42240	270-885-9011	R	1*	<.1
4166	Eagle Technology Inc (Mequon Wisconsin)—*Harshad Shah*	11019 N Towne Square R, Mequon WI 53092	262-241-3845	R	1*	<.1
4167	Permessa Corp—*Stefan Mehlhorn*	69 Hickory Dr, Waltham MA 02451	781-694-2200	R	1	<.1
4168	Ranac Corp—*Keith Pitzele*	4181 E 96th St Ste 280, Indianapolis IN 46240		R	1*	<.1
4169	Benefit Software Inc—*Larry Deblaf*	212 Cottage Grove Ave, Santa Barbara CA 93101		R	1*	<.1
4170	InfoValue Computing Inc—*Monsong Chen*	4 Westchester Plz Ste, Elmsford NY 10523	914-345-5980	R	1*	<.1
4171	AG Vision—*Jose Laracuente* DMI Computer Technologies	1601 N Ankeny Blvd, Ankeny IA 50023	515-964-0708	D	1*	<.1
4172	AskSam Systems—*Phil Schnyder*	PO Box 1428, Perry FL 32348	850-584-6590	R	1*	<.1
4173	AT Communication Corp—*William H Welling*	2041 Pioneer Ct Ste 20, San Mateo CA 94403	650-375-8198	R	1*	<.1
4174	Chadwick and Associates Management Systems Inc—*Alan Chadwick*	1201 Broadrick Dr, Dalton GA 30720	706-226-3801	R	1*	<.1
4175	Cortex Medical Management Systems Inc—*Stan Gordon*	2107 Elliott Ave Ste 2, Seattle WA 98121	206-812-6981	R	1*	<.1
4176	Custom Software Systems Inc—*Richie Wilkes*	7012 Westbelt Dr, Nashville TN 37209	615-350-8111	R	1*	<.1
4177	Data-Core Systems Inc—*Shyamal Choudhury*	1880 John F Kennedy Bl, Philadelphia PA 19103	215-243-1990	S	1*	<.1
4178	i2Gemini Inc—*Michael T Hills*	40 Cedar Ave, Hershey PA 17033	717-533-4973	R	1*	<.1
4179	JPMA Inc—*James P Magee*	1626 Cole Blvd Ste 250, Lakewood CO 80401	303-232-3700	R	1*	<.1
4180	Miller/Davis Co	310 Fourth Ave S Ste 1, Minneapolis MN 55415	612-312-1570	R	1*	<.1
4181	Mitas Group Inc—*Susan Mitas*	1575 Heritage Dr Ste 3, McKinney TX 75069		R	1*	<.1
4182	Scherrer Resources Inc—*Jim Scherrer*	PO Box 207, Uwchland PA 19480	484-875-1710	R	1*	<.1
4183	Sphere Health Systems Inc—*Florian Wieland*	22912 Mill Creek Rd St, Laguna Hills CA 92653		R	1*	<.1
4184	TrailBlazer Studios—*Tom Waring*	1610 Midtown Pl, Raleigh NC 27609	919-645-6600	R	1*	<.1
4185	Applied Information Management Sciences Inc—*Robert Canterbury*	235 DeSiard St, Monroe LA 71201	318-323-2467	R	1*	<.1
4186	WinWay Corp	PO Box 1097, Folsom CA 95763	916-965-7879	R	1*	<.1
4187	BEZ Systems Inc—*F Daniel Haley*	355 Congress St, Boston MA 02210	617-426-5105	R	1*	<.1
4188	Cel Corp—*Christopher K Schrichte*	1615 M St NW Ste 900, Washington DC 20005	202-331-5080	R	1*	<.1
4189	Ford Equity Research Inc—*Timothy R Alward* Mergent International Inc	11722 Sorrento Valley, San Diego CA 92121	858-755-1327	S	1*	<.1
4190	Munics Informations Systems Inc	2 Ridgedale Ave Ste 33, Cedar Knolls NJ 07927	973-778-7753	R	1*	<.1
4191	Autodocs LLC	8233 Old Courthouse Rd, Vienna VA 22182	703-532-9720	R	1*	<.1
4192	Interactive Systems Inc (North Billerica Massachusetts)	101 Billerica Ave 5 Bi, North Billerica MA 01862	978-670-2600	R	1*	<.1
4193	Dalcon Technologies Inc—*David Condra*	3401 West End Ave Ste, Nashville TN 37203	615-843-9000	S	1*	<.1
4194	Duxbury Systems Inc—*Joe Sullivan*	270 Littleton Rd Unit, Westford MA 01886	978-692-3000	R	1*	<.1
4195	Absoft Corp—*Wood Lotz*	2781 Bond St, Rochester Hills MI 48309	248-853-0050	R	1*	<.1
4196	Accelerated Computer Technologies Inc	245 5th Ave 17th Fl, New York NY 10016	212-213-0153	R	1*	<.1
4197	Advanced Technology Center Inc—*David Wohletz*	160 W Carmel Dr Ste 24, Carmel IN 46032	317-846-0491	R	1*	<.1
4198	Applications Systems Corp—*Richard W Smith*	262 Washington St 5th, Boston MA 02108	617-426-2918	R	1*	<.1
4199	Aptech Systems Inc—*Susan Ranney*	PO Box 250, Black Diamond WA 98010	360-886-7100	R	1*	<.1
4200	Athena Group Inc—*Monica Murphy*	408 W University Ave S, Gainesville FL 32601	352-371-2567	R	1*	<.1
4201	Big Sky Technologies Inc—*Bill Doll*	9325 Sky Park Ct Ste12, San Diego CA 92123	858-715-5000	R	1*	<.1
4202	Computer Support Inc—*Fred Nichols*	47 W Main St, Mechanicsburg PA 17055	717-691-6707	R	1*	<.1
4203	Dataweld Inc—*Jim Broughtom*	1909 Citizens Bank Dr, Bossier City LA 71111	318-746-6111	R	1*	<.1
4204	Direct Systems Inc—*Howard Worrell*	PO Box 13753, Richmond VA 23225	804-320-2040	R	1*	<.1
4205	Graphx Inc—*Joseph T Kowalik*	400 W Cummings Pk, Woburn MA 01801	781-932-0430	R	1	<.1
4206	Henschen and Associates Inc—*Bud Henschen*	432 W Gypsy Ln Rd, Bowling Green OH 43402	419-352-5454	R	1*	<.1
4207	Impact Solutions Inc—*John Keelin*	3810 McKnight East Dr, Pittsburgh PA 15237	412-367-8833	R	1*	<.1
4208	Integrated Design Inc—*Jim Carroll*	3768 Plaza Dr, Ann Arbor MI 48108	734-665-8470	R	1*	<.1
4209	Pixion Inc—*Mitch Diamond*	3180 Crow Canyon Pl, San Ramon CA 94583	925-328-1500	R	1*	<.1
4210	Plansmith Corp—*Craig D Hartman*	1827 Walden Office Sq, Schaumburg IL 60173	847-359-4045	R	1*	<.1
4211	Prosoft Inc—*Linda Everson*	6018 E Columbus Dr, Tampa FL 33619	813-626-8778	R	1*	<.1
4212	Sawtooth Software—*Rich Johnson*	1457 E 840 N, Orem UT 84097	801-477-4700	R	1*	<.1
4213	Scanco Inc—*Paul Heim*	470 Portage Lakes Dr S, Akron OH 44319	330-645-9959	R	1*	<.1
4214	Teacher's Pal Inc—*Karsten Solheim*	PO Box 37956, Phoenix AZ 85069	602-861-3440	R	1*	<.1
4215	Thermeon Corp—*Scott Samson*	1175 Warner Ave, Tustin CA 92780	714-731-9191	R	1*	<.1
4216	TL Ashford and Associates Inc—*John Pigott*	626 Buttermilk Pike, Crescent Springs KY 41017	859-291-7555	R	1*	<.1
4217	TL Data Corp—*Mark Mantese*	1539 River Oaks Rd E S, Elmwood LA 70123	504-731-2900	R	1*	<.1
4218	VDP Inc—*Janine Sotelo*	2010 E Lohman Ave, Las Cruces NM 88001	575-522-0003	R	1*	<.1
4219	WinSoft Corp—*Ehud Shany*	1932 E Deere Ave Ste 1, Santa Ana CA 92705	949-428-4844	R	1*	<.1
4220	Xytech Systems Corp—*Richard Gallagher*	15451 San Fernando Mis, Mission Hills CA 91345	818-698-4900	R	1*	<.1
4221	Bendan Technologies Inc—*John Dunn*	2236 Rutherford Rd Ste, Carlsbad CA 92008	760-929-7500	R	1*	<.1
4222	CallWare Technologies Inc—*Reino Kerttula*	9100 S 500 W, Sandy UT 84070	801-988-6800	R	1*	<.1
4223	Cedalion Corp—*Bill Thorpe*	338 S Sharon Amity Rd, Charlotte NC 28211	704-716-1400	R	1*	<.1
4224	DynoTech Software—*David W Carlson*	1448 Kent St, Saint Paul MN 55117	612-235-7253	R	1*	<.1
4225	Edibar Systems Inc—*Wayne Metcalfe*	51520 Regency Center D, Macomb MI 48042	586-677-8800	R	1*	<.1
4226	SARS Corp—*Frank Bonadio*	2462 Washington Rd, Washington IL 61571	309-427-5961	P	1	<.1
4227	Vertical Software Inc (Peoria Illinois)—*Patrick G Gilroy*	409 S Keller, Bartonville IL 61607	309-633-0700	R	1*	<.1
4228	AVL Looms Inc—*Bob Kruger*	2360 Park Ave, Chico CA 95928	530-893-4915	R	1*	<.1
4229	Black Ice Software LLC—*Allan Wolfson*	20 Broad St, Nashua NH 03064	603-882-7711	R	1	<.1
4230	Church Management Solutions—*William Pressprich* ParishSOFT	3300 Bass Lake Rd Ste, Brooklyn Center MN 55429	763-566-4212	D	1*	<.1
4231	ControlSoft Inc—*Tien L Chia*	5387 Avion Park Dr, Highland Heights OH 44143	440-443-3900	R	1*	<.1
4232	Knowles-McNiff—*Angel Bolden*	PO Box 6386, Garden Grove CA 92846		R	1*	<.1
4233	Anesis Group Inc—*Thom Mills*	2047 Castaic Ln, Knoxville TN 37932	865-531-0303	R	1*	<.1
4234	Applied Micro Inc—*Ron Hurst*	2304 Spring Ridge Dr S, Spring Grove IL 60081	815-675-9050	R	1*	<.1
4235	Avocet Systems Inc	PO Box 1347, Rockland ME 04841	207-596-7766	R	1*	<.1
4236	Bennet-Tec Information Systems Inc—*Jeff Bennett*	50 Jericho Tpke, Jericho NY 11753	516-997-5596	R	1*	<.1
4237	C Systems LLC—*Ray Ferraro*	510 Thornall St Ste 31, Edison NJ 08837	732-548-6100	R	1*	<.1
4238	CMS Construction Software—*Jeff Gerardi*	17065 Camino San Berna, San Diego CA 92127	858-312-8900	R	1*	<.1
4239	Constructive Computing Company Inc—*John Maultsby*	112 Terrace Trail S, Lake Quivira KS 66217		R	1*	<.1
4240	Cubix Software Limited Inc—*R Lee*	2705 Gilmer Rd, Longview TX 75604	903-297-7771	R	1*	<.1
4241	Database Systems Corp (Phoenix Arizona)	1118 E Missouri Ave, Phoenix AZ 85014	602-265-5968	R	1*	<.1
4242	Desaware Inc—*Dan Appleman*	3510 Charter Park Dr S, San Jose CA 95136	408-404-4760	R	1*	<.1
4243	DPD International Inc—*Tom Politowski*	19700 Fairchild Ste 30, Irvine CA 92612	714-695-1000	R	1*	<.1
4244	EXSYS Inc—*Dustin Huntington*	6301 Indian School Rd, Albuquerque NM 87110	505-888-9494	R	1	<.1
4245	IMA Technologies Inc	1816 Tribute Rd Ste 10, Sacramento CA 95815	916-446-1114	R	1*	<.1

Note: An asterisk (*) indicates an estimated financial figure. The company type code used is as follows: R = Private, P = Public, S = Private Subsidiary, B = Public Subsidiary, D = Division, J = Joint Venture, I = Investment Fund.

COMPANY RANKINGS BY SALES WITHIN 4-DIGIT SIC

Rank	Company Name—*Executive Officer*	Address, City, State, Zip	Phone	Type	Fin	Empls
4246	Information Presentation Technologies Inc	PO Box 12607, San Luis Obispo CA 93406	805-541-3000	R	1*	<.1
4247	Information Security Corp—*Thomas J Venn*	1141 Lake Cook Rd, Deerfield IL 60015		R	1*	<.1
4248	InterNetworX Systems Inc—*Don Fitzpatrick*	325 N Corporate Dr Ste, Brookfield WI 53045	262-792-0050	R	1*	<.1
4249	Medi Group Ltd—*Cynthia M McCarthy*	PO Box 839, Oaks PA 19456	610-666-1955	R	1*	<.1
4250	MIMICS Inc—*Maggie Merten*	10701 Lomas NE Ste 218, Albuquerque NM 87112	505-332-9220	R	1*	<.1
4251	Newpoint Technologies Inc—*Wally Martin*	5 Industrial Way Ste 2, Salem NH 03079	603-263-2014	S	1*	<.1
4252	Pegasus Disk Technologies Inc—*Roy Slicker*	18 Crow Canyon Ct, San Ramon CA 94583	925-314-1800	R	1*	<.1
4253	Prefab Software Inc—*Scott Lawton*	24 Colonial Dr, Chelmsford MA 01824	781-791-7593	R	1*	<.1
4254	Quality America Inc—*Dennis Nolan*	PO Box 31055, Tucson AZ 85751	520-722-6154	R	1*	<.1
4255	RiT Technologies Inc—*Doron Zinger*	900 Corporate Dr, Mahwah NJ 07430	201-512-1970	S	1*	<.1
4256	Scientific Software Tools Inc—*Rich Percell*	1023 E Baltimore Pke S, Media PA 19063	610-891-1640	R	1*	<.1
4257	Squarerigger Inc—*Edward Cooper*	9119 Ridgetop Blvd Nw, Silverdale WA 98383	360-698-3562	R	1*	<.1
4258	Stat-Ease Inc—*Mark J Anderson*	2021 E Hennepin Ave St, Minneapolis MN 55413	612-378-9449	R	1*	<.1
4259	TotalRewards Software Inc—*Ray O'Donnell*	2208 Plaza Dr Ste 120, Rocklin CA 95765	916-632-1000	R	1*	<.1
4260	User Solutions Inc—*David Ringstrom*	11009 Tillson Dr, South Lyon MI 48178	248-486-1934	R	1*	<.1
4261	Civilized Software Inc—*Gary Knott*	12109 Heritage Park Ci, Silver Spring MD 20906	301-962-3711	R	1	<.1
4262	Etek International Inc—*AIW Blair*	44 Inverness Dr E Bldg, Englewood CO 80112	720-545-9966	R	1*	<.1
4263	Relex Software Corp—*Jim Heppelmann*	540 Pellis Rd, Greensburg PA 15601	724-836-8800	S	1*	<.1
4264	Spectrum Software—*Andy Thompson*	1021 S Wolfe Rd Ste 13, Sunnyvale CA 94086	408-738-4387	R	1*	<.1
4265	Taurus Software Inc—*Cailean Sherman*	420 Brewster St, Redwood City CA 94063	650-482-2022	R	1*	<.1
4266	TS Partners Inc—*Benjamin Goldfield*	500 N Gulph Rd Ste 500, King of Prussia PA 19406	610-768-1100	R	1*	<.1
4267	UniBar Inc	7801 W 110th St, Overland Park KS 66210	913-696-4090	S	1*	<.1
4268	Abby Inc—*Ken Evans*	2865 Lesslie Hwy, Rock Hill SC 29730	803-909-4050	R	1*	<.1
4269	ACUGEN Software Inc—*Peter de Bruyn Kops*	379 Amherst St Ste 222, Nashua NH 03063	603-673-8392	R	1*	<.1
4270	Advanced Analytical Inc—*Dan Gimple*	621 Courtney Ct, Newbury Park CA 91320	805-375-7000	R	1*	<.1
4271	Allied Business Systems Inc—*Jerry Crespi*	18627 Brookhurst St St, Fountain Valley CA 92708	714-963-5554	R	1*	<.1
4272	Allison Systems Inc—*Alan Doyle*	W226N781 Eastmound Dr, Waukesha WI 53186	262-522-9800	R	1*	<.1
4273	Apiary Inc—*Gary Dowdy*	1170 15th Ave SE, Minneapolis MN 55414	612-788-5882	R	1*	<.1
4274	AS Thomas Inc—*EM Thomas*	355 Providence Hwy, Westwood MA 02090	781-329-9200	R	1*	<.1
4275	Automatic Forecasting Systems Inc—*David Reilly*	PO Box 563, Hatboro PA 19040	215-675-0652	R	1*	<.1
4276	Banyon Data Systems Inc—*Jeff Christensen*	101 W Burnsville Pkwy, Burnsville MN 55337	952-882-7730	R	1*	<.1
4277	BICC Systems Inc—*Phillip Kotas*	611 E Butterfield Rd S, Lombard IL 60148	630-629-2422	R	1*	<.1
4278	Brickhouse Software Inc—*Jonathan Matcho*	1661 US Hwy 22, Bound Brook NJ 08805	732-764-4100	R	1*	<.1
4279	CCS Computer Systems Inc—*Dan McCormick*	PO Box 6819, Lynnwood WA 98036		R	1*	<.1
4280	Chariot Software Group	2645 Financial Ct Ste, San Diego CA 92117	858-270-0202	R	1*	<.1
4281	CheckMark Software Inc—*Jim Mathre*	724 Whalers Way Bldg H, Fort Collins CO 80525	970-225-0522	R	1*	<.1
4282	Classic Solutions—*Kandi Christian*	22365 El Toro Rd Ste 4, Lake Forest CA 92630	949-309-2451	R	1*	<.1
4283	Commercial Business Systems Inc—*Mike McCarty*	PO Box 1439, Marion IN 46952	765-662-9851	R	1*	<.1
4284	ComputaLabel International Ltd—*Simone Urquhart*	80 Turkey Hill Rd, Newburyport MA 01950		R	1*	<.1
4285	Construction Information Systems Inc	PO Box 1205, Mill Valley CA 94942	415-785-7926	R	1*	<.1
4286	Creative Information Systems Co—*Charles Sereboff*	5305 Gulf Dr Ste 1, New Port Richey FL 34652		R	1*	<.1
4287	Data Management Assistance Corp—*Fred Tarbox*	15408 Scarlet St, Austin TX 78728	512-782-8193	R	1*	<.1
4288	Data Management Inc (San Angelo Texas)—*Jorge Ellis*	3322 W Loop 306, San Angelo TX 76904	325-223-9500	R	1*	<.1
4289	DataModes Inc—*Terry Brittanham*	4200 Perimeter Center, Oklahoma City OK 73112	405-947-3887	R	1*	<.1
4290	Datapax Inc	3233 W Peoria Ave Ste, Phoenix AZ 85029	602-274-1321	R	1*	<.1
4291	DataTech Software Inc—*Paul Endress*	4800 Linglestown Rd St, Harrisburg PA 17112	717-652-4344	R	1*	<.1
4292	Digimation Inc—*David Avgikos*	250 International Pky, Lake Mary FL 32746	407-833-0600	R	1*	<.1
4293	Donald B Cook and Associates—*Donald Cook*	1050 George St - 18M, New Brunswick NJ 08901	732-246-3600	R	1*	<.1
4294	Donald R Frey and Company Inc—*Donald Frey*	40 N Grand Ave Ste 303, Fort Thomas KY 41075	859-441-6566	R	1*	<.1
4295	Emerging Technology Solutions LLC—*Bud Brasier*	145 Sandy Hollow Trl S, Franktown CO 80116	303-688-1987	R	1*	<.1
4296	Entech Data Systems Inc—*Gene Brown*	PO Box 30055, Pensacola FL 32503	850-479-3773	R	1*	<.1
4297	Entrinsik Inc—*Doug Leupen*	7501 Creedmoor Rd Ste, Raleigh NC 27613	919-848-4828	R	1*	<.1
4298	Eric Systems—*Chris Chambers*	9833 NE 120th Pl Suite, Kirkland WA 98034		R	1*	<.1
4299	Evolution Robotics Inc—*Paolo Pirjanian*	1055 E Colorado Blvd S, Pasadena CA 91106	626-993-3300	R	1*	<.1
4300	FileStream Inc—*Chris Pirillo*	PO Box 93, Glen Head NY 11545	516-759-4100	R	1*	<.1
4301	FSI Automation Inc	22833 Bothell-Everett, Bothell WA 98021	425-486-3444	S	1*	<.1
4302	Hyperception Inc—*James Truchard* National Instruments Corp	11500 N Mopac Expy, Austin TX 78759	214-343-8525	S	1*	<.1
4303	Information Consultants Inc—*Rex Smith*	1320 Tower Rd Ste160, Schaumburg IL 60173	847-397-0088	R	1*	<.1
4304	Integra Information Inc—*Phil Burgess*	1640 Airport Rd Ste 11, Kennesaw GA 30144		D	1*	<.1
4305	Interactive CAD Systems	PO Box 4182, Santa Clara CA 95056	408-970-0852	R	1*	<.1
4306	Intrac Systems Inc—*Mike Mucciarone*	PO Box 76, Fairview PA 16415	814-474-4884	R	1*	<.1
4307	Isee Systems Inc—*Jack Templin*	31 Old Etna Rd Ste 7N, Lebanon NH 03766	603-448-4990	R	1*	<.1
4308	Larson Software Technology Inc—*Don Larson*	3352 Walnut Bend Ln, Houston TX 77042	713-977-4177	R	1*	<.1
4309	Learning Multi-Systems Inc—*Brad Oltrogge*	1402 Greenway Cross, Madison WI 53713	608-273-8060	R	1*	<.1
4310	Lieberman Technologies—*Philip Lieberman*	223 NW 2nd St Ste 300, Evansville IN 47708	812-434-6600	R	1*	<.1
4311	Logical Data Solutions Inc	31 Windward Isle, Palm Beach Gardens FL 33418	561-694-9229	R	1*	<.1
4312	Mabry Software Inc—*James Shields*	503 316th St NW, Stanwood WA 98292	360-629-9218	R	1*	<.1
4313	Manage Operations—*Jim Corrigan*	3608 Davis Dr Ste 356, Morrisville NC 27560	919-342-7016	R	1*	<.1
4314	MB Software and Consulting Inc—*Mike Boadway*	3105 Cold Springs Rd, Baldwinsville NY 13027	315-635-5880	R	1*	<.1
4315	Measurement Techniques Inc—*Clinton Battersby*	160 Old Maple St, Stoughton MA 02072	781-344-6230	R	1	<.1
4316	Micro Digital Inc—*Ralph Moore*	2900 Bristol St Ste G2, Costa Mesa CA 92626	714-437-7333	R	1*	<.1
4317	Molsoft LLC—*Crystal Crawford*	11199 Sorrento Valley, San Diego CA 92121	858-625-2000	R	1*	<.1
4318	Multidata Computer Systems Inc—*Susan Skaggs*	160 Broadway Ste 1010, New York NY 10038	212-967-6700	R	1*	<.1
4319	NetDIVE Inc	41 Sutter St Ste1142, San Francisco CA 94104	415-378-8200	R	1	<.1
4320	Networking Dynamics Corp—*Daniel Kingsbury*	101 N Garden Ave Ste 2, Clearwater FL 33755	727-446-4511	R	1*	<.1
4321	NewportWave Inc—*John Graves*	15 McLean, Irvine CA 92620	949-651-1099	R	1*	<.1
4322	NWinds Inc—*Randolph Krofick*	PO Box 1760, Greensburg PA 15601	724-838-8993	R	1*	<.1
4323	Pragma Systems Inc—*Quamrul Mina*	13809 Research Blvd St, Austin TX 78750		R	1*	<.1
4324	Property Management Systems Corp—*Christopher Campbell*	2800 28th St Ste 109, Santa Monica CA 90405	310-450-2566	R	1*	<.1
4325	Proprietary Software Systems Inc—*Richard Gilinsky*	218 15th St, Santa Monica CA 90402	310-394-5233	R	1*	<.1
4326	ProWorks LLC—*Gary Prothero*	1600 SW Western Blvd S, Corvallis OR 97333	541-752-9885	R	1*	<.1
4327	Quadbase Systems Inc—*Fred Luk*	275 Saratoga Ave Ste 1, Santa Clara CA 95050	408-982-0835	R	1*	<.1
4328	R:Base Technologies Inc—*A Razzak Memon*	3935 Old William Penn, Murrysville PA 15668	724-733-0053	R	1*	<.1
4329	RT Systems Inc	27620 Farmington Rd St, Farmington Hills MI 48334	734-662-7099	R	1*	<.1
4330	S4i Systems—*Spencer Elliott*	616 S El Camino Real S, San Clemente CA 92672	849-366-5234	S	1*	<.1
4331	Santronics Software—*Hector Santos*	15600 SW 288th St Ste3, Homestead FL 33033	305-248-3638	R	1*	<.1
4332	Smart Solutions LLC	6425 Middle Lake Rd, Clarkston MI 48348	248-620-5664	R	1*	<.1
4333	Software Magic Inc	3859 Wekiva Springs Rd, Longwood FL 32779	407-814-9474	R	1*	<.1
4334	SOLSOFT Inc—*Jea- Francis Dechant*	2085 Landings Dr, Mountain View CA 94043	650-428-2800	R	1	<.1
4335	Specialized Business Solutions—*Michael Gebb*	PO Box 2019, Dillon CO 80435	970-262-1720	R	1*	<.1

Rank	Company Name—Executive Officer	Address, City, State, Zip	Phone	Type	Fin	Empls
4336	Syware Inc—Sy Danberg	PO Box 425091, Cambridge MA 02142	617-497-1300	R	1*	<.1
4337	TBS Automation Systems Inc	122 Kings Hwy Ste 504, Maple Shade NJ 08052	856-424-3247	R	1*	<.1
4338	Thornberry Ltd—Tom Peth	2148 Embassy Dr, Lancaster PA 17603	717-283-0980	R	1	<.1
4339	TranSolutions Inc—Peter Celestina	PO Box 25876, Scottsdale AZ 85255	480-473-2453	R	1*	<.1
4340	Ventana Systems Inc—Laura Peterson	60 Jacob Gates Rd, Harvard MA 01451	508-651-0432	R	1*	<.1
4341	Visionary Legal Technologies—Timothy Piganelli	1555 Valwood Pky Ste 1, Carrollton TX 75006	214-370-4359	R	1*	<.1
4342	Vista Control Systems Inc—Peter Clout	2101 Trinity Dr Ste Q, Los Alamos NM 87544	505-662-2484	R	1*	<.1
4343	Ward Systems Group Inc—Steve Ward	5 Hillcrest Dr, Frederick MD 21703	301-662-7950	R	1*	<.1
4344	WebMaster Inc—Peter Moore	1601 Civic Ctr Dr Ste, Santa Clara CA 95050	408-243-5000	R	1*	<.1
4345	Advanced Lease Systems Inc—Dennis Szody	PO Box 493160, Redding CA 96049	530-378-6868	R	1*	<.1
4346	CenterSoft Corp—Michael McKean	68910 Adelina Rd, Cathedral City CA 92234	760-327-6618	R	1*	<.1
4347	Computer Investment Advice Inc—Greg McVay	505 Mill St, Coraopolis PA 15108	412-262-5661	R	1*	<.1
4348	Compututor Inc—William Conner	PO Box 687, Plymouth Meeting PA 19462	610-260-0300	R	1*	<.1
4349	Expert Object Corp—Nicholas Vitulli	222 Wisconsin Ave, Lake Forest IL 60045	847-615-8400	R	1*	<.1
4350	Garman Routing Systems Inc—Wayne Garman	PO Box 1126, Taylor TX 76574		R	1*	<.1
4351	GBS Inc—Richard Seale	2100 Central Ave Ste 1, Boulder CO 80301	303-449-4897	R	1*	<.1
4352	Genzlinger Associates Inc	5700 Crooks Rd Ste 212, Troy MI 48098	248-879-7070	R	1*	<.1
4353	Husdawg LLC	4364 Town Center Blvd, El Dorado Hills CA 95762	916-933-7622	R	1*	<.1
4354	INTECK Corp—Donald Jacobs	10830 Old Mill Rd, Omaha NE 68154	402-592-4414	R	1*	<.1
4355	Lode Data Systems Inc—Daniel Dawson	10609 W 159th St, Orland Park IL 60467		R	1*	<.1
4356	Muse Research Inc—Chris Halaby	970 Obrien Dr, Menlo Park CA 94025	650-326-5400	R	1*	<.1
4357	Nordic Software Inc—James Wrenholt	PO Box 5403, Lincoln NE 68506	402-489-1557	R	1*	<.1
4358	North American Software Inc—Robert Seal	1077 Celestial St Ste, Cincinnati OH 45202	513-258-2981	R	1*	<.1
4359	Ready-to-Run Software Inc—Jeff Moskow	212 Cedar Cove, Lansing NY 14882	607-533-8649	R	1*	<.1
4360	S4Software Inc	PO Box 178607, San Diego CA 92177	858-560-8112	R	1*	<.1
4361	Tenon Intersystems	232 Anacapa St Ste 2A, Santa Barbara CA 93101	805-963-6983	R	1*	<.1
4362	Aptitune Corp—Don Winterhalter	PO Box 7104, Portsmouth NH 03802	603-430-8300	R	1*	<.1
4363	Arcata Pet Software—Don Bradner	600 F St, Arcata CA 95521	707-822-6417	R	1*	<.1
4364	Arman Schroeder—Arman Schroeder	471 W 36th Ave Ste 200, Anchorage AK 99503	907-277-5007	R	1*	<.1
4365	Bare Bones Software Inc—Rich Siegel	PO Box 1048, Bedford MA 01730	978-251-0500	R	1*	<.1
4366	Buerg Software	139 White Oak Cir, Petaluma CA 94952	707-778-1811	R	1*	<.1
4367	Cadmax Corp—Louis Wohlmuth	11 Chartley Park Rd, Reisterstown MD 21136	410-526-0490	R	1*	<.1
4368	Cole Software LLC—David B Cole	736 Fox Hollow Rd, Afton VA 22920	540-456-8210	R	1*	<.1
4369	Computerized Fleet Analysis Inc—Mike Ohlinger	1020 W Fullerton Ave S, Addison IL 60101	630-543-1410	R	1*	<.1
4370	Creel Consulting LLC—Cliff Creel	33 Appledor Rd, Bedford NH 03110	603-472-0868	R	1*	<.1
4371	DataNOW LLC—Phillip Jones	PO Box 446, Twin Falls ID 83303	208-734-2245	R	1*	<.1
4372	EASI Computer Systems Inc	PO Box 590065, San Francisco CA 94159	415-386-6157	R	1*	<.1
4073	EDP System Services Inc—Ralph Cantrell	19905 Scriber Lake Rd, Lynnwood WA 98036	425-771-3796	R	1*	<.1
4374	Evolution Inc (Shawnee Mission Kansas)—Don Sprowl	10000 W 75th Ste 230-A, Shawnee Mission KS 66204	913-384-2654	R	1*	<.1
4375	FBS Systems Inc—Norm Brown	1855 55th Ave, Aledo IL 61231		R	1*	<.1
4376	Flowmaster USA Inc—Barry Fowell	800 Waukegan Rd Ste 20, Glenview IL 60025	847-901-4240	R	1*	<.1
4377	GRALIN associates Inc—Tim Watson	407 White Oak Branch R, Statesville NC 28625	704-871-2282	R	1	<.1
4378	GW Hannaway and Associates—Wyndham Hanaway	839 Pearl St, Boulder CO 80302	303-440-9631	R	1*	<.1
4379	Hatteras Software Inc—Kevin Sheehan	PO Box 110025, Research Triangle Park NC 27709	919-991-5440	R	1*	<.1
4380	HBG Systems Inc—Bert Gold	5961 Whitetail Ln, Jupiter FL 33458	561-741-3655	R	1*	<.1
4381	Lindo Systems Inc—Linus Schrage	1415 N Dayton St, Chicago IL 60622	312-988-7422	R	1*	<.1
4382	Management Sciences Inc—Marlene Blemel	6022 Constitution Ave, Albuquerque NM 87110	505-255-8611	R	1*	<.1
4383	Maxwell Resources Inc—Howard R Maxwell Jr	2457 Perkiomen Ave, Reading PA 19606	610-779-0522	R	1*	<.1
4384	Micromat Inc	1055 W College Ave, Santa Rosa CA 95401	707-566-3831	R	1*	<.1
4385	MIT Group Inc—Michael Mellott	5090 Dorsey Hall Rd, Ellicott City MD 21042	410-884-0225	R	1*	<.1
4386	Monico LLC—Doyle Taylor	3403 Chapel Sq Dr, Spring TX 77388	281-530-8751	R	1*	<.1
4387	North Ridge Software Inc	1305 11th St Ste 302, Bellingham WA 98225	360-676-5999	R	1*	<.1
4388	Sassafras Software Inc—Denis Devlin	PO Box 150, Hanover NH 03755	603-643-3351	R	1*	<.1
4389	See Corp—Richard Montoni	106 Apple St Ste 100, Tinton Falls NJ 07724	732-933-4040	R	1*	<.1
4390	Software Development Inc—Michael Richards	PO Box 1369, Maplewood NJ 07040	908-620-3030	R	1*	<.1
4391	Software Solutions (Evansville Indiana)—Bob Wheeler	6404 E Oak St, Evansville IN 47715	630-752-0220	R	1*	<.1
4392	Summit Software Inc—Joseph Kohnen	4242 Flagstaff Cove, Fort Wayne IN 46815	260-486-4357	S	1*	<.1
4393	Synaptec Software Inc—Philip L Homburger	4155 E Jewell Ave Ste, Denver CO 80222	303-320-4420	R	1*	<.1
4394	TBSP Inc—IN Botnick	3334 E Coast Hwy Ste 3, Corona Del Mar CA 92625		R	1*	<.1
4395	Vamp Inc—John Soluk	6753 Selma Ave, Los Angeles CA 90028	323-466-5533	R	1	<.1
4396	Virtual Training Company Inc—Mark Vernon	5395 Main St, Stephens City VA 22655	540-869-8686	R	1*	<.1
4397	WaveMetrics Inc—Larry Hutchinson	PO Box 2088, Lake Oswego OR 97035	503-620-3001	R	1*	<.1
4398	Young Minds Inc—David H Cote	700 E Redlands Blvd St, Redlands CA 92373	909-793-8261	R	1*	<.1
4399	a2b Tracking Solutions	207 High Point Ave, Portsmouth RI 02871	401-683-5215	R	1*	<.1
4400	Addsum Business Software Inc—Anthony Frates	PO Box 17284, Salt Lake City UT 84117	801-277-9240	R	1*	<.1
4401	Alternative System Concepts Inc—Jake Karrfalt	PO Box 128, Windham NH 03087	603-437-2234	R	1*	<.1
4402	Amicus Software—Ted Williford	916 Lakepointe St, Grosse Pointe Park MI 48230	313-417-9550	R	1	<.1
4403	Applied Computer Excellence Inc—Michael Fritz	5050 Hillside Dr, West Bend WI 53095		R	1*	<.1
4404	Astrolabe Inc—Gary Christen	PO Box 1750, Brewster MA 02631	508-896-5081	R	1*	<.1
4405	AT/SCAN Ltd	P O Box 152, Portsmouth RI 02871		R	1*	<.1
4406	Barke Group—Roy Barke	7607 Equitable Dr, Eden Prairie MN 55344	952-259-0539	R	1*	<.1
4407	Bluebox Communications Inc	10190 Parkwood Dr Ste, Cupertino CA 95014	408-480-0463	R	1*	<.1
4408	CDE Software—Patrick Lajko	4746 44th Ave SW Ste 2, Seattle WA 98116	206-937-8927	R	1*	<.1
4409	Cerious Software Inc—Phillip Crews	1515 Mockingbird Ln St, Charlotte NC 28209	704-529-0200	R	1*	<.1
4410	Classic Software Inc—John Morgan	7665 Athenia Dr, Cincinnati OH 45244	513-342-2212	R	1*	<.1
4411	Contegra Systems Inc—Rob Wiesenberg	200 Mamaroneck Ave Ste, White Plains NY 10601	914-328-2269	R	1*	<.1
4412	Data Concepts Inc (Nashville Tennessee)—Terry Woodson	187 Graylynn Dr, Nashville TN 37214	615-251-6200	R	1*	<.1
4413	DigiEffects—Robert Sharp	27 N Front St Ste 200, Wilmington NC 28401	910-473-5169	R	1*	<.1
4414	DJW Inc—Danial Yahdav	4460 Redwood Hwy Ste 1, San Rafael CA 94903	415-491-1616	R	1*	<.1
4415	eCaliper—Robert Vanzant	3400 Industrial Ln Ste, Broomfield CO 80020	303-469-3700	R	1*	<.1
4416	Encore Imaging Systems Inc—Lance Johnson	14675 Sw Millikan Way, Beaverton OR 97006	503-639-1528	R	1*	<.1
4417	Examiner Corp—Gary Brown	600 Marshall Ave Ste 1, Saint Paul MN 55102	651-451-7360	R	1*	<.1
4418	Exergetic Systems Inc—Fred D Lang	12 San Marino Dr, San Rafael CA 94901	415-455-0100	R	1*	<.1
4419	Foodco 6—Ron Wilkinson	PO Box 1269, Orem UT 84059	801-225-7907	R	1*	<.1
4420	Freedom Systems Corp—David Crist	2550 Eisenhower Ave, Norristown PA 19403		R	1*	<.1
4421	Geotech Computer Systems Inc—Toni Rich	12150 E Briarwood Ave, Centennial CO 80112	303-740-1999	R	1*	<.1
4422	GrayMatter Corp	1019 Pacific Ave Ste 8, Tacoma WA 98402	253-503-0523	R	1*	<.1
4423	GrayTech Software Inc—Kathryn Gray	2172 Menomini, Wheaton IL 60189	630-682-4030	R	1*	<.1
4424	Greenwich Software and Consulting Group Inc—Mark Dollar	20 Division St Ste B, Greenwich CT 06830	203-661-4777	R	1*	<.1
4425	HEM Data Corp—Ricky Walter	17320 Twelve Mile Rd, Southfield MI 48076	248-559-5607	R	1*	<.1

Note: An asterisk (*) indicates an estimated financial figure. The company type code used is as follows: R = Private, P = Public, S = Private Subsidiary, B = Public Subsidiary, D = Division, J = Joint Venture, I = Investment Fund.

COMPANY RANKINGS BY SALES WITHIN 4-DIGIT SIC

Rank	Company Name—*Executive Officer*	Address, City, State, Zip	Phone	Type	Fin	Empls
4426	Landmark Data Systems Inc—*Bill Skelton*	2 Old River Pl Ste L, Jackson MS 39202	601-362-0303	R	1*	<.1
4427	Matsch Financial Systems Ltd—*Bill Aho*	911 Division Ave N, Grand Rapids MI 49503		R	1*	<.1
4428	MicroControls International—*Dan Slaughter*	PO Box 3254, Rancho Cucamonga CA 91729		R	1*	<.1
4429	Micronet Systems Inc—*Alan Queen*	4411 Emerald Rd, Boise ID 83706	208-384-9137	R	1*	<.1
4430	Mountain Systems Inc—*Erik Udstuen*	4748 Norwood St SW, Roanoke VA 24018		R	1*	<.1
4431	Musick International Inc—*Sara Burns*	PO Box 1370, Buena Vista CO 81211	719-395-4124	R	1*	<.1
4432	Norman Data Defense Systems Inc—*Stein Surlien*	9302 Lee Hwy Ste 950A, Fairfax VA 22031	703-267-6109	S	1*	<.1
4433	Northeast Texas Online Inc—*Paul Starnes*	201 N Collegiate Dr St, Paris TX 75460	903-784-1582	R	1*	<.1
4434	NSC Inc—*Larry Nies*	428 W Ryan St, Brillion WI 54110	920-756-5305	R	1*	<.1
4435	PALOS Software—*David Altomare* JinTek LLC	5205 Kearny Villa Way, San Diego CA 92123	858-836-4400	S	1*	<.1
4436	PC Scale Inc—*Donald Tefft*	PO Box 98, Oxford PA 19363	610-932-4006	R	1*	<.1
4437	Pictographics International Corp—*Craig Huelskoetter*	151 W Burnsville Pkwy, Burnsville MN 55337	952-894-6247	R	1*	<.1
4438	Prairie Group Inc—*John Kirk*	PO Box 65820, West Des Moines IA 50265	515-225-3720	R	1*	<.1
4439	Shelko Consulting LLC—*Aric Shelko*	214 State St Ste 104, Hackensack NJ 07601	201-444-2089	R	1*	<.1
4440	Software Bisque Inc—*Stephen Bisque*	912 12th St, Golden CO 80401		R	1*	<.1
4441	Software Partners/32 Inc—*Phil Jamieson*	447 Old Boston Rd, Topsfield MA 01983	978-887-6409	R	1*	<.1
4442	StrayLight Corp—*Tony Asch*	16 Mount Bethel Rd Ste, Warren NJ 07059	908-580-0086	R	1*	<.1
4443	Tardis Systems Inc—*Christopher Ciarcia*	21632 High Rock Rd Bld, Monroe WA 98272		R	1*	<.1
4444	Tranxition Corp—*Jim Creech*	1231 NW Hoyt St Ste 20, Portland OR 97209		R	1*	<.1
4445	Visionary Solutions Inc—*Jordan Christoff*	2060 Alameda Padre Ser, Santa Barbara CA 93103	805-845-8900	R	1*	<.1
4446	Workstation Group—*John Cifonelli*	785 Oakwood Rd Ste E10, Lake Zurich IL 60047	847-540-3395	R	1*	<.1
4447	Academy Systems Inc—*Michael Hochman*	1343 E 10 St, Brooklyn NY 11230	718-645-2330	R	1*	<.1
4448	ASD/QMS Inc	PO Box 1454, Birmingham MI 48012	248-370-9919	R	1	<.1
4449	Bear Computer Systems Inc—*Larry Robertson*	12315 Califa St Ste 2, Valley Village CA 91607	818-203-4569	R	1*	<.1
4450	Chamber Data Systems Inc—*Forence Durant*	15221 Berry Trl Ste 50, Dallas TX 75248	972-233-1299	R	1*	<.1
4451	Conquest Systems Inc—*Richard Landry*	7617 Arllington Rd, Bethesda MD 20814	301-556-2455	R	1*	<.1
4452	Database Management Technology Inc	218 Delaware St Ste 40, Kansas City MO 64105	816-421-3500	R	1*	<.1
4453	Decision Support Technology Inc	PO Box 665, Ramsey NJ 07446	201-995-9500	R	1*	<.1
4454	Demand Wave Solutions'	1015 S Wall St Ste G, Calhoun GA 30701	706-625-4898	R	1*	<.1
4455	Digital ChoreoGraphics	PO Box 8268, Newport Beach CA 92658	949-548-1969	R	1*	<.1
4456	Elite Software Development Inc—*Bill Smith*	2700 Arrington Rd, College Station TX 77845		R	1	<.1
4457	Empirical Software	1151 Williams Dr, Aiken SC 29803	803-648-5931	R	1*	<.1
4458	Financial Accounting Systems Inc—*Doyle Castleberry*	1961 Royal View Dr, Placerville CA 95667	417-623-8647	R	1*	<.1
4459	Gary Bergman Associates Inc—*Gary Bergman*	14 Hickory Ln, North Brunswick NJ 08902	732-247-2727	R	1*	<.1
4460	Gimpel Software—*James Gimpel*	3207 Hogarth Ln, Collegeville PA 19426	610-584-4261	R	1	<.1
4461	Hanford Bay Associates Ltd—*Kenneth D Stanely*	275 Northpointe Pkwy S, Amherst NY 14228	716-636-0100	R	1*	<.1
4462	Kent Homeopathic Associates Inc—*David Warkentin*	454 Las Gallinas Ave S, San Rafael CA 94903	415-662-1005	R	1*	<.1
4463	Klynas Engineering—*Scott Klynas*	PO Box 1818, Santa Maria CA 93456	805-938-9988	R	1	<.1
4464	Micro Specialties Inc—*Gus Levesque*	430 Smith St, Middletown CT 06457	203-874-1832	R	1*	<.1
4465	Multimedia Graphic Network—*Gill Davis*	2533 S Hwy 101 Ste 206, Cardiff By The Sea CA 92007	760-753-6397	R	1*	<.1
4466	Nota Bene—*Anthony Lassman*	PO Box 160, Hastings on Hudson NY 10706	718-382-1500	R	1*	<.1
4467	Pettit and Company PC—*Larry Pettit*	12221 Merit Dr, Dallas TX 75251	972-437-2230	R	1*	<.1
4468	Piedmont Systems Inc—*Tom Hiers*	P O Box 2088, Advance NC 27006	336-998-2800	R	1*	<.1
4469	Pizer Inc—*Allen Peyser*	503 N 36th St Ste A, Seattle WA 98103	206-634-2808	R	1*	<.1
4470	Ray Ontko and Co—*Nathan Treadway*	822 E Main St, Richmond IN 47374	765-935-4283	R	1*	<.1
4471	RTP Group Inc—*Gary DeLong*	5100 E Anaheim Rd, Long Beach CA 90815	562-961-4100	R	1*	<.1
4472	Sammamish DataSystems Inc—*Robert Schweitzer*	PO Box 70382, Bellevue WA 98007	425-867-1485	R	1*	<.1
4473	SoftTech Solutions LLC—*Paul Violassi*	630 S Ortonville Rd, Ortonville MI 48462	248-627-8100	R	1*	<.1
4474	Software Computer Group Inc—*Butch Evans*	PO Box 3042, Charleston WV 25331	304-343-6480	R	1*	<.1
4475	SST Systems Inc—*G V Ranjan PE*	1798 Technology Dr Ste, San Jose CA 95110	408-452-8111	R	1*	<.1
4476	TAL Technologies Inc	2101 Brandywine St Ste, Philadelphia PA 19130	215-496-0222	R	1*	<.1
4477	Telepartner International Inc—*Dan Kokoruda*	1822 Main St, Glastonbury CT 06033	860-368-4550	R	1	<.1
4478	Ultramarine Inc—*Ray Nachlinger*	3100 S Gessner Ste 325, Houston TX 77063	713-975-8146	R	1*	<.1
4479	Adager Corp—*Alfredo Rego*	PO Box 3000, Sun Valley ID 83353	208-726-9100	R	1*	<.1
4480	Advanced Graphics Software Inc	PO Box 9281, Rancho Santa Fe CA 92067	760-634-8360	R	1*	<.1
4481	Alpine Data Inc—*Jesse A Tarshis*	62926 Hwy 90, Montrose CO 81403	970-249-1400	R	1*	<.1
4482	Andromeda Software Inc (Thousand Oaks California)—*Sumeet Pasricha*	699 Hampshire Rd Ste 1, Thousand Oaks CA 91361	805-379-4109	R	1*	<.1
4483	Applied Logic Systems Inc	PO Box 400175, Cambridge MA 02140	617-497-0100	R	1*	<.1
4484	Arbor Image Corp—*Tom Gray*	5651 Plymouth Rd, Ann Arbor MI 48105	734-741-8700	R	1*	<.1
4485	ARC Science Simulation Inc—*Thomas Ligon*	1122 N Denver Ave, Loveland CO 80537	970-667-1168	R	1*	<.1
4486	Automated Accounting Systems Inc	PO Box 436, Livingston AL 35470		R	1*	<.1
4487	Bokler Software Corp—*Jeff Bezos*	PO Box 261, Huntsville AL 35804	256-539-9901	R	1*	<.1
4488	Boston Business Computing Ltd—*David Pikcilingis*	PO Box 2316, Acton MA 01720	978-725-3222	R	1*	<.1
4489	Building Block Software Inc—*John Keklak*	12 West St, Sudbury MA 01776	978-443-6429	R	1*	<.1
4490	Business Forecast Systems Inc—*Bob Goodrich*	68 Leonard St, Belmont MA 02478	617-484-5050	R	1	<.1
4491	CADMAN Corp—*Delton J Rowe*	1413 Montgomery Rd, Thousand Oaks CA 91360	805-390-6978	R	1*	<.1
4492	Channel Trend Inc—*Allen F Campbell*	4400 Northcorp Pky, Palm Beach Gardens FL 33410	561-847-7174	R	1*	<.1
4493	Computer Business Solutions Inc—*Dennis Smith*	22 E Main St, Lititz PA 17543	717-627-1730	R	1*	<.1
4494	Computronics (Addison Illinois)—*Randal Styka*	4N165 Wood Dale Rd, Addison IL 60101	630-941-7767	R	1*	<.1
4495	CONDOR Computing Inc—*Tom Beasley*	PO Box 17276, Huntsville AL 35810	256-852-4490	R	1*	<.1
4496	CostFlex Systems Inc—*Jim Ryan*	4320 Blvd Park S Ste A, Mobile AL 36609	251-343-9595	R	1*	<.1
4497	Crescent Bay Software Corp—*Brian Brode*	10950 Washington Blvd, Culver City CA 90232	310-836-5183	R	1*	<.1
4498	Digitool Inc—*Steve Hain*	PO Box 335, Lancaster MA 01523	617-441-5000	R	1*	<.1
4499	DND Inc	2833 Duke St, Alexandria VA 22314	703-751-2666	R	1*	<.1
4500	Ferox Microsystems Inc	8403 Porter Ln, Alexandria VA 22308	703-780-2044	R	1*	<.1
4501	FFE Software Inc—*Lee Fesperman*	PO Box 1570, El Cerrito CA 94530	510-232-6800	R	1*	<.1
4502	Fuel Data Systems Inc—*Janice Brown*	772 Greenville Tpke, Middletown NY 10940	845-355-2051	R	1*	<.1
4503	G and Z Systems Inc—*Richard Zuckerman*	515 N State Rd, Briarcliff Manor NY 10510	914-345-5600	R	1*	<.1
4504	g4 Inc	2821 E Commercial Blvd, Fort Lauderdale FL 33308	954-229-0900	R	1*	<.1
4505	Gamma Software Inc—*Gary Mayfield*	PO Box 760, Medford OR 97501	541-770-5587	R	1*	<.1
4506	GBS Consultants Inc—*Richard Latham*	17714 Littleleaf Ct, Chesterfield MO 63005	636-530-1308	R	1*	<.1
4507	Generation Technologies Corp	6420 W 110th St Ste 10, Overland Park KS 66211	913-345-1012	R	1*	<.1
4508	GraphPad Software Inc—*Harvey Motulsky*	2236 Avenida de la Pla, La Jolla CA 92037	858-454-5577	R	1*	<.1
4509	HindSight Ltd—*Jeff Schewe*	PO Box 520, Lafayette CO 80026	303-791-3770	R	1*	<.1
4510	Hydrocomp Inc—*Norman Crawford*	2386 Branner Dr, Menlo Park CA 94025	650-561-9030	R	1*	<.1
4511	Insider Software Inc—*Bruce Mitchell*	208 Granada Way Ste 20, Los Gatos CA 95032	520-229-1212	R	1*	<.1
4512	International Software Engineering	2302 US Hwy 41 W, Marquette MI 49855	906-228-7800	R	1*	<.1
4513	Internet Programming and Consulting Inc—*Essandra Macedo*	PO Box 347, Glen Echo MD 20812	301-320-7080	R	1*	<.1

Rank	Company Name—*Executive Officer*	Address, City, State, Zip	Phone	Type	Fin	Empls
4514	InTrec Software Inc—*Jerry Cline*	3035 E Topaz Cir, Phoenix AZ 85028	602-992-1345	R	1*	<.1
4515	Irwin P Sharpe and Associates Business Research and Surveys Div	50 Greenwood Ave, West Orange NJ 07052	973-731-7800	D	1*	<.1
4516	JP Software Inc—*Rex Conn*	PO Box 328, Chestertown MD 21620		R	1*	<.1
4517	Linker Systems Inc—*Toni Poper*	13612 Onkayha Cir, Irvine CA 92620	949-552-1904	R	1*	<.1
4518	Malibu Software Group Inc	228 Commercial St Ste, Nevada City CA 95959	530-478-0500	R	1*	<.1
4519	Math Corp—*Michael Shohoney*	610 South St, Green Lake WI 54941	920-294-0180	R	1*	<.1
4520	MBA Software and Consulting—*John Stevenken*	5409 Nicollet Ave S, Minneapolis MN 55419	612-825-3315	R	1*	<.1
4521	Meat Handler Co—*Jay Hall*	1030 Beech St, Cleveland WI 53015	920-693-3141	R	1*	<.1
4522	Metagraphics Software Corp	PO Box 225, Woodinville WA 98072		R	1	<.1
4523	MGM Interactive Inc	10250 Constellation Bl, Los Angeles CA 90067	310-449-3000	S		<.1
4524	MicroGlyph Systems—*Charlotte Vote*	PO Box 474, Lexington MA 02420	781-861-0426	R	1*	<.1
4525	Microtab Inc—*Laurence G Hills Jr*	5505 Orchard Hill Terr, Cumming GA 30028	678-455-3161	R	1*	<.1
4526	MIX Software Inc—*Jim Sinamon*	1203 Berkeley Dr, Richardson TX 75081	972-231-0949	R	1*	<.1
4527	MKS Inc (Wayne Pennsylvania)—*Victor Hansen*	992 Old Eagle School R, Wayne PA 19087	610-989-9905	R	1*	<.1
4528	Mumford Micro Systems—*Bryan Mumford*	PO Box 156, Green Bank WV 24944	805-687-5116	R	1*	<.1
4529	NanoPac Inc—*Silvio Cianfrone*	4823 S Sheridan Rd Ste, Tulsa OK 74145	918-665-0329	R	1*	<.1
4530	Neal Nelson and Associates—*Neal Nelson*	222 N River St, East Dundee IL 60118	847-851-8900	R	1*	<.1
4531	Netlogic Inc—*Bret D Schlussman*	770 Broadway 2nd Fl, New York NY 10003	212-533-9090	R	1*	<.1
4532	Northern Computing Consultants—*Eric Mostrom*	18201 Sunrise Ridge Av, Poulsbo WA 98370	907-723-3386	R	1*	<.1
4533	Northern Software Inc—*Robert Hamen*	PO Box 309, Hancock MI 49930	906-932-9990	R	1*	<.1
4534	NovaTek Corp—*Gaston Oxman*	3837 Northdale Blvd St, Tampa FL 33624	813-968-7195	R	1*	<.1
4535	NP Systems Inc—*Howard Prussack*	6318 Amboy Rd, Staten Island NY 10309	718-966-1708	R	1*	<.1
4536	Omnitrend Software Inc	3 Stanwich Ln, Burlington CT 06013	860-673-8910	R	1*	<.1
4537	OpWare LLC—*James Nielson*	PO Box 310, Le Roy NY 14482	585-768-2282	R	1*	<.1
4538	Padus Inc—*Boghos Levon Zekiyan*	76 East Campbell Ave, Campbell CA 95008	408-370-0377	R	1*	<.1
4539	PAE Inc—*Peter O'Connor*	50 Masten Dr, Northwood NH 03261	603-548-5721	R	1*	<.1
4540	Page Technology Marketing Inc—*Robert Pooley*	3525 Del Mar Heights R, San Diego CA 92130	858-794-6884	R	1*	<.1
4541	Para Technologies—*Arthur Saltzman*	3273 Indiana Ave, Costa Mesa CA 92626	714-546-8619	R	1*	<.1
4542	PeleSoft—*Alex Soya* Logan Industries Inc (Palm Bay Florida)	2312 S Babcock St, Melbourne FL 32901	321-984-1627	D	1*	<.1
4543	Precision Data Systems Inc—*Robert Pollock*	13957 S Kostner Ave, Crestwood IL 60445	708-371-6555	R	1*	<.1
4544	Program Workshop Inc—*Michael Sanders*	301 Healthpark Blvd St, Saint Augustine FL 32086	904-829-6500	R	1*	<.1
4545	Qualitas Inc—*Mary Stanley*	PO Box 3299, Shepherdstown WV 25443	304-876-1856	R	1*	<.1
4546	QuantumWorks Corp—*Steve Tice*	5664 Mission Center Rd, San Diego CA 92108	619-295-9648	R	1*	<.1
4547	Qube Connections Inc—*Kent Greene*	7210 Estrella De Mar R, Carlsbad CA 92009	760-804-3721	R	1*	<.1
4548	Quick America Corp—*Jun Yamori*	708 3rd Ave Ste 1320, New York NY 10017	212-310-1960	R	1*	<.1
4549	RDR Inc (Portland Oregon)—*Robert Russell*	740 NW 114th Ave, Portland OR 97229	503-643-2723	R	1*	<.1
4550	RealData Inc—*Frank Gallinelli*	PO Box 691, South Norwalk CT 06854	203-816-8457	R	1*	<.1
4551	Response Technology Inc—*Phil Sensabaugh*	304 Main Ave S Ste 300, Renton WA 98057	425-254-8687	R	1*	<.1
4552	Scientific Computing Associates Corp—*Ching Liu*	525 N Lincoln Ave, Villa Park IL 60181	630-834-4567	R	1*	<.1
4553	Shekinah Studios—*Jason Hurdlow*	713 N Lincoln, Moscow ID 83843	208-596-4027	R	1*	<.1
4554	Sinclair Optics Inc—*Carl Wilson*	5 Lacoma Ln, Pittsford NY 14534	585-381-0205	R	1*	<.1
4555	Soft USE Inc—*Tulin Edev*	116 Old Padonia Rd, Hunt Valley MD 21030	410-561-4342	R	1*	<.1
4556	Software602 Inc (Jacksonville Florida)—*David Kusner*	351 15th Ave S Ste A, Jacksonville Beach FL 32250	904-642-5400	R	1*	<.1
4557	Spede Technologies—*Robert Bunsoy*	24864 Detriot Rd, Cleveland OH 44145	440-808-8888	R	1*	<.1
4558	SpeechSoft Inc	49 The Xing, Armonk NY 10504		R	1*	<.1
4559	Stand Alone Inc	522 N Ada, Chicago IL 60642		R	1	<.1
4560	Standardware Inc—*David Evans*	424 Pelham Manor Rd, Pelham NY 10803	914-738-6382	R	1*	<.1
4561	T-Cubed Systems Inc—*George Oram*	31220 La Baya Dr Ste 1, Westlake Village CA 91362	818-991-0057	R	1*	<.1
4562	Telenomics Inc—*Rick Hupe*	41120 Elm St Ste 221, Murrieta CA 92562	951-677-4714	R	1*	<.1
4563	Terra Data Inc—*Paul Pugliese*	6 Corwin Ct, Dix Hills NY 11746	631-462-6939	R	1*	<.1
4564	TexaSoft Mission Technologies—*Alan Elliiot*	PO Box 1169, Cedar Hill TX 75106	972-291-2115	R	1*	<.1
4565	Till Photography—*Mark Till*	6 Surrey Ln, Natick MA 01760	508-655-9595	R	1	<.1
4566	TOPS Engineering Corp—*Bill Rehring*	275 W Campbell Road St, Richardson TX 75080	972-739-8677	R	1*	<.1
4567	Tracer Technologies Inc (York Pennsylvania)—*Curtis Crowe*	PO Box 189, Windsor PA 17366	717-764-9240	R	1*	<.1
4568	!Trak-It Solutions Inc—*John Enyedy*	7523 W Crimson Sky Dr, Tucson AZ 85743	916-780-8767	R	1*	<.1
4569	TransWare Enterprises Inc—*Virginia Jones*	1565 Mediterranean Dr, Sycamore IL 60178	815-895-4700	R	1*	<.1
4570	TreeAge Software Inc—*Morris Raker*	1075 Main St, Williamstown MA 01267	413-458-0104	R	1*	<.1
4571	Twinbridge Software Corp—*Edward Chang*	1055 Corporate Ctr Dr, Monterey Park CA 91754	323-263-3926	R	1*	<.1
4572	UNI-SOURCE 2000 Inc	11040 Manchester Rd St, Saint Louis MO 63122	314-822-3735	R	1*	<.1
4573	Von Gunten Engineering Software Inc—*Michael Von Gunten*	363 W Drake Ste 10, Fort Collins CO 80526	970-223-8788	R	1*	<.1
4574	V-Technologies LLC—*Angelo Volta*	675 W Johnson Ave, Cheshire CT 06410	203-439-9060	R	1*	<.1
4575	Willies Computer Software Co	6215 Longflower Ln, Kingwood TX 77345	281-360-4232	R	1*	<.1
4576	Wincite Systems—*Don Smith*	19 S LaSalle St Ste 30, Chicago IL 60603	312-424-6420	R	1*	<.1
4577	Winworks Software—*Jennifer Folsom*	344 Placerville Dr Ste, Placerville CA 95667	530-621-3265	R	1*	<.1
4578	World Sharp Inc—*Bobby Anderson*	PO Box 841, Angel Fire NM 87710	575-445-2504	R	1*	<.1
4579	WritePro Corp—*Sol Stein*	43 S Highland Ave, Ossining NY 10562		R	1	<.1
4580	Young and Associates Ltd—*William J Young*	2625 Butterfield Rd St, Oak Brook IL 60523	630-573-2500	R	1*	<.1
4581	Zerious Electronic Publishing—*Jeff Starfield*	93 Park St, Beverly MA 01915	617-782-5884	R	1*	<.1
4582	Abbott Systems Inc—*Ken Abbott*	62 Mountain Rd, Pleasantville NY 10570	914-747-3116	R	1*	<.1
4583	Advanced Computer Innovations Inc—*Vasant Saini*	656 Kreag Rd, Pittsford NY 14534	585-385-3810	R	1*	<.1
4584	Advantage Solutions Inc—*Roger Hughes*	671 Paxton Pl, Carol Stream IL 60188	630-668-1598	R	1*	<.1
4585	Application Programming and Development Inc—*Mark Burnett*	1282 Smallwood Dr W St, Waldorf MD 20603	301-893-9115	R	1*	<.1
4586	Asset Systems Inc—*Alden Snyder*	24 W 500 Maple Ave, Naperville IL 60540	630-428-9898	R	1*	<.1
4587	Basic Solutions—*Victoria Brooks*	PO Box 50198, Long Beach CA 90815	562-972-1211	R	1*	<.1
4588	Business Applications Performance Corp—*John Peterson*	756 Herrman Ct, Liberty MO 64068		R	1*	<.1
4589	Carmel Software Inc—*Steve Roth*	1050 Northgate Dr Ste, San Rafael CA 94903		R	1*	<.1
4590	Catalyst Corp—*Tony McConn*	12322 Hwy 99 Ste 126, Everett WA 98204	425-485-0331	R	1*	<.1
4591	Centaur Systems Ltd—*Rob Latousek*	407 N Brearly St, Madison WI 53703	608-255-6979	R	1*	<.1
4592	Creative Approaches Inc—*Travis Piper*	PO Box 116, East Bloomfield NY 14443	585-657-6379	R	1*	<.1
4593	Critical Tools Inc—*Jim Spiller*	7308 W Rim Dr, Austin TX 78731	512-342-2232	R	1*	<.1
4594	Data Center Software Inc	70 Herrick St, Beverly MA 01915	978-922-5500	R	1*	<.1
4595	Data Intelligence Systems Corp—*Milan Dabcovich*	5 Shawsheen Ave Ste 4, Bedford MA 01730		R	1*	<.1
4596	Data Team Corp	5459 W 85th Ter, Prairie Village KS 66207		R	1*	<.1
4597	Database Services Inc	5415 Lake Howell Rd St, Winter Park FL 32792	407-679-1539	R	1*	<.1
4598	DesignSoft Co	P O Box 187, Trevor WI 53179		R	1*	<.1
4599	Digital Wisdom Inc—*David Broad*	PO Box 2070, Tappahannock VA 22560	804-443-9000	S	1*	<.1
4600	E-8 Publications Inc—*Patricia Mutkoski*	121 E Remington Rd, Ithaca NY 14850	607-257-7610	R	1*	<.1

Note: An asterisk (*) indicates an estimated financial figure. The company type code used is as follows: R = Private, P = Public, S = Private Subsidiary, B = Public Subsidiary, D = Division, J = Joint Venture, I = Investment Fund.

COMPANY RANKINGS BY SALES WITHIN 4-DIGIT SIC

Rank	Company Name—*Executive Officer*	Address, City, State, Zip	Phone	Type	Fin	Empls
4601	Econometric Modeling and Computing Corp—*William D Teeters*	10489 Haley St, Spring Hill FL 34608	352-688-7622	R	1*	<.1
4602	EDI Communications Corp	20380 Town Ctr Ln Ste, Cupertino CA 95014	408-996-1343	R	1*	<.1
4603	EDI Integration Corp—*Joseph Carley*	PO Box 4166, Crofton MD 21114	410-721-9744	R	1*	<.1
4604	ElectraSoft—*Jon Krahmer*	3207 Carmel Valley Dr, Missouri City TX 77459	281-261-0307	R	1*	<.1
4605	Enercomp Inc	1721 Arroyo Dr, Auburn CA 95603	530-885-9890	R	1*	<.1
4606	Exceller Software Corp—*Eric Fikri*	10999 Reed Hartman Hwy, Cincinnati OH 45242	513-792-9555	R	1*	<.1
4607	Fifth Wave—*John Dasher*	1627 Via Campo Verde, San Jose CA 95120	408-927-5108	R	1*	<.1
4608	FirmWorks—*William M Bradley*	4568 Darcelle Dr, Union City CA 94587	510-324-8510	R	1*	<.1
4609	Flexus International Corp—*Robert Wolfe*	PO Box 640, Bangor PA 18013	610-863-8400	R	1*	<.1
4610	Granville Publications Software—*Harvey A Goldstein*	4250 Ellenita Ave, Tarzana CA 91356		R	1	<.1
4611	Greenbriar Graphics LLC—*Paul McClung*	438 Lockbridge Rd, Meadow Bridge WV 25976	304-484-7034	R	1*	<.1
4612	Haleo Corp—*Leslie Hvostov*	PO Box 245, West Linn OR 97068	503-675-1675	R	1*	<.1
4613	Health Software of Mt Pleasant	1501 W Washington St, Mount Pleasant IA 52641	319-986-5131	R	1*	<.1
4614	InfoStar Inc—*Peter Greene*	7637 Farmington Way, Madison WI 53717	608-444-8061	R	1*	<.1
4615	Insight Software Solutions Inc—*Stan Jones*	PO Box 106, Kaysville UT 84037	801-927-5009	R	1*	<.1
4616	INTEDATA Systems—*Dean Muehler*	113 E 5th St, Mountain Home AR 72653	870-425-3838	R	1*	<.1
4617	Interactive Health Systems Inc—*Roger Gould*	1014 Moraga Dr, Los Angeles CA 90049	310-824-0622	R	1*	<.1
4618	Judson Rosebush Co—*Judson Rosebush*	630 9th Ave Ste 502, New York NY 10036	212-581-3000	R	1*	<.1
4619	KIS Information Systems Inc—*Carl Rogger*	PO Box 1694, Oroville WA 98844	250-490-8117	R	1*	<.1
4620	Logic Group Inc	1024 Patterson Rd, Austin TX 78733	512-263-0118	R	1*	<.1
4621	Medical Knowledge Systems Inc—*Creflo Mims*	440 Burroughs Ste 130, Detroit MI 48202	313-483-0955	R	1*	<.1
4622	Millennia Corp	PO Box 9410, Surprise AZ 85374	425-788-0932	R	1*	<.1
4623	MoneySoft Inc—*Bob Machiz*	1 E Camelback Rd Ste 5, Phoenix AZ 85012	602-266-7710	R	1*	<.1
4624	Monis Software Inc	340 Madison Ave, New York NY 10173	646-445-1018	S	1*	<.1
4625	Peak Horizons Inc—*Brad Hillyard*	473 E 1150 N, Logan UT 84341	435-753-0007	R	1*	<.1
4626	Professional Software Associates Inc	1526 W Pawnee Ln, Colbert WA 99005	509-466-9800	R	1*	<.1
4627	Purity Software Inc—*Nathan Nunn*	PO Box 151385, Austin TX 78715	512-328-2288	R	1*	<.1
4628	Quinn-Curtis Inc—*Richard Quinn*	18 Hearthstone Dr, Medfield MA 02052	508-359-6639	R	1*	<.1
4629	Rapid Output Co	1220 Kilkare Rd, Sunol CA 94586		R	1*	<.1
4630	Real Time Computer Services Inc—*David J Rosenbaum*	132 Euclid Ave, Ardsley NY 10502	914-693-7000	R	1*	<.1
4631	RJM Systems Inc—*Reece Schuler*	712 Madelyn Dr, Des Plaines IL 60016	847-228-1130	R	1*	<.1
4632	RR Software Inc—*Randall Brukardt*	PO Box 1512, Madison WI 53701	608-245-0375	R	1*	<.1
4633	Santa Maria Software Inc—*Vance Breese*	PO Box 1239, Nipomo CA 93444	805-929-8266	R	1*	<.1
4634	Schellenbach and Associates Inc—*Lee Bacall*	8041 Foothill Blvd, Sunland CA 91040	818-951-1891	R	1*	<.1
4635	Skyhound—*Greg Crinklaw*	PO Box 1182, Cloudcroft NM 88317	575-446-1221	R	1*	<.1
4636	SofDesign International Inc	3309 Buckethorn Ct, Garland TX 75044	972-316-8920	R	1*	<.1
4637	Softek Business Systems Inc—*Madhurima Kura*	PO BOX 158, Selkirk NY 12158	518-475-0700	R	1*	<.1
4638	Software Art Consulting—*Doug Spencer*	6830 Via Del Oro Ste 1, San Jose CA 95119	408-226-7321	R	1*	<.1
4639	Software Co-Op Inc—*Bruce Bender*	59 E Mill Rd Ste 1-103, Long Valley NJ 07853	908-867-7055	R	1*	<.1
4640	Solution Technology Inc—*Daniel Doczy*	1101 S Rogers Cir Ste, Boca Raton FL 33487	561-241-3210	R	1*	<.1
4641	Stanford Business Software Inc—*Mukund N Thapa*	PO Box 60398, Palo Alto CA 94306	650-856-1695	R	1*	<.1
4642	Steel Solutions Inc—*Ron Taylor*	PO Box 321425, Jackson MS 39232	304-493-6561	R	1*	<.1
4643	Synergetic Data Systems Inc	3976 Durock Rd Rm 102, Latrobe CA 95682	530-672-9970	R	1*	<.1
4644	Systems Effectiveness Associates Inc—*Peter Bachant*	20 Vernon St, Norwood MA 02062	781-762-9252	R	1*	<.1
4645	Thermal Analysis Systems Co—*Robert Cronfel*	725 Parkview Cir, Elk Grove Village IL 60007	847-439-5429	R	1*	<.1
4646	Torrid Technologies Inc—*Tim Turner*	1860 Sandy Plains Rd S, Marietta GA 30066	770-565-6405	R	1*	<.1
4647	Trix Systems Inc—*Jorgen Frilander*	68 Smith St, Chelmsford MA 01824	978-256-4445	S	1*	<.1
4648	Ultra-X Inc—*Steve Weitzner*	2075 De La Cruz Blvd S, Santa Clara CA 95050	408-261-7090	R	1*	<.1
4649	Utopia Software Solutions Inc—*Brian Earley*	51 Wraith Ave, Cumberland RI 02864		R	1*	<.1
4650	WILLIAMS Cadco	72 Via Sonrisa, San Clemente CA 92673	949-492-7862	R	1*	<.1
4651	WorksRight Software Inc—*Leon Stewart*	PO Box 1156, Madison MS 39110	601-856-8337	R	1*	<.1
4652	A Bit Better Corp—*Cathleen Belleville*	171 Main St Ste 171, Los Altos CA 94022		R	1*	<.1
4653	a/Soft Development Inc—*Kenneth Graf*	46-369 Haiku Rd H-8, Kaneohe HI 96744	808-754-7272	R	1*	<.1
4654	Ability Systems Corp—*Arthur Volta*	1422 Arnold Ave, Roslyn PA 19001	215-657-4338	R	1*	<.1
4655	AeroHydro Inc—*John Letcher*	PO Box 684, Southwest Harbor ME 04679	207-244-4100	R	1*	<.1
4656	AnaTek Corp	PO Box 1200, Amherst NH 03031	603-672-0172	R	1*	<.1
4657	Application Techniques Inc—*Daniel Case*	PO Box 484, Pepperell MA 01463	978-433-5201	R	1*	<.1
4658	Articulate Software Inc—*Adam Pease*	420 College Ave, Angwin CA 94508	707-965-2562	R	1*	<.1
4659	ARTS PDF—*Karl Deabrew*	4713 1st St Ste 200, Moraga CA 94556	925-931-1641	D	1*	<.1
4660	AS-Pro Software Inc—*Anthony Sebastian*	5601 Schooner Loop, Discovery Bay CA 95014	760-672-3309	R	1*	<.1
4661	Attorneys' Computer Network Inc—*Gerald W McFarren*	415 Marlboro Rd, Kennett Square PA 19348	610-347-1500	R	1*	<.1
4662	Auto FX Corp—*Cliff Weems*	141 Village St Ste 2, Birmingham AL 35242	205-980-0056	R	1*	<.1
4663	Beacon Hill Software—*Brad Lucas*	230 Park Ave Ste 1000, New York NY 10169	914-834-2820	R	1*	<.1
4664	BeCubed Software Inc—*Bill Locke*	7366 Bridle Dr, Nashville TN 37221		R	1*	<.1
4665	Bekemeier and Associates—*Mike Bekemeier*	4578 Georgia St, San Diego CA 92116	619-297-3306	R	1*	<.1
4666	Bharani Software Solutions Inc—*Arul Priya Balasubramanian*	1901 Carnegie Ave Ste, Santa Ana CA 92705	949-864-0734	R	1*	<.1
4667	Burton Systems Software Inc—*David Burton*	PO Box 4157, Cary NC 27519	919-481-0149	R	1*	<.1
4668	CADlink Technology Corp (Clinton Massachusetts)—*Jim Ramsden*	500 Main St, Clinton MA 01510	978-368-3353	R	1*	<.1
4669	Callaway Graphicsoftware LLC—*Bryan D Mullins*	232 S Ashland Ave, Lexington KY 40502	859-269-7512	R	1*	<.1
4670	CalWeb Internet Services Inc—*Robert Dugaue*	11465 Sunrise Gold Cir, Rancho Cordova CA 95742	916-641-9320	R	1*	<.1
4671	Carina Software	865 Ackerman Dr, Danville CA 94526	925-838-0695	R	1*	<.1
4672	ChemInnovation Software Inc—*Henry Li*	7966 Arjons Dr Ste A, San Diego CA 92126	858-780-0371	R	1*	<.1
4673	Christian Technologies Inc—*Michael Rusk*	PO Box 2201, Independence MO 64055	816-478-8320	R	1*	<.1
4674	CMG Inc—*Johnny Chan*	5171 Oswego Rd, Rome NY 13440	315-533-1849	R	1*	<.1
4675	Commercial Data Systems Corp—*Billy S Davis*	601 Woodlawn Dr NE Ste, Marietta GA 30067	770-971-8000	R	1*	<.1
4676	Computer Language Company Inc—*Alan Freedman*	5521 State Park Rd, Point Pleasant PA 18950	215-297-8082	R	1*	<.1
4677	Crosstech Systems Inc—*Ed Singer*	PO Box 740346, Boynton Beach FL 33474	561-880-0077	R	1*	<.1
4678	CryptoMetrics Inc—*Robert Barra*	73 Main St, Tuckahoe NY 10707	914-793-2053	R	1*	<.1
4679	Cybernetic Solutions Company Inc—*R Kent Francis*	3251 W 6610 S, Salt Lake City UT 84184	801-966-0999	R	1*	<.1
4680	CyberSoft Inc (Phoenix Arizona)—*Ed Prestwood*	3851 E Thunderhill Pl, Phoenix AZ 85044	480-626-2025	R	1*	<.1
4681	Data Techniques Inc (Burnsville North Carolina)—*John Davis*	5 CC Allen Rd, Burnsville NC 28714	828-682-4111	R	1*	<.1
4682	Daystar Software Inc—*Mark Florence*	8303 NW Hillside, Kansas City MO 64152	816-741-4310	R	1*	<.1
4683	Digimage Arts—*Keith Woodard*	PO Box 269, Winterset IA 50273	515-462-5930	R	1*	<.1
4684	Donnay Software Designs Inc—*Roger Donnay*	1486 S Loggers Pond Pl, Caldwell ID 83607	208-344-0108	R	1*	<.1
4685	EFG Software Inc—*Mark Gerlach*	200 W Bullard Ste A-3, Clovis CA 93612	559-323-9484	R	1*	<.1
4686	Enterprise Management Technology LLC	1 Penn Plz Ste 360025, New York NY 10119	212-835-1557	R	1*	<.1
4687	Experience In Software Inc—*Roy Nierenberg*	2029 Durant Ave, Berkeley CA 94704	510-644-0694	R	1	<.1
4688	Fitzgerald and Long Inc—*Jeff Fitzgerald*	12341 E Cornell Ave, Aurora CO 80014	303-755-1102	R	1*	<.1

Rank	Company Name—*Executive Officer*	Address, City, State, Zip	Phone	Type	Fin	Empls
4689	FontLab Ltd—*Ted Harrison*	403 S Lincoln St Ste 4, Port Angeles WA 98362	301-560-3208	R	1*	<.1
4690	Forob Inc—*Robert Simgleton*	8687 E Vie de Ventura, Scottsdale AZ 85258	480-946-8080	R	1*	<.1
4691	Gigasoft Inc—*Robert Dede*	206 Bear Hollow, Keller TX 76248	817-431-8470	R	1*	<.1
4692	Gill and Piette Inc—*Richard Gill*	6832 Old Dominion Driv, McLean VA 22101	703-639-0707	R	1*	<.1
4693	Gottaplay Interactive Inc—*Michael Rochetti*	114 West 47th St Ste 1, New York NY 10036	201-735-5454	P	1	<.1
4694	Gracion Software—*Paul A Collins*	1257 Tolman Creek Rd, Ashland OR 97520	541-538-2297	R	1*	<.1
4695	Graphical Dynamics Inc	2701 California Ave SW, Seattle WA 98116	206-935-6032	R	1*	<.1
4696	Handmade Software Inc—*Marcos H Woehrmann*	302 F Toyon Ave Ste258, San Jose CA 95127	510-252-0101	R	1	<.1
4697	Host Interface International Inc—*Bryant Kittleson*	PO Box 159, Yacolt WA 98675	425-746-4361	R	1*	<.1
4698	hSoft Consulting—*Dean Harrison*	11770 S Harrell's Ferr, Baton Rouge LA 70816	225-293-1264	R	1*	<.1
4699	Hybrid Systems Limited Inc—*Phil Loethen*	200 University Park Dr, Edwardsville IL 62025	618-692-4757	R	1*	<.1
4700	Illimite Inc—*Gwen Lynn*	PO Box 876, Lockport NY 14095	716-439-8600	R	1*	<.1
4701	ImageTrak Software Inc—*James Runde*	PO Box 26106, Greenville SC 29616	864-235-9216	R	1*	<.1
4702	Inductel Inc—*Allan Pekary*	17537 Blanchard Dr, Monte Sereno CA 95030	408-866-8016	R	1*	<.1
4703	Infopoint Systems Inc—*John Cole*	PO Box 795663, Dallas TX 75379	972-669-4700	R	1*	<.1
4704	Ingenuus Software Inc—*Christopher Williams*	6136 Frisco Sq Blvd St, Frisco TX 75034	469-252-1144	R	1*	<.1
4705	INPRO International Inc—*CRAIG VANHORN*	700 Lavaca St, Austin TX 78701	512-320-9107	R	1*	<.1
4706	IntegrityWare Inc—*David Gill*	13064 Trail Dust Ave, San Diego CA 92129	858-592-8884	R	1*	<.1
4707	Intrepid Systems—*Rich White*	701 Galer St Ste 504, Seattle WA 98109		R	1*	<.1
4708	John Grady Inc	33 Circle Dr, Chestertown NY 12817	518-494-5036	R	1*	<.1
4709	Linguistic Products Inc—*Susie Mallard*	PO Box 8263, The Woodlands TX 77387	281-409-3804	R	1*	<.1
4710	LynnSoft Inc—*Ott Sathngam*	1219 Airport Rd Ste 31, Destin FL 32541	850-650-2266	R	1*	<.1
4711	Macro Industries Inc—*Norris Luce*	1003 Putman Dr, Huntsville AL 35816	256-721-1120	R	1*	<.1
4712	MaeDae Enterprises LLC	5805 Prospero, Peyton CO 80831	719-683-5189	R	1*	<.1
4713	Magic Mouse Productions—*H Beck*	12615 Sir Francis Drak, Inverness CA 94937	415-669-7010	R	1	<.1
4714	MarshallSoft Computing Inc—*Mike Marshall*	PO Box 4543, Huntsville AL 35815	256-881-4630	R	1*	<.1
4715	McArthur Business Systems Inc—*Ken Mcarthur*	152 Chestnut Dr, Richboro PA 18954	215-355-1291	R	1*	<.1
4716	McQ Productions—*Lon McQuillin*	PO Box 1676, San Mateo CA 94401	650-678-4551	R	1*	<.1
4717	Mediabridge Infosystems—*Charles Thayer*	225 Lafayette St Ste 5, New York NY 10012	212-334-7745	R	1*	<.1
4718	Merdan Group Inc—*Gilbert J Huey Sr*	4010 Morena Blvd Ste 2, San Diego CA 92117		R	1*	<.1
4719	Miller Microcomputer Services—*Dick Miller*	61 Lake Shore Rd, Natick MA 01760	508-653-6136	R	1*	<.1
4720	MJM Software Design—*Michael J Mefford*	PO Box 129, Gleneden Beach OR 97388		R	1*	<.1
4721	MLM Software Solutions Inc—*Jeff Shafe*	72 Wessex Way, San Carlos CA 94070	650-594-9058	R	1*	<.1
4722	NetJumper Software LLC	PO Box 158, Bloomfield Hills MI 48303	248-353-5555	R	1*	<.1
4723	Northlake Software Inc—*David Kellerman*	3169 Royce Way, Lake Oswego OR 97034	503-228-3383	R	1*	<.1
4724	Northwest Geophysical Associates Inc—*Rowland French*	8366 SW Nimbus Ave Bld, Beaverton OR 97008	503-992-6723	R	1*	<.1
4725	Office Automation Consultants Inc—*Larry Breed*	3682 Johnstonville Rd, Forsyth GA 31029	478-994-3219	R	1*	<.1
4726	Olmsted Office Systems—*Michael R Olmsted*	PO Box 19968, South Lake Tahoe CA 96151	530-544-0231	R	1*	<.1
4727	Opttechcom—*Dennis Olenick*	2875 Idlewild Dr Apt 8, Reno NV 89509	775-348-8008	R	1*	<.1
4728	Out of Your Mindand Into the Marketplace—*Linda Pinson*	13381 White Sand Dr, Tustin CA 92780	714-544-0248	R	1*	<.1
4729	Partners for Growth—*Mark Free*	7829 Center Blvd SE St, Snoqualmie WA 98065	425-831-7915	R	1*	<.1
4730	Pathfinders Software—*Herb Rubin*	701 S Grant St, San Mateo CA 94402	650-343-4571	R	1*	<.1
4731	Performance Solutions Technology LLC—*Rodney Brim*	PO Box 2157, Tolovana Park OR 97145		R	1*	<.1
4732	Platte Canyon Multimedia Software Corp—*Jeff Rhodes*	8870 Edgefield Dr, Colorado Springs CO 80920	719-548-1110	R	1*	<.1
4733	Practical Computer Solutions Inc—*Randy Clark*	3082 Sandy Plains Rd, Marietta GA 30066	770-569-2900	R	1*	<.1
4734	ProtoNet—*David Reynolds*	PO Box 8781, Calabasas CA 91372	818-876-0636	S	1	<.1
4735	Pulse Metric Inc—*Shiu-Shin Chio*	2100 Hawley Dr, Vista CA 92084	760-842-8224	R	1*	<.1
4736	Quality Photographic Imaging	1520 S Lewis St, Anaheim CA 92805	714-300-0500	R	1*	<.1
4737	Quantum Films Software—*Emil Safier*	PO Box 480255, Los Angeles CA 90048	323-938-4912	R	1*	<.1
4738	Quest Business Systems Inc (Oakland California)	PO Box 715, Brentwood CA 94513	925-634-2670	R	1*	<.1
4739	Rambow Enterprises—*Dan Rambow*	15127 NE 24th St Ste 1, Redmond WA 98052	425-881-7243	R	1*	<.1
4740	Rasmussen Software Inc—*Bob Rasmussen*	10240 SW Nimbus Ave St, Portland OR 97223	503-624-0360	R	1*	<.1
4741	Raw Bandwidth Communications Inc—*Mike Durkin*	PO Box 1305, San Bruno CA 94066	650-802-8006	R	1*	<.1
4742	Reichard Software Corp	655 Metro Pl Ste 600, Dublin OH 43017	704-849-2773	R	1*	<.1
4743	Replica Technology—*James Smith*	4650 Langford Rd, North Collins NY 14111	716-337-0621	R	1*	<.1
4744	ReSoft International LLC—*Clive Horton*	PO Box 124, New Canaan CT 06840	203-972-8462	R	1*	<.1
4745	Revelar Corp—*Van Evans*	2607 Casto Ln, Salt Lake City UT 84117	801-278-7107	R	1*	<.1
4746	Rich Media Technologies—*Jason Rich*	1002 Lynes Ave, Savannah GA 31415		R	1*	<.1
4747	RootsMagic Inc—*Bruce Buzbee*	PO Box 495, Springville UT 84663		R	1*	<.1
4748	RS Pressman and Associates Inc—*Roger S Pressman*	7075 Mandarin Dr, Boca Raton FL 33433	561-213-6580	R	1*	<.1
4749	S and S Programming Inc—*Keith Schuman*	3601 Sagamore Pkwy N S, Lafayette IN 47904	765-423-4472	R	1*	<.1
4750	Santa Barbara Software Products Inc—*Robert Eisberg*	1400 Dover Rd, Santa Barbara CA 93103	805-963-4886	R	1*	<.1
4751	Sherwood Technologies Inc—*JD Hellman*	PO Box 579, Huntington NY 11743	631-692-4340	R	1*	<.1
4752	Shilstone Companies Inc—*James Shilstone*	1721 W Plano Pky Ste 2, Plano TX 75075	972-509-9501	R	1*	<.1
4753	Sierra Systems—*Larry Rosenthal*	6728 Evergreen Ave, Oakland CA 94611	510-339-1976	R	1*	<.1
4754	Sight Software Inc—*John Patton*	85 High Bridge Rd, Lyme NH 03768		R	1*	<.1
4755	Silver Soft Inc—*Carl Bergman*	1301 Geranium St NW, Washington DC 20012	202-291-8212	R	1*	<.1
4756	Software Store Products Inc—*Michael Colucci*	PO BOX 772092, Ocala FL 34477	352-237-0616	R	1*	<.1
4757	Sound Ideas of America Inc	HC 62 Box 67, Long Pond PA 18334	570-643-6611	R	1*	<.1
4758	Sparrow Corp (Daytona Beach Florida)	1179 Dominion Ct, Port Orange FL 32129		R	1*	<.1
4759	Sustainable Softworks Inc—*Peter Sichel*	13 Fieldside Dr, Cumberland RI 02864		R	1*	<.1
4760	Sydex Inc—*Charles Guzis*	PO Box 5700, Eugene OR 97405	541-683-6033	R	1*	<.1
4761	Sylvan Ascent Inc—*Roger Bedell*	PO Box 2478, Taos NM 87571		R	1*	<.1
4762	Synergistic Systems Inc—*Michael Marley*	70 Old Fairwood Rd, Bethany CT 06524	203-932-1440	R	1*	<.1
4763	TechPool Software—*Andy Schnoebelen*	PO Box 300128, Escondido CA 92030	760-737-9240	S	1*	<.1
4764	Textco BioSoftware Inc (West Lebanon New Hampshire)—*Robert H Gross SciQuest Inc*	27 Gilson Rd, West Lebanon NH 03784	603-643-1471	S	1*	<.1
4765	THINK Solutions Inc—*Dennis Van Geffen*	PO Box 8505, Metairie LA 70011	504-455-6330	R	1*	<.1
4766	Time America Inc—*Thomas Bednarik*	16425 N Pima Rd Ste 19, Scottsdale AZ 85260	480-374-7713	R	1*	<.1
4767	Trifox Inc—*Niklas Back*	2959 S Winchester Blvd, Campbell CA 95008	408-796-1590	R	1*	<.1
4768	True Audio—*John L Murphy*	387 Duncan Ln, Andersonville TN 37705	865-494-3388	R	1*	<.1
4769	Turtle Creek Software	625 W Buffalo St Rm 1, Ithaca NY 14850		R	1*	<.1
4770	Uhimchuk and Associates—*George A Uhimchuk*	2506 Wade Hampton Blvd, Greenville SC 29615	864-292-3711	R	1*	<.1
4771	Vertical Solutions Inc—*George Spengler*	203 11th Ave SW, Minot ND 58701	701-839-1195	R	1*	<.1
4772	ViComp Management Inc	88 Masonic Home Rd, Charlton MA 01507	508-434-2899	R	1*	<.1
4773	Virginia Systems Software Services Inc—*Philip Van Cleave*	5509 W Bay Ct, Midlothian VA 23112	804-739-3200	R	1*	<.1
4774	Vividata Inc—*Mark Liebman*	1300 66th St, Emeryville CA 94608	510-658-6587	R	1*	<.1
4775	Vizdom Software Inc	100 San Luis St Box 43, Avila Beach CA 93424	805-549-7400	R	1*	<.1
4776	Waverley Software Design Inc—*Matt Brown*	159 Waverley St, Palo Alto CA 94301	650-646-5333	R	1*	<.1

Note: An asterisk (*) indicates an estimated financial figure. The company type code used is as follows: R = Private, P = Public, S = Private Subsidiary, B = Public Subsidiary, D = Division, J = Joint Venture, I = Investment Fund.

COMPANY RANKINGS BY SALES WITHIN 4-DIGIT SIC

Rank	Company Name—Executive Officer	Address, City, State, Zip	Phone	Type	Fin	Empls
4777	Western Wares LLC—Rick Hollinbeck	Box C, Norwood CO 81423	970-327-4898	R	1*	<.1
4778	Weston and Muir—Steven Weston	338 E Fallbrook St Ste, Fallbrook CA 92028		R	1*	<.1
4779	White Crane Systems Inc—Guy C Gordon	8255 Overview Ct Ste 1, Roswell GA 30076	770-594-8180	R	1*	<.1
4780	World of Reading Ltd—Cindy Tracy	PO Box 13092, Atlanta GA 30324	404-233-4042	R	1*	<.1
4781	3k Associates Inc—Chris Bartram	6901 Old Keene Mill Rd, Springfield VA 22150	703-569-9189	R	1*	<.1
4782	Advanced Reserves Management Inc—Bill Chaffee	2237 Del Mar Scenic Pk, Del Mar CA 92014	858-755-8877	R	1	<.1
4783	Alterity Inc—Ron Souder	600 Six Flags Dr Ste 6, Arlington TX 76011	817-870-1311	R	1*	<.1
4784	AndersonBell Corp—Ed Anderson	PO Box 745160, Arvada CO 80006		R	1*	<.1
4785	ANDXOR Corp—Raffaello Galli	46-28 243 St, Douglaston NY 11362	917-683-1780	R	1*	<.1
4786	Animated Communications Inc—Darryl Freedman	PO Box 16907, Chapel Hill NC 27516		R	1*	<.1
4787	Animated Software Co—Russell D Hoffman	3575 Roosevelt St, Carlsbad CA 92008	760-720-7261	R	1*	<.1
4788	ARJ Software Inc—Susan Jung	PO Box 249, Norwood MA 02062		R	1*	<.1
4789	Arney Computer Systems—Chuck Arney	PO Box 382511, Duncanville TX 75138	972-296-6166	D	1*	<.1
4790	Artemis Software Inc—Brendan Patterson	4251 Madison Ave, Culver City CA 90232	310-945-5975	R	1*	<.1
4791	Ataman Software Inc—C Brian Sturgill	PO Box 271130, Fort Collins CO 80527	970-444-2866	R	1*	<.1
4792	Bader Technologies Inc—David Bader	2045 Westgate Dr, Bethlehem PA 18017	610-867-7798	R	1*	<.1
4793	Beach City Software Inc—James Gregg	2310 6th St Ste 3, Santa Monica CA 90405	310-310-3888	R	1*	<.1
4794	Birch Grove Software Inc—Herbert Axilrod	7434 Centenary Ave Ste, Dallas TX 75225	214-361-8060	R	1*	<.1
4795	Brother Wolf Inc—Sam Palahnuk	500 Hampton Rd, Burbank CA 91504	818-566-4479	R	1*	<.1
4796	Carnation Software Inc—Rich Love	PO Box 318, Driftwood TX 78619	512-858-9234	R	1*	<.1
4797	Clear and Simple Inc—Steve Sargent	PO Box 130, West Simsbury CT 06092	860-658-1204	R	1*	<.1
4798	CodeSource Software Corp—Mark Strachan	2219 E Thousand Oaks B, Thousand Oaks CA 91362		R	1*	<.1
4799	CompuQuilt—Linda Breshears	1732 Del Rey St, Woodland CA 95695	530-383-7689	R	1*	<.1
4800	Computer Assistance Inc—Myles Swift	82277 Weiss Rd, Creswell OR 97426	541-895-3347	R	1*	<.1
4801	Consensus Software Inc—Mary Kay Hannon	11304 Glade Dr, Reston VA 20191	703-648-2404	R	1*	<.1
4802	Cottonwood Software—Stan Spielbusch	PO Box 657, Litchfield Park AZ 85340		R	1*	<.1
4803	CSPS Pharmaceuticals Inc	6161 Arnoldson Ct, San Diego CA 92122	858-550-9636	R	1*	<.1
4804	Cypress Software Inc (Paradise Valley Arizona)	5539 S Wilkinson Rd, Langley WA 98260	360-341-4595	R	1*	<.1
4805	Cypress Technologies—James Hall	PO Box 41447, Bakersfield CA 93384	661-374-3102	R	1*	<.1
4806	Data Technologies Inc—Paul Smith	PO Box 5820, Lynnwood WA 98046	425-353-4161	R	1*	<.1
4807	Desktop Graphic Services—EricJon Oxenberg	PO Box 66456, Los Angeles CA 90066	310-391-5275	R	1	<.1
4808	Dolphin Interconnect LLC	PO Box 148, Woodsville NH 03785	603-747-4100	R	1*	<.1
4809	DP Directory Inc—Al Harberg	525 Goodale Hill Rd, Glastonbury CT 06033	860-659-1065	R	1*	<.1
4810	Dream House Software Inc—Alan Finke	21 C Orinda Way Ste 37, Orinda CA 94563		R	1*	<.1
4811	DWW Software Inc—Danny Weibling	5350 Commerce Blvd Ste, Rohnert Park CA 94928		R	1*	<.1
4812	Electronic Software Publishing Corp—Kenneth Churilla	1361 Shelby Creek Ct, San Jose CA 95120	408-323-3030	R	1*	<.1
4813	ETCAI Products	PO Box 1347, Collierville TN 38027	901-861-0232	R	1*	<.1
4814	eWalk Software Corp—Art Clark	16325 Greenwood Ln, Monte Sereno CA 95030		R	1*	<.1
4815	Excel Software—Harold Halbleib	515 N Racetrack Rd, Henderson NV 89015	702-445-7645	R	1*	<.1
4816	F1 Technologies—Mike Feltman	2108 Glenwood Ave, Toledo OH 43604	419-255-6366	R	1*	<.1
4817	FairBrothers Inc—Jim Fairbrother	2262 Marginella Dr, Reston VA 20191	703-620-2392	R	1*	<.1
4818	Flicks Software Inc—Kevin Flick	1443 Yeager Ave, Las Vegas NV 89123	702-263-3476	R	1*	<.1
4819	Free Play Productions—Stephen Nachmanovitch	PO Box 667, Ivy VA 22945	434-245-4084	R	1*	<.1
4820	Fundamental Objects Inc—Bill Shadish	800 Robert Dean Dr, Downingtown PA 19335	610-873-8022	R	1	<.1
4821	Fuzzy Systems Engineering and Actland Inc—F Martin McNeill	12223 Wilsey Way, Poway CA 92064	858-206-3517	R	1*	<.1
4822	Glick Associates Inc—Oren Glick PhD	3570 SW River Pkwy Ste, Portland OR 97239	503-278-7527	R	1*	<.1
4823	Golden Hawk Technology—L Griswold	32 Manchester St, Nashua NH 03064	603-577-5559	R	1*	<.1
4824	Green Mountain Software Corp—Lou Krieg	128 Lakeside Ave Ste 1, Burlington VT 05401	802-865-2728	R	1*	<.1
4825	H and H Servicco Corp—Barbara Hilliard	PO Box 9340, Saint Paul MN 55109	651-777-0152	R	1*	<.1
4826	Healthcare Programming and Management Services Inc—Kathleen Fuller	PO Box 288, East Derry NH 03041		R	1*	<.1
4827	High Regard Software Inc—Jeffrey P Anderson	1452 Ranch Rd, Encinitas CA 92024	619-573-4077	R	1*	<.1
4828	Hopkins Technology LLC—Carol Dunn	421 Hazel Ln, Hopkins MN 55343	952-931-9376	R	1*	<.1
4829	Husom and Rose Photographics—David Husom	W8484 162nd Ave, Hager City WI 54014	715-792-5556	R	1*	<.1
4830	Idea Works Inc—Edward Brent	100 W Briarwood Ln, Columbia MO 65203	573-445-4554	R	1*	<.1
4831	Independant Data Processing Corp	1100 Logger Ct Ste E10, Raleigh NC 27609	919-878-0204	R	1*	<.1
4832	Innovative Software/Firmware Products Inc—William J Bracken III	5255 Vista Montana, Yorba Linda CA 92886	714-693-0447	R	1*	<.1
4833	Instant Recall Inc—Rodger Knaus	8180 Greensboro Dr Ste, McLean VA 22102	703-714-1332	R	1*	<.1
4834	James Associates—Lawrence James	PO Box 601, Nederland CO 80466	303-258-0576	R	1*	<.1
4835	Jasteck Inc—Brian Jansen	1975 Linden Blvd Ste 4, Elmont NY 11003	516-285-1600	R	1*	<.1
4836	Kandu Software Corp—Dotti Lathan	PO Box 290363, Port Orange FL 32129	386-760-4568	R	1*	<.1
4837	Kings Mountain Software Engineering—Benjamin Melvin	PO Box 413, Kings Mountain NC 28086	704-734-5116	R	1*	<.1
4838	Klos Technologies Inc—Patrick Klos	12 Jewett Ave, Cortland NY 13045		R	1*	<.1
4839	Kubera Software Inc—Mehran Bazargan	1690 More Ave, Los Gatos CA 95032	408-460-7012	R	1*	<.1
4840	KyTek Inc—David Gamache	PO Box 338, Weare NH 03281	603-529-2512	R	1*	<.1
4841	Landrum Software Inc—Richard H Landrum	PO Box 842, Palm City FL 34991	772-286-1324	R	1*	<.1
4842	Leadtrack Software—Norman Koltys	10142 Brooks School Rd, Fishers IN 46037		R	1*	<.1
4843	Lev Software	693 Racquet Club Rd St, Weston FL 33326	954-385-1919	R	1*	<.1
4844	Linguist's Software Inc—David Baer	PO Box 580, Edmonds WA 98020	425-775-1130	R	1*	<.1
4845	Llamagraphics Inc—Catherine White	401 King St, Franklin MA 02038		R	1*	<.1
4846	Looking Glass Microproducts Inc—Pepper Forrest	PO Box 2981, Loveland CO 80539	303-886-8540	R	1*	<.1
4847	Lord Publishing Inc—Rebecca Lord-Ronstadt	PO Box 369, Gilmanton NH 03237	603-267-7349	R	1*	<.1
4848	M and R Technologies Inc (Palm Bay Florida)—Mike Raustad	PO Box 061298, Palm Bay FL 32906	321-951-2268	R	1	<.1
4849	M2 Software Inc (Santa Monica California)	6725 Sunset Blvd Ste 2, Los Angeles CA 90028	310-399-2728	R	1*	<.1
4850	Macon Systems Inc—Jerry L Macon	115 Glencrest Ct, Colorado Springs CO 80906	719-520-1555	R	1*	<.1
4851	Madison Technical Software Inc	15 Perwal St, Westwood MA 02090		R	1*	<.1
4852	MaintSmart Software Inc—Daniel Cook	66164 Homestead Rd, North Bend OR 97459	541-751-0450	R	1*	<.1
4853	Mentor Software Inc—Norm Olsen Autodesk Inc	7931 S Broadway PMB 13, Littleton CO 80122	303-277-9967	S	1*	<.1
4854	Merrill Consultants—Herbert Merrill	10717 Cromwell Dr, Dallas TX 75229	214-351-1966	R	1*	<.1
4855	Metron Time Clock Co—Susan Reed	86-56 Woodhaven Blvd 2, Woodhaven NY 11421	718-805-1273	R	1*	<.1
4856	MiBAC Music Software Inc—John Ellinger	PO Box 468, Northfield MN 55057	507-645-5851	R	1*	<.1
4857	MINEsoft Ltd—Mike Norred	PO Box 1140, Morrison CO 80465	303-980-5300	R	1*	<.1
4858	Mobilogic Inc—Susan Sarno	11605 J Tomahawk Creek, Leawood KS 66211	913-642-4883	R	1*	<.1
4859	NEOSOFT Corp—David Riley	PO Box 5667, Bend OR 97708	541-389-5489	R	1*	<.1
4860	Open Window—Dick Bryant	6862 N Solaz Segundo, Tucson AZ 85718	520-299-9341	R	1*	<.1
4861	Orbis Systems Inc—Randy Kriz	36381 N Tara Ct, Ingleside IL 60041	847-587-0800	R	1*	<.1
4862	Outlook Computing Inc—Mitch Cohen	PO Box 375, Deerfield IL 60015	847-236-1850	R	1*	<.1
4863	Page Studio Graphics—Roger Vershen	1404 E Ganymede Dr, Oro Valley AZ 85737	520-797-9348	R	1	<.1

Rank	Company Name—*Executive Officer*	Address, City, State, Zip	Phone	Type	Fin	Empls
4864	Parnassus Software—*John Waderman*	1923 Lyans Dr, La Canada CA 91011	818-952-8102	R	1*	<.1
4865	Pendock Mallorn Ltd—*Cleve Pendock*	3822 Bell St, Kansas City MO 64111		R	1*	<.1
4866	Personal Composer Inc—*Norman S James*	PO Box 33016, Tulsa OK 74153	918-742-3488	R	1*	<.1
4867	Precision Computer Methods Inc—*Peter Heinicke*	1800 W Hawthorne Ln St, West Chicago IL 60185	630-208-8000	R	1*	<.1
4868	Printing Communications Associates Inc—*Thomas F Divine*	4201 Brunswick Ct, Smyrna GA 30080	770-432-4580	R	1*	<.1
4869	ProVue Development Corp—*James Rea*	18685 Main St Rm A, Huntington Beach CA 92648		R	1*	<.1
4870	Real Pro-Jections Inc—*Sal Caldarone*	300 Carlsbad Village D, Carlsbad CA 92008	760-434-2180	R	1*	<.1
4871	Reportmill Software Inc—*Jeff Martin*	4504 Trotter Ln, Flower Mound TX 75028	214-513-1636	R	1*	<.1
4872	RFF Electronics—*Roger F Faaborg*	PO Box 1244, Loveland CO 80538	970-663-5767	R	1	<.1
4873	River City Software Development Inc—*Jim Murphy*	406 W Overlook Mountai, Buda TX 78610	512-295-5934	R	1*	<.1
4874	Safari Software Inc—*Robert Sean Walsh*	PO Box 1938, Sonoma CA 95476	707-939-9002	R	1*	<.1
4875	Salinon Corp—*Dan Stone*	7424 Greenville Ave St, Dallas TX 75231	214-692-9091	R	1*	<.1
4876	Satori Chiropractic Software Inc—*Tony Vince*	74 Ranch Dr, Novato CA 94945		R	1*	<.1
4877	Schema Research Corp—*Lowell Schneider*	2532 Santa Clara Ave S, Alameda CA 94501	510-903-1055	R	1*	<.1
4878	Scrutiny Inc—*Warren Chapman*	2202 W St NW, Auburn WA 98001	253-735-5500	R	1*	<.1
4879	Sensory Computer Systems LLC—*John Ream*	16 South St, Morristown NJ 07960	973-267-0065	R	1*	<.1
4880	Sequential Software Inc—*George Schmid*	576 Valley Rd Ste 294, Wayne NJ 07470	973-942-3440	R	1*	<.1
4881	Serious Accounting Software Inc—*Robert Pachner*	9988 Hibert St Ste 206, San Diego CA 92131	858-271-7703	R	1*	<.1
4882	SG Schoggen and Co—*Steve Schoggen*	PO Box 246, Little Silver NJ 07739	732-530-4659	R	1*	<.1
4883	SPAR Associates Inc—*Laurent C Deschamps*	927 West St, Annapolis MD 21401	410-263-8593	R	1*	<.1
4884	Statistical Designs—*Stan Deming*	9941 Rowlett Rd Ste 6, Houston TX 77075	713-947-1551	R	1*	<.1
4885	Stellar Software Inc—*Michael Lampton*	PO Box 10183, Berkeley CA 94709	510-845-8405	R	1*	<.1
4886	Strong Software Inc—*Dwight Strong*	145 Town Center Ste 63, Corte Madera CA 94925		R	1*	<.1
4887	Structural Data Inc	PO Box 146, Huntington Beach CA 92648	714-840-5570	R	1*	<.1
4888	Survivor Software Ltd—*Mike Farmer*	11222 La Cienega Blvd, Inglewood CA 90304	310-410-9527	R	1*	<.1
4889	Syntact Solutions Inc—*Marcia Potter*	PO Box 915, Murray Hill NJ 07974	908-464-7048	R	1*	<.1
4890	Ted Gruber Software Inc—*Ted Gruber*	PO Box 13408, Las Vegas NV 89112	702-735-1980	R	1*	<.1
4891	The Third Rail	3377 Cimarron Dr, Santa Ynez CA 93460	805-688-7370	R	1*	<.1
4892	Travel Software Consultants—*John Allen*	1963 Galena St, Aurora CO 80010	303-343-9516	R	1*	<.1
4893	Up Software Inc—*Jim Hurd*	722 Lombard St Ste 204, San Francisco CA 94133	415-921-4691	R	1*	<.1
4894	Update Software Inc—*Edward P Starr*	14620 S Hwy 101, Hopland CA 95449	707-744-1898	R	1*	<.1
4895	Vedder Software Group—*Steven Vedder*	630 Salvia Ln, Schenectady NY 12303	518-356-3698	R	1*	<.1
4896	Video Collage Inc	PO Box 2550, Boston MA 02130	617-524-7835	R	1*	<.1
4897	White Wolf Software Inc—*Pat Homelvig*	27 Honey Locust, Littleton CO 80127	303-906-6104	R	1*	<.1
4898	Woll2Woll Software—*Roy Woll*	3150 Reed Ave, Livermore CA 94550	925-371-1663	R	1*	<.1
4899	XSynergy Software Corp—*Dennis J Retherford*	PO Box 9327, Ontario CA 91762		R	1*	<.1
4900	Yacht Design Software—*Howard Young*	169 Winding Creek Dr, Oriental NC 28571	252-249-7230	R	1*	<.1
4901	Yuri Software Inc—*Yuri Diomin*	1463 Santa Marta Ct, Solana Beach CA 92075	858-755-9058	R	1*	<.1
4902	Absolute Software Company Inc—*Edward Colbert*	7040 Avenida Encinas S, Carlsbad CA 92011	760-929-0236	R	1*	<.1
4903	BetaData Systems Inc—*John H Moffatt*	3137 E Greenlee Rd, Tucson AZ 85716	520-917-1028	R	1*	<.1
4904	DC Software Design Inc—*David Ching*	239 Main St Ste E, Pleasanton CA 94566	408-482-6160	R	1*	<.1
4905	Dispatch Software Inc—*Don Weber*	1038 Hooker Rd, Sequim WA 98382	360-582-0202	R	1*	<.1
4906	Doceo Publishing Inc—*Jan Ozer*	412 W Stuart Dr, Galax VA 24333	276-238-9135	R	1*	<.1
4907	Dow Software Services Inc—*Peter Dow*	822 Lombard Dr, Redlands CA 92374	909-793-9050	R	1*	<.1
4908	Drawback Solutions Software Inc—*Brenton Ashworth*	PO Box 89, Modesto CA 95353	209-576-0010	R	1*	<.1
4909	Hamilton Laboratories—*Nicole Hamilton*	16645 NE 46th St, Redmond WA 98052	425-497-0102	R	1	<.1
4910	Hilbert Computing Inc—*Gary Murphy*	13632 S Sycamore Dr, Olathe KS 66062	913-780-5051	R	1*	<.1
4911	Information Dynamics LLC—*Thomas Corson*	2435 E Mayview Dr, Green Valley AZ 85614	520-225-0244	R	1*	<.1
4912	Information Transformation Services—*Louis Acts*	14175 W Indian School, Goodyear AZ 85338	602-357-4310	R	1*	<.1
4913	Jerry Jackson Associates Ltd—*Jerry Jackson*	PO Box 12340, College Station TX 77842	979-204-7821	R	1*	<.1
4914	KLC Enterprises—*Kit Christiansen*	6 Woodside Ct, San Anselmo CA 94960	415-485-0555	R	1*	<.1
4915	Logical Software Solutions Inc—*Becky Bazabal*	3713 E County 14 1/4 S, Yuma AZ 85365	928-502-9398	R	1*	<.1
4916	Mathemaesthetics Inc—*Douglas Mckenna*	PO Box 298, Boulder CO 80306	303-440-0707	R	1*	<.1
4917	Prescient Software jrd Inc—*John Dillavou*	23732 Hillhurst Ave, Laguna Niguel CA 92677	949-248-5788	R	1*	<.1
4918	Prous Science—*Vin Caraher*	1500 Market St 12th Fl, Philadelphia PA 19102	215-246-3441	S	1*	<.1
4919	Sequan Software—*Lee Inness-Brown*	15735 Lawson Valley Rd, Jamul CA 91935	619-659-9305	R	1*	<.1
4920	Serena Software—*Kevin E Gilbert*	PO Box 3076, Bloomington IN 47402	812-333-0823	R	1*	<.1
4921	T/Maker Research Co—*Peter Roizen*	830 W Parr Ave, Los Gatos CA 95030	408-370-0475	R	1	<.1
4922	Time Cycles Research—*Dennis Haskell*	PO Box 797, Waterford CT 06385	860-444-6641	R	1*	<.1
4923	CPR International—*Levent Sert*	PO Box 54512, Jacksonville FL 32245	904-220-0045	R	1	N/A
4924	Fourth World Media Corp—*Richard Gaskin*	620 Moulton Ave Ste101, Los Angeles CA 90031	323-225-3717	R	1	N/A
4925	MicroComputer Specialists—*Rodney B Murray*	18 Rosedale Rd, Wynnewood PA 19096	610-616-2199	R	1	N/A
4926	Praedea Solutions Inc—*James Graff*	477 Madison Ave Fl 18, New York NY 10022	212-206-8529	R	1*	<.1
4927	Plugged In LLC	8701 Shoal Creek Blvd, Austin TX 78757	512-380-0900	R	1*	<.1
4928	Dimension 5 Solutions Inc—*Lance Tressler*	300 Harding Blvd Ste 2, Roseville CA 95678	916-789-7007	R	1*	<.1
4929	Lode Data Corp—*Trygve Lode*	7200 S Alton Way Ste B, Centennial CO 80112	303-759-0100	R	1*	<.1
4930	A Micro Inc—*Doug Andrews*	PO Box 9474, Pasadena CA 91109	626-353-7216	R	1	<.1
4931	Microlite Corp—*D Podnar*	2315 Mill St, Aliquippa PA 15001	724-375-6711	R	1*	<.1
4932	MIS Construction Software Inc—*Thomas Moore*	8642 154th Ave Ne, Redmond WA 98052	425-882-3027	R	1*	<.1
4933	SuperSpeed Software Inc—*Eric Dickman*	327 Boston Post Rd, Sudbury MA 01776	978-443-5106	R	1	<.1
4934	Tampa Software Co—*Greg Stockford*	2521 W N St, Tampa FL 33614	813-930-8942	R	1*	<.1
4935	BlueWater Systems Inc	110 110th Ave NE Ste 2, Bellevue WA 98004	425-519-5900	S	1	<.1
4936	Northern Software Tools Inc—*Dave Mikkalson*	54945 210th Ln, Mankato MN 56001	507-388-4748	R	1*	<.1
4937	Pace Software Systems Inc—*Roger Pace*	PO Box 458, Fraser MI 48026	586-727-3189	R	1*	<.1
4938	Pico Publishing—*Gordon Waite*	450 Shrewsbury Plaza S, Shrewsbury NJ 07702	732-345-0220	R	1	<.1
4939	Roving Software Inc—*Gail F Goodman*	1601 Trapelo Rd Ste 24, Waltham MA 02451	781-472-8100	R	1	<.1
4940	Destiny Software Inc—*Desta Dickinson*	PO Box 827, Woodinville WA 98072	425-415-1777	R	1*	<.1
4941	Digital Manga Inc—*Hikaru Sasahara*	1487 W 178th St Ste 30, Gardena CA 90248	310-817-8010	R	1*	<.1
4942	S and H Computer Systems Inc—*Alan Keyes*	1027 17th Ave S, Nashville TN 37212	615-327-3670	R	1	<.1
4943	Trinity Animation Inc—*Jim Lammers*	672 SE Bayberry Ln Ste, Lees Summit MO 64063	816-525-0103	R	1	<.1
4944	Meadows Publishing Solutions Inc—*John Kriho*	1305 Remington Rd Ste, Schaumburg IL 60173	847-882-8202	R	1	N/A
4945	Aviation Software—*Gordon Rosen*	400 Rella Blvd Ste 205, Suffern NY 10901	845-504-0789	R	1*	<.1
4946	Xavier Electronics Inc—*Francis Mc Entee*	421 Magnolia Ave, Croydon PA 19021	215-788-7554	R	1*	<.1
4947	Zultner and Co—*Richard Zultner*	12 Wallingford Dr, Princeton NJ 08540	609-452-0216	R	1*	<.1
4948	Compumatics Group Inc—*Dennis Laibson*	8321 Old Courthouse Rd, Vienna VA 22182	703-748-4545	R	1*	<.1
4949	Extrasensory Software	PO Box 491232, Los Angeles CA 90049	310-478-4092	R	1	<.1
4950	Vqs Inc—*John Patton*	4343 Shallowford Rd H4, Marietta GA 30062	770-640-1715	R	1*	<.1
4951	Outhink Inc—*Dave Toole*	15732 Los Gatos Blvd S, Los Gatos CA 95032	408-377-2660	R	1*	<.1
4952	ASAP Inc (Los Angeles California)	13101 W Washington Blv, Los Angeles CA 90066	310-578-6766	R	1	<.1
4953	Trident Software Inc (Sausalito California)	1001 Bridgeway Ste 104, Sausalito CA 94965	415-332-0188	R	1	<.1

Note: An asterisk (*) indicates an estimated financial figure. The company type code used is as follows: R = Private, P = Public, S = Private Subsidiary, B = Public Subsidiary, D = Division, J = Joint Venture, I = Investment Fund.

COMPANY RANKINGS BY SALES WITHIN 4-DIGIT SIC

Rank	Company Name—*Executive Officer*	Address, City, State, Zip	Phone	Type	Fin	Empls
4954	Seaquest Software Inc—*Pete Mackie*	4200 NW Columbia Ave, Portland OR 97229	503-531-0252	R	1*	<.1
4955	Sophos Software Ltd	3449 N Druid Hills Rd, Decatur GA 30033	404-325-9494	R	1	N/A
4956	Zoo Entertainment Inc—*Mark Seremet*	3805 Edwards Rd Ste 40, Cincinnati OH 45209	513-824-8297	P	1	<.1
4957	NeXplore Corp—*Edward W Mandel*	708 3rd Ave 6th Fl, New York NY 10017	212-209-3849	P	1	<.1
4958	Simtrol Inc—*Oliver M Cooper III*	520 Guthridge Ct Ste 2, Norcross GA 30092	678-365-2315	P	1	<.1
4959	Bluebook International Holding Co—*Mark Josipovich*	21098 Bake Pkwy Ste 10, Lake Forest CA 92630	949-470-9534	P	1	<.1
4960	Arboretum Systems Inc—*Georges Jaroslaw*	484 Lake Park Ave Ste, Oakland CA 94610	510-444-0880	R	1	<.1
4961	Coastal Software and Consulting Inc—*Deryk Marien*	PO Box 872106, Vancouver WA 98687	360-891-6174	R	1*	<.1
4962	Real Estate Video Educational Institute Inc—*Richard Gould*	24007 Ventura Blvd Ste, Calabasas CA 91302	818-222-4515	R	1*	<.1
4963	Colour Matters International Inc—*William Tsao*	1040 First Ave Ste 359, New York NY 10022		R	1	<.1
4964	Trio Systems LLC—*Alan Bartholomew*	4 E Holly St Ste 211, Pasadena CA 91106	626-584-9706	R	1	<.1
4965	Element LLC—*Jeff Mcleod*	7829 Greenbriar Pkwy, Orlando FL 32819	407-472-1280	R	1*	<.1
4966	Rhode Island Soft Systems Inc—*Aaron Weber*	1900 Medical Arts Ave, Sartell MN 56377		R	1	<.1
4967	Visage Image Systems	270 Lafayette St, New York NY 10012	212-431-4804	R	1	<.1
4968	CadPlus Products Co	PO Box 620623, Charlotte NC 28262	704-547-9400	R	1*	<.1
4969	LinkPro Technologies Inc—*Frank Reinhart*	5319 University Dr Ste, Irvine CA 92612	949-833-3322	R	1	<.1
4970	Insight Manufacturing Software Inc	1935 S Plum Grove Rd S, Palatine IL 60067	847-241-4512	R	1	<.1
4971	Supply Chain Management Inc—*Bruce Hollingsworth*	2431 Nw 160th Ave, Beaverton OR 97006	503-617-1525	R	1*	<.1
4972	Visual Engineering Inc	164 Main St 2nd Fl, Los Altos CA 94022	650-949-5410	R	1*	<.1
4973	Data Enterprises Of The Northwest Inc—*D Brown*	9 Lake Bellevue Dr Ste, Bellevue WA 98005	425-688-8805	R	1*	<.1
4974	Gigacase Corp—*Teddy Wong*	4010 Valley Blvd Ste 1, Walnut CA 91789	909-595-8939	R	1*	<.1
4975	Legal Plus Software Group Inc—*Stephen Sooter*	6947 Coal Creek Pkwy S, Newcastle WA 98059	425-687-9001	R	1*	<.1
4976	Liberty Publishing Company Inc—*Jeff Little*	PO Box 4485, Deerfield Beach FL 33442	561-395-3750	R	1*	<.1
4977	Microsystems Development Technologies Inc	1177 Park Ave, San Jose CA 95126	408-280-1226	R	1	<.1
4978	Specialty Systems Inc (Louisville Kentucky)—*Frank Andersen*	3600 Chamberlain Ln St, Louisville KY 40241	502-425-3343	R	1	<.1
4979	Marietta Systems Inc—*Jack Dawson*	PO Box 71506, Marietta GA 30007	770-565-1560	R	1	<.1
4980	MEDformatics Inc—*Jeffrey Hertzberg*	128 Magnolia Ave, Fayetteville NC 28305	910-323-1748	R	1	<.1
4981	Montage Software Systems Inc—*James Alonso*	PO Box 7574, Wilton CT 06897	203-834-1144	R	1	<.1
4982	Tricon Systems Corp—*Richardson Sanderson*	880 SW 60th Ave, Plantation FL 33317	954-792-1112	R	1*	<.1
4983	DB-NET Inc	522 Hickory Ln Unit B, Howard OH 43028	740-397-9229	R	1*	<.1
4984	FontGear Inc—*John Morrison*	8124 Grahamson Ln Ste, Charlotte NC 28269	704-875-1337	R	1	<.1
4985	Milagro Systems Inc	1004 Willow St, San Jose CA 95125	408-293-4193	R	1	<.1
4986	REMedia Inc—*Rob Ranson*	16 Mckee Dr, Mahwah NJ 07430	201-529-4500	R	1*	<.1
4987	TechNovation Software	1025 S Main St, Corona CA 92882	951-736-1169	R	1*	<.1
4988	Barnard Software Inc—*Teri Barnard*	806 Silk Oak Ter, Lake Mary FL 32746	407-323-4773	R	1	<.1
4989	Circle Systems Inc	1001 4th Ave Ste 3200, Seattle WA 98154	206-682-3783	R	1	<.1
4990	Image Technology Laboratories Inc—*Lewis Edwards*	602 Enterprise Dr, Kingston NY 12401	845-338-3366	P	1	<.1
4991	Murphy Software Co	1000 Town Ctr Ste 1950, Southfield MI 48076	248-351-0900	R	1*	<.1
4992	Professional Automation Services Inc—*Brian Anderson*	1111 Kimbark St, Longmont CO 80501	970-532-4041	R	1	<.1
4993	Skylight Publishing—*Gary Litvin*	9 Bartlet St Ste 70, Andover MA 01810		R	1	<.1
4994	Crafted Smalltalk—*Terry Raymond*	80 Lazywood Ln, Tiverton RI 02878	401-624-4517	R	1	N/A
4995	DPE and Associates—*Douglas Ewen*	100 Coxe Ave Unit 302, Asheville NC 28801	828-712-8411	R	1	N/A
4996	Exeter Software	47 Rte 25A Ste 2, Setauket NY 11733	631-689-7838	R	1	N/A
4997	people for people	PO Box13221, San Luis Obispo CA 93406	805-544-7066	R	1	N/A
4998	Time Pilot Corp—*Douglas Marsh*	340 Mckee St, Batavia IL 60510	630-879-6400	R	<1*	<.1
4999	DiamondWare Ltd—*Keith Weiner*	4856 E Baseline Rd Ste, Mesa AZ 85206	480-380-1122	R	<1	<.1
5000	Tru-Truss Engineering	1783 Arroyo Vista Way, El Dorado Hills CA 95762	916-933-3478	R	<1	<.1
5001	Phase Three Logic Inc—*Chong Lee*	15201 NW Greenbrier Pk, Beaverton OR 97006	503-645-1551	R	<1	<.1
5002	Craig Systems Inc—*Shirley Craig*	16717 Monitor Ave, Baton Rouge LA 70817	225-756-0580	R	<1	<.1
5003	Personal Data Systems Inc—*Noel Runyan*	638 Sobrato Ln, Campbell CA 95008	408-866-1126	R	<1	<.1
5004	Intellicell Biosciences Inc—*Steven Victor*	30 E 76th St, New York NY 10012	212-249-3050	P	<1	N/A
5005	Ram Informatics Ltd—*Raman Pullakad*	36 Mill Plain Rd Ste 4, Danbury CT 06811	203-748-5700	R	<1*	<.1
5006	TLogic Inc—*Morgan Johnson*	9702 Harford Rd Ste C, Baltimore MD 21234	410-665-9244	R	<1	<.1
5007	Maynard Software Solutions Inc—*Joe Maynard*	180 E 200 S, Smithfield UT 84335	435-563-1840	R	<1*	<.1
5008	Proven Software Inc—*Mark Matt*	PO 476, Manlius NY 13104		R	<1	<.1
5009	Innovative Research Inc—*Suhas Patankar*	3025 Harbor Ln N Ste 3, Minneapolis MN 55447	763-519-0105	R	<1*	<.1
5010	Ashleywilde Inc—*Thomas Sawyer*	25301 Malibu Rd, Malibu CA 90265	310-456-1277	R	<1	<.1
5011	BonAmi Software Corp	34 Hammond St, Acton MA 01720	978-264-6641	R	<1	<.1
5012	Klever Marketing Inc—*Paul G Begum*	PO Box 711308, Salt Lake City UT 84171	801-847-6444	P	<1	<.1
5013	Devore Software and Consulting—*Michael Devore*	106 S Columbia, Naperville IL 60540	630-717-6369	R	<1	<.1
5014	Dynacomp Inc	4768 Rte 89, Romulus NY 14541	315-257-9303	R	<1	<.1
5015	Micro-Processor Services Inc—*Avi Nudelman*	92 Stone Hurst Ln, Dix Hills NY 11746	631-499-4461	R	<1	.1
5016	Textfyre Inc—*David Cornelson*	1144 E State St Ste A, Geneva IL 60134	630-803-4302	R	<1*	<.1
5017	PurchaseSoft Inc—*Steven A Flagg*	7514 Girard Ave Ste144, La Jolla CA 92037	949-263-0910	R	<1	<.1
5018	River City Software LLC—*Michelle Berk*	PO Box 128, Exeter NH 03833	603-686-5525	R	<1	<.1
5019	Brown Bear Software—*Micheal Gardner*	1405 Matterhorn Way, Anchorage AK 99508	907-278-1231	R	<1*	<.1
5020	August Software Corp	701 N Green Valley Pky, Henderson NV 89074	702-944-9794	R	<1	<.1
5021	DigitalTown Inc—*Richard Pomije*	11974 Portland Ave, Burnsville MN 55337	952-890-2362	P	<1	<.1
5022	Isys Business Systems—*Vernon Ikeler*	1230 Crenshaw Blvd Ste, Torrance CA 90501	310-224-4777	R	<1*	<.1
5023	Mind Media Inc—*Bruce Ehrlich*	9360 W Flamingo Rd PMB, Las Vegas NV 89147		R	<1	<.1
5024	Partek Inc—*Tom Downey*	12747 Olive Blvd Ste 2, Saint Louis MO 63141	314-878-2329	R	<1	<.1
5025	Patten Enterprises Inc—*David Patten*	PO Box 9777, Salt Lake City UT 84109	801-485-4992	R	<1	<.1
5026	Pixelan Software—*Michael Feerer*	2950 Newmarket Pl Ste, Bellingham WA 98226	360-647-0112	R	<1	<.1
5027	Publishers Software Systems Inc—*Wayne Zafft*	511 Washington St, Norwood MA 02062	781-326-3564	R	<1*	<.1
5028	Avista Design Systems—*Anil Valbh*	5353 Conroy Rd, Orlando FL 32811	407-581-9000	R	<1	<.1
5029	BusNet Inc	9099 Gould Rd, Eden Prairie MN 55347	952-934-3606	R	<1	<.1
5030	Crm Solutions Inc—*Christian Williams*	PO Box 5456, Milford CT 06460	203-882-9492	R	<1	<.1
5031	Forensic Logic Inc—*Robert Batty*	712 Bancroft Rd Ste 42, Walnut Creek CA 94598	415-810-2114	R	<1*	<.1
5032	Information Navigation Inc—*Tom Butters*	PO Box 2508, Durham NC 27715		R	<1	<.1
5033	MarWare—*Edward Martin*	2402 Hollywood Blvd, Hollywood FL 33020	954-927-6031	R	<1*	<.1
5034	Packageworks Inc—*Fred Levitt*	9 Cross Gate Rd, Wayne PA 19087	610-293-9076	R	<1	<.1
5035	Performance Trends Inc	PO Box 530164, Livonia MI 48153	248-473-9230	R	<1	<.1
5036	Sitcur Analysis—*Roger Curtis*	7916 Melrose Ave Ste 2, Los Angeles CA 90046	323-653-0311	R	<1	<.1
5037	Sub Systems Inc	3017 Convington Pl, Round Rock TX 78681	512-733-2525	R	<1	<.1
5038	Varatek Software Inc—*David Determan*	523 Winter St, North Andover MA 01845	978-685-7003	R	<1	<.1
5039	American Systems	PO Box 93747, Southlake TX 76092	817-485-6547	R	<1	N/A
5040	Bulova Technologies Group Inc—*Stephen L Gurba*	19337 US Hwy 19 N Ste, Clearwater FL 33764	727-536-6666	P	<1	N/A
5041	Desktop Solutions of Pennsylvania Inc—*Jerry Britton*	185 Newberry Commons, Etters PA 17319	717-938-4270	R	<1	N/A
5042	Syndesis Corp—*John Foust*	235 S Main St, Jefferson WI 53549	920-674-5200	R	<1	N/A
5043	Microdesk Inc—*Michael A DeLacey*	10 Tara Blvd Ste 420, Nashua NH 03062	603-657-3800	R	<1	.1

Rank	Company Name—*Executive Officer*	Address, City, State, Zip	Phone	Type	Fin	Empls
5044	Solutions X Global—*Rodger Smith*	3520 N University Ave, Provo UT 84604	801-224-4444	R	<1	<.1
5045	Brilliant Technologies Corp—*Allan Klepfisz*	211 Madison Ave Ste 28, New York NY 10016	212-532-2736	P	<1	<.1
5046	Quest Analytics LLC	17 Park Pl Ste 300, Appleton WI 54914	920-739-4552	R	<1*	<.1
5047	Shrink Nanotechnologies Inc—*Mark L Baum*	2038 Corte De Nogal St, Carlsbad CA 92011	760-804-8844	P	<1	<.1
5048	Startly Technologies LLC—*Randy Skeie*	PO Box 65580, West Des Moines IA 50265	515-221-1801	R	<1	<.1
5049	Tenberry Software Inc—*Terry Colligan*	PO Box 20050, Fountain Hills AZ 85269	480-767-8868	R	<1	<.1
5050	Kiwiboxcom Inc—*Andre S Scholz*	330 W 38th St Ste 1602, New York NY 10018	212-239-8210	P	<1	<.1
5051	ModelOffice Inc—*Amy Rudy*	804-C Rio Grande St, Austin TX 78701	512-457-1100	R	<1	<.1
5052	The Humanities Computing Laboratory—*Richard A Kunst*	PO Box 3231, Durham NC 27701	919-656-5915	R	<1	<.1
5053	Global Links Corp—*Frank L Dobrucki*	3571 E Sunset Rd, Las Vegas NV 89120	702-436-7007	P	<1	<.1
5054	Health Care Systems Corp—*Jeff Buhrt*	P O Box 284, Westfield IN 46074	317-843-4444	R	<1	<.1
5055	NetTech Inc—*Lori Farquhar*	PO Box 757, Monee IL 60449	708-570-0685	R	<1	<.1
5056	Oak Software Inc	PO Box 400, Indian Rocks Beach FL 33785	727-596-0262	R	<1	<.1
5057	ProText Mobility Inc—*Peter Charles*	6800 Jericho Tpke Ste, Syosset NY 11791	516-802-0223	P	<1	<.1
5058	StatPoint LLC—*Carolyn Chopek* Statistical Graphics Corp	560 Broadview Ave Ste, Warrenton VA 20186	540-428-0084	S	<1	<.1
5059	USA Video Interactive Corp—*Edwin Molina*	1224 Mill St Bldg 2 St, East Berlin CT 06023	860-828-2017	P	<1	<.1
5060	Cinovation Inc—*Steven Sashen*	1282 Elder Ave, Boulder CO 80304	303-786-7899	R	<1	<.1
5061	El Dorado Softworld—*Moquey Marquross*	35952 Carnahan Ln, Richland OR 97870	541-893-3032	R	<1	<.1
5062	SWK Holdings Corp—*John Nemelka*	5314 N River Run Dr St, Provo UT 84604		P	<1	<.1
5063	Imaja—*Greg Jalbert*	2409 Parker St Unit 2, Berkeley CA 94704	510-526-4621	R	<1	<.1
5064	Industrial Systems Laboratory—*James Dawson*	58 Logan Ave S, Renton WA 98057	425-226-7585	R	<1*	<.1
5065	Mansfield Software Group Inc—*Kevin Kearney*	PO Box 532, Storrs CT 06268	860-429-8402	R	<1	<.1
5066	Responsive Software—*Robyn Kay*	2887 S Katherine, Salt Lake City UT 84109		R	<1	<.1
5067	SET Laboratories Inc—*Bob Carpenter*	13810 Stafford Rd, Stafford TX 77477	281-403-0300	R	<1	<.1
5068	Teca Inc—*Michael Otey*	14600 SE Center St, Portland OR 97236	503-901-6335	R	<1	<.1
5069	Tech Five Inc—*Don Horst*	PO Box 318, Hamel MN 55340	763-473-6804	R	<1	<.1
5070	Webs Unlimited—*Mike Chafin*	17191 Oak Valley Rd, Crescent IA 51526	402-210-2204	R	<1	<.1
5071	Winsby Group LLC—*Doug Winsby*	11124 S Towne Sq Ste 1, Saint Louis MO 63123	314-487-8186	R	<1*	<.1
5072	EnXnet Inc—*Ryan Corley*	11333 E Pine St Ste 92, Tulsa OK 74116	918-592-0015	P	<1	<.1
5073	ICS Software Inc—*Manoj Chitre*	1784 W Andes Dr, Upland CA 91784	909-709-3015	R	<1	<.1
5074	Incompass Inc—*Ron Perry*	PO Box 75, Mountain Center CA 92561	714-742-1056	R	<1	<.1
5075	Infomark Software Corp—*Chet Leighton Amborn*	376 Raven Way, Petaluma CA 94954	503-348-6970	R	<1	<.1
5076	Integra Computing—*Richard Kelly*	910 Cobb Pl Manor Dr, Marietta GA 30066	770-426-5735	R	<1	<.1
5077	Jam Software Inc	PO Box 123, Tulsa OK 74104		R	<1	<.1
5078	Kazoo Software Inc—*Joseph Cardoza*	PO Box 2452, Santa Clara CA 95055	408-310-4670	R	<1	<.1
5079	Meredith Software Inc—*Michael G Meredith-Saunders*	3505 Paydirt Dr, Placerville CA 95667	916-203-5864	R	<1	<.1
5080	Open Field Software Inc—*Bob Cagle*	1347 Pacific Ave, Santa Cruz CA 95060	831-466-3000	R	<1	<.1
5081	Quadron Corp—*Paula Golus*	4919 Cervato Way, Santa Barbara CA 93111	805-680-5377	R	<1	<.1
5082	Quatrix Inc—*Edward Higginbotham*	8210 Coolshire Ln, Houston TX 77070	281-469-8847	R	<1*	<.1
5083	Software Spectra Inc—*Tony Noe*	14025 NW Harvest Ln, Portland OR 97229	503-690-2099	R	<1	<.1
5084	Strategic Software Technologies Inc	7451 Lower Troy Rd, Temple TX 76501	254-791-5191	R	<1	<.1
5085	Tipton Cole Co—*Tipton Cole*	PO Box 161563, Austin TX 78716	512 329 0060	R	<1	<.1
5086	Vendig Software Services Inc—*Betty Vendig*	5517 Cabrillow Way, Rocklin CA 95765		R	<1	<.1
5087	Viking Software—*Ned Bjorn*	37910 53rd Ave S, Auburn WA 98001	253-939-3290	R	<1*	<.1
5088	Advanced Voice Recognition Systems Inc—*Walter Geldenhuys*	7659 E Wood Dr, Scottsdale AZ 85260	480-704-4183	P	<1	N/A
5089	Calpian Inc—*Harold Montgomery*	500 N Akard St Ste 285, Dallas TX 75201	214-758-8600	P	<1	N/A
5090	Camelot Corp—*Jeffrey Rochlin*	17 Sutton Way, Township of Washington NJ 07676	201-970-4987	P	<1	N/A
5091	Exobox Technologies Corp—*Jacob Cukjati*	5780 Avenida Robledal, Pensacola FL 32504	850-384-3009	P	<1	N/A
5092	Formcap Corp—*Graham Douglas*	50 W Liberty St Ste 88, Reno NV 89501	775-322-0626	P	<1	N/A
5093	Granite Bear Development—*Stuart MacFaddin*	PO Box 1201, Avon CT 06001		R	<1	N/A
5094	Lecere Corp—*James B Morris*	519 SW 3rd Ave Ste 500, Portland OR 97204	503-781-4828	P	<1	N/A
5095	McRae Software International Inc—*Don McRae*	17180 Creighton Blvd, Chagrin Falls OH 44023	440-543-9242	R	<1	N/A
5096	MMedia Research Corp	1749 E Hallandale Beac, Hallandale FL 33009	954-927-4441	R	<1	N/A
5097	Objective Technologies Inc—*Eric Bergerson*	90-07 68th Ave, Forest Hills NY 11375	718-997-9741	R	<1	N/A
5098	Omen Technology Inc—*Chuck Forsberg*	PO Box 4681, Portland OR 97208	503-614-0430	R	<1	N/A
5099	Pacific Systems Group—*Robert Hahn*	PO Box 790, Lake Oswego OR 97034	503-675-5982	R	<1	N/A
5100	Petrobyte—*Scott Susen*	96 Inverness Dr E Unit, Englewood CO 80112	303-872-2086	R	<1	N/A
5101	Softstar Systems	PO Box 1360, Amherst NH 03031	603-672-0987	R	<1	N/A
5102	TGFIN Holdings Inc—*S Emerson Lybbert*	101 N Main St Ste B, Smithfield UT 84335	435-563-8080	P	<1	N/A
5103	VulcanSoft Ltd	1630 30th St A Ste 342, Boulder CO 80301	303-731-3143	R	<1	N/A
5104	Northrop Grumman Information Technology—*Linda A Mills*	7575 Colshire Dr, McLean VA 22102	703-713-4000	R	N/A	24.0
5105	NEC Corporation of America—*Takayuki Okada*	6535 N State Hwy 161, Irving TX 75039	214-626-2000	R	N/A	15.4
5106	Fredericksburg PC Users Group—*Raymond Pallock*	250 Butler Rd, Fredericksburg VA 22405	540-373-7929	R	N/A	.1
5107	BID2WIN Software Inc (Portsmouth New Hampshire)—*Paul J McKeon Jr*	1 New Hampshire Ave St, Portsmouth NH 03801	603-427-0440	R	N/A	<.1
5108	Silicomp America—*John Michel Gliner*	7011 Koll Ctr Pky Ste, Pleasanton CA 94566	925-931-4450	D	N/A	<.1
5109	Business Machines Systems Inc—*Richard Crews*	6101 S Shackleford Rd, Little Rock AR 72204	501-375-8380	R	N/A	<.1
5110	Oaktree Systems Inc	4062 Grumman Blvd Bldg, Calverton NY 11933	631-369-0094	R	N/A	<.1
5111	Lifeware TEK—*Michael DeLuca*	1301 Plantation Island, Saint Augustine FL 32080	904-794-7070	R	N/A	<.1
5112	Sitech Software—*John Simmons*	12913 Alton Sq Ste 314, Herndon VA 20170		R	N/A	<.1
5113	SNX Inc—*Allen Lubow*	257 Park Ave S 7th Fl, New York NY 10010	718-499-6293	R	N/A	<.1
5114	Star Technologies Inc (Potomac Maryland)—*Robert C Compton*	21351 Ridgetop Cir Ste, Dulles VA 20166	703-737-6717	R	N/A	<.1
5115	Personal TeX Inc—*Craig A Rubin*	722 Lombard St Ste 201, San Francisco CA 94133	415-296-7550	R	N/A	<.1
5116	Professional Business Computer Systems Inc—*Bruce Goetze*	7121 E Cholla St, Scottsdale AZ 85254	480-596-0922	R	N/A	<.1
5117	P22 Type Foundry Inc—*Leon Czolgosz*	PO Box 770, Buffalo NY 14213	716-885-4490	R	N/A	<.1
5118	Quetzal Info Systems—*John Byrd*	1708 E 4th St, Brooklyn NY 11223	718-375-1186	R	N/A	<.1
5119	Harmonic Software Inc	1982 S Pennslyvania St, Denver CO 80210		R	N/A	<.1
5120	Image Processing Software Inc—*Peggy Bostwick*	PO Box 5017, Madison WI 53705	608-233-5033	R	N/A	<.1
5121	ImageTech Corp—*Haresh Verma*	PO Box 847, Bloomfield Hills MI 48303	248-538-4321	R	N/A	<.1
5122	JinTek LLC	9606 Aero Dr Ste 1600, San Diego CA 92123	858-836-4455	R	N/A	<.1
5123	Marketing Decision Support Systems Inc—*Dale Pellman*	5833 N Post Rd Rm D, Indianapolis IN 46216	317-541-9740	R	N/A	<.1
5124	Myrick Computer Services Inc—*John Myrick*	1250 Tower Ln, Erie PA 16505	814-455-6610	R	N/A	<.1
5125	Research Software Design	617 SW Hume St, Portland OR 97219		R	N/A	<.1
5126	Sierra-Pacific Software—*Bill Wiltse*	2880 Fillmore Ave NW, Salem OR 97304	503-585-7022	R	N/A	<.1
5127	IF Software Inc—*Eric Hosick*	126 Oak Knoll Dr, Santa Cruz CA 95060		R	N/A	<.1
5128	IN/QUEST LLC	2051 Big Thompson Ave, Estes Park CO 80517	970-577-0789	R	N/A	<.1
5129	Inphinet Interactive Communications Inc—*Daniel G Budiac*	10437 Innovation Dr St, Milwaukee WI 53226	414-456-0500	R	N/A	<.1
5130	Integrated Software Technologies Inc	4184 E Choloa Canyon D, Phoenix AZ 85044	480-704-5066	R	N/A	<.1
5131	KDS Software and Consulting Inc—*Klaus-Dieter Spatz*	3715 Jefferson Ct, Redwood City CA 94062	650-365-0565	R	N/A	<.1

Note: An asterisk (*) indicates an estimated financial figure. The company type code used is as follows: R = Private, P = Public, S = Private Subsidiary, B = Public Subsidiary, D = Division, J = Joint Venture, I = Investment Fund.

COMPANY RANKINGS BY SALES WITHIN 4-DIGIT SIC

Rank	Company Name—Executive Officer	Address, City, State, Zip	Phone	Type	Fin	Empls
5132	Kutastha Software Solutions Inc—Naresh Sawhney	990 E El Camino Real S, Sunnyvale CA 94087	408-735-1138	R	N/A	<.1
5133	Labyrinth Software Solutions Inc—David Ireland	1503 Meadowlark Ln, Sunnyvale CA 94087	408-733-6223	R	N/A	<.1
5134	Lapel Software Inc—Emil Rojas	PO Box 683, Los Gatos CA 95031		R	N/A	<.1
5135	Logan Industries Inc (Palm Bay Florida)—Alex Soya	2312 S Babcock St, Melbourne FL 32901	321-984-1627	R	N/A	<.1
5136	Logical Decisions—Gary Smith	9206 St Marks Pl, Fairfax VA 22031	703-218-1801	R	N/A	<.1
5137	MICR Automation Inc—Richard E Illyes	2022 Hiwatha Ave, Saint Louis MO 63143	314-406-1654	R	N/A	<.1
5138	Minnow Bear Computers—Michael E Nunamaker	219 N Elmwood, Oak Park IL 60302	708-445-0807	R	N/A	<.1
5139	NCSS—Jerry Hintze PhD	329 N 1000 East, Kaysville UT 84037	801-546-0445	R	N/A	<.1
5140	NetHere Inc—Andrew Taubman	4993 Niagara Ave Ste 2, San Diego CA 92107	619-224-7610	R	N/A	<.1
5141	NetRep	1085 Murrieta Blvd Uni, Livermore CA 94550	925-215-1015	R	N/A	<.1
5142	Nine Eleven Software Inc—Kelly W Keifer	2144 Cromwell Ave, Clovis CA 93611	559-940-1460	R	N/A	<.1
5143	Oakland Software Inc—Francis Robbins Upton IV	484 Lake Park Ave, Oakland CA 94610	510-835-3123	R	N/A	<.1
5144	OPA Inc—Will Ozier	1706 Autumn Meadow Dr, Fairfield CA 94534	707-446-7897	R	N/A	<.1
5145	Porchdog Software Inc—Scott Herscher	555 Bryant St Ste 438, Palo Alto CA 94301	650-331-9085	R	N/A	<.1
5146	Professional Designers and Engineers Inc—Kent R Rieske	5086 Cottonwood Dr, Boulder CO 80301	303-927-6937	R	N/A	<.1
5147	Savard Software	PO Box 3955, Pasco WA 99302	509-585-5092	R	N/A	<.1
5148	Scientific Endeavors Corp—James A Rome	106 Oklahoma Ave, Oak Ridge TN 37830	865-482-9193	R	N/A	<.1
5149	Semarca Corp—Gereld H Smith	8213-A Shoal Creek Blv, Austin TX 78757	512-343-1049	R	N/A	<.1
5150	SLO Revo Inc—Steve Mann	1315 Palm St, San Luis Obispo CA 93401	805-784-9461	R	N/A	<.1
5151	Sparkology—Marty Brenneis	PO Box 3299, San Rafael CA 94912	415-485-4478	R	N/A	<.1
5152	STAZ Software Inc—Chris Stasny	320 Saint Charles St, Bay Saint Louis MS 39520	228-493-0227	R	N/A	<.1
5153	W Strahl's Software Consulting Corp—Bill Strahl	PO Box 26194, Santa Ana CA 92799	714-968-0346	R	N/A	<.1
5154	Windsor Technologies Inc	25 Bellam Blvd Ste 250, San Rafael CA 94901	415-456-2200	R	N/A	<.1
5155	Wine Technologies—Robert Parker	PO Box 67465, Chestnut Hill MA 02467	617-323-8745	R	N/A	<.1
5156	IdeaFisher Systems Inc—Mark Alan Effinger	815 E 20th St, Vancouver WA 98663		R	N/A	N/A
5157	iolo technologies LLC—Noah T Rowles	7470 N Figueroa St, Los Angeles CA 90041	323-257-8888	R	N/A	N/A
5158	John A Keane and Associates—John Keane	273 Jefferson Rd, Princeton NJ 08540	732-991-2256	R	N/A	N/A
5159	MCF Software LLC—Farokh Irani	300 W Rte 59, Nanuet NY 10954	845-735-0210	R	N/A	N/A
5160	Objectsoft Inc—Kevin Clark	3501 N Southport Ave S, Chicago IL 60657	773-755-8331	R	N/A	N/A

TOTALS: SIC 7372 Prepackaged Software
Companies: 5,160 — 446,758 — 1,048.0

7373 Computer Integrated Systems Design

Rank	Company Name—Executive Officer	Address, City, State, Zip	Phone	Type	Fin	Empls
1	Computer Sciences Corp—Michael W Laphen	3170 Fairview Park Dr, Falls Church VA 22042	703-876-1000	P	16,042	91.0
2	Computer Science Corporation Federal Sector—Michael Laphen Computer Sciences Corp	3170 Fairview Pk Rd, Falls Church VA 22042	703-876-1000	D	13,144*	92.0
3	SAIC Inc—Walter P Havenstein	1710 SAIC Dr, McLean VA 22102	703-676-4300	P	11,117	43.4
4	Avaya Inc—Kevin Kennedy	211 Mount Airy Rd, Basking Ridge NJ 07920	908-953-6000	R	5,060	18.9
5	Northrop Grumman Information Technology - Computing Systems Div—Jim White	7575 Colshire Dr, McLean VA 22102	703-556-1000	D	4,500	18.5
6	CACI International Inc—Paul M Cofoni	1100 N Glebe Rd, Arlington VA 22201	703-841-7800	P	3,578	13.7
7	Pricelinecom Inc—Jeffery H Boyd	800 Connecticut Ave, Norwalk CT 06854	203-299-8000	P	3,085	3.4
8	MedQuist—Peter Masanotti	9009 Carothers Pkwy St, Franklin TN 37067		R	2,845*	6.3
9	DuPont Fabros Technology Inc—Hossein Fateh	1212 New York Ave NW S, Washington DC 20005	202-728-0044	P	2,491	.1
10	Reynolds Vehicle Registration Inc—Lloyd G Waterhouse Reynolds and Reynolds Co	PO Box 2608, Dayton OH 45401	937-485-2000	S	2,125*	5.0
11	Cerner Corp—Neal L Patterson	2800 Rockcreek Pkwy, Kansas City MO 64117	816-201-1024	P	1,850	8.2
12	Reynolds and Reynolds Co—Robert Brockman	PO Box 1474, Dayton OH 45401	937-485-2000	R	1,477*	6.0
13	AllScripts-Misys Healthcare Solutions Inc—Vern Davenport	222 Merchandise Mart P, Chicago IL 60654	847-680-3515	P	1,449	6.0
14	Sykes Enterprises Inc—Charles E Sykes	400 N Ashley Dr Ste 28, Tampa FL 33602	813-274-1000	P	1,169	41.0
15	Sapient Corp—Alan J Herrick	131 Dartmouth St 3rd F, Boston MA 02116	617-621-0200	P	1,062	10.0
16	CACI Incorporated - COMMERCIAL—Paul M Cofoni CACI International Inc	1100 N Glebe Rd Ste 20, Arlington VA 22201	703-841-7800	S	1,062*	14.4
17	MICROS Systems Inc—A L (Tom) Giannopoulos	7031 Columbia Gateway, Columbia MD 21046	443-285-6000	P	1,008	5.0
18	Jack Henry and Associates Inc—John F Prim	PO Box 807, Monett MO 65708	417-235-6652	P	967	4.7
19	Mentor Graphics Corp—Walden C Rhines	8005 SW Boeckman Rd, Wilsonville OR 97070	503-685-7000	P	915	4.4
20	Forsythe Solutions Group Inc—William P Brennan	7770 Frontage Rd, Skokie IL 60077	847-213-7000	R	775*	.8
21	Intergraph Corp—Ola Rollen	PO Box 240000, Huntsville AL 35813	256-730-2000	S	774*	4.0
22	Verint Systems Inc—Dan Bodner	330 S Service Rd, Melville NY 11747	631-962-9600	P	727	.9
23	COMSYS Information Technology Services Inc—Larry Enterline	4400 Post Oak Pky Ste, Houston TX 77027	713-386-1400	S	660*	.7
24	Bernard C Harris Publishing Company Inc—Robert Gluck	1400A Crossways Blvd S, Chesapeake VA 23320		R	645*	2.0
25	Getronics—Klaas Wagenaar	290 Concord Rd, Billerica MA 01821	978-625-5000	D	618*	4.2
26	SARCOM Inc—Jim Garrity	8337-A Green Meadows D, Lewis Center OH 43035	614-854-1300	S	600*	1.5
27	NuVox Inc—Jeff Gardner	4001 Rodney Parham Rd, Little Rock AR 72212	501-754-7000	S	594*	1.3
28	Advanced Technology Laboratories Inc—Kenneth Fertner	1751 Loretta Ave, Feasterville Trevose PA 19053	215-355-8111	R	585*	.3
29	Bechtel Software Inc	PO Box 193965, San Francisco CA 94119	415-768-1234	S	500*	.3
30	BAE Systems (McLean Virginia)—Linda Hudson	8201 Greensboro Dr Ste, McLean VA 22102	703-847-5820	S	497*	1.3
31	Hobart West Group Inc—Alexander Gallo	25A Vreeland Rd, Florham Park NJ 07932	973-377-7750	R	455*	1.0
32	L-1 Identity Solutions Inc—Robert V LaPenta	296 Concord Rd, Billerica MA 01821	978-215-2400	S	450	1.4
33	FileNet Corp—Lee D Roberts	3565 Harbor Blvd, Costa Mesa CA 92626	714-327-3400	S	422	1.7
34	Berbee Information Networks Corp—Paul Shain	5520 Research Park Dr, Madison WI 53711	608-288-3000	S	375*	1.0
35	Quality Systems Inc—Steven T Plochocki	18111 Von Karman Ave S, Irvine CA 92612	949-255-2600	P	353	1.6
36	DealerTrack Holdings Inc—Mark F O'Neil	1111 Marcus Ave Ste M0, Lake Success NY 11042	516-734-3600	P	353	1.9
37	Solarcom Capital	1 Sun Ct, Norcross GA 30092	770-449-6116	S	350*	.4
38	Sirius Computer Solutions Inc—Joe Mertens	613 NW Loop 410 Ste 10, San Antonio TX 78216	210-369-8000	R	341*	.4
39	DLT Solutions Inc—Rick Marcotte	13861 Sunrise Valley D, Herndon VA 20171	703-709-7172	R	337*	.2
40	RadiSys Corp—Mike Dagenais	5435 NE Dawson Creek D, Hillsboro OR 97124	503-615-1100	P	331	1.0
41	Softlayer Technologies Inc—Lance Crosby	4849 Alpha Rd, Dallas TX 75244	214-442-0600	R	330	.4
42	MSI Systems Integrators Inc—Bill Fairfield	14301 FNB Pkwy Ste 400, Omaha NE 68154	402-965-2300	R	302*	.7
43	Datalink Corp—Paul F Lidsky	8170 Upland Cir, Chanhassen MN 55317	952-944-3462	P	294	.3
44	Calence / Insight Networking Solutions—Michael Fong	1560 W Fountainhead Pk, Tempe AZ 85282	480-889-9500	S	291*	.2
45	NetScout Systems Inc—Anil Singhal	310 Littleton Rd, Westford MA 01886	978-614-4000	P	291	.8
46	TRI-COR Industries Inc—Louis Gonzalez	4403 Forbes Blvd, Lanham MD 20706	301-731-6140	R	289*	.9
47	Sonata Software Ltd—B Ramaswamy	39300 Civic Center Dr, Fremont CA 94538	510-791-7220	S	274*	.9
48	Dynamics Research Corp—James P Regan	2 Tech Dr, Andover MA 01810	978-289-1500	P	272	1.3
49	Sonus Networks Inc—Raymond P Dolan	4 Technology Park Dr, Westford MA 01886	978-614-8100	P	260	1.1
50	NCI Information Systems Inc	11730 Plz America Dr, Reston VA 20190	703-707-6900	S	259*	2.2
51	Vero International Inc—Jack Thompson	30150 Telegraph Rd, Birmingham MI 48012	248-644-4956	R	250*	<.1
52	Goodman Networks Inc—John Goodman	6400 International Ste, Plano TX 75093	972-406-9692	R	242*	1.5

Rank	Company Name—*Executive Officer*	Address, City, State, Zip	Phone	Type	Fin	Empls
53	MicroAge Inc—*Jeffrey D McKeever*	8160 S Hardy Dr Ste 10, Tempe AZ 85284	480-366-2000	R	241	.2
54	Worldwide Techservices LLC—*Michael Tracy*	836 N St Unit 5, Tewksbury MA 01876	978-848-9000	R	241*	3.0
55	Mainline Information Systems Inc—*Richard S Kearney*	1700 Summit Lake Dr, Tallahassee FL 32317	850-219-5000	R	235*	.3
56	Scientific Games Holdings Corp—*Joseph Wright*	1500 Bluegrass Lakes P, Alpharetta GA 30004	770-664-3700	S	229	N/A
57	Telos Corp—*John B Wood*	19886 Ashburn Rd, Ashburn VA 20147	703-724-3800	P	226	.6
58	Scientific Games Royalty Corp—*A Lorne Weil*	1500 Bluegrass Lakes P, Alpharetta GA 30004	770-664-3700	S	215*	.6
59	Samsung Telecommunications America Inc—*Dale Sohn*	1301 E Lookout Dr, Richardson TX 75082	972-761-7000	S	212*	.6
60	Biometric Applications and Technology Inc—*Robert V LaPenta* Identix Inc	177 Broad St 12th Fl, Stamford CT 06901	203-504-1100	S	205*	.5
61	Centra Technology—*Harold Rosenbaum*	25 Burlington Mall Rd, Burlington MA 01803	781-272-7887	R	178*	.4
62	Integral Systems Inc—*Stuart Daughtridge*	6721 Columbia Gateway, Columbia MD 21046	443-539-5008	R	178	.7
63	SMS Data Products Group Inc—*Bert Rosecan*	1501 Farm Credit Dr, McLean VA 22102		R	175*	.2
64	MTM Technologies Inc—*Steven Stringer*	1200 High Ridge Rd, Stamford CT 06905	203-975-3700	P	175	.4
65	Telamon Corp—*Albert Chen*	1000 E 116th St, Carmel IN 46032	317-818-6888	R	164*	.3
66	ZT Group International Inc—*Frank Chang*	350 Meadowlands Pkwy, Secaucus NJ 07094	201-559-1000	R	161*	.1
67	Virtual Enterprises Inc—*David Sosnowski*	12405 Grant St, Thornton CO 80241	303-301-3000	R	160*	.1
68	Delta Technology LLC—*Nancy Damico*	1001 International Blv, Atlanta GA 30354	404-714-1500	R	151*	1.9
69	Analex Corp—*Michael G Stolarik*	2677 Prosperity Ave St, Fairfax VA 22031	703-852-4000	S	150	1.1
70	USinternetworking Inc—*Stephen A Mucchetti*	2500 Riva Rd, Annapolis MD 21401	410-897-4400	S	150	.7
71	Travelzoo Inc—*Christopher Loughlin*	590 Madison Ave 37th F, New York NY 10022	212-484-4900	P	148	.4
72	Strategic Products and Services—*John N Poole*	300 Littleton 2nd F, Parsippany NJ 07054	973-540-0600	R	147*	.4
73	Thomson Elite—*Kim Massana*	5100 W Goldleaf Cir St, Los Angeles CA 90056	323-642-5200	D	144*	.8
74	BOLData Technology Inc—*Eugene Kiang*	48363 Fremont Blvd, Fremont CA 94538		R	144*	<.1
75	BARRA Inc—*Henry Fernandez*	2100 Milvia St, Berkeley CA 94704	510-548-5442	S	142*	.5
76	Zygo International—*John Berg*	PO Box 448, Middlefield CT 06455	860-347-8506	R	141*	.3
77	Sumaria Systems Inc—*Venilal Sumaria*	99 Rosewood Dr Ste 140, Danvers MA 01923	978-739-4200	R	141*	.4
78	Datamatics Consultants Inc—*Jeetan Singh*	3505 Duluth Park Ln St, Duluth GA 30096	770-232-9460	R	137*	.3
79	Global Edge Software Inc—*MP Kumar*	1635A S Main St, Milpitas CA 95035	408-732-7324	S	135*	.3
80	CDO Technologies Inc—*Al Wofford*	5200 Springfield St St, Dayton OH 45431	937-258-0022	R	134*	.3
81	Tier Technologies Inc—*Alex P Hart*	11130 Sunrise Valley D, Reston VA 20191	571-382-1000	P	130	.2
82	Intelligroup Inc—*John McCain*	5 Independence Way Ste, Princeton NJ 08540	646-810-7400	S	127	2.1
83	Fujitsu Frontech North America Inc—*Yoshihiko Masuda*	25902 Towne Centre Dr, Foothill Ranch CA 92610	949-855-5500	R	126*	1.4
84	eInfochips Inc—*Pratul Shroff*	1230 Midas Way Ste 200, Sunnyvale CA 94085	408-496-1882	S	126*	.3
85	Noblestar Systems Corp—*Kenneth Lew*	PO Box 221196, Chantilly VA 20153	571-323-7800	R	126*	.3
86	Hitachi Computer Products (USA) Inc—*George Wilson*	1800 E Imhoff Rd, Norman OK 73071	405-360-5500	S	122	.6
87	Peirce-Phelps Inc—*Brian G Peirce*	2000 N 59th St, Philadelphia PA 19131	215-879-7000	R	122*	.3
88	Embarcadero Technologies Inc—*Wayne D Williams*	100 California St 12th, San Francisco CA 94111	415-834-3131	R	121*	.3
89	All Covered Inc—*Tim Mott*	101 Redwood Shores Pky, Redwood City CA 94065	650-486-5000	R	118*	.3
90	NYFIX Inc—*P Howard Edelstein*	100 Wall St 26th Fl, New York NY 10005	646-525-3000	S	118	.3
91	MRJ Technology Solutions Inc—*Edward P McMahon*	10560 Arrowhead Dr, Fairfax VA 22030	703-385-0700	R	111*	.8
92	Digital Intelligence Systems Corp—*Mahfuz Ahmed*	8270 Greensboro Dr Ste, Mc Lean VA 22102	703-752-7900	R	110*	1.5
93	Vasco Data Security International Inc—*T Kendall Hunt*	1901 S Meyers Rd Ste 2, Oakbrook Terrace IL 60181	630-932-8844	P	108	.3
94	Techlogix Inc—*Salman Akhtar*	800 W Cummings Park St, Woburn MA 01801	781-933-1846	R	105*	.3
95	Sonic Solutions—*Dave Habiger*	7250 Redwood Blvd Ste, Novato CA 94945	415-893-8000	S	104	.5
96	Patriot Communications LLC—*Dennis Holt*	1201 Alta Loma Rd, West Hollywood CA 90069		R	102	N/A
97	Custom Computor Specialists Inc—*Gregory Galdi*	70 Suffolk Ct, Hauppauge NY 11788	631-864-6699	R	101*	.3
98	AppSense—*Charles Sharland*	17 State St 19th Fl, New York NY 10004	212-597-5500	R	101*	.2
99	GoldenSource—*Michael Meriton*	22 Cortlandt St, New York NY 10007	212-798-7100	R	97*	.2
100	Accu-Weather Inc—*Joel Myers*	385 Science Park Rd, State College PA 16803	814-235-8770	R	96*	.4
101	IceptsTechnology Group Inc—*Less Adams Jr*	1301 Fulling Mill Rd, Middletown PA 17057	717-704-1000	R	95*	<.1
102	Innovative Logistics Techniques Inc—*Verle B Hammond*	4000 Legato Dr Ste 830, Fairfax VA 22033	703-766-1419	R	94*	.4
103	Wausau Financial Systems Inc—*Gary Cawthorne*	PO Box 37, Mosinee WI 54455	715-359-0427	R	94*	.4
104	Odyssey Group Of Cos—*George Kaplan*	11 Overlook Way, Setauket NY 11733	631-751-8400	R	93*	.1
105	Core Bts Inc—*Don Eckrod*	201 W 103rd St Ste 240, Indianapolis IN 46290	317-566-6200	R	93*	.3
106	Kroll Ontrack Inc—*Gregory A Olsen*	9023 Columbine Rd, Eden Prairie MN 55347	952-937-5161	S	92*	.6
107	TranTech Inc—*George J Pedersen*	4900 Seminary Rd Ste 2, Alexandria VA 22311	703-671-9873	S	91*	.2
108	Applied Intelligence Group—*Gregg Smith*	200 N Glebe Rd Ste 803, Arlington VA 22203	703-807-2401	R	90*	.2
109	Comstor—*Jon Pritchard*	14850 Conference Cente, Chantilly VA 20151	703-345-5100	D	90*	.1
110	Edgewater Technology Inc—*Shirley Singleton*	20 Harvard Mill Sq, Wakefield MA 01880	781-246-3343	P	89	.4
111	Thoughtworks Inc—*Trevor Mather*	200 E Randolph St 25th, Chicago IL 60601	312-373-1000	R	88*	.6
112	A10 Networks Inc—*Lee Chen*	2309 Bering Dr, San Jose CA 95131	408-325-8668	R	85*	.3
113	W Bradley Electric Inc—*Leslie Murphy*	90 Hill Rd, Novato CA 94945	415-898-1400	R	85*	.2
114	Artel Inc (Reston Virginia)—*Abbas Yazdani*	1893 Preston White Dr, Reston VA 20191	703-620-1700	R	84*	.2
115	ILS Technology LLC—*Fred Yentz*	5300 Broken Sound Blvd, Boca Raton FL 33487	561-982-9898	S	84*	.2
116	Mercury Data Systems Inc—*John E Taylor*	4214 Beechwood Dr Ste, Greensboro NC 27410	336-294-2828	R	84*	.2
117	Apogen Technologies—*Duane Andrews*	7450-B Boston Blvd, Springfield VA 22153	703-644-6433	S	82*	.5
118	Maryville Technologies Inc—*Joe Blomker*	540 Maryville Centre S, Saint Louis MO 63141	636-519-4100	S	82*	.1
119	Dynamix Group Inc—*Chuck Hawkins*	1905 Woodstock Rd Ste, Roswell GA 30075	912-756-9898	R	80	.1
120	Pulse EFT Association—*Dave Schneider*	1301 McKinney Ste 2500, Houston TX 77010	832-214-0100	R	76*	.2
121	OpSource Inc—*Treb Ryan*	5201 Great America Pkw, Santa Clara CA 95054	408-567-2000	R	76*	.2
122	Telsource Corp—*Vincent Sciarra*	30 Two Bridges Rd Ste, Fairfield NJ 07004	973-227-8040	R	75*	.3
123	Dimensions International Inc—*Russell T Wright*	2800 Eisenhower Ave St, Alexandria VA 22314	703-998-0098	S	75*	.6
124	Liquent Ltd—*Richard Riegel*	101 Gibraltar Rd Ste 2, Horsham PA 19044	215-328-4444	S	74*	.2
125	OfficeTiger—*Ken N Beyer*	7000 Central Pky Ste 8, Atlanta GA 30328		S	74*	.2
126	Identix Inc L-1 Identity Solutions Inc	5705 W Old Shakopee Rd, Bloomington MN 55437	952-932-0888	D	74	.5
127	CSP Inc—*Alexander R Lupinetti*	43 Manning Rd, Billerica MA 01821	978-663-7598	P	74	.1
128	JK Group Inc—*Roy Kaplan*	PO Box 7174, Princeton NJ 08543	609-799-7830	R	70*	.2
129	IVCi LLC—*Robert Swing*	601 Old Willets Path, Hauppauge NY 11788	631-273-5800	R	68*	.2
130	Avineon Inc—*Karlu Rambhalu*	4825 Mark Center Dr St, Alexandria VA 22311	703-671-1900	R	68*	.2
131	XP Systems—*Jeffrey Yabuki*	405 Science Dr, Moorpark CA 93021	805-532-9100	S	66*	.2
132	WTI Systems Ltd—*John Veradian*	1741 S Big Bend Blvd, Saint Louis MO 63117	314-754-1932	R	66*	.2
133	CompuGeek—*Martin A Joseph*	5241 Cleveland St Ste, Virginia Beach VA 23462	757-499-6761	R	66*	.1
134	SunGard HTE Inc—*Gil Santos*	1000 Business Center D, Lake Mary FL 32746	407-304-3235	S	66	.5
135	Crexendo Inc—*Steven G Mihaylo*	1615 S 52nd St, Tempe AZ 85281	801-227-0004	P	66	.4
136	Keane Federal Systems Inc	100 City Square, Boston MA 02129	617-241-9200	S	65*	.7
137	Computer Dynamics Inc—*G William Whitehurst*	7640 Pelham Rd, Greenville SC 29615	864-627-8800	R	63	.4
138	CALIBRE Systems Inc—*Joseph A Martore*	6354 Walker Ln Ste 300, Alexandria VA 22310	703-797-8500	R	61*	.4
139	Universal Hi-Tech Development Inc—*Jerry Lin*	1383 Piccard Dr, Rockville MD 20850	301-926-8000	R	60*	.3
140	Sunguard Availability Services—*Cristobal Conde*	680 E Swedesford Rd, Wayne PA 19087		R	60*	.1

Note: An asterisk (*) indicates an estimated financial figure. The company type code used is as follows: R = Private, P = Public, S = Private Subsidiary, B = Public Subsidiary, D = Division, J = Joint Venture, I = Investment Fund.

COMPANY RANKINGS BY SALES WITHIN 4-DIGIT SIC

Rank	Company Name—*Executive Officer*	Address, City, State, Zip	Phone	Type	Fin	Empls
141	Ungerboeck Systems International Inc—*Krister Ungerboeck*	100 Ungerboeck Pk, O Fallon MO 63368	636-300-5606	R	58*	.2
142	TekScape—*David Smith*	247 W 30th St, New York NY 10001	855-835-7227	R	58	<.1
143	Integrated Systems Analysts Inc—*C Micheal Gooden*	2001 N Beauregard St S, Alexandria VA 22311	703-824-0700	R	57*	.7
144	Progressive Software Computing Inc—*Christopher J O'Neill*	3505 Silverside Rd Plz, Wilmington DE 19810	302-479-9700	R	57*	.1
145	eWorkplace Solutions—*Sahib A Dudani*	24461 Ridge Rte Dr Ste, Laguna Hills CA 92653	949-583-1646	D	56*	.2
146	Mediware Information Systems Inc—*T Kelly Mann*	11711 W 79th St, Lenexa KS 66214	913-307-1000	P	56	.3
147	Solix Systems Inc—*Sai Gundavelli*	4500 Great American Pk, Santa Clara CA 95054	408-328-6400	R	55*	.4
148	Peak 10 Inc—*David Jones*	8910 Lenox Pointe Dr S, Charlotte NC 28273		R	54*	.2
149	Future Tech Enterprise Inc—*Bob Venero*	101 Colin Dr Unit 8, Holbrook NY 11741	631-472-5500	R	53†	.1
150	Cherokee Information Services Inc—*Robin E Gutridge*	1225 S Clark StSte 130, Arlington VA 22202	703-416-0720	R	53*	.6
151	COLOSSUS Inc—*Andrew Filipowski*	9990 Fairfax Blvd Ste, Asheville NC 28801	828-254-9876	R	53*	.2
152	Computer Software Innovations Inc—*Nancy K Hedrick*	900 E Main St Ste T, Easley SC 29640	864-855-3900	P	53	.2
153	Intermedia Group Inc—*Jason Denmark*	5 Hanover Sq, New York NY 10004	212-248-0100	R	52*	.2
154	Technica Corp—*Miguel Collado*	45245 Business Ct Ste, Dulles VA 20166	703-662-2000	R	52*	.2
155	Global Data Systems Inc—*Chuck Vincent*	537 Cajundome Blvd Ste, Lafayette LA 70503	337-291-6500	R	52*	.1
156	Versatile Systems Inc—*John Hardy*	100 Sterling Pkwy Ste, Mechanicsburg PA 17050	717-796-1936	R	52*	.1
157	Advanced Computer Concepts Inc	7927 Jones Branch Dr S, McLean VA 22102	703-276-7800	R	52*	<.1
158	Verso Technologies Inc—*Darryl S Dunaway*	400 Galleria Pky Ste 2, Atlanta GA 30339	678-589-3500	P	51	.3
159	ACS Dataline LP—*Terri Blackmore*	2535 Brockton Dr Ste 4, Austin TX 78758	512-837-4400	R	50*	.5
160	Acentron Technologies Inc—*Dan Springer*	PO Box 78378, Charlotte NC 28271	704-335-0030	R	50*	.2
161	Rightstar Inc—*Richard Stark*	1951 Kidwell Dr Ste 11, Vienna VA 22182	703-242-7200	R	49*	.1
162	ASA International Ltd—*Alfred C Angelone*	10 Speen St, Framingham MA 01701	508-626-2727	R	49*	.1
163	Healthcarecom Corp—*Matias de Tezanos*	3301 NE 1st Ave Ste PH, Miami FL 33137	786-472-2966	R	48	.2
164	Maverick Technologies—*Paul J Galeski*	PO Box 470, Columbia IL 62236	618-281-9100	R	48*	.5
165	Advanced Technical Solutions Inc	20 Main St, Acton MA 01720	978-849-0533	R	48*	.1
166	Millennial Media—*Paul Palmieri*	2400 Boston St Ste 201, Baltimore MD 21224	410-522-8705	R	48	.2
167	Imr Ltd—*Robert Chamberlain*	PO Box 1777, Harrisburg PA 17105	717-364-3700	R	48*	.1
168	GSE Systems Inc—*Jim Eberle*	1332 Londontown Blvd S, Sykesville MD 21784	410-970-7800	B	47	.2
169	Convergent Media Systems Corp—*Bryan Allen*	One Convergent Ctr 190, Alpharetta GA 30005	770-369-9000	R	47*	.3
170	Datamatic Inc—*Ken Kercher*	3600 K Ave, Plano TX 75074	972-234-5000	R	47*	.1
171	Catapult Technology Ltd—*Randy J Slager*	7500 Old Georgetown Rd, Bethesda MD 20814	240-482-2100	R	46*	.3
172	ManTech Systems Engineering Corp—*George J Pedersen*	11 Rt 235, Lexington Park MD 20653	301-862-2200	S	46*	.1
173	Pointe Technology Group Inc—*Jan Townsend*	8201 Corporate Dr Ste, Landover MD 20785	301-306-4400	R	46*	.1
174	United Technology	PO Box 8638, Rowland Heights CA 91748		S	46*	<.1
175	Employer Management Solutions Inc—*Elaine Myrback*	5550 W Executive Dr St, Tampa FL 33609	813-287-2486	R	45*	.1
176	SDI Networks Inc	127 W Antrim Dr, Greenville SC 29607	864-679-0006	S	45*	.1
177	Wireless Generation Inc—*Larry Berger*	55 Washington St Ste 9, Brooklyn NY 11201	212-796-2200	R	45*	.3
178	Ciber Enterprise Solutions—*David C Peterschmidt*	1401 Willow Pass RdSte, Concord CA 94520	925-671-0595	S	44*	.3
179	Strategic Business Systems of Virginia Inc—*Scott Podmilsak*	13241 Woodland Pk Dr 2, Herndon VA 20171	703-766-8950	R	44*	.1
180	Hughes-Calihan Corp—*Peter Calihan*	4730 N 16th, Phoenix AZ 85016	602-264-9631	R	43*	.3
181	Learningcom Inc—*William Kelly*	1620 SW Taylor St Ste, Portland OR 97205	503-284-0100	R	43*	.1
182	SS8 Networks Inc—*Dennis Haar*	750 Tasman Dr, Milpitas CA 95035	408-944-0250	R	42*	.1
183	P-Cube Inc—*John Chambers*	170 West Tasman Dr, San Jose CA 95134	408-720-7770	S	42*	.1
184	DocuTech Corp—*Howard Podgurski*	2049 Stout Dr Ste B-2, Ivyland PA 18974	215-672-7060	R	42*	.1
185	Manatron Inc—*Bill McKinzie*	510 E Milham Ave, Portage MI 49002	269-567-2900	S	42	.3
186	Computer Enterprises Inc—*Barry Zungre*	1910 Cochran Rd Ste 23, Pittsburgh PA 15220	412-341-3541	R	40*	.4
187	Professional Systems Corp (Valley Forge Pennsylvania)—*Joseph J Greco*	PO Box 703, Valley Forge PA 19482	610-650-3900	R	39*	.1
188	Identix Public Sector Inc—*Joseph Atick* Identix Inc	5705 W Old Shakope Rd, Bloomington MN 55437	952-932-0888	S	38*	.4
189	Techturn Ltd—*John Buller*	PO Box 143597, Austin TX 78714	512-997-7974	R	38*	.2
190	Mindshift Technologies—*Paul W Chisholm*	3975 Fair Ridge Dr Ste, Fairfax VA 22033	571-432-4000	R	38*	.1
191	ArrayNetworks Inc—*Michael Zhao*	1371 McCarthy Blvd, Milpitas CA 95035	408-240-8700	R	38*	.1
192	Nation Safe Drivers—*Frank Minton*	800 Yamato Rd Ste 100, Boca Raton FL 33431		R	38*	.1
193	Thinkmate - East Coast	159 Overland Rd, Waltham MA 02451		S	38	<.1
194	Paragon Development Systems Inc—*Craig Schiefelbein*	PO Box 128, Oconomowoc WI 53066		R	37*	.3
195	Siwel Consulting Inc—*Lewis Johnson*	71 W 23rd St Ste 1907, New York NY 10010	212-691-9326	R	37*	.1
196	Segue Software Inc—*Joseph Krivickas*	201 Spring St Ste 2, Lexington MA 02421	781-402-1000	S	36	.2
197	Global Science and Technology Inc—*Chieh-san Cheng*	7855 Walker Dr Ste 200, Greenbelt MD 20770	301-474-9696	R	36*	.3
198	MicroBilt Corp—*Walter Wojciechowski*	1640 Airport Rd Ste 11, Kennesaw GA 30144		D	35*	.3
199	Subsystem Technologies Inc—*Sam Malhotra*	2121 Crystal Dr 68, Arlington VA 22202	703-841-0071	R	35*	.3
200	Decisive Analytics Corp—*John Donnellon*	1235 S Clark St Ste 40, Arlington VA 22202	703-414-5033	R	35*	.2
201	Ms Inet LLC—*James Desilver*	270 Davidson Ave Fl 8, Somerset NJ 08873	732-469-2866	R	35*	.4
202	Essintal Enterprise Solutions—*Charles L McNew*	100 Sterling Pkwy Ste, Mechanicsburg PA 17050	717-610-3200	R	34	.3
203	Banklink USA—*Gary Kasik*	116 W 32nd St 10th Fl, New York NY 10001	212-419-3000	D	34*	.1
204	Jamcracker Inc—*KB Chandrasekhar*	4677 Old Ironsides Dr, Santa Clara CA 95054	408-496-5500	R	34*	.1
205	CipherMax—*Ray Kao*	3 Results Way, Cupertino CA 95014	408-861-3697	R	34*	.1
206	Narus Inc—*Greg Oslan*	570 Maude Ct, Sunnyvale CA 94085	408-215-4300	S	34*	.1
207	POSDATA Inc—*William Mccubbins*	PO Box 1305, Gig Harbor WA 98335		R	34*	.1
208	BDNA Corp—*Constantin Delivanis*	339 N Bernardo Ave Ste, Mountain View CA 94043	650-625-9530	R	34*	.1
209	Global Management Systems Inc—*Hilton Augustine*	2201 Wisconsin Ave NW, Washington DC 20007	202-471-4674	R	33*	.3
210	DataCert Inc—*James Tallman*	3040 Post Oak Blvd Ste, Houston TX 77056	713-572-3282	R	33*	.1
211	Lighthouse Computer Services Inc—*Thomas Mrva*	6 Blackstone Valley Pl, Lincoln RI 02865	401-334-0799	R	33*	.1
212	Schematic Inc—*Trevor Kaufman*	3457 S La Cienega Blvd, Los Angeles CA 90016	310-202-2900	R	33*	.3
213	Network Dynamics Inc—*James Bradshaw*	640 Brooker Creek Blvd, Oldsmar FL 34677	813-818-8597	R	33*	<.1
214	Health Management Systems Inc—*Bill Lucia*	401 Park Ave S, New York NY 10016	212-857-5000	S	32	N/A
215	ISG Novasoft—*Krishna Srinivasan*	3220 Tillman Dr Ste 30, Bensalem PA 19020	267-525-9400	R	32*	.4
216	CAM Commerce Solutions Inc—*Geoffrey D Knapp*	17075 Newhope St Ste A, Fountain Valley CA 92708	714-241-9241	R	32*	.2
217	Foresight Technology Group Inc—*Paul Shain*	6670 W Snowville Rd Un, Brecksville OH 44141	440-717-1800	R	32*	.1
218	Apex IT Inc—*Eric Steege*	860 Blue Gentian Rd St, Eagan MN 55121	651-287-2820	R	32*	.1
219	Corporate Technologies Inc—*Harry Kasparian*	3 Burlington Woods Dr, Burlington MA 01803	781-273-4100	R	32*	.1
220	Works Computing Inc—*Rick Anderson*	1801 American Blvd E S, Minneapolis MN 55425	952-746-1580	R	32*	<.1
221	Digimarc Corp—*Bruce Davis*	9405 SW Gemini Dr, Beaverton OR 97008	503-469-4800	P	31	.1
222	Buchanan Associates—*Jim Buchanan*	125 E John Carpenter F, Irving TX 75062	972-869-3966	R	31*	.3
223	451 Group—*Martin V McCarthy*	20 W 37th St 6th Fl, New York NY 10018	212-505-3030	R	31*	.1
224	Ascentium Corp—*James Beebe*	1005 N E 8th St Ste 13, Bellevue WA 98004	425-519-7700	R	30	.3
225	Wise Men Inc—*Juuhi Ahuja*	1500 S Dairy Ashford S, Houston TX 77077	281-679-6740	R	30*	.3
226	Advanced Resource Technology Inc—*Horace F Jones*	1555 King St Ste 400, Alexandria VA 22314	703-682-4740	R	30*	.2
227	MSN Communications Inc—*Doug Schuck*	20 Inverness Pl E, Englewood CO 80112	303-347-8303	R	30*	.1
228	System Development Integration LLC—*Duane Flowers*	33 W Monroe St Ste 400, Chicago IL 60603	312-580-7500	R	30*	.1

Rank	Company Name—*Executive Officer*	Address, City, State, Zip	Phone	Type	Fin	Empls
229	Teletracking Technologies Inc—*Anthony Sanzo*	336 4th Ave Fl 7, Pittsburgh PA 15222	412-391-7862	R	30*	.2
230	Attronica Computers Inc—*Atul Tucker*	15867 Gaither Dr, Gaithersburg MD 20877	301-417-0070	R	29*	<.1
231	Morphotrak Inc—*Daniel Vassy*	113 S Columbus St Ste, Alexandria VA 22314	703-797-2600	R	29*	.2
232	Fortent Americas Inc—*Sandra Jaffee*	99 Park Ave Rm 1102, New York NY 10016	212-661-1325	R	28*	.3
233	Telogis Inc—*David Cozzens*	85 Enterprise Ste 450, Aliso Viejo CA 92656	949-389-5500	R	28*	.2
234	InfoVision Consultants Inc—*Sean Yalamanchi*	800 E Campbell Rd Ste, Richardson TX 75081	972-234-0058	R	28*	.1
235	Packet360 Inc—*Kevin Gerber*	100 Eastshore Dr, Glen Allen VA 23059	804-545-4700	R	28*	.1
236	Encore Real Time Computing Inc—*Cal Morrell*	999 N Sepulveda Blvd S, El Segundo CA 90245	310-768-1800	S	27*	.1
237	iXP Corp—*Richard E Dale*	1249 S River Rd Ste 10, Cranbury NJ 08512	609-409-7272	R	27*	.1
238	SkyBitz Inc—*Homaira Akbari*	22455 Davis Dr Ste 100, Sterling VA 20164	703-318-8100	R	27*	.1
239	Perficient Meritage Inc—*Jack McDonald*	401 North Front St Ste, Columbus OH 43215	614-224-0500	S	26*	.2
240	K/Micro Inc—*Michael Sabourian*	2050 S Westgate Ave, Los Angeles CA 90002	310-442-3200	R	26*	.1
241	Blue Ridge Networks—*Mike Fumai*	14120 Parke Long Ct St, Chantilly VA 20151	703-631-0700	R	26*	.1
242	Advantage Business Computer Systems Inc—*Gregory K Matatall*	PO Box 421, Big Sandy TX 75755	903-636-5200	S	26*	.1
243	Preferred Systems Solutions Inc—*Scott Goss*	1945 Old Gallows Rd St, Vienna VA 22182	703-663-2777	R	25*	.3
244	Troy Group Inc—*Patrick J Dirk*	940 S Coast Dr Ste 200, Costa Mesa CA 92626	714-241-4760	R	25*	.1
245	TechSpace Inc—*James Watson*	65 Enterprise, Aliso Viejo CA 92656	949-389-5800	R	25*	.1
246	JDL Technologies Inc	5450 NW 33rd Ave Ste 1, Fort Lauderdale FL 33309	954-334-0650	S	25	<.1
247	CBE Technologies Inc—*John Mann*	200 Bulfinch Dr, Andover MA 01810	617-514-1700	R	24*	.2
248	Lowry Computer Products Inc—*Mike Lowry*	9420 Maltby Rd, Brighton MI 48116	810-229-7200	R	24*	.1
249	Integrated IT Solutions Inc—*David Yazdi*	159 Overland Rd, Waltham MA 02451	781-453-5100	R	24*	.1
250	M2S—*Greg Lange*	12 Commerce Ave, West Lebanon NH 03784	603-298-5509	R	24*	.1
251	Network Integration Company Partners Inc—*Franklin Spaeth*	11981 Jack Benny Dr St, Rancho Cucamonga CA 91739	909-919-2800	R	23*	<.1
252	Dynamic Concepts Inc (Washington DC)—*Pedro Alfonso*	1730 17th St NE, Washington DC 20002	202-944-8787	R	23*	.3
253	ISA Consulting—*Lou Polisano*	5 Valley Sq Ste 205, Blue Bell PA 19422	215-646-8676	R	23*	.1
254	HSQ Technology Corp—*Jeffrey M Levy*	PO Box 4557, Hayward CA 94540	510-259-1334	S	23*	.1
255	Vanteon—*Joseph L Burke*	255 Woodcliff Dr Ste 2, Fairport NY 14450	585-419-9555	R	23*	.1
256	Connecticut Computer Service Inc—*Ralph Carbone Jr*	101 E Summer St, Plantsville CT 06479	860-276-1285	R	23*	.1
257	Cintas Document Management Imaging Div—*Scott Farmer*	2850 S Lynhurst Dr, Indianapolis IN 46241	317-244-8772	R	23*	.1
258	NetWolves Technologies Corp—*Scott Foote* NetWolves Corp	4710 Eisenhower Blvd S, Tampa FL 33634	813-579-3200	S	23*	.1
259	Canvas Systems LLC—*Matt Blackburn*	3025 Northwoods Pkwy, Norcross GA 30071	770-662-1881	R	22*	.2
260	Skyline Network Engineering LLC—*Christine Bangerd*	6200 Georgetwn Blvd St, Sykesville MD 21784	410-795-2700	R	22*	.1
261	IKANO Communications Inc—*George Naspo*	124 N Charles Lindburg, Salt Lake City UT 84116	801-924-0900	R	22*	.3
262	NuWare Technology Corporation Inc—*Venk Krishnan*	100 Wood Ave S Ste 122, Iselin NJ 08830	732-494-0550	R	22*	.1
263	Ascent Media Systems and Technology Services—*Jose Royo*	100 Stonehurst Ct, Northvale NJ 07647	201-767-1200	S	22*	.1
264	PCnet Inc—*Camilo Soto*	100 Technology Dr, Trumbull CT 06611	203-452-8500	R	22*	.1
265	Single Source Systems Inc—*Tony Petrucciani*	9003 Technology Dr, Fishers IN 46038	317-596-3000	R	22*	.1
266	Enterprise Computing Solutions Inc—*David Butler*	26024 Acero, Mission Viejo CA 92691	949-609-1980	R	22*	.1
267	Clearpath Solutions Group—*Gary Vaughan*	13800 Coppermine Rd St, Herndon VA 20171		R	22	<.1
268	REI Systems Inc—*Veer V Bhartiya*	200 Fairbrook Dr Ste 1, Herndon VA 20170	703-480-9100	R	21*	.2
269	Alteryx Inc—*George Mathew*	230 Commerce Ste 250, Irvine CA 92602	714-516-2400	R	21*	.1
270	Merit Network Inc—*Don Welch*	1000 Oakbrook Dr Ste 2, Ann Arbor MI 48104	734-527-5700	R	21*	.1
271	Synergon Solutions Inc—*Gary E Bradley*	1335 Gateway Dr Ste 20, Melbourne FL 32901		R	21*	.1
272	US Internet Corp—*William J Milota*	12450 Wayzata Blvd Ste, Minnetonka MN 55305		R	21*	<.1
273	Iteq Integrated Technologies Inc—*Patricia De Aloia*	8757 Georgia Ave Ste 5, Silver Spring MD 20910	301-495-5545	R	21*	.3
274	Trivalent Group Inc—*Larry Andrus*	3145 Prairie St Sw Ste, Grandville MI 49418	616-222-9200	R	21*	.1
275	Dai Inc—*Mohammed Daher*	17735 Ne 65th St Ste 1, Redmond WA 98052	425-467-8000	R	20*	.2
276	Vital Network Services—*John Koehler*	14520 McCormick Dr, Tampa FL 33626	813-818-5100	R	20	.1
277	Fatpipe Networks Inc—*Ragula Bhaskar*	4455 S 700 East, Salt Lake City UT 84107	801-281-3434	R	20*	.1
278	Newtech Infosystems Inc—*Bill Yao*	9999 Muirlands Blvd, Irvine CA 92618	949-421-0720	R	20*	.1
279	InterNetworking Technologies Inc—*Allan Wagamon*	PO Box 852, Milford DE 19963	302-424-1855	R	20*	<.1
280	W-Industries of Louisiana LLC—*Michael Johnson* BrightStar Consulting Inc	PO Box 820, Maurice LA 70555	337-233-4537	S	19*	.3
281	Metters Industries Inc—*Samuel Metters*	8200 Greensboro Dr, McLean VA 22102	703-821-3300	R	19*	.2
282	Teros Inc	851 W Cypress Creek Rd, Fort Lauderdale FL 33309	954-267-3000	S	19*	.1
283	Key Information Systems Inc—*Leif Morin*	21700 Oxnard St Ste 25, Woodland Hills CA 91367	818-992-8950	R	19*	<.1
284	Viccs Inc—*Mellina Soheili*	11821 Parklawn Dr Ste, Rockville MD 20852	301-984-1355	R	19*	.3
285	Viatech Systems Inc—*Victor Kan*	7901 Jones Branch Dr S, Mc Lean VA 22102	703-917-0550	R	19*	.1
286	LabVantage Solutions Inc—*Jeff Ferguson*	265 Davidson Ave Ste 2, Somerset NJ 08873	908-707-4100	R	18	.2
287	Pacific Blue Micro Inc	16800 Aston St Ste 175, Irvine CA 92606	949-417-7000	R	18*	.1
288	Vertex Solutions Inc—*Jeff Kidwell*	7389 Lee Hwy Ste 301, Falls Church VA 22042	703-564-7100	S	18*	.1
289	NA Elmos Inc—*Simon Haider*	32255 Nw Hwy Ste 45, Farmington Hills MI 48334	248-865-3200	R	18*	<.1
290	Onstream Media Corp—*Randy S Selman*	1291 SW 29th Ave, Pompano Beach FL 33069	954-917-6655	P	18	.1
291	Streamline Health Solutions Inc—*Robert E Watson*	10200 Alliance Rd Ste, Cincinnati OH 45242	513-794-7100	P	18	.1
292	Future Information Technology Inc—*Daniele Wishnow*	1114 Benfield Blvd Ste, Millersville MD 21108	410-867-7199	R	17*	<.1
293	Alpha Data Corp—*Vercell Vance*	1326 Lewis Turner Blvd, Fort Walton Beach FL 32547	850-315-0417	R	17*	.1
294	Computer Resources—*Michael Christiansen*	125 B Maple St, Port Clinton OH 43452	419-734-6037	R	17*	.1
295	NetWolves Corp—*Scott Foote*	4710 Eisenhower Blvd S, Tampa FL 33634	813-579-3200	R	17*	<.1
296	Computac Inc—*John Hochreiter*	162 N Main St, West Lebanon NH 03784	603-298-5721	R	17*	<.1
297	Scientific Games Management Corp	750 Lexington Ave 25th, New York NY 10022	212-754-2233	S	17*	<.1
298	Advanced Technology Solutions Group Inc—*Tony Rametra*	1762 Central Ave, Albany NY 12205	518-452-3700	R	17*	<.1
299	Triumph Technologies Inc—*Steve Munroe*	12 Gill St, Woburn MA 01801	781-756-3700	S	17*	.1
300	On2 Technologies Inc—*Matthew Frost*	3 Corporate Dr Ste 100, Clifton Park NY 12065	518-348-0099	S	17	.1
301	Stroz Friedberg LLC—*John Fcurran*	32 Ave Of The Americas, New York NY 10013	212-981-6540	R	16*	.1
302	Able Microsystems Corp—*Richard Chan*	16533 Old Valley Blvd, La Puente CA 91744	626-723-7777	R	16*	<.1
303	First Tek Technologies—*Kumar Bhavanasi*	1551 S Washington Ave, Piscataway NJ 08854	732-745-0700	R	16*	.3
304	Intrasphere Technologies Inc—*Bill Karl*	3 Second Street Harbor, Jersey City NJ 07311	212-937-8200	R	16*	.1
305	Nuvo Network Management—*Richard Fournier*	5400 Opportunity Ct St, Hopkins MN 55343	952-933-4600	R	16*	.1
306	Commerce Controls Inc—*Harold Gardynik*	41069 Vincenti Ct, Novi MI 48375	248-476-1442	R	16*	.1
307	Automation Image Inc—*Indira Singla*	2650 Valley View Ln St, Dallas TX 75234	972-247-8816	R	16*	.1
308	Radiant Logic Inc—*Michael Prompt*	75 Rowland Way Ste 300, Novato CA 94945	415-209-6800	R	16*	<.1
309	Veraxx Engineering Corp—*Charlie Smith*	14221a Willard Rd Ste, Chantilly VA 20151	703-880-9000	R	16*	<.1
310	Nivis LLC—*Doug Johns*	1000 Cir 75 Pkwy Se St, Atlanta GA 30339	678-202-6800	R	16*	.1
311	Allin Corp—*Richard W Talarico*	381 Mansfield Ave, Pittsburgh PA 15220	412-928-8800	P	15	.1
312	Tritek Solutions Inc—*John Finnegan*	7617 Little River Tpke, Annandale VA 22003	703-333-3060	R	15*	.1
313	Advanced Systems Technology Inc (Lawton Oklahoma)—*Steve Webley*	PO Box 2305, Lawton OK 73502	580-248-0321	R	15*	.3
314	Gryphon Technologies LC—*PJ Braden*	6301 Ivy Ln Ste 300, Greenbelt MD 20770	240-387-1000	R	15*	.2

Note: An asterisk (*) indicates an estimated financial figure. The company type code used is as follows: R = Private, P = Public, S = Private Subsidiary, B = Public Subsidiary, D = Division, J = Joint Venture, I = Investment Fund.

COMPANY RANKINGS BY SALES WITHIN 4-DIGIT SIC

Rank	Company Name—*Executive Officer*	Address, City, State, Zip	Phone	Type	Fin	Empls
315	Innovative Systems LLC	1000 Innovative Dr, Mitchell SD 57301	605-995-6120	R	15*	.1
316	UPS Logistics Technologies Inc—*Len Kennedy*	849 Fairmount Ave Ste, Baltimore MD 21286	410-847-1900	D	15*	.1
317	Parallel Technologies Inc—*Dale Klein*	7667 Equitable Dr Ste, Eden Prairie MN 55344	952-920-7185	R	15*	.1
318	Telesoft Corp—*Thierry Zerbib*	3443 N Central Ave Ste, Phoenix AZ 85012	602-308-2100	R	15*	.1
319	Primus Global Services Inc—*Anil Kilaru*	1431 Greenway Dr Ste 7, Irving TX 75038	972-753-6500	R	15*	.1
320	Kline Process Systems Inc—*Robert Kline*	625 Spring St Ste 200, Reading PA 19610	610-371-0200	R	15*	<.1
321	Netfast Communications Inc—*Joe Asady*	989 Ave Of The America, New York NY 10018	212-792-5200	R	15*	<.1
322	Iron Brick Associates LLC—*Kevin Kiser*	8405 Greensboro Dr Ste, Mc Lean VA 22102	703-288-3874	R	15*	<.1
323	Lodestar Consulting LLC—*Diana Begley*	780 Newtown Yardley Rd, Newtown PA 18940	215-860-1223	R	15*	<.1
324	Summit Technologies Inc—*Paul Patel*	45 S Main St Ste 40, West Hartford CT 06107	860-570-0661	R	15*	.1
325	Axispoint Inc—*Daniel Disano*	350 Madison Ave Fl 4, New York NY 10017	212-920-2677	R	15*	.1
326	Selectica Inc—*Jason Stern*	2121 S El Camino Real, San Mateo CA 94403	650-532-1500	P	15	.1
327	Acma Computers Inc—*Jean Shih*	1505 Reliance Way, Fremont CA 94539	510-257-6800	R	15*	<.1
328	Fiberplus Federal Services Inc—*Carl Strobel*	8240 Preston Ct Ste C, Jessup MD 20794	301-317-3300	R	14*	.4
329	IronCAD—*Jan Tung*	700 Galleria Pky Ste 3, Atlanta GA 30339		R	14*	.2
330	TDC Systems Integration—*Tony Dozier*	2875 Spring Hill Pkwy, Smyrna GA 30080	770-805-9300	R	14*	.1
331	Pepperweed Consulting LLC—*Patrick Stewart*	1603 Carmody Ct, Sewickley PA 15143		R	14*	.1
332	Agency Technologies Inc—*Dennis Derringer*	PO Box 10057, Florence SC 29501		S	14*	<.1
333	ProTech Associates Inc—*Brian Bruffey*	5457 Twin Knolls Rd St, Columbia MD 21045	847-384-1838	R	14*	<.1
334	Personnel Data Systems Inc—*Charles Jefferies*	470 Norristown Rd Ste, Blue Bell PA 19422	610-238-4600	R	14*	<.1
335	WatchITcom—*Jim Fallon*	12 Skyline Dr, Hawthorne NY 10532	914-345-2620	D	14*	<.1
336	Planet Associates Inc—*William Spencer*	3535 Rte 66 Pky 100 -, Neptune NJ 07753	732-922-5300	R	14*	.1
337	Advanced Integration Technology Inc—*Edward Chalupa*	2805 E Plano Pkwy Ste, Plano TX 75074	972-423-8354	R	14*	.1
338	Document Security Systems Inc—*Patrick White*	28 Main St E Ste 1525, Rochester NY 14614	585-325-3610	P	13	.1
339	ENfrastructure Technologies Inc—*Daniel Pickett*	5 Enterprise Ave, Clifton Park NY 12065	518-664-3899	R	13*	.1
340	Helios and Matheson Information Technology Inc—*Divya Ramachandran*	200 Park Ave S Ste 901, New York NY 10003	212-979-8228	P	13	<.1
341	Clinicomp International Inc—*Chris Haudenschild*	9655 Towne Centre Dr, San Diego CA 92121	858-546-8202	R	13*	.1
342	SPADAC Inc—*Mark Dumas*	7921 Jones Branch Dr S, McLean VA 22102	703-893-3500	R	13*	.1
343	Hagerman and Company Inc—*Dennis Hagerman*	PO Box 139, Mount Zion IL 62549	217-864-2326	R	13*	.1
344	ASAP Systems—*Elie Jean Touma*	175 Bernal Rd Ste 240, San Jose CA 95119	408-227-2720	R	13*	<.1
345	Actify Inc—*David Opsahl*	150 Post St Ste 480, San Francisco CA 94108	415-227-3800	R	13*	<.1
346	CosaTech Inc—*Ann Le*	1415 W 22nd St Tower F, Oak Brook IL 60523	630-684-2331	R	13*	<.1
347	O2 Micro Inc—*Sterling Du*	3118 Patrick Henry Dr, Santa Clara CA 95054	408-987-5920	R	13*	.1
348	Voxware Inc—*Keith Phillips*	300 American Metro Blv, Hamilton NJ 08619	609-514-4100	R	13	.1
349	Synergis Technologies Inc—*David Sharp*	472 California Rd Ste, Quakertown PA 18951	215-529-9900	R	12*	.1
350	Plexsys Interface Products Inc—*John Ledoux*	4900 Nw Camas Meadows, Camas WA 98607	360-838-2500	R	12*	.1
351	Computer System Designers LLC	PO Box 7244, Oklahoma City OK 73153	405-604-3277	R	12*	.2
352	Innovative Management and Technology Services LLC—*Chirag Patel*	1000 Technology Dr Ste, Fairmont WV 26554	304-363-6757	R	12*	.2
353	International TechneGroup Inc—*Mike Lemon*	5303 DuPont Cir, Milford OH 45150	513-576-3900	R	12*	.2
354	AccessLine Communications Corp—*Doug Johnson*	11201 SE 8th St, Bellevue WA 98004	206-621-3500	S	12*	.1
355	netASPx Inc—*John Whiteside*	13530 Dulles Technolog, Herndon VA 20171	703-561-0450	S	12*	.1
356	Park City Group Inc (Park City Utah)—*Randy Fields*	3160 Pinebrook Rd, Park City UT 84098	435-645-2000	S	12*	.1
357	Cott Systems Inc—*Deborah Ball*	350 E Wilson Bridge Rd, Worthington OH 43085	614-847-4405	R	12*	.1
358	Thomas and Herbert Consulting LLC—*Rodney E Thomas*	1901 N Moore St Ste 70, Arlington VA 22209	703-248-8116	R	12*	.1
359	Versalign Inc—*Mark Greenberg*	1719 Delaware Ave, Wilmington DE 19806	302-225-7800	R	12*	.1
360	Design Analysis Associates Inc—*William Fletcher*	75 W 100 S, Logan UT 84321	435-753-2212	S	12*	<.1
361	COMPUtek Dental Systems—*Phillip A Tarver*	3825 E Mulberry St Ste, Fort Collins CO 80524	970-224-4022	R	12*	<.1
362	GSE Power Systems Inc—*Jim Eberle* GSE Systems Inc	1332 Londontown Blvd S, Sykesville MD 21784	410-970-7800	S	12*	<.1
363	BIAS Corp—*Jeff Harvey*	1100 Abernathy Rd NE S, Atlanta GA 30328	770-352-9920	R	12*	<.1
364	EIA Inc—*George Engel*	31-00 47th Ave Ste 113, Long Island City NY 11101	212-206-8850	R	12*	<.1
365	Allin Interactive Corp—*Richard W Talarico* Allin Corp	2841 W Cypress Creek R, Fort Lauderdale FL 33309	954-630-1020	S	12*	<.1
366	McBride and Associates Inc—*Johnathan E McBride*	1701 Pennsylvania Ave, Washington DC 20006	202-349-3663	R	12*	<.1
367	NTS Test Systems Engineering—*Steve Orton*	5200 Pasadena NE Ste A, Albuquerque NM 87113	505-345-9499	S	12*	<.1
368	Harmony Computers and Electronics Inc	1801 Flatbush Ave, Brooklyn NY 11210	718-692-2828	R	12*	<.1
369	Friendly Software Corp—*Bill Bales*	1628 Henthorne Dr Ste, Maumee OH 43537	419-868-6090	R	12*	<.1
370	Sawgrass Technologies Inc—*Nathan Hale*	2233 Hwy 17 N, Mount Pleasant SC 29466	843-884-1575	R	12*	.1
371	Simulations Plus Inc—*Walter S Woltosz*	42505 10th St W, Lancaster CA 93534	661-723-7723	P	12	<.1
372	Network Designs Inc—*James Hill*	501 Church St Ne Ste 2, Vienna VA 22180	703-255-2206	R	12*	<.1
373	Source Medical Solutions Inc—*Larry Mctavish*	866 N Main St Ext, Wallingford CT 06492	203-949-6290	R	11*	.1
374	Cyber-World Solutions Inc—*Sam Reddy*	2001 Butterfield Rd St, Downers Grove IL 60515	630-371-0530	R	11*	.1
375	Strategic Data Systems—*Donna Locke*	7777 Alvardo Rd Ste 52, La Mesa CA 91942	619-697-0025	R	11*	.1
376	DB Professionals Inc—*Shankar Viswanathan*	620 SW 5th Ave Ste 610, Portland OR 97204	503-226-6586	S	11*	.1
377	Stonebridge Technologies Oklahoma—*James Ivy*	4200 E Skelly Dr Ste 9, Tulsa OK 74135	918-663-8000	S	11*	.1
378	CSP Securities Corp CSP Inc	43 Manning Rd, Billerica MA 01821	978-663-7598	S	11*	<.1
379	Zeroid and Company Inc	15010 Broschart Rd, Rockville MD 20850	703-461-8383	S	11*	<.1
380	ComSpec International Inc	30800 Telegraph Rd Ste, Bingham Farms MI 48025	248-647-8841	R	11*	<.1
381	Global Systems and Strategies—*Kevin Connolly*	13512 Hunting Hill Way, Gaithersburg MD 20878	301-926-7610	R	11*	<.1
382	Passport Software Inc—*John Miller*	181 Waukegan Rd Ste 20, Northfield IL 60093	847-729-7900	R	11*	<.1
383	Performance Management Inc—*Dave Camner*	1103 Washington, Dearborn MI 48124	313-561-3700	R	11*	<.1
384	Schemers Inc—*Terry Kaufman*	7435 NW 4 St, Fort Lauderdale FL 33317	954-776-7376	R	11*	<.1
385	Valley Network Solutions Inc—*Daniel Duffy*	364 W Fallbrook Ave St, Fresno CA 93711	559-650-2600	R	11*	<.1
386	Vicon (Centennial Colorado)—*Douglas Reinke*	7388 S Revere Pkwy Ste, Centennial CO 80112	303-799-8686	S	11*	<.1
387	InfoSolutions Inc—*Jerry Junker*	2734 Chancellor Dr Ste, Crestview Hills KY 41017	859-331-7999	R	11*	<.1
388	Oakwood Systems Group Inc—*Charles Windsor*	2 Cityplace Dr Ste 10, Saint Louis MO 63141	314-824-3000	R	11*	.1
389	Zumasys Inc—*Paul Giobbi*	9245 Research Dr, Irvine CA 92618	949-334-0287	R	11*	.1
390	Axom Technologies Inc—*Matthew Norris*	10010 Junction Dr, Annapolis Junction MD 20701		R	11	.1
391	Integrated Computer Concepts Inc—*William Adams*	1334 Ashton Rd Ste A, Hanover MD 21076	443-270-5300	R	10*	.1
392	Secom International—*Ted Burton*	9610 Bellanca Ave, Los Angeles CA 90045	310-641-1290	R	10*	.1
393	Buckardt Technologies Inc—*Judith Buckardt*	2230 Point Blvd Ste 80, Elgin IL 60123	847-426-9355	R	10*	<.1
394	Alpine Consulting Inc—*Chris Millin*	1100 E Wdfield Rd Ste, Schaumburg IL 60173	847-605-0788	R	10*	.1
395	Paloma Systems Inc—*Isabel C Pedrozo*	11250 Waples Mill Rd S, Fairfax VA 22030	703-278-8999	R	10*	.1
396	SNVC—*Tom Dewitt*	12150 Monument Dr Ste, Fairfax VA 22033	703-952-7682	R	10*	.1
397	Minerva Networks Inc—*Mauro Bonomi*	2150 Gold St, Alviso CA 95002	408-567-9400	R	10*	.1
398	Asure Software Inc—*Pat Goepel*	110 Wild Basin Rd Ste, Austin TX 78746	512-437-2700	P	10	.1
399	Mainstream Data Inc—*Scott Calder*	375 Chipeta Way Ste B, Salt Lake City UT 84108	801-584-2800	R	10*	.1

Rank	Company Name—*Executive Officer*	Address, City, State, Zip	Phone	Type	Fin	Empls
400	Davlong Business Solutions LLC—*Tammy Garner*	PO Box 13486, Savannah GA 31416	912-355-3213	R	10*	<.1
401	OpenConnect Systems Inc—*Edward M Peters*	2711 LBJ Fwy Ste 700, Dallas TX 75234	972-484-5200	R	10*	<.1
402	SCT Inc—*Scott C Tippetts*	4830 Lawrenceville Hwy, Lilburn GA 30047	770-921-8436	R	10*	<.1
403	Computer World Services Corp—*Frank Hameed*	1100 G St NW Rm 625, Washington DC 20005	202-637-9699	R	10*	<.1
404	Ideas International Inc—*Stephen Bowhill*	800 Westchester Ave St, Rye Brook NY 10573	914-937-4302	D	10*	<.1
405	Fig Leaf Software Inc—*Steven Drucker*	1523 16th St Nw Apt 2, Washington DC 20036	202-797-7711	R	10*	<.1
406	JMark Business Solutions Inc—*Thomas Douglas*	601 N National Ave Ste, Springfield MO 65802	417-863-1700	R	10*	<.1
407	CERIS / NPIRS—*Eileen Luke*	1435 Win Hentschel Blv, West Lafayette IN 47906		R	10*	<.1
408	Paramount Computer Corp—*Steve Marshall*	4201 S Cngrtx Ave 316, Austin TX 78745	512-263-7010	R	10*	<.1
409	Germane Systems LC—*Doug Anderson*	3680 Centerview Dr Ste, Chantilly VA 20151	703-502-8890	R	10*	.1
410	Fisher Unitech Inc—*Gregory Fisher*	1150 Stephenson Hwy, Troy MI 48083	248-577-5100	R	10*	.1
411	Yeo and Yeo Computer Consulting LLC—*Jeff Mcculloch*	3023 Davenport Ave, Saginaw MI 48602	989-797-4075	R	10*	<.1
412	Advanced Systems Resources Inc—*Jeff Kinkead*	407 Lincoln Rd Ste 8M, Miami Beach FL 33139	305-531-9530	R	10	<.1
413	Zykronix Inc—*David Ghaemi*	188 Invrneco Dr W Ste, Englewood CO 80112	303-799-4944	R	10*	.1
414	Unitek Inc—*Jin Kim*	47333 Warm Springs Blv, Fremont CA 94539	510-623-8544	R	10*	.1
415	Kraft and Kennedy Inc—*Michael Kraft*	360 Lexington Ave Fl 1, New York NY 10017	212-986-4700	R	10*	.1
416	Competitive Computing Inc—*Carolyn Edwards*	354 Mountain Ave 400, Colchester VT 05446	802-764-1700	R	10*	.1
417	Computer Logic Group Inc—*Robert Springer*	33 Comac Loop Unit 8, Ronkonkoma NY 11779	631-738-1900	R	9*	.1
418	MPL Systems Inc—*Kelly Lavorgna*	95 Main Ave Ste 1, Clifton NJ 07014	973-256-8220	R	9*	.1
419	Fedvar Corporation—*Anthony Brown*	1025 Connecticut Ave N, Washington DC 20036	202-857-9770	R	9*	<.1
420	Pinnacle Software Inc—*Donald Potter*	2001 W Cyprefl Creek R, Fort Lauderdale FL 33309	954-938-8870	R	9*	.1
421	ProSoft Technology Group Inc—*Raj Gupta*	2001 Butterfield Rd St, Downers Grove IL 60515	630-725-1800	R	9*	.1
422	SP Systems Inc (Greenbelt Maryland)—*Swami Reddy*	7500 Greenway Center D, Greenbelt MD 20770	301-614-1322	R	9*	.1
423	Application Development Resources Inc—*Adil Choksey*	4555 Mansell Rd Ste 21, Alpharetta GA 30022	404-374-2331	R	9*	.1
424	Plexus Installations Inc	2520 Lord Baltimore Dr, Baltimore MD 21244	410-265-1818	R	9*	.1
425	Intuitive Research and Technology Corp—*Rey Almodovar*	5030 Bradford Dr Ste 2, Huntsville AL 35805	256-922-9300	R	9*	.1
426	UC4 Software—*Jason Liu*	14475 NE 24th St Ste 2, Bellevue WA 98007	425-644-2121	R	9*	.1
427	Intekras Inc—*Charles Williams*	21515 Ridgetop Cir Ste, Sterling VA 20166	703-547-3500	R	9*	<.1
428	Network Data Systems Inc—*Al Siders*	50 East Commerce Dr St, Schaumburg IL 60173	847-385-6700	R	9*	<.1
429	Direct Insite Corp—*Matthew E Oakes*	13450 West Sunrise Blv, Sunrise FL 33323	631-873-2900	P	9	<.1
430	ID Experts Corp—*Robert S Gregg*	10300 SW Greenburg Rd, Portland OR 97223		R	9	<.1
431	Accent Media (Burbank California)—*Greg Howard*	1011 W Alameda Ave Ste, Burbank CA 91506	818-973-7600	S	9*	<.1
432	Blackstone and Cullen Inc—*Lee Blackstone*	1125 Sanctuary Pkwy St, Alpharetta GA 30009	770-612-1550	R	9*	<.1
433	Evans Technology Inc—*Jay Evans*	1335 Northmeadow Pky S, Roswell GA 30076	770-751-9950	R	9*	.1
434	Foxit Corp	42840 Christy St Ste 2, Fremont CA 94538		R	9*	<.1
435	Revelex Corp—*David Goodis*	6405 Congress Ave Ste, Boca Raton FL 33487	561-988-5588	R	9*	.1
436	Trident Computer Resources Inc—*Scott Swain*	151 Industrial Way E A, Eatontown NJ 07724	732-544-9333	R	9*	.1
437	Automated Control Concepts Inc—*Michael Blechman*	3535 State Rte 66 Ste, Neptune NJ 07753	732-922-6611	R	9*	.1
438	Logistics Resources Inc—*William Erzig*	2600 Internationale Pk, Woodridge IL 60517	630-972-2892	R	9*	.1
439	Wireless Ronin Technologies Inc—*Scott W Koller*	5929 Baker Rd Ste 475, Minneapolis MN 55345	952-564-3500	P	9	.1
440	Aspyra Inc—*Ade Lawal*	4360 Park Terrace Dr S, Westlake Village CA 91361	818-880-6700	R	9	.1
441	InfoQuest Technologies Inc—*Norm Dallago*	471 JPL Wick Dr, Harrisburg PA 17111	717-541-9325	R	9	.1
442	Alitech Consulting LP—*Madona Crawford*	19627 Interstate 45, Spring TX 77388	281-433-0676	R	9*	<.1
443	Dox Electronics Inc—*Ruth Michael*	105 College Ave, Rochester NY 14607	585-473-7766	R	8*	.1
444	Milvets Systems Technology Inc—*Bobby Daniels*	2000 N Alafaya Trl Ste, Orlando FL 32826	407-207-2242	R	8*	.1
445	Bitwise Inc—*Salil Sakhardando*	1515 E Wdfield Rd Ste, Schaumburg IL 60173	847-969-1500	R	8*	.1
446	Electronic Consulting Services Inc—*Roy Kapani*	2750 Prosperity Ave St, Fairfax VA 22031	703-270-1540	R	8*	.1
447	Tanner Research Inc—*John Tanner*	825 S Myrtle Ave, Monrovia CA 91016	626-471-9700	R	8*	.1
448	CompuData Inc—*Angela Nadeau*	2701 Commerce Way, Philadelphia PA 19154	215-969-1000	R	8*	.1
449	Integrated Digital Systems/Scanamerica Inc—*Dharmesh Shin-gala*	10521 Rosehaven St, Fairfax VA 22030	703-368-2887	R	8*	<.1
450	Niscayah (Kansas City Missouri)—*Edward Meltzer*	8901 Washington St, Kansas City MO 64114	816-333-6299	R	8*	<.1
451	MICROS-Fidelio Southwest Inc—*Ryan Ritter* MICROS Systems Inc	1850 Crown Rd Ste 1107, Dallas TX 75234	972-831-8250	S	8*	<.1
452	Netsphere Inc—*Bill Pournaras*	6870 Elm St Ste 302, McLean VA 22101	703-748-0800	R	8*	<.1
453	Network Engineering Inc (Indianapolis Indiana)—*Dave Spilker*	4975 E 79th St, Indianapolis IN 46250	317-595-6387	R	8*	<.1
454	Rutter Networking Technologies Inc—*David Pearce*	187 Ballardvale St A13, Wilmington MA 01887	978-642-1000	R	8*	<.1
455	Katalyst Network Group—*Mark Johnson*	PO Box 1443, Hickory NC 28603	828-267-6450	R	8*	<.1
456	Compusoft Integrated Solutions—*Pratap Koganti*	31500 W 13 Mile Rd Ste, Farmington Hills MI 48334	248-538-9494	R	8*	.1
457	Saturn Business Systems Inc—*Ana Krieger*	228 E 45th St Rm 502, New York NY 10017	212-557-8134	R	8*	.1
458	Schwan's Technology Group Inc—*David Paskach*	5140 Moundview Dr, Red Wing MN 55066	651-388-1821	R	8*	.1
459	Durst Image Technology Us LLC—*Arthur Shufelt*	50 Methodist Hill Dr S, Rochester NY 14623	585-486-0340	R	8*	.1
460	SofTech Inc—*Joe Mullaney*	59 Lowes Way Ste 401, Lowell MA 01851	978-513-2700	P	8	.1
461	Marketing Direct Inc—*Dennis Barnes*	530 Maryville Centre D, Saint Louis MO 63141	314-590-8300	R	8*	.1
462	Aspen Systems Inc—*Steven Spring*	3900 Youngfield St, Wheat Ridge CO 80033	303-431-4606	R	8*	<.1
463	Eanytime Corp—*Laurence Cohn*	PO Box 5100, Huntington Beach CA 92615	614-842-7000	R	8*	<.1
464	Computer Services Group Inc—*Boris Khutoretsky*	22 W 38th St Fl 8, New York NY 10018	212-819-0122	R	7*	.1
465	L and E Associates Inc—*Lindberg Bing*	PO Box 532, Temple Hills MD 20757	301-567-7810	R	7*	.1
466	Saitech Inc—*Mangala Annambhotla*	10411 Motor City Dr St, Bethesda MD 20817	571-321-0664	R	7*	.1
467	Saxon Global Inc—*Jerry Heftler*	320 Greenway Dr Ste 66, Irving TX 75038	972-550-9346	R	7	.1
468	Ogre Partners Ltd—*John Capozzi*	PO Box 744275, Dallas TX 75374	214-575-4088	R	7*	.1
469	Phillip's Machine And Welding Company Inc—*Don Mckenna*	16125 Gale Ave, City Of Industry CA 91745	909-627-0055	R	7*	.1
470	ClearAccess—*Fred Lawrence*	501 SE Columbia Shores, Vancouver WA 98661	360-859-1780	R	7	<.1
471	Electronic Data Care—*Nabil Salem*	23670 Hawthrne Blvd St, Torrance CA 90505	310-373-2475	R	7*	.1
472	Vgs Systems Engineering USA Inc—*Paolo Moro*	4501 Vineland Rd Ste 1, Orlando FL 32811	407-370-2900	R	7*	.1
473	Icygen LLC	940 Dwight Way Ste 13b, Berkeley CA 94710	510-540-7122	R	7*	.1
474	MindLeaf Technologies—*Paresh K Shah*	19B Crosby Dr Ste 330, Bedford MA 01730	781-275-1845	R	7*	.1
475	Weather Decision Technologies Inc—*Michael Eilts*	201 David L Boren Blvd, Norman OK 73072	405-579-7675	R	7*	.1
476	PB Systems Inc—*Rao Prathipati*	230 Commerce Ste 180, Irvine CA 92602	714-573-1230	R	7*	.1
477	GoEngineer—*Ken Coburn*	1787 E Fort Union Ste, Salt Lake City UT 84121	801-359-6100	R	7*	.1
478	Hoppmann Communications Corp—*Charles Wheeler*	4170 Lafayette Ctr Dr, Chantilly VA 20151	703-502-4080	R	7*	<.1
479	Real Time Enterprises Inc—*Bob Ruppenthal*	160 Office Park Way, Pittsford NY 14534	585-383-1290	R	7	<.1
480	Schoollink Inc—*Eric Wells*	PO Box 36067, Fayetteville NC 28303		R	7*	<.1
481	Syscom Services Inc	1010 Wayne Ave Ste 720, Silver Spring MD 20910	301-768-1800	R	7*	<.1
482	Cascade Controls Inc—*John Bonchen*	1132 N 7th St, San Jose CA 95112	408-808-8000	R	7*	<.1
483	CHIPS Computer Consulting LLC—*Evan J Leonard*	5 Aerial Way Ste 400, Syosset NY 11791	516-377-6585	R	7*	<.1
484	Competitive Innovations LLC—*Michael Kennedy*	2724 Dorr Ave Ste 100G, Fairfax VA 22031	703-698-5000	R	7*	<.1
485	ExecUtron Computers Inc—*Daniel Mosier*	3094 Coffey Ln, Santa Hosa CA 95403		R	7*	<.1
486	GSE Erudite Software Inc—*Jim Eberle* GSE Systems Inc	1332 Londontown Blvd S, Sykesville MD 21784	410-970-7800	S	7*	<.1

Note: An asterisk (*) indicates an estimated financial figure. The company type code used is as follows: R = Private, P = Public, S = Private Subsidiary, B = Public Subsidiary, D = Division, J = Joint Venture, I = Investment Fund.

COMPANY RANKINGS BY SALES WITHIN 4-DIGIT SIC

Rank	Company Name—*Executive Officer*	Address, City, State, Zip	Phone	Type	Fin	Empls
487	Tab Computer Systems Inc—*Thomas Benoit*	29 Bissell St Ste 31, East Hartford CT 06108	860-289-8850	R	7*	<.1
488	Democrasoft Inc—*Richard A Lang*	50 Old Courthouse Sq S, Santa Rosa CA 95404		R	7*	<.1
489	eonBusiness Corp—*Dave Carlson*	7430 E Caley Ave Ste 2, Centennial CO 80111	303-850-9300	R	7*	<.1
490	Genesta Partnership—*Kelson Elam*	1850 Interstate 30, Rockwall TX 75087	972-771-1653	R	7*	<.1
491	C-Gull Technologies Inc—*Arti Carrandi*	635 Woodbrook Way, Melbourne FL 32940	321-253-4190	R	7*	<.1
492	Softronics Inc—*Scott Pierce*	5085 List Dr, Colorado Springs CO 80919	719-593-9540	R	7*	<.1
493	Premcom Corp—*John Diguiseppe*	85 Northpointe Pkwy St, Buffalo NY 14228	716-691-0791	R	7*	<.1
494	Electronic Vision Access Solutions—*Gerald Swerdlick*	39 Canal St, Westerly RI 02891	401-596-3155	R	7*	<.1
495	Software Decisions Inc—*Shawn Ramirtha*	5821 Suthwest Fwy Ste, Houston TX 77057	713-523-9911	R	7*	.1
496	Cadence Technologies Inc—*G Brink*	1006 Windward Ridge Pk, Alpharetta GA 30005	770-667-6250	R	7*	<.1
497	T-Rex Consulting Corp—*Gregory Wilby*	11495 Sunset Hills Rd, Reston VA 20190	703-742-0566	R	7*	<.1
498	Profit Concepts International Inc—*Vukan Ruzic*	4201 Long Beach Blvd S, Long Beach CA 90807	562-216-6000	R	7*	<.1
499	Frakes Engineering Inc—*James Frakes*	7950 Castleway Dr Ste, Indianapolis IN 46250	317-577-3000	R	7*	<.1
500	Alpha Networks Inc—*Hander Housing*	3945 Freedom Cir Ste 1, Santa Clara CA 95054	408-844-8850	R	7*	<.1
501	Jca Electron Co—*James Adams*	2543 Pony Peak Rd, Timbo AR 72680	870-746-4402	R	7*	<.1
502	Cohesive Automation Inc—*Robert Hudson*	3010 Story Rd W, Irving TX 75038	972-659-0401	R	6*	.1
503	Cyberdefenses Inc—*Randell Casey*	1205 Sam Bass Rd Ste 3, Round Rock TX 78681	512-255-3700	R	6*	<.1
504	iTrendz Inc—*Paul Silverstein*	399 Thornall St 8th Fl, Edison NJ 08837	732-777-1510	R	6	.1
505	Computer Information Specialist Inc—*Michele Dyson*	1010 Wayne Ave Ste 720, Silver Spring MD 20910	301-588-2977	R	6*	<.1
506	Great South Texas Corp—*Carolyn Labatt*	814 Arion Pkwy Ste 101, San Antonio TX 78216	210-369-0300	R	6*	<.1
507	Sytronics Inc—*Barrett Myers*	4433 Dayton Xenia Rd S, Beavercreek OH 45432	937-431-6100	R	6*	<.1
508	Advanced Technical Solutions LLC—*Denise Cutler*	PO Box 149, Scott Depot WV 25560	304-757-6542	R	6*	<.1
509	Comtrex Systems Corp—*Jeffrey C Rice*	1247 N Church St Ste 7, Moorestown NJ 08057	856-778-0090	R	6*	.1
510	Advanced Production Systems Inc—*Don Korfhage*	8016 Vine Crest Ave, Louisville KY 40222	502-423-0882	R	6*	.1
511	Networkd Corp—*Ashley Leonard*	3300 Irvine Ave Ste 26, Newport Beach CA 92660	949-222-2287	R	6*	<.1
512	Process Control and Instrumentation LLC—*Ivy Clay*	845 W Milwaukee St, Detroit MI 48202	313-874-5877	R	6*	<.1
513	Universal Mind Inc—*Brett Cortese*	94 N Elm St Ste 306, Westfield MA 01085	413-562-3630	R	6*	<.1
514	Condortech Services Inc—*Jorge Lozano*	3700 Wheeler Ave, Alexandria VA 22304	703-916-9200	R	6*	<.1
515	SDGblue LLC—*Glen Combs*	501 Darby Creek Rd Ste, Lexington KY 40509	859-263-7344	R	6*	<.1
516	Soaring Eagle Inc—*Craig Newbold*	114 W 5th St, East Liverpool OH 43920	330-385-5579	R	6*	<.1
517	Stone Technologies Inc—*Don Ulrich*	550 Spirit of St Louis, Chesterfield MO 63005	636-530-7240	R	6*	<.1
518	Graphics Systems Corp—*David Kasinskas*	W133n5138 Campbell Dr, Menomonee Falls WI 53051	262-790-1080	R	6*	<.1
519	Barquin And Associates Inc—*Ramon Barquin*	1707 L St Nw Ste 1030, Washington DC 20036	202-296-7147	R	6*	<.1
520	Affiliated Resource Group—*Mike Moran*	PO Box 491, Dublin OH 43017	614-889-6555	R	6	<.1
521	Reference Systems Inc—*Rand Mark Manasse*	5 Walden Hill, Chappaqua NY 10514	914-666-0830	R	6*	<.1
522	Terra Communications Inc—*Joe Echols*	675 Prgrega Ctr Ave St, Lawrenceville GA 30043	678-397-1470	R	6*	<.1
523	Legislative Demographic Services Inc—*Scott A Castleman* Identix Public Sector Inc	205 Pennsylvania Ave S, Fairfax VA 22033	703-259-5225	S	6*	<.1
524	Applied Automated Engineering Corp—*Charles G Everett*	65 S Main St Bldg C, Pennington NJ 08534	609-737-6800	R	6*	<.1
525	eAsic Corp—*Ronnie Vasishta*	2585 Augustine Dr Ste, Santa Clara CA 95054	408-855-9200	R	6*	<.1
526	Inlite Research Inc—*Gene Manheim*	615 Templeton Ct, Sunnyvale CA 94087	408-737-7092	R	6*	<.1
527	P and N Technologies—*Micheal Richmond*	6971 Exchequer Dr, Baton Rouge LA 70809	225-755-1258	R	6*	<.1
528	QED Information Systems—*Tony Cummings*	7201 Haven Ave Ste E-3, Rancho Cucamonga CA 91701	909-724-4876	R	6*	<.1
529	ComputerEase—*John Meibers*	6460 Harrison Ave, Cincinnati OH 45211	513-481-5800	R	6*	<.1
530	D and D Consulting Ltd—*Christopher Labatt-Simon*	3 Columbia Cir Washing, Albany NY 12203	518-478-8620	R	6*	<.1
531	Yancy and Associates Inc—*Linda Yancy*	3119 Martin L King Ave, Washington DC 20032	301-868-5410	R	6*	<.1
532	Information Sales Associates Inc—*John O'toole*	45 Walpole St Ste 2, Norwood MA 02062	781-551-5930	R	6*	<.1
533	Accessvia Inc—*Dean Sleeper*	3131 Western Ave Ste 5, Seattle WA 98121	206-285-4994	R	6*	<.1
534	Indusys Technology Inc—*Tony Lau*	210 Baypointe Pkwy, San Jose CA 95134	408-321-2888	R	6*	<.1
535	Amend John—*John Amend*	8150 N Control Expy St, Dallas TX 75206	214-696-3339	R	6*	.1
536	United Computer Sales And Services Inc—*Anthony Calabrese*	100 Dobbs Ln Ste 208, Cherry Hill NJ 08034	856-795-7330	R	6*	<.1
537	Gbl Systems Corp—*James Buscemi*	760 Paseo Camarillo St, Camarillo CA 93010	805-987-4345	Gbl	6*	<.1
538	Lan Utilities Electric Inc—*Sheri Hotton*	700 Broadhollow Rd Ste, Farmingdale NY 11735	631-651-8895	R	6*	<.1
539	Compusource Systems Inc—*Gary Gonzales*	110 John Muir Dr, Amherst NY 14228	716-636-3700	R	6*	<.1
540	Starnet Data Design Inc—*Steve Marks*	2659 Townsgate Rd Ste, Westlake Village CA 91361	805-371-0585	R	6*	<.1
541	Network 2000 LLC—*Anthony Pfaltzgraff*	2100 N Nimitz Hwy, Honolulu HI 96819	808-848-0000	R	6*	<.1
542	Blogher Inc—*Elizabeth Stone*	1301 Shoreway Rd Ste 3, Belmont CA 94002	650-551-1364	R	5*	<.1
543	Nms Imaging Inc—*Stephen Dring*	12041 Bournefield Way, Silver Spring MD 20904	301-622-4300	R	5*	<.1
544	Infiniti Systems Group Inc—*John L Bianco Sr*	6980 S Edgerton Rd, Brecksville OH 44141	440-546-9440	R	5	<.1
545	Drt Strategies Inc—*Susan Kidd*	4245 Fairfax Dr Ste 80, Arlington VA 22203	571-482-2500	R	5*	.1
546	Velquest Corp—*Kenneth Rapp*	35 S St Ste A, Hopkinton MA 01748	508-497-9911	R	5*	<.1
547	Yorel Integrated Solutions Inc—*Leroy Hill*	8520 Cliff Cameron Dr, Charlotte NC 28269	704-594-9870	R	5*	<.1
548	Computeran Systems Corp—*Myrna Yagoda*	100 1st St, Hackensack NJ 07601	201-489-7500	R	5*	.1
549	Staffing Alternatives Inc—*Patrick Stoup*	656 Quince Orchard Rd, Gaithersburg MD 20878	301-721-8900	R	5*	<.1
550	Base 2 Technologies Inc—*Marlin Newell*	707 Amelia Island Ct, Silver Spring MD 20905	301-421-1654	R	5*	<.1
551	Asc-Cubed LLC	13990 Parkeast Cir, Chantilly VA 20151	703-968-6300	R	5*	.2
552	CAS Severn—*Carson Soule*	6201 Chevy Chase Dr, Laurel MD 20707	301-776-3400	R	5*	.1
553	Accessnorthgeorgia—*Bill Wilson*	1102 Thompson Bridge R, Gainesville GA 30501	770-536-8020	R	5*	.1
554	Xc Networks—*Tomas Gomez*	4316 Bryan St Ste 11, Dallas TX 75204	214-515-1400	R	5*	.1
555	Infracell Inc—*Ian Ingram*	PO Box 3490, Tualatin OR 97062	503-885-7700	R	5*	<.1
556	Bordercomm Inc—*Thomas Spackman*	4316 Bryan St, Dallas TX 75204		R	5*	<.1
557	Intellicom Inc—*Dan Shundoff*	2701 Renaissance Blvd, King of Prussia PA 19406	610-731-0400	R	5*	<.1
558	Lodging and Gaming Systems Inc—*Steve Urie*	1865 Plumas St Ste 3, Reno NV 89509	775-688-4440	R	5*	<.1
559	Nextengine Inc—*Mark Knighton*	401 Wilshire Blvd Fl 9, Santa Monica CA 90401	310-883-1827	R	5*	<.1
560	Avatar Systems Ltd—*Edita Maier*	925 W Chicago Ave 300, Chicago IL 60642	312-432-4300	R	5*	<.1
561	Network Synergy Corp—*Dana Gargano*	126 Monroe Tpke Unit B, Trumbull CT 06611	203-261-2201	R	5*	<.1
562	Computer Assets Inc—*Abe Salzar*	PO Box 1364, Espanola NM 87532	505-747-1172	R	5*	<.1
563	Wavenet Technologies Inc—*Michael Catanese*	PO Box 4416, Fort Walton Beach FL 32549	850-439-0090	R	5*	<.1
564	Fds USA Inc—*Andreas Roubian*	18 W Ridgewood Ave, Paramus NJ 07652	201-670-1300	R	5*	<.1
565	Integrated Design Engineering Systems Corp—*Mike Kmetz*	PO Box 2131, Laramie WY 82073	307-742-9227	R	5*	<.1
566	Ili Infodisk Inc—*Peregrine Rowse*	610 Winters Ave Ste 3, Paramus NJ 07652	201-986-1131	R	5*	<.1
567	Autodraft Inc—*Julia Grant*	2815 Baird Rd, Fairport NY 14450	585-389-1900	R	5*	<.1
568	Coil Counts Ford and Cheney Inc—*George Kase*	150 E Huron Ave Ste 12, Chicago IL 60611	312-649-6300	R	5*	<.1
569	2M Technologies Inc—*James Mandler*	700 Veterans Memorial, Hauppauge NY 11788	631-231-3255	R	5*	<.1
570	Emergin Inc—*Frans van Houten*	6400 Congress Ave Ste, Boca Raton FL 33487	561-361-6990	S	5*	<.1
571	Micro Depot Inc—*Hamid Hashemi*	3190 Reps Miller Rd, Norcross GA 30071	770-263-0339	R	5*	<.1
572	Netis Technology Inc—*Susan Liang*	511 Montague Exwy, Milpitas CA 95035	408-263-0368	R	5*	<.1
573	MSHI Inc—*Jim Eberle* GSE Systems Inc	1332 Londontown Blvd S, Sykesville MD 21784	410-970-7800	S	5*	<.1
574	Facet Corp—*Jim Bryant*	5999 Summerside Drive, Dallas TX 75252	972-985-9901	R	5*	<.1

Rank	Company Name—*Executive Officer*	Address, City, State, Zip	Phone	Type	Fin	Empls
575	GP International Engineering and Simulation Inc—*Jim Eberle* GSE Systems Inc	1332 Londontown Blvd S, Sykesville MD 21784	410-970-7800	S	5*	<.1
576	Aalstec Data Corp—*Mark Lamon*	PO Box 43555, Detroit MI 48243	313-962-7790	R	5*	<.1
577	DMS Systems Corp—*Grady Davis*	PO Box 8049, Rocky Mount NC 27804	252-985-2500	R	5*	<.1
578	MH Software Inc—*George Sexton*	5023 W 120th Ave Ste 3, Broomfield CO 80020	303-438-9585	R	5*	<.1
579	SolidSpace LLC—*James H Capps III*	111 N Chestnut St Ste, Winston Salem NC 27101	336-201-5656	R	5*	<.1
580	Skillsnet Commercial Ltd—*Michael Brown*	310 W Jefferson St, Waxahachie TX 75165	972-923-2950	R	5*	<.1
581	Chesapeake TechLabs Inc—*Steve Leibholz*	2333 Huntingdon Pike, Huntingdon Valley PA 19006	215-938-7800	R	5*	<.1
582	CPI Solutions Inc—*Arnie Friedman*	5999 Ridgeview St Ste, Camarillo CA 93012	805-987-2222	R	5*	<.1
583	Cao Computer Technology—*Eve Hanwisai*	16057 Tampa Palms Blvd, Tampa FL 33647	813-610-3216	R	5*	<.1
584	Computer Systems Engineering Inc—*Edgar You*	5611 Byington Dr, Newark CA 94560	510-742-5573	R	5*	<.1
585	Conexus Communication Systems Inc—*Robert Irvin*	5600 Nw Central Dr Ste, Houston TX 77092	713-690-5656	R	5*	<.1
586	Patty Girardi—*Bill Shickling*	1511 Walnut St, Williamsport PA 17701	570-322-5001	R	5*	.1
587	Omnitrol Networks Inc—*Raj Saksena*	2025 Landings Dr, Mountain View CA 94043	650-625-1400	R	5*	.1
588	Phonefactor Inc—*Timothy Sutton*	7301 W 129th St Ste 20, Overland Park KS 66213	913-499-4100	R	5*	.1
589	Joseph Systems Inc—*Jeanette Joseph*	2521 Warren Dr Ste A, Rocklin CA 95677	916-303-7200	R	5*	<.1
590	Access It Group Inc—*David Hark*	20106 Valley Forge Cir, King Of Prussia PA 19406	610-783-5200	R	5*	<.1
591	Axcess International Inc—*Allan Griebenow*	16650 Westgrove Dr Ste, Addison TX 75001	972-407-6080	P	5	<.1
592	Alpha-Gamma Technologies Inc—*Anwar Shareef*	3301 Benson Dr Ste 535, Raleigh NC 27609	919-954-0033	R	5*	<.1
593	Holman's Of Nevada Inc—*Deric Hill*	4445 S Valley View Blv, Las Vegas NV 89103	702-222-1818	R	5*	<.1
594	Rkon Inc—*Jeff Mullarkey*	820 W Jackson Blvd Ste, Chicago IL 60607	312-654-0300	R	5*	<.1
595	Leeds Seitel and Associates Inc—*Matthew Kayes*	1200 Post Aly 2, Seattle WA 98101	206-283-4355	R	5*	<.1
596	Braintech Inc—*Frederick Weidinger*	1750 Tysons Blvd Ste 3, McLean VA 22102	703-637-9780	P	5	<.1
597	Telenotes Inc—*James Metcalf*	9500 S 500 W Ste 104, Sandy UT 84070	801-523-6300	R	5*	<.1
598	Venture Netcomm Inc—*Nathan Tyson*	1377 Capital Cir, Lawrenceville GA 30043	678-377-0007	R	5*	<.1
599	Sourcecode Inc—*Harold Fernandes*	120 White Plains Rd St, Tarrytown NY 10591	914-366-0216	R	5*	.1
600	Veridyne Inc—*Samuel Patterson*	370 Reed Rd Ste 105, Broomall PA 19008	610-328-7971	R	5*	.1
601	STI Group Inc—*David Walters*	30950 Rancho Viejo Rd, San Juan Capistrano CA 92675	949-373-7282	P	5	<.1
602	Coskey Television and Radio Sales and Service Inc—*Victor Coskey*	656 Georges Rd, North Brunswick NJ 08902	732-247-7098	R	5*	<.1
603	Distributed Information Technologies Inc—*Duane Graham*	3500 Victoria Ln, Davidsonville MD 21035	301-205-0106	R	5*	<.1
604	Datascan Systems Inc—*Darris Mccord*	3140 Martin Rd, Commerce Township MI 48390	248-624-8000	R	5*	<.1
605	Csic Corp—*George Biskup*	2400 Ogden Ave, Lisle IL 60532	630-852-1700	R	4*	<.1
606	Embee Computer Design Group Inc—*Luke Slymen*	16592 Millikan Ave, Irvine CA 92606	949-266-1700	R	4*	<.1
607	Ivs Computer Technology Inc—*Reginald Lie-A-Tjam*	1415 Mcdonald Way, Bakersfield CA 93309	661-831-3900	R	4*	<.1
608	Zeal Group—*Chris Dobkins*	720 Cool Springs Blvd, Franklin TN 37067	615-261-4100	R	4*	.1
609	Global Techpro LLC	8230 Boone Blvd Ste 45, Vienna VA 22182	703-288-4770	R	4*	.1
610	Metrosoft Inc—*Andrew Zejb*	299 Market St Ste 480, Saddle Brook NJ 07663	201-291-6555	R	4*	<.1
611	R And S Computers Inc—*Bart Nachimow*	1412 Broadway Rm 410, New York NY 10018	212-869-9300	R	4*	<.1
612	Baum Control Systems Inc—*Larry Baum*	15 Thornwood Dr Ste 4, Ithaca NY 14850	607-257-3524	R	4*	<.1
613	Tingley Network Services Corp—*Wayne Tingley*	31722 State Rd 52, San Antonio FL 33576	352-588-2250	R	4	<.1
614	Goodman Consulting and Technology LLC—*Tom Connelly*	272 Bendix Rd Ste 500, Virginia Beach VA 23452	757-457-6200	R	4*	<.1
615	Ease Technologies Inc—*Charles Bubeck*	10320 Little Patuxent, Columbia MD 21044	410-992-7268	R	4*	.1
616	Rcnet LP—*Kenny Frazier*	915 9th St Ste 100, Wichita Falls TX 76301	940-322-9990	R	4*	<.1
617	Awesome Technologies Inc—*Henry H Willcox IV*	740 Rowlee Rd, Fulton NY 13069	607-562-3620	R	4*	.1
618	InfoTech New York City—*Jay F McKeage*	7 Kingsbridge Rd, Fairfield NJ 07004	973-227-8772	D	4*	<.1
619	Emergisoft Corp—*Jordan Davis*	524 E Lamar Blvd Ste 1, Arlington TX 76011	817-855-1000	S	4*	<.1
620	Application Objects Inc	425 Walnut St Ste 2200, Cincinnati OH 45202	513-345-6670	R	4*	<.1
621	S3 Integration LLC—*Mike Behles*	1550 Caton Ctr Dr F, Baltimore MD 21227	410-536-1999	R	4*	<.1
622	Miles Consulting Corp—*Miles Feinberg*	193 Blue Ravine Rd Ste, Folsom CA 95630		R	4*	<.1
623	Network Outsource Inc—*Adam Mahoney*	135 Denton Ave, New Hyde Park NY 11040	516-488-5888	R	4*	<.1
624	Ellison Systems Inc—*Tony Ellison*	90 Broad St Ste 2000, New York NY 10004	212-619-3353	R	4*	<.1
625	Government Service Automation Inc—*Michael Boswell*	201 4th Ave N Ste 1220, Nashville TN 37219	615-742-3838	R	4*	<.1
626	Telemac Corp—*Kenin M Spivak*	13101 Washington Blvd, Los Angeles CA 90066	310-228-1506	R	4*	<.1
627	Thinsolutions LLC—*Michael Fischer*	1388 Riverside Dr, Cleveland OH 44107	216-685-3000	R	4*	<.1
628	Data Consultants Corp—*Abhijit Guha*	PO Box 6345, Aurora IL 60598	630-692-2700	R	4*	<.1
629	Beck Computer Systems—*Gary D Beck*	3530 Altlantic Ave Ste, Long Beach CA 90807	562-428-2894	R	4*	<.1
630	Comet Micro Systems Inc	390 Swift Ave Ste 24, South San Francisco CA 94080	650-615-9123	R	4*	<.1
631	First Information Technology Services Inc—*Kenneth Paige*	2461 S Clark St Ste 60, Arlington VA 22202	703-872-0500	R	4*	<.1
632	Dental Technology Designs Inc—*Paul Ponkratz*	1300 W Main Ave, De Pere WI 54115	920-330-0600	R	4*	<.1
633	Vibrant Technologies Inc—*Chris Radlicz*	15 Charter Oak Rd, Southbury CT 06488	203-267-7710	R	4*	<.1
634	GSE Services Company LLC—*Jim Eberle* GSE Systems Inc	1332 Londontown Blvd S, Sykesville MD 21784	410-970-7800	S	4*	<.1
635	SecurePay Inc—*MacAllister Smith*	1515 Hancock St Ste 30, Quincy MA 02169		S	4*	<.1
636	RegNow Digital River Inc—*Joel A Ronning*	9625 W 76th St, Eden Prairie MN 55344	952-646-5331	R	4*	<.1
637	BCS*A	385 Bel Marin Keys Blv, Novato CA 94949	415-382-4227	R	4*	<.1
638	CAI/SIS Co—*Tony Constable*	6 W 3rd St, Frederick MD 21701	301-840-5959	R	4*	<.1
639	ClinLab Inc—*Daniel Stewart*	2411 E Graves Ave Ste, Orange City FL 32763	386-774-0030	R	4*	<.1
640	Computer Insights Inc—*Dennis R Cowhey*	108 S Third St, Bloomingdale IL 60108		R	4*	<.1
641	DigiSpace Solutions LLC—*Amish Shah*	2323 Broadway Ste 202, San Diego CA 92102	619-684-6737	R	4*	<.1
642	Lexicom Computer Systems Inc—*Herman Roehm*	175 Kershaw Industrial, Montgomery AL 36117	334-215-4500	R	4*	<.1
643	MegaForce LLC—*Robert Thayer*	12880 Metcalf Ave, Overland Park KS 66213	913-402-0800	R	4*	<.1
644	Peerlis Inc—*Frank Wasinski*	2530 Superior AveE Ste, Cleveland OH 44114	216-378-0366	R	4*	<.1
645	Realtime Software Corp—*Tom Loftus*	24 Deane Rd, Bernardston MA 01337	847-803-1100	R	4*	<.1
646	REN Testing Corp—*Gary Roberts*	5900 S Perkins Rd, Stillwater OK 74077	405-533-2700	S	4*	<.1
647	WechTECH Inc—*Keith B Wechsler*	6000 N University Dr, Tamarac FL 33321	954-721-3536	R	4*	<.1
648	Image Information Inc—*William Johnson*	1100 Old Ellis Rd Ste, Roswell GA 30076	770-664-5329	R	4*	<.1
649	Runtime Design Automation Inc—*Andrea Casotto*	2700 Augustine Dr Ste, Santa Clara CA 95054	408-492-0940	R	4*	<.1
650	Controllink Inc—*Gary Dembski*	1650 Cambridge Dr, Elgin IL 60123	847-622-1100	R	4*	<.1
651	RTC Group LLC—*Neil Banerjee*	975 Cobb Pl Blvd Nw St, Kennesaw GA 30144	770-425-0401	R	4*	<.1
652	Network Access Products Inc—*Thomas Koll*	6230 Mckinley St Nw C2, Ramsey MN 55303	763-323-3041	R	4*	<.1
653	American Networks International LLC—*Josh Bartlett*	PO Box 638, New Britain CT 06050	860-229-0800	R	4*	<.1
654	Granger Telecom Corp—*Lonnie Tomerlin*	22 Corgey Rd, Pleasanton TX 78064	830-569-8088	R	4*	<.1
655	Janalent Corp—*Anne Chahal*	7582 Las Vegas Blvd S, Las Vegas NV 89123		R	4*	<.1
656	Americom Inc—*Dean Jakubowicz*	308 Lafayette Fwy, Saint Paul MN 55107	651-726-2200	R	4*	<.1
657	Lucas Systems Inc—*Lee Lucas*	123 Grace Dr, Easley SC 29640	864-527-0033	R	4*	<.1
658	Spongecell—*Ben Kartzman*	261 Madison Ave 14 Fl, New York NY 10016		R	4	<.1
659	Unapen Inc—*Joseph Walker*	2 Barnes Industrial Rd, Wallingford CT 06492	203-269-2111	R	4*	<.1
660	K-Form Inc—*Nathan Keen*	PO Box 497, Sterling VA 20167	703-450-4401	R	4*	<.1
661	Arservices Ltd—*Albert Spaulding*	7764 Armistead Rd Ste, Lorton VA 22079	703-824-6382	R	4*	<.1

Note: An asterisk (*) indicates an estimated financial figure. The company type code used is as follows: R = Private, P = Public, S = Private Subsidiary, B = Public Subsidiary, D = Division, J = Joint Venture, I = Investment Fund.

COMPANY RANKINGS BY SALES WITHIN 4-DIGIT SIC

Rank	Company Name—*Executive Officer*	Address, City, State, Zip	Phone	Type	Fin	Empls
662	Vinimaya Inc—*John Hutchinson*	10290 Alliance Rd, Blue Ash OH 45242	513-792-5100	R	4*	<.1
663	XI Techgroup Inc—*John Scott*	1901 S Harbor City Blv, Melbourne FL 32901	321-726-6483	R	4*	<.1
664	Central Desktop Inc—*Isaac Garcia*	129 N Hill Ave Ste 202, Pasadena CA 91106	626-689-4420	R	4	<.1
665	Hna Computers Systems Inc—*Jeffrey Hollander*	PO Box 15489, Brooksville FL 34604	352-796-3285	R	4*	<.1
666	Wheat Systems Integration LLC—*Tod Balsbaugh*	11551 Nuckols Rd Ste G, Glen Allen VA 23059	804-565-6700	R	4*	<.1
667	Nei Software Inc—*David Weinberg*	5555 Garden Grove Blvd, Westminster CA 92683	714-893-8503	R	4*	<.1
668	Omega Technologies Inc—*Patricia Williams*	PO Box 2368, Merrifield VA 22116	703-891-6630	R	4*	<.1
669	Geodesign Inc—*Theodore Rosenvinge*	984 Southford Rd Ste 9, Middlebury CT 06762	203-758-8836	R	4*	<.1
670	Amcom Data Processing Inc—*Steven Clary*	2 Annabel Ln Ste 130, San Ramon CA 94583	925-328-0322	R	4*	<.1
671	Associated Electronic Systems Inc—*Kenneth Charles*	35 Thomas St, East Hartford CT 06108	860-289-6876	R	4*	<.1
672	RDA Inc—*Richard Dator*	PO Box 49, Doylestown PA 18901	215-340-9514	R	4*	<.1
673	Protronix Inc—*Greg Price*	PO Box 481988, Charlotte NC 28269	704-921-9200	R	4*	<.1
674	Aumtech Inc—*Madhav Bhide*	710 Old Bridge Tpke, East Brunswick NJ 08816	732-254-6539	R	3*	<.1
675	Bazon-Cox And Associates Inc—*Anderson Cox*	1244 Executive Blvd B1, Chesapeake VA 23320	757-410-2128	R	3*	<.1
676	Eagle Design and Technology Inc—*Bruce Okkema*	55 E Roosevelt Ave, Zeeland MI 49464	616-748-1022	R	3*	<.1
677	Net Friends Inc—*David Scarborough*	PO Box 52723, Durham NC 27717	919-680-3763	R	3*	<.1
678	Lansolutions LLC—*Kenneth Bowes*	6359 Nancy Ridge Dr, San Diego CA 92121	858-587-8000	R	3*	<.1
679	Mon Valley Technologies LLC—*Robert Bishop*	3564 River Rd, Morgantown WV 26501	304-278-7773	R	3*	<.1
680	Argos Computer Systems Inc—*Aric Rosenbach*	110 W 32nd St Fl 7, New York NY 10001	212-594-5400	R	3*	<.1
681	Cargowise Inc—*Richard White*	1515 E Wdfield Rd Ste, Schaumburg IL 60173	847-364-5600	R	3*	<.1
682	Design Data Systems Inc—*Dennis Ruck*	7606 Lindbergh Dr, Gaithersburg MD 20879	301-921-6696	R	3*	<.1
683	Ingeniux Corp—*James Edmunds*	1601 2nd Ave Ste 500, Seattle WA 98101	206-788-4300	R	3*	<.1
684	Micro Technology Consultants Inc—*Randy Smith*	132 Osigian Blvd Ste 2, Warner Robins GA 31088	478-953-1921	R	3*	<.1
685	Netserve365 LLC—*Cherie Bergles*	1000 Cliffmine Rd, Pittsburgh PA 15275	412-722-0555	R	3*	<.1
686	Netgain Information Systems Co—*Michael Minnich*	PO Box 400, De Graff OH 43318	937-593-7177	R	3*	<.1
687	Qt Technologies LLC	1605 L B Johnson Fwy S, Dallas TX 75234	972-406-5989	R	3*	<.1
688	New Year Tech Inc—*Soy Chu*	12330 Pinecrest Rd Ste, Reston VA 20191	703-564-0290	R	3*	<.1
689	I360technologies Inc—*Michael Meyer*	13873 Park Ctr Rd 400s, Herndon VA 20171	703-476-4100	R	3*	<.1
690	Workspot Inc—*Greg Bryant*	555 Bryant St 345, Palo Alto CA 94301	650-814-8108	R	3*	<.1
691	Integrated Precision Systems Inc—*James Butkovic*	9321 Ravenna Rd Ste C, Twinsburg OH 44087	330-963-0064	R	3*	<.1
692	CMC Americas Inc—*Ramanathan Ramanan*	825 Maria Ln Apt 644, Sunnyvale CA 94086	408-342-3600	S	3*	<.1
693	Infuturo Technologies LLC—*Dennis Champion*	9155 Crestwyn Hills Dr, Memphis TN 38125	901-260-2600	R	3*	<.1
694	Computer Care Company Inc—*Joseph Mattausch*	247 S Main St, Adrian MI 49221	517-265-7872	R	3*	<.1
695	Sparkart Group Inc—*Naveen Jain*	1714 Franklin St Fl 2, Oakland CA 94612	510-420-0201	R	3*	<.1
696	Column Engineering LLC—*Kitty Daly*	1400 Opus Pl Ste 110, Downers Grove IL 60515	630-515-6610	R	3*	<.1
697	Amsys Inc—*Edward Heere*	900 Ethan Allen Hwy St, Ridgefield CT 06877	203-431-1500	R	3*	<.1
698	Comstructure LLC—*Chuck Divine*	5950 Canoga Ave Ste 50, Woodland Hills CA 91367	818-961-8000	R	3*	<.1
699	Kpg Global Enterprises LLC	PO Box 857, Fishers IN 46038	317-915-0671	R	3*	.1
700	Prometric Inc—*Michael Brannick*	1501 S Clinton St, Baltimore MD 21224	443-455-8000	S	3*	<.1
701	Lynx Network Services Inc—*Leonard Elfenbein*	1 Gatehall Dr Ste 5, Parsippany NJ 07054	973-244-8500	R	3*	<.1
702	Epitomione—*Liz Wiener*	4502 Chews Vineyard, Ellicott City MD 21043	443-540-2230	R	3*	<.1
703	Mercury Group LLC	270 N Ave Ste 709, New Rochelle NY 10801	914-633-8700	R	3*	<.1
704	Advanced Simulation Technology Inc—*James Norton*	500a Huntmar Park Dr, Herndon VA 20170	703-471-2104	R	3*	<.1
705	ConnectShip Inc—*Andy Locker*	8282 S Memorial Dr Ste, Tulsa OK 74133	918-461-4460	S	3*	<.1
706	Network Installation Services Inc—*Susan Walsh*	192 N Plains Industria, Wallingford CT 06492	203-294-4655	R	3*	<.1
707	Mid-Atlantic Computers Inc—*Gary Monagle*	PO Box 68, Phoenixville PA 19460	610-935-5570	R	3*	<.1
708	Anertec Holdings LLC—*Dawn Moore*	815 Rice Lake St Ste 1, Owatonna MN 55060	507-451-5430	R	3*	<.1
709	CDE Integrated Systems Inc—*Phillip Hutchins*	6 Twelve Oak Cir, Jackson MS 39209	601-960-8500	R	3*	<.1
710	Crossroads Technologies Inc—*Frank Greco*	55 Broad St Lbby, New York NY 10004	212-482-5280	R	3*	<.1
711	Detroit Engineered Products Inc—*Radha Krishnan*	560 Kirts Blvd Ste 103, Troy MI 48084	248-269-7130	R	3*	<.1
712	Intellisight LLC	483 N Semoran Blvd Ste, Winter Park FL 32792	407-647-3771	R	3*	<.1
713	Mitchell and Mccormick Inc—*John Fahey*	2165 W Park Ct Ste G, Stone Mountain GA 30087	770-465-1511	R	3*	<.1
714	Vysym Corp—*Steven Meissel*	PO Box 51660, Irvine CA 92619	949-452-0840	R	3*	<.1
715	Midstates Industrial Group Inc—*Arnold Jones*	21299 Carlo Dr, Clinton Township MI 48038	586-307-3414	R	3*	<.1
716	Diamond Visionics LLC—*Jason Gdovin*	400 Plz Dr Ste A, Vestal NY 13850	607-729-8526	R	3*	<.1
717	NetworkFloss—*Robert Marhamat*	PO Box 623, San Francisco CA 94104	415-658-6777	R	3*	<.1
718	Packet Digital LLC—*Joel Jorgenson*	201 5th St N 15th Fl, Fargo ND 58102	701-232-0661	R	3*	<.1
719	R-Computer	30 Golf Club Rd, Pleasant Hill CA 94523	925-798-4884	R	3*	<.1
720	Syscon Inc—*Robert Wilson*	94 Mcfarland Blvd, Northport AL 35476	205-758-2000	R	3*	<.1
721	NE Hospitality Management Services Inc—*Stephen Henry*	4 Augusta National Cir, Bedford NH 03110	603-629-9859	R	3*	<.1
722	Samcotime Inc—*Sandy Weiner*	24 River Rd Ste 201, Bogota NJ 07603	201-883-0400	R	3*	<.1
723	Pro-Tech Systems Inc—*Mark Headley*	123 E Waterloo Rd, Akron OH 44319	330-773-9828	R	3*	<.1
724	AZTEK Inc—*Evan Lippincott*	13765-F Alton Pky, Irvine CA 92618	949-770-8787	R	3*	<.1
725	Baker Motion Control Systems Inc	860 Waterman Ave Ste 3, East Providence RI 02914	401-435-3100	R	3*	<.1
726	Foundation Technologies Inc	PO Box 27045, Greenville SC 29616		R	3*	<.1
727	Micromedia Studios—*Robert Moore*	711 West St, Duxbury MA 02332		R	3*	<.1
728	NetObjective LLC	27 N Wacker Dr Ste 520, Chicago IL 60606	312-961-8330	R	3*	<.1
729	Pulse Inc—*Sal Constino*	909 Ridgebrook Rd Rm 1, Sparks MD 21152	508-660-0340	R	3*	<.1
730	Atlantic Computer Products Inc (Beltsville Maryland)—*Margaret Eerwanger*	6802 Industrial Dr Ste, Beltsville MD 20705	301-595-9700	R	3*	<.1
731	Logix Inc—*John R Massman*	11900 Farmington Rd, Livonia MI 48150	734-522-6900	R	3*	<.1
732	SysArc—*Tim Brennen*	11300 Rockville Pike S, Rockville MD 20852	301-231-5252	R	3*	<.1
733	LANspeed Systems Inc—*Chris Chirgwin*	100 N Hope Ave Ste 20, Santa Barbara CA 93110	805-682-9981	R	3*	<.1
734	Mideo Systems Inc—*Gary Crawford*	15206 Transistor Ln, Huntington Beach CA 92649	714-379-3760	R	3*	<.1
735	PowerScan Inc—*Robert Compton*	341 Manor Dr, Winchester VA 22602	540-877-9280	S	3*	<.1
736	Xelic Inc—*Mark Gibson*	1250 Pittsford-Victor, Pittsford NY 14534	585-415-2930	R	3*	<.1
737	Next View Software Inc	1401 N Batavia St, Orange CA 92867	714-881-5105	S	3*	<.1
738	Data Seek—*Ken Leininger*	41 E 30th St Frnt, New York NY 10016	212-683-7204	R	3*	<.1
739	Inelect Corp—*Robert Peterson*	5245 Taneytown Pke, Taneytown MD 21787	410-756-6960	R	3*	<.1
740	Turvac Inc	125 Settlmyre Rd, Oregonia OH 45054	513-932-2771	R	3*	<.1
741	See First Technology Inc—*James Martin*	22486 Rancho Ventura S, Cupertino CA 95014		R	3*	<.1
742	Arlotto Technologies Inc—*Raymond Wang*	48521 Warm Springs Blv, Fremont CA 94539	510-360-0788	R	3*	<.1
743	Astra Communications USA Inc—*Felipe Noguera*	114 E Hillcrest Blvd S, Inglewood CA 90301	310-809-6524	R	3*	<.1
744	Ase Technology Inc—*Judson Clift*	128 Holiday Ct Ste 103, Franklin TN 37067	615-595-8990	R	3*	<.1
745	Boise Office Equipment Inc—*John Wood*	574 Somerset St, North Plainfield NJ 07060	908-755-5544	R	3*	<.1
746	Integrated Technology Solutions Inc—*Debra Shapiro*	6325 Woodside Ct Ste 1, Columbia MD 21046	443-430-9014	R	3*	<.1
747	Experis Technology Group Inc—*Raymond Tuchman*	7272 Wisconsin Ave Ste, Bethesda MD 20814	240-223-0607	R	3*	<.1
748	Global American Sales Inc—*Nizar Jhaver*	17 Hampshire Dr Ste 3, Hudson NH 03051	603-886-3900	R	3*	<.1
749	AuthentiDate Holding Corp—*O'Connell Benjamin*	300 Connell Dr Ste 510, Berkeley Heights NJ 07922	908-787-1700	P	3	<.1
750	MIC Systems and Software Inc—*Richard Haasch*	2964 Airway Ave, Costa Mesa CA 92626	714-545-4444	R	3*	<.1

Rank	Company Name—*Executive Officer*	Address, City, State, Zip	Phone	Type	Fin	Empls
751	Rapid Systems Inc—*Tom Bardeen*	1080 W Ewing Pl Ste 30, Seattle WA 98119	206-784-0626	R	3*	<.1
752	Netxperts Inc—*Gary Nordine*	2680 Bishop Dr Ste 125, San Ramon CA 94583	925-806-0800	R	3*	<.1
753	RC and Jt Inc—*Andrea Thorell*	6185 Cornerstone Ct E, San Diego CA 92121	858-622-1100	R	3*	<.1
754	Benchmark Network Solutions Inc—*Scott Griffin*	1931 Evans Rd, Cary NC 27513	919-678-8595	R	3*	<.1
755	Gem Companies Inc—*Edward Espinosa*	2240 Blake St Ste 250, Denver CO 80205	720-974-0207	R	3*	<.1
756	Global Software Corp—*Jeff Pugh*	5001 N Pennsylvania Av, Oklahoma City OK 73112		D	3*	<.1
757	Penta Corp—*Rawley Penick*	325 Edwards Ave, New Orleans LA 70123	504-733-1700	R	3*	<.1
758	Local Biz U S A Inc—*Jeff Rosenberg*	201 State Rt 17 Ste 10, Rutherford NJ 07070	201-964-0400	R	3*	<.1
759	Dynamic Computer Solutions Of Topeka Inc—*Frances Miller*	2214 Sw 10th Ave, Topeka KS 66604	785-354-7000	R	3*	<.1
760	Vitalect Inc—*Pran Kurup*	82 Pioneer Way Ste 104, Mountain View CA 94041	650-210-3800	R	3*	<.1
761	Cadnetics Inc—*Terry Arrington*	1205 E Carson St, Pittsburgh PA 15203	412-642-2701	R	3*	<.1
762	Enhanced Network Solutions Group Inc—*Timothy Savage*	7224 Engle Rd, Fort Wayne IN 46804	260-432-1364	R	3*	<.1
763	Glw Specialty LLC	1954 W Race Ave, Chicago IL 60622		R	3*	<.1
764	Innovative Computer Concepts and Services Inc—*Anita Lambert*	1090 Vermont Ave Nw Pm, Washington DC 20005	202-399-9133	R	3*	<.1
765	Telecoast Communications LLC—*John Bathel*	1187 Coast Village Rd, Santa Barbara CA 93108	805-957-1660	R	3*	<.1
766	Microsys Information Systems Inc—*Sylvia Hobeika*	PO Box E, Wallingford PA 19086	610-716-7393	R	3*	<.1
767	Imagetech Inc—*Charles Lee*	1950 University Blvd N, Jacksonville FL 32211	904-745-4444	R	3*	<.1
768	Voxiva Inc—*Paul Meyer*	1990 K St Nw Ste 400, Washington DC 20006	202-419-0130	R	3*	.1
769	Multiprocess Computer Corporation Inc—*Serge Gravel*	PO Box 1020, Windham NH 03087	603-893-9090	R	3*	<.1
770	System Services Integration Corp—*Daniel Mory*	453 Lincoln St Ste 112, Carlisle PA 17013	717-541-0800	R	3*	<.1
771	Information Technology Architects Inc—*Tereva Strickland*	20 Nw 4th St Ste 301, Evansville IN 47708	812-423-1950	R	3*	<.1
772	Htmt Inc—*Ajit Chakravorti*	535 Madison Ave Fl 12, New York NY 10022	212-355-0755	R	3*	<.1
773	Liveprocess Corp—*Nathaniel Weiss*	271 Grove Ave Ste D, Verona NJ 07044	973-571-2531	R	3*	<.1
774	Kinetek Corp—*Neil Grossman*	10939 Northgreen Dr, Lake Worth FL 33449	561-304-4677	R	3*	<.1
775	Scott Sheldon LLC	1331 Kings Ridge Blvd, Wadsworth OH 44281	330-904-4947	R	3*	<.1
776	Computer Office Solutions Inc—*Faisal Mohammad*	PO Box 557909, Miami FL 33255	305-663-5518	R	3*	<.1
777	SF Research Corp—*Peter Shapiro*	8811 Hadley St, Shawnee Mission KS 66212	913-381-6189	R	3*	<.1
778	Idalica Corp—*Donald Ladwig*	1173 Warner Ave, Tustin CA 92780	714-235-2025	R	3*	<.1
779	Suite 224 Internet—*Tom Ticard*	224 State St, Conneaut OH 44030	440-593-7113	R	3*	<.1
780	Integrated Support Systems Inc—*Everett Thomas*	PO Box 1842, Clemson SC 29633	864-654-1284	R	3*	<.1
781	Digitech Publishing International Inc—*Ruth Sisson*	478 Thurston Rd, Rochester NY 14619	585-436-3100	R	3*	<.1
782	Ram Communication Inc—*Jesus Ramirez*	359 Lake Park Rd Ste 1, Lewisville TX 75057	972-221-3577	R	3*	<.1
783	Contract Data Services Inc—*Dodd Howell*	PO Box 70188, Myrtle Beach SC 29572	843-213-0285	R	3*	<.1
784	Future Solutions Inc—*Jack Schmelter*	73 Bunsen, Irvine CA 92618	949-250-1133	R	3*	<.1
785	Strategic Link Consulting Inc—*Robert Salcone*	999 W Chester Pke Ste, West Chester PA 19382	610-280-3660	R	3*	<.1
786	Data Systems Of Texas Inc—*Bob Mceachern*	720 N 64th St, Waco TX 76710	254-772-6301	R	3*	<.1
787	IT Remarketing Inc—*Michael Buckles*	6600 Long Point Rd Ste, Houston TX 77055	713-263-8800	R	3*	<.1
788	Netcomm Solutions Inc—*Mark Wilson*	5275 E Trindle Rd Ste, Mechanicsburg PA 17050	717-791-5275	R	3*	<.1
789	Turnkey Technology LLC	6030 Bethelview Rd Ste, Cumming GA 30040	678-845-0611	R	3*	<.1
790	Professional Accounting Solutions Inc—*William Euler*	1901 Res Blvd Ste 300, Rockville MD 20850	301-762-8208	R	3*	<.1
791	Semantic Research Inc—*Richard Harrison*	4922 N Harbor Dr, San Diego CA 92106	619-222-4050	R	3*	<.1
792	Link Medical Computing Inc—*William Nguyen*	200 Reservoir St Ste 1, Needham MA 02494	781-453-0300	R	3*	<.1
793	Dolik and Associates Inc—*Frank Dolik*	1250 W NW Hwy Ste 103, Mount Prospect IL 60056	847-342-8899	R	3*	<.1
794	Professional Data Systems Inc—*James Howlett*	664 SE Bayberry Ln Ste, Lees Summit MO 64063	816-554-3010	R	3*	<.1
795	Mnsg Acquisition Company LLC	112 S Main St, Bel Air MD 21014	410-838-1088	R	3*	<.1
796	BrightStar Consulting Inc—*Scott Bryden*	370 Wellesley Dr, Conway AR 72034	501-952-8110	R	2	<.1
797	Integration Technolgy Partners—*Ronald Cooke*	11 Penn Plz Bsmt 100, New York NY 10001	212-946-2820	R	2*	<.1
798	Agricultural Data Systems Inc—*Carl Gennaro*	24331 Los Arboles Dr, Laguna Niguel CA 92677	949-363-5353	R	2*	<.1
799	Crs Data Inc—*Matt Casey*	341 Troy Cir, Knoxville TN 37919	865-584-8017	R	2*	<.1
800	Raapnet Inc—*Allen Fahami*	5431 Industrial Dr, Huntington Beach CA 92649	714-903-8668	R	2*	<.1
801	Computer Services And Consulting Inc—*Caroline Crozier*	1613 S Michigan Ave, Chicago IL 60616	312-360-1100	R	2*	<.1
802	Millenium Cable and Wireless LLC—*Patty Divert*	21631 Red Rum Dr Ste 1, Ashburn VA 20147	703-726-1292	R	2*	<.1
803	Commsystems LLC—*Ronald Nitz*	10225 Barnes Canyon Rd, San Diego CA 92121	858-824-0056	R	2*	<.1
804	Funambol Inc—*Amit Chawla*	643 Bair Island Rd Ste, Redwood City CA 94063	650-587-4570	R	2*	<.1
805	Symbiont Inc—*James Ward*	1320 Fenwick Ln Ste 10, Silver Spring MD 20910	301-650-0069	R	2*	<.1
806	Computer Company Inc—*Eileen Hasson*	15 Commerce Dr, Cromwell CT 06416	860-635-0500	R	2*	<.1
807	Omni Information Systems Inc—*Fred Henck*	1130 Hurrcne Shls Rd 2, Lawrenceville GA 30043	678-377-5560	R	2*	<.1
808	Data Exchange Inc—*Ronald Zaba*	5157 Thatcher Rd, Downers Grove IL 60515	630-963-4424	R	2*	<.1
809	All-Tex Networking Solutions Inc—*Hurley Johnson*	1815 Mons Ave, Rosenberg TX 77471	281-232-9118	R	2*	<.1
810	Financial Institution Technologies Inc—*Duane Lankard*	1100 Sw Wanamaker Rd S, Topeka KS 66604	785-273-5578	R	2*	<.1
811	Vercom Software Inc—*Hussain Nasser*	5501 Lbj Fwy Ste 730, Dallas TX 75240	972-661-9336	R	2*	<.1
812	Istech Inc—*Marlin Yohn*	2121 Pennsylvania Ave, York PA 17404	717-764-5565	R	2*	<.1
813	Eastern Data Of Virginia Inc—*Kimball Hargis*	2798 Dean Dr Ste B, Virginia Beach VA 23452	757-498-1600	R	2*	<.1
814	Bar Code Integrators Inc—*Richard Teising*	11 N Skokie Hwy Ste 20, Lake Bluff IL 60044	847-615-2933	R	2*	<.1
815	Dynamic Computer Corp—*Fida Bohra*	23400 Industrial Park, Farmington Hills MI 48335	248-473-2200	R	3*	<.1
816	Sphinx International Inc—*Bahram Yusefzadeh*	2180 W State Rd 434 St, Longwood FL 32779	407-682-1894	R	2*	<.1
817	Lan Lab Communications—*Fakhri Ghrakhan*	1901 Carnegie Ave Ste, Santa Ana CA 92705	714-979-2121	R	2*	<.1
818	Intelution Inc—*Syed Hussain*	810 Trenton Rd, Fairless Hills PA 19030	215-269-0211	R	2*	<.1
819	Beyond Email Inc—*Malinda Pengelly*	416 Gallimore Dairy Rd, Greensboro NC 27409	336-851-0040	R	2*	<.1
820	Waterfield Technologies Inc—*J Waterfield*	1 W 3rd St Ste 1115, Tulsa OK 74103	918-858-6400	R	2*	<.1
821	Maximum Technology Corp—*Mickey Crutcher*	PO Box 11817, Huntsville AL 35814	256-864-7630	R	2*	<.1
822	E-Services Group Inc—*David Walsh*	5301 Buckeystown Pke S, Frederick MD 21704	301-698-1900	R	2*	<.1
823	Premier Network Solutions Inc—*Steven Immerman*	5070 Oaklawn Dr, Cincinnati OH 45227	513-631-6381	R	2*	<.1
824	Eos Systems Inc—*C Speliakos*	PO Box 778, Needham Heights MA 02494	781-453-2600	R	2*	<.1
825	Joseph Galliani—*Joseph Galliani*	449 Broadway Ste 14, Everett MA 02149	617-381-0340	R	2*	<.1
826	Galler Associates Inc—*Brian Carey*	12106 Old Colony Dr St, Upper Marlboro MD 20772	301-627-8100	R	2*	<.1
827	Cuttingedge Inc—*Brian Dorherty*	PO Box 3003, Tustin CA 92781	714-505-4901	R	2*	<.1
828	Tsr Solutions Inc—*Tim Radtke*	N106w13131 Bradley Way, Germantown WI 53022	262-512-4100	R	2*	<.1
829	Aae Systems Inc—*Javed Husain*	642 N Pastoria Ave, Sunnyvale CA 94085	408-732-1710	R	2*	<.1
830	Guro Enterprises LLC—*Shannon Vinzant*	430 Emery Dr Ste A, Birmingham AL 35244	205-733-9111	R	2*	<.1
831	Dataflow Systems LLC—*Peter Dewar*	PO Box 1193, Manassas VA 20108	703-393-2355	R	2*	<.1
832	Infosoft Technologies Inc—*Robert Nichols*	927 Horan Dr, Fenton MO 63026	636-600-4070	R	2*	<.1
833	Integrated Micro Systems Inc—*Jeffery Durante*	74 Lee Ave, Haledon NJ 07508	973-904-9700	R	2*	<.1
834	Artel Software Inc—*Boris Yamnitsky*	25 Thompson Pl 4th Fl, Boston MA 02210	508-573-5100	R	2*	<.1
835	Integrated Business Systems Inc (Cedar Grove New Jersey)—*David Yavorsky*	999 Riverview Dr, Totowa NJ 07512	973-575-4950	R	2*	<.1
836	Manufacturing Data Systems Inc—*Michael Tarr*	1026 Baker Rd, Dexter MI 48130		D	2*	<.1
837	Applied Software Technologies—*Edward D Garibian*	59 Interstate Dr, West Springfield MA 01089	413-739-7390	R	2*	<.1
838	Owera Inc—*Finn Backer*	245 1st St, Cambridge MA 02142	617-444-8647	R	2*	<.1

Note: An asterisk (*) indicates an estimated financial figure. The company type code used is as follows: R = Private, P = Public, S = Private Subsidiary, B = Public Subsidiary, D = Division, J = Joint Venture, I = Investment Fund.

COMPANY RANKINGS BY SALES WITHIN 4-DIGIT SIC

Rank	Company Name—*Executive Officer*	Address, City, State, Zip	Phone	Type	Fin	Empls
839	Sky Blue Factory Inc—*Gregory Cangialosi*	40 E Cromd St Ste 2, Baltimore MD 21230	410-230-0061	R	2*	<.1
840	Trenton Systems Inc—*Michael Bowling*	2350 Centennial Dr Ste, Gainesville GA 30504	770-287-3123	R	2*	<.1
841	VideoPropulsion Inc—*Carl A Pick*	255 Info Hwy, Slinger WI 53086	262-644-1000	R	2*	<.1
842	Computerworks Of Chicago Inc—*Jean Fishbeck*	5153 N Clark St Ste 20, Chicago IL 60640	773-275-4437	R	2*	<.1
843	Georetiary Networks Inc—*Douglas Lattman*	3956 Town Ctr Pmb 209, Orlando FL 32837	407-855-0200	R	2*	<.1
844	Chicago Financial Technology Inc—*Irek Koziol*	1556 S Michigan Ave 2, Chicago IL 60605	312-588-0006	R	2*	<.1
845	Cooper Software Inc—*Alan Cooper*	100 1st St 26th Fl, San Francisco CA 94105	415-267-3500	R	2*	<.1
846	Ciplex—*Josh Krane*	8981 Sunset Blvd Ste 3, West Hollywood CA 90069	310-461-0330	R	2*	<.1
847	Cmj Information Technology Inc—*Barry Schindelheim*	6924 Canby Ave Ste 109, Reseda CA 91335	818-700-6400	R	2*	<.1
848	GTX Corp—*Marviri Ling*	15333 N Pima Rd Ste 11, Scottsdale AZ 85260	480-889-8600	R	2*	<.1
849	One System Inc—*Stan Cabe*	1187 Coast Village Rd, Santa Barbara CA 93108	805-965-7007	R	2*	<.1
850	TTSS Interactive Products Inc—*Tim Fuller*	11910 Parklawn Dr Ste, Rockville MD 20852	301-230-1464	R	2*	<.1
851	ZMD Reining Inc—*Thilo von Selchow*	8413 Excelsior Dr Ste, Madison WI 53717	608-829-1987	S	2*	<.1
852	Cdt Micrographics Inc—*Diane Martin*	137 Water St, Exeter NH 03833	603-778-6140	R	2*	<.1
853	Office/Pro Technologies Inc—*Mary Locke*	336 McLaws Cir, Williamsburg VA 23185	757-253-8650	R	2*	<.1
854	Web-Hed Technologies Inc—*Juanita Gonzalez*	1617 E Commerce St Ste, San Antonio TX 78205	210-354-1661	R	2*	<.1
855	CapeCom Inc—*Vernon Grabel*	509 Falmouth Rd Ste 6, Mashpee MA 02649	508-539-9500	R	2*	<.1
856	Havens and Associates Inc—*Steve Havens*	14295 Sycamore Dr, Morgan Hill CA 95037	408-776-0593	R	2*	<.1
857	In Control Inc—*Kay Klemetsen*	10350 Jamestown St Ne, Minneapolis MN 55449	763-783-9500	R	2*	<.1
858	Infassure—*Tim Mcdonald*	2435 N Central Exwy St, Richardson TX 75080	972-680-7800	R	2*	<.1
859	RGB Technology Inc—*David W Chen*	590 Herndon Pky Ste 50, Herndon VA 20170	703-834-1500	R	2*	<.1
860	Solid Waste Technologies Inc—*Paul Schonfeld*	PO Box 548, East Brunswick NJ 08816	732-967-1070	R	2*	<.1
861	Tvc Inc—*Linda Tyring*	284 Constitution Ave, Portsmouth NH 03801	603-431-5251	R	2*	<.1
862	ZyLAB International Inc—*Pieter Varkevisser*	7918 Jones Branch Dr S, McLean VA 22102		S	2*	<.1
863	Data Technique Inc—*Terry Calloway*	PO Box 1301, Pittsburg KS 66762	620-235-1000	R	2*	<.1
864	Digica Inc—*Patrick Dolan*	Fox Hollow Business Ct, Branchburg NJ 08876	908-526-8488	S	2*	<.1
865	Datec Inc—*David Almonte*	364 Upland Dr, Tukwila WA 98188	206-575-1470	R	2*	<.1
866	Ahmed Corp—*Shakil Ahmed*	420 Keawe St, Honolulu HI 96813	808-537-1234	R	2*	<.1
867	Adi LLC—*Akram Sandhu*	200 Canal View Blvd St, Rochester NY 14623	585-239-6057	R	2*	<.1
868	Axis Microsystems Inc—*Brett Jaffe*	300 Unicron Pk Dr Fl 2, Woburn MA 01801	781-395-7014	R	2*	<.1
869	Copia International Ltd—*Steve Hersee*	1342 Avalon Ct, Wheaton IL 60189	630-388-6900	R	2*	<.1
870	Equinox Corp—*Lawrence Wolff*	9 W 57th St Ste 1650, New York NY 10019	212-421-2999	R	2*	<.1
871	GW Instruments—*Glenn Weinreb*	35 Medford St Ste 208, Somerville MA 02143	617-625-4096	R	2*	<.1
872	Netrate Systems Inc—*David Jordan*	3493 Woods Edge Ste 15, Okemos MI 48864	517-347-6739	R	2*	<.1
873	Ofm Distributors Inc—*Gene Bumgardner*	PO Box 4917, Charlottesville VA 22905	434-984-6190	R	2*	<.1
874	Pixel USA—*Tracy Bui*	3229 Stevens Creek Blv, San Jose CA 95117	408-293-8333	R	2*	<.1
875	Xinergy Microsystems—*George Sandoval*	278 Daniel Webster Hwy, Nashua NH 03060	603-888-8288	R	2*	<.1
876	Candela Controls Inc—*Steven Helliker*	751 Business Park Blvd, Winter Garden FL 34787	407-654-2420	R	2*	<.1
877	Network Presence LLC—*Leonard Liebowitz*	PO Box 606, Manhattan Beach CA 90267	310-216-6850	R	2*	<.1
878	Lumintel Corp—*Robert Esoda*	11260 Roger Bacon Dr, Reston VA 20190	703-435-6673	R	2*	<.1
879	Taylor Systems Engineering Corp—*Mark Taylor*	2929 Plymouth Rd Ste 2, Ann Arbor MI 48105	734-420-7447	R	2*	<.1
880	Automation Solutions Company LLC—*Shelly Hail*	PO Box 8, Walkerton VA 23177	804-769-0916	R	2*	<.1
881	Geneva Group Inc—*Glenn Ewing*	677 Strander Blvd Ste, Seattle WA 98188	206-575-0331	R	2*	<.1
882	ISRA Surface Vision Inc—*Brian Heil*	4470 Peachtree Lakes D, Duluth GA 30096	770-449-7776	S	2*	<.1
883	It Partshouse—*Gregory Maisel*	10400 Vintage Dr, Frisco TX 75035	972-987-6950	R	2*	<.1
884	Responsive Solutions Inc—*Frank Miller*	111 2nd Ave Ne Ste 350, Saint Petersburg FL 33701	727-456-1250	R	2*	<.1
885	Vertical Software Inc (Houston Texas)—*Robert Gemignani*	1217 W Loop N Ste 130, Houston TX 77055	713-680-1993	R	2*	<.1
886	Aera Products Div—*Hans-Georg Betz*	8601 Cross Park Dr Ste, Austin TX 78754	512-339-7100	D	2*	<.1
887	ASR Data Acquisition And Analysis LLC—*Meta Rosen*	3505 Cumberland Gap, Cedar Park TX 78613	512-918-9227	R	2*	<.1
888	New Frontiers Software Inc—*Keith Breton*	2428 Armstrong St, Livermore CA 94551	925-449-2029	R	2*	<.1
889	Standard Computer Inc—*Woody Stark*	10 Shackleford Plz Ste, Little Rock AR 72211	501-224-0050	R	2*	<.1
890	Tandem Data Resource Group Inc	25 Highland Park Villa, Dallas TX 75205		R	2*	<.1
891	Altara—*Helene Cole*	3430 American River Dr, Sacramento CA 95864	916-456-4346	R	2*	<.1
892	Baumark Accounting Software—*Fred Baumeister*	33873 Cyclone Hollow R, Wagoner OK 74467	918-485-8900	R	2*	<.1
893	CMS Research Inc—*John E Lenz*	1610 S Main St, Oshkosh WI 54902	920-235-3356	R	2*	<.1
894	Computer Performance Engineering Inc	PO Box 2125, Rolling Hills Estates CA 90274	310-541-6326	R	2*	<.1
895	Digital Lynks LLC—*Trish Duell*	12 Pheasant Run, Gladstone NJ 07934	908-902-0279	R	2*	<.1
896	Ideographix Inc—*Chan Yeh*	PO Box 696, Mountain View CA 94042	408-739-1290	R	2*	<.1
897	Integrated Solutions and Systems LLC—*Marilyn Bardash*	1510 Old North Gate Rd, Colorado Springs CO 80921	719-495-5866	R	2*	<.1
898	IT Pathworx Ltd—*Allen Schneid*	13223 Black Mountain R, San Diego CA 92129	858-484-7000	R	2*	<.1
899	NETiMAGE Inc—*Dale Whitney*	2 Corporate Dr Ste 930, Shelton CT 06484	203-242-1111	R	2*	<.1
900	Network Support Group—*Patricia Murakami*	2817 S McClellan St, Seattle WA 98144	206-721-0992	R	2*	<.1
901	OmniSoft Inc—*Gerald A Wilson*	2231 Faraday Ave Ste 1, Carlsbad CA 92008	760-931-8428	R	2*	<.1
902	Point 4 Data Corp—*Don Burden*	PO Box 991090, Redding CA 96099	714-755-6550	R	2*	<.1
903	Secant Technology Inc	PO Box6040, Sherwood AR 72124	501-835-6868	R	2*	<.1
904	Signature Systems Inc—*Tina Gerber*	2233 Walelia Pl, Koloa HI 96756	808-742-7207	R	2*	<.1
905	Visko Federal Systems Inc—*Amir Javed*	PO Box 151234, Alexandria VA 22315	703-871-5238	R	2*	<.1
906	Ada Business Computers—*Bruce R Huddleston*	PO Box 860, Ada OK 74821	580-436-2803	R	2*	<.1
907	Alternate Access Inc—*Kelly M Lumpkin*	5623 Duraleigh Rd Ste, Raleigh NC 27612	818-831-1860	R	2*	<.1
908	American Techsystems Corp—*Lawrence Menzin*	21 Volunteer Way, Lexington MA 02420		R	2*	<.1
909	Celestial Software Inc—*Bill Campbell*	PO Box 820, Mercer Island WA 98040	206-236-1676	R	2*	<.1
910	INTEKnet LLC—*Jim Tracy*	4678 Britcastle Dr, St Louis MO 63128	314-487-6008	R	2*	<.1
911	Intellicode Software Inc—*Peter Jolly*	PO Box 23382, San Jose CA 95153	408-629-3465	R	2*	<.1
912	CAD Systems Unlimited Inc	4936 Plz Escuela, Santa Clara CA 95054	408-988-3677	R	2	<.1
913	HoffTek Inc—*Scott Hoffman*	631 N Buckner St Ste 2, Derby KS 67037	316-789-9000	R	2*	<.1
914	Magik Technology Solutions—*Garrett Peck*	14703 Independence Dr, Plainfield IL 60544	847-348-1126	R	2*	<.1
915	Pacific Century Group Inc—*Max Mohan*	676 W Pullman Rd Ste 1, Moscow ID 83843	509-287-2029	R	2*	<.1
916	Printers Computers and Lans Inc—*John Darner*	7125 W Tidwell Rd Ste, Houston TX 77092	713-462-6474	R	2*	<.1
917	Dataweb Inc—*Richard Locke*	PO Box 236, Puyallup WA 98371	206-838-5940	R	2*	<.1
918	Mi16 Inc—*Darryl Vigil*	PO Box 65862, Albuquerque NM 87193	505-280-8176	R	2*	<.1
919	Creative Networking Concepts Inc—*Carmine Salierno*	PO Box 1130, Vernon NJ 07462	201-831-0109	R	2*	<.1
920	Granger John—*John Granger*	7345 Whitepine Rd, Richmond VA 23237	804-743-1860	R	2*	<.1
921	Alakai LLC—*Katie Tran*	1616 Anderson Rd Ste 1, Mc Lean VA 22102	703-288-6960	R	2*	<.1
922	Handshake Solutions—*Wouter Roost*	1109 Mckay Dr Fl 2, San Jose CA 95131	408-474-6248	R	2*	<.1
923	Adi Group Inc—*David Heile*	2004 N Hi Mount Blvd, Milwaukee WI 53208	414-546-2738	R	2*	<.1
924	Easy Computer Systems—*Mark Shainberg*	1800 Century Park E St, Los Angeles CA 90067	310-204-6134	R	2*	<.1
925	XM C Inc—*Robert Hamilton*	823 Exocet Dr Ste 109, Cordova TN 38018	901-795-9565	R	2*	<.1
926	Fluent Systems Inc—*Will Gibson*	PO Box 1731, Forney TX 75126	214-219-3200	R	2*	<.1
927	Columbus Data Technologies Inc—*Kevin Tapp*	4211 Anderson Mill Rd, Spartanburg SC 29301	864-595-1124	R	2*	<.1
928	International System Strategies Inc—*Clayton Bell*	2839 Paces Ferry Rd Se, Atlanta GA 30339	770-444-0470	R	2*	<.1

Rank	Company Name—*Executive Officer*	Address, City, State, Zip	Phone	Type	Fin	Empls
929	Creative Logistics Solutions Inc—*Richard Williams*	2135 Espey Ct Ste 1, Crofton MD 21114	410-793-0708	R	2*	<.1
930	Steel Vault Corp—*William J Caragol*	1690 S Congress Ave St, Delray Beach FL 33445	561-805-8000	S	2	<.1
931	Ranac Computer Corp—*Keith Pitzele*	4181 E 96th St Ste 280, Indianapolis IN 46240	317-844-0141	R	2*	<.1
932	Computer Tree Of Winston-Salem Inc—*Bob Young*	1760 Jonestown Rd Ste, Winston Salem NC 27103	336-768-9820	R	2*	<.1
933	Bizmate Consulting Inc—*Pearson Huang*	1251 Park Ave, Emeryville CA 94608	510-652-8283	R	2*	<.1
934	Ininet Inc—*Scott Vickery*	16 Church St Ste 1a, Keene NH 03431	603-352-7555	R	2*	<.1
935	Networkguys Inc—*Shiang Carney*	39355 California St St, Fremont CA 94538	510-713-8880	R	2*	<.1
936	Rco Systems Inc—*Dale Carroll*	251 James Jackson Ave, Cary NC 27513	919-319-3612	R	2*	<.1
937	Pinnacle Computer Services Inc—*Brian Ricci*	640 S Hebron Ave, Evansville IN 47714	812-476-6662	R	2*	<.1
938	KBS Computer Services Inc—*Anthony Kitchens*	15537 S 70th Ct, Orland Park IL 60462	708-444-8425	R	2*	<.1
939	Sypamore Inc—*Melissa Willison*	241 E 4th St Ste 204, Frederick MD 21701	301-668-4694	R	2*	<.1
940	Axios Systems Inc—*Michele Hudnall*	2214 Rock Hill Rd Ste, Herndon VA 20170	703-326-1357	R	2*	<.1
941	Netwar Defense Corp—*Paul Wells*	12403 Quarterhorse Dr, Bowie MD 20720	301-805-4355	R	2*	<.1
942	Computer Technical Services Inc (Las Vegas Nevada)—*Kathleen Sturek*	4275 W Bell Dr Ste 10, Las Vegas NV 89118	702-368-1885	R	2*	<.1
943	Modus Associates LLC	37 W 20th St Ste 304, New York NY 10011	212-255-6768	R	2*	<.1
944	Icomsys Inc—*Lee Padron*	55 W 9000 S, Sandy UT 15459	801-563-7999	R	2*	<.1
945	Inetz Corp—*Josie Gay*	1055 E 3900 S, Salt Lake City UT 84124	801-415-2500	R	2*	<.1
946	M Soft Inc—*Amnon Sarig*	6355 Topanga Canyon Bl, Woodland Hills CA 91367	818-716-7081	R	2*	<.1
947	Riley Industries International LLC—*Ester Ho*	1702 Willow Creek Rd A, Prescott AZ 86301	928-445-0700	R	2*	<.1
948	Northwest Network Inc—*Vicki Kahlke*	PO Box 2217, Kirkland WA 98083	425-488-6389	R	2*	<.1
949	Az Technology Inc—*Lynn Leeper*	7047 Old Madison Pke N, Huntsville AL 35806	256-837-9877	R	2*	<.1
950	Burgess Computer Decisions Inc—*Jeffrey Burgess*	333 Skokie Blvd Ste 11, Northbrook IL 60062	847-205-1922	R	2*	<.1
951	Computer Network Systems Inc—*Andrew Brenkus*	2702 Lighthouse Point, Baltimore MD 21224	301-931-3700	R	2*	<.1
952	Prime Computer Systems Inc—*Ahmad Ghaffari*	3100 Banksville Rd Ste, Pittsburgh PA 15216	412-344-5555	R	2*	<.1
953	Computer Systems Design Co—*John Nebel*	735 Highland Ave, Boulder CO 80302	303-447-8025	R	2*	<.1
954	Coretrace Corp—*Toney Jennings*	6500 River Pl Blvd, Austin TX 78730	512-592-4100	R	2*	<.1
955	Isi/Pss Group JV—*Yumi Cooper*	1201 15th St Nw Ste 20, Washington DC 20005	202-263-0863	R	2*	<.1
956	Probo Data Group Inc—*Patrick Dill*	1250 Oakmead Pkwy Ste, Sunnyvale CA 94085	408-501-8891	R	2*	<.1
957	Trinet Solutions Group Inc—*Louis Oliva*	5246 Regal Ct, Frederick MD 21703	301-662-7122	R	2*	<.1
958	Vipertech Corp—*Michael Davis*	7516 Slate Ridge Blvd, Reynoldsburg OH 43068	614-866-1472	R	2*	<.1
959	Mobiletec International Inc—*Reid Friedman*	14502 N Dale Mabry Hwy, Tampa FL 33618	813-876-8333	R	2*	<.1
960	Advanced Integrated Manufacturing Computer Solutions Inc—*Jeffrey Siciliano*	34673 Bennett, Fraser MI 48026	586-439-0300	R	2*	<.1
961	Quadzilla Performance Technologies Inc—*Quad Boenker*	6032 Lake Worth Blvd S, Fort Worth TX 76135	817-306-2444	R	2*	<.1
962	Vitalink—*Brian Frazee*	PO Box 100, Marklleysburg PA 15459	724-329-1516	R	2*	<.1
963	Automated Switching And Controls Inc—*Eric Maccalla*	6621 N Calle Eva Miran, Irwindale CA 91702	626-969-8441	R	2*	<.1
964	Marzik Inc—*Brad Willcockson*	116 Defense Hwy Ste 31, Annapolis MD 21401	410-571-9466	R	2*	<.1
965	Software Reproduction Technologies Inc—*Jeffrey Bitsimis*	100 Corporate Plz B-10, Islandia NY 11749	212-447-4475	R	2*	<.1
966	Digital One Networks Inc—*Yesenia Monsour*	915 W Oak Estates Dr, San Antonio TX 78260	210-481-3312	R	2*	<.1
967	Aquaveo LLC—*Laura White*	3210 N Canyon Rd Ste 3, Provo UT 84604	801-691-5528	R	2*	<.1
968	Soltech Inc—*Tim Smith*	3445 Peachtree Rd Ne S, Atlanta GA 30326	404-601-6000	R	2*	<.1
969	Clare Computer Solutions—*Anthony Barone*	2400 Camino Ramon Ste, San Ramon CA 94583	925-277-0690	R	2*	<.1
970	NeoMedia Technologies Inc—*Laura Marriott*	1360 Center Dr Ste 210, Dunwoody GA 30338	678-638-0460	P	2	<.1
971	Gencom Technology LLC—*Ross Knowles*	140 Dougherty Ave, Holbrook NY 11741	516-593-9300	R	2*	<.1
972	Laser Photo Tooling Services Inc—*John Leyva*	5081 N Dixie Hwy, Boca Raton FL 33431	561-393-4710	R	2*	<.1
973	MRA Technologies—*Pam Mcclure*	2502 Park Rd, Emerald Hills CA 94062	650-361-8140	R	2*	<.1
974	Inetsupport Inc—*Vijay Kaushik*	1814 Menesini Pl, Martinez CA 94553	925-957-0100	R	2*	<.1
975	Management Information Systems Co—*Michael Benbenek*	5856 W 74th St, Indianapolis IN 46278	317-295-4200	R	2*	<.1
976	Imagestream Internet Solutions Inc—*Jc Utter*	7900 8th Rd, Plymouth IN 46563	574-935-8484	R	2*	<.1
977	GCAS Inc—*C Savell*	1531 Grand Ave Ste A, San Marcos CA 92078	760-591-4227	R	2*	<.1
978	Baraka Inc—*Furat Abraham*	505 S Neil St Ste 3, Champaign IL 61820	217-356-7226	R	2*	<.1
979	Computer Integrated Solutions Inc—*Thomas Jividen*	1213 Culbreth Dr, Wilmington NC 28405	910-256-5353	R	2*	<.1
980	Bvc Systems Inc—*Suk-Man Wong*	43064 Christy St, Fremont CA 94538	510-683-6718	R	2*	<.1
981	James F Rigell—*James Rigell*	8611 Village Ter, Houston TX 77040	713-983-0696	R	2*	<.1
982	JES Hardware Solutions Inc—*James Sessions*	2138 Van Buren St Apt, Hollywood FL 33020	305-597-3980	R	2*	<.1
983	Archive Index Systems Inc—*Douglas Vogt*	PO Box 40135, Bellevue WA 98015	425-644-6449	R	2*	<.1
984	Alexander Cameron—*Alexander Cameron*	PO Box 3253, Fayville MA 01745	508-481-4067	R	2*	<.1
985	Shebesta Abest Inc—*W Shebesta*	1118 Ferris Rd Ste 2, Amelia OH 45102	513-943-4426	R	2*	<.1
986	Interplex International LLC—*Richard Kelsey*	7200 Us Hwy 50 E, Carson City NV 89701	775-885-0488	R	1*	<.1
987	T 3 Corp—*David Pujals*	PO Box 623, Nokesville VA 20182	304-368-9147	R	1*	<.1
988	N I C Group—*Michael Skomba*	1130 Us Hwy 202 E6, Raritan NJ 08869	908-253-8106	R	1*	<.1
989	Essexusa LLC—*Thomas Napolitano*	185 N State Rt 17 1, Paramus NJ 07652	201-576-0001	R	1*	<.1
990	Uptime Solutions Professional Services Group Inc—*Mark Mann*	3801 Gaskins Rd, Richmond VA 23233	804-836-1490	R	1*	<.1
991	Legal Technology Inc—*Rick Goldberg*	1301 Mckinney St Ste 3, Houston TX 77010	713-655-9393	R	1*	<.1
992	Computer Circuit Inc—*David Ramirez*	18105 La Salle Ave, Gardena CA 90248	310-515-0922	R	1*	<.1
993	Industrial Control and Design Inc—*Cliff Taylor*	3585 E Date Ave, Fresno CA 93725	559-498-0290	R	1*	<.1
994	Olmec Systems Inc—*Christopher Forte*	255 Us Hwy 46, Denville NJ 07834	973-586-6590	R	1*	<.1
995	Mid America Computer Corporation Inc—*David Goodwin*	11711 N College Ave St, Carmel IN 46032	317-846-3101	R	1*	<.1
996	Link Neighborhood Inc—*Don Bachner*	2546 15th St, Denver CO 80211	303-830-0123	R	1*	<.1
997	Three Phase Electric and Controls LLC	1171 Market St, Fort Mill SC 29708	803-548-5729	R	1*	<.1
998	Nk Technologies Inc—*Gregg Kaloust*	36 Brunswick Ave, Gardiner ME 04345	207-588-5000	R	1*	<.1
999	Trinity Government Systems A Private Company Inc—*Jerry Coker*	719 2nd St Ste 12, Davis CA 95616	530-759-2204	R	1*	<.1
1000	Fonix Corp—*Roger D Dudley*	387 S 520 W Ste 110, Lindon UT 84042	801-382-7997	P	1	.1
1001	Advintex Inc—*Renrick Halls*	3580 Pall Mall Dr, Jacksonville FL 32257	904-880-3669	R	1*	<.1
1002	Healthwise International LLC—*Shahnaz Abbasi*	1555 E Flamingo Rd Ste, Las Vegas NV 89119	702-510-7976	R	1*	<.1
1003	See-Technology Inc—*Carl Price*	12310 W Spring Lake Dr, Lockport IL 60491	708-710-2491	R	1*	<.1
1004	Melaphyre Inc—*J Suresh*	5807 Topanga Canyon Bl, Woodland Hills CA 91367	818-348-0432	R	1*	<.1
1005	Micromatic Electronic Distribution Inc—*Juhi Aswani*	3100 De La Cruz Blvd S, Santa Clara CA 95054	408-970-8566	R	1*	<.1
1006	Idc Global Inc—*Ben Clarke*	26 Broadway Ste 941, New York NY 10004	212-514-8186	R	1*	<.1
1007	International Telematics Corp—*Craig Marris*	311 W 43rd St Ste 304, New York NY 10036	646-688-2350	R	1*	<.1
1008	Visual Information Inc—*Joseph Burke*	700 17th St Ste 100, Denver CO 80202	303-825-0413	R	1*	<.1
1009	Asic Inc—*Chris Castel*	2834 S Sherwood Forest, Baton Rouge LA 70816	225-291-2742	R	1*	<.1
1010	Cim Concepts Inc—*Randall Herbein*	200 Continental Dr Ste, Newark DE 19713	302-613-5400	R	1*	<.1
1011	Ideas Incorporated Of Ohio—*Bradley Borne*	3755 Boettler Oaks Dr, Uniontown OH 44685	330-896-8215	R	1*	<.1
1012	Wertheim Inc—*Joshua Wertheim*	1430 Broadway Rm 1611, New York NY 10018	212-354-6180	R	1*	<.1
1013	Kelgun Enterprises Ltd—*Paul Kelly*	10211 S Blessen Rd, Amarillo TX 79119	806-467-1133	R	1*	<.1
1014	Advantage Technologies Inc—*Barry Malter*	9 E 38th St Ste 4, New York NY 10016	212-717-7700	R	1*	<.1
1015	Conceptual Systems and Software Inc—*Edward Andert*	PO Box 372, Chino Valley AZ 86323	928-636-2600	R	1*	<.1

Note: An asterisk (*) indicates an estimated financial figure. The company type code used is as follows: R = Private, P = Public, S = Private Subsidiary, B = Public Subsidiary, D = Division, J = Joint Venture, I = Investment Fund.

COMPANY RANKINGS BY SALES WITHIN 4-DIGIT SIC

Rank	Company Name—Executive Officer	Address, City, State, Zip	Phone	Type	Fin	Empls
1016	Secure Data Solutions Inc—Mark Bordelon	21613 Rhodes Rd, Spring TX 77388	281-719-5700	R	1*	<.1
1017	Source One Solutions Inc—Brian Jacobs	1065 Katella St, Laguna Beach CA 92651	949-494-1408	R	1*	<.1
1018	Sysnet Technologies LLC	PO Box 1125, South Windsor CT 06074	860-627-9192	R	1*	<.1
1019	Decker-Wright Corp—Marshall Wright	628 Shrewsbury Ave Ste, Tinton Falls NJ 07701	732-747-9373	R	1*	<.1
1020	Information Technology Engineering Inc—John Abdullah	11405 Bronzedale Dr St, Oakton VA 22124	703-934-6130	R	1*	<.1
1021	eDigital Corp—Alfred H Falk	16770 W Bernardo Dr, San Diego CA 92127	858-304-3016	P	1	<.1
1022	Integrated Information Solutions Inc—Loren Stormo	2425 W Central Ave Ste, Missoula MT 59801	406-728-0600	R	1*	<.1
1023	Rogers and Company Cpas PC—Eric Rogers	125 Jericho Tpke, Jericho NY 11753	516-338-9500	R	1*	<.1
1024	Dcsc Inc—Kirsten Austin	5257 Shaw Ave Ste 303, Saint Louis MO 63110	314-664-2200	R	1*	<.1
1025	Advatech Solutions Inc—Shane Cupps	PO Box 940803, Plano TX 75094	469-272-5000	R	1*	<.1
1026	21st Century Computer Systems—Robert Bullemer	PO Box 1419, Santa Barbara CA 93102	805-964-6677	R	1*	<.1
1027	Twin-State Tech Services Inc—Elizabeth Tinsman	3543 E Kimberly Rd, Davenport IA 52807	563-441-1504	R	1*	<.1
1028	Ourtech Solutions Inc—Robert Troyer	1010 N 96th St Ste 102, Omaha NE 68114	402-778-7999	R	1*	<.1
1029	Copia Technologies Inc—Pete Salucci	600 Anton Blvd Fl 11, Costa Mesa CA 92626	714-371-4053	R	1*	<.1
1030	JNJ Computer Inc—James Stiene	171 Madison Ave, Franklin Square NY 11010	516-358-0580	JNJ	1*	<.1
1031	Creative Web Inc—John Raomono	101 E Main St Bldg 13, Little Falls NJ 07424	973-812-5222	R	1*	<.1
1032	Focus 24 Inc—Vincent Dipippo	575 Park Ave, Cranston RI 02910	401-781-0300	R	1*	<.1
1033	Intelli-Mine Inc—Anio Suri	12 Trovita, Irvine CA 92620	714-505-4094	R	1*	<.1
1034	K-2 Engineering Group LLC—Bryan Goetzke	PO Box 280, Big Bend WI 53103	262-662-3452	R	1*	<.1
1035	Xtend Consulting LLC—Amy Ray	1825 Barrett Lakes Blv, Kennesaw GA 30144	770-771-5066	R	1*	<.1
1036	Intecon Inc—Brandon Spiker	1215 S Park Ln Ste 4, Tempe AZ 85281	480-892-1065	R	1*	<.1
1037	Dataware Inc—Marty Hain	5153 Exchange Dr, Flint MI 48507	810-732-3777	R	1*	<.1
1038	On The Move Technology Inc—Paul Rodriguez	23120 Alicia Pkwy Ste, Mission Viejo CA 92692	949-215-9073	R	1*	<.1
1039	Networks Inmocean Inc—Yau Hom	PO Box 910424, San Diego CA 92191	858-240-2642	R	1*	<.1
1040	Comconnexion—Joe Garrett	407 E Lantrip St, Kilgore TX 75662	903-983-1984	R	1*	<.1
1041	Greendragon Creations Inc—Howard Shere	PO Box 70, Water Valley MS 38965	662-473-9209	R	1*	<.1
1042	Vector Technology Inc—Steven Orszag	152 Bouvant Dr, Princeton NJ 08540	609-921-3660	R	1*	<.1
1043	Cds - Networks and Services Inc—Randy Hood	PO Box 6218, Kinston NC 28501	252-523-6664	R	1*	<.1
1044	Solutions Group LLC	6703 Lumsden St, Mc Lean VA 22101	703-790-6153	R	1*	<.1
1045	Syscomp Inc—Peggy Juhlin	3505 River Dr Ste C, Lawrenceville GA 30044	770-972-5992	R	1*	<.1
1046	Threewill LLC—Joe Markiewicz	4400 N Point Pkwy Ste, Alpharetta GA 30022	678-513-6930	R	1*	<.1
1047	Comstar LLC—Greg Eggold	2240 N Grandview Blvd, Waukesha WI 53188	262-524-9628	R	1*	<.1
1048	Comtech International Inc—Masroor Syed	45 Seusing Blvd, Hauppauge NY 11788	631-366-4045	R	1*	<.1
1049	Mverify Corp—Robert Binder	PO Box 977, Northbrook IL 60065	312-881-7337	R	1*	<.1
1050	Newdata Solutions Inc—Rick Freda	222 N Sepulveda Blvd S, El Segundo CA 90245	310-335-2026	R	1*	<.1
1051	Future Designs Inc—Kent Lowman	2702 Triana Blvd Sw St, Huntsville AL 35805	256-883-1240	R	1*	<.1
1052	Accelerated Technologies Inc—Richard Pelupessy	2161 Saturn Ct, Bakersfield CA 93308	661-393-5546	R	1*	<.1
1053	Personal Systems Plus Inc—Robert Hostutler	30432 Euclid Ave Ste 1, Wickliffe OH 44092	440-585-7013	R	1*	<.1
1054	Datamatrix Systems Inc—Henry Strohm	505 Lincoln Hwy, East McKeesport PA 15035	412-825-3600	R	1*	<.1
1055	Messaging Solutions LLC—Gail Smit	8203 Shoregrove Dr Ste, Humble TX 77346	281-852-1301	R	1*	<.1
1056	Sartell Group Inc—Pam Sartell	310 4th Ave S Ste 800, Minneapolis MN 55415	612-548-3101	R	1*	.1
1057	Trade American Card Corp—Michael Ames	17975 Sky Park Cir Bld, Irvine CA 92614	949-225-6000	R	1*	<.1
1058	Enterprise Integration Inc—Thomas Gulledge	5901 Kingstowne Villag, Alexandria VA 22315	703-236-0880	R	1*	<.1
1059	Noble House Funding Corp—Richard Mehan	828 Se 8th Ave, Deerfield Beach FL 33441	954-418-0828	R	1*	<.1
1060	SynaptiCAD Inc—Daniel Notestein	PO Box 10608, Blacksburg VA 24062	540-953-3390	R	1*	<.1
1061	Cipher Corp—Allen J Rembert	2 Centerview Dr, Greensboro NC 27407	336-855-8733	R	1*	<.1
1062	Jackson Digital Imaging Corp—Kevin Jackson	3055 Northern Ave, Kingman AZ 86409	928-757-8837	R	1*	<.1
1063	Engage Communication Inc—Mark Doyle	9565 Soquel Dr, Aptos CA 95003	831-688-1021	R	1*	<.1
1064	Newspaper Electronics Corp—Kelvin Perry	5737 Swope Pkwy, Kansas City MO 64130	816-523-5993	R	1*	<.1
1065	Thirdwave Corp—Roy Hernandez	11400 W Olympic Blvd, Los Angeles CA 90064	310-914-1480	R	1*	<.1
1066	Computer Creations LLC—Scott Beach	88 Westpark Rd, Dayton OH 45459	937-438-2777	R	1*	<.1
1067	C and J Computer Consulting Inc—James Mease	1916 Crain Hwy S Ste 1, Glen Burnie MD 21061	410-766-2070	R	1*	<.1
1068	Hitech Computers Of Ruston Inc—Richard Raue	715 W California Ave, Ruston LA 71270	318-255-1110	R	1*	<.1
1069	Intuitive Business Solutions Inc—Marc Liojegren	2119 Monroe St, Dearborn MI 48124	313-359-7000	R	1*	<.1
1070	Medical Systems Development Corp—Henry N Camp	620 Village Trace NE B, Marietta GA 30067	770-984-9550	R	1*	<.1
1071	Mountain State Information Systems Inc—Paul Garnett	PO Box 3738, Telluride CO 81435	970-708-7723	R	1*	<.1
1072	Website Connection—David Katlin	2655 W Guadalupe Rd, Mesa AZ 85202	480-775-1055	R	1*	<.1
1073	Bogdan Computer Services Inc—Edward Bogdan	9006 Yellow Brick Rd A, Baltimore MD 21237	410-780-3000	R	1*	<.1
1074	Computer Upgrade Corp—Scott Lamb	1901 Sampson Ave, Corona CA 92879		R	1*	<.1
1075	Conduit Systems Inc—David Cameron	14 Breakneck Hill Rd S, Lincoln RI 02865	401-722-5995	R	1*	<.1
1076	CyberResources Corp	1101 Bristol Rd, Mountainside NJ 07092	908-789-3000	R	1*	<.1
1077	PC One Professional Systems Inc—Bea Allen	300 N Crockett St, Granbury TX 76048	817-573-7011	R	1*	<.1
1078	Azar Computer Software Services Inc—Anthony Azar	1200 Regal Row, Austin TX 78748	512-476-5085	R	1*	<.1
1079	Catalyst Computer Services Inc—Richard Shaw	2271 Prosser Ave, Los Angeles CA 90064	310-441-4300	R	1*	<.1
1080	CPak Technology Solutions—Phillip Abbott	133 Main St, LaGrange GA 30240	706-883-7664	R	1*	<.1
1081	Elemco Software Integration Group Ltd—Louis Maggio	PO Box 1059, Central Islip NY 11722	631-234-3099	R	1*	<.1
1082	Global System Services Corp—Ron Herardian	650 Castro St Ste 120, Mountain View CA 94041	650-965-8669	R	1*	<.1
1083	Gravitate Design Studio	12808 Ne 95th St, Vancouver WA 98682	360-253-4387	R	1*	<.1
1084	Information Systems and Networks Corp—Roma Malkani	10411 Motor City Dr St, Bethesda MD 20817	301-469-0400	R	1*	<.1
1085	Integrated Custom Software Inc—Bryan Andrews	12 National Dr, Glastonbury CT 06033	860-657-3339	R	1*	<.1
1086	Light Speed Networks LLC—Mary Skrezec	1650 Rte 112, Port Jefferson Station NY 11776	631-642-2044	R	1*	<.1
1087	Nevalon Technologies LLC—Chad Lafon	12105 Ballybrook Ct, Raleigh NC 27614	919-844-8555	R	1*	<.1
1088	PC Audio Labs—Thomas Bolton	14141 Covello St Ste 5, Van Nuys CA 91405	818-986-2673	R	1*	<.1
1089	Qcera Inc—Margaret Kahn	1525 S Sepulveda Blvd, Los Angeles CA 90025	310-473-7988	R	1*	<.1
1090	Total Systems Approach Inc—Robert Mossanen	14817 Sutton St, Van Nuys CA 91403	818-789-2824	R	1*	<.1
1091	In-Sys Solutions Inc—Tim Harger	14048 W Petronella Dr, Libertyville IL 60048	847-996-0400	R	1*	<.1
1092	Network Management Inc—Rafiq Masri	8229 Boone Blvd Ste 25, Vienna VA 22182	703-848-9000	R	1*	<.1
1093	Network Resource Technologies Corp—John Wilson	4611 Assembly Dr Ste A, Lanham MD 20706	301-429-8842	R	1*	<.1
1094	Compunite Computers Inc	PO Box 362 - 39 Rte 46, Pine Brook NJ 07058	973-227-6008	R	1*	<.1
1095	Computer Information Enterprises Inc—David LaFrancis	2091 Business Ctr Dr S, Irvine CA 92612	949-263-0910	D	1*	<.1
1096	dESCO LLC—Dean Schreiner	44 Barkley Cir, Fort Myers FL 33907	239-275-1991	R	1*	<.1
1097	Microdata Group Inc—Glenn Mores	100 Cummings Ctr Ste 1, Beverly MA 01915	978-921-0990	R	1*	<.1
1098	Bavarian Computer Works Inc—Greg Schmitt	307 7th Ave Rm 2101, New York NY 10001	212-366-0436	R	1*	<.1
1099	Business Management Systems Inc—Adelard L Brault	10560 Main St Ste PH-1, Fairfax VA 22030	703-591-0911	R	1*	<.1
1100	Eagle Automation Corp—Alan Morgan	4455 S Padre Island Dr, Corpus Christi TX 78411	361-857-8446	R	1*	<.1
1101	Unilan Network Inc—Susan Yan	18856 Amar Rd Ste 6, Walnut CA 91789	626-854-8222	R	1*	<.1
1102	Datajet Services Inc—Bruce Green	5805 State Bridge Rd G, Duluth GA 30097	678-542-2212	R	1*	<.1
1103	First Option Inc—Paul Fuller	PO Box 365, Mansfield MA 02048	508-339-0588	R	1*	<.1
1104	FTA Computer Consultants Inc—Richard Taha	177 Bovet Rd Ste 600, San Mateo CA 94402	650-591-1781	R	1*	<.1
1105	Quikey Computer Systems Inc—Michael Stiller	520 S Main St Ste 2451, Akron OH 44311	234-542-4400	R	1*	<.1

Rank	Company Name—Executive Officer	Address, City, State, Zip	Phone	Type	Fin	Empls
1106	SSOE Systems Inc—Tony D Damon	1001 Madison Ave, Toledo OH 43604	419-255-3830	S	1*	<.1
1107	Actek Inc—Frederick Graham	PO Box 27128, Seattle WA 98165	206-363-0217	R	1*	<.1
1108	Airlink Network Corp—Grace Fang	1900 Proforma Ave Ste, Ontario CA 91761	909-598-5968	R	1*	<.1
1109	Applied Resource Technologies Inc—Scott Ryan	8350 N Central Expy St, Dallas TX 75206	214-550-2000	R	1*	<.1
1110	CableSoft Inc—Tom Reedy	PO Box 1417, Fairfield IA 52556	641-472-8393	R	1*	<.1
1111	Cadnet Services—Gregg Johnson	1 Sundial Ave Ste 418, Manchester NH 03103	603-296-2376	R	1*	<.1
1112	Datagroup Ltd—Daniel Drennan	7444 N Claremont Ste S, Chicago IL 60645	773-338-6020	R	1*	<.1
1113	Intelligent Machine Control Inc—Brent Woolston	423 Commerce Ln Unit 6, West Berlin NJ 08091	856-768-5370	R	1*	<.1
1114	American Commercial Terminals Inc	300 Dove Creek, McKinney TX 75071	972-837-4207	R	1*	<.1
1115	Hiltech Inc—Harry Lipkind	6124 Tuckerman Ln, Rockville MD 20852	301-571-1971	R	1*	<.1
1116	Mariette Systems International—Ernie Mariette	39 Ericson Rd, San Mateo CA 94402	650-344-1519	R	1*	<.1
1117	Media Group Inc	79 Alexander Ave Ste 3, Bronx NY 10454	718-585-6880	R	1*	<.1
1118	Milcom Corporation Inc	PO Box 472, Blackstone MA 01504		R	1*	<.1
1119	Project Planning and Support Inc—Chris Rose	101 W Grand Ave Ste 50, Chicago IL 60654	312-245-0101	R	1*	<.1
1120	ReproMax Inc—Rick Bosworth	16141 Swingley Ridge, Chesterfield MO 63017	636-537-0555	R	1*	<.1
1121	ABSolute Businesss Software Inc—Scott Gary	226 W 6th St, Panama City FL 32401	850-747-8788	R	1*	<.1
1122	AI Software Solutions Inc	10703 J St, Omaha NE 68127	402-339-9500	R	1*	<.1
1123	C and F Computers Inc—Joel Ciarochi	427 Oleander St, Duncanville TX 75137	972-296-0797	R	1*	<.1
1124	Coefficient LLC	165 D St, Independence OR 97351	503-606-9120	R	1*	<.1
1125	Insurance Systems Group—Charles Kerr	PO Box 50387, Raleigh NC 27650	919-834-4907	R	1*	<.1
1126	Mcshelle National Inc—Micheal Sheller	4212 Independence St, Rockville MD 20853	301-706-5095	R	1*	<.1
1127	SLPowers—Rory Sanchez	1254 Okeechobee Rd, West Palm Beach FL 33401	561-835-8351	R	1*	<.1
1128	Stok Software Inc—Glenn Stok	373 Nesconset Hwy Ste, Hauppauge NY 11788	631-232-2228	R	1*	<.1
1129	Versatility Software Inc—Eric Hoffert	349 Montrose Ave, South Orange NJ 07079	973-762-9323	R	1*	<.1
1130	4Dvision—Scot Susmann	9678 E Arapahoe Rd, Englewood CO 80112	303-785-8321	R	1*	<.1
1131	Amchi Software Company Inc—Uday Shingwekar	450 Lower Vintners Cir, Fremont CA 94539	510-440-1705	R	1*	<.1
1132	Batch Process Technologies Inc—James Cook	1291 Cumberland Ave, West Lafayette IN 47906		R	1*	<.1
1133	Consul Tec Inc—John Eilertsen	PO Box 964, Sparta NJ 07871	201-563-7800	R	1*	<.1
1134	Crider Consulting Inc—Tracy D Crider	4735 Clairemont Sq Ste, San Diego CA 92117	858-270-6577	R	1*	<.1
1135	Devers Group Inc—William Devers	1200 Central Ave Ste 3, Wilmette IL 60091	847-920-1678	R	1*	<.1
1136	Emanoncom Inc—Scott Morris	3805 Aria Ln, Lexington KY 40514	859-225-5349	R	1*	<.1
1137	Fusion Design—Steve Farnworth	764 Live Oak Ave, Menlo Park CA 94025	650-325-1398	R	1*	<.1
1138	Qualitech Computer Systems—Stan Zielinski	11055 Century Ln, Overland Park KS 66210	913-515-4037	R	1*	<.1
1139	Software Interphase Inc—Don Lambert	82 Cucumber Hill Rd, Foster RI 02825	401-397-4540	R	1*	<.1
1140	ULTRAsafe Security Specialists—Ronald Lander	PO Box 5530, Norco CA 92860	951-736-5234	R	1*	<.1
1141	Fourb Technologies Inc—Kami Ghadoushi	1544 Purdue Ave, Los Angeles CA 90025	310-444-1122	R	1*	<.1
1142	Pileated Pictures LLC—Michael Levine	350 March Rd, Shelburne Falls MA 01370	413-625-8551	R	1*	<.1
1143	Nationwide Value Computers Inc—David Cicchitti	401 E 4th St Ste 15, Bridgeport PA 19405	610-277-6500	R	1*	<.1
1144	Delta Network Services LLC	510 Highland Ave, Milford MI 48381	248-889-3530	R	1*	<.1
1145	Grove Networks Inc—Andrew Judge	2103 Coral Way Ste 810, Coral Gables FL 33145	305-448-6126	R	1*	<.1
1146	Kiva North America Inc—Michael Baker	40 S River Rd Unit 57, Bedford NH 03110	603-641-5482	R	1*	<.1
1147	Transition Management—Thomas Roginski	28 Deerfoot Trl, Harvard MA 01451	978-456-8512	R	1*	<.1
1148	Ethany Corp—Carole Dakin	19 Main St, Scottsville NY 14546	585-889-2586	R	1*	<.1
1149	Kore-Linq Co—Mike Khatibi	17 Appleseed Ln, Gaithersburg MD 20878	301-948-9494	R	1*	<.1
1150	Flex Resources Inc—Edward Clayo	PO Box 517, Brunswick OH 44212	330-273-1070	R	1*	<.1
1151	Intellisource Consulting Services Inc—George Thomas	5 Independence Way Ste, Princeton NJ 08540	609-514-5160	R	1*	<.1
1152	Synatronic Inc—Jim Liaw	2400 Lincoln Ave, Altadena CA 91001	626-296-6200	R	1*	<.1
1153	Sigma Data Systems Inc—H Spears	PO Box 9767, Newark DE 19714	302-453-8812	R	1*	<.1
1154	Datapoint USA Inc—John Perkins	8122 Datapoint Dr Ste, San Antonio TX 78229	210-614-9977	R	1*	<.1
1155	Meridian Service Group Inc—Robert Koupeny	8121 S Lemont Rd, Darien IL 60561	630-910-4970	R	1*	<.1
1156	Technicraft Inc—Michael Jordan	49 Depot St, Merrimack NH 03054	603-424-1955	R	1*	<.1
1157	Lns Technologies Inc—John Lorelle	17407 Bridge Hill Ct C, Tampa FL 33647	813-221-1315	R	1*	<.1
1158	Penn Computer Corp—Michael Jordon	1800 Mearns Rd Ste Aa, Warminster PA 18974	215-444-9999	R	1*	<.1
1159	Andrew Grygus—Andrew Grygus	4542 Pennsylvania Ave, La Crescenta CA 91214	818-248-2348	R	1*	<.1
1160	Bill West Inc—Bill West	887 Main St Ste D, Monroe CT 06468	203-261-6027	R	1*	<.1
1161	Comca Systems Inc—Mogens Jensen	3143 Pine Shadow Dr, Land O Lakes FL 34639	813-996-5922	R	1*	<.1
1162	Micro Madness Ltd—Vincent Liggio	11020 71st Ave Apt 718, Forest Hills NY 11375	212-741-4177	R	1*	<.1
1163	Cat Studios—Bill Levin	4925 N College Ave, Indianapolis IN 46205	317-923-8379	R	1*	<.1
1164	Indigo Pacific—Dave Bagell	2070 Woodglen Dr, San Jose CA 95130	408-866-2676	R	1*	<.1
1165	Steve Skelton—Steve Skelton	20 S Santa Cruz Ave St, Los Gatos CA 95030	408-354-7733	R	1*	<.1
1166	Integration and Automation Solutions Inc—Eugene Fellows	PO Box 5085, Phillipsburg NJ 08865	610-573-8980	R	1*	<.1
1167	Martronix Inc—Terry Mertell	118 W Streetsboro St S, Hudson OH 44236	330-655-2238	R	1*	<.1
1168	Sullivan Electric Group Inc—David Henle	3650 Roll Ave, Cincinnati OH 45223	513-241-5413	R	1*	<.1
1169	Alltek Services Inc—Samuel Bowles	PO Box 2355, Lakeland FL 33806	863-709-0709	R	1*	<.1
1170	Resolution Technology Inc—Diana Voigt	5990 Wilcox Pl Ste B, Dublin OH 43016	614-791-0045	R	1*	<.1
1171	Scm Products Inc—Michael Molack	155 Ricefield Ln, Hauppauge NY 11788	631-234-1304	R	1*	<.1
1172	Adjile Systems Inc—Bill Riggins	300 Harris Ave Ste A, Sacramento CA 95838	916-928-2590	R	1*	<.1
1173	Scio Consulting International LLC—Pedro Garza	6580 Via Del Oro, San Jose CA 95119	408-239-4020	R	1*	<.1
1174	Data Unlimited International Inc—Flora Kan	PO Box 10156, Gaithersburg MD 20898	240-631-7933	R	1*	<.1
1175	Slickfish Studios—Gordon Holman	408 Fore St Ste 5, Portland ME 04101	207-253-5557	R	1*	<.1
1176	Information Technology Solutions Inc—Robert Barnett	26415 212th Ave, Delhi IA 52223	563-922-3043	R	1*	<.1
1177	Straughn Computer Management Inc—Charles Straughn	PO Box 2546, Breckenridge CO 80424	863-666-9600	R	1*	<.1
1178	System Fabric Works Inc—Robert Pearson	9390 Res Blvd Ste Ii-4, Austin TX 78759	512-343-6101	R	1*	<.1
1179	Pj Doland Web Design Inc—P Doland	11591 Maple Ridge Rd, Reston VA 20190	202-265-1664	R	1*	<.1
1180	Eti Engineering Inc—Melvern Rushing	4219 Lafayette Ctr Dr, Chantilly VA 20151	703-318-7100	R	1*	<.1
1181	Martex Software Inc—Rusty Hancock	2201 Brookhollow 135, Arlington TX 76006	817-608-9511	R	1*	<.1
1182	Texas Cad Inc—R Dalton	527 Dow Ross Blvd, Duncanville TX 75116	972-296-6050	R	1*	<.1
1183	Comtech Network Systems Inc—Jeff Nagel	1320 Lincoln Ave Ste 4, Holbrook NY 11741	631-981-2694	R	1*	<.1
1184	Centella Consulting—John Woloshen	1916 Boothe Cir, Longwood FL 32750	407-398-0898	R	1*	<.1
1185	Corena USA Inc—Steen Hansen	40 Lake Bellevue Dr St, Bellevue WA 98005	425-643-7443	R	1*	<.1
1186	Bit By Bit Computing—Lance Smith	6951 Hickory Pl Ne, Minneapolis MN 55432	763-571-5088	R	1*	<.1
1187	Interactive Systems Worldwide Inc—Bernard Albanese	2 Andrews Dr 2nd Fl, West Paterson NJ 07424	973-256-8181	P	1	<.1
1188	VHGI Holdings Inc—Douglas P Martin	325 W Main St Ste 240, Lexington KY 40507	817-820-7080	P	1	<.1
1189	Riada Corp—Robin Adair	1101 Channelside Dr St, Tampa FL 33602	813-283-0075	R	1*	<.1
1190	Iba America LLC	6845 Shiloh Rd E Ste D, Alpharetta GA 30005	770-886-2318	R	1*	<.1
1191	Network Communications Group Inc—Robert Daniel	PO Box 1775, Colorado Springs CO 80901	719-520-5016	R	1*	<.1
1192	Program Automation Inc—Stan Simon	22706 Aspan St Ste 308, Lake Forest CA 92630	949-859-8200	R	1*	<.1
1193	Va Associates LLC—Virginia Callahan	8775 Cloudleap Ct Ste, Columbia MD 21045	410-872-0758	R	1*	<.1
1194	Micro Magic Inc—Terry Kraus	135 S Brooke St, Fond Du Lac WI 54935	920-929-9626	R	1*	<.1
1195	Modulus Data Systems Inc—George Liviakis	386 Main St Ste B, Redwood City CA 94063	650-365-3111	R	1*	<.1

Note: An asterisk (*) indicates an estimated financial figure. The company type code used is as follows: R = Private, P = Public, S = Private Subsidiary, B = Public Subsidiary, D = Division, J = Joint Venture, I = Investment Fund.

COMPANY RANKINGS BY SALES WITHIN 4-DIGIT SIC

Rank	Company Name—*Executive Officer*	Address, City, State, Zip	Phone	Type	Fin	Empls
1196	Plotter Pros Inc—*Peter Inshaw*	1068 The Alameda Frnt, San Jose CA 95126	408-299-0680	R	1*	<.1
1197	D Lawton Associates—*David Kahn*	17 Fox Hill Dr, Natick MA 01760	508-651-3112	R	<1*	<.1
1198	Brook Trout Technology Partners LLC—*Ann Kumpf*	2993 Wheatfield Rd, Finksburg MD 21048	410-499-1766	R	<1*	<.1
1199	Information Systems Laboratories Inc—*Jeff Nebeker*	2235 E 25th St Ste 100, Idaho Falls ID 83404	208-552-5727	R	<1*	<.1
1200	It Wizard Inc—*Praveen Annavarapu*	23035 Douglas Ct Ste 2, Sterling VA 20166	703-597-5167	R	<1*	<.1
1201	Systronix Inc—*Bruce Boyes*	939 Edison St, Salt Lake City UT 84111	801-534-1017	R	<1*	<.1
1202	Web Tech Services Inc—*Tammy Finch*	619 Taylor St, East Peoria IL 61611	309-699-2849	R	<1*	<.1
1203	Computer Network Technology Group Inc—*Ted Brandt*	6750 E Exposition Ave, Denver CO 80224	303-757-7181	R	<1*	<.1
1204	Microlaw Inc—*Ross Kodner*	2320 W Camden Rd, Milwaukee WI 53209	414-540-9433	R	<1*	<.1
1205	Solutions 2k LLC	6844 Pacific Ave, Stockton CA 95207	209-476-7100	R	<1*	<.1
1206	Adarose Inc—*George Holt*	1538 Vt Rte 66 Ste 220, Randolph VT 05060	802-728-9448	R	<1*	<.1
1207	Dot Bananatree Com—*Paul Mcvorn*	9228 Marysville Rd, Oregon House CA 95962	530-692-0800	R	<1*	<.1
1208	Dayton Scientific Inc—*Lamar Springer*	625 Nutt Rd, Dayton OH 45458	937-433-9600	R	<1*	<.1
1209	Sjs Cadd Inc—*Jon Howell*	4072 Us Hwy 62, Calvert City KY 42029	270-395-1851	R	<1*	<.1
1210	Sherwood Engineering Inc—*J Sherwood*	1268 S Ogden St, Denver CO 80210	303-722-2257	R	<1*	<.1
1211	Sign Systems Of Maine Inc—*Robert Verrier*	22 Free St Ste 303, Portland ME 04101	207-775-7110	R	<1*	<.1
1212	Accounting Machine—*Michael Mccormick*	1975 Drake Dr, Oakland CA 94611	510-339-3966	R	<1*	<.1
1213	American Syntactics Inc—*John Deim*	151 Weott Hts Rd Unit, Weott CA 95571	707-946-2443	R	<1*	<.1
1214	CAE Systems Inc—*Robert Slyh*	5909 W Lyn Haven Dr Se, Kentwood MI 49512	616-554-7900	R	<1*	<.1
1215	Dewitt Computer Technologies LLC—*Doug Smith*	1826 Hilltop Rd, Saint Joseph MI 49085	269-983-4011	R	<1*	<.1
1216	Jiku—*Hiroya Shirabe*	554 5th Ave Fl 3, New York NY 10036	212-869-3638	R	<1*	<.1
1217	Pro Bar Inc—*Robert Hobmann*	31324 Via Colinas Ste, Westlake Village CA 91362	818-707-2772	R	<1*	<.1
1218	Fluid Solutions Inc—*Thomas Nelson*	2650 NAPA Valley Corp, NAPA CA 94558	707-255-0123	R	<1*	<.1
1219	Pacific Power Systems Integration Inc—*Kytchener Whyte*	14729 Spring Ave, Santa Fe Springs CA 90670	562-281-0500	R	<1*	<.1
1220	Wyant Inc—*Thomas Wyant*	415 Munson Ave Ste 104, Traverse City MI 49686	231-946-5969	R	<1*	<.1
1221	Pro-Tech Controls Company Inc—*John Rizzolo*	332 Spider Lily Ln, Naples FL 34119	239-643-6596	R	<1*	<.1
1222	Netcast Media Corp—*Tom Nichols*	11104 W Airport Blvd S, Stafford TX 77477	281-564-4700	R	<1*	<.1
1223	Control Master Inc—*David Tomich*	PO Box 201129, Cleveland OH 44120	216-595-6990	R	<1*	<.1
1224	Grand Slam Designs—*Barb Geer*	655 2nd St N, Middle River MN 56737	218-222-3501	R	<1*	<.1
1225	Advanced Transportation Systems Inc—*Sam Powell*	PO Box 271027, Littleton CO 80127		R	<1*	<.1
1226	Gap Instrument Corp—*Lawrence Monahan*	244 Mill Rd, Yaphank NY 11980	631-924-1700	R	<1*	<.1
1227	iVoice Inc—*Jerome R Mahoney*	750 Hwy 34, Matawan NJ 07747	732-441-7700	P	<1	<.1
1228	Karisma Enterprises Inc—*Joseph Emington*	3483 Satellite Blvd St, Duluth GA 30096	770-446-0776	R	<1*	<.1
1229	Network Central—*Matthew Desario*	5617 Hollywood Blvd St, Los Angeles CA 90028	323-467-1336	R	<1*	<.1
1230	Octet Corp—*Tatiana Aleksa*	32 Broadway, New York NY 10004	212-475-6393	R	<1*	<.1
1231	Webspy USA Inc—*Jack Andrys*	137 7th Ave Ste 202, Kirkland WA 98033	425-828-4400	R	<1*	<.1
1232	SafeStitch Medical Inc—*Jeffrey P Spragens*	4400 Biscayne Blvd Ste, Miami FL 33137	305-575-4600	P	<1	<.1
1233	Mango Capital Inc—*Dennis Geott*	108 Village Sq Ste 315, Somers NY 10589	914-669-5333	P	<1	<.1
1234	Quest Business Systems Inc—*Thompson Elliott*	PO Box 715, Brentwood CA 94513	925-634-2670	R	<1*	<.1
1235	Accutech Tooling—*Paul Franklyn*	4367 Krystallee Dr, Muskegon MI 49442	231-767-2224	R	<1*	<.1
1236	Pdq PC Design Inc—*Kelly Wigington*	540 Edgewood Dr, Providence UT 84332	435-752-6796	R	<1*	<.1
1237	Benports Internetionel Inc—*Hector Benedi*	PO Box 43, Herndon VA 20172	703-742-6732	R	<1*	<.1
1238	JB Computer Consulting	80 Mariner Cir, Trumbull CT 06611	203-459-9132	R	<1	<.1
1239	Lans-R-Us—*Ron Thomas*	1358 Rawley Ridge Dr, Front Royal VA 22630	540-550-1061	R	<1	<.1
1240	Nuralnet Inc—*Vincent Isom*	14292 Foxhall Rd, Dowell MD 20629	703-598-1696	R	<1*	<.1
1241	openSynthesis	2667 170th Ave SE, Bellevue WA 98008	425-861-6700	R	<1	<.1
1242	Robocom Systems International Inc—*Irwin Balaban*	1111 Rte 110, Farmingdale NY 11735	631-753-2180	P	<1	N/A
1243	Chase Com Corp—*Herb Levitin*	2420 Selrose Ln, Santa Barbara CA 93109	805-963-4864	R	N/A	<.1
1244	Innovatek Microsystems Inc—*Dorothy Fitts*	349 Smithfield Rd, Millerton NY 12546	845-373-9003	R	N/A	<.1
1245	Luitporia Software Consultancy Inc—*Luna Bora*	3038 Lusitana Dr, Livermore CA 94550	925-606-5753	R	N/A	<.1
1246	OPtions Computer Consulting—*Tony Oppenheim*	2124 Edgehill Dr, Furlong PA 18925	215-794-8199	R	N/A	<.1

TOTALS: SIC 7373 Computer Integrated Systems Design
Companies: 1,246   108,416   515.2

7374 Data Processing & Preparation

Rank	Company Name—*Executive Officer*	Address, City, State, Zip	Phone	Type	Fin	Empls
1	First Data Corp—*Jonathan J Judge*	5565 Glenridge Connect, Atlanta GA 30342		S	10,380	24.5
2	Automatic Data Processing Inc—*Gary C Butler*	1 ADP Blvd, Roseland NJ 07068	973-974-5000	P	9,880	51.0
3	Affiliated Computer Services Inc—*Lynn R Blodgett*	2828 N Haskell, Dallas TX 75204	214-841-6111	S	6,523	74.0
4	SunGard Data Systems Inc—*Cristobal Conde*	680 E Swedesford Rd, Wayne PA 19087	484-582-2000	S	4,865	20.1
5	Fiserv Inc—*Wade Coleman*	PO Box 979, Brookfield WI 53008	262-879-5000	P	4,133	19.0
6	Dell Perot Systems—*Peter Altabef*	2300 W Plano Pky, Plano TX 75075	972-577-0000	S	2,779	23.1
7	Acxiom SDC Inc—*Rodger Kline* Acxiom Corp	PO Box 8180, Little Rock AR 72203	501-342-7799	S	2,310*	6.5
8	AOL Inc—*Tim Armstrong*	770 Broadway, New York NY 10003	212-652-6400	P	2,202	5.7
9	IMS Health Inc—*Ari Bousbib*	83 Wooster Heights Rd, Danbury CT 06810	203-448-4600	S	2,114*	7.0
10	Heartland Payment Systems Inc—*Robert O Carr*	90 Nassau St, Princeton NJ 08542	609-683-3831	P	1,997	2.7
11	First Data Resources Inc—*Michael D Capellas* First Data Corp	10825 Farnam Dr, Omaha NE 68154	402-777-3000	S	1,833*	6.0
12	Total System Services Inc—*Philip W Tomlinson*	PO Box 2567, Columbus GA 31902	706-649-2310	P	1,809	8.2
13	Ceridian Corp—*Stuart C Harvey Jr*	3311 E Old Shakopee Rd, Minneapolis MN 55425	952-853-8100	R	1,554*	8.8
14	Galileo International Inc—*Jeff Clarke*	Morris Corporate Cente, Parsippany NJ 07054	973-939-1000	S	1,494*	3.0
15	Verisk Analytics Inc—*Frank J Coyne*	545 Washington Blvd, Jersey City NJ 07310	201-469-3000	P	1,332	5.4
16	Acxiom Corp—*Scott Howe*	601 E 3rd St, Little Rock AR 72201	501-342-7799	P	1,160	6.6
17	ChoicePoint Inc—*Derek V Smith*	1000 Alderman Dr, Alpharetta GA 30005	770-752-6000	S	982*	5.0
18	Convergys Information Management Group—*Jeff Fox*	201 E 4th St, Cincinnati OH 45202	513-723-7000	S	748*	4.0
19	CSG Systems International Inc—*Peter E Kalan*	9555 Maroon Cir, Englewood CO 80112	303-796-2850	P	735	3.5
20	Alltel Information Services—*Roger Leitner*	13560 Morris Rd Ste 25, Alpharetta GA 30004	678-319-0199	R	663*	4.0
21	GPS Holding LP	10 Glen Lake Pkwy N Tw, Atlanta GA 30328	770-829-8000	S	619*	2.0
22	Healthserve LLC—*Jeff Loskowitz*	21 Fox St Ste 101, Poughkeepsie NY 12601	845-483-6706	R	547*	.1
23	TriZetto Group Inc—*Trace Devanny*	6061 S Willow Dr Ste 3, Denver CO 80111		R	533*	2.4
24	PSCU Financial Services Inc—*Mike Kelly*	560 Carillon Pkwy, Saint Petersburg FL 33716		R	487*	1.7
25	Arbitron Inc—*William T Kerr*	9705 Patuxent Woods Dr, Columbia MD 21046	410-312-8000	P	422	1.6
26	Macy's Systems and Technology—*Larry Lewark*	5985 State Bridge Rd, Duluth GA 30097	678-474-2000	S	388*	1.4
27	MedQuist Inc—*Roger L (Vern) Davenport*	9009 Carothers Pkwy St, Franklin TN 37067	615-798-6000	B	375	6.5
28	IC System Inc—*John Erickson*	PO Box 64444, Saint Paul MN 55164	651-483-8201	R	369*	1.1
29	Intersections Inc—*Michael R Stanfield*	PO Box 222455, Chantilly VA 20153	703-488-6100	P	364	.8
30	Boston Financial Data Services Inc—*Terry Metzger*	2000 Crown Colony Dr, Quincy MA 02169	617-483-7637	J	330*	2.0
31	Cable Services Group Inc—*Peter Kalan* CSG Systems International Inc	9555 Maroon Cir, Englewood CO 80112	303-796-2850	S	325*	1.8
32	Applied Card Systems—*Rocco Abessinio*	50 Applied Card Way, Glen Mills PA 19342	484-840-1700	S	317*	1.0

Rank	Company Name—*Executive Officer*	Address, City, State, Zip	Phone	Type	Fin	Empls
33	NetSpend Holdings Inc—*Daniel R Henry*	PO Box 2136, Austin TX 78768	512-532-8200	P	306	.5
34	CyberSource Corp—*Michael Walsh*	PO Box 8999, San Francisco CA 94128	650-432-7350	S	265	.1
35	RBS Lynk—*Wanda Darrah*	600 Morgan Falls Rd St, Atlanta GA 30350	770-396-1616	S	250*	1.3
36	InfoSpace Inc—*Willian J Ruckelshaus*	601 108th Ave NE Ste 1, Bellevue WA 98004	425-201-6100	P	247	.2
37	Intercept Inc	3150 Holcomb Bridge Rd, Norcross GA 30071	770-248-9600	S	206*	1.6
38	Vesta Corp—*Douglas M Fieldhouse*	11950 SW Garden Pl, Portland OR 97223	503-790-2500	R	190*	.6
39	Pegasus Solutions Inc—*Mike Kistner*	8350 N Central Expy St, Dallas TX 75206	214-234-4000	S	176*	1.0
40	Computer Services Inc—*Steven A Powless*	3901 Technology Dr, Paducah KY 42001		P	164	.9
41	iPass Inc—*Evan L Kaplan*	3800 Bridge Pky, Redwood City CA 94065	650-232-4100	P	156	.4
42	TSYS Debt Management—*Philip W Tomlinson* Total System Services Inc	PO Box 2567, Columbus GA 31902	706-644-6081	S	154*	.5
43	Incomm Holdings Inc—*M Brooks Smith*	250 Williams St Ste M-, Atlanta GA 30303		R	148*	.5
44	Genpact—*Frank Freeman*	PO Box 981077, El Paso TX 79998	915-225-2500	R	145*	2.5
45	CCRA International Reservation Center Inc	PO Box 7254, Fort Worth TX 76111	682-233-0909	S	143*	.5
46	Las Vegas Sports Consultants Inc—*Karol Lucan*	2575 S Highland Dr, Las Vegas NV 89109	702-361-2911	R	143*	<.1
47	APEX Data Services Inc—*Shashikant Gupta*	198 Van Buren St Ste 2, Herndon VA 20170	703-709-3000	R	138*	2.5
48	Accelerated Claims Processing Inc—*William Lucia*	401 Park Ave S, New York NY 10016	212-857-5000	S	138*	.6
49	Billing Services Group Ltd—*Gregory Mark Carter*	7411 John Smith Dr Ste, San Antonio TX 78229	210-949-7000	P	134	<.1
50	Merkle Direct Marketing Inc—*David Williams*	7001 Gateway Dr, Columbia MD 21046	443-542-4000	R	131*	.9
51	Carreker Corp—*John Carreker Jr*	4055 Valley View Ln, Dallas TX 75244	972-458-1981	R	120*	.5
52	Billscom Inc—*Brad Stroh*	1875 S Grant St Ste 40, San Mateo CA 94402		S	106	.6
53	Epocrates Inc—*Peter Brandt*	1100 Park Pl Ste 300, San Mateo CA 94403	650-227-1700	P	104	.3
54	Productive Data Systems—*Tom Sweetman*	7935 E Prentice Ave St, Greenwood Village CO 80111	303-220-7165	R	102*	.5
55	Nexxus Marketing Group LLC—*James Rao*	PO Box 2069, Danvers MA 01923	978-762-3900	R	102*	<.1
56	Specialized Loan Servicing LLC—*John Beggins*	PO Box 636005, Littleton CO 80163		S	100*	.3
57	Data2logistics LLC—*Gerry Burns*	4310 Metro Pky, Fort Myers FL 33916	239-936-2800	S	99*	.3
58	Questar InfoComm Inc	PO Box 45433, Salt Lake City UT 84145	801-324-5856	S	89*	.3
59	Ryzex Group—*Lorne Rubis*	4600 Ryzex Way, Bellingham WA 98226		R	87*	.3
60	Sunrise International Leasing Corp—*Peter King*	3001 Broadway St NE St, Minneapolis MN 55413		R	86*	.1
61	Aptara Inc—*Dev Ganesan*	3110 Fairview Park Dr, Falls Church VA 22042	703-352-0001	R	78*	4.5
62	Netsmart Technologies Inc—*Michael Valentine*	3500 Sunrise Hwy Ste D, Great River NY 11739	631-968-2000	R	70*	.4
63	CBSInteractive—*Michael Levy*	2200 W Cypress Rd, Fort Lauderdale FL 33309	954-489-4000	S	66*	.3
64	Epiq Systems (Portland Oregon)—*Tom Olofson*	10300 SW Allen Blvd, Beaverton OR 97005	503-350-5800	S	66*	.2
65	PM Liquidating Corp—*John Lettko*	1854 Shackleford Ct St, Norcross GA 30093	770-806-9918	R	66	.3
66	Innodata Isogen Inc—*Jack Abuhoff*	3 University Plz, Hackensack NJ 07601	201-371-8000	P	62	5.1
67	Gelco Information Network Inc	10700 Prairie Lakes Dr, Eden Prairie MN 55344	952-947-1500	S	59*	.4
68	Kroll Factual Data Inc—*Rod Bazzani*	5200 Hahns Peak Dr Ste, Loveland CO 80538	970-663-5700	S	58*	.3
69	Caelum Research Corp—*Diana Yeh*	1700 Research Blvd Ste, Rockville MD 20850	301-424-8205	R	58*	.2
70	Student Advantage Inc—*Shawn McCarthy*	280 Summer St, Boston MA 02210	617-912-2011	S	57	.3
71	Financial Services Inc—*Jack Schunke*	21 Harristown Rd, Glen Rock NJ 07452	201-652-6000	R	57*	.2
72	PRWT Services Inc—*Harold Epps*	1835 Market St Ste 800, Philadelphia PA 19103	215-569-8810	R	56*	.7
73	CSC Business Services—*Michael Laphen*	200 W Cesar Chavez, Austin TX 78701	469-499-8000	R	55*	.6
74	BNY Mellon Distributors Holdings Inc—*Steve Wynn*	301 Bellevue Pkwy, Wilmington DE 19809	302-791-2000	S	53*	4.4
75	Kleinschmidt Inc—*Harry Gaples*	450 Lake Cook Rd, Deerfield IL 60015	847-945-1000	R	48*	.1
76	Secured Digital Applications Inc—*Kamaruddin Dujang*	230 Park Ave 10th Fl, New York NY 10169	212-551-1747	S	48	<.1
77	LookSmart Ltd—*Jean-Yves Dexmier*	55 2nd St Ste 700, San Francisco CA 94105	415-348-7000	P	48	.1
78	Capario—*Jim Riley*	1901 E Alton Ste 100, Santa Ana CA 92705	949-852-3400	S	47*	.2
79	Workforce Software Inc—*Kevin Choksi*	38705 7 Mile Rd Ste 30, Livonia MI 48152	734-542-4100	R	45*	.2
80	Pro-Health Systems Inc Sandata Technologies Inc	26 Harbor Park Dr, Port Washington NY 11050	516-484-4400	S	44*	.2
81	IGN Entertainment Inc—*Mark A Jung*	625 2nd St 3rd Fl, San Francisco CA 94107	415-508-2000	S	43	.4
82	ProBusiness Services Inc—*Arthur F Weinbach* Automatic Data Processing Inc	4125 Hopyard Rd, Pleasanton CA 94588	925-737-3500	S	42*	.3
83	Data-Tronics Corp—*David Cogswell*	PO Box 10048, Fort Smith AR 72917	479-784-8400	S	41*	.3
84	Fiserv EFT Div—*Leslie Muma* Fiserv Inc	4550 SW MacAdam Ave, Portland OR 97239	503-224-9110	D	40*	.2
85	Evolution Benefits Inc—*Bob Patricelli*	22 Waterville Rd, Avon CT 06001	860-678-3400	S	37*	.1
86	Discovery Research Group Of Utah Inc—*Alison Castro*	6975 Union Park Ctr St, Midvale UT 84047	801-569-0107	R	36*	.6
87	Dice Inc—*Scot W Melland*	3 Park Ave 33rd Fl, New York NY 10016	212-725-6550	R	35*	.2
88	Input 1 LLC—*Todd B Greenbaum*	21820 Burbank Blvd, Woodland Hills CA 91367	818-713-2203	R	34*	.1
89	Life Quotes Inc—*Robert S Bland*	8205 S Cass Ave, Darien IL 60561	630-515-0170	R	33	.1
90	TSYS Acquiring Solutions Total System Services Inc	8320 S Hardy Dr, Tempe AZ 85284	480-333-7600	S	33*	.1
91	Centennial Bank—*Randy Simms*	PO Box 966, Conway AR 72033	501-328-4600	R	32*	.2
92	Sandsport Data Services Inc—*Harold S Blue* Sandata Technologies Inc	26 Harbor Park Dr, Port Washington NY 11050	516-484-4400	S	31*	.1
93	Standard Data Corp—*Tony Andretta*	26 Journal Sq, Jersey City NJ 07306	201-533-4433	R	29*	.1
94	Configuration Management Inc—*Zoraida Anderson*	100 Matawan Rd Ste 120, Matawan NJ 07747	732-450-1100	R	29*	.2
95	Arista Information Systems Inc—*Ron Camp*	2220 Northmont Pkwy St, Duluth GA 30096	678-473-1885	R	25*	.1
96	Geokinetics Processing Inc—*Richard Miles*	1500 CityWest Blvd Ste, Houston TX 77042	713-782-1234	S	24*	.1
97	Reservation Center Inc—*Richard Marxen*	29219 Canwood St Ste 1, Agoura Hills CA 91301	818-575-4300	R	23*	.1
98	Enalasys Corp—*Eric Taylor*	250 Avenida Campillo, Calexico CA 92231		R	23*	<.1
99	Cybrix Group Inc—*Tim Jones*	312 E 7th Ave, Tampa FL 33602	813-630-2744	R	22	<.1
100	Datagraphic Computer Services Inc—*Robert Silver*	6829 Lankershin Blvd, North Hollywood CA 91605	818-982-6423	R	22*	.1
101	First Community Services-Texas Inc—*Dave Epke*	4400 Swanner Loop, Killeen TX 76543	254-690-5185	R	21*	.2
102	Rising Medical Solutions Inc—*Jason Beans*	325 N La Salle Dr Ste, Chicago IL 60654	312-559-8445	R	20*	.2
103	First Health Services Corp—*Teresa DiMarco*	4300 Cox Rd, Glen Allen VA 23060	804-965-7400	S	20*	1.0
104	Verifi Inc—*Mathew Katz*	8391 Beverly Blvd Ste, Los Angeles CA 90048	323-655-5789	R	20*	.1
105	Sanrise Inc—*David Schneider*	7950 Dublin Blvd Ste 1, Dublin CA 94568	925-560-3900	R	20*	.2
106	Compushare Inc—*Romir Bosu*	3 Hutton Cntre Dr Ste, Santa Ana CA 92707	714-427-1000	R	20*	.1
107	Marketing Software Company A California Corp—*Larry Sacks*	6200 Canoga Ave Ste 10, Woodland Hills CA 91367	818-346-1600	R	19*	<.1
108	Powertek Corp—*Nancy Scott*	9420 Key W Ave Ste 210, Rockville MD 20850	301-795-0413	R	19*	.1
109	Microdynamics Corp—*Thomas Harter*	1400 Shore Rd, Naperville IL 60563	630-527-8400	R	19*	.2
110	Z57 Inc—*Steve Weber*	8445 Camino Santa Fe S, San Diego CA 92121	858-623-5577	R	18*	.2
111	Array Information Technology Inc—*Brian Leung*	7474 Greenway Center D, Greenbelt MD 20770	301-345-8188	R	18*	.1
112	Realmed Corp—*Philip Christianson*	510 E 96th St Ste 400, Indianapolis IN 46240	317-580-0658	R	17*	.1
113	GalleryWatchcom Inc—*Betty Otter-Nickerson*	50 F St Ste 700, Washington DC 20001	202-248-5300	R	16*	.1
114	ISTS Worldwide Inc—*Viren Rana*	39300 Civic Ctr Dr Ste, Fremont CA 94538	510-794-1400	R	15*	.3
115	Sandata Technologies Inc—*Herold Blue*	26 Harbor Park Dr, Port Washington NY 11050	516-484-4400	R	15*	.1

Note: An asterisk (*) indicates an estimated financial figure. The company type code used is as follows: R = Private, P = Public, S = Private Subsidiary, B = Public Subsidiary, D = Division, J = Joint Venture, I = Investment Fund.

COMPANY RANKINGS BY SALES WITHIN 4-DIGIT SIC

Rank	Company Name—*Executive Officer*	Address, City, State, Zip	Phone	Type	Fin	Empls
116	IMS Health Finance Ltd IMS Health Inc	83 Wooster Heights Rd, Danbury CT 06810	203-448-4600	S	15*	<.1
117	Image Api Inc—*Richard Griffith*	2670 W Executive Ctr C, Tallahassee FL 32301	850-222-1400	R	15*	.2
118	Viewpointe Archive Services LLC—*Lou Buglioli*	227 W Trade St Ste 200, Charlotte NC 28202	704-602-6650	R	14*	.1
119	Coordinated Management Systems Inc IMS Health Inc	83 Wooster Heights Rd, Danbury CT 06810	203-448-4600	S	14*	<.1
120	Enterprise Associates LLC IMS Health Inc	83 Wooster Heights Rd, Danbury CT 06810	203-448-4600	S	14*	<.1
121	IMS Health Licensing Associates LP—*Dave Carlucci* IMS Health Inc	901 Main Ave Ste 612, Norwalk CT 06851	203-845-5200	S	14*	<.1
122	Mailing House Inc—*David Willock*	5600 Bandini Blvd, Bell CA 90201	323-262-6000	R	13*	.1
123	DPF Data Services Group Inc—*John Walters*	1990 Swarthmore Ave, Lakewood NJ 08701	732-370-8840	R	13*	.1
124	Boloto Group Inc—*Robert Donnelli*	7373 E Doubletree Ranc, Scottsdale AZ 85258	480-281-1613	R	12*	.1
125	Cricket Technologies—*Arthur C Blades*	12310 Pinecrest Rd, Reston VA 20191	703-391-1020	R	12*	<.1
126	Provena Health—*Guy Wiebking*	19065 Hickory Creek Dr, Mokena IL 60448	708-478-6300	R	12*	.1
127	XyberNET Inc	10640 Scripps Ranch Bl, San Diego CA 92131	858-530-1900	R	11*	.1
128	Park City Group Inc—*Randall K Fields*	3160 Pinebrook Rd, Park City UT 84098	435-645-2000	P	11	.1
129	IDP Inc—*Bob Blitshtein*	PO Box 137, Wyncote PA 19095	215-885-2150	R	10*	.1
130	Hotspot Fxi Inc—*John H Eley*	545 Washington Blvd, Jersey City NJ 07310	212-209-1420	R	10*	<.1
131	Internet Advancement Inc—*Ken Committe*	11601 Willows Rd Ne, Redmond WA 98052	425-882-8838	R	9*	.1
132	LeadQual LLC—*Andrew Coleman*	6001 Shellmound St Ste, Emeryville CA 94608	510-653-3000	R	9*	.1
133	CFC Data Corp—*David B Ramaker*	127 Townsend St, Midland MI 48640	989-839-5375	S	9*	.1
134	Klik Technologies Corp—*Jonathan Gustave*	4 N Main St, Spring Valley NY 10977	845-573-0900	R	9*	.1
135	Integrated Marketing Technologies Inc—*Jeff Wood*	2945 Carquest Dr, Brunswick OH 44212	330-225-3550	R	9*	.1
136	Syphermedia International Inc—*Dennis Flaharty*	5455 Garden Grove Blvd, Westminster CA 92683	714-895-8801	R	9*	<.1
137	Laducer And Associates Inc—*James Laducer*	201 Missouri Dr, Mandan ND 58554	701-667-1980	R	8*	.2
138	Cdsnet Soft Inc—*Jon Park*	6053 W Century Blvd St, Los Angeles CA 90045	213-427-2000	R	8*	.1
139	Intelligent Mobile Solutions Inc—*Eduardo Kawas*	6303 Blue Lagoon Dr St, Miami FL 33126	786-866-8054	R	8	.3
140	Electronic Ink Inc—*Harold Hambrose*	1 S Broad St, Philadelphia PA 19107	215-922-3800	R	8*	.1
141	Ballista Securities LLC—*Todd Kenney*	875 3rd Ave 29th Fl, New York NY 10022		R	8*	<.1
142	Genesee Survey Services Inc—*Gary P Gleason*	3136 Winton Rd S, Rochester NY 14623	585-272-9944	R	8*	<.1
143	Identec Solutions Inc—*Gerhard Schedler*	5057 Keller Springs Rd, Addison TX 75001	972-535-4144	R	8*	<.1
144	LocatePLUS Holdings Corp—*Kenneth Kaiser*	100 Cummings Ctr Ste 2, Beverly MA 01915		P	8*	<.1
145	Esc Inc—*Maggie Harris*	8201 Corp Dr Ste 1105, Landover MD 20785	301-577-0056	R	8*	.1
146	Document Processing Solutions Inc—*Felipe Heras*	590 W Lambert Rd, Brea CA 92821	562-929-3311	R	8*	.1
147	US Dataworks Inc—*Charles E Ramey*	1 Sugar Creek Center B, Sugar Land TX 77478	281-504-8000	P	7	<.1
148	Neoscape Inc—*Robert Macleod*	330 Congress St Fl 3, Boston MA 02210	617-345-0330	R	7*	<.1
149	Renkim Corp—*Robert Swearingen*	13333 Allen Rd, Southgate MI 48195	734-374-8300	R	7*	.2
150	Avalon International Inc—*Seth Narayanan*	3550 Engineering Dr St, Norcross GA 30092	770-740-2211	S	7*	<.1
151	Teledraft Inc—*Al Slaten*	4625 S Wendler Dr Ste, Tempe AZ 85282	602-454-9575	R	7*	<.1
152	Dallas Data Processing Services Inc—*Sam Hocking*	4849 Greenville Ave St, Dallas TX 75206	214-638-2514	R	7	<.1
153	HSW International Inc—*Gregory Swayne*	6 Concourse Pkwy Ste 1, Atlanta GA 30328	404-926-0660	P	7	.1
154	Professional Data Dimensions Inc—*Wayne Patrick*	200 S Meridian St Ste, Indianapolis IN 46225	317-636-7355	R	7*	.1
155	Bma Management Support Corp—*Gary Matern*	2151 S 3600 W, Salt Lake City UT 84119	801-978-0200	R	6*	.1
156	Wts Inc—*Thomas Hughes*	1100 Olive Way Ste 110, Seattle WA 98101	206-436-3306	R	6*	.1
157	APR Consulting Inc—*Erlinda R Stone*	22632 Golden Springs D, Diamond Bar CA 91765	909-396-5375	R	6*	.1
158	Triangle Reprographics Inc—*Roger Garner*	850 S Hughey Ave, Orlando FL 32801	407-843-1492	R	6*	.1
159	Voip Carriers Inc—*Marc Lewis*	231 Jebavy Rd, Ludington MI 49431	616-855-2451	R	6*	.1
160	Conversion Technologies International Inc—*Yale Epstein*	7000 Atrium Way Ste 2, Mount Laurel NJ 08054	856-722-5588	R	6*	.1
161	Vaiilant Communication Inc—*Anthony Petraco*	110 Crossways Park Dr, Woodbury NY 11797	516-390-1100	R	6*	.1
162	Emphusion—*David Herron*	353 Sacramento St Ste, San Francisco CA 94111	415-776-0660	R	6*	<.1
163	Swift Technologiescom Inc—*Charles Walker*	2636 Walnut Hill Ln St, Dallas TX 75229	214-350-8202	R	6*	<.1
164	Aamonte Inc—*Steven Elefant*	PO Box 14363, Palm Desert CA 92255	760-776-4888	R	6*	<.1
165	NGH Enterprises LLC—*Michael Freckleton*	110 Broadway St Ste 19, San Antonio TX 78205	210-527-1390	R	5*	<.1
166	Pioneer Marketing Research Inc—*William Tyner*	3725 Da Vinci Ct Ste 3, Norcross GA 30092	770-455-0114	R	5*	.1
167	Diagnostic Imaging Associates—*Peter Ricci*	10700 E Geddes Ave Ste, Englewood CO 80112	303-761-9190	R	5*	<.1
168	Data Input Services Inc—*John Dion*	1720 28th St Ste A, West Des Moines IA 50266	515-256-4792	R	5	.4
169	Recom Technologies Inc—*Calbert Lai*	809 Cuesta Dr Ste B212, Mountain View CA 94040	650-966-1150	R	5*	<.1
170	Infovision 21 Inc—*Bapaiah Koneru*	6077 Frantz Rd Ste 105, Dublin OH 43017	614-761-8844	R	5*	<.1
171	AgriTech Analytics—*John M Meyer*	5545 Avenida de los Ro, Visalia CA 93291	559-738-5300	S	5*	<.1
172	Sitestar Corp—*Frank Erhartic Jr*	7109 Timberlake Rd, Lynchburg VA 24502	434-239-4272	P	5	<.1
173	Sweet Data Concepts—*Colby Harmon*	2301 W Anderson Ln, Austin TX 78757	512-458-9922	R	5*	<.1
174	Complex Litigation Integrators Inc	44 Gilbert St W, Tinton Falls NJ 07701		R	5*	<.1
175	Construction Resources Management Inc—*Kurt Bechthold*	PO Box 1632, Waukesha WI 53187	262-524-1717	R	5*	.1
176	Apple Valley Secretarial Service Inc—*Fran Greenfield*	7275 147th St W Ste 10, Saint Paul MN 55124	952-432-3467	R	5*	.1
177	Lake Data Center Inc—*Tony Saranita*	800 Lloyd Rd, Wickliffe OH 44092	440-944-2020	R	5*	.1
178	Universal Image Productions Inc—*Richard Gagnon*	20750 Civic Ctr Dr Ste, Southfield MI 48076	248-357-4160	R	5*	<.1
179	Lunar Cow Design Inc—*Ben Harris*	120 E Mill St Ste 415, Akron OH 44308	330-836-0911	R	5*	.1
180	Reality Systems LLC	2061 Exchange Dr, Saint Charles MO 63303	636-699-4063	R	5*	.1
181	Reliable Elections Systems Inc—*Robyn Ceppos*	2255 Centre Ave Ste 10, Bellmore NY 11710	516-679-1200	R	5*	.1
182	Nextcorp Ltd—*David Greer*	7701 Las Colinas Rdg, Irving TX 75063	214-574-6398	R	5*	<.1
183	BulbsCom Inc—*Michael Connors*	243 Stafford St, Worcester MA 01603	508-363-2800	R	4*	<.1
184	Document Imaging Systems Corp—*Bonnie Bodkin*	1717 Olive St Fl 3, Saint Louis MO 63103	314-436-2800	R	4*	.1
185	Tusker Group LLC—*Lakshmi Keshav*	100 Congress Ave Ste 2, Austin TX 78701	512-347-8812	R	4*	.1
186	Thinkgate LLC—*Eric Waynick*	PO Box 597, Woodstock GA 30188	678-480-3328	R	4*	<.1
187	Impact Technology Inc—*Randy Mechels*	608 7th St Ne, Long Prairie MN 56347	320-732-4900	R	4*	<.1
188	Payscape Advisors—*Leo Welf*	729 Lambert Dr, Atlanta GA 30324	404-350-6565	R	4*	<.1
189	Account Management Resources Inc—*Joseph Berardi*	3443 N Central Ave Ste, Phoenix AZ 85012	602-954-6554	R	4*	.1
190	Digital Pond—*Peter Hogg*	88 Arkansas St, San Francisco CA 94107	415-216-8200	R	4*	<.1
191	Fulcrum Analytics—*Richard Vermillion*	70 W 40th St 10th Fl, New York NY 10018	212-651-7000	R	4*	<.1
192	Acumen Data Systems Inc—*Ed Squires Sr*	2223 Westfield St, West Springfield MA 01089	413-737-4800	R	4*	.1
193	Incorporatetimecom Inc—*K Welsh*	173 N Main St Ste 400, Sayville NY 11782		R	4*	<.1
194	FullNet Inc FullNet Communications Inc	201 Robert S Kerr Ave, Oklahoma City OK 73102	405-236-8200	S	4*	<.1
195	AMB Enterprises Inc—*Ann Bundarin*	PO Box 398, Sunland CA 91041	818-353-7195	R	4*	<.1
196	Intercasting Corp—*Shawn Conahan*	5960 Cornerstone Ct W, San Diego CA 92121	858-450-4221	R	4*	.1
197	Data Shop Inc—*Gerald Machkovech*	1230 Plainfield Ave, Janesville WI 53545	608-752-2580	R	4*	.1
198	C3 Premedia Solutions Inc—*Alayne Jurgens*	2900 Gateway Dr Ste 60, Irving TX 75063	972-550-0600	R	4*	<.1
199	Direct Marketing Excellence Inc—*James Kennel*	10499 Bradford Rd, Littleton CO 80127	303-339-9300	R	4*	.1
200	Accesso LLC—*Stephen K Brown*	300 Colonial Center Pk, Lake Mary FL 32746	407-333-7311	R	4	N/A

Rank	Company Name—*Executive Officer*	Address, City, State, Zip	Phone	Type	Fin	Empls
201	Zekiah Technologies Inc—*Brianna Bowling*	103 Centennial St Ste, La Plata MD 20646	301-392-3788	R	4*	<.1
202	Bytemanagers Inc—*Sanjay Agarwal*	800 W Huron St Ste 200, Chicago IL 60642	312-243-1140	R	4*	.1
203	Mark Doman—*Mark Doman*	621 17th St N, Sartell MN 56377	320-203-9004	R	4*	.1
204	First Step Internet LLC—*Donna Latimer*	PO Box 9587, Moscow ID 83843	208-882-8869	R	4*	<.1
205	Fpl Services—*Joseph Sigler*	3539 Hampton Rd, Oceanside NY 11572	516-763-2000	R	4*	<.1
206	Revere Graphics Inc—*Richard Smith*	726 Se Grand Ave, Portland OR 97214	503-239-6098	R	4*	<.1
207	Campaign Mail and Data Inc—*John Simms*	7704 Leesburg Pke Ste, Falls Church VA 22043	703-790-8676	R	3*	<.1
208	Chesapeake Document Services LLC	PO Box 861, Waldorf MD 20604	301-870-1956	R	3*	<.1
209	Via Networks USA—*Patrick Gaul*	15 Piedmont Center Ne, Atlanta GA 30305	404-949-1057	R	3*	<.1
210	Razvi Inc—*Asad Razvi*	12657 Alcosta Blvd Ste, San Ramon CA 94583	925-242-1200	R	3*	<.1
211	Acsel Corp—*Phillip Redmond*	2876 Guardian Ln Ste 2, Virginia Beach VA 23452	757-463-5240	R	3*	<.1
212	Sonic Media Solutions Inc—*Gurvinder Bindra*	30 Bloomington St, Medford NY 11763	516-840-3660	R	3*	<.1
213	Ecommercepartners—*Gil Levy*	57 Franklin St, New York NY 10013	212-334-3390	R	3*	.1
214	Teledata Communications Inc—*William Nass*	185 Commerce Dr Ste 30, Hauppauge NY 11788	631-231-6700	R	3*	<.1
215	CW Mars Inc—*Tamson Ely*	67 Millbrook St Ste 20, Worcester MA 01606	508-755-3323	R	3*	<.1
216	Docs Etc Inc—*Laurence Abrams*	1010 Lamar St Ste Pl40, Houston TX 77002	713-658-1175	R	3*	<.1
217	Data Entry Company Inc—*G Maurice DuFour*	4920 Elm St Ste 200, Bethesda MD 20814	301-718-0703	R	3*	.2
218	Product Reports Inc—*Sheldon Manheim*	650 Wantagh Ave Ste 1, Levittown NY 11756	516-520-0000	R	3*	.1
219	Data Conversion Laboratory—*Mark Gross*	61-18 190th St 2nd Fl, Fresh Meadows NY 11365	718-357-8700	R	3*	<.1
220	Phoenix Legal LLC—*Bill Rioux*	901 South Mopac Barton, Austin TX 78746	512-327-0963	R	3*	<.1
221	Voxel Dot Net Inc—*Raul Martynek*	29 Broadway Fl 30, New York NY 10006	212-812-4190	R	3*	<.1
222	Push Media Group Inc—*Bob Holmes*	206 5th Ave Fl 2, New York NY 10010	212-353-1188	R	3*	<.1
223	Excel Technical Services Inc—*Bob Langieri*	30100 Town Ctr Dr Ste, Laguna Niguel CA 92677	949-240-0438	R	3*	<.1
224	AmpliFind Music Services Inc—*Andrew Stess*	11 Petaluma Blvd N Ste, Petaluma CA 94952	415-367-3566	R	3*	<.1
225	ToolWorx Information Products Inc—*Brad Oyster*	7994 Grand River Rd, Brighton MI 48114	810-220-5115	R	3*	<.1
226	Western Micro Services Inc—*Linda J Smith*	PO Box 1552, Bellevue WA 98009	425-451-9522	R	3*	<.1
227	Accudata Computer Services Inc—*Neil Khot*	25 Carlinville Plz, Carlinville IL 62626	217-854-3158	R	3*	<.1
228	First Banking Services Of The South Inc—*J Beasley*	15 Eglin Pkwy Ne, Fort Walton Beach FL 32548	850-796-2200	R	3*	<.1
229	Jetcommerce—*Adrine Sahakian*	6021 Etiwanda Ave, Tarzana CA 91356	818-705-1485	R	3*	<.1
230	Computer Systems LLC—*Gregory Graan*	PO Box 557, Shawano WI 54166	715-526-6125	R	3*	<.1
231	Natural Wireless LLC	23a Poplar St, East Rutherford NJ 07073	201-438-2865	R	3*	<.1
232	Compucorp Of South Florida—*Debbie Woerner*	2699 Stirling Rd Ste A, Fort Lauderdale FL 33312	954-966-2766	R	3*	.1
233	Technical Programming Services Inc—*Atef Iskander*	5544 S 104th E Ave, Tulsa OK 74146	918-254-9622	R	3*	<.1
234	Creata Vivendi Inc—*Randy Schrum*	PO Box 7343, York PA 17404	717-764-3911	R	3*	<.1
235	Dataflow Services—*Jeffery Wiggins*	15851 Dallas Pkwy Ste, Addison TX 75001	972-239-2571	R	3*	<.1
236	Ms Data Service Corp—*Maria Shores*	18 Richmond Hl, Laguna Niguel CA 92677	949-475-1430	R	3*	<.1
237	Data Center Inc—*Tim Tribble*	PO Box 368, Yadkinville NC 27055	336-463-1800	R	3*	<.1
238	Plot Multimedia Developers LLC—*Lise Berman*	222 E 44th St Fl 8, New York NY 10017	212-450-7900	R	3*	<.1
239	Team Tsi Corp	PO Box 1547, Albertville AL 35950	256-878-2132	R	2*	<.1
240	Atomic Playpen Inc—*Troy Venjohn*	701 Xenia Ave S Ste 20, Minneapolis MN 55416	763-231-3400	R	2*	<.1
241	Business Systems Processing Inc—*Evan Domingo*	7665 Redwood Blvd Ste, Novato CA 94945	415-878-2990	R	2*	<.1
242	Creative Alliance Inc—*Christophor Burke*	231 Arlington Ave, Clifton NJ 07011	212-461-1744	R	2*	<.1
243	Oliver Group LLC—*Debra Gluszczak*	595 Greenhaven Rd, Pawcatuck CT 06379	860-599-9700	R	2*	<.1
244	Groupee Inc—*Edward O'neill*	1904 3rd Ave Ste 525, Seattle WA 98101	206-283-5999	R	2*	<.1
245	Lorton Data Inc—*Ray Davey*	2 Pine Tree Dr, Saint Paul MN 55112	612-362-0200	R	2*	<.1
246	Information Data Services Inc—*Gary Abernathy*	1906 Swift Ave, Kansas City MO 64116	816-842-2611	R	2*	<.1
247	Systems Methodologies Inc—*Daniel Roth*	169 Maple Ave, Red Bank NJ 07701	732-842-2772	R	2*	<.1
248	Annapolis Technologies LLC	1100 Wicomico St Ste 5, Baltimore MD 21230	410-385-1892	R	2*	<.1
249	Megagate Broadband Inc—*Kevin Pack*	6184 U S Hwy 98 Ste 20, Hattiesburg MS 39402	601-450-5000	R	2*	<.1
250	Tierpoint LLC—*Nicki Kopelson*	23403 E Mission Ave, Liberty Lake WA 99019	509-688-2555	R	2*	<.1
251	Shirley Oberg Services—*Kari Morgan*	8607 219th St Se Ste N, Woodinville WA 98072	425-885-2221	R	2*	<.1
252	Geo Center Inc—*Sukhdev Hyare*	16800 Greenspoint Park, Houston TX 77060	281-443-8150	R	2*	<.1
253	A3 It Solutions LLC—*Jeff Lang*	338 N Elm St Ste 410, Greensboro NC 27401	336-389-1101	R	2*	<.1
254	Business Solution Providers—*Shirley Johnson*	44 Joshua Trl, Madison CT 06443	203-421-4287	R	2*	<.1
255	Identrust Services LLC—*Don Johnson*	PO Box 77186, San Francisco CA 94107	801-326-5400	R	2*	<.1
256	Novapointe LLC—*Adrienne Gioeli*	2060 E Francis St, Ontario CA 91761	909-947-2710	R	2*	<.1
257	Get Real Interactive—*Jeffrey Karlovitch*	PO Box 405, Kenilworth NJ 07033	908-497-0033	R	2*	<.1
258	Richa Inc—*Rita Vyas*	204 N Tryon St, Charlotte NC 28202	704-331-9744	R	2*	<.1
259	Infocon Corp—*Richard Bouch*	PO Box 568, Ebensburg PA 15931	814-472-6066	R	2*	<.1
260	Pipeline Interactive Inc—*Dennis Miller*	941 Cumberland St, Lebanon PA 17042	717-273-5665	R	2*	<.1
261	Accuimage LLC—*Tom Beasley*	2807 Biloxi Ave, Nashville TN 37204	615-242-7226	R	2*	<.1
262	H 4 Development LLC	12555 Biscayne Blvd St, North Miami FL 33181	305-893-6136	R	2*	<.1
263	Advanced Data Transcribing Center Inc—*Patty Kwan*	PO Box 1146, Rosemead CA 91770	626-571-1570	R	2*	.1
264	Rainbow Networking—*Anthony Chie*	688 Matsonia Dr, Foster City CA 94404	650-377-0913	R	2*	.1
265	Electronic Decontamination Specialists—*Mark Jensen*	13081 Minuteman Dr, Draper UT 84020	801-553-1087	R	2*	<.1
266	Automatic Funds Transfer Services Inc—*Eric Johnson*	PO Box 34108, Seattle WA 98124	206-254-0975	R	2*	<.1
267	Club Billing Services Inc—*Cathy Lowe*	PO Box 612563, Dallas TX 75261	972-756-9100	R	2*	<.1
268	Core Communications—*Ed Rattig*	PO Box 818, Corvallis OR 97339	541-758-0755	R	2*	<.1
269	Lazo Technologies Ltd—*Tom Lazo*	611 W Mockingbird Ln, Dallas TX 75247	214-652-9898	R	2*	<.1
270	Matrix Group International Inc—*Joanna Pineda*	2711 Jefferson Davis H, Arlington VA 22202	703-838-9777	R	2*	<.1
271	Netniques Corp—*Miguel Cardoso*	6175 Nw 167th St Ste G, Hialeah FL 33015	305-823-3803	R	2*	<.1
272	Eagle Data—*Judith Boyung*	7163 123rd Cir, Largo FL 33773	727-572-6200	R	2*	<.1
273	Internet Texoma Inc—*Larry Vaden*	PO Box 2543, Sherman TX 75091	903-813-4500	R	2*	<.1
274	Delphi Communications—*Alex Majthenyi*	36 Garth Rd, Scarsdale NY 10583	914-725-8000	R	2*	<.1
275	Montgomery Data Services Inc—*David Grigg*	355 Bilhen St, Troy NC 27371	910-572-3791	S	2*	<.1
276	Cace Technologies Inc—*Jerry Kennelly*	1949 5th St Ste 103, Davis CA 95616	530-758-2790	R	2*	<.1
277	Eds Corp	5400 Chevrolet Blvd, Cleveland OH 44130	216-265-5532	R	2*	<.1
278	Brown's Data Processing Service Center—*Wayne Brown*	PO Box 728, Woodstock IL 60098	815-338-1200	R	2*	<.1
279	Horan Data Services Inc	150 E 4th St, Cincinnati OH 45202	513-241-2382	R	2*	<.1
280	Managed Care Systems Inc—*Dan Beal*	32531 N Scottsdale Rd, Scottsdale AZ 85266	623-434-3881	R	2*	<.1
281	Nasuni Corp—*Andres Rodriguez*	313 Speen St, Natick MA 01760	508-651-0580	R	2*	<.1
282	Practicelink Ltd—*Ken Allman*	PO Box 100, Hinton WV 25951	304-466-5046	R	2*	<.1
283	Chase Agri Credit Systems Inc—*Lavern Boese*	PO Box 405, Chase KS 67524	620-938-2946	R	2*	<.1
284	Capital Graphics Inc—*Don Walters*	305 Se 17th St Ste C, Topeka KS 66607	785-233-6677	R	2*	<.1
285	ASK Technologies Inc—*Kirk Jackson*	325 Windsor St, Reading PA 19601	610-320-6400	R	2*	<.1
286	DNI Corp—*William Brennan*	701 Murfreesboro Rd, Nashville TN 37210	615-313-7000	R	2*	<.1
287	Digital Business Solutions Inc—*Jim Rodriguez*	133 S 4th St Ste 306, Springfield IL 62701	217-744-3271	R	2*	<.1
288	Jazz Review—*Maurice Blackwell*	10101 Hunt Club Cir, Mequon WI 53097	262-242-5277	R	2*	<.1
289	H20 Associates LLC—*Gary Heim*	6 W 18th St Fl 8, New York NY 10011	212-627-7652	R	2*	<.1
290	Innonet LLC—*Dee Bellaria*	2 Huntley Rd, Old Lyme CT 06371	860-339-1500	R	2*	<.1

Note: An asterisk (*) indicates an estimated financial figure. The company type code used is as follows: R = Private, P = Public, S = Private Subsidiary, B = Public Subsidiary, D = Division, J = Joint Venture, I = Investment Fund.

COMPANY RANKINGS BY SALES WITHIN 4-DIGIT SIC

Rank	Company Name—*Executive Officer*	Address, City, State, Zip	Phone	Type	Fin	Empls
291	Nozone Inc—*Karl Zimmerman*	350 E Cermak Rd Ste 24, Chicago IL 60616	312-602-2689	R	2*	<.1
292	Delaware Sunny Electrics Inc—*Anthony Jahangani*	2116 Wilshire Blvd Ste, Santa Monica CA 90403	310-828-1397	R	2*	<.1
293	Library Technologies Inc—*James Schoenung*	2300 Computer Rd Ste D, Willow Grove PA 19090	215-830-9320	R	2*	<.1
294	Go E BizCom—*Tom Salonek*	1020 Discovery Rd Ste, Saint Paul MN 55121	651-454-0013	R	2*	<.1
295	Netsolutions Group Inc—*Steve Wadhwa*	1641 N Milwaukee Ave S, Libertyville IL 60048	847-281-9300	R	2*	<.1
296	Pyron Technologies Inc—*Dave Pyron*	PO Box 8795, Missoula MT 59807	406-543-9211	R	2*	<.1
297	Virginia Interactive LLC—*Carol Amato*	1111 E Main St Ste 901, Richmond VA 23219	804-786-4718	R	2*	<.1
298	Active Micrographics Inc—*Nolasco Castillo*	PO Box 5214, Chatsworth CA 91313	818-998-2561	R	2*	<.1
299	New York Interactive Inc—*Jaime Hazan*	2350 Broadway House2, New York NY 10024	212-496-1890	R	2*	<.1
300	Zebec Data Systems Inc—*John Feltham*	2425 Fountain View Dr, Houston TX 77057	713-782-3480	R	2*	<.1
301	Patrina Corp—*Dan Roulet*	2 Wall St Ste 401, New York NY 10005	212-233-1155	R	2*	<.1
302	FullNet Communications Inc—*Timothy J Kilkenny*	201 Robert S Kerr Ave, Oklahoma City OK 73102	405-236-8200	P	2	<.1
303	Airborne Systems Inc—*Kas Eberahim*	17361 Armstrong Ave, Irvine CA 92614	714-634-3002	R	2*	<.1
304	Invision Power Services Inc—*Lindy Throgmartin*	PO Box 2365, Forest VA 24551	434-316-7201	R	2*	<.1
305	Hopkins Duley and Associates Inc—*Larry Hopkins*	1200 Mountain Creek Rd, Chattanooga TN 37405	423-877-1220	R	2*	<.1
306	Cornwell Data Services Inc—*Peter Cornwell*	352 Evelyn St, Paramus NJ 07652	201-261-1050	R	2*	<.1
307	Brandywine Cad Design Inc—*Donald Lloyd*	3204 Concord Pke, Wilmington DE 19803	302-478-8334	R	2*	<.1
308	Silverscape LLC—*Max Glantzman*	75 Broad St Fl 2, Boston MA 02109	617-338-8922	R	2*	<.1
309	Tigar Hare Studios Inc—*Charles Hare*	4485 Matilija Ave, Sherman Oaks CA 91423	818-907-6663	R	2*	<.1
310	Merdian M R I—*Amy Rice*	8805 N Meridian St Ste, Indianapolis IN 46260	317-706-7226	R	2*	<.1
311	Reol Services LLC—*Roley Green*	568 Broadway Rm 802, New York NY 10012	212-755-5544	R	2*	<.1
312	Business Equipment House Inc—*Harold Root*	5647 W Diversey Ave, Chicago IL 60639	773-889-9393	R	2*	<.1
313	Data Source of Overland Park LLC—*Debby Middleton*	6976 W 105th St, Shawnee Mission KS 66212	913-385-0800	R	2*	<.1
314	Alicomp Inc—*Arthur Kurek*	2 Christie Hts, Leonia NJ 07605	201-840-4900	R	2*	<.1
315	Citie Sites—*Ben Plumber*	1946 W 26th St Ste 14, Erie PA 16508	814-836-1000	R	2*	<.1
316	DEP S Inc—*Shobhana Davda*	100 E Campus View Blvd, Columbus OH 43235	614-547-0040	R	2*	<.1
317	Infotext Systems Inc—*John Dixon*	3001 St Rd, Bensalem PA 19020	215-639-9000	R	2*	<.1
318	Advance Graphix Imaging Solutns—*Karim Mojtahedi*	2082 E Gladwick St, Rancho Dominguez CA 90220	310-921-2424	R	2*	<.1
319	Borer Financial Communication LLC—*Paul Anastacio*	615 5th St Ste 210, Carlstadt NJ 07072	201-939-9297	R	2*	<.1
320	Acp-Tpf Inc—*Dianne Edmondson*	207 W Hickory St Ste 2, Denton TX 76201	940-565-0658	R	2*	<.1
321	Wasabi Inc—*Jorge Dagnessess*	15378 Sw 140th St, Miami FL 33196	305-252-0027	R	1*	<.1
322	Right Networks LLC	29 Riverside St Ste A, Nashua NH 03062	603-324-0403	R	1*	<.1
323	Akg Solutions—*Ronal Harper*	4333 Carl Dr Ste 101, Lisle IL 60532	630-271-0652	R	1*	<.1
324	Physicians Billing Management Inc—*Gregory Hummer*	20600 Chagrin Blvd Ste, Cleveland OH 44122	216-283-7999	R	1*	<.1
325	Cboss Inc—*Betty Jagnow*	PO Box 5038, Youngstown OH 44514	330-726-0429	R	1*	<.1
326	Cape Notary Services—*Melissa Capers*	PO Box 224, Olanta SC 29114	843-396-4367	R	1*	<.1
327	Mainxchange Inc—*Clay Stobaugh*	2000 Linwood Ave Apt 5, Fort Lee NJ 07024	201-461-7484	R	1*	<.1
328	Internet Ideas Work LLC	22611 Markey Ct Ste 10, Sterling VA 20166	703-450-1980	R	1*	<.1
329	J-W Labs Inc—*Jimmy Williams*	620 N W St, Raleigh NC 27603	919-832-6335	R	1*	<.1
330	Group Dynamic Inc—*Clifford Mohr*	411 Us Rte 1, Falmouth ME 04105	207-781-8800	R	1*	<.1
331	Business Recovery Services Inc—*Sharon David*	2694 Bishop Dr Ste 115, San Ramon CA 94583	925-277-3900	R	1*	<.1
332	Psj Enterprises Inc—*Donald Dorsey*	3111 4th St Apt 214, Santa Monica CA 90405	310-396-7356	R	1*	<.1
333	Western Computer Service Inc—*Katie Reeder*	9865 S State St, Sandy UT 84070	801-233-3213	R	1*	<.1
334	Fca Technologies LLC—*Linda King*	150 S Washington St St, Falls Church VA 22046	703-534-0166	R	1*	<.1
335	Datamax Solutions Inc—*Stacey Riska*	7431 Lindbergh Dr, Gaithersburg MD 20879	240-243-2200	R	1*	<.1
336	Oeuf Inc—*Matthias Kehder*	1010 Turquoise St Ste, San Diego CA 92109	858-488-0771	R	1*	<.1
337	Five Star Merchant's Service Inc—*Tahir Bhatti*	9703 Richmond Ave Ste, Houston TX 77042	713-490-3389	R	1*	<.1
338	Peachtree Data Inc—*Richard West*	2905 Premiere Pkwy Ste, Duluth GA 30097	678-987-4600	R	1*	<.1
339	High Resolutions Inc—*Paul Kedrow*	PO Box 2229, Knoxville TN 37901	865-523-3361	R	1*	<.1
340	Quicksilver Interactive Group Inc—*Steve Lee*	251 O Connor Ridge Blv, Irving TX 75038	214-999-0301	R	1*	<.1
341	Synergy Market Systems Inc—*Aaron Alonzo*	19370 Collins Ave Ste, Sunny Isles Beach FL 33160	786-316-2978	R	1*	<.1
342	Sophisticated Data Research Inc—*D Feldman*	PO Box 81038, Atlanta GA 30366	770-451-5100	R	1*	<.1
343	Applied DNA Sciences Inc—*James A Hayward*	25 Health Sciences Dr, Stony Brook NY 11790	631-444-6370	P	.1	<.1
344	American Resource Systems Inc—*Thomas Briggs*	7480 Bartlett Corp Cv, Bartlett TN 38133	901-382-9595	R	1*	<.1
345	Custom Computer Service Inc—*Robert Oratorio*	PO Box 689, New Castle DE 19720	302-325-5511	R	1*	<.1
346	PayChoice—*Robert Digby*	840 N Lenola Rd Ste 6, Moorestown NJ 08057	856-231-4667	R	1*	<.1
347	Versura Inc—*Lydia Marshall*	252 N Washington St St, Falls Church VA 22046	703-533-0347	R	1*	<.1
348	Overcoffee Productions LLC—*Ryp Walters*	PO Box 2042, Cedar Rapids IA 52406	319-398-7300	R	1*	<.1
349	Station The Web Inc—*Madjid Ebadi*	140 Hoffman Ln, Central Islip NY 11749	631-650-0000	R	1*	<.1
350	Research Enhanced Design—*Rushford Lee*	86 N University Ave St, Provo UT 84601	801-377-3954	R	1*	<.1
351	CCS and T Inc—*Charels Beauvais*	10600a Crestwood Dr, Manassas VA 20109	703-368-8046	R	1*	<.1
352	Interactive Graphics Inc—*Robert Schnorr*	10 Waterloo Ave Fl 2, Berwyn PA 19312	610-293-0755	R	1*	<.1
353	Iobjectsolutions Inc—*William Hale*	205 Curie Dr, Alpharetta GA 30005	678-341-1225	R	1*	<.1
354	Ladorn Systems Corp—*Hazel Chan*	2270 Beaver Rd Ste 227, Landover MD 20785	301-429-0003	R	1*	<.1
355	Timberline Interactive Inc—*Rick Fitzsimmons*	PO Box 992, Middlebury VT 05753	802-388-8377	R	1*	<.1
356	Abacus Inc—*Frank Combs*	169 Burt Rd Ste A, Lexington KY 40503	859-278-9241	R	1*	<.1
357	Carlton Computer Support Service Inc—*James Carlton*	10746 Tucker St Ste A, Beltsville MD 20705	301-595-5212	R	1*	<.1
358	Federal Information and News Dispatch Inc—*C Thorne*	5900 Princss Gdn Pkwy, Lanham MD 20706	301-429-5944	R	1*	<.1
359	Infoscan—*Dan Eckard*	1540 International Pkw, Lake Mary FL 32746	407-792-6115	R	1*	<.1
360	Indexing Research—*Frances Lennie*	620 Park Ave Ste 183, Rochester NY 14607	585-413-1819	R	1*	<.1
361	ReadyServe Computer Center—*Steven Romero*	5201 Great America Pkw, Santa Clara CA 95054	408-562-6044	R	1*	<.1
362	CareMaster Inc—*Frederick Wolfe*	10919 Candlelight Ln, Dallas TX 75204	214-219-7600	R	1*	<.1
363	Gulley Computer Associates—*Dale Gulley*	PO Box 700295, Tulsa OK 74170	918-744-0100	R	1*	<.1
364	Logos Systems International—*Brett K Nelson*	175 El Pueblo Rd, Scotts Valley CA 95066	831-600-6101	R	1*	<.1
365	Pwl/Bpc Joint Venture LLC—*Leslie Liu*	100 Custis St Ste 5, Aberdeen MD 21001	410-272-3308	R	1*	<.1
366	Royce Designs Inc—*Robert Royce*	2427 E Huber St Ste 1, Mesa AZ 85213	480-964-6022	R	1*	<.1
367	City County Data Center Commission—*Gerard Klein*	407 Grant St, Wausau WI 54403	715-261-6700	R	1*	<.1
368	Lille Corp—*Jordan Rosen*	7 Southwoods Blvd Ste, Albany NY 12211	518-432-7625	R	1*	<.1
369	Apollo Direct LLC	1050 Wall St W Ste 620, Lyndhurst NJ 07071	201-460-7050	R	1*	<.1
370	Blue Moose Litigation Support Inc—*Ray Sunday*	633 17th St Ste 120, Denver CO 80202	303-298-7114	R	1*	<.1
371	Defense Solutions Group Inc—*Russell Hague*	5597 Oak St, Fort Worth TX 76140	817-563-5661	R	1*	<.1
372	T4 Inc—*Carol Conway*	4426 Se 16th Pl Ste 4, Cape Coral FL 33904	239-542-8450	R	1*	<.1
373	Accurate Data Inc—*Beverly Ward*	PO Box 849, Palatine IL 60078	847-781-8120	R	1*	<.1
374	Lynswell Technologies Inc—*Bill Lin*	610 N 10th St, Camden NJ 08102	856-365-1711	R	1*	<.1
375	Event Streams LLC—*Sam Austin*	3109 Maple Dr Ne Ste 4, Atlanta GA 30305	404-816-1114	R	1*	<.1
376	Netchemistry Inc—*Chris Cruttenden*	4600 Campus Dr Ste 101, Newport Beach CA 92660	949-399-5380	R	1*	<.1
377	Advanced Imaging Services Inc—*Jamie Goble*	2320 N Grand River Ave, Lansing MI 48906	517-485-2440	R	1*	<.1
378	Griban Technologies Inc—*Joseph Weeks*	11034 W Flagler St, Miami FL 33174	305-226-6111	R	1*	<.1
379	Cadenza Group Inc—*Grant Cook*	PO Box 1865, Ann Arbor MI 48106	734-994-6121	R	1*	<.1

Rank	Company Name—*Executive Officer*	Address, City, State, Zip	Phone	Type	Fin	Empls
380	Government Intelligence and Proposal Resources Inc—*Christopher Stahl*	47097 Glenaire Ct, Sterling VA 20165	571-434-6016	R	1*	<.1
381	Breck Media Inc—*Ann Carr*	802 Avnue Of The Ameri, New York NY 10001	212-727-3020	R	1*	<.1
382	Enroute Networks Inc—*David Hampson*	3775 Roswell Rd, Marietta GA 30062	770-794-1115	R	1*	<.1
383	Baca Stein White and Associates—*Larry Baca*	801 Morton St, Richmond TX 77469	281-342-2646	R	1*	<.1
384	Beljan Limited Inc—*Faith Krug*	2870 Baker Rd, Dexter MI 48130	734-426-2415	R	1*	<.1
385	Vector Computer Systems Inc—*Alex Couto*	300 N Midland Ave, Saddle Brook NJ 07663	201-368-9670	R	1*	<.1
386	Electron Factory Inc—*Bruce Sauer*	873 E Baltimore Pke St, Kennett Square PA 19348	610-388-3690	R	1*	<.1
387	Odyssey Communication Group Inc—*Ron Grayson*	9441 Lbj Fwy Ste 510, Dallas TX 75243	972-997-9052	R	1*	<.1
388	Inamics Corp—*Al Harlow*	PO Box 2, Chagrin Falls OH 44022	216-916-0196	R	1*	<.1
389	Santeon Group Inc—*Ash Rofail*	1666 Garnet Ave Ste 31, San Diego CA 92109		B	1	<.1
390	Blue River Digital Inc—*David Thompson*	1624 Santa Clara Dr St, Roseville CA 95661	916-727-2700	R	1*	<.1
391	Internet Connections Inc—*Yvonne Cariveau*	PO Box 205, Mankato MN 56002	507-344-2280	R	1*	<.1
392	Internet Resource Center Inc—*Lee Warren*	3189 Powers Ford Se, Marietta GA 30067	770-933-3491	R	1*	<.1
393	Milestone Internet Marketing—*Benu Aggarwal*	2620 Augustine Dr Ste, Santa Clara CA 95054	408-492-9055	R	1*	<.1
394	Electric Word Inc—*Cherryl Austine*	26252 E Otero Dr, Aurora CO 80016	303-693-5642	R	1*	<.1
395	Lightpoint Colocation and Hosting LLC	625 Sw Stark St Ste 50, Portland OR 97205	503-224-6120	R	1*	<.1
396	Netcommerce LLC	1210 N Jefferson St St, Anaheim CA 92807	714-224-0450	R	1*	<.1
397	S Corporation Inc—*Phil Landreth*	303 S Broadway 200-177, Denver CO 80209	303-722-1263	R	<1*	<.1
398	Advanced Input Data Entry—*Marita Brengettcy*	2255 Honolulu Ave Ste, Montrose CA 91020	818-541-9155	R	<1*	<.1
399	Modern Creative Services Inc—*Dan Haskel*	580 Sylvan Ave Ste Mm, Englewood Cliffs NJ 07632	201-541-2300	R	<1*	<.1
400	SGA Business Systems Inc—*Wayne Scarano*	83 Haverford Ct, Hillsborough NJ 08844	908-359-4626	R	<1*	<.1
401	Datatex Media Dolls—*Katherine Sanders*	PO Box 38125, Cleveland OH 44138	216-598-1000	R	<1*	<.1
402	Spiralfx Interactive LLC—*Vanessa Siegal*	326 Allegheny Trl Ln, Garland TX 75043	214-497-6573	R	<1*	<.1
403	Fsv Payment Systems Inc—*Richard Savard*	15710 John F Kennedy B, Houston TX 77032	832-201-6500	R	<1*	<.1
404	Visionary Consulting—*Kathleen Brown*	240 Saint Paul St Ste, Denver CO 80206	303-860-0262	R	<1*	<.1
405	I Networld Marketing Group—*William Derrig*	84 Dundas Ave, Warwick RI 02889	401-737-3730	R	<1*	<.1
406	Weblife Inc—*Zack Johnson*	1362 Wabash Ave, Terre Haute IN 47807	812-234-5100	R	<1*	<.1
407	Flint Interactive LLC—*John Hyduke*	11 E Superior St Ste 5, Duluth MN 55802	218-740-3516	R	<1*	<.1
408	Ideasource Creative Marketng Services LLC—*Steven Miller*	1382 Teton Pt, Lafayette CO 80026	303-666-0690	R	<1*	<.1
409	Gem Of The Net LLC—*Bob Akbarie*	523 W 6th St Ste 1120, Los Angeles CA 90014	213-622-6622	R	<1*	<.1
410	Smart Web Design Corp—*Moshe Englander*	4109 12th Ave, Brooklyn NY 11219	718-972-9341	R	<1*	<.1
411	Fisher Technical Services Rentals Inc—*Scott Fisher*	6955 Spdway Blvd Unit, Las Vegas NV 89115	702-251-0700	R	<1*	<.1
412	Chappell Graphics—*Deborah Benz*	1410 Incarnation Dr St, Charlottesville VA 22901	434-971-7334	R	<1*	<.1
413	Resource Data Inc—*R Thomas*	305 Westover Dr, Asheville NC 28801	828-251-1658	R	<1*	<.1
414	Nebraska Digital—*John Rood*	PO Box 83871, Lincoln NE 68501	402-476-3438	R	<1*	<.1
415	Heart Graphics—*Randy Hjelmeir*	1230 Briarmede Rd, Lewisville NC 27023	336-760-8552	R	<1*	<.1
416	Lionfish Solutions Inc—*Glen Mattheus*	4616 E Bennington Ave, Castle Rock CO 80104	303-663-4130	R	<1*	<.1
417	Red Studio Design—*Kenneth Derouchie*	5602 Ne 72nd Ave, Vancouver WA 98661	360-326-3275	R	<1*	<.1
418	Wired City—*Martin Otterson*	2526 Sw 146th Ln, Burien WA 98166	206-988-5104	R	<1*	<.1
419	InfoCrossing Inc—*Martha Bejar*	2 Christie Heights St, Leonia NJ 07605	201-840-4700	S	N/A	.2
420	Solution Data Systems Inc—*Debbie Rowan*	1051 Cassens Industria, Fenton MO 63026	636-305-8400	R	N/A	.1
421	Montana Cancer Consortium Inc—*Amanda Dinsdale*	90 Poly Dr Ste 2, Billings MT 59101	406-259-2245	R	N/A	<.1
422	24Holdings Inc—*Arnold Kling*	133 Summit Ave Ste 22, Summit NJ 07901	973-635-4047	P	N/A	N/A

TOTALS: SIC 7374 Data Processing & Preparation
Companies: 422   71,798   362.8

7375 Information Retrieval Services

Rank	Company Name—*Executive Officer*	Address, City, State, Zip	Phone	Type	Fin	Empls
1	Time Warner Inc—*Jeffrey L Bewkes*	1 Time Warner Ctr, New York NY 10019	212-484-8000	P	28,974	34.0
2	Yahoo! Inc—*Alfred Amoroso*	701 First Ave, Sunnyvale CA 94089	408-349-3300	P	6,325	13.6
3	Media General Operations Inc—*Marshall N Morton*	333 E Franklin St, Richmond VA 23219	804-649-6000	S	3,770*	7.2
4	Travelport Ltd—*Jeff Clarke*	300 Galleria Pkwy, Atlanta GA 30339	770-563-7400	S	2,290	5.5
5	Cengage Learning Inc—*Ronald G Dunn*	PO Box 6904, Florence KY 41022	203-965-8600	S	1,876	5.5
6	Salesforcecom Inc—*Marc Benioff*	1 Market St Ste 300, San Francisco CA 94105	415-901-7000	P	1,657	5.3
7	Thomson Financial Inc—*Matthew Burkley*	195 Broadway, New York NY 10007	646-822-2000	S	1,543	7.6
8	Libraries Online Inc—*Alan Hagyard*	100 Riverview Ctr Ste, Middletown CT 06457	860-347-1704	R	1,317*	<.1
9	CareStepscom Inc—*Ban Leedle*	701 Cool Springs Blvd, Franklin TN 37067	615-665-1122	S	905*	2.5
10	United Online Inc—*Mark R Goldston*	21301 Burbank Blvd, Woodland Hills CA 91367	818-287-3000	P	898	1.5
11	FactSet Research Systems Inc—*Philip A Hadley*	601 Merritt 7 3rd Fl, Norwalk CT 06851	203-810-1000	P	727	2.8
12	Shark Holdings Inc—*Raymond D'Arcy*	22 Crosby Dr, Bedford MA 01730	781-687-8800	S	697*	1.7
13	First American Real Estate Information Services Inc	1 First American Wy, Westlake TX 76262	714-250-3000	S	660*	2.0
14	West Publishing Corp—*Peter Warwick*	PO Box 64833, Saint Paul MN 55164	651-687-7000	S	519*	.9
15	IIJ America Inc—*Koichi Kobayashi*	1211 Ave of the Americ, New York NY 10036	212-440-8080	S	490*	1.0
16	BAE Systems (Rockville Maryland)—*Linda Hudson*	1601 Research Blvd, Rockville MD 20850	301-838-6000	S	453*	.8
17	Dialog Corp—*Susanne BeDell*	2250 Perimeter Park Dr, Morrisville NC 27560	919-804-6400	S	380*	.7
18	Westlaw Business—*Richard Harrison* West Publishing Corp	1100 13th St NW Ste 30, Washington DC 20005	202-572-1997	D	346*	.3
19	NOVO 1—*George D Dalton*	20825 Swenson Dr, Waukesha WI 53186	262-717-0990	R	327*	1.0
20	Athenahealth Inc—*Jonathon Bush*	311 Arsenal St, Watertown MA 02472	617-402-1000	P	324	1.8
21	Travelocitycom LP—*Carl Sparks*	3150 Sabre Dr, Southlake TX 76092	210-521-5871	S	308*	1.6
22	Lycos Inc—*Jungwook Lim*	400-2 Totten Pond Rd, Waltham MA 02451	781-370-2700	S	291	.9
23	Factiva—*Rupert Murdoch*	2451 Cumberland Pkwy S, Atlanta GA 30339	609-627-2000	R	289*	.8
24	IAC Search and Media Inc—*Paul Gardi*	555 12th St Ste 500, Oakland CA 94607	510-985-7400	S	258*	.5
25	Oclc Online Computer Library Center Incorporate—*Robert Jordan*	6565 Kilgour Pl, Dublin OH 43017	614-764-6000	R	228*	1.0
26	Mobile Productivity Inc—*Les Silver*	3058 E Sunset Rd Ste 1, Las Vegas NV 89120		R	174*	.3
27	Quick Test Inc—*Adam Rodgers*	1061 E Indiantown Rd S, Jupiter FL 33477	561-748-0931	R	170*	1.0
28	Penton Internet Inc—*John French* Internet World Media Inc	1300 E 9th St, Cleveland OH 44114	216-696-7000	S	170*	.3
29	Data Transmission Network Corp—*Robert Gordon*	9110 W Dodge Rd Ste 20, Omaha NE 68114	402-390-2328	S	167	1.1
30	Iso Services Inc—*Frank Coyne*	545 Washington Blvd Fl, Jersey City NJ 07310	201-469-2000	R	155*	3.0
31	Pandora Media Inc—*Joe Kennedy*	2101 Webster St Ste 16, Oakland CA 94612	510-451-4100	P	138	.2
32	Amadeus Americas Inc—*David Jones*	3470 NW 82nd Ave Ste 1, Miami FL 33122	305-499-6000	S	134*	.8
33	Yahoo! Broadcast Services—*Jerry Yang* Yahoo! Inc	1680 N Glenville Dr, Richardson TX 75081	214-748-6660	D	130*	.3
34	New Edge Network Inc—*Cardi Prinzi*	3000 Columbia House Bl, Vancouver WA 98661	360-693-9009	R	125*	.3
35	Advanced Academics Inc—*Jeffrey A Elliott*	1 E California Ave Ste, Oklahoma City OK 73104		S	123*	.2
36	Homeaway Inc—*Brian Sharples*	1011 W 5th St Ste 300, Austin TX 78703	512-493-0382	P	120*	.6
37	STSN Inc—*David Garrison*	10757 S River Front Pk, South Jordan UT 84095	801-563-2000	R	118*	.2

Note: An asterisk (*) indicates an estimated financial figure. The company type code used is as follows: R = Private, P = Public, S = Private Subsidiary, B = Public Subsidiary, D = Division, J = Joint Venture, I = Investment Fund.

COMPANY RANKINGS BY SALES WITHIN 4-DIGIT SIC

Rank	Company Name—*Executive Officer*	Address, City, State, Zip	Phone	Type	Fin	Empls
38	Logical Technical Services Corp—*James R Bloomberg*	7250 Woodmont Ave Ste, Bethesda VA 20814	301-652-2121	R	117*	.2
39	AWS Convergence Technologies Inc—*Robert S Marshall*	12410 Milestone Center, Germantown MD 20876	301-250-4000	R	117*	.2
40	HealthAnswers Inc—*Michael Tague*	1140 Welsh Rd Ste 100, North Wales PA 19454	215-412-3900	R	114*	.4
41	Pegasus Business Intelligence LP	8350 N Central Exp, Dallas TX 75206	214-234-4000	S	108*	.3
42	Yellow Services Inc—*William D Zollars*	10990 Roe Ave, Overland Park KS 66211	913-344-3000	S	103*	.4
43	eSignalcom Inc—*Chuck Thompson*	3955 Point Eden Way, Hayward CA 94545	510-266-6000	S	103*	.3
44	Internet World Media Inc—*David Nussbaum*	18 S Main St, Norwalk CT 06854	203-945-2070	S	100*	.3
45	Wow! Business Solutions—*Colleen Abdoulah*	PO Box 5789, Evansville IN 47716	812-437-0345	J	100*	.1
46	Aboutcom Inc—*Janet L Robinson*	249 W 17th St 2nd Fl, New York NY 10011	212-204-4000	S	97	.3
47	Pac-West Telecomm Inc—*James F Hensel*	1776 W March Ln Ste 25, Stockton CA 95207		R	91	.3
48	Elsevier Science Inc Secondary Publishing Div—*Eric Engstrum*	360 Park Ave S, New York NY 10010		D	90*	.5
49	Juno Online Services United Online Inc	75 9th Ave, New York NY 10011	212-597-9000	S	86*	.3
50	MRG Document Technologies—*Michael Riddle*	717 N Harwood Ste 2400, Dallas TX 75201	214-220-6300	R	86*	.2
51	Localcom Corp—*Heath B Clarke*	7555 Irvine Center Dr, Irvine CA 92618	949-784-0800	P	84	.1
52	Pacific Internet—*Garry Hipsher*	105 West Clay St, Ukiah CA 95482	707-468-1005	R	80	N/A
53	ADP Screening and Selection Services—*Dean Suposs*	301 Remington St, Fort Collins CO 80524	970-484-7722	D	76*	.2
54	EasyLink Services Corp—*Thomas J Stallings*	33 Knightsbridge Rd, Piscataway NJ 08854	732-652-3500	S	74	.3
55	Newsbank Inc—*John McDowell*	5801 Pelican Bay Blvd, Naples FL 34108		R	74*	.3
56	Dataquick—*John Walsh*	9620 Towne Centre Dr, San Diego CA 92121	858-597-3100	R	73*	.2
57	First American Flood Data Services—*Vicki Chenault* First American Real Estate Information Services Inc	11902 Burnet Rd, Austin TX 78758	512-834-9595	D	72*	.4
58	LoopNet Inc—*Rich Boyle*	185 Berry St Ste 4000, San Francisco CA 94107	415-243-4200	P	71	.4
59	NEON Communications Group Inc—*Kurt Van Wagenen*	2200 W Park Dr, Westborough MA 01581	508-616-7800	S	66	.3
60	Infinite Computer Solutions Inc—*Upinder Zutshi*	5 Choke Cherry Rd, Rockville MD 20850	301-795-1260	R	64*	1.9
61	Bolt Media Inc—*Dan Pelson*	304 Hudson St 7th Fl, New York NY 10013	212-620-5900	R	63*	<.1
62	Automotive Information Systems Inc—*Jeff Sweet*	2714 Patton Rd, Saint Paul MN 55113	651-633-8007	S	62*	.1
63	NameMedia Inc—*Kelly Conlin*	230 3rd Ave, Waltham MA 02451	781-839-2800	R	60*	.1
64	Iserv Co—*Vic Shepherd*	5222 33rd St SE, Grand Rapids MI 49512	616-493-3720	R	60*	.1
65	ODesk Corp—*Gary Swart*	901 Marshall St Ste 20, Redwood City CA 94063	650-853-4100	R	60*	<.1
66	ChangingOurWorldcom—*Brian Crimmins*	220 E 42nd St 7th Fl, New York NY 10017	212-499-0866	R	58*	.2
67	NewsMax Media Inc—*Christopher Ruddy*	PO Box 20989, West Palm Beach FL 33416	561-686-1165	R	58*	.1
68	Reis Services LLC—*Lloyd Lynford*	5 W 37th St, New York NY 10018	212-921-1122	S	58*	.1
69	OneSource Information Services Inc—*Phil Garlick*	300 Baker Ave, Concord MA 01742	978-318-4300	D	57*	.3
70	Opinion Access Corp—*Jimmy Hoffman*	47-10 32nd Pl, Long Island City NY 11101	718-729-2622	R	57*	.1
71	Zinio Systems Inc—*Richard A Maggiatto*	139 Townsend St Ste 30, San Francisco CA 94107	415-494-2700	R	57*	.1
72	Zoom Information Inc—*Jonathan Stern*	307 Waverley Oaks Rd, Waltham MA 02452	781-693-7500	R	57*	.1
73	All Web Leads Inc—*Bill Daniel*	7300 FM 2222 Bldg 2 St, Austin TX 78730		R	57	<.1
74	Surescript Systems Inc—*Harry Totonis*	2800 Crystal Dr, Arlington VA 22202	703-921-2121	R	53*	.1
75	Askcom—*Jim Safka* IAC Search and Media Inc	555 12th St Ste 500, Oakland CA 94607	510-985-7400	S	51*	.1
76	Streaming Media Inc—*Dan Rayburn*	213 Danbury Rd, Wilton CT 06897	604-886-9378	S	49*	.1
77	Senior Market Sales Inc—*Milton M Kleinberg*	8420 W Dodge Rd Ste 51, Omaha NE 68114		R	48*	.1
78	Acquire Media Corp—*Lawrence Rafsky*	3 Becker Farm Rd Ste 4, Roseland NJ 07068	973-422-0800	R	46*	.1
79	Sterling Infosystems Inc—*William Greenblatt*	249 W 17th St Fl 6, New York NY 10011	212-736-5100	R	46*	.6
80	CH2M HILL Managed Services—*Jeff Akers*	6161 S Syracuse Way St, Greenwood Village CO 80111	303-706-0990	R	45	.4
81	GoRemote Internet Communications Inc—*Tom Thimot*	1421 McCarthy Blvd, Milpitas CA 95035	408-955-1920	S	45*	.2
82	Ethicspoint Inc—*David Childers*	6000 Meadows Rd Ste 20, Lake Oswego OR 97035	971-250-4100	R	45*	.1
83	Medsite Inc	111 8th Ave 7th FL, New York NY 10011	212-624-3700	S	45*	.1
84	Data Foundry Inc—*Ron Yokubaitis*	1044 Liberty Park Dr, Austin TX 78746	512-684-9000	R	44*	.1
85	ActiveVideo Networks Inc—*Jeff Miller*	333 W San Carlos St St, San Jose CA 95110	408-931-9200	R	40*	.1
86	MarketWatch Inc—*Larry S Kramer*	825 Battery St, San Francisco CA 94111	415-733-0500	S	39*	.3
87	GlobalMedia Group LLC—*Joel E Barthelemy*	15020 N 74th St, Scottsdale AZ 85260	480-922-0044	R	39*	.1
88	ChaCha Search Inc—*Scott Jones*	1020 W 116th St, Carmel IN 46032		R	35*	.1
89	Community of Science Inc—*Jeffrey Baer*	1 N Charles St Ste 230, Baltimore MD 21201	410-563-2378	R	34*	.1
90	nStreams Technologies Inc—*ML Lee*	209 E Java Dr, Sunnyvale CA 94089	408-734-8889	R	34*	.1
91	Reply! Inc—*Payam Zamani*	12667 Alcosta Blvd Ste, San Ramon CA 94583	925-983-3400	R	34*	<.1
92	Hostway Corp—*Lucas Roh*	PO Box 380, Chicago IL 60654		R	33*	.7
93	LexisNexisCourtLink Corp—*Andy Prozes*	13427 NE 16th St, Bellevue WA 98005	206-728-2275	S	32*	.1
94	Internet Broadcasting Systems Inc—*Elmer Baldwin*	355 Randolph Ave, Saint Paul MN 55102	651-365-4000	R	31*	.3
95	Megapath Networks Inc—*Jim Cragg*	555 Anton Blvd Ste 200, Costa Mesa CA 92626	714-327-2000	R	30*	.2
96	TWS Holdings Inc—*Rackesh Kaul*	Park 80 West Plz 2 Ste, Saddle Brook NJ 07663	201-291-2770	R	30*	.1
97	Zvents Inc—*Ethan Stock*	1875 S Grant St Ste 80, San Mateo CA 94402		R	30*	.1
98	Shoppingcom Ltd—*Andre Haddad*	8000 Marina Blvd, Brisbane CA 94005	650-616-6500	S	29*	.2
99	Chockstone Inc—*Jeffrey D Lipp*	326 SW Broadway Ste 40, Portland OR 97205	503-227-7600	S	29*	.1
100	ebrary Inc—*Christopher Warnock*	318 Cambridge Ave, Palo Alto CA 94306	650-475-8700	R	29*	.1
101	Goettler Associates—*John Goettler*	580 S High St, Columbus OH 43215	614-228-3269	R	29*	.1
102	Physicians World—*David Thompson*	200 Meadowlands Pkwy, Secaucus NJ 07094	201-271-6068	D	29*	.1
103	Tickle Inc—*James Currier*	222 Sutter St 5th Fl, San Francisco CA 94108		S	29*	.1
104	Walz Group Inc—*Mohan Tavorath*	27398 Via Industria, Temecula CA 92590	951-491-6800	R	29*	.1
105	Investor Force Inc—*Jim Morrissey*	640 Lee Road Ste 200, Wayne PA 19087	610-408-3700	R	28*	<.1
106	Reuters Loan Pricing Corp	3 Times Square, New York NY 10036	646-223-6890	S	27*	.1
107	U S Internet Corp—*William Milota*	12450 Wayzata Blvd Ste, Minnetonka MN 55305	651-222-4638	R	26*	<.1
108	Electronic Evidence Discovery Inc—*Dave McCAnn*	3933 Lake Washington B, Kirkland WA 98033	425-629-6777	R	26*	.1
109	Docusign Inc—*Steve King*	1301 2nd AveSte 2000, Seattle WA 98101	206-219-0200	R	26*	<.1
110	Craigslist Inc—*Jim Buckmaster*	1381 9th Ave, San Francisco CA 94122	415-566-6394	R	25*	<.1
111	SureScripts Inc—*Harry Totonis*	2800 Crystal Dr, Arlington VA 22202		R	23*	.1
112	LawInfocom—*Gunter Enz*	1782 La Costa Meadows, San Marcos CA 92078		R	22*	.1
113	Healthline Networks Inc—*West Shell III*	660 3rd St, San Francisco CA 94107	415-281-3100	R	22*	<.1
114	Knovel Corp—*Christopher Forbes*	489 5th Ave 9th Fl, New York NY 10017		R	22*	<.1
115	Luxury Link LLC—*Drew Marich*	5570 Lincoln Blvd, Los Angeles CA 90094	310-215-8060	R	22*	<.1
116	PropertyMaps Inc—*Jeff Chambers*	435 Aspen Dr, Austin TX 78737	512-791-3527	R	21*	<.1
117	Healthanswerscom Inc—*Louisa Holland* HealthAnswers Inc	1140 Welsh Rd Ste 100, North Wales PA 19454	215-412-3900	S	20*	.1
118	dataLOK Co—*Takashi Nakamura*	5990 Malburg Way, Los Angeles CA 90058	323-582-6100	R	19*	<.1
119	By Light Professional It Services—*Robert Donahue*	3101 Wilson Blvd Ste 8, Arlington VA 22201	703-224-1000	R	18*	<.1
120	Manta Media Inc—*Pamela Springer*	9200 Worthington Rd St, Westerville OH 43082	614-682-5103	R	18*	<.1
121	Pontiflex—*Zephrin Lasker*	45 Main St Ste 636, Brooklyn NY 11201		R	18*	<.1
122	CitySearch Inc—*Jay Herratti*	8833 Sunset Blvd, W Hollywood CA 90069	310-360-4500	S	17*	<.1
123	CourseAdvisor Inc	10 Presidential Way 2nd, Woburn MA 01801	781-683-3300	S	17*	<.1

Rank	Company Name—Executive Officer	Address, City, State, Zip	Phone	Type	Fin	Empls
124	Highbeam Research Inc—Patrick Spain	1 N State St Ste 900, Chicago IL 60602		S	17*	<.1
125	Weblogs Inc LLC	770 Broadway, New York NY 10003	212-652-6400	S	17*	<.1
126	Sensitech Inc—Eric Schultz	800 Cummings Ctr Ste 2, Beverly MA 01915	978-927-7033	R	16*	.2
127	ABG Capital Inc—Jeff Tapolci	8 Penn Ctr W Ste 101, Pittsburgh PA 15276	412-440-2070	R	16*	<.1
128	Rapid Reporting Co—Jay H Meadows	4100 International Plz, Fort Worth TX 76109		S	16*	<.1
129	TheFind Inc—Siva V Kumar	310 Villa St, Mountain View CA 94041	650-641-0127	R	15	<.1
130	Ohio Supercomputer Center—Steve Gordon	1224 Kinnear Rd, Columbus OH 43212	614-292-9248	R	15*	.2
131	Jeppesen DataPlan Inc	225 W Santa Clara St S, San Jose CA 95113	408-961-2825	S	15*	.1
132	Aptuit Informatics Inc—Michael Griffith	29219 Canwood St Ste 1, Agoura Hills CA 91301	818-879-0075	S	15*	.1
133	Fansonly Network—Richard Beedon	2035 Corte Del Nogal S, Carlsbad CA 92009	760-431-8221	S	15*	.1
134	LOGOS Communications Inc—Chris Tjotjos	26100 First St, Cleveland OH 44145	440-871-0777	R	15*	.1
135	Zixitcom Inc—Richard Spurr	2711 N Haskell Ave Ste, Dallas TX 75204	214-370-2000	S	14*	.3
136	Information Inc—Allen Carr	6707 Democracy Blvd, Bethesda MD 20817	301-215-4688	S	14*	.1
137	LoanPerformance—Dan Feshback	188 The Embarcadero 3r, San Francisco CA 94105	415-536-3500	R	14*	.1
138	Zoove Corp—Joseph Gillespie	2300 Geng RdSte 230, Palo Alto CA 94303	650-798-2700	R	14*	<.1
139	IA Global Inc—Brian Hoekstra	101 California St Ste, San Francisco CA 94111	415-946-8828	P	13	<.1
140	Digital Motorworks LP—Howard Gardner	8601 RR 2222 Bldg I St, Austin TX 78730	512-349-9360	S	13	.1
141	Intelligent Integration Systems Inc—Paul Davis	10 Post Office Sq 8th, Boston MA 02109	617-314-7872	R	13	<.1
142	Imaging Science and Services Inc—Phil Hodge	95 Executive Pkwy Ste, Hudson OH 44236	330-342-7760	R	12*	<.1
143	Aries Systems Corp—Lyndon Holmes	200 Sutton St, North Andover MA 01845	978-975-7570	R	12*	.1
144	icruisecom—Brett Howard	444 Merrick Rd Ste 230, Lynbrook NY 11563		R	12*	.1
145	CT Lien Solutions—Kenneth Kraus	2727 Allen Pkwy Ste 10, Houston TX 77019		R	12*	<.1
146	InsuranceAgentscom—Lev Barinskiy	309 S 4th St 4th Fl, Columbus OH 43215		R	12*	<.1
147	Dealnewscom Inc—Dan de Grandpre	103 Mountain Brook Blv, Madison AL 35758	256-971-6840	R	12*	<.1
148	zNET Internet Services Inc—Andy Taubman	4993 Niagara Ave Ste 2, San Diego CA 92107	619-221-7499	R	12*	<.1
149	Cqg Inc—Tim Mather	1050 17th St Ste 2000, Denver CO 80265	303-573-1400	R	11*	.1
150	Western Folder Distributing Company Inc—Bruce Brainerd	1549 Glenlake Ave, Itasca IL 60143	630-773-3377	R	11*	.1
151	Trojan Professional Services Inc—Ingrid Kidd	PO Box 1270, Los Alamitos CA 90720	714-816-7169	R	11*	.1
152	Granicus Inc—Tom Spengler	600 Harrison St Ste120, San Francisco CA 94107	415-357-3618	R	11*	.1
153	i365 Inc—Terry Cunningham	3101 Jay St Ste 110, Santa Clara CA 95054		S	11*	<.1
154	Internet Specialties West Inc—Drew J Kaplan	30077 Agoura Ct 1st Fl, Agoura Hills CA 91301	818-735-3000	R	11*	<.1
155	AutoTradercom LLC—Chip Perry III	5775 Peachtree Dunwood, Atlanta GA 30342	404-843-5000	S	11	<.1
156	SunGard Market Data Services—John Hyde	112 W Park Dr, Mount Laurel NJ 08054	856-235-7300	D	10	.1
157	Physician's Weekly Inc—Keith D'Orio HealthAnswers Inc	2445 Kuser Rd Ste 202, Hamilton NJ 08690	609-588-0370	D	10*	<.1
158	Software Tool and Die Inc—Barry Shein	PO Box 35555, Boston MA 02135		R	10*	<.1
159	BigBad Inc—Ty Glasgow	321 Summer St, Boston MA 02210	617-338-7770	R	10*	<.1
160	VitaminShoppecom—Jeffrey Horowitz	444 Madison Ave, New York NY 10022	212-308-6730	R	9*	.1
161	Servervault Corp—John Kraft	45240 Business Ct Ste, Dulles VA 20166	703-333-5900	R	9*	<.1
162	Telematch Inc—Peg Kuman	6883 Commercial Dr, Springfield VA 22151	703-658-8300	R	9*	<.1
163	Akademos Inc—John Squires	200 Connecticut Ave, Norwalk CT 06854	203-866-0190	R	9*	<.1
164	Hotelicopter—Adam Healey	103 W Main St, Charlottesville VA 22902	434-227-6728	R	9*	<.1
165	Safe Deposit Company Inc—Bill Cannon	515 S Lindbergh Blvd, Saint Louis MO 63131	314-991-3858	R	9*	<.1
166	Reprise Media Inc—Bant Breen	55 5th Ave 16th Fl, New York NY 10003	212-444-7474	R	8*	<.1
167	Globecot Inc—Robert Antoshak	3322 W End Ave Ste 550, Nashville TN 37203		R	8*	<.1
168	High Beam Resources LLC—Patrick J Spain	65 E Wacker Pl Ste 400, Chicago IL 60601	312-782-3900	R	8*	<.1
169	Realtimepublisherscom—Bailey Sory	300 Montgomery St Ste, San Francisco CA 94104	415-477-0100	R	8*	<.1
170	WinNet Business Internet—Michael Tague	1048 E Chestnut St 2nd, Louisville KY 40204	502-815-7000	R	8*	<.1
171	Townsend Polymer Services and Information—Ron Babinsky	523 Sam Houston Pkwy E, Houston TX 77060	281-873-8733	R	8*	<.1
172	Supernews Inc—Mark Ferrer	2 Harrison St, San Francisco CA 94105	415-541-2500	S	8	<.1
173	Xyvision Enterprise Solutions Inc—Kevin Duffy	101 Edgewater Dr, Wakefield MA 01880	781-756-4400	R	7*	.1
174	Switchboard Inc	PO Box 619810, Dallas TX 75261		S	7*	<.1
175	InfoSpace Sales LLC—William J Ruckelshaus	601 108th Ave NE Ste 1, Bellevue WA 98004	425-201-6100	S	7*	<.1
176	Saraide Inc—William Lansing	601 108th Ave NE Ste 1, Bellevue WA 98004	425-201-6100	S	7*	<.1
177	Insignis Inc—Peter W Dietz	1 N LaSalle St Ste 825, Chicago IL 60602	312-368-3630	R	7*	<.1
178	Adtrack Corp—Dan Rogers	6060 Huntington Ct Ne, Cedar Rapids IA 52402	319-395-9777	R	6*	.1
179	San Antonio Board Of Realtors Inc—Barbara Tarin	9110 W Ih 10 Ste 1, San Antonio TX 78230	210-593-1200	R	6*	<.1
180	Quepasa Corp—John C Abbott	224 Datura St Ste 1100, West Palm Beach FL 33401	561-491-4181	P	6	.1
181	Strategic Resources International Inc—Bharath Sreerangam	777 Washington Rd Ste, Parlin NJ 08859	732-887-4646	R	6*	<.1
182	Neubus Inc—Chris Albury	11700 Stnholw Dr Ste 1, Austin TX 78758	512-833-5339	R	6*	<.1
183	Agriculture—John Walter	1716 Locust St, Des Moines IA 50309	515-284-2917	D	6*	<.1
184	Justice Network Inc—Paul Ross	2430 Poplar Ave 3rd Fl, Memphis TN 38112	901-454-7880	R	6*	<.1
185	Polygon Network Inc—Louis Mousseau	PO Box 4806, Dillon CO 80435	450-463-8926	S	6*	<.1
186	4R Systems—Jiri M Nechleba	801 Cassatt Rd Ste 202, Berwyn PA 19312	610-644-1234	S	6*	<.1
187	ChemIndustrycom Inc—Daniel Fishman	730 E Cypress Ave, Monrovia CA 91016	626-930-0808	D	6*	<.1
188	Lexico Publishing Group LLC—Brian Kariger	65 Pine Ave, Long Beach CA 90802	562-432-3700	R	6*	<.1
189	WinNet Internet—Michael Tague	PO Box 4189, Louisville KY 40204	502-815-7000	R	6*	<.1
190	EducationDynamics LLC—Steven Isaac	5 Marine View Plz, Hoboken NJ 07030	201-377-3000	R	5*	<.1
191	VerusMed—Roscoe C Smith	8502 E Princess Dr Ste, Scottsdale AZ 85255		R	5*	<.1
192	Alexander Haas Martin and Partners Inc—David H King	3520 Piedmont Rd NE St, Atlanta GA 30305	404-832-9200	R	5*	<.1
193	Franchise Gator LLC—Farrah Kennedy	599 W Crossville Rd, Roswell GA 30075	678-748-3000	S	5*	<.1
194	OpenHire Inc—Andrew J Filipowski	102 W 3rd St Ste 250, Winston-Salem NC 27101	336-201-2100	S	5*	<.1
195	Accudata Technologies Inc—M Gregory Smith	800 N Watters Rd Ste 1, Allen TX 75013	972-390-2610	R	5*	<.1
196	Clickshare Service Corp—Richard Lerner	PO Box 376, Amherst MA 01004	413-458-7000	R	5*	<.1
197	Wintek Corp—Stephen E Belter	427 N 6th St Rm C, Lafayette IN 47901	765-742-8428	R	5*	<.1
198	Advanced Wireless Solutions—Micheal Huerta	4402 South Congress Av, Austin TX 78745	512-233-4638	R	5*	<.1
199	Forest2Market Inc—Peter Stewart	10030 Park Cedar Dr St, Charlotte NC 28210	704-357-0110	R	5*	<.1
200	Searchtec Inc—Marc Lovenworth	314 N 12th St Apt 201, Philadelphia PA 19107	215-963-0888	R	5*	<.1
201	Midwest Medical Copy Service Inc—Teresa Stewart	PO Box 129, Leo IN 46765	260-627-8742	R	5*	<.1
202	nFinanSe Inc—Jerry R Welch	PO Box 89233, Tampa FL 33689	813-367-4400	P	4	.1
203	Public Interest Data Inc—Michael Mac Leod	1800 Diagonal Rd Ste 4, Alexandria VA 22314	703-683-9500	R	4*	<.1
204	JuriSearchcom LLC—James Matison	1467 Greenbrier Pl, Charlottesville VA 22901	213-632-0336	R	4*	<.1
205	Comware International—David Retz	PO Box 410, Solvang CA 93463	805-686-1262	R	4*	<.1
206	Xedar Corp (Englewood Colorado)—Hugh H Williamson III	3772 Cherry Creek Nort, Denver CO 80209	303-377-0033	P	4	.1
207	US Data Security Corp—Paul Hrabal	PO Box 17073, Reno NV 89511	775-337-9300	R	4*	<.1
208	Pepperjam Network—Kristopher Jones	7 S Main St 3rd Fl, Wilkes Barre PA 18701		R	3	<.1
209	Yupi Internet Inc—Oscar Coen	1688 Meridian Ave 10th, Miami Beach FL 33139	305-604-0366	S	3	.3
210	Jackson Securities—Maynard Jackson	445 S Figueroa St, Los Angeles CA 90071	213-489-6872	R	3*	<.1
211	Archi-Tech Systems Inc—Paul Gray	275 Phillips Blvd Ste, Trenton NJ 08618	609-882-2447	R	3*	<.1
212	Catbird Networks Inc—Edmundo Costa	1800 Green Hills Rd St, Scotts Valley CA 95066		R	3*	<.1

Note: An asterisk (*) indicates an estimated financial figure. The company type code used is as follows: R = Private, P = Public, S = Private Subsidiary, B = Public Subsidiary, D = Division, J = Joint Venture, I = Investment Fund.

COMPANY RANKINGS BY SALES WITHIN 4-DIGIT SIC

Rank	Company Name—Executive Officer	Address, City, State, Zip	Phone	Type	Fin	Empls
213	Ignited Discovery LLC—Russ Kaulback	2020 14th St N 7th Fl, Arlington VA 22201	703-807-0710	S	3*	<.1
214	Rentbitscom—Dan Daugherty	6560 Greenwood Plz Ste, Englewood CO 80111	303-640-3160	R	3*	<.1
215	FreeRun Technologies Inc—Frank Forbes	550 Gateway Dr Ste 103, Napa CA 94558	707-265-1835	R	3*	<.1
216	Commodex—Philip Gotthelf	PO BOX 566, Closter NJ 07624	201-784-1235	R	3*	<.1
217	CenturyTel Interactive—Jack Doege	7502 Greenville Ave St, Dallas TX 75231	214-360-6280	S	3*	<.1
218	New Mexico Technet Inc—Terry Boulanger	924 Park Ave SW Rm D, Albuquerque NM 87102	505-345-6555	R	3*	<.1
219	RefCheck Information Services Inc—Zuni Corkerton	3962 Brown Park Dr Ste, Hilliard OH 43026	614-777-8844	R	3*	<.1
220	Adam's Career Transitions Inc—John Adams	423 New Karner Rd, Albany NY 12205	518-456-5216	R	3*	<.1
221	Teleshuttle Corp—Richard R Reisman	20 E 9th St, New York NY 10003	212-673-0225	R	3*	<.1
222	CANHELP LLC—Madeleen Herreshoff	PO Box 1678, Livingston NJ 07039		R	3*	<.1
223	Internet Business Systems Inc—David Heller	496 Salmar Ave, Campbell CA 95008	408-850-9246	R	3*	<.1
224	Lexiteria Corp—Robert Beard	2459 Smoketown Rd, Lewisburg PA 17837	570-522-0122	R	3*	<.1
225	QuipNet Inc—Bill Ball	1200 NW South Outer Rd, Blue Springs MO 64015	816-228-7200	R	3*	<.1
226	Industrial Television Services Inc—Brian Reynolds	3515 Martens St, Franklin Park IL 60131	847-671-4793	R	3*	<.1
227	Metalink Technologies Inc—Eric Merkel	PO Box 1121, Defiance OH 43512	419-782-3472	R	3*	<.1
228	U and X Group Inc—Boris Chait	1000 Rte 9 N Ste 203, Woodbridge NJ 07095	732-634-6304	R	3*	<.1
229	Tnt Information Services—Thanh Tran	1401 N Batavia St Ste, Orange CA 92867	714-538-4848	R	3*	<.1
230	Cybersearch Ltd—Craig Sherwood	800 E NW Hwy Ste 950, Palatine IL 60074	847-357-0200	R	2*	<.1
231	QuoteMedia Inc—R Keith Guelpa	17100 E Shea Blvd Ste, Fountain Hills AZ 85268	480-905-7311	P	2	.1
232	WeatherData Services Inc—Mike Smith	100 N Broadway Ste 750, Wichita KS 67202	316-266-8000	S	2*	<.1
233	Direct Mail Managers—Brent Harte	2642 N Sun Rd, Apache Junction AZ 85219	602-488-9389	R	2	<.1
234	Empress Software Inc—John Kornatowski	11785 Beltsville Dr, Beltsville MD 20705	301-220-1919	R	2*	<.1
235	Toolwire Inc—John Valencia	7031 Koll Center Parkw, Pleasanton CA 94566	925-227-8500	R	2*	<.1
236	E-Znet Inc—Tom Day	1119 Sibley Tower Bldg, Rochester NY 14604	716-262-2065	R	2	<.1
237	Information Processing Technology Inc—Robert Barzellato	1305 Fulton St, Rahway NJ 07065	732-396-0991	R	2*	<.1
238	STLtodaycom—Kevin Mowbray	900 N Tucker Blvd, Saint Louis MO 63101	314-657-3300	S	2*	<.1
239	Realty Computer Solutions Inc—James Lamar	13284 Pond Springs Rd, Austin TX 78729	512-459-8300	R	2*	<.1
240	Datasite Northwest Inc—Dale Mitchell	12000 Ne 8th St Ste 10, Bellevue WA 98005	425-455-1198	R	2*	<.1
241	Crescent Systems LLC—John Steele	25 Main Pl Ste 400, Council Bluffs IA 51503	712-388-2132	R	2*	<.1
242	IDT Hospitality Group—Harry Rivkin	161 Leverington Ave St, Philadelphia PA 19127	215-487-3102	R	2*	<.1
243	EOS Inc—Anthony Hopp	6900 Preston Dr, Springfield IL 62711	217-241-6000	R	2*	<.1
244	Information Sources Inc—Ruth Koolish	2175 Cactus Ct Ste 1, Walnut Creek CA 94595	925-891-4190	R	2*	<.1
245	PhotoSpin Inc—Val Gelineau	302 W 5th St Ste 100B, San Pedro CA 90731	310-548-5420	R	2*	<.1
246	Bellhawk Systems Inc—Emily Green	PO Box 300, Millbury MA 01527	508-865-8070	R	2*	<.1
247	Nysernet Inc—Timothy L Lance	100 S Salina St Ste 30, Syracuse NY 13202	315-413-0345	R	2*	<.1
248	Access Information Inc—Wanda McDavid	234 Columbine St Ste 3, Denver CO 80206	303-778-7677	R	2*	<.1
249	Training and Seminar Locators Inc—Margie Sweaney	719 Lakemont Pl Ste 2, San Ramon CA 94582	925-735-8275	R	2*	<.1
250	CheckRite of Kansas City Inc	3641 SW Plass Ave, Topeka KS 66611	785-266-3255	S	2*	<.1
251	CheckRite of Oklahoma Inc	123 W 7th Ste 203, Stillwater OK 74074	405-943-9199	S	2*	<.1
252	New Radio Star Inc—Bob Hamilton	225 Crossroads Blvd St, Carmel CA 93923	626-817-2346	R	2*	<.1
253	Cartoon Bank Inc—Robert Mankoff	1440 Broadway 11th Fl, New York NY 10018	212-630-2710	D	2*	<.1
254	Chase Solutions Inc—Dave Chase	PO Box 1116, Centerville MA 02632	508-790-2500	R	2*	<.1
255	Pioneer Teletechnologies LLC—Tony Mau	PO Box 67, Sergeant Bluff IA 51054	712-271-4000	R	2*	<.1
256	North Of Boston Library Exchange Inc—Ronald Gagnon	26 Cherry Hill Dr, Danvers MA 01923	978-777-8844	R	2*	<.1
257	Premiere Properties Inc—Joseph Grimes	530 E 76th St Office H, New York NY 10021	212-628-9735	R	2*	<.1
258	Anesis Inc—Chris Greely	15995 N Barkers Lndg 1, Houston TX 77079	281-597-6700	R	2*	<.1
259	Apk Net Inc—Macy Hallock	15166 Neo Pkwy, Cleveland OH 44128	440-710-1002	R	2*	<.1
260	Crowdgather Inc—Sanjay Sabnani	20300 Ventura Blvd Ste, Woodland Hills CA 91364	818-435-2472	P	2	<.1
261	Isp Associates Inc—Jerry Windham	PO Box 28, Ripley MS 38663	662-993-2000	R	2*	<.1
262	Reno Information Services—Rick Vandenberg	490 S Ctr St, Reno NV 89501	775-326-6664	R	1*	<.1
263	DigitalPost Interactive Inc—Michael Sawtell	4040 Barranca Pkwy Ste, Irvine CA 92604		P	1	<.1
264	Cobalius Solutions PLLC—Yves France	10201 W Lincoln Ave, Milwaukee WI 53227	414-546-2738	R	1*	<.1
265	Archives Security Inc—Paul Griffin	88 Green Springs Hwy, Homewood AL 35209	205-322-6197	R	1*	<.1
266	Tower Publishing—Michael Lyons	588 Saco Rd, Standish ME 04084	207-642-5400	R	1*	<.1
267	Document Center Inc—Claudia Bach	111 Industrial Way Ste, Belmont CA 94002	650-591-7600	R	1*	<.1
268	Internet Professionals Inc—Jason Kubasak	2302 W N Ave Ste 1w, Chicago IL 60647	773-292-1899	R	1*	<.1
269	C Stegman Company Inc—Eric Banister	PO Box 181491, Fairfield OH 45018	513-522-0111	R	1	<.1
270	readMedia—Colin Mathews	418 Broadway 4th Fl, Albany NY 12207	518-429-2800	R	1*	<.1
271	Mitchell Selling Dynamics Inc—John Mitchell	1360 Puritan Ave, Birmingham MI 48009	248-644-8092	R	1*	<.1
272	Airwirenet Inc—Donald Turek	PO Box 620, Melbourne FL 32902	321-752-4000	R	1*	<.1
273	HilSoft Inc—Laura Schultz	10300 SW Allen Blvd, Beaverton OR 97005	215-721-2120	S	1*	<.1
274	Spectrum Unlimited—John Ritter	2261 Market St Ste 276, San Francisco CA 94114	415-647-1070	R	1*	<.1
275	Digital Wise Inc—Heather Lukes	PO Box 361, Woodbridge VA 22194		R	1*	<.1
276	Street Software Technology Inc—Bret Black	230 Park Ave Ste 857, New York NY 10169	212-922-0500	R	1*	<.1
277	Document Retention Systems Inc—Robert Sorbonne	1619 Cotswold Cir, Sandy UT 84093	801-266-7711	R	1*	<.1
278	DataSource Corp—Terry Struthers	736 7th St, Boulder CO 80302	303-444-9194	R	1	<.1
279	Unet 2 Corp—James Monaco	80 E 11th St, New York NY 10003	212-777-5463	R	1*	<.1
280	DBS Systems Inc—Al Behrendt Clickshare Service Corp	PO Box 367, Williamstown MA 01267	413-458-8001	S	1*	<.1
281	Izzy Dot Net Inc—Judy Freedman	PO Box 1225, Ann Arbor MI 48106	734-213-5710	R	1*	<.1
282	Research on Demand Inc—Steve McIntosh	290 N Fairview Ave, Goleta CA 93117		R	1*	<.1
283	The Job Seeker—Bill Oakes	403 Oakwood St, Warrens WI 54666	608-378-4450	R	1*	<.1
284	Beyond Commerce Inc—Robert J McNulty	750 Coronado Ctr Dr St, Henderson NV 89052	702-952-9549	P	1*	<.1
285	Intellidyn Inc—Peter Harvey	8 Maple Dr, Sandy Hook CT 06482	203-426-5644	R	1*	<.1
286	Capitol District Information Services Inc—Kevin O'Mahony	471 H St NW, Washington DC 20001	202-265-1516	R	1*	<.1
287	Mlh Services LLC	315 Mount Evans Blvd, Pine CO 80470	303-816-7156	R	1*	<.1
288	Dataline Verification Company LLC	34 Preston Rd, Parsippany NJ 07054	973-887-0207	R	1*	<.1
289	Infinite Systems Support Inc—Ira Thompson	42w114 Retreat Ct, Saint Charles IL 60175	630-584-5609	R	1*	<.1
290	Iggys House Inc—Joseph Fox	1 S Wacker Dr Ste 1900, Chicago IL 60606		R	<1	<.1
291	Sandglass Systems—Andrew Fraser	3005 McComas Ave, Kensington MD 20895	301-942-8400	R	<1*	<.1
292	Tdnet Inc—Michael Markwith	PO Box 38, West Chester PA 19381	610-738-0280	R	<1*	<.1
293	Madison Ave Media Inc—Jim Lindsey	1515 S Federal Hwy Ste, Boca Raton FL 33432	561-549-3100	P	<1	<.1
294	FamilytravelCom—Lynn Hayes	9280 E Thompson Peak P, Scottsdale AZ 85255	480-556-6266	R	<1*	<.1
295	CrownNet Inc—Delores Bellar	6300 Melton Rd, Portage IN 46368	219-762-1431	R	<1*	<.1
296	KLAS Enterprises LLC—Adam Gale	630 E Technology Ave, Orem UT 84097	801-226-5120	R	<1	<.1
297	Businessvn Inc—Carlos Rosette	9449 Balboa Ave Ste114, San Diego CA 92123		P	<1	N/A
298	Intellidyn Corp—Peter Harvey	175 Derby St, Hingham MA 02043	781-741-5503	R	N/A	<.1
299	RadixNet Inc	6178 Oxon Hill Rd Ste, Oxon Hill MD 20745	301-567-9831	R	N/A	<.1

TOTALS: SIC 7375 Information Retrieval Services
Companies: 299

					62,890	128.1

Rank	Company Name—*Executive Officer*	Address, City, State, Zip	Phone	Type	Fin	Empls
	7376 Computer Facilities Management					
1	TekSystems Inc—*Keith Bozeman*	7437 Race Rd, Hanover MD 21076		R	7,636*	20.0
2	NJVC LLC—*Jody J Tedesco*	8614 Westwood Ctr Ste, Vienna VA 22182	703-556-0110	R	502*	1.3
3	BT Radianz—*Laurie Bowen*	575 Lexington Ave 12th, New York NY 10022	212-415-4600	R	382*	1.0
4	Broadstripe—*Gustavo Prilick*	13455 Noel Rd Ste 1310, Dallas TX 75240	972-663-6971	R	331*	.8
5	E Plus Technology—*Phillip Norton*	13595 Dulles Technolog, Herndon VA 20171	703-984-8400	S	266*	.7
6	Akibia Inc—*Thomas Tucker*	4 Technology Dr, Westborough MA 01581	508-621-4735	R	147*	.4
7	Perimeter Internetworking—*TIm Harvey*	440 Wheelers Farms Rd, Milford CT 06460		R	136*	.4
8	StoresOnlinecom Inc	1303 N Research Way Bl, Orem UT 84097	801-434-8582	S	115*	.3
9	OneNeck IT Services Corp—*Dawne L Britney*	5301 N Pima Rd Ste 100, Scottsdale AZ 85260	480-315-3000	R	95*	.2
10	Glasshouse Technologies Inc—*Patrick J Scannell Jr*	200 Crossing Blvd, Framingham MA 01702	508-879-5729	R	85*	.6
11	Telx Group Inc—*Eric Shepcaro*	1 State St 21st Fl, New York NY 10004	212-480-3300	R	84*	.2
12	Panasas Inc—*Faye Pairman*	969 W Maude Ave, Sunnyvale CA 94085	408-215-6800	R	51*	.1
13	SARCOM—*Jim Garrity*	19 Morgan, Irvine CA 92618	949-472-9000	S	49*	.1
14	Neohapsis Inc—*James Mobley*	215 First St Ste 005, Cambridge MA 02142	773-269-6300	R	45*	.1
15	dbaDirect Inc—*John Bostick*	7310 Turfway Rd Ste 30, Florence KY 41042		R	26*	.1
16	ORI Services Corp—*Tracy Walcott*	4565 Ruffner St Ste 20, San Diego CA 92111	858-576-4422	R	25*	.2
17	Mi8 Corp—*David Ehrhardt*	601 W 26th St, New York NY 10001	212-727-0911	D	22*	<.1
18	Electronic Environments Corp—*Kenneth Rapoport*	410 Forest St, Marlborough MA 01752	508-229-1400	R	21*	.1
19	Gaits Inc—*Tony Asefi*	11781 Lee Jackson Memo, Fairfax VA 22033	703-866-2400	R	19*	.3
20	Accelera Solutions Inc—*Chong Yi*	12150 Monument Dr Ste, Fairfax VA 22033		R	17*	<.1
21	Coresite LLC—*Robert Stuckey*	1050 17th St Ste 800, Denver CO 80265	303-405-1000	R	17*	.2
22	Infologics Inc—*Lowrie W McIntosh*	52 Robinwood Village, Saylorsburg PA 18353	570-922-3696	R	16*	<.1
23	WynnCom—*Jimmy Wynn*	419 Salem St, Lexington NC 27292		R	14*	.1
24	RTL Networks Inc—*Richard Lewis*	2460 W 26th Ave Ste 25, Denver CO 80211	303-757-3100	R	13	<.1
25	Five9 Inc—*Mike Burkland*	7901 Stoneridge Dr Ste, Pleasanton CA 94588	925-201-2000	R	11	.1
26	E Solutions Corp—*Richard Nicholas*	400 N Tampa St 16th Fl, Tampa FL 33602	813-301-2600	S	11*	<.1
27	Data Base Systems International Inc—*William Bachenberg*	3949 Schelden Cir, Bethlehem PA 18017	610-691-8811	R	9*	.1
28	Telehouse International Corporation of America—*Yasushi Kubota*	7 Teleport Dr, Staten Island NY 10311	718-355-2500	R	7*	.1
29	Castle Access—*Mark Hopperton*	9606 Aero Dr, San Diego CA 92123	858-836-0200	R	6*	<.1
30	Biz Net Technologies	1715 Pratt Dr Ste 3500, Blacksburg VA 24060	540-961-7560	R	5*	<.1
31	Imaging Solutions Inc (Wallingford Connecticut)—*Rick Smith*	860 N Main St Ext, Wallingford CT 06492	203-294-6300	R	5*	<.1
32	EZ Hi-Tech Services Inc—*Zeev Sela*	PO Box 1342, Springfield NJ 07081	908-317-8203	R	4*	<.1
33	US Billing Inc—*John Bernhoft*	10012 W Capitol Dr L10, Milwaukee WI 53222	414-461-1222	R	4*	<.1
34	NewAgeSys Inc—*Limy John*	231 Clarksville Rd Ste, Princeton Junction NJ 08550	609-919-9800	R	4	.1
35	Major Inc—*Joan Rizzo*	14220 Northbrook Dr St, San Antonio TX 78232	210-828-6081	R	4*	<.1
36	Ruland Associates Inc—*James Ruland*	PO Box 790, Charles Town WV 25414	304-728-6225	R	4*	<.1
37	ConQwest Inc—*Michelle Drolet*	615 Concord St, Framingham MA 01702	774-204-0700	R	4*	<.1
38	Interactive Payer Network LLC—*Nick Rosenstein*	5910 Landerbrook Dr St, Cleveland OH 44124	440-720-0700	R	3*	<.1
39	Zag Technical Services Inc—*Greg Gatzke*	2144 Bering Dr, San Jose CA 95131	408-436-2080	R	3*	<.1
40	Infolink Information Services Inc—*David Hillstrom*	3109 Grand Ave Ste 455, Miami FL 33133		R	3*	<.1
41	Facility Technology Services Inc—*Bobby Chandler*	PO Box 1381, Sterling VA 20167	571-203-0245	R	3*	<.1
42	Csam Marketing Inc—*Kash Mahna*	PO Box 20, Somerville NJ 08876	908-725-1373	R	3*	<.1
43	Enertron LLC—*Scott Venier*	24705 Mound Rd, Warren MI 48091	586-757-1200	R	2*	<.1
44	Jenkins-Lara Corp—*Antonio Jenkins-Lara*	PO Box 16641, Sugar Land TX 77496	281-208-3706	R	2*	<.1
45	Ism Services Inc—*Paul Williams*	103a W George St, Carmichaels PA 15320	724-415-9842	R	1*	<.1
46	NIlj Holdings Inc—*Brian Marcuzzo*	PO Box 45827, Omaha NE 68145	402-884-7967	R	1*	<.1
47	Libraries Of Middlesex Automation Consortium—*Eileen Palmer*	1030 St Grges Ave Ste, Avenel NJ 07001	732-750-2525	R	1*	<.1
48	Laurel Computer Systems Inc—*Ray Thomas*	PO Box 1085, Uniontown PA 15401	724-438-6601	R	1*	<.1
49	Computer Management and Support Services—*Tom Smith*	PO Box 11916, Costa Mesa CA 92627	626-533-3750	R	1*	<.1
50	Cmsolutions LLC—*Zoe Morno*	210 High St, Palo Alto CA 94301	650-289-1040	R	1*	<.1
51	Meridian Holdings Inc—*Anthony C Dike*	4477 W 118th St Ste 30, Hawthorne CA 90250	323-295-5062	P	<1	<.1
52	Arkay Engravers Inc—*Kenneth Kaplan*	10 Drew Ct Ste 3, Ronkonkoma NY 11779	631-467-7795	R	<1*	<.1
53	Burton Holmes Associates Inc—*Burton Holmes*	2 Grove St, New York NY 10014	212-989-0207	R	<1*	<.1
54	Star Lake Consulting Inc—*Patrick Mccaghren*	2515 Grand Point Cir, Birmingham AL 35226	205-979-8044	R	<1*	<.1

TOTALS: SIC 7376 Computer Facilities Management
    Companies: 54   10,219   27.8

Rank	Company Name—*Executive Officer*	Address, City, State, Zip	Phone	Type	Fin	Empls
	7377 Computer Rental & Leasing					
1	El Camino Resources International Inc—*David Harmon*	21300 Superior St, Chatsworth CA 91311	818-226-6600	R	750	1.3
2	California First National Bancorp—*Patrick E Paddon*	18201 Von Karman Ave S, Irvine CA 92612	949-255-0500	P	524	.2
3	Relational Funding Corp—*Jeff Ehlers*	3701 Algonquin Rd Ste, Rolling Meadows IL 60008	847-818-1700	R	332*	.4
4	Electro Rent Corporation Data Rentals/Sales Div—*William Weitzman*	6060 Sepulveda Blvd, Van Nuys CA 91411	818-787-2100	D	256*	.4
5	SmartSource Computer and Audio Visual Rentals—*Julian Sandler*	265 Oser Ave, Hauppauge NY 11788	631-273-8888	R	223*	.3
6	Insight Investments LLC—*John Ford*	600 City Pkwy W Ste 50, Orange CA 92868	714-939-2300	R	153*	.2
7	Balboa Capital Corp—*Phil Silva*	2010 Main St 11th Fl, Irvine CA 92614	949-756-0800	R	106*	.1
8	Winthrop Resources Corp—*Craig R Dahl*	11100 Wayzata Blvd Ste, Minnetonka MN 55305	952-936-0226	S	106*	.1
9	ePlus Group Inc	13595 Dulles Technolog, Herndon VA 20170	703-984-8400	S	64	.1
10	G/S Leasing Inc—*Dennis Cyrus*	3290 W Big Beavr Rd St, Troy MI 48084	248-649-5560	R	24*	<.1
11	MicroTek Inc (Oakbrook Terrace Illinois)—*Don Slivensky*	2001 Butterfield Rd Rm, Downers Grove IL 60515	630-719-0211	R	15*	.1
12	Macquarie Equipment Finance LLC—*Jeffrey M Peek*	2285 Franklin Rd Ste 1, Bloomfield Hills MI 48302	248-253-9000	S	8*	.1
13	Affordable Computer Rentals Inc—*Larry Gazdick*	PO Box 1891, Ashburn VA 20146	703-776-9320	R	7*	<.1
14	Technology Investment Partners LLC—*Scott Grady*	40950 Woodward Ave Ste, Bloomfield Hills MI 48304	248-593-3900	R	5*	<.1
15	Paragon Capital Corp—*J Thomas Williams*	2820 1st Ave N, St Petersburg FL 33713		R	5*	<.1
16	Rent-A-Bit Inc—*Thomas LaFree*	3920 Pendleton Way, Indianapolis IN 46226	317-334-0393	R	5*	<.1
17	US Financial Services Inc—*James Mcconnachie*	21599 W 11 Mile Rd Ste, Southfield MI 48076	248-356-4500	R	4*	<.1
18	Britannia Inc—*Peter Harrison*	1616 Directors Row, Fort Wayne IN 46808	260-482-6321	R	4*	<.1
19	Kingsbridge Holdings LLC	150 N Field Dr Ste 193, Lake Forest IL 60045	847-693-4100	R	4*	<.1
20	It Strategies International Corp—*Michael Beardslee*	4550 W Okley Blvd Ste, Las Vegas NV 89102	702-878-3828	R	4*	<.1
21	Visual Information Systems—*Alan Burgess*	16412 N 92nd St Ste 11, Scottsdale AZ 85260	480-968-5600	R	3*	<.1
22	Tno-Madymo North America Inc—*Bachar Aljundi*	38701 7 Mile Rd Ste 26, Livonia MI 48152	734-779-4850	R	3*	<.1
23	RAC Solutions—*Nancy Spencer*	4853 Cordell Ave Ste 2, Bethesda MD 20814		R	2*	<.1
24	AL Cunningham-B Corp—*James Cunningham*	PO Box 96, Wyandotte MI 48192	734-282-3830	R	2*	<.1
25	Navcor—*Tammy Shovelson*	16526 W 78th St 313, Eden Prairie MN 55346	952-906-2808	R	2*	<.1
26	Cgt Enterprise Inc—*Christopher Thompson*	PO Box 26716, Minneapolis MN 55426	952-944-8838	R	1*	<.1
27	Comdisco Holding Company Inc—*Randolph I Thornton*	PO Box 2133, Des Plaines IL 60017	847-698-3000	P	1	<.1

Note: An asterisk (*) indicates an estimated financial figure. The company type code used is as follows: R = Private, P = Public, S = Private Subsidiary, B = Public Subsidiary, D = Division, J = Joint Venture, I = Investment Fund.

COMPANY RANKINGS BY SALES WITHIN 4-DIGIT SIC

Rank	Company Name—*Executive Officer*	Address, City, State, Zip	Phone	Type	Fin	Empls
28	JTA Leasing Company LLC—*Robert Alfano*	2050 Center Ave Ste 60, Fort Lee NJ 07024	201-346-0444	R	1*	<.1
29	Encore Leasing Group LLC—*Pam Gaynor*	815 Mission Ave Ste 20, Oceanside CA 92054	760-721-9090	R	1*	<.1
30	Rac Tek Inc—*Dorothy Jennings*	5632 E Broadway Blvd, Tucson AZ 85711	520-292-6771	R	1*	<.1
31	Point Financial Inc—*Michael O'malley*	PO Box 50576, Phoenix AZ 85076	480-785-1113	R	1*	<.1
32	Governmentquotecom—*John Flores*	Hc 30 Box 80e, Caldwell WV 24925	304-645-7928	R	1*	<.1
33	R and J Randall Enterprises Inc—*Rick Randall*	5726 Harborside Way, Elk Grove CA 95758	916-479-3495	R	<1*	<.1

TOTALS: SIC 7377 Computer Rental & Leasing
Companies: 33

					2,617	3.6

7378 Computer Maintenance & Repair

Rank	Company Name—*Executive Officer*	Address, City, State, Zip	Phone	Type	Fin	Empls
1	Alorica Inc—*Andy Lee*	14726 Ramona Ave 3rd F, Chino CA 91710	909-606-3600	R	2,347*	20.0
2	DecisionOne Holdings Corp—*Neal Bibeau*	426 W Lancaster Ave, Devon PA 19333	610-296-6000	R	1,868*	4.5
3	DecisionOne Corp—*Neil Bibeau*	426 West Lancaster Ave, Devon PA 19333	610-296-6000	S	333*	2.5
4	Maintech—*Frank DAlessio*	4 Commerce Dr, Cranford NJ 07016	973-472-4572	D	199*	.6
5	Peripheral Computer Support Inc	47951 Westinghouse Dr, Fremont CA 94539	510-651-6077	R	55*	.2
6	Meridian IT—*Brad Illanfeld*	Nine Parkway N Ste 500, Deerfield IL 60015	847-964-2700	R	53*	.2
7	United Asset Coverage Inc—*Anthony J Parella*	1405 S Beltline Rd, Coppell TX 75019	972-462-5800	R	51*	.1
8	Dataprise Inc—*David E Eisner*	12250 Rockville Pike 2, Rockville MD 20852	301-945-0700	R	36*	.1
9	Cokeva Inc—*Anhtuyet Nguyen*	3387 Industrial Ave St, Rocklin CA 95765	916-543-7600	R	30*	.4
10	Tekserve Corp—*Dick Demenus*	119 W 23rd St, New York NY 10011	212-929-3645	R	26*	.2
11	Pulau Electronics Corp—*Walter Sunderlin*	12633 Challenger Pkwy, Orlando FL 32826	407-380-9191	R	23*	.2
12	Spartan Computer Services Inc—*Jack Steenhausen*	PO Box 2045, Greer SC 29652	864-848-3810	R	21*	.2
13	DRS Technical Services Inc—*Mark S Newman*	5 Sylvan Way, Parsippany NJ 07054	973-898-1500	S	19*	.1
14	WRG Services Inc—*Mike Stevenson*	38585 Apollo Pky, Willoughby OH 44094	440-942-8650	S	18*	<.1
15	Prism Pointe Technologies LLC—*Rock Lyke*	4605a Coates Dr, Fairburn GA 30213	678-610-4900	R	17*	.2
16	Accram Inc—*Bob Daquilante*	2901 W Clarendon Ave, Phoenix AZ 85017	602-264-0288	R	16*	.1
17	Networking Technologies and Support Inc—*Bernard Robinson*	14421 Justice Rd, Midlothian VA 23113	804-379-1800	R	16*	.1
18	Computer Gallery Inc—*Joseph Pauper*	73-965 Hwy 111, Palm Desert CA 92260	760-779-1001	R	15*	<.1
19	Signature Technology Group Inc—*Charles Layne*	2424 W Desert Cove Ave, Phoenix AZ 85029	602-427-4500	R	12*	.1
20	Electronic Systems Services Inc—*Bill Kisse*	22515 Gateway Ctr Dr, Clarksburg MD 20871	301-944-2300	R	12*	.1
21	InterTech Computer Products Inc—*Michael Novotny*	5225 S 39th St, Phoenix AZ 85040	602-437-0035	R	11*	<.1
22	Intratek Computer Inc—*Anthony Battey*	200 Sandpointe Ave Ste, Santa Ana CA 92707	714-892-0892	R	10*	.2
23	DriveSavers Inc—*Jay Hagan*	400 Bel Marin Keys Blv, Novato CA 94949	415-382-2000	R	10*	.1
24	Av Connection Inc—*Ajay Jalota*	24586 Hawthorne Blvd S, Torrance CA 90505	310-782-6500	R	10*	<.1
25	AA Computech Inc	29021 Ave Sherman Ste, Valencia CA 91355	661-257-6801	R	10*	<.1
26	OfficeCare Corp—*Howard Williams*	700 W Pete Rose Way, Cincinnati OH 45203	513-831-2813	R	10*	<.1
27	Retail Technology Group Inc—*Jeffrey Wolfangel*	PO Box 22438, Saint Louis MO 63126	636-600-4070	R	9*	<.1
28	CHE Consulting Inc—*David L York*	1576 Fencorp Dr, Fenton MO 63026		R	9*	.1
29	Amtek Computer Services—*Van H Boone*	1389 Calle Avanzado, San Clemente CA 92673		R	9*	<.1
30	Shermantic Computer Service—*Aaron Ashley*	600 Fairmont Ave, Fairmont WV 26554	304-367-0020	R	8*	.1
31	NextNine Inc—*Shmulik Aran*	75 Maiden Ln, New York NY 10038	212-405-2221	R	8*	<.1
32	Virtual Kreation Inc—*Roberto Alberdeston*	1210 Pinar Dr, Orlando FL 32825	407-208-9022	R	8*	<.1
33	Alquest Technologies Inc—*Henry Wojcik*	560 E Arrow Hwy, San Dimas CA 91773	909-592-8708	R	7*	.1
34	Ces Computers Inc—*Gerald Holt*	120 Bryant St Ste 101, Dubuque IA 52003	563-588-9020	R	7*	.1
35	D/I Laser Products Of Dallas Inc—*Tom Shambo*	PO Box 294273, Lewisville TX 75029	972-219-1300	R	7*	.1
36	Service Assurance Corp—*Mark Giannini*	6935 Appling Farms Pkw, Memphis TN 38133	901-382-2500	R	7*	.1
37	Domestic Securities Inc—*Mark Shefts*	160 Summit Ave, Montvale NJ 07645	201-782-0888	R	7*	<.1
38	Support Of Microcomputers Associates Inc—*Ed Blumenthal*	1819 Jfk Blvd Ste 460, Philadelphia PA 19103	215-496-0303	R	7*	<.1
39	Advanced Network Inc—*Robert Plunkett*	8940 Activity Rd Ste F, San Diego CA 92126	858-578-1533	R	7*	.1
40	Ener-Tel Services Inc—*Michael Favre*	PO Box 5290, San Angelo TX 76902	325-658-8375	R	7*	<.1
41	Micro Medics Computer/Printer Service Inc—*Matthew Sheasaby*	999 Forest Edge Dr, Vernon Hills IL 60061	847-955-1200	R	6*	.1
42	Network Management Resources Inc—*David Garcia*	201 Defense Hwy Ste 20, Annapolis MD 21401	410-573-0080	R	6*	.1
43	Somax Inc	490 Sun Valley Dr Ste, Roswell GA 30076	770-518-1514	R	6*	<.1
44	Evergreen Information Technology Services Inc—*Thelma Martin*	14900 Sweitzer Ln Ste, Laurel MD 20707	301-270-6200	R	6*	<.1
45	Cascade Computer Maintenance Inc—*Jim Mollett*	3240 Commercial St Se, Salem OR 97302	503-581-0081	R	6*	.1
46	Positive Business Solutions Inc—*Ray Cool*	11880 Kemper Springs D, Cincinnati OH 45240	513-772-2255	R	5*	.1
47	Mainstreet Technologies Inc—*Rufus Davis*	7125 Thomas Edison Dr, Columbia MD 21046	410-347-1277	R	5*	.1
48	Geeks On Call Holdings Inc—*Richard T Cole*	1081 19th St, Virginia Beach VA 23451	757-466-3448	P	5	.1
49	Forward Edge Inc—*Stan Gerlich*	3428 Hauck Rd Ste K, Cincinnati OH 45241	513-761-3343	R	5*	<.1
50	Arista Business Imaging Solutions Inc—*Lorrie Eysel*	5153 Commercial Cir St, Concord CA 94520	925-825-8400	R	5*	<.1
51	Compucharts Computer Products and Services Inc—*Bruce Byerly*	775 S Progress Dr, Medina OH 44256	330-725-0880	R	5*	<.1
52	Delcom Group LP—*Christine Delph*	PO Box 1988, Allen TX 75013	214-389-5500	R	5*	<.1
53	Acropolis Computers Inc—*Tracy Butler*	300 Hunter Ave Ste 103, Saint Louis MO 63124	314-890-2208	R	5*	<.1
54	Gryphon Group Ltd—*Constantine Potamianos*	25 E Wayne Ave Apt 110, Silver Spring MD 20901	301-585-8140	R	5*	<.1
55	Chip Inc—*Chip Meyer*	21060 Centre Pointe Pk, Santa Clarita CA 91350	661-260-3000	R	4	.1
56	Technology Specialist Inc—*Andrew Porch*	PO Box 1547, Albertville AL 35950	256-878-2121	R	4*	.1
57	MacMedics—*Dana Stibolt*	1131 Benfield Blvd Ste, Millersville MD 21108	410-987-8588	R	4*	<.1
58	Excalibur Data Recovery Inc—*Darlene Keough*	13 Branch St Ste 2078, Methuen MA 01844	978-681-1200	R	4*	<.1
59	Connexis LLC	1520 Kensington Rd Ste, Oak Brook IL 60523	630-413-5050	R	4*	.1
60	Laptop Service Center LLC—*Tom Clarke*	50 W Powhattan Ave Ste, Essington PA 19029	610-521-6100	R	4*	<.1
61	Computer Integrated Services Company Of New York LLC—*Claudette Faison*	561 7th Ave Fl 13, New York NY 10018	212-577-6033	R	3*	<.1
62	PC Professional Incorporation—*Dan Sanguinetti*	1615 Webster St, Oakland CA 94612	510-465-5700	R	3*	<.1
63	CBS Computers Inc—*Victor Salerno*	675 Grier Dr, Las Vegas NV 89119	702-735-4873	R	3*	<.1
64	Solbrekk Inc—*Steve Solbrack*	1000 Boone Ave N Ste 6, Golden Valley MN 55427	763-475-9111	R	3*	<.1
65	Consolidated Computer Services Inc—*Tim Rizer*	5509 Vine St, Alexandria VA 22310	703-922-2020	R	3	<.1
66	Hillside Electronic Corp—*William Chamberlin*	17 Buffington Hill Rd, Worthington MA 01098	413-238-5566	R	3*	<.1
67	AlterNative Technologies (Sheridan Wyoming)—*Steve Owen*	69 Dee Dr, Sheridan WY 82801	307-675-1010	R	3*	<.1
68	Systems Supply Inc—*John Cappello*	291 Rockland St Ste 10, Hanover MA 02339	781-878-8000	R	3*	<.1
69	Acclaim Networks Inc—*David Yandry*	754 Port America Pl St, Grapevine TX 76051	817-488-1030	R	3*	<.1
70	Dtidatacom Inc—*David Mohyla*	1155 Pasadena Ave S St, South Pasadena FL 33707	727-345-9665	R	3*	<.1
71	Tritech Solution—*Anthony Nguyen*	12802 Nutwood St, Garden Grove CA 92840	714-638-8487	D	3*	<.1
72	AccuNOC IT—*Jeffrey Bond*	29 Sullivan Way, East Brunswick NJ 08816	732-568-4669	R	3*	<.1
73	New Age Digital—*Dennis Pace*	318 N Arch Rd, Richmond VA 23236	804-340-1300	R	3*	<.1
74	OmniData Corp—*Larry McGovern*	2500 Townsgate Rd Ste, Westlake Village CA 91361	805-371-4400	R	3*	<.1
75	Xtras Inc—*Mike Schinkel*	4355J Cobb Pky Ste 264, Atlanta GA 30339	404-474-0148	R	3*	<.1
76	Israel Katcher—*Israel Ketchin*	122 Tompkins Rd, Lagrangeville NY 12540	845-677-5553	R	3*	<.1

Rank	Company Name—*Executive Officer*	Address, City, State, Zip	Phone	Type	Fin	Empls
77	Lan Solutions Inc—*Victor Kellan*	1430 Spring Hill Rd St, Mc Lean VA 22102	703-891-9628	R	3*	<.1
78	Surf Investment Ltd—*Julie Peterson*	17922 Sky Park Cir Ste, Irvine CA 92614	949-250-0744	R	3*	<.1
79	Frontier Vision Technologies Inc—*Yury Ruban*	705 N Mountain Rd A120, Newington CT 06111	860-953-0240	R	3*	.1
80	Infinite Systems Services Inc—*Donald Fitzgerald*	970 Bolger Ct, Fenton MO 63026	636-305-9200	R	3*	<.1
81	Gkc Total Solutions Inc—*Guy Mehring*	4904 Spring Rd, Oak Lawn IL 60453	708-425-3832	R	2*	<.1
82	American Video Service Inc—*Ken Lee*	855 Jarvis Dr, Morgan Hill CA 95037	408-778-5562	R	2*	<.1
83	Data Vista Inc—*Stephen Gifford*	122 Burrs Rd Ste A, Westampton NJ 08060	609-702-9300	R	2*	<.1
84	P and J Computers Inc—*Paul Joralemon*	1 Highland Ave, Colonie NY 12205	518-459-6712	R	2*	<.1
85	Cambyte Computer Services Inc—*Ndamukong Tangeh*	18410 Tall Cypress Dr, Spring TX 77388	281-353-4169	R	2*	<.1
86	Wal Greens—*Mike Tito*	2040 S Carboy Rd, Mount Prospect IL 60056	847-981-8863	R	2*	<.1
87	A-Tech Computer Service Inc—*Frank Suda*	296 Williams Pl, East Dundee IL 60118	847-428-9199	R	2*	<.1
88	Waypoint Business Solutions Gp LLC	10555 Cossey Rd, Houston TX 77070	281-847-1642	R	2*	<.1
89	Mx Consulting Services Inc—*George Kavgic*	544 Paramount Dr, Raynham MA 02767	508-821-5855	R	2*	<.1
90	Datatrek Xtreme Inc—*Roy Hykes*	1498 Reisterstown Rd, Pikesville MD 21208	410-527-9800	R	2*	<.1
91	CTS Services Inc—*Michelle Carlow*	260 Maple St, Bellingham MA 02019	508-528-7720	R	2*	<.1
92	Computer and Laser Services Inc—*Eric Lindo*	6006 S Central Ave, Chicago IL 60638	773-735-9199	R	2*	<.1
93	Word-Tech Inc—*Bruce Karlson*	5625 Foxridge Dr Ste 1, Shawnee Mission KS 66202	913-722-3334	R	2*	<.1
94	Brooks Technology Management Inc—*Randy Brooks*	509 2nd Ave S, Nashville TN 37210	615-254-5766	R	2*	<.1
95	Laptop and Desktop Repair LLC	4900 Ampere Dr Ste 102, Reno NV 89502	775-857-1878	R	2*	<.1
96	Southwestern Computer Technologies—*Clint Dewitt*	4626 E La Puente Ave, Phoenix AZ 85044	602-791-3575	R	2*	<.1
97	Landmark Systems Inc—*Steven Hothem*	1209 Chicago Rd, Troy MI 48083	248-589-9665	R	2*	<.1
98	Essential Technologies—*Drew Foster*	805 Virginia Dr, Orlando FL 32803	407-896-8155	R	2*	<.1
99	Crisis Computer Corp—*Larry Lehman*	PO Box 210060, San Jose CA 95151	408-270-1100	R	2*	<.1
100	Dominion Repair Service Inc—*Mike Burstein*	PO Box 30521, Alexandria VA 22310	703-768-3510	S	2*	<.1
101	Emergency Computer Technician LLC—*Matthew Matter*	305 N 2nd Ave, Upland CA 91786	909-297-3593	R	2*	<.1
102	TIS Communications of El Paso—*Patrick Cottman*	11394 James Watt Dr, El Paso TX 79936	915-590-8902	R	2*	<.1
103	Computer Medic Center of North Palm Beach Inc—*Dan Bukowski*	958 Northlake Blvd, Lake Park FL 33403	561-844-0707	R	2*	<.1
104	Integrated Office Solutions—*Rick Heist*	PO Box 90212, Santa Barbara CA 93190	805-965-0031	R	2*	<.1
105	Solo Business Group Inc—*Ann Solo*	11 Augusta Dr, Rancho Mirage CA 92270	760-324-6439	R	2*	<.1
106	Vanco Computing—*Sean Van Couwenberghe*	465 Stony Point Rd Ste, Santa Rosa CA 95401	707-578-5802	R	2*	<.1
107	Intelligent Solutions and Technologies LLC—*Brent Neal*	1320 E 53rd St Ste D, Anderson IN 46013	765-640-8455	R	2*	<.1
108	Netservices Inc—*Michael Stephens*	PO Box 1853, Maryland Heights MO 63043	314-323-1742	R	2*	<.1
109	Computer Specialists Inc—*Donald Weymer*	2101 Gaither Rd Ste 17, Rockville MD 20850	301-921-8660	R	2*	<.1
110	Westech Computer Systems Inc—*Tim Mcdonald*	2435 N Control Expy St, Richardson TX 75080	972-680-7800	R	2*	<.1
111	Liam Services Inc—*William Schade*	227 S White Horse Pke, Audubon NJ 08106	610-879-5800	R	2*	<.1
112	Quantex Industries Inc—*Todd Gunby*	3100 Medlock Bridge Rd, Norcross GA 30071	770-416-0301	R	2*	<.1
113	Edward Technology Group Inc—*G Naugle*	149 Northland Blvd, Cincinnati OH 45246	513-772-6000	R	2*	<.1
114	American Technology International—*James Piloco*	34 Shirley Ln, White Plains NY 10607	914-949-6429	R	2*	<.1
115	Gremark Technologies Inc—*Greg Jablonowski*	1400 Brook Dr, Downers Grove IL 60515	630-705-0900	R	2*	<.1
116	New York Computer Help LLC	53 E 34th St Fl 3, New York NY 10016	212-599-0339	R	2*	<.1
117	Printelogy Inc—*Michael Greenberg*	2137 S Birch St Fl 1, Denver CO 80222	303-757-1711	R	2*	<.1
118	Aegis Computer Services Inc—*Pamella Butler*	1310 Thomasville Rd, Tallahassee FL 32303	850-422-2661	R	2*	<.1
119	Business Information Solutions Inc—*Phillip Long*	21530 Professional Dr, Robertsdale AL 36567	251-943-1744	R	2*	<.1
120	El Dorado Trading Group Inc—*Lawrence Bach*	760 San Antonio Rd, Palo Alto CA 94303	650-494-6600	R	2*	<.1
121	Delta Automation Inc—*Robert Culley*	2704 Charles City Rd, Richmond VA 23231	804-236-2800	R	1*	<.1
122	Expert Services—*Scott Klever*	1335 Donaldson Hwy Ste, Erlanger KY 41018	859-371-9690	R	1*	<.1
123	Code Red Technologies LLC	74 Ritchie Rd, Capitol Heights MD 20743	301-560-7159	Π	1*	<.1
124	Performanceit Inc—*Michael Mittel*	6600 Peachtree Dunwood, Atlanta GA 30328	678-323-1300	R	1*	<.1
125	PC Depot Inc—*Thomas Moser*	2424 Franklin St Ste 2, Michigan City IN 46360	219-874-5600	R	1*	<.1
126	Icetech Inc—*William Hopson*	940 W N Ave, Baltimore MD 21217	410-225-3117	R	1*	<.1
127	Scsi Inc—*Robert Lowry*	PO Box 461267, San Antonio TX 78246	210-348-9310	R	1*	<.1
128	Hallmarks Laser Imaging Inc—*Scott Hallmark*	11011 Cutten Rd Ste 10, Houston TX 77066	281-583-7552	R	1*	<.1
129	Ink Impress USA Inc—*Roland Parker*	1718 Fry Rd Ste 315, Houston TX 77084	281-647-9977	R	1*	<.1
130	Micro Data Systems Inc—*Paul Boglino*	8730 Us Hwy 19, Port Richey FL 34668	727-847-6955	R	1*	<.1
131	Lka Computer Consultants Inc—*Lawrence Aikins*	9658 Baltimore Ave Ste, College Park MD 20740	301-345-7777	R	1*	<.1
132	Hyundai Information Service North America LLC—*Jeremy Kim*	111 Peters Canyon Rd, Irvine CA 92606	714-965-3939	R	1*	<.1
133	Orbit Electrical Services Corp—*Vladimer Schuster*	250 Union Ave, Moonachie NJ 07074	201-296-0101	R	1*	<.1
134	PC Outlet LLC	1435 N Mitchell St Ste, Cadillac MI 49601	231-779-5305	R	1*	<.1
135	Apresys Inc—*Wojtek Michalik*	3650 N Cicero Ave, Chicago IL 60641	773-545-7700	R	1*	<.1
136	Fsu Computer Store—*William Gargano*	199 Territory Way, Tallahassee FL 32306	850-644-7344	R	1*	<.1
137	Mobile Office Machines Inc—*Michael Volmert*	2223 S Brentwood Blvd, Saint Louis MO 63144	314-968-4322	R	1*	<.1
138	Disk Doctor Labs Inc—*Muhamed Aslam*	5555 Oakbrook Pkwy Ste, Norcross GA 30093	770-840-8402	R	1*	<.1
139	Maintenance Alternatives Inc—*Robert Field*	PO Box 751239, Petaluma CA 94975	707-765-1325	R	1*	<.1
140	Prodata Systems Inc—*Brian Goertz*	11007 Slater Ave NE, Kirkland WA 98033	425-296-4168	R	1*	<.1
141	Citation Technologies Inc—*Leilani Doyle*	5450 Nw Central Dr Ste, Houston TX 77092	713-895-8261	R	1*	<.1
142	B P Enterprises—*Paul Daigle*	PO Box 180548, Casselberry FL 32718	407-699-2108	R	1*	<.1
143	Fpctechnology Group Inc—*Steve Christman*	616 N Main St, Bluffton IN 46714	260-824-9160	R	1*	<.1
144	Bay Area Data Supply Inc—*Ron Starnes*	525 Del Rey Ave Ste G, Sunnyvale CA 94085	408-328-8680	R	1*	<.1
145	Pandya Computers Inc—*Himanshu Pandya*	650 Industrial Park Rd, Ebensburg PA 15931	814-472-6685	R	1*	<.1
146	Simple Solution Enterprises LLC—*Brian Kurfess*	3550 Executive Pkwy St, Toledo OH 43606	419-531-1170	R	1*	<.1
147	Drivetech Inc—*Bob Falco*	7 Windsor Ave, Acton MA 01720	978-263-0700	R	1*	<.1
148	MicroMat Computer Service—*Jeff Baudin*	5329 Skylane Blvd, Santa Rosa CA 95403	707-566-3831	R	1*	<.1
149	Cornice—*Tim R Carroll*	615 N Benson Ave Ste B, Upland CA 91786	909-985-8323	R	1*	<.1
150	DFW Mobile Tech—*William Carson*	7001 Preston Rd Ste 30, Dallas TX 75205	214-349-6972	R	1*	<.1
151	Double Eagle Services Inc—*Mark E James*	920 Leadville Dr, Arlington TX 76001	817-528-9146	R	1*	<.1
152	Integra Management Systems	2533 N Carson St Ste 3, Carson City NV 89706		S	1*	<.1
153	Noblitt PC Inc—*George Noblitt*	4015 Nowata Rd, Bartlesville OK 74006	918-331-2164	R	1*	<.1
154	Printech Enterprises Inc—*Gabriel Manea*	2048 Connolly Dr, Troy MI 48084	248-288-5800	R	1*	<.1
155	DPS Laser—*Mike Liebergesell*	145 Thompson St, Alpharetta GA 30004	770-751-1954	R	1*	<.1
156	Grove Solutions Inc—*Pedro Delgado*	6481 SW 6th St, Miami FL 33144	305-260-9305	R	1*	<.1
157	Microspy—*Peter Cohen*	2221 Ave U, Brooklyn NY 11229	718-616-1111	R	1*	<.1
158	Duffy PC—*John Duffy*	413 Main Ave, De Pere WI 54115	920-338-0291	R	1*	<.1
159	Markon Computer Science Inc—*Mark Esser*	25012 Narbonne Ave Ste, Lomita CA 90717	310-325-5610	R	1*	<.1
160	Moravits and Mazurek Inc—*James Mazurek*	1735 Babcock Rd, San Antonio TX 78229	210-349-0015	R	1*	<.1
161	Accurate Computer Technology Inc—*Anil Patel*	PO Box 17928, Irvine CA 92623	949-261-6677	R	1*	<.1
162	Washington Area Network Services LLC	PO Box 55309, Washington DC 20040	202-262-1851	R	1*	<.1
163	Totally You Inc—*Gina Clausen*	25 S Main St Ste 2, Munroe Falls OH 44262	330-686-5558	R	1*	<.1
164	Jupiternet Inc—*Gregory Tanner*	1221 S Clarkson St Ste, Denver CO 80210	303-777-7562	R	1*	<.1
165	Alaska Computer And Typewriter Service Inc—*Janet Miessner*	3601 Minnesota Dr, Anchorage AK 99503	907-276-5945	R	1*	<.1

Note: An asterisk (*) indicates an estimated financial figure. The company type code used is as follows: R = Private, P = Public, S = Private Subsidiary, B = Public Subsidiary, D = Division, J = Joint Venture, I = Investment Fund.

COMPANY RANKINGS BY SALES WITHIN 4-DIGIT SIC

Rank	Company Name—*Executive Officer*	Address, City, State, Zip	Phone	Type	Fin	Empls
166	Omega Electronic Instrument Inc—*Eric Weinstein*	198 S Dietz Mill Rd, Telford PA 18969	215-723-1776	R	<1*	<.1
167	Solutions By Design Inc—*Gary Robbins*	318 Delaware Ave Ste 1, Delmar NY 12054	518-478-0373	R	<1*	<.1
168	NJ Industrial Research Center Inc—*Mohammad Hamzeh*	1059 Main Ave, Clifton NJ 07011	973-773-7355	R	<1*	<.1
169	Twin Peaks Computer Inc—*Scott Pfauth*	PO Box 2039, Longmont CO 80502	303-678-7154	R	<1*	<.1
170	Hall and Associates Computing Inc—*Craig Hall*	301 Oak St, Quincy IL 62301	217-224-8535	R	<1*	<.1
171	Precision Pcb Services Inc—*Lan O'donnell*	1750 Mitchell Ave, Oroville CA 95966	530-534-1738	R	<1*	<.1
172	H Dh Consulting—*Steve Hackbarth*	11875 W 12th Ave, Lakewood CO 80401	303-374-0006	R	<1*	<.1
173	Printhead Specialists—*Bill Harrigan*	PO Box 240, Twain CA 95984	530-283-0538	R	<1*	<.1
174	Dcm Computer Sales And Service—*David Campbell*	2995 Chico Way Nw, Bremerton WA 98312	360-373-2014	R	<1*	<.1
175	MadmodcomputingCom—*David Mawdsley*	8 New Light Dr, Danbury CT 06810	203-748-2960	R	<1*	<.1
176	Steven Soemer—*Steven Soemer*	521 Laurel Ave, Mcallen TX 78501	956-630-1654	R	<1*	<.1
177	iYogi Inc—*Uday Challu*	12 Desbrosses St 3rd F, New York NY 10013		R	N/A	.6
178	MediaLinx—*Nir Slepack*	17 Magnolia Dr, Great Neck NY 11021	516-466-0788	R	N/A	<.1
179	Solid Technology—*Isaac Lavian*	5979 Nora Lynn Dr, Woodland Hills CA 91367	310-963-1881	R	N/A	<.1

TOTALS: SIC 7378 Computer Maintenance & Repair

Companies: 179					5,620	33.6

7379 Computer Related Services Nec

Rank	Company Name—*Executive Officer*	Address, City, State, Zip	Phone	Type	Fin	Empls
1	Google Inc—*Eric Shmidt*	1600 Amphitheatre Pkwy, Mountain View CA 94043	650-253-0000	P	29,321	24.4
2	Accenture Inc (New York New York)—*Pierre Nanterme*	1345 Ave of the Americ, New York NY 10105	917-452-4400	S	13,670*	2.0
3	Level 3 Communications Inc—*James Q Crowe*	1025 Eldorado Blvd, Broomfield CO 80021	720-888-1000	P	4,333	10.9
4	LPL Investment Holdings Inc—*Mark S Casady*	1 Beacon St 22nd Fl, Boston MA 02108	617-423-3644	P	3,479	2.7
5	World Wide Technology Holding Company Inc—*James P Kavanaugh*	60 Weldon Pkwy, Maryland Heights MO 63043	314-569-7000	R	3,286*	1.2
6	Day and Zimmermann Information Solutions—*Harold L Yoh III*	1500 Spring Garden St, Philadelphia PA 19130	215-299-8000	D	2,880*	24.0
7	LexisNexis Group—*Andrew Prozes*	PO Box 933, Dayton OH 45401	937-865-6800	D	2,746*	15.0
8	Elemica Inc—*Michael McGuigan*	222 Valley Creek Blvd, Exton PA 19341	610-786-1200	R	2,626*	5.0
9	Infor Global Solutions—*Charles Phillip*	13560 Morris Rd Ste 41, Alpharetta GA 30004	678-319-8000	R	2,200*	9.0
10	Westcon Group Inc—*Dean Douglas*	520 White Plains Rd St, Tarrytown NY 10591	914-829-7000	S	1,885*	1.0
11	BT INS Inc—*David Butze*	2160 E Grand Ave, El Segundo CA 90245	408-330-2700	R	1,600*	4.3
12	HCL America Inc—*Vineet Nayar*	330 Potrero Ave, Sunnyvale CA 94085	408-733-0480	S	1,377*	3.0
13	GSI Commerce Inc—*Paul Cataldo*	935 1st Ave, King of Prussia PA 19406	610-491-7000	S	1,358	5.3
14	IHS Inc—*Jerre L Stead*	15 Inverness Way E, Englewood CO 80112	303-790-0600	P	1,326	5.5
15	Verio Inc—*Kiyoshi Maeda*	8005 S Chester St Ste, Centennial CO 80112	303-645-1900	S	1,228*	2.6
16	Akamai Technologies Inc—*Paul Sagan*	8 Cambridge Ctr, Cambridge MA 02142	617-444-3000	P	1,159	2.4
17	Sybase Application Support Div	1 Sybase Dr, Dublin CA 94568	925-236-5000	D	1,026*	4.0
18	Rackspace Hosting Inc—*Lanham Napier*	5000 Walzem Rd, San Antonio TX 78218	210-312-4000	P	1,025	4.0
19	CIBER Associates Inc—*David C Peterschmidt*	6363 Fiddler's Green C, Greenwood Village CO 80111	303-220-0100	S	956	N/A
20	Conexant Spinco Inc—*Scott Mercer*	4000 MacArthur Blvd, Newport Beach CA 92660	949-483-4600	S	849*	1.5
21	Direct Data Capture (USA) Ltd—*Jan Trevalyan*	PO Box 589, Huntington Station NY 11746	631-547-5500	R	762*	2.1
22	Oxford Consulting Group Inc—*Michelle Abreu*	385 County Line Rd W S, Westerville OH 43082	614-310-2700	S	696*	1.5
23	24/7 Customer Inc—*Pv Kannan*	910 E Hamilton Ave Ste, Campbell CA 95008	650-385-2247	R	629*	9.0
24	Carahsoft Technology Corp—*Craig Abod*	12369 Sunrise Valley D, Reston VA 20191	703-871-8500	R	586*	.2
25	NCI Inc (Reston Virginia)—*Charles K Narang*	11730 Plaza America Dr, Reston VA 20190	703-707-6900	P	581	2.6
26	Bull HN Information Systems Inc (Billerica Massachusetts)—*Jonathan Burbank*	285 Billerica, Chelmsford MA 01824	978-294-6000	S	564*	1.2
27	Presidio Inc—*Joel A Schleicher*	1 Penn Plz 19th Fl Ste, New York NY 10119	212-652-5700	R	555*	1.2
28	iSky Inc—*Steve Newman*	1700 Pennsylvania Ave, Washington DC 20006	855-475-4759	R	545*	1.5
29	K12 Inc—*Ronald J Packard*	2300 Corporate Park Dr, Herndon VA 20171		P	522	2.5
30	Aston Group—*John Matterson*	7050 Jomar Dr, Whitmore Lake MI 48189	734-205-1900	S	520*	1.4
31	Priority Fulfillment Services Inc—*Mark C Layton*	500 N Central Expy Ste, Plano TX 75074	972-881-2900	S	519*	1.0
32	RCG Information Technology Inc—*Robert Simplot*	379 Thornall St Ste 60, Edison NJ 08837	732-744-3500	R	500*	1.0
33	Elcom Services Group Inc—*William Lock*	10 Oceana Way, Norwood MA 02062		S	486*	.2
34	Stanley Associates Inc—*Phil Nolan*	3101 Wilson Blvd Ste 7, Arlington VA 22201	703-684-1125	S	447*	.9
35	ValueClick Inc—*James R Zarley*	30699 Russell Ranch Rd, Westlake Village CA 91362	818-575-4500	P	431	1.1
36	Trinity Millennium Group Inc—*David Garza*	2424 Babcock Rd Ste 30, San Antonio TX 78229	210-615-1606	R	425*	.1
37	CNET Networks Inc—*Quincy Smith*	235 2nd St, San Francisco CA 94105	415-344-2000	S	406	2.7
38	Keane Inc—*John McCain*	100 City Square, Boston MA 02129		S	403*	12.5
39	Global Cash Access Inc	3525 E Post Rd Ste 120, Las Vegas NV 89120	702-855-3000	S	403	N/A
40	Ajilon LLC—*Bill DeMario*	317 Madison Ave Ste 50, New York NY 10017	212-661-8235	S	400*	4.0
41	Interactive Business Systems Inc—*Daniel T Williams*	2625 Butterfield Rd, Oak Brook IL 60523	630-571-9100	R	391*	.8
42	Network Solutions Inc—*Tim Kelly*	13861 Sunrise Valley D, Herndon VA 20171	703-742-0400	S	362*	.9
43	MarketAxess Holdings Inc—*Richard M McVey*	299 Park Ave 10th Fl, New York NY 10171	212-813-6000	P	350	.2
44	Demand Media Inc—*Richard M Rosenblatt*	1299 Ocean Ave Ste 500, Santa Monica CA 90401	310-394-6400	P	325	.6
45	Global Knowledge Inc—*Brian Branson*	PO Box 1039, Cary NC 27512	919-461-8600	S	319*	1.3
46	Element K Corp—*Stephen Hoffman*	500 Canal View Blvd, Rochester NY 14623	585-240-7500	R	285*	.8
47	Lockheed Martin Information Technology	1981 Snyder St Rm 124, Richland WA 99354	509-376-1090	S	285*	.6
48	EnerNOC Inc—*Timothy G Healy*	101 Federal St Ste 110, Boston MA 02110	617-224-9900	P	280	.5
49	Internap Network Services Corp—*Eric Cooney*	250 Williams St, Atlanta GA 30303	404-302-9700	P	245	.5
50	Birlasoft Inc—*J Ramachandran*	2035 Lincoln Hwy 2nd F, Edison NJ 08817	732-287-5000	R	242*	<.1
51	Agencycom Ltd—*Riccardo Zane*	488 Madison Ave 4th Fl, New York NY 10022	212-358-2600	S	240*	.5
52	Judge Group Inc—*Martin E Judge Jr*	300 Conshohocken State, West Conshohocken PA 19428	610-667-7700	R	238*	.6
53	Interdyn—*John Hendrickson*	875 6th Ave Ste 200, New York NY 10001	212-502-3900	R	234*	.5
54	Interdyn AKA—*Alan Kahn* Interdyn	875 6th Ave Ste 200, New York NY 10001	212-502-3900	S	234*	.5
55	Bureau van Dijk Electronic Publishing Inc—*Tom Baskind*	40 Wall St 27th Fl, New York NY 10005	212-797-3550	S	233*	.5
56	CTG HealthCare Solutions Inc—*Jim Boldt*	312 Plum St Ste 700, Cincinnati OH 45202	513-564-0909	S	232*	.5
57	Yodle Inc—*Court Cunningham*	50 W 23rd St 4th Fl, New York NY 10010		R	218*	.4
58	Genesis Corp—*Harley Lippman*	950 3rd Ave 26th Fl, New York NY 10022	212-688-5522	R	214*	.6
59	Excell Data Corp—*Jen Dixon*	1756 114th Ave SE Ste, Bellevue WA 98004	425-974-2000	S	213*	.5
60	RapidStream Inc—*Joe Wang*	505 Fifth Ave S Ste 50, Seattle WA 98104	206-613-6660	R	213*	.5
61	Larsen and Toubro Infotech Ltd—*Sudip Banerjee*	2035 Lincoln Hwy Ste 3, Edison NJ 08817	732-248-6111	S	212*	10.0
62	HealthLink Inc—*Ivo Nelson*	3800 Buffalo Speedway, Houston TX 77098	713-790-0800	S	210*	.6
63	iOne Technology Inc—*Charles Chen*	41656 Christy St, Fremont CA 94538	510-413-9018	R	210*	.6
64	24/7 Real Media Inc—*David J Moore*	132 W 31st St, New York NY 10001	212-231-7100	S	200	.4
65	ePartners Inc—*Michael McCarty*	1231 Greenway Dr Ste 2, Irving TX 75038	972-819-2700	R	200*	.4
66	Software Paradigms International Inc—*Sid Mookerji*	5 Concrs Pkwy Ne Ste 9, Atlanta GA 30328	404-582-6020	R	199*	1.3
67	Sword Intech Inc—*David Warren*	17 State St Fl 26, New York NY 10004	212-279-6734	R	164*	2.0
68	iTech US—*Kishor Khandavalli*	20 Kimball Ave Ste 303, South Burlington VT 05403	802-383-1500	R	164*	.4
69	Stefanini Techteam—*Antonio Moreira*	27335 W 11 Mile Rd, Southfield MI 48033	248-357-2866	R	156*	2.3

Rank	Company Name—Executive Officer	Address, City, State, Zip	Phone	Type	Fin	Empls
70	Abacus America Inc—Gaberial Murphy	7500 W 110th St Ste 40, Overland Park KS 66210	913-890-7700	R	151*	.3
71	Leader Communications Inc—Michael O Lyles	6421 S Air Depot Ste A, Oklahoma City OK 73135	405-622-2200	R	151*	.3
72	Phacil Inc—Rafael Collado	991 US Hwy 22 W Ste 20, Bridgewater NJ 08807	973-622-0544	R	150*	.1
73	Online Resources Corp—Joseph L Cowan	4795 Meadow Wood Ln, Chantilly VA 20151	703-653-3100	P	150	.6
74	Mgl Americas Inc—Sandy Chandra	1699 E Wdfield Rd Ste, Schaumburg IL 60173	847-619-5005	R	149*	2.4
75	ALLDATA LLC—Bret Easley	9412 Big Horn Blvd, Elk Grove CA 95758	916-684-5225	S	145*	.4
76	TesComm Inc—Ofer Albeck	3525 Piedmont Rd NE St, Atlanta GA 30305	678-250-1166	R	144*	.6
77	SmartDrive Systems Inc—Jason Palmer	9276 Scranton Rd Ste 5, San Diego CA 92121	858-225-5550	R	144*	.3
78	TABcom LLC—Alexander Tabibi	1 Maplewood Dr, Hazleton PA 18202	570-384-5555	R	144*	.2
79	Dotster Inc—Clint Page	PO Box 821066, Vancouver WA 98682	360-449-5900	R	142*	.3
80	IHS Energy (Englewood Colorado)—Jerre Stead	15 Inverness Way E, Englewood CO 80112	303-790-0600	S	138*	1.1
81	Engineering Geometry Systems—Glenn McMinn	275 E S Temple Ste 305, Salt Lake City UT 84111	801-575-6021	S	133*	<.1
82	Mindbank Consulting Group Inc—Neal S Grunstra	11400 Commerce Pk Dr S, Reston VA 20191		R	132*	.3
83	Stonesoft Inc—Ilkka Hiidenheimo	1050 Crown Point Pkwy, Atlanta GA 30338	770-668-1125	S	131*	.3
84	Sogeti USA LLC—Benassis Jacques	7735 Paragon Rd, Dayton OH 45459	937-291-8100	R	130*	1.9
85	Silver Peak Systems Inc—Rick Tinsley	4500 Great American Pk, Santa Clara CA 95054	408-935-1800	R	130*	.1
86	American NetLink—John Poss	PO Box 205, Good Hope GA 30641	770-266-7682	R	125*	.3
87	Zycron Inc—Steven Howard Smith	2620 Clarksville Pike, Nashville TN 37208	615-251-9588	R	125*	.3
88	Direct Alliance Corp—Judi Hand	8123 S Hardy Dr, Tempe AZ 85284	480-902-5900	S	124*	.8
89	Miracle Software Systems Inc—Prasad V Lokam	45625 Grand River Ave, Novi MI 48374	248-350-1515	R	123*	1.4
90	Force10 Networks Inc—Henry Wasik	350 Holger Way, San Jose CA 95134	408-571-3500	S	119*	.6
91	Paragon Computer Professionals Inc—Daniel OConnor	25 Commerce Dr 2nd Fl, Cranford NJ 07016	908-709-6767	R	118*	.3
92	Intelligent Decisions Inc—Harry Martin Jr	21445 Beaumeade Cir, Ashburn VA 20147	703-554-1600	R	116*	.3
93	Moorhead Electric Inc—Marty Eckren	3030 24th Ave S, Moorhead MN 56560	218-284-9500	S	116*	.3
94	PGP Corp (Palo Alto California)—Enrique Salem	200 Jefferson Dr, Menlo Park CA 94025		R	115*	.2
95	INCAT Systems Inc—Patrick McGoldrick	41050 W 11 mile Rd, Novi MI 48375	248-426-1482	S	112*	.6
96	Lockheed Martin Aspen Systems Inc—Robert J Steven Lockheed Martin Information Technology	2775 Research Blvd, Rockville MD 20850	301-519-5000	S	110*	1.7
97	Xceed—Teresa Freeborn	888 N Nash St, El Segundo CA 90245		R	108	.5
98	Eureka Networks—Michael Robinson	39 Broadway 19th Fl, New York NY 10006	212-404-5000	S	106*	.2
99	Heritage web Solutions—Brad Stone	1460 N Moonriver Dr, Provo UT 84604	801-655-1600	R	104*	.2
100	Viecore Inc—Paul Ricci	1111 Macarthur Blvd St, Mahwah NJ 07430		S	104*	.2
101	Z-Tech Corp—Sudhakar Kesavan	1803 Research Blvd Ste, Rockville MD 20850	301-315-2800	S	103*	.2
102	AuthorizeNet Holdings Inc	808 E Utah Valley Dr, American Fork UT 84003	801-492-6450	S	96	.2
103	CIBER International Inc—Tom van den Berg	6363 S Fiddler's Green, Greenwood Village CO 80111	303-220-0100	S	96	N/A
104	TechTarget Inc—Greg Strakosch	275 Grove St, Newton MA 02466	617-431-9200	P	95	.6
105	Global Financial Services Inc—William Gorman	212 S Tryon St Ste 105, Charlotte NC 28281	704-376-4022	S	95*	.2
106	CoreTech Consulting Group Inc—Yuki Tsaroya	500 N Gulph Rd Ste 110, King of Prussia PA 19406		S	93*	.2
107	Iron Mountain Off-Site Data Protection Inc—C Richard Reese	745 Atlantic Ave, Boston MA 02111	617-535-4766	S	91*	1.0
108	ConSol Consulting and Solutions Corp	PO Box 2925, Dublin CA 94568	925-479-1370	S	90*	.2
109	NETCONN Solutions—Judy York	108 Western Maryland P, Hagerstown MD 21740	301-739-9110	R	82*	.2
110	Interactive Technology Solutions LLC—Stefan Lalos	8757 Georgia Ave Ste 5, Silver Spring MD 20910	301-495-5545	R	79*	.5
111	Ockham Development Group Inc—James Baker	8000 Regency Pkwy Ste, Cary NC 27518	919-462-8867	R	79*	.2
112	Lloyd Lamont Design Inc—Joe Carlini	2941 Fairview Park Dr, Falls Church VA 22042	703-698-0461	R	78*	.2
113	FloodSource Corp—Russell Capper	1421 Wells Branch Pkwy, Pflugerville TX 78660		S	77*	<.1
114	Avesta Computer Services Ltd—Cyrus H Davierwalla	Harborside Financial P, Jersey City NJ 07310	201-369-9400	R	76*	.2
115	Prosum Inc—Ravi Chatwani	2321 Rosecrans Ave Ste, El Segundo CA 90245	310-426-0600	R	75*	.2
116	Vodium—Cameron Clarke	1629 K St NW Ste 950, Washington DC 20006	202-223-1800	R	75*	.2
117	Quilogy Inc	117 S Main St, Saint Charles MO 63301		S	74*	.3
118	Int Technologies—Richard Krause	2415 E Camelbck Rd Ste, Phoenix AZ 85016	602-508-6177	R	71*	.5
119	American Public Education Inc—Wallace E Boston Jr	111 W Congress St, Charles Town WV 25414	304-724-3700	P	69	1.8
120	Hireright Inc—Michael Petrullo	5151 California Ave, Irvine CA 92617	949-428-5800	S	69*	.4
121	EqualLogic Inc—Don Bulens	300 Innovative Way Ste, Nashua NH 03062	603-579-9762	S	68	.3
122	iVillage Inc—Deborah I Fine	500 7th Ave 14th Fl, New York NY 10018	212-664-4444	S	67	.2
123	Laurus Technologies Inc—John Udelhofen	1222 Hamilton Pkwy, Itasca IL 60143	630-875-9200	R	65*	.1
124	Software Management Consultants Inc—Spencer Karpf	500 N Brand Blvd Ste 1, Glendale CA 91203	818-240-3177	R	64*	.4
125	Tekmark Global Solutions LLC—Art Hall	100 Metroplex Dr Ste 1, Edison NJ 08817	732-572-5400	R	63*	.9
126	Revere Group Ltd—Michael Parks	325 N LaSalle St Ste 3, Chicago IL 60654	312-873-3400	R	62*	.5
127	CenterBeam Inc—A Kevin Francis	30 Rio Robles Dr, San Jose CA 95134	408-750-0500	R	62*	.2
128	Computer Express Inc—Maureen Harris	PO Box 308, Wakefield MA 01880	781-246-4477	R	61*	.2
129	Carbonite Inc—Dave Friend	177 Huntington Ave, Boston MA 02115	617-587-1100	P	61	.2
130	Alpine Web Media LLC—William Alexander	5997 Shelburne Rd, Shelburne VT 05482	802-233-3261	R	60*	.1
131	Windmill International Inc—Richard L Manganello	2 Robinson Rd, Nashua NH 03060	603-888-5502	R	56*	.2
132	SMC Networks Inc—Tod Babic	20 Mason, Irvine CA 92618	949-679-8000	S	56*	.1
133	TMP Worldwide Marketing—Michelle Abbey	4055 Valley View Ln St, Dallas TX 75244	972-728-3009	S	55*	1.1
134	The Generations Network Inc—Tim Sullivan	360 W 4800 N, Provo UT 84604	801-705-7000	R	55*	.2
135	Intelius Inc—Naveen Jain	500 108th Ave NE 22nd, Bellevue WA 98004	425-974-6100	R	55*	.1
136	iSuppli Corp—Derek Lidow IHS Inc	1700 E Walnut Ave Ste, El Segundo CA 90245		S	55*	.1
137	HostingCom Inc—Art Zeile	900 S Broadway Ste 400, Denver CO 80209	720-389-3800	R	54*	.3
138	Current Analysis Inc—Tim Dowd	21335 Signal Hill Plz, Sterling VA 20164	703-404-9200	R	54*	.1
139	Lancesoft Inc—Ramkumar Karuppusamy	13454 Sunrise Valley D, Herndon VA 20171	703-674-4500	R	52	.7
140	Boeing-SVS Inc	4411 The 25 Way NE Ste, Albuquerque NM 87109	505-449-4600	S	52*	.1
141	GeoTrust Inc	350 Ellis St Bldg J, Mountain View CA 94043	650-426-5010	S	52*	.1
142	Giftcertificatescom—Ian O'Brien	11510 Blondo St, Omaha NE 68164	402-445-2300	NE	52*	.1
143	Autobytel Inc—Jeffrey H Coats	18872 MacArthur Blvd S, Irvine CA 92612	949-225-4500	P	52	.1
144	Calence Inc—Michael Fong	1560 W Fountainhead Pk, Tempe AZ 85282	480-889-9500	S	51*	.2
145	Crown Partners LLC—Richard Hearn	7750 Paragon Rd, Dayton OH 45459	937-723-2300	R	51*	.1
146	Health Market Science Inc—Matt Reichert	2700 Horizon Dr Ste 20, King of Prussia PA 19406	610-940-4002	R	51*	.1
147	djmillernet Services—Daniel Miller	23617 Cedar Knoll Cir, Elkhart IN 46516	574-295-1051	R	51*	.1
148	Terremark Dallas—Kerri Baily	222 W Las Colinas Blvd, Irving TX 75039	972-869-0770	S	50*	.5
149	Magnum Technologies Inc	10340 Viking Dr Ste 10, Eden Prairie MN 55344	952-229-3500	S	50*	.2
150	Muze Inc—Fred Amaroso	2830 De La Cruz Blvd, Santa Clara CA 95050	408-562-8400	R	50*	.2
151	MacMastery—Dan Nolen	1800 Hickory Ridge Cov, Round Rock TX 78665	512-627-8379	R	50*	.1
152	Instantiations Inc—Mike Taylor	18101 SW Boones Ferry, Portland OR 97224	503-598-4900	R	49*	<.1
153	Skillstorm Inc—Hany Girgis	10105 Pacific Heights, San Diego CA 92121	858-551-9322	R	48*	.7
154	Mountain Hawk Corp—John Babson	106 Berwick Dr, Pittsburgh PA 15215	412-963-6180	R	48*	.1
155	IntermediaNET Inc—Serguei Solinski	156 W 56th St Ste 1601, New York NY 10019	212-375-6375	R	47*	.1
156	Logoworks—Paul Brockbank	333 S 520 W Ste 360, Lindon UT 84042	801-922-9932	R	47*	.1
157	Verifacts Automotive LLC—Farzam Afshar	1000 Bristol St N Ste, Newport Beach CA 92660		R	47*	.1

Note: An asterisk (*) indicates an estimated financial figure. The company type code used is as follows: R = Private, P = Public, S = Private Subsidiary, B = Public Subsidiary, D = Division, J = Joint Venture, I = Investment Fund.

COMPANY RANKINGS BY SALES WITHIN 4-DIGIT SIC

Rank	Company Name—*Executive Officer*	Address, City, State, Zip	Phone	Type	Fin	Empls
158	InScope International Inc—*Mike Bruce*	12018 Sunrise Valley D, Reston VA 20191	703-480-3200	R	47*	.1
159	ASAP Staffing LLC—*Roz L Alford*	3885 Holcomb Bridge Rd, Norcross GA 30092	770-246-1718	R	46*	.4
160	MedData—*Richard Bettison* Agdata Holdings Inc	2100 Rexford Rd Ste 30, Charlotte NC 28211	704-367-4615	D	46*	.1
161	On-Demand Software Consultants Inc—*Nigel P Gower*	190 Colonial Drive, Woodstock GA 30189	678-905-1290	R	46	.1
162	Management and Engineering Technologies International Inc—*Renard U Johnson*	8600 Boeing Dr, El Paso TX 79925	915-772-4975	R	45*	.4
163	Able Cable Inc—*Don Yager*	5115 N Douglas Fir Rd, Calabasas CA 91302	818-223-3600	R	45*	.2
164	Womencom—*Doug McCormick* iVillage Inc	500 7th Ave 14th Fl, New York NY 10018	212-600-6000	S	44*	.3
165	Information Technology Partners—*Lloyd B Solomon*	260 Madison Ave, New York NY 10016	212-403-6100	D	44*	.2
166	OptiMark Inc—*Robert Warshaw*	2500 Plz 5 Harborside, Jersey City NJ 07311	212-626-6814	S	44*	.1
167	IMVU Inc—*Cary Rosenzweig*	PO Box 390012, Mountain View CA 94039	650-321-8334	R	43*	.1
168	RedVision Systems Inc—*Brian Twibell*	1055 Parsippany Blvd S, Parsippany NJ 07054	973-854-9500	R	43	.5
169	AlphaMetrix LLC—*Aleks Kins*	181 W Madison 34th Fl, Chicago IL 60602	312-267-8400	R	42	.1
170	Mu Sigma Inc—*Dhiraj Rajaram*	3400 Dundee Rd Ste 160, Northbrook IL 60062	847-919-0445	R	42	.9
171	Heitech Services Inc—*Heidi Gerding*	8201 Corporate Dr Ste, Landover MD 20785	301-918-9500	R	42*	.2
172	Information Innovators Inc—*Debbie Ikirt*	7400 Fullerton Rd Ste, Springfield VA 22153	703-635-7088	R	41*	.1
173	Fedstore Corporation Inc—*Skip Trahern*	1 Research Ct Ste 450, Rockville MD 20850	240-715-4320	R	41*	<.1
174	Internet Montana—*Doug Dickey*	2511 Montana Ave, Billings MT 59101	406-255-9657	R	40*	.1
175	SecureLogix Corp—*Lee Sutterfield*	13750 San Pedro Ave St, San Antonio TX 78232	210-402-9669	R	40*	.1
176	Turing Smi LLC—*Phil Brooks*	260 Madison Ave Fl 8, New York NY 10016	646-216-2193	R	40*	.1
177	Carousel Industries of North America Inc—*Jeff Gardner*	659 S County Tr, Exeter RI 02822	401-284-1925	R	39*	.2
178	Nobel Systems Inc—*Micheal Samuel*	436 E Vanderbilt Way, San Bernardino CA 92408	909-890-5611	R	39*	.1
179	Grant Street Group—*Myles Harrington*	429 Forbes Ave Ste 180, Pittsburgh PA 15219	412-391-5555	R	39*	.1
180	Worldwide Information Network Systems Inc—*Ulysese Jefferson*	7404 Executive Place S, Seabrook MD 20706	301-982-4640	S	38*	.2
181	RealFoundations Inc—*Christopher Shaida*	14135 Midway Rd Ste 30, Addison TX 75001	214-292-7000	R	38*	.2
182	S1 Community and Regional eFinance Solutions Group—*James Mahan*	12401 Research Blvd Bl, Austin TX 78759	512-336-3000	S	38*	.1
183	SSH Communications Security Inc—*Jari Mieloen*	4410 El Camino Real St, Los Altos CA 94022	650-559-2220	R	38*	.1
184	IntelliNet Corp (Atlanta Georgia)—*Mark Seely*	2 Concourse Pky Ste 10, Atlanta GA 30328	404-442-8000	R	38*	.1
185	Rally Software Development Corp—*Tim Miller*	4001 Discovery Dr Ste, Boulder CO 80303	303-565-2800	R	38*	.1
186	EBSCO Publishing—*Tim Collins*	10 Estes St, Ipswich MA 01938	978-356-6500	S	36*	.3
187	Directpointe Inc—*Michael D Proper*	333 S 520 W Ste 200, Lindon UT 84042	801-805-9700	R	36*	.1
188	Inventory Locator Service LLC—*Eric Anderson*	8001 Centerview Pkwy S, Cordova TN 38018	901-794-5000	S	36*	.1
189	LUCRUM Inc—*John BostickDetzel*	7755 Montgomery Rd Ste, Cincinnati OH 45236	513-241-5949	R	36*	.1
190	3Cinteractive LLC—*John Duffy*	750 Park of Commerce B, Boca Raton FL 33487	561-443-5505	R	36*	.1
191	Hurwitz and Associates Inc—*Judith Hurwitz*	175 Highland Ave FL 3, Needham MA 02494	617-597-1724	R	36*	.1
192	Microtechnologies LLC—*Anthony Jimenez*	8330 Boone Blvd Ste 60, Vienna VA 22182	703-891-1073	R	35*	.3
193	Fujitsu Systems Business of America Inc—*Masami Yamamoto*	1250 E Arques Ave, Sunnyvale CA 94085	408-746-6200	S	35*	.2
194	Software Testing Services Inc—*Adam Irgon*	620 Cranbury Rd Ste 20, East Brunswick NJ 08816	732-257-9033	R	35*	.1
195	Southwest Stars Corp	1100 NW Loop 410 Ste 7, San Antonio TX 78213	210-858-5644	R	35*	.1
196	American Internet Services—*Tim Caulfield*	9725 Scranton Rd, San Diego CA 92121	858-576-4272	R	35*	.1
197	Varrow Inc—*Dan Weiss*	2618-A Battleground Av, Greensboro NC 27408		R	35*	<.1
198	Informative Technologies Limited Inc—*Joseph Seely*	204 Andover St Fl 3, Andover MA 01810	978-470-4550	R	35*	<.1
199	Ajasa Technologies Inc—*Anthony Williamson*	1710 Douglas Dr N Ste, Golden Valley MN 55422	763-381-0899	R	35*	.2
200	Us Tech Solutions Inc—*Rajesh Agarwal*	1 Exchange Pl Ste 902, Jersey City NJ 07302	201-524-9600	R	35*	.3
201	Lightsquared—*Sanjiv Ahuja*	10802 Parkridge Blvd, Reston VA 20191		R	35	.2
202	ComGlobal Systems Inc	7545 Metropolitan Dr, San Diego CA 92108	619-725-3700	S	34*	.2
203	ELance Inc—*Fabio Rosati*	510 Logue Ave, Mountain View CA 94043	650-316-7500	R	34*	.1
204	ZyQuest Inc—*Al Zeise*	1385 W Main Ave, De Pere WI 54115	920-499-0533	R	34*	.1
205	Klasky Csupo Inc—*Arlene Klasky*	6353 W Sunset Blvd, Hollywood CA 90028	323-463-0145	R	34*	.1
206	Neudesic LLC—*Parsa Rohani*	8105 Irvine Ctr Dr, Irvine CA 92618	949-754-4500	R	33*	.2
207	Odyssey Systems Consulting Group Ltd—*Michael Sweat*	201 Edgewater Dr Ste 2, Wakefield MA 01880	781-245-0111	R	33*	.2
208	DRS Sustainment Systems Inc—*Mark S Newman*	7780 Technology Dr, West Melbourne FL 32904	321-768-7977	R	33*	.1
209	Norvax Inc—*Brandon Cruz*	214 W Huron St, Chicago IL 60654	312-226-0027	R	33*	.1
210	Tagged Inc—*Greg Tseng*	110 Pacific Ave, San Francisco CA 94111	415-956-1377	R	33	.1
211	ExpressPoint Technology Services Inc—*David Anderson*	1109 Zane Ave N, Golden Valley MN 55422		R	32*	.3
212	Docudata—*J Coley Clark*	2701 E Grauwyler Rd, Irving TX 75061	972-821-4000	S	32*	.1
213	Quinnox Inc—*Udai Kumar*	2056 Westings Ave Ste, Naperville IL 60563	630-548-4800	R	32*	.6
214	HMS Technologies Inc—*Harry M Siegel*	1 Discovery Pl, Martinsburg WV 25403	304-596-5583	R	31	.1
215	JSMN International Inc—*Ravinder Thota*	591 Summit Ave Ste 522, Jersey City NJ 07306	201-792-6800	R	31*	.4
216	MicroTech—*Anthony Jimenez*	8330 Boone Blvd Ste 60, Vienna VA 22182	703-891-1073	R	31*	.2
217	CorePartners Inc—*Lisa Blagaich*	5 S Market St Ste 302, Frederick MD 21701	301-695-2673	R	31*	.1
218	VeriTest Inc—*Rory J Cowan*	3535 Factoria Blvd SE, Bellevue WA 98006	425-688-1000	S	31*	.1
219	Northern Light Technology LLC—*C David Suess*	10 Canal Park, Cambridge MA 02142	617-674-2074	R	31*	.1
220	Overture Networks Inc—*Jeff Reedy*	507 Airport Blvd Ste 1, Morrisville NC 27560	919-337-4100	R	30*	.2
221	Intellectual Ventures LLC—*C Venkataraman*	227 Bellevue Way Ne, Bellevue WA 98004	425-467-2300	R	30*	.5
222	American Unit Inc—*Devender Aerrabolu*	2801 Network Blvd Ste, Frisco TX 75034	214-872-4700	R	30*	.3
223	Visicu Inc—*Frank T Sample*	217 E Redwood St Ste 1, Baltimore MD 21202	410-276-1960	S	30*	.1
224	Enlightened Inc—*Antwanye Ford*	1100 15th St NW Ste 30, Washington DC 20005	202-728-7190	R	30*	.1
225	Alumni Consulting Group International Inc—*Jim Hertzel*	7600 E Orchard Rd Ste, Greenwood Village CO 80111	303-850-0073	R	30*	.1
226	Arsin Corp—*Danis Yadegar*	4800 Great America Pkw, Santa Clara CA 95054	408-653-4160	S	30*	.1
227	Certified Associates Inc—*Nancy K Warren*	16951 Feather Craft Ln, Houston TX 77058	281-280-9500	R	30*	.1
228	Merlin International Inc—*David Phelps*	4b Inverness Ct E Ste, Englewood CO 80112	303-221-0797	R	30*	.3
229	Technology Ventures Inc—*Constance Blair*	PO Box 337, Warren MI 48090	586-573-6000	R	29*	.1
230	IFX Corp—*Mike Shalom*	1930 Harrison St Ste 4, Hollywood FL 33020	305-512-1100	R	28	.4
231	Travco Inc—*Benjamin Krell*	2851 S Parker Rd Ste 5, Aurora CO 80014	303-755-6565	R	28*	.2
232	HTC Global Services Inc—*Madhava Reddy*	3270 W Big Beaver Rd, Troy MI 48084	248-786-2500	R	28*	.3
233	Netreflector Inc—*Rob Monster*	2101 4th Ave Ste 1530, Seattle WA 98121	206-462-4240	S	28*	.1
234	Consolidated Communications	121 South 17th Street, Mattoon IL 61938	724-933-9800	S	28*	.1
235	Link_A_Media Devices Corp—*Hemant K Thapar*	2550 Walsh Ave Ste 200, Santa Clara CA 95051	408-987-2400	R	28*	.1
236	iSeatzcom—*Kenneth Purcell*	643 Magazine St Ste100, New Orleans LA 70130		R	28*	<.1
237	Real Soft Inc—*Rajan Desai*	2540 Rte 130 Ste 118, Cranbury NJ 08512	609-409-3636	R	27*	.6
238	Washington Consulting Group—*Armando Chapelli Jr*	4915 Auburn Ave Ste 30, Bethesda MD 20814	301-656-2330	S	27*	.5
239	Context Integration Inc—*Stephen Sharp*	1 Van De Graaff Dr Ste, Burlington MA 01803	781-229-6500	R	27*	.3
240	NTS Inc (Culver City California)—*William McGinnis*	24007 Ventura Blvd Ste, Calabasas CA 91302		D	27*	.3
241	eSkye Solutions Inc—*J Smoke Wallin*	250 E 96th St Ste 415, Indianapolis IN 46240	317-574-6400	R	27*	.1
242	Paragon Solutions Group Inc—*Haydn Hirstine*	4700 S Syracuse St Ste, Denver CO 80237		S	27*	<.1

Rank	Company Name—*Executive Officer*	Address, City, State, Zip	Phone	Type	Fin	Empls
243	Achieve 3000 Inc—*Saki Dodelson*	1091 River Ave Ste 1, Lakewood NJ 08701	732-367-5505	R	27*	.1
244	Capricorn Systems Inc—*Murali Suddala*	3569 Habersham at Nort, Tucker GA 30084	678-514-1080	R	26*	.3
245	Integrated Archive Systems Inc—*Amy Rao*	1121 N San Antonio Rd, Palo Alto CA 94303	650-390-9995	R	26*	.1
246	Metaweb Technologies Inc—*Thomas Leyton*	631 Howard St Ste 400, San Francisco CA 94105	415-546-5700	R	26*	.1
247	Bristlecone Inc—*Ashok Santhanam*	488 Ellis St, Mountain View CA 94043	650-386-4000	R	26*	.1
248	Genius Inc—*Sam Weber*	1400 Fashion Island Bl, San Mateo CA 94404	650-212-2050	R	26*	.1
249	Mvp Consulting Plus Inc—*Ilakumari Patel*	435 New Karner Rd Ste, Albany NY 12205	518-218-1700	R	26*	<.1
250	Concept Solutions LLC—*Cari Piper*	11600 Sunrise Valley D, Reston VA 20191	703-889-8444	R	26*	.2
251	Command Systems Inc—*James A Cochran*	838 Third St, Oakmont PA 15139	412-820-9132	R	26	.3
252	Logistics Company Inc—*Lawrence Walsh*	3400 Walsh Pkwy, Fayetteville NC 28311	910-482-8084	R	25*	.1
253	Earth Resources Technology Inc—*Jingli Yang*	6100 Frost Pl Ste A, Laurel MD 20707	240-554-0161	R	25*	.3
254	STATE NET LexisNexis Group	2101 K St, Sacramento CA 95816	916-444-0840	S	25*	.2
255	Atlantic Data Services Inc—*William H Gallagher*	1 Batterymarch Pk, Quincy MA 02169	617-770-3333	R	25*	.1
256	Information Management Group—*Richard Knudson*	1001 Green Bay Rd St 2, Winnetka IL 60093	312-802-7948	R	25*	.1
257	Sans Consulting Services Inc—*Leo Kogan*	90 John St Rm 313, New York NY 10038	212-616-4800	R	25*	.1
258	Critical Mass (Chicago Illinois)—*Neil Clemmons*	225 N Michigan Ave Ste, Chicago IL 60601	312-288-2500	S	25*	.1
259	Marquis Software Solutions Inc—*Michael Bartoo*	5465 Legacy Dr Ste 750, Plano TX 75024		R	25*	.1
260	NewWave Technologies Inc—*Bill Cordell*	4635 Wedgewood Blvd St, Frederick MD 21703	301-624-5300	R	25*	.1
261	Centuria Corp—*Kevin M Burke*	11955 Democracy Dr Ste, Reston VA 20190	703-435-4600	R	25*	.2
262	MusicMatch Inc—*Terry Semel*	16935 W Bernardo Dr St, San Diego CA 92127	858-485-4300	S	24	.1
263	Creative Information Technologies Inc—*Sunil Kolhekar*	7799 Leesburg Pke Ste, Falls Church VA 22043	703-483-4300	R	24*	.2
264	AITOC Inc—*Sergei Rabotai*	113 Barksdale Professi, Newark DE 19711		R	24*	.1
265	CyrusOne—*David Ferdman*	4211 Southwest Fwy, Houston TX 77027	713-821-1260	R	24*	.1
266	Deep Blue Sea Inc—*Carlos Rondon*	2850 Tigertail Ave, Miami FL 33133	305-857-0943	R	24*	.1
267	Guidance Solutions Inc—*Jason Meugniot*	4134 Del Rey Ave, Marina del Rey CA 90292	310-754-4000	R	24*	.1
268	IT4LA—*Dirien Barcenas*	8033 Sunset Blvd Ste 2, Los Angeles CA 90046	323-936-4900	R	24*	.1
269	Lloyd Group Inc—*Adam L Eiseman*	263 W 38th St 7th Fl, New York NY 10018	212-221-3320	R	24*	.1
270	Sophisticated Systems Inc—*Dwight Smith*	2191 CityGate Dr, Columbus OH 43219	614-418-4600	R	23*	.1
271	ADVANCE2000 Inc—*Brian Maouad*	1140 Wehrle Dr, Buffalo NY 14221	761-631-5602	R	23*	.1
272	COMPRO Consulting Group Inc—*Lakshmi Rao*	7179 W 111th St, Worth IL 60482	708-598-5910	R	23*	.1
273	Redemtech Inc—*Robert Houghton*	4115 Leap Rd, Hilliard OH 43026	614-850-3366	R	23*	.3
274	Return Path Inc—*Matt Blumberg*	304 Park Ave S 7th Fl, New York NY 10010	212-905-5500	R	23	.1
275	Intelliswift Software Inc—*Bob Patel*	39120 Argonaut Way Ste, Fremont CA 94538	510-490-9240	R	22*	.3
276	Sai Systems International Inc—*Ramesh Wadhwani*	12 Progress Dr, Shelton CT 06484	203-929-0790	R	22*	.2
277	Dyonyx LP—*Kathleen Paluaea*	1235 N Loop W Ste 1220, Houston TX 77008	713-485-7000	R	22*	.1
278	Edcor Data Services—*Steven Corso*	888 Enterprise Dr, Pontiac MI 48341	248-530-4200	R	22*	.4
279	Technical and Project Engineering LLC—*Louisa L Jaffe*	5695 King Centre Dr St, Kingstowne VA 22315	703-924-5020	R	22*	.1
280	WebHouse Inc—*Daniel Kerning*	2365 Milburn Ave Bldg, Baldwin NY 11510	516-764-6300	R	22*	.1
281	Trekk Design—*Laura Terry*	134 N Main St Ste 101, Rockford IL 61101	815-962-2132	R	22*	<.1
282	Systems Engineering Services Corp—*Jeffrey Lutman*	12355 Sunrise Valley D, Reston VA 20191	703-716-0200	R	21*	.3
283	Succeed Corp—*Omar Sayed*	7119 E Shea Blvd Ste 1, Scottsdale AZ 85254		R	21	.2
284	Magenic Technologies Inc—*Greg Frankenfield*	4150 Olson Memorial Hw, Golden Valley MN 55422	763-398-4800	R	21	.2
285	Bayshore Technologies Inc—*Peter Anderson*	5461 W Waters Ave Ste, Tampa FL 33634	813-889-8324	R	21*	<.1
286	ACCESS Systems Inc—*Julie S Lee*	11710 Plz America Dr S, Reston VA 20190	703-464-6900	R	21*	.3
287	Comnet International Co—*Upinder Zutshi*	1 TransAm Plz Dr Ste 5, Oakbrook Terrace IL 60181	630-615-2000	S	21*	.2
288	Delivery Agent Inc—*Mike Fitzsimmons*	300 California St 3rd, San Francisco CA 94104	415-248-0082	R	21*	.1
289	Front Porch Digital Inc—*Michael Knaisch*	2011 Cherry St Ste 202, Louisville CO 80027	303-440-7930	R	21*	<.1
290	Gregory C Rigamer And Associates Inc—*Gregory Rigamer*	2021 Lakeshore Dr Ste, New Orleans LA 70122	504-304-2500	R	21*	.1
291	Cosaweb Technologies Inc—*Hieu Le*	1 Mid America Plz Fl 3, Oakbrook Terrace IL 60181	630-368-1234	R	21*	.4
292	Direct Pointe Inc—*Alan Taylor*	333 S 520 W Ste 200, Lindon UT 84042	801-805-9700	R	21*	.1
293	Atlas Data Systems LLC—*John Chmiel*	560 Springfield Ave St, Westfield NJ 07090	908-233-3443	R	20*	.2
294	Seal Consulting Inc—*Badal Patel*	105 Feldcrest Ave Ste, Edison NJ 08837	732-417-9595	R	20*	.2
295	Applied Data Trends Inc—*Derrick Copeland*	215 Wynn Dr Nw Ste 101, Huntsville AL 35805	256-319-0238	R	20*	.1
296	Frontline Consulting Services Inc—*Vikas Handa*	8701 Mallard Creek Rd, Charlotte NC 28262	704-510-1998	R	20*	.5
297	Southeastern Computer Consultants Inc—*Leo Harris*	3 Hillcrest Dr Rm A-20, Frederick MD 21703	301-695-5311	R	20*	.2
298	FlexPrint Inc—*Frank Gaspari*	1911 E 5th St, Tempe AZ 85281		R	20*	.1
299	Computer Systems Center Inc—*Linda La Roche*	PO Box 127, Springfield VA 22150	703-866-4000	R	20*	.1
300	emagination network LLC	6711 Columbia Gateway, Columbia MD 21046	443-285-0120	S	20*	.1
301	Overtone Inc—*Craig Brennan*	44 Montgomery St Ste 2, San Francisco CA 94104	760-517-4100	R	20*	.1
302	nCipher Inc (Milpitas California)—*Barbara Nelson*	1655 McCarthy Blvd, Milpitas CA 95035		S	20*	<.1
303	PPD Informatics	929 N Front St, Wilmington NC 28401	910-251-0081	D	20*	<.1
304	Svam International Inc—*Anil Kapoor*	233 E Shore Rd Ste 201, Great Neck NY 11023	516-466-6655	R	20*	.1
305	Beechwood Computing Ltd—*Maurice Ryan*	4677 Old Ironsides Dr, Santa Clara CA 95054	408-496-2900	R	19*	.2
306	eAcceleration Corp—*Clinton L Ballard*	1050 NE Hostmark St 10, Poulsbo WA 98370	360-779-6301	R	19*	.1
307	Futron Corp—*Joe Fuller Jr*	7315 Wisconsin Ave Ste, Bethesda MD 20814	301-913-9372	R	19*	.1
308	Corente—*James L Zucco Jr*	80 Morristown Rd Unit, Bernardsville NJ 07924		R	19*	.1
309	Design Strategy Corp—*Marsh Newmark*	805 3rd Ave 11th Fl, New York NY 10022	212-370-0000	R	19*	<.1
310	International Computer Negotiations Inc—*Joe Auer*	PO Drawer 2970, Winter Park FL 32790	407-740-0700	R	19*	<.1
311	Collins Consulting Inc—*Robert Collins*	999 N Plz Dr Ste 240, Schaumburg IL 60173	847-290-8775	R	19*	.2
312	Virtual Care Provider Inc—*Loren Claypool*	111 W Michigan St, Milwaukee WI 53203	414-908-8000	R	19*	.2
313	Definition 6 LLC—*Robby Ball*	2115 Monroe Dr Ne Ste, Atlanta GA 30324	404-870-0323	R	19*	.1
314	Verinon Technology Solutions Ltd—*Tewabe Ayenew*	3395 N Arlington Heigh, Arlington Heights IL 60004	847-577-5256	R	19	.3
315	Computer Network Solutions LLC	131 Hoffman Ln, Islandia NY 11749	516-937-0300	R	18*	.1
316	New Image Technology Corp—*Alex Friedman*	600 Bradley Hill Rd St, Blauvelt NY 10913	845-727-1827	R	18*	.2
317	Acclaim Systems Inc—*Kailash Kalantri*	203 E Pennsylvania Blv, Trevose PA 19053	215-354-1420	R	18*	.1
318	SecurityMetrics Inc—*Brad Caldwell*	1275 W 1600 N, Orem UT 84057	801-724-9600	R	18*	.3
319	Koger Inc—*George Sipko*	12 N State Rt 17 Ste 1, Paramus NJ 07652	201-291-7747	R	18*	.2
320	RBC Inc—*Rowland Bell*	100 N Pitt St Ste 300, Alexandria VA 22314	703-549-6921	R	18*	.2
321	DDC Advocacy—*BR McConnon III*	174 Waterfront St Ste, Oxon Hill MD 20745	703-684-9690	R	18*	.2
322	Jacer Corp—*Edgar Caburian*	10340 Democracy Ln Ste, Fairfax VA 22030	703-352-1964	R	18*	.1
323	Astir It Solutions Inc—*Kishore Ganji*	2 Austin Ave Fl 2, Iselin NJ 08830	732-694-6000	R	18*	.1
324	Mortgagebot LLC—*Scott Happ*	1000 W Donges Bay Rd S, Mequon WI 53092		R	18*	.1
325	KnowledgeStorm Inc—*Kelly Gay* TechTarget Inc	2520 Northwinds Pky St, Alpharetta GA 30004	770-290-8850	S	18*	.1
326	InfoPros Drakeley-Smith Inc—*Bernie Schneider*	12325 Oracle Blvd Ste, Colorado Springs CO 80921	719-593-7377	R	18*	.1
327	Freezecom LLC—*Robert J Weber*	1900 Medical Arts Ave, Sartell MN 56377	320-203-7157	R	18*	<.1
328	MBS Associates Inc—*Keith Rosnell*	10148 Commerce Park Dr, Cincinnati OH 45246	513-645-1600	R	18*	<.1
329	Retail Solutions Inc—*Jonathan Golovin*	2440 W El Camino Real, Mountain View CA 94040	650-390-6100	R	18	.2
330	Ironworks Consulting LLC—*Scott Mendenhall*	10900 Nuckols Rd Ste 4, Glen Allen VA 23060	804-967-9200	R	18*	.2

Note: An asterisk (*) indicates an estimated financial figure. The company type code used is as follows: R = Private, P = Public, S = Private Subsidiary, B = Public Subsidiary, D = Division, J = Joint Venture, I = Investment Fund.

COMPANY RANKINGS BY SALES WITHIN 4-DIGIT SIC

Rank	Company Name—Executive Officer	Address, City, State, Zip	Phone	Type	Fin	Empls
331	Valuemomentum Inc—Sridhar Koduri	3001 Hadley Rd Ste 8, South Plainfield NJ 07080	908-755-0050	R	18*	.2
332	Conversion Services International Inc—Lori Cohen	100 Eagle Rock Ave, East Hanover NJ 07936	973-560-9400	P	18	.1
333	Solid It Networks Inc—Oliver Newman	845 Fm 407 E, Argyle TX 76226	940-464-0608	R	18*	<.1
334	Business Control Systems LP—Bernard Francis	16415 Addison Rd Ste 1, Addison TX 75001	972-241-8392	R	18*	.2
335	Natchez Group Inc—Steven Laine	3100 Oak Rd Ste 205, Walnut Creek CA 94597	925-956-4200	R	18*	.1
336	SEI Information Technology—Chris Daly	51 Broadway Ste 301, Fargo ND 58102	701-293-2650	R	17*	.1
337	Location Labs Inc—Tasso Roumeliotis	5980 Horton St Ste 675, Emeryville CA 94608	510-601-7012	R	17	.1
338	Undertone Networks Inc—Michael Cassidy	101 Park Ave 17th Fl, New York NY 10178	212-685-8000	R	17*	<.1
339	Anadarko Industries LLC—Victoria Edgington	17625 El Cam Ste 410, Houston TX 77058	281-286-9200	R	17*	.2
340	S4 Inc—Chandu Shah	8 NE Executive Park St, Burlington MA 01803	781-273-1600	R	17	.1
341	Applied Integrated Technologies Inc—Kenneth Blake	6305 Ivy Ln Ste 520, Greenbelt MD 20770	301-614-9700	R	17*	.2
342	Isys Inc—Teresa Porter	801 W Mineral Ave Ste, Littleton CO 80120	303-290-8922	R	17*	.1
343	Sector 7 - USA Inc—Jonathan Power	6500 River Pl Blvd 2-2, Austin TX 78730	512-340-0606	R	17*	.2
344	Optitek Inc—Ricki Guire	2001 S Hanley Rd Ste 2, Saint Louis MO 63144	314-644-2880	R	16*	<.1
345	DeviceAnywhere—Faraz A Syed	1730 S Amphlett Blvd S, San Mateo CA 94402	650-655-6400	R	16*	.2
346	Apn Software Services Inc—Aslam Chandiwalli	39899 Balentine Dr Ste, Newark CA 94560	510-623-5050	R	16*	.1
347	Acclaim Technical Services Inc—Trever Neves	7777 Center Ave Ste 69, Huntington Beach CA 92647	714-596-8704	R	16*	.1
348	Everge Group Inc—Esteban Neely	4965 Preston Park Blvd, Plano TX 75093	972-608-1803	R	16*	.1
349	TOASTnet Internet Service—Kevin David	4841 Monroe St Ste 307, Toledo OH 43623	419-292-2200	R	16*	<.1
350	Nomadix Inc—Michael Keaney	30851 Agoura Rd Ste 10, Agoura Hills CA 91301	818-597-1500	S	16*	<.1
351	i-Pak DVD NA—John Chang	2385 Buena Vista St, Irwindale CA 91010	626-305-4288	R	16*	<.1
352	TCSN Inc—JoEllen Fitton	1306 Pine St, Paso Robles CA 93446	805-227-7000	R	16*	<.1
353	High Performance Technologies Inc—Victor Smith	PO Box 471393, Charlotte NC 28247	704-553-2335	R	16*	<.1
354	Apex Technology Group Inc—Sarvesh Dharayan	2703 Merrywood Dr, Edison NJ 08817	732-964-1300	R	16*	.1
355	V-Soft Consulting Group Inc—Radhika Veeramachaneni	2115 Stanley Gault Pkw, Louisville KY 40223	502-425-8425	R	16*	.2
356	Perceptis LLC—Shelly Stata	1250 Old River Rd Ste, Cleveland OH 44113	216-458-4122	R	16*	.2
357	Programmers' Consortium Inc—William Lupinacci	21711 Filigree Ct, Ashburn VA 20147	703-758-1500	R	15*	.2
358	Systime Computer Corp—Vishal Grover	595 Market St Ste 2400, San Francisco CA 94105	415-369-9900	R	15*	.1
359	Guidesoft Inc—Julie Bielawski	5875 Castle Creek Pkwy, Indianapolis IN 46250	317-578-1700	R	15*	.2
360	Seamast Inc—Bruce Glass	12330 Pinecrest Rd, Reston VA 20191	703-716-5000	R	15*	.1
361	Craig Technologies—Carol Craig	7195 Murrell Rd Ste 10, Melbourne FL 32940	321-752-0394	R	15*	.3
362	IPC Technologies Inc (Richmond Virginia)—Kenneth Banks	7200 Glen Forest Dr, Richmond VA 23226	804-285-9300	R	15*	.2
363	Laser Pros International—Steve Spencer	1 International Ln, Rhinelander WI 54501	715-369-5995	R	15*	.2
364	Lbi Us LLC—Frank Pedersen	295 Lafayette St, New York NY 10012	212-274-0470	R	15*	.2
365	Telmar Information Services Corp (New York New York)	470 Park Ave S 15th Fl, New York NY 10016	212-725-3000	R	15*	.2
366	Bluefish Wireless Management Inc—Michael Browning	6100 W 96th Ste 175, Indianapolis IN 46278	317-733-8300	R	15*	.1
367	InnoCentive LLC—Dwayne Spradlin	610 Lincoln St Ste 125, Waltham MA 02451	978-482-3300	R	15*	<.1
368	eCorp Inc—Richard Stegall	PO Box 441688, Indianapolis IN 46244	317-414-3751	R	15*	<.1
369	Imaginova Inc—Jay Kirsch	470 Park Ave S 9th Fl, New York NY 10022	212-703-5800	R	15*	<.1
370	Splice Communications Inc—Andy Coan	1900 S Norfolk Ste 350, San Mateo CA 94403	650-577-2304	R	15*	<.1
371	Kemtah Group Inc—Keith Harris	6565 Americas Pkwy Ne, Albuquerque NM 87110	505-346-4900	R	15*	.1
372	Synergetics Diversified Computer Services Inc—David Palmer	501 Hwy 12 W Ste 100, Starkville MS 39759	662-323-9484	R	15*	<.1
373	Kaegan Corp—Shirley Wolf	12000 Res Pkwy Ste 164, Orlando FL 32826	407-363-3636	R	15*	.1
374	Apex Technology Systems Inc—Jigen Patel	50 Cragwood Rd Ste 214, South Plainfield NJ 07080	908-821-9975	R	14*	.1
375	Printelligent Corp—Mark Crosby	2580 Decker Lake Blvd, Salt Lake City UT 84119	801-924-6200	R	14*	.1
376	Daticon Systems Inc—Tom Haug	11 Stott Ave, Norwich CT 06360	860-823-4400	R	14*	.4
377	Computech Inc—JD Murphy Jr	7735 Old Georgetown Rd, Bethesda MD 20814	301-656-4030	R	14*	.2
378	Enrich IT Inc—Arul Murugan	100 N Point Ctr E Ste, Alpharetta GA 30022	770-667-0510	R	14*	.2
379	Infosystems Inc—Tushar Patel	293 Executive Dr, Troy MI 48083	248-588-2321	R	14*	.2
380	Intuitive Technology Group LLC—Eric Ohlson	2001 Killebrew Dr Ste, Bloomington MN 55425	952-854-1663	R	14*	.2
381	Numbers Only Inc—Hari Polavarapu	1520 Us Hwy 130 Ste 20, North Brunswick NJ 08902	732-940-0033	R	14*	.1
382	Rolta Tusc Inc—Richard Niemiec	377 E Bttrfeld Rd Ste, Lombard IL 60148	630-960-2909	R	14*	.1
383	CareScience Inc—Susan DeVore	3600 Market St 7th Fl, Philadelphia PA 19104	215-387-9401	S	14*	.1
384	Gantech Inc—Thomas Laskowski	9175 Guilford Rd Ste 1, Columbia MD 21046	443-276-4760	R	14*	.1
385	ISite Design Inc—Paul Williams	115 NW 1st Ave Ste 500, Portland OR 97209		R	14*	.1
386	CyberData Technologies Inc—Amy Liu	455 Springpark Pl Ste, Herndon VA 20170	703-481-0888	R	14*	.1
387	Cyberitas Enterprises LLC—Bruce Covill	4736 N 12th St, Phoenix AZ 85014	602-381-0123	R	14*	<.1
388	Enterprise Information Management Inc—Bruce Lyman	1655 Ft Myer Dr Ste 50, Arlington VA 22209	703-527-7808	R	14*	<.1
389	Micro-Serv Corp—David Hoglund	6577 Edsall Rd, Springfield VA 22151	703-914-1300	R	14*	<.1
390	RCMS Group LLC—KP Reddy	640 10th St NW, Atlanta GA 30318	678-247-2300	R	14*	<.1
391	ScripNet Inc—Dennis M Sponer	PO Box 379037, Las Vegas NV 89137		R	14*	<.1
392	DMB Consulting Services LLC—Billy Whittington	1401 Shoal Creek Ste 2, Highland Village TX 75077	972-899-3460	R	14*	<.1
393	Connecting Point Computer Services—Mike Minarik	4328 George Washington, Yorktown VA 23692	757-873-1580	R	14*	<.1
394	S and P Solutions Inc—Gary Bates	35000 Chardon Rd Ste 2, Willoughby Hills OH 44094	440-918-9111	R	14*	.1
395	Adaequare Inc—Padma Rao	1183 E Lyons Rd, Dayton OH 45458	937-684-9220	R	14	.1
396	Catapult Consultants LLC—Anthony Fung	2300 Clarendon Blvd St, Arlington VA 22201	703-849-0960	R	13*	.2
397	Intecon LLC—Alan Omo	6775 Rangewood Dr, Colorado Springs CO 80918	719-597-2275	R	13*	.1
398	JDM Systems Consultants Inc—Jeffrey Magnell	PO Box 1893, Brighton MI 48116	248-324-1938	R	13*	.1
399	Advanced Systems Design Inc—John DuBard	2915 Kerry Forest Pkwy, Tallahassee FL 32309	850-385-5129	R	13*	.2
400	Innospire Systems Corp—Rajasekar Duraipandiyan	199 Main St Ste 12, Matawan NJ 07747	732-290-9651	R	13*	.1
401	Sensys Networks—Amine Haoui	2560 9th St Ste 219, Berkeley CA 94710	510-548-4620	R	13*	.1
402	clearAvenue LLC—Harini Kankanahalli	939 Elkridge Landing R, Linthicum MD 21090	410-999-6403	R	13*	<.1
403	Worknet Inc—John E Vaughan	600 E Diehl Rd Ste 100, Naperville IL 60563	630-536-0406	R	13*	<.1
404	VJ Studio Inc—Vladimir Jelnov	197 Rte 18 Ste 3000, East Brunswick NJ 08816		R	13*	<.1
405	SDV Solutions Inc—Mike McMahan	133 Waller Mill Rd Ste, Williamsburg VA 23185	757-903-2068	R	13*	<.1
406	SinglePoint—Gowri Shankar	600 108th Ave NE Ste 6, Bellevue WA 98004	425-638-4500	R	13*	<.1
407	CrossComm—Don Shin	207 N Church St, Durham NC 27701	919-667-9432	R	13*	<.1
408	Deltyme Corp—John Olinger	2858 Del Mar Heights R, Del Mar CA 92014	858-483-0497	R	13*	<.1
409	VOX Network Solutions—Scott Landis	250 E Grand Ave Ste 55, South San Francisco CA 94080	650-989-1000	R	13	.1
410	Cquest America Inc—Thomas Simonds	500 S 9th St, Springfield IL 62701	217-541-7460	R	13*	.1
411	Inergex Inc—Rick Muller	50 Fountain Plz Ste 92, Buffalo NY 14202	716-829-1000	R	13*	.1
412	Uni-Data And Communications Inc—Peter Striano	6521 Fresh Meadow Ln, Flushing NY 11365	718-445-5600	R	13*	.1
413	Trofholz Technologies Inc—Yvonne Glenn	2207 Plz Dr Ste 100, Rocklin CA 95765	916-577-1903	R	13*	.1
414	Round2 Technologies Inc—Ian Bagnall	6301 E Stassney Ln Bld, Austin TX 78744	512-342-8855	R	12*	.1
415	Terra Infotech Inc—Manoj Agarwal	1 Exchange Pl Ste 903, Jersey City NJ 07302	201-324-1960	R	12*	.1
416	Newberry Group Inc—Chris Steinbach	2510 Old Hwy 94 S Ste, Saint Charles MO 63303	636-928-9944	R	12*	.1
417	Flaggstaff Technology Group Inc—Eileen Flagg	8 Claremont Rd, Scarsdale NY 10583	914-722-6831	R	12*	.1
418	National Prosource—Patricia Davis	9494 Suthwest Fwy Ste, Houston TX 77074	713-272-8800	R	12*	.1
419	VARtek Services Inc—Michael Hosford	1785 S Metro Pkwy, Dayton OH 45459	937-438-3550	R	12*	<.1
420	Cloud Creek Systems Inc—Bryan F Coville	30101 Agoura Ct Ste 10, Agoura Hills CA 91301	818-865-2800	R	12*	<.1

Rank	Company Name—*Executive Officer*	Address, City, State, Zip	Phone	Type	Fin	Empls
421	Home Run Software Services Inc—*Patrick Brenden*	15562 Chemical Ln, Huntington Beach CA 92649	714-901-0109	R	12*	<.1
422	LIGATT Security International—*Gregory Evans*	6050 Peachtree Pky Ste, Norcross GA 30092		P	12*	<.1
423	Menlo Innovations—*Richard Sheridan*	410 N 4th Ave 3rd Fl, Ann Arbor MI 48104	734-665-1847	R	12*	<.1
424	Southern Design—*Bill Evans*	100 Paradise Dr, Mount Juliet TN 37122	615-773-7157	R	12*	<.1
425	Zetta Inc—*Ali Jenab*	1362 Borregas Ave, Sunnyvale CA 94089	650-590-0950	R	12*	<.1
426	ERP Analysts Inc—*Srikanth Gaddam*	425 Metro Pl N Ste 510, Dublin OH 43017	614-718-9222	R	12	.1
427	Genex Interactive—*Walter Schild*	9905 Jefferson Blvd, Culver City CA 90232	310-736-2000	R	12	.2
428	Namtra Business Solutions Inc—*Ayesha Khalid*	11800 Sunrise Valley D, Reston VA 20191	703-391-7071	R	12*	.1
429	Universal Consulting Services Inc—*Charu Dhumne*	3975 Fair Ridge Dr S40, Fairfax VA 22033	703-591-5100	R	12*	.1
430	Hjpc Corp—*Sriram Iyer*	1149 Tasman Dr, Sunnyvale CA 94089	408-747-1237	R	12*	.1
431	Intellex Consulting Services Inc—*Linda Bronson*	4 Apple Row, Kennett Square PA 19348	610-388-3939	R	11*	<.1
432	Connection Strategies Enterprises Inc—*Adonica Randall*	N28 W23050 Roundy Dr, Pewaukee WI 53072	262-650-6500	R	11*	.2
433	DOMA Technologies LLC—*Wesley Gibson*	2875 Sabre St Ste 500, Virginia Beach VA 23452	757-306-4920	R	11*	.2
434	DCL—*David Tu*	48641 Milmont Dr, Fremont CA 94538	510-651-5100	R	11*	.1
435	Dynamic Systems Resource Management Inc—*Rahul Shah*	500 Davis St Ste 801, Evanston IL 60201	847-328-6355	R	11*	.1
436	Integracore LLC—*Ted Broman*	6077 W Wells Park Rd, West Jordan UT 84081	801-975-9411	R	11*	.1
437	Solution Set LLC—*Jeff Haggin*	100 Shoreline Hwy, Mill Valley CA 94941	415-289-1110	R	11*	.1
438	Thrillistcom—*Ben Lerer*	560 Broadway, New York NY 10012		R	11*	.1
439	Belzon Inc—*Ron Klein*	6767 Old Madison Pke S, Huntsville AL 35806	256-461-6039	R	11*	.1
440	Global Business Consulting Services Inc—*Pradeep Nigam*	489 Plainfield Rd, Edison NJ 08820	732-548-4000	R	11*	.1
441	Keylogic Systems Inc—*Jon Hammock*	3168 Collins Ferry Rd, Morgantown WV 26505	304-296-9100	R	11*	.1
442	USBid Inc—*Gary Heyes*	2320 Commerce Park Dr, Palm Bay FL 32905	321-725-9565	R	11*	.1
443	GRT Corp—*Anna Rozinov*	777 Summer St, Stamford CT 06901	203-340-0277	R	11*	.1
444	Information Transport Solutions Inc—*Tomi Selby*	335 Jeanette Barrett I, Wetumpka AL 36092	334-567-1993	R	11*	.1
445	ParentWatch Inc—*Adam Aronson*	45 Kensico Dr, Mount Kisco NY 10549	914-919-1701	R	11*	<.1
446	CommonPlaces e-Solutions LLC—*Ben Bassi*	2 Village Green Rd Ste, Hampstead NH 03841	603-329-6760	R	11*	<.1
447	Knight Communications Inc—*KC Mouli*	427 N Yale Ave Rm 201, Claremont CA 91711	909-621-3559	R	11*	<.1
448	Linde Group—*Wolfgang Reitzle*	1331 7th St Ste G, Berkeley CA 94710	510-705-8910	R	11*	<.1
449	Mission E Commerce LLC—*Adam Pollicino*	15550 N 84th St Ste 10, Scottsdale AZ 85260	480-596-0610	R	11*	<.1
450	SilverTech Inc—*Nick Saggu*	196 Bridge St, Manchester NH 03104	603-669-6600	R	11*	<.1
451	Atrilogy Solutions Group Inc—*David Charest*	1 Jenner Ste 240, Irvine CA 92618	949-777-4700	R	11*	<.1
452	Foreground Security—*David Amsler*	801 International Pky, Lake Mary FL 32746	407-562-1925	R	11	<.1
453	Peri Software Solutions Inc—*Saravanan Periasamy*	PO Box 32188, Newark NJ 07102	973-735-9500	R	11*	.2
454	Lcg Systems LLC—*Peter Carothers*	6000 Executive Blvd St, Rockville MD 20852	301-984-4004	R	11*	.1
455	Orbit Systems Inc—*Stephen Mcfarland*	1333 Northland Dr Ste, Mendota Heights MN 55120	651-767-3322	R	10*	.1
456	Diaspark Inc—*Vipin Bhardwajv*	200 Metroplex Dr Ste 4, Edison NJ 08817	732-248-8333	R	10*	.2
457	Bass and Associates Inc—*Deb Bass*	6825 Pine St Ste 354, Omaha NE 68106	402-346-1505	S	10*	.1
458	Logic Trends Inc—*Ken Stone*	500 Colonial Center Pk, Roswell GA 30076	770-551-5050	R	10*	.1
459	Neoris DFW—*Claudio Muruzabal*	4055 International Plz, Fort Worth TX 76109	817-731-0995	S	10*	.1
460	Systems Service Enterprises Inc—*Elizabeth Niedringhaus*	77 W Port Plz Ste 500, Saint Louis MO 63146	314-439-4700	R	10*	.1
461	Covestic Inc—*John Schaffer*	5555 Lakeview Dr Ste 1, Kirkland WA 98033	425-803-9889	R	10*	.1
462	It People Corp—*SAI Nidamary*	1906 E NC Hwy 54 100f, Durham NC 27713	919-806-3535	R	10*	.1
463	DoubleStar Inc—*Harry Griendling*	1161 McDermott Dr Ste, West Chester PA 19380	610-719-1900	R	10*	.1
464	Netscaler Inc	851 W Cypress Creek Rd, Ft Lauderdale FL 33309	954-267-3000	S	10*	.1
465	Flash Networks Inc—*Liam Galin*	505 Thornall St Ste 20, Edison NJ 08837	732-205-9401	R	10*	.1
466	Newbury Consulting Group Inc—*John Weston*	PO Box 416, Byfield MA 01922	978-465-5103	R	10*	.1
467	Odesus Inc—*Robert Michaels*	11766 Wilshire Blvd St, Los Angeles CA 90025	310-473-4600	R	10*	.1
468	Management Information Consulting Inc—*Thomas Sonseca*	2800 S Shirlington Rd, Arlington VA 22206		R	10*	< 1
469	Mushkin Inc—*D George Stathakis*	317 Inverness Way S St, Englewood CO 80112	303-534-5306	S	10*	<.1
470	IFI/Plenum Data Corp—*Harry Allcock*	3202 Kirkwood Hwy Ste, Wilmington DE 19808	302-633-7200	S	10*	<.1
471	International Checkout Inc—*Saskia Strick*	7950 Woodley Ave Unit, Van Nuys CA 91406	310-601-8196	R	10*	<.1
472	DSW Group Ltd—*Terry Dietzler*	900 Circle 75 Pkwy Ste, Atlanta GA 30339	770-953-0393	R	10*	<.1
473	ReelPlaycom Inc—*Dennis Young*	11301 Olympic Blvd Ste, Los Angeles CA 90064		R	10*	<.1
474	StayHealthy Inc—*John Collins*	724 E Huntington Dr St, Monrovia CA 91016	626-256-6152	R	10*	<.1
475	Systems People Inc—*Nasir Ahmed*	1650 Tysons Blvd Ste 1, Mc Lean VA 22102	703-282-4359	R	10*	<.1
476	Tabor Communications Inc—*Thomas Tabor*	8445 Camino Santa Fe S, San Diego CA 92121	858-625-0070	R	10*	<.1
477	Ventana Health Services Inc—*Giovanni Colella*	695 Market St Ste 300, San Francisco CA 94107	415-671-4683	R	10*	<.1
478	Your-Site Virtual Servers—*Jean Ann Hatch*	PO Box 963, Hinsdale MA 01235	413-499-6690	R	10*	<.1
479	Broadleaf Group LLC—*Sam Mehta*	PO Box 816, Tomball TX 77377	832-295-7202	R	10*	<.1
480	Magex Corp—*Patrick Campbell*	520 Madison Ave Ste 20, New York NY 10022	917-639-7600	R	10*	.2
481	Jobs2web Inc—*Ken Holec*	10901 Red Circle Dr St, Minnetonka MN 55343	952-697-2900	R	10	.1
482	NextDocs Corp—*Zikria Syed*	500 N Gulph Rd Ste 240, King of Prussia PA 19406	610-265-9474	R	10	.1
483	Compri Consulting Inc—*Tom Melaragno*	2601 Blake St Ste 110, Denver CO 80205	303-860-1533	R	10	.1
484	Panache Resources and Systems Corp—*Sanjay Malik*	9 Campus Dr Ste 2, Parsippany NJ 07054	973-349-1800	R	10*	.1
485	Logic Planet Inc—*Sudhir Varma*	45 Brunswick Ave Ste 1, Edison NJ 08817	732-512-0009	R	10*	.1
486	Neutron Interactive—*Dan Caffee*	224 S 200 W Ste 210, Salt Lake City UT 84101	801-327-9090	R	10	.1
487	LIDP Consulting Services Inc—*William Schnittker*	8s70 Brenwood Dr, Naperville IL 60540	630-369-6832	R	9*	.1
488	Bankscom Inc—*Dan O'Donnell*	222 Kearny St Ste 550, San Francisco CA 94108	415-962-9700	P	9	<.1
489	Accuvant Federal Solutions	7467 Ridge Rd, Hanover MD 21076	410-855-8888	S	9	.1
490	Hawk Technologies Inc—*Michael Ibarra*	2 Spencer Pl Fl 62, Scarsdale NY 10583	914-725-6300	R	9*	<.1
491	Aplusnet—*Philip Spencer*	110 E Broward Blvd Ste, Fort Lauderdale FL 33301	858-410-6929	R	9*	.3
492	ENSCICON Corp—*Will Smith*	555 Zang St Ste 100, Lakewood CO 80228	303-980-8600	R	9*	.1
493	Treetop Technologies Inc—*Kriss Kirchhoss*	223 N 6th St Ste 320, Boise ID 83702	208-342-5668	R	9*	.1
494	ActioNet Inc—*Ashley W Chen*	2600 Park Tower Dr Ste, Vienna VA 22180	703-204-0090	R	9*	.1
495	Nixsol Inc—*Praveen Kari*	216 N Washington Ave S, Dunellen NJ 08812	732-762-3996	R	9*	.1
496	Pro Softnet Corp—*Raghu Kulkarni*	26115 Mureau Rd Ste A, Calabasas CA 91302	818-251-4200	R	9*	.1
497	WebMediaBrands Inc—*Alan M Meckler*	50 Washington St Ste 9, Norwalk CT 06854	203-662-2800	P	9	.1
498	Product Support Solutions Inc—*Todd Funk*	7172 Regional St 431, Dublin CA 94568	925-208-2403	R	9*	<.1
499	Empower Professionals Inc—*Laxmi Indukuri*	555 Donofrio Dr Ste 10, Madison WI 53719	608-827-5115	R	9*	<.1
500	Technatomy Corp—*Nadeem Butler*	3554 Chain Bridge Rd S, Fairfax VA 22030	703-268-5525	R	9*	<.1
501	Axis Group LLC—*Albert J Hughes*	400 Connell Dr Ste 720, Berkeley Heights NJ 07922	908-988-0200	R	9*	<.1
502	BizLand Inc—*Steve Sydness*	70 Blanchard Rd 3rd Fl, Burlington MA 01803	781-272-6470	R	9*	<.1
503	Advanced Legal Systems Inc—*Scott Randall*	121 SW Salmon St Ste 1, Portland OR 97204	503-227-5400	R	9*	<.1
504	Carpathia Hosting Inc—*Peter Weber*	43480 Yukon Dr Ste 200, Ashburn VA 20147	703-740-1730	R	9*	<.1
505	Comentum Corp—*Scott R Cohen*	6222 Ferris Sq, San Diego CA 92121	858-410-0700	R	9*	<.1
506	Dataway Inc—*Simon Lewis*	180 Redwood St Fl 3, San Francisco CA 94102	415-882-8700	R	9*	<.1
507	netCOMPONENTS Inc—*John Vassil*	100 E Linton Blvd Ste, Delray Beach FL 33483	561-274-6780	R	9*	<.1
508	Nethosting Corp—*Elaine Livingston*	1155 S 800 East, Orem UT 84097	801-223-9939	R	9*	<.1
509	New Media Communications—*Mike Connell*	3046 Brecksville Rd, Richfield OH 44286	330-659-7373	R	9*	<.1
510	O'Daniel Designs—*Gina O'Daniel*	17401 158th Ave SE, Renton WA 98058	425-277-5005	R	9*	<.1

Note: An asterisk (*) indicates an estimated financial figure. The company type code used is as follows: R = Private, P = Public, S = Private Subsidiary, B = Public Subsidiary, D = Division, J = Joint Venture, I = Investment Fund.

COMPANY RANKINGS BY SALES WITHIN 4-DIGIT SIC

Rank	Company Name—*Executive Officer*	Address, City, State, Zip	Phone	Type	Fin	Empls
511	Public Access Networks Corp—*Alexis Rosen*	134 W 29th St Ste 609, New York NY 10001	212-741-4400	R	9*	<.1
512	Tekmethods LLC—*Lori Sechio*	8466 Flagstone Dr, Tampa FL 33615	813-249-5674	R	9*	<.1
513	YellowBrix Inc—*Jeffrey Massa*	500 Montgomery St Ste, Alexandria VA 22314	703-548-3300	R	9*	<.1
514	Symbian Inc USA—*David Wood*	1051 E Hillsdale Blvd, Foster City CA 94404	650-645-7500	S	9*	<.1
515	Archimage Inc—*Richard Buday*	4100 Montrose Blvd Ste, Houston TX 77006	713-523-3425	R	9*	<.1
516	Ilinc Communications Inc—*James M Powers Jr*	2999 N 44th St Ste 650, Phoenix AZ 85018	602-952-1200	S	9	.1
517	Nova Datacom LLC—*Shana Cruz*	4501 Singer Ct Ste 350, Chantilly VA 20151	703-234-9000	R	9*	.1
518	Tpi Billing Solutions LLC—*John Pitts*	PO Box 472330, Tulsa OK 74147	918-664-0144	R	9*	.1
519	Hallmark Global Technologies Inc—*Neelima Elluri*	262 Chapman Rd Ste 102, Newark DE 19702	302-366-8960	R	9*	.1
520	Software Productivity Strategists Inc—*Hashmat Malik*	9420 Key W Ave Ste 220, Rockville MD 20850	301-838-2777	R	9*	<.1
521	Cardinal Technologies Inc (Bethesda Maryland)—*Earl M Furfine*	4695 MacArthur Ct 8th, Newport Beach CA 92660	949-975-1550	S	9	.1
522	New Technologies and Associates Inc—*John Kelly*	24 School St Fl Mezz, Boston MA 02108	617-624-3600	R	9*	.1
523	Merizon Group Inc—*Fredrick Merizon*	PO Box 147, Appleton WI 54912	920-739-4326	S	9*	.1
524	Drsdigital LLC	10 E 29th St Apt 21g, New York NY 10016	917-292-9069	R	9*	<.1
525	3i People Inc—*Raj Swami*	5755 N Point Pkwy Ste, Alpharetta GA 30022	404-551-5226	R	8*	.1
526	Compsat Technology Inc—*Richard Glisky*	25300 Telg Rd Ste 555, Southfield MI 48033	248-223-1020	R	8*	.1
527	Field Solutions Inc—*C Lewis*	5775 Wayzata Blvd Ste, Minneapolis MN 55416	952-288-2500	R	8*	<.1
528	Advanced Information Network Systems Inc—*Mohinder Goswami*	806 W Diamond Ave Ste, Gaithersburg MD 20878	301-670-2300	R	8*	.1
529	CT Male Associates PC—*Gary R Male*	PO Box 727, Latham NY 12110	518-786-7400	R	8*	.1
530	New York Technology Partners Inc—*Blake Bhatia*	75 Montgomery St Fl 5, Jersey City NJ 07302	201-521-0300	R	8*	.1
531	Seven Seas Technology Inc—*Dayakar Veerlapati*	720 Spirit 40 Park Dr, Chesterfield MO 63005	636-530-9286	R	8*	.1
532	Sparta Consulting Inc—*Lokesh Sikaria*	111 Woodmere Rd Ste 20, Folsom CA 95630	916-985-0300	R	8*	.1
533	Sierra Atlantic Inc—*Raju Reddy*	7979 Gateway Blvd #220, Newark CA 94560	510-742-4100	R	8*	.1
534	Vanguard Integrity Professionals Inc—*Ron Dailey*	6625 S Eastern Ave St, Las Vegas NV 89120	702-794-0014	R	8*	.1
535	ROME Corp—*David Achim*	901 S Mopac, Austin TX 78746	512-347-3200	R	8*	.1
536	PeopleAdmin Inc—*Susanne Bowen*	816 Congress Ave Ste 1, Austin TX 78701		R	8*	.1
537	Jouve Data Management Inc—*Geoffrey Godet*	17671 Cowan Ave Ste 20, Irvine CA 92614	949-474-4200	S	8*	<.1
538	Riata Technologies Inc—*Tommy Wald*	8001 Centre Park Dr St, Austin TX 78754	512-458-8226	R	8*	<.1
539	Cimdata Inc—*Ed Miller*	3909 Research Park Dr, Ann Arbor MI 48108	734-668-9922	R	8*	<.1
540	Unety Systems Inc—*Jim Fleming*	25W231 Oldham Rd Ste 1, Naperville IL 60563	630-955-9500	R	8*	<.1
541	DMB Group Inc—*Billy Whittington*	1401 Shoal Creek Ste 2, Highland Village TX 75077	972-899-3460	R	8*	<.1
542	Aenigma Inc—*Kenneth Foster*	212 Towne Village Dr, Cary NC 27513	919-244-8944	R	8*	<.1
543	PSS-Product Support Solutions—*Todd Funk*	7172 Regional St, Dublin CA 94568	925-208-2450	R	8	<.1
544	Computing Strategies Inc—*Mark A Schecter*	12182 Royal Valley Dr, Saint Louis MO 63141	314-644-6181	R	8*	<.1
545	Teksell Inc—*Michael Bourne*	3121 Bartlett Corporat, Bartlett TN 38133	901-758-8179	R	8	<.1
546	Valytics LLC	10758 Riverscape Run, Great Falls VA 22066	703-421-3484	R	8*	<.1
547	DPE Systems Inc	425 Pontius Ave N Ste, Seattle WA 98109	206-223-3737	R	8*	<.1
548	Cannella Response Television—*Robert Medved*	492 N Pine St, Burlington WI 53105	262-763-4810	R	8*	<.1
549	Sky Computer Services LLC—*Skye Southwick*	1100 Glendon Ave Ste 1, Los Angeles CA 90024	310-837-2525	R	8*	<.1
550	Wood River Technologies Inc—*Richard White*	371 Main St S, Ketchum ID 83340	208-726-5553	R	8*	<.1
551	Web Solutions Inc—*Tom Barton*	250 Pomeroy Ave Ste 20, Meriden CT 06450	203-235-7777	R	8*	<.1
552	GW WebDesign—*Gabriele Winckler*	4500 Hardscrabble Dr S, Columbia SC 29229	864-223-9629	R	8*	<.1
553	ARTISTdirect Recordings Inc—*Johnathan V Diamond*	10900 Wilshire Blvd St, Los Angeles CA 90024	310-208-8525	S	8*	<.1
554	Information Analytics Inc—*Kenneth Livingston*	134 S 13th St Ste 700, Lincoln NE 68508	402-477-8300	R	8*	<.1
555	Information Express	565 Middlefield Rd 2nd, Menlo Park CA 94025	650-812-3588	R	8*	<.1
556	Optial North America—*Chris O'Brien*	12600 Deerfield Park S, Alpharetta GA 30004	770-753-0128	R	8*	<.1
557	Powertest Software Sales Inc—*Tom Lynch*	336 Bon Air Center #43, Greenbrae CA 94904	415-778-0580	R	8*	<.1
558	Rose Business Solutions—*K Linda Rose*	5900 Wilshire Blvd Ste, Los Angeles CA 90036	323-634-7800	R	8*	<.1
559	CMS Consulting Inc—*Charles Lapadula*	4 Cornwall Dr Ste 225, East Brunswick NJ 08816	732-940-6700	R	8*	<.1
560	Simacor LLC—*Alisa Theis*	10700 Hwy 55 Ste 170, Minneapolis MN 55441	763-544-4415	R	8*	<.1
561	J2a Systems LLC	246 Federal Rd Ste C34, Brookfield CT 06804	203-740-2888	R	8*	<.1
562	Login Consulting Services Inc—*Elece Otten*	300 Continental Blvd, El Segundo CA 90245	310-607-9091	R	8*	.1
563	Corporate Systems Engineering LLC—*Chris Bennett*	1215 Brookville Way, Indianapolis IN 46239	317-375-3600	R	8*	<.1
564	ShareFile—*Jesse Lipson*	4140 Parklake Ave Ste, Raleigh NC 27612		S	8	<.1
565	Dua Computer Resources Inc—*Ammu Warrier*	6001 Broken Sound Pkwy, Boca Raton FL 33487	561-998-3737	R	8*	.1
566	Rs Interest Inc—*Art Romack*	PO Box 140129, Irving TX 75014	214-394-9817	R	8*	.1
567	Compass Solutions Corp—*Joompoj Thapanawat*	2760 Eisenhower Ave St, Alexandria VA 22314	703-373-6770	R	8*	.1
568	Prescient Development Inc—*Jeffery Scheper*	1025 Mountain Dr, Deerfield IL 60015	847-405-9417	R	8*	<.1
569	Qualsoft Group LLC	3097 Ziron Ave, Simi Valley CA 93065	818-231-6528	R	8*	.1
570	Abacus Solutions Group LLC—*Bill Branstetter*	1919 Oakwell Farms Pkw, San Antonio TX 78218	210-293-6400	R	7	.1
571	Advanced Reservation Systems Inc—*Alec House*	3750 Convoy St Ste 312, San Diego CA 92111	619-238-0900	R	7*	.1
572	K4 Solutions Inc—*Sumi Krishnan*	7702 Leesburg Pike Cen, Falls Church VA 22043	703-448-4860	R	7	.1
573	Db Access LLC—*Octavio Ballesta*	505 N Lake Shore Dr, Chicago IL 60611	312-404-6458	R	7*	.1
574	Hypermedia Systems Inc—*Michael Frick*	700 S Flower St Ste 32, Los Angeles CA 90017	213-908-2214	R	7*	.1
575	Secure-24 Inc—*Matthias Horch*	29355 Northwestern Hwy, Southfield MI 48034	248-784-1021	R	7	<.1
576	Charter Solutions Inc—*William Leonard*	3033 Campus Dr Ste N16, Minneapolis MN 55441	763-230-6100	R	7*	.1
577	Cetan Corp—*Bradley Scott*	1001 Scenic Pkwy Ste 2, Chesapeake VA 23323		R	7	<.1
578	Prithvi Information Solutions International LLC—*Shiva Bongu*	14711 Ne 29th Pl Ste 1, Bellevue WA 98007	425-451-7448	R	7*	.1
579	Court Square Data Group Inc—*Keith M Parent*	1350 Main St 5th Fl, Springfield MA 01103	413-746-0054	R	7*	.1
580	Educational Data Systems Inc—*Robert Schnierder*	15300 Commerce Dr N St, Dearborn MI 48120	313-271-2660	R	7*	.1
581	eVox Productions—*David Falstrup*	2363 E Pacifica Pl, Rancho Dominguez CA 90220	310-605-1400	R	7*	.1
582	Systemguru Inc—*Avnish Madan*	900 Rte 9 N Ste 400, Woodbridge NJ 07095	732-326-3951	R	7*	.1
583	Equipment Data Associates LLC—*Bill Ault*	1509 Orchard Lake Dr S, Charlotte NC 28270	704-845-5666	R	7*	.1
584	Infoexperience LLC—*Joseph Prats*	PO Box 522, Lake Oswego OR 97034	503-452-0723	R	7*	.1
585	Madison Hobbs Inc—*Gary Madison*	479 Dedham Ave, Needham MA 02492	781-444-4007	R	7*	.1
586	Digital Infuzion Inc—*Hemant Virkar*	656 Quince Orchard Rd, Gaithersburg MD 20878	301-948-4871	R	7*	<.1
587	Cynergies Consulting Inc—*Debbie Holy*	387 Golfview Lane Ste, Highland Heights OH 44143	440-918-9341	R	7*	<.1
588	Audio Video Systems Inc—*Peter Barthelson*	14566 Lee Rd, Chantilly VA 20151	703-263-1002	R	7*	<.1
589	Interactive Marketing Technologies—*Howard Buckland*	19800 MacArthur Blvd S, Irvine CA 92612	623-218-6572	R	7*	<.1
590	Knovalent Inc—*Matt Bresson*	3135 S State St Ste 30, Ann Arbor MI 48108	734-996-8300	R	7*	<.1
591	Music Bakery—*Jack Waldenmaier*	7522 Campbell Rd Ste 1, Dallas TX 75248	978-578-7863	R	7*	<.1
592	Quintum Technologies Inc—*Cheng Chen*	71 James Way, Eatontown NJ 07724		S	7*	<.1
593	Moneynet Inc—*Harold Arnem*	185 Franklin St Fl 2, New York NY 10013	212-334-2000	R	7*	<.1
594	ADR Data Recovery Inc	2300 W Sahara Ave Ste, Las Vegas NV 89102	702-949-9450	R	7*	<.1
595	AS Was—*Debbie Levitt*	PO Box 8676, San Jose CA 95155	408-416-3580	R	7*	<.1
596	DAG Online Inc—*John Paukulis*	23632 Calabasas Rd, Calabasas CA 91302	818-793-1000	R	7*	<.1
597	DomainIt Inc—*Paul Goldstone*	9525 Kenwood Rd Ste 32, Cincinnati OH 45242	513-351-4222	R	7*	<.1
598	Forbes Technology Group—*Siraj Bukhari*	1681McGaw Ave, Irvine CA 92614	949-756-2000	R	7*	<.1

Rank	Company Name—Executive Officer	Address, City, State, Zip	Phone	Type	Fin	Empls
599	Joseph Co (St Louis Missouri)—Susan Blake	5142 Dominion Dr Ste 8, Arnold MO 63010	636-282-7300	R	7*	<.1
600	Race Telecommunications Inc	101 Haskins Way, South San Francisco CA 94080	650-246-8900	R	7*	<.1
601	Square Tree Software—Bill Pennock	1016 N Market Blvd Ste, Sacramento CA 95834	916-925-8733	R	7*	<.1
602	Yesterday's Business Computers Inc—Tom Tsivgas	110 Clyde Rd, Somerset NJ 08873	732-271-7060	R	7*	<.1
603	Onelife Digital Inc—Chris Adams	PO Box 73430, San Clemente CA 92673	949-429-1269	R	7*	<.1
604	Istonish Inc—Annette Quintana	6400 S Fiddlers Green, Greenwood Village CO 80111	303-771-1765	R	7*	.1
605	Syscore Solutions International Inc—Bruce Gallager	15 Maiden Ln Frnt, New York NY 10038	212-619-5200	R	7*	.1
606	B2b Workforce LP—Brad Elster	200 Northpoint Ctr Eas, Alpharetta GA 30022	770-667-7200	S	7*	.1
607	Yash and Lujan Consulting Inc—Manoj Baheti	7550 W Ih 10 Ste 940, San Antonio TX 78229	210-340-0098	R	7*	.1
608	Burgiss Group LLC—Carlos Ibarra	111 River St Fl 10th, Hoboken NJ 07030	201-427-9600	R	7*	.1
609	Walker Systems Support Inc—Katherine Emery	20 Waterside Dr Ste 20, Farmington CT 06032	860-678-3530	R	7*	.1
610	Firestream Worldwide Inc—James Turner	12935 N 40 Dr Ste 200, Saint Louis MO 63141	314-434-4601	R	7*	.1
611	Spectrum Technology Services LLC—Joe Basile	8201 Greensboro Dr Ste, Mc Lean VA 22102	703-761-9490	R	7*	<.1
612	Local Splash—Steve Yeich	3611 S Harbor Blvd Ste, Santa Ana CA 92704		R	7	.1
613	Adea International Inc—Shouvik Bhattacharyya	14185 Dallas Pkwy Ste, Dallas TX 75254	972-764-1700	R	7*	.1
614	Professional Technology Services Inc—Bob Adams	PO Box 142, Seaford DE 19973	302-628-8898	R	7*	.1
615	PMH Enterprises Inc—Alastair Main	4893 W Waters Ave Ste, Tampa FL 33634	813-885-7974	R	7*	.1
616	Premier Consulting Group Inc—Madhu Madhavan	2279 State Hwy 33 Ste, Hamilton NJ 08690	609-631-0050	R	7*	.1
617	Integra Technology Consulting Corp—David Teplow	400 5th Ave Ste 100, Waltham MA 02451	781-890-0070	R	7*	<.1
618	Datasafe—Thomas Reese	37580 Filbert St, Newark CA 94560	510-713-3500	R	7*	.1
619	First Consulting Inc—Art Roberts	PO Box 20710, Rochester NY 14602	585-387-0302	R	7*	.1
620	Internal Data Resources Inc—Dale Deese	7000 Peachtree Dunwood, Atlanta GA 30328	770-671-0040	R	7*	.1
621	Business Microvar Inc—John Hendrickson	2277 Hwy 36 W Ste 300, Saint Paul MN 55113	651-639-0575	R	7*	.1
622	Valley Us Inc—Sunita Kumari	888 Saratoga Ave Ste 2, San Jose CA 95129	408-260-7342	R	6*	.1
623	Internetwork Services Inc—Charles Steiner	PO Box 473155, Charlotte NC 28247	704-540-5800	R	6*	.1
624	Ea Consulting Inc—Chin Wong	1024 Iron Point Rd, Folsom CA 95630	916-357-6588	R	6*	.1
625	Klc Consulting Inc—Keith Cricks	2239 Woodbine Dr, Tallahassee FL 32309	850-894-1952	R	6*	<.1
626	Computer Sykes Inc—Ramon Sykes	PO Box 13762, Atlanta GA 30324	404-634-9599	R	6*	<.1
627	Acumen Consulting Inc—Manu Jetley	1275 Bloomfield Ave St, Fairfield NJ 07004	973-227-1094	R	6*	.1
628	Walter Associates Inc—Jeffrey Walter	100 E Mi Ave Ste 200, Saline MI 48176	734-429-3892	R	6*	.1
629	Wright Solutions Inc—Lee Wright	7833 Walker Dr Ste 630, Greenbelt MD 20770	301-459-3552	R	6*	.1
630	Microtel Computer Systems Inc—Juliet Chui	19565 E Walnut Dr S B6, City Of Industry CA 91748	909-895-8828	R	6*	.1
631	Futuretech Consultants LLC—Anj Balusu	PO Box 922577, Norcross GA 30010	678-990-7777	R	6*	.1
632	Govolution Inc—Gregory Gentile	2000 14th St N Ste 600, Arlington VA 22201	703-894-5000	R	6*	.1
633	CCI (Milwaukee Wisconsin)—Christopher Carter	2156 S 4th St, Milwaukee WI 53207		R	6	<.1
634	Best Value Technology Inc—Daniel Zimmerman	15855 Parnell Ct, Haymarket VA 20169	703-229-4200	R	6*	<.1
635	GrubHubcom—Matt Maloney	2211 N Elston Ste 400, Chicago IL 60614		R	6*	.1
636	Advanced Systems Development Inc—Richard L Bennett	2800 Shirlington Rd St, Arlington VA 22206	703-998-3900	R	6*	.1
637	Vensai Technologies Inc—Kavitha Nimmgadda	2450 Atlanta Hwy Ste 1, Cumming GA 30040	770-888-4804	R	6*	.1
638	Parx Group Of New York Inc—Patricia Ruffino	4625 S Clyde Morris Bl, Port Orange FL 32129	386-763-1771	R	6*	.1
639	Dataserv LLC—Dave Preis	1630 Des Peres Rd Ste, Saint Louis MO 63131	314-842-1155	R	6*	.1
640	Jat Computer Consulting Inc—Jack Felicio	440 Us Hwy 22 Ste 102, Bridgewater NJ 08807	908-725-0111	R	6*	.1
641	Sekon Enterprise Inc—Angela Wilson	2250 Corp Park Dr Ste, Herndon VA 20171	703-463-3133	R	6*	.1
642	Bicitis Group Inc—Louis Cicitta	426 Herrick Dr, Dover NJ 07801	973-515-9280	R	6*	<.1
643	Wellfount Pharmacy Inc—Paul Leamon	5751 W 73rd St, Indianapolis IN 46278		R	6*	<.1
644	MIG and Co—Eric McGuardian	60 E 42nd St Ste 2137, New York NY 10165	212-681-1400	R	6*	<.1
645	RFIP Inc—Brandon Clark	100 W Wilshire Blvd St, Oklahoma City OK 73116	405-286-0928	R	6*	<.1
646	Tomorrow's Solutions Today Inc—Kevin Dziekonski	4956 Wyaconda Rd, Rockville MD 20852	301-881-8050	R	6*	<.1
647	Security by Design—Clark D Manus	269 Walker, Detroit MI 48207	313-259-2700	R	6*	<.1
648	StumbleUpon—Garrett Camp	301 Brannan St, San Francisco CA 94107	415-979-0640	R	6*	<.1
649	Enterprise Solutions Realized Inc—Dennis Christmas	2400 Longstone Ln Ste, Marriottsville MD 21104	410-442-5501	R	6	<.1
650	authsec—Marion Bischoff	6990 Columbia Gateway, Columbia MD 21046	443-285-0630	R	6*	<.1
651	Qualex Consulting Services Inc—Clive Pearson	4300 Biscayne Blvd Ste, Miami FL 33137	305-576-5447	R	6*	<.1
652	TechSoft Systems Inc—Clifford A Bailey	10296 Springfield Pike, Cincinnati OH 45215	513-772-5010	R	6*	<.1
653	Arsenal Acquisition Corp—David C Peterschmidt	6363 Fiddler's Green C, Greenwood Village CO 80111	303-220-0100	S	6*	<.1
654	Devine Systems Inc—John Devine	1 Perimeter Rd, Manchester NH 03103	603-626-3400	R	6*	<.1
655	All Star Consulting Inc—Pamela E Munn	1111 Oak St, San Francisco CA 94102	415-552-1400	R	6*	<.1
656	Zibiz Corp—Vanil Walia	50 Alexander Ct, Ronkonkoma NY 11779	631-738-1100	R	6*	<.1
657	BiT Group Inc—Steffan Berelowitz	29 Camp St, Cambridge MA 02140	617-876-8900	R	6*	<.1
658	CoVision Inc—Lenny Lind	567 Sutter St 3rd Fl, San Francisco CA 94102	415-563-2020	R	6*	<.1
659	Backbone Networks Inc—Thomas Mulanix	9061 Miller Rd Ste 9, Swartz Creek MI 48473	810-630-9200	R	6*	<.1
660	Night Kitchen Interactive—Matthew Fisher	411 S Second St Ste 20, Philadelphia PA 19147	215-629-9962	R	6*	<.1
661	Really Strategies Inc—Barry Bealer	2570 Blvd of the Gener, Norristown PA 19403	610-631-6770	R	6*	<.1
662	SearchKing Inc—Robert Massa	2400 NW 23rd, Oklahoma City OK 73107	405-231-1911	R	6*	<.1
663	Bowman Group—Joel M Bowman	1515 Dickey Dr, Atlanta GA 30322	404-727-6592	R	6*	<.1
664	Delphi International Software Inc—David Mastrandrea	PO Box 620729, Woodside CA 94062	650-802-9696	R	6*	<.1
665	MakeBuzz LLC—Christopher Skinner	3606 Magazine St, New Orleans LA 70115	707-709-8780	R	6*	<.1
666	Saylent Technologies Inc—Tyson Nargassans	500 Franklin Village D, Franklin MA 02038	508-570-2161	R	6*	<.1
667	Testware Associates Inc—Leslie Segal	21 East High St, Somerville NJ 08876	908-526-2900	R	6*	<.1
668	Trilogy Consulting—Barbara Baldwin	2021 Midwest Rd Ste 20, Oak Brook IL 60523	630-953-6278	R	6*	<.1
669	Webdesigns-Studio—Marina Lehmann	291 S La Cienega Blvd, Beverly Hills CA 90211	909-510-2002	R	6*	<.1
670	Innovative System Solutions Corp—Richard Huang	1601 N Kent St Ste 100, Arlington VA 22209	703-527-2009	R	6*	<.1
671	SCK Inc—Barb Cagley	2221 Professor Ave, Cleveland OH 44113	216-522-9740	R	6*	<.1
672	SpinWeb Internet Media Inc—Michael Reynolds	8500 Keystone Crossing, Indianapolis IN 46240	317-324-1100	R	6*	<.1
673	Cyber F/X Inc—Dick Cavdek	2940 N Naomi St, Burbank CA 91504	818-246-2911	R	6*	<.1
674	Telos Online Inc—John Wood	PO Box 740669, Arvada CO 80006	303-424-0770	R	6*	<.1
675	iFAX Solutions Inc—Darren Nickerson	161 Leverington Ave St, Philadelphia PA 19127	215-825-8700	R	6*	<.1
676	Aracaelum Corp—Gary Dsilva	402 Main St Ste 100-05, Metuchen NJ 08840	212-561-5887	R	6*	<.1
677	Misha Consulting Group Inc—Amardeep Misha	2 N 1st St Fl 4, San Jose CA 95113	408-654-7900	R	6*	<.1
678	Cara Group Inc—Daniel King	2215 York Rd Ste 510, Oak Brook IL 60523	630-574-2272	R	6*	.1
679	Fusion Learning Systems Inc—Bryan Menell	7600 N Capitol Of Texa, Austin TX 78731	512-853-8900	R	6*	.1
680	1 Edi Source Inc—John Onysko	PO Box 391466, Solon OH 44139	440-519-7800	R	6*	.1
681	Verecloud Inc—John Mccawley	6569 S Greenwood Ste 4, Englewood CO 80111		R	6*	<.1
682	Orpine Inc—Sridhar Marupudi	11785 Northfall Ln Ste, Alpharetta GA 30009	770-475-1445	R	6*	<.1
683	Applications Engineering Group Inc—Mark Church	12300 Old Tesson Rd, Saint Louis MO 63128	314-842-9110	R	6*	<.1
684	SIS - G Ltd—Sam Hassen	701 Carlyle Ct, Northbrook IL 60062	847-205-4085	R	6*	<.1
685	Mcinnis Consulting Services Corp—Robert Mcinnis	100 Prospect St, Norwell MA 02061	781-659-4922	R	6*	.1
686	Objectwave Corp—Sam Cinquegrani	333 W Wacker Dr Ste 18, Chicago IL 60606	312-269-0111	R	6*	<.1
687	Texas Govlink Inc—Mariano Camarillo	1304 W Ave Ste 200, Austin TX 78701	512-474-1847	R	6*	.1
688	U-Nav Microelectronics Corp—Russ Garcia	8 Hughes, Irvine CA 92618	949-453-2727	R	5*	.1

Note: An asterisk (*) indicates an estimated financial figure. The company type code used is as follows: R = Private, P = Public, S = Private Subsidiary, B = Public Subsidiary, D = Division, J = Joint Venture, I = Investment Fund.

COMPANY RANKINGS BY SALES WITHIN 4-DIGIT SIC

Rank	Company Name—*Executive Officer*	Address, City, State, Zip	Phone	Type	Fin	Empls
689	Telovations Inc—*Mark Swanson*	1410 N West Shore Blvd, Tampa FL 33607	813-321-1000	R	5	<.1
690	Pacific Northwest Gigapop—*Ed Lazowska*	93 S Jackson St Ste 30, Seattle WA 98104	206-727-9900	R	5*	<.1
691	Baytree Associates Inc—*Gregory Lovette*	13925 Ballantyne Corpo, Charlotte NC 28277	704-424-5641	R	5*	<.1
692	Unilava Corp—*Baldwin Yung*	353 Sacramento St Ste, San Francisco CA 94111	415-321-3490	P	5	<.1
693	Ookla—*Mike Apgar*	538 5th Ave E, Kalispell MT 59901	406-943-4473	R	5	<.1
694	Digicert Inc—*Ken Bretschneider*	355 S 520 W, Lindon UT 84042	801-701-9600	R	5*	.1
695	Macrosearch Inc—*Marjie Peterson*	2800 156th Ave Se Ste, Bellevue WA 98007	425-641-7252	R	5*	<.1
696	Monmouth Internet Corp—*Kenneth Leland*	10 Drs James Parker Bl, Red Bank NJ 07701	732-704-1000	R	5*	<.1
697	Sloan Limited Partners LLC	225 Abbe Rd, South Windsor CT 06074	860-432-3014	R	5*	<.1
698	King Technologies Inc—*Larry Matthews*	3760 Sports Arena Blvd, San Diego CA 92110	619-523-4977	R	5*	<.1
699	Dot Blue Solutions Inc—*Gary Blohm*	1900 Grant St Ste 1200, Denver CO 80203	303-674-3500	R	5*	<.1
700	Optimal Technologies International LLC	3361 Rouse Rd Ste 120, Orlando FL 32817	407-982-7660	R	5*	<.1
701	Link Solutions Inc—*Bhupesh Wadhawan*	12007 Sunrise Valley D, Reston VA 20191	703-707-6256	R	5	.1
702	Teracore—*Luis Perez*	3300 Holcomb Bridge Rd, Norcross GA 30092	770-454-9119	R	5*	.1
703	Capstone—*David C Turtletaub*	15770 Dallas Pkwy Ste, Dallas TX 75248	972-818-4433	R	5*	.1
704	Computer Evidence Specialists LLC—*Josh Jaspan*	4320 A1a S Ste 1, Saint Augustine FL 32080	904-461-8388	R	5*	.1
705	Morris Kimmel Corp—*Jason Kimmel*	7600 N Mineral Dr Ste, Coeur D Alene ID 83815	208-762-4575	R	5*	.1
706	Thuridion—*Patrick Hendry*	5619 Scotts Valley Dr, Scotts Valley CA 95066	831-439-7900	R	5*	.1
707	Tsymmetry Inc—*Philip Lowit*	1101 Penn Ave Nw Ste 8, Washington DC 20004	202-480-2020	R	5*	.1
708	Usability Sciences Corp—*Jeff Schueler*	909 Hidden Ridge Ste 5, Irving TX 75038	972-550-1599	R	5*	.1
709	A3 Technology Inc—*Karen Vargas*	327 W White Horse Pke, Egg Harbor City NJ 08215	609-652-7933	R	5*	<.1
710	Croyten LLC	275 Grove St Ste 2-400, Auburndale MA 02466	617-477-6888	R	5*	<.1
711	Customer Effective Inc—*Scott Millwood*	25 E Court St, Greenville SC 29601	864-250-2170	R	5	<.1
712	Health Hero Network Inc—*Derek Newell*	2400 Geng Road Ste 200, Palo Alto CA 94303	650-690-9100	R	5*	<.1
713	Syrinx Consulting Corp—*Andrew Gelina*	PO Box 920201, Needham MA 02492	781-487-7800	R	5*	<.1
714	Szanca Solutions Inc—*Mark Szanca*	100 E Pitt St Ste 300, Bedford PA 15522	814-624-0123	R	5*	<.1
715	Csols Inc—*Kyle Mcduffie*	131 Continental Dr Ste, Newark DE 19713	302-731-5290	R	5*	<.1
716	MVC Corp—*Lori Stroh*	203 N LaSalle St Ste 2, Chicago IL 60601	312-606-5555	R	5*	<.1
717	Spin Systems Inc—*Wael Al-Ali*	100 Carpenter Dr Ste 1, Sterling VA 20164	703-318-0803	R	5*	<.1
718	Vaultcom Inc—*Claude P Sheer*	132 W 31st St 15th Fl, New York NY 10001	212-366-4212	R	5*	<.1
719	Onlc Consulting—*Andy Williamson*	505 Carr Rd 101, Wilmington DE 19809	302-658-3026	R	5*	<.1
720	Eagle Consulting and Development Corp—*Bill Paone*	135 Kinnelon Rd Ste 20, Kinnelon NJ 07405	973-838-5006	R	5*	<.1
721	Level One LLC—*Ray Gaffney*	3 Great Valley Pkwy St, Malvern PA 19355	610-229-9200	R	5*	<.1
722	LoyaltyExpress Inc—*Jeffrey Doyle*	53 Commerce Way, Woburn MA 01801	781-938-1175	R	5*	<.1
723	Enterprise Warehousing Solutions Inc—*David Marco*	15 Spinning Wheel Rd S, Hinsdale IL 60521	630-920-0005	R	5*	<.1
724	AJ Boggs and Co—*Clark Anderson*	4660 S Hagadorn Rd Ste, East Lansing MI 48823	517-347-1100	R	5*	<.1
725	Evero Corp—*David Jacobson*	181 Hillside Ave Ste A, Williston Park NY 11596	516-747-4200	R	5*	<.1
726	Fantastic Network Solutions Inc—*Dennis O'leary*	5220 S University Dr S, Fort Lauderdale FL 33328	619-906-4104	R	5*	<.1
727	Partnersolve LLC	14 Fawn Ridge Rd, Ashland MA 01721	508-309-3230	R	5*	<.1
728	Sns One Inc—*Leon Stanley*	8850 Stanford Blvd, Columbia MD 21045	240-460-1111	R	5*	<.1
729	ERISS Corp	3809 Atrisco Dr Ste D, Albuquerque NM 87120		R	5*	<.1
730	GramTel LLC—*Tracy D Graham*	PO Box 720, South Bend IN 46624	574-472-4726	S	5*	<.1
731	Lkrg Consulting Group Inc—*Denise Kastenbaum*	295 Madison Ave Fl 12, New York NY 10017	212-679-0220	R	5*	<.1
732	MicroMega Systems Inc—*Charles Bornheim*	2 Fifer Ave Ste 120, Corte Madera CA 94925	415-924-4700	R	5*	<.1
733	Pearl Computer Services Inc—*Patrick Howard*	910 First Capitol Dr, Saint Charles MO 63301	636-949-8850	R	5*	<.1
734	Punch Networks Corp—*David Campbell*	3121 W Government Way, Seattle WA 98199	206-405-3337	R	5*	<.1
735	Triad Systems Engineering Inc—*Robert Rodger*	403 Glenn Dr Ste 2, Sterling VA 20164	703-404-0306	R	5*	<.1
736	Regional Technology Strategies Inc—*Stuart Rosenfeld*	205 Lloyd St Ste 210, Carrboro NC 27510	919-933-6699	R	5*	<.1
737	Nordonia Computer Services Inc—*Reinhold Krueger*	1617 Shirley Ave Unit, Akron OH 44310	330-633-3693	R	5*	<.1
738	American Micronics Inc—*Michael Kolsy*	17731 Irvine Blvd, Tustin CA 92780	714-544-1968	R	5*	<.1
739	Biltmore Technologies Inc—*John Orvis*	70 W Oakland Ave Ste 2, Doylestown PA 18901	215-489-9099	R	5*	<.1
740	Connexus Technology LLC—*Ruba Habtemical*	3225 Arch St, Philadelphia PA 19104		R	5*	<.1
741	Managed Care On-Line Inc—*Clive Riddle*	1101 Standiford Ave St, Modesto CA 95350	209-577-4888	R	5*	<.1
742	Metal Toad Media—*Joaquin Lippincott*	920 SW 3rd Ave Ste 200, Portland OR 97204	503-336-1658	R	5*	<.1
743	Amnet—*Trevor Dierdorff*	219 W Colorado Ave Ste, Colorado Springs CO 80903	719-442-6683	R	5*	<.1
744	Legal Computer Solutions Inc—*Neil Aresty*	107 Union Wharf, Boston MA 02135	617-227-4469	R	5*	<.1
745	Montana Banana—*Stewart McCullough*	1752 NW Market St Ste, Seattle WA 98107	206-686-3631	R	5*	<.1
746	A to A Studio Services Inc—*Allan Waller*	47 Euclid Ave, Stamford CT 06902	212-229-0800	R	5*	<.1
747	AccessPort—*David Acquistapace*	725 Farmers Ln Ste 17, Santa Rosa CA 95405	707-573-3500	R	5*	<.1
748	BitPusher LLC—*Daniel Lieberman*	737 Post St Apt 1026, San Francisco CA 94109	415-751-1055	R	5*	<.1
749	Computer Concern Inc—*David Dotson*	426 E Southern Ste 101, Tempe AZ 85282	480-921-9044	R	5*	<.1
750	Computer Physicians Inc—*Marc Leeka*	330 Arden Ave Ste 100, Glendale CA 91203	818-242-6480	R	5*	<.1
751	Computer Solutions 911—*Renee Nix*	PO Box 1406, Woodstock GA 30188	770-926-7930	R	5*	<.1
752	Digital Movers LLC—*Ken Konikowski*	PO Box 569, Mashpee MA 02649	973-742-7422	R	5*	<.1
753	Embed Inc—*Richard Fischer*	410 Great Rd, Littleton MA 01460	978-742-9014	R	5*	<.1
754	Graphic Systems Inc (Cambridge Massachusetts)—*Eric Teicholz*	56 John F Kennedy St 3, Cambridge MA 02138	617-492-1148	R	5*	<.1
755	Great Scott Enterprises Inc—*Scott Greene*	PO Box 42047, Tucson AZ 85733	520-795-7166	R	5*	<.1
756	Infolane Inc—*David Hillstrom*	2340 Powell St, Emeryville CA 94608	510-277-2399	R	5*	<.1
757	INOW Inc—*Mounir Kardosh*	1391 Woodside Rd Ste 2, Redwood City CA 94061	650-995-9300	R	5*	<.1
758	Interface Technologies Inc (Raleigh North Carolina)—*Kelly Campbell*	3120 Highwoods Blvd St, Raleigh NC 27604	919-876-1566	R	5*	<.1
759	IT Support Guys—*Roy Adamcik*	13101 Washington Blvd, Los Angeles CA 90066	424-672-9090	R	5*	<.1
760	Jobsoft Design and Development Inc—*Mark Bailey*	104 Arlington Place St, Franklin TN 37064	615-904-9559	R	5*	<.1
761	Knowledge Systems Corp—*Allen B Davis*	1143 Executive Cir Ste, Cary NC 27511	919-789-8549	R	5*	<.1
762	Marshall Network Services—*Richard Marshall*	PO Box 4492, Lexington KY 40503	859-276-3636	R	5*	<.1
763	Mega Star Media Inc—*Sandy Rowley*	297 Kingsbury Grade St, Lake Tahoe NV 89449	775-453-6120	R	5*	<.1
764	Monderacom Inc—*Fred Mouawad*	45 W 45th St Ste 808, New York NY 10036		R	5*	<.1
765	Panoptic Corp—*Paul Cirano*	Po Box 32, Wauconda IL 60084	847-487-2200	R	5*	<.1
766	Pasadena Computer Works—*Timothy Lugosi*	3202 E Foothill Blvd S, Pasadena CA 91107	626-449-4729	R	5*	<.1
767	preEmptive Solutions Inc—*Gabriel Torok*	767 Beta Dr Ste A, Mayfield Village OH 44143	440-443-7200	R	5*	<.1
768	Rhizome Internet LLC—*Lauren Cornell*	235 Bowery, New York NY 10002	212-219-1288	R	5*	<.1
769	RunTime Technologies—*James Killough*	515 Greenwich St Ste 5, New York NY 10013	212-462-2800	R	5*	<.1
770	Sierra Tech Computers—*Dean Fender*	6390 Clark Rd, Paradise CA 95969	530-877-8123	R	5*	<.1
771	Software Science Inc (San Rafael California)—*George Rothbart*	7 Mt Lassen Dr, San Rafael CA 94903	415-479-7286	R	5*	<.1
772	Veraciti Inc—*Frank Altieri Jr*	49 S Jefferson Rd, Whippany NJ 07981	973-887-8660	R	5*	<.1
773	webslingerz Inc—*Jeffrey Hoffman*	101 E Weaver St Ste G3, Carrboro NC 27510	919-933-1222	R	5*	<.1
774	Safe Systems Inc (Alpharetta Georgia)—*Darren Bridges*	11395 Old Roswell Rd, Alpharetta GA 30004	770-752-0550	R	5*	<.1
775	EmoryDay LLC—*Joe Jaap*	PO Box 176, Glenelg MD 21737		R	5	<.1

Rank	Company Name—*Executive Officer*	Address, City, State, Zip	Phone	Type	Fin	Empls
776	Emids Technologies—*Jerry Buchanan*	624 Grassmere Park Ste, Nashville TN 37211	615-866-6430	R	5*	<.1
777	Flagship Networks Inc—*John Blankley*	10 Doverton Dr, Greenwich CT 06831	203-869-2443	R	5*	<.1
778	Q A Technologies Inc—*Kenneth Bass*	222 S 15th St Ste 1404, Omaha NE 68102	402-391-9200	R	5*	<.1
779	Enterprise Systems Consulting Inc—*Chuck Calanni*	4199 Campus Dr Ste 550, Irvine CA 92612	949-509-6560	R	5*	<.1
780	Trade Ship Inc—*Surjit Jairath*	425 Broadhollow Rd Ste, Melville NY 11747	631-694-5400	R	5*	.1
781	Smx Services and Consulting Inc—*Richard Quevedo*	1000 Brickell Ave Ste, Miami FL 33131	305-463-7191	R	5*	.1
782	Strategic Information Group Inc—*Doug Novak*	8 E Arrellaga St, Santa Barbara CA 93101	805-963-8377	R	5*	.1
783	Coldcypress LLC—*Shanda Bissett*	100 Emerson Ln Ste 151, Bridgeville PA 15017	412-677-1500	R	5*	<.1
784	Istor Networks Inc—*Kevin Daly*	7585 Irvine Ctr Dr Ste, Irvine CA 92618	949-753-8999	R	5*	<.1
785	Bravo Interactive Inc—*Rebecca Ellis*	485 Alberto Way Ste 11, Los Gatos CA 95032	408-399-5075	R	5*	<.1
786	Woodbourne Solutions Inc—*John Fendrick*	12800 Middlebrook Rd, Germantown MD 20874	301-428-7620	R	5*	<.1
787	PayLease LLC—*Ty Kalklosch*	9330 Scranton Rd Ste 4, San Diego CA 92121	858-657-9391	R	5	.1
788	Training Education Development Solutions Inc—*Joseph Ellis*	PO Box 700, Atkins VA 24311	276-783-6991	R	5*	.1
789	Synergy Corporate Technologies Ltd—*James Beck*	518 Riverside Ave Bldg, Westport CT 06880	203-222-5200	R	5*	<.1
790	AvantLinkcom—*Scott Kalbach*	1200 Iron Horse Dr, Park City UT 84060		R	5	.1
791	El Camino Systems Inc—*David Beatty*	1430 Vantage Ct Ste 10, Vista CA 92081	760-597-1700	R	5*	.1
792	Communication Technology For Business Inc—*Coley Brown*	PO Box 66, Park Ridge NJ 07656	201-573-0682	R	5*	<.1
793	Media Systems Inc—*Shane Spiess*	100 Se Salmon St, Portland OR 97214	503-635-0205	R	5*	<.1
794	Rainbow Data Systems Inc—*John Kim*	2358 Lakeview Dr Ste A, Beavercreek OH 45431	937-431-8000	R	5*	<.1
795	Synteractive—*Paul Brubaker*	1100 H St NW Ste 900, Washington DC 20005	202-904-2165	R	5	<.1
796	Mindbank Consulting Group Of Denver LLC—*Judy Perrault*	15000 W 6th Ave Ste 40, Golden CO 80401	303-623-4700	R	5*	.1
797	Arisglobal LLC—*Ranjita Adur*	2777 Summer St Ste 701, Stamford CT 06905	203-588-3000	R	5*	.1
798	Professional Software Solutions Ne Inc—*Raymond Range*	175 S Montgomery St St, Walden NY 12586	845-778-3342	R	5*	<.1
799	Bay State Computers Inc—*Patricia Hill*	4201 Northview Dr Ste, Bowie MD 20716	301-352-7878	R	5*	<.1
800	Inetu Inc—*Dev Chanchani*	744 Roble Rd Ste 70, Allentown PA 18109	610-266-7441	R	5*	<.1
801	Micro Technology Groupe Inc—*Wayne Haslam*	200 Rittenhouse Cir 3-, Bristol PA 19007	215-788-6811	R	5*	<.1
802	Realtech Inc—*Ralph Jacobus*	301 Lindenwood Dr Ste, Malvern PA 19355	610-356-4401	R	5*	<.1
803	Santoso Associates—*Andy Santoso*	8875 Hidden River Pkwy, Tampa FL 33637	916-880-1560	R	4*	.1
804	Nemadji Research Corp—*Kim Bohnsack*	PO Box 100, Bruno MN 55712	320-838-3838	R	4*	<.1
805	Quest America Inc—*Soundaran Natarajan*	111 N Market St Ste 71, San Jose CA 95113	408-492-1650	R	4*	.1
806	Insyst Inc—*Arun Parikh*	271 Rte 46 W Ste A201, Fairfield NJ 07004	973-227-6582	R	4*	.1
807	Diminutive Network Solutions Inc—*Christine Mirro*	100 Lake Ave, Monroe NY 10950	845-818-3885	R	4*	<.1
808	Proceed Technical Resources Inc—*Edward Garcia*	PO Box 703775, Dallas TX 75370	972-769-0746	R	4*	.1
809	Transtech LLC—*Michael Serdiuk*	901 W Hawthorn Dr, Itasca IL 60143	630-250-8880	R	4*	.1
810	Csd Inc—*Clement Dang*	1302 Exchange Dr Ste 1, Richardson TX 75081	972-437-6455	R	4*	<.1
811	Highdata Software Corp—*Senraj Soundararajan*	2 Keewaydin Dr, Salem NH 03079	603-890-1251	R	4*	.1
812	Michael Gray and Associates Inc—*Michael Gray*	3000 Gulf To Bay Blvd, Clearwater FL 33759	727-791-7890	R	4*	.1
813	Qi Consulting LLC	3909 Artic Blvd Ste 20, Anchorage AK 99503		R	4*	<.1
814	Exeter Government Services LLC—*Thomas Green*	9841 Washingtonian Blv, Gaithersburg MD 20878	301-545-0977	R	4*	<.1
815	Cleveland Dovington Partners Inc—*Philip Carrier*	15 Spinning Wheel Rd S, Hinsdale IL 60521	630-325-8757	R	4*	.1
816	Overture Toohnologies Inc—*C Carlson*	6900 Wisconsin Ave Ste, Chevy Chase MD 20815	301-492-2140	R	4*	<.1
817	V-Link Solutions Inc—*Abbas Sadriwalla*	2755 E Oaklnd Prk Blvd, Fort Lauderdale FL 33306	954-566-0992	R	4*	<.1
818	Project Partners LLC—*P Shankar*	520 Purissima St, Half Moon Bay CA 94019	650-712-6200	R	4*	<.1
819	Hi-Tek Data Corp—*Alexander Hartley*	7 Broadway, Massapequa NY 11758	516-797-8800	R	4*	<.1
820	International Information Technology Team—*Balaji Ravi*	19 Longview Dr, Holmdel NJ 07733	732-417-9301	R	4*	<.1
821	Digital Consulting and Software Services Inc—*Patricia Patterson*	2277 Plaza Dr Ste 275, Sugar Land TX 77479	713-982-8030	R	4*	.1
822	Sygenex Inc—*Terry Magee*	4770 Eastgate Mall, San Diego CA 92121	858-455-5530	R	4*	.1
823	Computer Careers And Consulting Inc—*Srinivas Neela*	PO Box 84330, Pearland TX 77584	832-647-7324	R	4*	.1
824	Cymphonix Corp—*Brent Nixon*	8871 Sandy Pkwy Ste 15, Sandy UT 84070	801-938-1500	R	4*	<.1
825	Decypher Technologies Ltd—*Caroline Meador*	200 Concord Plaza Dr S, San Antonio TX 78216	210-735-9900	R	4*	<.1
826	Enertia Software—*Kevin Schmidt*	125 W Missouri Ave, Midland TX 79701	432-685-1753	R	4*	<.1
827	Abacuss Software Technologies LLC—*Ravindran Padmanabhan*	2200 Century Pkwy Ne S, Atlanta GA 30345	404-248-9293	R	4*	<.1
828	IntegriChain Inc—*Kevin Leininger*	100 Canal Pointe Blvd, Princeton NJ 08540	609-806-5005	R	4*	<.1
829	Project Assistants Inc—*Augustus Cicala*	3521 Silverside Rd Ste, Wilmington DE 19810	302-477-9711	R	4*	<.1
830	Winnertech Corp	75 W Front St, Red Bank NJ 07701	732-758-9500	R	4*	<.1
831	Tri-Analytics Inc—*Wayne S Copes*	134 Industry Ln Ste C, Forest Hill MD 21050	410-838-1144	R	4*	<.1
832	Optimum Technology Inc—*Jagdish Davda*	100 E Campus View Blvd, Columbus OH 43235	614-785-1110	R	4*	<.1
833	Applied Computer Technology—*Burt Gearhart*	602 Branch Hollow Cir, Garland TX 75043	214-774-4522	R	4*	<.1
834	Cyrus Innovation Inc—*Bruce Eckfeldt*	200 Varick St Ste 902, New York NY 10014	212-647-7186	R	4*	<.1
835	Corporate Services LLC	3801 Plz Tower Dr, Baton Rouge LA 70816	225-923-3767	R	4*	<.1
836	Bruner Consulting Associates Inc—*Linda Bruner*	1069 Briarwood Ave, Bridgeport CT 06604	203-366-8737	R	4*	<.1
837	Key Consulting Group Inc—*David Campbell*	30 Hackamore Ln Ste 12, Bell Canyon CA 91307	818-884-6080	R	4*	<.1
838	Logic20/20 Inc—*Sean Cunningham*	1505 Westlake Ave N St, Seattle WA 98109	206-576-0400	R	4*	<.1
839	Randa Solutions—*Marty Reed*	722 Rundle Ave, Nashville TN 37210	615-467-6387	R	4*	<.1
840	Reliant Enterprise LLC	9903 Santa Monica Blvd, Beverly Hills CA 90212	310-984-2008	R	4*	<.1
841	Sierra Computers Ltd—*Mike Christianson*	1900 Vassar St, Reno NV 89502	775-322-6455	R	4*	<.1
842	AccessCom Inc—*Jeff Giles*	1340 Poydras St Ste 35, New Orleans LA 70112	504-962-2000	R	4*	<.1
843	Antennas Direct—*Richard Schneider*	16388 Westwoods Busine, Ellisville MO 63021		R	4*	<.1
844	Blh Technologies Inc—*Benjamin Harris*	1803 Res Blvd Ste 615, Rockville MD 20850	240-399-8722	R	4*	<.1
845	Ear Ltd—*Evan Alford*	PO Box 470, Ashburn VA 20146	703-729-2227	R	4*	<.1
846	MICON Consulting—*Steven Dick*	1820 E Ray Rd Ste A209, Chandler AZ 85225	480-656-8393	R	4*	<.1
847	Cogentes Inc—*Bradley Rhine*	13275 Ga Hwy 231, Davisboro GA 31018	404-424-9347	R	4*	<.1
848	InterWorking Labs Inc—*Chris Wellens*	PO Box 66190, Scotts Valley CA 95067	831-460-7010	R	4*	<.1
849	Lumeon Software Corp—*Trey Gramann*	PO Box 340723, Austin TX 78734	512-732-7000	R	4*	<.1
850	MAS Consulting Inc—*Michael A Suglich*	300 S Wacker Dr Ste243, Chicago IL 60604	312-922-5511	R	4*	<.1
851	Mid-Atlantic Data System Inc—*Honore Sheridan*	845-D Quince Orchard B, Gaithersburg MD 20878	301-590-0666	R	4*	<.1
852	Sierra Tel Internet—*Harry H Baker*	PO Box 11, Oakhurst CA 93644	559-641-9000	S	4*	<.1
853	342 Media—*John Moore*	5410 Wilshire Blvd 10t, Los Angeles CA 90036	323-937-8009	R	4*	<.1
854	Analytic and Computational Research Inc	1931 Stradella Rd, Los Angeles CA 90077	310-471-3023	R	4*	<.1
855	ATC Enterprises LLC—*Jay Mehta*	PO Box 1024, Danville CA 94526		R	4*	<.1
856	Collaborative Strategies LLC—*David Coleman*	37 N Idaho St, San Mateo CA 94401		R	4*	<.1
857	Kurani Interactive Inc—*Dan Kurani*	25 Bridge Ave Ste 203, Red Bank NJ 07701	732-345-1700	R	4*	<.1
858	Plexus Web Creations—*Stephanie Sharp*	675 Pulaski St Ste 300, Athens GA 30601	706-353-2048	R	4*	<.1
859	ServerSide Inc—*Steve Oren*	10150 Lantern Rd Ste 2, Fishers IN 46037	317-596-5000	R	4*	<.1
860	Universal Certificate Group LLC—*Edward Brookshire*	307 5th Ave, New York NY 10016	212-252-8891	R	4*	<.1
861	WebWorqs—*Janet Laylor*	446 Girard St Ste 302, Gaithersburg MD 20877	202-415-1256	R	4*	<.1
862	CSI Networks—*Joe Brachle*	359 Interstate Blvd, Sarasota FL 34240	941-379-4747	R	4*	<.1
863	Websurf Internet—*Martin Inergrin*	PO Box 9104, Wichita KS 67277	316-945-7873	R	4*	<.1

Note: An asterisk (*) indicates an estimated financial figure. The company type code used is as follows: R = Private, P = Public, S = Private Subsidiary, B = Public Subsidiary, D = Division, J = Joint Venture, I = Investment Fund.

COMPANY RANKINGS BY SALES WITHIN 4-DIGIT SIC

Rank	Company Name—*Executive Officer*	Address, City, State, Zip	Phone	Type	Fin	Empls
864	Northlight Web Site Design Group Inc—*George Wardwell*	PO Box 721, Waldoboro ME 04572	207-832-7262	R	4*	<.1
865	PanTerra Networks Inc—*Arthur G Chang*	1153 Bordeaux Dr Ste 1, Sunnyvale CA 94089	408-702-2200	R	4	.1
866	Fabergent Inc—*Swarna Rao*	63 Ramapo Valley Rd St, Mahwah NJ 07430	201-378-0036	R	4*	<.1
867	Terra Technology LLC—*Robert Byrne*	20 Glover Ave, Norwalk CT 06850	203-847-4007	R	4*	<.1
868	Brazos Technology Corp—*Michael Mcaleer*	PO Box 10713, College Station TX 77842	979-690-2811	R	4	<.1
869	4c International LLC	1575 Old 122 Rd Nd, Lebanon OH 45036	513-934-2622	R	4*	.1
870	Whitegold Solutions Inc—*Jack Zoken*	43 Fernwood Way Ste 21, San Rafael CA 94901	415-456-4493	R	4*	.1
871	Supplyframe Inc—*Steve Flagg*	51 W Dayton St Ste 300, Pasadena CA 91105	626-793-7732	R	4*	<.1
872	Universal Conversion Technologies LLP—*Rae Albertini*	PO Box 141478, Irving TX 75014	214-348-2000	R	4*	<.1
873	Rentgrow Inc—*Michael Lapsley*	307 Waverley Oaks Rd S, Waltham MA 02452	781-890-5100	S	4*	<.1
874	Nveg Inc—*Derrick Morris*	3130 Fairview Park Dr, Falls Church VA 22042	703-280-3880	R	4*	<.1
875	Mainstreet Integration Services and Consulting Inc—*Sharon Moore*	2510 W Main St Ste 100, Grand Prairie TX 75050	469-733-1921	R	4*	<.1
876	Imagetek Inc—*Ted Kruzan*	1851 Se Miehe Dr, Grimes IA 50111	515-270-4858	R	4*	<.1
877	Data Services Corp—*Ailyn Popowski*	18503 Pines Blvd Ste 2, Pembroke Pines FL 33029	305-594-6933	R	4*	<.1
878	SomethingdigitalCom LLC—*James Idoni*	9 E 38th St Rm 8r, New York NY 10016	212-983-8373	R	4*	<.1
879	Objectcrafters Inc—*Raj Ratnakar*	1405 Granby Way, West Chester PA 19380	610-719-0989	R	4*	<.1
880	Clair Christo Corp—*Marlon Joe*	68 Alvin Sloan Ave, Washington NJ 07882	908-835-8601	R	4*	.1
881	Mark Technology Services—*Steven Baker*	156 N Jefferson St Ste, Chicago IL 60661	312-612-8203	R	4*	<.1
882	Sena Systems Inc—*Robert Levine*	379 Thornall St Ste 2, Edison NJ 08837	732-548-9408	R	4*	<.1
883	Jacobson Consulting Applications Inc—*Steven Jacobson*	575 8th Ave Fl 21, New York NY 10018	212-465-2336	R	4*	<.1
884	Micro Tech Computer Service Inc—*Brian Goreman*	PO Box 216, Weatogue CT 06089	860-651-8111	R	4*	.1
885	Terra Infosystems Inc—*Manoj Agarwai*	1 Exchange Pl Ste 907, Jersey City NJ 07302	201-324-1960	R	4*	.1
886	Infomatics Inc—*Rangarajan Raghunathan*	31313 Nw Hwy Ste 219, Farmington Hills MI 48334	248-865-0300	R	4*	<.1
887	Software International Associates Inc—*Alvaro Acosta*	80 Van Houton Ave, Chatham NJ 07928	973-635-3700	R	4*	<.1
888	Virtual Technology Services LLC—*A Tricia*	806 W Curtis Dr Ste A, Midwest City OK 73110	405-733-3500	R	4*	<.1
889	Macdonald Consulting Group Inc—*Ray Pearson*	1100 Johnson Ferry Rd, Atlanta GA 30342	404-841-6240	R	4	<.1
890	Adrem Systems Corp—*Patrick Birt*	1801 Robert Fulton Dr, Reston VA 20191	703-860-2233	R	4*	<.1
891	Applied Decision Support Inc—*Doug Charleston*	42 Reads Way, New Castle DE 19720	302-323-8145	R	4*	<.1
892	Dbnet Systems Inc—*Ganesh Karnik*	3602 Keenland Dr, Marietta GA 30062	770-509-3638	R	4*	<.1
893	Triteck Inc—*Michael Chu*	4523 Meyer Park Cir, Fremont CA 94536	510-791-0286	R	4*	<.1
894	Parrish Consulting—*Sabrena Parrish*	1001 Kayak Ave, Capitol Heights MD 20743	240-432-4466	R	3*	<.1
895	Select Solutions Group LLC—*William Tompkins*	28 Woodland Ave, Bronxville NY 10708	914-793-3506	R	3*	.1
896	Amensys Inc—*Lizamma Kappukattil*	101 E Park Blvd Ste 71, Plano TX 75074	972-801-9970	R	3*	<.1
897	Encore Development Of North America Inc—*Lesley Cormick*	5210 Belfort Rd Ste 30, Jacksonville FL 32256	904-245-7500	R	3*	<.1
898	Medaptus Inc—*Douglas Percy*	176 Federal St Lbby 3, Boston MA 02110	617-523-1221	R	3*	<.1
899	Global Link Solutions Inc—*Sang Kim*	46179 Westlake Dr Ste, Potomac Falls VA 20165	703-421-5193	R	3*	<.1
900	Apt Source Inc—*Mallika Viswanathan*	6043 Hudson Rd Ste 399, Saint Paul MN 55125	651-493-0039	R	3*	<.1
901	Intertech Training and Consulting Inc—*Mike Grobelch*	25 Barcelona Ste 200, Irvine CA 92614	949-852-1165	R	3*	<.1
902	Olr America Inc—*Kenneth Wehr*	1200 Washington Ave S, Minneapolis MN 55415	612-436-4970	R	3*	<.1
903	C/S Solutions Inc—*Gregory Young*	PO Box 11969, Spring TX 77391	281-376-0235	R	3*	<.1
904	Southeastern Technology Group Inc—*Robert Mcgirt*	14120 Ballentyne Corpo, Charlotte NC 28277	704-525-2022	R	3*	<.1
905	Triad Solutions—*Jerry Blake*	515 Washington Ave Ste, Bridgeville PA 15017	412-220-4063	R	3*	<.1
906	Wilson Technology Associates Inc—*Bruce Wilson*	2 Campus Blvd Ste 101, Newtown Square PA 19073	610-353-9879	R	3*	<.1
907	Datalex (USA) Inc—*Cormac Whelan*	1105 Lakewood Pkwy Ste, Alpharetta GA 30009	770-255-2400	R	3*	<.1
908	Thor Solutions Inc—*Oli Thordarson*	10 Corporate Park Ste, Irvine CA 92606	949-428-5000	R	3*	<.1
909	AB Star Group—*Atul Parikh*	39899 Balentine Dr Ste, Newark CA 94560	510-440-0240	R	3*	<.1
910	Seatech Consulting Group Inc—*Chairul Irawan*	609 Deep Valley Dr Ste, Rlng Hls Est CA 90274	310-356-6828	R	3*	.1
911	Campus Works Inc—*Lawrenc Schoenberg*	126 S Osprey Ave, Sarasota FL 34236	941-316-0308	R	3*	<.1
912	Kini Information Technologies Inc—*Rajendra Iyer*	75 Maiden Ln, New York NY 10038	212-571-0634	R	3*	<.1
913	Zerone Inc—*David Sossamon*	1120 Connecticut Ave N, Washington DC 20036	202-363-1360	R	3*	<.1
914	St Consulting International—*Tahir Mohammad*	132 W 36th St Rm 503, New York NY 10018	212-279-0440	R	3*	<.1
915	Exobase Corp—*Murali Gudala*	3150 De La Cruz Blvd S, Santa Clara CA 95054	408-235-8808	R	3*	<.1
916	Svr Group Inc—*Ravi Gulvindala*	750 Lexington Ave Fl 2, New York NY 10022	212-446-9077	R	3*	<.1
917	Insound LLC—*Seven Kleinverg*	61 Greenpoint Ave Ste, Brooklyn NY 11222	718-383-3456	R	3*	<.1
918	Agdata Holdings Inc—*James Thompson*	PO Box 221978, Charlotte NC 28222	704-364-2186	R	3*	<.1
919	APC Wireless—*Paul Greene*	11910 U Parklawn Dr, Rockville MD 20852	301-468-3090	R	3*	<.1
920	Systems Application Information Network Inc—*Parindra Ramnarayan*	64 W 48th St, New York NY 10036	212-376-4040	R	3*	<.1
921	Softech and Associates Inc—*David Nguyen*	1570 Corporate Dr Ste, Costa Mesa CA 92626	714-427-1122	R	3*	<.1
922	Interchange Technologies Inc—*Phillip Greene*	8130 Brentwood Industr, Saint Louis MO 63144	314-647-5440	R	3*	<.1
923	PrinciplesGroup LLC—*Mike Tierney*	PO Box 305, Liberty Corner NJ 07938	973-795-2232	R	3	<.1
924	Cbx Technologies Inc—*Christian D'Andrade*	8393 Capwell Dr Ste 17, Oakland CA 94621	510-729-7130	R	3*	<.1
925	Shooting Star Solutions LLC—*Mike Hess*	1959 Columbia Dr, Yuba City CA 95991	916-567-7827	R	3*	<.1
926	Migration Specialties International Inc—*Bruce Claremont*	217 W 2nd St, Florence CO 81226	719-784-9196	R	3*	.1
927	Pscomm LLC	1 Church St Ste 900, Rockville MD 20850	301-222-1420	R	3*	<.1
928	It Professional Recruiting LLC	3945 Shorewood Ct Sw, Grandville MI 49418	616-887-8027	R	3*	<.1
929	Technical Software Consulting Inc—*Sukhpal Dhillon*	33045 Hamilton Ct Ste, Farmington Hills MI 48334	248-848-1484	R	3*	<.1
930	United Solutions And Services LLC—*Lisa Burke*	49 Robin Ct, Hockessin DE 19707	302-239-4853	R	3*	<.1
931	Techsys Advanced Resources LLC—*Cliff Bogle*	1412 Main St Ste 2000, Dallas TX 75202	214-742-1068	R	3*	<.1
932	Infopeople Corp—*Shyam Gulati*	99 Wall St Ste 1702, New York NY 10005	212-232-0099	R	3*	<.1
933	Technology Recovery Group Ltd—*Sean Kennedy*	29307 Clemens Rd, Westlake OH 44145	440-250-9970	R	3*	<.1
934	Telophase Corp—*Jamil Husain*	2000 14th St N Ste 700, Arlington VA 22201	703-312-7550	R	3*	<.1
935	Vital Networks inc—*Doug Heestand*	2720 Gateway Oaks Dr S, Sacramento CA 95833	916-436-8757	R	3	<.1
936	Interactive Planet Inc—*Tomer Vardi*	1373 Broad St Ste 300, Clifton NJ 07013	973-779-6999	R	3*	<.1
937	Triad Web Design—*Geeta Punjabi*	3344 Six Forks Rd, Raleigh NC 27609		R	3	.1
938	Discount Computer Services—*Roland Sambolah*	7303 213th Pl Sw, Edmonds WA 98026	206-601-8682	R	3*	<.1
939	Systems Management Group—*Dennis Kommisky*	214 Saint Anselms Dr, Goffstown NH 03045	603-626-0685	R	3*	<.1
940	Organic People Inc—*Remmington Greene*	600 17th St Ste 2800s, Denver CO 80202	303-333-2036	R	3*	<.1
941	Sysconnect International Inc—*Dilip Luthra*	17 Barnyard Ct, Plainsboro NJ 08536	609-716-8800	R	3*	<.1
942	Maria Terra Corp—*Alemtsehay Bogale*	10621 Gramercy Pl Ste, Columbia MD 21044	443-668-2300	R	3*	<.1
943	Spindustry Systems Inc—*Michael Bird*	1370 NW 114th St Ste 3, Des Moines IA 50325	515-225-0920	R	3*	<.1
944	Centum Inc—*Graham Challis*	3321 Vincent Rd, Pleasant Hill CA 94523	925-946-5111	R	3*	<.1
945	Falkor Group LLC	549 W Randolph St Ste, Chicago IL 60661	312-602-6550	R	3*	<.1
946	NOREX Inc—*Ron Haberkorn*	5505 Cottonwood Ln SE, Prior Lake MN 55372	952-447-8898	R	3*	<.1
947	Group International Associates—*Henry Traendly*	98 Cuttermill Rd Ste 3, Great Neck NY 11021	516-482-2111	R	3*	<.1
948	Logica Advantage KBS Inc—*Eileen Weinstein*	1 Ethel Rd Ste 106B, Edison NJ 08817	732-287-2286	R	3	<.1
949	ProtoTest LLC—*Pete Dignan*	9137 E Mineral Cir Ste, Centennial CO 80112	303-703-1510	R	3*	<.1
950	Cities2Night Inc—*Brian Nagele*	441 N 5th St Ste 401, Philadelphia PA 19123	215-966-1535	R	3*	<.1
951	Intertech Software Consulting Inc—*Tom Salonek*	1020 Discovery Rd Ste, Eagan MN 55121	651-994-8558	R	3*	<.1

Rank	Company Name—*Executive Officer*	Address, City, State, Zip	Phone	Type	Fin	Empls
952	Data Distributors Inc—*Roger Challen*	46 Park St Ste 3, Framingham MA 01702	508-875-7511	R	3*	<.1
953	Directapps Inc—*Fred Michanie*	1430 Blue Oaks Blvd St, Roseville CA 95747	916-787-2201	R	3*	<.1
954	Harvard Consulting Group Inc—*Kimberly Scolieri*	1664 Plum Ln, Redlands CA 92374	909-307-8400	R	3*	<.1
955	Innovative Analytics Inc—*Patricia L Ruppel*	161 E Michigan Ave Hay, Kalamazoo MI 49007	269-488-3200	R	3*	<.1
956	Digital Documents LLC—*Pat Smith*	8000 Towers Crescent D, Vienna VA 22182	703-288-5555	R	3*	<.1
957	Cutter Information LLC—*Tom Bragg*	37 Broadway Ste 1, Arlington MA 02474	781-648-8700	R	3*	<.1
958	Inforeem Inc—*Bhal Deshpande*	1 Quality Pl Ste 200, Edison NJ 08820	732-494-4100	R	3*	<.1
959	Info-Matrix Corp—*Joseph Gondek*	1335 N Front St, Harrisburg PA 17102	717-260-9850	R	3*	<.1
960	Catalogcom Inc—*Bob Crull*	14000 Quail Springs Pk, Oklahoma City OK 73134	405-753-9300	R	3	<.1
961	Asset Recovery Specialists Inc	9707 Aero Dr, San Diego CA 92123	858-277-7555	R	3*	<.1
962	Comnexia Corp—*James Wilson*	590 W Crssvlle Rd Ste, Roswell GA 30075	678-323-5000	R	3*	<.1
963	Davalen LLC—*Kenya Claytor*	104 Archway Ct, Lynchburg VA 24502	978-443-5385	R	3*	<.1
964	AMI Strategies—*Jane Sydlowski*	34705 W 12 Mile Rd, Farmington Hills MI 48331	248-957-4200	R	3*	<.1
965	Group 3 Consultants Inc	1411 SW Morrison Ste 3, Portland OR 97205	503-224-4961	R	3	<.1
966	Pcmechanic—*Mark Anderson*	800 Westport Rd, Kansas City MO 64111	816-931-4005	R	3*	<.1
967	Brooks Logic LLC—*Lateefah Cobb*	9470 Annapolis Rd Ste, Lanham MD 20706	301-358-2600	R	3*	<.1
968	EurekaDIGITAL—*Mark Mathias*	PO Box 11029, Burbank CA 91510	818-295-2888	R	3*	<.1
969	Provectus Technology Inc—*Richard Blevins*	43407 Coton Commons Dr, Leesburg VA 20176	571-215-7368	R	3*	<.1
970	WebSafe Shield Inc—*David Highbarger*	1141 Catalina Dr Ste 2, Livermore CA 94550		R	3*	<.1
971	Primestream Corp—*Claudio Lisman*	PO Box 547053, Miami FL 33154	305-868-9085	R	3*	<.1
972	Enterprise Resource Procurement LLC—*Aaron Gage*	15224 S 14th Pl, Phoenix AZ 85048	480-982-2333	R	3*	<.1
973	Intercomp Design Inc—*Jeff V Pulver*	4 Richfield Ct, Branchburg NJ 08853	908-369-5633	R	3*	<.1
974	SimpleSoft Inc—*Sudhir Pendse*	257 Castro St Ste 220, Mountain View CA 94041	650-965-4515	R	3*	<.1
975	Adventures in Technology LLC—*George Hefter*	PO Box 3428, Tri Cities WA 99302	509-627-4808	R	3*	<.1
976	American Web Page LLC—*David Atwood*	31965 Schoolcraft Rd, Livonia MI 48150	734-266-2900	R	3*	<.1
977	Cds Consulting LLC	29 Golf Course Dr Ste, Suffern NY 10901	845-369-9080	R	3*	<.1
978	Media Net Link—*Ryan McGredy*	2010 Crow Canyon Pl St, San Ramon CA 94583	925-804-2500	R	3*	<.1
979	Meta Information Services—*Kent Hymas*	2012 H St Ste 100, Sacramento CA 95811	916-231-0608	R	3*	<.1
980	PagePoint—*Aaron Gobler*	1732 Rose St, Berkeley CA 94703	510-558-1534	R	3*	<.1
981	Plaudit Design—*Michael Schlotfeldt*	2470 University Ave W, Saint Paul MN 55114	651-646-0696	R	3*	<.1
982	Rainbow Computer Services Inc—*Betty Dinette*	PO Box 41783, Baton Rouge LA 70835	225-753-5644	R	3*	<.1
983	SCV Systems—*Scott C Virtes*	197 Woodland Pky Ste 1, San Marcos CA 92069	760-781-4021	R	3*	<.1
984	Thunderhawk Internet Systems—*Charles Bookman*	1085 Commonwealth Ave, Boston MA 02215	617-244-0988	R	3*	<.1
985	Accent Interactive—*Ken Kinard*	156 Westbury Rd, Lutherville MD 21093	410-321-9327	R	3*	<.1
986	Advanced Media Productions Inc—*Joop Rijk*	251 W Central St Ste 2, Natick MA 01760	508-647-5151	R	3*	<.1
987	Ancient Wisdom Productions—*Christoper Delcollo*	PO Box 6602, Ithaca NY 14851	607-277-2757	R	3*	<.1
988	DataMart Inc—*Bruce Jenkins*	3746 Cherry Rd, Memphis TN 38118	901-369-9476	R	3*	<.1
989	Datamax—*Dan Sommerville*	7777 Leesburg Pike Ste, Falls Church VA 22043	703-917-9400	R	3*	<.1
990	EZSolution Corp—*Tom Malesic*	111 Centerville Rd, Lancaster PA 17603	717-291-4689	R	3*	<.1
991	MDS Disk Service—*Gary Tacy*	3380 La Sierra Ave Ste, Riverside CA 92503	951-352-2425	R	3*	<.1
992	Siteit Web Design—*Todd Quatier*	PO Box 163, Rosholt SD 57260	605-323-1628	R	3*	<.1
993	tatnet Inc—*Mark Peck*	133 Defense Hwy Ste 20, Annapolis MD 21401	410-571-9462	R	3*	<.1
994	Technology Solutions of SC Inc—*Richard K Ellison*	PO Box 128, Seneca SC 29679	864-882-9194	R	3*	<.1
995	Abke Publishing and Graphic Services Inc—*Lisa Abke*	53522 Atherton, New Baltimore MI 48047	586-725-4038	R	3*	<.1
996	EscapeWire Solutions LLC—*Chris Hart-Nova*	617 Dingens St, Buffalo NY 14206	716-893-4984	R	3*	<.1
997	interbiznet—*John Sumser*	PO Box 637, Mill Valley CA 94942	415-377-2255	R	3*	<.1
998	Planet Blue—*Maury Rosenfeld*	1250 6th St Ste 102, Santa Monica CA 90401	310-899-3877	R	3*	<.1
999	Sitespring Inc—*Matthew Pattison*	4411 Bee Ridge Rd Ste, Sarasota FL 34233	941-351-3219	R	3*	<.1
1000	Spyder Byte Web Design LLC—*Russ Cuthrell*	47935 Ben Franklin Dr, Shelby Township MI 48315	586-260-1344	R	3*	<.1
1001	WA Rogers Software Engineering—*William Rogers*	7203 Cercis Cove, Austin TX 78759	512-335-6318	R	3*	<.1
1002	Web Sites by Interpol—*Dan Interpol*	816 Lancaster Rd, Ridgefield NJ 07657	201-289-2462	R	3*	<.1
1003	Web To Market Corp—*Cynthia Bhatnagar*	5416 S Tacoma Way Ste, Tacoma WA 98409		R	3*	<.1
1004	Whole Internet LLC—*Robert Wilson*	5834 E Bottlebrush Dr, Orange CA 92869	714-538-6657	R	3*	<.1
1005	Wesolve LLC—*Eddie Fowler*	PO Box 724995, Atlanta GA 31139	706-798-6783	R	3*	.1
1006	Topgrade Technology Corp—*Pierre Boisrond*	6100 Ohio Dr Apt 612, Plano TX 75024	832-344-9400	R	3*	<.1
1007	Everpoint Inc—*Chuck Schaeffer*	141 W Key Palm Rd, Boca Raton FL 33432	561-392-8992	R	3*	<.1
1008	Resqsoft Inc—*Tom Bragg*	8300 Boone Blvd Ste 50, Vienna VA 22182	703-868-8140	R	3*	<.1
1009	I3solutions Inc—*Christopher Johnson*	21630 Ridgetop Cir Ste, Sterling VA 20166	703-404-9595	R	3*	<.1
1010	Lsq Ii LLC	1403 W Colonial Dr Ste, Orlando FL 32804	407-206-0022	R	3*	<.1
1011	Infax Inc—*David Davis*	4250 River Green Pkwy, Duluth GA 30096	770-209-9925	R	3*	<.1
1012	International Consulting Group Inc—*Alberto Gross*	7235 Nw 19th St Ste A, Miami FL 33126	305-594-0848	R	3*	<.1
1013	Application Oriented Designs Inc—*Michael Byrne*	8550 Nw 33rd St Ste 20, Doral FL 33122	305-599-2531	R	3*	<.1
1014	Autoexec Computer Systems Inc—*John Comito*	64 Sand Ln, Staten Island NY 10305	718-442-1056	R	3*	<.1
1015	Esecuritytogo LLC—*Anthony Ruffolo*	1109 Quail St, Newport Beach CA 92660	949-261-5555	R	3*	<.1
1016	PetPlacecom—*Jon Rappaport*	20283 State Rd 7 Ste 4, Boca Raton FL 33498	561-237-2940	R	3	<.1
1017	MindSmack Inc—*Samuel Feuer*	311 W 43rd St, New York NY 10036	732-348-8785	R	3*	<.1
1018	Intelliquest Systems Inc—*Priti Parikh*	301 Grant St Ste 4300, Pittsburgh PA 15219	412-734-8440	R	3*	<.1
1019	Fti Inc—*Sheri Slezak*	869 E Schaumburg Rd 24, Schaumburg IL 60194	847-352-0130	R	3*	<.1
1020	Guru Inc—*Jeffrey Cheng*	704 Quince Orchard Rd, Gaithersburg MD 20878	301-987-8950	R	3*	<.1
1021	Talus Group Inc—*Georgia Andria*	19675 Near Mountain Bl, Excelsior MN 55331	952-544-2526	R	3*	<.1
1022	Odin Technologies Inc—*Patrick Sweeney*	21631 Red Rum Dr Ste 1, Ashburn VA 20147	703-968-0000	R	3*	<.1
1023	Paradigm Systems Integration Inc—*Harry Merrifield*	290 Hawkins Ave Ste E, Melville NY 11747	631-585-8102	R	3*	<.1
1024	Algonquin Studios Inc—*Stephen Kiernan*	403 Main St Ste 400, Buffalo NY 14203	716-842-1439	R	3*	<.1
1025	Nqueue Inc—*Richard Hellers*	7890 S Hardy Dr Ste 10, Tempe AZ 85284	602-426-1550	R	3*	<.1
1026	Keystone Consultants Inc—*James Joiner*	32 E Main St, Carnegie PA 15106	412-278-2100	R	3*	<.1
1027	Platinum Db Consulting Inc—*Anthony Derosa*	728 W Jackson Blvd Ste, Chicago IL 60661	312-906-8710	R	3*	<.1
1028	Robert M Consulting Inc—*Robert Myaskovsky*	28720 Roadside Dr Ste, Agoura Hills CA 91301	818-991-8230	R	3*	<.1
1029	Sentri Inc—*Alex Beletsky*	200 Friberg Pkwy Ste 3, Westborough MA 01581	508-616-7900	R	3*	<.1
1030	Information Management Forum—*Ted Williams*	10896 Crabapple Rd Ste, Roswell GA 30075	770-455-0070	R	3*	<.1
1031	Norland Group—*Mayling Liang*	292 Gibraltar Dr Ste 1, Sunnyvale CA 94089	408-541-1818	R	3*	.1
1032	Cmw And Associates Corp—*Charlene Turczyn*	122 W Pine St, Springfield IL 62704	217-522-0452	R	3*	.1
1033	Vb Computer Consulting Inc—*James Holmes*	445 S Moorland Rd Ste, Brookfield WI 53005	262-797-0400	R	3*	<.1
1034	Bhb Solutions—*Frank Manning*	2055 Andover Ct, Cinnaminson NJ 08077	856-829-1215	R	3*	<.1
1035	Startspot Mediaworks Inc—*Ian Hueck*	1033 University Pl Ste, Evanston IL 60201	847-866-1830	R	3*	<.1
1036	Ag Connections Inc—*Pete Clark*	1576 Killdeer Trl, Murray KY 42071	270-435-4369	R	3*	<.1
1037	Knowledge Mosaic Inc—*Jason Hinz*	3450 16th Ave W Ste 30, Seattle WA 98119	206-525-8395	R	3*	<.1
1038	Artech Consulting Group Inc—*Rohit Virmani*	PO Box 938712, Margate FL 33093	954-315-4745	R	3*	<.1
1039	Arris Systems Inc—*Gazo Namoglu*	650 E Swedesford Rd St, Wayne PA 19087	610-407-9800	R	3*	<.1
1040	Praxinet Inc—*Robert Bedard*	PO Box 1171, Ridgefield CT 06877	203-894-9000	R	3*	<.1
1041	Rhino Systems Inc—*Kevin Durkin*	118 S Adams St, Green Bay WI 54301	920-437-4466	R	3*	<.1

Note: An asterisk (*) indicates an estimated financial figure. The company type code used is as follows: R = Private, P = Public, S = Private Subsidiary, B = Public Subsidiary, D = Division, J = Joint Venture, I = Investment Fund.

COMPANY RANKINGS BY SALES WITHIN 4-DIGIT SIC

Rank	Company Name—Executive Officer	Address, City, State, Zip	Phone	Type	Fin	Empls
1042	Steel Beach Productions Inc—Bob Kenny	6551 Silver Glen Dr, Jacksonville FL 32258	904-296-2743	R	3*	<.1
1043	Nibbles and Bits Computer Technologies Corp—Scott Andreacci	855 Rte 206, Bordentown NJ 08505	609-291-9466	R	3*	<.1
1044	Powerteam Inc—Dean Jones	718 Washington Ave N S, Minneapolis MN 55401	612-339-3355	R	3*	<.1
1045	Dialect Technologies Inc—Sakis Karakitsos	48 Wall St Ste 1100, New York NY 10005		R	3	<.1
1046	Xfact Inc—Amit Banerji	120 Water St Ste 214, North Andover MA 01845	978-686-3180	R	3*	<.1
1047	Mavenspire Inc—Michael Tanenhaus	53 Old Slmns Isl Rd, Annapolis MD 21401	443-949-7868	R	3*	<.1
1048	Kandar Enterprises Inc	120 Fisherville Rd Ste, Concord NH 03303	603-715-5630	R	3*	<.1
1049	Argosy Group LLC	9737 Washingtonian Blv, Gaithersburg MD 20878	301-287-2700	R	3*	<.1
1050	Global Consolidated Services USA Inc—Bert Accomando	875 Sunrise Hwy Ste 10, Lynbrook NY 11563	516-881-0104	R	3*	<.1
1051	Softpro Itechnology Partners—Arun Chinnaraju	12 Roszel Rd Ste B101, Princeton NJ 08540	609-419-1890	R	3*	<.1
1052	Ziba Group—Chad Zucker	5953 Manchester Dr, Oakland CA 94618	510-654-9595	R	3*	<.1
1053	Truetandem LLC—Stuart Houten	11911 Freedom Dr 5, Reston VA 20190	703-889-6004	R	3*	<.1
1054	Inscitek Microsystems Inc—George Daddis	300 Main St Ste 11, East Rochester NY 14445	585-425-9000	R	3*	<.1
1055	Media Captioning Services Inc—Patricia Ferrier	2111 Palomar Airport R, Carlsbad CA 92011	760-431-2882	R	3*	<.1
1056	Powermetal Technologies Inc—Edward Hughes	2726 Loker Ave W, Carlsbad CA 92010	760-607-0404	R	3*	<.1
1057	Act Data Services Inc—Paul Meyer	17-10 River Rd Ste 2b, Fair Lawn NJ 07410	201-794-1114	R	3*	<.1
1058	Business Technical Consulting LLC—Nerissa Acar	3306 Executive Pkwy St, Toledo OH 43606	419-539-6922	R	3*	<.1
1059	Software Quality Management Services Inc—Paul Shellman	245 Kirkton Knls, Alpharetta GA 30022	770-664-1700	R	3*	<.1
1060	Linkedge Technologies Inc—Renu Chopra	18375 Ventura Blvd Ste, Tarzana CA 91356	818-700-2920	R	3*	<.1
1061	Doculabs—Kurt Grosser	13791 E Rice Pl, Aurora CO 80015	303-481-4284	R	3*	<.1
1062	Tom Kelly—Tom Kelly	204 7th St W, Northfield MN 55057	507-645-7464	R	3*	<.1
1063	All American Balianti Inc—Amir Arif	519 Standish Rd, Teaneck NJ 07666	201-392-1727	R	3*	<.1
1064	Lg Associates Inc—Lana Gertz	900 National Pkwy Ste, Schaumburg IL 60173	847-995-1300	R	3*	<.1
1065	MorevisibilityCom Inc—Dennis Pushkin	925 S Federal Hwy Ste, Boca Raton FL 33432	561-620-9682	R	3*	<.1
1066	Premier Technology Solutions Inc—Thomas Bradbury	232 Madison Ave Rm 150, New York NY 10016	212-576-1600	R	3*	<.1
1067	William James and Associates Ltd—James Pinckney	209 E Liberty Dr, Wheaton IL 60187	630-665-6669	R	3*	<.1
1068	Xtech—John Eaton	1275 Fairfax Ave Ste 2, San Francisco CA 94124	415-285-3292	R	3*	<.1
1069	Seventh Wave Technology Inc—David Fournier	2216 Ascott Valley Trc, Duluth GA 30097	770-495-2453	R	3*	<.1
1070	Hypercube LLC—Ronald Beaumont	3200 W Pleasant Run Rd, Lancaster TX 75146	469-727-1577	R	3*	<.1
1071	Trikaya Solutions LLC	2124 Oak Tree Rd, Edison NJ 08820	732-744-0777	R	3*	<.1
1072	Blue Oasis Technologies Inc—Paul Tartre	5375 Mira Sorrento Pl, San Diego CA 92121	858-525-0304	R	3*	<.1
1073	Pinebreeze Technologies Inc—Allan Nichols	3204 Long Prairie Rd, Flower Mound TX 75022	972-899-2366	R	3*	<.1
1074	Healthpac Computer Systems Inc—Burl Claborn	1010 E Victory Dr Ste, Savannah GA 31405	912-544-0829	R	3*	<.1
1075	Computer and Network Services Inc—Michael Payne	1217 Ne Burnside Rd St, Gresham OR 97030	503-492-5302	R	3*	<.1
1076	Management Systems Services Inc—Roy Igersheim	10411 Motor City Dr St, Bethesda MD 20817	301-222-0694	R	3*	<.1
1077	Castle Rock Computing Inc—Kreig Ecklund	PO Box 3610, Saratoga CA 95070	408-366-6540	R	3	<.1
1078	Group Three Systems LLC	40 Lake Bellevue Dr St, Bellevue WA 98005	425-562-4433	R	3*	<.1
1079	Kig Healthcare Solutions—C Keane	10777 Sunset Office Dr, Saint Louis MO 63127	314-966-4692	R	3*	<.1
1080	Small Business Technology And Communications Corp—Aaron Thomas	12160 Abrams Rd Ste 50, Dallas TX 75243	214-351-0988	R	3*	<.1
1081	Service-Vision Consulting Inc—Penny Schultz	11082 Whstling Straits, Las Vegas NV 89141	702-898-2080	R	3*	<.1
1082	Friendster Inc—Ganesh Kumar Bangah	568 Howard St, San Francisco CA 94105	415-618-0871	R	2	.1
1083	Cybrid Inc—Ravi Vaylay	1017 Mumma Rd Ste 105, Lemoyne PA 17043	717-541-5541	R	2*	<.1
1084	Forsythe Technology—Greg Fearing	5800 Granite Pkwy Ste, Plano TX 75024	972-543-6200	R	2*	<.1
1085	Cluen Corp—Andrew Shapiro	7 W 22nd St Fl 5, New York NY 10010	212-255-6659	R	2*	<.1
1086	Unit4 Coda Inc—Steve Pugh	1000 Elm St Ste 801, Manchester NH 03101	603-471-1700	R	2*	<.1
1087	Bryan Vincent Associates Inc—Bryan Vincent	1517 W Knudsen Dr, Phoenix AZ 85027	623-251-7000	R	2*	<.1
1088	Teknion Data Solutions Ltd—Steven Agee	1431 Greenway Dr Ste 4, Irving TX 75038	214-614-7600	R	2*	<.1
1089	Jba International LLC—John Wasmeier	1192 N Lake Ave, Pasadena CA 91104	626-844-1400	R	2*	<.1
1090	Patel International Inc—Samir Patel	30 N River Rd Ste 102, Des Plaines IL 60016	847-827-2475	R	2*	<.1
1091	Application Design Consultants Inc—Vinod Sachdeva	2614 Butterway Rd, Cleveland OH 44124	216-292-6636	R	2*	<.1
1092	Athena Investment Systems LLC—Scott Sykowski	47 Highland Rd, Boxford MA 01921	617-755-4001	R	2*	<.1
1093	Mth Information Solutions LLC—Chris Neal	828 E Main St, Spartanburg SC 29302	864-594-4580	R	2*	<.1
1094	Trioh Consulting Group Inc—Joseph Harry	4308 Lynbrook Dr Ste 1, Bethesda MD 20814	301-351-4695	R	2*	<.1
1095	Eric Reiter—Eric Reiter	5401 Chimney Rock Rd S, Houston TX 77081	713-667-5851	R	2*	<.1
1096	Performance Technology Partners LLC—Lynn Olson	11246 Gold Express Dr, Gold River CA 95670	916-791-8263	R	2*	<.1
1097	Peace Technology Inc—Andrew Chen	13685 Baltimore Ave, Laurel MD 20707	301-206-9696	R	2*	<.1
1098	Techquest International Inc—Kamal Gogineni	10420 S De Anza Blvd, Cupertino CA 95014	408-446-5373	R	2*	<.1
1099	Advanced Projects International—Garrett Hill	1333 N Mcdowell Blvd A, Petaluma CA 94954	707-283-8000	R	2*	<.1
1100	Case Partners Inc—Michael Kimball	750 Main St Ste 1312, Hartford CT 06103	860-527-0436	R	2*	<.1
1101	MK and Associates Inc—Thomas Mcdonald	5360 Cascade Rd Se, Grand Rapids MI 49546	616-532-5006	R	2*	<.1
1102	Insinc Corp—William Callahan	9 Kidder Rd, Chelmsford MA 01824	978-256-2296	R	2*	<.1
1103	Friendly Consultants Inc—Manohar Lokareddy	14 Washington Rd Ste 6, Princeton Junction NJ 08550	609-750-9157	R	2*	<.1
1104	Business Security Software Inc—Jack Sprouse	920 S 107th Ave Ste 41, Omaha NE 68114	402-933-7709	R	2*	<.1
1105	Disconnect Reconnect LLC—Brian Lawlor	3911 Old Lee Hwy Ste 4, Fairfax VA 22030	703-273-4020	R	2*	<.1
1106	Softtek Consultants—Emilio Rejas	2898 N University Dr, Coral Springs FL 33065	954-340-5991	R	2*	<.1
1107	Consultnet—Don Goldsberg	860 Hillview Ct Ste 30, Milpitas CA 95035	408-945-2966	R	2*	<.1
1108	Portal Solutions LLC—Daniel Cohen-Dumani	2301 Res Blvd Ste 105, Rockville MD 20850	240-450-2166	R	2*	<.1
1109	Alpha Technology Concepts Inc—Thomas Wilkerson	2122 Kratky Rd Ste 200, Saint Louis MO 63114	314-429-3311	R	2*	<.1
1110	Tech Heads Inc—Randy Richardson	16869 65th Ave Ste 166, Lake Oswego OR 97035	503-639-8542	R	2*	<.1
1111	Transparent Technologies Inc—Donald Baugh	2100 Riverside Pkwy St, Lawrenceville GA 30043	770-888-9800	R	2*	<.1
1112	Amaitis And Associates Inc—Edward Amaitis	810 Lively Blvd, Wood Dale IL 60191	630-595-8555	R	2*	<.1
1113	Blair Dubilier and Associates Inc—Greg Blair	4853 Cordell Ave St, Bethesda MD 20814	301-951-9131	R	2*	<.1
1114	Electronic Compliance Management Inc—Vincent Campione	755 Silver Cloud Cir U, Lake Mary FL 32746	850-443-2193	R	2*	<.1
1115	Hard Drive Productions Inc—Paul Pilcher	3402 N 26th Pl, Phoenix AZ 85016	602-852-0139	R	2*	<.1
1116	C-Edge Software Consultants LLC	10805 Sunset Office Dr, Saint Louis MO 63127	314-238-1347	R	2*	<.1
1117	Itfusion Inc—Jeff Henderson	3817 Northlake Creek D, Tucker GA 30084	770-934-9998	R	2*	<.1
1118	KPI Consulting—Kenneth Pounk	2900 Jazz St, Round Rock TX 78664	512-218-1001	R	2*	<.1
1119	Modus Technology Inc—Alex Coffey	1420 NW Gilman Blvd St, Issaquah WA 98027	425-313-5121	R	2*	<.1
1120	Plaza Information Technologies Inc—David Maher	101 S Hanley Rd Ste 30, Saint Louis MO 63105	314-726-0628	R	2*	<.1
1121	Reliance It Inc—Sim Batlanki	3010 Lbj Fwy Fl 1200, Dallas TX 75234	214-261-5600	R	2*	<.1
1122	Herzum (North America) Inc—Peter Herzum	175 N Franklin St Ste, Chicago IL 60606	312-602-1001	R	2*	<.1
1123	iGoDigital LLC—Eric Tobias	5252 E 82nd St Ste 300, Indianapolis IN 46250		R	2	<.1
1124	Appical Inc—Gavin Prior	222 Las Colinas Blvd W, Irving TX 75039		R	2*	<.1
1125	Digital Criterion Enterprises Inc—Micah Bergdale	275 7th Ave Rm 1501, New York NY 10001		R	2*	<.1
1126	Provion LLC—Sondra Wolfe	1415 Ritner Hwy, Carlisle PA 17013	717-240-0088	R	2*	<.1
1127	Abas - USA Inc—Allan Salton	21240 Ridgetop Cir Ste, Sterling VA 20166	703-444-2500	R	2*	<.1
1128	Heating Inc—Kermit Macaulay	3104 Ne Minnehaha St, Vancouver WA 98663	360-521-0815	R	2*	<.1
1129	Linden Group Corp—Ken Chen	419 Franklin Ave Ste 3, Rockaway NJ 07866	973-983-8809	R	2*	<.1

Rank	Company Name—*Executive Officer*	Address, City, State, Zip	Phone	Type	Fin	Empls
1130	All-In-One Network Solutions Inc—*Michael Ehrich*	PO Box 323, Succasunna NJ 07876	973-775-4000	R	2*	<.1
1131	Willco Technologies Inc—*Kevin Williams*	929 Walnut St Ste 600, Kansas City MO 64106	816-842-6262	R	2*	<.1
1132	Anderson Walker and Associates Inc—*Eric Anderson*	1000 Heritage Ctr Cir, Round Rock TX 78664	512-238-1111	R	2*	<.1
1133	Akt LLC	499 Ernston Rd Ste B9, Parlin NJ 08859	732-707-3112	R	2*	.1
1134	Microagility Inc—*Sajid Khan*	666 Plainsboro Rd Ste, Plainsboro NJ 08536	609-716-9020	R	2*	.1
1135	Mj Technologies of Nj Inc—*Saji Philip*	2301 Cottontail Ln, Somerset NJ 08873	732-855-1194	R	2*	<.1
1136	Alexander Consulting LLC—*Lorie Brocklehurst*	4405 Cox Rd Ste 145, Glen Allen VA 23060	804-934-9000	R	2*	<.1
1137	R and W Engineering Inc—*Mark Wirfs*	9615 SW Allen Blvd Ste, Beaverton OR 97005	503-292-6000	R	2*	<.1
1138	Future Advance Satellite Technology Inc—*Michael Betton*	22323 107th Ave, Queens Village NY 11429	718-434-0057	R	2*	<.1
1139	Achieve Internet—*Ron Huber*	1767 Grand Ave Ste 2, San Diego CA 92109	858-453-5760	R	2*	<.1
1140	Bluerange Technology Corp—*Jeff Mcfarlane*	9241 Globe Ctr Dr Ste, Morrisville NC 27560	919-544-9898	R	2*	<.1
1141	Infoserve Technology Corp (Glendale New York)—*Ko Fa Hsiang*	37 Cooper Ave Unit 79, Glendale NY 11385	718-326-8888	R	2*	<.1
1142	Interface Consulting Solutions Inc—*Desiree Green*	12007 Sunrise Valley D, Herndon VA 20191	703-262-9400	R	2*	<.1
1143	Nowmy Net Works LLC	92 Park Groton Pl, San Jose CA 95136	661-349-9234	R	2*	<.1
1144	Plexent LP—*Gordon Brown*	16479 Dallas Pkwy Ste, Addison TX 75001	972-381-0077	R	2*	<.1
1145	Delphi Systems Ltd—*Mike Yinger*	6740 Pennsylvania Ave, Kansas City MO 64113	816-333-6944	R	2*	<.1
1146	Emergency Power Services Inc—*Doretta Davies*	10835 Philadelphia Rd, White Marsh MD 21162	410-335-4575	R	2*	<.1
1147	Mapscom—*John Serpa*	120 Cremona Dr Ste H, Santa Barbara CA 93117	805-685-3100	R	2*	<.1
1148	Alliance Merchant Service Inc—*Casey Louche*	225 E Robinson St Ste, Orlando FL 32801	407-254-5252	R	2*	<.1
1149	Brainlink International Inc—*Sharon Goel*	8790 118th St, Richmond Hill NY 11418	718-805-6545	R	2*	<.1
1150	Beringer Associates Inc—*Craig Beringer*	1591 Hylton Rd Ste A, Pennsauken NJ 08110	856-910-7771	R	2*	<.1
1151	BurstNET Technologies Inc—*S Matthew Arcus*	PO Box 591, Scranton PA 18504	570-343-2200	R	2*	<.1
1152	Coptech Inc—*Tom Cherry*	100 Cummings Park, Woburn MA 01801	781-935-2679	R	2*	<.1
1153	Datech Solutions—*Sheila Ogorek*	57 Auerbach Ln, Lawrence NY 11559	516-569-5773	R	2*	<.1
1154	ion interactive Inc—*Justin Talerico*	124 E Boca Raton Rd, Boca Raton FL 33432	561-394-9484	R	2*	<.1
1155	Liquid Motors Inc—*Michael Daseke*	1755 N Collins Blvd St, Richardson TX 75080		R	2*	<.1
1156	Lockwood Technology Corp—*Bradford Vinecombe*	25 Constitution Dr Ste, Bedford NH 03110	603-472-2349	R	2*	<.1
1157	Qortex LLC—*Rick Cranston*	98 Inverness Dr E Ste, Englewood CO 80112	303-766-5040	R	2*	<.1
1158	Systems Solutions Inc—*Tony Kakar*	7712 N Moonlight Ln, Paradise Valley AZ 85253	602-955-5566	R	2*	<.1
1159	TNS Prognostics—*Dan Ryan*	4005 Miranda Ave suite, Palo Alto CA 94304	650-213-5102	S	2*	<.1
1160	Futureworld Technologies Inc—*Ernest Willis*	5740 Windmill Way Ste, Carmichael CA 95608	916-481-3156	R	2*	<.1
1161	Ciphertechs Inc—*Michael Quattrochi*	55 Broadway, New York NY 10006	212-897-6900	R	2*	<.1
1162	Comptel Inc—*Manu Khanna*	2114 Tysons Executive, Dunn Loring VA 22027	703-582-7819	R	2*	<.1
1163	Labrador Technology Inc—*Thomas Bradbury*	171 Madison Ave Rm 130, New York NY 10016	646-380-2800	R	2*	<.1
1164	Sycor Americas Inc—*James Marczak*	1 Penn Ctr W Ste 209, Pittsburgh PA 15276	412-788-9494	R	2*	<.1
1165	Bartimaeus Group LLC	1481 Chain Bridge Rd S, Mc Lean VA 22101	703-442-5023	R	2*	<.1
1166	Omni Data LLC—*Dennis O'neill*	11 Research Dr Ste 1, Woodbridge CT 06525	203-387-6664	R	2*	<.1
1167	EA Hunter Transportation Inc—*Neal Saling*	PO Box 1042, Springboro OH 45066	937-430-8087	R	2*	<.1
1168	Harpoon Technologies Inc—*Jay Meyer*	10805 Sunset Office Dr, Saint Louis MO 63127	314-238-1354	R	2*	<.1
1169	Internet Security Advisors—*Ira Winkler*	35 Sunset Dr, Severna Park MD 21146	410-544-3435	R	2*	<.1
1170	Wildon Solutions LLC *Dana Jones*	1508 N Capitol St NW, Washington DC 20002	202-234-1522	R	2*	<.1
1171	Wyant Data Systems Inc—*Rick Wyant*	245 Century Circle Ste, Louisville CO 80027	303-604-6254	R	2*	<.1
1172	Kaltech Int Corp—*Kimberly Kalke*	3965 Stone Village Ct, Duluth GA 30097	678-584-1940	R	2*	<.1
1173	MDJ Inc—*Dan Mcgalliard*	210 Lake Como Dr, Pomona Park FL 32181	386-649-1188	R	2*	<.1
1174	Coresphere LLC	13413 Bissel Ln, Potomac MD 20854	202-421-8284	R	2*	<.1
1175	Virtual Office Inc (Burbank California)—*Josh Touber*	2600 W Olive Ave Ste 5, Burbank CA 91505		R	2*	<.1
1176	Esage Group LLC—*Duane Bedard*	6838 Sw Maury Park Rd, Vashon WA 98070	206-463-6190	R	2*	<.1
1177	Island Tech Services LLC	PO Box 88, Brookhaven NY 11719	631-447-2442	R	2*	<.1
1178	Adept Engineering Solutions LLC—*Glades Adams*	3000 Green Rd 130443, Ann Arbor MI 48105	248-245-0861	R	2*	<.1
1179	Brain Power International Inc	PO Box 234, Aurora OR 97002	503-678-6643	R	2*	<.1
1180	Dickerson Engineering Inc—*Joe D Dickerson*	8101 N Milwaukee Ave, Niles IL 60714	847-966-0290	R	2*	<.1
1181	Infinity Solutions Group Inc—*Edward Ip*	132 Nassau St Rm 1402, New York NY 10038	212-404-6168	R	2*	<.1
1182	InnovaSafe Inc—*John Stulman*	28502 Constellation Rd, Valencia CA 91355		R	2*	<.1
1183	Network Consulting Solutions Inc—*Bruce Desmond*	181 Stedman St Ste 1, Lowell MA 01851	978-970-3155	R	2*	<.1
1184	Networld Solutions Inc—*Scott Herron*	8316 Clairemont Mesa B, San Diego CA 92111	858-874-0464	R	2*	<.1
1185	Altus Consulting Corp—*Jacob Porter*	38699 Old Wheatland Rd, Waterford VA 20197	703-929-4000	R	2*	<.1
1186	Premier Internet Inc	3814 W St Ste 201, Cincinnati OH 45227	513-561-6245	R	2*	<.1
1187	Agilepath Corporaton—*Eric Marks*	38 Merrimac St Unit 20, Newburyport MA 01950	978-462-5737	R	2*	<.1
1188	Computer Consulting Services of WNY Inc—*Paul Brynski*	7954 Transit Rd Ste 32, Williamsville NY 14221	716-691-3117	R	2*	<.1
1189	Film Finders Inc—*Sydney Levine*	10920 Ventura Blvd, Studio City CA 91604	310-300-2180	R	2*	<.1
1190	Russell Martin and Associates—*Lou Russell*	6326 Rucker Rd Ste E, Indianapolis IN 46220	317-475-9311	R	2*	<.1
1191	Tristate Network Integrators—*Tom Meadows*	1905 Newport Gap Pke, Wilmington DE 19808	302-225-0400	R	2*	<.1
1192	Jagr Holdings LLC	11 Wellington Pl, New Brunswick NJ 08901	732-208-2763	R	2*	<.1
1193	ComputerGraphics/Atlanta	645 Molly Ln Ste 130, Woodstock GA 30189	770-345-8907	R	2*	<.1
1194	VantagePoint Software Inc—*Larry Wilcox*	1619 E Lakeview Dr, Bountiful UT 84010	801-292-5344	R	2*	<.1
1195	Access2001—*Dario J Saal*	1881 NE 206 St, Miami FL 33179	305-494-0958	R	2*	<.1
1196	Computer Engineering Operations Inc—*Jamshid Javidi*	5435 Balboa Blvd Ste 1, Encino CA 91316	818-501-2281	R	2*	<.1
1197	CyberStrategies Inc—*Michael L Carroll*	112 Harvard Ave Ste 88, Claremont CA 91711	909-920-9154	R	2*	<.1
1198	EMusicquest—*Donald Reese*	PO Box 112, Lansdale PA 19446	215-855-0181	R	2*	<.1
1199	Gamasutra CMP Media LLC—*Simon Carless*	600 Harrison St 5th Fl, San Francisco CA 94107	415-947-6000	R	2*	<.1
1200	GSC Associates Inc—*George Carson*	2727 Xanthia Ct, Denver CO 80238	303-388-6355	R	2*	<.1
1201	Hinman Associates—*Jack Hinman*	PO Box 97, Nevada City CA 95959	530-265-2157	R	2*	<.1
1202	Hyperride Technologies Inc—*Kimberly Horvath*	3746 NW 124th Ave, Coral Springs FL 33065	954-369-4184	R	2*	<.1
1203	MainStreet Solutions Inc—*Matt Ammon*	13500 Midway Rd Ste 40, Dallas TX 75244	972-406-9900	R	2*	<.1
1204	Old Dominion Enterprises Corp—*Mike Burstein*	PO Box 30521, Alexandria VA 22310	703-672-1915	R	2*	<.1
1205	On-Site Solutions Inc—*Robert Ladan* Judge Group Inc	1251 W 9th St, Upland CA 91786	909-985-3249	S	2*	<.1
1206	OPTX International—*Brian Meyerpeter*	170 AirPark Blvd, Chico CA 95973	530-873-0265	R	2*	<.1
1207	Pair Networks Inc—*Kevin Martin*	2403 Sidney St Ste 210, Pittsburgh PA 15203	412-381-7247	R	2*	<.1
1208	Pragma Systems Corp—*Rebecca Bowerman*	PO Box 1427, Reston VA 20190	703-796-0010	R	2*	<.1
1209	Reifer Consultants Inc—*Donald Reifer*	14820 N Dragons Breath, Prescott AZ 86305	928-237-9060	R	2*	<.1
1210	ScoringAgcom—*Brunhilde Merker*	11711 Winding Woods Wa, Bradenton FL 34202	941-792-6405	D	2*	<.1
1211	Sculpt Image Studio—*Jerome Russell*	406 Milton St, Valparaiso IN 46385	219-707-0012	R	2*	<.1
1212	SOHO Prospecting Inc—*Dale R DeHart*	55 S Glenn Dr, Camarillo CA 93010	805-482-2170	R	2*	<.1
1213	Sonnar Internet Inc	4121 S Fremont Ave Ste, Springfield MO 65804		R	2*	<.1
1214	TenFold (Oakland California)—*Andrea Silvestri*	2330 7th Ave, Oakland CA 94606	510-596-2000	R	2*	<.1
1215	Web Ignite Corp—*Jeff Wilson*	250 Storke Rd Ste 16, Santa Barbara CA 93117	805-961-8735	R	2*	<.1
1216	WebSolutions Technology Inc—*Jeff Gahn*	3817 McCoy Dr Ste 105, Aurora IL 60504	630-375-6833	R	2*	<.1
1217	WhiteGyr—*Millard Hiner*	PO Box 394, Pierce ID 83546	208-464-1127	R	2*	<.1

Note: An asterisk (*) indicates an estimated financial figure. The company type code used is as follows: R = Private, P = Public, S = Private Subsidiary, B = Public Subsidiary, D = Division, J = Joint Venture, I = Investment Fund.

COMPANY RANKINGS BY SALES WITHIN 4-DIGIT SIC

Rank	Company Name—*Executive Officer*	Address, City, State, Zip	Phone	Type	Fin	Empls
1218	Alaskan Star Software—*Gonzalo Miranda*	405 Espanola Way Studi, Miami Beach FL 33139	305-673-8676	R	2*	<.1
1219	NETView Communications Inc—*Michael Shannon*	1177 Branham Ln Ste 39, San Jose CA 95118		R	2*	<.1
1220	New South Network Services—*Charles Hofacker*	3303 Dartmoor Dr, Tallahassee FL 32312	850-386-4318	R	2*	<.1
1221	OrangeSitescom—*Ludovic Goarin*	20251 Cape Coral Ln St, Huntington Beach CA 92646		R	2*	<.1
1222	RJS Software Systems—*Richard Schoen*	2970 Judicial Rd Ste 1, Burnsville MN 55337	952-736-5800	R	2*	<.1
1223	Soho Solutions Inc—*Larry Brinley*	11715 Fox Rd Ste 400, Indianapolis IN 46236	317-462-1280	R	2*	<.1
1224	Storsoft Technology Corp—*Jonathan Evans*	PO Box 297666, Miramar FL 33029	954-436-9292	R	2*	<.1
1225	Tommy Dew Design Inc—*Sally Dew*	5980 Horton St Ste 105, Emeryville CA 94608	510-652-7700	R	2*	<.1
1226	Web Results Inc—*Tim Wickstrom*	440 E Sample Rd Ste 20, Pompano Beach FL 33064	954-569-0200	R	2*	<.1
1227	Aufrance Associates—*Tom Aufrance*	PO Box 1600, Carson City NV 89702	775-841-1193	R	2*	<.1
1228	Aver Inc—*Byron Joslin*	74330 Magnesia Falls D, Palm Desert CA 92260	760-568-4351	R	2*	<.1
1229	Engineering Concepts (Fullerton California)—*J Scott Reynolds*	612 W Gage Ave, Fullerton CA 92832	714-525-3519	R	2*	<.1
1230	Gravcom	25480 Telegraph Rd Ste, Southfield MI 48033	248-283-0834	R	2*	<.1
1231	Intuitive Solutions—*Fito Kahn*	11536 Cedarcliffe Dr, Austin TX 78750	512-775-9270	R	2*	<.1
1232	Smoky Mountain Internet Services Inc—*Sam Fiske*	17 Smoky Mountain Dr, Franklin NC 28734	828-349-9541	R	2*	<.1
1233	Stochos Inc—*Don Holmes*	PO Box 247, Duanesburg NY 12056	518-895-2896	R	2*	<.1
1234	Webtyme Design and Hosting—*Don Mahnke*	1210 Cypress Ave, San Mateo CA 94401	650-401-6200	R	2*	<.1
1235	OverByte Computer Systems—*Scott Rainey*	PO Box 6500, Portland OR 97228	503-228-1100	R	2*	<.1
1236	SK Max Inc—*Scott Sampson*	1935 Stonegate Valley, Tyler TX 75703	903-245-4669	R	2*	<.1
1237	Studio Melizo	53 Meadow Ln, Levittown NY 11756	516-520-0366	R	2*	<.1
1238	World Technology Solutions Corp—*Inderjit Kocher*	21 Broadfield Pl, Glen Cove NY 11542	516-759-5701	R	2*	<.1
1239	Systech Computers—*Paul Ray*	319 N Shiawassee St, Corunna MI 48817	989-743-4296	R	2*	<.1
1240	Spectrum Informatics Inc—*Nigam Shah*	5565 Nw Barry Rd, Kansas City MO 64154	816-891-2591	R	2*	<.1
1241	Aeria Technology Services Inc—*Gary Ziolko*	PO Box 297, Waterman IL 60556	708-966-9402	R	2*	<.1
1242	Industrynext LLC	151 W 19th St Fl 7, New York NY 10011	212-542-8885	R	2*	<.1
1243	Certified Computer Service Inc—*Bill Anderson*	11601 Wilshire Blvd St, Los Angeles CA 90025	310-254-4983	R	2*	<.1
1244	Agility Integration Corp—*Brian Bush*	3350 Shelby St Ste 200, Ontario CA 91764	909-821-0796	R	2*	<.1
1245	Kpk Technologies Inc—*Kishan Donepudi*	26645 W 12 Mile Rd Ste, Southfield MI 48034	248-223-9826	R	2*	<.1
1246	Advanced Technologies Integration Inc—*Hong Huie*	7301 Ohms Ln Ste 500, Minneapolis MN 55439	952-832-0033	R	2*	<.1
1247	Samepage LLC—*Will Armentrout*	1099 Akron Rd, Wooster OH 44691	330-264-9892	R	2*	<.1
1248	Moore Computing LLP—*Kim Graman*	317 N 11th St Ste 502, Saint Louis MO 63101	314-621-5585	R	2*	<.1
1249	Advocate Consulting Group LLC—*Darren Hughes*	1560 Wall St Ste 105, Naperville IL 60563	630-388-1700	R	2*	<.1
1250	Clear Winds Technologies Inc—*Stan Sargent*	PO Box 1121, Pell City AL 35125	205-413-8330	R	2*	<.1
1251	Ims Inc—*Duane Severson*	PO Box 100, Hughson CA 95326	209-543-1800	R	2*	<.1
1252	International Solutions Group Inc—*Ravi Puli*	7915 14th St NW, Washington DC 20012	202-470-6846	R	2*	<.1
1253	Monks Associates Inc—*Robert Monks*	950 S Cherry St Ste 50, Denver CO 80246	303-860-8870	R	2*	<.1
1254	Business Integration Group—*Steve Drew*	644 Linn St Ste 830, Cincinnati OH 45203	513-723-1184	R	2*	<.1
1255	Extended Data Solutions Inc—*Scott Smith*	500 N Michigan Ave Ste, Chicago IL 60611		R	2*	<.1
1256	Aspen Networks Inc—*Sajit Bhaskaran*	3777 Stevens Creek Blv, Santa Clara CA 95051	408-246-4059	R	2*	<.1
1257	Citihub Inc—*Chris Allison*	757 3rd Ave Fl 20, New York NY 10017	212-878-8840	R	2*	<.1
1258	Computer Business Technologies Inc—*Joe Clayton*	5402 W Roosevelt St St, Phoenix AZ 85043	623-445-0055	R	2*	<.1
1259	Custom Systems Corp—*Thomas March*	334 Sparta Ave, Sparta NJ 07871	973-726-0202	R	2*	<.1
1260	Confio Corp—*Matt Larson*	4772 Walnut St Ste 100, Boulder CO 80301	303-938-8282	R	2*	<.1
1261	North Atlantic Networks LLC—*E Anderson*	PO Box 351, North Attleboro MA 02761	508-339-0482	R	2*	<.1
1262	Qxest Holdings LLC	9900 Greenbelt Rd Ste, Lanham MD 20706	240-334-4410	R	2*	<.1
1263	Satnam Data Systems Inc—*Parita Patel*	100 Davidson Ave Ste 1, Somerset NJ 08873	732-961-8383	R	2*	<.1
1264	Superior Information Systems Inc—*Bradly Moll*	3055 Old Hwy 8 Ste 190, Minneapolis MN 55418	612-217-7030	R	2*	<.1
1265	Tri Synergy Inc—*Shane Nestler*	21 Sturges Rd, Sharon MA 02067	781-884-2888	R	2*	<.1
1266	Kmk Consulting Inc—*Michael Karbachinskiy*	18 Smallbrook Cir, Randolph NJ 07869	973-895-5268	R	2*	<.1
1267	Compunet Consulting Group Inc—*Graham Mcgehee*	6535 Shiloh Rd Ste 300, Alpharetta GA 30005	678-965-6500	R	2*	<.1
1268	Resultz Staffing LLC	1045 Delaware Ave.Se S, Atlanta GA 30316	404-622-4852	R	2*	<.1
1269	Net Tech Inc—*David Watkins*	17910 158th Pl Se, Renton WA 98058	425-277-9806	R	2*	<.1
1270	Complete Computer Inc—*Yidis Landau*	685 Myrtle Ave, Brooklyn NY 11205	718-855-2022	R	2*	<.1
1271	Tangopoint Inc—*Frank Labedz*	407 S 27th Ave Fl 3, Omaha NE 68131	402-978-3087	R	2*	<.1
1272	Rdl Group Inc—*R Lee*	4840 N Adams Rd Ste 50, Oakland MI 48306	248-892-0276	R	2*	<.1
1273	Anovotek LLC	PO Box 971, Barnwell SC 29812	803-300-0687	R	2*	<.1
1274	Direct Services Miami Inc—*Oran Buck*	10390 USA Today Way, Miramar FL 33025	954-433-9810	R	2*	<.1
1275	Inlink International Inc—*Balaji Jilai*	41 Evergreen Ave, Poughkeepsie NY 12601	845-454-2584	R	2*	<.1
1276	Sterling Computer Consultants Inc—*Kurt Diederich*	275 E Big Beavr Rd Ste, Troy MI 48083	248-526-3333	R	2*	<.1
1277	Pr3 Systems Inc—*Rajeev Priyadarshi*	2909 Colton Ct, Lisle IL 60532	630-364-1469	R	2*	<.1
1278	Ami Technical Consultants Inc—*Jerry Golley*	PO Box 260468, Denver CO 80226	303-980-4500	R	2*	<.1
1279	Manhattan Scientifics Inc—*Emmanuel Tsoupanarias*	405 Lexington Ave The, New York NY 10174	212-541-2405	P	2	<.1
1280	Risk Technologies Inc—*Chuck Allen*	803 Stadium Dr Ste 109, Arlington TX 76011	817-477-2197	R	2*	<.1
1281	Micro Net Associates Inc—*Howard Lieberman*	PO Box 1755, Ashburn VA 20146	703-620-2075	R	2*	<.1
1282	Quikteks LLC—*Thomas Hussey*	333 Us Hwy 46 A, Fairfield NJ 07004	973-882-4644	R	2*	<.1
1283	Voice Data Solutions Inc—*Greg Ratica*	8024 Glenwood Ave Ste, Raleigh NC 27612	919-571-4300	R	2*	<.1
1284	Delta Consulting PA Inc—*Dieter Hotz*	PO Box 1556, Chadds Ford PA 19317	610-558-1730	R	2*	<.1
1285	Management Software Systems Inc—*Winston Mc Cleery*	PO Box 9365, Mobile AL 36691	251-345-9960	R	2*	<.1
1286	Taylor-Oden Enterprises Inc—*Leslie Taylor*	7426 Alban Station Blv, Springfield VA 22150	703-455-9019	R	2*	<.1
1287	Itscinc—*Francis Holder*	11519 N Star Dr, Fort Washington MD 20744	301-839-2016	R	2*	<.1
1288	Tigernet Systems Inc—*Amiram Soifer*	400 Main St Ste 809, Stamford CT 06901	203-316-0112	R	2*	<.1
1289	Burstabit Media Inc—*Frank Ouimette*	3130 W Maple Loop Dr G, Lehi UT 84043	801-331-6945	R	2*	<.1
1290	Maruva Technologies Inc—*Uma Murali*	780 Newtown Yardley Rd, Newtown PA 18940	817-564-2994	R	2*	<.1
1291	Omar Mc Call and Associates Inc—*Omar Call*	11325 Maryland Ave Ste, Beltsville MD 20705	301-937-7717	R	2*	<.1
1292	Techdrive Inc—*Raj Singh*	1028 N Monroe St, Arlington VA 22201	703-243-2068	R	2*	<.1
1293	Bulkregister LLC	10 E Baltimore St Ste, Baltimore MD 21202	410-234-3350	R	2*	<.1
1294	Goldtier Technologies LLC—*Gene Kozo*	100 Technology Way Ste, Mount Laurel NJ 08054	856-235-9600	R	2*	<.1
1295	Haitech LLC	1136 Park Pl, Brooklyn NY 11213	718-604-7184	R	2*	<.1
1296	IndustrialValley Consultants Inc—*Surender Nagireddy*	1430 Yankee Park Pl, Dayton OH 45458	937-660-4748	R	2*	<.1
1297	Kenneth L Kurz and Associates—*Kenneth Kurz*	325 Post Rd W, Westport CT 06880	203-227-8885	R	2*	<.1
1298	Silicon Interfaces America Inc—*Subhas Basu*	256 E Hamilton Ave Ste, Campbell CA 95008	408-871-0672	R	2*	<.1
1299	Business Computer Associates LLC—*Carline Augustin*	8813 Nw 23rd St, Doral FL 33172	305-477-9515	R	2*	<.1
1300	Polysort Inc—*John Dellagnese*	4000 Embassy Pkwy Ste, Akron OH 44333	330-665-5918	R	2*	<.1
1301	Novus Technic Inc—*Richard Kratz*	26893 Bouquet Canyon R, Saugus CA 91350	661-263-8317	R	2*	<.1
1302	4d Internet Solutions Inc—*Bruce Randall*	10 Liberty Ship Way St, Sausalito CA 94965	415-339-1831	R	2*	<.1
1303	Lan Systems Inc—*Mary Haster*	6015 Atlantic Blvd Ste, Norcross GA 30071	770-662-0312	R	2*	<.1
1304	Speastech Inc—*Gary Speas*	1527 S Bowman Rd Ste F, Little Rock AR 72211	501-219-9992	R	2*	<.1
1305	Technology Concepts Group Inc—*Avis Rivers*	67 Veronica Ave Ste 14, Somerset NJ 08873	732-659-6031	R	2*	<.1
1306	Evergreen Data Continuity Inc—*Robert Burns*	28 Green St Ste 4, Newbury MA 01951	978-499-7700	R	2*	<.1
1307	Aiis Inc—*Eleanor Redmond*	PO Box 69, King George VA 22485	540-220-1145	R	2*	<.1

Rank	Company Name—*Executive Officer*	Address, City, State, Zip	Phone	Type	Fin	Empls
1308	Codex Inc—*Neil Schmidt*	3641 Liberty Ln, Marietta GA 30062	678-361-4696	R	2*	<.1
1309	Eagle Collaborative Computing Services Inc—*George Wrightsman*	PO Box 1505, Stafford VA 22555	540-657-1286	R	2*	<.1
1310	Capstone Information Technologies Inc—*Sitima Fowler*	252 Plymouth Ave S, Rochester NY 14608	585-546-4120	R	2*	<.1
1311	Ip Elements LLC	3867 W Market St Ste 2, Akron OH 44333	330-315-2007	R	2*	<.1
1312	Nse Consulting—*Alexander Ma*	11432 S St Ste 392, Cerritos CA 90703	562-233-9285	R	2*	<.1
1313	Webspun Inc—*David Britton*	PO Box 1171, Mount Clemens MI 48046	586-954-3201	R	2*	<.1
1314	Smc Data Systems Inc—*Dan Kaplan*	2 Horatio St Apt 10a, New York NY 10014	212-807-0640	R	2*	<.1
1315	Computer Assistance For Subsidized Housing—*Phillip Deschaine*	6215 Oakpark Trl Ste 1, Haslett MI 48840	517-339-7555	R	2*	<.1
1316	Lieberman Group LLC—*Stewart Klipsch*	223 Nw 2nd St Ste 300, Evansville IN 47708	812-434-6600	R	1*	<.1
1317	Modulus Financial Engineering Inc—*Richard Gardener*	9375 E Shea Blvd Ste 1, Scottsdale AZ 85260		R	1*	<.1
1318	Dr William Turner—*William Turner*	1155 Concannon Blvd St, Livermore CA 94550	925-306-8217	R	1*	<.1
1319	Elgia Inc—*Stacey Scott*	11675 Rainwater Dr Ste, Alpharetta GA 30009	678-749-8000	R	1*	<.1
1320	Laptop Co-Op—*Robert Crawford*	1122 E Pke St Ste 418, Seattle WA 98122	206-810-0000	R	1*	<.1
1321	Paragon Solutions and Technologies Inc—*Eileen Trinh*	591 Camino De La Reina, San Diego CA 92108	619-819-9348	R	1*	<.1
1322	Thornberry Consulting LLC—*Robert Sinclair*	1604 Ridgeside Dr Ste, Mount Airy MD 21771	301-829-8570	R	1*	<.1
1323	Eleview International Inc—*Oleg Nayandin*	7406 Alban Station Ct, Springfield VA 22150	703-752-0559	R	1*	<.1
1324	C Forward Inc—*Brent Cooper*	5 W 5th St Ste 201, Covington KY 41011	859-442-7877	R	1*	<.1
1325	Expert Choice Inc—*Richard Dougherty*	1501 Lee Hwy Ste 302, Arlington VA 22209	703-243-5595	R	1*	<.1
1326	Infinium LLC	125 Trade Ct Ste 32f, Mooresville NC 28117	828-478-1130	R	1*	<.1
1327	Inone Technology LLC—*Linda Edwards*	190 Lake Front Dr, Cockeysville MD 21030	410-666-3800	R	1*	<.1
1328	Lumark Technologies Inc—*Luis Riesco*	4904 Tydfil Ct Ste 100, Fairfax VA 22030	703-278-8500	R	1*	<.1
1329	PC Assistance Inc—*Ben Thomas*	3200 S Shackleford Rd, Little Rock AR 72205	501-907-4722	R	1*	<.1
1330	Wheeler Inc—*Keith Wheeler*	320 E Washington St, Oswego IL 60543	630-554-0700	R	1*	<.1
1331	PC Helpers Inc—*Tim Guim*	331 S Black Horse Pke, Williamstown NJ 08094	856-740-3939	R	1*	<.1
1332	Gt Micro Corp—*Jeff Burns*	17300 SW Upper Boones, Portland OR 97224	503-924-1090	R	1*	<.1
1333	Power Resources Inc—*Gail Toracinta*	PO Box 537, Hope Valley RI 02832	401-539-8646	R	1*	<.1
1334	MLJ and Associates—*Mark Johnston*	13337 S St Ste 296, Cerritos CA 90703	562-292-2057	R	1*	<.1
1335	Settimo Group Inc—*Mike Sisk*	8490 Abby Ct, Springboro OH 45066	937-886-9580	R	1*	<.1
1336	Pike Online Inc—*Janice Bredhal-Hurwitz*	PO Box 337, Milford PA 18337	570-296-5993	R	1*	<.1
1337	ABN Technologies LLC	1000 Station Dr Ste 13, Dupont WA 98327	425-369-8323	R	1*	<.1
1338	Alp International Corp—*Andrew Pollner*	4350 E W Hwy Ste 550, Bethesda MD 20814	301-654-9200	R	1*	<.1
1339	Flying Bridge Technologies Inc—*Michael Kelly*	2709 Water Ridge Pkwy, Charlotte NC 28217	704-357-8011	R	1*	<.1
1340	Grace Equity It Resource Corp—*Michael Bilotta*	320 Goddard Ste 100, Irvine CA 92618	949-425-1125	R	1*	<.1
1341	Grainger Solutions—*Liz Grainger*	988 King John Way, El Dorado Hills CA 95762	916-939-1529	R	1*	<.1
1342	Nemertes Research Group Inc—*Johna Johnson*	19225 S Blackhawk Pkwy, Mokena IL 60448	815-469-3671	R	1*	<.1
1343	Sargon Consulting LLC	13 Galaxy Ct, Hillsborough NJ 08844	908-904-0749	R	1*	<.1
1344	Adler Consulting Group Inc—*Steven Adler*	1636 3rd Ave 405, New York NY 10128	212-883-6604	R	1*	<.1
1345	Ksb Consulting—*Simon Chan*	10505 Valley Blvd Ste, El Monte CA 91731	626-279-7227	R	1*	<.1
1346	B and T Enterprises Inc—*Steve Verhille*	PO Box 2338, Davenport IA 52809	563-388-9111	R	1*	<.1
1347	Burk Consulting Inc—*John Poo*	1400 Shipley Ferry Rd, Kingsport TN 37663	423-578-8000	R	1*	<.1
1348	Cms Duplication Inc—*Alan Gill*	8830 Rehco Rd Ste G, San Diego CA 92121	858-587-9756	R	1*	<.1
1349	Softech Consulting Inc—*Mitch Tanner*	22 Church St Ste 5, Ramsey NJ 07446	201-327-9737	R	1*	<.1
1350	Thomas/Gont Enterprises Inc—*Jesse Thomas*	4415 Harrison St Ste 4, Hillside IL 60162	708-449-3500	R	1*	<.1
1351	Tuscaloosa Computer Systems Inc—*William Biggs*	615 Queen City Ave, Tuscaloosa AL 35401	205-342-2422	R	1*	<.1
1352	Robert Ferrilli LLC—*John Trott*	117-119 N Olive St, Media PA 19063	484-319-6158	R	1*	<.1
1353	B and R Business Solutions LLC	315 State Rte 34 Ste 1, Colts Neck NJ 07722	732-845-5002	R	1*	<.1
1354	GAM Information Systems Inc—*Greg Metzger*	24 Merchants Way Ste 1, Colts Neck NJ 07722	732-462-5600	R	1*	<.1
1355	Bridge-X Technologies Inc—*Sundeep Nalgundwar*	379 Prnctn Hghtstwn 8, East Windsor NJ 08512	609-371-7101	R	1*	<.1
1356	Ntm Consulting Services Inc—*James Teipen*	39300 Civic Ctr Dr Ste, Fremont CA 94538	510-744-3901	R	1*	<.1
1357	Wiseoutlook Ii LLC	PO Box 10464, Tallahassee FL 32302	850-576-9473	R	1*	<.1
1358	Castlegarde Inc—*Jon Bebeau*	4911 Sw Shore Blvd, Tampa FL 33611	813-872-4844	R	1*	<.1
1359	Insynq Inc—*John P Gorst*	3312 Rosedale St Ste 2, Gig Harbor WA 98335	253-857-9400	P	1	<.1
1360	Digital Knowledge Inc—*Curt Fellke*	101 W Ohio St Ste 2000, Indianapolis IN 46204	317-575-6280	R	1*	<.1
1361	Next Technology Consulting Inc—*Regino Sanchez*	15165 Northwest77thave, Hialeah FL 33014	305-818-5915	R	1*	<.1
1362	Catalyst Technology Group Inc—*Neil Issa*	8888 Keystone Xing Ste, Indianapolis IN 46240	317-705-0333	R	1*	<.1
1363	Findskills Inc—*Gurvinder Sayal*	1612 Rte 27, North Brunswick NJ 08902	732-398-3987	R	1*	<.1
1364	Intelligent Enterprise Inc—*Gary Beechum*	7077 Orangewood Ave St, Garden Grove CA 92841	714-898-8195	R	1*	<.1
1365	Neteffect Technologies LLC—*John Campbell*	PO Box 411121, Charlotte NC 28241	704-504-9040	R	1*	<.1
1366	Computer Telephone Inc—*Alan Jones*	60 Alhambra Rd Ste 2, Warwick RI 02886	401-737-5300	R	1*	<.1
1367	Enterprise Accounting Solution LLC	851 E 12300 S Ste 503, Draper UT 84020	801-572-8927	R	1*	<.1
1368	Kms Consulting Services Inc—*Kevin Smith*	92 Broadway Ste 206, Greenlawn NY 11740	631-912-0200	R	1*	<.1
1369	Federico Consulting Inc—*Jim Federico*	333 W Shaw Ave Ste 104, Fresno CA 93704	559-224-5922	R	1*	<.1
1370	Meem Technologies Inc—*Nadeem Malik*	2704 Chanbourne Way, Vienna VA 22181	703-242-6336	R	1*	<.1
1371	Nflexion Consulting Service LLC	4111 E Molly Ln, Cave Creek AZ 85331	480-515-1891	R	1*	<.1
1372	Contactpc Inc—*Chip Roepke*	7600 Park Meadows Dr S, Lonetree CO 80124	720-348-0398	R	1*	<.1
1373	Tech Spectrum It Consulting Inc—*Jason Mazzaro*	119 E Rte 59 Ste 215, Nanuet NY 10954	845-638-6500	R	1*	<.1
1374	Embedded Plus Engineering LLC—*Cory Bialowas*	20 E University Dr Ste, Tempe AZ 85281	480-517-9200	R	1*	<.1
1375	Rtt Associates Inc—*Donald Cole*	PO Box 5771, Cordele GA 31010	229-271-9266	R	1*	<.1
1376	Ensync Interactive Solutions Inc—*Claude Jones*	83 S St Ste 202, Freehold NJ 07728	732-542-4001	R	1*	<.1
1377	Foresight Consulting Inc—*Mark Ricketts*	40 Shuman Blvd Ste 160, Naperville IL 60563	630-548-0509	R	1*	<.1
1378	Getsmart Solutions Inc—*Robert Wilborn*	7111 Dixie Hwy Ste 112, Clarkston MI 48346	248-670-1234	R	1*	<.1
1379	Interactive Business Technologies Inc—*Rick Sarmiento*	27832 Spruce Creek Cir, Valencia CA 91354	661-297-8277	R	1*	<.1
1380	Westtown Consulting Group Inc—*Daniel Hamm*	1512 W Chester Pke 165, West Chester PA 19382	610-918-9070	R	1*	<.1
1381	Mobile Software Inc—*Russell Karlberg*	437 D St Apt 6a, Boston MA 02210	617-443-8603	R	1*	<.1
1382	Jtl Technical Services LLC—*Charlie Mcdonnell*	113 Crosby Rd Ste 8, Dover NH 03820	603-427-2500	R	1*	<.1
1383	Perket Technologies Inc—*Carolyn Keane*	PO Box 492323, Lawrenceville GA 30049	770-881-7829	R	1*	<.1
1384	Questinghound Technology Partners LLC—*Rich Kent*	3155 Sw 10th St Ste N, Deerfield Beach FL 33442	954-727-2200	R	1*	<.1
1385	Retail Navigator—*Mike Marriner*	388 Jasmine St, Laguna Beach CA 92651	949-494-5473	R	1*	<.1
1386	Station 1 Internet Services Inc—*George Spanos*	2665 30th St Ste 214, Santa Monica CA 90405	310-581-4288	R	1*	<.1
1387	Technical Support International—*Gerard Louise*	10 Mechanic St, Foxboro MA 02035	508-543-6979	R	1*	<.1
1388	Andrew Gerard Group Inc—*Frank Petronick*	532 Oakridge Dr, Johnstown PA 15904	814-539-6899	R	1*	<.1
1389	CB Software Systems Inc—*Chad Barr*	20600 Chagrin Blvd Ste, Cleveland OH 44122	216-991-2277	R	1*	<.1
1390	Data-Rite Systems Group Inc—*Michael Feldman*	331 Madison Ave Fl 10, New York NY 10017	212-297-1242	R	1*	<.1
1391	Apexio Solutions Inc—*Beverly Rodriguez*	515 Sparkman Dr Nw Ste, Huntsville AL 35816	256-721-6567	R	1*	<.1
1392	Fabcad Inc—*Dave Filippi*	PO Box 13, White Stone VA 22578	804-862-8807	R	1*	<.1
1393	Pi Sigma Inc—*Rana Saad*	12216 Parklawn Dr Ste, Rockville MD 20852	301-881-9804	R	1*	.1
1394	RuleSpace Inc—*Paul Goodrich*	1925 NW AMBERGLEN PARK, Beaverton OR 97006	503-290-5100	R	1*	<.1
1395	Amtek Consulting LLC	18170 Dallas Pkwy Ste, Dallas TX 75287	972-931-7799	R	1*	<.1

Note: An asterisk (*) indicates an estimated financial figure. The company type code used is as follows: R = Private, P = Public, S = Private Subsidiary, B = Public Subsidiary, D = Division, J = Joint Venture, I = Investment Fund.

COMPANY RANKINGS BY SALES WITHIN 4-DIGIT SIC

Rank	Company Name—*Executive Officer*	Address, City, State, Zip	Phone	Type	Fin	Empls
1396	DigitalWork Inc—*Robert A Schultz*	1016 W Jackson, Chicago IL 60607	312-288-8640	R	1*	<.1
1397	Wisage Technology Inc—*Ipming Law*	438 Red Birch Ct, Ridgewood NJ 07450	201-882-2447	R	1*	<.1
1398	M 2 V P Inc—*Viktor Ohnjec*	804 Cobblestone Ct, West Chester PA 19380	610-918-2230	R	1*	<.1
1399	Oakland Management Services Inc	360 E Maple Rd, Troy MI 48083	248-583-9714	R	1*	<.1
1400	Access Innovations Inc—*Jay Ven Eman*	PO Box 8640, Albuquerque NM 87198	505-998-0800	R	1*	<.1
1401	BenchmarkQA Inc—*Larry Decklever*	7301 Ohms Ln Ste 590, Minneapolis MN 55439	952-392-2381	R	1*	<.1
1402	PARSEC Group—*Wayne Sauer*	999 18th St Ste 1725, Denver CO 80202	303-763-9600	R	1*	<.1
1403	Lifeguard Consulting LLC	860 Chelsea Ct, Aurora IL 60504	630-290-3419	R	1*	<.1
1404	Quantier Inc—*Thomas Holiday*	8050 Beckett Ctr Dr St, West Chester OH 45069	513-860-4470	R	1*	<.1
1405	Allframe Computer Services Inc—*Henry Pomponio*	34 Wood Hole Dr, Scarsdale NY 10583	914-723-0100	R	1*	<.1
1406	Genware Computer Systems—*Sherlock Holmes*	PO Box 4447, Wayne NJ 07474	973-633-6606	R	1*	<.1
1407	JDD Enterprises—*John Dyer*	1340 Treat Blvd Ste 18, Walnut Creek CA 94597	925-296-0680	R	1*	<.1
1408	Renaissance Services Inc—*Dan Sokol*	1 S Limestone St Ste 1, Springfield OH 45502	937-322-3227	R	1*	<.1
1409	Netmethods LLC—*Lisa Bonnecarre*	PO Box 24670, New Orleans LA 70184	504-208-4775	R	1*	<.1
1410	Bassco Incorporated Data Processing Consultants—*Robert Bass*	7770 Cooper Rd Ste 3b, Cincinnati OH 45242	513-791-7876	R	1*	<.1
1411	Blue Rock Technologies—*James Dibler*	800 Kirts Blvd Ste 600, Troy MI 48084	248-786-6100	R	1*	<.1
1412	Datalogistics Corp—*Etienne Terblanche*	3480 Preston Ridge Rd, Alpharetta GA 30005	678-339-9810	R	1*	<.1
1413	Financial Information Systems Inc—*William Ferguson*	PO Box 210426, Bedford TX 76095	512-858-0164	R	1*	<.1
1414	Micro Design Engineering Corp—*Angad Singh*	10701 Balantre Ln, Potomac MD 20854	301-299-3943	R	1*	<.1
1415	Software Leverage Inc—*Mike Ballentine*	411 Waverley Oaks Rd S, Waltham MA 02452	781-894-3399	R	1*	<.1
1416	Testa Consulting Services Inc—*Michael Testa*	108 Wingate Dr, Pittsburgh PA 15205	412-697-2000	R	1*	<.1
1417	Uti Inc—*Joseph Benyola*	11 Sayer Ave Ste 100, Cherry Hill NJ 08002	856-488-8448	R	1*	<.1
1418	Gmg Solutions LLC	PO Box 134, Mendenhall PA 19357	484-770-7000	R	1*	<.1
1419	RLRA Inc—*Ron L Russ*	3813 Easy St, Alvarado TX 76009	817-798-8122	R	1*	<.1
1420	Aps Group Inc—*Marc Asch*	2828 Kennedy St Ne, Minneapolis MN 55413	612-623-8118	R	1*	<.1
1421	ArtFact LLC	38 Everett St Ste 101, Allston MA 02134	617-746-9800	R	1*	<.1
1422	Brass Valley LLC	198 Inverary Dr, Watertown CT 06795	860-274-6761	R	1*	<.1
1423	Breakthrough Computer Technology Inc—*Ronald Lenox*	5 Duke St, Ewing NJ 08618	609-883-0441	R	1*	<.1
1424	Computech Support Services Inc—*Ariel Gozlan*	3272 Motor Ave Ste F, Los Angeles CA 90034	310-237-6065	R	1*	<.1
1425	Computer Instructors Corp—*Rick Shaddock*	3300 Fairfax Dr Ste A, Arlington VA 22201	703-486-2222	R	1*	<.1
1426	Hyperdigm Research LLC	21640 Frame Sq, Broadlands VA 20148	703-858-5869	R	1*	<.1
1427	James Scanlon—*James Scanlon*	123 Hoy St, State College PA 16801	814-238-5103	R	1*	<.1
1428	Strategic Enterprise Technology Inc—*Olaniyi Taiwo*	60 State St Ste 700, Boston MA 02109	617-854-7499	R	1*	<.1
1429	Utc Associates Inc—*Aziz Ahmad*	PO Box 172, Wickatunk NJ 07765	212-344-4111	R	1*	<.1
1430	VANTAGE Technologies Inc—*Randy Williams*	4 John Tyler St, Merrimack NH 03054	603-883-6249	R	1*	<.1
1431	Crystal Computer Consulting Inc—*Brian Lippincott*	51 S Jackson St, Janesville WI 53548	608-757-0710	R	1*	<.1
1432	Heide Wilson—*Joe Dyer*	355 W Olive Ave Ste 21, Sunnyvale CA 94086	408-733-5550	R	1*	<.1
1433	Henry A Bromelkamp and Co—*Henry Bromelkamp*	106 E 24th St, Minneapolis MN 55404	612-870-9087	R	1*	<.1
1434	NetAppl Inc—*Vipul Goel*	2415 San Ramon Valley, San Ramon CA 94583	925-265-4015	R	1*	<.1
1435	New Instruction LLC	615 Valley Rd, Montclair NJ 07043	973-746-7010	R	1*	<.1
1436	See The Matrix Inc—*Troy Rice*	2132 W Morehead St, Charlotte NC 28208	704-334-7893	R	1*	<.1
1437	Swift Technologies Inc—*John Bussert*	920 Davis Rd Ste 202, Elgin IL 60123	847-289-8339	R	1*	<.1
1438	Tukuru Technologies LLC—*Julie Fetzner*	6 Maiden Ln Fl 10, New York NY 10038	212-962-5790	R	1*	<.1
1439	Dallas Digital Services LLC	5316 Bransford Rd Unit, Colleyville TX 76034	817-577-8794	R	1*	<.1
1440	DDL Systems Inc—*Doug LaRocco*	PO Box 1831, Valparaiso IN 46384		R	1*	<.1
1441	Hightechnique Inc—*Philip Babb*	150 Grossman Dr Ste 20, Braintree MA 02184	781-848-9602	R	1*	<.1
1442	IAC Securetech Inc—*Aaron Hughes*	10700 N Fwy Ste 680, Houston TX 77037	832-615-3523	R	1*	<.1
1443	Ikon It Solutions Inc—*Swarna Latha*	1333 Corporate Dr Ste, Irving TX 75038	972-550-1100	R	1*	<.1
1444	Mekos Corp—*David Page*	7414 NE Hazel Dell Ave, Vancouver WA 98665	360-695-0386	R	1*	<.1
1445	Techsquare Inc—*Scott Blomquist*	PO Box 425831, Cambridge MA 02142	617-547-6046	R	1*	<.1
1446	Bardon Data Systems Inc—*Barry Smiler*	1164 Solano Ave Ste 41, Albany CA 94706	510-526-8470	R	1*	<.1
1447	Excel Program Inventions	375 Redondo Ave, Long Beach CA 90814	562-366-0083	R	1*	<.1
1448	Huff Technologies Inc—*Paula Huff*	9310 Old Kings Rd S St, Jacksonville FL 32257	904-396-4170	R	1*	<.1
1449	Ivascu Consulting LLC	495 E Rincon St Ste 20, Corona CA 92879	951-582-0994	R	1*	<.1
1450	Mequoda Group LLC—*Don Nicholas*	PO Box 253, Hopkinton MA 01748	978-440-8037	R	1*	<.1
1451	Onctek LLC	331 Newman Springs Rd, Red Bank NJ 07701		R	1*	<.1
1452	Sooner Technology Applications Inc—*Thomas Jaggers*	1507 Se 9th St, Wagoner OK 74467	918-485-3121	R	1*	<.1
1453	Compatibility Plus Corp—*Floyd Ashburn*	1013 Se 12th St, Brainerd MN 56401	218-828-1500	R	1*	<.1
1454	Total Integration Inc—*Patricia J Skurski*	PO Box 612, Lake Zurich IL 60047	847-719-2866	R	1*	<.1
1455	Alpha CD Imaging	1328 Michael Dr, Tracy CA 95377	209-833-9422	R	1*	<.1
1456	Chemical Systems International Inc—*Gerald Maurer*	3567 Blue Rock Rd, Cincinnati OH 45247	513-385-6688	R	1*	<.1
1457	Concisesoft Inc—*Anuradha Kola*	16424 Mulberry Way, Northville MI 48168	248-842-8989	R	1*	<.1
1458	Easyoffice Network Inc—*Kevin Kohut*	PO Box 4489, Sunland CA 91041	818-542-4440	R	1*	<.1
1459	Jcv Investment Systems—*Joseph Veneziano*	40 Mountain Rd Ste 45, Colchester CT 06415	860-537-6747	R	1*	<.1
1460	RMG Consultants Inc—*Rob McGee*	333 W North Ave Ste 39, Chicago IL 60610	312-321-0432	R	1*	<.1
1461	Rytech International Inc—*Jeff Whelan*	2 Stamford Landing Ste, Stamford CT 06902	203-357-7788	R	1*	<.1
1462	Schultz-Bernstein and Associates Inc—*Bradley Bernstein*	PO Box 872, Menomonee Falls WI 53052	262-644-2191	R	1*	<.1
1463	View by View Inc	1606 Stockton St, San Francisco CA 94133	415-391-2440	R	1*	<.1
1464	Withmomentum LLC—*Rudy Ordaz*	10801 National Blvd St, Los Angeles CA 90064	310-474-1398	R	1*	<.1
1465	Automatic Identification Systems Inc—*Michael J Nolan*	397 Venture Dr, Westerville OH 43081	614-431-3300	R	1*	<.1
1466	Harvey Spencer Associates Inc—*Harvey Spencer*	2 Penfield Dr, East Northport NY 11731	631-368-8393	R	1*	<.1
1467	Investment Systems Co—*Ronni Bialosky*	37840 Jackson Rd, Moreland Hills OH 44022	440-247-2865	R	1*	<.1
1468	Sysintegrators LLC—*Deepak Thandani*	4909 28th Ave, Woodside NY 11377	718-545-5055	R	1*	<.1
1469	Alacritech Inc—*Larry Boucher*	1995 N 1st St Ste 200, San Jose CA 95112	408-287-9997	R	1*	<.1
1470	Aurora Information Systems Inc—*Heidi Marsh*	PO Box 1175, Sanford FL 32771	407-708-1040	R	1*	<.1
1471	B-Squared Designs Inc—*Brad Banks*	1939 High House Rd Ste, Cary NC 27519	919-608-7054	R	1*	<.1
1472	Ciphersync—*Lee Ellis*	611 Pennsylvania Ave S, Washington DC 20003	202-489-3588	R	1*	<.1
1473	Corporate Performance Artists Corp—*Joseph Franklyn McElroy*	940 Garrison Ave, Bronx NY 10474	646-279-2309	R	1*	<.1
1474	Creative Analytics Inc—*Greg Fawcett*	10325 Courageous Dr, Indianapolis IN 46236	317-826-1657	R	1*	<.1
1475	Digital Resources—*Mitch Krayton*	24307 Magic Mountain P, Valencia CA 91355	661-310-2435	R	1*	<.1
1476	DVD International—*David Goodman*	PO Box 6243, West Caldwell NJ 07007	973-335-1837	R	1*	<.1
1477	Eclipse Media—*Joseph Krisberg*	2266 N Prospect Ave St, Milwaukee WI 53202	414-377-4877	R	1*	<.1
1478	Halsey Street Inc—*Robert Robinson*	6A Caldwell Ave, Summit NJ 07901	908-273-8203	R	1*	<.1
1479	Holzschu Jordan Schiff and Associates—*Michael Holzschu*	21546 Colwell Ste 101, Farmington Hills MI 48336	248-476-6907	R	1*	<.1
1480	IT Crown Services Inc—*Bella Bekker*	20 Beverly Rd, Great Neck NY 11021	516-829-9270	R	1*	<.1
1481	Mainsail Marketing Information Inc—*Mark White*	769 Center Blvd Ste 5, Fairfax CA 94930	415-256-8700	R	1*	<.1
1482	Netmar Inc—*Cengiz Akinli*	PO Box 71277, Durham NC 27722	919-641-2510	R	1*	<.1
1483	Ounce of Prevention Systems—*John Urbaniak*	1120 Perry Hwy, Pittsburgh PA 15237	412-488-0190	R	1*	<.1
1484	Reliable Sites LLC—*Douglas Arndt*	235 6th St E Ste 204, Saint Paul MN 55101	651-204-2054	R	1*	<.1

Rank	Company Name—*Executive Officer*	Address, City, State, Zip	Phone	Type	Fin	Empls
1485	Avtone Management Consulting	PO Box 104, Magalia CA 95954	530-873-3056	R	1*	<.1
1486	C-Double Web Development—*Cindy Curtis*	3208 La Entrada, Bakersfield CA 93306	661-872-2738	R	1	<.1
1487	Chilla Computer and Internet Services—*Debbie Cavins*	200 Cherokee Ln, Jacksboro TN 37757	423-566-1484	R	1*	<.1
1488	ComBase Communications—*Al Stephens*	117 W Alexander St Ste, Plant City FL 33563	813-681-9342	R	1*	<.1
1489	Comnet Consulting Inc—*David Kennedy*	PO Box 2227, Tijeras NM 87059	505-235-4187	R	1*	<.1
1490	Danielle's DesignCom Web Site Services—*Danielle Metcalf*	735 13th St, Clarkston WA 99403	509-295-1744	R	1*	<.1
1491	Davis Computing Solutions Inc—*Bruce Davis*	3984 Washington Blvd S, Fremont CA 94539		R	1*	<.1
1492	Electronic Corporate Pages Inc—*Tusher Patel*	12113 Roxie Dr Ste 200, Austin TX 78729	512-257-1077	R	1*	<.1
1493	Freeman Software—*Jan Miller*	3960 Broadway Blvd Ste, Garland TX 75043	972-840-0906	R	1*	<.1
1494	Ginsburg and Co—*Gerry Ginsburg*	800 Summer St Ste 315, Stamford CT 06901	203-359-2420	R	1*	<.1
1495	Global Data Systems	1031 USA 90 W, DeFuniak Springs FL 32433		R	1*	<.1
1496	Griffin Consulting—*Phillip H Griffin*	1625 Glenwood Ave, Raleigh NC 27608	919-291-0019	R	1*	<.1
1497	Heatscan Inc—*Gerhard Norman Thoen*	352 P G Sweet Rd, Kelso WA 98626	360-423-7167	R	1*	<.1
1498	I-Tul Design and Software Inc—*Amanda Hart*	3009 Douglas Blvd Ste, Roseville CA 95661	916-749-1500	R	1*	<.1
1499	Madaba Enterprises Inc—*Mary Ramirez*	PO Box 1964, Eustis FL 32727	352-217-1010	R	1*	<.1
1500	Monash Research Services—*Curt A Monash*	10 Beverly Rd, Acton MA 01720	978-266-1815	R	1*	<.1
1501	Montagar Software Concepts Inc—*David C*	PO Box 260772, Plano TX 75026	972-423-5224	R	1*	<.1
1502	NetTempo Inc—*Mike Hennahane*	594 Howard St Ste 202, San Francisco CA 94105	415-992-4900	R	1*	<.1
1503	Rudy Mantel and Associates Inc—*Rudy Mantel*	6885 NW 12th St, Plantation FL 33313	954-792-5703	R	1*	<.1
1504	Sarah Spencer Solutions LLC—*Sarah Spencer*	1971 Hillview Rd, Richmond VT 05477		R	1*	<.1
1505	ScottWorld—*Scott Rose*	874 Alandale Ave, Los Angeles CA 90036	323-954-1978	R	1*	<.1
1506	Sincere Design—*David Moore*	103 Santa Fe Ave, Point Richmond CA 94801	510-215-1139	R	1*	<.1
1507	Stylefish Inc—*Jennifer Caritas*	3109 W 50th St Rm 109, Minneapolis MN 55410	612-722-4400	R	1*	<.1
1508	Web Strategies Internet Solutions LLC—*Beth J Bates*	122 W 14th St Ste 329, Front Royal VA 22630	540-869-5991	R	1*	<.1
1509	Webflare Enterprises—*John Crow*	2151 Oakland Rd, San Jose CA 95131	408-324-1802	R	1*	<.1
1510	WebsiteMGT—*John Pepper*	8118 Isabella Ln, Brentwood TN 37027	615-370-1121	R	1*	<.1
1511	Coffman Software Inc—*John Coffman*	PO Box 12297, La Crescenta CA 91224	818-293-0472	R	1*	<.1
1512	Dark Moon Technologies—*Michael Parrill Sr*	PO Box 3094, Winchester VA 22604	540-667-2848	R	1*	<.1
1513	Dave's Custom Computers—*David T Stevens*	c/o Lehman College 250, Bronx NY 10468	347-579-3506	R	1*	<.1
1514	Dave's Web Dynamics—*David Schaafsma*	222 W 19th St, Upland CA 91784	909-982-2458	R	1*	<.1
1515	Digital Pursuit Inc—*Rene Curbelo*	339 Ives Dairy Rd Ste, Miami FL 33179	305-651-5777	R	1*	<.1
1516	Franklin Communications Services—*Sheryl Franklin*	PO Box 307, Phoenixville PA 19460	610-792-4597	R	1*	<.1
1517	Franklin Registration—*Sheryl Franklin*	PO Box 307, Phoenixville PA 19460	610-792-4597	R	1*	<.1
1518	Grizzly Designs—*Kenneth Gleason*	325 John Knox Rd Bldg, Tallahassee FL 32303	925-449-2174	R	1*	<.1
1519	Homestead Custom Computing—*Tony Hindman*	HC 70 PO Box 49, Hay Springs NE 69347	308-638-4690	R	1*	<.1
1520	HTF Solutions Inc—*Jeff Holman*	12305 S Boynton St, Oregon City OR 97045	503-246-8010	R	1*	<.1
1521	Internet Effective—*Justin Glavis-Bloom*	75 Waterman St Box 55, Providence RI 02912		R	1*	<.1
1522	Nancy Leffingwell Enterprises—*Nancy Leffingwell*	59 Oakford Ave, Richwood WV 26261	304-300-7475	R	1*	<.1
1523	Northeastern Wisconsin Results LLC—*Jeff Blackman*	2940 Gentle Hills Dr, De Pere WI 54115	920-246-8875	R	1*	<.1
1524	Nuance9—*Justin Pease*	PO Box 1111, Meridian ID 83680	208-991-0006	R	1*	<.1
1525	Tribal Core—*Tyler Suchman*	323 E Matilija St Ste, Ojai CA 93023	805-715-9694	R	1*	<.1
1526	WEB-2000 Inc—*Bret Ritchie*	5740 Parkcrest Dr, La Verne CA 91750	909-721-4111	R	1*	<.1
1527	Webstart Communications—*James E Donnelley*	2835 Bonvenue Ave, Berkeley CA 94705	510-548-4590	R	1*	<.1
1528	Aeroweb Services—*Gregg Kline*	300 Andover St, Peabody MA 01960	781-321-9238	R	1*	<.1
1529	Azcomp Technologies Inc—*Lance Foster*	890 W Elliot Rd Ste 10, Gilbert AZ 85233	480-730-3055	R	1*	<.1
1530	Ewitness LLC—*Elizabeth Davehall*	1902 Central Dr, Bedford TX 76021	817-509-1919	R	1*	<.1
1531	London Computer Systems Inc—*David Hegemann*	1007 Cottonwood Dr, Loveland OH 45140	513-583-1482	R	1*	<.1
1532	National Health Data Syst Inc—*Stephen Beller*	130 Hastings Ave, Croton On Hudson NY 10520	914-271-5434	R	1*	<.1
1533	Digital Root Inc—*Kumar Verma*	40 W 22nd St Fl 9, New York NY 10010	212-331-9890	R	1*	<.1
1534	Search Cactus LLC—*Aaron Weitzman*	176 N Old Woodward Ave, Birmingham MI 48009	248-816-7100	R	1*	<.1
1535	Tailor Made Software Ltd—*Scott Taylor*	11905 Se 277th St, Kent WA 98030	253-631-1513	R	1*	<.1
1536	Turn Key Technologies Inc—*Garry Togni*	5 Adler Dr Ste 3, East Syracuse NY 13057	315-437-4390	R	1*	<.1
1537	Micro Visions Inc—*Julie Lough*	262 Leonard St Nw Ste, Grand Rapids MI 49504	616-776-0400	R	1*	<.1
1538	Precision Consulting Inc—*Adam Schechter*	527 Tunxis Hill Rd Ste, Fairfield CT 06825	203-696-0005	R	1*	<.1
1539	Progressive Computing Inc—*Robert Cioffi*	909 Midland Ave, Yonkers NY 10704	914-375-3009	R	1*	<.1
1540	P and T Technologies—*Larry Porter*	20 Amherst Dr, Springfield IL 62702	217-546-8667	R	1*	.1
1541	Infrastructure Management Systems LLC—*Ethan Agai*	450 7th Ave Fl 28, New York NY 10123	212-244-8600	R	1*	<.1
1542	Velocitie Integration Inc—*Susan Heuvelmans*	1620 S Ashland Ave Ste, Green Bay WI 54304	920-432-1820	R	1*	<.1
1543	Enlightened Concepts LLC	2 Normandy Rd, Colonia NJ 07067	732-680-0123	R	1*	<.1
1544	Ats Commercial Group LLC	PO Box 260, Piper City IL 60959	815-686-2705	R	1*	<.1
1545	Data Monster LLC—*Bill Fox*	4222 E Thomas Rd Ste 2, Phoenix AZ 85018	602-808-4400	R	1*	<.1
1546	Linergroup Inc—*Richard Liner*	8000 E Prentice Ave A1, Greenwood Village CO 80111	303-721-7269	R	1*	<.1
1547	End Ii End Communications Inc—*John Dwyer*	2118 Water Ridge Pkwy, Charlotte NC 28217	704-423-9113	R	1*	<.1
1548	Linked Technologies Inc—*James Mahoney*	4324 N Saginaw Rd, Midland MI 48640	989-837-3060	R	1*	<.1
1549	Rb Balch And Associates Inc—*Rochelle Balch*	PO Box 10007, Glendale AZ 85318	623-561-9366	R	1*	<.1
1550	Onion Mountain Technology Inc—*Judith Sweeney*	74 Sextons Hollow Rd, Canton CT 06019	860-693-2683	R	1*	<.1
1551	Bcs Tech Center Inc—*Chris Cote*	627 S 48th St Ste 103, Tempe AZ 85281	480-731-9300	R	1*	<.1
1552	Colormetrix Technologies LLC—*James Raffel*	PO Box 70, Sussex WI 53089	262-820-1131	R	1*	<.1
1553	Softech Solutions Inc—*William Torrey*	300 N Ronald Reagan Bl, Longwood FL 32750	407-331-8324	R	1*	<.1
1554	Delk Inc—*Eugene Kushnir*	95 Samrose Dr, Novato CA 94945	415-722-4037	R	1*	<.1
1555	Pervigil Inc—*Gerald McGarvin*	17000 Dallas Pkwy Ste, Dallas TX 75248	972-267-0333	R	1*	<.1
1556	Sigma Technology Services—*Chris Urban*	7 Park Plz, Greenville SC 29607	864-329-0141	R	1*	<.1
1557	Bna Computing Inc—*Kevin Nylen*	28 Gulf St, Shrewsbury MA 01545	508-842-0844	R	1*	<.1
1558	Caveo Technology Inc—*George Mcnulty*	PO Box 22158, Minneapolis MN 55422	952-920-9425	R	1*	<.1
1559	Mondz Distribution—*Zack Mond*	9525 Berger Rd Ste N, Columbia MD 21046	443-539-1450	R	1*	<.1
1560	Change Sciences Group Inc—*Pamela Pavliscak*	11 Penn Plz Fl 5, New York NY 10001		R	1*	<.1
1561	Epistemic Corp—*Vidur Dhanda*	60 Village Dr, Longmeadow MA 01106	413-303-9765	R	1*	<.1
1562	International Teknologies LLC	28 E Jackson Blvd Ste, Chicago IL 60604	312-893-7546	R	1*	<.1
1563	Sierra Corp—*Rassul Hashemi*	7700 Leesburg Pke Ste, Falls Church VA 22043	703-847-3123	R	1*	<.1
1564	Britek Consulting Inc—*Charles Brier*	3501 N Southport Ave S, Chicago IL 60657	773-915-1027	R	1*	<.1
1565	Haber Group Inc—*Charles Haber*	29 W 36th St Rm 1100, New York NY 10018	212-609-8500	R	1*	<.1
1566	Informed Systems Inc—*Judith Kosek*	1710 Walton Rd Ste 206, Blue Bell PA 19422	610-940-9840	R	1*	<.1
1567	Business Solutions Unlimited Inc—*Igor Peysakhovich*	617 Academy Dr, Northbrook IL 60062	847-559-0992	R	1*	<.1
1568	Tahas Technologies Inc—*Deborah Smith*	139 Fulton St Rm 609, New York NY 10038	212-962-2849	R	1*	<.1
1569	Dp Systems Inc—*Dinesh Patel*	PO Box 11808, Richmond VA 23230	804-353-1900	R	1*	<.1
1570	ViewstreamCom Inc—*John Assalian*	300 Brannan St Ste 502, San Francisco CA 94107	415-975-8686	R	1*	<.1
1571	A2zunique Inc—*Aruna Gerendla*	1867 Snead St, Bolingbrook IL 60490	630-820-1581	R	1*	<.1
1572	Aces Of Jacksonville Inc—*Jesse Pina*	PO Box 17267, Jacksonville FL 32245	904-221-6278	R	1*	<.1
1573	Kramer Consulting Inc—*William Kramer*	7630 Fishel Dr N A, Dublin OH 43016	614-792-3900	R	1*	<.1
1574	Relevant Automation Corp—*Harry Shaugnessy*	12243 Capital Blvd Ste, Wake Forest NC 27587	919-554-1919	R	1*	<.1

Note: An asterisk (*) indicates an estimated financial figure. The company type code used is as follows: R = Private, P = Public, S = Private Subsidiary, B = Public Subsidiary, D = Division, J = Joint Venture, I = Investment Fund.

COMPANY RANKINGS BY SALES WITHIN 4-DIGIT SIC

Rank	Company Name—Executive Officer	Address, City, State, Zip	Phone	Type	Fin	Empls
1575	American Computer and Electronic Services—William Magedanz	2107 Nw Fillmore Ave, Corvallis OR 97330	541-752-5229	R	1*	<.1
1576	K MI It Consulting Inc—Mark Rossi	43119 Southern Mile Rd, Northville MI 48167	248-735-1952	R	1*	<.1
1577	UGM Enterprises Inc—Patricia Edouarde	5482 Wilshire Blvd 152, Los Angeles CA 90036	323-465-9115	R	1*	<.1
1578	Dativoci LLC—Robert Cordova	11902 Lackland Rd, Saint Louis MO 63146	314-743-2094	R	1*	<.1
1579	Mad Dad Inc—Lee Darby	17847 Sunrise Dr, Lutz FL 33549	813-909-9001	R	1*	<.1
1580	Xduce Corp—Sajar Acharya	15 Corporate Pl S Ste, Piscataway NJ 08854	732-465-9100	R	1*	<.1
1581	David Hoffman—David Hoffman	1325 G St Nw Ste 500, Washington DC 20005	484-733-4670	R	1*	<.1
1582	Ferrara Technology Partners Inc—Thomas Ferrara	611 Druid Rd E Ste 204, Clearwater FL 33756	727-442-5670	R	1*	<.1
1583	Enterprise Data Concepts LLC—Elise Gautreau	PO Box 52504, Lafayette LA 70505	337-235-7741	R	1*	<.1
1584	Baarns Consulting Group Inc—Don Baarns	13234 Lazard St, Sylmar CA 91342	818-362-9235	R	1	<.1
1585	On Site Service—Bernice Martin	PO Box 71952, Charleston SC 29415	843-308-0349	R	1*	<.1
1586	Allied Systems Design Inc—Louis Rodriguez	10455 Torre Ave, Cupertino CA 95014	408-268-2480	R	1*	<.1
1587	Grayson Technologies Inc—Steve Wittry	1897 Tribble Crest Dr, Lawrenceville GA 30045	770-822-2410	R	1*	<.1
1588	Princeton Resource Associates Inc—Shahid Ahmed	140 S Easton Rd Fl 2, Glenside PA 19038	215-576-5650	R	1*	<.1
1589	Kam Companies Inc—Robert Kaminski	PO Box 40208, Fort Wayne IN 46804	260-432-4432	R	1*	<.1
1590	Graphics Development International Inc—Tom Carter	PO Box 6167, San Rafael CA 94903	415-499-0545	R	1	<.1
1591	Rendercore Inc—Eun Choi	650 S Grand Ave Ste 50, Los Angeles CA 90017	213-627-3149	R	1*	<.1
1592	Soogatech Corp—Andrew Agoos	63 Woodridge Rd, Wayland MA 01778	508-358-6646	R	1	<.1
1593	Winter Corp—Richard Winter	245 1st St Ste 1800, Cambridge MA 02142	617-695-1800	R	1*	<.1
1594	Project Enterprises—Kyle Moran	5128 E Juniper Ave, Scottsdale AZ 85254	602-795-9074	R	<1*	<.1
1595	Tigra Organization—Tonya Russell	1220 Tiffany Ct, Indian Creek IL 60061	847-971-3105	R	<1*	<.1
1596	William A Grunnah Jr—William Grunnah	3026 Commerce St Apt 2, Dallas TX 75226	214-698-8608	R	<1*	<.1
1597	Anthelion Systems Inc—Terry Sadeghi	PO Box 5245, Katy TX 77491	281-698-8031	R	<1*	<.1
1598	EMS Professional Shareware Libraries—Eric R Engelmann	6829 Needwood Rd, Derwood MD 20855	240-683-5949	R	<1	<.1
1599	Acenes Technology Solutions Inc—James Valentine	8320 Old Courthouse Rd, Vienna VA 22182	703-903-0290	R	<1*	<.1
1600	Data Miners Inc—Michael Berry	PO Box 609, Amesbury MA 01913	617-742-4252	R	<1*	<.1
1601	Privo Inc—Denise Tayloe	6320 Augusta Dr Fl 10, Springfield VA 22150	703-569-0504	R	<1*	<.1
1602	Sunlink Systems Inc—Francois Antebi	701 N Alder Dr, Chandler AZ 85226	480-380-7977	R	<1*	<.1
1603	724 Inc—Edward York	416 E Ocean Ave, Lompoc CA 93436	805-740-6163	R	<1*	<.1
1604	Incorporated Inc—Marc Chow	330 W 11th St Apt 102, Los Angeles CA 90015	213-745-8880	R	<1*	<.1
1605	Infocation—Stephen Madeira	3333 Bowers Ave Ste 25, Santa Clara CA 95054	408-654-8051	R	<1*	<.1
1606	Maven Companies Inc—Manish Kochhar	1155 Kelly Johnson Blv, Colorado Springs CO 80920	719-434-4441	R	<1*	<.1
1607	Red Deer Ventures Inc—Teresa Peterson	1835 S Centre Cty Pkwy, Escondido CA 92025	760-781-1401	R	<1*	<.1
1608	Graphic Computer Consultants—Randall Blinn	10704 Burnt Oaks Ct, Louisville KY 40241	502-339-9500	R	<1*	<.1
1609	Visual Records Consulting Inc—Robert Baddorf	26323 Jefferson Ave St, Murrieta CA 92562	951-693-1350	R	<1*	<.1
1610	Global Strategic Solutions LLC	7817 Cooper Rd, Cincinnati OH 45242	513-891-1430	R	<1*	<.1
1611	Vara Technologies—Vijay Yerragudi	104 Industrial Blvd St, Sugar Land TX 77478	281-494-9685	R	<1*	<.1
1612	Computer Security Consulting Inc—James Scholz	509 Tracy Ln Ste 1b, Warrensburg MO 64093	816-463-3014	R	<1*	<.1
1613	Multimedia Data Storage LLC	278 Glandore Dr, Ballwin MO 63021	314-892-1610	R	<1*	<.1
1614	A Better Server—Gene Schallert	3598 Stallion Dr, Santa Rosa CA 95404	707-526-0580	R	<1*	<.1
1615	Emerson Cooke Associates—Elaine Russell	47 Brushy Hill Rd, Darien CT 06820	203-655-4427	R	<1*	<.1
1616	Hawa Enterprises Inc—Adan Doubass	23641 20th Ave S Apt J, Des Moines WA 98198	206-293-1234	R	<1*	<.1
1617	Home Media Technologies Inc—Roland Desjarlais	PO Box 1059, Belcourt ND 58316	701-477-7205	R	<1*	<.1
1618	Management Systems Consulting LLC	19901 SW Fwy Ste 109, Sugar Land TX 77479	281-635-4672	R	<1*	<.1
1619	Ftf Technologies Inc—Faisal Shah	391 N Ancestor Pl, Boise ID 83704	208-685-1751	R	<1*	<.1
1620	N-Telligent LLC	322 4th Ave, Pittsburgh PA 15222	412-512-3482	R	<1*	<.1
1621	Rob S Computer Services—Rob Szymendera	3443 Shelmire Ave, Philadelphia PA 19136	215-533-8713	R	<1*	<.1
1622	Storbase Corp—Thomas Macarthur	PO Box 98, North Chatham MA 02650		R	<1*	<.1
1623	Alphagen USA Inc—Rene Fauchet	358 Baker Ave Ste 4, Concord MA 01742	978-371-2250	R	<1*	<.1
1624	G2 Communications Inc—Darryl Gill	PO Box 4614, Saint Louis MO 63108	314-371-4577	R	<1*	<.1
1625	Sendthisfile Inc—Aaron Freeman	2116 N Mccomas St, Wichita KS 67203	316-942-4707	R	<1*	<.1
1626	Silhouette Management Services LLC—Bill Budde	PO Box 65, Unionville CT 06085		R	<1*	<.1
1627	Cmyk Corp—Christopher Song	587 Warren St 2, Brooklyn NY 11217	212-695-1838	R	<1*	<.1
1628	MP Consulting Inc—Michael Price	309 Elm St Fl 3, West Springfield MA 01089	413-747-2809	R	<1*	<.1
1629	Hard Drive 911 LLC—Marc Gittleman	7621 1/2 Norton Ave, West Hollywood CA 90046	323-988-1047	R	<1*	<.1
1630	ML Pfeffer Associates—Murray Pfeffer	447 E 14th St, New York NY 10009	212-677-0252	R	<1*	<.1
1631	Rafael Orozco—Rafael Orozco	926 S Main St, Santa Ana CA 92701	714-972-8880	R	<1*	<.1
1632	Xyber Technologies Inc—Mario Faucsse	10800 Nw 21st St Ste 1, Miami FL 33172		R	<1*	<.1
1633	Cammtech—Brian Taylor	635 Pulaski Blvd, Bellingham MA 02019	508-883-0307	R	<1*	<.1
1634	Ekuber Ventures Inc—Anita Srivastava	2443 Brch Cove Rd Ste, Herndon VA 20171	703-624-1473	R	<1*	<.1
1635	Usp LLC	13014 N Dale Mabry Hwy, Tampa FL 33618	813-908-1600	R	<1*	<.1
1636	Dna Productions LLC	12537 N Lake Ct, Fairfax VA 22033	703-222-5394	R	<1*	<.1
1637	Doctor Inc—Kevin Bouchonnet	8430 Los Robles Rd, Fishers IN 46038	317-598-9851	R	<1*	<.1
1638	Energetic Systems Inc—Michael S Maiten	136 Belvue Dr, Los Gatos CA 95032	408-356-3111	R	<1	<.1
1639	Glencairn Consulting Group Inc—Richard Graham	PO Box 929, Lorton VA 22199	703-909-3973	R	<1*	<.1
1640	I Train Technologies Ltd—Daniel Deitch	PO Box 13833, Atlanta GA 30324	404-876-1929	R	<1*	<.1
1641	Joseph Ford and Associates Inc—Joseph Ford	PO Box 1859, Olympia WA 98507	360-352-4434	R	<1*	<.1
1642	Next Step Computer Training LLC	8777 Purdue Rd Ste 115, Indianapolis IN 46268	317-875-6728	R	<1*	<.1
1643	Norco Technologies—Eric Jorgensen	18310 Montgomery Villa, Gaithersburg MD 20879	301-519-0557	R	<1*	<.1
1644	Precise Networks Inc—Patrick Hagen	250 W Ctr St Ste 113, Provo UT 84601	801-491-3331	R	<1*	<.1
1645	Susan Watson—Susan Watson	129 E Ctr St Ste 5, Manteca CA 95336	209-239-7580	R	<1*	<.1
1646	Sony Pictures Imageworks—Tim Sarnoff	9050 W Washington Blvd, Culver City CA 90232	310-840-8000	S	<1	.1
1647	Crosswise Corp—L Brian McGann	1545 1/2 Pacific Ave, Santa Cruz CA 95060	831-459-9060	R	<1	<.1
1648	OvisLink Technologies Corp	20266 Paseo Robles, Walnut CA 91789		R	<1	<.1
1649	GDT Tek Inc—Albert R Reda	2816 E Robinson St, Orlando FL 32803	407-574-4740	P	<1	<.1
1650	Pelland Advertising—Peter Pelland	25 Depot Rd, Haydenville MA 01039	413-268-0100	R	<1*	<.1
1651	All Fuels and Energy Co—Dean E Sukowatey	6165 NW 86th St, Johnston IA 50131	515-331-6509	P	<1	<.1
1652	Jumpstart Point Of Arrival LLC	9801 Fall Creek Rd, Indianapolis IN 46256	317-777-1995	R	<1*	<.1
1653	Magixsoft Technical Servi—Bob Hinman	12 Knode Rd, Sheridan WY 82801	307-672-2246	R	<1*	<.1
1654	Overseer Inc—Blair Habig	121 Ave A Frnt, New York NY 10009	212-253-0351	R	<1*	<.1
1655	Technique Consulting Group Inc—Shontrea Bazemore	PO Box 8266, Elkridge MD 21075	301-509-0947	R	<1*	<.1
1656	Zonecorp Inc—Ramon Guerrero	4017 Wallingford Dr, Garland TX 75043	214-770-5422	R	<1*	<.1
1657	Crisafulli Consulting Inc—Robert Crisafulli	6 Founders Ct, Damascus MD 20872	301-254-9405	R	<1*	<.1
1658	Elvish Consulting—Alan Avery	1408 S Noble Ave, Springfield IL 62704	217-698-8600	R	<1*	<.1
1659	Gunkie Company Inc—Scott Ghiz	PO Box 121, Carversville PA 18913	215-297-8262	R	<1*	<.1
1660	Humphrey Services—Clayton Humphrey	16114 Se 42nd St, Bellevue WA 98006	425-644-2512	R	<1*	<.1
1661	Impact Business Developers LLC	11970 Borman Dr Ste 25, Saint Louis MO 63146	314-434-4860	R	<1*	<.1
1662	Jax Industries—James Cox	3764 Ne Meadow Ln, Hillsboro OR 97124	503-648-2484	R	<1*	<.1
1663	Lake Kezar Computer—Alan Broyer	88 Shave Hill Rd, Lovell ME 04051	207-925-2322	R	<1*	<.1

Rank	Company Name—*Executive Officer*	Address, City, State, Zip	Phone	Type	Fin	Empls
1664	LandUse USA LLC—*Sharon Woods*	6971 Westgate Dr, Laingsburg MI 48848	517-290-5531	R	<1	<.1
1665	Media Etc—*Jaime Martorano*	570 Taxter Rd Fl 6, Elmsford NY 10523	914-769-0500	R	<1*	<.1
1666	Merck Technical Consulting Inc—*Jeffrey Merck*	PO Box 381031, Birmingham AL 35238	205-243-8467	R	<1*	<.1
1667	Mission Support Corp—*Glenn Tuley*	1991 Alma Dr, Melbourne FL 32904	321-223-3164	R	<1*	<.1
1668	Open Computer Systems—*Ringo Cheng*	14203 Torrey Vista Dr, Houston TX 77014	281-444-6488	R	<1*	<.1
1669	Raflex—*Elliot Goykhman*	244 Madison Ave 357, New York NY 10016	212-202-0220	R	<1*	<.1
1670	Rampart Systems Inc—*Malcolm Taylor*	32 Nutmeg Hill Rd, Hamden CT 06514	203-248-9418	R	<1*	<.1
1671	Ray Moses Co—*Ray Moses*	10119 Clubhouse Cir, Magnolia TX 77354	281-259-9276	R	<1*	<.1
1672	Rosetta Stone Consulting Group—*Rosetta Stone*	5545 W 46th St, Indianapolis IN 46254	317-297-5300	R	<1*	<.1
1673	S and E Consulting Inc—*Safi Alsadka*	1004 Nimitz Ct, Henderson NV 89002	702-566-1914	R	<1*	<.1
1674	Wendy Howard—*Wendy Howard*	3601 Adams Dr, Silver Spring MD 20902	301-946-5091	R	<1*	<.1
1675	West Mountain Systems Inc—*Bruce Preston*	120 Old W Mountain Rd, Ridgefield CT 06877	203-431-2920	R	<1*	<.1
1676	Xanadu Alpacas—*Pamela Ray*	669 Emerson St, Denver CO 80218	303-832-3478	R	<1*	<.1
1677	Wild Brain Inc—*Michael Polis*	660 Alabama St, San Francisco CA 94110	415-553-8000	R	N/A	.1
1678	SDG Corp—*Ajay Gupta*	65 Water St, Norwalk CT 06854	203-866-8886	R	N/A	<.1
1679	Kramis And Associates LLC—*Mary Kramis*	6742 Lendell St, San Antonio TX 78249	210-694-5500	R	N/A	<.1
1680	Jakob Metzger—*Jakob Metzger*	101 Stratford Area No, Houston TX 77006	713-568-8966	R	N/A	<.1
1681	Marketwizz Internet Solutions—*Dave Harris*	7 Sunview Ln, Eureka Springs AR 72631	479-696-9401	R	N/A	<.1
1682	Multimedia Ink Designs—*Rick Degelsmith*	14544 High Pine St, Poway CA 92064	858-679-8317	R	N/A	<.1
1683	NetTechs Inc—*Harold Larsen*	8406 Rives Ave, Downey CA 90240	714-398-8122	R	N/A	<.1
1684	Network Solutions International Inc—*Blair Brandenburg*	2629 Main St, Santa Monica CA 90405	310-314-7325	R	N/A	<.1
1685	Neuroscape Communications Resources—*Paul Raebalo*	PO Box 122, Eureka CA 95502	707-443-7825	R	N/A	<.1
1686	World-Link Group Inc—*Robert Wilkus*	150 N Michigan Ave Ste, Chicago IL 60601	312-474-7742	R	N/A	<.1
1687	Litigation Risk Analysis Inc—*Marc B Victor*	PO Box 1085, Kenwood CA 95452	707-833-1093	R	N/A	N/A

TOTALS: SIC 7379 Computer Related Services Nec
Companies: 1,687   114,007   302.0

7381 Detective & Armored Car Services

Rank	Company Name—*Executive Officer*	Address, City, State, Zip	Phone	Type	Fin	Empls
1	Pinkerton Consulting and Investigations—*Kevin Sandkuhler*	6850 Versar Center Ste, Springfield VA 22151	703-750-2519	S	16,066*	240.0
2	Wackenhut Corp—*Grahame Gibson*	4200 Wackenhut Dr Ste, West Palm Beach FL 33410	561-691-6610	S	2,768*	67.0
3	US Security Associates Inc—*Karen Deogracia*	200 Mansell Ct 5th Fl, Roswell GA 30076	770-625-1500	R	1,937*	26.0
4	Andrews International—*Randy Andrews*	27959 Smyth Dr, Valencia CA 91355	661-775-8400	R	1,470*	10.5
5	Guardsmark Inc—*Ira A Lipman*	10 Rockefeller Plz, New York NY 10020	212-765-8226	R	513*	18.0
6	American Commercial Security Services—*Henrik C Slipsager*	2135 Gulf Central Dr, Houston TX 77023	713-926-4453	D	398*	6.0
7	Akal Security Inc—*Ken Lieberman*	PO Box 1197, Espanola NM 87532	505-753-7832	R	363*	4.0
8	Elite Show Services Inc—*John Kontopuls*	2878 Camino del Rio S, San Diego CA 92108	619-574-1589	R	290*	2.0
9	Universal Protection Services Inc—*Steve Claton*	1551 N Tustin Ave Ste, Santa Ana CA 92705	714-619-9700	R	258*	4.0
10	Omniplex World Services Corp—*Terri J Wesselman*	14151 Park Meadow Dr, Chantilly VA 20151	703-652-3100	R	248*	3.5
11	MVM Inc—*Dario Marquez*	44620 Guilford Dr Ste, Ashburn VA 20147	571-223-4500	R	240*	4.0
12	Universal Protection Service LP—*Louis Boulgarides*	1551 N Tustin Ave Ste, Santa Ana CA 92705	714-619-9700	R	170*	8.0
13	Us Investigations Services LLC—*Randy Dobbs*	7799 Lsburg Pke Ste 40, Falls Church VA 22043	703-734-0232	R	149*	7.9
14	Command Security Corp—*Barry I Regenstein*	1133 Rte 55 Ste D, LaGrangeville NY 12540	845-454-3703	P	146	5.2
15	Coastal International Security Inc—*Curtis Wrenn*	PO Box 1197, Santa Cruz NM 88554	703-339-0233	R	143*	5.0
16	Argyle Security Inc—*Sam Youngblood*	12903 Delivery Dr, San Antonio TX 78247	210-495-5245	P	78	.4
17	Gateway Group One—*Kurus Elavia*	604-608 Market St, Newark NJ 07105	973-465-8006	R	76	3.5
18	Rsig Security Inc—*Michael Whittaker*	24209 Northwestern Hwy, Southfield MI 48075	248-357-9064	R	61*	3.0
19	Northwest Protective Service Inc—*Randy Neely*	801 S Fidalgo, Seattle WA 98121	206-448-4040	R	58*	.5
20	Kent Security Services—*Gil Neuman*	14600 Biscayne Blvd, Miami FL 33181	305-919-9400	R	54*	.9
21	Tri-S Security Corp—*Ronald G Farrell*	11675 Great Oaks Way S, Alpharetta GA 30022	678-808-1540	P	52	3.0
22	Budd Group—*Joseph R Budd*	2325 S Stratford Rd, Winston-Salem NC 27103	336-765-7690	R	42*	3.1
23	SOS Security Inc—*Edward B Silverman*	1915 Rte 46 E, Parsippany NJ 07054	973-402-6600	R	40*	2.0
24	J Diamond Group Inc—*Jeanette Diamond*	13101 Preston Rd Ste 2, Dallas TX 75240	972-788-1111	R	38*	.6
25	American Guard Services Inc—*Sherine Assal*	1299 E Artesia Blvd, Carson CA 90746	310-645-6200	R	36*	.5
26	Advance Security (Grand Rapids Michigan) US Security Associates Inc	123 Wealthy St SE, Grand Rapids MI 49503	616-774-4012	S	36*	.5
27	Imperial Guard And Detective Services Inc—*R Brewer*	2555 Poplar Ave, Memphis TN 38112		R	32*	2.0
28	Securitas Security Services USA Inc (Parsippany New Jersey)—*Thomas Hauck*	2 Campus Dr, Parsippany NJ 07054	973-267-5300	D	28*	1.4
29	Weiser Security Services Inc—*Michael Weiser*	3308 Tulane Ave, New Orleans LA 70119	504-949-7222	R	26*	.5
30	Vinson Guard Service Inc—*JD Vinson*	955 Howard Ave, New Orleans LA 70113	504-529-2260	R	25*	.2
31	Mc2 Security Inc—*Felix Cabreja*	615 Jackson Ave, Bronx NY 10455	718-401-4006	R	24*	1.2
32	Castlerock Security Inc	2101 S Arlington Heigh, Arlington Heights IL 60005	847-956-8650	S	21*	.2
33	Cauley Detective Agency Inc—*James Cauley*	5777 Baum Blvd Ste 1, Pittsburgh PA 15206	412-661-6000	R	17*	.8
34	Asset Protection and Security Services LP—*Ron Gates*	5502 Burnham Dr, Corpus Christi TX 78413	361-906-1552	R	16*	.8
35	Iidon Inc—*Hans Yoo*	4055 Valley View Ln St, Dallas TX 75244	972-620-2344	R	16*	.5
36	EM Security Services Inc—*Richard Estus*	785 King George Blvd, Savannah GA 31419	912-961-0040	R	16*	.1
37	United Security Inc—*Carmine Aquila*	4295 Arthur Kill Rd St, Staten Island NY 10309	718-967-6820	R	16*	.7
38	Master Security Company LLC—*Joy Strouse*	10946 Beaver Dam Rd, Cockeysville MD 21030	410-584-8789	R	15*	.2
39	Boyd and Associates—*Dan Boyd*	6319 Colfax Ave, North Hollywood CA 91606	818-752-1888	R	15*	.3
40	Loomis—*Jarl Dahlfors*	2500 Citywest Blvd Ste, Houston TX 77042	713-435-6700	S	15*	.1
41	Security One Inc—*J Castleberry*	3715 S Perkins Rd Ste, Memphis TN 38118	901-346-7746	R	15*	.5
42	Security Alliance Of Florida LLC—*Angel Rosado*	8323 Nw 12th St Ste 21, Doral FL 33126	305-670-6544	R	15*	.5
43	Watkins Security Agency Of DC Inc—*Richard Hamilton*	5325 E Capitol St Se, Washington DC 20019	202-581-2871	R	14*	.3
44	Security Management Of South Carolina LLC—*Randy Sturkey*	17 Broad St, Sumter SC 29150	803-775-1259	R	13*	.6
45	Superior Protection Service Inc—*Martyn Hammond*	PO Box 55646, Little Rock AR 72215	501-663-1633	R	13*	.3
46	Absolute Security Network Inc—*Gerry Lee*	333 Meadowlands Pkwy, Secaucus NJ 07094	201-864-4000	R	13*	.6
47	Triple Canopy Inc—*Lee Arsdale*	12018 Sunrise Valley D, Reston VA 20191	703-673-5000	R	12*	.6
48	Safeguard Security Services—*Mike Bradley*	8454 North 90th St, Scottsdale AZ 85258	480-609-6200	R	11*	.2
49	Esg Security Inc—*Joseph Robinson*	1060 N Capitol Ave E21, Indianapolis IN 46204	317-261-0866	R	11*	.6
50	Inner Parish Security Corp—*Mark Leto*	43222 Pecan Ridge Dr, Hammond LA 70403	985-542-7960	R	10*	.5
51	Cambridge Security Services Corp—*Ethan Lazar*	419 Park Ave S Rm 300, New York NY 10016	212-889-2111	R	10*	.5
52	Hana Group Inc—*David Cooper*	841 Bishop St Ste 1160, Honolulu HI 96813	808-522-7278	R	10*	.4
53	Starside Security and Investigation Inc—*Yvonne Coventry*	1930 S Brea Canyon Rd, Diamond Bar CA 91765	909-396-9999	R	9*	.3
54	Ira E Clark Detective Agency Inc—*Richard Curby*	PO Box 38, Evansville IN 47701	812-424-2448	R	9*	.5
55	American Heritage Protective Services—*Arthur Hannus*	5100 W 127th St, Alsip IL 60803	708-388-7900	R	9*	.5
56	CFS Security Inc—*Dennis Bernstein*	115 Mchenry Ave Ste 2a, Baltimore MD 21208	443-471-7000	R	9*	.5
57	Safeguard Security Holdings Inc—*Michael Lagow*	4801 Spring Valley Rd, Dallas TX 75244	214-393-6990	P	9	.4
58	Michael G Kessler and Associates Ltd—*Michael Kessler*	45 Rockefeller Plz 20t, New York NY 10111	212-286-9100	R	9*	.1
59	Total Protection Services Carolinas LLC	13850 Balntyn Corp Pl, Charlotte NC 28277	704-887-3434	R	9*	.2

Note: An asterisk (*) indicates an estimated financial figure. The company type code used is as follows: R = Private, P = Public, S = Private Subsidiary, B = Public Subsidiary, D = Division, J = Joint Venture, I = Investment Fund.

COMPANY RANKINGS BY SALES WITHIN 4-DIGIT SIC

Rank	Company Name—Executive Officer	Address, City, State, Zip	Phone	Type	Fin	Empls
60	First Response Inc—V Foglio	4970 Sw Griffith Dr St, Beaverton OR 97005	503-207-5300	R	9*	.2
61	Off Duty Services Inc—Sherry Rowley	PO Box 704, Fulshear TX 77441	281-346-2188	R	8*	.5
62	Gilbert Security Systems Inc—Fred Williams	8245 D Backwood Rd, Lorton VA 22079	703-550-8860	R	8*	.3
63	Buckeye Protective Service Inc—Richard Jacobsen	PO Box 6416, Canton OH 44706	330-456-2671	R	8*	.4
64	American Security Group LLC—Tom Combs	PO Box 18445, Richmond VA 23226	804-355-2000	R	8*	.3
65	Lantz Security Systems Inc—Jack Lantz	43440 Sahuayo St, Lancaster CA 93535	661-949-3565	R	8*	.5
66	L and R Security Services Inc—Annette Lawson	3930 Old Gentilly Rd, New Orleans LA 70126	504-943-3191	R	8*	.2
67	Njb Security Services Inc—Frank Maiolo	44 S W St, Mount Vernon NY 10550	914-237-8200	R	8*	.2
68	Guardian Eagle Security Inc—Hassan Galal	4311 Wilshire Blvd Ste, Los Angeles CA 90010		R	8*	.5
69	Silicon Valley Security and Patrol Inc—Ray Higdon	1131 Luchecai Dr Ste 2, San Jose CA 95118	408-978-2198	R	8*	.2
70	Arrow Security Inc—Alexander Caro	60 Knickerbocker Ave, Bohemia NY 11716	631-675-2430	R	7*	.3
71	General Security Service Inc—Brian Hanhart	9110 Meadow View Rd, Minneapolis MN 55425	952-858-5000	R	7*	.1
72	Kroll Inc—J Philip Casey	600 3rd Ave, New York NY 10016	212-593-1000	S	7*	<.1
73	Beach Cities Investigation and Protective Service Inc—Kevin Hackie	2500 Via Cabrillo Mari, San Pedro CA 90731	310-322-4724	R	7*	.3
74	Mike Garcia Merchant Security LLC—Alfredo Navarro	6000 Welch Ave Ste 11, El Paso TX 79905	915-772-7047	R	7*	.4
75	Executive Security Specialists Inc—Thomas Harwood	265 Stebbings Ct Ste 1, Bradley IL 60915	815-932-8800	R	7*	.2
76	Phelps Security Inc—E Phelps	2760 Colony Park Dr St, Memphis TN 38118	901-365-9728	R	7*	.2
77	Axel Protection Systems Inc—George Larson	9024 161st St Ste 1, Jamaica NY 11432	718-206-4800	R	7*	.2
78	Atwood Security Services Inc—Glen Grabowski	1346 Elm St, West Springfield MA 01089	413-788-0474	R	7*	.5
79	Executive Security Systems Incorporated Of America—F Coleman	PO Box 43, Addison TX 75001	972-480-0101	R	7*	.4
80	Merchants Security Service Of Dayton Oh Inc—James Houpt	PO Box 432, Dayton OH 45409	937-256-9373	R	7*	.3
81	Terrace Security Co—Earl Hailey	1055 Gessner Dr Ste A, Houston TX 77055	713-464-2280	R	6*	.3
82	Prestige Security—George Bernaba	5855 Green Valley Cir, Culver City CA 90230	310-670-5999	R	6*	.4
83	Star Detective and Security Agency—Vivian Wilson	813 E 75th St, Chicago IL 60619	773-874-1900	R	6*	.3
84	Wackenhut Services Inc—Steve Warner	PO Box 96027, Las Vegas NV 89193	702-295-1600	S	6*	.3
85	L Siracusa and Associates Inc—Louis Siracusa	PO Box 61867, Honolulu HI 96839	808-988-7077	R	6*	.2
86	Saratoga Security Guard Service—Edgar Young	248 50th St, Brooklyn NY 11220	718-439-0110	R	6*	.2
87	Marion Leigh Corp—Marion Phillips	PO Box 8624, Red Bank NJ 07701	732-530-7133	R	6*	.4
88	CR Dispatch Service Inc—Allison Misajon	PO Box 2073, Honolulu HI 96805	808-841-6137	R	6*	.1
89	Red Alert Group Inc—Timothy A Holly	1011 Maitland Ctr Comm, Maitland FL 32751		R	6*	<.1
90	Alanis Security Services Corp—Augustine Ajagbe	7220 Nw 36th St Ste 42, Miami FL 33166	305-593-8233	R	6*	.3
91	Professional Security Inc—David Purifoy	3610 Towson Ave Ste 3, Fort Smith AR 72901	479-785-9333	R	6*	.2
92	River City Security Services Inc—Constance Robertson	3728 Phillips Hwy Ste, Jacksonville FL 32207	904-346-0488	R	6*	.2
93	Danson Inc—Justin Dutro	3033 Robertson Ave, Cincinnati OH 45209	513-948-0066	R	6*	.2
94	Illinois Security Services Inc—Robert Schaller	PO Box 428010, Evergreen Park IL 60805	773-881-0044	R	6*	.2
95	Brewer Guard And Detective Service Inc—R Brewer	2555 Poplar Ave, Memphis TN 38112	901-327-1818	R	5*	.2
96	Elite Agency Inc—Ron Jones	5295 Vaughn Rd Ste 17, Montgomery AL 36116	334-260-5177	R	5*	.7
97	Swetman Security Service Inc—Cynthia Childers	180 Delauney St, Biloxi MS 39530	228-374-4528	R	5*	.2
98	Asi Security Inc—Robert Palmer	9 S 086 Frontenac Rd, Aurora IL 60504	630-978-1900	R	5*	.2
99	Citadel Security Inc—Brian Kelley	5199 E Pacific Cst Hwy, Long Beach CA 90804	562-248-2300	R	5*	.2
100	Safe Security Inc—James Webb	1835 Commerce St, Grenada MS 38901	662-227-1987	R	5*	.2
101	Apc Corporate Security Inc—David Zeldin	PO Box 1128, Bellmore NY 11710	516-781-1000	R	5*	.2
102	Quality Protection Services Inc—Mirjana Mirjanic	801 2nd Ave Fl 8, New York NY 10017	212-883-0009	R	5*	.1
103	Anderson Security Inc—Robert Anderson	4600 S Dixie Dr, Moraine OH 45439	937-294-1478	R	5*	.2
104	Fortress Protective Services Inc—Joel Leffler	10100 W Sample Rd Ste, Coral Springs FL 33065	954-757-3589	R	5*	.2
105	American Security and Protective Services Inc—Anthony Galante	4314 W Cheyenne Ave, North Las Vegas NV 89032	702-877-4006	R	5*	.1
106	Aloha Security Inc—Mark Lafita	400 Hualani St Ste 291, Hilo HI 96720	808-969-3300	R	5*	.1
107	Giddens Security Corp—Darrell Giddens	PO Box 37459, Jacksonville FL 32236	904-384-8071	R	5*	.3
108	Richard Hall—Richard Hall	3111 S Western Ave Fl, Los Angeles CA 90018	323-735-0275	R	5*	.3
109	Primary Security Services Inc—Richard Friedman	9131 Queens Blvd Ste 3, Elmhurst NY 11373	718-651-1808	R	5*	.1
110	Spartan Inc—George Papademetriou	2505 Brown Farm Ct, Brookeville MD 20833	301-899-1408	R	5*	.1
111	Twin City Security Inc—Larry Shrider	1660 S Albion St Ste 4, Denver CO 80222	303-574-0000	R	4*	.1
112	Brinks B0662 PA Service Robin—Cheryl Hreha	500 Vista Park Dr, Pittsburgh PA 15205	412-490-5153	R	4*	.1
113	A and I Security Inc—Vincent Ruffolo	PO Box 357, Blue Island IL 60406	708-388-3857	R	4*	.3
114	Southern Adjustment Services Inc—Samuel Corolla	4250 Sw 59th Ave, Davie FL 33314	954-797-9997	R	4*	.1
115	Blackwater Security Consulting LLC	PO Box 1029, Moyock NC 27958	252-435-1870	R	4*	.3
116	Griffiths Inc—Brenda Griffith	PO Box 3424, Hickory NC 28603	828-327-4354	R	4*	.3
117	Allpoints Security And Detective Inc—Sharon Benson	PO Box 496463, Chicago IL 60649	773-955-6700	R	4*	.2
118	Crescent Guardian Inc—Marian Pierre	4640 S Carrollton Ave, New Orleans LA 70119	504-483-7811	R	4*	.1
119	Clarence M Kelley and Associates Of Kansas City Inc—C Dupriest	7945 Flint St, Lenexa KS 66214	913-647-7700	R	4*	.1
120	Landmark Protection Inc—Dan Miranda	675 N 1st St Ste 800, San Jose CA 95112	408-293-6300	R	4*	.2
121	World Private Security Inc—Fred Youssif	16921 Parthenia St Ste, Northridge CA 91343	818-894-1800	R	4*	.2
122	Confidential Background Investigations Inc—Adam Kerbs	59 Cleveland Ave, Salt Lake City UT 84115	801-363-2604	R	4*	.2
123	Pdp Enterprises Inc—Dave Parker	PO Box 1184, Houston TX 77251	713-229-0200	R	4*	.1
124	Falken Industries LLC—Robert Ord	9510 Technology Dr, Manassas VA 20110	703-753-1158	R	4*	.1
125	Armadillo Security Service of Texas—Ronita Maynard	2855 Mangum Rd Ste 415, Houston TX 77092	713-645-2711	R	4*	.1
126	Information Network Associates Inc—Barry Ryan	PO Box 60515, Harrisburg PA 17106	717-599-5505	R	4*	.2
127	Mundi Corporate Inc—Philip Garcia	61 Audubon Ave Frnt 1, New York NY 10032	212-927-8521	R	4*	.1
128	Southern Security And Investigation Inc—Lilia Torres	6925 Nw 77th Ave, Miami FL 33166	305-592-2596	R	4*	.1
129	Great Lakes Maintenance and Security Corp—Leonard Waters	8734 S Cottage Grove A, Chicago IL 60619	773-994-1899	R	4*	.3
130	A and A Security Service Inc—Jonathan Adams	PO Box 477, Norton VA 24273	276-679-1622	R	4*	.1
131	Nationwide Security—John Montville	1551 21st Ave N Ste 17, Myrtle Beach SC 29577	843-448-7697	R	4*	.2
132	Pelican Real Estate Corp—Dario Ferrari	215 Mill St, Lawrence NY 11559	516-239-6141	R	4*	.1
133	Ranco Security Inc—Leonard Rancilio	36809 Groesbeck Hwy, Clinton Township MI 48035	586-792-3810	R	4*	.1
134	Richmond Security Service Inc—Larry Daniel	PO Box 4349, Lynchburg VA 24502	434-239-2609	R	3*	.2
135	Field Force Protective Services Corp—Mariana Rodriguez	6001 Nw 153rd St Ste 1, Hialeah FL 33014	305-827-8278	R	3*	.1
136	Chase Investigations Inc—Antonio Manzella	3349 Delaware Ave, Buffalo NY 14217	716-874-8397	R	3*	.1
137	Pro Quest Security Inc—Jeremiah O'shea	693 Broadway, Massapequa NY 11758	516-799-3382	R	3*	.1
138	Delta Security Inc—Betty Hughes	PO Box 2532, Port Arthur TX 77643	409-982-1477	R	3*	.2
139	Ada Security Inc—Mark Kwahara	PO Box 1300, Adrian MI 49221	517-265-7488	R	3*	.1
140	Events Services Inc—Mike Hendi	PO Box 13047, Reno NV 89507	775-626-3000	R	3*	.1
141	Roman Sentry Security Systems Inc—Loretta Mckenna	1005 Spring Garden St, Philadelphia PA 19123	215-236-7000	R	3*	.4
142	Secureone Inc—James McGovern	15374 Natalie Dr, Oak Forest IL 60452	708-687-6018	R	3*	.2
143	Samson Security Services—Charlie Grone	5210 Palmero Ct Ste 10, Buford GA 30518	770-932-3038	R	3*	.1
144	Bismarck-Mandan Security Inc—Jack Werner	PO Box 744, Bismarck ND 58502	701-223-2328	R	3*	.1
145	Air Security International Inc—Charile LeBlanc	2925 Briarpark Dr Ste, Houston TX 77042	713-430-7300	S	3*	<.1

Rank	Company Name—Executive Officer	Address, City, State, Zip	Phone	Type	Fin	Empls
146	Sentinel Group Inc—Kimberly Breining	245 E 93rd St Apt 33c, New York NY 10128	212-423-1044	R	3*	.1
147	Guard Force Inc—Leslie Nady	PO Box 2483, Bullhead City AZ 86430	928-754-3013	R	3*	.1
148	Custom Sound and Security Inc—Kenneth Cook	162 Riverwood Dr, Franklin NC 28734	828-524-9092	R	3*	.1
149	Neal And Associates Inc—Judy Neal	3614 Coal Heritage Rd, Bluefield WV 24701	304-589-3328	R	3*	.1
150	Top Guard Inc—Nicole Stuart	PO Box 284, Hampton VA 23669	757-722-3961	R	3*	.2
151	ADF Services Of America Inc—William Hull	PO Box 2003, Tucker GA 30085	404-370-0142	R	3*	.1
152	Westserve Inc—Jeffrey Cohen	PO Box 19358, Portland OR 97280	503-452-1050	R	3*	.1
153	Paramount Security Bureau Inc—Solomon Osa	PO Box 200529, South Ozone Park NY 11420	718-659-6764	R	3*	.1
154	Rancho Security Services LLC—Michele Jaroszynski	333 N Rancho Dr Ste 79, Las Vegas NV 89106	702-382-6150	R	3*	.1
155	Cdc Security Corp—William Hubbard	1403 Grand Concourse, Bronx NY 10452	718-590-9676	R	3*	.1
156	Anchor Security and Investigations Inc—Roman Gomaz	1 Fulton Ave Ste 14, Hempstead NY 11550	516-481-6800	R	3*	.1
157	B-House Security Consultants Inc—Robert Brennan	160 Schroeders Ave 14c, Brooklyn NY 11239	718-942-1369	R	3*	.1
158	Keith L Fontana—Keith Fontana	PO Box 11, Eastport NY 11941	631-878-4673	R	3*	<.1
159	Alliance Security Inc—Richard Waybright	100 N Charles St Frnt, Baltimore MD 21201	410-576-0290	R	2*	.1
160	Emerald Pi Inc—Anna Moore	4202 Spicewood Springs, Austin TX 78759	512-451-6970	R	2*	.1
161	AIM Security Services Inc—Thomas Frey	PO Box 630, Conyers GA 30012	770-388-3625	R	2*	.1
162	Intrepid Detective Agency Inc—Joseph Calabrese	600 S Poplar St, Hazleton PA 18201	570-455-1984	R	2*	.1
163	Al Rossy Investigations Inc—Alfred Rossy	Rr 46, Parsippany NJ 07054	973-335-4246	R	2*	.1
164	Prime Protective Services Inc—Terry English	26 Ct St Ste 709, Brooklyn NY 11242	718-254-0900	R	2*	.1
165	Titan International Security Services—Scott Duchene	1975 Sansburys Way Ste, West Palm Beach FL 33411	561-296-3893	R	2*	.1
166	Censor Security Inc—James Eckhardt	50 Woodstock Ave, Rutland VT 05701	802-773-4441	R	2*	.1
167	Crime Prevention Security Inc—Samantha Towler	2124 Lakeview Dr Apt 1, Ypsilanti MI 48198	734-480-2777	R	2*	.1
168	AWA Security Inc—Alejandro Gutrierrez	7901 W 25th Ave Unit 2, Hialeah FL 33016	305-822-4774	R	2*	.2
169	Bay Security Company LLC	2122 Hand Ave Ste D, Mobile AL 36612	251-330-0776	R	2*	.1
170	A1 Protective Services Inc—Paula Jones	1601 Donner Ave Ste 2, San Francisco CA 94124	415-671-1900	R	2*	.1
171	Barry Security Inc—Patrick Barry	317 Madison Ave Rm 920, New York NY 10017	212-730-6709	R	2*	.1
172	Icon Services Corp—Elijah Shaw	1043 Grand Ave Ste 312, Saint Paul MN 55105	651-695-8778	R	2*	<.1
173	Security Plus USA—Chris Stephens	4080 Burns Rd, Palm Beach Gardens FL 33410	561-691-8521	R	2*	<.1
174	Graham Security Police Inc—Jan Roddick	21 N 6th St, Emmaus PA 18049	610-967-2082	R	2*	.1
175	Madera Private Security Patrol—Michael Gonzalez	910 W Yosemite Ave, Madera CA 93637	559-662-1546	R	2*	.1
176	Park Place West Inc—Wesley Moore	PO Box 45043, Los Angeles CA 90045	310-477-2095	R	2*	.1
177	Davis Group Inc—Keith Davis	PO Box 52, Camden NJ 08101	856-338-0078	R	2*	.1
178	JI Special Investigations LLC	14401 Sylvan St Ste 21, Van Nuys CA 91401	818-781-5500	R	2*	<.1
179	Ir Mueller Corp—Leo Noe	789 Colvin Blvd, Kenmore NY 14217	716-876-9218	R	2*	.2
180	Guard Services Inc—Alma Mcwherter	1009 N Sheridan Rd, Peoria IL 61606	309-674-4321	R	2*	.1
181	Guardco Security Services—David Williams	1360 W 18th St, Merced CA 95340	209-723-4273	R	2*	.1
182	National Security Agency Inc—Ibriham Kiswani	343 S Drbrn St 1610 2, Chicago IL 60604	312-322-0000	R	2*	.4
183	Security Management Services Inc—Norman Barnard	13200 Sw 128th St Ste, Miami FL 33186	305-238-2981	R	2*	.1
184	Allied Protection Services Inc—Leon Brooks	1973 W 48th St, Los Angeles CA 90062	310-330-8314	R	2*	.1
185	Minuteman Security Inc—Michael Conlon	401 Lynn Fells Pkwy, Saugus MA 01906	781-231-7313	R	2*	.1
186	Pre-EmployCom Inc—Robert Mather	2301 Balls Ferry Rd, Anderson CA 96007	530-378-7680	R	2*	.1
187	Dlo Enterprises Inc—Dennis Olivor	41625 Eclectic St Ste, Palm Desert CA 92260	760-346-8033	R	2*	.1
188	Krayer Detective Agency Inc—Francis Jolly	PO Box 223, Dunmore PA 18512	570 347 6754	R	2*	.1
189	Taylor Made Security Inc—Pamela Smith	396 Ferry Rd, Saco ME 04072	207-282-8674	R	2*	.1
190	All State Security Inc—Robert Bond	114 Chestnut St Fl 4, Philadelphia PA 19106	215-829-9191	R	2*	.1
191	Portland Patrol Inc—John Hren	208 Nw 1st Ave, Portland OR 97209	503-224-7383	R	2*	.1
192	Eastern Investigational Services Inc—Edward Salek	39 Cannon Blvd, Staten Island NY 10306	718-351-0700	R	2*	.1
193	Peace Security Inc—Cang Huynh	489 Johnson Ave Ste 21, Bohemia NY 11716	631-563-2606	R	2*	.1
194	Sandra K Schmitz—Sandra Schmitz	3202 Brookside Dr, Dothan AL 36303	334-702-1702	R	2*	.1
195	Essential Security Group	635 Hauger Rd, Rockwood PA 15557	814-926-4141	R	2*	.1
196	Dunbar Cash Vault Services—Emando Mendez	6056 Westview Dr, Houston TX 77055	713-812-8320	R	2*	.1
197	Security Concepts Inc—Mike Gonzales	PO Box 536, Las Cruces NM 88004	575-526-4151	R	2*	.1
198	National Protective Services Inc—Victoria Sutton	4121 Plank Rd Ste 438, Fredericksburg VA 22407	703-379-7272	R	2*	.1
199	Baechler Investigative Services—Anthony Baechler	4910 70th St, San Diego CA 92115	619-303-0360	R	2*	.1
200	Allegiance Protection Group Inc—James Ricaurte	42 W 38th St Rm 1101, New York NY 10018	212-398-0200	R	2*	<.1
201	Security Operations and Solutions Inc—William Scharfenberg	3815 N Hwy 1 Ste 67, Cocoa FL 32926	321-636-8011	R	1*	.1
202	Iss/Wal LLC—B Whittemore	PO Box 3864, Dalton GA 30719	706-259-9942	R	1*	.1
203	Conley Group—Tom Conley	2867 104th St, Des Moines IA 50322	515-223-6319	R	1*	.1
204	Professional Protection Inc—Carlton Miles	PO Box 33217, Charlotte NC 28233	704-523-1107	R	1*	.1
205	Advantage Sentry And Protection Inc—Norman Llanes	1229 3rd Ave Ste E, Chula Vista CA 91911	619-425-2727	R	1*	.1
206	Buckland Security Services—Leonard Buckland	2 Survey Cir 2a, North Billerica MA 01862	978-667-5188	R	1*	.1
207	1992 International Ltd—Jim Murphy	110 Stewart Ave Ste 2a, Hicksville NY 11801	516-935-6650	R	1*	<.1
208	Metro One Lpsg—Lu Granda	1050 N State St Ste 5, Chicago IL 60610	312-475-1145	R	1*	.1
209	Tight Security Inc—John Deheer	3400 W 111th St Ste 45, Chicago IL 60655	773-445-6364	R	1*	.1
210	Aces Security Inc—James Calace	6237 W 59th St, Chicago IL 60638	773-582-1116	R	1*	.1
211	Double E's Security Unlimited—Edward Elliott	PO Box 384, La Canada Flintridge CA 91012	818-425-2524	R	1*	.1
212	Frederick Group Inc—Eleanor Amona	712 55th St Stop 1, Kenosha WI 53140	262-652-6831	R	1*	.1
213	Evans Private Security Inc—Delilah Taylor	2050 Shuttle Dr, Atwater CA 95301	209-725-3415	R	1*	.1
214	Security Associates International Ltd—Kevin Rychlik	PO Box 30, Manassas VA 20108	703-257-0292	R	1*	.1
215	Statewide Enterprises Inc—Deanna Baker	PO Box 246, Dania FL 33004	954-923-8900	R	1*	.1
216	Guardian Security Inc—Suzzane Gahagan	PO Box 80633, Billings MT 59108	406-656-8646	R	1*	.1
217	7/21 Quality Security Solutions Inc—Richard Dunmire	PO Box 6184, Ellicott City MD 21042	410-313-9076	R	1*	.1
218	J Waters Inc—Mary Waters	75 San Miguel Ave Ste, Salinas CA 93901	831-424-1946	R	1*	.1
219	International Protection Systems Inc—Michael Pasquale	210 Sylvan Ave Ste 29, Englewood Cliffs NJ 07632	201-894-5505	R	1*	<.1
220	Enterprise Protective Services Inc—Armand Aranda	7560 Monterey St Ste 2, Gilroy CA 95020	408-840-2680	R	1*	<.1
221	Gss Security Services Inc—John Smaragdakas	250 W 49th St Ste 703, New York NY 10019	212-764-5400	R	1*	<.1
222	Pacific River LLC	6300 Ne St Ja Ste 104, Vancouver WA 98663	360-772-1140	R	1*	.1
223	Sioux City Night Patrol Inc—Kurt Bornholtz	PO Box 3276, Sioux City IA 51102	712-252-3003	R	1*	.1
224	Bps Security LLC—Karby Melton	4800 N Classen Blvd, Oklahoma City OK 73118	405-848-7233	R	1*	.1
225	R and R Security Inc—Richard Thompson	28 Pky Cir, Mount Vernon NY 10552	914-664-0894	R	1*	<.1
226	Acme Security Service Inc—Jackie Teel	12702 Toepperwein Rd S, Live Oak TX 78233	210-599-3670	R	1*	<.1
227	Jack Boyd's Atlas Security Inc—Jack Boyd	12647 Victory Blvd, North Hollywood CA 91606	818-769-0395	R	1*	<.1
228	Trade Net Corp—Chen-Cho Tsang	18830 Norwalk Blvd, Artesia CA 90701	562-402-4519	R	1*	<.1
229	Craig S Stevenson—Craig Stevenson	PO Box 907, Alton NH 03809	603-524-5253	R	1*	<.1
230	Kevin P Carey and Associates Inc—Kevin Carey	5 Maple Ave Ste 2, Morristown NJ 07960	973-538-3711	R	1*	<.1
231	Select Personnel Investig—Patty Mcgowan	201 N Colorado St Unit, Whitney TX 76692	254-694-5917	R	1*	<.1
232	Fidelifacts—Thomas Norton	42 Broadway Ste 1548, New York NY 10004	212-425-1520	R	1*	<.1
233	Barefoot Private Investigations—Jan Barefoot	1011 E Morehead St Ste, Charlotte NC 28204	704-377-1000	R	1*	<.1
234	West Coast Detectives Group International Inc—Phil Little	16000 Ventura Blvd Ste, Encino CA 91436	818-501-8181	R	1*	<.1
235	Security Arts Corp—Matthew Elliott	1517 S 12th St, Sheboygan WI 53081	920-457-9008	R	1*	<.1

Note: An asterisk (*) indicates an estimated financial figure. The company type code used is as follows: R = Private, P = Public, S = Private Subsidiary, B = Public Subsidiary, D = Division, J = Joint Venture, I = Investment Fund.

COMPANY RANKINGS BY SALES WITHIN 4-DIGIT SIC

Rank	Company Name—*Executive Officer*	Address, City, State, Zip	Phone	Type	Fin	Empls
236	American Diversified Security Inc—*William Sunke*	25 Mitchell Blvd Ste 1, San Rafael CA 94903	415-472-6631	R	1*	<.1
237	Argus Security Group—*Patrick Pabouet*	52 Oakland Ave Ste H, East Hartford CT 06108	860-528-7700	R	1*	<.1
238	Roberts Security And Investigations Inc—*Betty Roberts*	14930 Laplaisance Rd S, Monroe MI 48161	734-242-5417	R	1*	.1
239	Pyratech Security Systems Inc—*Larry Teamer*	20150 Livernois Ave, Detroit MI 48221	313-345-2000	R	1*	<.1
240	Seaboard Security Inc—*Scott Baxter*	PO Box 910, Brewer ME 04412	207-991-9621	R	1*	<.1
241	Trachel Inc—*Fred Rast*	PO Box 100, Atlantic Highlands NJ 07716	732-291-4369	R	1*	<.1
242	Senica Security South Inc—*Joseph Senica*	PO Box 780, Brick NJ 08723	732-477-0096	R	1*	.1
243	National Detective Agency—*R Brewer*	2555 Poplar Ave, Memphis TN 38112	901-452-9930	R	1*	<.1
244	Preeminent Protective Services—*Lena Bell*	2607 Mary Pl, Fort Washington MD 20744	301-265-9420	R	1*	<.1
245	Fenguard Security Inc—*James Fenner*	12003 Provost Way, Germantown MD 20874	301-972-1866	R	1*	<.1
246	Scout Risk Management Inc—*Michael Kopp*	9265 Dowdy Dr Ste 213, San Diego CA 92126	858-530-0380	R	1*	<.1
247	North Coast Patrol Inc—*Gary Rice*	146 Eucalyptus Ave, Vista CA 92084	760-940-2776	R	1*	<.1
248	Cefaratti Investigation and Process Services Inc—*Arther Cefaratti*	4608 Saint Clair Ave, Cleveland OH 44103	216-694-4493	R	1*	<.1
249	Strategies Stern International LLC—*Sarah Johnson*	11 N Washington St Ste, Rockville MD 20850	301-279-6700	R	1*	<.1
250	East Coast Investigative Services Inc—*James Collins*	33 Central St Ste 1, Hingham MA 02043	781-849-3525	R	1*	<.1
251	Mcginnis Protective Services Inc—*David Mcginnis*	955 S Bethany Rd, Locust Grove GA 30248	770-898-3737	R	1*	<.1
252	Weatherford Security Services Inc—*Robert Galbreaith*	PO Box 2500, Weatherford TX 76086	817-613-9448	R	1*	<.1
253	Black Ice Security Services Inc—*Steven Collins*	PO Box 650277, Sterling VA 20165	703-591-4700	R	1*	<.1
254	Integral Protection Inc—*Joel Feder*	675 Hegenberger Rd Ste, Oakland CA 94621	510-633-1664	R	1*	<.1
255	Advanced Security Services Inc—*Charles Troccolo*	59 Federal Rd, Danbury CT 06810	203-797-8012	R	1*	<.1
256	Seattle Goon Squad—*Ryan Hughes*	6921 34th Ave Sw, Seattle WA 98126	206-423-5064	R	1*	<.1
257	Reel Security Corp—*Mario Ramirez*	4370 Tujunga Ave Ste 1, Studio City CA 91604	818-508-4750	R	1*	<.1
258	Argus Protective Service LLC—*Robert Murphy*	10 W 66th St Frnt 2, New York NY 10023	212-875-0010	R	1*	<.1
259	Calyptix Security Corp	8701 Mallard Creek Rd, Charlotte NC 28262	704-971-8989	R	<1*	<.1
260	CLS Security Services Inc—*George Slay*	400 N E Ave Lot 10, Panama City FL 32401	850-763-0097	R	<1*	<.1
261	Sallys Home Service—*Sally Senstinger*	1306 Se 16th Ter, Cape Coral FL 33990	239-573-6549	R	<1*	<.1
262	US Monitoring Inc—*Robert Forsythe*	PO Box 12660, Oklahoma City OK 73157		R	<1*	<.1
263	Southern Research Company Inc—*Thomas Ostendorff*	PO Box 1590, Shreveport LA 71165	318-227-9700	R	<1*	<.1
264	Pro Security Group Inc—*Denise Nicholson*	PO Box 878, Lorena TX 76655	254-753-7766	R	<1*	<.1
265	Adams Security—*Wayne Adams*	PO Box 462, Sapulpa OK 74067	918-224-6782	R	<1*	<.1
266	In Depth Leak Detection—*Gene Pullin*	830 Fernbrook Ct, Vacaville CA 95687	707-448-3260	R	<1*	<.1
267	Armada Security Group Inc—*Jaime Arizaga*	182 Culpepper Rd, South Mills NC 27976	252-207-1206	R	<1*	<.1
268	CT Holdings Inc (Los Angeles California)—*Valerie Vekkos*	PO Box 60016, San Diego CA 92166	323-966-5830	P	<1	<.1
269	LS Investigations—*R Lockhart*	PO Box 430872, Miami FL 33243	305-248-3558	R	<1*	<.1
270	Pinkerton Government Services Inc—*Kevin M Sandkuhler*	6850 Versar Ctr Ste 40, Springfield VA 22151	703-750-1098	R	N/A	200.0

TOTALS: SIC 7381 Detective & Armored Car Services
Companies: 270 26,838 671.3

7382 Security Systems Services

Rank	Company Name—*Executive Officer*	Address, City, State, Zip	Phone	Type	Fin	Empls
1	Tyco Fire and Security Services—*John Koch*	One Town Ctr Rd, Boca Raton FL 33486	561-988-3600	D	29,607*	100.0
2	Protection One Inc—*Tim Whall*	PO Box 49292, Wichita KS 67201	785-856-5500	S	354*	2.5
3	Red Hawk Industries—*Bipin Agarwal*	5690 DTC Blvd Ste 100, Greenwood Village CO 80111	303-779-6272	R	345*	1.1
4	Guardian Protection Services Inc—*Russell Cersosimo*	174 Thorn Hill Rd, Warrendale PA 15086		S	276*	1.0
5	Stanley Convergent Security Solutions Inc—*Brett Bontrager*	55 Shuman Blvd Ste 900, Naperville IL 60563	630-245-2500	R	254*	.8
6	Network Multifamily Corp	4221 W John Carpenter, Irving TX 75063		S	200*	.9
7	Monitronics International Inc—*Mike Haislip*	PO Box 814530, Dallas TX 75381	972-243-7443	R	178*	.6
8	Broadview Security Inc—*Robert Allen*	8880 Esters Blvd, Irving TX 75063	972-871-3500	R	172*	3.3
9	A and R Security Services Inc—*Vincent Ruffolo*	2552 W 135th St, Blue Island IL 60406	708-389-3830	R	79*	1.0
10	Statland Security Systems—*Paul Ferrara* Devcon Security Services Corp	1000 South Ave, Staten Island NY 10314	718-761-5700	S	60*	.3
11	Devcon International Corp—*Robert C Farenhem*	141 NW 20th St Ste G1, Boca Raton FL 33431	561-208-7200	S	56*	.6
12	RFI Communications and Security Systems—*Brad J Wilson*	360 Turtle Creek Ct, San Jose CA 95125	408-298-5400	R	52*	.2
13	ADT Advance Intergration (Norristown Pennsylvania)	2450 Blvd of the Gener, Norristown PA 19403	610-630-6790	D	50*	.1
14	Carter Brothers LLC—*John Carter*	100 Hartsfield Center, Atlanta GA 30354		R	47*	.2
15	Sword and Shield Enterprise Security—*John McNeely*	1431 Centerpoint Blvd, Knoxville TN 37932	865-244-3500	R	39*	<.1
16	Per Mar Security and Research Corp—*Jason Eicman*	1910 E Kimberly Rd, Davenport IA 52807	563-359-3200	R	34*	2.0
17	Bay Alarm Corp—*Mathew Westphal*	60 Berry Dr, Pacheco CA 94553	925-935-1100	R	34*	.6
18	Westec Intelligence Surveillance—*Kelby Hagar*	1089 Jordan Creek Pky, West Des Moines IA 50266	515-327-7200	R	32*	.3
19	Authentix Inc—*David Moxam*	4355 Excel Pkwy Ste 10, Addison TX 75001	469-737-4400	S	30*	.1
20	Videotronix Inc—*Thomas Asp*	401 W Travelers Trl, Burnsville MN 55337	952-894-5343	R	29*	.1
21	Electronic Technologies Corporation USA Inc—*Kaoru Yano*	43 Mill St, Dover Plains NY 12522		R	26*	.3
22	Rapid Response Monitoring Services Inc—*Russell Macdonnell*	400 W Division St Ste, Syracuse NY 13204	315-424-6794	R	24*	.4
23	Devcon Security Services Corp—*Robert Farenhem* Devcon International Corp	3880 N 28 Ter, Hollywood FL 33020	954-926-5200	S	23*	.3
24	Security One Systems—*Robert Newman*	5747 N Andrews Way, Fort Lauderdale FL 33309	954-351-1711	S	23*	.1
25	Elite Security Services Inc—*Michael Birchall*	495 W University Pkwy, Orem UT 84058		R	20*	.1
26	Safehome Security Inc—*Chad Christofferson*	4778 N 300 W Ste 230, Provo UT 84604	801-377-9111	R	20*	<.1
27	Crescent City Security Inc—*William Pendleton*	PO Box 144, Evansville IN 47701	812-426-2603	R	19*	.2
28	First Coast Security Services Inc—*E Cologne*	1 Independent Dr 1, Jacksonville FL 32202	904-598-1993	R	18*	.4
29	GDI LLC—*Andrew Gilmour*	150 S Wacker Dr Ste 45, Chicago IL 60606		R	15	.1
30	Managed Security Solutions Group—*Jeff Schmidt*	1600 Memorex Dr Rm 200, Santa Clara CA 95050	408-330-2860	R	15*	.1
31	Doyle Group Inc—*John Doyle*	792 Calkins Rd, Rochester NY 14623	585-244-3400	R	15*	.1
32	Industrial Defender—*Brian M Ahern*	16 Chestnut St Ste 300, Foxborough MA 02035	508-718-6700	R	14*	.1
33	Aronson Security Group Inc—*Phil Aronson*	1505 Westlake Ave N St, Seattle WA 98109	206-284-3553	R	13*	.1
34	Doyle Security Systems—*John Doyle* Doyle Group Inc	792 Calkins Rd, Rochester NY 14623	585-244-3400	D	13*	.1
35	Employer's Security Inc—*Nathan Soward*	PO Box 1045, Elkhart IN 46515	574-295-1020	R	13*	.3
36	Whitestone Group Inc—*John Clark*	4100 Regent St Ste C, Columbus OH 43219	614-501-7007	R	13*	.3
37	Philadelphia Protection Bureau Inc—*J Ladd*	197 Philips Rd, Exton PA 19341	610-903-4900	R	12*	.1
38	Guardian Security Services Inc	20800 Southfield Rd, Southfield MI 48075	248-423-1000	R	12*	.2
39	JSW Security Inc—*Stephen Coppola*	PO Box 25, Groveland MA 01834	978-373-9732	R	12*	.1
40	All American Private Security Inc—*Ashraf Salama*	101 N Orange Ave A, West Covina CA 91790	626-962-9620	R	11*	.3
41	Admiral Security Services Inc—*Mohamed Ahmed*	6536 Telg Ave Ste B102, Oakland CA 94609	510-557-0849	R	10*	.2
42	Sting Surveillance LLC—*Jonathan Fine*	5 Longevity Dr, Henderson NV 89014	702-737-8464	R	10	.1
43	Cooperative Choice LLC—*Lean Bran*	55 Satellite Blvd Nw, Suwanee GA 30024	770-963-0305	R	9*	<.1
44	Assured Information Security—*Charles Green*	PO Box 1182, Rome NY 13442	315-336-3306	R	9*	.1
45	Dallas Security Systems Inc	10731 Rockwall Rd, Dallas TX 75238	214-553-6103	R	9*	.1
46	Secure Mission Solutions LLC—*Mark Mcintosh*	1100 15th St Nw Ste 12, Washington DC 20005	202-783-4970	R	9*	.1
47	Fayette Electrical Service Inc—*James Reesor*	390 Blue Sky Pkwy, Lexington KY 40509	859-263-8620	R	9*	.1

Rank	Company Name—*Executive Officer*	Address, City, State, Zip	Phone	Type	Fin	Empls
48	Eid Passport Inc—*Jim Robell*	10450 Sw Nimbus Ave St, Portland OR 97223	503-924-5300	R	9*	.1
49	Sonitrol Communications Corp—*Todd Legget*	1000 Westlakes Dr Ste, Berwyn PA 19312	610-725-9706	S	8*	.1
50	Je Systems Inc—*Melanie Eakle*	PO Box 6246, Fort Smith AR 72906	918-626-4300	R	8*	.1
51	Apex Alarm LLC—*Diane Durfey*	5132 N 300 W, Provo UT 84604		R	8*	.1
52	Ultraguard Protective Systems Inc—*James Baker*	18 N Maple St, Woburn MA 01801	781-937-0555	R	8*	.1
53	Habitec Security Inc—*Nancy Smythe*	PO Box 352497, Toledo OH 43635	419-537-6768	R	8*	.1
54	Sonitrol Of Tallahassee Inc—*Doug Smith*	1136 Thomasville Rd, Tallahassee FL 32303	850-205-5000	R	8*	.1
55	Safetouch Security Systems Inc—*Lester Jackson*	9600 Sunbeam Ctr Dr, Jacksonville FL 32257	904-886-4664	R	7*	.1
56	Commercium Technology Inc—*Bill O'Brien*	148 Ave of Two Rivers, Rumson NJ 07760	732-933-0405	R	7*	<.1
57	Security Alarm Financing Enterprises Inc—*Paul Sargenti*	PO Box 5164, San Ramon CA 94583	925-830-4777	R	7*	.1
58	Kastle Systems Inc—*Piyush Sodha*	1501 Wilson Blvd, Arlington VA 22209		R	7*	.2
59	Emergency 24 Inc—*Dante Monteverde*	999 E Touhy Ste 500, Des Plaines IL 60018	773-777-0707	R	7*	.1
60	GBS Esecure LLC—*Brigitte Bailliez*	595 Blossom Rd Ste 312, Rochester NY 14610	585-506-4408	R	7*	<.1
61	Security Services Northwest Inc—*Joe D'amico*	PO Box 660, Port Townsend WA 98368	360-797-8480	R	7*	.1
62	Red Lion Group A Cintas Co—*Jeffrey Snellenburg*	21 Bon Air Dr, Warminster PA 18974	215-487-1000	R	7*	.1
63	Electro-Watchman Inc—*Brian Bertram*	1 Water St W Ste 110, Saint Paul MN 55107	651-227-8461	R	6*	.1
64	Mutual Central Alarm Services Inc—*Joel Cohen* Devcon Security Services Corp	10 W 46th St, New York NY 10036	212-768-0808	S	6*	<.1
65	Grey's Inc—*Hubert Grey*	1400 E 3rd St, Dayton OH 45403	937-461-3684	R	6*	.1
66	Nutech Fire And Security Inc—*Greg Detardo*	150 Candace Dr, Maitland FL 32751	407-629-7200	R	6*	.1
67	Affiliated Central Inc—*Stanley Oppenheim*	354 Neptune Ave, Brooklyn NY 11235	718-332-6100	R	6*	.1
68	Authorized Taxi Cab—*Behzad Bitaraf*	9468 Alverstone Ave, Los Angeles CA 90045	323-776-5324	R	6*	.1
69	Intervid Inc—*Collin Steyn*	4650 Wedgewood Blvd St, Frederick MD 21703	301-698-0086	R	6*	<.1
70	Infrasafe Inc—*Todd Flemming*	12612 Challenger Pkwy, Orlando FL 32826	407-859-3350	R	6*	.1
71	Sentry Surveillance Inc—*Steve Dimitrious*	840 Shallowford Rd Ne, Kennesaw GA 30144	770-592-0400	R	6*	.1
72	Sentinel Silent Alarm Company Inc—*Stanley Correia*	99-1036 Iwaena St, Aiea HI 96701	808-487-0088	R	6*	.1
73	Nefertiti Protective Services—*Shehab Abdelazim*	PO Box 361, Redlands CA 92373	909-384-9820	R	5*	.1
74	American Service Industries—*Stephen Kulp*	2930 W Imperial Hwy St, Inglewood CA 90303	323-779-4000	R	5*	.1
75	Protegrity USA Inc—*Suni Munshani*	5 High Ridge Park Ste, Stamford CT 06905	203-326-7200	R	5*	.1
76	Sos Systems Inc—*Thomas Smolinski*	3811 Harlem Rd Ste 1, Buffalo NY 14215	716-831-0151	R	5*	<.1
77	Midstate Security Company LLC—*Jim Salzwedel*	3945 Viaduct St Sw, Grandville MI 49418	616-257-1100	R	5*	.1
78	Smg Security Systems Inc—*John Reidy*	120 King St, Elk Grove Village IL 60007	847-593-0999	R	5*	.1
79	Sentinel Services Inc—*John Menter*	1765 Woodhaven Dr Ste, Bensalem PA 19020	215-633-7400	R	5*	.1
80	Communication Systems Inc—*Jim Landis*	415 N 3rd St, Allentown PA 18102	610-439-1600	R	5*	<.1
81	Snap Defense Systems LLC—*Oran Wolf*	1900 Campus Commons Dr, Reston VA 20191	703-766-6540	R	5*	<.1
82	Advanced Protection Industries Inc—*Michael Schubert*	26800 Laguna Hills Dr, Aliso Viejo CA 92656	949-215-8000	R	5*	.1
83	Talon Executive Services Inc—*Ronald William*	151 Kalmus Dr Ste A103, Costa Mesa CA 92626	714-434-7476	R	5*	.1
84	Jade Alarm Co—*Joe Pfefer*	7636 Troost Ave, Kansas City MO 64131	816-444-5233	R	5*	.1
85	Professionals LLC	1501 E Main St Ste 16, Meriden CT 06450		R	4*	<.1
86	Washington Alarm Inc—*John Woodman*	1253 S Jackson St, Seattle WA 98144	206-328-1800	R	4*	<.1
87	Safe-N-Sound Security Inc—*Ryan Torrence*	2833 Cleveland Ave Nw, Canton OH 44709	330-491-1148	R	4*	.1
88	Mcm Integrated Systems Inc—*Richard Mcmillan*	6961 Hayvenhurst Ave, Van Nuys CA 91406	818-780-3800	R	4*	<.1
89	Ontel Security Services Inc—*James Amato*	PO Box 579730, Modesto CA 05357	209-521-0200	R	4*	.1
90	California Security Alarms Inc—*Roger Carr*	PO Box 5445, San Mateo CA 94402	650-570-6500	R	4*	<.1
91	Electronic Security Systems Inc—*Martin Wietecha*	PO Box 220, Warren MI 48090	586-756-8400	R	4*	<.1
92	Gaston Security Inc—*Gregory Burns*	PO Box 219, Gasburg VA 23857	434-577-2716	R	4*	<.1
93	Secure System Inc—*Gregory Lawson*	1800 Bloomsbury Ave, Ocean NJ 07712	732-922-3609	R	4*	<.1
94	Integrated Security Technologies Inc—*Christine Lanning*	3375 Koapaka St Ste G3, Honolulu HI 96819	808-836-4094	R	4*	<.1
95	Dial One Security—*John Lindberg*	6114 Madison Rd, Cincinnati OH 45227	513-527-4400	R	4	<.1
96	Cymtec Systems Inc—*Andrew Rubin*	10845 Olive Blvd Ste 3, Saint Louis MO 63141	314-993-8700	R	4*	.1
97	S2 Security Corp—*John Moss*	50 Speen St Ste 300, Framingham MA 01701	508-663-2500	R	4*	.1
98	A and R Fixit Inc—*Jeffrey Nunberg*	1876 Nw 7th St, Miami FL 33125	305-324-8800	R	4*	<.1
99	Site Security Solutions Inc—*Shawn Rolison*	PO Box 131, Winder GA 30680		R	4*	.1
100	Safeguards Technology LLC—*Moshe Levy*	75 Atlantic St, Hackensack NJ 07601	201-488-1022	R	4*	<.1
101	Tactical Protection Corp—*Marlon Namorado*	PO Box 961408, Miami FL 33296	305-326-1175	R	4*	.1
102	USA Central Station Alarm Corp—*Bart Didden*	28 Willett Ave Fl 2, Port Chester NY 10573	914-939-6666	R	4*	.1
103	Digital Defense Inc—*Larry Hurtado*	9000 Tesoro Dr Ste 100, San Antonio TX 78217	210-822-2645	R	4*	<.1
104	Dickey Manufacturing Co—*Terry Mauger*	1315 E Main St, Saint Charles IL 60174	630-584-2918	R	3*	<.1
105	United Burglar Alarm Inc—*Martin Lane*	205 W Houston St, New York NY 10014	212-989-1700	R	3*	<.1
106	DJ Enterprises Incorporated Of Virginia—*David Jablonski*	2655 Duke St, Alexandria VA 22314	703-461-8100	R	3*	.1
107	Service Works Inc—*Stephen Govel*	95 Megill Rd, Farmingdale NJ 07727	732-919-7900	R	3*	<.1
108	All In 1 Security Services Inc—*Mary Parker*	3915 Cascade Rd Sw Ste, Atlanta GA 30331	404-691-4915	R	3*	.2
109	Amherst Alarm Inc—*Timothy Creenan*	435 Lawrence Bell Dr S, Buffalo NY 14221	716-632-4600	R	3*	<.1
110	Mcrobert's Protective Agency Inc—*Jesse Owens*	405 Atlantis Rd Ste A1, Cape Canaveral FL 32920	321-868-1876	R	3*	.1
111	Iep Ltd—*Charles Reader*	7701 E Gray Rd Ste 2, Scottsdale AZ 85260	480-951-3267	R	3*	<.1
112	United Central Control Inc—*Donald Munford*	8415 Datapoint Dr Ste, San Antonio TX 78229	210-477-1400	R	3*	.1
113	Bel Air Security Inc—*Carlos Sutton*	311 Robertson Blvd, Beverly Hills CA 90211	310-286-0010	R	3*	.1
114	Hawkeye Security Services LP—*Dallas Faulkner*	3201 W Benjamin Holt D, Stockton CA 95219	209-957-3333	R	3*	.1
115	Ibis USA Corp—*David Weekes*	1126 Elfin Ave, Capitol Heights MD 20743	202-812-9630	R	3*	<.1
116	Builder Security Group Inc—*Ronnie Evans*	12702 Cimarron Path, San Antonio TX 78249	210-877-1222	R	3*	<.1
117	Richmond Sprinkler Corp—*Sam Beach*	2540 Norcliff Rd, Richmond VA 23237	804-275-6800	R	3*	<.1
118	Huffman Security Company Inc—*Rex Huffman*	1312 Lonedell Rd, Arnold MO 63010	636-282-7233	R	3*	<.1
119	Oral Data Systems Inc—*Louis Weiss*	6955 Valjean Ave, Van Nuys CA 91406	818-994-6498	R	3*	<.1
120	Advanced Detection Technology LLC—*Dave Kesic*	618 N Carolina Ave, Maiden NC 28650	828-428-9569	R	3*	<.1
121	TEAM Technologies Inc (Cedar Falls Iowa)—*Mark Kittrell*	1205 Technology Pkwy, Cedar Falls IA 50613		R	3*	<.1
122	Bureau Workers Compensation	13430 Yarmouth Dr, Pickerington OH 43147	614-466-5109	R	3*	<.1
123	Sonitrol Of Hawaii Inc—*Ronald Jones*	PO Box 17928, Honolulu HI 96817	808-847-5966	R	3*	<.1
124	Mellon Security and Sound Systems Inc—*Harold Zeller*	7922 Coral St, Lantana FL 33462	561-395-2144	R	3*	<.1
125	Imac Group LLC	44 Wall St Fl 12, New York NY 10005	212-784-9143	R	3*	<.1
126	South West Sonitrol Inc—*Frank Stewart*	4042 Doniphan Dr, El Paso TX 79922	915-587-1000	R	3*	<.1
127	Certified Alarm Company Of Alabama Inc—*Edward Buckley*	PO Box 237, Sheffield AL 35660	256-383-1225	R	3*	<.1
128	Electraserve Inc—*Dyan Concannon-Nelso*	3744 Sw 30th Ave, Fort Lauderdale FL 33312	954-327-9475	R	3*	<.1
129	Clarke Security Services Inc—*Jim Buckalew*	1275 W Roosevelt Rd St, West Chicago IL 60185	630-293-4497	R	3*	<.1
130	Sensormatic Hawaii Inc—*Richard Osborne*	99-1285 Halawa Valley, Aiea HI 96701	808-484-4000	R	3*	<.1
131	Commercial Instruments and Alarm Systems Inc—*John Lombardi*	2 Summit Ct Ste 306, Fishkill NY 12524	845-473-2000	R	2*	<.1
132	Audio Central Alarm Inc—*Patricia Obrien*	PO Box 2427, Saginaw MI 48605	989-755-0911	R	2*	<.1
133	Metrodial Corp—*Peter Lowitt*	25 Bethpage Rd, Hicksville NY 11801	516-681-8877	R	2*	<.1
134	Aaep Inc—*Debbie Lugan*	PO Box 54, New Albany IN 47151	812-948-2601	R	2*	.1
135	X Strategy Inc—*Clifford Lewis*	PO Box 663, Harrison ME 04040	207-583-6700	R	2*	<.1

Note: An asterisk (*) indicates an estimated financial figure. The company type code used is as follows: R = Private, P = Public, S = Private Subsidiary, B = Public Subsidiary, D = Division, J = Joint Venture, I = Investment Fund.

COMPANY RANKINGS BY SALES WITHIN 4-DIGIT SIC

Rank	Company Name—*Executive Officer*	Address, City, State, Zip	Phone	Type	Fin	Empls
136	Elk Products Inc—*Joel Rosson*	PO Box 100, Hildebran NC 28637	828-397-4200	R	2*	<.1
137	Fidelity Telealarm LLC—*Jack Gulati*	2501 Kutztown Rd, Reading PA 19605	610-929-4200	R	2*	<.1
138	Safeco Alarm Systems Inc—*Paul Sistare*	PO Box 1849, Kingston NY 12402	845-338-4440	R	2*	<.1
139	Metro Communication Systems Inc—*David Cossu*	PO Box 1267, Grapevine TX 76099	972-621-8700	R	2*	<.1
140	Archambo Enterprises Inc—*Duane Archambo*	1798 Northern Star Dr, Traverse City MI 49696	231-922-5933	R	2*	<.1
141	Linstar Inc—*Mary Cornell*	430 Lawrence Bell Dr S, Buffalo NY 14221	716-631-9200	R	2*	<.1
142	Access Security Corp—*Daniel Cogan*	271 York Rd, Warminster PA 18974	215-443-8600	R	2*	<.1
143	Texguard Security Network Inc—*Kaj Berg*	7248 Gateway Blvd E, El Paso TX 79915	915-594-6664	R	2*	.1
144	Federal Alarm Inc—*Mary Omara*	PO Box 10040, Trenton NJ 08650	609-585-3912	R	2*	<.1
145	Silent Partner Security Systems Inc—*Samuel Rogers*	PO Box 445, Marshall VA 20116	540-364-3872	R	2*	<.1
146	Technintel Systems Inc—*Frank Stalzer*	766 Deltona Blvd Ste A, Deltona FL 32725	386-860-9600	R	2*	<.1
147	Vigilant Video Inc—*Shawn Smith*	2021 Las Positas Ct St, Livermore CA 94551	925-398-2079	R	2*	<.1
148	Absolute Security And Technologies Inc—*Richard Perini*	679 E Easy St Ste C, Simi Valley CA 93065	805-581-0771	R	2*	<.1
149	Alarm Masters—*Charles R Turner*	11285 Southwest Fwy St, Houston TX 77031		R	2*	<.1
150	Multilink Security Inc—*David Baker*	PO Box 461028, San Antonio TX 78246	210-494-9112	R	2*	<.1
151	Dataguise Inc—*Manmeet Bhasin*	2201 Walnut Ave Ste 26, Fremont CA 94538	510-824-1036	R	2*	<.1
152	Kelly Protection—*Patrick Kelly*	1317 N San Fernando Bl, Burbank CA 91504	818-363-7134	R	2*	<.1
153	San Angelo Security Service Inc—*James Mchellan*	4409 Crawford Dr, Abilene TX 79602	325-692-0480	R	2*	<.1
154	Patriot Alarm Systems Inc—*Edward O'hearn*	292 Bailey St, Canton MA 02021	781-821-2325	R	2*	<.1
155	Sanders Security Inc—*John Sanders*	1036 W Main St, Dothan AL 36301	334-673-2686	R	2*	<.1
156	Access Control Technologies Inc—*Randy Mann*	511 Fairground Ct, Nashville TN 37211	615-333-6300	R	2*	<.1
157	Community Alert Network Inc—*Kenneth Baechel*	255 Washington Ave Ext, Albany NY 12205	518-862-0987	R	2*	<.1
158	Security Claims Consultants—*David Gordon*	4822 Mcknight Rd, Pittsburgh PA 15237	412-366-5332	R	2*	<.1
159	Cms Development Group LLC	PO Box 454, Bellmawr NJ 08099	856-308-8890	R	2*	<.1
160	IHR Security LLC—*Renick E*	1107 12th St, Wichita Falls TX 76301	940-766-1553	R	2*	.1
161	Marker Security Inc—*Marshall Rodriguez*	395 May St 1, Worcester MA 01602	508-421-4849	R	2*	<.1
162	Transcontinental Security Inc—*Scott Moore*	1418 W I65 Service Rd, Mobile AL 36693	251-662-0500	R	1*	<.1
163	Blanket Security Inc—*Fred Sandefer*	6750 Poplar Ave Ste 11, Memphis TN 38138	901-756-5006	R	1*	<.1
164	Great Plains Security Inc—*Michael Perrin*	14340 Bradford Ct, Waverly NE 68462	402-786-5218	R	1*	<.1
165	Interstate Security—*Gary Rice*	1500 E Fourth Plain Bl, Vancouver WA 98661	360-750-9955	R	1*	<.1
166	Central Alarm Signal Inc—*Robert Hakim*	13400 W 7 Mile Rd, Detroit MI 48235	313-864-8900	R	1*	<.1
167	Georgia Security Systems—*Diane Freeland*	73 Lawrenceville St, Mcdonough GA 30253	678-432-3049	R	1*	<.1
168	Central Systems and Security Service—*Joe Weaver*	4545 Samuel St, Sarasota FL 34233	941-923-5233	R	1*	<.1
169	Alarm Monitoring Of Cincinnati Inc—*Nancy Conner*	4507 W 8th St, Cincinnati OH 45238	513-251-7511	R	1*	<.1
170	Commercial Technology Group Inc—*C Earle*	7001 Gibsonton Dr, Gibsonton FL 33534	813-671-3575	R	1*	<.1
171	D 3 Inc—*Don Friedrichs*	28800 Salmon River Hwy, Grand Ronde OR 97347	503-339-6447	R	1*	<.1
172	Ibs Electronic and Security Inc—*Jonathan Waitt*	225 Armory St, Springfield MA 01104	413-739-2271	R	1*	<.1
173	Icu Security LLC	128 Holiday Ct Ste 121, Franklin TN 37067	615-786-0912	R	1*	<.1
174	Protection Source LLC	404 W Broadway Rd Ste, Tempe AZ 85282	480-730-1466	R	1*	<.1
175	Priebe Security Services—*Katarzyna Priebe*	7940 Shoal Creek Blvd, Austin TX 78757	512-340-1555	R	1*	.1
176	Michael Stapleton Associates Ltd—*Michael O'neil*	9 Murray St Fl 2, New York NY 10007	212-509-1336	R	1*	<.1
177	United States Intelligence Agency Inc—*Larry Keffer*	PO Box 1177, Boca Raton FL 33429	813-930-2323	R	1*	<.1
178	Culpepper and Associates Security Services Inc—*Louis Culpepper*	1810 Water Pl SE Ste 1, Atlanta GA 30339	770-916-0060	R	1*	<.1
179	American Connection Information Systems Inc—*Eve Berliet*	17 High St, Norwalk CT 06851	203-945-2020	R	1*	<.1
180	New England Security Inc—*Jeffery A Morrone*	PO Box 562, Westerly RI 02891	401-596-0660	R	1*	<.1
181	Minatronics Corp—*Edwin P Wilson*	1 Trimont Ln 850-C, Pittsburgh PA 15211	412-488-6435	R	1*	<.1
182	Predictive Maintenance Inspection Inc—*F Scott Hoover*	PO Box 429, Madison AL 35758	256-721-0100	R	1*	<.1
183	Sirius Systems Inc—*Rob Giordano*	14795 N 78th Way No 10, Scottsdale AZ 85260	480-998-5157	R	1*	<.1
184	Fortress Security and Life Safety—*Jerrod Smith*	2000 E Randol Mill Rd, Arlington TX 76011	817-226-7233	R	1*	<.1
185	Centurion Alarm Services Inc—*Ralph Marchesano*	10223 Clodine Rd, Richmond TX 77407	281-277-7070	R	1*	<.1
186	Clarke Electric Company LLC	50 E Highland Rd, Northfield OH 44067	330-467-0232	R	<1*	<.1

TOTALS: SIC 7382 Security Systems Services
Companies: 186

					32,795	125.2

7383 News Syndicates

Rank	Company Name—*Executive Officer*	Address, City, State, Zip	Phone	Type	Fin	Empls
1	Bloomberg LP—*Daniel Doctoroff*	731 Lexington Ave, New York NY 10022	212-318-2000	R	6,250	12.4
2	Reuters America LLC—*Tom Glocer*	3 Times Sq, New York NY 10036	646-223-4000	S	854*	3.8
3	United Press International Inc—*Nicholas Chaiaia*	1510 H St NW, Washington DC 20005	202-898-8000	R	638*	.1
4	Associated Press—*Thomas Curley*	450 W 33rd St, New York NY 10001	212-621-1500	R	466*	3.7
5	Thomson Reuters (Markets) LLC—*Brian Vaughan*	3 Times Sq, New York NY 10036	646-223-4000	R	155*	2.5
6	PR Newswire Association Inc—*Ninah Chacko*	350 Hudson St Ste 300, New York NY 10014		S	54*	.3
7	Business Wire—*Cathy Baron Tamraz*	44 Montgomery St 39th, San Francisco CA 94104	415-986-4422	S	43*	.5
8	CONUS Communications Company LP	3415 University Ave, Saint Paul MN 55114	651-642-4645	S	33*	.3
9	New York Times Syndication Sales Corp—*William Abrams*	122 E 42nd St 14th Fl, New York NY 10168	212-499-3300	S	21*	.1
10	Tribune Media Services Inc—*David D Williams*	435 N Michigan Ave Ste, Chicago IL 60611	312-222-4444	S	20*	.5
11	Burrelle's/Luce—*Robert Waggoner*	75 E Northfield Rd, Livingston NJ 07039	973-992-6600	R	19*	.3
12	United Feature Syndicate Inc—*Douglas R Stern*	200 Madison Ave 4th Fl, New York NY 10016	212-293-8500	S	16*	.1
13	Mediacentrix Inc—*David Garrett*	10940 Wilshire Blvd, Los Angeles CA 90024	310-443-4193	R	5*	<.1
14	Network News Service LLC	524 W 57th St Ste 5380, New York NY 10019	212-974-6102	R	4*	.1
15	Dorf Feature Service Inc—*Sid Dorfman*	187 Mill Ln, Mountainside NJ 07092	908-789-3355	R	4*	<.1
16	Mediii News Service—*Mindy Trossman*	105 W Adams St Ste 200, Chicago IL 60603	312-503-4100	R	3*	.1
17	WYZZ Licensee Inc	3131 N University, Peoria IL 61604	309-688-3131	S	2*	<.1
18	Marshall News Messenger Inc—*Kay Dorman*	PO Box 730, Marshall TX 75671	903-935-7355	R	1*	<.1

TOTALS: SIC 7383 News Syndicates
Companies: 18

					8,587	24.8

7384 Photofinishing Laboratories

Rank	Company Name—*Executive Officer*	Address, City, State, Zip	Phone	Type	Fin	Empls
1	Shutterfly Inc—*Jeffrey Housenbold*	2800 Bridge Pkwy, Redwood City CA 94065	650-610-5200	P	473	1.0
2	Peeq Media LLC—*Jeff Sinaw*	3030 47th Ave Ste F200, Long Island City NY 11101	212-213-8310	R	45*	.3
3	Gamma Photo Labs—*Douglas Goddard*	314 W Superior St, Chicago IL 60654	312-337-0022	R	43*	.1
4	Qualex Inc—*Matthias Freund*	3404 N Duke St, Durham NC 27704	919-383-8535	S	30*	.3
5	H and H Color Lab Inc—*Wayne Haub*	8906 E 67th St, Raytown MO 64133	816-358-6677	R	19*	.3
6	Advanced Photographic Solutions LLC—*Bill Mcconkey*	PO Box 8019, Cleveland TN 37320	423-479-5481	R	18*	.3
7	DNP IMS America Corp	4524 Enterprise Dr NW, Concord NC 28027		S	13*	.1
8	PhotoWorks Inc	1 American Rd, Cleveland OH 44144		S	12*	.1
9	Mckenna Professional Imaging—*Kelly Kenna*	102 W Morten Ave, Phoenix AZ 85021	602-522-2708	R	11*	.4
10	Graphic Systems Group Inc—*William Hufstader*	33 E 17th St, New York NY 10003	212-242-8787	R	9*	.1
11	Cpq Colorchrome Inc—*Ronald Coppinger*	PO Box 8014, Cleveland TN 37320	423-479-6186	R	8*	.2
12	Great Big Pictures Inc—*Mary Chandler*	5701 Manufacturers Dr, Madison WI 53704	608-257-7071	R	8*	.1

Rank	Company Name—Executive Officer	Address, City, State, Zip	Phone	Type	Fin	Empls
13	Rekcut Photographic Inc—Leonard Tucker	PO Box 1928, Saint Augustine FL 32085	904-829-6541	R	7*	.1
14	Shiflet Imaging Inc—Charles Matchett	459 Franklin Ave 61, Aliquippa PA 15001	724-375-6674	R	7*	.1
15	Northwest Professional Color Inc—Arden Glanzer	PO Box 517, West Fargo ND 58078	701-282-3577	R	7*	.1
16	Photomation—Matt Hesketh	2551 W La Palma, Anaheim CA 92801	714-236-2121	R	7*	<.1
17	Harold's Photo Centers Inc—Robert Hanson	912 W 41st St, Sioux Falls SD 57105	605-336-0879	R	7*	.1
18	Filmet Color Laboratories Incorporated A Close Corp—Richard Bachelder	1051 Russellton Rd, Cheswick PA 15024	724-265-5500	R	6*	.1
19	Jones Photo Inc—Teri Tavour	2901 N Country Club Rd, Tucson AZ 85716	520-327-9521	R	5*	.1
20	Ez Prints Inc—James Bardin	1890 Beaver Ridge Cir, Norcross GA 30071	678-405-5500	R	5*	.1
21	30 Minute Photo Etc—Mitchell Goldstone	3 Corporate Park, Irvine CA 92606	949-474-3942	R	5*	<.1
22	Wilson Photofinishing Corp—Bruce Laumeister	254 Benmont Ave Ste 1, Bennington VT 05201	802-442-6371	R	5*	.1
23	Genti Studios Inc—Kiran Genti	1825 W Mockingbird Ln, Dallas TX 75235	214-951-9696	R	4*	.1
24	Portraits International of The Southwest Inc—James Kraxner	PO Box 6644, Houston TX 77265	713-780-4242	R	4*	<.1
25	5 Star Image Inc—Peter Fradin	2212 E McDowell, Phoenix AZ 85006	602-468-9970	R	3*	.1
26	Digichrome Imaging Inc—Ira Nutis	3487 E Fulton St, Columbus OH 43227	614-239-5200	S	3*	<.1
27	Burrell Professional Labs Inc—Gene Baldino	1311 Merrillville Rd, Crown Point IN 46307	219-663-3210	S	3*	<.1
28	JD Color Lab—Daphine Hicks	3018 Corunna Rd, Flint MI 48503	810-239-8671	R	3*	<.1
29	Capitol Filmworks Inc—Joan Brinsfield	PO Box 6999, Montgomery AL 36106	334-269-3456	R	3*	<.1
30	Baumgardner Imaging Inc—Richard Baumgardner	208 S 5th Ave, Yakima WA 98902	509-575-1770	R	3*	<.1
31	Photographic Works Inc—Mary Findysz	3550 E Grant Rd, Tucson AZ 85716	520-327-7291	R	3*	<.1
32	Cooper Enterprises Inc—Aida Cooper	4555 S Palo Verde Rd S, Tucson AZ 85714	520-748-9094	R	3*	<.1
33	Color Reflections Inc—Eric Berger	400 Green St, Philadelphia PA 19123	215-627-4686	R	3*	<.1
34	Photo Ad Inc—Jackie Koda	145 Prado Rd, San Luis Obispo CA 93401	805-543-4624	R	2*	<.1
35	Academy Productions Inc—Medford Greenstreet	6100 Orr Rd, Charlotte NC 28213	704-596-8121	R	2*	<.1
36	Colortek—James Rodgers	10401 Jefferson Blvd, Culver City CA 90232	310-202-1984	R	2*	<.1
37	Inder Lali Color Lab Inc—Inder Mahendru	1 W 22nd St, New York NY 10010	212-206-7733	R	2*	<.1
38	Quantity Photos—Knight Harris	726 N Cahuenga Blvd, Los Angeles CA 90038	323-467-6178	R	2*	<.1
39	Pacific Color Inc—Bob Paasch	7107 Woodlawn Ave NE S, Seattle WA 98115	206-524-7200	R	2*	<.1
40	ProDPI—Caitlin Lazo	3890 S Windermere St, Englewood CO 80110	855-416-9212	R	2*	<.1
41	Burris Photography Inc—Jeffery Burris	751 N Country Club Dr, Mesa AZ 85201	480-924-1945	R	2*	<.1
42	Professional Color Service Inc—Louis Darre	PO Box 55670, Metairie LA 70055	504-835-3551	R	2*	<.1
43	Vista Color Imaging Inc—Paul Gallo	2048 Fulton Rd, Cleveland OH 44113	216-651-2830	R	2*	<.1
44	HAS Images Inc—Harry Stiller	136 N Saint Clair St S, Dayton OH 45402	937-222-3856	R	2*	<.1
45	Specialty Photo Lab LLC—Randy Wright	230 E Cota St, Santa Barbara CA 93101	805-965-1832	R	2*	<.1
46	Vann Photo Services Inc—William Cleve	2420 Oak Valley Dr, Ann Arbor MI 48103	734-665-3686	R	2*	<.1
47	Abc Photo And Imaging Services Inc—Wesley Billstone	9016 Prince William St, Manassas VA 20110	703-369-1906	R	2*	<.1
48	East Greenwich Photo and Studio Inc—Susan Sundlun	50 Cliff St, East Greenwich RI 02818	401-884-0220	R	2*	<.1
49	LWB Corp—Bruce Laumeister	254 Benmont Ave Ste 1, Bennington VT 05201	802-442-3114	R	1*	<.1
50	Mrpc Inc—Kristine Johnson	1540 Lowell St, Elyria OH 44035	440-326-0234	R	1*	<.1
51	Azura Photo Albums LLC	6680 Jones Mill Ct, Norcross GA 30092	770-662-3935	R	1*	<.1
52	Mark Gordon Co—Mark Gordon	12200 W Olympic Blvd S, Los Angeles CA 90064	310-943-6401	R	1*	<.1
53	David Photo Service Inc—Kenneth Gallisdorfer	910 Niagara Falls Blvd, Buffalo NY 14223	716-835-4620	R	1*	<.1
54	Putnam Imaging Corp—William Mc Cann	4 Eagle Rd, Danbury CT 06810	203-790-9650	R	1*	<.1
55	Lenzart Inc—David Jaekle	1872 Hertel Ave, Buffalo NY 14214	716-834-0142	R	1*	<.1
56	Fast Foto Inc—Mark Patterson	612 S Truman Blvd, Festus MO 63028	636-933-0171	R	1*	<.1
57	Dale Laboratories Inc—Dale Farkas	2960 Simms St, Hollywood FL 33020	954-925-0103	R	1*	<.1
58	Perra and O'toole Inc—Patrick O'toole	10 Harvard St, Worcester MA 01609	508-752-1924	R	1*	<.1
59	Bradley Images and Photography Inc—Bradley Zisow	1498 Reisterstown Rd S, Pikesville MD 21208	410-902-6664	R	<1*	<.1

TOTALS: SIC 7384 Photofinishing Laboratories
Companies: 59

					826	4.7

7389 Business Services Nec

Rank	Company Name—Executive Officer	Address, City, State, Zip	Phone	Type	Fin	Empls
1	RGIS Inventory Specialists—Paul Street	2000 E Taylor Rd, Auburn Hills MI 48326	248-651-2511	R	28,506*	40.0
2	Waste Management Inc—Barry H Caldwell	1001 Fannin Ste 4000, Houston TX 77002	713-512-6200	P	21,476	42.8
3	Liberty Interactive Group—Gregory Maffei	12300 Liberty Blvd, Englewood CO 80112	720-875-5400	S	10,982	.1
4	Visa Inc—Joseph W Saunders	PO Box 8999, San Francisco CA 94128	415-932-2100	P	9,188	7.5
5	eBay Inc—John Donahoe	2065 Hamilton Ave, San Jose CA 95125	408-376-7400	P	8,541	17.7
6	SafeRent Inc—John Long	789 Sherman St Ste 385, Denver CO 80203		S	7,599*	35.4
7	Spectrum Group International Inc—Gregory N Roberts	1063 McGaw, Irvine CA 92614	949-955-1250	P	7,202	.2
8	MasterCard Inc—Ajay Banga	2000 Purchase St, Purchase NY 10577	914-249-2000	P	5,539	5.6
9	Fidelity National Information Services Inc—Frank R Martire	601 Riverside Ave, Jacksonville FL 32204	904-854-5000	P	5,270	33.0
10	Dci Marketing Inc—Joseph Asfour	PO Box 514010, Milwaukee WI 53203	414-228-7000	R	4,499*	.2
11	DynCorp International Inc—Steven F Gaffney	3190 Fairview Park Dr, Falls Church VA 22042	571-722-0210	S	3,387	23.0
12	Facebook Inc—Christopher Cox	156 University Ave, Palo Alto CA 94301	650-543-4800	R	3,313*	3.0
13	Alliance Data Systems Corp—Ed Heffernan	7500 Dallas Pkwy Ste 7, Plano TX 75024	214-494-3000	P	3,173	8.6
14	Belk Stores Services Inc—Thomas M Belk Jr	2801 W Tyvola Rd, Charlotte NC 28217	704-357-1000	S	2,969	23.2
15	West Corp—Thomas B Barker	11808 Miracle Hills Dr, Omaha NE 68154	402-963-1200	P	2,491	36.5
16	Convergys Corp—Philip A Odeen	PO Box 1638, Cincinnati OH 45201	513-723-7000	P	2,262	77.0
17	Freeman Cos—Joe Popolo	PO Box 660613, Dallas TX 75266	214-445-1000	R	2,259*	3.8
18	Zenta—Henry Hortenstine	3500 Maple Ave Ste 550, Dallas TX 75219	214-520-9615	S	2,174*	3.7
19	Lender Processing Services Inc—Jeffrey S Carbiener	601 Riverside Ave, Jacksonville FL 32204	904-854-5100	P	2,090	8.1
20	Transperfect Translations Inc—Elizabeth Elting	3 Park Ave 39th Fl, New York NY 10016	212-689-5555	R	2,069*	4.0
21	Software House International Inc—Thai Lee	33 Knightsbridge Rd, Piscataway NJ 08854	732-764-8888	R	2,051*	1.0
22	Summit Energy Services Inc—Steve Wilhite	10350 Ormsby Park Pl S, Louisville KY 40223	502-429-3800	R	2,000*	.2
23	Resolute Systems Inc—Ryan Hamilton	1550 N Prospect Ave, Milwaukee WI 53202	414-276-4774	R	1,980*	2.8
24	Avanade Inc—Adam Warby	818 Stewart St Ste 400, Seattle WA 98101	206-239-5600	R	1,959*	13.0
25	LiveBridge—Pat Hanlin	7303 SE Lake Rd, Portland OR 97267	503-652-6000	R	1,956*	3.0
26	Apptis Inc—Burt Notini	4800 Westfields Blvd, Chantilly VA 20151	703-745-6016	R	1,944*	1.5
27	Visa USA Inc—Joe Saunders Visa Inc	PO Box 8999, San Francisco CA 94128	650-432-3200	S	1,900*	3.6
28	Global Payments Inc—Paul R Garcia	10 Glenlake Pkwy NE No, Atlanta GA 30328	770-829-8000	P	1,860	3.8
29	Sitel—Dagoberto Quintana	2 American Center 3102, Nashville TN 37203	615-301-7100	S	1,700*	66.0
30	Presentation Services - Long Beach CA—Mike Mcilwain Audio Visual Services Corp	111 West Ocean Blvd St, Long Beach CA 90802	562-366-0620	S	1,397*	3.0
31	Maritz Performance Improvement Co—Steve Maritz	1000 Town Center Ste 1, Southfield MI 48075	248-948-4500	S	1,300*	.1
32	Freeman Decorating Co—Joseph V Popolo Jr Freeman Cos	8801 Ambassador Row, Dallas TX 75247	214-634-1463	S	1,202	31.2
33	Affinion Group Holdings Inc—Nathaniel J Lipman	6 High Ridge Pk, Stamford CT 06905	203-956-1000	S	1,200*	3.0

Note: An asterisk (*) indicates an estimated financial figure. The company type code used is as follows: R = Private, P = Public, S = Private Subsidiary, B = Public Subsidiary, D = Division, J = Joint Venture, I = Investment Fund.

COMPANY RANKINGS BY SALES WITHIN 4-DIGIT SIC

Rank	Company Name—Executive Officer	Address, City, State, Zip	Phone	Type	Fin	Empls
34	Phoenix International Freight Services Ltd—Stephane Rambaud	712 N Central Ave, Wood Dale IL 60191		R	1,189*	1.9
35	Marathon Cheese Corp—John Skoug	PO Box 185, Marathon WI 54448	715-443-2211	R	1,169*	2.0
36	Moneygram International Inc—Pamela H Patsley	1550 Utica Ave S, Saint Louis Park MN 55416	952-591-3000	P	1,167	2.3
37	InfoCision Management Corp—Carl Albright	325 Springside Dr, Akron OH 44333	330-668-1400	R	1,078*	4.1
38	Overstockcom Inc—Patrick M Byrne	6350 S 3000 E, Salt Lake City UT 84121	801-947-3100	P	1,054	1.5
39	Emdeon Business Services LLC—George I Lazenby	3055 Lebanon Pike, Nashville TN 37214	615-932-3000	P	1,003	3.0
40	SHI International—Thai Lee	290 Davidson Ave, Somerset NJ 08873		R	993*	1.7
41	Hotelscom—Cheryl Rosner	10440 N Central Expy S, Dallas TX 75231	469-335-5825	S	987*	1.2
42	Viad Corp—Paul B Dykstra	1850 N Central Ave Ste, Phoenix AZ 85004	602-207-4000	P	942	3.4
43	Maximus Inc—Richard A Montoni	11419 Sunset Hills Rd, Reston VA 20190	703-251-8500	P	930	7.1
44	SHPS Inc—Rishabh Mehrotra	9200 Shelbyville Rd, Louisville KY 40222		S	879*	1.5
45	ModusLink Global Solutions Inc—Joseph C Lawler	1100 Winter St Ste 460, Waltham MA 02451	781-663-5001	P	876	4.0
46	Getty Images Inc—Jonathan D Klein	601 N 34th St, Seattle WA 98103	206-925-5000	R	858*	1.9
47	NAVTEQ Corp—Judson C Green	425 W Randolph St, Chicago IL 60606	312-894-7000	S	853*	3.3
48	First Health Benefits Administrators Corp—George Bennett	3200 Highland Ave, Downers Grove IL 60515	630-737-7900	S	843	5.5
49	Macquarie Infrastructure Company LLC—James Hooke	125 W 55th St 22nd Fl, New York NY 10019	212-231-1825	B	841	1.7
50	Sotheby's—William F Ruprecht	1334 York Ave, New York NY 10021	212-606-7000	P	832	1.4
51	Acusis LLC—Ray Dyer	4 Smithfield St, Pittsburgh PA 15222	412-209-1300	R	796*	1.2
52	George P Reintjes Company Inc—Robert J Reintjes Sr	PO Box 410856, Kansas City MO 64141	816-756-2150	R	789*	3.0
53	Vertrue Inc—Gary A Johnson	20 Glover Ave, Norwalk CT 06850	203-324-7635	R	755*	2.4
54	Disaboom Inc—John Walpuck	7730 E Belleview Ave S, Greenwood Village CO 80111	720-407-6530	P	752	<.1
55	CBIZ Inc—Steven L Gerard	6050 Oak Tree Blvd S S, Cleveland OH 44131	216-447-9000	P	733	5.3
56	Georgia Tech Research Corp—G Wayne Clough	505 10th St, Atlanta GA 30318	404-894-6962	R	720*	1.1
57	iPayment Inc—Greg S Daily	40 Burton Hills Blvd S, Nashville TN 37215	615-665-1858	R	718*	.3
58	Kentucky Lottery Corp—Arthur L Gleason Jr	1011 W Main St, Louisville KY 40202	502-560-1500	R	718*	.2
59	GoIndustry Michael Fox International—David S Fox GoIndustry USA Inc	11425 Cronhill Dr, Owings Mills MD 21117	410-654-7500	D	714*	.3
60	RWD Technologies Inc—Laurens MacLure Jr	5521 Research Park Dr, Baltimore MD 21228	410-869-1000	R	710*	1.2
61	CT Charlton and Associates Inc—Christopher T Charlton	24000 Greater Mack Ave, Saint Clair Shores MI 48080	586-775-2900	R	700	.1
62	NGTS LLC—J Brian Burkhead	8150 N Central Expy St, Dallas TX 75206	214-365-0600	R	696*	<.1
63	Yahoo! Search Marketing—Carol Bartz	74 N Pasadena Ave 3rd, Pasadena CA 91103	626-685-5600	S	663*	.9
64	CareerBuilder LLC—Matt Ferguson	200 N LaSalle St Ste 1, Chicago IL 60601	773-527-3600	J	654*	1.8
65	Bob Rohrman Auto Group—Bob Rohrman	701 Sagamore Pky S, Lafayette IN 47905	765-448-1000	R	648*	.9
66	Cardtronics Inc—Steven Rathgaber	3250 Briarpark Dr Ste, Houston TX 77042	832-308-4000	P	625	.6
67	BT Infonet	2160 E Grand Ave, El Segundo CA 90245	310-335-2600	R	622	1.1
68	Fair Isaac Corp—Mark Greene	901 Marquette Ave Ste, Minneapolis MN 55402	612-758-5200	P	620	2.0
69	Converge Inc—Frank Cavallaro	4 Technology Dr, Peabody MA 01960	978-538-8000	R	600*	.3
70	OKS-Ameridial Inc—Vinit Khanna	4535 Strausser St NW, North Canton OH 44720	330-497-4888	R	570*	1.5
71	Digitas Inc—David W Kenny	33 Arch St, Boston MA 02110	617-369-8000	S	566	1.7
72	WebMD Health Corp—Wayne T Gattinella	111 8th Ave 7th Fl, New York NY 10011	212-624-3700	P	559	1.7
73	Provest LLC—Scott Strady	4520 Seedling Cir, Tampa FL 33614	813-877-2844	R	556*	1.0
74	Coinmach Service Corp—Robert M Doyle	303 Sunnyside Blvd Ste, Plainview NY 11803	516-349-8555	R	555*	2.0
75	Wright Express Corp—Michael E Dubyak	97 Darling Ave, South Portland ME 04106	207-773-8171	P	553	.9
76	Resources Connection Inc—Don Murray	17101 Armstrong Ave, Irvine CA 92614	714-430-6400	P	546	3.0
77	Cross Country Group Inc—Sidney Wolk	One Cabot Rd, Medford MA 02155	781-396-3700	R	544*	1.0
78	TCIM Services Inc—John Magee	1013 Centre Rd Ste 403, Wilmington DE 19805	302-633-3000	R	533*	2.0
79	Transaction Network Services—Henry H Graham Jr	11480 Commerce Park Dr, Reston VA 20191	703-453-8300	P	527	1.2
80	NeuStar Inc—Lisa A Hook	21575 Ridgetop Cir, Sterling VA 20166	571-434-5400	P	527	1.0
81	SOURCECORP BPS Inc SOURCECORP Inc	369 Inverness Pky, Englewood CO 80112	303-790-8300	S	524*	.8
82	iSeva Inc—Vaibhav Tewari	3979 Freedom Cir 6th F, Santa Clara CA 95054		R	513*	1.0
83	Team Inc—Philip J Hawk	PO Box 123, Alvin TX 77512	281-331-6154	P	508	3.5
84	PartMiner Worldwide Inc—David Churchill	7807 E Peakview Ave St, Centennial CO 80111	303-200-5500	R	501*	.3
85	Bad Boy Entertainment Inc—Sean Combs	1710 Broadway, New York NY 10019	212-381-1540	R	500*	.6
86	kgb—Robert Pines	655 Madison Ave 21st F, New York NY 10065	212-909-8282	R	499	9.0
87	Telecheck Services Inc (Houston Texas)—Charles Drucker	PO Box 4514, Houston TX 77210	713-599-7600	S	490*	1.3
88	Cubic Applications Inc—Jimmie Balentine	4550 3rd Ave SE, Lacey WA 98503	360-493-6275	S	479	.9
89	SDI Media—Walter Schonfeld	10950 Washington Blvd, Culver City CA 90232	323-602-5455	S	476*	.8
90	Elephant Group Inc—Benny Aboud	3303 W Commercial Blvd, Fort Lauderdale FL 33309	954-657-9600	R	469*	.8
91	Green Dot Corp—Steven Streit	605 E Huntington Dr St, Los Angeles CA 90016	626-775-3400	P	467	.5
92	Convergys Corp (Ogden Utah)—David Dougherty Convergys Corp	1400 W 4400 S, Ogden UT 84405	801-629-6423	S	463*	9.0
93	Harland Clarke—Stanley Hollen	5267 Program Ave, Mounds View MN 55112	651-604-5300	S	451*	.9
94	aQuantive Inc—Clark M Kokich	821 2nd Ave Ste 1800, Seattle WA 98104	206-816-8700	S	442	2.1
95	ViA Marketing Design—John R Coleman	619 Congress St, Portland ME 04101	207-221-3000	R	435*	.2
96	Voxeo Corp—Jonathan Taylor	189 S Orange Av Ste 20, Orlando FL 32801	407-418-1800	R	430*	.1
97	PSCU Service Centers Inc—Mike Yatros Payment Systems for Credit Unions Inc	560 Carillon Pkwy, Saint Petersburg FL 33716	727-572-8822	S	421*	1.7
98	Freightquotecom Inc—Timothy A Barton	16025 W 113, Lenexa KS 66219	913-642-4700	R	420*	.9
99	WebEx Communications Inc—Subrah Iyar	3979 Freedom Cir, Santa Clara CA 95054	408-435-7000	S	419*	2.4
100	SOURCECORP Inc—Ed H Bowman Jr	3232 McKinney Ave Ste, Dallas TX 75204	214-740-6500	R	415	4.2
101	MCS Group Inc—Rosemary Gould Esposito	1601 Market St Ste 800, Philadelphia PA 19103	215-246-0900	R	411*	.7
102	Kratos Defense and Security Solutions Inc—Eric M DeMarco	4820 Eastgate Mall Ste, San Diego CA 92121	858-812-7300	P	409	2.9
103	YUM! Restaurants International Inc—Graham Allan	14841 Dallas Pky, Dallas TX 75254	972-338-7700	S	407*	1.5
104	Lionbridge Technologies Inc—Rory J Cowan	1050 Winter St Ste 230, Waltham MA 02451	781-434-6000	P	405	4.5
105	Audio Visual Services Corp—Digby Davies	111 West Ocean Blvd St, Long Beach CA 90802	562-366-0620	R	401*	3.0
106	G1440 Holdings Inc—Larry Fiorino	2031 Clipper Park Rd S, Baltimore MD 21211	410-843-3800	S	397*	.6
107	Arbinet Corp—Shawn F O'Donnell	460 Herndon Pky Ste 15, Herndon VA 20170	703-456-4100	R	372*	.1
108	Claritas Inc	9276 Scranton Rd Ste 3, San Diego CA 92121	858-622-0800	S	368*	.6
109	Websense Inc—Gene Hodges	10240 Sorrento Valley, San Diego CA 92121	858-320-8000	P	364	1.5
110	HMS Holdings Corp—William Lucia	401 Park Ave S, New York NY 10016	212-857-5000	P	364	2.2
111	Jack Morton Inc—Josh McCall	919 3rd Ave 14th Fl, New York NY 10022	212-401-7000	R	355	.6
112	PRA International—Terrance J Bieker	4130 ParkLake Ave Ste, Raleigh NC 27612	919-786-8200	R	338*	2.7
113	Alta Resources Corp—James Bere	120 N Commercial St, Neenah WI 54956	920-751-5800	R	338*	.8
114	Safeguard Scientifics Inc—Peter J Boni	435 Devon Pk Dr Bldg 8, Wayne PA 19087	610-293-0600	P	337	<.1
115	Virtual Chip Exchange Inc—Michael Wood	140 Fell Ct, Hauppauge NY 11788	631-851-2808	S	332*	.4
116	APAC Customer Services Inc—Kevin T Keleghan	2201 Waukegan Rd Ste 3, Bannockburn IL 60015	847-374-4980	S	326	13.4
117	Eastern Sales and Marketing Co—Mike Freda	2 Van Riper Rd, Montvale NJ 07645	201-307-9100	R	325*	.6
118	DG FastChannel Inc—Neil Nguyen	750 W John Carpenter F, Irving TX 75039	972-581-2000	P	325	1.7

Rank	Company Name—*Executive Officer*	Address, City, State, Zip	Phone	Type	Fin	Empls
119	Global Healthcare Exchange LLC—*Bruce Johnson*	1315 W Century Dr, Louisville CO 80027	720-887-7000	R	316*	.5
120	Premier Global Services Inc—*Boland T Jones*	3280 Peachtree Rd NE S, Atlanta GA 30305	404-262-8400	R	315*	2.7
121	Astra Group (Overland Park Kansas)—*Shane Jones*	5913 Woodson, Mission KS 66202	913-378-1900	R	300*	.3
122	CCH Legal Information Services—*Richard Flynn*	3 Winners Circle, New York NY 12005	212-894-8940	D	298*	1.2
123	Precision Response Corp—*Steven Richards*	8151 Peters Rd Ste 300, Plantation FL 33324	954-693-3700	S	297*	9.0
124	Broadlane Inc—*Patrick Ryan*	13727 Noel Rd Ste 1400, Dallas TX 75240	972-813-7500	R	282*	.5
125	Advance Presort Service Inc—*Dennis Mac Harg*	4258 N Knox Ave, Chicago IL 60641	773-736-8333	R	278*	.4
126	PFSweb Inc—*Mark C Layton*	500 N Central Expy Ste, Plano TX 75074	972-881-2900	P	275	1.1
127	Quality Demonstration Services Inc—*Linda Moody*	7560 N Del Mar Ave, Fresno CA 93711	559-448-9173	R	271*	6.6
128	StarTek Inc—*Chad Carlson*	44 Cook St Ste 400, Denver CO 80206	303-262-4500	P	265	8.9
129	Master Translating Services Inc—*Martha Cordero-Esquivel*	10651 N Kendall Dr Ste, Miami FL 33176		R	256*	.4
130	Alliance Inspection Management—*Jim Yates*	330 Golden Shore Ste 4, Long Beach CA 90802	562-432-5050	R	255*	.5
131	Provide Commerce Inc—*Blake T Bilstad*	4840 Eastgate Mall, San Diego CA 92121	858-729-2800	S	253*	.3
132	ExlService Holdings Inc—*Rohit Kapoor*	280 Park Ave 38th Fl, New York NY 10017	212-277-7100	P	253	12.7
133	World Hotels AG—*Robert Hornman*	152 W 57th St 33rd Fl, New York NY 10019	212-956-0200	R	250*	.1
134	Norstan Inc (Minnetonka Minnesota)—*Donna Warner*	5101 Shady Oak Rd, Minnetonka MN 55343	952-303-8800	S	249*	1.2
135	Welocalize Inc—*E Smith Yewell*	241 E 4th Ste 207, Frederick MD 21701	301-668-0330	R	240*	.4
136	Icon International Inc—*John P Kramer*	4 Stamford Plz 15th Fl, Stamford CT 06902	203-328-2300	S	235*	.2
137	SITEL Insurance Marketing Services Inc—*David Garner* Sitel	2115 Windsor Spring Rd, Augusta GA 30906	706-796-7035	S	234*	.4
138	Intrado Inc—*George K Heinrichs* West Corp	1601 Dry Creek Dr, Longmont CO 80503	720-494-5800	S	226*	1.2
139	Fair Isaac International Corp—*Mark Greene* Fair Isaac Corp	200 Smith Ranch Rd, San Rafael CA 94903	415-446-6000	S	222*	.4
140	Garden City Group Inc—*David Isaac*	1985 Marcus Ave, Lake Success NY 11042	631-470-5000	S	217*	.4
141	Time-Life Customer Service Inc	PO Box 4002011, Des Moines IA 50340		R	217*	.4
142	Intuit Financial Services—*Brad Smith*	21215 Burbank Blvd Ste, Woodland Hills CA 91367		S	214	.8
143	Emtec Inc—*Dinesh R Desai*	11 Diamond Rd, Springfield NJ 07081	973-376-4242	P	212	.6
144	Durham Exchange Club Industries Inc—*Alan Wayne*	1717 Lawson St, Durham NC 27703	919-596-1341	R	207*	.4
145	Ross Marine LLC—*Arthur Swygert*	2676 Swygert Blvd, Johns Island SC 29455	843-559-0379	R	201*	<.1
146	Sonicwall Inc—*Matthew Medeiros*	1143 Borregas Ave, Sunnyvale CA 94089	408-745-9600	R	201	.8
147	American Systems Engineering Corp—*Gary Lisota*	PO Box 8988, Virginia Beach VA 23452	757-463-6666	J	200*	2.0
148	Market America Inc—*James H Ridinger*	1302 Pleasant Ridge Rd, Greensboro NC 27409	336-605-0040	R	198	.4
149	CoStar Group Inc—*Andrew C Florance*	1331 L St NW, Washington DC 20005	202-346-6500	P	193	1.5
150	Liquidity Services Inc—*William Angrick III*	1920 L St NW 6th Fl, Washington DC 20036	202-467-6868	P	192	.7
151	Payment Systems for Credit Unions Inc—*David J Serlo*	560 Carillon Pky, Saint Petersburg FL 33716	727-572-7723	R	190*	.8
152	Intraco Corp—*Nicola Antakli*	530 Stephenson Hwy, Troy MI 48083	248-585-6900	R	188*	.3
153	SupplyCore Inc—*Peter Provenzano*	303 N Main St Ste 800, Rockford IL 61101	815-964-7940	R	187*	.1
154	Limelight Networks Inc—*Jeffrey W Lunsford*	222 S Mill Ave, Tempe AZ 85281	602-850-5000	P	183	.2
155	Commission Junction Inc—*Tom Vadnaif*	530 E Montecito St, Santa Barbara CA 93103	805-730-8000	S	183*	.3
156	Excess Technologies LLC—*Joel Holtzman*	1050 Vintage Club Dr, Duluth GA 30097		R	180*	<.1
157	Dice Holdings Inc—*Scot W Melland*	1040 Avenue of the Ame, New York NY 10018	212-725-6550	P	179	.4
158	PayPal Inc—*Scott Thompson* eBay Inc	2211 N 1st St, San Jose CA 95131	408-967-1000	S	177*	.6
159	Classmates Media Corp—*Mark R Goldston*	21301 Burbank Blvd, Woodland Hills CA 91367	818-287-3000	S	177*	.3
160	Higher One Holdings Inc—*Dean Hatton*	25 Science Pk, New Haven CT 06511		P	176	.7
161	2 Places at 1 Time Inc—*Andrea Arena*	739 Trabert Ave Ste E, Atlanta GA 30318		R	176*	.3
162	Medeanalytics—*Michael E Gallagher*	5858 Horton St Ste 475, Emeryville CA 94608	510-379-3300	R	176*	.3
163	Percepta LLC—*James Barlett*	290 Town Ctr Dr Ste 61, Dearborn MI 48126		R	175*	4.5
164	Blue Water Finance and Insurance—*Troy Tiedeman*	5041 New Cntre Dr Ste, Wilmington NC 28403		R	175*	<.1
165	Western Reserve Care System	1350 E Market St, Warren OH 44483	330-841-9929	R	173*	<.1
166	Rosemount-Apple Valley And Eagan—*Jonathan Reppe*	14445 Diamond Path W, Rosemount MN 55068	651-423-7700	R	172*	6.0
167	Clarion Sales Corp—*Tom Hayashi*	661 W Redondo Beach Bl, Gardena CA 90247	310-327-9100	S	170*	.3
168	StarCite Inc—*Greg Dukat*	1650 Arch St 18th Fl, Philadelphia PA 19103	267-330-0500	R	168*	.3
169	Bankrate Inc—*Thomas R Evans*	11760 US Hwy 1 Ste200, North Palm Beach FL 33408	561-630-2400	B	167	.3
170	LawCrossing—*Harrison Barnes*	202 S Lake Ave Ste 250, Pasadena CA 91101	626-243-1801	R	164*	.3
171	American Alloy Sourcing Specialists LP—*Bob Covey*	PO Box 40469, Houston TX 77240	713-462-8081	R	163*	.2
172	Chex Systems Inc—*Paul Walsh* Fidelity National Information Services Inc	7805 Hudson Rd Ste 100, Woodbury MN 55125	651-361-2000	S	163*	.3
173	San Francisco Foundation—*Sandra Hernandez*	225 Bush St Ste 500, San Francisco CA 94104	415-733-8500	R	162*	.1
174	United Space Alliance LLC—*Jessie Harris*	Launch Equipment Suppo, Kennedy Space Center FL 32899	321-861-0733	R	162*	5.0
175	Ryt-Way Industries LLC—*David Finch*	21850 Grenada Ave, Lakeville MN 55044	952-469-1417	R	162*	.7
176	TeleSpectrum Worldwide Inc—*Zia Chishti*	1700 Pennsylvania Ave, Washington DC 20006	202-289-9898	R	158*	4.2
177	Interval International Inc—*Paul Rishell*	PO Box 431920, Miami FL 33243		S	158*	1.6
178	Excell Global Services Inc—*John Andrews*	7776 South Pointe Pkwy, Phoenix AZ 85044	602-808-1511	R	155	3.5
179	Warrantech Direct Inc Warrantech Corp	2200 Hwy 121 Ste 100, Bedford TX 76021	817-785-6601	S	155*	.3
180	Mastercard International Inc—*Ajay Banga*	2000 Purchase St, Purchase NY 10577	914-249-2000	R	154*	3.0
181	RedBack Networks Inc	300 Holger Way, San Jose CA 95134	408-750-5000	S	153	.5
182	University Of Nebraska Foundation—*Terry Fairfield*	PO Box 82555, Lincoln NE 68501	402-458-1100	R	151*	.1
183	San Diego Convention Center Corp—*Carol Wallace*	111 W Harbor Dr, San Diego CA 92101	619-525-5000	R	151*	.6
184	National Auction Group Inc—*William R Bone*	PO Box 149, Gadsden AL 35902	256-547-3434	R	150*	.2
185	Electronic Cash Systems Inc—*Fadi Cheikha*	27422 Portola Pkwy Ste, Foothill Ranch CA 92610	949-888-8580	R	149*	<.1
186	Warehouse Demo Services Inc—*Ted Koehn*	330 4th St, Kirkland WA 98033	425-897-2864	R	149*	4.0
187	Key Plastics LLC—*Terrence Gohl*	21700 Haggerty Rd Ste, Northville MI 48167	248-449-6100	R	148*	3.2
188	Figi's Inc—*James Krueger*	3200 S Central Ave, Marshfield WI 54449		S	148*	.3
189	Cosmopolitan and Associates Inc—*Halimo Said*	711 W Lake St, Minneapolis MN 55408	612-822-3830	R	147*	8.1
190	Marketing Research Services Inc—*Todd Earhart*	720 E Pete Rose Way St, Cincinnati OH 45202	513-579-1555	S	147*	.3
191	Performance Printing (Dallas Texas)—*Jeffrey Bainter*	2929 Stemmons Fwy, Dallas TX 75247	214-665-1000	R	145*	.3
192	PDI Inc (Upper Saddle River New Jersey)—*Nancy Lurker*	300 Interpace Pkwy Mor, Parsippany NJ 07054	862-207-7800	P	145	1.6
193	Interim Pastor Ministries Inc—*Robert Page*	PO Box 549, Walcott IA 52773	563-284-4151	R	144*	<.1
194	CRE America Corp—*John A Kanas*	255 Alhambra Cir, Coral Gables FL 33134	305-569-0327	S	144*	.3
195	Vertex Data Utility Services LLC—*Susie Buffam*	250 E Arapaho Rd Ste 1, Richardson TX 75081	214-576-1000	R	141*	.4
196	EMI Latin America Inc—*Rodolfo Negrete*	404 Wshington Ave Ste, Miami Beach FL 33139	305-695-6400	R	140*	5.0
197	OpenTable Inc—*Matthew Roberts*	799 Market St 4th Fl, San Francisco CA 94103	415-344-4200	P	140	.6
198	Action Without Borders/Idealistorg—*Ami Dar*	302 Fifth Ave 11th Fl, New York NY 10001	212-843-3973	R	139*	.2
199	Vestcom International Inc—*John Lawlor*	7304 Kanis Rd, Little Rock AR 72204	501-663-0100	R	136*	1.0
200	FTDcom Inc—*Robert S Apatoff*	3113 Woodcreek Dr, Downers Grove Il 60515	630-724-6200	S	134*	.1
201	LivePerson Inc—*Robert LoCascio*	462 7th Ave 3rd Fl, New York NY 10018	212-609-4200	P	133	.5
202	Bidzcom Inc—*David Zinberg*	3562 Eastham Dr, Culver City CA 90232	310-280-7373	P	132	.2

Note: An asterisk (*) indicates an estimated financial figure. The company type code used is as follows: R = Private, P = Public, S = Private Subsidiary, B = Public Subsidiary, D = Division, J = Joint Venture, I = Investment Fund.

COMPANY RANKINGS BY SALES WITHIN 4-DIGIT SIC

Rank	Company Name—Executive Officer	Address, City, State, Zip	Phone	Type	Fin	Empls
203	SumTotal Systems Inc—John Borgerding	2850 NW 43rd St Ste 20, Gainesville FL 32606	352-264-2800	S	127	.8
204	aNetorder Inc—Shane Randall	820 Frontenac Rd, Naperville IL 60563	630-579-8800	R	126*	.2
205	NaviSite Inc—R Brooks Borcherding	400 Minuteman Rd, Andover MA 01810	978-682-8300	S	126	.6
206	Exostar LLC—Kevin Loudermilk	13530 Dulles Technolog, Herndon VA 20171	703-793-7800	R	124*	.2
207	DynTek Inc—Ron Ben-Yishay	4440 Von Karman Ste 20, Newport Beach CA 92660	949-271-6700	P	124	.2
208	Warrantech Corp—Barry Zyskind	2200 Hwy 121 Ste 100, Bedford TX 76021	817-785-6601	S	123	.3
209	Mail Boxes Etc Inc—Stuart Mathis	6060 Cornerstone Ct W, San Diego CA 92121	858-455-8800	S	123*	.4
210	Avendra LLC—Dennis Baker	702 King Farm Blvd Ste, Rockville MD 20850	301-825-0500	S	122*	.2
211	OneCoast Network Corp—John Keiser	230 Spring St Ste 1800, Atlanta GA 30303		S	122*	.2
212	PSAV Presentation Services—Mike McIlwain	111 West Ocean Blvd St, Long Beach CA 90802	562-336-0620	R	120*	.4
213	OEConnection LLC—Charles Rotuno	4205 Highlander Pkwy, Richfield OH 44286	330-523-1800	R	120*	.2
214	Franklin Covey Services LLC	2200 W Parkway Blvd, Salt Lake City UT 84119	801-817-1776	S	120*	.2
215	Blackstone Technology Group—David Mysona	150 California St 9th, San Francisco CA 94111	415-837-1400	R	119*	.2
216	Global Traffic Network Inc—William C Yde III	880 3rd Ave 6th Fl, New York NY 10022	212-896-1255	P	117	<.1
217	Pacific Dental Services Inc—Stephen Thorne IV	2860 Michelle Dr 2nd F, Irvine CA 92606	714-508-3600	R	115*	1.8
218	ICM Holdings Inc—Nancy Josephson	825 8th Ave, New York NY 10019		R	115*	.3
219	Newtek Business Services Inc—Barry Sloane	212 W 35th St 2nd Fl, New York NY 10001	212-356-9500	P	113	.3
220	Beryl Cos—Paul Spiegelman	3600 Harwood Rd Ste A, Bedford TX 76021	817-785-5000	R	110*	.2
221	Kurtz Brothers Inc—John Kurtz	6415 Granger Rd, Independence OH 44131	216-986-9000	R	110*	.2
222	Synergy Brands Inc—Mair Faibish	223 Underhill Blvd, Syosset NY 11791	516-714-8200	P	109	<.1
223	Rewards Network Inc—Ronald L Blake	2 N Riverside Plz Ste, Chicago IL 60606		S	109	.4
224	Kipany Productions Ltd—Tiffany Hendry	32 E 39th St, New York NY 10016	212-883-8300	R	107*	<.1
225	Argent Associates Inc—Betty Manetta	140 Fieldcrest Ave, Edison NJ 08837	732-512-9009	R	107	.1
226	Storr Office Environments Inc—Tom Vande Guchte	PO Box 90639, Raleigh NC 27675	919-313-3700	R	106*	.2
227	Logistic Specialties Inc—Sean Slatter	1530 N Layton Hills Pk, Layton UT 84041	801-776-0062	R	106*	.2
228	Credit Solutions—Doug Van Arsdale	12700 Park Central Dr, Dallas TX 75251		R	105*	1.0
229	Ipower Distribution Group LLC—JD Sullivan	812 Huron Rd Ste 410, Cleveland OH 44115	216-535-4600	R	104*	.2
230	Keynote Systems Inc—Umang Gupta	777 Mariners Island Bl, San Mateo CA 94404	650-403-2400	P	103	.4
231	USfalcon Inc—Peter von Jess	1 Copley Pkwy Ste 200, Morrisville NC 27560	919-388-3778	R	103*	.2
232	Interclick Inc—Michael D Katz	11 W 19th St 10th Fl, New York NY 10011	646-722-6260	P	101	.1
233	RegisterCom Inc	575 8th Ave 11th Fl, New York NY 10018	212-798-9100	S	101	.5
234	Americorp Inc—Gail Plummer	7500 Dallas Pkwy Ste 3, Plano TX 75024	972-468-3000	R	101*	.2
235	BenefitMall—Bernard DiFiore	4851 LBJ Fwy Ste 100, Dallas TX 75244	469-791-3300	R	100*	.2
236	Internet Brands Inc—Robert N Brisco	909 N Sepulveda Blvd 1, El Segundo CA 90245		P	100	.6
237	Janel World Trade Ltd—James N Jannello	150-14 132nd Ave, Jamaica NY 11434	718-527-3800	P	99	.1
238	Marchex Inc—Russell C Horowitz	520 Pike St Ste 2000, Seattle WA 98101	206-331-3300	P	98	.4
239	Powersecure International Inc—Sidney Hinton	1609 Heritage Commerce, Wake Forest NC 27587	919-556-3056	P	98	.4
240	BSQUARE Corp—Brian T Crowley	110 110th Ave NE Ste 2, Bellevue WA 98004	425-519-5900	P	97	.3
241	Cass Information Systems Inc—Eric H Brunngraber	13001 Hollenberg Dr, Bridgeton MO 63044	314-506-5931	P	96	.9
242	Advance Insights	500 Atrium Dr, Somerset NJ 08873		D	96*	.2
243	Library of Natural Sounds—John Fitzpatrick	Cornell Laboratory of, Ithaca NY 14850	607-254-2473	R	96*	.2
244	ServiceMagic Inc—Michael J Beaudoin	14023 Denver W Pkwy Bl, Golden CO 80401	303-963-7200	S	95*	1.0
245	Wausau Papers Export Corp—Thomas J Howatt	100 Paper Pl, Mosinee WI 54455	715-693-4470	S	95	<.1
246	Transcend Services Inc—Larry Gerdes	1 Glenlake Pky Ste 132, Atlanta GA 30328	678-808-0601	P	94	2.0
247	Consonus Technologies Inc—Bob McCarthy	301 Gregson Dr, Cary NC 27511	919-379-8000	R	94*	.2
248	LexiCode Corp—Ed Bowman SOURCECORP Inc	PO Box 190, Ballentine SC 29002	803-749-9778	S	94*	.2
249	MPS Group Inc (Detroit Michigan)—Charlie Williams	2920 Scotten St, Detroit MI 48210	313-841-7588	R	94*	.2
250	Concord Payment Services Inc	2240 New Market Pkwy S, Marietta GA 30067	770-953-2664	S	93*	.4
251	Economic Research Services Inc—Sam N Kimelman SOURCECORP Inc	4901 Tower Ct, Tallahassee FL 32303	850-562-1211	S	93*	.2
252	Sparks Marketing Group Inc—Scott Tarte	2828 Charter Rd, Philadelphia PA 19154	215-676-6900	R	92*	.3
253	West Interactive Corp West Corp	11650 Miracle Hills Dr, Omaha NE 68154	402-963-1200	S	91*	14.0
254	comScore Media Metrix Inc—Magid M Abraham	5 Penn Plz 2nd Fl, New York NY 10001	212-497-1700	D	90*	.4
255	Franklin Covey Marketing Ltd	2200 W Parkway Blvd, Salt Lake City UT 84119	801-817-1776	S	90*	.2
256	Infologix Inc—David Gulian	101 E County Line Rd S, Hatboro PA 19040	215-604-0691	S	90	.2
257	Packaging Services Inc (Weyers Cave Virginia)—Bill Leith	PO Box 126, Weyers Cave VA 24486	540-234-9292	S	89*	.1
258	Encompass Group Affiliates Inc—Robert Gowens	775 Tipton Industrial, Lawrenceville GA 30046		P	88	.3
259	Cenergy Corp—June Ressler	1221 Lamar St Ste 1110, Houston TX 77010		R	88*	.2
260	ICR Inc—Thomas M Ryan	33 Broad Street, Boston MA 02109	617-956-6725	R	88*	.2
261	NewlineNoosh Inc—Ofer Ben-Shachar	1300 Island Dr Ste 201, Redwood City CA 94065	650-637-6000	R	87*	.1
262	AmeriNet Inc—Todd Edbert	PO Box 46930, Saint Louis MO 63146	314-878-2525	R	86*	.1
263	Credit Card Processing USA Inc—George Mayo	890 Mountain Ave Ste 2, New Providence NJ 07974	908-516-5900	R	85*	<.1
264	Dawson Subscription Service Inc—Vernon W Cain	1001 W Pines Rd, Oregon IL 61061	815-732-9001	S	85	.2
265	EB Morris Associates Inc—Alex Morris	PO Box 50440, Indianapolis IN 46250	317-554-9000	R	84*	.1
266	ICG Commerce Inc—Carl Guarino	211 S Gulph Rd Ste 500, King of Prussia PA 19406		S	83*	.1
267	Avesis Inc—Alan S Cohn	3030 N Central Ave Ste, Phoenix AZ 85012		P	83*	.1
268	Audible Inc—Donald R Katz	1 Washington Pk, Newark NJ 07102	973-837-2700	S	82	.2
269	HealthStream Inc—Robert A Frist Jr	209 10th Ave S Ste 450, Nashville TN 37203	615-301-3100	P	82	.5
270	StarGuide Digital Networks Inc—Ian A Lerner	6260 Sequence Dr, San Diego CA 92121	858-452-2010	S	82*	.2
271	Nielsen//NetRatings—William Pulver	120 W 45th St 35th Fl, New York NY 10036	212-703-5900	R	82	.4
272	Buxton Co (Fort Worth Texas)—Charles Wetzel	2651 S Polaris Dr, Fort Worth TX 76137	817-332-3681	R	80*	.1
273	Innotrac Corp—Scott D Dorfman	6465 E Johns Crossing, Duluth GA 30097	678-584-4000	P	80	1.2
274	Seaway Valley Capital Corp—Thomas W Scozzafava	213 W Main St, Sackets Harbor NY 13685	315-646-7101	P	80	.1
275	David Evans and Associates Inc—Ken Wightman	2100 SW River Pkwy, Portland OR 97201	503-223-6663	R	79*	.9
276	Product Line Inc—Dennis King	5000 Lima St, Denver CO 80239	720-374-3800	R	79*	.3
277	CoreLogic Inc—Steve Schroeder	4 1st American Way, Santa Ana CA 92707	714-250-6400	P	79*	.2
278	Logistics Engineering and Environmental Support Services Inc—Anita B Williams	4845 University Sq Ste, Huntsville AL 35816	256-971-7165	R	78*	1.0
279	Diversified Business Communications—Nancy Hasselback	PO Box 7437, Portland ME 04112	207-842-5500	S	78*	.1
280	iDine Restaurant Group Inc Rewards Network Inc	300 S Park Rd Ste 300, Hollywood FL 33021		S	77	.4
281	VertMarkets Inc—Tom Roberts	101 Gibraltar Rd Ste 1, Horsham PA 19044	215-675-1800	R	77*	.1
282	AFFINA Corp—Donna J Malone	2001 Ruppman Plz, Peoria IL 61614	309-685-5901	R	76*	2.0
283	Design Line Interiors Inc	1302 Camino Del Mar St, Del Mar CA 92014	858-309-6100	R	74*	.1
284	RubberNetworkcom LLC—John Garrison	1455 Lincoln Pkwy Ste, Atlanta GA 30346	678-514-3700	R	74*	.1
285	Results Technologies Inc—Alan Schein	499 E Sheridan St Fl 4, Dania FL 33004	954-688-2905	R	74*	.1
286	LinkShare Corp—Yasuhisa Iida	215 Park Ave S 9th Fl, New York NY 10003	646-943-8200	S	73*	.1
287	Traffix Inc—Jeffrey L Schwartz	PO Box 1665, Pearl River NY 10965	845-620-1212	S	73	.2

Rank	Company Name—*Executive Officer*	Address, City, State, Zip	Phone	Type	Fin	Empls
288	Merisel Inc—*Donald R Uzzi*	127 W 30th St 5th Fl, New York NY 10001	212-594-4800	P	72	.3
289	Impairment Resources LLC—*Christopher R Brigham*	8885 Rio San Diego Dr, San Diego CA 92108	619-299-7377	R	71*	<.1
290	Andesa Services Inc—*Frank Memmo*	3435 Winchester Rd Ste, Allentown PA 18104	610-821-8980	R	70*	.1
291	Telerx Marketing Inc—*Linda Schellenger*	723 Dresher Rd, Horsham PA 19044	215-347-5700	S	68*	1.4
292	Swisslog Logistics Inc—*Markus Schmidt*	161 Enterprise Dr, Newport News VA 23603	757-820-3400	R	67*	.1
293	Advanced Health Media LLC—*James Burgess*	420 Mountain Ave, New Providence NJ 07974	908-393-8700	R	67*	.9
294	ChemConnect Inc—*Micheal Ereli*	5925 Kirby Dr Ste E-47, Houston TX 77005	832-789-9619	R	67*	<.1
295	NDT Systems and Services (America) Inc—*Alfred Barbian*	PO Box 300248, Houston TX 77230	713-799-5430	R	66*	.2
296	Euro RSCG 4D DRTV—*Steve Netzley*	513 13th Ave 5th Fl, Portland OR 97209	503-228-5555	R	65*	.1
297	MG Design Associates Corp—*John Patten*	8778 100th St, Pleasant Prairie WI 53158	262-947-8890	R	65*	.1
298	Fortune Industries Inc (Indianapolis Indiana)—*Tena Mayberry*	6402 Corporate Dr, Indianapolis IN 46278	317-532-1374	P	64	.1
299	SPAR Group Inc—*Gary S Raymond*	560 White Plains Rd St, Tarrytown NY 10591	914-332-4100	P	63	10.0
300	On-Target Supplies and Logistics Ltd—*Albert Black*	1133 S Madison Ave, Dallas TX 75208	214-941-4885	R	63*	.2
301	eVisibility—*Danny DeMichele*	5650 El Camino Real St, Carlsbad CA 92008	760-431-8594	S	63*	.1
302	TriNet Group Inc—*Burton M Goldfield*	1100 San Leandro Blvd, San Leandro CA 94577	510-352-5000	R	63*	.1
303	Horizon Consulting Inc—*Wanda A Alexander*	44135 Woodridge Pkwy S, Lansdowne VA 20176	703-726-6430	R	62*	.1
304	Solutions Group Inc—*Sean O'Neal*	3757 State St Ste 306, Santa Barbara CA 93105	805-964-3344	P	62	.1
305	TPi Billing Solutions—*Ray Thomas*	PO Box 472330, Tulsa OK 74147	918-664-0144	R	62*	.1
306	Reed Exhibition Cos—*Chet Burchett*	383 Main Ave, Norwalk CT 06851	203-840-4800	D	61*	.1
307	Moody International Inc—*David Johnson*	24900 Pitkin Rd Ste 20, Spring TX 77386	281-367-8764	R	60*	.3
308	Pacific Event Productions Inc—*Larry Toll*	6989 Corte Santa Fe, San Diego CA 92121	858-458-9908	R	60*	.1
309	Triplefin LLC—*Gregory T LaLonde*	6000 Creek Rd Ste 2, Cincinnati OH 45242	513-794-9870	R	60*	.1
310	Rosemont Exposition Services Inc—*David Houston*	9291w Bryn Mawr Ave, Rosemont IL 60018	847-696-2208	R	59*	1.5
311	Juran Institute Inc—*Joseph A De Feo*	555 Heritage Rd Rm 100, Southbury CT 06488	203-267-3445	R	59*	.1
312	Service 800 Inc (Minneapolis Minnesota)—*Jean Mark Bredeson*	2190 W Wayzata Blvd, Long Lake MN 55356	952-475-3747	R	59*	.1
313	Lenderlive Network Inc—*Rick Seehausen*	710 South Ash St Ste 2, Glendale CO 80245		R	59*	.1
314	Warrantech Automotive Inc Warrantech Corp	2220 Hwy 121, Bedford TX 76021	817-785-6601	S	58*	.1
315	Davis Carter Scott Ltd—*Doug Carter*	1676 International Dr, Mc Lean VA 22102	703-556-9275	R	58*	.1
316	Qk4—*Davie Smith*	815 W Market St Ste 30, Louisville KY 40202	502-585-2222	R	58*	.1
317	Bowne Global Solutions Inc—*Jim Fagan* Lionbridge Technologies Inc	11400 W Olympic Blvd S, Los Angeles CA 90064		S	57*	.2
318	Carolane Propane Gas Inc—*CH Timberlake III*	339 S Main St, Lexington NC 27292	336-249-8981	S	57*	.1
319	Brede Exposition Service—*William C Casey III*	2211 Broadway St NE, Minneapolis MN 55413	612-331-4540	R	57*	.1
320	Carson Design Associates—*Jack Carson*	2325 Pointe Pkwy Ste 2, Carmel IN 46032	317-843-5979	R	57*	<.1
321	TRX Inc—*Shane Hammond*	2970 Clairmont Rd Ste, Atlanta GA 30329	404-929-6100	P	57	.8
322	Hargrove—*Timothy Mcgill*	1 Hargrove Dr, Lanham MD 20706	301-306-9000	R	57*	.2
323	Mintie Corp—*Kevin J Mintie*	1114 San Fernando Rd, Los Angeles CA 90065	323-225-4111	R	55*	.1
324	Ipsos-ASI Inc	301 Merritt 7, Norwalk CT 06851	203-840-3400	S	55*	.1
325	IronPlanet Inc—*Gregory J Owens*	4695 Chabot Dr Ste 102, Pleasanton CA 94588		R	55	<.1
326	Publicis Modem—*Richard Giannicchi*	1 Selleck St 2nd Fl, Norwalk CT 06855	203-295-0615	S	54*	.3
327	Employers Mutual Inc—*William McCreary*	700 Central Pkwy, Stuart FL 34004		S	54*	.1
328	Storr Office Environments of Florida Inc—*Kyle Doezema* Storr Office Environments Inc	5112 W Linebaugh Ave, Tampa FL 33624	813-418-3300	S	53*	.2
329	Logistics Management Solutions—*Dennis Schoemehl*	1 Cityplace Dr Ste 415, Saint Louis MO 63141	314-692-8886	R	53*	.1
330	FX Alliance LLC—*Philip Weisberg*	909 3rd Ave, New York NY 10022	646-268-9900	R	53*	.1
331	Central Payment—*Matthew Hyman*	2350 Kerner Blvd Ste 3, San Rafael CA 94901	415-462-0035	R	53	.1
332	AnswerNet Inc—*Gary A Pudles*	2325 Maryland Rd Ste 2, Willow Grove PA 19090		R	52*	2.0
333	Encore Productions Inc—*Bill Dayton*	5150 S Decatur Blvd, Las Vegas NV 89118	702-739-8803	S	52*	.2
334	Kanuga Conferences Inc—*Albert Gooch*	PO Box 250, Hendersonville NC 28793	828-692-9136	R	52*	.1
335	MoreDirect Inc—*Russell L Madris*	4800 T-Rex Ave Ste 300, Boca Raton FL 33431	561-237-3300	S	51*	.2
336	LaGrou Distribution Systems Inc—*Donald E Schimek*	3514 S Kostner Ave, Chicago IL 60632	773-523-0044	R	50*	.3
337	Health Grades Inc—*Kerry R Hicks*	999 18th St Ste 600, Denver CO 80202	303-716-0041	R	50*	.2
338	Devon Self Storage LLC—*Kenneth Nitzberg*	2000 Powell St, Emeryville CA 94608	510-450-1300	R	50*	.1
339	Access Communications Inc (Berkeley Heights New Jersey)—*Michael Mitrow Jr*	400 Connell Dr, Berkeley Heights NJ 07922	908-508-6700	R	50*	.1
340	Sb Capital Group LLC—*Jack Duffy*	4300 E 5th Ave, Columbus OH 43219	614-443-4080	R	50*	<.1
341	Impact Group—*Laura Herring*	12977 N Outer 40 Dr St, St Louis MO 63141	314-453-9002	R	49*	.2
342	CarFax Inc—*Dick Raines*	10304 Eaton Pl Ste 500, Fairfax VA 22030	703-934-2616	S	49*	.1
343	MD Systems/Clair Brothers—*Barry Clair*	3335 Ambrose Ave, Nashville TN 37207	615-227-6657	R	49*	.1
344	Computer Integration Technologies Inc—*Christopher Taylor*	2375 Ventura Dr Ste A, Woodbury MN 55125	651-450-0333	R	49*	.1
345	Seamlessweb Professional Solutions Inc—*Jonathan Zabusky*	232 Madison Ave, New York NY 10016		D	49*	<.1
346	Premier Payment Systems—*Drew Sementa*	2625 Butterfield Rd St, Oak Brook IL 60523		R	49*	<.1
347	Arnold Logistics	4410 Industrial Park R, Camp Hill PA 17011	717-731-4374	S	48*	1.0
348	Users Inc—*Joe Barry*	1250 Drummers Ln, Wayne PA 19087	610-687-9400	S	48*	.3
349	Martin Williams—*Mike Gray*	60 S 6th St, Minneapolis MN 55402	612-340-0800	R	48*	.2
350	Impact Unlimited Inc—*Kenneth Payne*	PO Box 558, Dayton NJ 08810	732-274-2000	R	48*	.2
351	McKesson Health Solutions	275 Grove St Ste 1-110, Newton MA 02466		D	48*	.1
352	US Script Inc—*Robert Bagdasarian*	2425 W Shaw, Fresno CA 93711	559-244-3700	R	48*	<.1
353	Better Life Mobility Centers—*Mo Abusham*	8130 Parkway Dr, La Mesa CA 91942	619-474-4072	R	48*	<.1
354	Employees Only Inc—*Mario Apruzzese*	3256 University Dr Ste, Auburn Hills MI 48326	248-276-0950	R	48*	<.1
355	IdenTrust DST	255 N Admiral Byrd Rd, Salt Lake City UT 84116	801-326-5400	S	47*	.1
356	United Information Services Inc—*David Smith* SOURCECORP Inc	4434 112th St, Des Moines IA 50322	515-251-7040	S	47*	.1
357	Telepoint Communications Inc—*Daniel Benenfeld*	8 Somerdale Sq, Somerdale NJ 08083	856-627-7100	R	47*	.1
358	Trans-Pak Inc—*Bert Inch*	520 Marburg Way, San Jose CA 95133	408-254-0500	R	46*	.2
359	Q Communication International Inc—*Dennis Andrews*	9350 S 150 E, Sandy UT 84070	801-617-1600	S	46	<.1
360	Advance Ross Corp—*Bill Fisher*	3000 E Marshall, Longview TX 75601	903-758-3395	R	46*	.1
361	eKairecom Inc—*Michael Lightfoot*	PO Box 2318, Goldenrod FL 32733		R	46*	.1
362	Korg USA Inc—*Michael Korvins*	316 S Service Rd, Melville NY 11747		R	46*	.1
363	Pipeline Data Inc—*Randall A McCoy*	4400 North Point Pky S, Alpharetta GA 30022	617-405-2600	P	46	.1
364	Tollgrade Communications Inc—*Edward H Kennedy*	493 Nixon Rd, Cheswick PA 15024	412-820-1400	R	46	.1
365	Mobility Services International LLC—*Timm Runnion*	260 Merrimac St Ste 4, Newburyport MA 01950	978-358-2000	R	45*	.1
366	Timeshare Relief Inc—*David MacMillan*	2239 W 190th St, Torrance CA 90504		R	45*	.1
367	Carolina Manufacturer's Service—*L David Mounts*	PO Box 1170, Winston Salem NC 27106	336-631-2500	S	45*	.1
368	BFI—*Dan Morley*	133 Rahway Ave, Elizabeth NJ 07202	908-355-3400	R	45*	.1
369	MoneyLine Lending Services Inc—*Taylor Woods*	15420 Laguna Canyon Rd, Irvine CA 92618		S	45*	.1
370	Star Trax Inc—*Geoff Kretchmer*	24463 W Ten Mile Rd, Southfield MI 48033	248-263-6300	R	45*	.1
371	Collectors Universe Inc—*Michael J McConnell*	1921 E Alton Ave, Santa Ana CA 92705	949-567-1234	P	44	.2

Note: An asterisk (*) indicates an estimated financial figure. The company type code used is as follows: R = Private, P = Public, S = Private Subsidiary, B = Public Subsidiary, D = Division, J = Joint Venture, I = Investment Fund.

COMPANY RANKINGS BY SALES WITHIN 4-DIGIT SIC

Rank	Company Name—*Executive Officer*	Address, City, State, Zip	Phone	Type	Fin	Empls
372	McNeil Technologies Inc—*Ron Thomas*	6564 Loisdale Ct Ste 9, Springfield VA 22150	703-921-1600	S	44*	.8
373	Allant Group Inc—*Terrence E McCarthy*	2056 Westings Ave Ste, Naperville IL 60563		R	44*	.2
374	Cordia Corp—*Kevin Griffo*	13275 W Colonial Dr, Winter Garden FL 34787	407-313-7000	P	44	.4
375	Acxiom Digital	1051 E Hillsdale Blvd, Foster City CA 94404	650-356-3400	S	44	.3
376	GA Wright Sales Inc—*Gary Wright*	PO Box 17188, Denver CO 80217	303-333-4453	R	43*	.1
377	Photolibrary Index Stock—*Glen Parker*	23 W 18th St 3rd Fl, New York NY 10011	212-929-4644	R	43*	.1
378	Enable Holdings Inc—*Patrick Neville*	1400 Thorndale Ave, Itasca IL 60143	773-272-5000	P	43	.1
379	Search123com Inc	30699 Russell Ranch Rd, Westlake Village CA 91362	818-575-4500	S	43*	.1
380	CreditCardscom Inc—*Christopher J Speltz*	8920 Business Park Dr, Austin TX 78759	512-996-8663	S	43*	<.1
381	Two Maids and A Mop—*Ron Holt*	33 Barber Ct Ste 109, Birmingham AL 35209	205-940-2292	R	43*	<.1
382	Allworld Language Consultants Inc—*Carlos Scandiffio*	PO Box 2128, Rockville MD 20847	301-881-8884	R	43*	.3
383	Electronic Payments Inc—*Michael Nardy*	1161 Scott Ave, Calverton NY 11933	631-822-1140	R	43*	<.1
384	InsWeb Corp—*Hussein A Enan*	10850 Gold Center Dr S, Rancho Cordova CA 95670	916-853-3300	P	42	.1
385	Weather Services International—*Mark Gildersleeve*	400 Minuteman Rd, Andover MA 01810	978-983-6300	S	42*	.2
386	Compass Knowledge Group Inc	2145 MetroCenter Blvd, Orlando FL 32835	407-573-2000	S	42*	.1
387	Cloverleaf Cold Storage Co—*William Feiges*	2800 Cloverleaf Ct, Sioux City IA 51111	712-279-8000	R	42*	.6
388	Access Direct Telemarketing Inc—*John G Hall*	4515 20th Ave SW Ste B, Cedar Rapids IA 52404	319-390-8200	R	41*	2.0
389	Masterplan—*Jerry Bowe*	21540 Plummer St, Chatsworth CA 91311	818-773-2647	R	41*	.4
390	Zierer Visa Service Inc	4301 Connecticut Ave N, Washington DC 20008		R	41*	.1
391	Keystone Automotive—*Joseph Holsten*	433 Crofton St SE, Grand Rapids MI 49507	616-452-2300	D	41*	.1
392	PartsBase Inc—*Robert A Hammond Jr*	905 Clint Moore Rd, Boca Raton FL 33487	561-953-0700	R	41*	.1
393	Spark Networks Inc—*Greg Liberman*	8383 Wilshire Blvd Ste, Beverly Hills CA 90211	323-658-3000	P	41	.1
394	American Medical Alert Corp—*Jack Rhian*	3636 33rd St, Long Island City NY 11106	516-536-5850	P	41	.6
395	Access Plans USA Inc—*David Huguelet*	4929 W Royal Ln Ste 20, Irving TX 75063	972-915-3200	D	41	.1
396	Woori USA Inc—*Kun Choi*	2475 Paseo De Las A St, San Diego CA 92154	619-662-3911	R	40*	<.1
397	Teleflora LLC—*Phil Kleweno*	PO Box 30130, Los Angeles CA 90030		S	40*	.3
398	MPLC Holdings LLC—*Burton Katz*	469 7th Ave 10th Fl, New York NY 10018	212-716-1977	P	40	<.1
399	SoundBite Communications Inc—*Jim Milton*	22 Crosby Dr, Bedford MA 01730	781-897-2500	P	40	.1
400	Blaine Kern Artists Inc—*Barry Kern*	PO Box 6307, New Orleans LA 70174	504-362-8211	R	39*	.3
401	vCustomer Corp—*Sanjay Kumar*	4040 Lake Washington B, Kirkland WA 98033	206-802-0200	R	39*	4.0
402	Wageworks Inc—*Joe Jackson*	1100 Park Pl 4th Fl, San Mateo CA 94403		R	39*	.7
403	US Searchcom Inc—*Jeff Pullen*	600 Corporate Pointe S, Culver City CA 90230	310-302-6300	S	39*	.3
404	Titanium Solutions Inc—*Michael Redeskey*	5225 Wiley Post Way St, Salt Lake City UT 84116	801-322-4442	R	39*	.2
405	WePackItAll—*Jack Bershtel*	2745 Huntington Dr, Duarte CA 91010	626-301-9214	R	39*	.1
406	Heritage Microfilm Inc—*Chris Gill*	4049 21st Ave SW, Cedar Rapids IA 52404		R	38*	.1
407	Composite Image Systems—*Don Fly*	1144 N Las Palmas Ave, Hollywood CA 90038	323-463-8811	R	38*	.1
408	RenewData Corp—*Steven Horan*	9500 Arboretum Blvd St, Austin TX 78759	512-276-5500	R	37*	.2
409	Q Interactive Inc—*Matthew Wise*	1 N Dearborn St 12th F, Chicago IL 60602	312-224-5000	S	37*	.1
410	IMCO Recycling of Illinois Inc—*Jonathon Markle*	400 E Lincoln Hwy, Chicago Heights IL 60411	708-758-8700	S	37*	.1
411	Publicis Meetings USA—*Patti Giles*	340 N Primrose Dr, Orlando FL 32803	407-513-3700	R	37*	.1
412	Petroleum Place Inc—*Gary R Vickers*	216 16th St Ste 1700, Denver CO 80202	303-390-9400	R	36*	.3
413	Palisades Media Group Inc—*Roger Schaffner*	1620 26th St Ste 200S, Santa Monica CA 90404	310-828-9100	R	36*	.1
414	Environments Group Company Inc—*Fred Schmidt*	303 E Wacker Dr Ste 80, Chicago IL 60601	312-644-5080	S	36*	.1
415	Vertro Inc—*Peter A Corrao*	143 Varick St, New York NY 10013	212-231-2000	P	36	<.1
416	Helm Inc—*Dennis Gusick*	14310 Hamilton Ave, Detroit MI 48203	313-865-5000	R	35*	.2
417	Five Point Capital Inc—*Greg Wells*	13280 Evening Creek Dr, San Diego CA 92128		R	35*	.1
418	InsWeb Insurance Services Inc InsWeb Corp	11290 Pyrites Way Ste, Gold River CA 95670	916-853-3300	S	35*	.1
419	Media Information Services—*Marianne Volpe*	353 Lexington Ave 7th, New York NY 10016	212-329-2200	R	35*	.1
420	Cal Western Packaging Corp—*Jim Felt*	2070 S 3rd St, Memphis TN 38109	901-947-4661	R	35*	.1
421	ConServit Integrated Teleservices—*Peter F Theis*	28 N Route 12, Fox Lake IL 60020	847-629-5567	R	35*	.1
422	Capital Growth Systems Inc—*Patrick C Shutt*	200 South Wacker Dr 16, Chicago IL 60606	312-673-2400	S	34	.1
423	360trainingcom—*Ed Sattar*	13801 N Mo-Pac Ste 100, Austin TX 78727	512-441-1097	R	34*	.2
424	Diversified Inspections-Independent Testing Laboratories—*Leland Bisbee III*	PO Box 39669, Phoenix AZ 85069	602-995-5800	R	34*	.1
425	Dale Corp—*Dale Jablonski*	28091 Dequindre Rd, Madison Heights MI 48071	248-542-2400	R	34*	.1
426	Cost Management Services Inc (Lafayette Louisiana)—*Tommy Huval*	102 Asma Blvd, Lafayette LA 70508		S	34*	.1
427	iLanguagecom Inc—*Marc J Bautil*	901 Wilshire Blvd Ste, Santa Monica CA 90401	310-899-6802	R	34*	.1
428	Telesource Inc—*Michael Woods*	1450 Highwood E, Pontiac MI 48340	248-335-3000	R	32*	.1
429	Switzer Group Inc—*Lou Switzer*	535 5th Ave 11th Fl, New York NY 10017	212-922-1313	R	32*	.1
430	Seafax Inc—*George Babeu*	PO Box 15340, Portland ME 04112	207-773-3533	R	32*	.1
431	IDG World Expo Corp—*Mary Dolaher*	3 Speen St Ste 320, Framingham MA 01701	508-879-6700	S	32*	.1
432	Accupac Inc—*Paul Alvater*	PO Box 200, Mainland PA 19451	215-256-6181	R	32*	.4
433	Official Payments Corp—*Ronald Rossetti*	2333 San Ramon Valley, San Ramon CA 94583	925-855-5000	R	31*	.1
434	Arthur Shuster Inc—*Chuck Shuster*	1995 Oakcrest Ave W, Saint Paul MN 55113	651-631-9200	R	31*	.1
435	FoodTrader International Inc—*Frank Tomasino*	1111 Brickell Ave Fl 1, Miami FL 33131	305-533-1126	R	31*	.1
436	Phoenix Advisory Partners LLC—*John Siemann*	110 Wall St 27th Fl, New York NY 10005	212-493-3910	S	31*	<.1
437	WWA Group Inc—*Eric Montandon*	700 Lavaca St Ste 1400, Austin TX 78701	480-505-0070	P	31	<.1
438	Sperry and Hutchinson Company Inc—*Ron Pedersen*	1625 S Congress Ave, Delray Beach FL 33445	561-454-7600	R	30	1.0
439	Dialogue Marketing Inc—*Alejandro Vargas*	3252 University Dr Ste, Auburn Hills MI 48326	248-836-2600	R	30*	.8
440	General Converters And Assemblers Inc—*George Stinson*	1325 16th St, Racine WI 53403	262-634-1942	R	30*	.2
441	CASCO International Inc—*Charles R Davis*	4205 E Dixon Blvd, Shelby NC 28152	704-482-9591	R	30*	.2
442	American Bank Note Holographics Inc—*Kenneth Traub*	2 Applegate Dr, Robbinsville NJ 08691	609-632-0800	S	30*	.1
443	SOURCECORP HealthSERVE Radiology Inc—*Stan Burch* SOURCECORP Inc	602 N English Station, Louisville KY 40223	502-244-0035	D	30*	.1
444	The Complex Studios—*Chris Cotone*	2323 Corinth Ave, Los Angeles CA 90064	310-477-1938	R	30*	.1
445	Meyer Associates Inc (Ardmore Pennsylvania)—*Norman Liedtke*	227 E Lancaster Ave, Ardmore PA 19003	610-649-8500	R	30*	.1
446	Sonnet-NewMarkets International Inc—*Timothy Cote*	1000 Broadway Ste 460, Oakland CA 94607		R	30*	.1
447	A Custom Brokerage Inc—*Gabriel Rodriguez*	5400 Nw 84th Ave, Doral FL 33166	305-805-6797	R	30*	<.1
448	Carman Productions Inc—*Tom Skeeter* Sound City Entertainment Group Inc	15456 Cabrito Rd, Van Nuys CA 91406		S	30*	<.1
449	ISR Group Inc—*Alfred Lumpkin*	670 Industrial Rd, Savannah TN 38372	731-926-4188	R	29	.2
450	BondDesk Group LLC—*Kim Bang*	1 Lovell Ave, Mill Valley CA 94941	415-383-4988	R	29*	.1
451	Explus Inc—*Duncan Burt*	44156 Mercure Cir, Dulles VA 20166	703-260-0780	R	29	.1
452	Indovance—*Sandesh Joshi*	412 Chime Ct, Cary NC 27519	919-238-4044	R	29*	.1
453	KPS Group Inc—*Gary Plosser Jr*	2101 1st Ave N, Birmingham AL 35203	205-251-0125	R	29*	.1
454	LeTip International Inc—*Kim Marie Branch-Pettid*	4838 E Baseline Rd Ste, Mesa AZ 85206	480-264-4600	R	29*	.1
455	MyLifecom Inc—*Jeffrey Tinsley*	2118 Wilshire Blvd, Santa Monica CA 90403	310-571-3144	R	29*	.1

Rank	Company Name—*Executive Officer*	Address, City, State, Zip	Phone	Type	Fin	Empls
456	The History Factory—*Bruce Weindruch*	14140 Parke Long Ct, Chantilly VA 20151	703-631-0500	R	29*	.1
457	SuperMarkets Online Inc	200 Carillon Pkwy, Saint Petersburg FL 33716	727-579-5000	S	29*	<.1
458	The Amacore Group Inc—*Jay Shafer*	485 N Keller Rd Ste 45, Maitland FL 32751	407-805-8900	P	29	.1
459	The March Group LLP—*Robert W Scarlata*	1375 Gateway Blvd, Boynton Beach FL 33426	469-619-5410	R	28*	.2
460	Tommy Boy Music—*Tom Silverman*	120 5th Ave 7th Fl, New York NY 10011	212-388-8300	R	28*	.1
461	Commercial Levin—*Murray R McClean*	PO Box 30, Burlington NC 27216	336-584-0333	D	28*	.1
462	Planning Design Research Corp—*Drew Patton*	909 Fannin St 39th Fl, Houston TX 77010	713-739-9050	R	28*	<.1
463	Reis Inc (New York New York)—*Llyod Lynford*	530 5th Ave 5th Fl, New York NY 10036	212-921-1122	P	28	.1
464	Landacorp Inc—*Eugene J Miller* SHPS Inc	500 Orient St Ste 110, Chico CA 95928	530-891-0853	S	27	.2
465	Premier Equipment Inc—*John Grabenau*	990 Sunshine Ln, Altamonte Springs FL 32714	407-786-2000	R	27*	<.1
466	ADP Employease Inc—*Philip Fauver*	3295 River Exchange Dr, Norcross GA 30092	770-325-7700	D	27*	.2
467	Interbrand—*Jez Frampton*	130 5th Ave 6th Fl, New York NY 10011	212-798-7500	S	27*	.2
468	Onvia Inc—*Henry Riner*	509 Olive Way Ste 400, Seattle WA 98101	206-282-5170	P	27	.1
469	Icor Partners LLC—*Anne Reed*	3101 Wilson Blvd Ste 5, Arlington VA 22201	703-684-1840	R	27*	.1
470	Joint Purchasing Corp—*Christopher C Moore*	11 Penn Plz 5th Fl, New York NY 10001		R	27*	.1
471	Messe Frankfurt Inc—*Roland Bleinroth*	1600 Parkwood Cir SE S, Atlanta GA 30339	770-984-8016	S	27*	.1
472	Telrex—*Robert Kapela*	8525 120th Ave NE Ste, Kirkland WA 98033	425-827-6156	R	27*	.1
473	College Financial Aid Services—*David Polino*	450 New Karner Rd Rm 1, Albany NY 12205	518-862-1850	R	27*	<.1
474	Global Domains International Inc—*Michael Stark*	701 Palomar Airport Rd, Carlsbad CA 92011	760-602-3000	R	27*	<.1
475	Surety LLC—*Tom Klaff*	12020 Sunrise Valley D, Reston VA 20191	571-748-5800	R	27*	<.1
476	Interni Design Inc—*Charles Colosimo*	100 W Broadway Ste 604, Long Beach CA 90802	562-980-9988	R	27*	<.1
477	EMA Services Inc—*Terry Brueck*	1970 Oakcrest Ave Ste, Saint Paul MN 55113	651-639-5600	S	26*	.3
478	Medical Security Card Company Inc—*Lori Bryant*	4911 E Broadway Ste 20, Tucson AZ 85711		R	26*	.2
479	Materials Management Group Inc—*Jim Fitzpatrick*	2763 Manitowoc Rd, Green Bay WI 54311	920-205-1384	S	26*	.1
480	RJ Pavlik Inc	3032 E Commercial Blvd, Fort Lauderdale FL 33308	954-523-3300	R	26*	.1
481	Thumbs-Up Telemarketing Inc—*Greg Johnston*	13545 Barrett Pky Dr S, Ballwin MO 63021	314-821-8111	R	26*	.1
482	FurnishNet Inc	9890 Towne Center Dr S, San Diego CA 92121		S	26*	.1
483	Hospital Solutions Inc—*Philip D Kryk*	8582 Katy Fwy Ste 220, Houston TX 77024	713-350-9900	R	26*	.1
484	Optimance—*Don Hanratty*	3608 Preston Rd Ste 22, Plano TX 75093	469-467-2800	R	26*	.1
485	RMC Property Trust Inc—*Mitchell Rice*	8902 N Dale Mabry Hwy, Tampa FL 33614	813-960-8154	R	26*	.1
486	Co-Operations Inc—*Patricia Granum*	20049 SW 112th Ave, Tualatin OR 97062	503-620-7977	R	26*	<.1
487	THW Design—*William R Witte*	2100 River Edge Pky NW, Atlanta GA 30328	404-252-8040	R	26*	<.1
488	ID Systems Inc—*Jeffrey M Jagid*	123 Tice Blvd Ste 101, Woodcliff Lake NJ 07677	201-996-9000	P	26	.1
489	360i LLC—*Bryan Wiener*	1545 Peachtree St Ste, Atlanta GA 30309	404-876-6007	R	26	.1
490	Auction Services Inc—*Alexis Jacobs*	4700 Groveport Rd, Obetz OH 43207	614-497-2000	R	25*	.7
491	Covisint LLC—*Robert Paul*	1 Campus Martius, Detroit MI 48226	313-227-7300	S	25*	.3
492	Jenco Productions Inc—*Jennifer Imbriani*	401 S J St, San Bernardino CA 92410	909-381-9453	R	25*	.3
493	AtLast Fulfillment Inc—*Ted Tanner*	22100 E 26th Ave Ste10, Aurora CO 80019		R	25*	.2
494	Here Media Inc—*Paul Colichman*	10990 Wilshire Blvd Pe, Los Angeles CA 90024	310-806-4288	R	25	.1
495	Niagara Falls Water Board—*Gerald Grose*	5815 Buffalo Ave, Niagara Falls NY 14304	716-283-9770	R	25*	.1
496	Rockhurst College Continuing Education Center Inc—*Susan Tuller*	PO Box 419107, Kansas City MO 64141	913-432-7755	R	25*	.1
497	Neptune Underwater Services (USA) LLC—*Bryan Nicholls*	PO Box 2168, Mansfield TX 76063	817-447-7321	R	25*	.1
498	Service Intelligence Inc—*Michael Gaffney*	1057 521 Corporate Cen, Fort Mill SC 29707	704-552-1119	S	25*	.1
499	Lynn Investment Corp—*William Lynch*	PO Box 10, South Plainfield NJ 07080	908-753-2200	R	25*	<.1
500	WQN Inc—*B Michael Adler*	14911 Quorum Dr Ste 14, Dallas TX 75254		P	25	<.1
501	Richard Bertram Inc—*George Jousma*	1445 SE 16th St, Fort Lauderdale FL 33316	954-462-5527	R	24*	.1
502	RL Deppmann Co—*Norman Hall*	20929 Bridge St, Southfield MI 48033	248-354-3710	R	24*	.1
503	Marine Engineering Systems Company Inc—*Agrifina H Hux*	5030 Old Kings Rd NW, Jacksonville FL 32254		R	24*	.1
504	International Museum Corp—*Tony Webber*	6399 Windfern Rd, Houston TX 77040	713-462-7754	R	24*	.1
505	Cleveland Corp—*Robert Kujawinski*	42810 N Green Bay Rd, Zion IL 60099	847-872-7200	R	24*	<.1
506	Dallas Fan Fares Inc—*Kaye Burkhardt*	5485 Beltline Rd Ste 2, Dallas TX 75254	972-239-9969	R	24*	<.1
507	Aeroxchange Ltd—*Albert Koszarek*	5221 N O'Connor Blvd S, Irving TX 75039	972-556-8543	R	24*	<.1
508	Choice Medical Management Services LLC—*Tom Barrett*	1408 N Westshore Blvd, Tampa FL 33607		D	24*	<.1
509	Greater Talent Network Inc—*Don R Epstein*	437 5th Ave, New York NY 10016	212-645-4200	R	24*	<.1
510	Hall-Erickson Inc—*Pete Erickson*	98 E Chicago Ave, Westmont IL 60559	630-434-7779	R	24*	<.1
511	Liberty Bell—*Nigel Alexander*	2460 W 26th Ave Ste 38, Denver CO 80211	303-831-1977	R	24*	<.1
512	Caterpillar World Trading Corp—*James Owens*	100 NE Adams St, Peoria IL 61629		S	24*	<.1
513	ERAI Inc—*Mark Snider*	3899 Mannix Dr Unit 42, Naples FL 34104	239-261-6268	R	24*	<.1
514	Legal Courier LCL—*Karlie Carlette*	58 South St, Morristown NJ 07960	973-422-1333	R	24*	<.1
515	Revenue Enhancement Group—*Bob Lockhart*	530 S Main St Ste 105, Orange CA 92868	714-543-4460	R	24*	<.1
516	Sightline Payments—*Kirk Sanford*	6871 S Eastern Ave Ste, Las Vegas NV 89119	702-851-4747	R	24*	<.1
517	TrustTone Communications Inc—*Hemant Thakkar*	4950 Hamilton Ave Ste, San Jose CA 95130	408-282-3563	R	24*	<.1
518	Medical Business Systems Inc—*Andrew Kluger* Med Bus Inc	70 Mitchell Blvd Ste 1, San Rafael CA 94903	415-479-6000	D	24*	<.1
519	DA Consulting Group Inc—*Steve Schloss*	900 E Hamilton Ave Ste, Campbell CA 95008	408-879-7310	R	24	.2
520	Eperformax Inc—*Teresa Hartsaw*	8001 Centerview Pkwy F, Cordova TN 38018	901-751-4800	R	23*	.6
521	Capitol LLC—*Lucas Mageno*	555 Capitol Mall Ste 5, Sacramento CA 95814	916-449-2820	R	23*	.4
522	Fasig-Tipton Company Inc—*Boyd T Browning Jr*	2400 Newtown Pike, Lexington KY 40511	859-255-1555	R	23*	.1
523	Global Axcess Corp—*Michael Connolly*	7800 Belfort Pkwy Ste, Jacksonville FL 32256	904-280-3950	P	23	.1
524	Century Payments Inc—*Robert Wechsler*	2601 Network Blvd Ste, Frisco TX 75034		R	23	.4
525	Interclick Ad Network—*Michael Mathews* Interclick Inc	11 W 19th St, New York NY 10011	646-722-6260	S	22	N/A
526	StarTek USA Inc—*Larry Jones* StarTek Inc	44 Cook St Ste 400, Denver CO 80206	303-262-4500	S	22*	.7
527	Opportunities Inc—*Barbara LeDuc*	200 E Cramer St, Fort Atkinson WI 53538	920-563-2437	R	22*	.2
528	Superior Home Services Inc—*David Cook*	15279 N Scottsdale Rd, Scottsdale AZ 85254	480-391-5500	R	22*	.1
529	Matrix Settles—*Carolyn Settles*	1005 N Glebe Rd, Arlington VA 22201	703-525-0424	R	22*	<.1
530	Howard M Schwartz Recording Inc—*Howard M Schwartz*	420 Lexington Ave Ste, New York NY 10170	212-687-4180	R	22*	<.1
531	VeenendaalCave Inc—*Edward A Cave III*	1170 Peachtree St NE S, Atlanta GA 30309	404-881-1811	R	22*	<.1
532	Mekus Studios Ltd—*Chris Mekus*	445 E Illinois St Ste, Chicago IL 60611	312-661-0778	R	22*	<.1
533	Ventura Associates Inc—*Marla Altberg*	1040 Ave of the Americ, New York NY 10018	212-302-8277	S	22*	<.1
534	Harry Davis and Co—*Stanford G Davis*	1725 Blvd of Allies, Pittsburgh PA 15219	412-765-1170	R	22*	<.1
535	MapQuest Inc—*Michael J Mulligan*	555 17th St Ste 1600, Denver CO 80202	303-486-4000	S	21*	.1
536	Caliendo-Savio Enterprises Inc—*Tom Savio*	PO Box 510941, New Berlin WI 53151	262-786-8400	R	21*	.1
537	Bookmasters Inc—*David Wurster*	30 Amberwood Pkwy, Ashland OH 44805	419-281-5100	R	21*	.3
538	Crossroad Services Inc—*Steven Scheiner*	2360 Alvarado St, San Leandro CA 94577	510-895-5055	R	21*	.4
539	Travisa Inc—*Jan Dvorak*	1731 21st St NW, Washington DC 20009	202-463-6166	R	21*	.1
540	Odyssey Marine Exploration Inc—*Gregory P Stemm*	5215 W Laurel St, Tampa FL 33607	813-876-1776	P	21	<.1

Note: An asterisk (*) indicates an estimated financial figure. The company type code used is as follows: R = Private, P = Public, S = Private Subsidiary, B = Public Subsidiary, D = Division, J = Joint Venture, I = Investment Fund.

COMPANY RANKINGS BY SALES WITHIN 4-DIGIT SIC

Rank	Company Name—Executive Officer	Address, City, State, Zip	Phone	Type	Fin	Empls
541	Hart Interior Design Ltd—Ken Zinser	15551 N Greenway-Hayde, Scottsdale AZ 85260	480-756-5200	R	21*	<.1
542	Analytical Solutions Inc—Mike Strizich	10401 Research Rd SE, Albuquerque NM 87123	505-299-1967	R	21*	<.1
543	SmartZip Analytics Inc—Tom Glassanos	6210 Stoneridge Mall R, Pleasanton CA 94588	925-271-6271	R	21*	<.1
544	Iron Mountain Information Management Inc—Bob Brennan	745 Atlantic Ave, Boston MA 02111	617-535-4766	S	21*	<.1
545	National Pharmaceutical Returns Inc—Amber Hollar	4164 NW Urbandale Dr, Urbandale IA 50322	515-252-7722	R	21*	<.1
546	Pipe and Tube Supply Inc—Mark Walker	1407 N Cypress St, North Little Rock AR 72114	501-372-6556	R	21*	<.1
547	Mid-Ship Marine Inc—Matthew DeLuca	145 Main St, Port Washington NY 11050	516-944-3500	R	21*	<.1
548	Aerofil Technology Inc—Gene Ivnik	225 Industrial Park Dr, Sullivan MO 63080	573-468-5551	R	21*	.5
549	NetCreations Inc—Matt Blumberg	379 W Broadway Ste 202, New York NY 10012	212-625-1370	S	21	<.1
550	Show Management Inc—Bill Burbank	1115 Ne 9th Ave, Fort Lauderdale FL 33304	954-764-7642	R	21*	.5
551	Merical Inc—Michael Schlinger	2995 E Miraloma Ave, Anaheim CA 92806	714-238-7225	R	20*	.3
552	Delex Systems Inc—Edmund F Driscoll II	13865 Sunrise Valley D, Herndon VA 20171	703-734-8300	R	20*	.3
553	Shiel Sexton Company Inc Interiors Div—Andy Shiel	PO Box 44107, Indianapolis IN 46244	317-423-6000	D	20*	.3
554	GeoLogics Corp—Fernando J Arroyo	5285 Shawnee Rd Ste 30, Alexandria VA 22312	703-750-4000	R	20*	.2
555	Crescent City Consultants—Patricia Denechaud	1010 Common St Ste 301, New Orleans LA 70112	504-561-1191	R	20*	.1
556	Activities 4 Less Inc—Robert Bluh	900 Front St Ste J20, Lahaina HI 96761	808-661-7300	R	20*	.1
557	Accurate Paper Recycling Corp—David Lasensky	508 E Baltimore Ave, Lansdowne PA 19050	610-623-7772	R	20	.1
558	Marts and Lundy Inc—Donald M Fellows	1200 Wall St W, Lyndhurst NJ 07071	201-460-1660	R	20*	<.1
559	Risk Management Services Corp—Jeff Rausch	PO Box 22989, Louisville KY 40252	502-326-5900	R	20*	<.1
560	Ct Investment Management Company LLC	410 Park Ave Fl 14, New York NY 10022	212-655-0240	R	20*	<.1
561	Island Def Jam Music Group—LA Reid	825 8th Ave 24th Fl, New York NY 10019	212-333-8000	S	20*	<.1
562	Sync Sound Inc—William Marino	450 W 56th St, New York NY 10019	212-246-5580	R	20*	<.1
563	Ipsos-Vantis—Ed Wolkenmuth Ipsos-ASI Inc	3130 Crow Canyon Pl St, San Ramon CA 94583	925-820-7350	D	20*	<.1
564	Schur Success Auction Services—Shannon M Schur	1042 W Baptist Rd Ste1, Colorado Springs CO 80921	719-667-1000	R	20*	<.1
565	Flamingo Surprise Inc—Rick Fazio	250 James St, Bensenville IL 60106	630-350-1280	R	20*	<.1
566	Alien Technology Corp—Peter Green	18220 Butterfield Blvd, Morgan Hill CA 95037	408-782-3900	R	20	.2
567	Diamond Paper Box Co—Karla Fichter	PO Box 23620, Rochester NY 14692	585-334-8030	R	20*	.2
568	EDGAR Online Inc—John M Connolly	11200 Rockville Pke St, Rockville MD 20852	301-287-0300	P	20	.1
569	Pacific Medical Inc—John Petlansky	PO Box 149, Tracy CA 95378		R	19*	.3
570	Aptimus Inc—Rob Wrubel	199 Fremont St Ste1800, San Francisco CA 94105	415-896-2123	S	19*	.1
571	Avesis Third Party Administrators Inc—Alan S Cohn Avesis Inc	3724 N 3rd StSte 300, Phoenix AZ 85012	602-240-9101	S	19*	<.1
572	Data Company Inc—Hal Ferrell	254 Court Ave 5th Fl, Memphis TN 38103	901-527-6623	R	19*	<.1
573	C and C Recycle—Debbie Cook	PO Box 1688, La Fayette GA 30728	706-638-0140	R	19*	<.1
574	SCA Enterprises Inc—Timothy Davis	PO Box 1455, Burbank CA 91507	818-845-7621	R	19*	.1
575	SmartPros Ltd—Alan S Greene	12 Skyline Dr, Hawthorne NY 10532	914-345-2620	P	19	.1
576	Exhibit Works Inc—Dominic Silvio	13211 Merriman Rd, Livonia MI 48150	734-525-9010	R	19*	.5
577	Ansatel Company Inc—Anthony Greenfield	PO Box 1, Moorestown NJ 08057	856-234-4100	R	19*	.3
578	General Theming Contractors LLC—Joe Barton	3750 Courtright Ct, Columbus OH 43227	614-252-6342	R	18*	.1
579	Mccormick Place Convention Center—Juan Ochoa	2301 S Lake Shore Dr, Chicago IL 60616	312-791-7900	R	18*	.6
580	National Packaging Company Inc—Joel Matthews	101 Lenwood Rd Se, Decatur AL 35603	256-350-7047	R	18*	.3
581	Perceptive Informatics Inc—Steve Kent	195 West St, Waltham MA 02451	781-487-9900	S	18*	.2
582	Merchant One Inc—Sandy Saka	524 Arthur Godfrey Rd, Miami Beach FL 33140		R	18*	.1
583	Sherwood Studios Inc—Mark Morganroth	6644 Orchard Lake Rd, West Bloomfield MI 48322	248-855-1600	R	18*	.1
584	E-Markets Inc—Scott Cavey	807 Mountain Ave Ste 2, Berthoud CO 80513		R	18*	<.1
585	Interior Systems Contract Group Inc—Marian Lavoy	28000 Woodward Ave, Royal Oak MI 48067	248-399-1600	R	18*	<.1
586	Hilco Appraisal Services LLC—Arnold Dratt	5 Revere Dr Ste 206, Northbrook IL 60062		S	18*	<.1
587	Hilco Industrial LLC—Robert Levy	31555 W Fourteen Mile, Farmington Hills MI 48334	248-254-9999	S	18*	<.1
588	Home Access Health Corp—Mary Vogt	2401 W Hassel Rd Ste 1, Hoffman Estates IL 60169	847-781-2500	R	18*	<.1
589	InfoPros—Bernie Schneider	12325 Oracle Blvd Ste, Colorado Springs CO 80921	719-593-7377	R	18*	<.1
590	Manning and Napier Information Services—Paul Tyborowski	500 University Corpora, Amherst NY 14226	716-862-0051	R	18*	<.1
591	Marketing Analysts Inc—Richard Serrins	238 Albemarle Rd, Charleston SC 29407	843-797-8900	R	18*	<.1
592	SJ Bashen Corp—Janet Emerson Bashen	1616 S Voss Ste 300, Houston TX 77057	713-780-8056	R	18*	<.1
593	Topitzes and Associates Inc—Nicholas Topitzes	124 Horizon Dr, Verona WI 53593	608-845-1850	R	18*	<.1
594	UGO Entertainment Inc—J Moses	670 Broadway Fl 2, New York NY 10012	212-624-3300	R	18*	<.1
595	Kelley's Personal Communications Inc	14240 Interurban Ave S, Tukwila WA 98168	206-682-1111	R	18*	<.1
596	Marc Truant and Associates Inc—Marc Truant	32 Warren St, Cambridge MA 02141	617-868-8630	R	18*	<.1
597	Accu-Tec Inc—Jeff Davis	1735 W Burnett Ave, Louisville KY 40210	502-339-7511	R	18*	.3
598	Swanke Hayden Connell and Partners LLP—George Alexander	295 Lafayette St Fl 6, New York NY 10012	212-226-9696	R	18*	.1
599	Solix Inc—John Parry	PO Box 685, Parsippany NJ 07054	973-581-5001	R	18*	.4
600	Order Express Inc—Jorge Miranda	685 W Ohio St, Chicago IL 60654	312-235-5200	R	18*	.3
601	Packaging Service Company Inc—Jean Baizan	1904 Mykawa Rd, Pearland TX 77581	281-485-1458	R	18*	.3
602	Genesee Packaging Inc—Willie Artis	PO Box 7716, Flint MI 48507	810-235-6120	R	18*	.3
603	DI Y/Group Inc—Finley Durham	2401 W 26th St, Muncie IN 47302	765-284-9000	R	18*	.3
604	In-Store Opportunities Inc—Leonard Rosinski	362 Industrial Park Rd, Middletown CT 06457	860-632-8880	R	17*	.4
605	Plastiflex Company Inc—David Mcivor	601 E Palomar St Ste 4, Chula Vista CA 91911	619-662-8792	R	17*	.2
606	Archimedes Global Inc	3001 N Rocky Point Dr, Tampa FL 33607		R	17	.1
607	FreightMatrix North America Inc—Mark Skoda	6799 Great Oaks Rd Ste, Memphis TN 38138	901-746-6200	S	17*	.1
608	Air Survey Corp—William J McKeague	45180 Business Ct, Dulles VA 20166	703-471-4510	S	17*	<.1
609	RTi-DFD—David Rothstein	1351 Washington Blvd, Stamford CT 06902	203-324-2420	R	17*	<.1
610	Taylor Studios Inc—Betty Brennan	1320 Harmon Dr, Rantoul IL 61866	217-893-4874	R	17*	<.1
611	Robert Coleman and Partners—Robert M Coleman III	3377 North Blvd, Baton Rouge LA 70806	225-387-4414	R	17*	<.1
612	Egg Strategy—Heather Dupre	1360 Walnut St Ste 102, Boulder CO 80302	303-546-9311	R	17*	<.1
613	Safer Textile Processing Corp—Albert Safer	1875 Mccarter Hwy, Newark NJ 07104	973-482-6400	R	17*	.4
614	Sunrise Credit Services Inc—Richard Doane	PO Box 9100, Farmingdale NY 11743	631-501-8500	R	17*	.2
615	LARK Industries Inc—Richard Scholten	4900 E Hunter Ave, Anaheim CA 92807	714-701-9200	R	16*	.2
616	ITEX Corp (Bellevue Washington)—Steven White	3326 160th Ave SE Ste, Bellevue WA 98008	425-463-4000	P	16	<.1
617	Fremont Grain Inspection Department Inc—David Reeder	603 E Dodge St, Fremont NE 68025	402-721-1270	R	16*	<.1
618	Griffith Inc—Brett Griffith	458 Pke Rd, Huntingdon Valley PA 19006	215-322-7010	R	16*	.2
619	Alpine Access Inc—Christopher M Carrington	1120 Lincoln St Ste 14, Denver CO 80203	303-279-0585	R	16*	5.0
620	Brennan Beer Gorman Monk/Interiors—Julia Monk	161 6th Ave 3rd Fl, New York NY 10113	212-888-7667	S	16*	.1
621	O'ryan Group Inc—Emmett O'ryan	4010 Pilot Dr Ste 108, Memphis TN 38118	901-794-4610	R	16*	.1
622	Aerial Cartographics of America Inc—Mark Detrick	1722 W Oak Ridge Rd, Orlando FL 32809	407-851-7880	S	16*	.1
623	Bailey Brand Consulting—Christopher K Bailey	200 W Germantown Pike, Plymouth Meeting PA 19462	610-940-9030	R	16*	<.1
624	American Voice Mail Inc	2310 S Sepulveda Blvd, Los Angeles CA 90064	310-478-4949	R	16*	<.1
625	Battery Studios—Barry Weiss	321 W 44th St 10th Fl, New York NY 10036	212-833-7373	D	16*	<.1
626	Hendrick Inc—Randy Seay	8 Piedmont Ctr Ste 300, Atlanta GA 30305	404-261-9383	R	16*	<.1
627	Hilco Merchant Resources LLC—Jeffrey Hecktman	5 Revere Dr Ste 206, Northbrook IL 60062	847-509-1100	S	16*	<.1
628	Burst Communications Inc—Kirk Basefsky	8200 S Akron Ste 10, Centennial CO 80112	303-649-9600	R	16*	<.1

Rank	Company Name—*Executive Officer*	Address, City, State, Zip	Phone	Type	Fin	Empls
629	Equitable Production Group Div—*Murry Gerber*	787 7th Ave, New York NY 10019	212-314-4000	S	16*	<.1
630	Recording Workshop—*Jim Rosebrook*	455 Massieville Rd, Chillicothe OH 45601	740-663-1000	R	16*	<.1
631	Global Financial Aid Services Inc—*Edward Addison*	10467 Corporate Dr, Gulfport MS 39503	228-523-1080	R	16*	.3
632	Dexter Hospitality Inc—*Mark Zimmerman*	3493 Lamar Ave, Memphis TN 38118	901-365-4742	R	16*	.2
633	Mountain Glacier LLC—*Jay Peterson*	709 Oak Hill Rd, Evansville IN 47711	812-423-1955	R	16*	.1
634	In Terminal Services Corp—*John Lanigan*	3111 167th St, Hazel Crest IL 60429	708-225-2400	R	15*	.3
635	Reo Allegiance Inc—*Lisa Levine*	111 Linnett St, Bayonne NJ 07002	201-823-4605	R	15*	.1
636	Military Sales and Service Co—*Roy Barber*	5301 S Westmoreland Rd, Dallas TX 75237	214-330-4621	R	15*	.8
637	Production Service Too LLC—*Louis Stone*	1319 N Broad St, Hillside NJ 07205	908-353-1500	R	15*	.4
638	Hirsch/Bedner International Inc—*Howard Pharr*	3216 Nebraska Ave, Santa Monica CA 90404	310-829-9087	R	15*	.4
639	Institutional Investor Inc—*Christopher Brown*	225 Park Ave S Fl 7, New York NY 10003	212-224-3300	S	15*	.3
640	Quick Check—*Dale Smith*	988 Main St, Roanoke AL 36274	334-863-5501	R	15*	.1
641	MJ Harden Associates Inc—*Doug Leibbrandt*	5700 Broadmoor St Ste, Mission KS 66202	913-981-9600	S	15*	.1
642	Exec-U-Net Inc—*David B Opton*	295 Westport Ave Ste 8, Norwalk CT 06851	203-750-1030	R	15*	.1
643	Propac Marketing Inc—*Charles Daigle*	PO Box 595, Addison TX 75001	972-733-3199	R	15*	<.1
644	Bodine Inc—*Eddie Miller*	2141 14th Ave S, Birmingham AL 35205	205-933-9100	R	15*	<.1
645	Interior Architects Inc—*Mick McCullough*	350 California St Ste, San Francisco CA 94104	415-434-3305	R	15*	<.1
646	Vasco Corp—*Ken Hunt*	1901 S Meyers Rd, Oakbrook Terrace IL 60181	630-932-8844	R	15*	<.1
647	BDH and Young Space Design Inc—*Jill Brecount*	7001 France Ave S Ste, Edina MN 55435	952-893-9020	R	15*	<.1
648	Kay Green Design and Merchandising Inc—*Kay Green*	859 Outer Rd, Orlando FL 32814	407-246-7155	R	15*	<.1
649	AvSupport Inc—*KC Hemelstrand*	1801 23rd Ave N Ste 11, Fargo ND 58102	701-271-9111	R	15*	<.1
650	Eimont Capital Group LLC	1410 Stark St, Lakewood NJ 08701	732-267-5137	R	15*	<.1
651	Futurex—*Brett Smith*	864 Old Boerne Rd, Bulverde TX 78163	830-980-9782	R	15*	<.1
652	GoIndustry USA Inc—*Jack Reinelt*	11425 Cronhill Dr, Owings Mills MD 21117	410-654-7500	D	15*	<.1
653	Medialynx Group—*Denise Hoff*	4529 Charing Cross Roa, Sarasota FL 34241	941-366-9396	R	15*	<.1
654	Ocean Tomo LLC—*Jake Geleerd*	200 W Madison 37th Fl, Chicago IL 60606	312-327-4400	R	15*	<.1
655	Corporate Design Group—*Carol Parra-Little*	2150 Douglas Blvd Ste, Roseville CA 95661	916-781-6543	R	15*	<.1
656	Datascension Inc—*Lou Persico*	532 Pima Canyon Ct, Las Vegas NV 89144	832-615-4777	P	15	1.0
657	Noram Capital Holdings Inc—*Anthony Renteria*	PO Box 9250, Dallas TX 75209		P	15	<.1
658	Constructioncom—*Robert D Stuono*	2 Penn Plz 9th Fl, New York NY 10121	212-904-3092	D	15	.1
659	Mission Of Mercy—*David Perkin*	PO Box 62600, Colorado Springs CO 80962	719-481-0400	R	15*	<.1
660	Contract Filling Inc—*William Lizzi*	10 Cliffside Dr, Cedar Grove NJ 07009	973-239-6608	R	14*	.2
661	Quality Associates Inc—*Delores Epps*	5121 Fishwick Dr, Cincinnati OH 45216	513-242-4477	R	14*	.3
662	Virtual-Agent Services—*Robert Camastro*	1920 N Thoreau Dr Ste, Schaumburg IL 60173	847-925-2340	R	14*	.6
663	Hilton Resort Palm Springs—*Aftab Dada*	400 E Tahquitz Canyon, Palm Springs CA 92262	760-320-6868	R	14*	.2
664	Aaron Thomas Company Inc—*Thomas Bacon*	7421 Chapman Ave, Garden Grove CA 92841	714-894-4468	R	14*	.2
665	Bay Microfilm Inc—*William D Whitney*	1115 E Arques Ave, Sunnyvale CA 94085	408-736-7444	R	14*	.2
666	mSpot Inc—*Daren Tsui*	455 Portage Ave Ste A, Palo Alto CA 94306	650-321-7000	R	14*	.1
667	Colorado Consumer Credit Counseling Services of Greater Denver Inc—*John Berglund*	PO Box 378050, Denver CO 80237	303-632-2100	R	14*	.1
668	Shuman Plastics Inc—*Ken Shuman*	35 Neoga St, Depew NY 14043	716-685-2121	R	14*	<.1
669	Courtesy Associates Inc—*Brad Weaber*	2025 M St NW Ste 800, Washington DC 20036	202-331-2000	S	14*	<.1
670	Patrick Henry Creative Promotions—*Patrick Henry*	11104 W Airport Blvd S, Stafford TX 77477	281-983-5500	R	14*	<.1
671	Royal Buying Group Inc—*Mike Zielinski*	2100 Western Ct Ste 35, Lisle IL 60532	630-353-7950	R	14*	<.1
672	Philpotts and Associates Inc—*Mary Philpotts McGrath*	40 S School St Ste 200, Honolulu HI 96813	808-523-6771	R	14*	<.1
673	Vervelife—*Justin Jarvinen*	625 N Michigan Ave Ste, Chicago IL 60611	312-893-7000	R	14*	<.1
674	Capitol Fiber Inc—*Margaret Abbott*	6610 Electronic Dr, Springfield VA 22151	703-658-0020	R	14*	<.1
675	Transite Technology Inc—*Geoff Comrie*	1008 Bullard Ct Ste 10, Raleigh NC 27615	919-802-1900	R	14*	<.1
676	Electronic Check Services—*Derron Winfrey*	1615 S Ingram Mill Rd, Springfield MO 65804		R	14*	<.1
677	L B Limited Inc—*Bruce Lewis*	120 S Dixie Hwy Ste 20, West Palm Beach FL 33401	561-833-8080	R	14*	<.1
678	Rancho Mesa Properties—*Alan Townsend*	4550 Kearny Villa Rd N, San Diego CA 92123		R	14*	<.1
679	OptiMark Holdings Inc—*Robert Warshaw*	2500 Plz 5 Harborside, Jersey City NJ 07311	212-626-6814	R	14	.1
680	EH Packing LLC	1929 S Arizona Ave Ste, Yuma AZ 85364	928-317-0183	R	14*	.5
681	Jonco Industries Inc—*Thomas Ryan*	2501 W Hampton Ave, Milwaukee WI 53209	414-449-2000	R	14*	.1
682	International Monetary Systems Ltd—*John E Strabley*	16901 W Glendale Dr, New Berlin WI 53151	262-780-3640	P	14	N/A
683	Wood Group Production Services Inc—*Rod Prinsep*	182 Equity Blvd, Houma LA 70360	985-868-4116	R	14*	.4
684	Associated Production Services Inc—*Debbie Belding*	PO Box 781, Doylestown PA 18901	215-364-0211	R	14*	.2
685	Southern Design Services Inc—*Danny Cash*	110 Carpet Dr, Spartanburg SC 29303	864-278-5000	R	14*	.3
686	Farm Progress Companies Inc—*Brian Mccarthy*	255 38th Ave Ste P, Saint Charles IL 60174	630-690-5600	R	14*	.2
687	Particle Measuring Systems Inc—*Paul Kelly*	5475 Airport Blvd, Boulder CO 80301	303-443-7100	R	14*	.2
688	Butterball Farms Inc—*Mark Peters*	1435 Buchanan Ave Sw, Grand Rapids MI 49507	616-243-0105	R	13*	.2
689	Wellsco Field Services LLC—*Kasy Isayeva*	PO Box 630906, Houston TX 77263	713-789-1650	R	13*	.4
690	Benchmark-Tech Corp—*Tom O'shea*	PO Box 2788, Santa Cruz CA 95063	831-475-5600	R	13*	.3
691	Mpb Group LLC—*Andrew Pryor*	3600 Harwood Rd Ste A, Bedford TX 76021	817-785-5073	R	13*	.3
692	Camping Companies Inc—*Kevin Camping*	PO Box 56037, Phoenix AZ 85079	602-864-7860	R	13*	.1
693	Genscape Inc—*Sean O'Leary*	445 E Market St Ste 20, Louisville KY 40202	502-583-3435	R	13*	.1
694	Specialized Housing Inc—*David Wizansky*	45 Bartlett Crescent, Brookline MA 02446	617-277-1805	R	13*	.1
695	Aero-Metric Incorporated Anchorage Div—*Anthony Follett*	2014 Merrill Field Dr, Anchorage AK 99501	907-272-4495	D	13*	.1
696	Metropolitan Presort Inc—*Richard Barton*	3506 NW 35th, Portland OR 97210	503-224-7230	R	13*	.1
697	Harry Walker Agency Inc—*Don Walker*	355 Lexington Ave 21st, New York NY 10117	646-227-4900	R	13*	<.1
698	VoiceLog LLC—*Gregory Carter*	580 Burbank St Ste 120, Broomfield CO 80020		R	13*	<.1
699	AIIM International Inc—*John Mancini*	1100 Wayne Ave Ste 110, Silver Spring MD 20910	301-587-8202	R	13*	<.1
700	ABJ Fire Protection Co—*Dennis Weller*	6500 New Venture Gear, East Syracuse NY 13057	315-423-9766	R	13*	<.1
701	MarketingSherpa Inc—*Anne Holland*	499 Main St, Warren RI 02885	401-247-7655	R	13*	<.1
702	Party Planners West Inc—*Patricia Ryan*	5730 Uplander Way Ste, Culver City CA 90230	310-305-1000	R	13*	<.1
703	Rotman Collectibles Inc—*Greg Rotman* Paid Inc	4 Brussels St, Worcester MA 01610	508-791-6710	S	13*	<.1
704	Yessick's Design Center—*Marsha Yessicks*	1926 Gunbarrel Rd, Chattanooga TN 37421	423-892-1785	R	13*	<.1
705	Telarus Inc—*Adam Edwards*	12401 S 450 E Unit D-1, Draper UT 84020	801-523-2100	R	13*	<.1
706	Architext Inc (Andover Massachusetts)—*Hans Fenstermacher*	Bldg 300 Brickstone Sq, Andover MA 01810	978-409-6112	D	13*	<.1
707	Business Network International—*Ivan Misner*	545 College Commerce W, Upland CA 91786	909-608-7575	R	13*	<.1
708	Newell Novelty Company Inc—*David B Newell*	PO Box 1098, Roxboro NC 27573	336-597-2248	R	13*	<.1
709	Input Technology Inc—*Don Monroe*	1470 S Vandeventer Ave, Saint Louis MO 63110	314-534-4375	R	13*	<.1
710	Imagine Fulfillment Services LLC—*Pablo Hernandez*	20100 S Vermont Ave, Torrance CA 90502	310-217-4610	R	13*	.3
711	Geotext Translations Inc—*Joseph Duncan*	259 W 30th St Fl 17, New York NY 10001	212-631-7432	R	13*	.1
712	Hill's Pool Service Inc—*Gerald Hill*	23 Edwards Ct, Burlingame CA 94010	650-342-2484	R	13*	<.1
713	Applied Textiles Inc—*John Schroeter*	555 76th St Sw Ste 4, Byron Center MI 49315	616-559-6100	R	13*	.2
714	P and L Development Of New York Corp—*Mitchell Singer*	200 Hicks St, Westbury NY 11590	516-986-1700	R	13*	.2
715	Dimensional Merchandising Inc—*Eugene Sylva*	86 N Main St, Wharton NJ 07885	973-328-1600	R	12*	.3
716	ARTISTdirect Inc—*Dimitri Villard*	1601 Cloverfield Blvd, Santa Monica CA 90404	310-956-3300	S	12	.1

Note: An asterisk (*) indicates an estimated financial figure. The company type code used is as follows: R = Private, P = Public, S = Private Subsidiary, B = Public Subsidiary, D = Division, J = Joint Venture, I = Investment Fund.

COMPANY RANKINGS BY SALES WITHIN 4-DIGIT SIC

Rank	Company Name—Executive Officer	Address, City, State, Zip	Phone	Type	Fin	Empls
717	Medusind Solutions Inc—Vipul Bansal	31103 Rancho Viejo Rd, San Juan Capistrano CA 92675	949-240-8895	R	12*	.9
718	You and Associates LLC—Doreen Baca	20770 N Hwy 281, San Antonio TX 78258	210-402-0062	R	12*	.2
719	BMI Imaging Systems Inc—William D Whitney Jr Bay Microfilm Inc	1115 E Arques Ave, Sunnyvale CA 94085	408-736-7444	D	12*	.1
720	Santa Barbara Applied Research Inc—Grace Vaswani	2151 Alessandro Dr Ste, Ventura CA 93001	805-643-7081	R	12*	.1
721	Palladian Partners Inc—Marion Barker	8484 Georgia Ave, Silver Spring MD 20910	301-650-8660	S	12*	.1
722	High Street Partners Inc—Larry Harding	222 Severn Ave Bldg 14, Annapolis MD 21403	410-263-7400	R	12*	.1
723	Customized Energy Solutions Ltd—Stephen Fernands	1528 Walnut St 22nd Fl, Philadelphia PA 19102	215-875-9440	R	12*	.1
724	Corporate Call Center Inc—Claudia Timbo	1400 Union Meeting Rd, Blue Bell PA 19422	215-283-4200	R	12*	<.1
725	Lee Group Inc—Michelle Jacobs	2006 Old Greenbriar Rd, Chesapeake VA 23320	757-420-8011	R	12*	<.1
726	Avatar Entertainment Corp—Kirk Imamura	441 W 53rd St, New York NY 10019	212-765-7500	R	12*	<.1
727	Engstrom Design Group Inc—Jennifer Johanson	1201 5th Ave, San Rafael CA 94901	415-454-2277	R	12*	<.1
728	Integrated Power Solutions Inc—David Knight	4165 Raphael St Sw, Covington GA 30014	770-385-3480	R	12*	<.1
729	Managed Care Professionals Inc—Tim Alfeirro SOURCECORP Inc	580 Old State Rd, Ballwin MO 63021	636-227-7919	S	12*	<.1
730	PowerSecure Inc Powersecure International Inc	1609 Heritage Commerce, Wake Forest NC 27587	919-556-3056	S	12*	<.1
731	Aero Studios Ltd—Thomas O'Brien	419 Broome St, New York NY 10013	212-966-4700	R	12*	<.1
732	Bernd Group Inc—Pilar Ricaurte-Bernd	1251 Pinehurst Rd, Dunedin FL 34698		R	12*	<.1
733	Capital Auto and Truck Auction Inc—Mark Loesberg	1905 Brentwood Rd NE, Washington DC 20018	202-269-3361	R	12*	<.1
734	Impulse Point—J David Robinson	6810 New Tampa Hwy Ste, Lakeland FL 33815	863-802-3738	R	12*	<.1
735	Liska and Associates—Steve Liska	610 N Fairbanks, Chicago IL 60611	312-867-1111	R	12*	<.1
736	Metal Suppliers Online LLC—Alan Gamble	PO Box 711, Hampstead NH 03841	603-329-0101	R	12*	<.1
737	Metropolitan Communication Services Inc—R Scott Harrell	914 E Palmetto Ave, Melbourne FL 32901	321-723-9300	R	12*	<.1
738	OneAero—Justin Spaulding	45 E 100 N, Alpine UT 84004	801-492-4070	J	12*	<.1
739	Wildfire Studios—Chris David	640 S San Vincente Blv, Los Angeles CA 90048	323-951-1700	R	12*	<.1
740	Alaric Compliance Services LLC—Guy F Talarico	150 Broadway Ste 302, New York NY 10038	212-243-5241	R	12*	<.1
741	Goodman Factors—Keith Reid	3010 LBJ Fwy, Dallas TX 75234	972-241-3297	R	12*	<.1
742	Fisher Auction Company Inc—Louis Fisher	619 E Atlantic Blvd, Pompano Beach FL 33060	954-942-0917	R	12*	<.1
743	Workhouse Publicity—Adam Nelson	133 West 25th St No 3W, New York City NY 10001	212-645-8006	R	12*	<.1
744	Inter-Faith Food Shuttle—Jill Bullard	PO Box 14638, Raleigh NC 27620	919-250-0043	R	12*	<.1
745	Identatronics Inc—William Bangston	165 N Lively Blvd, Elk Grove Village IL 60007	847-437-2654	R	12*	.2
746	Automated Presort Inc—Jerry Imbriani	1400 Centre Cir, Downers Grove IL 60515	630-620-7678	R	11*	.2
747	Visage Mobile Inc—Matthew Johnson	500 Sansome St Ste 300, San Francisco CA 94111	415-200-2888	R	11*	.2
748	Hawaii Convention Center—Neil Mullanaphy	1801 Kalakaua Ave, Honolulu HI 96815	808-943-3500	R	11*	.1
749	Bonded Services Inc—Glen Greene	3205 Burton Ave, Burbank CA 91504	818-848-9766	R	11*	.2
750	Argent Trading Corp—Rafael Corral	521 5th Ave Rm 2200, New York NY 10175	212-697-8800	R	11*	.2
751	Hartmann Studios Inc—Mark Guelfi	70 W Ohio Ave Ste H, Richmond CA 94804	510-232-5060	R	11*	.2
752	Active International—Sharon Marshall	1 Blue Hill Plz, Pearl River NY 10965	845-735-1700	R	11*	.3
753	Rsdc Of Michigan LLC—Joseph Mcdevitt	1775 Holloway Dr, Holt MI 48842	517-699-7732	R	11*	.3
754	Classmates Online Inc—Mark R Goldston Classmates Media Corp	2001 Lind Ave SW Ste 5, Renton WA 98057	425-917-5000	S	11*	.2
755	Intermap Technologies Inc—Todd Oseth	8310 S Valley Hwy Ste, Englewood CO 80112	303-708-0955	P	11*	.2
756	TestPak Inc—Uma Kastury	125 Algonquin Prky, Whippany NJ 07981	973-887-4440	R	11*	.1
757	Listencom Inc—Rob Glaser	2012 16th St, San Francisco CA 94103	415-934-2000	S	11*	<.1
758	Audio Messaging Solutions—Mitchell Keller	720 Brooker Creek Blvd, Oldsmar FL 34677	727-787-2440	R	11*	<.1
759	Auction Systems Auctioneers and Appraisers Inc—Deb Weidenhamer	951 W Watkins St, Phoenix AZ 85007	602-252-4842	R	11*	<.1
760	Teammates Commercial Interiors Inc—Mike Berkery	320 S Teller St Ste 25, Lakewood CO 80226	303-639-5885	R	11*	<.1
761	Higgenbotham Auctioneers International Limited Inc—Martin Higgenbotham	1666 Williamsburg Sq, Lakeland FL 33803	863-644-6681	R	11*	<.1
762	ForTheFarm Inc—Chris Houden	6417 Normandy Ln, Madison WI 53719	608-277-5952	R	11*	<.1
763	Mastermind Marketing Inc—Dan Dodson	1450 W Peachtree St, Atlanta GA 30309	678-420-4000	R	11*	<.1
764	American Security Shredding—Steve Schlake	PO Box 402, Oceanside NY 11572	516-766-2997	R	11*	<.1
765	Mailways Enterprises Inc—David Carson	6105 Factory Rd, Crystal Lake IL 60014	815-455-4850	R	11*	<.1
766	NHT Global Inc—Chris T Sharng	751 Canyon Dr Ste 150, Coppell TX 75019	972-241-4080	S	11*	<.1
767	Reiser Group—Paul Reiser	4723 Viking Dr, Bossier City LA 71111	318-549-1489	R	11*	<.1
768	Regency-Superior Ltd—David M Kols	229 N Euclid Ave, Saint Louis MO 63108	314-361-5699	R	11*	<.1
769	LE Seitz Associates Inc—Larry Seitz	PO Box 347348, Miami FL 33234	782-942-9173	R	11*	<.1
770	Crestcom International Ltd—Dan Bowers	6900 E Belleview Ave S, Greenwood Village CO 80111	303-267-8200	R	11*	<.1
771	Kemble Interiors Inc—Mimi McMakin	294 Hibiscus Ave, Palm Beach FL 33480	561-659-5556	R	11*	<.1
772	Syntes Language Groups Inc—Beatriz A Bonnet	7465 E Peakview Ave, Centennial CO 80111	303-779-1288	R	11*	<.1
773	Fox Paine and Company LLC—Saul A Fox	3500 Alameda de las Pu, Menlo Park CA 94025	650-235-2075	R	11*	<.1
774	Thurston County Fire Protection District 3—Nola Harrison	1231 Franz St SE, Lacey WA 98503	360-491-9555	R	11*	.1
775	PaymentMax—Tony Sharp	749 Lakefield Rd, Westlake Village CA 91361	805-497-2400	R	11	<.1
776	Listen Up Espanol Inc—Craig Handley	50 Monument Sq Ste 300, Portland ME 04101		R	11	.5
777	Bel Air Auto Auction Inc—Raymond Nichols	PO Box 516, Bel Air MD 21014	410-838-5880	R	11*	.2
778	Industrial Stitchtech Inc—Ed Perez	520 Library St, San Fernando CA 91340	818-365-1300	R	11*	.2
779	Metro Fire Safety Guards Inc—Charles Loiodice	588 Meacham Ave, Elmont NY 11003	516-352-4465	R	11*	.2
780	Skillpath Seminars Inc—Robb Garr	6900 Squibb Rd, Shawnee Mission KS 66202	913-362-3900	R	11*	.3
781	Msdsonline Inc—Glenn Trout	350 N Orleans St Ste 9, Chicago IL 60654	312-881-2000	R	11*	.1
782	Cip International Inc—Kathleen Huff	9575 Le Saint Dr, Fairfield OH 45014	513-874-9925	R	11*	.1
783	Language Connection—Michael Antonelli	12417 W Surrey Ave, El Mirage AZ 85335	623-842-4748	R	10*	.4
784	Scherzer International Corp—Larry Scherzer	6351 Owensmouth Ave St, Woodland Hills CA 91367	818-227-2770	R	10*	.1
785	Bronx Defenders—Robin Steinberg	860 Courtland Ave, Bronx NY 10451	718-838-7878	R	10*	.1
786	Nationwide Biweekly Administration Inc—Daniel Lipsky	855 Lower Bellbrook Rd, Xenia OH 45385	937-376-5800	R	10*	.1
787	Liberty Capital Group—Gregory B Maffei	12300 Liberty Blvd, Englewood CO 80112	720-875-5400	S	10	.1
788	Pro Pools Management Inc—Robert Shelton	3990 Fee Fee Rd, Bridgeton MO 63044	314-298-8000	R	10*	.2
789	Ideal Steel Inc—Ronald Duquette	90693 Link Rd, Eugene OR 97402	541-689-0901	R	10*	.1
790	Robert W Hunt Co—Greg Rzonca	2211 Butterfield Rd, Downers Grove IL 60515	630-795-3200	S	10*	.4
791	Willow Bend Communications Inc—Stephen L Thompson	PO Box 797485, Dallas TX 75379	972-248-0451	R	10	.2
792	Protocall Communications Inc—Scott Kleinknecht	312 Marshall Ave Ste 9, Laurel MD 20707	301-361-1111	R	10*	.2
793	National Arbitration Forum Inc—Edward Anderson	PO Box 50191, Minneapolis MN 55405	952-516-6400	R	10*	.2
794	Plant-N-Power Services LLP—Nichalos Brost	2711 Lilac St, Pasadena TX 77503	713-477-6006	R	10*	.1
795	The O'Brien's Group—Tim Perkins	2929 E Imperial Hwy St, Brea CA 92821	714-577-2100	S	10*	.1
796	Wolcott Architecture and Interiors—AJ Wilder	3859 Cardiff Ave, Culver City CA 90232	310-204-2290	R	10*	.1
797	Cook and Company Inc—Peter A Cook St	PO Box 1068, Marshfield MA 02050	781-837-7300	R	10*	<.1
798	Business Integra Inc—Prathiba Ramadoss	7229 Hanover Pky Ste D, Greenbelt MD 20770		R	10*	<.1
799	Rizzo Packaging Inc—Paul Rizzo	PO Box 278, Plainwell MI 49080	269-685-5808	R	10*	<.1
800	Strickland Packaging Company Inc—Bayard S Tynes Jr	481 Republic Cir, Birmingham AL 35214	205-798-3000	R	10*	<.1

Rank	Company Name—Executive Officer	Address, City, State, Zip	Phone	Type	Fin	Empls
801	FreightDesk Technologies LLC—Donald R Quartel	7925 Jones Branch Dr S, McLean VA 22102	703-356-5050	R	10*	<.1
802	Checkvelocity Inc—Ed Marcoe	PO Box 331047, Nashville TN 37203	615-321-2665	R	10*	<.1
803	Spear Corp—Brian Spear	PO Box 3, Roachdale IN 46172	765-522-1126	R	10*	<.1
804	Aloft Group Inc—Matt Bowen	26 Parker St, Newburyport MA 01950	978-462-0002	R	10*	<.1
805	Bittners Commerical Group—Claire Alagia	731 E Main St, Louisville KY 40202	502-584-6349	R	10*	<.1
806	Interior Design Associates Inc—Bonnie Manson	618 Church St Ste 400, Nashville TN 37219	615-320-7550	R	10*	<.1
807	Marcum Denver Inc Powersecure International Inc	1609 Heritage Commerce, Wake Forest NC 27587	919-556-3056	S	10*	<.1
808	Pyle Joe R Complete Auction Service—Joe Pyle	199 Gas Company Rd, Mount Morris PA 15349	724-324-9000	R	10*	<.1
809	Universal Exhibits—M Robert Bell	9517 E Rush St, South El Monte CA 91733	323-686-0562	R	10*	<.1
810	Atlanta Arrangements Inc—Susan Henderson	1197 Peachtree St Ste, Atlanta GA 30361	404-443-5959	R	10*	<.1
811	Computer Telecommunications Company Inc—William Bennett	3000 Scott Blvd Ste 11, Santa Clara CA 95054	408-727-3171	R	10	<.1
812	Probablistic Software Inc—Sonja J Friedman	4536 Indianola Way PSI, La Canada Flintridge CA 91011	818-790-6412	R	10*	<.1
813	Integrated Mortgage Solutions—Cheryl Lang	16225 Park Ten Pl Ste, Houston TX 77084	281-994-4500	R	10*	<.1
814	Insyght Interactive Inc—Rina Yasuda	11900 Olympic Blvd Ste, Los Angeles CA 90064	310-247-3840	R	10*	<.1
815	Sun Media Productions	5320 S Procyon St, Las Vegas NV 89118	702-597-1969	R	10*	<.1
816	Wells Design Group—Susan Wells	7700 Congress Ave Ste, Boca Raton FL 33487	561-417-8364	R	10*	<.1
817	Peoples Foreign Exchange Corp—Alami Binani	575 5th Ave Lobby 3, New York NY 10017	212-883-0550	R	10	<.1
818	Perimeter Digital Imaging and Supply—Gary Adams	5150 Peachtree Industr, Norcross GA 30071		R	10*	<.1
819	Digital-Ink Inc—John Nissley	PO Box 426, Dillsburg PA 17019	717-432-7766	R	10*	.1
820	Blue Chip Inventory Service Inc—Gerard Walsh	14852 Ventura Blvd Ste, Sherman Oaks CA 91403	818-461-1765	R	10*	.2
821	Hydrosol Inc—Alan Howarth	8407 S 77th Ave, Bridgeview IL 60455	708-598-7180	R	10*	.1
822	Industrial Appraisal Company Inc—Raymond Durkin	603 Stanwix St Ste 150, Pittsburgh PA 15222	412-471-2566	R	10*	.1
823	Aggressive Grinding Service Inc—Lester Sutton	4413 Rte 982, Latrobe PA 15650	724-537-7722	R	10*	.1
824	Eurpac—Michael Ruez	8220 Elmbrook Dr, Dallas TX 75247	214-630-8771	R	10*	.1
825	H CA S Of Florida Inc—Joseph Pores	4720 Nw Boca Raton Blv, Boca Raton FL 33431	561-994-3334	R	10*	.2
826	Expo Group LP—Ron Farrington	5931 Campus Cir Dr W, Irving TX 75063	972-580-9000	R	9*	.1
827	Knight Printing Co—Michael Wenaas	PO Box 2306, Fargo ND 58108	701-235-1121	R	9*	.1
828	ERepublic Inc—Dennis Mckenna	100 Blue Ravine Rd, Folsom CA 95630	916-932-1300	R	9*	.1
829	Founders Group—Julian Fruhling	15100 N 78th Way Ste 2, Scottsdale AZ 85260	480-367-8202	R	9*	<.1
830	Elite Exhibits LLC—Donna Nagy	PO Box 610, Flowery Branch GA 30542	770-718-9282	R	9*	<.1
831	Three-Dimensional Services Inc—Douglas Peterson	2547 Product Dr, Rochester Hills MI 48309	248-852-1333	R	9*	.2
832	Eei Global Inc—Derek Gentile	1400 S Livernois Rd, Rochester Hills MI 48307	248-601-9900	R	9*	.2
833	Gsa Design Inc—Grigor Grigoryan	4551 San Fernando Rd S, Glendale CA 91204	818-241-2558	R	9*	.2
834	Bdops LLC	4261 Park Rd, Ann Arbor MI 48103	734-663-1611	R	9*	.1
835	American Friends Of The Hebrew University Inc—Ira Sorkin	1 Battery Park Plz Fl, New York NY 10004	212-809-4430	R	9*	.1
836	Enterprise Events Group Inc—Matt Gillam	950 Northgate Dr, San Rafael CA 94903	415-499-4444	R	9*	.1
837	BServ Inc—David F Kvederis	8350 S Durango Dr, Las Vegas NV 89113	415-277-9900	R	9*	.1
838	American Micro Data—Tim Norris	4950 E 41st Ave, Denver CO 80216	303-322-4008	R	9*	<.1
839	Larrabee Sound Inc—Rachel Carpenter	4162 Lankershim Blvd, North Hollywood CA 91602	818-753-0717	R	9*	<.1
840	Nelson and Associates Inc—John Nelson Jr	222-230 Walnut St, Philadelphia PA 19106	215-925-6562	R	9*	<.1
841	Comtel Corp	39830 Grand River Ave, Novi MI 48375	248-888-4730	R	9*	<.1
842	Home Raters Inc—Stewart Zwang	512 Green Bay Rd, Highwood IL 60040	847-433-3450	R	9*	<.1
843	Signius Communications Inc—Robert Shaw	8 Marcella Ave, West Orange NJ 07052	973-731-6500	R	9*	<.1
844	Brookman Auto Parts Inc—William Brookman	4 Race St, Washington PA 15301	724-222-4260	R	9*	<.1
845	ComCam International—Don Gilbreath	1140 McDermott Dr Ste, West Chester PA 19380	610-436-8089	R	9*	<.1
846	Loan Toolbox—David Fournier	24 S Holmdel Rd, Holmdel NJ 07733		R	9*	<.1
847	Vivian-Nichols Associates Inc—Dierde Wilson	8070 Park Ln Ste 250, Dallas TX 75231	214-979-9050	R	9*	<.1
848	Arlene Semel and Associates Inc—Arlene Semel	223 W Erie Ste 7, Chicago IL 60610	312-640-0000	R	9*	<.1
849	Cenicola-Helvin Enterprises—Mark A Cenicola	6348 S Rainbow Blvd St, Las Vegas NV 89118	702-312-9444	R	9*	<.1
850	Creative Audio Enterprises Inc—Neil Fishman	955 Lincoln Ave, Glen Rock NJ 07452	201-444-6488	R	9*	<.1
851	Fisher Vista LLC—Mark Willaman	PO Box 10, Capitola CA 95010	831-685-9700	R	9*	<.1
852	Global Link Language Services Inc—Anthony Federico	71 Commercial St Ste 2, Boston MA 02109	617-451-6655	R	9*	<.1
853	Health Promotion Management Inc—Lisa Bailey	730 Burbank St, Broomfield CO 80020	303-297-0729	R	9*	<.1
854	Orlando Diaz-Azcuy Designs Inc—Orlando Diaz-Azcuy	201 Post St Fl 9, San Francisco CA 94108	415-362-4500	R	9*	<.1
855	Show Michigan Corp—John Loeks	2121 Celebration Dr NE, Grand Rapids MI 49525	616-447-2860	R	9*	<.1
856	U Edit Video—Laureen Benatar	1002 N Central Expwy S, Richardson TX 75080	972-690-3348	R	9*	<.1
857	Full Circle Studios LLC—Jerry MacKay	741 Main St, Buffalo NY 14203	716-875-7740	R	9*	<.1
858	Kornick Lindsay Inc—Joe Kornick	230 W Huron, Chicago IL 60610	312-280-8664	R	9*	<.1
859	Kratzenberg and Associates Inc—Thomas Kratzenberg	546 Wendel Rd, Irwin PA 15642	724-978-0300	R	9*	<.1
860	Moravia It Inc—Lorraine Grubwieser	199 E Thousand Oaks Bl, Thousand Oaks CA 91360	805-557-1700	R	9*	<.1
861	Telstrat International Ltd—Robert Carroll	6900 Ave K, Plano TX 75074	972-543-3500	R	9*	.1
862	Tacoma Recycling Company Inc—Silas Ceballos	PO Box 828, Puyallup WA 98371	253-474-9559	S	9	.1
863	Advance Testing Company Inc—James Smith	3348 Rte 208, Campbell Hall NY 10916	845-496-1600	R	9*	.1
864	Floralsource International LLC—Cynthia Hayes	PO Box 810, Eagle Point OR 97524	541-494-4041	R	9*	.1
865	Oasys Mobile Inc—Doug Dyer	8000 Regency Pkwy Ste, Cary NC 27518	919-807-5600	R	9	.1
866	Shelterlogic Holdings LLC	150 Callender Rd, Watertown CT 06795	860-945-6442	R	9*	.1
867	Kay Green Design Inc—Margaret Jennings	859 Outer Rd, Orlando FL 32814	407-246-7155	R	9*	<.1
868	Carlson Testing Inc—Douglas Leach	8430 Sw Hunziker St, Tigard OR 97223	503-684-3460	R	8*	.1
869	Clothing Depot Inc—Joe Wynn	24040 Camino Del Ave S, Dana Point CA 92629	949-743-1451	R	8*	<.1
870	Summit Sportswear Inc—Brian Haws	1460 Mcdonald St Ne, Salem OR 97301	503-587-7887	R	8*	.1
871	John Conti Coffee Co—John Conti	PO Box 18289, Louisville KY 40261	502-499-8600	R	8*	.1
872	Celestar Corp—Gregory J Celestan	9501 E US Hwy 92, Tampa FL 33610	813-627-9069	R	8	.1
873	Integrated Alliance LP—April Holsinger	5800 N I-35 Ste 200b, Denton TX 76207	940-565-9415	R	8*	.1
874	Ccb Packaging Inc—Dave Canfield	PO Box 220, Hiawatha IA 52233	319-378-0114	R	8*	.1
875	Marker Group Inc—Marlene Marker	13105 NW Fwy Ste 300, Houston TX 77040	713-460-9070	R	8*	.1
876	Fire Research Corp—John Loughlin	26 Southern Blvd, Nesconset NY 11767	631-724-8888	R	8*	.1
877	Adams Elevator Equipment Co—Robert Schreck	6310 W Howard St, Niles IL 60714	847-581-2900	S	8*	.1
878	Shares Inc—Clifford Strachman	1611 S Miller St, Shelbyville IN 46176	317-398-8218	R	8*	.2
879	Design Craftsmen LLC—Gerald Grieser	PO Box 2126, Midland MI 48641	989-496-3220	R	8*	.1
880	Qualified Presort Service LLC—Tom Lawrenz	PO Box 85010, Sioux Falls SD 57118	605-965-3200	R	8*	.1
881	MTVi Group Inc—Nicolas Butterworth	1515 Broadway 14th Fl, New York NY 10036	212-258-8000	S	8*	.2
882	Just Packaging Inc—Stephen Fischbein	450 Oak Tree Ave Ste 1, South Plainfield NJ 07080	908-753-6700	R	8*	.2
883	Coyotes Hockey LLC—Doug Cannon	6751 N Sunset Blvd E20, Glendale AZ 85305	623-772-3200	R	8*	.1
884	Shield Packaging Company Inc—George Bates	PO Box 190, Canton MA 02021	781-821-0400	R	8*	.1
885	Private Eyes Inc—Sandra James	190 N Wiget Ln Ste 220, Walnut Creek CA 94598	925-927-3333	R	8*	.1
886	Bill Bartmann Enterprises—Bill Bartmann	2488 E 81st St Ste 600, Tulsa OK 74137	918-388-3328	R	8	.1
887	Synoptck Inc—Timothy J Britt	1932 E Deere St Ste 15, Santa Ana CA 92705	949-241-8600	R	8*	.1
888	Printron Engravers Inc—Steven Barry	PO Box 627, Neenah WI 54957	920-725-3077	R	8*	.1
889	Charon Planning Corp—J Lawrence Hager	2600 Kelly Rd Ste 300, Warrington PA 18976	267-482-8300	S	8*	.1

Note: An asterisk (*) indicates an estimated financial figure. The company type code used is as follows: R = Private, P = Public, S = Private Subsidiary, B = Public Subsidiary, D = Division, J = Joint Venture, I = Investment Fund.

COMPANY RANKINGS BY SALES WITHIN 4-DIGIT SIC

Rank	Company Name—*Executive Officer*	Address, City, State, Zip	Phone	Type	Fin	Empls
890	Marc-Michaels Interior Design Inc—*Mark Tremblay*	720 W Morse Blvd, Winter Park FL 32789	407-629-2124	R	8*	.1
891	Pass Word Inc	1303 W First Ave, Spokane WA 99201	509-624-5235	R	8*	.1
892	Riverside Scrap Iron—*Daniel Frankel*	PO Box 5288, Riverside CA 92517	951-686-2120	R	8*	.1
893	Critical Mention Inc—*Sean Morgan*	1776 Broadway Fl 24, New York NY 10019	212-398-1141	R	8*	<.1
894	XS Inc—*Fulton Breen*	1500 Perimeter Park Dr, Morrisville NC 27560	919-379-3500	R	8*	<.1
895	Valuation Research Corp—*Neil Kelly*	330 E Kilbourn Ave Ste, Milwaukee WI 53202	414-271-8662	R	8*	<.1
896	California Closet Company Inc—*William Barton*	1000 4th St Ste 800, San Rafael CA 94901	415-256-8500	R	8*	<.1
897	Childs/Dreyfus Group—*Renee Pabon*	70 W Hubbard St Ste 21, Chicago IL 60610	312-222-0098	R	8*	<.1
898	HanoverTrade Inc—*John Burchett*	200 Metroplex Dr Ste 1, Edison NJ 08817	732-548-0101	R	8*	<.1
899	JSM Music Inc—*Joel Simon*	665 Broadway Ste 1201, New York NY 10012	212-627-2200	R	8*	<.1
900	Mid-Ship Logistics—*Matthew DeLuca*	145 Main St 1st Fl, Port Washington NY 11050	516-944-3500	R	8*	<.1
901	Reel Grobman and Associates—*Winfield Roney*	96 N 2nd St, San Jose CA 95113	408-288-7833	R	8*	<.1
902	Synchron Communications Inc—*Benjamin Cascio*	15095 W 116th St, Olathe KS 66062	913-338-4860	R	8*	<.1
903	Carlton Property Group Ltd—*Howard L Michaels*	560 Lexington Ave 10th, New York NY 10022	212-545-1000	R	8*	<.1
904	Max Rouse and Sons Inc—*Scott Rouse*	361 S Robertson Blvd, Beverly Hills CA 90211	310-360-9200	R	8*	<.1
905	Viking Systems Inc—*John Kennedy*	134 Flanders Rd, Westborough MA 01581	508-366-3668	P	8	<.1
906	Broadnet—*Steve Patterson*	1805 Shea Center Dr St, Highlands Ranch CO 80129		R	8*	<.1
907	Hp Industries Inc—*Steve Hansen*	PO Box 989, Kirksville MO 63501	660-627-2000	R	8*	<.1
908	University Subscription Service Inc	1213 Butterfield Rd, Downers Grove IL 60515	630-960-3233	R	8*	<.1
909	Adam D Tihany International Ltd—*Adam D Tihany*	135 W 27th St 9th Fl, New York NY 10001	212-366-5544	R	8*	<.1
910	Chase Design Group—*Chris Lowery*	2019 Riverside Dr, Los Angeles CA 90039	323-668-1055	R	8*	<.1
911	Paramount Convention Services Inc—*Thomas Kelly*	5015 Fyler Ave, Saint Louis MO 63139	314-621-6677	R	8*	<.1
912	Universal Promotions Inc—*Cathy Scanlon*	3561 Valley Dr, Pittsburgh PA 15234	412-831-8423	R	8*	<.1
913	Back Pocket Recording Studios Inc—*John Russo*	37 W 20th St 8th Fl, New York NY 10011	212-633-1175	R	8*	<.1
914	Environmental Soil Management Inc—*Robert Manns*	67 International Dr, Loudon NH 03307	603-783-0228	R	8*	<.1
915	Studio B Productions Inc—*David Rogelberg*	62 Nassau Dr, Great Neck NY 11021	516-829-2102	R	8*	<.1
916	Kathy Andrews Interiors Inc—*Kathy Andrews*	9464 Kirby Dr, Houston TX 77054	713-952-6400	R	8*	<.1
917	PepCom Inc—*Chris O'Malley*	955 NW 17th Ave Bldg L, Delray Beach FL 33445	561-278-5601	R	8*	<.1
918	Target Promotions and Marketing Inc—*Carl Vernetti*	1255 University Ave St, Rochester NY 14607	585-473-0750	S	8*	<.1
919	Astro Computing Services—*David Reecher*	334 Calef Hwy, Epping NH 03042	603-734-4300	R	8*	<.1
920	Moderns—*Janene James*	900 Broadway Ste 903, New York NY 10003	212-387-8852	R	8*	<.1
921	Rene Bates Auctioneers Inc—*Rene Bates*	4660 County Rd 1006, McKinney TX 75071	972-548-9636	R	8*	<.1
922	Consumers Periodical Service Inc—*Kent Shannon*	1300 Greenbrook Blvd S, Hanover Park IL 60133	630-837-0833	R	8*	<.1
923	VillageEDOCS Inc—*K Mason Conner*	1401 N Tustin Ave Ste, Santa Ana CA 92705	714-734-1030	P	8	.1
924	Convention Management Resources Inc—*Stefan Olsen*	33 New Montgomery St S, San Francisco CA 94105	415-905-0130	R	8*	.1
925	Sky Capital LLC—*Stephen Shea*	110 Wall St Ste 800, New York NY 10005	212-709-1900	R	8*	.1
926	East Baltimore Development Inc—*Christopher Shea*	1704 E Chase St, Baltimore MD 21213	410-342-6948	R	8*	.1
927	Academy Studios Inc—*Dean Weldon*	70 Galli Dr, Novato CA 94949	415-883-8842	R	8*	<.1
928	Compact Industries Inc—*Mike Brown*	3945 Ohio Ave, Saint Charles IL 60174	630-513-9600	R	8*	.1
929	Cce Services Inc—*Paul Lankford*	13933 Lynmar Blvd, Tampa FL 33626	813-854-3033	R	8*	<.1
930	I-K-I Manufacturing Company Inc—*Stanley Midtbo*	116 Swift St, Edgerton WI 53534	608-884-3411	R	8*	.1
931	Workstream Inc (Maitland Florida)—*John Long*	2200 Lucien Way Ste 20, Maitland FL 32751	407-475-5500	P	8	.1
932	Appletree Answering Services—*John Ratliff*	1521 Concord Pike Ste, Wilmington DE 19803		R	8	.4
933	Jubilee Embroidery Company Inc—*Charles Tracy*	PO Box 215, Lugoff SC 29078	803-438-2934	R	8*	.2
934	Silversun Technologies Inc—*Mark Meller*	5 Regent St Ste 520, Livingston NJ 07039	973-758-9555	P	8	<.1
935	Vgm Golf Inc—*Van Miller*	PO Box 1707, Waterloo IA 50704	319-232-5480	R	7*	.1
936	Air Land Express Courier And Trucking Service Inc—*Kathleen Porteus*	48 S Bayles Ave, Port Washington NY 11050	516-767-2255	R	7*	.1
937	Extek Inc—*Tom Bienias*	370 Summit Point Dr, Henrietta NY 14467	585-321-5000	R	7*	.1
938	Logistics Inc—*Paul Alberts*	6774 Brandt St, Romulus MI 48174	734-641-1600	R	7*	.1
939	North Bay Construction Inc—*James Manns*	25800 1st St Ste 1, Westlake OH 44145	440-835-1898	R	7*	<.1
940	Square Peg Packaging and Printing LLC—*Jack Kellogg*	12245 Kirkham Rd Ste 3, Poway CA 92064	858-486-6000	R	7	<.1
941	3d Exhibits Inc—*Eugene Faut*	2800 Lively Blvd, Elk Grove Village IL 60007	847-250-9000	R	7*	.1
942	Ultra Seal Corp—*Dennis Borrello*	521 Main St, New Paltz NY 12561	845-255-2490	R	7*	.1
943	Wilen Press LLC—*Vicky Argento*	3333 Sw 15th St, Deerfield Beach FL 33442	954-246-5000	R	7*	.1
944	Woodinville Fire and Life Safety	PO Box 2200, Woodinville WA 98072	425-483-2131	R	7*	.1
945	Broadcast International Inc—*Rodney M Tiede*	7050 Union Park Ctr St, Midvale UT 84047	801-562-2252	P	7	<.1
946	Liveworld Inc—*Peter Friedman*	4340 Stevens Creek Blv, San Jose CA 95129	408-871-5200	P	7	<.1
947	Henry Doneger Associates Inc—*Abraham Doneger*	463 7th Ave Fl 3, New York NY 10018	212-564-1266	R	7*	.1
948	BevaccessCom Inc	116 John St Fl 21, New York NY 10038	212-571-3232	R	7*	.1
949	Paid Inc—*Gregory Rotman*	236 Huntington Ave 5th, Boston MA 02115	617-861-6050	P	7	<.1
950	B-Line LLC—*Edward Barton*	2101 4th Ave Ste 900, Seattle WA 98121	206-239-1989	S	7*	.1
951	Hukill Chemical Corp—*Robert Hukill*	PO Box 15279, Lansing MI 48901	440-232-9400	R	7*	.1
952	United Way Of Lancaster County—*Susan Eckert*	630 Janet Ave Ste A100, Lancaster PA 17601	717-394-0731	R	7*	<.1
953	National Fire Services LLC—*Jim Turner*	PO Box 581050, Pleasant Prairie WI 53158	847-406-5097	R	7*	<.1
954	Pharmaceutical Research Plus—*Steven Peskin*	645 Baltimore Annapoli, Severna Park MD 21146	410-544-1601	R	7*	<.1
955	Chattanooga Labeling Systems Inc—*Marvin Smith*	PO Box 2492, Chattanooga TN 37409	423-825-2125	R	7*	.1
956	Gordon Technical Consultants Inc	2100 Lakeside Blvd Ste, Richardson TX 75082	972-616-1300	R	7*	<.1
957	Judicial Arbiter Group Inc	1601 Blake St Ste 400, Denver CO 80202	303-572-1919	R	7*	<.1
958	National Gym Supply Inc—*Jonathan Webster*	8511 Steller Dr, Culver City CA 90232	310-280-0931	R	7*	<.1
959	American Post Tension Inc—*Michael Abbott*	1179 Center Point Dr, Henderson NV 89074	702-565-7866	P	7	<.1
960	MAC II LLC—*Ken Gan*	3301 Brighton-Henriett, Rochester NY 14623	585-272-7700	R	7*	<.1
961	ACFN Franchised Inc—*Jeff Kerr*	96 N 3rd St Ste 600, San Jose CA 95112		R	7*	<.1
962	Express Visa Service Inc	1650 Tysons Blvd Ste 1, McLean VA 22102	202-337-2442	S	7*	<.1
963	Guy Chemical Company Inc—*Guy Berkebile*	150 Dominion Dr, Somerset PA 15501	814-443-9455	R	7*	<.1
964	Russ Kiko Associates Inc—*Richard T Kiko Jr*	2805 Fulton Dr NW, Canton OH 44718	330-455-9357	R	7*	<.1
965	Woodlist Inc	277 Linden St Ste 204, Wellesley MA 02482	781-283-5757	R	7*	<.1
966	Array Technology Group LLC—*Charles Schugart*	363 N Sam Houston Pkwy, Houston TX 77060		R	7*	<.1
967	Brandstand Group Inc—*Chris Peterson*	686 Yorktown Rd, Lewisberry PA 17339	717-932-4178	S	7*	<.1
968	Special Services Corp—*Jim Alexander*	54 Watson Aviation Rd, Greenville SC 29607	864-242-3383	R	7*	<.1
969	Trust Marketing and Communications Consortium—*Howard Robertson*	44 N 2nd St Ste 701, Memphis TN 38103	901-521-1300	R	7*	<.1
970	Wiredrive—*Tracy Smith*	500 E Court Ave Ste 31, Des Moines IA 50309	515-323-3468	S	7*	<.1
971	CommerceNet—*Robert Rodin*	169 University Ave, Palo Alto CA 94301	650-289-4040	R	7*	<.1
972	DK Realty Partners LLC—*David M Kaufman*	650 E Algonquin Rd Ste, Schaumburg IL 60173	847-397-8900	R	7*	<.1
973	Elements (Tampa Florida)—*Debra K Altenbernd*	600 S Magnolia Ave Ste, Tampa FL 33606	813-251-0565	R	7*	<.1
974	Image Generators—*Mike J Weiner*	18156 Darnell Dr, Olney MD 20832	301-924-5700	R	7*	<.1
975	JY Legner Associates Inc—*Josephine Legner*	PO Box 24331, Louisville KY 40224	502-585-9000	R	7*	<.1
976	One Planet Corp	850 Ridge Ave, Pittsburgh PA 15212	412-323-1050	R	7*	<.1
977	Palm Beach Jewelry and Antiques—*Kris Charamonde*	510 Evernia St, West Palm Beach FL 33401	561-822-5440	R	7*	<.1

Rank	Company Name—*Executive Officer*	Address, City, State, Zip	Phone	Type	Fin	Empls
978	Pincus Group—*Aileen Pincus*	309 Reserve Gate Terra, Silver Spring MD 20905	301-938-6990	R	7*	<.1
979	Dolphin MultiMedia Inc—*Serguey Kondratieff*	1660 Belleville Way, Sunnyvale CA 94087	650-354-0800	R	7*	<.1
980	Skyline Office Solutions—*Randy Carpenter*	4100 E Harmony Rd, Fort Collins CO 80525		R	7*	<.1
981	Lubbock Radio Paging Service Inc—*Dusty Earl*	PO Box 10127, Lubbock TX 79408	806-762-0811	R	7*	.1
982	Decorating Den Systems Inc—*James S Bugg Jr*	8659 Commerce Dr, Easton MD 21601		R	7	.1
983	PMG Mentors—*Ethan Willis*	5072 N 300 W, Provo UT 84604	801-371-0755	R	7*	.2
984	Amerigo Inc—*Cheri Hall*	PO Box 4668, Pocatello ID 83205	208-234-2181	R	7*	.1
985	Merchant Data Service Inc—*Gerald Phipps*	2275 E Central Ave, Miamisburg OH 45342	937-859-0237	R	7*	.1
986	Quality Control Inspection Inc—*Rick Capone*	40 Tarbell Ave, Cleveland OH 44146	440-359-1900	R	7*	.1
987	Restaurant Services Inc—*George Hoffman*	2 Alhambra Plz Ste 500, Coral Gables FL 33134	305-529-3400	R	7*	.1
988	Jack Onofrio Dog Shows LLC—*Kyle Robinson*	PO Box 25764, Oklahoma City OK 73125	405-427-8181	R	7*	.1
989	Capital Confirmation Inc—*Christopher F Schelhorn*	214 Centerview Dr Ste, Brentwood TN 37027	615-844-6222	R	7	.1
990	Boyett Enterprises LLC	PO Box 551261, Jacksonville FL 32255	904-448-8000	R	7*	.1
991	Kutol Products Company Inc—*Joseph Rhodenbaugh*	100 Partnership Way, Sharonville OH 45241	513-527-5500	R	7*	.1
992	BluePoint Data Inc—*Paul Sachse*	791 Park of Commerce B, Boca Raton FL 33487	561-417-0324	P	7	<.1
993	Kansas Grain Inspection Service Inc—*Thomas Meyer*	PO Box 750077, Topeka KS 66675	785-233-7063	R	7*	.1
994	Valley Inventory Service Inc—*Jeffrey Link*	PO Box 503, Fairfield CA 94533	707-422-6050	R	7*	.1
995	Cable Lock Inc—*Hank Deshazer*	2830 Renshaw St, Houston TX 77023	713-928-2325	R	7*	.1
996	Md7 LLC—*Michael Gianni*	10590 W Ocean Air Dr S, San Diego CA 92130	858-799-7850	R	7*	.1
997	Jerry Lee Chemical Company Inc—*Jerome Schwartz*	1016 Beal Pkwy Nw, Fort Walton Beach FL 32547	850-862-9432	R	7*	<.1
998	Schwartz and Company LLC—*Paul Schwartz*	PO Box 300140, Minneapolis MN 55403		R	7	<.1
999	Basic Line Corp—*David Shalom*	4500 District Blvd, Vernon CA 90058	323-588-1400	R	6*	.1
1000	Andrew and Associates—*Andrew Ybarra*	PO Box 450714, Houston TX 77245	713-471-0922	R	6*	.1
1001	COMTEX News Network Inc—*Chip Brian*	625 N Washington St St, Alexandria VA 22314	703-820-2000	P	6	<.1
1002	Hollywood Sports Park LLC—*Omar Pinuelas*	9030 Somerset Blvd, Bellflower CA 90706	562-867-9600	R	6*	.1
1003	Vegetable Juices Inc—*James Hurley*	7400 S Narragansett Av, Bedford Park IL 60638	708-924-9500	R	6*	.1
1004	Fdc Services Inc—*Pat Baldwin*	PO Box 1151, Saint Cloud MN 56302	320-656-8880	R	6*	.2
1005	Deanco Auction Company Of Mississippi Inc—*Donnie Dean*	1042 Holland Ave, Philadelphia MS 39350	601-656-9768	R	6*	.1
1006	Northwest Direct Teleservices Inc—*Tim Rote*	PO Box 29, West Linn OR 97068	503-722-1640	R	6*	.1
1007	Phone Bank Systems Inc—*Sarah Shaw*	4990 Northwind Dr Ste, East Lansing MI 48823	517-332-1500	R	6*	.1
1008	Aaa Restaurant Fire Control Inc—*Brent Patterson*	PO Box 3626, Hayward CA 94540	510-786-9555	R	6*	.1
1009	Haringa Inc—*Victoria Haringa*	PO Box 4707, Cerritos CA 90703	562-802-2765	R	6*	.1
1010	Stone Street Capital LLC—*David Friedman*	7316 Wisconsin Ave Ste, Bethesda MD 20814	301-951-8900	R	6*	.1
1011	Telesight Inc—*Cliff Knowles*	820 N Franklin St Ste, Chicago IL 60610	312-640-2500	R	6*	.4
1012	Consolidated Market Response Inc—*Robert J Currey*	700 W Lincoln Ave Ste, Charleston IL 61920	217-348-7050	S	6*	.2
1013	Crown Asset Management LLC—*Brian K Williams*	3355 Breckinridge Blvd, Duluth GA 30096	770-817-6700	R	6*	.2
1014	Pack and Process Inc—*Steven Ames*	PO Box 883, New Castle DE 19720	302-658-5148	R	6	.2
1015	Prosero Inc—*Mark Montanari*	1200 Ashwood Pky Ste 4, Atlanta GA 30338	678-731-8500	R	6*	.1
1016	Toll Packaging Group LLC	PO Box 456, Gibson City IL 60936	217-784-4238	R	6*	.1
1017	Profitfuel Inc—*David Rubin*	9300 United Dr Ste 180, Austin TX 78758	512-637-3000	R	6*	.1
1018	ABW Tulsa Inc—*Sherry Lewis*	4745 E 91st St Ste 100, Tulsa OK 74137	918-496-2252	R	6*	.1
1019	Cerida Investment Corp—*Gary Pudles*	2325 Maryland Rd Ste 2, Willow Grove PA 19090	267-942-6000	R	6*	.1
1020	Golder Ranch Fire District—*Vicky Cox-Golder*	3885 E Golder Ranch Dr, Tucson AZ 85739	520-825-9001	R	6*	.1
1021	Schooldude Com Inc—*Kent Hudson*	PO Box 1070, Charlotte NC 28201	919-816-8237	R	6*	.1
1022	Closson's Co	10100 Montgomery Rd, Cincinnati OH 45242	513-762-5500	R	6*	.1
1023	Cyracom International Inc—*Jeremy Woan*	5780 N Swan Rd, Tucson AZ 85718	520-745-9447	R	6*	.1
1024	Broadreach Partners Inc—*Scott Willard*	1266 E Main St Ste 2a, Stamford CT 06902	203-921-4400	R	6*	.1
1025	Edwin Schlossberg Inc—*Edwin Schlossberg*	111 5th Ave, New York NY 10003	212-989-3993	R	6*	.1
1026	Company of Dorosz and Drummer Inc—*Brian Dorosz*	300 W Chestnut St, Wauseon OH 43567		R	6*	<.1
1027	Stage Equipment and Lighting Inc—*Vivian Gill*	12250 NE 13th Ct, Miami FL 33161	305-891-2010	R	6*	<.1
1028	Accredited Auctioneers Inc—*Scott Varney*	207 N Livingston St, Madison WI 53703	608-255-7630	R	6*	<.1
1029	Barenbrug USA Production Div—*Don Obrist*	PO Box 820, Boardman OR 97818	541-481-4001	D	6*	<.1
1030	Device Dynamics Inc—*Jay Stebbins*	3401 Leonard Ct, Santa Clara CA 95054	408-919-1710	R	6*	<.1
1031	Directions in Design Inc—*Jane L Ganz*	1849 Craig Rd, Saint Louis MO 63146	314-205-2010	R	6*	<.1
1032	Leadmaster Operating Co—*Russell King*	885 Woodstock Rd, Roswell GA 30075	770-641-1162	R	6*	<.1
1033	Premier World Marketing Inc—*Claudio A Silvestri*	2600 SW 3rd Ave 3rd Fl, Miami FL 33129		R	6*	<.1
1034	Smart Courier Inc—*Nabih Kadri*	3209 Wellington Ct Ste, Raleigh NC 27615	919-827-6790	R	6*	<.1
1035	Aa Teleservices LLC	PO Box 1171, Ocean View DE 19970	302-541-4599	R	6*	<.1
1036	Central Paper Stock Company Inc—*David Robnak*	6665 Jonas Pl, St Louis MO 63134	314-521-8686	R	6*	<.1
1037	Five Star Speakers And Trainers LLC—*Barbara Byrnes*	7500 College Blvd Ste, Overland Park KS 66210	913-648-6480	R	6*	<.1
1038	David M and Peter J Mancuso Inc—*David M Mancuso*	PO Box 667, New Hope PA 18938	215-862-5828	R	6*	<.1
1039	OnlineMetalscom Inc—*John Byrum*	1138 W Ewing St, Seattle WA 98119	206-285-8603	R	6*	<.1
1040	Andover Consulting Group Inc—*Michael Syiek*	436 N Canal St Ste 8, South San Francisco CA 94080	415-537-6950	R	6*	<.1
1041	Direct Communications Corp—*Michael Brogna*	23 Court St, Rutland VT 05701	802-747-3322	R	6*	<.1
1042	Emil Pawuk and Associates Inc—*Emil Pawuk*	PO Box 535, Richfield OH 44286	330-659-9393	R	6*	<.1
1043	Global Electronic Music Marketplace Inc—*Roger Raffee*	PO Box 2186, La Jolla CA 92038		R	6*	<.1
1044	McLaughlin Associates Corp—*James B McLaughlin*	309 Morris Ave Ste D, Spring Lake NJ 07762	732-449-4004	R	6*	<.1
1045	Motivation Through Incentives Inc—*Vicki Krupp*	10400 W 103rd St Ste 1, Overland Park KS 66214	816-942-0122	R	6*	<.1
1046	National Online Registries LLC—*Deborah Luling*	9640 N Augusta St Ste, Carmel IN 46032	317-802-6040	S	6*	<.1
1047	Promusic Inc	35 W Dayton St, Pasadena CA 91105	626-304-1698	S	6*	<.1
1048	sellcom Inc—*Darren Dittrich*	PO Box 1330, Addison TX 75001	972-960-6060	R	6*	<.1
1049	Software Licensing Consultants Corp—*Edgardo Ramirez*	3413 Bermuda Ct, San Ramon CA 94582	925-968-0051	R	6*	<.1
1050	Susan Marinello Interiors—*Susan Marinello*	119 S Main St Ste 300, Seattle WA 98104	206-344-5551	R	6*	<.1
1051	Syncom Pharmaceuticals Inc—*James W DeCoursin*	125 Clinton Rd, Fairfield NJ 07004	973-787-2405	R	6*	<.1
1052	The Muller Group Inc—*Karl Muller*	PO Box 3031, Williamsburg VA 23187	757-566-4485	R	6*	<.1
1053	Unirec Inc—*Stan Levy*	552 Valley Rd, West Orange NJ 07052	973-325-9111	R	6*	<.1
1054	Dystel and Goderich Literary Management—*Jane Dystel*	One Union Sq W Ste 904, New York NY 10003	212-627-9100	R	6*	<.1
1055	Peggy Nye and Lodin Inc—*Dana Lodin*	777 Brickell Ave Ste 1, Miami FL 33131	305-374-6230	R	6*	<.1
1056	SoundImage NY—*Mark Barasch*	621 W 45th 10th Fl, New York NY 10036	212-986-6445	R	6*	<.1
1057	Salt Palace Convention Center—*Chris Peterson*	100 S W Temple, Salt Lake City UT 84101	801-534-4777	R	6*	.1
1058	Nnncc Ranch—*Richard Nicholas*	7602 Monson Ave, Orange Cove CA 93646	559-626-4890	R	6*	.1
1059	Aplicor Inc—*Charles Schaeffer*	1615 S Federal Hwy, Boca Raton FL 33432	561-347-0300	R	6*	.1
1060	Summit Inspection Services Inc—*Monte Nelson*	PO Box 721087, San Jose CA 95172	805-962-1777	R	6*	.1
1061	Forecast Product Development Corp—*Corey Weber*	2221 Rutherford Rd, Carlsbad CA 92008	760-929-9380	R	6*	.1
1062	Res Exhibit Services LLC—*Beverly Bailey*	435 Smith St, Rochester NY 14608	585-546-2040	R	6*	.1
1063	Renaissance Financial Corp—*Steven Kontz*	5700 Oakland Ave 4, Saint Louis MO 63110	314-569-2900	R	6*	.1
1064	Barnett Associates Inc—*Paul Barnett*	61 Hilton Ave Ste 24, Garden City NY 11530	516-877-2860	R	6*	.1
1065	Valk Industries Inc—*Nick Valk*	PO Box 668, Greeneville TN 37744	423-638-1284	R	6*	.1
1066	Schmid and Son Packaging Inc—*Mary Schmid*	7699 95th St S, Cottage Grove MN 55016	651-452-0588	R	6*	.1
1067	Clearpoint LP—*Peter Carpenter*	720 Olive Way Ste 1700, Seattle WA 98101	206-962-2000	R	6*	.1

Note: An asterisk (*) indicates an estimated financial figure. The company type code used is as follows: R = Private, P = Public, S = Private Subsidiary, B = Public Subsidiary, D = Division, J = Joint Venture, I = Investment Fund.

COMPANY RANKINGS BY SALES WITHIN 4-DIGIT SIC

Rank	Company Name—*Executive Officer*	Address, City, State, Zip	Phone	Type	Fin	Empls
1068	Millstone Medical Outsourcing LLC—*Chris Ramsden*	580 Commerce Dr, Fall River MA 02720	508-679-8384	R	6*	.1
1069	Telecomp Inc—*Kathy Pavelka*	3375 Brighton Henriett, Rochester NY 14623	585-272-1160	R	6*	.1
1070	Taylored Systems Inc—*William Taylor*	14701 Cumberland Rd St, Noblesville IN 46060	317-776-4000	R	6*	<.1
1071	Carter Street Corp—*Tim Riddle*	PO Box 6008, Chattanooga TN 37401	423-756-0001	R	6*	.1
1072	K Weilbaecher Enterprises Inc—*Kerry Weilbaecher*	21 Pin Oak Cir, Covington LA 70433	985-809-9258	R	6*	.1
1073	Third Dimension Inc—*Jeanette Jesus*	PO Box 309, Geneva OH 44041	440-466-4040	R	6*	.1
1074	Velo Corporation Of America—*Mark Macbain*	267 W 17th St Fl 3, New York NY 10011	212-463-7070	R	6*	.1
1075	Rush Index Tabs Inc—*Jay Cohen*	450 Murray Hill Pkwy C, East Rutherford NJ 07073		R	6*	<.1
1076	Accurate Binding Company Inc—*Jerry Baron*	468 Totowa Ave Ste 3, Paterson NJ 07522	973-720-1800	R	5*	.1
1077	Reliant Inventory Services Inc—*Barry Hoffman*	11050 Fancher Rd Lot 1, Westerville OH 43082	614-855-2960	R	5*	.1
1078	American Screen Art Inc—*Peter Carey*	1801 Midpark Rd, Knoxville TN 37921	865-584-0701	S	5*	.1
1079	Centrelink Insurance and Financial Services—*Barry Wolfe*	20750 Ventura Blvd Ste, Woodland Hills CA 91364	818-587-2001	R	5*	.1
1080	Compumail Information Services Inc—*Monte Bish*	PO Box 6756, Concord CA 94524	925-689-7100	R	5*	.1
1081	Boulevard Entertainment Inc—*Scott Jacobson*	PO Box 1188, Burbank CA 91507	818-840-6969	R	5*	.1
1082	Columbus It Partner USA Inc—*Jim Bretschneider*	351 Ballenger Ctr Dr S, Frederick MD 21703	203-705-4000	R	5*	.1
1083	Clarity Customer Management Inc—*Richard Barbato*	69 Cascade Dr Ste Ll2, Rochester NY 14614	585-298-9900	R	5*	.1
1084	Supreme Building Messengers Inc—*Gerry Herman*	11 Penn Plz Bsmt 107, New York NY 10001	212-268-6132	R	5*	.1
1085	Aurico Reports Inc—*Joel Goldberg*	116 W Eastman St Ste 1, Arlington Heights IL 60004	847-255-1852	R	5*	.1
1086	Louisiana Sewn Products Inc—*Daniel Schnaars*	1400 W Maple Ave, Eunice LA 70535	337-457-8800	R	5*	.1
1087	Saja Bankcard Services Inc—*Dewan Bachai*	11 Walter Ct, Commack NY 11725	631-864-4266	R	5*	.1
1088	Site Maintenance Inc—*Stephen Principe*	17435 Mill Branch Pl, Bowie MD 20716	301-464-7660	R	5*	.1
1089	Insco Corp—*David Ammen*	PO Box 489, Groton MA 01450	978-448-6369	R	5*	<.1
1090	Quintas Marketing LLC—*Tim Roth*	300 E 2nd St Ste 1310, Reno NV 89501	775-828-4006	R	5*	.1
1091	Patented Acquisition Corp—*Ken Mcnerney*	1630 E 2nd St, Dayton OH 45403	937-254-4023	R	5*	.1
1092	Call Centers India Inc—*Sandip Mehra*	701 5th Ave Ste 4200, Seattle WA 98104	206-441-7760	R	5*	.4
1093	USA 800—*Tom Davis*	9808 E 66th Terr, Kansas City MO 64133	816-358-1303	R	5*	.4
1094	Ranger Land Systems Inc—*Dennis Suggs*	2707 Artie St Sw Ste 1, Huntsville AL 35805	256-533-7538	R	5*	.3
1095	Rjm Enterprises Of Minnesota Inc—*Jim Lundeen*	6650 143rd Ave Nw, Anoka MN 55303	763-323-8389	R	5*	.2
1096	Orion Marketing Group Inc—*Joseph Seringer*	12000 Network Blvd Ste, San Antonio TX 78249	210-694-4114	R	5*	.2
1097	WorldRes Inc	15333 N Pima Rd Ste 24, Scottsdale AZ 85260	480-946-5100	R	5*	.1
1098	iSqFt—*Dave Conway*	4500 Lake Forest Dr St, Cincinnati OH 45242	513-645-8004	R	5*	.1
1099	Scottsdale Villa Mirage—*Terry Gunn*	7887 E Princess Blvd, Scottsdale AZ 85255	480-473-4000	R	5*	.1
1100	Skipco Financial Adjusters Inc—*Robert Blowers*	PO Box 606, Canal Fulton OH 44614	330-854-4900	R	5*	.1
1101	Digital International Corp—*Ed Ceja*	2424 N Ontario St, Burbank CA 91504	818-847-1157	R	5*	.1
1102	Dis Pack Corp—*Jorge Zavala*	6550 S Lavergne Ave, Chicago IL 60638	708-496-1750	R	5*	.1
1103	Elite Trade Show Sevices Inc—*Joseph Bello*	12461 S Industrial Dr, Plainfield IL 60585	815-439-8540	R	5*	.1
1104	Iron Data Solutions LLC Transportation Sector—*Jerry Rau*	3400 Players Club Pkwy, Memphis TN 38125		S	5*	.1
1105	800 Call-Kc Inc—*Roy Nafziger*	PO Box 33597, Kansas City MO 64120	816-231-4321	R	5*	.1
1106	Aesbus Co—*Edward Castor*	3707 Fm 1960 Rd W Ste, Houston TX 77068	281-720-5000	R	5*	.1
1107	Southwest Inspection And Testing—*Steven Godbey*	441 Commercial Way, La Habra CA 90631	562-941-2990	R	5*	.1
1108	Burgess Construction Consultants Inc—*Glenn W Burgess*	1255 W 15th St Ste 100, Plano TX 75075		R	5*	.1
1109	Contour360 Corp—*John Moller*	5 Industrial Way, Cornish ME 04020	207-625-4000	R	5*	<.1
1110	TechDisposal—*Sepp Rajaie*	320 Outerbelt St, Columbus OH 43213	614-755-5100	R	5*	<.1
1111	Channel Methods Partners LLC—*David Hirschfeld*	200 Atlantic Ave, Manasquan NJ 08736	732-292-4777	R	5*	<.1
1112	Writers House Inc—*Albert Zuckerman*	21 W 26th St, New York NY 10010	212-685-2400	R	5*	<.1
1113	Executive Coffee Service Inc—*Greg Fragakis*	PO Box 2326, West Palm Beach FL 33402	561-655-4700	R	5*	<.1
1114	Triple J Tomato Company LLC	PO Box 11458, Denver CO 80211	303-291-0683	R	5*	<.1
1115	Allan Industries—*A Allan*	PO Box 999, Wilkes Barre PA 18703	570-826-0123	R	5	<.1
1116	Franchise Solutions Inc—*Hunter Stokes*	222 International Dr S, Portsmouth NH 03801	603-427-0569	R	5*	<.1
1117	Huntsinger and Jeffer—*Vicki Lester*	809 Brook Hill Cir, Richmond VA 23227	804-266-2499	R	5*	<.1
1118	Media Event Concepts Inc—*Gordon Feller*	2036 Centimeter Cir, Austin TX 78758	512-832-1142	R	5*	<.1
1119	Ocean Corp—*John Wood*	10840 Rockley Rd, Houston TX 77099	281-530-0202	R	5	<.1
1120	Horizon Worldwide—*Gary M Seline*	1765 Stebbins Dr, Houston TX 77043	713-647-7400	R	5*	<.1
1121	Barone Design Group—*Ann Wagner*	13831 Northwest Fwy St, Houston TX 77040	713-460-0920	R	5*	<.1
1122	Buxbaum Group and Associates Inc—*Paul M Buxbaum*	28632 Roadside Drive S, Agoura Hills CA 91301	818-878-3900	R	5*	<.1
1123	Cyclone Surface Cleaning Inc—*Richard Rohrbacher*	1845 W 1st St Ste 101, Tempe AZ 85281	480-345-7733	R	5*	<.1
1124	Flyte Tyme Productions Inc—*Jimmy Harris*	PO Box 398045, Edina MN 55439	952-897-3901	R	5*	<.1
1125	National Community Development Services Inc—*Howard C Benson*	3155 Roswell Rd NE Ste, Atlanta GA 30305	404-231-0730	R	5*	<.1
1126	Oceanos Marketing—*Brian P Hession*	99 Derby St, Hingham MA 02043	781-804-1010	R	5*	<.1
1127	Polarity Post Productions—*Roger Wiersema*	69 Green St, San Francisco CA 94111	415-421-6622	R	5*	<.1
1128	Splash Graphics Inc	7001 S Adams St, Willowbrook IL 60527	630-230-5777	R	5*	<.1
1129	Telephone Look-Up Service Co—*Michael Schoedler*	301 Oxford Valley Rd S, Yardley PA 19067	215-321-0706	R	5*	<.1
1130	Contract Design Group Inc—*Jaime Henderson*	6301 SW 9th St, Topeka KS 66615	785-271-1188	R	5*	<.1
1131	Epic Multimedia	1741 S Cleveland Ave S, Sioux Falls SD 57103	605-271-2598	R	5*	<.1
1132	Gallery of History Auctions Inc—*Todd M Axelrod*	3601 W Sahara Ave Prom, Las Vegas NV 89102	702-364-1000	S	5*	<.1
1133	Sherman Gabus Inc—*Rayne Sherman*	3649 Atlantic Ave, Long Beach CA 90807	562-424-2227	R	5*	<.1
1134	Bestgen Typeworks Inc—*Paul Bestgen*	4405 Glenbrook Rd, Willoughby OH 44094	440-946-0700	R	5*	<.1
1135	One Stop Permits Inc—*Laura Norman*	PO Box 373311, Key Largo FL 33037	305-304-8086	R	5*	<.1
1136	Approval Payment Solutions Inc—*Allen Noe*	PO Box 446, Boonville IN 47601	812-897-4837	R	5*	.1
1137	Professional Sports Authenticator—*Steve Rochhi*	PO Box 6180, Newport Beach CA 92658	949-833-8824	R	5*	.1
1138	Crown Castle South—*John Kelly*	2000 Corporate Dr, Canonsburg PA 15317	724-416-2084	R	5*	.1
1139	VJ Associates Incorporated Of Suffolk—*Vijay Desai*	100 Duffy Ave Ste 303, Hicksville NY 11801	516-932-1010	R	5*	.1
1140	Wilcorp Industries Inc—*J Wilson*	PO Box 201, Billings MO 65610	417-744-4132	R	5*	.1
1141	Econtactlive Inc—*Julie Hutchings*	2000 W Briggsmore Ave, Modesto CA 95350	209-548-4300	R	5*	.1
1142	Isi Inspection Services Inc—*Leslie Sakai*	The Embrcdro Fl 2 Pier, San Francisco CA 94105	415-243-3265	R	5*	.1
1143	Europa Partners LLC—*Elizabeth Carden*	1 Europa Dr, Chapel Hill NC 27517	919-968-4900	R	5*	.1
1144	AdStar Inc—*Leslie Bernhard*	13428 Maxella Ave Ste, Marina Del Rey CA 90292	310-577-8255	P	5	<.1
1145	Unitech Solutions Inc—*Steven Glasberg*	5550 Touhy Ave Ste 400, Skokie IL 60077	847-675-1200	R	5*	.1
1146	Continental Pools Inc—*Michael Kinloch*	8520 Corridor Rd Ste B, Savage MD 20763	301-498-1000	R	5*	.1
1147	It Trailblazers LLC—*Padmaja Harisrikanth*	100 Jersey Ave Ste B10, New Brunswick NJ 08901	732-227-1772	R	5*	.1
1148	Town Of Weaverville—*Michael Boaz*	PO Box 338, Weaverville NC 28787	828-645-7116	R	5*	.1
1149	Apg Inc—*Paul Richardson*	PO Box 2988, Elkhart IN 46515	574-295-0000	R	5*	.1
1150	Dunbrooke Apparel Corp—*Matt Grey*	4200 Little Blue Pkwy, Independence MO 64057	816-795-7722	R	5*	.1
1151	Precision Inspection Company Inc—*Kelly Hislop*	1247 Main St, Newman CA 95360	209-862-9511	R	5*	.1
1152	Khan Enterprises Inc—*Ahmed Khan*	13200 Old Marlboro Pke, Upper Marlboro MD 20772	301-627-7575	R	5*	<.1
1153	Cbc Corporation Business Service—*R Cooper*	PO Box 400, Dallas OR 97338	503-623-3916	R	5*	.1
1154	Cutting Corp—*James Cutting*	4940 Hampden Ln Ste 30, Bethesda MD 20814	301-654-2887	R	5*	.1
1155	Hidalgo County Appraisal District—*Rolando Garza*	PO Box 208, Edinburg TX 78540	956-565-2461	R	5*	.1
1156	Trispec Offshore Corp—*Graham Evans*	12436 Fm 1960 Rd W, Houston TX 77065	713-453-7143	R	5*	.1

Rank	Company Name—*Executive Officer*	Address, City, State, Zip	Phone	Type	Fin	Empls
1157	Wittern Group Inc—*John Bruntz*	PO Box 1333, Des Moines IA 50306	515-274-3641	R	5*	.1
1158	Kent Warehouse And Labeling LLC—*Richard Friedman*	22615 64th Ave S, Kent WA 98032	253-437-5110	R	5*	.1
1159	Oak Ridge Foundation Inc—*Robert Holcombe*	PO Box 498, Oak Ridge NC 27310	336-643-4131	R	5*	.1
1160	Christopher Chadbourne And Associates Inc—*Christopher Chadbourne*	129 Portland St Fl 2, Boston MA 02114	617-305-1000	R	5*	<.1
1161	Commonwealth Industrial Services Inc—*Larry Gunnin*	PO Box 479, Hopewell VA 23860	804-458-9844	R	5*	<.1
1162	Valley Packaging Indutries Inc—*Robert Russo*	110 N Kensington Dr, Appleton WI 54915	920-749-5840	R	5*	1.0
1163	Conde Systems Inc—*William Gross*	5600 Commerce Blvd E, Mobile AL 36619	251-633-5704	R	5*	.1
1164	Arga Computer and Mailing Services Inc—*William Nims*	33 Business Park Dr, Branford CT 06405	203-483-3001	R	5*	.1
1165	Ocean Way Recording—*Allen Sides*	6050 W Sunset Blvd, Los Angeles CA 90028	323-467-9375	R	5*	<.1
1166	Professional Planning Group—*Edwin Mahoney*	PO Box 1328, Roseville CA 95678	916-774-8601	R	5*	<.1
1167	East Bay Innovations—*Tom Heinz*	303 W Joaquin Ave Ste, San Leandro CA 94577	510-618-1580	R	4*	.1
1168	Med-Tech Resource Inc—*Michael Knowles*	2252 Nw Pkwy Se Ste D, Marietta GA 30067	770-955-7292	R	4*	.1
1169	A Call Nurse—*Marty Norman*	1900 S Hawthorne Rd 76, Winston Salem NC 27103	336-718-0050	R	4*	.1
1170	Apartment and Corporate Relocation Service—*Crawford Sanders*	775 Woodruff Rd Ste A, Greenville SC 29607	864-297-5690	R	4*	.1
1171	Dahill Packaging Inc—*David Hillhouse*	717 William Leigh Dr, Bristol PA 19007	215-547-7006	R	4*	.1
1172	James Alexander Corp—*Francesca Fazzolari*	845 State Rte 94, Blairstown NJ 07825	908-362-9266	R	4*	.1
1173	Registration Control Systems Inc—*Edgar Bolton*	1833 Portola Rd Unit B, Ventura CA 93003	805-654-0171	R	4*	.1
1174	Commercial Interiors Of Jacksonville Inc—*Daren Hoffman*	4501 Irvington Ave, Jacksonville FL 32210	904-388-6625	R	4*	.1
1175	Banner Service Corp—*Mark Redding*	494 E Lies Rd, Carol Stream IL 60188	630-653-7500	R	4*	.1
1176	Adams Evens and Ross Inc—*Wilson Cole*	1301 Shiloh Rd Ste 811, Kennesaw GA 30144		R	4	<.1
1177	Stetson Convention Services Inc—*William Sandherr*	2900 Stayton St, Pittsburgh PA 15212	412-223-1090	R	4*	<.1
1178	Suburban Hospital Integrated Physician Service LLC—*Segmus O'harlooran*	6430 Rockledge Dr Ste, Bethesda MD 20817	301-896-2800	R	4*	.1
1179	Miami-Dade Housing Agency—*Donald Lavoy*	1401 Nw 7th St, Miami FL 33125	305-644-5100	R	4*	.1
1180	Miller-Marek Inc—*Shawn Marek*	Rr 1 Box 54b, Oklahoma City OK 73131	405-350-0850	R	4*	.1
1181	Presentation Group Inc	2702 E Robinson St, Orlando FL 32803	407-894-4760	R	4	.1
1182	Credit Unions Chartered In Sta—*Bonnette Dawson*	PO Box 431, Old Hickory TN 37138	615-847-4043	R	4*	.1
1183	Fortis Investment Management USA Inc—*Will Braman*	75 State St Ste 27, Boston MA 02109	617-478-7200	R	4*	.1
1184	Elegant Fashions Inc—*Peter Ting*	257 W 38th St Fl 3, New York NY 10018	212-869-2699	R	4*	.1
1185	County Packaging Inc—*Jack Kent*	13600 Kildare Ave, Crestwood IL 60445	708-597-1100	R	4*	.1
1186	Dungarvin Group Inc—*Timothy Madden*	690 Cleveland Ave S, Saint Paul MN 55116	651-699-0206	R	4*	.1
1187	Stairway 9 LLC—*David Rosen*	575 Lexington Ave Fl 2, New York NY 10022	212-752-3348	R	4*	.1
1188	Plantscapes Inc—*Terry Posner*	1127 Poplar Pl S, Seattle WA 98144	206-623-7100	R	4*	.1
1189	Trailblazer Technologies—*Rich Brownstein*	4100 W Burbank Blvd Fl, Burbank CA 91505	818-848-0575	R	4*	.1
1190	LaborLawCenter Inc—*Kelly Petersen*	12534 Valley View St S, Garden Grove CA 92845		R	4	<.1
1191	Enhance A Colour Corp—*Jim O'conor*	17-19 Marble Ave, Pleasantville NY 10570	914-747-5111	R	4*	<.1
1192	Addesso-Madden Inc	211-49 26th Ave, Bayside NY 11360	718-224-4880	S	4	N/A
1193	Oxford Obg-Waterton Skokie Hotel Property Co—*Jose Acosta*	9599 Skokie Blvd, Skokie IL 60077	847-329-4383	R	4*	.1
1194	G and H Telephone Answering Service Inc—*Dave Raynard*	247 Harbor Dr S, Venice FL 34285	941-488-4332	R	4*	.1
1195	Exodus Inc—*Duc Nguyen*	2318 Eisenhower St, Tallahassee FL 32310	850-575-9729	R	4*	.1
1196	Service Graphics Inc—*Michael Burks*	8350 Allison Ave, Indianapolis IN 46268	317-471-8246	R	4*	.1
1197	Design Works By Dave And Mike Inc—*Michael Roffino*	3869 Steele St Ste D, Denver CO 80205	720-941-7440	R	4*	.1
1198	Rand Whitney Packaging Corp—*Robert Kraft*	150 Grove St, Worcester MA 01605	508-890-7001	R	4*	.1
1199	Opportunity Center Inc—*Dennis Dapolito*	PO Box 254, Wilmington DE 19899	302-762-0300	S	4*	.1
1200	International Packaging Inc—*Jon Butkovich*	8921 Wyoming Ave N, Minneapolis MN 55445	763-315-6200	R	4*	.1
1201	A2z Global LLC—*Peter Landgren*	230 E Cuthbert Blvd, Haddon Township NJ 08108	856-833-0220	R	4*	.1
1202	Us Interior Surface Mining Reclamation and Enforcement—*Brent Walquist*	3 Pky Ctr, Pittsburgh PA 15220	412-937-2146	R	4*	.1
1203	MC Pack Inc—*Scott Miller*	412 Van Buren St, Newark NY 14513	315-226-1000	R	4*	.1
1204	Professional Communications Network LP—*Diann Johnston*	PO Box 20409, Riverside CA 92516	951-275-9149	R	4*	.1
1205	Slifer Designs Inc—*Elizabeth Slifer*	24 Sprint St, Edwards CO 81632	970-926-8200	R	4*	.1
1206	Triton Diving Services Inc—*Karen Stall*	8 Greenway Plz, Houston TX 77046	713-963-9599	R	4*	.1
1207	United Merchant Services of California Inc—*Joyce L Gaines*	750 Fairmont Ave Ste 2, Glendale CA 91203	818-246-6767	R	4*	.1
1208	Buyseasons Inc—*Dan Haight* Liberty Interactive Group	5915 S Moreland Rd, New Berlin WI 53151	262-901-2000	S	4*	.1
1209	Enablx Inc—*James Riff*	675 Rt 10 E, Randolph NJ 07869	973-361-7770	R	4*	.1
1210	Sms Industries Inc—*Leslie Hamerschlag*	80 Maiden Ln Rm 905, New York NY 10038	212-293-1971	R	4*	.1
1211	Bizsellbrokers Inc—*Ron Hottes*	2293 W 190th St, Torrance CA 90504	310-539-8300	R	4*	<.1
1212	First Advantage Recruiting Solutions—*LeRoy Robbins*	12395 First American W, Poway CA 92064		S	4*	<.1
1213	Walker Group Inc—*Daniel Walker*	PO Box 572, Fairfield IA 52556	641-469-5900	R	4*	<.1
1214	Yates-Silverman Inc—*Charles Silverman*	4045 Dean Martin Dr, Las Vegas NV 89103	702-791-5606	R	4*	<.1
1215	Deco West Inc—*Melvin Kerr*	80 N Mojave Rd Ste 190, Las Vegas NV 89101	702-644-8839	R	4*	<.1
1216	Interprise Inc—*Katie Berg*	5080 Spectrum Dr Ste, Addison TX 75001	972-385-3991	R	4*	<.1
1217	Pacific Shredco LLC—*Don Kiele*	PO Box 59505, Renton WA 98058	425-264-0073	R	4*	<.1
1218	Street Legal Industries Inc—*Lisa Bisese*	102 Jefferson Ct, Oak Ridge TN 37830	865-483-6373	R	4*	<.1
1219	Tower Inspection Inc—*Gary Lehman*	PO Box 709, Muskogee OK 74402	918-683-8915	R	4*	<.1
1220	Genco Industries Inc—*Steve Dombrock*	209 Wilmont Dr, Waukesha WI 53189	262-548-8890	R	4*	<.1
1221	American Micro Co—*Mark Zecy*	1933 Troost Ave, Kansas City MO 64108	816-221-0123	R	4*	<.1
1222	Trade Exchange of America Inc—*Fred Detwiler*	23200 Coolidge Hwy, Oak Park MI 48237	248-544-1350	R	4*	<.1
1223	RKS Design Inc—*Ravi Sawhney*	350 Conejo Ridge Ave, Thousand Oaks CA 91361	805-370-1200	R	4*	<.1
1224	Insight Sourcing Group Inc—*Tom Beaty*	5555 Triangle Pkwy Ste, Norcross GA 30092	770-481-3027	R	4*	<.1
1225	Annex Design Service Inc—*Tom Srigley*	41150 Technology Pk Dr, Sterling Heights MI 48314	586-254-5880	R	4*	<.1
1226	Checkcare (Louisville Kentucky)—*Joseph E Caruso*	4102 Cadillac Ct, Louisville KY 40213	502-473-4000	R	4*	<.1
1227	Evansville Auto Parts Inc—*David Dazey*	9000 N Kentucky Ave, Evansville IN 47725	812-867-9900	R	4*	<.1
1228	Grenald Waldron Associates—*Lee Waldron*	PO Box 525, Narberth PA 19072	610-667-6330	R	4*	<.1
1229	Griffiths and Associates—*Penny Griffith*	808 S Windsor Blvd, Los Angeles CA 90005	323-939-5529	R	4*	<.1
1230	Messe Dusseldorf North America—*Tom Mitchell*	150 N Michigan Ave Ste, Chicago IL 60601	312-781-5180	S	4*	<.1
1231	William Beson Interior Design—*William Beson*	275 Market St Ste 530, Minneapolis MN 55405	612-338-8187	R	4*	<.1
1232	Cranston Textile Services—*George Shuster*	1381 Cranston St, Cranston RI 02920	401-943-4800	D	4*	<.1
1233	Pandisc Music Corp—*Bo Crane*	247 SW 8th St Ste 349, Miami FL 33131	305-557-1914	R	4*	<.1
1234	Electron Technologies Corp—*Richard H Plank*	PO Box 316, South Windsor CT 06074	860-289-7451	R	4*	<.1
1235	Hubbuch and Co—*John A Hubbuch*	324 W Main St, Louisville KY 40202	502-583-2713	R	4*	<.1
1236	Serving by Irving Inc—*Irving Botwinick*	233 Broadway Ste 2201, New York NY 10279	212-233-3346	R	4*	<.1
1237	Bethe Cohen Design Associates—*Bethe Cohen*	150 E Campbell Ave Ste, Campbell CA 95008	408-379-4051	R	4*	<.1
1238	SelectForce Inc—*Tammi Didlot*	200 NW 66th St Ste 972, Oklahoma City OK 73116	405-842-2088	S	4*	<.1
1239	Farrington Design Group Ltd—*Frank Farrington*	1447 Peachtree St NE S, Atlanta GA 30309	404-836-3000	R	4*	<.1
1240	Barrington Multi Media—*Mike Barrington*	9337 Heritage Pkwy, West TX 76691	254-826-3455	R	4*	<.1
1241	Brown Corrosion Services Inc—*Jerry Brown*	PO Box 940638, Houston TX 77094	832-327-0965	R	4*	<.1

Note: An asterisk (*) indicates an estimated financial figure. The company type code used is as follows: R = Private, P = Public, S = Private Subsidiary, B = Public Subsidiary, D = Division, J = Joint Venture, I = Investment Fund.

COMPANY RANKINGS BY SALES WITHIN 4-DIGIT SIC

Rank	Company Name—Executive Officer	Address, City, State, Zip	Phone	Type	Fin	Empls
1242	Kamen Entertainment Group Inc—Roy Kamen	701 7th Ave 6th Fl, New York NY 10036	212-575-4660	R	4*	<.1
1243	Specialty Trade Shows Inc—Jeff Yunis	3939 Hardie Rd, Coconut Grove FL 33133	305-663-6635	R	4*	<.1
1244	Texeira Inc—Glenn Texeira	717 N La Cienega Blvd, Los Angeles CA 90069	310-358-7280	R	4*	<.1
1245	Bartlett and Picarella—Anita Bartlett-Picarella	9 Alden Pl, Bronxville NY 10708	914-961-4443	R	4*	<.1
1246	Collier Communications Inc	PO Box 190988, Dallas TX 75219	972-395-7754	R	4*	<.1
1247	Complete Telecommunications Inc—Vincent M Cordero	2816 Rowena Ave Ste 2, Los Angeles CA 90039		R	4*	<.1
1248	Honolulu Information Service—Jo Kamae Byrne	PO Box 2390, Honolulu HI 96804	808-524-4488	R	4*	<.1
1249	Infinity Management—Ron Contarino	PO Box 2410, Flemington NJ 08822	908-782-7396	R	4*	<.1
1250	ITCS Inc—Brian Hood	1013 E Main St, Salem VA 24153	540-387-2101	S	4*	<.1
1251	Rocky Mountain Recorders—Paul Vastola	1250 W Cedar Ave, Denver CO 80223	303-777-3648	R	4*	<.1
1252	Serafine Inc—Frank Serafine	PO Box 1798, Simi Valley CA 93062	310-399-9279	R	4*	<.1
1253	Cotton Hill Studios Inc—Ray Rettig	13 Walker Way, Albany NY 12205	518-869-1968	R	4*	<.1
1254	Meyer and Associates Inc—Bruce Meyer	2130 Freeport Rd Ste C, Natrona Heights PA 15065	724-224-1440	R	4*	<.1
1255	Rigsby Hull—Lana Rigsby	2309 University Blvd, Houston TX 77005	713-660-6057	R	4*	<.1
1256	U-Fix-It Appliance Parts Inc—Jim Plummer	9919 Garland Rd, Dallas TX 75218	214-321-7054	R	4*	<.1
1257	Godfrey Design Consultants Inc—Betsey Godfrey	124 E Welborne Ave, Winter Park FL 32789		R	4	<.1
1258	Gray and Walter Associates—Kenneth Walter	1018 11th St, Wilmette IL 60091	847-853-1940	R	4*	<.1
1259	National Auction Co—George Richards	1325 S Congress Ave St, Boynton Beach FL 33426	561-364-7004	R	4*	<.1
1260	Traffic Builders Inc—Michael O'Connell	65 Parker St Unit 11, Newburyport MA 01950	978-499-3700	R	4*	<.1
1261	Zen Music Inc—Julie Dansky	45 W 21st St 6th Fl, New York NY 10010	718-237-2768	R	4*	<.1
1262	Feather Larson and Synhorst—Scott Miller	12181 Margo Ave S Ste, Hastings MN 55033	651-480-0123	S	4*	.1
1263	Cable Doctors Inc—Morton Carey	8677 Villa La Jolla Dr, La Jolla CA 92037	619-595-4650	R	4*	.1
1264	Issues Management Inc—Craig Lawrence	4502 N Lewis Ave, Sioux Falls SD 57104	605-978-2000	R	4*	.1
1265	Dittrich Specialties Inc—Robert Dittrich	PO Box 755, New Ulm MN 56073	507-359-2927	R	4*	.1
1266	Picerne Construction/Fm LLC—Craig Constant	4467 Leonard Wood Ave, Fort Meade MD 20755	410-672-4570	R	4*	.1
1267	M Rogers Design Inc—Michael Rogers	3400 W Lake Ave, Glenview IL 60026	847-564-5033	R	4*	.1
1268	Pro-Tech Auction Inc—Gary Lisowski	13000 Haggerty Rd, Belleville MI 48111	734-697-5679	R	4*	.1
1269	Staffelbach Inc—Jo Staffelbach	2525 Mckinnon St Ste 8, Dallas TX 75201	214-747-2511	R	4*	.1
1270	Klocke Of America Inc—Carsten Klocke	14201 Jetport Loop W, Fort Myers FL 33913	239-561-5800	R	4*	.1
1271	Thermo-Pak—Daniel Simpson	360 Balm Ct, Wood Dale IL 60191	630-860-1303	R	4*	.1
1272	Wdt World Discount Telecommunications Co—Roman Talis	13644 Neutron Rd, Dallas TX 75244	214-890-7700	R	4*	.1
1273	Wise Payment Systems Inc—William Wise	8481 Fishers Ctr Dr, Fishers IN 46038		R	4*	<.1
1274	Dig Safe System Inc—Dan Cote	331 Montvale Ave Ste 4, Woburn MA 01801	781-721-0990	R	4*	<.1
1275	Texas Exclusive Five Star Enterprises Inc—Greg Morse	4817 Colorado Blvd, Fort Worth TX 76180	214-272-0389	R	4*	<.1
1276	S and S Promotional Group Inc—Bradley Ness	PO Box 2923, Fargo ND 58108	701-280-1916	R	4*	<.1
1277	Prn Health Solutions Inc—Sammy Molvi	996 Nw Cir Blvd Ste 20, Corvallis OR 97330	541-752-1543	R	4*	.1
1278	Star-Lite Manufacturing Company Inc—Charles Soponski	201 James E Casey Dr, Buffalo NY 14206	716-827-7091	R	4*	.1
1279	Bobb Corp—Daryl Bobb	6640 Ammendale Rd, Beltsville MD 20705	301-595-1010	R	4*	.1
1280	Kobey Corporation Inc—Kimberly Pretto	PO Box 81492, San Diego CA 92138	619-523-2700	R	4*	.1
1281	Pegasus Steel LLC—Brent Dillion	1 Alliance Dr E Creek, Goose Creek SC 29445	843-737-9900	R	4*	.1
1282	Dw Direct Inc—David Daniels	174 Passaic St Ste 1, Garfield NJ 07026	973-591-1411	R	4*	.1
1283	R Brooks Associates Inc—Raymond Brooks	6546 Pound Rd, Williamson NY 14589	315-589-4000	R	4*	.1
1284	Optimal Ltd—Jason Murphy	12701 Directors Dr, Stafford TX 77477	832-886-5300	R	4*	.1
1285	Decimal Inc—Chad Parks	530 Bush St Fl 9, San Francisco CA 94108	415-477-8800	R	4*	.1
1286	Walker Brothers Machinery Moving Inc—David Walker	3839 E Coronado St, Anaheim CA 92807	714-630-5957	R	4*	.1
1287	Superior Expo Ltd—Joe Mecca	4819 Woodall St, Dallas TX 75247	469-341-1130	R	4*	<.1
1288	Validation Experts Inc—Kenneth Bean	70 Arrowhead Rd, Eastham MA 02642	508-240-7015	R	4*	.1
1289	Moline Postal Service—George Van Voren	514 17th St, Moline IL 61265	309-764-5011	R	4*	.1
1290	Western Pacific Packaging Inc—Andrew Martin	2715 Adelaida Rd, Paso Robles CA 93446	805-239-1188	R	4*	.1
1291	Quality Companies Inc—David Pulsifer	1491 Quality Way, Tallahassee FL 32303	850-576-4880	R	4*	.1
1292	Anserve Inc—Nancy Ward	1250 State Rt 23 Ste 4, Butler NJ 07405	973-283-2000	R	4*	.1
1293	Sanders Sanders and Block PC—Stanley Sanders	100 Herricks Rd Ste 10, Mineola NY 11501	516-741-5252	R	4*	.1
1294	South Atlantic Services Inc—Frank Hamilton	PO Box 1886, Wilmington NC 28402	910-763-3496	R	4*	.1
1295	Sanford L Alderfer Auction Company Inc—Sanford Alderfer	501 Fairgrounds Rd, Hatfield PA 19440	215-393-3000	R	4*	.1
1296	Dillon Works Inc—Mike Dillon	11775 Harbour Reach Dr, Mukilteo WA 98275	425-493-8309	R	4*	<.1
1297	Pro-Tech Design and Manufacturing Inc—Pamela Master	14561 Marquardt Ave, Santa Fe Springs CA 90670	562-207-1680	R	4*	.1
1298	Resource One International LLC—Rose Stafford	2225 Bohm Dr, Little Chute WI 54140	920-788-1550	R	4*	.1
1299	Qualfax Inc—Jim Wolf	3605 Long Beach Blvd S, Long Beach CA 90807	562-989-9902	R	4*	.1
1300	Tlk Industries Inc—Douglas Sarrazine	130 Prairie Lake Rd St, East Dundee IL 60118	847-359-3200	R	4*	.1
1301	20-20 Technologies Commercial Corp—Jean Mignault	550 3 Mile Rd Nw Ste A, Grand Rapids MI 49544	616-454-0000	R	4*	.1
1302	Phoenix Rising Industries Inc—Ali Haq	150 N Wiget Ln Ste 111, Walnut Creek CA 94598	925-295-1200	R	4*	.1
1303	Americall International Inc—Scott Hager	PO Box 1393, Tacoma WA 98401	253-272-4111	R	4*	.1
1304	Getco LLC—Katherine Makstenieks	141 W Jackson Blvd Ste, Chicago IL 60604	312-931-2200	R	4*	.1
1305	CIC Associates Inc—Carol Garrett	2145 Unity Trl Nw, Marietta GA 30064	770-426-9050	R	4*	<.1
1306	Arc Water Treatment Company Of Maryland Inc—David Gold- stein	10620 Riggs Hill Rd St, Jessup MD 20794	410-880-0706	R	4*	<.1
1307	Winter People Inc—Carol Bouton	125 Us Rte 1, Freeport ME 04032	207-865-6636	R	4*	<.1
1308	Preferred Community Services—Jeff Brooks	5778 W 74th St, Indianapolis IN 46278	317-295-1548	R	4*	.2
1309	Plum Healthcare Group LLC—Shuang Bai	1620 W Fern Ave, Redlands CA 92373	909-793-2609	R	4*	.1
1310	University Language Services Inc—Victor Hertz	15 Maiden Ln Fl 3, New York NY 10038	212-766-4187	R	4*	.1
1311	David Santos Farming—David Santos	720 Jefferson Ave, Los Banos CA 93635	209-826-1065	R	4*	.1
1312	A Mm Company Holdings LLC—Ron Spoltore	16539 S Main St, Gardena CA 90248	310-323-2000	R	4*	.1
1313	Affiliated Communications Inc—Richard Starr	PO Box 5720, Ventura CA 93005	805-650-4949	R	4*	.1
1314	Incomm Solutions Inc—Bill Martin	208 Harristown Rd Ste, Glen Rock NJ 07452	201-612-9696	R	4*	.1
1315	Premium Marketing Systems Inc—William Stephansen	5816 W Cermak Rd, Cicero IL 60804	708-652-7500	R	4*	.1
1316	Public Auto Auction Inc—John Sharp	2400 S Broadway, Denver CO 80210	303-783-9090	R	4*	.1
1317	Data Image Inc—Dennis Barrett	3752 W 2270 S Ste B, Salt Lake City UT 84120	801-977-0066	R	4*	<.1
1318	Twi Of South Florida Inc—Michael Gattuso	PO Box 4357, North Fort Myers FL 33918	239-731-1900	R	4*	<.1
1319	Miller Jones Corp—Jamila Robinson	174 W Lincoln Ave 518, Anaheim CA 92805	714-782-6426	R	4*	<.1
1320	Alpha Brokers Corp—Sergio Lozano	2875 Nw 82nd Ave, Doral FL 33122	305-594-9290	R	4*	<.1
1321	Harris Fire Protection Company Inc—Lawrence Ceislak	50 Kane St, Baltimore MD 21224	410-285-7272	R	4*	<.1
1322	Brooks Beal Center—Betty Bush	100 Beal Pkwy Nw, Fort Walton Beach FL 32548	850-244-9814	R	3*	.1
1323	NCS—George Bush	701 S Courthouse Rd Co, Arlington VA 22204	703-607-6125	R	3*	.1
1324	Alert Telephone Answering Service Inc—Sherry Lindsey	1230 Central Ave, Albany NY 12205	518-374-3388	R	3*	.1
1325	Dr Joseph L Curtis Associates Builders and Contractors Inc— Joseph Curtis	3911 24th Ave, Temple Hills MD 20748	301-894-7538	R	3*	.1
1326	Ticketing Technologies Corp—Melissa Carlston	12202 Airport Way Ste, Broomfield CO 80021	303-876-4100	R	3*	.1
1327	Fuller Communications Ltd—Linda Fuller	PO Box 3696, Bloomington IL 61702	309-827-0777	R	3*	.1
1328	Small Wonders Preschool Childc—Lynette Lein	1401 Oak Mnor Ave S St, Fargo ND 58103	701-235-7149	R	3*	.1
1329	Custom Moulding and Accessories Ltd—Ron Cole	26511 I 45 N, The Woodlands TX 77380	281-681-3800	R	3*	.1

Rank	Company Name—*Executive Officer*	Address, City, State, Zip	Phone	Type	Fin	Empls
1330	File Rite Inc—*Lucille Laoni*	1 Sprague Rd, Clinton MA 01510	978-368-8027	R	3*	.1
1331	Menke And Associates Inc—*John Menke*	255 California St Fl 1, San Francisco CA 94111	415-277-1245	R	3*	.1
1332	Np Sterling Labs Inc—*Cynthia Bitting*	PO Box 4309, Chesterfield MO 63006	636-530-1779	R	3*	.1
1333	Sally White and Associates Inc—*Sally White*	4131 N Central Expy St, Dallas TX 75204	214-219-7115	R	3*	.1
1334	Darco Enterprises Inc—*John Friedman*	5200 W 73rd St, Bedford Park IL 60638	708-496-1696	R	3*	.1
1335	Entravision Communications Corp—*Veronica Modeno*	801 N Jackson Rd, Mcallen TX 78501	956-687-4848	R	3*	.1
1336	Corporate Claims Management Inc—*Bob Martines*	PO Box 2308, Warminster PA 18974	215-396-1991	R	3*	<.1
1337	Paytel Communications Inc—*Vincent Townsend*	PO Box 8179, Greensboro NC 27419	336-852-7419	R	3*	<.1
1338	Great Lakes Scrip Center Inc—*Jack Smith*	PO Box 8158, Grand Rapids MI 49518	616-827-8180	R	3*	<.1
1339	Spectra-Tech Inc—*Anne Reutimann*	995 Muirfield Dr, Hanover Park IL 60133	630-539-4190	R	3*	<.1
1340	Atlantic Studios Inc—*Donald Filippelli*	661 4th St, Newark NJ 07107	973-481-9242	R	3*	<.1
1341	Greater Des Moines Convention And Visitors Bureau Inc—*Greg Edwards*	400 Locust St Ste 265, Des Moines IA 50309	515-286-4960	R	3*	<.1
1342	Market Builder Inc—*Keith Lawson*	5135 E Ingram St Ste 2, Mesa AZ 85205	480-641-6200	R	3*	<.1
1343	Metro Education and Entertainment Inc—*Harold Queen*	17534 Royalton Rd, Cleveland OH 44136	440-238-8588	R	3*	.1
1344	Quality Containment Solutions Inc—*Samir Olabi*	6044 Oakman Blvd, Dearborn MI 48126	313-215-6539	R	3*	.1
1345	Southwest Gem and Minerals—*Paul Able*	220 Kingsman St, Converse TX 78109	210-658-8920	R	3*	.1
1346	Wilmay Inc—*Wilbur Mayhew*	893 Oak Ave, Fillmore CA 93015	805-524-2603	R	3*	.1
1347	Kenneth Bordewick Interior Designs Inc—*Kenneth Bordewick*	415 N Cresford Dr, Los Angeles CA 90046	323-650-7663	R	3*	.1
1348	Home Of Fine Decorators LLC	2200 Sw 45th St Ste 10, Fort Lauderdale FL 33312	954-456-6000	R	3*	.1
1349	Hpi Products Inc—*William Garvey*	PO Box 997, Saint Joseph MO 64502	816-233-1237	R	3*	.1
1350	Future Pak Ltd—*Steven Mead*	28115 Lakeview Dr, Wixom MI 48393	248-486-0045	R	3*	.1
1351	Boshart Automotive Testing Services Inc—*Ken Boshart*	1175 N Del Rio Pl, Ontario CA 91764	909-466-1602	R	3*	.1
1352	Scai Inc—*Cecil Almand*	2819 Woodcliffe St Ste, San Antonio TX 78230	210-561-8700	R	3*	.1
1353	Contract Packaging Resources Inc—*Betty Wade*	8009 Industrial Villag, Greensboro NC 27409	336-665-1300	R	3*	.1
1354	Industrial Terminal Systems Inc—*Michael Steimer*	PO Box 4127, New Kensington PA 15068	724-335-9837	R	3*	.1
1355	Lab Gaynes Engineering Co—*William Noonan*	1549 Ardmore Ave, Itasca IL 60143	630-595-4288	R	3*	.1
1356	Pacmoore Products Inc—*William Moore*	PO Box 1299, Hammond IN 46325	219-932-2666	R	3*	.1
1357	Universal Laminating Ltd—*Scott Mahalick*	560 Territorial Dr, Bolingbrook IL 60440	630-759-6240	R	3*	.1
1358	National Relocation Services Inc—*Irene Ito*	2671 Pomona Blvd, Pomona CA 91768	909-869-5748	R	3*	<.1
1359	Engenuity Financial—*Garrett Gunderson*	9890 S 300 W Ste 300, Sandy UT 84070	801-304-7730	R	3	<.1
1360	Embroidery Industries Inc—*Farid Kahen*	3022 S Grand Ave, Los Angeles CA 90007	213-747-6226	R	3*	.1
1361	Personalized Communications Inc—*Stanley Gardner*	205 E Ctr St, Duncanville TX 75116	214-361-6684	R	3*	.1
1362	Charlotte Scott—*Charlotte Scott*	2309 Inverrary Cir, Austin TX 78747	512-282-0270	R	3*	.1
1363	Langenfelder Marine Inc—*James Matters*	400 Pier Ave, Stevensville MD 21666	410-643-5560	R	3*	.1
1364	Skeletech Inc—*Christopher Jerome*	22011 30th Dr SE, Bothell WA 98021	425-424-2663	R	3*	.1
1365	Cherry Avenue Auction Inc—*William Mitchell*	4640 S Cherry Ave, Fresno CA 93706	559-266-9856	R	3*	.1
1366	Deco Productions Inc—*Sharon Siegel*	7711 W 22nd Ave, Hialeah FL 33016	305-558-0800	R	3*	.1
1367	General Council On Finance And Admin Of The United Methodist Church—*Moses Kumar*	1 Music Cir N, Nashville TN 37203	615-369-2353	R	3*	.1
1368	Applied Resources Inc—*Joseph Salontai*	205 S Mckemy Ave, Chandler AZ 85226	480-961-7673	R	3*	<.1
1369	Pioneer Service Inc—*Umar Muthana*	542 W Factory Rd, Addison IL 60101	630-628-0249	R	3*	<.1
1370	Aaron Pallet Corp—*Walter Desmond*	88 Benson St, Fitchburg MA 01420	978-343-4000	R	3*	<.1
1371	G and E Delivery—*Kevin Leary*	PO Box 5872, Burlington VT 05402	802-578-2762	R	3*	.1
1372	Woodruff Agency—*Frank Woodruff*	10101 Reunion Pl Ste 9, San Antonio TX 78216	210-384-5346	R	3*	.1
1373	Plus Relocation Services Inc—*Lloyd Lee*	600 Hwy 169 S Ste 500, Minneapolis MN 55426	952-512-5500	R	3*	.1
1374	BHS Design Group—*J Bedard*	375 Commerce Dr, Amherst NY 14228	716-691-8080	R	3*	.1
1375	Hrm Recruitment Firm Inc—*Jacqueline Najeeullah*	2205 Point Blvd, Elgin IL 60123	847-783-4628	R	3*	.1
1376	M P and A Fibers Inc—*Bill Crosby*	1024 Commerce Dr, Grafton OH 44044	440-926-1074	R	3*	.1
1377	Communication Centre Inc—*Roger Elkins*	PO Box 1700, Calumet City IL 60409	708-862-2000	R	3*	.1
1378	Pandora Manufacturing LLC—*Ralph Whetsel*	157 W Main St, Ottawa OH 45875	419-384-3241	R	3*	.1
1379	Orbit Industries Inc—*Robert Aleksandrovic*	6840 Lake Abrams Dr, Cleveland OH 44130	440-243-3311	R	3*	.1
1380	Citipak Delivery System Inc—*Rose Campozano*	1270 Broadway Rm 201, New York NY 10001	212-265-9080	R	3*	.1
1381	Universal Meeting Management Inc—*Kathy Truelove*	3201 Glenwood Ave Ste, Raleigh NC 27612	919-846-1397	R	3*	<.1
1382	Champion International Moving Ltd—*Ronald Smith*	1 Champion Way, Canonsburg PA 15317	724-873-8000	R	3*	<.1
1383	Commerce Technologies Inc—*Frank Poore*	255 Fuller Rd Ste 327, Albany NY 12203	518-810-0700	R	3*	<.1
1384	Business Move Solutions Inc—*David Greenblatt*	11 Boulden Cir, New Castle DE 19720	302-324-0080	R	3*	<.1
1385	Northwest Traffic Control Inc—*Patricia Marti*	12005 Ne Marx St, Portland OR 97220	503-262-6500	R	3*	.1
1386	Michigan Message Ctr Inc—*Larry Gignac*	341 W Lovell St, Kalamazoo MI 49007	269-382-2800	R	3*	.1
1387	Restaurantcom Inc—*Cary Chessick*	1500 W Shure Dr Ste 20, Arlington Heights IL 60004		R	3*	.1
1388	Generations Home Care LLC—*Teri Vance*	8601 Se Causey Ave Ste, Portland OR 97086	503-652-0753	R	3*	.1
1389	Managed Care Network Inc	PO Box 696, Niagara Falls NY 14303	716-285-5710	R	3*	.1
1390	Tri-Data Inc—*Dan Smirl*	1601 Washington Ave, Huntington WV 25704	304-429-8007	R	3*	.1
1391	Kyle Jones Enterprise Inc—*Kyle Jones*	PO Box 62763, Phoenix AZ 85082	602-234-0111	R	3*	.1
1392	Academy Answering Service Inc—*Daniel Day*	1446 Som Ctr Rd Ste 7, Cleveland OH 44124	440-442-8500	R	3*	.1
1393	Button's Inventory Service Inc—*Luis Carter*	7910 Westglen Dr Ste 1, Houston TX 77063	713-781-0805	R	3*	.1
1394	California Credits Group LLC—*Dave Finley*	234 E Colorado Blvd St, Pasadena CA 91105	626-584-9800	R	3*	.1
1395	Carlson Auction Service Inc—*Daniel Carlson*	11048 Sw Us Hwy 40, Topeka KS 66615	785-478-4250	R	3*	.1
1396	ImproveNet Inc—*Rodney Rice* ServiceMagic Inc	10799 N 90th St Ste 20, Scottsdale AZ 85260	480-346-0000	S	3	.1
1397	Knickerbocker Construction LLC—*Marc Altheim*	155 Ave of The Amrcs 3, New York NY 10013	212-620-0500	R	3*	.1
1398	Lange Financial Corp—*William Lange*	17 Corporate Plaza Dr, Newport Beach CA 92660	949-640-4950	R	3*	.1
1399	Stoney Creek Roadhouse—*Bob Macray*	3000 26 Mile Rd, Shelby Township MI 48316	586-781-9108	R	3*	.1
1400	B and F Technical Code Services Inc—*Wanda Piccolo*	PO Box 957648, Hoffman Estates IL 60195	847-490-1443	R	3*	<.1
1401	Nicoletti Hornig and Sweeney—*Larry Munck*	88 Pine St Ste 704, New York NY 10005	212-220-3830	R	3*	<.1
1402	Rowland Associates Inc—*Sallie Rowland*	701 E New York St, Indianapolis IN 46202	317-636-3980	R	3*	<.1
1403	Ace Cleaners And Reconditioners Of Athletic Equipment Inc—*William Homnick*	PO Box 775, Washington PA 15301	724-225-8710	R	3*	<.1
1404	Answer Fort Smith Inc—*Hugh Jones*	1623 N A St, Fort Smith AR 72901	479-782-1100	R	3*	<.1
1405	Heritage Laboratories International—*Ken Stelzer*	1111 W Hwy 56, Olathe KS 66061	913-764-1045	S	3*	<.1
1406	Image Ink Ltd—*Brian Weinstein*	365 Criss Cir, Elk Grove Village IL 60007	847-631-2600	R	3*	<.1
1407	Airways Systems Inc—*Harris L Rothenberg*	106 Gateway Rd, Bensenville IL 60106	630-595-4242	R	3*	<.1
1408	Alphase Interiors Inc—*Maurine Lewis*	PO Box 73940, Puyallup WA 98373	253-840-4911	R	3*	<.1
1409	Broadbents Inc—*James D Broadbent*	39-45 Industrial Hwy, Essington PA 19029	610-521-0330	R	3*	<.1
1410	Fishero and Associates—*Clancey Fishero*	5291 Charles Ct, Carmel IN 46033	317-844-1274	R	3*	<.1
1411	Franke's Unlimited Inc—*Bill Franke*	825 Collins Ave, Marysville OH 43040	937-642-0706	R	3*	<.1
1412	National Marine Consultants Inc—*Ghulam Suhrawardi*	236 Ernston Rd Ste 3, Parlin NJ 08859	732-553-9210	R	3*	<.1
1413	Clearing House Auction Galleries Inc—*Thomas Le Clair*	207 Church St, Wethersfield CT 06109	860-529-3344	R	3*	<.1
1414	Fluid Conditioning Products Inc—*Karl Reinhart*	PO Box 407, Lititz PA 17543	717-627-1550	R	3*	<.1
1415	Commodity Systems Inc—*Bob Pelletier*	200 W Palmetto Park Rd, Boca Raton FL 33432	561-392-8663	R	3*	<.1

Note: An asterisk (*) indicates an estimated financial figure. The company type code used is as follows: R = Private, P = Public, S = Private Subsidiary, B = Public Subsidiary, D = Division, J = Joint Venture, I = Investment Fund.

COMPANY RANKINGS BY SALES WITHIN 4-DIGIT SIC

Rank	Company Name—Executive Officer	Address, City, State, Zip	Phone	Type	Fin	Empls
1416	Aqua Leisure Pool and Spa Inc—J Crawl	143 S Central Ave Ste, Elmsford NY 10523	914-347-5226	R	3*	<.1
1417	Fabritec Industries Inc—Doris Conner	708 Hwy U, Butterfield MO 65623	417-442-3543	R	3*	<.1
1418	Moore Coal Company Inc—Jimmy Moore	129 N 4th St, Bessemer AL 35020	205-424-2705	R	3*	<.1
1419	New York City Design Co—Maia Chiat	1412 Broadway Rm 1210, New York NY 10018	212-302-5551	R	3*	<.1
1420	Noelle Couture—Noelle Vazzano	3350 Barham Blvd, Los Angeles CA 90068	323-496-9868	R	3*	<.1
1421	B and C Fire Safety Inc—Walter Alligood	823 Navy St, Fort Walton Beach FL 32547	850-862-7812	R	3*	<.1
1422	Drykef Inc—Dennis Young	PO Box 10985, Fort Irwin CA 92310	760-380-5898	R	3*	<.1
1423	Ohio-Kentucky Steel Corp—Christopher Fiora	2001 Commerce Ctr Dr, Franklin OH 45005	937-743-4600	R	3*	<.1
1424	Cole Martinez Curtis and Associates—Jill I Cole	4040 Del Rey Ave Rm B, Marina Del Rey CA 90292	310-827-7200	R	3*	<.1
1425	Health Science Associates—Howard Spielman	10771 Noel St, Los Alamitos CA 90720	714-220-3922	R	3*	<.1
1426	Record Plant Inc—Rick Stevens	1032 N Sycamore Ave, Los Angeles CA 90038	323-993-9300	R	3*	<.1
1427	Wear The Best Inc—Rich Shanley	32 Henry St Ste 2, Bethel CT 06801	203-744-8336	R	3*	<.1
1428	W Ray Wallace and Associates—W Ray Wallace	3460 Preston Ridge Rd, Alpharetta GA 30005		R	3*	<.1
1429	Party By Design Inc—Franny Andahazy	530 W St Ste 1, Braintree MA 02184	781-848-1665	R	3*	<.1
1430	Food Technology Service Inc—Richard G Hunter	502 Prairie Mine Rd, Mulberry FL 33860	863-425-0039	P	3	<.1
1431	S Group Inc—Gary Peck	308 SW 1st Ave Ste 200, Portland OR 97204	503-328-0160	R	3*	<.1
1432	TeamPlay USA—Todd O Davis	7950 E Acoma Dr Ste 10, Scottsdale AZ 85260	480-443-9800	R	3*	<.1
1433	Holiday Models Convention Services—Kami Griffith Oisboid	3651 Lindell Rd Ste D1, Las Vegas NV 89103	702-735-7353	R	3*	<.1
1434	Gerald Zakim Associates LLC—Gerald Zakim	PO Box 2129, Wayne NJ 07474	973-633-1130	R	3*	<.1
1435	Hannover Fairs USA Inc—Art Paredes	2 Research Way, Princeton NJ 08540	609-987-1202	S	3*	<.1
1436	Mooney Industrials Inc—Pat Parmelle	16162 Beach Blvd Ste 2, Huntington Beach CA 92647	714-841-7902	R	3*	<.1
1437	Strategic Alliance Group—Pete Severens	PO Box 88824, Atlanta GA 30356	770-671-0404	R	3*	<.1
1438	Dashe and Thomson Inc—Jon Matejcek	401 N 3rd St Ste 500, Minneapolis MN 55401	612-338-4911	R	3*	<.1
1439	Contract Office Group—Leonard Alvarado	931 Cadillac Ct, Milpitas CA 95035	408-262-6400	R	3*	<.1
1440	Mactivity Inc—Paul Kent	15466 Los Gatos Blvd S, Los Gatos CA 95032	408-356-8585	R	3*	<.1
1441	Very Special Events Inc—Nancy R Walters	12182 Royal Birkdale R, San Diego CA 92128	858-485-1171	R	3*	<.1
1442	buyCastings Inc—Robert Dzugan	2411 Crosspointe Dr, Miamisburg OH 45342	937-247-9194	R	3	<.1
1443	Western Contract Interiors—Bob Mahowald	298 Jackson St, San Jose CA 95112	408-275-9600	R	3*	<.1
1444	Hopkins Foodservice Specialists Inc—Richard Hopkins	7906 MacArthur Blvd, Cabin John MD 20818	301-320-9200	R	3*	<.1
1445	Integrated Trade Systems Inc—Tom Glasgow	2200 S Main St Ste 103, Lombard IL 60148	630-781-8890	R	3*	<.1
1446	Lohr Design Inc—Marcus D Lohr III	27 E 9th St, Indianapolis IN 46204	317-237-5610	R	3*	<.1
1447	Pacific Stock—Barbara Brundage	7192 Kalanianaole Hwy, Honolulu HI 96825	808-394-5100	R	3*	<.1
1448	Print Resource Inc—David Sears	1500 W Park Dr Ste 215, Westborough MA 01581	508-433-4600	R	3*	<.1
1449	ShowHomes of America—Bert Lyles	2110 Blair Blvd, Nashville TN 37212	615-292-0892	R	3*	<.1
1450	Annex Research Inc—Bob Djurdjevic	8183 E Mountain Spring, Scottsdale AZ 85255	602-532-7789	R	3*	<.1
1451	Bridgeman Art Library International—Edward Whitley	65 E 93rd St, New York NY 10128	212-828-1238	S	3*	<.1
1452	Capitol Services—David Kalb	1225 8th St Ste 580, Sacramento CA 95814	916-443-0657	R	3*	<.1
1453	Carol Franklin Associates Inc—Carol Franklin	433 Highwood Ave, Leonia NJ 07605	201-461-7770	R	3*	<.1
1454	Chamness Relocation Services Inc—Darla Chamness	25 S Arizona Pl Ste 40, Chandler AZ 85225	480-899-7222	R	3*	<.1
1455	Design Works Inc—Diane Gote	392 Morris Ave, Summit NJ 07901	908-277-2522	R	3*	<.1
1456	Designing Women Inc—Mary Capobianco	801 73rd St, Des Moines IA 50312	515-222-0510	R	3*	<.1
1457	Exchange Enterprises Inc—Sharon Connelly	919-7 Stratford Ave, Stratford CT 06615	203-386-9466	R	3*	<.1
1458	Hadco International Appraisal Services—Harvey A Davis	PO Box 1465, Conroe TX 77305	936-760-1220	R	3*	<.1
1459	Imprima Management Services Inc—Frank Goovaerts	62 Burton St, Bristol RI 02809	401-396-9977	R	3*	<.1
1460	Interior Space Design Inc—Suzette Schultz	2109 Post Office St, Galveston TX 77550	409-737-1500	R	3*	<.1
1461	Intermountain Voice Messaging Systems Inc—Jerry K Nerdin	490 E 1000 N, North Salt Lake UT 84054	801-292-8190	R	3*	<.1
1462	Nassi Group LLC—Albert Nassi	340 N Westlake Blvd St, Westlake Village CA 91362	805-497-8900	R	3	<.1
1463	Paul McInnis Inc—Paul McInnis	1 Juniper Rd, North Hampton NH 03862	603-964-1301	R	3*	<.1
1464	Pexx Inc—Palmer L Greene	PO Box 210, Plantersville TX 77363	832-237-5888	R	3*	<.1
1465	Reunited Inc—Johnathan Miller	PO Box 2258, Evergreen CO 80437		R	3*	<.1
1466	Route Brokers Inc—Ken Sussman	107 Northern Blvd, Great Neck NY 11021	516-482-8250	R	3*	<.1
1467	Slot 1 Recording Studios Inc—Rick Denzien	PO Box 567, Ambler PA 19002	215-643-1313	R	3*	<.1
1468	Miller and Jedrziewski Associates—Vivian Miller	395 E 3900 S, Salt Lake City UT 84107	801-363-6229	R	3*	<.1
1469	Marketplace Productions LLC—Altin Paulson	1885 University AveW S, Saint Paul MN 55104	651-645-6061	R	3	<.1
1470	Plantmobile Inc—Janelle Johnson	6507 N Pleasant Ave, Fresno CA 93711	559-432-1816	R	3*	<.1
1471	Advanced Microfilm Systems Inc—Peter Gallagher	11833 New Halls Ferry, Florissant MO 63033	314-837-4000	R	3*	.1
1472	Eight Crossings Inc—Patrick Maher	PO Bx 188913, Sacramento CA 95816	916-444-0002	R	3	.1
1473	Green Valley Security—Jeffrey Sellers	PO Box 531606, Henderson NV 89053	702-261-0440	R	3*	.1
1474	PHR Design—Paul Rothstein	4134 Kraft Ave, Studio City CA 91604	818-760-1065	R	3*	.1
1475	Twentyfirst Century Auction—Jeff Lienkaemper	1748 Alviso St, Simi Valley CA 93065	805-341-4944	R	3*	.1
1476	Micro Brew I Inc—Victor Rallo	1171 Hooper Ave, Toms River NJ 08753	732-244-7566	R	3*	.1
1477	Pb Car Movers—Jose Desiderio	5510 W 120th St, Hawthorne CA 90250	310-283-2741	R	3*	.1
1478	Fts Inc—John Fiore	PO Box 2091, Ponca City OK 74602	580-762-0032	R	3*	.1
1479	Hudson And Marshall Inc—Benjamin Hudson	PO Box 38, Bolingbroke GA 31004	478-743-1511	R	3*	.1
1480	3psc LLC—Susan Powell	7099 N Atlantic Ave, Cape Canaveral FL 32920	321-799-3329	R	3*	.1
1481	Atlas O LLC—Tom Haedrich	378 Florence Ave, Hillside NJ 07205	908-687-9590	R	3*	.1
1482	Creative Coatings Of Carolina Inc—Ronald Sewell	5020 W Wt Harris Blvd, Charlotte NC 28269	704-598-5822	R	3*	.1
1483	Ruspak Corp—Timothy Brickle	PO Box 29, Lyons NY 14489	315-946-9777	R	3*	.1
1484	Technicom Services Inc—Thomas Pearson	11401 Allison Ct, Huntley IL 60142	847-669-7530	R	3*	.1
1485	Telemed Inc—Betty Neisler	PO Box 20015, Atlanta GA 30325	404-355-1555	R	3*	.1
1486	FL Haus Co—Francis Haus	921 Ridge Ave, Pittsburgh PA 15212	412-231-7700	R	3*	<.1
1487	New World Environmental Inc—Michael Butler	448 Commerce Way, Livermore CA 94551	925-443-7967	R	3*	<.1
1488	A Spacios Design Group Inc—Cecilia Alvarez	7370 Nw 36th Ave, Miami FL 33147	305-696-1766	R	3*	<.1
1489	Dotcom Distrubution Corp—William Follett	300 Nixon Ln, Edison NJ 08837	732-287-2300	R	3*	<.1
1490	Onbrand 24 Inc—Mark Fichera	100 Cummings Ctr Ste 3, Beverly MA 01915	978-524-8777	R	3*	<.1
1491	Sweeney Steel Service Corp—Michael Sweeney	PO Box 851, Buffalo NY 14240	716-877-7100	R	3*	<.1
1492	Corporate Language Services—Victor Hertz	15 Maiden Ln Ste 300, New York NY 10038	212-766-4187	R	3*	<.1
1493	Boucher Family LP—Norman Boucher	73 Woodview Dr, Doylestown PA 18901	215-348-8592	R	3*	.1
1494	Rave Inc—Albert Bluemle	940 River Rd, North Tonawanda NY 14120	716-695-1110	R	3*	.1
1495	Hudson Microimaging Inc—Stephen Fisher	PO Box 640, Port Ewen NY 12466	845-338-5785	R	3*	.1
1496	Societe Intertionale De Telecm—Rudy Laija	2250 E Imperial Hwy St, El Segundo CA 90245	310-647-7912	R	3*	.1
1497	Vendor Managed Solutions Inc—Rumia Burbank	850 Stephenson Hwy, Troy MI 48083	248-658-4600	R	3*	.1
1498	Cast Pac Inc—Donald Caldwell	200 Cascade Dr Ste E, Allentown PA 18109	610-264-8131	R	3*	<.1
1499	ManufacturingCom Inc—David Free	2700 Cumberland Pkwy S, Atlanta GA 30339	770-444-9686	R	3*	<.1
1500	Instrumentation And Controls Inc—Joyce Raines	100 Industrial Dr, Bridgeton PA 18901	215-348-4304	R	3*	<.1
1501	Burdorf-Kessler Inc—Allan Morris	3939 Shelbyville Rd, Louisville KY 40207	502-719-9700	R	3*	<.1
1502	Mystic Assembly and Decorating Company Inc—Jerry Doyle	19 Vincent Cir, Warminster PA 18974	215-957-0280	R	3*	<.1
1503	First Financial Credit Union—Greg Forch	PO Box 104360, Jefferson City MO 65110	573-636-9198	R	3*	<.1
1504	Mainstream Commercial Divers Inc—Craig Fortenbery	322 Cc Lowry Dr, Murray KY 42071	270-753-9654	R	3*	<.1
1505	Continental Aerial Surveys Inc—Freddie Nix	3356 Regal Dr, Alcoa TN 37701	865-970-3115	R	3*	<.1

Rank	Company Name—*Executive Officer*	Address, City, State, Zip	Phone	Type	Fin	Empls
1506	Miller Mining And Engineering Technologies // Oregon LLC	PO Box 2636, Grants Pass OR 97528	541-956-1519	R	3*	.1
1507	All Star Corrugated—*Kimberly Stephens*	208 Hiddenglen St, Burleson TX 76028	817-454-8640	R	3*	.1
1508	GFD Courier Corp—*Gary Demsak*	63 Flushing Ave Unit 2, Brooklyn NY 11205	718-222-7444	R	3*	.1
1509	Mckesson Packaging Services	7101 Weddington Rd Nw, Concord NC 28027	704-784-4301	R	3*	.1
1510	Enhanced Tele-Services Inc—*Kristine Gallagher*	5550 S 138th St, Omaha NE 68137	402-894-0282	R	3*	.1
1511	American Sign Language Services Corp—*Angela Roth*	3700 Commerce Blvd Ste, Kissimmee FL 34741	407-518-7900	R	3*	.1
1512	Airosol Company Inc—*Carl Stratemeier*	PO Box 120, Neodesha KS 66757	620-325-2666	R	3*	.1
1513	7 West Secretarial/Answering Service Inc—*Karen Podany*	7525 Mitchell Rd Ste 3, Eden Prairie MN 55344	952-936-4000	R	3*	.1
1514	Web Industries Fort Wayne Inc—*Don Romine*	3925 Ardmore Ave, Fort Wayne IN 46802	260-432-0027	R	3*	<.1
1515	Absolute Resolutions Corp—*Michael Bendickson*	PO Box 880306, San Diego CA 92168	619-295-1200	R	3*	<.1
1516	Liquid Engineering Corp—*Wayne Dykstra*	PO Box 80230, Billings MT 59108	406-651-0105	R	3*	<.1
1517	Richmond Commercial Services Inc—*Montie Harper*	PO Box 27976, Richmond VA 23261	804-358-4035	R	3*	<.1
1518	Parvin-Clauss Sign Company Inc—*Robert Clauss*	165 Tubeway Dr, Carol Stream IL 60188	630-510-2020	R	3*	<.1
1519	Genie Manufacturing Corp—*Jeffrey Gleason*	999 Rush Henrietta Tow, Rush NY 14543	585-359-4100	R	3*	<.1
1520	Janklow and Nesbit Associates—*Morton Janklow*	445 Park Ave Fl 13, New York NY 10022	212-421-1700	R	3*	<.1
1521	Market Channels Inc—*Robert Clarke*	125 Old Gate Ln Ste 1, Milford CT 06460	203-874-6140	R	3*	<.1
1522	Northeast Laser and Electropolish Inc—*Richard Rosselli*	246c Main St, Monroe CT 06468	203-268-7238	R	3*	<.1
1523	Personal Mail International Inc—*Peter Fehnel*	PO Box 311, Mendham NJ 07945	973-543-6001	R	3*	<.1
1524	Image Teleproducts Inc—*Ronald Zate*	6689 Orchard Lake Rd S, West Bloomfield MI 48322	248-737-3000	R	3*	<.1
1525	Meredith Enterprises Inc—*Cynthia Meredith*	8585 Sw Beaverton Hill, Portland OR 97225	503-292-8931	R	3*	<.1
1526	Linda Viviani Touring Company Inc—*Linda Viviani*	20800 Jefferson St, Napa CA 94558	707-938-2100	R	3*	<.1
1527	Systems Technology Inc—*Melvin Farnaby*	2830 Holmestown Rd, Myrtle Beach SC 29588	843-650-2225	R	3*	<.1
1528	QSGI Inc—*Marc Sherman*	70 Lake Dr, Hightstown NJ 08520	609-426-4666	P	3	.1
1529	National Handicapped Workshop—*Cheryl Guinn*	5900 W Kilgore Ave, Muncie IN 47304	765-287-8331	R	3*	.1
1530	Genoveva Chavez Community Center—*Martin Lujan*	3221 Rodeo Rd, Santa Fe NM 87507	505-955-4001	R	3*	.1
1531	Glass City Black Brothers United—*Earl Landry*	1001 Indiana Ave Ste 3, Toledo OH 43607	419-242-9438	R	3*	.1
1532	Tim Jones—*Tim Jones*	5008 Curtis Ln, New Iberia LA 70560	337-364-3235	R	3*	.1
1533	ME Productions—*Jim Edgen*	2000 Sw 30th Ave, Fort Lauderdale FL 33309	954-458-7050	R	3*	.1
1534	Glouster Township—*Gabe Busa*	1729 Erial Rd, Blackwood NJ 08012	856-228-3144	R	3*	.1
1535	Carroll's Creek Fire Protection District	PO Box 735, Northport AL 35476	205-333-1156	R	3*	.1
1536	Falcon Messenger Service—*William Micotra*	1201 Corbin St Fl 2, Elizabeth NJ 07201	908-282-0060	R	3*	.1
1537	Infopro Group Inc—*Richard Collins*	229 Furys Ferry Rd Ste, Augusta GA 30007	706-724-1555	R	3*	.1
1538	Polysi Technologies Inc—*Ann Luther*	5108 Rex Mcleod Dr, Sanford NC 27330	919-775-4989	R	3*	.1
1539	Breakdown Services Ltd—*Gary Marsh*	2140 Cotner Ave, Los Angeles CA 90025	310-276-9166	R	3*	<.1
1540	Coleman Assembly and Packaging Inc—*S Goldberg-Arguij*	208 Coleman St, Gardner MA 01440	978-632-3807	R	3*	<.1
1541	Chapter 13 Trustee—*Jan Cooper*	600 University St Ste, Seattle WA 98101	206-624-5124	R	3*	<.1
1542	Guy Brown Fire and Safety Inc—*Guy Brown*	310 W Commerce St, Dallas TX 75208	214-653-1100	R	3*	<.1
1543	Asi Show Inc—*Matthew Cohn*	4800 E St Rd Ste 100a, Feasterville Trevose PA 19053	215-953-4800	R	3*	<.1
1544	Boulder Rural Fire Protection District—*Dana Dolan*	5075 Jay Rd, Boulder CO 80301	303-530-9575	R	3*	<.1
1545	Digital Graphics Inc—*Rob Noller*	PO Box 950240, Oklahoma City OK 73195	405-682-4385	R	3*	<.1
1546	International Convention And Event Services—*Donald Takaki*	1004 Makepono St, Honolulu HI 96819	808-832-2430	R	3*	<.1
1547	Staurt Mill Capital Acquisition Partners—*Cathy Conti*	PO Box 158, Greene NY 13778	607-656-4107	R	3*	<.1
1548	JMBZ Inc—*Jon Griffith*	1250 S Wilson Way Ste, Stockton CA 95205	209-465-0177	R	3*	<.1
1549	Charity Auction Services LLC	11175 Redwood Ave, Fontana CA 92337	909-829-7320	R	3*	<.1
1550	Dynamic Consultants Inc—*Michelle Craig*	1300 Space Park Way, Mountain View CA 94043	650-967-6982	R	3*	<.1
1551	Laurel Adjustment Bureau Inc—*William Johns*	PO Box 185, Lanham MD 20703	301-459-6660	R	3*	<.1
1552	Prana Inc—*Julia Ray*	PO Box 2728, Hallandale FL 33008	954-457-5595	R	3*	.3
1553	Your Selling Team Inc—*Lezlie Gallaway*	224 N Main St, Ainsworth NE 69210	308-432-8700	R	3*	.1
1554	Richlands Piggly Wiggly—*Ward Sylvester*	108 Franck St, Richlands NC 28574	910-324-3333	R	3*	.1
1555	Dallas Metroplex Wiley College Alumni Association Inc—*E Shaw*	1009 Glenda St, Terrell TX 75160	972-524-6116	R	3*	.1
1556	Cafe Pacific Inc—*David Knouse*	24 Highland Park Villa, Dallas TX 75205	214-526-1170	R	3*	.1
1557	Davis Interiors Ltd—*Rexanne Metzger*	3300 Azalea Garden Rd, Norfolk VA 23513	757-853-0968	R	3*	.1
1558	Riley's Ready Pack Inc—*Clyde Riley*	PO Box 150026, Dallas TX 75315	214-745-5588	R	3*	.1
1559	Ecg Management Consultants—*Andrew Macdonald*	1111 3rd Ave Ste 2700, Seattle WA 98101	206-689-2200	R	3*	.1
1560	Roseview Heights Mutual Water Company Inc—*Tim Satcher*	12450 Mount Hamilton R, San Jose CA 95140	408-258-4796	R	3*	.1
1561	Soft Line Interior Design Inc—*Michael Stein*	1135 Brighton Beach Av, Brooklyn NY 11235	718-646-0441	R	3*	<.1
1562	United Enterprise Co—*Robert Henkel*	10913 E Cir, Omaha NE 68137	402-597-1700	R	3*	<.1
1563	American Barricade Rental Inc—*Janet Tisdall*	3537 Delgany St, Denver CO 80216	303-298-8407	R	3*	<.1
1564	Contract Packaging Associates Inc—*Dennis Favale*	3003 W Hirsch St, Melrose Park IL 60160	708-865-2600	R	3*	<.1
1565	Direct Line Inc—*Ruth Goldenburg*	2847 Shattuck Ave, Berkeley CA 94705	510-843-3900	R	3*	<.1
1566	Brevard Water Conditioning Inc—*Michael Carey*	PO Box 9307, Daytona Beach FL 32120	386-274-5036	R	3*	<.1
1567	Rewardsnow Inc—*Steven Fleet*	383 Central Ave Ste 35, Dover NH 03820	603-516-3440	R	3*	<.1
1568	CWA Manufacturing Company Inc—*Frank Walker*	PO Box 10, Mount Morris MI 48458	810-686-3030	R	3*	<.1
1569	Donnally Vujcic Associates LLC—*Richard Donnally*	400 Professional Dr St, Gaithersburg MD 20879	301-590-8900	R	3*	<.1
1570	KO Enterprises—*Kevin O'brien*	6005 N Lindbergh Blvd, Hazelwood MO 63042	314-521-4151	R	3*	<.1
1571	Revere Data LLC—*Michael Engmann*	100 Pine St Ste 600, San Francisco CA 94111	415-782-0454	R	3*	<.1
1572	Riekes International LP—*Jesse Lindenstein*	3455 Edison Way, Menlo Park CA 94025	650-364-2509	R	3*	<.1
1573	Product Ventures Ltd—*Peter Clarke*	55 Walls Dr Ste 400, Fairfield CT 06824	203-319-1119	R	3*	<.1
1574	Henschel Coating and Laminating Company Inc—*Warren Henschel*	15805 W Overland Dr, New Berlin WI 53151	262-786-1750	R	3*	<.1
1575	Southwest Bio-Labs Inc—*John Byrd*	401 N 17th St Ste 11, Las Cruces NM 88005	575-524-8917	R	3*	<.1
1576	Industrial Design Innovations Inc—*Chuck Mchugh*	10611 Haggerty St, Dearborn MI 48126	313-846-6601	R	3*	<.1
1577	Concept Design Productions—*James Leverton*	718 S Primrose Ave, Monrovia CA 91016	626-932-0082	R	3*	<.1
1578	JKP Enterprises Inc—*Jerry Payne*	5847 San Felipe St Ste, Houston TX 77057	713-785-0677	R	3*	<.1
1579	Kincaid Auction Service House Inc—*Johnny Kincaid*	1905 Cottonwood St, Abilene TX 79601	325-676-4077	R	3*	<.1
1580	Motif Designs Inc—*Lyn Peterson*	718 S Fulton Ave Ste 5, Mount Vernon NY 10550	914-633-1170	R	3*	<.1
1581	David Judge—*David Judge*	1600 Park Ave Ste 301, New York NY 10029	212-305-6283	R	2*	.1
1582	Morris and Associates—*Robert Morris*	6605 Jefferson Hwy, Baton Rouge LA 70806	225-215-2332	R	2*	.1
1583	Ed Bertholet And Associates Inc—*Edward Bertholet*	2801 Bertholet Blvd St, Valparaiso IN 46383	219-462-0325	R	2*	.1
1584	Greater St Louis Agility	200 Dana Dr, Collinsville IL 62234	618-345-5899	R	2*	.1
1585	Performance Tradeshow Group Inc—*Phillip Doughty*	3315 E Russell Rd Ste, Las Vegas NV 89120	702-436-5180	R	2*	.1
1586	West Coast Now Inc—*David Ramos*	2381 Elan Ln, San Ramon CA 94582	415-515-4359	R	2*	.1
1587	Rankin Fitness Group Ltd—*Kim Simmonds*	336 Crossgates Blvd, Brandon MS 39042	601-825-9181	R	2*	.1
1588	Dutelle Enterprises LLC	5263 Ridge Rd, Glenville NY 12302	518-399-0057	R	2*	.1
1589	Advance Communications Inc—*Ron Schlossberg*	10 Melrose Dr Unit 2, Farmington CT 06032	860-677-0091	R	2*	.1
1590	Advanced Fulfillment Inc—*Wayne Vanderlaan*	955 Godfrey Ave Sw, Grand Rapids MI 49503	616-245-3636	R	2*	.1
1591	H and R General Contractor And Custodian Services Inc—*Richard Landes*	1219 Stoneburner St, Staunton VA 24401	540-885-1454	R	2*	.1
1592	Sunset Farm—*Greg Burris*	PO Box 188, Loxley AL 36551	251-964-6464	R	2*	.1

Note: An asterisk (*) indicates an estimated financial figure. The company type code used is as follows: R = Private, P = Public, S = Private Subsidiary, B = Public Subsidiary, D = Division, J = Joint Venture, I = Investment Fund.

COMPANY RANKINGS BY SALES WITHIN 4-DIGIT SIC

Rank	Company Name—*Executive Officer*	Address, City, State, Zip	Phone	Type	Fin	Empls
1593	Ambs Message Center Inc—*Richard Ambs*	PO Box 1325, Jackson MI 49204	517-787-6470	R	2*	<.1
1594	Divcon LLC—*Heidi Eschliman*	8120 Hwy 182 E, Morgan City LA 70380	985-385-9911	R	2*	<.1
1595	Audio Properties Inc—*Alan Kubicka*	232 E Ohio St Fl 1, Chicago IL 60611	312-822-9333	R	2*	<.1
1596	Jet Pay LLC—*David Lantz*	3361 Boyington Dr Ste, Carrollton TX 75006	972-503-8900	R	2*	<.1
1597	East Lake Tarpon Special Fire Control District	3375 Tarpon Lake Blvd, Palm Harbor FL 34685	727-784-8668	R	2*	<.1
1598	Metal Processing Corp—*Frank Eberwein*	201 Mississippi St, Gary IN 46402	219-883-5722	R	2*	<.1
1599	Meyer Design Inc—*Norman Vievtke*	227 E Lancaster Ave, Ardmore PA 19003	610-649-8500	R	2*	<.1
1600	Mulliniks Recycling Inc—*Billy Mulliniks*	5937 Soutel Dr, Jacksonville FL 32219	904-764-3644	R	2*	<.1
1601	Non-Profit Services Inc—*Debra Foster*	PO Box 291585, Nashville TN 37229	615-385-4444	R	2*	<.1
1602	Ohio Laminating and Binding Inc—*Jim Ondecko*	4364 Reynolds Dr, Hilliard OH 43026	614-771-4868	R	2*	<.1
1603	Reliable Runners Courier Service Inc—*Marc Coben*	8624 Station St, Mentor OH 44060	440-578-7000	R	2*	<.1
1604	Sign On A Sign Language Interpreting Resource Inc—*Karen Graham*	130 Nickerson St Ste 1, Seattle WA 98109	206-632-7100	R	2*	<.1
1605	Environmental Security Inc—*Christopher Smith*	29 Diana Ct, Cheshire CT 06410	203-699-2458	R	2*	<.1
1606	Professional Water Services Inc—*Keith Borochaner*	2902 New Rodgers Rd, Bristol PA 19007	215-788-8881	R	2*	<.1
1607	Voice Genesis Inc—*Timothy Bender*	8748 Brecksville Rd St, Brecksville OH 44141	440-717-1017	R	2*	<.1
1608	88 Trading Corp—*Shelly Tseng*	5829 48th St, Maspeth NY 11378	718-326-1699	R	2*	<.1
1609	Oklahoma City National Memorial Foundation—*Kari Watkins*	PO Box 323, Oklahoma City OK 73101	405-235-3313	R	2*	<.1
1610	Sri Monogramming Inc—*Charlotte O'reilly*	PO Box 2383, Round Rock TX 78680	512-388-4989	R	2*	<.1
1611	ASU Indian Club Inc—*David Strafford*	PO Box 2219, State University AR 72467	870-972-2401	R	2*	<.1
1612	Selco Inc—*Joel Selber*	4715 Steiner Ranch Blv, Austin TX 78732	512-266-4232	R	2*	.1
1613	Ballantyne Leasing LLC	13860 Ballantyne Corp, Charlotte NC 28277	704-248-2000	R	2*	.1
1614	Consumerlink Inc—*Deirdre Cechin*	721 Cedar Glen Dr, Weldon Spring MO 63304	636-441-8780	R	2*	.1
1615	Feather Larson and Synhorst	11225 N 28th Dr Ste C1, Phoenix AZ 85029	602-333-0590	R	2*	.1
1616	Village Of Northfield—*Anne Kane*	1800 Winnetka Ave, Northfield IL 60093	847-441-3800	R	2*	.1
1617	Recycled Baseball Items—*Frank Galan*	5401 Mitchelldale St, Houston TX 77092	713-682-0475	R	2*	.1
1618	Integrated Financial Group—*Donald Patrick*	6600 Dnwoody Peachtree, Atlanta GA 30328	770-353-6317	R	2*	.1
1619	Message Center Communication Inc—*Gary Schaumann*	6779 Mesa Ridge Rd Ste, San Diego CA 92121	858-974-7419	R	2*	.1
1620	Sonoma County Fairgrounds-Santa Rosa—*Glenn Stubblefield*	PO Box 1536, Santa Rosa CA 95402	707-545-4203	R	2*	<.1
1621	Bharat H Barai Associates—*Bharat Barai*	9903 Twin Creek Blvd, Munster IN 46321	219-924-4145	R	2*	<.1
1622	Organicare Inc—*Anthony Lawson*	12814 Sagamore Forest, Reisterstown MD 21136	410-517-2880	R	2*	<.1
1623	Dependable Medical Directory LLC—*Brian Curdy*	PO Box 36308, Phoenix AZ 85067	602-266-2557	R	2*	<.1
1624	Exhibit Services Group Inc—*Amanda Helgemoe*	2627 Farrington St, Dallas TX 75207	214-752-7075	R	2*	<.1
1625	Financial Courier Service Inc—*V Myers*	6099 Mount Moriah Rd 1, Memphis TN 38115	901-761-4555	R	2*	<.1
1626	Naples Pool Service Inc—*Pete Roeser*	6455 Airport Pulling R, Naples FL 34109	239-597-7114	R	2*	<.1
1627	Mitchell Associates Inc—*Louis Rosenberg*	1 Ave Of The Arts Ste, Wilmington DE 19801	302-594-9400	R	2*	<.1
1628	3b Media Inc—*Bashar Barazi*	2140 W Fulton St, Chicago IL 60612	312-242-1793	R	2*	<.1
1629	Custom Pak Illinois Inc—*Daniel Chapin*	PO Box 550, Hampshire IL 60140	847-683-3388	R	2*	<.1
1630	BXC Products Inc—*Ester Yip*	39 E 31st St Fl 4, New York NY 10016	212-532-9428	R	2*	<.1
1631	Interactive Games And Creations Inc—*Michael Hellyar*	1467 Lidcombe Ave, El Monte CA 91733	626-453-0003	R	2*	<.1
1632	Pro-Grind Inc—*Carl Stringer*	5637 Hogue St, Houston TX 77087	713-645-2966	R	2*	<.1
1633	Benrich Service Company Inc—*Peter Bendheim*	3190 Airport Loop Dr S, Costa Mesa CA 92626	714-241-0284	R	2*	<.1
1634	Penegon West Inc—*Trevor Finn*	9176 W Sunset Blvd, Los Angeles CA 90069	310-274-5133	R	2*	<.1
1635	Total Reclaim Inc—*Craig Lorch*	PO Box 24996, Seattle WA 98124	206-343-7443	R	2	<.1
1636	NorthStar Business and Property Brokers	20 Peachtree Ct, Holbrook NY 11741	631-676-4076	R	2	<.1
1637	Normco Supply Company Inc—*Norman Schmotzer*	3665 E Industrial Way, Riviera Beach FL 33404	561-848-8640	R	2*	.1
1638	Bail Bonds Now Inc—*Don Dekker*	PO Box 1249, Flippin AR 72634	870-453-4357	R	2*	.1
1639	Belle Interiors—*Frank Zandella*	309 Montauk Hwy, East Moriches NY 11940	631-874-2181	R	2*	.1
1640	Ag World Support Systems LLC—*Adelle Calvert*	PO Box 1696, Moses Lake WA 98837	509-765-0698	R	2*	.1
1641	Aztec Messenger Inc—*Joseph Mei*	240 S Main St Ste L, South Hackensack NJ 07606	201-342-8088	R	2*	.1
1642	Bhatti Enterprises Inc—*Santokh Bhatti*	8045 Vegas Cir, West Chester OH 45069	513-886-6000	R	2*	.1
1643	National Publishers Marketing Center Inc—*Louis Carbonaro*	1383 S Missouri Ave, Clearwater FL 33756	727-467-9207	R	2*	.1
1644	Project Packaging Inc—*Ken Franklin*	20001 Euclid Ave Ste 1, Euclid OH 44117	216-451-7878	R	2*	.1
1645	Skyblue Sewing Manufacturing Inc—*Huang Zhem*	960 Mission St Fl 2, San Francisco CA 94103	415-777-9978	R	2*	.1
1646	Fonseca Citrus Harvesting LLC	PO Box 2109, Lake Placid FL 33862	863-465-3466	R	2*	<.1
1647	Daco Enterprises—*Dale Cooley*	21309 Hill Rd, Colton CA 92324	909-825-7547	R	2*	<.1
1648	Flexopak Inc—*Anna Tsai*	17989 Arenth Ave, City of Industry CA 91748	626-196-7265	R	2*	<.1
1649	Kim Zeder—*Kim Zeder*	3720 S Santa Fe Ave, Vernon CA 90058	323-583-5404	R	2*	<.1
1650	Alexander Pft Inc—*John Keefner*	3250 E Grant St, Long Beach CA 90755	562-595-1741	R	2*	<.1
1651	Destination South USA Inc—*Cynthia Alford*	959b Piedmont Ave Ne, Atlanta GA 30309	404-815-3010	R	2*	<.1
1652	Sub Source Inc—*Kristen Reinhardt*	600 18th Ave, Rockford IL 61104	815-968-7800	R	2*	<.1
1653	Ajr Enterprises Inc—*Jacob Rukel*	3635 Swenson Ave, Saint Charles IL 60174	630-377-8886	R	2*	<.1
1654	Secured Fibres—*James Kaup*	4751 Vandenberg Dr, North Las Vegas NV 89081	702-643-5718	R	2*	<.1
1655	Future Innovations Inc—*Mark Frohnen*	4495 Stoneridge Dr, Pleasanton CA 94588	925-485-2000	R	2*	<.1
1656	Imageseller LLC—*Tim Griffiths*	1855 Blake St Ste 201, Denver CO 80202	303-215-1066	R	2*	<.1
1657	Interior Plant Design Inc—*Jerry Gates*	1950 Monterey Hwy, San Jose CA 95112	408-286-1367	R	2*	<.1
1658	Perfect Cut-Off Inc—*Michael Picciano*	29201 Anderson Rd, Wickliffe OH 44092	440-943-0000	R	2*	<.1
1659	Precept Financial Solutions—*Robert Ward*	PO Box 740126, Dallas TX 75374	972-788-8126	R	2*	<.1
1660	Segtel Inc—*Steven Goldsmith*	PO Box 610, Lebanon NH 03766	603-643-5883	R	2*	<.1
1661	Textilemaster LLC	PO Box 2816, Norcross GA 30091	770-368-4111	R	2*	<.1
1662	Applied Laser Technology Inc—*Hossein Karamooz*	14155 Sw Brigadoon Ct, Beaverton OR 97005	503-641-4400	R	2*	<.1
1663	T and T Transit Products—*Andra Thacker*	PO Box 709, Alexandria AL 36250	256-892-1604	R	2*	<.1
1664	Valley Forge Press Inc—*Michael Parella*	2570 Blvd Of The Gener, Norristown PA 19403	610-854-3770	R	2*	<.1
1665	Apollo Transfer Company LLC—*Emil Rakovich*	422 S Madison Dr Ste 1, Tempe AZ 85281	480-966-7777	R	2*	<.1
1666	Infrared Testing Inc—*Terry Malagoli*	445 W Erie St Ste 106, Chicago IL 60654	312-670-5005	R	2*	<.1
1667	Pacific Dimensions Inc—*Jennifer Elling*	201 Continental Blvd S, El Segundo CA 90245	310-335-1800	R	2*	<.1
1668	Maury Boyd and Associates Inc—*Richard Boyd*	6330 E 75th St Ste 212, Indianapolis IN 46250	317-849-6110	R	2*	<.1
1669	Creative Native Inc—*Jeri Garrett*	PO Box 3009, South Padre Island TX 78597	956-761-7771	R	2*	<.1
1670	Brooke Industries Inc—*David Thornburg*	1257 Industrial Pkwy, Fond Du Lac WI 54937	920-924-3020	R	2*	.2
1671	Richardson Industries Inc—*Judy Richardson*	PO Box 178, Vevay IN 47043	812-427-2550	R	2*	.1
1672	Glenwood Financial Group Inc—*Frank Meyer*	225 W Washington St St, Chicago IL 60606	312-443-8414	R	2*	.1
1673	Severn Trent Envirotest—*Robert Ferrera*	53 Southampton Rd Ste, Westfield MA 01085	413-572-4000	R	2*	.1
1674	Douglas Tahoe Fire Protection—*Tim Allison*	PO Box 919, Zephyr Cove NV 89448	775-588-3591	R	2*	.1
1675	Anderson Birtcher Investors LLC	31910 Del Obispo St St, San Juan Capistrano CA 92675	949-545-0526	R	2*	.1
1676	CFI Delivery Service—*Martha Shelton*	PO Box 1393, San Antonio TX 78295	512-320-5446	R	2*	.1
1677	CIA LLC	4111 Fremont Ave N, Seattle WA 98103	206-547-4111	R	2*	.1
1678	Cleanpack—*Steve Drozdow*	600 Orange St, Millville NJ 08332	856-825-4026	R	2*	.1
1679	Ellermedia Group—*Tim Fedarko*	8466 Eastwood Rd, Saint Paul MN 55112	612-369-5612	R	2*	.1
1680	Homesights By Design LLC—*Robert Campbell*	6573 Ridgeview Cir, Dallas TX 75240	972-392-3495	R	2*	.1
1681	Legend Merchant Group Inc—*Chip Unsworth*	201 Micaion St Ste 230, San Francisco CA 94105	415-957-9555	R	2*	.1

Rank	Company Name—*Executive Officer*	Address, City, State, Zip	Phone	Type	Fin	Empls
1682	Detroit Metro Convention And Visitors Bureau Inc—*Larry Alexander*	211 W Fort St Ste 1000, Detroit MI 48226	313-202-1952	R	2*	<.1
1683	Jaypar Inc—*Jay Parekh*	10500 Littl Patuxent 7, Columbia MD 21044	410-997-9080	R	2*	<.1
1684	Business Couriers Inc—*Mark Freneaux*	PO Box 78272, Baton Rouge LA 70837	225-261-1500	R	2*	<.1
1685	Eagle Delivery Systems Inc—*Raymond Maynard*	PO Box 64396, Los Angeles CA 90064	310-475-6111	R	2*	<.1
1686	Capital Inventory Inc—*Duran Dunn*	PO Box 1081, Woodstock GA 30188	770-928-7202	R	2*	<.1
1687	Appraisal Economics Inc—*Lawrence Goldberg*	140 E Ridgewood Ave 38, Paramus NJ 07652	201-265-3333	R	2*	<.1
1688	Dot Passkey Com Inc—*Greg Pesik*	180 Old Colony Ave Fl, Quincy MA 02170	617-328-4800	R	2*	<.1
1689	Notify Md—*Sue Eaves*	9484 Lewis And Clark B, Saint Louis MO 63136	314-868-6600	R	2*	<.1
1690	Quality Inventory Services Inc—*John Boullear*	5427 Johnson Dr Ste 30, Shawnee Mission KS 66205	913-888-7700	R	2*	<.1
1691	South Pointe Center Inc—*George Stratton*	200 Gurler Rd, Dekalb IL 60115	815-758-5636	R	2*	<.1
1692	Boyt John Industrial Sewing Inc—*John Boyt*	3101 Justin Dr, Urbandale IA 50322	515-252-8680	R	2*	<.1
1693	Hazeltownship Fire Rescue Inc—*Dennis Calarco*	And 27 Rr 309, Hazleton PA 18201	570-454-3411	R	2*	<.1
1694	Constant Communications Answering Service Inc—*Terry Griffin*	4139 W 123rd St, Chicago IL 60803	708-489-2600	R	2*	<.1
1695	Kendor Steel Rule Die Inc—*Kenneth Eltringham*	31275 Fraser Dr, Fraser MI 48026	586-293-7111	R	2*	<.1
1696	Health Facility Solutions Co—*Michele Pauli*	124 Oakwell Farms Pkwy, San Antonio TX 78218	210-375-4465	R	2*	<.1
1697	B C Products—*Andre Coltrin*	503 W Larch Rd Ste A, Tracy CA 95304	209-832-1704	R	2*	<.1
1698	Best Signs Inc—*Jesse Cross*	1550 S Gene Autry Trl, Palm Springs CA 92264	760-320-3042	R	2*	<.1
1699	Bodypoint Designs Inc—*David Hintzman*	558 1st Ave S Ste 300, Seattle WA 98104	206-405-4555	R	2*	<.1
1700	Ibb Management Inc—*Beth Rafferty*	5798 Genesis Ct, Frisco TX 75034	214-618-6600	R	2*	<.1
1701	Messenger Corp—*William Davis*	37 S Hudson St, Seattle WA 98134	206-623-4525	R	2*	<.1
1702	National Meeting Company Inc—*Douglas Daggett*	6360 Ne M L King Blvd, Portland OR 97211	503-232-6666	R	2*	<.1
1703	Carrel Forwarding Inc—*Juan Carranza*	835 Hallmark Dr, Laredo TX 78045	956-724-4531	R	2*	<.1
1704	Indiana Precision Grinding Inc—*David Cox*	3101 Bertha St, Indianapolis IN 46222	317-634-9620	R	2*	<.1
1705	Nefra Communication Center Inc—*Frances Courtright*	3433 E Market St, York PA 17402	717-755-1112	R	2*	<.1
1706	AcquireLists—*Andrew F Robinson*	1971 Western Ave, Albany NY 12203		R	2	.2
1707	Consero Global Solutions LLC—*Scott Tynes*	106 E Sixth St Ste 912, Austin TX 78701		R	2*	.1
1708	Kaizen Direct Inc—*Jeff Rogers*	111 Humboldt St, Rochester NY 14609	585-760-2200	R	2*	.1
1709	SJ Manufacturing Inc—*Robert Jaron*	148 Townsend St, San Francisco CA 94107	415-597-7500	R	2*	.1
1710	Brogden Mills Of Smithfield Inc—*Allen Westbrook*	PO Box 1596, Smithfield NC 27577	919-934-4218	R	2*	.1
1711	A To Z Couriers Inc—*Adam Dally*	106 Ridge St Frnt 2, New York NY 10002	212-505-5936	R	2*	.1
1712	American Volkssport Associates—*Ed Masloob*	4710 Aboite Lake Dr, Fort Wayne IN 46804	260-432-9370	R	2*	.1
1713	Brooklyn Fire and Ems Protection District	104 S Rutland St, Brooklyn WI 53521	608-455-3812	R	2*	.1
1714	Paradigm Tax Group—*Doug Coby*	1831 Tapo St Ste B, Simi Valley CA 93063	805-433-0351	R	2*	.1
1715	Potomac Hills Fire Station—*Jeff Decatur*	749 Widewater Rd, Stafford VA 22554	540-720-3288	R	2*	.1
1716	SorcityCom Inc—*Wes Guillemaud*	5550 Lyndon B Johnson, Dallas TX 75240	972-612-1411	R	2*	.1
1717	Contract Labeling Services Inc—*Duane Johnson*	4881 E Airport Dr, Ontario CA 91761	909-937-0344	R	2*	<.1
1718	Baltimore County Building Inspection	111 W Chesapeake Ave S, Towson MD 21204	410-887-3953	R	2*	<.1
1719	Carroll Distributing Co—*Joanne Eubank*	1553 Silicon, Melbourne FL 32940	321-636-2377	R	2	<.1
1720	Infinitec Inc—*Ron Davis*	1007 W 27th St, Hays KS 67601	785-625-3570	R	2*	<.1
1721	Michael Nash Interiors Inc—*Sonny Nazemian*	8630 Lee Hwy Ste C, Fairfax VA 22031	703-560-5900	R	2*	<.1
1722	Metroplex Printing And Finishing Inc—*Eric Swanson*	PO Box 7012, Dallas TX 75209	972-318-0809	R	2*	<.1
1723	PHI Service Agency Inc—*Sam Paschal*	1103 Paulsun St, San Antonio TX 78219	210-224-1665	R	2*	<.1
1724	Quality Solutions Group LLC	2296 Kenmore Ave, Buffalo NY 14207	716-875-8223	R	2*	<.1
1725	Schmidt Sign Service Inc—*K Schmidt*	1265 S 300 W, Salt Lake City UT 84101	801-486-0193	R	2*	<.1
1726	Tero Tek International Inc—*William Aldrich*	PO Box 310, Delano CA 93216	661-725-1135	R	2*	<.1
1727	Apak Inc—*Edwin Raynor*	850 Tower Rd, Mundelein IL 60060	847-566-9595	R	2*	<.1
1728	Bay Area Medical Exchange Of Florida Inc—*Cynthia Baur*	PO Box 40750, Saint Petersburg FL 33743	727-346-4400	R	2*	<.1
1729	Berger Devine Yaeger Inc—*Carl Yaeger*	7780 W 119th St, Overland Park KS 66213	913-742-8000	R	2*	<.1
1730	Custom Faberkin Inc—*Michael Krueger*	PO Box 1065, Fond du Lac WI 54936	920-921-5660	R	2*	<.1
1731	Hunt Products Inc—*Jo Hunt*	5417 Detroit Ave, Cleveland OH 44102	216-281-1125	R	2*	<.1
1732	Logobranders Inc—*Terry Southern*	1161 Lagoon Business L, Montgomery AL 36117	334-277-1144	R	2*	<.1
1733	Presort Plus Inc—*William Ragen*	PO Box 47, Fairmont WV 26555	304-363-1194	R	2*	<.1
1734	Recreational Marketing Inc—*Michael Howell*	2627 W Birchwood Cir S, Mesa AZ 85202	480-557-7379	R	2*	<.1
1735	Gasper T Puccio Jr Inc—*Gasper Puccio*	1910 Highland Ave, Rockdale TX 76567	512-446-8115	R	2*	<.1
1736	Mississippi Coast Coliseum Commission—*William Holmes*	PO Box 4676, Biloxi MS 39535	228-594-3700	R	2*	<.1
1737	Nu-Fone Secretarial Service Inc—*Joann Plumb*	715 Lake St Ste 100, Oak Park IL 60301	708-484-4950	R	2*	<.1
1738	Riggs Company Incorporated A—*Matthew Riggs*	578 Woodruff Rd, Greenville SC 29607	864-676-9400	R	2*	<.1
1739	Abigail H Hess Interiors Inc—*Abigail Hess*	308 E 79th St, New York NY 10075	212-288-2058	R	2*	<.1
1740	Gardan Inc—*Dan Verbeten*	221 Industrial Park Av, Hortonville WI 54944	920-779-0256	R	2*	<.1
1741	Tasone Services Inc—*Gordon Mott*	4009 Market St Unit E, Upper Chichester PA 19014	484-766-7500	R	2*	<.1
1742	Med Bus Inc—*Andrew Kluger*	70 Mitchell Blvd Ste 1, San Rafael CA 94903	415-479-6000	R	2*	<.1
1743	Rj Torching Inc—*Gerald Roughton*	5061 Energy Dr, Flint MI 48505	810-785-9759	R	2*	<.1
1744	A-Cti Answerconnect Inc—*Michael Payne*	PO Box 80040, Portland OR 97280	503-245-5572	R	2*	<.1
1745	Eved Services Inc—*Talia Mashiach*	4811 Oakton St Ste 250, Skokie IL 60077	773-764-7000	R	2*	<.1
1746	First Choice Messenger Inc—*Alee Shariffi*	3225 Fletcher Dr, Los Angeles CA 90065	323-255-6800	R	2*	<.1
1747	Martinez Corp—*Tony Martinez*	8011 34th AveS Ste C47, Bloomington MN 55425	952-698-0230	R	2*	<.1
1748	Moises G Duenas—*Moises Duenas*	1106 N Howland St, Porterville CA 93257	559-781-4276	R	2*	<.1
1749	Tom's Installation Company Inc—*Tom Slusser*	PO Box 30, Celina OH 45822	419-584-1218	R	2*	<.1
1750	All Ways Communications—*Anthony Zandy*	22 E N Ave, Hagerstown MD 21740	301-733-1100	R	2*	<.1
1751	Communication Business Services Inc—*Cheryl Chandler*	2985 Gordy Pkwy Ste 10, Marietta GA 30066	770-977-2402	R	2*	<.1
1752	Art-Tech Decorating I Inc—*Henry Steinberg*	PO Box 187, East Northport NY 11731	718-278-9428	R	2*	<.1
1753	Clear Choice Lien Service Inc—*Val L'heureux*	PO Box 159009, San Diego CA 92175	619-583-2123	R	2*	<.1
1754	Lesley Roy Designs LLC—*Lesley Roy*	845 Whalley Ave, New Haven CT 06515	203-389-7410	R	2*	<.1
1755	Nationwide Homes Network Inc—*Steve Nickerson*	5424 E Grand River Ave, Howell MI 48843	517-540-0000	R	2*	<.1
1756	Lafayette Grinding LLC—*Gopal Sharma*	115 Banker St Fl 1, Brooklyn NY 11222	718-388-5973	R	2*	<.1
1757	Chuck Bohn and Associates Inc—*Chuck Bohn*	PO Box 3233, Englewood CO 80155	303-340-2422	R	2*	<.1
1758	Contract Furniture Installations—*Darla Vegenski*	4526 Transport Dr, Tampa FL 33605	813-247-6622	R	2*	<.1
1759	Crossbow Group LLC—*Jay Bower*	136 Main St, Westport CT 06880	203-222-2244	R	2*	<.1
1760	Devries Bar Grinding Inc—*David Devfreies*	2433 Minnehaha Ave, Minneapolis MN 55404	612-729-9313	R	2*	<.1
1761	Louisville Corporate Services Inc—*Gary Riley*	401 S 4th St Ste 1200, Louisville KY 40202	502-583-2956	R	2*	<.1
1762	Navigational Construction Inc—*Kimberlie Hollinger*	PO Box 1245, Redmond OR 97756	541-504-7840	R	2*	<.1
1763	Nustone Industry Inc—*Joseph J Lombardi*	195 State St, North Haven CT 06473	203-288-7491	R	2*	<.1
1764	Packaging Services Inc (Ivyland Pennsylvania)—*Michael Schmidt*	PO Box 2204, Ivyland PA 18974	215-322-5588	S	2*	<.1
1765	Pipeline Video Inspection LLC—*Chris Nmihalecos*	1616 S 31st Ave, Phoenix AZ 85009	602-237-0292	R	2*	<.1
1766	Tarrant Inc—*Johnny Tarrant*	217 Pennsylvania St, Wichita KS 67214	316-942-2208	R	2*	<.1
1767	Sugar Beach Interiors Inc—*Karen Waterfield*	11974 Us Hwy 98 W, Destin FL 32550	850-837-5157	R	2*	<.1
1768	Cimarron Office Furniture Services Inc—*Gary Sleege*	3132 Dwight Rd, Elk Grove CA 95758	916-391-4480	R	2*	<.1
1769	Class Encounters Co—*Greg Hollander*	PO Box 254678, Sacramento CA 95865	916-489-1992	R	2*	<.1

Note: An asterisk (*) indicates an estimated financial figure. The company type code used is as follows: R = Private, P = Public, S = Private Subsidiary, B = Public Subsidiary, D = Division, J = Joint Venture, I = Investment Fund.

COMPANY RANKINGS BY SALES WITHIN 4-DIGIT SIC

Rank	Company Name—*Executive Officer*	Address, City, State, Zip	Phone	Type	Fin	Empls
1770	Inter Plan Design Group Inc—*Lawrence Lake*	7373 N Scottsdale Rd S, Scottsdale AZ 85253	480-443-3400	R	2*	<.1
1771	Sun Studio—*John Schorr*	706 Union Ave, Memphis TN 38103	901-521-0664	R	2*	<.1
1772	Promark Co/OI Partners Inc—*Tim Schoonover*	Baldwin 200 625 Eden P, Cincinnati OH 45202	513-768-6500	R	2*	<.1
1773	Direct Mail of Texas—*Kimberly Hendrick*	5121 69th St Ste A4, Lubbock TX 79424	806-748-1000	R	2*	<.1
1774	Alexander Associates (Brooklyn New York)—*Mimi Alexander*	2607 Nostrand Ave, Brooklyn NY 11210	718-253-9400	R	2*	<.1
1775	HUM Music and Sound Design—*Jeff Koz*	1547 9th St, Santa Monica CA 90401	310-260-4949	R	2*	<.1
1776	Nb Finishing Inc—*Bruce Nichols*	1075 Morse Ave, Schaumburg IL 60193	847-895-0900	R	2*	<.1
1777	Recovered Capital Corp—*Russell P Hann*	PO Box 3455, Mooresville NC 28117		R	2*	<.1
1778	Steve Ford Music Inc—*Steve Ford*	610 N Fairbanks Court, Chicago IL 60611	818-828-0567	R	2*	<.1
1779	Triangle Sales Co—*Dave Shank*	1128 S St, Noblesville IN 46060	317-773-5480	R	2*	<.1
1780	Toxguard Fluid Technologies Inc—*Dan Cook*	11942 Western Ave, Stanton CA 90680	714-698-3400	R	2*	<.1
1781	Aumens Asner Inc—*Karen Auman*	100 N Charles St Ste 9, Baltimore MD 21201	410-837-2767	R	2*	<.1
1782	Court Reporter's Clearinghouse Inc—*Paula Babin*	2929 Carlisle St Ste A, Dallas TX 75204	214-954-0352	R	2*	<.1
1783	JIL Design Group Inc—*Irit Winston*	1147 Eastern Ave, Sacramento CA 95864	916-485-7077	R	2	<.1
1784	Kallman Associates Inc—*Jerry Kallman Jr*	20 Harrison Ave, Waldwick NJ 07463	201-652-7070	R	2*	<.1
1785	National Risk Services Inc—*Montgomery Gale*	266 Harristown Rd Ste, Glen Rock NJ 07452	201-689-4040	R	2*	<.1
1786	Pamela Stavroff Design Associates Inc—*Pamela Stavroff*	101 Liberty St, Columbus OH 43215	614-233-5300	R	2*	<.1
1787	Blackman and Holberton Move Planning Services—*Barbara Blackman*	201 Wilshire Blvd Ste, Santa Monica CA 90401	310-458-8898	R	2*	<.1
1788	Main Point Productions—*Will R Stanton*	295 Lobachsville Rd, Oley PA 19547	610-987-9320	R	2*	<.1
1789	Paradigm Interiors Inc—*Gail S Ackermann*	11098 Marin St, Coral Gables FL 33156	305-667-7113	R	2*	<.1
1790	Thomas Transcription Services Inc—*Dee Thomas*	PO Box 26613, Jacksonville FL 32226	904-751-5058	R	2	<.1
1791	Bordelon Design Associates Inc—*Maria Bordelon*	675 Bering Dr Ste 140, Houston TX 77057	713-789-9681	R	2*	<.1
1792	Designs of Elegance—*Leslie Carlseen*	3750 Greenbriar Dr, Stafford TX 77477	281-242-0116	R	2*	<.1
1793	Digital Music Products Inc	175 Dolphin Cove Rd, Stamford CT 06902	203-327-3810	R	2*	<.1
1794	Elaine Lewis Ltd—*Elaine Lewis*	420 E 61st St, New York NY 10021	212-755-0466	R	2*	<.1
1795	Florage by Gayle Christie—*Gayle Christie*	6401 Woodway Dr, Houston TX 77057	713-266-5707	R	2*	<.1
1796	Innovative Leisure Inc—*Terry Foley*	PO Box 16208, West Palm Beach FL 33416	561-969-2420	R	2*	<.1
1797	Internet Customer Solutions—*Toon Six*	239 New Rd Unit B103, Parsippany NJ 07054	973-244-1470	R	2*	<.1
1798	Jack M Zufelt—*Jack M Zufelt*	3228 E Phillips Dr, Littleton CO 80122	303-741-9025	R	2*	<.1
1799	REFAC Optical Group—*J David Pierson*	1 Bridge Plaza Ste 550, Fort Lee NJ 07024	201-585-0600	S	2*	<.1
1800	Winter Associates Inc—*Linda Stamm*	PO Box 823, Plainville CT 06062	860-793-0288	R	2*	<.1
1801	Architectural Arts Co—*Sharon Leeber*	6410 Dykes Way, Dallas TX 75230	972-392-2121	R	2*	<.1
1802	BroadbandReports.com—*Justin Beech*	1636 Third Ave Ste 408, New York NY 10128		R	2*	<.1
1803	Business Success Center—*Daniel Diener*	7600 Burnet Rd No 130, Austin TX 78758	512-933-1983	R	2*	<.1
1804	GS Beckham Design Associates Inc—*Geoff Beckham*	3199 Airport Loop Dr S, Costa Mesa CA 92626	714-556-9802	R	2*	<.1
1805	Martha Weems Ltd—*Deborah J Dunn Chipouras*	374 Maple Ave E Ste 20, Vienna VA 22180	703-281-6344	R	2*	<.1
1806	Pat Kuleto Restaurant Development and Management Co—*Bob Burke*	55 Francisco St Rm 430, San Francisco CA 94133	415-474-9669	R	2	<.1
1807	Peace Design—*William B Peace*	349 Peach Tree Hills A, Atlanta GA 30305	404-237-8681	R	2*	<.1
1808	Sound City Entertainment Group Inc—*Tom Skeeter*	15456 Cabrito Rd, Van Nuys CA 91406	818-787-3722	R	2*	<.1
1809	Willis Henry Auctions Inc—*Willis Henry*	22 Main St, Marshfield MA 02050	781-834-7774	R	2*	<.1
1810	ACE Collateral Inspections Inc—*William E Meade*	1340 S Jason St, Denver CO 80223	303-886-4195	R	2*	<.1
1811	Art Horizons International Inc—*Lisa Hahn*	420 Riverside Dr Ste 1, New York NY 10025	212-969-9410	R	2*	<.1
1812	Business Brokerage Group Inc—*Edward A Granka*	421 New Karner Rd, Albany NY 12205	518-869-5444	R	2*	<.1
1813	Criterium-Liszkay Engineers—*Donald W Liszkay*	110 N High St, Gahanna OH 43230	614-418-7200	R	2*	<.1
1814	Design Concepts and Associates Inc—*Roger C Hall Jr*	214 S Armenia Ave, Tampa FL 33609	813-251-5472	R	2*	<.1
1815	Haigh Architects—*Paul Haigh*	2 Bowling Pl, Greenwich CT 06830	203-869-5445	R	2*	<.1
1816	HealthBlocks Inc—*Darin Greaham*	402 W Wheatland Rd Ste, Duncanville TX 75116	972-298-4044	R	2*	<.1
1817	Information Impact International Inc—*Larry P English*	871 Nialta Ln Ste 100, Brentwood TN 37027	615-837-1211	R	2*	<.1
1818	International Trade Information Inc—*Stephanie Selesnick*	6233 Randi Ave, Woodland Hills CA 91367	818-591-2255	R	2*	<.1
1819	IOR Technologies Inc—*Nicholas Noor*	75 Pershing Ave, Carteret NJ 07008	732-802-0090	R	2*	<.1
1820	Kozacko Enterprises Inc—*Richard L Kozacko*	800 Underwood Ave, Elmira NY 14905	607-733-7138	R	2*	<.1
1821	Marks and Salley Inc—*E Carol Salley*	5120 Woodway Dr Ste 40, Houston TX 77056	713-622-9333	R	2*	<.1
1822	Marks Design Group Inc—*Kimberly A Marks*	150 W Sunset Rd, San Antonio TX 78209	210-227-2400	R	2*	<.1
1823	Premier Events and Design—*Kathryn Loos*	5401 Longley Ln Blds B, Reno NV 89505	775-825-4561	R	2*	<.1
1824	Quantum Leap Productions Inc—*Dennis Ford*	6910 E 5th Ave, Scottsdale AZ 85251	480-990-7988	R	2*	<.1
1825	Reflection Sound Productions Inc—*Wayne Jernigan*	1018 Central Ave, Charlotte NC 28204	704-377-4596	R	2*	<.1
1826	Richardson Munson and Weir—*John Munson*	3901 W 86th St Ste 370, Indianapolis IN 46268	317-872-0100	R	2*	<.1
1827	Showstopper Exhibits Inc	7301 Boulder View Ln, Richmond VA 23225	804-643-4044	S	2*	<.1
1828	Sunshine Permit Service—*Margaret Jackson*	8678 Sky Rim Dr, Lakeside CA 92040	619-559-1704	R	2*	<.1
1829	Visual Resources International Inc—*Julia O'Connor*	PO Box 17155, Richmond VA 23226	804-355-7800	R	2*	<.1
1830	Wooding Design Ltd—*Peter Wooding*	369 Ives St, Providence RI 02906	401-454-1744	R	2*	<.1
1831	Absolute Music Inc—*Johnny Hagen*	410 N 2nd St, Minneapolis MN 55401	612-339-6758	R	2*	<.1
1832	Pope And Associates—*Robert Pope*	2629 Manhattan Ave Ste, Hermosa Beach CA 90254	310-937-6120	R	2*	<.1
1833	Little Wing Productions Inc—*Larry Schaffer*	423 N Main St, Tulsa OK 74103	918-865-8770	R	2*	.1
1834	Usgs Water Resources Discipline—*Marie Stewart*	5338 Montgomery Blvd N, Albuquerque NM 87109	505-830-7906	R	2*	.1
1835	Acs Integrated Doc Inc—*Jeff Hennen*	680 Transfer Rd, Saint Paul MN 55114	651-999-5400	R	2*	.1
1836	Central Cass County Fire Protection District	PO Box 668, Harrisonville MO 64701	816-380-6744	R	2*	.1
1837	Coeur D Alene Answering Service—*Rodney Bacon*	1919 N 3rd St, Coeur D Alene ID 83814	208-769-6000	R	2*	.1
1838	Eastcoast Trading—*Jeff Archer*	434 N Columbia St Ste, Covington LA 70433	985-875-0739	R	2*	.1
1839	Mach I Packaging Inc—*Frank Massa*	406 Kesco Dr, Bristol IN 46507	574-848-1410	R	2*	.1
1840	Mar Leen Inc—*Preston Hickman*	PO Box 70, Millville NJ 08332	856-327-8281	R	2*	.1
1841	National Strategy Group Inc—*Brent Esken*	2950 Colorful Ave 400, Longmont CO 80504	970-674-0363	R	2*	.1
1842	Property Inventory Auditor	600 Dexter Ave Ste S10, Montgomery AL 36130	334-242-7010	R	2*	.1
1843	Belardi/Ostroy Alc LLC—*Andy Ostroy*	16 W 22nd St Fl 11, New York NY 10010	212-924-1300	R	2*	.1
1844	Feeding Frenzy Inc—*Frank Amadeo*	420 Jefferson Ave, Miami Beach FL 33139	305-534-4330	R	2*	<.1
1845	San Fernando Swap Meet and Flea Market—*William Hannon*	585 Glenoaks Blvd, San Fernando CA 91340	818-361-1431	R	2*	<.1
1846	Santa Clara Convention Center—*Susan Grover*	5001 Great America Pkw, Santa Clara CA 95054	408-748-7000	R	2*	<.1
1847	Ans Wood Manufacturing—*Antonio Saucedo*	2538 E 115th St, Los Angeles CA 90059	323-569-5077	R	2*	<.1
1848	Doctor's Exchange Inc—*Ron Richardson*	PO Box 1330, Madisonville LA 70447	504-454-7382	R	2*	<.1
1849	Glenside Fire Protection District—*Nicholas Kosiara*	1608 Bloomingdale Rd, Glendale Heights IL 60139	630-668-5323	R	2*	<.1
1850	Advantage Information Management Solutions LLC—*Trisha Hop*	1025 33rd Ave Sw, Cedar Rapids IA 52404	319-363-5266	R	2*	<.1
1851	Deaf Inter-Link Inc—*Alta Bradshaw*	PO Box 510, Florissant MO 63032	314-837-7757	R	2*	<.1
1852	Telephone Exchange—*Cynthia Downing*	PO Box 1071, Fresno CA 93714	559-228-6140	R	2*	<.1
1853	Ken Morgan Enterprises Inc—*Ken Morgan*	3705 Aurora Loop, Rocklin CA 95677	916-316-5471	R	2*	<.1
1854	AIE Inc—*Lorraine Abbott*	PO Box 1072, Portland ME 04104	207-767-6004	R	2*	<.1
1855	Answerfone Inc—*Conner Limerick*	610 Rock St, Little Rock AR 72202	501-376-3121	R	2*	<.1
1856	Action Mail Service Inc—*Jeffrey Scott*	1904 Premier Row, Orlando FL 32809	407-855-9277	R	2*	<.1

Rank	Company Name—*Executive Officer*	Address, City, State, Zip	Phone	Type	Fin	Empls
1857	Canton Twp Public Works Inc—*Jake Dingledey*	4847 S Sheldon Rd, Canton MI 48188	734-397-1019	R	2*	<.1
1858	Gw Limited 40 LLC—*Shan Bauder*	2150 Cabot Blvd W, Langhorne PA 19047	215-295-1670	R	2*	<.1
1859	Hennessey Capital Solutions Inc—*Thomas Cross*	26321 Woodward Ave Ste, Huntington Woods MI 48070	248-658-1100	R	2*	<.1
1860	Designshop Display Communications Inc—*E Hughes*	4654 35th St, Orlando FL 32811	407-251-1800	R	2*	<.1
1861	Peak Service Corp—*Gerrard Farese*	PO Box 2329, Cinnaminson NJ 08077	856-787-1400	R	2*	<.1
1862	Ttj Enterprises LP—*Tim Watkins*	3609 Conflans Rd, Irving TX 75061	972-399-1303	R	2*	<.1
1863	Addax Telecom Inc—*Joe Carroll*	PO Box 291263, Nashville TN 37229	615-345-5050	R	2*	<.1
1864	Member Home Lending Services Inc—*David Vettraino*	PO Box 470, Howell MI 48844	517-552-7235	R	2*	<.1
1865	Remedios Siembieda Inc—*Peter Remedios*	400 Oceangate Ste 1100, Long Beach CA 90802	562-437-5444	R	2*	<.1
1866	Car Tech Auction Inc—*Lou Rapuano*	87 Randolph Ave, Avenel NJ 07001	732-541-7500	R	2*	<.1
1867	Hogan Steel Erectors Inc—*C Hogan*	PO Box 1051, Orange TX 77631	409-883-8208	R	2*	<.1
1868	Shaw Steel Inc—*Harry Sulzer*	25701 N Lakeland Blvd, Euclid OH 44132	216-289-2840	R	2*	<.1
1869	Alternative Business Accommodations—*Frank Laufer*	1650 Broadway Ste 501, New York NY 10019	212-445-0494	R	2*	<.1
1870	Network Interpreting Service Inc—*Clifford Hanks*	1650 Overland Ave Ste, Burley ID 83318	208-878-2642	R	2*	<.1
1871	Operations Rod Permian LC—*Fred Huston*	PO Box 12907, Odessa TX 79768	432-367-4149	R	2*	<.1
1872	California Style Plant Service Inc—*Larry Charrlin*	5410 W Roosevelt Rd, Chicago IL 60644	773-626-0300	R	2*	<.1
1873	Bolke - Miller Co—*Janine Bolke*	1585 S Lakeside Dr, Waukegan IL 60085	847-693-7230	R	2*	<.1
1874	Thermotest Inc—*Norman Eisenberg*	600 Martin Ave Ste 206, Rohnert Park CA 94928	415-453-7200	R	2*	<.1
1875	Cyios Corp—*Timothy W Carnahan*	1300 Pennsylvania Ave, Washington DC 20004	202-204-3006	P	2	<.1
1876	Phoenix Language Services Inc—*William Martin*	PO Box 6070, Philadelphia PA 19114	215-632-9000	R	2*	.2
1877	18 Mile Emergency Services Association Inc—*Rick Traut*	1922 W Bay Ter, Ship Bottom NJ 08008	609-548-9869	R	2*	.1
1878	A-1 Bail Bonds Inc—*Judy Miller*	20 S Detroit St, Xenia OH 45385	937-372-2400	R	2*	.1
1879	Frankie Foundation—*Howard William*	2471 Watering Pl, Morganton NC 28655	828-439-2414	R	2*	.1
1880	Plus 2 Recording Studio—*Lavonne Nipper*	603 Broad St 1, Bennettsville SC 29512	843-479-3896	R	2*	.1
1881	Amateur Artist Development—*Eric Ansley*	7940 Runnymede Dr, Jonesboro GA 30236	770-603-0008	R	2*	<.1
1882	Chesterfeild County Treasurers	PO Box 70, Chesterfield VA 23832	804-748-1287	R	2*	<.1
1883	Consumer Protection Services—*John Carroll*	1232 Washingtn Ave Ste, Saint Louis MO 63103	314-621-7646	R	2*	<.1
1884	Hexagon Metrology Services Inc—*William Gruber*	250 Circuit Dr, North Kingstown RI 02852	401-886-2000	R	2*	<.1
1885	Skybar—*Scott Gertner*	3400 Montrose Blvd Fl, Houston TX 77006	713-520-9688	R	2*	<.1
1886	Translations Incorporated Corporate—*Mary Gawlicki*	77 Hartland St Ste 210, East Hartford CT 06108	860-450-0405	R	2*	<.1
1887	Aqua Rama Pool Spas and Service Inc—*Bennett Frey*	565 Powder Springs St, Marietta GA 30064	770-422-6291	R	2*	<.1
1888	Ariel Enterprises Inc—*Scott Rabe*	PO Box 17869, Honolulu HI 96817	808-484-2258	R	2*	<.1
1889	Bank-A-Count Corp—*Scott Blanke*	1666 Main St, Rudolph WI 54475	715-435-3131	R	2*	<.1
1890	Callstar Inc—*Cynthia Baur*	PO Box 40750, Saint Petersburg FL 33743	727-346-4400	R	2*	<.1
1891	Faust Goetz Schenker and Blee—*Robert Schenker*	2 Rector St Fl 20, New York NY 10006	212-363-6900	R	2*	<.1
1892	Hicks Convention Services Inc—*Billy Hicks*	935 Rayner St, Memphis TN 38114	901-272-1171	R	2*	<.1
1893	Home Labor Associates Inc—*Leonard Frits*	299 Duke St, Northumberland PA 17857	570-473-1145	R	2*	<.1
1894	Houston Manufacturing and Design Inc—*Shirley Houston*	PO Box 1798, Richmond IN 47375	765-935-0446	R	2*	<.1
1895	Purchasing Management International LP—*Linda Fltzerman*	4055 Valley View Ln St, Dallas TX 75244	972-239-5555	R	2*	<.1
1896	Rosen Group Inc—*Wendy Rosen*	3000 Chestnut Ave Ste, Baltimore MD 21211	410-889-2933	R	2*	<.1
1897	United States Crane Certification Bureau Inc—*Richard Gridley*	PO Box 593290, Orlando FL 32859	407-859-6000	R	2*	<.1
1898	Texas Star Document Services Inc—*Clark Ross*	400 W 15th St Ste B30, Austin TX 78701	512-474-8411	R	2*	<.1
1899	Asi Packaging Co—*Margaret Costa*	3019 Airpark Dr N, Flint MI 48507	810-239-0644	R	2*	<.1
1900	Frontline Data Inc—*Michael Blackstone*	397 Eagleview Blvd, Exton PA 19341	610-722-9745	R	2*	<.1
1901	S and S Auction Inc—*Stephen Shivers*	62 Repaupo Station Rd, Swedesboro NJ 08085	856-467-3778	R	2*	<.1
1902	Consumer Profiles Inc—*Henry Cowles*	111 Venture Dr, Dover NH 03820	603-742-4000	R	2*	<.1
1903	Stitches Embroidery Inc—*Cynthia Kearney*	1600 Marys Ave 2, Pittsburgh PA 15215	412-781-7046	R	2*	<.1
1904	Arctic Falls Spring Water Inc—*Frank Lipari*	58 Sand Park Rd, Cedar Grove NJ 07009	973-857-3000	R	2*	<.1
1905	Coffee-Serv Inc—*Jack Kirshner*	250 S 18th St Apt 802, Philadelphia PA 19103	215-848-8400	R	2*	<.1
1906	Knight Technologies Inc—*Craig Knight*	201 W Lakeway Rd Ste 2, Gillette WY 82718	307-682-8547	R	2*	<.1
1907	All Access Music Group Inc—*Joel Denver*	28955 Pcfc Cst Hwy 210, Malibu CA 90265	310-457-6616	R	2*	<.1
1908	Lamcraft Inc—*Robert Sabin*	4131 Ne Port Dr, Lees Summit MO 64064	816-795-5505	R	2*	<.1
1909	Thelamco Inc—*David Mcfall*	PO Box 456, Benton Harbor MI 49023	269-926-6101	R	2*	<.1
1910	2nd Chance Credit Solutions Inc—*Carlos Rodriguez*	6625 Mami Lkes Dr Ste, Hialeah FL 33014	305-779-8580	R	2*	<.1
1911	Winfield Community Volunteer Fire Company Inc—*Norman Zepp*	1320 W Old Liberty Rd, Sykesville MD 21784	410-795-1333	R	2*	.1
1912	American Society Of Interior Designers—*Lori Schiefen*	408 Ne Wild Rose Ln, Lees Summit MO 64064	816-373-3305	R	2*	.1
1913	Answertel Corp—*Span Gardner*	205 Centre St, Dallas TX 75208	214-349-1700	R	2*	.1
1914	Elkhart Gamma Associate U—*Jo Engber*	51281 Maplewood Dr, Elkhart IN 46514	574-848-1430	R	2*	.1
1915	Todd Services Inc—*Todd Blake*	PO Box 222, Corbett OR 97019	503-695-5364	R	2*	.1
1916	Wolfe Security Group—*William Wolfe*	4444 Omaha Ave, Medford OR 97501	541-890-2163	R	2*	.1
1917	Dairy Queen Of Harrodsburg—*Richard Ballando*	945 N College St, Harrodsburg KY 40330	859-734-0252	R	2*	<.1
1918	Edgewood Fire Protection District—*John Bailey*	1127 Orchard Ave, Louisville KY 40213	502-964-6011	R	2*	<.1
1919	Malibu's—*Marianne Beard*	165 Barton Blvd, Rockledge FL 32955	321-636-5090	R	2*	<.1
1920	Randall Cloud—*Randy Cloud*	PO Box 7229, Colorado Springs CO 80933	719-380-8599	R	2*	<.1
1921	Sun Inventory Company Inc—*John Shepherd*	8339 Holly Hill Cv, Jacksonville FL 32221	904-781-0275	R	2*	<.1
1922	Prince Security Services Inc—*Curtis Prince*	8701 Georgia Ave Ste 6, Silver Spring MD 20910	301-563-3333	R	2*	<.1
1923	Camelot Limited Inc—*William Wheeler*	173 W Station Dr Nw, Kennesaw GA 30144	770-516-8500	R	2*	<.1
1924	Alternative Home Care Solutions Inc—*L Daniels*	157 Blue Bell Rd, Greensboro NC 27406	336-370-9400	R	2*	<.1
1925	Fox Imports—*Jane Fox*	180 Grant Ave, Auburn NY 13021	315-253-7341	R	2*	<.1
1926	Phoenix LLC—*Jason Berry*	1415 N Royal Ave, Evansville IN 47715	812-422-1888	R	2*	<.1
1927	Community Answering Service Inc—*Thomas Wingo*	433 S Rose St, Kalamazoo MI 49007	269-382-8500	R	2*	<.1
1928	Verdigris Fire Protection District—*Tony Williams*	25707 S Hwy 66, Claremore OK 74019	918-266-3217	R	2*	<.1
1929	Huntington Testing and Technology Inc—*Mike Skeens*	1200 Airport Rd, Huntington WV 25704	304-453-6111	R	2*	<.1
1930	Balloon Haven Inc—*George Quintero*	13867 Central Ave, Chino CA 91710	909-591-8449	R	2*	<.1
1931	Ely Services Inc—*Beverly Ely*	PO Box 197103, Louisville KY 40259	502-452-6014	R	2*	<.1
1932	Hillstroms Aircraft Services—*William Schuler*	106 Bristol Dr, Vacaville CA 95687	707-446-9034	R	2*	<.1
1933	Midamerica Printing—*Jeffrey Fouse*	5601 N NW Hwy, Chicago IL 60646	773-631-0100	R	2*	<.1
1934	Remington Support Services Inc—*Netia Pyles*	PO Box 590147, Houston TX 77259	713-473-6755	R	2*	<.1
1935	Summit Primary Care PLLC—*Judy Derryberry*	3939 Central Pke Ste 3, Hermitage TN 37076	615-883-2331	R	2*	<.1
1936	Tonyson Financial Group LLC	12280 Dixie, Redford MI 48239	313-541-5200	R	2*	<.1
1937	Upstate Detailing Inc—*Daniel Walsh*	PO Box 389, Burnt Hills NY 12027	518-399-0205	R	2*	<.1
1938	Computer Embroidery Specialists Inc—*Anita Malapas*	17312 Gillette Ave, Irvine CA 92614	949-852-8888	B	2*	<.1
1939	Iverson Language Associates Inc—*Steven Iverson*	PO Box 511759, Milwaukee WI 53203	414-271-1144	R	2*	<.1
1940	Media Services Inc—*Mike Pettid*	206 S 19th St Ste 500, Omaha NE 68102	402-537-4499	R	2*	<.1
1941	Title Check LLC	516 W S St, Kalamazoo MI 49007	269-226-2600	R	2*	<.1
1942	Grind Lap Services Inc—*John Gallichio*	1045 National Ave, Addison IL 60101	630-458-1111	R	2*	<.1
1943	Premier Companies LLC—*Rodney Berg*	415 N Prince St Ste 20, Lancaster PA 17603	717-581-1231	R	2*	<.1
1944	Vialanguage Inc—*Chanin Ballance*	700 Sw Taylor St Ste 3, Portland OR 97205	503-243-2007	R	2*	<.1
1945	Pacific Embroidery LLC	1189 N Kraemer Blvd, Anaheim CA 92806	714-630-4757	R	2*	<.1

Note: An asterisk (*) indicates an estimated financial figure. The company type code used is as follows: R = Private, P = Public, S = Private Subsidiary, B = Public Subsidiary, D = Division, J = Joint Venture, I = Investment Fund.

COMPANY RANKINGS BY SALES WITHIN 4-DIGIT SIC

Rank	Company Name—*Executive Officer*	Address, City, State, Zip	Phone	Type	Fin	Empls
1946	Airborne 1 Corp—*Todd Stennett*	300 N Sepulveda Blvd, El Segundo CA 90245	310-414-7400	R	2*	<.1
1947	Commercial Grinding Company Inc—*Gale Sturdevant*	6829 Walthall Way, Paramount CA 90723	562-531-9970	R	2*	<.1
1948	Fsr Construction Inc—*Paul Qualls*	3490 Union St Ste A, Fremont CA 94538	510-490-7911	R	2*	<.1
1949	Mc Millen Inc—*Louis Ray*	155 E 56th St Fl 5, New York NY 10022	212-753-5600	R	2*	<.1
1950	University Business Interiors Inc—*Daniel Rose*	23231 Industrial Park, Farmington Hills MI 48335	248-426-0100	R	2*	<.1
1951	West Courier Express Inc—*Marc West*	314 Boren Ave S, Seattle WA 98144	206-322-1597	R	2*	<.1
1952	Mississippi One Call System—*Sam Johnson*	5258 Cedar Park Dr Ste, Jackson MS 39206	601-362-4322	R	2*	<.1
1953	Ocean Spray Pool Services Inc—*Joseph Musnicki*	97 Old Riverhead Rd, Westhampton Beach NY 11978	631-288-6006	R	2*	<.1
1954	Future Now Group Inc—*Greg Goldberg*	80 Mountain Laurel, Fairfield CT 06824		P	2	<.1
1955	Automated Edm Inc—*Walter Pelto*	6231 Mckinley St Nw, Anoka MN 55303	763-576-6946	R	2*	<.1
1956	Hyacinth Technology Inc—*Noberto Tecson*	155 New Boston St L, Woburn MA 01801	781-937-0619	R	2*	<.1
1957	Sew Team No 3—*Mike Bernhagen*	4540 W State Hwy 31, Corsicana TX 75110	903-641-0738	R	2*	.1
1958	Form-Co Inc—*Allen Shaffer*	33112 Hwy 31, Spanish Fort AL 36527	251-443-5212	R	2*	.1
1959	Unique/Multidec—*Leonard Clineman*	30 Moffitt St, Stratford CT 06615	203-378-7713	R	2*	<.1
1960	Rochester Telemessaging Center—*Herbert Chinoski*	1130 Tienken Ct Ste 11, Rochester Hills MI 48306	248-651-9181	R	2*	<.1
1961	Antonio Collis—*Antonio Collis*	38 Montvale Ave Ste 36, Stoneham MA 02180	781-438-3875	R	2*	<.1
1962	Answerfirst Communications Inc—*M Herron*	2112 W Kennedy Blvd, Tampa FL 33606	813-882-5307	R	2*	<.1
1963	Kapowsin Water District	PO Box 45, Kapowsin WA 98344	360-879-5620	R	2*	<.1
1964	Tristar Group Inc—*Robert Harrison*	5220 Spring Valley Rd, Dallas TX 75254	972-392-2848	R	2*	<.1
1965	Hppi LLC—*Sue Adams*	PO Box 140909, Irving TX 75014	972-830-0147	R	2*	<.1
1966	Fitch Enterprises Inc—*William Fitch*	PO Box 610, Holly Springs MS 38635	662-252-8855	R	2*	<.1
1967	All Pro Answering Bureau—*Catherine Collier*	612 S Harbor Blvd, Anaheim CA 92805	714-991-9595	R	2*	<.1
1968	Allied Marine Inc—*Dwight Tracy*	1445 Se 16th St, Fort Lauderdale FL 33316	954-462-7424	R	2*	<.1
1969	CBI Corp—*Clifford Bregstone*	855 S Fiene Dr, Addison IL 60101	630-543-0055	R	2*	<.1
1970	International Transcription—*Clifford Molin*	3800 Lakeside Ave E, Cleveland OH 44114	216-361-5910	R	2*	<.1
1971	Jmw Industries—*Betty Holyfield*	PO Box 3271, Burlington NC 27215	336-226-2866	R	2*	<.1
1972	KS Fashion—*Henriette Baissari*	1060 S Broadway Ste 90, Los Angeles CA 90015	213-749-9097	R	2*	<.1
1973	Med Com Inc—*Clyde Jackson*	3818 River Dr, Columbia SC 29201	803-779-6660	R	2*	<.1
1974	Olympic Metals Inc—*Doug Russell*	PO Box 11112, Knoxville TN 37939	865-522-1700	R	2*	<.1
1975	Paradigm Alliance Inc—*Steve Mcgaffin*	PO Box 9123, Wichita KS 67277	316-554-9225	R	2*	<.1
1976	Ridgeview Manufacturing Inc—*Kevin Boghigian*	PO Box 3073, Nashua NH 03061	603-883-9877	R	2*	<.1
1977	Super Auctions Inc—*Robert Storment*	2116 E Walnut Ave Ste, Fullerton CA 92831	714-535-7000	R	2*	<.1
1978	Tejas Supreme Meat—*Sue Rosen*	222 E Cevallos, San Antonio TX 78204	210-224-9672	R	2*	<.1
1979	Terra Point USA Inc—*Bruce Nelson*	25216 Grogans Park Dr, The Woodlands TX 77380	281-364-4080	R	2*	<.1
1980	Tourist Bureau Marketing Inc—*Pete Bertenshaw*	1125 W Pinnacle Pk Rd, Phoenix AZ 85027	602-952-2106	R	2*	<.1
1981	Tri Green Interstate Equipment Inc—*Richard Green*	1499 Us Hwy 42 Ne, London OH 43140	614-879-7731	R	2*	<.1
1982	Your Town Yellow Pages LLC—*Barb Anderson*	3790 Arapaho Rd, Addison TX 75001	972-242-1101	R	2*	<.1
1983	Century Mold and Tool Co—*Peter Varhegyi*	855 Touhy Ave, Elk Grove Village IL 60007	847-364-5858	R	2*	<.1
1984	Coburn and Saleeby LLP—*Sean Cobourn*	PO Box 5888, Spartanburg SC 29304	864-699-4000	R	2*	<.1
1985	Equity Technologies Corp—*Cathy Anderson-Giles*	2301 Perimeter Rd, Mobile AL 36615	251-432-7784	R	2*	<.1
1986	First Business Solutions Inc—*Wayne Orkin*	2700 Dawson Ave, Signal Hill CA 90755		R	2*	<.1
1987	Dcd Investments Inc—*Ann Garrett*	2448 E 81st St Ste 230, Tulsa OK 74137	918-492-9227	R	2*	<.1
1988	Design Central Inc—*Gregg Davis*	6464 Presidential Gate, Columbus OH 43231	614-890-0202	R	2*	<.1
1989	Global Health Management Systems Inc—*Annette Austin*	PO Box 66982, Baton Rouge LA 70896	225-261-0160	R	2*	<.1
1990	Sullivan Fire Protection LLC—*Darlene Ness*	1345 Pine Way, Sanford FL 32773	407-302-9632	R	2*	<.1
1991	Aksia LLC—*Joseph Larucci*	599 Lexington Ave Fl 4, New York NY 10022	212-907-6662	R	2*	<.1
1992	Allen Commercial Industries Inc—*Troy Allen*	11301 Mosier Valley Rd, Euless TX 76040	817-267-4919	R	2*	<.1
1993	Bron-Shoe Co—*Robert Kaynes*	1313 Alum Creek Dr, Columbus OH 43209	614-252-0967	R	2*	<.1
1994	Groundscare Ltd—*Lewis Kriegel*	PO Box 1106, New City NY 10956	845-639-4400	R	2*	<.1
1995	Intermark Design Group Inc—*Rick Thomas*	4602 Pkwy Commerce Blv, Orlando FL 32808	407-426-9975	R	2*	<.1
1996	Longhorn Pool Service Inc—*Michael Hurosky*	PO Box 2625, Austin TX 78768	512-832-5676	R	2*	<.1
1997	Mark Iv Enterprises Inc—*Carl Mark*	PO Box 30387, Portland OR 97294	503-234-3459	R	2*	<.1
1998	Ohio Steel Slitters Inc—*Warren Selinsky*	PO Box 80168, Canton OH 44708	330-477-6741	R	2*	<.1
1999	Peoria Area Convention And Visitors Bureau—*Bob Marx*	456 Fulton St Ste 300, Peoria IL 61602	309-676-0303	R	2*	<.1
2000	Sunfish Express Inc—*Frank Yomoutpor*	6401 Hwy 10 Nw, Anoka MN 55303	763-433-8383	R	2*	<.1
2001	Timberland Group Inc—*Kevin Kelly*	PO Box 26721, Minneapolis MN 55426	952-924-9070	R	2*	<.1
2002	Todd's Ltd—*Alan Niedermeier*	PO Box 4821, Des Moines IA 50305	515-266-2276	R	2*	<.1
2003	Bartlett Hackett Feinberg PC—*Edward Bartlett*	155 Federal St Fl 9, Boston MA 02110	617-422-0200	R	2*	<.1
2004	Basic Metals Inc—*Todd Fogel*	PO Box 757, Germantown WI 53022	262-255-9034	R	2*	<.1
2005	Demert and Dougherty Inc—*Yasav Samarah*	1300 North St, Coal City IL 60416	815-634-2302	R	2*	<.1
2006	Ka Custom Design Inc—*Kenneth Alpert*	595 Madison Ave Fl 8, New York NY 10022	212-223-0314	R	2*	<.1
2007	Lopez Chaff and Wiesman Associates Inc—*Bill Chaff*	130 Parker St Unit 20, Lawrence MA 01843	978-689-8822	R	2*	<.1
2008	CIM Tech Corp—*Stephen Teed*	40 Corporate Park Dr, Hopewell Junction NY 12533	845-897-3060	R	2*	<.1
2009	3-D Technical Services Inc—*David Brahm*	255 Industrial Dr, Franklin OH 45005	937-746-2901	R	2*	<.1
2010	Rehkemper Invention and Design Inc—*Steve Rehkemper*	1300 W Washington Blvd, Chicago IL 60607	312-421-1300	R	2*	<.1
2011	Klarity Multimedia Inc—*Gary Coull*	PO Box 160, North Vassalboro ME 04962	207-873-3911	R	2*	<.1
2012	Lithographic Services Inc—*Hubert Neil*	4887 Victor St, Jacksonville FL 32207	904-367-0002	R	2*	<.1
2013	Cppg Inc—*Louis Torres*	3905 E Miraloma Ave, Anaheim CA 92806	714-572-3662	R	2*	<.1
2014	Sports and Exhibition Authority Of Pittsburgh And Allegheny County—*Mary Conturo*	425 6th Ave Ste 2750, Pittsburgh PA 15219	412-393-0200	R	2*	<.1
2015	Viper Networks Inc—*Farid Shouekani*	189 E Big Beaver Ste 2, Troy MI 48083	248-724-1300	P	2	<.1
2016	Total Marketing Outbound Inc—*Randall Davila*	1320 Central Park Blvd, Fredericksburg VA 22401	703-490-8115	R	2*	.1
2017	Inland Desert Security And Communications—*Robert Beecham*	PO Box 830, Rialto CA 92377	909-875-2560	R	2*	.1
2018	Contact One Call Center Inc—*Judy Wood*	818 W Miracle Mile, Tucson AZ 85705	520-292-9222	R	2*	<.1
2019	Accredited Language Services—*Victor Hertz*	18 John St Ste 300, New York NY 10038	914-761-0615	R	2*	<.1
2020	Ppsb Warehouse—*Terry Mills*	1341 Olds St, Sandusky OH 44870	419-621-4591	R	2*	<.1
2021	Be Connected USA—*Cynthia Fritz*	1702 Meridian Ave Ste, San Jose CA 95125	408-885-1169	R	2*	<.1
2022	Woodland Avenue Fire Protection District—*Mike Passassalaqua*	3300 Woodland Ave, Modesto CA 95358	209-524-4239	R	2*	<.1
2023	Exchange Network Inc—*Alan Hamer*	101 Billerica Ave 5-20, North Billerica MA 01862	978-663-4515	R	2*	<.1
2024	Automated Mailing Systems Inc—*George Summers*	PO Box 12246, Roanoke VA 24024	540-343-1156	R	2*	<.1
2025	Eclipse Messenger Service—*Paul Carthy*	2400 S Grand Ave Ste 1, Santa Ana CA 92705	714-391-9732	R	2*	<.1
2026	Maritime and Seafood Industry Museum—*Robin Krohn-David*	PO Box 1907, Biloxi MS 39533	228-435-6320	R	2*	<.1
2027	Timberlake Fire Protection District—*Sam Scheu*	PO Box 810, Athol ID 83801	208-683-3333	R	2*	<.1
2028	Big Monster Toys LLC—*Maryann Kotowicz*	21 S Racine Ave, Chicago IL 60607	312-829-8697	R	2*	<.1
2029	Design Continuum Inc—*Norwood Faust*	3565 Piedmont Rd Ne 2-, Atlanta GA 30305	404-266-0095	R	2*	<.1
2030	Webb Devlam Chicago LLP—*Hugh Burton*	1032 W Fulton Market S, Chicago IL 60607	312-575-0700	R	2*	<.1
2031	Advanced Civil Design Inc—*Thomas Warner*	422 Beecher Rd, Columbus OH 43230	614-428-7750	R	2*	<.1
2032	Applied Research Laboratories Inc—*Alan Sukert*	5371 Nw 161st St, Hialeah FL 33014	305-624-4800	R	2*	<.1
2033	Oak Cliff Family Healthcare PA—*Steven Fenyves*	129 W 9th St, Dallas TX 75208	214-941-0032	R	2*	<.1

Rank	Company Name—*Executive Officer*	Address, City, State, Zip	Phone	Type	Fin	Empls
2034	Orion Payment Systems Inc—*Walter Raines*	14340 Torrey Chase Blv, Houston TX 77014	832-286-9000	R	2*	<.1
2035	Quad City Salvage Auction Inc—*John Lindle*	PO Box 138, Eldridge IA 52748	563-285-2100	R	2*	<.1
2036	Business Voice Inc—*Gerald Brown*	1600 Madison Ave Fl 4, Toledo OH 43604	419-473-9000	R	2*	<.1
2037	Diversified Design and Drafting Services Inc—*Pamela Nobles*	2374 Capital Cir Ne, Tallahassee FL 32308	850-385-1133	R	2*	<.1
2038	Preferred Quality Services Inc—*Marc Keizer*	11382 1st Ave Nw, Grand Rapids MI 49534	616-453-9577	R	2*	<.1
2039	Red Rover Trading Company LLC	9216 W 107th Mews, Westminster CO 80021	303-298-8620	R	2*	<.1
2040	River Mills Outfitters—*Patrick Fahey*	2375 Lincoln Ave, Hayward CA 94545	510-781-3900	R	2*	<.1
2041	Scottsdale Pool Service Inc—*Gavin Milliken*	PO Box 12845, Scottsdale AZ 85267	480-948-2001	R	2*	<.1
2042	Solis Jr Manuel E—*Manuel Solis*	6657 Navigation Blvd, Houston TX 77011	713-844-2700	R	2*	<.1
2043	Sundberg-Ferar Inc—*Curtis Bailey*	4359 Pineview Dr, Commerce Township MI 48390	248-360-3800	R	2*	<.1
2044	Nrai Corporate Services Inc—*Charles Baclet*	2875 Michelle Ste 100, Irvine CA 92606	949-955-9585	R	2*	<.1
2045	Eds Enterprises Inc—*Drew Schildwachter*	508 Providence Hwy, Norwood MA 02062	617-731-0150	R	2*	<.1
2046	River City Fire Equipment Company Inc—*Alex Bastedo*	PO Box 980305, West Sacramento CA 95798	916-374-8295	R	2*	<.1
2047	Sri Inc—*Jim Hughes*	8082 Bash St, Indianapolis IN 46250	317-842-5818	R	2*	<.1
2048	West Meade Pool Inc—*Eddie Porter*	404 American Rd, Nashville TN 37209	615-356-7086	R	2*	<.1
2049	Long Island Cauliflower Association—*Carl Key*	139 Marcy Ave, Riverhead NY 11901	631-727-2212	R	2*	<.1
2050	Snorgrass Auction Co—*Ron Snorgrass*	689 Barlow St, Clearfield UT 84015	801-725-0041	R	2*	<.1
2051	Suburban Grinding Co—*Larry Ludwig*	PO Box 473, Tualatin OR 97062	503-692-6188	R	2*	<.1
2052	Advanced Records Storage Inc—*Deadra Goodin*	1720 E Hwy 264, Springdale AR 72764	479-751-8120	R	2*	<.1
2053	Applied Microimage Corp—*John Doherty*	PO Box 540494, Waltham MA 02454	781-893-7863	R	2*	<.1
2054	Gesco Inc—*John Jasko*	711 4th St, Beaver Falls PA 15010	724-846-8700	R	2*	<.1
2055	Panef Corp—*George Walker*	5700 W Douglas Ave, Milwaukee WI 53218	414-464-7200	R	2*	<.1
2056	Eveready Products Corp—*Daniel Harrington*	1101 Belt Line Ave, Cleveland OH 44109	216-661-2755	R	2*	<.1
2057	Sara Weems Home Interiors—*Sara Weems*	108 Barrington Ct, Hardy VA 24101	540-890-3912	R	1*	<.1
2058	Pac Group—*Terry Taugher*	1400 Weiss St, Saginaw MI 48602	989-754-4712	R	1*	<.1
2059	Alabama Skills USA—*John Scott*	5226 Gordon Persons Bl, Montgomery AL 36130	334-242-9112	R	1*	<.1
2060	Epi-Hab Phoenix Inc—*Matthew Redmann*	2125 W Fillmore St, Phoenix AZ 85009	602-254-7027	R	1*	<.1
2061	Bramacint LLC	PO Box 1361, Rowlett TX 75030	972-226-3402	R	1*	<.1
2062	Curtis Manfredo Associates LLC	18 Warncke Rd, Wilton CT 06897	203-834-8588	R	1*	<.1
2063	Aero Properties LLC—*Sharon Keen*	8345 Blue Gill Dr, Peyton CO 80831	719-683-4778	R	1*	<.1
2064	Builders Interior Designs Inc—*Jennifer Johnson*	22 Violet Ct Ste 1a, Dallas GA 30132	678-363-8101	R	1*	<.1
2065	Desert Marketing Publications—*Daniel Stewart*	1720 W Suthern Ave Ste, Mesa AZ 85202	480-655-8787	R	1*	<.1
2066	Hawkeye Inc—*Si Luong*	12321 Denholm Dr, El Monte CA 91732	626-823-4405	R	1*	<.1
2067	Ruiz Enterprises LLC—*Jose Jalio*	11009 N 56th St, Temple Terrace FL 33617	813-985-2392	R	1*	<.1
2068	Raney Recording Studio and Print Inc—*Zyndall Raney*	110 S Front St, Drasco AR 72530	870-668-3222	R	1*	<.1
2069	Holbert Engineering Company Inc—*Erik Holbert*	750 Chapin St, South Bend IN 46601	574-287-2377	R	1*	<.1
2070	Sunshine Flag Car Service—*Thomas Alexander*	PO Box 262, Hershey PA 17033	717-534-1213	R	1*	<.1
2071	B and R Services For Professionals—*Frederic Blum*	235 S 13th St, Philadelphia PA 19107	215-546-7400	R	1*	<.1
2072	Dorian Ltd—*Emil Ionaiscu*	7269 Huntcliff, West Bloomfield MI 48322	248-788-3493	R	1*	<.1
2073	Els Surveying and Mapping—*E Sarton*	2004 Grande Blvd, Tyler TX 75703	903-581-2631	R	1*	<.1
2074	Fail Safe Testing Inc—*George Nirenberg*	PO Box 272, Monmouth Beach NJ 07750	732-728-0739	R	1*	<.1
2075	Fun Land Theatre and Swap Shop Inc—*Lauren Durren*	PO Box 11188, Tampa FL 33680	813-237-0886	R	1*	<.1
2076	Gardner Auction Service Inc—*Davar Gardner*	PO Box 958, Kalispell MT 59903	406-752-7682	R	1*	<.1
2077	Ices Production Hawaii—*Don Takaki*	1004 Marepono St, Honolulu HI 96819	808-832-2430	R	1*	<.1
2078	La Belle Exchange—*Herb Rose*	501 French St, Santa Ana CA 92701	714-547-8346	R	1*	<.1
2079	National Financial Corp—*George Franco*	1021 W National Ave 2, Milwaukee WI 53204	414-289-9140	R	1*	<.1
2080	Shared Financial Services—*Tom Mcfaden*	1000 Ridc Plz Ste 504, Pittsburgh PA 15238	412-968-1178	R	1*	<.1
2081	Timmerman Supper Club—*Mark Hayes*	PO Box 196, East Dubuque IL 61025	815-747-3316	R	1*	<.1
2082	West Office Exhibition Design—*Andrew Kramer*	225 3rd St, Oakland CA 94607	510-251-9633	R	1*	<.1
2083	Logical Source Microfilming Inc—*Jon Demarest*	PO Box 349, Wayne NJ 07474	973-523-9300	R	1*	<.1
2084	Perceptionist Inc—*Tiger Downey*	1010 Taylor Station Rd, Columbus OH 43230		R	1*	<.1
2085	Alabama Liquidation And Auction Inc—*James Langford*	PO Box 70878, Tuscaloosa AL 35407	205-758-3068	R	1*	<.1
2086	American Asia Express Corp—*Sean Jin*	35 W 39th St, New York NY 10018	212-302-8113	R	1*	<.1
2087	Credentials Inc—*Thomas Mckechney*	436 W Frontage Rd Ste, Northfield IL 60093	847-716-3000	R	1*	<.1
2088	D and G Packaging Co—*Keith Reierson*	12039 Riverwood Dr, Burnsville MN 55337	952-890-7525	R	1*	<.1
2089	Daily Bread Co—*Ron Murry*	703 S River Farm Dr, Alpharetta GA 30022	770-368-4016	R	1*	<.1
2090	General Printing and Design Inc—*Douglas Dratch*	22 Ledge Hill Rd, Southborough MA 01772	781-326-4449	R	1*	<.1
2091	Gordon Haskett and Co—*Jeff Braswell*	115 E Putnam Ave Ste 2, Greenwich CT 06830	203-862-5100	R	1*	<.1
2092	Great Lakes Production Support LLC—*Breanne Rozek*	152 S Rose St, Mount Clemens MI 48043	586-868-0305	R	1*	<.1
2093	King Communications Inc—*Carl King*	334 S Water St, Saginaw MI 48607	989-752-5678	R	1*	<.1
2094	Marcel S Garrigues Co—*Ronald Garrigues*	560 3rd St, San Francisco CA 94107	415-421-0371	R	1*	<.1
2095	Mobile's Answer Service Inc—*Kay Hirsch*	PO Box 180501, Mobile AL 36618	251-639-0371	R	1*	<.1
2096	Orlando Resort Development Group Inc—*Nicholas Kosmas*	4999 Kyngs Heath Rd, Kissimmee FL 34746	407-397-1058	R	1*	<.1
2097	Park Translations LLC	134 W 29th St Fl 5, New York NY 10001	212-581-8870	R	1*	<.1
2098	Primary Care Partners—*Donald Cohen*	8125 S Walker Ave Ste, Oklahoma City OK 73139	405-632-6000	R	1*	<.1
2099	Tom's Pole Buildings Inc—*Thomas Wehrly*	4050 Industrial Dr, Harrison MI 48625	989-539-3556	R	1*	<.1
2100	Unimeddirect LLC—*Jennifer Deleon*	5068 W Plano Pkwy Ste, Plano TX 75093	972-931-5100	R	1*	<.1
2101	You Inc—*George Smith*	130 Elm St, Millbury MA 01527	508-865-0533	R	1*	<.1
2102	Eastern Instrument Laboratories Inc—*Mildred Brandt*	416 Landmark Dr, Wilmington NC 28412	910-392-2490	R	1*	<.1
2103	Mbm Logistech LLC	931 Seville Rd, Wadsworth OH 44281	330-335-4300	R	1*	<.1
2104	Murphy W E Special Events Management—*Hank Zemola*	2023 W Carroll Ave Ste, Chicago IL 60612	312-226-1350	R	1*	<.1
2105	Security Recovery Inc—*Linda Raines*	PO Box 72540, Baltimore MD 21237	410-574-4840	R	1*	<.1
2106	Valley Exposition Service Inc—*Michael Nelson*	4950 American Rd, Rockford IL 61109	815-873-1500	R	1*	<.1
2107	Agenda Kansas City Inc—*Alton Hagen*	5290 Foxridge Dr, Shawnee Mission KS 66202	913-268-4466	R	1*	<.1
2108	Lanard Toys Inc—*Elizabeth Momaco*	2011 Auto Ctr Dr Ste 2, Oxnard CA 93036	805-278-0628	R	1*	<.1
2109	Lange Grinding Inc—*Richard Lange*	10165 Philipp Pkwy, Streetsboro OH 44241	330-463-3500	R	1*	<.1
2110	Visalia Sales Yard Inc—*Karen Green*	29660 Rd 152, Visalia CA 93292	559-734-9092	R	1*	<.1
2111	Bob's Pool Service Inc—*Jim Atkisson*	5014 Hwy 80 E, Pearl MS 39208	601-939-3388	R	1*	<.1
2112	Global Environmental Assurance Inc—*John Beach*	PO Box 337, Saint George SC 29477	843-563-8916	R	1*	<.1
2113	Hire Solutions Inc—*David Hooper*	70 E Lake St Fl 7, Chicago IL 60601	312-541-9432	R	1*	<.1
2114	Nevada Business Management Inc—*Rhett Long*	10 Hardy Dr, Sparks NV 89431	775-358-1066	R	1*	<.1
2115	Abc Legal Messengers—*Chris Horgan*	633 Yesler Way, Seattle WA 98104	206-625-9063	R	1*	<.1
2116	Advertising Resources Inc—*Richard Ehrie*	11601 S Central Ave, Alsip IL 60803	708-293-1926	R	1*	<.1
2117	All Seasons Distributors Inc—*Douglas Mayhall*	9135 W 135th St, Orland Park IL 60462	708-349-2222	R	1*	<.1
2118	Arge Inc—*Jerry Giannakaris*	224 Delaware St, Thorofare NJ 08086	856-848-4441	R	1*	<.1
2119	Brandt and Hochman Literary Agents Inc—*Gail Hochman*	1501 Broadway Ste 2310, New York NY 10036	212-840-5760	R	1*	<.1
2120	Creativity Inc—*Charles Albert*	990 Terminal Way, San Carlos CA 94070	650-508-3000	R	1*	<.1
2121	Desmond Marcello and Amster Inc—*Aaron Amster*	6060 Ctr Dr Ste 825, Los Angeles CA 90045	310-216-1400	R	1*	<.1
2122	Infoshred LLC	3 Craftsman Rd, East Windsor CT 06088	860-627-5800	R	1*	<.1
2123	Mtm Communications Inc—*Steven Melhorn*	350 Holly St, Junction City OR 97448	541-998-6148	R	1*	<.1

Note: An asterisk (*) indicates an estimated financial figure. The company type code used is as follows: R = Private, P = Public, S = Private Subsidiary, B = Public Subsidiary, D = Division, J = Joint Venture, I = Investment Fund.

COMPANY RANKINGS BY SALES WITHIN 4-DIGIT SIC

Rank	Company Name—*Executive Officer*	Address, City, State, Zip	Phone	Type	Fin	Empls
2124	Plastilam Inc—*James Mcguire*	PO Box 2057, Salem MA 01970	978-745-5563	R	1*	<.1
2125	Windham House Inc—*Megan Deroulet*	PO Box 888, Locust Valley NY 11560	516-621-7722	R	1*	<.1
2126	Batrow Inc—*Phyllis Batrow*	28 Stone St, Branford CT 06405	203-488-0039	R	1*	<.1
2127	American Accessories Of Pensacola Inc—*Michael Mulcahy*	7804 Sears Blvd, Pensacola FL 32514	850-477-4804	R	1*	<.1
2128	EM Basile and Associates Inc—*Emilio Basile*	9855 Aldea Ave, Northridge CA 91325	661-294-7030	R	1*	<.1
2129	Iei Group Ltd—*Rosemary Espanol*	428 N 2nd St, Philadelphia PA 19123	215-413-3700	R	1*	<.1
2130	Imaging and Microfilm Access Inc—*Mitchell Davis*	150 Knickerbocker Ave, Bohemia NY 11716	631-589-8100	R	1*	<.1
2131	Silicon Valley Cable Company Inc—*Bajram Madzar*	14424 New Jersey Ave, San Jose CA 95124	408-238-7000	R	1*	<.1
2132	Cisco City Shop—*Leon Boles*	PO Box 110, Cisco TX 76437	254-442-2113	R	1*	<.1
2133	Remac Information Corp—*Peter Maucher*	300 Professional Dr St, Gaithersburg MD 20879	301-948-4550	R	1*	<.1
2134	Ab Dan Felton Broker Notary—*Dan Felton*	860 E Lewelling Blvd, Hayward CA 94541	510-317-8687	R	1*	<.1
2135	Cadyville Firehouse—*Charles Chadwick*	2122 State Rte 3, Cadyville NY 12918	518-293-8326	R	1*	<.1
2136	Mountain Management Inc—*Norma Londe*	PO Box 151, Placerville CA 95667	530-295-0225	R	1*	<.1
2137	Earth-Core Inc—*Monty Fisher*	PO Box 32, Bowie TX 76230	940-872-8300	R	1*	<.1
2138	Action Communications and Secretarial Service—*Carol Sonn*	1017 Walnut St, Linden NJ 07036	908-964-4444	R	1*	<.1
2139	Barton Malow Design- Build JV—*George Houhanisin*	26500 American Dr, Southfield MI 48034	248-436-5000	R	1*	<.1
2140	Bay Answerphone Inc—*George Biddle*	1100 Beck Ave, Panama City FL 32401	850-763-1763	R	1*	<.1
2141	Cannon Kevin Law Offices—*Kevin Cannon*	PO Box 140005, Orlando FL 32814	407-839-1040	R	1*	<.1
2142	Fredricks Design—*Bruce Fredricks*	44675 Helm Ct, Plymouth MI 48170	734-459-9848	R	1*	<.1
2143	Gil Sewing Corp—*Michael Khakhan*	3500 N Kostner Ave, Chicago IL 60641	773-545-0990	R	1*	<.1
2144	Intt America—*Ana Mahoney*	22451 Shaw Rd, Sterling VA 20166	703-421-4157	R	1*	<.1
2145	Ltl Management Inc—*Don Williams*	1050 W Ppeline Rd Ste, Hurst TX 76053	817-284-2991	R	1*	<.1
2146	Phoenix Testing Inspection LLC—*Ibet Rodriguez*	3635 S 43rd Ave, Phoenix AZ 85009	602-272-2688	R	1*	<.1
2147	Praxis Technology Group—*Bill Adamowski*	275 Ne Venture Dr, Waukee IA 50263	515-327-5581	R	1*	<.1
2148	Ra-Tech Industries Inc—*Robert Wadsworth*	10653 W 181st Ave, Lowell IN 46356	219-696-5225	R	1*	<.1
2149	Rietta Flea Market—*Ronald Vesque*	PO Box 35, Hubbardston MA 01452	978-632-0559	R	1*	<.1
2150	Smallwood Reynolds Stewart Stewart Interiors Inc—*Howard Stewart*	3565 Piedmont Rd Ne 1-, Atlanta GA 30305	404-233-5453	R	1*	<.1
2151	Voice Link Of Columbus Inc—*Glynn Fussell*	PO Box 1653, Columbus GA 31902	706-323-6733	R	1*	<.1
2152	Wilson Kc and Associates—*K Wilson*	23232 Peralta Dr Ste 1, Laguna Hills CA 92653	949-470-3960	R	1*	<.1
2153	Allegis Group Aerotek—*Paul Bowie*	9600 Sw Barnes Rd Ste, Portland OR 97225	503-205-3420	R	1*	<.1
2154	Answer Incorporated of Corpus Christi—*Lester Lothman*	PO Box 2407, Corpus Christi TX 78403	361-884-6388	R	1*	<.1
2155	Itasca Fire Protection District 1—*James Burke*	520 W Irving Park Rd, Itasca IL 60143	630-773-1223	R	1*	<.1
2156	Argent Group LLC	10701 River Front Pkwy, South Jordan UT 84095	801-446-0110	R	1*	<.1
2157	Global Real Estate Investors and Financial Services Inc—*Ngozi Gbemudu*	468 N Camden Dr Ste 37, Beverly Hills CA 90210	310-860-7585	R	1*	<.1
2158	Air Pre Employment Screening Services Inc—*Philip Davis*	11403 Cronridge Dr Ste, Owings Mills MD 21117	410-654-5665	R	1*	<.1
2159	Alternative Micrographics Inc—*Mike Baker*	PO Box 506, Spicer MN 56288	320-796-2599	R	1*	<.1
2160	Biz Auction Corp—*Jake Ptasznik*	1510 Corporate Ctr Dr, San Diego CA 92154	619-325-1966	R	1*	<.1
2161	Cambridge Taxi Company Inc—*Joseph Silva*	76 Hampshire St, Cambridge MA 02139	617-547-3000	R	1*	<.1
2162	Cli Graphics Inc—*Kevin Bannan*	5 Pond Park Rd Ste 2, Hingham MA 02043	781-836-5185	R	1*	<.1
2163	Cps Of Ny Inc—*Sy Weisman*	247 W 35th St Fl 8, New York NY 10001	212-971-9444	R	1*	<.1
2164	Hoffmann's Green Industries Inc—*Barbara Hoffmann*	8141 E 21st St N, Wichita KS 67206	316-634-1500	R	1*	<.1
2165	Isovac Engineering Inc—*George Neff*	614 Justin Ave, Glendale CA 91201	818-552-6200	R	1*	<.1
2166	Keys Complete Inc—*Calvin Keys*	25950 E Us Hwy 50, Pueblo CO 81006	719-583-7999	R	1*	<.1
2167	Laiben Holdings Inc—*Richard Laiben*	8773 Commercial Blvd, Pevely MO 63070	636-479-5400	R	1*	<.1
2168	Mosquito Fire Protection District—*Mary Joseph*	8801 Rock Creek Rd, Placerville CA 95667	530-626-9017	R	1*	<.1
2169	OnesourceCom Inc—*Geroge Dalton*	1350 W 200 S, Lindon UT 84042	801-796-7777	R	1*	<.1
2170	Pro-Active Communications Inc—*Gerald Clifton*	10391 E Lylewood Way, Clovis CA 93619	559-291-3343	R	1*	<.1
2171	RSD Systems Inc—*Richard Dietz*	1547 Los Angeles Ave S, Ventura CA 93004	805-642-7665	R	1*	<.1
2172	So Cool Events Inc—*Dean Holderman*	2632 Nw 21st Ter, Miami FL 33142	305-635-8088	R	1*	<.1
2173	Town Of Cumberland—*Grace Heck*	PO Box 29155, Indianapolis IN 46229	317-894-3580	R	1*	<.1
2174	Cape Care For Women LLC—*Ann Behrends*	150 S Mount Auburn Rd, Cape Girardeau MO 63703	573-339-1166	R	1*	<.1
2175	Etched Images—*Stu Mcfarland*	1758 Industrial Way St, Napa CA 94558	707-252-5450	R	1*	<.1
2176	Industrial Finishing Services Inc—*Phillip Smith*	2517 W Schneidman Dr S, Quincy IL 62305	217-224-4374	R	1*	<.1
2177	Atlanta Custom Coach Inc—*Todd Lay*	7940 Bowen Rd, Palmetto GA 30268	770-463-5624	R	1*	<.1
2178	Culver Tool and Engineering Inc—*David Winrotte*	PO Box 970, Plymouth IN 46563	574-935-9611	R	1*	<.1
2179	Hippo Studios Inc—*Martin Gleitsman*	27 Bank St, Warwick RI 02888	401-521-5676	R	1*	<.1
2180	American Pegboard Printing Inc—*Carl Bradshaw*	2210 College Dr, Lake Havasu City AZ 86403	928-680-3841	R	1*	<.1
2181	Bernard Laboratories Inc—*Boyd Piper*	1738 Townsend St, Cincinnati OH 45223	513-681-7373	R	1*	<.1
2182	New York State Theatre For Opera and Ballet/Subscription—*Nadia Stone*	20 Lincoln Center Plz, New York NY 10023	212-870-5580	R	1*	<.1
2183	Plant Span Inc—*Paula Blanton*	PO Box 610302, Dallas TX 75261	817-379-5425	R	1*	<.1
2184	Soest and Associates Inc—*Maria Vansoest*	6682 Doolittle Ave, Riverside CA 92503	951-359-4906	R	1*	<.1
2185	Steel Slitting Company Inc—*Rich Brunnemer*	PO Box 102, Elwood IN 46036	765-552-5021	R	1*	<.1
2186	Travamerica Inc—*Louis Barberi*	4505 Peachtree Lake Dr, Duluth GA 30096	770-448-7700	R	1*	<.1
2187	Alexander Haas Martin and Partners—*Del Martin*	3520 Piedmont Rd Ne St, Atlanta GA 30305	404-525-7575	R	1*	<.1
2188	Crimson Cup Inc—*Greg Ubert*	700 Alum Creek Dr Ste, Columbus OH 43205	614-252-3335	R	1*	<.1
2189	Planning and Development Services Inc—*Patricia Joiner*	8588 Katy Fwy Ste 441, Houston TX 77024	713-463-8200	R	1*	<.1
2190	Total Media Technologies Inc—*Greg Hilz*	1565 Hotel Cir S Fl 2, San Diego CA 92108	619-574-0376	R	1*	<.1
2191	Absolute Print Graphics Inc—*Kevin Mergens*	7379 Washington Ave S, Minneapolis MN 55439	952-746-8839	R	1*	<.1
2192	Amerimerchant LLC	475 Park Ave S Fl 16, New York NY 10016		R	1*	<.1
2193	Auctions By The Bay Inc—*Allen Michaan*	PO Box 489, Alameda CA 94501	510-740-0220	R	1*	<.1
2194	Blanton Studio Inc—*David Jackson*	15720 Crabbs Branch Wa, Derwood MD 20855	301-840-8044	R	1*	<.1
2195	Cartruck Packaging Inc—*Sam Sharaba*	7315 Associate Ave, Cleveland OH 44144	216-631-7225	R	1*	<.1
2196	Crown Packaging LLC—*Margaret Leggin*	88b N Main St, Wharton NJ 07885	973-361-3717	R	1*	<.1
2197	Ctg Inc—*Thomas Dicampo*	449 Boston Post Rd E S, Marlborough MA 01752	508-787-0555	R	1*	<.1
2198	Eastern James Inc—*Jim O'donnell*	610 S Read St, Cinnaminson NJ 08077	856-786-8988	R	1*	<.1
2199	Enterprise Courier Inc—*Louis Green*	26893 Bouquet Canyon R, Santa Clarita CA 91350	661-296-1685	R	1*	<.1
2200	GES Contractors LLC—*Guy Stockstill*	1108 Fifth Ave, Picayune MS 39466	601-798-3731	R	1*	<.1
2201	Hadrian Corp—*Diana O'niell*	3120 Suthwest Fwy Ste, Houston TX 77098	713-522-3945	R	1*	<.1
2202	Infinity Products Inc—*Linda Scott*	141 Casco Dr, Avon IN 46123	317-272-3435	R	1*	<.1
2203	Integrity Recovery Inc—*Karl Moss*	PO Box 2473, Heath OH 43056	740-522-1111	R	1*	<.1
2204	Jet Brew Inc—*John Ventura*	187 Cortlandt St, Belleville NJ 07109	973-751-1800	R	1*	<.1
2205	JL Honberger Company Inc—*Joni Honberger*	883 S Chiques Rd, Manheim PA 17545	717-898-7787	R	1*	<.1
2206	Masterpieces Of Central Florida Inc—*Mitchell Burke*	2101 Premier Row, Orlando FL 32809	407-857-9987	R	1*	<.1
2207	Medical Couriers Inc—*Stephen Reiff*	1282 Montgomery Ave, San Bruno CA 94066		R	1*	<.1
2208	Punchgini Inc—*Pragnesh Desai*	217 E 49th St, New York NY 10017	212-888-2839	R	1*	<.1
2209	Qtechnology International Inc—*Raymon Bacchus*	6009 Raina Dr, Centreville VA 20120	703-899-8590	R	1*	<.1
2210	Rice's Market Inc—*Robert Blanche*	6326 Greenhill Rd, New Hope PA 18938	215-297-5993	R	1*	<.1

Rank	Company Name—*Executive Officer*	Address, City, State, Zip	Phone	Type	Fin	Empls
2211	Suben Dougherty Partnership—*Michael Azarian*	233 Spring St Rm 801, New York NY 10013	212-524-8512	R	1*	<.1
2212	Sullivan Corp—*Jerome Sullivan*	460 Cardinal Ln, Hartland WI 53029	262-369-7200	R	1*	<.1
2213	THEM Of Maryland Inc—*Robert Lipsky*	4030 Benson Ave Frnt, Baltimore MD 21227	410-247-5656	R	1*	<.1
2214	Wilcorp Enterprises—*Wanda Willard*	1830 Northwestern Ave, Gurnee IL 60031	847-263-6411	R	1*	<.1
2215	Wire To Wire Communications Inc—*Cathy Knight*	9017 Reseda Blvd, Northridge CA 91324	818-727-9940	R	1*	<.1
2216	Q-Peak Inc—*George Caledonia*	135 S Rd Ste 2, Bedford MA 01730	781-275-9535	R	1*	<.1
2217	Barbara Barry Inc—*Barbara Barry*	9526 W Pico Blvd, Los Angeles CA 90035	310-276-9977	R	1*	<.1
2218	Mjo Services LLC	1101 Business Pkwy S, Westminster MD 21157	410-840-9104	R	1*	<.1
2219	Rayken Inc—*Thomas Kennedy*	900 Shady Ln B, Kissimmee FL 34744	407-870-2822	R	1*	<.1
2220	H G Roebuck and Son Inc—*Charles Roebuck*	4987 Mercantile Rd, Baltimore MD 21236	410-931-3300	R	1*	<.1
2221	Answer Net Montana—*Debra Rogers*	735 Grand Ave, Billings MT 59101	406-248-2337	R	1*	<.1
2222	Security Couriers Inc—*Ron Porat*	12828 Victory Blvd, North Hollywood CA 91606	818-509-9500	R	1*	<.1
2223	Integrated Packaging and Fastener Inc—*Jill Rozehon*	1678 Carmen Dr, Elk Grove Village IL 60007	847-439-5730	R	1*	<.1
2224	Centennial Lending LLC—*Brett Bridge*	PO Box 30228, Lincoln NE 68503	402-476-5105	R	1*	<.1
2225	Cheryl A Mangio Inc—*Cheryl Mangio*	520 Pke St Ste 1213, Seattle WA 98101	206-622-6875	R	1*	<.1
2226	Crimson Life Sciences—*Marc Miller*	2181 Fillmore St, San Francisco CA 94115	415-563-8663	R	1*	<.1
2227	West Coast Courier—*Stephen Shaughnessey*	26081 Merit Cir Ste 10, Laguna Hills CA 92653	949-587-1678	R	1*	<.1
2228	Tandem Design Inc—*Maury Bonas*	1846 W Sequoia Ave, Orange CA 92868	714-978-7272	R	1*	<.1
2229	Madonna's Bail Bonds—*Terry Finn*	PO Box 189, San Carlos CA 94070	650-366-9111	R	1*	<.1
2230	Miracle Place International Church—*Veronica Jefferson*	8228 S Green St, Chicago IL 60620	312-285-3272	R	1*	<.1
2231	Career Development—*Betty Thompson*	2201 Murfreesboro Pke, Nashville TN 37217	615-207-7441	R	1*	<.1
2232	Charter Financial Inc—*Leland Vonsyring*	5555 Mrnngside Dr Ste, Houston TX 77005	713-432-0030	R	1*	<.1
2233	Long Island Materials Testing Labs Inc—*Robert Barnett*	PO Box 560233, College Point NY 11356	718-445-8300	R	1*	<.1
2234	Mercy Center At Madison—*Genie Guterch*	PO Box 191, Madison CT 06443	203-245-0401	R	1*	<.1
2235	Resource Design—*Ron Hudnall*	316 S 1st St, Rogers AR 72756	479-633-8181	R	1*	<.1
2236	Lone Star Exhibits Inc—*E Hoppens*	9433 Kirby Dr, Houston TX 77054	713-797-1994	R	1*	<.1
2237	Pure Touch LLC	425 Broadway Fl 4, New York NY 10013	212-680-4240	R	1*	<.1
2238	Impact Telecom Inc—*Bob Beaty*	9250 E Costilla Ave St, Greenwood Village CO 80112	303-779-5700	R	1*	<.1
2239	Sunset Sound Recorders Inc—*Paul Carmarata*	6650 W Sunset Blvd, Los Angeles CA 90028	323-469-1186	R	1*	<.1
2240	Coded Systems LLC	608 Hwy 71, Spring Lake NJ 07762	732-775-2300	R	1*	<.1
2241	Global Lion Group Inc—*May Lau*	PO Box 1069, Rosemead CA 91770	626-307-6423	R	1*	<.1
2242	Montrose Fire Protection District—*Steve Ellis*	441 S Uncompahgre Ave, Montrose CO 81401	970-249-9181	R	1*	<.1
2243	Cdc Pool Specialties LLC—*Katy Grant*	2364 S Airport Blvd St, Chandler AZ 85286	480-539-7700	R	1*	<.1
2244	Audit Logistics LLC	258 S Taylor Ave, Louisville CO 80027	303-951-9000	R	1*	<.1
2245	Clearsky Mobile Media Inc—*William Poellmitz*	390 N Orange Ave Ste 1, Orlando FL 32801	407-515-9000	R	1*	<.1
2246	Contract Support Group—*Donald Bergeron*	PO Box 958, Belmont NH 03220	603-267-8225	R	1*	<.1
2247	Docublue—*Lue Yat*	7154 N University Dr S, Tamarac FL 33321	954-933-9819	R	1*	<.1
2248	Exact Cutting Service Inc—*Jerry Narduzzi*	6892 W Snwvlle Rd Ste, Brecksville OH 44141	440-546-1319	R	1*	<.1
2249	Express Sixty Minute Delivery Service Inc—*Lynn Clayton*	3301 E Randol Mill Rd, Arlington TX 76011	817-336-5333	R	1*	<.1
2250	Hung Thai Dental Corp—*Hung Thai*	1111 Story Rd Ste 1037, San Jose CA 95122	408-999-0480	R	1*	<.1
2251	M2m Data Corp—*Alan Forbes*	8668 Concord Ctr Dr, Englewood CO 80112	303-768-0064	R	1*	<.1
2252	Modern Mailers Inc—*Karen Biggs*	PO Box 5376, Tallahassee FL 32314	850-877-0613	R	1*	<.1
2253	Munivest Financial Group LLC—*Amily Jones*	20355 Northwestern Hwy, Southfield MI 48034		R	1*	<.1
2254	Petro-Canada America Lubricant Inc—*Thomas Watson*	980 N Michigan Ave Ste, Chicago IL 60611	708-784-1885	R	1*	<.1
2255	Philcord Packaging Inc—*Greg Acord*	9121 Sibley Hole Rd, Little Rock AR 72209	501-455-0000	R	1*	<.1
2256	Tag Diamond and Label—*Tony Oliva*	100 Hankes Ave, Aurora IL 60505	630-844-9395	R	1*	<.1
2257	Tss Disrtibutions Services—*James Allen*	1150 Valencia Ave, Tustin CA 92780	714-259-0300	R	1*	<.1
2258	Gastonian—*Melanie Bliss*	220 E Gaston St, Savannah GA 31401	912-232-2869	R	1*	<.1
2259	Lamit Industries Inc—*Stephen Mihaly*	710 Marion Rd, Columbus OH 43207	614-444-3010	R	1*	<.1
2260	Museum Arts Inc—*Phillip Paramore*	2639 Freewood Dr, Dallas TX 75220	214-357-5644	R	1*	<.1
2261	Dimensional Validation Incorporated DVI—*Michael Ryan*	5971 E Executive Dr, Westland MI 48185	734-729-9190	R	1*	<.1
2262	Balas Inc—*Alan Drag*	1080 Kingsland Dr, Batavia IL 60510	630-406-7971	R	1*	<.1
2263	Power Select Inc—*Todd Milby*	11660 Western Ave, Stanton CA 90680	714-901-3900	R	1*	<.1
2264	Signature Print Services—*Meifang Xu*	PO Box 32464, San Jose CA 95152	408-982-0888	R	1*	<.1
2265	Hilton Engineering Co—*Jim Berei*	5900 Page Pl, Rockford IL 61101	815-968-5030	R	1*	<.1
2266	Aaa Storage—*Todd Gardere*	PO Box 958, Kalispell MT 59903	406-752-7682	R	1*	<.1
2267	Kensington Design and Build LLC—*Stanley Buden*	4507 Faroe Pl, Rockville MD 20853	301-933-0072	R	1*	<.1
2268	Sentor Technologies Inc—*Bijan Khazai*	1612 W King St, Chesterfield MO 63006	314-497-8629	R	1*	<.1
2269	Telephone Answering—*Laverne Turpin*	1113 6th St, Alexandria LA 71301	318-484-3000	R	1*	<.1
2270	Anthony Gizzi Appraiser—*Anthony Gizzi*	4415 Metro Pkwy Ste 11, Fort Myers FL 33916	239-437-6262	R	1*	<.1
2271	Executive Resources Group—*Victor Klein*	6030 Daybreak Cir Ste, Clarksville MD 21029	410-375-6837	R	1*	<.1
2272	Midwest Paralegal Services Inc—*Shawn Olley*	7625 S Howell Ave, Oak Creek WI 53154	414-764-2772	R	1*	<.1
2273	Albuquerque Council For International Visitors—*John Hooker*	6000 Menaul Blvd Ne St, Albuquerque NM 87110	505-888-1867	R	1*	<.1
2274	Ams Metal Slitting Corp—*Stan Szaflarski*	1710 N 25th Ave, Melrose Park IL 60160	708-681-1850	R	1*	<.1
2275	Ats Parkridge Exchange Inc—*Robert Castle*	3223 W Ridge Rd, Rochester NY 14626	585-723-6600	R	1*	<.1
2276	Quality Telecommunications Services Inc—*Frank Feldhaus*	612 S Harbor Blvd, Anaheim CA 92805	714-635-6700	R	1*	<.1
2277	Velvet Hammer Music Group	9014 Melrose Ave, West Hollywood CA 90069	310-657-6161	R	1*	<.1
2278	Barona Fire Protection District	1112 Barona Rd, Lakeside CA 92040	619-390-2794	R	1*	<.1
2279	Bonnamy and Associates LLC	PO Box 3491, Carefree AZ 85377	630-357-7899	R	1*	<.1
2280	Ghesquiere Plastic Testing Inc—*Michael Ghesquiere*	20450 Harper Ave, Harper Woods MI 48225	313-885-3535	R	1*	<.1
2281	Jain Malkin Inc—*Jain Malkin*	5070 Santa Fe St Ste C, San Diego CA 92109	858-454-3377	R	1*	<.1
2282	Lakeshore Document Services—*Garry Olson*	6522 Schamber Dr, Norton Shores MI 49444	231-798-8756	R	1*	<.1
2283	Lingua Science Corp—*Sue Aitken*	921 W Washington St Ap, Ann Arbor MI 48103	734-930-1553	R	1*	<.1
2284	Norcom Systems Inc—*John Newman*	1055 W Germantown Pke, Norristown PA 19403	610-592-0167	R	1*	<.1
2285	Rice Village Animal Hospital—*James Bray*	2348 Rice Blvd, Houston TX 77005	713-527-0489	R	1*	<.1
2286	Sound/Video Impressions Inc—*Bill Hultane*	110 S River Rd, Des Plaines IL 60016	847-297-4360	R	1*	<.1
2287	All Points Inspection Services Inc—*Alayne Johnson*	6448 E Hwy 290 Ste C11, Austin TX 78723	512-272-5056	R	1*	<.1
2288	Tetra Tech HEI—*Greg Rudy*	1009 Commerce Park Dr, Oak Ridge TN 37830	865-483-7007	R	1*	<.1
2289	Sujac Sewing Contractors—*Jack Friedlander*	PO Box 1840, Moultrie GA 31776	229-890-1150	R	1*	<.1
2290	Twin Lakes Pool Corp—*Earl Snapp*	9964 Griffin Rd, Cooper City FL 33328	954-434-5700	R	1*	<.1
2291	Stroud Diving and Hydrography Div—*Will F Hux* Marine Engineering Systems Company Inc	5030 Old Kings Rd NW, Jacksonville FL 32254	904-355-1777	D		
2292	Translatus Inc—*Matthew Miodonski*	333 N Michigan Ave Ste, Chicago IL 60601	312-443-0887	R	1*	<.1
2293	Beaufort Ems Inc—*Michael Foreman*	PO Box 950, Beaufort NC 28516	252-728-3255	R	1*	<.1
2294	Reliance Fire Protection Inc—*Nancy Hammond*	PO Box 428, Preston WA 98050	206-682-6636	R	1*	<.1
2295	Barry Design Associates Inc—*Robert E Barry*	10780 Santa Monica Blv, Los Angeles CA 90025	310-474-7050	R	1*	<.1
2296	Dlp Enterprises Inc—*Denise Paige*	820 Greenbrier Cir Ste, Chesapeake VA 23320	757-420-5886	R	1*	<.1
2297	Hart Foundation—*Kenneth Johnson*	4914 Dale Dr, Columbia SC 29203	803-309-2247	R	1*	<.1
2298	Hartford Auction Group Inc—*Michael Ferrara*	PO Box 52, Portland CT 06480	860-342-1699	R	1*	<.1
2299	Tepper Galleries Inc—*Kenneth Hutter*	110 E 25th St, New York NY 10010	212-677-5300	R	1*	<.1

Note: An asterisk (*) indicates an estimated financial figure. The company type code used is as follows: R = Private, P = Public, S = Private Subsidiary, B = Public Subsidiary, D = Division, J = Joint Venture, I = Investment Fund.

COMPANY RANKINGS BY SALES WITHIN 4-DIGIT SIC

Rank	Company Name—*Executive Officer*	Address, City, State, Zip	Phone	Type	Fin	Empls
2300	Answerone LLC	3121 Ctr Point Dr, Edinburg TX 78539	956-994-6500	R	1*	<.1
2301	Intercoastal Diving Inc—*Stanley Rudd*	6101 Diamond Shamrock, Castle Hayne NC 28429	910-675-9215	R	1*	<.1
2302	Encino Pool And SpA—*Jeff Schulte*	5150 Collett Ave, Encino CA 91436	818-789-6295	R	1*	<.1
2303	Design Collective Inc (Columbus Ohio)—*Eugene McHugh*	151 E Nationwide Blvd, Columbus OH 43215	614-464-2880	R	1*	<.1
2304	Eagle International Software—*Scott Swarm*	6405 Kinzua Ave, Chicago IL 60646	773-594-1472	R	1*	<.1
2305	ADS Courier and Messenger Service Inc—*Terry Mummert*	PO Box 868, York PA 17405	717-751-0000	R	1*	<.1
2306	Advanced Automotive Technologies Inc—*Steve Pasteiner*	1763 W Hamlin Rd, Rochester Hills MI 48309	248-852-2900	R	1*	<.1
2307	Call America Inc—*Jeffrey Buckingham*	PO Box 3310, San Luis Obispo CA 93403	805-549-7800	R	1*	<.1
2308	Certified Grinding and Machine Inc—*Robert Rock*	850 Saint Paul St Ste, Rochester NY 14605	585-423-0990	R	1*	<.1
2309	Choice Money Transfer Inc—*Kevin Neuschatz*	350 5th Ave Ste 1016, New York NY 10118	212-268-9290	R	1*	<.1
2310	Coppinger Exhibits Inc—*Mike Coppinger*	9955 Westpoint Dr Ste, Indianapolis IN 46256	317-913-1400	R	1*	<.1
2311	Eai Acquisition Company LLC	7750 Montgomery Rd, Cincinnati OH 45236	513-792-5414	R	1*	<.1
2312	Marguerite Rodgers Ltd—*Marguerite V Rodgers*	2131 N American St, Philadelphia PA 19122	215-634-7888	R	1*	<.1
2313	MarTel International Inc—*Annette Burke*	11038 N Harrison St, Kansas City MO 64155	816-734-0400	R	1*	<.1
2314	Mccartan—*Colum Mccartan*	416 W 13th St Ste 206, New York NY 10014	212-957-1815	R	1*	<.1
2315	Meditext Inc—*Wendy Whitehurst*	PO Box 8502, Greenville NC 27835	252-329-8300	R	1*	<.1
2316	MWC Management Corp—*Michael Coleman*	451 Park Ave S Lbby, New York NY 10016	212-447-9018	R	1*	<.1
2317	DAT/EM Systems International	8240 Sandlewood Pl Ste, Anchorage AK 99507	907-522-3681	R	1*	<.1
2318	McKeever Services Corp—*James McKeever*	10505 Judicial Dr Ste, Fairfax VA 22030	703-691-1100	R	1*	<.1
2319	Trackwise Inc—*Fran Bowelen*	630 9th Ave Ste 416, New York NY 10036	212-627-7700	R	1*	<.1
2320	Whereoware LLC—*Eric M Dean*	505 Huntmar Park Dr St, Herndon VA 20170	703-821-7448	R	1*	<.1
2321	B and D Packaging Inc—*Brad Yaker*	35569 Industrial Rd St, Livonia MI 48150	734-427-9010	R	1*	<.1
2322	Straub's Inventory Control Inc—*Jack Beinhower*	873 Clare Ln, York PA 17402	717-774-2323	R	1*	<.1
2323	Clayton Aquariums Inc—*Steve Clayton*	13256 Northup Way, Bellevue WA 98005	425-644-7222	R	1	<.1
2324	Compliance Services International Inc—*Bernalyn D Mc-Gaughey*	7501 Bridgeport Way W, Lakewood WA 98499	253-473-9007	R	1*	<.1
2325	HipLink Software—*Anthony N LaPine*	718 University Ave Ste, Los Gatos CA 95032	408-399-6120	R	1	<.1
2326	Beverly Clark Enterprises LLC—*Danielle Blackwell*	114 E Haley St Ste K, Santa Barbara CA 93101	805-560-3604	R	1*	<.1
2327	Consulting Coop	1837 Newfield Ave, Stamford CT 06903	203-653-3556	R	1	<.1
2328	Elias Design Group Inc—*Brad Elias*	226 E 54th St 9th Fl, New York NY 10022	212-826-8702	R	1*	<.1
2329	Flow Safe Inc—*Eileen Klees*	30 Broad St Ste 3, Denville NJ 07834	973-627-8553	R	1*	<.1
2330	HoustonStreet Inc—*Frank W Getman Jr*	1 New Hampshire Ave St, Portsmouth NH 03801	603-766-8716	R	1*	<.1
2331	NAME-IT	4546 El Camino Real St, Los Altos CA 94022	650-948-2990	R	1*	<.1
2332	National Center For Dispute Settlement LLC—*John Holloran*	105 Decker Ct Ste 350, Irving TX 75062	972-652-3400	R	1*	<.1
2333	Roommate Express—*Dennis Smith*	3100 S Rural Rd #1, Tempe AZ 85282	480-966-4126	R	1*	<.1
2334	Trademark Express—*Chris DeMassa*	1065 K St Ste D, Arcata CA 95521	707-822-7050	R	1*	<.1
2335	Customer Perspectives—*Judith Ann Hess*	213 W River Rd, Hooksett NH 03106	603-647-1300	R	1*	<.1
2336	Liberty Opportunities—*Daniel F Kostecky*	2395 Prince St, Conway AR 72034		R	1*	<.1
2337	Vanderbyl Design—*Michael Vanderbyl*	171 2nd St 2nd Fl, San Francisco CA 94105	415-543-8447	R	1*	<.1
2338	Guernsey's—*Arlan Ettinger*	108 E 73rd St, New York NY 10021	212-794-2280	R	1*	<.1
2339	Interior Design Force Inc—*Stephen Thompson*	636 Broadway, New York NY 10012	212-777-0999	R	1*	<.1
2340	June Roesslein Interiors Inc—*June Roesslein*	10411 Clayton Rd Ste 2, Frontenac MO 63131	636-394-1465	R	1*	<.1
2341	Justice Electronics Training Services Inc—*Lucy Justice*	5850 TG Lee Blvd Ste 2, Orlando FL 32822	407-850-0205	R	1*	<.1
2342	Alliance Artists Ltd—*Robert Geddes*	1825 Lockeway Dr Rm 20, Alpharetta GA 30004	770-663-4240	R	1*	<.1
2343	Claire/Alden Inc—*Patricia Claire*	6 W 20th St 9th Fl, New York NY 10011	212-255-2252	R	1*	<.1
2344	CyberEdge Informaton Services—*Ben Delaney*	407 Martin Luther King, Oakland CA 94607	510-419-0800	R	1*	<.1
2345	David Michael Miller Associates—*David Miller*	7034 E 1st Ave, Scottsdale AZ 85251	480-425-7545	R	1*	<.1
2346	Don Grind Associates Inc—*Don Grind*	PO Box 2441, Placerville CA 95667	530-622-0630	R	1*	<.1
2347	Juan Montoya Design Corp—*Juan Montoya*	330 E 59th St 2nd Fl, New York NY 10022	212-421-2400	R	1*	<.1
2348	Mama's Garden Design Studio—*Jo Ann Villalobos*	104 W Cedar St, Bertrand MO 63823	310-428-1099	R	1	<.1
2349	Partners 4 Design—*John Idstrom II*	275 Market St, Minneapolis MN 55405	612-927-4444	R	1*	<.1
2350	Robert A Siegel Auction Galleries Inc—*Scott R Trepel*	60 E 56th St 4th Fl, New York NY 10022	212-753-6421	R	1*	<.1
2351	Source Systems Inc—*Robert Martin*	2307 E Aurora Rd Ste B, Twinsburg OH 44087	330-963-1001	R	1*	<.1
2352	Celebrity Source Inc—*Rita Tateel*	8033 Sunset Blvd Ste 2, Los Angeles CA 90046	323-651-3300	R	1*	<.1
2353	Impulse Communications Inc—*Eric Borgos*	14525 SW Millikan Ste, Beaverton OR 97005	503-828-9050	R	1*	<.1
2354	Interior Space Management of Michigan Inc—*Martha Brooks*	2081 Heide St, Troy MI 48084	248-362-4950	R	1	<.1
2355	Kaufman Partnership Ltd—*Don Kaufman*	233 S 6th St Ste702, Philadelphia PA 19106	215-592-9709	R	1*	<.1
2356	Loyd-Paxton Inc—*Loyd Taylor*	3137 Irving Blvd Ste 3, Dallas TX 75247	214-521-1521	R	1*	<.1
2357	BZ/Rights and Permissions Inc—*Barbara Zimmerman*	145 W 86th St, New York NY 10024	212-924-3000	R	1*	<.1
2358	Career Control Group Inc—*Don Hanratty Optimance*	3608 Preston Rd Ste 22, Plano TX 75093	469-467-2800	S	1*	<.1
2359	International Meeting Planners Ltd—*Audrye Bird*	4863 Hampshire Ct Ste, Naples FL 34112	239-775-1467	R	1*	<.1
2360	Marcia Davis and Associates Inc—*Marcia Davis*	5064 Roswell Rd NE Ste, Atlanta GA 30342	404-255-5600	R	1*	<.1
2361	Maxcy Design—*Marcia Maxcy*	31 Redondo Ct, Saint Helena CA 94574	707-968-9299	R	1	<.1
2362	Metro Bay Associates Inc—*Larry Register*	2106 Drew St Ste104, Clearwater FL 33765	727-442-1225	R	1*	<.1
2363	Winslow Group Inc—*David Winslow*	PO Box 10973, Winston Salem NC 27108	336-722-7982	R	1*	<.1
2364	Brickhouse of NY Inc—*Randy DeVaul*	7573 E Rte 20, Westfield NY 14787	716-326-6262	R	1*	<.1
2365	Camelot Technologies Group LLC—*Michael L Weaver*	17231 Camelot Ct, Land O Lakes FL 34638	813-920-8725	R	1*	<.1
2366	Checkmatic Recovery Systems—*Chris Tipton*	P O Box 130021, The Woodlands TX 77393	281-288-5450	R	1*	<.1
2367	COLORCOM—*Jill Morton*	3905-C Maunahilu Pl, Honolulu HI 96816	707-709-8988	R	1*	<.1
2368	Creative Concept Unlimited—*Cynthia Minor*	PO Box 801, Liberty NY 12754		R	1*	<.1
2369	Denise Marcil Literary Agency Inc—*Denise M Marcil*	156 5th Ave Ste 625, New York NY 10010	212-337-3402	R	1*	<.1
2370	Extreme Connection—*Ann Krcik*	38 Miller Ave Ste 231, Mill Valley CA 94941	415-388-0416	S	1*	<.1
2371	Got Clicks—*Sarah Spencer*	PO Box 882, Richmond VT 05477		S	1*	<.1
2372	GreaterValue—*Greg Blomberg*	2293 Willow Way W, La Crosse WI 54601	608-769-3579	R	1*	<.1
2373	Hurricane Moving and Transfers—*Hillery Capes*	1120 Lake View Dr, Altamonte Springs FL 32714	321-231-1993	R	1*	<.1
2374	InfoSports—*Albert Gross*	PO Box 890384, Temecula CA 92589	909-308-1663	R	1*	<.1
2375	Inland Empire Consultants—*Joe Mabry*	PO Box 6052, San Bernardino CA 92412	909-800-0108	R	1*	<.1
2376	Inner Space Design Inc—*Charlin S Devanney*	2128 Madison Rd, Cincinnati OH 45208	760-717-6005	R	1*	<.1
2377	Marshall Long Acoustics—*Marshall Long*	13636 Riverside Dr, Sherman Oaks CA 91423	818-981-8005	R	1	<.1
2378	Metro Music Production—*Randy Wachtler*	1030 16th Ave S, Nashville TN 37212	615-244-6515	S	1*	<.1
2379	OmniTranslations—*Myung-Hee Kim*	41-29 41 St Ste 6A, Sunnyside NY 11104	718-729-6115	R	1*	<.1
2380	Precision Cartographics Inc—*Gary D Joiner*	1029 Blanchard Pl, Shreveport LA 71104	318-222-6112	R	1*	<.1
2381	Rachel Carter PR—*Rachel Carter*	564 Garen Rd Ste 4, Charlotte VT 05445	802-425-4886	R	1*	<.1
2382	Rein Nomm and Associates Inc—*Rein Nomm*	PO Box 700613, Plymouth MI 48170	734-420-3174	R	1*	<.1
2383	River City Sound Productions—*Bob Pierce*	PO Box 750786, Memphis TN 38175	901-274-7277	R	1*	<.1
2384	Southwestern Textile Restoration Inc—*Ben Leroux*	2505 Ingalls St, Edgewater CO 80214	303-232-7504	R	1*	<.1
2385	Staton Institute Inc—*Mary Staton*	2431 Hartmill Ct, Charlotte NC 28226	704-365-2122	R	1*	<.1
2386	Academ Consulting Services—*Stan Barber*	PO Box 300481, Houston TX 77230	713-747-7270	R	1*	<.1
2387	CareerWise Inc—*Estelle Newman*	4 Susan Ct, Owings Mills MD 21117	410-746-3651	R	1*	<.1

Rank	Company Name—Executive Officer	Address, City, State, Zip	Phone	Type	Fin	Empls
2388	Discovery Computing Inc—Allen L Wyatt	PO Box 2145, Mesa AZ 85214	480-629-4160	R	1*	<.1
2389	English Motion Media Inc—Henry English	243 Riverside Dr Ste 5, New York NY 10025	212-865-7242	R	1*	<.1
2390	Florida Properties of Jacksonville Inc	3705 W Memorial Rd Bld, Oklahoma City OK 73134	904-389-0331	R	1*	<.1
2391	Fullstream DVD—Jay Rydman	9419 Hillview Dr, Dallas TX 75231	214-207-9080	R	1*	<.1
2392	Golden Eagle Technologies LLC—Greg Black	14280 W 50th Pl, Golden CO 80403	303-278-9268	R	1*	<.1
2393	INTELLIGENCE—Edward Rosenfeld	PO Box 20008, New York NY 10025	212-222-1123	R	1*	<.1
2394	Jakubson Telecommunications Inc—Joel E Jakubson	30 Sunrise Ct Ste 100, Menlo Park CA 94025	415-309-1678	R	1*	<.1
2395	Kari and Associates—Kari Sable Burns	PO Box 7126, Olympia WA 98507	360-637-4043	R	1*	<.1
2396	Lafayette Development Corp—Ken Harwood	PO Box 133, Darlington WI 53530	608-776-8080	S	1*	<.1
2397	Michael Levine Music Inc—Michael Levine	1531 14th St, Santa Monica CA 90404	310-401-7101	R	1*	<.1
2398	New Century Marketing Concepts—Robert Villegas	1243 Priority Pl, Indianapolis IN 46227	317-881-3826	R	1*	<.1
2399	Sunday Productions Inc—Hilary Lipsitz	1501 Broadway, New York NY 10036	212-302-6888	R	1*	N/A
2400	Edwards Answering Service Inc—Gary Edwards	230 Hartford Tpke Ste, Vernon Rockville CT 06066	860-646-5080	R	1*	<.1
2401	On Letterhead—Vince Dragovic	PO Box 350426, Toledo OH 43635	419-724-0228	R	1*	<.1
2402	Aaa Bail Bonding Company Inc—R Newman	413 S President St Ste, Jackson MS 39201	601-948-4105	R	1*	<.1
2403	Ambassador Financial Group—Samir Rasdedie	15188 N 75th Ave, Peoria AZ 85381	623-815-1921	R	1*	<.1
2404	Appr A Ze Co—David Harper	1910 E 14th St, Tucson AZ 85719	520-798-1785	R	1*	<.1
2405	Atlantic-Pacific Processing Systems Inc—Robyn Hickman	17220 Newhope St, Fountain Valley CA 92708	714-241-1402	R	1*	<.1
2406	Caid Solutions LLP—Jane Propst	7155 W Campo Bello Dr, Glendale AZ 85308	623-582-1516	R	1*	<.1
2407	Charles Norris—Charles Norris	25539 John R Rd, Madison Heights MI 48071	248-548-1900	R	1*	<.1
2408	Colorado Accurate Inventory—David Luther	1540 S Zenobia St, Denver CO 80219	303-936-5352	R	1*	<.1
2409	Professional Communication Services—Kay Mills	260 Sheridan Ave Ste 2, Palo Alto CA 94306	650-688-0495	R	1*	<.1
2410	Relocation Center—Scott Nelson	9350 S 150 E Ste 500, Sandy UT 84070	801-563-7708	R	1*	<.1
2411	SH Lee Corp—James Lee	2700 Carl Blvd, Elk Grove Village IL 60007	630-860-4607	R	1*	<.1
2412	William Bunch H Auctioneers and Appraiser LLC	1 Hillman Dr, Chadds Ford PA 19317	610-558-1800	R	1*	<.1
2413	Integbusiness Services Inc—Clayton Uyehara	1050 Bishop St Ste 500, Honolulu HI 96813	808-599-4998	R	1*	<.1
2414	BioImmune Inc—Arnold Takemoto	8300 N Hayden Rd Ste A, Scottsdale AZ 85258	480-778-1618	R	1	<.1
2415	Concierge Technologies Inc—David W Neibert	3615 Superior Ave Ste, Cleveland OH 44114		P	1	N/A
2416	Nextech Solutions Inc—Tony Di Napoli	10480 Markison Rd, Dallas TX 75238	214-343-5300	P	1	N/A
2417	Premier Facility Group Inc—Brian Nielsen	125 Mansell Pl Ste 207, Roswell GA 30076	770-521-2224	R	1*	.1
2418	New Mexico Communications Inc—Louis Curley	PO Box 81347, Albuquerque NM 87198	505-266-5551	R	1*	<.1
2419	Joe Pippin Auctioneers—Joseph Pippin	PO Box 165331, Irving TX 75016	972-256-3830	R	1*	<.1
2420	1 800 Tax Lws Inc—Joseph Greco	899 Hwy 34, Matawan NJ 07747	732-290-2400	R	1*	<.1
2421	BK Solutions Inc—Bryan Keith	6111 Quiet Village Ct, Houston TX 77053	713-857-1533	R	1*	<.1
2422	Glc Partners	623 5th Ave Fl 2901, New York NY 10022	646-573-9009	R	1*	<.1
2423	Khojna Technologies—Ganesh Rajapan	770 L St Ste 950, Sacramento CA 95814		R	1*	<.1
2424	Language Solutions	16400 Avondale Rd Ne, Woodinville WA 98077	206-919-1367	R	1*	<.1
2425	Modular Building Sales Inc—Colin Mclean	419 Sudden Valley, Bellingham WA 98229	360-738-0281	R	1*	<.1
2426	Phoenix Promotions Inc—Will Nonnamaker	7195 Arlington Rd, Massillon OH 44646	330-854-1279	R	1*	<.1
2427	Smokestack Records—Monica Brown	PO Box 288375, Chicago IL 60628	773-264-2552	R	1*	<.1
2428	Tri-State Consulting Services—Jeff Cooke	PO Box 160, Cropwell AL 35054	205-338-1060	R	1*	<.1
2429	KCM Holdings Corp—Ed Kang	6729 Lebanon Rd Ste 14, Frisco TX 75034	972-523-1680	P	1	<.1
2430	Center Line Tool Inc—Wes Cyphert	106 5th St, Freeport PA 16229	724-295-2440	R	1*	<.1
2431	Middletown Adolescent Leaders Achieve—Sharon Bogan	PO Box 1314, Middletown OH 45042	513-423-0795	R	1*	<.1
2432	Access Inc—Villie Mcdaniel	1441 Lincoln Ave, Louisville KY 40213	502-367-1881	R	1*	<.1
2433	Kutter Products Inc—Bill Gregory	1340 Quebec St, Kansas City MO 64116	816-221-2274	R	1*	<.1
2434	Rice Hydro Inc—Kenneth Alexander	3500 Arrowhead Dr, Carson City NV 89706	775-885-1280	R	1*	<.1
2435	Alesis Semiconductor Corp—Kathy Moniz	12555 W Jefferson Blvd, Los Angeles CA 90066	310-301-0780	R	1*	<.1
2436	Pioneer Design Inc—Terry Jackson	3829 Long Meadow Ln, Lake Orion MI 48359	248-437-0920	R	1*	<.1
2437	Sungard Institutional Brokerage Inc—Scott Frank	4 Cityplace Dr Ste 225, Saint Louis MO 63141	314-983-9216	R	1*	<.1
2438	View Systems Inc—Gunther Than	1550 Caton Center Dr S, Baltimore MD 21227	410-242-8439	P	1	<.1
2439	Monster Offers—Paul Gain	PO Box 1092, Bonsall CA 92003	760-208-4905	P	1	N/A
2440	Wiscraft Inc—Bill Piernot	5316 W State St, Milwaukee WI 53208	414-778-5800	R	1*	<.1
2441	Ocean Answer—Stephan Kenny	6500 Coastal Hwy Ste D, Ocean City MD 21842	410-520-2000	R	1*	<.1
2442	Camp Courageous Of Iowa—Charles Becker	PO Box 418, Monticello IA 52310	319-465-5916	R	1*	<.1
2443	County Property Appraisers Office—Ronnie Hawkins	209 N Florida St Ste 2, Bushnell FL 33513	352-793-0210	R	1*	<.1
2444	Eagle Hurst Ranch—John Butz	9700 Mackenzie Rd, Saint Louis MO 63123	314-638-3382	R	1*	<.1
2445	Garcia Packaging Inc—Joseph Garcia	26721 C Dr N, Albion MI 49224	269-857-8542	R	1*	<.1
2446	Julie Fund Inc—Peter Mcavinn	PO Box 620657, Newton MA 02462	781-431-7687	R	1*	<.1
2447	Visitor Center Of Lexington—Jean Clark	106 E Washington St, Lexington VA 24450	540-463-3777	R	1*	<.1
2448	Datum Industries Inc—William Salvesen	PO Box 227, North Bergen NJ 07047	201-943-8870	R	1*	<.1
2449	Chicago Multilingua Graphics Inc—Lizhe Sun	990 Grove St Ste 303, Evanston IL 60201	847-864-3230	R	1*	<.1
2450	Identifax Of Greater Orlando Inc—Pamela Aicher	PO Box 98, Winter Park FL 32790	407-740-0005	R	1*	<.1
2451	International Language Services Inc—Irene Gross	60 E 42nd St Ste 1329, New York NY 10165	212-856-9848	R	1*	<.1
2452	Skyline Exhibits West Inc—Jeff Johnson	4101 Guardian St, Simi Valley CA 93063	805-915-0280	R	1*	<.1
2453	Intersol Inc—Susana Turbitt	3 Pointe Dr Ste 301, Brea CA 92821	714-671-9180	R	1*	<.1
2454	Colt Tech LLC—Robert Lynn	PO Box 4710, Olathe KS 66063	913-322-9230	R	1*	<.1
2455	Techniart Inc—Gary Cardillo	PO Box 500, Collinsville CT 06022	860-693-8697	R	1*	<.1
2456	Race On Motor Sports—John Ballinger	3638 Fite Rd, Memphis TN 37501	901-527-6174	R	1*	<.1
2457	Roy Coggins—Roy Coggins	5904 Robertson Ave, Nashville TN 37209	615-356-0564	R	1*	<.1
2458	Bagolitas By Janice LLC—Ron Meyer	315 W Cherry St 2, North Liberty IA 52317	319-626-2906	R	1*	<.1
2459	Special Service Systems Inc—Gary Drummond	2007 E 11th St, Tulsa OK 74104	918-582-7777	R	1*	<.1
2460	American Printing Finishers Inc—Donald Trotter	1707 Stone Ridge Dr, Stone Mountain GA 30083	770-934-9228	R	1*	<.1
2461	Green Valley Manufacturing Co—Edward Kosanovic	PO Box 236, Cameron WV 26033	304-686-3312	R	1*	<.1
2462	Acoustilog Inc—Alan Fierstein	19 Mercer St Office A, New York NY 10013	212-925-1365	R	1*	<.1
2463	Twin City Engraving Company Inc—Jeffrey Jones	PO Box 85, Saint Joseph MI 49085	269-983-0601	R	1*	<.1
2464	Surgical Technologies Inc—Timothy Scanlan	292 E Lfytte Frntage R, Saint Paul MN 55107	651-298-0997	R	1*	<.1
2465	Solutions Staffing Services Inc—Eduardo Vargas	PO Box 526404, Miami FL 33152	305-477-6220	R	1*	<.1
2466	Trade Show Alliance Inc—Eric Britt	PO Box 93412, Las Vegas NV 89193	702-361-1898	R	1*	.1
2467	J and L Microfilm Service Inc—Howard Olson	2707 Golf Ave, Racine WI 53404	262-632-4550	R	1*	<.1
2468	Multilingual Communications Corp—Charles Kostecki	PO Box 7164, Pittsburgh PA 15213	412-621-7450	R	1*	<.1
2469	Musicol Inc—John Hull	780 Oakland Park Ave, Columbus OH 43224	614-267-3133	R	1*	<.1
2470	Storm Crankshaft Grinding And Welding Corp—Ray Obrien	511 Homestead Ave, Mount Vernon NY 10550	914-664-3563	R	1*	<.1
2471	Robert Long—Robert Long	13111 Glen Mill Rd, Rockville MD 20850	301-424-6830	R	<1*	.1
2472	Hampstead Stage Co—Michael Phillips	1053 N Barnstead Rd, Center Barnstead NH 03225	603-776-6044	R	<1*	<.1
2473	Conversa Language Center Inc—Jerry Thiemann	817 Main St Ste 600, Cincinnati OH 45202	513-651-5679	R	<1*	<.1
2474	Quick Caption Antha Ward	2374 Arroyo Dr, Riverside CA 92506	951-536-0850	R	<1*	<.1
2475	Kard Inc—Rajah Menon	955 Msschstls Ave Ste, Cambridge MA 02139	978-921-4125	R	<1*	<.1
2476	Data Design Group—Stephen Roberts	PO Box 3318, La Jolla CA 92038	858-454-5234	R	<1*	<.1
2477	Innovative Software Technologies Inc—Michael Hester	911 Ranch Rd N Ste 204, Austin TX 78734	813-387-3304	R	<1	<.1

Note: An asterisk (*) indicates an estimated financial figure. The company type code used is as follows: R = Private, P = Public, S = Private Subsidiary, B = Public Subsidiary, D = Division, J = Joint Venture, I = Investment Fund.

COMPANY RANKINGS BY SALES WITHIN 4-DIGIT SIC

Rank	Company Name—*Executive Officer*	Address, City, State, Zip	Phone	Type	Fin	Empls
2478	Cash Technologies Inc—*Bruce R Korman*	1434 W 11th St, Los Angeles CA 90015	213-745-2000	R	<1	<.1
2479	Quality Inspection and Containment Company Inc—*James Middleton*	PO Box 66, Dayton OH 45409	937-439-9950	R	<1*	<.1
2480	Mormax Inc—*Glenn Henry*	1219 Morningside Dr, Manhattan Beach CA 90266	310-546-5789	R	<1*	<.1
2481	Quality Unlimited LLC—*Debbie Mcguffin*	104 Twenty Nine Ct, Williamston SC 29697	864-847-1620	R	<1*	<.1
2482	Tax Prep Inc—*Mike Bitet*	13303 Crossbay Blvd, Ozone Park NY 11417	718-738-4500	R	<1*	<.1
2483	Lakeshore Roller World Inc—*Robert Saleem*	PO Box 161, Stevensville MI 49127	269-429-7700	R	<1*	<.1
2484	Arkados Group Inc—*Andreas Typaldos*	256 Central Ave, West Caldwell NJ 07006	972-815-2340	P	<1	<.1
2485	King Centerless Grinding Company Inc—*Gerald King*	29800 Stephenson Hwy, Madison Heights MI 48071	248-542-1615	R	<1*	<.1
2486	Trod Nossel Productions and Recording Studios Inc—*Thomas Cavalier*	PO Box 57, Wallingford CT 06492	203-269-4465	R	<1*	<.1
2487	Retail Design Group Inc—*Al Ranyak*	13709 Gamma Rd, Dallas TX 75244	972-701-9095	R	<1*	<.1
2488	IVI Communications Inc—*Kurt Jensen*	1818 N Farwell Ave, Milwaukee WI 53202	414-727-2699	P	<1*	<.1
2489	Diversity Group International Inc—*Kevin Bobryk*	375 Park Ave Ste 2607, New York NY 10152	305-515-5610	P	<1	N/A
2490	XCel Brands Inc—*Robert W D'Loren*	475 10th Ave 4th Fl, New York NY 10018	347-632-5891	P	<1	N/A
2491	Nationalease Of Maine Inc—*Thomas Thonton*	PO Box 1169, Bangor ME 04402	207-945-6451	R	<1*	.1
2492	Sivers Auctions Inc—*Theodore Sivers*	7112 State Rte 104, Oswego NY 13126	315-343-3325	R	<1*	<.1
2493	uVuMobile Inc—*Scott Hughes*	3870 Peachtree Industr, Duluth GA 30096	678-682-9663	P	<1	<.1
2494	Rutland Industries Inc—*Ted Tarisi*	PO Box 6264, Rutland VT 05702	802-775-7638	R	<1*	<.1
2495	Finest Engraving LLC	5 Bunker Hill Rd, Andover CT 06232	860-643-1778	R	<1*	<.1
2496	Illinois Audio Productions Inc—*Charles Filippi*	3906 Turner Ave, Plano IL 60545	630-552-9600	R	<1*	<.1
2497	Zippi Networks Inc—*Robert Rositano Jr*	1821 S Bascom Ave, Campbell CA 95008	408-884-2006	P	<1	<.1
2498	Contek Design and Products Inc—*Nicholas Liu*	14619 Woonsockett Dr, Silver Spring MD 20905	301-989-0662	R	<1*	<.1
2499	GMI Sound Corp—*David Weiss*	39 S 5th St, Brooklyn NY 11249	718-384-7625	R	<1*	<.1
2500	Mark Design Associates—*Kathleen Glynn*	3615 Ivanhoe Ave, Boynton Beach FL 33436	561-731-1701	R	<1*	<.1
2501	Equipment Development Services—*Frank Olshefsky*	3578 Guilderland Ave, Schenectady NY 12306	518-356-7841	R	<1*	<.1
2502	Bluegate Corp—*Stephen J Sperco*	701 N Post Oak Rd Ste, Houston TX 77024	713-686-1100	P	<1	N/A
2503	Glastonbury Press LLC—*Misty Forsman*	454 Las Gallinas Ave S, San Rafael CA 94903	415-492-2140	R	<1	N/A
2504	United Business Service of NY—*Joseph DeSimone*	3715 Church Ave, Brooklyn NY 11203	718-941-5100	R	<1	N/A
2505	Complete Logistics Co—*Robert Rains*	1670 E Etiwanda, Ontario CA 91761	931-361-1158	R	<1	.2
2506	True Product ID Inc—*Michael J Antonoplos*	1615 Walnut St, Philadelphia PA 19102	610-687-7668	P	<1	<.1
2507	Sunnydale Industries Inc—*Dean Corridan*	PO Box 65665, West Des Moines IA 50265	573-682-2128	P	<1*	<.1
2508	Magnum D'Or Resources Inc—*Joseph J Glusic*	2850 W Horizon Ridge P, Henderson NV 89052	303-536-4581	P	<1	<.1
2509	Debt Resolve Inc—*James Brakke*	150 White Plains Rd St, Tarrytown NY 10591	914-949-5500	P	<1	<.1
2510	Euthenics Inc—*Gene Collins*	1005 1st Ave N, Saint Petersburg FL 33705	727-823-6633	R	<1	<.1
2511	MSGI Security Solutions Inc—*Jeremy Barbera*	575 Madison Ave 10th F, New York NY 10022	212-605-0245	P	<1	<.1
2512	Spratronics Inc—*Fred Oligschlaeger*	20403 80th Ave Se, Snohomish WA 98296	360-668-2548	R	<1*	<.1
2513	Schimatic Cash Transactions Networkcom Inc—*Bernard F McHale*	7757 Foredawn Dr, Las Vegas NV 89123	702-778-4784	P	<1	<.1
2514	Bio-Matrix Scientific Group Inc—*David R Koos*	8885 Rehco Rd, San Diego CA 92121	619-398-3517	P	<1	<.1
2515	eDoorways Corp—*Gary F Kimmons*	820 W 3rd St Ste 1103, Austin TX 78701		P	<1	<.1
2516	Fuelstream Inc—*John Thomas*	10757 S River Front Pk, South Jordan UT 84095	801-816-2500	P	<1	<.1
2517	General Metals Corp—*Daniel Forbush*	615 Sierra Rose Dr Ste, Reno NV 89511	775-583-4636	P	<1	<.1
2518	Video Walls USA Inc—*Poulo Ginobbi*	5491 Cow Town Ln, Las Vegas NV 89118	702-873-4306	R	<1*	<.1
2519	Water Front Inc—*Arthur Young*	14 Maine St Uppr, Brunswick ME 04011	207-729-0378	R	<1*	<.1
2520	Ascendant Solutions Inc—*David E Bowe*	16250 Knoll Trail Dr S, Dallas TX 75248	972-250-0945	R	<1	N/A
2521	Maydao Corp—*Paul Roszel*	PO Box 58228, Salt Lake City UT 84158	801-531-0404	P	<1	N/A
2522	Medical Makeover Corporation of America—*Jason Smart*	2101 Vista Pkwy Ste292, West Palm Beach FL 33411	561-228-6148	P	<1	N/A
2523	Subjex Corp—*Andrew D Hyder*	3240 Aldrich Ave S Ste, Minneapolis MN 55408	612-382-5566	P	<1	N/A
2524	Vois Inc—*William R Marginson*	951 Yamato Rd Ste 201, Boca Raton FL 33431	516-998-3882	P	<1	N/A
2525	Employer Services Corp—*John D Hawkins*	20 Pineview Dr, Amherst NY 14228	716-691-4455	R	N/A	3.5
2526	Kruse Asset Management—*Daniel Kruse*	11202 Disco Dr Ste 100, San Antonio TX 78216	210-499-0777	R	N/A	<.1
2527	PowerSpring Inc Powersecure International Inc	1609 Heritage Commerce, Wake Forest NC 27587	919-556-3056	S	N/A	<.1
2528	Sales Opportunity Services Inc—*Paul Yohn*	PO Box 951, Altoona PA 16603	814-949-3327	R	N/A	<.1
2529	National Telecommunications Services Inc—*Mac Hansbrough*	122 C St NW Ste 640, Washington DC 20001	202-638-4500	R	N/A	<.1
2530	Trade Show Solution Center LLC—*Laura McLeod*	200 Broadhollow Rd Ste, Melville NY 11747	631-393-5079	R	N/A	<.1
2531	Rights International Group—*Robert Hazaga*	500 Paterson Plank Rd, Union City NJ 07087	201-863-4500	R	N/A	N/A

TOTALS: SIC 7389 Business Services Nec
Companies: 2,531   252,209   993.1

7513 Truck Rental & Leasing Without Drivers

Rank	Company Name—*Executive Officer*	Address, City, State, Zip	Phone	Type	Fin	Empls
1	Penske Corp—*Roger S Penske*	2555 S Telegraph Rd, Bloomfield Hills MI 48302	248-648-2000	R	10,000*	34.0
2	Ryder System Inc—*Gregory T Swienton*	11690 NW 105th St, Miami FL 33178	305-500-3726	P	6,051	27.5
3	Penske Truck Leasing Company LP—*Brian Hard*	PO Box 563, Reading PA 19603		J	4,020*	20.0
4	United Rentals Inc—*Michael J Kneeland*	5 Greenwich Office Pk, Greenwich CT 06831	203-622-3131	P	2,611	7.5
5	AMERCO—*Edward J Shoen*	1325 Airmotive Way Ste, Reno NV 89502	775-688-6300	P	2,241	16.6
6	Fastenal Company Leasing—*Willard Oberton*	2001 Theurer Blvd, Winona MN 55987	507-454-5374	S	579*	1.0
7	Aim National Lease—*Thomas Fleming*	1500 Trumbull Ave, Girard OH 44420	330-759-0438	R	354*	1.1
8	Star Truck Rentals Inc—*William Bylenga*	3940 Eastern Ave SE, Grand Rapids MI 49508	616-243-7033	R	308*	.3
9	Western Truck Parts and Equipment—*Frank Anglin*	1441 Richards Blvd, Sacramento CA 95814	916-441-6151	R	300*	.1
10	Mendon Leasing Corp—*Roger Palazzo*	362 Kingsland Ave, Brooklyn NY 11222	718-391-5300	R	183*	.2
11	PHH Vehicle Management Services LLC—*George Kilroy*	940 Ridgebrook Rd, Sparks MD 21152	410-771-1900	S	169*	1.2
12	Idealease Services Inc—*William Kennedy*	430 N Rand Rd, Barrington IL 60010	847-304-6000	R	120*	<.1
13	Salem Leasing Corp—*Thomas L Teague*	PO Box 24788, Winston-Salem NC 27114		R	80*	.3
14	Interstate NationaLease Inc—*Jack Zolomy*	2700 Palmyra Rd, Albany GA 31707	229-883-7250	S	66*	.2
15	Lily Transportation Corp—*John Simourian II*	145 Rosemary St, Needham MA 02494		R	59*	.5
16	Leasing Associates Inc	12600 N Featherwood Dr, Houston TX 77034	832-300-1300	R	55*	.1
17	Brody Transportation Company Inc—*Steve Brody*	621 S Bentalou St, Baltimore MD 21223	410-789-4050	R	26	.1
18	Edart Truck Rental Corp—*EM Siegal* Ryder System Inc	PO Box 234, Hartford CT 06141	860-527-8274	S	23*	.2
19	De Carolis Truck Rental Inc—*Michael Margarone*	333 Colfax St, Rochester NY 14606	585-254-1169	R	14*	.2
20	US Rents It—*James V Rau*	1513 Industrial Dr, Jefferson City MO 65109	573-635-6171	R	11*	<.1
21	Benedict Enterprises Inc—*Arnold Benedict*	PO Box 370, Monroe OH 45050	513-539-9216	R	5*	.1

TOTALS: SIC 7513 Truck Rental & Leasing Without Drivers
Companies: 21   27,274   111.1

7514 Passenger Car Rental

Rank	Company Name—*Executive Officer*	Address, City, State, Zip	Phone	Type	Fin	Empls
1	Enterprise Rent-A-Car Co—*Andrew C Taylor*	600 Corporate Park Dr, Saint Louis MO 63105	314-512-5000	R	10,100*	65.0
2	Avis Group Holdings Inc—*Ronald L Nelson*	6 Sylvan Way, Parsippany NJ 07054	973-496-3500	S	3,903*	19.3

Rank	Company Name—*Executive Officer*	Address, City, State, Zip	Phone	Type	Fin	Empls
3	Dollar Thrifty Automotive Group Inc—*Scott L Thompson*	5330 E 31st St, Tulsa OK 74135	918-660-7700	P	1,549	5.9
4	Budget Rent A Car System Inc—*F Robert Salerno*	6 Sylvan Way, Parsippany NJ 07054	973-496-4700	S	1,312*	.5
5	Auto Europe Inc	PO Box 7006, Portland ME 04112	207-842-2000	R	246*	.3
6	Ace Rent-A-Car Inc—*Richard Radzis*	4529 W 96th St, Bloomington IN 47404	812-727-2004	R	97*	.2
7	National Car Rental System Inc—*Greg Stubblefield*	6929 N Lakewood Ave St, Tulsa OK 74117		S	83*	.7
8	Thrifty Car and Truck Rental—*Steve Sternberg*	3902 Crittenden Dr, Louisville KY 40209	502-367-9733	R	64*	.1
9	Griffin's Hub Chrysler Jeep Dodge—*James Lecher*	5700 S 27th St, Milwaukee WI 53221	414-325-3333	R	58*	.1
10	Air Brook Limousine Inc—*Donald M Petroski*	PO Box 123, Rochelle Park NJ 07662	201-843-6100	R	9*	.1
11	JDR Franchises LLC—*Jennifer Richardson*	PO Box 1098, Mukilteo WA 98275	425-353-8213	R	7*	<.1
12	Auto Service Company Inc—*John Hill*	1000 Cadillac Ct, Fairbanks AK 99701	907-456-6217	R	6*	.1

TOTALS: SIC 7514 Passenger Car Rental
Companies: 12   17,434   92.1

7515 Passenger Car Leasing

Rank	Company Name—*Executive Officer*	Address, City, State, Zip	Phone	Type	Fin	Empls
1	Hertz Corp—*Mark P Frissora*	225 Brae Blvd, Park Ridge NJ 07656	201-307-2000	S	7,469	32.2
2	Automotive Resources International—*Carl Ortell*	9000 Midlantic Dr, Mount Laurel NJ 08054	856-778-1500	S	3,932*	1.8
3	Wheels Inc—*Jim Frank*	666 Garland Pl, Des Plaines IL 60016	847-699-7000	R	2,000*	.5
4	American Honda Finance Corp—*Kunio Endo*	20800 Madrona Ave, Torrance CA 90503	310-781-4100	S	1,087*	1.0
5	Automotive Rentals Inc—*William McKee*	PO Box 5039, Mount Laurel NJ 08054	856-778-1500	R	930*	.5
6	Major Fleet and Leasing Corp	43-40 Northern Blvd, Long Island City NY 11101	718-937-3700	S	594*	.5
7	Allstate Leasing Inc—*Brent Baron*	9428 Reisterstown Rd, Owings Mills MD 21117	410-363-6500	R	243*	.1
8	Executive Car Leasing Co—*Sam Goldman*	7807 Santa Monica Blvd, Los Angeles CA 90046		R	150*	.2
9	Jake Sweeney Auto Leasing Inc—*David Loper*	8755 Fields Ertel Rd, Cincinnati OH 45249	513-489-5253	R	53*	<.1
10	Sutliff Capital Ford Inc—*Greg Sutliff*	5001 Jonestown Rd, Harrisburg PA 17112		R	34*	.1

TOTALS: SIC 7515 Passenger Car Leasing
Companies: 10   16,492   36.9

7519 Utility Trailer Rental

Rank	Company Name—*Executive Officer*	Address, City, State, Zip	Phone	Type	Fin	Empls
1	GE Trailer Fleet Services—*Joe Artuso*	530 E Swedesford Rd, Wayne PA 19087	484-254-0100	S	545*	2.0
2	XTRA Lease—*Jordan Ayers*	1632 Park 370 Court, Hazelwood MO 63042	314-209-0504	S	477	.7
3	Mobile Mini Inc—*Steven G Bunger*	PO Box 79149, Phoenix AZ 85062	480-894-6311	P	364	1.6
4	National Trailer Center Of Michigan Inc—*Craig Howell*	38600 Ford Rd, Westland MI 48185	734-729-6767	R	15*	<.1
5	E and J Trailer Sales and Service Inc—*Edward Focke*	610 Wayne Park Dr Ste, Cincinnati OH 45215	513-563-2550	R	1*	<.1

TOTALS: SIC 7519 Utility Trailer Rental
Companies: 5   1,402   4.4

7521 Automobile Parking

Rank	Company Name—*Executive Officer*	Address, City, State, Zip	Phone	Type	Fin	Empls
1	Central Parking Corp—*Emanuel Eads*	2401 21st Ave S Ste 20, Nashville TN 37212	615-297-4255	R	1,109*	18.9
2	Standard Parking Corp—*James A Wilhelm*	900 N Michigan Ave Ste, Chicago IL 60611		P	721	12.0
3	Interpark Inc—*J Marshall Peck*	549 Peachtree St Ste 1, Atlanta GA 30308	404-658-9053	R	647*	2.0
4	Imperial Parking (US) Inc—*Charles Huntzinger*	510 Walnut St Ste 420, Philadelphia PA 19106	215-574-0830	R	172*	3.5
5	AMPCO System Parking—*Rich Kindorf*	808 S Olive St, Los Angeles CA 90014	213-624-6065	D	165*	8.0
6	Park Towne Ltd—*Jerry South*	1 Park Pl Ste 200, Annapolis MD 21401	410-267-6111	R	150*	6.9
7	Diamond Parking Inc—*Joel Diamond*	605 First Ave Ste 600, Seattle WA 98104	206-284-3100	R	72*	1.2
8	SJW Land Co—*W Richard Roth*	PO Box 229, San Jose CA 95103	408-279-7800	S	59*	.2
9	Colonial Parking Inc—*Jed Hatfield*	715 Orange St, Wilmington DE 19801	302-651-3600	R	17*	.3
10	Alco Parking Corp—*Merrill Stabile*	501 Martindale St, Pittsburgh PA 15212	412-323-4455	R	13*	.2
11	Allright New York Parking Inc—*Monroe Carell* Central Parking Corp	36 Main St W, Rochester NY 14614	585-232-3411	S	12*	<.1
12	Central Parking System Inc—*Brandon Smith* Central Parking Corp	700 E Franklin St Ste, Richmond VA 23219	804-648-2155	S	4*	.2
13	Allright Colorado Inc—*Monroe Carell* Central Parking Corp	475 17th St Ste 750, Denver CO 80202	303-893-9402	S	3*	<.1
14	Allright Boston Parking Inc—*Monroe Carell* Central Parking Corp	125 Lincoln St, Boston MA 02110	617-426-6748	S	3*	<.1
15	USA Parking Systems Inc—*Lou Francos* Central Parking Corp	1325 Carnegie Ave Fl 1, Cleveland OH 44115	216-621-9255	S	3*	<.1
16	Allright Shreveport Inc—*Monroe Carell* Central Parking Corp	1520 Kings Hwy, Shreveport LA 71103	318-424-6408	S	2*	<.1
17	Allright Baton Rouge Inc—*Monroe Carell* Central Parking Corp	210 Laurel St, Baton Rouge LA 70802	225-344-4142	S	1*	<.1

TOTALS: SIC 7521 Automobile Parking
Companies: 17   3,154   53.5

7532 Top & Body Repair & Paint Shops

Rank	Company Name—*Executive Officer*	Address, City, State, Zip	Phone	Type	Fin	Empls
1	Three-C Body Shop Inc—*Robert Juniper*	2300 Briggs Rd, Columbus OH 43223	614-274-8245	R	52*	.1
2	Earl Scheib Inc—*Christian K Bement*	15206 Ventura Blvd Ste, Sherman Oaks CA 91403	818-981-9992	S	43	.8
3	Midwest Bus Corp—*Daniel Morrill*	PO Box 787, Owosso MI 48867	989-723-5241	R	30*	.1
4	Miracle Auto Painting Inc—*Les Thayer*	2343 Lincoln Ave, Hayward CA 94545	510-887-2211	R	27	.1
5	1-Day Paint and Body Centers Inc—*Javier R Uribe*	PO Box 3037, Torrance CA 90510	310-328-8900	R	23*	.5
6	Accurate Autobody and Glass Inc—*Nathan Hostetler*	5550 S Garnett Rd, Tulsa OK 74146	918-443-4948	R	12*	<.1
7	Us Vantage Company LLC—*David Eaton*	5202 S 28th Pl, Phoenix AZ 85040	602-243-2700	R	8*	.1
8	Associated Partnership Ltd—*Du Wade Harris*	6591 Hwy 13 W, Savage MN 55378	952-890-7851	R	6*	.1
9	Diversatech Plastics Group LLC—*Curt Dubois*	PO Box 701, Winchester TN 37398	931-967-7418	R	6*	.1
10	Van Majestic Corp—*Bryan Bivins*	8297 Gratiot Rd, Saginaw MI 48609	989-781-0985	R	4*	.1
11	Advantage Mobility Outfitters Inc—*Joe Rickard*	3990 2nd St, Wayne MI 48184	734-595-4400	R	3*	<.1
12	Schneider Graphic's Inc—*Ward Schneider*	PO Box 8246, Des Moines IA 50301	515-289-4464	R	3*	<.1
13	Hillside Recycling Equipment Corp—*Vito Vittorio*	5025 71st St, Woodside NY 11377	718-898-0407	R	2*	<.1
14	Precision Body and Frame—*Rick Bender*	1509 Post Ave, Schofield WI 54476	715-359-9655	R	2*	<.1

TOTALS: SIC 7532 Top & Body Repair & Paint Shops
Companies: 14   221   2.1

7533 Automobile Exhaust System Repair Shops

Rank	Company Name—*Executive Officer*	Address, City, State, Zip	Phone	Type	Fin	Empls
1	Monro Muffler Brake Inc—*Robert Gross*	200 Holleder Pkwy, Rochester NY 14615	585-647-6400	P	637	5.0

7534 Tire Retreading & Repair Shops

Rank	Company Name—*Executive Officer*	Address, City, State, Zip	Phone	Type	Fin	Empls
1	Tire Distribution Systems Inc—*Janet Sichterman*	PO Box 17287, Nashville TN 37217	615-833-7900	S	878*	1.7
2	Wingfoot Commercial Tire Systems LLC	PO Box 48, Fort Smith AR 72902	479-788-6400	S	252*	2.8

Note: An asterisk (*) indicates an estimated financial figure. The company type code used is as follows: R = Private, P = Public, S = Private Subsidiary, B = Public Subsidiary, D = Division, J = Joint Venture, I = Investment Fund.

COMPANY RANKINGS BY SALES WITHIN 4-DIGIT SIC

Rank	Company Name—*Executive Officer*	Address, City, State, Zip	Phone	Type	Fin	Empls
3	Mcgriff Industries Inc—*Barry Mcgriff*	PO Box 1148, Cullman AL 35056	256-739-0710	R	110*	.7
4	Service Tire Truck Center Inc—*Ronald Bennett*	2255 Ave A, Bethlehem PA 18017	610-954-8473	R	81*	.5
5	Purcell Tire and Rubber Company Inc—*Dennis Flynn*	PO Box 100, Potosi MO 63664	573-438-2131	R	40*	1.0
6	Bergson Tire Company Inc—*James Wood*	PO Box 1258, Vernon Rockville CT 06066	860-872-7729	R	3*	<.1

TOTALS: SIC 7534 Tire Retreading & Repair Shops
Companies: 6 — 1,363 — 6.7

7536 Automotive Glass Replacement Shops

Rank	Company Name—*Executive Officer*	Address, City, State, Zip	Phone	Type	Fin	Empls
1	Safelite Glass Corp—*Tom Feeney*	PO Box 2000, Columbus OH 43216		S	740*	7.0
2	Henderson Glass Inc—*Carlton Ostdiek*	715 S Blvd E, Rochester MI 48307	248-829-4800	S	388*	.4
3	Glassworks Plus Inc—*Brian Chriss*	2244 N Wilson Rd, Columbus OH 43228	614-771-7111	R	57*	<.1
4	Speedy Auto Glass Inc—*Allan Skidmore*	9675 SE 36th St, Mercer Island WA 98040	206-232-9500	S	28*	.3
5	Guardian Glass Co (Westerville Ohio)—*William Davidson*	2300 Harmon Rd, Auburn Hills MI 48326	248-340-1800	D	20*	.2

TOTALS: SIC 7536 Automotive Glass Replacement Shops
Companies: 5 — 1,233 — 7.9

7537 Automotive Transmission Repair Shops

Rank	Company Name—*Executive Officer*	Address, City, State, Zip	Phone	Type	Fin	Empls
1	Specialties Clutch Inc—*Pete Webster*	2490 Performance Cir, Bessemer AL 35022	205-491-8581	R	2*	<.1
2	Rockland Standard Gear Inc—*Michael Weinberg*	150 Rte 17, Sloatsburg NY 10974	845-753-2005	R	2*	<.1

TOTALS: SIC 7537 Automotive Transmission Repair Shops
Companies: 2 — 5 — <.1

7538 General Automotive Repair Shops

Rank	Company Name—*Executive Officer*	Address, City, State, Zip	Phone	Type	Fin	Empls
1	Lucor Inc—*Stephen P Conway*	790 Pershing Rd, Raleigh NC 27608	919-828-9511	R	2,027*	2.0
2	McCombs Enterprises Inc—*BJ 'Red' McCombs*	755 E Mullberry Ave St, San Antonio TX 78212	210-821-6523	R	1,015*	1.4
3	US Logistics Inc—*Michael Boyce*	4200 Morganton Rd Ste, Fayetteville NC 28314	910-339-5050	S	728*	.7
4	Somerset Tire Service Inc—*Bill F Caulin*	400 W Main St, Bound Brook NJ 08805	732-356-8500	R	258*	.8
5	Dobbs Tire and Auto Center Inc—*David Dobbs*	1983 Brennan Plz, High Ridge MO 63049	636-677-2101	R	202*	.7
6	McCarthy Tire Service Co—*John McCarthy Sr*	340 Kidder St, Wilkes Barre PA 18702	570-822-3151	R	171*	.6
7	Caliber Collision Centers Inc—*Steve Grimshaw*	17771 Cowan Ave Ste 10, Irvine CA 92614	949-224-0300	S	161*	1.5
8	SpeeDee Oil Change and Tune-Up	159 Hwy 22 E, Madisonville LA 70447	985-624-2261	S	81*	<.1
9	Expressway Lube Centers—*Al Chance*	25 Main St 4th Fl, Hartford CT 06106		R	78*	.2
10	Tires Plus Total Car Care—*Stu Watterson*	2021 Sunnydale Blvd, Clearwater FL 33765	727-796-2322	R	52*	.1
11	Foreign Auto Preparation Services Inc—*Gary LoBue*	371 Craneway St, Newark NJ 07114	973-589-5656	R	30*	.4
12	La Crosse Truck Center Inc—*Stephen T Heuslein*	PO Box 1176, La Crosse WI 54602	608-785-0800	R	18*	.1
13	Collision King Inc—*Pete Sapp*	2529 W Reno Rd, Oklahoma City OK 73107	405-232-5236	R	14*	<.1
14	Slagle Jack L Fire Equipment And Supply Company Inc—*Barry Slagle*	1100 Bill Tuck Hwy, South Boston VA 24592	434-575-7905	R	11*	<.1
15	Beckwith's Car Care—*Lynn Beckwith*	1919 FM 1960 Bypass Ea, Humble TX 77338	281-540-2000	R	10*	<.1
16	Cobra Auto—*Eliad Dela Jr*	6221 N 55th Ave No 7, Glendale AZ 85301	623-915-0674	R	10*	<.1
17	Great American Tire and Auto Service Center—*Renee Lippolis*	5670 Greenwood Plz Blv, Greenwood Village CO 80111	720-346-5000	R	8*	<.1
18	Midway Muffler Inc—*Elden Lattea*	649 Leona St, Elyria OH 44035	440-324-7484	R	8*	<.1
19	Grooms Engines-Parts-Machining Inc—*Jeff Lacroix*	PO Box 101009, Nashville TN 37224	615-242-2410	R	7*	.1
20	Minn-Dak Co—*Ron Ristvedt*	PO Box 11057, Fargo ND 58106	701-293-9133	R	5*	.1
21	P And H Auto Electric Inc—*Lanny Hatfield*	PO Box 25889, Baltimore MD 21224	410-282-1830	R	5*	.1
22	Pelletrox Inc—*Charlie Tindall*	2606 N Newark St Ste A, Portland OR 97217	503-279-2602	R	5*	<.1
23	Eleven Mile Truck Frame and Axle Inc—*Milan Krstich*	1750 E 11 Mile Rd, Madison Heights MI 48071	248-399-7536	R	5*	.1
24	Jones Automotive Engine Inc—*Robert Jones*	817 N Lincoln St, Spokane WA 99201	509-838-3625	R	4*	<.1
25	Grant Iron And Motors Inc—*Ronald Shreve*	3815 N 21st St, Saint Louis MO 63107	314-421-5585	R	4*	<.1
26	Gardner Chevrolet Inc—*John Gardner*	PO Box 668, Manahawkin NJ 08050	609-597-1161	R	4*	<.1
27	Jgb Industries Inc—*Joseph Baker*	1310 Roseneath Rd, Richmond VA 23230	804-864-6800	R	4*	<.1
28	Interstate Truck Equipment Inc—*Robin Baughman*	12821a Salem Ave, Hagerstown MD 21740	301-733-1707	R	3*	<.1
29	Northeast Machine And Motor Supply Inc—*Robert Dee*	71 Two Mile Creek Rd, Tonawanda NY 14150	716-695-3760	R	3*	<.1
30	Salta's Tire Company Inc—*William Salta*	PO Box 69, Laconia NH 03247	603-524-9030	R	3*	<.1
31	Bonded Rebuilders Inc—*Thomas Abruzese*	29 Agar St, Yonkers NY 10701	914-965-6000	R	3*	<.1
32	H and H Diesel Service Inc—*Jackie Holmes*	407 Porter Way Unit A, Milton WA 98354	253-922-8786	R	3*	<.1
33	Jlg Enterprises Inc—*Darla Greene*	1401 Harding Ct, Indianapolis IN 46217	317-784-3740	R	2*	<.1
34	Quality Cylinder Head Repair Corp—*Jeff Learn*	PO Box 425, West Sacramento CA 95691	916-371-4302	R	2*	<.1
35	Dover's Cylinder Head Service Inc—*Earl Dover*	2929 Calhoun Ave, Chattanooga TN 37407	423-624-5161	R	2*	<.1
36	Berger and Sons Inc—*Jesse Berger*	43320 N Gratiot Ave, Clinton Township MI 48036	586-468-6301	R	2*	<.1
37	Wagamon Brothers Inc—*Perry Wagamon*	3719 3rd St Ne, Minneapolis MN 55421	763-789-7227	R	2*	<.1
38	Gregg Bruce Auto and Performance—*Gregg Bruce*	601 High St, Baldwin KS 66006	785-594-4088	R	2*	<.1
39	Continental Diesel Inc—*Tony Arellano*	2734 W Palm Ln, Phoenix AZ 85009	602-278-7270	R	2*	<.1
40	Curts Truck And Diesel Service—*Curtis Johnson*	370 24th Ave Nw, Owatonna MN 55060	507-451-1326	R	2*	<.1
41	Creek Diesel Services Inc—*Mike Bronson*	2490 Van Ommen Dr, Holland MI 49424	616-399-2970	R	2*	<.1

TOTALS: SIC 7538 General Automotive Repair Shops
Companies: 41 — 4,958 — 9.2

7539 Automotive Repair Shops Nec

Rank	Company Name—*Executive Officer*	Address, City, State, Zip	Phone	Type	Fin	Empls
1	Walt's Radiator and Muffler Inc—*Doug Danstrom*	2588 Pacific Hwy E, Tacoma WA 98424	253-531-2200	R	109*	.2
2	Millennium Plastics Technologies LLC—*Mario Murillo*	1305 Henry Brennan Dr, El Paso TX 79936	915-834-2700	R	67*	.1
3	Southeastern Trailer and Container Repairs Inc—*Angel Dones*	7500 Nw 82nd Pl, Medley FL 33166	305-670-1033	R	32*	.1
4	CARSTAR Franchise Systems Inc—*Richard Hunter Cross III*	8400 W 110th Ste 200, Overland Park KS 66210	913-451-1294	R	8*	<.1
5	Gcm Medical—*Seanus Meaghr*	1350 Atlantic St, Union City CA 94587	510-475-0404	R	8*	.1
6	All Florida Staffing Inc—*Dave Swann*	2111 Garden St, Titusville FL 32796	321-269-6700	R	4*	.1
7	Hill John M Machine Company Inc—*Bart Hill*	233 Farview Rd, Hamburg PA 19526	610-562-8690	R	4*	<.1
8	Wegner Motor Sports Inc—*Carl Wegner*	N2258 Hilltop Rd, Markesan WI 53946	920-394-3557	R	3*	<.1
9	Landmark Signs and Electrical Maintenance Corp—*Anthony Calvano*	1501 Broadway Ste 704, New York NY 10036	212-262-3699	R	3*	<.1
10	Kranz Automotive Body Co—*Eugene Kohler*	300 Russell Blvd, Saint Louis MO 63104	314-776-3787	R	2*	<.1
11	Croft Trailer Supply Inc—*Sandra Jones*	PO Box 300320, Kansas City MO 64130	816-861-1001	R	2*	<.1
12	Metro Trailer Repair Company Inc—*Orlando Scelsi*	904 30th St N, Birmingham AL 35203	205-323-2877	R	2*	<.1
13	Caldwell Corp—*Joseph Caldwell*	PO Box 230, Emporium PA 15834	814-486-3493	R	2*	<.1
14	Action Equipment Co—*Mark Ellingson*	2350 Arrowhead Rd, Moundridge KS 67107	620-345-2811	R	2*	<.1
15	GS Automation Builder Inc—*George Solomon*	35740 Stanley Dr, Sterling Heights MI 48312	586-979-1850	R	2*	<.1
16	Globe Mechanical and Electrical LLC—*Matthew Barlow*	PO Box 541, Fredonia AZ 86022		R	2*	.1
17	Tri-Gon Precision Inc—*George Gonzales*	820 Sahwatch St, Colorado Springs CO 80903	719-473-2635	R	1*	<.1
18	North Star Auto Electric Inc—*Brett Norton*	PO Box 867, Macedon NY 14502	315-986-4451	R	1*	<.1
19	Atlas Spring Service—*Ernesto Herrera*	3535 E 7th St, Austin TX 78702	512-385-3661	R	1*	<.1

Rank	Company Name—*Executive Officer*	Address, City, State, Zip	Phone	Type	Fin	Empls
20	Hurst Auto-Truck Electric Ltd—*Thomas Hurst*	9004 Madison Ave, Cleveland OH 44102	216-961-1800	R	<1*	<.1
21	Ebs Auto Electric Inc—*Kevin Sexton*	901 Lakeview Rd, Clearwater FL 33756	727-461-1488	R	<1*	<.1
22	Badger State Rebuilders Inc—*Dean Lusk*	PO Box 172, New Franken WI 54229	920-866-9347	R	<1*	<.1

TOTALS: SIC 7539 Automotive Repair Shops Nec
Companies: 22 — 253 — 1.0

7542 Car Washes

1	Colonial Full Service Car Wash Inc—*Mark Norega*	3022 S Cooper, Arlington TX 76015	817-467-0623	S	53*	<.1
2	Super Wash Inc—*Robert D Black*	PO Box 188, Morrison IL 61270	815-772-2111	R	12*	.1
3	Beheydt's Auto Wrecking—*Maxwell Beheydt*	15475 Serfass Rd, Doylestown OH 44230	330-658-6109	R	1*	.1
4	Gentle Touch Auto Wash—*Danny Martin*	1921 Sherwood Way, San Angelo TX 76901	325-653-4860	R	1*	<.1

TOTALS: SIC 7542 Car Washes
Companies: 4 — 68 — .2

7549 Automotive Services Nec

1	Kelley Automotive Group Inc—*Thomas Kelley*	633 Ave of Autos, Fort Wayne IN 46804	260-434-4700	R	850*	1.2
2	Bridestone/Firestone Research—*Gary Garfield*	1200 Firestone Pkwy, Akron OH 44317	330-379-7000	D	475*	1.1
3	United Road Services Inc—*Michael A Wysocki*	10701 Middlebelt Rd, Romulus MI 48174	734-947-7900	S	332*	2.3
4	McCormick Paints—*Casey McCormick*	2355 Lewis Ave, Rockville MD 20851	301-770-3235	S	156*	.2
5	LMS International—*Marc Boonen*	5755 New King St, Troy MI 48098	248-952-5664	R	100*	.5
6	Lube Stop Inc—*Jerry Forstner*	140 Sheldon Rd, Berea OH 44017	440-891-2378	R	83*	.3
7	Allied Gardens Towing Inc	3821 Calle Fortunada #, San Diego CA 92123	619-563-4060	S	69*	.2
8	Smith-System Driver Improvement Institute Inc—*Tony Douglas*	2201 Brookhollow Plz D, Arlington TX 76006	817-652-6969	R	38*	.1
9	Interstate National Dealer Services Inc—*Shawn Feterstone*	6120 Powersferry Rd NW, Atlanta GA 30339	678-894-3500	R	32*	.1
10	Ackerman Wrecker Service Inc—*Glenn Smith*	900 11th St, Macon GA 31201	478-742-0221	R	18*	<.1
11	Randy's High Country Towing Inc—*Randy Schranz*	1205 E Las Vegas St, Colorado Springs CO 80903	719-596-6067	R	17*	<.1
12	Ziebart International Corp—*Thomas Wolfe*	PO Box 1290, Troy MI 48007	248-588-4100	R	16*	.1
13	Arrow Wrecker Service Inc—*Al Muzny*	700 N Villa Ave, Oklahoma City OK 73107	405-943-1800	R	16*	<.1
14	Coleman's Towing and Recovery Inc—*Jeffrey I Badgley*	1871 Birchwood Dr, Troy MI 48083	248-680-0540	R	16*	<.1
15	Automotive Testing And Development Services Inc—*Larry Smith*	400 Etiwanda Ave, Ontario CA 91761	909-390-1100	R	14*	.2
16	Central Valley Towing Inc—*Eric Foster*	8240 14th Ave, Sacramento CA 95826	916-457-4000	R	13*	<.1
17	Allied Towing and Recovery Inc—*Harold Gibble*	4937 S 45th W Ave, Tulsa OK 74107	918-437-2835	R	10*	<.1
18	Speedemissions Inc—*Richard A Parlontieri*	1015 Tyrone Rd Ste 220, Tyrone GA 30290	770-306-7667	P	9	.1
19	Robbins Auto Top LLC	PO Box 5567, Oxnard CA 93031	805-604-3200	R	8*	.1
20	Grease Monkey International Inc—*Rex Utsler*	7100 E Belleview Ave S, Greenwood Village CO 80111	303-308-1660	R	8*	.1
21	Cedar Bluff 24 Hour Towing Inc—*Randy Hinton*	623 Simmons Rd, Knoxville TN 37932	865-675-4918	R	7*	<.1
22	Trailstar Manufacturing Corp—*David Barker*	PO Box 3820, Alliance OH 44601	330-821-9900	R	5*	.1
23	Golden West Towing Equipment Inc—*Donna Coe*	4920 E La Palma Ave, Anaheim CA 92807	714-979-6000	R	5*	<.1
24	Bob Vincent and Sons Wrecker Service Inc—*Hubert Mosby*	4611 Pinewood Rd, Louisville KY 40218	502-961-0555	R	4*	<.1
25	Team Towing and Recovery Inc—*William Gratzianna*	2139 N Mannheim Rd, Melrose Park IL 60164	847-451-8001	R	3*	<.1
26	Anderson Towing Service Inc—*John Klitzke*	PO Box 285, Walla Walla WA 99362	509-525-3693	R	2*	<.1
27	Gresham Driving Aids Inc—*Gerald Gresham*	PO Box 930334, Wixom MI 48393	248-624-1533	R	1*	<.1
28	Interstate Truckers Inc—*Lou Louiso*	16053 Myakka Rd, Sarasota FL 34240	941-322-1669	R	1*	<.1

TOTALS: SIC 7549 Automotive Services Nec
Companies: 28 — 2,309 — 7.0

7622 Radio & T.V. Repair

1	Contec—*Frank Hickey*	1011 State St, Schenectady NY 12307	518-382-8000	R	66*	.5
2	Electra-Sound Inc—*Robert Masa Jr*	5260 Commerce Parkway, Parma OH 44130	216-433-9600	R	26*	.1
3	Intertech Digital Entertainment Inc—*James Stephen*	6523 S Transit Rd, Lockport NY 14094	716-625-8555	R	8*	.1
4	Television-Electronics Co—*Gwendolyn Mitchell-Beard*	PO Box 93726, Atlanta GA 30377	404-875-9316	R	5*	<.1
5	Glessner Protective Services Inc—*Neil Glessner*	1216 Sherman Ave, Hagerstown MD 21740	301-797-1280	R	4*	<.1
6	Aerotronics Inc—*Steve Vold*	1651 Aviation Pl, Billings MT 59105	406-259-5006	R	4*	<.1
7	Tfmcomm Inc—*Douglas Flair*	125 Sw Jackson St, Topeka KS 66603	785-233-2343	R	3*	<.1
8	Vid-Air Services Inc—*Mario Irizarry*	120 Craft Ave, Inwood NY 11096	516-239-5400	R	2*	<.1
9	Action Antenna Service Company Inc—*Roger Spurgeon*	4128 Washington Blvd, Baltimore MD 21227	410-242-0440	R	1*	<.1
10	Freeland Products Inc—*Joel Freeland*	75412 Hwy 25, Covington LA 70435	985-893-1243	R	1*	<.1
11	Hoyt Stereo Inc—*Robert Wing*	1927 Beach Blvd, Jacksonville Beach FL 32250	904-247-9001	R	1*	<.1
12	Caldwell Electronics Inc—*James Caldwell*	988 Cherokee Rd, Alexander City AL 35010	256-329-8000	R	<1*	<.1

TOTALS: SIC 7622 Radio & T.V. Repair
Companies: 12 — 119 — 1.0

7623 Refrigeration Services Repair

1	Grunau Corp—*Larry Loomis*	1100 W Anderson Ct, Oak Creek WI 53154	414-216-6900	R	200*	.8
2	MISCOR Group Ltd—*Michael P Moore*	800 Nave Rd SE, Massillon OH 44646	330-830-3500	P	46	.3
3	Magnetech Industrial Services Inc—*Michael P Moore* MISCOR Group Ltd	800 Nave Rd SE, Massillon OH 44646	330-830-3500	S	27*	.3
4	Tampa Bay Systems Sales Inc—*Douglas Cohn*	PO Box 18547, Tampa FL 33679	813-877-8251	R	22*	.2
5	Century Service Systems Inc—*Gary Langbaum*	1055 Sw 30th Ave, Deerfield Beach FL 33442	954-421-3344	R	19*	.2
6	Western Allied Service Co—*Steve Kieve*	PO Box 3628, Santa Fe Springs CA 90670	562-944-6341	R	15*	.3
7	Pride Air Conditioning and Appliance Inc—*Barry Pearl*	2150 Nw 18th St, Pompano Beach FL 33069	954-977-7433	R	13*	.1
8	Tecogen Inc—*Robert Panora*	45 1st Ave, Waltham MA 02451	781-466-6400	R	12*	.1
9	Ctou Inc—*Mike Deputy*	PO Box 25415, Salt Lake City UT 84125	801-973-4040	R	11*	<.1
10	Wiegold and Sons Inc—*Dave Borowski*	4380 Enterprise Ave, Naples FL 34104	239-597-8774	R	8*	<.1
11	Ascosta Heating and Cooling—*Ezequiel Acosta*	3915 Stuart Andrew Blv, Charlotte NC 28217	704-357-6900	R	4*	<.1
12	Air-Rite Inc—*David Harris*	1290 W 117th St, Cleveland OH 44107	216-228-8200	R	4*	<.1
13	Compressor Parts and Repair Inc—*Robert Harwood*	1501 Peck Rd, El Monte CA 91733	626-444-4521	R	3*	<.1
14	Fraley and Quattlebaum Inc—*Robert Quattlebaum*	PO Box 3365, Columbia SC 29230	803-754-4831	R	2*	<.1
15	Allegheny Refrigeration Service Co—*Robert Radzevich*	1228 Brighton Rd, Pittsburgh PA 15233	412-321-6626	R	2*	<.1
16	Sahara Air Conditioning and Heating Inc—*Robert Haas*	2718 S Highland Dr, Las Vegas NV 89109	702-796-9677	R	2*	<.1
17	Houston Hermetics Inc—*Doyle Janner*	4443 W 12th St, Houston TX 77055	713-681-0685	R	1*	<.1

TOTALS: SIC 7623 Refrigeration Services Repair
Companies: 17 — 391 — 2.4

7629 Electrical Repair Shops Nec

1	Communications Test Design Inc—*Leo Parsons*	1373 Enterprise Dr, West Chester PA 19380	610-436-5203	R	741*	3.8
2	GE Capital Rail Services—*Joe Lattazio*	161 N Clark St 7th Fl, Chicago IL 60601	312-853-5000	S	153*	1.0

Note: An asterisk (*) indicates an estimated financial figure. The company type code used is as follows: R = Private, P = Public, S = Private Subsidiary, B = Public Subsidiary, D = Division, J = Joint Venture, I = Investment Fund.

COMPANY RANKINGS BY SALES WITHIN 4-DIGIT SIC

Rank	Company Name—Executive Officer	Address, City, State, Zip	Phone	Type	Fin	Empls
3	SIMCO Electronics—Lee M Kenna Jr	1178 Bordeaux Dr, Sunnyvale CA 94089	408-734-9750	R	59*	.3
4	Wilhelmsen Callenberg Inc—Avraham Tal	4130 Sw 28th Way, Fort Lauderdale FL 33312	954-585-5800	R	25*	.1
5	Electrical South Inc—Jeff George	PO Box 49239, Greensboro NC 27419	336-668-4848	S	25*	.2
6	AJR International Inc—James Oesterrich	300 Regency Dr, Glendale Heights IL 60139	630-832-0222	R	24*	.1
7	Peek Traffic Signal Maintenance Inc—Moshe Meidar	2283 Via Burton St, Anaheim CA 92806	714-563-4000	S	21*	.1
8	Dbk Concepts Inc—Danny Katz	12905 Sw 129th Ave, Miami FL 33186	305-596-7226	R	12*	.1
9	International Systems Of America LLC—Michale Apperson	1812 Cargo Ct, Louisville KY 40299	502-499-9485	R	11*	.1
10	Longo Electrical-Mechanical Inc—Joseph Longo	PO Box 511, Wharton NJ 07885	973-537-0400	R	11*	.1
11	Illinois Electric Works Inc—Dale Hamil	2161 Adams St, Granite City IL 62040	618-451-6900	R	10*	.1
12	Walco Electric Co—Ellis Waldman	303 Allens Ave, Providence RI 02905	401-467-6500	R	10*	.1
13	Belyea Company Inc—Robert Belyea	2200 Northwood Ave Uni, Easton PA 18045	610-515-8775	R	10*	<.1
14	Test Technology Inc—Joseph Connell	4 E Stow Rd Ste 2, Marlton NJ 08053	856-596-0900	R	9*	.1
15	Central Armature Works Inc—Robert Dorr	1200 3rd St Ne, Washington DC 20002	202-544-0500	R	7*	.1
16	Hansome Energy Systems Inc—Selma Rossen	365 Dalziel Rd, Linden NJ 07036	908-862-9044	R	7*	.1
17	Precision Measurements Inc—Richard Ayala	333 Moffett Park Dr, Sunnyvale CA 94089	408-733-8600	R	6*	.1
18	Hayden Electric Inc—James Hayden	561 Sw 9th Ter, Pompano Beach FL 33069	954-946-9220	R	6*	.1
19	Applied Dynamics Corp—David Manning	36 Butternut St, Greenfield MA 01301	413-774-7268	R	6*	<.1
20	D and S Communications Inc—Jason Kaubasak	1355 N Mclean Blvd, Elgin IL 60123	847-468-8082	R	6*	.1
21	Thompson Electric Service Inc—Gary Thompson	70 River Rd, Logan WV 25601	304-752-6070	R	5*	.1
22	Midwest Service Center LLC—Peter Tournis	408 S Shelby St, Hobart IN 46342	219-942-8585	R	5*	.1
23	Straton Industries Inc—Edward Cremin	180 Surf Ave, Stratford CT 06615	203-375-4488	R	5*	.1
24	Usherwood Business Equipment Inc—Louis Usherwood	1005 W Fayette St Ste, Syracuse NY 13204	315-472-0050	R	5*	.1
25	Trans East Inc—L Corning	PO Box 127, Dunn NC 28335	910-892-1081	R	5*	.1
26	On-Site LaserMedic Corp—Gail Solomon	21540 Prairie St Ste D, Chatsworth CA 91311	818-772-6911	R	5	<.1
27	Word Processing Services Inc—Vincent Dellaposta	14500 Byers Rd, Hagerstown MD 21742	301-797-1399	R	4*	.1
28	Aviation Network Services LLC—Del Chapman	2000 Sullivan Rd Ste H, Atlanta GA 30337		R	4*	.1
29	Northwest Transformer Company Inc—Gene Stanley	8 Sw 29th St, Oklahoma City OK 73109	405-636-1454	R	3*	<.1
30	Dolphin Machine Inc—Daniel Dicello	2939 Brooks Park Dr, North Las Vegas NV 89030	702-642-0075	R	3*	<.1
31	Dynamic Office Systems Inc—Patrick Gorman	PO Box 4437, Wichita Falls TX 76308	940-691-3962	R	3*	<.1
32	Electric Service Company Inc—Helen Snyder	5331 Hetzell St, Cincinnati OH 45227	513-271-1752	R	3*	<.1
33	Dte Inc—Rob Nelson	110 Baird Pkwy, Mansfield OH 44903	419-522-3428	R	3*	<.1
34	Sotis Business Equipment Ltd—Michael Curaba	242 W 36th St Rm 801, New York NY 10018	212-227-9838	R	3*	<.1
35	Merrimack Valley Business Machines Inc—Ronald Miller	PO Box 336, North Chelmsford MA 01863	978-251-7877	R	2*	<.1
36	N/C Servo Technology Corp—Eddie Harmon	38422 Webb Dr, Westland MI 48185	734-326-6666	R	2*	<.1
37	Affordable Appliance Repair Inc—Lori Tudhope	PO Box 14157, Bradenton FL 34280	941-795-0097	R	2*	<.1
38	Leak Meter Services Inc—Bruce A Magruder	11925 Ramah Church Rd, Huntersville NC 28078	704-875-1922	R	2*	<.1
39	Printer Wizard—Peter Gaines	1816 Firmona Ave, Redondo Beach CA 90278	310-528-7159	R	2*	<.1
40	Caltronix Inc—Peter Dulmage	100 Town Centre Dr Ste, Rochester NY 14623	585-359-3780	R	2*	<.1
41	Regal Business Machines Inc—Robert Goldsmith	1140 W Washington Blvd, Chicago IL 60607	312-666-4700	R	2*	<.1
42	Leader Business System's Inc—Mark Macken	20900 Hubbell St, Oak Park MI 48237	248-967-1000	R	2*	<.1
43	Kissler and Company Inc—Jerry Kissler	770 Central Blvd, Carlstadt NJ 07072	201-896-9600	R	2*	<.1
44	Aa-Plus Imaging Systems Inc—Tim Cataldi	7610 Philadelphia Rd, Baltimore MD 21237	410-325-2222	R	2*	<.1
45	Conductive Systems Inc—Bruce Page	31 Mozzone Blvd, Taunton MA 02780	508-880-3880	R	2*	<.1
46	Brothers Ii Business Machines Of LI Inc—William Cavallo	1350 Lincoln Ave Ste 1, Holbrook NY 11741	631-585-0684	R	2*	<.1
47	Pacific Electronic Enterprises Inc—Robert Taddeo	7471 Talbert Ave, Huntington Beach CA 92648	714-848-9091	R	1*	<.1
48	Teletec Communications LLC—Marie Golden	PO Box 9436, Columbus MS 39705	662-328-8474	R	1*	<.1
49	Serial Scene Inc—Steven Robinson	410 Wilmot Rd, Deerfield IL 60015	847-948-0224	R	1*	<.1
50	St Lawrence-Troy LLC—Colin Myles	32399 Milton Ave, Madison Heights MI 48071	248-585-7733	R	1*	<.1
51	Advanced Teleco USA Inc—Rick Bowman	29842 Cabo Del Oeste, Highland CA 92346	909-425-1233	R	1*	<.1
52	Partners of Progress Inc (Troy Michigan)—Linda Stoup	999 Chicago Rd, Troy MI 48083	248-733-9944	R	1*	<.1
53	Tricounty Business Machines—Steve Holder	125 Turner St, Southern Pines NC 28387	910-692-4374	R	1*	<.1
54	Interface Logic Systems Inc—Eli Sneward	3311 E Livingston Ave, Columbus OH 43227	614-236-8388	R	1*	<.1
55	Transtel Group Inc—Reiner Gerdes	5555 Okbrook Pkwy Ste, Norcross GA 30093	770-368-8343	R	1*	<.1
56	GFA Electronics Inc—Bill Allen	205 Overby Dr, Antioch TN 37013	615-781-2443	R	1*	<.1
57	Motion-Tronix Inc—Truman Jarva	7265 Jurupa Ave, Riverside CA 92504	951-358-0777	R	1*	<.1
58	Hartel Industries Inc—Henry Dodson	9449 Maltby Rd Ste 1, Brighton MI 48116	810-220-2121	R	<1*	<.1
59	Instrument And Control Systems Inc—Ira Martin	10088 6th St Ste F, Rancho Cucamonga CA 91730	909-987-4488	R	<1*	<.1
60	Instrument Control Company LLC	2633 Louisiana Ave S, Saint Louis Park MN 55426	952-285-4202	R	<1*	<.1

TOTALS: SIC 7629 Electrical Repair Shops Nec
Companies: 60

					1,246	7.4

7631 Watch, Clock & Jewelry Repair

Rank	Company Name—Executive Officer	Address, City, State, Zip	Phone	Type	Fin	Empls
1	Peoples Jewelry Company Inc—David Perlmutter	245 23rd St, Toledo OH 43604	419-241-4191	R	10*	.4

7641 Reupholstery & Furniture Repair

Rank	Company Name—Executive Officer	Address, City, State, Zip	Phone	Type	Fin	Empls
1	Raw Skate Parks Inc—Robert Fisher	1640 Berryessa Rd Ste, San Jose CA 95133	408-437-1700	R	4*	<.1

7692 Welding Repair

Rank	Company Name—Executive Officer	Address, City, State, Zip	Phone	Type	Fin	Empls
1	JV Industrial Companies Ltd—John Durham	4040 Red Bluff Rd, Pasadena TX 77503	713-568-2600	R	163*	2.5
2	Industry Products Co—Linda Cleveland	500 W Statler Rd, Piqua OH 45356	937-778-0585	R	36*	.4
3	Miller Welding And Machine Co—David Miller	PO Box G, Brookville PA 15825	814-849-3061	R	26*	.2
4	Johnstown Welding And Fabrication Inc—William Polacek	PO Box 1286, Johnstown PA 15907	814-539-6922	R	26*	.3
5	Major Tool And Machine Inc—J Weyreter	1458 E 19th St, Indianapolis IN 46218	317-636-6433	R	23*	.3
6	Bay Area Industrial Contractors LP—Chris Morgin	PO Box 966, La Porte TX 77572	281-471-0400	R	14*	.2
7	Magic Metals Inc—Garry Griggs	3401 Bay St, Union Gap WA 98903	509-453-1690	R	12*	.1
8	WALCO Tool and Engineering—William Bucciarelli	18954 Airport Rd, Lockport IL 60441	815-834-0225	R	11*	.1
9	Amc Manufacturing Inc—Kevin Koepp	10584 Middle Ave, Elyria OH 44035	440-458-5165	R	11*	.1
10	Mah Machine Co—Martin Hozjan	3301 S Central Ave, Cicero IL 60804	708-656-1826	R	10*	.1
11	Ebtec Corp—John Leveille	120 Shoemaker Ln, Agawam MA 01001	413-786-0393	R	10*	.1
12	Byron Products Inc—Mark Byron	3781 Port Union Rd, Fairfield OH 45014	513-870-9111	R	8*	.1
13	Cumberland Machine Company Inc—Raymond Lane	1305 4th Ave N, Nashville TN 37208	615-255-7373	R	7*	.1
14	K and R Enterprises I Inc—Karl Renner	28128 Gray Barn Ln, Lake Barrington IL 60010	847-502-3371	R	6*	.1
15	Hollis Line Machine Company Inc—John Siergiewicz	295 S Merrimack Rd, Hollis NH 03049	603-465-2251	R	6*	.1
16	Ingleside Machine Company Inc—Jan Venomett	1120 Hook Rd, Farmington NY 14425	585-924-3046	R	6*	.1
17	Baron Machine Company Inc—Kim Baron	40 Primrose Dr, Laconia NH 03246	603-524-6800	R	5*	.1
18	Craig Welding And Manufacturing Inc—Donald Craig	5158 N 825 E, Mentone IN 46539	574-353-7912	R	5*	<.1
19	Mack Energy Corporation Welding Shop—Mack Chase	PO Box 960, Artesia NM 88211	575-746-8658	R	5*	.1
20	Jerl Machine Inc—Robert Brossia	11140 Ave Rd, Perrysburg OH 43551	419-873-0270	R	5*	.1
21	Campbell Incorporated Press Repair—Peter Campbell	925 River St, Lansing MI 48912	517-371-1034	R	5*	<.1
22	Welco Services Inc—Robert Cullon	1426 13th Ave, Mcpherson KS 67460	620-241-3000	R	5*	<.1

Rank	Company Name—*Executive Officer*	Address, City, State, Zip	Phone	Type	Fin	Empls
23	Montgomery Machine Company Inc—*Leon Bond*	1005 Mae Dr, Houston TX 77015	713-453-6381	R	4*	.1
24	Acro Manufacturing Corp—*Kenneth Packingham*	5429 N Towne Pl Ne, Cedar Rapids IA 52402	319-393-2537	R	4*	.1
25	Bryant Industrial Maintenance Inc—*Dalton Bryant*	915 Mcentire Ln, Decatur AL 35601	256-353-8643	R	4*	.1
26	Laser Cladding Services Ltd—*Theron Metz*	5675 Guhn Rd, Houston TX 77040		S	4*	<.1
27	Precision Metal Crafters Ltd—*Doug Phillips*	220 Huff Ave Ste 700, Greensburg PA 15601	724-837-2511	R	4*	<.1
28	Production Machine and Tool Co—*Mark Mcmullen*	2450 Burkburnett Rd, Wichita Falls TX 76306	940-592-2186	R	4*	<.1
29	Sumiton Machine Inc—*Floyd Burton*	PO Box 556, Sumiton AL 35148	205-648-3259	R	3*	<.1
30	P and S Machining And Fabrication Inc—*Michael Scoggins*	2900 Tucker St, Burlington NC 27215	336-227-0151	R	3*	<.1
31	Specialty Engineering Corp—*Bruce Miller*	PO Box 245, Dexter MO 63841	573-624-3521	R	3*	<.1
32	Welding Technologies Inc	1975 Delta Dr, Gainesville GA 30501	770-297-6441	D	3*	<.1
33	Creative Mold And Machine Inc—*Ray Lyons*	PO Box 323, Newbury OH 44065	440-564-7545	R	3*	<.1
34	Nashville Welding and Machine Works Inc—*Oscar Ellis*	2356 Firestone Pkwy Ne, Wilson NC 27893	252-243-0113	R	3*	<.1
35	W and M Welding Inc—*Gary Mcmullin*	202 Industrial Rd, Sedalia MO 65301	660-826-3705	R	3*	<.1
36	Hub Machine and Tool Inc—*Sherrill Pettus*	PO Box 1508, Graham TX 76450	940-549-0155	R	2*	<.1
37	Tifton Machine Works Inc—*Roy Jackson*	PO Box 731, Tifton GA 31793	229-382-6406	R	2*	<.1
38	Thornburg Machine and Supply Company Inc—*B Lineberger*	PO Box 981, Lincolnton NC 28093	704-735-5421	R	2*	<.1
39	J and L Welding and Machine Company Inc—*Jeff Amero*	19-25 Arthur St, Gloucester MA 01930	978-283-3388	R	2*	<.1
40	North East Welding And Fabrication Inc—*Leo Roche*	928 Minot Ave, Auburn ME 04210	207-786-2446	R	2*	<.1
41	Hafemeister Machine Corp—*Louis Hafemeister*	PO Box 1048, Neenah WI 54957	920-722-3368	R	2*	<.1
42	LM Gill Welding and Manufacturing LLC—*Francis Benison*	1422 Tolland Tpke, Manchester CT 06042	860-647-9931	R	2*	<.1
43	Emmert Welding And Manufacturing Company Inc—*Stephen Emmert*	23500 E State Rte 78, Independence MO 64056	816-796-4000	R	2*	.2
44	Dubois Production Services Inc—*Kathleen Dubois*	PO Box 209, Comstock Park MI 49321	616-785-0088	R	2*	<.1
45	Plastic Sales and Service Inc—*Ruben Rael*	6870 Woodlawn Ave Ne, Seattle WA 98115	206-524-8312	R	2*	<.1
46	Anderson Welding and Machine Service Inc—*Raymond Anderson*	PO Box 1055, Seminole TX 79360	432-758-5744	R	2*	<.1
47	Rettig Machine Shop Inc—*Franz Rettig*	PO Box 7460, Redlands CA 92375	909-793-7811	R	2*	<.1
48	B-G Machine Inc—*Patrick Wathen*	2990 New Haven Rd, Bardstown KY 40004	502-348-9061	R	2*	<.1
49	Ultima Nashua Industrial Corp—*Anoosh Kia*	1 Pine St Ext 135a, Nashua NH 03060	603-882-8174	R	2*	<.1
50	Allen Tool Phoenix Inc—*Cheryl Maines*	6821 Ellicott Dr, East Syracuse NY 13057	315-463-7533	R	2*	<.1
51	Waggoner Manufacturing Company Inc—*Luther Waggoner*	1065 Hall Rd, Mount Ulla NC 28125	704-278-2000	R	2*	<.1
52	S and T Welding Inc—*Betty Stevens*	PO Box 39, Pineville WV 24874	304-732-7605	R	2*	<.1
53	Electric and Machine Services Inc—*Sam Patterson*	PO Box 2243, Tupelo MS 38803	662-842-2807	R	2*	<.1
54	Alloyweld Inspection Company Inc—*Edward Piecko*	796 Maple Ln, Bensenville IL 60106	630-595-2145	R	2*	<.1
55	Corry Laser Technology Inc—*Scott Brady*	1530 Enterprise Rd, Corry PA 16407	814-664-7212	R	2*	<.1
56	J and J Welding Inc—*Dorothy Smith*	PO Box 579, Mount Vernon IN 47620	812-838-4391	R	1*	<.1
57	Accurate Welding Inc—*Charles Starks*	41301 Production Dr, Harrison Township MI 48045	586-465-5033	R	1*	<.1
58	L and W Machine Corp—*David Little*	3301 Lafayette Blvd, Norfolk VA 23513	757-857-4145	R	1*	<.1
59	Jack Garner and Sons Inc—*Jack Garner*	1901 Landis Rd, Mount Joy PA 17552	717-367-2638	R	1*	<.1
60	Titus Inc—*Thomas Read*	9887 6b Rd, Plymouth IN 46563	574-936-3345	R	1*	<.1
61	Lagasse Works Inc—*Daniel Lagasse*	5 Old Rte 31, Lyons NY 14489	315-946-9202	R	1*	<.1

TOTALS: SIC 7692 Welding Repair
Companies: 61   494   6.3

7694 Armature Rewinding Shops

Rank	Company Name—*Executive Officer*	Address, City, State, Zip	Phone	Type	Fin	Empls
1	Brandon and Clark Inc—*Walton Clark*	3623 Interstate 27, Lubbock TX 79404	806-771-5600	R	102*	.2
2	National Electric Coil Inc—*Robert Barton*	PO Box 370, Columbus OH 43216	614-488-1151	R	30*	.5
3	Western States Machine Co	PO Box 327, Hamilton OH 45012	513-863-4758	R	19*	.1
4	Wazee Company LLC—*Trevor Armstrong*	4224 E B St, Pasco WA 99301	509-547-1691	R	10*	<.1
5	Auburn Armature Inc—*Michael Capocefalo*	PO Box 870, Auburn NY 13021	315-253-9721	R	9*	.1
6	Kiemle-Hankins Co—*Timothy Martindale*	PO Box 507, Toledo OH 43697	419-666-0660	R	9*	.1
7	Bradleys' Inc—*Jimmie Williams*	PO Box 308, Gregory TX 78359	361-882-4381	R	7*	.1
8	Mcbroom Electric Company Inc—*Richard Mcbroom*	800 W 16th St, Indianapolis IN 46202	317-926-3451	R	6*	.1
9	Electric Motor and Supply Inc—*Patrick Illig*	PO Box 152, Altoona PA 16603	814-946-0401	R	6*	<.1
10	Catch and Release Inc—*Michael Schaldecker*	PO Box 10045, Cedar Rapids IA 52410	319-393-1230	R	6*	<.1
11	Warfield Electric Company Inc—*Jerome Warfield*	175 Industry Ave, Frankfort IL 60423	815-469-4094	R	6*	.1
12	Soles Electric Company Inc—*Charles Tucker*	1552 Tulip Ln, Fairmont WV 26554	304-363-2058	R	6*	.1
13	Mid-America Taping and Reeling Inc—*Barbara Pauls*	121 Exchange Blvd, Glendale Heights IL 60139	630-629-6646	R	6*	.1
14	Pennsylvania Electric Motor Service Inc—*Joe Pugliese*	4693 Iroquois Ave, Erie PA 16511	814-898-1555	R	5*	.1
15	Grayson Armature Large Motor Division Inc—*Leon Huggins*	1910 Jasmine Dr, Pasadena TX 77503	713-743-4201	R	5*	.1
16	Hibbs Electromechanical Inc—*Ryan Senter*	1300 Industrial Rd, Madisonville KY 42431	270-821-5216	R	5*	.1
17	Jasper Electric Motors Inc—*Robert Ross*	PO Box 1494, Jasper AL 35502	205-384-6071	R	5*	.1
18	Calumet Armature And Electric LLC—*Hugh Scott*	1050 W 134th St, Riverdale IL 60827	708-841-6880	R	4*	<.1
19	Keystone Acquisition Company Inc—*Christopher Bentz*	2807 Annapolis Rd, Baltimore MD 21230	410-539-1730	R	4*	.1
20	Industrial Maintenances and Engineering Corp—*Robert Robinson*	1531 Jp Hennessy Dr, La Vergne TN 37086	615-641-9474	R	3*	.1
21	Davis Electric Company Inc—*Mark Tarley*	PO Box 1997, Fairmont WV 26555	304-363-8730	R	3*	<.1
22	Red Stick Armature Works Inc—*E Howard*	PO Box 310, Saint Francisville LA 70775	225-635-0443	R	3*	<.1
23	Industrial Motor Service Inc—*David Napier*	PO Box 13378, Anderson SC 29624	864-226-2893	R	3*	<.1
24	Eurton Electric Company Inc—*John Buchanan*	PO Box 2113, Santa Fe Springs CA 90670	562-946-4478	R	3*	<.1
25	MR Glenn Electric Inc—*Michael Glenn*	9700 197th St, Mokena IL 60448	708-479-9200	R	3*	<.1
26	Mid-Ohio Electric Co—*Cynthia Langhirt*	1170 Mckinley Ave, Columbus OH 43222	614-274-8000	R	2*	<.1
27	Hobgood Electric and Machinery Company Inc—*Herbert Hobgood*	PO Box 3249, Columbia SC 29230	803-754-8700	R	2*	<.1
28	Martin Electric Company Inc—*Kenneth Martin*	1504 W Jackson St, El Campo TX 77437	979-543-6421	R	2*	<.1
29	Delmarva Electric Motors and Machine Inc—*Gary Brown*	111 Gordy Rd, Salisbury MD 21804	410-749-1377	R	2*	<.1
30	Southern Electric and Machine Company Inc—*John Meade*	PO Box 419, Narrows VA 24124	540-726-7444	R	2*	<.1
31	Electro-Mechanical Systems Group Inc—*Gregory Barker*	PO Box 503, Grand Island NY 14072	716-297-8484	R	2*	<.1
32	Fife Pearce Electric Co—*Roger Pearce*	20201 Sherwood St, Detroit MI 48234	313-369-2560	R	2*	<.1
33	Lange Electric Company Inc—*Michael Lange*	2626 W Patapsco Ave, Baltimore MD 21230	410-644-3500	R	2*	<.1
34	Huntingdon Electric Motor Service Inc—*Leon Hopkins*	PO Box 542, Huntingdon PA 16652	814-643-3921	R	1*	<.1
35	Harvey Brothers Inc—*Gary Harvey*	2181 Grand Ave, Galesburg IL 61401	309-342-3137	R	1*	<.1
36	Altek Electrical Services Inc—*Karl Koch*	PO Box 262, Princeton IN 47670	812-385-2561	R	1*	<.1

TOTALS: SIC 7694 Armature Rewinding Shops
Companies: 36   285   2.2

7699 Repair Services Nec

Rank	Company Name—*Executive Officer*	Address, City, State, Zip	Phone	Type	Fin	Empls
1	International Airmotive Holding Company Inc—*Hugh McElory*	900 Nolen Dr Ste 100, Grapevine TX 76051	214-956-3000	R	46,008*	1.6
2	Puma Industries Inc—*Yin Lai*	1992 Airways Blvd, Memphis TN 38114	901-744-7979	R	800*	<.1

Note: An asterisk (*) indicates an estimated financial figure. The company type code used is as follows: R = Private, P = Public, S = Private Subsidiary, B = Public Subsidiary, D = Division, J = Joint Venture, I = Investment Fund.

COMPANY RANKINGS BY SALES WITHIN 4-DIGIT SIC

Rank	Company Name—Executive Officer	Address, City, State, Zip	Phone	Type	Fin	Empls
3	Triumph Air Repairs Inc—Elizabeth Rakestraw	4010 S 43rd Pl, Phoenix AZ 85040	602-437-1144	S	449*	.2
4	CMF of Kansas LLC—Fred Adams	625 Ave K, Chase KS 67524	620-938-2300	S	388	1.5
5	L-3 Communications AeroTech LLC—Ed Boyington	555 Industrial Dr S, Madison MS 39110	601-856-2274	S	385*	.5
6	Kone Inc—Vance Tang	1 Kone Ct, Moline IL 61265	309-764-6771	R	273*	4.1
7	Vortex Industries Inc—Mike Kattan	3198-M Airport Loop, Costa Mesa CA 92626	714-434-8000	R	209*	.3
8	Roto-Rooter Inc	255 E 5th St Ste 2500, Cincinnati OH 45202	513-762-6690	S	192	2.4
9	Signal International LLC—Rob Busby	PO Box 7007, Pascagoula MS 39568	228-762-0010	R	180*	2.8
10	U S Tool Grinding Inc—Bruce Williams	701 S Desloge Dr, Desloge MO 63601	573-431-3856	R	161*	.5
11	Trimedx LLC—Greg Ranger	6325 Digital Way Ste 4, Indianapolis IN 46278	317-275-5501	R	148*	.5
12	Aaron's Automotive Products Inc—Keith Wright	2707 N Farm Rd 123, Springfield MO 65803	417-831-5257	S	145*	.8
13	Chalmers and Kubeck—Dennis Kubeck	PO Box 2447, Aston PA 19014	610-494-4300	R	142*	.2
14	First Aviation Services Inc—Aaron Hollander	15 Riverside Ave, Westport CT 06880	203-291-3300	P	129	.2
15	Brake Supply Company Inc—David Koch	5501 Foundation Blvd, Evansville IN 47725	812-467-1000	S	115*	.2
16	Phillips Service Industries Inc—Scott Phillips	11878 Hubbard, Livonia MI 48150	734-853-5000	R	92*	.7
17	Southern Elevator Group Inc—Rodney Pitts	130 O'Conner St, Greensboro NC 27406	336-274-2401	R	71*	.1
18	Sasker Repair—Robert Sasker	27535 460th Ave, Chancellor SD 57015	605-647-5766	R	69*	2.0
19	Columbia Helicopters Inc—Michael Fahey	PO Box 3500, Portland OR 97208	503-678-1222	R	65*	.8
20	Allied Power Group—Keith Marler	10131 Mills Rd, Houston TX 77070	281-444-3535	R	64*	.1
21	Phillips Machine Service Inc—Jack Phillips	367 George St, Beckley WV 25801	304-255-0537	R	63*	.1
22	Logistic Services International Inc—Charlie Johns	6200 Lake Gray Blvd, Jacksonville FL 32244	904-771-2100	R	55*	.5
23	Frank Lill and Son Inc	656 Basket Rd, Webster NY 14580	585-265-0490	R	53*	.1
24	Hoober Inc—Charlie Hoober	PO Box 518, Intercourse PA 17534	717-768-8231	R	48*	.2
25	Rail Systems Inc—Jody Lefort	114 Capital Blvd, Houma LA 70360	985-223-7300	S	45*	<.1
26	GPX Inc (Zelienople Pennsylvania)—David L Greb	60 Progress Ave, Cranberry Township PA 16066	724-779-9000	R	41*	.1
27	Bae Systems Hawaii Shipyards Inc—Roger Kubischta	PO Box 30989, Honolulu HI 96820	808-836-7776	S	40*	.2
28	Schumacher Elevator Co—Marvin Schumacher	PO Box 393, Denver IA 50622	319-984-5676	R	31*	.2
29	Loss Mitigation Services Inc—Don Preston	925 S Hwy 19/24, Paris TX 75462	903-784-3559	R	30*	<.1
30	Exline Inc—Robert Exline	PO Box 1487, Salina KS 67402	785-825-4683	R	26*	.2
31	Tecniflex Inc—Walt Wasyliw	931 N Walnut Ave, Republic MO 65738	417-732-7238	R	24*	.4
32	Perform Air International Inc—Cindy Mcgown	463 S Hamilton Ct, Gilbert AZ 85233	480-610-3500	R	23*	.1
33	Plant Maintenance Service Corp—Robert Baker	PO Box 280883, Memphis TN 38168	901-353-9880	R	21*	.2
34	Scales Industrial Technologies Inc—William Scalchunes	110 Voice Rd, Carle Place NY 11514	516-248-9096	R	20*	.2
35	Four Guys Stainless Tank and Equipment Inc—Alma Lauver	PO Box 90, Meyersdale PA 15552	814-634-8373	R	19*	.1
36	PS Marcato Elevator Inc—David Marcato	4411 11th St, Long Island City NY 11101	718-392-6400	R	18*	.2
37	Stereo Lab Service Inc—Thomas Goodwin	4532 Indianola Ave, Columbus OH 43214	614-268-5500	R	18*	<.1
38	Timken Bearing Inspection Inc—Michael Arnold	4422 Corporate Center, Los Alamitos CA 90720	714-484-2400	S	17*	.1
39	Electric Motor Repair Co—H Kauffman	9100 Yellow Brick Rd H, Baltimore MD 21237	410-467-8080	R	17*	.2
40	Hannon Hydraulics LP—Tami Beckham	625 N Loop 12, Irving TX 75061	972-438-2870	R	16*	.1
41	Atm Solutions Inc—Paul Scott	551 Northland Blvd, Cincinnati OH 45240	513-742-4900	R	15*	.2
42	Southern Elevator Company Inc Southern Elevator Group Inc	130 O'Connor St, Greensboro NC 27406	336-274-2401	S	15*	.1
43	Alfred Conhagen Inc—Alfred Conhagen	2035 State Rte 27 Ste, Edison NJ 08817	732-287-4565	R	14*	.1
44	Peggs Company Inc—John Peggs	PO Box 907, Mira Loma CA 91752	951-360-9170	R	14*	.1
45	Bay Container Repairs Of New Jersey Inc—Alvina Hojnacki	99 Chapel St, Newark NJ 07105	973-589-2188	R	14*	.1
46	Specialty Machine and Supply Inc—Charles Maurice	PO Box 1530, Scott LA 70583	337-232-8198	R	14*	.2
47	F and E Aviation Holdings Inc—Fred Murphy	PO Box 660707, Miami Springs FL 33266	305-871-3758	R	14*	.2
48	Diehl Aerospace Inc—Jean-Noel Barrere	12001 Hwy 280, Sterrett AL 35147	205-678-7101	R	13*	<.1
49	Power Pallet Inc—Sam Donadio	4715 State Hwy 30, Amsterdam NY 12010	518-843-3100	R	13*	.1
50	Total Cleaning Systems—Chad Berges	W145n5800 Shawn Cir, Menomonee Falls WI 53051	262-790-5600	R	13*	.1
51	Helicomb International Inc—William Cole	1402 S 69th E Ave, Tulsa OK 74112	918-835-3999	S	11*	.1
52	Airtek Construction Inc—John Roberts	PO Box 388, Troy AL 36081	334-566-7400	R	11*	.2
53	Besco Inc—Daniel Bowater	6555 Trade Ctr Dr, Jacksonville FL 32254	904-783-4504	R	11*	.1
54	Aero-Mach Laboratories Inc—Charles Perkins	7707 E Funston St, Wichita KS 67207	316-682-7707	R	10*	.1
55	R4 Technical Center North Carolina LLC—Larry Powell	1309 Buck Shoals Rd, Hamptonville NC 27020	336-659-6958	R	10*	.1
56	United Shoe Machinery Corp—Frank Kirby	32 Stevens St, Haverhill MA 01830	978-374-0303	R	10*	.1
57	Firewall Forward Inc—Mark Seader	5212 Cessna Dr, Loveland CO 80538	970-669-6185	R	10*	<.1
58	Offshore Inland Services Of Alabama Inc—Robin Roberts	3521 Brookdale Dr S, Mobile AL 36618	251-479-6081	R	9*	.1
59	Missouri Machinery and Engineering Co—Bruce Fleissig	1228 S 8th St, Saint Louis MO 63104	314-231-9806	R	9*	<.1
60	Ted Levine Drum Co—Ozzie Levine	PO Box 3246, South El Monte CA 91733	626-579-1084	R	9*	.1
61	National Hydraulics Inc—Frank Brush	PO Box 20, Scottdale PA 15683	724-547-9222	R	9*	.1
62	Southern Metal Processing Company Inc—James Ulrey	PO Box 3327, Oxford AL 36203	256-831-8130	R	8*	.1
63	Bristol Manufacturing Corp—Brent Davis	2020 E Dale St, Springfield MO 65803	417-862-3545	R	8*	.1
64	Pallet Consultants Of Georgia Inc—Gustavo Gutierrez	2555 Moreland Ave Se, Atlanta GA 30315	404-622-4500	R	8*	.1
65	Francis Enterprises Inc—Mark Cyphert	PO Box 2284, Morgantown WV 26502	304-296-8331	R	8*	.1
66	Iowa Machinery and Supply Company Inc—Darrell Randall	PO Box 50, Mossville IL 61552	515-288-0123	R	7*	.1
67	Andrew Belmont Sargent Business Products Inc—Charles Andrew	10855 Medallion Dr, Cincinnati OH 45241	513-769-7800	R	7*	.1
68	Zabatt Engine Services Inc—Jose Sabatier	4612 Hwy Ave, Jacksonville FL 32254	904-384-4505	R	7*	.1
69	Industrial Pump Services Of North Carolina Inc—Willard Seguin	PO Box 780, Leland NC 28451	910-371-2711	R	7*	<.1
70	Bonded Filter Co—Matthew Ashwood	304 Oldham St, Nashville TN 37213	615-724-0105	R	7*	.1
71	Magone Marine Service Inc—Daniel Magone	PO Box 920247, Dutch Harbor AK 99692	907-581-1400	R	7*	<.1
72	Allied Valve Inc—James Knox	1019 W Grand Ave, Chicago IL 60642	312-226-1506	R	7*	.1
73	Am Machining Inc—Frank Amador	7422 Walnut Ave, Buena Park CA 90620	714-367-0830	R	7*	<.1
74	Hfw Industries Inc—Jon Watson	PO Box 8, Buffalo NY 14207	716-875-3380	R	6*	.1
75	York Goltens-New Corp—Norman Golten	160 Van Brunt St, Brooklyn NY 11231	718-855-7200	R	6*	.1
76	Nelson Machine and Welding Corp—Gordon Robertson	1206 Parkview Rd, Green Bay WI 54304	920-337-1926	R	6*	<.1
77	Biotronics Inc—Daniel Drawbaugh	1370 Beulah Rd Fl 2, Pittsburgh PA 15235	412-473-6870	S	6*	.1
78	Auxier Welding Inc—Burton Auxier	PO Box 99, Belva WV 26656	304-632-1201	R	6*	.1
79	Ben's Precision Instruments Inc—Robert Overmars	4813 Pacific Hwy E, Fife WA 98424	253-883-5040	R	6*	.1
80	Titan Machine Corp—Carlos Escobar	4211 9th St, Long Island City NY 11101	718-361-7848	R	6*	<.1
81	Allied Crane Inc—David Costa	855 N Parkside Dr, Pittsburg CA 94565	925-427-9200	R	6*	<.1
82	Astrotech Space Operations LP—Thomas B Pickens III	401 Congress Ave, Austin TX 78701	512-485-9530	S	6*	<.1
83	Southern Stainless Equipment Company Inc—Robert Rouse	1400 Hopeman Pkwy, Waynesboro VA 22980	540-943-8000	R	6*	.1
84	Atlas Welding and Boiler Repair Inc—Sanford Blaser	173 Beechwood Ave, New Rochelle NY 10801	718-293-3300	R	6*	.1
85	Melton Sales and Service—John Melton	1723 Jacksonvlle Brlng, Bordentown NJ 08505	609-699-4800	R	6*	.1
86	Hydraulic Service Company Inc—John Short	3215 Victory Blvd, Portsmouth VA 23702	757-487-2513	R	5*	<.1
87	Taylor's Oilfield Manufacturing Inc—Clyde Taylor	PO Box 100, Broussard LA 70518	337-837-4084	R	5*	.1
88	Power Construction and Maintenance Inc—Jk Germaine	PO Box 719, Altavista VA 24517	434-309-1046	R	5*	<.1
89	Speed-O-Tach Inc—Donald Russel	4090 Pke Ln, Concord CA 94520	925-691-4090	R	5*	<.1

Rank	Company Name—*Executive Officer*	Address, City, State, Zip	Phone	Type	Fin	Empls
90	Dalhart R and R Machine Works Inc—*Wade Wood*	PO Box 1330, Dalhart TX 79022	806-244-5686	R	5*	<.1
91	Beverage Control Inc—*James Young*	5060 N Royal Atlanta D, Tucker GA 30084	770-939-9637	R	5*	.1
92	Metso Wyesco Service Center Inc—*Jukka Tiitinen*	PO Box 266, Zachary LA 70791	225-654-5654	R	5*	<.1
93	Rome Ltd—*Michael Weaver*	PO Box 186, Sheldon IA 51201	712-324-5391	R	5*	<.1
94	McCann Electronics—*Gerry McCann*	100 Division St, Metairie LA 70001	504-837-7272	R	5*	<.1
95	Foremost Pump and Well Services LLC—*Roy Jensen*	PO Box 3111, Union Gap WA 98903	509-966-0814	R	5*	<.1
96	Marine Technical Services Inc—*Diane Hawke*	PO Box 1301, San Pedro CA 90733	310-549-8030	R	5*	.1
97	Country Saw And Knife Inc—*Stanley Glista*	PO Box 887, Salem OH 44460	330-332-1611	R	5*	<.1
98	Machinery Maintenance Inc—*Richard Kotecki*	PO Box 1127, La Salle IL 61301	815-223-4058	R	5*	.1
99	Cs Industries Inc—*Terry White*	2375 Stonebridge Cir S, West Bend WI 53095	262-334-7777	R	5*	.1
100	Ditch Witch Of Illinois Inc—*Earl Harbaugh*	124 N Schmale Rd, Carol Stream IL 60188	630-665-5600	R	5*	.1
101	FMG Enterprises—*Gary Govola*	1125 Memorex Dr, Santa Clara CA 95050	408-982-0110	R	5*	<.1
102	Muncie Reclamation And Supply Company—*Robert Heaney*	3720 S Madison St, Muncie IN 47302	765-288-1971	R	5*	.1
103	Saunders Engine And Equipment Company Inc—*John Fitzgerald*	PO Box 1790, Orange Beach AL 36561	251-981-3700	R	5*	.1
104	Dover Hydraulics Inc—*Robert Sensel*	PO Box 2239, Dover OH 44622	330-364-1617	R	5*	.1
105	H and S Valve Inc—*Les Littlejohn*	6704 N County Rd W, Odessa TX 79764	432-362-0486	R	5*	.1
106	Action Door Repair Corp—*Joseph Jaifre*	5420 Malabar St, Huntington Park CA 90255	323-583-1026	R	5*	<.1
107	Interstate Cash Register Inc—*Scott Doody*	961 Norfolk Sq, Norfolk VA 23502	757-461-1600	R	5*	<.1
108	Red Top Rentals Inc—*John Dowden*	1815 Kentucky Ave, Indianapolis IN 46221	317-686-1100	R	4*	<.1
109	Becker Machine Company Inc—*Mark Becker*	N51w13270 Brahm Ct, Menomonee Falls WI 53051	262-781-6009	R	4*	<.1
110	Shannahan Crane and Hoist Inc—*William Shannahan*	PO Box 790379, Saint Louis MO 63179	314-965-2800	R	4*	<.1
111	Tri State Business Machines Inc—*Jim Jambois*	PO Box 1807, La Crosse WI 54602	608-781-2100	R	4*	<.1
112	Sweco Products Inc—*Maria Ziegenmeyer*	PO Box 259, Sutter CA 95982	530-673-8949	R	4*	<.1
113	Process Systems and Components Inc—*Mark Townshend*	5321 W Crenshaw St, Tampa FL 33634	813-888-6300	R	4*	<.1
114	Harter Industries Inc—*William Hinski*	401 W Gemini Dr, Tempe AZ 85283	480-345-9595	R	4*	<.1
115	Fraser's Boiler Service Inc—*Bruce Fraser*	PO Box 13186, San Diego CA 92170	619-233-0195	R	4*	<.1
116	Mcginnis Brothers Inc—*Roger Hinchman*	PO Box 2047, Huntington WV 25720	304-523-6428	R	4*	<.1
117	Kuhar Metallizing Company Inc—*Gary Montgomery*	3824 Fremont Ave, Kansas City MO 64129	816-921-3400	R	4*	<.1
118	Nuell Inc—*Darlene Holsclaw*	PO Box 55, Warsaw IN 46581	574-453-4900	R	4*	<.1
119	Paragon Technologies Inc (Warren Michigan)—*Leonard Yurkovic*	5775 Ten Mile Rd, Warren MI 48091	586-756-9100	R	4*	<.1
120	Press Repair Engineering Sales And Services Inc—*Jack Miner*	PO Box 1381, Morristown TN 37816	423-586-2406	R	4*	<.1
121	Lead Screws International Inc—*David Busch*	2101 Precision Dr, Traverse City MI 49686	231-947-4124	R	4*	<.1
122	National Recovery Technologies Inc—*Ed Sommer*	566 Mainstream Dr Ste, Nashville TN 37228	615-734-6400	R	4*	<.1
123	IPC Inc—*Carl Padilla*	505 Rd 350, Farmington NM 87401	505-632-0977	R	4*	<.1
124	General Conveyor Inc—*William Braund*	13385 Estelle St, Corona CA 92879	951-734-3460	R	4*	<.1
125	Power Plant Service Inc—*Donald Akey*	2500 W Jefferson Blvd, Fort Wayne IN 46802	260-432-6716	R	4*	<.1
126	Signal Machine Company Inc—*Thomas Hall*	PO Box 5427, Fort Oglethorpe GA 30742	706-866-9885	R	4*	<.1
127	Padgett-Swann Machinery Company Inc—*Tad Humphreys*	5128 36th Ave S, Tampa FL 33619	813-247-3478	R	4*	<.1
128	B and A Marine Company Inc—*Bill Crokos*	75 Huntington St, Brooklyn NY 11231	718-875-6700	R	4*	.1
129	Matrix Machine And Repair Inc—*Shawn Lednick*	2901 Danese St, Jacksonville FL 32206	904-633-5001	R	4*	<.1
130	Renew Valve and Machine Company Inc—*Tim Rorick*	PO Box 298, Carleton MI 48117	734-654-2201	R	3*	<.1
131	Popp Machine and Tool Inc—*James Popp*	1463 S Brook St, Louisville KY 40208	502-635-5259	R	3*	<.1
132	Apph Wichita Inc—*Dan Kilby*	1445 S Sierra Dr, Wichita KS 67209	316-943-5752	R	3*	.1
133	Ken Cal Ltd—*Steve Simonson*	18150 E 32nd Pl Ste E, Aurora CO 80011	303-698-2249	R	3*	<.1
134	Armstrong Services Inc—*Pat Armstrong*	2409 Princeton Dr Ne, Albuquerque NM 87107	505-345-6390	R	3*	<.1
135	Hydraulic Sales and Service Inc—*Cleveland Jones*	PO Box 260188, Miami FL 33126	305-633-4677	R	3*	<.1
136	Emerald Tool Inc—*Gary Walker*	PO Box 80312, Seattle WA 98108	206-767-5670	R	3*	<.1
137	Wolfe Machinery Co—*Michelle Wolfe*	6300 Nw Beaver Dr, Johnston IA 50131	515-270-2766	R	3*	<.1
138	Bama Fluid Power Inc—*A Mc Vay*	540 Carson Rd N, Birmingham AL 35217	205-520-1220	R	3*	<.1
139	Bay Diesel Corp—*J Wheeler*	PO Box 7009, Portsmouth VA 23707	757-485-0075	R	3*	<.1
140	Grand Rapids Machine Repair Inc—*Ronald Brow*	4000 Eastern Ave Se, Grand Rapids MI 49508	616-245-9102	R	3*	<.1
141	Smith Hamilton Shop Inc—*John Mac Laren*	4401 Nw 37th Ave, Miami FL 33142	305-633-6372	R	3*	<.1
142	Alpha Services Ii Inc—*Richard Elliott*	PO Box 1045, Marion IL 62959	618-997-9999	R	3*	<.1
143	Hub Energy Services Inc—*Willie Hess*	PO Box 192, Belle Chasse LA 70037	504-392-9321	R	3*	<.1
144	Industrial Machine and Tool Company Inc—*Robert Chilton*	88 Polk Ave, Nashville TN 37210	615-242-2596	R	3*	<.1
145	Dyno One Inc—*Bill Willis*	14671 N 250 W, Edinburgh IN 46124	812-526-0500	R	3*	<.1
146	Tulsa Aircraft Engines—*Sam Thompson*	9311 E 44th St N, Tulsa OK 74115	918-838-8532	R	3*	<.1
147	Graphic Tech Service LLC—*Don Nichols*	17047 Ohara Dr, Port Charlotte FL 33948	941-855-0024	R	3*	<.1
148	Mid-South Engine Systems Inc—*Christophe Lytle*	5145 Taravella Rd, Marrero LA 70072	504-347-2470	R	3*	<.1
149	Glm Inc—*Mike Schilling*	420 N Willow St, Kenai AK 99611	907-283-7556	R	3*	<.1
150	Dewar of Virginia Inc—*Shelby Akers*	PO Box 125, Falls Mills VA 24613	276-322-5322	R	3*	<.1
151	Evansville Association For The Blind Inc—*Karla Horrell*	PO Box 6445, Evansville IN 47719	812-422-1181	R	3*	.1
152	Waters Equipment Company Inc—*Judy Waters*	PO Box 5179, Maryville TN 37802	865-982-6256	R	3*	<.1
153	American Diesel Equipment Inc—*Joaquin Sampedro*	604 Time Saver Ave, Harahan LA 70123	504-734-5300	R	3*	<.1
154	Disgraf Services Inc—*William Sharp*	720 N Agnes Ave, Kansas City MO 64120	816-474-3884	R	3*	<.1
155	Kasgro Rail Corp—*Joe Crawford*	121 Rundle Rd, New Castle PA 16102	724-658-9061	R	3*	.2
156	Tech Pro Inc—*John Putman*	3030 Gilchrist Rd, Akron OH 44305	330-923-3546	R	3*	<.1
157	Rocky Mountain Tool Manufacturing Inc—*Michael Lemon*	50 E 200 N, Hyrum UT 84319	435-245-5021	R	3*	<.1
158	Saw Menominee And Supply Company Inc—*Felix Mroz*	900 16th St, Menominee MI 49858	906-863-2609	R	3*	<.1
159	Five Star Hydraulics—*Timothy Bowgren*	1210 Crisman Rd, Portage IN 46368	219-762-1619	R	3*	<.1
160	Torque-A-Matic Inc—*Michael Hall*	PO Box 14106, Spokane Valley WA 99214	509-928-0535	R	3*	<.1
161	Lemac Mine Service—*Lester Mullens*	166 Distributor Dr, Morgantown WV 26501	304-292-6163	R	3*	<.1
162	Colley Elevator Co—*Ray Zomchek*	226 William St, Bensenville IL 60106	630-766-7230	R	3*	<.1
163	Graphic Systems Services Inc—*Daniel Green*	400 S Pioneer Blvd, Springboro OH 45066	937-746-0708	R	2*	<.1
164	Baker Valve and Machine Service Inc—*Mart Richardson*	PO Box 564, Zachary LA 70791	225-654-0928	R	2*	<.1
165	Princeton Machinery Service Inc—*William Stafford*	171 Athens Rd, Princeton WV 24740	304-425-4991	R	2*	<.1
166	Anchor Sales And Service Company Inc—*Dave Whistance*	106 W 31st St, Independence MO 64055	816-836-5900	R	2*	<.1
167	Florida Plating and Machining Inc—*Joan Lawson*	1555 Centennial Blvd, Bartow FL 33830	863-533-8868	R	2*	<.1
168	Coastal Environmental Operations Inc—*Randy Boudreaux*	PO Box 6062, Lake Charles LA 70606	337-775-5881	R	2*	<.1
169	USA Services Inc—*James Beale*	PO Box 12103, Norfolk VA 23541	757-855-2233	R	2*	<.1
170	Allegheny Manufacturing and Electrical Service Inc—*Andrew Stager*	107 Station St, Johnstown PA 15905	814-288-1597	R	2*	<.1
171	Carr Enterprises Inc—*John Car*	PO Box 1329, Longview TX 75606	903-753-8421	R	2*	<.1
172	Sara Mana Business Products Inc—*James Dean*	1618 Barbara Rd, Sarasota FL 34240	941-379-9999	R	2*	<.1
173	Bailey Machine Co—*Thomas Bailey*	1516 Morrell Ave, Connellsville PA 15425	724-628-4730	R	2*	<.1
174	Ruch Carbide Burs Inc—*Robert Huch*	PO Box 252, Willow Grove PA 19090	215-657-3660	R	2*	<.1
175	Wisconsin Hydraulics Inc—*Kenneth Kersten*	1666 S Johnson Rd, New Berlin WI 53146	262-547-8550	R	2*	<.1
176	Mowrey Elevator Company Inc—*Timothy Mowrey*	4518 Lafayette St, Marianna FL 32446	850-526-4111	R	2*	<.1

Note: An asterisk (*) indicates an estimated financial figure. The company type code used is as follows: R = Private, P = Public, S = Private Subsidiary, B = Public Subsidiary, D = Division, J = Joint Venture, I = Investment Fund.

COMPANY RANKINGS BY SALES WITHIN 4-DIGIT SIC

Rank	Company Name—*Executive Officer*	Address, City, State, Zip	Phone	Type	Fin	Empls
177	Air Mac Inc—*James Keller*	8901 Directors Row, Dallas TX 75247	214-879-1010	R	2*	<.1
178	Industrial Hydraulics Inc—*Ron Dilley*	1005 Western Dr, Indianapolis IN 46241	317-247-4421	R	2*	<.1
179	Hypar Machine Co—*John Sleven*	PO Box 446, Hurricane WV 25526	304-562-6450	R	2*	<.1
180	Big B'z Machine Shop—*Donald Nicely*	PO Box 2315, Mills WY 82644	307-266-5552	R	2*	<.1
181	Dick Farrell Industries Inc—*Tim Farrell*	4821 Chino Ave, Chino CA 91710	909-613-9424	R	2*	<.1
182	Patient Equipment Rebuild Inc—*Terry Patient*	PO Box 806, Atwood IL 61913	217-578-3014	R	2*	<.1
183	Commercial Honing Company Inc—*Robert Haislett*	8606 Sultana Ave, Fontana CA 92335	909-829-1211	R	2*	<.1
184	Crematory Manufacturing and Service Inc—*Lawrence Stuart*	PO Box 371, Tulsa OK 74101	918-446-1475	R	2*	<.1
185	US Machines Inc—*James Seremetis*	100 10th St, Fairmont WV 26554	304-366-0734	R	2*	<.1
186	Cascade Hydraulics And Machine Inc—*David Fleming*	PO Box 2787, Longview WA 98632	360-423-1082	R	2*	<.1
187	Lucas Precision LP—*Darrell Bonney*	13020 Saint Clair Ave, Cleveland OH 44108	216-451-5588	R	2*	<.1
188	Warren Elevator Corp—*Kenneth Seiferth*	227 Eagle St, Brooklyn NY 11222	718-389-1234	R	2*	<.1
189	Southwest Industrial Motors Inc—*Delbert Harrod*	PO Box 14133, Humble TX 77347	281-987-8972	R	2*	<.1
190	Aggressive Tool And Die Inc—*Roger Geary*	PO Box 335, Buckner KY 40010	502-222-5555	R	2*	<.1
191	Patented Systems Inc—*Andrew Jackson*	16810 Barker Springs R, Houston TX 77084	281-647-9770	R	2*	<.1
192	Annapolis Outboard Repair Co—*Cliff Dean*	2756 Riverview Dr, Riva MD 21140	443-852-0896	R	2*	<.1
193	Harvard House—*David Alvarado*	90 E Escalon Ave Ste 1, Fresno CA 93710	559-432-9071	R	2*	<.1
194	James Manufacturing Inc—*James Shanahan*	PO Box 125, Corsicana TX 75151	903-872-6251	R	2*	<.1
195	Delhomme Industries Inc—*Alfred Delhomme*	PO Box 9662, New Iberia LA 70562	337-365-5476	R	2*	<.1
196	Fortune Tool and Machine Inc—*Donna Dancik*	29650 Beck Rd, Wixom MI 48393	248-669-9119	R	2*	<.1
197	Nearhoof Machine Inc—*Charles Nearhoof*	PO Box 127, Osceola Mills PA 16666	814-339-6621	R	2*	<.1
198	Hyseco Inc—*Dick Wagoner*	5900 Almeda Genoa Rd, Houston TX 77048	713-991-4240	R	2*	<.1
199	R and N Hydraulics Inc—*Ronnie Hill*	PO Box 269, Bryant AR 72089	501-847-2816	R	2*	<.1
200	Mine-Safe Electronics Inc—*Charles Pryor*	PO Box 281, Sturgis KY 42459	270-333-5581	R	2*	<.1
201	Pavyer Printing Machine Works Inc—*Charles Koyn*	3306 Washington Ave, Saint Louis MO 63103	314-535-0774	R	2*	<.1
202	MDK Inc—*Kathryn Donnelly*	6018 Smoke Ranch Rd, Las Vegas NV 89108	702-647-4451	R	2*	<.1
203	Hyval Industries Inc—*Brian Tinder*	898 Widgeon Rd, Norfolk VA 23513	757-855-2026	R	2*	<.1
204	Cindex Industries Inc—*Dennis Lefebvre*	42 Perimeter Rd, Ludlow MA 01056	413-589-9151	R	2*	<.1
205	United Changers Inc—*James Balsano*	108 Robinson Ave, Medford NY 11763	631-654-1230	R	2*	<.1
206	Iselann Moss Industries Inc—*Mark Wolstenholme*	41 Slater Rd, Cranston RI 02920	401-463-5950	R	2*	<.1
207	Jacobs Boiler and Mechanical Industries Inc—*Matthew Jacobs*	6632 W Diversey Ave, Chicago IL 60707	773-525-9013	R	2*	<.1
208	Liquid Solids Control Inc—*Paul Bonneau*	PO Box 259, Upton MA 01568	508-529-3377	R	2*	<.1
209	St Gabriel Valve Service LLC—*Johnny Downs*	PO Box 106, Saint Gabriel LA 70776	225-642-5468	R	2*	<.1
210	Field System Machining Inc—*Dusan Radakovic*	720 Schneider Dr, South Elgin IL 60177	847-468-1313	R	2*	<.1
211	Huntington Plating Inc—*Thomas Houvouras*	625 Monroe Ave, Huntington WV 25704	304-522-0381	R	2*	<.1
212	Hydraulic Service And Manufacturing Inc—*Greg Zajackowski*	W165n5760 Ridgewood Dr, Menomonee Falls WI 53051	262-703-4476	R	2*	<.1
213	Dearborn Crane And Engineering Co—*Larry Dunville*	1133 E 5th St, Mishawaka IN 46544	574-259-2444	R	2*	<.1
214	Independent Web Inc—*Joe Abdale*	66 Nancy St Unit D, West Babylon NY 11704	631-249-7544	R	2*	<.1
215	Boyd Machine and Repair Company Inc—*Larry Boyd*	PO Box 93, Wolflake IN 46796	260-635-2195	R	2*	<.1
216	Reedy Manufacturing and Repair Service Inc—*Jerry Reedy*	PO Box 2413, Odessa TX 79760	432-362-8711	R	2*	<.1
217	Micro Quality Calibration Inc—*Lera Gontmaher*	20743 Marilla St, Chatsworth CA 91311	818-701-4969	R	2*	<.1
218	T and L Sharpening Inc—*Thomas All*	PO Box 338, Monticello IN 47960	574-583-3868	R	2*	<.1
219	River City Valve Service Inc—*George Leblanc*	10020 Mammoth Ave, Baton Rouge LA 70814	225-928-4457	R	2*	<.1
220	Rocky Mountain Air And Lubrication Inc—*Victor Stark*	2244 Main St, Billings MT 59105	406-248-9038	R	2*	<.1
221	International Valve and Instrument Corp—*Marianne Brodeur*	PO Box 2649, Springfield MA 01101	413-736-3682	R	2*	<.1
222	Leitelt Iron Works—*Douglas Kesler*	2301 Turner Ave Nw, Grand Rapids MI 49544	616-363-3817	R	2*	<.1
223	Corbett Industries Inc—*Richard Geier*	PO Box 212, Waldwick NJ 07463	201-445-6311	R	2*	<.1
224	Automated Machinery Inc—*Mark Sackett*	2002 Ford Cir Ste G, Milford OH 45150	513-965-9644	R	2*	<.1
225	Comprehensive Control Systems Inc—*Thomas Kennedy*	16902 Von Karman Ave B, Irvine CA 92606	714-669-8603	R	2*	<.1
226	Five Rivers Hydraulics Inc—*Clay French*	1006 W Old A J Hwy, New Market TN 37820	865-475-4731	R	2*	<.1
227	All Power Battery Inc—*William Ferris*	1387 Clarendon Ave Sw, Canton OH 44710	330-453-5236	R	2*	<.1
228	Sharpening Specialists LC—*Julian Reyes*	PO Box 13322, Wichita KS 67213	316-945-0593	R	1*	<.1
229	Republic Valve Service Inc—*Diane Bardwell*	PO Box 1035, Port Allen LA 70767	225-343-0680	R	1*	<.1
230	Dugan Tool And Die Inc—*Mark Willmore*	41 E Macarthur Dr, Cottage Hills IL 62018	618-259-1351	R	1*	<.1
231	K and J Machine Inc—*Homer Luyster*	326 Fairmont Ave, Barnesville OH 43713	740-425-3282	R	1*	<.1
232	Rms Precision Inc—*Timothy Lazzari*	30105 State Hwy 59, Loxley AL 36551	251-964-6688	R	1*	<.1
233	Dmo Food Equipment Service Inc—*Dennis Ozarchuk*	8400 Sweet Valley Dr S, Cleveland OH 44125	216-328-0600	R	1*	<.1
234	Hydraulic Specialty Company Inc—*Richard Haarstad*	1131 72nd Ave Ne, Minneapolis MN 55432	763-571-3072	R	1*	<.1
235	J and A Grinding Inc—*Jeff Coffin*	307 Markus Ct, Newark DE 19713	302-368-8760	R	1*	<.1
236	Repair Technology Inc—*Ken Morehead*	PO Box 80426, Seattle WA 98108	206-762-6221	R	1*	<.1
237	American Welding And Press Repair Inc—*Norman Jinerson*	26500 W 8 Mile Rd, Southfield MI 48033	248-358-2050	R	1*	<.1
238	FS Repair Inc—*Floyd Sitzman*	PO Box 478, Kingsley IA 51028	712-378-2522	R	1*	<.1
239	Acu Grind Tool Works Inc—*Anthony Antony*	PO Box 68, Bradenton FL 34206	941-758-6963	R	1*	<.1
240	Mayo Manufacturing Company Inc—*Mason Mayo*	PO Box G, Holden WV 25625	304-855-5947	R	1*	<.1
241	Bulldog Fire Apparatus Inc—*Jeffrey Mazza*	PO Box 58, Woodville MA 01784	508-435-4200	R	1*	<.1
242	Pungo Machine Shop Inc—*Michael Ahearn*	PO Box 188, Pantego NC 27860	252-943-6363	R	1*	<.1
243	Meta Tec Development Inc—*Leon Adcock*	125 N Commercial St, Lacon IL 61540	309-246-2960	R	1*	<.1
244	J and L Honing Company Inc—*Timothy Putney*	4150 S Nevada St, Saint Francis WI 53235	414-744-9500	R	1*	<.1
245	Advanced Recycling Systems Inc—*Gus Lyras*	4000 Mccartney Rd, Lowellville OH 44436	330-536-8210	R	1*	<.1
246	Incineration Recycling Services Inc—*Ron Fogel*	PO Box 563, Blackwood NJ 08012	856-963-5200	R	1*	<.1
247	Amatco USA Inc—*James Creighton*	2000 Des Moines St, Des Moines IA 50317	515-276-4528	R	1*	<.1
248	Lake Charles Instruments Inc—*Frank Carpenter*	PO Box 3051, Lake Charles LA 70602	337-433-6900	R	1*	<.1
249	Phoenix Instruments Inc—*James Jordan*	65 N Plains Industrial, Wallingford CT 06492	203-269-4331	R	1*	<.1
250	Nor Cal Marine Service LLC—*Nicolas Parker*	5851 Alder Ave Ste A, Sacramento CA 95828		R	1*	<.1
251	Westcoast Helicopter and Accessories—*Robert Valencia*	915 Wall St No 6, Redding CA 96002	530-722-0400	R	1*	<.1
252	Travelite Inc—*Peter Pitts*	PO Box 98, Wellington OH 44090	440-647-3670	R	1*	.1
253	Heftee Industries LLC—*Nona Sveum*	PO Box 218, Oregon IL 61061	815-732-7540	R	1*	<.1
254	Artisan Grinding Service Inc—*Carolyn Buechly*	1300 Stanley Ave, Dayton OH 45404	937-461-1405	R	1*	<.1
255	D and J Pallet Inc—*Dennis Hammitt*	3665 S Hwy 85 87, Colorado Springs CO 80906	719-576-0111	R	1*	<.1
256	Fleetwood Lock Company Inc—*Paul Romano*	1085 Yonkers Ave, Yonkers NY 10704	914-237-1073	R	1*	<.1
257	Global Turbine Support LLC	2890 Tyler Rd, Ypsilanti MI 48198	734-485-1276	R	1*	<.1
258	Mhr Inc—*Gordon Breuker*	78 Veterans Dr, Holland MI 49423	616-394-0191	R	1*	<.1
259	Ergonomic Design Inc—*Jack Hicks*	7185 Newton St Ste A, Westminster CO 80030	303-452-8006	R	1*	<.1
260	Fibrenetics Inc—*Herbert Segars*	PO Box 632, Woodbridge NJ 07095	732-636-5670	R	1*	<.1
261	First Coast Pallet Inc—*Kevin Crump*	PO Box 1647, Yulee FL 32041	904-786-2886	R	1*	<.1
262	Hosokawa Service Company Inc—*Rob Vorhees*	10 Chatham Rd, Summit NJ 07901	908-273-6360	R	1*	<.1
263	Systems Engineering Inc—*Sylvia Scott*	3824 Aurora Ave N, Seattle WA 98103	206-633-4972	R	1*	<.1
264	Lehigh Precision Company Inc—*Mark Biederman*	PO Box 214, Elizabeth NJ 07207	908-351-6600	R	1*	<.1
265	Mcfarlands Inc—*James Mcfarland*	4528 Hillsborough Rd, Durham NC 27705	919-383-7760	R	<1*	<.1
266	Philbin Manufacturing Co—*Anthony Neisz*	28 N Russell St, Portland OR 97227	503-287-1710	R	<1*	<.1

Rank	Company Name—*Executive Officer*	Address, City, State, Zip	Phone	Type	Fin	Empls
267	Compu-Lock Inc—*Gail Sanders*	29 Harwich Cir, Westwood MA 02090	781-440-9900	R	<1*	<.1

TOTALS: SIC 7699 Repair Services Nec
Companies: 267 —— 51,572 —— 31.0

					51,572	31.0

7812 Motion Picture & Video Production

Rank	Company Name—*Executive Officer*	Address, City, State, Zip	Phone	Type	Fin	Empls
1	Merrill Lynch Video Network Co—*Stan O Neal*	4 World Finance Ctr, New York NY 10281	212-449-1000	R	135,279*	50.6
2	Walt Disney Co—*Robert A Iger*	500 S Buena Vista St, Burbank CA 91521		P	40,893	156.0
3	Liberty Media Corp—*Gregory B Maffei*	12300 Liberty Blvd, Englewood CO 80112	720-875-5400	P	10,982	24.1
4	Warner Brothers—*Barry Mayer*	4000 Warner Blvd, Burbank CA 91522	818-954-6000	D	6,971*	7.9
5	Sony Pictures Entertainment Inc—*Michael Lynton*	10202 W Washington Blv, Culver City CA 90232	310-244-4000	S	4,534*	2.5
6	Fox Filmed Entertainment Fox Entertainment Group Inc	10201 W Pico Blvd, Los Angeles CA 90035	310-369-1000	S	4,498*	3.7
7	Universal Orlando—*Bob Golf*	1000 Universal Studios, Orlando FL 32819	407-363-8000	R	3,376*	12.0
8	News America Inc	1211 Ave of the Americ, New York NY 10036	212-852-7000	S	2,571*	12.0
9	Metro-Goldwyn-Mayer Inc—*Gary Barber*	10250 Constellation Bl, Los Angeles CA 90067	310-449-3000	R	1,725	1.4
10	Lions Gate Entertainment Corp—*Jon Feltheimer*	2700 Colorado Ave Ste, Santa Monica CA 90404	310-449-9200	P	1,583	.5
11	PDI/Dreamworks Inc—*Jeffery Katzenberg* DreamWorks Animation SKG Inc	3101 Park Blvd, Palo Alto CA 94306	650-846-8100	S	1,069*	.4
12	Lucasfilm Ltd—*Micheline Chau*	PO Box 29901, San Francisco CA 94129	415-662-1800	R	875*	1.5
13	New Line Cinema Corp—*Barry Meyer*	888 7th Ave 19th Fl, New York NY 10106	212-649-4900	S	855*	.5
14	DreamWorks LLC—*Jeffrey Katzenberg*	1000 Flower St, Glendale CA 91201	818-695-5000	R	736*	1.2
15	ABC Family Worldwide Inc—*Michael Riley*	500 S Buena Vista St, Burbank CA 91521	818-560-1000	R	724	1.2
16	DreamWorks Animation SKG Inc—*Jeffrey Katzenberg*	1000 Flower St, Glendale CA 91201	818-695-5000	P	706	2.1
17	Twentieth Century Fox Film Corp—*Hutch Parker* Fox Entertainment Group Inc	PO Box 900, Beverly Hills CA 90213	310-277-2211	S	666*	2.0
18	NBA Entertainment—*Rich Gotham*	100 Plz Dr, Secaucus NJ 07094	201-865-1500	S	604*	.3
19	Resolution Inc—*William Schubart*	327 Holly Ct, Williston VT 05495	802-862-8881	R	586*	.3
20	Paramount Pictures Corp—*Brad Grey*	5555 Melrose Ave, Los Angeles CA 90038	323-956-5000	S	560*	4.0
21	World Wrestling Entertainment Inc—*Vincent McMahon*	1241 E Main St, Stamford CT 06902	203-352-8600	P	478	.6
22	Broadcast Video Inc—*Gonzalo Rodriquez*	1750 Coral Way, Miami FL 33145	305-250-9997	R	402*	.2
23	Second City—*Andrew Alexander*	1616 N Wells St, Chicago IL 60614	312-664-4032	R	396*	.2
24	Fremantle Media North America Inc—*Cecile Frot-Coutaz*	11500 W Olympic Blvd, Los Angeles CA 90064	310-806-9610	S	380*	.2
25	Rush Communications of New York Inc—*Russell Simmons*	512 Fashion Ave Fl 43-, New York NY 10018	212-840-9399	R	320*	.2
26	Pixar Animation Studios—*Ed Catmull* Walt Disney Co	1200 Park Ave, Emeryville CA 94608	510-752-3000	S	281	.9
27	Gaiam Inc—*Lynn Powers*	PO Box 3095, Boulder CO 80307	303-222-3600	P	274	.6
28	CKX Inc—*Michael G Ferrel*	650 Madison Ave, New York NY 10022	212-838-3100	S	274	.5
29	Grace and Wild Inc—*Harvy Grace*	23689 Industrial Park, Farmington Hills MI 48335	248-471-6010	R	268*	.2
30	Associated Television International—*David McKenzie*	4401 Wilshire Blvd, Los Angeles CA 90010	323-556-5600	R	247*	.1
31	MGM-UA Inc—*Paula Wagner* Metro-Goldwyn-Mayer Inc	10250 Constellation Bl, Los Angeles CA 90067	310-449-3000	S	245*	.8
32	Hallmark Entertainment Inc—*Donald J Hall Jr*	PO Box 2116, New York NY 10019	212-977-9001	S	235*	.2
33	Industrial Light and Magic Div—*Chrissie England*	PO Box 2459, San Rafael CA 94912	415-448-9000	D	214*	.7
34	Second City Communications—*Tom Yorton* Second City	1616 N Wells St, Chicago IL 60614	312-784-1101	D	198*	.1
35	Hello and Co—*Michael Karbelnikoff*	1641 N Ivar Ave, Hollywood CA 90028	323-465-9494	R	196*	.1
36	KSN News—*John Dawson*	833 N Main, Wichita KS 67203	316-265-3333	R	189*	.1
37	Imaginary Forces—*Danixa Diaz*	6526 Sunset Blvd, Hollywood CA 90028	323-957-6868	R	189*	.1
38	LearnKey Inc—*John T Clemons*	35 N Main, Saint George UT 84770	435-674-9733	R	189*	.1
39	JPM Productions Inc—*Jay Peter Mitchell*	7115 Oak Ridge Pky Ste, Austell GA 30168	770-941-0543	R	164*	.3
40	Walt Disney Records Direct—*Alan Bergman*	500 S Buena Vista St, Burbank CA 91521	818-560-1000	R	154*	3.0
41	iMemories—*Mark Rukavina*	9181 E Bell Rd Ste 101, Scottsdale AZ 85260	480-767-2510	R	139*	.1
42	Creative Technology (Akron Ohio)—*Roger Berk*	137 Heritage Woods Dr, Akron OH 44321	330-668-7777	R	135*	.1
43	Northstar Studios—*Grant Barbre*	3201 Dickerson Pike, Nashville TN 37207	615-650-6000	R	103*	<.1
44	Chicago Story—*Mark Androw*	401 W Superior St, Chicago IL 60610	312-642-3173	R	100*	.3
45	EUE/Screen Gems Ltd—*George Cooney*	222 E 44th St, New York NY 10017	212-450-1600	R	100*	.3
46	Morgan Creek Music Group	10351 Santa Monica Blv, Los Angeles CA 90025	310-432-4848	R	92*	<.1
47	Stone and Company Entertainment—*Scott A Stone*	1040 N Las Palmas Ave, Hollywood CA 90038	323-960-2599	R	88*	.2
48	Click 3X Inc—*Peter Corbett*	16 W 22nd St 4th Fl, New York NY 10010	212-627-1900	R	84*	<.1
49	Tix Corp—*Mitchell J Francis*	12711 Ventura Pl Ste 3, Studio City CA 91604	818-761-1002	P	82	.2
50	Playboy Entertainment Group Inc—*Christie Hefner*	2706 Media Center Dr, Los Angeles CA 90065	310-246-4000	S	73*	.2
51	Dick Clark Productions Inc—*Orly Adelson*	2900 Olympic Blvd, Santa Monica CA 90404	310-255-4600	S	70*	.7
52	Lot—*Greg Harless* Warner Brothers	1041 N Formosa Ave, West Hollywood CA 90046	323-850-3180	D	67*	<.1
53	Saul Zaentz Co—*Saul Zaentz*	2600 10th St, Berkeley CA 94710	510-549-1528	R	59*	.1
54	Harmony Gold USA Inc—*Frank Agrama*	7655 Sunset Blvd, Los Angeles CA 90046	323-851-4900	R	56*	<.1
55	Sheffield Audio-Video Production—*John Ariosa*	13816 Sunnybrook Rd, Phoenix MD 21131	410-628-7260	R	53*	<.1
56	Euro RSCG Tyee MCM—*Steve Netzley*	915 SW Stark St 2nd Fl, Portland OR 97205	503-228-5555	R	52*	.1
57	Miramax Film Corp—*Mike Lang* Walt Disney Co	161 Ave of the America, New York NY 10013	917-606-5500	D	50*	.2
58	BD Fox Independent—*Brian D Fox*	23307 Bocana St, Malibu CA 90265	310-456-7190	R	50*	.1
59	Colorado Production Group—*Frank Matson*	2800 Speer Blvd Ste 10, Denver CO 80211	303-455-5200	R	49*	<.1
60	Film Roman Inc—*Dana Booton*	2950 North Hollywood W, Burbank CA 91505	818-748-4000	S	48*	.3
61	Nest Family LLC—*Ernest Z Frausto*	1461 S Beltline Rd Ste, Coppell TX 75019	972-402-7100	R	43*	.1
62	Cornerstone Studios Inc—*Steve Falke*	2475 N Coolidge Ave, Wichita KS 67204	316-263-4464	R	42*	.1
63	Mad River Post Inc	2415 Main St, Santa Monica CA 90405	310-392-1577	R	40*	.1
64	Colorado Film and Television Studios Inc—*Philip Garvin*	8269 E 23rd Ave, Denver CO 80211	303-388-8500	R	39*	.1
65	Cutters Production Inc—*Vicki Payne*	8349 Arrow Ridge Blvd, Charlotte NC 28273	704-522-9900	R	39*	<.1
66	Cramer Production Company Inc—*Thomas Martin*	425 University Ave, Norwood MA 02062	781-255-8400	R	38*	.2
67	Cinecraft Productions Inc—*Maria Keckan*	2515 Franklin Blvd, Cleveland OH 44113	216-781-2300	R	37*	<.1
68	MVP Communications Inc—*Roger Gullickson*	1751 E Lincoln Ave, Madison Heights MI 48071	248-591-5100	R	37*	<.1
69	Texas Video and Post—*Jack Hattingh*	8964 Kirby Dr, Houston TX 77054	713-667-5000	R	37*	<.1
70	Seals Communications Corp—*E Lamar Seals III*	3340 Peachtree Rd NE S, Atlanta GA 30326	404-230-9600	R	36*	<.1
71	David Naylor and Associates Inc—*David Naylor*	6535 Santa Monica Blvd, Hollywood CA 90038	323-463-2826	R	34*	<.1
72	@radicalmedia Inc—*Jon Kamen*	435 Hudson St 6th Fl, New York NY 10014	212-462-1500	R	33*	.1
73	Immersion Medical Inc—*Victor Veigas*	801 Fox Ln, San Jose CA 95131	408-467-1900	S	32*	<.1
74	Manga Entertainment LLC—*Kaoru Mfaume* Liberty Media Corp	727 N Hudson Ave Ste 1, Chicago IL 60610		S	32*	<.1
75	Big Fish Films Inc Robert Latorre Productions Inc	5626 Alta Ave, Dallas TX 75206	214-887-3474	S	32*	<.1
76	Curious Pictures Corp—*Richard Winkler*	440 Lafayette St 6th F, New York NY 10003	212-674-1400	R	31*	.1

Note: An asterisk (*) indicates an estimated financial figure. The company type code used is as follows: R = Private, P = Public, S = Private Subsidiary, B = Public Subsidiary, D = Division, J = Joint Venture, I = Investment Fund.

COMPANY RANKINGS BY SALES WITHIN 4-DIGIT SIC

Rank	Company Name—*Executive Officer*	Address, City, State, Zip	Phone	Type	Fin	Empls
77	Kartemquin Films Ltd—*Gordon Quinn*	1901 W Wellington St, Chicago IL 60657	773-472-4366	R	31*	<.1
78	White Star Video—*Dennis Hedlund* Kultur International Films Ltd	195 Hwy 36, West Long Branch NJ 07764		D	31*	<.1
79	Culver Studios—*James Cella* Sony Pictures Entertainment Inc	9336 W Washington Blvd, Culver City CA 90232	310-202-1234	S	29*	.1
80	Alan Weiss Productions Inc—*Alan Weiss*	270 White Plains Road, Eastchester NY 10709	212-974-0606	R	29*	<.1
81	Medcom Inc—*Larry Gorum*	6060 Phyllis Dr, Cypress CA 90630		R	28*	.1
82	Post Group Inc—*Vincent Lyons*	1415 N Cahuenga Rd, Hollywood CA 90028	323-462-2300	R	27*	.2
83	Worldvision Home Video Inc—*Bob Sigman*	1700 Broadway, New York NY 10019	212-261-2900	S	27*	.1
84	Lyon Video Inc—*Robert S Lyon*	2091 Arlington Ln, Columbus OH 43228	614-297-0001	R	27*	<.1
85	MacGuffin Films Ltd—*Michael Salzer*	411 Lafayette St, New York NY 10003	212-529-3100	R	27*	<.1
86	Mediastar Inc	702 Mangrove Ave #221, Chico CA 95926	530-826-3342	R	26*	<.1
87	White Hawk Pictures Inc—*Charlie U Barth*	567 Bishopgate Ln, Jacksonville FL 32204	904-634-0500	R	26*	<.1
88	Central City Productions Inc—*Don Jackson*	212 E Ohio Ste 300, Chicago IL 60611	312-654-1100	R	26*	<.1
89	Bedford Falls Co—*Richard Solomon*	409 Santa Monica Blvd, Santa Monica CA 90401	310-394-5022	S	26*	<.1
90	Transvideo Studios—*Raymond Clark*	990 Villa St, Mountain View CA 94041	650-965-4898	R	25*	.1
91	Gail and Rice Productions Inc—*Jeff Bouchard*	21301 Civic Center Dr, Southfield MI 48076	248-799-5000	R	24*	.1
92	Castle Rock Entertainment Inc—*Martin Shafer*	335 N Maple Dr Ste 350, Beverly Hills CA 90210	310-285-2300	S	23*	<.1
93	Landmark Media Inc—*Michael Hartogs*	3450 Slade Run Dr, Falls Church VA 22042	703-241-2030	R	22*	<.1
94	JM-RM Mack Corp—*Robert N Mack*	223 W Erie St 4NW, Chicago IL 60654	312-427-3395	R	21*	<.1
95	Kino International Corp—*Donald Krim*	333 W 39th St Ste 503, New York NY 10018	212-629-6880	R	21*	<.1
96	Broadview Institute Inc—*Jeffrey D Myhre*	8147 Globe Dr, Woodbury MN 55125	651-332-8000	P	21	.2
97	Criterion Collection Inc	215 Park Avenue South, New York NY 10003	212-756-8822	R	20	<.1
98	Weston Woods Studio Inc—*Linda Lee*	143 Main St, Norwalk CT 06851	203-845-0197	S	20*	<.1
99	Broad Street Productions Inc—*Mark Baltazar*	20 W 22 12th Fl, New York NY 10010	212-780-5700	R	20*	<.1
100	Maslow Media Group Inc—*Linda Maslow*	2233 Wisconsin Ave Nw, Washington DC 20007	202-965-1100	R	19*	.1
101	A Taste of New York—*Patricia Maiti*	10 Roberta Ln, Syosset NY 11791	516-677-0239	R	18*	<.1
102	Moving Pictures Video and Film Inc—*Steve Lovelace*	200 Court St, Middletown CT 06457	860-704-6900	R	18*	<.1
103	Atlantic Video Inc—*Ed Miligan*	650 Massachusetts Ave, Washington DC 20001		R	17*	.1
104	Jaffe/Braunstein Films Ltd—*Micheal Jaffe*	12301 Wilshire Blvd St, Los Angeles CA 90025	310-207-6600	R	17*	<.1
105	Silicon Mountain Holdings Inc—*Rudolph Cates III*	4755 Walnut St, Boulder CO 80301	303-938-1155	P	16	<.1
106	Big Deahl Productions Inc—*David Deahl*	1450 N Dayton St, Chicago IL 60622	312-573-0733	R	16*	<.1
107	MTI Home Video Inc—*Larry Brahms*	14216 SW 136th St, Miami FL 33186	305-255-8684	R	16*	<.1
108	Moxie Media Inc—*Martin Glenday*	PO Box 10203, New Orleans LA 70181	504-733-6907	R	16*	<.1
109	Jay Silverman Productions Inc—*Jay Silverman*	1541 N Cahuenga Blvd, Hollywood CA 90028	323-466-6030	R	16*	<.1
110	Blackside Inc—*Judi Hampton*	46 Plympton St, Boston MA 02118	617-482-2195	R	15*	.1
111	Lucky Duck Productions Inc—*Linda Ellerbee*	96 Morton St 4th Fl, New York NY 10014	212-463-0029	R	15*	.1
112	Radar Pictures Inc—*Ted Field*	10900 Wilshire Blvd St, Los Angeles CA 90024	310-208-8525	R	15*	.1
113	Robert Latorre Productions Inc—*Robert Latorre*	5626 Alta Ave, Dallas TX 75206	214-887-3474	R	15*	<.1
114	Mills-James Inc—*Cameron James*	3545 Fishinger Blvd, Hilliard OH 43026	614-777-9933	R	14*	.1
115	Tel Systems—*Karl Couyoumjian*	7235 Jackson Rd, Ann Arbor MI 48103	734-761-4506	R	14*	<.1
116	Great Southern Studios—*Phil Gillan*	15221 NE 21st Ave, North Miami Beach FL 33162	305-944-2464	R	14*	<.1
117	Script to Screen Inc—*Barbara Kerry*	200 N Tustin Ave Ste 2, Santa Ana CA 92705	714-558-3971	R	13*	.1
118	Kultur International Films Ltd—*Dennis Hedlund*	195 Hwy 36, West Long Branch NJ 07764	732-229-2343	R	13*	<.1
119	Media Communication Inc—*Mark A Kramer*	9700 Southern Pines Bl, Charlotte NC 28273	704-527-8853	R	12*	.1
120	Warren Miller Entertainment—*Kurt Miller*	2540 Frontier Ave Ste, Boulder CO 80301	303-442-3430	S	12*	<.1
121	American Zoetrope—*Francis Ford Coppola*	916 Kearny St, San Francisco CA 94133	415-788-7500	R	12*	<.1
122	Cinergi Productions Inc—*Andrew Vajna*	2308 Broadway St, Santa Monica CA 90404	310-315-6000	R	12*	<.1
123	Mind Over Media—*Jospeh Wittkoski*	2425 Liberty Ave, Pittsburgh PA 15222	412-391-2900	R	12*	<.1
124	Studios at Las Colinas Ltd—*Justin Muller*	6301 Riverside Dr Bldg, Irving TX 75039	972-869-0700	S	12*	<.1
125	Multi Image Productions Inc—*Fred Ashman*	8829 Complex Dr, San Diego CA 92123	858-560-8383	R	12*	<.1
126	Aptinet Videos—*Ollie Faraji*	130 W 42nd St 10th Fl, New York NY 10036	212-725-7255	R	12*	<.1
127	Winkler Films Inc—*Irwin Winkler*	211 S Beverly Dr Ste 2, Beverly Hills CA 90212	310-858-5780	R	12*	<.1
128	On the Scene Productions Inc—*Madeline DiNonno*	5900 Wilshire Blvd 14t, Los Angeles CA 90036	323-930-1030	R	11*	<.1
129	Bonneau Production Services—*Terry Bonneau*	9135 N Meridian St, Indianapolis IN 46260	317-846-8965	R	11*	<.1
130	Kushner-Locke Co	280 S Beverly Dr Ste 2, Beverly Hills CA 90212	310-275-7508	R	11*	<.1
131	A and V Company Of The Triad—*Tony Tajalli*	4238 Piedmont Pkwy, Greensboro NC 27410	336-292-9700	R	10*	<.1
132	Scene Three Inc—*Marc W Ball*	2600 Franklin Rd, Nashville TN 37204	615-345-3000	R	10*	.1
133	Kurtz and Friends Animation—*Bob Kurtz*	2312 W Olive Ave, Burbank CA 91506	818-841-8188	R	10*	<.1
134	Video Technics Inc—*Mark Rivers*	PO Box 14247, Atlanta GA 30324	404-327-8300	R	10*	<.1
135	Geomatrix Productions—*Cathie Reese*	270 Amity Rd, Woodbridge CT 06525	203-389-0001	R	10*	<.1
136	Media Images Inc—*Adam Grover*	1010 Taylor Station Rd, Columbus OH 43230	614-410-3000	R	10*	<.1
137	National Lampoon Inc—*Daniel S Laikin*	8228 Sunset Blvd, Los Angeles CA 90046	310-474-5252	P	10	<.1
138	Decker Communications Inc—*Bert Decker*	575 Market St Ste 1925, San Francisco CA 94105	415-543-8100	R	9*	.1
139	CineTel Films Inc—*Paul Hertzberg*	8255 W Sunset Blvd, West Hollywood CA 90046	323-654-4000	R	9*	.1
140	Cubist Media Group Ltd—*John Ballentyne*	234 Market St, Philadelphia PA 19106	267-765-7000	R	9*	<.1
141	Enter-Space Inc—*Robert Collier*	PO Box 265, Moss Landing CA 95039	831-633-3171	R	9*	<.1
142	Martin Brinkerhoff Associates Inc—*Martin Brinkerhoff*	17732 Cowan, Irvine CA 92614	949-660-9396	R	9*	<.1
143	Lopes Picture Company Inc—*Rob Lopes*	29 E 19th St 7th Fl, New York NY 10003	212-477-1114	R	9*	<.1
144	Pix Video Film and Multimedia Inc—*Ridgie Barton*	1805 E Dyer Rd, Santa Ana CA 92705	949-250-1749	R	9*	<.1
145	Vanguard Films—*John H Williams*	8703 W Olympic, Los Angeles CA 90035	310-888-8020	R	9*	<.1
146	Broadcast News Networks Inc—*Michael Hill*	75 Broad St 15th Fl, New York NY 10004	212-747-0601	R	8	.1
147	Information Television Network—*Edward Lerner*	6650 Park of Commerce, Boca Raton FL 33487	561-997-7771	R	8*	<.1
148	Showscan Entertainment Inc	468 N Camden Dr Ste 20, Beverly Hills CA 90210	310-858-5589	R	8	<.1
149	Davis Entertainment Co—*John A Davis*	2121 Avenue of the Sta, Los Angeles CA 90067	310-556-3550	R	8*	<.1
150	DJM Films Inc—*Edward Friedman*	4 E 46th St, New York NY 10017	212-687-0111	R	8*	<.1
151	Whitehouse Post Productions—*Carrie Holecek*	54 W Hubbard St Ste 50, Chicago IL 60610	312-822-0888	R	8*	<.1
152	Brentwood Communications Inc—*Michael Hattem*	2508 S Barrington Ave, Los Angeles CA 90064	310-476-6363	R	8*	<.1
153	Oliver Productions Inc—*John McLaughlin*	1717 Rhode Island Ave, Washington DC 20036	202-457-0870	R	8	<.1
154	PCTV Inc—*Matt Cookson*	PO Box 286, Keene NH 03431	603-863-9322	R	8*	<.1
155	Gelber Television—*Charles Gelber*	1697 Broadway Ste 404, New York NY 10019	212-262-6260	R	8*	<.1
156	Kalish Communications—*Karen Kalish*	2120 S St NW, Washington DC 20008		R	8*	<.1
157	Lacy Street Production Center	2630 Lacy St, Los Angeles CA 90031	323-222-8872	R	8*	<.1
158	Richter Productions Inc—*Robert Richter*	330 W 42nd St 24 Fl, New York NY 10036	212-947-1395	R	8*	<.1
159	Dsi Entertainment Systems Inc—*Eric Thies*	6955 Hayvenhurst Ave, Van Nuys CA 91406	818-906-9940	R	8*	<.1
160	West Glen Communications Inc—*Ed Lamoureaux*	1430 Broadway 9th Fl, New York NY 10018	212-921-2800	R	7*	<.1
161	MEE Productions Inc—*Ivan J Juzang*	5070 Parkside Ave Ste, Philadelphia PA 19131	215-829-4920	R	7*	<.1
162	L and P Media—*Paul Madelone*	255 River St, Troy NY 12180	518-880-0300	R	7*	<.1

Rank	Company Name—*Executive Officer*	Address, City, State, Zip	Phone	Type	Fin	Empls
333	Spicer Productions Inc—*Bill Spicer*	3820 Wards Chapel Rd, Marriottsville MD 21104	410-750-8822	R	N/A	<.1
334	Pelican Pictures Inc—*Bobbie Westerfield*	614 E Rutland St, Covington LA 70433	504-608-8097	R	N/A	<.1
335	Word Pictures Inc—*Craig Handley*	24752 Forterra Dr, Warren MI 48089	586-757-4601	R	N/A	<.1
336	YL Communications Inc—*Michael Yada*	1253 Vine St Ste 21 A, Hollywood CA 90038	323-461-1616	R	N/A	<.1
337	Hollywood Visual Productions—*Bob Iovinerla*	90 W Campbell Rd Ste 1, Schenectady NY 12306	518-370-2119	R	N/A	<.1

TOTALS: SIC 7812 Motion Picture & Video Production
Companies: 337 — 229,046 — 314.1

7819 Services Allied to Motion Pictures

Rank	Company Name—*Executive Officer*	Address, City, State, Zip	Phone	Type	Fin	Empls
1	Universal Studios Inc—*Ron Meyer*	100 Universal City Plz, Universal City CA 91608	818-777-1000	S	1,932*	14.0
2	Todd-AO Studios East Inc	1619 Broadway 8th Fl, New York NY 10019	212-265-6225	S	662*	.9
3	Ascent Media Group LLC—*William R Fitzgerald*	520 Broadway 5th Fl, Santa Monica CA 90401	310-434-7000	S	564*	4.0
4	Technicolor Video Services Inc—*Frederic Rose*	3233 Mission Oaks Blvd, Camarillo CA 93012	805-445-1122	R	500*	5.0
5	Genius Products Inc—*Trevor Drinkwater*	3301 Exposition Ste 10, Santa Monica CA 90404	310-401-2200	P	474	.2
6	Century Park Pictures Corp—*Thomas K Scallen*	4701 IDS Ctr, Minneapolis MN 55402	612-338-5100	R	255*	.4
7	RealD Inc—*Michael V Lewis*	100 N Crescent Dr Ste, Beverly Hills CA 90210	310-385-4000	P	246	.1
8	Lucas Digital Limited LLC—*Lynwen Brennan*	PO Box 2459, San Rafael CA 94912	415-746-3000	D	243*	1.0
9	NFL Films—*Steve Sabol*	1 NFL Plz, Mount Laurel NJ 08054	856-222-5675	R	179*	.4
10	Laser-Pacific Media Corp—*Bill Roberts*	809 N Cahuenga Blvd, Hollywood CA 90038	323-462-6266	S	170*	.2
11	Broadway Video Inc—*Jack Sullivan*	1619 Broadway, New York NY 10019	212-265-7600	R	168*	.2
12	Soundelux Entertainment Group—*Jeffrey Edell* Ascent Media Group LLC	7080 Hollywood Blvd St, Hollywood CA 90028	323-603-3200	S	144*	.2
13	WaxWorks Inc—*Terry Woodward*	325 E 3rd St, Owensboro KY 42303	270-926-0008	R	120	.3
14	Modern Videofilm Inc—*Moshe Barkat*	2300 W Empire, Burbank CA 91504	818-840-1700	R	96*	.4
15	Image Entertainment Inc—*Theodore S Green*	20525 Nordhoff St Ste, Chatsworth CA 91311	818-407-9100	P	89	.1
16	Technicolor Videocassette Of Michigan Inc—*Lanni Ormonvo*	36121 Schoolcraft Rd, Livonia MI 48150	734-853-3800	R	85*	2.0
17	Pacific Film Laboratories—*Bill Roberts* Laser-Pacific Media Corp	823 Seward St, Los Angeles CA 90038	323-461-9921	S	75*	.2
18	Corporate Disk Co—*Bill Mahoney*	4610 Prime Pkwy, McHenry IL 60050	815-331-6000	R	65*	.1
19	Allied Vaughn (Minneapolis Minnesota)—*Dennis Walden*	7951 Computer Ave, Minneapolis MN 55435	952-832-3100	R	59*	.3
20	Technicolor Inc	4050 Lankershim Blvd, North Hollywood CA 91604	818-769-8500	S	54*	.4
21	Universal Studios Home Video—*Craig Kronblau* Universal Studios Inc	10 Universal City Plz, Universal City CA 91608	818-777-1000	D	54*	.2
22	Cine Magnetics Inc—*Joseph Barber*	100 Business Park Dr, Armonk NY 10504	914-273-7500	R	49*	.2
23	Henninger Media Services Inc—*Rob Henninger*	2601 Wilson Blvd Unit, Arlington VA 22201	703-243-3444	R	44*	.2
24	Todd-AO Studios	900 Seward St, Los Angeles CA 90038	323-962-4000	S	40*	.3
25	Radium—*Gary Gertulla*	2115 Colorado Ave, Santa Monica CA 90404	310-264-6440	R	39*	.1
26	GoLive! Mobile—*Asher Delug*	10940 S Parker Rd Ster, Parker CO 80134		R	36	.1
27	Point360—*Haig S Bagerdjian*	2777 N Ontario St, Burbank CA 91504	818-565-1400	P	35	.3
28	Video Post and Transfer Inc—*Neil Feldman*	2727 Inwood Rd, Dallas TX 75235	214-350-2676	R	35*	<.1
29	Cutters Inc—*Tim McGuire*	515 N State St 25th Fl, Chicago IL 60654	312-644-2500	R	31*	.1
30	Video Monitoring Services of America LP—*David Stephens*	1500 broadway, New York NY 10036	212-736-2010	R	28*	.4
31	Chapman/Leonard Studio Equipment Inc—*Leonard Chapman*	12950 Raymer St, North Hollywood CA 91605	818-764-6726	R	25*	.2
32	Duplication Factory Inc—*Pete McCarthy*	4275 Norex Dr, Chaska MN 55318	952-448-9912	R	25*	.1
33	Raleigh TV and Film Studios—*Michael Moore*	5300 Melrose Ave, Hollywood CA 90038	323-466-3111	R	25*	.1
34	EFILM—*Joe Matza*	1146 N Las Palmas Ave, Hollywood CA 90038	323-463-7041	R	24*	.1
35	Daily Planet Ltd—*Scott Marvel*	720 N Franklin St Ste, Chicago IL 60654	312-640-7447	R	23*	<.1
36	Midnight Media Group—*David Emmerling*	45 E Willow St, Millburn NJ 07041	973-379-5959	R	22*	<.1
37	Hollywood Rental Company Inc—*Kelly Coskella*	12800 Foothill Blvd, Sylmar CA 91342	818-407-7800	S	20*	.1
38	American Multimedia Inc—*Bill Brit*	2609 Tucker St, Burlington NC 27215	336-229-5554	R	17*	.3
39	Video Tape Associates—*Ken Chambliss*	1575 Sheridan Rd NE, Atlanta GA 30324	404-634-6181	R	17*	.1
40	Crash and Sue's—*Heidi Habben*	510 Marquette Ave Ste6, Minneapolis MN 55402	612-338-7947	R	17*	<.1
41	Optimus Inc—*Tom Duff*	161 E Grand Ave Fl 1, Chicago IL 60611	312-321-0880	R	16*	.1
42	Downstream—*Tim Larsen*	1650 NW Naito Pky Ste, Portland OR 97209	503-226-1944	R	15*	<.1
43	Texas Pacific Film Video—*Richard Kooris*	501 N IH 35, Austin TX 78702	512-485-3000	R	12*	.1
44	DVC Inc—*Brent McClarnon*	7301 E 46th St, Indianapolis IN 46226	317-544-2150	R	11*	<.1
45	Framerunner—*Keith Shapiro*	555 W 57th St Ste 1710, New York NY 10019	212-246-4224	R	11*	<.1
46	Blair and Associates Ltd—*Robert Blair*	11333 E 60th Pl, Tulsa OK 74146	918-254-6337	R	11*	<.1
47	Todd-AO Studios West Inc	3000 Olympic Blvd, Santa Monica CA 90404	310-315-5000	S	10*	<.1
48	Crew Connection Inc—*Heidi McLean*	PO Box 2101, Evergreen CO 80437	303-526-4900	R	10*	<.1
49	Motion Picture Laboratories Inc—*Diane Towe*	621 Mainstream Dr Ste, Nashville TN 37228	615-256-1675	R	8*	.1
50	Manhattan Transfer Edit Co—*Dan Rosen*	545 5th Ave 2nd Fl, New York NY 10017	212-907-1200	S	8*	<.1
51	Playback Technologies Inc—*Steve Irwin*	135 N Victory Blvd, Burbank CA 91502	818-556-5030	R	8*	<.1
52	Great Lakes Media Technology Inc—*Brian Axtman*	6501 W Donges Bay Rd, Mequon WI 53092	262-512-0100	R	7*	<.1
53	Interface Media Group—*Jeff Weingarten*	1233 20th St NW, Washington DC 20036	202-861-0500	R	7*	<.1
54	Modern Digital Inc—*Rich Fassio*	1921 Minor Ave, Seattle WA 98101	206-623-3444	R	7*	<.1
55	Santa Clarita Studio Corp—*Mike Delorenzo*	25135 Anza Dr, Santa Clarita CA 91355	661-294-2000	R	7*	<.1
56	Newart Miami—*George Oneil*	2850 Tigertail Ave, Coconut Grove FL 33133	305-857-0350	J	6*	<.1
57	High Technology Video Inc—*Jim Hardy*	3575 Chnga Blvd W Ste, Los Angeles CA 90068	323-969-8822	R	5*	.1
58	Lost Planet Inc—*Hank Corwin*	113 Spring St 4th Fl, New York NY 10012	212-226-5678	R	5*	<.1
59	Crew Cuts Film and Tape Inc—*Clayton Hemmert*	28 W 44th St 22nd Fl, New York NY 10036	212-302-2828	R	5*	<.1
60	Media City Teleproduction Center—*Marty Giller*	2525 N Naomi St, Burbank CA 91504	818-848-5800	R	5*	<.1
61	Castle Hill Productions—*Julian Schlossberg*	36 W 25th St 2nd Fl, New York NY 10010	212-242-1500	R	5*	<.1
62	Synergy Films—*George Watkins*	1735 Peachtree St NE S, Atlanta GA 30309	404-888-9393	R	5*	<.1
63	Imtek Inc—*David Lesniak*	2075 High Hill Rd, Bridgeport NJ 08014	856-467-0047	R	5*	.1
64	Tri State Metrovision Inc—*Steve Masseau*	271 Us Hwy 46 F108, Fairfield NJ 07004	973-276-8000	R	4*	<.1
65	Have Inc—*Nancy Gordon*	350 Power Ave, Hudson NY 12534	518-828-2000	R	4*	<.1
66	501 Post Inc Texas Pacific Film Video	501 N Interstate Hwy 3, Austin TX 78702	512-476-3876	S	4*	<.1
67	Cutting Vision Co—*Jeff Beckerman*	665 Broadway Ste 1201, New York NY 10012	212-533-9400	R	4*	<.1
68	Gilbert Group Inc—*Bill Gilbert*	6801 W 76th Ter, Overland Park KS 66204		R	4*	<.1
69	Greenwich Studio Inc—*Carlene Tiederman*	12100 16th Ave, North Miami FL 33161	305-899-9467	R	4*	<.1
70	BlahUSA—*Andy Arkin*	1 Union Sq W Ste 205, New York NY 10003	212-627-8700	R	4*	<.1
71	Chace Productions Inc—*Bob Heiber*	201 S Victory Blvd, Burbank CA 91502	818-842-8346	S	3*	.1
72	Northern Lights Post Inc—*Mark Littman*	135 W 27th St 8th Fl, New York NY 10001	212-274-1199	R	3*	<.1
73	Filmcore Editorial San Francisco LLC—*Jon Ettinger*	500 Sansome St 7th Fl, San Francisco CA 94111	415-392-6300	S	3*	<.1
74	Bride Media International Inc—*James H Bride II*	39 Glenridge Rd, Dedham MA 02026	781-608-5817	R	3*	<.1
75	Rex Production Services Inc—*Roy McFarland*	610 SW 17th Ave, Portland OR 97205	503-238-4525	R	2*	<.1
76	Piper Media Services Inc—*Daniel B Piper*	904 W Kenosha, Broken Arrow OK 74012	918-251-0477	R	2*	<.1

Note: An asterisk (*) indicates an estimated financial figure. The company type code used is as follows: R = Private, P = Public, S = Private Subsidiary, B = Public Subsidiary, D = Division, J = Joint Venture, I = Investment Fund.

COMPANY RANKINGS BY SALES WITHIN 4-DIGIT SIC

Rank	Company Name—*Executive Officer*	Address, City, State, Zip	Phone	Type	Fin	Empls
77	Video Communications Inc—*Robert Blair*	11333 E 60th Pl, Tulsa OK 74146	918-254-6337	R	2*	<.1
78	Chicago Studio City—*John Crededio*	5660 W Taylor St, Chicago IL 60644	773-261-3400	R	2*	<.1
79	Pi Edit	23 E 22nd 2nd Fl, New York NY 10010	212-254-0202	R	2*	<.1
80	Harmonic Ranch—*Brooks Williams*	59 Franklin St Ste 303, New York NY 10013	212-966-3141	R	2*	<.1
81	Katina Productions LLC—*Simon Nuchtern*	34 Macdougal St, New York NY 10012	212-228-2393	R	2*	<.1
82	Rio Vista Media—*Jonathan Davis*	1851 W Indiantown Rd S, Jupiter FL 33458	561-602-9222	R	2*	<.1
83	Wings Wildlife Production Inc—*Gary Gero*	2 Mclaren Ste A, Irvine CA 92618	949-830-7845	R	2*	<.1
84	Doug Smith Production Consultants—*Douglas Smith*	2235 Defoor Hills Rd N, Atlanta GA 30318	404-609-9001	R	2*	<.1
85	Ntt Enterprises Inc—*Nelson Tyler*	14218 Aetna St, Van Nuys CA 91401	818-989-4420	R	1*	<.1
86	Continental Video Productions Inc—*Derard Richer*	2777 Allen Pkwy Ste 60, Houston TX 77019	713-522-7585	R	1*	<.1
87	Edge Films—*Ken Nahoum*	55 Vandam St 16th Fl, New York NY 10013	949-494-3900	R	1*	<.1
88	CitiCam Video Productions Inc—*Scott Morette*	515 W 57th St, New York NY 10019	212-315-4855	R	1*	<.1
89	Duplication Specialists—*Ray Nieves*	843 Merrick Rd, Baldwin NY 11510	516-867-7300	R	1*	<.1
90	Pacific Grip and Lighting Inc—*Doug Boss*	6550 NE Portland Hwy, Portland OR 97218	503-233-4747	R	1*	<.1
91	Fincannon and Associates Inc—*Craig Fincannon*	1235 N 23rd St, Wilmington NC 28405	910-251-1500	R	1*	<.1
92	Studio Bard Inc—*Linda Bard*	807 NE Couch, Portland OR 97232	503-273-2273	R	1*	<.1
93	Terry Fryer Music Inc—*Terry Fryer*	1120 Forest Ave, Evanston IL 60202	847-328-3787	R	1*	<.1
94	Bob Shelley's Special Effects International—*Bob Shelley*	550 Marksmen Ct, Fayetteville GA 30214		R	1*	<.1
95	Fresh Music Library—*Charlie Conquest*	320 South St, Agawam MA 01001	413-786-1450	R	1*	<.1
96	SlingShot Entertainment Inc—*JD Sussman*	15030 Ventura Blvd Ste, Sherman Oaks CA 91403	818-755-8888	R	1*	<.1
97	Camelot Entertainment Group Inc—*Robert P Atwell*	10 Universal City Plz, Universal City CA 91608	818-308-8858	P	<1	<.1
98	OSL Holdings—*Eli Feder*	6019 Olivas Park Dr St, Ventura CA 93003	805-650-6749	P	<1	<.1
99	Today Video Inc—*David Seeger*	555 W 57th St Ste 1420, New York NY 10019	212-307-0707	R	N/A	<.1

TOTALS: SIC 7819 Services Allied to Motion Pictures
Companies: 99

					7,048	34.3

7822 Motion Picture & Tape Distribution

Rank	Company Name—*Executive Officer*	Address, City, State, Zip	Phone	Type	Fin	Empls
1	BBC Worldwide America Inc—*Herb Scannell*	1120 Ave of the Americ, New York NY 10036	212-705-9300	R	775*	.2
2	Buena Vista Pictures Distribution—*Chuck Viane*	500 S Buena Vista St, Burbank CA 91521	818-560-5900	R	754*	.2
3	CBS Television Distribution—*John Nogawski*	2401 Colorado Ave Ste, Santa Monica CA 90404	310-264-3300	S	684	.4
4	Harpo Inc—*Oprah Winfrey*	110 N Carpenter St, Chicago IL 60607	312-633-1000	R	421*	.5
5	Harpo Productions Inc—*Oprah Winfrey*	110 N Carpenter St, Chicago IL 60607	312-633-1000	R	385*	.4
6	Preservation Resources—*Robert Jordan*	9 S Commerce Way, Bethlehem PA 18017	610-758-8700	R	298*	.1
7	WT Cox Subscriptions—*Cynthia Heniford*	201 Village Rd, Shallotte NC 28470		R	220*	.1
8	Jump Jump Music—*Dan Berkman*	7005 NE Prescott St, Portland OR 97218	503-284-4828	R	178*	<.1
9	Hallmark Channel—*Henry Schlieff*	12700 Ventura Blvd Ste, Studio City CA 91604	818-755-2300	D	171*	.2
10	Rentrak Corp—*Bill Livek*	7700 NE Ambassador Pl, Portland OR 97220	503-284-7581	P	97	.3
11	Royal Electronics—*Shawn Rad*	15829 Stagg St, Van Nuys CA 91406	818-781-6300	R	79*	<.1
12	Jack of All Games—*Kevin Connelly*	9271 Meridian Way, West Chester OH 45069	513-326-3020	D	68*	.2
13	DAP Distributed Art Publishers—*Sharon Gallagher*	155 Sixth Ave 2nd FL, New York NY 10013	212-627-1999	R	62*	<.1
14	New Frontier Media Inc—*Michael Weiner*	7007 Winchester Cir St, Boulder CO 80301	303-444-0900	P	49	.2
15	Master Communications Inc—*Selina Yoon*	4480 Lake Forest Dr St, Cincinnati OH 45242	513-563-3100	R	47*	<.1
16	American Overseas Book Co Inc—*Suzanne Gaffney*	550 Walnut St, Norwood NJ 07648	201-767-7600	R	39*	<.1
17	Compact Media Inc—*Ko Byeong*	1714-A Ringwood Ave, San Jose CA 95131	408-573-1011	R	39*	<.1
18	Sell My DVDscom—*Dave Sparks*	350 S Lake Ave Ste 112, Pasadena CA 91101	626-578-7282	R	25*	<.1
19	Wellspring Media Inc—*Trevor Drinkwater*	419 Park Ave S 20th Fl, New York NY 10016	212-686-6777	S	24*	.1
20	Facets Multimedia Inc—*Milos Stehlik*	1517 W Fullerton Ave, Chicago IL 60614	773-281-9075	R	23*	.1
21	Distribution Video and Audio Inc—*Brad Kugler*	133 Candy Ln, Palm Harbor FL 34683	727-447-4147	R	22*	<.1
22	MPI Media Group—*Malik Ali*	16101 S 108th Ave, Orland Park IL 60467	708-460-0555	R	20*	.1
23	Music Video Distributors Inc—*Tom Seaman*	PO Box 280, Oaks PA 19456	610-650-8200	R	18*	<.1
24	Surplus Sourcing Group Inc—*Tony Shah*	21040 Nordhoff St, Chatsworth CA 91311	818-407-0200	R	17*	<.1
25	Ambrose Video Publishing Inc—*William Ambrose*	145 W 45th St Ste 1115, New York NY 10036	212-768-7373	R	16*	<.1
26	Questar Inc (Chicago Illinois)—*Albert J Nader*	307 N Michigan Ave Ste, Chicago IL 60601	312-266-9400	R	14*	<.1
27	Library Video Co—*Andrew Schlessinger*	PO Box 580, Wynnewood PA 19096	610-645-4000	R	13*	.1
28	Water Bearer Films Inc—*Michael Stimler*	3239 Gateway Circle, Charlottesville VA 22911	434-923-8686	R	13*	<.1
29	Hollywood Edge—*Ken Statemen*	7080 Hollywood Blvd St, Hollywood CA 90028	323-603-3252	S	12*	<.1
30	VIEW Video Inc—*Bob Karcy*	PO Box 77, Saugerties NY 12477	845-246-9955	R	8*	<.1
31	Omega Entertainment Ltd—*Nico Mastorakis*	315 S Beverly Dr Ste 2, Beverly Hills CA 90212	310-855-0516	R	7*	<.1
32	International Historic Films Inc—*Peter P Bernotas*	PO Box 5796, Chicago IL 60680	773-927-2900	R	7*	<.1
33	Vide-O-Go Inc/That's Infotainment!—*Dean Stevens*	PO Box 2994, Princeton NJ 08543	609-716-1989	R	7*	<.1
34	Q Up Arts Sample Collections—*Doug Morton*	PO Box 521481, Salt Lake City UT 84152		R	5*	<.1
35	Pyramid Films Corp—*Randolph Wright*	PO Box 1048/WEB, Santa Monica CA 90406	310-398-6149	R	4*	<.1
36	Video Placement Worldwide—*Dan Kater*	25 2nd St N, Saint Petersburg FL 33701	727-823-9595	R	3*	<.1
37	Bedford Entertainment Inc—*Larry Brahms*	14216 SW 136th St, Miami FL 33186	305-255-8684	R	2*	<.1
38	York Pictures Inc—*Tanya York*	13101 Washington Blvd, Culver City CA 90066	818-788-4050	R	2	<.1
39	Video Learning Library LLC—*Arlene M Spencer*	15838 N 62nd St, Scottsdale AZ 85254	480-596-9970	R	1*	<.1
40	PC Mac Connections—*Patricia Gallup*	730 Milford Rd Rte 101, Merrimack NH 03054	603-355-6100	S	N/A	1.6
41	Buena Vista International Inc	500 S Buena Vista St, Burbank CA 91521	818-560-6971	S	N/A	.4

TOTALS: SIC 7822 Motion Picture & Tape Distribution
Companies: 41

					4,629	5.2

7829 Motion Picture Distribution Services

Rank	Company Name—*Executive Officer*	Address, City, State, Zip	Phone	Type	Fin	Empls
1	EastCoast Entertainment Inc—*Lee Moore*	703 Southlake Blvd, Richmond VA 23236	804-355-2178	R	31*	.1
2	Concepts TV Productions Inc—*Collette Liantonio*	328 W Main St, Boonton NJ 07005	973-331-1500	R	2*	<.1

TOTALS: SIC 7829 Motion Picture Distribution Services
Companies: 2

					33	.1

7832 Motion Picture Theaters Except Drive-In

Rank	Company Name—*Executive Officer*	Address, City, State, Zip	Phone	Type	Fin	Empls
1	National Amusements Inc—*Shari Redstone*	PO Box 9126, Dedham MA 02027	781-461-1600	R	36,437*	121.7
2	Regal Entertainment Group—*Amy E Miles*	7132 Regal Ln, Knoxville TN 37918	865-922-1123	P	2,682	20.7
3	AMC Entertainment Inc—*Gerardo I (Gerry) Lopez*	920 Main St, Kansas City MO 64105	816-221-4000	R	2,432	17.9
4	Cinemark Holdings Inc—*Alan W Stock*	3900 Dallas Pkwy Ste 5, Plano TX 75093	972-665-1000	P	2,280	14.0
5	Regal Cinemas Corp—*Michael L Campbell* Regal Entertainment Group	7132 Regal Ln, Knoxville TN 37918	865-922-1123	S	1,166	12.6
6	American Multi-Cinema Inc—*Gerardo Lopez* AMC Entertainment Inc	PO Box 725489, Atlanta GA 31139	816-221-4000	S	658*	9.5
7	United Artists Theatre Circuit Inc—*Kurt Hall* Regal Entertainment Group	7132 Regal Ln, Knoxville TN 37918	865-922-1123	S	582*	24.6
8	Carmike Cinemas Inc—*S David Passman*	PO Box 391, Columbus GA 31902	706-576-3400	P	491	6.2
9	AMC-GCT Inc—*Richard Smith* American Multi-Cinema Inc	27 Boylston St, Chestnut Hill MA 02467	617-277-2500	S	358	3.9

Rank	Company Name—*Executive Officer*	Address, City, State, Zip	Phone	Type	Fin	Empls
10	Pacific Theatres Corp—*Cristopher S Forman*	120 N Robertson Blvd 3, Los Angeles CA 90048	310-657-8420	R	327*	3.0
11	Kerasotes ShowPlace Theaters LLC—*Tony Kerasotes*	224 N Des Plaines, Chicago IL 60661	312-756-3360	R	176*	2.5
12	Century Theaters—*Raymond W Syufy*	150 Pelican Wy, San Rafael CA 94901		R	164*	2.8
13	Metropolitan Theatres Corp—*Bruce Corwin*	8727 W 3rd St 3rd Fl, Los Angeles CA 90048	310-858-2800	R	164*	.4
14	Wallace Theater Holdings Inc—*Scott Wallace*	919 Sw Taylor St Ste 8, Portland OR 97205	503-221-7090	R	155*	1.3
15	Malco Theatres Inc—*Steve Lightman*	5851 Ridgeway Center P, Memphis TN 38120	901-761-3480	R	110*	.6
16	Eastern Federal Corp—*Carter Meiselman*	901 East Blvd, Charlotte NC 28203	704-377-3495	R	101*	.6
17	Harkins Amusement Enterprises Inc—*Dan Harkins*	7511 E McDonald Dr, Scottsdale AZ 85250	480-627-7777	R	79*	1.2
18	Jack Loeks Theaters Inc—*John D Loeks*	2121 Celebration Dr NE, Grand Rapids MI 49525	616-530-7469	R	76*	.4
19	Landmark Theatre Corp—*Ted Mundorff*	2222 S Barrington Ave, Los Angeles CA 90064	310-473-6701	S	39	1.0
20	Iwerks Entertainment Inc—*Gary J Matus*	4520 W Valerio St, Burbank CA 91505	818-841-7766	S	25*	.1
21	Cinema Grill Systems Inc—*Steven Swin*	13682 E Alameda Ave, Aurora CO 80012	303-344-3456	R	18*	<.1
22	City Cinemas—*Robert Smerling* Pacific Theatres Corp	1001 Third Ave, New York NY 10022	212-758-5600	S	10*	.1
23	ITEC Attractions Inc—*Paul M Bluto*	3562 Shepherd of the H, Branson MO 65616	417-335-3533	R	5*	.1
24	Angelika Film Centers LLC—*Jessica Saleh*	18 W Houston St, New York NY 10012	212-995-2570	S	5	<.1
25	Liberty Theaters Inc	500 Citadel Dr Ste 300, Commerce CA 90040	213-235-2240	S	5*	<.1
26	Minetta Live LLC	500 Citadel Dr Ste 300, Commerce CA 90040	213-235-2240	S	5*	<.1

TOTALS: SIC 7832 Motion Picture Theaters Except Drive-In
Companies: 26 — 48,549 — 245.1

7833 Drive-In Motion Picture Theaters

Rank	Company Name—*Executive Officer*	Address, City, State, Zip	Phone	Type	Fin	Empls
1	Nationwide Theatres Corp—*Christopher Forman*	120 N Robertson Blvd F, Los Angeles CA 90048	310-657-8420	R	175*	3.0
2	De Anza Land and Leisure Corp—*William Oldknow*	1615 Cordova St, Los Angeles CA 90007	323-734-9951	R	41*	.5
3	Summit Media Inc—*Scott Gentry*	450 Fremont St Ste 310, Las Vegas NV 89101	702-258-0039	R	2*	<.1

TOTALS: SIC 7833 Drive In Motion Picture Theaters
Companies: 3 — 218 — 3.5

7841 Video Tape Rental

Rank	Company Name—*Executive Officer*	Address, City, State, Zip	Phone	Type	Fin	Empls
1	Blockbuster LLC—*Michael Kelly*	1201 Elm St, Dallas TX 75270	214-854-3000	S	3,241	25.0
2	Movie Gallery Inc—*Wes Sand*	9275 SW Peyton Ln, Wilsonville OR 97070	503-570-1700	R	2,452	5.9
3	Netflix Inc—*Reed Hastings*	100 Winchester Cir, Los Gatos CA 95032	408-399-3700	P	2,163	2.2
4	Hollywood Entertainment Corp—*JT Malugen* Movie Gallery Inc	9275 SW Peyton Ln, Wilsonville OR 97070	503-570-1600	S	1,782*	30.6
5	MG Midwest Inc—*Sherif Mityas* Movie Gallery Inc	900 W Main St, Dothan AL 36301	334-677-2108	S	1,385	N/A
6	Oregon Entertainment Corp—*Tracy B Lakeslee*	3137 NE Sandy Blvd, Portland OR 97232	503-239-6505	R	26*	.1
7	DVDPlay Inc—*Charles Piper*	695 Campbell Technolog, Campbell CA 95008	408-583-1300	R	19*	.1
8	Movie Exchange Inc—*Brian Ward*	PO Box 394, Oaks PA 19456	610-631-9180	R	4*	<.1
9	International Film and Video Center Inc—*Bahman Maghsoud-lou*	PO Box 1012, Township of Washington NJ 07676	201-666-6772	R	1*	<.1

TOTALS: SIC 7841 Video Tape Rental
Companies: 9 — 11,073 — 63.9

7922 Theatrical Producers & Services

Rank	Company Name—*Executive Officer*	Address, City, State, Zip	Phone	Type	Fin	Empls
1	International Management Group—*Theodore Forstmann*	767 5th Ave, New York NY 10153	212-355-5656	S	1,300*	3.0
2	Shubert Theater Organization Inc—*Phillip Smith*	234 W 44th St, New York NY 10036	212-944-3700	R	534*	1.5
3	Feld Entertainment Inc—*Kenneth Feld*	8607 Westwood Center D, Vienna VA 22182	703-448-4000	R	528*	1.7
4	Tihati Productions Ltd—*Jack Thompson*	3615 Harding Ave Ste 5, Honolulu HI 96816	808-735-0292	R	383*	1.0
5	Dial Global Inc—*Spencer Brown*	220 W 42nd St, New York NY 10036	212-419-2900	P	363	1.0
6	New Line Home Video Inc—*Toby Emmerich*	116 N Robertson Blvd, Los Angeles CA 90048	310-854-5811	S	327*	1.5
7	William Morris Agency Inc—*Dave Wirtschafter*	1325 Ave of the Americ, New York NY 10019	212-586-5100	R	96*	.5
8	House of Blues Entertainment Inc	7060 Hollywood Blvd 11, Hollywood CA 90028	323-769-4600	S	95*	.3
9	Atlantic Recording Group—*Craig Kallman*	1290 Ave of the Americ, New York NY 10104	212-707-2000	S	90	.3
10	Raycom Sports—*Ken Haines*	1900 W Morehead St, Charlotte NC 28208	704-378-4400	S	75*	.1
11	Carolina Opry Gilmore Entertainment Group LLC	PO Box 7576, Myrtle Beach SC 29572	843-913-1400	S	69	.2
12	Capitol Steps Productions Inc—*Elaina Newport*	210 N Washington St, Alexandria VA 22314	703-683-8330	R	61*	<.1
13	Elite Model Management Corp—*Niel Hamel*	404 Park Ave S9th Fl, New York NY 10016	212-529-9700	R	61*	<.1
14	Talent Plus Inc—*Kimberly Rath*	1 Talent Plus Way, Lincoln NE 68506	402-489-2000	R	53*	.1
15	Creative Artists Agency Inc—*Richard Lovett*	2000 Avenue of the Sta, Los Angeles CA 90067	424-288-2000	R	51	.5
16	Rhino Records Inc—*Richard Foos*	1250 Connecticut Ave, Washington DC 20036		R	42*	.1
17	ABC Sports Inc—*George Bodenheimer*	47 W 66th St, New York NY 10023	212-456-7777	D	38*	.1
18	Carnegie Hall Corp—*Clive Gillinson*	881 7th Ave, New York NY 10019	212-903-9600	R	34*	.3
19	Kimmel Center Inc—*Anne Eyers*	260 S Broad St Ste 901, Philadelphia PA 19102	215-790-5800	R	32*	.7
20	Gilmore Entertainment Group LLC—*Calvin Gilmore*	PO Box 7576, Myrtle Beach SC 29572	843-913-1400	R	32*	.2
21	Metropolitan Tickets Inc—*Richard Baker*	527 N Grand Blvd, Saint Louis MO 63103	314-534-1111	R	22*	.1
22	On Stage Entertainment Inc	333 Orville Wright Ct, Las Vegas NV 89119	702-253-1333	R	22	.4
23	Knitting Factory Entertainment—*Morgan Margolis*	361 Metropolitan Ave, Brooklyn NY 11211	347-529-6696	R	19*	.1
24	One Reel—*Norman Langill*	PO Box 9750, Seattle WA 98109	206-281-7788	R	19*	.1
25	Nederlander Producing Company of America Inc—*James M Nederlander*	1450 Broadway Fl 6, New York NY 10018	212-840-5577	R	18*	.1
26	BRC Imagination Arts—*Bob Rogers*	2711 Winona Ave, Burbank CA 91504	818-841-8084	R	16*	.1
27	Dale Morris and Associates Inc—*Dale Morris*	818 19th Ave S, Nashville TN 37203	615-327-3400	R	16*	<.1
28	Higher Octave Music Inc—*David Nightheart*	4650 N Port Washington, Milwaukee WI 53212	414-961-8350	R	15*	.1
29	Keppler Speakers—*Jim Keppler*	4350 Fairfax Dr Ste 70, Arlington VA 22203	703-516-4000	R	15*	<.1
30	Pacific Northwest Ballet Foundation—*D Brown*	301 Mercer St, Seattle WA 98109	206-441-9411	R	15*	.2
31	United Talent Agency Inc—*James Berkus*	9560 Wilshire Blvd Ste, Beverly Hills CA 90212	310-273-6700	R	14*	.3
32	Bargemusic Ltd—*Mark Peskanov*	Fulton Ferry Landing, Brooklyn NY 11201		R	13*	<.1
33	Monterey Peninsula Artists Inc—*Dan Weiner*	509 Hartnell St, Monterey CA 93940	831-375-4899	R	12*	<.1
34	Curtis Brown Ltd—*Timothy Knowlton*	10 Astor Pl, New York NY 10003	212-473-5400	R	11*	<.1
35	Matador Records Inc—*Patrick Amory*	304 Hudson St 7th Fl, New York NY 10013	212-995-5882	R	11*	<.1
36	Leading The Way With Dr Michael Youssef Inc—*Michael Youssef*	PO Box 20100, Atlanta GA 30325	404-841-0100	R	11*	<.1
37	Lyric Opera of Kansas City—*Evan Luskin*	1029 Central Ave, Kansas City MO 64105	816-471-4933	R	10*	<.1
38	Eastern Educational Television Network Inc—*Robert Fleming*	55 Summer St Fl 4, Boston MA 02110	617-338-4455	R	9*	<.1
39	Musson Theatrical Inc—*Robert Downs*	890 Walsh Ave, Santa Clara CA 95050		R	8*	<.1
40	Elliot Amusement Co—*Robert Nederlander*	231 S Old Woodward Ave, Birmingham MI 48009	248-644-3456	R	8*	.2

Note: An asterisk (*) indicates an estimated financial figure. The company type code used is as follows: R = Private, P = Public, S = Private Subsidiary, B = Public Subsidiary, D = Division, J = Joint Venture, I = Investment Fund.

COMPANY RANKINGS BY SALES WITHIN 4-DIGIT SIC

Rank	Company Name—*Executive Officer*	Address, City, State, Zip	Phone	Type	Fin	Empls
41	Bgw Design Limited Inc—*Barton Weiss*	5061 Biscayne Blvd, Miami FL 33137	305-576-8888	R	8*	.2
42	Gersh Agency Inc—*Robert Gersh*	9465 Wilshire Blvd Fl, Beverly Hills CA 90212	310-274-6611	R	8*	.1
43	Metro Meadows Associates Inc—*Leroy Mobley*	11445 Stagg St, North Hollywood CA 91605	818-759-1224	R	7*	<.1
44	RA Reed Productions Inc—*Rick Reed*	955 N Columbia Blvd Bl, Portland OR 97217	503-735-0003	R	6*	<.1
45	North American Theatrix Ltd—*Jeff Mele*	60 Industrial Dr, Southington CT 06489	860-863-4112	R	6*	<.1
46	ACE Entertainment Inc—*J Allen Collier*	261 Friend St 5th Fl, Boston MA 02114	617-557-4400	R	6*	<.1
47	Troika Company Inc—*Nicholas Howey*	818 W Diamond Ave Ste, Gaithersburg MD 20878	301-208-2080	R	6*	.2
48	Palace Theater—*Tom Dolan*	1420 Celebrity Cir, Myrtle Beach SC 29577	843-448-9224	R	5*	.2
49	Media Theatrical Services Inc—*Tim Kohlmeyer*	7510 Burlington St, Omaha NE 68127	402-592-5522	R	5*	<.1
50	Dick Orkin's Creative Services Inc—*Dick Orkin*	13440 Ventura Blvd, Sherman Oaks CA 91423	818-465-0150	R	5*	<.1
51	Professional Sports Planning Inc—*Kevin D Poston*	909 Fannin St, Houston TX 77010	713-659-2255	R	5*	<.1
52	Triangle Talent Inc—*David H Snowden*	10424 Watterson Tr, Louisville KY 40299	502-267-5466	R	5*	<.1
53	Celebrity Series Of Boston Inc—*Marth Jones*	20 Park Plz Ste 1032, Boston MA 02116	617-482-6661	R	4*	<.1
54	Harmonia Mundi USA Inc—*Richard Rodzinski*	1117 Chestnut St, Burbank CA 91506	818-333-1500	R	4*	<.1
55	Television Production Service Inc—*Roger Zobel*	3988 Flowers Rd Ste 69, Atlanta GA 30360	770-452-8700	R	4*	<.1
56	Dattner Dispoto and Associates—*Fay Dattner*	10635 Santa Monica Blv, Los Angeles CA 90025	310-474-4585	R	4*	<.1
57	Law Actors Inc—*Ian Harris*	6171 N Sheridan Rd Ste, Chicago IL 60660	773-761-7738	R	4*	<.1
58	Pacific Talent Inc—*Andy Gilbert*	PO Box 19145, Portland OR 97239	503-228-3620	R	4*	<.1
59	Cavalry Security Gear and System—*Patrick Garvey*	PO Box 10127, Fairfield NJ 07004	973-276-6070	R	4*	.1
60	Alaska Center For The Performing Arts Inc—*Nancy Harbour*	621 W 6th Ave, Anchorage AK 99501	907-263-2900	R	3*	<.1
61	Electric Factory Concerts Inc—*Larry Magid*	421 North 7th St, Philadelphia PA 19123	215-569-9400	S	3*	<.1
62	Go West Presents—*Steve West*	PO Box 24545, Nashville TN 37202	615-256-6151	R	3*	<.1
63	Steven Scott Productions—*Stuart White*	400 Crossways Park Dr, Woodbury NY 11797	516-682-0080	D	3*	<.1
64	PSX Inc—*Jeffrey Borne*	17587 Hard Hat Dr, Covington LA 70435	985-809-8001	R	3*	<.1
65	Artists International Management Inc—*Steve Green*	2901 Clint Moore Rd St, Boca Raton FL 33496	561-498-1300	R	3*	<.1
66	Country Tonite Theatre—*Jeff Taylor*	129 Showplace Blvd, Pigeon Forge TN 37863	865-453-2193	R	2*	.1
67	Star Tickets Inc—*Brad Meyer*	6034 W Courtyard Dr St, Austin TX 78730	512-469-7469	R	2*	.1
68	Industry Entertainment Partners—*Phil Traill*	955 Carrillo Dr Ste 30, Los Angeles CA 90048	323-954-9000	R	2*	<.1
69	NS Bienstock Inc—*Richard Leibner*	250 W 57th St Ste 333, New York NY 10107	212-765-3040	R	2*	<.1
70	T Skorman Productions Inc—*Ted Skorman*	5156 S Orange Ave, Orlando FL 32809	407-895-3000	R	2*	<.1
71	Delicious Vinyl Inc—*Michael Ross*	6607 W Sunset Blvd, Los Angeles CA 90028	323-465-2700	R	2*	<.1
72	CorporateMagic—*Jim Kirk*	1925 Cedar Springs Rd, Dallas TX 75201	972-869-1919	S	2*	<.1
73	Soundscapes Inc—*Brent Walker*	3422 Old Cantrell Rd, Little Rock AR 72202	501-661-1765	R	2*	<.1
74	JestMaster Productions Inc—*Jon Koons*	434 Tenafly Rd, Englewood NJ 07631	201-568-7782	R	2*	<.1
75	Directors Co—*Micheal Parva*	311 W 43rd St Ste 409, New York NY 10036	212-246-5877	R	2*	<.1
76	Roger Richman Agency Inc—*Roger Richman*	9777 Wilshire Blvd Ste, Beverly Hills CA 90212	310-276-7000	S	2*	<.1
77	Dolores Robinson Ward Entertainment—*Dolores Robinson*	2554 Hutton Dr, Beverly Hills CA 90210	310-777-8777	R	2*	<.1
78	Nationwide Entertainment Services Inc—*AJ Sagman*	2756 N Green Valley Pk, Las Vegas NV 89104	702-451-8090	R	2*	<.1
79	Willy Bietak Productions Inc—*Willy Bietak*	1404 3rd St Promenade, Santa Monica CA 90401	310-576-2400	S	2*	<.1
80	Jm Associates Inc—*Jerry Kinnis*	1200 Scott St, Little Rock AR 72202	501-372-6544	R	2*	<.1
81	David Fee Is Magic Inc—*David Fee*	PO Box 1453, Pigeon Forge TN 37868	865-428-5222	R	1*	<.1
82	Management 360—*Doug Johnson*	9111 Wilshire Blvd, Beverly Hills CA 90210	310-272-7000	R	1*	<.1
83	KC Productions Inc—*Marcy Tuttle*	PO Box 2447, Kernersville NC 27285	336-993-9073	R	1*	<.1
84	Great Seats Inc—*Enrique Matta*	7338 Baltimore Ave 108, College Park MD 20740	301-985-6250	R	1*	<.1
85	American Talent Management—*Herb Rothman*	928 Broadway Ste 506, New York NY 10010	212-951-7341	R	1*	<.1
86	Buddy Lee Attractions Inc—*Donna Lee*	38 Music Sq E Ste 300, Nashville TN 37203	615-244-4336	R	1*	<.1
87	Franklin Designs Inc—*Robert Franklin*	208 Industrial Dr, Ridgeland MS 39157	601-853-9005	R	1*	<.1
88	Ticketsage Inc—*Stephen Cassar*	112 W Ctr St Ste 300, Fayetteville AR 72701	479-587-8336	R	1*	<.1
89	Modern Options Inc—*Robert R Walker*	PO Box 757, Temecula CA 92593	760-716-6295	R	1*	<.1
90	International Renaissance Festivals Ltd—*Jules Smith Sr*	PO Box 315, Crownsville MD 21032	410-266-7304	R	1*	<.1
91	Kingsland Entertainment Agency—*Norman E Land*	PO Box 4360, Pineville LA 71361	318-640-5555	R	1*	<.1
92	Stone City Attractions Inc—*Jack Orbin*	13300 Old Blanco Rd St, San Antonio TX 78216	210-493-3900	R	1*	<.1
93	Thea Dispeker Artists Management—*Kathryn Takach*	59 E 54th St Ste 81, New York NY 10022	212-421-7676	R	1*	<.1
94	Ariza Inc—*Jeff Callender*	1928 Boothe Cir, Longwood FL 32750	407-332-0011	R	1*	<.1
95	HighNote Records Inc—*Barney Fields*	106 W 71st St, New York NY 10023	212-873-2020	R	1*	<.1
96	Grand Entertainment Group Inc—*Joe Meador*	20 Music Sq W Ste 200, Nashville TN 37203	615-742-8080	R	1*	<.1
97	JJ Sedelmaier Productions Inc—*JJ Sedelmaier*	199 Main St, White Plains NY 10601	914-949-7979	R	1*	<.1
98	Oregon Cabaret Theatre Inc—*Craig Hudson*	PO Box 1149, Ashland OR 97520	541-488-8349	R	1*	<.1
99	Main Street Music Hall Inc—*Judy Blair*	1048 Main St, Osage Beach MO 65065	573-348-0588	R	1*	<.1
100	Milwaukee Public Theatre—*Jill Haaf*	626 E Kilbourn Ave Ste, Milwaukee WI 53202	414-347-1685	R	1*	<.1
101	Advanced Audio—*Robert Cap*	PO Box 305, Gilbert MN 55741	218-749-4056	R	<1*	<.1
102	Sibling Entertainment Group Holdings Inc—*Stephen Carlson*	333 Hudson St Ste 901, New York NY 10013	212-414-9600	P	<1	N/A
103	Just Voices Inc—*Maureen Kelly*	62 W 45th St 10th Fl, New York NY 10036	212-944-0992	R	N/A	<.1
104	Alan Wasser Associates—*Alan Wasser*	1650 Broadway Ste 800, New York NY 10019	212-307-0800	R	N/A	N/A

TOTALS: SIC 7922 Theatrical Producers & Services
Companies: 104 — 4,715 / 16.4

7929 Entertainers & Entertainment Groups

Rank	Company Name—*Executive Officer*	Address, City, State, Zip	Phone	Type	Fin	Empls
1	Warner Music Group Corp—*Edgar Bronfman Jr*	75 Rockefeller Plz, New York NY 10019	212-275-2000	P	554	3.7
2	Cove Marketing Inc—*Keith Horita*	1860 Ala Moana Blvd St, Honolulu HI 96815	808-842-5911	R	33*	.2
3	Music on the Move Plus Inc—*Taj Jordan*	6600 Industrial Loop, Greendale WI 53129	414-282-3866	R	24*	.1
4	Advanced Radio Network Studios—*Dave Graveline*	18165 NW 62nd Ct, Miami FL 33015		R	11*	<.1
5	World Classic Productions Inc—*George E Runquist*	PO Box 10, Whites Creek TN 37189	615-876-6100	R	9*	<.1
6	Steven Scott Orchestra Inc—*Joey Mills*	400 Crossways Park Dr, Woodbury NY 11797		R	8*	.1
7	Chicago City Limits—*Paul Zuckerman*	318 W 53rd St, New York NY 10019	212-888-5233	R	3*	<.1
8	Oglio Entertainment Group—*Carl Caprioglio*	PO Box 404, Redondo Beach CA 90277	310-791-8600	R	3*	<.1
9	Celebrity Suppliers	2756 Green Valley Pkwy, Las Vegas NV 89104	702-451-8090	D	2*	<.1
10	W Colston Leigh Inc—*William Leigh*	92 E Main St Ste 200, Somerville NJ 08876	908-253-8600	R	1*	<.1
11	Stratus Media Group Inc—*Paul Feller*	3 E De La Guerra St 2n, Santa Barbara CA 93101	805-884-9977	P	<1	N/A
12	Tip Quiet Entertainment Co—*Debra Phelps*	6607 Claridge St, Philadelphia PA 19111	215-342-2272	R	<1*	<.1

TOTALS: SIC 7929 Entertainers & Entertainment Groups
Companies: 12 — 649 / 4.2

7933 Bowling Centers

Rank	Company Name—*Executive Officer*	Address, City, State, Zip	Phone	Type	Fin	Empls
1	AMF Bowling Mexico Holding Inc—*Fredrick R Hipp* AMF Bowling Worldwide Inc	8100 AMF Dr, Mechanicsville VA 23111	804-730-4000	S	1,763*	10.0
2	Boliches AMF Inc—*Fredrick R Hipp* AMF Bowling Worldwide Inc	8100 AMF Dr, Mechanicsville VA 23111	804-730-4000	S	1,763*	10.0
3	AMF Bowling Centers International Inc—*Fredrick A Hipp* AMF Bowling Worldwide Inc	8100 AMF Dr, Mechanicsville VA 23111	804-730-4000	S	1,447*	10.0

Rank	Company Name—*Executive Officer*	Address, City, State, Zip	Phone	Type	Fin	Empls
4	AMF Bowling Worldwide Inc—*Frederick Hipp*	7313 Bell Creek Rd, Mechanicsville VA 23111	804-730-4000	S	405*	8.8
5	Bowl America Inc—*Leslie H Goldberg*	PO Box 1288, Springfield VA 22151	703-941-6300	P	27	.6
6	Western Bowl Inc—*Larry Schmitlou*	6383 Glenway Ave, Cincinnati OH 45211	513-574-2222	R	10*	.2

TOTALS: SIC 7933 Bowling Centers
Companies: 6   **5,415**   **39.6**

7941 Sports Clubs, Managers & Promoters

Rank	Company Name—*Executive Officer*	Address, City, State, Zip	Phone	Type	Fin	Empls
1	San Diego Padres Baseball Club LP—*Jeffrey Moorad*	9449 Friars Rd, San Diego CA 92108	619-881-6500	R	15,900*	.2
2	Spectator Management Group—*Wes Westley*	300 Conshohocken State, West Conshohocken PA 19428	610-729-7900	R	809*	1.4
3	Pro-Football Inc—*Daniel M Snyder*	21300 Redskin Park Dr, Ashburn VA 20147	703-726-7000	R	345	.3
4	Pittsburgh Associates—*Kevin McClatchy*	115 Federal St, Pittsburgh PA 15212	412-323-5000	R	284*	.5
5	KSA Industries Inc—*Kenneth S Adams Jr*	PO Box 844, Houston TX 77001	713-881-3400	R	283*	.4
6	Indianapolis Colts	7001 W 56th St, Indianapolis IN 46254	317-297-2658	R	248	.1
7	Los Angeles Dodgers Inc—*Bob Graziano*	1000 Elysian Park Ave, Los Angeles CA 90012	323-224-1500	R	246	.4
8	Major League Baseball—*Allan H Selig*	245 Park Ave 31st Fl, New York NY 10167	212-931-7800	R	196*	.3
9	Washington Nationals Baseball Club LLC	1500 S Capitol St SE, Washington DC 20003	202-675-6287	R	180	.1
10	Debartolo Inc—*Marie Debartoloyork*	7620 Market St, Youngstown OH 44512	330-965-2000	R	162*	6.0
11	Rocket Ball Ltd—*Thaddeus B Brown*	1510 Polk St, Houston TX 77002	713-758-7200	R	153	.3
12	NBA Inc—*Joel M Litvin*	645 5th Ave 19th Fl, New York NY 10022	212-407-8000	R	152*	.6
13	LA Lakers—*Frank Mariani*	555 N Nash St, El Segundo CA 90245	310-426-6000	R	152	<.1
14	Oakland Raiders—*Amy Trask*	1220 Harbor Bay Pkwy, Alameda CA 94502	510-864-5000	R	149	N/A
15	San Antonio Spurs LLC	1 AT and T Pkwy, San Antonio TX 78219	210-444-5000	R	139	N/A
16	Jazz Basketball Investors Inc	301 W South Temple, Salt Lake City UT 84101	801-325-2500	R	121	.1
17	AZPB LP—*Derrick Hall*	PO Box 2095, Phoenix AZ 85001	602-462-6500	R	81*	.3
18	Professional Basketball Club LLC	2 Leadership Square 21, Oklahoma City OK 73102	405-208-4800	R	80	.1
19	Bobcat Sports and Entertainment LLC—*Robert Johnson*	333 E Trade St, Charlotte NC 28202	704-688-8600	R	79*	.1
20	Athletics Investment Group—*Michael Crowley*	7000 Coliseum Way, Oakland CA 94621	510-638-4900	R	67*	.1
21	Dreams Entertainment Inc	2 S University Dr Ste, Plantation FL 33324	954-377-0002	S	58*	.1
22	Collegiate Licensing Co—*Pat Battle*	290 Interstate North C, Atlanta GA 30339	770-956-0520	R	57*	.1
23	Harlem Globetrotters International Inc—*Mannie L Jackson*	400 E Van Buren St Ste, Phoenix AZ 85004	602-258-0000	R	54*	.1
24	Detroit Pistons Basketball Co—*Tom Wilson*	4 Championship Dr, Auburn Hills MI 48326	248-377-0100	R	20*	.3
25	Indiana Sports Corp—*Susan Williams*	201 S Capitol Ave Ste, Indianapolis IN 46225	317-237-5000	R	17*	<.1
26	Kemper Lesnik Integrated Communications—*Steven Skinner*	444 N Michigan Ave Ste, Chicago IL 60611	312-755-3500	R	16*	.1
27	American Junior Golf Association Inc—*Jonah Beck*	1980 Sports Club Dr, Braselton GA 30517	770-868-4200	R	10*	.1
28	NHL Enterprises Inc—*Gary Bettman*	1251 Ave of the Americ, New York NY 10020	212-789-2000	R	10*	.4
29	Momentum- NA Inc—*John Armstrong*	161 Avenue Of The Amer, New York NY 10013	212-367-4500	S	10*	.1
30	Baseball Jax Inc—*Peter Bragan Sr*	PO Box 4756, Jacksonville FL 32201	904-358-2846	R	9*	<.1
31	Quicken Loans Arena—*Len Komoroski*	1 Center Ct, Cleveland OH 44115	216-420-2000	R	8*	.1
32	Main Events Inc—*Kathy Duva*	772 Union Blvd, Totowa NJ 07512	973-200-7050	R	8*	<.1
33	Suns Legacy Partners LLC—*Jennifer Irish*	PO Box 1369, Phoenix AZ 85001	602-379-7900	R	8*	.2
34	Orlando Predators Entertainment Inc—*Brett Bouchy*	302 S Graham Ave, Orlando FL 32803	407-447-3300	R	6*	.1
35	Don King Productions Inc—*Don King*	501 Fairway Dr, Deerfield Beach FL 33441	954-418-5800	R	5*	<.1
36	Championship Group Inc—*Ardy Arani*	1954 Airport Rd Ste 20, Atlanta GA 30341	770-457-5777	R	3*	<.1
37	Tom Collins Enterprises Inc—*Tom Collins*	3500 W 80th St #190, Minneapolis MN 55431	952-831-2237	R	3*	<.1
38	Career Sports and Entertainment Inc—*Lonnie Cooper*	600 Galleria Pkwy Se S, Atlanta GA 30339	770-955-1300	R	2*	.1
39	Louisville Baseball Club Inc—*Gary Ulmer*	PO Box 36407, Louisville KY 40233	502-212-2287	R	2*	.1
40	Sports Management Network Inc—*John P Caponigro*	1668 S Telegraph Rd St, Bloomfield Hills MI 48302	248-335-3535	R	1*	<.1
41	Athletic Resource Management Inc—*Jimmy Sexton*	6060 Poplar Ave Ste 47, Memphis TN 38119	901-763-4900	S	1*	<.1
42	Promotion Company Inc—*C Hubley*	838 N Delaware St, Indianapolis IN 46204	317-236-6515	R	1*	<.1
43	Horrow Sports Ventures Inc—*Rick Horrow*	6800 SW 40th St Ste 17, Miami FL 33155	561-743-6408	R	<1	<.1
44	SimplePons Inc—*C Leo Smith*	3960 N Andrews Ave, Oakland Park FL 33309	561-367-1055	P	<1	N/A

TOTALS: SIC 7941 Sports Clubs, Managers & Promoters
Companies: 44   **20,135**   **12.9**

7948 Racing Including Track Operations

Rank	Company Name—*Executive Officer*	Address, City, State, Zip	Phone	Type	Fin	Empls
1	Penn National Gaming Inc—*Peter M Carlino*	825 Berkshire Blvd Ste, Wyomissing PA 19610	610-373-2400	P	2,742	16.7
2	Dover Downs International Speedway Inc—*Denis McGlynn* Dover Motorsports Inc	PO Box 1412, Dover DE 19901	302-674-4600	S	1,160	N/A
3	International Speedway Corp—*Lesa France Kennedy*	PO Box 2801, Daytona Beach FL 32120	386-254-2700	P	630	.9
4	Churchill Downs Inc—*Robert L Evans*	700 Central Ave, Louisville KY 40208	502-636-4400	P	585	2.0
5	Speedway Motorsports Inc—*O Bruton Smith*	PO Box 600, Concord NC 28026	704-455-3239	P	502	1.1
6	MTR Gaming Group Inc—*Jeffrey J Dahl*	PO Box 356, Chester WV 26034	304-387-8000	P	435	2.5
7	Boomtown Biloxi Casino—*Chett Harrison* Penn National Gaming Inc	PO Box 369, Biloxi MS 39530	228-435-7000	S	359*	1.5
8	Sportsystems Corp—*Rick Abramson*	40 Fountain Plz, Buffalo NY 14202	716-858-5000	S	357*	1.1
9	Los Angeles Turf Club Inc—*Frank Stronach*	PO Box 60014, Arcadia CA 91066	626-574-7223	R	328*	1.6
10	Fair Grounds Race Course and Slots—*Tim Bryant* Churchill Downs Inc	1751 Gentilly Blvd, New Orleans LA 70119	504-944-5515	S	235*	.9
11	Delta Downs Racing Association Inc—*Steve Kuypers*	2717 Delta Downs Dr, Vinton LA 70668		R	148*	1.2
12	Charles Town Races and Slots Inc—*Jim Buchanan*	100 Hollywood Dr, Charles Town WV 25414		R	130*	1.1
13	Twin River Casino—*Craig Sculos*	100 Twin River Rd, Lincoln RI 02865	401-723-3200	R	124*	1.0
14	Churchill Downs Management Co Churchill Downs Inc	700 Central Ave, Louisville KY 40208	502-636-4400	S	71*	.3
15	Dover Motorsports Inc—*Denis McGlynn*	PO Box 843, Dover DE 19903	302-883-6500	P	63	.1
16	Southland Racing Corp—*Jeremy Jacobs*	PO Box 2088, West Memphis AR 72303	870-735-3670	S	61*	.5
17	Calder Race Course Inc—*C Kenneth Dunn*	PO Box 1808, Miami FL 33055	305-625-1311	R	59*	1.0
18	Scioto Downs Inc—*Ed Ryan* MTR Gaming Group Inc	PO Box 07823, Columbus OH 43207	614-491-2515	S	45*	.2
19	Mile High Racing and Entertainment—*Steve Rose*	10750 E Iliff Ave, Aurora CO 80014	303-751-5918	R	43*	.4
20	Canterbury Park Holding Corp—*Randall D Sampson*	1100 Canterbury Rd, Shakopee MN 55379	952-445-7223	P	40	.5
21	Sunland Park Racetrack—*Stan Fulton*	1200 Futurity Dr, Sunland Park NM 88063	575-874-5200	R	39*	.6
22	Hawthorne Race Course—*Tim Carey*	3501 S Laramie Ave, Cicero IL 60804	708-780-3700	R	35*	<.1
23	Brainerd International Raceway and Resort Inc—*Jed Copham*	5523 Birchdale Rd, Brainerd MN 56401	218-824-7223	H	28*	.1
24	Mile High Greyhound Racing at Wembly Park—*Bruce Frazier*	10750 E Iliff Ave, Aurora CO 80014	303-751-5918	R	24*	.2
25	World Racing Group Inc—*Brian Carter*	7575 West Winds Blvd S, Concord NC 28027	704-795-7223	P	23	.1
26	Turf Paradise Inc—*Jerry Simms*	1501 W Bell Rd, Phoenix AZ 85023	602-942-1101	R	17	.5
27	Westwood Group Inc—*Richard P Dalton*	190 VFW Pky, Revere MA 02151	781-284-2600	R	13*	.4
28	600 Racing Inc—*Ken Ragan* Speedway Motorsports Inc	5245 Hwy 49 S, Harrisburg NC 28075	704-455-3896	S	10*	<.1

Note: An asterisk (*) indicates an estimated financial figure. The company type code used is as follows: R = Private, P = Public, S = Private Subsidiary, B = Public Subsidiary, D = Division, J = Joint Venture, I = Investment Fund.

COMPANY RANKINGS BY SALES WITHIN 4-DIGIT SIC

Rank	Company Name—*Executive Officer*	Address, City, State, Zip	Phone	Type	Fin	Empls
29	Oaklawn Jockey Club Inc—*Charles Cella*	2705 Central Ave, Hot Springs AR 71901	501-623-4411	R	8*	.1
30	Dogwood Stable Inc—*W Cothran Campbell*	PO Box 1549, Aiken SC 29802	803-642-2972	R	8*	<.1
31	Retama Entertainment Group Inc—*Bryan Brown* Call Now Inc	PO Box 47535, San Antonio TX 78265	210-651-7000	S	6*	.2
32	Atlanta Motor Speedway Inc—*Ed Clark* Speedway Motorsports Inc	PO Box 500, Hampton GA 30228	770-946-4211	S	6*	.1
33	Walker Racing Inc—*Bernie Ecclestone*	4035 Championship Dr, Indianapolis IN 46268	317-387-1500	R	6*	.1
34	Indy Indoor Sports Inc—*George Klein*	6382 W 34th St, Indianapolis IN 46224	317-291-2729	R	6*	<.1
35	Memphis International Motorsports Corp Dover Motorsports Inc	5500 Victory Ln, Millington TN 38053	901-358-7223	S	6*	<.1
36	Call Now Inc—*Thomas Johnson*	PO Box 47535, San Antonio TX 78265	210-651-7145	P	4	.3
37	Red Mile Inc—*Joe Costa*	1200 Red Mile Rd, Lexington KY 40504	859-255-0752	R	4*	<.1
38	Team Valor Inc—*Barry Irwin*	PO Box 1048, Versailles KY 40383		R	2*	<.1
39	Mi-Jack Promotions LLC—*John Lanigan*	3111 167th St, Hazel Crest IL 60429	708-596-5200	R	<1*	<.1

TOTALS: SIC 7948 Racing Including Track Operations
Companies: 39   8,363   37.2

7991 Physical Fitness Facilities

Rank	Company Name—*Executive Officer*	Address, City, State, Zip	Phone	Type	Fin	Empls
1	Bally Total Fitness Corp—*Michael Shehan*	8700 W Bryn Mawr Ave, Chicago IL 60631	773-380-3000	S	728*	16.3
2	Cree Employee Services Co	4600 Silicon Dr, Durham NC 27703	919-313-5300	S	275*	1.3
3	Planet Fitness Inc—*Mike Grondahl*	26 Fox Run Rd, Newington NH 03801	603-750-0001	R	157	.2
4	New York Health and Racquet Club Inc—*Howard Brodsky*	24 E 13th St, New York NY 10003	212-924-4600	R	91*	.4
5	Cooper Aerobics Enterprises—*Rob Nelson*	12200 Preston Rd, Dallas TX 75230	972-560-2667	R	46*	.5
6	Lucille Roberts Health Spas—*Lucille Roberts*	925 Kings Hwy, Brooklyn NY 11223	718-339-0990	R	42*	.5
7	Brick Bodies Fitness Services Inc—*Victor Brick*	201 Old Padonia Rd, Cockeysville MD 21030	410-252-8058	R	19*	.2
8	Physique 57—*Jennifer Vaughan Maanavi*	24 W 57th St Ste 805, New York NY 10019	212-399-0570	R	8	.1
9	Liebenow and Torok Inc—*Susan Liebenow*	7309 Arlington Blvd St, Falls Church VA 22042	703-204-1355	R	8*	.3
10	Corporate Sports Unlimited Inc—*Bob Carignan*	6400 Highlands Pky SE, Smyrna GA 30082	770-432-0100	R	5*	.1
11	Spectrum Club Co—*John S Aylsworth*	2425 Olympic Blvd Ste, Santa Monica CA 90404	310-829-4995	R	5*	<.1
12	Seattle Gym—*Kari Anderson*	3811 NE 45th St, Seattle WA 98105	206-524-9246	R	4*	<.1
13	Leisure World Health Clubs	9 Collinsport Dr, Collinsville IL 62234	618-344-3095	R	4*	<.1
14	Aspire Kid Sports Center—*Scott Barclay*	50 S Hearthstone Way, Chandler AZ 85226	480-820-3774	R	3*	<.1
15	Racquet Club of Columbus Ltd—*Jim Hendrix*	1100 Bethel Rd, Columbus OH 43220	614-457-5671	R	3*	<.1
16	Health and Fitness Management Corp—*Denise Johnson*	3200 Westown Pkwy, West Des Moines IA 50266	515-223-5111	R	2*	<.1
17	Fitness Firm—*Ann Richards Schot*	Edgar Town Vineyard Ha, Edgartown MA 02539	508-627-3398	R	2*	<.1
18	Osmosis Partners Ltd—*Michael Stusser*	209 Bohemian Hwy, Freestone CA 95472	707-823-8231	R	1*	<.1
19	Colarossi Associates—*Glenn Colarossi*	75 3rd St, Stamford CT 06905	203-357-7555	R	1*	<.1
20	Cardiac Carr Co—*Margaret Carr*	34976 Aspenwood Ln, Willoughby OH 44094	440-946-7888	R	1*	<.1
21	Carolina Woman—*Meredith Fagen*	17036 Kenton Dr, Cornelius NC 28031	704-895-4482	R	1*	<.1
22	Inches-A-Weigh USA LLC—*Scott Simcik*	2850 West Horizon Ridg, Henderson NV 89052		R	N/A	<.1
23	Pee Wee Workout Inc—*Margaret Carr* Cardiac Carr Co	34976 Aspenwood Ln, Willoughby OH 44094	440-946-7988	S	N/A	<.1
24	Reform LLC—*Dorene Remo*	136 S Barrington Pl, Los Angeles CA 90049	310-471-8139	R	N/A	<.1

TOTALS: SIC 7991 Physical Fitness Facilities
Companies: 24   1,405   19.9

7992 Public Golf Courses

Rank	Company Name—*Executive Officer*	Address, City, State, Zip	Phone	Type	Fin	Empls
1	American Golf Corp—*Paul Major*	2951 28th St, Santa Monica CA 90405	310-664-4000	R	660*	20.0
2	Evergreen Alliance Golf Ltd—*Joe R Munsch*	4851 LBJ Fwy Ste 600, Dallas TX 75244	214-722-6000	R	284*	3.0
3	Wsg Parent Golf Iv LP—*Greg Adarr*	5080 Spectrum Dr, Addison TX 75001	972-419-1400	R	174*	5.0
4	Kemper Sports Management Inc—*Stephen Skinner*	500 Skokie Blvd Ste 44, Northbrook IL 60062	847-291-9666	S	150*	4.0
5	NTS Development Co—*Brian F Lavin*	10172 Linn Station Rd, Louisville KY 40223	502-426-4800	S	46*	.4
6	Cog Hill Second Inc—*Frank Jemsek*	12294 Archer Ave, Lemont IL 60439		R	24*	.3
7	Back O' Beyond Inc—*Maurice Greenberg*	Federal Hill Rd, Brewster NY 10509	845-279-7179	R	1*	<.1
8	Birchwood Farms Inc—*Thomas R Prewitt*	2126 Cypress Lake Rd, Hope Mills NC 28348	910-483-0359	R	1	<.1
9	Cherry Creek Golf Course—*Peter Quaresima*	PO Box 146, Youngwood PA 15697	724-925-8665	D	1*	<.1

TOTALS: SIC 7992 Public Golf Courses
Companies: 9   1,341   32.7

7993 Coin-Operated Amusement Devices

Rank	Company Name—*Executive Officer*	Address, City, State, Zip	Phone	Type	Fin	Empls
1	Caesars Entertainment Inc—*Gary Loveman*	3930 Howard Hughes Pkw, Las Vegas NV 89109	702-699-5000	S	5,888*	70.0
2	Barona Casino—*Carol Schoen*	1932 Wildcat Canyon Rd, Lakeside CA 92040	619-443-2300	R	4,320*	2.8
3	Sycuan Gaming Center—*Sheila Howe*	5469 Casino Way, El Cajon CA 92019	619-445-6002	R	3,230*	2.2
4	Commerce Casino—*George Tumanjan*	6131 E Telegraph Rd, Commerce CA 90040	323-721-2100	R	1,475*	2.5
5	Muckleshoot Indian Casino—*Peter Valentine*	2402 Auburn Way S, Auburn WA 98002	253-939-7484	R	718*	1.7
6	Seneca Gaming Corp—*Cathy Walker*	310 Fourth St, Niagara Falls NY 14303	716-299-1100	R	621*	4.0
7	Par-A-Dice Gaming Corp—*Keith E Smith*	21 Blackjack Blvd, East Peoria IL 61611	309-699-7711	S	563*	1.1
8	Hollywood Park Casino—*Taro Ito*	3883 W Century Blvd, Inglewood CA 90303	310-330-2800	R	538*	1.0
9	Little Six Inc—*Ed Stevenson*	2400 Mystic Lake Blvd, Prior Lake MN 55372	952-445-9000	R	330*	4.0
10	Mystic Lake Casino Hotel—*Edward Stevenson* Little Six Inc	2400 Mystic Lake Blvd, Prior Lake MN 55372	952-445-9000	S	330*	4.0
11	Belterra Resort Indiana LLC—*Anthony Sanfilippo*	777 Belterra Dr, Florence IN 47020	812-427-7777	S	280*	1.1
12	Dover Downs Gaming and Entertainment Inc—*Dennis McGlynn*	PO Box 843, Dover DE 19903	302-674-4600	P	238	1.3
13	Fitzgeralds Gaming Corp—*Don H Barden*	163 Madison Ave Ste 20, Detroit MI 48226	313-496-2900	S	202	3.2
14	Alton Gaming Co—*Richard Glasier*	219 Piasa St, Alton IL 62002	618-474-7500	S	86*	.9
15	Aztar Indiana Gaming Company LLC—*Thomas Dindman*	421 NW Riverside Dr, Evansville IN 47708		S	82	1.8
16	Fitzgeralds Tunica—*Chuck Miller* Fitzgeralds Gaming Corp	711 Lucky Ln, Robinsonville MS 38664		S	77*	1.2
17	Lady Luck Casino (Caruthersville Missouri)	PO Box 1135, Caruthersville MO 63830	573-333-6000	S	75*	.5
18	Lucky Eagle Casino—*Jphn Fetterstrom*	12888 188th Ave SW, Rochester WA 98579	360-273-2000	R	70*	.6
19	Century Casinos Inc—*Erwin Haitzmann*	2860 S Circle Dr Ste 3, Colorado Springs CO 80906	719-527-8300	P	61	.9
20	Rainbow Casino	122 S Water St, Henderson NV 89015	702-565-7977	R	23*	.2
21	Vacationland Vendors Inc—*David Gussel*	PO Box 177, Wisconsin Dells WI 53965	608-254-8515	R	8*	<.1
22	Southern Amusement Co—*John Lineberry*	3770 Progress Rd, Norfolk VA 23502	757-857-6211	R	7*	.1
23	Global Casinos Inc—*Clifford L Neuman*	1507 Pine St, Boulder CO 80302	303-449-2100	P	6	.1
24	Premier Amusements Inc—*Philip Wood*	6420 Wuliger Way Ste A, Fort Worth TX 76180	817-577-0638	R	4*	.1
25	Doc Holiday Inc—*Terry Houk*	PO Box 639, Central City CO 80427	303-582-1400	R	3*	<.1
26	Mc Donald's Amusements Inc—*Jimmy Mcdonald*	1965 Great Falls Hwy, Lancaster SC 29720	803-286-5676	R	2*	.1

TOTALS: SIC 7993 Coin Operated Amusement Devices
Companies: 26   19,236   105.3

Rank	Company Name—*Executive Officer*	Address, City, State, Zip	Phone	Type	Fin	Empls
7996 Amusement Parks						
1	Disney-MGM Studios—*Al Weiss*	PO Box 10000, Lake Buena Vista FL 32830	407-824-4321	R	8,522*	60.0
2	Busch Entertainment Corp—*Keith Kasen*	231 South Bemisstan St, Clayton MO 63105	314-613-6040	S	7,500*	15.0
3	Walt Disney Parks and Resorts—*James Rasulo*	500 S Buena Vista St, Burbank CA 91521	818-560-1000	S	6,319*	25.0
4	Walt Disney World Co—*Robert A Igar*	PO Box 10000, Lake Buena Vista FL 32830	407-824-2222	S	5,820*	60.0
5	Cedar Fair LP—*Matthew A Ouimet*	PO Box 5006, Sandusky OH 44870	419-627-2233	P	1,029	38.7
6	Six Flags Entertainment Corp—*James Reid-Anderson*	924 Ave J E, Grand Prairie TX 75050	972-595-5000	P	1,013	28.9
7	Dollywood Co—*Dan Rohman*	2700 Dollywood Park Bl, Pigeon Forge TN 37863	865-428-9488	R	769*	3.0
8	Knott's Berry Farm Foods Inc—*Jack Salsas*	8039 Beach Blvd, Buena Park CA 90620	714-220-5200	S	655*	3.0
9	Six Flags Theme Parks Inc—*Mark Shapiro* Six Flags Entertainment Corp	1540 Broadway 15th Fl, New York NY 10036	212-652-9403	S	600	.5
10	Six Flags Services of Texas Inc—*Mark Shapiro* Six Flags Entertainment Corp	2201 Rd to Six Flags, Arlington TX 76011	817-640-8900	S	458*	2.0
11	Elitch Gardens LP—*Rod Rakin*	2000 Elitch Cir, Denver CO 80204	303-595-4386	S	446*	1.5
12	Lagoon Corp—*David Freed*	PO Box 696, Farmington UT 84025	801-451-8000	R	436*	2.0
13	Six Flags Over Texas Inc—*Alexander Weber Jr* Six Flags Entertainment Corp	2201 Rd to Six Flag St, Arlington TX 76011	817-640-8900	S	413*	1.3
14	Six Flags California—*Jay Thomas* Six Flags Entertainment Corp	PO Box 5500, Valencia CA 91355	661-255-4100	S	296*	.3
15	Herschend Family Entertainment Corp—*Jack Herschend*	5445 Triangle Pkwy Ste, Norcross GA 30092	770-441-1940	R	284*	2.0
16	Silver Dollar City Inc—*Joel Manby*	399 Indian Point Rd, Branson MO 65616		R	284*	2.0
17	SeaWorld San Diego—*Andy Fichthorn* Busch Entertainment Corp	500 Seaworld Dr, San Diego CA 92109	619-226-3901	S	257*	3.5
18	Six Flags St Louis Inc—*Dave Roemer* Six Flags Theme Parks Inc	PO Box 60, Eureka MO 63025	636-938-5300	S	251*	.3
19	Sea World of Florida Inc—*Keith Kasen* Busch Entertainment Corp	7007 Sea World Dr, Orlando FL 32821	407-351-3600	S	240*	3.0
20	Seaworld Parks and Entertainment Inc—*James Atchison*	9205 Southprk Cntr Loo, Orlando FL 32819	407-226-5080	R	147*	3.5
21	Morey's Piers—*Will Morey*	3501 Boardwalk, Wildwood NJ 08260	609-522-3900	R	71*	1.1
22	Nickels and Dimes Inc—*Ron Kostelny*	4534 Old Denton Rd, Carrollton TX 75010	972-939-4220	R	68*	.5
23	Castle Park Amusement Co—*Jeff Moody*	3500 Polk St, Riverside CA 92505	951-785-3000	R	50*	.4
24	Malibu Entertainment Worldwide Inc—*Robert A Whitman*	717 N Harwood St Ste 1, Dallas TX 75201	214-210-8701	R	42	.9
25	Adventure Lands of America Inc—*Jack F Krantz*	305 34th Ave NW, Altoona IA 50009	515-266-2121	R	29*	.2
26	Shepherd of the Hills Homestead and Outdoor Theatre—*Gary Snadon*	5586 W Hwy 76, Branson MO 65616	417-334-4191	R	26*	.2
27	Venice Amusement Corp—*Robert Bennett*	800 Ocean Ter, Seaside Heights NJ 08751	732-793-6469	R	23*	.2
28	Kennywood Entertainment Co—*Richard Golding*	4800 Kennywood Blvd, West Mifflin PA 15122	412-461-0500	S	22*	.1
29	Mountain Creek—*Frank DeBerry*	200 Rte 94, Vernon NJ 07462	973-864-8128	R	20*	2.6
30	HH Knoebels Sons Inc—*Richard Knoebel*	PO Box 317, Elysburg PA 17824	570-672-2572	R	19*	1.4
31	Adventureland Park—*John F Krantz*	PO Box 3355, Des Moines IA 50316	515-266-2121	R	19*	.2
32	Gatorland—*John C Atz*	14501 S Orange Blossom, Orlando FL 32837	407-855-5496	R	17*	.1
33	Fun-Plex Inc—*Frank Khan*	13700 Beechnut St, Houston TX 77083	281-530-7777	R	14*	.1
34	Clabrook Farms Inc—*Jacob Kagan*	26205 E Hwy 50, Christmas FL 32709	407-568-2885	R	13*	<.1
35	Dutch Wonderland—*Rick Stammel*	2249 Lincoln Hwy E, Lancaster PA 17602	717-386-2839	R	10*	<.1
36	Lakeside Park Co—*Rhoda Krasner*	4601 Sheridan Blvd, Denver CO 80212	303-477-1621	R	9*	.1
37	Santa's Enchanted Forest Inc—*Steven Brian Shechtman*	7900 SW 40th St, Miami FL 33155	305-893-0090	R	7*	.1
38	Scandia Amusement Park—*Scott Larson*	1155 S Wanamaker Ave, Ontario CA 91761	909-390-3092	R	7*	.1
39	Consign LLC—*Todd Twigg*	PO Box 1297, Severna Park MD 21146	410-987-2097	R	1*	<.1

TOTALS: SIC 7996 Amusement Parks
Companies: 39

					36,205	263.6

Rank	Company Name—*Executive Officer*	Address, City, State, Zip	Phone	Type	Fin	Empls
7997 Membership Sports & Recreation Clubs						
1	24 Hour Fitness Worldwide Inc—*Carl Liebert III*	PO Box 2689, Carlsbad CA 92018	925-543-3100	S	1,096*	20.0
2	Bally Total Fitness Holding Corp—*Mike Sheehan*	8700 W Bryn Mawr Ave 2, Chicago IL 60631	773-380-3000	R	1,059*	19.2
3	Life Time Fitness Inc—*Bahram Akradi*	2902 Corporate Pl, Chanhassen MN 55317	952-947-0000	P	913	19.0
4	ClubCorp Inc—*Eric Affeldt*	PO Box 819012, Dallas TX 75381	972-243-6191	S	779*	14.0
5	Ponte Vedra Corp—*Dale Haney*	200 Ponte Vedra Blvd, Ponte Vedra Beach FL 32082	904-285-1111	S	462*	.7
6	Wsg Pecan Grove Iv LP—*Greg Adarr*	5080 Spectrum Dr Fl 11, Addison TX 75001	972-490-2785	R	150*	<.1
7	Harrah's Aviation Inc—*Gary W Loveman*	1 Harrahs Ct, Las Vegas NV 89119	702-407-6000	S	71	N/A
8	Sports Club Company Inc—*Rex A Licklider*	11151 Missouri Ave, Los Angeles CA 90025	310-479-5200	P	64	2.6
9	Club One Inc—*Jim Mizes*	555 Market St 13th Fl, San Francisco CA 94105	415-477-3000	R	57*	1.6
10	Anytime Fitness Inc—*Jeff Klinger*	12181 Margo Ave S, Hastings MN 55033	651-438-5000	R	40*	.1
11	Snap Fitness—*Peter Taunton*	2411 Galpin Ct Ste 110, Chanhassen MN 55317	952-474-5422	R	26*	.1
12	Green Valley Recreation Inc—*Anndrea Blackshear*	1070 Calle De Las Casi, Green Valley AZ 85614	520-625-3440	R	8*	.1
13	Buffalo Athletic Club Southtown LLC—*John Schiffhauer*	3035 Union Rd, Orchard Park NY 14127	716-675-9353	R	3*	.1
14	Cherokee Recreation and Parks Authority—*J Biello*	7545 Main St Bldg 200, Woodstock GA 30188	770-924-6689	R	2*	<.1
15	Sanyo Foods Corporation Of America—*Jun Ida*	11955 Monarch St, Garden Grove CA 92841	714-891-3671	R	2*	<.1

TOTALS: SIC 7997 Membership Sports & Recreation Clubs
Companies: 15

					4,732	77.5

Rank	Company Name—*Executive Officer*	Address, City, State, Zip	Phone	Type	Fin	Empls
7999 Amusement & Recreation Nec						
1	Bob Evans Farms Inc (Rio Grande Ohio)—*Steven A Davis*	791 Farmview Dr, Bidwell OH 45614	740-245-5305	S	38,238*	42.0
2	Rancho Station LLC	2400 N Rancho Dr, Las Vegas NV 89130	702-631-7000	S	10,117*	11.0
3	Wynn Resorts Ltd—*Stephen A Wynn*	3131 Las Vegas Blvd S, Las Vegas NV 89109	702-770-7555	P	4,185	16.4
4	Harrah's Cherokee Casino and Hotel	777 Casino Dr, Cherokee NC 28719	828-497-7777	S	2,532*	2.3
5	Harrah's Laughlin Inc—*Gary Loveman*	2900 S Casino Dr, Laughlin NV 89029	702-298-4600	S	2,355*	3.0
6	Boyd Gaming Corp—*Keith E Smith*	3883 Howard Hughes Pkw, Las Vegas NV 89169	702-792-7200	P	2,141	21.3
7	Boyd Tunica Inc—*William Boyd* Boyd Gaming Corp	5111 Boulder Hwy, Las Vegas NV 89122	702-456-7777	S	1,995*	1.8
8	Green Valley Ranch Gaming LLC—*Tim Wright* GV Ranch Station Inc	2300 Paseo Verde Pkwy, Henderson NV 89052	702-617-7777	S	1,863*	2.0
9	Sunset Station Inc	1301 W Sunset Rd, Henderson NV 89014	702-547-7777	S	1,863*	2.0
10	Durango Station Inc—*Frank J Fertitta*	2411 W Sahara Ave, Las Vegas NV 89126	702-367-2411	S	1,862*	2.0
11	GV Ranch Station Inc—*Tim Wright*	2300 Paseo Verde Pkwy, Henderson NV 89052	702-617-7777	S	1,862*	2.0
12	Lake Mead Station Holdings LLC—*Frank J Fertitta* Station Holdings Inc	777 W Lake Mead Dr, Henderson NV 89015	702-558-7000	S	1,862*	2.0
13	Texas Station LLC—*Richard St Jean*	2101 Texas Star Ln, North Las Vegas NV 89032	702-631-1000	S	1,397*	1.5

Note: An asterisk (*) indicates an estimated financial figure. The company type code used is as follows: R = Private, P = Public, S = Private Subsidiary, B = Public Subsidiary, D = Division, J = Joint Venture, I = Investment Fund.

COMPANY RANKINGS BY SALES WITHIN 4-DIGIT SIC

Rank	Company Name—Executive Officer	Address, City, State, Zip	Phone	Type	· Fin	Empls
14	Ameristar Casinos Inc—Gordon Kanofsky	3773 Howard Hughes Pky, Las Vegas NV 89169	702-567-7000	P	1,215	7.2
15	Vail Resorts Inc—Robert A Katz	PO Box 7, Vail CO 81658	303-404-1800	P	1,167	4.3
16	Pinnacle Entertainment Inc—Anthony M Sanflippo	8918 Spanish Ridge Ave, Las Vegas NV 89148	702-784-7777	P	1,141	7.5
17	Blue Chip Casino LLC—William Boyd	777 Blue Chip Dr, Michigan City IN 46360	219-879-7711	S	1,109*	1.0
18	Isle of Capri Casinos Inc—Virginia McDowell	600 Emerson Rd Ste 300, Saint Louis MO 63141	314-813-9200	P	1,005	8.6
19	Lake Mead Station Inc—Frank J Feritta III	777 W Lake Mead Dr, Henderson NV 89015	702-558-7000	S	932*	1.0
20	Palm Station LLC—Frank Feritta III	4321 W Flamingo Rd, Las Vegas NV 89103	702-942-7777	S	932*	1.0
21	Tropicana Station Inc—Frank J Feritta III	3330 W Tropicana Ave, Las Vegas NV 89103	702-740-0000	S	932*	1.0
22	Centerline Holdings LLC—Frank J Fertitta III	2411 W Sahara Ave, Las Vegas NV 89102	702-367-2411	S	931*	1.0
23	Fiesta Station Holdings LLC—Frank J Fertitta Station Holdings Inc	2400 N Rancho Dr, Las Vegas NV 89130	702-631-7000	S	931*	1.0
24	Station Holdings Inc—Frank J Fertitta	2411 W Sahara Ave, Las Vegas NV 89102	702-367-2411	S	931*	1.0
25	Station Online Inc—Frank J Fertitta	2411 W Sahara Ave, Las Vegas NV 89102	702-367-2411	S	931*	1.0
26	Station Technology LLC—Frank J Fertitta	2411 W Sahara Ave, Las Vegas NV 89102	702-367-2411	S,	931*	1.0
27	Vista Holdings LLC—Frank J Fertitta	2411 W Sahara Ave, Las Vegas NV 89102	702-367-2411	S	931*	1.0
28	Aztar Corp—Robert M Haddock	2390 E Camelback Rd St, Phoenix AZ 85016	602-381-4100	S	921	9.8
29	Scientific Games Corp—A Lorne Weil	750 Lexington Ave, New York NY 10022	212-754-2233	P	879	3.5
30	Four Queens Hotel and Casino Inc—Terry Caudill	202 Fremont St, Las Vegas NV 89101	702-385-4011	R	855*	.8
31	Boyd Louisiana LLC—William Boyd Boyd Gaming Corp	5050 Williams Blvd, Kenner LA 70065	504-443-8000	S	795*	1.0
32	Bally Technologies Corp—Richard M Haddrill	6601 S Bermuda Rd, Las Vegas NV 89119	702-584-7700	P	758	2.8
33	Harrah's Kansas Casino Corp—Gary Loveman	12305 150th Rd, Mayetta KS 66509	785-966-7777	S	711*	.9
34	Harrah's Phoenix Ak-Chin Casino—Gary Loveman	15406 N Maricopa Rd, Maricopa AZ 85139	480-802-5000	S	632*	.8
35	MLB Advanced Media LP—Robert A Bowman	75 9th Ave 5th Fl, New York NY 10011	212-485-3444	R	622*	.6
36	Skagit Valley Casino Resort—Don Guglialnimo	5984 Darrk Ln, Bow WA 98232	360-724-7777	R	536*	.5
37	Coast Resorts Inc—Michael J Gaughan	4500 W Tropicana Ave, Las Vegas NV 89103	702-365-7469	R	526	7.3
38	Alpine Meadows of Tahoe Inc—Matt Janney	PO Box 5279, Tahoe City CA 96145	530-583-4232	S	492*	.1
39	Harrah's Operating Company Memphis Inc	1023 Cherry Rd, Memphis TN 38117	901-762-8600	S	460*	.5
40	Hollywood Casino Corp—Gary Luderitz	777 Hollywood Blvd, Grantville PA 17028	717-469-2211	S	458	4.7
41	Ringling Brothers and Barnum and Bailey Circus and Combined Shows Inc	8607 Westwood Center D, Vienna VA 22182	703-448-4000	S	409*	3.0
42	Treasure Island Inc (Red Wing Minnesota)—Kim Pang	PO Box 75, Red Wing MN 55066		R	408*	1.5
43	Jacobs Entertainment Inc—Jeffrey P Jacobs	26 Allendale Dr, Rye NY 10580		R	257	1.0
44	Boomtown Inc—Daniel Lee Pinnacle Entertainment Inc	PO Box 399, Verdi NV 89439	775-345-6000	S	226*	2.8
45	Stubhub Inc—Chris Tsakalakis	199 Fremont St Fl 4, San Francisco CA 94105	415-222-8400	S	199*	.3
46	H Ski Corp—Kirk Hanna	PO Box 280, Government Camp OR 97028	503-272-3206	R	197*	.2
47	Harrah's Interactive Investment Co—Gary W Loveman	1 Harrah's Ct, Las Vegas NV 89119	702-407-6000	S	189*	.2
48	Western Regional Off-Track Betting Corp—Micheal D Kane	8315 Park Rd, Batavia NY 14020	585-343-1423	R	180*	.5
49	American Wagering Management Company Inc—Victor J Salerno American Wagering Inc	675 Grier Dr, Las Vegas NV 89119	702-735-5529	S	178*	.2
50	Boca Resorts Inc—H Wayne Huizenga	501 E Camino Real, Boca Raton FL 33432	561-447-5300	R	163*	2.2
51	Ticketmaster Group Inc	3701 Wilshire Blvd Fl, Los Angeles CA 90010	213-381-2000	S	149	N/A
52	Arabian Nights—Mark M Miller	3081 Arabian Nights Bl, Kissimmee FL 34747	407-239-9223	R	144*	.1
53	Deadwood Gulch Resort and Gaming Corp	PO Box 643, Deadwood SD 57732	605-578-1294	R	116*	.1
54	Laurel Highlands River Tours Inc—Mark McCarty	PO Box 107, Ohiopyle PA 15470	724-329-8531	R	109*	.1
55	Steamboat Ski and Resort Corp—Christopher S Diamond	2305 Mt Werner Cir, Steamboat CO 80487	970-879-6111	S	104*	1.8
56	Playnetwork Inc—Lon Troxel	8727 148th Ave NE, Redmond WA 98052	425-497-8100	R	96*	.1
57	HCAL Corp—Gary W Loveman	1 Harrah's Ct, Las Vegas NV 89119	702-407-6000	S	90*	.1
58	Orlando Jai Alai	6405 S Hwy 17-92, Fern Park FL 32730	407-339-6221	R	89*	.2
59	New York Skyline Inc Skyline Multimedia Entertainment Inc	350 5th Ave 2nd Fl, New York NY 10118	212-279-9777	S	88*	.1
60	Peninsula Gaming Company LLC—Brent Stevens	600 Star Brewery Dr, Dubuque IA 52001	563-690-4975	R	87*	.7
61	Skerbeck Brothers Shows Inc—Joseph Skerbeck	PO Box 1062, Escanaba MI 49829	616-550-3147	R	84	.1
62	Cheer Ltd—Gwen P Holtsclaw	118 Ridgeway Dr Ste 10, Fayetteville NC 28311	910-488-2600	R	82*	.1
63	Carson Nugget Inc—Brian Smith	507 N Carson St, Carson City NV 89701	775-882-1626	R	80*	.6
64	United Skates of America Inc—David Feitel	3362 Refugee Rd, Columbus OH 43232	614-239-7202	R	74*	.6
65	155 East Tropicana LLC—Neil Kiefer	115 E Tropicana Ave, Las Vegas NV 89109	702-739-9000	R	72	N/A
66	Epoch Holding Corp—William W Priest	640 5th Ave 18th Fl, New York NY 10019	212-303-7200	P	71	.1
67	Harrah's Michigan Corp—Gary W Loveman	1 Harrahs Ct, Las Vegas NV 89119	705-407-6000	S	68*	.1
68	Challenge Park Xtreme LLC—Ray Dagnino	2903 Schweitzer Rd, Joliet IL 60436	815-726-2800	S	64*	.1
69	Nolan Amusement Co—Christi Nolan	3600 Moxahala Pl, Zanesville OH 43701	740-452-3398	R	58*	.1
70	Sailboats Inc—Jack Culley	250 Marina Dr, Superior WI 54880	715-392-7131	R	57*	.1
71	Ticketscom Inc—John Walker MLB Advanced Media LP	555 Anton Blvd Fl 11, Costa Mesa CA 92626	714-327-5400	S	56	.9
72	VCG Holding Corp—Troy H Lowrie	390 Union Blvd Ste 540, Lakewood CO 80228	303-934-2424	S	55	.9
73	Harrah's Crescent City Investment Co—Gary W Loveman	1 Harrah's Ct, Las Vegas NV 89119	705-407-6000	S	54*	.1
74	Sally Corp—John Wood	745 W Forsyth St, Jacksonville FL 32204	904-355-7100	R	49*	<.1
75	Nevada Gold and Casinos Inc—Robert Sturges	50 Briar Hollow Ln Ste, Houston TX 77027	713-621-2245	P	48	1.4
76	Premier Exhibitions Inc—Christopher J Davino	3340 Peachtree Rd NE S, Atlanta GA 30326	404-842-2600	P	45	.1
77	Big Apple Circus—Wendy Siegel	505 8th Ave 19th Fl, New York NY 10018	212-268-2500	R	41*	.3
78	Janus Hotels and Resorts Inc—Louis S Beck	2300 Corporate Blvd NW, Boca Raton FL 33431	561-997-2325	R	40	2.1
79	Cumberland Valley Shows Inc—Terry Stafford	PO Box 702, Lebanon TN 37087	615-566-7430	R	40*	.3
80	Ray Cammack Shows Inc—Guy Leavitt	4950 W Southern Ave, Laveen AZ 85339	602-237-3333	R	40*	.3
81	GameTech International Inc—Kevin Painter	8850 Double Diamond Pk, Reno NV 89521		P	35	.1
82	Trans World Corp—Rami Ramadan	545 5th Ave Ste 940, New York NY 10017	212-983-3355	P	34	.6
83	Ripley Entertainment Inc	7576 Kingspointe Pky S, Orlando FL 32819	407-345-8010	S	34*	.2
84	Full House Resorts Inc—Andre M Hilliou	4670 S Fort Apache Rd, Las Vegas NV 89147	702-221-7800	P	33	<.1
85	Amtote International Inc—Steve Keech	11200 Pepper Rd, Hunt Valley MD 21031	410-771-8700	R	32*	.3
86	Tupelo Furniture Market Inc—VM Cleveland	1879 N Coley Rd, Tupelo MS 38801	662-842-4442	R	30*	<.1
87	Greeters of Hawaii Ltd—Peter Fithian	PO Box 29638, Honolulu HI 96820	808-836-0161	R	28*	.1
88	Harrah's Wheeling Corp—Gary W Loveman	1 Harrahs Ct, Las Vegas NV 89119	702-407-6000	S	28*	<.1
89	Davis Amusement Cascadia Inc—Michael Davis	PO Box 1585, Clackamas OR 97015	503-632-6104	R	28*	<.1
90	Lakes Entertainment Inc—Lyle Berman	130 Cheshire Ln Ste 10, Minnetonka MN 55305	952-449-9092	P	25	<.1
91	Archon Corp—Paul W Lowden	2200 S Casino Dr, Laughlin NV 89029	702-732-9120	P	23	.3
92	MDI Entertainment Inc—Steve Saferin	1500 Bluegrass Lakes P, Alpharetta GA 30004	770-664-3700	S	23*	<.1
93	Leroy's Horse and Sports Place—Victor J Salerno American Wagering Inc	675 Grier Dr, Las Vegas NV 89119	702-735-0101	S	21*	.2
94	New Orleans Paddlewheels Inc	610 S Peters St Ste 10, New Orleans LA 70130		R	20*	.2

Rank	Company Name—*Executive Officer*	Address, City, State, Zip	Phone	Type	Fin	Empls
95	Myers International Midways Inc—*Bobby Myers*	PO Box 1929, Gibsonton FL 33534	813-677-2787	R	20*	.1
96	Loon Mountain Recreation Corp—*George Gillette Jr*	60 Loon Mountain Rd, Lincoln NH 03251	603-745-8111	R	15*	.7
97	Winter Sports Inc—*Daniel Graves*	PO Box 1400, Whitefish MT 59937	406-862-1900	R	15*	.1
98	Paintball Dave's Inc—*Dave Rudig*	203 N Broadway, Milwaukee WI 53202	414-271-3004	R	15*	<.1
99	Venture Up Inc—*Teresa Lengyel*	1938 E Medlock Dr, Phoenix AZ 85016	602-955-9100	R	15*	<.1
100	Blue Grass Shows Inc—*James J Murphy Sr*	PO Box 75244, Tampa FL 33675	813-247-4431	R	14*	.2
101	Farrow Amusement Company Inc—*James M Williams*	PO Box 6747, Jackson MS 39282	601-371-1203	R	14	.2
102	Pyrotex Inc—*Randy Beckham*	4368 FM 1553, Leonard TX 75452	903-587-8000	R	14*	<.1
103	Tracy's Karate Studios—*Tim Golby*	10220 Manchester Rd, Kirkwood MO 63122	314-821-0555	R	13*	<.1
104	Alta Ski Lifts Company Inc—*David Davenport*	PO Box 8007, Alta UT 84092	801-359-1078	R	12	.5
105	American Wagering Inc—*Victor J Salerno*	675 Grier Dr, Las Vegas NV 89119	702-735-5529	P	12	.2
106	Nbo Systems Inc—*Keith Guevara*	3676 California Ave D, Salt Lake City UT 84104	801-746-8000	R	12*	<.1
107	Global Entertainment Corp—*Richard Kozuback*	1600 N Desert Dr Ste 3, Tempe AZ 85281	480-994-0772	P	11	.2
108	Bear Valley Mountain Resort—*Martin Wegenstein*	PO Box 5038, Bear Valley CA 95223	209-753-2301	R	11*	.4
109	Absolute Amusements—*David Peters*	11100 Astronaut Blvd, Orlando FL 32837	407-856-3866	R	.11*	<.1
110	Body Construction Personal Fitness Trainers—*Roy Taylor*	4504 W Kennedy Blvd, Tampa FL 33609	813-289-7867	R	10*	<.1
111	New Orleans Tourism Marketing Corp—*Sandra S Shilstone*	365 Canal St Ste1120, New Orleans LA 70130	504-524-4784	R	10*	<.1
112	Littlefield Corp—*Jeffrey Minch*	2501 N Lamar Blvd, Austin TX 78705	512-476-5141	P	10	.1
113	Florida Gaming Corp—*W Bennett Collett*	3500 NW 37th Ave, Miami FL 33142	305-633-6400	P	9	.1
114	Pyro Shows Inc—*Lansden E Hill*	PO Box 1776, LaFollette TN 37766	423-566-5729	R	9*	<.1
115	Florida Radio Rental Inc	2700 Davie Rd, Davie FL 33314	954-581-4437	S	8*	<.1
116	Bombard Society Inc—*Buddy Bombard*	605 Belvedere Rd Ste 1, West Palm Beach FL 33401	561-837-6610	R	8*	<.1
117	Skyline Multimedia Entertainment Inc—*Michael Leeb*	350 5th Ave Ste 324, New York NY 10118	212-279-9777	P	8	.1
118	Royal Gorge Bridge Co—*Mike Bandera*	PO Box 549, Canon City CO 81215	719-275-7507	R	7*	.2
119	Pump It Up—*Grant Beem*	1249 Quarry Ln, Pleasanton CA 94566	925-397-1300	R	7*	<.1
120	Peter Hughes Diving Inc—*Wayne B Brown*	15291 NW 60th Ave Ste, Miami Lakes FL 33014	305-669-9391	R	7*	<.1
121	Kissel Brothers Shows Inc—*Barbara Kissel*	6104 Rose Petal Dr, Cincinnati OH 45247	513-741-1080	R	6*	<.1
122	Kramer Entertainment Agency Inc—*Robert A Kramer*	3849 Lake Michigan Dr, Grand Rapids MI 49534	616-791-0095	R	6	<.1
123	Counter Attactics Inc—*Bob Thurman*	PO Box 35, Lees Summit MO 64063	816-525-3717	R	6*	<.1
124	My Pony Party Inc	595 Buena Vista Ave, Gilroy CA 95020	408-847-6424	R	6*	<.1
125	Van Tents Co—*Peter Manfredi*	1191 Zara Rd, Pottstown PA 19464	610-495-1433	R	6*	<.1
126	AIMS Worldwide Inc—*Thomas W Cady*	10400 Eaton Pl Ste 203, Fairfax VA 22030	703-621-3875	P	6	<.1
127	Resort Golf Group LLC—*John Fechter*	8300 East Raintree Dr, Scottsdale AZ 85260	480-505-3210	R	5*	.1
128	EveryTicketcom—*John Marshall*	1874 West Ave, Miami Beach FL 33139	305-534-5983	R	5*	<.1
129	Windy City Amusements Inc—*Tony Salerno Sr*	914 W Main St, Saint Charles IL 60174	630-443-4547	R	5*	<.1
130	Mid-America Festivals Inc—*James H Peterson*	1244 Canterbury Rd S S, Shakopee MN 55379	952-445-7361	R	4*	<.1
131	Jack's Diving Locker Inc—*Jack Clothier*	74-5813 Alii Dr, Kailua Kona HI 96740	808-329-7585	R	4	<.1
132	Cloud 9 Living LLC—*John Augst*	4999 Pearl East Cir St, Boulder CO 80301	303-443-8777	R	4*	<.1
133	Appalachian Outfitters—*Ben LaChance*	2084 S Chestatee, Dahlonega GA 30533	706-864-7117	R	4*	<.1
134	Boys Club Of Mount Kisco Inc—*Brian Skanes*	351 E Main St, Mount Kisco NY 10549	914-666-8069	R	3*	.1
135	Air Combat USA Inc—*Mav Blackstone*	PO Box 2726, Fullerton CA 92837	714-522-7590	R	3*	<.1
136	Table Trac Inc—*Glenn J Goulet*	6101 Baker Rd Ste 206, Minnetonka MN 55345	952-548-8877	P	3	<.1
137	Jo/Don Farms Inc—*Don J Meyer*	5907 Nicholson Rd, Franksville WI 53126	262-835-2777	R	3*	<.1
138	Bates Amusement Inc—*Geary Bates*	1292 Bantam Ridge Rd, Steubenville OH 43953	740-266-3120	R	2*	.1
139	Independent Divers Inc—*H Merrihue*	PO Box 23123, New Orleans LA 70183	504-466-2900	R	2*	<.1
140	Grandfather Mountain Inc—*Penn Dameron*	PO Box 129, Linville NC 28646	828-733-2013	R	2*	<.1
141	Bates Brothers Amusement Co—*Eric Bates*	1506 Fernwood Rd, Wintersville OH 43953	740-266-2950	R	2*	<.1
142	Fathom Five Divers Inc—*Jeannette Thompson*	PO Box 907, Koloa HI 96756	808-742-6991	R	2*	<.1
143	Have Trunk Will Travel—*Gary Johnson*	27575 State Hwy 74, Perris CA 92570	951-943-9227	R	2*	<.1
144	Ocean Quest Dive Center—*Vicky Roberts*	84801 State Rd 4A, Islamorada FL 33036	305-664-4401	R	2*	<.1
145	Sea Sense Inc—*Carol Cuddyer*	PO Box 1961, Saint Petersburg FL 33731	727-289-6917	R	2*	<.1
146	Music Caterer—*John Comstock*	PO Box 1688, Evergreen CO 80439	303-674-3901	R	2*	<.1
147	American Fitness Professionals and Associates Inc—*Mark Oc-chipint*	PO Box 214, Ship Bottom NJ 08008	609-978-7583	R	2*	<.1
148	Dvorak Kayak and Rafting Expeditions Inc—*William D Dvorak*	17921 US Hwy 285, Nathrop CO 81236	719-539-6851	R	1*	<.1
149	Napa Valley Balloon Inc—*Kim Kleist*	PO Box 2860, Yountville CA 94599	707-944-0228	R	1*	<.1
150	Breeze Hawaii Diving Adventures Corp—*Shinichi Yoshimiya*	3014 Kaimuki Ave, Honolulu HI 96816	808-735-1857	R	1*	<.1
151	Ocean Divers Inc—*Robert Schweinler*	522 Caribbean Dr, Key Largo FL 33037	305-451-1113	R	1*	<.1
152	Blue Ridge Arsenal Inc—*Earl Curtis*	14725 Flint Lee Rd Ste, Chantilly VA 20151	703-818-0230	R	1*	<.1
153	SkyDance SkyDiving Inc—*Ray Ferrell*	24390 Aviation Ave, Davis CA 95616	530-753-2651	R	1*	<.1
154	Great White Shark Enterprises Inc—*Barry Maranta*	2041 Vista Prky Level, West Palm Beach FL 33411	561-640-7000	R	1*	<.1
155	Christiansen Amusements Inc—*Buzz Christiansen*	PO Box 997, Escondido CA 92033	760-741-7552	R	1*	<.1
156	Silent World Dive Center Inc—*Chris Brown*	PO Box 2363, Key Largo FL 33037	305-451-3252	R	1*	<.1
157	Animal Rentals Inc	5742 W Grand Ave, Chicago IL 60639	773-237-1710	R	1*	<.1
158	South Seas Aquatics—*Masao Nakagawa*	2155 Kalakaua Ave Ste, Honolulu HI 96815	808-922-0852	R	1*	<.1
159	Creekside Golf Dome—*Tonny Latell*	1300 N State St, Girard OH 44420	330-545-5000	R	1*	<.1
160	Scores Holding Company Inc—*Robert M Gans*	533-535 W 27th St, New York NY 10001	212-421-3763	P	1	<.1
161	Diamondhead Casino Corp—*Deborah A Vitale*	1301 Seminole Blvd Ste, Largo FL 33770	727-674-0055	P	<1	<.1
162	Myriad Entertainment and Resorts Inc—*Nick Lopardo*	PO Box 100, Tunica MS 38676		R	<1	<.1
163	Green Valley Station Inc—*Tim Wright*	2300 Paseo Verde Pkwy, Henderson NV 89052	702-617-7777	S	N/A	1.0
164	Boulder Outdoor Center Inc—*Eric Bader*	2525 Arapahoe Ave Ste, Boulder CO 80302	303-444-8420	R	N/A	<.1

TOTALS: SIC 7999 Amusement & Recreation Nec
Companies: 164

					100,392	210.2

8011 Offices & Clinics of Medical Doctors

	Company	Address	Phone	Type	Fin	Empls
1	Heartland Health—*Alfred L Purcell*	5325 Faraon St, St Joseph MO 64506	816-271-6000	R	6,439*	3.6
2	WellQuest Medical and Wellness Corp—*Steve Swift*	3400 SE Macy Rd Ste 8, Bentonville AR 72712	479-845-0880	P	3,674	<.1
3	Molina Healthcare Inc—*J Mario Molina*	200 Oceangate Ste 100, Long Beach CA 90802	562-435-3666	P	1,652	5.2
4	MDVip Inc—*Dan Hecht*	6001 Broken Sound Pkwy, Boca Raton FL 33487		R	1,427*	.5
5	Pediatrix Medical Group of Florida Inc—*Roger J Medel MD*	PO Box 559001, Fort Lauderdale FL 33355	954-384-0175	S	1,106*	1.5
6	AmSurg Corp—*Christopher A Holden*	20 Burton Hills Blvd S, Nashville TN 37215	615-665-1283	P	787	5.5
7	Radiological Associates of Sacramento Medical Group Inc—*Mark H Leibenhaut*	1500 Expo Pkwy, Sacramento CA 95815	916-646-8300	R	722*	.9
8	Georgia Cancer Specialists PC—*Bruce A Feinberg*	2712 Lawrenceville Hwy, Decatur GA 30033	770-496-5555	R	384*	.5
9	Total Health Care Inc—*Dennis Cherot*	1501 Division St, Baltimore MD 21217	410-383-8300	R	369*	.5
10	Metropolitan Health Networks Inc—*Michael M Earley*	777 Yamato Rd Ste 510, Boca Raton FL 33431	561-805-8500	P	368	.2
11	Medical Clinic of North Texas—*Karen Kennedy*	9003 Airport Freeway S, North Richland Hills TX 76180	817-514-5200	R	353*	.5
12	Symbion Inc—*Richard Francis*	40 Burton Hills Blvd S, Nashville TN 37215	615-234-5900	R	302*	2.6
13	IntegraMed America Inc—*Jay Higham*	2 Manhattanville Rd, Purchase NY 10577	914-253-8000	P	243	1.4

Note: An asterisk (*) indicates an estimated financial figure. The company type code used is as follows: R = Private, P = Public, S = Private Subsidiary, B = Public Subsidiary, D = Division, J = Joint Venture, I = Investment Fund.

COMPANY RANKINGS BY SALES WITHIN 4-DIGIT SIC

Rank	Company Name—*Executive Officer*	Address, City, State, Zip	Phone	Type	Fin	Empls
14	JSA Healthcare Corp—*Lorie Glisson*	111 2nd Ave NE Ste1500, Saint Petersburg FL 33701	727-824-0780	R	213*	.4
15	Unmc Physicians—*Rod Markin*	988101 Nebraska Med Ct, Omaha NE 68198	402-559-9700	R	204*	1.2
16	Woodland Health Care—*Kevin Vaziri*	1325 Cottonwood St, Woodland CA 95695	530-662-3961	S	186*	1.0
17	Methodist Medical Center	1410 Centerpoint Blvd, Knoxville TN 37932	865-374-6864	R	179*	<.1
18	Pacific Medical Center Clinic—*William Reilly*	1200 12th Ave S Ste G1, Seattle WA 98144	206-621-4466	R	179*	1.1
19	Kansas University Physicians Inc—*Jim Albertson*	3901 Rainbow Blvd, Kansas City KS 66103	913-588-5000	R	178*	.5
20	Children's Hospital Pediatric Associates Inc—*William Tarvainen*	20 Overland St, Boston MA 02215	617-919-2822	R	177*	<.1
21	Mountain - Pacific Quality Health Foundation - Wyoming—*Janice Connors*	409 S 4th St, Glenrock WY 82637	307-436-8733	R	176*	<.1
22	West Suburban Medical Center—*Maria Chon*	414 S Oak Park Ave Ste, Oak Park IL 60302	708-358-0776	R	176*	<.1
23	Wellspan Medical Group—*Tom Mcgann*	PO Box 2767, York PA 17405	717-851-6515	S	173*	.7
24	Va Hospital—*George Moore*	510 E Stoner Ave, Shreveport LA 71101	318-221-8411	R	172*	.1
25	Cook Children's Physician Network—*Mark Laney Ms*	PO Box 9044, Belfast ME 04915	682-885-6800	R	171*	.8
26	Central Mississippi Medical Center—*Glenn Silverman*	1850 Chadwick Dr, Jackson MS 39204	601-376-1000	R	170*	1.2
27	Greater Rochester Independent Practice Association Inc—*Gregg Coughlin*	60 Carlson Rd, Rochester NY 14610	585-922-1529	R	170*	<.1
28	Sansum Clinic—*Kurt Ransohoff*	PO Box 1200, Santa Barbara CA 93102	805-681-7500	R	166*	.9
29	A and M Green Power Group LC—*Randy Mccunn*	PO Box 71, Glenwood IA 51534	712-623-4440	R	165*	.2
30	Ajay Patel Md—*Ajay Patel*	450 2nd St, Saint Albans WV 25177	304-746-7244	R	164*	<.1
31	Medical Clinic of Houston—*Karen Rainey*	1701 Sunset Blvd, Houston TX 77005	713-526-5511	R	161*	.3
32	San Joaquin General Hospital—*Cleona Cash*	PO Box 1020, Stockton CA 95201	209-468-6000	R	161*	<.1
33	Colorado Access—*Marshall Thomas*	10065 E Harvard Ave St, Denver CO 80231	720-744-5100	R	158*	.3
34	Corizon Health Inc—*Richard Hallworth*	105 Westpark Dr Ste 20, Brentwood TN 37027	615-373-3100	R	158*	2.6
35	Scottsdale Healthcare Family Practice—*Thomas J Sadvary*	7301 E Second St Ste 2, Scottsdale AZ 85251	480-882-4000	R	157*	.2
36	US Healthworks Inc—*Daniel Crowley*	25124 Springfield Ct, Valencia CA 91355	661-678-2600	R	154*	2.2
37	Community Premier Plus Inc—*Harris Lampert*	534 W 135th St, New York NY 10031	212-491-2333	R	151*	.1
38	Iowa Physicians Clinic Medical Foundation—*Eric Crowell*	8101 Birchwood Ct Unit, Johnston IA 50131	515-241-6212	R	151*	1.0
39	America's Health Choice Medical Plans Inc—*Walter Janke*	PO Box 110, Tallahassee FL 32302	772-794-0030	R	150*	.1
40	Illinois Bone And Joint Institute LLC—*Wayne Goldstein*	8930 Waukegan Rd Ste 2, Morton Grove IL 60053	847-375-3000	R	147*	.7
41	Moffitt Cancer Center—*William Dalton*	12902 Usf Magnolia Dr, Tampa FL 33612	813-972-8438	R	145*	3.0
42	Faith Regional Health Services—*Diane Mouchka*	PO Box 869, Norfolk NE 68702	402-371-4880	R	145*	<.1
43	Centracare Clinic—*Hallen Horn*	1200 6th Ave N, Saint Cloud MN 56303	320-252-5131	R	145*	.7
44	Mercy Care Management Inc—*Lee Lui*	PO Box 786, Cedar Rapids IA 52406	319-398-6011	R	144*	2.2
45	Physicians Health Plan Of Northern Indiana Inc—*Jay Gilbert*	8101 W Jefferson Blvd, Fort Wayne IN 46804	260-432-6690	R	143*	.1
46	Tch Pediatric Associates Inc—*Ayse Mccraken*	8080 N Stadium Dr Ste, Houston TX 77054	832-824-6626	R	143*	<.1
47	New Lexington Clinic PSC—*Andrew Henderson*	1221 S Broadway, Lexington KY 40504	859-258-4000	R	140*	1.1
48	Paradigm Health Corp—*John Penrose*	1001 Galaxy Way Ste 30, Concord CA 94520		R	136*	.2
49	Buffalo Cardiology and Pulmonary Associates PC—*Gina Gray*	6460 Main St, Williamsville NY 14221	716-634-5100	R	128*	.2
50	Urgent Care Holdings Inc—*Frank Alderman*	1751 Earl L Core Rd, Morgantown WV 26505	304-225-2500	R	115*	1.0
51	Aspen Medical Group PA—*Tom Holets*	1021 Bandana Blvd E St, Saint Paul MN 55108	612-262-4200	R	102*	.9
52	Lomax Companies LP—*Walter P Lomax*	200 Highpoint Dr Ste 2, Chalfont PA 18914	215-822-1550	R	94*	.1
53	Laser Vision Centers Inc—*Steve Rasch*	540 Maryville Centre D, Saint Louis MO 63141	636-534-2300	S	80*	.1
54	AmSurg Holdings Inc—*Christopher Holden* AmSurg Corp	20 Burton Hills Blvd S, Nashville TN 37215	615-665-1283	S	69*	.1
55	Houston Eye Associates PC—*Jeffrey Lanier*	2855 Gramercy St, Houston TX 77025	713-668-6828	R	68*	.4
56	Diagnostic Clinic Medical Group PA—*H Charles Campbell*	1301 2nd Ave SW, Largo FL 33770	727-581-8767	R	60*	.5
57	Blue Ridge/Clemson Orthopaedic ASC LLC AmSurg Holdings Inc	10630 Clemson Blvd Ste, Seneca SC 29678	864-324-0466	S	57*	.1
58	Coast Dental Services Inc—*Thomas J Marler*	4010 W Boy Scout Blvd, Tampa FL 33607	813-288-1999	R	56	.7
59	AmSurg Glendale Inc AmSurg Corp	607 N Central Ave Ste, Glendale CA 91203	818-956-1010	S	54*	.1
60	Glendale Opthalmology Inc—*Christopher Holden* AmSurg Glendale Inc	607 N Central Ave Ste, Glendale CA 91203	818-956-1010	S	54*	.1
61	Dermatology Associates of Atlanta—*Edmond Griffin*	5555 Peachtree Dunwood, Atlanta GA 30342	404-256-4457	R	47*	.1
62	Valley Healthcare Systems Inc—*Sarah Lang*	1315 Delauney Dr Ste 2, Columbus GA 31901	706-322-9599	R	44*	.1
63	Premier Practice Management—*Richard A Norling*	12255 El Camino Real S, San Diego CA 92130	858-481-2727	S	43*	.4
64	Managed HealthCare Northwest Inc—*Dolores Russell*	PO Box 4629, Portland OR 97208	503-413-5800	S	43*	<.1
65	Kauai Medical Clinic	3-3420 Kuhio Hwy Ste B, Lihue HI 96766	808-245-1500	S	42*	.3
66	PAPP Clinic PC—*Carol E Alenander*	PO Box 609, Newnan GA 30264	770-253-6616	R	42*	.3
67	AHC Physicians Corp—*JW Stucki* American HealthChoice Inc	4300 Windsor Centre Tr, Flower Mound TX 75028	817-837-8000	S	36*	<.1
68	Plastic Surgery Center—*John Osborn MD*	95 Scripps Dr, Sacramento CA 95825	916-929-1833	R	36*	<.1
69	Phoenix Medical Management Inc—*Stefani Daniels*	1401 S Ocean Blvd, Pompano Beach FL 33062	954-941-6505	R	36*	<.1
70	Delphi Healthcare Partners Inc—*David Joyce*	170 Southport Dr Ste 2, Morrisville NC 27560	919-655-1305	R	35*	.1
71	Gastrointestinal Associates PC AmSurg Corp	PO Box 59002, Knoxville TN 37950	865-588-5121	S	32*	<.1
72	Amsurg Encino Inc AmSurg Corp	18425 Burbank Blvd Ste, Tarzana CA 91356	818-708-6050	S	31*	<.1
73	Ocala Endoscropy ASC LP—*Fay McCrocklin* AmSurg Ocala Inc	1160 SE 18th Pl, Ocala FL 34471	352-261-0499	S	31*	<.1
74	Medcost LLC—*Michelle Shoaf*	165 Kimel Park Dr, Winston Salem NC 27103	336-760-3090	R	30*	.3
75	Mountain West Endoscopy Center AmSurg Holdings Inc	6360 S 3000 E Ste 320, Salt Lake City UT 84121	801-944-3166	S	30*	<.1
76	Aurora Medical Group Inc—*Nick Turkal*	3000 W Montana St, Milwaukee WI 53215	414-647-3000	D	28*	.2
77	Cardiovascular Associates PSC—*Timothy J Higgins*	6420 Dutchmans Pkwy St, Louisville KY 40205	502-891-8300	R	28*	.2
78	Galichia Medical Group PA—*Gregory R Boxberger*	PO Box 47668, Wichita KS 67201	316-684-3838	R	28*	.2
79	Mid-America Cardiology Associates PC—*Tracy Rasmussen*	3901 Rainbow Blvd, Kansas City KS 66160	913-588-1227	R	27*	.2
80	AmSurg-Las Vegas LLC AmSurg Holdings Inc	2575 Lindell Rd, Las Vegas NV 89146	702-367-7874	S	27*	<.1
81	South Denver Endoscopy Center—*Christopher A Holden* AmSurg Holdings Inc	499 E Hampden Ave Ste, Englewood CO 80113	303-874-0350	S	27*	<.1
82	Atlanta Obstetrics and Gynecology Associates PC—*Renea Haskett*	275 Collier Rd STE 100, Atlanta GA 30309	404-355-0320	R	26*	<.1
83	Citrus Surgery and Endoscopy Center AmSurg Corp	6412 W Gulf to Lake Hw, Crystal River FL 34429	352-563-0223	S	26*	<.1
84	Carolina Cardiology Consultants—*John Kelly*	3324 Six Forks Rd, Raleigh NC 27609	919-781-7772	R	24*	<.1
85	Eye Surgery Center of Paducah AmSurg Holdings Inc	100 Medical Center Dr, Paducah KY 42003	270-442-1024	S	24*	<.1
86	Orion HealthCorp Inc—*Terrence L Bauer*	1805 Old Alabama Rd St, Roswell GA 30076	678-832-1800	R	23	.4
87	Naples Endoscopy ASC LP—*Ken P McDonald*	150 Tamiami Trail N St, Naples FL 34102	239-262-8306	S	22*	<.1

Rank	Company Name—*Executive Officer*	Address, City, State, Zip	Phone	Type	Fin	Empls
88	Valley Endoscopy Center LP Amsurg Encino Inc	18425 Burbank Blvd Ste, Tarzana CA 91356	818-708-6050	S	22*	<.1
89	Meridian Medical Associates—*Robert S Schubert*	2100 Glenwood Ave, Joliet IL 60435	815-725-2121	R	21*	.1
90	Healthcor Inc—*Bryan Schefman*	17117 W 9 Mile Rd Ste, Southfield MI 48075	248-559-5656	R	20*	.2
91	Florham Park Endoscopy ASC LLC AmSurg Holdings Inc	195 Columbia Tpke, Florham Park NJ 07932	973-947-7511	S	20*	<.1
92	New West Physicians—*Ruth Benton*	1707 Cole Blvd Ste 250, Golden CO 80401	303-763-4900	R	19*	.3
93	Tennessee Endoscopy Center AmSurg Corp	1706 E Lamar Alexander, Maryville TN 37804	865-983-0073	S	19*	<.1
94	Santa Monica Bay Physicians Health Services Inc—*Eileen Mcgrath*	6029 Bristol Pkwy Ste, Culver City CA 90230	310-417-5900	R	19*	.2
95	Koch Eye Associates—*Peter A Koch*	566 Tollgate Rd, Warwick RI 02886	401-738-4800	R	18*	.1
96	AmSurg Burbank Inc—*Christopher Holden* AmSurg Corp	2829 W Burbank Blvd, Burbank CA 91505	818-567-0348	S	18*	<.1
97	Burbank Opthalmology ASC LP AmSurg Burbank Inc	2829 W Burbank Blvd St, Burbank CA 91505	818-567-0348	S	18*	<.1
98	Chevy Chase ASC LLC AmSurg Holdings Inc	5530 Wisconsin Ave Ste, Chevy Chase MD 20815	301-654-8020	S	18*	<.1
99	Ft Myers Digestive Health and Pain ASC LLC AmSurg Holdings Inc	12700 Creekside Ln Ste, Fort Myers FL 33919	239-489-4454	S	18*	<.1
100	Louisville Endoscopy Center AmSurg Holdings Inc	1400 Poplar Level Rd S, Louisville KY 40217	502-442-7303	S	18*	<.1
101	Metairie Opthalmology ASC LLC AmSurg Holdings Inc	3900 Veterans Memorial, Metairie LA 70002	504-455-1550	S	18*	<.1
102	Montgomery Eye Surgery Center LLC—*Christopher A Holden* AmSurg Holdings Inc	2752 Zelda Rd, Montgomery AL 36106	334-270-9677	S	18*	<.1
103	Reproductive Genetics In Vitro Inc—*George Henry MD*	455 S Hudson St Level, Denver CO 80246	303-399-5393	R	18*	<.1
104	Sonoma County Indian Health Project Inc—*Molin Malicay*	144 Stony Point Rd, Santa Rosa CA 95401	707-521-4545	R	17*	.2
105	Tidewater Physicians Multispecialty Group—*Linda Gatewood*	860 Omni Blvd Ste 101, Newport News VA 23606	757-223-9794	R	16*	.1
106	Jackson Opthalmology ASC LLC—*Kim Haynes* AmSurg Holdings Inc	207 Stonebridge Blvd, Jackson TN 38305	731-661-6340	S	16*	<.1
107	Sarasota Opthalmology ASC LLC—*Christopher A Holden* AmSurg Holdings Inc	3920 Bee Ridge Rd Bldg, Sarasota FL 34233	941-925-0000	S	16*	<.1
108	Henry J Austin Health Center Inc—*Walter Isaacs*	321 N Warren St, Trenton NJ 08618	609-278-5900	R	15*	.1
109	AmSurg EC Washington Inc—*Christopher A Holden* AmSurg Corp	2021 K St NW Ste T-115, Washington DC 20006	202-775-0574	S	15*	<.1
110	Endoscopy Center of Washington DC LP—*Christopher A Holden* AmSurg EC Washington Inc	2021 K St NW Ste T-115, Washington DC 20006	202-775-0574	S	15*	<.1
111	Las Vegas Opthalmology ASC LLC—*Christopher A Holden* AmSurg Holdings Inc	3575 Pecos McLeod, Las Vegas NV 89121	702-731-2088	S	15*	<.1
112	Surgery and Laser Center AmSurg Holdings Inc	3744 State Rte 257, Seneca PA 16346	814-677-6700	S	15*	<.1
113	Dover Opthalmology ASC LLC—*Jackie Tiller* AmSurg Holdings Inc	655 Bay Rd Ste 5B, Dover DE 19901	302-678-4688	S	15*	<.1
114	Radiology Alliance—*Henry Howerton*	PO Box 440166, Nashville TN 37244	615-312-0600	R	15*	.2
115	Martin Luther King Jr Community Health Center—*P Wong*	1556 Straight Path, Wyandanch NY 11798	631-854-1700	R	14*	.1
116	Waldorf Endoscopy ASC LLC AmSurg Holdings Inc	11340 Pembrooke Sq Sto, Waldorf MD 20603	301-638-5354	S	14*	<.1
117	EyeCare Consultants Surgery Center LLC AmSurg Holdings Inc	101 NW 1st St Ste 104, Evansville IN 47708	812-435-2372	S	14*	<.1
118	University Endoscopy Center—*Christopher A Holden* AmSurg Holdings Inc	9275 Montgomery Rd Ste, Cincinnati OH 45242	513-936-4518	S	14*	<.1
119	Northwest Ohio Endoscopy Center AmSurg Holdings Inc	4841 Monroe St Ste 111, Toledo OH 43623	419-474-3949	S	13*	<.1
120	Sarasota Endoscopy ASC LLC—*Christopher A Holden* AmSurg Holdings Inc	2800 Bahia Vista Ste 3, Sarasota FL 34239	941-373-9808	S	13*	<.1
121	Arizona Gastroenterology Ltd—*FA Klein*	1521 E Tangerine Rd St, Oro Valley AZ 85755	520-742-4139	R	13*	<.1
122	GI Endoscopy Center AmSurg Holdings Inc	257 N Breiel Blvd, Middletown OH 45042	513-422-5990	S	13*	<.1
123	Miami ASC LP—*Christopher A Holden* AmSurg Miami Inc	5101 SW Eighth St Firs, Miami FL 33134	305-461-1881	S	13*	<.1
124	Center For Orthopedic And Research Excellence Inc—*David Jacofsky*	14520 W Granite Valley, Sun City West AZ 85375	623-537-5600	R	12*	.2
125	Eye Health Services Inc—*Neal Snebold*	1900 Crown Colony Dr S, Quincy MA 02169	617-770-4400	R	12*	.2
126	Block Vision Holdings Corp—*Andy Alcorn*	700 939 Elkridge Landi, Linthicum MD 21090	410-752-0121	R	12*	.1
127	AmSurg EC Topeka Inc AmSurg Corp	2200 SW 6th St Ste 103, Topeka KS 66606	785-354-1254	S	12*	<.1
128	Oak Grove Institute Foundation Inc—*Tamara Wilson*	24275 Jefferson Ave, Murrieta CA 92562	951-677-5599	R	12*	.2
129	Medical Transcription Corp—*Phyllis Uchin*	PO Box 757, Reading MA 01867	781-938-5000	R	11*	.1
130	American HealthChoice Inc—*Joseph W Stucki*	4300 Windsor Centre Tr, Flower Mound TX 75022	817-837-8000	R	11	.1
131	Newark Endoscopy ASC LLC AmSurg Holdings Inc	1090 Old Churchmans Rd, Newark DE 19713	302-892-2710	S	11*	<.1
132	AmSurg Miami Inc—*Christopher A Holden* AmSurg Corp	5101 SW Eighth St Firs, Miami FL 33134	305-461-1881	S	10*	<.1
133	Associates In Digestive Health—*James Wolper*	2721 Del Prado Blvd St, Cape Coral FL 33904	239-772-3636	R	10*	<.1
134	Atlantic Coastal Surgery Center LLC AmSurg Holdings Inc	301 Central Ave Ste A, Egg Harbor Township NJ 08234	609-653-9000	S	10*	<.1
135	Mercer County Surgery Center LLC AmSurg Holdings Inc	3120 Princeton Pke 2nd, Lawrenceville NJ 08648	609-895-0290	S	10*	<.1
136	Surgery Center of Coral Gables LLC—*Laura Lilburn*	1097 SW 42nd Ave 2nd F, Coral Gables FL 33134	305-461-1300	R	10*	<.1
137	Med7 Urgent Care Center Medical Group—*Meryl O'Brien*	4156 Manzanita Ave, Carmichael CA 95608	916-483-5400	R	9*	.1
138	Akron Endoscopy ASC LLC AmSurg Holdings Inc	1037 N Main St Ste B, Akron OH 44310	330 940-3000	S	9*	<.1
139	AmSurg EC Sante Fe Inc AmSurg Corp	1650 Hospital Dr Ste 9, Santa Fe NM 87505	505-988-3373	S	9*	<.1
140	AmSurg Suncoast Inc—*Theressa Long* AmSurg Corp	3621 E Forest Dr, Inverness FL 34453	352-637-2787	S	9*	<.1
141	Suncoast Endoscopy ASC LP—*Teressa Long* AmSurg Suncoast Inc	3621 E Forest Dr, Inverness FL 34453	352-637-2787	S	9*	<.1

Note: An asterisk (*) indicates an estimated financial figure. The company type code used is as follows: R = Private, P = Public, S = Private Subsidiary, B = Public Subsidiary, D = Division, J = Joint Venture, I = Investment Fund.

COMPANY RANKINGS BY SALES WITHIN 4-DIGIT SIC

Rank	Company Name—*Executive Officer*	Address, City, State, Zip	Phone	Type	Fin	Empls
142	Seven Hills Womens Health Centers—*Joseph Sclafani*	2060 Reading Rd Ste 15, Cincinnati OH 45202	513-721-3200	R	8*	.1
143	Endoscopy Center of South Bay LP—*Elaine Campos*	23560 Madison St Ste 1, Torrance CA 90505	310-325-6331	S	8*	<.1
144	DR Systems Inc—*Richard Porritt*	10140 Mesa Rim Rd, San Diego CA 92121	858-625-3344	R	7*	.1
145	Medical Park Family Care—*Bill Burton*	2211 E Northern Lights, Anchorage AK 99508	907-279-8486	R	7*	.1
146	AmSurg Palmetto Inc AmSurg Corp	2140 W 68th St Ste 102, Hialeah FL 33016	305-512-8220	S	7*	<.1
147	Endoscopy Center of Meridian AmSurg Holdings Inc	13313 N Meridian Bldg, Oklahoma City OK 73120		S	7*	<.1
148	Palmetto ASC LP AmSurg Palmetto Inc	2140 W 68th St Ste 102, Hialeah FL 33016	305-512-8220	S	7*	<.1
149	AmSurg Melbourne Inc—*Christopher A Holden* AmSurg Corp	1401 S Apollo Ste B, Melbourne FL 32901	321-725-5151	S	7*	<.1
150	AmSurg Ocala Inc—*Christopher A Holden* AmSurg Corp	1160 SE 18th Pl, Ocala FL 34471	352-732-8905	S	7*	<.1
151	Endoscopy Center of Centennial LP—*Christopher Holden*	2400 Patterson St Ste, Nashville TN 37203	615-327-2111	S	7*	<.1
152	Surgical Eye Care Ltd—*Steven B Siepser*	860 E Swedesford Rd, Wayne PA 19087		R	6*	.1
153	El Paso ASC LP	1300 Murchison Dr Ste, El Paso TX 79902	915-544-5000	S	6*	<.1
154	Columbia ASC LLC AmSurg Holdings Inc	2739 Laurel St Ste 1-B, Columbia SC 29204	803-254-9588	S	6*	<.1
155	Rami E Geffner MD PA—*Rami Geffner*	PO Box 4979, Toms River NJ 08754	732-244-4703	R	6*	.1
156	Columbia ASC Northwest LLC AmSurg Holdings Inc	1510 1/2 Hatcher Ln, Columbia TN 38401		S	5*	<.1
157	Food Allergy and Anaphylaxis Network—*Julia Bradsher*	11781 Lee Jackson Memo, Fairfax VA 22033	703-691-3179	R	5*	<.1
158	Advantage Health Care—*Wendy Keehan*	155 S Executive Dr Ste, Brookfield WI 53005	262-432-0220	R	5*	.1
159	Umhs Physician Services—*William Berry*	700 Km S Pl, Ann Arbor MI 48108	734-647-5299	R	4*	.1
160	Cascade Orthopaedics Properties LLC—*Virgil Becker*	122 3rd St Ne, Auburn WA 98002	253-833-7762	R	4*	<.1
161	East County Urgent Care Industrial Medical Clinic Inc—*Jack Wolfe*	1625 E Main St Ste 100, El Cajon CA 92021	619-442-9896	R	4*	<.1
162	Capital Nephrology Medical Group—*Melony Askew*	77 Cadillac Ste130, Sacramento CA 95825	916-929-8564	R	4*	<.1
163	Alexandria Opthalmology ASC LLC—*Christopher A Holden* AmSurg Holdings Inc	4100 Parliament Dr, Alexandria LA 71303	318-487-8342	S	4*	<.1
164	AmSurg La Jolla Inc—*Lisa Weath* AmSurg Corp	9850 Genesee Ave Ste 9, La Jolla CA 92037	858-453-7525	S	4*	<.1
165	AmSurg Weslaco Inc—*Christopher A Holden* AmSurg Corp	1402 E 6th St, Weslaco TX 78596	956-968-6155	S	4*	<.1
166	La Jolla Endoscopy Center LP—*Lisa Weath* AmSurg La Jolla Inc	9850 Genesee Ave Ste 9, La Jolla CA 92037	858-453-7525	S	4*	<.1
167	US Medical Group Inc—*Thomas F Winters*	1406 S Orange Ave Ste, Orlando FL 32806	407-849-2288	R	3	<.1
168	Collis Group—*Mark Janack*	1 Eagle Valley Ct, Broadview Heights OH 44147	440-746-1055	R	3*	<.1
169	Carolina Kids Pediatric Associates—*Lori Pote*	2605 Blue Ridge Rd Ste, Raleigh NC 27607	919-881-9009	R	3*	<.1
170	Penn Diagnostic Center Inc—*Lawrence K Spitz*	1801 Market St Ste 200, Philadelphia PA 19103	215-569-9500	R	3*	<.1
171	Northside Gastroeneroloty Endoscopy Center LLC AmSurg Holdings Inc	8424 Naab Rd Ste 3G, Indianapolis IN 46260	317-871-7308	S	3*	<.1
172	Derf Corp—*Brian Coe*	2250 W Campbell Park D, Chicago IL 60612	312-243-0600	R	3*	<.1
173	Women's Specialists of Houston—*Edward Yosowitz*	6624 Fannin Ste 1800, Houston TX 77030		R	2*	<.1
174	Milwaukee Endoscopy Center AmSurg Holdings Inc	8585 W Forest Home Ave, Greenfield WI 53228	414-427-5138	S	2*	<.1
175	Eye Center Of Racine Ltd—*Kanwar Singh*	3805b Spring St Ste 13, Mount Pleasant WI 53405	262-637-2402	R	2*	<.1
176	Dermac Labs Inc—*John Simpson*	PO Box 5268, Salem OR 97304	503-399-8181	R	2*	<.1
177	Cardiostaff Corp—*Timothy Lohman*	4014 Medical Pkwy, Austin TX 78756	512-419-1755	R	2*	<.1
178	Lehigh Valley Health Network—*Ronald Swinfard*	PO Box 689, Allentown PA 18105	610-402-2273	R	2	N/A
179	Georgia Plastic Surgery PC—*Sheldon Licenberg*	1 Glenlake Pkwy Ste 95, Atlanta GA 30328	770-730-8222	R	1*	<.1
180	Dynacq Healthcare Inc—*Chiu Moon Chan*	10304 Interstate 10 E, Houston TX 77029	713-378-2000	P	<1	.1

TOTALS: SIC 8011 Offices & Clinics of Medical Doctors
Companies: 180   26,290   57.4

8021 Offices & Clinics of Dentists

Rank	Company Name—*Executive Officer*	Address, City, State, Zip	Phone	Type	Fin	Empls
1	SmileCare Dental Group—*Daniel D Crowley*	PO Box 18917, Irvine CA 92602	714-708-5300	R	218*	.8
2	Dental Health Resources Inc—*Rick Workman*	1200 Network Centre Dr, Effingham IL 62401	217-540-5100	R	159*	.8
3	OrthoSynetics Inc—*David J Marks*	222 W Las Colinas Blvd, Irving TX 75039		R	130*	3.1
4	American Dental Partners of California LLC—*Edgar Rouhe*	7251 Magnolia Ave, Riverside CA 92504	909-689-5031	S	89*	.2
5	Allcare Dental Management Inc—*David Pennington*	1740 Walden Ave Ste 10, Buffalo NY 14225		S	77	.8
6	American Dental Partners of Oklahoma LLC—*Gregory Serrao*	4801 Richmond Sq, Oklahoma City OK 73118	405-840-5600	S	30*	.1
7	Prosthodontics Intermedica—*Thomas J Balshi*	467 Pennsylvania Ave, Fort Washington PA 19034	215-646-6334	R	24*	.1
8	Godwin Corp—*Marcus Balogun*	PO Box 1482, Laurel MD 20725	301-434-3111	R	23*	.4
9	HealthDrive Medical and Dental Practices—*Steven Charlap*	25 Needham St, Newton MA 02461	617-964-6681	R	15*	.3
10	American Dental Partners of Tennessee LLC—*Greg Sierrao*	878 Willow Tree Cir, Memphis TN 38108	901-754-0191	S	14*	<.1
11	American Dental Partners of Maryland LLC—*Gregory Serrao*	5005 Signal Bell Ln St, Clarksville MD 21029	301-843-9330	S	7*	<.1
12	Rose Dental Associates—*Robert Santoro*	5 Pine W Plaza Washing, Albany NY 12205	518-456-7673	R	7*	<.1
13	American Dental Partners of Alabama LLC—*Gregory Serrao*	7703 Crestwood Blvd, Birmingham AL 35210	205-595-2273	S	7*	<.1
14	American Dental Partners of New York LLC—*Gregory Serrao*	Mezzanine Level Statle, Buffalo NY 14202	716-854-5543	S	6*	<.1
15	American Dental Partners of North Carolina LLC—*Linda Marler*	8430 University Execut, Charlotte NC 28262	704-549-1164	S	5*	.1
16	American Dental Partners of Louisiana LLC—*Gregory Serrao*	3000 W Esplanade Ave, Metairie LA 70002	504-833-3200	S	5*	<.1
17	Castle Dental Centers of Florida Inc—*Steven C Bilt*	27066 US Hwy 19 N, Clearwater FL 33761	727-723-3357	S	4*	<.1
18	American Dental Partners of Wisconsin LLC—*Gregory Serrao*	9052 North Deerbrook T, Milwaukee WI 53223	414-357-2040	S	4*	<.1
19	Castle Dental Centers of Tennessee Inc—*Steven C Bilt*	1010 Murfreesboro Rd, Franklin TN 37064	615-794-0402	S	4*	<.1
20	Northpark Dental Group LLC—*Greg Serrao* American Dental Partners of Wisconsin LLC	9052 North Deerbrook T, Milwaukee WI 53223	414-357-2040	S	3*	.1
21	Adult and Implant Dentistry of Ventura County—*Richard Gagne*	1350 W Gonzales Rd Ste, Oxnard CA 93036	805-485-2777	R	3*	<.1
22	Union Dental Holdings Inc—*George D Green*	1700 University Dr Ste, Coral Springs FL 33071	954-575-2252	P	3	<.1
23	Wayne Witt Dds Inc—*Wayne Witt*	PO Box 4969, Maryville TN 37802	865-983-8630	R	2*	.1
24	American Mobile Dental Corp—*Charles D Randolph*	875 Mamaroneck Ave Ste, Mamaroneck NY 10543	914-835-6001	P	2	<.1
25	Tanya Manyak DDS—*Tanya Manyak*	100 S Ellsworth Ave St, San Mateo CA 94401	650-342-9941	R	2*	<.1

TOTALS: SIC 8021 Offices & Clinics of Dentists
Companies: 25   843   6.8

8041 Offices & Clinics of Chiropractors

Rank	Company Name—*Executive Officer*	Address, City, State, Zip	Phone	Type	Fin	Empls
1	AHC Chiropractic Clinics Inc—*JW Stucki*	4300 Windsor Centre Tr, Flower Mound TX 75028	817-837-8000	S	692*	<.1
2	New Orleans East Chiropractic Clinics Inc	200 S Broad St, New Orleans LA 70119	504-822-6383	S	636*	<.1
3	United Chiropractic Clinics of Uptown Inc	807 S Carrollton Ave, New Orleans LA 70118	504-861-1600	S	636*	<.1

Rank	Company Name—Executive Officer	Address, City, State, Zip	Phone	Type	Fin	Empls
4	Valley Family Health Center LLC—JW Stucki	4300 Windsor Centre Tr, Flower Mound TX 75028	817-837-8000	S	566*	<.1
5	Active Posture Chiropractic—Jason Shumard	6904 Miramar Rd Ste 21, San Diego CA 92121	858-564-7081	R	34*	<.1
6	Hall Chiropractic Inc—Curtis J Hall	914 W Anderson Ln, Austin TX 78757	512-454-4072	R	2*	<.1

TOTALS: SIC 8041 Offices & Clinics of Chiropractors
Companies: 6 — 2,566 — .2

8042 Offices & Clinics of Optometrists

1	Primary Eyecare Associates—Jeffery Ahrns	1086 Fairington Dr, Sidney OH 45365	937-492-9197	R	2*	<.1
2	Eagle Vision and Eye Clinic—Clark Blackwood	2080 Main St, Longmont CO 80501	303-651-2020	R	1*	<.1

TOTALS: SIC 8042 Offices & Clinics of Optometrists
Companies: 2 — 4 — <.1

8043 Offices & Clinics of Podiatrists

1	Texas Podiatry Group LLC—Richard Weiner	4523 W Lovers Ln, Dallas TX 75209	214-351-2180	R	2*	<.1

8049 Offices of Health Practitioners Nec

1	Sutter Health—Patrick Fry	2200 River Plaza Dr, Sacramento CA 95833	916-733-8800	R	8,772*	48.0
2	US Physical Therapy Inc—Christopher J Reading	1300 W Sam Houston Pkw, Houston TX 77042	713-297-7000	P	211	1.9
3	Burger Physical and Rehabilitation Agency Inc—Carol Burger	1301 E Bidwell St Ste, Folsom CA 95630	916-983-5900	R	69*	.3
4	Plus One Holdings Inc—Chris Ciatto	75 Maiden Ln Ste 801, New York NY 10038	212-791-2300	R	48*	1.5
5	A Full Life Agency Inc—Don Gross	233 E Locust Ave, Coeur D Alene ID 83814	208-762-9835	R	36*	.7
6	Diagnostic Imaging Services Inc	1516 Cotner Ave, Los Angeles CA 90025	310-479-0399	S	22*	.2
7	FEI Behavioral Health—Hunter Atkins	11700 W Lake Park Dr, Milwaukee WI 53224		R	22*	.1
8	American Healthways Services Inc—Ben Leedler	701 Cool Springs Blvd, Franklin TN 37067	615-665-1122	S	18*	.2
9	Burger Rehabilitation Systems Inc—Carol Burger	1301 E Bidwell St Ste, Folsom CA 95630	916-983-5900	R	14*	.3
10	Phoenix Rehabilitation and Health Services Inc—David D Watson	520 Philadelphia St, Indiana PA 15701	724-463-7478	R	14*	.1
11	Coastal Clinical And Management Services Inc—Julia Mutch	919 Conestoga Rd Bldg, Bryn Mawr PA 19010	484-380-2080	R	9*	.2
12	NovaCare Outpatient Rehabilitation (Indianapolis Indiana)	1048 N Shadeland Ave, Indianapolis IN 46219	317-298-9746	S	8*	.1
13	OptimumCare Corp—Edward A Johnson	30011 Ivy Glenn Dr Ste, Laguna Niguel CA 92677	949-495-1100	P	8	.1
14	Advanced Physical Therapy PC—Joanne Jonathon	5949 West Raymond St, Indianapolis IN 46241	317-390-5590	R	6*	.1
15	Aquatic Rehabilitation Center Inc—Stephen Kempf	10567 Montgomery Rd, Cincinnati OH 45242	513-793-5525	R	6*	<.1
16	Care Dynamix LLC—Jim Greiff	235 Hembree Park Dr St, Roswell GA 30076	770-512-8566	R	5	<.1
17	Community Care Services Inc—Cindy Wheeler	PO Box 645, Mangham LA 71259	318-248-2377	R	5*	.1
18	Nationwide Sports and Injury Inc—JW Stucki	4300 Windsor Centre Tr, Flower Mound TX 75028	817-837-8000	S	4*	<.1
19	Kingston Anesthesia LLC	601 Wyoming Ave, Kingston PA 18704	570-288-7405	S	4*	<.1
20	BaySport Inc—Doug Emery	987 University Ave Ste, Los Gatos CA 95032	408-395-7300	R	3*	.2
21	St Charles Sports and Physical Therapy Inc—Dennis Roth	939 Hwy K, O Fallon MO 63366	636-240-7000	R	3*	<.1
22	Naples Endoscopy Anesthesia LLC—Christopher A Holden	150 Tamiami Trail N St, Naples FL 34102	239-262-8306	S	3*	<.1
23	Corporate Psychology Resources Inc—Frank M Merritt	1275 Peachtree St NE S, Atlanta GA 30309	404-266-9368	R	3*	<.1
24	Lloyd-Silber Prosthetics Inc—Robert Hrynko	315 W James St Ste 101, Lancaster PA 17603		R	3*	<.1
25	MDA Leadership Consulting—Sandra Davis	150 S 5th St Ste 3300, Minneapolis MN 55402	612-332-8182	R	2*	<.1
26	Associates For Women's Health—David Horne	825 Ne 10th St Ste 330, Oklahoma City OK 73104	405-271-5239	R	2*	.1
27	Staff Quest—Jason Gibbs	201 W Ellison St Ste 2, Burleson TX 76028	817-426-0224	R	1*	<.1
28	Berman Center Inc—Laura Berman	211 E Ontario Ste 800, Chicago IL 60611	312-255-8088	P	1	<.1
29	West Florida Urology PLC Brian Hale	35095 US 19 N Ste 202, Palm Harbor FL 34684	727-771-0600	S	1*	<.1
30	Novacare—Dan Bradley	680 American Ave Ste 2, King of Prussia PA 19406		D	1*	<.1
31	Prather Wellness Center—Robert Prather	8902 N Meridian St, Indianapolis IN 46260	317-848-8048	R	1*	<.1
32	Comprehensive Health Services Inc (Phoenix Arizona)—Kevin Cameron	3543 N 7th St, Phoenix AZ 85014	602-263-8484	R	1*	<.1
33	Sport Clinic of Greater Milwaukee Inc—John Crowe	11904 W North Ave, Wauwatosa WI 53226	414-453-8616	R	1*	<.1
34	American Network Services Inc (Incline Village Nevada)—Ray Mulry	PO Box 107, The Sea Ranch CA 95497	775-833-3400	R	1*	<.1
35	Pine Street Chinese Benevolent Association—Michael Broffman	124 Pine St, San Anselmo CA 94960	415-485-0484	R	<1*	<.1

TOTALS: SIC 8049 Offices of Health Practitioners Nec
Companies: 35 — 9,308 — 54.3

8051 Skilled Nursing Care Facilities

1	HCR ManorCare—Paul A Ormond	PO Box 10086, Toledo OH 43699	419-252-5500	S	3,643*	60.0
2	Country Villa Service Corp—Steven Riseman	5120 W Goldleaf Cir St, Los Angeles CA 90056	310-574-3733	R	2,538*	1.8
3	Genesis HealthCare Corp—George V Hager Jr	101 E State St, Kennett Square PA 19348	610-444-6350	R	2,144*	43.0
4	Sun Healthcare Group Inc—William A Mathies	18831 Von Karman Ste 4, Irvine CA 92612	949-255-7100	P	1,930	28.7
5	Capital Living and Rehabilitation Centres—Patrick R Martone	26 N Broadway, Schenectady NY 12305	518-346-9640	R	1,472*	1.0
6	Sunrise Senior Living Inc—Mark S Ordan	7900 Westpark Dr Ste T, McLean VA 22102	703-273-7500	P	1,312	31.6
7	Five Star Quality Care Inc—Bruce J Mackey Jr	400 Centre St, Newton MA 02458	617-796-8387	P	1,282	25.6
8	SavaSeniorCare LLC—Tony Ogolsby	1 Ravinia Dr Ste 1400, Atlanta GA 30346	770-829-5100	R	1,270	22.0
9	Chicagoland Christian Village Inc—Mitch Beam	6685 E 117th Ave, Crown Point IN 46307	219-662-0642	R	1,252*	.1
10	Central Management Company Inc—Teddy R Price	PO Box 638-4116 , Winnfield LA 71483	318-628-4116	R	1,142*	.8
11	Skilled Healthcare Group Inc—Boyd W Hendrickson	27442 Portola Pkwy Ste, Foothill Ranch CA 92610	949-282-5800	B	870	13.8
12	National HealthCare Corp—Robert Adams	100 E Vine St, Murfreesboro TN 37130	615-890-2020	P	774	12.7
13	Ensign Group Inc—Christopher R Christensen	27101 Puerta Real Ste, Mission Viejo CA 92691	949-487-9500	P	758	N/A
14	Evergreen House Health Center—Jessica Moreale	1 Evergreen Dr, East Providence RI 02914	401-438-3250	S	465*	.2
15	Centennial HealthCare Corp—Patrick Duplantis	303 Perimeter Ctr N St, Atlanta GA 30346	770-698-9040	S	379	11.2
16	Advocat Inc—William R Council III	1621 Galleria Blvd, Brentwood TN 37027	615-771-7575	P	290	5.6
17	Harborside Healthcare Corp—Stephen L Guillard	101 Sun Ave NE, Albuquerque NM 87109	505-821-3355	S	233*	6.0
18	Capital Senior Living Corp—Lawrence A Cohen	14160 Dallas Pkwy Ste, Dallas TX 75254	972-770-5600	P	212	4.2
19	Nowata Nursing Center Inc—Jason Bell	436 S Joe St, Nowata OK 74048	918-273-2236	R	178*	<.1
20	Extendicare Facilities Inc—Mel Rhinelander	111 W Michigan St, Milwaukee WI 53203	414-908-8000	S	172*	4.6
21	Nehalom Valley Care Center—Herald Delmarter	280 Rowe St, Wheeler OR 97147	503-368-5171	R	172*	<.1
22	Promise Regional Medical Center - Hutchinson Inc—Linda Harrison	1701 E 23rd Ave, Hutchinson KS 67502	620-665-2000	R	168*	1.0
23	Quinton Manor	1209 W Main, Quinton OK 74561	918-469-2753	R	162*	N/A
24	Hcf Management Inc—Jim Unverferth	1100 Shawnee Rd, Lima OH 45805	419-999-2010	R	160*	3.1
25	Volunteers Of America National Services—Charles Gould	7530 Market Pl Dr, Eden Prairie MN 55344	952-941-0305	R	160*	3.0
26	Tendercare Inc—Timothy Lukenda	111 W Michigan St, Milwaukee WI 53203		R	155*	3.1
27	Epoch SL Vi Inc—Lawrence Gerber	51 Sawyer Rd Ste 500, Waltham MA 02453	781-891-0777	R	154*	3.0
28	Shc Holding Inc—Robert Fusco	311 Park Pl Blvd, Clearwater FL 33759	727-533-9700	R	150*	2.0

Note: An asterisk (*) indicates an estimated financial figure. The company type code used is as follows: R = Private, P = Public, S = Private Subsidiary, B = Public Subsidiary, D = Division, J = Joint Venture, I = Investment Fund.

COMPANY RANKINGS BY SALES WITHIN 4-DIGIT SIC

Rank	Company Name—*Executive Officer*	Address, City, State, Zip	Phone	Type	Fin	Empls
29	Interwest Medical Corp—*Arch B Gilbert*	3221 Hulen St Ste C, Fort Worth TX 76107	817-731-2743	R	150*	.2
30	Care Initiatives—*Hulon Walker*	1611 W Lakes Pkwy, West Des Moines IA 50266	515-224-4442	R	147*	3.0
31	NHCOP LP—*W Adams*	PO Box 1398, Murfreesboro TN 37133	615-890-2020	R	142*	3.0
32	Beverly Enterprises - Wisconsin Inc—*David Banks*	One Thousand Beverly W, Fort Smith AR 72919	479-201-2000	R	142*	2.9
33	West View Health Care Center—*Antonio Guerro*	239 Legris Ave, West Warwick RI 02893	401-828-9000	R	128*	.2
34	Cherry Hill Manor Nursing Ctr—*Hugh Hall*	2 Cherry Hill Rd, Johnston RI 02919	401-231-3102	R	108*	.2
35	HUSA Liquidating Corp—*Joseph Luzinski*	1250 Northpoint Pky, West Palm Beach FL 33407		B	84	.5
36	Trilogy Health Services LLC—*Randall J Bufford*	1650 Lyndon Farm Ct St, Louisville KY 40223	502-412-5847	R	69*	2.0
37	Brandywine Nursing and Rehabilitation Center Inc—*Harry Tractman*	505 Greenbank Rd, Wilmington DE 19808	302-998-0101	R	63*	.2
38	Hunter Woods Nursing and Rehabilitation Center—*James Krob*	620 Tom Hunter Rd, Charlotte NC 28213	704-598-5136	R	60*	.1
39	Ovid Healthcare Center—*Nancy Henderson*	9480 E M 21, Ovid MI 48866	989-834-2228	R	59*	.1
40	Prestige Care Inc—*Harold Delamarter*	7700 NE Pkwy Dr Ste 30, Vancouver WA 98662	360-735-7155	R	55*	2.0
41	Gateway Nursing Center—*William Dietz*	2030 Harper Ave NW, Lenoir NC 28645	828-754-3888	R	55*	.1
42	Lighting Science Group Corp—*James Haworth*	1227 S Patrick Dr Bldg, Satellite Beach FL 32937	321-779-5520	P	53	.2
43	Medicalodges Inc—*Garen Cox*	PO Box 509, Coffeyville KS 67337	620-251-6700	R	51*	2.5
44	Pinewood Care Center Centennial HealthCare Corp	2514 N 7th St, Coeur D Alene ID 83814	208-664-8128	S	50	.1
45	Cary Health and Rehabilitation Center—*Marcia Sabo*	6590 Tryon Rd, Cary NC 27518	919-851-8000	R	42*	.1
46	Harts Harbor Health Care	11565 Harts Rd, Jacksonville FL 32218	904-751-1834	S	39*	.1
47	Pine River Healthcare Center—*Carl Bassett*	1149 W Monroe Rd, Saint Louis MI 48880	989-681-2124	R	35*	.1
48	Woonsocket Health and Rehabilitation Center—*Norma M Pezzelli*	262 Poplar St, Woonsocket RI 02895	401-765-2100	R	32*	.2
49	Eger Health Care and Rehabilitation Center—*David Rose*	140 Meisner Ave, Staten Island NY 10306	718-979-1800	R	29*	.6
50	Behavioral Health Group—*Andrew Love*	209 Woody Trl, Lake Dallas TX 75065		R	26	.3
51	SavaSeniorCare—*Harry Grunstein*	1 Ravinia Dr Ste 1500, Atlanta GA 30346	310-255-3577	S	26*	.1
52	Sunrise Riverside Assisted Living LP—*Paul Klassen* Sunrise Senior Living Inc	7902 Westpark Dr, McLean VA 22102	703-273-7500	S	25*	.1
53	Brookdale Place of Fall Creek LLC	5011 Kessler Blvd E, Indianapolis IN 46220	317-251-1300	S	22*	.1
54	Sunrise Willow Lake Assisted Living LLC Sunrise Senior Living Inc	2725 Lake Circle Dr, Indianapolis IN 46268	317-334-9400	S	22*	.1
55	Sunrise Shaker Heights Assisted Living LLC Sunrise Senior Living Inc	16333 Chagrin Blvd, Cleveland OH 44120	216-751-0930	S	20*	.1
56	Sunrise Hamilton Assisted Living LLC Sunrise Senior Living Inc	896 NW Washington Blvd, Hamilton OH 45013	513-893-9000	S	19*	.1
57	Mt Carmel Health and Rehabilitation Center—*Darrin Hull*	5700 W Layton Ave, Milwaukee WI 53220	414-281-7200	S	18*	.7
58	Sunnyside Rehabilitation And Nursing Center Inc—*Judy Narloda*	22617 S Vermont Ave, Torrance CA 90502	310-320-4130	R	17*	.2
59	Garden Manor Extended Care Center Inc—*Sam Boymel*	6898 Hamilton-Midltn S, Middletown OH 45044	513-424-5321	R	17*	.3
60	Sunrise North Farmington Hills Assisted Living LLC Sunrise Senior Living Inc	29681 Middlebelt Rd, Farmington Hills MI 48334	248-538-9200	S	16*	.1
61	VTA Management Services Inc—*Richard LaCourse*	3041 Ave U, Brooklyn NY 11229	718-615-0049	R	12*	<.1
62	Greek American Rehabilitation And Care Centre Inc—*Eleni Bousis*	220 N 1st St, Wheeling IL 60090	847-459-8700	R	11*	.2
63	Ingleside Homes Inc—*Lawerence Cessna*	1005 N Franklin St, Wilmington DE 19806	302-575-0250	R	11*	.3
64	Clear Creek Centers Inc—*Bob Dallas*	7481 Knox Pl, Westminster CO 80030	303-427-7101	R	8*	.1
65	Cadbury Corp—*Victor Amey*	2150 Rte 38 Ofc, Cherry Hill NJ 08002	856-667-4550	R	8*	.3
66	Friendly Home Inc—*Kathryn Epp*	303 Rhodes Ave, Woonsocket RI 02895	401-769-7220	R	8*	.2
67	Ollie Steele Burden Manor Inc—*Barbara Arceneaux*	4250 Essen Ln, Baton Rouge LA 70809	225-926-0091	R	7*	.2
68	Waterview Villa Inc—*Garrett Sullivan*	1275 S Broadway, East Providence RI 02914	401-438-7020	R	7	.2
69	Langdon Place Of Dover Inc—*Katrina Andrade*	60 Middle Rd, Dover NH 03820	603-743-4110	R	7*	.1
70	St Paul's Home For The Aged Inc—*Kimberly Cornell*	1021 W E St, Belleville IL 62220	618-233-2095	R	7*	.2
71	Tri-County Care Center—*Shirley Whetstine*	601 N Galloway Rd, Vandalia MO 63382	573-594-6467	R	6*	.1
72	Little Sisters Of The Poor Of Saint Paul—*Sister Mary Sylvia Kar*	330 Exchange St S, Saint Paul MN 55102	651-227-0336	R	6*	.1
73	St Ann's Home—*Molly Wooldridge*	9400 Saint Ann Dr, Oklahoma City OK 73162	405-728-7888	R	6*	.1
74	Stebbins Five Cos—*Dick Stebbins*	600 E Whaley St, Longview TX 75601	903-757-5360	R	5*	<.1
75	Trinity Village Inc—*James Ness*	PO Box 1265, Pine Bluff AR 71613	870-879-3113	R	5*	.1
76	United Nursing International LLC	4051 Vtrns Memrl Blvd, Metairie LA 70002	504-888-8641	R	4*	.1
77	Ryan Health Centers—*David Ryan*	359 Broad St, Providence RI 02907	401-751-3800	R	3*	.1
78	Seaford Retirement and Rehabilitation Center Genesis HealthCare Corp	1100 Norman Eskridge H, Seaford DE 19973	302-629-3575	S	3*	.1
79	Extendicare Health Facilities Inc—*Timothy Lukenda*	111 W Michigan St, Milwaukee WI 53203	414-908-6720	S	2*	20.0
80	Clear Creek Care Center—*Jay Moscowitz*	7481 Knox Pl, Westminster CO 80030	303-427-7101	R	2*	.2
81	Hattie Ide Chaffee Home—*Deborah Griffin*	200 Wampanoag Trl, East Providence RI 02915	401-434-1520	R	2*	.1

TOTALS: SIC 8051 Skilled Nursing Care Facilities
Companies: 81 — 25,546 — 331.3

8052 Intermediate Care Facilities

Rank	Company Name—*Executive Officer*	Address, City, State, Zip	Phone	Type	Fin	Empls
1	GGNSC Holdings LLC—*Neil Kurtz*	7160 Dallas Pkwy Ste 4, Dallas TX 75024	479-201-2000	R	13,529*	41.0
2	Kindred Healthcare Inc—*Paul J Diaz*	680 S 4th St, Louisville KY 40202	502-596-7300	P	5,522	51.1
3	Brookdale Senior Living Inc—*Bill E Sheriff*	111 Westwood Pl Ste 40, Brentwood TN 37027	615-221-2250	P	2,458	46.4
4	Life Care Centers of America Inc—*Beecher Hunter*	PO Box 3480, Cleveland TN 37320	423-472-9585	R	2,290*	31.0
5	Community Alternatives Nebraska Inc	9901 Linn Station Rd, Louisville KY 40223	502-394-2100	S	1,433	N/A
6	National Surgical Care—*Sami S Abbasi*	191 N Wacker Dr Ste 92, Chicago IL 60606	312-419-1033	R	323*	.5
7	Lexington Nursing Home Inc—*Gerald Lawson*	632 Se 3rd St, Lexington OK 73051	405-527-6531	R	158*	.1
8	Miller's Health Systems Inc—*Patrick Boyle*	PO Box 4377, Warsaw IN 46581	574-267-7211	R	147*	3.0
9	National Health Management—*Rick Irwin*	4415 5th Ave, Pittsburgh PA 15213	412-578-7800	R	67*	.4
10	NorthStar Healthcare Investors Inc—*David T Hamamoto*	399 Park Ave 18th Fl, New York NY 10022	212-547-2600	R	65	<.1
11	Sullivan County Chapter Of The Nys Association For Retarded Children Inc—*Stephen Miller*	162 E Broadway, Monticello NY 12701	845-796-1350	S	31*	.4
12	American Hospitality Group—*Robert Leatherman*	200 W Smokerise Dr Ste, Wadsworth OH 44281	330-336-6684	R	12*	.1
13	East Central Missouri Behavioral Health Services Inc—*Terry Mackey*	321 W Promenade St, Mexico MO 65265	573-582-1234	R	3*	.1
14	Mann Health Services Inc—*Charles H Mann III*	750 Park Ave 26 West, Atlanta GA 30326	404-250-9300	R	2*	<.1

TOTALS: SIC 8052 Intermediate Care Facilities
Companies: 14 — 26,041 — 173.8

8059 Nursing & Personal Care Nec

Rank	Company Name—*Executive Officer*	Address, City, State, Zip	Phone	Type	Fin	Empls
1	Horizon West Inc—*Larry Bear*	4020 Sierra College Bl, Rocklin CA 95677	916-624-6230	R	1,545*	2.5

Rank	Company Name—*Executive Officer*	Address, City, State, Zip	Phone	Type	Fin	Empls
2	Emeritus Corp—*Granger Cobb*	3131 Elliott Ave Ste 5, Seattle WA 98121	206-298-2909	P	1,007	29.3
3	Golden State Health Centers Inc—*David B Weiss*	13347 Ventura Blvd, Sherman Oaks CA 91423	818-385-3200	R	435*	1.6
4	Assisted Living Concepts Inc—*Laurie Bebo*	W140 N8981 Lilly Rd, Menomonee Falls WI 53051	262-257-8888	P	233	4.2
5	Young Adult Institute Inc—*Joel Levy*	460 W 34th St Fl 11, New York NY 10001	212-563-7474	R	174*	5.0
6	Lifespace Communities Inc—*Scott Harrison*	100 E Grand Ave Ste 20, Des Moines IA 50309	515-288-5805	R	160*	1.9
7	South Park East—*William Taylor*	225 Sw 35th St, Oklahoma City OK 73109	405-631-7444	R	155*	N/A
8	Unlimited Care Inc—*Marcia Birnbaum*	333 Westchester Ave G0, White Plains NY 10604	914-428-4300	R	148*	2.5
9	K and C LLC—*Mary Taylor*	204 W 1st St, Heavener OK 74937	918-653-2464	R	143*	<.1
10	VMP Inc—*Jim Enlund*	3023 S 84th St, West Allis WI 53227	414-607-4100	R	130*	.5
11	Epic MedStaff Services—*Matt Peterson*	1349 Empire Central, Dallas TX 75247	214-637-1300	R	84*	.2
12	Kendall Healthcare Properties Inc—*Jacob Shaham*	11355 SW 84th St, Miami FL 33173	305-270-7000	R	63*	.2
13	Visiting Nursing Association of Western New York Inc—*Larry Zielinski*	2100 Wehrle Dr, Williamsville NY 14221	716-630-8000	R	53*	.4
14	Cambridge Home Health Care Inc—*Nancy Diller-Shively*	4085 Embassy Pky, Akron OH 44333	330-668-1922	R	46*	1.6
15	Fairview Ministries Inc—*William Myers*	250 Village Dr, Downers Grove IL 60516	630-769-6000	R	43*	.3
16	MedAire Inc—*Grant Jeffrey*	1250 W Washington St S, Tempe AZ 85281	480-333-3700	R	31	.2
17	Home Instead Inc—*Paul Hogan*	13330 California St St, Omaha NE 68154		R	30*	.1
18	Community Residences Inc—*Jill Gruver*	14160 Newbrook Dr, Chantilly VA 20151	703-841-0607	R	20*	.4
19	Carmel Community Living Corp—*Julius Monge*	3030 Sterling Cir, Boulder CO 80301	303-444-0573	R	15*	.2
20	Community Care Center Inc—*Peter Bennett*	2335 Mountain Ave, Duarte CA 91010	626-357-3207	R	13*	.2
21	Presbyterian Special Services Inc—*Martin Favif*	3395 Grand Ave, Deland FL 32720	386-734-2874	R	8*	.3
22	Mid-America Health Centers—*Chuck Wurth*	200 W Douglas Ave, Wichita KS 67202	316-262-4206	R	8*	.1
23	Fps Enterprises LP—*Dale Kanath*	4138 Market St Ne, Salem OR 97301	503-364-3383	R	8*	.1
24	Faith Hope And Charity Inc—*Cindy Wiemold*	PO Box 243, Storm Lake IA 50588	712-732-5127	R	8*	.2
25	Kankakee Terrace Operator LLC—*Randy Levo*	100 Belle Aire Ave, Bourbonnais IL 60914	815-939-0910	R	4*	.1
26	Consumer Support Services Inc—*Daniel Swickard*	2040 Cherry Valley Rd, Newark OH 43055	740-788-8260	R	3*	.1
27	Aromaland Inc—*Elizabeth Bezzerides*	1326 Rufina Cir, Santa Fe NM 87507	505-438-0402	R	1*	<.1
28	Omnilife Health Care Systems Inc—*Robert Banasik*	PO Box 8309, Columbus OH 43201	614-299-3100	R	1*	<.1

TOTALS: SIC 8059 Nursing & Personal Care Nec
Companies: 28   **4,566**   **52.0**

8062 General Medical & Surgical Hospitals

Rank	Company Name—*Executive Officer*	Address, City, State, Zip	Phone	Type	Fin	Empls
1	HCA Holdings Inc—*Richard M Bracken*	PO Box 550, Nashville TN 37202	615-344-9551	B	30,683	194.0
2	Orlando Health—*John Hillenmeyer*	1414 Kuhl Ave, Orlando FL 32806	321-843-7000	R	23,857*	16.0
3	Advocate Health Care—*Jim Skogsbergh*	2025 Windsor Dr, Oak Brook IL 60523		R	17,489*	20.0
4	Tenet HealthSystem Holdings Inc—*Trevor Fetter* Tenet Healthcare Corp	1445 Ross Av suite 140, Dallas TX 75202	469-893-2200	S	14,043*	113.9
5	Emory Healthcare—*John T Fox*	1440 Clifton Rd NE, Atlanta GA 30322	404-778-5000	R	13,290*	9.0
6	Community Health Systems Inc—*Wayne T Smith*	PO Box 217, Franklin TN 37065	615-465-7000	P	12,987	87.0
7	Banner Health System—*Peter S Fine*	1441 N 12th St, Phoenix AZ 85006	602-495-4000	R	11,815*	22.0
8	Tenet Healthcare Corp—*Trevor Fetter*	PO Box 139003, Dallas TX 75313	469-893-2000	P	9,205	56.6
9	University of Pittsburgh Medical Center—*Jeffrey A Romoff*	200 Lothrop St, Pittsburgh PA 15213	412-647-8762	R	8,333*	50.0
10	Indiana University Health—*Daniel F Evans Jr*	PO Box 1367, Indianapolis IN 46206	317-962-2000	R	7,256	23.0
11	Carolinas HealthCare System—*Michael C Tarwater*	PO Box 32861, Charlotte NC 28232	704-355-2000	R	6,503*	44.0
12	Gwinnett Health System Inc—*Philip R Wolfe*	1000 Medical Center Bl, Lawrenceville GA 30045	678-312-1000	R	6,209*	4.1
13	Partners HealthCare System Inc—*Gary Gottlieb*	800 Boylston St Ste 11, Boston MA 02199	617-278-1000	R	5,852*	50.0
14	Health Management Associates Inc—*Gary D Newsome*	PO Box 770621, Naples FL 34107	239-598-3131	P	5,805	40.6
15	North Shore Long Island Jewish Health System—*Michael Dowling*	102-01 66th Rd, Forest Hills NY 11375		R	5,630	43.0
16	Mount Sinai Medical Center—*Kenneth L Davis*	1 Gustave L Levy Pl, New York NY 10029	212-241-6500	R	5,619*	3.5
17	Community Hospitals—*Bryan Mills*	1500 N Ritter Ave, Indianapolis IN 46219	317-355-1411	R	5,573*	10.7
18	Universal Health Services Inc—*Alan B Miller*	PO Box 61558, King of Prussia PA 19406	610-768-3300	P	5,568	65.1
19	Banner Health—*Peter S Fine* Banner Health System	1441 N 12th St, Phoenix AZ 85006	602-495-4000	D	4,677	35.0
20	Oakwood Healthcare System Inc—*Gerald Fitzgerald*	1633 Fairlane Cir Ste, Allen Park MI 48101	313-294-1104	R	4,400*	9.0
21	Catholic Healthcare Partners—*Michael D Connelly*	615 Elsinore Pl, Cincinnati OH 45202	513-639-2800	R	4,086	36.9
22	Baptist Health System Inc—*Shane Spees*	3201 Fourth Ave S, Birmingham AL 35222	205-715-5000	R	3,398*	6.5
23	Intermountain Health Care Inc—*Charles Sorenson*	36 S State St Fl 22, Salt Lake City UT 84111	801-442-2000	R	3,185*	32.0
24	LifePoint Hospitals Inc—*William F Carpenter III*	103 Powell Ct Ste 200, Brentwood TN 37027	615-372-8500	P	3,026	23.0
25	Allina Health System Inc—*Kenneth Paulus*	PO Box 43, Minneapolis MN 55440	612-775-5000	R	2,903*	24.0
26	Texas Health Resources Inc—*Douglas D Hawthorne*	612 E Lamar Blvd, Arlington TX 76011	682-236-7900	R	2,900*	20.5
27	IASIS Healthcare LLC—*W Carl Whitmer*	117 Seaboard Ln Bldg E, Franklin TN 37067	615-844-2747	R	2,787	14.3
28	Aurora Health Care Inc—*Nick Turkal*	PO Box 341880, Milwaukee WI 53215	414-647-3000	R	2,734*	24.0
29	Loudoun Healthcare Inc—*Knox Singleton*	44045 Riverside Pkwy, Leesburg VA 20176	703-858-6000	R	2,685*	1.5
30	Southcoast Health System—*John Day*	101 Page St, New Bedford MA 02740	508-961-5000	R	2,269*	5.5
31	Inova Health System—*Knox Singleton*	8110 Gatehouse Rd, Falls Church VA 22042	203-289-2000	R	2,250*	16.0
32	Sharp Healthcare—*Michael W Murphy*	8695 Spectrum Center B, San Diego CA 92123	858-499-2000	R	2,100*	14.0
33	William Beaumont Hospital—*Kenneth Matzick*	3601 W 13 Mile Rd, Royal Oak MI 48073	248-551-5000	R	2,061*	15.0
34	BJC Healthcare—*Steven H Lipstein*	4444 Forest Park Ave, Saint Louis MO 63108	314-747-9322	R	1,984*	27.0
35	Fairview Health Services—*Mark A Eustis*	2450 Riverside Ave, Minneapolis MN 55454	612-672-6000	R	1,983	18.0
36	Medstar Health—*Kenneth A Samet*	5565 Sterrett Pl, Columbia MD 21044	410-772-6500	R	1,850*	22.1
37	New York - Presbyterian Hospital—*Herbert Pardes*	654 W 170th St, New York NY 10021	212-821-0500	R	1,850	13.3
38	Reston Hospital Center LLC—*Bill Adams* HCA Holdings Inc	1850 Town Center Pky, Reston VA 20190	703-689-9000	S	1,748*	2.0
39	Adventist Health—*Robert G Carmen*	2100 Douglas Blvd, Roseville CA 95661	916-781-2000	R	1,571*	17.5
40	Norton Healthcare Inc—*Stephen A Williams*	200 E Chestnut St, Louisville KY 40202	502-629-8000	R	1,488*	9.0
41	Detroit Medical Center—*Michael E Duggan*	3663 Woodward Ave, Detroit MI 48201	313-578-2000	R	1,452*	16.5
42	Mednax Inc—*Roger J Medel*	PO Box 559001, Fort Lauderdale FL 33355	954-384-0175	P	1,402	6.3
43	Davis Hospital and Medical Center Inc—*Michael Jensen* IASIS Healthcare LLC	1600 W Antelope Dr, Layton UT 84041	801-807-1000	S	1,355*	.9
44	Wheaton Franciscan Services Inc—*John D Oliverio*	PO Box 667, Wheaton IL 60187	630-909-6900	R	1,273*	22.1
45	Memorial Health Services Inc—*Barry Arbuckle*	2801 Atlantic Ave, Long Beach CA 90806	562-933-2000	R	1,166*	5.0
46	Sparrow Health System—*Dennis Swan*	1215 E Michigan Ave, Lansing MI 48912	517-364-3935	R	1,008	10.0
47	Orlando Regional Healthcare System Inc—*Sherrie Sitarik*	1414 Kuhl Ave, Orlando FL 32806	407-841-5111	R	971*	13.0
48	Straub Clinic and Hospital Inc—*Raymond Vara*	888 S King St, Honolulu HI 96813	808-522-4000	R	884*	1.8
49	Methodist Healthcare—*Paula Jacobs*	1265 Union Ave Ste 700, Memphis TN 38104	901-516-7000	R	855*	10.2
50	MeritCare Health System—*Roger Gilbertson MD*	PO BOX MC, Fargo ND 58122	701-234-6000	R	659*	6.6
51	Lake Cumberland Regional Hospital LLC—*William F Carpenter III* LifePoint Hospitals Inc	PO Box 620, Somerset KY 42501	606-679-7441	S	645*	1.2

Note: An asterisk (*) indicates an estimated financial figure. The company type code used is as follows: R = Private, P = Public, S = Private Subsidiary, B = Public Subsidiary, D = Division, J = Joint Venture, I = Investment Fund.

COMPANY RANKINGS BY SALES WITHIN 4-DIGIT SIC

Rank	Company Name—Executive Officer	Address, City, State, Zip	Phone	Type	Fin	Empls
52	Adventist HealthCare—William Robertson	1801 Research Blvd Ste, Rockville MD 20850	301-315-3030	R	599*	7.2
53	United Surgical Partners International Inc—William H Wilcox	15305 Dallas Pky Ste 1, Addison TX 75001	972-713-3500	R	579	5.5
54	PeaceHealth—Alan Yordy	14432 SE Eastgate Way, Bellevue WA 98007	425-747-1711	R	549*	6.7
55	Heart Hospital of BK LLC—John T Casey MedCath Corp	3001 Sillect Ave, Bakersfield CA 93308	661-316-6000	S	482*	.3
56	United Health Services Inc—Matthew Salanger	33-57 Harrison St, Johnson City NY 13790	607-763-6000	R	471*	5.2
57	Integrated Healthcare Holdings Inc—Kenneth K Westbrook	1301 N Tustin Ave, Santa Ana CA 92705	714-953-3652	P	458	3.1
58	Tempe St Luke's Hospital LP—Ed Myers IASIS Healthcare LLC	1500 S Mill Ave, Tempe AZ 85281	480-784-5500	S	440*	.9
59	Putnam Community Medical Center LLC—Daniel P McLean LifePoint Hospitals Inc	PO Box 778, Palatka FL 32178	386-328-5711	S	439*	.5
60	South Shore Hospital—Richard Aubut	55 Fogg Rd, South Weymouth MA 02190	781-624-8000	S	383*	3.8
61	Clarent Hospital Corp	12337 Jones Rd Rm 218, Houston TX 77067	281-970-5104	R	369	4.7
62	Good Samaritan Health System—Paul Beaupre	2425 Samaritan Dr, San Jose CA 95124	408-559-2011	R	344*	2.8
63	Ingalls Health System—Kurt Johnson	1 Ingalls Dr, Harvey IL 60426	708-333-2333	R	333*	3.0
64	Via Christi Health System Inc—Randall L Peterson	929 N St Francis, Wichita KS 67214	316-268-5000	R	332*	4.0
65	Baptist Hospitals and Health Systems Inc—Dennis Knox	2000 W Bethany Home Rd, Phoenix AZ 85013	602-249-0212	R	330	4.1
66	Tampa General Healthcare—Ron Hytoff	PO Box 1289, Tampa FL 33601	813-844-8100	R	314*	3.8
67	University Health Inc—James R Davis	1350 Walton Way, Augusta GA 30901	706-722-9011	R	309*	3.0
68	St Joseph Health System LLC Community Health Systems Inc	700 Broadway, Fort Wayne IN 46802	260-425-3000	S	308*	1.1
69	Salt Lake Regional Medical Center Inc—Jeff Frandsen IASIS Healthcare LLC	1050 E S Temple, Salt Lake City UT 84102	801-350-4111	S	269*	.6
70	Jackson Purchase Medical Center—William F Carpenter III LifePoint Hospitals Inc	1099 Medical Center Ci, Mayfield KY 42066	270-251-4100	S	269*	.5
71	CHRISTUS Santa Rosa Healt Care—Don Beeler	333 N Santa Rosa St, San Antonio TX 78207	210-704-2011	R	265*	3.2
72	Children's Hospital and Medical Center—Gary Perkins	8200 Dodge St, Omaha NE 68114	402-955-5400	R	264	2.3
73	John C Lincoln Health Network—Rhonda Forsyth	9200 N 3rd St Ste 5, Phoenix AZ 85020	602-870-6309	R	260*	3.7
74	Arkansas Heart Hospital—Mark Hartman MedCath Corp	1701 S Shackleford Rd, Little Rock AR 72211	501-219-7000	S	238*	.5
75	Alexian Brothers Medical Center—Roger Johnson	800 Biesterfield Rd, Elk Grove Village IL 60007	847-437-5500	R	236*	2.0
76	Saint Luke's Health System Inc—Richard Hastings	10920 Elm Ave, Kansas City MO 64134	816-932-6220	R	235*	5.0
77	Citrus Valley Health Partners Inc—Robert Curry	210 W San Bernardino R, Covina CA 91723	626-331-7331	R	225*	3.0
78	Pioneer Valley Hospital Inc—Bryanie Swilley IASIS Healthcare LLC	3460 S Pioneer Pkwy, West Valley City UT 84120	801-964-3100	S	205*	.4
79	SunLink Health Systems Inc—Robert M Thornton Jr	900 Circle 75 Pky Ste, Atlanta GA 30339	770-933-7000	P	181	1.4
80	La Grange Troup County Hospital Authority—Gerald Fulke	PO Box 1567, Lagrange GA 30241	706-882-1411	R	180*	1.3
81	Center The Community Medical—Theodore Topolewski	1822 Mulberry St, Scranton PA 18510	570-969-8000	R	180*	1.3
82	Columbia Hospital At Medical City Dallas Subsidiary LP—Jane Alberiko	7777 Forest Ln Ste C84, Dallas TX 75230	972-566-7000	S	180*	2.6
83	West Florida Hospital—Jeff Amerson	8383 N Davis Hwy, Pensacola FL 32514	850-494-6503	R	179*	<.1
84	Everett Hospital—Jerry Maier	PO Box 26307, Oklahoma City OK 73126	405-271-4700	R	179*	2.8
85	Underwood Memorial Hospital Inc—Eileen Cardile	509 N Broad St, Woodbury NJ 08096	856-845-0100	R	179*	1.7
86	St Luke's Cornwall Hospital—Allan Atzrott	70 Dubois St, Newburgh NY 12550	845-561-4400	R	178*	1.5
87	Mercy Anderson Hospital Inc—Patrica Shroer	7500 State Rd, Cincinnati OH 45255	513-624-4500	R	177*	.8
88	Regional Medical Center Of Orangeburg and Calhoun Counties—Thomas Dandridge	3000 Saint Matthews Rd, Orangeburg SC 29118	803-533-2200	R	177*	1.2
89	Grand View Hospital—Stuart Fine	PO Box 902, Sellersville PA 18960	215-453-4000	R	177*	1.6
90	Vhs Sinai-Grace Hospital Inc—Conrad Mallett	6071 W Outer Dr, Detroit MI 48235	313-966-3300	R	176*	2.3
91	Franklin Regional Hospital Association—Thomas Clairmont	15 Aiken Ave, Franklin NH 03235	603-934-2060	R	176*	.3
92	Medical Center At Princeton New Jersey—Barry Rabner	253 Witherspoon St Ste, Princeton NJ 08540	609-497-4000	R	176*	2.3
93	Cobb Hospital Inc—Eunice Staffer	3950 Austell Rd, Austell GA 30106	770-792-7600	S	176*	2.4
94	Vhs Huron Valley-Sinai Hospital Inc—Joanne Bellairre	1 William Carls Dr, Commerce Township MI 48382	248-937-3300	R	175*	1.0
95	Manchester Memorial Hospital Inc—Marc Lory	71 Haynes St, Manchester CT 06040	860-646-1222	R	175*	1.1
96	St Elizabeth Hospital—Katia Richard	PO Box 5405, Beaumont TX 77726	409-892-7171	S	175*	2.5
97	Henry Medical Center Inc—Charles Scoot	1133 Eagles Landing Pk, Stockbridge GA 30281	678-604-1001	R	174*	1.1
98	Jupiter Medical Center Inc—Seldon Taub	PO Box 8350, Jupiter FL 33468	561-747-2234	R	174*	1.5
99	St Charles Hospital And Rehabilitation Center—James O'connor	200 Belle Terre Rd, Port Jefferson NY 11777	631-474-6000	R	174*	1.4
100	Sisters Of Charity Hospital Of Buffalo New York—Harry Smith	2157 Main St, Buffalo NY 14214	716-862-1000	R	174*	1.3
101	St Michaels Hospital Inc—Jeffery Martin	PO Box 4753, Tulsa OK 74159	715-346-5000	R	173*	1.9
102	St Mary's Health Care System Inc—Don Mckenna	1230 Baxter St, Athens GA 30606	706-389-3000	S	173*	1.4
103	Mcallen Medical Center LP—Cesar Matos	1400 W Trenton Rd, Edinburg TX 78539	956-632-4003	R	173*	2.5
104	Denton Regional Medical Center Inc—Robert Haley	3535 S Interstate 35 E, Denton TX 76210	940-384-3535	S	173*	.9
105	Williamsport Hospital—Steven Johnson	777 Rural Ave, Williamsport PA 17701	570-321-1000	R	172*	1.2
106	St Joseph Hospital—Peter Davis	172 Kinsley St, Nashua NH 03060	603-882-3000	R	172*	1.2
107	Samaritan Medical Center—Thomas Carman	830 Washington St, Watertown NY 13601	315-785-4000	R	171*	1.3
108	Marymount Hospital Inc—David Kilarski	12300 Mccracken Rd, Cleveland OH 44125	216-581-0500	R	171*	.5
109	St Francis Hospital Inc—Debra Standridge	PO Box 343921, Milwaukee WI 53234	414-647-5000	R	170*	1.6
110	Saint Francis Memorial Hospital—John Williams	900 Hyde St, San Francisco CA 94109	415-353-6000	R	170*	.8
111	Baptist Memorial Hospital - North Mississippi Inc—Don Hutson	PO Box 946, Oxford MS 38655	662-232-8100	R	170*	.9
112	Kishwaukee Community Hospital—Renee Simons	PO Box 707, Dekalb IL 60115	815-756-1521	R	170*	.9
113	Summa Health System—Penny Agner	PO Box 2090, Akron OH 44309	330-375-3000	R	169*	7.4
114	Denver Health And Hospitals Authority Inc—Patricia Gabow	12201 W 38th Ave, Wheat Ridge CO 80033	303-436-4600	R	169*	3.5
115	Beaufort Memorial Hospital—Thomas Deems	955 Ribaut Rd, Beaufort SC 29902	843-522-5163	R	167*	N/A
116	MedCath Corp—J Arthur Parker	10720 Sikes Pl Ste 300, Charlotte NC 28277	704-708-6600	B	167	.4
117	Roger Williams Hospital—Robert Urciuoli	825 Chalkstone Ave, Providence RI 02908	401-456-2000	R	167*	1.4
118	Goshen Hospital Association Inc—James Dague	PO Box 139, Goshen IN 46527	574-533-2141	R	167*	.7
119	St Joseph Hospital—Joseph Mark	2700 Dolbeer St, Eureka CA 95501	707-445-8121	R	167*	.9
120	Hca Health Services Of Tennessee Inc—Jeff Whitehorn	5655 Frist Blvd, Hermitage TN 37076	615-316-3000	R	167*	1.2
121	Athens Regional Medical Center Inc—John Drew	1199 Prince Ave, Athens GA 30606	706-475-7000	R	167*	2.3
122	Logan Regional Medical Center—William F Carpenter III LifePoint Hospitals Inc	20 Hospital Dr, Logan WV 25601	304-831-1101	S	166*	.3
123	Saint Francis Hospital—Jeff Murphy	355 Ridge Ave, Evanston IL 60202	847-316-4000	S	166*	1.4
124	Wuesthoff Health Systems Inc—Emil Miller	PO Box 565002, Rockledge FL 32956	321-636-2211	R	165*	2.4
125	Fayette Community Hospital Inc—W Cutts	1255 Hwy 54 W, Fayetteville GA 30214	770-719-7070	R	165*	1.0
126	White River Health System Inc—Gary Bebow	PO Box 2197, Batesville AR 72503	870-262-1200	R	165*	1.5
127	Erie-Austin Investors Inc—David Cecero	3 Erie Ct, Oak Park IL 60302	708-383-6200	R	164*	2.3
128	Theda Clark Memorial Hospital—Dean Gruner	130 2nd St, Neenah WI 54956	920-729-3100	R	164*	1.2

Rank	Company Name—*Executive Officer*	Address, City, State, Zip	Phone	Type	Fin	Empls
129	Hospital Service District—*Phyllis Peoples*	PO Box 6037, Houma LA 70361	985-873-4141	R	164*	1.4
130	Roger Williams Medical Center—*Kenneth Belcher*	825 Chalkstone Ave, Providence RI 02908	401-456-2000	R	162*	1.5
131	Salmon Legacy Creek Hospital—*Lee Domanico*	2211 Ne 139th St, Vancouver WA 98686	360-487-1000	S	162*	.7
132	Columbia-Csa/Hs Greater Canton Area Healthcare Systems LP—*Jack Topoleski*	1320-30 Mercy Dr, Canton OH 44708	330-489-1000	R	162*	2.3
133	Sound Shore Medical Center Of Westchester—*John Spicer*	16 Guion Pl, New Rochelle NY 10801	914-365-3636	R	162*	1.4
134	Regional West Medical Center—*Todd Sorensen*	4021 Ave B, Scottsbluff NE 69361	308-635-3711	R	162*	1.1
135	Livingston Regional Hospital LLC—*William Carpenter III* LifePoint Hospitals Inc	315 Oak St, Livingston TN 38570	931-823-5611	S	161*	.3
136	Habor Ucla Medical Center Inc—*Miguel Ortiz*	1000 W Carson St 2, Torrance CA 90502	310-222-2906	R	161*	3.0
137	Dameron Hospital Association Inc—*Christopher Arismendi*	525 W Acacia St, Stockton CA 95203	209-944-5550	R	161*	1.0
138	Our Lady Bellefonte Hospital Inc—*Kevin Halter*	PO Box 789, Ashland KY 41105	606-833-3333	R	160*	1.1
139	Phelps County Regional Medical Center—*Denise Pinson*	1000 W 10th St, Rolla MO 65401	573-458-8899	R	160*	1.2
140	Ahs Hillcrest Medical Center LLC—*Jason Fahrlander*	1120 S Utica Ave, Tulsa OK 74104	918-584-1351	R	160*	2.1
141	Avera Mckennan Hospital and University Center—*Fredrick Slunecka*	PO Box 5045, Sioux Falls SD 57117	605-322-8000	R	159*	2.3
142	Community Hospital Of San Bernardino—*Diane Nitta*	1805 Medical Ctr Dr, San Bernardino CA 92411	909-887-6333	R	159*	1.4
143	St Marys Hospital—*Michael Sniffen*	350 Blvd, Passaic NJ 07055	973-365-4300	R	159*	<.1
144	Chippenham and Johnston-Willis Hospitals Inc—*Peter Marmerstein*	7101 Jahnke Rd, Richmond VA 23225	804-320-3911	S	158*	2.4
145	Sturdy Memorial Hospital Inc—*Linda Shyavitz*	PO Box 2963, Attleboro MA 02703	508-222-5200	R	158*	1.1
146	St Elizabeth Hospital Inc—*Travis Andersen*	1506 S Oneida St, Appleton WI 54915	920-738-2000	R	158*	1.4
147	Good Samaritan Hospital Of Lebanon Pennsylvania—*Robert Longo*	PO Box 1281, Lebanon PA 17042	717-270-7500	R	157*	.1
148	Massachusetts General Hospital—*Peter Slecin*	55 Fruit St, Boston MA 02114	617-726-2000	R	157*	10.2
149	Cheshire Medical Center—*Arthur Nichols*	580 Ct St, Keene NH 03431	603-352-4111	R	156*	1.0
150	Forrest S Chilton Iii Memorial Hosp—*Edwin Wills*	242 W Pky Fl 2, Pompton Plains NJ 07444	973-831-0717	R	156*	N/A
151	Rockledge Hma LLC—*Emil Miller*	PO Box 565002, Rockledge FL 32956	321-636-2211	R	156*	2.5
152	Poplar Bluff Regional Medical Center Inc—*Bruce Eady*	2620 N Westwood Blvd, Poplar Bluff MO 63901	573-785-7721	R	156*	<.1
153	Hima San Pablo Fajardo—*Jose Carballo*	PO Box 1028, Fajardo PR 00738	787-863-0505	R	156*	4.0
154	Milford Regional Healthcare Foundation Inc—*Francis Saba*	14 Prospect St, Milford MA 01757	508-473-1190	R	155*	1.8
155	St Charles Hospital Of Oregon Ohio Inc—*Davis Ameen*	2600 Navarre Ave, Oregon OH 43616	419-696-7200	R	155*	1.9
156	Saint Mary's Health Care Corp—*Larry O'brien*	235 W 6th St, Reno NV 89503	775-770-3000	R	155*	2.3
157	Camden-Clark Memorial Hospital Corp—*Thomas Corder*	PO Box 718, Parkersburg WV 26102	304-424-2111	R	154*	1.6
158	Verde Valley Medical Center—*Mike Young*	269 S Candy Ln, Cottonwood AZ 86326	928-634-2251	R	154*	.5
159	Mercy Hospital Of Scranton PA—*James May*	746 Jefferson Ave, Scranton PA 18510	570-348-7100	S	154*	1.5
160	Hayward Sister Hospital—*Michael Mahoney*	27200 Calaroga Ave, Hayward CA 94545	510-264-4000	R	154*	.9
161	Capella Healthcare Inc—*Tom Anderson*	501 Corporate Centre D, Franklin TN 37067	615-764-3000	R	153*	2.7
162	Baptist Health—*Russell Tyner*	PO Box 244001, Montgomery AL 36124	334-273-4217	R	153*	2.3
163	Vail Clinic Inc—*Greg Repetti*	PO Box 40000, Vail CO 81658	970-476-2451	R	153*	.6
164	Iredell Memorial Hospital Inc—*Ed Rush*	PO Box 1828, Statesville NC 28687	704-873-5661	R	153*	1.4
165	Oroville Hospital—*Robert Wentz*	2767 Olive Hwy, Oroville CA 95966	530-533-8500	R	153*	1.4
166	St Vincent's Medical Center—*William Riordan*	2800 Main St, Bridgeport CT 06606	203-576-6000	R	152*	1.9
167	Forest Hills Hospital—*Gerelyn Raendazzo*	10201 66th Rd, Forest Hills NY 11375	718-830-4000	R	152*	.9
168	Orange Coast Memorial Medical Center—*Marcia Manker*	9920 Talbert Ave, Fountain Valley CA 92708	714-962-4677	R	152*	1.0
169	Satilla Health Services Inc—*Robert Trimm*	PO Box 139, Waycross GA 31502	912-283-3030	R	151*	1.3
170	Putnam Hospital Center Foundation Inc—*Donna Mcgregor*	670 Stoneleigh Ave, Carmel NY 10512	845-279-5711	R	151*	1.0
171	Methodist Medical Center Of Oak Ridge—*Mike Belbeck*	PO Box 2529, Oak Ridge TN 37831	865-835-1000	S	150*	1.5
172	Metropolitan Hospital Center Inc—*Dennis Gowie*	1901 1st Ave, New York NY 10029	212-423-6898	R	150*	3.0
173	Alexian Brothers Of San Jose Inc—*Steven Barron*	225 N Jackson Ave, San Jose CA 95116	408-259-5000	R	150*	1.2
174	West Orange Healthcare District Inc—*Richard Irwin*	10000 W Colonial Dr Of, Ocoee FL 34761	407-296-1000	R	150*	1.3
175	Winona Health Services—*Rachelle Schultz*	PO Box 5600, Winona MN 55987	507-454-3650	R	150*	.9
176	Hanford Community Hospital—*Rick Rawson*	PO Box 240, Hanford CA 93232	559-582-9000	R	149*	.7
177	Conway Hospital Inc—*Philip Clayton*	PO Box 829, Conway SC 29528	843-347-7111	R	149*	1.2
178	Trident Medical Center LLC—*Robin Phillips*	9330 Medical Plz Dr, Charleston SC 29406	843-797-7000	R	149*	2.0
179	Holy Name Medical Center Inc—*Michael Maron*	718 Teaneck Rd, Teaneck NJ 07666	201-833-3000	R	149*	2.0
180	Bon Secours - Depaul Medical Center Inc—*Daniel Duggan*	150 Kingsley Ln, Norfolk VA 23505	757-889-5000	R	148*	1.4
181	St Rose Dominican Hospital—*Rod Davis*	102 E Lake Mead Pkwy, Henderson NV 89015	702-492-8789	R	148*	.8
182	Seton Health System Inc—*Carol Crucetti*	1300 Massachusetts Ave, Troy NY 12180	518-268-5000	R	148*	1.3
183	Kimball Medical Center—*Joanne Carrocino*	600 River Ave, Lakewood NJ 08701	732-886-4419	R	148*	1.5
184	Mennonite General Hospital Inc—*Ruben Santos*	PO Box 373130, Cayey PR 00737	787-535-1001	R	148*	1.2
185	Mary Greeley Medical Center—*Brian Dieter*	1111 Duff Ave, Ames IA 50010	515-239-2011	R	147*	.1
186	Empire Health Centers Group—*Jeff Nelson*	PO Box 248, Spokane WA 99210	509-458-7960	R	147*	2.0
187	Legacy Meridian Park Hospital—*Anthony Bilotti*	19300 Sw 65th Ave, Tualatin OR 97062	503-692-1212	R	147*	.5
188	Baptist Memorial Hospital-Golden Triangle Inc—*Joseph Powell*	PO Box 1307, Columbus MS 39703	662-244-1000	R	146*	1.1
189	Holy Caritas Family Hospital Inc—*Thomas Sager*	70 E St, Methuen MA 01844	978-687-0151	S	146*	1.7
190	St Francis' Hospital Poughkeepsie New York—*Robert Savage*	241 N Rd, Poughkeepsie NY 12601	845-471-2000	R	146*	1.5
191	Adventist Health System/Sunbelt Inc—*Donald Jernigan*	111 N Orlando Ave, Winter Park FL 32789	407-647-4400	R	145*	44.0
192	Mercy Health Partners—*Tom Urban*	4600 Mcauley Pl Ste A, Blue Ash OH 45242	513-981-6251	S	145*	2.9
193	Columbus Regional Hospital Inc—*James Bickel*	2400 17th St, Columbus IN 47201	812-379-4441	R	145*	1.5
194	Greater Lafayette Health Services Inc—*Terry Wilson*	1501 Hartford St, Lafayette IN 47904	765-423-6011	S	145*	2.7
195	Olmsted Medical Center—*Roy Yawn*	210 9th St Se, Rochester MN 55904	507-288-3443	R	144*	1.0
196	Little Company Of Mary Hospital Of Indiana Inc—*Raymond Snowden*	800 W 9th St, Jasper IN 47546	812-482-2345	R	144*	1.0
197	Baxter County Regional Hospital Inc—*Ron Peterson*	624 Hospital Dr, Mountain Home AR 72653	870-508-1000	R	144*	1.2
198	North Fulton Medical Center Volunteer Services Organization Inc—*Debbie Keel*	3000 Hospital Blvd, Roswell GA 30076	770-751-2500	R	143*	1.0
199	Central Peninsula General Hospital Inc—*Ryan Smith*	250 Hospital Pl, Soldotna AK 99669	907-714-4404	R	143*	.4
200	Western Plains Regional Hospital LLC—*William F Carpenter III* LifePoint Hospitals Inc	PO Box 1478, Dodge City KS 67801	620-225-8400	S	143*	.3
201	St Luke's Health System—*Wayne Gower*	1800 E Van Buren St, Phoenix AZ 85006	602-251-8100	S	143*	1.6
202	Southeastern Ohio Regional Medical Center—*Jim Keller*	PO Box 610, Cambridge OH 43725	740-439-3561	R	143*	.8
203	Hutzel Hospital—*Mike Duggin*	3980 John R St, Detroit MI 48201	313-745-7555	R	142*	1.9
204	St Clare Hospital—*Jean Clark*	11315 Bridgeport Way S, Tacoma WA 98499	253-588-1711	R	142*	.5
205	Blount Memorial Hospital Inc—*Jane Andrews*	907 Elmar Alexander Pk, Maryville TN 37804	865-983-7211	R	142*	2.1
206	Singing River Health System—*Chris Anderson*	PO Box 1597, Gautier MS 39553	228-809-5251	R	142*	2.1
207	Williamson County Hospital District Inc—*Dennis Miller*	4321 Carothers Pkwy, Franklin TN 37067	615-435-5000	R	142*	1.1
208	St Barnabas Community Enterprises—*Victor Wright*	4422 3rd Ave, Bronx NY 10457	718-960-6100	R	142*	2.0
209	York Hospital—*Jud Knox*	15 Hospital Dr, York ME 03909	207-363-4321	R	142*	.5
210	Memorial Hermann Katy Hospital—*Dan Wolterman*	23900 Katy Fwy, Katy TX 77494	281-644-7000	S	141*	N/A

Note: An asterisk (*) indicates an estimated financial figure. The company type code used is as follows: R = Private, P = Public, S = Private Subsidiary, B = Public Subsidiary, D = Division, J = Joint Venture, I = Investment Fund.

COMPANY RANKINGS BY SALES WITHIN 4-DIGIT SIC

Rank	Company Name—Executive Officer	Address, City, State, Zip	Phone	Type	Fin	Empls
211	Presbyterian Medical Care Corp—Carl Armato	1500 Mtthews Twnship P, Matthews NC 28105	704-384-6500	S	141*	.4
212	Boca Raton Community Hospital Physicians Group—Gary Strack	800 Meadows Rd, Deerfield Beach FL 33441	561-395-7100	R	141*	1.9
213	Bon Secours-Memorial Regional Medical Center Inc—Michael Robinson	8260 Atlee Rd Ste 1203, Mechanicsville VA 23116	804-764-6000	R	141*	2.0
214	Yukon-Kuskokwim Health Corp—Gene Peltola	PO Box 528, Bethel AK 99559	907-543-6300	R	141*	1.8
215	Mercy Health Partners—Kevin Cook	746 Jefferson Ave, Scranton PA 18510	570-348-7100	R	140*	2.3
216	Ball Memorial Hospital Inc—Michael Haley	2401 W University Ave, Muncie IN 47303	765-747-3111	R	140*	3.0
217	Integris Rural Health Inc—Stan Hupfeld	3366 Nw Expy St Ste 80, Oklahoma City OK 73112	405-949-3011	R	140*	1.9
218	Falmouth Hospital Association Inc—Mike Connors	100 Ter Heun Dr, Falmouth MA 02540	508-548-5300	S	140*	1.0
219	Southern Tennessee Medical Center LLC—William Carpenter III LifePoint Hospitals Inc	185 Hospital Rd, Winchester TN 37398	931-967-8200	S	134*	.3
220	Hillside Hospital LLC—Jim Edmondson LifePoint Hospitals Inc	1265 E College St, Pulaski TN 38478	931-363-7531	S	121*	.3
221	CareGroup Inc—Paul F Levy	375 Longwood Ave, Boston MA 02215	617-975-5000	R	120*	15.0
222	Arizona Heart Hospital LLC—Don Jaffee MedCath Corp	1930 E Thomas Rd, Phoenix AZ 85016	602-532-1000	S	114*	.3
223	Heart Hospital IV LP—Kerry R Hicks MedCath Corp	3801 N Lamar Blvd, Austin TX 78756	512-407-7000	S	114*	.3
224	Nanticoke Memorial Hospital Inc—Steve Rose	801 Middleford Rd, Seaford DE 19973	302-629-6611	R	113*	1.2
225	Logan Memorial Hospital LLC—William F Carpenter III LifePoint Hospitals Inc	PO Box 10, Russellville KY 42276	270-726-4011	S	107*	.2
226	Heart Hospital of DTO LLC—John T Casey MedCath Corp	2222 Philadelphia Dr, Dayton OH 45406	937-278-2612	S	104*	.3
227	Crockett Hospital LLC—William F Carpenter III LifePoint Hospitals Inc	PO Box 847, Lawrenceburg TN 38464	931-762-6571	S	81*	.2
228	Bartow Healthcare System Ltd—William F Carpenter III LifePoint Hospitals Inc	103 Powell Ct Ste 200, Brentwood TN 37027	615-372-8500	S	74*	.2
229	Ashley Valley Medical Center LLC—William F Carpenter III LifePoint Hospitals Inc	150 W 100 N, Vernal UT 84078	435-789-3342	S	64*	.1
230	CHCA Conroe LP—Jerry A Nash HCA Holdings Inc	504 Medical Center Blv, Conroe TX 77304	936-539-1111	S	55*	1.2
231	Castleview Hospital LLC—William F Carpenter III LifePoint Hospitals Inc	300 N Hospital Dr, Price UT 84501	435-637-4800	S	54*	.1
232	Russellville Hospital LLC—Christine Stewart LifePoint Hospitals Inc	PO Box 1089, Russellville AL 35653	256-332-1611	S	54*	.1
233	Smith County Memorial Hospital LLC—William F Carpenter III LifePoint Hospitals Inc	158 Hospital Dr, Carthage TN 37030	615-735-1560	S	54*	.1
234	First Physicians Capital Group Inc—David Hirschhorn	9663 Santa Monica Blvd, Beverly Hills CA 90210	301-260-2501	P	40	<.1
235	Piedmont Hospital Inc—Robert Maynard	1968 Peachtree Rd NW, Atlanta GA 30309	404-605-5000	R	31*	3.0
236	Cataract Eye Center—Samuel M Salamon	2322 E 22nd St Ste 307, Cleveland OH 44115	216-574-8900	R	31*	<.1
237	Pacer Corp—Rainier Gonzalez	14100 Palmetto Frontag, Miami Lakes FL 33016	305-828-7660	R	30	.5
238	Meadows Holdings LP—Betty Hanson	1655 N Tegner St, Wickenburg AZ 85390	928-684-4026	R	16*	.2
239	Southern Coos Hospital and Health Center—Jim Wathen	900 11th St Se, Bandon OR 97411	541-347-2426	R	15*	.1
240	Columbia/Alleghany Regional Hospital Inc—Greg Madsen HCA Holdings Inc	PO Box 7, Low Moor VA 24457	540-862-6011	S	15*	.4
241	Bjc Health Clincal Asset Management—Larry Mcwhirter	1537 Larkin Williams R, Fenton MO 63026	636-717-3600	R	11*	.1
242	Sanford Health—Kelby K Krabbenhoft	PO Box 5039, Sioux Falls SD 57117	605-333-1000	R	8*	18.0
243	Lovejoy Surgicenter Inc—Kayla Reich	933 NW 25th Ave, Portland OR 97210	503-221-1870	R	2*	<.1
244	Mission Health System—Ronald Paulus	509 Biltmore Ave, Asheville NC 28801	828-213-1111	R	1*	7.0
245	Ancilla Systems Inc—Toni Mola	1419 S Lake Park Ave, Hobart IN 46342	219-947-8500	R	1*	<.1
246	Sentara Healthcare—David L Bernd	6015 Poplar Hall Dr, Norfolk VA 23502	757-455-7540	R	<1	17.0
247	Promedica Health System Inc—Alan W Brass	2142 N Cove Blvd, Toledo OH 43606	419-291-4602	R	<1	11.7
248	University of Arkansas for Medical Sciences—Tim E Hunt	4301 W Markham St, Little Rock AR 72205	501-686-8000	R	<1	10.6
249	UMass Memorial Health Care—John O'Brien	Biotech One 365 Planta, Worcester MA 01605	508-334-1000	R	<1	10.0
250	Franciscan Missonaries of Our Lady Health System Inc—John Finan Jr	4200 Essen Lane, Baton Rouge LA 70809	225-923-2701	R	<1	9.0

TOTALS: SIC 8062 General Medical & Surgical Hospitals
Companies: 250

					298,532	1,774.0

8063 Psychiatric Hospitals

Rank	Company Name—Executive Officer	Address, City, State, Zip	Phone	Type	Fin	Empls
1	Ardent Health Services LLC—David T Vanderwater	1 Burton Hills Blvd St, Nashville TN 37215	615-296-3000	S	5,007*	7.8
2	Magellan Health Services Inc—Rene Lerer MD	55 Nod Rd, Avon CT 06001		P	2,156	4.8
3	MHM Correctional Services Inc—Mike Pinkert Mental Health Management Inc	1593 Spring Hill Rd St, Vienna VA 22182	703-749-4600	S	1,627*	2.0
4	Magellan Behavioral Health Inc Magellan Health Services Inc	6950 Columbia Gateway, Columbia MD 21046		S	1,024*	6.1
5	FHC Health Systems Inc—Ronald I Dozoretz	240 Corporate Blvd, Norfolk VA 23502	757-459-5100	R	612*	3.1
6	CRC Health Corp—Andrew Eckert	20400 Stevens Creek Bl, Cupertino CA 95014	408-998-7260	R	470	N/A
7	Rye Hospital Center—Jack C Schoenholtz	754 Boston Post Rd, Rye NY 10580	914-967-4567	R	285*	.1
8	Gulf Coast Treatment Center Inc—Jeffrey M Kaplan	1015 Mar Walt Dr, Fort Walton Beach FL 32547	850-863-4160	S	241*	.3
9	Mental Health Management Inc—Michael S Pinkert	1593 Spring Hill Rd St, Vienna VA 22182	703-749-4600	R	196*	2.0
10	Heartland Behavioral Health Services Inc—Allison Wyson-Harder	1500 W Ashland St, Nevada MO 64772	417-667-2666	R	161*	.2
11	Telecare Corp—Anne Bakar	1080 Marina Village Pk, Alameda CA 94501	510-337-7950	R	152*	2.1
12	Bountiful Psychiatric Hospital Inc—Joey A Jacobs	6640 Carothers Parkway, Franklin TN 37067	615-312-5711	S	80*	.1
13	Prairie View Inc—Mel Goering	PO Box 467, Newton KS 67114	316-283-2400	R	30*	.4
14	Naperville Psychiatric Ventures—Neil Gupta	801 S Washington St, Naperville IL 60540	630-305-5500	R	29*	.2
15	Comprehensive Behavioral Care Inc—Clark A Marcus	3405 W Dr Martin Luthe, Tampa FL 33607	813-288-4808	S	24*	.1
16	Hillside Inc—Teresa Stoker	PO Box 8247, Atlanta GA 31106	404-875-4551	R	11*	.2
17	Core Health Care—Eric McKowski	PO Box 419, Dripping Springs TX 78620	512-894-0801	R	10*	.1
18	Texarkana Behavioral Associates LC—Angela Klinikowski	PO Box 9240, Fayetteville AR 72703	479-521-5731	R	9*	.1
19	Colorado Boy's Ranch Foundation Inc—Charles Thompson	PO Box 681, La Junta CO 81050	719-384-5981	R	7*	.2

TOTALS: SIC 8063 Psychiatric Hospitals
Companies: 19

					12,131	29.8

8069 Specialty Hospitals Except Psychiatric

Rank	Company Name—Executive Officer	Address, City, State, Zip	Phone	Type	Fin	Empls
1	Bon Secours Health System Inc—Richard J Statuto	1505 Marriottsville Rd, Marriottsville MD 21104	410-442-5511	R	13,391*	21.0
2	Consulate Management Co—Joseph Conte	800 Concourse Pkwy S S, Maitland FL 32751	407-571-1550	R	8,292*	12.0

Rank	Company Name—*Executive Officer*	Address, City, State, Zip	Phone	Type	Fin	Empls
3	University of Texas MD Anderson Cancer Center—*Ronald A DePinho*	1515 Holcombe Blvd, Houston TX 77030	713-792-6161	R	3,043*	17.0
4	Bronson Healthcare Group Inc—*Frank Sardone*	1 Healthcare Plz, Kalamazoo MI 49007		R	1,994*	3.0
5	Cincinnati Children's Hospital Medical Center—*Michael Fisher*	3333 Burnet Ave, Cincinnati OH 45229	513-636-4200	R	1,465*	12.4
6	RehabCare Group Inc—*John H Short*	7733 Forsyth Blvd Ste, Saint Louis MO 63105		R	1,329	18.8
7	Nationwide Children's Hospital—*Steve Allen*	700 Children's Dr, Columbus OH 43205	614-722-2000	R	1,171*	8.5
8	Children's Medical Center of Dallas—*Christopher Durovich*	1935 Medical District, Dallas TX 75235	214-456-7000	R	912	5.6
9	Palms of Pasadena Hospital LP—*Brian Flynn*	1501 Pasadena Ave, Saint Petersburg FL 33707		S	737*	1.2
10	Odessa Regional Hospital LP—*Stacey Gerig*	520 E 6th St, Odessa TX 79761	432-582-8200	S	335*	.5
11	ReMed Recovery Care Centers—*Joanne Finegar*	16 Industrial Blvd Ste, Paoli PA 19301	484-595-9300	R	285*	.4
12	Columbia Health System Inc—*Leo P Brideau*	2025 E Newport Ave, Milwaukee WI 53211	414-961-3300	R	196	1.4
13	East Tennessee Children's Hospital Association Inc—*Keith Goodwin*	PO Box 15010, Knoxville TN 37901	865-541-8000	R	170*	1.5
14	Hospital For Special Care—*David Crandall*	2150 Corbin Ave, New Britain CT 06053	860-223-2761	R	145*	<.1
15	Central Baptist Hospital Foundation Inc—*John Barton*	1740 Nicholasville Rd, Lexington KY 40503	859-260-6670	R	145*	2.5
16	Oklahoma Heart Hospital LLC—*Kris Kimmel*	4050 W Memorial Rd, Oklahoma City OK 73120	405-608-3200	R	144*	.4
17	Lakeview Center Inc—*Gary Bembry*	1221 W Lakeview Ave, Pensacola FL 32501	850-432-1222	R	144*	1.9
18	Gillette Children's Specialty Healthcare—*Margaret Perryman*	200 University Ave E, Saint Paul MN 55101	651-291-2848	R	140*	.6
19	Southboro Medical Group Inc—*Marvin Ostrousky*	24 Newton St, Southborough MA 01772	508-481-5500	R	46*	.4
20	MD Anderson Cancer Center—*Clarence Brown MD*	1400 S Orange Ave, Orlando FL 32806	407-648-3800	S	30*	.3
21	Compass Intervention Center LLC—*Al Smith*	7900 Lowrance Rd, Memphis TN 38125	901-758-2002		8*	.1
22	MileStone Healthcare—*Charles Allen*	2435 N Central Expy St, Richardson TX 75080		S	1*	<.1
23	Urban Child Institute—*Eugene K Cashman Jr*	600 Jefferson Ave Ste, Memphis TN 38105	901-523-9199	S	1*	<.1

TOTALS: SIC 8069 Specialty Hospitals Except Psychiatric
Companies: 23

					34,123	109.6

8071 Medical Laboratories

Rank	Company Name—*Executive Officer*	Address, City, State, Zip	Phone	Type	Fin	Empls
1	Quest Diagnostics Inc—*Surya N Mohapatra*	3 Giralda Farms, Madison NJ 07940	973-520-2700	P	7,369	42.0
2	AmeriPath Inc	7111 Fairway Dr Ste 40, Palm Beach Gardens FL 33418	561-845-1850	S	3,176*	1.9
3	Silliker Inc—*Russell Flowers*	111 E Wacker Dr Ste 23, Chicago IL 60601	312-938-5151	R	2,448*	.6
4	CDI Management Corp—*Robert Baumgartner*	5775 Wayzata Blvd Ste, Minneapolis MN 55416	952-543-6500	R	717*	.5
5	Bio-Reference Laboratories Inc—*Marc D Grodman PhD*	481 Edward H Ross Dr, Elmwood Park NJ 07407	201-791-2600	P	559	2.4
6	RadNet Inc—*Howard G Berger*	1510 Cotner Ave, Los Angeles CA 90025	310-445-2800	P	549	4.6
7	Alliance Healthcare Services—*Paul Viviano*	100 Bayview Cir Ste 40, Newport Beach CA 92660	714-688-7100	B	479	2.0
8	MQ Associates Inc—*Chris Winkle*	3480 Preston Ridge Rd, Alpharetta GA 30005	770-300-0101	R	277*	1.6
9	InSight Health Services Corp—*Louis E Hallman III*	26250 Enterprise Ct St, Lake Forest CA 92630	949-282-6000	R	254*	1.9
10	Cardium Therapeutics Inc—*Christopher Reinhard*	12255 El Camino Real S, San Diego CA 92130	858-436-1000	P	245	<.1
11	Sierra Medical Center—*Mary Pavia*	1625 Medical Ctr Dr, El Paso TX 79902	915-747-4000	R	178*	<.1
12	Genomic Health Inc—*Kimberly J Popovits*	301 Penobscot Dr, Redwood City CA 94063	650-556-9300	P	178	.5
13	National Dentex Corp—*Josh Green*	2 Vision Dr, Natick MA 01760	508-907-7800	R	161	1.7
14	Cooperative Health Services Inc—*Jeffrey Barber*	PO Box 20007, Owensboro KY 42304	270-688-3075	S	160*	3.2
15	Dynacare Laboratories Inc—*Osama Sherif*	740 E Campbell Rd, Richardson TX 75081	281-227-2727	S	158*	3.0
16	Medical Resources Inc—*John Valla*	1455 Broad St 4th Fl, Bloomfield NJ 07003	973-707-1100	R	158*	1.1
17	St Charles Hospital Port Jefferson New York—*Carol Salisbury*	200 Belle Terre Rd, Port Jefferson NY 11777	631-474-1572	R	154*	<.1
18	Puget Sound Blood Center and Program—*Bob Gleeson*	921 Terry Ave, Seattle WA 98104	206-292-6500	R	150*	.8
19	Stern Cardiovascular Center—*Debbie Eddlestone*	8060 Wolf River Blvd, Germantown TN 38138	901-271-1000	R	149*	.1
20	Dihydro Services Inc Dihydro Analytical Services Div—*Danny Hutchins*	40833 Brentwood Dr, Sterling Heights MI 48310	586-978-0425	S	128*	.1
21	Bostwick Laboratories Inc—*David G Bostwick*	4355 Innslake Dr, Glen Allen VA 23060	804-967-9225	R	103	.8
22	Enzo Biochem Inc—*Elazar Rabbani*	527 Madison Ave, New York NY 10022	212-583-0100	P	102	.6
23	MEDTOX Scientific Inc—*Richard J Braun*	402 W County Rd D, Saint Paul MN 55112	651-636-7466	P	97	.6
24	LipoScience Inc—*Richard O Brajer*	2500 Sumner Blvd, Raleigh NC 27616	919-212-1999	R	97*	.2
25	DIANON Systems Inc—*Thomas P MacMahon*	1 Forest Parkway, Shelton CT 06484	203-926-7100	S	62*	.5
26	Lipomics Technologies Inc—*Steven Watkins*	3410 Industrial Blvd S, West Sacramento CA 95691	916-371-7974	R	50*	<.1
27	Medtox Laboratories Inc MEDTOX Scientific Inc	402 W County Rd D, Saint Paul MN 55112	651-636-7466	D	42*	.4
28	Health Network Laboratories LP—*David Beckwith*	2024 Lehigh St, Allentown PA 18103	610-530-0809	R	36*	.7
29	PharmChem Inc—*Joseph W Halligan*	2411 E Loop 820 N, Fort Worth TX 76118	817-590-2537	P	24*	.2
30	Psychemedics Corp—*Raymond C Kubacki Jr*	125 Nagog Pk Ste 200, Acton MA 01720	978-206-8220	P	20	.1
31	Clinical Reference Laboratory Inc—*Robert Stout*	8433 Quivira Rd, Lenexa KS 66215	913-492-3652	R	20*	.4
32	Enzo Clinical Labs Inc—*Elazar Rabbani* Enzo Biochem Inc	60 Executive Blvd, Farmingdale NY 11735	631-755-5500	S	19*	.2
33	American Shared Hospital Services—*Ernest A Bates*	4 Embarcadero Ctr Ste, San Francisco CA 94111	415-788-5300	P	17	<.1
34	Legacy Laboratory Services—*George J Brown*	1120 NW 19th Suite 111, Portland OR 97209	503-413-5000	S	16*	.2
35	Orchid GeneScreen Inc	2600 Stemmons Frwy Ste, Dallas TX 75207	214-631-8152	S	15	.2
36	Aerotech Laboratories Inc—*David Fetveit*	1501 W Knudsen Dr, Phoenix AZ 85027	623-780-4800	S	15*	.2
37	Cell Signaling Technology Inc—*Michael Comb*	3 Trask Ln, Danvers MA 01923	978-867-2300	R	13*	.2
38	Signature Genomic Laboratories LLC—*Lisa G Shaffer*	2820 N Astor St, Spokane WA 99207	509-474-6840	R	13*	.1
39	Architectural Testing Inc—*Henry Taylor*	130 Derry Ct, York PA 17406	717-764-7700	R	12*	.2
40	Vista Imaging Services Inc—*Jeffery Perry*	3941 Park Dr Ste 20-46, El Dorado Hills CA 95762	415-272-3925	R	9	<.1
41	Bodycote Materials Testing Inc—*D Northington*	9240 Santa Fe Springs, Santa Fe Springs CA 90670	562-948-2225	R	8*	<.1
42	Precision Optical Group Inc—*Michael Tamerius*	PO Box 369, Creston IA 50801	641-782-6685	R	7*	.1
43	Clinical Research Laboratories Inc—*Bruce E Kanengiser*	371 Hoes Ln Rm 1, Piscataway NJ 08854	732-981-1616	R	6*	.1
44	Virginia Radiology Associates Inc—*H Keith Hellem Jr*	8629 Sudley Rd Ste 102, Manassas VA 20110	703-361-3030	R	6*	.1
45	GeneLink Inc—*Bernard Kasten Jr*	317 Wekiva Springs Rd, Longwood FL 32779		P	6	<.1
46	Community Mobile Diagnostics LLC—*Fipe Mose*	1700 150th Ave, San Leandro CA 94578	510-278-9030	R	6*	.1
47	SpectraCell Laboratories Inc—*William B Stanberry Jr*	10401 Townpark Dr, Houston TX 77072	713-621-3101	R	5*	.1
48	Bioscience Laboratories Inc—*Daryl Paulson*	PO Box 190, Bozeman MT 59771	406-587-5735	R	4*	<.1
49	Forensic Fluids Laboratories—*Bridget Lorenz Lemberg*	225 Parsons St, Kalamazoo MI 49007		R	4*	<.1
50	Accura Analytical Laboratory Inc—*Shaker Reddy*	6017 Financial Dr, Norcross GA 30071	770-449-8800	R	4*	<.1
51	Golf Diagnostic Imaging Center—*Parvez Shirazi*	9680 Golf Rd, Des Plaines IL 60016	847-296-5366	R	3*	<.1
52	Meretek Inc—*Ryuiche Kishigami*	2440 Research Blvd, Rockville MD 20850	720-479-6400	S	3*	<.1
53	Biotronic—*Gene Balzer*	812 Avis Dr, Ann Arbor MI 48108	734-213-3920	R	2*	<.1
54	Laborde Diagnostics Inc—*Jeffrey LaBorde MD*	309 St Julien Ave Ste, Lafayette LA 70506	337-237-3424	R	2*	<.1
55	Cranford Diagnostic Imaging	25 S Union Ave, Cranford NJ 07016	908-709-1323	S	2*	<.1
56	Gilpin Testing Service—*Richard Gilpin*	P O Box 7555, Gaithersburg MD 20898	301-948-4121	D	2*	<.1
57	Thora-Test Laboratories Inc—*Marius Teodorescu*	1111 N Main St, Lombard IL 60148	630-627-6069	R	1*	<.1
58	Physicians Reference Laboratory—*Spencer K Kerly*	7800 W 110th St, Overland Park KS 66210	913-338-4070	R	1*	.4
59	BG Medicine Inc—*Pieter Muntendam*	610 Lincoln St N, Waltham MA 02451	781-890-1199	P	I	<.1

Note: An asterisk (*) indicates an estimated financial figure. The company type code used is as follows: R = Private, P = Public, S = Private Subsidiary, B = Public Subsidiary, D = Division, J = Joint Venture, I = Investment Fund.

COMPANY RANKINGS BY SALES WITHIN 4-DIGIT SIC

Rank	Company Name—*Executive Officer*	Address, City, State, Zip	Phone	Type	Fin	Empls
60	Walnut Creek Heartscan LLC—*Kate Kim*	2161 Ygnacio Valley Rd, Walnut Creek CA 94598	925-939-3003	R	N/A	<.1

TOTALS: SIC 8071 Medical Laboratories
Companies: 60 — — — — 18,499 — 74.5

8072 Dental Laboratories

Rank	Company Name—*Executive Officer*	Address, City, State, Zip	Phone	Type	Fin	Empls
1	InterDent Inc—*Ivar Chinna*	9800 S La Cienega Blvd, Inglewood CA 90301	310-765-2400	R	212*	1.8
2	James R Glidewell Dental Ceramics Inc—*James Glidewell*	4141 Macarthur Blvd, Newport Beach CA 92660	949-440-2600	R	120*	1.9
3	Bright Now! Dental—*Steven C Bilt*	201 E Sandpointe Ste 8, Santa Ana CA 92707	714-668-1300	R	35*	.3
4	Dental Arts Laboratory Inc—*Terry Knueppel*	216 Ne Perry Ave, Peoria IL 61603	309-674-8191	R	19*	.3
5	BSML Inc—*Jeffery Nourse*	7777 Glades Rd Ste 100, Boca Raton FL 33434		P	18	.1
6	Oral Arts Laboratory Inc—*Thomas Winstead*	PO Box 413, Huntsville AL 35804	256-533-6670	R	10*	.2
7	Ottawa Dental Labs Inc—*Lucian Caruso*	1304 Starfire Dr, Ottawa IL 61350	815-434-0655	R	8*	.1
8	Edmonds Dental Prosthetics Inc—*Bob Edmonds*	PO Box 10387, Springfield MO 65808	417-881-8572	R	6*	.1
9	United Dental Laboratories Inc—*Richard Delapa*	187 W Exchange St, Akron OH 44302	330-253-1810	R	6*	.1
10	Harold A Burdette Dental Laboratories Inc—*Chris Waldrop*	PO Box 364, Birmingham AL 35201	205-916-0887	R	6*	.1
11	Mason Dental Midwest Inc—*Gary Lockwood*	12752 Stark Rd Ste 1, Livonia MI 48150	734-525-1070	R	5*	.1
12	Associated Dental Laboratories Of America Inc—*Chris Morris*	PO Box 34188, Louisville KY 40232	502-451-2200	R	5*	<.1
13	Andrea's Prosthesis Inc—*Andrea Bonafiglia*	PO Box 121209, Melbourne FL 32912	321-724-6722	R	4*	.1
14	Perry and Young Inc—*Mac Perry*	14100 E Evans Ave, Aurora CO 80014	303-671-0903	R	4*	<.1
15	Myron's Dental Laboratories Inc—*Timothy Sigler*	PO Box 171458, Kansas City KS 66117	913-281-5552	R	4*	.1
16	Artistic Dental Studio Inc—*Jerry Ulaszek*	470 Woodcreek Dr, Bolingbrook IL 60440	630-679-8686	R	3*	<.1
17	Roe Dental Laboratory Inc—*Bruce Kowalski*	9565 Midwest Ave, Cleveland OH 44125	216-663-2233	R	3*	.1
18	Dental Prosthetic Services Inc—*Christine Cleve*	PO Box 2939, Cedar Rapids IA 52406	319-393-1990	R	3*	<.1
19	Bay View Dental Laboratory Inc—*Vernon Shafer*	1207 Volvo Pkwy, Chesapeake VA 23320	757-583-1787	R	3*	<.1
20	Albensi Dental Laboratory Inc—*Donald Albensi*	1061 Main St Ste 21, Irwin PA 15642	724-864-8880	R	3*	<.1
21	Hootman Dental Laboratories Inc—*Robert Farrar*	PO Box 708, Rockford IL 61105	815-964-8932	R	3*	<.1
22	Jackson Spah Dental Studio Inc—*Gerald Jackson*	PO Box 9659, Minneapolis MN 55440	763-785-2435	R	3*	<.1
23	Bertram Dental Laboratory—*William Bertram*	PO Box 1853, Appleton WI 54912	920-731-1483	R	2*	.1
24	Tincher Dental Laboratory—*George Obst*	PO Box 18057, Charleston WV 25303	304-744-4671	R	2*	<.1
25	Saylors Dental Laboratory Inc—*Robert Sayors*	PO Box 410, Manassas VA 20108	703-631-1875	R	2*	<.1
26	Williams Dental Laboratory Inc—*Randy Tuggle*	5001 World Dairy Dr, Madison WI 53718	608-256-5477	R	2*	<.1
27	Encore Crown and Bridge Inc—*Steven Schilling*	PO Box 1699, Plymouth MA 02362	508-746-6025	R	2*	<.1
28	Thompson Suburban Dental Laboratories Inc—*William Grill*	PO Box 4115, Lutherville Timonium MD 21094	410-453-9600	R	2*	<.1
29	Dental Arts Laboratories and Supply Company Inc—*Jackie Fischer*	8415 Us 42, Florence KY 41042	859-647-6100	R	2*	<.1
30	Dental Services Group—*Bob Ditta*	5775 Wayzata Blvd Ste, Minneapolis MN 55416	952-345-6314	R	2*	<.1
31	Somer Inc—*Larry Sowinski*	11707 N Michigan Rd, Zionsville IN 46077	317-873-1111	R	2*	<.1
32	Oratech Inc—*Norman Ross*	PO Box 13486, Springfield IL 62791	217-793-2735	R	2*	<.1
33	Allen Dental Laboratory Inc—*Stanley Ferguson*	1405 E Berry St, Fort Wayne IN 46803	260-424-4846	R	2*	<.1
34	Dental Professional Laboratories Inc—*Michael Suris*	8040 Cleveland Pl, Merrillville IN 46410	219-769-6225	R	2*	<.1
35	Saunders Dental Laboratory LLC—*Marie Muncy*	PO Box 13866, Roanoke VA 24037	540-345-7319	R	2*	<.1
36	Jochim Chrome Laboratory Inc—*Ron Dixon*	PO Box 4058, Concord CA 94524	925-676-9200	R	2*	<.1
37	Littman Dental Laboratory Inc—*Ronald Gill*	1209 Greenwood Rd, Baltimore MD 21208	410-486-0666	R	1*	<.1
38	O'Guinn Corp—*Howard O'Guinn*	10609 N Park Ave, Indianapolis IN 46280	317-848-1414	R	1*	<.1

TOTALS: SIC 8072 Dental Laboratories
Companies: 38 — — — — 510 — 5.9

8082 Home Health Care Services

Rank	Company Name—*Executive Officer*	Address, City, State, Zip	Phone	Type	Fin	Empls
1	Parkview Home Health and Hospice—*Kristine Hepler*	1900 Carew St Ste 5, Fort Wayne IN 46805	260-373-9800	S	4,237*	7.0
2	Chartwell Community Services Inc—*Roy Serpa* Chartwell Diversified Services Inc	PO Box 1387, Mount Vernon TX 75457		S	2,174*	13.0
3	Chartwell Home Therapies LP—*Roy Serpa* Chartwell Diversified Services Inc	PO Box 1387, Mount Vernon TX 75457		S	2,174*	13.0
4	Chartwell Care Givers Inc—*Roy Serpa* Chartwell Diversified Services Inc	PO Box 1387, Mount Vernon TX 75457	972-735-8606	S	1,698*	13.0
5	Amedisys Inc—*William F Borne*	5959 S Sherwood Forest, Baton Rouge LA 70816	225-292-2031	P	1,470	16.5
6	Gentiva Health Services Inc—*Tony Strange*	3350 Riverwood Pky Ste, Atlanta GA 30339	770-951-6450	P	1,447	15.4
7	Chemed Corp—*Kevin J McNamara*	255 E 5th St, Cincinnati OH 45202	513-762-6900	P	1,356	13.8
8	Chartwell Diversified Services Inc—*Judith Rooney*	14295 Midway Rd Ste 40, Addison TX 75001	972-713-3400	R	1,326*	8.1
9	LHC Group Inc—*Keith G Meyers*	420 W Pinhook Rd Ste A, Lafayette LA 70503	337-233-1307	P	635	8.0
10	American Nursing Service Inc—*Mary Lee Kammer*	1 Galleria Blvd Ste 22, Metairie LA 70001	504-833-3100	R	395*	2.5
11	Pediatric Home Nursing Services Inc—*Jim McCurry* Pediatric Services of America Inc	310 Technology Pkwy, Norcross GA 30092	770-441-1580	S	300*	3.5
12	VITAS Healthcare Corp—*David Wester* Chemed Corp	100 S Biscayne Blvd St, Miami FL 33131	305-374-4143	S	272*	8.0
13	Addus HomeCare Corp—*Mark S Heany*	2401 S Plum Grove Rd, Palatine IL 60067	847-303-5300	P	272	13.3
14	Allied Healthcare International Inc—*Sandy Young*	245 Park Ave, New York NY 10167	212-750-0064	S	271	1.2
15	American HomePatient Inc (Brentwood Tennessee)—*Joseph F Furlong III*	5200 Maryland Way Ste, Brentwood TN 37027	615-221-8884	S	236	2.3
16	Willcare Inc—*Todd Brason*	344 Delaware Ave, Buffalo NY 14202	716-856-7500	R	188*	1.5
17	Centura Health at Home—*Erin Denholm*	1391 Speer Blvd Ste 60, Denver CO 80204	303-561-5000	R	181*	1.4
18	Bon Secours - St Francis Medical Center Inc—*Peter Gallagher*	13700 St Francis Blvd, Midlothian VA 23114	804-594-7780	R	178*	N/A
19	1199seiu Nbf For Home Care Employees	PO Box 842, New York NY 10108	646-473-6020	R	171*	N/A
20	Hospice Of The Valley—*Susan Levine*	1510 E Flower St Bldg, Phoenix AZ 85014	602-530-6900	R	170*	1.6
21	Walgreens Infusion Services Inc—*Rajat Rai*	485 E Half Day Rd Ste, Buffalo Grove IL 60089	847-465-2100	R	163*	4.2
22	Bayada Nurses Inc—*J Baiada*	290 Chester Ave, Moorestown NJ 08057	856-231-1000	R	162*	6.0
23	Ephraim Mcdowell Health Inc—*Vicki Darnell*	217 S 3rd St, Danville KY 40422	859-239-1000	R	161*	1.7
24	Pediatric Services Holding Corp	310 Technology Pkwy, Norcross GA 30092	770-441-1580	R	156*	3.9
25	New Partners Inc—*Richard Flender*	1250 Broadway Fl 10, New York NY 10001	212-609-7700	S	151*	4.4
26	Loving Care Agency Inc—*Robert Creamer*	611 Rte 46 W Ste 200, Hasbrouck Heights NJ 07604	201-403-9300	R	150*	3.5
27	Advanced Home Care Inc—*Joel Mills*	PO Box 18049, Greensboro NC 27419	336-878-8950	R	143*	1.5
28	Pediatric Services of America Inc—*Daniel Kohl*	310 Technology Pky, Norcross GA 30092	770-441-1580	R	119*	1.3
29	National Home Health Care Corp—*Steven Fialkow*	700 White Plains Rd St, Scarsdale NY 10583	914-722-9000	R	111	3.7
30	BrightStar Care—*Shelly Sun*	1790 Nations Dr Ste 10, Gurnee IL 60031	847-693-2026	R	99	.1
31	SpectraCare Inc—*Richard Hogan*	9000 Wessex Pl Ste 100, Louisville KY 40222	502-429-4550	S	95*	.8
32	HomeCall Incorporated McCulloh Home Health Agency—*Gretchen Murzda*	1080 W Patrick St Ste, Frederick MD 21703		R	92*	1.0
33	ATC Healthcare Inc—*David Savitsky*	1983 Marcus Ave Ste E1, Lake Success NY 11042	516-750-1600	P	89	7.1
34	Medical Resources Home Health Corp National Home Health Care Corp	433 Watertown St, Newton MA 02458	617-969-7517	S	62*	.1

Rank	Company Name—*Executive Officer*	Address, City, State, Zip	Phone	Type	Fin	Empls
35	American Caresource Holdings Inc—*Kenneth S George*	5429 Lyndon B Johnson, Dallas TX 75240	972-308-6830	P	61	.1
36	Cooperative Home Care Associates Inc—*Carlos Rivera*	349 E 149th St 5th Fl, Bronx NY 10451	718-993-7104	R	60	.8
37	PHC Inc—*Bruce A Shear*	200 Lake St Ste 102, Peabody MA 01960	978-536-2777	P	53*	.7
38	Home Health Corporation of America Inc—*David S Gellar*	620 Freedom Business C, King of Prussia PA 19406	610-205-2740	R	50	1.0
39	Sunalliance Healthcare Services Inc—*Richard K Matros*	101 Sun Ave NE, Albuquerque NM 87109	505-821-3355	S	50*	.4
40	Allied Home Health—*Helen Dichoso*	2403 Dunstan, Houston TX 77005	713-522-5773	R	46*	.4
41	Lincare Inc—*John P Byrnes*	1490 N Belcher Rd Ste, Clearwater FL 33765	727-733-2927	S	46*	.4
42	New York Health Care Inc—*Murry England*	20 E Sunrise Hwy Ste 2, Valley Stream NY 11581	718-375-6700	P	44	1.5
43	Binson's Home Health Care Centers—*James Binson*	26834 Lawrence, Center Line MI 48015	586-755-2300	R	44*	.4
44	Evergreen Homes Inc—*Denise Brougham*	101 Ross Ave, Ford City PA 16226	724-763-3125	R	38*	.2
45	Ambulatory Infusion Therapy Specialist Inc	10304 I 10 E Ste 369, Houston TX 77029		S	37*	.3
46	Baptist Trinity Health Care Services—*Stephen C Reynolds*	350 N Humphreys Blvd, Memphis TN 38120	901-767-6767	S	33*	.3
47	Fornance Physician Services Inc—*Steve Kirkpatrick*	15 W Wood St Ste 300, Norristown PA 19401	610-270-2344	R	30*	<.1
48	Tender Loving Care Health Care Services Inc—*Wes Perry* ATC Healthcare Inc	1983 Marcus Ave, Lake Success NY 11042	516-750-1600	S	29*	.8
49	Preferred Homecare—*Kevin Gardner RPh*	13621 Inwood Rd Ste 42, Dallas TX 75244	214-866-2700	S	27*	.2
50	Medical Systems Inc	133 Mayfair Rd, Hattiesburg MS 39402	601-544-2903	R	26*	.3
51	HomeCall Inc LHC Group Inc	1446 W Patrick St Ste, Frederick MD 21702	240-215-4668	S	25	.8
52	Remedi Senior Care—*Michael Bronfein*	9006 Yellow Brick Rd S, Baltimore MD 21237	443-927-8400	R	20*	.2
53	Critical Homecare Solutions Holdings Inc—*Robert A Cucuel*	One Fayette St Ste 150, Conshohocken PA 19428	610-825-2061	S	18*	2.0
54	Caremark Therapeutic Services—*John Henry*	1127 Bryn Mawr Ave Ste, Redlands CA 92374	909-796-7171	S	16*	.2
55	Egan Healthcare Services Inc—*Peter Egan*	3121 21st St, Metairie LA 70002	504-835-4474	R	16*	.1
56	Correctional Healthcare Solutions Inc—*Michael Traina*	200 Highpoint Dr, Chalfont PA 18914	215-822-1050	R	15	.3
57	American Nursing Care Inc—*Daniel Dietz*	1000 Summit Dr Ste 300, Milford OH 45150	513-576-0262	S	15*	.1
58	Accent on Independence—*Carol Bouchard*	11949 W Colfax Ave, Lakewood CO 80215	303-331-0818	R	13*	.1
59	Trinity Homecare LLC—*William McMichael*	11402 15th Ave, College Point NY 11356		S	12*	.1
60	ATS Health Services of Jacksonville—*C Fred Toney*	6820 Southpoint Pkwy, Jacksonville FL 32216	904-398-9098	R	12*	<.1
61	Visiting Nurse and Hospice Care Of South West CT—*Anne Rich*	1266 E Main St, Stamford CT 06902	203-276-3000	R	10*	.1
62	Sleepcare Diagnostics Inc—*Jim Snider*	4780 Socialville-Foste, Mason OH 45040	513-459-7750	R	10*	.1
63	Star Multi Care Services Inc—*Stephen Sternbach*	115 Broad Hollow RD ST, Melville NY 11747	631-423-6689	R	9*	.1
64	Visiting Nurse Service Inc—*John L Pipas*	4701 N Keystone Ave, Indianapolis IN 46205	317-722-8200	R	7*	.2
65	Medical Team Inc—*Leslie Pembrook*	1850 Centennial Pk Dr, Reston VA 20191	703-390-2300	R	7*	.1
66	Supplemental Health Care Services Ltd—*Janet Elkin*	1640 Redstone Center D, Park City UT 84098	435-645-0788	H	6*	.6
67	Home Health Outreach	1460 Walton Blvd, Rochester Hills MI 48309	248-656-6757	R	6*	.2
68	Camelot Lake Inc—*Melissa Moore*	5099 Camelot Dr, Fairfield OH 45014	513-829-8992	R	6*	.1
69	Family HomeCare Inc—*Gina Ragland*	3636 S I-10 Service Rd, Metairie LA 70001	504-835-0934	R	6*	.1
70	MGR HOMECARE Inc—*L Jack Clark*	PO Box 630, Griffin GA 30224	770-228-6371	R	6*	<.1
71	Drew County Developmental Disability Council Inc—*Sandra Patrick*	PO Box 359, Monticello AR 71657	870-367-6825	R	5*	.3
72	LifeMatters USA—*Scott Thompson*	7768 Woodmont Ave, Bethesda MD 20814	301-652-7212	R	5*	.3
73	Camellia Home Health and Hospice—*WA Payne* Medical Systems Inc	133 Mayfair Rd, Hattiesburg MS 39402	601-268-0408	S	5*	.1
74	Entrum Care Inc	PO Box 1265, Haughton LA 71037	318-949-1828	R	5*	<.1
75	Coram Inc—*Dan Greenleaf*	1675 Broadway Ste 900, Denver CO 80202	303-292-4973	S	4*	2.1
76	Older Adults Care Management—*Cheri Jackson*	3335 Birch St, Palo Alto CA 94306	650-329-1411	R	4*	.2
77	Medical Services Of Northwest Florida Inc—*Eva White*	8074 Navarro Pkwy, Navarre FL 32566	850-936-0400	R	4*	.1
78	Amedisys Home Health Incorporated of Florida—*William F Borne* Amedisys Inc	101 W Main St Ste140, Lakeland FL 33815	863-682-2293	S	4*	<.1
79	Brookside Home Health Care—*Kim Wilson*	460 McLaws Cir, Williamsburg VA 23185	757-253-2536	R	4*	<.1
80	Experts In Home Health Management Inc—*Rohit Gandhi*	19148 E 10 Mile Rd, Eastpointe MI 48021	586-585-0201	R	4*	.1
81	Family Service Organization of Worcester Inc—*Chris Macwade*	31 Harvard St, Worcester MA 01609	508-756-4646	R	4*	.1
82	Health Services District Of Northern Larimer County—*Joe Hendrickson*	120 Bristlecone Dr, Fort Collins CO 80524	970-224-5209	R	3*	.1
83	South Mississippi Home Health Inc—*Sorten Berry*	PO Box 16929, Hattiesburg MS 39404	601-268-1842	R	3*	.1
84	Patient Care Inc—*Bob Nixon*	100 Executive Dr Ste 1, West Orange NJ 07052	973-243-5900	R	3*	<.1
85	Lincare New York Inc—*John P Byrnes*	4 Main St, Ballston Lake NY 12019	518-384-0202	S	3*	<.1
86	America's Nursing Inc—*Maria Crespo*	4216 Evergreen Ln Ste, Annandale VA 22003	703-998-8900	R	3*	<.1
87	Miss Daisy's Home Care LLC	1 Ravenwood Dr, Weston CT 06883	203-454-1812	R	3*	<.1
88	Lighthouse Medical Staffing Inc—*James Burk*	3970 Brown Park Dr Ste, Hilliard OH 43026	614-777-5950	R	3*	.1
89	Area Homecare Family Services Inc—*Gordon Mccollester*	1320 Woodbury Ave, Portsmouth NH 03801	603-436-9059	R	2*	.1
90	A and D Home Health Solutions—*Dan Fisher*	85 Market Sq, Newington CT 06111	860-667-2275	R	2*	.1
91	Angel's Touch Nursing Care Inc—*Bonnie Perrino*	3619 Harrison, Cincinnati OH 45211		R	1*	<.1
92	UltraStaff—*Jolyn Scheirman*	1818 Memorial Dr Ste 2, Houston TX 77007	713-522-7100	R	1*	<.1
93	Senior Solutions for South Florida Inc—*Ronnee Rosen*	1117 E Hallandale Beac, Hallandale Beach FL 33009	954-456-8984	R	1*	<.1
94	Elderly Home Health Care Inc—*C Ray*	FM 1960 West, Houston TX 77068	713-956-8183	R	1*	<.1
95	Health Design Plus—*Ruth Coleman*	1755 Georgetown Rd, Hudson OH 44236	330-656-1072	D	1*	<.1
96	Instructive Visiting Nurse Association—*Jim Beckner*	5008 Monument Ave Fl 2, Richmond VA 23230	804-355-7100	R	1*	.2

TOTALS: SIC 8082 Home Health Care Services
Companies: 96

					21,893	199.2

8092 Kidney Dialysis Centers

Rank	Company Name—*Executive Officer*	Address, City, State, Zip	Phone	Type	Fin	Empls
1	DaVita Inc—*Kent J Thiry*	1551 Wewatta St, Denver CO 80202	303-405-2100	P	6,447	36.5
2	American Renal Associates Inc—*Joseph Carlucci*	66 Cherry Hill Dr, Beverly MA 01915	978-922-3080	R	583*	.2
3	National Renal Alliance—*Mike Klein*	730 Cool Springs Blvd, Franklin TN 37067	615-771-4400	R	75*	.5
4	Caridianbct Inc—*Kevin Smith*	14143 Denver W Pkwy, Lakewood CO 80401	303-232-6800	R	24*	.4
5	DCA of Carlisle Inc	101 Noble Blvd Ste 103, Carlisle PA 17013	717-258-3099	S	11*	<.1
6	DCA of Wellsboro Inc	223 Tioga St, Wellsboro PA 16901	570-724-3188	S	9*	<.1
7	DCA of Mechanicsburg LLC	120 S Filbert St, Mechanicsburg PA 17055	717-790-6080	S	8*	<.1
8	DCA of Chambersburg Inc	765 Fifth Ave Ste A, Chambersburg PA 17201	717-263-9300	S	7*	<.1
9	DCA of Cincinnati LLC	7600 Affinity Dr, Mount Healthy OH 45231	513-931-7900	S	7*	<.1
10	DCA Medical Services Inc	1302 Concourse Dr Ste, Linthicum MD 21090	410-694-0500	S	4*	<.1

TOTALS: SIC 8092 Kidney Dialysis Centers
Companies: 10

					7,176	37.6

8093 Specialty Outpatient Facilities Nec

Rank	Company Name—*Executive Officer*	Address, City, State, Zip	Phone	Type	Fin	Empls
1	US Oncology Inc—*Bruce Broussard*	10101 Woodloch Forest, The Woodlands TX 77380	281-863-1000	S	3,512	9.7

Note: An asterisk (*) indicates an estimated financial figure. The company type code used is as follows: R = Private, P = Public, S = Private Subsidiary, B = Public Subsidiary, D = Division, J = Joint Venture, I = Investment Fund.

COMPANY RANKINGS BY SALES WITHIN 4-DIGIT SIC

Rank	Company Name—Executive Officer	Address, City, State, Zip	Phone	Type	Fin	Empls
2	Select Medical Holdings Corp—Robert A Ortenzio	4714 Gettysburg Rd, Mechanicsburg PA 17055	717-972-1100	P	2,805	28.8
3	HEALTHSOUTH Corp—Jay Grinney	3660 Grandview Pkwy St, Birmingham AL 35243	205-967-7116	P	1,999	23.0
4	Psychiatric Solutions Inc—Joey A Jacobs	6640 Carothers Pkwy St, Franklin TN 37067	615-312-5700	S	1,334*	17.0
5	Concentra Operating Corp—James M Greenwood	5080 Spectrum Dr Ste 1, Addison TX 75001	972-364-8000	S	1,299	11.6
6	Correctional Health Services Inc—Richard Hallworth	105 Westpark Dr Ste 20, Brentwood TN 37027	615-373-3100	S	1,119*	3.8
7	Hanger Orthopedic Group Inc—Thomas F Kirk	10910 Domain Dr Ste 30, Austin TX 78758	512-777-3800	P	919	4.4
8	Prison Health Services Inc—Richard Hallworth	105 Westpark Dr Ste 20, Brentwood TN 37027	615-373-3100	S	833*	3.8
9	Continucare Corp—Richard C Pfenniger	7200 Corporate Center, Miami FL 33126	305-500-2000	P	334	.9
10	Critical Care Systems Inc—Tom Martin	61 Spit Brook Rd Execu, Nashua NH 03060	603-888-1500	S	282	.7
11	Aptiem Oncology—Peter H Jessup	8201 Beverly Blvd, Los Angeles CA 90048	323-966-3400	S	209*	1.4
12	HealthTronics Inc—James SB Whittenburg	9825 Spectrum Dr Bldg, Austin TX 78717	512-328-2892	S	185	.6
13	Watson Clinic LLP—Louis C Saco	PO Box 95000, Lakeland FL 33804	863-680-7000	R	153*	1.5
14	Northern Arizona Regional Behavioral Health Authority Inc—Michael Pattinson	1300 S Yale St, Flagstaff AZ 86001	928-774-7128	R	147*	.1
15	Theracare Of New York Inc—John Calderon	116 W 32nd St Fl 8, New York NY 10001	212-564-2350	R	143*	2.3
16	LCA-Vision Inc—David Thomas	7840 Montgomery Rd, Cincinnati OH 45236	513-792-9292	P	100	.4
17	UCI Medical Affiliates Inc—D Michael Stout MD	1818 Henderson St, Columbia SC 29201	803-782-4278	R	87	1.1
18	United Behavioral Health—Jim Hudak	425 Market St Fl 27, San Francisco CA 94105		S	72*	2.3
19	Fedcap Rehabilitation Services Inc—Mike Brenne	211 W 14th St, New York NY 10011	212-727-4200	R	70*	1.5
20	Mid Rockland Imaging Partners Inc	18 Squadron Blvd, New City NY 10956	845-634-9729	S	68*	.4
21	Community Imaging Partners Inc—Mark Casner	4110 Aspen Hill Rd Ste, Rockville MD 20853	301-438-5011	R	62*	.4
22	Spectrum Diagnostics Imaging—Richard Kampa	4400 Rockside Rd Ste 1, Independence OH 44131	216-584-2900	R	56*	.3
23	IDE Imaging Partners Inc	2263 S Clinton Ave, Rochester NY 14618	585-241-6400	S	53*	.3
24	Mental Health Network Inc—Kevin Middleton	PO Box 209010, Austin TX 78720	512-347-7900	R	39*	.1
25	Sma Behavioral Health Services Inc—W Bell	1220 Willis Ave, Daytona Beach FL 32114	386-236-3200	R	38*	.3
26	FONAR Corp—Raymond V Damadian	110 Marcus Dr, Melville NY 11747	631-694-2929	P	33	.2
27	California Pharmaceutical Services Inc	16825 Northchase Dr St, Houston TX 77060	832-601-8766	R	17*	.1
28	Starkey Inc—Carolyn Hill	4500 W Maple St, Wichita KS 67209	316-942-4221	R	13*	.3
29	Macon Resources Inc—Dreux Lewandoski	PO Box 2760, Decatur IL 62524	217-875-1910	R	13*	.2
30	Chaddock—Gene Simon	205 S 24th St, Quincy IL 62301	217-222-0034	R	13*	.2
31	Contact Behavioral Health Services—Jay T Roundy	1400 E Southern Ste 80, Tempe AZ 85282		S	12*	.1
32	Transylvania Vocational Services Inc—Nancy Stricker	11 Mountain Industrial, Brevard NC 28712	828-884-3195	R	11*	.1
33	Pacific Sports Medicine—Diane Cecchettini	3124 S 19th St Ste 340, Tacoma WA 98405	253-459-7000	R	11*	.1
34	Alcohol And Drug Recovery Centers Inc—Ronald Fleming	500 Blue Hills Ave Fl, Hartford CT 06112	860-714-3701	R	10*	.2
35	Metro Therapy Inc—Barbara Kupferman Select Medical Holdings Corp	PO Box 6005, Hauppauge NY 11788		S	10*	<.1
36	Northpoint-Pioneer Inc—Beth Combs	6024 W Maple Rd Ste 10, West Bloomfield MI 48322	248-539-0899	S	9*	.1
37	PHC of Michigan Inc—Sari Abromovich	35031 23 Mile Rd, New Baltimore MI 48047	586-725-5777	S	9*	.1
38	PHC of Utah Inc—Robert Beatty	7309 S 180 W, Midvale UT 84047	801-569-2153	S	9*	.1
39	PHC of Virginia Inc—Gail Basham	405 Kimball Ave, Salem VA 24153	540-389-4761	S	9*	.1
40	Change Point Inc—Richard Drandoff	PO Box 92067, Portland OR 97292	503-253-5954	R	9*	<.1
41	Sunrise House Foundation Inc—Phillip Horowitz	PO Box 600, Lafayette NJ 07848	973-383-6300	R	9*	.1
42	Harmony Healthcare—Margie Koch	1701 W Charleston Blvd, Las Vegas NV 89102	702-251-8000	R	8*	.1
43	Valley Imaging Partners Inc—Howard G Berger	3031 Tisch Way Ste 400, San Jose CA 95128	408-244-2100	S	8*	<.1
44	Supervised Lifestyles Inc—Alfred Bergman	2505 Carmel Ave Ste 21, Brewster NY 10509	845-279-5994	R	6*	.1
45	Alamo Group Inc (San Antonio Texas)—Ronald A Robinson	1627 East Walnut, Seguin TX 78155	830-379-1480	R	5*	<.1
46	Tradewinds Services Inc—Jon Gold	5901 W 7th Ave, Gary IN 46406	219-949-4000	R	4*	.2
47	Hudson Physical Therapy Services Inc—Ed Miersch Select Medical Holdings Corp	65 Sip Ave, Jersey City NJ 07306	201-792-2582	S	4*	<.1
48	Coreance Inc—Chris West	2935 Baseline Rd Ste 3, Boulder CO 80303	303-444-2951	R	4*	<.1
49	Lynchburg Sheltered Industries Inc—Cecil Kendrick	PO Box 10905, Lynchburg VA 24506	434-847-4488	R	4*	.2
50	Pro Active Therapy of Ahoskie Inc—Susan Vick Select Medical Holdings Corp	2413 Professional Dr, Rocky Mount NC 27804	252-443-6627	S	3*	<.1
51	US Neurosurgical Inc—Alan Gold	1899 Sawyer Ln, Alva FL 33920	239-872-1272	P	3	<.1
52	Women's Center—Vicki Kirkbride	133 Park St Ne Fl 2, Vienna VA 22180	703-281-2657	R	2*	.1
53	Unipsych Corp—Dov Charney	9606 N Mopac Expy Ste, Austin TX 78759	954-704-8686	R	2*	<.1
54	Northside Physical Therapy Inc—Debbie Peterson Select Medical Holdings Corp	6821 N Country Homes B, Spokane WA 99208	509-325-6776	S	2*	<.1
55	Med-Staff Inc—Elizabeth Halsey	PO Box 2454, Davenport IA 52809	563-359-1933	R	1*	<.1
56	Center for Applied Sciences—Terence T Gorski	6147 Deltona Blvd, Spring Hill FL 34606	352-596-8000	R	1*	<.1
57	Questar Duluth Inc	1527 London Rd, Duluth MN 55812	218-724-5040	S	1*	<.1
58	Questar Los Alamitos Inc—Howard G Berger	4281 Katella Ave Ste 1, Los Alamitos CA 90720	714-816-0134	S	1*	<.1
59	Questar Victorville Inc—Howard G Berger	12276 Hesperia Rd Ste, Victorville CA 92395	760-843-0995	S	1*	<.1
60	Michigan Hand Rehabilitation Center Inc—Edward Burke	22731 Newman St Ste 10, Dearborn MI 48124	313-791-0616	R	1*	<.1
61	Sagemark Companies Ltd—Cathy Bergman	1221 Ave of the Americ, New York NY 10020	212-921-5733	P	<1	N/A
62	Meier Clinics—Nancy Meier Brown	2099 N Collins Blvd St, Richardson TX 75080	972-437-4698	R	N/A	.8

TOTALS: SIC 8093 Specialty Outpatient Facilities Nec
Companies: 62   16,174   120.0

8099 Health & Allied Services Nec

Rank	Company Name—Executive Officer	Address, City, State, Zip	Phone	Type	Fin	Empls
1	Lincare Holdings Inc—John Byrnes	19387 US 19 N, Clearwater FL 33764	727-530-7700	P	1,848	10.8
2	Triple-S Management Corp—Ramon M Ruiz-Comas	PO Box 363628, San Juan PR 00936	787-749-4949	P	1,759	2.3
3	Team Health Holdings Inc—Greg Roth	265 Brookview Centre W, Knoxville TN 37919	865-693-1000	P	1,745	6.8
4	Accredo Health Inc—Steven R Fitzpatrick	1640 Century Ctr Pky, Memphis TN 38134	901-385-3600	S	1,517	2.5
5	Duffy and Associates Physical Therapy Corp—Gregg Lehman Health Fitness Corp	1650 W 82nd St Ste 110, Minneapolis MN 55431	952-831-6830	S	1,253*	3.0
6	Medlink Management Services Inc—Jerry Noyce Health Fitness Corp	3600 American Blvd W S, Bloomington MN 55431	952-831-6830	S	1,253*	3.0
7	Horizon Behavioral Services Inc—Matthew Rosenberg Horizon Health Corp	113 Lakeside Park, Southampton PA 18966	215-355-9707	S	752*	1.8
8	Specialty Rehab Management Inc—Frank Bowman Horizon Health Corp	2941 S Lake Vista Dr, Lewisville TX 75067		S	752*	1.8
9	Health First Inc—Michael D Means	6450 US Hwy 1, Rockledge FL 32955	321-434-4300	R	732*	6.0
10	Healthways Inc—Ben R Leedle Jr	701 Cool Springs Blvd, Franklin TN 37067	615-614-4929	P	720	2.8
11	Monarch Dental Corp Smile Brands Group Inc	201 E Sandpointe Ste 8, Santa Ana CA 92707	714-668-1300	S	690*	1.5
12	AMN Healthcare Services Inc—Susan Salka	12400 High Bluff Dr, San Diego CA 92130		P	689	1.8
13	Corizon Inc—Richard Hallworth	105 Westpark Dr Ste 20, Brentwood TN 37027	615-373-3100	B	630	3.3
14	Accretive Health Inc—Mary A Tolan	401 N Michigan Ave Ste, Chicago IL 60611	312-324-7820	P	606*	2.0
15	IPC the Hospitalist Company Inc—Adam D Singer MD	4605 Lankershim Blvd S, North Hollywood CA 91602	818-766-3502	P	458	2.0

Rank	Company Name—*Executive Officer*	Address, City, State, Zip	Phone	Type	Fin	Empls
16	Smile Brands Group Inc—*Steven C Bilt*	8105 Irvine Center Dr, Irvine CA 92618	714-668-1300	S	445	1.8
17	StayWell Health Management Systems Inc—*Paul Terry*	3000 Ames Crossing Rd, Saint Paul MN 55121	651-454-3577	S	329*	.4
18	American Dental Partners Inc—*Gregory A Serrao*	401 Edgewater Pl Ste 4, Wakefield MA 01880	781-224-0880	P	286	2.7
19	National Government Services Inc—*Sandy Miller*	8115 Knue Rd, Indianapolis IN 46250	317-841-4400	S	260*	2.0
20	One Call Medical Inc—*Don Duford*	PO Box 614, Parsippany NJ 07054		S	234*	.5
21	Horizon Health Corp—*Joey Jacobs*	2941 S Lake Vista Dr, Lewisville TX 75067	972-420-8200	R	198*	2.1
22	Sterigenics International Inc—*David E Meyer*	2015 Spring Rd Ste 650, Oak Brook IL 60523	630-928-1700	S	198*	1.1
23	Simplex Healthcare Inc—*Doug Hudson*	6840 Carothers Pky Ste, Franklin TN 37067		R	193*	.3
24	Schaller Anderson Inc—*Thomas L Kelly*	4645 E Cotton Center B, Phoenix AZ 85040	602-659-1100	S	182*	1.6
25	Labor Health and Wel Trust Fndne CA	220 Campus Ln, Fairfield CA 94534	707-864-2800	R	175*	<.1
26	Facey Medical Foundation—*Bill Gil*	15451 San Fernando Mis, Mission Hills CA 91345	818-365-9531	R	173*	1.2
27	Priority Health Government Programs Inc	1231 E Beltline Ave Ne, Grand Rapids MI 49525	616-942-0954	R	173*	<.1
28	Hooper Holmes Inc—*Ransom J Parker*	170 Mt Airy Rd, Basking Ridge NJ 07920	908-766-5000	P	166	1.7
29	NightHawk Radiology Holdings Inc—*David M Engert* Virtual Radiologic Corp	4900 N Scottsdale Rd S, Scottsdale AZ 85251		S	162	.5
30	Ut Medicine San Antonio	PO Box 29810, San Antonio TX 78229	210-257-1512	R	158*	<.1
31	National Cancer Coalition LLC—*Robert Landry*	225 Hillsborough St St, Raleigh NC 27603	919-821-2182	R	152*	<.1
32	Examination Management Services Inc—*Mark Davis*	3050 Regent Blvd Ste 4, Irving TX 75063	214-689-3600	S	152*	2.5
33	Ssm Employee Health Care Fund	477 N Lindbergh Blvd, Saint Louis MO 63141	314-997-7800	R	149*	<.1
34	Broadspire Services Inc—*Kenneth Martino*	PO Box 189089, Fort Lauderdale FL 33318	954-452-4000	R	147*	2.2
35	Baxter County Regional Hospitl	21 Medical Plz, Mountain Home AR 72653	870-424-1940	R	143*	<.1
36	Med3000—*Patrick Hampson*	680 Andersen Dr Foster, Pittsburgh PA 15220	412-937-8887	R	131*	1.7
37	Virtual Radiologic Corp—*Robert Kill*	11995 Singletree Ln St, Eden Prairie MN 55344	952-392-1100	R	121	.2
38	MedWare Inc—*Donald Flannery*	2250 Lucien Way Ste 30, Maitland FL 32751		R	120*	.6
39	Suncare Respiratory Services Inc—*Angel Arciero*	4656 SW 74th Ave, Miami FL 33155	305-663-7389	S	112*	4.5
40	Gulf Coast Regional Blood Center—*Doug Mcclain*	1400 La Concha Ln, Houston TX 77054	713-790-1200	R	109*	.6
41	Coalition America Inc—*Scott Smith*	2 Concourse Pkwy Ste 3, Atlanta GA 30328	404-459-7201	R	107*	.1
42	Amedex USA Medical Services Corp—*David Maltbi*	7001 SW 97th Ave, Miami FL 33173	305-275-1400	S	106*	.3
43	Health Dialog Services Corp—*James Tugendhat*	60 State St Ste 1100, Boston MA 02109	617-406-5200	S	102*	.8
44	Sterling Medical Associates Inc—*Richard Blatt*	411 Oak St, Cincinnati OH 45219	513-984-1800	R	97*	.1
45	Health Resources Inc—*David L Dalton*	10 E Baltimore St Ste, Owings Mills MD 21202	410-347-1541	R	92*	.1
46	Health Fitness Corp—*Paul Lotharius*	1650 W 82nd St Ste 110, Minneapolis MN 55431	952-831-6830	S	89*	4.0
47	Health Diagnostics—*Bradford Peters*	8 Corporate Center Dr, Melville NY 11747	631-396-1050	R	84*	.8
48	Biomedical Systems Corp—*Timothy Barrett*	77 Progress Pkwy, Maryland Heights MO 63043	314-576-6800	R	68*	.1
49	Birner Dental Management Services Inc—*Frederic WJ Birner*	1777 S Harrison St Ste, Denver CO 80210	303-691-0680	P	64	.7
50	beBetter Networks Inc—*Ralph Gaines*	109 Capitol St, Charleston WV 25301	304-345-6800	R	53*	.1
51	Isomedix Inc—*Robert Moss*	9 Apollo Dr, Whippany NJ 07981	973-887-2754	S	46*	.4
52	UM Holdings Inc—*John Aglialoro*	PO Box 200, Haddonfield NJ 08033	856-354-2200	R	46*	.2
53	Medcor Inc—*Philip Seeger*	4805 Prime Pkwy, Mchenry IL 60050	815-363-9500	R	44*	.8
54	BioPartners In Care Inc—*Steven R Fitzpatrick* Accredo Health Inc	201 Great Circle Rd, Nashville TN 37228	615-352-2500	S	42*	.1
55	Healthhelp LLC—*Cherrill Farnsworth*	654 N Sam Houston Pky, Houston TX 77060	281-447-7000	R	32*	.2
56	HealthForce Partners Inc—*Jack L Siemering*	11805 N Creek Pkwy S S, Bothell WA 98011	425-806-5700	R	32*	.1
57	HemaCare Corp—*Pete van der Wal*	15350 Sherman Way Ste, Van Nuys CA 91406	818-226-1968	P	30	.3
58	Reed Group Ltd—*Michael Sayre*	10155 Westmoor Dr Ste, Westminster CO 80021	303-247-1860	R	30*	.1
59	Griffith Micro Science Inc—*Kevin Swan*	8550 Bryn Mawr Ave Ste, Chicago IL 60601	630-571-1280	R	26*	.1
00	DHS Management Services Inc Diagnostic Health Services Inc	5055 Keller Springs Rd, Addison TX 75001	214-242-8500	S	26*	<.1
61	The Henried Center—*John Hernried*	2825 J St Ste 435A, Sacramento CA 95816	916-978-0300	R	25*	<.1
62	Creative Care Corp—*Walter Powers*	4747 S Emporia St Lowr, Wichita KS 67216	316-262-2273	R	23*	.3
63	Health Fitness Rehab Inc—*Gregg Lehman* Health Fitness Corp	1650 W 82nd St Ste 110, Bloomington MN 55431		S	21*	<.1
64	Medical Mutual Group—*Dale Jenkins*	PO Box 98028, Raleigh NC 27624	919-872-7117	R	20*	.1
65	American Correctional Solutions—*Barry Goldstein*	1588 N Batavia St Ste1, Orange CA 92867	714-538-0200	R	16*	.1
66	Sleep Disorders Center of Georgia—*James Wellman*	PO Box 198840, Atlanta GA 30384	404-256-6545	R	15*	<.1
67	Concord Inc (Philadelphia Pennsylvania)—*Stephen Rosenz-weig*	1835 Market St Ste 120, Philadelphia PA 19103		R	14*	<.1
68	Clinical Resource Network LLC—*Nicki Norris*	One Parkway North Blvd, Deerfield IL 60015	847-215-0437	R	14*	<.1
69	Ed Necco and Associates Inc—*Ed Necco*	1130 County Rd 18, South Point OH 45680	740-894-4360	R	12*	.1
70	OPNET Inc—*Rebecca Hast*	1375 Piccard DrSte300, Rockville MD 20850		S	11*	<.1
71	Nanostring Technologies Inc—*H Perry Fell*	530 Fairview Ave N Ste, Seattle WA 98109	206-378-6266	R	11*	<.1
72	Implantable Provider Group Inc—*James J Ethridge Jr*	2520 Northwinds Pkwy B, Alpharetta GA 30009	770-753-0046	R	11	<.1
73	Correctional Medical Associates Inc—*Sandra Baccus*	201 17th St Nw Ste 300, Atlanta GA 30363	404-760-0296	R	11*	.1
74	SpringBoard Inc—*Gavin Hays*	2525 W Carefree Hwy Bl, Phoenix AZ 85085	623-516-8001	R	10*	.2
75	Medex Assistance Corp—*Bruce Kirby*	PO Box 19056, Baltimore MD 21284	410-453-6300	S	10*	.1
76	Lauren Corp—*Thomas H Fortner*	11990 Grant St Ste 310, Northglenn CO 80233	303-813-9585	R	10*	<.1
77	Blood Bank of Delmarva—*Robert L Travis*	100 Hygeia Dr, Newark DE 19713	302-737-8400	R	8*	.2
78	IgG America Inc	514 Progress Dr, Linthicum Heights MD 21090		S	8*	<.1
79	Test Country—*Serhart Pala*	6310 Nancy Ridge Dr St, San Diego CA 92121	858-784-6904	R	8*	<.1
80	Mediscan Diagnostic Services Inc—*Val Serebryany*	21050 Califa St Ste 10, Woodland Hills CA 91367	818-758-4224	R	8*	.1
81	Medical-Dental Bureau Inc—*Robert Johnson*	263 E Market St, York PA 17403	717-843-3861	R	8*	<.1
82	ProCare One Nurses LLC	4041 MacArthur Blvd St, Newport Beach CA 92660	949-251-1950	S	7*	<.1
83	DSP Clinical Research LLC—*Darlene Panzitta*	300 Interpace Pkwy Bld, Parsippany NJ 07054	973-265-1060	R	7*	<.1
84	Remote Medical International—*Andrew Cull*	4259 23rd Ave W Ste 20, Seattle WA 98199	206-686-4878	R	7	.1
85	Atlanta Pediatric Therapy Inc—*George Rosero*	675 Seminole Ave Ste T, Atlanta GA 30307	404-575-4000	R	6*	.1
86	Texas Physical Therapy Specialists—*Andrew Bennett*	3453 N IH 35 Ste 211, San Antonio TX 78219		R	6*	.1
87	Diagnostic Health Services Inc—*Christopher Turner*	5055 Keller Springs Rd, Addison TX 75001	214-242-8500	R	6*	.1
88	Private Secretary Inc—*Earle Truesdell*	1921 S Alma School Rd, Mesa AZ 85210	480-899-4110	R	6*	.1
89	System13—*Robert Reid*	1648 State Farm Blvd, Charlottesville VA 22911	434-977-0000	R	5*	<.1
90	Rocky Mountain Prostate Thermotherapy LLC—*Sam B Humphries*	2319 W 17th St, Greeley CO 80634		S	5*	<.1
91	MEDIVAN Inc—*Christine Geiger*	4953 S Packard Ave, Cudahy WI 53110	414-483-8267	R	5*	<.1
92	Salt Lake Physical Therapy Associates Inc	4888 S Highland Dr, Holladay UT 84117	801-264-9855	S	5	N/A
93	Spine and Sport—*Erick C Bull*	135 Goshen Rd Ext Ste2, Rincon GA 31326	912-826-3797	R	4*	.1
94	Mental Health Outcomes Inc—*David White* Horizon Health Corp	2941 S Lake Vista Dr, Lewisville TX 75067	972-420-8200	R	4*	<.1
95	Thrombovision Inc—*Edward Teitel*	8036 El Rio St, Houston TX 77054	713-491-4449	R	4*	<.1
96	Galen Healthcare Solutions—*Stephen McQueen*	PO Box 36715, Grosse Pointe MI 48236		R	4	<.1
97	DSS Funding Inc	1105 Brookstown Ave, Winston Salem NC 27101	336-724-1000	S	3	.1
98	Advanced Weight Loss Clinics—*Anita Gibson*	3324 Independence Dr S, Birmingham AL 35209	205-670-5355	R	3*	.1

Note: An asterisk (*) indicates an estimated financial figure. The company type code used is as follows: R = Private, P = Public, S = Private Subsidiary, B = Public Subsidiary, D = Division, J = Joint Venture, I = Investment Fund.

COMPANY RANKINGS BY SALES WITHIN 4-DIGIT SIC

Rank	Company Name—*Executive Officer*	Address, City, State, Zip	Phone	Type	Fin	Empls
99	Pharma-Care Inc—*Harlan Martin*	136 Central Ave, Clark NJ 07066	732-574-9015	R	3*	.1
100	Corridor Group Inc—*Katheen J Dodd*	6405 Metcalf Ste 108, Overland Park KS 66202	913-362-0600	R	3*	<.1
101	Sw Florida Regional Mri Inc	329 E Olympia Ave, Punta Gorda FL 33950	941-637-1100	R	3*	.1
102	SironaHealth—*Jeff Forbes*	500 Southborough Dr, South Portland ME 04106	207-775-2600	R	3	.2
103	GenMark Diagnostics Inc—*Hany Massarany*	5964 La Place Ct Ste 1, Carlsbad CA 92008	760-448-4300	P	3	.1
104	Cryobanks International Inc—*Dwight Brunoehler*	270 S North Lake Blvd, Altamonte Springs FL 32701	407-834-8333	R	2*	<.1
105	Xytex Corp—*Michael Tucker*	1100 Emmett St, Augusta GA 30904	706-733-0130	R	2*	<.1
106	Fertility Solutions Inc—*Susan Rothmann*	11811 Shaker Blvd Ste, Cleveland OH 44120	216-491-0030	R	2*	<.1
107	TMG Health—*John Tighe III*	455 S Gulph Rd Ste 307, King of Prussia PA 19406	610-878-9111	R	1*	1.0
108	Idant Laboratories Div—*Joseph Feldschuh*	350 5th Ave Ste 7120, New York NY 10118	212-244-0555	D	1*	<.1
109	Biogenetics Corp—*Albert Anouna*	187 Mill Ln, Mountainside, NJ 07092	908-654-8836	R	1*	<.1
110	Electronic Transmission Corp—*Friedrich T Elliott*	15400 Knoll Trail Dr, Dallas TX 75248	972-980-0900	R	1*	<.1
111	CNS Response Inc—*George Carpenter*	85 Enterprise Ste 410, Aliso Viejo CA 92656	949-420-4400	P	1	<.1
112	ExamWorks Group Inc—*James K Price*	3280 Peachtree Rd NE S, Atlanta GA 30305	404-952-2400	P	<1	1.9
113	Catasys Inc—*Terren S Peizer*	11150 Santa Monica Blv, Los Angeles CA 90025	310-444-4300	P	<1	<.1
114	Pics Inc—*Albert Behar*	PO Box 2400, Reston VA 20195	703-758-1795	R	<1*	<.1
115	We Care Physicals LLC—*Lillian Willis*	1201 Franklin St NE St, Washington DC 20017	202-526-5972	R	<1	<.1
116	Ingen Technologies Inc—*Scott R Sand*	35193 Ave A, Yucaipa CA 92399	909-790-7180	P	<1	<.1
117	National Quality Care Inc—*Robert Snukal*	2431 Hill Dr, Los Angeles CA 90041	323-254-2014	P	<1	N/A

TOTALS: SIC 8099 Health & Allied Services Nec
Companies: 117 — 21,674 — 94.8

8111 Legal Services

Rank	Company Name—*Executive Officer*	Address, City, State, Zip	Phone	Type	Fin	Empls
1	Skadden Arps Slate Meagher and Flom LLP and Affiliates—*Eric Friedman*	4 Times Sq, New York NY 10036	212-735-3000	R	2,147*	4.6
2	Hogan Lovells US LLP—*Warren Gorrell*	555 Thirteenth St NW, Washington DC 20004	202-637-5600	R	1,800	3.0
3	Latham and Watkins LLP—*Robert M Dell*	885 3rd Ave, New York NY 10022	212-906-1200	R	1,755*	4.5
4	Baker and McKenzie—*John Conroy*	130 E Randolph Dr Ste, Chicago IL 60601	312-861-8000	R	1,522*	8.5
5	Mayer Brown LLP—*Herbert W Krueger*	71 S Wacker Dr, Chicago IL 60606	312-782-0600	R	1,402*	5.5
6	Morgan Lewis and Bockius LLP—*Francis Milone*	1701 Market St, Philadelphia PA 19103	215-963-5000	R	1,343*	3.0
7	Davis Polk—*John Ettinger*	450 Lexington Ave, New York NY 10017	212-450-4000	R	1,323*	2.0
8	Kirkland and Ellis LLP	300 N LaSalle, Chicago IL 60654	312-862-2000	R	1,150	3.4
9	White and Case LLP—*Hugh Verrier*	1155 Ave of the Americ, New York NY 10036	212-819-8200	R	1,081*	1.9
10	Holland and Knight LLP—*Bradford Kimbro*	100 N Tampa St Ste 410, Tampa FL 33602	813-227-8500	R	1,075*	2.6
11	Weil Gotshal and Manges LLP—*Stephen J Dannhauser*	767 5th Ave, New York NY 10153	212-310-8000	R	949*	2.8
12	Jones Day—*Stephen J Brogan*	901 Lakeside Ave, Cleveland OH 44114	216-586-3939	R	924*	5.4
13	Holme Roberts and Owen LLP—*Randy Miller*	1700 Lincoln St Ste 41, Denver CO 80203	303-861-7000	R	830*	.5
14	Paul Hastings Janofsky and Walker LLP—*Greg Nitzkowski*	75 E 55th St 1st Fl, New York NY 10022	212-318-6000	R	814*	2.6
15	Gibson Dunn and Crutcher—*Kenneth M Doran*	333 S Grand Ave, Los Angeles CA 90071	213-229-7000	R	770*	1.7
16	Cleary Gottlieb Steen and Hamilton—*Mark Leddy*	1 Liberty Plz 38th Fl, New York NY 10006	212-225-2000	R	769*	2.8
17	Goodwin Procter LLP—*Regina Pisa*	53 State St, Boston MA 02109	617-570-1000	R	658*	.8
18	Sidley Austin LLP—*Thomas A Cole*	1 S Dearborn, Chicago IL 60603	312-853-7000	R	557*	1.7
19	Wilson Sonsini Goodrich and Rosati—*Larry Sonsini*	650 Page Mill Rd, Palo Alto CA 94304	650-493-9300	R	537*	1.3
20	Pepper Hamilton LLP—*Nina M Gusssack*	3000 Two Logan Sq, Philadelphia PA 19103	215-981-4000	R	498*	1.1
21	Shearman and Sterling—*John Madden*	599 Lexington Ave, New York NY 10022	212-848-4000	R	490*	1.9
22	Wilmer Cutler Pickering Hale and Dorr LLP—*Scott Green*	399 Park Ave, New York NY 10022	212-230-8800	R	462*	1.0
23	Kilpatrick Stockton LLP—*Dorris Williams*	1100 Peachtree St Ste, Atlanta GA 30309	404-815-6500	R	452*	1.3
24	Wilson Elser Moskowitz Edelman and Dicker LLP—*Thomas Wilson*	150 E 42nd St, New York NY 10017	212-490-3000	R	446*	1.6
25	Quinn Emanuel Urquhart Oliver and Hedges LLP—*John Quinn*	865 S Figueroa St 10th, Los Angeles CA 90017	213-443-3000	R	385*	.9
26	Andrews and Kurth LLP—*William R Livesay Jr*	600 Travis St Ste 4200, Houston TX 77002	713-220-4200	R	379*	.9
27	Manatt Phelps and Phillips—*William T Quicksilver*	11355 W Olympic Blvd, Los Angeles CA 90064	310-312-4000	R	350*	.4
28	Simpson Thacher and Bartlett—*Richard I Beattie*	425 Lexington Ave, New York NY 10017	212-455-2000	R	347*	1.0
29	Bingham McCutchen—*Jay S Zimmerman*	150 Federal St, Boston MA 02110	617-951-8000	R	346*	1.0
30	Justice 900 Inc—*Harland Stonecipher*	PO Box 145, Ada OK 74821	580-436-1234	S	342*	.8
31	Morrison and Foerster LLP—*Keith C Wetmore*	425 Market St, San Francisco CA 94105	415-268-7000	R	338*	2.0
32	Womble Carlyle Sandridge and Rice PLLC—*Keith Vaughan*	1 W 4th St, Winston Salem NC 27101	336-721-3600	R	338*	1.8
33	Dickstein Shapiro LLP—*Michael Nannes*	1825 Eye St NW, Washington DC 20006	202-420-2200	R	331*	.8
34	King and Spalding—*Robert Hays*	1180 Peachtree St NE, Atlanta GA 30309	404-572-4600	R	331*	.8
35	K and L Gates LLC—*Michael J Sullivan*	210 6th Ave, Pittsburgh PA 15222	412-355-6500	R	330*	2.0
36	Winston and Strawn—*Dan Webb*	35 W Wacker Dr, Chicago IL 60601	312-558-5600	R	320*	1.0
37	Fulbright and Jaworski LLP—*Steven B Pfeiffer*	1301 McKinney St Ste 5, Houston TX 77010	713-651-5151	R	319*	1.7
38	K and L Gates—*Henry W Flint*	214 N Tryon St 47th Fl, Charlotte NC 28202	704-331-7400	R	312*	1.9
39	Charles River Associates Inc—*Paul A Maleh*	200 Clarendon St T-33, Boston MA 02116	617-425-3000	P	305	.5
40	Drinker Biddle and Reath LLP—*Alfred Putnam*	1 Logan Sq Ste 2000, Philadelphia PA 19103	215-988-2700	R	299*	.7
41	Dechert LLC—*Daniel O'Donnell*	2929 Arch St, Philadelphia PA 19104	215-994-4000	R	294*	.9
42	Stroock and Stroock and Lavan—*Thoms E Heftler*	180 Maiden Ln, New York NY 10038	212-806-5400	R	288*	.8
43	Carlton Fields Ward Emmanuel Smith and Cutler—*Gary L Sasso*	4221 W Boy Scout Blvd, Tampa FL 33607	813-223-7000	R	276*	.6
44	Barnes and Thornburg—*Tim Shaw*	11 S Meridian St, Indianapolis IN 46204	317-236-1313	R	275*	.7
45	Willkie Farr and Gallagher LLP—*Henry Kennedy*	787 7th Ave, New York NY 10019	212-728-8000	R	274*	.6
46	Sutherland Asbill and Brennan (Washington DC)—*Mark Wasserman*	1275 Pennsylvania Ave, Washington DC 20004	202-383-0100	R	269*	.6
47	Baker and Botts LLP—*Walter J Smith*	910 Lousiana St, Houston TX 77002	713-229-1234	R	258*	1.6
48	Fried Frank Harris Shriver and Jacobson LLP—*Justin Spend-love*	1 New York Plz, New York NY 10004	212-859-8000	R	252*	.3
49	O'Melveny and Myers LLP—*Michael Masin*	400 S Hope St, Los Angeles CA 90071	213-430-6000	R	248*	1.0
50	Ice Miller LLP—*Phillip L Bayt*	1 American Sq Ste 3100, Indianapolis IN 46282	317-236-2100	R	248*	.6
51	Jackson Walker LLP—*David Moran*	901 Main St Ste 6000, Dallas TX 75202	214-953-6000	R	248*	.6
52	Quarles and Brady LLP (Chicago Illinois)—*John J Peterburs*	300 N LaSalle St Ste 4, Chicago IL 60654	312-715-5000	R	240*	.6
53	Miller Canfield Paddock and Stone PLC—*Michael W Hartman*	150 W Jefferson Ste 25, Detroit MI 48226	313-963-6420	R	232*	.8
54	Arnold and Porter—*Michael N Sohn*	555 12th St NW, Washington DC 20004	202-942-5000	R	230*	.5
55	Kelley Drye and Warren LLP—*Seunghwan Kim*	101 Park Ave, New York NY 10178	212-808-7800	R	224*	.8
56	Squire Sanders and Dempsey LLP—*William Kwiatkowski*	4900 Key Tower 127 Pub, Cleveland OH 44114	216-479-8500	R	223*	1.6
57	Schnader Harrison Segal and Lewis LLP—*David Smith*	1600 Market St Ste 360, Philadelphia PA 19103	215-751-2000	R	223*	.8
58	Dewey Ballantine LLP—*Morton Pierce*	1301 Ave of the Americ, New York NY 10019	212-259-8000	R	222*	1.1
59	Cozen and O'Connor—*Thomas Decker*	1900 Market St, Philadelphia PA 19103	215-665-2000	R	222	.8
60	Arent Fox PLLC—*William R Charyk*	1050 Connecticut Ave N, Washington DC 20036	202-857-6000	R	220*	.5
61	Proskauer Rose LLP—*Arthur Gurwitz*	1585 Broadway, New York NY 10036	212-969-3000	R	218*	1.2
62	Cadwalader Wickersham and Taft—*Charles Adelman*	One World Financial Ct, New York NY 10281	212-504-6000	R	217*	.9

Rank	Company Name—*Executive Officer*	Address, City, State, Zip	Phone	Type	Fin	Empls
63	Stinson Morrison Hecker LLP—*Mark S Foster*	1201 Walnut Ste 2900, Kansas City MO 64106	816-842-8600	R	216*	.7
64	Paul Weiss Rifkind Wharton and Garrison LLP—*Brad S Karp*	1285 Ave of the Americ, New York NY 10019	212-373-3000	R	213*	.9
65	Troutman and Sanders LLP—*Stephen E Lewis*	600 Peachtree St NE St, Atlanta GA 30308	404-885-3000	R	213*	.7
66	Luce Forward Hamilton and Scripps—*Richard C Bigelow*	600 W Broadway Ste 260, San Diego CA 92101	619-236-1414	R	209*	.6
67	Steptoe and Johnson LLP—*Robert Jordan*	1330 Connecticut Ave N, Washington DC 20036	202-429-3000	R	209*	.6
68	McDermott Will and Emery—*Edward H McDermott*	600 13th St NW, Washington DC 20005	202-756-8000	R	209*	.5
69	McCarter and English—*Andrew T Berry*	100 Mulberry St, Newark NJ 07102	973-622-4444	R	208*	.6
70	Lowenstein Sandler PC—*Gary M Wingens*	65 Livingston Ave, Roseland NJ 07068	973-597-2500	R	207*	.6
71	Gardner Carton and Douglas—*David Abernethy* Drinker Biddle and Reath LLP	191 N Wacker Dr Ste 37, Chicago IL 60606	312-569-1000	S	206*	.5
72	Riker Danzig Scherer Hyland and Perretti LLP—*Jack Berkowitz*	1 Speedwell Ave, Morristown NJ 07960	973-538-0800	R	206*	.5
73	Adams and Reese LLP—*Charles P Adams*	450 Laurel St Ste 1900, Baton Rouge LA 70801	225-336-5200	R	202*	.5
74	Greenberg and Traurig PA—*John Lessner*	1007 N Orange St Ste 1, Wilmington DE 19801	302-661-7000	R	196*	.6
75	Buchanan Ingersoll PC—*John Barbour*	301 Grant St 20th Fl, Pittsburgh PA 15219	412-562-8800	R	193*	1.0
76	McGuireWoods LLP—*John Coghill*	1 James Ctr 901 E Cary, Richmond VA 23219	804-775-1000	R	193*	.8
77	Phillips Lytle LLP—*David J McNamara*	1 HSBC Ctr Ste 3400, Buffalo NY 14203	716-847-8400	R	192*	.5
78	Bryan Cave LP—*Robert L Newmark*	211 N Broadway Ste 360, Saint Louis MO 63102	314-259-2000	R	190*	1.3
79	Stites and Harbison—*Kennedy Helm III*	400 W Market St Ste 18, Louisville KY 40202	502-587-3400	R	186*	.5
80	Coughlin Stoia Geller Rudman Robbins LLP—*Ramzi Abadou*	655 W Broadway Ste 190, San Diego CA 92101	619-231-1058	R	186*	.5
81	Winstead Sechrest and Minick PC—*Tom Forestier*	910 Travis St Ste 2400, Houston TX 77002	713-650-8400	R	183*	.7
82	Linebarger Goggan Blair and Sampson LLP—*Brian Brown*	2700 Via Fortuna Dr St, Austin TX 78746	512-447-6675	R	180*	.7
83	Phelps Dunbar LLP—*Richard N Dicharry*	365 Canal St Ste 2000, New Orleans LA 70130	504-566-1311	R	180*	.5
84	Strasburger and Price LLP—*Daniel L Butcher*	901 Main St Ste 4400, Dallas TX 75202	214-651-4300	R	175*	.4
85	Debevoise and Plimpton LLP—*Emily Thall*	919 3rd Ave Lbby 3, New York NY 10022	212-909-6000	R	174*	2.1
86	BuchalterNemer LLC—*Rick Cohen*	1000 Wilshire Blvd Ste, Los Angeles CA 90017	213-891-0700	R	174*	.5
87	Sullivan and Cromwell LLP—*Sylvia Sanchez*	125 Broad St Lowr Sc1, New York NY 10004	212-558-4000	R	172*	1.9
88	Jenner and Block—*Susan C Levy*	353 N Clark St, Chicago IL 60654	312-222-9350	R	171*	.4
89	Seyfarth Shaw—*David J Rowland*	131 S Dearborn St Ste, Chicago IL 60603	312-460-5000	R	170*	.8
90	Husch Blackwell LLP—*David Fenley*	4801 Main St Ste 1000, Kansas City MO 64112	816-983-8000	R	170*	.6
91	Stoel Rives LLP—*E Walter Van Valkenburg*	900 SW 5th Ave Ste 260, Portland OR 97204	503-224-3380	R	168*	.9
92	Honigman Miller Schwartz and Cohn LLP—*David Fulton*	2290 First National Bl, Detroit MI 48226	313-465-7000	R	167*	.6
93	Nelson Mullins Riley and Scarborough—*David Dukes*	1320 Main St 17th Fl, Columbia SC 29201	803-799-2000	R	167*	.6
94	Chapman and Cutler—*Richard Cosgrove*	111 W Monroe St, Chicago IL 60603	312-845-3000	R	166*	.6
95	Lathrop and Gage LC—*Joel Voran*	2345 Grand Blvd, Kansas City MO 64108	816-292-2000	R	166*	.6
96	Godfrey and Kahn—*Richard Bliss*	780 N Water St, Milwaukee WI 53202	414-273-3500	R	166*	.4
97	Foley and Lardner LLP—*Jay O Rothman*	777 E Wisconsin Ave, Milwaukee WI 53202	414-271-2400	R	165*	1.0
98	Broad and Cassel—*C David Brown II*	390 N Orange Ave Ste 1, Orlando FL 32801	407-839-4200	R	165*	.4
99	Wilentz Goldman and Spitzer PA—*Steve Varcan*	PO Box 10, Woodbridge NJ 07095	732-636-8000	R	165*	.4
100	Gibson Dunn and Crutcher LLP—*Jonathan Dickey*	333 S Grand Ave Ste 44, Los Angeles CA 90071	213-229-7000	R	164*	1.9
101	Moore and Van Allen—*Matt Gillespie*	100 N Tryon St Ste 470, Charlotte NC 28202	704-331-1000	R	164*	.6
102	Saul Ewing LLP—*David Antzis*	500 E Pratt St Ste 900, Baltimore MD 21207	410-332-8600	R	159*	.6
103	Foley Hoag LLP—*Robert S Sanoff*	155 Seaport Blvd, Boston MA 02210	617-832-1000	R	159*	.4
104	Perkins Coie LLP—*Robert Giles*	1201 3rd Ave Ste 4800, Seattle WA 98101	206-359-8000	R	157*	1.4
105	Porter Wright Morris and Arthur LLP—*Robert Trafford*	41 S High St Ste 2800, Columbus OH 43215	614-227-2000	R	157*	.6
106	Blank Rome LLP—*Patrick O Cavanaugh*	One Logan Sq 130 N 18t, Philadelphia PA 19103	215-569-5500	R	156*	.6
107	Truck Underwriters Association—*Leonard Gelfand*	PO Box 2478, Los Angeles CA 90051	323-932-3200	R	155*	2.8
108	Chadbourne and Parke LLP—*Charles K O'Neill*	30 Rockefeller Plz, New York NY 10112	212-408-5100	R	154	1.0
109	Akin Gump Strauss Hauer and Feld LLP—*R Bruce McLean*	1333 New Hampshire Ave, Washington DC 20036	202-887-4000	R	153*	.9
110	Dechert LLP—*Judith Tellefsen*	2929 Arch St Ste 400, Philadelphia PA 19104	215-994-4000	R	152*	1.8
111	Hunton and Williams LLP—*Barry D Koval*	951 E Byrd St, Richmond VA 23219	804-788-8200	R	151*	.9
112	Cahill Gordon and Reindel—*Jay Geiger*	80 Pine St, New York NY 10005	212-701-3000	R	151*	.6
113	Vorys Sater Seymour and Pease LLP—*Robert E Werth*	PO Box 1008, Columbus OH 43216	614-464-6400	R	150*	.9
114	Brown Rudnick Berlack Israels—*Joseph F Ryan*	1 Financial Ctr, Boston MA 02111	617-856-8200	R	150*	.4
115	Loeb and Loeb LLP—*Michael A Mayerson*	110100 Santa Monica Bl, Los Angeles CA 90067	310-282-2000	R	149*	.5
116	King and Spalding LLP—*Robert Hays*	1180 Peachtree St Ne S, Atlanta GA 30309	404-572-4600	R	149*	1.9
117	Frost Brown Todd LLC—*John Crocket III*	201 E 5th St Ste 2200, Cincinnati OH 45202	513-651-6800	R	147*	.5
118	Morrison Mahoney LLP—*Mark P Harty*	250 Summer St, Boston MA 02210	617-439-7500	R	147*	.4
119	Gray Plant Mooty PA	500 IDS Ctr 80 S 8th S, Minneapolis MN 55402	612-632-3000	R	146*	.4
120	Faegre Baker and Daniels—*Philip S Garon*	90 S 7th St, Minneapolis MN 55402	612-766-7000	R	145*	1.0
121	Bowles Rice McDavid Graff and Love LLP—*P Nathan Bowles Jr*	600 Quarrier St, Charleston WV 25301	304-347-1100	R	145*	.4
122	Dickinson Wright PLLC—*Dennis W Archer*	500 Woodward Ave Ste 4, Detroit MI 48226	313-223-3500	R	145*	.4
123	Montgomery McCracken Walker and Rhoads LLP—*Stephen A Madva*	123 S Broad St, Philadelphia PA 19109	215-772-1500	R	145*	.4
124	Thompson Coburn LLP—*Thomas J Minogue*	1 US Bank Plaza, Saint Louis MO 63101	314-552-6000	R	145*	.4
125	Mintz Levin Cohn Ferris Glovsky and Popeo PC—*Peter Biagetti*	1 Financial Ctr, Boston MA 02111	617-542-6000	R	144*	.9
126	Heller Ehrman White and McAuliffe LLP—*Susan Leberman*	333 Bush St, San Francisco CA 94104		R	142*	1.0
127	Bracewell and Giuliani LLP—*Patrick C Oxford*	711 Louisiana St Ste 2, Houston TX 77002	713-223-2300	R	141*	.9
128	Dykema Gossett PLLC—*Peter Kellett*	400 Renaissance Ctr, Detroit MI 48243	313-568-6800	R	141*	.5
129	Akerman Senterfitt PA—*Mark A Cassanego*	420 S Orange Ave Ste12, Orlando FL 32801	407-423-4000	R	140*	.5
130	Epstein Becker and Green PC—*George P Sape*	250 Park Ave, New York NY 10177	212-351-4500	R	139*	.4
131	Fowler White Boggs Banker—*Rhea F Law*	501 E Kennedy Blvd Ste, Tampa FL 33602	813-228-7411	R	139*	.4
132	Sonnenschein Nath and Rosenthal LLP—*Elliottl Portnoy*	233 S Wacker Dr Ste 78, Chicago IL 60606	312-876-8000	R	138*	.7
133	Altheimer and Gray	10 S Wacker Dr Ste 380, Chicago IL 60606	312-715-4080	R	138*	.5
134	Saul Ewing LLP—*David Antzis*	Centre Sq W 1500 Marke, Philadelphia PA 19102	215-972-7777	R	136*	.3
135	Finnegan Henderson Farabow Garrett and Dunner LLP—*Richard Racine*	901 New York Ave NW, Washington DC 20001	202-408-4000	R	134*	.8
136	Harter Secrest and Emery LLP—*Maureen Alston*	1600 Bausch and Lomb P, Rochester NY 14604	585-232-6500	R	134*	.3
137	Covington and Burling LLP—*John Waters*	1201 Pennsylvania Ave, Washington DC 20004	202-662-6000	R	133*	.8
138	Locke Lord LLP—*Marc Watts*	600 Travis St 2800 JP, Houston TX 77002	713-226-1200	R	133*	.7
139	Snell and Wilmer—*John J Bouma*	1200 17th St Ste 1900, Denver CO 80202	303-634-2000	R	132*	.4
140	Clifford Chance LLP—*John Carroll*	31 W 52nd St, New York NY 10019	212-878-8000	R	130*	.9
141	Cummings and Lockwood—*Johnathan Mills*	6 Landmark Sq, Stamford CT 06901	203-327-1700	R	128*	.3
142	Ford and Harrison LLP—*John Monroe*	271 17th St NW Ste 190, Atlanta GA 30363	404-888-3800	R	128*	.3
143	Gray Robinson PA—*Byrd F Marshall Jr*	301 E Pine St Ste 1400, Orlando FL 32801	407-843-8880	R	127*	.5
144	Quarles and Brady LLP (Milwaukee Wisconsin)—*John J Petersburs*	411 E Wisconsin Ave St, Milwaukee WI 53202	414-277-5000	R	125*	.5
145	Wiggin and Dana LLP—*Robert W Benjamin*	PO Box 1832, New Haven CT 06508	203-498-4400	R	125*	.3
146	Patterson Belknap Webb and Tyler LLP—*Robert P Lobue*	1133 Avenue of the Ame, New York NY 10036	212-336-2000	R	123*	.4

Note: An asterisk (*) indicates an estimated financial figure. The company type code used is as follows: R = Private, P = Public, S = Private Subsidiary, B = Public Subsidiary, D = Division, J = Joint Venture, I = Investment Fund.

COMPANY RANKINGS BY SALES WITHIN 4-DIGIT SIC

Rank	Company Name—*Executive Officer*	Address, City, State, Zip	Phone	Type	Fin	Empls
147	Haynes and Boone LLP—*Robert E Wilson*	2323 Victory Ave Rm 70, Dallas TX 75219	214-651-5000	R	122*	.8
148	Cravath Swaine and Moore—*EvanR Chesler*	825 Eighth AveFl 38, New York NY 10019	212-474-1000	R	121	1.4
149	Rutan and Tucker LLP—*Thomas Crane*	611 Anton Blvd Ste 140, Costa Mesa CA 92626	714-641-5100	R	121*	.4
150	Bond Schoeneck and King PLLC—*Richard Hole*	1 Lincoln Ctr, Syracuse NY 13202	315-218-8000	R	120*	.4
151	Benesch Friedlander Coplan and Aronoff—*George N Aronoff*	200 Public Sq Ste 2300, Cleveland OH 44114	216-363-4500	R	120*	.3
152	California Casualty Management Co—*Beau Brown*	PO Box M, San Mateo CA 94402	650-574-4000	R	119*	1.0
153	Thompson and Knight LLP—*Jeffrey Zlotky*	1722 Routh St Ste 1500, Dallas TX 75201	214-969-1700	R	117*	.4
154	Kramer Levin Naftalis and Frankel LLP—*Paul Pearlman*	1177 Ave of the Americ, New York NY 10036	212-715-9100	R	116*	.6
155	Kutak Rock—*David Jacobson*	1650 Farnam St, Omaha NE 68102	402-346-6000	R	115*	.3
156	Cooley Godward Kronish LLP—*Joe Conroy*	101 California St 5th, San Francisco CA 94111	415-693-2000	R	114*	.6
157	Briggs and Morgan PA—*Alan H Maclin*	80 S 8th St 2200 IDS C, Minneapolis MN 55402	612-977-8400	R	113*	.4
158	Stradley Ronon Stevens and Young—*Jeffrey A Lutsky*	PO Box 2170, Wilmington DE 19899	302-576-5850	R	113*	.3
159	Nutter McClennen and Fish LLP—*Donald Kondub*	155 Seaport Blvd, Boston MA 02210	617-439-2000	R	112*	.4
160	Gardere Wynne Sewell LLP—*Steve Good*	1601 Elm St Ste 3000, Dallas TX 75201	214-999-3000	R	112*	.3
161	Dorsey and Whitney LLP—*Marianne D Short*	50 S 6th St Ste 1500, Minneapolis MN 55402	612-340-2600	R	109*	.8
162	Miller Nash LLP—*Don Burns*	3400 US Bancorp Tower, Portland OR 97204	503-224-5858	R	109*	.3
163	Locke Lord Bissell and Liddell LLP—*Jerry K Clements*	111 S Wacker Dr, Chicago IL 60606	312-443-0700	R	108*	.7
164	Fragomen Del Rey Bernsen and Loewy PC	1101 15th St NW Ste 70, Washington DC 20005	202-223-5515	R	106*	.5
165	Lane Powell Spears Lubersky LLP—*Lewis Horowitz*	1420 5th Ave Ste 4100, Seattle WA 98101	206-223-7000	R	105*	.7
166	Brown McCarroll LLP—*Adam Hauser*	111 Congress Ave Ste14, Austin TX 78701	512-472-5456	R	104*	.3
167	Robinson and Cole	1055 Washington Blvd, Stamford CT 06901	203-462-7500	S	104*	.3
168	Ungaretti and Harris LLP—*Thomas M Fahey*	70 W Madison Ste 3500, Chicago IL 60602	312-977-4400	R	103*	.3
169	Williams Kastner and Gibbs PLLC—*Sheryl Willert*	PO Box 21926, Seattle WA 98111	206-628-6600	R	102*	.3
170	Orrick Herrington and Sutcliffe LLP—*Ralph Baxter*	405 Howard St, San Francisco CA 94105	415-773-5700	R	100*	.8
171	Venable LLP—*Sterling Chadwick*	750 E Pratt St, Baltimore MD 21202	410-244-7400	R	100*	.6
172	Crowell and Moring LLP—*Kent Gardinier*	1001 Pennsylvania Ave, Washington DC 20004	202-624-2500	R	100*	.6
173	Davis Graham and Stubbs LLP—*Chris Richardson*	1550 17th St Ste 500, Denver CO 80202	303-892-9400	R	100*	.2
174	Greensfelder Hemker and Gale PC—*Timothy Thornton*	10 S Broadway St Ste 2, Saint Louis MO 63102	314-241-9090	R	98*	.4
175	Nixon Peabody LLP—*Andrew I Glincher*	100 Summer St, Boston MA 02110	617-345-1000	R	98*	.4
176	Whyte Hirschboeck Dudek SC—*Paul J Eberle*	555 E Wells St Ste 190, Milwaukee WI 53202	414-273-2100	R	98*	.3
177	Davis Wright Tremaine LLP—*Ron Drake*	1201 3rd Ave Ste 2200, Seattle WA 98101	206-622-3150	R	97*	.5
178	Jacoby and Meyers Law Offices LLP—*Leonard Jacoby*	222 Broadway 18th Fl, New York NY 10038	212-445-7000	R	97*	.5
179	Schulte Roth and Zabel LLP—*Gary Fievert*	919 3rd Ave, New York NY 10022	212-756-2000	R	97*	.5
180	Munger Tolles and Olson LLP	355 S Grand Ave 35th F, Los Angeles CA 90071	213-683-9100	R	96*	.3
181	Duane Morris LLP—*Wayne Mack*	30 S 17th St, Philadelphia PA 19103	215-979-1000	R	95*	.7
182	Choate Hall and Stewart LLP—*William P Gelnaw Jr*	2 International Pl, Boston MA 02110	617-248-5000	R	95*	.5
183	Cohen and Grigsby PC—*Jack W Elliott*	625 Liberty Ave, Pittsburgh PA 15222		R	95*	.2
184	Baker Donelson Bearman Caldwell and Berkowitz PC (Memphis TN)—*Charles Tuggle Jr*	165 Madison Ave Ste 20, Memphis TN 38103	901-526-2000	R	94*	.2
185	Bagatelos Law Firm—*Peter Bagatelos*	380 W Portal Ave Ste F, San Francisco CA 94127	415-242-8830	R	94*	<.1
186	Bricker and Eckler LLP—*Kurt Tunnell*	100 S 3rd St, Columbus OH 43215	614-227-2300	R	93*	.3
187	Reed Smith LLP—*Gregory B Jordan*	225 5th Ave, Pittsburgh PA 15222	412-288-3131	R	92*	.6
188	Fredrikson and Byron PA—*John M Koneck*	200 S 6th St Ste 4000, Minneapolis MN 55402	612-492-7000	R	92*	.3
189	Oppenheimer Wolff and Donnelly LLP—*Brad Keil*	Plaza VII Ste 3300 45, Minneapolis MN 55402	612-607-7000	R	91*	.1
190	Hinshaw and Culbertson LLP—*J William Roberts*	222 N LaSalle St, Chicago IL 60601	312-704-3000	R	90*	.9
191	Lewis Brisbois Bisgaard and Smith LLP—*Timothy Graves*	221 N Figueroa St Ste, Los Angeles CA 90012	213-250-1800	R	90*	.5
192	Stark and Stark—*Lewis J Pepperman*	PO Box 5315, Princeton NJ 08543	609-896-9060	R	90*	.3
193	Michael Best and Friedrich LLP—*David A Krutz*	100 E Wisconsin Ave St, Milwaukee WI 53202	414-271-6560	R	89*	.5
194	Gallop Johnson and Neuman LC—*Thomas J Campbell*	101 S Hanley Ste 1700, Saint Louis MO 63105	314-615-6000	R	89*	.2
195	Kitch Drutchas Wagner Valitutti and Sherbrook—*Richard A Kitch*	1 Woodward Ave Ste 24t, Detroit MI 48226	313-965-7900	R	87*	.2
196	Greenberg Glusker Fields Claman Machtinger LLP—*Kimberly Lahs*	1900 Ave of the Stars, Los Angeles CA 90067	310-553-3610	R	87*	.2
197	Hiscock and Barclay LLP—*John P Langan*	2000 HSBC Plz 100 Ches, Rochester NY 14604	585-295-4400	R	87*	.2
198	Irell and Manella LLP—*Elliot Brown*	1800 Ave of the Stars, Los Angeles CA 90067	310-277-1010	R	86*	.6
199	Dickie McCamey and Chilcote PC—*James Miller*	2 PPG Place Ste 400, Pittsburgh PA 15222	740-284-1682	R	85*	.3
200	Herzfeld and Rubin PC—*Herbert Rubin*	40 Wall St, New York NY 10005	212-471-8500	R	84*	.3
201	Ulmer and Berne LLP—*Kip Reader*	1660 W 2nd St Ste 1100, Cleveland OH 44113	216-583-7000	R	84*	.3
202	Wiley Rein LLP—*Daniel Standish*	1776 K St NW, Washington DC 20006	202-719-7000	R	83*	.5
203	Ruden McClosky Smith Schuster and Russell PA—*Carl Schuster*	PO Box 1900, Fort Lauderdale FL 33302	954-764-6660	R	83*	.4
204	Gunster Yoakley and Stewart PA—*Donald J Beuttenmuller Jr*	777 S Flagler Dr Ste 5, West Palm Beach FL 33401	561-655-1980	R	83*	.2
205	Howard Rice Nemerovski Canady Falk and Rabkin—*Lawrence B Rabkin*	3 Embarcadero Ctr 7th, San Francisco CA 94111	415-434-1600	R	83*	.2
206	Keller and Heckman LLP—*Jerome Heckman*	1001 G St NW Ste 500 W, Washington DC 20001	202-434-4100	R	83*	.2
207	Reinhart Boerner Van Deuren SC—*Jerome Janzer*	PO Box 2965, Milwaukee WI 53201	414-298-1000	R	83*	.2
208	Sedgwick Detert Moran and Arnold LLP—*Michael A TanenbaumBerry*	1 Market Plaza Steuart, San Francisco CA 94105	415-781-7900	R	80*	.7
209	Wachtell Lipton Rosen and Katz—*Herbert Wachtell*	51 W 52nd St, New York NY 10019	212-403-1000	R	79*	.4
210	Miller Johnson Snell and Cummiskey—*Craig Mutch*	250 Monroe Ave NW Ste, Grand Rapids MI 49503	616-831-1700	R	79*	.2
211	Curtis Mallet-Prevost Colt and Mosle LLP	101 Park Ave, New York NY 10178	212-696-6000	R	78*	.3
212	Hinckley Allen and Snyder LLP—*Michael DeFanti*	50 Kennedy Plz Ste 150, Providence RI 02903	401-274-2000	R	78*	.3
213	Hughes Hubbard and Reed—*Candace Beinecke*	1 Battery Park Plz, New York NY 10004	212-837-6000	R	77*	.6
214	Bullivant Houser Bailey PC—*John Bennett*	888 SW 5th Ave Ste 300, Portland OR 97204	503-228-6351	R	77*	.4
215	Best Best and Krieger LLP—*Eric L Garner*	PO Box 1028, Riverside CA 92502	909-686-1450	R	77*	.2
216	Thompson Hine LLP—*David J Hooker*	127 Public Sq, Cleveland OH 44114	216-566-5500	R	76*	1.0
217	Bose McKinney and Evans LLP—*Jeff Gaither*	111 Monument Cir Ste 2, Indianapolis IN 46204	317-684-5000	R	76*	.3
218	Clark Thomas and Winters PC	PO Box 1148, Austin TX 78767	512-472-8800	R	75*	.3
219	Keating Muething and Klekamp—*Paul Muething*	1 E 4th StSte 1400, Cincinnati OH 45202	513-579-6400	R	74*	.3
220	Banner and Witcoff Ltd—*Thomas K Pratt*	1100 13th St NW Ste 12, Washington DC 20005	202-824-3000	R	74*	.2
221	Baron and Budd PC	3102 Oak Lawn Ave Ste, Dallas TX 75219	214-521-3605	R	72*	.3
222	Sirote and Permutt PC—*John H Cooper*	PO Box 55727, Birmingham AL 35255	205-930-5100	R	71*	.3
223	Miller and Chevalier—*Marianna G Dyson*	655 15th St NW Ste 900, Washington DC 20005	202-626-5800	R	70*	.3
224	Rivkin Radler LLP—*Paul Czeladnicki*	21 Main St Ste 158, Hackensack NJ 07601	201-287-2460	R	70*	.3
225	Bradley Arant Rose and White LLP—*Beau Grenier*	1819 5th Ave N, Birmingham AL 35203	205-521-8000	R	70*	.2
226	Cox Castle and Nicholson LLP—*Phillip R Nicholson*	2049 Century Park E 28, Los Angeles CA 90067	310-284-2200	R	70	.2
227	Foster Pepper and Shefelman PLLC—*Robert Kunold Jr*	1111 3rd Ave Ste 3400, Seattle WA 98101	206-447-4400	R	69*	.3
228	Hopkins and Carley—*Arthur Bernstein*	PO Box 1469, San Jose CA 95113	408-286-9800	R	69*	.2
229	Palmer and Dodge—*John Gosnell*	111 Huntington Ave, Boston MA 02199	617-239-0100	R	68*	.4
230	Bur And Forman LLP—*William Thuston*	420 N 20th St Ste 3400, Birmingham AL 35203	205-251-3000	R	68*	.2

Rank	Company Name—*Executive Officer*	Address, City, State, Zip	Phone	Type	Fin	Empls
231	Hawkins and E-Z Messenger Legal Support Providers LLC—*Steve Ezell*	10 W Madison, Phoenix AZ 85003	602-258-8081	R	68*	.2
232	Baker and Hostetler LLP	1900 E 9th St Ste 3200, Cleveland OH 44114	216-621-0200	R	67*	.4
233	Taft Stettinius and Hollister LLP—*Thomas Terp*	425 Walnut St Ste 1800, Cincinnati OH 45202	513-381-2838	R	67*	.4
234	Freeborn and Peters LLP—*Michael Kelly*	311 S Wacker Dr Ste 30, Chicago IL 60606	312-360-6000	R	67*	.2
235	Bingham McHale LLP—*Toby McClamroch*	10 W Market St Flr 27, Indianapolis IN 46204	317-635-8900	R	65*	.2
236	Harris Beach PLLC—*Patrick J Dalton*	99 Garnsey Rd, Pittsford NY 14534	585-419-8800	R	64*	.2
237	Sandler Travis and Rosenberg PA—*Thomas Travis*	5200 Blue Lagoon Dr St, Miami FL 33126	305-267-9200	R	63*	.3
238	Constangy Brooks and Smith LLP—*James Gillespie*	230 Peachtree St NW St, Atlanta GA 30303	404-525-8622	R	63*	.2
239	Debevoise and Plimpton—*Rick Evans*	919 Third Ave, New York NY 10022	212-909-6000	R	62*	.4
240	Brown and James PC—*Donald L James*	1010 Market St 20th Fl, Saint Louis MO 63101	314-421-3400	R	61*	.2
241	Graydon Head and Ritchey LLP—*Monica Kohnen*	PO Box 6464, Cincinnati OH 45202	513-621-6464	R	61*	.1
242	Lewis and Roca LLP	40 N Central Ave Ste 1, Phoenix AZ 85004	602-262-5311	R	60*	.4
243	Torys LLP—*Les M Viner*	237 Park Avenue, New York NY 10017	212-880-6000	R	60*	.1
244	Farella Braun and Martel LLP—*Steve Lowenthal*	235 Montgomery St 17th, San Francisco CA 94104	415-954-4400	R	59*	.3
245	Wildman Harrold Attorneys and Counselors—*Robert Shuftan*	225 W Wacker Dr Ste 30, Chicago IL 60606	312-201-2000	R	59*	.3
246	Holland and Hart LLP—*Cliff Stricklin*	555 17th St Ste 3200, Denver CO 80202	303-295-8000	R	58*	.6
247	Mitchell Silberberg and Knupp—*Thomas Lambert*	11377 W Olympic Blvd, Los Angeles CA 90064	310-312-2000	R	58*	.4
248	Crowe and Dunlevy PC—*Roger Stong*	20 N Broadway Ste 1800, Oklahoma City OK 73102	405-235-7700	R	58*	.3
249	Cox and Smith Inc—*James B Smith*	112 E Pecan St Ste 180, San Antonio TX 78205	210-554-5500	R	58*	.1
250	Wicker Smith Tutan O'Hara McCoy and Ford PA—*Jackson F McCoy*	2800 Ponce de Leon Blv, Coral Gables FL 33134	305-448-3939	R	57*	.2
251	Shutts and Bowen LLP—*Fred Omalley*	201 S Biscayne Blvd St, Miami FL 33132	305-358-6300	R	56*	.2
252	Brownstein Hyatt and Farber PC—*Steven W Farber*	410 17th St 22nd Fl, Denver CO 80202	303-223-1100	R	56*	.2
253	Barack Ferrazzano Kirschbaum and Nagelberg LLP—*Howard J Kirschbaum*	200 W Madison St Ste 3, Chicago IL 60606	312-984-3100	R	56*	.2
254	Greenbaum Rowe Smith Ravin Davis and Himmel LLT—*Paul Rowe*	PO Box 5600, Woodbridge NJ 07095	732-549-5600	R	56*	.2
255	Hanna Brophy McLean McAleer and Jensen—*Richard Brophy*	PO Box 12488, Oakland CA 94604	213-943-4800	R	56*	.2
256	Jeffer Mangels Butler and Mitchell LLP—*Bruce P Jeffer*	1900 Ave of the Stars, Los Angeles CA 90067	310-203-8080	R	55*	.2
257	Lester Schwab Katz and Dwyer LLP—*Michael McDonagh*	120 Broadway 38th Fl, New York NY 10271	212-946-6611	R	55*	.2
258	Stearns Weaver Miller Weissler Alhadeff and Sitterson PA—*Ron Weaver*	150 W Flagler St Ste 2, Miami FL 33130	305-789-3200	R	55*	.2
259	Graham and Dunn PC—*K Michael Fandel*	2801 Alaskan Way Ste 3, Seattle WA 98121	206-624-8300	R	54*	.1
260	Smith Currie and Hancock LLP—*Thomas Kelleher*	1023 W Morehead St Ste, Charlotte NC 28208	704-334-3459	R	54*	.1
261	Fennemore Craig PC—*Kathy Hancock*	3003 N Central Ave Ste, Phoenix AZ 85012	602-916-5000	R	53*	.3
262	Groom Law Group Chartered—*Jon Breyfogle*	1701 Pennsylvania Ave, Washington DC 20006	202-857-0620	R	53*	.1
263	Cowles and Thompson—*Jim E Cowles*	901 Main St Ste 3900, Dallas TX 75202	214-672-2000	R	52*	.2
264	Varnum Riddering Schmidt and Howlett—*William Lawrence*	PO Box 352, Grand Rapids MI 49501	616-336-6000	R	51*	.3
265	Gunderson Dettmer Stough Villeneuve Franklin and Hachigian—*Robert Gunderson*	1200 Seaport Blvd, Redwood City CA 94063	650-321-2400	R	51*	.2
266	Meyer Unkovic and Scott LLP—*Patricia Dodge*	535 Smithfield St Ste, Pittsburgh PA 15222	412-456-2800	R	51*	.1
267	Neal Gerber and Eisenberg—*Jerry Biederman*	2 N LaSalle St Ste 220, Chicago IL 60602	312-269-8000	R	50*	.3
268	Berlinger Cohen—*Jerold A Reiton*	10 Almaden Blvd 11th F, San Jose CA 95113	408-286-5800	R	50*	.2
269	Shartsis Friese LLP—*Arthur J Shartsis*	1 Maritime Plz 18th Fl, San Francisco CA 94111	415-421-6500	R	50*	.1
270	Seed Intellectual Property Law Group PLLC—*Karl Hermann*	701 5th Ave Ste 6300, Seattle WA 98104	206-622-4900	R	49*	.2
271	Richards Layton and Finger—*Gregory Williams*	PO Box 551, Wilmington DE 19899	302-651-7700	R	48*	.3
272	Haynsworth Sinkler Boyd PA—*Martin McWilliams*	PO Box 11889, Columbia SC 29211	803-779-3080	R	47*	.1
273	Post and Schell—*Brian M Peters*	1600 John F Kennedy Bl, Philadelphia PA 19103	215-587-1000	R	46*	.2
274	Mitchell Williams Selig Gates and Woodyard PLLC—*Harry Hamlin*	425 W Capitol Ave Ste, Little Rock AR 72201	501-688-8800	R	46*	.1
275	Carter Ledyard and Milburn LLP—*Richard G Pierson*	2 Wall St, New York NY 10005	212-732-3200	R	46*	.1
276	Glaser Weil Fink Jacobs Howard Archen and Shapiro LLP—*Peter Weil*	10250 Constellation Bl, Los Angeles CA 90067	310-553-3000	R	45*	.2
277	Beveridge and Diamond PC—*Karla Monroe*	1350 I St NW Ste 700, Washington DC 20005	202-789-6000	R	45*	.2
278	Smith Anderson Blount Dorsett Mitchell and Jernigan LLP—*John Jernigan*	PO Box 2611, Raleigh NC 27602	919-821-1220	R	45*	.1
279	Hall and Evans—*Kenneth Lyman*	1125 17th St Ste 600, Denver CO 80202	303-628-3300	R	45*	.1
280	Hill Wallack Attorneys at Law—*Robert Bacso*	202 Carnegie Ctr, Princeton NJ 08540	609-924-0808	R	45*	.1
281	Spencer Fane Britt and Browne LLP—*Michael F Saunders*	1000 Walnut St Ste 140, Kansas City MO 64106	816-474-8100	R	45*	.1
282	Carlsmith Ball LLP—*Joanne L Grimes*	1001 Bishop St Ste 220, Honolulu HI 96813	808-523-2500	R	45*	.1
283	Hyman Phelps and McNamara PC—*Paul M Hyman*	700 13th St NW Ste 120, Washington DC 20005	202-737-5600	R	45*	.1
284	Morris Manning and Martin LLP—*Robert E Saudek*	3343 Peachtree Rd NE, Atlanta GA 30326	404-233-7000	R	44*	.3
285	Shannon Gracey Ratliff and Miller LLP—*Victor Anderson Jr*	777 Main St Ste 3800, Fort Worth TX 76102	817-336-9333	R	44*	.2
286	Walsworth Franklin and Bevins and McCall LLP—*Mary Watson Fisher*	1 City Blvd W 5th Fl, Orange CA 92868	714-634-2522	R	44*	.2
287	Robinson Bradshaw and Hinson PA—*Robert G Griffin*	101 N Tryon St Ste 190, Charlotte NC 28246	704-377-2536	R	43*	.2
288	Rodey Dickason Sloan Akin and Robb PA—*Monty R Morton*	PO Box 1888, Albuquerque NM 87103	505-765-5900	R	43*	.2
289	Sheehan Phinney Bass and Green—*Jospeh A DiBrigida*	PO Box 3701, Manchester NH 03105	603-668-0300	R	43*	.2
290	Brice Vander Linden and Wernick PC—*Lance J Vander Linden*	9441 LBJ Fwy Ste 250, Dallas TX 75243	214-550-3955	R	43*	.1
291	Goodell DeVries Leech and Dann LLP—*Linda Woolf*	1 South St 20th Fl, Baltimore MD 21202	410-783-4000	R	43*	.2
292	Howard and Howard Attorneys PC—*Frederick Hoffman*	450 W 4th St, Royal Oak MI 48067	248-645-1483	R	42*	.2
293	Corboy and Demetrio—*Philip H Corboy*	33 N Dearborn St, Chicago IL 60602	312-346-3191	R	42*	.1
294	Kronick Moskovitz Tiedemann and Girard—*Robert H Brumfield III*	400 Capitol Mall 27th, Sacramento CA 95814	916-321-4500	R	42*	.1
295	Jaffe Raitt Heuer and Weiss PC—*Jeffrey G Heuer*	27777 Franklin Rd Ste, Southfield MI 48034	248-351-3000	R	41*	.1
296	Keesal Young and Logan—*Terry Ross*	PO Box 1730, Long Beach CA 90801	562-436-2000	R	41*	.1
297	Kemp and Smith LLP—*Jack Chapman*	PO Box 2800, El Paso TX 79999	915-533-4424	R	41*	.1
298	Smith Gambrell and Russell—*Steve Forte*	1230 Peachtree St NE S, Atlanta GA 30309	404-815-3500	R	40*	.3
299	Kelly Hart and Hallman LLP—*Dee Kelly Jr*	201 Main St Ste 2500, Fort Worth TX 76102	817-332-2500	R	40*	.2
300	Lemle and Kelleher LLP—*Ernest L Edwards*	601 Poydras St Fl 21, New Orleans LA 70130	504-586-1241	R	40*	.2
301	Shefsky and Froelich—*Cesar M Froelich*	111 E Wacker Ste 2800, Chicago IL 60601	312-527-4000	R	40*	.1
302	Perona Langer BeckSerbin and Mendoza—*Major Langer*	300 E San Antonio Dr, Long Beach CA 90807	562-426-6155	H	40*	.1
303	Gallagher and Kennedy PA—*Michael L Gallagher*	2575 E Camelback Rd, Phoenix AZ 85016	602-530-8000	R	39*	.2
304	Johnson and Bell Ltd—*William Johnson*	33 W Monroe St Ste 410, Chicago IL 60603	312-372-0770	R	39*	.2
305	Krieg DeVault LLP—*Michael E Williams*	1 Indiana Sq Ste 2800, Indianapolis IN 46204	317-636-4341	R	39*	.1
306	Strauss and Troy—*William V Strauss*	150 E 4th St, Cincinnati OH 45202	513-621-2120	R	39*	.1
307	Chamberlain Hrdlicka White Williams and Aughtry—*David Aughtry*	1200 Smith St Ste 1400, Houston TX 77002	713-658-1818	R	38*	.3

Note: An asterisk (*) indicates an estimated financial figure. The company type code used is as follows: R = Private, P = Public, S = Private Subsidiary, B = Public Subsidiary, D = Division, J = Joint Venture, I = Investment Fund.

COMPANY RANKINGS BY SALES WITHIN 4-DIGIT SIC

Rank	Company Name—Executive Officer	Address, City, State, Zip	Phone	Type	Fin	Empls
308	White and Williams LLP—George J Hartnett	1650 Market St Ste 180, Philadelphia PA 19103	215-864-7000	R	38*	.2
309	Vedder Price Kaufman and Kammholz—Michael Nemeroff	222 N LaSalle St, Chicago IL 60601	312-609-7500	R	38*	.2
310	Ryley Carlock and Applewhite PA—Rodolfo Parga Jr	1 N Central Ave Ste 12, Phoenix AZ 85004	602-258-7701	R	38*	.2
311	Ball Janik LLP—Irene Ringwood	655 15th St NW Ste 225, Washington DC 20005	202-638-3307	R	38*	.1
312	Wendel Rosen Black and Dean LLP—Howard Lind	PO Box 2047, Oakland CA 94604	510-834-6600	R	38*	.1
313	Lane and Waterman—Robert Van Vooren	220 N Main St Ste 600, Davenport IA 52801	563-324-3246	R	38*	.1
314	Rackemann Sawyer and Brewster—Thomas J Corcoran	160 Federal St Ste 415, Boston MA 02111	617-542-2300	R	37*	.1
315	Linowes and Blocher LLP—Richard M Zeidman	7200 Wisconsin Ave Ste, Bethesda MD 20814	301-654-0504	R	37*	.1
316	Riemer and Braunstein LLP—Stanley J Riemer	3 Center Plz 6th Fl, Boston MA 02108	617-523-9000	R	36*	.1
317	Jennings Strouss and Salmon PLC—John C West	201 E Washington St 11, Phoenix AZ 85004	602-262-5911	R	35*	.2
318	Cooper and Dunham LLP—Peter Murray	30 Rockefeller Plz 20t, New York NY 10112	212-278-0400	R	35*	.1
319	Crabbe Brown and James LLP—Jeffrey Brown	500 S Front St Ste 120, Columbus OH 43215	614-228-5511	R	35*	.1
320	Fisher Rushmer Werrenrath Keiner Wack and Dickson PA—Russell K Dickson	PO Box 712, Orlando FL 32802	407-843-2111	R	35*	.1
321	Allen Matkins Leck Gamble and Mallory LLP	515 S Figueroa St 9th, Los Angeles CA 90071	213-622-5555	R	34*	.2
322	Barger and Wolen—Andrew S Williams	633 W 5th St 47th Fl, Los Angeles CA 90071	213-680-2800	R	34*	.2
323	Rawle and Henderson LLP—James C Stroud	1339 Chestnut St 1 S P, Philadelphia PA 19107	215-575-4200	R	34*	.2
324	Severson and Werson Inc—James Werson	1 Embarcadero Ctr Ste, San Francisco CA 94111	415-398-3344	R	34*	.1
325	Stolar Partnership—Harvey Harris	911 Washington Ave 7th, Saint Louis MO 63101	314-231-2800	R	34*	.1
326	Fox Rothschil LLP—Paul Straub	2000 Market St, Philadelphia PA 19103	215-299-2000	R	34*	.1
327	Gust Rosenfeld	1 E Washington Ste 160, Phoenix AZ 85004	602-257-7422	R	34*	.1
328	Hurwitz and Fine—Robert Fine	1300 Liberty Bldg, Buffalo NY 14202	716-849-8900	R	34*	.1
329	Morrison Cohen LLP—David A Scherl	909 Third Ave, New York NY 10022	212-735-8600	R	34*	.1
330	Van Ness Feldman PC (Washington DC)—Willam Van Ness	1050 Thomas Jefferson, Washington DC 20007	202-298-1800	R	34*	.1
331	Pietragallo Gordon Alfano Bosick and Raspanti LLP—William Pietragallo	1 Oxford Ctr 38th Fl, Pittsburgh PA 15219	412-263-2000	R	34*	.1
332	Parker Milliken Clark O'Hara and Samuelian—Richard Robins	555 S Flower St 30th F, Los Angeles CA 90071	213-683-6500	R	34*	.1
333	McElroy Deutsch Mulvaney and Carpenter LLP—Edward B Deutsch	PO Box 2075, Morristown NJ 07962	973-993-8100	R	33*	.2
334	McNees Wallace and Nurick—Richard C Burrnett	PO Box 1166, Harrisburg PA 17108	717-232-8000	R	33*	.2
335	Sommers Schwartz Law Offices—Charles R Ash III	2000 Town Ctr Ste 900, Southfield MI 48075	248-355-0300	R	33*	.2
336	Ropers Majeski Kohn and Bentley—Richard K Wilson	1001 Marshall St Ste 3, Redwood City CA 94063	650-364-8200	R	33*	.2
337	Jones Waldo Holbrook and McDonough—Kevin P Rowe	170 S Main St Ste 1500, Salt Lake City UT 84101	801-521-3200	R	33*	.1
338	Maynard Cooper and Gale PC—Mark L Drew	1901 6th Ave N Ste 240, Birmingham AL 35203	205-254-1000	R	33*	.1
339	Carlile Patchen and Murphy—Robert Barnett Jr	366 E Broad St, Columbus OH 43215	614-228-6135	R	33*	.1
340	Kacal and FreehanPC—Jerry Kacal	675 Bering Dr, Houston TX 77057	713-529-3992	R	33*	.1
341	Lewis Rice and Fingersh LC—John K Pruellage	600 Washington Ave Ste, Saint Louis MO 63101	314-444-7600	R	32*	.3
342	Kerr Russell and Weber—Bob Russell	500 Woodward Ave Ste 2, Detroit MI 48226	313-961-0200	R	32*	.1
343	Wood Herron and Evans LLP—Greg Ahrens	441 Vine St, Cincinnati OH 45202	513-241-2324	R	32*	.1
344	Southern Poverty Law Center Inc—J Cohen	PO Box 548, Montgomery AL 36101	334-956-8200	R	32*	.1
345	Rhoads and Sinon—Charles Ferry	PO Box 1146, Harrisburg PA 17108	717-233-5731	R	31*	.1
346	Ball and Weed PC	10001 Reunion Pl Rm 60, San Antonio TX 78216	210-731-6300	R	31*	.1
347	Kominiarek Presler Harvick and Gudmundson LLC—Michael Kominiarek	33 N Dearborne St Ste, Chicago IL 60602	312-322-1111	R	31*	.1
348	Tressler Soderstrom Maloney and Priess—Daniel Formeller	233 S Wacker Dr Sears, Chicago IL 60606	312-627-4000	R	30*	.2
349	Williams and Anderson LLP—W Jackson Williams	111 Center St 22nd Fl, Little Rock AR 72201	501-372-0800	R	30*	.1
350	Buckingham Doolittle and Burroughs LLP—Nicholas T George	3800 Embassy Pkwy Ste, Akron OH 44333	330-376-5300	R	29*	.3
351	Bodman LLC—Laura A Collins	1901 Saint Antoine St, Detroit MI 48226	313-259-7777	R	29*	.2
352	Bowman and Brooke LLP—Mark V Berry	879 W 190th St Ste 700, Gardena CA 90248	310-768-3068	R	29*	.2
353	Carroll Burdick and McDonough—Doris Alexander	44 Montgomery St Ste 4, San Francisco CA 94104	415-989-5900	R	29*	.2
354	Kegler Brown Hill and Ritter Company LPA—Michelle Kondas	65 E State St Ste 1800, Columbus OH 43215	614-462-5400	R	29*	.2
355	Mastagni Holstedt and Chiurazzi—David P Mastagni	1912 I St, Sacramento CA 95811	916-446-4692	R	29*	.2
356	Procopio Cory Hargreaves and Savitch LP—James Perkins	530 B St Ste 2100, San Diego CA 92101	619-238-1900	R	29*	.2
357	Sherman and Howard LLC—R Michael Sanchez	633 17th St Ste 3000, Denver CO 80202	303-297-2900	R	29*	.2
358	Van Ness Feldman PC (Seattle Washington)—Howard J Feldman	Millenium Tower 719 Se, Seattle WA 98104	206-623-9372	R	29*	.1
359	Rose Law Firm—Steve Joiner	120 E 4th St, Little Rock AR 72201	501-375-9131	R	29*	.1
360	Boardman Suhr Curry and Field—Donna Hurd	PO Box 927, Madison WI 53701	608-257-9521	R	28*	.1
361	Casey Ciklin Lubitz Martens and O'Connell—Bruce G Alexander	515 N Flagler Dr Ste 1, West Palm Beach FL 33401	561-832-5900	R	28*	.1
362	Cochran Firm—Jock M Smith	4929 Wilshire Blvd Ste, Los Angeles CA 90010	323-931-6200	R	28*	.1
363	Gordon Feinblatt Rothman Hoffberger and Hollander LLC—Barry F Rosen	233 E Redwood St, Baltimore MD 21202	410-576-4156	R	28*	.1
364	Jacob Medinger and Finnegan LLP—Peter A Cross	1270 Ave of the Americ, New York NY 10020	212-524-5000	R	28*	.1
365	Thomas Thomas and Hafer—James K Thomas II	PO Box 999, Harrisburg PA 17108	717-237-7100	R	28*	.1
366	Gipson Hoffman and Pancione—Robert E Gipson	1901 Ave of the Stars, Los Angeles CA 90067	310-556-4660	R	28*	.1
367	John G Phillips and Associates—Stephen Phillips	161 N Clark St Ste 492, Chicago IL 60601	312-346-4262	R	28*	<.1
368	Von Briesen and Roper SC—Randall Crocker	PO Box 3262, Milwaukee WI 53202	414-276-1122	R	27*	.2
369	Downey Brand LLP	621 Capitol Mall 18th, Sacramento CA 95814	916-444-1000	R	27*	.1
370	Ater Wynne LLP Attorneys At Law—John Ater	1331 NW Lovejoy Ste 90, Portland OR 97209	503-226-1191	R	27*	.1
371	Helsell Fetterman LLP—Scott Collins	PO Box 21846, Seattle WA 98111	206-292-1144	R	27*	.1
372	Thompson Coe Cousins and Irons—Jack M Cleaveland Jr	700 N Pearl 25th Fl, Dallas TX 75201	214-871-8200	R	26*	.2
373	Snow Christensen and Martineau—David Slaughter	PO Box 45000, Salt Lake City UT 84145	801-521-9000	R	26*	.1
374	Schneider Kleinick Weitz and Damashek—Phil Damashek	233 Broadway 5th Fl, New York NY 10279	212-553-9000	R	26*	.1
375	Tripp Scott—James A Scott	110 SE 6th St 15th Fl, Fort Lauderdale FL 33301	954-525-7500	R	26*	.1
376	Discovision Associates—Dennis Fishcel	1925 E Dominguez, Long Beach CA 90810	310-952-3300	R	26*	.1
377	Law Weathers PC—John Huff	333 Bridge St NW Ste 8, Grand Rapids MI 49504	616-459-1171	R	26*	.1
378	Reminger and Reminger Company LPA—Mario C Ciano	101 Prospect Ave W Ste, Cleveland OH 44115	216-687-1311	R	25*	.3
379	Davis and Kuelthau SC—Ann Rieger	111 E Kilbourn Ave Ste, Milwaukee WI 53202	414-276-0200	R	25*	.2
380	Wright Lindsey and Jennings LLP—Edwin Lowther	200 W Capitol Ave Ste, Little Rock AR 72201	501-371-0808	R	25*	.2
381	Cavanagh Law Firm—Kerry M Griggs	1850 N Central Ave Ste, Phoenix AZ 85004	602-322-4000	R	25*	.1
382	White and Steele PC—John Craver	600 17th St Ste 600 N, Denver CO 80202	303-296-2828	R	25*	.1
383	McDowell Rice Smith and Buchanan PC—Pete Smith	605 W 47th St Ste 350, Kansas City MO 64112	816-753-5400	R	25*	.1
384	Barley Snyder LLC—Timothy Dietrich	126 E King St, Lancaster PA 17602	717-299-5201	R	25*	.1
385	Hennigan Bennett and Dorman LLP—Robert Palmer	865 S Figueroa St Rm 2, Los Angeles CA 90017	213-694-1200	R	24*	.1
386	Morris Polich and Purdy—Donald Ridge	1055 W 7th St Ste 2400, Los Angeles CA 90017	213-891-9100	R	24*	.1
387	Dean Mead Edgerton Bloodworth Capouano and Bozarth PA—Scott Wendel	800 N Magnolia Ave Ste, Orlando FL 32803	407-841-1200	R	24*	.1
388	Watanabe Ing LLP—James Ing	999 Bishop St 23rd Fl, Honolulu HI 96813	808-544-8300	R	24*	.1

Rank	Company Name—*Executive Officer*	Address, City, State, Zip	Phone	Type	Fin	Empls
389	Tompkins McGuire Wachenfeld and Barry LLP—*William B McGuire*	100 Mulberry St 4 Gate, Newark NJ 07102	973-622-3000	R	24*	.1
390	Chaffe McCall LLP—*Corrine Morrison*	2300 Energy Centre 110, New Orleans LA 70163	504-585-7000	R	23*	.2
391	Haight Brown and Bonesteel—*S Christian Stouder*	6080 Center Dr Ste 800, Los Angeles CA 90045	310-215-7100	R	23*	.2
392	McCorriston Miller Mukai MacKinnon—*William McCorriston*	PO Box 2800, Honolulu HI 96803	808-529-7300	R	23*	.1
393	Gray and Associates LLP	16345 W Glendale Dr, New Berlin WI 53151	414-224-8404	R	23*	.1
394	Orgain Bell and Tucker LLP—*Joe Ben*	470 Orleans St Ste 400, Beaumont TX 77701	409-838-6412	R	23*	.1
395	Susman Godfrey LLP—*Stephen D Susman*	1000 Louisiana St Ste, Houston TX 77002	713-651-9366	R	23*	.1
396	Law Offices of Bernard P Wolfsdorf—*Bernard Wolfsdorf*	1416 2nd St, Santa Monica CA 90401	310-570-4088	R	23*	.1
397	Bickel and Brewer—*John W Bickel II*	1717 Main St Ste 4800, Dallas TX 75201	214-653-4000	R	22*	.1
398	Smith Hulsey and Busey—*Stephen D Busey*	225 Water St Ste 1800, Jacksonville FL 32202	904-359-7700	R	22*	.1
399	Gold and Associates PA—*Mark Gold*	1580 S Federal Hwy, Fort Lauderdale FL 33316	305-858-9390	R	22*	.1
400	Kurtzman Carson Consultants LLC—*Eric S Kurtzman*	2335 Alaska Ave, El Segundo CA 90245	310-823-9000	R	22*	.1
401	Keker and Van Nest LLP—*Christopher C Kearney*	710 Sansome St, San Francisco CA 94111	415-391-5400	R	22*	.1
402	Grogan Graffam PC—*Dennis A Watson*	4 Gateway Ctr 12th Fl, Pittsburgh PA 15222	412-553-6300	R	22*	.1
403	Gordon Thomas Honeywell LLP—*William Holt*	1201 Pacific Ave Ste 2, Tacoma WA 98402	253-620-6500	R	22*	.1
404	Mariscal Weeks McIntyre and Friedlander—*Gary L Birnbaum*	2901 N Central Ste 200, Phoenix AZ 85012	602-285-5000	R	21*	.1
405	Cobb and Cole—*Ryan Kamachan*	PO Box 2491, Daytona Beach FL 32115	386-255-8171	R	21*	.1
406	Ireland Stapleton Pryor and Pascoe PC—*Libby Mosher*	1675 Broadway Ste 2600, Denver CO 80202	303-623-2700	R	21*	.1
407	Merchant and Gould PC—*Randy King*	191 Peachtree St NE St, Atlanta GA 30303	404-954-5100	R	20*	.2
408	Maslon Edelman Borman and Brand LLP—*Mary Jo Welter*	90 S 7th St, Minneapolis MN 55402	612-672-8200	R	20*	.1
409	Rhoades McKee—*Bruce W Neckers*	161 Ottawa Ave NW Ste, Grand Rapids MI 49503	616-235-3500	R	20*	.1
410	Best and Flanagan LLP—*James C Diracles*	225 S 6th St Ste 4000, Minneapolis MN 55402	612-339-7121	R	20*	.1
411	Niles Barton and Wilmer—*Matthew Kimball*	111 S Calvert St Ste 1, Baltimore MD 21202	410-783-6300	R	20*	.1
412	Lieff Cabraser Heimann and Bernstein LLP—*Robert L Lieff*	275 Battery St 29th Fl, San Francisco CA 94111	415-956-1000	R	20*	.1
413	Trenam Kemker Scharf Barkin Frye O'Neill and Mullis—*Harold Mullis Jr*	PO Box 1102, Tampa FL 33601	813-223-7474	R	19*	.1
414	Burch Porter and Johnson—*David Harris*	130 N Court Ave, Memphis TN 38103	901-524-5000	R	19	.1
415	Karr Tuttle Campbell	1201 3rd Ave Ste 2900, Seattle WA 98101	206-223-1313	R	19*	.1
416	Middleberg Riddle and Gianna—*Michael Riddle*	717 N Harwood Ste 2400, Dallas TX 75201	214-220-6300	R	19*	.1
417	Tucker Arensberg PC—*Richard Tucker III*	1500 1 PPG Pl, Pittsburgh PA 15222	412-566-1212	R	19*	.1
418	Zelle Hofmann Voelbel Mason and Gette LLP—*Mark J Feinberg*	500 Washington Ave S S, Minneapolis MN 55415	612-339-2020	R	19*	.1
419	Carr McClellan Ingersoll Thompson and Horn—*Mark A Cassanejo*	216 Park Rd, Burlingame CA 94010	650-342-9600	R	19*	.1
420	Kennedy Childs PC—*Steve Michalek*	633 17th St Ste 2200, Denver CO 80202	303-825-2700	R	19*	.1
421	Montgomery Little Soran and Murray PC—*James Soran III*	5445 DTC Pkwy Ste 800, Greenwood Village CO 80111	303-773-8100	R	19*	.1
422	Shumaker Loop and Kendrick LLP—*Gregory Alexander*	1000 Jackson St, Toledo OH 43624	419-241-9000	R	18*	.4
423	Mette Evans and Woodside—*Michael Mixell*	PO Box 5950, Harrisburg PA 17110	717-232-5000	R	18*	.1
424	Shernoff Bidart and Darras LLP—*William M Shernoff*	600 S Indian Hill Blvd, Claremont CA 91711	909-621-4935	R	18*	.1
425	McDonald Sanders PC—*Rick Sorenson*	777 Main St Ste 1300, Fort Worth TX 76102	817-336-8651	R	18*	.1
426	Lee Smart P3 Inc—*Todd S Arkley*	701 Pike St 1800 One C, Seattle WA 98101	206-624-7990	R	18*	<.1
427	McGinnis Lochridge and Kilgore LLP—*Campbell McGinnis*	600 Congress Ave Ste 2, Austin TX 70701	512-495-6000	R	17*	.2
428	Munsch Hardt Kopf Harr PC—*Glenn Callison*	500 N Akard St 3800 Li, Dallas TX 75201	214-855-7500	R	17*	.2
429	Cook and Franke SC—*Margaret Lund*	660 E Mason St, Milwaukee WI 53202	414-271-5900	R	17*	.1
430	VanCott Bagley Cornwall and McCarthy—*Steve Swindle*	36 S State St Ste 1900, Salt Lake City UT 84111	801-532-3333	R	17*	.1
431	Pellettieri Habstein and Altman—*Gary E Altman*	100 Nassau Park Blvd S, Princeton NJ 08540	609-520-0900	R	17*	.1
432	Bloom Hergott Diemer and Cook LLP—*Jake Bloom*	150 S Rodeo Dr, Beverly Hills CA 90212	310-859-6800	R	17*	.1
433	Brown Eassa and McLeod LLP—*Eugene Brown Jr*	1999 Harrison St 18th, Oakland CA 94612	510-444-3131	R	17*	.1
434	Whitfield and Eddy PLC—*Megan Antenucci*	317 6th Ave Ste 1200, Des Moines IA 50309	515-288-6041	R	17*	.1
435	Dewey and LeBoeufs—*James R Woods*	1 Montgomery St Ste 35, San Francisco CA 94104	415-951-1100	R	17*	.1
436	Rendigs Fry Kiely and Dennis LLP—*Edward R Goldman*	1 West 4th St Ste 900, Cincinnati OH 45202	513-381-9200	R	17*	.1
437	Saltzburg Ray and Bergman LLP	12121 Wilshire Blvd St, Los Angeles CA 90025	310-481-6700	R	17*	.1
438	Clark Hill PLC—*John J Hern Jr*	500 Woodward Ave Ste 3, Detroit MI 48226	313-965-8300	R	16*	.2
439	Schwabe Williamson and Wyatt—*David Bartz*	1211 SW 5th St Ste1900, Portland OR 97204	503-222-9981	R	16*	.2
440	Montgomery Barnett Brown Read Hammond and Mintz LLP—*Dan Lund*	1100 Poydras St Ste 32, New Orleans LA 70163	504-585-3200	R	16	.1
441	Otten Johnson Robinson Neff and Ragonetti—*Mike Westover*	950 17th St Ste 1600, Denver CO 80202	303-825-8400	R	16*	.1
442	Sanders and Parks PC—*Frank Parks*	3030 N Third St Rm 130, Phoenix AZ 85012	602-532-5600	R	16*	.1
443	Countess Gilbert Andrews—*Sharon Myers*	135 N George St, York PA 17401	717-848-4900	R	16*	.1
444	Bartlett Pontiff Stewart and Rhodes PC—*J Lawrence Paltrowitz*	PO Box 2168, Glens Falls NY 12801	518-792-2117	R	16*	.1
445	Kozyak Tropin and Throckmorton PA—*Harley Tropin*	2525 Ponce De Leon 9th, Coral Gables FL 33134	305-372-1800	R	16*	<.1
446	Duckor SpradlingMetzger and Wynne—*Gary Spradling*	3043 4th Ave, San Diego CA 92103	619-209-3000	R	16*	<.1
447	Burch and Cracchiolo PA	702 E Osborn Rd Ste 20, Phoenix AZ 85014	602-274-7611	R	15*	.1
448	Hill Farrer and Burrill LLP—*Arthur B Cook*	300 S Grand Ave 37th F, Los Angeles CA 90071	213-620-0460	R	15*	.1
449	Mika Meyers Beckett and Jones PLC—*Claude Vanderploeg*	900 Monroe Ave NW, Grand Rapids MI 49503	616-632-8000	R	15*	.1
450	Nisen and Elliott LLC—*Paul Gerbosi*	200 W Adams St Ste 250, Chicago IL 60606	312-346-7800	R	15*	.1
451	Dreyer Babich Buccola and Callaham and Wood LLP—*Roger Dreyer*	20 Bicentennial Cir, Sacramento CA 95826	916-379-3500	R	15*	.1
452	Beus Gilbert PLLC—*Leo Beus*	4800 N Scottsdale Rd S, Scottsdale AZ 85251	480-429-3000	R	14*	.1
453	Torkildson Katz MooreHetherington and Harris—*Robert Katz*	700 Bishop St 15th Fl, Honolulu HI 96813	808-523-6000	R	14*	.1
454	Sheehy Ware And Pappas PC—*Richard Sheehy*	909 Fannin St Ste 2500, Houston TX 77010	713-951-1000	R	14*	.1
455	DeCotiis Fitzpatrick and Cole LLP—*Joseph DeCotiis*	500 Frank W Burr Blvd, Teaneck NJ 07666	201-928-1100	R	14*	.1
456	Hartman Underhill and Brubaker—*Alexander Henderson*	221 E Chestnut St, Lancaster PA 17602	717-299-7254	R	14*	.1
457	Cummins and White LLP—*James Wakefield*	2424 SE Bristol St Ste, Newport Beach CA 92660	949-852-1800	R	14*	.1
458	Goldberg Katzman and Shipman PC	PO Box 1268, Harrisburg PA 17108	717-234-4161	R	14*	.1
459	Long and Levit LLP—*Joseph McMonigle*	465 California St 5th, San Francisco CA 94104	415-397-2222	R	14*	.1
460	Meltzer Lippe Goldstein and Breitstone LLP—*Lewis S Meltzer*	190 Willis Ave, Mineola NY 11501	516-747-0300	R	14*	.1
461	Stein and Lubin LLP—*Robert S Stein*	600 Montgomery St 14th, San Francisco CA 94111	415-981-0550	R	14*	.1
462	Di Renzo and Bomier—*Robert C Di Renzo*	PO Box 788, Neenah WI 54957	920-725-8464	R	14*	<.1
463	Higgs Fletcher and Mack LLP—*John Morrell*	401 W A St Ste 2600, San Diego CA 92101	619-236-1551	R	13*	.1
464	Garvey Schubert and Barer—*John K Hoerster*	1191 2nd Ave 18th Fl, Seattle WA 98101	206-464-3939	R	13*	.1
465	Meyer Darragh Buckler Bebenek and Eck PLLC—*Carl A Eck*	600 Grant StSte 4850, Pittsburgh PA 15219	412-261-6600	R	13*	.1
466	King and Ballow—*Frank S King*	315 Union St 1100 Unio, Nashville TN 37201	615-259-3456	R	13*	.1
467	Blakinger Byler and Thomas PC—*James H Thomas*	28 Penn Sq, Lancaster PA 17603	717-299-1100	R	13*	.1
468	Barber McCaskill Jones and Hale PA—*Glenn Jones*	400 W Capital Ste 2700, Little Rock AR 72201	501-372-6175	R	13*	.1
469	Price Heneveld Cooper DeWitt and Litton—*Randy Litton*	PO Box 2567, Grand Rapids MI 49501	616-949-9610	R	13*	.1
470	Shigemura and Harakal—*Gary Y Shigemura*	745 Fort St Ste 700, Honolulu HI 96813	808-531-9711	R	13*	<.1
471	Urish Popeck and Company LLC—*Brian Deutch*	401 Liberty Ave Ste 24, Pittsburgh PA 15222	412-391-1994	R	13*	<.1
472	Ford Nassen and Baldwin PC—*John Nassen*	8080 North Central Exp, Dallas TX 75206	214-523-5100	R	13*	<.1

Note: An asterisk (*) indicates an estimated financial figure. The company type code used is as follows: R = Private, P = Public, S = Private Subsidiary, B = Public Subsidiary, D = Division, J = Joint Venture, I = Investment Fund.

COMPANY RANKINGS BY SALES WITHIN 4-DIGIT SIC

Rank	Company Name—*Executive Officer*	Address, City, State, Zip	Phone	Type	Fin	Empls
473	McDonald Toole and Wiggins PA—*Michael J Wiggins*	485 N Keller Rd Ste 40, Orlando FL 32810	407-246-1800	R	13*	<.1
474	Hawkins Parnell Thackston and Young LLP—*Albert H Parnell*	4000 SunTrust Plz 303, Atlanta GA 30308	404-614-7400	R	12*	.1
475	Danning Gill Diamond and Kollitz LLP—*Richard Diamond*	2029 Century Park E 3r, Los Angeles CA 90067	310-277-0077	R	12*	.1
476	Trainor Fairbrook—*Candice B Harper*	980 Fulton Ave, Sacramento CA 95825	916-929-7000	R	12*	.1
477	Cooper Erving and Savage LLP—*Terrance P Christenson*	39 N Pearl St, Albany NY 12207	518-618-4082	R	12*	.1
478	Baach Robinson and Lewis PLLC—*Martin R Baach*	1201 F St NW Ste 500, Washington DC 20004	202-833-8900	R	12*	<.1
479	Decker Jones McMackin McClane Hall and Bates PC—*Charles Milliken*	801 Cherry St Ste 2000, Fort Worth TX 76102		R	12*	<.1
480	Warner Smith and Harris PLC—*Douglas O Smith Jr*	PO Box 1626, Fort Smith AR 72902	479-782-6041	R	12*	<.1
481	Davis Cowell and Bowe—*Barry Jellison*	595 Market St Ste 1400, San Francisco CA 94105	415-597-7200	R	12*	<.1
482	General Code LLC—*Gary Domenico*	781 Elmgrove Rd, Rochester NY 14624	585-328-1810	R	11*	.1
483	Burnham and Brown—*John Verber*	PO Box 119, Oakland CA 94604	510-444-6800	R	11*	.1
484	Keller Rohrback LLP—*Lynn Levin*	1201 3rd AveSte 3200, Seattle WA 98101	206-623-1900	R	11*	.1
485	Axley Brynelson LLP—*Michael Anderson*	PO Box 1767, Madison WI 53701	608-257-5661	R	11*	.1
486	Gordon Arata McCollam Duplantis Eagan LLP—*Tim Eagan*	201 St Charles Ave Ste, New Orleans LA 70170	504-582-1111	R	11*	.1
487	Williams Montgomery and John Ltd—*Lloyd E Williams Jr*	233 S Wacker Dr Ste 61, Chicago IL 60606	312-443-3200	R	11*	<.1
488	Cohen and Wolf PC—*Austin K Wolf*	1115 Broad St, Bridgeport CT 06604	203-368-0211	R	11*	<.1
489	Law Snakard and Gambill PC—*Jay Garrett*	1600 W 7th St Ste 500, Fort Worth TX 76102	817-335-7373	R	11*	<.1
490	Rosenfeld Meyer and Susman LLP—*Michael E Meyer*	9601 Wilshire Blvd Ste, Beverly Hills CA 90210	310-858-7700	R	11*	<.1
491	Legal Research Center Inc—*Christopher Ljungkull*	310 4th Ave S Ste 1100, Minneapolis MN 55415		P	11*	<.1
492	Ramey and Kampf PA—*Mark Ramey*	400 North Ashley St St, Tampa FL 33602	813-241-0123	R	11*	<.1
493	Roach Brown McCarthy and Gruver—*Daniel T Roach*	424 Main St Rm 1620, Buffalo NY 14203	716-852-0400	R	11*	<.1
494	James Hoyer and Newcomer PA—*John Newcomer*	4830 W Kennedy Blvd #5, Tampa FL 33609	813-397-2300	R	10*	<.1
495	Appel and Yost—*Harry Yost*	33 N Duke St, Lancaster PA 17602	717-394-0521	R	10*	<.1
496	Angino and Rovner—*Richard Angino*	4503 N Front St, Harrisburg PA 17110	717-238-6791	R	10*	<.1
497	Springer Bush and Perry	500 Cherrington Pkwy S, Coraopolis PA 15108	412-281-4200	R	10*	<.1
498	Finz and Finz PC—*Stuart L Finz*	100 Jericho Quadrangle, Jericho NY 11753	516-433-3000	R	10*	<.1
499	Magavern Magavern and Grimm LLP—*William J Magavern II*	1100 Rand Bldg 14 Lafa, Buffalo NY 14203	716-856-3500	R	10*	<.1
500	Rosenthal Siegel Muenkel and Maloney LLP—*Jay Rosenthal*	300 Main St, Buffalo NY 14202	716-854-1300	R	10*	<.1
501	Hill Gilstrap PC—*Frank Hill*	1400 W Abram St, Arlington TX 76013	817-261-2222	R	10*	<.1
502	Smith Murphy and Schoepperle LLP—*Dennis P Mescall*	295 Main St Ste 786, Buffalo NY 14203	716-852-1544	R	10*	<.1
503	Disability Group Inc—*Ronald Miller*	6033 W Century Blvd, Los Angeles CA 90045		R	9	.1
504	Moser and Marsalek PC—*David Zwart*	200 N Broadway Ste 700, Saint Louis MO 63102	314-282-2625	R	9*	.1
505	Pearl Law Group—*Julie Pearl*	315 Montgomery St Ste, San Francisco CA 94104	415-771-7500	R	9*	<.1
506	Tobin and Tobin John H Hall Esq—*Molly Barton*	500 Sansome St, San Francisco CA 94111	415-433-1400	R	9*	<.1
507	Dover Dixon Horne PLLC—*Darrell D Dover*	425 W Capitol Fl 37, Little Rock AR 72201	501-375-9151	R	9*	<.1
508	Lippes Mathias Wexler Friedman LLP—*William Mathias*	665 Main St Ste 300, Buffalo NY 14203	716-853-5100	R	9*	<.1
509	Quirk and Quirk—*Martin Quirk*	6000 Lake Forrest Dr N, Atlanta GA 30328	404-252-1425	R	9*	<.1
510	Brown and Ruprecht	911 Main St Ste 2300, Kansas City MO 64105	816-292-7000	R	9*	<.1
511	Cohen and Lombardo—*Richard Blewett*	343 Elmwood Ave, Buffalo NY 14222	716-881-3010	R	8*	<.1
512	Jack Lyon and Jones PA—*Donald Jack*	2800 Cantrell Rd Ste 5, Little Rock AR 72202	501-375-1122	R	8*	<.1
513	Bassett Law Firm—*Woodson Bassett III*	PO Box 3618, Fayetteville AR 72702	479-521-9996	R	8*	<.1
514	Dunwody White and Landon PA—*Robert DW Landon II*	550 Biltmore Way Ste81, Coral Gables FL 33134	305-529-1500	R	8*	<.1
515	Jones Gregg Creehan and Gerace LLP—*John P Corcoran Jr*	411 7th Ave Ste 1200, Pittsburgh PA 15219	412-261-6400	R	8*	<.1
516	Black Helterline—*Robert Donaldson*	805 SW Broadway Ste 19, Portland OR 97205	503-224-5560	R	8*	<.1
517	Fisher Boyd Brown and Huguenard LLP—*Jim Huguenard*	2777 Allen Pky 14th Fl, Houston TX 77019	713-400-4000	R	8*	<.1
518	Amigone Sanchez and Mattrey LLP—*Vincent J Sanchez*	350 Main St, Buffalo NY 14202	716-852-1300	R	8*	<.1
519	Galland Kharasch Greenberg Fellman and Swirsky PC—*Keith G Swirsky*	1054 31st St NW Canal, Washington DC 20007	202-342-5200	R	8*	<.1
520	Osborn Maledon PA—*Scott Rodgers*	2929 N Central Ave 21s, Phoenix AZ 85012	602-640-9000	R	7*	.1
521	Pryor Johnson Montoya Carney and Karr PC—*Peter Pryor*	5619 DTC Pwy, Greenwood Village CO 80111	303-773-3500	R	7*	<.1
522	Hefner Stark and Marois—*Mike Cook*	2150 River Plz Dr Ste, Sacramento CA 95833	916-925-6620	R	7*	<.1
523	Bridges Young Matthews and Drake PLC—*Steve Matthews*	PO Box 7808, Pine Bluff AR 71611	870-534-5532	R	7*	<.1
524	Laser Law Firm—*Sam Laser*	101 S Spring St Ste 30, Little Rock AR 72201	501-376-2981	R	7*	<.1
525	Lukas Nace Gutierrez and Sachs—*David Nace*	8300 Greensboro Dr Ste, Mc Lean VA 22102	703-584-8678	R	7*	<.1
526	Haas LewisDifiorey and Amos—*Raymond Haas*	PO Box 1700, Tampa FL 33634	813-253-5333	R	7*	<.1
527	Brooks Tom Quitiquit and Cheewatts—*Robert Brooks*	841 Bishop St Ste 2125, Honolulu HI 96813	808-526-3011	R	7*	<.1
528	Bochetto and Lentz PC—*Gavin Lentz*	1524 Locust St, Philadelphia PA 19102	215-735-3900	R	7*	<.1
529	Epstein Tabor and Schorr—*Bruce Schorr*	650 Smithfield St Ste, Pittsburgh PA 15222	412-261-2245	R	7*	<.1
530	The Margolis Law Firm—*Martin G Margolis*	5 Becker Farm Rd 4th F, Roseland NJ 07068	973-239-3000	R	7*	<.1
531	Legal Aid Bureau Of Buffalo Inc—*David Schopp*	237 Main St Ste 1602, Buffalo NY 14203	716-853-9555	R	6*	.1
532	Arnzen Wentz Molloy Laber and Storm PSC—*Mark Arnzen*	600 Greenup St, Covington KY 41011	859-431-6100	R	6*	<.1
533	Elias Matz Tiernan and Herrick LLP—*Timothy Matz*	734 15th St NW 11th Fl, Washington DC 20005	202-347-0300	R	6*	<.1
534	Sidney D Torres III Law Offices—*Sidney D Torres III*	8301 W Judge Perez Dr, Chalmette LA 70043	504-271-8422	R	6*	<.1
535	Bolling Walter and Gawthrop—*Michael Keby*	PO Box 255200, Sacramento CA 95865	916-369-0777	R	6*	<.1
536	Kilgore and Kilgore PLLC—*Theodore Anderson*	3109 Carlisle St, Dallas TX 75204	214-969-9099	R	6*	<.1
537	Kline Keppel and Koryak PC—*Criag A Koryak*	425 6th Ave Ste250, Pittsburgh PA 15219	412-281-1901	R	6*	<.1
538	Muller Muller Richmond Harms and Myers PC—*John Muller*	PO Box 3026, Birmingham MI 48012	248-645-2440	R	6*	.1
539	Waldman Inc—*Hal K Waldman*	1326 Freeport Rd Ste 1, Pittsburgh PA 15238	412-338-1000	R	5*	.3
540	Guaranteed Subpoena Service Inc—*Philip Geron*	PO Box 2248, Union NJ 07083	908-687-0056	R	5*	.1
541	Schwartz Manes and Ruby—*Dennis Manes*	2900 Carew Tower 441 V, Cincinnati OH 45202	513-579-1414	R	5*	<.1
542	Hollyer Brady Smith and Hines LLP—*A Rene Hollyer*	60 E 42nd St Ste 1825, New York NY 10165	212-706-0248	R	5*	<.1
543	Kesler and Rust—*Joseph Rust*	McIntyre Bldg 2nd Floo, Salt Lake City UT 84101	801-532-8000	R	5*	<.1
544	Shrager Spivey and Sachs—*Wayne Spivey*	2005 Market St Ste 230, Philadelphia PA 19103		R	5*	<.1
545	Tsukazaki Yeh and Moore—*Thomas Yeh*	85 W Lanikaula St, Hilo HI 96720	808-961-0055	R	5*	<.1
546	Leason Ellis LLP—*Peter Sloane*	One Barker Ave 5th Fl, White Plains NY 10601		R	5*	<.1
547	Spray Gould and Bowers LLP—*Robert Dean*	15139 Woodlawn Ave, Tustin CA 92780	714-258-1550	R	5*	<.1
548	Tolbert Beadle and Musgrave LLC—*Terry Tolbert*	3010 E Battlefield Rd, Springfield MO 65804	417-887-3010	R	5*	<.1
549	Axiom Legal—*Mark Harris*	75 Spring St 8th Fl, New York NY 10012	917-237-2900	R	4*	.2
550	Lamm Rubenstone Totaro and David LLC—*Anthonay Lamb*	3600 Horizon Blvd Ste, Feasterville Trevose PA 19053	215-638-9330	R	4*	<.1
551	Silver Freedman and Taff LLP—*Sidney J Silver*	3299 K St NW Ste 100, Washington DC 20007	202-295-4500	R	4*	<.1
552	Dunn Nutter and Morgan LLP—*Winford L Dunn Jr*	3601 Richmond Rd, Texarkana TX 75503	903-793-5651	R	4*	<.1
553	Gillin Jacobson Ellis and Larsen—*Andrew Gillin*	2 Theatre Sq Ste 230, Orinda CA 94563	925-253-5800	R	4*	<.1
554	MPEG LA—*Lawrence A Horn*	6312 S Fiddlers Green, Greenwood Village CO 80111	303-331-1880	R	4*	<.1
555	Authors Registry Inc—*Letty Cottin Pogrebin*	31 E 23rd St 7th Fl, New York NY 10016	212-563-6920	R	4*	<.1
556	Gwilliam Ivary Chiosso Cavalli and Brewer—*Gary Gwilliam*	PO Box 2079, Oakland CA 94604	510-291-4888	R	4*	<.1
557	Law Offices of Pat Maloney PC—*Pat Maloney Jr*	239 E Commerce St, San Antonio TX 78205	210-226-8888	R	4*	<.1
558	Love Scherle and Bauer—*Thomas J Love*	310 Grant St Ste 1020, Pittsburgh PA 15219	412-281-8270	R	4*	<.1
559	Deutch and Weiss—*Alan Deutch*	7670 N Port Washington, Glendale WI 53217	414-247-9958	R	4*	<.1
560	Michael R Panter and Associates—*Michael R Panter*	30 N LaSalle St Ste 15, Chicago IL 60602	312-782-0933	R	4*	<.1

Rank	Company Name—*Executive Officer*	Address, City, State, Zip	Phone	Type	Fin	Empls
561	Miyagi Tscuchida Inc—*Melvin Miyagi*	1001 Bishop St 1200 Pa, Honolulu HI 96813	808-524-2466	R	4*	<.1
562	Dennis C Gaughan—*Dennis C Gaughan*	6161 S Park Ave, Hamburg NY 14075	716-648-8000	R	4*	<.1
563	Rochlin Settleman and Dobres PA—*Paul Rochlin*	201 N Charles St Ste 7, Baltimore MD 21201	410-539-3070	R	4*	<.1
564	Law Offices of William W Price PA—*William Price*	320 Fern St, West Palm Beach FL 33401	561-659-3212	R	4*	<.1
565	Mays Byrd and Associates—*Richard L Mays Sr*	415 Main St, Little Rock AR 72201	501-372-6303	R	4*	<.1
566	The Trademark Co—*Matthew H Swyers*	344 Maples Ave W Ste 1, Vienna VA 22180		R	3	<.1
567	Braverman and Associates—*Robert Braverman*	331 Madison Ave, New York NY 10017	212-682-2900	R	3*	<.1
568	Davis Clark ButtCarithers and Taylor PLC—*Sidney P Davis Jr*	PO Box 1688, Fayetteville AR 72702	479-521-7600	R	3*	<.1
569	Sanford Holshouser Economic Development Consulting—*Ernest C Pearson*	4141 Parklake Ave Ste, Raleigh NC 27612	919-653-7805	S	3*	<.1
570	Tamburello and Hanlon—*Anthony Tamburello*	214 Duboce Ave, San Francisco CA 94103	415-431-4500	R	3*	<.1
571	Iandiorio Teska and Coleman—*Joseph S Iandiorio*	260 Bear Hill Rd, Waltham MA 02451	781-890-5678	R	3*	<.1
572	Kershner and Moreno—*Kenneth Moreno*	3720 Holland Rd Ste 10, Virginia Beach VA 23452	757-486-1938	R	3*	<.1
573	Ruff Bond Cobb Wade and McNair LLP—*Robert Adden*	831 E Morehead St Ste, Charlotte NC 28282	704-377-1634	R	3*	<.1
574	Gale and Vallance—*Andrew Gale*	1820 W Orangewood Ave, Orange CA 92868	714-634-1414	R	3*	<.1
575	Executive Reporting Service—*Diane T Emery*	111 Second Ave NE Ste, St Petersburg FL 33701	727-823-4155	R	3*	<.1
576	King Hershey PC—*Marvin Clark*	2345 Grand Blvd Ste 21, Kansas City MO 64108	816-842-3636	R	3*	<.1
577	Carroll Guido and Groffman A LLP—*Rosemary Carroll*	1790 Broadway Fl 20, New York NY 10019	212-759-2300	R	2*	<.1
578	Cooper and Kirk PLLC	1523 New Hampshire Ave, Washington DC 20036	202-220-9600	R	2*	<.1
579	McAndrews Held and Malloy Ltd—*Jack Sauer*	500 W Madison St 34th, Chicago IL 60661	312-775-8000	R	2*	.2
580	Holahan Gumpper and Dowling—*Edward Holahan Jr*	PO Box 320177, Fairfield CT 06825	203-384-1385	R	2*	<.1
581	American Patent and Trademark Law Center—*Donn K Harms*	12702 Via Cortina Ste, Del Mar CA 92014	858-509-1400	R	2*	<.1
582	Pelletreau and Pelletreau—*Brian T Egan*	475 E Main St Ste 114, Patchogue NY 11772	631-447-8100	R	2*	<.1
583	John T Fields and Associates LLC—*John T Fields*	15700 W Bluemound Rd, Brookfield WI 53005	262-782-8322	R	2*	<.1
584	Kenoff and Machtinger LLP—*Jay Kenoff*	1801 Century Park E St, Los Angeles CA 90067	310-552-0808	R	2*	<.1
585	Lamson and Cutner PC—*David A Cutner*	9 E 40th St, New York NY 10016	212-759-1818	R	2*	<.1
586	Legal Club of America Corp—*Brett Merl*	7771 W Oakland Park Bl, Sunrise FL 33351	954-377-0222	R	2	<.1
587	Smythe Masterson and Judd Inc—*Mark Henley*	551 Madison Ave Fl 17, New York NY 10022	212-286-0003	R	2*	<.1
588	William E Gottfred	979 N Main St, Rockford IL 61103	815-968-8851	R	1*	<.1
589	Querrey and Harrow Ltd—*Michael B Stillman*	175 W Jackson Blvd Ste, Chicago IL 60604	312-540-7000	R	1*	.3
590	Swanson Midgley LLC—*Daniel V Hiatt*	4600 Madison Ave Ste 1, Kansas City MO 64112	816-842-6100	R	1	<.1
591	Hanna and Morton LLP—*Ed Renwick*	444 S Flower St Ste 15, Los Angeles CA 90071	213-628-7131	R	1*	<.1
592	Hughes Law LLC—*Tommy Hughes*	PO Box 1610, Albuquerque NM 87103	505-842-6700	R	1*	<.1
593	Russin and Vecchi LLP—*J Frederick Berg*	260 Madison Avenue FL1, New York NY 10106	212-279-3500	R	1*	<.1
594	Sheldon Miller and Associates—*Sheldon L Miller*	31731 Northwestern Hwy, Farmington MI 48334	248-538-3400	R	1*	<.1
595	Kathleen D Crane A Law Corp—*Kathleen D Crane*	21535 Hawthorne Blvd S, Torrance CA 90503	310-540-9111	R	1*	<.1
596	Law Offices of George G Braunstein Co—*George Braunstein*	11755 Wilshire Blvd St, Los Angeles CA 90025	310-914-4999	R	1*	<.1
597	Andrew D Woll Law Office—*Andrew D Woll*	550 Main St Ste B1B, Placerville CA 95667	530-626-7654	R	1*	<.1
598	Clearance Unlimited Inc—*Suzy Vaughan*	6848 Firmament Ave, Van Nuys CA 91406	818-988-5599	R	1*	<.1
599	Richard Henshaw Group—*Richard Henshaw*	22 West 23rd St 5th Fl, New York NY 10010	212-414-1172	R	1*	<.1
600	Vinson and Elkins LLP—*Marie Yates*	First City Twr 1001 Fa, Houston TX 77002	713-758-2222	R	N/A	1.6
601	Schuyler Roche and Zwirner PC—*Richard Michaels*	130 E Randolph St Ste, Chicago IL 60601	312-565-2400	R	N/A	.1
602	McKenna Storer Rowe White and Farrug—*Samuel A Purves*	33 N La Salle St Ste 1, Chicago IL 60602	312-558-3900	R	N/A	<.1
603	Lofton and Jennings—*William Lofton*	225 Bush St Ste 16, San Francisco CA 94105	415-772-1900	R	N/A	N/A

TOTALS: SIC 8111 Legal Services
Companies: 603

					64,520	232.5

8211 Elementary & Secondary Schools

Rank	Company Name—*Executive Officer*	Address, City, State, Zip	Phone	Type	Fin	Empls
1	Nobel Learning Communities Inc—*George H Bernstein*	1615 W Chester Pike St, West Chester PA 19382	484-947-2000	P	232	4.7
2	Dayton Board Of Education—*Sharen Thornton*	115 S Ludlow St, Dayton OH 45402	937-461-3000	R	180*	3.5
3	Merion Lower School District Inc—*Victor Fedeli*	301 E Montgomery Ave, Ardmore PA 19003	610-645-1800	R	180*	1.6
4	School District Of Indian River County—*Larry Harrah*	1990 25th St, Vero Beach FL 32960	772-564-3000	R	180*	2.0
5	Palm Springs Unified School Dist—*John Biggie*	980 E Tahquitz Canyon, Palm Springs CA 92262	760-416-8000	R	179*	2.4
6	Elkhart Community Schools Building Corp	2720 California Rd, Elkhart IN 46514	574-262-5563	R	178*	1.7
7	Davenport Community School District—*Scott Martin*	1606 Brady St Ste 100, Davenport IA 52803	563-336-5000	R	177*	2.5
8	Sachem Central School District At Holbrook—*Stephen Shadbolt*	245 Union Ave, Holbrook NY 11741	631-471-1300	R	177*	2.5
9	Board Of Education Of Carroll County—*Nancy Codner*	125 N Ct St Ste 101, Westminster MD 21157	410-751-3000	R	177*	2.5
10	Hampton City School District—*Tom Sawyer*	1 Franklin St Fl 2, Hampton VA 23669	757-728-5142	R	176*	3.0
11	School District 5 Of Lexington and Richland Counties—*Brenda Ellisor*	1020 Dutch Fork Rd, Irmo SC 29063	803-476-8000	R	176*	2.5
12	Allen Independent School District—*Greg Suttle*	PO Box 13, Allen TX 75013	972-727-0510	R	176*	1.7
13	Weslaco Independent School District—*Arnoldo Canche*	PO Box 266, Weslaco TX 78599	956-969-6500	R	175*	2.0
14	Appleton Area School District—*Sue Martin*	PO Box 2019, Appleton WI 54912	920-832-6161	R	174*	1.4
15	Edmond Public Schools—*Cordell Ehrich*	1001 W Danforth Rd, Edmond OK 73003	405-340-2800	R	174*	2.3
16	Bridgeport City School District—*Arnold Barnes*	45 Lyon Ter, Bridgeport CT 06604	203-576-7302	R	174*	2.3
17	Board Of Education Of The City Of Trenton—*Everett Collins*	108 N Clinton Ave, Trenton NJ 08609	609-656-4900	R	173*	2.4
18	Green Bay Area Public Schools—*Jean Marsch*	PO Box 23387, Green Bay WI 54305	920-448-2101	R	173*	2.6
19	Renton School District 403—*Alice Heuschel*	300 Sw 7th St, Renton WA 98057	425-204-2340	R	173*	1.5
20	Independent School District 281—*Judy Lund*	4148 Winnetka Ave N, Minneapolis MN 55427	763-504-8000	R	172*	1.7
21	Leon County School District—*Diane Johnson*	2757 W Pensacola St, Tallahassee FL 32304	850-487-7100	R	172*	4.0
22	Reorganized School District No 4 Of Jackson County Mo—*Tanya Bomar*	1801 Nw Vesper St, Blue Springs MO 64015	816-224-1300	R	171*	1.7
23	Harnett County Board Of Education—*John Biratch*	PO Box 1029, Lillington NC 27546	910-893-8151	R	171*	2.1
24	Pennsbury School District—*Paul Long*	PO Box 338, Levittown PA 19058	215-428-4100	R	170*	2.0
25	Harlingen Consolidated Independent School District—*Joel Cruz*	1409 E Harrison Ave, Harlingen TX 78550	956-427-3400	R	169*	2.4
26	Lynwood Unified School District—*Michael Lett*	11321 Bullis Rd, Lynwood CA 90262	310-886-1600	R	169*	1.7
27	Hartford School District—*Wilda Torres*	960 Main St Fl 9, Hartford CT 06103	860-695-8400	R	169*	2.8
28	Waco Independent School District—*Craig Finley*	PO Box 27, Waco TX 76703	254-752-8341	R	168*	3.0
29	Saint Johns County School Board—*Rosalind Lundell*	40 Orange St, Saint Augustine FL 32084	904-547-7500	R	168*	2.5
30	Rock Hill School District 3—*Brian Vaughn*	PO Box 10072, Rock Hill SC 29731	803-981-1000	R	167*	1.8
31	Pocono Mountain School District—*Butch Pisko*	PO Box 200, Swiftwater PA 18370	570-839-7121	R	167*	1.5
32	Clarke County School District—*Cathy Benson*	PO Box 1708, Athens GA 30603	706-546-7721	R	166*	1.9
33	Warwick Public Schools—*David Laplante*	34 Warwick Lake Ave, Warwick RI 02889	401-734-3000	R	165*	2.4
34	Millard Public Schools—*Victoria Hoskovec*	5606 S 147th St, Omaha NE 68137	402-715-8200	R	165*	2.5
35	ABC Unified School District—*Celia Spitzer*	16700 Norwalk Blvd, Cerritos CA 90703	562-926-5566	R	165*	2.3
36	Pearland Independent School District—*David Holland*	PO Box 7, Pearland TX 77588	281-485-3203	R	164*	1.2
37	Nashau School District	PO Box 687, Nashua NH 03061	603-966-1000	R	162*	2.0
38	Park Hill School District—*Jim Rich*	7703 Nw Barry Rd, Kansas City MO 64153	816-359-4040	R	162*	1.5

Note: An asterisk (*) indicates an estimated financial figure. The company type code used is as follows: R = Private, P = Public, S = Private Subsidiary, B = Public Subsidiary, D = Division, J = Joint Venture, I = Investment Fund.

COMPANY RANKINGS BY SALES WITHIN 4-DIGIT SIC

Rank	Company Name—*Executive Officer*	Address, City, State, Zip	Phone	Type	Fin	Empls
39	Lafourche Parish School Board Inc—*Floyd Benoit*	PO Box 879, Thibodaux LA 70302	985-446-5631	R	161*	2.2
40	Topeka Unified School District 501—*Larry Ribbons*	624 Sw 24th St, Topeka KS 66611	785-295-3082	R	160*	3.2
41	Roanoke County Public Schools	5937 Cove Rd, Roanoke VA 24019	540-562-3700	R	160*	N/A
42	Commack Union Free School District 10—*Brenda Lentsch*	PO Box 150, Commack NY 11725	631-912-2000	R	159*	1.5
43	Oceanside Unified School District—*Mike Valles*	2111 Mission Ave, Oceanside CA 92058	760-966-4000	R	158*	2.2
44	Rankin County School District—*Pam Hopkins*	1220 Apple Park Pl, Brandon MS 39042	601-825-5590	R	158*	2.2
45	Board Of Education City Of Paterson—*Micheal Maglio*	90 Delaware Ave, Paterson NJ 07503	973-881-6000	R	157*	3.1
46	Wilson County Board Of Education—*Mitch Fox*	351 Stumpy Ln, Lebanon TN 37090	615-444-3282	R	156*	2.5
47	Ventura Unified School District—*Dave Marshall*	255 W Stanley Ave Ste, Ventura CA 93001	805-641-5000	R	156*	2.0
48	Reading School District—*William Knowles*	800 Washington St, Reading PA 19601	610-371-5611	R	156*	1.9
49	Upper Darby School District—*Patrick Grant*	4611 Bond Ave, Drexel Hill PA 19026	610-789-7200	R	155*	1.5
50	Catawba County Board Of Education—*Joyce Spencer*	PO Box 1010, Newton NC 28658	828-464-8333	R	154*	2.2
51	Gary Community School Corp—*Erma Patton*	620 E 10th Pl, Gary IN 46402	219-886-6400	R	153*	3.3
52	Independent School District 833—*Laurel Dalluhn*	7362 E Point Douglas R, Cottage Grove MN 55016	651-458-6300	R	153*	2.5
53	Portsmouth City School Board—*Elizabeth Hudgins*	801 Crawford St Fl 3, Portsmouth VA 23704	757-393-8751	R	153*	3.0
54	Dougherty County School System—*David Maschke*	PO Box 1470, Albany GA 31702	229-431-1285	R	152*	2.5
55	Livingston Parish School District—*Keith Martin*	PO Box 1130, Livingston LA 70754	225-686-7044	R	152*	2.4
56	Thurston North Public Schools—*Cindi Carey*	305 College St Ne, Lacey WA 98516	360-412-4400	R	152*	1.4
57	Kyrene School District 28—*David Wheeler*	8700 S Kyrene Rd, Tempe AZ 85284	480-783-4000	R	151*	2.0
58	County Of Santa Rosa Board Of Public Instruction—*Marlyn Brown*	5086 Canal St, Milton FL 32570	850-983-5018	R	150*	2.2
59	Davidson County Board Of Education—*Wynn Conrad*	PO Box 2057, Lexington NC 27293	336-249-8181	R	150*	2.5
60	Boone County Board Of Education—*Todd Obanion*	8330 Us Hwy 42, Florence KY 41042	859-283-1003	R	150*	1.9
61	Nash-Rocky Mount Schools—*Susan Blackwell*	930 Eastern Ave, Nashville NC 27856	252-459-5220	R	149*	2.7
62	Roman Catholic Diocese Of Paterson—*Arthur Serratelli*	777 Valley Rd, Clifton NJ 07013	973-777-8818	R	149*	2.0
63	Vallejo City Unified School District—*Becky Oraboni*	665 Walnut Ave, Vallejo CA 94592	707-556-8921	R	149*	2.0
64	Bartow County Board Of Education—*Dan Knowles*	PO Box 200007, Cartersville GA 30120	770-606-5800	R	147*	1.9
65	Independent School District No 271	1350 W 106th St, Minneapolis MN 55431	952-681-6400	R	147*	N/A
66	Pueblo School District No 60—*Casey Mahon*	315 W 11th St, Pueblo CO 81003	719-253-6025	R	146*	2.5
67	Clover Park School District 400—*Linda Gallagher*	10903 Gravelly Lake Dr, Lakewood WA 98499	253-583-5000	R	146*	1.1
68	Niagara Falls City School District—*Robert Keveangin*	630 66th St, Niagara Falls NY 14304	716-286-4205	R	145*	1.2
69	Sunnyside Unified School District 12—*Richard Oros*	2238 E Ginter Rd, Tucson AZ 85706	520-545-2024	R	145*	1.7
70	Racine Unified School District—*Glenn Scheuffner*	2220 Northwestern Ave, Racine WI 53404	262-635-5600	R	144*	2.5
71	Eastern Los Angeles Regional Center	PO Box 7916, Alhambra CA 91802	626-299-4700	R		N/A
72	San Bernardino County School District—*Carollyn Alvino*	601 N E St, San Bernardino CA 92415	909-386-2417	R	144*	1.7
73	Eastern Los Angeles Regional C	10946 Groveland Ave, Whittier CA 90603	562-947-5876	R	144*	N/A
74	Antioch Unified School District—*Sheri Gamba*	510 G St, Antioch CA 94509	925-706-4100	R	144*	1.8
75	Downingtown Area School District—*Lee Snodgrass*	126 Wallace Ave, Downingtown PA 19335	610-269-8460	R	144*	1.3
76	Wayne Board Of Education—*Tim Carlin*	50 Nellis Dr, Wayne NJ 07470	973-633-3000	R	144*	2.0
77	Cartwright School District 83—*Michaco Martinez*	3401 N 67th Ave, Phoenix AZ 85033	623-691-4100	R	144*	1.9
78	Eagle Pass Independent School District—*Cecilia Garza*	1420 Eidson Rd, Eagle Pass TX 78852	830-773-5181	R	144*	2.5
79	Kenai Peninsula Borough School District—*Doris Cannon*	PO Box 409, Seward AK 99664	907-714-8888	R	143*	1.3
80	Franklin Township Public School District Of Somerset—*John Roberts*	1755 Amwell Rd, Somerset NJ 08873	732-873-2400	R	143*	1.0
81	Bryan Independent School District—*Sandra Davis*	101 N Texas Ave, Bryan TX 77803	979-209-1000	R	143*	2.1
82	Campbell County School District 1—*Andy Mravlja*	PO Box 3033, Gillette WY 82717	307-682-5171	R	143*	1.4
83	Chaffey Joint Union High School District—*Bill Brod*	211 W 5th St, Ontario CA 91762	909-988-8511	R	143*	1.9
84	Lawton Public School District I-008—*Patti Cargill*	PO Box 1009, Lawton OK 73502	580-357-6900	R	142*	2.2
85	Highland Park Independent School District—*Emily Bowers*	7015 Westchester Dr, Dallas TX 75205	214-780-3000	R	142*	.7
86	Bridgewater Raritan Board Of Education—*Patti Wilson*	PO Box 6030, Bridgewater NJ 08807	908-685-2777	R	142*	1.2
87	Metropolitan School District Wayne Township—*Lisa Baize*	1220 S High School Rd, Indianapolis IN 46241	317-243-8251	R	141*	2.2
88	Waterford School District—*Randy Portwood*	1150 Scott Lake Rd, Waterford MI 48328	248-682-7800	R	141*	1.9
89	Citrus County School District—*John Colasanti*	1007 W Main St, Inverness FL 34450	352-726-1931	R	141*	2.1
90	East Stroudsburg Area School District—*Marie Goodry*	PO Box 298, East Stroudsburg PA 18301	570-424-8500	R	141*	1.2
91	Paramount Unified School District—*Cynthia Ditaola*	15110 California Ave, Paramount CA 90723	562-602-6000	R	140*	1.8
92	La Mesa-Spring Valley School District—*Chris Benker*	4750 Date Ave, La Mesa CA 91942	619-668-5700	R	140*	1.8
93	Fauquier County Public Schools—*Greg Livesay*	320 Hospital Dr Ste 40, Warrenton VA 20186	540-351-1000	R	140*	1.7
94	Inglewood Unified School District—*Carren Newton*	401 S Inglewood Ave, Inglewood CA 90301	310-419-2700	R	140*	1.6
95	Industry School Dist 621	350 Hwy 96 W, Saint Paul MN 55126	651-621-6000	R	140*	1.5
96	Community Unit School District 220—*Tom Campagna*	310 James St, Barrington IL 60010	847-381-6300	R	140*	1.1
97	Eagle Mountain-Saginaw Independent School District—*Lucia Campuzano*	1200 Old Decatur Rd, Fort Worth TX 76179	817-232-0880	R	140*	.1
98	National Heritage Academies Inc—*Jeff Clark*	3850 Broadmoor Ave SE, Grand Rapids MI 49512		R	125*	1.2
99	Mosaica Education Inc—*Michael J Connelly*	42 Broadway Ste 1039, New York NY 10004	404-841-2305	R	84*	1.2
100	Leona Group LLC—*William Coats*	4660 S Hagadorn Rd Ste, East Lansing MI 48823	517-333-9030	R	40*	1.2
101	United Cerebral Palsy Of Queens Inc—*Charles Houston*	8115 164th St, Jamaica NY 11432	718-380-3000	R	34*	.6
102	Julia Dyckman Andrus Memorial Inc—*Nancy Ment*	1156 N Broadway, Yonkers NY 10701	914-965-3700	R	27*	.3
103	St Coletta's Of Illinois Inc—*Wayne Kottmeyer*	18350 Crossing Dr, Tinley Park IL 60487	708-342-5200	R	15*	.3
104	Pikes Peak Boces—*Dave Thompson*	4825 Lorna Pl, Colorado Springs CO 80915	719-570-7474	R	9*	.1
105	Blue Island Citizens For Persons With Developmental D—*Ron Blouin*	2155 Broadway St, Blue Island IL 60406	708-389-6578	R	6*	.1
106	Aspire Inc—*Jennifer Gray*	607 N 4th St, Aberdeen SD 57401	605-229-0263	R	6*	.2
107	Willowood Industries Inc—*Curtis Alford*	1635 Boling St, Jackson MS 39213	601-366-0123	R	3*	.1
108	Preparatory Rehabilitation For Individual and Emp Inc—*Jean Goldsberry*	3 Maple St, Taunton MA 02780	508-823-7134	R	2*	<.1
109	Blind And Vision Rehabilitation Services Of Pittsburgh—*Erika Abrogast*	1800 W St, Homestead PA 15120	412-368-4400	R	2*	.1

TOTALS: SIC 8211 Elementary & Secondary Schools

	Companies: 109				15,643	196.9

8221 Colleges & Universities

1	Apollo Group Inc—*Charles B Edelstein*	4025 S Riverpoint Pkwy, Phoenix AZ 85040	480-966-5394	P	4,733	37.7
2	Education Management Corp—*Todd S Nelson*	210 6th Ave 33rd Fl, Pittsburgh PA 15222	412-562-0900	P	2,888	14.5
3	Corinthian Colleges Inc—*Jack Massimino*	6 Hutton Centre Dr Ste, Santa Ana CA 92707	714-427-3000	P	1,764	16.6
4	Strayer University Inc—*Joel Nwagbaraocha* Strayer Education Inc	1133 15th St NW Ste 20, Washington DC 20005	202-408-2400	S	860*	.6
5	Bridgepoint Education Inc—*Andrew S Clark*	13500 Evening Creek Dr, San Diego CA 92128	858-668-2586	P	713	3.0
6	Strayer Education Inc—*Robert S Silberman*	1100 Wilson Blvd Ste 2, Arlington VA 22209	703-247-2500	P	627	2.1
7	Capella Education Co—*J Kevin Gilligan*	225 S 6th St, Minneapolis MN 55402	612-339-8650	P	430	2.9
8	Grand Canyon Education Inc—*Brian Mueller*	PO Box 11097, Phoenix AZ 85061	602-639-7500	P	427	2.6

Rank	Company Name—*Executive Officer*	Address, City, State, Zip	Phone	Type	Fin	Empls
9	Learning Annex LP—*Bill Zanker*	443 Park Avenue S Ste, New York NY 10016	212-371-0280	R	268*	.1
10	Art Institute of Colorado Inc—*David C Zorn* Education Management Corp	1200 Lincoln St, Denver CO 80203	303-837-0825	S	202*	.1
11	Montana State University Inc—*Waded Cruzado*	PO Box 172440, Bozeman MT 59717	406-994-4361	R	180*	2.5
12	University Of Southern Mississippi—*Shelby Thames*	PO Box 5143, Hattiesburg MS 39406	601-266-4111	R	179*	4.5
13	Corporation Of Gonzaga University—*Robert Spitzer*	502 E Boone Ave, Spokane WA 99258	509-328-4220	R	178*	.7
14	Florida State College At Jacksonville—*Steven Wallace*	501 W State St, Jacksonville FL 32202	904-632-3251	R	176*	2.4
15	University Of Maryland Baltimore County—*Freeman Hrabowski*	1000 Hilltop Cir, Baltimore MD 21250	410-455-1503	S	175*	3.9
16	Sacred Heart University Inc—*John Petillo*	5151 Park Ave, Fairfield CT 06825	203-371-7999	R	167*	.6
17	Eastern Kentucky University—*Robert Watts* Eastern Kentucky University	91 Lilley Cornett Br, Hallie KY 41821	606-633-5828	S	165*	<.1
18	Andrews University Inc—*Niels-Erik Andreasen*	4150 Aministration Dr, Berrien Springs MI 49104	269-471-7771	R	163*	2.3
19	Kean University—*Dawood Farahi*	1000 Morris Ave Ste 1, Union NJ 07083	908-527-2000	R	162*	1.9
20	South Dakota State University—*David Chicoina*	PO Box 2201, Brookings SD 57007	605-688-6101	S	161*	2.0
21	College Of Charleston—*P Benson*	66 George St, Charleston SC 29424	843-953-5570	R	160*	1.8
22	Midwestern University—*Kathleen Goeppinger*	555 31st St, Downers Grove IL 60515	630-515-7145	R	159*	.7
23	Vassar College—*Frances Fergusson*	PO Box 12, Poughkeepsie NY 12602	845-437-7000	R	158*	1.0
24	Rowan University—*Donald Farish*	201 Mullica Hill Rd, Glassboro NJ 08028	856-256-4000	R	156*	1.9
25	Eastern Illinois University—*William Perry*	600 Lincoln Ave, Charleston IL 61920	217-581-5000	R	156*	2.2
26	Towson University—*Robert Caret*	8000 York Rd, Baltimore MD 21252	410-704-2000	R	156*	2.5
27	Eastern Kentucky University—*Charles Whitlock*	521 Lancaster Ave, Richmond KY 40475	859-622-2101	R	155*	2.1
28	West Chester University Of Pennsylvania Of The System Of Higher Education—*Madeleine Adler*	PO Box 2500, West Chester PA 19380	610-436-1000	R	154*	1.2
29	Pomona College—*David Oxtoby*	550 N College Ave, Claremont CA 91711	909-621-8135	R	153*	.5
30	Western Washington University—*Karen Morse*	516 High St, Bellingham WA 98225	360-650-3000	R	152*	.5
31	Georgia Southern University—*Brooks Keel*	PO Box 8014, Statesboro GA 30460	912-681-5224	R	151*	1.7
32	New Jersey Institute Of Technology—*Robert Altenkirch*	323 Martin Luther, Newark NJ 07102	973-596-3000	R	150*	1.0
33	Monmouth University—*Paul Gaffney*	400 Cedar Ave 213, West Long Branch NJ 07764	732-571-3400	R	145*	1.0
34	Arcadia University—*Jerry Greiner*	450 S Easton Rd, Glenside PA 19038	215-572-2900	R	143*	.4
35	Houston Sam State University—*James Gaertner*	PO Box 2027, Huntsville TX 77341	936-294-1111	R	141*	2.2
36	American InterContinental University Inc—*Peter Correa*	6600 Peachtree-Dunwood, Atlanta GA 30328		R	116*	.5
37	ITT Technical Institutes—*Patricia Corrales-Toy*	9511 Angola Ct, Indianapolis IN 46268		R	115*	.1
38	National American University Holdings Inc—*Ronald L Shape*	5301 S Hwy 16 Ste 200, Rapid City SD 57701	605-721-5220	P	107	.7
39	Concorde Career Colleges Inc—*Timothy P Cole*	5800 Foxridge Dr Ste 5, Mission KS 66202	913-831-9977	R	88	1.0
40	University of Phoenix Inc—*William J Pepicello* Apollo Group Inc	4615 E Elwood St, Phoenix AZ 85040	480-804-7600	S	78*	2.0
41	Art Institute of Atlanta LLC—*Jo Ann Koch* Education Management Corp	6600 Peachtree Dunwood, Atlanta GA 30328	770-394-8300	S	50*	.3
42	Art Institute of Los Angeles Inc—*Laura Soloff* Education Management Corp	2900 31st St, Santa Monica CA 90405	310-752-4700	S	34*	.2
43	Art Institute of Seattle Inc Education Management Corp	2323 Elliott Ave, Seattle WA 98121	206-448-6600	S	34*	.2
44	Jones Knowledge Group Inc—*Glen Jones*	9697 E Mineral Ave, Centennial CO 80112	303-792-3111	S	26	.3
45	Colorado Technical University Inc—*Marijane Paulsen*	4435 N Chestnut St, Colorado Springs CO 80907	719-598-0200	R	26*	.2
46	Art Institute of Charlotte LLC—*Maurice Lee* Education Management Corp	Three LakePoint Plz 21, Charlotte NC 28217	704-357-8020	S	22*	.1
47	Gibbs College—*Karen Silva*	85 Garfield Ave, Cranston RI 02920	401-824-5300	S	21*	.1
48	St Meinrad Archabbey—*Justin Duvall*	200 Hill Dr, Saint Meinrad IN 47577	812-357-6611	R	20*	.4
49	LeCordon Bleu Colledge of culinary Arts in Portland—*Jon Alberts*	600 SW 10th Ave Ste 40, Portland OR 97205	503-223-2245	S	18*	.1
50	Art Institute of Fort Lauderdale Inc—*Chuck Nagele* Education Management Corp	1799 SE 17th St, Fort Lauderdale FL 33316	954-463-3000	S	17*	.1
51	Art Institute of Las Vegas Inc—*Steven E Brooks* Education Management Corp	2350 Corporate Circle, Henderson NV 89074	702-369-9944	S	17*	.1
52	Art Institute of Los Angeles - Orange County Inc—*Gregory J Marick* Education Management Corp	3601 W Sunflower Ave, Santa Ana CA 92704	714-830-0200	S	17*	.1
53	Art Institute of Phoenix Inc—*Kevin LaMountain* Education Management Corp	2233 W Dunlap Ave, Phoenix AZ 85021	602-331-7500	S	17*	.1
54	Art Institute of Washington Inc—*George Sebolt* Education Management Corp	1820 N Fort Myer Dr, Arlington VA 22209	703-358-9550	S	17*	.1
55	Art Institutes International at San Francisco Inc—*Byron Chung* Education Management Corp	1170 Market St, San Francisco CA 94102	415-865-0198	S	17*	.1
56	Art Institutes International Minnesota Inc—*Jeffrey S Allen* Education Management Corp	15 S 9th St, Minneapolis MN 55402	612-332-3361	S	17*	.1
57	Art Institute of Houston Inc—*Larry Horn* Education Management Corp	4140 Southwest Fwy, Houston TX 77027	713-623-2040	S	16*	.1

TOTALS: SIC 8221 Colleges & Universities
Companies: 57 — 17,793 — 128.4

8222 Junior Colleges

1	Education America Inc—*Jack Forrest*	500 International Pkwy, Lake Mary FL 32746	407-562-5500	R	176*	1.2

8231 Libraries

1	Harry Kahn Associates Inc—*William Mumma*	13126 Pa Ave Ste 104, Hagerstown MD 21742	301-797-3390	R	1*	<.1

8243 Data Processing Schools

1	Learning Tree International USA Inc—*David C Collins*	1831 Michael Faraday D, Reston VA 20190	310-417-9700	S	68*	.1
2	ExecuTrain Corp—*Axel Leblois*	2500 Northwinds Pkwy S, Alpharetta GA 30009	770-521-1964	R	40*	.5
3	Ascolta LLC—*Irene Kinoshita*	2351 McGaw Ave, Irvine CA 92614	949-477-2000	R	36*	<.1
4	Canterbury Consulting Group Inc—*Kevin J McAndrew*	PO Box 109, Bordentown NJ 08505	609-298-3500	R	20*	.1
5	Next Level Solutions LLC—*Michael C Hill*	1101 30th St NW Ste 50, Washington DC 20007	202-625-4343	R	12*	<.1
6	LinuxCertified Inc—*Chander Kant*	349 Cobalt Way Ste 304, Sunnyvale CA 94085	408-314-6700	R	10*	<.1
7	training etc Inc—*Michael Saltzman*	7150 Riverwood Dr Ste, Columbia MD 21046	410-290-8383	R	10*	<.1
8	Webucator Inc—*Nathaniel Dunn*	4933 Jamesville Rd, Jamesville NY 13078	315-849-2724	R	10*	<.1
9	ITSM Academy Inc—*Jayne Groll*	100 W Cypress Creek Rd, Fort Lauderdale FL 33309	954-491-3442	R	7*	<.1
10	Jacobson Computer Inc—*Gary Jacobson*	1900 Indian Wood Cir S, Maumee OH 43537	419-885-0082	R	4*	<.1
11	NetMasters Inc—*Mark Pedigo*	102 Chestnut St, Gaithersburg MD 20877	301-840-5922	R	4*	<.1
12	Soft-Train Inc—*Richard Pasqualino*	2932 Daimler St, Santa Ana CA 92705	949-242-3600	R	4*	<.1

Note: An asterisk (*) indicates an estimated financial figure. The company type code used is as follows: R = Private, P = Public, S = Private Subsidiary, B = Public Subsidiary, D = Division, J = Joint Venture, I = Investment Fund.

COMPANY RANKINGS BY SALES WITHIN 4-DIGIT SIC

Rank	Company Name—*Executive Officer*	Address, City, State, Zip	Phone	Type	Fin	Empls
13	Kamper Inc—*John Kamper*	5701 E Glenn Ste 90, Tucson AZ 85712	520-751-0061	R	3*	<.1
14	West Pro—*Dave West*	2274 Hampton Way, Clovis CA 93611	559-322-9561	R	3*	<.1
15	International Software Integration Services Inc—*Patricia Luzi*	1905 Laguna St, San Francisco CA 94115	415-563-4747	R	1*	<.1
16	Kurtus Technologies—*Ron Kurtus*	94 Wheatherstone Pl, Lake Oswego OR 97035	503-699-4139	R	1*	<.1
17	Tropaion Inc—*Bruce Meyer*	PO Box 1230, Mountainside NJ 07092	908-654-3870	R	<1*	<.1

TOTALS: SIC 8243 Data Processing Schools
Companies: 17 — 233 / .9

8244 Business & Secretarial Schools

Rank	Company Name—*Executive Officer*	Address, City, State, Zip	Phone	Type	Fin	Empls
1	International Quality and Productivity Center—*Richard Worden*	535 Fifth Ave 8th Fl, New York NY 10017	646-378-6026	S	514*	1.7
2	Bryant and Stratton Business Institute Inc—*Angela Erie*	465 Main St Ste 400, Buffalo NY 14203	716-884-9120	R	235*	1.1
3	New Horizons Computer Learning Centers Inc—*Mark Miller*	1900 S State College B, Anaheim CA 92806	714-940-8000	S	73*	.2
4	Dale Carnegie and Associates Inc—*Peter V Handal*	290 Motor Pkwy, Hauppauge NY 11788	631-415-9300	R	50*	.3
5	Linda Christas—*Ronald Bernard*	1731 37th St, Sacramento CA 95816	916-798-1304	R	22	.3
6	New Horizon Computer Learning Center (Miami Florida)—*Tom Bresnan* New Horizons Computer Learning Centers Inc	7757 W Flagler St Ste, Miami FL 33144		S	3*	<.1

TOTALS: SIC 8244 Business & Secretarial Schools
Companies: 6 — 897 / 3.6

8249 Vocational Schools Nec

Rank	Company Name—*Executive Officer*	Address, City, State, Zip	Phone	Type	Fin	Empls
1	Career Education Corp—*Gary E McCullough*	231 N Martingale Rd, Schaumburg IL 60173	847-781-3600	P	1,885	14.6
2	ITT Educational Services Inc—*Kevin M Modany*	13000 N Meridian St, Carmel IN 46032	317-706-9200	P	1,500	10.0
3	Lincoln Educational Services Corp—*Shaun E McAlmont*	200 Executive Dr Ste 3, West Orange NJ 07052	973-736-9340	B	640	4.5
4	Board Of Cooperative Educational Services	201 E Sunrise Hwy, Patchogue NY 11772	631-289-2200	R	153*	2.5
5	Vatterott Educational Centers Inc—*Pamela Bell*	PO Box 28269, Saint Louis MO 63132	314-264-1500	R	140*	1.0
6	Lincoln Technical Institute Inc—*David Carney*	200 Executive Dr, West Orange NJ 07052	973-736-9340	R	128*	1.0
7	Monroe 2-Orleans BOCES—*George Howard*	3599 Big Ridge Rd, Spencerport NY 14559	585-352-2400	R	115*	.9
8	General Physics Corp—*Scott N Greenberg*	6095 Marshalee Dr Ste, Elkridge MD 21075	410-379-3600	S	108	1.3
9	Instructional Systems Div—*Bruce N Whitman*	8900 Trinity Blvd, Hurst TX 76053		D	35*	.2
10	Airline Training Center Arizona Inc—*Mapphias Kippenbert*	1658 S Litchfield Rd, Goodyear AZ 85338	623-932-1600	R	25*	.2
11	Black Hills Workshop And Training Center Inc—*Bradley Saathoff*	PO Box 2104, Rapid City SD 57709	605-343-4550	R	17*	.4
12	Professional Photographers Of America Inc—*David Trust*	229 Peachtree St Ne, Atlanta GA 30303	404-522-8600	R	7*	<.1
13	Truby's Writers Studio—*John Truby*	664 Brooktree Rd, Santa Monica CA 90402	310-573-9630	R	3*	<.1
14	Studio Productions Inc—*Edward Petersen*	5609 Fishers Ln Ste 14, Rockville MD 20852	301-230-9100	R	3*	<.1
15	Goodwill Industries Of Rhode Island—*Jeffrey Machado*	100 Houghton St, Providence RI 02904	401-861-2080	R	2*	.1
16	Knowledge Development Centers—*Jeff Tuomi*	7000 Central Parkway S, Atlanta GA 30328	678-935-4500	R	2*	<.1
17	InterVISTAS Consulting Group—*Gerry Bruno*	7200 Wisconsin Ave Ste, Bethesda MD 20814	301-941-1400	R	2*	<.1
18	Tectrix Inc—*Kirsten Sitnick*	10025 Governor Warfiel, Columbia MD 21044	410-788-2209	R	1*	<.1
19	Travel Resource Center Inc—*Mary Long Harvey*	1630 SE Rex St, Portland OR 97202	503-232-5362	R	N/A	<.1

TOTALS: SIC 8249 Vocational Schools Nec
Companies: 19 — 4,765 / 36.7

8299 Schools & Educational Services Nec

Rank	Company Name—*Executive Officer*	Address, City, State, Zip	Phone	Type	Fin	Empls
1	Kaplan Professional—*Andrew Rosen* Kaplan Inc	888 7th Ave, New York NY 10106	212-492-5800	D	3,265*	6.4
2	PCS Edventures!com Inc—*Valerie L Grindle*	345 Bobwhite Ct Ste 20, Boise ID 83706	208-343-3110	P	1,839	<.1
3	Laureate Education Inc—*Douglas Becker*	650 S Exeter St, Baltimore MD 21202	410-843-6100	R	1,420*	28.5
4	Universal Technical Institute Inc—*Kimberly J McWaters*	20410 N 19th Ave Ste 2, Phoenix AZ 85027	623-445-9500	P	452	2.3
5	Edison Schools Inc—*Terry L Stecz*	521 5th Ave 11th Fl, New York NY 10175	212-419-1600	R	426*	6.3
6	Berlitz International Inc—*Mike Kashani*	31D Hulfish Street, Princeton NJ 08542	609-514-3400	R	401*	5.0
7	INVESTools Inc—*Fredrick Tomczyk*	4211 S 102nd St, Omaha NE 68127	402-597-8464	S	372	.7
8	Argosy Education Group Inc—*Gregory O'Brien*	2 First National Plz 2, Chicago IL 60603	312-899-9900	S	306*	.5
9	Stanislaus County Office Of Education—*Kurtiz Carr*	1100 H St, Modesto CA 95354	209-238-1900	R	151*	1.0
10	CareerTrack Inc—*Phil Love*	5700 Broadmoor St Ste, Mission KS 66202	913-967-8599	D	134*	.4
11	Learning Tree International Inc—*David c Collins*	1805 Library St, Reston VA 20190	703-709-9119	P	134	.5
12	Excelligence Learning Corp—*Ronald C Elliott*	2 Lower Ragsdale Dr St, Monterey CA 93940	831-333-2000	R	133	.4
13	Ambassador Programs Inc—*Jeffrey Thomas*	1956 Ambassador Way, Spokane WA 99224	509-568-7000	S	108*	.2
14	Tigrent Inc—*Steven C Barre*	1612 Cape Coral Pky St, Cape Coral FL 33904	239-542-0643	P	103	.2
15	Imagine Schools Inc—*Dennis Bakke*	1005 North Glebe Rd St, Arlington VA 22201	703-527-2600	R	100	.7
16	GovConnection Inc—*Robert Howard*	732 Milford Rd, Merrimack NH 03054		S	97*	.2
17	Delta Connection Academy Inc—*Gary Beck*	2700 Flightline Ave, Sanford FL 32773	407-330-7020	S	93*	.3
18	Youth Services International Inc—*James F Slattery*	6000 Cattleridge Dr St, Sarasota FL 34232	941-953-9199	R	90*	1.5
19	Center For Creative Leadership Inc—*John Ryan*	PO Box 26300, Greensboro NC 27438	336-288-7210	R	86*	.6
20	San Diego County Office Of Education—*Michele Fort-Merrill*	6401 Linda Vista Rd 50, San Diego CA 92111	858-292-3500	R	84*	1.4
21	SimuFlite Training International—*Tom Stelter*	Box 619119, Dallas TX 75261	972-456-8000	D	75*	.4
22	EVCI Career Colleges Holding Corp—*John J McGrath*	1 Van Der Donck St, Yonkers NY 10701	914-623-0700	B	65	.7
23	Northwest Evaluation Association—*Matt Chapman*	121 Nw Everett St, Portland OR 97209	503-624-1951	R	65*	.2
24	EduTrades Inc—*Ronald Simon* Tigrent Inc	5245 College Dr, Murray UT 84123		S	61*	.1
25	Ambassadors Group Inc—*Jeffrey D Thomas*	1956 Ambassador Way, Spokane WA 99224	509-568-7000	P	57	.2
26	eCollegecom—*Matthew Leavy*	2154 E Commons Ave Ste, Centennial CO 80122	303-658-1000	S	52	.5
27	Management Concepts Inc—*Thomas Dungan*	8230 Leesburg Pke Ste, Vienna VA 22182	703-790-9595	R	49*	.2
28	Scientific Learning Corp—*D Andrew Myers*	300 Frank H Ogawa Plz, Oakland CA 94612	510-444-3500	B	43	.2
29	Questar Assessment Inc—*Roy Lipner*	PO Box 382, Brewster NY 10509		P	43	.1
30	Alpine Ascents International—*Tom Burleson*	109 W Mercer St, Seattle WA 98119	206-378-1927	R	36*	.1
31	Archipelago Learning Inc—*Tim McEven*	3232 McKinney Ave, Dallas TX 75204		R	34*	.2
32	New Horizons Worldwide Inc—*Earle W Pratt*	1 W Elm St Ste 125, Conshohocken PA 19428	484-567-3000	P	34	.2
33	Peoples Education Holdings Inc—*Brian T Beckwith*	PO Box 513, Saddle Brook NJ 07663	201-712-0900	P	31	.1
34	Training Associates (Westborough Massachusetts)—*Victor Melfa*	287 Turnpike Rd Ste 30, Westborough MA 01581	508-890-8500	R	27*	.1
35	Diplomatic Language Services Inc—*Jim Bellas*	1901 N Ft Myer Dr 6th, Arlington VA 22209	703-243-4855	R	26*	.2
36	Kansas City Aviation Center Inc—*David Armacost*	PO Box 1850, Olathe KS 66063	913-782-0530	R	24*	.1
37	Apangea Learning Inc—*Mark DeSantis*	925 Liberty Ave Fl 3, Pittsburgh PA 15222		R	19*	<.1
38	DDI Enterprises Inc—*John Lessard*	99 Hollywood Dr, Smithtown NY 11787	631-366-2900	R	17*	1.7
39	Merex Corp (Tempe Arizona)	2101 E Broadway Rd Ste, Tempe AZ 85282	480-921-7877	R	17*	<.1
40	California Culinary Academy Inc—*Peter Lee*	350 Rhode Island St, San Francisco CA 94103	415-771-3500	S	16*	.4
41	Schoolwires Inc—*Edward Marflak*	320 Rolling Ridge Dr S, State College PA 16801	814-689-1046	R	16*	.1

Rank	Company Name—*Executive Officer*	Address, City, State, Zip	Phone	Type	Fin	Empls
42	Xinnix—*Casey Gonzalez Cunningham*	1 Glenlake Pkwy Ste 30, Atlanta GA 30328	678-325-3500	R	15*	<.1
43	GlobalSim Inc—*Scott M Huntsman*	12577 S 265 W Ste3A, Draper UT 84020	801-571-9094	R	15*	<.1
44	National Safety Commission—*Ken Underwood*	PO Box 3359, Ponte Vedra Beach FL 32004	904-688-2300	R	14*	.1
45	Learning Voyage Inc—*Christopher Dirksing*	10737 Medallion Dr Ste, Cincinnati OH 45241	513-881-7055	R	14*	<.1
46	MindIQ Corp—*Louis H Bernstein*	7742 Spalding Dr Ste 2, Norcross GA 30092	770-248-0442	R	14*	<.1
47	Quest Continuing Education Solutions—*Alan Krenke*	10850 W Park Pl Ste 10, Milwaukee WI 53224	414-375-3400	R	13*	<.1
48	Phoenix East Aviation Inc—*Chassan Resian*	561 Pearl Harbor Dr, Daytona Beach FL 32114	386-258-0703	R	11*	.1
49	Color Me Mine Enterprises Inc—*James Warner*	3722 San Fernando Rd, Glendale CA 91204	818-291-5900	R	11*	<.1
50	RealtyU Group—*Stefan JM Swanepoel*	223785 El Toro Rd Rm 4, Lake Forest CA 92630	949-349-9394	R	11*	<.1
51	FortuneBuilders Inc—*Than Merrill*	4655 Cass St, San Diego CA 92109	858-270-8600	R	10	<.1
52	Presidium Inc—*Greg Davies*	1810 Samuel Morse Dr, Reston VA 20190		R	10*	.3
53	Proliteracy Worldwide—*David Harvey*	1320 Jamesville Ave, Syracuse NY 13210	315-422-9121	R	10*	<.1
54	Advanced Health Education Center Ltd—*Marilyn Sackett*	8502 Tybor Dr, Houston TX 77074	713-772-0157	R	10*	<.1
55	Acclaim Training—*Linda Levy*	5200 Nome Ave, El Paso TX 79924	915-759-9814	R	10*	<.1
56	Uaw-Chrysler Skill Development And Training Program—*Jimmy Davis*	2211 E Jefferson Ave F, Detroit MI 48207	313-567-3300	R	9*	.2
57	Educational Service Unit 9—*Kevin Krueger*	PO Box 2047, Hastings NE 68902	402-463-5611	R	9*	.1
58	Christiansen Aviation Inc—*William Christiansen*	PO Box 702412, Tulsa OK 74170	918-299-2687	R	9*	<.1
59	CEA Global Education—*Brian Boubek*	2005 W 14th St Ste 113, Tempe AZ 85281	480-557-7900	R	8*	.1
60	Educational Services Inc—*Susan F Dixon*	4350 East West Hwy Ste, Bethesda MD 20814	240-744-7000	R	7*	.1
61	Kaplan Inc—*Andrew S Rosen*	395 Hudson St, New York NY 10014	212-492-5800	S	6*	.4
62	Sequoia System International—*Edward J Sierawski*	1515 Legacy Cir, Naperville IL 60563	630-955-6030	R	6*	<.1
63	TRACOM Corp—*John R Myers*	8878 S Barrons Blvd, Highlands Ranch CO 80129	303-470-4900	S	5*	<.1
64	Safe Passage International Inc—*Alan Resler*	333 Metro Park, Rochester NY 14623	585-292-4910	R	5*	<.1
65	Wishart Safety Training Inc—*Donna Wishart*	4302 Henderson Blvd, Tampa FL 33629	813-902-8001	R	5*	<.1
66	Arachne Internet Solutions—*Grant Fraga*	601 Montgomery St Unit, San Francisco CA 94111	415-392-8024	R	5*	<.1
67	Massachusetts Continuing Legal Education Inc—*Janice Bassil*	10 Winter Pl, Boston MA 02108	617-482-2205	R	5*	<.1
68	Powerspeak—*Robert Blair*	1682 W 820 N, Provo UT 84601	801-373-3973	R	4*	<.1
69	E and A Information Inc—*Etta Enow*	6 St Charles Ct, Stafford VA 22556	540-720-9660	R	4*	<.1
70	EZ-REF Courseware—*Henry Vandermeir*	51 Valmont Way, Ladera Ranch CA 92694	949-218-6344	R	4	N/A
71	Shelburne Farms—*Alexander Webb*	1611 Harbor Rd, Shelburne VT 05482	802-985-8686	R	4*	<.1
72	From The Top Inc—*Gerald Slavet*	295 Huntington Ave Ste, Boston MA 02115	617-437-0707	R	4*	<.1
73	Ncme Holding Corp—*Paul Gersh*	1 Harmon Plz Ste 603, Secaucus NJ 07094		R	3*	.1
74	Shakespeare Squared LLC—*Kim Kleeman*	626 Academy Dr, Northbrook IL 60062	847-998-0535	R	3*	<.1
75	Pragmatic Marketing Inc—*Craig Stull*	8910 E Raintree Dr, Scottsdale AZ 85260	480-515-1411	R	3*	<.1
76	Professional Registry Of Nursing Inc—*Jerry Crosby*	10828 Gravelly Lake Dr, Lakewood WA 98499	253-840-1909	R	2*	<.1
77	Be Bilingual Inc—*Elizabeth Thrush*	8588 Katy Fwy Ste 353, Houston TX 77024	713-789-6338	R	2*	<.1
78	I Understand—*Noah Salzman*	6363 Longcroft Dr Ste, Oakland CA 94611		R	2*	<.1
79	Accelebrate Inc—*Steve Heckler*	925B Peachtree St NE, Atlanta GA 30309	678-648-3113	R	2*	<.1
80	Language Intelligence Ltd—*Irene White*	16 N Goodman St Ste 10, Rochester NY 14607	585-244-5578	R	1*	<.1
81	Instructivision Inc	PO Box 2004, Pine Brook NJ 07058	973-575-9992	R	1*	<.1
82	Answer Quest Technologies Inc—*Linda Link*	PO Box 43494, Baltimore MD 21236	410-538-3698	R	1*	<.1
83	CYSIP—*Andreas Spanias*	PO Box 242, Tempe AZ 85284	480-756-2520	R	1*	<.1
84	Hyper/Word Services—*Neil Perlin*	101 Emily Rd, Tewksbury MA 01876	978-657-5464	R	1*	<.1
85	Nuthatch Information Technologies Inc—*William E Holden*	PO Box 5159, Lancaster PA 17606	717-371-8605	R	N/A	<.1

TOTALS: SIC 8299 Schools & Educational Services Nec

Companies: 85					10,889	64.7

8322 Individual & Family Services

Rank	Company Name—*Executive Officer*	Address, City, State, Zip	Phone	Type	Fin	Empls
1	Community Behavioral Health Inc—*Estelle Richmond*	801 Market St Ste 7000, Philadelphia PA 19107	215-413-3100	R	453*	.3
2	Pgba LLC—*Mike Skarupa*	I-20 Alpine Rd, Columbia SC 29219	803-788-3860	R	270*	2.2
3	San Andreas Regional Center—*Santi Rogers*	PO Box 50002, San Jose CA 95150	408-374-9960	R	258*	.3
4	Kidspeace National Centers For Kids In Crisis Inc—*C O'donnell*	5300 Kidspeace Dr, Orefield PA 18069		R	169*	3.6
5	San Gabriel/Pomona Valleys Developmental Services Inc—*R Penman*	761 Corporate Ctr Dr, Pomona CA 91768	909-620-7722	R	168*	.3
6	County Of Fauquier—*Tom Pazelko*	70 Culpeper St, Warrenton VA 20186	540-422-8080	R	165*	<.1
7	New York State Industries For The Disabled Inc—*Larry Barker*	11 Columbia Cir, Albany NY 12203	518-463-9706	R	159*	.1
8	Harvest Time International Inc—*Arthur Murphy*	225 N Kennel Rd, Sanford FL 32771	407-328-0667	R	159*	.1
9	Active Services Corp—*Peter Harris*	400 Redland Ct Ste 114, Owings Mills MD 21117	443-548-2200	R	159*	1.5
10	Stavros Center For Independent Living Inc—*Jim Kruidenier*	210 Old Farm Rd, Amherst MA 01002	413-256-0473	R	151*	.1
11	Dallas County Indigent Care Corp	1441 Acapulco Dr, Dallas TX 75232	469-272-0758	R	150*	<.1
12	Eastern Los Angeles Regional Center For The Developmentally Disabled Inc—*Gloria Wong*	PO Box 7916, Alhambra CA 91802	626-299-4700	R	144*	.3
13	Community Coordinated Care For Children Inc—*Scott Wall*	3500 W Colonial Dr, Orlando FL 32808	407-522-2252	R	144*	.3
14	Coastal Developmental Services Foundation—*Michael Danneker*	5901 Green Valley Cir, Culver City CA 90230	310-258-4000	R	141*	<.1
15	Care Wisconsin First Inc—*Karen Musser*	PO Box 14017, Madison WI 53708	608-240-0020	R	140*	.5
16	Kern Regional Center—*Michal Clark*	PO Box 2536, Bakersfield CA 93303	661-327-8531	R	136*	.2
17	Focus On The Family Inc—*James Daly*	8605 Explorer Dr, Colorado Springs CO 80920	719-531-3400	R	134*	.8
18	Community Food Bank Of New Jersey Inc—*Richard Brody*	31 Evans Terminal, Hillside NJ 07205	908-355-3663	R	76*	.1
19	Leake and Watts Services Inc—*William Kirk*	463 Hawthorne Ave, Yonkers NY 10705	914-375-8700	R	55*	.9
20	Greater Lynn Senior Services Inc—*Vincent Lique*	8 Silsbee St, Lynn MA 01901	781-599-0110	R	45*	.5
21	Urban League Of Philadelphia Inc—*Pat Coulter*	121 S Broad St Fl 9, Philadelphia PA 19107	215-985-3220	R	45*	.1
22	Community Action Project Of Tulsa County Inc—*Steven Dow*	4606 S Garnett Rd Ste, Tulsa OK 74146	918-382-3200	R	45*	.3
23	Essex County Welfare Board Inc—*Bruce Nigro*	18 Rector St Ste 9, Newark NJ 07102	973-733-3326	R	39*	1.0
24	United Home Care Services Inc—*Jose Fox*	5255 Nw 87th Ave Ste 4, Doral FL 33178	305-477-0440	R	38*	.6
25	St Johnland Nursing Center Inc—*Mary Weber*	395 Sunken Meadow Rd, Kings Park NY 11754	631-269-5800	R	35*	.4
26	Jefferson Rehabilitation Center Inc—*Daniel Stern*	PO Box 41, Watertown NY 13601	315-788-2730	S	35*	.6
27	Advanced Behavioral Health Inc—*Samuel Moy*	213 Ct St, Middletown CT 06457	860-638-5309	R	34*	.2
28	Central Boston Elder Services Inc—*Perry Smith*	2315 Washington St, Roxbury MA 02119	617-277-7416	R	33*	.1
29	Illinois Action For Children—*Maria Whelan*	4753 N Broadway St Ste, Chicago IL 60640	312-823-1100	R	33*	.4
30	Sunbelt Human Advancement Resources Inc—*Willis Crosby*	1200 Pendleton St, Greenville SC 29611	864-269-0700	R	32*	.4
31	North Metro Community Services Incorporated—*Roxanne Pinneo*	1001 W 124th Ave, Westminster CO 80234	303-457-1001	R	30*	.3
32	Southwest Human Development Inc—*Virginia Ward*	2850 N 24th St, Phoenix AZ 85008	602-468-3400	R	30*	.2
33	Kintock Group Of New Jersey Inc—*Diane Barri*	2010 Renaissance Blvd, King Of Prussia PA 19406	610-687-1336	R	29*	.5
34	N Penn Comprehensive Health Services—*Elaine Herstek*	101b W Ave, Wellsboro PA 16901	570-723-0500	R	26*	.5
35	Center For Disability Rights Inc—*Bruce Darling*	497 State St, Rochester NY 14608	585-546-7510	R	26*	.1

Note: An asterisk (*) indicates an estimated financial figure. The company type code used is as follows: R = Private, P = Public, S = Private Subsidiary, B = Public Subsidiary, D = Division, J = Joint Venture, I = Investment Fund.

COMPANY RANKINGS BY SALES WITHIN 4-DIGIT SIC

Rank	Company Name—*Executive Officer*	Address, City, State, Zip	Phone	Type	Fin	Empls
36	Brook Beech—*Bari Goggins*	3737 Lander Rd, Cleveland OH 44124	216-831-2255	R	25*	.5
37	In-Roads Creative Programs Inc—*Sharon Barton*	7955 Webster St Ste 14, Highland CA 92346	909-864-1551	R	24*	.8
38	Monadnock Developmental Services Inc—*Alan Greene*	121 Railroad St, Keene NH 03431	603-352-1304	R	24*	.3
39	Catholic Charities Of Santa Clara County—*Gregory Kepferle*	2625 Zanker Rd Ste 200, San Jose CA 95134	408-468-0100	R	24*	.5
40	Drew Child Development Corporation Inc—*Michael Jackson*	1770 E 118th St, Los Angeles CA 90059	323-249-2950	R	24*	.2
41	National Able Network Inc—*Grace Jenkins*	567 W Lake St Ste 1150, Chicago IL 60661	312-994-4200	R	24*	.2
42	Casa Pacifica Centers For Children And Families—*Steven Elson*	1722 S Lewis Rd, Camarillo CA 93012	805-445-7800	R	22*	.4
43	Pathways To Housing Inc—*Sam Tsmemberis*	186 E 123rd St Fl 3, New York NY 10035	212-289-0000	R	22*	.2
44	Otsego County Chapter Association For Retarded Children—*Joe Judd*	PO Box 490, Oneonta NY 13820	607-432-8595	S	21*	.3
45	In-Home Supportive Services Consortium of San Francisco—*Margaret Baran*	1453 Mission St Ste 52, San Francisco CA 94103	415-255-2079	R	21*	.5
46	Glade Run Lutheran Services—*Charles Lockwood*	PO Box 70, Zelienople PA 16063	724-452-4453	R	21*	.5
47	Advance Inc—*Sylvia Garcia*	4281 Dacoma St, Houston TX 77092	713-812-0033	R	21*	.3
48	Fayette Resources Inc—*Kathy Morris*	1313 Connellsville Rd, Lemont Furnace PA 15456	724-437-6461	R	21*	.1
49	Cen-Clear Child Services Inc—*Eugene Kephart*	1633 Phlpsburg Bigler, Philipsburg PA 16866	814-342-5678	R	20*	.5
50	Arc Of Jefferson County Inc—*William Hoehle*	215 21st Ave S, Birmingham AL 35205	205-503-4040	R	20*	.5
51	Community Action Organization—*Jerralynn Ness*	1001 Sw Baseline St, Hillsboro OR 97123	503-648-6646	R	20*	.3
52	Community Action Agency Of South Central Michigan—*Nancy Macfarlane*	PO Box 1026, Battle Creek MI 49016	269-965-7766	R	20*	.3
53	University Settlement Society Of New York Inc—*Michael Zisser*	184 Eldridge St, New York NY 10002	212-674-9120	R	20*	.1
54	American Corrective Counseling Services Inc—*Michael Schreck*	180 Avenida La Pata, San Clemente CA 92673	949-369-6210	R	19*	.3
55	Exceptional Persons Inc—*Christopher Sparks*	PO Box 4090, Waterloo IA 50704	319-232-6671	R	19*	.4
56	Jacksonville Urban League Inc—*Richard Danford*	903 Union St W, Jacksonville FL 32204	904-356-8336	R	19*	.4
57	Seamen's Society For Children and Families—*Nancy Vomero*	50 Bay St, Staten Island NY 10301	718-447-7740	R	18*	.2
58	Southwestern Pennsylvania Area Agency On Aging Inc—*Karen Bennett*	305 Chamber Plz, Charleroi PA 15022	724-489-8080	R	18*	.1
59	Volunteers Of America Colorado—*Dianna Kunz*	2660 Larimer St, Denver CO 80205	303-297-0408	R	18*	.3
60	Goodwill Industries Rehabilitation Center Inc—*Ken Weber*	408 9th St Sw, Canton OH 44707	330-454-9461	R	18*	.3
61	Pro Action Of Steuben And Yates Inc—*David Hill*	117 E Steuben St Ste 1, Bath NY 14810	607-776-2125	R	17*	.3
62	Metropolitan New York Coordinating Council On Jewish Poverty Inc—*William Rapfogel*	80 Maiden Ln Fl 21, New York NY 10038	212-453-9500	R	17*	.3
63	Hias Inc—*Gideon Aronoff*	333 7th Ave Rm 1600, New York NY 10001	212-967-4100	R	17*	.1
64	Downtown Emergency Service Center—*William Hobson*	515 3rd Ave, Seattle WA 98104	206-464-1570	R	17*	.4
65	Catholic Charities Foundation Of Northeast Kansas—*Jan Lewis*	2220 Central Ave, Kansas City KS 66102	913-621-1504	R	16*	.2
66	Individual Advocacy Group Inc—*Charlene Bennett*	1289 Windham Pkwy, Romeoville IL 60446	815-372-8950	R	16*	.4
67	Greater New Bedford Community Health Center Inc—*Stuart Forman*	874 Purchase St, New Bedford MA 02740	508-992-6553	R	16*	.1
68	Baby Fold' 'the—*Dale Strassheim*	PO Box 327, Normal IL 61761	309-452-1170	R	16*	.3
69	Forestdale Inc—*Anstiss Agnew*	6735 112th St, Forest Hills NY 11375	718-263-0740	R	15*	.1
70	Child Care Resource and Referral Inc—*Patrick Gannon*	126 Woodlake Dr Se, Rochester MN 55904	507-287-2020	R	15*	.2
71	NEW Curative Rehabilitation Inc—*John Bloor*	PO Box 8027, Green Bay WI 54308	920-468-1161	R	15*	.3
72	Eliza Bryant Village—*Harvey Shankman*	7201 Wade Park Ave, Cleveland OH 44103	216-361-6141	R	15*	.3
73	Somerville Cambridge Elder Services Corp—*Ligia Taylor*	61 Medford St, Somerville MA 02143	617-628-2601	R	14*	.1
74	Camillus House Inc—*Paul Ahr*	PO Box 11829, Miami FL 33101	305-374-1065	R	14*	.2
75	Claddagh Commission Inc—*Barbara Lamoreaux*	PO Box 266, Derby NY 14047	716-947-5857	R	14*	.4
76	South Shore Elder Services Inc—*Constance Doolittle*	159 Bay State Dr, Braintree MA 02184	781-848-3910	R	14*	.1
77	Community Living Alliance Inc—*Sara Roberts*	1414 Macarthur Rd, Madison WI 53714	608-242-8335	R	14*	1.0
78	Threshold Rehabilitation Services Inc—*Ronald Williams*	1000 Lancaster Ave, Reading PA 19607	610-777-7691	R	13*	.3
79	Eihab Human Services Inc—*Fatma Abboud*	16818 S Conduit Ave St, Jamaica NY 11434	718-276-6101	R	13*	.2
80	Weingart Center Association Inc—*Gregory Scott*	566 S San Pedro St, Los Angeles CA 90013	213-627-9000	R	13*	.2
81	Oak Crest Homes Inc—*Charles Schipper*	7811 Cottonwood Dr, Jenison MI 49428	616-457-5869	R	13*	.3
82	Home For Jewish Parents—*Janice Corran*	4000 Camino Tassajara, Danville CA 94506	925-648-2800	R	12*	.2
83	Child and Family Center—*Elizabeth Seipel*	21545 Centre Pointe Pk, Santa Clarita CA 91350	661-259-9439	R	12*	.1
84	Bradley Cleveland Services Inc—*Lucas Queen*	PO Box 29, Cleveland TN 37364	423-472-5268	R	12*	.5
85	Hadassah Medical Relief Association Inc—*June Walker*	50 W 58th St, New York NY 10019	212-355-7900	R	11*	.3
86	Hillcroft Services Inc—*Debbie Bennett*	114 E Streeter Ave, Muncie IN 47303	765-284-4166	R	11*	.2
87	Family Empowerment Council Inc—*Joseph O'connell*	225 Dolson Ave Ste 403, Middletown NY 10940	845-343-8100	R	11*	.1
88	Jewish Community Center Of The Greater Palm Beaches Inc—*Michelle Lobovits*	8500 Jog Rd, Boynton Beach FL 33472	561-740-9000	R	11*	.1
89	Council On Aging Silicon Valley Inc—*Stephen Schmoll*	2115 The Alameda, San Jose CA 95126	408-296-8290	R	11*	.1
90	Senior Services Inc—*Robert Littke*	918 Jasper St, Kalamazoo MI 49001	269-382-0515	R	11*	<.1
91	Juvenile Justice Center Of Philadelphia—*Richard Chapman*	100 W Coulter St, Philadelphia PA 19144	215-849-2112	R	10*	.2
92	Cleveland Society For The Blind—*Stephen Friedman*	PO Box 1988, Cleveland OH 44106	216-791-8118	R	10*	.1
93	Lunchtime Solutions Inc—*Michael Cranny*	PO Box 2022, North Sioux City SD 57049	605-235-0939	R	10*	.4
94	Maryhurst Inc—*Judith Lambeth*	1015 Dorsey Ln, Louisville KY 40223	502-245-1576	R	10*	.2
95	Child and Family Services Of Eastern Virginia Inc—*Edward Welp*	222 W 19th St, Norfolk VA 23517	757-622-7017	R	10*	.1
96	Metropolitan Inter-Faith Association—*Margaret Craddock*	PO Box 3130, Memphis TN 38173	901-527-0208	R	10*	.3
97	D A Blodgett For Children—*Sharon Loughridge*	805 Leonard St Ne, Grand Rapids MI 49503	616-451-2021	R	10*	.2
98	Kelly Restaurant Group LLC—*Tom Kelley*	401 Moltke Ave Frnt, Scranton PA 18505	570-969-2188	R	10*	.2
99	Colorado West Recovery Center—*Kenneth Stein*	711 Grand Ave, Glenwood Springs CO 81601	970-945-8439	R	10*	.4
100	Crittenton Womens Union—*Elizabeth Babcock*	1 Washington Mall Lbby, Boston MA 02108	617-536-5651	R	10*	.1
101	Ketchikan Indian Corp—*Norman Arriola*	2960 Tongass Ave, Ketchikan AK 99901	907-228-4945	R	9*	.2
102	Child and Family Support Services Inc—*Tim Penrod*	4700 S Mcclintock Dr S, Tempe AZ 85282	480-635-9944	S	9*	.2
103	Project Open Hand—*Loura Smith*	730 Polk St Fl 3, San Francisco CA 94109	415-447-2300	R	9*	.1
104	Open Door Center—*Mary Simonson*	129 3rd Ave Ne, Valley City ND 58072	701-845-1124	R	9*	.2
105	Scan Inc—*Rachel Tobin-Smith*	500 W Main St, Fort Wayne IN 46802	260-421-5000	R	9*	.1
106	Child Guidance Center Inc—*Veronica Valentine*	5776 Saint Augustine R, Jacksonville FL 32207	904-448-4700	R	9*	.2
107	Lifestream Services Inc—*Kenneth Adkins*	1701 S Pilgrim Blvd, Yorktown IN 47396	765-759-1121	R	9*	.2
108	Catholic Charities Of The Diocese Of Worcester—*Catherine Loessler*	10 Hammond St, Worcester MA 01610	508-798-0191	R	9*	.3
109	Seniors First Inc—*Marsha Lorenz*	5395 L B Mcleod Rd, Orlando FL 32811	407-292-0177	R	9*	.2
110	New Canaan Community Ymca Inc—*Gene Weil*	564 S Ave, New Canaan CT 06840	203-966-4528	R	9*	.1
111	Resources For Child Caring Inc—*Barbara Yates*	10 Yorkton Ct, Saint Paul MN 55117	651-641-0305	R	9*	.1
112	Scioto County Counseling Center Inc—*Ed Hughes*	1634 11th St, Portsmouth OH 45662	740-354-6685	R	9*	.1
113	Children's Community Programs Of Ct Inc—*Brian Lynch*	446a Blake St 100, New Haven CT 06515	203-786-6403	R	9*	.1
114	Opportunities For Chenango Inc—*Craig Cashman*	PO Box 470, Norwich NY 13815	607-334-7114	R	9*	.1

Rank	Company Name—*Executive Officer*	Address, City, State, Zip	Phone	Type	Fin	Empls
115	Western New York Independent Living Inc—*Douglas Usiak*	3108 Main St, Buffalo NY 14214	716-836-0822	R	8*	.2
116	Catholic Comprehensive Services For Children Child Center-Marygrove—*Sr Negri*	2705 Mullanphy Ln, Florissant MO 63031	314-837-1702	R	8*	.2
117	Glove House Inc—*John Treahy*	220 Franklin St, Elmira NY 14904	607-734-5238	R	8*	.2
118	Learning Disabilities Association Of The Genesee Valley Inc—*Colin Garwood*	339 E Ave Ste 420, Rochester NY 14604	585-263-3323	R	8*	.2
119	Aids Action Committee Of Massachusetts Inc—*Rebecca Haag*	294 Washington St Fl 5, Boston MA 02108	617-437-6200	R	8*	.1
120	Alternative Community Mental Health Center Inc—*Yvonne Chase*	1251 Muldoon Rd Ste 11, Anchorage AK 99504	907-274-4055	R	8*	.1
121	Marathon Infants And Toddlers Inc—*Bernard Esrig*	22018 Horace Harding E, Flushing NY 11364	718-423-0056	R	8*	<.1
122	Saint Vincent's Home—*Joe Lavoritano*	1509 Church St, Philadelphia PA 19124	215-624-5600	R	8*	.2
123	Tcn Behavioral Health Services Inc—*James George*	452 W Market St, Xenia OH 45385	937-376-8700	R	8*	.2
124	Children's Foundation Inc—*Lisa Pieper*	403 S State St, Bloomington IL 61701	309-827-0374	R	8*	.1
125	Operation Breakthrough Inc—*Corita Bussanmas*	3039 Troost Ave, Kansas City MO 64109	816-756-3511	R	8*	.1
126	Midland Community Center Inc—*Chris Tointon*	2205 Jefferson Ave, Midland MI 48640	989-832-7937	R	8*	.7
127	Boys and Girls Clubs Of Greater Fort Worth Inc—*Daphne Barlow*	3218 E Belknap St, Fort Worth TX 76111	817-834-4711	R	8*	.2
128	Mid Island Y Jewish Community Center Inc—*Bruce Nuzie*	45 Manetto Hill Rd, Plainview NY 11803	516-822-3535	R	8*	.1
129	Interfaith Older Adult Programs Inc—*Carol Eschner*	600 W Virginia St Ste, Milwaukee WI 53204	414-291-7500	R	8*	.3
130	U Tellurian CA N Inc—*Kevin Florek*	300 Femrite Dr, Monona WI 53716	608-222-7311	R	7*	.2
131	Family Resources Community Action—*B Lessing*	245 Main St, Woonsocket RI 02895	401-766-0900	R	7*	.1
132	Arbor Rehabilitation And Healthcare Services Inc—*Robert Vadas*	PO Box 99, Gates Mills OH 44040	440-423-0206	R	7*	.3
133	Community Action Commission Of Belmont County—*Gary Obloy*	153 1/2 W Main St, Saint Clairsville OH 43950	740-695-0293	R	7*	.1
134	Bridges Community Support Services Inc—*Barry Larson*	3114 Sutton Blvd, Saint Louis MO 63143	314-781-7900	R	7*	.1
135	Civicorps Schools—*Rebecca Grove*	101 Myrtle St, Oakland CA 94607	510-992-7800	R	7*	.3
136	Point Loma Rehabilitation Center LLC—*Mac Rodriguez*	3202 Duke St, San Diego CA 92110	619-224-4141	R	7*	.1
137	Mecosta Osceola Area Rehabilitation Center—*Janet Wood*	PO Box 66, Paris MI 49338	231-796-4801	R	7*	.2
138	Open Doors Inc—*Lin Preston*	PO Box 709, Lewisburg WV 24901	304-645-2130	R	7*	.1
139	His House Inc—*Jean Gonzalez*	PO Box 170239, Hialeah FL 33017	305-430-0085	R	7*	.1
140	Crisis Intervention And Recovery Center Inc—*Bernard Jesiolowski*	832 Mckinley Ave Nw, Canton OH 44703	330-455-9407	R	7*	.1
141	Community Services Of Stark County Inc—*Daniel Fuline*	625 Cleveland Ave Nw, Canton OH 44702	330-455-0374	R	7*	.1
142	Highfields Inc—*James Hines*	PO Box 98, Onondaga MI 49264	517-628-2287	R	6*	.2
143	Community Support Services—*Jhan Hurn*	2312 Annie Baxter Ave, Joplin MO 64804	417-624-4515	R	6*	.2
144	Wacosa—*Steve Howard*	PO Box 757, Waite Park MN 56387	320-251-0087	R	6*	.1
145	Tableland Services Inc—*Jeffrey Masterson*	535 E Main St Ste 1, Somerset PA 15501	814-445-9628	R	6*	.1
146	Philadelphia Developmental Disabilities Corp—*John Felt*	2350 W Westmoreland St, Philadelphia PA 19140	215-229-4550	R	6*	.1
147	Transitional Living Communities—*John Schwary*	PO Box 1586, Mesa AZ 85211	480-833-0143	R	6*	.1
148	Philmat Inc—*James Kelly*	1000 Howard Ave Ste 80, New Orleans LA 70113	504-523-3755	R	6*	.2
149	Queen's Parent Resource Center Inc—*James Magalee*	8850 165th St Ste B, Jamaica NY 11432	718-523-6953	R	6*	.1
150	Sterling Area Services Inc—*Kevin Orindeen*	72 S Main St, White River Junction VT 05001	802-888-7602	R	6*	.1
151	Family Resource Center—*Greg Echele*	3309 S Kingshighway Bl, Saint Louis MO 63139	314-534-9350	R	6*	.2
152	Jewish Community Center Of Richmond—*Alan Sataloff*	5403 Monument Ave, Richmond VA 23226	804-288-6091	R	6*	.2
153	St Johns County Council On Aging Inc—*Catherine Brown*	180 Marine St, Saint Augustine FL 32084	904-823-4810	R	6*	.1
154	Bridge Family Center Of Atlanta Inc—*Tom Russel*	1559 Johnson Rd Nw, Atlanta GA 30318	404-792-0070	R	6*	.1
155	Yjcc Of Bergen County—*Harold Benus*	605 Pascack Rd, Twp Washinton NJ 07670	201-666-6610	R	6*	.1
156	MR Home Care Inc—*Scott Rosado*	PO Box 2758, Bristol CT 06011	860-583-1541	R	6*	.1
157	Schooner Retirement Community Inc—*Gail Sasseville*	200 Stetson Rd, Auburn ME 04210	207-784-2900	R	6*	.1
158	Village At Duxbury Homeowners Cooperative Corp—*Carrie Alexander*	290 Kingstown Way Ofc, Duxbury MA 02332	781-585-2334	R	6*	.1
159	Youth In Action—*Keith Rawlings*	1269 Avery Ct, Saint Louis MO 63122	314-821-4042	R	6*	.2
160	May Center For Adult Services—*Alan Harchik*	1111 Elm St Ste 2, West Springfield MA 01089	413-734-0300	R	6*	.2
161	Family Service Inc—*Allen Thomas*	29 N Hamilton St Ste 1, Poughkeepsie NY 12601	845-452-1110	R	6*	.2
162	Florence Crittenton Agency Inc—*Nancy Christian*	1531 Dick Lonas Rd Bld, Knoxville TN 37909	865-602-2021	R	6*	.1
163	Malcolm Eaton Enterprises—*Sue Swanson*	570 W Lamm Rd, Freeport IL 61032	815-235-7181	R	6*	.1
164	Janet Pomeroy Center—*Henry Woo*	207 Skyline Blvd, San Francisco CA 94132	415-665-4100	R	5*	.2
165	Southgate At Shrewsbury Inc—*Stephen Flanagan*	30 Julio Dr, Shrewsbury MA 01545	508-842-8331	R	5*	.1
166	Jewish Community Centers Of South Broward Inc—*Mark Sherman*	5850 S Pine Island Rd, Davie FL 33328	954-434-0499	R	5*	.1
167	Salvation Army—*Donna Manning*	PO Box 76, Guntersville AL 35976	256-582-0536	R	5*	.1
168	Alaska Family Services Inc—*Donn Bennice*	1825 S Chugach St, Palmer AK 99645	907-746-4080	R	5*	.1
169	Economic Opportunity Committee Of St Clair County Inc—*Melinda Johnson*	302 Michigan St, Port Huron MI 48060	810-982-8541	R	5*	.1
170	Fargo Youth Commission Inc—*Rob Kuenenman*	2500 18th St S, Fargo ND 58103	701-235-2147	R	5*	.1
171	Community Access Inc—*Jeff Spangler*	PO Box 154, Lawton OK 73502	580-353-2045	R	5*	.2
172	House Of Ruth Maryland Inc—*Carole Alexander*	PO Box 64036, Baltimore MD 21264	410-889-0840	R	5*	.1
173	Parent and Child Together For West Central Illinois—*Denise Conkright*	PO Box 231, Mount Sterling IL 62353	217-773-3903	R	5*	.1
174	Valley Emergency Communication Center—*William Harry*	5360 Ridge Village Dr, West Valley City UT 84118	801-840-4100	R	5*	.1
175	Turning Point Enterprises Inc—*C Evans*	2418 N Wheeling Ave, Tulsa OK 74110	918-551-7740	R	5*	.2
176	Urban Renewal Corp—*Lane Jacobs*	224 Sussex Ave, Newark NJ 07103	973-483-2882	R	5*	.1
177	Amberleigh Retirement Community—*Frank Miosi*	2330 Maple Rd Apt 321, Williamsville NY 14221	716-689-4555	R	5*	.1
178	Spring Of Tampa Bay Inc—*Joanne Lighter*	PO Box 5147, Tampa FL 33675	813-247-5433	R	5*	.1
179	Rutherford County Adult Activity Center—*Betty Mcneely*	1130 Haley Rd, Murfreesboro TN 37129	615-890-4389	R	5*	.1
180	Orange County Rehabilitative And Developmental Services Inc—*William Smith*	PO Box 267, Paoli IN 47454	812-723-4486	R	5*	.1
181	Lima Head Start—*Nancy Redding*	540 S Central Ave, Lima OH 45804	419-227-9953	R	5*	.1
182	Arc Of Southington Inc—*Gail Ford*	201 W Main St, Plantsville CT 06479	860-628-9220	R	4*	.1
183	Wantagh Seaford Police Boys Club—*Maureen Roach*	PO Box 122, Wantagh NY 11793	516-783-8464	R	4*	.1
184	Lincoln And Lancaster County Child Guidance Center Inc—*Carol Crumpacker*	2444 O St, Lincoln NE 68510	402-475-7666	R	4*	.1
185	Arc Of Fayette County Inc—*Ninos Thomas*	80 Old New Salem Rd, Uniontown PA 15401	724-438-9042	R	4*	.1
186	Arc Butte County Inc—*Michael Mcginnis*	PO Box 3697, Chico CA 95927	530-891-5865	R	4*	.3
187	Alpha Opportunities Inc—*Betsy Broderson*	PO Box 824, Jamestown ND 58402	701-252-0162	R	4*	.1
188	Visiting Nurses Association—*Jacqalyn Flemming*	PO Box 368, Webster MA 01570	508-943-0612	R	4*	.1
189	Community Resources Inc—*Joan Wright*	208 W Bay Dr Nw, Olympia WA 98502	360-943-6257	R	4*	.1
190	Cdm In Home Care Services—*Eric Erickson*	11818 Se Mill Plain Bl, Vancouver WA 98684	360-896-9695	R	4*	.2

Note: An asterisk (*) indicates an estimated financial figure. The company type code used is as follows: R = Private, P = Public, S = Private Subsidiary, B = Public Subsidiary, D = Division, J = Joint Venture, I = Investment Fund.

COMPANY RANKINGS BY SALES WITHIN 4-DIGIT SIC

Rank	Company Name—Executive Officer	Address, City, State, Zip	Phone	Type	Fin	Empls
191	Crossroads For Youth—Janet Peek	PO Box 9, Oxford MI 48371	248-628-2561	R	4*	.1
192	Visiting Nurse and Homemaker Service Inc—Wayne Wayland	1603 Rte 38, Lumberton NJ 08048	609-267-7417	R	4*	.1
193	Arizona Baptist Children's Services—Cathy Orr	PO Box 35637, Phoenix AZ 85069	602-346-2300	R	4*	.1
194	Neighbors Organized For Adequate Housing—Edna Mcclendon	601 Covenant Dr, Belle Glade FL 33430	561-996-0131	R	4*	.1
195	Central Virginia Area Agency On Aging Inc—Andy Dooley	PO Box 1390, Lynchburg VA 24505	434-385-9070	R	4*	.1
196	Project HOME Community Development Corp—Sister Scullion	1515 Fairmount Ave, Philadelphia PA 19130	215-232-7272	R	4*	.2
197	Arc Of Clairborne County Inc—Scott Ferguson	1214 Cedar Fork Rd, Tazewell TN 37879	423-626-6757	R	4*	.1
198	Lgar Health and Rehabilitation—Shirley Vozar	800 Elsie St, Turtle Creek PA 15145	412-825-9000	R	4*	.1
199	Daytop Family Association—Keith Pollaci	2075 New York Ave, Huntington Station NY 11746	631-351-7112	R	4*	.1
200	Marshalltown Ymca-Ywca—Carol Hibbs	108 Washington St, Marshalltown IA 50158	641-752-8658	R	4*	.1
201	Domestic Violence Intervention Services Inc—Felicia Correia	4300 S Harvard Ave Ste, Tulsa OK 74135	918-585-3143	R	4*	<.1
202	Allentown Jewish Community Center—Carol Kranigz	702 N 22nd St, Allentown PA 18104	610-435-3571	R	4*	.1
203	Bridges USA Inc—James Boyd	477 N 5th St, Memphis TN 38105	901-454-5600	R	4*	.1
204	Rehabilitation Associates Ltd—Nancy Richman	1268 Sheridan Rd, Highland Park IL 60035	847-432-3833	R	4*	.1
205	Neighborhood Service Resource Center—Diane Cline	PO Box 68, Lafayette TN 37083	615-666-4141	R	4*	.1
206	Independent Options—Dennis Mattson	2532 Santa Catalina Dr, Costa Mesa CA 92626	714-434-1175	R	4*	.1
207	Arc Of Harrison County—George Harrington	PO Box 764, Clarksburg WV 26302	304-624-3641	R	4*	.1
208	John Hope Settlement House—Peter Lee	7 Thomas P Whitten Way, Providence RI 02903	401-421-6993	R	4*	.1
209	Polk County Youth Services Inc—Brian Boyer	1548 Hull Ave, Des Moines IA 50316	515-286-3221	R	4*	.1
210	Job Squad Inc—Brenda Hellwig	102 2nd St, Bridgeport WV 26330	304-848-0850	R	3*	.1
211	Community Services Inc—Kathy Taylor	PO Box 242, Tipp City OH 45371	937-667-8631	R	3*	.1
212	Magnolia Shrewsbury—Paulette Cali	307 Shrewsbury Rd, New Orleans LA 70121	504-731-1310	R	3*	.1
213	Pender Adult Services Inc—Wesley Davis	PO Box 1251, Burgaw NC 28425	910-259-9119	R	3*	.2
214	Baton Rouge Developmental Centers Inc—Michael Welch	7324 Alberta Dr Ste A, Baton Rouge LA 70808	225-767-2234	R	3*	.1
215	Bucks County Fire Dispatch—Brent Wigians	55 E Ct St, Doylestown PA 18901	215-547-5225	R	3*	.1
216	Falconer Street Group Home—Donald Trayner	299 Falconer St, Jamestown NY 14701	716-664-1897	R	3*	.1
217	Child Abuse and Neglect—Gaynell West	142 S Dean St Ste 104, Spartanburg SC 29302	864-596-2333	R	3*	.1
218	Womens Law Center—Richard Gilbert	950 W 17th St Ste D, Santa Ana CA 92706	714-667-1038	R	3*	.1
219	Launchability—Cathy Packard	4350 Sigma Rd Ste 100, Dallas TX 75244	972-991-6777	R	3*	<.1
220	Columbia Lighthouse For The Blind—Jed Babbin	1825 K St Nw Ste 1103, Washington DC 20006	202-454-6400	R	3*	<.1
221	Care and Share Of Erie Count Inc—Daniel Ward	241 Jackson St, Sandusky OH 44870	419-624-1411	R	3*	.1
222	American Learning Corp—Gary Gelman	1 Jericho Plz, Jericho NY 11753	516-938-8000	P	3	.1
223	East Baton Rouge Council On Aging Inc—Johnny Dykes	5790 Florida Blvd, Baton Rouge LA 70806	225-923-8000	R	3*	.1
224	Lewis County Senior Citizens Center Inc—Dinah Mills	171 W 2nd St, Weston WV 26452	304-269-5738	R	3*	.1
225	Saint Peter Counseling Center—Dave Compton	1711 Sheppard Dr, Saint Peter MN 56082	507-934-9612	R	3*	.1
226	Hispanic Human Resources Council Inc—Jorge Avellana	1427 S Congress Ave, West Palm Beach FL 33406	561-641-7400	R	3*	.1
227	Arc Of Washington-Holmes Counties Inc—Mavis Smith	1335 S Blvd, Chipley FL 32428	850-638-7517	R	3*	.1
228	Aunt Martha's Youth Service Center Inc—Gary Leofanti	718 N Bridge St Ste C, Yorkville IL 60560	630-553-1400	R	3*	.1
229	National Council On Family Violence—Sheryl Cates	PO Box 161810, Austin TX 78716	512-794-1133	R	3*	.2
230	Cabell County Community Services Organization Inc—Robert Roswall	724 10th Ave, Huntington WV 25701	304-529-4952	R	3*	.1
231	Independent Living Inc—Rita Giovannoni	815 Forward Dr, Madison WI 53711	608-274-7900	R	3*	.1
232	All Care Services Inc—Lynn Stevens	17671 Irvine Blvd Ste, Tustin CA 92780	714-669-1148	R	3*	.1
233	Youth Emergency Services and Shelter Of Iowa—Michael Fritz	918 Se 11th St, Des Moines IA 50309	515-282-9377	R	3*	.1
234	Methodist Childrens Home—Bobby Gilliam	1111 Herring Ave, Waco TX 76708	254-753-0181	R	2*	.3
235	Port City Development Center—Rebekah Cardwell	2124 N Williams Ave, Portland OR 97227	503-236-9515	R	2*	.1
236	Cherokee County Disabilities and Special Needs—H Cooper	PO Box 340, Gaffney SC 29342	864-487-4190	R	2*	.1
237	Community Housing Options Integrated Community Emp Social Servs Inc—Joseph Donofrio	135 E Live Oak Ave Ste, Arcadia CA 91006	626-447-5477	R	2*	.1
238	Millionair Club Charity Inc—Jim Osborn	2515 Western Ave, Seattle WA 98121	206-728-5627	R	2*	<.1
239	Sherwood Community Services—Mike Sink	402 91st Ave Ne, Everett WA 98205	425-334-4071	R	2*	.1
240	Information And Referral Network Inc—William Koss	3901 N Meridian St Ste, Indianapolis IN 46208	317-920-4850	R	2*	<.1
241	Floc—Linda Wright-Fuller	1763 Columbia Rd Nw St, Washington DC 20009	202-462-8686	R	1*	.1
242	Charleston Area Senior Citizens Service Inc—Sandra Clair	259 Meeting St, Charleston SC 29401	843-722-4127	R	1*	.2
243	Family Service Agency—Sue Plote	14 Health Services Dr, Dekalb IL 60115	815-758-8616	R	1*	<.1
244	Sugar Plum Inc—Thad Nowak	1353 Laskin Rd, Virginia Beach VA 23451	757-422-3913	R	1*	<.1
245	Living Ways Inc—Fiorella Spalvieri	626 Reed Ave, Kalamazoo MI 49001	269-343-6355	R	<1*	.2
246	District Iii Governmental Coop—Mike Guy	4453 Lee Hwy, Marion VA 24354	276-783-8157	R	<1*	.2
247	Horizon House Of Illinois Valley Inc—Jim Monterastelli	2000 Plank Rd, Peru IL 61354	815-223-4488	R	<1*	.2
248	Pddc A R C—Donald White	2350 W Westmoreland St, Philadelphia PA 19140	215-229-4550	R	<1*	.1
249	Arc Of East Central Iowa—Delaine Petersen	680 2nd St Se Ste 200, Cedar Rapids IA 52401	319-365-0487	R	<1*	.3

TOTALS: SIC 8322 Individual & Family Services
Companies: 249 | | | | | 5,568 | 53.9

8331 Job Training & Related Services

Rank	Company Name—Executive Officer	Address, City, State, Zip	Phone	Type	Fin	Empls
1	Global Knowledge Network Inc—Brian K Branson	PO Box 1039, Cary NC 27512	919-461-8600	S	400*	1.7
2	Hope Rehabilitation Services—John Christensen	30 Las Colinas Ln, San Jose CA 95119	408-284-2850	R	261*	.5
3	North Bay Developmental Disabilities Services Inc—Nancy Gardner	PO Box 3360, Napa CA 94558	707-256-1100	R	146*	.2
4	Myers Recording Studio—Robert Sirota	120 Claremont Ave Rm 2, New York NY 10027	212-749-2802	R	144*	.3
5	Abilities Unlimited Of Hot Springs Arkansas Inc—Steve Corbell	PO Box 3420, Hot Springs AR 71914	501-767-8400	R	119*	.2
6	SW Resources Inc—Gloria Cox	1007 Mary St, Parkersburg WV 26101	304-428-6344	R	119*	.2
7	Sacramento Employment and Training Agency—Kathy Kossick	925 Del Paso Blvd, Sacramento CA 95815	916-263-3800	R	106*	.6
8	Easter Seal New Hampshire Inc—Larry Gammon	555 Auburn St, Manchester NH 03103	603-624-5401	R	103*	2.0
9	PureSafety—William A Grana Jr	730 Cool Springs Blvd, Franklin TN 37067	615-367-4404	R	87*	.2
10	MTCI—Kent Milliken	3800 Fettler Park Dr S, Dumfries VA 22025		R	82*	.2
11	Orc Industries Inc—Barbara Barnard	PO Box 218, La Crosse WI 54602	608-781-7727	R	75*	.4
12	MIC Communications LLC—Frank F Brett	101 Huntington Ave, Boston MA 02199	617-406-4000	S	75*	.1
13	Pearl Buck Production Services—Jan Aho Pearl Buck Center Inc	3690 W 1st Ave, Eugene OR 97402	541-484-4666	D	75*	.1
14	Hope Enterprises Inc—James F Campbell	PO Box 1837, Williamsport PA 17703	570-326-3745	R	64*	.5
15	Lighthouse For The Blind Inc—Kirk Adams	PO Box 14959, Seattle WA 98114	206-322-4200	R	52*	.4
16	Goodwill Industries Of Northern New England—Micheal Coughlin	PO Box 8600, Portland ME 04104	207-774-6323	R	51*	1.2
17	VisionQuest National Ltd—Peter Ranalli	PO Box 12906, Tucson AZ 85732	520-881-3950	R	44*	1.0
18	Mankato Rehabilitation Center Inc—Pamela Year	PO Box 328, Mankato MN 56002	507-386-5600	R	42*	3.0
19	Southeastern Kentucky Rehabilitation Industries Inc—Norman Bradley	PO Box 1692, Corbin KY 40702	606-528-7490	R	42*	.6
20	Didlake Inc—Rexford Parr	8641 Breeden Ave Ste 1, Manassas VA 20110	703-361-4195	R	42*	1.1
21	Knowlgy Corp—Hassan Jugeh	1934 Old Gallows Rd, Vienna VA 22182	703-532-1000	R	40*	.1

Rank	Company Name—*Executive Officer*	Address, City, State, Zip	Phone	Type	Fin	Empls
22	Blessing/White Inc—*Christopher Rice*	23 Orchard Rd, Skillman NJ 08558	908-904-1000	R	40*	.1
23	Tualatin Valley Workshop Inc—*Dan Aberg*	6615 SE Alexander St, Hillsboro OR 97123	503-649-8571	R	37*	.3
24	Easter Goodwill Seals Miami Valley—*Amy Lyttrell*	1511 Kuntz Rd, Dayton OH 45404	937-461-4800	R	34*	.8
25	Pearl Buck Center Inc—*Edward F McDunn*	3690 W 1st Ave, Eugene OR 97402	541-484-4666	R	32*	.1
26	Haywood Vocational Opportunities Inc—*George Marshall*	PO Box 7, Hazelwood NC 28738	828-456-4455	R	31*	.3
27	Lott Industries Inc—*Jeff Holland*	3350 Hill Ave, Toledo OH 43607	419-536-5564	R	30*	1.0
28	Opportunity Partners Inc—*Jon Thompson*	5500 Opportunity Ct, Hopkins MN 55343	952-938-5511	R	29*	.5
29	Consortium For Worker Education Inc—*Barry Feinstein*	275 7th Ave Rm 1801, New York NY 10001	212-647-1900	R	29*	.5
30	Rappahannock Goodwill Industries Inc—*C Van Valkenburg*	PO Box 905, Fredericksburg VA 22404	540-371-3070	R	28*	.4
31	Goodwill Industries Of Central Florida Inc—*William Oakley*	7531 S Orange Blossom, Orlando FL 32809	407-857-0659	R	28*	.6
32	Work Services Corp—*Gerald Bettenhausen*	3401 Armory Rd, Wichita Falls TX 76302	940-766-3207	R	26*	.7
33	Goodwill Industries Of Hawaii Inc—*Laura Robertson*	2610 Kilihau St, Honolulu HI 96819	808-836-0313	R	26*	.5
34	Southeast Enterprises Package—*Paul Spears*	PO Box 9473, Kansas City MO 64133	816-353-2704	R	26*	.2
35	Board Of Cooperative Educational Services Of Chautauqua County—*Richard Miga*	9520 Fredonia Stockton, Fredonia NY 14063	716-672-4371	R	25*	.4
36	Anthony Wayne Rehabilitation Center For Handicapped And Blind Inc—*William Swiss*	8515 Bluffton Rd, Fort Wayne IN 46809	260-744-6145	R	24*	1.3
37	Huntsville Rehabilitation Foundation Inc—*Bryan Dodson*	2939 Johnson Rd Sw, Huntsville AL 35805	256-880-0671	R	24*	.4
38	Livingston-Wyoming County Chapter Nysarc—*Cindy Huether*	18 Main St, Mount Morris NY 14510	585-658-2828	S	23*	.4
39	Community Workshop Inc—*Stuart Rosenblatt*	PO Box 303, Glens Falls NY 12801	518-793-4700	R	23*	.3
40	Nysarc Incorporated Ontario County Chapter—*William Castiglione*	3071 County Complex Dr, Canandaigua NY 14424	585-394-7500	S	22*	.4
41	Goodwill Industries of Greater Detroit—*Lorna Utley*	3111 Grand River Ave, Detroit MI 48208	313-964-3900	R	22*	.2
42	Colorado Bluesky Enterprises—*Lawrence Velasco*	115 W 2nd St, Pueblo CO 81003	719-546-0572	R	21*	.3
43	Rolling Hills Progress Center—*Peter R Hermes*	PO Box 85, Lanark IL 61046	815-493-2321	R	21*	<.1
44	Coastal Enterprises Of Jacksonville Inc—*John Glover*	2715 Commerce Rd, Jacksonville NC 28546	910-455-2131	R	21*	.4
45	Cardinal Services Incorporated Of Indiana—*N Greene*	504 N Bay Dr, Warsaw IN 46580	574-267-3823	R	21*	.6
46	Infomentis Inc—*Wendy Reed*	1750 Founders Pkwy Ste, Alpharetta GA 30004	770-667-5352	R	19*	<.1
47	Kreider Services Inc—*Arlan Mcclain*	PO Box 366, Dixon IL 61021	815-288-6691	R	18*	.3
48	Arc Bridges Inc—*Kris Prohl*	2650 W 35th Ave, Gary IN 46408	219-884-1138	R	17*	.5
49	Brevard Achievement Center Inc—*Dayle Olsen*	1845 Cogswell St, Rockledge FL 32955	321-632-8610	R	17*	.5
50	Svrc Industries Inc—*Thomas Holmes*	919 Veterans Memorial, Saginaw MI 48601	989-752-6176	R	17*	.2
51	Assets Inc—*Rob Shoas*	2330 Nichols St, Anchorage AK 99508	907-279-6617	R	16*	.4
52	Helping Hand Of Goodwill Industries—*Larry Jones*	1817 Campbell St, Kansas City MO 64108	816-842-7425	R	16*	.3
53	Pathfinder Services Inc—*John Niederman*	PO Box 1001, Huntington IN 46750	260-356-0500	R	16*	.4
54	Goodwill Industries Of Akron Ohio Inc—*Nancy Mcclenaghan*	570 E Waterloo Rd, Akron OH 44319	330-724-6995	R	16*	.3
55	Mid-Michigan Industries Inc—*Alan Shilling*	2426 Parkway Dr, Mount Pleasant MI 48858	989-773-6918	R	15*	.1
56	Proact Inc—*Steven Ditschler*	3195 Neil Armstrong Bl, Saint Paul MN 55121	651-686-0405	R	15*	.2
57	Fairbanks Resource Agency Inc—*Emily Ennis*	805 Airport Way, Fairbanks AK 99701	907-456-8901	R	14*	.3
58	Lambs Farm Inc—*Dianne Yaconetti*	PO Box 520, Libertyville IL 60048	847-362-4636	R	14*	.1
59	Clearbrook—*Carl Lamell*	1835 W Central Rd, Arlington Heights IL 60005	847-870-7711	R	14*	.5
60	Corporate Source Inc—*Michael Kramer*	460 W 34th St Fl 11, New York NY 10001	212-273-6148	R	13*	.2
61	Knox County ARC—*Michael Carney*	2525 N 6th St, Vincennes IN 47591	812-895-0059	R	13*	.5
62	Southeast Community Work Center Inc—*Judith Shamley*	181 Lincoln St, Depew NY 14043	716-683-7100	R	12*	.5
63	Human Technologies Corp—*Richard Sebastian*	2260 Dwyer Ave, Utica NY 13501	315-724-9891	R	12*	.3
64	Gateway Community Industries—*Francoise Dunefsky*	PO Box 5002, Kingston NY 12402	845-331-1261	R	12*	.2
65	Cedar Valley Services Inc—*James Mueller*	2111 4th St Nw, Austin MN 55912	507-433-2303	R	12*	.5
66	Wall Street Mission—*John Hantla*	PO Box 1438, Sioux City IA 51102	712-258-4511	R	12*	.5
67	Star Incorporated Lighting The Way—*Jack Mcfadden*	PO Box 470, Norwalk CT 06852	203-846-9581	R	12*	.2
68	Sertoma Centre Inc—*Bob Straz*	4343 W 123rd St, Alsip IL 60803	708-371-9700	R	12*	.3
69	Waltham Committee Inc—*Nancy Hargreaves*	135 Beaver St Fl 3, Waltham MA 02452	781-899-8220	R	12*	.1
70	Michael Dunn Center—*Mike Mcelhinney*	629 Gallaher Rd, Kingston TN 37763	865-376-3416	R	11*	.3
71	Ability Building Center—*Steve Hill*	PO Box 6938, Rochester MN 55903	507-281-6262	R	11*	.3
72	Kansas Elks Training Center For The Handicapped Inc—*Ron Pasmore*	1006 E Waterman St, Wichita KS 67211	316-383-8700	R	11*	.3
73	Evansville Arc Inc—*Deidra Conner*	PO Box 4089, Evansville IN 47724	812-428-4500	R	11*	.2
74	Bosma Industries For The Blind Inc—*Lou Moneymaker*	8020 Zionsville Rd, Indianapolis IN 46268	317-684-0600	R	11*	.1
75	Arc San Francisco—*Timothy Hornbecker*	1500 Howard St, San Francisco CA 94103	415-255-7200	R	10*	.5
76	Oswego Industries Inc—*Cave Vickery*	7 Morrill Pl, Fulton NY 13069	315-598-3108	R	10*	.5
77	Lincoln Training Center and Rehabilitation Workshop—*Caron Nunez*	2643 Loma Ave, South El Monte CA 91733	626-442-0621	R	10*	.1
78	San Antonio Lighthouse For The Blind—*Mike Gilliam*	2305 Roosevelt Ave, San Antonio TX 78210	210-533-5195	R	10*	.3
79	Linden Resources—*Charles Richman*	750 23rd St S, Arlington VA 22202	703-521-4441	R	10*	.3
80	Arrowhead West Inc—*Lori Pendergast*	PO Box 1417, Dodge City KS 67801	620-227-8803	R	10*	.2
81	Opportunity Resources Inc—*Jack Chambers*	2821 S Russell St, Missoula MT 59801	406-721-2930	R	10*	.2
82	Kenosha Achievement Center Inc—*Paula Williams*	1218 79th St, Kenosha WI 53143	262-658-9500	R	10*	.6
83	Midwest Janitorial Services—*Kerny Waites*	100 Smoky Ln, Vicksburg MS 39180	601-638-2761	R	10*	.2
84	Urban Corps Of San Diego—*Sam Duran*	PO Box 80156, San Diego CA 92138	619-235-6884	R	10*	.1
85	Midwest Special Services Inc—*Lyth Hartz*	900 Ocean St, Saint Paul MN 55106	651-778-1000	R	9*	.4
86	Arnold Center Inc—*Michael Shea*	400 Wexford Ave, Midland MI 48640	989-631-9570	R	9*	.1
87	Center For Alternative Sentencing And Employment—*Joel Copperman*	346 Broadway Rm 3w, New York NY 10013	212-732-0076	R	9*	.2
88	Goodwill Industries Of Southwestern Michigan—*John Dillworth*	420 E Alcott St, Kalamazoo MI 49001	269-382-0490	R	9*	.2
89	Emory Valley Center—*Dick Jernigan*	PO Box 6854, Oak Ridge TN 37831	865-483-4385	R	9*	.2
90	Adapt Inc—*Thomas Kramer*	PO Box 190, Coldwater MI 49036	517-279-7531	R	9*	.1
91	AWS Inc—*David Kronstain*	1275 Lakeside Ave E, Cleveland OH 44114	216-861-0250	R	8*	2.4
92	Cornerstone Ondemand Inc—*Adam Miller*	1601 Cloverfield Blvd, Santa Monica CA 90404	310-752-0200	R	8*	.3
93	Jewish Vocational Services—*Peter Bloch*	4300 Rossplain Dr, Blue Ash OH 45236	513-985-0515	R	8*	.1
94	Bobby Dodd Institute Inc—*Wayne Mcmillan*	2120 Marietta Blvd Nw, Atlanta GA 30318	678-365-0071	R	8*	.1
95	Boone Center Inc—*Chuck Blossim*	200 Trade Ctr Dr W, Saint Peters MO 63376	636-978-4300	R	8*	.2
96	Lifequest—*Daryl Kilstrom*	804 N Mentzer St, Mitchell SD 57301	605-996-2032	R	8*	.2
97	Workshop Inc—*Richard Bennett*	339 Broadway, Menands NY 12204	518-465-5201	R	8*	.4
98	Aspiro Inc—*Mike Duschene*	1673 Dousman St, Green Bay WI 54303	920-498-2599	R	8*	.1
99	Community Workshop And Training Center Inc—*Gail Leiby*	3215 N University St, Peoria IL 61604	309-686-3300	R	8*	.5
100	Ardmore Enterprises Inc—*Donalda Lovelace*	3000 Lottsford Vista R, Mitchellville MD 20721	301-577-2575	R	7*	.2
101	Productive Alternatives Inc—*Steve Skauge*	1205 N Tower Rd, Fergus Falls MN 56537	218-998-5630	R	7*	.2
102	Tazewell County Resource Centers Inc—*Ron Hale*	21310 State Rte 9, Tremont IL 61568	309-347-7148	R	7*	.2
103	Spring Dell Center Inc—*Donna Retzlaff*	6040 Radio Station Rd, La Plata MD 20646	301-934-4561	R	7*	.2
104	Renewal Unlimited Inc—*Orwin Eilertson*	2900 Red Fox Run, Portage WI 53901	608-742-5329	R	7*	<.1
105	Shelby County Community Services Inc—*Richard Gloede*	PO Box 650, Shelbyville IL 62565	217-774-5587	R	7*	.2

Note: An asterisk (*) indicates an estimated financial figure. The company type code used is as follows: R = Private, P = Public, S = Private Subsidiary, B = Public Subsidiary, D = Division, J = Joint Venture, I = Investment Fund.

COMPANY RANKINGS BY SALES WITHIN 4-DIGIT SIC

Rank	Company Name—*Executive Officer*	Address, City, State, Zip	Phone	Type	Fin	Empls
106	Skyline Center Inc—*John Robinson*	PO Box 3064, Clinton IA 52732	563-243-4065	R	7*	.1
107	Lum Inc—*Anik Singal*	100 Lakeforest Blvd St, Gaithersburg MD 20877	240-252-4228	R	7*	.1
108	Ability Counts Inc—*Roger Cox*	775 Trademark Cir Ste, Corona CA 92879	951-734-6595	R	7*	.5
109	Work Skills Corp—*Rodney Jones*	100 Summit St, Brighton MI 48116	810-227-4868	R	7*	.4
110	Kaskaskia Workshop Inc—*Greg Shaver*	PO Box 1946, Centralia IL 62801	618-533-4423	R	7*	.2
111	Employment Horizons Inc—*Jurate Fiory*	10 Ridgedale Ave, Cedar Knolls NJ 07927	973-538-8822	R	7*	.2
112	Pueblo Diversified Industries Inc—*Karen Lillie*	2828 Granada Blvd, Pueblo CO 81005	719-564-0000	R	7*	.3
113	Tobosa Development Services—*Joe Madrid*	110 E Summit St, Roswell NM 88203	575-624-1025	R	6*	.2
114	Southern Indiana Resource Solutions Inc—*Kelly Mitchell*	1579 S Folsomville Rd, Boonville IN 47601	812-897-4840	R	6*	.2
115	Life's Work Of Western PA—*Everett Mc Elveen*	1323 Forbes Ave, Pittsburgh PA 15219	412-471-2600	R	6*	.1
116	Will Good Industries Inc—*John Owen*	2961 S Port Ave, Corpus Christi TX 78405	361-888-5268	R	6*	.2
117	Telecomm Research Associates—*Steve Wages*	505 Bertrand Ave, Saint Marys KS 66536	785-437-2000	R	6*	<.1
118	Suncom Industries Inc—*Peggy Vitale*	PO Box 46, Northumberland PA 17857	570-473-8352	R	6*	.6
119	Goodwill Industries Vocational Enterprises Inc—*Marg Bray*	700 Garfield Ave Ste 1, Duluth MN 55802	218-722-6351	R	6*	.3
120	Rauch Inc—*Bettye Dunham*	845 Park Pl, New Albany IN 47150	812-945-4063	R	6*	.1
121	Vocational Visions—*Kathryn Hebel*	26041 Pala, Mission Viejo CA 92691	949-837-7280	R	6*	.1
122	Columbia Industries—*Rich Foeppel*	PO Box 7346, Kennewick WA 99336	509-582-4142	R	6*	<.1
123	Development Workshop Inc—*Michael O'bleness*	555 W 25th St, Idaho Falls ID 83402	208-524-1550	R	6*	.3
124	Vip Services Inc—*Cynthia Simonsen*	530 E Centralia St, Elkhorn WI 53121	262-723-4043	R	6*	.1
125	Palm Beach Habilitation Center Inc—*Tina Philips*	4522 S Congress Ave, Lake Worth FL 33461	561-965-8500	R	6*	.1
126	Do-All Inc—*Christopher Girard*	PO Box 858, Bay City MI 48707	989-894-2851	R	5*	.2
127	Chicago Lighthouse For People Who Are Blind Or Visually Impaired—*Janet Szlyk*	1850 W Roosevelt Rd St, Chicago IL 60608	312-666-1331	R	5*	.2
128	Alabama Goodwill Industries Inc—*Don Smith*	2350 Green Springs Hwy, Birmingham AL 35205	205-323-6331	R	5*	.2
129	East Texas Employment and Training—*Martha Boston*	4100 Troup Hwy, Tyler TX 75703	903-561-8131	R	5*	.1
130	Ser-Jobs For Progress Of The Texas Gulf Coast Inc—*Nory Angel*	201 Broadway St, Houston TX 77012	713-773-6000	R	5*	<.1
131	Putnam County Comprehensive Services Inc—*Charles N Schroeder*	630 Tennessee St, Greencastle IN 46135	765-653-9763	R	5*	.3
132	Challenge Industries Inc—*Patrick Mckee*	950 Danby Rd Ste 179, Ithaca NY 14850	607-272-8990	R	5*	.1
133	Foley-Belsaw Co—*Richard J Hentges*	6300 Equitable Rd, Kansas City MO 64120		R	5*	<.1
134	Knowledge Tek—*Nicholas Kondur*	8620 Wolff Ct Ste 110, Westminster CO 80031	303-465-1800	R	5*	<.1
135	ARC Services Of Macomb Inc—*Joseph Tinsmen*	44050 N Gratiot Ave, Clinton Township MI 48036	586-469-1600	R	5*	.1
136	Diversified Inc—*Tiffany Mack*	13008 Beverly Park Rd, Mukilteo WA 98275	425-355-1253	R	5*	.1
137	Marshall-Starke Development Center Inc—*Michael Lintner*	PO Box 160, Plymouth IN 46563	574-936-9400	R	5*	.2
138	Illinois Growth Enterprises Inc—*Dale Sanders*	7200 Clinton Rd, Loves Park IL 61111	815-962-8333	R	5*	.5
139	Tahmc Associates—*Scott Rapp*	1545 Tacoma Ave S, Tacoma WA 98402	253-627-7980	R	5*	.2
140	Behavorial Technologies Corp—*David Bradish*	2601 E University Ave, Des Moines IA 50317	515-263-9109	R	5*	.1
141	Northwest Essex Community Health Care Network Inc—*Mauro Tucci*	83 Walnut St, Montclair NJ 07042	973-744-7733	R	5*	.1
142	Portage Industries Inc—*Philip Miller*	7008 State Rte 88, Ravenna OH 44266	330-296-2839	R	5*	.2
143	Futures Unlimited Inc—*Jeanne Gernentz*	210 E Torrance Ave, Pontiac IL 61764	815-842-1122	R	5*	.1
144	Op Shop Inc—*Jan Smith*	316 Columbia St, Fairmont WV 26554	304-366-5737	R	4*	.1
145	L E Phillips Career Development Center Inc—*Terry Peterson*	PO Box 600, Eau Claire WI 54702	715-834-2771	R	4*	.3
146	West Central Industries Inc—*Charles Oakes*	1300 22nd St Sw, Willmar MN 56201	320-235-5310	R	4*	.1
147	Joplin Workshops Inc—*Ron Sampson*	501 S School Ave, Joplin MO 64801	417-781-2862	R	4*	.2
148	Integrated Resources Inc—*Earl Smith*	PO Box 835, Mullens WV 25882	304-294-5610	R	4*	.2
149	Southwest Community Services Inc—*Mary Ambrosino*	6775 Prosperi Dr, Tinley Park IL 60477	708-429-1260	R	4*	.1
150	Hire Methods Inc—*Clint Drawdy*	7807 Baymeadows Rd E S, Jacksonville FL 32256	904-398-4133	R	4*	<.1
151	Gotham Writers' Workshop—*Andre Becker*	555 8th Ave Ste 1402, New York NY 10018	212-974-8377	R	4*	<.1
152	Industrial Aid Inc—*Mark Stroud*	4417 Oleatha Ave, Saint Louis MO 63116	314-773-3200	R	4*	.2
153	Lakeside Curative Services Inc—*Mary Popchock*	2503 Lincolnwood Ct, Racine WI 53403	262-598-0098	R	4*	.2
154	North East Placement Service Inc—*Rick Roy*	PO Box 185, South Woodstock CT 06267	860-963-2555	R	4*	.2
155	Alpha Group Of Delaware Inc—*Joseph Leonard*	1000 Alpha Dr, Delaware OH 43015	740-368-5810	R	4*	.2
156	New Horizons Corp—*Marva Greenwood*	5221 Harding Pl, Nashville TN 37217	615-360-8595	R	4*	.1
157	Holiday House Of Manitowoc County Inc—*Thomas Keil*	PO Box 579, Manitowoc WI 54221	920-682-4663	R	4*	.3
158	Mission Mountain Enterprises Inc—*Graden Mall*	330 Main St Sw, Ronan MT 59864	406-676-2563	R	4*	.1
159	Nci Affiliates Inc—*Jason Cybelski*	496 Linne Rd, Paso Robles CA 93446	805-238-6630	R	4*	.1
160	Community Workshops Inc—*Serena Powell*	174 Portland St Ste 20, Boston MA 02114	617-720-2233	R	4*	<.1
161	Rehabilitation Opportunities Inc—*Rory Brett*	5100 Philadelphia Way, Lanham MD 20706	301-731-4242	R	4*	.2
162	New Horizons Rehabilitation Inc—*Marie Dausch*	PO Box 98, Batesville IN 47006	812-934-4528	R	4*	.1
163	Rlcb Inc—*Janet Griffey*	3200 Bush St, Raleigh NC 27609	919-256-4220	R	4*	.1
164	Career Transition Center—*Brian Rogers*	3447 Atlantic Ave Ste, Long Beach CA 90807	562-570-3702	R	4*	.1
165	Springfield Workshop Inc—*Raymond Mcmenamy*	2835 W Bennett St, Springfield MO 65802	417-866-2339	R	3*	.2
166	Barbara Olson Central Of Hope Inc—*Barbara Olson*	3206 N Central Ave, Rockford IL 61101	815-964-9275	R	3*	.1
167	Skills Unlimited Inc—*Dave Rubin*	405 Locust Ave, Oakdale NY 11769	631-567-3320	R	3*	.1
168	Portal Industries Inc—*Carole Stuede*	420 10th Ave, Grafton WI 53024	262-377-4410	R	3*	.1
169	Winona ORC Industries Inc—*William Harris*	1053 E Mark St, Winona MN 55987	507-452-1855	R	3*	.4
170	Friendship Industries Inc—*David Flick*	801 Friendship Dr, Harrisonburg VA 22802	540-434-9586	R	3*	.2
171	Acts Of South Carolina Inc—*David Stuard*	PO Box 429, New Ellenton SC 29809	803-652-8600	R	3*	.1
172	Opportunity Workshop Of Lexington Inc—*David Boggs*	650 Kennedy Rd, Lexington KY 40511	859-254-0576	R	3*	.1
173	Lark Enterprises Inc—*Alice Sankey*	315 Green Ridge Rd Ste, New Castle PA 16105	724-658-5676	R	3*	.1
174	Nw Works Inc—*John Brauer*	3085 Shawnee Dr, Winchester VA 22601	540-667-0809	R	3*	.1
175	Elm City Rehabilitation Center Inc—*Tom Frederick*	1314 W Walnut St, Jacksonville IL 62650	217-245-9504	R	3*	<.1
176	Career TEAM LLC—*Christopher J Kuselias*	250 State StUnit C2, North Haven CT 06473	203-407-8800	R	3	<.1
177	Lower Shore Enterprises Inc—*Mike Perkey*	PO Box 1692, Salisbury MD 21802	410-749-6183	R	3*	.2
178	West Central Iowa Sheltered Workshop—*Floyd Klocke*	PO Box 340, Denison IA 51442	712-263-6141	R	3*	.2
179	Abilities Services Inc	1237 N Concord Rd, Crawfordsville IN 47933	765-362-4020	R	3*	.1
180	CompTutor-Computer Tutoring—*John Mitrano*	539 Northfield Ave, West Orange NJ 07052	973-736-7973	R	3*	<.1
181	South Texas Lighthouse For The Blind—*Regis Barber*	PO Box 9697, Corpus Christi TX 78469	361-883-6553	R	3*	.2
182	Worksource Enterprises—*Charles Mcelroy*	1311 Carlton Ave, Charlottesville VA 22902	434-972-1730	R	3*	.2
183	Functional Industries Inc—*Rodney Pederson*	PO Box 336, Buffalo MN 55313	763-682-4336	R	3*	.4
184	Trico Opportunities Inc—*Dale Frei*	PO Box 2610, Iron Mountain MI 49802	906-774-5718	R	3*	.3
185	Handishop Industries Inc—*Joe Greene*	1411 N Superior Ave, Tomah WI 54660	608-372-3289	R	3*	.1
186	Quadco Rehabilitation Center Inc—*Bruce Abell*	427 N Defiance St, Stryker OH 43557	419-682-1011	R	3*	.4
187	Lafayette Work Center Inc—*Rob Libera*	179 Garwood Dr, Ballwin MO 63021	636-227-5666	R	3*	.2
188	Expanco Inc—*David Dodson*	3005 Wichita Ct, Fort Worth TX 76140	817-293-9486	R	3*	.2
189	Work Force Development Board Incorporated Bcvb—*Todd Gustasson*	499 W Main St, Benton Harbor MI 49022	269-927-1064	R	3*	.1

Rank	Company Name—*Executive Officer*	Address, City, State, Zip	Phone	Type	Fin	Empls
190	National Plastering Industries Joint Apprenticeship Trust Fund—*William Roger*	8400 Corporate Dr Ste, Landover MD 20785	301-429-3123	R	3*	.1
191	Ross Training Center Inc—*Brian Reimes*	36 County Rd 32 S, Bellefontaine OH 43311	937-592-2009	R	3*	.1
192	Great Bay Services Inc—*Ruth Carney*	2061 Woodbury Ave, Newington NH 03801	603-436-2014	R	3*	.1
193	Habilitation Inc—*Robert Stclair*	1755 W Market St, Pottsville PA 17901	570-628-5316	R	3*	.1
194	Helena Industries Inc—*Wallace Melcher*	1325 Helena Ave, Helena MT 59601	406-442-8632	R	3*	.1
195	Work Opportunities Inc—*Phillip Mcconnel*	6515 202nd St Sw, Lynnwood WA 98036	425-778-2156	R	3*	.1
196	Northern Transitions Inc—*Patricia Shimmens*	1401 W Easterday Ave, Sault Sainte Marie MI 49783	906-635-5681	R	3*	<.1
197	Employment Connection—*Brenda Mahr*	2838 Market St, Saint Louis MO 63103	314-652-0360	R	2*	.1
198	Crowder Industries Inc—*Fred Gardner*	3707 Howard Bush Dr, Neosho MO 64850	417-451-5075	R	2*	.2
199	Northeastern Michigan Rehabilitation And Opportunity Center—*David Szydlowski*	800 Bolton St, Alpena MI 49707	989-356-6141	R	2*	.1
200	Belco Works Inc—*Anne Haning*	340 Fox Shannon Pl, Saint Clairsville OH 43950	740-695-0500	R	2*	.4
201	Work Opportunity Center Inc—*Alan Skole*	PO Box 481, Agawam MA 01001	413-786-8830	R	2*	.1
202	Jdwi—*Mike Bieleinva*	PO Box 6087, Galena IL 61036	815-777-2211	R	2*	.1
203	Madison Avenue Family Life Center—*Devin Brown*	2100 Eutaw Pl, Baltimore MD 21217	410-523-1828	R	2*	.1
204	Hanover-Adams Rehabilitation And Training Center Inc—*Lloyd Sterner*	PO Box 397, New Oxford PA 17350	717-624-4323	R	2*	.2
205	Industries Inc—*Kris Nally*	500 Walnut St S, Mora MN 55051	320-679-2354	R	2*	.1
206	Tri County Industries Inc—*Brenda Cogdell*	1250 Atlantic Ave, Rocky Mount NC 27801	252-977-3800	R	2*	.1
207	Shepard's Industrial Training Systems Inc—*Jim Shephard*	PO Box 341033, Bartlett TN 38184	901-382-5507	R	2*	<.1
208	Workshop And Rehabilitation Facilities For The Blind And Disabled Inc—*James Crim*	4244 3rd Ave S, Birmingham AL 35222	205-592-9683	R	2*	.3
209	Fontana Rehabilitation Workshop Inc—*Joseph Mitchell*	PO Box 848, Fontana CA 92334	909-428-3833	R	2*	.1
210	Vocation Plus Inc—*Judy Rogers*	5271 N 1st St, Fresno CA 93710	559-221-8983	R	2*	.1
211	Burnley Workshop Of The Poconos Inc—*Conrad Bergo*	4219 Manor Dr, Stroudsburg PA 18360	570-992-6616	R	2*	.1
212	Community Rehabilitation Industries Inc—*Rebecca Tschirgi*	3447 Atlantic Ave Ste, Long Beach CA 90807	562-591-0539	R	2*	<.1
213	Achieva—*Marsha Blanco*	711 Bingham St, Pittsburgh PA 15203	412-995-5000	R	2*	.6
214	Medina County Sheltered Industries Inc—*Jim Brown*	150 Quadral Dr Ste D, Wadsworth OH 44281	330-334-4491	R	2*	.3
215	Double S Industries—*Allison Young*	4405 Galloway Rd, Sandusky OH 44870	419-626-1048	R	2*	.1
216	Occupational Services Inc—*Sam Noble*	17 Redwood St, Chambersburg PA 17201	717-263-9293	R	2*	.1
217	Murray Ridge Production Center Inc—*Jenny Buschur*	1091 Infirmary Rd, Elyria OH 44035	440-284-2720	R	2*	.5
218	Southeast Enterprises Inc—*Dee Stock*	PO Box 9473, Kansas City MO 64133	816-353-2704	R	2*	.2
219	Hatcher Center Inc—*Chris Wright*	7180 U S Hwy 29, Blairs VA 24527	434-836-3272	R	2*	.1
220	Futures Rehabilitation Center Inc—*William Leven*	1 Futures Way, Bradford PA 16701	814-368-4101	R	2*	<.1
221	Professional Resource Associates Inc—*Pamela Petitpren*	201 Broadway St Ste 1, Marine City MI 48039	810-765-1181	R	2*	<.1
222	Florissant Valley Sheltered—*Steve Frank*	143 Mcdonnell Blvd B, Hazelwood MO 63042	314-731-1771	R	2*	.2
223	Knox New Hope Industries Inc—*Clare Bartlett*	1375 Newark Rd, Mount Vernon OH 43050	740-397-4601	R	2*	.2
224	Thumb Industries Inc—*Rhonda Wisenbaugh*	1263 Sand Beach Rd, Bad Axe MI 48413	989-269-9229	R	1*	<.1
225	Wabash Area Vocational Enterprises Inc—*David Roberts*	PO Box 487, Mount Carmel IL 62863	618-262-8614	R	1*	<.1
226	Frankfort Habilitation Inc—*Patty Graham*	3755 Lawrenceburg Rd, Frankfort KY 40601	502-227-9529	S	1	<.1
227	Capitol Projects Inc—*Ken Wagner*	2001 E Mccarty St, Jefferson City MO 65101	573-634-3660	R	1*	.1
228	Goodwill Industries Of Wayne And Holmes Counties Inc—*Judy Delaney*	PO Box 1188, Wooster OH 44691	330-264-1300	R	1*	.1
229	Sandco Industries—*Donald Nalley*	1101 Castalia St, Fremont OH 43420	419-334-9090	R	1*	.1
230	Arc Of North Webster—*Terri Simmons*	PO Box 351, Sarepta LA 71071	318-847-4356	R	1*	.1
231	Jackson County Developmental Center Inc *Craig Greening*	270 Jack Burlingame Dr, Millwood WV 25262	304-273-9311	R	1*	<.1
232	Donald L Mooney Enterprises LLC—*Charlotte Guilmenot*	924 Coronado Blvd, Universal City TX 78148	210 566 0995	R	1*	<.1
233	Rooc Inc—*Greg Bush*	PO Box 487, Roscommon MI 48653	989-275-9555	R	1*	.2
234	Foundation Workshop Inc—*Harry Jacoby*	12600 3rd St, Grandview MO 64030	816-763-7822	R	1*	.1
235	Arc Of Northern Rhode Island Inc—*Robert Carl*	80 Siaban St 1 Sox Ri, Woonsocket RI 02895	401-765-3700	R	1*	1.1
236	Indianhead Enterprises Of Menomonie Inc—*Michael Beauppe*	1426 Indianhead Dr E, Menomonie WI 54751	715-232-6460	R	1*	.1
237	Business By Phone Inc—*Art Sobczak*	13254 Stevens St, Omaha NE 68137	402-895-9399	R	1*	<.1
238	Gnome Digital Media—*Bruce Nazarian*	3727 W Magnolia Blvd S, Burbank CA 91505	818-563-6539	R	1*	<.1
239	Cetc Inc—*Leroy Evans*	PO Box 611, Havelock NC 28532	252-638-2177	R	1*	.1
240	Longwood Industries—*Renee Fisher*	PO Box 1025, Bedford VA 24523	540-586-1430	R	1*	.1
241	Innovative Industries Inc—*Larry Cooper*	421 W Centennial Ave, Carthage MO 64836	417-358-6891	R	1*	.1
242	Jeffco Subcontracting Inc—*Edgar Stolle*	2065 Pomme Rd, Arnold MO 63010	636-296-6211	R	1*	.1
243	Starlight Enterprises Inc—*Cassie Elvin*	638 Commercial Ave Sw, New Philadelphia OH 44663	330-339-3578	R	1*	.2
244	Growth and Opportunity Inc—*James Hutchinson*	525 S Ct St, Lapeer MI 48446	810-664-8504	R	1*	.2
245	Atco Inc	21 Campbell St, Athens OH 45701	740-592-6659	R	1*	.2
246	Learnwright Inc—*Frank Taylor*	4157 Oakdale Dr, Ayden NC 28513	252-746-4510	R	1*	<.1
247	Key Opportunities Inc—*Jane Munson*	400 Hillsdale St, Hillsdale MI 49242	517-437-4469	R	<1*	.2
248	Licco Inc—*Kyle Miller*	600 Industrial Pkwy, Newark OH 43056	740-522-8345	R	N/A	.3
249	Hopewell Industries Inc—*Lynn Tramomtano*	637 Chestnut St, Coshocton OH 43812	740-622-3563	R	N/A	.2

TOTALS: SIC 8331 Job Training & Related Services

Companies: 249					3,934	63.8

8351 Child Day Care Services

Rank	Company Name—*Executive Officer*	Address, City, State, Zip	Phone	Type	Fin	Empls
1	LPA Holding Corp—*Gary Graves*	21333 Haggerty RdSte 3, Novi MI 48375	248-697-9000	R	11,340*	13.0
2	Childcare Network Inc—*J Scott Cotter*	PO Box 2708, Columbus GA 31902	706-562-8600	R	1,278*	2.9
3	Knowledge Learning Corp—*Peter Maslen*	PO Box 6760, Portland OR 97228	503-872-1300	S	811*	41.0
4	Bright Horizons Family Solutions Inc—*David Lissy*	200 Talcott Ave S, Watertown MA 02472	617-673-8000	R	779*	18.5
5	KinderCare Learning Centers Inc—*Thomas Heymann* Knowledge Learning Corp	650 NE Holliday Ste 14, Portland OR 97232	503-872-1300	S	749*	21.0
6	La Petite Academy Inc Learning Care Group Inc	21333 Haggerty Rd Ste, Novi MI 48375		S	377*	13.0
7	Learning Care Group Inc—*William D Davis*	21333 Haggerty Rd Ste, Novi MI 48375	248-697-9000	S	212	7.5
8	Community Development Institute Head Start—*Carolyn Miller*	10065 E Harvard Ave St, Denver CO 80231	720-747-5100	R	160*	3.3
9	Ward North Center Inc—*Stephen Adubato*	346 Mount Prospect Ave, Newark NJ 07104	973-481-0415	R	18*	.2
10	New Horizon Kids Quest Inc—*William M Dunkley*	3405 Annapolis Lane No, Plymouth MN 55446		R	17	.6
11	Youth In Need—*James Braun*	1815 Boones Lick Rd, Saint Charles MO 63301	636-946-2303	R	16*	.3
12	Montgomery Community Action Committee and Cdc Inc—*Tom Gardner*	1066 Adams Ave, Montgomery AL 36104	334-263-3474	R	12*	.3
13	Harmonium Inc—*Rosa Lozada*	9245 Activity Rd Ste 1, San Diego CA 92126	858-684-3080	R	12*	.8
14	Two Rivers Head Start Agency—*Jane Whitaker*	1661 Landmark Rd, Aurora IL 60506	630-264-1444	R	10*	.1
15	Maryvale Day Care Center—*Linda Cahill*	PO Box 1039, Rosemead CA 91770	626-280-6510	R	9*	.2
16	Riverdale Ym-Ywha—*Vicki Matalon*	5625 Arlington Ave, Bronx NY 10471	718-548-8200	R	9*	.2
17	Hoyleton Youth And Family Services—*Christopher Cox*	PO Box 218, Hoyleton IL 62803	618-493-7382	R	8*	.1

Note: An asterisk (*) indicates an estimated financial figure. The company type code used is as follows: R = Private, P = Public, S = Private Subsidiary, B = Public Subsidiary, D = Division, J = Joint Venture, I = Investment Fund.

COMPANY RANKINGS BY SALES WITHIN 4-DIGIT SIC

Rank	Company Name—*Executive Officer*	Address, City, State, Zip	Phone	Type	Fin	Empls
18	Plea Inc—*Deborah Ferraro*	733 S Ave, Pittsburgh PA 15221	412-243-3464	R	6*	.1
19	Mid Columbia Children's Council Inc—*Suzanne Orman*	1100 E Marina Way Ste, Hood River OR 97031	541-386-2010	R	6*	.1
20	Sharon Baptist Board Of Directors Inc—*E Velasquez*	1925 Bathgate Ave, Bronx NY 10457	718-466-1604	R	6*	.1
21	First Assembly Of God—*Terri Richards*	2725 Merle Hay Rd, Des Moines IA 50310	515-279-2938	R	6*	.1
22	Bedford Stuyvesant Early Childhood Development Center Inc—*Ruth Cherry*	275 Marcus Garvey Blvd, Brooklyn NY 11221	718-453-0500	R	6*	.1
23	Lutheran Care Center—*Pat Gatewood*	702 W Cumberland Rd, Altamont IL 62411	618-483-6136	R	5*	.1
24	4 C's Council—*Alfredo Villasenor*	2515 N 1st St, San Jose CA 95131	408-487-0747	R	5*	.1
25	Capital Area Head Start—*Joe Pepper*	3700 Vartan Way Fl 2, Harrisburg PA 17110	717-541-1795	R	4*	.1
26	Early Childhood Centers Of Greater Springfield Inc—*Wayman Lee*	PO Box 90222, Springfield MA 01139	413-732-9518	R	4*	.1
27	Early Childhood Alliance Inc—*Madeleine Baker*	3320 Fairfield Ave, Fort Wayne IN 46807	260-745-2501	R	4*	<.1
28	Diane Adair Day Care Centers Inc—*Diane Carbine*	5780 Lewis Way, Concord CA 94521	925-672-1942	R	4*	.2
29	SeekingSitters—*Adrianne Kallweit*	3144 S Winston Ave, Tulsa OK 74135	918-749-3588	R	4*	<.1
30	Ruach Day Camp—*David Teichman*	2611 Ave Z, Brooklyn NY 11235	718-646-0009	R	4*	.1
31	Union Child Day Care Center Inc—*Leface Haris*	30 Manhattan Ave, White Plains NY 10607	914-761-6134	R	4*	.1
32	Carolyn E Wylie Center For Children Youth and Families—*Connie Beasley*	7177 Potomac St, Riverside CA 92504	951-784-0020	R	3*	.1
33	County Of Macomb—*Kathleen Nicosia*	21885 Dunham Rd Ste 10, Clinton Township MI 48036	586-469-5215	R	3*	.1
34	New Horizon Enterprises Inc—*Susan K Dunkley*	3405 Annapolis Ln N St, Plymouth MN 55447	763-557-1111	R	3*	.1
35	PRIDE Head Start—*Anna Farrell*	PO Box 1346, Logan WV 25601	304-752-5344	R	3*	.1
36	Aeoa Headstart—*Norman Ferris*	702 S 3rd Ave, Virginia MN 55792	218-749-5856	R	2*	.1
37	South Coast Head Start—*Dale Helland*	PO Box 239, Coos Bay OR 97420	541-888-3717	R	2*	.1
38	Orchard Valley Learning Center Inc—*Bradford Bennett*	15100 E Orchard Rd, Centennial CO 80016	303-699-2233	R	2*	.1
39	New Life Discovery Schools Inc—*Lynette Ferguson*	3097 Willow Ave Ste 14, Clovis CA 93612	559-292-8687	R	2*	<.1
40	Tripada Inc—*Donna Todd*	740 Middlesex Ave, Metuchen NJ 08840	732-321-5558	R	1*	.1
41	Child Saving Institute Foundation Inc—*Peg Harriott*	4545 Dodge St, Omaha NE 68132	402-553-6000	R	1*	.1
42	Blackfeet Head Start—*Susan Carlson*	615 S Piegan, Browning MT 59417	406-338-7370	R	<1*	<.1

TOTALS: SIC 8351 Child Day Care Services
Companies: 42   15,906   125.0

8361 Residential Care

Rank	Company Name—*Executive Officer*	Address, City, State, Zip	Phone	Type	Fin	Empls
1	Res-Care Inc—*Ralph Gronefeld*	9901 Linn Station Rd, Louisville KY 40223	502-394-2100	S	1,558*	45.0
2	Lutheran Home-Hickory Inc—*Ted Goins*	PO Box 947, Salisbury NC 28145	704-637-2870	R	1,011*	.2
3	Res-Care Inc Persons with Disabilities Div—*Ralph Gronefeld* Res-Care Inc	9901 Linn Station Rd, Louisville KY 40223	502-394-2100	D	694*	29.0
4	Elder Care Services Inc—*Frank Romano*	51 Summer St, Rowley MA 01969	978-948-7383	R	223*	.8
5	Ohio Presbyterian Retirement Services—*David Kaasa*	1001 Kingsmill Pkwy, Columbus OH 43229	614-888-7800	R	170*	2.8
6	Trinity Senior Living Community—*Ken Robibns*	PO Box 9184, Farmington Hills MI 48333	734-542-8300	R	159*	1.8
7	Jewish Home and Hospital For Aged—*Audrey Weiner*	120 W 106th St, New York NY 10025	212-870-4809	R	145*	2.2
8	Phineas Corp—*George Spelios*	9040 Sunset Dr, Miami FL 33173	305-596-9040	R	115*	2.0
9	Ann's Choice Inc—*Joseph Locascio*	10000 Anns Choice Way, Warminster PA 18974	215-443-3801	R	73*	.7
10	Children's Village—*Jeremy Kohomban*	Echo Hls, Dobbs Ferry NY 10522	914-693-0600	R	62*	.7
11	New England Center For Children Inc—*L Strully*	33 Tpke Rd, Southborough MA 01772	508-481-1015	R	51*	.7
12	Cal Farley's Boys Ranch—*Dan Adams*	PO Box 1890, Amarillo TX 79174	806-372-2341	R	39*	.7
13	George Junior Republic In Pennsylvania—*Richard Losasso*	PO Box 1058, Grove City PA 16127	724-458-9330	R	32*	.7
14	Buckeye Ranch Inc—*Richard Rieser*	5665 Hoover Rd, Grove City OH 43123	614-875-2371	R	32*	.4
15	Central City Concern—*George Sheldon*	232 Nw 6th Ave, Portland OR 97209	503-294-1681	R	32*	.5
16	Restore Therapy Services Ltd—*Alan Parker*	245 Cahaba Valley Pkwy, Pelham AL 35124	205-942-6820	R	29*	.7
17	Community Access Unlimited Inc—*Sidney Blanchard*	80 W Grand St Ste 2, Elizabeth NJ 07202	908-354-3040	R	28*	.4
18	Cal Farleys Girlstown USA—*Dan Adams*	PO Box 1890, Amarillo TX 79174	806-372-2341	R	27*	.6
19	Glenridge On Palmer Ranch Inc—*Howard Crowell*	7333 Scotland Way, Sarasota FL 34238	941-552-5300	R	27*	.3
20	Saratoga County Chapter Nysarc Inc—*Valerie Muratori*	2902 Rte 9, Ballston Spa NY 12020	518-587-0723	S	27*	.4
21	Clinton County Arc—*Theresa Garrow*	PO Box 826, Plattsburgh NY 12901	518-563-0930	S	26*	.5
22	Paul's Run Inc—*Luanna Fisher*	9896 Bustleton Ave Frn, Philadelphia PA 19115	215-934-3000	R	26*	.3
23	Way Station Inc—*Scott Rose*	PO Box 3826, Frederick MD 21705	301-662-0099	R	24*	.4
24	St Aemilian-Lakeside Inc—*Robert Sowinski*	8901 W Capitol Dr, Milwaukee WI 53222	414-463-1880	R	24*	.3
25	J Arthur Trudeau Memorial Center—*Mary Madden*	PO Box 7789, Warwick RI 02887	401-739-2700	R	22*	.9
26	Marianna Sunland Facility—*J Sherrel*	3700 Williams Dr, Marianna FL 32446	850-482-9484	R	22*	.8
27	Arcadia Retirement Residence—*Emmet White*	1434 Punahou St, Honolulu HI 96822	808-941-0941	R	22*	.3
28	Chapel Hill Residential Retirement Center Inc—*James Copeland*	PO Box 2121, Chapel Hill NC 27515	919-968-4511	R	22*	.3
29	Black Hills Special Services Co-Operative—*Ron Rosenboom*	PO Box 218, Sturgis SD 57785	605-347-4467	R	21*	.6
30	Partnerships In Community Living Inc—*Zellee Allen*	PO Box 129, Monmouth OR 97361	503-838-2403	R	20*	.5
31	Friends Retirement Concepts Inc—*Robert Kiser*	100 Monroe St Ste 1, Bridgewater NJ 08807	908-595-6600	R	20*	.2
32	Life Care Ponte Vedra Inc—*Milton Fulton*	1000 Vicars Landing Wa, Ponte Vedra Beach FL 32082	904-273-1700	R	19*	.2
33	Church Home Of Hartford Inc—*John Mobley*	200 Seabury Dr, Bloomfield CT 06002	860-286-0243	R	18*	.3
34	Vista Maria—*Cameron Hosner*	20651 W Warren St, Dearborn Heights MI 48127	313-271-3050	R	18*	.3
35	Florence Crittenton Services Of Orange County Inc—*Joyce Capelle*	PO Box 9, Fullerton CA 92836	714-680-9000	R	18*	.3
36	Brethren Hillcrest Homes—*Charles Cable*	2705 Mountain View Dr, La Verne CA 91750	909-593-4917	R	18*	.2
37	Orchard Place—*Brock Wolff*	PO Box 35425, Des Moines IA 50315	515-244-2267	R	18*	.3
38	John E Andrus Memorial Inc—*Betsy Biddle*	185 Old Broadway, Hastings On Hudson NY 10706	914-478-3700	R	18*	.3
39	Marrakech Housing Options Inc—*Francis Mccarthy*	6 Lunar Dr Ste 1, Woodbridge CT 06525	203-389-2970	R	17*	.3
40	Evergreen Center Inc—*Robert Littleton*	345 Fortune Blvd, Milford MA 01757	508-473-3422	R	17*	.3
41	Frederick Mennonite Community—*John Hendrickson*	PO Box 498, Frederick PA 19435	610-754-7878	R	17*	.3
42	Kidspeace National Centers For Kids In Crisis Of New England—*C Odonnell*	PO Box 787, Ellsworth ME 04605	207-667-2021	R	16*	.1
43	Parry Center For Children—*Kim Scott*	3415 Se Powell Blvd, Portland OR 97202	503-234-9591	R	16*	.2
44	Evangelical Retirement Homes Of Greater Chicago Inc—*David Loop*	350 W Schaumburg Rd St, Schaumburg IL 60194	847-884-5000	R	16*	.6
45	Carolina Village Inc—*Doley Bell*	600 Carolina Village R, Hendersonville NC 28792	828-692-6275	R	16*	.2
46	Cinnamon Hills Inc—*Jack Williams*	770 E Saint George Blv, Saint George UT 84770	435-674-0984	R	16*	.2
47	Senior Residential Care Inc—*Elena Black*	17 Chipman Way, Kingston MA 02364	781-585-4100	R	15*	.3
48	Glenkirk—*Alan Spector*	3504 Commercial Ave, Northbrook IL 60062	847-272-5111	R	15*	.3
49	Oconomowoc Developmental Training Center Of Wisconsin LLC	PO Box 278, Dousman WI 53118	262-569-5515	R	15*	.3
50	Lincoln Child Center—*Chris Mertz*	4368 Lincoln Ave, Oakland CA 94602	510-531-3111	R	15*	.2
51	Mid-Step Services Inc—*Gary Turbes*	4303 Stone Ave, Sioux City IA 51106	712-274-2252	R	15*	.4
52	California Friends Homes—*Charles Hise*	12151 Dale Ave, Stanton CA 90680	714-530-9100	R	14*	.3

Rank	Company Name—Executive Officer	Address, City, State, Zip	Phone	Type	Fin	Empls
53	St Mary's Manor—Michael Parke	701 Lansdale Ave, Lansdale PA 19446	215-368-0900	R	14*	.2
54	Valleylife—Cletus Thiebeau	1100 N Hamilton St, Chandler AZ 85225	602-371-0806	R	14*	.4
55	New Hope Village Inc—Chuck Clark	PO Box 887, Carroll IA 51401	712-792-5500	R	14*	.4
56	Carey Services Inc—Mark Draves	2724 S Carey St, Marion IN 46953	765-668-8961	R	14*	.4
57	Cunningham Childrens Home—Marlin Livingston	PO Box 878, Urbana IL 61803	217-367-3728	R	13*	.3
58	Redwoods A Community Of Seniors—Barbara Solomon	40 Camino Alto, Mill Valley CA 94941	415-383-2741	R	13*	.1
59	Development Homes Inc—Sandi Marshall	3880 S Columbia Rd, Grand Forks ND 58201	701-335-4000	R	13*	.3
60	Concern For Independent Living Inc—Ralph Fasano	PO Box 358, Medford NY 11763	631-758-0474	R	13*	.1
61	Logan Community Resources Inc—Daniel Harshman	PO Box 1049, South Bend IN 46624	574-289-4831	R	13*	.3
62	Progress Industries—Dan Skokan	PO Box 1449, Newton IA 50208	641-792-6119	R	12*	.3
63	Village At Waterman Lake Lld—Peter Sangermano	715 Putnam Pke Ofc, Greenville RI 02828	401-949-1333	R	12*	.2
64	Transitional Living Services Inc—Robert Wrenn	1040 S 70th St, Milwaukee WI 53214	414-476-9631	R	12*	.2
65	St Anne's Maternity Home—Tony Walker	155 N Occidental Blvd, Los Angeles CA 90026	213-381-2931	R	12*	.2
66	Lake Lad Inc—Gary Erdmann	PO Box 158, Dousman WI 53118	262-965-2131	R	12*	.2
67	Pioneer Center For Human Services—Lorraine Kopczynski	4001 W Dayton St, Mchenry IL 60050	815-344-1230	R	12*	.5
68	Rawhide Inc—John Solberg	7475 E Rawhide Rd, New London WI 54961	920-982-6100	R	12*	.1
69	Child Development Center Inc—Peter Howard	4620 17th St, Sarasota FL 34235	941-371-8820	R	12*	.3
70	Leroy Haynes Center For Children And Family Services Inc—Daniel Maydeck	PO Box 400, La Verne CA 91750	909-593-2581	R	12*	.2
71	Eastern Christian Children's Retreat Inc—William Bushman	700 Mountain Ave, Wyckoff NJ 07481	201-848-8005	R	12*	.3
72	Norwalk Rehabilitation Services Inc—Antonia Leonard	37 N Ave Ste 5, Norwalk CT 06851	203-845-8000	R	12*	.2
73	Boston Health Care Systems Inc—Jeffrey Boston	1865 Old Hudson Rd, Saint Paul MN 55119	651-501-2378	R	11*	.2
74	Travelers Haven—Elia Wallen	425 S Cherry St Ste 84, Denver CO 80246	720-833-5333	R	11	<.1
75	Beaverbrook Step Inc—Stanley Kruszewski	125 Walnut St Ste 202, Watertown MA 02472	617-926-1113	R	11*	.2
76	Larkin Center—Don Graf	1212 Larkin Ave, Elgin IL 60123	847-695-5656	R	10*	.2
77	Women's Treatment Center—Jewell Oates	140 N Ashland Ave, Chicago IL 60607	312-850-0050	R	10*	.2
78	Cenneidigh Inc—Russ Cenneidigh	402 Heritage Pl, Faribault MN 55021	507-334-4347	R	10*	.3
79	Comprehensive Systems Inc—Mark Stanton	PO Box 457, Charles City IA 50616	641-228-4842	R	10*	.5
80	Westminster Village Muncie Inc—Elizabeth Devoe	5801 W Bethel Ave, Muncie IN 47304	765-288-2155	R	10*	.2
81	Washoe Medical Center South Meadow—Alan Olive	10101 Double R Blvd, Reno NV 89521	775-982-7000	R	10*	.3
82	Pibly Residential Programs Inc—Thomas Jennings	2415 Westchester Ave, Bronx NY 10461	718-863-4100	R	10*	.1
83	Barium Springs Home For Children Inc—John Koppelmeyer	PO Box 1, Barium Springs NC 28010	704-872-4157	R	10*	.3
84	New Hampshire Odd Fellows Home—Kenneth Brochu	200 Pleasant St, Concord NH 03301	603-225-6644	R	9*	.2
85	Canton Christian Home Inc—Pam Knight	2550 Cleveland Ave Nw, Canton OH 44709	330-456-0004	R	9*	.2
86	Home For Aged Women-Minquadale Home Inc—Harvey Smith	1101 Gilpin Ave, Wilmington DE 19806	302-654-4486	R	9*	.2
87	Acton Medical Investors LP—Maik Persudy	1 Great Rd, Acton MA 01720	978-263-9101	R	9*	.2
88	Covenant House California—George Lozano	1325 N Western Ave, Los Angeles CA 90027	323-461-3131	R	9*	.2
89	Harmony Hill School Inc—Alfred Vuono	63 Harmony Hill Rd, Chepachet RI 02814	401-949-0690	R	9*	.1
90	Summit Childrens Residence—Bruce Goldsmith	339 N Broadway, Nyack NY 10960	845-358-7772	R	9*	.1
91	Somerset Community Services Inc—Roland Adkins	5574 Tulls Corner Rd, Marion Station MD 21838	410-623-2261	R	9*	.2
92	Pathway Homes Inc—Joel Mcnair	10201 Fairfax Blvd Ste, Fairfax VA 22030	703-876-0390	R	9*	.1
93	Good Shepherd-Fairview Home Inc—Michael Keenan	80 Fairview Ave, Binghamton NY 13904	607-724-2477	R	9*	.2
94	Cape Retirement Community Inc—Lynne Spriggs	3120 Independence St, Cape Girardeau MO 63703	573-335-1281	R	9*	.2
95	Mcbride Quality Care Services Inc—Alberta Mcbride	209 E Chippewa St, Mount Pleasant MI 48858	989-772-1261	R	9*	.5
96	Masonic Home For Children At Oxford Inc—Charles Ingram	600 College St, Oxford NC 27565	919-693-5111	R	9*	.1
97	Glenmeadow Inc—Tim Cotz	24 Tabor Xing Ste D34, Longmeadow MA 01106	413-567-7800	R	8*	.2
98	William Breman Jewish Home Inc—Deborah Beads	3150 Howell Mill Rd Nw, Atlanta GA 30327	404-351-8410	R	8*	.2
99	My Own Place Inc—Kim Scott-Hopkins	817 Varnum St Ne Ste 1, Washington DC 20017	202-636-2985	R	8*	.1
100	Baddour Memorial Center Inc—Parke Pepper	PO Box 97, Senatobia MS 38668	662-562-0100	R	8*	.3
101	Christian Haven Inc—John Fulkerson	12501 N State Rd 49, Wheatfield IN 46392	219-956-3125	R	8*	.1
102	Appleridge At Bethany Village—Grant Schumway	3005 Watkins Rd, Horseheads NY 14845	607-796-0430	R	8*	.3
103	Youth Campus—James Guidi	733 N Prospect Ave, Park Ridge IL 60068	847-823-5161	R	8*	.2
104	Bashor Home Of The United Methodist Church Inc—Donald Phillips	PO Box 843, Goshen IN 46527	574-875-5117	R	8*	.1
105	Saint Joseph's Home For The Elderly Of The Little Sisters Of The Poor—Gerard O'connor	140 Shepherds Ln Ste 1, Totowa NJ 07512	973-942-0300	R	8*	.1
106	Hillcrest Terrace—Kenneth Lorden	200 Alliance Way Ofc, Manchester NH 03102	603-645-6500	R	8*	.1
107	Youth For Tomorrow -- New Life Center Inc—Gary Jones	11835 Hazel Cir Dr, Bristow VA 20136	703-368-7995	R	8*	.1
108	Hope Network SE—Pat Crandall	35 W Huron St Ste 302, Pontiac MI 48342	248-334-3454	R	8*	.3
109	Oe Enterprises Inc—Kathy Bryan	348 Elizabeth Brady Rd, Hillsborough NC 27278	919-732-8124	R	8*	.1
110	Promesa Behavioral Health—Lisa Weigant	7475 N Palm Ave Ste 10, Fresno CA 93711	559-439-5437	R	7*	.2
111	Pilgrim Manor Inc—Steve Kauffman	2000 Leonard St Ne, Grand Rapids MI 49505	616-458-1133	R	7*	.1
112	Rosemont Center Inc—Robert Marx	2440 Dawnlight Ave, Columbus OH 43211	614-471-2626	R	7*	.1
113	Behavior Training Research Inc—Clay Hill	PO Box 307, Lake Jackson TX 77566	281-489-0317	R	7*	.1
114	Victoria Home For Retired Men And Women Inc—Elaine Jensen	25 N Malcolm St, Ossining NY 10562	914-941-2450	R	7*	.1
115	Childrens Home Inc—George Bryan	1001 Reynolda Rd, Winston Salem NC 27104	336-721-7600	R	7*	.1
116	Developmental Enterprises Corp—Susan Golec	333 E Airy St, Norristown PA 19401	610-277-3122	R	7*	.2
117	Hanna Boys Center—John Crews	PO Box 100, Sonoma CA 95476	707-996-6767	R	7*	.2
118	Springbridge Rehab and Wellness Ctr—Cameron Hodges	550 White Rd, Chesterfield MO 63017	314-469-1200	R	7*	.1
119	St Joseph's Children's Home—Bob Mayor	PO Box 1117, Torrington WY 82240	307-532-3494	R	7*	.1
120	Golfview Developmental Center Inc—Anthony Miner	9555 Golf Rd, Des Plaines IL 60016	847-827-6628	R	7*	.1
121	Pleasant Living Healthcare Inc—Randy Kropp	155 Blake Blvd, Pinehurst NC 28374	910-295-2294	R	7*	.1
122	Lutheran Housing Of Erie Inc—Tanya Moyer	149 W 22nd St, Erie PA 16502	814-452-3271	R	7*	.1
123	Dac Inc—Todd Seifert	1710 E Maple St, Maquoketa IA 52060	563-652-5252	R	7*	.1
124	Forum At The Woodlands Inc—Mary Parada	5055 W Panther Creek D, The Woodlands TX 77381	281-292-2600	R	7*	.2
125	Rha Community Services Of Utah—Brian Coates	645 S 1300 E, Salt Lake City UT 84102	801-582-1457	R	7*	.2
126	St Joseph Catholic Orphan Society—Pam Cotton	2823 Frankfort Ave, Louisville KY 40206	502-893-0241	R	7*	.1
127	Odyssey House Inc—Eric Schmidt	344 E 100 S Ste 301, Salt Lake City UT 84111	801-428-3406	R	7*	.1
128	Hilton East Assisted Living—Lori Curran	231 E Ave, Hilton NY 14468	585-392-7171	R	7*	.1
129	Health Resources Of Glastonbury Inc—Daniel Strauss	72 Salmon Brook Dr, Glastonbury CT 06033	860-633-5244	R	7*	.1
130	Abraham And Laura Lisner Home For Aged Women—Sharon Swann	5425 Western Ave Nw, Washington DC 20015	202-966-6667	R	7*	.1
131	Alpha Homes Of Wisconsin Inc—Valerie Duffeck	6216 Washington Ave St, Mount Pleasant WI 53406	262-886-3328	R	7*	.1
132	Midwest Health Services Inc—Joseph Knetzer	11 Lincoln Way W Ste 5, Massillon OH 44647	330-828-0779	R	6*	.1
133	Nexus Recovery Center Inc—A Crowell	8733 La Prada Dr, Dallas TX 75228	214-321-0156	R	6*	.1
134	Golden Pond Resident Care Corp—Larry Kunst	50 W Main St Ste 1, Hopkinton MA 01748	508-435-1250	R	6*	.1
135	Covenant Place Of Sumter Inc—Jack Richardson	2825 Carter Rd, Sumter SC 29150	803-469-7007	R	6*	.1
136	Children's Home Of Stockton—Mark Phelps	PO Box 201068, Stockton CA 95201	209-466-0853	R	6*	.1

Note: An asterisk (*) indicates an estimated financial figure. The company type code used is as follows: R = Private, P = Public, S = Private Subsidiary, B = Public Subsidiary, D = Division, J = Joint Venture, I = Investment Fund.

COMPANY RANKINGS BY SALES WITHIN 4-DIGIT SIC

Rank	Company Name—*Executive Officer*	Address, City, State, Zip	Phone	Type	Fin	Empls
137	Kensington Community Corporation For Individual Dignity—*Maku Warrakah-Ali*	9150 Marshall St Ste 9, Philadelphia PA 19114	215-288-9797	R	6*	.1
138	Springhouse Inc—*Anne Marchetta*	44 Allandale St Ofc, Jamaica Plain MA 02130	617-522-0043	R	6*	.1
139	Gibson County Area Rehabilitation Center Inc—*George Rehnquist*	PO Box 5, Princeton IN 47670	812-386-6312	R	6*	.2
140	Seattle Children's Home Inc—*Don Burdine*	2142 10th Ave W, Seattle WA 98119	206-283-3300	R	6*	.2
141	Mur-Ci Homes Inc—*Terry Kopansky*	PO Box 735, Antioch TN 37011	615-641-6446	R	6*	.1
142	Vi Casa—*Ann Walp*	PO Box 150, Westbrook ME 04098	207-879-6165	R	6*	.2
143	Cookson-Hill Community Action Foundation Inc—*Cleon Harrell*	PO Box 648, Sallisaw OK 74955	918-456-0571	R	6*	.2
144	Seventy Five State Street—*Tony Forgione*	75 State St Apt 524, Portland ME 04101	207-774-4447	R	6*	.2
145	National Church Residences Of Denver—*Joe Kasberg*	2335 N Bank Dr, Columbus OH 43220	614-451-2151	R	6*	.1
146	Garden Valley Retirement Village Inc—*Kenny Shafer*	1505 E Spruce St, Garden City KS 67846	620-275-9651	R	6*	.2
147	Indiana United Methodist Childrens Home Inc—*Gary Davis*	515 W Camp St, Lebanon IN 46052	765-482-5900	R	6*	.1
148	Spring Meadows Health Care Center LLC—*Margaret Childress*	220 Hwy 76, Clarksville TN 37043	931-552-0181	R	6*	.1
149	Arundel Lodge Inc—*Michael Drummond*	2600 Solomons Island R, Edgewater MD 21037	443-433-5900	R	6*	.1
150	Wilson Care Inc—*Bryan Barrish*	4544 N Hazel St, Chicago IL 60640	773-561-7241	R	6*	.1
151	Independent Opportunities Of Michigan Inc—*Leslie Salvani*	45199 Cass Ave, Utica MI 48317	586-739-2911	R	5*	.3
152	Lakeway Center For The Handicapped Inc—*Jerry Hammontree*	320 Industrial Ave, Morristown TN 37813	423-586-2196	R	5*	.2
153	Denver Children's Home—*Jerry Yager*	1501 Albion St, Denver CO 80220	303-399-4890	R	5*	.2
154	Able Inc—*Carletta Decker*	653 19th St W, Dickinson ND 58601	701-456-3000	R	5*	.2
155	Sertoma Center Inc—*Rebecca Massey*	1400 E 5th Ave, Knoxville TN 37917	865-524-5555	R	5*	.2
156	Easter Seal Society Inc—*Gordon Hauge*	PO Box 1206, Mandan ND 58554	701-663-6828	R	5*	.1
157	John C Proctor Endowment Home—*William Christison*	2724 W Reservoir Blvd, Peoria IL 61615	309-685-6580	R	5*	.1
158	One Organization For The Needs For Elderly—*William Daniel*	17400 Victory Blvd, Van Nuys CA 91406	818-708-6371	R	5*	<.1
159	Children's Home Of Lubbock And Family Service Agency Inc—*Lynn Harms*	PO Box 2824, Lubbock TX 79408	806-762-0481	R	5*	.1
160	Saint Ann's Infant And Maternity Home—*Sister Bader*	4901 Eastern Ave, Hyattsville MD 20782	301-559-5500	R	5*	.1
161	Bittersweet Inc—*Vicki Obee-Hilty*	12660 Archbold Whthuse, Whitehouse OH 43571	419-875-6986	R	5*	.1
162	Livhome Corp—*Mike Nicholson*	5900 Wilshire Blvd Ste, Los Angeles CA 90036	323-932-1300	R	5*	<.1
163	Veterans Of Foreign Wars National Home For Children—*Dana Huffy*	3573 S Waverly Rd, Eaton Rapids MI 48827	517-663-1521	R	5*	.1
164	Thornwell Home For Children—*Robert Stansell*	PO Box 60, Clinton SC 29325	864-833-1232	R	5*	.1
165	Twin Valley Developmental Services Inc—*Edgar Henry*	PO Box 42, Greenleaf KS 66943	785-747-2251	R	5*	.1
166	Davis-Stuart Inc—*Mark Spangler*	RR 2 Box 188a, Lewisburg WV 24901	304-647-5577	R	5*	.1
167	Hermitage House Youth Services Inc—*Ray Overholt*	25493 Hwy 99, Cambridge Springs PA 16403	814-734-4951	R	5*	.1
168	Mizpah Healthcare Inc—*Cathy Childrey*	510 Banner Ave, Greensboro NC 27401	336-273-2380	R	5*	.1
169	Llrien Inc—*Nancy Target*	6336 Cedar Ln Ofc, Columbia MD 21044	410-531-6000	R	4*	.1
170	B and D Hotel Corp—*Joseph Magit*	321 N Central Ave, Chicago IL 60644	773-626-2300	R	4*	.1
171	New Horizons Of Northwest Florida—*Casandra Baker*	10050 Hillview Dr, Pensacola FL 32514	850-474-0667	R	4*	.1
172	Washington County Community Residential Services Inc—*Ronald Bennett*	409 W Walnut St, Johnson City TN 37604	423-928-2752	R	4*	.1
173	Assisted Living Inc—*Frankie Lafleur*	1400 W Magnolia Ave, Eunice LA 70535	337-550-7200	R	4*	.1
174	Vantage Place Inc—*Lori Summerville*	6355 Woodside Ct, Columbia MD 21046	410-381-1500	R	4*	.1
175	Friends And Family Inc—*Buddy Smith*	PO Box 406, Romeo MI 48065	586-752-0372	R	4*	.1
176	Common Sense Housing Inc—*Randall Chretien*	15 Riverside Dr, Eddington ME 04428	207-989-1303	R	4*	.1
177	Veranda Preston Hollow—*John Berg*	11409 N Central Expy, Dallas TX 75243	214-363-5100	R	4*	.1
178	Virginia Home For Boys And Girls—*Christopher Schultz*	8716 W Broad St, Richmond VA 23294	804-270-6566	R	4*	.1
179	Arc Of The District Of Columbia Inc—*Mary Maccariello*	415 Mchgan Ave Ne Ste, Washington DC 20017	202-636-2957	R	4*	.2
180	Reynolds Road Ira—*Jeannie Liepis*	6 Reynolds Rd, Monroe NY 10950	845-774-7184	R	4*	.1
181	Coosa Valley Youth Services—*Michael Rollins*	PO Box 4519, Anniston AL 36204	256-237-2881	R	4*	.1
182	Southern Iowa Resources For Families Inc—*Rae Tucker*	PO Box 106, Creston IA 50801	641-782-4170	R	3*	.1
183	Hanover Juvenile Correctional Center—*Don Driscoll*	7093 Broad Neck Rd, Hanover VA 23069	804-537-5316	R	3*	.1
184	Whispering Pines West—*Kelly Bellmore*	N16 003 Main St, Powers MI 49874	906-497-5580	R	3*	.1
185	Connie Maxwell Children's Home—*Ben Davis*	PO Box 1178, Greenwood SC 29648	864-942-1400	R	3*	.1
186	Easter Seals Children's Development Center—*Steve Guedet*	650 N Main St, Rockford IL 61103	815-965-6745	R	3*	.1
187	Pleasant Living Inc—*Thomas Nobel*	11535 Fulton St E Ste, Lowell MI 49331	616-897-8413	R	2*	<.1
188	Children's Home Of Easton Inc—*Gregg Dowty*	2000 S 25th St, Easton PA 18042	610-258-2831	R	2*	.1
189	Powell Valley Assisted Living And Alsheimer's Community—*Kim Boggs*	4001 Se 182nd Ave Apt, Gresham OR 97030	503-665-2496	R	2*	.1
190	Jawonio Inc—*Jefferey Keahon*	260 N Little Tor Rd, New City NY 10956	845-634-4648	R	2*	.7
191	Fulton County Rehabilitation—*Rex Lewis*	500 N Main St, Canton IL 61520	309-647-6510	R	2*	.1
192	Cioffi Enterprises Inc—*Mary Cioffi*	973 Arnold Way, Alpine CA 91901	619-445-5291	R	1*	<.1
193	Wayne Wicks and Associates Investigations—*Wayne Wicks*	110 Broadway Ste C, La Porte TX 77571	713-439-1896	R	1*	<.1
194	Childrens Home Of Wheeling Inc—*Edward Pennington*	1 Orchard Rd, Wheeling WV 26003	304-233-2367	R	1*	.1
195	Connecticut Society To Prevent Blindness Inc—*Kathryn Garre-Ayars*	101 Whitney Ave Ste A, New Haven CT 06510	203-772-4653	R	<1*	.8
196	Klingberg Family Centers Inc—*Cathline Sullivan*	370 Linwood St, New Britain CT 06052	860-832-5542	R	<1*	.4
197	West Haven Foundation—*Tony Thomas*	20575 Ctr Ridge Rd Ste, Rocky River OH 44116	440-356-2330	R	N/A	.1

TOTALS: SIC 8361 Residential Care

	Companies: 197				6,147	124.9

8399 Social Services Nec

Rank	Company Name—*Executive Officer*	Address, City, State, Zip	Phone	Type	Fin	Empls
1	Legacy Health System—*Lee Dominqou*	1919 NW Lovejoy, Portland OR 97209	503-415-5600	R	1,364*	10.0
2	Baystate Health Systems Inc—*Mark R Tolosky*	280 Chestnut St, Springfield MA 01199	413-794-0000	R	940*	10.0
3	Providence Service Corp—*Fletcher Jay McCusker*	64 E Broadway Blvd, Tucson AZ 85701	520-747-7108	P	880	7.0
4	Almost Family Inc—*William B Yarmuth*	9510 Ormsby Station Rd, Louisville KY 40223	502-891-1000	P	340	9.0
5	CoMed Communications Inc—*Lorna Weir*	601 Walnut St Ste 250-, Philadelphia PA 19106	215-592-1363	S	261*	.1
6	VistaCare Inc—*Robert A Lefton*	717 N Harwood St Ste 1, Dallas TX 75201	214-922-9711	S	241	2.1
7	Stark County Community Action Agency—*Rodney Reasonover*	1366 Market Ave N, Canton OH 44714	330-454-1676	R	159*	.2
8	Polish National Alliance—*Frank J Spula*	6100 N Cicero Ave, Chicago IL 60646	773-286-0500	R	145*	.1
9	Medecins Sans Frontieres USA Inc—*Darin Portnoy*	333 7th Ave Fl 2, New York NY 10001	212-679-6800	R	145*	.1
10	Providence Saint John Foundation Inc—*Michael Dorsey*	8929 Parallel Pkwy, Kansas City KS 66112	913-596-4835	R	144*	.1
11	eHarmonycom Inc—*Jeremy Verba*	300 N Lake Ave Ste 111, Pasadena CA 91101	626-795-4814	R	133*	.2
12	Ipas—*Elizabeth Maguire*	300 Market St Ste 200, Chapel Hill NC 27516	919-967-7052	R	38*	.1
13	Educational Alliance Inc—*Richard Cantor*	197 E Broadway, New York NY 10002	212-780-2300	R	34*	1.0
14	Help At Home Inc—*Frank Guerrieri*	1 N State St Ste 800, Chicago IL 60602	312-	P	34	.2
15	Livingston Oakland Human Service Agency—*Ronald Borngesser*	PO Box 430598, Pontiac MI 48343	248-209-2600	R	30*	.5
16	Village For Families and Children—*William Baker*	1680 Albany Ave, Hartford CT 06105	860-236-4511	R	22*	.1

Rank	Company Name—*Executive Officer*	Address, City, State, Zip	Phone	Type	Fin	Empls
17	Upper East Tennessee Human Development Agency—*Lois Smith*	PO Box 46, Kingsport TN 37662	423-246-6180	R	21*	.3
18	Cherokee Boys Club Inc—*Mark Crowe*	PO Box 507, Cherokee NC 28719	828-497-9101	R	20*	.6
19	United Way Of Central Oklahoma Inc—*Robert Spinks*	PO Box 837, Oklahoma City OK 73101	405-236-8441	R	16*	<.1
20	Baltimore Healthcare Access Inc—*Kathleen Westcoat*	201 E Baltimore St Ste, Baltimore MD 21202	410-649-0521	R	7*	.1
21	Our Lady Of Victory Homes Of Charity Inc—*Paul Burkard*	780 Ridge Rd, Lackawanna NY 14218	716-828-9500	R	7*	.1
22	Residential Care Services Inc—*Beth Monteverde*	2400 Ardmore Blvd Ste, Pittsburgh PA 15221	412-271-2990	R	6*	.1
23	Jewish Community Federation Of Louisville Inc—*Alan Engel*	3630 Dutchmans Ln, Louisville KY 40205	502-451-8840	R	5*	<.1
24	United Way Of Genesee County—*Ronald Buttler*	PO Box 949, Flint MI 48501	810-232-8121	R	5*	<.1
25	Rocmond Area Youth Services—*Robert Spadden*	PO Box 912, Vinita OK 74301	918-256-7518	R	4*	.1
26	InfoQuest Inc	101 N 4th St Ste 105, Sandpoint ID 83864		R	4*	<.1
27	Arc Inc—*Tresa Ball*	PO Box 1016, Boise ID 83701	208-343-5583	R	2*	.1
28	Black River Industries Inc—*William Hrabe*	650 Jensen Dr, Medford WI 54451	715-748-2950	R	1*	<.1
29	Rockwest Training Company Inc—*Starla Hirszhkors*	4646 Ridge Dr Ne, Salem OR 97301	503-390-7355	R	1*	.1
30	District Xi Human Resource Council—*Jim Morton*	1801 S Higgins Ave, Missoula MT 59801	406-728-3710	R	<1*	.1

TOTALS: SIC 8399 Social Services Nec
Companies: 30

					5,008	42.4

8412 Museums & Art Galleries

Rank	Company Name—*Executive Officer*	Address, City, State, Zip	Phone	Type	Fin	Empls
1	Andreas Enterprises Inc—*George C Andreas*	PO Box 8, Middleburg VA 20118	540-687-8282	R	2*	<.1

8422 Botanical & Zoological Gardens

Rank	Company Name—*Executive Officer*	Address, City, State, Zip	Phone	Type	Fin	Empls
1	Zoological Society Of San Diego—*Berit Durler*	PO Box 120551, San Diego CA 92112	619-231-1515	R	173*	2.3
2	Houston Aquarium Inc	410 Bagby St, Houston TX 77002	713-315-5158	S	36*	.3
3	Florida Cypress Gardens Inc—*Kent Buescher*	6000 Cypress Gardens B, Winter Haven FL 33884	863-324-2111	R	27*	.3

TOTALS: SIC 8422 Botanical & Zoological Gardens
Companies: 3

					236	2.9

8711 Engineering Services

Rank	Company Name—*Executive Officer*	Address, City, State, Zip	Phone	Type	Fin	Empls
1	Fluor Corp—*David T Seaton*	6700 Las Colinas Blvd, Irving TX 75039	469-398-7000	P	20,849	39.2
2	Fluor Enterprises Inc—*Alan Boeckmann* Fluor Corp	3 Polaris Way, Aliso Viejo CA 92698	949-349-2000	S	14,747*	30.0
3	KBR Inc—*William P 'Bill' Utt*	601 Jefferson St Ste 3, Houston TX 77002	713-753-3011	P	10,099	35.0
4	URS Corp—*Martin M Koffel*	600 Montgomery St 26th, San Francisco CA 94111	415-774-2700	P	9,177	27.0
5	Mustang Engineering Inc—*Paul Redmon*	16001 Park Ten Pl, Houston TX 77084	713-215-8000	S	6,000*	5.0
6	CH2M Hill Companies Ltd—*Lee A McIntire*	9191 S Jamaica St, Englewood CO 80112		R	5,555	30.0
7	Earth Tech Inc—*Alan Krusi*	300 Oceangate Ste 700, Long Beach CA 90802	562-951-2000	S	4,195*	4.7
8	Golder Associates Inc (Atlanta Georgia)—*Hugh Golder*	3730 Chamblee Tucker R, Atlanta GA 30341	770-496-1893	R	3,978*	7.0
9	Bodycote Taussig Inc—*Ian Nichols*	7530 Frontage Rd, Skokie IL 60077	847-676-2100	R	3,580*	.2
10	Parsons Infrastructure and Technology Group Inc—*Charles L Harrington*	100 W Walnut St, Pasadena CA 91124	626-440-2000	R	2,865*	3.0
11	Plexus Services Corp—*Dean Foate*	PO Box 156, Neenah WI 54957	920-722-3451	S	2,704*	5.5
12	Tetra Tech Inc—*Dan L Batrack*	3475 E Foothill Blvd, Pasadena CA 91107	626-351-4664	P	2,573	13.0
13	Professional Service Industries Inc—*Murray Savage*	1901 S Meyers Rd Ste 4, Oakbrook Terrace IL 60181	630-691-1490	R	2,442*	2.5
14	Camp Dresser and McKee Inc—*Richard D Fox*	50 Hampshire St, Cambridge MA 02139	617-452-6000	R	2,373*	4.5
15	Black and Veatch Holding Co—*Len C Rodman*	11401 Lamar Ave, Overland Park KS 66211	913-458-2000	R	2,167*	9.6
16	Parsons Brinckerhoff Inc—*George J Piorcon*	1 Penn Plz, New York NY 10119	212-465-5000	R	2,144*	14.0
17	Teledyne Technologies Inc—*Robert Mehrabian*	1049 Camino Dos Rios, Thousand Oaks CA 91360	805-373-4545	P	1,942	8.9
18	Louis Berger Group Inc—*Larry Walker*	412 Mount Kemble Ave, Morristown NJ 07960	973-407-1000	R	1,558*	3.0
19	MWH Global Inc—*Robert B Uhler*	380 Interlocken Cresce, Broomfield CO 80021	303-533-1900	R	1,070*	7.0
20	Creare Inc—*James J Barry*	PO Box 71, Hanover NH 03755	603-643-3800	R	1,064*	1.9
21	Gannett Fleming Inc—*William M Stout*	PO Box 67100, Harrisburg PA 17106	717-763-7211	S	1,001*	1.9
22	Henningson Durham Richardson Inc—*George Little*	8404 Indian Hills Dr, Omaha NE 68114	402-399-1000	R	898*	7.8
23	VSE Corp—*Maurice A Gauthier*	2550 Huntington Ave, Alexandria VA 22303	703-960-4600	P	866	2.9
24	Stanley Group—*Gregs G Thomopulos*	225 Iowa Ave, Muscatine IA 52761	563-264-6600	R	845*	1.0
25	Chemtex International Inc—*Pedro Losa*	1979 Eastwood Rd, Wilmington NC 28403	910-509-4400	S	766*	.9
26	SBA Communications Corp—*Bill Bates*	5900 Broken Sound Pky, Boca Raton FL 33487	561-995-7670	P	698	.8
27	S and B Engineers and Constructors Ltd—*James G Slaughter Jr*	7825 Park Place Blvd, Houston TX 77087	713-645-4141	R	644*	4.0
28	DLZ Corp—*VV Rajadhyaksha*	6121 Huntley Rd, Columbus OH 43229	614-888-0040	R	624*	.7
29	Chapman Corp (Washington Pennsylvania)—*Art Hathaway*	331 S Main St, Washington PA 15301	724-228-1900	R	621*	1.2
30	Greenman-Pedersen Inc—*Steven Greenman*	325 W Main St, Babylon NY 11702	631-587-5060	R	607*	1.1
31	Gonzalez Design and Engineering Inc—*Gary Gonzalez*	29401 Stephenson Hwy, Madison Heights MI 48071	248-548-6010	R	576*	1.2
32	Day and Zimmermann International Inc—*Mick Mcareavy*	1500 Spring Garden St, Philadelphia PA 19130	215-299-8000	R	558*	6.0
33	Vanadium Group—*Matthew Schneider*	134 Three Degree Rd, Pittsburgh PA 15237	412-367-6060	R	540*	1.0
34	Greenhorne and O'Mara Inc—*Frank R Finch*	6110 Frost Pl, Laurel MD 20707	301-982-2800	R	537*	.6
35	Ecology and Environment Engnrng PC Ecology and Environment Inc	368 Pleasant View Dr, Lancaster NY 14086	716-684-8060	S	525*	1.0
36	BE and K/Terranext LLC—*Kim Martin*	155 S Madison St Ste 3, Denver CO 80209	303-399-6145	S	523*	2.8
37	Ralph M Parsons Co—*Charles Harrington*	100 W Walnut St, Pasadena CA 91124	626-440-2000	S	514*	4.0
38	Thornton-Tomasetti Group Inc—*Thomas Z Scarangello*	51 Madison Ave, New York NY 10010	917-661-7800	R	513*	1.5
39	Belcan Engineering Group Inc—*Ralph Anderson*	11591 Goldcoast Dr, Cincinnati OH 45249	513-489-4300	S	500*	7.5
40	Hill International Inc—*Irvin E Richter*	303 Lippincott Ctr, Marlton NJ 08053	856-810-6200	P	452	3.1
41	Jacobs-Sirrine Engineers Inc—*Craig Martin*	PO Box 5456, Greenville SC 29606	864-676-6000	R	451*	.5
42	KPFF Consulting Engineers Inc—*Jeff Asher*	1601 5th Ave Ste 1600, Seattle WA 98101	206-622-5822	R	423*	.8
43	Ardaman and Associates Inc—*Anwar E Z Wissa*	8008 S Orange Ave, Orlando FL 32809	407-855-3860	R	421*	.4
44	Foster Wheeler International Corp—*J Kent Masters*	53 Frontage Rd, Hampton NJ 08827	908-730-4000	S	420*	1.3
45	Burns and McDonnell—*Greg Graves*	9400 Ward Pky, Kansas City MO 64114	816-333-9400	R	371*	3.0
46	SNC-Lavalin America Inc—*Pierre Duhaime*	6585 Penn Ave, Pittsburgh PA 15206	412-363-9000	S	370*	2.0
47	Patton Harris Rust and Associates PC—*Thomas D Rust*	14532 Lee Rd, Chantilly VA 20151	703-449-6700	R	364*	.4
48	Strand Associates Inc—*Theodore Richards*	910 W Wingra Dr, Madison WI 53715	608-251-4843	R	346*	.4
49	STV Environmental—*Dominick Servedio* STV Group Inc	205 W Welch Dr, Douglassville PA 19518	610-385-8200	S	339*	1.4
50	MISTRAS Group Inc—*Sotirios Vahaviolos*	195 Clarksville Rd, Princeton Junction NJ 08550	609-716-4000	P	339	2.7
51	Thermal Solutions Inc (Hampton New Hampshire)—*Amin J Khoury*	216 Lafayette Rd, North Hampton NH 03862	603-964-9780	R	330*	.6
52	Gray Construction—*Stephen Gray*	10 Quality St, Lexington KY 40507	859-281-5000	R	329*	.3
53	Barrios Technology Inc—*Sandra G Johnson*	16441 Space Center Blv, Houston TX 77058	281-280-1900	R	325*	.6
54	Engineering Consulting Services Ltd—*Henry Lucas*	14026 Thunderbolt Pl S, Chantilly VA 20151	703-471-8400	R	324*	.6

Note: An asterisk (*) indicates an estimated financial figure. The company type code used is as follows: R = Private, P = Public, S = Private Subsidiary, B = Public Subsidiary, D = Division, J = Joint Venture, I = Investment Fund.

COMPANY RANKINGS BY SALES WITHIN 4-DIGIT SIC

Rank	Company Name—*Executive Officer*	Address, City, State, Zip	Phone	Type	Fin	Empls
55	L Robert Kimball and Associates—*Jeff Kimball*	615 W Highland Ave, Ebensburg PA 15931	814-472-7700	R	322*	.6
56	Fesco Inc—*Bill Findley*	1000 Fesco Ave, Alice TX 78332	361-661-7000	R	321*	.7
57	ENGlobal Corp—*Edward L Pagano*	654 N Sam Houston Pkwy, Houston TX 77060	281-878-1000	P	321	2.0
58	Elgin National Industries Inc—*Peter Walier*	2001 Butterfield Rd St, Downers Grove IL 60515	630-434-7200	R	320*	.6
59	Amec Earth and Environmental Inc—*Hisham Mahmoud*	3800 Ezell Rd Ste 100, Nashville TN 37211	615-333-0630	S	306*	3.9
60	Sargent and Lundy LLC—*Alan W Wendorf*	55 E Monroe St, Chicago IL 60603	312-269-2000	R	289*	1.8
61	Macaulay-Brown Inc—*Sidney Fuchs*	4021 Executive Dr, Beavercreek OH 45430	937-426-3421	R	285*	2.0
62	Turner Collie and Braden Inc—*James F Thompson*	5757 Woodway Ste 101 W, Houston TX 77057	713-780-4100	S	266*	.5
63	Parsons Transportation Inc—*Charles L Harrington*	100 M St SE Ste 1200, Washington DC 20003	202-775-3300	S	265*	1.4
64	Merrick and Co—*Ralph W Christie Jr*	2450 S Peoria St, Aurora CO 80014	303-751-0741	R	264*	.5
65	Comsearch Holdings Inc—*Chris Hardy*	19700 Janelia Farm Blv, Ashburn VA 20147	703-726-5500	S	258*	.1
66	LGE (Old Co) Inc—*Fred M Brune* CH2M Hill Companies Ltd	PO Box 491, Spartanburg SC 29304	864-578-2000	S	255*	2.5
67	Brown and Caldwell—*Craig Goehring*	PO Box 8045, Walnut Creek CA 94596	925-937-9010	R	244*	1.5
68	Abacus Technology Corp—*Dennis J Yee*	5454 Wisconsin Ave Ste, Chevy Chase MD 20815	301-907-8500	R	241*	.4
69	Kimley-Horn and Associates Inc—*John C Atz*	PO Box 33068, Raleigh NC 27636	919-677-2000	R	240*	1.5
70	George G Sharp Inc—*Allen Chin*	22 Cortlandt St 10th F, New York NY 10007	212-732-2800	R	238*	.5
71	Geomatrix Consultants Inc—*Anthony D Daus*	2101 Webster St 12th F, Oakland CA 94612	510-663-4100	R	237*	.5
72	Hazen and Sawyer PC—*James Fagan*	498 7th Ave 11th Fl, New York NY 10018	212-777-8400	R	235*	.4
73	Sotera Defense Solutions Inc—*John F Hillen III*	1501 Farm Credit Dr St, McLean VA 22102	703-738-2840	P	233	1.1
74	Terracon Consultants Inc—*David Gaboury*	18001 W 106th St Ste 3, Olathe KS 66061	913-599-6886	R	230*	2.5
75	Cubellis Inc—*Lenord G Cubellis*	281 Summer St 4th Fl, Boston MA 02210	617-338-0009	R	221*	.4
76	GDA Technologies Inc—*Isaac Sundarajan*	1010 Rincon Cir, San Jose CA 95131	408-432-3090	R	221*	.4
77	Science Management Corp—*Paul J Hoeper* Versar Inc	6850 Versar Ctr Ste 1, Springfield VA 22151	703-750-3000	S	217*	.4
78	Rettew Associates Inc—*George Rettew*	3020 Columbia Ave, Lancaster PA 17603	717-394-3721	R	201*	.2
79	CH2M Hill Inc (Bellevue Washington)—*Lee McIntire* CH2M Hill Companies Ltd	PO Box 91500, Bellevue WA 98009	425-453-5000	D	199*	.4
80	Moffatt and Nichol Engineers—*Robert D Nichol*	3780 Kilroy Airport Wa, Long Beach CA 90806	562-590-6500	R	191*	.5
81	Det Norske Veritas Holding (USA) Inc—*Kenneth Vareide*	1400 Ravello Dr, Katy TX 77449	281-396-1000	R	180*	.7
82	Washington Mining—*Robert Zaist*	PO Box 5888, Denver CO 80217	303-843-2000	D	179*	.8
83	Parsons Engineering Science Inc	100 W Walnut St, Pasadena CA 91124	626-440-2000	D	177*	1.5
84	STV Group Inc—*Dominick M Servedio*	205 W Welsh Dr, Douglassville PA 19518	610-385-8200	R	174*	1.2
85	Blasland Bouck and Lee Inc—*Steve Blake*	630 Plaza Dr Ste 200, Highlands Ranch CO 80129	720-344-3500	S	170	.9
86	Ecology and Environment Inc—*Kevin S Neumaier*	368 Pleasant View Dr, Lancaster NY 14086	716-684-8060	P	169	1.1
87	Skelly and Loy Inc—*Sandra Loy Bell*	449 Eisenhower Blvd St, Harrisburg PA 17111	717-232-0593	R	166*	.2
88	Wsa Group Inc—*Stevenson Smith*	PO Box 92, Columbia SC 29202	803-758-4500	R	165*	1.3
89	Florence and Hutcheson—*Robert Echols Jr*	2550 Irvin Cobb Dr, Paducah KY 42003	270-444-9691	S	163*	.3
90	Greeley and Hansen LLC—*Thomas J Sullivan*	100 S Wacker Dr Ste 14, Chicago IL 60606	312-558-9000	R	162*	.3
91	MSA Professional Services Inc—*Jim Owen PE*	1230 South Blvd, Baraboo WI 53913	608-356-2771	R	162*	.3
92	Consoer Townsend Envirodyne Engineers Inc—*Bob Fischer*	303 E Wacker Dr Ste600, Chicago IL 60601	312-938-0300	S	161*	1.0
93	Aero-Metric Inc—*Patrick M Olson*	4020 Technology Pky, Sheboygan WI 53083	920-457-3631	R	161*	.3
94	Bionetics Corp—*Charles J Stern*	101 Production Dr Ste, Newport News VA 23606	757-873-0900	R	160*	1.0
95	National Security Technologies LLC—*Stephen Younger*	PO Box 98521, Las Vegas NV 89193	702-295-2162	R	158*	2.5
96	Dugan Kinetics LLC	PO Box 1116, Carnation WA 98014	360-674-2113	R	157*	.1
97	Jt3 LLC—*Thomas Nunley*	821 Grier Dr, Las Vegas NV 89119	702-492-2100	R	157*	2.0
98	Vt Milcom Inc—*Walter Yourstone*	532 Viking Dr, Virginia Beach VA 23452	757-463-2800	S	154*	1.0
99	GAI Consultants—*Gary DeJidas*	385 E Waterfront Dr, Homestead PA 15120	412-476-2000	R	152*	.8
100	Kennedy/Jenks Consultants Inc	303 2nd St Ste 300 S, San Francisco CA 94107	415-243-2150	R	149*	.3
101	Jacobs Engineering Group Medical Plan Trust	PO Box 7084, Pasadena CA 91109	626-578-3500	R	149*	<.1
102	KCI Technologies Inc—*Terry F Neimeyer*	936 Ridgebrook Rd, Sparks MD 21152	410-316-7800	R	146*	1.0
103	Braun Intertec Corp—*George Kluempke*	11001 Hampshire Ave S, Minneapolis MN 55438	952-995-2000	R	144*	.3
104	Sasaki Associates Inc—*Ken Bassett*	64 Pleasant St, Watertown MA 02472	617-926-3300	R	144*	.3
105	Applied Research Associates Inc—*Neil Higgins*	4300 San Mateo Blvd NE, Albuquerque NM 87110	505-881-8074	R	142*	1.2
106	Mei Technologies Inc—*Ed Muniz*	2525 Bay Area Blvd Ste, Houston TX 77058	281-283-6200	R	142*	.9
107	Bahnson Inc—*T Whitener*	3901 Westpoint Blvd St, Winston Salem NC 27103	336-760-3111	S	140*	1.0
108	Roberts and Schaefer Co—*David Carter*	222 S Riverside Plz St, Chicago IL 60606	312-236-7292	R	138*	.2
109	Versar Inc—*Anthony L Otten*	6850 Versar Ctr, Springfield VA 22151	703-750-3000	P	138	.6
110	Reynolds Smith and Hills Inc—*Leerie T Jenkins Jr*	PO Box 4850, Jacksonville FL 32201	904-256-2500	R	136*	.9
111	MorganFranklin Corp—*Robert Morgan*	1753 Pinnacle Dr Ste 1, McLean VA 22102	703-564-7525	R	135*	.3
112	Roebbelen Contracting Inc—*Terence J Street*	1241 Hawks Flight Ct, El Dorado Hills CA 95762	916-939-4000	R	133*	.4
113	Syska and Hennessy Inc—*Cyrus Izzo*	1515 Broadway, New York NY 10036	212-921-2300	R	131*	.3
114	Shaw Solid Waste Management—*JM Bernhard Jr*	4 Commerce Dr S, Harriman NY 10926	845-492-3100	S	130	1.1
115	Ford Bacon and Davis Inc—*Rick Moore*	4001 Jackson St, Monroe LA 71202	318-323-9000	R	130*	.6
116	Andrews Group—*Frank J Andrews*	PO Box 250, Fairfield CA 94533	707-422-4844	R	125*	.2
117	Columbia Group Inc—*Rod Buck*	PO Box 531, Oakton VA 22124	202-546-1435	R	120*	.3
118	Smith Roberts Baldischwiler LLC—*Glen W Smith*	100 NE 5th St, Oklahoma City OK 73104	405-840-7094	R	116*	.1
119	GeoEngineers Inc—*Kurt Fraese*	600 Stewart St Ste 170, Seattle WA 98101	206-728-2674	R	115*	.5
120	Wilbur Smith Associates Inc—*Hollis A Walker*	PO Box 92, Columbia SC 29202	803-758-4500	R	113*	1.0
121	Aerospace Testing Alliance—*Rogers Starr*	600 William Northern B, Tullahoma TN 37388	931-454-4397	R	112*	2.1
122	Edwards and Kelcey Inc—*Kevin McMahon*	PO Box 1936, Morristown NJ 07962	973-267-0555	S	110*	1.1
123	KEYW Holding Corp—*Leonard Moodispaw*	1334 Ashton Rd Ste A, Hanover MD 21076	443-270-5300	P	108	.7
124	Engineering/Remediation Resources Group Inc—*Cynthia A Liu*	4585 Pacheco Blvd Ste, Martinez CA 94553	925-969-0750	R	108*	.2
125	Clough Harbour and Associates LLP—*Raymond Kinley*	PO Box 5269, Albany NY 12205	518-453-4500	R	107*	.7
126	SpanPro Inc—*Craig Wheeler*	5495 North Bend Rd Ste, Burlington KY 41005		R	106*	.2
127	Psomas—*Blake Murillo*	555 S Flower St Ste 44, Los Angeles CA 90071	213-223-1400	R	102*	.4
128	Global Water Technologies Inc—*Erik Hromadka*	351 W 10th St Ste537, Indianapolis IN 46202	317-452-4488	P	101	.2
129	WK Dickson and Company Inc—*David L Peeler*	616 Colonnade Dr, Charlotte NC 28205	704-334-5348	R	99*	.2
130	Benatec Associates Inc—*Wayne Willey*	200 Airport Rd Capital, New Cumberland PA 17070	717-901-7055	R	99*	.1
131	BEI Corp (Pasadena Texas)—*FD Bandini*	3741 Red Bluff Rd Ste, Pasadena TX 77503	713-475-2424	R	97*	.2
132	Systems Engineering Solutions Inc—*Alisha Williams*	2301 Gallows Rd Ste 20, Dunn Loring VA 22027	703-573-4366	R	97*	.2
133	PACE Resources Inc—*RE Horn Jr*	PO Box 15055, York PA 17405	717-852-1300	R	96*	.6
134	Parkhill Smith and Cooper Inc—*Joseph Rapier*	4222 85th St, Lubbock TX 79423	806-473-2200	R	96*	.2
135	Bechtel National Inc	PO Box 193965, San Francisco CA 94119	415-768-1234	S	95*	.5
136	Maguire Group Inc—*Carlos Duart*	1 Ct St, New Britain CT 06051	860-224-9141	R	95*	.2
137	3D-International Inc—*Charles Harrington*	1900 W Loop S Ste 400, Houston TX 77027	713-871-7000	R	94*	.5
138	Ref-Chem Construction Corp—*Harvey Page*	PO Box 262507, Houston TX 77207	713-477-4471	S	94*	.5
139	Capstone Corp—*William J Moore III*	635 Slaters Ln Ste 100, Alexandria VA 22314	703-683-4220	R	92*	.5
140	Computer Technology Associates Inc—*Tom Velez*	12530 Parklawn Dr Ste, Rockville MD 20852	301-581-3200	R	92*	.5
141	Kilohana Corp—*Russell Figueiroa*	2024 N King St Ste 200, Honolulu HI 96819	808-842-1133	R	91*	.2

Rank	Company Name—*Executive Officer*	Address, City, State, Zip	Phone	Type	Fin	Empls
142	Zin Technologies Inc—*Daryl Laisure*	6745 Engle Rd, Cleveland OH 44130	440-625-2200	R	90*	.2
143	Emcor Government Services—*Mike Shelton*	2800 Crystal Dr Ste 60, Arlington VA 22202	703-553-7500	S	90	N/A
144	Tcom Limited Partnership A/K/A Tcom LP—*Donald Spritzer*	7115 Thomas Edison Dr, Columbia MD 21046	410-312-2400	R	89*	.3
145	Newcomb and Boyd—*Stephen M Sessler*	303 Peachtree Center A, Atlanta GA 30303	404-730-8400	R	87*	.2
146	Ayres Associates—*Thomas Pulse*	3433 Oakwood Hills Pkw, Eau Claire WI 54701	715-834-3161	R	83*	.3
147	Power Engineers Inc—*Jack Hand*	PO Box 1066, Hailey ID 83333	208-788-3456	R	82*	1.0
148	FPMI Solutions Inc—*Joseph Sapanaro*	101 Quality Cir NW Ste, Huntsville AL 35806	256-539-1850	R	81*	.7
149	Stantec Consulting Corp—*Robert Gomes*	PO Box 230, Redmond WA 98073	425-372-1600	R	81*	.8
150	Engineering and Professional Services Inc—*Francesco Musor-rafitt*	78 Apple St, Tinton Falls NJ 07724	732-747-8277	R	79*	.6
151	Berger/ABAM Engineers Inc—*Arnfinn Rusten*	33301 9th Ave S Ste 30, Federal Way WA 98003	206-431-2300	R	79*	.2
152	Triumph Aerospace Systems - Newport News—*William Jacobson*	703 Middle Ground Blvd, Newport News VA 23606	757-873-1344	S	79*	.2
153	Willdan Group Inc—*Mark Risco*	2401 E Katella Ave Ste, Anaheim CA 92806	714-940-6300	P	78	.5
154	SE Technologies Inc—*Roger Dhoanu*	98 Vanadium Rd Bldg D, Bridgeville PA 15017	412-221-1100	R	76*	1.0
155	Moreland Altobelli Associates Inc—*Thomas D Moreland*	2211 Beaver Ruin Rd St, Norcross GA 30071	770-263-5945	R	76*	.4
156	Buchart-Horn—*Brian Funkhouser* PACE Resources Inc	PO Box 15040, York PA 17405	717-852-1400	S	73*	.3
157	ERM-Southwest Inc—*Peter T Regan*	15810 Park Ten Pl Ste, Houston TX 77084	281-579-8999	R	73*	.1
158	RMT Inc (Madison Wisconsin)—*Steven Johannsen*	PO Box 8923, Madison WI 53708	608-831-4444	S	72*	.6
159	McMahon Associates Inc—*Dennis Lamers* McMahon Group	PO Box 1025, Neenah WI 54957	920-751-4200	S	71*	.1
160	Applied Engineering Management Corp—*Sharon deMonsabert*	14030 Thunderbolt Pl S, Chantilly VA 20151	703-464-7030	R	70*	.1
161	Vollmer Associates LLP—*Gerald V Nielsten*	50 W 23rd St 8th Fl, New York NY 10010	212-366-5613	S	69*	.6
162	Freese and Nichols Inc—*Robert F Pence*	PO Box 96, Cedar Hill TX 75106	817-735-7300	R	68*	.4
163	Wilson and Company Incorporated Engineers and Architects—*Steven D Watt*	4900 Lang Ave NE, Albuquerque NM 87109	505-348-4000	R	67*	.4
164	Eichleay Engineers Incorporated of California—*Russell Miller*	1390 Willow Pass Rd St, Concord CA 94520	925-689-7000	R	67*	.1
165	Burgess and Niple Ltd—*Kenneth R Davis Jr*	5085 Reed Rd, Columbus OH 43220	614-459-2050	R	65*	.8
166	Boyle Engineering Corp—*Phil Petrocelli*	PO Box 7350, Newport Beach CA 92658	949-476-3300	S	65*	.6
167	Emteq Inc—*Jerry Jendusa*	5349 S Emmer Dr, New Berlin WI 53151	262-679-6170	R	64*	.4
168	Environmental Co—*Richard Heiderstadt*	PO Box 5127, Charlottesville VA 22905	434-295-4446	R	63*	.1
169	GeoTrans Inc—*Charles R Faust* Tetra Tech Inc	21335 Signal Hill Plaz, Sterling VA 20164	703-444-7000	S	62*	.3
170	Shafer Kline and Warren Inc—*Ron Petering*	11250 Corporate Ave, Lenexa KS 66219	913-888-7800	R	61*	.3
171	Hal-Tec Corp—*Robert Hales*	405 N Reo St Ste 240, Tampa FL 33609	813-289-4119	R	60*	.1
172	RBF Consulting—*S Robert Kallenbaugh*	14725 Alton Pkwy, Irvine CA 92618	949-472-3505	S	59*	.5
173	MSE Inc—*Donald R Peoples*	PO Box 4078, Butte MT 59701	406-494-7100	R	59*	.1
174	Fugro USA Inc	PO Box 740010, Houston TX 77274	713-778-5500	S	58*	.1
175	Electrosonic Inc—*James Bowie*	3320 N San Fernando Bl, Burbank CA 91504	818-333-3600	R	57*	.2
176	A Epstein and Sons International Inc—*Sidney Epstein*	600 W Fulton St, Chicago IL 60661	312-454-9100	R	57*	.4
177	GRW Engineers Inc—*Ron Gilkerson*	801 Corporate Dr, Lexington KY 40503	859-223-3999	R	57*	.2
178	Government Systems Technologies Inc	3159 Schrader Rd, Dover NJ 07801	973-607-4080	R	57*	.1
179	Coon Engineering Inc—*Bryan E Coon*	2832 W Wilshire Blvd S, Oklahoma City OK 73116	405-842-0363	R	57*	.1
180	D3 Technologies Inc—*Ryan Bogan*	4838 Ronson Ct, San Diego CA 92111	858-571-1685	R	56*	.1
181	Rincon Research Corp—*Michael Taylor*	101 N Wilmot Rd Ste 10, Tucson AZ 85711	520-519-4600	R	56*	.2
182	McMahon Group—*Dennis J Lamers*	PO Box 1025, Neenah WI 54957	920-751-4200	R	55*	.1
183	Techno-Sciences Inc—*Jean-Luc Abaziou*	11750 Beltsville Dr 3r, Deltsville MD 20705	240-790-0600	R	54*	<.1
184	Portage Inc (Idaho Falls Idaho)—*Nick Stanisich*	1075 S Utah Ave Ste 20, Idaho Falls ID 83402	208-528-6608	R	54*	.4
185	IMS Co (Brea California)—*Joe Renton*	2929 E Imperial Hwy St, Brea CA 92821	714-854-8600	R	54*	.1
186	M and H Vincotte Partnership—*Dave Costello*	2900 Wilcrest Dr Ste30, Houston TX 77042	713-974-3627	R	54*	.1
187	Proconex Inc—*John Weekley*	PO Box 13700-1259, Philadelphia PA 19191	610-495-1835	R	54*	.1
188	Alan Plummer and Associates Inc—*Alan H Tucker*	1320 S University Dr S, Fort Worth TX 76107		R	53*	.1
189	Gwin Dobson and Foreman Inc—*Mark Glenn*	3121 Fairway Dr Ste B, Altoona PA 16602	814-943-5214	R	53*	.1
190	Lea Elliott Inc—*Jack Norton*	2505 N State Hwy 360 S, Grand Prairie TX 75050	972-890-9800	R	53*	.1
191	Vertex Engineering Services Inc—*James O'Brien* Tetra Tech Inc	400 Libbey Pky, Weymouth MA 02189	781-952-6000	S	52*	.1
192	HSA Engineers and Scientists—*Nicholas Albergo*	4019 E Fowler Ave, Tampa FL 33617	813-971-3882	R	51*	.3
193	K and M Engineering and Consulting Corp—*Michael H Kappaz*	PO Box 9865, McLean VA 22102	202-861-5632	R	50*	.4
194	Navarro Research and Engineering Inc—*Susana Navarro-Valenti*	669 Emory Valley Rd, Oak Ridge TN 37830	865-220-9650	R	50*	.4
195	Wood Group Pratt and Whitney Industrial Turbine Services LLC—*Karen Christensen*	1460 Blue Hills Ave, Bloomfield CT 06002	860-286-4600	R	50*	.2
196	Process Plus LLC—*Jim Wendle*	1340 Kemper Meadow Dr, Cincinnati OH 45240	513-742-7590	R	50*	.1
197	Tempco Engineering Inc—*Pablo Ontiveros*	8866 Laurel Canyon Blv, Sun Valley CA 91352	818-767-2326	S	50*	.1
198	Engineers and Constructors International Inc—*Bob Armstrong*	PO Box 86030, Baton Rouge LA 70879	225-293-7768	S	50*	.1
199	Applied Research Associates Transportation Div—*Robert Sues* Applied Research Associates Inc	100 Trade Center Dr St, Champaign IL 61820	217-356-4500	D	49*	.1
200	Omitron Inc—*Bruce Larsen*	7051 Muirkirk Meadows, Beltsville MD 20705	301-474-1700	R	49*	.1
201	SENTEL Corp—*Darrel L Crapps*	1101 King St Ste 550, Alexandria VA 22314	703-739-0084	S	48*	.4
202	Pacific Scientific Oeco Corp—*Dorinda Walton*	4607 SE International, Milwaukie OR 97222	503-659-5999	D	48*	.3
203	CV International Inc—*Robert Tatge*	2771 Plaza Del Amo Sui, Torrance CA 90503	310-328-8550	R	48*	.1
204	Haley and Aldrich Inc—*Bruce E Beverly*	465 Medford St Ste 220, Boston MA 02129	617-886-7400	R	47*	.4
205	Hubbell Inc Kellems Wiring Device Div—*Timothy H Powers*	40 Waterview Dr, Shelton CT 06484	475-882-4800	S	46*	.4
206	MWH—*Robert Uhler*	2353 130th Ave NE Ste, Bellevue WA 98005	425-882-2455	R	46*	.1
207	Microcosm Inc—*James R Wertz*	4940 W 147th St, Hawthorne CA 90250	310-219-2700	R	46*	.1
208	Chiyoda International Corp	1177 W Loop S Ste 680, Houston TX 77027	713-965-9005	S	46	<.1
209	Herbert Rowland and Grubic Inc—*Robert C Grubic*	369 E Park Dr, Harrisburg PA 17111	717-564-1121	R	45*	.1
210	Skyline Windows LLC—*Steven Kraus*	220 E 138th St, Bronx NY 10451	212-491-3000	R	44*	.3
211	Foth and Van Dyke and Associates Inc—*Tim Weyenberg*	PO Box 19012, Green Bay WI 54307	920-497-2500	R	44*	.5
212	GZA GeoEnvironmental Technologies Inc—*William Beloff*	202 Kent Pl, Newmarket NH 03857	603-659-3559	R	44*	.5
213	Robert E Lee and Associates—*Lee Novak*	4664 Golden Pond Park, Oneida WI 54155	920-662-9641	R	44*	<.1
214	Garver LLC—*Dian Barton*	4701 Northshore Dr, North Little Rock AR 72118	501-376-3633	R	43*	.3
215	WH Pacific Inc—*David Williams*	12100 NE 195th St Ste, Bothell WA 98011	425-951-4800	S	43*	.3
216	MS Consultants Inc—*Thomas E Mosure*	333 E Federal St, Youngstown OH 44503	330-744-5321	R	43*	.2
217	Assurance Technology Corp—*H Renfroe*	84 S St, Carlisle MA 01741	978-369-8848	R	42*	.3
218	Middough Associates Inc—*Ronald R Ledin*	1901 E 13th St, Cleveland OH 44114	216-367-6000	R	42*	.6
219	Harris Group Inc—*Jim Gabriel*	300 Elliott Ave W Ste, Seattle WA 98119	206-494-9400	R	42*	.4
220	Transnuclear Inc—*Tara Neider*	7135 Minstrel Way Ste, Columbia MD 21045	410-910-0900	S	42*	.1
221	Belt Collins and Associates Ltd—*Anne Li Mapes*	2153 N King St Ste 200, Honolulu HI 96819	808-521-5361	R	42*	.1

Note: An asterisk (*) indicates an estimated financial figure. The company type code used is as follows: R = Private, P = Public, S = Private Subsidiary, B = Public Subsidiary, D = Division, J = Joint Venture, I = Investment Fund.

COMPANY RANKINGS BY SALES WITHIN 4-DIGIT SIC

Rank	Company Name—*Executive Officer*	Address, City, State, Zip	Phone	Type	Fin	Empls
222	Heath Consultants Inc—*Graham Midgley*	9030 W Monroe Rd, Houston TX 77061	713-844-1300	R	42*	.5
223	Structural—*Peter Emmons*	7455 New Ridge Rd Ste, Hanover MD 21076	410-850-7000	R	41*	.1
224	ANGI International LLC—*Andrew Grimmer*	15 Plumb St, Milton WI 53563	608-868-4626	S	41*	.1
225	Quanta Systems LLC—*Philip M Blackmon*	213 Perry Pky, Gaithersburg MD 20877	301-590-3300	S	41*	.1
226	Stanley Consultants Inc Stanley Group	225 Iowa Ave, Muscatine IA 52761	563-264-6600	S	40*	.6
227	Wade-Trim—*Doug Watson*	500 Griswold Ave Ste 2, Detroit MI 48226	313-961-3650	R	40*	.4
228	Chemical and Industrial Engineering Inc—*Jamie Ghazi*	1930 Bishop Ln Ste 800, Louisville KY 40218	502-451-4977	R	40*	.3
229	Williams Fire and Hazard Control Inc—*Dwight Williams*	PO Box 1359, Mauriceville TX 77626	409-727-2347	R	40*	.1
230	Nissan Technical Center North America Inc—*Shigeo Ishida*	PO Box 9200, Farmington Hills MI 48333	248-488-4123	R	40*	.5
231	Grant Geophysical Inc—*Richard Miles*	PO Box 219950, Houston TX 77218	713-850-7600	R	39*	1.0
232	Affiliated Engineers Inc—*David S Odegard*	PO Box 44991, Madison WI 53744	608-238-2616	R	39*	.4
233	Evergreen Engineering Inc—*Richard Bernhardt*	PO Box 21530, Eugene OR 97402	541-484-4771	R	39*	.2
234	Dannenbaum Engineering Corp—*Len Waterworth*	3100 W Alabama St, Houston TX 77098	713-520-9570	R	38*	.2
235	Grubbs Hoskyn Barton and Wyatt Inc—*Mark Wyatt*	PO Box 55105, Little Rock AR 72215	501-455-2536	R	38*	.1
236	Barr Engineering Co—*Doug Connell*	4700 W 77th St Ste 200, Minneapolis MN 55435	952-832-2600	R	37*	.4
237	Facility Group—*James Strack*	2233 Lake Park Dr, Smyrna GA 30080	770-437-2700	R	37*	.2
238	Aker Solutions US Inc—*Oyvind Eriksen*	3600 Briarpark, Houston TX 77042	713-988-2002	D	36*	.2
239	Lurgi PSI Inc—*Kurt Torster*	1790 Kirby Pky Ste 300, Memphis TN 38138	901-756-8250	R	36*	.1
240	Lja Engineering and Surveying Inc—*Calvin Ladner*	2929 Briarpark Dr Ste, Houston TX 77042	713-953-5200	R	36*	.3
241	Davidson Technologies Inc—*Julian Davidson*	530 Discovery Dr Nw, Huntsville AL 35806	256-922-0720	R	35*	.2
242	ENGlobal Constant Power Inc ENGlobal Corp	654 N Sam Houston Pkwy, Houston TX 77060	281-878-1000	S	35*	.1
243	Us Auctions Live Corp—*Cornelius Theron*	1688 Hull Ct, West Palm Beach FL 33414	561-337-6009	R	35*	.4
244	Future Research Corp—*Jesse Nunn*	675 Discovery Dr Nw 2s, Huntsville AL 35806	256-430-4304	R	34*	.2
245	Srf Consulting Group Inc—*Randall Geerdes*	1 Carlson Pkwy N Ste 1, Minneapolis MN 55447	763-475-0010	R	34*	.3
246	PPM Consultants Inc—*L Todd Perry*	2508 Ticheli Rd, Monroe LA 71202	318-325-7270	R	33*	.3
247	Systems Engineering and Management Co—*William M Tincup*	1430 Vantage Ct, Vista CA 92081	760-727-7800	R	33*	.1
248	Amos and Andrews Inc—*Frank J Andrews* Andrews Group	1801 Walters Ct, Fairfield CA 94533	707-422-4844	S	33*	.1
249	Columbus Technologies And Services Inc—*Ajay Handa*	225 S Lake Ave Ste 101, Pasadena CA 91101	626-795-3556	R	32*	.4
250	Perigon PA—*Harvey Mason*	931 Industrial Dr, Matthews NC 28105	704-246-2000	R	32*	.2
251	International Steel Services Inc—*Walter Sieckman*	661 Andersen Dr Ste 3, Pittsburgh PA 15220	412-922-9100	R	32*	.1
252	Eberspaecher North America Inc—*Heinrich Baumann*	29101 Haggerty Rd, Novi MI 48377	248-994-7010	S	32*	.1
253	Barge Waggoner Sumner and Cannon—*Robert Higgins*	211 Commerce St Ste 60, Nashville TN 37201	615-254-1500	R	31*	.4
254	Crawford Murphy and Tilly Inc—*Brian Whiston*	2750 W Washington St, Springfield IL 62702	217-787-8050	R	31*	.3
255	RLE International—*Gerd Zimmerman*	31701 Research Park Dr, Madison Heights MI 48071	248-498-5200	R	31*	.1
256	Orbital Engineering Inc—*Robert J Lewis*	1344 5th Ave, Pittsburgh PA 15219	412-261-9100	R	30*	.3
257	Duos Technologies Inc—*Gianni Arcaini*	6622 Southpoint Dr S S, Jacksonville FL 32216	904-296-2807	R	30*	.1
258	Kta-Tator Inc—*Kenneth Tator*	115 Technology Dr, Pittsburgh PA 15275	412-788-1300	R	30*	.2
259	Bowyer-Singleton and Associates Inc—*Raymond Bradick*	520 S Magnolia Ave, Orlando FL 32801	407-843-5120	R	29*	.2
260	Larson Design Group Inc—*Keith Kuzio*	PO Box 487, Williamsport PA 17703	570-323-6603	R	29*	.2
261	Nana/Colt Engineering LLC—*Greg Cooke*	700 G St Fl 5, Anchorage AK 99501	907-273-3900	R	29*	.4
262	Ctl Engineering Inc—*C Satyapriya*	PO Box 44548, Columbus OH 43204	614-276-8123	R	29*	.3
263	Quasar Engineering Inc—*Massy Kadivar*	111-C Independence Dr, Menlo Park CA 94025	650-289-2610	R	29*	<.1
264	Automation Precision Technology Inc—*Joe Murphy*	4535 E Princess Anne R, Norfolk VA 23502	757-499-6802	R	28*	.4
265	Urban Engineers Inc—*Edward M D'Alba*	530 Walnut St 14th Fl, Philadelphia PA 19106	215-922-8080	R	28*	.4
266	Bonestroo Rosene Anderlik and Associates Inc—*Marvin L Sorvala*	2335 Hwy 36 W, Saint Paul MN 55113	651-636-4600	R	28*	.3
267	Halff Associates Inc—*Martin Molloy*	1201 North Bowser Rd, Richardson TX 75081	214-346-6200	R	28*	.3
268	MTS Technologies Inc—*Daniel T Perkins*	2800 S Shirlington Rd, Arlington VA 22206	703-575-2900	R	28*	.2
269	Denham Blythe Company Inc—*Denis G Steiner*	100 Trade St, Lexington KY 40511	859-255-7405	R	28*	.2
270	Lockwood Kessler and Bartlett Inc—*Andre Haddad*	1 Aerial Way, Syosset NY 11791	516-938-0600	R	28*	.2
271	Anderson Engineering Consultants Inc—*Scott Anderson*	10205 W Rockwood Rd, Little Rock AR 72204	501-455-4545	R	28*	.1
272	Sterling Staffing Inc—*Dolores Connolly*	977 N Oaklawn Ave, Elmhurst IL 60126	630-993-3400	R	27*	.4
273	WTI Inc (Phoenix Arizona)—*James E Warne III*	3737 E Broadway Rd, Phoenix AZ 85040	602-437-8979	R	27*	.4
274	Infoscitex Corp—*Stu Haber*	303 Bear Hill Rd, Waltham MA 02451	781-890-1338	R	27*	.1
275	Applied Control Engineering Inc—*Timothy Cole*	700 Creek View Rd, Newark DE 19711	302-738-8800	R	27*	.1
276	BE and K-Houston/MEI Consultants Inc—*William Utt*	14701 St Mary's Ln Ste, Houston TX 77079	713-753-4523	S	27*	.1
277	Calty Design Research Inc—*Kevin Hunter*	2810 Jamboree Rd, Newport Beach CA 92660	949-759-1701	S	27*	.1
278	DeciBel Research Inc—*Baosem Mahafza*	325 Bob Heath Dr, Huntsville AL 35806	256-716-0787	R	27*	.1
279	Joseph D Fail Engineering Company Inc—*Robert Sandhaus*	PO Box 925, Bay Springs MS 39422	601-764-2195	R	27*	.1
280	Evans Mechwart Hambleton and Tilton Inc—*Nelson Kohman*	5500 New Albany Rd, New Albany OH 43054	614-775-4500	R	27*	.3
281	Hodges Transportation Inc—*Henry Hodges*	PO Box 234, Carson City NV 89702	775-629-2000	R	27*	.2
282	Pro-Inspect Inc—*Juanita Jones*	1710 Sens Rd, La Porte TX 77571	281-470-7783	R	26*	.2
283	Environmental Systems Corp—*Jack Missimer*	200 Tech Ctr Dr, Knoxville TN 37912	865-688-7900	R	26*	.2
284	Patterson and Dewar Engineers Inc—*Michael Kline*	PO Box 2808, Norcross GA 30091	770-453-1410	R	26*	.1
285	Fay Spofford and Thorndike Inc—*Emile J Hamwey*	5 Burlington Woods, Burlington MA 01803	781-221-1000	R	26*	.2
286	SEI Group Inc—*Eloy J Torrez*	303 Williams Ave Ste 1, Huntsville AL 35801	256-533-0500	R	26*	.1
287	Select Energy Services Inc—*James Redden*	24 Prime Pky, Natick MA 01760	508-653-0456	S	26*	.1
288	McGill Smith Punshon Inc—*Craig Rambo*	3700 Park 42 Dr Ste 19, Cincinnati OH 45241	513-759-0004	R	26*	.1
289	Technical Automation Services Company Ltd—*John Burkland*	2000 Nasa Pkwy, Seabrook TX 77586	281-474-3232	R	26*	.2
290	Bohannan-Huston Inc—*Brian Burnett*	7500 Jefferson St Ne, Albuquerque NM 87109	505-823-1000	R	26*	.2
291	Houston County Public Works Dept—*Tommy Stolnaker*	2018 Kings Chapel Rd, Perry GA 31069	478-987-4280	R	25*	.5
292	Pape-Dawson Consulting Engineers Inc—*Sam Dawson*	555 E Ramsey Rd, San Antonio TX 78216	210-375-9000	R	25*	.3
293	Bucher Willis and Ratliff Corp—*Larry White*	903 E 104th St Ste 900, Kansas City MO 64131	816-363-2696	R	25*	.3
294	Taylor and Hill Inc—*Raymond Nunez*	9941 Rowlett Rd, Houston TX 77075	713-941-2671	R	25*	.2
295	Heinz Corp—*Andrew Hidalgo*	804 Lebanon Dr, Saint Louis MO 63104	314-231-1200	S	25*	.1
296	Loyola Enterprises Inc	2984 S Lynnhaven Rd St, Virginia Beach VA 23452	757-498-6118	R	25*	<.1
297	Interop JV—*Wallace Ricks*	400 W Fry Blvd Ste 13, Sierra Vista AZ 85635	520-538-5134	R	25*	.3
298	Siemens Oil Gas And Marine—*Patrick Berwanger*	4615 Suthwest Fwy Ste, Houston TX 77027	713-570-2900	R	24*	.2
299	Hirata Corporation Of America—*Hiroshi Yoshida*	5625 Decatur Blvd, Indianapolis IN 46241	317-856-8600	R	24*	<.1
300	Bowman Consulting Group Ltd—*Gary Bowman*	3863 Centerview Dr Ste, Chantilly VA 20151	703-464-1000	R	24*	.3
301	Keith and Schnars PA—*Martin King*	6500 N Andrews Ave, Fort Lauderdale FL 33309	954-776-1616	R	24*	.2
302	Martin/Martin Inc—*Gary Thomas* John A Martin and Associates Inc	PO Box 151500, Lakewood CO 80215	303-431-6100	S	24*	.2
303	Dvirka and Bartilucci Consulting Engineers—*Henry J Chlupsa*	330 Crossways Park Dr, Woodbury NY 11797	516-364-9890	R	24*	.1
304	Landmark Entertainment Group—*Tony Christopher*	3900 W Alameda Ave Rm, Burbank CA 91505	818-569-4900	R	24*	.1
305	Mickle Wagner Coleman Inc—*Patrick J Mickle*	3434 Country Club Ave, Fort Smith AR 72903	479-649-8484	R	24*	<.1

Rank	Company Name—*Executive Officer*	Address, City, State, Zip	Phone	Type	Fin	Empls
306	Forte and Tablada Incorporated Consulting Engineers—*Ann Trappey*	9107 Interline Ave, Baton Rouge LA 70809	225-927-9321	R	24*	<.1
307	Rovisys Co—*John Robertson*	1455 Danner Dr, Aurora OH 44202	330-562-8600	R	23*	.2
308	Computer Sciences Parsons LLC—*Randy Hamlin*	PO Box 921001, Fort Worth TX 76121	405-734-4358	R	23*	.4
309	Lopezgarcia Group—*Wendy Lopez* URS Corp	1950 N Stemmons Fwy St, Dallas TX 75207	214-741-7777	D	23*	.2
310	Integrex—*Jack Saltich*	1600 N Desert Dr, Tempe AZ 85281	602-389-8600	R	23*	.1
311	American Consulting Services Inc—*Terry Swor*	550 Cleveland Ave N, Saint Paul MN 55114	651-659-9001	R	22*	.3
312	Wood Patel and Associates Inc—*Darrel Wood*	2051 W Northern Ave St, Phoenix AZ 85021	602-335-8500	R	22*	.1
313	George Butler Associates Inc—*Michael Smith*	9801 Renner BlvdSte 30, Lenexa KS 66219	913-492-0400	R	22*	.2
314	BL Companies Inc—*Carolyn Stanworth*	355 Research Pky, Meriden CT 06450	203-630-1406	R	22*	.2
315	Ws Atkins Inc—*Martin Grant*	920 Mmrial City Way St, Houston TX 77024	713-576-8500	R	22*	.1
316	Daxcon Engineering Inc—*Michael Daxenbichler*	5607 Washington St, Peoria IL 61607	309-697-5975	R	22*	.2
317	Test and Experimentation Services Co—*Jeffrey Larson*	Bldg Ca007 Warehouse R, Fort Hood TX 76544	254-288-1179	R	21*	.5
318	C and S Companies Inc—*Orrin B MacMurray*	499 Col Eileen Collins, North Syracuse NY 13212	315-455-2000	R	21*	.3
319	Bsk Associates—*Richard Johnson*	567 W Shaw Ave Ste C1, Fresno CA 93704	559-497-2880	R	21*	.2
320	EMAX Laboratories Inc—*Kam Y Pang*	1835 W 205th St, Torrance CA 90501	310-618-8889	R	21*	.1
321	McGoodwin Williams and Yates Inc—*Carl Yates*	302 E Millsap Rd, Fayetteville AR 72703	479-443-3404	R	21*	<.1
322	Omni-Means Ltd—*H Ross Ainsworth*	943 Reserve Dr, Roseville CA 95678	916-782-8688	R	21*	<.1
323	Alexander and Associates Company Inc—*Thomas Luebbe*	360 Mclean Dr, Cincinnati OH 45237	513-731-7800	R	20*	.1
324	Simpson Gumpertz and Heger Inc—*Glenn R Bell*	41 Seyon St Ste 500 Bl, Waltham MA 02453	781-907-9000	R	20*	.2
325	Tighe and Bond Inc—*David G Healey*	53 Southampton Rd, Westfield MA 01085	413-562-1600	R	20*	.2
326	MPR Associates Inc—*Robert Coward*	320 King St Ste 400, Alexandria VA 22314	703-519-0200	R	20*	.1
327	Communications Products Inc—*Cliff Arellano*	7301 E 90th St Ste 111, Indianapolis IN 46256	317-595-7863	R	20*	.1
328	Tj Cross Engineers Inc—*Lisa Wong*	200 New Stine Rd Ste 2, Bakersfield CA 93309	661-831-8782	R	20*	.1
329	Arnold and O'Sheridan Inc—*Brian Hanson*	1111 Deming Way Ste 20, Madison WI 53717	608-821-8500	R	20*	.1
330	Hope Engineers Inc—*William W Hope Sr*	322 N Market St, Benton AR 72015	501-315-0786	R	20*	<.1
331	Myers Houghton and Partners Inc—*Garry Myers*	4500 E Pacific Coast H, Long Beach CA 90804	562-985-3200	R	20*	<.1
332	ARSEE Engineers Inc—*Fritz Herget*	9715 Kincaid Dr Ste 10, Fishers IN 46037	317-594-5152	R	20*	<.1
333	Southern California Soil And Testing Inc—*Kimberly Fregoe*	PO Box 600627, San Diego CA 92160	619-280-4321	R	20*	.1
334	Louis Perry and Associates Inc—*Louis Perry*	165 Smokerise Dr, Wadsworth OH 44281	330-334-1585	R	20*	.1
335	Ort Tool and Die Corp—*Robert Milano*	PO Box 5008, Toledo OH 43611	734-848-6845	R	19*	.1
336	William F Cosulich Associates Inc—*Nicholas Bartilucci*	330 Crossways Park Dr, Woodbury NY 11797	516-364-9890	R	19*	.1
337	Miller Legg and Associates Inc—*David L John*	5747 N Andrews Way, Ft Lauderdale FL 33309	954-436-7000	R	19*	.1
338	TH Hill Associates Inc—*Thomas Wadsworth*	7676 Hillmont St Ste 3, Houston TX 77040	713-934-9215	R	19*	<.1
339	Barton and Loguidice PC—*S Alston*	PO Box 3107, Syracuse NY 13220	315-457-5200	R	19*	.1
340	Distron Corp—*Robert Donovan*	87 John L Dietsch Sq, North Attleboro MA 02763	508-695-8786	R	18*	.1
341	Product Development Technologies Inc—*Mark Schwartz*	One Corporate Dr Ste 1, Lake Zurich IL 60047	847-821-3000	S	18	.1
342	Arkel International Inc—*George Knost*	PO Box 4621, Baton Rouge LA 70821	225-343-0525	R	18*	.5
343	Mark Thomas and Company Inc—*Richard Tanaka*	1960 Zanker Rd, San Jose CA 95112	408-453-5373	R	18*	.2
344	Techma USA Inc—*Joseph Maurelli*	PO Box 340, Gretna VA 24557	434-656-3003	S	18*	.2
345	Mnemonics Inc—*Harry Thompson*	PO Box 219, Melbourne FL 32902	321-254-7300	R	18*	.1
346	CS Davidson Inc—*David M Davidson Jr*	38 N Duke St, York PA 17401	717-846-4805	R	18*	.1
347	Robert Derector PE PC—*Robert Derector*	19 W 44th St Fl 10, New York NY 10036	212-764-7272	R	18*	.1
348	Biohabitats Inc—*Keith Bowers*	2081 Clipper Park Rd, Baltimore MD 21211	410-554-0156	R	18*	<.1
349	Yamas Environmental Systems Inc—*Greg Hill*	5030 Hillsdale Circle, El Dorado Hills CA 95762	916-933-7750	R	18*	<.1
350	Modelwerks Inc—*Jon Stamm*	655 S Andover St, Seattle WA 98108	206-340-6007	R	18*	<.1
351	Anatec International Inc—*Blaine Curtis*	PO Box 73190, San Clemente CA 92673	949-498-3350	R	18*	.1
352	Nashville Machine—*Don Orr*	PO Box 101603, Nashville TN 37224	615-244-6620	R	17*	.3
353	Vantage Systems Inc—*Joseph Polk*	10210 Greenbelt Rd Ste, Lanham MD 20706	301-459-6007	R	17*	.1
354	Raydar and Associates Inc—*Mark Roberts*	13991 E State Rd 558, Odon IN 47562	812-854-7041	R	17*	.2
355	Cameron Engineering and Associates LLP—*John Cameron*	100 Sunnyside Blvd Ste, Woodbury NY 11797	516-827-4900	R	17*	.1
356	Michaud Cooley Erickson and Associates Inc—*Dean Rafferty*	333 S 7th St Ste 1200, Minneapolis MN 55402	612-339-4941	R	17*	.1
357	Mcdonough Associates Inc—*Feroz Nathani*	130 E Randolph St Ste, Chicago IL 60601	312-946-8600	R	16*	.1
358	RJN Group Inc—*Alan J Hollenbeck*	200 W Front St, Wheaton IL 60187	630-682-4700	R	16*	.2
359	McLaren Performance Technologies Inc—*Phil Guys*	32233 W 8 Mile Rd, Livonia MI 48152	248-477-6240	S	16*	.1
360	Techshot—*Mark S Deuser*	7200 Hwy 150, Greenville IN 47124	812-923-9591	R	16*	<.1
361	GKY and Associates Inc—*Stuart Stein*	4229 Lafayette Center, Chantilly VA 20151	703-870-7000	R	16*	<.1
362	PowerComm Engineering Inc—*Mike Leahy*	5025 W Grace St, Tampa FL 33607	813-287-8008	S	16*	<.1
363	SBA Properties Inc—*Jeffrey A Stoops*	5900 Broken Sound Pkwy, Boca Raton FL 33487		S	16*	<.1
364	SBA Sites Inc—*Jeffrey A Stoops*	5900 Broken Sound Pkwy, Boca Raton FL 33487		S	16*	<.1
365	SBA Towers Inc—*Jeffrey A Stoops*	5900 Broken Sound Pkwy, Boca Raton FL 33487		S	16*	<.1
366	Solusia Inc—*Christopher Moccia*	3343 Peachtree Rd NE S, Atlanta GA 30326	404-601-1100	R	16*	<.1
367	Fugro Geoservices Inc—*Thomas Hamilton*	PO Box 740010, Houston TX 77274	713-369-5800	R	16*	.1
368	N and P Engineers and Land Surveyor PLLC—*Chris Schmidt*	572 Walt Whitman Rd, Melville NY 11747	631-427-5665	R	16*	.1
369	United Consulting Group Ltd—*Reza Abree*	625 Holcomb Bridge Rd, Norcross GA 30071	770-209-0029	R	16*	.1
370	Peter Basso Associates Inc—*Tao Wang*	5145 Livernois Rd, Troy MI 48098	248-879-5666	R	16*	.1
371	Pierson Construction Corp—*Richard Pierson*	222 S 52nd St Ste 1, Tempe AZ 85281	480-966-4424	R	16*	<.1
372	Gstek Inc—*Burhl Strother*	1100 Madison Plz Ste A, Chesapeake VA 23320	757-548-1597	R	16*	.2
373	Fujitsu Semiconductor America Inc—*Hiroyuki Hojo*	1250 E Arques Ave, Sunnyvale CA 94085	408-737-5600	R	15*	.1
374	McKim and Creed PA—*Michael W Creed*	243 N Front St, Wilmington NC 28401	910-343-1048	R	15*	.2
375	HJ Ford Associates Inc—*Barry Aldrich*	2900 Presidential Dr S, Fairborn OH 45324	937-427-1300	S	15*	.2
376	Innovation Associates Inc—*Mary Reno*	627 Field St, Johnson City NY 13790	607-798-9376	R	15*	.1
377	Sidney B Bowne and Son LLP—*Frank Antetomaso*	235 E Jericho Tpke, Mineola NY 11501	516-746-2350	R	15	.1
378	Brockette Davis Drake Inc—*Robert Hill*	4144 N Cntl Expy Ste 1, Dallas TX 75204	214-824-3647	R	15*	.1
379	Midrex Corp—*James McClaskey*	2725 Water Ridge Pkwy, Charlotte NC 28217	704-373-1600	S	15*	.1
380	SBA Network Services Inc—*Jeffrey A Stoops*	5900 Broken Sound Pkwy, Boca Raton FL 33487		S	15*	<.1
381	Patrick Energy Services Inc—*Daniel Dietzler*	4970 Varsity Dr, Lisle IL 60532	630-795-7200	R	15*	.1
382	Mackin Engineering Co—*Italo Mackin*	117 Industry Dr, Pittsburgh PA 15275	412-788-0472	R	15*	.1
383	Facchina Global Services LLC—*Douglas Dick*	102 Centennial St Ste, La Plata MD 20646	301-539-4400	R	14*	.1
384	Diversitech Inc (Cincinnati Ohio)—*Lucretia Clifton*	110 Boggs Ln Ste 230, Cincinnati OH 45246	513-772-4447	R	14*	.2
385	Walter Dorwin Teague Inc—*John Barratt*	2727 Western Ave Ste 2, Seattle WA 98121	206-838-4200	R	14*	.2
386	Isothermal Systems Research—*Jeff Severs*	2218 N Molter Rd, Liberty Lake WA 99019	509-232-3600	R	14*	.1
387	Pyramid Systems Inc—*Gwo Ching Jeff Hwan*	9302 Lee Hwy Ste 1200, Fairfax VA 22031	703-553-0800	R	14*	.1
388	Camp Dresser and McKee Federal Programs Corp—*V L Wimberley* Camp Dresser and McKee Inc	14420 Albemarle Point, Chantilly VA 20151	703-968-0920	S	14*	.1
389	Huitt-Zollars Inc—*Robert L Zollars*	3131 McKinney Ave, Dallas TX 75204	214-871-3311	R	14*	.1
390	Eiffel Software—*Jacques Stern*	5949 Hollister Ave, Goleta CA 93117	805-685-1006	R	14*	<.1
391	HESI—*Roland Marquardt*	11200 Crosseto Dr, Las Vegas NV 89141	702-578-0790	R	14*	<.1

Note: An asterisk (*) indicates an estimated financial figure. The company type code used is as follows: R = Private, P = Public, S = Private Subsidiary, B = Public Subsidiary, D = Division, J = Joint Venture, I = Investment Fund.

COMPANY RANKINGS BY SALES WITHIN 4-DIGIT SIC

Rank	Company Name—*Executive Officer*	Address, City, State, Zip	Phone	Type	Fin	Empls
392	Cerami and Associates—*Victoria Cerami*	404 Fifth Ave, New York NY 10018	212-370-1776	R	14*	<.1
393	EDD Inc—*David Hermann*	2941 W State Rd 434 St, Longwood FL 32779	407-774-7776	R	14*	.2
394	Integrated Management Services PA—*John D Calhoun*	126 E Amite St, Jackson MS 39201	601-968-9194	R	14	<.1
395	Richard A Alaimo Associates—*Richard Alaimo*	200 High St, Mount Holly NJ 08060	609-267-8310	R	14*	.1
396	Withers and Ravenel Holdings PA—*Sam Ravenel*	111 Mackenan Dr, Cary NC 27511	919-469-3340	R	13*	.1
397	Esys Corp—*Chris Marcus*	1670 N Opdyke Rd, Auburn Hills MI 48326	248-754-1900	R	13*	.1
398	Zeppelin Systems USA Inc—*Robert Anderson*	13330 Byrd Dr, Odessa FL 33556	813-920-7434	S	13*	.1
399	Classic Design Inc—*Ken Kareta*	665 Elmwood Dr, Troy MI 48083	248-588-2738	R	13*	.1
400	Ventech Engineers Inc—*Herbert Long*	PO Box 4261, Pasadena TX 77502	713-477-0201	R	13*	.1
401	Ken Thompson Inc—*Ken Thompson*	PO Box 749, Cypress CA 90630	714-995-1371	R	13*	.1
402	Icon Mechanical Construction and Engineering LLC—*Michael F Bieg*	1610 Delmar Ave, Granite City IL 62040	618-452-0035	R	13*	<.1
403	Abate Associates Engineers and Surveyors PC—*Ralph Abate*	PO Box 218, Buffalo NY 14225	716-632-2300	R	13*	<.1
404	GHH Engineering Inc—*Gary H Hall*	11960 Heritage Oak Pl, Auburn CA 95603	530-886-3100	R	13*	<.1
405	Romeo Engineering Inc—*Frank Romeo*	4217 Hahn Blvd, Fort Worth TX 76117	817-656-0048	R	13*	<.1
406	Fleet-Fisher Engineering Inc—*Fred Fleet*	4250 E Camelback Rd St, Phoenix AZ 85018	602-264-3335	R	13*	.1
407	Professional Engineering Consultants Inc—*Tom Kelley*	PO Box 530008, Debary FL 32753	407-422-8062	R	13*	.1
408	Optimetrics Inc—*Frederick Smith*	3115 Professional Dr, Ann Arbor MI 48104	734-973-1177	R	12*	.1
409	Century Engineering Inc—*Francis Smyth*	10710 Gilroy Rd, Hunt Valley MD 21031	443-589-2400	R	12*	.2
410	Remington and Vernick Engineers—*Edward Vernick*	232 Kings Hwy E, Haddonfield NJ 08033	856-795-9595	R	12*	.1
411	Kirkham Michael and Associates Inc—*Roger Helgoth*	PO Box 542030, Omaha NE 68154	402-393-5630	R	12*	.1
412	Osborn Engineering Co—*E Baxendale*	1300 E 9th St Ste 1500, Cleveland OH 44114	216-861-2020	R	12*	.1
413	Tristar Fire Protection Inc—*Gary Wolf*	PO Box 701728, Plymouth MI 48170	734-454-1350	R	12*	.1
414	Bricmont Inc—*David Gilbert*	500 Technology Dr, Canonsburg PA 15317	724-746-2300	R	12*	.1
415	Speck Product Design Inc—*Elisa Jagerson*	3221 Porter Dr, Palo Alto CA 94304	650-462-9080	R	12*	<.1
416	Onsite Energy Corp—*Richard T Sperberg*	2701 Loker Ave W Ste 1, Carlsbad CA 92010	760-931-2400	R	12*	<.1
417	Mobilerobots Inc—*Jeanne Dietsch*	10 Columbia Dr, Amherst NH 03031	603-881-7960	R	12*	<.1
418	Spaceclaim Corp—*Chris Randles*	150 Baker Ave, Concord MA 01742	978-482-2100	R	12*	<.1
419	Zahl-Ford Inc—*Steven J Ford*	8411 S Walker Ave, Oklahoma City OK 73139	405-634-3393	R	12*	<.1
420	Stationary Power Services Inc—*Bill Maher*	4902 113th Ave N, Clearwater FL 33760	727-576-2330	R	12*	<.1
421	I-Con Systems Inc—*Shawn Bush*	3100 Camp Rd, Oviedo FL 32765	407-365-6241	R	12*	<.1
422	Advanced Technology and Research Corp—*Jackson Yang*	6650 Eli Whitney Dr, Columbia MD 21046	443-766-7888	R	12*	.1
423	Flemington Instrument Company Inc—*Ralph Migliaccio*	PO Box 298, Ringoes NJ 08551	908-782-4229	R	12*	.1
424	TL Industries Inc—*Theodore Stetschulte*	2541 Tracy Rd, Northwood OH 43619	419-666-8144	R	12*	.1
425	SSP Offshore (USA) Inc—*Gary Quenan*	10370 Richmond Ave Ste, Houston TX 77042	713-461-0044	R	12*	.1
426	Leech Industries Inc—*Dean Leech*	PO Box 748, Meadville PA 16335	814-336-2141	R	11*	.1
427	Analytical Design Service Corp—*Dilip K Nigam*	540 Avis Dr Ste E, Ann Arbor MI 48108	734-761-2626	R	11*	.1
428	CET Engineering Services—*Jeff Wendle*	1240 N Mountain Rd, Harrisburg PA 17112	717-541-0622	R	11*	<.1
429	Biothane Corp—*Robert I Sax*	2500 Broadway, Camden NJ 08104	856-541-3500	R	11*	<.1
430	Pettit and Pettit Consulting Engineering Inc—*Sam Cummings*	201 E Markham St Ste 4, Little Rock AR 72201	501-374-3731	R	11*	<.1
431	ICSN Inc—*Joon Lee*	1826 Pomona Rd, Corona CA 92880	951-687-8818	R	11	<.1
432	Camcast Corp—*Ed Campbell*	11231 N Memorial Dr, Owasso OK 74055	918-371-9966	R	11*	.1
433	Mazda Research And Development Of North America Inc—*Debby Feeney*	1421 Reynolds Ave, Irvine CA 92614	949-852-8898	R	11*	.1
434	H H Holmes Testing Laboratories Inc—*Scott Nelson*	170 Shepard Ave Ste A, Wheeling IL 60090	847-541-4040	R	10*	.1
435	Spotts Stevens and McCoy Inc—*J Carlton Godlove II*	PO Box 6307, Reading PA 19610	610-621-2000	R	10*	.1
436	Design Teams Inc—*FM Latham*	20 Ridgely Ave Ste 311, Annapolis MD 21401	410-269-0534	R	10*	.1
437	Atcs Services LLC—*Eric Basore*	2553 Dulles View Dr St, Herndon VA 20171	703-430-7500	R	10*	.1
438	Design Services Group—*Criag Herkert*	6533 Flying Cloud Dr S, Eden Prairie MN 55344	952-914-5670	S	10*	.1
439	Optech LLC—*Ronia Kruse*	PO Box 1857, Troy MI 48099	313-962-9000	R	10*	.1
440	Setpoint Systems Inc—*Mike Thompson*	2835 Commerce Way, Ogden UT 84401	801-621-4117	R	10*	<.1
441	American Industrial Insulation LLC—*Mae Kato*	91-505 Awakumoku St, Kapolei HI 96707	808-682-5750	R	10*	.1
442	Dimensions Consulting Inc—*Zaid Ayoub*	3350 Scott Blvd Bldg 5, Santa Clara CA 95054	408-988-6800	S	10*	<.1
443	Taeus International Corp—*Arthur M Nutter*	1155 Kelly Johnson Blv, Colorado Springs CO 80920	719-325-5000	R	10*	<.1
444	Ambient Engineering Inc—*Bruce Bruns*	PO Box 243, Rocky Hill NJ 08553	609-279-6888	S	10*	<.1
445	Blaylock Threet Engineers Inc—*Carl Meurer*	1501 Market St, Little Rock AR 72211	501-224-3922	R	10*	<.1
446	Global Power Technology Inc—*Joseph Gonzalez Rivas*	PO Box 4019, Edison NJ 08818	732-287-3680	R	10*	.1
447	Lumos and Associates Inc—*Charles Macquarie*	800 College Pkwy, Carson City NV 89706	775-883-7077	R	10*	.1
448	Optimal Computer Aided Engineering Inc—*Song Young*	14492 N Sheldon Rd Ste, Plymouth MI 48170	734-414-7933	R	10*	.1
449	Micro Industries Corp—*Michael Curran*	8399 Green Meadows Dr, Westerville OH 43081	740-548-7878	R	10*	.1
450	Dinegy Inc—*Steve Furbacher*	1000 La St Ste 6400, Houston TX 77002	713-507-6400	R	9*	.1
451	Van Zelm Heywood and Shadford Inc—*Thomas Wunder*	10 Talcott Notch Rd St, Farmington CT 06032	860-284-5064	R	9*	.1
452	Espo Engineering Corp—*Eugene Esposito*	855 Midway Dr, Willowbrook IL 60527	630-789-2525	R	9*	.1
453	Spectrum Engineers Inc—*Stewart Greene*	324 S State St Ste 400, Salt Lake City UT 84111	801-328-5151	R	9*	.1
454	MacKay and Somps Civil Engineers Inc—*James C Ray*	5142 Franklin Dr Ste B, Pleasanton CA 94588	925-225-0690	R	9*	.1
455	Erdman Anthony Associates Inc—*Russell J Bullock*	2165 Brighton-Henriett, Rochester NY 14623	585-427-8888	R	9*	.1
456	Sam O Hirota Inc—*Dennis Hirota*	864 S Beretania St, Honolulu HI 96813	808-537-9971	R	9*	<.1
457	Moore Control Systems Inc—*Jae Moore*	PO Box 677, Katy TX 77492	281-392-7747	R	9*	.1
458	Bechdon Co—*William Turley*	300 Commerce Dr, Upper Marlboro MD 20774	301-249-0900	R	9*	.1
459	Crew Corp—*Kathy Reehling*	7439 Woodland Dr Ste X, Indianapolis IN 46278	317-713-7715	R	9*	.1
460	Redzone Robotics Inc—*Eric Close*	91 43rd St 250, Pittsburgh PA 15201	412-476-8980	R	8*	.1
461	West Point Foundry And Machine Company Inc—*Pate Huguley*	PO Box 589, West Point GA 31833	706-643-2174	R	8*	.1
462	AWGM Inc—*Warren Myers*	667 Industrial Park Rd, Ebensburg PA 15931	814-472-7980	R	8*	.1
463	Thar Technologies Inc—*Lalit Chordia*	730 William Pitt Way, Pittsburgh PA 15238	412-435-0200	R	8*	<.1
464	Campbell Grinder Co—*Mark Lorencz*	1226 Pontaluna Rd, Norton Shores MI 49456	231-798-6464	R	8*	.1
465	Eta Engineering Consultants psc Inc—*Ralph Jackson*	5802 Brown Ln, Catlettsburg KY 41129	606-739-6805	R	8*	.1
466	ADS Engineers—*Michael Ambrosino*	275 7th Ave, New York NY 10001	212-645-6060	R	8*	<.1
467	Alphaport Inc—*Rosella Miranda*	18013 Cleveland Pkwy S, Cleveland OH 44135		R	8*	<.1
468	MacArthur Associated Consultants LLC—*Sam Pappas*	3033 NW 63rd St Ste 25, Oklahoma City OK 73116	405-848-2471	R	8*	<.1
469	AirPol Inc—*Frank E Hsu PE*	199 Pomeroy Rd, Parsippany NJ 07054	973-599-4418	S	8*	<.1
470	Bay-Tec Engineering—*John Justus*	5130 Fulton Dr Ste X, Fairfield CA 94534	707-252-6575	R	8*	.1
471	NIKA Technologies—*Kabir Chaudhary*	451 Hungerford Dr 4th, Rockville MD 20850	301-770-3520	R	8	<.1
472	Summit Engineering Corp—*Thomas Gallagher*	5405 Mae Anne Ave, Reno NV 89523	775-747-8550	R	8*	.1
473	Gus Perdikakis Associates Inc—*Gus Perdikakis*	PO Box 498612, Cincinnati OH 45249	513-583-0900	R	7*	.1
474	Engeo Inc—*Uri Eliahu*	2010 Crow Canyon Pl St, San Ramon CA 94583	925-866-9000	R	7*	.1
475	Northern Industrial Services Inc—*Stewart Wagner*	1843 Central Ave Ste 2, Albany NY 12205	518-456-2566	R	7*	.1
476	ROV Technologies Inc—*John Judge*	49 Bennett Dr, Brattleboro VT 05301	802-254-9353	R	7*	<.1
477	Ditron Manufacturing Inc—*John Dinovo*	2020 W Quail Ave, Phoenix AZ 85027	623-581-3118	R	7*	.1
478	Allen and Hoshall Inc—*David L Nicholson*	1661 International Dr, Memphis TN 38120	901-820-0820	R	7*	.1
479	Integrated Science Solutions Inc—*Cecelia McCloy*	1777 N California Blvd, Walnut Creek CA 94596	925-979-1535	R	7*	.1

Rank	Company Name—*Executive Officer*	Address, City, State, Zip	Phone	Type	Fin	Empls
480	Xvei Inc—*Mark Smith*	143e Spring Hill Dr, Grass Valley CA 95945	530-272-2448	R	7*	.1
481	Henry F Teichmann Inc—*Arch Mcintyre*	3009 Washington Rd, McMurray PA 15317	724-941-9550	R	7*	<.1
482	Glitsch Technology Corp—*Pinti Wang*	1001 S Dairy Ashford R, Houston TX 77077	281-597-4800	S	7*	<.1
483	Autotec Engineering Co—*Thomas Ballay*	7345 Sylvania Ave, Sylvania OH 43560	419-885-2529	R	7*	<.1
484	Affiliated Engineers Inc (Hot Springs Arkansas)—*Jerrod Schuett*	PO Box 1299, Hot Springs AR 71902	501-624-4691	R	7*	<.1
485	Aspen Banner Engineering—*Roger Strube*	PO Box 550, Laramie WY 82070	307-745-7366	R	7*	<.1
486	LSI Adapt Inc	10000 Alliance Rd, Cincinnati OH 45242	513-793-3200	S	7*	<.1
487	ZRHD PC—*Randy Ragsdale*	1318 N Robinson Ave, Oklahoma City OK 73106	405-942-8475	R	7*	<.1
488	Systems Engineering Technologies Corp—*Jose Diaz*	6121 Lincolnia Rd Ste, Alexandria VA 22312	703-941-7887	R	7*	.1
489	Spaan Tech Inc—*Smita Shah*	311 S Wacker Dr Ste 24, Chicago IL 60606	312-277-8800	R	7*	.1
490	Comdel Inc—*Theodore Johnson*	11 Kondelin Rd, Gloucester MA 01930	978-282-0620	R	7*	.1
491	K-Line Industries Inc—*Thomas Knowles*	315 Garden Ave, Holland MI 49424	616-396-3564	R	7*	.1
492	Midpoint International Corp—*Ghazi Hijer*	8044 Ray Mears Blvd St, Knoxville TN 37919	865-691-5657	R	6*	.1
493	Indesign LLC—*Thomas Nielsen*	8225 E 56th St Ste A, Indianapolis IN 46216	317-377-5450	R	6*	.1
494	Innovative Control Solutions Inc—*Bill Downs*	840 F Ave Ste 100, Plano TX 75074	972-509-2979	R	6*	<.1
495	Dwfritz Automation Inc—*Synthia Fritz*	17750 Sw Uppr Bnes Fry, Portland OR 97224	503-598-9393	R	6*	<.1
496	Kinney Industries Inc—*Steven Westbrook*	2514 Hall Ave Nw, Huntsville AL 35805	256-533-5580	R	6*	.1
497	3D Research Corp—*Lisa Williams*	360D Quality Cir rm 45, Huntsville AL 35806	256-705-5410	R	6*	.1
498	McCrone Inc Design Teams Inc	20 Ridgely Ave Ste 201, Annapolis MD 21401	410-267-8621	S	6*	.1
499	Englekirk and Sabol Inc—*Thomas A Sabol*	2116 Arlington Ave, Los Angeles CA 90018	323-733-6673	R	6*	.1
500	Eisenmann Corp—*Mark West*	150 E Dartmoor Dr, Crystal Lake IL 60014	815-455-4100	R	6*	.1
501	Bentley Austin—*Gregory Bentley*	5918 W Courtyeard Dr S, Austin TX 78730	512-338-1711	S	6*	<.1
502	Industrial Accessories Company Inc—*Glenn Smith*	4800 Lamar Ave, Mission KS 66202	913-384-5511	R	6*	<.1
503	Ride and Show Engineering Co—*Roland Feuer*	279 E Arrow Hwy, San Dimas CA 91773	909-592-5575	R	6*	<.1
504	Infinigy Engineering—*John Stevens*	11 herbert Dr, Latham NY 12110	518-690-0790	R	6*	<.1
505	Epcon International Inc—*Oliver Siebert*	16225 Park Ten Pl Ste, Houston TX 77084	281-398-9400	R	6*	<.1
506	James W Bunger and Associates Inc—*James W Bunger*	PO Box 520037, Salt Lake City UT 84152	801-975-1456	R	6*	<.1
507	EVE USA Inc—*Luc Burgan*	2290 N First St, San Jose CA 95131	408-855-3200	S	6*	<.1
508	Illgen Simulation Technologies—*John Illgen*	130 Robin Hill Rd Ste, Goleta CA 93117	805-692-2333	R	6*	.1
509	Azimuth Inc—*Craig Hartzell*	3741 Morgantown Indust, Morgantown WV 26501	304-292-3700	R	6*	.1
510	Fec Technologies Inc—*Frederick Lepage*	PO Box 427, Manchester PA 17345	717-764-5959	R	6*	<.1
511	American Gnc Corp—*Ching-Fang Lin*	888 E Easy St, Simi Valley CA 93065	805-582-0582	R	6*	.1
512	Emi Technologies Inc—*Jose Alvarez*	2200 N Telshor Blvd, Las Cruces NM 88011	575-532-9190	R	6*	.1
513	Argus and Associates Inc—*Bryan Swarthout*	28064 Ctr Oaks Ct B, Wixom MI 48393	248-344-8700	R	6*	.1
514	East Group PA—*D Smith*	324 Evans St, Greenville NC 27858	252-758-3746	R	5*	.1
515	Advanced Engineering Solutions Inc—*Teressa Bush*	250 Advanced Dr, Springboro OH 45066	937-743-6900	R	5*	.1
516	Edison Industrial Systems Center—*David Beck*	5555 Airport Hwy Ste 1, Toledo OH 43615	419-535-6000	R	5*	.1
517	Michigan Mechanical Services Inc—*Scott Smith*	25445 Brest, Taylor MI 48180	734-946-9948	R	5*	<.1
518	Cawley Gillespie and Associates Inc—*Aaron Cawley*	306 W 7th St Ste 302, Fort Worth TX 76102	817-336-2461	R	5*	<.1
519	Tom Synnott Associates Inc—*Andrew J Synnott*	PO Box 44145, Pittsburgh PA 15205	412-787-0980	R	5*	<.1
520	DW Smith Associates LLC—*Tim Lurie*	149 Yellowbrook Rd Ste, Farmingdale NJ 07727	732-363-5850	R	5*	<.1
521	Precise Engineering Corp—*Patrick Quinlan*	683 Lincoln Lake Ave S, Lowell MI 49331	616-897-8977	R	5*	<.1
522	Brandir International Inc—*Steven Levine*	521 5th Ave 17th Fl, New York NY 10175	212-505-6500	R	5*	<.1
523	Dynamic Engineering Inc (Houston Texas)—*Joe Ausikaitis*	654 N Sam Houston Pkwy, Houston TX 77060	281-617-0099	R	5*	<.1
524	Fluidized Bed Technologies Inc—*Robert Vncent*	1 Northgate Park Ste, Chattanooga TN 37415	423-877-0871	R	5*	<.1
525	Thoroughbred Technology and Telecommunications Inc—*Danny Smith*	1200 Poachtroo St NE, Atlanta GA 30309	404-962-5541	S	5*	.1
526	HOAG Electronics Inc—*Tom E Hoag*	6602 127th Pl SE, Bellevue WA 98006	425-614-2603	R	5*	<.1
527	Jonal Laboratories Inc—*Marc Nemeth*	PO Box 743, Meriden CT 06450	203-634-4444	R	5*	.1
528	Applied Chemical Technology Inc—*Curtis Lewey*	4350 Helton Dr, Florence AL 35630	256-760-9600	R	5*	<.1
529	Demark Inc—*Mark Inserra*	604 Rookery Ln, Joliet IL 60431	815-725-7481	R	5	<.1
530	Microbes Inc—*Alan Warren*	1330 Lake Robbins Dr S, Spring TX 77380	281-367-7500	R	5*	<.1
531	Lucidyne Technologies Inc—*George Carman*	155 Sw Madison Ave, Corvallis OR 97333	541-753-5111	R	5*	<.1
532	B and F Design Inc—*Raymond Forgione*	187 Stamm Rd, Newington CT 06111	860-665-0062	R	5*	<.1
533	Ls Research LLC—*Kimberly Dexter*	W66n220 Commerce Ct, Cedarburg WI 53012	262-421-4071	R	5*	<.1
534	Stork Climax Research Services Inc—*Ca Noall*	51229 Century Ct, Wixom MI 48393	248-960-4900	R	5*	<.1
535	Stratos Product Development LLC—*Mark Ando*	2401 Elliott Ave Ste 5, Seattle WA 98121	206-448-1388	R	5*	<.1
536	North Star Scientific Corp—*James Stamm*	91-238 Kalaeloa Blvd A, Kapolei HI 96707	808-682-4100	R	5*	<.1
537	Hms Company Inc—*Stefan Wanczyk*	13231 23 Mile Rd, Shelby Township MI 48315	586-726-4300	R	4*	.1
538	Ernie Elliott Inc—*Ernie Elliott*	PO Box 476, Dawsonville GA 30534	706-265-1346	R	4*	.1
539	Powerspan Corp—*Frank Alix*	PO Box 219, New Durham NH 03855	603-859-2500	R	4*	.1
540	UAI Inc—*S Chauhan*	307 Wynn Dr NW, Huntsville AL 35805	256-327-3495	R	4*	.1
541	PAI Corp—*Doan L Phung*	116 Milan Way, Oak Ridge TN 37830	865-483-0666	R	4*	.1
542	Select Engineering Inc—*Scott Hastings*	1717 S Boulder Ave Ste, Tulsa OK 74119	918-592-1133	R	4*	<.1
543	Knight Piesold and Co—*Barbara Filas*	1580 Lincoln St ste 10, Denver CO 80203	303-629-8788	R	4*	<.1
544	Manufacturing and Engineering Excellence Inc—*Steve Curtis*	1380 Piper Dr, Milpitas CA 95035	408-382-1900	R	4*	<.1
545	Professional Electronics Company Inc—*Grace Worsham*	150 Airpark Industrial, Alabaster AL 35007	205-664-5555	R	4*	<.1
546	Solekai Systems Corp—*Martin Caniff*	3398 Carmel Mountain R, San Diego CA 92121	858-436-2040	R	4*	<.1
547	Ansol Inc—*Brian Cheripko*	PO Box 82044, San Diego CA 92138	858-538-0128	R	4*	<.1
548	CEC Consultants Inc—*John R Puskar*	11699 Brookpark Rd, Cleveland OH 44130	216-749-2992	R	4*	<.1
549	I5 Wireless LLC—*Zenovy Mogilevsky*	1984 Raymond Dr, Northbrook IL 60062	847-562-1888	R	4*	<.1
550	White Engineering Associates Inc—*Ronald White*	5500 N Western Ave Ste, Oklahoma City OK 73118	405-208-8700	R	4*	<.1
551	Allison-Ide Structural Engineers LLC—*John S Allison*	900 Fort St Mall Ste 1, Honolulu HI 96813	808-536-2108	R	4*	<.1
552	LECORP Inc—*Danny Crane*	PO Box 7508, Paducah KY 42002	270-554-9653	R	4*	<.1
553	V Soft Inc—*Ashwin Vora*	888 Saratoga Ave Ste 2, San Jose CA 95129	408-342-1700	R	4*	<.1
554	E and M Engineers and Surveyors PC—*Glenn D Cooley*	482 S Cascade Dr, Springville NY 14141	716-592-2851	R	4*	<.1
555	Integrated Technologies Inc (Danville Vermont)—*Peter Gallerani*	552 Peacham Rd, Danville VT 05828	802-284-1016	R	4*	<.1
556	Stronghold Engineering Inc—*Beverly A Bailey*	2000 Market St, Riverside CA 92501	951-684-9303	R	4*	<.1
557	Extended Enterprise Engineering and Design LLC—*Brian Lambka*	2851 High Meadow Cir, Auburn Hills MI 48326	248-852-5955	R	4*	.1
558	Analysis And Measurement Services Corp—*H Hashemian*	9119 Cross Park Dr, Knoxville TN 37923	865-691-1756	R	4*	.1
559	Q Comp Technologies Inc—*Tom Doyle*	W6564 Quality Dr, Greenville WI 54942	920-757-0775	R	4*	<.1
560	PT Systems Inc—*Peter Chan*	1980 Olivera Rd Ste A, Concord CA 94520	925-676-0709	R	4*	<.1
561	Materials Handling Systems Inc—*Matt Sourney*	8715 Bollman Pl, Savage MD 20763	240-568-9898	R	4*	<.1
562	Polyfusion Electronics Inc—*Alan Pearce*	30 Ward Rd, Lancaster NY 14086	716-681-3040	R	4*	<.1
563	Birket Engineering Inc—*Glenn Birket*	PO Box 770370, Winter Garden FL 34777	407-290-2000	R	4*	<.1
564	Shenandoah Engineering Services Inc—*Louis Ioia*	PO Box 189, Harrisonburg VA 22803	540-434-0406	R	4*	<.1

Note: An asterisk (*) indicates an estimated financial figure. The company type code used is as follows: R = Private, P = Public, S = Private Subsidiary, B = Public Subsidiary, D = Division, J = Joint Venture, I = Investment Fund.

COMPANY RANKINGS BY SALES WITHIN 4-DIGIT SIC

Rank	Company Name—*Executive Officer*	Address, City, State, Zip	Phone	Type	Fin	Empls
565	Digital Design Inc—*Edward Gerri*	67 Sand Park Rd, Cedar Grove NJ 07009	973-857-9500	R	4*	<.1
566	Quality Engineering Services Inc—*Richard Addy*	122 N Plains Industria, Wallingford CT 06492	203-269-5054	R	4*	<.1
567	Staneco Corp—*Stanley Dworak*	901 Sheehy Dr, Horsham PA 19044	215-672-6500	R	4*	<.1
568	Lathrop Engineering Inc—*Robert Lathrop*	1101 S Winchester Blvd, San Jose CA 95128	408-260-2111	R	4*	<.1
569	Flow Systems Inc—*Mike Carter*	220 Bunyan Ave, Berthoud CO 80513	970-532-0617	R	4*	<.1
570	Trisect Engineering and Consulting Corp	7675 Oak Ridge Hwy, Knoxville TN 37931	865-342-8333	R	4*	.1
571	Clark Testing Services LLC—*Saul Siegel*	821 E Front St, Buchanan MI 49107	269-697-8632	R	4*	<.1
572	Horne International Inc—*Evan Auld-Susott*	3975 University Dr Ste, Fairfax VA 22030		P	3	<.1
573	Sturman Industries Inc—*Carol Sturman*	1 Innovation Way, Woodland Park CO 80863	719-686-6000	R	3*	<.1
574	Brunsing Associates Inc—*Thomas Brunsing*	PO Box 588, Windsor CA 95492	707-838-3027	R	3*	<.1
575	Claudius Peters Americas Inc—*Ralph Parks*	445 W President George, Richardson TX 75080	972-715-7825	R	3*	<.1
576	Enerco Energy Services Inc—*Charles Paul*	PO Box 4527, Salisbury NC 28145	704-637-7410	R	3*	<.1
577	Seaworthy Systems Inc—*Andrew Marsh*	22 Main St, Centerbrook CT 06409	860-767-9061	R	3*	<.1
578	Cqs Innovation Inc—*Gordon Kilgore*	2390 Pipestone Rd, Benton Harbor MI 49022	269-926-2148	R	3*	<.1
579	Tjm Electronic Associates Inc—*Thomas Mccarthy*	2924 New Rodgers Rd, Bristol PA 19007	215-788-2278	R	3*	<.1
580	Computer Age Engineering Inc—*Mike Bartrom*	PO Box 3268, Marion IN 46953	765-674-8551	R	3*	<.1
581	AmeriResource Technologies Inc—*Delmar A Janovec*	3440 E Russell Rd Ste, Las Vegas NV 89120	702-214-4249	P	3	<.1
582	Strategic Power Systems Inc—*Salvatore Della Villa*	11016 Rushmore Dr Ste, Charlotte NC 28277	704-544-5501	R	3*	<.1
583	Aegir Systems Inc—*Ella Williams*	2151 Alessandro Dr Ste, Ventura CA 93001	805-648-2660	R	3*	<.1
584	Bw Resources LLC—*Mike Basos*	PO Box 1600, Whitney TX 76692	254-694-5846	R	3*	.1
585	Underground Services Inc—*Robert Milliken*	24 Hagerty Blvd Ste 11, West Chester PA 19382	610-738-8762	R	3*	<.1
586	Nemeth Engineering Associates Inc—*Peter Nemeth*	5901 W Hwy 22, Crestwood KY 40014	502-241-1502	R	3*	<.1
587	Mp Technologies Inc—*Paul Takacs*	8000 Snowville Rd, Cleveland OH 44141	440-838-4466	R	3*	<.1
588	Howell-Summers Engineering Inc—*Ray Howell*	4101 N Classen Blvd St, Oklahoma City OK 73118	405-525-9030	R	3*	<.1
589	Geotechnical Group Inc—*John P Sullivan*	100 Crescent Rd, Needham MA 02494	781-449-6450	R	3*	<.1
590	WDB Engineering Inc—*David Wyatt*	6330 SE 74th, Oklahoma City OK 73135	405-741-7090	R	3*	<.1
591	DL Adams Associates Ltd	970 N Kalaheo Ave Ste, Kailua HI 96734	808-254-3318	R	3*	<.1
592	Robert J Jenkins Co—*Robert Jenkins*	906 Medical Ctr Blvd, Webster TX 77598	281-332-3566	R	3*	<.1
593	Tera Research Inc—*Sam Verona*	1945 Old Gallows Rd St, Vienna VA 22182	408-734-3096	R	3*	.1
594	Machine And Process Design Inc—*Stanley Davis*	820 Mckinley St, Anoka MN 55303	763-427-9991	R	3*	<.1
595	Unitrack Industries Inc—*Clayton Marchetti*	967 E Masten Cir, Milford DE 19963	302-424-5050	R	3*	<.1
596	Henshaw Inc—*Dave Clark*	100 Shaffer Dr, Romeo MI 48065	586-752-0700	R	3*	<.1
597	Wiltec—*Moses Wilson*	610 N Lake Ave, Pasadena CA 91101	626-564-1944	R	3*	<.1
598	Second Source Inc—*Mark Sedore*	2070 Rte 52, Hopewell Junction NY 12533	845-226-8710	R	3*	<.1
599	Manchester Corp—*Irving Morrow*	280 Ayer Rd, Harvard MA 01451	978-772-2900	R	2*	<.1
600	Mjs Designs Inc—*Jerry Mohney*	4130 E Wood St Ste 100, Phoenix AZ 85040	602-437-5068	R	2*	<.1
601	Glex Inc—*Elba Larco*	12900 Fm 529 Rd, Houston TX 77041	713-849-4985	R	2*	<.1
602	Advanced Navigation and Postioning Corp—*Jeff Mains*	11 3rd St, Hood River OR 97031	541-386-1747	R	2*	<.1
603	Aero-Vac Service Corp—*Stanley Levin*	262 Twin Ln E, Wantagh NY 11793	516-679-9774	R	2*	<.1
604	Production Systems Automation Inc—*Edward Robson*	1 Crozerville Rd, Aston PA 19014	610-358-0500	R	2*	<.1
605	Studio Red Inc—*Philip Bourgeois*	115 Independence Dr, Menlo Park CA 94025	650-324-2244	R	2*	<.1
606	Elcon Technologies Inc—*Fredrick Kim*	2014 Babcock Blvd Ste, Pittsburgh PA 15209	412-822-8250	R	2*	<.1
607	Northwest Cad Services Inc—*Shaun Twyman*	1650 Nw Naito Pkwy Ste, Portland OR 97209	503-295-1808	R	2*	.1
608	Damrow Co—*Cynthia Farvour*	PO Box 750, Fond du Lac WI 54936	920-922-1500	R	2*	<.1
609	Futura Design Service Inc—*Dennis Tresslar*	6001 N Dixie Dr, Dayton OH 45414	937-890-5252	R	2*	<.1
610	Silicon Designs Inc—*John Cole*	1445 Nw Mall St, Issaquah WA 98027	425-391-8329	R	2*	<.1
611	Automation Systems Inc—*Carl Schanstra*	9960 Pacific Ave, Franklin Park IL 60131	847-671-9515	R	2*	<.1
612	Tec Engineering Inc—*Rolland Eakins*	2233 S W St Ct, Wichita KS 67213	316-838-9100	R	2*	<.1
613	Precision Blasting Services—*Calvin J Konya*	PO Box 189, Montville OH 44064	440-474-6700	D	2*	<.1
614	Roussey Associates Inc—*Robert Roussey*	436 Creamery Way Ste 2, Exton PA 19341	610-524-1346	R	2*	<.1
615	D'Appolonia	275 Center Rd, Monroeville PA 15146	412-856-9440	R	2*	<.1
616	Schultz Engineering Services Inc—*Stanley J Schultz*	4800 West Blvd, Poplar Bluff MO 63901	573-686-0806	R	2*	<.1
617	Serralta Rebull Serig Inc—*Ignacio Serralta*	5001 SW 74 Rm 201, Miami FL 33155	305-817-3393	R	2*	<.1
618	Compunetics Inc—*Donald Bernier*	3863 Rochester Rd, Troy MI 48083	248-524-6376	R	2*	<.1
619	Latanick Equipment Inc—*Richard Poorman*	720 River Rd, Huron OH 44839	419-433-2200	R	2*	<.1
620	Xytel Corp—*Jay Khadye*	4220 S Church St Ext, Roebuck SC 29376	864-576-9777	S	2*	<.1
621	Engineering Diagnostics Inc—*David H Nicastro*	6150 Richmond Ave Ste, Houston TX 77057	713-772-6300	R	2*	<.1
622	Abm Test Inc—*Michael Maslana*	47810 Westinghouse Dr, Fremont CA 94539	510-490-4600	R	2*	<.1
623	Dressler Consulting Engineers Inc—*Don Dressler*	PO Box 7450, Overland Park KS 66207	913-341-5575	R	2*	<.1
624	Axiom Design Inc—*Robert L Kranson*	5117 Johnson Dr, Pleasanton CA 94588	925-416-2000	R	2*	<.1
625	Riddick Engineering Corp—*Edgar Riddick*	4600 W Markham, Little Rock AR 72205	501-666-7300	R	2*	<.1
626	Durand Interstellar Inc—*Gerald Durand*	219 Oak Wood Way, Los Gatos CA 95032	408-356-3886	R	2*	<.1
627	Edinger Engineering Inc—*Mark McKinney*	105 N Hudson Ave Ste 5, Oklahoma City OK 73102	405-232-6315	R	2*	<.1
628	Environmental Control Systems Inc—*Barbara Lippmann*	950 Sussex Blvd, Broomall PA 19008	610-328-2880	R	2*	<.1
629	PAR Marketing Inc—*Bill Fletemeyer*	205 Ave I Ste 5, Redondo Beach CA 90277	310-316-8959	R	2*	<.1
630	SiteTech Inc—*Bernie Mayer*	8061 Church St, Highland CA 92346	909-864-3180	R	2*	<.1
631	United Enviromental Network—*Zhendong Liu*	46 Longview Dr, Emerson NJ 07630	201-265-7684	R	2*	<.1
632	Hicks Electronic Design Inc—*Steve Hicks*	460 S Link Ln, Fort Collins CO 80524	970-225-0955	R	2*	<.1
633	Graybill's Tool and Die Inc—*H Graybill*	147 W High St, Manheim PA 17545	717-665-5546	R	2*	<.1
634	Peoplequest Inc—*Tiffany Graef*	401 N Brand Blvd Ste 8, Glendale CA 91203	818-507-5845	R	2*	<.1
635	Mas Air Systems Inc—*Gary Miller*	2008 County Line Rd, New Castle PA 16101	724-652-1367	R	2*	<.1
636	Control Masters Inc—*Carl Horn*	5235 Katrine Ave, Downers Grove IL 60515	630-968-2390	R	2*	<.1
637	Philadelphia Scientific Int'l Inc—*William Jones*	207 Progress Dr, Montgomeryville PA 18936	215-616-0390	R	2*	<.1
638	Rkf Engineering Solutions LLC—*Ted Kaplan*	1229 19th St Nw, Washington DC 20036	202-463-1567	R	2*	<.1
639	Remote Control Systems Inc—*Betty Smith*	75 Pennsylvania Ave, Irwin PA 15642	724-864-7100	R	2*	<.1
640	Tucker Induction Systems Ltd—*Denny Martin*	50550 Rizzo Dr, Shelby Township MI 48315	586-247-9100	R	2*	<.1
641	Kem Equipment Inc—*Travis Garske*	PO Box 546, Tualatin OR 97062	503-692-5012	R	2*	<.1
642	Sycon Instruments Inc—*Donald Fifolt*	6757 Kinne St, East Syracuse NY 13057	315-463-5297	R	2*	<.1
643	Advanced Manufacturing Systems Inc—*Ray Landis*	3110 Sexton Rd Se, Decatur AL 35603	256-350-8386	R	2*	<.1
644	Neologic International Inc—*Marcos Delgado*	6600 Westwind Dr, El Paso TX 79912	915-584-3651	R	2*	<.1
645	Southwest Image and Graphics Inc—*Rick Snell*	4625 S Ash Ave Ste J-3, Tempe AZ 85282	480-966-8866	R	2*	<.1
646	Patten Tool And Engineering Inc—*Kevin Stine*	22 Rte 236, Kittery ME 03904	207-439-1555	R	2*	<.1
647	Electro Mechanical Engineering Corp—*Glenn Olesen*	1197 Baltmor Annapolis, Arnold MD 21012	410-544-8563	R	2*	<.1
648	RG Research Inc—*James Jiranek*	2216 Greenspring Dr, Lutherville Timonium MD 21093	410-561-7777	R	2*	<.1
649	Industrial Systems Inc—*Terry Loznak*	14841 Keel St, Plymouth MI 48170	734-455-2610	R	1*	<.1
650	Arion Technologies Inc—*Denis Sheehy*	1121 Waterbury Rd Apt, Cheshire CT 06410	203-272-7743	R	1*	<.1
651	Mercury Iron and Steel—*Michael Rainer*	3401 Virginia Rd, Cleveland OH 44122	216-831-1000	R	1*	<.1
652	R and L Engineering Inc—*Neal Stevens*	PO Box 3970, Albany GA 31706	229-883-6052	R	1*	<.1
653	Us Digital Designs Inc—*Todd Smith*	1835 E 6th St Ste 27, Tempe AZ 85281	602-828-6965	R	1*	<.1
654	Mechanical Engineering Controls Automation Corp—*Jim Bour*	PO Box 519, Elkhart IN 46515	574-294-7580	R	1*	<.1

Rank	Company Name—*Executive Officer*	Address, City, State, Zip	Phone	Type	Fin	Empls
655	Mec Water Resources Inc—*Trent Sober*	1123 Wilkes Blvd Ste 4, Columbia MO 65201	573-443-4100	R	1*	<.1
656	Aircraft Lighting International Inc—*Nicholas Michelinakis*	PO Box 638, Mount Sinai NY 11766	631-474-2254	R	1*	<.1
657	Signal Engineering Inc—*John Thompson*	6370 Lusk Blvd Ste F20, San Diego CA 92121	858-552-8131	R	1*	<.1
658	Shoreham Graphics Inc—*Benedict Matheis*	299 Hawkins Ave Ste 15, Ronkonkoma NY 11779	631-981-2308	R	1*	<.1
659	Get Control Inc—*Rick Weber*	1530 N Hobson St Ste 1, Gilbert AZ 85233	480-539-0478	R	1*	<.1
660	Structural Integrity Associates Inc—*Laney Bisbee*	5215 Hellyer Ave Ste 2, San Jose CA 95138	408-978-8200	R	1*	.3
661	Evans Environmental and Geosciences—*Timothy Gipe*	14505 Commerce Way, Miami Lakes FL 33016	305-374-8300	R	1*	.1
662	Dodson and Associates Inc—*Brian Delaney*	5629 FM 1960 W Ste 314, Houston TX 77069	281-440-3787	R	1*	<.1
663	United International Engineering Inc—*David C Chou*	2201 Buena Vista Dr SE, Albuquerque NM 87106	505-242-9200	R	1*	<.1
664	Top-Vu Technology Inc—*Thomas Vu*	2650 14th St Nw, Saint Paul MN 55112	651-633-5925	R	1*	<.1
665	Ackenheil Engineers Inc—*Susan Ackenheil-Snow*	1000 Banksville Rd, Pittsburgh PA 15216	412-531-7111	R	1*	<.1
666	Creatone Inc—*Arun Patel*	1011 Us Hwy 22 Ste 1, Mountainside NJ 07092	908-789-8700	R	1*	<.1
667	D Singer Engineering Inc—*Claire Singer*	12117 Julius Ave, Downey CA 90242	562-927-6068	R	1*	<.1
668	Envision Wireless Inc—*Robert Joslin*	6550 N Wickham Rd Ste, Melbourne FL 32940	321-674-9010	R	1*	<.1
669	Web Engineering Associates Inc—*William Baird*	104 Longwater Dr Ste 1, Norwell MA 02061	781-878-7766	R	1*	<.1
670	David L Adams Associates Inc—*David L Adams*	1701 Boulder St, Denver CO 80211	303-455-1900	R	1*	<.1
671	Alpha Automation Inc—*Paul Bamburak*	127 Walters Ave, Ewing NJ 08638	609-882-0366	R	1*	<.1
672	Jentec Inc—*Jarl Jensen*	20 Charles St Ste C, Northvale NJ 07647	201-784-8511	R	1*	<.1
673	Dynamic Computer Resources Inc	13089 Peyton Dr Ste C4, Chino Hills CA 91709	909-548-0465	R	1*	<.1
674	Advantec Engineering LLC—*Fred Anderson*	219 Stagecoach Rd, Avon CT 06001	860-977-3099	R	1*	<.1
675	kbd/Technic Inc—*Gerry A Lanham*	3131 Disney St, Cincinnati OH 45209	513-351-6200	S	1*	<.1
676	Ra-Nav Laboratories Inc—*Don Perry*	PO Box 12224, Oklahoma City OK 73157	405-947-3361	R	1*	<.1
677	Sieler Design Products—*Patrice Sieler*	1310 W 130th St, Gardena CA 90247	310-324-9663	R	1*	<.1
678	Geospatial Holdings Inc—*Mark A Smith*	229 Howes Run Rd, Sarver PA 16055	724-353-3400	P	1	.1
679	Davis Technologies Inc—*Robert Dillon*	837 W Main St, Alliance OH 44601	330-823-2544	R	1*	<.1
680	Innovative Technologies Group And Co—*Robert Wilt*	8017 Dorsey Run Rd Ste, Jessup MD 20794	443-755-0870	R	1*	<.1
681	International Mechanical Design Inc—*Frank Ascenzo*	2015 Bellaire Ave, Royal Oak MI 48067	248-546-5740	R	1*	<.1
682	Kaltec Of Minnesota Inc—*Bruce Kallevig*	9766 Fallon Ave Ne Ste, Monticello MN 55362	763-295-2360	R	1*	<.1
683	Inovent Engineering Inc—*P Hungerford*	PO Box 39541, Cleveland OH 44139	440-248-2100	R	1*	<.1
684	Magnum International and Inc—*Dionne Povlitz*	318 Irwin Ave, Pontiac MI 48341	248-335-9520	R	1*	<.1
685	Technalithics Inc—*Steve Scott*	PO Box 8883, Waco TX 76714	254-776-7994	R	1*	<.1
686	Temple Systems Inc—*Thomas Temple*	6228 Webster St, Dayton OH 45414	937-264-0709	R	1*	<.1
687	Electronic Systems Design Inc—*Michael Stern*	1010 N Maclay Ave, San Fernando CA 91340	818-365-0864	R	<1*	<.1
688	Dunegan Engineering Company Inc—*Harold Dunegan*	PO Box 61803, Midland TX 79711	432-563-0178	R	<1*	<.1
689	Wettekin Electronics—*Charles Wettekin*	4506 W 12th St, Erie PA 16505	814-838-9184	R	<1*	<.1
690	Tom Saliga—*Tom Saliga*	12918 Commodity Pl, Tampa FL 33626	813-855-4778	R	<1*	<.1
691	Patriot Engineering Co—*Barbara Jensen*	16937 Munn Rd, Chagrin Falls OH 44023	440-543-3100	R	<1*	<.1
692	Applied Technology Solutions Inc—*Giorgio Belvassori*	10332 Main St 315, Fairfax VA 22030	703-277-9611	R	<1*	<.1
693	Automation and Controls Engineering Ltd—*Bob Holman*	5775 Wayzata Blvd Ste, Minneapolis MN 55416	952-525-9593	R	<1*	<.1
694	F and F Consultants Inc—*Frank Luisi*	PO Box 287, Tarentum PA 15084	724-224-4593	R	<1*	<.1
695	Leghart Associates Inc—*Michael Leghart*	PO Box 9239, Canton OH 44711	330-453-5595	R	<1*	<.1
696	Bowlin Company Inc—*Charles Bowlin*	PO Box 3007, Shreveport LA 71133	318-635-5344	R	<1*	<.1
697	Kelyniam Global Inc—*James Ketner*	97 River Rd, Canton CT 06019		P	<1	N/A
698	John A Martin and Associates Inc—*John A Martin Sr*	950 S Grand Ave, Los Angeles CA 90015	213-483-6490	R	<1	.4
699	Magnum Opus Inc—*Robert Galanty*	284 Kennedy St, Iselin NJ 08830	732-283-4925	R	<1	<.1
700	Thermal Energy Storage Inc—*Richard A McCormack*	6362 Ferris Sq Ste C, San Diego CA 92121	858-453-1395	P	<1	N/A
701	O'Brien and Gere Engineers Inc—*Terry L Brown*	PO Box 4873, East Syracuse NY 13057	315-437-6100	S	N/A	.8

TOTALS: SIC 8711 Engineering Services

Companies: 701					**144,114**	**444.0**

8712 Architectural Services

Rank	Company Name—*Executive Officer*	Address, City, State, Zip	Phone	Type	Fin	Empls
1	Modjeski and Mastes Inc—*John M Kulicki*	PO Box 2345, Harrisburg PA 17105	717-790-9565	R	5,653*	.2
2	Howard Needles Tammen and Bergendoff—*Ken Graham*	PO Box 419299, Kansas City MO 64146	816-472-1201	R	468*	2.7
3	RTKL International Ltd—*Lance K Josal* RTKL Associates Inc	901 S Bond St, Baltimore MD 21231	410-537-6000	S	352*	1.0
4	SSOE Inc—*Tony Damon*	1001 Madison Ave, Toledo OH 43604	419-255-3830	R	351*	1.0
5	RTKL Associates Inc—*Lance Josal*	901 S Bond St, Baltimore MD 21231	410-537-6000	S	341*	1.0
6	Heery International Inc—*Bill Heitz*	999 Peachtree St NE, Atlanta GA 30309	404-881-9880	S	293*	.8
7	NBBJ Design—*Doug Parris*	1555 Lake Shore Dr, Columbus OH 43204	614-224-7145	R	260*	.8
8	Gresham Smith and Partners—*James Bearden*	1400 Nashville City Ct, Nashville TN 37219	615-770-8100	R	246*	.7
9	Ellstreet Corp Perkins and Will Inc	2100 M St NW Ste 800, Washington DC 20037	202-737-1020	S	243*	1.0
10	OWP/P—*Michael J Sullivan* Cannon Design	111 W Washington Ste 2, Chicago IL 60602	312-332-9600	S	241*	1.0
11	Ganflec Architects and Engineers Inc—*Joseph Botchie*	209 Senate Ave, Camp Hill PA 17011	717-763-7220	R	217*	.8
12	Skidmore Owings and Merrill LLP—*William F Baker*	224 S Michigan Ave Ste, Chicago IL 60604	312-554-9090	R	202*	.8
13	Dewberry Cos—*Donald E StoneJr*	8401 Arlington Blvd, Fairfax VA 22031	703-849-0100	R	182*	.6
14	Hellmuth Obata and Kassabaum Inc—*William Hellmuth*	211 N Broadway Ste 700, Saint Louis MO 63102	314-421-2000	R	178*	1.8
15	Austin Co—*William Melsop*	6095 Parkland Blvd, Cleveland OH 44124	440-544-2600	R	175*	.3
16	M Arthur Gensler Jr and Associates Inc—*M Gensler*	2 Harrison St Fl 4, San Francisco CA 94105	415-433-3700	R	174*	2.3
17	Smithgroup Companies Inc—*Carl Roehling*	500 Griswold St Fl 170, Detroit MI 48226	313-983-3600	R	166*	.7
18	A/E Ellerbe Becket Co—*Rick Lincicome*	800 Lasalle Ave, Minneapolis MN 55402	612-376-2000	S	157*	.6
19	Wiss Janney Elstner Associates Inc—*William Nugent*	330 Pfingsten Rd, Northbrook IL 60062	847-272-7400	R	149*	.4
20	CSA Group Inc—*Guido Conegliano*	6100 Blue Lagoon Dr St, Miami FL 33126	305-461-5484	R	144*	.4
21	Ghafari Associates Inc	17101 Michigan Ave, Dearborn MI 48126	313-441-3000	R	128*	.4
22	Leo A Daly Co—*Leo A Daly III*	8600 Indian Hills Dr, Omaha NE 68114	402-391-8111	R	119*	1.1
23	NBBJ—*Scott W Wyatt*	223 Yale Ave N, Seattle WA 98109	206-223-5555	R	115*	.8
24	Cannon Design—*Mark Mendell*	2170 Whitehaven Rd, Grand Island NY 14072	716-773-6800	R	106*	1.0
25	Callison Architecture Inc—*John Jastrem*	1420 5th Ave Ste 2400, Seattle WA 98101	206-623-4646	R	103*	.6
26	STV Architects—*Milo Riverso*	205 W Welsh Dr, Douglassville PA 19518	610-385-8200	S	103*	.3
27	Lockwood Andrews and Newnam Inc—*Dennis W Petersen* Leo A Daly Co	2925 Briarpark Dr, Houston TX 77042	713-266-6900	S	94*	1.1
28	Wight and Co—*Mark Wight*	2500 N Frontage Rd, Darien IL 60561	630-969-7000	R	94*	.1
29	HLW International LLP—*Ted Hammer*	115 Fifth Ave 5th Fl, New York NY 10003	212-353-4600	R	88*	.3
30	Swanke Hayden Connell Ltd—*Peter Gross*	295 Lafayette St, New York NY 10012	212-226-9696	R	88*	.3
31	Del Ciotto Architects Inc—*Joseph J Del Ciotto Jr*	309 N Sumneytown Pike, North Wales PA 19454	215-699-6901	R	88*	.1
32	Flad and Associates—*William Bulla*	644 Science Dr, Madison WI 53711	608-238-2661	R	85*	.3
33	R W Armstrong and Assoc Inc—*James Wade*	300 S Meridian St, Indianapolis IN 46225	317-786-0461	R	76*	.2
34	Woolpert LLP—*Michael Flannery*	4454 Idea Ctr Blvd, Dayton OH 45430	937-461-5660	R	74*	.8

Note: An asterisk (*) indicates an estimated financial figure. The company type code used is as follows: R = Private, P = Public, S = Private Subsidiary, B = Public Subsidiary, D = Division, J = Joint Venture, I = Investment Fund.

COMPANY RANKINGS BY SALES WITHIN 4-DIGIT SIC

Rank	Company Name—Executive Officer	Address, City, State, Zip	Phone	Type	Fin	Empls
35	Einhorn Yaffee Prescott Architecture and Engineering PC—Tom Birdsey	257 Fuller Rd 1st Fl, Albany NY 12203	518-795-3800	R	74*	.4
36	Zimmer Gunsul Frasca Partnership—Robert Zimmerman	1223 SW Washington St, Portland OR 97205	503-224-3860	R	73*	.4
37	Anshen and Allen—Roger Swanson	901 Market St, San Francisco CA 94103	415-882-9500	R	72*	.4
38	KBJ Architects Inc—Will Morris	510 N Julia St, Jacksonville FL 32202	904-356-9491	R	71*	<.1
39	Kling—Robert Thompson	2301 Chestnut St, Philadelphia PA 19103	215-569-2900	R	70*	.4
40	STUDIOS Architecture—Todd Degarmo	405 Howard St Ste 588, San Francisco CA 94105	415-398-7575	R	69*	.2
41	Shw Group LLP—David Hickman	5717 Legacy Dr Ste 250, Plano TX 75024	214-473-2400	R	67*	.3
42	Waldemar S Nelson And Company Inc—Charles Nelson	1200 Saint Charles Ave, New Orleans LA 70130	504-523-5281	R	65*	.3
43	Moody-Nolan Limited Inc—Curtis J Moody	300 Spruce St Ste 300, Columbus OH 43215	614-461-4664	R	63*	.2
44	Perkins Eastman Architects PC—L Bradford Perkins	115 5th Ave 3rd Fl, New York NY 10003	212-353-7200	R	62*	.7
45	TPG Architecture LLP—James G Phillips	360 Park Ave S, New York NY 10010	212-768-0800	R	60*	.3
46	TY Lin International (San Francisco California)—Alvaro Piedra-hita	2 Harrison St Ste 500, San Francisco CA 94105	415-291-3700	R	56*	1.0
47	NewGround—Kevin Blair	15450 S Outer Forty Dr, Chesterfield MO 63017	636-898-8100	R	54*	.2
48	Earl Swensson Associates Inc—Richard Miller	2100 W End Ave Ste 120, Nashville TN 37203	615-329-9445	R	54*	.2
49	Pickering Inc—Mike Pohlman	6775 Lenox Centre Ct S, Memphis TN 38115	901-726-0810	R	54*	.2
50	Jeter Cook and Jepson Architects Inc—Peter Stevens	38 Prospect St, Hartford CT 06103	860-247-9226	R	54*	.1
51	Lionakis Design Group—Bruce Starkweather	1919 19th St, Sacramento CA 95814	916-558-1900	R	52*	.2
52	Smith Group Inc—Carl Roehling	500 Griswold St Ste 17, Detroit MI 48226	313-983-3600	R	50*	.5
53	Kaplan/McLaughlin/Diaz—Roy Latka	222 Vallejo St, San Francisco CA 94111		R	50	.2
54	Vickrey Ovresat Awsumb Associates Inc—Rebel Roberts	224 S Michigan Ave Ste, Chicago IL 60604	312-554-1400	R	49*	.2
55	Hayes Seay Mattern and Mattern Inc—John M Dionisio	PO Box 13446, Roanoke VA 24034	540-857-3100	R	47*	.6
56	Ballinger—William R Gustafson	833 Chestnut St Ste 14, Philadelphia PA 19107	215-446-0900	R	44*	.2
57	Tsoi/Kobus and Associates Inc—Ed Tsoi	PO Box 9114, Cambridge MA 02238	617-475-4000	R	44*	.1
58	NTD Architecture	9655 Granite Ridge Dr, San Diego CA 92123	858-565-4440	R	43*	.3
59	Hobbs and Black Associates Inc—William Hobbs	100 N State St, Ann Arbor MI 48104	734-663-4189	R	43*	.1
60	Corgan Associates Inc—Robert Morris	401 N Houston St, Dallas TX 75202	214-748-2000	R	42*	.3
61	Weidlinger Associates Inc—Raymond Daddazio	375 Hudson St 12th Fl, New York NY 10014	212-367-3000	R	42*	.2
62	Beyer Blinder Belle LLP—John H Beyer	41 E 11th St, New York NY 10003	212-777-7800	R	41*	.2
63	Freeman White Inc—Alan Baldwin	8845 Red Oak Blvd, Charlotte NC 28217	704-523-2230	R	40*	.2
64	Page Southerland Page—Lawrence Speck	400 W Ceasar Chavez St, Austin TX 78701	512-472-6721	R	39*	.3
65	Gould Evans Affiliates—Robert E Gould	4041 Mill St, Kansas City MO 64111	816-931-6655	R	39*	.2
66	Langdon Wilson Architects	1055 Wilshire Blvd Ste, Los Angeles CA 90017	213-250-1186	R	39*	.1
67	Payette Associates Inc—James H Collins Jr	285 Summer St, Boston MA 02210	617-895-1000	R	38*	.1
68	BWBR Architects—Stephen Patrick	380 Saint Peter St Ste, Saint Paul MN 55102	651-222-3701	R	38*	.1
69	DiLeonardo International Inc—James Lehouiller	2348 Post Rd Ste 501, Warwick RI 02886	401-732-2900	R	38*	.1
70	Perkins and Will Inc—Phil Harrison	330 N Wabash Ste 3600, Chicago IL 60611	312-755-0770	R	38*	.1
71	Looney Ricks Kiss Architects Inc—Frank Ricks	175 Toyota Plz Ste 600, Memphis TN 38103	901-521-1440	R	38*	.1
72	Harley Ellis Devereaux Corp—Gary Skog	26913 Nw Hwy Ste 200, Southfield MI 48033	248-262-1500	R	37*	.2
73	Pierce Goodwin Alexander and Linville—Jeffrey P Gerber	3131 Briarpark Ste 200, Houston TX 77042	713-622-1444	R	36*	.2
74	FRCH Design Worldwide—James R Tippmann	311 Elm St Ste 600, Cincinnati OH 45202	513-241-3000	R	36*	.2
75	S/L/A/M Collaborative Architects—Robert Pulito	80 Glastonbury Blvd, Glastonbury CT 06033	860-657-8077	R	35*	.2
76	Beyer Blinder Belle Architects And Planners LLP—John Belle	41 E 11th St Fl 2, New York NY 10003	212-777-7800	R	35*	.1
77	Eppstein Uhen Architects Inc—Greg Uhen	333 East Chicago St, Milwaukee WI 53202	414-271-5350	R	35*	.1
78	Bermello Ajamil and Partners Inc—Woody Bermello	2601 S Bayshore Dr, Miami FL 33133	305-859-2050	R	35*	.1
79	Pelli Clarke Pelli Architects—Cesar Pelli	1056 Chapel St, New Haven CT 06510	203-777-2515	R	35*	.1
80	Foit-Albert Associates Architects and Engineers PC—Beverly Foit-Albert	763 Main St, Buffalo NY 14203	716-856-3933	R	34*	.1
81	EwingCole—Joseph Kelly	100 N 6th St, Philadelphia PA 19106	215-923-2020	R	32*	.3
82	Brennan Beer Gorman/Architects—David Beer	161 6th Ave 3rd Fl, New York NY 10113	212-888-7667	R	32*	.1
83	EI Associates—Guy P Cipriano	8 Ridgedale Ave, Cedar Knolls NJ 07927	973-775-7777	R	30*	.2
84	Kirksey and Partners Architects Inc—John Kirksey	6909 Portwest Dr, Houston TX 77024	713-850-9600	R	30*	.1
85	Baker and Barrios Architects Inc—Tim Baker	189 S Orange Ave Ste 1, Orlando FL 32801	407-926-3000	R	29*	.1
86	Bernard Johnson Young Inc	9050 N Capital of Texa, Austin TX 78759	512-331-8900	R	29*	.1
87	Peckham Guyton Albers and Viets Inc	200 N Broadway Ste 100, Saint Louis MO 63102	314-231-7318	R	29*	.1
88	Gale Associates Inc—John Lindberg	PO Box 890189, Weymouth MA 02189	781-335-6465	R	29*	.1
89	Harriman Associates—Clifton Greim	46 Harriman Dr, Auburn ME 04210	207-784-5100	R	29*	.1
90	C H Guernsey and Co—Patrick Carroll	5555 N Grand Blvd Ste, Oklahoma City OK 73112	405-416-8100	R	28*	.2
91	Little Diversified Architectural Consulting Inc—Phillip Kuttner	5815 Westpark Dr, Charlotte NC 28217	704-525-6350	R	27*	.3
92	Winzler and Kelly Consulting Engineers Inc—Iver Skavdal	495 Tesconi Cir, Santa Rosa CA 95401	707-523-1010	R	27*	.3
93	LPA Inc—Robert Kupper	5161 California Ave St, Irvine CA 92617	949-261-1001	R	27*	.2
94	Multatech-Freese and Nichols JV—Alfred Saenz	1407 Texas St Ste 200, Fort Worth TX 76102	817-877-5571	R	26*	.4
95	Rogers Lovelock and Fritz Inc—Steven Hingtgen	PO Box 730, Winter Park FL 32790	407-647-1039	R	26*	.1
96	VITETTA Architects and Engineers—Alan Hoffmann	4747 S Broad St, Philadelphia PA 19112	215-218-4747	R	26*	.2
97	SERA Architects and Interiors—Bing Sheldon	338 NW 5th Ave, Portland OR 97209	503-445-7372	R	26*	.1
98	Stubbins Associates Inc—Bradford White	1 Broadway, Cambridge MA 02142	617-491-6450	R	26*	.1
99	WorthGroup—Douglas Worth	9400 Gateway Dr Ste B, Reno NV 89521	775-852-3977	R	26*	<.1
100	Reed Westlake Leskosky Ltd—Roger Chang	925 Euclid Ave Ste 190, Cleveland OH 44115	216-522-1350	R	26*	.1
101	Ruprecht Schroeder Hoffman Architects—Arthur R Ruprecht	363 Vanadium Rd, Pittsburgh PA 15243	412-429-1555	R	25*	.1
102	Bbg Technical Services Inc—Louis Hedgecock	350 5th Ave Fl 25, New York NY 10118	212-888-7663	R	25*	.2
103	Elkus/Manfredi Architects Ltd—Howard F Elkus	300 A St Ste 3, Boston MA 02210	617-426-1300	R	24*	.2
104	Cooper Carry and Associates Inc—Kevin Cantley	3520 Piedmont Rd Ste 2, Atlanta GA 30305	404-237-2000	R	24*	.1
105	FKP Architects Inc—John Crane	8 Greenway Plz Ste 300, Houston TX 77046	713-621-2100	R	24*	.1
106	Orcutt/Winslow Partnership—Paul Winslow	3003 N Central Ave 16, Phoenix AZ 85012	602-257-1764	R	24*	.1
107	Pei Cobb Freed and Partners—IM Pei	88 Pine St, New York NY 10005	212-751-3122	R	23*	.1
108	Nadel Architects Inc—Herbert Nadel	1990 S Bundy Dr 4th Fl, Los Angeles CA 90025	310-826-2100	R	23*	.1
109	CSO Schenkel Schultz—Allen Tucker	280 E 96th St Ste 200, Indianapolis IN 46240	317-848-7800	R	23*	.1
110	GMB Architects-Engineers—Harm Perdok	85 E 8 St Ste 200, Holland MI 49423	616-796-0200	R	23*	.1
111	Zeigler Cooper Inc—R Scott Zeigler	600 Travis St Ste 1200, Houston TX 77002	713-374-0000	R	23*	.1
112	Oz Architecture—Bud Thompson	1805 29th St Unit 2054, Boulder CO 80301	303-449-8900	R	22*	.3
113	Kennedy Associates/Architects Inc—Michael E Kennedy	211 N Broadway Ste 190, Saint Louis MO 63102	314-241-8188	R	22*	.1
114	Crump Firm Inc—Metcalf Crump	81 Monroe Ave, Memphis TN 38103	901-525-7744	R	22*	.1
115	FWA Group—Randall Larsen	500 East Blvd, Charlotte NC 28203	704-332-7004	R	22*	.1
116	BSA Lifestructures—Sam Reed	9365 Counselors Row, Indianapolis IN 46240	317-819-7878	R	21*	.1
117	Hixson Inc—J Wickliffe Ach	659 Van Meter St, Cincinnati OH 45202	513-241-1230	R	21*	.1
118	Smallwood Reynolds Stewart Stewart and Associates Inc—Howard Stewart	3565 Piedmont Rd Ste 3, Atlanta GA 30305	404-233-5453	R	21*	.1
119	Hellmuth Obata and Kassabaum Inc Sports Facilities Group	300 Wyandotte St, Kansas City MO 64105	816-221-1500	R	20*	.3
120	RSP Architects Ltd—David C Norback	1220 Marshall St NE, Minneapolis MN 55413	612-677-7100	R	20*	.3

Rank	Company Name—Executive Officer	Address, City, State, Zip	Phone	Type	Fin	Empls
121	Weihe Design Group PLC—M Durwood Dixon	1025 Connecticut Ave N, Washington DC 20036	202-857-8300	R	20*	.1
122	Davis (Tempe Arizona)—Mike R Davis	60 E Rio Salado Pkwy S, Tempe AZ 85281	480-638-1100	R	20*	.1
123	Stull and Lee Inc—Donald L Stull	33-41 Farnsworth St, Boston MA 02111	617-426-0406	R	20*	.1
124	Rosser International Inc—Noah Long	524 W Peachtree St, Atlanta GA 30308	404-876-3800	R	19*	.1
125	Champlin/Haupt Architects—Michael Battoclette	424 E 4th St St 400, Cincinnati OH 45202	513-241-4474	R	19*	.1
126	Loebl Schlossman and Hackl Inc—Donald Hackl	233 N Michigan Ave Ste, Chicago IL 60601	312-565-1800	R	19*	.1
127	Neumann/Smith and Associates—Joel Smith	400 Galleria Office Ce, Southfield MI 48034	248-352-8310	R	19*	.1
128	Ka Inc—James Heller	1468 W 9th St Ste 600, Cleveland OH 44113	216-781-9144	R	19*	.1
129	Watkins Hamilton Ross Architects Inc—David H Watkins	1111 Louisiana 26th Fl, Houston TX 77002	713-665-5665	R	18*	.1
130	Casco Corp—James Alberts	10877 Watson Rd, Saint Louis MO 63127	314-821-1100	R	18*	.1
131	Kuhlmann Design Group Inc—John Kuhlmann	66 Progress Pky, Maryland Heights MO 63043	314-434-8898	R	18*	.1
132	Murphy-Jahn Inc—Helmut Jahn	35 E Wacker Dr Ste 300, Chicago IL 60601	312-427-7300	R	18*	.1
133	Merritt and Pardini—Ellen Watson	1119 Pacific Ave Ste 1, Tacoma WA 98402	253-383-8700	S	18*	.1
134	SGPA/Architecture and Planning—Dave Reinker	1545 Hotel Cir S Ste 2, San Diego CA 92108	619-297-0131	R	18*	.1
135	Lawrence Group Inc—Stephen Smtih	319 N 4th St Ste 1000, Saint Louis MO 63102	314-231-5700	R	18*	.2
136	Moody-Nolan Inc—Curtis Moody	300 Spruce St Ste 300, Columbus OH 43215	614-461-4664	R	17*	.2
137	Karlsberger Cos—Mitchel R Levitt	99 E Main St, Columbus OH 43215	614-461-9500	R	17*	.2
138	Granary Associates	1500 Spring Garden Ste, Philadelphia PA 19130	215-665-7000	S	17*	.1
139	BaMo Inc—Pamela Babey	500 3rd St, San Francisco CA 94107	415-979-9880	R	17*	.1
140	Ware Malcomb—Lawrance Armstrong	10 Edelman, Irvine CA 92618	949-660-9128	R	17*	.2
141	Odell Associates Inc—Robert Griffin	800 W Hill St 3rd Fl, Charlotte NC 28208	704-414-1000	R	16*	.2
142	Schenkel and Shultz Inc—Michael S Gouloff	111 E Wayne St Ste 555, Fort Wayne IN 46802	260-424-9080	R	16*	.1
143	Reese Lower Patrick and Scott Ltd—Michael J Martin	1910 Harrington Dr, Lancaster PA 17601	717-560-9501	R	16*	.1
144	Sheladia Associates Inc—Manish Kothari	15825 Shady Grove Rd S, Rockville MD 20850	301-590-3939	R	16*	.1
145	Plunkett Raysich Architects LLP—David Schneider	11000 W Park Pl, Milwaukee WI 53224	414-359-3060	R	16*	.1
146	Solomon Cordwell Buenz and Associates Inc—Thomas Humes	625 N Michigan Ave Ste, Chicago IL 60611	312-896-1100	R	16*	.2
147	Hanbury Evans Wright Vlattas and Co—Jane C Wright	120 Atlantic St, Norfolk VA 23510	757-321-9600	R	15*	.1
148	VLK Architects Inc—Steven Aloway	2821 W 7th St Ste 300, Fort Worth TX 76107	817-633-1600	R	15*	.1
149	Hermes Architects Inc—Bob Bellomy	1177 W Loop S Ste 500, Houston TX 77027	713-785-3644	R	15*	.1
150	Margulies Perruzzi Architects—Marc Margulies	308 Congress St, Boston MA 02210	617-482-3232	R	15*	.1
151	Array Architects—Douglas Lindsey	2520 Renaissance Blvd, King of Prussia PA 19406	610-270-0599	R	15*	<.1
152	LWPB Architects and Planners PC—Daniel Pruitt	5909 NW Expwy Ste 600, Oklahoma City OK 73132	405-722-7270	R	14*	.1
153	Kell Munoz Architects Inc—Henry Munoz III	PO Box 90209, San Antonio TX 78209	210-349-1163	R	14*	.1
154	Bernardon Haber Holloway Architects PC—Arthur Bernardon	425 McFarlan Rd Ste 20, Kennett Square PA 19348	610-444-2900	R	14*	<.1
155	Design Partnership LLP—John Boerger	1412 Van Ness Ave, San Francisco CA 94109	415-777-3737	R	14*	<.1
156	Klipp Colussy Jenks DuBois Architects PC—Brian R Klipp	1512 Larimer St, Denver CO 80202	303-893-1990	R	14*	<.1
157	Kke Architects Inc—Gregory Hollenkamp	300 1st Ave N Ste 500, Minneapolis MN 55401	612-339-4200	R	14*	.2
158	Pei Cobb Freed and Partners LLP—Ian Bater	88 Pine St Lbby 1, New York NY 10005	212-751-3122	R	13*	.1
159	Schmidt Associates Inc—Wayne Schmidt	320 E Vermont St, Indianapolis IN 46204	317-263-6226	R	13*	.1
160	Martin Ac Partners Inc—Christopher Martin	444 S Flower St Ste 12, Los Angeles CA 90071	213-683-1900	R	13*	.1
161	Setter Leach and Lindstrom Inc—Robert Egge	730 2nd Ave S Ste 1100, Minneapolis MN 55402	612-338-8741	R	13*	.1
162	Mithun Partners Inc—Bert Gregory	Pier 56 1201 Alaskan W, Seattle WA 98101	206-623-3344	R	13*	.1
163	Kideney Architects/Laping Jaeger Associates PC—Thomas E Jaeger	200 John James Audubon, Buffalo NY 14228	716-636-9700	R	13*	.1
164	Valerio Dewalt Train Associates Inc—Mark Dewalt	500 N Dearborn Ste 900, Chicago IL 60654	312-260-7300	R	13*	<.1
165	Alfonso Architects Inc—Carlos J Alfonso	1705 N 16th St, Tampa FL 33605	813-247-3333	R	13*	<.1
166	Ford Powell and Carson Inc—Boone Powell	1138 E Commerce St, San Antonio TX 78205	210-226-1246	R	13*	<.1
167	Lorenzi Dodds and Gunnill Inc—James Lorenzi	3475 Leonardtown Rd St, Waldorf MD 20602	301-843-6255	R	13*	<.1
168	Sizeler Thompson Brown Architects—William Sizeler	300 Lafayette St Ste 2, New Orleans LA 70130	504-523-6472	R	13*	<.1
169	Flansburgh Associates Inc—David Soleau	77 N Washington St Ste, Boston MA 02114	617-367-3970	R	13*	.1
170	Ktgy Group Inc—Tricia Esser	17922 Fitch, Irvine CA 92614	949-851-2133	R	12*	.1
171	Des Architects Engineers Inc—Thomas Gilman	PO Box 3599, Redwood City CA 94064	650-364-6453	R	12*	.1
172	Cromwell Architects Engineers Inc—Charlie Penix	101 S Spring St Ste 10, Little Rock AR 72201	501-372-2900	R	12*	.1
173	Mclarand Vasquez Emsiek and Partners Inc—Carl Mclarand	1900 Main St Ste 800, Irvine CA 92614	949-809-3388	R	12*	.1
174	Widom Wein Cohen O'Leary Terasawa—Chester A Widom	3130 Wilshire Blvd 6th, Santa Monica CA 90403	310-828-0040	S	12*	.1
175	Fisher and Arnold Inc—Jeff Arnold	9180 Crestwyn Hills Dr, Memphis TN 38125	901-748-1811	R	12*	.1
176	Daniel Cook And Associates—Daniel Cook	2909 Washington Blvd, Ogden UT 84401	801-621-4781	R	12*	.1
177	Esherick Homsey Dodge and Davis Architects Inc—Charles Davis	500 Treat Ave Ste 201, San Francisco CA 94110	415-285-9193	R	12*	.1
178	Aumiller Youngquist PC	208 S Jefferson St 1st, Chicago IL 60661	312-377-8109	R	12*	.1
179	Engberg Anderson Design Partnership Inc—Charles Engberg	320 E Buffalo St Ste 5, Milwaukee WI 53202	414-944-9000	R	12*	.1
180	Gilbert Architects—Thomas W Gilbert	626 N Charlotte St, Lancaster PA 17603	717-291-1077	R	12*	.1
181	Peter Schwabe Inc—Daniel Schwabe	PO Box 215, Big Bend WI 53103	262-662-5551	R	12*	.1
182	Ross Barney Architects—Carol Ross Barney	10 W Hubbard St, Chicago IL 60610	312-832-0600	R	12*	.1
183	Loving and Campos Architects Inc—Carl Campos	245 Ygnacio Valley Rd, Walnut Creek CA 94596	925-944-1626	R	12*	<.1
184	Davis Brody Bond LLP—Grace Bailey	315 Hudson St Fl 9, New York NY 10013	212-633-4700	R	12*	.1
185	Bradley Steffian Architects—Kurt Rockstroh	100 Summer St Ste 900, Boston MA 02110	617-305-7100	R	12*	.1
186	Davis Partnership PC—Gary Adams	2301 Blake St Ste 100, Denver CO 80205	303-861-8555	R	12*	.1
187	Destefano And Partners Ltd—Phyllis Anderson	330 N Wabash Ave Ste 3, Chicago IL 60611	312-836-4321	R	12*	.1
188	William Hezmalhalch Architects Inc—William Hezmalhalch	2850 Red Hill Ave Ste, Santa Ana CA 92705	949-250-0607	R	12*	.1
189	Solomon Cordwell Buenz and Associates Inc—John Lahey	625 N Michigan Ave Fl, Chicago IL 60611	312-896-1100	R	11*	.1
190	Hnedak Bobo Group Inc—L Bobo	104 S Front St, Memphis TN 38103	901-525-2557	R	11*	.1
191	Hardy Holzman Pfeiffer Associates LLP—Hugh Hardy	902 Broadway 19th Fl, New York NY 10010	212-677-6030	R	11*	.1
192	Luckett and Farley Architects Engineers And Construction Managers Inc—Edward Jerdonek	737 S 3rd St, Louisville KY 40202	502-585-4181	R	11*	.1
193	John Portman and Associates—John C Portman III	303 Peachtree Center A, Atlanta GA 30303	404-614-5555	S	11*	.1
194	Goettsch Partners—James Goettsch	224 S Michigan Ave 17t, Chicago IL 60604	312-356-0600	R	11*	.1
195	BraytonHughes Design Studios—Richard Brayton	639 Howard St 2nd Fl, San Francisco CA 94105	415-291-8100	R	11*	.1
196	Jack Rouse Associates—Jack Rouse	600 Vine St Ste 1700, Cincinnati OH 45202	513-381-0055	R	11*	.1
197	Boynton Williams and Associates—Clarence Williams	900 36th Ave NW Ste 10, Norman OK 73072	405-329-0423	R	11*	<.1
198	Lauer Manguso and Associates Architects—James W Manguso	4080 Ridge Lea Rd, Buffalo NY 14228	716-837-0833	R	11*	<.1
199	Triplett Office Essentials—Dick Triplett	3553 109th St, Urbandale IA 50322	515-270-9150	R	11*	<.1
200	Clark/Kjos	333 NW 5th Ave Ste 800, Portland OR 97209	503-224-4848	R	11*	<.1
201	DEI Inc—Richard Grow	1550 Kemper Meadow Dr, Cincinnati OH 45240	513-825-5800	R	11*	.1
202	Armstrong Torseth Skold And Rydeen Inc—Paul Erickson	8501 Golden Valley Rd, Minneapolis MN 55427	763-545-3731	R	10*	.1
203	Niles Bolton Associates Inc—G Niles Bolton	3060 Peachtree Rd NW S, Atlanta GA 30305	404-365-7600	R	10*	.1
204	RMW Architecture and Interiors—Thomas B Gerfen	40 S Market St 4th Fl, San Jose CA 95113	408-294-8000	R	10*	.1
205	MARATHON Engineers/Architects/Planners LLC (Appleton Wisconsin)—Larry Lando	PO Box 8028, Appleton WI 54912	920-954-2000	R	10*	.1
206	Simon Martin-Vegue Winkelstein Moris—Cathy Simon	185 Berry St Ste 5000, San Francisco CA 94107	415-546-0400	R	10*	<.1

Note: An asterisk (*) indicates an estimated financial figure. The company type code used is as follows: R = Private, P = Public, S = Private Subsidiary, B = Public Subsidiary, D = Division, J = Joint Venture, I = Investment Fund.

COMPANY RANKINGS BY SALES WITHIN 4-DIGIT SIC

Rank	Company Name—*Executive Officer*	Address, City, State, Zip	Phone	Type	Fin	Empls
207	Benson Hlavaty Architects Inc—*Martti Benson*	3141 Hood St Ste 420, Dallas TX 75219	214-521-8500	R	10*	<.1
208	CUBE 3 Studio—*Nicholas Adam Middleton*	360 Merrimack St Bldg, Lawrence MA 01843	978-989-9900	R	10	<.1
209	Butler Rogers Baskett Architects PC—*Charles Baskett*	330 W 34th St Ste 1800, New York NY 10001	212-792-4600	R	9*	.1
210	Foreman Program and Construction Managers Inc—*Phillip G Foreman*	PO Box 189, Zelienople PA 16063	724-452-9690	R	9*	<.1
211	JPC Architects LLC—*Roger Merritt*	909 112th Ave NE Ste 2, Bellevue WA 98004	425-641-9200	R	9*	<.1
212	Jackson and Ryan Architects—*Guy Jackson*	2370 Rice Blvd Ste 210, Houston TX 77005	713-526-5436	R	9*	<.1
213	Rogers Burgun Shahine and Deschler Inc—*Mahmoud F Agha*	161 William St, New York NY 10038	212-571-0788	R	9*	<.1
214	Rodriguez and Quiroga Architects Chartered—*Raul L Rodriguez*	2100 Ponce De Leon Blv, Coral Gables FL 33134	305-448-7417	R	9*	<.1
215	Meyer Scherer and Rockcastle Ltd—*Jack Polind*	710 S 2 St 7 Fl, Minneapolis MN 55401	612-375-0336	R	8*	.1
216	WalkerGroup/CNI—*Kenneth Walker*	95 Morton St, New York NY 10014	212-462-8000	S	8*	.1
217	BETA Design Group Inc—*Doug Brant*	70 Ionia SW Ste 400, Grand Rapids MI 49503	616-235-6220	R	8*	<.1
218	Jova/Daniels/Busby Inc—*Henri V Jova*	1201 Peachtree St NE S, Atlanta GA 30361	404-892-2890	R	8*	<.1
219	DRS Architects—*Philip Hundley*	1 Gateway Ctr 17th Fl, Pittsburgh PA 15222	412-391-4850	R	8*	<.1
220	Franz Jeanes Lazo Cora Associates Inc	4055 International Plz, Fort Worth TX 76109	817-737-9922	R	8*	<.1
221	Chiodini Associates Inc—*Louis G Chiodini*	1401 S Brentwood Ste 4, Saint Louis MO 63144	314-725-5588	R	8*	<.1
222	Duckett Design Group Inc—*Karen I Duckett*	1632 Ware Ave, Atlanta GA 30344	404-592-4539	R	8*	<.1
223	Minnesota Architectural Alliance Inc—*Thomas Deangelo*	400 Clifton Ave, Minneapolis MN 55403	612-871-5703	R	8*	.1
224	Fugleberg Koch Architects Inc—*Lyle Fugleberg*	2555 Temple Trl Ste 10, Winter Park FL 32789	407-629-0595	R	7*	.1
225	Ratio Architects Inc—*Bill Browne*	107 S Pennsylvania St, Indianapolis IN 46204	317-633-4040	R	7*	.1
226	Carrier Johnson—*Gordon Carrier*	1301 3rd Ave, San Diego CA 92101	619-239-2353	R	7*	.1
227	Scott Partnership Architecture Inc—*Ray Scott*	423 S Keller Rd Ste 20, Orlando FL 32810	407-660-2766	R	7*	.1
228	Rothenberg Sawasy Architects Inc—*Mark Rothenberg*	953 E 3rd St, Los Angeles CA 90013	213-225-7201	R	7*	<.1
229	BEA International Inc—*Bruno Elias Ramos*	3075 NW South River Dr, Miami FL 33142	305-461-2053	R	7*	<.1
230	Boccard Suddell Construction Corp—*George Suddell*	202-11 E Shore Rd, Huntington NY 11743	631-421-2595	R	7*	<.1
231	Murray Associates Architects PC—*D Michael Frye*	1600 N 2nd St, Harrisburg PA 17102	717-234-2581	R	7*	<.1
232	CE Fleming Corp—*Charles E Fleming*	440 N 4th St, Saint Louis MO 63102	314-241-9550	R	7*	<.1
233	Cshqa A PA—*Jeffrey Shneider*	250 S 5th St Ste 600, Boise ID 83702	208-343-4635	R	7*	.1
234	OPX LLC—*Steve Polo*	21 Dupont NW, Washington DC 20036	202-822-9797	R	6*	.1
235	Spector Group	220 Crossways Park Wes, Woodbury NY 11797	516-365-4240	R	6*	.1
236	RBB Architects Inc—*Joseph Balbona*	10980 Wilshire Blvd, Los Angeles CA 90024	310-473-3555	R	6*	<.1
237	Acai Associates Inc—*Adolfo Cotilla Jr*	2937 W Cypress Creek R, Fort Lauderdale FL 33309	954-484-4000	R	6*	<.1
238	Apostolou Associates—*Paul Apostolou*	47 Bailey Ave, Pittsburgh PA 15211	412-381-1400	R	6*	<.1
239	Judd Brown Designs Inc—*Judd Brown*	700 School St, Pawtucket RI 02860	401-721-0977	R	6*	<.1
240	McKinney Partnership Architects—*Richard McKinney*	3600 W Main Ste 200, Norman OK 73072	405-360-1400	R	6*	<.1
241	Quorum Architects Inc—*Bill Blankenship*	707 W Vickery Blvd Ste, Fort Worth TX 76104	817-738-8095	R	6*	<.1
242	Ray Group Inc—*Michael R Patton*	127 E Orange St, Lancaster PA 17602	717-392-6502	R	6*	<.1
243	Architectural Partnership—*John Ward*	415 N Broadway Ave, Oklahoma City OK 73102	405-232-8787	R	6*	<.1
244	Morrison Kattman Menze Inc—*George D Morrison*	119 W Wayne St, Fort Wayne IN 46802	260-422-0783	R	6*	<.1
245	Minuta Architecture PLLC—*Joseph J Minuta*	345 Windsor Hwy Ste 10, New Windsor NY 12553	845-565-0055	R	6*	<.1
246	ARCTURIS—*Patricia D Whitaker*	720 Olive Ste 200, Saint Louis MO 63101	314-206-7100	R	5*	.1
247	Christner Inc—*John R Reeve*	168 N Meramec Ste 400, Saint Louis MO 63105	314-725-2927	R	5*	<.1
248	Stottler Stagg and Associates Architects Engineers Planners Inc—*Richard H Stottler Jr*	1802 S Fiske Blvd Ste, Rockledge FL 32955	321-338-2902	R	5*	<.1
249	Clark Nexsen PC—*Chris Stone*	6160 Kempsville Cir St, Norfolk VA 23502	757-455-5800	R	5*	<.1
250	Lehman-Smith and McLeish PLLC—*James Black McLeish*	1212 Banks NW, Washington DC 20007	202-295-4800	R	5*	<.1
251	Thompson Hancock Witte and Associates Inc—*William R Witte*	2100 Riveredge Pkwy St, Atlanta GA 30328	404-252-8040	R	5*	<.1
252	HMR Architects Inc—*Eric M Mifkovic*	2130 21st St, Sacramento CA 95818	916-736-2724	R	5*	<.1
253	Philip Johnson/Alan Ritchie Architects—*Alan Ritchie*	841 Broadway, New York NY 10003	212-319-5880	R	5*	<.1
254	Valentour English Bodnar and Howell—*Bob Bodnar*	470 Washington Rd, Pittsburgh PA 15228	412-561-7117	R	5*	<.1
255	Ross Schonder Sterzinger Cupcheck PC—*Ralph J Sterzinger*	5500 Brooktree Rd Ste, Wexford PA 15090	724-933-9100	R	5*	<.1
256	B Five Studio LLP—*Ronald Bentley*	30 West 24th St 8th Fl, New York NY 10010	212-255-7827	R	5*	<.1
257	Freyer Collaborative Architects—*Warren Freyer*	37 E 18th St 10th Fl, New York NY 10003	212-598-0900	R	5*	<.1
258	FTL Design Engineering Studio—*Nic Goldsmith*	44 E 32nd St 3rd Fl, New York NY 10016	212-732-4691	S	5*	<.1
259	Gorman Richardson Architects Inc—*Michael T Gorman*	77 Main St, Hopkinton MA 01748	508-497-2590	R	5*	<.1
260	Krisken Electronics Corp—*Gordon Wolfe*	17432 Devonshire St, Northridge CA 91325	818-360-3107	R	5*	<.1
261	Celli-Flynn Brennan Architects and Planners—*Thomas Celli*	606 Liberty Ave, Pittsburgh PA 15222	412-281-9400	R	5*	<.1
262	Digiorgio Costantini Partnership—*Mike Costantini*	24 Ne 24th Ave Ste 102, Pompano Beach FL 33062	954-785-0034	R	5*	<.1
263	Nelson—*Mitchell Cohen*	55 W Wacker DrSte 600, Chicago IL 60601	312-263-6605	R	4*	.1
264	James Harb Architects—*James Harb*	230 W 17th St 5th Fl, New York NY 10011	212-645-3600	R	4*	<.1
265	Ahearn-Schopfer and Associates PC—*Patrick Ahearn*	160 Commonwealth Ave S, Boston MA 02116	617-266-1710	R	4*	<.1
266	Cuyahoga Company Inc—*Diane Wagner*	13427 Madison Ave, Cleveland OH 44107	216-228-4700	R	4*	<.1
267	Mitchell Carlson Stone Inc—*Keith Carlson*	3221 W Alabama St, Houston TX 77098	713-522-1054	R	4*	<.1
268	Rosenberg Kolb Architects PC—*Eric J Rosenberg*	226 E 79th St, New York NY 10175	212-996-3099	R	4*	<.1
269	Beck Associates Architects—*Donald K Beck*	110 W 7th St Ste 710, Tulsa OK 74119	918-583-5300	R	4*	<.1
270	Jonathan Cohen and Associates—*Jonathan Cohen*	65 Acacia Ave, Berkeley CA 94708	510-558-8154	R	4*	<.1
271	Papadatos Partnership LLP—*Steven Papadatos*	27 W 24th St, New York NY 10010	212-604-9444	R	4*	<.1
272	Scholz Design Inc—*Christopher Gibson*	6546 Weatherfield Ct S, Maumee OH 43537	419-531-1601	R	4*	<.1
273	Solar Design Associates Inc—*Steven Strong*	PO Box 242, Harvard MA 01451	978-456-6855	R	4*	<.1
274	Aston Pereira and Associates—*Aston Pereira*	909 Montgomery St Ste, San Francisco CA 94133	415-982-6015	R	4*	<.1
275	Frank Betz Associates Inc—*Russell Moody*	3550 George Busbee Pkw, Kennesaw GA 30144	770-431-0888	R	4*	<.1
276	Kubala Washatko Architects Inc—*Thomas Kubala*	W61n617 Mequon Ave, Cedarburg WI 53012	262-377-6039	R	3*	<.1
277	Advance Manufacturing Co—*David Craig*	3890 Homewood Rd, Memphis TN 38118	901-365-8500	R	3*	<.1
278	SMPC Architects PA—*Chris Willadsen*	115 Amherst Dr SE, Albuquerque NM 87106	505-255-8668	R	3*	<.1
279	CT Hsu and Associates Inc—*Chu-tzu Hsu*	820 Irma Ave, Orlando FL 32803	407-423-0098	R	3*	<.1
280	RPGA Design Group Inc—*Robert Garza*	101 S Jennings Ste 100, Fort Worth TX 76104	817-332-9477	R	3*	<.1
281	William E Johnson Associates Inc—*William E Johnson*	127 Peachtree St Ste 1, Atlanta GA 30303	404-525-5400	R	3*	<.1
282	Cameron Alread Architects Inc—*Cameron Alread Jr*	209 W 8th St, Ft Worth TX 76102	817-332-6231	R	3*	<.1
283	Carlson Group Inc (Irvine California)—*William Fraser*	34 Executive Pk Ste 23, Irvine CA 92614	949-251-0455	R	3*	<.1
284	DMS Architects Inc—*Raymond L Darrow*	300 College Ave, Fort Worth TX 76104	817-570-2000	R	3*	<.1
285	Moed de Armas and Shannon Architects PC—*Leon Moed*	80 Broad St, New York NY 10004	212-809-0100	R	3*	<.1
286	Charles Rose Architects—*Charles Rose*	115 Willow Ave, Somerville MA 02144	617-628-5033	R	3*	<.1
287	Hanrahan Meyers Architects—*Thomas Hanrahan*	347 W 36th St Ste 1101, New York NY 10018	212-989-6026	R	3*	<.1
288	Kitchens by Krengel Inc—*Lauri Jo Krengel*	1688 Grand Ave, Saint Paul MN 55105	651-698-0844	R	3*	<.1
289	Kersey and Kersey Inc—*Cheryl Kersey*	839 E Gray St, Louisville KY 40204	502-583-0094	R	3*	<.1
290	McCleary/German Associates Inc—*Scott Clanton*	14800 St Marys Ln Ste, Houston TX 77027	713-552-0707	R	3*	<.1
291	Daroff Design Inc—*Karen Daroff*	2121 Market St, Philadelphia PA 19103	215-636-9900	R	2*	<.1
292	Shea Architects Inc—*David Shea*	100 N 6th St Ste 650C, Minneapolis MN 55403	612-339-2257	R	2*	<.1
293	Collman and Karsky Architects—*Rodney Collman*	4301 Anchor Plz Pkwy S, Tampa FL 33634	813-884-2000	R	2	<.1

Rank	Company Name—*Executive Officer*	Address, City, State, Zip	Phone	Type	Fin	Empls
294	Kerns Group Architects PC—*Thomas L Kerns*	4600 N Fairfax Dr Ste, Arlington VA 22203	703-528-1150	R	2*	<.1
295	Peacock and Lewis Architects and Planners Inc—*Brian D Idle*	11770 US Hwy 1 Ste 102, North Palm Beach FL 33408	561-626-9704	R	2*	<.1
296	JT Nakaoka Associates Architects—*James T Nakaoka*	10390 Santa Monica Blv, Los Angeles CA 90025	310-286-9375	R	2*	<.1
297	Janko Rasic Associates Architects—*Janko Rasic*	109 E 37th St 2nd Fl, New York NY 10016	212-685-9500	R	2	<.1
298	MA Architecture LLC—*Paul B Meyer*	4000 N Classen Blvd St, Oklahoma City OK 73118	405-525-8806	R	2*	<.1
299	Lauster Radu Architects—*Chuck Lauster*	104 W 27th St 10th Fl, New York NY 10001	212-691-1711	R	2	<.1
300	Rotwein and Blake Associated Architects PA—*Lance Blake*	16 Microlab Rd, Livingston NJ 07039	973-740-9755	R	2*	<.1
301	Youngman and Company Inc—*Michael Youngman*	11 S Lasalle St Ste 27, Chicago IL 60603	312-263-2670	R	2*	<.1
302	Terry M Harden Architects—*Terry M Harden*	110 Manhattan Plz 6850, Fort Worth TX 76120	817-446-1484	R	2*	<.1
303	Cornerstone Architects Inc—*Tom Nemitz*	440 Bridge St NW, Grand Rapids MI 49504	616-774-0100	R	2*	<.1
304	Jeffrey Parker Architects—*Jeffrey Parker*	855 28th St SE, Grand Rapids MI 49508	616-241-0090	R	2*	<.1
305	Manley Architecture Group—*Patrick Manley*	3820 N High St, Columbus OH 43214	614-545-1147	R	2*	<.1
306	Spiers McDonald Bharucha and Royal Inc—*Darius S Bharucha*	150 Corporate Center D, Camp Hill PA 17011	717-975-3620	R	2*	<.1
307	Turett Collaborative Architects—*Wayne Turett*	277 Broadway Ste 1300, New York NY 10007	212-965-1244	R	2*	<.1
308	Amie Gross Architectural PC—*Amie Gross*	380 Lexington Ave 17th, New York NY 10168	212-755-4010	R	2*	<.1
309	Dunwody/Beeland Architects—*Eugene Cox Dunwody*	PO Box 306, Macon GA 31202	478-742-5321	R	2*	<.1
310	Architronics Inc—*Edward T Vermurlen*	5090 60th St SE, Grand Rapids MI 49512	616-554-0577	R	2*	<.1
311	Manufacturing And Design Technology Inc—*Gerhard Marxrieser*	1033 Cavalier Blvd, Chesapeake VA 23323	757-485-8924	R	1*	<.1
312	Strada Architecture LLC—*Alan Cuteri*	925 Liberty Ave, Pittsburgh PA 15222	412-263-3800	R	1*	<.1
313	Harris Design Associates Inc—*Olaf Harris*	3535 Travis St Ste 265, Dallas TX 75204	214-526-8621	R	1*	<.1
314	Ward/Hall Associates AIA PLC—*GT Ward*	14900 Conferencer Cntr, Chantilly VA 20151	703-961-1755	R	1*	<.1
315	Colimore Thoemke Architects Inc—*James Colimore Jr*	1240 Key Hwy, Baltimore MD 21230	410-752-3720	R	1*	<.1
316	L Bogdanow Partners Architects PC—*Larry Bogdanow*	33 Greene St Rm 5W, New York NY 10013	212-966-0313	R	1*	<.1
317	SRK Architects—*S Neil Schlosser*	1225 Spring St, Philadelphia PA 19107	215-568-1090	R	1*	<.1
318	Eberhard Architects LLC—*William T Eberhard AIA IIDA*	2587 University Blvd, University Heights OH 44118	216-513-1300	R	1*	<.1
319	Mesher Shing and Associates—*Robert Mesher*	808 E Roy St, Seattle WA 98102	206-622-4981	R	1*	<.1
320	Terry J Martin Associates—*Terry Martin*	61 E Main St Ste D, Los Gatos CA 95030	408-395-8016	R	1*	<.1
321	Aaron Cohen Associates Ltd—*Aaron Cohen*	159 Teatown Rd, Croton On Hudson NY 10520	914-271-8170	R	1*	<.1
322	HSE Architects—*Dan Skaggs*	914 N Broadway Ste 200, Oklahoma City OK 73102	405-526-1300	R	1*	<.1
323	KSA Inc—*Kenneth Adams*	4400 Post Oak Pkwy Ste, Houston TX 77027	713-881-3400	R	1*	<.1
324	Otto/Walker Architects Inc—*Richard Otto*	2200 Park Ave Ste C201, Park City UT 84098	435-649-6373	R	1*	<.1
325	Timothy R Winters Architect—*Timothy R Winters*	8009 New LaGrange Rd S, Louisville KY 40222	502-412-1210	R	1*	<.1
326	Althouse Martin and Associates Inc—*Aldel Stoltzfus*	3008 Columbia Ave, Lancaster PA 17603	717-291-5928	R	1*	<.1
327	Hanno Weber and Associates—*Hanno Weber*	11 E Adams St Ste 702, Chicago IL 60603	312-922-5589	H	1*	<.1
328	Rex Nichols Architect International PA—*Rex Nichols*	101 Plaza Real S Ste 2, Boca Raton FL 33432	561-368-9445	R	1*	<.1
329	Gardner Partnership Architects—*Ray Gardner*	PO Box 549, Cedar City UT 84721	435-586-9494	R	1*	<.1
330	Pouw and Associates Inc—*Stanley Pouw*	7417 Grandview Ave, Arvada CO 80002	303-296-4343	R	1*	<.1
331	Acanthus Architects—*Henry Alpass*	1608 Buchanan St NW, Washington DC 20011	202-966-7900	R	1*	<.1
332	Renner Architects LLC—*Peter Renner*	643 E Erie St, Milwaukee WI 53202	414-273-6637	R	N/A	<.1
333	Robert P Davis Architects—*Robert P Davis*	7710 Moondance Ln, Houston TX 77071	713-291-6023	R	N/A	<.1

TOTALS: SIC 8712 Architectural Services
Companies: 333

					16,523	52 1

8713 Surveying Services

Rank	Company Name—*Executive Officer*	Address, City, State, Zip	Phone	Type	Fin	Empls
1	Carson Helicopters Inc—*Franklin Carson*	952 Blooming Glen Rd, Perkasie PA 18944	215-249-3535	R	24*	.2
2	Quantapoint Inc—*John R Wilson*	2650 Fountain View Dr, Houston TX 77057	713-574-1444	R	15*	.1
3	Golden Field Services Inc—*Jerry Jeffries*	10830 E 45th St Ste 40, Tulsa OK 74146	918-010-0014	R	15*	.2
4	Intech Inc (Chattanooga Tennessee)—*Sam Crabtree*	2802 Belle Arbor Ave, Chattanooga TN 37406	423-622-3700	S	13*	<.1
5	Advanced Imaging Systems Inc—*Madeleine Solomon*	10617 Southern Loop Bl, Pineville NC 28134	704-525-4392	R	7*	.1
6	Stewart Geo Technologies—*Pat Vader*	5730 Northwest Pkwy, San Antonio TX 78249	210-684-2147	S	6*	<.1
7	Tactical TeleSolutions Inc—*Laura Hylton*	550 Kearny St Ste 210, San Francisco CA 94108	415-788-8808	R	4*	.2
8	Thomas C Merritts Land Surveyor PC—*Thomas C Merritts*	394 Bedford Rd, Pleasantville NY 10570	914-769-8003	R	2*	<.1
9	Laser Scan Inc—*Steven Cox*	45945 Ctr Oak Plz Ste, Sterling VA 20166	703-444-9488	R	2*	<.1
10	Landmark Engineering Ltd—*Jeff Olhausen*	3521 W Eisenhower Blvd, Loveland CO 80537	970-667-6286	R	1*	<.1

TOTALS: SIC 8713 Surveying Services
Companies: 10

					88	.7

8721 Accounting, Auditing & Bookkeeping

Rank	Company Name—*Executive Officer*	Address, City, State, Zip	Phone	Type	Fin	Empls
1	PricewaterhouseCoopers LLP—*Bob Moritz*	300 Madison Ave 24th F, New York NY 10017	646-471-4000	R	29,200	168.7
2	McGladrey and Pullen LLP—*Joe Adler*	3600 American Blvd W 3, Bloomington MN 55431	952-921-7700	R	27,425*	6.5
3	Ernst and Young LLP—*James Turley*	5 Times Sq, New York NY 10036	212-773-3000	R	22,900	152.0
4	Deloitte Touche Tohmatsu—*Barry Salzberg*	1633 Broadway, New York NY 10019	212-489-1600	R	11,000*	44.4
5	Crowe Chizek and Company LLP (Indianapolis Indiana)—*Charles Allen*	10 W Market St Ste 200, Indianapolis IN 46204	317-632-1100	R	9,806*	1.7
6	Deloitte and Touche LLP—*Barry Salzberg*	1633 Broadway, New York NY 10019	212-489-1600	R	9,252*	44.0
7	Rothstein Kass—*Steven A Kass*	1350 Ave of the Americ, New York NY 10019	212-997-0500	R	5,982*	1.0
8	CDR Associates Inc—*Jeff Donnelly*	307 International Cir, Hunt Valley MD 21030	410-560-6700	S	5,408*	1.4
9	Eide Bailly LLP—*Jerry Topp*	1850 N Central Ave Ste, Phoenix AZ 85004	602-264-5844	R	5,363*	1.1
10	Wiss and Company LLC—*Jeffrey Campo*	354 Eisenhower Pkwy, Livingston NJ 07039	973-994-9400	R	4,985*	.1
11	Saltmarsh Cleaveland and Gund—*Ronald E Jackson*	900 N 12th Ave, Pensacola FL 32501	850-435-8300	R	3,631*	.1
12	Stone Carlie and Company LLC—*Jeffery Ward*	101 S Hanley Rd Ste 80, Clayton MO 63105	314-889-1100	R	3,212*	.1
13	KolbCo—*Tom Luken*	13400 Bishops Ln Ste 3, Brookfield WI 53005	262-754-9400	R	2,918*	.1
14	Thompson Dunavant PLC—*Steve Dunavant*	5100 Poplar Ave 30th F, Memphis TN 38137	901-685-5575	R	2,869*	.1
15	Israeloff Trattner and Company CPA's PC—*Michael J Garibaldi*	350 Fifth Ave, New York NY 10118	212-239-3300	R	2,861*	.1
16	Gifford Hillegass and Ingwersen—*Steve Baldwin*	6 Concourse Pkwy Rm 60, Atlanta GA 30328	770-396-1100	R	2,698*	.1
17	Hannis T Bourgeois LLP—*Randy Bonnecaze*	2322 Tremont Dr, Baton Rouge LA 70809	225-928-4770	R	2,520*	.1
18	KPMG LP—*John B Veihmeyer*	345 Park Ave, New York NY 10154	212-758-9700	R	2,450*	19.6
19	Boston Safe Deposit and Trust Co—*James Palermo*	1 Boston Pl Fl 15, Boston MA 02108	617-722-7000	S	2,315*	.6
20	Clayton and McKervey PC—*Donald H Clayton*	2000 Town Center Ste 1, Southfield MI 48075	248-208-8860	R	2,161*	.1
21	BGBC Partners LLP—*Steve Eichenberger*	300 N Meridian St Ste, Indianapolis IN 46204	317-633-4700	R	2,159*	.1
22	Stambaugh Ness PC—*Steven H Klunk*	2600 Eastern Blvd Ste, York PA 17402	717-757-6999	R	2,143*	.1
23	Green Hasson and Janks LLP—*Leon C Janks*	10990 Wilshire Blvd 16, Los Angeles CA 90024	310-873-1600	R	2,141*	.1
24	Paychex Inc—*Martin Mucci*	911 Panorama Trl S, Rochester NY 14625	585-385-6666	P	2,084	12.4
25	Washington Services—*Dennis R Washington*	PO Box 16630, Missoula MT 59808	406-523-1300	R	2,000	10.0
26	Barnes Wendling CPA Inc—*Jeffrey D Neuman*	1215 Superior Ave Ste, Cleveland OH 44114	216-566-9000	R	1,800*	.1
27	Buffamante Whipple Buttafaro PC—*Tom Buffamante*	PO Box 1170, Orchard Park NY 14127	716-664-5104	R	1,800*	.1
28	Simon Lever and Co—*Marlin Benedict*	444 Murry Hill Cir, Lancaster PA 17601	717-569-7081	R	1,784*	.1
29	Keefe McCullough and Company LLP—*Joseph Leo*	6550 N Federal Hwy Ste, Fort Lauderdale FL 33308	954-771-0896	R	1,781*	.1

Note: An asterisk (*) indicates an estimated financial figure. The company type code used is as follows: R = Private, P = Public, S = Private Subsidiary, B = Public Subsidiary, D = Division, J = Joint Venture, I = Investment Fund.

COMPANY RANKINGS BY SALES WITHIN 4-DIGIT SIC

Rank	Company Name—Executive Officer	Address, City, State, Zip	Phone	Type	Fin	Empls
30	Grant Thornton International—Edward Nusbaum	175 West Jackson Blvd, Chicago IL 60604	312-856-0200	R	1,700	21.9
31	CBIZ McClain Accounting Tax and Advisory Inc	200 S Biscayne Blvd St, Miami FL 33131	305-371-2731	S	1,603	<.1
32	Pyramid Healthcare Solutions Inc—Lawrence E Hynek	14141 46th St N Ste 12, Clearwater FL 33762	727-431-3000	R	1,533*	.3
33	Williams Benator and Libby—Bruce V Benator	1040 Crown Pointe Pkwy, Atlanta GA 30338	770-512-0500	R	1,460*	<.1
34	White Nelson and Co—David P Doran	2875 Michelle Drive St, Irvine CA 92606	714-978-1300	R	1,448*	<.1
35	Albright Crumbacker Moul and Itell—John P Itell	1110 Professional Ct S, Hagerstown MD 21740	301-739-5300	R	1,428*	<.1
36	Cherry Bekaert and Holland—Jerry P Fox	PO Box 27127, Richmond VA 23261	804-673-4224	R	1,400*	.7
37	Freed Maxick Group—Robert Glaser RSM McGladrey Inc	424 Main St Ste 800, Buffalo NY 14202	716-847-2651	S	1,206*	.3
38	Grant Thornton LLP—Stephen Chipman	175 W Jackson Blvd 20t, Chicago IL 60604	312-856-0200	R	1,200*	3.6
39	Katz Sapper and Miller LLP—David A Resnick	PO Box 40857, Indianapolis IN 46240	317-580-2000	R	1,171*	.3
40	RA Mercer and Co—Roger Lis	6455 Lake Ave, Orchard Park NY 14127	716-675-4270	R	1,079*	<.1
41	Ennis Pellum and Associates PA—Robert Ennis	5150 Belfort Rd S Bldg, Jacksonville FL 32256	904-396-5965	R	1,043*	<.1
42	Schowalter and Jabouri PC—James Torti	11777 Gravois Rd, Saint Louis MO 63127	314-842-2929	R	1,036*	<.1
43	Brock Schecter and Polakoff LLP—Tom Grogan	726 Exchange St Ste 82, Buffalo NY 14210	716-854-5034	R	971*	<.1
44	Helmholdt and Co—Ed Timmer	5940 Tahoe Dr SESte 10, Grand Rapids MI 49546	616-949-7250	R	931*	<.1
45	Mohler Nixon and Williams—Bill Kelleher	635 Campbell Technolog, Campbell CA 95008	408-369-2400	R	913*	.2
46	RubinBrown LLP—James M Castellano	1 N Brentwood Blvd, Saint Louis MO 63105	314-290-3300	R	912*	.3
47	Martin Werbelow LLP—David P Beringer	300 N Lake Ave Ste 930, Pasadena CA 91101	626-577-1440	R	905*	<.1
48	Blum Shapiro and Co—Carl R Johnson	29 S Main St 4th Fl, West Hartford CT 06127	860-561-4000	R	897*	.2
49	Dolinka Van Noord and Co—Robert Brouwer	360 E Beltline NE Ste, Grand Rapids MI 49506	616-459-2233	R	894*	<.1
50	MSI Barnes and Associates—Joseph B Barnes	2929 E Commercial Blvd, Fort Lauderdale FL 33308	954-491-1950	R	892*	<.1
51	Philip R Friedman and Associates LLP—David Klunk	1601 S Queen St, York PA 17403	717-843-3804	R	892*	<.1
52	Mitchell and Titus LLP—Tony Kendall	1 Battery Park Plz 27t, New York NY 10004	212-709-4500	R	874*	.2
53	Lipsey Youngren Means Ogren and Sandberg LLP—Robert H Lipsey	525 B St Ste 1750, San Diego CA 92101	619-234-0877	R	855*	<.1
54	Finley and Cook PLLC—Richard Finley	601 N Broadway, Shawnee OK 74802		R	843*	.2
55	Beers and Cutler PLLC—Matt Hallam	8219 Leesburg Pike Ste, Vienna VA 22182	703-923-8300	R	806*	.2
56	Padgett Strateman and Company LLP—John Wright	100 NE Loop 410 Ste 11, San Antonio TX 78216	210-828-6281	R	804*	.2
57	Bee Berguall and Co—James L Bee	PO Box 640, Warrington PA 18976	215-343-2727	R	736*	<.1
58	Isler and Co—John A Chambers	1300 SW 5th Ave Ste 29, Portland OR 97201	503-224-5321	R	730*	<.1
59	Miller Kaplan Arase and Company LLP—Mannon Kaplan	4123 Lankershim Blvd, North Hollywood CA 91602	818-769-2010	R	717*	.2
60	Brody Weiss Zucarelli and Urbanek—Philip Brody	2495 Kensington Ave, Buffalo NY 14226	716-839-2024	R	717*	<.1
61	Edward White and Co—Mariane Bakic	21700 Oxnard St 40, Woodland Hills CA 91367	818-716-1120	R	713*	<.1
62	Hoffman McCann PC- Tofias New England Div—Tracy Gallagher	350 Massachusetts Ave, Cambridge MA 02139	617-761-0600	R	654*	.2
63	Moore Stephens Tiller LLC—Bill Lankford	780 Johnson Ferry Rd S, Atlanta GA 30342	404-256-1606	R	640*	.1
64	Hein and Associates LLP—Larry D Unruh	717 17th St Ste 1600, Denver CO 80202	303-298-9600	R	611*	.1
65	Scheffel and Co—Richard Scheffel	143 N Kansas, Edwardsville IL 62025	618-656-1206	R	604*	.1
66	CBIZ Southern California Inc—Steven Gerard	10474 Santa Monica Blv, Los Angeles CA 90025	310-268-2040	S	598*	.1
67	Lane Gorman Trubitt PLLC—Bob Knight	2626 Howell St Ste 700, Dallas TX 75204		R	594*	.1
68	BDO Seidman LLP—Jack Weisbaum	130 E Randolph Ste 280, Chicago IL 60601	312-240-1236	S	585	2.5
69	Barnes Dennig and Company Ltd—William Cloppert	441 Vine St Ste 2000, Cincinnati OH 45202	513-241-8313	R	581*	.1
70	Rampell and Rampell PA—Richard Rampell	223 Sunset Ave Ste 200, Palm Beach FL 33480	561-655-5855	R	540*	<.1
71	Maryanov Madsen Gordon and Campbell PC—David Suss	PO Box 1826, Palm Springs CA 92263	760-320-6642	R	534*	<.1
72	Seligman Friedman and Company—James Smeltzer	96 S George St Ste 350, York PA 17401	717-843-0040	R	523*	.1
73	Ceridian Small Business Solutions Div—Stuart C Harvey	34 Maple Ave, Pine Brook NJ 07058	973-808-0500	D	522*	.1
74	Surepayroll Inc—Michael Alter Paychex Inc	2350 Ravine Way Ste 10, Glenview IL 60025	847-676-8420	S	513*	.1
75	Trout Ebersole and Groff LLC—Barry Huber	1705 Oregon Pike, Lancaster PA 17601	717-569-2900	R	492*	.1
76	Grassi and Company CPAs PC—Louis C Grassi	50 Jericho Quadrangle, Jericho NY 11753	516-256-3500	R	483*	.1
77	tpbs LLP—Michael J Beggs	1545 River Park Dr Ste, Sacramento CA 95815	916-929-1006	R	474*	<.1
78	Envision Pharmaceutical Services Inc—Kevin M Nagle	2181 E Aurora Rd Ste 2, Twinsburg OH 44087	330-405-8080	R	469*	.1
79	Smith Elliott Kearns and Co—Steven Kaufman	19 Brookwood Ave Ste10, Carlisle PA 17013	717-243-9104	R	455*	.1
80	Cole and Reed PC—James H Denny	531 Couch Dr Ste 200, Oklahoma City OK 73102	405-239-7961	R	453*	.1
81	Miller Wagner and Company PLLC—Joel Kramer	3101 N Central Ave Ste, Phoenix AZ 85012	602-264-6835	S	449*	.1
82	Windes and McClaughry Accountancy Corp—John L Di Carlo	PO Box 87, Long Beach CA 90801	562-435-1191	R	444*	.1
83	Ahmad Associates Ltd—Shad Ahmad	8230 Old Courthouse Rd, Vienna VA 22182	703-893-9644	R	443*	<.1
84	Bruner-Cox LLP—Steven O Pittman	4505 Stephen Cir NW St, Canton OH 44718	330-497-2000	R	434*	.1
85	Moore Stephens Lovelace PA—Bill Miller	311 Park Pl Blvd Ste 1, Clearwater FL 33759	727-531-4477	R	433*	.1
86	Lumsden and McCormick LLP—John P Schiavone	403 Main St Ste 430, Buffalo NY 14203	716-856-3300	R	428*	.1
87	Baker Spindler and Holtz—Lon J Baker	161 Ottawa Ave NW Ste, Grand Rapids MI 49503	616-458-1835	R	427*	<.1
88	Pearce Bevill Leesburg and Moore PC—Jackie Wray Pearce	110 Office Park Dr Ste, Birmingham AL 35223	205-323-5440	R	421*	.1
89	McKonly and Asbury—Terry Harris	PO Box 1331, Harrisburg PA 17105	717-761-7910	R	415*	.1
90	Teal Becker and Chiaramonte—John A Chiaramonte	7 Washington Sq, Albany NY 12205	518-456-6663	R	391*	.1
91	Sellers Richardson Holman and West LLP—J Allen Dunn II	3500 Blue Lake Dr Ste, Birmingham AL 35243	205-278-0001	R	385*	.1
92	Cornerstone Accounting Group LLP—Stanley R Perla	750 3rd Ave 27th Fl, New York NY 10017	646-845-3533	R	382*	.1
93	Advanced Information Management Systems LLC—EJ Nelson	PO Box 1150, Collierville TN 38027	901-854-5777	S	370*	.1
94	Core3 Inc—Gregg Scoresby	3600 E University Dr S, Phoenix AZ 85034	602-643-1300	R	367*	.1
95	Atlantic Services Inc—S Bailey	1445 N Rock Rd Ste 200, Wichita KS 67206	316-634-2183	R	361*	<.1
96	Heaton Adams and Co—Bob Heaton	PO Box 1026, Waterloo IA 50704	319-232-1943	R	359*	<.1
97	The Salt Group—Harlan J Hall	874 Harper Rd Ste 101, Kerrville TX 78028	830-257-1290	R	343*	.1
98	Outsourcing Solutions Inc—Michael Barrist	390 S Woods Mill Rd St, Chesterfield MO 63017	314-576-0022	R	342*	5.0
99	Groner Boyle and Quillin—Darci Congrove	230 West St Ste 700, Columbus OH 43215	614-221-1120	R	336*	.1
100	GHP Financial Group—Steven Levy	1670 Broadway Ste 3000, Denver CO 80202	303-831-5000	S	331*	.1
101	Hagen Kurth Perman and Company PS—Donald Kurth	601 Union St Ste 2700, Seattle WA 98101	206-682-9200	R	330*	.1
102	Norman Jones Enlow and Co—Nancy Lee Watts	226 N 5th St Ste 500, Columbus OH 43215	614-228-4000	R	327*	.1
103	Withum Smith and Brown LLC—William Hagaman Jr	5 Vaughn Dr, Princeton NJ 08540	609-520-1188	R	311*	.1
104	Hogan Taylor LLP—Bob L Slovacek	11600 Broadway Ext Ste, Oklahoma City OK 73114	405-848-2020	R	308*	.1
105	ACI Billing Services Inc—Patrick J Haynes III	7411 John Smith Dr, San Antonio TX 78229		S	302*	.1
106	Co-Advantage Resources Inc—Clinton Burgess	111 W Jefferson St, Orlando FL 32801	407-422-8448	R	300*	.2
107	Jones and Roth PC—Jens A Andersen	PO Box 10086, Eugene OR 97440	541-687-2320	R	285*	.1
108	Pannell Kerr Forster of Texas PC—Kenneth Guidry	5847 San Felipe Ste 24, Houston TX 77057	713-860-1400	R	282*	.1
109	Watkins Uiberall PLLC—William H Watkins Jr	6584 Poplar Ave Ste 20, Germantown TN 38138	901-761-2720	R	282*	.1
110	Goldstein Schecter Price Lucas Horwitz and Co—Lauri J Adler	2121 Ponce De Leon Blv, Coral Gables FL 33134	305-442-2200	R	266*	.1
111	Accume Partners—Fred Nitting	80 Broad St 34th Fl, New York NY 10004	646-375-9500	R	261*	.1
112	Universal Accounting Center—Allen B Bostrom	5188 S Commerce Dr, Salt Lake City UT 84107	801-265-3777	R	257*	.1
113	Birnbrey Minsk and Minsk—Warren Morrison	1801 Peachtree St NE S, Atlanta GA 30309	404-355-3870	R	254*	.1
114	Talbot Korvola and Warwick LLP—Craig Vagt	4800 SW Macadam Ave St, Portland OR 97201		R	250*	.1
115	Harrison Associates PC—Doane Harrison	131 E Main St Ste 201, Norman OK 73069	405-329-3110	R	250*	<.1

Rank	Company Name—*Executive Officer*	Address, City, State, Zip	Phone	Type	Fin	Empls
116	YFF and Scholma PC—*Daniel Yff*	688 Cascade W Pkwy SE, Grand Rapids MI 49546	616-942-6530	R	250*	<.1
117	Frazer Frost LLP—*Jeffrey Jones*	PO Box 3949, City of Industry CA 91744	714-990-1040	R	248*	.1
118	Innovative Employee Solutions Inc—*Elizabeth M Rice*	9665 Granite Ridge Dr, San Diego CA 92123	858-715-5100	R	238*	.1
119	Hay Group Inc—*Chris Matthews*	100 Penn Sq E, Philadelphia PA 19107	215-861-2000	R	234*	2.6
120	Mize Houser and Company PA—*Terry Kimes*	534 S Kansas Ave Ste 7, Topeka KS 66603	785-233-0536	R	227*	.1
121	Boyum and Barenscheer—*Thomas P Margarit*	4801 Hwy 61 Ste 201, White Bear Lake MN 55110	651-777-1331	R	224*	.1
122	Grijalva and Allen PC—*Antonio R Grijalva*	4801 Woodway Ste 210 W, Houston TX 77056	713-784-1181	R	222*	.1
123	Jeffrey Phillips Mosley and Scott PA—*Jim Phillips*	11300 Cantrell Rd Ste, Little Rock AR 72212	501-227-5800	R	221*	.1
124	Gursey Schneider and Company LLP—*Stanley Schneider*	1888 Century Park E St, Los Angeles CA 90067	310-552-0960	R	219*	.1
125	Vrakas Blum and Co—*James Holmes*	445 S Moorland Rd Ste, Brookfield WI 53005	262-797-0400	R	216*	.1
126	May and Co—*John Paris*	PO Box 821568, Vicksburg MS 39182	601-636-4762	R	216*	.1
127	Atkinson and Company Ltd—*Henry South*	6501 Americas Pky NE S, Albuquerque NM 87110	505-843-6492	R	213*	.1
128	Stuart Maue Mitchell and James Ltd—*Harry J Maue*	3840 McKelvey Rd, Bridgeton MO 63044	314-291-3030	R	213*	.1
129	Baird Kurtz and Dobson—*John Wanamaker*	PO Box 1190, Springfield MO 65801	417-865-8701	R	211*	2.0
130	Troconi Segarra and Associates LLP—*James Segarra*	6390 Main St Ste 200, Williamsville NY 14221	716-633-1373	R	210*	<.1
131	Charles L Marvin and Company PC—*Kevin J McCoy*	11 British American Bl, Latham NY 12110	518-785-0134	R	205*	.1
132	Sol Schwartz and Associates PC—*Sol Schwartz*	7550 Interstate 10 Ste, San Antonio TX 78229	210-384-8000	R	200*	<.1
133	Simpson and Simpson CPA—*Brainard C Simpson*	3600 Wilshire Blvd Ste, Los Angeles CA 90010	213-736-6664	R	197*	<.1
134	Smith Jackson Boyer and Bovard PLLC—*James A Smith*	9400 N Central Express, Dallas TX 75231	214-373-8900	R	197*	<.1
135	Firley Moran Freer and Eassa—*Andrew Eassa*	5010 Campuswood Dr Ste, East Syracuse NY 13057	315-472-7045	R	192*	<.1
136	Schechter Dokken Kanter Andrews and Selcer Ltd—*Herbert Schechter*	100 Washington Ave S S, Minneapolis MN 55401	612-332-5500	R	187*	.1
137	Crawford Pimentel and Company Inc—*Tony Pimental*	2150 Trade Zone Blvd S, San Jose CA 95131	408-942-6888	R	187*	<.1
138	Eisner and Lubin LLP—*Hirsch Levine*	1411 Broadway 9th Fl, New York NY 10018	212-751-9100	R	186*	<.1
139	Dworken Hillman LaMorte and Sterczala PC—*Erin N Hendlin*	4 Corporate Dr Ste 488, Shelton CT 06484	203-929-3535	R	185*	<.1
140	PRGX Global Inc—*Romil Bahl*	600 Galleria Pkwy, Atlanta GA 30339	770-779-3900	P	184	1.5
141	Epiq Systems - Bankruptcy Solutions—*Lorenzo Mendizabal*	757 Third Ave 3rd Fl, New York NY 10017	646-282-2500	S	180*	.1
142	Sattell Johnson Appel and Co—*Michael Sattell*	800 Woodland Prime, Menomonee Falls WI 53051	414-273-0500	R	180*	<.1
143	Tait Weller and Baker—*James Mahoney*	1818 Market St, Philadelphia PA 19103	215-979-8800	R	178*	<.1
144	JH Cohn LLP—*Thomas J Marino*	4 Becker Farm Rd, Roseland NJ 07068	973-228-3500	R	175*	.7
145	LB Carpenter PA—*LB Carpenter*	420 S Dixie Hwy 2B, Coral Gables FL 33146	305-661-7729	R	172*	<.1
146	Plante and Moran LLP—*Gordon Krater*	2155 Point Blvd Ste 20, Elgin IL 60123	847-697-6161	R	170*	1.5
147	RSM McGladrey Inc—*CE Andrews*	3600 American Blvd W 3, Bloomington MN 55431	952-921-7700	S	168*	3.0
148	Media Services Solution Contor Inc	500 S Sepulveda Blvd F, Los Angeles CA 90049	310-440-9600	R	165*	<.1
149	Winter Kloman Moter and Repp SC—*John Winter*	235 N Executive Dr Ste, Brookfield WI 53005	262-797-9050	R	164*	<.1
150	Geller Ragans James Oppenheimer and Creel—*Janet H Rapp*	111 N Orange Ave Ste 1, Orlando FL 32801	407-425-4636	R	161*	<.1
151	Smith Brooks Bolshoun and Company LLP—*Kenneth H Saliman*	2680 18th St Ste 200, Denver CO 80211	303-480-1200	R	161*	<.1
152	Loyola University Physician Foundation—*Stephen Valerio*	2 Westbrook Corporate, Westchester IL 60154	708-216-5626	R	160*	.1
153	Brooks Lodden PC—*Telford A Lodden*	1441 29th St Ste 305, West Des Moines IA 50266	515-223-7300	R	160*	<.1
154	Bdo USA LLP—*Ken Mooney*	130 E Randolph St Ste, Chicago IL 60601	312-240-1236	R	157*	2.2
155	Dixon Hughes PLLC—*Kenneth Hughes*	PO Box 3049, Asheville NC 28802	828-254-2254	R	157*	1.2
156	Washburn Ellingwood Sheeler Thaisz and Pinnoloy CPA's PC—*Robert F Thaisz*	112 S Broadway, Saratoga Springs NY 12866	518-587-5111	R	157*	<.1
157	Larson Allen Weishair and Co—*Gordon Viere*	220 S 6th St Ste 300, Minneapolis MN 55402	612-376-4500	R	153*	1.8
158	Whittemore Dowen and Ricciardelli LLP—*Paul Dowen*	333 Aviation Rd Bld B, Queensbury NY 12804	518-792-0926	R	148*	<.1
159	Faulk and Winkler LLC—*Bert Faulk*	6811 Jefferson Hwy, Baton Rouge LA 70806	225-927-6811	R	143*	<.1
160	Gerald T Reilly and Co—*Anthony Smeriglio*	424 Adams St, Milton MA 02186	617-696-8900	R	142*	<.1
161	Ocariz Gitlin and Zomerfeld LLP—*Raymond Zomerfeld*	999 Ponce De Leon Blvd, Coral Gables FL 33134	305-444-8288	R	141*	<.1
162	Saltzman Hamma Nelson Massaro LLP—*Gregory Osborn*	1660 Lincoln St Ste 20, Denver CO 80264	303-698-1883	R	141*	<.1
163	Simplified Business Solutions Inc—*Dean Lucente*	PO Box 51090, Phoenix AZ 85076	480-763-5900	R*	140*	6.0
164	Clifton Gunderson LLC—*Krista McMasters*	PO Box 2886, Oshkosh WI 54903	920-231-5890	R	137*	1.9
165	Waddell Smith Magoon and Freeman—*Gary C Waddell*	10892 Crabapple Rd Ste, Roswell GA 30075	770-993-6818	R	136*	<.1
166	Smith Carney and Company PC—*Kenneth L Carney*	5100 N Brookline Ave S, Oklahoma City OK 73112	405-272-1040	R	136*	<.1
167	Reilly Penner and Benton LLP—*Steve Barney*	1233 N Mayfair Rd Ste, Milwaukee WI 53226	414-271-7800	R	135*	<.1
168	Zielinski and Associates PC—*William Zielinski*	2150 Hampton Ave, Saint Louis MO 63139	314-644-2150	R	134*	<.1
169	Bland Garvey Eads Medlock and Deppe PC—*John Garvey*	1202 Richardson Dr Ste, Richardson TX 75080	972-231-2503	R	129*	<.1
170	Glass Jacobson PA—*Edward J Jacobson*	10711 Red Run Blvd Ste, Owings Mills MD 21117	410-356-1000	R	129*	<.1
171	Tull Forsberg and Olson PLLC—*John Tull*	5225 N Central Ave Ste, Phoenix AZ 85012	602-277-5447	R	126*	<.1
172	Dwight Darby and Co—*Brad Tushaus*	611 S Magnolia Ave, Tampa FL 33606	813-251-2411	R	119*	<.1
173	Echelbarger Himebaugh Tamm and Co—*David Echelbarger*	5136 Cascade Rd SE Ste, Grand Rapids MI 49546	616-575-3482	R	116*	<.1
174	Baune Dosen and Company LLP—*Jim Dosen*	600 South Hwy 169 Ste, Minneapolis MN 55426	952-473-2002	R	115*	<.1
175	Santora CPA Group—*William Santora*	220 Continental Dr Ste, Newark DE 19713	302-737-6200	R	113*	<.1
176	Physicians Practice Group—*Michael Herbert*	PO Box 730, Augusta GA 30903	706-724-6100	R	108*	.3
177	Lucas Horsfall Murphy and Pindroh LLP—*Michael Amerio*	100 E Corson St Ste 20, Pasadena CA 91103	626-744-5100	R	108*	<.1
178	Scearce Satcher and Jung PA—*Kenneth Scearce*	PO Box 3060, Winter Park FL 32790	407-647-6441	R	104*	<.1
179	Huselton and Morgan PC—*Susan Adams*	12221 Merit Dr Ste 180, Dallas TX 75251	972-404-1010	R	102*	<.1
180	Johanson and Yau Accountancy Corp—*Fred U Leonard*	160 W Santa Clara St S, San Jose CA 95113	408-288-5111	R	102*	<.1
181	Card Palmer Sibbison and Co—*James E Stroh*	4545 Hinckley Pkwy, Cleveland OH 44109	216-621-6100	R	100*	1.0
182	Correll Porvin Associates—*Bruce Correll*	26026 Telegraph Rd Ste, Southfield MI 48033	248-355-5151	R	93*	<.1
183	Hughes Welch and Milligan CPA's Ltd—*Robert Hughes*	PO Box 2094, Batesville AR 72503	870-793-5231	R	92*	<.1
184	Orlando Mitts Moore and Company—*Lou Mitts*	675 N 1st St Ste1200, San Diego CA 95112	408-278-0300	R	90*	<.1
185	DelConte Hyde Annello and Schuch PC—*Bruce M Del Conte*	6 Executive Dr Ste 111, Farmington CT 06032	860-676-9020	R	89*	<.1
186	Spielman Koenigsberg and Parker LLP	888 7th Ave 35th Fl, New York NY 10106	212-453-2500	R	89*	<.1
187	Stone Rudolph and Henry CPA—*Thomas M Henry*	124 Center Pointe Dr, Clarksville TN 37040	931-648-4786	R	87*	<.1
188	Timmins Kroll Jacobson LLP—*Don Timmins*	10550 New York Ave Ste, Des Moines IA 50322	515-270-8080	R	87*	<.1
189	House Park and Dobratz PC—*Stanley H House*	605 W 47th St Ste 301, Kansas City MO 64112	816-931-3393	R	83*	<.1
190	Sterling and Tucker—*Judith Sterling*	820 Mililani St 4th Fl, Honolulu HI 96813	808-531-5391	R	83*	<.1
191	KMJ/Corbin and Co—*Mike Faddoul*	555 Anton Blvd Ste 100, Costa Mesa CA 92626	714-380-6565	R	82*	<.1
192	Monroe Sweeris and Tromp PC—*Walter Monroe*	6617 Crossing Dr SE, Grand Rapids MI 49508	616-554-5800	R	82*	<.1
193	Arthur Place and Company PC—*Arthur Place*	1218 Central Ave Ste 4, Albany NY 12205	518-459-8395	R	82*	<.1
194	Fineman West and Company LLP—*Gary Fineman*	801 S Figueroa Rm 1000, Los Angeles CA 90017	310-888-1880	R	81*	<.1
195	Freyberg Hinkle Ashland Powers and Stowell SC—*James M Ashland*	15420 W Capitol Dr, Brookfield WI 53005	262-784-6210	R	81*	<.1
196	TM Byxbee Co—*Edward Cleary*	PO Box 187169, Hamden CT 06518	203-281-4933	R	78*	<.1
197	CJ Schlosser and Company LLC—*David Kamler*	PO Box 416, Alton IL 62002	618-465-7717	R	76*	<.1
198	Peachin Schwartz and Weingardt PC—*Michael Potter*	9449 W Priority Way Dr, Indianapolis IN 46240	317-574-4280	R	73*	<.1
199	Hartman Blitch and Gartside—*James R Karpowicz*	4929 Atlantic Blvd, Jacksonville FL 32207	904-396-9802	S	72*	<.1
200	Weinberg and Co—*Bruce Weinberg*	6100 Glades Rd 314, Boca Raton FL 33434	561-487-5765	R	72*	<.1
201	Allied Tax Service Inc—*Stephen Kasper*	17114 Lorain Ave, Cleveland OH 44111	216-252-5400	R	72*	<.1

Note: An asterisk (*) indicates an estimated financial figure. The company type code used is as follows: R = Private, P = Public, S = Private Subsidiary, B = Public Subsidiary, D = Division, J = Joint Venture, I = Investment Fund.

COMPANY RANKINGS BY SALES WITHIN 4-DIGIT SIC

Rank	Company Name—*Executive Officer*	Address, City, State, Zip	Phone	Type	Fin	Empls
202	Cardoni Waddell LLC—*Robert Cardoni*	8850 Stanford Blvd Ste, Columbia MD 21045	410-290-0770	R	70*	<.1
203	Seely Mullins and Associates PC—*Larry Eickman*	7141 N 51stAve Ste C, Glendale AZ 85301	623-939-7581	R	70*	<.1
204	Stuedle Spears and Francke PSC—*Joseph Stuedle*	2821 S Hurstbourne Pky, Louisville KY 40220	502-491-5253	R	69*	<.1
205	McCahan Helfrick Thiercof and Butera Accountancy Corp—*Charles W Helfrick*	1655 Willow St, San Jose CA 95125	408-266-4755	R	67*	<.1
206	Stulmaker Kohn and Richardson LLP—*Ronald Kohn*	296 Washington Ave Ext, Albany NY 12203	518-436-1040	R	67*	<.1
207	Engelkes Connor and Davis Ltd—*Tommy Davis*	PO Box 1167, Conway AR 72033	501-329-5613	R	64*	<.1
208	Grant Bennett Accountants—*Dawn Brenner*	1375 Exposition Blvd S, Sacramento CA 95815	916-922-5109	R	63*	<.1
209	Johnson Harris and Goff PLLC	8777 E Via De Ventura, Scottsdale AZ 85258	480-948-0060	R	63*	<.1
210	Semanchin and Wetter—*Thomas Semanchin*	6245 Sheridan Dr Ste 1, Williamsville NY 14221	716-633-7607	R	61*	<.1
211	Warinner Gesinger and Associates LLC—*William J Warinner*	10561 Barkley Ste 550, Overland Park KS 66212	913-599-3236	R	60*	<.1
212	Janice W Lake and Associates CPA—*Janice W Lake*	71 S Dixie Hwy, Saint Augustine FL 32084	904-824-1521	R	60*	<.1
213	Novogradac and Company LLP—*Christopher Jones*	246 1st St Fl 5, San Francisco CA 94105	415-356-8032	R	59*	.4
214	DeChants Fuglein and Johnson LLP—*Louis Dechant*	4 Avis Dr, Latham NY 12110	518-785-1211	R	58*	<.1
215	Berdon LLP—*Stanley H Freundlich*	360 Madison Ave, New York NY 10017	212-832-0400	R	56*	.4
216	Martin Bircher Buller and Flynn PC—*Robert Martin*	11400 98th Ave NE Ste, Kirkland WA 98033	425-827-3041	R	56*	<.1
217	Vander Ploeg Bergakker and Associates—*John Vander Ploeg*	3635 29th St SE, Grand Rapids MI 49512	616-957-0691	R	54*	<.1
218	Baker and Company PC—*Stephen A Baker*	220 Broadway Ste 405, Lynnfield MA 01940	781-593-5330	R	53*	<.1
219	Educational Credit Business Inc—*Edward Redhair*	3401 E Truman Rd, Kansas City MO 64127	816-483-4600	R	53*	<.1
220	Toski and Co Inc—*Ronald Toski*	300 Essjay Rd Ste 115, Williamsville NY 14221	716-634-0700	R	52*	<.1
221	Weaver and Tidwell LLP—*Tommy D Lawler*	2821 W Seventh Street, Fort Worth TX 76107	817-332-7905	R	51	.2
222	Gillispie and Ogilbee—*Walter Gillispie*	4400 N Meridian Ave, Oklahoma City OK 73112	405-947-3030	R	51*	<.1
223	Clark and Koller CPA—*Charles Koller*	1325 Union Rd, West Seneca NY 14224	716-674-4459	R	51*	<.1
224	John Gerlach and Co—*TJ Conger*	37 W Broad St, Columbus OH 43215	614-224-2164	R	51*	<.1
225	Tokumoto Yamamoto and Ichishita Inc—*Paul Kuramoto*	333 Queen St Ste 800, Honolulu HI 96813	808-523-0471	R	51*	<.1
226	Smith and Just PS—*Chuck Just*	401 Second Ave S Ste 5, Seattle WA 98104	206-624-8075	R	50*	<.1
227	Steakley and Gilbert PC—*Steve Steakley*	110 N Robinson Ave Ste, Oklahoma City OK 73102	405-235-4400	R	50*	<.1
228	Johnson Mackowiak and Associates LLP—*Richard S Johnson*	70 E Main St, Fredonia NY 14063	716-672-4770	R	49*	<.1
229	Clumeck Stern Schenkelberg and Getzoff—*Larry Clumeck*	17404 Ventura Blvd Fl, Encino CA 91316	818-906-2230	R	47*	<.1
230	Francis and Company PLLC—*Horace Francis*	701 Dexter Ave N Ste 4, Seattle WA 98109	206-282-3720	R	47*	<.1
231	Halt Buzas and Powell LTD—*Steve Halt*	1199 N Fairfax St 10th, Alexandria VA 22314	703-836-1350	R	47*	<.1
232	Main Amundson and Assoc—*James Main*	PO Box 1200, Las Vegas NV 89125	702-259-6222	R	46*	<.1
233	Arledge and AssociatesPC—*Jim DentonArledge*	309 N Bryant, Edmond OK 73034	405-348-0615	R	46*	<.1
234	CertiPay America LLC—*Grant Lacerte*	199 Ave B NW Ste 270, Winter Haven FL 33881	863-299-2400	R	45*	<.1
235	Compupay Inc—*Charlie Lathrop*	3450 Lakeside Dr Ste 4, Miramar FL 33027	954-874-4800	R	45*	.7
236	L Cotton Thomas and Co—*Mike Schaufele*	620 W 3rd St Ste 400, Little Rock AR 72201	501-375-9187	R	44*	<.1
237	Wipfli Ullrich Bertelson LLP—*Rick Dreher*	11 Scott St, Wausau WI 54403	715-845-3111	R	43*	.7
238	Engelbach Roberts and Co—*Jay H Engelbach*	4000 Classen Ctr Ste 1, Oklahoma City OK 73118	405-528-4000	R	42*	<.1
239	Lee Sperling Hisamune Accountancy Corp—*Frank M Saito*	550 N Brand Blvd Ste 5, Glendale CA 91203	818-507-6645	R	42*	<.1
240	Yoder and Co—*Doyle E Yoder*	3451 Longview Dr Ste 1, Sacramento CA 95821	916-488-5900	R	42*	<.1
241	Moss Adams LLP—*Rich Anderson*	999 Third Ave Ste 2800, Seattle WA 98104		R	39*	.3
242	Ashland Partners and Company LLP—*Melvin Ashland*	525 Bigham Knoll, Jacksonville OR 97530	541-857-8800	R	39*	<.1
243	Curosh Law Group PLLC—*William J Curosh*	12434 N 62nd St, Scottsdale AZ 85254	480-315-1010	R	37*	<.1
244	Bryan and PatersonPC—*Scott Bryan*	5944 Luther Ln Ste 950, Dallas TX 75225	214-361-2755	R	37*	<.1
245	Onstott and Associates—*Charles Onstott Jr*	6 NE 63rd Ste 240, Oklahoma City OK 73105	405-848-1099	R	36*	<.1
246	Kroll Zolfo Cooper Inc—*Michael Cherasky*	8 Penn Ctr, Philadelphia PA 19103	215-568-8090	R	34*	.3
247	Cummins Faber PC—*Richard Cummins*	750 Front St NW Riverw, Grand Rapids MI 49504	616-454-6555	R	34*	<.1
248	Blackman Kallick—*Dan Fensin*	10 S Riverside Plz 9th, Chicago IL 60606	312-207-1040	R	33*	.3
249	FD Thompson and Company PLC—*Frankie Thompson*	13320 N MacArthur Blvd, Oklahoma City OK 73142	405-603-6400	R	33*	<.1
250	Tel-Adjust Inc—*Karen Gaudette*	29000 Inkster Rd Ste 1, Southfield MI 48034	248-208-1600	R	33*	<.1
251	ParenteBeard LLC—*Robert Ciaruffoli*	46 Public Sq Ste 400, Wilkes Barre PA 18701	570-820-0100	R	32*	.4
252	TRILLIUM FINANCIAL SERVICES PC—*TG Howerzyl*	4060 White St SW, Grandville MI 49418	616-530-1810	R	32*	<.1
253	Pierce Riesbeck and Associates LLP—*Gregory Pierce*	16W485 S Frontage Rd S, Burr Ridge IL 60527	630-323-0340	R	30*	<.1
254	Bregman and Company PC—*Herbert Bregman*	350 Bedford St Ste 203, Stamford CT 06901	203-325-4155	R	29*	<.1
255	Curtis Sallee and Co—*Les Curtis*	200 W Mercer St Ste 41, Seattle WA 98119	206-284-6208	R	29*	<.1
256	Ross Buehler Falk and Co—*Jeffrey S Bleacher*	1500 Lititz Pike, Lancaster PA 17601	717-393-2700	R	28*	<.1
257	TAG Employer Services LLC—*Jack Biltis*	20815 N Cave Creek Rd, Phoenix AZ 85024	623-580-4900	R	27*	<.1
258	Suby Von Haden and Associates SC—*Jack Cotton*	PO Box 44966, Madison WI 53744	608-831-8181	R	26*	.4
259	Gales and Associates—*Nick Gales*	13312 N McArthur, Oklahoma City OK 73142	405-728-2727	R	26*	<.1
260	Olson Neaves and Co—*Forrest Olson*	1900 NW Expressway St, Oklahoma City OK 73118	405-842-4418	R	26*	<.1
261	Osu Surgery LLC	700 Ackerman Rd Ste 35, Columbus OH 43202	614-947-3700	R	25*	.2
262	Thompson Cobb Bazilio and Associates PC—*Ralph Bazilio*	1101 15th St Nw Ste 40, Washington DC 20005	202-778-3421	R	25*	.2
263	Lattimore Black Morgan and Cain PC—*David Morgan*	PO Box 1869, Brentwood TN 37024	615-377-4600	R	24*	.4
264	Mayer Hoffman McCann PC—*William Hancock*	One City Pl Dr Ste 570, Saint Louis MO 63141	314-968-6649	R	24	.2
265	Preferred Billing Management Services Inc—*Judy Pinner*	PO Box 4462, Rock Hill SC 29732	803-329-6570	R	24*	<.1
266	Clark Schaefer Hackett and Co—*Carl Cobur*	160 N Breiel Blvd, Middletown OH 45042	513-424-5000	R	23*	.3
267	Hawkins and Co—*Michael Hawkins*	824 Burton St SE, Grand Rapids MI 49507	616-241-1110	R	23*	<.1
268	Rosen Seymour Shapss Martin and Company LLP—*Burgman Connolly*	757 3rd Ave Fl 6, New York NY 10017	212-303-1800	R	23*	.2
269	Aronson LLC—*Lisa Cines*	805 King Farm Blvd Ste, Rockville MD 20850	301-231-6200	R	22*	.2
270	Friedman LLP—*Ricki Birner*	1700 Broadway Fl 23, New York NY 10019	212-582-1600	R	21*	.3
271	Siegfried Group LLP—*Robert Siegfried Jr*	1201 N Market St Ste 7, Wilmington DE 19801	302-984-1800	R	21*	.5
272	Baros and Co—*David Baros*	1314 E Santara Blvd, San Antonio TX 78258	210-366-9444	R	21*	<.1
273	Bolger and Associates—*John P Bolger*	8340 Plainfield Rd, Cincinnati OH 45236	513-793-6267	R	21*	<.1
274	Owen and Thorp Inc—*William E Owen*	1900 NW Expy Ste 300, Oklahoma City OK 73118	405-840-2232	R	21*	<.1
275	Tice Brunell and Baker CPA's Co—*Kenneth E Tice Jr*	14 Corporate Woods Blv, Albany NY 12211	518-482-1887	R	21*	<.1
276	Bonadio and Company LLP—*Claudia Groenevelt*	171 Sullys Trl Ste 201, Pittsford NY 14534	585-381-1000	R	21*	.3
277	Executive Charge Inc—*John Acierno*	1440 39th St, Brooklyn NY 11218	718-438-1100	R	21*	.3
278	Brown Smith Wallace LLC—*Ken Herold*	1050 N Lindbergh Blvd, Saint Louis MO 63132	314-983-1200	R	20*	.2
279	SingerLewak—*Harvey A Goldstein*	10960 Wilshire Blvd St, Los Angeles CA 90024	310-477-3924	R	20*	.2
280	TAG—*Robert Scherer*	2150 W Washington St S, San Diego CA 92110	619-225-9322	R	20	<.1
281	LeMaster and Daniels PLLC—*Scott Dietzen*	601 W Riverside Ave No, Spokane WA 99201	509-624-4315	S	19*	.2
282	Miller Cooper and Company Ltd—*Ross S Pearlstein*	1751 Lake Cook Rd Ste, Deerfield IL 60015	847-205-5000	R	19*	.2
283	Citrin Cooperman and Co—*Steven Winchester*	529 5th Ave, New York NY 10017	212-697-1000	R	19*	.1
284	Raich Ende Malter and Co LLP—*Charles Raich*	1375 Broadway, New York NY 10018	212-944-4433	R	19*	.1
285	Kessler and Associates Inc—*Charles P Kessler*	31800 Northwestern Hwy, Farmington Hills MI 48334	248-855-4224	R	19*	<.1
286	O'Connor Davies Munns and Dobbins LLP—*Kevin Keane*	60 E 42nd St Fl 36, New York NY 10165	212-286-2600	R	18*	.2
287	Margolin Winer and Evens LLP—*Teddy Selinger*	400 Garden City Plz 5t, Garden City NY 11530	516-747-2000	R	18*	.1
288	Allison and Chumney PC—*Jerry Allison*	5050 Poplar Ave Ste 31, Memphis TN 38157	901-761-4335	R	18*	<.1
289	Goodlander and Co—*Larry Goodlander*	3900 Costa Ave NE, Grand Rapids MI 49525	616-361-1896	R	18*	<.1

Rank	Company Name—Executive Officer	Address, City, State, Zip	Phone	Type	Fin	Empls
290	InfoSync Services—Dale Hoyer	1938 N Woodlawn Ste 11, Wichita KS 67208	316-685-1622	R	17	.3
291	Cohen and Co—Randy Myeroff	1350 Euclid Ave Ste 80, Cleveland OH 44115	216-579-1040	R	17*	.2
292	Accurecord Inc—George Chave	100 Executive Dr Ste G, Brentwood NY 11717	631-243-6400	R	17*	.1
293	Paychex Business Solutions Inc—Jonathan J Judge Paychex Inc	911 Panorama Trail Sou, Rochester NY 14625		S	16*	.1
294	TravisWolff Independent Advisors and Accountants—Harold Gaar	15950 Dallas Pkwy Ste, Dallas TX 75240	972-661-1843	R	15*	.1
295	Knorr and Associates PC—Robert Knorr	1776 S Jackson St, Denver CO 80210	303-756-3111	R	15*	<.1
296	Frost PLLC—Greg Flesher	425 W Capitol Ave Ste, Little Rock AR 72201	501-376-9241	R	14*	.2
297	Bowman and Company LLP—Kirk Applegate	601 White Horse Rd, Voorhees NJ 08043	856-435-6200	R	14*	.1
298	ProfitLine Inc—Bruce Myers	9920 Pacific Heights B, San Diego CA 92121	858-452-6800	S	14*	.2
299	Seiler and Company LLP—James GB DeMartini III	3 Lagoon Dr Ste 400, Redwood City CA 94065	650-365-4646	R	14*	.1
300	Skoda Minotti and Co—Michael Minotti	6685 Beta Dr, Mayfield Village OH 44143	440-449-6800	R	14*	.1
301	Thom-Dobson-Womack Inc—John S Dobson	6408-B N Santa Fe Ave, Oklahoma City OK 73116	405-842-0212	R	14*	<.1
302	Pierini Clark—Edward J Pierini	9845 Horn Rd Ste 280, Sacramento CA 95827	916-363-1010	R	14*	<.1
303	Armds Inc—Ken Reiher	400 Broadacres Dr Ste, Bloomfield NJ 07003	973-614-9100	R	14*	.2
304	Celergo LLC—Michele Honomichl	750 Estate Dr Ste 110, Deerfield IL 60015	847-512-2600	R	14	.1
305	American Pacesetters Enterprises LLC—Bill Robbins	1280 S Country Club Dr, Mesa AZ 85210	480-784-2270	R	13*	.2
306	Redw Technologies LLC—Michelle Wiegmann	6401 Jefferson St Ne, Albuquerque NM 87109	505-998-3200	R	13*	.1
307	Wolf and Company PC—Daniel P Devasto	99 High St, Boston MA 02110	617-439-9700	R	13*	.1
308	Mohler Nixon and Williams Accountancy Corp—Gregory Finley	635 Campbell Technolog, Campbell CA 95008	408-369-2400	R	13*	.1
309	Optimal Billing Solutions LLC—Eugene Dauchert	6400 Atlantic Blvd, Jacksonville FL 32211	904-805-1300	R	12*	.2
310	TMP/Hudson Global Resources—Stephan Carter	595 Market St Ste 2500, San Francisco CA 94105	415-659-5100	D	12*	.2
311	Argy Wiltse and Robinson PC—Paul Argy	8405 Greensboro Dr Ste, McLean VA 22102	703-893-0600	R	12*	.2
312	Horovitz Rudoy and Roteman—Paul K Rudoy	436 7th Ave 6th Fl, Pittsburgh PA 15219	412-391-2920	R	12*	<.1
313	A D Computer Corp—C Antich	3939 W Dr, Center Valley PA 18034	610-797-9500	R	12*	.1
314	Feeley and Driscoll PC—Thomas Feeley	200 Portland St Ste 50, Boston MA 02114	617-742-7788	R	11*	.1
315	Advantage Payroll Services Inc—Rolande Truchon Paychex Inc	PO Box 1330, Auburn ME 04211	207-784-0178	S	11*	.2
316	Henry and Horne LLP	2055 E Warner Rd Ste 1, Tempe AZ 85284	480-839-4900	R	11*	.1
317	Business Publications Audit of Circulation Inc—Glenn J Hansen	Two Corporate Dr Ste 9, Shelton CT 06484	203-447-2800	R	11*	.1
318	Peters and Chandler PC—Roy Chandler	2601 NW Expwy Ste 600E, Oklahoma City OK 73112	405-843-9371	R	11*	<.1
319	Practicare Medical Management Inc—Jim Antonacci	4567 Crossroads Park D, Liverpool NY 13088	315-434-9307	R	10*	.1
320	Paycor Inc—Bob Coughlin	644 Linn St Ste 200, Cincinnati OH 45203	513-381-0505	R	10*	.2
321	Solo W-2 Inc—James Ziegler	1355 Willow Way Ste 24, Concord CA 94520	925-680-0200	R	10*	.1
322	Paylocity Corp—Steve Beauchamp	3850 N Wilke Rd, Arlington Heights IL 60004	847-956-4850	R	10*	.1
323	Financial Intelligence LLC—Arnold Freilich	4410 El Camino Real St, Los Altos CA 94022		R	10*	<.1
324	Paul Scherer and Company LLP—David Tous	1440 Broadway Fl 12, New York NY 10018	212-588-2200	R	10*	.1
325	Ifpc Worldwide Inc—James Fruin	5440 N Cumberland Ave, Chicago IL 60656	773-714-9090	R	10*	.1
326	Arrow Funding Corp—Mark Arrow	37 W 26th St Frnt 1, New York NY 10010	212-803-7199	R	10*	.1
327	Insurance Data Services Inc—William Norris	PO Box 2327, Grand Rapids MI 49501	616-532-8000	R	9*	.1
328	Cotton and Co—Matthew Johnson	635 Slaters Ln 4th Fl, Alexandria VA 22314	703-836-6701	R	9*	.1
329	Apple Growth Partners—David Gaino	1540 W Market St, Akron OH 44313	330-867-7350	R	9*	.1
330	Billing Concepts Inc—Gregory Carter	7411 John Smith Dr Ste, San Antonio TX 78229	210-949-7000	S	9*	.1
331	Payroll 1 Inc—Elaine Kelly	34100 Woodware Ave Ste, Birmingham MI 48009		R	9*	.1
332	Sensiba San Filippo LLP—John Sensiba	1075 N 10th St, San Jose CA 95112	408-286-7780	R	9*	.1
333	Medical Health Care Solutions Inc—Stephen Brighton	PO Box 3160, Andover MA 01810	978-474-8885	R	9*	.1
334	Berger Lewis Accountancy Corp—Frank Minuti	55 Almaden Blvd Ste 60, San Jose CA 95113	408 491-1200	R	9*	.1
335	Snyder Cohn Collyer Hamilton and Associates PC—Edward Snyder	11200 Rockville Pike S, Rockville MD 20852	301-652-6700	R	9*	.1
336	Gumbiner Savett Inc—Louis H Savett	1723 Cloverfield Blvd, Santa Monica CA 90404	310-828-9798	R	9*	.1
337	Managed Business Services Inc—William Rosado	6410 S Eastern Ave, Las Vegas NV 89119	702-735-4819	R	9*	<.1
338	Lowrey Powell and Stevens—Charles Lowrey Padgett Strateman and Company LLP	931 Proton Rd, San Antonio TX 78258	210-490-2222	D	9*	<.1
339	Arrington and Co—Lee Arrington	2487 Aloma Ave Ste 200, Winter Park FL 32792	407-677-7372	R	9*	<.1
340	Ciproms Inc—Wayne Halpern	3600 Woodview Trce Ste, Indianapolis IN 46268	317-870-0480	R	9*	.1
341	Cbiz Duitch Franklin Parks Palmer—Michael Palmer	11601 Wilshire Blvd St, Los Angeles CA 90025	310-207-2777	R	8*	.1
342	Postlethwaite and Netterville—Bill Balhoff	8550 United Plaza Blvd, Baton Rouge LA 70809	225-922-4600	R	8*	.2
343	Morrison Brown Argiz and Farra LLP—Tony Argiz	1001 Brickell Bay Dr 9, Miami FL 33131	305-373-5500	R	8*	.1
344	Perelson Weiner LLP—John Lieberman	1 Dag Hammarskjold Plz, New York NY 10017	212-605-3100	R	8*	.1
345	Haskell and White LLP—Wayne Pinnell	8001 Irvine Ctr Dr Ste, Irvine CA 92618	949-450-6200	R	8*	.1
346	Geffen Mesher and Company PC—Kelly Coburn	888 SW 5th Ave Ste 800, Portland OR 97204	503-221-0141	R	8*	.1
347	Kushner La Graize—Ernie Gelpi	3330 W Esplanade Ave S, Metairie LA 70002	504-838-9991	R	8*	.1
348	Philip Vogel and Company PC—Bernard Raden	12400 Coit Rd Ste 1000, Dallas TX 75251	214-346-5800	R	8*	<.1
349	Al's Services—Al Afrouzian	3300 McKee Rd, Bakersfield CA 93313	661-836-8382	S	8*	<.1
350	Edwards Consulting—Dirk Edwards	4004 Kruse Way Pl Ste, Lake Oswego OR 97035	503-222-4708	R	8*	<.1
351	Envision Tax and Accounting Services—Cindy Rand	PO Box 72195, Orlando FL 32872	407-951-1492	R	8*	<.1
352	Kenneth M Weinstein CPA—Kenneth M Weinstein	1450 Niagara Falls Blv, Tonawanda NY 14150	716-837-2525	R	8*	<.1
353	ChiroNET LLC	2821 Lackland Rd Ste 1, Fort Worth TX 76116	817-886-8891	R	7	<.1
354	Deming Malone Livesay and Ostroff—Jennifer Hughes	9300 Shelbyville Rd St, Louisville KY 40222	502-426-9660	R	7*	.1
355	Conrad Government Services—Ronald L Conrad Mayer Hoffman McCann PC	2301 DuPont Dr Ste 200, Irvine CA 92612	949-474-2020	D	7*	.1
356	Nanas Stern Biers Neinstein and Co—Kenneth A Miles	9454 Wilshire Blvd 4th, Beverly Hills CA 90212	310-273-2501	R	7*	.1
357	Tanner Mainstain Blatt and Glynn—William H Tanner	10866 Wilshire Blvd 10, Los Angeles CA 90024	310-446-2700	R	7*	.1
358	Teal Becker and Chiaramonte CPA's PC—John A Chiaramonte	7 Washington Sq, Albany NY 12205	518-456-6663	R	7*	.1
359	Huber Ring Helm and Company PC—Thomas S Helm	PO Box 89, Saint Louis MO 63166	314-962-0300	R	7*	.1
360	Wegmann-Dazet and Co—Robert Watkins	111 Veterans Blvd Ste, Metairie LA 70005	504-837-8844	R	7*	.1
361	Abrams Foster Nole and Williams PA—Arnold Williams	2 Hammel Rd Ste 241 W, Baltimore MD 21210	410-433-6830	R	7*	<.1
362	Physicians' Service Center Inc—Kathryn Canny	520 E 22nd St, Lombard IL 60148	630-960-9222	R	7*	.1
363	Whitaker Physician Billing Services Inc—Libby Boyd	PO Box 2078, Huntington WV 25720	304-523-0746	R	7*	.1
364	Whipple and Company PC—Pat Early	PO Box 40368, Indianapolis IN 46240	317-469-7776	R	6*	.1
365	Successabilities Inc—Gina Murdza	PO Box 316, Rutland MA 01543	508-792-0622	R	6*	.1
366	Prost Mueller PC—Doug Muller	1034 S Brentwood Blvd, Saint Louis MO 63117	314-862-2070	R	6*	.1
367	Anders Minkler and Diehl LLP—Robert Minkler Sr	705 Olive St 10th Fl, Saint Louis MO 63101	314-655-5500	R	6*	.1
368	Albrecht Viggiano Zureck PC—Lawrence Lucarelli	25 Suffolk Ct, Hauppauge NY 11788	631-434-9500	R	6*	.1
369	TE Lott and Co—Mike Harkins	PO Box 471, Columbus MS 39703	662-328-5387	R	6*	.1
370	Bruno and Tervalon—Michael B Bruno	4298 Elysian Fields Av, New Orleans LA 70122	504-284-8733	R	6*	.1
371	Drucker and Scaccetti—Ronald H Drucker	1600 Market St 33rd Fl, Philadelphia PA 19103	215-665-3960	R	6*	.1
372	Reynolds Bone and Griesbeck PLC—John M Griesbeck	5100 Wheelis Dr Ste 30, Memphis TN 38117	901-682-2431	R	6*	.1
373	Pisenti and Brinker LLP—William A Robotham	3562 Round Barn Cir St, Santa Rosa CA 95403	707-542-3343	R	6*	.1

Note: An asterisk (*) indicates an estimated financial figure. The company type code used is as follows: R = Private, P = Public, S = Private Subsidiary, B = Public Subsidiary, D = Division, J = Joint Venture, I = Investment Fund.

COMPANY RANKINGS BY SALES WITHIN 4-DIGIT SIC

Rank	Company Name—*Executive Officer*	Address, City, State, Zip	Phone	Type	Fin	Empls
374	Distribution Data Inc—*Robert Hartig*	16101 Snow Rd Ste 200, Cleveland OH 44142	216-362-3009	R	6*	.1
375	Abbott Stringham and Lynch Accountancy Corp—*Ray Schaefer*	1550 Leigh Ave, San Jose CA 95125	408-377-8700	R	5*	.1
376	McLean Koehler Sparks and Hammond—*Terry W Weller*	11311 McCormick Rd Ste, Hunt Valley MD 21031	410-296-6200	R	5*	.1
377	Bader Martin Ross and Smith PS—*Walter Smith*	1000 2nd Ave 34th Fl, Seattle WA 98104	206-621-1900	R	5*	.1
378	Councilor Buchanan and Mitchell PC—*Vincent Crescenzi*	7910 Woodmont Ave Ste, Bethesda MD 20814	301-986-0600	R	5*	.1
379	Freed Maxick Battaglia PC—*Robert M Glaser* Freed Maxick Group	1 Evans St, Batavia NY 14020	585-344-1967	S	5*	.1
380	Wilkerson Guthmann and Johnson Ltd—*Randall Kroll*	55 E 5th St Ste 1300, Saint Paul MN 55101	651-222-1801	R	5*	.1
381	Johnston Gremaux and Rossi LLP—*Timothy F Brophy*	333 Civic Dr, Pleasant Hill CA 94523	925-944-1881	R	5*	<.1
382	LM Henderson and Company PC—*William Blaser*	450 E 96th St Ste 200, Indianapolis IN 46240	317-566-1000	R	5*	<.1
383	BKR Fordham Goodfellow LLP—*Lester Fordham*	233 SE 2nd Ave, Hillsboro OR 97123	503-648-6651	R	5*	<.1
384	dLs Consulting LLC—*Diana Smith*	26 Brighton Terr, Parsippany NJ 07054	973-808-6461	R	5*	<.1
385	Dca Services Inc—*Bill Bricking*	300 N Meridian Ave 200, Oklahoma City OK 73107	405-951-9300	R	5*	.1
386	Hudson Co—*William Hudson*	PO Box 220425, Saint Louis MO 63122	314-965-1929	R	4*	<.1
387	Roth Bookstein and Zaslow LLP—*Ken Coelho*	11755 Wilshire Blvd St, Los Angeles CA 90025	310-478-4148	R	4*	.1
388	Duplantier Hrapmann Hogan and Maher—*Guy L Duplantier*	1615 Poydras St Ste 21, New Orleans LA 70112	504-586-8866	R	4*	.1
389	Heard McElroy and Vestal LLP—*John W Dean*	333 Texas St Ste 1525, Shreveport LA 71101	318-429-1525	R	4*	.1
390	Carneiro Chumney and Company LC—*Robert M McAdams*	40 NE Loop 410 Ste 200, San Antonio TX 78216	210-342-8000	R	4*	.1
391	On-Site Financial Inc—*Hank Heath*	205 SE Spokane St Rm 3, Portland OR 97202	503-224-0797	R	4*	.1
392	Glickstein Laval Carris—*T Shepard Burr*	PO Box 940849, Maitland FL 32794	407-645-4775	R	4*	<.1
393	Kiefer Bonfanti and Company LLP—*Chris Bonfanti*	701 Emerson Rd Ste 201, Saint Louis MO 63141	314-812-1100	R	4*	<.1
394	Mather Hamilton and Co—*Bruce Smith*	9100 Shelbyville Rd St, Louisville KY 40222	502-429-0800	R	4*	<.1
395	Gray Gray and Gray LLP—*Joseph Ciccarello*	34 SW Park, Westwood MA 02090	781-407-0300	R	4*	<.1
396	Grossberg Company LLP	6500 Rock Spring Dr St, Bethesda MD 20817	301-571-1900	R	4*	<.1
397	Kushner Smith Joanou and Gregson LLP—*Robert Kushner*	8105 Irvine Center Dr, Irvine CA 92618	949-261-2808	R	4*	<.1
398	Wolfe Nilges Nahorski PC—*Dennis Nilges*	1630 Des Peres Rd Ste, Saint Louis MO 63131	314-835-4400	R	4*	<.1
399	Callaghan and Associates PCA—*John Callaghan*	4 Terry Dr Ste 7A, Newtown PA 18940	215-968-9500	R	4*	N/A
400	Carter Associates Inc—*Edmond Carter*	333 N Oxford Valley Rd, Fairless Hills PA 19030	215-945-4484	R	4*	N/A
401	Paul D Taylor CPA—*Paul D Taylor*	8620 N New Braunfels A, San Antonio TX 78217	210-340-3132	R	4*	N/A
402	Gensoft Systems Inc—*Scott Rubins*	319 Jf Edwards Dr, Geneseo IL 61254	309-944-8875	R	3*	<.1
403	Gaines Kriner Elliott LLP—*Rocco Surace*	100 Corporate Pkwy Ste, Amherst NY 14226	716-250-6600	R	3*	.1
404	Pattison Koskey Howe and Bucci CPA's PC—*Michael Bucci*	502 Union St, Hudson NY 12534	518-828-1565	R	3*	.1
405	Gordon Advisors PC—*Andrew Malec*	1301 W Long Lake Rd St, Troy MI 48098	248-952-0200	R	3*	.1
406	Causey Demgen and Moore Inc—*Bob Eichberg*	1801 California St Ste, Denver CO 80202	303-296-2229	R	3*	.1
407	Greenstein Rogoff Olsen and Co LLP—*Alan Olsen*	39159 Paseo Padre Pky, Fremont CA 94538	510-797-8661	R	3*	.1
408	Stockton Bates LLP—*Terry Hancock* Clifton Gunderson LLC	1617 JFK Blvd Ste 1005, Philadelphia PA 19103	215-241-7500	S	3*	.1
409	Casey Peterson and Associates Ltd—*Casey C Peterson*	505 Kansas City St, Rapid City SD 57701	605-348-1930	R	3*	<.1
410	Abrams Little-Gill Tishman and Witty PC—*Ronald L Loberfeld*	1330 Boylston St, Chestnut Hill MA 02467		R	3*	<.1
411	Benson and McLaughlin PS—*James R Erne*	2201 6th Ave Ste 1400, Seattle WA 98121	206-441-3500	R	3*	<.1
412	Pauly Rogers and Co—*Roy R Rogers*	12700 SW 72nd Ave, Tigard OR 97223	503-620-2632	R	3*	<.1
413	Andaloro Smith and Krueger LLP—*Michael Andaloro*	N19 W24400 Riverwood D, Waukesha WI 53188	262-544-2000	R	3*	<.1
414	Citrin Cooperman—*Larry Feldman*	37 North Ave, Norwalk CT 06851	203-847-4068	R	3*	<.1
415	Lesley Thomas Schwarz and Postma—*John Postma II*	2 San Joaquin PlzSte 2, Newport Beach CA 92660	949-650-2771	R	3*	<.1
416	Hanson and Company CPA/Consultant—*Ed Drummond*	4100 E Mississippi Ave, Denver CO 80246	303-388-1010	R	3*	<.1
417	DeLeon and Stang CPA—*Allen Deleon*	100 Lakeforest Blvd Rm, Gaithersburg MD 20877	301-948-9825	R	3*	<.1
418	Bredeweg and Zylstra PLC—*Dean M Adams*	4665 Broadmoor SE Ste, Grand Rapids MI 49512	616-698-2000	R	3*	<.1
419	Malcolm M Dienes and Co—*John W Theriot*	701 Metairie Rd Ste 2A, Metairie LA 70005	504-588-9288	R	3*	<.1
420	Kaptein Dykstra and Company PC—*Gary Kaptein*	4095 Chicago Dr SW, Grandville MI 49418	616-530-8712	R	3*	<.1
421	CASD Inc—*Michael Loehr*	PO Box 800883, Dallas TX 75380	469-298-4400	R	3*	<.1
422	LaPorte Sehrt Romig and Hand—*William T Mason III*	111 Veterans Blvd Ste, Metairie LA 70005	504-835-5522	R	2*	.1
423	Atlas Traffic Consultants Corp—*Robert M Silverman*	18-42 College Point Bl, Flushing NY 11356	718-461-0555	R	2*	.1
424	Petrinovich Pugh and Company LLP—*Mark Parkinson*	333 W Santa Clara St S, San Jose CA 95113	408-287-7911	R	2*	<.1
425	Judd Thomas Smith and Company Inc—*Judy M Durbin*	12222 Merit Dr Ste 190, Dallas TX 75251	214-296-0900	R	2*	<.1
426	Dunbar Cook and Shepard PC—*Ron Cook*	8250 Woodfield Crossin, Indianapolis IN 46240	317-469-0169	R	2*	<.1
427	Glenn M Gelman and Associates—*Glenn M Gelman*	1940 E 17th St, Santa Ana CA 92705	714-667-2600	R	2*	<.1
428	Metcalf Davis—*Arthur Metcalf II*	3340 Peachtree Rd NE S, Atlanta GA 30326	404-264-1700	R	2*	<.1
429	Schmidt Westergard and Company PLLC—*James A Schmidt*	77 W University Dr, Mesa AZ 85201	480-834-6030	R	2*	<.1
430	Scribner Cohen and Co—*Michael Friedman*	400 E Mason St Ste300, Milwaukee WI 53202	414-271-1700	R	2*	<.1
431	Shechtman Marks Devor PC—*Charles Shechtman*	2000 Market St Ste 500, Philadelphia PA 19103		R	2*	<.1
432	Whalen and Co—*Richard D Crabtree*	250 W Old Wilson Bridg, Worthington OH 43085	614-396-4200	R	2*	<.1
433	Alten Sakai and Co—*Nelson Rutherford*	1815 SW Marlow Ave Ste, Portland OR 97225	503-297-1072	R	2*	<.1
434	Varney and Associates PA—*Janice A Marks*	120 N Juliette St, Manhattan KS 66502	785-537-2202	R	2*	<.1
435	Feld Schumacher and Co—*DuWayne Schumacher*	PO BOX 270407, West Allis WI 53227	414-327-2320	R	2*	<.1
436	Midwestern Audit Services Inc—*Brad Busselle*	PO Box 1707, Troy MI 48099	248-928-2000	R	2*	<.1
437	Ritz Holman Butala Fine LLP—*Dean R Goetter*	330 E Kilbourn Ave Ste, Milwaukee WI 53202	414-271-1451	R	2*	<.1
438	Saddington Shusko LLP—*Alexander Shusko*	18201 Von Karman Ave S, Irvine CA 92612	949-475-5800	R	2*	<.1
439	Ross Lane and Co—*Mark Weinstein*	7000 Peachtree Dunwood, Atlanta GA 30328	770-804-8044	R	2*	<.1
440	Malloy Montague Karnowski Radosevich and Company PA—*James H Eichten*	5353 Wayzata Blvd Ste, Minneapolis MN 55416	952-545-0424	R	2*	<.1
441	RBM LLP—*Ash Hutchison*	624 Travis St Ste 800, Shreveport LA 71101	318-221-3615	R	2*	<.1
442	Ronald A Kawahara and Company CPA's Inc—*Ronald A Kawahara*	841 Alua St Ste 102, Wailuku HI 96793	808-244-9021	R	2*	<.1
443	Beemer Pricher Kuehnhackl and Heidbrink PA—*Kurt Kuehnhackl*	1560 N Orange Ave Ste, Winter Park FL 32789	407-998-9000	R	2*	<.1
444	LeGlue and Company CPA's—*Terrell Leglue*	1100 Poydras St Ste 28, New Orleans LA 70163	504-586-0581	R	2*	<.1
445	Jarrard Seibert Pollard and Co—*Jerry Pollard*	1800 Blankenship Rd St, West Linn OR 97068	503-723-7600	R	2*	<.1
446	Hamilton and Associates Inc—*Carl Hamilton*	3617 N Meridian, Oklahoma City OK 73112	405-946-8500	R	2*	<.1
447	Tackman Pilla Arnone and Company PC—*James F Beardsley*	84 W Park Pl, Stamford CT 06901	203-325-9771	R	2*	<.1
448	Wallace and Associates Inc—*Robert Wallace*	711 University Ave, Sacramento CA 95825	916-648-9838	R	2*	<.1
449	Prangley Marks LLP—*Leslie N Prangley III*	333 Bridge St NW 11th, Grand Rapids MI 49504	616-774-9004	R	2*	<.1
450	Equity Protection Services Inc—*Mike Murphy*	PO Box 733, Filer ID 83328	208-326-5936	R	2*	<.1
451	Martin W Cohen and Company PC—*Martin W Cohen*	8111 LBJ Fwy Ste 1440, Dallas TX 75251	214-953-3000	R	2*	<.1
452	Pepperman Emboulas Schwartz and Todaro—*Larry Emboulas*	1815 Clearview Pkwy, Metairie LA 70001	504-837-4555	R	2*	<.1
453	Rosenbloom and Associates CPAs PC—*Jeffrey B Rosenbloom*	1445 Research Blvd Ste, Rockville MD 20850	301-762-7755	R	2*	<.1
454	Payne Todd Sulak and Co—*Russ Payne*	101 Summit Ave Ste 806, Fort Worth TX 76102	817-335-2366	R	2*	<.1
455	Physicians Programs Inc—*Pete Levine*	4438 Oakbridge Dr Ste, Flint MI 48532	810-733-6260	R	2*	<.1
456	Emergency Physicians Dictation Services—*Robert Croft*	300 N Meridian Ave 120, Oklahoma City OK 73107	405-946-0003	R	1*	<.1
457	Medispec Management Services—*Glenda Edwards*	124 Dorchester Sq S, Westerville OH 43081	614-523-2266	R	1*	<.1
458	Wermer Rogers Doran and Ruzon CPA—*James A Ruzon*	755 Essington Rd, Joliet IL 60435	815-730-6250	R	1*	<.1

Rank	Company Name—*Executive Officer*	Address, City, State, Zip	Phone	Type	Fin	Empls
459	Serotta Maddocks Evans and Co—*Abram Serotta*	701 Greene St Ste 200, Augusta GA 30901	706-722-5337	R	1*	<.1
460	Waggoner Frutiger and Daub—*Timothy Waggoner*	5006 E Trindle Rd Ste, Mechanicsburg PA 17050	717-506-1222	R	1*	<.1
461	Kirsch Kohn and Bridge LLP—*Melvyn Kohn*	15910 Ventura Blvd Ste, Encino CA 91436	818-907-6500	R	1*	<.1
462	Pryba Tobin and Company PC—*Robert A Pryba Jr*	40 British American Bl, Latham NY 12110	518-783-3100	R	1*	<.1
463	Sobul Prime and Schenkel—*Richard Schenkel*	12100 Wilshire Blvd St, Los Angeles CA 90025	310-826-2060	R	1*	<.1
464	The Ewbank Group PC—*Thomas Ewbank*	16475 Dallas Pky Ste 7, Addison TX 75001	972-931-5777	R	1*	<.1
465	Fitzgerald Snyder and Company PC—*Gary P Fitzgerald*	7900 Westpark Dr SteT6, McLean VA 22102	703-847-4600	R	1*	<.1
466	Candy and Schonwald LLP—*Jerry Candy*	3116 Live Oak St, Dallas TX 75204	214-826-6660	R	1*	<.1
467	Mukai Greenlee and Co—*Louie Mukai Jr*	2600 N Central Ave Ste, Phoenix AZ 85004	602-279-2600	R	1*	<.1
468	People Lease Inc—*Larry Lewis*	PO Box 3303, Ridgeland MS 39158	601-987-3025	R	1*	<.1
469	Raines and Fischer—*Alan P Raines*	555 5th Ave 9th Fl, New York NY 10017	212-953-9200	R	1*	<.1
470	Scott and Baldwin CPAs PC—*Richard Scott*	1490 Stone Point Dr St, Roseville CA 95661	916-722-2524	R	1*	<.1
471	Lee Sperling Hisamune A/C—*Frank M Saito*	550 N Brand Blvd Ste 5, Glendale CA 91203	818-507-6645	R	1*	<.1
472	Netting and Pace CPA—*Conrad J Netting*	7373 Broadway St Ste 4, San Antonio TX 78209	210-738-3888	R	1*	<.1
473	Ceasar and Smilow LLP—*Alvin Smilow*	60 Cutter Mill Rd Ste, Great Neck NY 11021	516-466-5280	R	1*	<.1
474	Ross Rigby and Patten LLP—*Thomas J Ross*	PO Box 4750, Queensbury NY 12804	518-792-6595	R	1*	<.1
475	Rossmann MacDonald and Benetti Inc—*Ray Benetti*	3838 Watt Ave Ste E-50, Sacramento CA 95821	916-488-8360	R	1*	<.1
476	CFOToday—*John Harrison*	545 E Tennessee St, Tallahassee FL 32308	850-681-1941	R	1*	<.1
477	Pailet Meunier and LeBlanc LLP—*Kenneth Pailet*	3421 N Causeway Blvd S, Metairie LA 70002	504-837-0770	R	1*	<.1
478	Yerkes and Michels CPA LLC—*John D Carroll*	PO Box 707, Independence KS 67301	620-331-4600	R	1*	<.1
479	Branch Richards and Co—*Don W Busch*	155 NE 100th St Ste 41, Seattle WA 98125	206-729-0114	R	1*	<.1
480	Rosenthal and Kaplin—*Jeff Kaplin*	1117 Perimeter Ctr W S, Atlanta GA 30338	770-551-8665	R	1*	<.1
481	Bohlmann and Co—*Kenneth Bohlmann*	9200 Watson Rd Ste 120, Saint Louis MO 63126	314-843-7700	R	1*	<.1
482	Bolon Hart and Buehler Inc—*Edward B Hart*	100 E Broad St Ste 245, Columbus OH 43215	614-228-2691	R	1*	<.1
483	Konner Harbus and Schwartz PC—*Melvin Konner*	80 E Rte 4 Ste 408, Paramus NJ 07652	201-556-1311	R	1*	<.1
484	David J Bailey and Company PC—*Joseph G Davis III*	6243 W IH 10 Ste 650, San Antonio TX 78201	210-344-5000	R	1*	<.1
485	McDevitt and Andreason—*Chris McDevitt*	330 Dayton St Ste 2, Edmonds WA 98020	425-774-5300	R	1*	<.1
486	Warren Associates Incorporated Of Colorado—*Roy Warren*	4505 S Broadway, Englewood CO 80113	303-761-5226	R	1*	<.1
487	Doeren Mayhew and Company PC—*Mark Crawford*	755 W Big Beaver Rd St, Troy MI 48084	248-244-3000	R	N/A	.2
488	Witt Mares and Company PLC—*Alan Witt*	701 Town Center Dr Ste, Newport News VA 23606	757-873-1587	R	N/A	.2
489	Dean Dorton Ford PSC—*Douglas Dean*	106 W Vine St Ste 600, Lexington KY 40507	859-255-2341	R	N/A	.1
490	Hemming Morse Inc—*Stuart Harden*	160 Spear St Ste 1900, San Francisco CA 94105	415-836-4000	R	N/A	.1
491	Schechter Dokken Kanter—*John Lawson*	100 Washington Ave S S, Minneapolis MN 55401	612-332-5500	R	N/A	.1
492	Kuntz Lesher Capital LLC—*Sarah Young Fisher*	PO Box 8408, Lancaster PA 17604	717-399-1700	R	N/A	.1
493	Higdon and Hale CPA PC—*John P Martin*	6310 Lamar Ave Ste 110, Overland Park KS 66202	913-831-7000	R	N/A	<.1

TOTALS: SIC 8721 Accounting, Auditing & Bookkeeping

Companies: 493					249,614	553.9

8731 Commercial Physical Research

Rank	Company Name—*Executive Officer*	Address, City, State, Zip	Phone	Type	Fin	Empls
1	Bristol-Myers Squibb Co—*Lamberto Andreotti*	345 Park Ave, New York NY 10154	212-546-4000	P	19,484	27.0
2	Siemens Information and Communication Networks Inc	900 Broken Sound Pky, Boca Raton FL 33487	561-923-5000	S	11,400	53.0
3	PPD Development—*Raymond H Hill* Pharmaceutical Product Development Inc	929 N Front St, Wilmington NC 28401	910-251-0081	S	4,280*	9.0
4	Edwards Lifesciences Japan Holdings Inc—*Mike Mussallem*	1 Edwards Way, Irvine CA 92614	949-250-2500	S	2,615*	5.0
5	Covance Inc—*Joseph Herring*	210 Carnegie Ctr, Princeton NJ 08540	609-419-2240	P	2,236	10.5
6	Quintiles Transnational Corp—*Dennis B Gillings*	4820 Emperor Blvd, Durham NC 27703	919-998-2000	R	2,099*	20.0
7	Aerospace Corp—*Wanda Austin*	PO Box 92957, Los Angeles CA 90009	310-336-5000	R	1,961*	3.5
8	BD Biosciences Systems and Reagents Inc—*Vincent A For-lenza*	2350 Qume Dr, San Jose CA 95131		D	1,694*	3.0
9	Syngenta Crop Protection Inc—*Michael Mack*	PO Box 18300, Greensboro NC 27419	336-632-6000	D	1,532*	4.6
10	Pharmaceutical Product Development Inc—*Fredric N Eshelman*	929 N Front St, Wilmington NC 28401	910-251-0081	S	1,471*	11.0
11	Dow Automotive—*Steve Henderson*	1250 Harmon Rd, Auburn Hills MI 48326	248-391-6300	R	1,430*	2.0
12	PAREXEL International Corp—*Josef H von Rickenbach*	195 West St, Waltham MA 02451	781-487-9900	P	1,212	10.6
13	Elan Pharmaceuticals—*Kelly Martin*	800 Gateway Blvd, South San Francisco CA 94080	650-877-0900	S	1,113	1.3
14	Reactive NanoTechnologies Inc—*Joseph Grzyb*	34 Robinson Rd, Clinton NY 13323	315-853-4900	S	1,033*	2.0
15	Northrop Grumman Space Technology	1 Space Park Dr, Redondo Beach CA 90278	310-812-4321	S	1,000*	9.3
16	Pacific NorthWest National Laboratory—*Michael Kluse*	PO Box 999, Richland WA 99352	509-375-2121	R	938*	4.9
17	Edwards Lifesciences Financing LLC	1 Edwards Way, Irvine CA 92614	949-250-2500	S	932	5.0
18	Edwards Lifesciences LLC	1 Edwards Way, Irvine CA 92614	949-250-2500	S	932	5.0
19	Edwards Lifesciences US Inc	1 Edwards Way, Irvine CA 92614	949-250-2500	S	932	5.0
20	Edwards Lifesciences World Trade Corp	1 Edwards Way, Irvine CA 92614	949-250-2500	S	932	5.0
21	Reichhold Inc—*John S Gaither*	PO Box 13582, Research Triangle Park NC 27709	919-990-7500	R	865*	1.6
22	Alion Science and Technology Corp—*Bahman Atefi*	1750 Tysons Blvd Ste 1, McLean VA 22102	703-918-4480	R	802	3.7
23	Alion Science and Technology Corp Live and Environmental Technology—*Bahman Atefi* Alion Science and Technology Corp	1750 Tysons Blvd Ste 1, McLean VA 22102	703-918-4480	S	738	N/A
24	Omnicare Clinical Research Inc—*James M Pusey*	630 Allendale Rd, King of Prussia PA 19406	484-679-2400	S	674*	1.2
25	Edwards Lifesciences Asset Management Corp	1 Edwards Way, Irvine CA 92614	949-250-2500	S	628*	1.2
26	Instrumentation Laboratory Co—*Jose Manent*	180 Hartwell Rd, Bedford MA 01730	781-861-0710	S	500*	.6
27	PharmaNet Development Group Inc—*Jeffrey P McMullen*	504 Carnegie Ctr, Princeton NJ 08540	609-951-6800	R	470*	2.6
28	Agouron Pharmaceuticals Inc—*Kent Snyder*	10350 N Torrey Pines R, La Jolla CA 92037	858-622-3000	S	470*	1.0
29	Kendle International LLC	441 Vine St Ste 500, Cincinnati OH 45202	513-381-5550	R	448	3.1
30	ViroPharma Inc—*Vincent J Milano*	730 Stockton Dr, Exton PA 19341	610-458-7300	P	439	.2
31	Advanced Technology Materials Inc—*Doug Neugold*	7 Commerce Dr, Danbury CT 06810	203-794-1100	P	390	.8
32	GE Corporate Research and Development Center—*Scott Don-nelly*	1 Research Cir, Niskayuna NY 12309	518-387-5000	D	359*	2.5
33	Colsa Corp—*Francisco J Collazo*	6728 Odyssey Dr, Huntsville AL 35806	256-964-5555	R	349*	.6
34	Myriad Genetic Laboratories Inc	320 Wakara Way, Salt Lake City UT 84108	801-582-3600	S	311*	.6
35	Affymetrix Inc—*Frank Whitney*	3420 Central Expy, Santa Clara CA 95051	408-731-5000	P	311	.9
36	IDEO Product Development Inc—*Tim Brown*	100 Forest Ave, Palo Alto CA 94301	650-289-3400	R	310*	.5
37	Exelixis Inc—*Michael M Morrissey*	PO Box 511, South San Francisco CA 94083	650-837-7000	P	290	.2
38	Onyx Pharmaceuticals Inc—*N Anthony Coles*	249 E Grand Ave S, San Francisco CA 94108	650-266-0000	P	265	.3
39	Life Sciences Research Inc—*Andrew Baker*	PO Box 2360, East Millstone NJ 08875	732-649-9961	R	242	1.6
40	Genzyme Genetics Corp—*Jon Hart*	3400 Computer Dr, Westborough MA 01581	508-898-9001	S	228*	5.5
41	MIT Lincoln Laboratory—*Eric D Evans*	244 Wood St, Lexington MA 02420	781-981-5500	MA	216*	2.5
42	AAIPharma Services Corp—*Patrick Walsh*	2320 Scientific Park D, Wilmington NC 28405	910-254-7000	R	215	.9
43	Genoptix Inc—*Tina S Nova PhD*	1811 Aston Ave, Carlsbad CA 92008	760-268-6200	S	209*	.5
44	Sharp Laboratories of America Inc—*Jon Clemens*	5750 NW Pacific Rim Bl, Camas WA 98607	360-817-8400	S	209	.3
45	General Atomics—*James Blue*	PO Box 85608, San Diego CA 92186	858-455-3000	R	209*	2.0

Note: An asterisk (*) indicates an estimated financial figure. The company type code used is as follows: R = Private, P = Public, S = Private Subsidiary, B = Public Subsidiary, D = Division, J = Joint Venture, I = Investment Fund.

COMPANY RANKINGS BY SALES WITHIN 4-DIGIT SIC

Rank	Company Name—Executive Officer	Address, City, State, Zip	Phone	Type	Fin	Empls
46	Stiefel Laboratories Inc—Charles W Stiefel	255 Alhambra Cir, Coral Gables FL 33134	305-443-3800	S	206*	1.5
47	Albany Molecular Research Inc—Thomas E D'Ambra	28 Corporate Cr, Albany NY 12203	518-212-2000	P	198	1.4
48	Luminex Corp—Patrick J Balthrop Sr	12212 Technology Blvd, Austin TX 78727	512-219-8020	P	184	.6
49	LifeCell Corp—Lisa N Colleran	1 Millennium Way, Branchburg NJ 08876	908-947-1100	S	172*	.4
50	Aurora Diagnostics Inc—James C New	11025 RCA Center Dr St, Palm Beach Gardens FL 33410	561-626-5512	R	172	1.0
51	Univera Inc—Stuart Ochiltree	2660 Willamette Dr NE, Lacey WA 98516	360-486-7500	S	170*	.2
52	Pacific Biosciences Inc—Hugh Martin	1380 Willow Rd, Menlo Park CA 94025	650-521-8000	R	168*	.3
53	Incorporated Research LLC—James Ogle	3201 Beechleaf Ct Ste, Raleigh NC 27604	919-876-9300	R	166*	2.0
54	Scientific Research Corp—Michael L Watt	2300 Windy Ridge Pkwy, Atlanta GA 30339	770-859-9161	R	166*	1.4
55	Ktech Corp—Steven Downie	10800 Gibson Blvd SE, Albuquerque NM 87123	505-998-5830	R	164*	.3
56	Dynetics Inc—Marc Bendickson	1002 Explorer Blvd, Huntsville AL 35806	256-922-9230	R	160*	.8
57	Sanofi Pasteur Biologics Co—Wayne Pisano	38 Sidney St, Cambridge MA 02139	617-761-4200	R	159*	.3
58	GE Nuclear Energy—Mark Savoff	175 Curtner Ave, San Jose CA 95125	408-925-1000	S	143	1.0
59	Geodigm Corp—Andrew Hofmeister	1630 Lake Dr W, Chanhassen MN 55317	952-556-5657	R	142*	2.0
60	Wincup Holdings LP—George William Wurtz III	7980 W Buckeye Rd, Phoenix AZ 85043		R	133*	.2
61	BAE Systems Advanced Information Technologies—Julie Cohen	6 New England Executiv, Burlington MA 01803	781-273-3388	S	125*	.3
62	Covance Periapproval Services Inc / Covance Inc	1 Radnor Corporate Ctr, Wayne PA 19087	610-832-8877	S	117*	.2
63	Codexis Inc—Alan Shaw	200 Penobscot Dr, Redwood City CA 94063	650-421-8100	P	107	.3
64	Able Laboratories Inc	270 Prospect Plains Rd, Cranbury NJ 08512	609-495-2800	S	103	.4
65	Infinia Corp—JD Sitton	6811 W Okanogan Pl, Kennewick WA 99336	509-735-4700	R	101*	.1
66	ENSCO Inc—Gregory Young	3110 Fairview Park Dr, Falls Church VA 22042	703-321-9000	R	100	.8
67	Maxwell Technologies Systems Division Inc—Edward Caudill	9244 Balboa Ave, San Diego CA 92123	858-503-3300	S	99*	.2
68	Lundbeck Research USA Inc—Claus Braestrup	215 College Rd, Paramus NJ 07652	201-261-1331	S	97	N/A
69	Incyte Corp—Paul A Friedman	Experimental Sta Rte 1, Wilmington DE 19880	302-498-6700	P	94	.4
70	Macrogenics Inc—Scott K Koenig	1500 E Gude Dr, Rockville MD 20850	301-251-5172	R	94*	.1
71	Acceleron Pharma Inc—John Knopf	128 Sidney St, Cambridge MA 02139	617-649-9200	R	87*	.2
72	Chemstar Products Co—Paul Werler	3915 Hiawatha Ave, Minneapolis MN 55406	612-722-0079	R	86*	.1
73	Nokia Mobile Phones	12278 Scripps Summit D, San Diego CA 92131	858-831-5000	R	86*	.6
74	Jackson Laboratory—Richard P Woychik	600 Main St, Bar Harbor ME 04609	207-288-6000	R	84*	1.4
75	DuPont Automotive	950 Stephenson Hwy, Troy MI 48083	248-583-8000	S	83*	.5
76	Shionogi USA Inc—John Keller	300 Campus Dr, Florham Park NJ 07932	973-966-6900	S	81*	.1
77	TargetRx Inc	220 Gibraltar Rd Ste 2, Horsham PA 19044	215-444-8700	S	79*	.2
78	Exelixis Plant Sciences Inc—Michael M Morrissey PhD / Exelixis Inc	16160 SW Upper Boones, Portland OR 97224	503-670-7702	S	79*	.1
79	Hazen Research Inc—Nick Hazen	4601 Indiana St, Golden CO 80403	303-279-4501	R	77*	.1
80	National Research Corp—Michael D Hays	1245 Q St, Lincoln NE 68508	402-475-2525	P	76	.3
81	TKL Research Inc—Jon C Anderson	365 W Passaic St, Rochelle Park NJ 07662	201-587-0500	R	74*	.1
82	Transcept Pharmaceuticals Inc—Glenn A Oclassen	1003 W Cutting Blvd St, Richmond CA 94804	510-215-3500	P	74	N/A
83	Science Systems And Applications Inc—Om Bahethi	10210 Greenbelt Rd Ste, Lanham MD 20706	301-867-2000	R	73*	.6
84	Solvay Pharmaceuticals Inc—Stephen Hill	901 Sawyer Rd, Marietta GA 30062	770-578-9000	S	67	.5
85	iBiquity Digital Corp—Robert Struble	6711 Columbia Gateway, Columbia MD 21046	443-539-4290	R	65*	.1
86	Teledyne Controls—George Simmons	501 Continental Blvd, El Segundo CA 90245	310-765-3600	D	63*	.5
87	CVRx Inc—Nadim Yared	9201 W Broadway Ave St, Minneapolis MN 55445	763-416-2840	R	62*	.1
88	Cold Spring Harbor Laboratory—Bruce Stillman	PO Box 100, Cold Spring Harbor NY 11724	516-367-8397	R	60*	.8
89	Mascoma Corp—William J Brady	67 Etna Rd Ste 300, Lebanon NH 03766	603-676-3320	R	59*	.1
90	Specialized Technology Resources Inc—Dennis Jilot	10 Water St, Enfield CT 06082	860-749-8371	R	56*	.1
91	Intelligent Automation Inc—Joseph E Schwartz	15400 Calhoun Dr Ste 4, Rockville MD 20855	301-294-5200	R	55*	.1
92	NeoSan Pharmaceutical Inc—James G Martin / AAIPharma Services Corp	2320 Scientific Park D, Wilmington NC 28405	910-254-7000	S	54*	.1
93	BRL Screening Inc—Jack Lief	6154 Nancy Ridge Dr, San Diego CA 92121	858-453-7200	S	52*	.1
94	Prolexys Pharmaceuticals Inc—Sudhir Sahasrabudhe	2150 W Dauntless Ave, Salt Lake City UT 84116	801-303-1700	R	52*	.1
95	Dyax Corp—Gustav A Christensen	300 Technology Sq, Cambridge MA 02139	617-225-2500	P	51	.1
96	Evans Analytical Group—David A Lahar	810 Kifer Rd, Sunnyvale CA 94086	408-530-3500	R	50*	.1
97	Pharmalinkfhi—Albert J Siemens	4309 Emperor Blvd Ste, Durham NC 27703	919-484-1921	R	47*	.1
98	Celldex Therapeutics Inc—Anthony S Marucci	119 4th Ave, Needham MA 02494	781-433-0771	P	47	.1
99	DCS Corp—James T Wood	1330 Braddock Pl, Alexandria VA 22314	703-683-8430	R	46*	.5
100	Solid State Chemical Info—Sarah R Byrn	3065 Kent Ave, West Lafayette IN 47906	765-463-0112	R	46*	.1
101	Kraft Food Ingredients Corp—Bob Herron	8000 Horizon Center Bl, Memphis TN 38133	901-381-6500	R	46*	.1
102	Mds Pharma Services Us Inc—Douglas Squires	22011 30th Dr Se, Bothell WA 98021	425-487-8200	R	45*	.1
103	Siemens Corporate Research Inc—Klaus Kleinfeld	755 College Rd E, Princeton NJ 08540	609-734-6500	S	44*	.3
104	Osiris Therapeutics Inc—CRandal Mills Phd	7015 Albert Einstein D, Columbia MD 21046	443-545-1800	P	43	.1
105	Acadia Pharmaceuticals Inc—Uli Hacksell	3911 Sorrento Valley B, San Diego CA 92121	858-558-2871	P	42	<.1
106	Redcom Laboratories Inc—Klaus Gueldenpfennig	1 Redcom Ctr, Victor NY 14564	585-924-7550	R	41*	.2
107	Calvert Preclinical Services Inc—Allen N Reiss	Scott Technology Park, Olyphant PA 18447	570-586-2411	S	41*	.1
108	Chugai Pharma USA LLC—David Mazzo	300 Connell Drive Ste, Berkeley Heights NJ 07922	908-516-1350	R	40*	.1
109	Poten and Partners Inc—Michael Tusiani	805 3rd Ave, New York NY 10022	212-230-2000	R	40*	.1
110	Metrics Inc—William Hodges	1240 Sugg Pkwy, Greenville NC 27834	252-752-3800	R	39*	.1
111	Analytcal B Chemistry Laboratory Inc—Byron Hill	7200 E Abc Ln, Columbia MO 65202	573-797-6000	R	39*	.3
112	Penford Food Ingredients Co—John Randall	7094 S Revere Pkwy, Englewood CO 80112	303-649-1900	S	39*	.1
113	Snbl USA Ltd—Ryoichi Nagata	6605 Merrill Creek Pkw, Everett WA 98203	425-407-0121	R	38*	.2
114	Portola Pharmaceuticals Inc—Williams Lis	270 E Grand Ave Ste 22, South San Francisco CA 94080	650-246-7000	R	38*	.1
115	Priority One Services Inc—Jose Figueroa	6600 Fleet Dr, Alexandria VA 22310	703-971-5504	R	38*	.5
116	Lee Rj Group Inc—Richard Lee	350 Hochberg Rd, Monroeville PA 15146	724-325-1776	R	38*	.3
117	Maxygen Inc—James R Sulat	515 Galveston Dr, Redwood City CA 94063	650-298-5300	P	38	.1
118	Centurum Inc—Robert Matteucci / TECHPLAN Corp	7930 Jones Branch Dr S, Mc Lean VA 22102	703-415-9300	S	37*	.1
119	Radiant Research Inc—Julie McHugh	11500 Northlake Dr Ste, Cincinnati OH 45249	513-247-5500	R	36*	.4
120	Genesis Plastic Welding—Tom Ryder	720 E Broadway St, Fortville IN 46040	317-485-7887	R	36*	<.1
121	Allos Therapeutics Inc—Paul L Berns	11080 CirclePoint Rd S, Westminster CO 80020	303-426-6262	P	35	.2
122	Membrane Technology And Research Inc—Hans Wijmans	1360 Willow Rd Ste 103, Menlo Park CA 94025	650-328-2228	R	35*	.1
123	Luna Innovations Inc—My E Chung	1 Riverside Cr Ste 400, Roanoke VA 24016	540-769-8400	P	35	.2
124	New York State Energy Research And Development Author-ity—Francis Murray	17 Columbia Cir, Albany NY 12203	518-862-1090	R	34*	.2
125	Glycomed Inc—John L Higgins	10275 Science Center D, San Diego CA 92121	858-550-7410	S	34*	.1
126	Advanced Energy—Robert K Koger	909 Capability Dr Ste, Raleigh NC 27606	919-857-9000	R	32*	<.1
127	ReSearch Pharmaceutical Services Inc—Daniel M Perlman	520 Virginia Dr, Fort Washington PA 19034	215-540-0700	R	31*	.6
128	Ricerca Bioscience LLC—R Ian Lennox	7528 Auburn Rd, Concord TWP OH 44077	440-357-3300	R	31*	.3
129	Bend Research Inc—Jim Nightingale	64550 Research Rd, Bend OR 97701	541-382-4100	R	31*	.2

Rank	Company Name—*Executive Officer*	Address, City, State, Zip	Phone	Type	Fin	Empls
130	Physical Sciences Inc—*B David Green*	20 New England Bus Ctr, Andover MA 01810	978-689-0003	R	31*	.2
131	Orion International Technologies Inc—*Miguel Rios*	2201 Buena Vista Dr Se, Albuquerque NM 87106	505-998-4000	R	31*	.3
132	North American Science Associates Inc—*John Gorski*	6750 Wales Rd, Northwood OH 43619	419-666-9455	R	31*	.4
133	Bright Pharmaceutical Services Inc—*Alison Macpherson*	4570 Van Nuys Blvd Ste, Sherman Oaks CA 91403	818-981-9100	R	30*	.1
134	Kensey Nash Holding Co—*Joseph W Kaufmann*	735 Pennsylvania Dr, Exton PA 19341	484-713-2100	S	29*	.1
135	Senomyx Inc—*Kent Snyder*	4767 Nexus Center Dr, San Diego CA 92121	858-646-8300	P	29	.1
136	Hitachi Internetworking—*Masao Hisda*	2000 Sierra Point Pkwy, Brisbane CA 94005		D	29	.2
137	Novalar Pharmaceuticals Inc—*Donna Janson*	12555 High Bluff Dr St, San Diego CA 92130	858-436-1100	R	28*	.1
138	Amira Pharmaceuticals Inc—*Robert Baltera Jr*	9535 Waples St Ste 100, San Diego CA 92121	858-228-4650	R	28*	.1
139	KineMed Inc—*David M Fineman*	5980 Horton St Ste 400, Emeryville CA 94608	510-655-6525	R	28*	.1
140	Mpex Pharmaceuticals Inc—*Daniel D Burgess*	11535 Sorrento Valley, San Diego CA 92121	858-875-2840	R	28*	.1
141	Mortara Instrument Inc—*David Mortara*	7865 N 86th St, Milwaukee WI 53224	414-354-1600	R	28*	.2
142	Anesta Corp—*J Kevin Buchi*	4745 Wiley Post Way St, Salt Lake City UT 84116	801-595-1405	S	27*	.2
143	NextWave Pharmaceuticals Inc—*Jay Shephard*	20450 Stevens Creek Bl, Cupertino CA 95014	408-342-1300	R	27*	.1
144	Sicel Technologies Inc—*Michael D Riddle*	3800 Gateway Centre Bl, Morrisville NC 27560	919-465-2236	R	27*	.1
145	XenoBiotic Laboratories Inc—*Jinn Wu*	107 Morgan Ln, Plainsboro NJ 08536	609-799-2295	S	26*	.1
146	EFTEC North America LLC—*U Bonkat*	20219 Northline Rd, Taylor MI 48180	248-585-2200	R	26*	.1
147	Prochem Inc—*Barry Shelley*	5100 Enterprise Dr, Elliston VA 24087	540-268-9884	R	26*	.1
148	Priority Designs Inc—*Paul Kolada*	501 Morrison Rd, Columbus OH 43230	614-337-9979	R	26*	<.1
149	ReproSource Inc—*Benjamin Leader*	300 Trade Ctr Ste 6540, Woburn MA 01801	781-937-8893	R	26*	<.1
150	Universal Energy Systems—*Jim Clifford*	4401 Dayton-Xenia Rd, Dayton OH 45432	937-426-6900	R	25*	.2
151	TECHPLAN Corp	2120 Washington Blvd S, Arlington VA 22204	703-415-9300	R	25*	.1
152	Archaeological Consulting Services Ltd—*Margerie Green*	424 W Broadway Rd, Tempe AZ 85282	480-894-5477	R	24*	<.1
153	Prochem Analytical Inc—*Cheryl Daniel* Prochem Inc	PO Box 904, Salem VA 24153	540-268-9884	D	24*	<.1
154	KaloBios Pharmaceuticals Inc—*David W Pritchard*	260 E Grand Ave, South San Francisco CA 94080	650-243-3100	R	24*	<.1
155	BIOQUAL Inc—*John C Landon*	9600 Medical Center Dr, Rockville MD 20850	301-251-2801	P	23	
156	Sierra Research Inc—*Thomas Austin*	1801 J St, Sacramento CA 95814	916-444-6666	R	23*	<.1
157	Pure-Seed Testing Inc—*Bill Rose*	PO Box 449, Hubbard OR 97032	503-263-0742	R	22*	<.1
158	Galaxy Scientific Corp—*Renato DiPentima*	3120 Fire Rd, Egg Harbor Township NJ 08234	609-645-0980	S	21*	.5
159	Viacyte—*Alan J Robins*	3550 General Atomics C, San Diego CA 92121	858-455-3708	R	21*	<.1
160	Genaissance Pharmaceuticals Inc	5 Science Pk, New Haven CT 06511	203-773-1450	S	21	.2
161	Annapolis Micro Systems Inc—*Jane Donaldson*	190 Admiral Cochrane D, Annapolis MD 21401	410-841-2514	R	20*	.1
162	EnVivo Pharmaceuticals Inc—*Kees Been*	500 Arsenal St, Watertown MA 02472	617-225-4250	R	20*	<.1
163	Satiety Inc—*Eric Reuter*	2470 Embarcadero Way, Palo Alto CA 94303	650-320-2100	R	20*	<.1
164	Chromatin Inc—*Daphne Preuss*	3440 S Dearborn St Ste, Chicago IL 60616	312-235-3610	R	20*	<.1
165	Fate Therapeutics Inc—*Paul Grayson*	3535 General Atomics C, San Diego CA 92121	858-875-1800	R	20*	<.1
166	Medical Device Technologies Inc—*Jason Armstrong*	3600 Sw 47th Ave, Gainesville FL 32608	352-338-0440	R	20*	.2
167	Keith Manufacturing Co—*R Foster*	PO Box 1, Madras OR 97741	541-475-3802	R	19*	.2
168	CTLGroup—*Jeff Garrett*	5400 Old Orchard Rd, Skokie IL 60077	847-965-7500	R	18*	.2
169	AntiCancer Inc—*Andrew Perry*	7917 Ostrow St, San Diego CA 92111	858-654-2555	R	18*	<.1
170	Martek Biosciences Boulder Corp	4909 Nautilus Ct N Ste, Boulder CO 80301	303-381-8100	S	17*	.1
171	Baxter Healthcare Corp (Norwood Massachusetts)—*Robert Parkinson*	220 Norwood Park S, Norwood MA 02062	781-440-0100	S	17*	<.1
172	PhotoThera—*Arthur T Taylor*	5925 Priestly Dr Ste 1, Carlsbad CA 92008	760-496-3700	R	17*	<.1
173	Advanced Biologics LLC—*Louis Boccumini*	580 Union Sq Dr, New Hope PA 18938	267-744-6200	R	16*	.1
174	454 Life Sciences—*Severin Schwan*	15 Commercial St, Branford CT 06405	203-871-2300	S	16*	.2
175	Cellport Systems Inc—*Pat Kennedy*	885 Arapahoe Ave, Boulder CO 80302	303-541-0722	R	16*	<.1
176	Cylene Pharmaceuticals Inc—*William G Rice PhD*	5820 Nancy Ridge Rd St, San Diego CA 92121	858-875-5100	R	16*	<.1
177	Health Craft Inc—*Charles Knight*	PO Box 262502, Tampa FL 33685	813-885-5244	R	16*	<.1
178	Novum Pharmaceutical Research Services—*Chris Hendy*	5900 Penn Ave, Pittsburgh PA 15206	412-363-3300	R	16*	<.1
179	Buckshire Corp—*Sharon Hursh*	PO Box 155, Perkasie PA 18944	215-257-0116	R	16*	<.1
180	Dese Research Inc—*Wallace Kirkpatrick*	315 Wynn Dr Nw Ste 2, Huntsville AL 35805	256-837-8004	R	16*	.1
181	Cleveland BioLabs Inc—*Michael Fonstein*	73 High St, Buffalo NY 14203	716-849-6810	P	15	.1
182	Anaspec Inc—*Anita Hong*	34801 Campus Dr, Fremont CA 94555	510-791-9560	R	15*	.1
183	Nereus Pharmaceuticals Inc—*Kobi M Sethna*	10480 Wateridge Cir, San Diego CA 92121	858-587-4090	R	15*	<.1
184	Stanley Engineering / Alpha Analytical Laboratories—*Kelth L Stanley*	2700 NW 39th St, Oklahoma City OK 73119	405-948-6505	R	15*	<.1
185	Intertek CM-USA-Deer Park Lab	1114 Seaco Ave, Deer Park TX 77536	713-844-3200	D	14*	.1
186	Immuno Laboratories Inc	6801 Powerline Rd, Fort Lauderdale FL 33309		R	14*	<.1
187	Industrial Technology Research—*John Clymer*	817 W Broad St, Bethlehem PA 18018	610-867-0101	R	14*	.1
188	METALAST International LLC—*David Semas*	2241 Park Pl, Minden NV 89423	775-782-8324	R	14*	<.1
189	KAI Pharmaceuticals Inc—*Steven P James*	270 Littlefield Ave, South San Francisco CA 94080	650-244-1100	R	14*	<.1
190	Akron Rubber Development Laboratory Inc—*C Samples*	2887 Gilchrist Rd, Akron OH 44305	330-794-6600	R	14*	.1
191	Troxler Electronic Laboratories Inc—*William Troxler*	PO Box 12057, Durham NC 27709	919-549-8661	R	13*	.1
192	University Of Wyoming Research Corp—*Donald Collins*	365 N 9th St, Laramie WY 82072	307-721-2011	R	13*	.1
193	Philips Research USA—*Gerard Kleisterlee*	345 Scarborough Rd, Briarcliff Manor NY 10510	914-945-6000	D	13*	.1
194	Terratek Inc—*Rory Hokanson*	1935 Fremont Dr, Salt Lake City UT 84104	801-584-2400	R	13*	.1
195	Health Decisions Inc—*Michael Rosenberg*	2510 Merridian Pky, Durham NC 27713	919-967-1111	R	13*	<.1
196	W-L Research Inc—*Chris Wendorf*	PO Box 8112, Madison WI 53708	608-295-3566	R	13	<.1
197	Inter Coastal Electronics Inc—*C Kirk Patrick*	5750 E Mckellips Rd 10, Mesa AZ 85215	480-981-6898	R	12*	.1
198	Clinipace Worldwide—*Jeff L Williams*	3800 Paramount Pky Ste, Morrisville NC 27560	919-224-8800	R	12	<.1
199	Radiant Aviation Services Inc—*David Speirs*	2041 Niagara Falls Blv, Niagara Falls NY 14304		S	12*	<.1
200	Northwest Research Associates Inc—*Joan Oltman-Shay*	PO Box 3027, Bellevue WA 98009	425-556-9055	R	12*	.1
201	Mymic LLC—*Jason Call*	1040 University Blvd S, Portsmouth VA 23703	757-391-9200	R	12*	.1
202	Hmi Systems LLC	45 Locust St, Hartford CT 06114	860-982-4212	R	11*	<.1
203	ARCTECH Inc—*Daman Walia*	14100 Park Meadow Dr, Chantilly VA 20151	703-222-0280	R	11*	<.1
204	Light Sciences Oncology Inc—*Llew Keltner* Light Sciences Corp	15405 SE 37th St Ste 1, Bellevue WA 98006	425-957-8900	S	11*	<.1
205	Aptuit Inc—*Timothy Tyson*	2 Greenwich Office Pk, Greenwich CT 06831	203-422-6600	R	11*	<.1
206	NuGen Technologies Inc—*Elizabeth A Hutt*	201 Industrial Rd, San Carlos CA 94070	650-590-3600	R	11*	<.1
207	Energy Independence of America Corp—*Albert Calderon*	PO Box 126, Bowling Green OH 43402	419-354-4632	R	11*	<.1
208	Micro Encoder Inc—*Gary Olson*	11533 Ne 118th St, Kirkland WA 98034	425-821-3906	R	11*	.1
209	Pacific Biomarkers Inc—*Ronald R Helm*	220 W Harrison St, Seattle WA 98119	206-298-0068	P	11	.1
210	Sangamo BioSciences Inc—*Edward Lanphier*	Point Richmond Tech Ct, Richmond CA 94804	510-970-6000	P	10	.1
211	Prevention Research Inc—*Susan Curry*	1747 W Roosevelt Rd, Chicago IL 60608	312-996-7222	R	10*	.1
212	Prudent Technologies Inc—*Samuel Mudumala*	8080 Ward Pky Ste 405, Kansas City MO 64114	816-363-3703	R	10*	.1
213	Charles F Day and Associates LLC—*Charles F Day*	131 W 3rd St Ste 101, Davenport IA 52801	563-324-1670	R	10*	.1
214	WaterWorks America—*Bruce Wirtanen*	5005 Rockside Rd, Independence OH 44131		R	10*	.1
215	Continuum Dynamics Inc—*Alan J Bilanin*	34 Lexington Ave, Trenton NJ 08618	609-538-0444	R	10*	<.1

Note: An asterisk (*) indicates an estimated financial figure. The company type code used is as follows: R = Private, P = Public, S = Private Subsidiary, B = Public Subsidiary, D = Division, J = Joint Venture, I = Investment Fund.

COMPANY RANKINGS BY SALES WITHIN 4-DIGIT SIC

Rank	Company Name—Executive Officer	Address, City, State, Zip	Phone	Type	Fin	Empls
216	Enterprise Integration Group Inc—Rex Stringham	3767 Crow Canyon Rd, San Ramon CA 94582	925-735-1700	R	10*	<.1
217	GEOSPAN Corp—Ted Lachinski	10900 73rd Ave Ste 136, Osseo MN 55369	763-493-9320	R	10*	<.1
218	Light Sciences Corp—Llew Keltner	15405 SE 37th St, Bellevue WA 98006	425-957-8900	R	10*	<.1
219	Intellimed International Inc—Art Layne	1825 E Northern Ave St, Phoenix AZ 85020	602-889-7530	R	10*	<.1
220	Energy Ventures Analysis Inc—Seth Schwartz	1901 N Moore St Ste 12, Arlington VA 22209	703-276-8900	R	10*	<.1
221	Radant Technologies Inc—Jean Sureau	255 Hudson Rd, Stow MA 01775	978-562-3866	R	10*	.1
222	Complete Genomics Inc—Clifford Reid	2071 Stierlin Ct, Mountain View CA 94043	650-943-2800	P	9	.1
223	Cgmp Validation LLC—Jesse Gillikin	10314 Shawnee Miksion, Shawnee KS 66203	913-384-2221	R	9*	.1
224	Cir—Dan Collins	1745 Celeste Dr, San Mateo CA 94402	650-574-6900	R	9*	.1
225	Houston Advanced Research Center—Robert Harriss	4800 Research Forest D, The Woodlands TX 77381	281-367-1348	R	9*	.1
226	Neurion Pharmaceuticals Inc—William L Robbins	1 W Mountain St Ste 10, Pasadena CA 91103	626-791-0011	R	9*	<.1
227	LC Technologies Inc	10363 A Democracy Ln, Fairfax VA 22030	703-385-7133	R	9*	<.1
228	Lambda Optical Systems—Irfan Ali	960 Holmdel Rd Ste 1, Holmdel NJ 07733	732-946-7400	R	9*	.1
229	Spire Biomedical Inc—Roger G Little	1 Patriots Park, Bedford MA 01730	781-275-6000	S	8	N/A
230	Biocontrol Systems Inc—Phillip Feldsine	12822 Se 32nd St Ste 1, Bellevue WA 98005	425-603-1123	R	8*	.1
231	Applied Molecular Evolution Inc—Thomas F Bumol	10300 Campus Point Dr, San Diego CA 92121	858-597-4990	S	8*	.1
232	Air Quality Sciences Inc—Anthony Worthan	2211 Newmarket Pkwy St, Marietta GA 30067	770-933-0638	R	8*	.1
233	Stellartech Research Corp—Roger Stern	1346 Bordeaux Dr, Sunnyvale CA 94089	408-331-3000	R	8*	.1
234	Tanabe Research Laboratories USA Inc—Masaki Yamada	4540 Towne Centre Ct, San Diego CA 92121	858-622-7000	R	8	<.1
235	United Memories Inc—Robert L Gower	4815 List Dr Ste 109, Colorado Springs CO 80919		R	8*	<.1
236	Alvitae Pharmaceuticals Inc—Augustine Lin	2056 Feathermint Dr, San Ramon CA 94582		R	8*	<.1
237	M and L Pharmaceutical Inc—Jorge Molina	765 S Gifford Ave Ste, San Bernardino CA 92408	909-384-0591	R	8*	<.1
238	International Lubrication and Fuel Consultants Inc—Nancy Kitchen	PO Box 15212, Rio Rancho NM 87174	505-892-1666	R	8*	<.1
239	Marine Research Specialists—Eiji Imamura	3140 Telegraph Rd Ste, Ventura CA 93001	805-289-3920	R	8*	<.1
240	Nucleic Assays Corp—R Kevin Pegg	2432 Lynndale Rd, Fernandina Beach FL 32034	904-261-9039	R	8*	<.1
241	Cary Institute Of Ecosystem Studies Inc—William Schlesinger	PO Box Ab, Millbrook NY 12545	845-677-5343	R	8*	<.1
242	Merck Research Laboratories—William Comer	3535 Gerard Atomics Ct, San Diego CA 92121	858-452-5882	R	7	.1
243	BD Technologies—Charles Goldstein	PO Box 12016, Durham NC 27709	919-549-8641	D	7*	.1
244	Integrated DNA Technologies Inc—Joseph Walder	1710 Commercial Park, Coralville IA 52241	319-626-8400	R	7*	.1
245	Oceanit Laboratories Inc—Patrick K Sullivan	1001 Bishop St Ste 297, Honolulu HI 96813	808-531-3017	R	7*	.1
246	Prc Liquidating Corp—Patricia Monteforte	358 S Warminster Rd, Hatboro PA 19040	215-293-4900	R	7*	.1
247	Hawaii Biotech Inc—David Watumull	99-193 Aiea Heights Dr, Aiea HI 96701	808-486-5333	R	7*	.1
248	Ceregene Inc—Jeffrey M Ostrove	9381 Judicial Dr Ste 1, San Diego CA 92121	858-458-8800	R	7*	.1
249	Macleod Pharmaceuticals Inc—Michael Pay	2600 Canton Ct Ste C, Fort Collins CO 80525	970-482-7254	R	7*	<.1
250	Separation Technologies LLC—Randy Dunlap	PO Box 549, Daleville VA 24083	540-966-6847	S	7	<.1
251	Triangle Research and Development Corp—Victoria F Haynes	PO Box 12194, Research Triangle Park NC 27709	919-485-2666	R	7*	<.1
252	Anacapa Sciences Inc—Douglas H Harris	PO Box 519, Santa Barbara CA 93102	805-966-6157	R	7*	<.1
253	DesigneRx Pharmaceuticals Inc	4941 Allison Pkwy Ste, Vacaville CA 95688	707-451-0441	R	7*	<.1
254	Alvine Pharmaceuticals Inc—Abhay Joshi	75 Shoreway Rd Ste B, San Carlos CA 94070	650-632-1645	R	7*	<.1
255	Cerimon Pharmaceuticals Inc—James S Shannon	701 Gateway Blvd Ste 2, South San Francisco CA 94080	650-827-4000	R	7*	<.1
256	PAR Environmental Services Inc—Mary Maniery	PO Box 160756, Sacramento CA 95816	916-739-8356	R	7*	<.1
257	Aries Scientific Inc—Ryan Foust	PO Box 744065, Dallas TX 75374	972-783-7083	R	7*	<.1
258	Mcnc—Freddo So	PO Box 12889, Durham NC 27709	919-248-1900	R	6*	.1
259	Materials and Electrochemical Research Corp—James C Withers	7960 S Kolb Rd, Tucson AZ 85706	520-574-1980	R	6*	.1
260	Eltron Research and Development Inc—Paul Grimmer	4600 Nautilus Ct S, Boulder CO 80301	303-530-0263	R	6*	<.1
261	Bexel Pharmaceuticals Inc—Bishwajit Nag	32990 Alvarado Niles R, Union City CA 94587	510-324-0015	R	6*	<.1
262	Ecoair Corp—Peter Knudsen	4 Industrial Cir, Hamden CT 06517	203-230-3000	R	6*	<.1
263	Kolano and Saha Engineers Inc—Richard A Kolano	3559 Sashabaw Rd, Waterford MI 48329	248-674-4100	R	6*	<.1
264	OptiComp Corp—Peter Guilfoyle	PO Box 10779, Zephyr Cove NV 89448	775-588-4176	R	6*	<.1
265	SustainX Inc—Dax Kepshire	21 Technology Dr, West Lebanon NH 03784	603-276-3393	R	6*	<.1
266	Bivio Networks Inc—Elan Amir	4457 Willow Rd Ste 200, Pleasanton CA 94588	925-924-8600	R	6*	.1
267	Technology Assessment And Transfer Inc—Larry Fehrenbacher	133 Defense Hwy Ste 21, Annapolis MD 21401	410-224-3710	R	6*	.1
268	Iap Research Inc—John Barber	2763 Culver Ave, Dayton OH 45429	937-296-1806	R	6*	.1
269	Tavis Corp—John Tavis	3636 State Hwy 49 S, Mariposa CA 95338	209-966-2182	R	6*	.1
270	Analytical Resources Inc—Brian Bebee	4611 S 134th Pl Ste 10, Tukwila WA 98168	206-957-7120	R	6*	<.1
271	Accustandard Inc—Michael Bolgar	125 Market St, New Haven CT 06513	203-786-5290	R	5*	.1
272	EXACT Sciences Corp—Kevin T Conroy	441 Charmany Dr, Madison WI 53719	608-284-5700	P	5	<.1
273	Piasecki Aircraft Corp—John Piasecki	PO Box 360, Essington PA 19029	610-521-5700	R	5*	.1
274	Kinnetic Laboratories Inc—Mary Kinney	307 Washington St, Santa Cruz CA 95060	831-457-3950	R	5*	.1
275	GeoVax Labs Inc—Robert McNally	1900 Lake Park Dr Ste, Smyrna GA 30080	678-384-7220	P	5	<.1
276	Chemical Research and Licensing Inc—Philip K Asherman	10100 Bay Area Blvd, Pasadena TX 77507	281-474-0600	R	5*	.1
277	BioTrove Inc—Albert A Luderer	12 Gill St, Woburn MA 01801	781-721-3600	R	5*	.1
278	Pacific Vascular Inc—Keith Fujioka	11714 N Creek Pkwy N S, Bothell WA 98011	425-486-8868	R	5*	.1
279	Delta Research Inc—Lou Weiner	996 Explorer Blvd, Huntsville AL 35806	256-895-0881	R	5*	.1
280	Giner Inc—Anthony B LaConti	89 Rumford Ave, Newton MA 02466	781-529-0500	R	5*	.1
281	Guild Associates Inc—Sal Di Novo	PO Box 8013, Dublin OH 43016	614-798-8215	R	5*	.1
282	Ciencia Inc—Salvador Fernandez	111 Roberts St Ste K, East Hartford CT 06108	860-528-9737	R	5*	<.1
283	Cogentus Pharmaceuticals Inc—Mark A Goldsmith	1891 Page Mill Rd Ste, Palo Alto CA 94304	650-543-4730	R	5*	<.1
284	Humanetics Corp—Ronald Zenk	10400 Viking Dr Ste 10, Eden Prairie MN 55344	952-937-7660	R	5*	<.1
285	AVAX America Inc AVAX Technologies Inc	2000 Hamilton St Ste 2, Philadelphia PA 19130	215-241-9760	S	5*	<.1
286	Conatus Pharmaceuticals Inc—Stephen J Mento	4365 Executive Dr Ste, San Diego CA 92121	858-457-7221	R	5*	<.1
287	Mili Pharmaceuticals Inc—Minh Van Nguyen	1611 California Ave, Corona CA 92881	951-736-5317	R	5*	<.1
288	Potter Drilling Inc—Jared Potter	599 Seaport Blvd, Redwood City CA 94063	650-701-1737	R	5*	<.1
289	Constellation Technology Corp—William Swartz	7887 Bryan Dairy Rd St, Seminole FL 33777	727-547-0600	R	5*	<.1
290	Ptrl West Inc—Luis Ruzo	625b Alfred Nobel Dr, Hercules CA 94547	510-741-3000	R	5*	<.1
291	Advantest America R and D Center Inc—Robert Sauer	3201 Scott Blvd, Santa Clara CA 95054	408-727-2222	R	4*	<.1
292	Ophir Corp—Martin O'brien	10184 W Belleview Ave, Littleton CO 80127	303-933-2200	R	4*	<.1
293	Samaritan Pharmaceuticals Inc—Janet Greeson	101 Convention Center, Las Vegas NV 89109	702-735-7001	P	4	<.1
294	Biological Research Associates Inc—Richard J Callahan	3905 Crescent Park Dr, Riverview FL 33578	813-664-4500	R	4*	.1
295	Northeast Analytical Inc—Robert E Wagner	2190 Technology Dr, Schenectady NY 12308	518-346-4592	R	4*	<.1
296	Ultra Scientific Inc—William Russo	250 Smith St, North Kingstown RI 02852	401-294-9400	R	4*	<.1
297	Inotek Pharmaceuticals Corp—Paul Howes	100 Cummings Ctr Ste 4, Beverly MA 01915	978-232-9660	R	4*	<.1
298	Dyadic International Inc—Mark Emalfarb	140 Intracoastal Point, Jupiter FL 33477	561-743-8333	R	4*	<.1
299	FL Viscosity Oil Co—Jeff Hoch	600-H Joliet Rd, Willowbrook IL 60527	630-850-4000	S	4*	<.1
300	Pulse Sciences Inc—David Price	2700 Merced St, San Leandro CA 94577	510-357-4610	D	4*	<.1
301	Avera Pharmaceuticals Inc—Dinu Sen	4350 La Jolla Village, San Diego CA 92122		R	4*	<.1
302	3DM Inc—Keiji Nagano	245 1st St 18th Fl, Cambridge MA 02142		S	4*	<.1

Rank	Company Name—*Executive Officer*	Address, City, State, Zip	Phone	Type	Fin	Empls
303	APT Pharmaceuticals Inc—*Stephen Dilly*	700 Airport Blvd Ste 3, Burlingame CA 94010	650-931-1666	R	4*	<.1
304	BioMarker Pharmaceuticals Inc—*Charles Garvin*	5941 Optical Ct, San Jose CA 95138	408-257-2000	R	4*	<.1
305	Acuity Pharmaceuticals Inc—*Dale Pfost*	3701 Market St, Philadelphia PA 19104	215-966-6191	R	4*	<.1
306	MedSource Consulting Inc—*Eric Lund*	16902 El Camino Real, Houston TX 77058	281-286-2003	R	4*	<.1
307	Novelix Pharmaceuticals Inc—*Burkhard Jansen MD*	8008 Girard Ave Ste 33, La Jolla CA 92037	858-454-3245	R	4*	<.1
308	Orphagen Pharmaceuticals—*Scott Thacher*	11494 Sorrento Valley, San Diego CA 92121	858-481-6191	R	4*	<.1
309	Access Mortgage Research and Consulting Inc—*David Olson*	6140 Jerrys Dr, Columbia MD 21044	410-772-1161	R	4*	<.1
310	American Life Science Pharmaceuticals Inc—*Michael D Pier-schbacher*	3030 Bunker Hill St St, San Diego CA 92109	858-273-3900	R	4*	<.1
311	Biofield Corp—*David M Long Jr*	1025 9 N Dr Ste M, Alpharetta GA 30004	770-740-8180	R	4*	<.1
312	Interferometrics Inc—*Telisa Kidd*	13454 Sunrise Valley D, Herndon VA 20171	703-222-5800	R	4*	<.1
313	Spentech Inc—*Scott Seidel*	701 16th Ave, Seattle WA 98122	206-329-7220	R	4*	<.1
314	Zinfi Technologies Inc—*Sugata Sanyal*	6200 Stoneridge, Pleasanton CA 94588	925-251-0332	R	4*	<.1
315	Jeneil Biotech Inc—*N Gandhi*	400 N Dekora Woods Blv, Saukville WI 53080	262-268-6815	R	4*	<.1
316	JL Analytical Services Inc—*Richard Jacobs*	PO Box 576185, Modesto CA 95357	209-538-8111	R	3*	<.1
317	Meredith-Springfield Associates Inc—*Melvin C OLeary Jr*	321 Moody St, Ludlow MA 01056	413-583-8600	R	3*	.1
318	Herguth Laboratories Inc—*William Herguth*	101 Corporate Pl, Vallejo CA 94590	707-554-4611	R	3*	<.1
319	Applied Sciences Inc—*Max Lake*	PO Box 579, Cedarville OH 45314	937-766-2020	R	3*	<.1
320	High-Technology Corp—*Veronica Alroy*	144 S St, Hackensack NJ 07601	201-488-0010	R	3*	<.1
321	Gustavson Associates Inc—*Edwin Moritz*	5757 Central Ave Ste D, Boulder CO 80301	303-443-2209	R	3*	<.1
322	Aerosance Inc—*Stephen Smith*	1000 Camino Dos Rios, Thousand Oaks CA 91360	805-873-4545	S	3*	<.1
323	Visidyne Inc—*Jack Carpenter*	99 S Bedford St Ste 10, Burlington MA 01803	781-273-2820	R	3*	<.1
324	Digitec Inc—*Dan Pickerill*	PO Box 726, Milford NE 68405	402-761-3382	R	3*	<.1
325	Chemat Technology Inc—*Haixing Zheng*	9036 Winnetka Ave, Northridge CA 91324	818-727-9786	R	3*	<.1
326	Calando Pharmaceuticals Inc—*Christopher Anzalone*	225 S Lake Ave 3rd Fl, Pasadena CA 91101	626-304-3400	R	3*	<.1
327	DisplaySearch Inc—*Tim Bush*	101 W 6th St Ste 517, Austin TX 78701	512-687-1510	S	3*	<.1
328	Veldona USA Inc—*Joseph Cummins* Amarillo Biosciences Inc	4134 Business Park Dr, Amarillo TX 79110	806-376-1741	S	3*	<.1
329	Adamas Pharmaceuticals Inc—*Gregory Went*	1900 Powell St Ste 105, Emeryville CA 94608	510-450-3500	R	3*	<.1
330	Chemokine Pharmaceutical Inc—*Ziwei Huang*	10931 N Torrey Pine Rd, La Jolla CA 92037	858-866-0158	R	3*	<.1
331	Edison Pharmaceuticals Inc—*Guy Miller MD PhD*	350 N Bernardo Ave, Mountain View CA 94043	650-641-9200	R	3*	<.1
332	Elite Laboratories Inc—*Jerry Treppel*	165 Ludlow Ave, Northvale NJ 07647	201-750-2646	S	3*	<.1
333	LKT Laboratories Inc—*Luke Lam*	2233 University Ave W, Saint Paul MN 55114	651-644-8424	R	3*	<.1
334	Mitos Pharmaceuticals Inc—*Chris Bowman*	3 San Joaquin Plz Ste, Newport Beach CA 92660	949-467-2730	R	3*	<.1
335	Petro Probe Investigations Inc—*Mark Lynch*	940 Lone Star Dr, O Fallon MO 63366	636-379-0765	S	3*	<.1
336	Pherin Pharmaceuticals Inc—*Julian Stern*	4962 El Camino Real St, Los Altos CA 94022	650-961-2703	R	3*	<.1
337	Tousimis Research Corp—*Anastasios Tousimis*	2211 Lewis Ave, Rockville MD 20851	301-881-2450	R	3*	<.1
338	Optra Inc—*James Engel*	461 Boston St Ste E6, Topsfield MA 01983	978-887-6600	R	3*	<.1
339	XenoPort Inc—*Ronald W Barrett*	3410 Central Expwy, Santa Clara CA 95051	408-616-7200	P	3	.1
340	Superior Transmission Parts Inc—*Dennis Erickson*	3770 Hartsfield Rd, Tallahassee FL 32303	850-575-0788	R	3*	<.1
341	Oakwood Products Inc—*Richard Tracey*	1741 Old Dunbar Rd, West Columbia SC 29172	803-739-8800	R	3*	<.1
342	STI Optronics Inc—*William Thayer*	2755 Northup Way, Bellevue WA 98004	425-827-0460	R	3*	<.1
343	Compucyte Corp—*Elena Holden*	385 University Ave, Westwood MA 02090	781-801-1500	R	2*	<.1
344	H P White Laboratory Inc—*Eric Dunn*	3114 Scarboro Rd, Street MD 21154	410-838-6550	S	2*	<.1
345	Itronics Inc—*John W Whitney*	6490 S McCarran Blvd B, Reno NV 89509	775-689-7696	P	2	<.1
346	General Oceanics Inc—*Regis Cook*	PO Box 694301, Miami FL 33269	305-621-2882	R	2*	<.1
347	Inhand Electronics Inc—*Knut Skaro*	30 W Gude Dr Ste 550, Rockville MD 20850	240-558-2014	R	2*	<.1
348	Doltronics LLC—*Michelle Romanella*	65-4 N Branford Rd, Branford CT 06405	203 488 8766	R	2*	<.1
349	Deltagen Inc—*Robert J Driscoll*	1900 S Norfolk St Ste, San Mateo CA 94403	650-345-7602	P	2	.3
350	MSE Technology Applications—*Donald R Peoples*	PO Box 4078, Butte MT 59701	406-494-7100	S	2*	.1
351	diaDexus Inc—*James P Panek*	343 Oyster Point Blvd, South San Francisco CA 94080	650-246-6400	R	2*	.1
352	Agvise Laboratories Inc—*Robert Wallace*	PO Box 510, Northwood ND 58267	701-587-6010	R	2*	<.1
353	VLSI Research Inc—*G Dan Hutcheson*	2880 Lakeside Dr Ste 3, Santa Clara CA 95054	408-453-8844	R	2*	<.1
354	MBC Applied Environmental Sciences—*Charles Mitchell*	3000 Red Hill Ave, Costa Mesa CA 92626	714-850-4830	R	2*	<.1
355	Atlantic Coastal Electronics Inc—*Debbie Fogleman*	1875 Lake Mrkham Prsrv, Sanford FL 32771	407-328-1040	R	2*	<.1
356	Intracel Corp—*John Kenward*	550 Highland St Ste 41, Frederick MD 21701	301-668-8300	R	2*	<.1
357	Toxics Targeting Inc—*Walter Hang*	215 N Cayuga St, Ithaca NY 14850	607-273-3391	R	2*	<.1
358	Bioprogress Technology International Inc—*Richard Trevillion*	PO Box 500127, Atlanta GA 31150	770-649-1183	R	2*	<.1
359	Morter HealthSystem—*Milton T Morter Jr*	215 W Poplar St, Rogers AR 72756	479-636-9291	R	2*	<.1
360	Quest Integrated Inc—*Milton Altenberg*	19823 58th Pl S, Kent WA 98032	253-872-9500	R	2*	<.1
361	Research Technologies International Div—*Jerry G Singh*	31628 Glendale St, Livonia MI 48150	734-422-8000	R	2*	<.1
362	Umpqua Research Co—*Jim Atwater*	PO Box 609, Myrtle Creek OR 97457	541-863-7770	R	2*	<.1
363	Bio-Technical Resources LP—*Tom Jerrell*	1035 S 7th St, Manitowoc WI 54220	920-684-5518	S	2*	<.1
364	Potomac Photonics Inc—*Lori Beer*	4445 Nicole Dr, Lanham MD 20706	301-459-3031	R	2*	<.1
365	Geo-Microbial Technologies Inc—*Daniel C Hitzman*	PO Box 132, Ochelata OK 74051	918-535-2281	R	2*	<.1
366	Iris Technologies Inc—*Jerry Salandro*	413 Avonlea Ct, Gibsonia PA 15044	724-449-1041	R	2*	<.1
367	Biocoat Inc—*Djoerd Hoekstra*	211 Witmer Rd, Horsham PA 19044	215-734-0888	R	2*	<.1
368	OmniGene Bioproducts Inc—*Janice Pero*	25K Olympia Ave, Woburn MA 01801	781-938-1966	R	2*	<.1
369	Angstrom Pharmaceuticals Inc—*Malcolm Finlayson*	990 Highland Dr Ste 31, Solana Beach CA 92075	858-314-2356	R	2*	<.1
370	Auritec Pharmaceuticals Inc—*Thomas Smith*	15 Braeburn Rd, Hyde Park MA 02136	617-361-5434	R	2*	<.1
371	BioMed Systems LLC—*Erum Naqvi*	1501 Lincoln Way Ste 2, McKeesport PA 15131	412-678-1628	R	2*	<.1
372	Auspex Pharmaceuticals Inc—*Lawrence C Fritz PhD*	1261 Liberty Way Ste C, Vista CA 92081	760-599-1800	R	2*	<.1
373	Clean Coal Technologies Inc—*Robin Eves*	12518 West Atlantic Bl, Coral Springs FL 33071	954-344-2727	R	2*	<.1
374	Omnitech Robotics Inc—*David Parish*	3067 N 3422 E, Kimberly ID 83341	208-423-6281	R	2*	<.1
375	Antenen Research Company Inc—*Steve Antenen*	4300 Dues Dr, Cincinnati OH 45246	513-860-8800	R	2*	<.1
376	Terronics Development Corp—*Eduardo Escallon*	7565 W 900 N, Elwood IN 46036	765-552-0808	R	2*	<.1
377	High Technology Corp—*Mujeeb Malik*	101 Edgewood Ct, Yorktown VA 23692	757-898-3698	R	2*	<.1
378	Adaptive Micro-Ware Inc—*Robert Kniskern*	6917 Innovation Blvd, Fort Wayne IN 46818	260-489-0046	R	2*	<.1
379	Parish Chemical Company Inc—*W Parish*	PO Box 277, Orem UT 84059	801-226-2018	R	2*	<.1
380	Phase Iv Engineering Inc—*Robert Mueller*	2820 Wilderness Pl Ste, Boulder CO 80301	303-443-6611	R	2*	<.1
381	Miille Applied Research Co—*Jerry Miille*	PO Box 87634, Houston TX 77287	713-472-6272	R	2*	<.1
382	Martinsound Inc—*Joe Martinson*	1151 W Valley Blvd, Alhambra CA 91803	626-281-3555	R	1*	<.1
383	International Advanced Materials Inc—*Rodger Cary*	2 N Cole Ave, Spring Valley NY 10977	845-352-5800	R	1*	<.1
384	Redpoint Bio Corp—*F Raymond Salemme*	5501 Old York Rd, Philadelphia PA 19141	215-456-2312	P	1	<.1
385	Vermillion Inc—*Gail S Page*	12117 Bee Caves Rd Bld, Austin TX 78738	512-519-0400	P	1	<.1
386	Fluorochem Inc—*Kurt Baum*	680 S Ayon Ave, Azusa CA 91702	626-334-6714	R	1*	<.1
387	Calspan Corp—*Louis H Knotts*	4455 Genesee St, Buffalo NY 14225	716-632-7500	R	1*	.3
388	Astron Wireless Technologies—*James Jalbert*	22560 Glenn Dr Ste 114, Sterling VA 20164	703-450-5517	R	1*	<.1
389	ADA Technologies Inc—*Clifton H Brown Jr*	8100 Shaffer Pky Ste 1, Littleton CO 80127	303-792-5615	R	1*	<.1
390	Nielsen Engineering and Research Inc—*Michael Mendenhall*	2700 Augustine Dr Ste2, Santa Clara CA 95054	480-727-1428	R	1*	<.1

Note: An asterisk (*) indicates an estimated financial figure. The company type code used is as follows: R = Private, P = Public, S = Private Subsidiary, B = Public Subsidiary, D = Division, J = Joint Venture, I = Investment Fund.

COMPANY RANKINGS BY SALES WITHIN 4-DIGIT SIC

Rank	Company Name—*Executive Officer*	Address, City, State, Zip	Phone	Type	Fin	Empls
391	Cougar Electronics Corp—*Robert Cowles*	10 Lyman St, New Haven CT 06511	203-562-6545	R	1*	<.1
392	Boston Microsystems Inc—*Richard Mlcak*	30 6th Rd Ste H, Woburn MA 01801	781-933-5100	R	1*	<.1
393	EcoSphere Associates Ltd—*Dan Harmony*	4421 N Romero Rd, Tucson AZ 85705	520-888-0084	R	1*	<.1
394	Octamer Inc—*Jeffrey S Price*	392 Cecilia Way, Tiburon CA 94920	415-381-1602	R	1*	<.1
395	PRI Research and Development Corp—*William Shih*	25500 Hawthorne Blvd S, Torrance CA 90505	310-378-0286	R	1*	<.1
396	International Solar Electric Technology Inc—*Vijay Kapur*	20600 Plummer St, Chatsworth CA 91311	818-882-8687	R	1*	<.1
397	Enviro Sciences Inc—*Paul Fletcher*	2501 Mayes Rd Ste 100, Carrollton TX 75006	972-242-2479	R	1*	<.1
398	Bio Online Inc—*Lee Jensen PhD*	1900 Powell St Ste 230, Emeryville CA 94608	510-601-7194	R	1*	<.1
399	Magna-lastic Devices Inc—*Lawrence T Rupert*	7401 W Wilson Ave, Chicago IL 60706	708-867-6777	S	1*	<.1
400	Sonex Research Inc—*Andrew A Pouring*	23 Hudson St, Annapolis MD 21401	410-266-5556	R	1*	<.1
401	Janus Pharmaceuticals Inc—*Norifumi Nakamura*	1111 S Arroyo Pkwy Ste, Pasadena CA 91105	626-568-0762	J	1*	<.1
402	Acumen Pharmaceuticals Inc—*William F Goure*	4435 N 1st St Ste 360, Livermore CA 94551	925-368-8508	R	1*	<.1
403	Astro-Geo-Marine Inc—*Tom Fenole*	2186 Knoll Dr Ste B, Ventura CA 93003	805-654-8300	R	1*	<.1
404	Research Frontiers Inc—*Joseph M Harary*	240 Crossways Park Dr, Woodbury NY 11797	516-364-1902	P	1	<.1
405	ZIOPHARM Oncology Inc—*Jonathan Lewis*	1180 Ave of the Americ, New York NY 10036	646-214-0700	P	1	.1
406	Enviro Voraxial Technology Inc—*Alberto Di Bella*	821 NW 57th Pl, Ft Lauderdale FL 33309	954-958-9968	P	1	<.1
407	AVAX Technologies Inc—*Francois R Martelet MD*	2000 Hamilton St Ste 2, Philadelphia PA 19130	215-241-9760	P	1	<.1
408	Arrowhead Research Corp—*Christopher Anzalone*	225 S Lake Ave 3rd Fl, Pasadena CA 91101	626-304-3400	P	1	<.1
409	Lescarden Inc—*William E Luther*	420 Lexington Ave Ste, New York NY 10170	212-687-1050	P	1	<.1
410	Generics Group Inc—*Martin Frost*	Reservoir Pl 1601 Trap, Waltham MA 02451		S	1	<.1
411	Touch Scientific Inc—*Michael Touch*	3209 Gresham Lake Rd S, Raleigh NC 27615	919-872-4445	R	1*	<.1
412	Daniel K Jackson—*Daniel Jackson*	2143 Se 55th Ave, Portland OR 97215	503-232-2232	R	1*	<.1
413	Hollis Electronics Company LLC—*Roxanne Angavine*	5 Northern Blvd Ste 13, Amherst NH 03031	603-598-4640	R	<1*	<.1
414	Anacor Pharmaceuticals Inc—*David Perry*	1020 E Meadow Cir, Palo Alto CA 94303	650-543-7500	P	<1	.1
415	Napo Pharmaceuticals Inc—*Lisa Conte*	185 Berry St Ste 1300, San Francisco CA 94107	415-371-8300	R	<1	<.1
416	Mera Pharmaceuticals Inc—*Gregory F Kowal*	73-4460 Queen Ka'ahuma, Kailua Kona HI 96740	808-326-9301	P	<1	<.1
417	Vehicle Research And Development Inc—*Larry Bruzzese*	31925 Van Dyke Ave, Warren MI 48093	810-798-3911	R	<1*	<.1
418	Buck Research Instruments LLC	PO Box 19498, Boulder CO 80308	303-442-6055	R	<1*	<.1
419	Protein Polymer Technologies Inc—*James McCarthy*	11494 Sorrento Valley, San Diego CA 92121	858-558-6064	P	<1	<.1
420	Aastrom Biosciences Inc—*Timothy Mayleben*	PO Box 376, Ann Arbor MI 48106	734-930-5555	P	<1	<.1
421	Advance Nanotech Inc	400 Rella Blvd Ste 160, Suffern NY 10901	212-583-0080	P	<1	<.1
422	Commonwealth Biotechnologies Inc—*Richard Freer*	601 Biotech Dr, Richmond VA 23235	804-648-3820	P	<1	<.1
423	Anthera Pharmaceuticals Inc—*Paul F Truex*	25801 Industrial Blvd, Hayward CA 94545	510-856-5600	P	<1	<.1
424	Advaxis Inc—*Thomas A Moore*	305 College Rd E, Princeton NJ 08540	609-452-9814	P	<1	<.1
425	Amazon Biotech Inc—*Chaim Lieberman*	43 W 33rd St, New York NY 10001	212-444-1019	P	<1	<.1
426	Alseres Pharmaceuticals Inc—*Peter G Savas*	239 South St, Hopkinton MA 01748	508-497-2360	P	<1	<.1
427	Amarillo Biosciences Inc—*Joseph M Cummins*	4134 Business Park Dr, Amarillo TX 79110	806-376-1741	P	<1	<.1
428	Senesco Technologies Inc—*Lesley J Browne*	303 George St Ste 420, New Brunswick NJ 08901	732-296-8400	P	<1	<.1
429	OXIS International Inc—*Anthony J Cataldo*	468 N Camden Dr 2nd Fl, Beverly Hills CA 90210	310-860-5184	P	<1	<.1
430	Power3 Medical Products Inc—*Helen R Park*	26022 Budde Rd, The Woodlands TX 77380	281-298-7944	P	<1	<.1
431	Renewable Corp—*Andy Badolato*	2033 Main St Ste 400, Sarasota FL 34237	941-487-7560	P	<1	<.1
432	Magna-Lab Inc—*Lawrence A Minkoff*	6800 Jericho Tpke Ste, Syosset NY 11791	516-393-5874	P	<1	N/A
433	AAI International—*Patrick Walsh* AAIPharma Services Corp	2320 Scientific Park D, Wilmington NC 28405	910-254-7000	S	N/A	.1
434	Randers Engineers and Constructors—*Bruce Borurdon*	3597 Henry St Ste 200, Muskegon MI 49441	231-780-1200	R	N/A	<.1

TOTALS: SIC 8731 Commercial Physical Research

	Companies: 434				78,384	273.9

8732 Commercial Nonphysical Research

Rank	Company Name—*Executive Officer*	Address, City, State, Zip	Phone	Type	Fin	Empls
1	Westat Inc—*Joseph A Hunt*	1600 Research Blvd, Rockville MD 20850	301-251-1500	R	1,277*	2.0
2	Market Strategies International—*Andrew Morrison*	17430 College Pky, Livonia MI 48152	734-542-7600	R	1,087*	1.6
3	Millward Brown Inc—*Eileen Campbell*	11 Madison Ave 12th Fl, New York NY 10010	212-548-7200	S	921*	1.5
4	Nielsen Media Research—*David Calhoun*	770 Broadway, New York NY 10003	646-654-8300	S	723*	4.0
5	Information Resources Inc—*John Freeland*	150 N Clinton St, Chicago IL 60661	312-726-1221	R	555	4.4
6	JD Power and Associates—*Finbarr O'Neill*	2625 Townsgate Rd, Westlake Village CA 91361	805-418-8000	S	512*	.6
7	AUS Inc—*John L Ringwood*	155 Gaither Dr, Mount Laurel NJ 08054	856-234-9200	R	432*	.7
8	Research Data Design Inc—*John Stepleton*	8959 SW Barbur Blvd St, Portland OR 97219	503-223-7166	R	233*	.4
9	ComScore Inc—*Magid M Abraham*	11950 Democracy Dr Ste, Reston VA 20190	703-438-2000	P	232	1.0
10	SRI International—*Curtis Carlson*	333 Ravenswood Ave, Menlo Park CA 94025		R	195*	1.6
11	Opinion Research Corp—*Mark Litvinoff*	PO Box 183, Princeton NJ 08542	609-452-5400	S	190*	1.1
12	Lieberman Research Worldwide Inc—*David Sackman*	1900 Ave of the Stars, Los Angeles CA 90067	310-553-0550	R	182*	.3
13	Informa Research Services Inc—*Michael E Adler*	26565 Agoura Rd Ste 30, Calabasas CA 91302	818-880-8877	S	180*	.3
14	Maritz Research Inc—*Steve Maritz*	1375 N Hwy Dr, Fenton MO 63026	636-827-8865	S	164*	.7
15	Research International USA Inc—*Lorna Walters*	222 Merchandise Mart P, Chicago IL 60654	312-787-4060	R	163*	2.3
16	Akebono Corp (Elizabethtown Kentucky)—*Tsuyoshi Kashiwagi*	310 Ring Rd, Elizabethtown KY 42701	270-234-5500	R	160*	2.1
17	Mathematica Inc—*Paul Decker*	PO Box 2393, Princeton NJ 08543	609-799-3535	R	149*	1.2
18	Idc Research Inc—*Kirk Campbell*	PO Box 9015, Framingham MA 01701	508-872-8200	R	146*	1.5
19	RAND Corp—*James A Thomson*	PO Box 2138, Santa Monica CA 90407	310-393-0411	M	144*	1.6
20	Synovate Inc—*Robert Philpott*	222 S Riverside Plz St, Chicago IL 60606	312-526-4000	S	143*	1.5
21	Cardiac Science Corp—*Dave Marver*	3303 Monte Villa Pkwy, Bothell WA 98021	425-402-2000	B	141*	.5
22	RMC Research Corp—*Everett Barns*	1000 Market St Bldg 2, Portsmouth NH 03801	603-422-8888	R	138*	.2
23	Bridgewater Associates Inc—*Hope Woodhouse*	1 Glendinning Pl, Westport CT 06880	203-226-3030	R	120*	.2
24	Cna Corp—*Robert Murray*	4825 Mark Ctr Dr Ste 1, Alexandria VA 22311	703-824-2000	R	118*	.7
25	NPD Group Inc—*Tod Johnson*	900 W Shore Rd, Port Washington NY 11050	516-625-0700	R	112*	.8
26	Palo Alto Research Center Inc—*Mark Bernstein*	3333 Coyote Hill Rd, Palo Alto CA 94304	650-812-4000	S	109*	.2
27	Synovate—*Adrian Chedore*	222 S Riverside Plz St, Chicago IL 60606	312-526-4000	S	95*	.2
28	Digital Marketing Services Inc—*Dennis E Gonier*	1305 S State Hwy 121 S, Lewisville TX 75067	214-222-6133	S	90*	.5
29	Graham and Associates Inc—*James C Jager*	2100 Riverchase Center, Birmingham AL 35244	205-443-5399	R	79*	.1
30	National Economic Research Associates Inc—*Andrew Carron*	50 Main St 14th Fl, White Plains NY 10606	914-448-4000	S	77*	.4
31	idEXEC Inc—*Clare Hart*	300 Baker Ave Ste 370, Concord MA 01742	978-318-4300	S	77*	.2
32	Creative and Response Research Services Inc—*Robbin Jacklin*	500 N Michigan Ave, Chicago IL 60611	312-828-9200	R	75*	.4
33	Datamonitor—*Mark Meek*	52 Vanderbilt Ave 7th, New York NY 10017	212-686-7400	R	70*	.1
34	TheMarketscom LLC—*David Eisner*	810 7th Ave, New York NY 10019	212-812-4630	R	67*	.1
35	NFO Migliara/Kaplan—*Lorna Walters*	9 Park Center Ct, Owings Mills MD 21117	410-581-8188	R	55*	.2
36	Covente Inc—*Simon Boardman*	2727 Paces Ferry Rd SE, Atlanta GA 30339	404-287-3400	R	47*	.1
37	Guideline Inc—*Marc Litvinoff*	625 Ave of the America, New York NY 10011	212-645-4550	S	46	.2
38	MORPACE International Inc—*Frank J Ward*	31700 Middlebelt Rd St, Farmington Hills MI 48334	248-737-5300	R	46*	.3
39	Management Science Associates Inc (Pittsburgh Pennsylvania)—*Cathy Opsitnick*	6565 Penn Ave, Pittsburgh PA 15206	412-362-2000	R	42*	.9

Rank	Company Name—Executive Officer	Address, City, State, Zip	Phone	Type	Fin	Empls
40	Market Strategies Inc—Andrew Morrison	17430 College Parkway, Livonia MI 48152	734-542-7600	R	41*	.6
41	Decision Support Systems LP—Michelle Dodd	4150 International Plz, Fort Worth TX 76109	817-665-7000	R	41*	.3
42	House Party Inc—Kitty Kolding	1 Bridge St Ste 3, Irvington NY 10533		R	40*	.1
43	Clinical Research Management Inc—Victoria Tifft	1265 Ridge Rd Ste 2, Hinckley OH 44233	330-278-2343	R	35*	.2
44	National Corporate Research Ltd—Bruce Jacobi	10 E 40th St Fl 10, New York NY 10016	212-947-7200	R	31*	.2
45	Input Inc—Catherine Morales	2291 Wood Oak Dr, Herndon VA 20171	703-707-3500	S	29*	.2
46	Tmr-West Inc—Tom Ramsburg	450 Park Way Ste 106, Broomall PA 19008	610-359-1190	R	27*	.4
47	Colography Group Inc—Theodore R Scherck	1900 The Exchange SE S, Atlanta GA 30339	678-385-2500	R	27*	<.1
48	Michigan Development Corp—Kenneth Baker	3520 Green Ct Ste 300, Ann Arbor MI 48105	734-302-4600	R	23*	.3
49	TRA Inc—Mark Lieberman	52 Vanderbilt Ave 17th, New York NY 10017	212-286-7810	R	23*	<.1
50	Bibliographical Center For Research Rocky Mountain Region Inc—Brenda Hainer	PO Box 440626, Aurora CO 80044	303-751-6277	R	21*	<.1
51	IT Services Marketing Association—David C Munn	420 Bedford St Ste 110, Lexington MA 02420	781-862-8500	R	21*	<.1
52	Marketing and Research Resources—David Vershel	7101 Guilford Dr Ste 1, Frederick MD 21704	301-694-2800	R	21*	.2
53	Kalorama Information—Steven Heffner	38 E 29th St 6th Fl, New York NY 10016	212-807-2660	D	20*	<.1
54	International Data Collection Inc—Luis Durazo	1380 Clljn Segovia, Chula Vista CA 91910	619-271-7158	R	19*	.2
55	Sgs USTesting Company Inc—Christian Jilch	291 Fairfield Ave, Fairfield NJ 07004	973-575-5252	R	19*	.1
56	Q Research Solutions Inc—Patti Nelson	3548 Rte 9 Fl 2, Old Bridge NJ 08857	732-952-0000	R	18*	.2
57	Advanced Technologies International Inc—John Knight	367 Sinclair Frontage, Milpitas CA 95035	408-942-1780	R	17*	.2
58	Customer Research International Inc—Sanjay Vrudhula	135 S Guadalupe St, San Marcos TX 78666	512-757-8100	R	17*	.2
59	Novozymes Inc—Ejner Jensen	1445 Drew Ave, Davis CA 95618	530-757-8100	R	16*	.1
60	Corporate Research International—Michael Mallett	130 E Sandusky St, Findlay OH 45840	419-422-3196	R	16*	.2
61	Ideas International—Stephen Bowhill	800 Westchester Ave St, Rye Brook NY 10573	914-937-4302	S	16*	<.1
62	Market Force Information Inc—Karl Maier	248 Centennial Pky Ste, Louisville CO 80027	303-402-6920	R	16*	<.1
63	Blackstone Group Inc—Ashref Hashim	360 N Michigan Ave Ste, Chicago IL 60601	312-419-0400	R	15*	.2
64	New York Public Interest Research Group Fund Inc—Jay Halfon	9 Murray St Fl 3, New York NY 10007	212-349-6460	R	14*	.1
65	Wilkins Research Services Inc—Lisa Wilkins	1730 Gunbarrel Rd, Chattanooga TN 37421	423-894-9478	R	14*	.1
66	Toray Industries America Inc—Yusuke Orito	461 5th Ave Fl 9, New York NY 10017	212-697-8150	R	13*	.2
67	Widener-Burrows and Associates Inc—Steve Markenson	2191 Defense Hwy Ste 4, Crofton MD 21114	410-721-0500	R	13*	.1
68	International Communications Research Inc—Gilbert Barrish AUS Inc	53 W Baltimore Pike, Media PA 19063	484-840-4300	S	13*	.1
69	National Research LLC—Becky Craig	4201 Connecticut Ave N, Washington DC 20008	202-686-2406	R	13*	.2
70	Gallup Inc—James Clifton	901 F St NW, Washington DC 20004	202-715-3030	R	12*	2.0
71	Walker Information Inc—Steven F Walker	301 Pennsylvania Pky, Indianapolis IN 46280	317-843-3939	R	12*	.2
72	International Strategy and Investment Group Inc—Ed Hayman	40 W 57th 18th Fl, New York NY 10019	212-446-5600	R	12*	<.1
73	Moses Anshell Inc—Jos Anshell	20 W Jackson St, Phoenix AZ 85003	602-254-7312	R	12*	<.1
74	Carma International Inc—Albert J Barr	1615 M St NW Ste 750, Washington DC 20036	202-842-1818	R	12*	<.1
75	Smartanalyst Inc—Manu Bammi	9 E 38th St 12th Fl, New York NY 10016	212-331-0010	R	11*	<.1
76	Mountain West Research Center—Jared Schiers	675 Yellowstone Ave St, Pocatello ID 83201	208-232-1818	R	11*	.1
77	Seaman and Associates Inc—E Seaman	9845 Hedden Rd, Evansville IN 47725	812-214-2068	R	11*	.1
78	Clinilabs Inc—Gary Zammit	423 W 55th St Fl 4, New York NY 10019	212-994-5100	R	10*	.1
79	Global Intelligence Network LLC—Peter Maheu	3950e Patrick St Ste 1, Las Vegas NV 89120	702-891-0500	R	9*	.1
80	Thoroughbred Research Group Inc—Harold Busack	1941 Bishop Ln Ste 101, Louisville KY 40218	502-459-3133	R	9*	.1
81	Micron Optics Inc—Jeffrey Miller	1852 Century Pl Ne Ste, Atlanta GA 30345	404-325-0005	R	9*	<.1
82	Delta Information Systems Inc—Gary Thom	300 Welsh Rd Bldg 3-12, Horsham PA 19044	215-657-5270	R	9*	.1
83	Maryland Marketing Source Inc—Barbara Bridge	9936 Liberty Rd, Randallstown MD 21133	410-922-6600	R	8*	<.1
84	Merrill Research and Associates LLC—Patrick Merrill	1300 S El Camino Real, San Mateo CA 94402	650-341-4411	R	8*	<.1
85	Vertical Inc—Michael J Keating	1644 N Honore St Ste 1, Chicago IL 60622	773-278-6300	R	8*	<.1
86	Emarketer Inc—Geoffrey Ramsey	75 Broad St Fl 31, New York NY 10004	212-763-6010	R	7*	.1
87	Arthur Consulting Group Inc—Scott McGadden	31355 Oak Crest Dr Ste, Westlake Village CA 91361	818-735-4800	R	7*	<.1
88	Strategic Vision Inc—Darrel Edwards	PO Box 420429, San Diego CA 92142	858-576-7141	R	7*	<.1
89	Mannsville Chemical Products Corp—Douglas Lumley	PO Box 220, Adams NY 13605	315-232-5050	R	7*	<.1
90	Geneva Global Inc—Doug Balfour	595 E Lancaster Ave St, St Davids PA 19087		R	6*	<.1
91	TrimTabs Investment Research—Charles Biderman	1505 Bridgeway Ste 121, Sausalito CA 94965	415-331-4400	R	6*	.1
92	Strategic Analysis Inc—Frode Nordhoy	2208 Quarry Dr Ste 100, Reading PA 19609	610-320-6100	R	6*	.1
93	Quantum Research Services Inc—Frank Schaller	5505 Central Ave Ste L, Boulder CO 80301	303-786-9500	R	5*	.2
94	InfoTrends—Jeff Hayes	97 Libbey Industrial P, Weymouth MA 02189	781-616-2100	R	5*	.1
95	Public Priority Systems Inc—Roger Alban	6167 Deeside Dr, Dublin OH 43017	614-890-1573	R	5*	<.1
96	CDS Market Research—R Kent Dussair	1001 S Dairy Ashford S, Houston TX 77079		R	5*	<.1
97	Pioneer Consulting LLC—Howard Kidorf	60 State St Ste 700, Boston MA 02109	978-357-3605	R	5*	<.1
98	Research Dimensions Inc—Ann Parker Maust	801 E Main St Ste 1102, Richmond VA 23219	804-643-1082	R	5*	<.1
99	Etymotic Research Inc—Mark Piepenbrink	61 Martin Ln, Elk Grove Village IL 60007	847-228-0006	R	4*	<.1
100	In-Stat Inc—Mike Kirstein	6909 E Greenway Pkwy S, Scottsdale AZ 85254	480-483-4440	R	4	<.1
101	Ball Group—Wes Ball	307 Harvest Dr, Lititz PA 17543	717-627-0405	R	4*	<.1
102	Optronic Laboratories LLC—Alex Fong	4632 36th St, Orlando FL 32811	407-422-3171	R	4*	<.1
103	Pacific Market Research—Mark Rosenkranz	15 S Grady Way Ste 620, Renton WA 98057	425-271-2300	R	3*	.2
104	Scanner Applications Inc—Robert Gibson	400 Milford Pkwy, Milford OH 45150	513-248-5588	R	3*	<.1
105	Collective Intellect Inc—Don Springer	2040 14th St Ste 200, Boulder CO 80302	720-259-3600	R	3*	<.1
106	ath Power Consulting Corp—Frank J Aloi	9 Bartlett St, Andover MA 01810	978-474-6464	R	3*	<.1
107	CBRE Econometric Advisors—William Wheaton	260 Franklin St Ste 40, Boston MA 02110	617-912-5200	S	3*	<.1
108	Altamira—Richard Rapp	25 Sylvan Rd S Ste D, Westport CT 06880	203-227-1445	R	3*	<.1
109	Information Technology Trends Inc—Ian Teh	8378 Moller Ranch Dr, Pleasanton CA 94588	925-462-1202	R	3*	<.1
110	Rockwall Economic Development Corp—Sheri Franza	PO Box 968, Rockwall TX 75087	972-772-0025	R	3*	<.1
111	Princeton Data Source LLC—Laura Baron	65 Barrett Heights Rd, Stafford VA 22556	540-658-0148	R	3*	.1
112	Humancentric Technologies Inc—Barry Beith	200 Mackenan Dr, Cary NC 27511	919-481-0565	R	3*	<.1
113	Kadence (USA) Inc—Owen Jenkins	1 Clarks Hl Ste 302, Framingham MA 01702	508-620-1222	R	3*	<.1
114	Sms Research and Marketing Services Inc—Hersh Singer	1042 Fort St Mall Ste, Honolulu HI 96813	808-537-3356	R	2*	<.1
115	Bases Services and Durables—Ed Wolkenmuth	3130 Crow Canyon Pl St, San Ramon CA 94583	925-820-7350	R	2*	<.1
116	Barnes Research Inc—Sona Barnes	4920 Plnfeld Ave Ne St, Grand Rapids MI 49525	616-363-7643	R	2*	<.1
117	Delahaye Medialink—Laurence Moskowitz	800 Connecticut Ave 1s, Norwalk CT 06854	203-899-1600	S	2*	<.1
118	GRA Inc—Frank J Berardino	115 West Ave Ste 201, Jenkintown PA 19046	215-884-7500	R	2*	<.1
119	Darnell Group Inc—Jeff Shepard	1159-B Pomona Rd, Corona CA 92882	951-279-6684	R	2*	<.1
120	DataStream Market Intelligence Inc—Dan Davis	PO Box 1348, Owasso OK 74055	918-376-2724	R	2*	<.1
121	Science and Technology International Inc—Nicholas Susner	4275 Executive Sq Ste, La Jolla CA 92037	808-540-4700	R	2*	<.1
122	Research Network Inc—Marc Gertz	1560 Hickory Ave, Tallahassee FL 32303	850-681-9955	R	2*	.1
123	Emag Technologies Inc—Kazem Sabet	775 Technology Dr 100a, Ann Arbor MI 48108	734-996-3624	R	2*	<.1
124	Textwise LLC—Mike Colson	401 S Salina St Ste 5, Syracuse NY 13202	315-426-9311	R	1*	<.1
125	Mentor Technologies Inc—Sun Cho	5000 College Ave Ste 2, College Park MD 20740	301-277-4801	R	1*	<.1
126	CJ Olson Market Research—Tianna Ramaker	901 N 3rd St Ste 218, Minneapolis MN 55401	612-378-5040	R	1*	<.1

Note: An asterisk (*) indicates an estimated financial figure. The company type code used is as follows: R = Private, P = Public, S = Private Subsidiary, B = Public Subsidiary, D = Division, J = Joint Venture, I = Investment Fund.

COMPANY RANKINGS BY SALES WITHIN 4-DIGIT SIC

Rank	Company Name—Executive Officer	Address, City, State, Zip	Phone	Type	Fin	Empls
127	Charlton Research Co—Charles F Rund	333 Limpy Creek Rd, Grants Pass OR 97527	541-476-4050	R	1*	<.1
128	Scotti Research Inc—Nancy Matheis	1118 N Sheridan Rd, Peoria IL 61606	309-673-6194	R	1*	<.1
129	Pacific Media Associates—William L Coggshall	1060 Siskiyou Dr, Menlo Park CA 94025	650-561-9020	R	1*	<.1
130	Dan T Moore Co—Dan Moore	127 Public Sq Ste 2700, Cleveland OH 44114	216-771-8444	R	1*	<.1
131	Woods End Research Laboratory Inc—Will Brinton	PO Box 297, Mount Vernon ME 04352	207-293-2457	R	1*	<.1
132	CMC Associates—Colleen M McGrath	176 Roxbury Rd, Stamford CT 06902	203-968-9419	R	1	<.1

TOTALS: SIC 8732 Commercial Nonphysical Research
Companies: 132 — 10,355 — 45.5

8733 Noncommercial Research Organizations

Rank	Company Name—Executive Officer	Address, City, State, Zip	Phone	Type	Fin	Empls
1	South Carolina Research Authority Inc—Bill Mahoney	PO Box 12025, Columbia SC 29211	843-760-3200	R	172*	.2
2	Amgen Pharmaceuticals Inc—Gordon Binder	1 Amgen Ctr Dr, Thousand Oaks CA 91320	805-447-1000	R	164*	4.2
3	Rockefeller University Faculty And Sudents Club Inc—Paul Nurse	1230 York Ave, New York NY 10065	212-327-8078	R	151*	1.7
4	Wang Jing—John Mendelsohn	1400 Hermann Pressler, Houston TX 77030	713-794-4190	R	149*	5.0
5	Virginia Tech Corporate Research Center Inc—Joseph Meredith	1715 Pratt Dr Ste 1000, Blacksburg VA 24060	540-961-3600	R	146*	.1
6	Noblis Inc—Amr Elsawy	3150 Fairview Park Dr, Falls Church VA 22042	703-610-2000	R	145*	.8
7	Analytic Services Inc—Ruth David	2900 S Quincy St Ste 8, Arlington VA 22206	703-416-2000	R	139*	.6
8	WestStart-CALSTART—John Boesel	48 S Chester Ave, Pasadena CA 91106	626-744-5600	R	129*	.1
9	Abbott Molecular	1300 E Touhy, Des Plaines IL 60018		S	96*	.6
10	American Type Culture Collection Inc—Raymond Cypess	10801 University Blvd, Manassas VA 20110	703-365-2700	R	86*	.4
11	Oak Ridge Associated Universities Inc—Harry Page	PO Box 117, Oak Ridge TN 37831	865-576-3000	R	76*	.6
12	Education Development Center Inc—Luther Luedtke	55 Chapel St, Newton MA 02458	617-969-7100	R	69*	.5
13	Oklahoma Medical Research Foundation—Stephen Prescott	825 Ne 13th St, Oklahoma City OK 73104	405-271-6673	R	64*	.7
14	American Water Works Association—Terry Rolan	6666 W Quincy Ave, Denver CO 80235	303-794-7711	R	53*	.2
15	Otsuka America Pharmaceutical Inc—Hiromi Yoshikawa	2440 Research Blvd Ste, Rockville MD 20850	301-990-0030	R	47*	.6
16	NEC Laboratories Inc—Robert Millstein	4 Independence Way Ste, Princeton NJ 08540	609-520-1555	S	26*	.1
17	American Technology Research Inc	1290 Ave of the Americ, New York NY 10104	212-273-7178	S	16*	<.1
18	Cubrc Inc—Thomas Mcmahon	4455 Genesee St, Buffalo NY 14225	716-204-5100	R	15*	.1
19	i3 Statprobe—Lora H Schwab	5430 Data Ct Ste 200, Ann Arbor MI 48108	734-769-5000	R	15*	.3
20	Seattle Institute For Biomedical And Clinical Research—Eileen Lennon	1660 S Columbian Way 1, Seattle WA 98108	206-764-2730	R	14*	.1
21	Cooperative Educational Services—Max Luft	4216 Balloon Park Rd N, Albuquerque NM 87109	505-344-5470	R	13*	.2
22	Boston Biomedical Research Institute Inc—Charles Emerson	64 Grove St, Watertown MA 02472	617-658-7700	R	11*	.1
23	Carnegie Institution of Washington—Richard A Meserve	1530 P St NW, Washington DC 20005	202-387-6400	R	11*	<.1
24	Brookhaven Science Associates LLC—Lanny Bates	2 Ctr St, Upton NY 11973	631-344-8000	R	11*	.1
25	Ichauway Inc—P Hardin	3998 Jones Ctr Dr, Newton GA 39870	229-734-4706	R	8*	.1
26	R Tech Laboratories—Ed Arnold	PO Box 64101, Saint Paul MN 55164	651-481-2207	R	8*	.1
27	Haskins Laboratories Inc—Philip Rubin	300 George St Ste 900, New Haven CT 06511	203-865-6163	R	7*	.1
28	Houston Tomorrow—David Crossley	3015 Richmond Ave Ste, Houston TX 77098	713-523-5757	R	3*	<.1
29	Applied Health Physics Inc—Robert G Gallagher	2986 Industrial Blvd, Bethel Park PA 15102	412-835-9555	R	3*	<.1
30	Public Citizen Inc—Joan Claybrook	1600 20th St Nw, Washington DC 20009	202-588-1000	R	3*	.1
31	Krell Development—Wally Maschuga	5n373 Andrene Ln, Itasca IL 60143	630-773-0164	R	3*	<.1
32	Universities Research Association Inc—Frederick Bernthal	1111 19th St Nw Ste 40, Washington DC 20036	202-293-1382	R	2*	3.3
33	Research Planning Inc—Jacqueline Michel	PO Box 328, Columbia SC 29201	803-256-7322	R	2*	<.1
34	Cotton Foundation—Bill Norman	PO Box 783, Cordova TN 38088	901-274-9030	R	2*	.4
35	Engelmann-Becker Corp—Sigfried Engelmann	PO Box 10459, Eugene OR 97440	541-485-1163	R	2*	<.1
36	Webbs Machine Design Inc—John Webb	2251 Montclair Rd, Clearwater FL 33763	727-799-1768	R	2*	<.1
37	Aphios Corp—Trevor Castor	3 Gill St, Woburn MA 01801	781-932-6933	R	1*	<.1
38	Vision Sciences Research Corp—Arthur Ginsburg	130 Ryan Industrial Ct, San Ramon CA 94583	925-837-2083	R	1*	<.1
39	M and R Consulting Services Inc—Henri Maget	10633 Roselle St Ste E, San Diego CA 92121	858-552-0781	R	1*	<.1
40	Home Care Research Of Rochester Inc—Louise Woerner	85 Metro Park, Rochester NY 14623	585-272-1930	R	<1*	.5
41	Manatee River Laboratories Inc—John Roesel	1245 Mill Creek Rd, Bradenton FL 34212	941-746-6346	R	<1*	<.1
42	Sensors For Medicine And Science Inc—Marc Schneebaum	20451 Seneca Meadows P, Germantown MD 20876	301-515-7260	R	N/A	<.1

TOTALS: SIC 8733 Noncommercial Research Organizations
Companies: 42 — 1,866 — 22.1

8734 Testing Laboratories

Rank	Company Name—Executive Officer	Address, City, State, Zip	Phone	Type	Fin	Empls
1	Seminis Vegetable Seeds Inc—Kerry Preete	PO Box 1235, Twin Falls ID 83303	208-733-2667	S	1,028*	4.0
2	Charles Stark Draper Laboratory Inc—James Shields	555 Technology Sq, Cambridge MA 02139	617-258-1000	R	493*	1.1
3	GAB Robins Inc—Jim Girard	9 Campus Dr, Parsippany NJ 07054	973-993-3400	S	469*	3.3
4	Core Laboratories Inc—David M Demshur	6316 Windfern Rd, Houston TX 77040	713-328-2673	S	427	4.0
5	Radiation Therapy Services Inc—Daniel E Dosoretz	2234 Colonial Blvd, Fort Myers FL 33907	239-931-7275	R	294	1.3
6	Olympus America Inc—Mark Gumz	PO Box 610, Center Valley PA 18034	484-896-5000	S	259*	1.7
7	Tyree Organization Inc—Stephen Tyree	2702 Cindel Dr Ste 7, Riverton NJ 08077	856-303-2203	R	200*	.7
8	eResearchTechnology Inc—Jeffrey Litwin	1818 Market St Ste 100, Philadelphia PA 19103	215-972-0420	P	185	.7
9	Wyle Laboratories Inc—George Melton	1960 E Grand Ave Ste 9, El Segundo CA 90245		R	150*	.2
10	Promega Corp—William A Linton	2800 Woods Hollow Rd, Madison WI 53711	608-274-4330	R	145*	1.2
11	National Technical Systems Inc—William C McGinnis	24007 Ventura Blvd Ste, Calabasas CA 91302	818-591-0776	P	144	1.1
12	Landauer Inc—William E Saxelby	2 Science Rd, Glenwood IL 60425	708-755-7000	P	120	.6
13	Hoffman Engineering Corp—Andrew Sadlon	PO Box 4430, Stamford CT 06907	203-425-8900	R	102*	.1
14	WuXi AppTec Inc—Ge Li	2540 Executive Dr, St Paul MN 55120	615-675-2000	S	100*	.3
15	Unified Testing Services Inc—Don Uptain	PO Box 37, Woodstock AL 35188	205-938-3313	R	93*	.1
16	Genova Diagnostics—Ted Hull	63 Zillicoa St, Asheville NC 28801	828-253-0621	R	84*	.3
17	BioClinica Inc—John Blank	826 Newtown-Yardley Rd, Newtown PA 18940	267-757-3000	P	84	.5
18	HC Nutting Co—Jack Scott	611 Lunken Park Dr, Cincinnati OH 45226	513-321-5816	R	67*	.2
19	Orchid Cellmark Inc—Thomas A Bologna	4390 US Rte 1, Princeton NJ 08540	609-750-2200	P	64	.5
20	US Laboratories Inc—Dickerson Wright	7895 Convoy Ct Ste 18, San Diego CA 92111	858-715-5800	S	52*	.7
21	Froehling and Robertson Inc—Samuel Kirby	3015 Dumbarton Rd, Richmond VA 23228	804-264-2701	R	49*	.4
22	Southern Petroleum Laboratory Inc—Herman Brown	8880 Interchange Dr, Houston TX 77054	713-660-0901	R	44*	.1
23	Miltec Corp—Don Miller	678 Discovery Dr, Huntsville AL 35806	256-428-1301	S	42	N/A
24	Columbia Analytical Services Inc—Steve Vincent	1317 S 13th Ave, Kelso WA 98626	360-577-7222	R	41*	.4
25	Accutest Laboratories—Vincent J Pugliese	2235 US Hwy 130, Dayton NJ 08810	732-329-0200	R	40*	.3
26	Rjlg Ventures Inc—Richard Lee	350 Hochberg Rd, Monroeville PA 15146	724-325-1776	R	39*	.3
27	Twining Laboratories Of Southern California Inc—Brian Kramer	2883 E Spring St Ste 3, Long Beach CA 90806	562-426-3355	R	37*	.2
28	Nelson Laboratories Inc—Jeff Nelson	PO Box 571830, Salt Lake City UT 84157	801-290-7500	R	37*	.4
29	Evans East	104 Windsor Ctr Dr Ste, East Windsor NJ 08520	609-371-4800	S	34*	.1
30	Soil Consultants Engineering Inc—Donn Smith	9303 Center St, Manassas VA 20110	703-366-3000	R	33*	.1
31	Tanknology-NDE International Inc—Allen Porter	11000 N MoPac #500, Austin TX 78759	512-380-7220	R	32*	.2

Rank	Company Name—*Executive Officer*	Address, City, State, Zip	Phone	Type	Fin	Empls
32	Alere Toxicology Services Inc—*John Peterson*	1111 Newton St, Gretna LA 70053	504-361-8989	S	32*	.2
33	International Semiconductor Engineering Laboratories—*Tien Wu*	46800 Bayside Pky, Fremont CA 94538	510-687-2500	S	32*	.1
34	Universal Engineering Sciences Inc—*Seymour Israel*	3532 Maggie Blvd, Orlando FL 32811	407-423-0504	R	32*	.6
35	Smithers Viscient North America—*Donald Surprenant*	790 Main St, Wareham MA 02571	508-295-2550	S	31*	.2
36	Qc Inc—*Allen Schopbach*	PO Box 514, Southampton PA 18966	215-355-3900	R	30*	.2
37	Lifecodes Corp—*Walter O Fredericks* Orchid Cellmark Inc	550 West Ave, Stamford CT 06902	203-328-9500	S	30*	.2
38	Integrium LLC—*David Smith*	14351 Myford Rd, Tustin CA 92780	714-541-5591	R	30*	.1
39	Bode Technology Group Inc—*Barry Watson*	10430 Furnace Rd Ste 1, Lorton VA 22079	703-646-9740	S	29*	.1
40	Radisphere National Radiology Group—*Scott Seidelmann*	23625 Commerce Park St, Beachwood OH 44122	216-255-5700	R	29*	.1
41	Triad Engineering Inc—*Randy Moulton*	4980 Teays Valley Rd, Scott Depot WV 25560	304-755-0721	R	28*	.2
42	Mde International Inc—*Jeffrey Koch*	4033 S Ctr Rd, Burton MI 48519	810-743-5980	R	28*	.2
43	MEC Analytical Systems Inc—*Patrick G McCann*	2433 Impala Dr, Carlsbad CA 92010	760-795-6900	S	27*	.1
44	TUV Product Services—*Karstan Xander*	1775 Old Hwy 8 NW Ste, New Brighton MN 55112	651-631-2487	S	26*	.2
45	Integra Technologies—*John Titizian*	321 Coral Cir, El Segundo CA 90245	310-606-0855	R	26*	.1
46	Westmoreland Mechanical Testing and Research Inc—*Donald Rossi*	PO Box 388, Youngstown PA 15696	724-537-3131	R	26*	.2
47	Magna Chek Inc—*Waleed Hijazin*	32701 Edward Ave, Madison Heights MI 48071	248-597-0089	R	25*	.2
48	Spectrum Analytical Inc—*Hanibal Tayeh*	11 Almgren Dr, Agawam MA 01001	413-789-9018	R	23*	.2
49	Microbac's Wilson Division—*Richard Higby*	3809 Airport Dr, Wilson NC 27896	252-237-4175	D	22*	.1
50	Tektronix Service Solutions	PO Box 500, Beaverton OR 97077	410-842-1000	S	22*	.1
51	Mineral Labs Inc—*Edwin Lyon*	PO Box 549, Salyersville KY 41465	606-349-6145	R	21*	.2
52	USA Environmental Management Inc—*George W Woods*	8436 Enterprise Ave, Philadelphia PA 19153	215-365-5810	R	20*	.1
53	GEOMET Technologies Inc—*Ted Prociv*	20251 Century Blvd Ste, Germantown MD 20874	301-428-9898	S	20*	<.1
54	Kett Engineering Corp—*Eric Stromsborg*	15500 Erwin St Ste 102, Van Nuys CA 91411	818-908-5388	R	19*	.5
55	SD Myers Inc—*Scott Myers*	180 S Ave, Tallmadge OH 44278	330-630-7000	R	19*	.2
56	Specialized Technology Resources Inc (Canton Massachusetts)	85 John Rd, Canton MA 02021	781-821-2200	S	19*	.1
57	SGS Northview Laboratories Inc—*Martin Spalding*	1880 Holste Rd, Northbrook IL 60062	847-564-8181	R	18*	.1
58	Incon Processing LLC	970 Douglas Rd, Batavia IL 60510	630-761-1180	R	17*	<.1
59	Certified Testing Laboratories Inc—*Joseph Citardi*	PO Box 705, Bordentown NJ 08505	609-298-3255	R	16*	.1
60	Defiance Testing and Engineering Services Inc—*Peter Dodd*	1628 Northwood Dr, Troy MI 48084	248-458-5900	S	15*	.2
61	Midwest Laboratories Inc—*Ken Pohlman*	13611 B St, Omaha NE 68144	402-334-7770	R	15*	.1
62	Moore Twining Associates Inc—*Harry Moore*	PO Box 1472, Fresno CA 93716	559-268-7021	R	15*	.1
63	Charles River Malvern—*Douglas Rogers*	358 Technology Dr, Malvern PA 19355	610-640-4550	D	15*	.1
64	Compass Water Solutions Inc—*Daniel Grommersch*	1732 Mcgaw Ave, Irvine CA 92614	949-222-5777	R	15*	.1
65	Curtis-Straus LLC—*John Curtis*	527 Great Rd, Littleton MA 01460	978-486-8880	R	15*	.1
66	PARC Technical Services Inc—*Geoffrey Geoff*	100 William Pitt Way, Pittsburgh PA 15238	412-423-1120	S	15*	.1
67	ASAT Inc—*Eric Thompson*	490 N McCarthy Blvd St, Milpitas CA 95035	408-964-7400	R	15*	.1
68	Detroit Testing Laboratory Inc—*Earl Smith*	27485 George Merrelli, Warren MI 48092	586-754-9000	R	15*	.1
69	ABC Laboratories Inc—*Byron E Hill*	7200 E ABC Ln, Columbia MO 65202		R	12*	.2
70	Patriot Engineering and Environmental Inc—*William Dubois*	6330 E 75th St Ste 216, Indianapolis IN 46250	317-576-8058	R	11*	.2
71	Pathology Associates International Corp—*Mark Butt*	15 Wormans Mill Ct Ste, Frederick MD 21701	301-663-1644	S	11*	.2
72	Analysts Inc—*Michael Forgeron*	3401 Jack Northrop Ave, Hawthorne CA 90250	310-219-5000	R	11*	.2
73	Lawrence Ripak Company Inc—*Lawrence Ripak*	165 Field St, West Babylon NY 11704	631-249-4585	R	11*	.1
74	American Analytical Chemistry Laboratories Corp—*Charlie Li*	711 Parkland Ct, Champaign IL 61821	217-352-6060	S	11*	<.1
75	The Testing Group—*Lauren Evers*	1265 Los Angeles St St, Glendale CA 91204	818-241-7373	R	11*	<.1
76	American Reliability Labs Inc—*Richard Guarani*	150 Charles St, Malden MA 02148	781-321-7401	R	11*	.1
77	Test America Analytical Testing Corp—*Gary Steube*	17461 Derian Ave Ste 1, Irvine CA 92614	949-261-1022	R	10*	.1
78	General Testing and Inspection Inc—*Jay Haber*	8427 Atlantic Ave, Cudahy CA 90201	323-583-1653	R	10*	.1
79	De Par Inc—*Tito Parola*	806 N Batavia St, Orange CA 92868	714-771-6900	R	10*	.1
80	Mayes Testing Engineers—*Mike Mayes*	20225 Cedar Valley Rd, Lynnwood WA 98036	425-742-9360	R	10*	.1
81	Graham-Massey Analytical Laboratories Inc—*Matt Leahy*	60 Todd Rd, Shelton CT 06484	203-926-1100	R	10*	<.1
82	Plastic Technologies Inc—*Thomas Brady*	PO Box 964, Holland OH 43528	419-867-5400	R	10*	.1
83	BC Laboratories Inc—*Carolyn Jackson*	4100 Atlas Ct, Bakersfield CA 93308	661-327-4911	R	10*	.1
84	Dickson Testing Company Inc—*Robert Lyddon*	11126 Palmer Ave, South Gate CA 90280	562-862-8378	R	9*	.1
85	Minnesota Valley Testing Laboratories Inc—*Thomas R Berg*	1126 N Front St, New Ulm MN 56073	507-354-8517	R	9*	<.1
86	Bioscreen Testing Services Inc—*Bradford Rope*	3904 Del Amo Blvd Ste, Torrance CA 90503	310-214-0043	R	9*	.1
87	Edward S Babcock and Sons Inc—*Larry Chrystal*	PO Box 432, Riverside CA 92502	951-653-3351	R	8*	.1
88	Northwest EMC—*Dean Ghizzone*	22975 NW Evergreen Pky, Hillsboro OR 97124	503-844-4066	R	8*	<.1
89	Aircraft Xray Laboratories Inc—*Donald Johnson*	5216 Pacific Blvd, Huntington Park CA 90255	323-587-4141	R	8*	.1
90	Environmental Treatment and Technology Inc—*Edgar Caballero*	PO Box 92797, Long Beach CA 90809	562-989-4045	R	8*	.1
91	Garwood Laboratories Inc—*Jim Armstrong*	7829 Industry Ave, Pico Rivera CA 90660	562-949-2727	R	8*	.1
92	Sgs Life Science Services—*Jeff Mcdonald*	616 Heathrow Dr, Lincolnshire IL 60069	847-821-8900	S	8*	.1
93	Southern Soil Environmental Inc—*Kenny Jenkins*	PO Box 777, Haughton LA 71037	318-949-3436	R	7*	<.1
94	American Assay Laboratories Inc—*George Burke*	1500 Glendale Ave, Sparks NV 89431	775-356-0606	R	7*	.1
95	Fruit Growers Laboratory Inc—*Kelly Dunnahoo*	853 Corporation St, Santa Paula CA 93060	805-392-2000	R	7*	.1
96	Delta Testing and Inspection Inc—*William H Brenner*	1855 Mason Ave, Baton Rouge LA 70805	225-356-4355	S	7*	.1
97	Adirondack Environmental Services Inc—*Paul Batista*	314 N Pearl St, Albany NY 12207	518-434-4546	R	7*	<.1
98	Western Environmental Services and Testing Inc—*Alan Roylance*	913 Foster Rd, Casper WY 82601	307-234-5511	R	7*	<.1
99	Magnetic Inspection Laboratory Inc—*Bob Schiewe*	1401 Greenleaf Ave, Elk Grove Village IL 60007	847-437-4488	R	6*	.1
100	Mar-Test Inc—*Steven Etter*	1245 Hill Smith Dr, Cincinnati OH 45215	513-326-3821	R	6*	<.1
101	Wave Systems Corp (Sunnyvale California)—*Steven Sprague*	1159 Sonora Ct, Sunnyvale CA 94086	408-524-8630	R	6*	.1
102	National Everclean Services Inc—*John Mcshane*	28632 Roadside Dr Ste, Agoura Hills CA 91301		R	6*	.1
103	New Jersey Micro Electronic Testing Inc—*Giacomo Federico*	1240 Main Ave, Clifton NJ 07011	973-546-5393	R	6*	.1
104	Delisle Inc—*Robert Delisle*	PO Box 69, South Windsor CT 06074	860-289-8225	R	6*	.1
105	Abc Research Corp—*George Baker*	3437 Sw 24th Ave, Gainesville FL 32607	352-372-0436	R	6*	.1
106	West Penn Non-Destructive Testing Inc—*N Campbell*	1010 Industrial Blvd, New Kensington PA 15068	724-334-1900	R	6*	.1
107	Apex Instruments Inc—*William Howe*	204 Technology Park Ln, Fuquay Varina NC 27526	919-557-7300	R	6*	<.1
108	Huggins Metal Finishing Inc—*Jim Wand*	995 N Service Rd W, Sullivan MO 63080	573-468-8049	R	5*	.1
109	Link Testing Laboratories Inc—*Roy Link*	43855 Plymouth Oaks Bl, Plymouth MI 48170	734-453-0800	R	5*	.1
110	Celsis Laboratory Group—*Jay LeCoque*	6200 S Lindbergh Blvd, Saint Louis MO 63123	314-487-6776	D	5*	.2
111	Testing Engineers Inc—*Gary Snyder*	2811 Teagarden St, San Leandro CA 94577	510-835-3142	R	5*	.1
112	Texas Research International Inc—*Micheal Dingus*	9063 Bee Caves Rd, Austin TX 78733		R	5	.1
113	Truesdail Laboratories Inc—*John Hill*	14201 Franklin Ave, Tustin CA 92780	714-730-6239	R	5*	.1
114	Centauri Laboratories LLC—*Joe Hernandez*	7210A Corporate Ct, Frederick MD 21703	240-575-1150	R	5*	<.1
115	Hi-Rel Laboratories Inc—*Trevor Devaney*	6116 N Freya St, Spokane WA 99217	509-325-5800	R	5*	<.1
116	Chromalab Inc—*Eric Tam*	1220 Quarry Ln, Pleasanton CA 94566	925-484-1919	R	5*	<.1

Note: An asterisk (*) indicates an estimated financial figure. The company type code used is as follows: R = Private, P = Public, S = Private Subsidiary, B = Public Subsidiary, D = Division, J = Joint Venture, I = Investment Fund.

COMPANY RANKINGS BY SALES WITHIN 4-DIGIT SIC

Rank	Company Name—Executive Officer	Address, City, State, Zip	Phone	Type	Fin	Empls
117	Penniman and Browne Inc—Louis Wittenberg	PO Box 65309, Baltimore MD 21209	410-825-4131	R	5*	<.1
118	Praxair Services Inc—Stephen F Angel	39 Old Ridgebury Rd, Danbury CT 06810		S	5*	<.1
119	ClinAssure Inc—Stacey Pittman	19200 Von Karman Ste 8, Irvine CA 92612	949-502-6001	R	5*	<.1
120	The M and P Lab—Frank E Anderson	PO Box 724, Schenectady NY 12301	518-382-0082	S	5*	<.1
121	Anmar Metrology Inc—Martin Bakker	7726 Arjons Dr, San Diego CA 92126	858-621-2630	R	5*	<.1
122	Solecon Laboratories Inc—Dave Dickey	770 Trademark Dr, Reno NV 89521	775-853-5900	R	5*	<.1
123	Michelson Laboratories Inc—Jack Michelson	6280 Chalet Dr, Commerce CA 90040	562-928-0553	R	5*	.1
124	St Louis Testing Laboratories Inc—Willard Trowbridge	2810 Clark Ave, Saint Louis MO 63103	314-531-8080	R	4*	<.1
125	Environmental Testing and Consulting Inc—Nathan Pera	2790 Whitten Rd, Memphis TN 38133	901-213-2400	R	4*	<.1
126	Integrated Paper Services Inc—Bruce Shafer	3211 E Capitol Dr, Appleton WI 54911	920-749-3040	R	4*	<.1
127	Retlif Testing Laboratories—Walter A Poggi	795 Marconi Ave, Ronkonkoma NY 11779	631-737-1500	R	4*	<.1
128	RWTUV USA—Hans Groothuis	11 Red Roof Ln Ste 1B, Salem NH 03079	973-773-8880	S	4*	<.1
129	American Interplex Corporation Laboratories—Asa Morton	8600 Kanis Rd, Little Rock AR 72204	501-224-5060	R	4*	<.1
130	Stork East-West Technology Corp—David Lichtman	15814 Corporate Cir, Jupiter FL 33478	561-776-7339	R	4*	<.1
131	Trace laboratories Inc	1150 W Euclid Ave, Palatine IL 60067	847-934-5300	S	4*	<.1
132	Kellco Services Inc—Bonnie L Kellogg	3137 Diablo Ave, Hayward CA 94545	510-786-9751	R	4*	<.1
133	Vascular Associates Laboratory Inc—Don Varnado	8595 Picardy Ave, Baton Rouge LA 70809	225-769-4266	R	4*	<.1
134	Martel Laboratories JDS Inc—Joseph Wolfkill	1025 Cromwell Bridge R, Baltimore MD 21286	410-825-7790	R	4*	<.1
135	United States Drug Testing Laboratories Inc—Douglas Lewis	1700 S Mount Prospect, Des Plaines IL 60018	847-375-0770	R	4*	<.1
136	International Hydronics Corp—Bruce Bruns	PO Box 243, Rocky Hill NJ 08553	609-921-9216	R	4*	<.1
137	Flood Testing Laboratories Inc—Walter Flood	1945 E 87th St, Chicago IL 60617	773-721-2200	R	4*	<.1
138	Dnb Engineering Inc—Al Broaddus	3535 W Commonwealth Av, Fullerton CA 92833	714-870-7781	R	4*	<.1
139	Acz Laboratories Inc—Bradley Craig	2773 Downhill Dr, Steamboat Springs CO 80487	970-879-6590	R	4*	<.1
140	Katech Inc—John Kayl	24324 Sorrentino Ct, Clinton Township MI 48035	586-791-4120	R	4*	<.1
141	Fitzco Inc—June Fitz	4300 Shoreline Dr, Spring Park MN 55384	952-471-1185	R	4*	<.1
142	Monarch Analytical Laboratories Inc—Dennis Brengartner	349 Tomahawk Dr, Maumee OH 43537	419-897-9000	R	4*	<.1
143	Cmt Laboratories Inc—Frank Welsh	2701 Carolean Industri, State College PA 16801	814-231-8845	R	4*	<.1
144	QC Laboratories Inc—R Stickler	2870 Stirling Rd, Hollywood FL 33020	954-925-0499	R	3*	<.1
145	Chemir Analytical Services Inc—Shri Thanedar	PO Box 502832, Saint Louis MO 63150	314-291-6620	R	3*	.1
146	Atlas Testing Laboratories Inc—H Norton	9820 6th St, Rancho Cucamonga CA 91730	909-373-4130	R	3*	<.1
147	Durkee Testing Laboratories Inc—John Durkee	PO Box 1401, Paramount CA 90723	562-531-7111	R	3*	.1
148	Inspection Services Inc—Doug Stewart	7820 S 210th St Ste 11, Kent WA 98032	206-764-8123	R	3*	<.1
149	JT Adams Company Inc—Tim Adams	4520 Willow Pkwy, Cleveland OH 44125	216-641-3290	R	3*	<.1
150	Liberty Laboratories Inc—Gary Caywood	484 Vista Way, Milpitas CA 95035	408-262-6633	R	3*	<.1
151	Ardl Inc—Valerie Jenkins	PO Box 1566, Mount Vernon IL 62864	618-244-3235	R	3*	<.1
152	TRI Environmental Inc—Micheal Dingus Texas Research International Inc	9063 Bee Caves Rd, Austin TX 78733	512-263-2101	S	3*	.1
153	Lambda Research Inc—Paul S Prevey	3929 Virginia Ave, Cincinnati OH 45227	513-561-0883	R	3*	<.1
154	A and L Southern Agricultural Labs Inc—Lynn Griffith	1199 W Newport Ctr Dr, Deerfield Beach FL 33442	954-571-2103	R	3*	<.1
155	Oneida Research Services Inc—Thomas J Rossiter	8282 Halsey Rd, Whitesboro NY 13492	315-736-5480	R	3*	<.1
156	Turbine Trend Analysis Inc—Jon Anderson	PO Box 642, Clovis CA 93613		R	3*	<.1
157	Gaudet Associates Inc—Joseph E Gaudet	3021 Jupiter Park Cir, Jupiter FL 33458	561-748-3040	R	3*	<.1
158	Control Automation Technologies—Michael Watson	PO Box 6598, Williamsburg VA 23188	804-966-7585	R	3*	<.1
159	Analytical Laboratories Inc—Mike Moore	1804 N 33rd St, Boise ID 83703	208-342-5515	R	3*	<.1
160	Industrial Testing Laboratory—Shri Phanedar	2672 Metro Blvd, Maryland Heights MO 63043	314-738-9600	R	3*	<.1
161	Savant Inc—Theodore Selby	4800 James Savage Rd, Midland MI 48642	989-496-2301	R	3*	<.1
162	Morse Laboratories LLC—Kevin Clark	1525 Fulton Ave, Sacramento CA 95825	916-481-3141	S	3*	<.1
163	Cal Testing Services Inc—Larry Kondrat	PO Box 1510, Highland IN 46322	219-923-9800	R	3*	<.1
164	Alpha Spectra Inc—Frank Wilkinson	715 Arrowest Ct, Grand Junction CO 81505	970-243-4477	R	2*	<.1
165	Industrial Laboratories Company Inc—Mark Wong	4046 Youngfield St, Wheat Ridge CO 80033	303-287-9691	R	2*	<.1
166	Dyess-Peterson Testing Laboratory Inc—Dalana Peterson	PO Box 30699, Amarillo TX 79120	806-372-4911	R	2*	<.1
167	James Rilott Enterprises Inc—Scott Twigg	9865 N Alpine Rd, Machesney Park IL 61115	815-877-0880	R	2*	<.1
168	Primary Instruments Inc—Alan Ganner	9553 Vassar Ave, Chatsworth CA 91311	818-993-4971	R	2*	<.1
169	Tetra Tech Inc (Kansas City Kansas)—Dan Batrack	721 S Packard St, Kansas City KS 66105	913-321-8100	R	2*	.1
170	BTC Laboratories Inc—Scott Moors US Laboratories Inc	2978 Seaborg Ave, Ventura CA 93003	805-656-6074	S	2*	<.1
171	Construction Engineering Consultants Inc—Joseph Artuso	2018 Waverly St, Pittsburgh PA 15218	412-351-6465	R	2*	<.1
172	Ledoux and Company Inc—Bruce Peterson	359 Alfred Ave, Teaneck NJ 07666	201-387-7160	R	2*	<.1
173	O'Brien and Gere Laboratories Inc—Leland Davis	PO Box 4873, Syracuse NY 13221	315-437-6100	D	2*	<.1
174	Alfred H Knight North America Ltd—Graham Walls	PO Box 3504, Spartanburg SC 29304	864-595-1903	R	2*	<.1
175	Delsen Testing Laboratories Inc—John Moylan	1024 Grand Central Ave, Glendale CA 91201	818-247-4106	R	2*	<.1
176	Joliet Metallurgical Laboratories Inc—Wylie Mullen	PO Box 2489, Joliet IL 60434	815-725-9500	R	2*	<.1
177	AmTest Air Quality—Steve Fryberger	PO Box 525, Preston WA 98050	425-222-7746	S	2*	<.1
178	Rsa Industries Inc—Roger Arnold	870 N Batavia St, Orange CA 92868	714-997-0291	R	2*	<.1
179	SEAL Laboratories—Arun Kumar	250 N Nash St, El Segundo CA 90245	310-322-2011	S	2*	<.1
180	Environmental Micro Analysis Inc	40 N East St, Woodland CA 95776	530-666-6890	R	2*	<.1
181	CAP Index Inc—Steven K Aurand	150 John Robert Thomas, Exton PA 19341	610-903-3000	R	2*	<.1
182	Turner Laboratories Inc—Nancy D Turner	2445 N Coyote Dr, Tucson AZ 85745	520-882-5880	R	2*	<.1
183	Advanced Fuel Research Inc—James R Markham	87 Church St, E Hartford CT 06108	860-528-9806	R	2*	<.1
184	Alamo Analytical Lab—Karen Oldham	10526 Gulfdale, San Antonio TX 78216	210-340-8121	R	2*	<.1
185	Specialized Vehicles Inc—Michael Koran	2468 Industrial Row Dr, Troy MI 48084	248-280-2000	R	2*	<.1
186	Micro Tracers Inc—David Eisenberg	1370 Van Dyke Ave, San Francisco CA 94124	415-822-1100	R	2*	<.1
187	Sterilchek Sterilizer Management Services—Lonna Bernhard-Calas	PO Box 65139, Seattle WA 98155	206-367-5998	R	2*	<.1
188	Toy Tips Inc—Marianne M Szymanski	3611 Jerelin Dr, Franklin WI 53132	414-421-9668	R	2*	<.1
189	Envirometrics Inc—Michael Ruby	4128 Burke Ave N, Seattle WA 98103	206-633-4456	R	2*	<.1
190	Pro-Pack Testing Laboratory Inc—Manuel Rosa Jr	2385 Amann Dr, Belleville IL 62220	618-277-1160	R	2*	<.1
191	Surfaces Research and Applications Inc—Barbara J Kinzig	8330 Melrose Dr, Lenexa KS 66214	913-541-1221	R	2*	<.1
192	Advanced Systems Research Inc—Kevin Redmond	3399 Sw 42nd Ave, Palm City FL 34990	772-287-5802	R	2*	<.1
193	Ultratest International Inc—Robert Scoggins	7326 Craigshire Ave, Dallas TX 75231	214-340-5252	R	2*	<.1
194	Gonzales Industrial X Ray Inc—Ronald Williams	PO Box 481, Prairieville LA 70769	225-673-6600	R	2*	<.1
195	Cascade Technical Sciences Inc—Douglas Barrett	5245 Ne Elam Young Pkw, Hillsboro OR 97124	503-648-1818	R	2*	<.1
196	Geoanalytical Laboratories Inc—Donna Keller	2300 Maryann Dr, Turlock CA 95380	209-669-0900	R	2*	<.1
197	Spherix Inc—Claire L Kruger	6430 Rockledge Dr Ste, Bethesda MD 20817	301-897-2540	P	1	<.1
198	Ems Laboratories Inc—Bernadine Kolk	117 W Bellevue Dr, Pasadena CA 91105	626-568-4065	R	1*	<.1
199	Progreen Properties Inc—Jan Telander	380 North Old Woodward, Birmingham MI 48009	248-530-0725	P	1	<.1
200	Elliott Laboratories—Eddie Pavlu National Technical Systems Inc	684 W Maude Ave, Sunnyvale CA 94085	408-245-7800	S	1*	<.1
201	Flow Dynamics Inc—Christopher Royan	15555 N 79th Pl, Scottsdale AZ 85260	480-948-3789	R	1*	<.1
202	Inspection Specialists Inc—Rodney C Dufour	5201 Taravella Rd, Marrero LA 70072	504-347-5600	R	1*	<.1

Rank	Company Name—*Executive Officer*	Address, City, State, Zip	Phone	Type	Fin	Empls
203	Rhein Tech Laboratories Inc—*Desmond Fraser*	360 Herndon Pkwy Ste 1, Herndon VA 20170	703-689-0368	R	1*	<.1
204	Micron Inc—*James F Ficca Jr*	3815 Lancaster Pke, Wilmington DE 19805	302-998-1184	R	1*	<.1
205	EnHealth Environmental Inc—*James Litrides*	1409 SE 1st Ave, Fort Lauderdale FL 33316	954-522-5040	R	1*	<.1
206	Optical Data Associates LLC—*Michael Ray Jacobson*	5237 E 7th St, Tucson AZ 85711	520-748-7333	R	1*	<.1
207	Protegga LLC—*Amy Fogarty*	730 E Park Blvd Ste 21, Plano TX 75074	214-988-9240	R	1*	<.1
208	Compliance Worldwide Inc—*Larry Stillings*	357 Main St, Sandown NH 03873	603-887-3903	R	1	<.1
209	ADVENTRX Pharmaceuticals Inc—*Brian M Culley*	12390 El Camino Rd Ste, San Diego CA 92130	858-552-0866	P	1	<.1

TOTALS: SIC 8734 Testing Laboratories
Companies: 209   **6,442**   **36.2**

8741 Management Services

Rank	Company Name—*Executive Officer*	Address, City, State, Zip	Phone	Type	Fin	Empls
1	Christus Health Inc—*Ernie Sadau*	6363 N Hwy 161 Ste 450, Irving TX 75038	214-492-8500	R	224,138*	35.0
2	Chubb and Son Inc—*John D Finnegan*	15 Mountain View Rd, Warren NJ 07059	908-903-2000	D	11,634*	10.4
3	Concentra Inc—*James Greenwood*	5080 Spectrum Dr Ste 1, Addison TX 75001	972-364-8000	S	10,000*	100.0
4	PHH Corp—*Jim Egan*	PO Box 5452, Mount Laurel NJ 08054	856-917-1744	P	9,777	5.7
5	CT Corporation System—*Christopher Cartwright*	111 8th Ave Fl 13, New York NY 10011	212-894-8940	S	4,119*	1.5
6	ServiceMaster Co—*Hank Mullany*	860 Ridge Lake Blvd, Memphis TN 38120	901-597-1400	R	3,750	52.0
7	JA Jones Inc—*JP Bolduc*	8206 Providence Rd Ste, Charlotte NC 28277	704-553-3000	R	3,300	12.0
8	ManTech International Corp—*George J Pedersen*	12015 Lee Jackson Hwy, Fairfax VA 22033	703-218-6000	P	2,870	9.3
9	O'Brien and Gere Technical Services Inc—*James A Fox*	PO Box 4873, Syracuse NY 13221	315-437-6100	S	2,762*	.9
10	Saunders Hotels Group—*Jeffrey Saunders*	240 Newbury St, Boston MA 02116	617-861-9000	R	2,303*	.6
11	CACI Field Services Inc	1100 N Glebe Rd, Arlington VA 22201	703-841-7800	S	2,252*	5.7
12	Georgia Baptist Health Care System Inc—*Frank Upchurch*	6405 Sugarloaf Pkwy, Duluth GA 30097	770-497-4170	R	1,517*	1.3
13	Gartner Inc—*Eugene A Hall*	56 Top Gallant Rd, Stamford CT 06904	203-964-0096	P	1,469	5.0
14	Ohio Health—*David Blum*	180 E Broad St, Columbus OH 43215	614-544-4455	R	1,457*	15.3
15	Raytheon Technical Services Company LLC—*John D Harris II*	22265 Pacific Blvd, Dulles VA 20166	571-250-3399	S	1,330*	9.5
16	Hunt Construction Group Inc—*Robert G Hunt* Hunt Corp (Scottsdale Arizona)	6720 N Scottsdale Rd S, Scottsdale AZ 85253	480-368-4700	S	1,310*	.7
17	Hunt Corp (Scottsdale Arizona)—*Robert G Hunt*	6720 N Scottsdale Rd S, Scottsdale AZ 85253	480-368-4700	R	1,300*	.7
18	Geisinger Health System—*Glenn D Steele Jr MD PhD*	100 N Academy Ave, Danville PA 17822	570-271-6211	R	1,293*	8.4
19	Lifespan Corp—*George Vecchione*	167 Point St, Providence RI 02903	401-444-3500	R	1,284*	12.0
20	Evanston Northwestern Healthcare—*Mark R Neaman*	2650 Ridge Ave, Evanston IL 60201	847-570-2000	R	1,273*	9.0
21	Oce Business Services—*Joseph Marciano*	460 W 34th St 6th Fl, New York NY 10001	212-502-2100	D	1,222*	5.5
22	Property Insight LLC—*John Walsh*	4050 Calle Real, Santa Barbara CA 93110		S	1,222*	.5
23	CH2M Hill Industrial Design Corp	2020 SW 4th Ave, Portland OR 97201		S	1,070*	.7
24	Vanir Group of Companies—*Patricia Green*	290 N D St 9th Fl, San Bernardino CA 92401	909-884-9477	R	1,018*	.4
25	Fringe Benefits Management Co—*Lorraine Strickland*	PO Box 1878, Tallahassee FL 32303	850-425-6200	R	967*	.4
26	Zirmed Inc—*Jerry Merritt*	888 W Market St Ste 40, Louisville KY 40202	502-473-7709	R	865*	.3
27	Kirby Pines Estates—*Michael Escamilla*	3535 Kirby Rd, Memphis TN 38115	901-365-3665	R	817*	.3
28	Daniel O'Connell's Sons Inc—*Robert I McCullough* O'Connell Companies Inc	480 Hampden St, Holyoke MA 01040	413-534-5667	S	700*	3.0
29	Jeffrey M Brown Associates Inc—*Jeffrey M Brown*	2337 Philmont Ave Ste, Huntingdon Valley PA 19006	215-938-5000	R	690*	.2
30	Fox Associates LLC—*Richard Baker*	527 N Grand Blvd, Saint Louis MO 63103	314-534-1678	R	652*	.2
31	Michael Baker Corp—*Bradley Mallory*	PO Box 12259, Pittsburgh PA 15231	412-269-6300	P	499	2.9
32	O'Connell Companies Inc—*Richard J Hanson*	480 Hampden St, Holyoke MA 01040	413-534-5667	R	439*	.2
33	CBIZ Benefits and Insurance Services Inc	1 City Pl Dr Ste 570, Saint Louis MO 63141	314-692-2249	S	432*	.1
34	Universal Technical Resource Services Inc—*Jerry Wright*	950 N Kings Hwy Ste 20, Cherry Hill NJ 08034	856-667-6770	R	421*	.2
35	EmCare Holdings Inc—*Todd G Zimmerman*	1717 Main St Ste 5200, Dallas TX 75201	214-712-2000	S	413*	5.0
36	Clark Construction Company Inc—*Charles J Clark*	PO Box 40087, Lansing MI 48901	517-372-0940	R	412*	.2
37	Health Management Corporation of America—*Raymond Damadian*	110 Marcus Dr, Melville NY 11747	631-694-2816	S	402*	.2
38	HMCM Inc—*Raymond Damadian*	110 Marcus Dr, Melville NY 11747	631-694-2929	S	402*	.2
39	Brainstorm Logistics LLC—*Marc Farbstein*	PO Box 2024, Pine Brook NJ 07058	973-227-5844	R	400*	.2
40	Wheaton Franciscan Healthcare—*John D Oliveiro*	400 W River Woods Pkwy, Glendale WI 53212	414-465-3000	R	371*	9.0
41	Strategic Outsourcing Inc—*Bob Fotsh*	PO Box 241448, Charlotte NC 28224	704-523-2191	S	363*	.1
42	Louisiana Lottery Corp—*Rose I ludson*	555 Laurel St, Baton Rouge LA 70801	225-297-2000	R	339*	.2
43	Bad Boy Worldwide Entertainment Group—*Sean Combs*	1710 Broadway, New York NY 10019	212-381-1540	R	300*	.6
44	Advisory Board Co—*Robert M Musslewhite*	2445 M St NW, Washington DC 20037	202-266-5600	P	290	1.6
45	Tennis Corporation of America—*Steven Schwartz*	3611 N Kedzie Ave, Chicago IL 60618	773-463-1234	R	280*	1.7
46	Music Center Operating Co—*Andrea L Vander Kamp*	135 N Grand Ave, Los Angeles CA 90012	213-972-7211	R	270*	.1
47	Talon (Princeton New Jersey)—*Daniel Reynolds*	202 Carnegie Center Dr, Princeton NJ 08540	609-924-8900	R	270*	.1
48	Virtual Meeting Strategies Inc—*Andrea Heslin Smiley*	8425 Woodfield Crossin, Indianapolis IN 46240	317-805-6600	R	270*	.1
49	CBIZ Benefits and Insurance Services of Maryland Inc—*Steven Gerard*	9755 Patuxent Woods Dr, Columbia MD 21046	410-647-4200	S	270*	.1
50	ISS Solutions—*Peter Brooks*	2010 Cabot Blvd W, Langhorne PA 19047	215-752-2221	R	264*	.1
51	Alvin H Butz Inc—*Greg Butz*	PO Box 509, Allentown PA 18105	610-395-6871	R	259*	.1
52	Alden Systems Inc—*William Johnson*	10 Inverness Center Dr, Birmingham AL 35242	205-978-2400	R	251*	.1
53	Network Global Logistics—*Ray J Garcia*	320 Interlocken Pkwy S, Broomfield CO 80021		R	235*	1.0
54	Gentle Dental Service Corp—*Norman Huffaker*	9800 S La Cienega Blvd, Inglewood CA 90301	310-765-2400	S	226*	.2
55	Rhs Corp—*James Holmes*	PO Box 3391, Redlands CA 92373	909-335-5500	R	222*	1.5
56	Akron General Health System—*Michael West*	400 Wabash Ave, Akron OH 44307	330-384-6000	R	220*	5.0
57	Drury Development Corp—*Timothy Drury*	8315 Drury Industrial, Saint Louis MO 63114	314-423-6698	R	201*	.1
58	Gourmet Services Inc—*Nathaniel Goldston*	82 Piedmont Ave, Atlanta GA 30303	404-876-5700	R	196*	2.0
59	International Services Inc—*Gregg M Steinberg*	1250 Barclay Blvd, Buffalo Grove IL 60089	847-808-5590	R	180*	1.8
60	American Physicians Insurance Agency Inc—*W Stancil Starnes*	1301 S Capital of Texa, Austin TX 78746	512-328-0888	S	180*	.1
61	APS Insurance Services Inc—*W Stancil Starnes*	1301 S Capital of Texa, Austin TX 78746	512-328-0888	R	180*	.1
62	Labovitz Enterprises Inc—*Mark Labovitz*	202 W Superior St Ste, Duluth MN 55802	218-727-7765	R	179*	.5
63	Valenti Mid-Atlantic Management LLC—*Peter Grant*	3450 Buschwood Park Dr, Tampa FL 33618	813-935-8777	R	179*	4.5
64	Trinity Health System—*Fred Brower*	PO Box 24, Steubenville OH 43952	740-264-8000	R	179*	1.6
65	Baycare Health System Inc—*Steve Mason*	16255 Bay Vista Dr, Clearwater FL 33760	727-820-8200	R	179*	1.1
66	Potomac Hospital Foundation—*William Flannagan*	2300 Opitz Blvd, Woodbridge VA 22191	703-670-1313	R	177*	<.1
67	Prime Healthcare Services Inc—*Lex Reddy*	3300 E Guasti Rd Ste 3, Ontario CA 91761	909-235-4400	R	175*	4.0
68	Washington Healthcare Mary—*Fred Rankin*	2300 Fall Hill Ave Ste, Fredericksburg VA 22401	540-741-2507	R	175*	4.0
69	Ag Holdings Inc—*Ann Dobric*	4000 Hollywood Blvd, Hollywood FL 33021	954-987-7180	R	174*	3.0
70	Newton-Wellesley Health Care System Inc—*John Bihldorff*	2014 Washington St, Newton MA 02462	781-681-1000	R	174*	<.1
71	Sphs Corp—*Vincent Mccorcell*	PO Box 9012, Springfield MA 01102	413-748-9000	S	172*	4.0
72	Wexford Health Sources Inc—*Mark Hale*	425 Holiday Dr, Pittsburgh PA 15220	412-937-8590	R	172*	1.5
73	Cooper Health Care—*Dr christopher Olivia*	1 Cooper Plz Ste 504, Camden NJ 08103	856-342-2000	R	171*	4.5
74	Hca Midwest Div—*Steve Corbeil*	903 E 104th St Ste 500, Kansas City MO 64131	816-508-4000	R	170*	6.0

Note: An asterisk (*) indicates an estimated financial figure. The company type code used is as follows: R = Private, P = Public, S = Private Subsidiary, B = Public Subsidiary, D = Division, J = Joint Venture, I = Investment Fund.

COMPANY RANKINGS BY SALES WITHIN 4-DIGIT SIC

Rank	Company Name—Executive Officer	Address, City, State, Zip	Phone	Type	Fin	Empls
75	Nursecore Management Services LLC—Brenda King	PO Box 201925, Arlington TX 76006	817-649-1166	R	164*	4.2
76	Mercy Memorial Hospital Foundation—Richard Hiltz	PO Box 67, Monroe MI 48161	734-240-8400	R	159*	<.1
77	Parsons Brinckerhoff Construction Services Inc—C Herndon	465 Springpark Pl, Herndon VA 20170	703-742-5700	R	158*	.6
78	Lockheed Martin Government Services Inc—Gene Loftus	2339 Rte 70 W, Cherry Hill NJ 08002	856-486-5891	R	158*	5.0
79	St Johns Mercy Health Care—Alastair Wood	645 Maryville Centre D, Saint Louis MO 63141	314-364-2400	S	157*	N/A
80	NovaMed Inc—Thomas S Hall	333 W Wacker Dr Ste 10, Chicago IL 60606	312-664-4100	S	156	.8
81	Lea Williams Inc—Justin Barton	1 Dag Hammarskjold Plz, New York NY 10017	212-351-9000	S	154*	3.0
82	Harman-Management Corp—James Olson	199 1st St Ste 212, Los Altos CA 94022	650-941-5681	R	153*	4.0
83	Yale-New Haven Health Services Corp—Marna Borgstrom	789 Howard Ave, New Haven CT 06519	203-688-4608	R	150*	.5
84	Alfatech Cambridge Group Gp—Jeff Fini	345 S California Ave S, Palo Alto CA 94306	650-543-3030	R	150*	.1
85	Lifemark Corp—RC Jelinek	7600 N 16th St Ste 150, Phoenix AZ 85020	602-331-5100	S	150	.8
86	Trammell Crow Company (Dallas Texas)—George Lippe	2001 Ross Ave Ste 3400, Dallas TX 75201	214-863-3000	R	145*	3.4
87	American Industrial Acquisition Corp—Leonard Levie	1465 E Putnam Ave Ste, Greenwich CT 06830	203-698-9595	R	145*	5.4
88	Southwestern Vermont Health Care Corp—Cynthia Murphy	100 Hospital Dr, Bennington VT 05201	802-442-6361	R	142*	1.2
89	Our Lady Of Lourdes Health Care Services Inc—Alex Hatala	1600 Haddon Ave, Camden NJ 08103	856-757-3500	S	142*	3.5
90	Hercules Drilling LLC—Michael Donaldson	9 Greenway Plz Ste 220, Houston TX 77046	713-350-5100	R	141*	2.2
91	Sterling Healthcare—Robert J Bunker	6400 Atlantic Blvd, Jacksonville FL 32211	919-383-0355	R	141*	1.3
92	Marriott Worldwide Sales And Marketing Inc—J Marriott	10400 Fernwood Rd, Bethesda MD 20817	301-380-3000	R	140*	3.6
93	Kitchell CEM—Gregory Denk	1707 E Highland Ave, Phoenix AZ 85016	602-264-4411	S	134*	.1
94	Conner Partners—Patrick Litre	1230 W Peachtree St NW, Atlanta GA 30309	404-564-4800	R	131*	<.1
95	Mancor-Sc Inc—Art Church	397a Hwy 601 S, Lugoff SC 29078	803-438-6845	R	130*	.2
96	Vantage Hospitality Group Inc—Roger Bloss	3300 N University Dr S, Coral Springs FL 33065	954-575-2668	R	130*	<.1
97	Management Training Scientific Support Services Inc—Randall N Scott	12500 Fair Lakes Cir S, Fairfax VA 22033	703-227-0900	R	128*	.1
98	Access America Service Corp	6600 W Broad St, Richmond VA 23230	804-285-3300	S	119*	.3
99	nFrame Inc—Robert Alcorn	701 Congressional Blvd, Carmel IN 46032	317-805-3759	S	117*	<.1
100	CBIZ Colorado Inc	8181 E Tufts Ave Ste 6, Denver CO 80237	720-200-7000	S	110*	.1
101	ARAMARK Correctional Services Inc—Joseph L Neubauer	1801 S Meyers Rd Ste 3, Villa Park IL 60181	630-568-2500	S	101*	5.5
102	Conti Enterprises Inc—Patrick Hogan	One Cragwood Rd Ste 2C, South Plainfield NJ 07080	908-791-4800	R	100	.4
103	Kleinfelder Inc—Bill Siegel	5015 Shoreham Pl, San Diego CA 92122	858-320-2000	R	100*	N/A
104	Sheridan Healthcare Inc—Mitchell Eisenberg	1613 N Harrison Pky Bl, Sunrise FL 33323	954-838-2371	R	98	.8
105	JA Jones Management Services Inc—Charlie Davidson JA Jones Inc	8206 Providence Rd Ste, Charlotte NC 28277	704-553-6600	S	93*	2.0
106	Castle Dental Centers Inc—Stephen C Bilt	201 E Sandpointe Ste 8, Santa Ana CA 92707	714-668-1300	S	92*	1.0
107	Jtd Health Systems Inc—Joan Clark	200 Saint Clair Ave, Saint Marys OH 45885	419-394-3335	R	90*	.6
108	LF Driscoll Company LLC—John J Donnelly	9 Presidential Blvd, Bala Cynwyd PA 19004	610-668-0950	R	81*	.2
109	URS Construction Services Inc—Fred C Kreitzberg	600 Montgomerty St 26t, San Francisco CA 94111	415-774-2700	S	78*	.7
110	Science Management Company LLC—James A Skidmore	745 Routes 202 206, Bridgewater NJ 08807	908-722-0300	R	78*	.2
111	Storage International Inc—Michelle S Lee	99 Canal Center Plaza, Alexandria VA 22314	703-578-6030	R	77*	1.2
112	Liberty Construction Corp—Armen Kalaydjian	25480 Telegraph Rd, Southfield MI 48033	248-356-4060	R	75*	.1
113	Premier Inc (Charlotte North Carolina)—Susan D DeVore	13034 Ballantyne Corpo, Charlotte NC 28277	704-357-0022	R	74*	1.0
114	Asset Plus Corp—Michael S McGrath	675 Bering Dr Ste 200, Houston TX 77057	713-782-5800	R	74*	.8
115	Healthcare Ratings Inc	500 Golden Ridge Rd St, Golden CO 80401	303-716-0041	S	73*	.1
116	Burt and Associates—Jerry Curtis	6700 Pinecrest Dr Ste, Plano TX 75024	469-368-6400	R	72*	<.1
117	McCormick Construction Management Co—Michael McCormick	2507 Empire Ave, Burbank CA 91504	818-843-2010	R	70*	.1
118	Allen Health Systems Inc—John Knox	1825 Logan Ave, Waterloo IA 50703	319-235-3941	S	68*	1.8
119	Robbins-Gioia Inc—Mike Sledge	11 Canal Center Plz, Alexandria VA 22314	703-548-7006	R	67*	.6
120	White Mountain Apache Tribe—Ronnie Lupe	PO Box 700, Whiteriver AZ 85941	928-338-4346	R	62*	1.5
121	Policy Studies Inc—Margaret Laub	1515 Wynkoop St Ste 40, Denver CO 80202	303-863-0900	R	62*	1.3
122	The Long Co—Bill Zimmerman	20 N Clark St Ste 650, Chicago IL 60602	312-726-4606	R	61*	<.1
123	Construction Planning and Management Inc—Jerry Williams	10053 N Hague Rd, Indianapolis IN 46256	317-842-8040	R	61*	<.1
124	AmeriNet Central—Todd Ebert	500 Commonwealth Dr, Warrendale PA 15086		R	59*	.2
125	Zenith Management Co—Kenneth Goldfine	2305 W Superior St, Duluth MN 55806	218-723-8433	R	59*	<.1
126	McLane Advanced Technologies LLC—David F Mitchell	4001 Central Pointe Pk, Temple TX 76504		R	58*	.3
127	Dial Cos—Donald F Day	11506 Nicholas St Ste, Omaha NE 68154	402-493-2800	R	58*	.1
128	Trinidad Management Inc—Ronald J Tassinari American Vantage Cos	4735 S Durango Dr Ste, Las Vegas NV 89147	702-227-9800	S	58*	<.1
129	Chief Supermarkets Inc—Rose Richardson	705 Deatrick St, Defiance OH 43512	419-782-9156	R	55*	.9
130	CBIZ Benefits and Insurance Services of Florida Inc	2290 Lucien Way Ste 15, Maitland FL 32751	407-475-1765	S	54*	<.1
131	Liberty Geneva Steel Ltd—Rae Holmstrom	PO Box 6124, Youngstown OH 44501	330-740-0103	R	53*	.1
132	Electronic Training Solutions Inc—Maria Mogollon	PO Box 457, Cocoa FL 32923	321-636-2212	R	53*	<.1
133	Christman Co—Steven Roznowski	208 N Capitol Ave, Lansing MI 48933	517-482-1488	R	52*	.1
134	Dhg Management Company LLC—Benjamin Denihan	551 5th Ave Fl 10, New York NY 10176	212-465-3740	R	51*	1.2
135	Centrum Management LLC—Robert Couch	21400 Ridgetop Cir Ste, Sterling VA 20166	703-406-3471	R	50*	.2
136	Marathon Management Inc—Robert G Johnson	30050 SW Town Center L, Wilsonville OR 97070	503-582-8282	R	50	.1
137	Intelisyn Inc—Marc Strange	2281 W 190th St Ste 10, Torrance CA 90504	310-939-7777	R	49*	<.1
138	Skillman Corp—Harold A SSkillman	3834 S Emerson Ave Bld, Indianapolis IN 46203	317-783-6151	R	48*	.1
139	Genus Technologies LLC—Dave Fetters	6600 France Ave S Ste, Minneapolis MN 55435	952-844-2644	R	48*	<.1
140	Epsilon Systems Solutions Inc—Bryan B Min	9242 Lightwave Ave Ste, San Diego CA 92123	619-702-1700	R	47*	.3
141	SingleSource Property Solutions—Brian Cullen	333 Technology Dr Ste, Canonsburg PA 15317		R	47*	.2
142	Kaseman LLC—Donald Kerr	1600 Tysons Blvd Ste 1, Mc Lean VA 22102	703-676-3200	R	47*	.2
143	Pmhcc Inc—Bernard Borislow	123 S Broad St Fl 22a, Philadelphia PA 19109	215-546-0300	R	46*	.2
144	Northern Illinois Health Plan—Dennis Hamilton	1045 W Stephenson St, Freeport IL 61032	815-599-6361	R	46*	1.2
145	Diversified Restaurant Holdings Inc—Michael Ansley	27680 Franklin Rd, Southfield MI 48034	248-223-9160	P	45	1.1
146	Vanir Construction Management Inc—Mansour M Aliabadi Vanir Group of Companies	4540 Duckhorn Dr, Sacramento CA 95834	916-575-8888	S	45*	.3
147	ProKarma Inc—Vivek Kumar	8705 SW Nimbus Ave Ste, Beaverton OR 97008	503-521-1915	R	45	N/A
148	Unidine Corp—Richard Schenkel	1 Gateway Ctr Ste 751, Newton MA 02458	617-467-3700	R	43*	.9
149	Rainmaker Systems Inc—Michael Silton	900 E Hamilton Ave Ste, Campbell CA 95008	408-626-3800	P	43	1.5
150	Ecohomos Properties Inc—Nick Economos	4000 N Federal Hwy Ste, Boca Raton FL 33431	561-361-2504	R	42*	1.5
151	Renaissance Medical Management Co—Barry P Green	487 Devon Park Dr Ste, Wayne PA 19087	610-254-7662	R	42*	<.1
152	Damon G Douglas Co—Sam Prisco	245 Birchwood Ave, Cranford NJ 07016	908-272-0100	R	40*	.1
153	Fairmount Long Term Care—Herbert Long	2100 W Girard Ave, Philadelphia PA 19130	215-685-0800	R	37*	.5
154	Medsynergies Inc—Frank Marshall	909 Hidden RDG Ste 300, Irving TX 75038	972-791-1224	R	36*	.3
155	Alliance For Sustainable Energy LLC—Daniel Arvizu	1617 Cole Blvd, Lakewood CO 80401	303-275-3000	R	35*	1.2
156	J and D P/M Diversified Inc—Joshua Moore	12832 Valley View St S, Garden Grove CA 92845	714-891-7048	R	35*	.4
157	Safeguard Properties Inc—Robert Klein	7887 Safeguard Cir, Cleveland OH 44125	216-739-2900	R	34*	.8
158	Keiro Services—Shawn Miyake	325 S Boyle Ave, Los Angeles CA 90033	323-263-1007	R	33*	.5
159	Foundation Source Inc—Daniel M Schley	55 Walls Dr 3rd Fl, Fairfield CT 06824		R	33*	<.1
160	St Joseph Preferred Healthcare Inc—Michael Harrington	2500 Harbor Blvd, Port Charlotte FL 33952	941-625-4122	R	33*	1.4

Rank	Company Name—*Executive Officer*	Address, City, State, Zip	Phone	Type	Fin	Empls
161	Global Med Technologies Inc—*Michael I Ruxin*	12600 W Colfax Ste C-4, Lakewood CO 80215	303-238-2000	S	32	.2
162	Hall Management Corp—*Stacy Hampton*	759 S Madera Ave, Kerman CA 93630	559-846-7382	R	31*	2.0
163	Mitsui Sumitomo Marine Management (USA) Inc—*Tetsuro Kihara*	15 Independence Blvd S, Warren NJ 07059	908-604-2900	R	31*	.4
164	Bentley Co (Milwaukee Wisconsin)—*Thomas Bentley III*	4080 N Port Washington, Milwaukee WI 53212	414-967-8000	R	30*	.2
165	FGI Research Inc—*Archie Purcell*	PO Box 3767, Chapel Hill NC 27514	919-929-7759	R	30*	.2
166	Ijkg Opco LLC—*Penny Bond*	29 E 29th St, Bayonne NJ 07002	201-858-5000	R	29*	.7
167	OnCURE Medical Corp—*L Duane Choate*	188 Inverness DrW Ste, Englewood CO 80112	303-643-6500	S	29*	.2
168	Reserves Network Inc—*Donald Stallard*	22021 Brookpark Rd, Fairview Park OH 44126	440-779-1419	R	28*	.3
169	LevelTen Interactive—*Tom McCracken*	4228 N Central Expy St, Dallas TX 75206		R	28*	<.1
170	United Medical Resources Inc—*Jay Anliker*	5151 Pfeiffer Road ML4, Cincinnati OH 45242	513-619-3000	S	27*	.4
171	Retrievex Holdings Corp—*J Pierce*	4 1st Ave, Peabody MA 01960	978-539-3350	R	27*	.2
172	DSSI LLC—*BP Thacker*	26261 Evergreen Rd Ste, Southfield MI 48076	248-208-8303	R	26*	<.1
173	Jst Enterprises—*Joe Thomson*	5120 Summerhill Rd, Texarkana TX 75503	903-794-3743	R	25*	1.0
174	SmithBucklin Corp—*Henry S Givray*	401 N Michigan Ave Ste, Chicago IL 60611	312-644-6610	R	25*	.3
175	Pro Em LLC	1450 E Grant St, Phoenix AZ 85034	480-507-0999	R	25*	.2
176	Triumvirate Environmental—*John McQuillan*	61 Inner Belt Rd, Somerville MA 02143		R	25*	.1
177	Crown NorthCorp Inc—*Ronald E Roark*	1251 Dublin Rd, Columbus OH 43215	614-488-1169	P	24	.1
178	ForeRunner Corp—*Creg Hughes*	7125 W Jefferson Ave S, Lakewood CO 80235	303-969-0223	R	24*	.2
179	Four Flags Health Ventures Inc—*Dennis Mack*	PO Box 458, Niles MI 49120	269-684-0259	S	23*	.7
180	Ncdr LLC—*Scott Hornbuckle*	1090 Northchase Pkwy S, Marietta GA 30067	770-916-9000	R	22*	.5
181	Cadence Network Inc—*Jeff Hart*	600 Vine St Ste 1600, Cincinnati OH 45202	513-763-3100	R	20*	.1
182	Implementation Specialists—*Jeffrey Uliano*	30 Two Bridges Rd Ste, Fairfield NJ 07004		R	19*	.2
183	Schaffer Partners Inc—*Mary Anne Commotto*	6545 Carnegie Ave, Cleveland OH 44103		R	18*	.1
184	US Energy Services Inc—*Bill Bathe*	605 N Hwy 169 Ste 1200, Plymouth MN 55441	763-543-4600	R	18	.1
185	Prohealth Physicians Inc—*Jack Reed*	4 Farm Springs Rd, Farmington CT 06032	860-284-5200	R	17*	.4
186	Trade Center Management Associates LLC—*Craig Albright*	PO Box 14580, Washington DC 20044	202-312-1300	R	16*	.4
187	Boucher Brothers Miami Beach LLC—*Cesar Albarez*	420 Lincoln Rd Ste 265, Miami Beach FL 33139	305-535-8177	R	16*	.3
188	Internet Transaction Solutions Inc—*Joseph Cowen*	7720 Rivers Edge Dr, Columbus OH 43235	614-310-6714	R	16*	.6
189	Westford Group Inc—*W Rapp*	48 Junction Sq Dr, Concord MA 01742	978-369-8600	R	16*	.3
190	Geary Darling Lessee Inc—*Michael Depatie*	501 Geary St, San Francisco CA 94102	415-292-0100	R	16*	.2
191	Investors Capital Management Group—*Edward Lindor*	10390 Santa Monica Blv, Los Angeles CA 90025	310-553-5175	R	16*	.3
192	Middlesex Hospital Inc—*Robert Kiely*	28 Crescent St, Middletown CT 06457	860-344-6000	R	16*	.2
193	Remington Employers Corp—*Monty Bennett*	14185 Dallas Pkwy Ste, Dallas TX 75254	972-980-2700	R	15*	.5
194	El Jay Poultry Corp—*Leo Rubin*	PO Box 778, Voorhees NJ 08043	856-435-0900	R	15*	.3
195	Daja International LLC—*Chuck Maggio*	111 Pine St Ste 1400, San Francisco CA 94111	415-956-4029	R	15*	.3
196	Smart Management and Cos—*Tony Lutsi*	1501 Corp Way Ste 200, Sacramento CA 95831	916-392-3000	R	14*	.4
197	Exports of Washington Inc—*Kristine Moe*	435 Martin St Ste 4000, Blaine WA 98230	360-332-5239	R	14*	.2
198	Hawk Associates Inc—*Frank Hawkins*	227 Atlantic Blvd, Key Largo FL 33037	305-451-1888	R	14*	<.1
199	Midway Products Group Inc—*James Hoyt*	PO Box 737, Monroe MI 48161	734-241-7242	R	14*	.4
200	Headrick Companies Inc—*Richard Headrick*	1 Freedom Sq, Laurel MS 39440	601-649-1977	R	14*	.1
201	Bluegrass Cellular Inc—*Ron Smith*	PO Box 5012, Elizabethtown KY 42702	270-769-0339	R	13*	.3
202	Sweeney Hotels International Inc—*Charles Sweeney*	301 Lauberge Ln, Sedona AZ 86336	928-282-1661	R	13*	.3
203	HRH Construction Corp—*Brad Singer*	50 Main St 15th Fl, White Plains NY 10606	914-993-5500	R	13*	.1
204	PMA Literary and Film Management Inc—*Peter Miller*	PO Box 1817, New York NY 10010	212-929-1222	R	13*	<.1
205	Cdc Management Co—*Paul Jenkins*	4949 Fwy Dr E, Columbus OH 43229	614-781-0216	R	13*	.3
206	Harris Golf Management Inc—*John Harris*	4725 Piedmont Row Dr S, Charlotte NC 28210	704-556-1717	R	12*	.2
207	Pasadena Center Operating Co—*Micheal Ross*	300 E Green St, Pasadena CA 91101	626-793-2122	R	12*	.1
208	Central Group Management Co—*Robert Pace*	215 Park Ave S Ste 200, Saint Cloud MN 56301	320-654-6307	R	12*	.3
209	Wing Memorial Hospital—*Charles Cavagnaro*	40 Wright St, Palmer MA 01069	413-283-7651	R	12*	.4
210	Military Car Sales Inc—*David Goldring*	175 Crossways Park Dr, Woodbury NY 11797	516-921-2800	R	11*	.2
211	Prime Retail Services Inc—*Donald Bloom*	135 Maple St Ste 200, Gainesville GA 30501	770-297-0480	R	11*	.2
212	Executive Director Inc—*Kay Whalen*	555 E Wells St Ste 110, Milwaukee WI 53202	414-276-6445	R	11*	.1
213	Smarsh Inc—*Stephen Marsh*	921 SW Washington St S, Portland OR 97205	503-946-5980	R	11*	.1
214	Golden Bear Golf Inc—*Jack Nicklaus*	11780 US Hwy 1 Ste 500, North Palm Beach FL 33408	561-626-3900	R	11*	<.1
215	Clover Corporate Service LLC—*Thressa Jones*	16225 Park Ten Pl Ste, Houston TX 77084	713-225-6837	R	11*	.1
216	Riverview Health And Rehabilitation Center Inc—*Jackie Bryant*	6711 La Roche Ave, Savannah GA 31406	912-354-8225	R	10*	.3
217	Archives Management Corp—*Harlan Shapers*	1945 Carroll Ave, San Francisco CA 94124	415-468-5600	R	10*	.2
218	LTC Corp—*Lisa Cole*	1104 Teaneck Rd, Teaneck NJ 07666	201-837-9600	R	10*	.2
219	Garlin Hotel Corp—*Gary Gillis*	1500 N Military Hwy St, Norfolk VA 23502	757-466-8000	R	10*	.2
220	Regent Pacific Management Corp—*Stephen M Race*	433 California St Ste, San Francisco CA 94104	415-391-8500	R	10*	<.1
221	Balfour Concord—*Alan McKinney*	7810 Ballantyne Common, Charlotte NC 28277	704-319-2210	R	10*	<.1
222	Fisher Hotel Group Inc—*Donald Sagaria*	674 Thayer Rd, West Point NY 10996	845-446-1144	R	10*	.2
223	Group Enterprise Of North America Inc—*Barry George*	10509 Rte 68, Rimersburg PA 16248	814-473-3362	R	10*	.3
224	Merlin Management Company Inc—*William Zammer*	311 Gifford St, Falmouth MA 02540	508-548-2300	R	9*	.2
225	Consolidated Food Management Inc—*John Franks*	7429 Se 27th St, Mercer Island WA 98040	206-232-9771	R	9*	.2
226	Amberley Management Inc—*Gary Williams*	7501 Greenway Center D, Greenbelt MD 20770	301-474-6200	R	9*	.2
227	All In One Inc—*Janice Howroyd*	PO Box 29048, Glendale CA 91209	310-538-3374	R	9*	.1
228	University Physicians Services Inc—*Scott Griffin*	3800 Woodward Ave Ste, Detroit MI 48201	313-262-1500	R	9*	.1
229	Vna Home Health Services Inc—*Michelle Quirolo*	540 White Plains Rd Fl, Tarrytown NY 10591	914-666-7079	R	9*	.1
230	Pathfinder LLC—*Louis J Cabano*	11 Allison Dr, Cherry Hill NJ 08003	856-424-7100	R	9*	.1
231	Abide International Inc—*Marty Rapozo*	PO Box 348, Sonoma CA 95476	707-935-1577	R	9*	<.1
232	Washington Soldier's Home and Colony—*David Devore*	PO Box 199, Orting WA 98360	360-893-4501	R	9*	.2
233	Kerrington Health Systems Inc—*Howard Sipe*	2923 Hamilton Mason Rd, Hamilton OH 45011	513-863-0360	R	9*	.2
234	MZI Group Inc—*Arthur Miller*	2251 W Grand Ave, Chicago IL 60612	312-492-8740	R	9	<.1
235	Healthcare Shop Of North Central Indiana LLC—*Carolyn Kochert*	PO Box 4699, Lafayette IN 47903	765-447-8133	R	8*	.2
236	Tofte Management Company LLC—*Mary Henry*	PO Box 2125, Tofte MN 55615	218-663-7296	R	8*	.1
237	Icms Holdings Inc—*Dean Willard*	100 Central Park S 12d, New York NY 10019	212-246-9806	R	8*	.2
238	Inland Management Corp—*Harry Patten*	665 Simonds Rd, Williamstown MA 01267	413-458-5220	R	8*	.1
239	Midwest Medical Management Inc—*Ronald Leach*	3645 S East St, Indianapolis IN 46227	317-783-7474	R	8*	.1
240	Bacompt Systems Inc—*Bud Stanley*	12742 Hamilton Crossin, Carmel IN 46032	317-574-7474	R	8*	<.1
241	River Port Truck Stop LLC	940 Lobdell Ext S, Port Allen LA 70767	225-334-0670	S	8*	<.1
242	Peter Brown Associates—*David Shatz*	601 W 5th St Ste 220, Los Angeles CA 90071	213-627-7770	R	8*	<.1
243	Port Authority Of San Antonio—*Bruce Miller*	907 Billy Mitchell Rd, San Antonio TX 78226	210-362-7800	R	8*	.1
244	Pak Technologies Holding Company Inc—*Kevin Schuele*	7025 W Marcia Rd, Milwaukee WI 53223	414-438-8600	R	7*	.1
245	Ric-Man Construction Inc—*Steven Mancini*	6850 19 Mile Rd, Sterling Heights MI 48314	586-739-5210	R	7*	.1
246	Maritime Management Services—*Trevor Stabbert*	19600 International Bl, Seatac WA 98188	206-824-8500	R	7*	.1
247	Burrus Investment Group Inc—*George Newton III*	401 Veterans Memorial, Metairie LA 70005	504-455-7600	R	7*	<.1
248	H and R Services Inc—*Hope Hall*	1428 Weatherly Rd Se, Huntsville AL 35803	256-885-5960	R	7*	.1

Note: An asterisk (*) indicates an estimated financial figure. The company type code used is as follows: R = Private, P = Public, S = Private Subsidiary, B = Public Subsidiary, D = Division, J = Joint Venture, I = Investment Fund.

COMPANY RANKINGS BY SALES WITHIN 4-DIGIT SIC

Rank	Company Name—*Executive Officer*	Address, City, State, Zip	Phone	Type	Fin	Empls
249	American Access Care LLC—*Eva Blietz*	182 Industrial Rd, Glen Rock PA 17327	717-235-0181	R	7*	.1
250	Ozarks Methodist Manor—*Fred Royer*	PO Box 403, Marionville MO 65705	417-258-2573	R	7*	.1
251	Hialeah Hotel Inc—*Arthur Greenberg*	1950 W 49th St, Hialeah FL 33012	305-823-2000	R	7*	.1
252	Cedarwood Construction Company Inc—*Anthony Petrarca*	1765 Merriman Rd, Akron OH 44313	330-836-0721	R	7*	.1
253	Ohio Valley Bistro's Inc—*James Rigger*	5803 Mariemont Ave, Cincinnati OH 45227	513-271-2349	R	7*	.1
254	People Network Inc—*S Anderson*	1080 Holcomb Bridge Rd, Roswell GA 30076	770-558-1700	R	7*	.1
255	Atma Hotel Group Inc—*Manish Atma*	6121 Farrington Rd, Chapel Hill NC 27517	919-969-2728	R	7*	.2
256	Regent Care Center Of Laredo LP—*Francisca Medina*	7001 Mcpherson Rd, Laredo TX 78041	956-723-7001	R	6*	.1
257	Prestige Management Services Inc—*Joseph Dockery*	400 Sette Dr, Paramus NJ 07652	201-265-7800	R	6*	.1
258	Halcyon Offshore Asset Management LLC—*Lourine Ross*	477 Madison Ave Fl 8, New York NY 10022	212-303-9400	R	6*	.1
259	Robocom Us LLC—*Kathleen Poulos*	1111 Broadhollow Rd St, Farmingdale NY 11735	631-861-2045	R	6*	<.1
260	Hogan Services Inc—*David Hogan*	PO Box 7521, Saint Louis MO 63106	314-421-6000	S	6*	.1
261	Mid Atlantic Health Management Inc—*Harold Mcbee*	1220 Butterworth Ct, Stevensville MD 21666	410-643-3393	R	6*	.1
262	C and I Management Corp—*Latisia Moscrat*	123 S Illinois St, Indianapolis IN 46225	317-634-3000	R	6*	.1
263	Sahaj Management Corp—*Chintan Patel*	1230 Se Maynard Rd Ste, Cary NC 27511	919-468-1397	R	6*	.1
264	Rio Grande Valley Dme—*Johnny Walker*	2209 N 23rd St, Mcallen TX 78501	956-683-1655	R	5*	.3
265	Addison-Harrington Inc—*Peter Harrington*	13370 Branch View Ln S, Dallas TX 75234	214-317-4224	R	5*	.1
266	cPrime Inc—*Zubin Irani*	4100 E Third Ave, Foster City CA 94404	650-931-1650	R	5*	<.1
267	Physicans Services Corporation Of Southern Il—*Robert Gebhardt*	413 Main St, Mount Vernon IL 62864	618-242-7486	R	5*	.1
268	Gracy Woods Ii Nursing Center—*Hearther Guerin*	12042 Bittern Holw, Austin TX 78758	512-836-4241	R	5*	.1
269	North American Medical Management-Desert Region Inc—*Sherif Abdou*	PO Box 95638, Las Vegas NV 89193	702-318-2400	R	5*	.1
270	Whitbread Management Inc—*Randy Opliger*	4700 Belleview Ave Ste, Kansas City MO 64112	816-448-2300	R	5*	.1
271	Alliance For Children Inc—*Austin Smith*	1871 Woodslee Dr, Troy MI 48083	248-205-7214	R	5*	.1
272	Za Management—*Alexander Zaks*	250 N Robertson Blvd S, Beverly Hills CA 90211	310-271-2200	R	5*	.1
273	Zidell Management Company Inc—*Michael Zidell*	5421 Alpha Rd Ste 200, Dallas TX 75240	214-239-9800	S	4*	.1
274	Trihealth Inc—*John Prout*	619 Oak St, Cincinnati OH 45206	513-569-6141	R	4*	.7
275	Innkeepers Hospitality Florida Inc—*Jeffery Fisher*	340 Ryl Poinciana Way, Palm Beach FL 33480	561-655-9001	R	4*	.1
276	EmCare Inc—*Todd G Zimmerman* EmCare Holdings Inc	1717 Main St Ste 5200, Dallas TX 75201	214-712-2000	S	4*	4.5
277	St Vincent Health Services Inc—*William Riordan*	2800 Main St, Bridgeport CT 06606	203-576-6000	R	4*	2.0
278	Service Care Of America Inc—*James Long*	2050 Marconi Dr Ste 30, Alpharetta GA 30005	678-455-9009	R	4*	.4
279	Pacific Management Inc—*Patrick Somers*	20 S Clark St Ste 3000, Chicago IL 60603	312-855-9444	R	4*	.1
280	PHI Group Inc (Huntington Beach California)—*Henry D Fahman*	17011 Beach Blvd Ste 1, Huntington Beach CA 92647	714-843-5450	P	4	<.1
281	Anthony Mason Associates Inc—*Anthony Mason*	11766 Wilshire Blvd St, Los Angeles CA 90025	310-312-6603	R	4*	<.1
282	Masten-Wright Inc—*Gregory Wright*	282 State St, North Haven CT 06473	203-230-4130	R	4*	<.1
283	Stegeman and Kastner Inc—*Fritz W Kastner*	2601 Ocean Park Blvd S, Santa Monica CA 90405	310-450-9010	R	4*	<.1
284	Logik—*Andy Wilson*	707 G St NW, Washington DC 20001		R	4*	<.1
285	Atlas Management Corp—*Warren Sawyers*	750 Old Hickory Blvd 1, Brentwood TN 37027	615-371-6153	R	3*	.1
286	Western Medical Management LLC—*Baruch Fogel*	3333 Michelson Dr Ste, Irvine CA 92612	949-260-6507	R	3*	.1
287	Point Six Inc—*John Compton*	161 Prosperous Pl Ste, Lexington KY 40509	859-266-3606	R	3*	<.1
288	Onenet USA Inc—*Robert Brunmeier*	4445 W 77th St Ste 106, Minneapolis MN 55435	952-960-1000	R	3*	<.1
289	Innovative Health Care Concepts Inc—*Lona Smith*	790 S Holmes Ave, Idaho Falls ID 83401	208-529-8526	R	3*	<.1
290	Fertitta Enterprises—*Victoria Fertitta*	10801 W Charleston Blv, Las Vegas NV 89135	702-221-4700	R	2*	<.1
291	Ink Impressions Inc—*Terry Rainey*	PO Box 6306, Albuquerque NM 87197	505-891-0525	R	2*	<.1
292	Richfield Hospitality Services Inc—*Greg Mount*	7600 E Orchard Rd Ste, Greenwood Village CO 80111	303-220-2000	S	2*	<.1
293	RZO Productions LLC	250 W 57th St Ste 1101, New York NY 10107	212-307-1088	R	2*	<.1
294	Washington Compost LLC—*Robin Wright*	2810 34th St, Everett WA 98201	425-259-5115	R	1*	<.1
295	A and A Resources Inc—*Geroge Adams*	PO Box 350, Lapeer MI 48446	810-245-6622	R	1*	<.1
296	Benni 5848 LP—*Amer Hammoud*	600 Round Rock W Dr St, Round Rock TX 78681	512-310-2144	R	1*	.3
297	Talkie Tooter—*Neil Rohenbuhler*	524 Rhodes Rd, Sedro Woolley WA 98284	360-856-0836	S	1*	<.1
298	St Claire Inc—*David Austin*	37440 Hills Tech Dr, Farmington Hills MI 48331	248-553-2474	R	1*	<.1
299	Cole Financial Service Inc—*Patricia A Cole*	3170 E Lafayette Blvd, Detroit MI 48207	313-962-7055	R	1	<.1
300	Learning Communications LLC—*Lloyd W Singer*	5520 Trabuco Blvd, Irvine CA 92620		R	1*	<.1
301	Pinnell/Busch Inc—*Steve Pinnell*	6420 SW Macadam Ave St, Portland OR 97239	503-293-6280	R	1*	<.1
302	Critical Care Systems Inc—*Wendy Marx*	5000 Hollywood Blvd St, Hollywood FL 33021	954-989-4400	R	1*	<.1
303	American Vantage Cos—*Ronald J Tassinari*	PO Box 81920, Las Vegas NV 89180	702-227-9800	P	<1	<.1
304	Bublitz Machinery Co—*Jeffrey Bublitz*	703 E 14th Ave, Kansas City MO 64116	816-221-7335	R	<1*	<.1
305	Encompass Holdings Inc—*Scott Webber*	316 California Ave Ste, Reno NV 89509	415-259-4108	P	<1	<.1
306	Baker Engineering Inc—*Bradley Mallory* Michael Baker Corp	100 Airside Dr Airside, Moon Township PA 15108	412-269-6300	S	N/A	2.9
307	Michael Baker International Inc—*Bradley Mallory* Michael Baker Corp	100 Airside Dr, Moon Township PA 15108	412-269-6300	S	N/A	2.9
308	VHA Inc—*Curtis W Nonomaque*	PO Box 140909, Irving TX 75014	972-830-0000	R	N/A	1.0
309	Meeting Expectations Inc—*Brian R Meyer*	3535 Piedmont Center R, Atlanta GA 30305	404-240-0999	R	N/A	<.1
310	Hospitality Unlimited Investments Co—*Peter Hui*	13950 Cerritos Corpora, Cerritos CA 90703	562-926-0128	R	N/A	<.1

TOTALS: SIC 8741 Management Services
Companies: 310   4,318,856   489.7

8742 Management Consulting Services

1	Xerox Global Services Inc	PO Box 4505, Norwalk CT 06856	203-968-3000	S	21,320*	32.0
2	Symphony Technology Group LLC—*Romesh Wadhwani*	2475 Hanover St, Palo Alto CA 94304	650-935-9500	R	6,815*	10.0
3	Arthur D Little Inc—*Micheal Tram*	125 High St 28 FL, Boston MA 02110	617-532-9550	R	6,600*	10.0
4	Booz Allen Hamilton Holding Corp—*Ralph W Shrader*	8283 Greensboro Dr, McLean VA 22102	703-902-5000	P	5,591	25.0
5	McKinsey and Company Inc—*Donminic Barton*	55 E 52nd St 21st Fl, New York NY 10055	212-446-7000	R	4,434*	17.0
6	Aon Hewitt—*Baljit Dail* Aon Consulting Worldwide Inc	100 Half Day Rd, Lincolnshire IL 60069	847-295-5000	S	3,876*	29.0
7	HDR Engineering Inc—*George A Little*	8404 Indian Hills Dr, Omaha NE 68114	402-399-1000	R	3,361*	5.2
8	Lockheed Martin Technology Services—*Robert Stevens*	2339 Marlton Pike W, Cherry Hill NJ 08002	856-486-5400	D	3,300*	30.0
9	BearingPoint—*Peter Mockler*	100 Crescent Ct Ste 70, Dallas TX 75201	214-459-2770	S	3,197	15.2
10	Towers Watson Inc—*John J Haley*	875 3rd Ave, New York NY 10022	212-725-7550	P	3,180	14.0
11	Peppers and Rogers Group / Marketing 1to1—*Don Peppers*	901 Main Ave Ste 212, Norwalk CT 06850	203-642-5121	S	3,132*	.2
12	RBC Dain Rauscher Inc—*John Taft*	60 S Sixth St, Minneapolis MN 55402	612-371-2711	S	3,095*	5.0
13	Knight Management Services Inc—*Kevin P Knight*	5601 W Buckeye Rd, Phoenix AZ 85043	602-269-2000	S	2,722*	4.0
14	Insperity Inc—*Paul J Sarvadi*	19001 Crescent Springs, Kingwood TX 77339	281-358-8986	P	1,976	122.1
15	Boston Consulting Group Inc—*Hans-Paul Burkner*	1 Exchange Pl 31st Fl, Boston MA 02109	617-973-1200	R	1,760*	4.4
16	AT Kearney Inc—*Paul Laudicina*	222 W Adams St, Chicago IL 60606	312-648-0111	R	1,718*	2.7
17	Northern Trust Services Inc—*Frederick Waddell*	50 S La Salle St, Chicago IL 60603	312-630-6000	S	1,625*	5.0

Rank	Company Name—*Executive Officer*	Address, City, State, Zip	Phone	Type	Fin	Empls
18	FTI Consulting Inc—*Jack B Dunn IV*	777 S Flagler Dr Ste 1, West Palm Beach FL 33401	561-515-1900	P	1,567	3.8
19	RJE Telecom Inc—*Gary Hall*	8191 College Pky, Fort Myers FL 33919		S	1,353*	2.1
20	ARCADIS—*Steve Blake*	630 Plz Dr Ste 200, Highlands Ranch CO 80129	720-344-3500	S	1,312*	3.5
21	William M Mercer Companies Inc—*Michelle Burns*	1166 Ave of the Americ, New York NY 10036	212-345-7000	S	1,294*	4.0
22	Scottrade Inc—*Rodger Riney*	12800 Corporate Hill D, Saint Louis MO 63131	314-965-1555	R	1,236*	2.4
23	Quorum Health Resources LLC—*James L Horrar*	105 Continental Pl, Brentwood TN 37027	615-371-7979	R	1,122*	14.3
24	Maritz Inc—*W Stephen Maritz*	1375 N Hwy Dr, Fenton MO 63026	636-827-4000	R	1,100*	3.3
25	inVentiv Health Inc—*Paul Meister*	1 Van de Graaff Dr, Burlington MA 01803		R	1,072	6.4
26	Harte-Hanks Direct Marketing/Fullerton Inc	2337 W Commonwealth Av, Fullerton CA 92833	714-738-5478	S	1,030*	6.4
27	MarketStar Corp—*Dave Treadway*	PO Box 1031, Ogden UT 84402	801-393-1155	R	930	3.0
28	Swissport USA Inc—*Richard van Bruygom*	45025 Aviation Dr Ste, Dulles VA 20166	703-742-4300	R	915*	7.0
29	Altair Engineering Inc—*James Scapa*	1820 E Big Beaver Rd, Troy MI 48083	248-614-2400	R	880*	1.3
30	IW Group Inc—*Bill Imada*	8687 Melrose Ave Ste G, West Hollywood CA 90069	310-289-5500	R	868*	.1
31	Barry-Wehmiller Companies Inc—*Phil Ostapowicz*	8020 Forsyth Blvd, Saint Louis MO 63105	314-862-8000	R	802	4.2
32	Management Technology Inc—*Pauline C Brooks*	6710 Oxon Hill Rd Ste, Oxon Hill MD 20745	301-265-8900	R	800*	.4
33	Navigant Consulting Inc—*William M Goodyear*	30 S Wacker Ste 3100, Chicago IL 60606	312-583-5700	P	785	2.5
34	ICF International Inc—*Sudhakar Kesavan*	9300 Lee Hwy, Fairfax VA 22031	703-934-3603	P	765	3.7
35	ZS Associates Inc—*Andris Zoltners*	1800 Sherman Ave Ste 7, Evanston IL 60201	847-492-3600	R	675*	1.0
36	Aon Consulting Worldwide Inc—*Kathryn Haley*	200 E Randolph St, Chicago IL 60601	312-381-4844	S	656*	5.7
37	Capgemini US LLC—*Lanny Cohen*	623 Fifth Ave 33rd Fl, New York NY 10022	212-314-8000	S	583*	5.0
38	Premium Retail Services Inc—*Ronald Travers*	618 Spirit Dr Ste 200, Chesterfield MO 63005	636-728-0592	R	538*	4.0
39	Aspen Marketing Services—*Patrick O'Rahilly*	1240 North Ave, West Chicago IL 60185	630-293-9600	R	537*	.6
40	Milliman Inc—*Patrick Grannan*	1301 5th Ave Ste 3800, Seattle WA 98101	206-624-7940	R	472*	2.0
41	Duke Energy Trading and Marketing LLC—*Kate Perez*	5400 Westhiemer Ct, Houston TX 77056		S	469*	.4
42	John Snow Inc—*Joel Lamstein*	44 Farnsworth St 7th F, Boston MA 02210	617-482-9485	R	464*	1.6
43	International Data Corp—*Kirk Campbell*	5 Speen St Ste 1, Framingham MA 01701	508-872-8200	S	461*	.7
44	Drake Beam Morin Inc—*Robert Gasparini*	750 Third Ave 28th Fl, New York NY 10017	212-692-7700	R	456*	.7
45	ARC Worldwide—*Richard Stoddart*	35 W Wacker Dr, Chicago IL 60601	312-220-3200	D	455*	1.3
46	iCrossing—*Don Scales*	15169 N Scottsdale Rd, Scottsdale AZ 85254	480-505-5800	R	454*	.6
47	Corporate Executive Board Co—*Thomas L Monahan III*	1919 N Lynn St, Arlington VA 22209	571-303-3000	P	439	1.9
48	Pinnacle Technical Resources Inc—*Nina Vaca*	5501 Lyndon B Johnson, Dallas TX 75240	214-740-2424	R	411*	.6
49	Colerant Consulting Inc—*Ian Clarkson*	45 Hayden Ave, Lexington MA 02421	781-674-0400	S	383*	.6
50	Right Management Consultants Inc—*Owen J Sullivan*	1818 Market St 33rd Fl, Philadelphia PA 19103	215-988-0150	R	382*	3.5
51	CSC Consulting Group—*Mike Laphen*	404 Wyman St, Waltham MA 02451	781-890-7446	D	375*	3.0
52	Spencer Stuart Management Consultants NV—*David S Daniel*	353 N Clark, Chicago IL 60654	312-822-0088	R	375*	1.6
53	Applied Management Sciences Group—*Frank Burke*	2277 Research Blvd, Rockville MD 20850	301-519-5000	R	360*	1.0
54	Industrial Services of America Inc—*Harry Kletter*	PO Box 32428, Louisville KY 40232	502-367-7100	P	343	.2
55	Mercer Human Resource Consulting Inc—*M Michele Burns*	1166 Ave of the Americ, New York NY 10036	212-345-7000	S	338*	.5
56	Willis North America Inc—*Vic Krauze*	26 Century Blvd Ste 10, Nashville TN 37214	615-872-3700	D	337*	.5
57	BI (Minneapolis Minnesota)	7630 Bush Lake Rd, Minneapolis MN 55439	952-835-4800	R	334*	1.1
58	GP Strategies Corp—*Scott N Greenberg*	6095 Marshalee Dr Ste, Elkridge MD 21075	410-379-3600	P	333	2.5
59	Carestream Dental LLC—*Kevin J Hobert* PracticeWorks Inc	1765 The Exchange SE, Atlanta GA 30339		S	333*	.5
60	GMR Marketing LLC—*Gary Reynolds*	5000 S Towne Dr, New Berlin WI 53151	262-786-5600	S	319*	.5
61	ADEX Corp—*Gary P McGuire*	1035 Windward Ridge Pk, Alpharetta GA 30005	678-393-7900	R	309*	.5
62	Carlson Marketing—*Jeff Balagna*	1405 Xenium Ln N Ste 1, Minneapolis MN 55441	763-445-3000	D	285*	3.0
63	Collabera—*Hiten Patel*	25 Airport Rd, Morristown NJ 07960	973-889-5200	R	280*	4.5
64	Lewin Group Inc *Lisa Chimento*	3130 Fairview Park Dr, Falls Church VA 22042	703-269-5500	S	280*	.1
65	Exponent Inc—*Paul Johnston*	149 Commonwealth Dr, Menlo Park CA 94025	650-326-9400	P	272	.9
66	AOS-USA—*David Pfleeger*	3414 Peachtree Rd Ste, Atlanta GA 30326	770-393-4700	R	271*	.4
67	Los Alamos Technical Associates Inc—*Phil Reinig*	999 Central Ave Ste 30, Los Alamos NM 87544	505-662-9080	R	270*	.4
68	Haggin Marketing Inc—*Jeff Haggin*	100 Shoreline Hwy, Mill Valley CA 94941	415-289-1110	R	264*	.4
69	Pitney Bowes Inc Mailing Systems Div—*Murray Martin*	1 Elmcroft Rd, Stamford CT 06926	203-356-5000	D	250*	.8
70	Forum Corp—*Ed Boswell*	265 Franklin St, Boston MA 02110	617-523-7300	R	235*	.4
71	Alvarez and Marsal LLC	600 Lexington Ave 6th, New York NY 10022	212-759-4433	R	231*	.4
72	Hackett Group Inc—*Ted A Fernandez*	1001 Brickell Bay Dr 3, Miami FL 33131	305-375-8005	P	225	.9
73	FishNet Security—*Gary Fish*	1710 Walnut St, Kansas City MO 64108	816-421-6611	R	221*	.3
74	Owl Cos—*Sheri Bovino*	2465 Campus Dr, Irvine CA 92612	949-797-2001	R	219*	2.1
75	NIC Inc—*Harry H Herington*	25501 W Valley Pky Ste, Olathe KS 66061	913-498-3468	P	181	.7
76	Flik International Corp—*Scott Davis*	3 International Dr Ste, Port Chester NY 10573	914-935-5300	R	179*	3.3
77	Linc Logistics Co—*H Wolfe*	11355 Stephens Rd, Warren MI 48089	586-467-1500	R	178*	1.5
78	1 Source Consulting Inc—*William R Teel Jr*	1250 H St NW Ste 575, Washington DC 20005	202-624-0800	R	178*	.3
79	Booz and Company Inc—*Shumeet Banerji*	101 Park Ave Fl 18, New York NY 10178	212-697-1900	R	174*	3.5
80	Development Dimensions International Inc—*William Byham*	1225 Wash Pke Ste 200, Bridgeville PA 15017	412-257-0600	R	172*	1.1
81	Mobile Mex-Media Group—*Mark Kowsikie*	8424 Great Circle Dr S, California City CA 93505	310-341-6731	R	172*	.3
82	Parsons Worley International—*Robert Edwardes*	6330 W Loop S Ste 200, Bellaire TX 77401	713-407-5000	R	171*	4.5
83	Island Hospitality Management Inc—*Jeffrey Fisher*	50 Cocoanut Row Ste 20, Palm Beach FL 33480	561-655-9001	R	170*	4.0
84	Rosetta LLC—*Roy Bielewicz*	100 American Metro Blv, Hamilton NJ 08619	609-689-6100	R	170*	1.1
85	Lightspeed Research Inc—*David Day*	3 Mountain View Rd 3rd, Warren NJ 07059	908-605-4500	S	168*	.3
86	Kurt Salmon Associates Inc—*Jerry Black*	1355 Peachtree St NE S, Atlanta GA 30309	404-892-0321	R	167*	1.0
87	Synavant Inc—*Wayne P Yetter*	3445 Peachtree Rd Ste, Atlanta GA 30326	404-841-4005	S	166*	1.3
88	Harris Interactive Inc—*Al Angrisani*	161 6th Ave, New York NY 10013	585-272-8400	P	165	.7
89	Jsi Research And Training Institute Inc—*Joel Lamstein*	44 Farnsworth St Fl 7, Boston MA 02210	617-482-9485	R	164*	.1
90	Logistics Insight Corp—*H Wolfe*	11355 Stephens Rd, Warren MI 48089	586-467-1500	R	160*	2.8
91	Logistics and Environmental Support Services Corp—*Anita Williams*	4845 University Sq Ste, Huntsville AL 35816	256-971-7165	R	158*	.2
92	Oliver Wyman Co—*John Drizik*	99 Park Ave, New York NY 10016	212-541-8100	S	157*	2.9
93	Icf Macro Inc—*Jeanne Townend*	11785 Bltsvlle Dr Ste, Beltsvlle MD 20705	301-572-0200	S	155*	.6
94	Finca International Inc—*Rupert Scofield*	1101 14th St Nw Fl 11, Washington DC 20005	202-682-1510	R	154*	.1
95	Rosé Management Services—*Jeffrey Henley*	29 Friends Ln, Newtown PA 18940	215-579-9220	R	153*	5.0
96	Christus Health Gulf Coast—*Bryan Higginbotham*	2707 N Loop W Ste 900, Houston TX 77008	281-599-5700	R	150*	2.8
97	Astadia Inc—*Steven Horwitz*	2839 Paces Ferry Rd St, Atlanta GA 30339	678-589-7670	R	149*	.2
98	Meadowbrook Golf Group Inc—*Ron Jackson*	8390 Champions Gate Bv, Lakeland FL 33801	407-589-7200	R	146*	2.7
99	Ventiv Health Inc—*Eran Broshy* Health Products Research Inc	200 Cottontail Ln Ste, Somerset NJ 08873	732-537-4800	S	145*	2.8
100	Health Products Research Inc—*Norman Stalsberg*	500 Atrium Dr Ste 100, Somerset NJ 08873	908-524-4148	R	143*	2.8
101	Datatrac Information Services Inc—*Jose Jimenez*	3170 Fairview Park Dr, Falls Church VA 22042	703-876-1000	R	143*	2.0
102	American Healthcare Administrative Services Inc—*Grover Lee*	2217 Plz Dr Ste 100, Rocklin CA 95765	916-773-7227	R	140*	.1
103	Apex Environmental Inc—*Peter T Young*	15860 Crabbs Branch Wa, Rockville MD 20855	301-417-0200	R	136*	.2
104	Accruent Inc—*Mark Friedman*	1601 Cloverfield Blvd, Santa Monica CA 90404	310-526-5700	R	136*	.2

Note: An asterisk (*) indicates an estimated financial figure. The company type code used is as follows: R = Private, P = Public, S = Private Subsidiary, B = Public Subsidiary, D = Division, J = Joint Venture, I = Investment Fund.

COMPANY RANKINGS BY SALES WITHIN 4-DIGIT SIC

Rank	Company Name—*Executive Officer*	Address, City, State, Zip	Phone	Type	Fin	Empls
105	Corporate VAT Management—*John Powell*	122 S Jackson Ste 330, Seattle WA 98104	206-292-0300	R	134*	.2
106	Avizent—*Tom Watson*	PO Box 182364, Columbus OH 43216	614-793-8000	R	132*	.5
107	Blackhawk Management Corp—*Linda Moorehead*	1335 Regents Park Ste, Houston TX 77058	281-286-5751	R	132*	.4
108	Cimco Communications Inc—*Bill Jr Capraro*	1901 S Meyers Rd Ste 7, Oakbrook Terrace IL 60181	630-691-8080	D	132*	.2
109	Diversified Pharmaceutical Services Inc—*George Paz*	6625 W 78th St, Minneapolis MN 55439	952-820-7000	S	130	1.0
110	Deloitte Consulting (Chadds Ford Pennsylvania)	2 Braxton Way, Glen Mills PA 19342	610-479-3900	D	130*	.4
111	DL Ryan Companies Ltd—*David L Ryan*	PO Box 800, Wilton CT 06897	203-210-3000	R	129*	.3
112	Complete Rx Ltd—*Terry Andrus*	3100 S Gessner Rd Ste, Houston TX 77063	713-355-1196	R	125*	.4
113	ColleMcVoy—*Christine Fruechte*	400 1st Ave N Ste 700, Minneapolis MN 55401	612-305-6000	R	124*	.2
114	Wexford Group International Inc	8618 Westwood Center D, Vienna VA 22182	703-852-9569	S	121*	.2
115	CTPartners Executive Search Inc—*Brian Sullivan*	1166 Avenue of the Ame, New York NY 10036	212-588-3500	P	118	.3
116	Red Ventures LLC—*Ric Elias*	1101 521 Corporate Cen, Fort Mill SC 29707	704-971-2300	R	117*	.5
117	ICG Group Inc—*Walter W Buckley III*	690 Lee Rd Ste 310, Wayne PA 19087	610-727-6900	P	116	<.1
118	Lacek Group—*Bill Baker*	900 2nd Ave S Ste1800, Minneapolis MN 55402	612-359-3700	S	113*	.2
119	Creative Associates International Inc—*M Charito Kruvant*	5301 Wisconsin Ave NW, Washington DC 20015	202-966-5804	R	110*	.3
120	George S May International Co—*Kerry Sam Jacobs*	303 S Northwest Hwy, Park Ridge IL 60068	847-825-8806	R	109*	1.2
121	Global Insight Inc—*Scott C Key*	24 Hartwell Ave, Lexington MA 02421	781-301-9200	S	109*	.7
122	Premier Inc—*Susan D de Vore*	13034 Ballantyne Corpo, Charlotte NC 28277	704-357-0022	R	108*	1.2
123	OR Colan Associates Inc—*Catherine Colan Muth*	4651 Charlotte Park Dr, Charlotte NC 28217	704-529-3115	R	103*	.2
124	Access Development Corp—*Larry Maxfield*	PO Box 27563, Salt Lake City UT 84127		R	102*	.2
125	Coding Source LLC—*Greg J Sinaiko*	3415 S Sepulveda Blvd, Los Angeles CA 90034	310-622-1001	R	102*	.2
126	Ryan Management Group—*Dan Sullivan* DL Ryan Companies Ltd	PO Box 800, Wilton CT 06897	203-210-3000	S	100*	.3
127	Harte-Hanks Direct Marketing/Baltimore Inc—*Larry Franklin*	6701 Baymeadow Dr, Glen Burnie MD 21060	410-424-2050	S	100*	.2
128	J Brown/LMC Group—*Jon Kramer*	1010 Washington Blvd F, Stamford CT 06902	203-352-0800	R	100*	.2
129	SiloSmashers Inc—*Angela Drummond*	2677 Prosperity Ave St, Fairfax VA 22031	703-797-5600	R	99*	.2
130	Ventana Research—*Mark Smith*	2603 Camino Ramon Ste, San Ramon CA 94583	925-242-2579	R	99*	.2
131	SM and A—*Kevin Reiners*	4695 MacArthur Ct 8th, Newport Beach CA 92660	949-975-1550	R	98*	.4
132	Miller Zell Inc—*Harmon B Miller III*	4715 Frederick Dr, Atlanta GA 30336	404-691-7400	R	97*	.3
133	Ayzenberg Group—*Eric Ayzenberg*	49 E Walnut St, Pasadena CA 91103	626-584-4070	R	96	.1
134	Harry Fox Agency Inc—*Gary L Churgin*	601 W 26th St Ste 500, New York NY 10001	212-834-0100	R	95*	.1
135	Smith-Emery Co—*James Partridge*	791 E Wash Blvd Fl 2, Los Angeles CA 90021	213-749-3411	R	95*	.2
136	Wellness Power Management LLC—*John Danowski*	2055 W Army Trl Rd Ste, Addison IL 60101	630-570-2600	R	91*	1.9
137	A'viands LLC—*Terri Brooks*	1751 County Rd B W Ste, Saint Paul MN 55113	651-631-0940	R	91*	1.9
138	Execupharm Inc—*Maria Larson*	500 N Gulph Rd Ste 120, King Of Prussia PA 19406	610-272-8771	R	90*	.8
139	Point B—*Mike Pongon*	1420 5th Ave Ste 2200, Seattle WA 98101	206-517-5000	R	89	.4
140	Mattersight Corp—*Kelly D Conway*	200 S Wacker Dr Ste 82, Chicago IL 60606	847-582-7000	P	88	.4
141	PracticeWorks Inc—*Richard Hirschland*	1765 The Exchange Ste, Atlanta GA 30339	770-850-5006	S	87*	.7
142	Landor Associates—*Charlie Wrench*	1001 Front St, San Francisco CA 94111	415-365-1700	S	83*	.8
143	Dairy One Cooperative—*Jamie Zimmerman*	730 Warren Rd, Ithaca NY 14850	607-257-1272	R	81*	.2
144	University Research Company LLC—*Barbara N Turner*	7200 Wisconsin Ave Ste, Bethesda MD 20814	301-654-8338	R	80*	.6
145	RHR International LLP—*Thomas J Saporito*	220 Gerry Dr, Wood Dale IL 60191	630-766-7007	R	80*	.1
146	Adea Solutions Inc—*Abid H Abedi*	545 E John Carpenter F, Irving TX 75062	972-764-1700	S	78*	1.1
147	EA Engineering Science and Technology Inc—*Ian D MacFarlane*	11019 McCormick Rd, Hunt Valley MD 21031	410-584-7000	R	76*	.5
148	Fortress International Group Inc—*Thomas A Rosato*	7226 Lee DeForest Dr S, Columbia MD 21046	410-423-7438	P	75	.1
149	EL Hamm Associates Inc—*Edward L Hamm Jr*	4801 Columbus St, Virginia Beach VA 23462	757-497-5000	R	72*	.2
150	Creative Group Inc	619 North Lynndale Dr, Appleton WI 54914	920-739-8850	R	72*	.1
151	Swanson Sinkey Ellis Inc—*Dave Hanson*	1222 P St, Lincoln NE 68508	402-437-6400	R	71*	.1
152	Customer Value Partners—*Anirudh Kulkarni*	3701 Pender Dr Ste 200, Fairfax VA 22030	703-345-9100	R	71*	.1
153	Career Partners International LLC—*Rayann Burnham*	6340 Quadrangle Dr Ste, Chapel Hill NC 27517	919-401-4260	R	70*	1.6
154	Parson Group LLC—*Kevin Parry*	333 W Wacker Dr Ste 16, Chicago IL 60606	312-578-1170	S	70*	.7
155	Dean and Co—*Dean Wilde*	8065 Leesburg Pike 5th, Vienna VA 22182	703-506-3900	R	70*	.1
156	Convio Inc—*Gene Austin*	11501 Domain Dr Ste 20, Austin TX 78758	512-652-2600	P	70	.4
157	Aegis Communications Group Inc—*Sandip Sen*	8201 Ridge Point Dr, Irving TX 75063	972-830-1800	S	69	3.7
158	Productivity Inc—*Thomas L Jackson*	4 Armstrong Rd 3rd Fl, Shelton CT 06484	203-225-0451	R	68*	.1
159	RM Towill Corp—*Russell Figueiroa*	2024 N King St, Honolulu HI 96819	808-842-1133	S	68*	.1
160	Management Network Group Inc—*Richard Nespola*	7300 College Blvd Ste, Overland Park KS 66210	913-345-9315	P	67	.4
161	Adair Greene Inc—*Warren Greene*	1575 Northside Dr NW B, Atlanta GA 30318	404-351-8424	R	67*	.1
162	Linkage Inc—*Phillip J Harkins*	200 Wheeler Rd, Burlington MA 01803	781-402-5400	R	67*	.1
163	HealthCo Information Systems Inc—*Mike Cooper*	7657 SW Mohawk, Tualatin OR 97062	503-612-1666	R	66*	.1
164	Carbon Healthcare—*Darlene Dobry*	420 Interpace Pkwy, Parsippany NJ 07054	973-352-3500	S	65*	.1
165	Myers-Holum Inc—*Mark Myers*	244 Madison Ave Ste 21, New York NY 10016	212-753-5353	R	65*	.1
166	Visionary Integration Professionals LLC—*Jonna A Ward*	80 Iron Point Cir Ste, Folsom CA 95630	916-985-9625	R	64*	.1
167	Agilex Technologies Inc—*Robert Larose*	5155 Parkstone Dr, Chantilly VA 20151		R	63*	.1
168	Frost and Sullivan Inc—*Krishna Srinivasan*	7550 W IH-10 Ste 400, San Antonio TX 78229	210-348-1000	R	62*	.7
169	Kepner-Tregoe Inc—*Andrew Graham*	PO Box 704, Princeton NJ 08542	609-921-2806	R	62*	.2
170	Yankee Group—*Terry Waters*	1 Liberty Sq 7th Fl, Boston MA 02109	617-598-7200	R	62*	.2
171	Shay Investment Services Inc—*Roger Shay Jr*	1000 Brickell Ave Ste, Miami FL 33131	305-379-6656	R	61*	.1
172	Vitalsmarts LLC—*Andrew Shimberg*	282 W River Bend Ln St, Provo UT 84604	801-765-9600	R	61*	.1
173	Hibbert Group (Denver Colorado)—*Timothy J Moonan*	2399 Blake St Ste 120, Denver CO 80205		S	60	.8
174	Scientech Inc (Milford Connecticut)—*Larry Brodsky*	143 W Ave, New Milford CT 06776		S	60	.3
175	Optimum Group Inc—*Michael Halldrand*	9745 Mangham Dr, Cincinnati OH 45215	513-577-7000	S	59*	.2
176	WA Wilde Co—*Thomas A Wilde*	200 Summer St, Holliston MA 01746	508-429-5515	R	59	.4
177	Studeo Interactive Direct—*Scott Kenall*	6405 S 3000 E Ste 200, Salt Lake City UT 84121	801-993-2300	R	57*	.1
178	Executive Consulting Group Inc—*Andrew McDonald*	1111 3rd Ave Ste 2700, Seattle WA 98101	206-689-2200	R	56*	.2
179	Triage Consulting Group—*Brian Neece*	221 Main St Ste 1100, San Francisco CA 94105	415-512-9400	R	56*	.3
180	Proudfoot Consulting—*Luiz Carvalho*	11621 Kew Gardens Ave, West Palm Beach FL 33410	561-624-4377	S	55*	.1
181	Link America Inc—*Andres Ruzo*	3002 Century Dr, Rowlett TX 75088	972-463-0050	R	55	<.1
182	Hinda Incentives—*Michael Arkes*	2440 W 34th St, Chicago IL 60608	773-890-5900	R	54*	.1
183	Lippincott—*Rick Wise*	499 Park Ave, New York NY 10022	212-521-0000	S	54*	.1
184	Triple-I Corp—*Perry A Puccetti*	6330 Lamar Ave Ste 230, Overland Park KS 66202	913-563-7200	R	54*	.1
185	Greenwich Associates—*Joseph Herbert*	6 High Ridge Park, Stamford CT 06905	203-629-1200	R	53*	.2
186	TWC Group—*Terry Williams*	2570 Blvd of the Gener, Audubon PA 19403	610-635-0101	R	53*	.1
187	RW Lynch Company Inc—*Randy Lynch*	2333 San Ramon Valley, San Ramon CA 94583	925-837-3877	R	52*	.2
188	Code Consultants Inc—*Gregory R Miller*	2043 Woodland Pky Ste, St Louis MO 63146	314-991-2633	R	52*	.1
189	MSI International East Inc—*Paul J Strasser*	650 Park Ave, King of Prussia PA 19406	610-265-2000	R	52*	.1
190	Widepoint Corp—*Steven L Komar*	18W100 22nd St Ste 124, Oakbrook Terrace IL 60181	630-629-0003	P	51	.1
191	Range Online Media—*Misty Locke*	131 E Exchange Ave Ste, Fort Worth TX 76164	817-625-4157	R	50*	.1
192	Thobe Group Inc—*Deborah J Thobe*	2727 Raintree Dr, Carrollton TX 75006	972-245-9444	R	49*	.1

Rank	Company Name—*Executive Officer*	Address, City, State, Zip	Phone	Type	Fin	Empls
193	Accent Marketing Services Inc—*Tim Searcy*	400 Missouri Ave Ste 1, Jeffersonville IN 47130	812-206-6200	R	48*	1.0
194	North Highland Co—*Dan Reardon*	550 Pharr Rd NE Ste 85, Atlanta GA 30305	404-233-1015	R	48*	.7
195	Zyman Group LLC—*Scott Miller*	303 Peachtree Center A, Atlanta GA 30303	404-682-5400	R	47*	.1
196	Hildebrandt Baker Robbins—*Ian Dinwiddie*	200 Cottontail Ln, Somerset NJ 08873	732-560-8888	S	46*	.1
197	Sibson Consulting Group—*Howard Fluhr*	1009 Lenox Drive Suite, Lawrenceville NJ 08648	609-482-2300	S	46*	.2
198	Knowledge Systems and Research Inc—*Rita Reicher*	120 Madison St 15th Fl, Syracuse NY 13202	315-470-1350	R	45*	.3
199	Omega Performance Corp—*John Golden*	8701 Red Oak Blvd Ste, Charlotte NC 28217	704-672-1400	R	45*	.3
200	Incentive Concepts LLC—*Jeffery Reinberg*	2645 Metro Blvd, Maryland Heights MO 63043	314-801-1504	R	45*	<.1
201	Zempleo Inc—*Ramiro Zeron*	1331 N California Blvd, Walnut Creek CA 94596	925-284-5414	R	45*	<.1
202	Vcst Inc—*Vivian Wheaton*	13854 Lakeside Cir 201, Sterling Heights MI 48313	586-685-1747	R	44*	1.0
203	Convergenz LLC—*Greg McGuire*	8260 Greensboro Dr 5th, McLean VA 22102	703-584-3700	R	44*	.4
204	Epsilon Data Management LLC	1000 Summit Dr Ste 200, Milford OH 45150	513-707-6800	S	44*	.2
205	Axiom Resource Management Inc—*A Douglas Peardon Jr*	5203 Leesburg Pke Ste, Falls Church VA 22041	703-998-0327	R	43*	.5
206	TBM Consulting Group Inc—*Anand Sharma*	4400 Ben Franklin Blvd, Durham NC 27704	919-471-5535	R	43*	.1
207	Creditron Financial Corp—*Joyce Covatto*	PO Box 3368, Erie PA 16508	814-868-4824	R	42*	.7
208	1 Touch Marketing LLC—*Michael Decespedes*	123 Nw 13th St Ste 300, Boca Raton FL 33432	561-368-5067	R	42*	1.0
209	Quantech Services Inc—*Jim Monopoli*	91 Hartwell Ave 3rd Fl, Lexington MA 02421	781-271-9757	R	42*	.3
210	Alan B Whitson Company Inc—*Alan Whitson*	PO Box 9229, Newport Beach CA 92658	949-955-1200	R	41*	.8
211	Generational Equity Co—*Dwight Jacobs*	14241 Dallas Pkwy Ste, Dallas TX 75254		R	41*	.2
212	Bridge Integrated Communications—*Jay Woffington*	302 W 3rd St Ste 900, Cincinnati OH 45202	513-381-1380	R	41*	.1
213	Pioneer Health Services Inc—*Joseph Mcnulty*	PO Box 1100, Magee MS 39111	601-849-6440	R	40*	.2
214	Eagle Systems And Services Inc—*Rhonda Clemmer*	6223 W Gore Blvd, Lawton OK 73505	580-355-6023	R	40*	.8
215	Clinical Resources For Equipment Support Technology Services Inc—*Brian Montgomery*	735 Plz Blvd Ste 210, Coppell TX 75019	214-488-9301	R	40*	.2
216	Wastren Advantage Inc—*Steve Moore*	1571 Shyville Rd, Piketon OH 45661	740-443-7924	R	40*	.1
217	Condor Earth Technologies Inc—*Robert Job*	21663 Brian Ln, Sonora CA 95370	209-532-0361	R	40*	.1
218	Visionary Solutions LLC—*Cavanaugh Mims*	111-B Union Valley Rd, Oak Ridge TN 37830	865-482-8670	R	40*	.1
219	Pohlad Cos—*Robert Pohlad*	60 S 6th St Ste 3700, Minneapolis MN 55402	612-661-3700	R	39*	.7
220	Channel Marketing Corp—*David M Goldstein*	5200 Keller Springs Rd, Dallas TX 75248	972-960-0800	R	37*	<.1
221	Your Recruiting Company Inc—*John Jaeger*	3877 Fairfax Ridge Rd, Fairfax VA 22030	703-995-9600	R	37*	.3
222	Campbell Alliance Group Inc—*John J Campbell*	8045 Arco Corporate Dr, Raleigh NC 27617	919-844-7100	R	36*	.1
223	Hospitality Automation Consultants Ltd—*Lester I Spielman*	5013 Wilkinson Ave, Valley Village CA 91607	818-763-4449	R	36*	.1
224	CPAlead—*Peter Tarr*	6845 S Escondido St St, Las Vegas NV 89119		R	35	<.1
225	Capital H Group—*Jim Tapper*	130 W 42nd St Ste 1002, New York NY 10036	312-416-0700	R	35*	.2
226	Rexnord Technical Services—*Bill Ryan*	5101 W Beloit Rd, Milwaukee WI 53214	414-643-3067	D	35*	.1
227	ADS Financial Services Solutions—*William H Gallagher*	1 Batterymarch Pk, Quincy MA 02169	617-770-3333	R	34	.1
228	Med-Vantage Inc—*Geof Baker*	111 Sutter St 14th Fl, San Francisco CA 94104	415-814-7100	S	34*	.1
229	Program Planning Professionals Inc—*Adrian Balfour*	3923 Ranchero Dr, Ann Arbor MI 48108	734-741-7770	R	33*	.4
230	Bridge Design Inc—*Bill Evans*	375 Alabama St Ste 410, San Francisco CA 94110	415-487-7100	R	33*	.1
231	Access Worldwide Communications Inc—*Shawkat Raslan*	6402 Arlington Blvd 4t, Falls Church VA 22042	571-384-7000	P	33	1.0
232	Calnet Inc—*Kaleem S Shah*	12359 Sunrise Valley D, Reston VA 20191	703-547-6800	R	32*	.7
233	Premier Environmental Services Inc—*Earl Scott*	1880 W Oak Pky Bldg 10, Marietta GA 30062		R	32*	.2
234	Bahadur Balan and Kazerski Ltd—*William G Diehl*	300 Galleria Officentr, Southfield MI 48034	248-356-0800	R	32*	.1
235	Telwares Communications LLC—*Charlotte Yates*	7901 Stoneridge Dr Ste, Pleasanton CA 94588	925-224-7800	S	32*	.1
236	BioPharm Systems—*Alex Sefanov*	2000 Alameda de las Pu, San Mateo CA 94403		R	32*	.1
237	First Class Solutions Inc—*Rose T Dunn*	11426 Dorsett Rd, Maryland Heights MO 63043	314-209-7800	R	31*	<.1
238	Kingfisher Systems Inc—*Pete Howton*	3110 Fairview Park Dr, Falls Church VA 22042	703-820-7970	R	31*	<.1
239	Intouoh Solutions Inc—*Faruk Capan*	10975 Benson St Ste 20, Overland Park KS 66210	913-317-9700	R	30*	.2
240	Calvert Holdings Inc—*Allan N Reiss*	1225 Crescent Green St, Cary NC 27518	919-854-4453	R	30*	.1
241	Firefly Millward Brown—*Cheryl Stallworth-Hooper*	274 Riverside Ave, Westport CT 06880	203-221-0411	S	30*	.1
242	Astyra Corp—*Ken Ampy*	Linden Tower 116 E Fra, Richmond VA 23219	804-433-1100	R	30*	<.1
243	Shannon and Wilson Inc—*Gerard Buechel*	400 N 34th St, Seattle WA 98103	206-632-8020	R	29*	.3
244	Clinical Marketing Consortium—*Leonard S Schleifer*	777 Old Saw Mill River, Tarrytown NY 10591	914-345-9009	R	29*	<.1
245	Sentigy Inc—*Cindy Boyd*	3 Riverway Ste 1430, Houston TX 77056	713-481-3340	R	29*	<.1
246	SEOmoz—*Rand Fishkin*	119 Pine St Ste 400, Seattle WA 98101	206-632-3171	R	29*	<.1
247	Travelclick—*Larry Kutscher*	300 N Martingale Rd St, Schaumburg IL 60173	847-969-0820	R	28*	.5
248	Xtreme Consulting Group Inc—*Greg Rankich*	4014 148th Ave NE, Redmond WA 98052	425-861-9460	R	28	.2
249	Management Consulting and Research LLC—*Vincent J Kiernan Albert*	2010 Corporate Ridge S, McLean VA 22102	703-506-4600	R	27	.3
250	Morgan Borszcz Consulting—*Christine Morgan*	42395 Ryan Road Ste 11, Brambleton VA 20148		R	27*	.2
251	Paradigm Learning Inc—*Raymond D Green*	100 2nd Ave S 12th Fl, Saint Petersburg FL 33701	727-471-3170	R	27*	<.1
252	Blackstone Consulting Inc—*Ronald Blackstone*	11726 San Vicente Blvd, Los Angeles CA 90049	310-826-4389	R	27*	.5
253	Interflight Services Inc—*Fredrick Parsons*	515 116th Ave Ne Ste 1, Bellevue WA 98004	425-462-5700	R	26*	.5
254	Issues and Answers Network Inc—*Peter McGinnis*	5151 Bonney Rd Ste 100, Virginia Beach VA 23462	757-456-1100	R	26*	.6
255	Futuredontics Inc—*Alfred Joyal*	PO Box 45005, Los Angeles CA 90045	310-215-6400	R	26*	.3
256	WL Ross and Company LLC—*Wilbur L Ross Jr*	1166 Ave Of The Americ, New York NY 10036	212-826-1100	S	26*	<.1
257	Hicks And Associates Inc	1710 SAIC Dr Ste 1300, McLean VA 22102	703-676-4300	S	25*	<.1
258	Analytical Management Solutions Inc—*L Alex Staley*	9911 W Pico Blvd Ste 5, Los Angeles CA 90035	310-785-9470	R	25*	<.1
259	Performance Assessment Network Inc—*David T Pfenninger*	11590 N Meridian St St, Carmel IN 46032	317-566-3270	S	25	N/A
260	Revenue Production Management Inc—*Hamid Mirafzali*	991 Oak Creek Dr, Lombard IL 60148	847-257-3000	R	25*	.2
261	Stron International Inc—*Douglas Smith*	PO Box 36497, Pensacola FL 32516	850-453-0437	R	24*	.7
262	Roux Associates Inc—*Paul H Roux*	209 Shafter St, Islandia NY 11749	631-232-2600	R	24*	.3
263	HMS Inc (Arlington Virginia)—*Ted Spilman*	1235 S Clark St Ste 12, Arlington VA 22202	703-412-9394	R	24*	<.1
264	Integrated Healthcare Strategies—*Robert Erra*	700 W 47th St Ste 400, Kansas City MO 64112	816-795-1947	R	24*	<.1
265	GMAC Global Relocation Services—*Steve Phillips*	465 South St 2nd Fl E, Morristown NJ 07960		R	24*	<.1
266	Gerstman Harvey and Associates Inc—*Harvey Gerstman*	439 Oak St, Garden City NY 11530	516-594-4400	R	24*	.3
267	Specialized Health Management Co—*Nancy Nager*	246 Walnut St Ste 104, Newton MA 02460	617-244-3322	R	23*	.1
268	Control Systems International Inc—*Nelson Shirley*	8040 Nieman Rd, Lenexa KS 66214	913-599-5010	R	22*	.2
269	KSJ and Associates Inc—*Kasey S Jarosz*	5203 Leesburg Pike Ste, Falls Church VA 22041	703-824-7802	R	22*	.1
270	Kenesis Corporate and Information Consulting LLC—*Jonathan Terrell*	1100 New York Ave NW S, Washington DC 20005	202-772-2300	R	22*	<.1
271	Linium LLC—*Eduardo Arroyo*	187 Wolf Rd Ste 210, Albany NY 12205	518-689-3100	R	22*	.2
272	Michaelson Connor and Boul—*Joan Held*	5312 Bolsa Ave Ste 200, Huntington Beach CA 92649	714-230-3600	R	22*	.2
273	Octo Consulting Group—*Mehul Sanghani*	8000 Towers Cres Dr 13, Vienna VA 22182	703-847-3621	R	22	.1
274	Magnacare LLC—*Andrea Clark*	825 E Gate Blvd Ste 10, Garden City NY 11530	516-282-8000	R	21*	.3
275	Nursing Home and Hospital Consultant Corp—*S Andersen*	1913 N Pearl St, Jacksonville FL 32206	904-254-1341	R	21*	.1
276	Mountain Services Inc—*Joseph Hosmer*	19 Yarmouth Dr, New Gloucester ME 04260	207-688-6200	R	21*	<.1
277	Crescent Solutions—*Brian Fischbein*	1702 S Dixie Hwy Ste 2, Lake Worth FL 33460	561-585-1700	R	21*	<.1
278	AJ Higgins Search Group LP—*Bruce Long*	17440 N Dallas Pkwy St, Dallas TX 75287	972-267-3200	R	21*	<.1
279	Renaissance At South Shore—*Robert Hartman*	2425 E 71st St, Chicago IL 60649	773-721-5000	R	21*	.3

Note: An asterisk (*) indicates an estimated financial figure. The company type code used is as follows: R = Private, P = Public, S = Private Subsidiary, B = Public Subsidiary, D = Division, J = Joint Venture, I = Investment Fund.

COMPANY RANKINGS BY SALES WITHIN 4-DIGIT SIC

Rank	Company Name—Executive Officer	Address, City, State, Zip	Phone	Type	Fin	Empls
280	Personnel Decisions International Inc—RJ Heckman	33 S 6th St Ste 4900, Minneapolis MN 55402	612-339-0927	R	20*	.3
281	Wilson Learning Corp—Ed Emde	8000 W 78th St Ste 200, Edina MN 55439	952-944-2880	R	20*	.1
282	Project Management Solutions Inc—J Kent Crawford	1788 Wilmington Pike, Glen Mills PA 19342	610-853-3679	R	20*	.1
283	Training Associates Corp—Victor Melfa	287 Tpke Rd, Westborough MA 01581	508-890-8500	R	20*	.1
284	PrimeNet Marketing Services Inc—Mark Keefe	2100 Palmetto St Ste A, Clearwater FL 33765	727-447-6245	R	20*	.1
285	International Resources Group Ltd—Asif M Shaikh	1211 Connecticut Ave N, Washington DC 20036	202-289-0100	R	20*	.1
286	Aleri Inc—Don DeLoach	2 Prudential Plz, Chicago IL 60601	312-540-0100	R	20*	<.1
287	A10 Clinical Solutions Inc—Leah Brown	2000 Regency Pky Ste 6, Cary NC 27518	919-465-3366	R	20	.3
288	Advertising Checking Bureau Inc—Brian McShane	2 Park Ave 18th Fl, New York NY 10016	212-684-3377	R	19*	.3
289	Cenergy LLC—Chuck King	PO Box 455, Milton WV 25541	304-743-4250	R	19*	.1
290	Campus Dimensions Inc—Edward Solomon	1880 John F Kennedy Bl, Philadelphia PA 19103	215-568-1700	R	19*	.1
291	Consumer Resource Network LLC	9800 S La Cienega Blvd, Inglewood CA 90301		R	19*	.3
292	Promo Works LLC—Jon Bos	300 N Martingale Rd, Schaumburg IL 60173	847-310-2600	R	19*	.4
293	Administrative Services Cooperative Inc—Raymond Mcgreevy	2129 W Rosecrans Ave, Gardena CA 90249	310-715-1968	R	18*	.2
294	Professional Research Consultants Inc—Joe Inguanzo	11326 P St, Omaha NE 68137	402-592-5656	R	18*	.4
295	Net Matrix Solutions—Pankaj Maheshwari	10235 W Little York Rd, Houston TX 77040	281-598-2600	R	18*	.2
296	Big Communications Inc—Brad Oleshansky	1200 Woodward Hts, Ferndale MI 48220	248-246-5200	R	18*	.1
297	Data Consulting Group Inc—Wayne Wheeler	965 E Jefferson Ave, Detroit MI 48207	313-963-7771	R	18*	.1
298	Jancyn—Jan Pelletriere	PO Box 26934, San Jose CA 95159	408-267-2600	R	18*	<.1
299	Marden-Kane Inc—Paul Goldman	1055 Franklin Ave Ste, Garden City NY 11530	516-365-3999	R	18*	<.1
300	Phillip Townsend Associates Inc—Dave Bohmbach	523 N Sam Houston Pky, Houston TX 77060	281-873-8733	R	18*	<.1
301	P3S Corp—Mary Ellen Londrie	13750 San Pedro Ste 64, San Antonio TX 78232	210-496-6934	R	18	.3
302	Chesley Brown International Inc—Brent Brown	1190 Winchester Pkwy S, Smyrna GA 30080	770-436-3097	R	17*	.4
303	Sertec Corp—Steve Mitchell	2100 Powers Ferry Rd S, Atlanta GA 30339	770-916-6700	R	17*	.3
304	Manfredi and Associates Inc—Frank Manfredi	20934 W Lakeview Pkwy, Mundelein IL 60060	847-949-9080	R	17*	<.1
305	One Source Industries LLC—Laural Dimock	185 Technology Dr Ste, Irvine CA 92618	949-784-7700	S	17*	<.1
306	Suntiva Executive Consulting LLC—Michael Dow	7600 Leesburg Pke Ste, Falls Church VA 22043	703-462-8470	R	17	.1
307	Infinity Direct Inc—Tom Harding	13220 County Rd 6 Ste, Minneapolis MN 55441	763-559-1111	R	17*	<.1
308	Spectraforce Technologies Inc—Amit Singh	5511 Capital Center Dr, Raleigh NC 27606	919-233-4466	R	16*	.5
309	Revel Consulting Inc—Vikas Kamran	4020 Lake Washington B, Kirkland WA 98033	206-407-3173	R	16*	.1
310	Corwin Toyota Inc—Tim Corwin	201 SW 40th St, Fargo ND 58103	701-282-8425	R	16*	.1
311	MarketerNet LLC—Richard Scolio	233 S Wacker Dr Ste 18, Chicago IL 60606	312-229-5800	R	16*	.1
312	Permedion—Thomas Schultz	350 Worthington Rd Ste, Westerville OH 43082	614-895-9900	S	16*	.1
313	US RE Corp—Tal P Piccione	1 Blue Hill Plz, Pearl River NY 10965	845-920-7100	R	16*	<.1
314	Bolton Partners Inc—Robert Bolten	100 Light St FL9, Baltimore MD 21202	410-547-0500	R	16*	<.1
315	ImageOne Inc—Lee Reams Sr	PO Box 141580, Grand Rapids MI 49514		R	16*	<.1
316	ETG Inc—Sameer Kishore	2 Christie Heights St, Leonia NJ 07605	201-840-4700	S	16*	<.1
317	Supply Chain Edge—John DuBiel	1505 Brightwater Ct St, Raleigh NC 27614	440-937-5151	R	16*	<.1
318	His Manna Inc—Gordon Agrella	PO Box 1527, Santa Cruz CA 95061	831-429-8609	R	16*	.2
319	Direct Technologies Inc—David Jacobson	PO Box 3955, Suwanee GA 30024	678-288-1700	R	16*	.1
320	Corporate Fitness Works Inc—Sheila Drohan	18558 Office Park Dr, Montgomery Village MD 20886	301-417-9697	R	16*	.3
321	Federated Funeral Directors Of America Inc—John Rodenburg	PO Box 19244, Springfield IL 62794	217-525-1712	R	16*	.2
322	Control Associates/ Constantin Group LP—Chris Mitrovich	525 Washington Blvd Fl, Jersey City NJ 07310	201-377-7652	R	15*	.2
323	Resource Ventures Ltd—Anu Hariharan	343 N Front St Ste 300, Columbus OH 43215	614-621-2888	R	15*	.3
324	Applied Manufacturing Technologies Inc—Michael Jacobs	219 Kay Industrial Dr, Orion MI 48359	248-409-2000	R	15*	.3
325	Dodson Group Inc—Jim R Dodson	201 N Illinois St Ste, Indianapolis IN 46204	317-489-9008	R	15	<.1
326	Scientific Certification Systems Inc—Stanley Rhodes	2200 Powell St Ste 725, Emeryville CA 94608	510-452-8000	R	15*	<.1
327	Akoya—Bonnie Rack-Wildner	2325 E Carson St, Pittsburgh PA 15203	412-481-9800	R	15*	<.1
328	E3 Consulting LLC—Paul Plath	3333 S Bannock St Ste, Englewood CO 80110	303-762-7060	R	15*	<.1
329	Corporate Team Professionals—Denis Bruncak	4000 Venture Ct, Columbus OH 43228	614-850-7070	R	15*	<.1
330	Wilhelmina International Inc—Mark E Schwarz	200 Crescent Ct Ste 14, Dallas TX 75201	214-661-7488	P	15	.1
331	School Innovations And Advocacy Inc—Jeffrey Williams	11130 Sun Ctr Dr, Rancho Cordova CA 95670	916-669-0888	R	15*	.2
332	XT Global—Ramarao Mullapudi	18170 Dallas Pky Ste 2, Dallas TX 75287	972-755-1800	R	14	.3
333	Information International Associates Inc—Bonnie Carroll	PO Box 4219, Oak Ridge TN 37831.	865-481-0388	R	14*	.2
334	Willbros Engineers Inc—Robert Harl	PO Box 701650, Tulsa OK 74170	918-496-0400	S	14*	.2
335	Communispond—Bill Rosenthal	5 Lauras Ln, East Hampton NY 11937	631-907-8010	R	14*	.1
336	Stern and Associates—Gerry Stern	11260 Overland Ave Apt, Culver City CA 90230	310-838-0551	R	14	.1
337	Cura Group Inc—Frank Masie	3000 Atrium Wy, Mount Laurel NJ 08054	856-439-1113	R	14*	.1
338	Pragmatek Consulting Group Ltd—Steve Bloom	8500 Normandale Lake B, Bloomington MN 55437	612-333-3164	R	14*	.1
339	Jenkins Construction Inc—James B Jenkins	985 E Jefferson Ave St, Detroit MI 48207	313-625-7200	R	14*	<.1
340	Cumberland Group—Michael F Guibord	PO Box 46927, Cincinnati OH 45246	513-777-2800	R	14*	<.1
341	Jassin O'Rourke—Andrew Jassin	1370 Broadway Rm 1002, New York NY 10018	212-382-0045	R	14*	<.1
342	Mann Consulting—Harold Mann	282 2nd St 4th Fl, San Francisco CA 94105	415-546-6266	R	14*	<.1
343	Marx Layne and Co—Fredrick Marx	31420 Northwestern Hwy, Farmington Hills MI 48334	248-855-6777	R	14*	<.1
344	Practice Management Group LLC (Murrells Inlet South Carolina)—Michael Mitchell	5127 Ocean Hwy, Murrells Inlet SC 29576		R	14*	<.1
345	Trout and Partners Ltd—Jack Trout	8 Wahneta Rd, Old Greenwich CT 06870	203-637-7001	R	14*	<.1
346	East West Connection Inc—Ralph Weaver	389 Pittstown Rd, Pittstown NJ 08867	908-713-9655	R	14*	<.1
347	Specialized Services and Personnel—Jennifer Mcgill	301 N Sycamore St, Aberdeen NC 28315	910-944-8125	R	14*	.3
348	Matt Construction Corp—Paul Matt	9814 Norwalk Blvd Ste, Santa Fe Springs CA 90670	562-903-2277	R	14*	.1
349	Shepardson Stern and Kaminsky—Rob Shepardson	88 Pine St 30th Fl, New York NY 10005	212-274-9500	R	13*	.1
350	RJ Gordon and Co—Richard J Gordon	444 S Flower St Ste 18, Los Angeles CA 90071	213-986-4411	R	13*	.1
351	Broadstreet Inc—Mark Baltazar	20 W 22nd St Fl 12, New York NY 10010	212-780-5700	R	13*	<.1
352	Analytics Operations Engineering Inc—Mitchell Burman	111 Devonshire St 8th, Boston MA 02109	617-303-3600	R	13*	<.1
353	Harte-Hanks Data Services LLC—Larry Franklin	200 Concord Plz Dr Ste, San Antonio TX 78216	210-829-9000	S	13*	<.1
354	Innovation Group (New Orleans Louisiana)—Steven Rittvo	400 N Peters St Ste 20, New Orleans LA 70130	504-523-0888	R	13*	<.1
355	Medtech Insight LLC—Sharon O'Reilly	1 Technology Dr Bldg J, Irvine CA 92618	949-453-0071	S	13*	<.1
356	Battle Resource Management—Mike Battle	5525 Adams Ridge Rd, Clarksville MD 21029	202-449-3763	R	13*	<.1
357	Focus Environmental Inc—William Troxler	9050 Executive Park Dr, Knoxville TN 37923	865-694-7517	R	13*	<.1
358	International Quality Consultants Inc—Thomas Paserba	106 Freeport Rd, Butler PA 16002	724-284-3738	R	13*	.1
359	Ifc Holdings Inc—Lynn Niedermeier	8745 Tenderson Rd Ste, Tampa FL 33634	813-289-0722	R	13*	.3
360	Sierra Financial Services Inc—Scott Priesmeyer	380 Interlocken Cresce, Broomfield CO 80021	303-530-7770	R	13*	.2
361	ALK Technologies Inc—Barry J Glick	1000 Herrontown Rd Ste, Princeton NJ 08540	609-683-0220	R	12*	.2
362	Zoyto Inc—Chris Hollis	433 Northpark Central, Houston TX 77073	713-300-3000	R	12*	.1
363	ITA International LLC—Mike Melo	111 Cybernetics Way St, Yorktown VA 23693	757-246-6781	R	12*	.1
364	PetroSkills—W Dennis Wing	PO Box 35448, Tulsa OK 74153	918-828-2500	R	12*	.1
365	Glenture Group LLC—Dmitry Faybysh	155 Pfingsten Rd Ste 3, Deerfield IL 60015	847-656-8888	R	12*	.1
366	ALATEC Inc—Larry Anderson	650 C Pratt Ave NW, Huntsville AL 35801	256-489-0061	R	12	.1
367	Dan Carter Inc—Tim Omer	PO Box 282, Richfield WI 53076	262-677-3407	R	12*	.1
368	Dynamic Corporate Solutions Inc—Suzanne K Lemen	1543 Kingsley Ave Bldg, Orange Park FL 32073	904-278-5383	R	12*	<.1

Rank	Company Name—Executive Officer	Address, City, State, Zip	Phone	Type	Fin	Empls
369	Maximation Inc—Ron Brown	2257A Westbrooke Dr Bl, Columbus OH 43228	614-777-2082	R	12*	<.1
370	Advan International Corp—Kenzo Sudo	47817 Fremont Blvd, Fremont CA 94538	510-490-1005	R	12*	<.1
371	Burton and Associates Inc (Jacksonville Beach Florida)—Michael E Burton	200 Business Park Cir, Saint Augustine FL 32095	904-247-0787	R	12*	<.1
372	Dewolff Boberg and Associates Inc—Michael Owens	12750 Merit Dr Ste 250, Dallas TX 75251	972-233-5209	R	12*	.2
373	Simplicity Consulting Inc—Lisa Hufford	105 Central Way Ste 20, Kirkland WA 98033	425-968-2492	R	12	.1
374	Bob Saks and Associates—Robert Saks	345 Claremont Ave Apt, Montclair NJ 07042	973-824-8600	R	11*	.2
375	Vistage International Inc—Ken Jacobson	11452 El Camino Real S, San Diego CA 92130	858-523-6800	R	11*	.1
376	BETAH Associates Inc—Michelle Taylor	7910 Woodmont Ave Ste, Bethesda MD 20814	301-657-4254	R	11*	.1
377	Austin Chemical Company Inc—Samuel M Ponticelli	1565 Barclay Blvd, Buffalo Grove IL 60089	847-520-9600	R	11*	<.1
378	Jordan Edmiston Group—Wilma H Jordan	150 E 52nd St 18th Fl, New York NY 10022	212-754-0710	R	11*	<.1
379	Ceto and Associates—Nicholas Ceto	3325 Paddocks Pkwy Ste, Suwanee GA 30024	678-297-1151	R	11*	<.1
380	Giuliani Partners LLC—Rudolph W Giuliani	1251 Avenue of the Ame, New York NY 10020	212-931-7300	R	11*	<.1
381	Promedica International—Ellen Palo	3100 Bristol St Ste 25, Costa Mesa CA 92626	714-460-7363	R	11*	<.1
382	White and Baldacci—Mathew White	13665 Dulles Technolog, Herndon VA 20171	703-793-3000	R	11*	<.1
383	iMapDatacom Inc—Laurence J DeFranco	1615 L St NW Ste 540, Washington DC 20036	703-760-9729	R	11*	<.1
384	Sugarloaf Mountain Works Inc—George R Verdier	19807 Executive Park C, Germantown MD 20874	301-990-1400	R	11*	<.1
385	Leopard Communications Inc—Sherri Leopard	555 17th St Ste 300, Denver CO 80202	303-516-9401	R	11*	.1
386	Pursuit of Excellence Inc—Marie Diaz	10440 N Central Expy S, Dallas TX 75231	214-452-7881	R	11	.2
387	Kennedy Homes LP—John Emigh	14 Executive Ct, South Barrington IL 60010	847-756-2100	R	11*	.1
388	Creative Events Enterprises—Frank Biedka	4872 Topanga Canyon Bl, Woodland Hills CA 91364	818-610-7000	R	11*	.2
389	Dennis Millican and Associates Inc—Dennis Millican	5850 Coral Ridge Dr St, Coral Springs FL 33076	954-963-1771	R	11*	.1
390	Vintage Health Resources Inc—H Nichols	2032 Exeter Rd Ste 2, Germantown TN 38138	901-757-8899	R	11*	.1
391	Avalere Health LLC—Daniel Mendelson	1350 Connecticut Ave N, Washington DC 20036	202-207-1300	R	11*	.1
392	U S Merchandising Inc—Mark Gibbon	11781 Lee Jackson Memo, Fairfax VA 22033	703-385-0020	R	10*	.1
393	Clayton L Scroggins Associates Inc—Paul Trenz	200 Northland Blvd, Cincinnati OH 45246	513-771-7070	R	10*	.1
394	Cejka Search Inc—Karen Endsor	4 City Place Dr Ste 30, Saint Louis MO 63141	314-726-1603	S	10*	.1
395	Robert E Nolan Company Inc—Dennis B Sullivan	17746 Preston Rd, Dallas TX 75252	972-248-3727	R	10*	.1
396	COMPASS America Inc—David Whitmore	700 Commerce Dr Ste 40, Oak Brook IL 60523	630-955-0999	S	10*	<.1
397	Management Potentials Inc—Andrew Schwartz	PO Box 330, Grafton WI 53024		R	10*	<.1
398	Laughlin International USA—Aaron Young	2533 N Carson St, Carson City NV 89706	775-883-8484	R	10*	<.1
399	Arketi Group—Michael Neumeier	2801 Buford Hwy, Atlanta GA 30329	404-929-0091	R	10*	<.1
400	College Connections—Jeannie Borin	3551 Caribeth Dr, Encino CA 91436		R	10*	<.1
401	Hunt Howe Partners LLC—Sandra Rupp	1 Dag Hammarskjold Pl, New York NY 10017	212-758-2800	R	10*	<.1
402	Integrated Medical Solutions LLC—Jerry Heftler	99 Regency Pky Ste 307, Mansfield TX 76063	817-477-0400	R	10*	<.1
403	Logistechs Inc	7975 N Hayden Rd Ste A, Scottsdale AZ 85258	480-778-1393	S	10*	<.1
404	Reservation Connection Inc	4735 S Durango Dr Ste, Las Vegas NV 89147	702-227-9800	S	10*	<.1
405	Royal Reservation Inc	4735 S Durango Dr Ste, Las Vegas NV 89147	702-227-9800	D	10*	<.1
406	Stopka and Associates—Bruce Stopka	22 E Dundee Ste 4, Barrington IL 60010	847-381-5577	R	10*	.1
407	Charfen Institute—Alex Charfen	1122 S Capital of Texa, Austin TX 78746		R	10	.1
408	CRAssociates Inc—Charles H Robbins	8580 Cinderbed Rd Ste, Newington VA 22122	703-550-8145	R	10	.9
409	Shugoll Research Inc—Mark Shugoll	7475 Wisconsin Ave Ste, Bethesda MD 20814	301-656-0310	R	10*	.1
410	Talk Marketing LLC—Margot Teleki	2 Sylvan Way Ste 203, Parsippany NJ 07054	973-540-8333	R	10*	.1
411	Business Expansion Consulting Corp—George Naddaff	255 Washington St Ste, Newton MA 02458	617-244-5303	R	10*	.1
412	Ecco Select Corp—Jeanette Prenger	1301 Oak St Ste 400, Kansas City MO 64106	816-960-3800	R	10*	.1
413	Restmark Inc—Ann Jennings	5605 Green Cir Dr Ste, Minnetonka MN 55343	952-922-2205	R	9*	.2
414	Estate Assurance Systems Inc—John Moore	PO Box 1255, Saluda VA 23149	804-758-3414	R	9*	.1
415	Triumph Enterprises Inc (Fairfax Virginia)—MN Scott Ulvi	11325 Random Hills Rd, Fairfax VA 22030		R	9	.1
416	Geo-Solutions Inc—Chris Ryan	1250 Fifth Ave, New Kensington PA 15068	724-335-7273	R	9	<.1
417	Home Run Inn Inc—Joseph Perrino	1300 Internationale Pk, Woodridge IL 60517	630-783-9696	R	9*	.1
418	Utility Integration Solutions Inc—Ali Vojdani	24 Benthill Ct, Lafayette CA 94549	925-939-0449	R	9	<.1
419	Deluxe Marketing Inc—Jeremy Larson	101 Convention Center, Las Vegas NV 89109		R	9	<.1
420	IE Discovery—Chris May	13640 Briarwick Dr Ste, Austin TX 78729	512-498-7400	R	9*	.2
421	Foundry Partners LLC—Kris Ruther	295 E Dougherty St, Athens GA 30601	706-433-1927	R	9*	.1
422	Engauge LLC—Janet Rubio	11401 Century Oaks Ter, Austin TX 78758	512-220-7400	R	9*	.1
423	Dedicated Technologies Inc—Jeffrey Dalton	580 N 4th St Ste 280, Columbus OH 43215	614-460-3200	R	9*	.1
424	Motivation Excellence Inc—Greg A Lewis	1834 Walden Office Squ, Schaumburg IL 60173	847-839-5500	R	9*	<.1
425	EM Advertising—Michael L Medico	462 7th Ave 8th Fl, New York NY 10018	212-981-5921	R	9*	<.1
426	Ferrilli Information Group—Robert Ferrilli	414 W State St, Media PA 19063		R	9*	<.1
427	Brookwoods Group Inc—John Sweney	1225 N Loop W Ste 1111, Houston TX 77008	713-934-0532	R	9*	.1
428	Communicators Group—Jeff Whitcomb	9 Church St, Keene NH 03431	603-357-5678	R	9*	<.1
429	Settlement Funding LLC—Jim Terlizzi	3301 Quantum Blvd Fl 2, Boynton Beach FL 33426	561-962-3900	R	9*	.1
430	McFarland Hanson Inc—Tony Mcfarland	2501 4th Ave, Anoka MN 55303	763-421-9554	R	9*	.1
431	Spear Group Inc—Sean Durkin	4487 S Old Peachtree R, Norcross GA 30071	770-447-0267	R	9*	.1
432	Cask LLC—Elizabeth Guezzale	5151 Shoreham Plz Ste, San Diego CA 92112		R	9	<.1
433	Provideo Management Inc—Guillermo Calvo	46631 Winterset Ct, Sterling VA 20165	703-731-7694	R	9	.1
434	David Gooding Inc—David Gooding	173 Spark St, Brockton MA 02302	508-894-2000	R	9*	.1
435	Nexeon International Corp—Prasad Karcherla	1250 E Diehl Rd Ste 40, Naperville IL 60563	630-596-0401	R	8*	.1
436	Global Security Inc—Ed Page	8 Seclusion Woods, Festus MO 63028	636-931-6905	R	8*	.2
437	Viverae—Michael Nadeau	10670 N Central Expy S, Dallas TX 75231	214-827-4400	R	8	.1
438	American Flood Research Inc—Patrick Catalano	1820 Preston Park Blvd, Plano TX 75093	972-490-8667	R	8*	.1
439	Management Industrial Solutions SA de CV—Victor Gonzalez	910 E Redd Rd Ste 528k, El Paso TX 79912	915-613-9201	R	8*	.2
440	Organization Resources Counselors Inc—Robert J Freedmon	500 5th Ave, New York NY 10110	212-719-3400	R	8*	.1
441	Rhg Group Inc—Reginald Laurent	915 5th St Nw, Washington DC 20001	202-789-0039	R	8*	.1
442	Broadband Specialists Inc—Gerard Locke	1700 S Peachtree Rd St, Mesquite TX 75180	972-329-1280	R	8*	.1
443	Sage Management Enterprise LLC—W Andrew Glasscock	6731 Columbia Gateway, Columbia MD 21046	443-259-9960	R	8*	.1
444	Global Energy Inc (Cincinnati Ohio)—Harry Graves	312 Walnut St Ste 2300, Cincinnati OH 45202	513-621-0077	R	8	<.1
445	ServVaas Factories Inc—Paul ServVaas	5240 Walt Rd, Indianapolis IN 46254	317-633-2020	R	8*	<.1
446	iVision Technology Services—Gabe Damiani	1430 W Peachtree St NW, Atlanta GA 30309	678-999-3002	R	8*	.1
447	ABI Inc—Alan B Isacson	29 Broadway Ste 1300, New York NY 10006	212-529-4500	R	8*	<.1
448	Investor Relations International Inc—Haris Tajyar	15260 Ventura Blvd Ste, Sherman Oaks CA 91403	818-382-9700	R	8*	.2
449	George E Runquist Enterprises Inc—George E Runquist	PO Box 10, Whites Creek TN 37189	615-876-6100	R	8*	.1
450	Consensus Research Group Inc—Robert J Perkins	100 Park Ave Ste 1600, New York NY 10017	212-867-3383	R	8*	<.1
451	Ervin Marketing Creative Communications Inc—Sallie Ervin	5615 Pershing Ave Ste, St Louis MO 63112	314-994-1155	R	8*	.1
452	Kennedy Communications Inc—Andrew Kennedy	1730 M St NW Ste 1010, Washington DC 20036	202-333-7889	R	8*	.1
453	Tacna International Corp—Ross Baldwin	1401 Air Wing Rd, San Diego CA 92154	619-661-1261	R	8*	<.1
454	Prosper Business Development Corp—Gary Drenik	450 W Wilson Bridge St, Worthington OH 43085	614-846-0146	R	8*	<.1
455	Talent Connections LLC—Tom Darrow	175 Inverness Approach, Roswell GA 30075	770-552-1550	R	8*	<.1
456	Financial Industry Technical Services Inc—Henry Lange	400 Morris Ave Ste 264, Denville NJ 07834	973-586 8877	R	8*	.1
457	Unlimited Services Group - Hawaii LLC—Ron Bethel	300 Rodgers Blvd Unit, Honolulu HI 96819	808-834-0184	R	8*	.1

Note: An asterisk (*) indicates an estimated financial figure. The company type code used is as follows: R = Private, P = Public, S = Private Subsidiary, B = Public Subsidiary, D = Division, J = Joint Venture, I = Investment Fund.

COMPANY RANKINGS BY SALES WITHIN 4-DIGIT SIC

Rank	Company Name—*Executive Officer*	Address, City, State, Zip	Phone	Type	Fin	Empls
458	Shl Inc—*Frank Landy*	2555 55th St Ste 201, Boulder CO 80301	303-442-5607	R	8*	.1
459	CWCN Inc—*Michelle Harris*	PO Box 223, Allenhurst NJ 07711	732-918-9299	R	8*	.1
460	Secure Wrap Of Miami Inc—*Radames Villalon*	4050 Nw 29th St, Miami FL 33142	305-870-9720	R	8*	.1
461	Human Service Group Inc—*Melvin Estrin*	7200 Wisconsin Ave Ste, Bethesda MD 20814	301-941-8600	R	8*	.1
462	Dalbar Inc—*Louis Harvey*	600 Atlantic Ave Ste 3, Boston MA 02210	617-723-6400	R	8*	.1
463	Medical Connections Holdings Inc—*Jeffrey Rosenfeld*	4800 T Rex Ave Ste 310, Boca Raton FL 33431	561-353-1110	P	8	<.1
464	Ologie LLC—*Charles Cribbs*	447 E Main St, Columbus OH 43215	614-221-1107	R	8*	.1
465	Arc Aspicio LLC—*Lynn Ann Casey*	3318 Lorcom Ln, Arlington VA 22207	703-465-2060	R	8	<.1
466	Innovative Technologies Corp—*Ramesh Mehan*	1020 Woodman Dr Ste 10, Dayton OH 45432	937-252-2145	R	8*	.1
467	Lockwood Financial Group Inc—*Len Reinhardt*	10 Valley Stream Pkwy, Malvern PA 19355	610-695-9150	R	7*	.1
468	Kristel Marketing Ltd—*Steve Maclaskey*	PO Box 796, Blakeslee PA 18610	570-646-6885	R	7*	.1
469	Smart Design Inc—*Davin Stowell*	601 W 26th St Rm 1820, New York NY 10001	212-807-8150	R	7*	.1
470	Wfs Services Inc—*Deborah Shapiro*	1 Harmon Meadow Blvd S, Secaucus NJ 07094	201-617-7100	R	7*	.1
471	Ambulance Service Management Corp—*B Pino*	PO Box 237, Indiana PA 15701	724-349-5511	R	7*	.1
472	Ingram and Associates LLC—*Richard Goostree*	1720 General George Pa, Brentwood TN 37027	615-778-4500	R	7*	.1
473	Freedom Marketing Corp—*Joshua Sunshine*	2522 W Geneva Dr, Tempe AZ 85282	602-258-6400	R	7*	.1
474	Dbd Management Inc—*Michael Peter*	3425 N Federal Hwy, Fort Lauderdale FL 33306	954-566-0643	R	7*	.1
475	Information Systems Engineering Inc—*John Kempen*	PO Box 121, Oconomowoc WI 53066	262-567-9240	R	7*	.1
476	Strategic Decisions Group—*Carl Spetzler*	745 Emerson St, Palo Alto CA 94301	650-475-4400	R	7*	.1
477	Terradigm Inc—*Richard Krett* Management Consulting and Research LLC	6001 Indian School Rd, Albuquerque NM 87110	505-265-5765	S	7*	<.1
478	Culmen International LLC—*Daniel V Berkin*	99 Canal Center Plz, Alexandria VA 22314	703-224-7000	R	7*	<.1
479	Westover Consultants Inc—*Faye Coleman*	4340 E W Hwy Ste 900, Bethesda MD 20814	301-657-5800	R	7*	<.1
480	Pilko and Associates LP—*George Pilko*	700 Louisiana St Ste 4, Houston TX 77002	713-357-1000	R	7*	<.1
481	Winvale Group—*Brian R Dunn*	1012 14th St NW 5th Fl, Washington DC 20005	202-296-5505	R	7*	<.1
482	HPC Development LLC—*Marc Anderson*	46 Mill Plain Rd 2nd F, Danbury CT 06811	203-797-1112	R	7*	<.1
483	Estrela Marketing Solutions—*Adam Taub*	477 S Rosemary Ave Ste, West Palm Beach FL 33401	561-274-4443	R	7*	<.1
484	G2 Inc—*John D Sinsley*	289 Olmsted Blvd, Pinehurst NC 28374	910-215-9990	R	7*	<.1
485	Kei Advisors LLC—*Deborah K Pawlowski*	12 Fountain Plz, Buffalo NY 14202	716-843-3853	R	7*	<.1
486	Med-Vision LLC—*Daniel Ross*	PO Box 342006, Tampa FL 33694	813-962-7436	R	7*	<.1
487	Onset Marketing LLC—*Jim Graziano*	28525 Beck Rd No 125, Wixom MI 48393	248-596-9788	R	7*	<.1
488	Rafte and Co—*Dena Rafte*	945 McKinney St Ste 26, Houston TX 77002	713-993-9637	R	7*	<.1
489	TH Enterprises Inc—*Ted Hoisington*	310 E Interstate 30 St, Garland TX 75043	972-226-9311	R	7*	<.1
490	Nde Quality Systems Inc—*David Peterson*	397 N Sam Houston Pkwy, Houston TX 77060	281-847-4300	R	7*	.2
491	Motivation Marketing and Communications Inc—*Roland Mracek*	143 Thunder Cir, Bensalem PA 19020	215-752-7337	R	7*	.1
492	Tecmer Inc—*Thomas Drake*	132 Hurrcn Shoals Rd C, Lawrenceville GA 30046	770-237-5949	R	7*	<.1
493	Sage Group Consulting Inc—*Vijay Gupta*	100 Village Ct Ste 302, Hazlet NJ 07730	732-767-0010	R	7*	.1
494	Trade Ranger Us Inc—*Kees Linse*	10777 Westheimer Rd St, Houston TX 77042	713-332-6900	R	7*	.1
495	Pinnacle Management Group Inc—*Steve Hays*	4515 S Harvard Ave, Tulsa OK 74135	918-743-7935	R	7*	.1
496	White Glove Service Inc—*Shelly Green*	226 Broadway 3, Providence RI 02903	401-331-5800	R	7*	.1
497	Mdi Imaging and Mail LLC	21721 Filigree Ct Ste, Ashburn VA 20147	703-858-1200	R	7*	.1
498	Systems Technology International Inc—*Bailochan Behera*	39555 Orchard Hill Pl, Novi MI 48375	248-735-3900	R	7*	.1
499	Bpc Acquisition Co—*Thomas Thompson*	1218 Pontaluna Rd, Norton Shores MI 49456	231-798-1310	R	7*	.1
500	International Registries Inc—*William Gallagher*	11495 Commerce Park Dr, Reston VA 20191	703-620-4880	R	6*	.1
501	Rede—*Hubert Glover*	5700 Bullard Ave Ste 3, New Orleans LA 70128	504-834-0264	R	6*	.1
502	Bluemountain Capital Management LLC—*Jay Bryant*	280 Park Ave Fl 5e, New York NY 10017	212-905-3900	R	6*	.1
503	IndSoft Inc—*Anji Buche*	3755 E Main St Ste 180, St Charles IL 60174	630-324-0006	R	6*	.1
504	Imperial Corporate Training and Development—*Edward E Gordon*	220 E Walton Pl Unit 8, Chicago IL 60611	312-664-5196	R	6*	.1
505	Planalytics—*Frederic Fox*	920 Cassatt Rd Ste 300, Berwyn PA 19312	610-640-9485	R	6*	.1
506	TeraThink Corp—*Paul V Lombardi*	11955 Freedom Dr Ste 7, Reston VA 20190	703-773-6232	R	6*	.1
507	Reynolds Dewalt Corp—*Peter Dewalt*	186 Duchaine Blvd, New Bedford MA 02745	508-995-5118	R	6*	<.1
508	Weatherly Consulting Inc—*Sally Weatherly*	13911 Ridgedale Dr Ste, Minnetonka MN 55305	952-746-7910	R	6*	<.1
509	MoreVisibility—*Dennis Pushkin*	925 S Federal Hwy Ste, Boca Raton FL 33432	561-620-9682	R	6*	<.1
510	Resource Assistance Inc—*David Heath*	1934 Raritan Rd, Scotch Plains NJ 07076	908-317-2880	R	6*	<.1
511	Eworld Enterprise Solutions Inc—*Siu Yau*	841 Bishop St Ste 1830, Honolulu HI 96813	808-587-7763	R	6*	<.1
512	CallFire—*Dinesh Ravishanker*	1335 Fourth St Ste 200, Santa Monica CA 90401		R	6*	<.1
513	Praendex Inc—*Nancy Martini*	16 Laurel Ave Ste 10, Wellesley Hills MA 02481	781-235-8872	R	6*	<.1
514	BauerFinancial Inc—*Karen Dorway*	PO Box 143520, Coral Gables FL 33134	305-445-9500	R	6*	<.1
515	Entertainment Marketing and Communications International—*William J Kosovitch*	123 5th Ave, New York NY 10003	212-420-9898	R	6*	<.1
516	Florida Distributing Source—*Karen Eaton*	14038 63rd Way N, Clearwater FL 33760	727-531-0899	R	6*	<.1
517	Mostad and Christensen Inc—*Arvid Mostad*	PO Box 1709, Oak Harbor WA 98277	360-679-4164	R	6*	<.1
518	Mustang Marketing and Advertising—*Scott Harris*	1090 Calle Arroyo, Thousand Oaks CA 91360	805-498-8718	R	6*	<.1
519	Advisory Group of Denver Inc—*Ralf Garrison*	678 S Franklin, Denver CO 80209	303-722-7346	R	6*	<.1
520	Tarnow Associates—*Emil Vogel*	551 Park Ave Ste 4, Scotch Plains NJ 07076	908-288-7700	R	6*	<.1
521	Eppic—*William Brown*	6525 Morrison Blvd Ste, Charlotte NC 28211	704-442-0010	R	6*	.1
522	Re Max Elite Properties Inc—*Charlie Bangel*	5641 Burke Centre Pkwy, Burke VA 22015	703-250-8500	R	6*	.1
523	Linoma Software Inc—*Bob Luebbe*	1409 Silver St, Ashland NE 68003	402-944-4242	R	6*	.1
524	Leadnomics—*Stephen Gill*	2929 Arch St Cira Cent, Philadelphia PA 19104	215-987-4392	R	6	<.1
525	Brooks Group Inc—*Luigi Damasceno*	7108 Fairway Dr Ste 33, Palm Beach Gardens FL 33418	561-214-8800	R	6*	.1
526	Momentum Information Technology Inc—*Laura Guzzetta-Parfim*	2951 Marina Bay Dr Ste, League City TX 77573	281-413-6053	R	6*	.1
527	Malikco LLC—*Jan Button*	900 E Hamilton Ave Ste, Campbell CA 95008	408-879-7447	R	5*	.1
528	Forte Automation Systems Inc—*Toby Henderson*	8155 Burden Rd, Machesney Park IL 61115	815-633-2300	R	5*	.1
529	Acacia Holdings LLC	1139 9th Ave Apt 1204, Honolulu HI 96816	808-396-0400	R	5*	<.1
530	FutureBrand Company Inc—*Patrick Smith*	300 Park Ave S 7th Fl, New York NY 10010	212-931-6016	D	5*	.1
531	Richards and Southern Inc—*Terry Calonge*	PO Box 37, Goodlettsville TN 37070	615-859-4121	R	5*	.1
532	Spectra Marketing Systems Inc	200 W Jackson Blvd Ste, Chicago IL 60606	312-583-5100	S	5*	<.1
533	Construction Executive Online—*Kevin Carney*	1201 N Orange St No 74, Wilmington DE 19801	302-288-5656	R	5	<.1
534	ASK Associates Inc—*Kenneth Martinez*	PO Box 3885, Lawrence KS 66046	785-841-8194	R	5*	<.1
535	Integrity Management Consulting Inc—*Christopher Romani*	2000 Corporate Ridge S, McLean VA 22102	703-349-3394	R	5*	<.1
536	Performance Strategies Inc—*Jim Adams*	6862 Hillsdale Ct, Indianapolis IN 46250	317-842-0393	R	5*	<.1
537	MMC and P Retirement Benefit Services Inc—*John Parks*	1016 E Carson St, Pittsburgh PA 15219	412-394-9300	D	5*	<.1
538	NatCom Marketing Communications Inc—*Bob Bauer*	80 SW 8th St Ste 2230, Miami FL 33130	786-425-0028	R	5*	<.1
539	ODT Inc—*Howard Bronstein*	PO Box 134, Amherst MA 01004	413-549-1293	R	5*	<.1
540	XCEND Group—*Ron Schoenherr*	732 W Grand River Ave, Brighton MI 48116	810-494-7144	R	5*	<.1
541	RampRate LLC—*Anthony Greenberg*	1427 3rd StPromenade S, Santa Monica CA 90401	310-802-3702	R	5*	<.1
542	MarkeTech Group—*Christian P Renaudin*	502 Mace Blvd Ste 15, Davis CA 95618	530-792-8400	R	5*	<.1
543	The Amend Group—*John T Amend*	1445 Ross Ave, Dallas TX 75202	214-696-6900	R	5*	<.1
544	Utek-Ekms Inc—*Asa Lanum*	2109 E Palm Ave, Tampa FL 33605	813-754-4330	D	5*	<.1

Rank	Company Name—*Executive Officer*	Address, City, State, Zip	Phone	Type	Fin	Empls
545	Intetnational Marking Group—*David Bruno*	PO Box 379, Utica NY 13503	315-735-7591	R	5*	<.1
546	Market-Based Solutions Inc—*Jon Owyang*	PO Box 29486, Los Angeles CA 90029	818-543-5925	R	5*	<.1
547	Plas-Tool Co—*John Holdt*	7430 N Croname Rd, Niles IL 60714	847-647-8120	R	5*	<.1
548	Hillard Heintze LLC—*Arnette Heintze*	30 S Wacker Dr Ste 173, Chicago IL 60606	312-869-8500	R	5	.1
549	Slingshot SEO Inc—*Jay Love*	8900 Keystone Crossing, Indianapolis IN 46240	317-575-8852	R	5	.1
550	Mid-America Business Systems And Equipment Inc—*Gilbert Roscoe*	2500 Broadway St Ne St, Minneapolis MN 55413	612-378-3800	R	5*	<.1
551	Tab Boards International Inc—*Alan Fishman*	11031 Sheridan Blvd, Westminster CO 80020	303-839-1200	R	5*	<.1
552	Velocity Solutions Inc—*Mike Bender*	1710 Dawson St, Wilmington NC 28403	910-254-9383	R	4*	<.1
553	Employment Source Inc—*Annette Snyder*	1815 Grant St, Bettendorf IA 52722	563-355-4473	R	4*	.1
554	Community Support Resource—*C Roberson*	3124 Zebulon Rd, Rocky Mount NC 27804	252-972-2200	R	4*	.1
555	AdaQuest—*Hiram Machado*	14450 NE 29th Pl Ste 2, Bellevue WA 98007	425-284-7800	R	4	<.1
556	Restaurant Partners Inc—*David George Manuchia*	1030 N Orange Ave Ste, Orlando FL 32801	407-839-5070	R	4*	.3
557	BackTrack Inc—*Bob Gandee*	8850 Tyler Blvd, Mentor OH 44060	440-205-8280	R	4*	.1
558	GyanSys Inc—*Raj Una*	8440 Woodfield Crossin, Indianapolis IN 46240	317-580-4200	R	4*	<.1
559	Deep Water Point LLC—*Howard Seeger*	8300 Greensboro Dr Ste, McLean VA 22102	443-517-7820	R	4*	<.1
560	TechCFO—*Kent Elmer*	75 5th St Ste 354, Atlanta GA 30308	678-636-0004	R	4*	<.1
561	Five Nines Technology Group—*Nick Bock*	1560 S 70th St, Lincoln NE 68506	402-817-2630	R	4*	<.1
562	NeteSolutions Corp—*Jolly Vasani*	8280 Greensboro Dr Ste, McLean VA 22102	703-893-6383	R	4*	<.1
563	Camp Bow Wow International Inc—*Heidi Ganahl*	1877 Broadway St Ste 1, Boulder CO 80302		R	4*	<.1
564	Scientific Marketing Services Inc—*Robert W Norton*	PO Box 600, Minotola NJ 08341	856-697-1257	R	4*	<.1
565	Round Table Group Inc—*Robert Hull*	1 N Dearborn Ste 500, Chicago IL 60602	312-635-7877	D	4*	<.1
566	Crocker Flanagan—*Scott Crocker*	6313 Elvas Ave, Fair Oaks CA 95628	916-552-7971	S	4*	<.1
567	Morse Richard Weisenmiller and Associates Inc—*William Monsen*	1814 Franklin St Ste 7, Oakland CA 94612	510-834-1999	R	4*	<.1
568	Banking Spectrum Inc—*Carlos P Naudon*	1430 Broadway St Ste 1, New York NY 10018	212-819-1922	R	4*	<.1
569	Trinity Marketing Inc—*Dan Logan*	180 Canal St, Boston MA 02114	617-292-7300	R	4*	<.1
570	Agrivisor Services Inc—*Rob Huston*	1701 Towanda Ave, Bloomington IL 61701	309-557-3147	R	4*	<.1
571	Chicago Consulting—*Terry Harris*	8 S Michigan Ave Ste 3, Chicago IL 60603	312-346-5080	R	4*	<.1
572	Silico Corp—*John Cachat*	19702 Center Ridge Rd, Rocky River OH 44116	440-333-9900	R	4*	<.1
573	Synaptic Decisions Inc—*Robert A Endres*	340 N Sam Houston Pkwy, Houston TX 77060	832-300-9800	R	4*	<.1
574	Benefits Resource Group LLC	130 Wylderose Dr, Midlothian VA 23113	804-320-3602	R	4*	.1
575	Trident One Stop Career Center—*Angela Bryant*	1930 Hanahan Rd Ste 20, Charleston SC 29406	843-574-1800	R	4*	.1
576	CFO Selections LLC—*Tom Varga*	14432 SE Eastgato Way, Bellevue WA 98007	206-686-4480	R	4	<.1
577	Ali International LLC—*Ali Brown*	2029 Century Park E St, Los Angeles CA 90067		R	4	<.1
578	Falex Corp—*Andrew Faville*	1020 Airpark Dr, Sugar Grove IL 60554	630-556-3669	R	4*	<.1
579	Venator Holdings LLC—*Scott Foley*	3001 W Big Beaver Rd S, Troy MI 48084	248-269-0000	R	4*	.1
580	Gould and Associates Global Services Inc—*Stephen Gould*	612 Joseph Cir Ste A, Golden CO 80403	216-831-0135	R	4*	.1
581	Thomas Group Inc—*Michael N Romeri*	5221 N O'Connor Blvd S, Irving TX 75039	972-869-3400	P	4	<.1
582	Kvt Koenig LLC—*Jennifer Rolando*	73 Defco Park Rd Ste 6, North Haven CT 06473	203-245-1100	R	3*	<.1
583	Med Evolve Inc—*Emmett Moore*	17300 Chenal Pkwy Ste, Little Rock AR 72223	501-821-4949	R	3*	<.1
584	Project Resources Inc—*Frank Loscavio*	6385 S Rainbow Blvd, Las Vegas NV 89118	858-505-1000	R	3*	<.1
585	Carolina By-Products Co—*C Culling*	2410 Randolph Ave, Greensboro NC 27406	336-333-3030	R	3*	<.1
586	DLS Electronic Systems Inc—*Donald Sweeney*	1250 Peterson Dr, Wheeling IL 60090	847-537-6400	R	3*	<.1
587	Legend Technical Services Of Arizona Inc—*Cheryl Sykora*	17631 N 25th Ave, Phoenix AZ 85023	602-324-6100	R	3*	<.1
588	Newcogen Group Inc—*Noubar Afeyan*	1 Memorial Dr Ste 4, Cambridge MA 02142	617-497-2233	R	3*	<.1
589	Systems Integration Inc—*Bernhard Fritz*	PO Box 150287, Arlington TX 76015	817-468-1494	R	3*	<.1
590	Maracor Software and Engineering Inc—*Thomas Morgan*	PO Box 418, Middletown MD 21769	301-371-3260	R	3*	<.1
591	First Intermark Corp—*Kasha Kelley*	400 S Summit St, Arkansas City KS 67005	620-442-2460	R	3*	<.1
592	Customer Communications Group Inc—*Sandra Gudat*	12600 W Cedar Dr, Lakewood CO 80228	303-986-3000	R	3*	<.1
593	Cowan and Associates Inc—*Brian Cowan*	2316 S Eads St, Arlington VA 22202	703-920-2282	R	3*	<.1
594	Newcomb Print Communications Inc—*J Newcomb*	PO Box A, Michigan City IN 46361	219-874-3201	R	3*	<.1
595	Harkcon Inc—*Kevin Harkins*	1390 Chain Bridge Rd S, McLean VA 22101		R	3*	<.1
596	Roberts Communications and Marketing Inc—*Colleen Chappel*	1715 E 9th Ave, Tampa FL 33605	813-281-0088	R	3*	<.1
597	Angarai—*Venkat AR Subramanian*	1100 Mercantile Ln Ste, Largo MD 20774	301-583-4653	R	3*	<.1
598	TCI Companies Inc—*Linda Higgison*	818 Connecticut Ave NW, Washington DC 20006	202-457-0315	R	3*	<.1
599	Leancor LLC—*Terry Foster*	7660 Turfway Rd Ste 20, Florence KY 41042	859-283 9933	R	3*	<.1
600	Resource Management Systems Inc—*Clifford J Earl*	30 5th Ave Rm 4-G, New York NY 10011	212-633-2001	R	3*	<.1
601	Actuarial Data Inc—*Charles W Day III*	102 Broadway Ave Ste 2, Carnegie PA 15106	412-429-8700	R	3*	<.1
602	Engineering Center TEC—*Stanley D Elkerton*	1 Walnut St, Boston MA 02108	617-227-5551	R	3*	<.1
603	Handsome Dog Consulting Group—*Luke Croghan*	80 SW 8th St Ste 2000, Miami FL 33130	772-546-9228	R	3*	<.1
604	Executive Visions Inc—*Michael I Marto*	7000 Miller Ct E, Norcross GA 30071	770-416-6100	R	3*	<.1
605	Healthcare Forecasting Inc—*Janice Udesen Cohen*	PO Box 1663, Sanibel FL 33957	860-659-4077	R	3*	<.1
606	Communications 21 Inc—*Sharon L Goldmacher*	834 Inman Village Pkwy, Atlanta GA 30307	404-814-1330	R	3*	<.1
607	Infotech Management Inc—*Russ Choyce*	5601 Bridge St Ste 300, Fort Worth TX 76112		R	3*	<.1
608	Joint Venture Marketing—*Chris Napolitano*	10003 Derekwood Ln Ste, Lanham MD 20706	301-577-0887	R	3*	<.1
609	Potentials—*Ann Van Eron*	195 N Harbor Dr Ste 37, Chicago IL 60601		R	3*	<.1
610	Princeton Polymer Laboratories—*Peter Wachtel*	521 Lehigh Ave, Union NJ 07083	908-678-7033	R	3*	<.1
611	Small Business Advisory Group Inc—*Cindy Leddicotte*	1865 Herndon Ave Ste K, Clovis CA 93611	559-298-7585	R	3*	<.1
612	Worth Ethic Corp—*Kate Ludeman*	23 Hull Cir Dr, Austin TX 78746	512-330-9574	R	3*	<.1
613	ArtsMarket Inc—*Louise K Stevens*	1125 W Kagy Blvd Ste 1, Bozeman MT 59715	406-582-7466	R	3*	<.1
614	Mercatus Energy Advisors LLC—*Mike Corley*	3333 Richmond Ave Ste, Houston TX 77098	713-970-1003	R	3*	<.1
615	TeleChoice Inc (Richmond Virginia)—*Danny Briere*	PO Box 17858, Richmond VA 23226	804-288-6864	R	3*	<.1
616	Gillespie Corp—*Pe Macuga*	PO Box 359, Ware MA 01082	413-967-4980	R	3*	<.1
617	Ci2i Services Inc—*Anjali Sikka*	2018 156th Ave NE, Bellevue WA 98007	425-818-0560	R	3	<.1
618	Portage Area Regional Transportation Authority—*John Drew*	2000 Summit Rd, Kent OH 44240	330-678-1287	R	3*	.1
619	AnswerLab—*Amy Buckner*	160 Spear St Ste 700, San Francisco CA 94105	415-814-9910	R	3	<.1
620	Nexxio Group Ltd—*Wendy Vannoy*	25 Highland Park Villa, Dallas TX 75205	214-526-0014	R	3*	<.1
621	Printing Images Corp—*Thomas Mc Kiernan*	855 Brookside Rd, Pottstown PA 19464	610-327-1234	R	3*	<.1
622	TRE Communications Ltd—*Jim Bouzaglou*	11333 Chandler Blvd, North Hollywood CA 91601	818-509-0339	R	3*	<.1
623	Kingsley Kranzler Communications Ltd—*Wayne Kranzler*	PO Box 693, Bismarck ND 58502	701-255-3067	R	3*	<.1
624	Global Management Company LLC	3150 E Pico Blvd, Los Angeles CA 90023	323-261-8114	R	3*	.1
625	Beaird Inc—*Debra Beaird*	236 S Washington St St, Naperville IL 60540	630-637-0430	R	3*	.1
626	Christian Schools International—*David Koetje*	3350 E Paris Ave Se, Grand Rapids MI 49512	616-957-1070	R	3*	<.1
627	Infoway Software Inc—*Dan Mandan*	388 Washington Rd Ste, Sayreville NJ 08872	732-238-2122	R	3	<.1
628	Warm Thoughts Communications Inc—*Richard Goldberg*	200 Meadle Ln Fl 2, Secaucus NJ 07094	201-330-9276	R	3*	<.1
629	Dat Optic Inc—*Cuong Quach*	1815 E Wilshire Ave St, Santa Ana CA 92705	714-558-1808	R	3*	<.1
630	Steel Related Industries Quality System Registrar Inc—*Christopher Lake*	300 Nrthpinte Cir Ste, Seven Fields PA 16046	724-934-9000	R	2*	<.1
631	Innovative Utility Products Corp—*John Smith*	PO Box 1667, Van Buren AR 72957	479-410-2098	R	2*	<.1

Note: An asterisk (*) indicates an estimated financial figure. The company type code used is as follows: R = Private, P = Public, S = Private Subsidiary, B = Public Subsidiary, D = Division, J = Joint Venture, I = Investment Fund.

COMPANY RANKINGS BY SALES WITHIN 4-DIGIT SIC

Rank	Company Name—*Executive Officer*	Address, City, State, Zip	Phone	Type	Fin	Empls
632	Intech Enterprises Inc—*Tom Cunning*	3825 Grant St, Washougal WA 98671	360-835-8785	R	2*	<.1
633	JSymmetric Inc—*Chris Delgado*	2002 Summit Blvd Ste 3, Atlanta GA 30319	404-460-5535	R	2	<.1
634	Fedresults Inc—*Alan Balutis*	PO Box 346, Herndon VA 20172	703-318-8000	R	2*	<.1
635	Packiq LLC—*Mark Rainosek*	160 Alliance Pkwy, Williamston SC 29697	864-231-8908	R	2*	<.1
636	Pace and Partners Inc—*Dennis Pace*	1223 Turner St Ste 101, Lansing MI 48906	517-267-9800	R	2*	<.1
637	Fg Squared Multimedia Corp—*Steven Golab*	621 E 6th St Ste 200, Austin TX 78701	512-481-8831	R	2*	<.1
638	Pipeline Contractors Inc—*Ron Denmark*	PO Box 189, Starke FL 32091	904-964-2019	R	2*	.1
639	Marketshare Partners Inc—*Wes Nichols*	11100 Santa Monica Blv, Los Angeles CA 90025	310-914-5677	R	2*	<.1
640	Spectrum Marketing Inc—*David Ratchford*	1349 E Garrison Blvd B, Gastonia NC 28054	704-865-6300	R	2*	<.1
641	Innerspec Technologies Inc—*Borja Lopez*	PO Box 11986, Lynchburg VA 24506	434-847-2023	R	2*	<.1
642	Timberco Inc—*Steve Winistorfer*	1507 Matt Pass Ste 2, Cottage Grove WI 53527	608-403-4197	R	2*	<.1
643	Sims Consulting Group Inc—*Edward Phillips*	1525 Elmwood Dr NE, Lancaster OH 43130	740-654-1091	R	2*	<.1
644	Seam LLC—*John Nash*	6055 Primacy Pkwy Ste, Memphis TN 38119	901-374-0374	R	2*	<.1
645	Meeting Management Associates Inc—*Janis Bays*	PO Box 723, Sherburne NY 13460	607-674-2666	R	2*	<.1
646	CVM Inc—*Charles Veth*	149 Durham Rd, Madison CT 06443	203-245-4504	R	2*	<.1
647	LarsonO'BrienAcumen—*Ron Larson*	733 Washington St, Pittsburgh PA 15228	412-571-1600	R	2*	<.1
648	O'Connor and Partners Inc—*Ronald T O'Connor*	2010 S 8th St, St Louis MO 63104	314-772-0010	R	2*	<.1
649	Psi Long Island LLC—*Danielle Beiu*	663 Old Willets Path B, Hauppauge NY 11788	631-234-5900	R	2*	<.1
650	Concept Group USA -Strategic Brand Consultants—*Tom Kelley*	1133 14th St NW Ste 60, Washington DC 20005	760-688-0717	R	2*	<.1
651	Industrial Products Sales Inc—*Jeff Jacobs*	7659 Montgomery Rd, Cincinnati OH 45236	513-791-8055	R	2*	<.1
652	Woodend Nessel and Friends Inc—*Reed Nessel*	12526 High Bluff Dr St, San Diego CA 92130	858-792-3624	R	2*	<.1
653	AJ Environmental Inc—*Doug Picanso*	4800 Easton Dr Ste 101, Bakersfield CA 93309	661-327-7429	R	2*	<.1
654	Bottom Line Inc—*Robert Sturan*	168 S 19th St, Pittsburgh PA 15203	412-481-0400	R	2*	<.1
655	Pioneer Management Possibilities Inc—*Mark Stein*	31000 Telegraph Rd Ste, Bingham Farms MI 48025	248-647-9290	R	2*	<.1
656	Agile Strategy Institute—*Michael Lurie*	3525 Del Mar Heights R, San Diego CA 92130	858-792-2633	R	2*	<.1
657	De Novo Strategy Inc—*Wendell Brock*	201 Lake Village Dr, McKinney TX 75071	469-424-2888	R	2*	<.1
658	Windermere Associates—*Donald V Potter*	1100 Moraga Way Ste 20, Moraga CA 94556	925-377-2020	R	2*	<.1
659	Kasi Demos/Kirby Demos and Merchandising—*Trey Kirby*	13030 Memorial Dr, Houston TX 77079	281-933-3366	R	2*	<.1
660	Koenig Advertising and Public Relations—*Stewart Koenig*	309 S Franklin St Ste, Syracuse NY 13202	315-475-1603	R	2*	<.1
661	Kord Technologies Inc—*Tom Young*	701 Pratt Ave Nw Ste 1, Huntsville AL 35801	256-489-2346	R	2*	<.1
662	TBD Consulting—*Jonena Relth*	PO Box 35579, Phoenix AZ 85069	602-263-1961	R	2*	<.1
663	Legler Systems Co—*William S Legler*	23 Charles Hill Rd, Orinda CA 94563	925-254-1264	R	2*	<.1
664	Ogando Associates Inc—*Monika Ogando*	2860 Somerset Dr Ste K, Fort Lauderdale FL 33311		R	2*	<.1
665	Sullivan International Inc—*Barbara Sullivan*	110 Pine Ave Ste 700, Long Beach CA 90802	562-590-0512	R	2*	<.1
666	Fayette Cos—*Michael Boyle*	PO Box 1346, Peoria IL 61654	309-671-8005	R	2*	.4
667	Securance LLC—*Paul Ashe*	6922 W Linebaugh Ave S, Tampa FL 33625		R	2*	<.1
668	American Cybernetic Corp—*Harry Steinberg*	1 Research Ct Ste 450, Rockville MD 20850	301-216-3810	R	2*	<.1
669	Pinnacle Solutions Inc—*Ralph Carbone*	673 Morris Ave Ste 1, Springfield NJ 07081	973-258-0909	R	2*	<.1
670	Advanced Retail Merchandising—*James Hall*	PO Box 24539, Lakeland FL 33802	863-648-5708	R	2*	<.1
671	Acc Technical Services Inc—*Steven Oad*	PO Box 2635, Liverpool NY 13089	315-484-4500	R	2*	<.1
672	La Pash Inc—*Ted Hageni*	4412 Loveland St Ste A, Metairie LA 70006	504-885-0783	R	2*	<.1
673	Dantronics Inc—*Daniel Donohoo*	3175 Hafner Ct, Saint Paul MN 55126	651-484-2108	R	2*	<.1
674	Dynamic Consulting—*Cynthia Dai*	569 Andover St Ste 100, San Francisco CA 94110	415-285-4855	R	2*	<.1
675	Campus Party Inc—*Charles Murray*	444 N 3rd St Ste 3, Philadelphia PA 19123	215-320-1810	R	2*	<.1
676	Vanguard Computer Systems—*John Allen*	PO Box 1041, Ames IA 50014	515-232-3040	R	1*	<.1
677	Food and Beverage International—*Michael Walsh*	108 Walker St, Gardnerville NV 89410	707-284-1008	R	1*	<.1
678	Pro-Pac Inc—*Linda Sarna*	PO Box 369, Hayward WI 54843	262-642-9473	R	1*	<.1
679	Image Innovations Inc—*Winston Yonan*	4 Maclynn Rd, Excelsior MN 55331	952-474-8178	R	1*	<.1
680	Jdi Contracts Inc—*Roger Hoyum*	PO Box 698, Grand Rapids MN 55744	218-328-0040	R	1*	<.1
681	Automated Logic Marietta Control—*Emmet Creamer*	1805 124th St, College Point NY 11356	718-445-8400	R	1*	<.1
682	Frequent Flyer Services—*Randy Petersen*	1930 Frequent Flyer Po, Colorado Springs CO 80915	719-597-8889	R	1*	<.1
683	Managed Business Solutions—*Richard Noe*	12325 Oracle Blvd Ste, Colorado Springs CO 80921	719-314-3400	S	1*	<.1
684	Interglobal Partners LLC—*Robert Heuermann*	9648 Olive Blvd Ste 11, Saint Louis MO 63132	314-432-4811	R	1	<.1
685	V-Tip Inc—*James Hall*	4699 Hydraulic Rd, Rockford IL 61109	815-968-5885	R	1*	<.1
686	Southern Data Solutions—*Joe Richter*	PO Box 3065, Cumming GA 30028	770-886-9232	R	1*	<.1
687	Scott Yaw Associates LLC—*Scott Yaw*	1074 Park Ave, Wycombe PA 18980	215-598-9977	R	1*	<.1
688	Alpha Medical Products Inc—*Rafat Saman*	1827 E Chapman Ave, Orange CA 92867		R	1*	<.1
689	Bennett Marketing Group Inc—*Joan Bennett*	PO Box 124, Saline MI 48176	734-944-2209	R	1*	<.1
690	Hard Chrome Plating Consultant Inc—*Clarence Peger*	PO Box 44082, Cleveland OH 44144	216-631-9090	R	1*	<.1
691	Cross River Publishing Consultants Inc—*Thomas Woll*	3 Holly Hill Ln, Katonah NY 10536	914-232-6708	R	1*	<.1
692	Fred Cohen and Associates—*Fred Cohen*	572 Leona Dr, Livermore CA 94550	925-454-0171	R	1*	<.1
693	Grassfed Livestock Alliance—*Don Davis*	PO Box 122, Tarpley TX 78883	830-562-2333	R	1*	<.1
694	Harris/Ragan Management Group—*Godfrey Harris*	520 S Sepulveda Blvd S, Los Angeles CA 90049	310-476-6374	R	1*	<.1
695	Herrera and Assoc—*John Herrera*	27485 Chippewa Paws Ln, Pennington MN 56663	612-385-7562	R	1*	<.1
696	Synergistic Systems Inc—*Gary Lane*	9572 Mammoth Ave, Baton Rouge LA 70814	225-924-0099	R	1*	<.1
697	Total Business Services Inc—*Billy Richardson*	PO Box 5529, Waco TX 76708	254-757-1709	R	1*	<.1
698	Value Strategies LLC—*Duane Varnum*	6826 Morrhen Pl, Carlsbad CA 92011	760-602-0278	R	1	<.1
699	Ashton Metzler and Associates Inc—*Sarah Ashton*	PO Box 1640, Sanibel FL 33957	239-395-3152	R	1*	<.1
700	TLS Marketing Consultants—*Tracy Schneider*	3623 48th Ave SW, Seattle WA 98116	206-935-9283	R	1*	<.1
701	Chagrin Consulting Services Inc—*Ann Allard*	24800 Chagrin Blvd Ste, Cleveland OH 44122	216-514-3301	R	1*	<.1
702	Triad Solutions Inc—*John Anderson*	1025 N Demaree St, Visalia CA 93291	559-625-4800	R	1*	<.1
703	Transcendent Management—*Brandon Russell*	2201 Sw Adams St, Peoria IL 61602	309-966-3363	R	1*	<.1
704	Green Globe International Inc—*Christopher M Kimmes*	442 W Esplanade Ave St, San Jacinto CA 92583		P	1	N/A
705	Encotech Inc—*Paul Roediger*	PO Box 714, Schenectady NY 12301	518-374-0924	R	1*	<.1
706	PC Workshop Inc—*Chris Gonzales*	PO Box 390, Paulding OH 45879	419-399-4805	R	<1*	.1
707	Maxima Group LLC	PO Box 1089, Bothell WA 98041	425-486-2488	R	<1*	<.1
708	Eurotek Inc—*Jack Ross*	94 Buena Vista Ave, Rumson NJ 07760	732-224-9977	R	<1*	<.1
709	Fundcom Inc—*Greg Webster*	14 Wall St 20th Fl, New York NY 10005	212-818-1633	P	<1	<.1
710	Rapp Systems Corp—*Tod Rapp*	358 S Monroe St, Xenia OH 45385	937-376-5445	R	<1*	<.1
711	Circa Corp—*Mark Glazier*	1330 Fitzgerald Ave, San Francisco CA 94124	415-822-1600	R	<1*	<.1
712	Miguel Tejera Enterprises—*Miguel Tejera*	PO Box 194086, San Juan PR 00919	787-761-2982	R	<1	<.1
713	Intelligent Staffing Solutions—*Abigail Mambola*	2985 S Citrus St, West Covina CA 91791	626-966-5022	R	<1*	<.1
714	Paychest Inc—*Peter Coorey*	570 E La Cadena Dr Ste, Riverside CA 92507		P	<1	N/A
715	ProSidian Consulting—*Adrian Woolcock*	5500 Open Book Ln, Charlotte NC 28270		R	<1	<.1
716	GlobalOptions Group Inc—*Harvey Schiller*	75 Rockefeller Pl 27th, New York NY 10019	212-445-6262	P	<1	<.1
717	In Mind Communications LLC—*Charlie Cook*	3 West End Ave, Old Greenwich CT 06870	203-637-1118	R	<1	<.1
718	Marine Systems Technology Inc—*William Mcelroy*	PO Box 1507, North Falmouth MA 02556	508-548-0012	R	<1*	<.1
719	Visiblenet Inc—*Glenn Jones*	14953 NE 95th St, Redmond WA 98052		R	N/A	.1
720	Optima Direct—*Jim Lyons*	8618 Westwood Ctr Dr S, Vienna VA 22182	703-918-9000	D	N/A	<.1
721	Garner Consulting Inc—*John C Garner*	630 North Rosemead Blv, Pasadena CA 91107	626-351-2300	R	N/A	<.1

Rank	Company Name—*Executive Officer*	Address, City, State, Zip	Phone	Type	Fin	Empls
722	J Brooks Potter Marketing—*Jack Potter*	PO Box 1693, Clearwater FL 33757	949-636-6382	R	N/A	N/A
723	Performance Methods Inc—*Richard G Phelps*	2245 74th Ave SE, Mercer Island WA 98040	206-232-1790	R	N/A	N/A

TOTALS: SIC 8742 Management Consulting Services
Companies: 723   128,511   583.2

8743 Public Relations Services

Rank	Company Name—*Executive Officer*	Address, City, State, Zip	Phone	Type	Fin	Empls
1	Ketchum Inc—*Raymond Kotcher*	1285 Ave of the Americ, New York NY 10019	646-935-3900	S	1,075	1.2
2	Burson-Marsteller—*Mark Penn*	230 Park Ave S, New York NY 10003	212-614-4000	S	917*	2.0
3	Cohn Wolfe Read Poland and Associates—*Donna Imperato*	200 5th Ave, New York NY 10010	212-798-9700	R	400*	1.0
4	Financial Relations Board Inc—*Michael Kempner* MWW Group	875 North Michigan Ave, Chicago IL 60611	312-266-7800	S	395*	12.0
5	Manning Selvage and Lee Inc—*Juin Tsokanos*	1675 Broadway, New York NY 10019	212-468-4200	R	331*	1.0
6	Fleishman-Hillard Inc—*Dave Senay*	200 N Broadway, Saint Louis MO 63102	314-982-1700	S	211*	2.0
7	Edelman—*Richard Edelman*	200 E Randolph Dr 63rd, Chicago IL 60601	312-240-3000	R	183*	.4
8	Food Employers Labor Rels Assoc & United Food & Comm Works H & W Fund	911 Ridgebrook Rd, Sparks MD 21152	410-683-6500	R	172*	<.1
9	BioSpace Inc—*David Mott*	90 New Montgomery St S, San Francisco CA 94109	239-659-0100	R	160*	.4
10	Hill and Knowlton Inc—*Jack Martin*	825 3rd Ave, New York NY 10022	212-885-0300	S	152*	1.5
11	Barkley Evergreen and Partners Inc Public Relations Div—*Jeff King*	1740 Main St, Kansas City MO 64108	816-842-1500	D	152*	.3
12	Cohn and Wolfe—*Donna Imperato*	200 Fifth Avenue, New York NY 10010	212-798-9700	R	125*	.4
13	Deposit Computer Services Inc—*Frank G Fiumera*	PO Box 275, Deposit NY 13754	607-467-4600	R	123*	.3
14	Howard J Rubenstein Associates Inc—*Howard J Rubenstein*	1345 Ave of the Americ, New York NY 10105	212-843-8000	R	115*	.3
15	Waggener Edstrom Worldwide Inc—*Claire Lematta*	Civica North Tower 225, Bellevue WA 98004	425-638-7000	R	112	.8
16	Ken Blanchard Co—*Tom McKee*	125 State Pl, Escondido CA 92029	760-489-5005	R	101*	.2
17	The Marketing Arm—*Ray Clark*	1999 Bryan St, Dallas TX 75201	214-259-3200	R	101*	.2
18	Public Strategies Inc—*Dan Bartlett*	98 San Jacinto Blvd St, Austin TX 78701	512-474-8848	R	88*	.2
19	Rubenstein Associates Inc—*Howard Rubenstein*	1345 Ave of the Americ, New York NY 10105	212-843-8000	R	87*	.2
20	Positive Promotions Inc—*Nelson Taxel*	PO Box 18021, Hauppauge NY 11788	631-648-1200	R	80*	.3
21	Martin Thomas Inc—*Martin K Pottle*	42 Riverside Dr, Barrington RI 02806	401-245-8500	R	80*	.2
22	Ruder Finn Inc—*Kathy Bloomgarden*	301 E 57th St, New York NY 10022		R	70*	.6
23	Fogarty Klein Monroe—*Scott Brown*	1800 West Loop S Ste 2, Houston TX 77027	713-862-5100	S	69*	.2
24	Ogilvy Public Relations Worldwide—*Paul B Hicks III*	636 11th Ave, New York NY 10036	212-880-5200	S	67*	1.2
25	Calysto Communications Inc—*Laura Borgstede*	3577 Chamblee Tucker R, Atlanta GA 30341	404-266-2060	R	62*	.1
26	McNeil-Wilson Communications Inc—*David R McNeil*	1003 Bishop St Ste 950, Honolulu HI 96813	808-521-0244	R	60*	.1
27	Schwartz Communications Inc—*Bryan Scanlon*	300 5th Ave, Waltham MA 02451	781-684-0770	R	58*	.2
28	Euro RSCG Magnet—*Lisa Sepulveda*	200 Madison Ave 2nd Fl, New York NY 10016	212-367-6800	S	56*	.1
29	Lois Paul and Partners—*Lois Paul*	150 Presidential Way, Woburn MA 01801	781-782-5000	R	55*	.1
30	Strategy XXI Group Ltd—*Harriet Mouchly-Weiss*	515 Madison Ave 34th F, New York NY 10022	212-935-0210	R	54*	.2
31	Weber Shandwick Inc—*Harris Diamond*	919 3rd Ave, New York NY 10022	212-445-8000	S	54*	.1
32	Matlock and Associates Inc—*Kent Matlock*	107 Luckie St NW, Atlanta GA 30303	404-872-3200	R	49*	<.1
33	Golin/Harris International—*Fred Cook*	111 E Wacker Dr Fl 11, Chicago IL 60601	312-729-4000	S	48*	.1
34	Brodeur Partners—*Andrea Coville*	855 Boylston St, Boston MA 02116	617-587-2800	S	45*	.4
35	Padilla Speer Beardsley Inc—*Lynn Casey*	1101 W River Pkwy Ste4, Minneapolis MN 55415	612-455-1700	R	45*	.1
36	Dan Klores Communications—*Sean Cassidy*	261 Fifth Avenue, New York NY 10016	212-685-4300	R	34*	.1
37	Feinstein Kean Healthcare—*Marcia Kean* Ogilvy Public Relations Worldwide	245 1st St 14th Fl, Cambridge MA 02142	617-577-8110	S	32*	.1
38	Charles Ryan Associates Inc—*Patrick Gallagher*	1813 E Broad St, Richmond VA 23223	804-643-3820	R	31*	.1
39	Widmeyer Communications—*Scott Widmeyer*	1129 20th St NW Ste 20, Washington DC 20036	202-667-0901	R	31*	.1
40	Eventz Extraordinaire Inc—*Phillip Ramsden*	22691 Lambert St Ste 5, Lake Forest CA 92630	949-460-0888	R	31*	.3
41	Alan Taylor Communications—*Tony Signore*	350 5th Ave Ste 3800, New York NY 10118	212-714-1280	R	30*	.1
42	PBN Co—*David Herbert*	1150 18th St NW Ste 32, Washington DC 20036	202-466-6210	R	29*	.1
43	Pointclear LLC—*Dan McDade*	680 Engineering Dr Ste, Norcross GA 30092	678-533-2700	R	29*	.1
44	Eprize LLC—*Matt Wise*	1 Eprize Dr, Pleasant Ridge MI 48069	248-543-6800	R	26	.1
45	The Ardell Group—*David Stowe*	495 NW Flagline Dr, Bend OR 97701	619-925-8191	R	25*	.1
46	PepperCom Inc—*Edward Moed*	470 Park Ave S 5th Fl, New York NY 10016	212-931-6100	R	23*	.1
47	Fisher and Associates Inc—*Robert J Fisher*	4607 Lakeview Canyon R, Westlake Village CA 91361	805-496-5386	R	23*	.1
48	Horn Group Inc—*Sabrina Horn*	612 Howard St, San Francisco CA 94105	415-905-4000	R	23*	.1
49	Zorch International Inc—*Nicole Loftus*	223 W Erie St Ste 3NW, Chicago IL 60654	312-751-8010	R	23*	<.1
50	A and R Edelman—*Bob Angus* Edelman	201 Baldwin Ave, San Mateo CA 94401	650-762-2800	S	21*	.1
51	Shift Communications LLC—*Amy Lyons*	275 Washington St Ste, Newton MA 02458	617-779-1800	R	21*	.1
52	Rasky Baerlein Strategic Communications Inc—*Ann Carter*	70 Franklin St 3rd Fl, Boston MA 02110	617-443-9933	R	21*	<.1
53	All State Promotions Inc—*Cathy Halstead*	20 Cedar St Ste 304, New Rochelle NY 10801	914-637-7300	R	20*	.2
54	Dix and Eaton Inc—*Scott Chaikin*	200 Public Sq Ste 1400, Cleveland OH 44114	216-241-0405	R	20*	.1
55	Dresner Corporate Services Inc—*Steven D Carr*	20 N Clark St Ste 3550, Chicago IL 60602	312-726-3600	R	20*	.1
56	Kekst and Co—*Gershon Kekst*	437 Madison Ave, New York NY 10022	212-521-4800	S	20*	<.1
57	Harris Massey and Herinckx—*Ed Henrickx*	1800 SW 1st Ave Ste 25, Portland OR 97201	503-295-1922	R	20*	<.1
58	Gmmb Inc—*James Margolis*	1010 Wiscnsn Ave 800, Washington DC 20007	202-338-8700	R	20*	.2
59	Makovsky and Company Inc—*Ken Makovsky*	16 E 34th St, New York NY 10022	212-508-9600	R	19*	.1
60	PRR—*Rita Brogan*	1109 1st Ave Ste 300, Seattle WA 98101	206-623-0735	R	18*	<.1
61	CorpComm Inc—*Linda Polonsky-Hillmer*	2300 Fall Hill Ave Ste, Fredericksburg VA 22401	540-834-2467	R	18*	<.1
62	Design Image Group Inc—*Thomas J Strauch*	100 Tower Dr Ste 240, Burr Ridge IL 60527	630-789-8991	R	18*	<.1
63	Sard Verbinnen and Co—*George Sard*	630 3rd Ave 9th Fl, New York NY 10017	212-687-8080	R	17*	<.1
64	MWW Group—*Michael W Kempner*	1 Meadowlands Plz 6th, East Rutherford NJ 07073	201-507-9500	S	16*	.2
65	Powell Tate—*Pam Jenkins* Weber Shandwick Inc	700 13th St NW Ste 800, Washington DC 20005	202-383-9700	D	16*	.1
66	Bender/Helper Impact—*Lee Helper*	11500 W Olympic Blvd S, Los Angeles CA 90064	310-473-4147	R	16*	.1
67	Nerland Agency Inc—*Rick Nerland*	808 E St, Anchorage AK 99501	907-274-9553	R	16*	<.1
68	Amplify Public Affairs—*Robin Strongin*	1750 K St NW 7th Fl, Washington DC 20006	202-263-2900	R	15*	<.1
69	Podesta Group—*Kimberley Fritts*	1001 G St NW Ste 900 E, Washington DC 20001	202-393-1010	R	15*	<.1
70	Rogers and Cowan Inc—*Tom Tardio* Weber Shandwick Inc	8687 Melrose Ave 7th F, Los Angeles CA 90069	310-854-8100	S	14*	.1
71	Communications-Pacific Inc—*Kitty Lagareta*	745 Fort St, Honolulu HI 96813	808-521-5391	R	14*	<.1
72	Harrison and Shriftman—*Lara Shriftman*	141 W 36th St 12th Fl, New York NY 10018	917-351-8600	R	14*	<.1
73	LeGrand Hart—*DeeDee LeGrand*	1625 Broadway Ste 200, Denver CO 80204	303-298-8470	R	14*	<.1
74	Fleishman Hillard Inc (Cleveland Ohio)—*David T Senay*	1350 Euclid Ave Ste 20, Cleveland OH 44115	216-566-7019	R	13*	<.1
75	Hager Sharp Inc—*Garry Curtis*	1030 15th St NW Rm 600, Washington DC 20005	202-842-3600	R	13*	<.1
76	Karlitz and Co—*Herbert Karlitz*	95 Madison Ave, New York NY 10016	646-289-8900	R	13*	<.1

Note: An asterisk (*) indicates an estimated financial figure. The company type code used is as follows: R = Private, P = Public, S = Private Subsidiary, B = Public Subsidiary, D = Division, J = Joint Venture, I = Investment Fund.

COMPANY RANKINGS BY SALES WITHIN 4-DIGIT SIC

Rank	Company Name—*Executive Officer*	Address, City, State, Zip	Phone	Type	Fin	Empls
77	Paul Werth Associates Inc—*Sandra W Harbrecht*	10 N High StSte 300, Columbus OH 43215	614-224-8114	R	13*	<.1
78	Vanguard Communications of Falls Church Inc—*Maria Rodriquez*	2121 K St NW Ste 300, Washington DC 20037	202-331-4323	R	13*	<.1
79	Jumpstart Inc—*Raymond Leach*	737 Bolivar Rd Ste 300, Cleveland OH 44115	216-363-3400	R	12*	<.1
80	Telco Communications Inc—*Mark Hayes Sr*	21 Industrial Ct, Seekonk MA 02771	508-336-6633	R	12*	.1
81	SK Communications LLC—*J Greg Sherry*	10 Wilmot St, Morristown NJ 07960	973-267-5605	R	12*	<.1
82	Cushman/Amberg Communications Inc—*Thomas L Amberg*	1 E Wacker Dr Ste 3750, Chicago IL 60601	312-263-2500	R	12*	<.1
83	Rowland Worldwide Inc—*Sheri Smith*	1675 Broadway 3rd Fl, New York NY 10019	212-527-8800	D	12*	<.1
84	Sterling Communications Inc—*Marianne OConnor*	750 University Ave Ste, Los Gatos CA 95032	408-395-5500	R	12*	<.1
85	Media Two Interactive—*Michael Hubbard*	319 W Martin St Ste 20, Raleigh NC 27601	919-553-1246	R	12*	<.1
86	Hershey-Philbin Associates Inc—*Robert J Philbin*	2101 Orchard Rd Ste 3, Camp Hill PA 17011	717-975-2148	R	12*	<.1
87	Hoffman Agency—*Lou Hoffman*	70 N 2nd St, San Jose CA 95113	408-286-2611	R	11*	.1
88	Cooney/Waters Group—*Lenore Cooney*	90 5th Ave 8th Fl, New York NY 10011	212-886-2200	R	11*	<.1
89	Walt and Co—*Robert Walt*	2105 South Bascom Ave, Campbell CA 95008	408-369-7200	R	11*	<.1
90	Alexander Ogilvy Public Relations—*Marcia Silverman*	1111 19th St Nw Fl 10, Washington DC 20036	202-729-4000	R	11*	.2
91	CRT/tanaka—*Mark Raper*	101 W Commerce Rd, Richmond VA 23224	804-675-8100	R	10	N/A
92	MBI Gluckshaw Group—*Clark W Martin*	212 W State St, Trenton NJ 08608	609-392-3100	R	10*	<.1
93	Engage PR—*Jeantte Bitz*	1321 Harbor Bay Pkwy S, Alameda CA 94502	510-748-8200	R	10*	<.1
94	TransMedia Public Relations—*Glen Calder*	240 W Palmetto Park Rd, Boca Raton FL 33432	561-750-9800	R	10*	<.1
95	CKC Communications Inc—*Carnie Connors*	7 W 22nd St, New York NY 10010	212-798-1411	R	10*	<.1
96	Devillier Communications Inc—*Linda Devillier*	3315 Fessenden St NW, Washington DC 20008	202-362-4429	R	10*	<.1
97	Duffey Communications Inc—*Sherri Fallin*	3379 Peachtree Rd NE 7, Atlanta GA 30326	404-266-2600	R	10*	<.1
98	Sharon Merrill Associates Inc—*Sharon F Merrill*	77 Franklin St, Boston MA 02110	617-542-5300	R	10*	<.1
99	Blanc and Otus—*Richard Weber* Hill and Knowlton Inc	1001 Front St, San Francisco CA 94111	415-856-5100	S	9*	.1
100	Lippert/Heilshorn and Associates Inc—*Keith L Lippert*	800 3rd Ave Ste 1701, New York NY 10022	212-838-3777	R	9*	.1
101	Mathis Earnest and Vandeventer—*Bryan Earnest*	6711 Chancellor Dr, Cedar Falls IA 50613	319-268-9151	R	9*	<.1
102	Wall Street Group Inc (New York New York)—*Donald Kirsch*	1 Edward Hart Dr, Jersey City NJ 07305	201-333-4784	R	9*	<.1
103	J Stokes and Associates—*Jim Stokes*	1444 N Main St, Walnut Creek CA 94596	925-933-1624	R	9*	<.1
104	Porcaro Communications Inc—*Mike Porcaro*	433 W 9th Ave, Anchorage AK 99501	907-276-4262	R	9*	<.1
105	Rosenberg Communications—*Jeffrey Rosenberg*	451 Hungerford Dr Ste, Rockville MD 20850	301-545-1141	R	9*	<.1
106	CHN Inc—*Bonnie Arnouville*	1500 River Oaks Rd W, New Orleans LA 70123	504-734-7734	R	8*	.1
107	Keeble Cavaco and Duka—*Julie Mannion*	450 W 15th St Ste 604, New York NY 10011	212-590-5100	R	8*	<.1
108	Jaffe Associates Inc—*Jay M Jaffe*	1300 Pennsylvania Ave, Washington DC 20004		R	8*	<.1
109	Michael A Burns and Associates Inc—*Michael A Burns*	3333 Lee Pkwy, Dallas TX 75219	214-521-8596	R	8*	<.1
110	Solters and Digney Public Relations—*Lee Solters*	1680 N Vine St Ste 110, Hollywood CA 90028	323-993-3000	R	8*	<.1
111	Cheryl Andrews Marketing Communications Inc—*Cheryl Andrews*	331 Almeria Ave, Coral Gables FL 33134	305-444-4033	R	8*	<.1
112	Coffin Communications Group—*Crocker Coulsen*	10960 Wilshire Ste 205, Los Angeles CA 90024	310-477-9800	R	8*	<.1
113	Beuerman Miller Fitzgerald—*Virginia Miller*	748 Camp St, New Orleans LA 70130	504-524-3342	R	8*	<.1
114	DPR Group—*Dan Demaree*	12850 Middlebrook Rd, Germantown MD 20874	240-686-1000	R	8*	<.1
115	Fineman PR—*Michael Fineman*	330 Townsend St Ste 11, San Francisco CA 94107	415-392-1000	R	8*	<.1
116	Kaye Public Relations Inc—*David Kaye*	12740 Deon Pl, Granada Hills CA 91344	818-368-8212	R	8*	<.1
117	Stewart Agency—*H Donald Stewart*	Po Box 351, Trenton NJ 08609	856-299-2171	R	8*	<.1
118	Organic Dyestuffs Corp—*Greg Gormley*	PO Box 14258, East Providence RI 02914	401-434-3300	R	8*	.1
119	Wexler and Walker Public Policy Associates—*Dale Snape* Hill and Knowlton Inc	1317 F St NW Ste 600, Washington DC 20004	202-638-2121	S	7*	<.1
120	John Adams Associates Inc—*A John Adams*	750 National Press Bld, Washington DC 20045	202-737-8400	R	7*	<.1
121	Barton-Gilanelli and Associates Inc—*Frank Gilanelli*	51 N Mascher St, Philadelphia PA 19106	215-592-8601	R	7*	<.1
122	Alliant Group Inc—*Steve Eames*	5400 Westheimer Ct Ste, Houston TX 77056	713-877-9600	R	7*	<.1
123	Franco Public Relations Group—*Dan Ponder*	400 Renaissance Ctr St, Detroit MI 48243	313-567-2300	R	7*	<.1
124	Funk Luetke Skunda Marketing Inc—*Mark Luetke*	405 Madison Ave Ste 15, Toledo OH 43604	419-241-1244	R	7*	<.1
125	GA Creative—*Wally Lloyd*	10900 NE 8th St Ste, Bellevue WA 98004	425-454-0101	R	7*	<.1
126	Broydrick and Associates—*Bill Broydrick*	400 E Wisconsin Ave St, Milwaukee WI 53202	414-224-9393	R	7*	<.1
127	Fearey Group Inc—*Pat Fearey*	1809 7th Ave Ste 1111, Seattle WA 98101	206-343-1543	R	7*	<.1
128	Graze Public Relations—*Gregory G Graze*	3333 Lee Pky Ste 600, Dallas TX 75219	214-792-9955	R	7*	<.1
129	Pan Communications Inc—*Philip A Nardone Jr*	300 Brickstone Sq 7th, Andover MA 01810	978-474-1900	R	6*	.1
130	Falhgren Mortine—*Kathleen Obert*	1100 Superior Ave Rm 1, Cleveland OH 44114	216-781-2400	R	6*	.1
131	Nuffer Smith Tucker Inc—*Bill Trumpfheller*	707 Broadway 19th Fl, San Diego CA 92101	619-296-0605	R	6*	<.1
132	Peck Madigan Jones and Stewart Inc—*Jeff Peck*	1300 Connecticut Ave N, Washington DC 20036	202-775-8116	R	6*	<.1
133	Revell Communications—*Dennis C Revell*	1121 L St Ste 806, Sacramento CA 95814	916-443-3816	R	6*	<.1
134	Fingerhut Powers and Associates—*Frank Powers*	1925 K St NW Ste250, Washington DC 20006	202-331-3700	R	6*	<.1
135	Adient—*Matt Giegerich*	155 Rt 46 W, Wayne NJ 07470	973-785-2000	S	6*	<.1
136	Caryl Communications Inc—*Caryl Bixon-Gordon*	40 Eisenhower Dr Ste 2, Paramus NJ 07652	201-796-7788	R	6*	<.1
137	Silverman Media and Marketing Group Inc—*Ira H Silverman*	2761 Ellen Rd, Bellmore NY 11710	516-781-1668	R	6*	<.1
138	Blaze Co—*John Davies*	225 Santa Monica Blvd, Santa Monica CA 90401	310-395-5050	R	6*	<.1
139	Coles Media and Public Relations—*Barbara Coles*	3950 Priority Way S Dr, Indianapolis IN 46240	317-571-0051	R	6*	<.1
140	Brustman and Carrino Public Realations—*Susan Brustman*	4500 Biscayne Blvd Ste, Miami FL 33137	305-573-0658	R	6*	<.1
141	DRA Strategic Communications—*Denise D Resnik*	717 E Maryland Ave Ste, Phoenix AZ 85014	602-956-8834	R	6*	<.1
142	Nancy Scott Jones and Associates—*Nancy S Jones*	120 W Mistletoe Ave, San Antonio TX 78212	210-365-5200	R	6*	<.1
143	Brylski Co—*Cheron Brylski*	3418 Coliseum St, New Orleans LA 70115		R	6*	<.1
144	Printmark Industries Inc—*Alexander Sloot*	600 S Poplar St, Hazleton PA 18201	570-455-7000	R	6*	.1
145	Geneva Worldwide Inc—*Joel Buckstein*	261 W 35th St Ste 700, New York NY 10001	212-255-8400	R	5*	.6
146	Tunheim Group—*Kathy Tunheim*	8009 34th Ave S, Minneapolis MN 55425	952-851-1600	R	5*	<.1
147	Media Relations Inc—*Lonny Kocina*	350 W Burnsville Pkwy, Burnsville MN 55337	612-798-7200	R	5*	<.1
148	NCG Porter Novelli	7 World Trade Center 2, New York NY 10007	212-601-8000	S	5*	<.1
149	Health Care Communications Group—*Frank S Kilpatrick*	909 N Sepulveda Blvd S, El Segundo CA 90245	310-606-5700	R	5*	<.1
150	Bouchard Communications Group—*Ann Bouchard*	1430 Blue Oaks Blvd St, Roseville CA 95747	916-783-6161	S	5*	<.1
151	CFM Strategic Communications Inc—*Gary Conkling*	1100 SW 6th Ave Ste 14, Portland OR 97204	503-294-9120	R	5*	<.1
152	Coltrin and Associates—*Stephen H Coltrin*	1212 Avenue of the Ame, New York NY 10036	212-221-1616	R	5*	<.1
153	Dancie Perugini Ware Public Relations	711 Louisiana Ste 2050, Houston TX 77002	713-224-9115	R	5*	<.1
154	Linden Alschuler and Kaplan Inc—*Lisa Linden*	1251 Ave of the Americ, New York NY 10020	212-575-4545	R	5*	<.1
155	Marshall Communications Inc—*Nancy Marshall*	PO Box 317, Augusta ME 04332	207-623-4177	R	5*	<.1
156	Vista Group (Van Nuys California)—*Martin L Shenk*	200 Tim Ct Ste 104, Danville CA 94526	925-831-8402	R	5*	<.1
157	Groundfloor Media Inc—*Laura Love*	1923 Market St, Denver CO 80202	303-865-8110	R	5*	<.1
158	Interprose Inc (Reston Virginia)—*Vivian Kelly*	2635 Steeplechase Dr, Reston VA 20191	703-860-0577	R	5*	<.1
159	Frank Wilson and Associates Inc—*Frank Wilson*	30900 Rancho Viejo Rd, San Juan Capistrano CA 92675	949-218-1850	R	5*	<.1
160	Giles Communications LLC—*Peter N Giles*	2975 W Westchester Ave, Purchase NY 10577	914-644-3500	R	5*	<.1
161	Heying and Associates—*Jan E Heying*	2531 State St, San Diego CA 92101	619-295-9262	R	5*	<.1

Rank	Company Name—*Executive Officer*	Address, City, State, Zip	Phone	Type	Fin	Empls
162	Karen Weiner Escalera Associates Inc—*Karen Weiner Escalera*	75 SW 15th Rd, Miami FL 33129	305-476-5424	R	5*	<.1
163	Renee Sacks Associates Inc—*Renee Sacks*	545 Madison Ave, New York NY 10022	718-646-2799	S	5*	<.1
164	Ronald Trahan Associates Inc—*Ronald Trahan*	940 High St Ste 386, Westwood MA 02090	508-359-4005	R	5*	<.1
165	Sease Gerig and Associates—*Gene Sease*	101 W Ohio St Ste 1800, Indianapolis IN 46204	317-634-1171	R	5*	<.1
166	Stuart Newman Associates—*Stuart G Newman*	2140 S Dixie Hwy Ste 2, Miami FL 33133	305-461-3300	R	5*	<.1
167	Jampole Communications Inc—*Marc Jampole*	428 Forbes Ave Ste 414, Pittsburgh PA 15219	412-471-2463	R	5*	<.1
168	Laer Pearce and Associates—*Laer Pearce*	22892 Mill Creek Dr, Laguna Hills CA 92653	949-599-1212	R	5*	<.1
169	Spelling Communications—*Daniel Spelling*	865 S Figuero St Ste 1, Los Angeles CA 90017	213-415-7400	R	5*	<.1
170	Bates Associates—*Elizabeth R Bates*	4380 Georgetown Sq, Atlanta GA 30338	770-451-0370	R	5*	<.1
171	Brothers and Company Of Oklahoma—*Paul Brothers*	4860 S Lewis Ave Ste 1, Tulsa OK 74105	918-743-8822	R	5*	<.1
172	Performance Communications Group Ltd—*Tom Trainor*	35 E Wacker Dr Ste 400, Chicago IL 60601	312-419-0735	R	4*	<.1
173	Fusion Public Relations Inc—*Jordan Chanofsky*	570 Fashion Ave Fl 9, New York NY 10018	212-651-4200	R	4*	<.1
174	The Bohle Co—*Sue Bohle*	11601 Wilshire Blvd St, Los Angeles CA 90025	310-785-0515	R	4*	.1
175	Morgan and Myers Inc—*Tim Oliver*	N16 W23233 Stone Ridge, Waukesha WI 53188	262-650-7260	R	4*	<.1
176	Publicis Dialog Chicago—*Deborah Zdobinski*	950 6th Ave, New York NY 10001	212-279-5550	R	4*	<.1
177	Pierpont Communications Inc—*Phillip A Morabito*	1800 West Loop S Ste 8, Houston TX 77027	713-627-2223	R	4*	<.1
178	McQuerter Group Inc—*Gregory McQuerter*	5752 Oberlin Dr Ste 10, San Diego CA 92121	858-450-0130	R	4*	<.1
179	Eisbrenner Public Relations Inc—*Ray D Eisbrenner*	2950 W Sq Lake Rd Ste, Troy MI 48098	248-641-1446	R	4*	<.1
180	New Media Strategies Inc—*Pete Snyder*	1100 Wilson Blvd Ste 1, Arlington VA 22209	703-253-0050	R	4*	<.1
181	Lane Marketing Communications Inc—*Wendy Lane*	905 SW 16th Ave, Portland OR 97205	503-221-0480	R	4*	<.1
182	Rockey Company Inc—*Randy Pepple* Hill and Knowlton Inc	2121 5th Ave, Seattle WA 98121	206-728-1100	S	4*	<.1
183	Thorp and Co—*Patricia A Thorp*	150 Alhambra Cir Ste 9, Coral Gables FL 33134	305-446-2700	R	4*	<.1
184	Karwoski and Courage—*Glenn J Karwoski*	60 S 6th St Ste 2800, Minneapolis MN 55402	612-342-9649	D	4*	<.1
185	Strategies A Marketing Communications Corp—*Tara Stoutenborough*	13681 Newport Ave Ste, Tustin CA 92780	714-957-8880	R	4*	<.1
186	Herman Associates Public Relations—*Paula Herman*	261 Madison Ave Ste 15, New York NY 10016	212-616-1190	R	4*	<.1
187	Kaufer Miller Communications Inc—*Pam Miller*	1750 112th Ave NE Ste, Bellevue WA 98004	425-450-9965	R	4*	<.1
188	Porter Le Vay and Rose Inc—*Michael J Porter*	7 Penn Plz Ste 810, New York NY 10001	212-564-4700	R	4*	<.1
189	Sheridan Group Ltd—*Tom Sheridan*	1224 M St NW Ste 300, Washington DC 20005	202-628-7770	R	4*	<.1
190	Armanasco Public Relations Inc—*David Armanasco*	456 Washington St, Monterey CA 93940	831-372-2259	R	4*	<.1
191	BJ Communications Inc—*Sara DeMichele*	650 N 6th Ave, Phoenix AZ 85003	602-277-9530	R	4*	<.1
192	Silverman Heller Associates—*Eugene G Heller*	1100 Glendon Ave 17th, Los Angeles CA 90024	310-208-2550	R	4*	<.1
193	Thompson and Co—*Jennifer Thompson* Porcaro Communications Inc	445 W 9th Ave, Anchorage AK 99501	907-561-4488	D	4*	<.1
194	Wondergem Consulting Inc—*Timothy C Wondergem*	15 Ionia Ave SW Ste 40, Grand Rapids MI 49503	616-235-7467	R	4*	<.1
195	MRB Public Relations Inc—*Michael Becce*	2 E Main St 3rd Fl, Freehold NJ 07728	732-758-1100	R	4*	<.1
196	Quinn/Brein Public Relations—*Jeff Brein*	403 Madison Ave N Ste, Bainbridge Island WA 98110	206-842-8922	R	4*	<.1
197	Adler Public Affairs Inc—*Jeff Adler*	1995 Molino Avenue #20, Signal Hill CA 90755	562-961-6960	R	4*	<.1
198	Bassett and Bassett Inc—*Leland K Bassett*	660 Woodward Ave, Detroit MI 48226	313-965-3010	R	4*	<.1
199	Curley and Pynn Public Relations Management Inc—*Roger Pynn*	258 Southhall Ln Ste 1, Maitland FL 32751	407-423-8006	R	4*	<.1
200	Roher Public Relations Inc—*Richard S Roher*	427 Bedford Rd, Pleasantville NY 10570	914-741-2256	R	4*	<.1
201	Shank Public Relations Counselors Inc—*David L Shank*	2611 Waterfront Pkwy E, Indianapolis IN 46214	317-293-5590	R	4*	<.1
202	Brian S Hickey Associates—*Brian S Hickey*	9 Park St Ste 500, Boston MA 02108	617-248-9772	R	4*	<.1
203	Galli Associates Inc—*Anthony P Galli* Hill and Knowlton Inc	PO Box 7175, Princeton NJ 08543	609-291-0015	S	4*	<.1
204	Vollrath Associates Inc—*Marilyn Vollrath*	839 N Jefferson Ste 50, Milwaukee WI 53202	414-221-0210	R	4*	<.1
205	First Class Inc (Atlanta Georgia)—*Bunnie Jackson-Ransom*	PO Box 110090, Atlanta GA 30311	404-505-8188	R	4*	<.1
206	Carol Reed Associates Inc—*Carol Reed*	3232 McKinney Ave Ste, Dallas TX 75204	214-871-0783	R	4*	<.1
207	Rogers Group—*Ronald Rogers*	1875 Century Park E St, Los Angeles CA 90067	310-552-6922	R	4*	<.1
208	Cision US Inc—*Joe Bernardo*	332 S Michigan Ave Ste, Chicago IL 60604		S	3*	.1
209	Vollmer Public Relations—*Helen Vollmer*	808 Travis St Ste 501, Houston TX 77002	713-970-2100	R	3*	<.1
210	News USA Inc—*Richard D Smith*	2841 Hartland Rd, Falls Church VA 22043		R	3*	<.1
211	Sittercity Inc—*Genevieve Thiers*	222 Merchandise Mart P, Chicago IL 60654		R	3*	<.1
212	GS Schwartz and Company Inc—*Jerry Schwartz*	470 Park Ave S 10th Fl, New York NY 10016	212-725-4500	R	3*	<.1
213	LC Williams and Associates—*Kim Dahlborn*	150 N Michigan Ave Ste, Chicago IL 60601	312-565-3900	R	3*	<.1
214	Bonner and Associates—*Jack Bonner*	1101 17th St NW, Washington DC 20036	202-463-8880	R	3*	<.1
215	Lages and Associates Inc—*Beverly J Lages*	15635 Alton Pkwy Ste 1, Irvine CA 92618	949-453-8080	R	3*	<.1
216	Brandon Associates Inc—*Donald Flanagan*	29 Commonwealth Ave St, Boston MA 02116	617-695-8949	R	3*	<.1
217	Brotman Winter Fried Communications—*Charlie J Brotman*	111 Park Pl, Falls Church VA 22046	703-534-4600	R	3*	<.1
218	Epoch 5 Marketing Inc—*Katherine Heaviside*	755 New York Ave Ste 4, Huntington NY 11743	631-427-1713	R	3*	<.1
219	Everett Clay Associates Inc—*Melissa Mendez Chantres*	6161 Blue Lagoon Dr St, Miami FL 33126	305-261-6222	R	3*	<.1
220	LeBlanc and Schuster Public Relations Inc—*Byron LeBlanc*	PO Box 9214, Metairie LA 70055	504-833-5703	R	3*	<.1
221	Parry Romani DeConcini and Symms—*Romano Romani*	517 C St NE, Washington DC 20002	202-547-4000	R	3*	<.1
222	Paige Hendricks Public Relations Inc—*Paige Hendricks*	1255 W Magnolia, Fort Worth TX 76104	817-924-2300	R	3*	<.1
223	AD Adams Advertising Inc—*Connie Adams*	560 Sylvan Ave 3rd Fl, Englewood Cliffs NJ 07632	201-541-3111	R	3*	<.1
224	GA Kraut Company Inc—*Gary Kraut*	485 Madison Ave 4th Fl, New York NY 10016	212-696-5600	R	3*	<.1
225	Hermanoff Public Relations—*Sandra Hermanoff*	31500 W 13 Mile Rd Ste, Farmington Hills MI 48334	248-851-3993	R	3*	<.1
226	Market Pathways Financial Relations Inc—*Shannon Squyres*	17595 Harvard Ave Ste, Irvine CA 92614	949-955-0107	R	3*	<.1
227	Northstar Counselors Inc—*Joseph M McCarthy*	101 Lake St W Ste 210, Wayzata MN 55391	952-475-9000	R	3*	<.1
228	Sutter Group (Lanham Maryland)—*Karen Sutter*	4384 Lottsford Vista R, Lanham MD 20706	301-459-5445	R	3*	<.1
229	HMA Public Relations—*Scott Hanson*	3610 N 44th St Ste 110, Phoenix AZ 85018	602-957-8881	R	3*	<.1
230	Philosophy Communication Inc—*Jennifer Lester*	209 Kalamath St Ste 2, Denver CO 80223	303-394-2366	R	3*	<.1
231	Stapleton Communications Inc—*Deborah Stapleton*	3453 Ashton Ct, Palo Alto CA 94306	650-470-0200	R	3*	<.1
232	Epiphany Marketing Inc—*Ron Marcus*	10855 Sorrento Valley, San Diego CA 92121	858-866-0070	R	3*	<.1
233	Matter Communications Inc—*Scott Signore*	50 Water St Mill 3 The, Newburyport MA 01950	978-499-9250	R	3*	<.1
234	Renaissance House International—*Barbara Langham*	800 Berring Dr Ste 310, Houston TX 77057	713-961-7400	R	3	<.1
235	The Adler Network Inc	947 Clint Moore Rd, Boca Raton FL 33487	561-206-6081	R	3*	<.1
236	A Brown-Olmstead Associates Inc—*Amanda Brown-Olmstead*	274 W Paces Ferry Rd N, Atlanta GA 30305	404-659-0919	R	3*	<.1
237	Brown Nelson Public Relations—*George Nelson*	PO Box 461, Johnson City TX 78636	713-784-6200	R	3*	<.1
238	Karen Bakula and Company Inc—*Karen Bakula*	1722 J St Ste 11, Sacramento CA 95814	916-442-0957	R	3*	<.1
239	Landmark Communication Inc—*Mark Rountree*	11300 Atlantis Pl Ste, Alpharetta GA 30022	770-813-1000	R	3*	<.1
240	Maximum Exposure Public Relations—*Renee Sall*	50 Tice Blvd, Woodcliff Lake NJ 07677	201-573-0300	R	3*	<.1
241	Redington Inc (Westport Connecticut)—*Thomas Redington*	49 Richmondville Ave S, Westport CT 06880	203-222-7399	R	3*	<.1
242	Wernick Marketing Group—*Sandie Wernick*	1690 Broadway, San Francisco CA 94109	415-928-7414	R	3*	<.1
243	Gallior and Wittenberg Inc—*Martha Gallier*	717 N Harwood, Dallas TX 75201	214-979-0430	R	3*	<.1
244	Wepco Vintek LLC—*Kevin Colvin*	1903 E Jensen St Ste 1, Mesa AZ 85203	480-833-3390	R	3*	<.1

Note: An asterisk (*) indicates an estimated financial figure. The company type code used is as follows: R = Private, P = Public, S = Private Subsidiary, B = Public Subsidiary, D = Division, J = Joint Venture, I = Investment Fund.

COMPANY RANKINGS BY SALES WITHIN 4-DIGIT SIC

Rank	Company Name—*Executive Officer*	Address, City, State, Zip	Phone	Type	Fin	Empls
245	Bernstein and Associates Inc (Houston Texas)—*Patricia H Bernstein*	6300 W Loop S Ste 218, Bellaire TX 77401	713-838-8400	R	3*	<.1
246	Greenbaum Public Relations—*Stuart Greenbaum*	1783 11 Ave Ste 45, Sacramento CA 95818	916-443-3464	R	3*	<.1
247	Borshoff Inc—*Myra Borshoff Cook*	47 S Pennsylvania St S, Indianapolis IN 46204	317-631-6400	R	2*	<.1
248	FSA Association—*David Cawood*	455 S 4th St Ste 650, Louisville KY 40202	502-583-3783	S	2*	<.1
249	MCA Inc (Mountain View California)—*Marie Labrie*	2119 Landings Dr, Mountain View CA 94043	650-968-8900	R	2*	<.1
250	Metzger Associates Inc—*John Metzger*	5733 Central Ave, Boulder CO 80301	303-786-7000	R	2*	<.1
251	Prize Performance Inc—*Robert Kowalski*	4 Jangling Plain Rd, Newtown CT 06470	203-426-7112	R	2*	<.1
252	PRx Inc—*Steve Mangold*	991 W Hedding St STE 2, San Jose CA 95126	408-287-1700	R	2*	<.1
253	Schneider and Associates Inc—*Joan D Schneider*	2 Oliver St Ste 901, Boston MA 02109	617-536-3300	R	2*	<.1
254	Ackermann Public Relations and Marketing—*Cathy G Ackermann*	1111 Northshore Dr Ste, Knoxville TN 37919	865-584-0550	R	2*	<.1
255	DWJ Television—*Daniel Johnson*	1 Robinson Ln, Ridgewood NJ 07450	201-445-1711	R	2*	<.1
256	Gladstone International Inc—*Joan Gladstone*	1278 Glenneyre St Ste, Laguna Beach CA 92651	949-633-9900	R	2*	<.1
257	McGrath/Power Public Relations Inc—*Jonathan Bloom*	333 W San Carlos St St, San Jose CA 95110	408-727-0351	R	2*	<.1
258	PondelWilkinson Inc—*Roger S Pondel*	1880 Century Park E St, Los Angeles CA 90067	310-279-5980	R	2*	<.1
259	Primetime Publicity and Media Inc—*Reed Trencher*	30 Hamilton Ln, Mill Valley CA 94941	415-332-0000	R	2*	<.1
260	Sturges and Word Communications and Design Inc—*Melissa Sturges*	810 Baltimore Ave, Kansas City MO 64105	816-221-7500	R	2*	<.1
261	Townsend Raimundo Besler and Usher—*Sharon Usher*	1717 I St, Sacramento CA 95814	916-444-5701	R	2*	<.1
262	TRIAD Inc—*Dave Keller*	371 County Line Rd W, Westerville OH 43082	614-846-8761	R	2*	<.1
263	Publicom Inc—*Lisa O'Conner*	333 Albert Ave, East Lansing MI 48823	517-487-3700	R	2*	<.1
264	Design At Work Corp—*John Lowery*	3701 Kirby Dr Ste 1050, Houston TX 77098	832-200-8200	R	2*	<.1
265	Lane and Coady Inc—*Suzanne Lane*	1790 Broadway Ste 1701, New York NY 10019	212-757-6880	R	2*	<.1
266	Sterling Creative—*Jo Sterling*	555 University Ave, Sacramento CA 95825	916-923-9400	R	2*	<.1
267	Trylon SMR Inc—*Lloyd P Trufelman*	41 E 11th St, New York NY 10003	212-905-6060	R	2*	<.1
268	Jefferson Waterman International LLC—*Charles Waterman*	1401 K St NW Ste 400, Washington DC 20005	202-216-2200	R	2*	<.1
269	Hecht Spencer and Associates Inc—*William H Hecht*	499 S Capital St SW St, Washington DC 20003	202-554-2881	R	2*	<.1
270	Survey Analytics LLC—*Vivek Bhaskaran*	3518 Fremont Ave N Ste, Seattle WA 98103		R	2*	<.1
271	Casey Communications Inc—*Marie A Casey*	8301 Maryland Ave Ste, St Louis MO 63105	314-721-2828	R	2*	<.1
272	Executive Media Communications Consultants Inc (Indianapolis Indiana)—*David Dawson*	101 W Ohio St Ste 720, Indianapolis IN 46204	317-231-7000	R	2*	<.1
273	Wilson Group Communications Inc—*Steve Wilson*	PO Box 21877, Columbus OH 43221	614-461-1333	R	2*	<.1
274	3 Point Partners—*Don Martin*	1221 S Mopac Expy Ste, Austin TX 78746	512-328-4055	R	2*	<.1
275	BABB/Houston Public Relations—*Paul Babb*	1200 Smith St Ste 1600, Houston TX 77056	713-622-4213	R	2*	<.1
276	Cataldi Public Relations Inc—*Sal Cataldi*	143 W 29th St Ste 904, New York NY 10001	212-244-9797	R	2*	<.1
277	Chartrand Communications Group—*David Chartrand*	12710 S Pflumm Rd Ste, Olathe KS 66062	913-768-4700	R	2*	<.1
278	Corbett Associates Inc—*William J Corbett Jr*	111 S Tyson Ave, Floral Park NY 11001	516-775-0435	R	2*	<.1
279	Foley/Freisleben LLC—*Gerald S Freisleben*	15233 Ventura Blvd Ste, Sherman Oaks CA 91403	818-788-0010	R	2*	<.1
280	Hughey and Associates—*Byron R Hughey*	1200 St Charles Ave St, New Orleans LA 70130	504-524-8843	R	2*	<.1
281	JDI Communications Inc—*Rivian Bell*	611 W 6th St Ste 1880, Los Angeles CA 90017	213-612-4927	R	2*	<.1
282	Lucinda Hall Public Relations—*Lucinda Hill*	5115 Maryland Way, Brentwood TN 37027	615-377-0771	R	2*	<.1
283	McRae Agency—*Elizabeth McRae*	5685 N Scottsdale Rd, Scottsdale AZ 85250	480-990-0282	R	2*	<.1
284	Media West Communications Inc—*John Samford*	4305 S Bowen Rd, Arlington TX 76016	817-417-7711	R	2*	<.1
285	Structured Information Inc—*Jerry Fireman*	16 Russell Pl, Arlington MA 02474	781-674-2300	R	2*	<.1
286	Vander Houwen Public Relations Inc—*Boyd Vander Houwen*	8575 SE 76th Pl, Mercer Island WA 98040	206-949-4364	R	2*	<.1
287	Benson Marketing Group—*Jeremy Benson*	2700 Napa Valley Corpo, Napa CA 94558	707-254-9292	R	2*	<.1
288	Klute Communications—*Peter P Klute*	6625 E North Ln, Scottsdale AZ 85253	480-951-6525	R	2*	<.1
289	Opinion Research Associates Inc—*Ernest J Oakleaf*	1501 N University Ave, Little Rock AR 72207	501-663-2414	R	2*	<.1
290	Patterson and Murphy Public Relations—*Tessie Patterson*	PO Box 980974, Houston TX 77098	713-520-7111	R	2*	<.1
291	Rountree Group Inc—*Neva D Rountree*	11680 Great Oaks Pkwy, Alpharetta GA 30022	770-645-4545	R	2*	<.1
292	Booker/Hancock and Associates LLC—*Lynn Hancock*	675 Bering Dr Rm 395, Houston TX 77057	713-782-7502	R	2*	<.1
293	Cato and Newby Inc—*Marylee Cato*	55 Battery Park Dr, Bridgeport CT 06605	203-336-5257	R	2*	<.1
294	Flatt and Associates Ltd—*Joanie L Flatt*	623 W Southern Ave Ste, Mesa AZ 85210	480-835-9139	R	2	<.1
295	G Cole Davis and Associates—*G Cole Davis*	1667 Vann Ct, El Cajon CA 92020	619-579-1630	R	2*	<.1
296	Meredith and Hall Inc—*Judith Meredith*	30 Winter St 7th Fl, Boston MA 02108	617-338-0954	R	2*	<.1
297	Oppidan Group Inc—*Tom Andrzejewski*	50 Public Sq 25th Fl, Cleveland OH 44113	216-771-9988	R	2*	<.1
298	Pat Paton Public Relations—*Pat Paton*	4319 W 112th St, Leawood KS 66211	913-491-4000	R	2*	<.1
299	Pamela A Keene Public Relations Inc—*Pamela A Keene*	6256 Mount Salem Cir, Flowery Branch GA 30542	770-965-3340	R	2*	<.1
300	Jeffrey Group Inc—*Jorge Ortega*	1111 Lincoln Rd, Miami FL 33139	305-860-1000	R	1*	<.1
301	Kortenhaus Communications Inc—*Lynne Kortenhaus*	29 Commonwealth Ave, Boston MA 02116	617-536-5352	R	1*	<.1
302	Susan Magrino Agency—*Susan Magrino*	352 Park Ave S 13 Fl, New York NY 10010	212-957-3005	R	1*	<.1
303	LaBreche LLC—*Beth LaBreche*	500 Washington Ave S S, Minneapolis MN 55415	612-338-0901	R	1*	<.1
304	Bitner Goodman—*Gary Bitner*	701 W Cypress Creek Rd, Fort Lauderdale FL 33309	954-730-7730	R	1*	<.1
305	Public Affairs Associates Inc—*Thomas Hoisington*	120 N Washington Sq St, Lansing MI 48933	517-371-3800	R	1*	<.1
306	Aker Partners Inc—*Sanda Pecina*	2801 M St NW, Washington DC 20007	202-719-8062	R	1*	<.1
307	Berkshire Marketing Group Inc—*Darrell J Berman*	256 Broadway, Troy NY 12180	518-274-0414	R	1*	<.1
308	Boardroom Communications Inc—*Julie Silver*	1776 N Pine Island Rd, Plantation FL 33322	954-370-8999	R	1*	<.1
309	Guthrie/Mayes and Associates Inc—*Clair Nichols*	710 W Main St, Louisville KY 40202	502-584-0371	R	1*	<.1
310	International Communications and Marketing Inc—*Piers J Lishman*	PO Box 185, Stone Ridge NY 12484	845-687-4082	R	1*	<.1
311	Landau Public Relations—*Howard C Landau*	700 W St Clair Ave Ste, Cleveland OH 44113	216-696-1686	S	1	<.1
312	Ronald Levitt Public Relations Associates Inc—*Howard Levitt*	2573 Eagle Run Ln, Weston FL 33327	954-349-2596	R	1*	<.1
313	Anne Klein Communications Group—*Anne Sceia Klein*	1000 Atrium Way Ste 10, Mount Laurel NJ 08054	856-866-0411	R	1*	<.1
314	Firestone Associates—*Jeff Wolfman*	420 5th Ave 26th Fl, New York NY 10018	212-221-3399	R	1*	<.1
315	Kalt Rosen and Company LLC—*Howard Kalt*	388 Market St Ste 1400, San Francisco CA 94111	415-541-0750	R	1*	<.1
316	Rodheim Marketing Group Inc—*Ralph Rodheim*	125 E Baker St Ste 260, Costa Mesa CA 92626	714-557-5100	R	1*	<.1
317	VPE Public Relations Inc—*John A Echeveste*	1605 Hope St Ste 250, South Pasadena CA 91030	626-403-3200	R	1*	<.1
318	MMC Communications—*Scott Steinwert*	244 Capitol Mall Compl, Sacramento CA 95814	916-658-0180	R	1*	<.1
319	Barker Pacific Group—*Micheal D Barker*	3 Hamilton Landing Ste, San Francisco CA 94134	415-884-9977	R	1*	<.1
320	Samluk Communications Inc—*Donna Samluk*	PO Box 2997, Danville CA 94506	925-736-7301	R	1*	<.1
321	Whelan Communications Inc—*Edward Whelan*	1422 Euclid Ave Ste 62, Cleveland OH 44115	216-574-4330	R	1*	<.1
322	Fastforward Communications Inc—*Adam Handler*	401 Columbus Ave, Valhalla NY 10595	914-741-0555	R	1*	<.1
323	Fineberg Publicity Inc—*Erica Fineberg*	276 Fifth Ave Ste 701, New York NY 10001	212-686-7820	R	1*	<.1
324	Henry and Germann Public Affairs LLC—*Kelly Henry*	1669 Edgewood Rd Ste 2, Yardley PA 19067	215-493-1426	R	1*	<.1
325	Marken Communications Inc—*Gideon A Marken*	3375 Scott Blvd Ste 23, Santa Clara CA 95054	408-986-0100	R	1*	<.1
326	de La Garza Public Relations—*Henry A de La Garza*	5300 Memorial Dr Ste 2, Houston TX 77007	713-622-8818	R	1*	<.1
327	FiComm Inc—*Heidi A Flannery*	2572 NW Shields Dr, Bend OR 97701	541-322-0230	R	1*	<.1
328	Larry Lubenow and Associates Inc—*Larry Lubenow*	3102 Lombardi Way, Cedar Park TX 78613	512-335-9233	R	1*	<.1
329	Lauricella Public Relations Co—*Mary Ann Lauricella*	26 SpiceBush Ln, Williamsville NY 14221	716-683-2990	R	1*	<.1

Rank	Company Name—*Executive Officer*	Address, City, State, Zip	Phone	Type	Fin	Empls
330	Wirz and Associates Inc—*Robert A Wirz*	665-A North Trail, Stratford CT 06614		R	1*	<.1
331	Wools of New Zealand—*Wes Connelly*	PO Box 669273, Marietta GA 30066	770-977-1440	R	1*	<.1
332	Abrams Productions Inc—*Al Abrams*	4647 Caritina Dr, Tarzana CA 91356	818-343-6365	R	1*	<.1
333	Hal Copeland Company Inc—*Hal Copeland*	5646 Milton St Ste 336, Dallas TX 75206	214-361-8788	R	1*	<.1
334	Jensen and Walker Inc—*Keith H Walker*	8802 Ashcroft Ave, Los Angeles CA 90048	310-273-8696	R	1*	<.1
335	Kaiser Associates—*Stephen D Kaiser*	1201 Connecticut Ave N, Washington DC 20036	202-454-2000	R	1*	<.1
336	Kathy Barnum Public Relations—*Kathy Barnum*	26961 Avenida Las Palm, Capistrano Beach CA 92624	949-493-5281	R	1*	<.1
337	Knowledge in a Nutshell—*Audrey Reichblum*	1420 Centre Ave, Pittsburgh PA 15219	412-765-2020	R	1	<.1
338	Mountain Marketing Inc—*Craig A Altschul*	PO Box 17810, Tucson AZ 85731	520-290-4569	R	1*	<.1
339	Proby and Associates Inc—*Bay Proby*	7300 N Kendall Dr Ste, Miami FL 33156	305-251-3671	R	1*	<.1
340	Radcliffe and Associates Inc—*Donald Radcliffe*	575 Madison Ave Ste 10, New York NY 10022	212-605-0201	R	1*	<.1
341	Andrea Blain Public Relations Inc—*Andrea Blain*	9750 Crawford Ave, Skokie IL 60076	847-933-9884	R	1*	<.1
342	Publicity Matters—*Matt Amodeo*	14644 McKnew Rd Ste 20, Burtonsville MD 20866	301-385-2090	R	1*	<.1
343	Wordman Inc—*Steve Lewis*	215 Tawneywood Way, Alpharetta GA 30022	770-442-9805	R	1*	<.1
344	Barbara Nicol Public Relations—*Barbara Nicol*	4025 Queen Ave S, Minneapolis MN 55410	612-920-2279	R	1	N/A
345	Hasgo Power Equipment Sales Inc—*Jim O'neil*	PO Box 400, Le Roy NY 14482	585-768-8500	R	1*	<.1
346	Levin Public Relations and Marketing Inc—*Donald M Levin*	147 Rockland Ave, Larchmont NY 10538	914-834-5919	R	<1	<.1
347	Ross-Campbell Inc—*Ted Ross*	1912 F St, Sacramento CA 95814	916-446-4744	R	N/A	<.1
348	Janet Diederichs and Associates Inc—*Janet Diederichs*	208 S LaSalle St Ste 1, Chicago IL 60604	312-346-7886	R	N/A	<.1

TOTALS: SIC 8743 Public Relations Services
Companies: 348 — 7,931 — 36.0

8744 Facilities Support Services

Rank	Company Name—*Executive Officer*	Address, City, State, Zip	Phone	Type	Fin	Empls
1	Sodexo Inc—*John M Bush*	9801 Washingtonian Blv, Gaithersburg MD 20878	301-987-4431	S	49,828*	120.0
2	IAP Worldwide Services Inc—*Mike Williams*	7315 N Atlantic Ave, Cape Canaveral FL 32920	321-784-7100	R	2,005*	7.0
3	Corrections Corporation of America—*Damon Hininger*	10 Burton Hills Blvd, Nashville TN 37215	615-263-3000	P	1,736	16.8
4	GEO Group Inc—*George C Zoley*	621 NW 53rd St Ste 700, Boca Raton FL 33487	561-893-0101	P	1,613	18.9
5	Echo Global Logistics Inc—*Douglas R Waggoner*	600 W Chicago Ave Ste, Chicago IL 60654		P	426	.7
6	DEL-JEN Inc—*Edward Delane*	4465 Guthrie Hwy, Clarksville TN 37040	931-552-0232	S	390*	2.6
7	Inmar Inc—*Joe Odonell*	2601 Pilgrim Court Rd, Winston-Salem NC 27106	336-770-3500	R	265*	1.3
8	Call Henry Inc—*Henry L Foster*	308 Pine St, Titusville FL 32796	321-267-9808	R	188*	.5
9	Chugach World Services Inc—*Scott Davis*	3800 Centerpoint Dr St, Anchorage AK 99503	907-563-8866	R	177*	1.1
10	Carolina Rha/North Mr Inc—*John West*	1200 Rdgfeld Blvd Ste, Asheville NC 28806	828-232-6844	R	176*	2.0
11	ABM Engineering Services—*Mike Laphan*	5200 S Eastern Ave, Commerce CA 90040	323-887-5100	S	166*	2.5
12	Chugach Management Services Inc—*Matthew Hayes*	3800 Centerpoint Dr St, Anchorage AK 99503	907-563-8866	R	166*	1.0
13	Trax International Corp—*F Wilson*	8337 W Sunset Rd Ste 2, Las Vegas NV 89113	702-216-4455	R	156*	.5
14	Uniserve Corp—*Sam Hwang*	550 S Hope St Ste T200, Los Angeles CA 90071		R	155*	.8
15	SSI Services Inc—*Matt Schneider*	134 Three Degree Rd, Pittsburgh PA 15237	412-367-6060	S	125*	.8
16	KIRA Inc—*Carlos Garcia*	PO Box 1438, Boulder CO 80306	303-402-1526	R	120*	.4
17	Whittmanhart—*Paul Wimer*	150 N Michigan, Chicago IL 60601	312-981-6000	D	84*	.4
18	Joule Inc—*Emanuel N Logothetis*	1245 Rte 1 S, Edison NJ 08837	732-548-5444	R	69*	.2
19	Southern Corrections Systems Avalon Correctional Services Inc	13401 Railway Dr, Oklahoma City OK 73114	405-752-8802	S	68*	.3
20	Sentinel Benefits Group Inc—*John A Carnevale*	PO Box 5000, Reading MA 01867		R	41*	.2
21	Yoh Services LLC—*Lori Schultz*	1500 Spring Garden St, Philadelphia PA 19130	215-656-2650	S	40*	.6
22	Dzsp 21 LLC	1818 Market St Fl 22, Philadelphia PA 19103	215-299-8139	R	39*	.5
23	CMI Management Inc—*Abe Abraham*	5285 Shawnee Rd Ste 40, Alexandria VA 22312	703-738-5300	R	33*	.4
24	Ouzerne County Correctional Facility—*James Larson*	99 Water St, Wilkes Barre PA 18702	570-820-7741	R	30*	.3
25	Shamrock Companies Inc—*Robert Troop*	24090 Detroit Rd, Westlake OH 44145	440-899-9510	R	27*	.1
26	Avalon Correctional Services Inc—*Donald E Smith*	13401 Railway Dr, Oklahoma City OK 73114	405-752-8802	P	26	.1
27	Millennium Group Of Delaware Inc—*Dermot Murphy*	106 Apple St Ste 207, Tinton Falls NJ 07724	732-741-4870	R	25*	.4
28	Cubic Worldwide Technical Services Inc—*Walter J Zable*	9333 Balboa Ave, San Diego CA 92123	858-277-6780	S	24*	.3
29	US Inspect LLC—*William Bowman*	3650 Concorde Pkwy Ste, Chantilly VA 20151	703-293-1400	R	22*	.2
30	American Operations Corp—*L Field*	14030 Thunderbolt Pl S, Chantilly VA 20151	703-375-4333	R	22*	.2
31	Total Resource Management Inc—*Garner Bennett*	510 King St Ste 300, Alexandria VA 22314		R	19*	.1
32	Support Associates Inc—*John Shadwick*	22901 Mill Creek Dr, Laguna Hills CA 92653	949-580-1911	R	19*	.2
33	Argus Management Company LLC	1045 S Atl Ave Ste 705, Long Beach CA 90813	562-491-9673	R	18*	.3
34	Progressive Employer Services Inc—*Steve Herrig*	6407 Parkland Dr, Sarasota FL 34243		R	17*	.1
35	Selecttech Services Corp—*Robert Finch*	8045 Washington Villag, Centerville OH 45458	937-438-9905	R	14*	.1
36	Logistics 2020 Inc—*Michael Topp*	13203 N Enon Church Rd, Chester VA 23836	804-748-0042	R	13*	.2
37	Witt Fiala Flannery and Associates—*Robert Hardy*	211 S Jefferson, Saint Louis MO 63103		R	12*	.8
38	Kenny Industrial Services LLC—*Michael G Rothman*	414 N Orleans St Ste 2, Chicago IL 60610	312-645-0990	R	12*	.1
39	Envirotech Remediation Services Inc—*Dave Sobaski*	3000 84th Ln Ne, Minneapolis MN 55449	763-746-0670	R	11*	.1
40	Configuration Inc—*Christopher Powell*	3015 V St Ne, Washington DC 20018	202-526-8500	R	11*	.1
41	Virtue Group—*Raja Kalidindi*	5755 N Point Pkwy Ste, Alpharetta GA 30022	678-578-4555	R	9*	.1
42	American Services Technology Inc—*Moses L Harvin*	1028 Harvin Way Ste 12, Rockledge FL 32955	321-631-8771	R	8*	.1
43	Scientific and Commercial Systems Corp—*Vernon Stansbury*	7600 Leesburg Pke Ste, Falls Church VA 22043	703-917-9171	R	8*	.3
44	Alliance Logistics Inc—*James E Bedeker*	1170 James Savage Rd, Midland MI 48640	989-839-8100	R	7*	<.1
45	Chugach Industrials Inc—*Roberto Nevarez*	57 G St, Roswell NM 88203	575-347-5414	R	6*	.1
46	MG West Co—*Andrew Sullivan*	PO BOx 7231, San Francisco CA 94105	415-284-4800	R	6*	<.1
47	Portable Church Industries—*Pete van der Harst*	1923 Ring Dr, Troy MI 48083	248-585-9540	R	6*	<.1
48	Precis Corp—*William McGlouckton*	1400 Mercantile Ln, Largo MD 20774	301-341-6623	R	5*	.1
49	Enviromental Systems Products Holdings Inc—*Bob Tamburrino*	2002 N Forbes Blvd, Tucson AZ 85745	520-617-2539	R	4*	.1
50	Specialty Risk Services LLC—*Joe Boures*	55 Farmington Ave Ste, Hartford CT 06105	860-520-2500	S	<1	1.5
51	TLC Staffing—*Judith Lawton*	8788 Balboa Ave, San Diego CA 92123	858-569-6260	R	<1	.3
52	Government Contracting Resources Inc—*J Albritton*	315 Page Rd 7, Pinehurst NC 28374	910-215-1900	R	N/A	.2

TOTALS: SIC 8744 Facilities Support Services
Companies: 52 — 58,444 — 185.8

8748 Business Consulting Services Nec

Rank	Company Name—*Executive Officer*	Address, City, State, Zip	Phone	Type	Fin	Empls
1	National Shopping Service—*Matt Wozniak*	PO Box 1557, Rocklin CA 95677	916-781-6776	R	6,073*	16.0
2	Kantar Group—*Eric Salama*	501 Kings Hwy E 4th Fl, Fairfield CT 06825	203-330-5200	S	4,345*	9.6
3	Newmark Knight Frank—*Barry M Gosin*	125 Park Ave, New York NY 10017	212-372-2000	S	3,465*	7.0
4	L-3 Aeromet Communications—*Micheal T Strianese*	112 Beechcraft Dr, Tulsa OK 74132	918-299-2621	S	3,453*	6.2
5	Daymon Worldwide—*Carla Cooper*	700 Fairfield Ave, Stamford CT 06902	203-352-7500	R	3,178*	5.0
6	ICF International (Sacramento California)—*Sudhakar Kesavan*	630 K St Ste 400, Sacramento CA 95814	916-737-3000	S	1,723*	3.7
7	Protocol Marketing Group—*Don Norsworthy*	2805 Fruitville Rd, Sarasota FL 34237	847-236-3400	R	1,436*	3.4
8	Foundstone Inc—*Bill Hau*	27201 Puerta Real, Mission Viejo CA 92691	949-297-5600	D	987	3.3
9	Development Alternatives Inc—*James Boomgard*	7600 Wisconsin Ave, Bethesda MD 20814	301-771-7600	R	935*	2.5

Note: An asterisk (*) indicates an estimated financial figure. The company type code used is as follows: R = Private, P = Public, S = Private Subsidiary, B = Public Subsidiary, D = Division, J = Joint Venture, I = Investment Fund.

COMPANY RANKINGS BY SALES WITHIN 4-DIGIT SIC

Rank	Company Name—*Executive Officer*	Address, City, State, Zip	Phone	Type	Fin	Empls
10	Post Buckley Schuh and Jernigan Inc	2001 NW 107th Ave, Miami FL 33172	305-592-7275	S	842*	4.0
11	Environmental Resources Management Group Inc—*John Alexander*	350 Eagleview Blvd Ste, Exton PA 19341	610-524-3500	S	681	4.0
12	Huron Consulting Group Inc—*James H Roth*	550 W Van Buren St, Chicago IL 60607	312-583-8700	P	605	1.8
13	Experient Inc—*Jeff Price*	2500 E Enterprise Pky, Twinsburg OH 44087	330-425-8333	R	436*	.8
14	Exponent Environmental Group Inc—*Paul Johnson*	15375 SE 30th Pl Ste 2, Bellevue WA 98007	425-519-8700	S	428*	.9
15	Buck Consultants Inc—*Mike Roberts*	245 Park Avenue 23rd F, New York NY 10167	212-330-1000	S	416*	3.0
16	TRC Environmental Corp	21 Griffin Rd N, Windsor CT 06095	860-298-9692	S	401	2.6
17	Bensussen Deutsch and Associates Inc—*Jay Deutsch*	15525 Woodinville-Redm, Woodinville WA 98072	425-492-6111	R	263*	.5
18	NUS Consulting Group—*Richard Soultanian*	PO Box 712, Park Ridge NJ 07656	201-391-4300	R	218*	.5
19	Televerde—*James H Hooker*	4636 E University Dr S, Phoenix AZ 85034	480-736-8137	R	216*	.4
20	Ryan LLC—*G Brint Ryan*	3 Galleria Twr 13155 N, Dallas TX 75240	972-934-0022	R	213*	.9
21	Science Applications International Corp (Linthicum Maryland)	1306 Concourse Dr Ste, Linthicum MD 21090	410-691-5200	S	204*	.5
22	Jacobs Constructors Inc—*Craig L Martin*	PO Box 98033, Baton Rouge LA 70898	225-769-7700	S	195	.5
23	National Asset Recovery Services Inc—*Christopher Buehrle*	16253 Swingley Ridge R, Chesterfield MO 63017	636-530-7985	R	195*	3.3
24	Total Safety US Inc—*David Fanta*	11111 Wilcrest Green D, Houston TX 77042	713-353-7100	S	179*	1.5
25	TPI Inc—*Michael Connors*	10055 Grogans Mill Rd, The Woodlands TX 77380	281-465-5700	R	179*	.3
26	Dynetech Corp—*Laurence J Pino*	111 N Magnolia Ave Ste, Orlando FL 32801	407-206-6500	R	177*	.5
27	Ensr International Corp—*Robert Weber*	2 Technology Park Dr, Westford MA 01886	978-589-3000	R	176*	2.6
28	Environmental Resources Management Inc—*Michael Shaughnessy*	1701 Golf Rd Ste 1-100, Rolling Meadows IL 60008	847-258-8900	R	167*	3.5
29	Abt Associates Inc—*Kathleen L Flanagan*	55 Wheeler St, Cambridge MA 02138	617-492-7100	R	160	1.0
30	Atlanta Global Resources Inc—*Tony Akpele*	PO Box 1294, Tucker GA 30085	770-696-1507	R	160*	<.1
31	Community Counselling Service Company Inc—*Robert Kissane*	461 5th Ave 3rd Fl, New York NY 10017	212-695-1175	R	158*	.4
32	Sault Sainte Marie Tribe Of Chippewa Indians—*Aaron Payment*	523 Ashmun St, Sault Sainte Marie MI 49783	906-635-6050	R	152*	3.0
33	Gordon E And Betty I Moore Foundation—*Lewis Coleman*	1661 Page Mill Rd, Palo Alto CA 94304	650-210-9110	R	151*	.1
34	Anchorage Advisors LLC—*Kevin Ulrich*	610 Broadway, New York NY 10012	212-432-4600	R	150*	.1
35	EquaTerra Inc—*Mark Toon*	3 Riverway Ste 1290, Houston TX 77056	713-470-9812	R	146*	.3
36	Lexecon LLC—*Daniel Fischel*	332 Michigan Ave Ste 1, Chicago IL 60604	312-322-0200	S	140*	.3
37	USI Consulting Group—*William M Tremko*	95 Glastonbury Blvd, Glastonbury CT 06033	860-633-5283	R	138*	.3
38	Study Island LLC—*Tim McEwen*	3232 McKinney Ave Ste, Dallas TX 75204		R	118*	.2
39	Tech-Pro—*Dave Vadis*	3000 Centre Pointe Dr, Roseville MN 55113	651-634-1400	R	115*	.3
40	Nek Advanced Securities Group Inc—*Bruce Parkman*	110 S Sierra Madre St, Colorado Springs CO 80903	719-634-5523	R	112*	.2
41	Dynamac Corp—*W Dennis Lauchner*	2275 Research Blvd Ste, Rockville MD 20850	301-417-9800	R	111*	.4
42	Tetra Tech FW Inc—*Donald I Rogers*	1000 The American Rd, Morris Plains NJ 07950	973-630-8000	S	106*	1.0
43	Excellence in Motivation Inc—*Bob Miller*	National City Ctr 6 N, Dayton OH 45402	937-222-2900	R	95*	.2
44	ConsultNet LLC—*Don Goldberg*	10813 S River Front Pk, South Jordan UT 84095	801-208-3700	R	92*	.2
45	FA Bartlett Tree Expert Co—*Robert A Bartlett Jr*	PO Box 3067, Stamford CT 06905	203-323-1131	R	91*	2.0
46	Harbor Payments Inc—*Ashish Bahl*	400 Galleria Pkwy, Atlanta GA 30339	404-267-5000	S	88*	.2
47	Blackbird Technologies Inc—*Peggy Styer*	13900 Lincoln Park Dr, Herndon VA 20171	703-796-1420	R	86*	.2
48	Nordis Direct—*Ronnie Selinger*	4401 NW 124th Ave, Coral Springs FL 33065	954-323-5500	R	84*	.2
49	BP Barber	PO Box 1116, Columbia SC 29202	803-254-4400	S	83*	.2
50	Sparta Inc—*Robert Sepucha*	25531 Commercentre Dr, Lake Forest CA 92630	949-768-8161	R	83*	.1
51	Intervoice Services Inc—*David Brandenberg*	17811 Waterview Pkwy, Dallas TX 75252	972-454-8000	R	80*	.6
52	Operational Technologies Corp—*Max Navarro*	4100 NW Loop 410 Ste 2, San Antonio TX 78229	210-731-0000	R	80*	.2
53	Stearns Conrad and Schmidt Engineers Inc—*Jim Walsh*	3900 Kilroy Airport Wa, Long Beach CA 90806	562-426-9544	R	79*	.6
54	Decision Analyst Inc—*Jerry W Thomas*	604 E Ave H, Arlington TX 76011	817-640-6166	R	79*	.2
55	System Planning Corp—*Ronald Easley*	3601 Wilson Blvd, Arlington VA 22201	703-351-8200	R	75*	.2
56	LandDesign Inc—*Dale Stewart*	223 N Graham St, Charlotte NC 28202	704-333-0325	R	68*	.3
57	Client Network Services Inc—*B Chatterjee*	702 King Farm Blvd Fl, Rockville MD 20850	301-634-4600	R	67*	.5
58	Torres Advanced Enterprise Solutions—*Jerry Torres*	2111 Wilson Blvd Ste 2, Arlington VA 22201	703-527-8088	R	66*	.4
59	LD Astorino Companies—*Louis D Astorino*	227 Fort Pitt Blvd, Pittsburgh PA 15222	412-765-1700	R	66*	.2
60	Pevarnik Brothers Inc—*James L Pevarnik*	1302 Memorial Dr, Latrobe PA 15650	724-539-3516	R	63*	.2
61	Primary Energy Recycling Corp—*John D Prunkl*	2215 S York Rd Ste 202, Oak Brook IL 60523	630-230-1313	B	61	N/A
62	RESPEC—*Thomas J Zeller*	3824 Jet Dr, Rapid City SD 57703	605-394-6400	P	60*	.1
63	Rosetta Marketing Group LLC—*Christopher Kuenne*	100 American Metro Blv, Hamilton NJ 08619	609-689-6100	R	59*	.1
64	Contract Environmental Services Inc—*Ed Massey*	636 Powdersville Rd, Easley SC 29642	864-306-7785	R	59*	1.2
65	Passport Health Communications Inc—*Scott MacKenzie*	720 Cool Springs Blvd, Franklin TN 37067	615-661-5657	R	58*	.3
66	NetOps Information Solutions—*William H Swanson*	4601 N Fairfax Dr Ste, Arlington VA 22203	703-284-8700	S	57*	.1
67	A-T Solutions Inc—*Dennis Kelly*	11905 Bowman Dr Ste 51, Fredericksburg VA 22408	540-373-9542	R	54	.3
68	WTech Inc—*Robert Sheldon*	1568 Spring Hill Rd St, McLean VA 22185	703-847-4748	R	53*	<.1
69	Xenergy Inc—*Rich Barnes*	67 S Bedford Ste 201 E, Burlington MA 01803	781-273-5700	S	52*	.3
70	Sysmind LLC—*Kavita Gorty*	38 Washington Rd, Princeton Junction NJ 08550	609-897-9670	R	52*	.1
71	Remington Group Inc—*William Connor*	351 E Conestoga Rd, Wayne PA 19087		R	51*	.1
72	Ibbotson Associates Inc—*Peng Chen*	22 W Washington St, Chicago IL 60602	312-696-6000	R	50*	.1
73	McKean Defense Group LLC—*Joseph L Carlini*	3 Crescent Dr Ste 410, Philadelphia PA 19112	215-271-6108	R	49	.3
74	Business Development Group (Wayzata Minnesota)—*Peter C Lytle*	PO Box 652, Wayzata MN 55391	952-473-3831	R	48*	.1
75	St Charles Consulting Group LLC—*Philip Davis*	1121 E Main St Ste 220, Saint Charles IL 60174		R	48*	.1
76	Ala Inc—*Bill Galvin*	101 Turtle Creek Blvd, Dallas TX 75207	214-658-9000	R	48*	<.1
77	Armando Montelongo Co—*Armando Montelongo*	2935 Thousand Oaks Ste, San Antonio TX 78247	210-501-0077	R	47	.1
78	Bill Me Later Inc—*Gary Marino*	9690 Deereco Rd 7th Fl, Timonium MD 21093	443-921-1900	S	46*	.1
79	Matrix Information Consulting Inc—*Sharon Olzerowicz*	365 W Passaic St, Rochelle Park NJ 07662	201-587-0777	R	46*	.1
80	Pursuant Group Inc—*Matt Frazier*	5151 Beltline Rd Ste 9, Dallas TX 75254	214-866-7700	R	45*	.1
81	Morgan Joseph and Co—*John A Morgan*	600 Fifth Ave 19th Fl, New York NY 10020	212-218-3700	R	44*	.1
82	Inteq Group Inc—*James Proctor*	4425 S Mopac Expy Ste, Austin TX 78735	512-899-9600	R	44*	<.1
83	Joint Commission Resources Inc—*Paula Wilson*	1515 W 22nd St Ste 130, Oak Brook IL 60523	630-268-7400	R	44*	.2
84	CLEAResult Consulting Inc—*Glenn Garland*	4301 Westbank Dr Bldg, Austin TX 78746	512-327-9200	R	44	.3
85	Synechron Inc—*Faisal Husain*	15 Corporate Pl S Ste4, Piscataway NJ 08854	732-562-0088	R	41*	.8
86	Paladin Consulting Inc—*Enoch Timothy*	PO Box 581, Colleyville TX 76034	972-783-1995	R	40*	.7
87	Celerity IT LLC—*Michael Berkman*	8401 Greensboro Dr Ste, McLean VA 22102	703-848-1900	R	40*	.3
88	Miller Heiman Inc—*Sam Reese*	10509 Professional Cir, Reno NV 89502	775-827-4411	S	40*	.1
89	Benchmark Consulting International—*Peter Jobst*	14 Piedmont Center NE, Atlanta GA 30305	404-442-4100	R	38*	.1
90	Rosen Group Inc—*Scott Rosen*	2301 Evesham Rd Ste 11, Magnolia NJ 08049	856-470-1400	R	38*	.1
91	BAI—*Deborah L Bianucci*	115 S LASALLE ST STE 3, Chicago IL 60603	312-683-2464	R	38*	.1
92	Claraview Inc—*Dan Ross*	11400 Commerce Park Dr, Reston VA 20191	703-269-1500	R	38*	.1
93	John M Floyd and Associates—*John M Floyd*	125 N Burnet Dr, Baytown TX 77520	281-424-3800	R	38*	.1
94	Disaster Management Inc—*Douglas M Henderson*	1531 SE Sunshine Ave, Port Saint Lucie FL 34952	772-337-2985	R	38*	<.1
95	Empyrean Services LLC—*Sushil C Jain*	1108 Ohio River Blvd S, Sewickley PA 15143	412-528-1573	R	37*	.2
96	Binary Group—*Rose Wang*	1911 Fort Myer Dr Ste, Arlington VA 22209	571-480-4444	R	37*	.1

Rank	Company Name—Executive Officer	Address, City, State, Zip	Phone	Type	Fin	Empls
97	Segal Co—Joseph LoCicero	333 W 34th St, New York NY 10001	212-251-5000	R	36*	.8
98	Invizion Inc—Steven Johnson	7900 Westpark Dr Ste A, McLean VA 22102	703-226-5000	R	36*	.4
99	DynamicLogic Inc—Jean Robinson	11 Madison Ave 12th Fl, New York NY 10022	212-844-3700	D	36*	.1
100	SGI—Jack Burns	8350 Allison Ave, Indianapolis IN 46268	317-471-8246	R	35*	.1
101	York Enterprise Solutions—Bill Carr	1 Westbrook Corporate, Westchester IL 60154		R	34*	.1
102	ValueOptions Inc—Heyward R Donigan	240 Corporate Blvd, Norfolk VA 23502	757-459-5100	S	33*	.1
103	Perkins and Company PC—Gary Reynolds	1211 SW 5th Ave Ste 10, Portland OR 97204	503-221-0336	R	32*	.1
104	Krazan and Associates—Dean Alexander	215 W Dakota Ave, Clovis CA 93612	559-348-2200	R	32*	.3
105	Petra Geotechnical Inc—Siamak Jafroudi	3185-A Airway Ave, Costa Mesa CA 92626	714-549-8921	R	31*	.1
106	Clayton Holdings Inc—Paul Bossidy	2 Corporate Dr Ste 800, Shelton CT 06484	203-926-5600	R	30*	.4
107	Technet Resources Inc—Lynn Knox	4080 McGinnis Ferry Rd, Alpharetta GA 30005	678-527-1440	R	30*	<.1
108	nFusion Group LLC—John Ellett	5000 Plz On The Lake S, Austin TX 78746	512-716-7500	R	29*	.1
109	Liquidhub Inc—Jonathan Brassington	500 E Swedesford Rd St, Wayne PA 19087	484-654-1400	R	29*	.5
110	DuCharme McMillen and Associates Inc—Dave Meinika	6610 Mutual Dr, Fort Wayne IN 46825		R	28*	.3
111	Marketing and Planning Systems—John White	850 Winter St, Waltham MA 02451	781-642-6277	S	28*	.1
112	Momentum Market Intelligence—Doss Struse	220 NW 2nd Ave Ste 600, Portland OR 97209	503-241-9199	R	28*	.1
113	Environmental Engineering and Consulting Services—Timothy Gipe	14505 Commerce Way Ste, Miami Lakes FL 33016	305-374-8300	R	28*	.1
114	DS3 Computing Solutions Inc—Davis Sylvester III	1108 Summit Ave Ste 5, Plano TX 75074	972-379-2600	R	28*	<.1
115	Principle Solutions Group—Josh Nazarian	990 Hammond Dr NE Ste, Atlanta GA 30328	770-399-4500	R	28	.3
116	Computer Consultants of America Inc—Nicole Meathe	24901 Northwestern Hwy, Southfield MI 48075	248-353-0830	R	27	.2
117	Ospey The SAP Division of NIIT Technologies—Arvind Thakur	1050 Crown Pointe Pkwy, Atlanta GA 30338	770-551-9494	D	27*	.1
118	Towers Perrin Reinsurance—William Eyre	1500 Market St, Philadelphia PA 19102	215-246-6000	R	26*	.2
119	SyApps LLC—Bala Sundar	13800 Coppermine Rd, Herndon VA 20171	703-234-7800	R	25	.2
120	Schnabel Engineering Associates Inc—Gordon Matheson	1054 Technology Park D, Glen Allen VA 23059	804-264-3222	R	25*	.3
121	Firmlogic LLC—Lori Shields	PO Box 21668, Winston Salem NC 27120	336-607-8200	R	24*	.2
122	Adayana—Charley Grady	3905 Vincennes Rd Ste, Indianapolis IN 46268	952-830-0600	R	24*	.3
123	Zephyr Environmental Corp—Joe Zupan	1515 S Capital of Texa, Austin TX 78746	512-329-5544	R	24*	.1
124	Acumen Solutions Inc—David Joubran	1660 International Dr, Mclean VA 22102	703-600-4000	R	24*	.3
125	ICS—Shehraze Shah	2650 Park Tower Dr Ste, Vienna VA 22180	703-342-4260	R	23*	.2
126	Multivision Inc (Fairfax Virginia)—Srikanth Ramachandran	10565 Fairfax Blvd Ste, Fairfax VA 22030	703-225-1000	R	22*	.3
127	CenTauri Solutions LLC—James Kelly	675 N Washington St St, Alexandria VA 22314	703-647-2753	S	22*	.1
128	SBG Technology Solutions Inc—Carlos Del Toro	2 Brittany Ln, Stafford VA 22554	703-299-9093	R	22	<.1
129	Premier Integrity Solutions Inc—Brian Walters	PO Box 2279, Russell Springs KY 42642	270-866-3144	R	21*	.5
130	The Intersect Group Inc—Wayde Hughes	10 Glenlake Pky Ste 30, Atlanta GA 30328	770-500-3636	R	21*	.2
131	Pariveda Solutions Inc—Bruce Ballengee	2811 McKinney Ave Ste, Dallas TX 75204	214-777-4600	R	21*	.1
132	TechLaw Inc—Patricia Brown-Derocher	14500 Avion Pkwy Ste 3, Chantilly VA 20151	703-818-1000	R	21	.1
133	Nims and Associates—Patrick L Nims	1445 Technology Ln, Petaluma CA 94954	415-382-6300	R	21*	<.1
134	Gradient Corp—Teresa Bowers	20 University Rd, Cambridge MA 02138	617-395-5000	R	20*	<.1
135	Venue Management Services Inc—Charles Mcintyre	500 N 1st Ave Ste 4, Arcadia CA 91006	626-445-6000	R	20*	.3
136	RBA Consulting—Rick Born	100 W Lake St, Wayzata MN 55391	952-404-2676	R	19	.1
137	Netlink (Madison Heights Michigan)—Dilip Dupey	999 Tech Row, Madison Heights MI 48071		R	19*	1.2
138	HT Harvey and Associates—Ron Duke	983 University Ave Bld, Los Gatos CA 95032	408-458-3200	R	19*	<.1
139	Plan Consulting Group LLC	800 Oliver Ave, Indianapolis IN 46225	317-713-1399	S	19*	<.1
140	Veteran Corps of America—William G Wheeler	220 E State St Suite 2, O'Fallon IL 62269	703-691-8387	R	19	<.1
141	Warner Power LLC—Scott Rogers	40 Depot St, Warner NH 03278	603-456-3111	R	19*	.2
142	Phase One Consulting Group	99 Canal Center Plz St, Alexandria VA 22314	703-888-4800	R	19	.1
143	Bower Enterprises Inc—John Bower Cpa-Cpc	210 Town Ctr Dr, Troy MI 48084	248-205-7200	R	18*	.6
144	ZHA Inc (Orlando Florida)—Richard W Zipperly	221 NE Ivanhoe Blvd 2n, Orlando FL 32804	407-422-7487	R	18*	.1
145	Advanced System Designs—David Johnson	100 Yordy Rd, Morton IL 61550	309-263-7944	R	18*	<.1
146	American Background Information Services Inc	629 Cedar Creek Grade, Winchester VA 22601	540-665-8056	S	18*	<.1
147	Loughlin Meghji and Co—James J Loughlin	220 W 42nd St 9th Fl, New York NY 10036	212-340-8420	R	18*	<.1
148	Pangea3 LLC—Sanjay Kamlani	530 5th Ave 7th Fl, New York NY 10036	212-689-3819	S	17*	.6
149	American Fuji Seal Inc—Takato Sonoda	1051 Bloomfield Rd, Bardstown KY 40004	502-348-9211	R	17*	.4
150	Sparrow Manufacturing Co—John Jones	4179 Vansant Rd, Douglasville GA 30135	770-489-4775	R	17*	<.1
151	Mediaspace Solutions—Scott Jagodzinski	101 Merritt 7 3rd Fl, Norwalk CT 06851	203-849-8855	R	17*	<.1
152	Summit Group—Ari Sternberg	48 Wall St Fl 4, New York NY 10005	212-328-2500	R	17*	<.1
153	Superior Environmental Corp—Vaughn Quince	1128 Franklin Ct, Marne MI 49435		R	17*	<.1
154	Deal LLC—Kevin Worth	20 Broad St Fl 6, New York NY 10005	212-313-9200	R	17*	.2
155	Tenderloin Neighborhood Development Corp—Chris Gouig	201 Eddy St, San Francisco CA 94102	415-776-2151	R	16*	.2
156	Oak Grove Technologies—Mark Gross	7200 Stonehenge Dr Ste, Raleigh NC 27613	919-845-1038	R	16*	.2
157	Master Key Consulting—Jonathan Wilbur	4915 St Elmo Ave Ste 1, Bethesda MD 20814	301-907-8789	R	16*	.1
158	LogiSolve LLC—Jim McCleary	12866 Hwy 55, Minneapolis MN 55441	763-383-1000	R	16*	.1
159	ReSource Pro LLC—Dan Epstein	1180 Avenue of the Ame, New York NY 10036		R	16	.8
160	Technical Education Research Centers Inc—Arthur Nelson	2067 Mass Ave Ste 26, Cambridge MA 02140	617-547-0430	R	15*	.1
161	Improving Enterprises—Curtis Hite	16633 Dallas Pky Ste 1, Addison TX 75001	214-613-4444	R	15	.1
162	CareNet (San Antonio Texas)—John Erwin	11845 IH 10 W Ste 400, San Antonio TX 78230		R	15*	.2
163	CyberStaff America Ltd—Barbara Blair	1 Gateway Ctr Ste 2600, Newark NJ 07102	212-244-2300	R	15*	.1
164	AspireHR Inc—Joseph Hillesheim	2701 N Dallas Pkwy Ste, Plano TX 75093	214-880-0099	R	15*	.1
165	Strategic Equity Group Inc—Michael T Ellington	9841 Airport Blvd Ste, Los Angeles CA 90045	310-568-9380	R	15*	<.1
166	DAL Inc—Dominick A Longhi	PO Box 162, Clifton Heights PA 19018	610-623-1400	R	15*	<.1
167	Financial Design Group Inc—Andrew Rohrer	8010 Excelsior Dr Ste, Madison WI 53717	608-828-9800	R	15*	<.1
168	Hallmark Data Systems LLC—Jim Kuchinsky	7300 Linder Ave, Skokie IL 60077	847-983-2000	R	15*	.2
169	Ventera Corp—Robert Acosta	1881 Campus Commons Dr, Reston VA 20191	703-760-4600	R	14*	.1
170	AK Environmental LLC—Amy Gonzales	850 Bear Tavern Rd Ste, West Trenton NJ 08628	609-771-1730	R	14	.1
171	Kemron Environmental Services Inc—Juan Gutierrez	8521 Leesburg Pike Ste, Vienna VA 22182	703-893-4106	R	14*	.1
172	The C and L Group LLC—Dan Liebman	380 Lexington Ave Ste, New York NY 10168	646-257-5559	R	14*	.1
173	Enspiria Solutions Inc—Charles (Chip) Scott	5613 DTC Pky Ste 700, Greenwood Village CO 80111	303-741-8400	S	14*	.1
174	Lexicon Consulting Inc—Jamie Arundell-Latshaw	124 W Main St Ste 270, El Cajon CA 92020	619-792-1530	R	14	.1
175	Mindwave Research Inc	4412 Spicewood Springs, Austin TX 78759	512-469-7998	R	14*	<.1
176	BroadSource Inc—Michael Lustig	5901C Peachtree Dunwoo, Atlanta GA 30328	678-507-1220	R	14*	<.1
177	Qps LLC—Livia Gorini	3 Innovation Way, Newark DE 19711	302-369-5601	R	14*	.2
178	Incentive Technology Group Inc—Michelle Samad	1568 Spring Hill Rd St, McLean VA 22102	703-847-0125	R	14	.1
179	Life Win Inc—Peter Lowe	4710 Eisenhower Blvd B, Tampa FL 33634	813-884-7200	R	14*	.2
180	Southern California Association Of Governments—Hasan Ikhrata	818 W 7th St Ste 1200, Los Angeles CA 90017	213-236-1800	R	14*	.1
181	Interim Solutions for Government LLC—Gerald Williams	2224 NW 50th St Ste 29, Oklahoma City OK 73112	405-286-0915	R	13	<.1
182	Pyxis Solutions LLC—Shaffiu Sharma	55 Broad St Rm 28b, New York NY 10004	212-363-2828	R	13*	.2
183	Raba-Kistner Consultants Inc—Carl F Raba Jr	12821 W Golden Ln, San Antonio TX 78249	210-699-9090	R	13*	.4
184	Delan Associates Inc—Michael Chung	30 S Ocean Ave Ste 104, Freeport NY 11520	516-442-0040	R	13*	.2

Note: An asterisk (*) indicates an estimated financial figure. The company type code used is as follows: R = Private, P = Public, S = Private Subsidiary, B = Public Subsidiary, D = Division, J = Joint Venture, I = Investment Fund.

COMPANY RANKINGS BY SALES WITHIN 4-DIGIT SIC

Rank	Company Name—Executive Officer	Address, City, State, Zip	Phone	Type	Fin	Empls
185	Ross and Associates Environmental Consulting Ltd—Bill Ross	1218 3rd Ave Ste 1207, Seattle WA 98101	206-447-1805	R	13*	<.1
186	AFMS LLC—Mike Erickson	10260 SW Greenburg Rd, Portland OR 97223	503-246-3521	R	13*	<.1
187	HCItasca—Kathy Sikora	111 3rd Ave S Ste 450, Minneapolis MN 55401	612-371-4711	R	13*	<.1
188	Logistic Dynamics Inc—Dennis Brown	1140 Wehrle Dr, Buffalo NY 14221	716-250-3477	R	13	<.1
189	Solar Testing Laboratories Inc—George Ata	1125 Valley Belt Rd, Brooklyn Heights OH 44131	216-741-7007	R	12*	.1
190	Tpg Companies Inc—Elizabeth Procaccianti	1140 Reservoir Ave, Cranston RI 02920	401-946-4600	R	12*	.1
191	Infovision Technologies Inc—Krishna Lakamsani	2550 US Hwy 1, North Brunswick NJ 08902	732-398-1000	R	12*	.2
192	Normandeau Associates Inc—Pamela S Hall	25 Nashua Rd, Bedford NH 03110	603-472-5191	R	12*	.1
193	Knight Point Systems—Robert Eisiminger	1775 Wiehle Ave Ste 10, Reston VA 20190	703-657-7050	R	12*	.1
194	PriceSpective LLC—Steve Slovick	460 Norristown Rd Ste, Blue Bell PA 19422	310-869-1440	R	12*	.1
195	Sextant Search Partners LLC—Steven B Potter	521 Fifth Ave 43rd St, New York NY 10175	212-366-8600	R	12*	<.1
196	eTERA Consulting LLC—Scott Holec	1100 17th St NW Ste 60, Washington DC 20036	202-349-0177	R	12	<.1
197	Woodbridge Group LLC—Robert M Koenig	264 Amity Rd Ste 106, New Haven CT 06525	203-389-8400	R	12*	<.1
198	Rennhack Marketing Services Inc—James Gresham	752 Port America Pl St, Grapevine TX 76051	817-481-6516	R	12*	<.1
199	Vantage Technology Consulting Group—Richard Bussell	201 Continental Blvd S, El Segundo CA 90245	310-536-7676	R	12*	<.1
200	TM Technology Partners Inc—Tom Morley	250 W 39th St, New York NY 10018	212-398-2424	R	12*	<.1
201	Isi Telemanagement Solutions Inc—Richard Wilkus	1051 Perimeter Dr Ste, Schaumburg IL 60173	847-995-0002	R	12*	.1
202	East Central Planning and Development Inc—J Thrash	PO Box 499, Newton MS 39345	601-683-2007	R	12*	.1
203	Commdex Consulting LLC—Prince Niyyar	655 Engineering Dr Ste, Norcross GA 30092	770-349-0400	R	12*	.1
204	FranNet—Steven A Rosen	10302 Brookridge Villa, Louisville KY 40291	502-753-2380	R	12	<.1
205	Business Strategy Inc—Charles Fayon	944 52nd St Se, Grand Rapids MI 49508	616-261-2200	R	11*	.1
206	20/20 Financial Consulting Inc—Brian Biffle	11800 Ridge Pkwy Ste 4, Broomfield CO 80021	303-938-9981	R	11*	.1
207	Strategic Systems Inc—Jyothsna Vadada	485 Metro Pl S Ste 270, Dublin OH 43017	614-717-4774	R	11	.1
208	MaxisIT Inc—Maulik Shah	203 Main St, Metuchen NJ 08840	732-494-2005	R	11*	.1
209	GS5 LLC—Bobby Blackwell	17323 Jefferson Davis, Dumfries VA 22026	703-221-2555	R	11	.1
210	Billtrust—Flint A Lane	1095 Cranbury South Ri, Jamesburg NJ 08831	609-235-1010	R	11*	.1
211	Douglas Consulting and Computer Services Inc—James M Douglas Jr	3108 Lord Baltimore Dr, Baltimore MD 21244	410-298-3812	R	11*	<.1
212	Sanford Cohen and Associates—Sanford Cohen	1608 Spring Hill Rd St, Vienna VA 22182	703-893-6600	R	11*	<.1
213	Decision Strategies Inc—Chris Reinsvold	10260 Westheimer Ste 2, Houston TX 77042	713-465-1110	R	11*	<.1
214	SciMetrika—Jean Orelien	100 Capitola Dr Ste 10, Durham NC 27713	919-354-5200	R	11	.1
215	Alabama-Tombigbee Regional Commission—John Riggs	107 Broad St, Camden AL 36726	334-682-4234	R	11*	.2
216	Royal Eagle Services LLC—Henry Daigle	PO Box 3364, Morgan City LA 70381	985-329-2559	R	11*	.2
217	Carchex—Jason Goldsmith	10950 Gilroy Rd Ste D, Hunt Valley MD 21031	410-527-9280	R	11	.1
218	Fairfield Service Group Inc—Virginia Price	PO Box 31468, Knoxville TN 37930	865-531-3654	R	11*	<.1
219	Texas Test Fleet Inc—Michael Kloppe	PO Box J, Devine TX 78016	830-665-5555	R	10*	.1
220	Forensic Analytical Specialities Inc—David Kahane	3777 Depot Rd Ste 409, Hayward CA 94545	510-887-8828	R	10*	.1
221	Hart Crowser Inc—Michael Bailey	1700 Welake Ave N Ste, Seattle WA 98109	206-324-9530	R	10*	.1
222	So Do It LLC—Lisa Wehr	13561 S W Bay Shore Dr, Traverse City MI 49684	231-922-9977	R	10*	<.1
223	Sarofim Realty Advisors—C A Galpern	8115 Preston Rd Ste 40, Dallas TX 75225	214-692-4200	S	10*	<.1
224	Bankers Training and Certification Center—Deborah Bianucci BAI	12250 Weber Hill Rd St, Saint Louis MO 63127	314-843-5656	S	10*	<.1
225	Wolf Technical Services Inc—Mike Pepe	9855 Crosspoint Blvd S, Indianapolis IN 46256	317-842-6075	R	10*	<.1
226	Convergence Technology Consulting—Larry Letow	808 Landmark Dr Ste 21, Glen Burnie MD 21061	301-860-1960	R	10*	<.1
227	EDC Consulting LLC—Uli Werner	1104 Good Hope Rd SE, Washington DC 20020	703-637-0068	R	10	.1
228	Lenric Corp—Leonard Eisen	44 Simon St, Nashua NH 03060	603-886-6772	R	9*	.1
229	Insignia Technology Services LLC—David La Clair	610 Thimble Shoals Blv, Newport News VA 23606	757-591-2111	R	9*	.1
230	Orbis Clinical—Roland Norton	100 Unicorn Park Dr 2n, Woburn MA 01801	781-569-0607	R	9*	.1
231	Danter Company Inc—Ken Danter	2760 Airport Dr Ste 13, Columbus OH 43219	614-221-9096	R	9*	<.1
232	Biddle Consulting Group Inc—Daniel H Biddle	193 Blue Ravine Rd Ste, Folsom CA 95630	916-294-4250	R	9*	<.1
233	Wyvern Consulting Ltd—Jim Betlyon	PO Box 7299, Trenton NJ 08628	609-671-9300	R	9*	<.1
234	Isis Corp—Andrew Lohr	169 Ramapo Valley Rd S, Oakland NJ 07436	201-337-8115	R	9*	.1
235	KameddataCom Inc—Niels Andersen	4400 Bayou Blvd Ste 12, Pensacola FL 32503	850-477-2475	R	9*	.2
236	Industrial Economics Inc—Gail Coad	2067 Mass Ave Ste 4, Cambridge MA 02140	617-354-0074	R	9*	.1
237	Pizza Brothers East Ii Inc—Mark Eden	2813 University Blvd W, Kensington MD 20895	301-942-8896	R	9*	.1
238	Conference America Inc—Robert Pirnie	PO Box 241188, Montgomery AL 36124	334-260-9999	R	8*	.1
239	Vesta-Camden Urban Renewal LLC	245 Hopmeadow St, Weatogue CT 06089	860-408-5400	R	8*	.1
240	Innovative Foods Inc—Chris Collias	330 Ballardvale St, Wilmington MA 01887	781-596-0070	R	8*	.2
241	Spinnaker Management Group LLC—Robert Benson	231 Milwaukee St Ste 2, Denver CO 80206	720-457-5500	R	8*	.1
242	Ceteris Inc—Marlene Shaffer	604 N Milwaukee Ste 20, Libertyville IL 60048	847-247-9220	R	8*	.1
243	Summit Tech Consulting—Sally Gozder	772 Charles Allen Dr, Atlanta GA 30308	404-441-4050	R	8*	<.1
244	MBS Dev Inc—Laura Guillaume	9800 Mt Pyramid Ct Ste, Englewood CO 80112	303-469-2346	R	8*	<.1
245	Insight Resource Group Inc—Scott Mollahan	3 Altarinda Rd Ste 301, Orinda CA 94563	925-254-4114	R	8*	<.1
246	Integrated Environmental Solutions Inc—Mike Gurr	47 Fifth St NW, Winter Haven FL 33881	863-292-0600	R	8*	<.1
247	Wikler and Company Inc—Janet Wikler	128 Central Park S, New York NY 10019	212-333-2603	R	8*	<.1
248	Miro Consulting Inc—Scott D Rosenberg	167 Main St, Woodbridge NJ 07095	732-738-8511	R	8*	<.1
249	San Joaquin Valley A PC D—David Crow	1990 E Gettysburg Ave, Fresno CA 93726	559-230-6000	R	8*	.1
250	West Central Indiana Economic Development District Inc—Mervin Nolot	1718 Wabash Ave, Terre Haute IN 47807	812-238-1561	R	8*	.1
251	JeffreyM Consulting Inc—Jeffrey McCannon	10900 NE 4th St Ste 23, Bellevue WA 98004	425-885-3071	R	8	.1
252	Diamond Mind Business Services—Katherine Novikov	10220 River Rd Ste 306, Potomac MD 20854	240-898-1817	R	8	<.1
253	GlowTouch Technologies—V Ravichandran	4360 Brownsboro Rd Ste, Louisville KY 40207	502-410-1732	R	8	.8
254	Soft Tech Consulting Inc—Christine Do	4229 Lafayette Center, Chantilly VA 20151	703-348-1673	R	8	.1
255	Westest Engineering Corp—Robert Lessmann	810 Shepard Ln, Farmington UT 84025	801-451-9191	R	7*	<.1
256	Vinculums—Bart van Aardenne	350 Fischer Ave, Costa Mesa CA 92626	714-277-3959	R	7*	.1
257	Training and Development Systems Inc—Barry Hardy	16902 El Camino Real, Houston TX 77058	281-488-1128	R	7*	.1
258	Logical Innovations Inc—Chris Peters	2550 Centennial Blvd, Jeffersonville IN 47130	502-379-4100	R	7*	<.1
259	Material In Motion Inc—Ted Salah	1110 La Avenida, Mountain View CA 94043	650-967-3300	R	7*	<.1
260	Abelson Group Inc—Jennifer Abelson	200 Broadhollow Rd Ste, Melville NY 11747	917-445-4454	R	7*	<.1
261	Identification Technology Partners Inc—Paul Collier	12 S Summit Ave, Gaithersburg MD 20877	301-990-9061	R	7*	<.1
262	Gsm Systems Of New York Inc—Frederick Knox	349 Broadway, New York NY 10013	212-431-4763	R	7*	<.1
263	Winstin Ventures LLC—Tommy Winston	20562 Rawhide Flats Rd, Wellington CO 80549	970-494-0400	R	7*	<.1
264	Jpm Global Services Inc—John Maass	130 W Main St Ste 144, Trappe PA 19426	610-999-3180	R	7*	.1
265	Turning Basin Service Inc—Ed Hearon	PO Box 24398, Houston TX 77229	713-674-0567	R	7*	.1
266	Avian Engineering LLC—Jeff Sherman	22111 Three Notch Rd, Lexington Park MD 20653	301-866-2070	R	7	.1
267	Success Projects Inc—Toufic Simaan	8039 Rural Retreat Ct, Orlando FL 32819	407-354-3399	R	7*	.1
268	Andromeda Systems Inc—John H Kobelski	641 Lynnhaven Pky Ste, Virginia Beach VA 23452	757-340-9070	R	7	.1
269	Optimal Strategix Group Inc—R Sukumar	140 Terry Dr Ste 118, Newtown PA 18940	215-867-1880	R	7	<.1
270	Morton Consulting—Mark Morton	4701 Cox Rd Ste 135, Glen Allen VA 23060	804-290-4272	R	6	.1
271	Als International Inc—Victor Hertz	18 John St Ste 300, New York NY 10038	212-766-0247	R	6*	.1

Rank	Company Name—*Executive Officer*	Address, City, State, Zip	Phone	Type	Fin	Empls
272	The Retail Outsource Inc—*Brett Beveridge*	75 Valencia Ave Ste 80, Coral Gables FL 33134	305-539-3810	R	6*	.2
273	Root Learning Inc—*James Haudan*	5470 Main St Ste 100, Sylvania OH 43560	419-874-0077	R	6*	.1
274	Abso Inc—*David Dickson*	3009 Douglas Blvd, Roseville CA 95661		S	6*	.1
275	Harris Miller Miller and Hanson Inc—*Mary Ellen Eagan*	77 S Bedford St, Burlington MA 01803	781-229-0707	R	6*	.1
276	IZ Technologies Inc—*Donna Dacier*	44081 Pipeline Plz Ste, Ashburn VA 20147	703-724-7500	R	6*	<.1
277	Bryant Christie Inc—*James Christie*	500 Union St Ste 701, Seattle WA 98101	206-292-6340	R	6*	<.1
278	Universal Business Solutions Inc—*Abraham Thomas*	90 John St 5th Fl, New York NY 10038	212-643-4808	R	6*	<.1
279	Lexicon Branding Inc—*David Placek*	30 Liberty Ship Way St, Sausalito CA 94965	415-332-1811	R	6*	<.1
280	Ecocion Inc—*Gregory George*	7951 E Maplewood Ave S, Greenwood Village CO 80111	720-305-0050	R	6*	<.1
281	Asia Pacific Ventures—*Will Stewart*	3000 Sand Hill Rd Bldg, Menlo Park CA 94025	650-641-2838	R	6*	<.1
282	Black Mountain Group—*Mark Matuscak*	125 South Wacker, Chicago IL 60606	312-606-4800	R	6*	<.1
283	DRM Labs Inc—*Jeff Mankoff*	5950 Berkshire Ste 550, Dallas TX 75225	214-891-1800	R	6*	<.1
284	Kraft Group LLC—*Charles Kraft*	2425 Fountainview Ste, Houston TX 77057	713-627-3133	R	6*	<.1
285	LemmonTree Enterprises Inc—*Nicolette Lemmon*	3010 S Priest Dr Ste 1, Tempe AZ 85282	480-967-1405	R	6*	<.1
286	Downtown Partnership of Baltimore Inc—*J Fowler*	217 N Charles St Ste 1, Baltimore MD 21201	410-244-1030	R	6*	.1
287	Actionlink LLC—*Dianne Sink*	4100 Embassy Pkwy, Akron OH 44333	330-665-1660	R	6*	.1
288	Talented IT Inc—*Timothy Bennett*	800 W 5th Ave Ste 208A, Naperville IL 60563	630-364-4112	R	6	<.1
289	Wrb Communications Inc—*Sylvia Williams*	4200 Lafayette Ctr Dr, Chantilly VA 20151	703-449-0520	R	6*	.1
290	Warning Lites Incorporated Of Colorado—*Barbara Barron*	2200 W Bates Ave, Englewood CO 80110	303-936-2990	R	5*	.1
291	Cable Systems of North Haven Inc—*Anthony Buono*	500 Washington Ave Ste, North Haven CT 06473	203-234-1250	R	5*	<.1
292	Seifert and Group Inc—*Tim Seifert*	2323 Nave Rd Se, Massillon OH 44646	330-833-2700	R	5*	.1
293	Speridian Technologies LLC—*Girish Panicker*	2021 Girard Blvd SE St, Albuquerque NM 87106	505-217-3725	R	5*	.1
294	MasterPlans—*Bryan Howe*	1311 NW Lovejoy St Ste, Portland OR 97209		R	5*	<.1
295	International Executive Service Corp—*Spencer King*	1900 M St NW Ste 500, Washington DC 20036	202-589-2600	R	5*	<.1
296	Avankia LLC—*Reena Gupta*	750 Old Hickory Blvd B, Brentwood TN 37027	615-371-6191	R	5*	<.1
297	ScienceLogic LLC—*David F Link*	10700 Parkridge Blvd S, Reston VA 20191	703-354-1010	R	5*	<.1
298	Integrated Secure LLC—*Anne McMillan*	9595 Six Pines Dr Ste, The Woodlands TX 77380	281-465-9414	R	5*	<.1
299	Solutience Inc—*Julia Fowler*	640 S Main St Ste 200, Greenville SC 29601	864-242-6302	R	5*	<.1
300	Veterans Enterprise Technology Solutions Inc—*Jim Case*	2057 Woodford Rd Ste 2, Vienna VA 22182	703-801-8171	R	5*	<.1
301	Du-All Safety—*Terry McCarthy*	45950 Hotchkiss St, Fremont CA 94539	510-651-8289	R	5*	<.1
302	Runway Inc	10575 Virginia Ave, Culver City CA 90232	310-636-2000	S	5*	<.1
303	Apro Technology LLC—*Lisa Harris*	PO Box 820237, Vicksburg MS 39182	601-638-0545	R	5*	<.1
304	AbleCommerce—*Mike Randolph*	PO Box 873249, Vancouver WA 98687	360-571-5839	R	5*	<.1
305	EAS Engineering Inc—*Edward A Swakon*	55 Almoria Ave, Coral Gables FL 33134	305-445-5553	R	5*	<.1
306	InTech Group Inc—*Ernest E Holling*	305 Exton Commons, Exton PA 19341	610-524-8400	R	5*	<.1
307	McCulley Cuppan LLC—*Robert A Whitman*	970 Murray Holladay Rd, Salt Lake City UT 84117	801-685-7717	R	5*	<.1
308	Semico Research Corp—*Jim Feldhan*	PO Box 9850, Phoenix AZ 85068	602-997-0337	R	5*	<.1
309	Synergy Investment Inc—*Daniel Gould*	200 Friberg Pkwy Ste 4, Westborough MA 01581	508-366-0200	R	5*	<.1
310	Tefen USA Ltd—*Aaron Lichtenstein*	3 Park Ave 20th Fl, New York NY 10016		R	5*	<.1
311	Winkenwerder Company LLC—*Bill Winkenwerder*	330 John Carlyle St St, Alexandria VA 22314	703-836-1035	R	5*	<.1
312	Vinakom Inc—*Komal Patel*	860 Remington Rd, Schaumburg IL 60173		R	5*	.1
313	Animation Technologies Inc—*Lawrence Collins*	69 Canal St Ste 3, Boston MA 02114	617-723-6040	R	5*	<.1
314	California Traffic Safety Institute—*Wanda Paulson*	209 E Ave K8 Ste 210, Lancaster CA 93535	661-940-1907	R	5*	.2
315	Image Technologies Corp—*Thomas Kuntz*	523 Hanley Industrial, Saint Louis MO 63144	314-646-1800	R	5*	.1
316	Best Practice Systems Inc—*Clint Waite*	PO Box 3335, Parker CO 80134		R	5	<.1
317	Access Data Supply Inc—*Andrea Logans*	PO Box 56002, Houston TX 77256	713-439-0370	R	5*	<.1
318	Advanced Systems Group A Corp—*Bruce Greene*	1124 Broadway, Tacoma WA 98402	253-779-8030	R	5*	.1
319	Aqiwo Inc—*Stephen Mills*	1225 S Clark St Ste 13, Arlington VA 22202	703-416-8590	R	4*	<.1
320	Tahoe Partners LLC—*Billy Heintz*	770 N Halsted St Ste 5, Chicago IL 60642	312-491-3000	R	4*	.1
321	MMC Systems Inc—*Meena Roopdaska*	13800 Coppermine Rd 3r, Herndon VA 20171		R	4*	.1
322	Maxil Technology Solutions Inc—*Kalyan Reddy*	2625 Butterfield Rd St, Oak Brook IL 60523	630-472-7335	R	4*	.1
323	Mystikal Solutions LLC—*Ricky D White*	431 Wolfe Rd Ste 102, San Antonio TX 78216	210-979-9300	R	4*	.1
324	Keen Infotek Inc—*Suresh Alokam*	710 E Ogden Ave Ste 10, Naperville IL 60563		R	4*	.1
325	Deemsys Inc—*Tom Blue*	800 Cross Pointe Rd St, Gahanna OH 43230	614-322-9928	R	4*	<.1
326	A Harold and Associates LLC—*Andrew E Harold Jr*	11200 St Johns Industr, Jacksonville FL 32246	904-265-1940	R	4*	<.1
327	LuxSpan International Inc—*Maxine Wang*	900 E Hamilton Ave Ste, Campbell CA 95008	408-850-0116	R	4*	<.1
328	eSolution Architects Inc—*Bill Woodhouse*	3325 Kessinger Dr, Montgomery AL 36116	334-324-1262	R	4	<.1
329	Xcel Communications Intl—*Raymond Cox*	1853 S Acoma St, Denver CO 80223	303-766-1218	R	4*	<.1
330	Abovo Group Inc—*Karen See*	5 Concourse Pkwy Ste 1, Atlanta GA 30328	678-597-3000	R	4*	<.1
331	Insurance Resources Group Cos—*Richard Shoemaker*	PO Box 2527, Orangevale CA 95662	916-721-5511	R	4*	<.1
332	Kathy Casey Food Studios Inc—*Kathy Casey*	5130 Ballard Ave NW, Seattle WA 98107	206-784-7840	R	4*	<.1
333	Kalba International Inc—*Kas Kalba*	116 McKinley Ave, New Haven CT 06515	203-397-2199	R	4*	<.1
334	Genusys Group Inc—*Richard Elroy*	67 Beaver Ave Ste 27, Annandale NJ 08801	908-735-2188	R	4*	<.1
335	Workforce Solutions Group Inc—*Pamela K Jung*	22431 Antonio Pkwy Ste, Rancho Santa Margarita CA 92688	949-588-5812	R	4	<.1
336	Performance Support Inc—*Debra Watkins*	5775 Carmichael Pkwy, Montgomery AL 36117	334-244-9797	R	4*	.1
337	Teletec Corp—*Harry Taji*	5617 Departure Dr Ste, Raleigh NC 27616	919-954-7300	R	4*	<.1
338	Mcl Industries Inc—*Sharon Petty*	PO Box 170, Syracuse NY 13209	315-422-5010	R	4*	<.1
339	Biosonics Inc—*Tim Acker*	4027 Leary Way Nw, Seattle WA 98107	206-782-2211	R	4*	<.1
340	NPE LLC—*Sean Greeley*	3208 E Colonial Dr Ste, Orlando FL 32803		R	4*	<.1
341	Monterey Consultants Inc—*Gary Munoz*	5335 Far Hills Ave Ste, Dayton OH 45429	937-436-4536	R	3*	<.1
342	Research Associates Inc (New York New York)—*Sung Lee*	12 Desbrosses St, New York NY 10013	212-868-5100	R	3	<.1
343	Marathon Consulting—*Al Moore*	505 S Independence Blv, Virginia Beach VA 23452	757-427-6999	R	3	<.1
344	N-Tech Solutions Inc—*Haritha Pendli*	6170 Hunt Club Rd, Elkridge MD 21075		R	3	<.1
345	BCCUSA—*Ramesh Rahau*	1506 Bostn Provdnc Tpk, Norwood MA 02062	781-551-9759	R	3*	<.1
346	PCN Strategies—*Mike Rosinbum*	1115 Massachusetts Ave, Washington DC 20005	202-962-3980	R	3*	.1
347	SalesQuest LLC—*Mimi Evans*	16 Haverhill St, Andover MA 01810	978-749-9999	R	3*	<.1
348	Rimm Kaufman Group LLC—*George Michie*	PO Box 8025, Charlottesville VA 22906	434-978-4300	R	3*	<.1
349	Aqua Perfect Of Arizona LLC—*Stephen Kindt*	455 W 21st St Ste 108, Tempe AZ 85282	480-596-2100	R	3*	<.1
350	Spatial Integrated Systems Inc—*Ali Farsaie*	2815 Rouse Rd Ext, Kinston NC 28504	252-522-1456	R	3*	<.1
351	IC Interactive Inc—*Bernie Schneider*	12325 Oracle Blvd Ste, Colorado Springs CO 80921	719-593-7377	R	3*	<.1
352	Fleetweather Inc—*Tore Jakobsen*	2566 State Rte 52, Hopewell Junction NY 12533	845-226-8300	R	3*	<.1
353	Facility Engineering Associates PC—*James P Whittaker*	1270 Fair Lakes Cir St, Fairfax VA 22033	703-591-4855	R	3*	<.1
354	TGaS Advisors—*Stephen Gerard*	301 E Germantown Pke, Norristown PA 19401	610-233-1210	R	3	<.1
355	Technovant Inc—*Sridhar Gummadi*	11875 Dublin Blvd Ste, Dublin CA 94568	925-803-1117	R	3*	<.1
356	DynaLabs LLC—*Scott Glover*	3830 Washington Blvd S, Saint Louis MO 63108	314-533-1660	R	3*	<.1
357	DMC Consultants Inc—*Darshita Chaudhary*	13500 Foley St, Detroit MI 48227	313-491-1815	R	3*	<.1
358	ForeclosuresDailycom—*Mike Kane*	12600 Belcher Rd Ste 1, Largo FL 33773	727-683-1145	R	3*	<.1
359	Tres Design Group Inc—*Stephen Melamed*	435 N Lasalle St Ste 2, Chicago IL 60610	312-670-6880	R	3*	<.1
360	CBIZ Actuarial and Benefit Consultants Inc—*Neil Malhotra*	8181 E Tufts Ave Ste 6, Denver CO 80237	303-790-0825	D	3*	<.1
361	Kore Federal Inc—*Andrea Stygar*	7600 Leesburg Pke Ste, Falls Church VA 22043		R	3*	<.1

Note: An asterisk (*) indicates an estimated financial figure. The company type code used is as follows: R = Private, P = Public, S = Private Subsidiary, B = Public Subsidiary, D = Division, J = Joint Venture, I = Investment Fund.

COMPANY RANKINGS BY SALES WITHIN 4-DIGIT SIC

Rank	Company Name—Executive Officer	Address, City, State, Zip	Phone	Type	Fin	Empls
362	Onstott Group—Joe Onstott	55 William St Ste G40, Wellesley MA 02481	781-235-3050	R	3*	<.1
363	RJS and Associates—Bob Simmons	25151 Clawiter Rd, Hayward CA 94545	510-670-9111	R	3*	<.1
364	Wood Group Inc—Michael D Wood	601 Carlson Pkwy Ste 1, Minnetonka MN 55305	952-546-6997	R	3*	<.1
365	J Scott International Inc—Joy Scott	3 Neshaminy Interplex, Trevose PA 19053	215-245-2958	R	3*	<.1
366	MI-Comply—Dawn Hreben	PO Box 426, South Lyon MI 48178		R	3*	<.1
367	Stein Trending Branding Design LLC—Sanford B Stein	801 Washington Ave N S, Minneapolis MN 55401	612-338-3339	R	3*	<.1
368	101 Financial Group LLC—Alan Akina	PO Box 101, Kahuku HI 96731		R	3*	<.1
369	H2 Performance Consulting Inc—Hazel Wiggington	222 W Main St, Pensacola FL 32502	850-474-0844	R	3	<.1
370	Broadband Communication Services Inc—Joseph D'Agostino	11 Broadway Ste 404, New York NY 10004	212-514-9266	R	3*	<.1
371	Alpha Technology Group Inc—Samuel Klatt	4658 Leonardtown Rd, Waldorf MD 20601	301-632-5581	R	3*	<.1
372	Baseline People LLC—Michael Crisafi	15030 Ventura Blvd Ste, Sherman Oaks CA 91403	818-906-7638	R	3*	<.1
373	Ameritel—Scott Murphy	8910 Quartz Ave, Northridge CA 91324	818-734-7400	R	3*	<.1
374	Main Resource Inc—Suzan Elichaa	PO Box 6849, Portland ME 04103	207-797-8410	R	3*	<.1
375	Mid-Hudson Communications Inc—James Reynolds	3 Ecomm Sq Ste 1, Albany NY 12207	518-694-8700	R	2*	<.1
376	D C M Corp—Joyce Nohowel	8120 Woodmont Ave Ste, Bethesda MD 20814	301-367-0754	R	2*	<.1
377	MedValue Offshore Solutions Inc—Raj Vaswani	1415 West 22nd St Towe, Oak Brook IL 60523	630-299-7370	R	2	.2
378	Gunning and Associates Marketing Inc—Patrick Gunning	1001 Ford Cir, Milford OH 45150	513-688-1370	R	2*	<.1
379	Edward W Face Company Inc—Catherine Waldrop	PO Box 6300, Norfolk VA 23508	757-624-2121	R	2*	<.1
380	MCG LLC—Clark Guo	68 Dorrance St Ste 324, Providence RI 02903	401-331-6360	R	2	<.1
381	RM Electric Inc—Carol Mccrackin	16037 Grove Rd, Lansing MI 48906	517-323-7580	R	2*	<.1
382	Cygnet Controls Inc—Robert Hunter	8123 S Lemont Rd, Darien IL 60561	630-985-2400	R	2*	<.1
383	MediGain Inc—Hunter Howard	3523 McKinney Ave Ste, Dallas TX 75204	214-682-0168	R	2*	.3
384	International Banking Technologies LLC—Mylle Mangum	1770 Indian Trail Rd S, Norcross GA 30093	770-381-2023	S	2*	.1
385	Information Ventures Inc—Bruce H Kleinstein	42 S 15th St Ste 700, Philadelphia PA 19102	215-569-2300	R	2*	<.1
386	Ageatia Technology Consultancy Services Inc—Chandra Srinivasan	850 E Higgins Rd Ste 1, Schaumburg IL 60173	847-517-8415	R	2*	<.1
387	FTrans Corp—Daniel Drechsel	75 Fifth St NW Ste 440, Atlanta GA 30308	678-268-4000	R	2*	<.1
388	Mobius Communications Co—Tonya Mayer	PO Box 246, Hemingford NE 69348	308-487-5500	R	2*	<.1
389	Segnet Technologies Inc—Steve Goldsmith	PO Box 610, Lebanon NH 03766	603-643-5883	R	2*	<.1
390	Safeguard Protection Systems Inc—Mike Jackson	6191 Atlantic Blvd Ste, Norcross GA 30071	770-368-0123	R	2*	<.1
391	Baber Graphic Systems Inc—Michael Baber	3135 Millbranch Rd, Memphis TN 38116	901-332-6300	R	2*	<.1
392	CLC Construction Group Inc—Dan Payne	5940 E Shields Ave Ste, Fresno CA 93727	559-277-8555	R	2*	<.1
393	IData Inc—Brian Parish	1908 Mt Vernon Ave 2nd, Alexandria VA 22301	703-378-2110	R	2*	<.1
394	Computer Security Products Inc—Scott Anderson	PO Box 7549, Nashua NH 03060	603-889-9899	R	2*	<.1
395	Avmark Inc—Barbars Lynn Beyer	415 Church St NE Ste 2, Vienna VA 22180	240-582-0119	R	2*	<.1
396	Maxcam Corp—Robert Vosika	4205 White Bear Pkwy S, Saint Paul MN 55110	651-653-0969	R	2*	<.1
397	Environeering Inc—Tim White	810 S Hwy 6 Ste 200, Houston TX 77079	281-493-9005	R	2*	<.1
398	Qlog Corp—J Warden	33 Standen Dr, Hamilton OH 45015	513-874-1211	R	2*	<.1
399	Checktech Financial Corp—Brian Boyd	PO Box 5360, Santa Fe NM 87502	505-474-9550	R	2*	<.1
400	Vista Training Inc—Bruce K Rabe	721 Cornerstone Crossi, Waterford WI 53185	262-514-2886	R	2*	<.1
401	John L Adams and Company Inc—John L Adams	8925 SW 148 St Ste 110, Miami FL 33176	305-251-2203	R	2*	<.1
402	Promar International—Nick Young	333 N Fairfax St Ste 2, Alexandria VA 22314	703-739-9090	R	2*	<.1
403	Apogee Engineering Associates Inc—Byron Dearixon	8203 Willow Pl South S, Houston TX 77070	281-469-3662	R	2*	<.1
404	Huffman Communications—Don Huffman	PO Box 5512, Napa CA 94581	707-257-2585	R	2*	<.1
405	New Millennium Communications Inc—Daniel Mack	1332 Pearl St, Boulder CO 80302	303-444-1476	R	2*	<.1
406	Precision Blasting Inc—Calvin Konya	PO Box 189, Montville OH 44064	440-474-6700	R	2*	<.1
407	B and B Test Solutions Inc—David Burke	3040 Venture Ln Unit 1, Melbourne FL 32934	303-678-9898	R	2*	<.1
408	Conrad Pharmaceutical Consultants Inc—Kenneth A Conrad MD	4916 Smith Canyon Ct, San Diego CA 92130	858-509-0075	R	2*	<.1
409	Livingston Wilson and Associates Inc—Clark Wilson	26811 Chelsea, Laguna Hills CA 92653	949-348-8587	R	2*	<.1
410	Bactee Systems Inc—Rich Becker	PO Box 5192, Grand Forks ND 58206	701-775-8775	R	2*	<.1
411	Proffesional Resource Group Inc—Ramesh Akula	1039 Sterling Rd Ste 2, Herndon VA 20170	703-435-7500	R	2*	<.1
412	Law Forum LLC—Linda Molinari	35 Thorpe Ave Ste 101, Wallingford CT 06492	203-265-2424	R	2*	<.1
413	Aris Associates West Inc—Irwin Berry	5295 Commerce Dr Ste G, Salt Lake City UT 84107	801-262-0077	R	2*	<.1
414	Sparknotes LLC—Alan Kahn	122 5th Ave, New York NY 10011	212-633-3330	R	2*	<.1
415	Jami Enterprises Inc—Jack Tompkins	5338 Peters Creek Rd D, Roanoke VA 24019	540-265-7670	R	2*	<.1
416	Distribution Postal Consultants Inc—Louis Haber	PO Box 11738, Baltimore MD 21206	410-488-1002	R	2*	<.1
417	Scanning Electron Analysis Laboratories Inc—Arun Kumar	250 N Nash St, El Segundo CA 90245	310-322-2011	R	2*	<.1
418	Employment Practices Solutions Inc—Laurie Jones	502 N Carroll Ave Ste, Southlake TX 76092	817-329-8460	R	2*	<.1
419	Metal-Mation Inc—Robert Nagel	2391 W 38th St, Cleveland OH 44113	216-651-1083	R	2*	<.1
420	Advanced Chemistry Labs Inc—Nicolette Andros	PO Box 88610, Atlanta GA 30356	770-409-1444	R	2*	<.1
421	Asi Consulting Group LLC—Michael Kuppe	30200 Telg Rd Ste 100, Bingham Farms MI 48025	248-530-1395	R	1*	<.1
422	Celergy Networks Inc—Art Cormier	4918 N Harbor Dr Ste 2, San Diego CA 92106	760-268-1913	R	1*	<.1
423	Renquist Associates Inc—Gary Swetsch	2300 Washington Ave, Racine WI 53405	262-634-2351	R	1*	<.1
424	Broma Information Technology LLC	3411 Perkins Ave Ste 3, Cleveland OH 44114	216-426-9995	R	1*	<.1
425	Wordmark Associates Inc—Ryan Bernard	3730 Kirby Dr Ste 1200, Houston TX 77098	713-600-2403	R	1*	<.1
426	Sirius Technology Corp—Bruce Knox	PO Box 341, Mentor OH 44061	440-205-9200	R	1*	<.1
427	Business Automation Services Inc—George Vitti	636 Plank Rd Ste 207, Clifton Park NY 12065	518-371-6869	R	1*	<.1
428	Advanced Chemical Sensors Inc—Larry Locker	101 Glades Rd Ste B, Boca Raton FL 33432	561-338-3116	R	1*	<.1
429	Health Research Associates Corp—Diane Hatfeild	PO Box 1233, Kennesaw GA 30156	678-797-9470	R	1*	.3
430	Baymark Inc—Gregory Kappers	638 Beechwood Ave, Carnegie PA 15106	412-276-1935	R	1*	.1
431	Accounting Management Solutions Inc (Waltham Massachusetts)—James Bourdon	800 South St Ste 195, Waltham MA 02453	781-419-9200	R	1*	.1
432	Sound Visions Corp—Greg Turner	1184-A W Corporate Dr, Arlington TX 76006	817-640-7300	R	1*	<.1
433	ESI Technology Corp—Brenda Wiechmann	211 Vaughn Hill Rd, Bolton MA 01740	978-779-0257	R	1*	<.1
434	PolyDyne Software Inc—David Tabb	9390 Research Blvd Ste, Austin TX 78759	512-343-9100	R	1*	<.1
435	Ensoco Inc—John Connor	2323 S Voss Rd Ste 490, Houston TX 77057	713-278-2326	R	1*	<.1
436	A Dualdraw LLC	5900 E 58th Ave Unit A, Commerce City CO 80022	303-853-4083	R	1*	<.1
437	Lander International LLC—Richard Tuck	PO Box 1370, El Cerrito CA 94530	510-232-4264	R	1*	<.1
438	Quarterwave Corp—Steven Price	1300 Valley House Dr S, Rohnert Park CA 94928	707-793-9105	R	1*	<.1
439	PEPP Unlimited—John Perry	252 W Swamp Rd Ste 1, Doylestown PA 18901	215-348-3112	R	1*	<.1
440	Educational Enhancements Inc—David Banchiu	2200 N Squirrel Rd, Rochester MI 48309	248-648-4690	R	1*	<.1
441	Educational Equity Concepts Inc—Merle Froschl	100 5th Ave 8th Fl, New York NY 10011	212-243-1110	R	1*	<.1
442	Fairfax Management Group Ltd—Dave Campell	9800 Shelard Pkwy Ste, Minneapolis MN 55441	763-541-9898	R	1*	<.1
443	Whitney and Whitney Inc—John W Whitney	PO Box 10725, Reno NV 89510	775-689-7696	S	1*	<.1
444	Richardson Researches Inc—Terry Richardson	1136 Robert Mondavi In, Davis CA 95616	530-754-9813	R	1*	<.1
445	Appleby Software Corp—Peter Appleby	26 Snapdragon, Irvine CA 92604	949-552-5444	R	1*	<.1
446	Warm Haven Enterprises—Miriam Moore	PO Box 222061, Newhall CA 91322	661-295-8665	R	1*	<.1
447	Ansin Technology Group—Leonard Ansin	38 Lovett Rd, Newton MA 02459	617-332-4500	R	1*	<.1
448	DemandPoint—Jerry Goldberg	6825 S Galena St Ste 2, Englewood CO 80112	303-792-8300	R	1*	<.1

Rank	Company Name—*Executive Officer*	Address, City, State, Zip	Phone	Type	Fin	Empls
449	Discerning Software Corp—*Mark D Anderson*	2116 18th St, San Francisco CA 94107		R	1*	<.1
450	Jeff Kagan—*Jeffrey Kagan*	PO Box 670562, Marietta GA 30066	770-579-5810	R	1*	<.1
451	Atterbury Consultants Inc—*Toby Atterbury*	3800 Sw Cedar Hills Bl, Beaverton OR 97005	503-646-5393	R	1*	<.1
452	Aradiant Corp—*Joseph Burgio*	101 N Harrison St, Palmyra PA 17078	717-838-7220	R	1*	<.1
453	Application Support Company Inc—*John Blackshire*	PO Box 860, Naperville IL 60566	630-355-6297	R	1*	<.1
454	Nr Systems Inc—*Cynthia Johnson*	165 E 500 S, Logan UT 84321	435-752-4200	R	1*	<.1
455	Videocenters Inc—*Michael Tricarchi*	23632 Mercantile Rd St, Cleveland OH 44122	216-765-1524	R	1*	<.1
456	Data Fm Inc—*Marshall Bandy*	PO Box 429, Ringgold GA 30736	706-935-2875	R	<1*	<.1
457	CruiseCam International Inc—*D Scott Watkins*	901 S Federal Hwy Ste, Fort Lauderdale FL 33316	336-218-1033	R	<1	<.1
458	Kane Engineering Group Inc—*David Kane*	4873 Riemen Ct Se, Grand Rapids MI 49508	616-281-5858	R	<1*	<.1
459	Bay Zinc Company Inc—*Richard Camp*	PO Box 167, Moxee WA 98936	509-248-4911	R	<1*	<.1
460	Montessori Home Inc—*Robert Korngold*	25 Roxbury Rd, Scarsdale NY 10583	914-472-9849	R	<1*	<.1
461	MD Buyline Inc—*Larry Malcolmson*	5910 N Central Expy St, Dallas TX 75206	214-891-6700	R	<1	.1
462	McKee Network Inc—*Adrian McKee*	2N500 Bernice Ave, Glen Ellyn IL 60137	630-752-1909	R	<1*	<.1
463	Steel Structures Technology Center Inc—*Robert E Shaw Jr*	5277 Leelanau Ct, Howell MI 48843	734-878-9560	R	<1	<.1
464	Alsbridge Inc—*Ben Trowbridge*	3535 Travis St Ste 105, Dallas TX 75204	214-696-6410	R	N/A	.2
465	VeraCentra—*Constance Hill*	690 Airpark Rd, Napa CA 94558	707-224-6161	R	N/A	<.1
466	Monsoon Inc—*Kanth Gopalpur*	520 NW Davis St Ste 30, Portland OR 97209	503-239-1055	R	N/A	<.1

TOTALS: SIC 8748 Business Consulting Services Nec
Companies: 466   40,027   137.1

8999 Services Nec

Rank	Company Name—*Executive Officer*	Address, City, State, Zip	Phone	Type	Fin	Empls
1	Boston Medical Center—*Kate Walsh*	1 Boston Medical Ctr P, Boston MA 02118	617-638-8000	R	7,533*	5.0
2	Beth Israel Deaconess Medical Center—*Eric Buehrens*	330 Brookline Ave, Boston MA 02215	617-667-7000	R	7,321*	6.0
3	EnergySolutiuons LLC—*Val J Christenson*	423 W 300 South Ste 20, Salt Lake City UT 84101		R	5,572*	5.0
4	Geneve Corp—*Edward Netter*	60 Thread Needle Ln, Stamford CT 06902	203-358-0800	S	4,804*	2.0
5	Belo Interactive—*Robert W Desherd*	400 S Record St, Dallas TX 75202	214-977-8200	S	3,289*	3.4
6	Knights of Columbus—*Carl A Anderson*	PO Box 1966, New Haven CT 06509	203-752-4000	R	1,794	13.7
7	L and W Supply Corp—*John Meister*	550 W Adams St, Chicago IL 60661	312-672-7722	S	1,656*	5.0
8	Knowledge Networks Inc—*Simon Kooyman*	2100 Geng Rd Ste 210, Palo Alto CA 94303	650-289-2000	R	1,555*	1.0
9	Marshfield Clinic Inc—*Karl J Ulrich*	1000 N Oak Ave, Marshfield WI 54449	715-387-5511	R	967*	6.6
10	Veolia Environmental Serivces North America Corp—*Jim Bell*	700 E Butterfield Rd S, Lombard IL 60148	630-218-1600	S	900*	9.0
11	Military Personnel Services Corp—*John L Jones*	6066 Leesburg Pike, Falls Church VA 22041	571-481-4000	R	762*	.7
12	Metro Networks Inc—*Chuck Bortnick*	2800 Post Oak Blvd Ste, Houston TX 77056	713-407-6000	S	738*	2.1
13	Plantronics e-Commerce Inc—*Ken Kannappan*	345 Encinal St, Santa Cruz CA 95060	831-426-5858	S	614	3.0
14	Kammann Machines Inc	330 W State St Ste 200, Geneva IL 60134	630-513-8091	R	513*	.5
15	Farner-Bocken Co—*John J Norgaard*	PO Box 368, Carroll IA 51401	712-792-3503	R	476*	.9
16	Precyse Solutions LLC—*Jeffrey Levitt*	1275 Drummers Ln Ste 2, Wayne PA 19087	610-688-2464	R	419*	.4
17	Interval Leisure Group Inc—*Craig M Nash*	6262 Sunset Dr, Miami FL 33143	305-666-1861	P	409	2.9
18	American Insurance Services Group Inc—*Frank J Coyne*	545 Washington Blvd, Jersey City NJ 07310	201-469-2000	D	349*	2.0
19	Chemonics International Inc—*Richard Dreiman*	1717 H St NW, Washington DC 20006	202-955-3300	R	334*	.5
20	DigitalGlobe Inc—*Jeffrey R Tarr*	1601 Dry Creek Dr Ste, Longmont CO 80503	303-684-4000	P	322	.6
21	Hayneedle Inc—*Doug Nielson*	9394 W Dodge Rd Ste 30, Omaha NE 68114		R	305*	.3
22	Language Line Services Inc—*Louis Provenzano*	1 Lower Ragsdale Dr Bl, Monterey CA 93940	831-648-5800	R	299	4.5
23	Penson Worldwide Inc—*Philip A Pendergraft*	1700 Pacific Ave Ste 1, Dallas TX 75201	214-765-1100	P	288	1.0
24	Nebraska Educational Telecommunications—*Rod Bates*	1800 N 33rd St, Lincoln NE 68503		R	288*	.3
25	Northern Leasing Systems Inc—*Jay Cohen*	132 W 31stStreet 14th, New York NY 10001		R	251*	.2
26	Forrester Research Inc—*George F Colony*	400 Technology Sq, Cambridge MA 02139	617-613-5730	P	251	1.1
27	Matchcom LP—*Gregory R Blatt*	8300 Douglas Ave, Dallas TX 75225	214-576-9352	S	227*	.1
28	Metal Storm Inc—*Lee Finniear*	4350 N Fairfax Dr Ste, Arlington VA 22203	703-248-8218	S	226*	<.1
29	AG View FS Inc—*Mark Orr*	22069 US Hwy 34 E, Princeton IL 61356	815-875-2800	R	197*	.2
30	HealthPort Inc—*Michael J Labedz*	925 North Point Pkwy S, Alpharetta GA 30005	770-670-2150	R	188*	3.7
31	Invention Cos—*Martin Brown*	217 9th St, Pittsburgh PA 15222	412-288-1300	R	185*	.2
32	Riverside Physician Services Inc	608 Denbigh Blvd, Williamsburg VA 23185	757-442-6600	R	161*	<.1
33	CareCall Inc—*Jim Christensen*	200 14th Ave E, Sartell MN 56377	320-253-7800	R	158*	.1
34	Project Leadership Associates Inc—*Daniel Porcaro*	200 W Adams St Ste 250, Chicago IL 60606	312-441-0077	R	157*	.2
35	Delphi Technology Inc (Boston Massachusetts)—*Sam Fang*	1 Washington Mall 3rd, Boston MA 02108	617-259-1200	R	147*	.2
36	ATC Associates Inc—*Robert Toups*	221 Rue De Jean Ste 20, Lafayette LA 70508	337-234-8777	R	145*	1.6
37	Newgistics Inc—*Bill Razzouk*	2700 Via Fortuna, Austin TX 78746	512-225-6000	R	142*	.1
38	Thermacore Inc—*Jerry Toth*	780 Eden Rd, Lancaster PA 17601	717-569-6551	R	134*	.3
39	Fox International Limited Inc—*Murray G Fox*	23600 Aurora Rd, Bedford Heights OH 44146		S	133*	.1
40	Nth Degree Global LLC—*John Yohe*	2675 Beckinridge Blvd, Duluth GA 30096	404-296-5282	R	105*	.1
41	Ventraq Inc—*Dave Sellers*	817 E Gate Dr Ste 101, Mount Laurel NJ 08054	856-866-1000	R	98*	.1
42	Professional Bull Riders Inc—*Jim Hayworth*	101 W Riverwalk, Pueblo CO 81003	719-242-2800	S	95*	.1
43	iProspect—*Robert Murray*	200 Clarendon St 23rd, Boston MA 02116	617-449-4300	S	90*	.1
44	Bijoux Terner LP—*Gabriel Bottazzi*	6950 NW 77th Ct, Miami FL 33166	305-500-7500	R	88	.4
45	Salo LLC—*John Folkestad*	20 S 13th St Ste 200, Minneapolis MN 55403	612-230-7256	R	87*	.4
46	Dawson Logistics—*Doug Dawson*	431 N Vermillion St, Danville IL 61832	217-442-7036	R	82*	.1
47	Edisto Electric Cooperative Inc—*David Felkel*	PO Box 547, Bamberg SC 29003	803-245-5141	R	82*	.1
48	International Transport Solutions Inc—*William Gensburg*	310 Paterson Plank Rd, Carlstadt NJ 07072	201-549-1500	R	79*	.1
49	WeatherBank Inc—*Steven A Root*	1015 Waterwood Pkwy St, Edmond OK 73034	405-359-0773	R	64*	<.1
50	Nationwide Exchange Services Inc—*Michael Halloran*	50 W San Fernando St S, San Jose CA 95113		R	61*	.1
51	Tescom (USA) Software Systems Testing Inc—*Ofer Albeck*	7840 Roswell Rd Bldg 1, Atlanta GA 30350	678-250-1200	R	60*	.1
52	Cactus Stone and Tile Inc—*Don Bender*	401 S 50th St, Phoenix AZ 85034	602-275-6400	R	58*	.1
53	Hoefler Consulting Group—*Brian G Hoefler*	3401 Minnesota Dr Ste, Anchorage AK 99503	907-563-2137	R	55*	.1
54	Information Systems of Florida—*J Thomas Solana*	9550 Regency Sq Blvd S, Jacksonville FL 32225	904-724-2277	R	55*	.3
55	Ideal Innovations Inc—*Robert W Kocher*	950 N Glebe Rd Ste 800, Arlington VA 22203	703-528-9101	R	54*	.3
56	AdCare Health Systems Inc—*Boyd P Gentry*	5057 Troy Rd, Springfield OH 45502	937-964-8974	P	53	2.2
57	Bergaila and Associates Inc—*Chris Bergaila*	1880 S Dairy Ashford S, Houston TX 77077	281-496-0803	R	53*	.1
58	Zoosk Inc—*Shayan Ghazizadeh*	130 Battery St, San Francisco CA 94111	301-641-4319	R	52*	.1
59	NDR Energy Group LLC—*Ken Harris*	525 N Tryon St Ste 160, Charlotte NC 28202	704-248-0583	R	52*	.1
60	Simplified Logistics LLC—*David Klugman*	PO Box 40088, Bay Village OH 44140	440-250-8912	R	52*	<.1
61	Graef Anhalt Schloemer and Associates Inc—*Richard Bub*	125 S 84th St, Milwaukee WI 53214	414-259-1500	R	51*	.3
62	DeLorme Publishing Co—*David DeLorme*	PO Box 298, Yarmouth ME 04096		R	50*	.3
63	REC Solar Inc—*Angiolo Laviziano*	775 Fiero Ln Ste 200, San Luis Obispo CA 93401	805-528-9705	R	50*	.3
64	Visionary Services Inc—*David Safris*	300 E Locust St Ste 25, Des Moines IA 50309	515-369-3545	R	48*	<.1
65	Analysis Group LLC—*Patrick Curry*	300 N Washington St St, Falls Church VA 22046	703-241-7819	R	47*	.1
66	CUI Global Inc—*William J Clough*	20050 SW 112th Ave, Tualatin OR 97062	503-612-2300	P	41	.1
67	Compendium Inc—*Kobi Yamada*	600 N 36th St Ste 400, Seattle WA 98103	206-812-1640	R	38*	<.1

Note: An asterisk (*) indicates an estimated financial figure. The company type code used is as follows: R = Private, P = Public, S = Private Subsidiary, B = Public Subsidiary, D = Division, J = Joint Venture, I = Investment Fund.

COMPANY RANKINGS BY SALES WITHIN 4-DIGIT SIC

Rank	Company Name—*Executive Officer*	Address, City, State, Zip	Phone	Type	Fin	Empls
68	Olivia Cruises and Resorts—*Judith Dlugacz*	434 Brannan St, San Francisco CA 94107	415-962-5700	R	34*	<.1
69	Destination Wedding Travel Inc—*Quentin Carmichael*	1253 Worcester Rd Ste, Framingham MA 01701	508-879-4500	R	29*	<.1
70	Marketing Informatics—*Robert Massie*	5739 Professional Circ, Indianapolis IN 46241	317-788-4440	R	28*	.1
71	Borrego Solar Systems Inc—*Mike Hall*	1810 Gillespie Way Ste, El Cajon CA 92020		R	28*	.1
72	All Star Directories Inc—*Douglas Brown*	2200 Alaskan Way Ste 2, Seattle WA 98121	206-436-7500	R	27*	.1
73	Toyota Motor Corporate Services of North America Inc—*Toshiaki Taguchi*	601 Lexington Ave, New York NY 10022	212-223-0303	S	27*	<.1
74	Sisterson and Company LLP—*William E Troup*	310 Grant St Ste 2100, Pittsburgh PA 15219	412-281-2025	R	26*	.1
75	JibJab Media Inc—*Gregg Spiridellis*	228 Main St Ste 4, Venice CA 90291	310-664-1971	R	25*	<.1
76	ESC Select Inc—*Gregory M Bauer*	20 Pineview Dr, Amherst NY 14228	716-691-4455	R	25*	.1
77	Ahura Scientific Inc—*Douglas Kahn*	46 Jonspin Rd, Wilmington MA 01887	978-657-5555	S	24*	.1
78	Zerowait Corp—*Michael Linett*	707 Kirkwood Hwy, Wilmington DE 19805	302-266-9408	R	24*	<.1
79	BOSH Global Services Inc—*Robert Fitzgerald*	1 Compass Way Ste 250, Newport News VA 23606	757-271-3428	R	23*	.1
80	Barron Collier Co—*Lamar Gable*	2600 Golden Gate Pkwy, Naples FL 34105	239-262-2600	R	22*	.1
81	ARI Network Services Inc—*Roy W Olivier*	10850 W Park Pl Ste 12, Milwaukee WI 53224	414-973-4300	P	21	.1
82	LPL Financial Retirement—*William R Chetney*	33272 Valle Rd Ste 100, San Juan Capistrano CA 92675	419-636-4677	R	20*	.1
83	Albar Precious Metal Refining—*Jeff Aronson*	2800 Gateway Dr, Pompano Beach FL 33069		R	20*	<.1
84	Broadway Party and Tent Rental—*Terry Jean St Martin*	7409 Jolly Ln, Brooklyn Park MN 55428	763-424-6155	R	20*	<.1
85	Effective UI Inc—*Rebecca Flavin*	2162 Market St, Denver CO 80205	778-995-0661	R	20	.1
86	Tech Conferences Inc	731 Main St Ste D3, Monroe CT 06468		S	18*	.1
87	Binghamton Simulator Company Inc—*E Terry Lewis*	151 Court St, Binghamton NY 13901	607-722-6177	R	18*	<.1
88	Teksavers Inc—*Juan Staalenburg*	2128 W Braker Ln Ste 1, Austin TX 78758	512-491-5304	R	17*	<.1
89	Artbeats—*Phil Bates*	PO Box 709, Myrtle Creek OR 97457	541-863-4429	R	17*	<.1
90	Cryo-Cell International Inc—*David I Portnoy*	700 Brooker Creek Blvd, Oldsmar FL 34677	813-749-2100	P	16	.1
91	T Coombs and Associates LLC—*Tony Coombs*	6551 Loisdale Ct Ste 5, Springfield VA 22150	703-822-8228	R	16*	.1
92	MotionPoint Corp—*Will Fleming*	4661 Johnson Rd Ste14, Coconut Creek FL 33073	954-421-0890	R	16*	.1
93	InterSoft Group	26380 Curtiss Wright P, Richmond Heights OH 44143	216-765-7351	R	16*	<.1
94	Iwerks Touring Technologies Inc—*Michael J Needham*	4520 W Valerio St, Burbank CA 91505	818-841-7766	S	15*	<.1
95	Verisae—*Dan Johnson*	100 N 6th St Ste 710A, Minneapolis MN 55403	612-455-2300	R	14*	<.1
96	Asset International—*Jim Casella*	1055 Washington Blvd, Stamford CT 06901	203-595-3200	R	14*	<.1
97	Skipping Stone Inc—*Greg Lander*	83 Pine St Ste 101, West Peabody MA 01960	978-717-6100	R	14*	<.1
98	Advanced Planning Services Inc—*Debra Fitzpatrick*	1500 State St Ste 220, San Diego CA 92101	619-220-8116	R	14*	<.1
99	Bethel Plastics Inc—*Sang Chung Lee*	1900 Raymer Ave, Fullerton CA 92833	714-533-8500	R	14*	<.1
100	Global Wedge Inc—*Rao Marella*	3267 Larkspur St, Tustin CA 92782	951-413-1482	R	14*	<.1
101	Smart Destinations Inc—*Kevin McLaughlin*	85 Merrimac St Ste 300, Boston MA 02114	617-671-1016	R	13*	<.1
102	Myriad Development—*Chris Roussell*	6300 Bridgepoint Pky B, Austin TX 78730	512-302-3262	R	13*	<.1
103	Wendel Energy Services LLC—*Scott Smith*	140 John James Audubon, Amherst NY 14228	716-688-0766	R	13*	<.1
104	Classic Coffee Concepts Inc—*Victor Kung*	1016 Montana Dr, Charlotte NC 28216	704-596-3661	R	13*	<.1
105	Flipswap Inc—*Dave StritzingerFarudi*	2610 Columbia St Ste A, Torrance CA 90503	424-237-1500	R	12	<.1
106	Relevante Inc—*William Brassington*	1400 N Providence Rd S, Media PA 19063	610-832-0430	R	12	1.1
107	TCE Inc—*C Gail Bassette*	5801 Allentown Rd Ste, Camp Springs MD 20746	301-316-0501	R	12*	<.1
108	Smalls Electrical Construction Inc—*Jeffrey J Smalls*	63 Flushing Ave Unit 3, Brooklyn NY 11205	718-254-0009	R	12*	<.1
109	JBCStyle—*Bryan Zaslow*	108 W 39th St 7th Fl, New York NY 10018	212-355-3197	R	12*	<.1
110	MacArtney Offshore Inc—*Chris Howerter*	2901 W Sam Houston Pkw, Houston TX 77043	713-266-7575	R	12*	.1
111	Reeves Exploration and Technologies—*Derek Reeves*	498 Curtis Rd, Burleson TX 76028	817-447-8056	R	12*	<.1
112	GeBBS Healthcare Solutions—*Nitin Thakor*	560 Sylvan Ave Ste 205, Englewood Cliffs NJ 07632	201-227-0088	R	12	1.4
113	Projectline Services Inc—*Mike Kichline*	562 1st Ave S Ste 400, Seattle WA 98104	206-382-2025	R	11*	.1
114	Dunbar Bender and Zapf Inc—*Mark K Dunbar*	437 Grant St, Pittsburgh PA 15219	412-263-0102	R	11*	.1
115	Doba LLC—*Jeremy Hanks*	1530 N Technology Way, Orem UT 84097	801-765-6101	R	10*	.1
116	Myweddingcom—*Woddy Pastorius*	363 Tormey Ln Ste 200, Bainbridge Island WA 98110	206-855-7000	R	10*	<.1
117	SNACC Distributing Co—*Gary Krummen*	2105 Central Ave, Cincinnati OH 45214	513-723-1777	R	10*	<.1
118	Counsel on Call Inc—*Jane Hanner Allen*	112 Westwood Place Ste, Brentwood TN 37027	615-467-2388	R	10*	<.1
119	Integrated Wave Technologies Inc—*Timothy McCune*	4042 Clipper Ct, Fremont CA 94538	510-353-0260	R	10*	<.1
120	Marlin Co—*Frank Kenna*	10 Research Pkwy, Wallingford CT 06492	203-294-9800	R	9*	.1
121	Engineering Analysis Associates Inc—*John B Blystone*	5800 Enterprise Ct, Warren MI 48092	586-582-5828	S	9*	.3
122	Optimal Solutions Group LLC—*Mark Turner PhD*	8100 Professional Plac, Hyattsville MD 20785	301-306-1170	R	9*	<.1
123	Cottman Transmission Systems Inc—*Todd P Leff*	201 Gibraltar Rd Ste 1, Horsham PA 19044	215-643-5885	S	9*	<.1
124	Oil Data Inc	1888 Stebbins Dr, Houston TX 77043	713-461-7178	D	9*	<.1
125	Merrell Brothers Inc—*Ted Merrell*	8811 W 500 N, Kokomo IN 46901	574-699-7782	R	9*	<.1
126	Emoto—*Paul Schultz*	1615 16th St, Santa Monica CA 90404	310-399-6900	R	9*	<.1
127	Dahl-Morrow International—*Andy Steinem*	1821 Michael Faraday D, Reston VA 20190	703-787-8117	R	9*	<.1
128	Power Pro-Tech Services Inc—*Robert Byrne*	240 Circle Dr, Maitland FL 32751	407-628-8186	R	8*	.1
129	Promopeddler Inc—*Lewis Amicone III*	555 Bryant Street #402, Palo Alto CA 94301		R	8*	<.1
130	SafetyForumcom—*Russwin Francisco*	1711 Connecticut Ave N, Washington DC 20009	202-483-3400	R	8*	<.1
131	Testronic Labs—*Seith Hallen*	111 N 1st St Ste 304, Burbank CA 91502	818-845-3223	S	8*	.1
132	Optionomics Corp—*Scott Gordon*	1467 N Cherry Blossom, Farmington UT 84025	801-447-3300	R	8*	<.1
133	Single Path LLC—*Rob Koch*	905 Parkview Blvd, Lombard IL 60148	630-812-2300	R	8	<.1
134	VST Consulting Inc—*Suresh Chatakondu*	200 Middlesex Essex Tp, Iselin NJ 08830	732-404-0025	R	7*	.1
135	ReliableRemodelercom Inc—*Eric Doebele*	9305 SW Nimbus Ave, Beaverton OR 97008	503-574-3372	R	7*	.1
136	Sambazon Inc—*Ryan Black*	1160 Calle Cordillera, San Clemente CA 92673		R	7*	.1
137	TM Studios—*R David Graupner*	2002 Academy Ln Ste 11, Dallas TX 75234	972-406-6823	S	7*	<.1
138	Microlab-FXR—*Paul Genova*	25 Eastmans Rd, Parsippany NJ 07054	973-386-9696	S	7*	<.1
139	Sonicbids Corp—*Panos Panay*	500 Harrison Ave 4th F, Boston MA 02118	617-502-1388	R	7*	<.1
140	Hunt Consulting—*Henry Hunt*	9015 Maier Rd Ste B, Laurel MD 20723	301-490-3355	R	7	<.1
141	Medinitiatives—*Matthew Simas*	10901 Gold Center Dr, Rancho Cordova CA 95670	916-861-7770	R	7*	<.1
142	Velocity Networks Inc—*Christopher Eck*	70 James St Ste 111b, Worcester MA 01603	508-798-8121	R	7*	<.1
143	Communications Creative Inc—*Kathleen Losurdo*	3050 Metro Dr Ste 112, Bloomington MN 55425	952-851-7111	R	7*	<.1
144	KEEP Co—*Tom Kehoe*	803 Gateway Pkwy, Marble Falls TX 78654	830-693-5599	R	7*	<.1
145	Raj India Autoparts Outsourcing—*Dinesh Chhabra*	4001 - 134th St NE, Marysville WA 98271	360-658-1855	S	7*	<.1
146	Moebs Services Inc—*Michael Moebs*	21 N Skokie Hwy Ste 20, Lake Bluff IL 60044		R	7*	<.1
147	Stewart Acoustical Consultants—*Noral Stewart*	7330 Chapel Hill Rd, Raleigh NC 27607	919-858-0899	R	7*	<.1
148	Bryan Pendleton Swats and Mcallister-Wells Fargo LLC—*Jim Kurowski*	5301 Virginia Way Ste, Brentwood TN 37027	615-665-1640	R	7*	.1
149	Dexter Field Services—*Lucas Albrecht*	1844 IH-10 S Ste 202, Beaumont TX 77707	409-838-4800	R	6	.1
150	ProfitPoint Inc—*Vaden Landers*	4 Rockbourne Rd 4th Fl, Clifton Heights PA 19018		R	6*	.1
151	Nxtbook Media—*Michael Biggerstaff*	480 New Holland Ave St, Lancaster PA 17602	717-735-9740	R	6*	.1
152	Eau Claire Cooperative Oil Co—*Lynn Thompson*	PO Box 368, Fall Creek WI 54742	715-876-6422	R	6*	<.1
153	Colsky Media Inc—*Richard Colsky*	2740 Van Ness Ave Ste, San Francisco CA 94109	415-673-5400	R	6*	<.1
154	Granard Pharmaceutical Sales and Marketing—*Stephen Flood*	2317 Hwy 34 Ste 1E, Manasquan NJ 08736	732-292-2661	R	6*	<.1
155	Sales Partnerships Inc—*Fred Kessler*	9035 Wadsworth Pkwy St, Westminster CO 80021		R	5*	.1

Rank	Company Name—*Executive Officer*	Address, City, State, Zip	Phone	Type	Fin	Empls
156	Austin GeoModeling Inc—*Tron Isaksen*	6500 River Place Blvd, Austin TX 78730	512-257-8820	R	5*	<.1
157	Sub Pop Ltd—*Jonathan Poneman*	2013 4th Ave 3rd Fl, Seattle WA 98121	206-441-8441	R	5*	<.1
158	John Hayes and Sons—*John F Hayes III*	30 Potuccos Ring Rd, Wolcott CT 06716	203-879-4616	R	5*	<.1
159	Spectrum Technologies USA Inc—*Clyde D Keaton*	112 Erie Blvd Ste 3, Schenectady NY 12305	518-382-0056	D	5*	<.1
160	Reuseitcom—*Vincent Cobb*	3944 S Morgan St, Chicago IL 60609		R	5*	<.1
161	Damar Group Ltd—*David S Murphy*	6030-M Marshalee Dr, Elkridge MD 21075	410-461-5366	R	5*	<.1
162	Lake Products Company Inc—*Mark Youngberg*	PO Box 2248, Maryland Heights MO 63043	314-770-2299	R	5*	<.1
163	ThinkTank Holdings LLC—*Scott Blum*	PO Box 8378, Jackson WY 83002	307-734-9800	R	5*	<.1
164	Joe Kane Productions Inc—*Joseph Kane*	12526 Otsego St, Valley Village CA 91607	818-505-9829	R	5*	<.1
165	Dirt Pros EVS—*Marcell D Haywood*	PO Box 16453, Plantation FL 33318	954-318-2477	R	5	.3
166	Bridge Business and Property Brokers Inc—*AJ Caro*	60 Knickerbocker Ave, Bohemia NY 11716		R	4*	.3
167	Clearlink—*Phil Hansen*	5202 W Douglas Corriga, Salt Lake City UT 84116	801-424-0018	R	4*	.2
168	Transcontinents Record Sales Inc—*Leonard Silver*	1762 Main St, Buffalo NY 14208	716-883-9520	R	4*	<.1
169	American Bancard LLC—*Sam Zietz*	1081 Holland Dr, Boca Raton FL 33487	561-961-1353	R	4*	<.1
170	B and L Associates Inc—*Bryce Kramer*	220 Reservoir St Ste 1, Needham MA 02494	781-444-1404	R	4*	<.1
171	Gear Holdings Inc—*Bettye M Musham*	142 E 30th St, New York NY 10016	212-459-0050	R	4*	<.1
172	Delaware Valley Wholesale Florist—*Jack Chidester*	520 N Mantua Blvd, Sewell NJ 08080	856-468-7000	R	4*	<.1
173	Agnew Tech-II—*Irene Agnew*	741 Lakefield Rd Ste C, Westlake Village CA 91361	805-494-3999	R	4*	<.1
174	Badger Technical Services Inc—*Hal Butler*	10025 W Greenfield Ave, Milwaukee WI 53214	414-453-3313	R	4*	<.1
175	Visibility Factor Inc—*Jeff Wilson*	250 Storke Rd Ste 16, Santa Barbara CA 93117	805-961-8735	R	4*	<.1
176	String Real Estate Information Services—*Prashant Kothari*	3003 Van Ness St Ste W, Washington DC 20008	202-470-0648	R	3	.4
177	Hatch Mott MacDonald Operating Services Inc—*Peter J Wickens*	27 Bleeker St, Millburn NJ 07041	973-379-3400	R	3*	10.0
178	College Hunks Hauling Junk Inc—*Omar Soliman*	4836 W Gandy Blvd, Tampa FL 33611		R	3*	.1
179	InTouch Inc—*Brian Carroll*	2 Pine Tree Dr, Arden Hills MN 55112	651-255-7700	R	3*	.1
180	Access International LLC—*Malika C Bounaira*	5959 W Century Blvd St, Los Angeles CA 90045	310-258-9480	R	3*	<.1
181	Brian Taylor International LLC—*Brian Taylor*	100 Cheshire Dr, Griffin GA 30223	770-294-4653	R	3*	<.1
182	Sourcentra Inc—*Daniel Gonyea*	150 Speen St, Framingham MA 01701	508-405-2605	R	3*	<.1
183	R and B Films Ltd—*Rich Casey*	1057 Lakeville Rd, New Hyde Park NY 11040	516-327-0512	R	3*	<.1
184	Source Abroad Inc—*Caro Krissman*	405 N Oak St, Inglewood CA 90302	310-672-5862	R	3*	<.1
185	Lightsense Corp—*Lawrence Ring*	25852 McBean Pky Ste 1, Valencia CA 91355	949-463-1092	R	3*	<.1
186	Summit Research Associates Inc—*Francie Mendelsohn*	7728 Warbler Ln, Rockville MD 20855	301-670-0980	R	3*	<.1
187	Code Shred Ltd—*Michael Milillo*	1 Industrial Plaza Bld, Valley Stream NY 11581	516-431-5484	R	3	<.1
188	Aubrey Group Inc—*Tom Allen*	6 Cromwell Ste 100, Irvine CA 92618	949-581-0188	R	3	.1
189	Active Lawyers Referral Service—*Paul Mehdizadeh*	9301 Wilshire Blvd Ste, Beverly Hills CA 90210	310-247-0425	R	3*	.1
190	Metritech Inc—*Samuel Krug*	PO Box 6479, Champaign IL 61826	217-398-4868	R	2*	.1
191	Experts Inc—*Thomas E Hoshko*	2400 E Commercial Blvd, Fort Lauderdale FL 33308	954-493-8040	R	2*	.4
192	Lyrix Design Inc—*Jeff Graham*	900 Chelmsford St, Lowell MA 01851	978-442-3000	R	2*	<.1
193	Chesapeake Solar LLC—*Richard Deutschmann*	7761 Waterloo Rd, Jessup MD 20794	443-733-1221	R	2*	<.1
194	ElJet Aviation Services—*Ben Schusterman*	110 S Fairfax Ave Ste, Los Angeles CA 90036		R	2*	<.1
195	Byron Folse Associates Inc—*Byron Folse*	2275 Westpark Ct Ste 2, Euless TX 76040	817-267-3596	R	2*	<.1
196	Identek Corp	1072 N Kraemer Pl, Anaheim CA 92806	714-666-2025	R	2*	<.1
197	Butler Mailing Service Inc—*Todd Butler*	9060 Sutton Pl, Hamilton OH 45011	513-870-5060	R	2*	<.1
198	Weather Watch Inc—*Craig Berthiaume*	119 N 4th St, Minneapolis MN 55401	612-630-2555	R	2*	<.1
199	Tricom Communications Inc—*Gary Evans*	1301 Corp Ctr Dr Ste 1, Saint Paul MN 55121	651-686-9000	R	1*	<.1
200	Starkey Printing Company Inc—*George Millan*	PO Box 71869, Chattanooga TN 37407	423-629-4366	R	1*	<.1
201	Topaz Publications Inc—*Thomas Burke*	7445 Morgan Rd Ste 5, Liverpool NY 13090	315-451-2293	R	1*	<.1
202	Deaf Services Inc—*Dawn Melendez*	8733 Sigan Ln, Baton Rouge LA 70810	225-756-5339	R	1*	<.1
203	Reality Publishing Co—*Michael Miller*	11757 Katy Fwy Ste 210, Houston TX 77079	281-558-9101	R	1*	<.1
204	Integrated Environmental Restoration Services Inc—*Michael Hogan*	PO Box 7559, Tahoe City CA 96145	530-581-4377	R	1*	<.1
205	Talk Marketing Inc—*Taryn Letterman*	2 Sylvan Way, Parsippany NJ 07054	973-540-8333	R	1*	<.1
206	Mesoscale Environmental Simulation and Operations Inc—*John W Zack*	185 Jordan Rd Ste 8, Troy NY 12180	518-283-5169	R	1*	<.1
207	Science Regulatory Services International Corp—*John Todhunter*	7700 Leesburg Pike Ste, Falls Church VA 22043	703-821-0157	R	1*	<.1
208	Tampa Bay Plumbers LLC—*Brad Kalis*	PO Box 2377, Middleburg FL 32050		R	1*	<.1
209	Jonathan Helfand Music—*Johnathon Alliston*	11 W25th St 11th Fl, New York NY 10010	212-647-9500	R	1*	<.1
210	Mirage Studios—*Peter Laird*	PO Box 486, Northampton MA 01061	413-586-7066	R	1*	<.1
211	No Soap Productions—*Daniel Aron*	936 Broadway 4th Fl, New York NY 10010	212-581-5572	R	1*	<.1
212	Advanced Surface Microscopy Inc—*Donald A Chernoff*	3250 N Post Rd Ste 120, Indianapolis IN 46226	317-895-5630	R	1*	<.1
213	Aphco International Inc—*Philipee Cornu*	PO Box 22796, Lake Buena Vista FL 32830	407-256-8886	R	1*	<.1
214	Upshaw and Associates—*Lynn Upshaw*	101 Lucas Valley Rd St, San Rafael CA 94903	415-507-9193	R	1*	<.1
215	Accurate Metal Sawing Service Co—*Tom Blue*	8989 Tyler Blvd, Mentor OH 44060	440-974-6179	R	1*	<.1
216	Femto Tech Inc—*Edward Burgess*	PO Box 8257, Carlisle OH 45005	937-746-4427	R	1*	<.1
217	Nocopi Technologies Inc—*Michael A Feinstein*	9C Portland Rd, West Conshohocken PA 19428	610-834-9600	P	1	<.1
218	Siler Studios—*Buzz Siler*	2801 Lakeview Blvd, Lake Oswego OR 97035	503-969-0009	R	1*	<.1
219	Arpy Inc—*Ron Albert*	PO Box 1358, Mcallen TX 78505	956-682-6091	R	1*	<.1
220	Gallery of History Inc—*Todd M Axelrod*	3601 W Sahara Ave, Las Vegas NV 89102	702-364-1000	P	<1	<.1
221	Creative Solutions Editorial Inc—*KD Sullivan*	506 Kansas St, San Francisco CA 94107	415-621-0465	R	<1	N/A
222	NYLIFE Inc—*Ted Mathas*	51 Madison Ave, New York NY 10010	212-576-7000	R	N/A	12.1
223	PK Controls Inc—*Matt Patel*	8000 Corporate Blvd, Plain City OH 43064	614-733-0979	R	N/A	<.1

TOTALS: SIC 8999 Services Nec
Companies: 223

					47,341	119.8

Note: An asterisk (*) indicates an estimated financial figure. The company type code used is as follows: R = Private, P = Public, S = Private Subsidiary, B = Public Subsidiary, D = Division, J = Joint Venture, I = Investment Fund.

Company Name	SIC	Rank
1 800 Tax Lws Inc	7389	2420
1 Cab LLC	4121	6
1 Cochran Inc	5511	254
1 Drake Place	5087	95
1 Edi Source Inc	7379	680
1 Nation Investment Corp	5065	199
1 PC Network Inc	3669	285
1 Quality Electric Inc	1731	1405
1 Source Consulting Inc	8742	78
1 Stop Electronics Center Inc	5734	334
1 Touch Marketing LLC	8742	208
101 Financial Group LLC	8748	368
101 Pipe and Casing Inc	5051	228
1010data Inc	7371	748
1013 Integrated	7812	204
101communications LLC	2741	42
1079 Mix	4832	125
1099 Pro	5734	121
1105 Media Inc	2721	96
1199seiu Greater Ny Benefit Fund	6733	5
1199seiu Nbf For Home Care Employees	8082	19
123 E Doty Corp	5812	414
12th Avenue Graphics Copy Service	2752	1445
12zCD	3695	127
1316 Commonwealth Ave Corp	2082	56
1366 Technologies Inc	3674	418
14 Carats Ltd	5094	42
140 North Beacon LP	6513	5
155 East Tropicana LLC	7999	65
16500 Sixteen Five Hundred	5063	452
1660 Group LLC	3599	233
1776 Housekeeping Associates LLC	7349	417
18 Mile Emergency Services Association Inc	7389	1877
180 Connect Inc	4813	4
1-800 CONTACTS Inc	5995	4
1-800 FLOWERS Team Services Inc	5992	1
1-800-Flowerscom Inc	5992	3
1800mattresscom	6794	50
180s LLC	2389	20
1992 International Ltd	7381	207
1-Day Paint and Body Centers Inc	7532	5
1mage Software Inc	7372	2295
1N Bank	6712	250
1st Call Electronics Inc	5065	866
1ST Century Bancshares Inc	6021	228
1st Colonial Bancorp Inc	6021	238
1st Colonial National Bank	6021	334
1st Constitution Bancorp	6035	101
1st Electric Inc	1731	203
1st Express Inc	4213	1679
1st Farm Credit Services ACA	6159	44
1st Federal Federal Credit Union	6062	95
1st Franklin Financial Corp	6141	43
1st Patriots Federal Credit Union	6061	106
1st Rate Fixtures	5932	15
1st Run Computer Services	3695	64
1st Source Bank	6022	68
1st Source Corp	6022	44
1st Street Graphics Inc	2752	1010
1SYNC Inc	7372	2024
2 Places at 1 Time Inc	7389	161
20/20 Financial Consulting Inc	8748	206
20/20 Window Care Inc	7349	496
200 Park Inc	3585	212
2020 Exhibits Inc	7319	101
2020 Properties LLC	6531	19
20-20 Technologies	7372	3335
20-20 Technologies Commercial Corp	7389	1301
21st Amendment Inc	5921	2
21st Century Casualty Co	6331	21
21st Century Christian Inc	5192	34
21st Century Communications Of Mi-damerican Inc	5065	710
21st Century Computer Inc	5045	1029
21st Century Computer Systems	7373	1026
21st Century Film Company LLC	5043	42
21st Century Group LLC	6799	183

Company Name	SIC	Rank
21st Century Holding Co	6719	94
21st Century Insurance Co	6331	139
21st Century Plastics Corp	3089	774
21st Century Software Inc	7371	1235
21st Century Systems Inc	7371	83
21st Century Tile Inc	5032	85
22 Squared	7311	123
220 Laboratories Inc	2844	72
234 Culpepper Inc	5013	224
24/7 Customer Inc	7379	23
24/7 Real Media Inc	7379	64
24 Hour Co	7336	226
24 Hour Fitness Worldwide Inc	7997	1
24Holdings Inc	7374	422
2828 Clinton Inc	3532	54
2ab Nc	7372	4129
2INTERACTIVE LLC	4813	577
2ls Inc	3449	15
2m Associates Inc	7371	854
2-M Manufacturing Co	3599	1464
2m Oilfield Group Inc	3599	834
2M Technologies Inc	7373	569
2nd Avenue Design	3645	22
2nd Chance Credit Solutions Inc	7389	1910
2nd Sight Software Inc	7372	1873
2nd Swing Inc	5091	30
2Wire Inc	3577	83
0 D Cam Ino	3089	1601
3 Day Blinds Inc	5719	18
3 G Electric Inc	1731	2353
3 Point Partners	8743	274
3 Rivers D B S Inc	4841	141
3 Rivers Telephone Cooperative Inc	4813	247
3 S Industries	5999	254
3 Sixty Manufacturing	3678	74
3 Y Power Technology Inc	3679	186
30 Minute Photo Etc	7384	21
300 Below Inc	3398	25
300 North Capital LLC	6282	329
31 Inc	3011	19
32 Ford Mercury Inc	5511	149
321 Plumbing Inc	1711	235
3300 South Associates LLC	2064	129
342 Media	7379	853
345 Franklin LLC	6513	6
360 Services International	3699	149
360 Systems	3651	183
360 Vantage LLC	5045	921
360i LLC	7389	489
360trainingcom	7389	423
38 Caliber	7372	3763
38 Studios LLC	2741	36
3a Composites USA Inc	3334	2
3b Media Inc	7389	1628
3C Software Inc	7372	3131
3CI Complete Compliance Corp	4953	129
3Cinteractive LLC	7379	190
3d Exhibits Inc	7389	941
3d Farms and Machine LLC	3625	403
3d Incorporated Of Federal Way	7371	1773
3D Instruments LLC	5084	66
3D Joe Corp	7319	143
3d Medical Staffing LLC	7363	370
3D Nature LLC	7372	2838
3d Plus USA Inc	3823	460
3-D Polymers	3069	279
3D Research Corp	8711	497
3D Systems Corp	7372	221
3-D Technical Services Inc	7389	2009
3-Day Envelopes Inc	2752	1473
3DIcon Corp	3669	318
3D-International Inc	8711	137
3DM Inc	8731	302
3DT LLC	3559	412
3DTV Corp	3577	541
3E Co	7372	1077
3e Technologies International Inc	5045	115
3f Utility Construction Inc	1623	779
3form Inc	2899	32

Company Name	SIC	Rank
3-i Infotech Inc	7371	115
3i People Inc	7379	525
3-J Fuels Inc	4213	991
3k Associates Inc	7372	4781
3k Computers LLC	3575	27
3K Technologies LLC	7371	866
3KB Transportation Inc	4213	1169
3m Automotive Woodville	3089	1387
3M Cogent Inc	3695	10
3M Co	2672	1
3M Health Information Systems	7372	29
3M Label Materials	2671	18
3M Occupational Health and Safety Products	3842	37
3M Pacific Security Systems Inc	1731	2568
3M Precision Optics Inc	3827	3
3M Purification Inc	3569	10
3M Scientific Anglers	3949	149
3M Touch Systems	3577	124
3M Visual Systems Div	3861	24
3PAR Inc	3572	16
3PD Inc	4213	433
3PL Software Inc	7372	2933
3psc LLC	7389	1480
3R Inc	4213	1658
3R of Charleston Inc	4213	2946
3rd Angle Technologies Inc	7371	1391
3rd Coast Technologies LLC	7371	1719
3rd Wave Solutions Inc	5065	209
3s Group Inc	3695	143
3s Inc	5099	72
3s Realserv	7371	740
3sg Inc	5094	66
3SI Security Systems Inc	3669	202
3tier Environmental Forecast Group Inc	7371	629
3v Inc	2869	46
3W Internet Corp	6282	602
4 Consulting Inc	7371	757
4 C's Council	8351	24
4 D Printing Inc	2752	576
4 Guys Web Design Group	7336	98
4 Peaks Satellite And Sound Inc	4841	127
401k Datawarehouse LLC	4813	724
4086 Advisors Inc	6282	90
424 Holdings LLC	2752	1244
451 Group	7373	223
454 Life Sciences	8731	174
49er Federal Credit Union	6061	123
4C Controls Inc	3812	225
4c International LLC	7379	869
4-D Engineering Inc	3599	2104
4D Inc	7372	3075
4d Internet Solutions Inc	7379	1302
4-D Neuroimaging	3841	326
4D Vision LLC	7372	2112
4Dvision	7373	1130
4Front Engineered Solutions Inc	3599	2
4Kids Entertainment Inc	6794	73
4Life Research LC	5963	12
4-M Industries Inc	3544	240
4M Systems Inc	3669	116
4medica Inc	4813	275
4mf LLC	7371	1498
4R Systems	7375	186
4skware Technologies Inc	7372	4082
4-Star Bulk Transport Inc	4213	1355
4-Star Trailers Inc	3715	23
5 B's Inc	2339	33
5 Day Business Forms Manufacturing Inc	2752	389
5 Metacom	7311	508
5 Seasons Brewing LLC	2082	65
5 Star Image Inc	7384	25
501 Post Inc	7819	66
51 Entertainment Group LLC	2741	156
511 Inc	5699	10
5280 Solutions	7371	1043
5Linx Enterprises Inc	5963	17
600 Racing Inc	7948	28

Company Name	SIC	Rank
615 Productions Inc	7812	165
7/21 Quality Security Solutions Inc	7381	217
7 Hills Transport Inc	4213	1349
7 West Secretarial/Answering Service Inc	7389	1513
724 Inc	7379	1603
76 Lubricants Co	2992	38
77 Deerhurst Corp	7349	133
7-Eleven Inc	5499	1
7-Sigma Inc	3069	109
7th Sense Inc	5199	112
80/20 Inc	3354	48
800 Call-Kc Inc	7389	1105
800-JR Cigar Inc	5194	5
80-20 Software Inc	7371	897
814 Americas Inc	2013	179
84 Lumber Co	5211	6
88 Trading Corp	7389	1608
888 Digital Inc	5065	344
8x8 Inc	4813	123
911 VehicleCom Inc	1731	2123
926 Partners Inc	2064	101
9278 Communications Inc	4813	58
944 Media LLC	2711	322
949 Web Presence Management	7311	290
99 Cents Only Stores	5331	12
radicalmedia Inc	7812	72
A 1 Packaging Products Inc	5162	65
A 1 Quality Electric Inc	1731	1910
A 1 Tremendous Temporaries LLC	7361	222
A 2 Z Computers Inc	5045	694
A A Jansson Inc	5084	914
A All Pro Roofing Inc	5033	62
A American High Tech Transcription And Reporting Inc	7338	53
A Anastasio and Sons Trucking Co	4213	262
A and A Boltless Rack and Shelving	5084	910
A and A Electric Inc	1731	1973
A and A Electronics Assembly Inc	3672	158
A and A Engineering	3823	431
A and A Facility Services Inc	7349	361
A and A Fire and Security Inc	5063	459
A and A Global Industries	3581	5
A and A Industries Inc	3462	61
A and A Jewelry Supply	5999	46
A and A Machine and Development Company Inc	3451	119
A and A Machine And Welding LLC	3599	2039
A and A Machine Company Inc	3599	1300
A and A Magnetics Inc	3542	104
A and A Manufacturing Company Inc	3499	28
A and A Mechanical Inc	5074	90
A and A Printing Inc	2752	1290
A and A Resources Inc	8741	295
A and A Security Service Inc	7381	130
A and A Tank Truck Co	4213	1022
A and A Telecom Group Inc	5065	642
A and A Transfer and Storage Inc	4213	1800
A and A Trucking Inc	4213	2356
A and B Audio Video Sales Corp	5064	116
A and B Auto Body Supply Inc	5013	322
A and B Auto Electric Inc	5013	378
A and B Communication Inc	5999	209
A and B Construction Corp	1731	2511
A and B Construction Development Inc	1521	139
A and B Electric Company Inc	1731	506
A and B Electric Inc	1731	2211
A and B Freight Line Inc	4213	1763
A and B Label and Printing Inc	2759	385
A and B Leasing Inc	4213	2152
A and B Machine Inc	3545	256
A and B Manufacturing Company Inc	3599	950
A and B Packing Equipment Inc	5083	98
A and B Precision Metals Inc	3444	169
A and B Process Systems Corp	1799	14
A and B Tube Benders Inc	3429	136
A and C Auto Parts and Wrecking Company Inc	5093	202
A and C Communications Corp	1623	471
A And C Electronics	3672	227
A and C Maintenance	7349	524
A and C Metals-Sawing Inc	5051	329
A and C Mold Company Inc	3544	572
A and C Welding Inc	3444	239
A and D Home Health Solutions	8082	90
A and D Plastics Inc	3544	821
A and D Precision Machining Inc	3599	726
A and D Precision Manufacturing Inc	3599	1286
A and E Electrical Services And Parts Inc	5064	170
A and E Grinding Inc	3599	453
A and E Inc	3423	26
A and E International Inc	5063	727
A and E Leasing and Construction	1623	826
A and E Machine Shop Inc	3599	631
A and E Mailers Inc	7331	169
A and E Manufacturing Company Inc	3444	107
A and E Plastics Inc	3089	1441
A and E Printers And Mailers Inc	2752	982
A and E Products Group LP	3089	66
A and E Stores Inc	5632	8
A and F Electric Company Inc	1731	418
A and F Machine Products Co	3561	167
A and G Coal Corp	1221	34

Company Name	SIC	Rank
A and G Machine Inc	3429	61
A and G Manufacturing Company Inc	3599	454
A and G Trucking Inc	4213	588
A and H Electrical Services Inc	1731	1154
A and H Inc	4213	1594
A and H Industries Inc	3545	206
A and H Lithoprint Inc	2752	1298
A and H Sportswear Company Inc	2339	22
A and H Tool Engineering Corp	3541	213
A and I Security Inc	7381	113
A and J Automation Inc	3569	258
A and J Electric Company Inc	1731	894
A and J Industries LLC	3089	1799
A and J Precision Sheetmetal Inc	3599	1718
A and J Printing Inc	2752	918
A and J Washroom Accessories Inc	3261	5
A and Jay Automotive Warehouse Inc	5013	351
A and K Development Co	3556	90
A and K Railroad Materials Inc	5051	87
A and K Transport Company Inc	4213	2725
A and L Cable Service Inc	4841	101
A and L Distributing Co	5064	79
A and L Laboratories Inc	2842	99
A and L Litho Inc	2752	1304
A and L Potato Co	5148	82
A and L Sales Inc	5087	93
A and L Shielding Inc	3842	313
A and L Southern Agricultural Labs Inc	8734	154
A and M Cartage of Tinley Park	4213	1893
A and M Cheese Co	2022	48
A and M Data Systems Inc	7371	1800
A and M Donuts Inc	5461	21
A and M Electrical Contractors Inc	1731	1125
A and M Electronics Inc	3672	231
A and M Electronics Supply Inc	5065	771
A and M Engineering Plastics Inc	3089	1826
A and M Farm Center Inc	5083	129
A and M Green Power Group LC	8011	29
A and M Industries Inc	3599	706
A and M Tool and Die Company Inc	3544	252
A and M Tool C Inc	3469	301
A and M Tool Molding Division Inc	3089	1295
A and M Transport Inc	4213	962
A and M Truck Equipment And Fabrication	5046	296
A and N Corp	3494	52
A and N Electric Coop	4911	364
A and O Electric Inc	1731	2076
A and O Inc	7349	387
A and O Mold And Eng Inc	3544	425
A and P Enterprises Inc	5045	870
A and P Properties Ltd	6519	1
A and P Recycling Inc	5093	196
A and P Tool Inc	3541	161
A and R Construction Inc	1541	301
A and R Edelman	8743	50
A and R Engineering Company Inc	3599	903
A and R Fixit Inc	7382	98
A and R Security Services Inc	7382	9
A and R Transport	4213	2993
A and R Transport Inc	4213	206
A and S Building Systems LP	3448	16
A and S Electric Supply Inc	5063	599
A and S Electronics Inc	5045	957
A and S Fabricating Co	3449	37
A and S Mold and Die Corp	3089	645
A and S Of Modesto Inc	5093	104
A and S Pharmaceutical Corp	2834	346
A and S Supply Company Inc	5074	143
A and T Systems Inc	7372	718
A and V Company Of The Triad	7812	131
A and W Bottling Company Inc	2086	130
A and W Contractors Inc	1623	216
A and W Electric Of Hollywood Inc	1731	1316
A and W Oil Company Inc	5171	77
A and W Products Company Inc	2678	13
A and W Restaurants Inc	5812	255
A Angonoa Inc	2051	41
A Arnold and Sons Transfer and Storage Company Inc	4789	18
A B C Electric Company Inc	1731	607
A B Carter Inc	3552	8
A B Property Services Inc	5032	33
A Bar Code Business Inc	2679	82
A Bee C Service Inc	7349	199
A Better Industrial Temporary Inc	7363	213
A Better Server	7379	1614
A Bit Better Corp	7372	4652
A Boesch Corporation Electric	1731	1373
A Boy Electric Dolan Design	3645	59
A Brown-Olmstead Associates Inc	8743	236
A Business Computer Consulting Firm	7371	1841
A C Company Of South Lousiana Inc	7359	225
A C Furniture Company Inc	2521	16
A C Houston Lumber Co	2439	6
A C Miller Concrete Products Inc	3272	75
A California Labchoice Inc	5049	118
A Call Nurse	7389	1169
A Camacho Inc	5149	110
A Caring Experience Nursing Services Inc	7361	202
A/Coe Electric Corp	1731	944
A Colarusso And Son Inc	2951	32
A Custom Brokerage Inc	7389	447

Company Name	SIC	Rank
A D Computer Corp	8721	313
A D Electric Inc	1731	1155
A D M Corp	2393	10
A Daigger and Company Inc	5169	57
A Dan America Inc	5045	575
A Diamond Production Inc	5712	90
A Dualdraw LLC	8748	436
A Duda and Sons Inc	0161	3
A/E Ellerbe Becket Co	8712	18
A E Randles Company Inc	3565	168
A E Shull and Co	1623	511
A Eicoff and Co	7311	138
A Engineering and Fabrication Inc	3441	281
A Epstein and Sons International Inc	8711	176
A F and G Company Inc	3544	565
A F Industries Inc	1389	58
A F Lorts Company Inc	2511	43
A Federal Credit Union	6061	39
A Finkl and Sons Co	3544	1
A Forbes Company Inc	2752	1681
A Full Life Agency Inc	8049	5
A G Miller Company Inc	3444	204
A G Systems LLC	5084	805
A/G Technologies Inc	4789	9
A George Diack Inc	2542	15
A Give-Em Brake Safety Inc	7359	248
A H Electrical Service Inc	1731	2354
A Harold and Associates LLC	8748	326
A' Homestead Shoppe Inc	3645	61
A I E Company Inc	5084	468
A J Funk and Co	2842	157
A J Inc	7359	193
A J Manufacturing Inc	3442	79
A J R Industries Inc	3544	181
A J Rose ManufacturingCo	3465	26
A J Weller Corp	3441	212
A Jaffe Inc	3911	28
A J's Power Source Inc	5063	881
A/K/A Services Inc	1623	435
A Klein and Company Inc	2652	12
A L Eastmond and Sons Inc	3443	129
A L Lee Corp	3532	31
A L Pickens Company Inc	5063	911
A L Schutzman Company Inc	2068	20
A La Cart Inc	3589	158
A La Mode Inc	7372	1003
A Lakhany International Inc	2211	24
A Lindberg and Sons Inc	1442	34
A Liss and Company Inc	5084	700
A Loss Prevention System By Sonitrol	5063	444
A M Mailing Services Inc	7331	145
A M Ortega Construction Inc	1731	183
A M Todd Co	2087	18
A Marinelli And Sons Inc	5032	90
A Micro Inc	7372	4930
A Mm Company Holdings LLC	7389	1312
A Moresi Foundry Inc	3322	3
A Murphy Inc	1731	495
A One Cleaning Services Inc	7349	326
A Pest Control Inc	7342	90
A Pick Time Inc	3823	463
A Plus International Inc	5047	86
A Plus Letter Service Inc	7331	23
A Plus Medical and Mobility	5047	87
A Pomerantz and Co	5021	80
A Prompt Corp	5045	850
A Qc Group Corp	3861	56
A R Wilfley and Sons Inc	3561	87
A Randy's Electric Inc	1731	486
A Ray Lite Inc	5063	1049
A Rifkin Co	2393	15
A Santini Storage Company Inc	4213	1918
A Schonbek and Company Inc	3645	17
A Schulman Inc	3087	1
a/Soft Development Inc	7372	4653
A Sort Inc	7331	152
A Spacios Design Group Inc	7389	1488
A Special Electric Service And Supply Co	5063	829
A Taste of New York	7812	101
A Teichert and Son Inc	3273	16
A Terrycable California Corp	3714	415
A to A Studio Services Inc	7379	746
A To Z Couriers Inc	7389	1711
A To Z Drying	2879	47
A To Z Kosher Meat Products Company Inc	2011	143
A To Z Looseleaf Inc	2782	61
A To Z Machine Company Inc	3599	368
A To Z Machining Service LLC	3599	1931
A To Z Offset Printing and Publishing Inc	2752	1391
A To Z Portion Control Meats Inc	5147	96
A Trace Matic Corp	3599	231
A Tube Bending Corp	5051	371
A Usdf California Corp	2261	18
A W Chesterton Co	3053	8
A Wealthy Place Arts and Theater Company Inc	3648	87
A Williams Trucking and Trenching Inc	1794	22
A/Z Corp	1731	38
A Zahner Co	3444	7
A Zerega's Sons Inc	2098	5
A Zimmer Ltd	2711	448

Company Name	SIC	Rank
A-1 Air Compressor Corp	5084	568
A-1 Babbitt Company Inc	5085	459
A-1 Bail Bonds Inc	7389	1878
A-1 Coast Rentals Inc	7359	124
A-1 Components Inc	3585	40
A1 Contract Cleaning Inc	7349	512
A1 Datacom Supply Co	5045	475
A-1 Delivery Company Inc	4212	59
A-1 Digital Imaging	2796	27
A-1 Eastern-Home-Made Pickle Company Inc	2035	49
A-1 Electric Of Lake City Inc	1731	1584
A-1 Electric Service Inc	1731	1683
A-1 Electrical Contractors Inc	1731	1406
A-1 Excavating Inc	1623	112
A-1 Express Delivery Service Inc	4215	19
A-1 Freeman	4213	1828
A-1 Jay's Machining Inc	3599	403
A-1 Machine Inc	3599	1973
A-1 Machining Co	3724	62
A-1 Mechanical Lansing Inc	1731	449
A-1 Perfection Of Northwest Illinois Inc	4953	140
A-1 Pioneer Moving and Storage	4213	2491
A-1 Printing Service Inc	2752	1291
A-1 Production Inc	3599	1297
A1 Protective Services Inc	7381	170
A1 Radiator Repair Inc	5013	330
A-1 Scale Service	5046	48
A-1 Scale Service Inc	5046	259
A-1 Shower Door Co	3231	70
A1 Stop Non-Stop Scuba Training	5091	111
A1 Technologies Inc	3599	785
A-1 Technology Inc	7372	1617
A-1 Wholesale Sandwich Co	2099	225
A-1 Wire Tech Inc	3357	45
A10 Clinical Solutions Inc	8742	287
A10 Networks Inc	7373	112
A123 Systems Inc	3691	8
A2 Technologies LLC	3826	72
a2b Tracking Solutions	7372	4399
A2b Tracking Solutions Inc	5045	679
a2i Communications	4899	228
A2Z Cables Inc	5734	66
A2z Computers Inc	3571	243
A2z Global LLC	7389	1201
A-2-Z Solutions Inc	5734	238
A2zunique Inc	7379	1571
A3 It Solutions LLC	7374	253
A3 Technology Inc	7379	709
A5com LLC	4813	693
Aa/Acme Locksmiths Inc	1731	333
AA Adjustment Company Inc	6411	286
AA Anderson and Company Inc	5084	297
A-A Blueprint Company Inc	2791	20
Aa Circuit Tech Inc	3672	355
AA Computech Inc	7378	25
Aa Electric Ltd	1731	1637
AA Electric SE Inc	5063	243
AA Macpherson Company Inc	5063	502
Aa One Litho Inc	2752	1126
AA Precisioneering Inc	3544	587
AA Samuels Sheet Metal Company Inc	1711	225
Aa Southern Pest Control Inc	7342	30
Aa Teleservices LLC	7389	1035
AAA Aircraft Supply LLC	3452	70
Aaa Architectural	3299	13
AAA Auto Club South	6331	323
Aaa Bail Bonding Company Inc	7389	2402
Aaa Building Services Corp	7349	374
AAA Cooper Transportation	4213	61
AAA Digital Imaging Inc	2752	379
AAA Employment Agency Inc	7361	255
Aaa Exterminating Inc	7342	70
AAA Financial Inc	6162	131
Aaa Industries Inc	3451	112
Aaa Key-Lock Company Inc	5099	66
AAA Mine Service Inc	3599	540
AAA Pool Services Inc	1799	122
Aaa Printing and Graphics Inc	2759	536
Aaa Quality Maintenace Corp	7349	426
AAA Restaurant Equipment and Supplies	5046	322
Aaa Restaurant Fire Control Inc	7389	1008
Aaa Sales and Engineering Inc	3599	71
Aaa Storage	7389	2266
Aaa Technology And Specialties Company Inc	3498	83
AAA Transfer Inc	4213	1326
AAA Travel (Cincinnati Ohio)	4724	16
AAAdvantage Auto Transport	4213	2080
Aabbill Adhesives Inc	2891	21
A-Able Inc	7342	12
AAC Associates Inc	7372	230
AAC Enterprises LLC	5531	63
AAC Group Holding Corp	3911	7
AACOA Inc	3471	13
Aacom Inc	1731	2529
Aadast Co	4813	690
Aae Systems Inc	7373	829
AAEON Technology Inc	3571	23
Aaep Inc	7382	134
Aafp Systems Inc	1731	1357
AAI Corp	3679	66
AAI International	8731	433

Company Name	SIC	Rank
Aaim Controls Inc	3625	329
AAIPharma Services Corp	8731	42
Aakron Rule Corp	2499	17
Aaladin Industries Inc	3589	110
Aalstec Data Corp	7373	576
Aamco Transmissions Inc	5013	54
Aamonte Inc	7374	164
AAMP of America	3679	74
AAM-RO Corp	3599	2032
AandD Technology Inc	3825	64
AandE Television Networks	4833	32
AAON Coil Products Inc	3498	15
AAON Inc	3585	27
Aap International Inc	5085	471
AAP St Marys Corp	5013	21
Aapco Automotive Co	5013	346
Aaper Alcohol And Chemical Co	2869	91
Aa-Plus Imaging Systems Inc	7629	44
AAR Airframe and Accessories Group Inc	4581	15
AAR Corp	3721	9
AAR Defense Systems	3812	7
AAR Manufacturing Inc	3728	8
Aarco Equipment Inc	4213	2700
Aardvark Record Mastering	3695	115
Aardvark Software Inc	7372	2701
Aargon Agency Inc	7323	19
Aargus Plastics Inc	2673	21
Aarhus Karlshamn USA Inc	2079	7
Aaron And Company Inc	5074	41
Aaron Cohen Associates Ltd	8712	321
Aaron Corp	2339	36
Aaron Engineered Process Equipment Inc	3531	196
Aaron Equipment Company Inc	5084	251
Aaron Inc	3465	71
Aaron Industries Inc	2834	202
Aaron Pallet Corp	7389	1370
Aaron Thomas Company Inc	7389	664
Aaron Tool Inc	3599	2321
Aaron's Automotive Products Inc	7699	12
Aaron's Inc	5712	1
Aaron's Rental Purchase	7359	213
Aaron's Rental Purchase Div	7359	22
Aarubco Rubber Company Inc	3052	29
Aas Holding Co	5147	12
Aaseby Industrial Machining Inc	3599	1291
Aasent Mortgage Corp	6162	137
Aastra USA Inc	3661	29
Aastrom Biosciences Inc	8731	420
Aatfab Corp	5065	872
Aatrix Software Inc	7372	1281
Aatronics Ino	1731	782
Aavolyn Corp	3563	46
Aayco Pallet Systems LLC	5031	421
AB and B Auto Parts Inc	5015	24
A-B and C Enterprises Inc	2752	1634
AB and I	3321	22
AB and T Financial Corp	6712	636
AB Athens Inc	7334	88
AB Computer LLC	5734	303
Ab Dan Felton Broker Notary	7389	2134
AB Electrical Wires Inc	3641	33
Ab Electronics Inc	3672	250
AB Heller Inc	3599	205
A-B International Truck Inc	5012	178
AB Mclauchlan Company Inc	3599	181
AB Munroe Dairy Inc	2026	72
Ab Plastics Inc	3089	765
AB Star Group	7379	909
ABA Packaging Corp	5085	156
ABACAB Software Inc	7372	1558
Abacad Inc	5045	833
Abacus 21 Inc	7371	1176
Abacus 24-7 LLC	5734	165
Abacus America Inc	7379	70
Abacus Automation Inc	3549	71
Abacus Business Systems Inc	7372	3851
Abacus Data Systems	7372	2388
Abacus Data Systems Inc	7372	3475
Abacus FSB	6035	96
Abacus Inc	7374	356
Abacus Industries Inc	5065	350
Abacus Software Inc	2731	121
Abacus Solutions Group LLC	7379	570
Abacus Technology Corp	8711	68
Abacus Travel Inc	4724	7
Abacuss Software Technologies LLC	7379	827
ABA-PGT Inc	3089	169
Abaris Inc	7371	349
Abarta Inc	2086	21
Abas - USA Inc	7379	1127
Abate Associates Engineers and Surveyors PC	8711	403
Abatix Corp	5084	82
Abatron Inc	2821	195
Abaxis Inc	3829	20
Ahazias Inc	3911	44
ABB Automation Analytical Div	3826	20
ABB Energy Ventures	4911	479
ABB Flexible Automation Inc	3569	1
ABB Incorporated Automation Technologies Div	3444	64
ABB Inc Process Analytics Div	3826	19

Company Name	SIC	Rank
ABB Incorporated Small Power Transformers	3612	16
ABB Industrial Systems Inc	3829	14
ABB Instrumentation	3823	173
ABB Power T and D Company Inc	3613	1
Abba Optical Inc	3851	109
Abbacus Injection Molding Inc	3089	1565
ABBASOFT Technologies Inc	7372	3573
Abbett Electric Corp	1731	299
Abbey Carpet Co	6794	76
Abbey Color Inc	2865	19
Abbey Co	6531	117
Abbey Conception	2752	382
Abbey Mecca and Company Inc	7311	808
Abbey Party Rents Of San Diego And Riverside Counties Inc	7359	146
Abbott Ambulance Inc	4119	8
Abbott and Associates Professional Placement Inc	7361	261
Abbott Ball Company Inc	3399	6
Abbott Capital Management Inc	6282	332
Abbott Diabetes Care	3841	1
Abbott Enterprises Inc	3824	45
Abbott Furnace Co	3625	92
Abbott Gage Inc	5049	153
Abbott Industries Inc	3496	8
Abbott Industries Inc (Paterson New Jersey)	3085	33
Abbott Laboratories	2834	5
Abbott Laboratories Diagnostic Div	3826	10
Abbott Laboratories Ross Products Div	2834	23
Abbott Molecular	8733	9
Abbott Plastics and Supply Co	3089	1098
Abbott Printing Co	2752	560
Abbott Products Inc	3451	146
Abbott Stringham and Lynch Accountancy Corp	8721	375
Abbott SYSCO Transportation	4213	1268
Abbott Systems Inc	7372	4582
Abbott Technologies Inc	3677	42
Abbott Tool And Die Inc	3544	903
Abbott Tool Inc	3469	300
Abbott's Candy And Gifts Inc	2064	134
Abbott's Custom Printing	7334	53
Abbott's Premium Ice Cream Inc	5143	38
Abbottstown Industries Inc	3544	429
Abby Bindery Company Inc	2789	131
Abby Inc	7372	4268
Abbyland Foods Inc	2013	29
Abbyson Corp	2273	17
ABBYY USA Software House Inc	7372	1559
ABC Appliance Inc	5731	6
Abc Boring Company Inc	3541	126
Abc Building Service Corp	7349	355
ABC Cable and International Broadcast Group	4841	31
ABC Carpet Company Inc	5713	2
Abc Communications Corp	1731	968
ABC Compounding Company Inc	2841	11
ABC Control Systems Inc	3669	267
Abc Corp	2841	39
Abc Die Cutting And Embossing Inc	3544	720
Abc Electric Service Inc	1731	854
ABC Enterprise Systems Inc	5045	944
ABC Fabricators Inc	3672	402
ABC Family Worldwide Inc	7812	15
ABC Fine Wine and Spirits	5921	1
ABC Fry-Wagner Inc	4213	1421
ABC Global Rigging	4212	9
ABC Imaging LLC	2752	55
Abc Imaging Of Washington Inc	2759	51
ABC Laboratories Inc	8734	69
Abc Legal Messengers	7389	2115
ABC Metals Inc	5051	302
Abc Minneapolis LLC	5012	100
Abc Orthotics and Prosthetics Inc	5999	310
ABC Phones of North Carolina Inc	4812	13
Abc Photo And Imaging Services Inc	7384	47
Abc Printing Inc	2752	1333
Abc Research Corp	8734	105
Abc Restaurant Supplies and Equipment Inc	5046	307
Abc Sanitation and Septic Inc	7359	240
Abc School Equipment Inc	5049	38
ABC School Supply Inc	5943	26
Abc Sign Products Inc	5051	400
ABC Sports Inc	7922	17
Abc Technical Solutions Inc	5045	987
ABC Transportation Inc	4213	1170
ABC Unified School District	8211	35
ABC Window Co	3442	33
ABC Worldwide Chauffeured Transportation	4119	18
ABC-Clio Inc	2731	202
ABCD Transportation Company Inc	4213	2812
Abco Automation Inc	3569	85
Abco Builders Inc	1542	380
Abco Corp	5046	160
Abco Fire Protection Inc	5099	76
Abco Laboratories Inc	2099	155
ABCO Maintenance Inc	7349	246
Abco Manufacturing Inc	2842	124
ABCO Products Inc	5087	2
ABCO Refrigeration Supply Corp	5078	6

Company Name	SIC	Rank
Abco Tool and Die Inc	3544	622
Abdallah Inc	5145	11
Abdite Industries Inc	3724	74
Abdon Callais Offshore LLC	4499	3
Abe Utilities Inc	1623	521
Abec Inc	3556	26
Abeco Die Casting Inc	3363	33
Abekas Inc (Menlo Park California)	3651	161
Abel Automatics Inc	3451	96
Abel Enterprises Inc	7353	31
Abel Holdings Inc	3451	62
Abela Pharmaceuticals Inc	2834	384
Abelconn LLC	3678	18
Abell Corp	5191	35
Abel's Quik Shops	5411	246
Abelson Communications Inc	7371	1678
Abelson Group Inc	8748	260
Abel-Womack Integrated Handling Solutions	5084	106
Abercrombie and Fitch Co	5651	6
Aberdeen Asia Pacific Income Fund Inc	6726	9
Aberdeen Australia Equity Fund Inc	6726	63
Aberdeen Janitorial Service Inc	5087	163
Aberdeen LLC	5045	236
Aberdeen Machine Tool Inc	3542	75
Abernathy Co	2841	7
Abernathy-Thomas Engineering Co	5085	332
Abe's Auto Recyclers Inc	5015	21
Abex Display Systems Inc	2653	82
ABF Freight System Inc	4213	25
Abf Health Services Inc	7352	48
Abf Packing Inc	0751	10
Abg Acquisition Corp	2752	136
ABG Capital Inc	7375	127
Abi	3571	211
ABI Inc	8742	447
Abi International Group Corp	5045	678
Abi Packaging Inc	3086	162
Abide International Inc	8741	231
Abigail H Hess Interiors Inc	7389	1739
Abigail Kirsch at Tappan Hill Inc	5812	266
Abigal Press Inc	2759	111
Abilene Boot Company Inc	3144	7
Abilene Machine Inc	5083	51
Abilene Motor Express	4213	813
Abilene News Co	2711	222
Abilene Printing and Stationery Company Inc	5021	178
Abilities Services Inc	8331	179
Abilities Unlimited Of Hot Springs Arkansas Inc	8331	5
Ability Building Center	8331	71
Ability Counts Inc	8331	108
Ability Engineering Technology Inc	3441	224
Ability Metal Co	3812	135
Ability Plastics Inc	5162	52
Ability Systems Corp	7372	4654
Abimex LLC	3089	1163
Abington Group Inc	1799	20
Abington Pharmacy Inc	5912	42
Abington Saving Bank (Jenkintown Pennsylvania)	6036	44
Abisco Products Co	2782	60
ABIT Computer Corp USA	3672	41
Abita Springs Water Company Inc	2086	59
ABItalia Inc	3089	1032
AbitibiBowater Newsprint	2621	12
Abitibi-Consolidated Corp	2621	26
ABJ Enterprises Inc	5159	12
ABJ Fire Protection Co	7389	700
Abkco	3695	24
Abkco Music and Records Inc	3652	29
Abke Publishing and Graphic Services Inc	7379	995
Abke Trucking Inc	4213	2927
Abl Lights Inc	3648	64
Able 2 Products Company Inc	3648	29
Able Builders Equipment	3559	75
Able Cable Inc	7379	163
Able Coil And Electronics Co	3677	66
Able Energy Inc	5983	5
Able Exterminators Inc	7342	29
Able Fab Co	3443	201
Able Inc	8361	154
Able Industrial Products Inc	5085	258
Able Laboratories Inc	8731	64
Able Manufacturing LLC	3713	21
Able Microsystems Corp	7373	302
Able Software Corp	7372	2113
Able Software Inc	7372	891
Able Steel Equipment Company Inc	2542	75
Able Tool Company Inc	3599	1238
Able Tool Corp	3599	1415
Able Torco Pest Control	7342	57
Able-Age Inc	3679	259
Ablecomm Inc	1731	1713
AbleCommerce	8748	304
Ablenet Inc	5961	175
Ablest Inc	7361	35
ABM Engineering Services	8744	11
Abm Equipment and Supply LLC	5013	155
ABM Industries Inc	7349	3
Abm International Inc	3552	20
ABM Janitorial Services	7349	11
Abm Test Inc	8711	622
ABN AMRO Inc	6153	19
ABN Technologies LLC	7379	1337
Abner Herrman and Brock Inc	6282	438
Abnote USA Inc	3081	23
ABODA Inc	7299	31
Abode Building Materials Co	5031	388
ABOL Software Inc	7372	2441
About Learning Inc	7372	897
About Time Machining Inc	3599	1396
Aboutcom Inc	7375	46
Aboutgolf Ltd	3577	328
Above Board Electronics Inc	5065	290
Above Telecommunications Inc	4813	222
AboveNet Inc	3357	10
Abovo Group Inc	8748	330
Abp Corp	5461	2
ABR Information Services Inc	6411	151
Abracadata Ltd	7372	4078
Abraham And Laura Lisner Home For Aged Women	8361	130
Abraham Technical Services Inc	5045	367
Abrahams Oriental Rugs	5023	95
Abram Cleason Company Inc	5032	159
Abrams Foster Nole and Williams PA	8721	361
Abrams Little-Gill Tishman and Witty PC	8721	410
Abrams Power Inc	1541	139
Abrams Productions Inc	8743	332
Abrams Properties Inc	6552	305
Abrasive Blast Systems Inc	3569	270
Abrasive Diamond Tool Company Inc	3545	342
Abrasive Tool Specialties	5084	643
Abrasive-Form Inc	3599	90
Abrasive-Tool Corp	5084	301
Abraxas Petroleum Corp	1311	128
Abraxis BioScience Inc	2834	77
Abrisa Industrial Glass Inc	3211	11
ABRY Partners LLC	6211	163
ABS Associates Inc	7371	704
ABS Computer Technologies Inc	3571	28
ABS Data Systems Inc	3571	233
ABS Fax Technologies Inc	4822	17
ABS Global Inc	0751	4
ABS Graphics Inc	2752	197
ABS Imaging Systems Inc	5046	137
ABS Med Inc	5047	229
ABS Software Inc	7372	3293
ABS Ventures	6799	279
Absec USA Inc	3577	275
Absecon Mills Inc	2211	26
Abselcom Inc	4813	643
Abso Inc	8748	274
Absoft Corp	7372	4195
Absolute Amusements	7999	109
ABSolute Businesss Software Inc	7373	1121
Absolute Custom Extrusions Inc	3082	30
Absolute Fire Protection Inc	1711	255
Absolute Investments Inc	3554	48
Absolute Maintenace Inc	7349	405
Absolute Music Inc	7389	1831
Absolute Print Graphics Inc	7389	2191
Absolute Process Instruments Inc	3679	479
Absolute Quality Manufacturing Inc	3089	1873
Absolute Resolutions Corp	7389	1515
Absolute Security And Technologies Inc	7382	148
Absolute Security Network Inc	7381	46
Absolute Software Company Inc	7372	4902
Absolute Technologies	7371	1812
Absolute Turnkey Services Inc	3672	237
Absolute Windows Inc	2431	132
Absorbent Ink	5092	38
Absorption Corp	2842	22
Abstract Janitorial Services Inc	7349	155
Abt Associates Inc	8748	29
Abtec Inc	3089	579
ABTRE Inc	3089	42
ABV Electronics Inc	3577	268
ABW Technologies Inc	3441	101
ABW Tulsa Inc	7389	1018
Ab-Wey Machine and Die Company Inc	3599	2473
ABX Logistics (USA) Inc	4731	45
Abyx Business Systems Inc	5065	761
AC and T Company Inc	5983	19
AC Atel Electronics Corp	5065	452
A-C Brake Co	5013	294
Ac Cetera Inc	3651	222
AC Electrical Contractor Inc	1731	2351
AC Gentrol Inc	3613	107
Ac Inc	3769	17
AC International Inc	3751	28
Ac Label LLC	2759	175
AC Leasing Co	4213	2040
AC Legg Inc	2099	145
AC Lister and Company Inc	5046	272
Ac Marketing Inc	5045	858
AC Moore Arts and Crafts Inc	5945	5
AC Moore Inc	5945	7
AC Printing	2759	66
Ac Systems Inc	5045	667
Ac Technology Corp	3566	11
AC Tool and Machine Company Inc	3599	1364
AC Trucking Inc	4213	2497
AC Widenhouse Inc	4213	2151
AC Wright Trucking Inc	4213	2411
ACA Industries Inc	7349	76
Acacia Holdings LLC	8742	529
Acacia Home and Garden Inc	5712	114
Acacia Media Technologies Corp	3663	81
Acacia Research Corp	6794	22
Academ Consulting Services	7389	2386
Academic Communication Associates Inc	2731	258
Academic Management Services Corp	6141	26
Academic Performance Institute Inc	7371	1444
Academic Press Inc	2731	38
Academic Software Inc	7372	2630
Academic Therapy Publications	2731	256
AcademixDirect Inc	7372	1751
Academy Acquisition Corp	3081	154
Academy Answering Service Inc	7389	1392
Academy Chicago Publishers	2731	310
Academy Communications Inc	4813	303
Academy Graphic Communication Inc	2752	1136
Academy Group	3679	43
Academy Ltd	5941	8
Academy Mortgage Corp	6163	21
Academy Productions Inc	7384	35
Academy Roofing and Sheet Metal Co	1761	19
Academy Sports Outdoors	5091	1
Academy Studios Inc	7389	927
Academy Systems Inc	7372	4447
Academy Tent And Canvas Inc	7359	73
Acadia Industries Inc	2393	17
Acadia Insurance Co	6411	19
Acadia Pharmaceuticals Inc	8731	105
Acadia Power Partners LLC	4911	177
Acadia Realty Trust	6798	112
Acadian Advertising Inc	7311	773
Acadian Asset Management LLC	6282	424
Acadian Bakery Inc	2051	303
Acadian Fine Foods LLC	3556	113
Acadiana Fisherman's Company Op	5146	49
Acadiana Rubber and Gasket Co	5085	303
AcAe	7372	443
Acai Associates Inc	8712	237
Acal Universal Grinding Co	3599	2146
Acamard Technologies Inc	5065	614
Acanthus Architects	8712	331
ACC Construction Company Inc	1541	251
ACC Corp	4813	47
ACC Inc	5045	775
Acc Technical Services Inc	8742	671
Accede Mold and Tool Company Inc	3544	179
Accel Management Company Inc	6799	283
Accela	4213	1748
Accela Inc	7372	480
Accelebrate Inc	8299	79
Accelera Romar Corp	7372	1792
Accelera Solutions Inc	7376	20
Accelerate Software Inc	7372	2934
Accelerated Care Plus Inc	3845	84
Accelerated Claims Processing Inc	7374	48
Accelerated Computer Technologies	7371	1422
Accelerated Computer Technologies Inc	7372	4196
Accelerated Courier Inc	4213	1683
Accelerated Data Systems Inc	5045	878
Accelerated Genetics	5191	25
Accelerated Moving and Storage Inc	4214	23
Accelerated Technologies Inc	7373	1052
Accelerator Systems Inc	3679	879
Acceleron Pharma Inc	8731	71
Accel-KKR	6799	174
Accellent Corp	3357	9
Acceller Inc	7371	461
Accelr8 Technology Corp	3826	142
Accelrys Inc	7372	407
Accent Fabrics Inc	2257	12
Accent Human Resource Specialists	7361	218
Accent Industries Inc	2541	44
Accent Interactive	7379	985
Accent Lighting Inc	5063	533
Accent Marble Company Inc	3431	10
Accent Marketing Services Inc	8742	193
Accent Media (Burbank California)	7373	431
Accent on Independence	8082	58
Accent Plastics Inc	3089	561
Accent Publications	2731	92
Accent Surfaces LLC	5031	213
Accent Technologies Inc	7371	1017
Accentia BioPharmaceuticals Inc	2834	207
Accento Plastics Inc	5199	80
Accents Unlimited Inc	3299	10
Accentuate Staffing	7361	120
Accenture Inc (New York New York)	7379	2
Acceptance Insurance Companies Inc	6331	250
ACCES I/O Products Inc	3577	436
Accesories That Matter	5199	109
Access America Service Corp	8741	98
Access America Transport	4213	292
Access and Video Integration Corp	1731	2283
Access Business Group LLC	2834	421
Access Center Soke Shop	7352	37
Access Communications Inc (Berkeley Heights New Jersey)	7389	339
Access Computer Systems Corp	1731	2474

Company Name	SIC	Rank
Access Control Consultants Inc	5065	423
Access Control Technologies Inc	7382	156
Access Data Network Solutions Inc	1731	890
Access Data Supply Inc	8748	317
Access Development Corp	8742	124
Access Direct Systems Inc	7331	30
Access Direct Telemarketing Inc	7389	388
Access Drywall Supply Company Inc	5032	120
Access Energy Coop	4911	459
Access Financial Services Inc	6282	623
Access Group Inc	6331	318
Access Hardware Supply Inc	5072	117
Access Highway Inc	4813	663
Access Inc	7389	2432
Access Information Inc	7375	248
Access Information Technologies Inc	5932	18
Access Innovations Inc	7379	1400
Access Intelligence LLC	2741	108
Access International	7372	2758
Access International Group Inc	7372	1477
Access International Inc	7372	2807
Access International LLC	8999	180
Access It Group Inc	7373	590
Access Mortgage Research and Consulting Inc	8731	309
Access National Bank	6021	131
Access National Corp	6712	357
Access National Leasing Corp	7359	90
Access Office Electronics Inc	5065	955
Access One Inc	4832	82
Access Pharmaceuticals Inc	2834	442
Access Plans Inc	7331	20
Access Plans USA Inc	7389	395
Access Pos LLC	3578	34
Access Security Corp	7382	142
Access Softek Inc	2741	118
ACCESS Systems Inc	7379	286
Access Technology Inc	4813	322
Access Technology Solutions	4731	61
Access to Money Inc	7334	3
Access US	4899	135
Access Worldwide Communications Inc	8742	231
Access2001	7379	1195
AccessCom Inc	7379	842
Accessible Archives Inc	7372	1628
Accessible Products Co	3086	135
AccessLine Communications Corp	7373	354
Accessnorthgeorgia	7373	553
Accesso LLC	7374	200
Accessories For Electronics Inc	3678	70
AccessoRize 4 Less	5531	67
Accessory Exchange LLC	5137	29
Accessory Store Inc	4812	133
AccessPort	7379	747
Accessvia Inc	7373	533
Accidental Software	7372	3852
Accipiter Inc	7372	2248
Acclaim Electronics LLC	5065	739
Acclaim Networks Inc	7378	69
Acclaim Software	7372	2702
Acclaim Systems Inc	7379	317
Acclaim Technical Services Inc	7379	347
Acclaim Training	8299	55
Acclarent Inc	3841	104
Acclivity	7372	2529
ACCO Brands Corp	3452	3
Accord Electric Co	1731	2124
Accord Electric Corp	1731	969
Accord Human Resources Inc	7363	39
Accord Industries LLC	3084	13
Accord Services Inc	4213	2701
Account Abilities Inc	7361	245
Account Management Corp	6282	534
Account Management Resources Inc	7374	189
Account Receivable Management of Flordia	7299	40
Account Ware Inc	7372	3253
Accountant's Edge Software Services Inc	7372	3975
Accountants World LLC	5734	61
Accountemps	7361	77
Accounting and Finance Personnel Inc	7361	251
Accounting Connections	7363	322
Accounting Machine	7373	1212
Accounting Management Solutions Inc (Waltham Massachusetts)	8748	431
Accountix Inc	7372	3305
AccountMate Software Corp	7372	3207
Accounts Receivable Management Inc	7322	35
Accoutrements	5092	33
Accra Industries Inc	3087	27
Accra Manufacturing Inc	3728	116
Accrabond Corp	2891	110
Accraline Inc	3599	1262
Accram Inc	7378	16
Accraply Inc	3565	24
Accratronics Seals Corp	3679	307
Accra-Wire Controls Inc	3549	122
Accredical Software Inc	7372	2485
Accredited Auctioneers Inc	7389	1028
Accredited Building Services Inc	7349	51
Accredited Home Lenders Holding Co	6162	14
Accredited Home Lenders Inc	6162	31
Accredited Language Services	7389	2019

Company Name	SIC	Rank
Accredited Lock and Door Hardware Co	5099	35
Accredo Health Inc	8099	4
Accredo's Hemophilia Health Services Inc	5912	37
Accretech USA Inc	3674	352
Accretive Health Inc	8099	14
Accretive Solutions Inc	7363	41
Accrotool Inc	3498	40
Accrued Equities Inc	6282	517
Accruent Inc	8742	104
Accsys Technology Inc	3699	190
Accu Die and Mold Inc	3544	383
Accu Laser Technologies Inc	3544	392
Accu Rx Inc	3851	96
Accu Systems Inc	3553	2
Accu Tek Inc	3599	2352
Accubuilt Inc	3711	59
Accuchrome Tool and Mold Inc	3544	573
AccuCode Inc	5045	288
Accu-Cut Diamond Tool Company Inc	3545	88
AccuData America	7331	70
Accudata Computer Services Inc	7374	227
Accudata Technologies Inc	7375	195
Accudyn Products Inc	3089	868
Accu-Fab And Construction Inc	3441	200
Accu-Fab Inc (Ithaca New York)	3549	93
Accuforce Staffing Services LLC	7363	155
Accu-Form Polymers Inc	3089	1193
Accu-Glass LLC	3231	43
Accu-Glass Products Inc	3679	785
Accuimage LLC	7374	261
Accuity Inc	7372	635
Accuma Corp	3089	463
Accumark Inc	2759	379
Accume Partners	8721	111
Accu-Med Services LLC	7372	840
Accumed Technologies Inc	5047	58
Accumedic Computer Systems Inc	7372	3165
Accumetric LLC	5085	149
Accumetrics Associates Inc	3674	420
Accu-Mold and Tool Company Inc	3089	1326
Accu-Mold LLC	3089	453
Accunet Solutions Inc	5734	229
Accunex Inc	1731	639
AccuNOC IT	7378	72
Accupac Inc	7389	432
Accuprobe Inc	3825	197
Accura Analytical Laboratory Inc	8071	50
Accura Industries Inc	3599	2508
Accura Precision Inc	3599	1215
Accura Software Inc	7372	3174
Accurate Autobody and Glass Inc	7532	6
Accurate Binding Company Inc	7389	1076
Accurate Bit Copy Inc	7371	814
Accurate Business Mailers Inc	7331	187
Accurate Cabling Inc	1731	2199
Accurate Chemical and Scientific Corp	5122	106
Accurate Circuit Engineering Inc	3672	207
Accurate Communications Corp	4813	487
Accurate Computer Technology Inc	7378	161
Accurate Corrosion Control Inc	5065	464
Accurate Data Inc	7374	373
Accurate Die Cutting Inc	2653	116
Accurate Electric Inc	1731	2468
Accurate Electric NW Inc	1731	1176
Accurate Energetic Systems LLC	2892	5
Accurate Engineering Inc	3672	344
Accurate Gas Control Systems	3823	415
Accurate Industrial Machining Inc	3599	1999
Accurate Machine and Tool Corp	3545	262
Accurate Machine Products Corp	3559	298
Accurate Mailings Inc	7331	126
Accurate Measurement Controls Inc	3829	200
Accurate Metal Machining Inc	3599	196
Accurate Metal Sawing Service Co	8999	215
Accurate Mold Inc	3089	1637
Accurate Molded Products Inc	3089	1379
Accurate Paper Recycling Corp	7389	557
Accurate Paper Recycling Inc	5093	153
Accurate Patterns Inc	1611	230
Accurate Products Inc	3069	223
Accurate Products Manufacturing Corp	3429	91
Accurate Screwmachine Corp	3451	16
Accurate Steel Rule Cutting Die Inc	3544	430
Accurate- Superior Scale Co	5084	658
Accurate Technologies Inc	3825	105
Accurate Technology Manufacturing	3599	559
Accurate Telecom Inc	5999	154
Accurate Temperature Control Corp	5063	995
Accurate Threaded Fasteners Inc	3452	27
Accurate Tool and Die Inc	3599	1661
Accurate Tool and Manufacturing Corp	3544	784
Accurate Welding Inc	7692	57
Accuratus Ceramic Corp	3545	268
Accuray Inc	3841	36
Accur-Cut Machine Company Inc	3599	2167
Accurecord Inc	8721	292
AccuRev Inc	7372	1973
Accuride Corp	3714	42
Accuride International Inc	3429	11
Accurite Industries Inc	3549	76
Accurite Technologies Inc	3572	60
Accu-Router Inc	3553	48

Company Name	SIC	Rank
Accuscan Imaging LLC	3845	98
Accusemble Electronics Inc	3672	242
Accu-Sembly Inc	3672	110
Accusentry Inc	3669	120
Accu-Shape Die Cutting Inc	2675	31
Accushim Inc	3825	276
Accusoft Pegasus	7372	1607
Accu-Sort Systems Inc	3577	177
Accusplit Inc	3873	22
Accu-Sport International Inc	3829	256
Accustandard Inc	8731	271
Accu-Tec Inc	7389	597
Accutec Systems Inc	3089	1230
Accutech Films Inc	2673	34
Accutech (Hudson Massachusetts)	3823	154
Accutech LLC	3841	312
Accutech Packaging Inc	3089	702
Accutech Tooling	7373	1235
Accutek Microcircuit Corp	3674	436
Accutek Packaging Equipment Co	3565	71
Accutest Laboratories	8734	25
Accu-Therm Inc	3634	24
Accu-Time Systems Inc	3873	11
Accutome Inc	3827	56
Accutrex Products Inc	3053	25
Accuturn Corp	3599	1684
Accu-Turn Inc	3599	2361
Accu-Turn Tool Company Inc	3559	516
Accuvant Federal Solutions	7379	489
Accu-Weather Inc	7373	100
Accuweb Inc	3625	157
AccuZip Inc	7372	3254
ACD Inc	3561	84
ACD LLC	3561	10
ACDNet Inc	3577	443
Ace Air Manufacturing	3728	208
Ace Answering Service Inc	4899	215
Ace Asphalt and Paving Co	2951	27
Ace Auto Lease Inc	5511	497
Ace Baking Co	2051	101
Ace Boat Lifts LLC	3536	42
Ace Bolt and Screw Company Of San Antonio Inc	5072	196
ACE Business Solutions Inc	5999	59
ACE Cash Express Inc	6099	17
Ace Cleaners And Reconditioners Of Athletic Equipment Inc	7389	1403
Ace Clearwater Enterprises Inc	3728	80
Ace Coffee Bar Inc	5962	6
ACE Collateral Inspections Inc	7389	1810
Ace Communications Group	4813	104
Ace Composites Inc	3089	1842
Ace Computers and Telecom Inc	5734	296
Ace Controls Inc	0714	302
Ace Designs Inc	7319	131
Ace Doran Hauling and Rigging Co	4213	140
Ace Drill Corp	5051	491
Ace Drive Products and Servics Inc	5013	289
ACE Duraflo Systems LLC	1711	156
Ace Educational Supplies Inc	5049	45
Ace Electric Company Inc	1731	749
Ace Electric Service Company LLC	1731	1498
Ace Electrical Contractors Inc	1731	286
Ace Electrical Service of North Florida Inc	1731	1770
ACE Entertainment Inc	7922	46
Ace Equipment Company Inc	3713	54
Ace Fat Inc	3695	98
Ace Fixture Company Inc	5046	203
Ace Forms Of Kansas Inc	2752	877
Ace Graphics Inc	2752	1404
Ace Group Inc	2791	26
Ace Hardware Corp	5072	1
Ace Hobby Distributors Inc	3691	30
Ace Holdings Inc	3911	24
Ace Industries Inc	3599	1672
Ace Label Systems Inc	2759	399
Ace Machine and Fabrication Inc	3599	513
Ace Machine and Metal Sales Co	3599	27
Ace Machine Shop Inc	3599	371
Ace Machining Technologies Ltd	3599	2298
Ace Mailing Service Inc	7331	81
Ace Manufacturing And Parts Co	3714	326
Ace Manufacturing Co	3599	1103
ACE Marketing and Promotions Inc	7311	902
Ace Mart Restaurant Supply Co	5099	23
Ace Metal Kraft Company Inc	3599	1670
Ace Packaging Systems Inc	2653	94
Ace Paving Company Inc	1611	161
Ace Precision Industries Inc	3599	1383
Ace Precision Machining Corp	3599	83
Ace Printing Company Inc	2752	1672
Ace Production Technologies Inc	3548	33
Ace Property And Casualty Insurance Co	6321	63
Ace Publishing Inc	2721	455
Ace Pump Corp	3561	149
Ace Rent-A-Car Inc	7514	6
Ace Reprographic Service Inc	7334	33
Ace Software Inc	7372	3509
ACE Software Solutions Inc	7372	1010
Ace Stamping and Machine Company Inc	3469	276
Ace Surgical Supply Company Inc	3841	204

Company Name	SIC	Rank
Ace Tank and Equipment Co	5084	337
ACE Tempest Re USA Inc	6411	135
Ace Tool Co	5072	31
Ace Tooling Inc	3544	742
Ace Transport Ltd	4213	1509
Ace Wire and Cable Company Inc	5063	83
ACECAD Inc	3577	546
Aceco Precision Industrial Knives	3559	140
Ace-Lon Corp	2673	66
AcelRx Pharmaceuticals Inc	2834	460
Acenes Technology Solutions Inc	7379	1599
Acentron Technologies Inc	7373	160
A-Ceptional Inc	7349	285
Acer America Corp	3571	7
Acer American Holdings Corp	3577	98
Acer Latin America Inc	3679	127
Aces A/C Supply Inc	5075	57
Aces Of Jacksonville Inc	7379	1572
Aces Security Inc	7381	210
Acess411	7372	1097
Acetech Communication Inc	7361	375
Aceto Corp	5169	16
Acetylene Gas Co	2813	21
ACF Components and Fasteners Inc	5072	71
Acf General Media Corp	7319	155
ACFN Franchised Inc	7389	961
Acg Systems Inc	5065	127
ACH Food Co's Inc	2079	2
Achates International Inc	5172	154
Achenbach's Pastry Inc	5461	39
Achen-Gardner Inc	1521	57
Acheson Colloids Co	3479	7
Achieva	8331	213
Achieve 3000 Inc	7379	243
Achieve Internet	7379	1139
Achieveit New York Inc	5045	670
Achilles USA Inc	3081	43
Achillion Pharmaceuticals Inc	2834	395
ACI Billing Services Inc	8721	105
Aci Building Systems Inc	3448	20
ACI Capital	6799	177
Aci Communications Inc	3663	241
ACI Distribution	5039	4
Aci Industries Inc	3599	999
Aci Industries Ltd	5051	458
ACI Mechanical Inc	1731	166
ACI Media	7371	1741
ACI Motor Freight Inc	4213	483
Aci Parts Warehousing Inc	5013	167
Aci Services Inc	3563	51
ACI Worldwide	7372	479
ACI Worldwide Inc	7372	117
ACI Worldwide Inc (Riverside Rhode Island)	7372	267
Acist Medical Systems	3841	161
Ack Controls Inc	5013	62
Ack Technologies Inc	3728	225
Ackenheil Engineers Inc	8711	665
Acker Drill Company Inc	3532	48
Ackerman and Co	6552	165
Ackerman McQueen	7311	77
Ackerman Wrecker Service Inc	7549	10
Ackermann Public Relations and Marketing	8743	254
Ackermans Icu Software	7371	728
Ackley Machine Corp	3555	81
Ackner Fuels Inc	5983	28
Acl Computers Inc	5045	991
ACL Equipment Corp	3993	193
Acloche LLC	7363	282
ACM Holdings Corp	3299	1
Acm Machining Inc	3599	457
Acm Plastic Products Inc	3089	1001
Acma Computers Inc	7373	327
Acma USA Inc	3565	28
ACMAT Corp	6351	46
Acme Alliance LLC	3363	35
Acme Auto Electric Inc	5013	312
Acme Bookbinding Company Inc	2789	23
ACME Bread Co	2051	106
Acme Bread Co	2051	164
Acme Brick And Supply Co	5031	408
Acme Brick Company Inc	3251	1
Acme Building Brands	3251	20
Acme Building Maintenance Company Inc	7349	64
Acme Carbide Die Inc	3544	777
ACME Communications Inc	4833	148
Acme Construction Company Inc (Modesto California)	1542	292
Acme Cryogenics Inc	3559	103
ACME Distribution Centers Inc	4214	1
Acme Dynamics Inc	3561	175
Acme Electric Co	1731	300
Acme Electric Corp	3612	27
Acme Electric Corp (Lumberton North Carolina)	3629	16
Acme Electric Inc	1731	1874
Acme Engineering and Manufacturing Corp	3564	23
Acme Engraving Company Inc	2796	43
Acme Filmworks Inc	7812	268
Acme Finishing Company Inc	3479	42
Acme Furniture Industry Inc	5021	75

Company Name	SIC	Rank
Acme Galvanizing Inc	3471	48
Acme Gear Company Inc	3566	31
Acme Graphics Inc	2678	19
Acme Grinding and Manufacturing Inc	3599	2283
Acme Grooving Tool Co	3545	408
Acme Industrial Sales	5084	676
Acme Industries Inc	3599	69
Acme Iron and Metal Company Inc	5093	159
Acme Laundry Products Inc	2326	20
Acme Linen Co	5131	30
Acme Machine Co	3599	1610
Acme Manufacturing Co (Auburn Hills Michigan)	3559	270
Acme Manufacturing Company Inc	3429	86
ACME Manufacturing Company Inc (Philadelphia Pennsylvania)	3444	33
Acme Masking Company Inc	3069	212
Acme Mechanical Contractors Inc	3443	221
Acme Mills Co	5023	16
Acme Packet Inc	3577	64
Acme Pallet Company Inc	2448	41
Acme Paper and Supply Company Inc	5113	9
Acme Portable Machines Inc	3571	139
Acme Printing Company Inc	2752	308
Acme Products And Engineering Inc	5084	819
Acme Refrigeration of Baton Rouge Inc	5075	24
Acme Screw Co	3452	54
Acme Security Service Inc	7381	226
Acme Service Group LLC	7349	367
Acme Sign Hanger Inc	3993	89
Acme Smoked Fish Corp	2091	13
Acme Sponge and Chamois Company Inc	5199	75
Acme Stores Inc	5411	139
Acme Systems Inc	5083	150
Acme Television Of Tennessee LLC	4833	205
Acme Truck Line Inc	4213	357
Acme United Corp	3423	14
Acme Vial and Glass Company Inc	3221	10
AcmelitesCom Inc	5063	725
Acme-Machell Company Inc	3069	76
ACMI Corp	3999	28
Acn-International Corp	4812	62
Aco Optical Lab	5048	35
ACO Pacific Inc	3829	443
A-Com Enterprises Inc	7363	251
Acom Solutions Inc	5045	407
A-Com Telephone Company Inc	5999	290
Acon Inc	3679	370
Acopian Technical Co	3679	248
Acor Orthopaedic Inc	3842	147
Acorda Therapeutics Inc	2834	104
Acorn Electrical Specialists Inc	1731	949
Acorn Energy Inc	7371	246
Acorn Media Group Inc	7812	231
Acorn Metal Service Inc	5051	450
Acorn Paper Products Company Inc	2653	34
Acorn Petroleum Inc	5171	58
Acorn Plastics Inc	3089	1897
Acorn Products Company LLC	5139	25
Acorn Products Inc (Columbus Ohio)	3423	10
Acoustech Mastering	3695	37
Acousti Engineering Company of Florida	1742	3
Acoustic Standards LLC	3625	408
Acoustic Technology Inc	3613	93
Acoustic Ventures LLC	6799	190
Acoustical Material Services	5039	1
Acoustical Solutions Inc	3448	48
Acousticom Corp	3663	290
Acoustilog Inc	7389	2462
Acp Interactive LLC	4813	476
Acpi Systems Inc	1731	960
Acp-Tpf Inc	7374	320
Acquest Development LLC	6552	243
Acquire Direct Marketing Inc	7331	221
Acquire Media Corp	7375	78
AcquireLists	7389	1706
Acquirgy Inc	4899	94
Acr Electronics Inc	3648	13
ACR Group Inc	5075	4
ACR Systems Inc	7372	1616
Acra Electric Inc	1731	756
Acra Grinding Company Inc	3599	838
Acra-Cut Inc	5047	261
Acramold Inc	3089	1849
Acree-Daily Corp	1731	646
Acrendo Software Inc	7372	2921
Acrilex Inc	5162	36
Acro Industries Inc	3444	61
Acro Labels Inc	2672	66
Acro Machining Inc	3599	718
Acro Manufacturing Corp	7692	24
Acro Tool and Die Co	3544	196
Acroamatics Inc	3663	260
Acrodyne Communications Inc	3663	135
Acromag Inc	3625	63
Acromil Corp	3728	94
Acronis Inc	7371	109
Acrontos Manufacturing Inc	3469	284
Acropolis Computers Inc	7378	53
Acroprint Time Recorder Co	7372	1598
Acrotech Industries Inc	2992	30
Acrowood Corp	3531	128

Company Name	SIC	Rank
Acry Fab Inc	3089	742
Acrylic Design Associates Inc	3993	84
AcryMed Inc	3842	287
ACS Dataline LP	7373	159
ACS Government Systems Inc	7372	1200
Acs Inc	5065	439
Acs Integrated Doc Inc	7389	1835
ACS International Resources Inc	7372	419
Acs Northwest Inc	3531	243
ACS Security Systems Inc	1731	1331
ACS Software Inc	7372	3586
ACS Technologies	7372	1235
ACS Technologies Corp	3559	427
Acsel Corp	7374	211
Acsis Inc	7372	207
ACS-MIDAS	7371	395
Acstar Holdings Inc	6351	56
Acstar Insurance Co	6351	57
Acsys Inc	7361	281
Act Acquisitions LLC	3578	15
Act Data Services Inc	7379	1057
Act Electric Co	1731	978
Act Iii Office Supplies LLC	5045	1012
ACT Janitorial Services Company Inc	7349	213
Act Technologies Inc	3069	173
ACT Teleconferencing Inc	4899	68
ACT Teleconferencing Services Inc	4813	126
ACT Transportation	4213	1101
Act-1 Personnel Service	7361	12
Acta Technology Inc	7372	1079
Actall Corp	3842	273
Actant Inc	7371	1202
Actco Tool and Manufacturing Co	3544	404
Actek Inc	7373	1107
Actelis Networks Inc	3351	10
Acteras US Liquid Measurement Div	3824	14
A-Cti Answerconnect Inc	7389	1744
Actify Inc	7373	345
Actimize Inc	7371	100
Action Antenna Service Company Inc	7622	9
Action Bag and Cover Inc	2393	13
Action Blueprint And Supplies LLC	5049	218
Action Box Company Inc	2653	86
Action Business Furniture Inc	5021	144
Action Communications and Secretarial Service	7389	2138
Action Communications Inc	5731	190
Action Computers Inc	5734	205
Action Couriers Inc	4213	2628
Action Delivery Inc	4213	2751
Action Door Repair Corp	7699	106
Action Electric Sales Co	5063	237
Action Electrical Contracting Company Inc	1731	1395
Action Embroidery Corp	2399	19
Action Equipment Co	7539	14
Action Equipment Company Inc	3535	129
Action Express Inc	4213	1739
Action Fabricators Inc	3053	52
Action Floor Systems LLC	2426	29
Action Inc	3199	5
Action International Marketing Inc	5045	216
Action Labor	7363	275
Action Labs Inc	3679	662
Action Labs Inc (Placentia California)	5122	123
Action Mail Service Inc	7389	1856
Action Manufacturing Company Inc	3483	4
Action Mortgage Co	6162	107
Action Moving and Storage Inc	4213	2947
Action Packaging Automation Inc	3565	180
Action Pipeline Contractors Inc	1623	781
Action Plastics Inc	3089	1257
Action Plumbing Supply Co	5074	67
Action Precision Products Inc	3599	2000
Action Printers LLC	2752	1358
Action Printing Of Norman Inc	2752	1392
Action Products Co	3089	436
Action Products International Inc	3944	35
Action Pump Co	3561	177
Action Radio and Communications Inc	5731	231
Action/Reaction Techniques	5046	385
Action Rental And Sales Inc	7359	182
Action Rental Center Inc	7353	89
Action Resources Inc	4213	1116
Action Rotary Die Inc	3544	376
Action Services Group Inc	1731	522
Action Temporary Service Inc	7363	181
Action Tool and Machine Inc	3544	518
Action Tool and Manufacturing Inc	3469	289
Action Tool Service Inc	3541	192
Action Travel and Tours	4724	83
Action Windows Inc	3089	588
Action Without Borders/Idealistorg	7389	198
Actional Corp	7371	106
Actioneer Inc	7372	1805
ActioNet Inc	7379	494
Actionlink LLC	8748	287
Action-Pak Inc	4783	21
ActionTec Electronics Inc	3672	26
Activant Solutions Holdings Inc	7372	204
Activar Technical Products Group	3577	322
Activate Inc	3949	116
Activated Metals and Chemicals Inc	2819	103
Active Aero Charter LLC	4522	13

Company Name	SIC	Rank	Company Name	SIC	Rank	Company Name	SIC	Rank
Active Electrical Supply Co	5063	222	Ada Enterprises Inc	3523	219	Adchem Corp	2672	31
Active Endpoints	5045	854	Ada Feed and Seed Inc	0723	27	Adchemy Inc	4813	311
Active Grinding and Manufacturing Co	3545	425	Ada Metal Products Inc	3465	68	Adco Circuits	3679	213
Active Grinding Inc	3599	161	Ada Security Inc	7381	139	Adco Electric Inc	1731	516
Active Ink Software Inc	7372	3807	ADA Technologies Inc	8731	389	Adco Global Inc	2819	16
Active Interest Media Inc	2721	133	Adac Plastics Inc	3089	93	Adco Inc	2842	72
Active International	7389	752	Adacel Systems Inc	7372	3453	Adco International Plastics Corp	2821	137
Active Lawyers Referral Service	8999	189	Adaco Hospitality Solutions	7372	3587	Adco Manufacturing	5084	207
Active Machine and Tool Co	3545	277	Ad-A-Day Company Inc	2759	274	Adco Products Inc	2393	1
Active Manufacturing Corp	3541	169	Adaequare Inc	7379	395	ADCO Products Inc (Michigan City Michigan)	2891	24
Active Media Corp	7311	889	ADA-EX Inc	3822	18	ADCO South Medical Supplies Inc	3842	294
Active Micrographics Inc	7374	298	Adager Corp	7372	4479	ADCO Surgical Supply Inc	5047	139
Active Network Inc	7372	156	Adair	2732	28	Adcole Corp	3829	60
Active Parenting Publishers Inc	7812	255	Adair Greene Inc	8742	161	Adcolor Screenprinting Inc	2396	32
Active Posture Chiropractic	8041	5	Adair Progress Inc	2711	820	Adcom Communications Inc	7311	265
Active Power Inc	3629	19	Adalet	3699	59	Adcom Express Inc	4513	13
Active Services Corp	8322	9	Adam and Gillian's Sensual Whips and Toys	3999	205	Adcomm Inc	3679	253
Active USA Inc / ATC Leasing	4213	176	Adam D Tihany International Ltd	7389	909	Adcomp Systems Inc	5045	720
Active Web Services LLC	7371	973	Adam Electronics Inc	3629	88	Adcon Engineering Company Inc	5063	687
Active Window Products	3442	125	ADAM Inc	7372	1020	Adcor Industries Inc	3599	309
Activeaid	3842	218	Adam Matthews Inc	2051	260	Adcraft Decals Inc	2759	331
Activestrategy Inc	7372	2500	Adam Shelton Electric Inc	1731	1317	Adcraft Inc	2759	270
ActiveVideo Networks Inc	7375	85	Adamas Pharmaceuticals Inc	8731	329	Adcraft Printers Inc	2752	1797
Activeworlds Inc	7372	992	Adamation Inc (Newton Massachusetts)	3589	157	ADD Marketing Inc	7311	755
Actividentity Corp	7372	651				Add on Software Inc	7372	1728
Activision Blizzard Inc	7372	7	Adamis Pharmaceuticals Corp	2834	319	Add On Systems Inc	7371	1212
Activities 4 Less Inc	7389	556	Adampac Inc	4783	30	Add Staff Inc	7363	274
Activities Press Inc	2752	688	Adams and Co	5719	30	Add2net Inc	4813	250
Actix Inc	7371	351	Adams and Reese LLP	8111	73	Add-A-Tech Inc	7363	364
Acton Medical Investors LP	8361	87	Adams and Smith Inc	1622	29	Addax Inc	3714	378
Acton Technologies Inc	3081	68	Adams Apple Distributing LP	5199	89	Addax Telecom Inc	7389	1863
Acts Of South Carolina Inc	8331	171	Adam's Career Transitions Inc	7375	220	Adder Corp	3577	581
Actuality Systems Inc	3575	51	Adams Columbia Electric Coop	4911	305	Addesso-Madden Inc	7389	1192
Actuant Corp	3589	3	Adams Concrete Products Corp	3273	97	Addicks Engineering And Product Development Co	3089	1283
Actuarial Data Inc	8742	601	Adams County National Bank	6712	329	Addington Oil Corp	5172	142
Actuate Corp	7372	341	Adams Electric Inc	1731	265	Addison Biological Laboratory Inc	2836	75
Actuate International Corp	7372	88	Adams Electric Coop	4911	558	Addison Machine Engineering Inc	3547	10
Actus Manufacturing Inc	3625	211	Adams Electric Cooperative Inc	4911	337	Addison Meggitt Inc	3728	105
Acu Grind Tool Works Inc	7699	239	Adams Electric Inc	1731	1564	Addison Olian Inc	7311	621
Acucorp Inc	7372	1524	Adams Electronics Inc	3699	300	Addison Precision Manufacturing Corp	3599	443
Acucote Inc	2672	36	Adams Elevator Equipment Co	7389	877	Addison Press Inc	2711	821
ACUGEN Software Inc	7372	4269	Adams Evens and Ross Inc	7389	1176	Addison Truss And Building Supply Inc	5039	55
Acuity Brands Inc	3645	2	Adams Express Co	6799	43	Addison-Harrington Inc	8741	265
Acuity Brands Lighting Inc	3645	1	Adams Fairacre Farms	5191	31	Addition Technology Inc	3851	85
Acuity Mutual Insurance Co	6321	43	Adams Foam Rubber Co	5199	85	Addlestone International Corp	5093	213
Acuity Pharmaceuticals Inc	8731	305	Adams Golf Direct Response Ltd	3949	66	Addmaster Corp	3577	194
Aculis Inc	7371	304	Adams Golf Inc	3949	46	Add-On Computer Peripherals LLC	5045	650
Acumark Inc	7331	46	Adams Inc	7361	404	Add-On Data	7371	437
Acumed Pharmaceuticals Inc	2834	354	Adams Investment Co	2761	15	Addonics Technologies Corp	3575	15
Acumen Consulting Inc	7379	627	Adams Lithographing Company Inc	2759	275	Addressing Machines and Supply Company Inc	3579	51
Acumen Data Systems Inc	7374	192	Adams Manufacturing Co	3585	231	
Acumen International	7372	2114	Adams Manufacturing Corp	3089	236	Addsum Business Software Inc	7372	4400
Acumen Pharmaceuticals Inc	8731	402	Adam's Mark Hotels and Resorts	7011	57	Addtronics Business Systems	3089	1738
Acumen Solutions Inc	8748	124	Adams McClure Inc	3993	98	Addus HomeCare Corp	8082	13
Acumen Systems Inc	7372	3647	Adams Media Corp	7372	692	Addvantage Technologies Group Inc	5046	30
Acumen Technologies Inc	5065	678	Adams Motor Express Inc	4213	2207	Addventures Inc	7311	967
Acument Global Technologies Inc	3714	25	Adams National Bank	6021	313	Addwest Minerals International Ltd	1041	14
Acumentrics Corp	3629	51	Adams Outdoor Advertising Inc	7312	2	ADE Corp	3825	18
Acumeter Laboratories Inc	3554	38	Adams Outdoor Advertising Of Kalamazoo LP	7312	30	Ade Inc	3086	129
AcuNetx Inc	3841	395				Adea International Inc	7379	613
Acuo Technologies LLC	5045	252	Adams Produce Co	5148	62	Adea Solutions Inc	8742	146
Acupowder International LLC	3399	8	Adams Products Co	3272	36	Ad-Ease Communications Inc	7311	598
Acupower Inc	1731	2571	Adams Ralph and Paul Inc	2013	87	A-Dec Inc	3843	6
Acuprint Technology Inc	3577	433	Adams Resources and Energy Inc	5172	8	Adecco Inc	7361	3
Acura of Bellevue	5511	949	Adams Rite Manufacturing Co	3429	75	Adeia Technologies Inc	4813	645
Acura Pharmaceuticals Inc	2834	378	Adams Security	7381	265	Adel Wholesalers Inc	5074	157
Acura SpA Systems Inc	5999	282	Adams Telephone Coop	4813	407	Adele Knits Inc	2257	8
Acushnet Co	3949	6	Adams Tv Rental Of New Hampshire	7359	116	Adelita Tortilla Factory	2099	349
Acusis LLC	7389	51	Adam's Used Auto Parts	5013	407	Adell Plastics Inc	2295	9
Acusphere Inc	2834	389	Adams Wood Products Inc	2426	42	Adelman Sand and Gravel Inc	5032	123
AcuSport Corp	5091	5	Adams-Burch Inc	5087	26	Adelman Travel Group	4724	26
Acutec Precision Machining Inc	3599	81	Adamson Motors Inc	5511	243	AdelWiggins Group	3429	59
Acutek Adhesive Specialties Inc	3069	175	Adapt Inc	8331	90	Adema Technologies Inc	5065	594
Acutek Inc	3089	1870	Adapt Plastics Inc	5162	43	Adena Tool Corp	3544	238
Acu-Tek Solutions Inc	5045	899	ADAPT Software Applications Inc	7372	3045	Adenine Press Inc	2791	65
Acutrack Inc	3695	41	Adaptive Computing	7371	751	Adenna Inc	5047	129
Acutransformers Inc	3677	90	Adaptive Controls Inc	5064	154	Adept Corp	3083	36
Acutronic USA Inc	3812	117	Adaptive Inc	7372	3402	Adept Engineering Solutions LLC	7379	1178
Acx Inc	1731	2582	Adaptive Micro Systems Inc	3993	22	Adept International Inc	5013	384
Acxiom Corp	7374	16	Adaptive Micro-Ware Inc	8731	378	Adept Process Services Inc	3732	81
Acxiom Digital	7389	375	Adaptive Networks Inc	3661	204	Adept Technology Inc	3559	58
Acxiom SDC Inc	7374	7	Adaptive Optics Associates Inc	3827	39	Adeptron Technologies USA Inc	3672	303
A-C-Y Communications Contractors Inc	1731	1743	Adaptive Optics Associates Inc (Cambridge Massachusetts)	3669	33	Ader Inc	3559	550
Acz Laboratories Inc	8734	139				Aderis Pharmaceuticals Inc	2834	381
AD Adams Advertising Inc	8743	223	Adaptive Planning Inc	7371	319	ADESA Birmingham Inc	5511	152
Ad Color Inc	3861	71	Adaptive Research	7372	2819	ADESA Inc	5012	20
AD Conner Inc	4213	865	Adaptive Switch Laboratories Inc	3842	224	Adesa St Louis	5012	120
Ad Graphics Inc	7336	155	Adaptive Technologies Inc	3829	354	Adesso Inc	3577	352
AD Huesing Corp	5149	79	Adaptix Inc	4899	125	Adesta Communications Inc	3829	23
Ad Industries Inc	2782	18	Adapto Storage Products	2542	68	ADEX Corp	8742	61
Ad Methods Inc	7311	513	AdaQuest	8742	555	Adexa Inc	7372	643
Ad Results Inc	7311	582	Adarose Inc	7373	1206	ADF Services Of America Inc	7381	151
AD Sutton and Sons Inc	3171	3	ADAX Inc	7372	2590	Adf Systems Ltd	3589	199
Ad Systems Inc (Wake Forest North Carolina)	7372	3294	Adayana	8748	122	Ad-Fax Media Marketing Inc	2741	328
			ADB Systems International ASA	7372	1682	Adflex Corp	2796	36
Ad Tracker	7319	160	AdBrite Inc	7311	273	Adgo Inc	3613	119
AD Transport Express Inc	4213	275	Adc Acquisition Company Inc	2821	140	Adgravers Inc	2796	41
AD Weaver Service Inc	4213	2868	ADC Broadband Access Systems Inc	3001	12	Adh Health Products Inc	5122	82
AD Wynne Company Inc	5021	42	Adc Custom LLC	3441	241	Adherex Technologies Inc	2834	458
AD1 Agency	7311	730	Adc Diecasting LLC	3363	29	Adhesa-Plate Manufacturing Co	3993	157
AD2 Inc	2741	206	ADC Legal Systems Inc	7372	1702	Adhesive Applications Inc	2891	41
Ada Business Computers	7373	906	ADC Software Systems USA Inc	7372	14	Adhesive Packaging Specialties Inc	2671	32
Ada Coca-Cola and Dr Pepper Bottling Co	2086	89	AdCare Health Systems Inc	8999	56			

Company Name	SIC	Rank
Adhesive Products Corp	2891	118
Adhesive Systems Inc	2891	48
Adhesive Systems Inc (Detroit Michigan)	2891	52
Adhesive Systems Technology Corp	3823	297
Adhesive Technologies Inc	2891	57
Adhesives Research Inc	2891	11
Adhost	7371	438
Adi Electronics Inc	3678	68
Adi Group Inc	7373	923
Adi LLC	7373	867
Adidas America Inc	5139	7
Adidas Golf USA Inc	5136	21
Adient	8743	135
Adil Business Systems Inc	7371	750
ADINA R and D Inc	7372	2413
Adir International LLC	5311	39
Adirondack Beverages Inc	2086	49
Adirondack Cabling Inc	1731	547
Adirondack Environmental Services Inc	8734	97
Adirondack Plastics And Recycling Inc	3089	1476
Adis International Inc	2741	63
Aditi Technologies Private Ltd	7371	394
Adiva Corp	7371	1744
Adjile Systems Inc	7373	1172
Adjustable Clamp Co	3429	85
Adkin and Son Associated Food Products Inc	0171	3
Adkins and Associates Ltd	7361	408
Adkins Co	5211	255
Adkins Printing Co	2752	1543
AdKnowledge Inc	7372	786
Adko Inc	3544	564
ADL Data Systems Inc	7372	2371
Adler Consulting Group Inc	7379	1344
Adler Norco Inc	3444	288
Adler Public Affairs Inc	8743	197
Adleta Corp	5023	29
Adlife Marketing and Communications Company Inc	7336	48
Adlink	4822	5
Adlucent	7311	841
ADM Cocoa	2066	10
ADM Farmland Grain	5153	13
ADM Grain	5153	7
ADM/Growmark River Systems Inc	5153	1
ADM Investors Services Inc	6221	11
ADM Milling Co	2041	45
ADM Productions Inc	7336	50
ADM Tronics Unlimited Inc	2891	120
ADM Trucking Inc	4213	355
Ad-Mail Inc	7331	84
Admail West	7331	35
Adman Electric Inc	1731	135
Admark Graphic Systems Inc	2396	31
Ad-Mart Attractions Inc	3993	94
Ad-Mast Publishing Co	2711	356
AdMasters Inc	7311	849
AdMax Media Inc	7319	79
Admc Inc	2531	39
AdMedia Partners Inc	6282	188
Administrative Services Cooperative Inc	8742	293
Admins Inc	7372	2658
Admiral Broach Company Inc	3545	313
Admiral Craft Equipment Corp	5046	50
Admiral Engineering and Manufacturing Co	3599	1342
Admiral Exchange Company Inc	5141	137
Admiral Heating and Ventilating Inc	1711	151
Admiral Insurance Co	6331	205
Admiral Linen and Uniform Service Inc	7218	1
Admiral Merchants Motor Freight Inc	4212	25
Admiral Metals Servicenter Company Inc	5051	189
Admiral Moving and Storage Inc	4213	1799
Admiral Packaging Inc	3081	78
Admiral Products Company Inc	2752	1001
Admiral Sales Co	5065	697
Admiral Security Services Inc	7382	41
Admiral Steel LLC	5051	317
Admiral Transport Corp	4213	434
Admiral Wine and Liquor Co	5182	23
ADMMicro Inc	3629	28
Admor Restaurant And Equipment Supplies	5046	177
Admore Inc	2679	31
Adobe Electric Inc	1731	1190
Adobe Equipment Holdings	5084	160
Adobe Lumber Inc	5211	290
Adobe Systems Inc	7372	11
Adolf Meller Co	3827	72
Adolfson and Peterson Inc	1542	103
Adolor Corp	2834	198
Adom Engineering Inc	3599	1763
Adometry Inc	7371	720
Adonix	7371	544
ADP Employease Inc	7389	466
ADP Hayes-Ligon	2741	173
ADP Screening and Selection Services	7375	53
ADP TotalSource Group Inc	7363	23
Adpac Corp	7372	2631
ADPI Enterprises Inc	3089	1132
ADR Bookprint Inc	2789	55

Company Name	SIC	Rank
ADR Data Recovery Inc	7379	594
Adray Appliance and Photo Center Inc	5722	11
Adrem Systems Corp	7379	890
Adriaansen Trucking Inc	4213	1917
Adrian Carriers Inc	4213	1466
Adrian Homes	2452	12
Adrian Steel Co	3496	5
Adrian Tool Corp	3441	244
Adrian Trucking Inc	4213	2631
Adrianna Papell Ltd	2331	9
Adrienne's Gourmet Foods	2052	49
Adroit Medical Systems Inc	2834	197
Adron Inc	2869	119
Adron Tool Corp	3599	581
Adronics/Elrob Manufacturing Corp	3647	8
ADS Courier and Messenger Service Inc	7389	2305
ADS Engineers	8711	466
ADS Financial Services Solutions	8742	227
Ads Group	2741	54
ADS Machinery Corp	3549	28
ADS Media Group Inc	7331	184
Ads Up LLC	4813	565
Ad-Sell Co	2752	307
AdSell Marketing and Communications Group	7331	52
Adserts Inc	7331	155
AdStar Inc	7389	1144
ADT Advance Intergration (Norristown Pennsylvania)	7382	13
ADT Engineering and Machine	3559	61
ADT Security Services Inc	5065	1
Adtec Digital Inc	3669	45
Adtec Staffing Services	7363	290
Ad-Tech Medical Instrument Corp	3845	75
ADTI Media LLC	6794	129
Adtrack Corp	7375	178
ADTRAN Inc	3661	8
Adtron Corp	3572	40
Aduddell Industries	1761	5
Adult and Implant Dentistry of Ventura County	8021	21
ADVA Optical Networking	3357	23
Advacare Home Services Inc	5047	146
Adval Communications Inc	4822	15
Advan International Corp	8742	370
Advan LLC	2874	5
Advance America Cash Advance Centers Inc	6141	37
Advance Auto Parts Inc	5531	1
Advance Automation Co	3593	51
Advance Bank (Baltimore Maryland)	6022	473
Advance Bronze Inc	3366	17
Advance Business Systems	5044	27
Advance Cable Company LLC	1731	2560
Advance Carbon Products Inc	3624	21
Advance Communications Inc	7389	1589
Advance Computer Solutions Inc	3577	646
Advance Controls Inc	5063	375
Advance Data Communications Inc	1731	2438
Advance Data Technology Inc	3674	419
Advance Electric Inc	1731	2396
Advance Electrical Supply Co	5063	150
Advance Energy Technologies Inc	3585	201
Advance Engineering and Manufacturing Co	3544	502
Advance Engineering Co	3465	23
Advance Engineering Corp	3824	30
Advance Equipment Co	5082	152
Advance Finishing And Display Corp	3993	143
Advance Fixture Mart Inc	5046	103
Advance Food Service Company Inc	3589	49
Advance Gift Enterprises Inc	5063	604
Advance Graphic Systems Inc	3993	118
Advance Graphics Equipment Of York Inc	3555	73
Advance Graphix Imaging Solutns	7374	318
Advance Hydraulics Inc	3511	38
Advance Inc	8322	47
Advance Industrial Machine A Wisconsin LP	3599	737
Advance Insights	7389	242
Advance Insurance Co	6311	266
Advance Laundry Systems Inc	7359	160
Advance Management Corp	3569	82
Advance Manufacturing Co	8712	277
Advance Manufacturing Company Inc	3599	194
Advance Manufacturing Corp	3599	789
Advance Media	4832	280
Advance Metalworking Co	3715	60
Advance Mold and Manufacturing Inc	3544	91
Advance Nanotech Inc	8731	421
Advance Notice Inc	7311	324
Advance Packaging Corp	2653	48
Advance Paper Box Co	2653	24
Advance Paper Co	5113	63
Advance Personnel	7363	388
Advance Petroleum Distributing Company Inc	5172	131
Advance Pharmaceutical Inc	2834	330
Advance Plastics Unlimited Inc	3085	28
Advance Presort Service Inc	7389	125
Advance Print and Graphics Inc	2752	1405
Advance Printing Inc	2752	1127

Company Name	SIC	Rank
Advance Products Corp	3545	164
Advance Publications Inc	2711	4
Advance Reproductions Corp	3861	59
Advance Research Chemicals Inc	2819	83
Advance Ross Corp	7389	360
Advance Scale Company Inc	5046	122
Advance Security (Grand Rapids Michigan)	7381	26
Advance Sign Company LLC	5999	234
Advance Solutions	5045	804
Advance Synthetic Products Inc	3599	1197
Advance Technical Sales Inc	5065	336
Advance Testing Company Inc	7389	863
Advance Transport Inc	4213	2404
ADVANCE2000 Inc	7379	271
Advancecom Technologies Inc	7371	1842
Advanced Academics Inc	7375	35
Advanced Access	7371	500
Advanced Acoustic Concepts LLC	7371	353
Advanced Adhesive Technologies Inc	2891	100
Advanced Aero Safety Inc	3669	314
Advanced Aerospace	3585	106
Advanced Alarm Service Inc	1731	1493
Advanced Analogic Technologies Inc	3674	110
Advanced Analytical Inc	7372	4270
Advanced Analytical Technologies Inc	2834	124
Advanced Animations	3999	200
Advanced Asphalt Co	1611	233
Advanced Audio	7922	101
Advanced Audio Technology Inc	3652	52
Advanced Auto Trends Inc	3089	646
Advanced Automotive Technologies Inc	7389	2306
Advanced Barcode Technology Inc	3577	449
Advanced Battery Systems Inc	5999	304
Advanced Battery Technologies Inc	3691	9
Advanced Behavioral Health Inc	8322	27
Advanced Beverage Solutions Inc	3585	166
Advanced Biologics LLC	8731	173
Advanced Business Computers Of America Incorpor	7371	971
Advanced Business Fulfillment LLC	7331	90
Advanced Business Group Inc	7336	97
Advanced Business Information Systems Inc	7371	1093
Advanced Business Software Inc	7372	2935
Advanced Business Systems Inc	3571	202
Advanced Business Technologies Inc	7372	3476
ADVANCED BusinessLink Corp	5045	494
Advanced Cable Connection Inc	3496	114
Advanced Calibration Designs	3829	410
Advanced Cast Stone Inc	3272	101
Advanced Cell Technology Inc	2834	438
Advanced Chemical Co	2899	110
Advanced Chemical Sensors Inc	8748	428
Advanced Chemistry Labs Inc	8748	420
Advanced Chimney Inc	7349	489
Advanced Circuits Inc	3672	31
Advanced Civil Design Inc	7389	2031
Advanced Cleaning Systems Inc	7349	338
Advanced Cleanup Technologies Inc	4959	3
Advanced Combustion Systems Inc	3567	83
Advanced Communication Design Inc	3661	149
Advanced Communications Group Inc	1731	1872
Advanced Communications Systems Inc (North Olmsted Ohio)	7371	1691
Advanced Component Technologies Inc	2531	16
Advanced Components Inc	3829	360
Advanced Components Manufacturing	3599	1935
Advanced Composites Technology LLC	5013	182
Advanced Computer Concepts Inc	7373	157
Advanced Computer Connections Inc	5045	592
Advanced Computer Graphics Inc	7319	46
Advanced Computer Innovations Inc	7372	4583
Advanced Computer Products Inc	5734	201
Advanced Concept Technologies	7372	307
Advanced Concepts Inc	7372	3588
Advanced Concepts Inc (Columbia Maryland)	3661	22
Advanced Containment Systems Inc	3589	43
Advanced Control Systems Corp	3625	369
Advanced Control Technologies Inc	3822	61
Advanced Controls Corp	3822	56
Advanced Controls Inc	3613	134
Advanced Cosmetic Research Labs Inc	3999	153
Advanced Cutting Systems Corp	3599	21
Advanced Cutting Systems Inc	3291	26
Advanced Data Capture Corp	5112	59
Advanced Data Exchange	7372	1178
Advanced Data Management Inc	7372	2442
Advanced Data Marketing Inc	5065	265
Advanced Data Services Inc	3578	18
Advanced Data Transcribing Center Inc	7374	263
Advanced DC Motors Inc	3621	20
Advanced Delivery Systems Inc	4213	733
Advanced Delphi Systems	7371	1001
Advanced Design And Control Corp	3625	278
Advanced Design and Manufacturing Inc	3679	380
Advanced Design Corp	2741	286
Advanced Design Industries Inc	3559	402
Advanced Design Products Inc	3499	131
Advanced Designs Corp	3829	369
Advanced Detection Systems Inc	1731	1744

Company Name	SIC	Rank
Advanced Detection Technology LLC	7382	120
Advanced Digital Data Inc	7372	933
Advanced Digital Logic Inc	5045	561
Advanced Digital Media	3565	84
Advanced Digital Research Inc	3575	48
Advanced Displays In Plastic Inc	3083	57
Advanced Drainage Systems Inc	3083	1
Advanced Electric Company Inc	1731	1478
Advanced Electrical Services Inc	1731	876
Advanced Electrical Solutions Inc	1731	556
Advanced Electrical Systems Inc	1731	1318
Advanced Electro Mechanical Sales Inc	5063	593
Advanced Electrocircuits Corp	3672	339
Advanced Electromagnetics Inc	3823	193
Advanced Electronics Systems Inc	3629	109
Advanced Energy	8731	126
Advanced Energy Industries Inc	3679	39
Advanced Energy Voorhees Inc	3825	5
Advanced Engineering Corp	5065	848
Advanced Engineering Solutions Inc	8711	515
Advanced Environmental Recycling Technologies Inc	2431	21
Advanced Equipment Corp	2542	47
Advanced Equities Financial Corp	6722	17
Advanced Facilities Services International Inc	7349	104
Advanced Fibermolding Inc	3089	1197
Advanced Filtration Systems Inc	3599	116
Advanced Fire and Security Systems Inc	5065	679
Advanced Foam Inc	3086	103
Advanced Fresh Concepts Corp	2032	17
Advanced Fuel Research Inc	8734	183
Advanced Fulfillment Inc	7389	1590
Advanced Global Communications Inc	4813	584
Advanced Graphic Products Inc	2789	34
Advanced Graphics Software Inc	7372	4480
Advanced Green Components LLC	3562	33
Advanced Green Technologies Inc	7336	2
Advanced Health Education Center Ltd	8299	54
Advanced Health Media LLC	7389	293
Advanced Heating and Cooling Inc	5074	152
Advanced Home Care Inc	8082	27
Advanced Illumination Inc	3559	263
Advanced Imaging Concepts Inc	5045	518
Advanced Imaging Services Inc	7374	377
Advanced Imaging Systems Inc	8713	5
Advanced Industrial And Marine Services Inc	5084	561
Advanced Industrial Services	4213	395
Advanced Industrial Tech	3829	67
Advanced Industries Inc	3355	10
Advanced Information Management Systems LLC	8721	93
Advanced Information Network Systems Inc	7379	528
Advanced Information Services Inc	7372	1876
Advanced Input Data Entry	7374	398
Advanced Input Devices Inc	3577	139
Advanced Instrument Development Inc	3844	23
Advanced Integrated Manufacturing Computer Solutions Inc	7373	960
Advanced Integration Technology Inc	7373	337
Advanced Interactive Systems Inc	7372	35
Advanced Interconnections Corp	3679	237
Advanced International Technology LLC	3559	517
Advanced Internet Technologies Inc	7372	950
Advanced Labelworx Inc	2759	115
Advanced Lease Systems Inc	7372	4345
Advanced Legal Systems Inc	7379	503
Advanced Life Sciences Holdings Inc	2834	433
Advanced Lighting and Sound Inc	1731	2057
Advanced Lighting Inc	5063	641
Advanced Lighting Technologies Inc	3641	3
Advanced Linear Devices Inc	3674	225
Advanced Logic Solutions Inc	7372	3589
Advanced Looseleaf Technologies Inc	2782	49
Advanced Machine and Engineering Company Inc	3599	235
Advanced Machine and Stretchform International Inc	3728	114
Advanced Machine and Tool Corp	3599	237
Advanced Machine And Tool Inc	3599	635
Advanced Machine Design Company Inc	3541	254
Advanced Machine Works Inc	3561	157
Advanced Machining and Fabricating Inc	3599	1576
Advanced Machining and Tool Inc	3441	182
Advanced Management Solutions Inc	7372	3654
Advanced Manufacturing Inc	3679	614
Advanced Manufacturing Service Inc	3672	290
Advanced Manufacturing Systems Inc	8711	643
Advanced Manufacturing Technology For Bottles Inc	3535	89
Advanced Marketing and Distribution Inc	5064	133
Advanced Marketing Telecommunications Inc	5063	1031
Advanced Materials Group Inc	3086	50
Advanced Media Integration	3695	105
Advanced Media Post	7371	819
Advanced Media Productions Inc	7379	986
Advanced Media Services Inc	3651	146
Advanced Medical Center Inc	5047	196
Advanced Medical Concepts Inc	5047	214
Advanced Medical Instruments Inc	3841	155
Advanced Medical Psychiatric Software Inc	7372	3853
Advanced Medical Systems	7372	2594
Advanced Metal Components Inc	3444	123
Advanced Micro Controls Inc	3625	123
Advanced Micro Devices Inc	3674	8
Advanced Micro Devices Inc - Personal Connectivity Div	3674	231
Advanced Micro Solutions Inc	7372	1726
Advanced Micro Systems Inc	3679	810
Advanced Microelectronics Inc	3672	244
Advanced Microfilm Systems Inc	7389	1471
Advanced Microsensors Inc	3861	69
Advanced Microtechnology Inc	3825	250
Advanced Mold and Tooling Inc	3544	471
Advanced Mold Technology Inc	3544	754
Advanced Molding Technologies	3089	580
Advanced National Electronic Technologies 1 Inc	5734	363
Advanced Navigation and Postioning Corp	8711	602
Advanced Network Inc	7378	39
Advanced Network Marketing Inc	2721	192
Advanced Neuromodulation Systems Inc	3841	52
Advanced Nutrient Science LLC	5499	23
Advanced Nutritional Technology Inc	2833	70
Advanced Office Automation Inc	5044	154
Advanced Office Interiors Inc	1542	302
Advanced Oxygen Technologies Inc	6512	86
Advanced Personnel Systems	7372	2922
Advanced Phone Solutions Inc	4813	435
Advanced Photo Copy Services	7334	90
Advanced Photographic Solutions LLC	7384	6
Advanced Photonix Inc	3674	191
Advanced Physical Therapy PC	8049	14
Advanced Planning Services Inc	8999	98
Advanced Plastic Corp	3082	8
Advanced Plastic Molding Inc	3089	1752
Advanced Plastics Inc	5162	17
Advanced Plastiform Inc	3089	1261
Advanced Polymer Compounding	3087	13
Advanced Polymer Technology	3089	1365
Advanced Power Designs Inc	3679	162
Advanced Power Services LLC	5084	566
Advanced Power Systems International Inc	5084	824
Advanced Precision Machining Inc	3599	2192
Advanced Precision Manufacturing Inc	3599	100
Advanced Probing Systems Inc	3825	140
Advanced Process	5049	166
Advanced Processing and Imaging Inc	5045	726
Advanced Production Systems Inc	7373	510
Advanced Products Technology Inc	3599	2455
Advanced Programs Group LLC	7371	283
Advanced Programs Inc	3571	101
Advanced Projects International	7379	1099
Advanced Protection Industries Inc	7382	82
Advanced Protection Technologies Inc	5063	233
Advanced Radio Network Studios	7929	4
Advanced Receiver Research	3663	408
Advanced Records Storage Inc	7389	2052
Advanced Recycling Systems Inc	7699	245
Advanced Rehabilitation Technologies	5047	201
Advanced Relational Technology Inc	7372	3447
Advanced Relay Corp	7372	3336
Advanced Research and Development Corp	3672	343
Advanced Research Instruments Corp	3826	166
Advanced Reservation Systems Inc	7379	571
Advanced Reserves Management Inc	7372	4782
Advanced Resource Technology Inc	7373	226
Advanced Resources LLC	7361	193
Advanced Retail Management Systems Inc	3578	29
Advanced Retail Merchandising	8742	670
Advanced Rotocraft Technology Inc	7371	1086
Advanced Safety Systems Inc	5063	505
Advanced Scientifics Inc	3069	43
Advanced Sealing International LLC	3053	98
Advanced Security Services Inc	7381	255
Advanced Security Systems Of New Jersey	1731	1334
Advanced Semiconductor Materials America	3559	45
Advanced Simulation Technology Inc	7373	704
Advanced Software Applications Corp	7372	3510
Advanced Software Development Corp	7372	647
Advanced Software Products Group Inc	7372	1800
Advanced Software Talent LLC	7361	60
Advanced Solder Tech Inc	3699	207
Advanced Solutions International Inc	7372	969
Advanced Space Systems	3489	8
Advanced Specialty Lighting Inc	3646	22
Advanced Specialty Products	5082	147
Advanced Storage Concepts Inc	3577	612
Advanced Superabrasives Inc	3545	294
Advanced Surface Microscopy Inc	8999	212
Advanced System Designs	8748	145
Advanced Systems And Controls Inc	3829	223
Advanced Systems Concepts Inc (Hoboken New Jersey)	7372	2405
Advanced Systems Consultants Inc	7372	2897
Advanced Systems Design Inc	7379	399
Advanced Systems Development Inc	7379	636
Advanced Systems Group A Corp	8748	318
Advanced Systems Research Inc	8734	192
Advanced Systems Resources Inc	7373	412
Advanced Systems Technology	5083	44
Advanced Systems Technology Inc (Lawton Oklahoma)	7373	313
Advanced Teaching Resources Inc	7372	2192
Advanced Tech Sales Inc	5065	598
Advanced Technical Materials	3679	450
Advanced Technical Solutions Inc	7373	165
Advanced Technical Solutions LLC	7373	508
Advanced Technical Systems Inc	1731	2550
Advanced Technologies	7372	580
Advanced Technologies and Services Inc	7372	3655
Advanced Technologies Group Inc	7371	650
Advanced Technologies Group Ltd	6799	370
Advanced Technologies Integration Inc	7379	1246
Advanced Technologies International Inc	8732	57
Advanced Technologies Research Group Inc	5045	882
Advanced Technology and Research Corp	8711	422
Advanced Technology Center Inc	7372	4197
Advanced Technology Distributors Inc	5045	533
Advanced Technology Group Inc	3679	530
Advanced Technology Laboratories Inc	7373	28
Advanced Technology LLC	1731	2435
Advanced Technology Marketing Inc (Orlando Florida)	3674	414
Advanced Technology Materials Inc	8731	31
Advanced Technology Solutions Group Inc	7373	298
Advanced Technology Ventures	6799	250
Advanced Teleco USA Inc	7629	51
Advanced Telemetry Systems International Inc	1731	2420
Advanced Textile Composites Inc	2211	36
Advanced Thermal Products Inc	3086	71
Advanced Thermal Solutions Inc	3823	196
Advanced Thin Films LLC	3699	225
Advanced Tooling	3559	569
Advanced Tooling Inc	3541	177
Advanced Tooling Systems Inc	3544	65
Advanced Tracking Technologies Inc	3577	399
Advanced Transportation Systems Inc	7373	1225
Advanced Tubing Technology Inc	3498	31
Advanced Turf Trucking LLC	5091	89
Advanced Vacuum Company Inc	3823	156
Advanced Vehicle Technologies Inc	3826	159
Advanced Vending Systems Inc	5962	5
Advanced Ventures In Technology Inc	3559	370
Advanced Video Inc	5044	118
Advanced Video Surveillance Inc	1731	2397
Advanced Vision Research Inc	2834	313
Advanced Vision Science Inc	3827	128
Advanced Voice Recognition Systems Inc	7372	5088
Advanced Waste Carriers Inc	4213	2492
Advanced Waterjet Cutting Inc	3449	29
Advanced Web Offset Inc	2759	144
Advanced Weight Loss Clinics	8099	98
Advanced Window Corp	3089	764
Advanced Wireless Solutions	7375	198
Advanced Wireless Solutions Inc	4812	111
Advanced Wireworks Inc	1731	2418
Advanced Workstations In Education Inc	7371	1154
Advanced World Products	5046	163
Advanced Xerographics Imaging Systems Inc	2759	156
AdvancedMD Software Inc	7372	588
AdvanSource Biomaterials Corp	2834	412
Advanstar Communications Inc	2721	10
Advanstar Inc	2721	29
Advanswers PHD	7311	34
Advant Services Inc	7349	225
Advantage Bank	6035	236
Advantage Business Computer Systems Inc	7373	242
Advantage Chevrolet Inc	5511	289
Advantage Controls LLC	5084	430
Advantage Data Inc	7372	2610
Advantage Electronics Inc	3625	270
Advantage Engineering Inc	3822	29
Advantage Federal Resourcing Inc	7363	210
Advantage Fixtures Inc	5046	222
Advantage Food Marketing Corp	5141	192
Advantage Ford	5511	1183
Advantage Health Care	8011	158
Advantage Industries Inc	3543	24
Advantage Information Management Solutions LLC	7389	1850
Advantage Insurers Inc	6411	171
Advantage Laser Products Inc	5943	19
Advantage Leasing Corp	7359	110

Company Name	SIC	Rank	Company Name	SIC	Rank	Company Name	SIC	Rank
Advantage Marketing Group Inc	7311	1023	AEC Design Group	7372	2820	Aerodynamic Engineering Inc	3599	1025
Advantage Media Group	7311	531	Aec Electric Inc	1731	2592	Aerodynamics Inc	5088	35
Advantage Medical Electronics Inc	3679	485	AEC Electrical Contractors Inc	1731	1239	Aerodyne Alloys LLC	5051	91
Advantage Metal Services Inc	5051	379	Aec Engineering	3823	387	Aerodyne Industries LLC	3599	1178
Advantage Mobility Outfitters Inc	7532	11	AEC Inc	3585	30	Aero-Electric Connector Inc	3643	34
Advantage Payroll Services Inc	8721	315	AEC Software Inc	7372	3170	Aerofab Company Inc	3069	185
Advantage Pharmaceuticals Inc	5912	74	AECOM Technology Corp	7361	4	Aerofil Technology Inc	7389	548
Advantage Plastic Products Inc	3089	1715	Aee Solar Inc	5063	106	Aerofin Corp	3443	65
Advantage Plastics and Engineering Inc	3089	1505	Aegean Apparel International Inc	5131	37	Aeroflex Colorado Springs	3674	170
Advantage Print Solutions LLC	2752	1810	Aegerion Pharmaceuticals Inc	2834	463	Aeroflex Holding Corp	3679	33
Advantage Recovery System Inc	7322	185	Aegir Systems Inc	8711	583	Aeroflex International Inc	3728	66
Advantage Sales and Marketing LLC	5141	173	Aegis Assisted Living	6514	2	Aeroflex Laboratories Inc	3621	39
Advantage Security Integration Ltd	1731	2125	Aegis Communications Group Inc	8742	157	Aeroflex Powell	3823	132
Advantage Sentry And Protection Inc	7381	205	Aegis Computer Services Inc	7378	118	AeroGo Inc	3714	364
Advantage Sign Supply Inc	5044	42	Aegis Electronic Group Inc	5065	254	Aerogroup International Inc	5139	1
Advantage Solutions Inc	7372	4584	Aegis Lending Corp	6141	24	AeroGrow International Inc	3524	20
Advantage Systems	7372	3808	Aegis Sales and Engineering Inc	3599	2082	AeroHydro Inc	7372	4655
Advantage Tank Lines	4213	420	Aegis Semiconductor Inc	3674	246	Aero-Instruments Company LLC	3812	127
Advantage Technologies Inc	7373	1014	Aegis Software Corp	7372	1560	Aerojet	3769	2
Advantage Technology Group Inc	7371	1226	Aegistech Inc	7372	1541	Aero-K	3599	694
Advantage Telecommunications Corp	4813	670	AEGON USA Inc	6311	65	Aerolite Extrusion Co	3354	31
Advantage Truck Accessories Inc	5013	241	AEGON USA Realty Advisors Inc	6282	22	Aero-Mach Laboratories Inc	7699	54
Advantageware Inc	7372	841	Aehr Test Systems	3825	89	Aeromation Inc	3672	495
Advantec Engineering LLC	8711	674	AEI Services LLC	4939	2	Aeromatrix Inc	5045	960
Advantech Corp	5045	119	Aeltus Investment Management Inc	6282	52	Aero-Med Molding Technologies Inc	3089	1211
Advantech International Inc	5013	364	Aemetis Inc	2869	131	Aeromet Industries Inc	3599	574
Advantech Manufacturing Inc	3841	292	Aenigma Inc	7379	542	Aero-Metric Inc	8711	93
AdvanTel Inc	5065	278	Aeoa Headstart	8351	36	Aero-Metric Incorporated Anchorage Div	7389	695
Advantest America R and D Center Inc	8731	291	Aeolus Pharmaceuticals Inc	2834	474	Aeromix Systems Inc	3589	122
Advantis Global Inc	7363	120	Aeon Nexus Corp	7371	1452	Aero-Mod Inc	3589	115
Advantis Medical Inc	3841	154	aeonware Inc	7372	870	Aeronautical Electric Co	3644	48
Advantor Systems Corp	5063	125	Aeoroflex New Century	3769	10	Aeronautical Instrument And Radio Co	3812	134
Advantus	7323	16	AEP Industries Inc	4213	32	Aeronca Inc	3724	49
Advatech Solutions Inc	7373	1025	Aep Networks Inc	4813	444	Aeronet Worldwide	4215	5
Advaxis Inc	8731	424	AEP River Operations LLC	4449	18	Aeroparts Manufacturing and Repair Inc	4581	39
Advent Business Systems	7372	81	Aequor Healthcare Services LLC	7361	179	Aero-Plastics Inc	3089	1284
Advent Capital Management LLC	6282	268	Aequus Property Management Co	6531	317	Aeropostale Inc	5699	1
Advent Design Corp	3569	107	Aer Control Systems LLC	3677	118	Aeropres Corp	2813	19
Advent Inc	4491	18	Aer Travel	4724	97	Aeropulse LLC	3564	161
Advent International Corp	6799	63	Aera Products Div	7373	886	Aerosance Inc	8731	322
Advent International Financial Service Inc	6722	75	Aeration Industries International Inc	3589	166	AeroSoft Inc	7372	3687
Advent Machine Tool Inc	3554	68	AERC Broker of Texas Inc	6798	51	Aerosonic Avionics Specialties Inc	3823	80
Advent Security Inc	1731	1314	AERC Oak Bend Inc	6798	17	Aerosonic Corp	3812	60
Advent Software Inc	7371	35	Aerco	3695	176	Aerospace	3679	465
Advent Tool and Mold Inc	3089	344	Aer-Dan Precision	3599	1019	Aerospace America Inc	3589	230
Adventek Corp	3089	1485	Aeria Technology Services Inc	7379	1241	Aerospace and Commercial Technologies Inc	3812	108
Adventist Health	8062	39	Aerial Cartographics of America Inc	7389	622	Aerospace Coatings International Inc	3728	132
Adventist Health System/Sunbelt Inc	8062	191	Aerial Company Inc	5087	8	Aerospace Corp	8731	7
Adventist HealthCare	8062	52	Aerial Contractors Inc	1731	102	Aerospace Fasteners Inc	5088	97
ADVENTRX Pharmaceuticals Inc	8734	209	Aerial Lift Of Connecticut Inc	3531	119	Aerospace Inc	3599	1302
Adventure in Food Trading Company Inc	5149	214	Aerial Machine and Tool Corp	3429	76	Aerospace Materials Corp	5065	211
Adventure Lands of America Inc	7996	25	AERIES Software Inc	7372	1699	Aerospace Optics Inc	3679	384
Adventure Lighting Supply Ltd	5063	566	Aerio Software Inc	7372	4031	Aerospace Products International	5088	16
Adventure Web Productions	7319	75	Aerionx Inc	5045	879	Aerospace Systems	3714	217
Adventureland Park	7996	31	Aeris Corp	3812	210	Aerospace Testing Alliance	8711	121
AdventureLink Inc	4725	34	Aero Assemblies Inc	3496	105	Aerospec Inc	3599	905
AdVentures	6211	364	Aero Astro Inc	3761	8	Aerostar Aerospace Manufacturing Inc	3599	544
Adventures Aloft	4522	37	Aero Bulk Carrier Inc	4213	1510	Aerostar International Inc	3993	36
Adventures in Technology LLC	7379	975	Aero Chip Inc	3599	389	Aerostar Services	7349	290
Advercolor Press Inc	2741	380	Aero Cnc Inc	3728	178	Aerostructures Corp	3769	4
Advertiser Co	2711	102	Aero Components Inc	3599	1301	AeroSurf Wireless Internet Inc	4813	325
Advertiser Printers Inc	2752	542	Aero Contractors Ltd	7359	83	Aerosystems International Inc	7371	1228
Advertisers Duplicating Inc	2752	1221	Aero Controls Avionics Inc	5088	11	Aero-Tag Inc	7319	179
Advertisers Press Inc	2761	25	Aero Corp	3069	156	Aero-Tec Industries Inc	3728	226
Advertising Associates International	7311	916	Aero Design and Manufacturing Inc	3599	139	Aero-Tech Communications Inc	5065	795
Advertising Checking Bureau Inc	8742	288	Aero Direct Inc	5045	623	Aerotech Inc	3699	79
Advertising Company Of America Inc	7311	742	Aero Drapery Corp	2391	9	Aerotech Inc (Lansing Michigan)	3564	26
Advertising Distributors Of America Inc	7331	49	Aero Electrical Contractors Inc	1731	1009	Aerotech Laboratories Inc	8071	36
Advertising Holding Inc	7311	696	Aero Filter Inc	3564	90	Aerotech World Trade Corp	3728	32
Advertising Pam Jacobs	7311	963	Aero Fulfillment Services Corp	4225	25	Aerotechnic Corp	3699	175
Advertising Resources Inc	7389	2116	Aero Gear Inc	3728	68	Aeroterm	6519	16
Advertising Services International LLC	7336	324	Aero Graphics Inc	7335	19	Aerotronics Inc	7622	6
Advertising Specialty Institute Inc (Trevose Pennsylvania)	2721	38	Aero Grinding Inc	5084	358	Aerotron-Repco Sales Inc	5065	587
Advertising Strategies Inc	7311	636	Aero K A P Inc	5063	1038	Aero-Vac Service Corp	8711	603
Advertisingcom Inc	7319	26	Aero Manufacturing Company Inc	3589	107	Aerovironment Inc	3721	17
Advicon Inc	7371	548	Aero Metals Inc	3324	9	Aerovox Division PPC	3675	6
ADVICS North America Inc	3714	24	Aero Mobility Inc	3714	338	Aeroweb Services	7379	1528
Advin Systems Inc	3674	474	Aero Mold and Manufacturing Corp	2821	182	Aeroxchange Ltd	7389	507
Advintex Inc	7373	1001	Aero Precision Products Inc	3599	332	Aertech Machining and Manufacturing Inc	3599	1239
Adviso Group Ltd	6282	498	Aero Precision Repair and Overhaul Company Inc	4581	30	Aerus LLC	3635	6
Advisor Group Inc	6282	355	Aero Products Research Inc	3812	198	Aervoe Industries Inc	2851	53
Advisor Software Inc	7372	1869	Aero Properties LLC	7389	2063	Aes Corp	3699	143
Advisory Board Co	8741	44	Aero Propulsion Support Inc	3463	19	AES Corp	4911	10
Advisory Group of Denver Inc	8742	519	Aero Rubber Company Inc	3069	159	Aes Electric Supply Inc	5063	614
AdvizeX Technologies LLC	7371	159	Aero Simulation Inc	3699	114	AES Warrior Run LLC	1629	86
ADVIZOR Solutions Inc	7372	2506	Aero Space Tooling and Machining	3599	1132	Aesbus Co	7389	1106
Advocat Inc	8051	16	Aero Specialties Material Corp	5051	473	Aesco Electronics Inc	5065	113
Advocate Communications Inc	4841	91	Aero Spring and Manufacturing Company Inc	3495	26	AESOPS Inc	3822	86
Advocate Consulting Group LLC	7379	1249	Aero Studios Ltd	7389	731	AESP Inc	3577	276
Advocate Health Care	8062	3	Aero Surveys Of Georgia Inc	2741	488	AET Films	3089	27
Adwest Technologies Inc	3564	46	Aero Systems Engineering Inc	3825	29	Aetea Information Technology Inc	5045	54
Adwire Inc	7371	1813	Aero Tec Laboratories Inc	3069	166	Aether Dbs LLC	1731	267
Adwood Corp	5084	774	Aero Thermic Shields	3089	1700	Aethlon Medical Inc	3826	171
Adworks Inc (Washington DC)	7311	291	Aero Toy Store LLC	5088	59	Aethra Inc	5065	590
AdWriter Inc	7372	2115	Aero Transporters Inc	4213	2228	Aetna Freight Lines Inc	4213	1793
AE Litho Offset Printers Inc	2752	375	Aeroantenna Technology Inc	3812	80	Aetna Inc	6324	2
AE Staley Manufacturing Co	2046	1	Aerobee Electric Inc	1731	2338	Aetna Insulated Wire Co	3357	22
Ae Techron Inc	3651	177	Aerobics Inc	2284	5	Aetna Life Insurance Company of America	6311	10
AEA Investors Inc	6211	185	AeroCentury Corp	7359	56			
Aearo Technologies Inc	3842	18	AeroComm Inc	3669	101	Aetna Plastics Corp	5162	19
			Aerocomputers Inc	7371	956			
			Aero-Data Metal Crafters Inc	3444	111			

Company Name	SIC	Rank	Company Name	SIC	Rank	Company Name	SIC	Rank
Aetrex Worldwide Inc	3842	60	Ag Press Inc	2711	483	Agm Container Controls Inc	3429	84
Aetrium Inc	3825	80	AG Processing Inc	2075	4	Agm Electronics Inc	3571	164
AEW Capital Management LP	6282	277	Ag Services By Associated Tagline	2875	31	Agm Entertainment Inc	5731	141
AF Machine Inc	3599	1399	Corp			AGM Financial Services Inc	6162	136
Afa Foods Inc	2013	20	AG Spanos Cos	1542	14	Agmet LLC	5093	68
AFA Protective Systems Inc	5063	12	AG Spanos Cos	1531	11	Agnati America Inc	3554	40
Afassco Inc	3841	283	Ag Spray Equipment Inc	3523	132	Agnew Tech-II	8999	173
AFC Cable Systems Inc	3357	24	AG Systems Inc (Hutchinson Min-	3523	288	Agnity Inc	7371	143
AFC (Chatfield Minnesota)	3089	86	nesota)			AGO Insurance Software Inc	5734	173
Afc Electric Inc	1731	358	AG Trucking Inc	4213	2000	Agora Leather Products	3089	252
AFC Enterprises Inc	5812	206	AG View FS Inc	8999	29	Agostino Passanante Brothers	5499	8
Afc Finishing Systems	3448	50	AG Vision	7372	4171	Agouron Pharmaceuticals Inc	8731	28
AFC Industries LLC	3743	7	Ag World Support Systems LLC	7389	1640	AGP Grain Coop	5153	78
AFC Insurance Inc	6411	204	Aga LLC	5064	210	Agr Of Florida Inc	5099	119
Afc-Holcroft LLC	3567	33	Against All Odds Productions	7372	1232	Agralite Electric Coop	4911	518
Afco Electronics	6512	88	Agama Systems Inc (Houston Texas)	5045	254	Agraquest Inc	2879	25
Afco Inc	2653	19	Agape Plastics Inc	3089	404	Agrecolor Inc	2752	1093
Afco Industries Inc	3354	19	Agar Corporation Inc	3823	150	Agree LP	6531	342
Afco Systems Inc	2522	41	Agar Supply Inc	5147	7	Agree Realty Corp	6798	173
Afcon Products Inc	3559	417	Agate Software Inc	7371	1033	Agren Blando Court Reporting and	7338	27
Afe Victory Inc	3585	81	Agati Inc	2521	58	Video Inc		
Affholder Inc	1623	59	Ag-Bag International Ltd	3089	39	Agri Beef Co	0211	4
Affiliate Media Inc	7311	424	Agbest Cooperative Inc	5191	129	Agri Business International Inc	3523	274
Affiliated Bank	6061	133	AGC America Inc	3211	2	Agri Drain Corp	2821	132
Affiliated Business Consultants Inc	7311	951	Agc Electric Inc	1731	571	Agri Machinery and Parts Inc	3523	245
Affiliated Central Inc	7382	67	Agc Flat Glass North America Inc	3211	4	Agri Ventilation Systems LLC	3564	152
Affiliated Communications Inc	7389	1313	AGC Inc	3728	79	AgriBank FCB	6111	8
Affiliated Computer Services Inc	7374	3	AGC Life Insurance Co	6311	83	Agribusiness Management Company	6798	80
Affiliated Control Equipment Company	5085	199	Agc Manufacturing Services Inc	3621	150	LLC		
Inc			AGCO Corp	3523	2	Agricor Inc	2041	29
Affiliated Engineers Inc	8711	232	Agdata Holdings Inc	7379	918	Agricultural Data Systems Inc	7373	798
Affiliated Engineers Inc (Hot Springs	8711	484	Agdia Inc	2835	52	Agricultural Distributing Inc	3568	86
Arkansas)			Age Logistics Corp	3569	174	Agricultural Electronics Corp	3826	158
Affiliated Financial Services Inc	6211	288	Age Manufacturers Inc	3999	144	Agricultural Installations Inc	7359	275
Affiliated Foods Inc	5141	49	Ageatia Technology Consultancy	8748	386	Agricultural Supply Inc	0711	1
Affiliated Foods Midwest	5141	46	Services Inc			Agricultural Transportation Association	4213	2757
Affiliated Management Services Inc	7322	199	Agencias Condado Travel Inc	4724	82	Agriculture	7375	183
Affiliated Managers Group Inc	6282	35	Agency for Instructional Technology	2731	64	Agri-Data Systems Inc	7372	1195
Affiliated Manufacturers Inc	3555	95	Agency Mechanical Services Inc	5065	889	Agri-Education Inc	7812	251
Affiliated Metals	5051	240	Agency Software Inc	7372	725	Agri-Empire	0134	1
Affiliated Products Inc	3679	462	Agency Technologies Inc	7373	332	Agri-Fine Inc	2076	3
Affiliated Resource Group	7373	520	Agencycom Ltd	7379	51	Agrifos Fertilizer LP	1479	6
Affiliated Sports Management	4813	653	Agencysacks	7311	308	Agri-Industrial Plastics Co	3089	770
Company Inc			Agenda Kansas City Inc	7389	2107	Agriland FS Inc	5172	69
Affilisys LLC	4813	654	Agent Software Corp	7372	3854	Agri-Lines Irrigation Inc	5083	111
AFFINA Corp	7389	282	Agent Systems Inc	7372	3688	AgriLogic Inc	7372	499
Affinia Group Intermediate Holdings Inc	3714	22	Agent Video Intelligence	3812	148	Agri-Mark Inc	2026	28
Affinion Group Holdings Inc	7389	33	Agentek Inc	7372	2611	Agrinorthwest	0191	1
Affinity Custom Molding Inc	3089	1277	AgentlifeCom LLC	4813	530	Agri-Nutrients Company Inc	5162	34
Affinity Displays and Expositions Inc	3993	39	Agentrics LLC	7371	128	AgriPride FS Inc	5191	10
Affinity Express Inc	7336	15	Aget Manufacturing Co	3564	131	Agri-Products Inc	3523	257
Affinity Federal Credit Union	6061	12	AGETEC Inc	7372	2936	Agri-Sales Associates Inc	5191	20
Affinity Internet Inc	4899	180	Agfa Construction Inc	1731	1604	AgriSoft CMC	7372	1877
Affinity Network Inc	4813	318	Agfa Corp (Ridgefield Park New	3555	1	Agrisource Inc	5153	192
Affinity Wealth Management	6282	619	Jersey)			AgriStar Global Networks Ltd	4899	225
Affinnova Inc	7372	590	Agfa Materials Corp	3845	20	Agri-Systems Inc	1542	312
Affirmative Insurance Holdings Inc	6331	189	AGFirst Farm Credit Bank	6111	7	AgriTech Analytics	7374	171
Afford Building Maintenance Company	7349	375	Agfirst Farmers Coop (Brookings South	5153	95	Agritek Industries Inc	3523	135
Inc			Dakota)			Agri-Tronix Corp	3823	363
Affordable Appliance Repair Inc	7629	37	Aggio Medical Inc	5047	84	Agrium Inc (Denver Colorado)	2879	15
Affordable Computer Rentals Inc	7377	13	Aggregate Innovations LC	7371	1874	Agrivisor Services Inc	8742	570
Affordable Health Insurance Inc	6321	77	Aggregate Machinery Inc	3532	33	Agrizzi Enterprises Corp	5045	208
Affordable Interior Systems Inc	2522	23	Aggregate Plant Products Co	3443	38	Agro Land and Cattle Company Inc	5812	234
Affordable Warehouse Equipment Inc	5046	310	Aggregates Equipment Inc	3535	92	Agru/America Inc	3081	104
Affy Tapple LLC	2064	74	Aggressive Engineering Corp	3544	702	Ags Technology Inc	3663	173
Affymax Inc	2834	130	Aggressive Grinding Service Inc	7389	823	Agt Technologies Inc	5065	826
Affymetrix Inc	8731	35	Aggressive Industries Inc	3089	1005	Agtek Development Company Inc	7371	860
Afi Cybernetics Corp	3625	184	Aggressive Systems Inc	3823	227	AGV Products Inc	5084	243
AFL Quality Inc	2752	137	Aggressive Tool And Die Inc	7699	190	Ag-Valley Co-op	5191	18
AFLAC Inc	6321	3	Aggressive Tool and Machine	3545	384	AgVantage FS Inc	5191	98
AFMS LLC	8748	186	Company Inc			AgVantage Software Inc	7372	1791
Afp Industries Inc	5084	134	Aggressive Tooling Inc	3544	364	Agvise Laboratories Inc	8731	352
AFP Transformers LLC	3612	29	Agi American Grippers Inc	3679	663	AgWater Technologies Inc	3589	206
Afr Apparel International Inc	2341	14	Agi Industries Inc	5084	287	AGY Holding Corp	3089	80
African American Corp	2752	1599	AGI Media	3565	40	AH Belo Corp	2711	40
African Travel Inc	4725	49	Agi Publishing Inc	2741	61	AH Furnico Inc	5023	183
Afro-American Newspaper	2711	404	AGI Rubber Co	3069	142	AH Newman Inc	4213	2464
AFS and Associates Inc	1521	163	Agile Global Solutions Inc	7372	3088	AH Schreiber Company Inc	2339	11
AFS Technologies Inc (Phoenix	7372	2040	Agile Manufacturing LLC	3523	215	AH Systems Inc	3825	238
Arizona)			Agile Network LLC	3695	80	Ahac Inc	7361	62
Aft Corp	2796	62	Agile Strategy Institute	8742	656	Ahaus Tool and Engineering Inc	3599	334
After Market Technologies Corp	5013	392	Agile View Software Inc	7372	2328	AHC Chiropractic Clinics Inc	8041	1
After Six Inc	2325	17	Agilent Technologies Inc	3825	2	AHC Physicians Corp	8011	67
Afton Chemical Corp	2819	70	Agilepath Corporaton	7379	1187	Ahead Communications Systems Inc	3661	138
Afton Pumps Inc	3561	95	AgileThought Inc	7371	1066	Ahead Headgear Inc	2353	6
Afton Scientific Corp	2834	386	Agilex Flavor Div	2087	36	Ahead Magnetics Inc	3679	414
AG Bisset and Company Inc	6282	632	Agilex Flavors and Fragrances	2844	80	Ahearn-Schopfer and Associates PC	8712	265
AG Computer Center Inc	5734	403	Agilex Technologies Inc	8742	167	Ahf Industries Inc	2086	84
Ag Connections Inc	7379	1036	Agiliance Inc	7371	679	AHI International	4725	31
Ag Crystal Lighting Inc	5063	778	Agility Integration Corp	7379	1244	Ahlstrom Filtration Inc	2621	27
AG Davis Gage and Engineering Co	3545	71	Agility Manufacturing Inc	3672	238	Ahlstrom Mount Holly Springs LLC	2621	59
A-G Devices Of Colorado Inc	3357	85	Agiltron	3669	176	Ahlstrom West Carrollton Inc	2621	48
Ag Electrical Contractors Inc	1731	2365	Agilysys Inc	5065	18	Ahlstrom-Schaeffer Electric Corp	1731	785
Ag Electrical Specialists	3621	141	Ag-Industrial Manufacturing	3523	184	AHM Graves Company Incorporated	6531	381
Ag Engineering and Development Inc	3523	261	AgION Technologies LLC	2899	115	Realtors		
AG Gaston Construction Inc	1542	436	Agissar Corp	3579	34	Ahmad Associates Ltd	8721	83
Ag Holdings Inc	8741	69	Agistix Inc	7371	1102	Ahmed Corp	7373	866
AG Interactive Inc	2771	1	Agi-Vr/Wesson Inc	3541	121	Ahn Enterprises LLC	3677	106
Ag Leader Technology Inc	3829	81	AGL Resources Inc	4924	1	Aho Construction I Inc	1531	62
Ag Machining and Industries Inc	3444	173	AGL Services Co	3663	356	Ahold USA Inc	5411	6
Ag Partners Coop	2048	21	AGL Welding Supply Company Inc	5084	83	Ahrberg Milling Of Cushing Inc	2048	116
Ag Partners Cooperative Inc	5153	42	Agland Cooperative Inc	5191	63	Ahresty Wilmington Corp	3363	22
Ag Partners LLC	5153	29	Agland Inc	5172	58	Ahs Hillcrest Medical Center LLC	8062	140
Ag Partners LLC	5153	117	Agm Automotive Inc	3711	56	Ahura Scientific Inc	8999	77

Company Name	SIC	Rank
Ai Control Systems Inc	3613	149
ai Design Group Inc	7336	133
AI Friedman	5999	25
Ai Industries LLC	3471	76
AI Root Co	3999	66
AI Software Solutions Inc	7373	1122
Ai Squared (Manchester Center Vermont)	7372	3648
AIA Plastics Inc	3089	738
Aibus Corp	7336	214
AIC Inc	2851	120
Aicent Inc	4899	42
AICO Arena International Corp	7372	1582
Aidells Sausage Co	2013	101
Aids Action Committee Of Massachusetts Inc	8322	119
AIE Inc	7389	1854
AIE Pharmaceuticals Inc	2834	250
AIG American General	6371	1
Aig Global Asset Management Holdings Corp	6722	213
AIG SunAmerica Inc	6282	8
Aigner Index Inc	2679	78
AIIM International Inc	7389	699
Aiis Inc	7379	1307
Aiken Chemical Company Inc	5013	222
Aim Aerospace Inc	3728	104
AIM Basic Balanced B Fund	6722	245
AIM Charter Fund C	6722	198
AIM Constellation Fund	6722	50
Aim Electronics Distributors Inc	5063	716
AIM Energy Fund	6722	152
AIM Financial Services Fund	6722	221
AIM Global Growth B Fund	6722	207
AIM High Yield Fund	6722	252
AIM Income Fund	6722	264
Aim Industrial Maintenance Inc	7349	358
AIM International Growth B Fund	6722	246
AIM Investment Services Inc	6211	20
AIM Management Group Inc	6211	13
AIM Municipal Bond B Fund	6722	272
Aim National Lease	7513	7
AIM Security Services Inc	7381	161
Aim Services Inc	7371	950
AIM Software Systems Inc	7372	3590
AIM Summit Fund Inc	6722	112
Aim Transportation Inc	4213	915
AIM US Government B Fund	6722	231
AIM Weingarten Fund	6722	95
AimaSoft Inc	7372	2839
Aimbridge Group	6159	60
Aimet Technologies Inc	3089	974
Aimm Technologies Inc	7349	94
Aimpar Inc	3089	43
AIMS Worldwide Inc	7999	126
Aimtron Corp	3679	656
Ainslie Corp	3599	1200
Ainsworth Electric Inc	1731	1785
AIQ Systems Div	7372	3639
Air Academy Associates LLC	7372	2191
Air America Jet Charter	4522	39
Air and Process Systems Inc	3567	106
Air Bozeman Rental LLP	5083	113
Air Brook Limousine Inc	7514	10
Air Cargo Transit Inc	4213	1537
Air Check Manufacturing Company Inc	3089	1137
Air Cleaning Systems Inc	5075	90
Air Combat USA Inc	7999	135
Air Comfort Corp	1711	186
Air Compressor Products Inc	5084	865
Air Conditioning by Luquire Inc	1711	170
Air Conditioning Installations By Rusher Inc	5075	77
Air Conditioning Products Co	3444	142
Air Conditioning Store Inc	1711	269
Air Conveying Corp	3535	141
Air Cooled Engines	5082	94
Air Craftors Engineering Inc	3599	2267
Air Craftsman Inc	3564	158
Air Cruisers Company LLC	2531	7
Air Cryo Inc	3569	166
Air Duct Aseptics Inc	5075	86
Air Duct Systems Manufacturing Co	3444	250
Air Electro Inc	5065	83
Air Engineers Inc	3585	158
Air Engineers LLC	5075	85
Air Equipment Sales and Service Inc	5084	926
Air Evac Services Inc	4522	15
Air Filter Engineers Inc	5075	89
Air Filter Sales and Service Of Denver Inc	5085	365
Air Filter Sales and Service-Denver Inc	3564	50
Air Filter Service Company Inc	5085	338
Air Filtration Systems LLC	3677	114
Air Flow Technology Inc	3714	311
Air Frame Manufacturing and Supply Company Inc	5088	84
Air Ground Xpress Inc	4213	782
Air Hollywood	7336	17
Air Industries Group Inc	2834	208
Air Instruments and Measurements LLC	3823	402
Air Land Express Courier And Trucking Service Inc	7389	936

Company Name	SIC	Rank
Air Land Transport Inc	4213	1606
Air Liquide America LP	2813	1
Air Liquide Industrial US LP	2813	11
Air Logic Power Systems Inc	3823	189
Air Logistics Corp	3089	1468
Air Louver and Damper Inc	3822	64
Air Mac Inc	7699	177
Air Master Systems Corp	3821	49
Air Masters Inc	1711	268
Air Methods Corp	4522	8
Air Monitor Corp	3822	35
Air One Equipment Inc	5099	81
Air Orlando Aviation Inc	4522	32
Air Power Dynamics LLC	3543	2
Air Power Systems Company Inc	3443	187
Air Pre Employment Screening Services Inc	7389	2158
Air Products and Chemicals Inc	2813	3
Air Products and Controls Inc	3669	104
Air Products Equipment Co	5075	45
Air Quality Engineering Inc	3564	85
Air Quality Sciences Inc	8731	232
Air Relief Inc	3569	69
Air Security International Inc	7381	145
Air Serv South West	3581	16
Air Solutions Heating And Cooling Inc	3585	234
Air Structures American Technologies Inc	2394	22
Air Survey Corp	7389	608
Air System Components LP	3433	9
Air Systems Components	3651	9
Air Systems Distributors Inc	5075	122
Air Systems LLC	5084	574
Air T Inc	4513	10
Air/Tak Inc	3585	211
Air Technical Industries Inc	3537	97
Air Tek Inc	1731	2513
Air Tite Inc	3643	128
Air Touch Powder Coating Inc	3479	79
Air Transport Group Holdings Inc	6719	200
Air Transport International LLC	4512	27
Air Transport Services Group Inc	4513	3
Air Van northAmerica	4213	1278
Air Vegas Airlines	4512	62
Air Vent Inc	3564	10
Air Water International Corp	3585	246
Air Waves Inc	2752	108
Air Way Automation Inc	3549	69
Air Weld Inc	1623	412
Air Wisconsin Airline Corp	4512	39
Air2Web Inc	7372	1179
Airband Communications Inc	4899	73
Airbiquity Inc	3577	185
Airborne 1 Corp	7389	1946
Airborne Health	5122	31
Airborne Power	3679	365
Airborne Systems Group	2395	1
Airborne Systems Inc	7374	303
Airboss Polymer Products Corp	4225	33
Airboss Stock Footage	7336	306
Airbourne Reconnaisance Low	3669	167
Aircanopy Internet Services Inc	4813	461
Aircap Industries Corp	2752	94
Aircastle Ltd	4789	4
Airco Mechanical Inc	1711	83
Aircom Manufacturing Inc	3089	421
Aircon Corp	3564	55
Aircon Filter Sales and Service Co	3564	92
Aircorps Inc	3585	220
Aircraft Cylinders Of America Inc	3599	1936
Aircraft Designs Inc	7372	3976
Aircraft Finance Trust	7359	33
Aircraft Gear Corp	3714	144
Aircraft Industries Inc	2399	29
Aircraft Instrument And Radio Company Inc	5088	87
Aircraft Instruments Co	3812	200
Aircraft Lighting International Inc	8711	656
Aircraft Service International Group	4581	6
Aircraft Technical Publishers	2741	167
Aircraft Xray Laboratories Inc	8734	89
Air-Cure Acquisitions Corp	3312	104
Airdefense Inc	5045	107
Airdusco Inc	5075	99
Airdyne Ltd	5084	312
Aireko Construction Corp	1542	127
Aire-Master of America Inc	2842	34
Aireps Inc	5046	60
Airespace Inc	5045	74
Airetel Staffing Inc	7363	294
Airflex Industrial Inc	3446	33
AirFlite Inc	4581	45
Airflo Cooling Technologies LLC	3564	115
Air-Flo Manufacturing Company Inc	3531	87
Airflow Products Company Inc	3564	43
Airflow Systems Inc	5084	355
Airfoils Impellers Corp	3365	46
Airforce Federal Credit Union	6061	52
Airframe Business Software Inc	7372	2116
Airgain Inc	3577	41
Airgas Carbonic Inc	2813	9
Airgas Dry Ice	2097	4
Airgas Inc	5169	4
Airgas Incorporated Nor-Pac North	5251	3

Company Name	SIC	Rank
Airgas Intermountain Inc	3548	6
Airgas Mid South Inc	2813	5
Airgas North Central	2813	20
Airgas Rutland Tool and Supply Company Inc	5072	22
Airgas South	2813	6
Airgas West Inc	5084	60
Airgas-Nor Pac Inc	2813	12
Air-Hydraulics Co	3542	97
Air-Hydraulics Inc	3542	99
Airimba Wireless Inc	4899	110
Airjet Inc	3564	71
Air-Land Transport Service	4213	829
Airline Hydraulics Corp	5084	95
Airline Tariff Publishing Co	2721	124
Airline Training Center Arizona Inc	8249	10
Airline Transportation Specialists	4213	1297
Airlink Network Corp	7373	1108
Air-Lock Inc	3728	186
Airmall	5999	262
Airmar Technology Corp	3825	59
Airmate Company Inc	3829	286
Airmax International Inc	3564	162
Airmec Inc	3069	264
AirNet Systems Inc	4513	8
Airo Graphics Inc	2752	1120
Air-Oil Systems Inc	5084	764
Airolite Company LLC	3446	34
Airosol Company Inc	7389	1512
Airotech Environmental Inc	3822	89
Airpath Instrument Co	3812	131
airPharma	2834	385
AirPol Inc	8711	469
Airport Mechanical Services Inc	1731	2161
Airpot Corp	3499	123
AirPro Holdings Inc	3585	142
Air-Rite Inc	7623	12
Air-Rite Service	1711	165
Airsan Corp	3564	159
Air-Scent International	2842	106
Air-Sea Forwarders Inc	4731	50
Airspan Networks Inc	3663	54
Airspeed LLC	7371	1042
Airstream Inc	3792	3
Airtek Construction Inc	7699	52
AirTemp Inc	1711	117
Airtex Consumer Product Div	3086	42
Airtex Manufacturing LLP	3585	67
Airtex Products LP	5013	29
Airtherm LLC	3585	129
Airtite Contractors Inc	1742	18
AirTran Airways Inc	4512	49
AirTran Holdings Inc	4512	16
Airtrol Components Inc	3823	277
Airtrol Inc	1711	258
Airtronics Metal Products Inc	3444	42
Airtube Service Company LLC	3535	199
Air-Vac Engineering Company Inc	3548	37
Airvac Inc	1711	161
Airvana Inc	3661	39
Airversent Inc	7371	606
Air-Way Manufacturing Company Inc	3492	10
Airway Sheet Metal Company Inc	1761	41
Airway Technologies Inc	5065	157
Airways Electric Inc	1731	1666
Airways Systems Inc	7389	1407
Airwirenet Inc	7375	272
Airxcel Inc	3585	45
Ai-Shreveport LLC	3714	105
Aisin Brake and Chassis Inc	3714	76
Aisin Holdings of America Inc	3714	199
Aisin World Corporation of America	5013	55
AIT Worldwide Logistics	4731	26
Aitech Defense Systems Inc	3699	50
AITech International Corp	3577	334
Aitkin Iron Works Inc	3599	764
AITOC Inc	7379	264
Aiw-Alton Inc	3599	2026
AIX Media Group	3695	73
AJ Bart Inc	2752	264
AJ Boggs and Co	7379	724
AJ Environmental Inc	8742	653
AJ Giannattasio Electrical Contractors Inc	1731	2001
Aj Images Inc	2759	359
AJ Jersey Inc	5084	182
AJ Johns Inc	1629	82
AJ Kirkwood and Associates Inc	1731	1204
AJ Martini Inc	1541	169
AJ Oster West Inc	3444	223
AJ Parent Corp	2759	155
AJ Peachey and Sons Inc	0751	9
AJ Petrunis Inc	5983	30
AJ Rhem and Associates Inc	7371	1524
AJ Riggins Search Group LP	8742	278
AJ Rinella and Company Inc	5148	69
AJ Schrafel Paper Corp	5113	69
AJ Smoy Company Inc	3677	119
AJ Tool Company Inc	3544	551
AJ Tuck Co	3599	1764
AJ Walker Construction Co	1611	200
AJ Weigand Inc	4213	705
Aja International Inc	3829	198
Aja Landscaping And Maintenance Inc	7349	164

Company Name	SIC	Rank
AJACOM Corp	7372	3255
Ajasa Technologies Inc	7379	199
Ajax Building Corp	1542	315
Ajax Electric Co	3567	111
Ajax Industries Inc	3545	369
Ajax Manufacturing Co	3542	38
Ajax Metal Products Inc	3444	295
Ajax School and Office Source LLC	5049	206
Ajax Tool Inc	3544	904
Ajax - United Patterns and Molds Inc	3089	471
Ajax Window Corp	3442	133
Ajay Chemicals Inc	2834	366
Ajay Patel Md	8011	30
AJC International Inc	5141	112
Ajc Printing Inc	2759	352
AJD Forest Products LP	2421	96
Ajettix Inc	7361	310
Ajilon Finance	7361	30
Ajilon LLC	7379	40
Ajinomoto Frozen Foods USA Inc	2038	23
AJJ Trucking Company Inc	4213	2900
Ajk Electric Company Inc	5063	944
AJL Manufacturing Corp	3544	5
AJM Shrink Wrap Co	3565	149
Ajr Enterprises Inc	7389	1653
Ajr Flooring LLC	5023	69
AJR International Inc	7629	6
AJS Bancorp Inc	6712	606
AJS Publishing Inc	7372	3809
AJT Enterprises Inc	2752	1600
AK Allen Inc	3541	21
AK Environmental LLC	8748	170
AK Industries Inc	3089	641
AK Steel Corp	3312	6
AK Steel Holding Corp	3312	4
AKA Direct Inc	7331	91
AKA Michaelangelo Stairbuilder LLC	2431	98
Aka Printing and Mailing	7331	167
Akademos Inc	7375	163
AKAI Professional	5099	27
Akal Security Inc	7381	7
Akamai Technologies Inc	7379	16
Akdo Intertrade Inc	5032	87
Akebono Brake Corp	3714	78
Akebono Corp (Elizabethtown Kentucky)	8732	16
Aker Partners Inc	8743	306
Aker Solutions US Inc	8711	238
Akerman Construction Company Inc	1623	186
Akerman Senterfitt PA	8111	129
Akers Biosciences Inc	3829	279
Akers Packaging Service Inc	2653	31
Akerue Industries LLC	3448	47
Akg Solutions	7374	323
Aki Inc	5999	4
Akibia Inc	7376	6
Akimbo Systems Inc	7372	2361
Akin Gump Strauss Hauer and Feld LLP	8111	109
Akiwa Technology Inc	3572	73
Akkerman Inc	3531	124
Akm Enterprise Inc	1382	73
AKM LLC	1541	167
Akon Inc	3999	91
Akoo International Inc	3651	74
Akorn Inc	2834	144
Akorn Inc (Somerset New Jersey)	2834	289
Akorri Networks	7371	329
Akoya	8742	327
Akr Enterprises LLC	3699	232
Akra Plastic Products Inc	3089	1388
Akrion Inc	3559	48
Akro-Mils Corp	3089	349
Akron Auto Auction Inc	5012	13
Akron Brass Co	3429	28
Akron Cotton Products Inc	2211	39
Akron Dispersions Inc	2819	121
Akron Endoscopy ASC LLC	8011	138
Akron Foundry Co	3369	9
Akron Gasket and Packaging Enterprises Inc	3053	97
Akron General Health System	8741	56
Akron Hg Inc	2048	38
Akron Paint and Varnish Inc	2851	62
Akron Polymer Products Inc	3089	1069
Akron Porcelain and Plastics Co	3089	638
Akron Rubber Development Laboratory Inc	8731	190
Akron Special Machinery Inc	3599	836
Akron Steel Fabricators Co	3491	49
Akropois Marble And Granite LLC	5032	188
Akshay Software International Inc	7372	1981
Aksia LLC	7389	1991
Akt LLC	7379	1133
Akzo Nobel Coatings Inc	2851	6
Akzo Nobel Inc	2819	39
Al and John Inc	2013	67
Al Asher and Sons Inc	5511	1217
AL Bazzini Company Inc	2068	6
AL Cunningham-B Corp	7377	24
AL Damman Co	5251	7
Al Dente Inc	2099	359
Al Dia Newspaper Inc	2711	892
Al Forte Inc	4213	802

Company Name	SIC	Rank
AL Garey and Associates Inc	3444	153
AL Gilbert Co	5191	28
AL Huber and Son Inc	1542	342
Al Jeff Corp	5013	195
Al Knoch Interiors Inc	2273	36
Al Kramp Specialties	3648	80
Al Lasher Electronics	5999	313
Al Mar Building Maintenance Inc	7349	472
Al Neyer Inc	6552	186
Al Paul Lefton Company Inc	7311	185
al Punto Advertising Inc	7311	483
Al Rossy Investigations Inc	7381	163
Al Serra Chevrolet Inc	5511	177
AL Smith Trucking Inc	4213	1669
AL Systems Inc	7372	1966
Al T Inc	3569	296
Al Thompson Trucking Inc	4213	1963
Ala Inc	8748	76
Ala Wai Marine Ltd	3599	941
Alaark Tooling and Automation Inc	3544	246
Alabama Aircraft Industries Inc	3721	20
Alabama and Florida Railway Company Inc	4011	26
Alabama Bolt and Supply Inc	5072	155
Alabama Business Forms Inc	2759	452
Alabama Catfish Inc	2091	10
Alabama Coca-Cola Bottling Co	5149	65
Alabama Converter Corporation Inc	3441	239
Alabama Copper Bronze Company Inc	3365	34
Alabama Crown Distributing Co	5182	10
Alabama Dynamics Inc	3599	1502
Alabama Electric Company Incorporated Of Dothan	1731	199
Alabama Electric Motor Services LLC	5063	580
Alabama Farmers Coop	2041	5
Alabama Food Service Inc	4213	1451
Alabama Gas Corp	4924	24
Alabama Goodwill Industries Inc	8331	128
Alabama Graphics and Engineering Supply Inc	7334	28
Alabama Industrial LLC	5085	376
Alabama Interforest Corp	2426	27
Alabama Janitorial Services Inc	7349	347
Alabama Lighting Associates Inc	5063	1080
Alabama Liquidation And Auction Inc	7389	2085
Alabama Motor Express Inc	4213	102
Alabama Plastics Inc	3089	658
Alabama Power Co	4911	121
Alabama Railroad Co	4011	53
Alabama River Newsprint Co	2621	53
Alabama Skills USA	7389	2059
Alabama Specialty Products Inc	3829	44
Alabama Web Press Inc	2752	157
Alabama-Tombigbee Regional Commission	8748	215
ALAC Contracting Corp	5082	210
Alacer Corp	2834	140
Alacer Gold Corp	1021	6
Alaco Of Mississippi Inc	3086	124
Alacritech Inc	7379	1469
Alacron Inc	3571	138
Aladdin Bakers Inc	2051	94
Aladdin Electric Inc	1731	932
Aladdin Graphics Inc	2752	1761
Aladdin Knowledge Systems Inc	7372	1780
Aladdin Label Inc	2672	59
Aladdin Petroleum Corp	1311	242
Aladdin Steel Inc	5051	175
Aladdin Temp-Rite LLC	3589	7
Aladdin Travel and Meeting Planners	4724	102
Aladdin's Baking Company Inc	5149	148
Aladdin's Electrical	1731	1681
Alain's Originals In Wood Inc	3553	54
Alakai LLC	7373	921
Alaka'i Mechanical Corp	1711	32
Alakef Coffee Roasters Inc	5149	220
Alamac American Knits LLC	2257	3
Alamana County Maintenance	5087	188
Alambic Inc	2084	126
Alambry Funding Inc	6162	60
Alamo Aircraft Ltd	5088	33
Alamo Analytical Lab	8734	184
Alamo Capital Inc	6282	36
Alamo Group Inc (San Antonio Texas)	8093	45
Alamo Group Inc (Seguin Texas)	3523	10
Alamo Group Inc USA	3523	15
Alamo Group SMC Inc	3523	47
Alamo Lumber Co	5211	134
Alamo Marble Ltd	3281	32
Alamo Service Company Inc	5078	37
Alamo Tamale Company LP	2099	325
Alamo Title Co	6411	51
Alamo Title Holding Co	6411	43
Alamo Transformer Supply Co	5063	317
Alamo Transportation Services Co	4213	3000
Alamo Travel Group Inc	4724	39
Alan B Glazen Inc	7812	167
Alan B Lancz and Associates Inc	6282	370
Alan B Whitson Company Inc	8742	210
Alan Baird Industries Inc	2298	12
Alan Good Shop	5032	141
Alan Gordon Enterprises Inc	5946	16
Alan Gorzlancyk Enterprises Inc	2448	27

Company Name	SIC	Rank
Alan I Harris Group	2741	408
Alan Industries Inc	3679	529
Alan Jeffrey Corporation Communications	7336	207
Alan Manufacturing Inc	3444	255
Alan Plummer and Associates Inc	8711	188
Alan Ritchey Inc	4213	81
Alan Taylor Communications	8743	41
Alan Wasser Associates	7922	104
Alan Weiss Productions Inc	7812	80
Alan Wire Co	3351	21
Alanco Technologies Inc	3572	46
Alandale Industries Inc	3552	60
Alanis Security Services Corp	7381	90
Alaniz LLC	7331	37
Alante Corp	5045	1055
Alar Leasing Co	7359	243
Alare Capital Partners LLC	6282	261
Alaric Compliance Services LLC	7389	740
Alarm Components Distributing Corp	5063	1050
Alarm Controls Corp	3669	241
Alarm Digital Telecommunications Corp	5063	898
Alarm Masters	7382	149
Alarm Monitoring Of Cincinnati Inc	7382	169
Alarm Security	5063	722
Alarmco	3651	252
Alarms Unlimited Inc	1731	1960
AlarmSoft Inc	7372	1878
Alas Inc	7372	622
Alaska Air Group Inc	4512	11
Alaska Airlines Inc	4512	13
Alaska Center For The Performing Arts Inc	7922	60
Alaska Communications Systems Group Inc	4813	50
Alaska Computer And Typewriter Service Inc	7378	165
Alaska Electric Light and Power	4931	45
Alaska Family Services Inc	8322	168
Alaska Garden And Pet Supply Inc	2048	40
Alaska Instrument Company Inc	5065	686
Alaska Metal Recycling Co	5093	219
Alaska Pacific Bancshares Inc	6712	637
Alaska Pacific Bank	6035	184
Alaska Power and Telephone Co	4911	496
Alaska Pump and Supply Inc	5084	598
Alaska Quality Publishing Inc	2721	427
Alaska R and C Communications Inc	5064	148
Alaska Railroad Corp	4011	22
Alaska Sales and Service Inc	5511	770
Alaska Sausage Company Inc	2091	25
Alaska Seafood Company Inc	2092	101
Alaska Ship And Drydock Inc	3731	42
Alaska Wild Berry Products Inc	2033	110
Alaskan Brewing LLC	2082	62
Alaskan Copper Companies Inc	5051	208
Alaskan Star Software	7379	1218
ALATEC Inc	8742	366
Alba Editorial Inc	7372	3855
Alba International Inc	2048	149
Alba Manufacturing Inc	3535	94
Alban Service Industries LLC	7349	119
Albanese Confectionery Group Inc	2064	45
Albank Corp	6712	236
Albano Systems Inc	7371	673
Albany Auto Auction Inc	5012	110
Albany Bank and Trust Company NA	6021	116
Albany Bank and Trust NA	6022	246
Albany Foam And Supply Inc	5087	65
Albany Herald Publishing Co	2711	299
Albany Industries Inc	2512	16
Albany International Corp	2221	2
Albany International Corp (Menasha Wisconsin)	2221	27
Albany Molecular Research Inc	8731	47
Albany Steel Inc	5051	237
Albany Word Processing Services and One Plus Mail Inc	7338	56
Albany-Chicago Company LLC	3363	11
Albar Industries Inc	3089	493
Albar Precious Metal Refining	8999	83
Albarell Electric Inc	1731	230
Albarrie Technical Fabrics Inc	3569	251
Albaugh Inc	2879	3
Alba-Wheels Up International Inc	4731	63
Albax Inc	2394	34
Albco Sales Inc	5051	122
Al-Be Industries Inc	3599	78
Albee Appliances Inc	5722	19
Albemarle Corp	2821	9
Albemarle Electric Membership Corp	4911	478
Albemarle International Corp	2821	8
Albemarle Orthotics and Prosthetics Inc	3842	323
Albeni Falls Building Supply Inc	5031	284
Albensi Dental Laboratory Inc	8072	20
Albercorp	3825	119
Alberg Software Inc	7372	2010
Alberici Constructors	1542	267
Alberici Corp	1542	26
Albers Sheetmetal And Ventilating Inc	1711	132
Albert and Marc Kaufman Inc	2371	2
Albert Basse Associates Inc	2759	228
Albert D Phelps Inc	6531	263

Company Name	SIC	Rank
Albert D Seeno Construction Co	1521	29
Albert E Erickson Co	3599	1483
Albert Farms Inc	4213	1193
Albert G Ruben and Company Inc	6399	10
Albert Guarnieri Company Inc	5194	13
Albert H Notini and Sons Inc	5194	8
Albert M Higley Co	1541	105
Albert R Serviss	3089	1594
Albert S Smyth Company Inc	5944	19
Albert Shaffer Trucking Inc	4213	1785
Albert Trostel and Sons Co	3111	1
Albert W Sisk and Son Inc	4789	19
Albert Webster Engineering Co	3599	1738
Alberta Crowe Letter Service Inc	7331	265
Alberto-Culver Co	2844	8
Albert's Organics Inc	5148	15
Albert's Screen Print Inc	2759	107
Albertson and Hein Inc	3599	1863
Albertson's LLC	5411	3
Albertsons LLC	5411	290
Albertsons Mill	2541	31
Albertville Quality Foods Inc	2015	24
Albest Metal Stamping Corp	3469	219
Albia Newspapers Inc	2711	845
Albies Foods Inc	2053	23
Albin Engineering Services Inc	7361	116
Albina Community Bancorp	6712	678
Albina Community Bank	6022	639
Albino Construction Inc	1731	119
Albinson Reprographics LLC	5199	66
Albion Devices Inc	3829	489
Albion Industries Inc	3429	89
Albion Internation Inc	2048	66
Albion Telephone Co	4813	267
Albion-Holley Pennysaver Inc	2791	22
Albis Plastics Corp	5162	53
Albrecht Sand and Gravel Co	1442	26
Albrecht Viggiano Zureck PC	8721	368
Albright Crumbacker Moul and Itell	8721	35
Albright Electric Inc	1731	1911
Albright's Mill LLC	5153	195
Albritton Electrical Service Inc	1731	1319
Albumx Corp	2782	24
Albuquerque Council For International Visitors	7389	2273
Albuquerque Publishing Company Inc	2711	172
Albuquerque Tortilla Company Inc	2099	133
Alcan Baltek Corp	2493	13
Alcan Cable Div	3355	2
Alcan Foil Products Div	3353	14
Al-Cast Mold and Pattern Inc	3543	40
Alcat Inc	3083	60
Alcatel Lucent Submarine Network Inc	3661	10
Alcatel-Lulcent	3669	50
Alc-Collegedale LLC	2521	29
Alchem Limited Lllp	2869	109
Alchimisti Group Inc	3825	320
Alco Industries Inc	2879	10
Alco Machine Company Inc	3599	970
Alco Machine Corp	3599	2391
Alco Parking Corp	7521	10
Alco Plastics Inc	3089	536
Alcoa	3444	4
Alcoa Building Products Inc	3444	199
Alcoa Howmet	3324	4
Alcoa Inc	3334	1
Alcoa Steamship Company Inc	4412	22
Alco-Chem Inc	5087	78
Alcohol and Drug Addiction Services	2721	116
Alcohol And Drug Recovery Centers Inc	8093	34
Alcohol Monitoring Systems Inc	5047	74
Alcom Printing Group Inc	2752	166
Alcon Inc	3643	99
Alcon Industries Inc	3325	24
Alcon Laboratories Inc	2834	63
Alcona Tool and Machine Inc	3544	328
Alcone Company Inc	2844	140
Alcone Marketing Group	7311	106
Alconox Inc	2841	54
Alcore Inc	3469	187
Alcorn County Electric Power Association	4911	472
Alcorn Exploration Inc	1382	52
Alcorn Fence Co	1799	46
Alcotec Wire Corp	3355	6
Alcott Group Inc	7363	72
Aldag/Honold Mechanical Inc	1711	61
Aldagen Inc	2836	85
Aldajo Inc	2599	39
Aldan Electric Supply Inc	5063	412
Aldan Sundries Inc	5087	198
Aldas LLC	2841	52
Aldea Communications Inc	7319	97
Aldebaron Inc	7372	3640
Aldec Inc	7372	1510
Alden and Ott Printing Inks Co	2893	18
Alden Shoe Company Inc	3143	13
Alden State Bank	6022	504
Alden Systems Inc	8741	52
Alden Tool Company Inc	3545	222
Alder Construction Co	1541	113
Alderbrook Vineyards and Winery LLC	2084	132
Alderfer Inc	2013	100

Company Name	SIC	Rank
Aldila Inc	3949	55
Aldine Inc (New York New York)	2752	448
Aldinger Inc	7331	203
Aldon Electric Inc	1731	750
Aldon Food Corp	2099	166
Aldonex Inc	3612	109
Aldrico Inc	3433	60
Aldridge Jordan Inc	1623	713
Alds Inc	5013	243
Ale House Management Inc	5812	466
ALE Hydraulic Machinery Company LLC	3599	2193
Ale-8-One Bottling Co	2086	105
Alea Systems Inc	3571	230
Aleev Inc	5999	280
Alem Computer Software Inc	7372	3856
Alenco Holding Corp	3442	13
Alene Candles LLC	3999	88
Alenet Inc	4813	745
Alepo USA	5045	566
Aleratec Inc	5045	672
Alere Inc	2835	2
Alere Toxicology Services Inc	8734	32
Aleri Inc	8742	286
Aleris International Inc	3341	1
Alert Alarm System Inc	1731	1438
Alert Communications	5999	296
Alert Electric Inc	1731	1638
Alert Security Services By Kiser Group Inc	1731	1144
Alert Stamping and Manufacturing Company Inc	3699	186
Alert Technologies	3812	201
Alert Telephone Answering Service Inc	7389	1324
Alerus Financial Corp	6712	303
Alesis Semiconductor Corp	7389	2435
Alessi Manufacturing Corp	3511	35
Alethea's Chocolates Inc	2066	35
Alex E Paris Contracting Company Inc	1541	156
Alex Lee Inc	5141	25
Alex Orthopedic Inc	3842	307
Alex Products Inc	3599	66
Alex Silk Company Inc	2221	49
Alexander and Associates Company Inc	8711	323
Alexander and Baldwin Inc	4424	1
Alexander and Hornung Inc	2013	198
Alexander and Pamaro Inc	2752	1826
Alexander Associates (Brooklyn New York)	7389	1774
Alexander Binzel Corp	3548	51
Alexander Cameron	7373	984
Alexander Chemical Corp	2899	127
Alexander City Flying Service Inc	4111	17
Alexander Clark Inc	2752	553
Alexander Communities	6552	267
Alexander Company Inc	6552	178
Alexander Constructors Inc	1542	107
Alexander Consulting LLC	7379	1136
Alexander Dodds Co	3553	55
Alexander Doll Company Inc	3942	12
Alexander Electric Inc	1731	856
Alexander Global Promotions Inc	3944	33
Alexander Haas Martin and Partners	7389	2187
Alexander Haas Martin and Partners Inc	7375	192
Alexander International	4731	14
Alexander LAN Inc	7372	3591
Alexander Law Firm PC	6282	591
Alexander Lumber Co	5031	202
Alexander Marketing Services Inc	7311	243
Alexander Moulding Mill Co	2431	119
Alexander Ogilvy Public Relations	8743	90
Alexander Pft Inc	7389	1650
Alexander Plastics Inc	3999	130
Alexander Utility Engineering Inc	7372	2570
Alexander Wall Corp	7349	167
Alexander's Inc	6798	109
Alexander's Machine and Maintenance Service Company Inc	3599	1733
Alexander's of Brooklyn Inc	6512	69
Alexanders Print Stop Inc	2752	424
Alexander's Printing Company Inc	2759	607
Alexander's Restaurants of Texas Inc	5812	295
Alexandria Acquisition Company LLC	3354	44
Alexandria Moulding Inc	2431	61
Alexandria Opthalmology ASC LLC	8011	163
Alexandria Pro-Fab Company Inc	3599	493
Alexandria Real Estate Equities Inc	6798	44
Alexian Brothers Medical Center	8062	75
Alexian Brothers Of San Jose Inc	8062	173
Alexion Pharmaceuticals Inc	2834	48
Alexis Fire Equipment Co	3711	61
Alexy Associates Inc	3699	304
Alf Christianson Seed Co	0181	16
Alfa Aesar	2833	18
Alfa Color Inc	3861	39
Alfa Corp	6331	121
Alfa General Insurance Corp	6331	32
Alfa Insurance Corp	6331	31
Alfa International Corp	5046	113
Alfa Laval Inc	3443	166
Alfa Laval Inc (Warminster Pennsylvania)	3569	35

Company Name	SIC	Rank
Alfa Life Insurance Corp	6311	43
Alfa Machine and Tool Company Inc	3599	1818
Alfa Tec Manufacturing Company Inc	1796	38
Alfa Transformer Co	5063	1063
Alfa Travelgear Inc	5099	82
Alfab Inc	3441	103
Alfalfa Electric Cooperative Inc	4911	384
Alfalight Inc	3674	211
Alfa-Pet Inc	2048	89
alfaQuest Technology	3577	468
Alfatech Cambridge Group Gp	8741	84
Alfieri-Proctor Associates Trust	5075	76
Alfonso Architects Inc	8712	165
Alfonso Vastola	5045	807
Alford Advertising Inc	7311	800
Alfred Conhagen Inc	7699	43
Alfred Conhagen Incorporated Of California	5085	265
Alfred Dunhill of London Inc	5611	23
Alfred Envelope Co	2752	1685
Alfred H Knight North America Ltd	8734	174
Alfred Manufacturing Co	3469	174
Alfred Nickles Bakery Inc	2051	11
Alfred Technology Resources Inc	3821	63
Alfredo Malatesta Inc	1731	2024
Alfred's Pictures Frames Inc	3089	1072
Algae-X International	3823	303
Algas-Sdi International LLC	3569	178
Algen Design Services Inc	3679	381
Alger Company Inc	3645	68
Alger Equipment Company Inc	3843	89
Alger Manufacturing LLC	3451	20
Algoma Lumber Company Inc	2421	116
Algon Services Inc	7349	526
Algonquin Gas Transmission Co	4922	9
Algonquin Studios Inc	7379	1024
Algor Inc	7372	1950
Algorithmic Implementations Inc	5734	208
Algus Packaging Inc	3089	771
ALH Group Inc	7371	1181
Alhambra Productions Inc	5065	890
Alhern-Martin Industrial Furnace Co	5074	203
Ali International LLC	8742	577
Alianza Building Services Inc	7349	419
Alibris Inc	5961	132
Alice Corp	2051	240
Alice Manufacturing Company Inc	2211	18
Aliceblue	7335	18
Alico Inc	0174	5
Alicomp Inc	7374	314
Alief Electro Mechanical Inc	1731	2212
Alien Skin Software LLC	7372	3592
Alien Technology Corp	7389	566
Alienware Corp	3651	34
Alight Electric	1731	1917
Align Technology Inc	3842	27
Aligned Development Strategies Inc	7371	1423
AlignMark	7372	2447
Alimak Hek Inc	5084	163
Alin Machining Company Inc	3599	142
Alinabal Inc	3469	49
Aline Components Inc	3089	1461
A-Line Products Corp	2851	168
Alion Science and Technology Corp	8731	22
Alion Science and Technology Corp Live and Environmental Technology	8731	23
Aliroo America Inc	7371	1099
Alison Control Inc	3669	226
Alitech Consulting LP	7373	442
ALJ Regional Holdings Inc	7319	20
Aljo Precision Products Inc	3599	1058
Aljo-Gefa Precision Manufacturing LLC	3674	285
Al-Jon Manufacturing LLC	3523	64
ALK Technologies Inc	8742	361
Alkab Contract Manufacturing Inc	3599	1343
Alkat Electrical Contractors Inc	1731	1020
Alken-Murray Corp	2899	241
Alken-Ziegler Inc	5015	6
Alkermes Inc	2834	101
Alki Software Corp	7372	3383
AL-KO KOBER Corp (Elkhart Indiana)	3799	13
Alkota Cleaning Systems Inc	3589	92
All 1 Service Inc	7349	364
All 4-Pcb North America Inc	5065	893
All About People Inc	7361	112
All About Signs N Print Inc	2752	1025
All Access Music Group Inc	7389	1907
All Action Architectural Metal and Glass	1793	12
All American Amputee	3842	258
All American Arkansas Poly Corp	2673	41
All American Balianti Inc	7379	1063
All American Containers Inc	3411	10
All American Crafts Inc	2721	276
All American Forms Manufacturing Inc	2759	429
All American Hardwood Inc	5023	174
All American Home Center Inc	5251	10
All American Homes LLC	2452	5
All American Inc	5091	128
All American Packaging	2657	5
All American Pharmaceutical	2833	28
All American Poly Corp	3081	44
All American Private Security Inc	7382	40
All American Products Co	3366	3
All American Publishing Limited Co	2752	1374

Company Name	SIC	Rank
All American Racers Inc	3751	16
All American Scales Inc	5046	170
All American Seasonings Inc	2099	243
All American Semiconductor Inc	5065	43
All Appliance Parts Inc	5085	370
All Arctic Sheet Metal Inc	1711	198
All Book Covers Arizona Inc	3172	9
All Book Covers Inc	2678	8
All Care Services Inc	8322	232
All Chemical Disposal Inc	4953	99
All Chemical Transport Corp	4213	1901
All City Electric	1731	116
All Coast Communications Inc	1731	1205
All Communications Inc	4813	388
All Copy Products Inc	5999	100
All Covered Inc	7373	89
All Diameter Grinding Inc	3599	346
All Electric and Specialty Systems Inc	5063	630
All Erection and Crane Co	7353	5
All Five Tool Company Inc	3544	496
All Flex Flexible Circuits LLC	3672	98
All Florida Staffing Inc	7539	6
All Foam Products Co	3086	178
All Foils Inc	5051	250
All Freight Systems Inc	4213	830
All Fuels and Energy Co	7379	1651
All In 1 Security Services Inc	7382	108
All In One Inc	8741	227
All Industrial Electric Inc	1731	970
All Island Electrical Contracting Inc	1731	2487
All Kitchens Inc	5141	200
All Luminum Products Inc	2514	7
All Major Appliances Inc	5064	99
All Manufacturers Inc	3724	30
All Metal Sales Inc	5051	420
All Metals Industries Inc	5051	109
All Metals Processing Of San Diego Inc	3471	40
All Metals Service and Warehousing Inc	4225	10
All Nails and More	5087	193
All Natural Botanicals Inc	2844	171
All Phase Electrical Contractors	1731	1397
All Phase Video-Security Inc	5065	911
All Plastics And Fiberglass Inc	2821	149
All Plastics Molding Company Inc	3089	1218
All Points Equipment Inc	5511	1237
All Points Inspection Services Inc	7389	2287
All Pool and Spa Inc	1521	90
All Poolside Services Inc	5999	131
All Power Battery Inc	7699	227
All Pro Answering Bureau	7389	1967
All Pro Electrical Contractors Inc	1731	2319
All Pro Roofing	1761	50
All Pro Sales Inc	5063	853
All Pro Solutions Inc	3577	418
All Products Automotive Inc	5013	139
All Purpose Contracting Inc	1623	672
All Road Barricades Inc	7353	90
All Season Nails Div	2844	121
All Seasons Distributors Inc	7389	2117
All Secure Technologies Inc	5039	62
All Service Electric Inc	1731	1258
All Service Telecommunications	4813	586
All Sign Systems Inc	3993	174
All Southern Fabricators Inc	3469	247
All Star Apparel	5085	200
All Star Audio-Video Inc	5731	138
All Star Awards and Ad Specialties Inc	5999	172
All Star Consulting Inc	7379	655
All Star Corrugated	7389	1507
All Star Directories Inc	8999	72
All Star Electrical Services Inc	1731	2073
All Star Funds Inc	2741	270
All Star Lighting Supplies Inc	5063	854
All Star Maintenance Inc	7349	55
All Star Moving and Storage Inc	4213	2629
All Star Wireless	4812	93
All State Manufacturing Company Inc	5087	176
All State Promotions Inc	8743	53
All State Security Inc	7381	190
All Steel Products Inc	5051	216
All Systems Colour Inc	2732	57
All Systems Designed Solutions Inc	1731	649
All Systems Integrated	3629	118
All Technics Products Inc	3575	34
All Teriors Floor Covering Inc	5713	16
All That Ink and Computer Produc	5734	472
All Things Digital Inc	3679	668
All Tile Inc	5023	35
All Tool Company Inc	3599	2137
All Travel Inc	4724	104
All Truck Transportation Co	4213	698
All Used Transmission Parts Inc	5013	249
All Valley Washer Service Inc	7215	3
All Ways Communications	7389	1750
All Ways Moving and Storage	4213	2844
All Web Leads Inc	7375	73
All West Plastics Inc	3089	838
All West Utah Inc	5999	149
All World Machinery Supply Inc	5084	442
All World Travel Inc	4724	105
Alladin Investments Inc	3089	1129
Allamakee-Clayton Electric Cooperative Inc	4911	553
All-American Asphalt and Aggregates Inc	2951	37
All-American Co-Op	5153	175
All-American Engineering and Manufacturing Inc	3599	829
All-American Printing Services Corp	7334	39
All-American Services Inc	7342	67
All-American SportPark Inc	5999	246
Allan A Myers Inc	1622	5
Allan Brooks and Associates Inc	5112	87
Allan Co	5093	37
Allan Industries	7389	1115
Allan R Hackel Organization Inc	7311	619
Allant Group Inc	7389	373
Allbrite Electrical Contractors Inc	1731	403
Allbritton Communications Co	4833	12
AllBusiness	7363	198
Allcable Inc	5063	961
AllCapital/GPT Properties LLC	6798	152
Allcare Dental Management Inc	8021	5
AllChem Industries	2899	36
Allchem Services Inc	5169	147
All-City Computers Inc	3571	137
Allcom Electric Inc	1623	582
Allcomm Technologies Inc	5064	193
Allcraft Printing Inc	2752	1798
ALLDATA LLC	7379	75
Alleghany Corp	6361	2
Allegheny Bar Association Inc	2711	509
Allegheny City Electric Inc	1731	613
Allegheny Engineering Co	5075	96
Allegheny Fabricating and Supplies Inc	5021	146
Allegheny Financial Group Ltd	6282	442
Allegheny Iron and Metal Co	5093	137
Allegheny Manufacturing and Electrical Service Inc	7699	170
Allegheny Metal Corp	5051	440
Allegheny Plastics Inc	3089	556
Allegheny Plywood Company Inc	5031	163
Allegheny Refrigeration Service Co	7623	15
Allegheny Technologies Inc	3312	7
Allegheny Valley Bancorp Inc	6712	507
Allegheny Valley Bank of Pittsburgh	6022	139
Allegheny-Wagner Industries Inc	3589	159
Allegiance Inc	5731	215
Allegiance Industries Inc	7349	80
Allegiance Protection Group Inc	7381	200
Allegiant Networks LLC	4813	393
Allegiant Travel Co	4512	30
Allegis Group Aerotek	7389	2153
Allegis Group Inc	7361	2
Allegra Network	2752	643
Allegro Microsystems Inc	3674	54
Allegro Resorts Market Corp	7011	109
Allegro Software Development Corp	7372	3218
All-Electric Construction and Communication LLC	1731	1191
Allen and Allen Company Inc	5031	126
Allen and Cowley Urban Trading Company LLC	5149	160
Allen and Gerritsen	7311	168
Allen and Hoshall Inc	8711	478
Allen and O'Hara Inc	6552	286
Allen And Webb	5085	186
Allen and Whalen Company Incorporated Of Md	1731	2207
Allen Brothers Inc	2013	82
Allen Brothers Milling Company Inc	2041	55
Allen C Ewing and Co	6211	393
Allen C Ewing Financial Services Inc	6211	276
Allen C Ewing Mortgage and Realty	6211	254
Allen Commercial Industries Inc	7389	1992
Allen Communication Inc	7372	1862
Allen Company Inc	1611	176
Allen D Ormond	1623	478
Allen Datagraph Systems Inc	3577	401
Allen Dental Laboratory Inc	8072	33
Allen Electric Co	1731	2030
Allen Electric Company Inc	1731	2126
Allen Engineering Corp	3531	91
Allen Extruders Inc	3081	45
Allen Field Company Inc	3089	1030
Allen Filters Inc	3569	273
Allen Foods Inc	5141	171
Allen Freight Services Inc	4213	1184
Allen Gauge and Tool Co	3823	249
Allen Health Systems Inc	8741	118
Allen Independent School District	8211	12
Allen Industrial Supply LP	5072	156
Allen Industries Inc	3993	26
Allen Interactions Inc	7372	926
Allen L Bender Inc	1542	231
Allen Lumber Company Inc	5211	110
Allen Lund Company Inc	4731	40
Allen Machine Products Inc	3469	252
Allen Matkins Leck Gamble and Mallory LLP	8111	321
Allen Millwork Inc	5031	104
Allen Morris Co	6552	140
Allen Organ Co	3931	8
Allen Orton LLC	5085	289
Allen Press Inc	2721	97
Allen Printing Company Inc	2752	1042
Allen Roche Group Inc	7311	626
Allen Samuels Auto Group	5511	26
Allen Samuels Chevrolet Inc	5511	222
Allen Samuels Chevrolet Mercedes	5511	532
Allen Samuels Dodge Hyundai	5511	657
Allen Screen Printing	2759	209
Allen Stromberg And Co	2752	683
Allen Tate Company Inc	6531	73
Allen Tel Products Inc	3661	143
Allen Tool Phoenix Inc	7692	50
Allenair Corp	3494	50
Allendale Gravel Company Inc	1611	234
Allen-Edmonds Shoe Corp	3143	10
Allen-Mitchell and Co	3599	1347
Allen's Blueberry Freezer Inc	2037	43
Allens Inc	2033	16
Allen's of Hastings Inc	5311	49
Allens Steel Products Inc	1791	15
Allen-Sherman-Hoff	3494	23
Allensville Planing Mill Inc	5211	155
Allentown Beverage Company Inc	5181	100
Allentown Inc	3444	28
Allentown Jewish Community Center	8322	202
Allentown Optical Corp	5048	25
Allerdice Building Supply Inc	5072	150
Allergan Inc	2834	13
Allergan USA Inc	2834	112
Allergy Laboratories Inc	2836	64
Allergy Laboratories Of Ohio	2834	406
Allergy Research Group Inc	5122	76
Allermed Laboratories Inc	2833	67
Allerton Heneghan and O'Neill	7361	252
Alleson Of Rochester Inc	2329	27
ALLETE Inc	4931	30
Alley-Cassetty Companies Inc	5032	8
Allfast Fastening Systems Inc	3429	54
All-Fill Corp	3565	57
Allframe Computer Services Inc	7379	1405
Allgood Construction Company Inc	1623	143
Allgood Services Of Georgia Inc	7342	10
Allgress Inc	7371	1302
Alliance Artists Ltd	7389	2342
Alliance Bancorp Incorporated of Pennsylvania	6035	125
Alliance Bank and Trust Co	6022	597
Alliance Bank Corp	6022	271
Alliance Bank NA	6021	152
Alliance Bank of Arizona	6022	452
Alliance Bankshares Corp	6712	455
Alliance California Municipal Income Fund Inc	6722	229
Alliance Carolina Tool and Mold Corp	3089	584
Alliance Consulting Group Associates Inc	7372	504
Alliance Creative Group Inc	4729	9
Alliance Data Systems Corp	7389	13
Alliance Display and Packaging	3993	8
Alliance Distributors Holding Inc	3577	148
Alliance Dynamic Group Inc	3599	1427
Alliance Energy Services LLC	5172	52
Alliance Entertainment Corp	5099	4
Alliance Fiber Optic Products Inc	3674	149
Alliance Financial Corp	6712	244
Alliance Foods Inc	5141	104
Alliance For Children Inc	8741	271
Alliance For Sustainable Energy LLC	8741	155
Alliance FSB	6035	227
Alliance Grain Co	5153	63
Alliance Hardware and Supply	5072	182
Alliance Healthcare Services	8071	7
Alliance Hni LLC	3826	74
Alliance Holdings GP LP	1221	8
Alliance Holdings Inc	6719	114
Alliance Homes Inc	2452	33
Alliance Industrial Corp	3535	159
Alliance Industries Inc	3544	513
Alliance Innovative Manufacturing Inc	3549	47
Alliance Inspection Management	7389	130
Alliance Land Co	6552	203
Alliance Laundry Systems LLC	3582	1
Alliance Logistics Inc	8744	44
Alliance Machine Tool Company Inc	3599	1900
Alliance Maintenance and Services Inc	5084	606
Alliance Management Inc	6531	308
Alliance Manufacturing Inc	3589	213
Alliance Merchant Service Inc	7379	1148
Alliance New York Municipal Income Fund	6722	242
Alliance of Professionals and Consultants Inc	7363	83
Alliance One International Inc	5159	3
Alliance Pattern Inc	3544	616
Alliance Peripheral Systems Inc	3572	24
Alliance Pharmaceutical Corp	2835	79
Alliance Plastics Inc	3089	106
Alliance Press Inc	2752	1214
Alliance Printing and Publishing Inc	2752	1500
Alliance Printing LP	2752	726
Alliance Productions Inc	7812	224
Alliance Products LLC	3556	148
Alliance Publishing and Marketing Inc	2731	299
Alliance Publishing Company Inc	2711	162
Alliance Remanufacturing Inc	3593	29

Company Name	SIC	Rank
Alliance Resource Partners LP	1221	10
Alliance Riggers and Constructors Ltd	1791	16
Alliance Rubber Company Inc	3069	63
Alliance Security Inc	7381	159
Alliance Semiconductor Corp	3674	508
Alliance Service and Control Specialists Inc	1731	1126
Alliance Shippers Inc	4731	21
Alliance Specialty Motors Inc	5063	418
Alliance Steel Inc	5051	249
Alliance Supply Management Ltd	5088	63
Alliance Systems and Programming Inc	7371	1263
Alliance Technology Ventures LP	6799	330
Alliance Telecommunications Contractors Inc	1731	508
Alliance Underwriters AP Benefits Div	6311	230
Alliance Winding Equipment Inc	3559	191
Alliance Wireless Technologies Inc	5065	483
AllianceBernstein Balanced Shares A	6722	175
AllianceBernstein Global Thematic Growth Fund	6722	143
AllianceBernstein Holding LP	6282	28
AllianceBernstein Income Fund Inc	6726	14
AllianceBernstein Small/Mid Cap Growth A	6722	188
Alliant Ammunition and Powder Company LLC	3489	4
Alliant Defense LLC	3489	1
Alliant Energy Corp	4911	38
Alliant Energy Transportation Inc	4011	46
Alliant Group Inc	8743	122
Alliant Healthcare Products	2836	53
Alliant Holdings LLC	3489	2
Alliant Insurance Services Inc	6411	198
Alliant Lake City Small Caliber Ammunition Company LLC	3482	1
Alliant Resources Group	6311	176
Alliant Systems LLC	1731	134
Alliant Techsystems Inc	3489	3
Allianz Global Investors	6282	506
Allianz Insurance Co	6331	105
Allianz Life Insurance Company of North America	6311	19
Allianz of America Inc	6331	276
Allianz Sweeper Co	3711	53
Allianz Underwriters Insurance Co	6331	334
Allid-Baltic Rubber Inc dba Zhongding	3069	41
Allied Advertising	7311	383
Allied Advertising Agency	7311	56
Allied Advertising Agency Inc	7336	209
Allied Aerofoam Products LLC	3086	22
Allied Air Enterprises	3585	46
Allied Automotive Group	5088	2
Allied Battery Systems	5063	846
Allied Binders And Packaging Inc	2782	51
Allied Bindery LLC	2789	57
Allied Building Products Corp	5039	2
Allied Building Stores Inc	5031	50
Allied Business Accounts Inc	7322	179
Allied Business Systems Inc	7372	4271
Allied Chucker And Engineering Co	3599	82
Allied Collection Service Inc	7322	154
Allied Collections and Credit Bureau Inc	7322	198
Allied Components International	3677	75
Allied Construction Services Inc	1742	17
Allied Contracting Company Inc	1623	490
Allied Controls Inc	3679	788
Allied Converters Inc	2673	65
Allied Crane Inc	7699	81
Allied Crawford Inc (Lakeland Florida)	5051	370
Allied Decals-Fla Inc	2759	566
Allied Defense Group Inc	3489	23
Allied Die Casting Corp	3364	29
Allied Electric Supply Co	5063	578
Allied Electrical Contractors Inc	1731	425
Allied Electronics Trading Inc	5734	407
Allied Engineering And Production Corp	3599	917
Allied Envelope Company Inc	5112	41
Allied Financial Corp	6159	84
Allied Finishing Inc	3471	33
Allied Fire and Security Inc	5999	72
Allied Fire Protection	1711	157
Allied Foods Inc (Scranton Pennsylvania)	2013	72
Allied Gardens Towing Inc	7549	7
Allied General Fire and Security Inc	5063	1005
Allied Graphics Inc	3555	98
ALLIED Group Inc	6331	38
Allied Group Inc	2782	16
Allied Group Inc (Bellevue Washington)	6531	259
Allied Healthcare International Inc	8082	14
Allied Healthcare Products Inc	3842	74
Allied High Tech Products Inc	5085	207
Allied Holdings	4213	1550
Allied Home Health	8082	40
Allied Home Medical Inc	5999	88
Allied Industrial Distributors Inc	3589	253
Allied Industrial Equipment Corp	5084	117
Allied Industrial Equipment Inc	5084	396
Allied Insurance	6331	331
Allied Lithographing Company Inc	2752	963
Allied Locke Industries Inc	3496	6
Allied Machine and Engineering Corp	3545	23
Allied Machine Inc	3599	1503
Allied Machine Tool and Design Inc	3599	1719
Allied Mailing and Printing Inc	7331	256
Allied Marine Inc	7389	1968
Allied Marine Industries Inc	4492	4
Allied Marketing Group Inc	5961	106
Allied Metal Spinning Corp	3469	227
Allied Metals Inc	5051	105
Allied Mineral Products Inc	3297	4
Allied Molded Products LLC	3229	23
Allied Motion Technologies Inc	3825	26
Allied Moulded Products Inc	3089	327
Allied Network Solutions Inc	5045	270
Allied Pallet Co	2448	12
Allied Partners Inc	6371	13
Allied Plastics Holdings LLC	3081	75
Allied Power Group	7699	20
Allied Precision Industries Inc	3634	22
Allied Pressroom Products Inc	2899	180
Allied Printing and Mailing Inc	7331	263
Allied Printing Services Inc	2396	8
Allied Protection Services Inc	7381	184
Allied Purchasing	5085	282
Allied Realty Co	5714	1
Allied Reliability Inc	7349	143
Allied Security Alarms	1731	1959
Allied Security Innovations Inc	3069	202
Allied Solutions Group Inc	7371	436
Allied Solutions LLC	6399	4
Allied Specialty Foods Inc	2013	118
Allied Specialty Insurance Inc	6331	278
Allied Specialty Precision Inc	3728	142
Allied Steel Rule Dies Inc	3544	703
Allied Structural Lumber Products Inc	5031	319
Allied Supply Company Inc	5078	18
Allied Systems Co	3531	61
Allied Systems Design Inc	7379	1586
Allied Systems Inc	5074	198
Allied Tax Service Inc	8721	201
Allied Technologies Food Equipment Inc	5046	323
Allied Telecom Group LLC	4813	367
Allied Telesyn International Corp	3577	54
Allied Tool and Die Company LLC	3469	130
Allied Tool And Machine Co	3549	72
Allied Tools Inc	5085	448
Allied Towing and Recovery Inc	7549	17
Allied Trade Group Inc	5063	180
Allied Trading Inc	5063	1041
Allied Tube and Conduit Corp	3312	24
Allied Uniking Corporation Inc	3535	110
Allied Universal Corp	5169	75
Allied Valve Inc	7699	72
Allied Vaughn Communications	3695	5
Allied Vaughn (Minneapolis Minnesota)	7819	19
Allied Ventilation Inc	1711	227
Allied Waste Industries of Illinois Inc	4953	12
Allied Waste Industries of Northwest Indiana Inc	4953	8
Allied Waste of California Inc	4953	9
Allied Waste Services of Phoenix	4953	42
Allied Welding Inc	3599	185
Allied Wire and Cable Inc	5063	97
Alliedus Corp	5065	873
Alligator Technologies Inc	7371	1307
Allin Corp	7373	311
Allin Interactive Corp	7373	365
Allina Health System Inc	8062	25
Alling Henning Associates Inc	7311	627
Allingham Corp	7353	67
All-In-One Network Solutions Inc	7379	1130
Allion Healthcare Inc	5122	28
Allisa's Bridal	5699	20
Allis-Chalmers Energy Inc	1389	13
Allison Abrasives Inc	3291	13
Allison and Chumney PC	8721	288
Allison Corp	2211	19
Allison Payment Systems LLC	2752	148
Allison Systems Corp	3555	117
Allison Systems Inc	7372	4272
Allison-Ide Structural Engineers LLC	8711	551
Allison-Smith Co	1731	157
Allister Fabricating Inc	3443	191
All-Lift Systems Inc	5085	222
All-Line Equipment Inc	5046	297
AllMax Professional Solutions Inc	7372	2439
Allmet Building Products LP	3444	10
Allmetal Inc	3442	75
All-Mode Communications Inc	1731	659
Allnet Services Inc	4813	505
Allon Industries Inc	3599	1303
Allor Manufacturing Inc	3535	15
Allos Therapeutics Inc	8731	121
Alloso Technologies LLC	7371	1349
Alloy and Stainless Fasteners Inc	5085	136
Alloy Carbide Co	3599	304
Alloy Casting Company Inc	3365	43
Alloy Die Casting Co	3363	23
Alloy Engineering Company Inc	3823	237
Alloy Entertainment Inc	5961	44
Alloy Extrusion Co	3061	54
Alloy Hardfacing And Engineering Co	3443	194
Alloy Inc	5961	66
Alloy Industrial Contractors Inc	1771	37
Alloy Marketing and Promotions	5961	103
Alloy Polymers Inc	2821	51
Alloy Polymers Texas LP	3089	1664
Alloy Surfaces Company Inc	3489	16
Alloy Tool Steel Inc	5051	510
Alloy Welding Corp	3444	228
Alloyweld Inspection Company Inc	7692	54
Allpac Inc	3565	139
Allpak Co	5162	54
Allpak Container Inc	2653	75
All-Pak Manufacturing Corp	2653	114
Allparts Music Corp	5099	136
Allpetscom Inc	5961	78
All-Phase Electric Supply Co	5063	567
Allpoints Security And Detective Inc	7381	117
Allpoints Warehousing Equipment Co	5084	527
All-Pro Transport Company Inc	4213	1804
Allright Baton Rouge Inc	7521	17
Allright Boston Parking Inc	7521	14
Allright Colorado Inc	7521	13
Allright New York Parking Inc	7521	11
Allright Shreveport Inc	7521	16
Allright Tool Company Inc	3544	519
Allrout Inc	3823	429
Allsafe Security Systems Inc	4812	98
Allsafe Technologies Inc	3089	854
Allsale Electric Inc	5063	265
AllScripts-Misys Healthcare Solutions Inc	7373	13
Allstaff LLC	7361	270
Allstaff Management Inc	7363	79
Allstaff Services Inc	7361	94
Allstar Communications Inc	5065	514
Allstar Fasteners Inc	3452	74
All-Star Group Companies Inc	7363	100
Allstar Magnetics LLC	5065	291
Allstar Microelectronics Inc	3572	78
All-Star Sales Inc	5112	55
Allstar Staffing Inc	7361	241
All-Star Transportation Inc	4213	1398
Allstate Building Maintenance	7349	287
Allstate Corp	6331	8
Allstate Delivery Service Co	4213	2386
Allstate Electric Company Inc	1731	1145
Allstate Electric Inc	1731	879
Allstate Energy Inc	1731	745
Allstate Equipment Company Inc	5084	836
Allstate Insurance Co	6331	4
Allstate Leasing Inc	7515	7
Allstate Life Insurance Co	6311	4
Allstate Plastics Inc	3082	14
Allstate Printing Packaging Inc	5084	313
Allstate Services Inc	7342	28
Allstate Tool And Die Inc	3544	157
All-States Equipment Inc	3499	127
Allstates Worldcargo Inc	3845	41
Allsteel Inc	2522	4
All-Tech Electric Inc	1731	1398
Alltech Inc	2869	37
All-Tech Inc	5084	429
All-Tech Machine and Engineering Inc	3469	224
Alltech Manufacturing Ltd	3599	908
Alltek Services Inc	7373	1169
Alltel Cellular	4812	34
ALLTEL Corp	4813	6
ALLTEL Florida Inc	4813	76
Alltel Information Services	7374	20
ALLTEL Missouri Inc	4813	23
All-Tex Networking Solutions Inc	7373	809
Alltrista Industrial Plastics Co	3089	241
All-Type Welding And Fabrication Inc	3599	846
Allume Systems Inc	7372	1820
Allure Home Creation Company Inc	5023	34
Allured Publishing Corp	2741	274
Allway Tools Inc	3423	37
All-Ways Advertising Co	7311	268
AllWealth Federal Credit Union	6061	148
Allworld Language Consultants Inc	7389	382
Ally Financial Inc	6141	3
Allyn Corp	5085	197
Allyn Partners Inc	7311	850
Allyn Welch Holdings Inc	3841	27
Alm Enterprises Inc	7311	575
ALM Properties Inc	2741	13
Alma Plantation Ltd	2061	5
Alma Products Co	3585	78
Alma Tractor and Equipment Inc	5083	65
Almac Building Maintenance Inc	7349	323
ALMART Enterprises Inc	5049	8
Almatron Electronics Inc	3672	283
Almco Inc	3549	55
Almeda Times Star	2711	496
Almega Enterprises Inc	2431	124
Almega/Tru-Flex Inc	3679	495
Almet Inc	3441	155
Almira's Bakery	5461	47
Almo Corp	5045	90
Almond Brothers Lumber Co	2421	117
Almont:MediaLAB	3669	229
Almore Dye House Inc	2269	12
Almost Family Inc	8399	4
Alna Envelope Company Inc	2754	31
Alnye Trucking	4213	1502

Company Name	SIC	Rank
Alnylam Pharmaceuticals Inc	2834	148
Aloe Gator Suncare Co	5122	119
Aloette Cosmetics Inc	2844	83
Aloft Group Inc	7389	804
Alogent Corp	7372	1385
Aloha Airgroup Inc	4512	61
Aloha Restaurants Inc	5812	348
Aloha Security Inc	7381	106
Aloha Shoyu Company Ltd	2035	30
Aloha Tofu Factory Inc	2099	317
Alois J Binder Bakery Inc	2051	236
Alom Technologies Corp	7372	2213
Alon Brands Inc	5399	2
Alon USA Energy Inc	2911	20
Along Came Mary Productions Inc	5812	360
Alorica Inc	7378	1
Aloris Tool Co	3545	245
ALOS Micrographic Corp	3672	306
Alp International Corp	7379	1338
Alpa Precision Machine Works Inc	3823	229
Alpan Lighting Products Inc	5063	311
Alpena Oil Company Inc	5171	53
Alpena Supply Co	5013	181
Alpena Wholesale Grocery Co	5141	124
Alpert and Alpert Iron and Metal Inc	5051	88
Alpha Acme Electric Inc	1731	1501
Alpha and Omega Computer Corp	3577	386
Alpha Associates Inc	2295	10
Alpha Audio Systems Inc	1731	2375
Alpha Automation Inc	8711	671
Alpha Banco Inc	6712	710
Alpha Base Systems Inc	5045	963
Alpha Brokers Corp	7389	1320
Alpha Capital Partners Ltd	6799	276
Alpha Carb Enterprises Inc	3544	319
Alpha Card Services Inc	6159	52
Alpha CD Imaging	7379	1455
Alpha Chemical Services Inc	2842	114
Alpha Circuit Corp	3672	480
Alpha Coatings Inc	3479	43
Alpha Computers Inc	5734	26
Alpha Consulting Corp	7361	157
Alpha Data Corp	7373	293
Alpha Data Systems Inc	5734	108
Alpha Dyno Nobel	5169	103
Alpha Equipment Leasing	6159	70
Alpha Grainger Manufacturing Inc	3451	12
Alpha Graphics Inc	2791	64
Alpha Group Of Delaware Inc	8331	155
Alpha Homes Of Wisconsin Inc	8361	131
Alpha Imaging Inc	5047	211
Alpha Industries Inc	3544	848
Alpha Industries Inc (Knoxville Tennessee)	2311	7
Alpha Investment Consulting Group LLC	6282	587
Alpha Lehigh Tool and Machine Company Inc	3599	1324
Alpha Lex	7336	237
Alpha Liberty Co	5049	209
Alpha Manufacturing Company Inc	3545	285
Alpha Medical Products Inc	8742	688
Alpha Medical Resources Inc	7352	45
Alpha Mills Corp	2254	3
Alpha Mold West Inc	3544	443
Alpha Natural Resources Inc	1221	1
Alpha Natural Resources Virginia LLC	1241	4
Alpha Networks Inc	7373	500
Alpha Novatech Inc	5063	325
Alpha Office Supplies Inc	5021	41
Alpha Omega Publications Inc	2731	167
Alpha Opportunities Inc	8322	187
Alpha Packaging (Ypsilanti Michigan)	3085	26
Alpha Plastics Co	3089	1524
Alpha Plastics Inc	3085	8
Alpha Power and Technology LLC	3621	132
Alpha Precision Inc	3229	32
Alpha Printing Inc	3555	131
Alpha Products Inc	3678	59
Alpha Publishing Inc	2741	424
Alpha Radio Products LLC	3825	315
Alpha Rae Personnel Inc	7361	32
Alpha Recycling Inc	5093	189
Alpha Research and Technology Inc	3571	100
Alpha Resources Inc	5049	59
Alpha Scale Company Inc	3596	1
Alpha Scientific Electronics Inc	3679	730
Alpha Scrip Inc	7319	82
Alpha Sensors Inc	3829	216
Alpha Services Ii Inc	7699	142
Alpha Sintered Metals	3399	12
Alpha Software Inc	7372	3175
Alpha Sound International Inc	5731	191
Alpha Source Inc	5063	477
Alpha Spectra Inc	8734	164
Alpha Star Corp	7371	1164
Alpha Star Tool and Mold Inc	3544	614
Alpha Systems Fire Protection	5099	80
Alpha Systems Inc	5033	27
Alpha Technical Services Corporaton	7349	480
Alpha Technologies Inc	3663	57
Alpha Technology Concepts Inc	7379	1109
Alpha Technology Corp	3364	8
Alpha Technology Group Inc	8748	371
Alpha Technology Inc	3578	16
Alpha Telecom Incorporated USA	3577	315
Alpha Tile Distributors Inc	5032	7
Alpha Trx Inc	5012	195
Alpha Wire Co	3496	23
Alphabet Inc	3612	5
Alpha-Gamma Technologies Inc	7373	592
Alphagen USA Inc	7379	1623
AlphaMetrix LLC	7379	169
Alpha-Omega Industries Inc	3599	2094
Alpha-Omega Software Technologies Inc	7372	3857
Alphapage LLC	4812	87
Alphaport Inc	8711	467
Alphase Interiors Inc	7389	1408
AlphaSoft Marketing International	7372	4050
AlphaSoft Services Corp	7372	1523
Alphastaff Inc	7363	178
Alphatec Holdings Inc	3841	41
Alphatest Corp	3559	373
Alpheus Communications LP	4899	47
Alphi Manufacturing Inc	3714	313
Alphi Technology Corp	3672	407
Alpin Surgical Specialties Inc	5047	210
Alpine Access Inc	7389	619
Alpine Air Express Inc	4522	30
Alpine Armoring Inc	3711	70
Alpine Aromatics International Inc	2844	142
Alpine Ascents International	8299	30
Alpine Associates Inc	5085	275
Alpine Aviation Inc	4512	50
Alpine Bank of Illinois	6022	441
Alpine Banks of Colorado	6021	392
Alpine Broadcasting Corp	4832	265
Alpine Building Maintence Inc	7349	389
Alpine Cheese Co	2022	29
Alpine Consulting Inc	7373	394
Alpine Data Inc	7372	4481
Alpine Development Inc	1623	827
Alpine Electric Corp	1731	984
Alpine Electric Inc	1731	1080
Alpine Group Inc	3357	19
Alpine Meadows of Tahoe Inc	7999	38
Alpine Precision LLC	3599	1678
Alpine Printing Inc	2752	1723
Alpine Research Optics LLC	3827	96
Alpine Solutions Inc	5046	23
Alpine Staffing Inc	7361	300
Alpine Systems Inc	7299	27
Alpine Water Systems LLC	5074	154
Alpine Web Media LLC	7379	130
Alpine Wurst and Meathouse Inc	5812	454
Alpla Inc	3085	14
Alps Electric	3577	2
Alps Electric USA Inc	5961	80
ALPS Fund Services Inc	6211	140
Alps South Corp	2869	73
Alps Technologies Inc	2431	129
Alquest Technologies Inc	7378	33
ALR Systems and Software Inc	7372	2414
Alrajs Inc	2051	194
Alro Machine Tool And Die Company Inc	3599	1556
ALRO Steel Corp	5051	29
Alrs Inc	2512	31
ALS Inc	5147	94
Als International Inc	8748	271
Al's Leasing Inc	4213	2016
Al's Services	8721	349
Alsbridge Inc	8748	464
Alsco Inc	5113	16
Alsco Industries Inc	3089	954
Alseres Pharmaceuticals Inc	8731	426
Alside Inc	3442	4
Alsoft Inc	7372	3511
Alson's Corp	3432	16
Alsterda Cartage and Construction Company Inc	1623	476
Alstom Power Conversion	3569	27
ALSTOM Power Inc	3433	2
Alstom Signaling Inc	3743	13
Alston Machine Company Inc	3599	2071
Alston Tascom Inc	3661	182
Alta Communications Inc	6799	235
Alta Computer Services LLC	7371	1745
Alta Industries Limited LP	6719	178
Alta It Services LLC	7371	365
Alta Photographic Inc	3861	118
Alta Resources Corp	7389	113
Alta Robbins Inc	3491	56
Alta Ski Lifts Company Inc	7999	104
Altadis USA Inc	2121	2
Altair Corp	3555	15
Altair Engineering Inc	8742	29
Altair Nanomaterials Inc	1099	5
Altair Nanotechnologies Inc	2899	166
Altamaha Electric Membership Corp	4911	333
Altamira	8732	108
AltaOne Federal Credit Union	6061	76
AltaPacific Bancorp	6022	656
Altapacific Bank (Santa Rosa California)	6029	31
Altara	7373	891
Altaria Inc	3679	796
Altec Datacom LLC	4841	169
Altec Electrical Inc	1731	1502
Altec Engineering Inc	3089	808
Altec Equipment Inc	5049	203
Altec Hiline LLC	3531	132
Altec Industries Inc	3531	29
Altec Systems Inc	1731	2372
Altech Controls Corp	3822	73
Altegris Investments Inc	2741	119
Altek Corp	3577	405
Altek Electrical Services Inc	7694	36
Altek Electronics Inc	3825	76
Altek Systems Inc	3643	144
Altel Systems Inc	1731	558
Alten Sakai and Co	8721	433
Altendorf Express Inc	4213	2901
Altenloh Brinck and Company Inc	3452	46
Alter Barge Line Inc	4449	19
Alter Communications Inc	2711	517
Alter Trading Corp	5093	29
Altera Corp	3674	23
Altercom Website Design and Host Inc	7336	250
Alterian Inc	7371	1136
Alteris Renewables Inc	4939	13
Alterity Inc	7372	4783
Alternate Access Inc	7373	907
Alternate E-Components LLC	3679	585
Alternate Marketing Networks Inc	7319	58
Alternative Business Accommodations	7389	1869
Alternative Business Suppliers Inc	5044	145
Alternative Care Providers Inc	7352	29
Alternative Community Mental Health Center Inc	8322	120
Alternative Computer Technology Inc	5045	615
Alternative Energy Store LLC	5211	191
Alternative Home Care Solutions Inc	7380	1924
Alternative Manufacturing Inc	3672	80
Alternative Micrographics Inc	7389	2159
Alternative Petroleum	2869	36
Alternative Publications Inc	2721	319
Alternative Staffing Inc	7363	342
Alternative System Concepts Inc	7372	4401
Alternative Technologies	1311	263
AlterNative Technologies (Sheridan Wyoming)	7378	67
Alternative Technology Corp	3661	218
Alternative Telecommunications Corp	4813	143
Alternators Starters Etc	3694	47
Alteryx Inc	7373	269
Altex Engineered Electronic Solutions	5065	235
Altex Industries Inc	1311	265
Altheimer and Gray	8111	133
Altherm Inc	5074	188
Althouse Martin and Associates Inc	8712	326
Altia Inc	7372	2415
Altico Advisors LLC	5734	362
Alticor Inc	5963	1
AltiGen Communications Inc	3661	99
Altima Technologies Inc	7372	1989
Altimate Electric Inc	1731	2248
Altior Inc	5065	705
Altira Inc	3085	20
Altisys Communications	3661	236
Altium Inc	7372	934
Altivia Corp	2819	45
ALTL Inc	4213	735
Altman Manufacturing Company Inc	3544	896
Altman Printing Company Inc	2752	1698
Altman Stage Lighting Company Inc	3648	19
Altmeyer Home Stores Inc	5719	21
Altnet Inc	7371	549
Alto Bella Hair Products Inc	2844	192
Alto Consulting and Training	7371	1087
Alto Development Corp	3841	216
Alto Palo Broadcasting Co	7371	1392
Alto Precision Inc	3559	400
Alto Products Corp	3568	12
Altom Transport Inc	4213	1577
Alton/Aztec	3585	179
Alton Bean Trucking Inc	4213	1580
Alton Delivery Service Co	4213	2412
Alton Gaming Co	7993	14
Alton Manufacturing Inc	3469	141
Alton Winlectric Co	5063	648
Altoros Systems	7372	581
Alto's Express Inc	4213	2726
Altos Federal Group Inc	7361	18
Alto-Shaam Inc	3589	19
Altra Holdings Inc	3569	8
Altratek Plastics Inc	3089	1819
Altres Inc	7363	3
Altria Group Inc	2111	2
Altron Automation Inc	3535	87
Altron Inc	3672	76
Altronic Research Inc	3676	23
Altronix Corp	3699	97
Alt's Tool and Machine Inc	3599	545
Altschul Group Corp	7812	193
Altuglas International	3679	5
Altura Ventures LLC	7372	2307
Alturdyne	3511	18
Alturnamats Inc	3559	293
Altus Consulting Corp	7379	1185

Company Name	SIC	Rank
Altus Group Inc (Phildadelphia Pennsylvania)	7311	365
Altus Technologies Inc	7371	1261
Altwood Roll Label Company Inc	2754	33
Aluchem Inc	3295	4
Alumacraft Boat Co	3732	39
Aluma-Form Inc	3429	51
Alum-A-Lift Inc	3537	72
Alumapro Inc	3651	199
Aluminum and Stainless Inc	5051	155
Aluminum Blanking Company Inc	3469	164
Aluminum Coil Anodizing Corp	3471	21
Aluminum Components Ent Corp	3365	42
Aluminum Die Casting Company Inc	3363	42
Aluminum Extruded Shapes Inc	3354	32
Aluminum Fabricators Inc	3599	1662
Aluminum Finishing Of Georgia Corp	3471	61
Aluminum Frame Company Of America	5023	114
Aluminum Ladder Co	3499	37
Aluminum Line Products Co	5013	80
Aluminum Plus	5082	159
Aluminum Precision Products Inc	3463	4
Aluminum Recycling Of Mississippi Inc	5093	182
Aluminum Shapes LLC	3365	3
Aluminum Supply Company Inc	5051	462
Alumni Consulting Group International Inc	7379	225
Alva Allen Industries	3549	118
Alva/Amco Pharmacal Companies Inc	2834	350
Alva Electric Inc	1731	1335
Alvarado Construction Inc	1541	86
Alvarado Manufacturing Company Inc	3829	106
Alvarez and Bremer Travel	4724	116
Alvarez and Marsal LLC	8742	71
Alvarez Electric Inc	1731	981
Alva-Tech Inc	3089	1856
Alvellan Inc	3599	1377
Alventive Inc	7372	2320
Alvin and Company Inc	5049	24
Alvin E Benike Inc	1541	214
Alvin H Butz Inc	8741	51
Alvin J Bart and Sons Inc	2759	95
Alvin Wynn Electric Company Inc	1731	2310
Alvine Pharmaceuticals Inc	8731	254
Alvitae Pharmaceuticals Inc	8731	236
Alvord Systems Inc	3844	35
Alvord-Polk Inc	3545	84
Alward Electric Inc	1711	265
Always Equipment Inc	5046	153
Always In Mind Inc	3993	140
Alwin Manufacturing Company Inc	3469	182
AM and S Transportation Co	4213	1538
AM Best Company Inc	7323	12
AM Bickley Inc	5159	25
AM Castle and Co	5051	18
Am Cleaning Inc	7349	363
AM Express Inc	4213	940
AM General Corp	3711	16
Am General Holdings LLC	3711	36
Am Kwlc	4832	179
AM La Salle Electric Inc	1731	933
Am Machining Inc	7699	73
AM Networks Inc	3663	35
AM News Corp	2711	686
AM Precision Machine Inc	3599	585
A-M Systems LLC	3842	300
AM Tool and Die	3544	359
Am Trade Systems Inc	5063	1068
Am Wdef Fm Radio	4832	255
AMA Capital Partners	6722	183
AMA Plastics	3089	181
Ama Precision Screening Inc	2759	518
Ama Printing / Finishing Inc	3652	28
AMA Transportation Company Inc	4213	790
Amac Enterprises Inc	3398	7
Amacoil Inc	3549	80
Amacpi Corp	5088	62
Amada Manufacturing America Inc	3542	32
Amada Wasino America Inc	3541	255
Amadas Industries Inc	3531	104
Amadeus Americas Inc	7375	32
Amadeus Multimedia Technologies Ltd	7336	99
Amadeus Revenue Integrity Inc	7372	2840
AMAG Pharmaceuticals Inc	2835	18
Amag Technology Inc	3577	345
Amailcenter Franchise Corp	6794	153
Amaitis And Associates Inc	7379	1112
Amak Brake LLC	3714	87
Amalga Composites Inc	3084	39
Amalgamated Bank	6141	23
Amalgamated Bank of Chicago	6036	30
Amalgamated Culture Work Inc	2261	27
Amalgamated Life Insurance Co	6311	157
Amalgamated Software of North America Inc	7371	1296
Amalgamet Inc	5169	129
AmalgaTrust Company Inc	6091	17
Amalie Oil Co	4226	5
Amamco Tool and Supply Company Inc	3541	78
Aman Inc	2752	1843
Amanda Bent Bolt Co	3496	62
Amanda Company Inc	7372	2486
Amano Cincinnati Inc	3579	17

Company Name	SIC	Rank
Amano Mcgann Inc	5046	57
Amante Marketing Corp	5499	21
Amar Precision Corp	3541	194
Amarillo Biosciences Inc	8731	427
Amarillo Hardware Co	5072	43
Amarillo Mop and Broom Company Inc	3751	27
Amarillo National Bank Inc	6712	83
Amarillo Road Co	1611	149
Amarillo Utility Contractors Inc	1623	620
Amarillo Winnelson Co	5074	147
A-Mark Financial Corp	5094	1
A-Mark Precious Metals Inc	5094	16
AMAS Securities	6282	608
Amash Imports Inc	5072	126
Amatco USA Inc	7699	247
Amatech/Polycel LLC	3089	1150
Amateur Artist Development	7389	1881
Amateur Electronic Supply LLC	5731	34
Amato International Inc (Miami Florida)	5147	148
Amatrol Inc	3569	100
Amax Engineering Corp	3571	45
A-Max Wire and Cable Inc	5063	793
Amay Inc	5722	25
Amay's Bakery and Noodle Company Inc	2052	48
Amazing Beverages Inc	2086	144
Amazing Maid Services	7349	520
Amazing Man Inc	1623	643
Amazing! Smart Card Technologies Inc	3577	264
Amazon Biotech Inc	8731	425
Amazon Hose and Rubber Company Of Tampa Inc	3069	124
Amazon Technologies Co	7371	1353
Amazoncom Inc	5961	2
AMB Enterprises Inc	7374	195
AMB Financial Corp	6035	188
AMBAC Financial Group Inc	6351	2
Ambac International Corp	3714	335
Ambase Corp	6512	90
Ambassadair Travel Club Inc	4724	41
Ambassador Advertising Agency	7311	692
Ambassador Capital Management Inc	6282	422
Ambassador Construction Company Inc	1542	386
Ambassador Financial Group	7389	2403
Ambassador Press	2752	418
Ambassador Programs Inc	8299	13
Ambassadors Group Inc	8299	25
Ambassadors International Inc	4789	12
Ambath LLC	6719	163
Ambco Electronics	3825	301
AmBec Inc	3535	2
Amber Diagnostics Inc	5047	204
Amber Engineering And Manufacturing Co	3549	39
Amber Industries Inc	3679	653
Amberleigh Retirement Community	8322	177
Amberley Management Inc	8741	226
Amberwave Systems Corp	3674	158
Ambex Inc	5046	193
Ambient Corp	4813	194
Ambient Digital Media Inc	7371	820
Ambient Engineering Inc	8711	444
Ambient LLC	5063	571
Ambient Sound Inc	1731	1202
Ambit Energy Holdings LLC	4911	144
Ambit Pacific Recycling Inc	5093	40
Ambler Surgical Corp	5048	38
Amboy Aggregates	5032	24
Amboy National Bank	6021	84
Ambric Inc	3674	185
Ambrit Engineering Corp	3544	159
Ambrose Air Inc	5075	91
Ambrose Employer Group LLC	7363	268
Ambrose Printing Co	2752	276
Ambrose Video Publishing Inc	7822	25
Ambrosia Software Inc	7372	2898
Ambry International Ltd	5045	826
Ambs Investment Counsel LLC	6282	652
Ambs Message Center Inc	7389	1593
Ambulance Service Management Corp	8742	471
Ambulatory Infusion Therapy Specialist Inc	8082	45
AMC Entertainment Inc	7832	3
AMC Inc	6531	331
Amc Manufacturing Inc	7692	9
AMC Networks Inc	4841	22
AMC Technology LLC	7372	1804
Amcal Group of Cos	6552	253
Amcan Beverages Inc	2086	76
Am-Can Transport Service Inc	4213	534
Amcat	5045	139
AMC-GCT Inc	7832	9
Amchel Communications Inc	1623	233
Amchi Software Company Inc	7373	1131
Amclo Group Inc	3469	168
Amco Manufacturing Inc	3523	166
Amco Precision Tools Inc	3845	106
Amco Products Inc	3451	103
AMCOL International Corp	1459	1
Amcol Systems Inc	7322	50
Amcom Data Processing Inc	7373	670
AMCOM Software Inc	7372	777
Amcon Block and Precast Inc	3271	18

Company Name	SIC	Rank
AMCON Distributing Co	5141	44
Amcor Flexibles Inc	2671	12
AMCOR Sunclipse	2679	4
Amcore Bank NA	6021	38
AMCWE Advertising Sales	7311	947
Amdec Inc	3999	25
Amdex Corp	7371	250
Amdocs Inc	7372	15
AME Corp	3069	200
AME Software Products Inc	7372	3046
Amec Earth and Environmental Inc	8711	59
Amedex USA Medical Services Corp	8099	42
Amedisys Home Health Incorporated of Florida	8082	78
Amedisys Inc	8082	5
Amedore Homes Inc	1521	68
Amega Scientific Corp	3822	67
Amega Tool Works Inc	3542	61
Amegy Bank NA	6021	402
Amegy Corp	6712	90
Amelex Inc	5063	470
Amen Packaging Inc	5099	121
AMEN Properties Inc	5172	120
Amend John	7373	535
Amende and Schultz Corp	5146	59
Amensys Inc	7379	896
Amer Electric Inc	1731	1281
Amer Electric Motion Inc	5063	1090
Amer Sports Co	3949	2
Amera Cosmetics Inc	2844	189
Ameracash Solutions Inc	7322	186
Ameraflex Rubber and Gasket Company Inc	5085	210
Amerchol Corp	2899	76
AMERCO	7513	5
Amerco Real Estate Co	6519	15
Ameren Corp	4931	5
Ameren Missouri	4911	47
AmerenCIPS	4939	8
AmerenIP	4931	33
Amerequip Corp	3523	37
Ameresco Inc	3822	3
Amerex Group Inc	5137	4
Amerhart Ltd	5031	46
Ameri Source Manufacturing Inc	3823	393
Ameriana Bancorp	6712	494
Ameriana Bank and Trust SB	6036	62
America California Bank	6022	603
America First Properties Management Company LLC	6513	13
America First Tax Exempt Investors LP	6799	152
America Hears Inc	5999	52
America II Electronics	5065	28
America Press Inc	2721	309
America Shredding	3589	48
America Tent Rentals Inc	7359	241
Americable International Inc	4841	81
Ameri-Cad Inc	5045	945
Americad Technology Corporat	3089	1144
Americall Communications Company Inc	4813	644
Americall International Inc	7389	1303
American 2 Way Radio Inc	3663	292
American Access Care LLC	8741	249
American Access Controls Inc	1731	2558
American Access Systems Inc	3699	288
American Accessories Of Pensacola Inc	7389	2127
American Accurate Components Inc	5065	453
American Achievement Corp	3911	2
American Achievement Group Holding Corp	3911	8
American Acrylic and Injection Inc	3088	27
American Acrylic Corp	3083	40
American Ad Bag Company Inc	2759	151
American Adhesive Coatings LLC	2672	74
American Aerospace Controls Inc	3679	431
American Aerospace Technical Castings Inc	3324	16
American Air Filter Snydergeneral Corp	5085	403
American Air Liquide Holdings Inc	2813	7
American Airlines Employees Federal Credit Union	6061	162
American Airlines Inc	4512	5
American Alarm Company Inc	1731	548
American Alarm Systems Inc	5999	119
American Alarms Inc	1731	1254
American Alloy Sourcing Specialists LP	7389	171
American Almond Products Company Inc	2087	49
American Alpha Inc	3672	150
American Aluminum Co	3444	74
American Aluminum Extrusions Of Ohio LLC	3354	36
American Analytical Chemistry Laboratories Corp	8734	74
American and Efird Inc	2284	1
American and Schoen Machinery Co	3559	341
American Apparel Inc	2321	5
American Appraisal Associates Inc	6531	193
American Arium	7372	2372
American Art Clay Company Inc	3295	6
American Ash Recycling Corp	4953	59
American Asia Express Corp	7389	2086

Company Name	SIC	Rank
American Asphalt Paving Co	2951	30
American Assay Laboratories Inc	8734	94
American Assets Trust Inc	6798	127
American Atelier Inc	2511	61
American Augers Inc	3541	44
American Auto Accessories Inc	3429	5
American Auto Wire Systems Inc	5063	728
American Autogard Corp	3566	22
American Automated Engineering Inc	3769	20
American Axle and Manufacturing Holdings Inc	3714	15
American Azide Corp (Cedar City Utah)	2819	52
American Babbitt Bearing Inc	3599	1747
American Background Information Services Inc	8748	146
American Backplane Inc	3672	256
American Bag and Burlap Co	2393	18
American Balanced Fund	6722	8
American Baler Co	3559	219
American Bancard LLC	8999	169
American Bank and Trust Co	6022	394
American Bank Inc	6021	215
American Bank Note Holographics Inc	7389	442
American Bank of Oklahoma	6021	327
American Bank of St Paul	6022	234
American Bank (Silver Spring Maryland)	6035	173
American Bank Systems Inc	2752	1050
American Banking Co	6022	381
American Banknote Corp	2759	20
American Barricade Rental Inc	7389	1563
American Battery Charging Inc	3629	90
American Battery Corp	5063	871
American Beef Co	0751	5
American Belt Co	2387	4
American Beverage Corp	6799	32
American Beverage Corp Daily Juice Products Div	2033	44
American Beverage Equipment Company Inc	3432	36
American Bible Sales	7372	1748
American Biltrite Far East Inc	3089	44
American Biltrite Inc	3089	64
American Biltrite Sales Corp	3089	45
American Binding Company Inc	5112	70
American Bio Medica Corp	2834	309
American Bio Tech Inc	3559	32
American Biological Technologies Inc	2835	63
American Biophysics Corp	3999	29
American Blower Supply Inc	5085	418
American Bluegrass Marble Inc	3281	30
American Blueprinting and Supply Inc	7334	23
American Board Assembly Inc	3672	90
American Bolt Corp	5072	100
American Braiding and Manufacturing	3053	108
American Broach and Machine Company Inc	3541	131
American Broadband Nebraska Inc (Blair Nebraska)	4813	127
American Broadcasting Companies Inc	4833	6
American Brochure and Catalogue Company Inc	2752	679
American Brush Company Inc	3991	25
American Builders and Contractors Supply Company Inc	5033	1
American Building Components Co (Nicholasville Kentucky)	3272	80
American Building Components Inc	3089	1833
American Building Janitorial Inc	7349	482
American Building Maintenance Of Louisiana Inc	7349	191
American Building Services LLC	5031	273
American Building Supply Inc	5211	132
American Buildings Co	3448	6
American Business Bank (Los Angeles California)	6022	168
American Business Information Systems	1731	2355
American Business Network Inc	5045	395
American Business Networking Inc	5734	350
American Business Printing Inc	2761	47
American Business Services Corp	4731	62
American Business Systems Inc	7372	2809
American Business Technology	3861	67
American Cabin Supply	2759	186
American Cable Co	3714	192
American Cable Inc	5731	232
American Campus Communities Inc	6798	79
American Capacitor Corp	3675	39
American Capital Agency Corp	6798	20
American Capital Financial Services	6282	45
American Capital Ltd	6282	17
American Capital Partners LLC	6282	174
American Caresource Holdings Inc	8082	35
American Carrier Equipment Inc	3715	51
American Cast Iron Pipe Co	3321	3
American Central Transport Inc	4213	597
American Century Balanced Investors	6722	173
American Century Companies Inc	6282	68
American Century Growth Investors	6722	70
American Century Select Investors	6722	109
American Century Target Mat 2010	6722	206
American Century Target Mat 2020	6722	211
American Certified Equipment Inc	5082	59

Company Name	SIC	Rank
American Changer Corp	3578	20
American Chartered Bancorp Inc	6022	592
American Chartered Bank	6022	589
American Chemet Corp	2819	64
American Chemical Technologies Inc	5172	143
American Circuit Services Inc	3672	485
American Circuit Systems Inc	3672	384
American Circuit Technology Inc	3672	276
American Circuits Inc	3672	340
American City Business Journals Inc	2711	17
American Civil Constructors	1611	15
American Classified Inc	2711	645
American Classifieds	2741	377
American Cleaner Inc	5087	184
American Cleaning Service Company Inc	7349	210
American Coal Co	1222	4
American Colloid Co	3295	22
American Colorscans Inc	7335	30
American Combustion Industries Inc	3585	34
American Commerce Solutions Inc	3559	385
American Commercial Lines Inc	4449	10
American Commercial Lines LLC	4449	12
American Commercial Security Services	7381	6
American Commercial Terminals Inc	7373	1114
American Commodities Inc	4953	100
American Communications	3661	214
American Community Properties Trust	6552	111
American Compaction Equipment Inc	3569	118
American Compressed Steel Corp	5093	138
American Computer and Electronic Services	7379	1575
American Computer And Telephone Inc	7371	677
American Computer Development Inc	3669	51
American Computer Resources Inc	5045	848
American Concrete Products Inc	3272	7
American Connection Information Systems Inc	7382	179
American Connector LLC	5065	318
American Connectors Inc	5063	880
American Consolidated Industries Inc	5051	269
American Consolidated Manufacturing Co	3843	66
American Construction Supply Inc	1794	18
American Consulting and Distribution Corp	5045	200
American Consulting Services Inc	8711	311
American Consumers Inc	5411	222
American Container Transport	4213	2698
American Contract Assembly Corp	3651	188
American Contractors Equipment Co	5082	166
American Converters Inc	3086	56
American Conveyor Corp	3535	151
American Copak Corp	0723	12
American Copper and Brass Inc	5074	53
American Correctional Solutions	8099	65
American Corrective Counseling Services Inc	8322	54
American Corrugated Products Inc	2653	78
American Country Insurance Co	6331	274
American Country Underwriting Agency Inc	6411	114
American Covers Inc	2844	81
American Crane and Equipment	3536	9
American Crane And Hoist Corp	3536	26
American Crane Corp	3536	19
American Critical Care Services Inc	7363	187
American Crystal Sugar Co	2063	1
American Custodial Inc	7349	458
American Custom Drying Co	0723	17
American Cybernetic Corp	8742	668
American Deburring Inc	3599	2177
American Defense Services Inc	1731	2589
American Dehydrated Foods Inc	2015	33
American Delivery Service Inc	4213	1267
American Density Materials	3823	472
American Dental Association	2741	38
American Dental Coop	5047	153
American Dental Partners Inc	8099	18
American Dental Partners of Alabama LLC	8021	13
American Dental Partners of California LLC	8021	4
American Dental Partners of Louisiana LLC	8021	16
American Dental Partners of Maryland LLC	8021	11
American Dental Partners of New York LLC	8021	14
American Dental Partners of North Carolina LLC	8021	15
American Dental Partners of Oklahoma LLC	8021	6
American Dental Partners of Tennessee LLC	8021	10
American Dental Partners of Wisconsin LLC	8021	18
American Dental Professional Services LLC	8021	111
American Detection Systems Inc	1731	2466
American Diagnostica Inc	2865	14
American Die Corp	3544	552
American Die Technology Inc	3544	100

Company Name	SIC	Rank
American Diesel Equipment Inc	7699	153
American Digital Cartography Inc	5045	796
American Digital Corp	3577	425
American Distillation Inc	5169	164
American Distilling Inc	2085	19
American Diversified Security Inc	7381	236
American Douglas Metals Inc	5051	194
American Drapery Blind and Carpet Inc	2591	10
American Drew	2511	16
American Drill Bushing Co	3545	113
American Drilling Co	3599	277
American Drilling Inc	3599	773
American Driver Leasing Inc	7361	159
American Dryer Corp	3582	2
American Durable Inc	3599	2464
American Dynamics Video Products Div	3669	103
American Eagle Airlines Inc	4512	42
American Eagle Outfitters Inc	5651	7
American Eagle Systems Inc	5045	598
American Eagle Tankers Incorporated Ltd	4424	7
American Education Corp	7372	1852
American Educational Products Inc	3999	60
American Electric Company Inc	1731	1192
American Electric Equipment Inc	3629	73
American Electric Of Virginia Inc	1731	1986
American Electric Power Company Inc	4911	5
American Electric Supply Inc	5063	755
American Electric Technologies Inc	3629	25
American Electrical Contracting Inc	1731	1801
American Electronic Materials Inc	3679	345
American Electronic Supply Company Inc	5065	450
American Electronic Systems Inc	5063	962
American ELTEC Inc	5084	708
American Empire Insurance Co	6331	185
American Empire Surplus Lines Insurance Co	6331	178
American Encoder Repair Servic	5063	355
American Energy Group Ltd	1311	276
American Energy Services Inc	3494	70
American Engineering Services Inc	3589	208
American Envircon Inc	3585	219
American Environmental Supply LLC	5084	457
American Environmental Systems Inc	3564	132
American Epoxy And Metal Inc	2821	208
American Equipment and Fabricating Corp	7353	100
American Equipment Company Inc	5082	1
American Equipment Inc	5084	311
American Equity Investment Life Holding Co	6311	38
American Essentials Inc	2251	12
American Exchange Bank	6022	503
American Exhibition Services LLC	7311	581
American Express Co	6211	1
American Express Credit Corp	6153	26
American Express Investment Advisors	6282	597
American Express Publishing	2721	80
American Express Retirement Services	6022	71
American Express Trucking Co	4213	2271
American Extrusion International Corp	3556	127
American Fabricators Inc	3444	43
American Family Financial Services Inc	6163	13
American Family Life Assurance Company of Columbus	6311	45
American Family Mutual Insurance Co	6311	56
American Fan Co	3564	33
American Farm Implement And Specialty Company Inc	3523	177
American Fasteners Inc	5072	63
American Federal Corp	6712	571
American Feed Industry Insurance Co	6399	24
American Felt and Filter Company Inc	3569	131
American Fiber and Finishing Inc	2211	15
American Fiber Systems Inc	3357	8
American Fiberglass Inc	3089	1774
American Fiberglass Products Inc	3272	121
American Fibertech Corp	2448	9
American Fibertek Inc	3679	372
American Fidelity Group	6399	3
American Fidelity Property Co	6552	215
American Financial Group Inc	6331	22
American Financial Printing Inc	2752	303
American Fire and Casualty Co	6331	279
American Fire Equipment Sales and Service Corp	1731	274
American Fire Protection Group Inc	3569	44
American Fish and Seafood Inc	5142	28
American Fitness Professionals and Associates Inc	7999	147
American Fitting Corp	5063	450
American Fixture and Display Corp	5046	157
American Flood Research Inc	8742	438
American Fluorescent Corp	3645	18
American Flux and Metal	3313	7
American Foam Corp	3086	101
American Foam Products Inc	3086	122
American Food Equipment Company Inc	3556	94
American Foods Group LLC	2011	5
American Foods Inc	5141	205
American Foodservice Distributors Inc	5141	101

Company Name	SIC	Rank
American/Foothill Publishing Company Inc	2759	243
American Forest Products LLC	5031	165
American Founders Bancorp Inc	6712	296
American Friends Of The Hebrew University Inc	7389	835
American Frozen Foods Inc	5411	199
American Fruits And Flavors	2087	41
American FSB	6035	192
American FSB (East Grand Forks Minnesota)	6035	73
American Fuji Seal Inc	8748	149
American Fun Food Company Inc	5046	186
American Funds AMCAP A	6722	23
American Funds American Mutual A	6722	33
American Funds Bond Fund of Amer 529A	6722	14
American Funds Capital Inc Builder 529F	6722	6
American Funds Capital World G/I A	6722	248
American Funds EuroPacific Gr A	6722	10
American Funds Group US Government Securities Fund	6722	65
American Funds Incorporated Fund of Amer 529B	6722	233
American Funds Intermediate Bond Fund of America	6722	58
American Funds Investment Company of America A	6722	18
American Funds SMALLCAP World A	6722	15
American Funds Tax-Exempt Bond A	6722	34
American Funds Tax-Exempt Fund CA A	6722	107
American Funds Tax-Exempt Fund of Virginia	6722	185
American Funds Washington Mutual A	6722	12
American Future Technology Corp	5045	455
American Gas Group	2869	54
American Gasket Technologies Inc	3053	69
American General Corp	6331	9
American General Financial Services	6141	14
American General Life and Accident Insurance Co	6311	277
American General Life Insurance Co	6311	27
American General Life Insurance Company of New York	6311	241
American General Supplies Inc	5088	24
American Gfm Corp	3542	17
American Girl LLC	2721	25
American Glass Research Inc	3823	72
American Gnc Corp	8711	511
American Golf Corp	7992	1
American Gorwood Corp	3714	387
American Granby Inc	3432	22
American Graphic Systems Inc	2759	288
American Green Cross Inc	7363	361
American Greenwood Inc	3993	75
American Greetings Corp	2771	3
American Grinding and Machine Co	3443	130
American Group LLC	7372	2493
American Growth Fund Inc	6282	278
American Guard Services Inc	7381	25
American Gypsum Co	3275	5
American Gypsum Marketing Co	3275	6
American Handle Co	3089	1620
American Handling Systems Inc	3536	8
American Hardware Mutual Insurance Co	6331	109
American Hardwood Industries	2439	2
American Hardwood Industries LLC	2426	6
American Health and Life Insurance Co	6321	37
American Health Care Software Enterprises Inc	7372	2416
American Health Lawyers Association	2721	194
American Health Systems Inc	3841	401
American Healthcare Administrative Services Inc	8742	102
American HealthChoice Inc	8011	130
American Healthways Services Inc	8049	8
American Hearing Systems Inc	5047	77
American Heritage Life Insurance Co	6311	166
American Heritage Protective Services	7381	55
American Heritage Securities Inc	6211	272
American High-Income Trust	6722	38
American Hofmann Corp	3545	89
American Hollow Boring Co	3462	76
American Home Health Care Inc	7352	36
American HomePatient Inc (Brentwood Tennessee)	8082	15
American Homestar Corp	2452	6
American Honda Finance Corp	7515	4
American Honda Motor Company Inc	3711	3
American Hospitality Group	8052	12
American Hotel Register Co	5023	3
American House Spinning Inc	2281	13
American Hydro Corp	3511	22
American Hydrotherm Corp	3585	249
American Hytech Corp	7372	2756
American Implement Inc	5083	70
American Income Life Insurance Co	6311	168
American Inc	1731	57
American Indemnity Financial Corp	6331	335
American Independence Corp	6411	113

Company Name	SIC	Rank
American Independent Paper Mills Supply Company Inc	5093	183
American Industrial Acquisition Corp	8741	87
American Industrial Cleaning Company Inc	7349	49
American Industrial Equipment Corp	3699	235
American Industrial Insulation LLC	8711	441
American Industrial Partners	6799	258
American Industrial Plant Services Inc	3443	174
American Industrial Plastics Inc	3082	18
American Industrial Supply	5087	182
American Industrial Werks Inc	4231	4
American Information Technology Solutions LLC	5734	251
American Infoserv Inc	5045	666
American Infrastructure	2752	769
American Innotek Inc	3089	524
American Institute Of Aeronautics And Astronautics Inc	2731	116
American Insulated Panel Company Inc	3585	174
American Insurance Services Group Inc	8999	18
American Integrity Corp	3089	1006
American InterContinental University Inc	8221	36
American Interiors Inc	2522	42
American International Auto Parts Inc	5013	325
American International Exports Inc	5064	118
American International Group Inc	6719	2
American International Industries	5122	61
American International Industries Inc	6799	316
American International Management Corp	5075	8
American International Management Inc	7371	1376
American International Manufacturing Co	3523	194
American International Moving	4213	2523
American International Ventures Inc	1041	28
American Internet Services	7379	196
American Interplex Corporation Laboratories	8734	129
American Invsco Realty Corp	6531	101
American Iron and Steel Company Inc	5093	82
American Iron Works Inc	3441	159
American Iron-Steel Manufacturing Company Inc	3535	190
American Italian Pasta Co	2099	13
American Jetway Corp	2842	179
American Junior Golf Association Inc	7941	27
American Knitting Corp	2281	23
American Labelmark Company Incorporated Labelmaster	2759	44
American Land and Leisure Inc	7349	466
American Land Development US Inc	6552	55
American Land Lease Inc	6798	163
American Landfill Inc	4953	87
American Lawyer Media LLC	2721	43
American Lawyer Media - Philadelphia	2731	349
American Leak Detection Inc	6794	68
American Learning Corp	8322	222
American Leather Inc	2512	33
American Leather Products	3161	15
American Lecithin Co	5199	140
American Led-Gible Inc	3993	190
American Legal Publishing Corp	2731	245
American Legal Search LLC	7361	356
American Liba Inc	5084	851
American Liberty Corp	5047	285
American Licorice Co	2064	21
American Life Insurance Co	6311	227
American Life Science Pharmaceuticals Inc	8731	310
American Lifts Corp	3569	109
American Light Bulb Manufacturing Inc	3641	30
American Light Co	5063	501
American Linc Corp	3599	1304
American Liquid Packaging Systems Inc	5963	16
American List Counsel Inc	7331	14
American Lithe and Publishing Inc	2752	1631
American Little Swan Inc	5065	773
American Loan and Savings Association	6035	261
American Locker Group Inc	2599	22
American Locker Security Systems Inc	2542	11
American Logistic Management International Supply	3612	88
American Louver Co	2673	29
American Lumber Company Inc	5031	242
American Lumber Company LP	5031	229
American Lumber Corp	5031	328
American Machine Works Inc	3599	2315
American Machining and Welding Inc	3599	1416
American Mailers - Illinois Inc	7331	51
American Mailing and Printing Service Inc	7331	266
American Mailing Service Inc	7331	231
American Manufacturing and Equipment Inc	3559	498
American Manufacturing and Machine Inc	3589	95
American Manufacturing Company Inc	2298	1

Company Name	SIC	Rank
American Manufacturing Company Inc (Manassas Virginia)	3613	131
American Manufacturing Network Inc	3599	1561
American Manufacturing Services Inc	5065	538
American Map Inc	2741	384
American Maplan Corp	3559	174
American Marazzi Tile Inc	3253	2
American Marble Products Inc	3281	61
American Marine Transport	4213	1390
American Marketing Services Inc	2711	414
American Massage Products Inc	2514	18
American Mast Inc	3568	74
American Material Handling Company Inc	5046	267
American Media Inc	2721	19
American Media International Ltd	3695	11
American Media Investments Inc	4832	118
American Medical Alert Corp	7389	394
American Medical Association	2741	65
American Medical Industries Inc	3841	230
American Medical Response	4119	2
American Medical Sales Inc	3844	26
American Medical Security Group Inc	6324	50
American Medical Specialties Inc	3841	365
American Medical Supplies And Equipment Inc	5047	226
American Medical Systems Holdings Inc	3842	19
American Megatrends Inc	3674	100
American Metal Bearing Co	3562	38
American Metal Fab Inc	3444	184
American Metal Fibers Inc	3399	28
American Metal Wash Inc	3559	87
American Metalcraft Inc	3469	158
American Metals Company Inc	5093	100
American Metals Corp	3479	21
American Meta's Pack Company Inc	3559	551
American Micro Co	7389	1221
American Micro Data	7389	838
American Micronics Inc	7379	738
American Microsemiconductor Inc	5065	357
American Microsystems Ltd	3577	314
American Millennium Corporation Inc	4813	705
American Millwork Corp	2431	101
American Mine Research Inc	3532	58
American Minority Business Forms Inc	5112	66
American Mobile Dental Corp	8021	24
American Modern Insurance Group Inc	6331	167
American Modular Systems Inc	2452	37
American Moistening Company Inc	3585	238
American Mold Service	3544	822
American Molded Products LLC	3061	24
American Molding Technologies Inc	3089	1494
American Momentum Bank	6022	564
American Monorail Of California LP	5084	807
American Motor Lines Inc	4213	1003
American Moulding and Millwork Co	2511	45
American Multi-Cinema Inc	7832	6
American Multimedia Inc	7819	38
American Music and Sound LLC	5099	38
American Name Plate and Metal Decorating Co	3993	156
American National Bank	6021	114
American National Bank and Trust Co (Danville Virginia)	6021	115
American National Bank (Oakland Park Florida)	6021	280
American National Bank of Texas	6021	74
American National Bankshares Inc	6021	122
American National Carbide Co	3541	76
American National Corp (Omaha Nebraska)	6712	492
American National Insurance Co	6311	46
American National Property and Casualty Co	6331	226
American Natural Energy Corp	1311	246
American Ndt Inc	3829	375
American NetLink	7379	86
American Netronic Inc	5045	803
American Network Insurance Co	6321	72
American Network Services Inc (Incline Village Nevada)	8049	34
American Networks International LLC	7373	653
American NTN Bearing Manufacturing Corp	3562	18
American Nuclear Resources Inc	7361	200
American Nursing Care Inc	8082	57
American Nursing Service Inc	8082	10
American of Martinsville	2531	14
American Office Equipment Company Inc	5021	46
American Office Machines Inc	5112	42
American Oil and Supply Co	2992	67
American Operations Corp	8744	30
American Opinion Publishing Inc	2721	86
American Orthopedics Inc	3842	223
American Outdoor Products Inc	5141	206
American Overseas Book Co Inc	7822	16
American Overseas Marine Corp	4449	16
American Pacesetters Enterprises LLC	8721	305
American Pacific Corp	2819	27
American Pacific Financial Corp	6799	268
American Pacific Forwarders	4213	1005
American Packaging Machinery Inc	3565	159

Company Name	SIC	Rank
American Packaging Products Inc	5199	143
American Pan and Engineering Company Inc	1771	21
American Pan Co	3469	111
American Panel Corp	3585	114
American Paper and Supply Co	5113	56
American Paper Recycling Corp	2611	7
American Patent and Trademark Law Center	8111	581
American Pavers Consultants Inc	3251	17
American Pegboard Printing Inc	7389	2180
American Phoenix Inc	3069	82
American Photocopy Equipment Company of Pittsburgh	5044	20
American Physicians Assurance Corp	6351	25
American Physicians Capital Inc	6324	31
American Physicians Insurance Agency Inc	8741	60
American Physicians Service Group Inc	6331	343
American Pie LLC	2099	58
American Pipe and Supply Company Inc	5085	83
American Plant Food Corp	2875	3
American Plastic Card Co	3089	714
American Plastic Molding Corp	3089	695
American Plastic Products Inc	3544	154
American Plastic Profiles Inc	2821	158
American Plastic Supply and Manufacturing Inc	3081	163
American Plastic Toys Inc	3944	16
American Plastics Company Inc	3081	119
American Plastics Group Inc	3089	751
American Plastics Inc	3089	1590
American Platform and Scaffolding Inc	7353	77
American Plumbing Supply Co	3645	44
American Pneumatic Tool Inc	3546	43
American Polymers Inc	2821	94
American Polystyrene Corp	2821	180
American Polywater Corp	2992	57
American Pop Corn Co	2099	106
American Post Tension Inc	7389	959
American Poultry International Ltd	5144	32
American Power Connection Systems Inc	3643	151
American Power Conversion Corp	3629	1
American Power Devices Inc	3674	371
American Power Pull Corp	3423	82
American Precision Electronics Inc	3679	249
American Precision Inc	3444	248
American Precision Industries	3677	2
American Precision Machining Inc	3599	2157
American Precision Manufacturing LLC	3599	1084
American Press Inc	2752	89
American Pride Coop	5541	17
American Printers Exchange Inc	2752	1253
American Printing and Advertising Inc	7311	950
American Printing and Envelope Co	2752	1587
American Printing and Envelope Inc	2752	1222
American Printing and Lithographing Company Inc	2791	40
American Printing Co	2752	1733
American Printing Finishers Inc	7389	2460
American Printing House For The Blind	2731	187
American Probe and Technologies Inc	3825	307
American Process Lettering Inc	2396	10
American Processing Co	4953	122
American Producers Supply Company Inc	5085	134
American Product Distributors Inc	5099	16
American Products Company Inc	3491	41
American Products Inc	3679	235
American Products LLC	3444	13
American Profol Inc	3081	79
American Progressive Circuits	3672	385
American Pro-Mold Inc	3069	252
American Promotional Events Inc	2899	176
American Protectors Inc	3084	40
American Proteins Inc	2048	6
American Psychiatric Press Inc	2731	273
American Psychiatric Publishing Inc	2721	95
American Public Education Inc	7379	119
American Public Life Insurance Co	6321	49
American Publishing Co	2711	360
American Pulverizer Co	3535	49
American Punch Company Inc	3599	1713
American Purpac Technologies LLC	2086	112
American Quality Manufacturing Inc	3599	1117
American Quality Tools Inc	5085	336
American Radar Components Inc	3679	786
American Radiolabeled Chemicals Inc	2899	143
American Radionic Company Inc	3629	38
American Rag CIE	2339	35
American Railcar Industries Inc	3743	9
American Ramp Transit Inc	4213	2219
American Realty Investors	6531	85
American Realty Investors Inc	6519	4
American Recordable Media	3695	74
American Recreation Products Inc	3949	49
American Recycling Center Inc	3069	201
American Red Ball Transit Co	4213	807
American Reinforced Plastics Inc	3088	35
American Relays Inc	3625	304
American Reliability Labs Inc	8734	76

Company Name	SIC	Rank
American Reliance Inc	3571	83
American Renal Associates Inc	8092	2
American Renolit Corp	5162	71
American Rental Management Co	6552	56
American Reprographics Co	7349	14
American Research and Development Corp	6799	349
American Residential Services LLC	1711	2
American Resource Systems Inc	7374	344
American Ring Company Inc	3961	4
American River Bankshares	6712	436
American River Transportation Co	4449	5
American River-PackageOne Inc	2653	39
American Riviera Bank	6022	609
American Road Machinery Co	3531	156
American Rock Salt Company LLC	1499	2
American Roller Company LLC	3069	28
American Safety Casualty Insurance Co	6411	84
American Safety Indemnity Co	6411	85
American Safety Insurance Holdings Ltd	6411	27
American Safety Insurance Services Inc	6411	86
American Safety Utility Corp	5099	71
American Sales and Service	5084	845
American Satellite and Entertainment Inc	5731	46
American Savings Bank FSB (Honolulu Hawaii)	6035	34
American Savings Bank FSB (Portsmouth Ohio)	6035	159
American Savings FSB	6035	204
American Scale Corp	5046	251
American Science and Engineering Inc	3844	4
American Scientific Resources Inc	3841	417
American Scitec Inc	5065	636
American Screen Art Inc	7389	1078
American Seafood Co	2092	20
American Seafoods Group LLC	2092	5
American Seating Co	2522	12
American Security and Protective Services Inc	7381	105
American Security Bank	6022	304
American Security Group LLC	7381	64
American Security LLC	4213	224
American Security Products Co	3499	36
American Security Resources Corp	3621	164
American Security Shredding	7389	764
American Sensors Corp	3823	339
American Service Industries	7382	74
American Services Technology Inc	8744	42
American Sewer Services Inc	1623	623
American Shaft Co	3451	135
American Shared Hospital Services	8071	33
American Shield Refining Co	2911	42
American Shoreline Inc	1381	41
American Shower and Bath Corp	3431	5
American Sign Language Services Corp	7389	1511
American Skandia Life Assurance Corp	6351	6
American Skin LLC	2096	53
American Sleeve Bearing LLC	3568	64
American Society Of Interior Designers	7389	1912
American Software Inc	7372	478
American Soil Products Inc	5261	16
American Soil Technologies Inc	2879	57
American Solar Electric	3568	43
American Sound and Electronics Inc	5065	356
American Southern Insurance Co	6411	182
American Soy Products Inc	2075	11
American Specialty Advertising And Printing Co	2752	1841
American Specialty Grinding Company Inc	3541	165
American Specialty Window and Door Inc	5031	444
American Spectrum Realty Inc	6798	145
American Spirit Graphics Corp	2752	46
American Spool and Packaging	2655	10
American Spoon Foods Inc	2033	99
American Sporting Systems	5091	143
American Spring Wire Corp	3315	13
American Stainless and Supply LLC	5051	119
American Stairway Inc	2431	114
American Standard Circuits Inc	3672	148
American Standard Co	3469	308
American Standard Inc	3585	2
American Standard Inc Plumbing Div	3432	4
American Standox Inc	5198	11
American State Bank	6022	126
American State Financial Corp	6712	284
American States Utility Services Inc	4941	57
American States Water Co	4941	5
American Steamship Co	4432	1
American Steel LLC	3325	12
American Steel Treating Inc	3398	15
American Stitchco Inc	2396	16
American Stock Exchange Inc	6231	10
American Stock Transfer and Trust Co	6289	7
American Storage and Transport	4213	2311
American Student List LLC	7331	43
American Sub-Assembly Producers	3679	631
American Sunroof Co	3714	79

Company Name	SIC	Rank
American Superconductor Corp	3621	16
American Surgical Sponges LLC	3842	212
American Surplus Inc	5084	513
American Suzuki Motor Corp	5012	41
American Syntactics Inc	7373	1213
American Systems	7372	5039
American Systems Corp	5045	13
American Systems Engineering Corp	7389	147
American Talent Management	7922	85
American Tank and Fabricating Co	3443	33
American Tank Inc	1623	774
American Tar Co	2952	15
American Taximeters and Communications Inc	5531	68
American Technical Ceramics Corp	3679	96
American Technical Solutions Inc	2221	35
American Technology and Research Industries Inc	1799	140
American Technology International	7378	114
American Technology Network Corp	3827	71
American Technology Research Inc	8733	17
American Technology Services	3672	422
American Technology Solutions Inc	5045	663
American Techsystems Corp	7373	908
American Telecare Inc	7363	289
American Telecasting Inc	4841	66
American Telecom Solutions LLC	5065	750
American Telecommunications Corp	5065	1005
American Telecommunications Systems Inc	4813	357
American Teleconnect Inc	4899	194
American Telephone and Data Inc	4813	260
American Telesis Inc	4813	547
American Teletimer Corp	3625	212
American Television and Appliance of Madison Inc	5731	5
American Tenant Screen Inc	7323	43
American Tennis Courts Inc	1542	425
American Tent and Awning Company Inc	7359	190
American Testing Laboratories Inc	2421	67
American Textile Co	2261	5
American Thermoform Corp	3579	15
American Thermoplastic Extrusion Co	3089	424
American Tile Supply Inc	5032	2
American Time and Signal Co	3873	13
American Tire Distributors Holdings Inc	5014	1
American Tool and Engineering Inc	3544	264
American Tool and Machining Company Inc	3544	714
American Tool and Mold Inc	3544	30
American Tool Co	3599	1765
American Tooling Center Inc	3544	114
American Torch Tip Co	3548	23
American Tower Corp	4899	4
American Tower International Inc	3699	52
American Tower Management Inc	4899	16
American Traders Inc	1795	8
American Trading and Production Corp	1311	24
American Trading and Production Corp Hazel Div	5943	8
American Traffic Solutions Inc	3577	103
American Transparent Plastic Corp	3081	136
American Transport Group LLC	4213	309
American Trim LLC	3469	8
American Trust and Savings Bank	6036	103
American Trutzschler Inc	3552	14
American Tubing Inc	3351	19
American Type Culture Collection Inc	8733	10
American Ultraviolet West Inc	3535	181
American Underwater Products	3949	99
American Uniform Co	2326	9
American Unit Inc	7379	222
American United Mutual Insurance Holding Co	6311	53
American Urethane Inc	3531	126
American Utility Corporation Inc	1623	131
American Valve Inc	3494	59
American Vanguard Corp	2879	7
American Vantage Cos	8741	303
American Video Equipment	3663	254
American Video Service Inc	7378	82
American Viking Enterprises of Florida Inc	7372	4090
American Voice Mail Inc	7389	624
American Volkssport Associates	7389	1712
American Wagering Inc	7999	105
American Wagering Management Company Inc	7999	49
American Waste Management Services Inc	4953	102
American Water Heater Co	3639	1
American Water Works Association	8733	14
American Water Works Company Inc	4941	1
American Wax Inc	2843	15
American Web Inc	2752	176
American Web Page LLC	7379	976
American Weigh Scales Inc	5046	101
American Welding And Engineering LLC	3599	1330
American Welding and Gas	5084	367
American Welding And Press Repair Inc	7699	237
American West Bank NA	6021	381

Company Name	SIC	Rank
American West Homes Inc	1521	15
American Wholesale Insurance Group Inc	6411	107
American Wholesale Supply Inc	3564	166
American Window And Glass Inc	3089	495
American Window Products Inc	3089	1052
American Wire Tie Inc	3599	87
American Woodmark Corp	2439	3
American Woodmark Corp (Kingman Arizona)	2434	21
American Woolen Company Inc	2231	2
American Xtal Technology Inc	3674	109
American Zoetrope	7812	121
Americana Art China Co	3231	35
American-Canadian Fisheries Inc	2091	29
American-Iowa Manufacturing Inc	3523	218
American-Metric Corp	3568	47
American-Republican Inc	2711	207
American's Christian Credit Union	6062	75
American-Tel-A-Systems Inc	3661	41
Americantours International LLC	4725	26
AmericanWest Bancorp	6712	221
Americare Staffing Service Inc	7361	208
America's Business Software	7371	1861
America's Career Opportunities Inc	7363	152
America's Car-Mart Inc	5511	61
America's Choice Healthplans Inc	6324	117
America's Classic Foods LLC	5046	309
America's Collectibles Network Inc	5961	19
America's Drive-in Trust	6733	2
America's Finest Products Corp	2841	48
America's Gardening Resource Inc	5961	141
Americas Group	2731	350
America's Health Choice Medical Plans Inc	8011	39
America's Incredible Pizza Co	5812	259
America's Media Marketing Inc	7319	73
America's Nursing Inc	8082	86
America's Service Line Inc	4213	821
America's Staffing Associates Inc	7361	169
Americas United Bank	6029	28
Americast Metal Products Inc	3559	43
Americ-Evolved Manufacturing LLC	3652	27
Americhem Engineering Services	3559	416
Americhem Inc	2865	3
Americhem Systems Inc	3999	154
AmeriChoice Corp	6324	55
AmeriChoice of Pennsylvania Inc	6324	76
AmericInn International LLC	7011	147
Americlock Inc	3579	55
Ameri-Co Carriers Inc	4213	1089
Americo Financial Life and Annuity Insurance Co	6311	151
Americo Life Inc	6311	177
Americold Logistics LLC	4222	1
Americom Imaging Systems Inc	5045	736
Americom Inc	7373	656
Americom Telecommunications Inc (Houston Texas)	1731	1912
Americomm Direct Marketing Co	7331	26
Americor Electronics Ltd	3679	57
Americor Mortgage Inc	6162	119
Americorp Inc	7389	234
Americraft Carton Inc	2657	34
AmeriCredit Financial Services Inc	6141	29
Ameridrives International LLC	3568	6
Amerifax Services Corp	7372	2703
Amerifilm Converters LLC	5162	62
Ameriflex Inc	3494	55
Ameriflight LLC	4512	47
AmeriGas Eagle Parts and Service Inc	5984	11
AmeriGas Eagle Propane LP	4925	4
AmeriGas Inc	4925	2
AmeriGas Partners LP	5999	3
AmeriGas Propane LP	4925	1
AmeriGas Propane Parts and Service Inc	5984	1
Amerigo Inc	7389	984
Amerigon Inc	3711	39
Amerigroup Corp	6324	24
AMERIGROUP Florida Inc	6324	57
AMERIGROUP Illinois Inc	6324	101
AMERIGROUP New Jersey Inc	6324	88
Amerijet International Inc	4513	5
Ameri-Kart Corp Ohio Div	3083	24
Ameriken Die Supply Inc	3544	95
Ameriklean Inc	7349	110
Amerikohl Mining Inc	1221	25
Amerikooler Inc	3585	108
Amerilab Technologies Inc	2834	298
Ameri-Line Inc	4213	2576
Amerimac Cal-West Financial	6794	82
Amerimade Technology Inc	3089	962
Amerimail Corp	7331	251
AmeriMark Direct LLC	5961	46
Amerimax Home Products Inc	3444	6
Amerimerchant LLC	7389	2192
Amerimex Communications Corp	4813	259
Amerimold Tech Inc	5085	290
Amerind Oil Company Ltd	1382	37
Amerine Systems Inc	0781	15
Amerine Utilities Construction Inc	1623	569
AmeriNet Central	8741	124
AmeriNet Inc	7389	262

Company Name	SIC	Rank
Amerinex Applied Imaging Inc	7372	368
AmeriPath Inc	8071	2
AmeriPoint Title Inc	6361	35
Ameripride Services Inc	7213	2
AmeriPride Uniform Services	7213	8
Ameriprint Graphics Inc	2752	966
Ameriprise Financial Inc	6282	11
Ameripure Processing Company Inc	2091	19
Ameriqual Group LLC	2099	22
AmeriQuest Transportation and Logistics Resources	4731	29
AmeriResource Technologies Inc	8711	581
Ameris Bancorp	6712	152
AMERISAFE Inc	6331	163
AmeriServ Financial Bank	6022	778
AmeriServ Financial Inc	6712	334
Ameriserv Inc	2759	534
AmeriServ Life Insurance Co	6411	53
AmeriServ Trust and Financial Services Co	6022	658
Ameri-Shred Corp	3559	357
AmeriSource Corp (Paducah Kentucky)	5122	25
Amerisource Funding Inc	6159	61
AmerisourceBergen Corp	5122	2
Ameristar Casinos Inc	7999	14
Ameristar Fence Products Inc	3446	10
Ameristar Financial Co	6141	36
Amerisure Inc	6331	223
Amerisure Insurance Co	6331	112
Amerisure Mutual Insurance Co	6331	162
Ameritac Inc	7349	86
Ameritas Investment Advisors Inc	6282	436
Ameritas Investment Corp	6211	355
Ameritas Life Insurance Corp	6311	54
Ameritec Corp	3661	90
Ameritec Machining Inc	3549	33
Ameri-Tech Dist Inc	2325	12
Ameri-Tech Equipment Co	3531	140
Ameri-Tech Termite and Pest Control Inc	7342	31
Ameritek Lasercut Dies Inc	3544	347
Ameritel Inc	8748	373
Ameri-Tool Industries Inc	3544	837
Ameritrans Capital Corp	6722	259
Amerityre Corp	3011	22
Ameriwaste Inc	5064	145
Ameriwest Industries Inc	5072	112
Ameriwood Industries	2511	17
Amerlux Inc	3646	20
Ameron Fiberglass Composite Pipe Div	3084	10
Ameron International Corp	3272	29
Ameron International Water Transmission Group	5051	483
Ameron Pole Products Div	3441	117
Amerx Health Care Corp	2834	391
Ames Company Inc	3494	46
Ames Computer Forms Inc	2761	49
Ames Engineering Inc	3829	129
Ames International Inc	2064	59
Ames Metal Products Co	3356	39
Ames National Corp	6712	330
Ames Rubber Corp	3069	39
Ames Rubber Manufacturing Company Inc	3061	49
Ames Safety Envelope Co	7371	125
Ames Supply Co	5112	63
Ames True Temper	3423	9
AME's Uniforms Inc	2326	19
Amesbury Group Inc	3053	13
Amest Corp	3674	457
Ametco Manufacturing Corp	3315	32
AMETEK Aerospace Inc	3825	55
AMETEK Automation and Process Technologies	3625	72
Ametek Drexelbrook	3625	18
AMETEK Inc	3621	5
AMETEK Lamb Electric	3621	19
AMETEK Process and Analytical Instruments	3823	96
Ametek Rotron	3629	23
AMETEKVehicular Instrumentation Systems	3714	183
Ametherm Inc	3676	18
Ametrade Inc	5065	354
AMEX Assurance Co	6331	80
Amex Die Cutting Service Inc	2675	28
Amf Anaheim LLC	3444	91
AMF Bakery Systems	3556	29
AMF Beverage Company of Oregon Inc	3949	3
AMF Bowling Centers Holdings Inc	3949	4
AMF Bowling Centers Inc	3949	1
AMF Bowling Centers International Inc	7933	3
AMF Bowling Mexico Holding Inc	7933	1
AMF Bowling Products Inc	3949	90
AMF Bowling Worldwide Inc	7933	4
Amf Electrical Contractors Inc	1731	293
Amf Facility Services Inc	7349	247
Amf Support Surfaces Inc	2515	12
AMF Worldwide Bowling Centers Holdings Inc	3949	5
Amfan Corp	3599	638
Amfit Inc	5047	178
AMG Engineering and Machining Inc	3599	724

Company Name	SIC	Rank
Amg Forwarding Corp	5085	326
Amg Inc	3599	383
Amg Industries Corp	3312	70
Amg Industries Inc	3465	43
AMG Media Group	3695	84
Amgen Inc	2834	8
Amgen Pharmaceuticals Inc	8733	2
Amgraf Inc	7371	1617
Amgraph Packaging Inc	2671	20
AMGRO Inc	6153	15
Amherst Alarm Inc	7382	109
AmherstMadison	4449	11
AMHN Inc	7319	178
Amhof Trucking Inc	4213	416
Ami Acquisition Corp	7331	125
AMI Arc Machines Inc	3566	14
AMI/Coast Magnetics Inc	3677	87
Ami Corp	5045	912
Ami Entertainment Network Inc	3999	80
Ami Imaging Systems Inc	5044	82
AMI Inc	3639	22
AMI Metals Inc	5051	209
AMI Strategies	7379	964
Ami Technical Consultants Inc	7379	1278
Amica Mutual Insurance Co	6331	100
Amicalola Electric Membership	4911	222
Amick Sound Inc	5065	762
Amico Scientific Corp	5049	154
Amicus Inc	7372	1071
Amicus Software	7372	4402
Amicus Therapeutics Inc	2834	263
Amie Gross Architectural PC	8712	308
Amiee Lynn Accessories	2387	3
Amies Communications	7311	487
Amigo Business Computers	5045	630
Amigo Custom Screen Prints LLC	2759	432
Amigo Mobility International Inc	3842	161
Amigone Sanchez and Mattrey LLP	8111	518
Amin Food Inc	5149	189
Aminteron Systems Inc	3672	487
Amir Amirfar and Associates Inc	1521	112
Amir Foods Inc	5141	230
Amira Pharmaceuticals Inc	8731	138
Amiram Dror Inc	2051	261
Amis Materials Co	1429	11
Amistad Cattle Co	0211	14
Amistar Corp	3559	580
Amitron Inc	3672	78
Amity Die and Stamping Co	3469	305
Amity Packing Company Inc	5147	41
Amity Unlimited Inc	7331	140
Amjems Inc	2676	8
Amken Orthopedics Inc	3842	237
Amko Building Services Inc	7349	325
Amkor Technology Inc	3674	15
Amkus Inc	3569	201
AML International Inc	5146	34
Amli Residential Properties LP	6531	29
Amli Residential Properties Trust	6798	63
Amlings Flowerland	5992	7
Ammadis LLC	5045	703
Ammark Corp	7331	232
Ammcon Corp	3599	660
AMN Healthcare Services Inc	8099	12
Amneal Pharmaceuticals Of New York LLC	2834	113
Amnet	7379	743
Amnis	3669	59
Amodex Products Inc	2842	140
Amogha Solutions LLC	7371	1791
Amorim Cork Composites Inc	2499	29
Amoroso's Baking Co	2051	72
Amorphous Materials Inc	3339	22
Amos and Andrews Inc	8711	248
Amos Data Systems Inc	5045	641
Amos Press Inc	2721	150
Amos Townsend and Associates Inc	7311	900
Amos-Hill Associates Inc	2435	19
Amot Controls Corp	3823	97
Amp Check Electric	1731	2536
AMP Electric Vehicles Inc	3711	57
Amp Information Services Inc	7361	391
AMP King Battery Company Inc	5063	435
AMP Manufacturing And Supply Inc	3612	53
Amp Residential Services LLC	7363	347
Ampac Enterprises Inc	3231	40
AMPAC Farms Inc	2819	68
Ampac Holdings LLC	2673	1
Ampacet Corp	2816	2
Ampac-Isp Corporation LLC	3764	3
Amparts International Inc	5012	19
Ampco Metal Inc	3365	12
Ampco Products LLC	2431	13
AMPCO System Parking	7521	5
Ampco UES Sub Inc	3561	34
Ampco-Pittsburgh Corp	3561	28
Ampel Inc	3672	211
Ampem Electronics and Services Inc	5045	1034
Amperage Electrical Supply Inc	5063	419
Amperite Company Inc	3679	526
Ampersand Ventures Management Corp	6799	285
Ampex Co	7371	1471
Ampex Corp	3663	69

Company Name	SIC	Rank
Ampex Data System Corp	3572	27
AmPharmCo	2836	66
Amphastar Pharmaceuticals Inc	2834	163
Amphenol Borisch Technologies	3679	170
Amphenol Corp	3678	3
Amphenol Interconnect Products Corp	3357	33
Amphenol Sine Systems Pyle Connectors Corp	3643	38
Amplas Compounding Inc	3089	1689
Ample Industries Inc	2672	67
Amplexus Corp	7372	3689
Amplifier Research Corp	3663	65
AmpliFind Music Services Inc	7374	224
Amplify Public Affairs	8743	68
AmpliPhi Biosciences	2836	46
Amplitech Inc	3663	230
Amplitude Technical Sales	3679	856
Amplivox Sound Systems LLC	3663	234
Amplyx Pharmaceuticals Inc	2834	429
AMPM Inc	7311	398
Ampp Inc	3444	70
Ampride	5171	55
Ampro ADLINK Technology America Inc	3577	351
Ampronix Inc	5047	80
Amptech Inc	3679	231
AMR Advertising and Marketing	7311	535
AMR Corp	4512	4
AmREIT Inc	6798	170
AMRESCO Commercial Finance Inc	6162	64
AMRESCO Inc (Solon Ohio)	2899	57
Amrex-Zetron	3699	195
Amro Fabricating Corp	3728	115
Amron Stair Works Inc	2431	112
Ams Acquisition Corp	3674	99
Ame Car Stereo Inc	5731	147
Ams Controls Inc	5084	592
AMS Group Inc	5047	207
AMS Health Sciences Inc	5099	61
Ams Inc	3599	2100
AMS Inc (American Falls Idaho)	3829	190
Ams Metal Slitting Corp	7389	2274
Ams Of Indiana Inc	5031	296
AMS Plastics Inc	3089	113
Ams Temporaries Inc	7363	237
Ams Vans Inc	5511	1240
Amscan Holdings Inc	2679	2
AMSCO Inc	6531	273
Amsco School Publications Inc	2731	164
Amsco Steel Co	5051	214
Amsco Steel Products Co	5051	486
Amsco Transportation Inc	4213	2648
Amsco US Inc	3679	305
Amsco Windows	3442	40
Amsher Collection Services Inc	7322	63
Amsoil Inc	2992	18
Am-Source LLC	3089	1104
Amspec Chemical and Custom Compounding	2819	50
AMST Inc	4213	1866
Amstan Logistics Inc	4213	264
Amsted Industries Inc	3321	2
AmSurg Burbank Inc	8011	96
AmSurg Corp	8011	6
AmSurg EC Sante Fe Inc	8011	139
AmSurg EC Topeka Inc	8011	127
AmSurg EC Washington Inc	8011	109
Amsurg Encino Inc	8011	72
AmSurg Glendale Inc	8011	59
AmSurg Holdings Inc	8011	54
AmSurg La Jolla Inc	8011	164
AmSurg Melbourne Inc	8011	149
AmSurg Miami Inc	8011	132
AmSurg Ocala Inc	8011	150
AmSurg Palmetto Inc	8011	146
AmSurg Suncoast Inc	8011	140
AmSurg Weslaco Inc	8011	165
AmSurg-Las Vegas LLC	8011	80
Amsys Inc	7373	697
AMT Datasouth Corp	3577	305
Amt Labs Inc	2833	54
Amt Systems Inc	1731	923
AMTA	4724	117
Amtec Communications Inc	5065	215
Amtec Systems Corp	7371	1818
Amtech Electrocircuits Inc	3672	451
AMTECH Inc (Bensalem Pennsylvania)	7372	1831
Amtech Lighting Services	7349	24
Amtech LLC	3679	146
Amtech Microelectronics Inc	3679	402
Amtech Systems Inc	3559	24
Amtek Computer Services	7378	29
Amtek Consulting LLC	7379	1395
Amtek Electronic Inc	3571	159
Amtekco Industries Inc	3469	65
Amtel Security Systems Inc	3699	192
Amtel Systems Corp	3661	173
AmTest Air Quality	8734	177
Am-Tex Electric Inc	1731	762
Amtex Enterprises Inc	7371	1030
Amtex Inc	3429	70
Amtex Systems Inc	7371	216
Amtico International Inc	3069	40
Amtote International Inc	7999	85
Amtrak/Lirr JV	1731	769
Amtrend Corp	2541	29
Amtrol Inc	3411	7
Amtrust Financial Services Inc	6331	99
AMTRUST Inc	6022	188
Amtrust Mortgage Corp	6162	116
AMTSystems Inc	7372	2110
Amurcon Corp	6531	299
Amusement Management Inc	5092	42
Amusement Products LLC	3949	158
Amvac Chemical Corp	2879	14
AMVC Management Services	0213	12
Amw Cuyuna Engine Company Inc	3519	36
Amway Corp	5963	2
Amway Hotel Corp	7011	30
Amway International Inc	5169	13
Amwell Machine and Fabrication Inc	3599	2001
Amwest Surety Insurance Co	6351	12
Amy Food Inc	2038	59
Amylin Pharmaceuticals Inc	2834	55
Amyris Biotechnologies Inc	2899	42
Amy's Kitchen Inc	2038	12
Amyway North America	5963	6
Amzac Enterprises Inc	4213	1654
Amzi! Inc	7371	1720
AN Deringer Inc	4731	38
AN Webber Inc	4213	652
Ana Molinari	5087	104
Ana Trading Corporation USA	5084	378
Anaba Group Inc	5099	103
Anacapa Sciences Inc	8731	252
Anachemia Chemicals Inc	2819	96
Anaco Inc	3321	11
Anacom General Corp	3577	373
Anacom Inc	3663	152
Anacom Systems Inc	3663	190
Anaconda Foundry Fabrication Company Inc	3321	54
Anaconda Press Inc	2752	1000
Anacondabookscom	5961	192
Anacor Pharmaceuticals Inc	8731	414
Anadarko Industries LLC	7379	339
Anadarko Petroleum Corp	1311	10
ANADIGICS Inc	3674	85
Anadrill Schlumberger	1381	2
Anadyne Inc	3679	871
Anadys Pharmaceuticals Inc	2834	455
Anaheim Automation Inc	3625	294
Anaheim Custom Extruders Inc	3089	1041
Anaheim Extrusion Company Inc	3354	37
Anakam Inc	5734	56
Analab Inc	2899	203
Analex Corp	7373	69
Analog Devices Inc	3674	14
Analog Digital International	3695	106
Analogic Corp	3825	8
Analysis and Information Services Inc	7372	3858
Analysis And Measurement Services Corp	8711	558
Analysis Group LLC	8999	65
Analysts Inc	8734	72
Analysts International Corp	7371	96
Analytcal B Chemistry Laboratory Inc	8731	111
Analytic and Computational Research Inc	7379	854
Analytic Associates	5045	631
Analytic Concepts Inc	7371	1721
Analytic Investors Inc	6282	404
Analytic Plastic Inc	3089	1665
Analytic Services Inc	8733	7
Analytical Design Service Corp	8711	427
Analytical Graphics Inc	7372	839
Analytical Group Inc	7372	916
Analytical Instruments Corp	3823	307
Analytical Laboratories Inc	8734	159
Analytical Management Solutions Inc	8742	258
Analytical Resources Inc	8731	270
Analytical Scientific Instruments Inc	3826	98
Analytical Sensors and Instruments Ltd	3826	45
Analytical Services Co	5049	157
Analytical Services Inc	7372	298
Analytical Software	7372	2704
Analytical Solutions Inc	7389	542
Analytical Spectral Devices	3826	97
Analytical Technologies Inc	3826	162
Analytics Operations Engineering Inc	8742	352
Analytiks International Inc	7371	1368
Analyze Software Inc	7372	2937
Anaren Inc	3663	36
Anark Corp	7371	959
Anasazi Instruments Inc	3826	110
Anaspec Inc	8731	182
Anastasi Development Company LLC	6552	104
Anatec International Inc	8711	351
Anatech Electronics Inc	3679	467
Anatech Ltd	2835	70
AnaTek Corp	7372	4656
Anatomical Chart Co	3083	32
Anaya Gems Inc	5094	8
Anbakam Metals LLC	3321	17
Anbro Electric Company Inc	1731	1358
ANCA Inc (Wixom Michigan)	5084	45
Anchen Pharmaceuticals Inc	2834	119
Anchor BanCorp Wisconsin Inc	6712	141
Anchor Bolt and Screw Co	3452	48
Anchor Brewing Co	2082	32
Anchor Capital Advisors LLC	6282	115
Anchor Coatings Of Leesburg Inc	2851	172
Anchor Computer Inc	7372	4142
Anchor Coupling Inc	3429	35
Anchor Gasoline Corp	5411	260
Anchor Glass Container Corp	3221	4
Anchor Insulation Company Inc	1742	11
Anchor Investment Services Inc	6411	196
Anchor Lamina America Inc	3545	22
Anchor Lumber Company Inc	5211	171
Anchor Packaging Inc	3086	19
Anchor Paint Manufacturing Co	2851	69
Anchor Paper Co	5111	19
Anchor Products Co	3841	227
Anchor Sales And Service Company Inc	7699	166
Anchor Scientific Inc	3823	259
Anchor Security and Investigations Inc	7381	156
Anchor Subaru LLC	5511	1211
Anchor Tool and Die Co	3465	24
Anchor Tool And Plastics Inc	3089	575
Anchorage Advisors LLC	8748	34
Anchorage Municipal Light and Power	4911	131
AnchorBank FSB	6036	10
Anchor-Harvey Components LLC	3463	13
AnchorPad Security Inc	3429	40
AnchorPoint	7372	361
Ancient Wisdom Productions	7379	987
Ancilla Systems Inc	8062	245
Ancira Enterprises Inc	5511	53
Ancira Winton Chevrolet Inc	5511	67
Anco Engineering Inc	3441	125
Anco Fine Foods	5961	84
Anco Products Inc	3444	170
Ancol	3571	123
Ancom Communications Inc	5065	806
Ancon Transportation Services Inc	4213	1675
An-Cor Industrial Plastics Inc	3089	692
Ancra International LLC	3537	23
Anda Inc	5122	7
Andale Farmers Cooperative Co	5153	46
Andaloro Smith and Krueger LLP	8721	413
Andantex U S A Inc	3568	82
Andari Fashion Inc	2329	30
Andavo Travel	4724	75
Andco Inc	5511	1186
And-Dell Corp	3634	34
Andeen-Hagerling Inc	3825	268
Andela Products Ltd	3559	406
Andera Inc	7372	2222
Ander-Beacon Corp	2051	219
Anderberg Innovative Print Solutions Inc	2759	220
Anderco Inc	2431	111
Andermac Inc	3841	379
Anders Minkler and Diehl LLP	8721	367
Andersen Construction Company Inc	1542	62
Andersen Corp	2431	2
Andersen Dairy Inc	2026	60
Andersen Manufacturing Inc	3663	213
Andersen Services Inc	1731	374
Andersen Sterilizers Inc	3841	263
Andersen Wrecking Co	5093	227
Anderson Advertising	7311	961
Anderson and Middleton Co	2421	32
Anderson and Murison Inc	6411	233
Anderson and Strudwick Inc	6211	49
Anderson and Vreeland Inc	5043	7
Anderson Automatics Inc	3451	70
Anderson Birtcher Investors LLC	7389	1675
Anderson Brothers Construction Company Of Brainerd Inc	1771	17
Anderson Brothers Storage and Moving	4213	2948
Anderson Chemical Co	2842	48
Anderson Clayton Corp	0724	2
Anderson Cleaning Systems	7349	474
Anderson Columbia Company Inc	1611	67
Anderson Communications Inc	7311	206
Anderson Concrete Corp	3273	52
Anderson Contracting Inc	1623	739
Anderson Copper and Brass Co	3432	15
Anderson Dairy Inc	2026	33
Anderson Development Company Inc	2821	55
Anderson Die and Manufacturing Co	3089	1471
Anderson Electric Controls Inc	3625	208
Anderson Electric Inc	1731	200
Anderson Electronics Inc	5065	244
Anderson Engineering Consultants Inc	8711	271
Anderson Equipment Co	5082	31
Andorcon Fabrics Inc	2392	31
Anderson Forest Products Inc	2448	36
Anderson Global Inc	3543	4
Anderson Home Health Supply	5047	241
Anderson House Tours	4725	58
Anderson Imaging Group Inc	7372	1618
Anderson Industries Inc	3679	787
Anderson International Corp	3556	44
Anderson Lock Company Ltd	5072	76
Anderson Machinery Co	5049	136
Anderson Machinery Company Inc	5082	130
Anderson Machining Service Inc	3599	264

Company Name	SIC	Rank
Anderson Manufacturing Company Inc	3452	69
Anderson Manufacturing Company Inc (St Paul Minnesota)	3812	205
Anderson Marketing Group	7311	287
Anderson Moulds Inc	3089	1753
Anderson Pacific Corp	6211	358
Anderson Partners	7311	757
Anderson Perlstein Ltd	7336	54
Anderson Piping Contractors Inc	1623	356
Anderson Precision Inc	3451	53
Anderson Products Inc	3296	11
Anderson Rentals Inc	7359	262
Anderson Security Inc	7381	103
Anderson Services LLC	4212	18
Anderson Solid Waste Inc	4953	117
Anderson Tool and Die Corp	3841	255
Anderson Tool and Engineering Company Inc	3559	157
Anderson Towing Service Inc	7549	26
Anderson Transfer Inc	4213	3071
Anderson Transportation Co *	4213	2498
Anderson Truck Line Inc	4213	1745
Anderson Trucking Service Inc	4213	263
Anderson Truss Company Inc	2439	48
Anderson Valley Brewing Inc	2082	58
Anderson Walker and Associates Inc	7379	1132
Anderson Welding and Machine Service Inc	7692	46
Anderson Wood Products Co	2426	12
AndersonBell Corp	7372	4784
Anderson-Bolds Inc	5063	472
Anderson-Cook Inc	3542	9
Anderson-DuBose Co	5141	113
Anderson-Erickson Dairy Co	0241	1
Anderson-Martin Machine Co	3565	125
Anderson-Moore Construction Corp	1542	147
Anderson's Candies Inc	2064	120
Anderson's Candy Shop Inc	2066	44
Anderson's Grocery A Family Tradition Inc	5411	283
Andersons Inc	5153	4
Anderson-Tully Co	2421	26
Andes Manufacturing LLC	2064	18
Andesa Services Inc	7389	290
Andex Industries Inc	2671	47
Andhus Technologies Inc	7371	1120
Andin International Inc	3911	6
Andis Co	3999	63
Andlinger and Company Inc	6719	143
Andon Electronics Corp	3679	482
Andor Design Corp	3829	460
Andover Company Inc	6531	244
Andover Consulting Group Inc	7389	1040
Andover Corp	3827	86
Andover Healthcare Inc	3479	27
Andrade and Ashworth Inc	3842	296
Andre Bollier Ltd	5812	446
Andrea Aromatics Inc	2842	105
Andrea Blain Public Relations Inc	8743	341
Andrea by Sadek	5023	7
Andrea Electronics Corp	3663	215
Andrea Systems LLC	3669	206
Andreae Team Inc	3564	150
Andreas Enterprises Inc	8412	1
Andrea's Prosthesis Inc	8072	13
Andreini and Co	6411	127
Andrepont Printing Inc	2752	1690
Andresen-Ryan Coffee Co	5141	203
Andrew and Associates	7389	1000
Andrew and Williamson Sales Co	5148	25
Andrew Automotive Inc	5511	390
Andrew Belmont Sargent Business Products Inc	7699	67
Andrew Corp	3357	4
Andrew D Woll Law Office	8111	597
Andrew General Contractors Inc	1541	296
Andrew Gerard Group Inc	7379	1388
Andrew Grygus	7373	1159
Andrew Kolb and Son Ltd	3231	57
Andrew Roby General Contractor Inc	1521	72
Andrew T Johnson Company Inc	7334	75
Andrew Technologies Inc	3679	502
Andrew Tool and Machining Company Inc	3599	1490
Andrews and Kurth LLP	8111	26
Andrews Candy Company Inc	2064	124
Andrews Caramel Apples Inc	2064	122
Andrews Distributing Company of North Texas	5181	4
Andrews Filter And Supply Corp	3564	100
Andrews Glass Company Inc	3231	55
Andrews Group	8711	116
Andrews International	7381	4
Andrews Laser Works Corp	3444	187
Andrews Metal Works Inc	3441	236
Andrews Paper and Chemical Co	5169	126
Andrews Steel Rule Die Company Inc	2679	75
Andrews Termite and Pest Control	7342	76
Andrews Transport LP	4213	476
Andrews University Inc	8221	18
Andrews Van Lines Inc	4213	1843
Andrex Inc	3599	2252
Andrex Systems Inc	3679	872

Company Name	SIC	Rank
Andromeda Software Inc (Thousand Oaks California)	7372	4482
Andromeda Systems Inc	8748	268
Andronico's Market	5411	179
Androscoggin Bank	6036	35
Andrus Transportation Services	4213	510
ANDXOR Corp	7372	4785
Andy Gump Inc	7359	32
Andy Klein Electrical Contracting Inc	1731	921
Andy Mohr Truck Center	5511	950
Andy's Electrical Service Inc	3625	253
Andy's Seasoning Inc	2099	230
Anemostat	3564	36
Anertec Holdings LLC	7373	708
Anesis Group Inc	7372	4233
Anesis Inc	7375	258
Anesta Corp	8731	142
aNetorder Inc	7389	204
Anfinsen Plastic Moulding Company Inc	3089	1495
ANG Federal Credit Union	6061	144
Angarai	8742	597
Angeion Corp	3841	102
Angel Air Repair and Specialty Company Inc	5084	793
Angel Lithographing Co	2752	1314
Angel Staffing Inc	7361	66
Angel Touch Commercial Cleaning	7349	521
Angel Vincent Inc	5063	858
Angelica Brothers Electrical Contracting Inc	1731	974
Angelica Corp	7219	1
Angelika Film Centers LLC	7832	24
Angeli's Central Market	5411	210
Angelo Gordon and Co	6722	35
Angelo Gordon and Company LP	6282	177
Angelo Iafrate Cos	1611	254
Angelo Nieto Inc	3532	71
Angeloni Electric Inc	1731	1832
Angelo's Italian Ices	2024	62
Angel's Bakeries Inc	2051	197
Angel's Cleaning Service Inc	7349	403
Angel's Touch Nursing Care Inc	8082	91
Angelus Corp	5063	282
Angelus Pacific Company Inc	2752	1709
Angelus Sanitary Can Machine Co	3565	13
Angelus Shoe Polish Company Inc	2842	164
Angelvision Technologies Inc	7311	697
Anger Associates Inc	5084	935
ANGI International LLC	8711	224
Angie's List Inc	7299	28
Angino and Rovner	8111	496
AngioCare Corp	3845	35
AngioDynamics Inc	3841	37
Angle Park	2741	409
Angle Tower Corp	1623	864
Angler Boat Corp	3732	76
Anglo-Dutch Petroleum International Inc	1311	200
Angstrom Graphics Inc	2721	101
Angstrom Graphics Incorporated Midwest	2752	45
Angstrom Lighting	5063	274
Angstrom Pharmaceuticals Inc	8731	369
Angstrom Precision Metals	3599	48
Angstrom Sciences Inc	5052	14
Angstrom Technologies Inc	2899	16
Angstrom USA LLC	3317	57
Anguil Environmental Systems Inc	5075	49
Angus Chemical Co	2899	155
Angus Industries Inc	3537	17
Angus-Campbell Inc	5162	64
Angy's Food Products Inc	5142	41
Anheuser Marketing Inc	5199	95
Anheuser-Busch Companies Inc	2082	1
Anheuser-Busch Employees Credit Union	6062	62
Anheuser-Busch Inc	2082	10
ANI Pharmaceuticals Inc	2834	171
Anika Therapeutics Inc	3841	78
Anillo Industries Inc	3452	82
Anilox Roll Company Inc	2759	393
Animal Health Holdings Inc	5191	9
Animal Pest Management Services Inc	7342	36
Animal Rentals Inc	7999	157
Animal Science Products Inc	2048	91
Animas Corp	3841	70
Animated Communications Inc	7372	4786
Animated Software Co	7372	4787
Animation Technologies Inc	8748	313
Animax Interactive LLC	7371	610
AniMEDIA	2741	473
Ani's Inc	2051	230
Anita Santiago Advertising Inc	7311	263
Anita's Mexican Foods Corp	2096	25
Anixter Holdings Inc	5063	22
Anixter Inc	5063	5
Anixter International Inc	5063	1
Anjana Software Solutions Inc	7372	621
Anjin Computing	5045	355
Anjon Inc	3842	278
Anka Tool and Die Inc	3544	412
Anker Trucking Inc	4213	2752
Ankim Enterprises Inc	3678	71

Company Name	SIC	Rank
Ankmar LLC	3442	83
Anko Products Inc	3621	110
Anmar Electrical Contractor	1731	814
Anmar Metrology Inc	8734	121
Anmar Precision Components Inc	3728	215
Ann Arbor Credit Bureau Inc	7323	25
Ann Arbor Distribution	4213	1303
Ann Arbor Observer Co	2721	371
ANN Automation Inc	7372	3477
ANN INC	5621	5
Anna Quarries Inc	1411	17
Anna Young Assoc Ltd	3089	443
Annabelle Candy Company Inc	2064	60
Annalee Mobilitee Dolls Inc	5092	17
Annaly Capital Management Inc	6798	4
Annandale Contracting Inc	1623	619
Annandale Foods LLC	2099	253
Annandale Millwork And Allied Systems Corp	2431	66
Annapolis Bancorp Inc	6712	495
Annapolis Micro Systems Inc	8731	161
Annapolis Outboard Repair Co	7699	192
Annapolis Technologies LLC	7374	248
Anna's Linen Co	5719	8
Anne and Molly's Inc	2051	121
Anne Arundel County Employee Federal Credit Union	6061	128
Anne Klein Communications Group	8743	313
Anne Reid Capital Inc	5085	357
Annette Island Co	5146	23
Annette LLC	1731	1712
Annex Design Service Inc	7389	1225
Annex Manufacturing LLC	3585	199
Annex Research Inc	7389	1450
Annexus Data Systems	3661	228
Annie Maid Inc	7349	296
Annie Sez	5311	53
Annieglass Inc	3229	25
Annin and Co	2399	4
Anning-Johnson Co	1742	5
Anniston Pump Shop Inc	3561	146
Annmar Industries Inc	3089	1830
Annona Manufacturing Co	2431	76
Ann's Bakery Inc	5461	55
Ann's Choice Inc	8361	9
Annual Reviews	2731	157
Annwil Inc	3949	153
Ano-Coil Corp	2796	19
Anodes Nc Inc	2899	124
Anoka Motors LLC	5511	701
Anomatic Corp	3471	11
Anorad Corp	3827	32
Anotek Inc	2731	314
Anovotek LLC	7379	1273
Anpec Industries Inc	3451	115
ANR Pipeline	4922	21
Anritsu Co	3825	13
Anro Inc	2752	363
Anrod Screen Cylinder Co	3496	98
Ans Advanced Network Services LLC	1731	492
ANS International	3695	116
Ans Wood Manufacturing	7389	1847
Ansaldo Energy Inc	5063	882
Ansaldo STS USA	3669	2
Ansam Metals Corp	3341	23
Ansatel Company Inc	7389	577
Anschutz Corp	1382	40
Ansco and Associates Inc	1623	11
Ansco Machine Co	3599	695
Ansell Healthcare Products Inc	3842	58
Ansell Sandel Medical Solutions LLC	3842	226
Anseri Corp	3812	166
Anserve Inc	7389	1292
Anshen and Allen	8712	37
Ansin Technology Group	8748	447
Ansoft Corp	7372	467
Ansol Inc	8711	547
Anson Industries Inc	1542	154
Anson Machine Works Inc	3545	343
Anson Mold and Manufacturing Inc	3089	1809
Ansonia Copper and Brass Inc	3351	15
Ansonics Inc	5084	943
Anstro Manufacturing Inc	3965	3
Ansul Inc	3669	34
Answer Excellence Inc	4822	20
Answer Fort Smith Inc	7389	1404
Answer Incorporated of Corpus Christi	7389	2154
Answer Net Montana	7389	2221
Answer Network Paging Inc	5065	508
Answer Quest Technologies Inc	8299	82
Answer Quick Telecommunications Inc	4813	218
Answer Software Corp	7371	1692
Answer-All Secretarial Service Inc	7338	35
Answerfirst Communications Inc	7389	1962
Answerfone Inc	7389	1855
AnswerLab	8742	619
AnswerNet Inc	7389	332
Answerone LLC	7389	2300
Answers Corp	7372	2738
AnswersMedia Inc	4899	81
Answertel Corp	7389	1913
ANSYS Inc	7372	91
Ant USA Inc	7371	1549
Antaeus Fashions LLC	2329	24

Company Name	SIC	Rank
Antares Pharma Inc	3841	181
Antea Group	4953	62
Antec Inc	3577	374
Anteebo Publishers Inc	2711	580
Antelope Valley Bank	6022	389
Antelope Valley Newspapers Inc	2711	68
Antenen Research Company Inc	8731	375
Antenex Inc	3663	128
Antenna and Radome Research Associates Corp	3679	334
Antenna and Satellite Technology Inc	3663	369
Antenna Associates Inc	3812	140
Antenna Concepts Inc	3663	358
Antenna Products Corp	3663	186
Antenna Research Associates Inc	3663	166
Antenna Sites Inc	4899	224
Antenna Software Inc	7372	2534
Antennas Direct	7379	843
Antennas For Communications Ocala Fl Inc	3663	227
Antennas Unlimited Inc	1731	2482
Anter Corp	3829	227
Antex Electronics Corp	3577	340
Anthelion Systems Inc	7379	1597
Anthem Blue Cross Blue Shield (Richmond Virginia)	6321	79
Anthem Blue Cross of California	6324	20
Anthem Insurance Companies Inc	6324	11
Anthem Media LLC	2741	183
Anthera Pharmaceuticals Inc	8731	423
Anthony and Sylvan Pools Corp	1799	12
Anthony Augliera Inc	4213	2220
Anthony Business Forms Inc	5112	91
Anthony California Inc	5063	316
Anthony Construction Company Inc	1623	361
Anthony Farmers Cooperative and Elevator Co	5153	62
Anthony Farms Inc	0134	2
Anthony Gizzi Appraiser	7389	2270
Anthony Group Inc	7311	917
Anthony M Brida Inc	4213	2096
Anthony Mason Associates Inc	8741	281
Anthony Ray International Inc	7353	36
Anthony Thomas Candy Co	2064	26
Anthony Timberlands Inc	2421	16
Anthony Underwood Automotive	5511	1085
Anthony Wayne Rehabilitation Center For Handicapped And Blind Inc	8331	36
Anthony Wayne Vending Company Inc	7359	151
Anthony-Ross Co	3554	22
Anthony's Caribbean Cafe Inc	5812	456
Anthony's Seafood Group	5812	312
Anthracite Capital Inc	6708	66
Anthrobytes Consulting	7338	51
Antibodies Inc	2835	62
Antibus Scales and Systems Inc	5046	78
AntiCancer Inc	8731	169
Antietam Answering Service Inc	4812	105
Antigenics Inc	2836	70
Antigenics Inc (Lexington Massachusetts)	2836	45
Antigua Group Inc	2329	14
Antill Pipeline Construction Company Inc	1623	431
Antioch Building Materials Co	3273	32
Antioch Unified School District	8211	74
Anti-Pest Company Inc	7342	87
Antique Apparatus Co	3651	54
Antique Automobile Radio Inc	3612	135
Antique Warehouse Of Arkansas Inc	5099	104
Anton Electric Inc	1731	2366
Anton Systems Inc	5045	655
Antone's Records and Tapes	3652	36
Antonian Inn and Suites	7011	238
Antoniello and Company Inc	5032	127
Antonini Enterprises LLC	4213	1126
Antonini Freight Express Inc	4213	1637
Antonio Collis	7389	1961
Antonio Mozzarella Factory Inc	2022	60
Antrim Machine Co	3599	2131
Antrim Machine Products Inc	3599	2101
Antron Engineering and Machine Company Inc	3599	732
Ants Software Inc	7371	685
Antwerp Diamond Distributing Inc	3915	3
A-Nuh-Tha Level Of Louisiana Inc	7359	245
Anulex Technologies Inc	3842	192
Anver Corp	3599	473
AnviCom Inc	7371	221
Anvil Cases Inc	3161	1
Anvil Holdings Inc	2253	3
Anvita Health	7372	1624
Anworth Mortgage Asset Corp	6726	2
Anwright Corp	3451	124
Any Domest Work Inc	7349	263
Any Mountain The Great Outdoor Store	5091	141
AnyDoc Software Inc	7372	1416
Anysolv Technologies Inc	3571	218
Anysystem Group Holdings LLC	5045	618
Anytime Fitness Inc	7997	10
Anyware Technology Inc	7372	3574
Anzac Computer Equipment Corp	3577	255
AO Smith Corp	3621	7

Company Name	SIC	Rank
AO Smith Engineered Storage Products Co	3523	35
AO Smith Water Products Co	3639	8
AO Smith Water Products Corp	3639	5
AOG Inc	4581	2
A-Ok Wholesale Appliances and Electronics Inc	5064	139
AOL Inc	7374	8
Aon Consulting Washington DC	6411	152
Aon Consulting Worldwide Inc	8742	36
Aon Corp	6321	13
Aon Group Inc	6411	3
Aon Hewitt	8742	6
AON Re Inc	6411	70
Aon Re Worldwide Inc	6411	75
Aon Risk Services Central Inc	6411	133
Aon Risk Services Companies Inc	6411	5
Aon Risk Services Incorporated of Florida	6411	112
Aon Services Group Inc	6411	36
A-One Manufacturing LLC	3556	130
Aonix Corp	7372	975
AOPA Insurance Agency Inc	6331	228
AOS-USA	8742	66
Aot Electronics Inc	3577	270
Aot Inc	3559	240
Ap and G Company Inc	2879	28
Ap Exhaust Products Inc	3714	266
AP Hubbard Wholesale Lumber Corp	5031	338
AP Pharma Inc	2821	201
AP Seedorff and Company Inc	3625	316
APAC Customer Services Inc	7389	116
Apac Mid-South Inc	1475	1
APAC-Carolina Inc Barrus Div	2951	9
APAC-Central Inc	2951	15
Apacer Memory America Inc	5065	544
APAC-Georgia Inc	1611	59
Apache Corp	1311	9
Apache Design Solutions Inc	3674	164
Apache Enterprises Inc	3728	191
Apache Hose and Belting Company Inc	3496	38
Apache Mills Inc	2273	21
Apache Nitrogen Products Inc	2873	9
Apache Oxy-Med Inc	7352	43
Apache Rental LLC	5999	307
Apache Stainless Equipment Corp	3556	34
Apache Truck Lines Inc	4213	2201
Apacheta Corp	7371	1207
A-Packaged Parties	7359	268
APAC-Kansas Inc	2951	8
APAC-Mississippi Inc	3273	12
APAC-Southeast Inc	2951	10
APAC-Tennessee Inc	2951	12
Apago Inc	7372	3789
Apahouser Inc	3444	253
Apak Inc	7389	1727
Apangea Learning Inc	8299	37
Apani Networks	7372	2417
Apani Southwest Inc	2086	151
Apartment and Corporate Relocation Service	7389	1170
Apartment Express Corporate Housing Inc	7011	221
Apartment Housebuilders Inc	1522	25
Apartment Hunters	7299	13
Apartment Investment and Management Co	6798	40
Apason Distributors	5961	195
APB Financial LLC	6221	14
Apc Corporate Security Inc	7381	101
Apc International Ltd	3679	392
APC Upgrades and Services Inc	5734	470
APC Warehouse Co	4225	23
APC Wireless	7379	919
Apco Graphics Inc	3993	17
Apco Oil and Gas International Inc	1311	111
Apco Products	3496	107
APCON Inc	3577	354
Apelles LLC	7322	136
Aperio Technologies Inc	3826	33
Aperture Technologies Inc	7372	1597
Apex Airtronics Inc	3663	310
Apex Alarm LLC	7382	51
Apex Analytix	7372	114
Apex at Home LLC	5311	45
Apex Bolt and Machine Co	3599	864
Apex Broaching Systems Inc	3541	248
Apex Bulk Commodities Inc	4213	421
Apex Circuits Inc	3613	141
Apex Computers Inc	5045	660
Apex Conveyor Manufacturing LLC	3496	101
APEX Data Services Inc	7374	47
Apex Data Systems Inc	5045	415
Apex Die Corp	2675	12
Apex Digital Inc (Walnut California)	3651	69
Apex Digital LLC (Sturgis Kentucky)	1623	33
Apex Electric	1731	400
Apex Embedded Systems	3571	170
Apex Engineering Products Corp	2042	169
Apex Environmental Inc	8742	103
Apex Graphics LLC	7336	217
Apex Group LLC	1751	14
Apex Homes Inc	2452	19
Apex Industrial Equipment Inc	5084	852

Company Name	SIC	Rank
Apex Industry Service Inc	5731	237
Apex Instruments Inc	8734	107
Apex IT Inc	7373	218
Apex Learning Inc	2741	174
Apex Machine Tool Co	3599	438
Apex Manufacturing Services Ltd	1731	1601
Apex Marine Inc	3069	193
Apex Medical Corp	3089	1
Apex Microtechnology Corp	3629	47
Apex Mold and Die Corp	3544	645
Apex Mold and Engineering Inc	3544	185
Apex Oil Company Inc	5172	3
Apex Pharmaceuticals Inc	2834	329
Apex Piping Systems Inc	3498	55
Apex Plastics Inc	3085	25
Apex Precision Technologies Inc	3714	307
Apex Resource Technologies Inc	3089	907
Apex Systems Inc	7361	20
Apex Technology Group Inc	7379	354
Apex Technology Systems Inc	7379	374
Apex Tool and Manufacturing Inc	3599	1994
Apex Tool Works Inc	3544	280
Apex Venture Partners	6799	287
Apex Voice Communications Inc	7372	1610
Apex-Cooper Tools Div	3423	18
Apexical Inc	2899	195
Apexio Solutions Inc	7379	1391
Apexon Inc	7372	664
APEXteriors	1799	93
Apexx Omni-Graphics Inc	3555	56
APG Inc	2752	1354
Apg Inc	7389	1149
Apgar Brothers Inc	4213	1385
APH Enterprises Inc	3599	2329
Aphco International Inc	8999	213
Aphelion Procision Technologies Corp	3599	696
Aphios Corp	8733	37
API Advertising	7311	193
API Electric Co	1731	79
API Electronics Inc	3674	221
Api Foils Inc	3497	6
API Group Inc	1742	1
API Heat Transfer Inc	3443	88
Api Inc	5085	372
Api Inc	3691	39
Api Industries Inc	2673	11
API International Inc	7372	3690
Api International Inc	5013	211
Api Precision Machining Inc	3599	2216
Api Systems Inc	3672	82
Api Systems Inc	5734	27
Apian Software Inc	7372	3512
Apiary Inc	7372	4273
Apicellas Bakery Inc	5149	218
Apk Net Inc	7375	259
Apl Electric Inc	1731	1747
APL Ltd	4412	2
APL Logistics Freight Systems	4213	822
APL Logistics Ltd	4225	2
Aplicor Inc	7389	1059
Aplin Uno Creative	7336	233
Aplix Inc	3965	12
Aplusnet	7379	491
APM Hexseal Corp	3679	531
APN Consulting Inc	7361	96
Apn Software Services Inc	7379	346
APO Holdings Inc	5084	379
Apogee Coal Co	1221	24
Apogee Controls Inc	3679	471
Apogee Data Systems	5045	808
Apogee Designs Ltd	3089	1281
Apogee Engineering Associates Inc	8748	403
Apogee Enterprises Inc	3231	6
Apogee Interactive Inc	7372	199
Apogee Labs Inc	3679	609
Apogee Search	7311	809
Apogee Software Inc	7372	2938
Apogee Technology Inc	3674	506
Apogen Technologies	7373	117
Apollo Advisors LP	6722	88
Apollo Antenna and Sales Inc	3999	147
Apollo Colors Inc	2865	6
Apollo Commercial Real Estate Finance Corp	6798	222
Apollo Corp	3088	29
Apollo Design Technology Inc	3648	52
Apollo Direct LLC	7374	369
Apollo Display Technologies LLC	3674	326
Apollo Electric	1731	205
Apollo Enterprise Solutions LLC	7371	439
Apollo Group Inc	8221	1
Apollo Hosting Inc	4813	445
Apollo Industries Inc	2042	26
Apollo Investment Corp	6799	22
Apollo Motor Express Inc	4213	1749
Apollo Plating Inc	3471	28
Apollo Precision Machining Inc	3599	1819
Apollo Press Inc	2791	33
Apollo Printing and Graphics Center Inc	2759	464
Apollo Propane Inc	5023	165
Apollo Ship Chandlers Inc	5149	103
Apollo Tool and Engineering Inc	3545	374
Apollo Tool Inc	3544	324

Company Name	SIC	Rank
Apollo Transfer Company LLC	7389	1665
Apollo Travel Agency	4724	66
Apollo Van Lines Inc	4213	1926
Aponte Construction Company Inc	1623	512
Apostolou Associates	8712	238
Apotheca Inc	5122	108
Apothecary Products Inc	2834	152
Appairent Technologies Inc	3663	208
Appalachian Brewing Company Inc	2082	59
Appalachian Electric Coop	4911	304
Appalachian Electrical Supply Inc	5063	928
Appalachian Freight Carriers	4213	1299
Appalachian Machine Inc	3599	1859
Appalachian Mine Sales Inc	3532	45
Appalachian Outfitters	7999	133
Appalachian Piping Products Inc	3084	47
Appalachian Plastics Inc	3229	29
Appalachian Root And Herb Co	5159	34
Appalachian Stone Company Inc	5032	154
Appalachian Technology LLC	3678	57
Appalachian Tool and Machine Inc	3599	2511
Appalachian Wood Floors Inc	2491	19
Appalachian Wood Products Inc	2426	18
Appalaphian	2435	27
AppaNeta	7371	152
Apparel Business Systems Inc	7372	547
Apparel Business Systems LLC	5045	668
Apparel Finishing America Inc	7211	2
Apparel Machinery and Supply Co	5084	740
Apparel Ventures Inc	2339	20
Appareo Systems LLC	7371	696
AppAssure Software Inc	7372	2318
APPCO Premium Finance Inc	6411	169
Appeal-Democrat Inc	2711	164
Appel and Yost	8111	495
Appel Uniforms	2326	2
Appen Newspapers Inc	2711	739
Apperson Print Resources Inc	2761	17
Appertain Corp	5093	203
Appertain Inc	5039	42
Appert's Food Inc	2013	44
Appetito Provisions Company Inc	2013	127
Appetizers Made Easy Inc	2038	75
AppFinity Software Corp	7372	3859
Appgen Business Software Inc	7372	3152
Apph Wichita Inc	7699	132
Appian Corp (Vienna Virginia)	7372	1002
Appian Logistics Software Inc	7372	3513
Appical Inc	7379	1124
AppIntelligence Inc	6282	245
Apple and Eve LLC	2033	74
Apple Baking Company Inc	5149	161
Apple Bank for Savings	6719	23
Apple Corporate Technologies Inc	5065	867
Apple Electric Inc	1731	1479
Apple Farm	0175	10
Apple Food Sales Company Inc	5141	227
Apple Ford (Lynchburg Virginia)	5511	139
Apple Growth Partners	8721	329
Apple Inc	3571	2
Apple Machine and Supply Co	3599	1574
Apple Press Ltd	2752	947
Apple Rubber Products Inc	3069	80
Apple Scientific Inc	5049	84
Apple Steel Rule Die Company Inc	3544	70
Apple Valley Secretarial Service Inc	7374	176
Apple Valley Woodworks LLC	5031	195
Applebee's International Inc	5812	54
Appleby Software Corp	8748	445
Applegate Drayage Co	4213	1693
Applegate Insulation Systems Inc	2499	35
Applegate Livestock Equipment Inc	3523	13
AppleOne Inc	7361	9
Appleridge At Bethany Village	8361	102
Appleseed's Holding Inc	5621	28
Appleton Area School District	8211	14
Appleton Papers Inc	2621	15
Appleton Partners Inc	6282	303
Appleton Supply Company Inc	3444	72
Appletree Answering Services	7389	932
Applewood Controls Inc	3823	440
Applewood Lumber Co	5211	208
Appliance City Inc	5064	175
Appliance Controls Of Texas Corp	3625	154
Appliance Recycling Centers of America Inc	5719	14
Appliance Solutions By Brock's Appliance Inc	5064	63
Appliance Specialty Of Florida Inc	5064	187
Appliance Zone Inc	5722	16
ApplianceWare Inc	7372	1703
Applica Inc	3634	5
Applicad Inc	3672	202
Application Consultants Inc	5045	1013
Application Consulting Group	7372	1704
Application Design Consultants Inc	7379	1091
Application Design Group Inc	7371	378
Application Development Consultants Inc	7371	1168
Application Development Resources Inc	7373	423
Application Engineering Inc	3559	181
Application Link Inc	7372	1727
Application Objects Inc	7373	620

Company Name	SIC	Rank
Application Oriented Designs Inc	7379	1013
Application Programming and Development Inc	7372	4585
Application Security Inc	7372	1527
Application Support Company Inc	8748	453
Application Techniques Inc	7372	4657
Applications Engineering Group Inc	7379	683
Applications Plus Software Services Inc	5045	709
Applications Software Inc	7372	2705
Applications Systems Corp	7372	4198
Applied Aerospace Structures Corp	3728	56
Applied Art and Technology	7336	59
Applied Automated Engineering Corp	7373	524
Applied Automation Techologies Inc	7372	2939
Applied Biochemists Inc	2899	130
Applied Biomathematics Corp	7372	3764
Applied Business Services Inc	7372	3427
Applied Business Software Inc	7372	4092
Applied Card Systems	7374	32
Applied Cardiac Systems Inc	3841	212
Applied Ceramics Inc	3674	240
Applied Chemical Technology Inc	8711	528
Applied Chemometrics Inc	5045	1014
Applied Circuit Technology Inc	3672	59
Applied Communication Services Inc	7372	1639
Applied Communications Group Inc	1731	784
Applied Composite Technology Inc	3842	198
Applied Composites Engineering Inc	3544	283
Applied Computer Engineering	3579	68
Appleo Computer Excellence Inc	7372	4403
Applied Computer Online Services	5961	148
Applied Computer Systems Inc (Knoxville Tennessee)	7372	2659
Applied Computer Technology	7379	833
Applied Control Concepts Inc	3625	312
Applied Control Engineering Inc	8711	275
Applied Conveyor Technology Inc	5085	238
Applied Data Sciences Inc	3577	533
Applied Data Trends Inc	7379	295
Applied Decision Support Inc	7379	891
Applied Digital	3625	139
Applied DNA Sciences Inc	7374	343
Applied Drilling Technology Inc	1381	29
Applied Dynamics Corp	7629	19
Applied Dynamics International Inc	3571	97
Applied Educational Systems Inc	7372	1705
Applied Electric Inc	1731	1288
Applied Electronics	3679	368
Applied Electronics Corp	3613	140
Applied Energetics Inc	3812	99
Applied Energy Company LLC	3594	8
Applied Engineering Management Corp	8711	160
Applied Expert Systems Inc	7372	2793
Applied Extrusion Technologies Inc	3081	8
Applied Global Technologies	7372	1038
Applied Graphics Inc	3479	76
Applied Health Physics Inc	8733	29
Applied Home Healthcare Equipment Inc	3569	181
Applied Hydraulic Systems Inc	3536	3
Applied Ideas Inc	7372	3810
Applied Image Inc	3826	120
Applied Imaging Corp	3841	113
Applied Industrial Machining Inc	3599	464
Applied Industrial Technologies Inc	5082	2
Applied Information Group	7372	277
Applied Information Management Inc	7372	3514
Applied Information Management Sciences Inc	7372	4185
Applied Information Sciences Inc	7371	302
Applied Information Systems Inc (Chapel Hill North Carolina)	7372	2940
Applied Information Technologies Inc	7372	3247
Applied Innovation Inc	3661	78
Applied Instruments Corp	5049	199
Applied Insurance Research Inc	7372	794
Applied Integrated Technologies Inc	7379	341
Applied Integration Corp	3577	387
Applied Intelligence Group	7373	108
Applied Knowledge Systems Int'l Ltd	7371	1629
Applied Laboratories Inc	2834	173
Applied Laser Technology Inc	7389	1662
Applied Logic Inc	7371	1520
Applied Logic Systems Inc	7372	4483
Applied Machine and Motion Control Inc	5063	883
Applied Magic	3669	138
Applied Management Sciences Group	8742	53
Applied Manufacturing Technologies Inc	8742	324
Applied Materials Inc	3674	4
Applied Maths Inc	7371	1540
Applied Media Technologies Corp	3661	103
Applied Medical Resources Corp	3845	52
Applied Medical Technology Inc	3841	290
Applied Micro Circuits Corp	3674	80
Applied Micro Inc	7372	4234
Applied Microimage Corp	7389	2053
Applied Minerals Inc	1041	22
Applied Molecular Evolution Inc	8731	231
Applied Motor Controls Ltd	3625	361
Applied Nanotech Holdings Inc	3669	165
Applied Nanotech Inc	3669	100

Company Name	SIC	Rank
Applied Physics Systems	3829	165
Applied Plastic Machining Inc	3599	1340
Applied Plastic Technology Inc	3089	1447
Applied Plastics Company Inc	3082	7
Applied Polymer Systems Inc	2821	146
Applied Power Systems Inc	3679	590
Applied Precision LLC	3825	68
Applied Printing Technologies LP	2759	41
Applied Process Inc	3398	20
Applied Products No 1 Inc	5065	714
Applied Quality Test Inc	5063	670
Applied Recovery Systems Inc	5084	653
Applied Research Associates Inc	8711	105
Applied Research Associates Transportation Div	8711	199
Applied Research Laboratories Inc	7389	2032
Applied Resource Technologies Inc	7373	1109
Applied Resources Corp	3679	651
Applied Resources Inc	7389	1368
Applied Roller Technology Inc	3829	364
Applied Science Products Inc	3812	219
Applied Sciences Inc	8731	319
Applied Separations Inc	3826	99
Applied Signal Technology Inc	3669	23
Applied Software Inc	7372	3754
Applied Software Technologies	7373	837
Applied Solar Inc	3674	299
Applied Specialties Of California Inc	5065	400
Applied Systems and Technologies Inc	7372	4032
Applied Systems Engineering Inc	3663	110
Applied Systems Inc (Deerfield Beach Florida)	3674	464
Applied Systems Inc (University Park Illinois)	7372	608
Applied Systems Technology and Resources	5045	329
Applied Technical Services Corp	3672	58
Applied Technical Systems Inc	1731	502
Applied Technology Solutions Inc	8711	692
Applied Testing and Technology Inc	7372	2660
Applied Textiles Inc	7389	713
Applied Thermal Systems Inc	3674	499
Applied Thin-Film Products	3679	273
Applied Underwriters Inc	7371	62
Applied Vision Company LLC	3861	93
Applied Visions Inc	7372	1781
Applied Visual Sciences	2399	35
Applied Wave Research Inc	7372	262
Applied Wireless Inc	3674	438
Appling Boring Company Inc	1623	344
Applus AutoLogic LLC	3829	91
Appolis Inc	7371	1559
Appr A Ze Co	7389	2404
Appraisal Economics Inc	7389	1687
Apprise Media LLC	6799	12
Appriss Inc	7372	1325
Appro International Inc	3572	44
Appro Systems Inc	7372	2755
Approach Resources Inc	1311	131
Appropriate Solutions Inc	5045	471
Appropriate Technical Resources Inc	5049	91
Approva Corp	5045	63
Approval Payment Solutions Inc	7389	1136
Approved Aircraft Accessories Inc	3724	75
Approved Lightning Protection Company Inc	5063	1091
AppSense	7373	98
APPTECH Inc	7372	2899
Apptio	7372	857
Apptis Inc	7389	26
Apptix ASA	7372	808
Apptricity Corp	7371	743
APPX Software Inc	7372	3765
APR Consulting Inc	7374	157
Apr Plastic Fabricating Inc	3089	1165
APR Supply Co	5074	58
Apresys Inc	7378	135
Apria Healthcare Group Inc	7352	1
Apricorn	3577	430
Apricot Designs Inc	3841	386
Apricot Medical Services Inc	7372	2941
Aprima Medical Software Inc	5047	20
Aprimo Inc	7372	691
Apriso Corp	7372	1288
Apro Technology LLC	8748	303
Aprotek Inc	3577	641
APS Asset Management Inc	6282	51
APS Corp	1731	1302
APS Financial Corp	6282	133
Aps Group Inc	7379	1420
APS Insurance Services Inc	8741	61
Aps-Materials Inc	3479	29
Apt Electronics Inc	3672	105
APT Pharmaceuticals Inc	8731	303
Apt Source Inc	7379	900
Apta Software	7372	2593
Aptar	3561	47
Aptar Pharma	3089	34
Aptara Inc	7374	61
AptarGroup Inc	3089	15
APTE Inc	7372	1990
Aptech Computer Systems Inc	7372	3176
Aptech Systems Inc	7372	4199
Aptek Inc	7372	3248

Company Name	SIC	Rank
Aptek Industries Inc	3674	380
Aptera Motors Inc	3711	60
Aptiem Oncology	8093	11
Aptify	7372	1599
Aptima Inc	7372	1184
Aptimise Composites LLC	3089	1125
Aptimus Inc	7389	570
Aptinet Videos	7812	126
Aptitune Corp	7372	4362
Aptos Corp	3674	384
Aptron Corp	5045	446
Aptuit Inc	8731	205
Aptuit Informatics Inc	7375	132
APTwater Inc	3589	21
Apunix Computer Services Inc	7372	1879
APV Americas	3556	2
APW Mayville LLC	2522	18
APW/Wyott	3556	33
APX Inc (Santa Clara California)	4911	239
APX Logistics	4213	34
Apx Technologies Inc	3679	647
Aqiwo Inc	8748	319
Aql Quality Arson Test Labs	3568	89
Aqp Holdings LP	6141	62
AQS Inc	5045	99
Aqua America Inc	4941	2
Aqua Bath Company Inc	3088	26
Aqua Blox LLC	2086	153
Aqua Glass Corp	3949	19
Aqua Illinois Inc	4941	3
Aqua Leisure Pool and SpA Inc	7389	1416
Aqua Maine	4941	50
Aqua Massage International Inc	3634	31
Aqua Measure Instrument Co	3829	280
Aqua New Jersey	4941	33
Aqua North Carolina Inc	4941	22
Aqua Ohio Inc	4941	36
Aqua Pellet	0211	17
Aqua Perfect Of Arizona LLC	8748	349
Aqua/Process Inc	2869	111
Aqua Rama Pool Spas and Service Inc	7389	1887
Aqua Science Inc	2899	72
Aqua Smart Inc	2899	200
Aqua Solutions Inc	2899	157
Aqua Spas	7359	185
Aqua Sun Ozone International	5999	316
Aqua Superstore	5092	16
Aqua Tool LLC	3599	1901
Aqua Treatment Services Inc	3589	155
Aqua Xtremes Inc	3949	159
Aquafine Corp	3589	84
Aqua-Flo LLC	3561	88
Aquagenix Inc	4959	19
Aqua-Leisure Industries Inc	5092	28
Aqualogic Inc	3589	231
Aquamar Inc	2091	21
aQuantive Inc	7389	94
Aquarion Water Co	4941	37
Aquarion Water Company of Connecticut	4941	19
Aquascape Inc	0781	4
Aquasol Controllers Inc	3823	85
AquaTec Inc	3589	205
Aquatech Inc	5083	156
Aquatech International Corp	3589	32
Aquatech Of Birmingham Inc	2097	19
Aquathin Corp	3589	229
Aquatic and Wetland Consultants Inc	0781	14
Aquatic Rehabilitation Center Inc	8049	15
Aquatrol Inc	2048	143
Aquatrols Corporation Of America	2879	35
Aqua-Tronics Inc	3812	202
Aquaventures LLC	5091	125
Aquaveo LLC	7373	967
Aque Computers Inc	5734	142
Aquilex WSI	3548	11
Aquiline Capital Partners LLC	6799	94
Aquionics Inc	5074	223
Aquire	7372	1028
Aquis Communications Group Inc	4812	55
Aquitec Inc	7371	636
AR Communication	5065	938
A-R Editions Inc	2731	113
AR Group Inc	7372	868
Ar Kalmus Corp	3663	161
Ar Media Inc	2741	262
AR Merante Corp	1542	449
AR Neubauer Inc	5063	925
AR Paquette and Company Inc	4213	2047
AR Schmeidler and Company Inc	6282	145
AR Traffic Consultants Inc	7372	3153
Ara Food Corp	2096	34
Ara Pharmaceuticals Inc	2834	355
ARA Portfolio Management Company LLC	6282	249
Araban Coffee Company Inc	2095	50
Arabian American Development Co	2911	46
Arabian Nights	7999	52
Arabie Brothers Trucking Inc	4213	974
Aracaelum Corp	7379	676
Arachne Internet Solutions	8299	66
Arachnid Inc	3949	129
Aradiant Corp	8748	452
Aradigm Corp	3845	101

Company Name	SIC	Rank
ARAG Group	6411	98
Araize Inc	7372	3860
Arakelian Inc	5023	112
Aram Inc	5112	26
Aram Michael Inc	5023	151
Aram Precision Tool Die Inc	3599	2350
ARAMARK Corp	5812	5
ARAMARK Correctional Services Inc	8741	101
ARAMARK Healthcare Support Services Inc	5812	39
ARAMARK Refreshment Services Inc	5812	52
ARAMARK Sports and Entertainment Services Inc	5812	78
ARAMARK Uniform and Career Apparel Inc	7218	3
Aramco Inc	3559	395
Aramco Services Co	1311	73
Aramedia Group	5734	408
Aramsco Inc	5085	102
Aran Laboratories	3564	149
Aranda Tooling Inc	3599	398
Aranda's Tortilla Factory	2099	160
Arandell Corp	2752	15
Arango Inc	5947	1
Ararat Rock Products Co	1423	7
Aras Corp	7372	2117
Arasan Chip Systems Inc	3674	105
Arawak Paving Company Inc	1611	242
Araz Group	6324	123
ARB Inc (Paramount California)	1541	252
ARBA Retail Systems Corp	7372	3306
Arbco Industries Inc	3089	1209
Arbe Machinery Inc	3559	475
Arbill Industries Inc	7218	6
Arbin Corp	3559	62
Arbinet Corp	7389	107
Arbitech LLC	5045	91
Arbiter Systems Inc	3825	175
Arbitron Inc	7374	25
Arbon Inc	5065	916
Arbon Steel and Service Company Inc	5051	257
Arbor Commercial Mortgage LLC	6162	95
Arbor EnTech Corp	6799	366
Arbor Image Corp	7372	4484
Arbor Material Handling Inc	5084	278
Arbor Networks Inc	5045	98
Arbor Press LLC	2752	493
Arbor Realty Trust Inc	6798	108
Arbor Rehabilitation And Healthcare Services Inc	8322	132
Arboretum Systems Inc	7372	4960
ArborText Inc	7372	1168
Arborview LLC	6798	15
ArborWay Inc	5045	710
Arbuckle Coffee Co	2095	46
Arbus Inc	3571	240
Arby's Restaurant Group Inc	6794	35
Arc Aspicio LLC	8742	465
Arc Bridges Inc	8331	48
Arc Butte County Inc	8322	186
Arc Drilling Inc	3829	363
Arc Electric Company Inc	1731	409
ARC Electric Construction Company Inc	1731	831
Arc Equipment Inc	3069	186
Arc Fastener Supply and Manufacturing	5085	142
Arc Inc	8399	27
Arc Industries Inc	3544	144
Arc International North America (AINA)	3231	7
Arc International North America Inc	5099	11
Arc Light Efx Inc	3648	91
Arc Manufacturing Company Inc	3599	1059
Arc Of Clairborne County Inc	8322	197
Arc Of East Central Iowa	8322	249
Arc Of Fayette County Inc	8322	185
Arc Of Harrison County	8322	207
Arc Of Jefferson County Inc	8322	50
Arc Of North Webster	8331	230
Arc Of Northern Rhode Island Inc	8331	235
Arc Of Southington Inc	8322	182
Arc Of The District Of Columbia Inc	8361	179
Arc Of Washington-Holmes Counties Inc	8322	227
ARC One LLC	3442	76
Arc Plastics Inc	3089	1625
Arc Rubber Inc	3069	280
Arc San Francisco	8331	75
ARC Science Simulation Inc	7372	4485
ARC Services Of Macomb Inc	8331	135
Arc Systems Inc	3621	111
ARC Technical Resources Inc	5065	1010
ARC Technologies Corp	3613	146
Arc Underground Inc	1623	695
Arc Water Treatment Company Of Maryland Inc	7389	1306
ARC Wireless Solutions Inc	4899	186
ARC Worldwide	8742	45
ARCA Biopharma Inc	2835	75
Arcade Lithographing Corp	2752	921
Arcade Printing Co	2752	487
Arcadia Components LLC	5065	609
Arcadia Dairy Farms Inc	2033	123
Arcadia Inc	3355	4

Company Name	SIC	Rank
Arcadia Limestone Co	5032	167
Arcadia Retirement Residence	8361	27
Arcadia University	8221	34
Arcadian Networks Inc	7371	247
ARCADIS	8742	20
Arcaine Technology	3555	128
Arcapita Inc	6211	45
Arcata Pet Software	7372	4363
Arcelormittal Plate LLC	3312	19
Arcelormittal Steelton LLC	3312	53
Arcelormittal Tailored Blanks Americas Corp	3465	19
Arcelormittal Tubular Products USA Corp	3317	18
ARCH Air Medical Service Inc	4522	17
Arch Chemicals Inc	2899	13
Arch Coal Inc	1221	4
Arch Coal Sales Company Inc	1222	3
Arch Crown Inc	2759	378
Arch Environmental Equipment	3589	181
Arch Lighting Group Inc	3646	80
Arch Reinsurance (USA) Co	6331	251
Arch Specialty Chemicals Inc	2842	7
Arch Venture Partners	6799	240
Arch Wood Protection Inc	2861	1
Archaeological Consulting Services Ltd	8731	152
Archambo Enterprises Inc	7382	140
Archangel Systems Inc	3812	147
Archbold Health Services Inc	5047	30
Archemix Corp	2836	58
Archer Daniels Midland Co	2076	1
Archer/Malmo Advertising Inc	7311	220
Archer Manufacturing Corp	3469	311
Archer Tool Co	3423	81
Archetype 3d Images Inc	3999	201
Archibald Frozen Desserts	3556	72
ARCHIBUS Inc	7372	1551
Archie Comic Publications Inc	2721	173
Archilla Transportation Inc	4213	2790
Archimage Inc	7379	515
Archimedes Global Inc	7389	606
Archimica Inc	2834	268
Archipelago Learning Inc	8299	31
Archi-Tech Systems Inc	7375	211
Architects Leasing Inc	7359	138
Architectural Area Lighting Inc	3645	20
Architectural Arts Co	7389	1801
Architectural Cathode Lighting Inc	3648	88
Architectural Computer Services Inc	7372	2071
Architectural Control Systems Inc	3699	196
Architectural Designs Inc	2741	463
Architectural Division 8 Inc	5031	214
Architectural Door And Millwork Inc	5031	395
Architectural Doors Inc	5031	219
Architectural Fiberglass Corp	2295	21
Architectural Graphics Inc	3993	9
Architectural Interior Products Inc	5039	22
Architectural Millwork Manufacturing Co	5031	315
Architectural Partnership	8712	243
Architectural Polymers Inc	3081	147
Architectural Sales and Illumination Inc	5063	695
Architectural Sales Inc	5031	131
Architectural Signing Inc	3993	91
Architectural Specialty Products Inc	5031	428
Architectural Stone Sales Inc	1411	24
Architectural Testing Inc	8071	39
Architectural Tile and Stone Ltd	5032	133
Architectural Utilities Inc	1541	76
Architectural Woodworking Co	2541	34
Architext Inc	7371	940
Architext Inc (Andover Massachusetts)	7389	706
Architronics Inc	8712	310
Archive Index Systems Inc	7373	983
Archives Management Corp	8741	217
Archives Security Inc	7375	265
Archon Corp	7999	91
Archon Distribution Inc	5045	1015
Archon Vitamin Corp	2833	29
Archonix Systems LLC	7371	997
Archos Technology	5045	69
Archstone Communities LLC	6798	189
Archstone-Smith Trust	6798	22
Archway Systems Inc	7372	3755
Archway Technology Partners Inc	7371	923
Arcilla Mining And Land Company LLC	1455	6
Arcis Co The	5045	188
ARCLITE Lab - Brigham Young University	7371	684
ARCLOGIX Inc	7372	2418
Arco Auto and Marine Products	3699	7
ARCO Construction Company Inc	1541	188
Arco Electronics Inc	3675	32
Arco Metals Inc	3469	384
Arcoa Industries LLC	3589	258
Arcobasso Foods Inc	2035	45
Arcom Systems Inc	1731	934
Arcorp Properties	4482	1
Arcos Industries LLC	3699	137
Arcot Systems Inc	7372	976
arcplan Inc	7372	2620
ArcRon	3441	48
ARCS Commercial Mortgage Company LP	6162	38

Company Name	SIC	Rank
Arcservices Inc	7363	292
ArcSight LLC	7372	265
ArcSoft Inc	7372	1170
ARCTECH Inc	8731	203
Arctic Cat Inc	3799	4
Arctic Falls Spring Water Inc	7389	1904
Arctic Glacier Oregon Inc	2097	15
Arctic Industries Inc	3585	124
Arctic Office Machine Inc	5112	25
Arctic Slope Regional Corp	1311	21
Arctic Slope Telephone Association Cooperative Inc	4813	214
Arctic Slope World Services Inc	4522	16
Arctic Star Refrigeration Manufacturing Co	3585	205
ArcticShield Inc	2269	14
Arc-Tronics Inc	3672	55
ARCTURIS	8712	246
Arcturus Marine Systems	3511	24
Arcube Multimedia Inc	3695	34
Arcy Plastic Laminates Inc	2541	55
Ardaman and Associates Inc	8711	43
Ardax Systems Inc	3663	350
Ardea Biosciences Inc	2834	245
Ardel Engineering and Manufacturing Inc	3599	873
Arden Asset Management LLC	6282	105
Arden Cos	2392	4
Arden Group Inc	5411	120
Arden Realty Inc	6798	23
Arden-Mayfair Inc	5411	158
Ardent Health Services LLC	8063	1
Ardent Systems Inc	3672	313
Ardenwood Sound and DVD	3695	150
Ardex Laboratories Inc	2841	30
Ardisam Inc	3546	17
Ardl Inc	8734	151
Ardmore Enterprises Inc	8331	100
Ardmore Manufacturing Inc	2325	9
Ardmore Production and Exploration Co	1381	39
Ardmore Telephone Company Inc	4813	335
Ard's Trucking Company Inc	4213	1153
Ardsley Partners	6282	383
Ardus Medical Inc	5047	120
ARE Inc	3713	25
ARE Manufacturing Inc	3599	770
Area 51 Snowboards	5091	115
Area Diesel Service Inc	5531	52
Area Electronics Systems Inc	5045	611
Area Homecare Family Services Inc	8082	89
Area Iron and Steel Works Inc	5051	416
Area Temps Inc	7363	55
Area Tool and Manufacturing Inc	3544	864
Area Utilities Inc	1731	1272
Arehart Consulting	7372	3861
Arel Communications and Software (USA) Ltd	7372	264
Aremac Associates Inc	3599	1146
Aremco Products Inc	2759	398
Arena Communications LLC	7331	290
Arena Distributors Inc	5072	68
Arena Offshore LP	1382	45
Arena Pharmaceuticals Inc	2834	285
Arena Solutions Inc	7371	598
Arends Brothers Inc	5083	52
Arends Brothers LLC	5083	146
Arens Controls Company LLC	3568	18
Arens Corp	2711	808
Arens Electric Inc	1731	817
Arenson Office Furnishings Inc	5712	45
Arent Fox PLLC	8111	60
Ares Capital Corp	6726	3
Ares Management LLC	6799	15
Ares Printing And Packaging Corp	2752	139
Arete Associates	7372	385
Arete Construction Corp	1623	573
Arete Image Software	7372	3214
Arete Industries Inc	1311	266
AR-EX Ltd	2844	174
Arga Computer and Mailing Services Inc	7389	1164
Arga Controls Inc	3823	348
Argan Inc	1731	33
Argc LLC	2522	47
Arge Inc	7389	2118
Argee Corp	3089	780
Argen Corp	3339	14
Argen Inc	5074	181
Argent - A A A Credit Servicing Inc	7322	53
Argent Associates Inc	7389	225
Argent Chemical Laboratories Inc	2899	209
Argent Group LLC	7389	2156
Argent International Inc	2672	30
Argent Software Inc	7372	4144
Argent Trading Inc	7389	750
Argentine Federal Savings	6035	253
Argo and Company Inc	2842	142
Argo Data Resources Inc	7372	1330
Argo Envelope Corp	2759	191
Argo International Corp	5088	15
Argo Products Co	3496	40
Argon Corp	3571	155
Argon Office Supplies	5734	111

Company Name	SIC	Rank
Argon ST Inc	3812	15
Argonaut Constructors Inc	1623	44
Argonaut Great Central Insurance Co	6331	296
Argonaut Group Inc	6331	103
Argonaut Inflatable Research And Engineering Inc	5551	7
Argontech Global	2761	79
Argos Computer Systems Inc	7373	680
Argos Inc	3366	18
Argos Software	7372	3515
Argos Technologies Inc	5049	155
Argosy Capital	6798	142
Argosy Cruises	4725	10
Argosy Education Group Inc	8299	8
Argosy Group LLC	7379	1049
Argosy Publishing Inc	2791	17
Argus and Associates Inc	8711	513
Argus Avante Graphic Comunications	2752	499
Argus Camera Company LLC	3861	83
Argus Corp	3544	520
Argus Electric Inc	1731	2406
Argus Hillsboro Inc	2711	469
Argus International Inc	3567	86
Argus Management Company LLC	8744	33
Argus Press Co	2711	531
Argus Protective Service LLC	7381	258
Argus Research Group Incorporated Del	6282	375
Argus Security Group	7381	237
Argus Technologies Inc	5065	572
Argy Wiltse and Robinson PC	8721	311
Argyle Security Inc	7381	16
Argyll Technology Inc	3575	43
ARI Industries	3643	71
ARI Network Services Inc	8999	81
Ari Products Inc	1752	5
ARIAD Pharmaceuticals Inc	2836	32
Ariadne Genomics Inc	7371	682
Arial Software LLC	7372	3766
Arias Industries Inc	3714	401
Ariat International Inc	3199	10
Ariba Inc	7372	124
Aribex Inc	3844	21
Aricent Inc	7372	12
Aridi Computer Graphics Inc	2741	464
Ariel Capital Management LLC	6722	262
Ariel Corp (Mount Vernon Ohio)	3563	4
Ariel Design Inc	5045	1039
Ariel Enterprises Inc	7389	1888
Aries Acrylic Manufacturing Inc	3088	34
Aries Inc	3544	588
Aries Industries Inc	3663	39
Aries Network Inc	4813	210
Aries Party Rental Company Inc	7359	187
Aries Research Inc	3577	567
Aries Scientific Inc	8731	257
Aries Systems Corp	7375	143
Aries Technology Inc	7371	502
Arika Metals Inc	5051	308
Ari-Med Pharmaceuticals	2834	407
Arinc Inc	4899	12
Aring Equipment Company Inc	5082	90
Arion Technologies Inc	8711	650
Aris Associates West Inc	8748	413
Aris Corporation of America Inc	6282	475
Aris Corporation Spectrum Financial Network	6282	253
Aris Horticulture Inc	0181	9
Arise Virtual Solutions Inc	4813	169
Arisen Corp	7372	3307
Arisglobal LLC	7379	797
Arista Business Imaging Solutions Inc	7378	50
Arista Enterprises	3669	73
Arista Information Systems Inc	7374	95
Arista Insurance Co	6321	69
Arista Investors Corp	6411	278
Arista Tubes Inc	3082	23
Aristech Acrylics LLC	2821	25
Aristo-Craft Inc	3691	40
Aristocrat Technologies Inc	3578	5
Ariston Capital Management Corp	6282	388
Aristotle Electric	1731	2029
Aristotle International Inc	7372	1863
Aritronix Limited Inc	3699	291
Arity Corp	7372	3862
Ariza Cheese Co	2022	22
Ariza Inc	7922	94
Arizona Archery Enterprises Inc	3089	50
Arizona Auto and Truck Parts Inc	5531	56
Arizona Baptist Children's Services	8322	193
Arizona Beverage Analyst	2721	435
Arizona Boiler Company Inc	5074	165
Arizona Building Systems Inc	1541	201
Arizona Business Forms Inc	5112	83
Arizona Cactus Ranch	2032	48
Arizona Capacitors Inc	3629	92
Arizona Chemical Company Inc	2869	14
Arizona Commercial Printing Inc	2759	450
Arizona Components Company Inc	5065	170
Arizona Coral Point Apartments LP	6513	20
Arizona Dental Insurance Service Inc	6324	71
Arizona Domestic and Banquet Rentals and Sales Inc	7359	263
Arizona Electric Power Cooperative Inc	4911	146

Company Name	SIC	Rank
Arizona Embossing and Die Cutting Inc	2759	281
Arizona Federal Credit Union	6061	40
Arizona Gastroenterology Ltd	8011	121
Arizona Grain Inc	5153	75
Arizona Heart Hospital LLC	8062	222
Arizona Ice Man Inc	2097	10
Arizona Instrument LLC	3823	133
Arizona Machinery Group Inc	5083	29
Arizona Materials LLC	3273	70
Arizona Microtek Inc	3679	814
Arizona Natural Resources Inc	3999	52
Arizona Oxides LLC	2865	22
Arizona Pacific Transport Logistics	4213	1977
Arizona Portland Cement Co	3241	26
Arizona Precision Sheet Metal Inc	3444	25
Arizona Public Service Co	4911	48
Arizona Recycling Corp	5093	74
Arizona Road Specialties Inc	1623	686
Arizona Scrap Iron and Metals Inc	5093	233
Arizona Sun Products Inc	2844	162
Arizona Traffic Signal Inc	1731	905
Arizona-American Water Co	4941	40
ARJ Software Inc	7372	4788
Ar-Jay Building Products Inc	5031	197
Arjay Search Inc	7361	418
Arjay Telecom	5731	24
Arjay Telecommunications Inc	5999	35
ArjoHuntleigh	3842	15
Ark Operating Corp	5812	221
ARK -Ramos Foundry And Manufacturing Co	3366	14
Ark Restaurants Corp	5812	211
Ark Seal International	3531	238
ARK Solutions Inc	7371	632
Ark Technologies Inc	3495	10
Arkadin Inc	4899	18
Arkados Group Inc	7389	2484
Arkansas Best Corp	4213	22
Arkansas Blue Cross and Blue Shield	6321	15
Arkansas Capital Corp	6153	22
Arkansas Copier Center Inc	5999	145
Arkansas Data Services Inc	7372	3058
Arkansas Electric Cooperative Corp	4911	147
Arkansas Electrical Outlet Inc	5063	1001
Arkansas Federal Credit Union	6061	37
Arkansas Glass Container Corp	3144	2
Arkansas Graphics Inc	2752	807
Arkansas Heart Hospital	8062	74
Arkansas Independent Millwrights	3535	214
Arkansas Inet LLC	4813	659
Arkansas Lamp Manufacturing Company Inc	3641	19
Arkansas Packaging Products Inc	5085	147
Arkansas Printing Company Of Pine Bluff	2752	1724
Arkansas Steel Associates LLC	3312	33
Arkansas Times Inc	2711	561
Arkansas Tool and Die Inc	3544	431
Arkansas Valley Electric Co-operative Corp	4911	112
Arkansas Valley Publishing Company Inc	2711	508
Arkansas Water Products LLC	5085	416
Arkansas Western Gas Co	4924	18
Arkay Engravers Inc	7376	52
Arkay Packaging Corp	2657	13
Arkeia Corp	7372	2362
Arkel International Inc	8711	342
Arkema Inc	2899	15
Arketi Group	8742	399
Ark-Plastics Products Inc	3082	25
Arkray USA Inc	3841	146
Arktel Inc	5063	310
Arkwin Industries Inc	3728	85
Arkwright Advanced Coating Inc	2679	26
Arland Tool and Manufacturing Inc	3499	48
Arledge and AssociatesPC	8721	233
Arlene Semel and Associates Inc	7389	848
Arlin Curtiss Trucking Inc	4213	2869
Arlin Manufacturing Company Inc	3081	165
Arlinghaus Builders Inc	1521	99
Arlington Asset Investment Corp	6798	135
Arlington Capital Partners	6799	251
Arlington Coal and Lumber Co	5211	83
Arlington Hat Company Inc	2353	13
Arlington Industries Inc	3644	5
Arlington Machine and Tool Co	3599	201
Arlington Metals Corp	5051	274
Arlington Plating Co	3471	25
Arlington Printing And Stationers Inc	2761	32
Arlington Properties Inc	6531	79
Arlington Sample Book Company Inc	2399	36
Arlington Truck Co	4213	2791
Arlotto Technologies Inc	7373	742
Arlyn Tool and Manufacturing Company Inc	3545	318
ARM Inc	7372	178
Arm National Food Inc	5141	213
ARM Solutions	7322	81
Armaclad Inc	3442	128
Armada/Hoffler Construction Inc	1541	120
Armada Rubber Manufacturing Co	3069	128
Armada Security Group Inc	7381	267
Armadillo Security Service of Texas	7381	125

Company Name	SIC	Rank
Armaly Sponge Co	3089	1103
Arman Schroeder	7372	4364
Armanasco Public Relations Inc	8743	190
Armand Manufacturing Inc	3089	301
Armand Products Co	2812	8
Armando G Martinez	2099	262
Armando Montelongo Co	8748	77
Armanino Foods of Distinction Inc	2038	38
Armasi Inc	7372	2706
Armastrong Industries Inc	5047	269
Armatron International Inc	3812	100
Armatures Inc	3621	157
Armbrust International Ltd	3911	34
Armco Financial Services Corp	6159	89
Armds Inc	8721	303
Armed Forces Insurance Exhange	6331	336
Armedia LLC	7371	305
Armel Electronics Inc	3644	36
Armellini Express Lines Inc	4213	382
Armen of Ardmore	5511	865
Armil/Cfs Inc	3567	70
Armin Tool And Manufacturing Co	3544	289
Armite Laboratories Inc	2992	63
Armor All/STP Products Co	2842	25
Armor Deck Inc	1771	38
Armor Property Maintenance Inc	7349	461
Armortex Inc	3842	210
Armour and Sons Electric Inc	1731	121
Arms Etc Inc	7349	522
Armstong MacIntyre and Severns Inc	6282	315
Armstrong Electric Company Inc	1731	770
Armstrong Family Industries Inc	2752	1305
Armstrong Ford Inc	5511	876
Armstrong Holdings	6719	116
Armstrong International Inc	3491	17
Armstrong Landon Company Inc	5031	368
Armstrong Lumber Co	5211	265
Armstrong Machine Company Inc	3561	166
Armstrong McCall	5122	73
Armstrong Medical Industries Inc	5047	70
Armstrong Mold Corp	3089	518
Armstrong Moving and Storage Co	4213	1545
Armstrong Pharmaceuticals Inc	2834	141
Armstrong Services Inc	7699	134
Armstrong Torseth Skold And Rydeen Inc	8712	202
Armstrong Utilities Inc	4841	94
Armstrong Wood Products Inc	2499	15
Armstrong World Industries Inc	3089	11
Army and Air Force Exchange Service	2389	32
Army Hawaii Family Housing LLC	6531	140
Arnco	2822	7
Arnel Inc	3829	345
Arnet Pharmaceutical Corp	2833	42
Arnett Electric Inc	1731	1156
Arnette Pattern Company Inc	3599	550
Arney Computer Systems	7372	4789
Arnhold and S Bleichroeder Advisers LLC	6282	407
Arnie Bauer Cadillac-GMC Trucks Co	5511	849
Arnim Tool Inc	3544	829
Arnold A Semler Inc	3661	92
Arnold and O'Sheridan Inc	8711	329
Arnold and Porter	8111	54
Arnold Center Inc	8331	86
Arnold Electronics Inc	3672	458
Arnold Engineering Co	3452	22
Arnold Fabricating And Machine Inc	3441	214
Arnold Furniture Manufacturerss Inc	2521	51
Arnold Integrated Solutions	7311	676
Arnold Investment Counsel Inc	6282	216
Arnold L Barris Trucking Inc	4213	2928
Arnold Logistics	7389	347
Arnold Machinery Co (Salt Lake City Utah)	5082	26
Arnold Magnetic Technologies Corp	3679	176
Arnold Motor Supply Co	5013	66
Arnold Palmer Golf Management	3949	10
Arnold S Welding Service Inc	5084	589
Arnold Steel Company Inc	3441	144
Arnold Supply Inc	5085	272
Arnold Technical Sales Inc	5065	979
Arnold Tool and Die Co	3599	707
Arnold Transportation Service Inc	4214	9
Arnold Worldwide LLC	7311	15
Arnold-Gonsalves Inc	3599	1263
Arnold's Meat Food Products Inc	2013	215
Arnone and Sons	5141	231
Arnzen Wentz Molloy Laber and Storm PSC	8111	532
ARO Corp	3561	38
Aro Welding Technologies Inc	3548	27
A-Rod LP	5013	282
Aroma Vera	2844	69
Aromaland Inc	8059	27
Aromatic Fusion	2844	150
Aromatic Technologies Inc	2844	76
Aron Streit Inc	2052	52
Aronson and Partners	6282	331
Aronson LLC	8721	269
Aronson Security Group Inc	7382	33
Aronson-Campbell Industrial Supply Inc	5084	292
A-Roo Company LLC	5199	74
Aroplax Corp	3089	1066

Company Name	SIC	Rank
Arose Inc	1731	820
Arotech Corp	3691	12
Around The Clock Freightliner Group LLC	5012	36
Around The World Travel Inc	4724	93
Arox Land Development Corp	1623	648
Arpac LP	3565	19
Arpin Group Inc	4213	156
Arps Dairy Inc	2026	77
Arpy Inc	8999	219
Arq Electronics Manufacturing Services Inc	3678	58
ArQule Inc	2834	189
Arr Maz Custom Chemicals	2879	38
Arr Tech Manufacturing	5084	652
Arraid Inc	3572	99
Arrakis Systems Inc	3663	285
Array Architects	8712	151
Array Biopharma Inc	2834	155
Array Connector Corp	3678	34
Array Information Technology Inc	7374	111
Array Technology Group LLC	7389	966
ArrayComm Inc	7372	644
Arrayit Corp	3826	112
ArrayNetworks Inc	7373	191
Arrel Enterprises Inc	1731	2584
Arrelle Fine Linens Inc	5719	35
Arrgh Manufacturing Company Inc	3625	328
Arrhythmia Research Technology Inc	3845	62
Arri Inc	5043	2
Arribas Brothers Company Inc	5947	17
Arrington and Co	8721	339
Arrington Lumber And Pallet Company Inc	2448	20
Arris Builders Inc	1542	446
ARRIS Group Inc	3669	7
Arris Interactive LLC	3663	33
Arris Systems Inc	7379	1039
Arrival Communications Inc	4813	158
Arro Tool and Die Inc	3544	755
Arrow Air Inc	4512	46
Arrow Battert Edco	5063	712
Arrow Chemical Corp	2842	152
Arrow Communications Inc	1731	2173
Arrow Concrete Co	4213	359
Arrow Diversified Tooling Inc	3544	530
Arrow ECS	5045	198
Arrow Electric Company Inc	1731	78
Arrow Electronics Inc	5065	3
Arrow Electronics Incorporated Commercial Systems Group	5045	3
Arrow Exterminating Company Inc	7342	25
Arrow Financial Corp	6712	200
Arrow Financial Services LLC	7322	12
Arrow Ford Inc	5511	333
Arrow Freight Management Inc	4213	944
Arrow Funding Corp	8721	326
Arrow Gear Co	3724	31
Arrow Glass and Mirror Inc	1793	9
Arrow Grinding Inc	3599	2083
Arrow International Inc	3841	24
Arrow Machining Company Inc	3599	1572
Arrow Pneumatics Inc	3563	8
Arrow Pointo Federal Credit Union	6062	99
Arrow Printing Company Inc	2752	1602
Arrow Resources Development Inc	0811	8
Arrow Road Construction Co	1611	150
Arrow Scrap Corp	5093	234
Arrow Screw Products Inc	3599	1642
Arrow Security Inc	7381	70
Arrow Services Inc	7342	27
Arrow Shed LLC	3448	12
Arrow Shopper	2741	443
Arrow Specialties Inc	3451	148
Arrow Striping and Manufacturing Inc	1721	6
Arrow Tank and Engineering Co	3443	72
Arrow Thompson Metals Inc	5051	347
Arrow Tool and Stamping Company Inc	3499	104
Arrow Tool Die and Machine Company Inc	3544	843
Arrow Tools Fasteners and Saw Inc	5072	86
Arrow Truck Sales Inc	5511	73
Arrow Trucking Co	4213	168
Arrow Tru-Line Inc	3429	80
Arrow United Industries	3444	36
Arrow Valve and Instrument Inc	5084	729
Arrow Wrecker Service Inc	7549	13
Arrowhead Community Bank	6022	672
Arrowhead Co	6712	711
Arrowhead Conveyor Corp	3535	27
Arrowhead Mountain Spring Water Co	2086	16
Arrowhead Plastic Engineering Inc	3089	813
Arrowhead Press Inc	2752	1043
Arrowhead Products Corp	3728	46
Arrowhead Research Corp	8731	408
Arrowhead West Inc	8331	80
Arrow-Magnolia International Inc	2899	202
Arrowpoint Capital Corp	6331	130
Arrow-Tech Inc	3829	268
Ars Direct Mail	7331	268
ARS eCommerce LLC	7319	123
Ars International Consulting	7371	1709
ARS National Services Inc	7322	15
ARS Nova Software	7371	1109

Company Name	SIC	Rank
ARSEE Engineers Inc	8711	332
Arsenal Acquisition Corp	7379	653
Arsenal Credit Union	6062	30
Arsenal Digital Solutions Worldwide Inc	5045	134
Arsenault Associates Inc	7371	1127
Arservices Ltd	7373	661
Arsin Corp	7379	226
Art and Logic Inc	7372	1120
Art Bindery Inc	2789	103
Art Bookbinders Of America Inc	7334	48
Art Cathedral Metal Company Inc	3499	49
Art Chinese Gallery Inc	5023	103
Art Classics LLC	2741	334
Art Coco Chocolate Co	2064	132
Art Colbar Inc	5199	139
Art Communication Systems Inc	2752	1302
Art Design Concrete	5032	112
Art Dreams Home Inc	2752	322
Art Finished Inc	7336	118
Art Floor Inc	5023	102
Art Guild Binders Inc	2782	63
Art Horizons International Inc	7389	1811
Art Institute of Atlanta LLC	8221	41
Art Institute of Charlotte LLC	8221	46
Art Institute of Colorado Inc	8221	10
Art Institute of Fort Lauderdale Inc	8221	50
Art Institute of Houston Inc	8221	57
Art Institute of Las Vegas Inc	8221	51
Art Institute of Los Angeles Inc	8221	42
Art Institute of Los Angeles - Orange County Inc	8221	52
Art Institute of Phoenix Inc	8221	53
Art Institute of Seattle Inc	8221	43
Art Institute of Washington Inc	8221	54
Art Institutes International at San Francisco Inc	8221	55
Art Institutes International Minnesota Inc	8221	56
Art Klopfenstein Equipment Inc	3269	18
Art Machine LLC	7336	188
Art Materials Service Inc	3469	184
Art Moehn Chevrolet Co	5511	316
Art O Lite Electric Company Inc	1731	2498
Art Optical Contact Lens Inc	3851	32
Art Pape Transfer Inc	4213	1809
Art Phoenix Group Inc	5199	83
ART Plus Technology Inc	7372	3129
Art Research Institute Ltd	3861	123
Art Technologies Inc	3568	46
Art Technology Group Inc (Cambridge Massachusetts)	7372	268
Art Van Furniture Inc	5712	10
Art Wilson's Studio Inc	2759	176
Artagrafik	7311	791
Art-American Printing Plates Inc	2796	55
Artbeats	8999	89
Artbeats Software Inc	7372	3570
Artco Offset Inc	2752	519
Artco-Bell Corp	2531	24
Artcom Inc	2759	8
Artcraft Company Inc	2759	252
Artcraft Engraving and Printing Inc	2752	1406
Artcraft Fabricators Inc	3599	392
Artcraft Inc	2752	1144
Artcraft Machine And Tool Corp	3599	1566
Artcraft Optical Company Inc	3851	28
Artcraft Press Inc	2791	54
Artcraft Printers Inc	2752	341
Arte De Mexico Inc	2522	25
Arte Publico Press	2731	221
Artech Consulting Group Inc	7379	1038
Artech Diversified Inc	3544	571
Artech Industries Inc	3679	472
Artech Information Systems LLC	7371	47
Artek Inc	3089	991
Artel Electrical Contractors Inc	1731	1320
Artel Inc	3845	100
Artel Inc (Reston Virginia)	7373	114
Artel Software Inc	7373	834
Artel Video Systems Inc	3661	81
Artemis International Solutions Corp	7372	775
Artemis Rubber Technology Inc	3061	50
Artemis Software Inc	7372	4790
Artemis Woman LLC	5999	133
Arteriocyte Medical Systems Inc	3845	69
Artery Group LLC	6552	268
Artesia Sawdust Products Inc	2421	129
Artesian Resources Corp	4941	15
Artex Aircraft Supplies Inc	5088	40
Artex Inc	4213	1807
Artex Knitting Mills Inc	2253	16
ArtFact LLC	7379	1421
Artfx Inc	2399	12
Arthrex Inc	3841	95
ArthroCare Corp	3845	11
Arthrocare Medical Corp	3841	260
Arthur A Watson and Company Inc	6411	178
Arthur Asfar	3069	275
Arthur B Myr Industries Inc	3444	105
Arthur Consulting Group Inc	8732	87
Arthur Corp	3089	835
Arthur D Little Inc	8742	3
Arthur Diefenbach Inc	1731	2333
Arthur E Selnick Associates Inc	5064	192

Company Name	SIC	Rank
Arthur J Gallagher and Co	6411	20
Arthur J Gallagher and Company of Kentucky Inc	6411	220
Arthur J Gallagher and Company of Michigan Inc	6411	259
Arthur J Gallagher and Company of Mississippi Inc	6411	39
Arthur J Gallagher and Company of Oklahoma Inc	6411	118
Arthur J Rogers and Co	6531	128
Arthur L Davis Publishing Agency Inc	2721	247
Arthur Lumber Trading Co	5031	128
Arthur Murray International Inc	6794	146
Arthur Place and Company PC	8721	193
Arthur Rutenberg Homes Inc	1521	17
Arthur Sanderson and Sons North America Ltd	5131	20
Arthur Shuster Inc	7389	434
Arthur Weisburg Enterprises Inc	5063	23
Arthur Wells Inc	4213	1489
Arthurmade Plastics Inc	3089	594
Artic Express Inc	4213	5
Artic Tool and Engineering Company LLC	3599	2387
Artic-Temperature Inc	3585	196
Articulate Software Inc	7372	4658
Artifex Software Inc	7372	2900
Artifice Inc	7372	3691
Artime Group	7311	1017
Artimex Iron Company Inc	1791	12
Artio Global Investors Inc	6282	118
Artis And Associates Inc	7371	1031
Artisan Columbia Printing	2752	1355
Artisan Controls Corp	3625	219
Artisan Equipment Inc	3599	2434
Artisan Grinding Service Inc	7699	254
Artisan Industries Inc	3559	149
Artisan Nameplate And Awards Corp	2759	295
Artisan Power LLC	5063	1062
Artisan Press Inc	2752	1103
Artisan Tool and Die Inc	3544	721
Artisan's Bank	6022	333
Artisans' Guild Inc	2531	47
Artisans Inc	2396	21
Artisans Public Relations	7319	139
ARTISTdirect Inc	7389	716
ARTISTdirect Recordings Inc	7379	553
Artistic Accent Inc	3499	128
Artistic Dental Studio Inc	8072	16
Artistic Granite and Marble Inc	5032	125
Artistic Homes Inc	1531	8
Artistic Lighting And Electric	1731	532
Artistic Plastic And Fixtures Inc	3089	1089
Artistic Stairs Inc	2431	126
Artistic Tape and Label Printers	2752	1184
Artists International Management Inc	7922	65
Artlite Office Supply and Furniture Co	5021	62
Armor Plastics Corp	3089	1890
ARTnews LLC	2721	81
Artone LLC	2522	33
Artos Engineering Co	3549	22
Arts and Letters Corp	7371	1643
Art's Elegance Inc	5094	39
Art's Mexican Products Inc	2099	358
ARTS PDF	7372	4659
Art's Rental Equipment Inc	7359	101
ARTSCI Inc	2741	410
Artscroll Printing Corp	2759	419
ArtsMarket Inc	8742	613
Art's-Way Manufacturing Company Inc	3523	53
Art-Tech Decorating I Inc	7389	1752
Artvision Media Services	7812	189
Artwork Conversion Software Inc	7371	1387
Artwork Systems	7372	1249
Arty Imports Inc	5193	18
Aruba Networks Inc	3674	61
Arundel Lodge Inc	8361	149
Arva-Hudson Inc	5065	337
Arveda LLC	3842	231
Arvest Bank	6712	253
Arvest Holdings Inc	6022	826
Arvig Communications Systems	4813	202
Arvin International Holdings LLC	3714	46
Arvin Sango Inc	3714	45
ArvinMeritor OE LLC	3714	2
Arvo Communications Inc	7311	774
Arvon Staffing LLC	7363	211
Arvron Inc	2821	100
Arway Confections Inc	2064	43
Arwood Machine Corp	3599	294
Arxan Technologies Inc	7372	1256
Arya Corp	5112	100
Arylessence Inc	2869	71
Arzberger Engravers Inc	2754	44
Arzel Technology Inc	3823	163
AS Horner Construction Company Inc	1622	31
A-S Hospitality Div	2761	23
AS Pindel Corp	3451	75
AS Software Inc	7371	927
AS/SURE Software	7372	2707
AS Thomas Inc	7372	4274
AS Was	7379	595
ASA Computers Inc	5045	180
ASA Corp	3651	40

Company Name	SIC	Rank
ASA Engineering Inc	3571	142
ASA International Ltd	7373	162
ASA International Ltd Business Systems Div	7372	952
Asa Publication Incorporated Mt	2721	324
Asa Solutions Inc	7371	1403
ASA Tire Systems	7372	2095
Asael Farr and Sons Co	2024	15
Asahi/America Inc	3089	220
Asahi Kasei Plastics North America Inc	2821	36
Asahi Tec America Corp	3555	10
Asahi Thermofil Inc	3083	6
Asante Networks Inc	5045	249
Asap Consultants Inc	7361	403
ASAP Express Inc	4213	2405
ASAP Inc (Los Angeles California)	7372	4952
ASAP Screen Printing	2759	377
ASAP Staffing LLC	7379	159
ASAP Systems	7373	344
Asarco Inc	1021	3
ASAT Inc	8734	67
Asay Publishing Co	2741	311
Asb Properties LLC	7359	259
Asbestos Removal Technologies Inc	4953	136
Asbill Electric Service Inc	1731	2289
Asbuilt Construction Inc	1623	828
Asbury Automotive Group Inc	5511	9
Asbury Automotive Group LLC	5511	1207
Asbury Graphite Mills Inc	3624	11
Asbury Louisiana Inc	3624	10
Asbury Machine Corp	3532	75
Asbury Park Press Inc	2711	18
Asbury Syrup Company Inc	5145	38
Asbury Trucking	4213	2036
ASC Capacitors	3675	17
ASC Industries Inc (Arlington Texas)	5088	56
ASC International Inc	5088	17
Asc Machine Tools Inc	3554	7
ASC Securities Corp	6289	9
Ascar Business Systems	7372	2448
Asc-Cubed LLC	7373	551
Ascedia Inc	4813	695
Ascella Technologies Inc	7372	3408
Ascena Retail Group Inc	5621	2
Ascend Geo LLC	3829	307
Ascend HR Solutions	7361	414
Ascend Intelligence LLC	7371	929
Ascend Media	5192	11
Ascend Pharmaceuticals Inc	5912	60
Ascend Software Inc	7372	1982
Ascend Technologies Inc	5999	302
Ascend Venture Group LLC	6799	146
Ascendant Solutions Inc	7389	2520
Ascendent Telecommunications Inc	4812	96
Ascendix Technologies Inc	5045	572
Ascension Insurance Services Inc	6411	212
Ascent Capital Group Inc	3695	8
Ascent Logic Corp	7371	291
Ascent Media DVD	3695	3
Ascent Media Group LLC	7819	3
Ascent Media Systems and Technology Services	7373	263
Ascent Solar Technologies Inc	3674	390
Ascent Technology Inc	7372	3469
Ascent Venture Partners	6799	104
Ascentis Sofware Corp	7372	781
Ascentium Corp	7373	224
Ascert LLC	7372	4139
Aschinger Electric Co	1731	133
ASCI	3669	247
ASCI Corp	7371	1015
ASCII Group Inc	5045	394
ASCO	3491	2
Asco Division of Win Craft Inc	2399	9
Ascolta LLC	8243	3
Ascom Wireless Solutions Inc	4822	2
ASCOR Inc	3679	352
Ascosta Heating and Cooling	7623	11
ASD/QMS Inc	7372	4448
Ase Industries Inc	3599	568
Ase Technology Inc	7373	744
Ase (US) Inc	5065	137
Asea Brown Boveri Inc	3621	4
ASEC International Inc	7371	821
Asemblon Inc	2819	90
Asemco Inc	3674	356
Asentinel LLC	5045	495
Asentria Inc	2542	63
Aseptico Inc	3843	21
Aserdiv Inc	5045	531
Ash Gear Supply Corp	5085	428
Ash Grove Aggregates Inc	1422	31
Ash Grove Cement Co	3241	2
Ash Grove Texas LP	3241	23
Ash Industries Inc	3089	1221
Ash Love-Less Company Inc	3635	10
Ash Meadows Zeolite LLC	1446	10
Ash Millworks Inc	2431	127
Ash Stevens Inc	2834	296
Ashbrook Simon-Hartley Operations LP	3589	63
Ashby and Ashby Inc	7334	69
Ashby Cross Company Inc	3559	279
Ashby Dillon Inc	7311	599

Company Name	SIC	Rank
Ashby Industries Inc	3577	568
Ashby Manufacturing Company Inc	3312	131
Ashe Converting Equipment	3554	37
Ashe Industries Inc	3554	34
Asheboro Piedmont Printing Inc	2752	1169
Asher Management Group Ltd	5013	64
Asheville Waste Paper Company Inc	5093	185
Ashland Electric Products Inc	3621	128
Ashland Graphic Arts Inc	7336	327
Ashland Hardware Systems	3089	319
Ashland Inc	2911	17
Ashland Industries Inc	5084	506
Ashland Partners and Company LLP	8721	242
Ashland Publishing Co	2711	363
Ashland Roller Mills Inc	2041	57
Ashland Screening Corp	2759	588
Ashland Services LLC	7363	266
Ashland Shirt Inc	2321	15
Ashlar-Vellum	7371	440
Ashley Brooks	3523	224
Ashley Electric Inc	1731	2295
Ashley F Ward Inc	3451	1
Ashley Furniture Industries Inc	2511	1
Ashley Industrial Molding Inc	3089	429
Ashley Lighting Inc	3646	81
Ashley Resin Corp	2821	142
Ashley Salvage Co	5093	144
Ashley Sling Inc	3496	74
Ashley Transport Inc	4213	2101
Ashley Valley Medical Center LLC	8062	229
Ashley W George	4785	4
Ashley Welding and Machine Co	3441	266
Ashley-Martin Manufacturing LLC	2048	130
Ashley's Quality Care Inc	7363	222
Ashleywilde Inc	7372	5010
Ashling Broadcasting	4832	246
Ashly Audio Inc	3663	159
Ashman Distributing Co	2035	60
Ashmore Brothers Inc	1611	168
Ashpaugh Electric Inc	1731	2427
Ashta Chemicals Inc	2812	10
Ashtech Corp	3535	153
Ashton Company Inc	1629	16
Ashton Metzler and Associates Inc	8742	699
Ashton Residential LLC	1531	25
Ashwell Label Dies Inc	2865	30
Ashwood Computer Company Inc	5045	469
Ashworth's Inc	5571	9
ASI Computer Systems Inc	5045	106
ASI Computer Technologies Inc	5045	17
ASI Constructors Inc	1629	50
Asi Consulting Group LLC	8748	421
ASI Corp	5045	16
Asi Datamyte Inc	3823	109
ASI Electronics Inc	3625	347
ASI Instruments Inc	3829	482
ASI Investments Holding Co	6719	45
Asi Of Miami Inc	7349	182
Asi Packaging Co	7389	1899
Asi Security Inc	7381	98
Asi Show Inc	7389	1543
Asi Systems	5999	312
ASI Technologies Inc	3566	36
ASI Technologies Inc (Milwaukee Wisconsin)	3442	45
Asia America Enterprise Inc	2752	1488
Asia General Corp	5064	188
Asia Green Agriculture Corp	0161	20
Asia Network Enterprise Inc	4833	222
Asia Pacific Ventures	8748	281
Asia Star Broadcasting Inc	4833	214
Asia Tigers Fund Inc	6726	90
Asian Pacific Ltd	5065	518
Asiana Cuisine Enterprises Inc	2099	68
Asic Inc	7373	1009
Asinni 2000 Records Inc	3652	39
ASK Associates Inc	8742	534
ASK Foods Inc	2038	30
ASK Plastics Inc	3089	172
ASK Technologies Inc	7374	285
ASKA Co	3089	1701
Askcom	7375	75
Asko Processing Inc	3471	69
AskSam Systems	7372	4172
ASM International	5942	10
ASM Lithography Holding Inc	3559	8
ASMO North America LLC	3714	72
Asmo North Carolina Inc	3519	10
Asn Inc	2759	550
Aspect 1	7372	3656
Aspect Medical Systems Inc	3845	29
Aspect Software Inc	7371	15
Aspect Systems Inc	5065	96
Aspen Banner Engineering	8711	485
Aspen Diversified Industries Inc	7363	236
Aspen Electronics Inc	3679	599
Aspen Electronics Manufacturing Inc	3672	118
Aspen Graphics Inc	2752	1320
Aspen Imaging International Inc	3955	9
Aspen Leaf Software Inc	7372	3657
Aspen Manufacturing Inc	6719	35
Aspen Marketing Services	8742	39
Aspen Masonry Inc	3241	17
Aspen Medical Group PA	8011	51

Company Name	SIC	Rank
Aspen Medical Products	3841	151
Aspen Networks Inc	7379	1256
Aspen Press Company LC	2752	765
Aspen Products Inc	2674	4
Aspen Publishers Inc	2731	39
Aspen Research Group Ltd	7372	2766
Aspen Skiing Co	7011	142
Aspen Solutions Inc	5065	954
Aspen Sports Inc	5941	26
Aspen Systems Inc	7373	462
Aspen Technology Inc	7371	59
Aspen Test Engineering Inc	7371	1563
Aspen Transportation Service	4213	3025
AspenMedia	7336	295
Aspetuck Systems Inc	7372	3593
Asphalt Contractors Inc	1611	167
Asphalt Cutbacks Inc	2952	23
Asphalt Drum Mixers Inc	3531	77
Asphalt Equipment and Service Co	3531	175
Asphalt Equipment Company Inc	3531	173
Asphalt Patching Inc	1611	252
Asphalt Paving Co	1611	177
Asphalt Zipper Inc	3531	111
Aspire Inc	8211	106
Aspire Kid Sports Center	7991	14
AspireHR Inc	8748	164
Aspirin Software Inc	7372	3977
Aspiro Inc	8331	98
Asplin Excavating Inc	5032	65
Asplund Coffee LLC	5149	224
Asplundh Construction Corp	1623	43
Asplundh Tree Expert Co	0783	1
AS-Pro Software Inc	7372	4660
Aspyra Inc	7373	440
ASQ Technology Inc	3679	822
ASR Data Acquisition And Analysis LLC	7373	887
Assemblers Inc	3999	106
Assembly and Automation Technologies Inc	3549	124
Assembly and Design Inc	3672	436
Assembly and Test Worldwide Inc	3549	5
Assembly Automation Industries	3549	65
Assembly International Inc	3672	369
Assembly Plus LLC	3672	176
Assembly Specialists Inc	3549	115
Assembly Technologies Inc	3672	383
Assem-Tech Inc	3679	385
Asset Acceptance Capital Corp	7322	8
Asset Exchange Ltd	5065	835
Asset International	8999	96
Asset Management Associates	6722	237
Asset Management Concepts Inc	7371	1100
Asset Management Outsourcing Inc	7322	10
Asset Management Services	5065	107
Asset Management Services Inc	7322	118
Asset Management Technologies Inc	7372	572
Asset Plus Corp	8741	114
Asset Preservation Inc	6282	365
Asset Protection and Security Services LP	7381	34
Asset Protection Partnership Ltd	1731	2127
Asset Recovery Center LLC	5065	741
Asset Recovery Group Inc	7322	92
Asset Recovery Specialists Inc	7379	961
Asset Strategies Portfolio Services Inc	6282	514
Asset Systems Inc	7372	4586
AssetExchange Inc	6211	265
Assets Inc	8331	51
AssetWorks Inc	7372	258
Assi Fabricators LLC	2541	52
Assisted Living Concepts Inc	8059	4
Assisted Living Inc	8361	173
Assistex Inc	2752	1170
Assmann Corporation Of America	3089	1308
Assmann Electronics Inc	3577	590
Associate Engineering Corp	3563	37
Associated Acc International Ltd	1752	14
Associated Advertising Agency Inc	7311	593
Associated Aircraft Supply Company Inc	5088	79
Associated Bag Co	3081	35
Associated Banc-Corp	6712	35
Associated Bank	6022	261
Associated Bank Gladstone-Norwood	6022	703
Associated Bank Green Bay NA	6021	13
Associated Bank Madison	6022	731
Associated Bank Milwaukee	6022	211
Associated Bank-Chicago	6712	465
Associated Battery Co	5063	868
Associated Broach Corp	3545	321
Associated Building Maintenance Company Inc	7349	89
Associated Business Publications Company Ltd	2721	280
Associated Carriers LP	4213	2702
Associated Chemists Inc	2869	96
Associated Companies Inc	1731	437
Associated Computer Systems Ltd	7372	2624
Associated Content Inc	2741	93
Associated Couriers Inc	4213	1572
Associated Credit Union	6062	56
Associated Creditors Exchange Inc	7322	47
Associated Creditors Inc	7334	31

Company Name	SIC	Rank
Associated Dental Laboratories Of America Inc	8072	12
Associated Desert Shoppers Inc	2741	20
Associated Development Corp	5048	23
Associated Electric Cooperative Inc	4911	125
Associated Electrical Contractors Inc	1731	2153
Associated Electrical Services LLC	1731	1136
Associated Electro-Mechanics Inc	5084	431
Associated Electronic Systems Inc	7373	671
Associated Environmental Systems	3826	109
Associated Equipment Corp	3629	67
Associated Estates Realty Corp	6798	131
Associated Finishing Inc	3479	64
Associated Food Stores Inc	5141	48
Associated Fuel Pump Systems Corp	3714	248
Associated Global Systems	4731	16
Associated Grocers Inc (Baton Rouge Louisiana)	5141	56
Associated Grocers of Florida Inc	5141	57
Associated Grocers of Maine Inc	5141	106
Associated Grocers of New England Inc	5141	108
Associated Grocers of the South Inc	5141	79
Associated Healthcare Systems Inc	5047	68
Associated Home Health Nurses Of America Inc	7361	341
Associated Industries	5065	67
Associated Marine and Industrial Staffing Inc	7361	185
Associated Material Handling Industries Inc	5084	24
Associated Materials Holdings Inc	6719	68
Associated Materials LLC	3089	33
Associated Mechanical Erectors Company Inc	1389	36
Associated Medical	5047	52
Associated Milk Producers Inc	5143	3
Associated Music Publishers Inc	2741	231
Associated Packaging Inc	5084	67
Associated Packaging Technologies Inc	5113	4
Associated Pallets Inc	2448	30
Associated Partnership Ltd	7532	8
Associated Petroleum Carriers	4213	742
Associated Pipe Line Contractors Inc	1623	56
Associated Plastics Corp	3089	875
Associated Potato Growers Inc	5148	73
Associated Press	7383	4
Associated Printing Professionals Inc	2752	1682
Associated Production Services Inc	7389	684
Associated Rack Corp	3443	122
Associated Research Inc	3825	132
Associated Rubber Inc	3061	41
Associated Sign Co	3993	175
Associated Spring	3495	1
Associated Steel Company Inc	5051	446
Associated Systems Inc	7372	3575
Associated Technologies Inc	3769	22
Associated Television International	7812	30
Associated Textile Converters Inc	2211	9
Associated Thermoforming Inc	3089	815
Associated Welding and Machine Works Inc	3599	1144
Associated Wholesalers Inc	5141	37
Associated X-Ray Corp	5047	245
Associates Engraving Co	2796	22
Associates For Women's Health	8049	26
Associates In Digestive Health	8011	133
Associates In Medical Marketing Company Inc	2741	285
Associates in Software International	5045	621
Association Computer Services Inc	7371	1722
Association Of Medical Device Reprocessors	3671	25
Assumption Cooperative Grain Co	5153	113
Assurance Group	7361	435
Assurance Manufacturing Company Inc	3469	114
Assurance Systems Inc	7372	4114
Assurance Technologies Inc	3829	388
Assurance Technology Corp	8711	217
AssuranceAmerica Corp	6331	306
Assurant Health	6321	80
Assurant Inc	6321	6
Assurant Solutions	6399	2
Assured Aggregates Company Inc	4213	1618
Assured Computing Technologies Inc	3575	56
Assured Guaranty	6351	3
Assured Guaranty Corp	6351	17
Assured Information Security	7382	44
Assurity Life Insurance Co	6311	274
AssurX Inc	7372	1967
AST Engineering Services Inc	7372	3516
AST Products Inc	3829	298
Asta Funding Inc	6153	27
Astadia Inc	8742	97
Astar Air Cargo Inc	4513	7
Astar Inc	3089	1212
Astaro Corp	7372	555
Astea International Inc	7372	1196
Astec Industries Inc	3531	4
Astec Mobile Screens Inc	3569	92
Aster Investment Management Company Inc	6282	633
Astera Software Inc	7372	1976
Asteroid Grinding Co	3599	1409

Company Name	SIC	Rank
Astex Pharmaceuticals Inc	2834	183
Asthmatx Inc	3841	168
Asti Corp	3679	330
Astir It Solutions Inc	7379	323
Aston Group	7379	30
Aston Pereira and Associates	8712	274
Astonish SEO	7371	1326
Astor Products Inc	2841	2
Astoria Federal SLA	6035	16
Astoria Financial Corp	6035	10
Astoria Ford Inc	5511	1109
Astoria Imports Inc	5021	154
Astoria Software Inc	5045	191
Astoria-Pacific Inc	3999	140
Astra Associates Incorporated dba Mid-West Instrument	3545	198
Astra Communications USA Inc	7373	743
Astra Group (Overland Park Kansas)	7389	121
Astra Products Company Incorporated Of Tampa	3651	131
Astra Products Of Ohio Ltd	3089	687
Astra Tech Inc	3845	6
Astra Tool and Instrument Manufacturing Corp	3841	336
Astral Airlines Inc	4512	8
Astral Industries Inc	3995	8
Astralite	3674	466
Astralloy Steel Products Inc	3599	885
Astrata Group Inc	3829	105
AstraZeneca LP	2834	61
AstraZeneca Pharmaceuticals LP	2834	26
Astro Aerospace	3769	16
Astro American Chemical Company Inc	2819	116
Astro Apparel Inc	2325	13
Astro Cap Manufacturing-West Inc	3792	23
Astro Chemical Company Inc	2891	96
Astro Company Inc	1731	1571
Astro Computing Services	7389	919
Astro Flight Inc	3691	44
Astro Gaming	3669	157
Astro Labs Inc	3679	387
Astro Machine Corp	3579	40
Astro Machine Works Inc	3599	681
Astro Molding Inc	3061	43
Astro Moving and Storage Co	4213	1794
Astro Precision Machine Inc	3599	2140
Astro Seal Inc	3679	487
Astro Shapes Inc	3354	28
Astro Technical Services Inc	5063	373
Astro Tool and Die Company Inc	3469	333
Astro Tool and Machine Company Inc	3599	1412
Astrocom Corp	3577	654
Astrocom Electronics Inc	3661	141
Astro-Craft Inc	3599	1698
Astrofoam Molding Company Inc	3089	1729
Astro-Geo-Marine Inc	8731	403
AstroGraph Software Inc	7372	3863
Astrokam	5065	13
Astrolabe Inc	7372	4404
Astrolabe Pictures	2741	399
Astro-Med Inc	3577	129
Astron Wireless Technologies	8731	388
Astronautics Corporation Of America	3812	21
Astronic	3672	91
Astronics Corp	3728	28
Astro-Physics Inc	3827	140
Astroseal Products Manufacturing Corp	3053	130
Astrosystems Inc	5063	408
Astrotech Corp	3761	6
Astrotech Space Operations LP	7699	82
Astro-Tronics Inc	3669	302
Astrup Drug Inc	5912	17
Asturies Manufacturing Company Inc	3728	192
Astute Inc	7372	1853
Astute Networks Inc	3674	162
Astyra Corp	8742	242
ASU Indian Club Inc	7389	1611
Asure Software Inc	7373	398
Asurion	4812	4
Asus Computer International Inc	5045	332
ASV Distribution Inc	3531	33
ASW Services Inc	1541	93
ASYM Technologies	5734	245
Asynchrony Solutions Inc	7372	1118
A-Systems Corp	7372	3978
A-Systems Inc	3629	108
AT and G Co	3451	95
AT and T Alascom	4813	115
AT and T Inc	4813	1
AT and T Software Solutions	7372	61
AT Clayton and Company Inc	5111	11
AT Communication Corp	7372	4173
AT Cross Co	3951	2
AT Information Products Inc	3555	101
AT Kearney Inc	8742	16
At Last Naturals Inc	2834	425
At Once Cleaning Services Inc	7349	121
AT Parker/Solar Electronics	3825	236
AT Reynolds and Sons Inc	2097	6
AT/SCAN Ltd	7372	4405
A-T Solutions Inc	8748	67
A-T Surgical Manufacturing Company Inc	3842	243
AT Systems East Inc	4213	1368

Company Name	SIC	Rank
AT Systems Northwest Inc	4213	751
AT Williams Oil Co	5541	13
ATA Holdings Corp	4522	3
Atac	7371	507
Ataco Steel Products Corp	3469	104
Atacs Products Inc	3728	221
Atalanta Corp	5146	2
Atalanta/Sosnoff Capital Corp	6159	75
Atalanta/Sosnoff Management Corp	6289	26
Atalasoft Inc	7371	803
Atalla Corp	3577	212
Ataman Software Inc	7372	4791
Atap Inc	3537	42
Atari Inc	7372	507
Atash Fire and Safety Equipment Company Inc	5063	587
ATC Associates Inc	8999	36
ATC Companies Inc	3822	58
ATC Enterprises LLC	7379	855
ATC Healthcare Inc	8082	33
ATC Inc	3599	2002
ATC Leasing Co	4424	2
Atc Lighting and Plastics Inc	3647	10
Atc Power Systems Inc	3679	429
Atc Staffing Services Inc	7361	34
ATC Travel Inc	4724	110
Atchafalaya Crawfish Processing LLC	2092	67
Atco Inc	8331	245
Atco Investment Co	6282	568
Atco Manufacturing Co	2842	47
Atco Plastics Inc	3089	1014
ATCO Products Inc	3585	66
Atco Properties and Management Inc	6512	21
Atco Rubber Products Inc	3443	14
Atcs Services LLC	8711	437
ATD-American Co	5131	14
Atec Inc (Stafford Texas)	5084	43
A-Tech Computer Service Inc	7378	87
A-Tech Consulting Inc	4899	118
A-Tech Corp	3823	47
Ateeco Inc	2038	37
Ateez Corp	3812	161
Atek Manufacturing LLC	3499	12
Atek Plastics Inc	2821	98
Atek Products LLC	3674	394
Atel Cash Distribution Fund Vi LP	7359	184
Atempo Inc	5045	46
ATEN Technology Inc	7372	58
Ater Wynne LLP Attorneys At Law	8111	370
Atex Media Solutions Inc	7371	134
ath Power Consulting Corp	8732	106
Athan Corp	3599	2509
Athana International Inc	3572	89
Athea Laboratories Inc	2842	50
Athearn Inc	3944	23
Athena Brands Inc	3559	306
Athena Controls Inc	3823	139
Athena Diagnostics Inc	2835	27
Athena Group Inc	7372	4200
Athena Investment Systems LLC	7379	1092
Athenahealth Inc	7375	20
Athens Baking Company LLC	2051	91
Athens First Bank and Trust Co	6022	226
Athens Regional Medical Center Inc	8062	121
Athens Technical Specialists Inc	3669	271
Atheros Communications Inc	3674	41
Athersys Inc	2834	321
Atherton Construction Inc	1542	260
Atherton Grain Co	5153	147
Athlete's Foot Group Inc	5661	8
Athletic Business Publications Inc	2721	291
Athletic Resource Management Inc	7941	41
Athletic Supply Of California	5091	114
Athletics Investment Group	7941	20
Athoc Inc	7371	415
Athol Press Inc	2711	540
ATI Casting Service	3321	37
ATI Firth Sterling	3297	2
Ati Industrial Automation Export Co	3823	95
ATI Ladish LLC	3469	7
ATI Metalworking Products	3545	5
Ati Oldco Inc	3713	38
Ati Performance Products Inc	3714	365
Ati Titanium LLC	3339	11
ATI (Trabuco Canyon California)	4812	67
ATI Wah Chang	2899	55
Atiam Technologies LP	5734	73
Atic LLC	5999	266
Atis Ltd	3669	290
Atk Foods Inc	2013	176
ATK Space Systems	3489	5
Atkins and Pearce Inc	2299	5
Atkins Nutritionals Inc	5149	41
Atkins Printing Service Inc	2752	1254
Atkinson and Company Ltd	8721	127
Atkinson Candy Co	2064	35
Atkinson Construction Company Inc	1541	303
Atkinson Electronics Inc	5084	374
Atkinson Freight Lines	4213	266
Atkinson Industries Inc	3699	75
Atkinson Milling Co	2041	41
Atkinson Mullen and Rosso	4725	13
Atl Coca-Cola Btl Company Att Acct	2086	131
ATL Courier Inc	4213	3099

Company Name	SIC	Rank
Atlanco Inc	5199	36
Atlanta Arrangements Inc	7389	810
Atlanta Attachment Co	3639	15
Atlanta Beck Inc	7336	75
Atlanta Belting Co	3052	22
Atlanta Beverage Co	5181	12
Atlanta Bin and Shelving Corp	1796	28
Atlanta Brewing Co	2082	81
Atlanta Capital Management Company LLC	6282	240
Atlanta Computer Group Inc	5044	131
Atlanta Custom Coach Inc	7389	2177
Atlanta Datacom Inc	4813	153
Atlanta Fixture and Sales Company Inc	5046	34
Atlanta Fuel Company Inc	5172	133
Atlanta Gas Light Co	4924	23
Atlanta Global Resources Inc	8748	30
Atlanta Ice Company Inc	5199	128
Atlanta Latino Newspaper	2711	803
Atlanta Life Financial Group Inc	6311	217
Atlanta Lightning Protection Inc	3643	148
Atlanta Metropolitan Publishing Inc	2721	366
Atlanta Motor Speedway Inc	7948	32
Atlanta Nypro Inc	3089	243
Atlanta Obstetrics and Gynecology Associates PC	8011	82
Atlanta Pediatric Therapy Inc	8099	85
Atlanta Wupa Cw	4833	187
Atlantagrotnes Machine Co	3542	55
Atlantech Online Inc	4813	378
Atlantex Corporation Inc	3089	1521
Atlantic Advisors Inc	7322	191
Atlantic Aero Inc	4522	27
Atlantic American Corp	6311	205
Atlantic American Properties Trust	6798	206
Atlantic and Pacific Freightways	4213	396
Atlantic Aviation	5172	7
Atlantic Bank	6022	62
Atlantic Bay Mortgage Group LLC	6163	33
Atlantic Bingo Supply Inc	5092	27
Atlantic Bookbinders Inc	2789	139
Atlantic Broadband Inc	4899	27
Atlantic Builders Supply Inc	5031	254
Atlantic Business Communications Of Orlando Inc	5065	368
Atlantic Capital Bank	6022	294
Atlantic Carriers Inc	4213	1344
Atlantic Casting and Engineering Corp	3365	20
Atlantic Chemical And Equipment Co	2899	222
Atlantic City Sewerage Co	4952	7
Atlantic City Showboat Inc	7011	76
Atlantic Coast Asphalt Co	2951	17
Atlantic Coast Cabinet Distributors	5031	343
Atlantic Coast Federal Corp	6035	87
Atlantic Coast Fulfillment Inc	2789	69
Atlantic Coast Media Group LLC	7311	87
Atlantic Coast Orthopaedic Medical Supplies Inc	5047	134
Atlantic Coastal Electronics Inc	8731	355
Atlantic Coastal Surgery Center LLC	8011	134
Atlantic Coastal Trucking Co	4213	1453
Atlantic Companies Inc	6531	430
Atlantic Components Inc	5065	366
Atlantic Computer Products Inc	5045	509
Atlantic Computer Products Inc (Beltsville Maryland)	7373	730
Atlantic Container Line Inc	4412	17
Atlantic Control Systems Inc	3613	182
Atlantic Controls Corp	5063	613
Atlantic Corporate Interiors Inc	5021	68
Atlantic Credit and Finance Inc	7322	26
Atlantic Custom Processors LLC	4222	18
Atlantic Data Services Inc	7379	255
Atlantic Detroit Diesel Allison LLC	5084	63
Atlantic Digital Inc	5734	187
Atlantic Distribution Systems	4213	111
Atlantic Electric Supply Corp	5063	377
Atlantic Engineer Products LLC	3537	101
Atlantic Express Coachways	4724	2
Atlantic Express Transportation Group Inc	4151	3
Atlantic Filter Corp	3589	183
Atlantic Food Mart Inc	5411	143
Atlantic Good Services Inc	4213	3091
Atlantic Graphic Services Inc	2752	615
Atlantic India Rubber Co	5085	313
Atlantic Information Services Inc	2741	238
Atlantic Internet Technologies Inc	4813	702
Atlantic List Company Inc	7331	281
Atlantic List Marketing Div	7331	130
Atlantic Magnetics Inc	3677	70
Atlantic Maintenance Corp	7349	220
Atlantic Metal Products Inc	3441	251
Atlantic Metro Communications	4899	185
Atlantic Microwave Corp	3679	214
Atlantic Montana Corp	5063	822
Atlantic Monthly Group	2721	146
Atlantic Mutual Insurance Co	6331	201
Atlantic Optical Company Inc	5048	9
Atlantic Ordinance International Inc	1731	2320
Atlantic Pacific Automotive LP	5013	103
Atlantic Pork and Provisions Inc	2013	183
Atlantic Power and Light Company Inc	1731	832
Atlantic Precision Inc	3599	855

Company Name	SIC	Rank
Atlantic Premium Brands Ltd	5149	20
Atlantic Publication Group LLC	2721	423
Atlantic Realty Companies Inc	6531	93
Atlantic Recording Group	7922	9
Atlantic Relocation Systems	4213	199
Atlantic Rentals and Sales Corp	7359	159
Atlantic Reps	5064	189
Atlantic Sales Company LLC	5085	373
Atlantic Scale Company Inc	5046	73
Atlantic Scientific Corp	3699	119
Atlantic Securities Inc	6211	327
Atlantic Services Inc	8721	95
Atlantic Southeast Airlines Inc	4512	31
Atlantic Southern Financial Group Inc	6035	79
Atlantic Star Trucking Inc	4213	2221
Atlantic States Cast Iron Pipe Company Inc	3312	48
Atlantic States Insurance Co	6331	248
Atlantic Stewardship Bank	6022	383
Atlantic Studios Inc	7389	1340
Atlantic Telecom Inc	5063	298
Atlantic Teleconnect Inc	3496	12
Atlantic Tele-Network Inc	4813	32
Atlantic Telephone and Data Solutions Inc	5063	666
Atlantic Tool and Die Company Inc	3469	45
Atlantic Tooling And Fabricating Company Inc	3545	286
Atlantic Track and Turnout Co	5088	25
Atlantic Ultraviolet Corp	3589	128
Atlantic Veal and Lamb Inc	2011	104
Atlantic Veneer International Corp	2436	16
Atlantic Video Inc	7812	103
Atlantic Wood Industries Inc	2491	8
Atlantic Zeiser Co	3579	13
AtlantiCare Health Plans	6324	78
AtlantiCare Health System	6324	9
Atlantic-Meeco Inc	1629	81
AtlanticNet Broadband Inc	4813	294
AtlanticNet Internet Services Inc	4899	160
Atlantic-Pacific Capital Inc	6799	50
Atlantic-Pacific Processing Systems Inc	7389	2405
Atlantis Adventures LLC	4725	7
Atlantis Equipment Corp	3599	582
Atlantis Software Inc	5045	818
Atlantix Global Systems	5045	58
Atlas Air Inc	4512	19
Atlas Air Worldwide Holdings Inc	6719	51
Atlas Blue Print and Supply Co	7334	58
Atlas Bus Sales Inc	5013	288
Atlas Business Solutions Inc	7372	2661
Atlas Carpet Mills Inc	2273	9
Atlas Concrete Batching Corp	3273	82
Atlas Construction Specialties Company Inc	5032	107
Atlas Container Corp	2653	53
Atlas Copco CMT USA Inc	3532	16
Atlas Copco Hurricane LLC	3563	30
Atlas Copco Mafi-Trench Company LLC	3564	35
Atlas Copco Tools and Assembly Systems LLC	5072	208
Atlas Copco USA Holdings Inc	6722	220
Atlas Data Systems LLC	7379	293
Atlas Development Corp	7371	806
Atlas Electric Company Inc	1731	178
Atlas Energy Inc	4939	6
Atlas Energy LP	4922	12
Atlas Energy Resources LLC	1311	45
Atlas Fibre Co	3083	46
Atlas Foam Products Inc	3086	121
Atlas Food Systems And Services Inc	5962	7
Atlas Foundry Company Inc	3321	33
Atlas Industrial Holdings LLC	1796	3
Atlas Industries Holdings LLC	6719	136
Atlas Instrument Company Inc	3827	160
Atlas Instrument Supply Company Inc	3533	132
Atlas Lift Truck Rentals	5084	12
Atlas Lighting Products Inc	3645	26
Atlas Lithograph Co	2752	1375
Atlas Lock and Tool Inc	5013	416
Atlas Machine And Supply Inc	3599	115
Atlas Machining and Welding Inc	3599	667
Atlas Management Corp	8741	285
Atlas Manufacturing Company Inc	5084	455
Atlas Manufacturing Inc	3523	236
Atlas Match LLC	3999	104
Atlas Material Testing Technology LLC	3823	26
Atlas Merchandising Co	5194	19
Atlas Metal and Iron Corp	5093	64
Atlas Metal Working Corp	3443	234
Atlas Minerals and Chemicals Inc	2891	20
Atlas Model Railroad Company Inc	3944	30
Atlas Motor Express Inc	4213	2017
Atlas O LLC	7389	1481
Atlas Pacific Engineering Co	3556	8
Atlas Peat and Soil Inc	3295	16
Atlas/Pellizzari Electric Inc	1731	553
Atlas Pipeline Partners LP	4613	3
Atlas Putty Products Co	2851	91
Atlas Railroad Construction Co	1629	83
Atlas Recycling Company Inc	5093	239
Atlas Refinery Inc	2843	6
Atlas Roofing Corp	2952	5

Company Name	SIC	Rank
Atlas Software Technologies Inc	7372	1425
Atlas Specialized Transport Inc	4213	2870
Atlas Spring Service	7539	19
Atlas Stamping and Manufacturing Corp	3469	320
Atlas Steel Products Co	5051	95
Atlas Supply Inc	5085	126
Atlas Switch Company Inc	3613	95
Atlas Tag and Label Inc	2672	21
Atlas Technologies Inc	3599	73
Atlas Testing Laboratories Inc	8734	146
Atlas Thread Gage Inc	5131	54
Atlas Tool and Die Works Inc	3469	210
Atlas Traffic Consultants Corp	8721	423
Atlas Transfer and Storage Co	4213	1419
Atlas Van Lines Inc	4213	76
Atlas Venture	6799	129
Atlas Waste Paper Corp	5093	220
Atlas Welding and Boiler Repair Inc	7699	84
Atlas World Group Inc	6719	80
AtLast Fulfillment Inc	7389	493
Atlas-Tuck Concrete Inc	3272	8
Atlaz International Ltd	3577	560
Atlee Of Delaware Inc	3643	100
Atlite Inc	3645	51
ATM Express Inc	5044	37
Atm Solutions Inc	7699	41
Atm Systems Corp	5049	64
Atma Hotel Group Inc	8741	255
Atma-Sphere Music Systems	3651	220
Atmel Corp	3674	29
ATMI Packaging Inc	3565	42
Atmos Corp	3442	96
Atmos Energy Corp	4924	6
Atoka Trailer And Manufacturing LLC	3715	55
Atomatic Manufacturing Co	3599	2378
Atometron	5065	859
Atomic City Tool Inc	3599	2243
Atomic Playpen Inc	7374	240
Atomic Screen Printing and Embroidery	3953	20
Atotech USA Inc	2819	22
Atp Electronics Inc	3572	33
ATP Manufacturing LLC	3089	472
ATP Oil and Gas Corp	1311	59
Atr Distrubiting Inc	5734	276
ATR International Inc	7363	135
ATR Sales Inc	3568	80
ATR Supply Co	5074	99
ATR Systems Inc	5063	1035
A-Trac Computer Sales and Service Inc	5734	329
Atrenta Inc	5045	15
Atrex Inc	1623	32
Atric Technology Inc	5734	392
AtriCure Inc	3841	77
Atrilogy Solutions Group Inc	7379	451
Atrinsic Inc	4899	83
Atrion Corp	3841	55
Atrion Medical Products	3089	455
Atrion Networking Corporation Inc	5065	201
Atritech Inc	3841	311
Atrium Companies Inc	2499	6
Atrium Door And Window Company Of The Rockies	3089	417
Atrium Hr Boston LLC	7363	377
Atrium Medical Corp	3842	45
Atrix International Inc	3579	43
Atronix Sales Inc	3577	317
Ats Commercial Group LLC	7379	1544
ATS Computers Inc	3571	133
ATS Health Services of Jacksonville	8082	60
ATS Medical Inc	3842	59
Ats Parkridge Exchange Inc	7389	2275
Ats Sortimat USA LLC	3569	149
ATS Systems	3555	13
Ats Systems Oregon Inc	3569	62
Ats Workholding Inc	3545	91
Atsco Remanufacturing Inc	3714	213
Atscott Manufacturing Company Inc	3599	17
Atta Boy Automation Inc	3625	391
Attachmate Corp	7371	29
Attainment Company Inc	3999	145
AtTask Inc	7371	410
Attaway Inc	5943	29
Attbar Inc	3089	1198
ATTC Manufacturing Inc	3321	8
Attco Machine Products Inc	3728	158
Attebury Grain Inc	4221	5
Attend Software Corp	7372	3337
Attends Healthcare Products	2676	1
Attensity Corp	7372	1698
Attention Software Inc	7372	1098
Attentive Personnel Inc	7363	284
Atterbury Consultants Inc	8748	451
Attero Tech LLC	7371	867
Attest Systems Inc	7372	2519
Attica Hydraulic Exchange Corp	3594	17
Attitude Drinks Inc	5149	43
ATTO Technology Inc	3577	227
Attorney's Briefcase	5045	519
Attorneys' Computer Network Inc	7372	4661
Attorneys Software Inc	7372	2449
Attorney's Title Guaranty Fund Inc	6361	17

Company Name	SIC	Rank
Attorneys Title Insurance Fund Inc	6361	10
Attronica Computers Inc	7373	230
Attune Systems	3577	229
Attunity Inc	7372	1376
Attwood Corp	3089	177
ATV Bakery Inc	2051	180
Atw Companies Inc	6719	157
Atw Electronics Inc	3677	104
ATW Manufacturing Company Inc	3081	120
Atwater Inc	2282	6
Atwater-General Corp	1446	13
Atwood Adhesives Inc	2891	122
Atwood Corp	3556	131
Atwood Distributing Inc	5399	9
Atwood Hunter Co	1381	21
Atwood Mobile Products	3714	124
Atwood Oceanics Inc	1381	16
Atwood Security Services Inc	7381	78
Atwood Tool and Machine Inc	3545	335
ATX Communications Inc	4813	52
ATX Group Inc	4899	67
ATX/Kleinrock	7372	657
ATX Technologies Inc	3669	20
Atypon Systems Inc	7372	1755
Atzenhoffer Chevrolet Company Inc	5511	214
Aubrey Group Inc	8999	188
Aubrey Organics Inc	2844	127
Aubrey Silvey Enterprises Inc	1629	76
Auburn Armature Inc	7694	5
Auburn Bean and Grain	0723	14
Auburn Buick Pontiac GMC	5511	658
Auburn Electrical Construction Company Inc	1731	249
Auburn Gear Inc	3714	271
Auburn Journal Inc	2711	81
Auburn National Bancorporation Inc	6022	213
Auburn Supply Co	5074	130
Auburn Vacuum Forming Company Inc	3563	56
Aucilla Inc	3089	1356
AUCOTEC Inc	7372	3063
Auction Services Inc	7389	490
Auction Software Inc	7371	1638
Auction Systems Auctioneers and Appraisers Inc	7389	759
AuctionPay	7372	1540
Auctions By The Bay Inc	7389	2193
Auctor Corp	3674	465
Audax Group LP	6726	66
Audax Management Company LLC	6799	71
Audi of America Inc	5012	38
Audible Inc	7389	268
Audience Science	7372	1216
Audienco Voting Inc	3577	562
Audient Inc	3699	290
Audigy Group LLC	6324	112
Audina Hearing Instruments Inc	3842	169
Audio Accessories Inc	3663	205
Audio Amateur Inc	2721	330
Audio Authority Corp	3613	76
Audio Central Alarm Inc	7382	132
Audio Command Systems Inc	1731	388
Audio Connection Inc	5731	129
Audio Craft Company Inc	5731	17
Audio Direct LLC	5731	206
Audio Elite Inc	5731	247
Audio Encounters Inc	5731	133
Audio Equipment Co	5044	161
Audio Ethics Inc	5731	21
Audio Images Corp	5731	216
Audio Installation Company LLC	5731	109
Audio Intervisual Design Inc	5045	411
Audio Journal Inc	4832	295
Audio Messaging Solutions	7389	758
Audio Precision Inc	3829	153
Audio Productions Inc	3652	54
Audio Properties Inc	7389	1595
Audio Sounds Electronics Inc	5065	560
Audio Technology Inc	3669	193
Audio Video Caribe Inc	5731	230
Audio Video Color Corp	2671	40
Audio Video Communication Store Inc	5731	262
Audio Video International Ltd	5731	245
Audio Video Lifestyles Inc	5731	220
Audio Video Systems Inc	7379	588
Audio Vision Inc	5731	182
Audio Visions South Inc	5731	130
Audio Visual Aids Co	5043	35
Audio Visual Mart Inc	7359	67
Audio Visual Services Corp	7389	105
Audio West	1731	2356
Audio Xcellence Inc	5731	80
Audiobahn Inc	5065	110
AudioDev USA Inc	3669	37
Audiodontics Inc	3669	283
Audiology Online Inc	4813	660
AudiomidiCom	5734	72
Audion Automation Ltd	3565	154
Audiophile Systems Inc	5731	52
Audioplex Technology Inc	3083	55
Audioscribe Corp	5045	953
Audio-Sears Corp	3661	139
Audio-Technica US Inc	5065	223
Audio-Video Corp	5064	62
Audio-Video Supply Inc	5099	111

Company Name	SIC	Rank
Audiovisual Consultations Inc	5731	219
Audiovisual Inc	5731	18
Audissey	5065	284
Audiss-Thorsen Inc	1731	2577
Audit Logistics LLC	7389	2244
Audit Systems Inc	7322	124
Auditec of St Louis	3679	802
Audix Corporation USA	3651	166
Audrey Golden Associates Ltd	7361	351
Audrey Morris Cosmetics International Incorpora	5122	100
Audubon Media Corp	2752	780
Audubon Metals LLC	3341	11
Auer Precision Stamping Inc	3469	131
Auerbach Grayson and Company Inc	6211	136
Aufderworld Corp	1799	121
Aufrance Associates	7379	1227
Auger Enterprises Inc	6513	26
Augerscope Inc	3423	55
Auglaize-Erie Machine	3599	1611
Augme Technologies Inc	7371	1135
Augmentix Inc	5045	237
AuGrid Global Holdings Corp	3674	505
Augsburg Fortress Publishers	3443	46
August Home Publishing Co	2721	143
August Lang and Husak	7311	509
August Lotz Company Inc	2541	64
August Pensa Modern Movers Corp	4213	2949
August Schell Brewing Co	2082	70
August Software Corp	7372	5020
August Transport Inc	4213	2174
August Winter and Sons Inc	1711	10
Augusta Fiberglass Coatings Inc	3089	117
Augusta Focus Inc	2711	427
Augusta Ready Mix Inc	5032	34
Augusta Sportswear Inc	2329	35
Augusta Transportation Inc	4213	772
Augusta Wine Inc	2084	123
Augustus Barnett Advertising/Design	7311	995
Aui Contractors LLC	1542	236
Auld Co	3993	145
Aulds and Garner Tele-Com Services Inc	1731	816
Ault Electric Company Inc	1731	671
Ault Inc	3629	26
Aumens Asner Inc	7389	1781
Aumiller Youngquist PC	8712	178
Aumtech Inc	7373	674
Aunt Beth's Products Inc	2052	87
Aunt Lizzie's Cheese Straws Inc	2022	44
Aunt Martha's Youth Service Center Inc	8322	228
Aunt Sarahs LLC	5812	359
Auntie Anne's Inc	2096	17
Aura Energy Corp	6519	24
Aura Systems Inc	3827	122
Auralog SA	7372	993
Aureus Solutions Inc	7371	1823
AurGroup Financial Credit Union	6062	20
Aurico Reports Inc	7389	1085
AuriQ Systems Inc	7372	3594
Auritec Pharmaceuticals Inc	8731	370
Auritt Communications Group	7311	569
Aurora and Quanta Productions	2741	204
Aurora Bearing Co	3568	24
Aurora Blacktop Inc	1611	45
Aurora Capital Group	6799	198
Aurora Casket Company Inc	3995	3
Aurora Circuits LLC	3672	193
Aurora Communications	4832	219
Aurora Computer Systems Inc	3571	208
Aurora Contractors Inc	1629	38
Aurora Cooperative Elevator Co	5153	135
Aurora Diagnostics Inc	8731	50
Aurora Electric Inc	1731	895
Aurora Flight Sciences Corp	3721	19
Aurora Hardwoods Inc	5023	96
Aurora Health Care Inc	8062	28
Aurora Imaging Technology Inc	3841	158
Aurora Information Systems	5045	520
Aurora Information Systems Inc	7379	1470
Aurora Logistics Inc	4213	2296
Aurora Medical Group Inc	8011	76
Aurora Metals Division LLC	3364	12
Aurora Networks Inc	3669	63
Aurora Pump	3561	57
Aurora Research Company Inc	3572	87
Aurora Software Inc	7371	1174
Aurora Specialty Chemistries Corp	2899	182
Aurora Technical Services Ltd	3829	490
Aurum Assembly Plus Inc	3672	326
AUS Inc	8732	7
Ausco Products Inc	3714	297
Ausmus Corp	4213	1770
Auspex Inc	7372	3979
Auspex Pharmaceuticals Inc	8731	372
Austell Box Board Corp	2652	16
Aus-Tex Duplicators Inc	2752	324
Austin Air Systems Ltd	3564	72
Austin American Technology Corp	3679	611
Austin Architectural Graphics Inc	3993	169
Austin Chemical Company Inc	8742	377
Austin Chronicle Corp	2711	507
Austin Commercial Inc	1541	27
Austin Co	8712	15

Company Name	SIC	Rank
Austin Company Of Greensboro	3644	16
Austin Digital Inc	3812	163
Austin Electric Co	1731	2027
Austin General Contracting Inc	1542	360
Austin GeoModeling Inc	8999	156
Austin Hardware and Supply Inc	5013	38
Austin Horn Collection	2269	11
Austin Industries Inc	1542	11
Austin International Inc	5084	404
Austin Jet Corp	5599	22
Austin/Lawrence Group	7311	648
Austin Mac Haik Ford Lincoln Mercury Ltd	5511	158
Austin Newspapers Inc	2711	633
Austin Packaging Co	2099	117
Austin Powder Co	2892	3
Austin Pump and Supply Co	5084	249
Austin Resources Corp	1382	69
Austin Telecommunications and Electrical Inc	1731	1426
Austin Tri-Hawk Automotive Inc	3469	97
Austin Trust Co	6091	11
Austin Urethane Inc	2821	99
Austin/Westran	3714	263
Austin White Lime Co	3274	2
Austin-Abbott Inc	3089	1695
Austin-Mac Inc	3535	160
Austin's Bestline Inc	4813	603
Austin's Tropical Plant Leasing Inc	7359	222
Austin-Westran LLC	3715	31
Austrian Machine Corp	3555	90
Austro Mold Inc	3089	891
Autec Inc	3559	193
AuthenTec Inc	3674	152
AuthentiDate Holding Corp	7373	749
Authentix Inc	7382	19
Authoria Inc	7372	1146
Authority Domains Inc	4813	726
Authority For Educational Television Kentucky	4833	144
Authorized Earmold Labs	3842	202
Authorized Taxi Cab	7382	68
AuthorizeNet Holdings Inc	7379	102
Authors Registry Inc	8111	555
authsec	7379	650
Auto Appearance Specialists	5013	268
Auto Body Panels Inc	5012	44
Auto Butler Inc	3589	79
Auto Chlor System Inc	5064	28
Auto/Con Corp	3549	27
Auto Craft Radiators	5013	355
Auto Craft Tool and Die Co	3544	302
Auto Crane Co	3713	39
Auto Electric and Battery Inc	3694	54
Auto Europe Inc	7514	5
Auto FX Corp	7372	4662
Auto Locator	5511	1247
Auto Mall Inc	5511	1024
Auto Master	5013	373
Auto Metal Craft Inc	3465	60
Auto Meter Products Inc	3824	11
Auto Page Inc	5063	758
Auto Parts Employees Credit Union	6062	120
Auto Physics LLC	3679	865
Auto Recyclers Inc	5015	34
Auto Service Company Inc	7514	12
Auto Shop Equipment Company Inc	5013	335
Auto Sounds	5731	139
Auto Tran Inc	3829	282
Auto Warehousing Co	4226	2
Auto Wares Inc	5013	22
AutoAccessoriesGaragecom	5531	65
AutoAlliance International Inc	3711	15
Autobase Inc	7371	409
Autobody Products Inc	5013	152
Autobooks Inc	5085	391
Autobytel Inc	7379	143
Autocam Corp	3714	118
AutoCell Laboratories Inc	3669	85
Autochart Inc	5045	985
Auto-Comm Engineering Corp	3663	88
AutoComm Inc	3993	178
Autocraft Manufacturing Company Inc	3714	403
Autocrat LLC	2087	16
AutoData Systems	7372	2380
Autodesk Inc	7372	28
AutoDesSys Inc	7372	2821
Autodocs LLC	7372	4191
Autodraft Inc	7373	567
Autoexec Computer Systems Inc	7379	1014
Autoform Tool and Manufacturing Inc	3561	83
Auto-Gas Systems Inc	3578	25
AutoGenomics Inc	2835	69
AutoGraph International Inc	7372	3980
Autographics Inc	2752	1713
Auto-Graphics Inc	7372	2508
AutoInfo Inc	4215	2
Autoliv ASP Inc	3714	17
Autologue Computer Systems Inc	7371	796
Automanager Inc	7371	1440
Automart International Inc	5013	217
Automaster Motor Company Inc	5511	446
Automate Tech Inc	3559	542
Automated Accounting Systems Inc	7372	4486

Company Name	SIC	Rank
Automated Assembly Corp	3663	210
Automated Blasting Systems Inc	3559	532
Automated Building Components Inc	2431	34
Automated Building Components Mill-work Div	2431	35
Automated Business Products Inc	5999	239
Automated Business Resources Inc	5044	72
Automated Cable Services Inc	1731	1883
Automated Case Management Systems Inc	7372	3308
Automated Circuit Technology Inc	3679	476
Automated Collection Services Inc	7322	89
Automated Control Concepts Inc	7373	437
Automated Control Logic Inc	3674	439
Automated Controls Inc	1731	953
Automated Conveyor Systems Inc	3535	30
Automated Data Systems Inc	5044	162
Automated Direct Mail Inc	7331	211
Automated Direct Mail Service Center Inc	7331	205
Automated Edm Inc	7389	1955
Automated Energy Controls Inc	1731	1970
Automated Entry Systems Inc	1731	1324
Automated Equipment Co	3446	49
Automated Financial Systems Inc	7372	680
Automated Financial Technologies LLC	3578	35
Automated Finishing Inc	3582	15
Automated Industrial Machine Inc	3569	242
Automated Industrial Motion	3823	283
Automated Industrial Systems Inc	3953	19
Automated Installment Systems	6159	88
Automated License Systems Inc	7372	138
Automated Logic Design Company Inc	7372	717
Automated Logic Marietta Control	8742	681
Automated Lumber Handling Inc	3553	61
Automated Machinery Inc	7699	224
Automated Mailing Systems Inc	7389	2024
Automated Media Inc	7371	233
Automated Medical Products Corp	3841	419
Automated Molding Corp	3089	449
Automated Power Co	5063	558
Automated Power Technologies	5045	379
Automated Precision Inc	3826	70
Automated Presort Inc	7389	746
Automated Process Equipment Corp	3556	120
Automated Processes Inc	3651	147
Automated Production Machining Inc	3599	2398
Automated Products Inc	2439	35
Automated Programming Technologies Inc	7372	3658
Automated Quality Technologies Inc	3829	259
Automated Resources Group Inc	5045	186
Automated Routing Inc	2499	26
Automated Switching And Controls Inc	7373	963
Automated Systems Engineering Inc	3822	92
Automated Systems Inc	3535	145
Automated Systems Inc (Lincoln Nebraska)	7371	267
Automated Systems Of Tacoma LLC	3599	611
Automated Systems Technology Inc	3555	70
Automated Tech Tools Inc	7371	1453
Automated Technology Equipment Consultants Inc	3011	27
Automated Teller Accessories Inc	7349	163
Automated Trading Desk LLC	7372	984
Automated Training Systems Inc	7372	1548
Automated Vision LLC	3577	540
Automated Wheel	3471	9
Automatic Bakery Machine Inc	5113	60
Automatic Control Electronics Company Inc	3823	378
Automatic Control Systems Inc	5063	884
Automatic Controls Co	5084	704
Automatic Data Processing Inc	7374	2
Automatic Door Service Of Grand Rapids Inc	5063	950
Automatic Door Systems LLC	1731	2020
Automatic Electric Inc	1731	2112
Automatic Entrances Of Wisconsin Inc	5063	442
Automatic Equipment Manufacturing Co	3523	84
Automatic Feed Co	3549	11
Automatic Feeder Company Inc	3569	206
Automatic Fire Sprinklers Inc	1711	102
Automatic Firing Inc	3823	286
Automatic Forecasting Systems Inc	7372	4275
Automatic Funds Transfer Services Inc	7374	266
Automatic Ice Machine Company Inc	5078	36
Automatic Identification Systems Inc	7379	1465
Automatic Inspection Systems Inc	3827	105
Automatic Irrigation Supply Company Indiana Inc	5083	125
Automatic Laundry Services Company Inc	7359	147
Automatic Machine Products Sales Co	3494	58
Automatic Mail Services Inc	7331	207
Automatic Pool Covers Inc	5999	180
Automatic Power Inc	3812	76
Automatic Printing Company Inc	2396	38
Automatic Products Company Inc	3451	91
Automatic Products Corp	3599	199
Automatic Spring Products Corp	3493	3
Automatic Tool Control And Management Systems Inc	3829	224

Company Name	SIC	Rank
Automating Peripherals Inc	5045	203
Automation and Control Services Inc	3625	239
Automation And Control Technology Inc	3829	173
Automation and Controls Engineering Ltd	8711	693
Automation And Mechanical Services Inc	3625	390
Automation and Modular Components Inc	3535	105
Automation Associates Inc	3541	273
Automation Center Inc	5085	406
Automation Components Inc	3822	25
Automation Control Company Inc	5063	794
Automation Devices Inc	3569	159
Automation Displays Inc	3669	253
Automation Dynamics LLC	3581	13
Automation Graphics Inc	5112	72
Automation Image Inc	7373	307
Automation International Inc	3548	38
Automation ONSPEC Software Inc	7372	2270
Automation Plastics Corp	3089	921
Automation Precision Technology Inc	8711	264
Automation Printing Co	2752	825
Automation Resources Inc	7371	594
Automation Services Company Inc	7371	1229
Automation Solutions Company LLC	7373	880
Automation Specialists Inc	3549	116
Automation Systems and Control Inc	3625	373
Automation Systems and Services	5063	1092
Automation Systems Inc	8711	611
Automation Technologies Inc	7371	578
Automation Technology Inc	3829	341
Automation Tool and Die Inc	3544	267
Automation Tool Co	3569	84
Automation West Inc	3599	2253
Automec Inc	3549	95
Automecha International Ltd	3579	23
Autometrics	5012	160
Automobile Club of Michigan	6331	85
Automobile Consumer Services Inc	5511	1027
Automobile Protection Corp	6399	5
Automoco LLC	3714	342
Automotion Inc	3535	25
Automotive Business Management Consultants Inc	5734	63
Automotive Business Management Consulting Inc	7372	1476
Automotive Finance Corp	6159	20
Automotive Importing Manufacturing Inc	3694	10
Automotive Information Systems Inc	7375	62
Automotive International Inc	5169	56
Automotive Investment Group Inc (Phoenix Arizona)	5511	6
Automotive Manufacturing and Supply Company Inc	5013	180
Automotive Parts Headquarters Inc	5013	97
Automotive Parts Sales Inc	5013	206
Automotive Precision Machinery Inc	5084	654
Automotive Rentals Inc	7515	5
Automotive Resources International	7515	2
Automotive Servicenter Inc	3599	981
Automotive Services Inc	7312	34
Automotive Supply Associates Inc	5013	32
Automotive Supply Co	5013	40
Automotive Systems Warehouse Inc	5013	271
Automotive Testing And Development Services Inc	7549	15
Automundo Productions Inc	2721	393
AutoNation Inc	5511	1
Autonnic Manufacturing Inc	3825	337
Autonomy etalk	3661	113
Autonomy Inc	7372	964
Autonomy Interwoven Inc	7372	195
Autonomy Technology Inc	5063	312
Auto-Owners Insurance Co	6411	6
Autoparts Holdings Ltd	3714	108
Autopower Corp	7372	2612
Autoquip Corp	3537	27
Autoroll Print Technologies LLC	3555	105
Autosem Inc	3679	734
Autosig Systems Inc	7372	2942
Autosound and Security Inc	5731	144
Autosplice Inc	3643	22
Auto-Swage Products Inc	3599	1341
Auto-Systems and Service Inc	3559	415
Autotec Engineering Co	8711	483
Autotest Co	5961	119
Autotool Inc	3559	299
Autotote Lottery Corp	5045	22
AutoTradercom LLC	7375	155
Auto-trol Technology Corp	7372	2023
Auto-Tronic Control Co	3613	147
Autotronic Controls Corp	3694	19
Autotronics Inc	3625	264
AutoTruck Federal Credit Union	6061	108
Auto-Turn Manufacturing Inc	3599	766
Autrey Furniture Manufacturing Inc	5712	100
Autronics Corp	3679	294
Autry Greer and Sons Inc	5411	100
Autumn Enterprises Inc	7361	205
Autumn Transport Inc	4213	1300
Autumn-Harp Inc	2844	113
Auvi Coll Inc	7322	128

Company Name	SIC	Rank
Auvil Fruit Company Inc	0175	3
Auxier Welding Inc	7699	78
Auxilium Pharmaceuticals Inc	2834	96
Auxis Inc	7371	213
Av Connection Inc	7378	24
AV Systems Inc	7372	3309
AV Transportation Inc	4213	2632
Ava Electric Company Inc	1731	431
Ava Electronics Corp	3643	132
Ava Industries Inc	2295	23
Avab America Inc	3625	241
AVAC of Myrtle Beach Inc	5731	76
Available Plastics Inc	3089	678
Avalara Inc	7372	215
Avalere Health LLC	8742	391
Avalign Technologies Inc	3842	106
Avalon Acoustics Inc	5731	167
Avalon and Tahoe Manufacturing Inc	3732	60
Avalon Correctional Services Inc	8744	26
Avalon Digital Marketing Systems Inc	7311	883
Avalon Equipment Corp	7359	139
Avalon Global Group Inc	6719	60
Avalon Group Ltd	6211	341
Avalon Holdings Corp	4953	71
Avalon Home Cleaning Inc	7349	462
Avalon International Inc	7374	150
Avalon Laboratories LLC	3069	77
Avalon Place Trinity	7363	288
Avalon Vision Solutions LLC	3823	376
AvalonBay Communities Inc	6798	35
Avanade Inc	7389	24
Avanel Industries Inc	3825	267
AVANIR Pharmaceuticals Inc	2834	306
Avankia LLC	8748	296
Avanquest Global Software Publishing	7372	210
Avanquest North America Inc	7371	528
Avans Machine Inc	3549	60
Avantair Inc	4724	30
Avantcom Corp	7371	1851
Avantec Vascular Corp	3841	280
Avant-Garde Technology Inc	3678	80
Avanti Circuits Inc	3672	206
Avanti Destinations Inc	4725	39
Avanti Engineering Inc	5072	197
Avanti Foods Co	2022	64
Avanti Linens Inc	2395	3
Avanti Polar Lipids Inc	2833	51
Avanti Press Inc	2771	17
Avanti Resources LLC	3625	354
AvantLinkcom	7379	790
Avantor Performance Materials Inc	2899	52
Avantstar Inc	5045	725
Avatar Corp	2843	8
Avatar Entertainment Corp	7389	726
Avatar Holdings Inc	1531	78
Avatar NuMedia	2741	470
Avatar Properties Inc	6531	161
Avatar Realty Inc	6531	332
Avatar Retirement Communities Inc	1522	21
Avatar Studios Inc	7812	198
Avatar Systems Ltd	7373	560
Avatier Corp	7372	1008
AVAX America Inc	8731	285
AVAX Technologies Inc	8731	407
Avaya Inc	7373	4
Avb Inc	2051	190
Avco Meat Company Inc	0751	11
Avco Supply Inc	5074	200
AvCom International	2731	308
Avcom Smt Inc	3672	424
Avcon Industries	3721	21
Avcor Health Care Products Inc	3842	143
Ave Electric Inc	1731	1186
Ave Maria Press Inc	2731	293
Avebe America Inc	5169	151
Avectra Inc	7372	144
Aved Electronics Inc	3357	48
Avedis Zildjian Co	3931	14
Avedon Engineering Inc	3089	428
Avela Corp	7336	100
AVEMCO Insurance Co	6331	319
Avendra LLC	7389	210
Aventine Renewable Energy Holdings Inc	2899	27
Avenue A/NYC LLC	7311	253
Avenue A/Razorfish	7311	169
Avenue Code LLC	7371	550
Avenue Energy Inc	1311	177
Avenue Group Inc	1311	272
Avenue Inc (Troy Ohio)	5621	35
Avenue Tv Cable Service Inc	4841	131
AVEO Pharmaceuticals Inc	2834	194
AvePoint Inc	7372	762
Aver Inc	7379	1228
Avera Mckennan Hospital and University Center	8062	141
Avera Pharmaceuticals Inc	8731	301
Averitt Express Inc	4213	10
AVerMedia Technologies Inc	5045	377
Avers Machine and Manufacturing Inc	3599	2105
Avery Dennison Corp	2891	2
Avery Manufacturing LLC	5084	939
Avery Publishing Group Inc	2731	287
AVES Audio Visual Systems Inc	5064	219

Company Name	SIC	Rank
Avesis Inc	7389	267
Avesis Third Party Administrators Inc	7389	571
Avesta Computer Services Ltd	7379	114
Aveva Engineering IT	5045	687
Avex Electronics Corp	3691	36
Avexxis Corp	7371	622
Avfuel Corp	5172	97
Avg Advanced Technologies LP	3672	40
AVG Technologies USA Inc	7371	441
AVI BioPharma Inc	2834	241
Avi Communications Inc	3663	383
Aviad Corp	7319	48
Aviagen Group	0251	2
Aviall Inc	5084	5
Aviall Product Repair Services Inc	4581	9
Avian Engineering LLC	8748	266
A'viands LLC	8742	137
Aviat Aircraft Inc	3721	35
Aviat Networks Inc	3663	18
Aviation Brake Services Inc	5088	83
Aviation Capital Group Corp	4522	19
Aviation Leasing Group	4522	23
Aviation Network Services LLC	7629	28
Aviation Software	7372	4945
Aviation Technology Inc	3829	264
Aviation Week Group	2741	77
Avibank Manufacturing Inc	3965	2
Avid Identification Systems Inc	3674	217
Avid Media Venture Inc	2721	418
Avid Technology Inc	3861	5
Avid Technology Worldwide Inc	3651	18
Avidex Industries LLC	5099	51
Avidian Technologies Inc	7371	1372
Avilar Technologies Inc	7372	1257
Avila's Garden Art	3272	99
Avineon Inc	7373	130
Avio-Diepen Inc	5088	81
Avion Graphics Inc	2752	1092
Avionic Instruments Inc	3629	34
Avionics Interface Technologies LLC	3829	134
Avioserv San Diego Inc	5088	30
Avis Budget Group Inc	6794	2
Avis Ford Inc	5511	247
Avis Group Holdings Inc	7514	2
Avis Industrial Corp	3429	3
Avis Roto-Die Co	3544	81
Avisio Inc (Riverside California)	3577	658
Avision Labs Inc	3577	70
Avista Capital Holdings LP	6799	113
Avista Corp	4931	23
Avista Design Systems	7372	5028
Avista Inc	7371	148
Avistar Communications Corp	3577	245
Aviston Lumber Co	2439	19
Aviva Life and Annuity Co	6311	143
Aviva Petroleum Inc	1311	282
Avizent	8742	106
AVK Industries Inc	3829	444
Avl Instrumentation and Test Systems Inc	3823	73
AVL Looms Inc	7372	4228
AVM Enterprises Inc	5046	77
AVM Instrument Company Ltd	3663	405
Avmark Inc	8748	395
AvMed Health Plans	6324	34
Avnet Inc	5065	2
Avnet Memec	3674	27
Avocent Corp	3577	28
Avocet Systems Inc	7372	4235
Avolution Ltd	5045	604
Avon Books	2731	124
Avon Broach and Production Company LLC	3599	1509
Avon Custom Mixing Services Inc	3069	237
Avon Engineered Fabrications Inc	3443	164
Avon Plastic Products Inc	3089	993
Avon Products Inc	2844	1
Avon Workshop Inc	2512	87
Avondale Partners LLC	6799	54
Avondale Trucking Div	4213	886
Avon-Dixon Agency LLC	6321	60
Avontus Software Corp	7372	3338
Avotec Inc	3845	122
Avow Systems Inc	7371	1748
Avox Systems Inc	3728	26
Avrett Free and Ginsberg Advertising Inc	7311	64
AVS Group Inc	5087	133
AVS Supply Inc	5089	1865
AVST	3577	186
AvSupport Inc	7389	649
Avtec Corp	7371	1811
Avtec Finishing Systems Inc	3471	62
Avtec Homes	1521	133
Avtech Corp	3728	86
Avtech Inc	3625	246
AVTECH Software Inc	7372	1801
Avtone Management Consulting	7379	1485
Avtron Aerospace Inc	3825	57
Avure Technologies LLC	3556	66
Avw Equipment Company Inc	3589	201
AVX Corp	3675	2
AVX Tantalum Corp	3675	5
AW Bohanan Company Inc	5084	622

Company Name	SIC	Rank
Aw Carbide Fabricators Inc	3545	397
AW Coulter Trucking	4213	502
AW Die Engraving Inc	3544	482
AW Faber-Castell USA Inc	5092	26
AW Imported Auto Parts Inc	5013	266
AW Marshall Co	5194	18
AW Mercer Inc	3444	93
Aw Sheepscot Holding Company Inc	3571	140
AW Technical Center USA Inc	3714	188
AWA Security Inc	7381	168
Awad Brothers LLC	5064	105
Award/VisionPs Inc	2759	602
Aware Electronics Corp	3577	66
Aware Inc	3674	199
Aware Products LLC	2844	67
Aware Security Corp	6211	90
Aware Systems Inc	7371	1067
Awareness Technology Inc	3827	22
AWB Industries Inc	3546	27
A-Web Internet Marketing Services Corp	4813	683
Awerkamp Machine Co	3599	711
Awesome Technologies Inc	7373	617
Aweta-Autoline Inc	3523	141
AWGM Inc	8711	462
Awh Corp	2599	11
Awi Inc	5065	259
AWM Mold Service US Inc	3669	286
Awp Copperfield Inc	6163	35
Awp Industries Inc	3315	18
AWS Convergence Technologies Inc	7375	39
AWS Inc	8331	91
Aws Industries Inc	3728	161
Awtec USA Inc	3714	114
AXA Art Insurance Corp	6331	255
AXA Distributors LLC	6411	55
AXA Equitable Life Insurance Co	6411	10
AXA Financial Inc	6311	3
AXA Roseberg Investment Management LLC	6282	29
Axcel Photonics Inc	3652	26
Axcelerate Networks Inc	3825	300
Axcelis Technologies Inc	3559	23
Axcess Broadcast Services Inc	7313	34
Axcess International Inc	7373	591
Axcess Technology Source LLC	5065	1000
Axeda Corp	7372	1653
Axel Plastics Research Laboratories Inc	2992	51
Axel Protection Systems Inc	7381	77
Axelgaard Manufacturing Company Ltd	3823	68
Axeon Water Technologies	3589	134
Axes Technologies Inc	3577	419
Axesstel Inc	3613	24
Axiam Inc	3825	157
Axic Inc	3559	502
Axil Corp	3061	30
Axiom Design Inc	8711	624
Axiom Electronics Inc	3679	292
Axiom Hr Solutions Inc	7363	362
Axiom Industries Inc	2821	202
Axiom International Services Inc	7372	719
Axiom Legal	8111	549
Axiom Marketing Inc	7311	758
Axiom Resource Management Inc	8742	205
Axiom Software Laboratories Inc	7372	376
Axiom Systems Inc	7371	951
Axiom Technology Inc (Chino California)	5045	10
Axiom Technology Inc (Madison Alabama)	7372	1233
AxioMed Spine Corp	3841	366
Axion Corp	3599	1191
Axion International Holdings Inc	3086	171
Axion Power International Inc	3699	239
Axios Inc (Grand Rapids Michigan)	7363	140
Axios Products Inc	7372	2943
Axios Systems Inc	7373	940
Axis Business Solutions Ltd	5045	440
Axis Clinical Software Inc	7371	1279
Axis Communications Inc	5045	49
Axis Computer Systems Inc	7372	372
Axis Group LLC	7379	501
Axis Microsystems Inc	7373	868
Axis Products Inc	3714	257
Axis Welding and Machine Works Inc	3599	804
Axispoint Inc	7373	325
Axletree Media Inc	4813	639
Axley Brynelson LLP	8111	485
AXM Pharma Inc	2834	402
AxoGen Inc	3845	135
Axom Technologies Inc	7373	390
Axon Aerospace Inc	2851	108
Axon Circuit Inc	3672	235
Axon LLC	3565	109
Axonix Corp	3577	525
Axper Corp	3571	209
AXSA Document Solutions Inc	5044	21
Axson North America Inc	2821	163
AXS-One Inc	7372	1593
AXSYS Technologies Inc	3827	6
Axsys Technologies Inc Precision Machined Products Div	3679	187
Axton Candy and Tobacco Co	5194	12

Company Name	SIC	Rank
Axure Software Solutions Inc	7372	3047
Axxis Network and Telecommunications Inc	1731	450
Axya Medical Inc	3841	293
Ay Machine Co	3599	2299
AY McDonald Industries Inc	3432	6
AY McDonald Manufacturing Co	3432	19
AY McDonald Supply Company Inc	5074	44
Aya Associates Inc	7372	2944
Ayala Corp	7361	171
Ayala Electric Company Inc	1731	1971
Ayantra Inc	3661	198
Aydin Displays Inc	3661	43
Aylward Enterprises Inc	3565	43
Ayoka	7371	514
Ayre Acoustics Inc	3651	150
Ayres Associates	8711	146
Ayuda Management Corp	1541	210
Ayzenberg Group	8742	133
Az Department Transportation Equipment Services	5046	288
AZ Industries Inc	3499	120
A-Z Manufacturing Inc	3599	1168
Az Security and Equipment Inc	5063	1075
Az Technology Inc	7373	949
AZ Used Computers Inc	5734	404
Azadi Television Inc	4833	165
Azalea Capital	6799	87
Azalea Software Inc	7372	3864
Azar Computer Software Services Inc	7373	1078
Azar Electric Inc	1731	1572
Azar's Natural Foods Inc	2099	333
Azco Inc	1629	49
Azcomp Technologies Inc	7379	1529
Azego Technology Services Inc (Ramsey New Jersey)	3559	466
Azentek LLC	5045	752
Azimuth Custom Extrusions LLC	3081	122
Azimuth Electronics Inc	3825	269
Azimuth Inc	8711	509
Azimuth Systems Inc	5045	171
Azimuth Unlimited LLC	3663	384
AZMY Thinkware Inc	7372	1127
Aznet	3699	185
AZO Inc	3559	170
Azonic Products Inc	3677	128
Azonix Corp	3829	59
AZPB LP	7941	17
Aztalan Engineering Inc	3599	447
Aztar Corp	7999	28
Aztar Indiana Gaming Company LLC	7993	15
Aztec Capital LLC	5999	185
Aztec Electronics Inc	3672	349
Aztec Group Inc	6162	80
Aztec Machinery Co	3567	66
Aztec Manufacturing Corp	3714	132
Aztec Mechanical Inc	1711	241
Aztec Messenger Inc	7389	1641
Aztec Products Inc	3589	228
Aztec Rental Center No 2 Inc	7353	40
Aztec Supply Co	5162	70
Aztec Systems Corp	7336	259
Azteca Communications Inc	4832	247
Azteca Enterprises Inc	1542	159
Azteca Foods Inc	2096	10
Azteca Milling Co	2041	12
Azteca Restaurant Enterprises Inc	5812	87
Aztech Labs Inc	3577	244
Aztech Rentals Of San Antonio Inc	7359	137
Az-Tech Software Inc	7372	3865
AZTEK Inc	7373	724
Aztek Tool Company Inc	3089	1603
Aztron Chemical Services Inc	2842	173
AzTx Cattle Co	0211	5
Azumano Travel Service Inc	4724	73
Azura Photo Albums LLC	7384	51
Azuro Inc	7371	583
AZZ Inc	3648	1
B and A Construction Inc	1623	701
B and A Friction Materials Inc	5013	287
B and A Hyder Trucking Company Inc	4213	1607
B and A Manufacturing Co	3545	142
B and A Marine Company Inc	7699	128
B and B Adcrafters Inc	2759	544
B and B ARMR Corp	3441	21
B and B Auto Parts Inc	5013	173
B and B Collections Inc	7322	98
B and B Concrete Company Inc	1771	13
B and B Corporate Holdings Inc	5411	244
B and B Designed Systems Inc	1731	629
B and B Electric Inc	1731	1240
B and B Electronics Manufacturing Co	3825	36
B and B Equipment and Supply Inc	5046	126
B and B Equipment Sales Inc	5013	371
B and B Excavating Inc	3273	24
B and B International Inc	5049	202
B and B Land Clearing Company Inc	1623	532
B and B Lighting Inc	5063	980
B and B Lighting Supply Inc	5719	37
B and B Lingerie Company Inc	3842	324
B and B Lumber Company Inc	2448	22
B and B Machine and Grinding Service Corp	3599	616
B and B Machine and Tool Inc	3599	752
B and B Manufacturing Inc	3599	2401
B and B Marble Inc	5032	111
B and B Office Supply Inc	5943	45
B and B Paper Converters Inc	2621	68
B and B Pipe And Tool Co	3599	621
B and B Poultry Company Inc	2015	41
B and B Precision Inc	3599	2430
B and B Precision Manufacturing Inc	3545	282
B and B Precision Tool Co	3544	805
B and B Printers Inc	2752	992
B and B Printing Company Inc	2752	267
B and B Sooner Inc	5082	185
B and B Surplus Inc	5051	171
B and B Technology Inc	3564	87
B and B Test Solutions Inc	8748	407
B and B Tool and Die Company Inc	3544	294
B and B Tool And Die Inc	3399	38
B and B Tool Co	3599	1820
B and B Transformer Inc	3612	99
B and B Tritech Inc	2842	116
B and B Trucking Inc	4213	2950
B and C Computer Vision and Atari Sales and Service	5046	109
B and C Construction Company Inc	1623	242
B and C Data Systems	5045	476
B and C Fire Safety Inc	7389	1421
B and C Machine Company LLC	3599	155
B and C Machining Inc	3599	1766
B and C Management Systems Inc	7372	3310
B and C Trucking Inc	4213	2577
B and D Electric Inc	1731	1720
B and D Electrical Contractors Inc	1731	645
B and D Hotel Corp	8361	170
B and D Industrial And Mining Services Inc	3599	297
B and D Litho of Arizonia	2761	28
B and D Machine Inc	3599	1685
B and D Manufacturing Inc	3585	186
B and D Marine And Industrial Boilers Inc	3731	43
B and D Packaging Inc	7389	2321
B and D Precision Tools Inc	3544	512
B and D Sales Inc	5063	1076
B and D Threadrolling	3452	29
B and E Aqatics Inc	1623	775
B and E Communications Inc	1731	1651
B and E Industries LLC	7311	552
B and E Tool Company Inc	3728	87
B and F Design Inc	8711	532
B and F Plastics Inc	3081	105
B and F System Inc	5023	37
B and F Technical Code Services Inc	7389	1400
B and G Auto Sales Inc	5012	177
B and G Equipment Inc	5012	129
B and G Foods Inc	2035	3
B and G Machine Inc	3599	820
B and G Manufacturing Company Inc	3452	28
B and G Optics Inc	3851	64
B and G Supply Company Inc	4213	542
B and G Transportation Inc	4213	2208
B and H Foods Inc	2013	131
B and H Freight Lines Inc	4213	2687
B and H Machine Sales Inc	5084	597
B and H Manufacturing Company Inc	3565	37
B and H Manufacturing Inc	3523	165
B and H Pattern Inc	3543	13
B and H Technical Ceramics	3599	1864
B and H Toolworks Inc	3544	78
B and J Food Service Equipment Of Missouri Inc	5046	118
B and J Machine Works Inc	3599	2307
B and J Machinery Company Inc	3552	40
B and J Seafood LLC	5146	25
B and J Specialty Inc	5084	423
B and J Trucking Service Inc	4213	1727
B and J Wire Inc	3496	88
B and K Electric Wholesale	5063	73
B and K Electrical and Mechanical Contractors Inc	1731	1529
B and K Installations Inc	3441	205
B and K Machine Products Inc	3599	1567
B and K Precision Corp	5063	506
B and K Transportation Inc	4213	1311
B and L Associates Inc	8999	170
B and L Auto Parts Inc	5013	270
B and L Cremation Systems Inc	3567	51
B and L Financial Service	2711	240
B and L Mechanical Inc	1711	210
B and L Sales Inc	5013	295
B and L Sound Inc	5731	178
B and M Imports Inc	5094	34
B and M Precision Inc	3841	170
B and M Telecom Inc	1623	761
B and O Saws Inc	3541	101
B and P Lamp Supply Company Inc	5023	139
B and P Plastics Inc	3089	486
B and P Process Equipment And Systems LLC	3559	142
B and Q Distribution Service Inc	4213	1201
B and R Business Solutions LLC	7379	1353
B and R Electronics Inc	5065	912
B and R Machine Inc	3599	1612
B and R Plastics Inc	3089	724
B and R Scenery Inc	3999	192
B and R Services For Professionals	7389	2071
B and R Sheet Metal Inc	3535	156
B and R Stores Inc	5411	160
B and S Electric Supply Company Inc	5063	244
B and S Graphics Inc	2759	572
B and S Insulation Inc	5033	45
B and S International Inc	5065	86
B and S Machine Tool Inc	3599	1821
B and S Plastics Inc	3089	189
B and T Enterprises Inc	7379	1346
B and T Mail Service Inc	4213	549
B and T Tool and Engineering Inc	3545	292
B and W Engineering Corp	3825	340
B and W Equipment Company Inc	5082	196
B and W Farm Center Inc	5191	178
B and W Mechanical Contractors Inc	1711	39
B and Z Co	1623	395
B and Z Manufacturing Company Inc	3599	788
B Andrews Inc	5046	366
B B Robertson Co	3589	154
B Barine Inc	3999	170
B Braun Inc (Irvine California)	2834	56
B Braun Of America Inc	6719	93
B Bunch Company Inc	3555	71
B C Industrial Supply Inc	5051	461
B C Products	7389	1697
B Com Wireless Inc	5999	221
B Creative Services Inc	7311	675
B D B Inc	1731	931
B Dalton Bookseller Inc	5942	8
B Del Toro and Sons Inc	5141	225
B Drive Inc	7371	1446
B/E Aerospace Machined Products Inc	3724	4
B/E Aerospace Services Inc	3728	73
B Electric Inc	1731	1605
B Five Studio LLP	8712	256
B Frank Inc	5064	216
B Frank Joy Company Inc	1623	38
B G Peck Company Inc	3053	107
B G Service Company Inc	3694	36
B Harding Harry and Son Inc	2752	1732
B J Tidwell Industries Inc	2434	14
B Jacqueline And Associates Inc	7371	455
B L Makepeace Inc	5999	98
B Lipman and Associates Inc	1731	1311
B Mayfield Mccraw And Brenda Mccraw	3273	89
B Olinde and Sons Company Inc	5181	37
B P Enterprises	7378	142
B Peters Associates Inc	5045	280
B/R Instrument Corp	3821	62
B Riley and Company Inc	6282	111
B Robert Our Company Inc	1623	299
B/T Western Corp	5013	33
B Tech	3363	52
B To B Vision LLC	7371	1491
B United International Inc	5181	108
B W B Controls Inc	3492	25
B W Byrd Metal Fabricators Inc	3441	253
B W Implement Co	3523	214
B W Sinclair Inc	3535	135
B100 Kbea - Studio	4832	137
B2b Technologies LLC	7371	752
B2b Workforce LP	7379	606
B3O EnviroTek	5251	47
BA Box Tank and Supply Inc	5084	916
BA Die Mold Inc	3544	802
BA Miller and Sons Trucking Co	4213	2571
Baach Robinson and Lewis PLLC	8111	478
Baader Food Processing Machinery Inc	3556	51
Baader-Brown Manufacturing Co	3647	20
Baam Inc	2353	23
Baap Inc	3841	409
Baarns Consulting Group Inc	7379	1584
Baarts Trucking Inc	4213	2369
BAB Inc	2051	213
BAB Operations Inc	5461	11
BAB Systems Inc	6794	89
BABB/Houston Public Relations	8743	275
Babb Inc	6411	194
Babbitt Bearing Company Inc	3599	1433
Babbitt Bearings Inc	3599	430
Babbitt International Corp	5084	923
Babbitt Steam Specialty Co	5085	361
Babbitting Service Inc	3341	31
Babcock and Brown Holdings LP	6211	6
Babcock and Wilcox Co	3443	5
Babcock Inc	3677	3
Babcock Lumber Co	2426	4
Babcock Power Inc	3511	8
Babcox Publications Inc	2721	128
Babe Winkelman Productions Inc	2731	240
Babeco Inc	3599	2097
Baber Graphic Systems Inc	8748	391
Babich and Associates Inc	7361	288
Babies "R" Us	5641	1
Babler Brothers Inc	1611	219
Babson Capital Management LLC	6282	122
Baby Bee Bright Corp	2741	501
Baby Beepers	4812	114
Baby Fold' 'the	8322	68
Baby Togs Inc	2361	4
BabyCenter LLC	5961	85
BabyEarth	5999	102

Company Name	SIC	Rank
Baby's Dream Furniture Inc	2511	85
Baca Stein White and Associates	7374	383
Bacardi Bottling Corp	2085	10
Bacardi Corp	2085	8
Bacchus Press Inc	2752	752
Bacchus Video Releasing	5099	93
Bacco Construction Co	1611	8
Bacharach Inc	3829	57
Bachem Bioscience Inc	2833	26
Bachem Inc	2836	33
Bachman Co	2052	26
Bachman Machine Co	3599	148
Bachman Tool and Die Co	3599	1264
Bachrach Clothing Inc	5611	10
Back Acre Hop Farms Inc	0139	6
Back Alley Printers Inc	2261	20
Back and Middle River Savings and Loan	6035	259
Back Bay Restaurant Group Inc	5812	59
Back O' Beyond Inc	7992	7
Back Pocket Recording Studios Inc	7389	913
Back Yard Burgers Inc	5812	289
Backbone Entertainment	7372	2389
Backbone Networks Inc	7379	659
Backcountry Store Inc	5961	158
Backdraft Brewing Co	2082	38
Backe Digital Brand Marketing Inc	7311	454
Backer's Potato Chip Co	2096	33
Backgrounds Unlimited Inc	5049	86
BackJoy Orthotics	5999	104
Back-Mueller Inc	3842	264
BackOffice Associates LLC	7371	158
Backsoft Corp	7372	1182
BackTrack Inc	8742	557
Backup Communications	7363	333
Backyard Broadcasting Inc	4832	93
Baco Controls Inc	5063	945
Baco Exterminating Services LLC	7342	24
Bacompt Systems Inc	8741	240
Bacon Industries Inc	2891	103
Bacon Printing Inc	2752	1337
Bacon Products Company Inc	2879	48
Bacon Signs Inc	3993	139
Bacova Guild Ltd	2241	5
Bactee Systems Inc	8748	410
Bactolac Pharmaceutical Inc	2834	176
Bactolac Pharmaceutical Inc (Hauppauge New York)	2834	150
Bad Animals/Seattle	3695	101
Bad Boy Enterprises LLC	5561	13
Bad Boy Entertainment Inc	7389	85
Bad Boy Worldwide Entertainment Group	8741	43
Bada Networks	7371	716
Baddour Memorial Center Inc	8361	100
Badeco Inc	1799	124
Bader Corp	5734	154
Bader Martin Ross and Smith PS	8721	377
Bader Rutter and Associates Inc	7311	167
Bader Technologies Inc	7372	4792
Badertscher Communications Inc	7311	978
Badge Machine Products Inc	3599	1305
Badge Parts Inc	3965	27
Badge-A-Minit Ltd	5199	106
Badger Air Brush Co	3952	8
Badger Barrels Inc	3599	2072
Badger Building Maintenance	7349	401
Badger Corrugating Co	5033	12
Badger Express Inc	4213	406
Badger Federal Services Inc	4213	1293
Badger Fire Protection	3999	68
Badger Foundry Co	3321	38
Badger Graphics Systems Of Madison Inc	5112	43
Badger Herald Inc	2711	903
Badger Ladder Inc	5082	199
Badger Liquor Company Inc	5182	26
Badger Machine Inc	3599	2295
Badger Magnetics Inc	3677	47
Badger Meter Inc	3824	2
Badger Packaging Corp	2653	115
Badger Plug Co	3089	528
Badger Press Inc	2752	613
Badger State Ethanol LLC	2869	33
Badger State Rebuilders Inc	7539	22
Badger State Western Inc	4213	1191
Badger Tag And Label Corp	2672	72
Badger Technical Services Inc	8999	174
Badger Technologies Inc	3679	275
Badger Truck Center Inc	5012	55
Badger West Wine and Spirits LLC	5182	20
Badgerland Car Wash Equipment Company Inc	5087	96
Badgett Constructors LLC	1542	225
Badgley Phelps	6282	283
Badorf Shoe Company Inc	3149	28
BAE Industries Inc	3465	27
BAE Systems Advanced Information Technologies	8731	61
BAE Systems Aircraft Controls	3812	31
BAE Systems Composite Structures Inc	3624	7
Bae Systems Container Solutions Inc	2448	16
Bae Systems Hawaii Shipyards Inc	7699	27

Company Name	SIC	Rank
BAE SYSTEMS Integrated Defense Solutions	3728	13
BAE Systems (McLean Virginia)	7373	30
BAE Systems Mission Solutions	3825	12
Bae Systems Norfolk Ship Repair Inc	3731	15
BAE Systems Platform Solutions	3769	5
BAE Systems (Rockville Maryland)	7375	16
Bae Systems San Francisco Ship Repair Inc	3731	37
BAE Systems Ship Repair	3731	2
Bae Systems Ship Repair Inc	3731	12
Bae Systems Southeast Shipyards Alabama LLC	3731	20
Baechler Investigative Services	7381	199
Baerlocher Production USA LLC	2819	59
Baers Furniture Company Inc	5712	50
Baf Industries	2842	85
Bag Connection Inc	2673	52
Bag Makers Inc	2673	25
Bag One Arts Inc	6794	140
Bagatelos Law Firm	8111	185
Bagby Electric Of Virginia Inc	1731	589
Bagby Elevator Company Inc	3534	8
Bagcraft Packaging LLC	2673	4
Bagcraftpapercon III LLC	2671	3
Bagdad Roller Mills Inc	2048	100
Bagel Boy Inc	2051	142
Bagel Grove Inc	2051	304
Bagelry Inc	2051	134
Bagels and Blenderz	5461	48
Bagels Forever Inc	2051	275
Baggett Transportation Co	4213	435
Bagley Electric LLC	1731	2013
Bagnall Electric Inc	1731	1455
Bagolitas By Janice LLC	7389	2458
Bags Inc	2673	61
Bags Unlimited Inc	2673	72
Bagshaw Trucking Inc	4213	1802
Bahadur Balan and Kazerski Ltd	8742	234
Bahco North America	3541	69
Bahen Inc	7349	280
Bahia 21 Corp	3571	221
Bahl and Gaynor Investment Council Inc	6282	321
Bahnson Environmental Specialties LLC	3826	58
Bahnson Inc	8711	107
BAI	8748	91
Baicy Communications Inc	2752	1514
Baier and Baier Inc	3679	226
Baierl Chevrolet Inc	5511	204
Bail Bonds Now Inc	7389	1638
Bailard Biehl and Kaiser Inc	6282	275
Bailey Banks and Biddle	5944	9
Bailey Brand Consulting	7389	623
Bailey Co	5812	398
Bailey Company Inc	5084	137
Bailey County Electric Coop	4911	492
Bailey Foods LLC	2011	141
Bailey Lauerman	7311	269
Bailey Machine Co	7699	173
Bailey Nurseries Inc	5193	2
Bailey Printing and Publishing Inc	2759	594
Bailey Publishing and Communications Inc	2711	576
Bailey Quarries Inc	1422	37
Bailey Street Bakery LLC	2051	57
Bailey-Parks Urethane Inc	3083	44
Bailey's Express Inc	4213	982
Baillio's Electronic and Appliance Connection	5734	15
Baily International Inc	2098	8
Bain Capital LLC	6211	87
Bainbridge Post Searchlight Inc	2752	1049
Baines Management Corp	5411	259
Bainum Bancorp	6712	642
Baird and Warner Inc	6531	164
Baird Contracting Company Inc	1623	445
Baird Display	3993	101
Baird Kurtz and Dobson	8721	129
Baird Oil Company Inc	1311	208
Baird Patrick and Company Inc	6211	218
Baird-Neece Packing Corp	0723	19
Baise Enterprises Inc	2752	1725
Baish Electric Company Ltd	1731	1157
Baity Screw Products Inc	3599	895
Baja Foods LLC	5142	39
Baja Products Ltd	3842	182
Bakalars Sausage Company Inc	5142	30
BakBone Software Inc	7372	614
Bakemark Ingredients USA	5149	21
BakeMark-Youngstown OH	5149	101
Baker and Barrios Architects Inc	8712	85
Baker and Botts LLP	8111	47
Baker and Company PC	8721	218
Baker and Hostetler LLP	8111	232
Baker and McKenzie	8111	4
Baker and Sons Equipment Company Inc	5082	191
Baker and Taylor Acquisitions Corp	2731	35
Baker and Taylor Inc	5192	2
Baker Atlas	7372	24
Baker Book House Co	2731	69
Baker Boyer Bancorp	6712	478

Company Name	SIC	Rank
Baker Boyer National Bank	6021	126
Baker Brownie Inc	2051	173
Baker Cheese Factory Inc	2022	40
Baker Chevrolet	5511	999
Baker Company Inc	3821	15
Baker Concrete Construction Inc	1771	3
Baker Distributing Co	5078	2
Baker Donelson Bearman Caldwell and Berkowitz PC (Memphis TN)	8111	184
Baker Drywall Fort Worth Ltd	1742	15
Baker Electric Inc	1731	539
Baker Energy	3511	23
Baker Engineering Inc	8741	306
Baker Equipment And Materials Ltd	7359	164
Baker Graphics Corp	7334	86
Baker Group Iowa	1711	110
Baker Hill Corp	7372	1410
Baker Hosiery Inc	2252	25
Baker Hughes Inc	3533	1
Baker Hughes INTEQ	3533	8
Baker Implement Co	5083	23
Baker Inc	3568	85
Baker Instrument Co	3825	62
Baker Jewelers of Virginia Beach Inc	5944	35
Baker Maid Products Inc	5149	142
Baker Manufacturing Company LLC	3321	21
Baker Marine Corp	1389	56
Baker Metal Products Inc	3449	7
Baker Motion Control Systems Inc	7373	725
Baker Nye Investments LP	6799	267
Baker Oil Tools	3533	11
Baker Outlet	5063	847
Baker Perkins Inc	3556	7
Baker Petrolite Corp	2821	32
Baker Printing Company Inc	2752	731
Baker Rock Resources	1611	159
Baker Spindler and Holtz	8721	87
Baker Street Partners Advertising Inc	7331	208
Baker Transfer and Storage Co	4213	2817
Baker Truck Equipment Co	5012	154
Baker Truck Services Inc	4213	1339
Baker Underground and Construction LLC	1623	673
Baker Valve and Machine Service Inc	7699	164
Baker-Bohnert Rubber Company Inc	5084	817
Bakercorp	7353	12
Baker-Hill Industries Inc	3599	1099
Bakers Best/Trotter Soft Prtzl	2099	152
Bakers Choice Co	2052	59
Bakers Footwear Group Inc	5661	9
Baker's Ice Company Inc	2097	17
Bakers Jewelry and Gifts	5632	10
Bakers Pride Oven Company Inc	3556	42
Baker's Supermarkets	5411	133
Baker's Transportation Service of Lakeland	4213	2871
Baker's Waste Equipment Inc	3443	154
Bakersfield Californian	2711	134
Bakersfield Machine Company Inc	3599	532
Bakersfield Pipe And Supply Inc	5051	174
Bakery De France Inc	2051	144
Bakery Equipment Service	5046	255
Bakery Express Of Central Texas LP	2051	157
Bakery Express-Mid Atlantic Inc	2051	87
Bakery Management Corp	2051	265
Bakton Enterprises	3463	24
BAL Associates Inc	7363	151
Bal Seal Engineering Inc	3495	9
Balance Bar Co	2099	41
Balance Staffing	7361	187
Balance Systems Inc	3442	39
Balance Technology Inc	3829	76
Balanced Rock Electric Inc	1731	1172
Balancing Company Inc	3599	1397
Balas Inc	7389	2262
Balax Inc	3545	46
Balboa Capital Corp	7377	7
Balboa Dessert Co	2051	46
Balboa Software	7372	3692
Balboa Travel Inc	4724	37
Balboa Water Group Inc	3625	23
Balchem Corp	2899	31
Balco Enterprises Inc	5045	872
Balcrank Products Inc	3569	15
Baldan Inc	5065	308
Baldauf Enterprises Inc	3444	120
Baldinger Baking Company LP	2051	73
Baldor Electric Co	3621	8
Baldor of Texas LP	5063	153
Baldridge Electric Inc	1731	1748
Baldridge Lumber and Supply Inc	5211	302
Baldwin and Lyons Inc	6331	179
Baldwin and Shell Construction Co	1542	216
Baldwin Asia Pacific Corp	3555	45
Baldwin County Electric Membership Corp	4911	502
Baldwin Distribution Services Ltd	4213	965
Baldwin Filters	3714	41
Baldwin Hackett and Meeks Inc	7372	1121
Baldwin Kansa Corp	3555	12
Baldwin Piano Inc	3931	5
Baldwin Portable Toilets And Septic Tanks Inc	7359	210
Baldwin Precision Inc	3714	392

Company Name	SIC	Rank
Baldwin Press Inc	2752	1376
Baldwin Richardson Foods Co	2087	22
Baldwin Richardson Foods Co	2024	9
Baldwin Supply Co	5063	191
Baldwin Technology Company Inc	3555	6
Baldwin Transfer Company Inc	4231	2
Bale Chevrolet Geo Co	5511	212
Baleco International Inc	5091	76
Balenz Software Inc	7372	3866
Bales Continental Commission Co	5154	4
Bales for Food Inc	5411	278
Bales Services Inc	7342	96
Balestra Capital Management	6282	588
Balfour Industries Inc	3009	1328
Balfour Concord	8741	221
Balfour Lumber Company Inc	2421	97
Balian Ice Cream CoInc	2024	63
Balihoo Inc	7371	904
Balise Motor Sales Co	5511	851
Balkema Excavating Inc	1623	194
Ball Aerospace and Technologies Corp	3769	1
Ball and Ball LLP	3429	135
Ball And Prier Tire Inc	5014	44
Ball and Weed PC	8111	346
Ball Corp	3411	3
Ball Group	8732	101
Ball Homes Inc	6552	66
Ball Horticultural Co	5193	4
Ball Janik LLP	8111	311
Ball Memorial Hospital Inc	8062	216
Ball Park Brand	2013	21
Ball Plastic Container Operations Div	3221	3
Ball Publishing Company Inc	2711	624
Ball S Machine and Manufacturing Company Inc	3599	2254
Ball Screws and Actuators Company Inc	3568	41
Ball Systems Inc	3825	248
Ball Trading Corp	5093	198
Ballantine Inc	5082	154
Ballantine Laboratories Inc	3825	220
Ballantyne Leasing LLC	7389	1613
Ballantyne Strong Inc	3861	19
Ballard Bratsberg Inc	7311	981
Ballard Rural Telephone Cooperative Corporation Inc	4813	231
Ballard Technology Inc	3825	178
Ballek Die Mold Inc	3544	908
Ballenger Div	1611	95
Ballentine Equipment Company Inc	5046	124
Ballinger	8712	56
Ballista Securities LLC	7374	141
Ballistic Recovery Systems Inc	3728	143
Balloon Aviation	4522	33
Balloon Haven Inc	7389	1930
Balloonatics Inc	5947	29
Ballqube Inc	3089	1674
Ballreich Brothers Inc	2096	43
Ballston SpA Bancorp Inc	6712	524
Ballston SpA National Bank	6021	134
Balluff Inc	3625	37
Bally Bead Company Inc	5094	88
Bally Block Co	2599	31
Bally Refrigerated Boxes Inc	3585	64
Bally Ribbon Mills	2241	6
Bally Technologies	3999	30
Bally Technologies Corp	7999	32
Bally Total Fitness Corp	7991	1
Bally Total Fitness Holding Corp	7997	2
Bally United Produce Ltd	2015	66
Bally's Park Place Inc	7011	8
Balmac Inc	3829	346
Balmar Printing and Graphics Inc	2759	32
Balmoral Group International Inc	3533	45
Balon Corp	3494	22
Balsams Corp	7011	155
Balsys Technology Group Inc	3663	376
Balt Inc	2521	20
Baltec Corporation	5084	645
Baltek Inc	2436	2
Baltic Trading Ltd	4449	20
Baltimore Color Plate Inc	2796	39
Baltimore Contractors LLC	1542	431
Baltimore County Building Inspection	7389	1718
Baltimore County Savings Bank	6035	106
Baltimore Door And Frame Inc	5031	167
Baltimore Financial LLC	6163	37
Baltimore Gas and Electric Co	4911	67
Baltimore Healthcare Access Inc	8399	20
Baltimore Life Co	6311	174
Baltimore Life Insurance Co	6311	159
Baltimore Office Supply Company Inc	2796	53
Baltimore Publishing Group	2711	205
Baltimore Scrap Corp	5093	94
Baltimore Sound Engineering Inc	5065	313
Baltimore Sun Co	2711	13
Baltimore Tank Lines Inc	4213	1097
Baltimore Window Factory Inc	3089	1067
Balzer Pacific Equipment Co	5082	84
Bam Shields Corp	5091	71
Bama Companies Inc	2053	1
Bama Fluid Power Inc	7699	138
Bama Plastics Corp	3089	1742
Bama Sea Products Inc	5146	21

Company Name	SIC	Rank
Bamal Corp	5072	77
Bamar Plastics Inc	3089	1391
Bambeck Systems Inc	3823	241
Bamjak Inc	5013	394
Bamko	7311	338
BaMo Inc	8712	139
Bana Electric Corp	1731	268
Banana Republic	5651	28
Banc Affiliated Inc	6712	698
Banc of America Insurance Services Inc	6311	251
BancFirst	6022	60
BancFirst Corp	6712	114
Banchi Trucking LLC	4213	3051
Bancinsurance Corp	6331	286
BancLease	7372	2308
Banco Popular de Puerto Rico	6022	12
Banco Popular Inc	6712	668
Banco Popular NA	6021	340
BancOklahoma Mortgage Corp	6091	9
BancoPopular Illinois	6022	542
Bancorp Inc	6021	52
Bancorp of Southern Indiana	6712	572
Bancorp Rhode Island Inc	6712	226
BancorpSouth Capital Trust I	6099	1
BancorpSouth Inc	6712	61
Bancroft and Sons Transportation	4213	120
Bancroft Bag Inc	2674	5
Bancroft Corp	3548	65
Bancshares of Gleason Inc	6712	595
BancTec Inc	3577	50
BancTrust Financial Group Inc	6712	191
Bancvue Ltd	7371	163
BancWest Corp	6712	25
BancWest Inc	6712	697
Band Pro Film and Digital Inc	5731	78
Bandag Licensing Corp	3011	18
BandCon	4899	143
Bandel Manufacturing Inc	3469	359
Bandit Industries Inc	5082	69
BAND-IT-IDEX Inc	3429	65
BandNcom Holding Corp	5961	8
Bandspeed Inc	5045	612
Bandwidthcom Inc	4899	141
Bandy Carroll Hellige Advertising	7311	259
Bane Barham and Holloway Assets Management Inc	6282	371
Bane-Clene Corp	7217	4
Banesco USA	6022	678
Banfe Products Inc	2875	32
Banfi Products Corp	2084	9
Banfill Supply Inc	5032	195
Bangers LP	5091	40
Bangert Computer Systems Inc	5045	836
Bangor Bancorp Mhc	6712	661
Bangor Hydro-Electric Co	4911	448
Bangor Motor Sports Inc	5571	11
Bangor Pipe and Supply Inc	5074	138
Bangor Plastics Inc	3089	1706
Bangor Publishing Co	2711	302
Bangor Steel Service Inc	5051	460
Banister Tool Inc	3541	124
Bank and Office Interiors	5021	14
Bank and Trust - Del Rio	6022	470
Bank Leumi USA	6022	49
Bank Midwest NA	6021	85
Bank Mutual	6022	88
Bank Mutual Corp	6712	171
Bank of Agriculture and Commerce	6022	386
Bank of Akron	6022	588
Bank of Alameda	6022	448
Bank of Amador	6022	722
Bank of America Corp	6021	1
Bank of America Investment Services Inc	6211	76
Bank of America (Phoenix Arizona)	6022	37
Bank of America Securities LLC	6211	30
Bank of America Speciality Group	6141	30
Bank of America Texas NA	6021	394
Bank of Arizona	6022	602
Bank of Belle Glade	6022	552
Bank of Belton	6029	13
Bank of Blue Valley	6022	734
Bank of Castile	6022	432
Bank of Charles Town	6022	397
Bank of Choice (Denver Colorado)	6022	747
Bank of Clarke County	6022	669
Bank of Commerce and Trust Co (Wellington Kansas)	6022	649
Bank of Commerce Holdings	6022	177
Bank of Coweta	6022	569
Bank of Delmarva NA	6022	744
Bank of Eastern Oregon	6029	22
Bank of Essex	6022	158
Bank of Fayette County	6035	254
Bank of Fayetteville	6021	303
Bank of Floyd	6022	565
Bank of Georgetown	6022	707
Bank of Georgia (Peachtree Georgia)	6022	375
Bank of Glen Burnie	6036	82
Bank of Grain Valley	6022	784
Bank of Granite Corp	6712	323
Bank of Greene County	6036	77
Bank of Hampton Roads	6022	121

Company Name	SIC	Rank
Bank of Hawaii Corp	6712	62
Bank of Hawaii Insurance Services Inc	6411	117
Bank of Hazlehurst	6022	768
Bank of Idaho	6022	474
Bank of Internet USA	6029	14
Bank of Jamestown	6022	691
Bank of Kentucky Financial Corp	6035	47
Bank of Lancaster	6022	219
Bank of Landisburg	6022	457
Bank of Laramie	6021	393
Bank of Las Vegas	6022	642
Bank of Little Rock	6022	635
Bank of Louisiana	0022	344
Bank of Manhattan NA	6021	365
Bank of Marin	6022	178
Bank of Marin Bancorp	6022	142
Bank of Marion	6022	263
Bank of Marquette	6712	703
Bank of McKenney	6021	298
Bank of Napa NA	6021	355
Bank of Naples	6022	643
Bank of Nashville	6022	314
Bank Of Nevada	6022	595
Bank of New York	6022	2
Bank of New York Mellon Corp	6712	6
Bank of North Dakota	6022	421
Bank of Northumberland Inc	6022	752
Bank of Oak Ridge	6021	226
Bank of O'Fallon	6022	466
Bank of Oklahoma NA	6021	23
Bank of Rockbridge	6022	159
Bank of Sacramento	6022	657
Bank of St Petersburg	6022	322
Bank of Santa Clarita	6022	499
Bank of South Carolina Corp	6712	579
Bank of Southern California (San Diego California)	6021	306
Bank of Southside Virginia	6712	379
Bank of Springfield	6022	396
Bank of Sturgeon Bay Building Corp	6022	150
Bank of Texas Lake Worth	6021	55
Bank of Texas Trust Company NA	6091	19
Bank of the Commonwealth	6022	204
Bank of the Orient	6022	224
Bank of the Ozarks Inc	6712	143
Bank of the Pacific	6022	243
Bank of the Rockies NA	6021	373
Bank of the Sierra	6022	239
Bank of the West	6022	3
Bank of the West (Thomas Oklahoma)	6022	687
Bank Of Tokyo Mitsubishi Ufj Ltd	6022	587
Bank of Tuscaloosa	6022	454
Bank of Utah	6022	196
Bank of Virginia	6029	21
Bank of Walnut Creek	6022	342
Bank of Washington	6022	398
Bank of Willits	6022	718
Bank of Wisconsin Dells	6022	233
Bank of Wonewoc	6022	812
Bank of Zachary	6022	606
Bank Rhode Island	6036	23
Bank Street Telecom Funding Corp	6799	173
Bank Vault Service and Equipment	5065	827
BANK'34	6035	169
Bank-A-Count Corp	7389	1889
BankAnnapolis Inc	6022	360
BankAtlantic Bancorp Inc	6712	120
BankAtlantic FSB	6035	11
Bankcrafters Inc	3585	141
Bankers Bancorp	6712	684
Bankers Bank (Oklahoma City Oklahoma)	6022	689
Bankers Fidelity Life Insurance Co	6311	253
Bankers Life and Casualty Co	6411	18
Bankers Life Insurance Company of Illinois	6311	78
Bankers Security Safe and Vault Co	3499	93
Bankers Small Business Community Development Corp	6163	15
Bankers Supply Inc	5049	147
Bankers Training and Certification Center	8748	224
Bankers Trust Co (Des Moines Iowa)	6022	91
Bankers Trust (Wilmington Delaware)	6022	153
BankFinancial	6021	207
BankFinancial Corp	6035	51
Bankhead Enterprises Inc	1799	19
Bankier Companies Inc	3089	523
Banking Spectrum Inc	8742	568
BankLiberty	6035	128
Banklink USA	7373	203
Banknorth Connecticut	6022	236
Banknorth Insurance Agency Inc/MA	6311	93
Ban-Koe Systems Inc	5044	44
Bankrate Inc	7389	169
Bankruptcy Creditors' Service Inc	2721	469
Banks Electric Inc	1731	993
Banks Oil Co	1311	249
Bankscom Inc	7379	488
Bankston Chevrolet Dallas	5511	262
Bankston Construction Inc	1623	602
BankTennessee	6022	337
BankTrust	6022	463
BankTrust (Brewton Alabama)	6021	176

Company Name	SIC	Rank
BankUnited Capital	6153	4
BankUnited Capital II	6153	5
BankUnited Capital III	6153	6
BankUnited Financial Corp	6712	53
BankUnited Inc	6036	4
BankUnited Mortgage Corp	6162	27
BankWest of Nevada	6022	93
Banner Aerospace Inc	5088	5
Banner and Witcoff Ltd	8111	220
Banner Bank	6712	72
Banner Corp	6712	122
Banner Engineering and Sales Inc	3585	225
Banner Engineering Corp	3625	35
Banner Equipment Co	3585	138
Banner Health	8062	19
Banner Health System	8062	7
Banner Machine Company Inc	3599	1577
Banner Metals Group Inc	3469	226
Banner Mold and Die Company Inc	3544	558
Banner Moulded Products	3555	77
Banner News Publishing Company Inc	2711	779
Banner Plumbing Supply Company Inc	5074	100
Banner Security Systems Inc	1731	2213
Banner Service Corp	7389	1175
Banner Supply Co	5031	233
Banner Systems Of Massachusetts Inc	5087	53
Banner Welder Inc	3548	36
Banner Wholesale Grocers Inc	5141	147
Banta Foods Inc	5141	146
Banta Global Turnkey Ltd	3577	94
Banterra Corp	6712	281
Bantry Components Inc	3676	15
Bantu Inc	7372	562
Banyan Air Service Inc	4581	27
Banyan International Corp	3841	321
Banyan Rail Services Inc	6726	44
Banyon Data Systems Inc	7372	4276
Banzai Research Institute Inc	7371	1468
Baptist Credit Union	6062	116
Baptist Health	8062	162
Baptist Health System Inc	8062	22
Baptist Hospitals and Health Systems Inc	8062	65
Baptist Memorial Hospital - North Mississippi Inc	8062	111
Baptist Memorial Hospital-Golden Triangle Inc	8062	188
Baptist Trinity Health Care Services	8082	46
Bar Code Integrators Inc	7373	814
Bar Harbor Bank and Trust Co	6022	171
Bar Harbor Bankshares	6712	279
Bar S Machine Inc	3599	1400
Bar Scan Inc	7372	3219
Bar Technologies LLC	3316	31
Bar Tie Reinforcing Inc	5051	469
Baraboo Bancorporation Inc	6712	375
Baraboo Candy Co	2066	42
Baraboo National Bank	6021	142
Baraboo Tent and Awning Inc	2394	30
Barack Ferrazzano Kirschbaum and Nagelberg LLP	8111	253
Baraka Inc	7373	978
Barakat Associates Ltd	5052	13
Baran Telecom Inc	4813	286
Barbara Barry Inc	7389	2217
Barbara Creations Inc	5048	7
Barbara Nicol Public Relations	8743	344
Barbara Olson Center Of Hope Inc	8331	166
Barbara's Bakery Inc	2096	21
Barbco Inc	3531	165
Barbee-Neuhaus Implement Co	5083	17
Barbeques Galore Inc	5722	9
Barber Brothers Contracting Company Inc	1611	136
Barber Coins and Collectibles Inc	5094	82
Barber Electric Manufacturing Company Inc	3469	334
Barber Foods	2015	26
Barber Manufacturing Company Inc	3493	10
Barber McCaskill Jones and Hale PA	8111	468
Barber Milk Inc	2026	8
Barber Packaging Co	3086	94
Barber Welding And Manufacturing Co	3443	207
Barberino Brothers Inc	5511	1033
Barber-Nichols Inc	5063	342
Barber's Poultry Inc	4222	16
Barber-Webb Company Inc	3081	139
Barbey Electronics Corp	5065	128
Barbizon Capitol Inc	5063	320
Barbizon International Inc	6794	94
Barbosa Cabinets Inc	2599	17
Barbour Corp	3429	24
Barbour Publishing Inc	5942	34
Barbron Corp	3569	255
Barc Electric Coop	4911	373
Barcelo Crestline Corp	7011	13
Barcelona Nut Company Inc	2068	18
Barcelona West Inc	5091	55
Barclay Communications Inc	7319	114
Barclay Dean	5021	44
Barclay Enterprises Inc	5999	259
Barclay Home Products Corp	2392	8
Barclay Machine Inc	3312	114
Barclay Mechanical Services Inc	1796	32

Company Name	SIC	Rank
Barclay Water Management Inc	2899	137
Barclays American Mortgage Corp	6159	21
Barclays Global Investors	6282	41
Barclay's International Realty Inc	6531	211
BARCO Projection Systems America	3679	86
Barco Stamping Co	3469	132
Barco Uniforms Inc	2311	5
Barcoding Inc	3669	114
BarControl Systems and Services Inc	7372	3595
Bard Access Systems Inc	3841	48
Bard Business Systems Inc	5046	269
Bard Peripheral Vascular Inc	3842	73
Bardahl Manufacturing Corp	2992	33
Bardane Manufacturing Co	3363	36
Barden Companies Inc	4832	7
Barden Corp	3562	15
Bardes Plastics Inc	3089	1239
Bardes Products Inc	3089	1669
Bardex Corp	3569	58
Bardon Data Systems Inc	7379	1446
Bardons and Oliver Inc	3549	12
Bardot Plastics Inc	3089	676
Bardwil Industries Inc	2392	14
Bare Bones Software Inc	7372	4365
Bare Escentuals	2844	12
Bare Escentuals Beauty Inc	5999	24
Barebo Inc	3569	176
Barefoot Private Investigations	7381	233
Bareman Dairy Inc	2026	26
Barenbrug USA Inc	0139	5
Barenbrug USA Production Div	7389	1029
Barex World Trade Corp	6221	8
Barfield Fence and Wall Inc	5039	63
Barfield Miami	3812	45
BargainLockscom	3999	94
Barge Terminal Trucking Inc	4213	2153
Barge Waggoner Sumner and Cannon	8711	253
Bargemusic Ltd	7922	32
Barger And Son Construction Company Incorporated Charles W	3273	87
Barger and Wolen	8111	322
Barger Packaging Corp	2657	6
Bargo Engineering Inc	3559	237
Bargreen Coffee Company Inc	2095	58
Bargreen Ellingson Of Hawaii Inc	5046	155
Bargreen-Ellingson Inc	5046	13
Baril Coatings	1799	145
Barile Precision Grinding Inc	3599	2237
Baring Asset Management Inc	6282	183
Barington Capital Group LP	6211	312
Barium Springs Home For Children Inc	8361	83
Barix Technology Inc	3577	360
Bark River Transit Inc	4213	2979
Barke Group	7372	4406
Barker and Williamson Corp	3663	344
Barker Blue Digital Imaging Inc	7334	32
Barker Campbell and Farley	7311	281
Barker Controls Inc	3824	48
Barker Lumber Co	5211	188
Barker Pacific Group	8743	319
Barker Specialty Co	7311	295
Barker Steel LLC	3449	2
Barker-Jennings Corp	5072	124
Barkley Evergreen and Partners Inc Public Relations Div	8743	11
Barkley Truck Line Inc	4213	3037
Barksdale Inc	3492	4
Barkus Oil Corp	5171	85
Barlean's Organic Oils LLC	2079	8
Barletta and Associates Inc	6531	321
Barley Snyder LLC	8111	384
Bar-Lo Carbon Products Inc	3545	275
Barlo Signs International Inc	3993	106
Barlovento LLC	1623	128
Barlow Chevrolet and Oldsmobile Inc	5511	468
Barlow Truck Lines Inc	4213	939
Barloworld USA	5084	14
Barna Log Homes LLC	2452	27
Barnaby Inc	2752	1814
Barnard Manufacturing Company Inc	3599	204
Barnard Nut Company Inc	2099	207
Barnard Software Inc	7372	4988
Barnes Aerospace/Advanced Fabrications Div	3724	38
Barnes Aerospace Corp	3769	6
Barnes Aerospace Lansing Div	3769	18
Barnes and Noble College Booksellers Inc	5942	5
Barnes and Noble Inc	5942	2
Barnes and Powell Electrical Company Inc	1731	221
Barnes and Thornburg	8111	44
Barnes Dennig and Company Ltd	8721	69
Barnes Distribution	5085	10
Barnes Financing LLC	6153	13
Barnes Group Finance Co	6153	14
Barnes Group Inc	6719	57
Barnes Group LLC	3495	21
Barnes Holdings Inc	5084	905
Barnes Industries Inc	3568	52
Barnes International Inc	3541	84
Barnes Motor and Parts Company Inc	5531	61
Barnes Nursery Inc	5261	7
Barnes Plastics Inc	3081	144

Company Name	SIC	Rank
Barnes Research Inc	8732	116
Barnes Transportation Services Inc	4213	1700
Barnes Wendling CPA Inc	8721	26
Barnesandnoblecom Inc	5942	9
Barnet Levinson Design	7336	318
Barnet's Express Inc	4213	3006
Barnets Inc	4213	687
Barnett and Company Inc	6282	665
Barnett and Ramel Optical Company Of Nebraska	3851	61
Barnett Associates Inc	7389	1064
Barnett Auto Group	5511	239
Barnett Chrysler-Plymouth-Jeep-Kia	5511	970
Barnett Inc	5074	11
Barnett International Inc	3949	124
Barnett Millworks Inc	2431	37
Barnett Transportation Inc	4213	983
Barnette Construction Inc	1623	539
Barnette Industries Inc	3829	322
Barney Holland Oil Co	5171	54
Barney Trucking Inc	4213	320
Barney's Bakery Inc	2052	76
Barney's New York	5651	20
Barnhart	7311	228
Barnhart And Son Inc	1623	649
Barnhart Crane and Rigging Co	4213	402
Barnhart Inc	1542	38
Barnhart Press	2752	564
Barnhart Printing Corp	2752	1588
Barnhill Contracting Co	1611	4
Barno Electronics Corp	5065	451
Barnstead-Thermolyne Corp	3841	49
Barnum Printing and Publishing Co	2711	675
Barnwell Hawaiian Properties	6211	237
Barnwell Industries Inc	1311	147
Barnwell Kona Corp	1381	37
Baroco Electric Construction Co	1731	251
Barole Trucking Inc	4213	2048
Baron and Baron Inc	7336	114
Baron and Budd PC	8111	221
Baron Glass Inc	3229	10
Baron Machine Company Inc	7692	17
Baron Manufacturing Company LLC	3429	144
Baron Services Inc	3829	85
Baron Technology Inc	2759	221
Barona Casino	7993	2
Barona Fire Protection District	7389	2278
Barone Design Group	7389	1121
Barone Inc	3589	193
Baroni Designs	5094	86
Baros and Co	8721	272
Barquin And Associates Inc	7373	519
Barr Air Patrol LLC	7363	228
Barr Engineering Co	8711	236
Barr Lumber Company Inc	5211	41
Barr Pharmaceuticals Inc	2834	22
Barr Systems Inc	3577	240
BARRA Inc	7373	75
Barracudaware	7372	373
Barrage	3639	30
Barrango	3999	161
Barratt Edwards International Corp	7372	3125
Bar-Ray Products Inc	3842	247
Barrco Automotive Warehouse Distributors Inc	5013	208
Barrel O' Fun Snack Foods Co	2096	4
Barrel Reconditioning Industries Inc	3542	101
Barrel Service Co	3599	1133
Barrett Business Services Inc	7363	42
Barrett Capital Corp	7359	129
Barrett Carpet Mills Inc	2273	35
Barrett Moving and Storage Co	4213	746
Barrett Paving Materials Inc	1611	32
Barrett Technology Inc	3569	223
Barrett Trucking Company Inc	4213	1070
Barrett-Crofoot Inc	0211	7
Barrette Outdoor Living Inc	3086	7
Barrettemps Inc	7363	366
Barretts Inc	5731	63
Barricade Books Inc	2731	378
Barrick Enterprises	5411	274
Barrie House Coffee Company Inc	2095	28
Barrier Corp	3296	18
Barrier Electric Company Inc	1731	243
Barrier Motors Inc	5511	84
Barrington Associates	6211	168
Barrington Automation Ltd	3535	169
Barrington Enterprises Inc	5045	961
Barrington Multi Media	7389	1240
Barrington Research Associates Inc	6282	273
Barrios Technology Inc	8711	53
Barrister Executive Suites Inc	6531	379
Barr-Mullin Inc	3553	31
Barr-Nunn Transportation Inc	4213	159
Barron Collier Co	8999	80
Barron Communications Inc	5065	874
Barron Fan Technology Inc	5075	60
Barron Machine and Fabrication Inc	3599	2003
Barron Metal Products Inc	3544	779
Barron's Educational Series Inc	2731	155
Barrons Enterprises Inc	5211	146
Barron's Wholesale Tire LLC	5014	26
Barrow Hanley Mewhinney and Strauss Inc	6282	437

Company Name	SIC	Rank
Barrow Industries Inc	5131	5
Barrow Investment Management Inc	6282	675
Barry And Sewall Industrial Supply Co	5085	293
Barry Avenue Plating Company Inc	3471	68
Barry Bashore Inc	4213	2474
Barry Bunker Chevrolet Cadillac	5511	551
Barry Communications Inc	1731	918
Barry County Lumber Company Inc	5211	163
Barry County Telephone Co	4813	295
Barry Cran Inc	5091	66
Barry Design Associates Inc	7389	2295
Barry Electric Coop	4911	536
Barry Graham Oil Service LLC	4489	6
Barry Industries Inc	3625	91
Barry Metals Company Inc	5093	193
Barry of San Angelo	3142	2
Barry Optical Laboratories Inc	5048	16
Barry Sales Engineering Inc	5084	411
Barry Security Inc	7381	171
Barry Trucking Inc	4213	2321
Barry-Wehmiller Companies Inc	8742	31
Bar-S Foods Co	2013	22
Bar's Products Inc	2899	132
Bart Larsen Trucking Inc	4213	1919
Barta-Schoenewald Inc	3621	71
Bartash Printing Inc	2759	64
Bartech Group Inc	7363	48
Bartek Construction Co	1629	100
Bartell Drug Co	5912	28
Bartell Machinery Systems LLC	3549	14
Barth Electric Company Inc	1731	47
Barth Electronics Inc	3679	729
Barth Industries Company LP	3541	64
Bartholomew County Rural Electric Membership Coop	4911	528
Bartimaeus Group LLC	7379	1165
Bartizan Data Systems LLC	3575	20
Bartlett and Co (Cincinnati Ohio)	6282	102
Bartlett and Co (Kansas City Missouri)	2041	6
Bartlett and Picarella	7389	1245
Bartlett Brainard Eacott Inc	1541	151
Bartlett Cocke Inc	1542	29
Bartlett Fund Management Co	6282	542
Bartlett Hackett Feinberg PC	7389	2003
Bartlett Instrument Company Inc	3825	317
Bartlett Pontiff Stewart and Rhodes PC	8111	444
Bartley Bob Electric Inc	1731	1597
Bartley Machine and Manufacturing Company Inc	3599	1955
Bartlo Packaging Inc	4783	22
Bartlow Brothers Inc	2011	116
Bartoli Electric Co	1731	1407
Barton and Cooney LLC	7331	276
Barton and Loguidice PC	8711	339
Barton Birks Chevrolet Cadillac	5511	918
Barton County Electric Coop	4911	529
Barton Creek Conference Resort Inc	7011	174
Barton Inc	2085	9
Barton Industries Inc	2752	1506
Barton Leasing Inc	5032	23
Barton Malow Co	1541	15
Barton Malow Design- Build JV	7389	2139
Barton Manufacturing	3599	448
Barton Medical Corp	2599	20
Barton Nelson Inc	2759	30
Barton Precision Components LLC	3451	72
Barton Solvents Inc	4213	344
Barton-Gilanelli and Associates Inc	8743	121
Barton's Club 93 Inc	7011	78
Bartow County Board Of Education	8211	64
Bartow Ethanol Of Florida LC	2085	24
Bartow Healthcare System Ltd	8062	228
Bartunek Group Inc	7361	389
Bartush-Schnitzius Foods Co	2035	38
Barudan America Inc	3552	35
BAS Recycling Inc	3011	24
Basalite Concrete Products LLC	3271	3
Basalite Div	3271	17
Bascom Global Internet Services Inc	7371	1801
Bascom Maple Farms Inc	5149	165
Bascom-Turner Instruments Inc	5085	88
Bascon Inc	1541	255
Basden Steel And Erection Inc	3312	73
Base 10 Inc	2844	170
Base 2 Corp	7371	1819
Base 2 Technologies Inc	7373	550
Base Manufacturing Inc	3499	50
Baseball America Inc	2711	281
Baseball Jax Inc	7941	30
Baseline Data Systems Inc	7371	1644
Baseline Engineering Inc	7361	92
Base-Line Ii Inc	3861	98
Base-Line Inc	2621	39
Baseline People LLC	8748	372
Baseline Tool Company Inc	3543	51
Bases Services and Durables	8732	115
BASF Corp	2899	3
Basha Equipment Leasing Co	7359	112
Basham Industries	2331	14
Bashas' Inc	5411	69
Bashian Brothers Inc	5023	129
Bashlin Industries Inc	3842	119
Bashor Home Of The United Methodist Church Inc	8361	104
Basic Adhesives Inc	2891	62
Basic American Foods Inc	2034	1
Basic American Medical Products Inc	5047	16
Basic Components Inc	5039	40
Basic Concepts Inc	2399	31
Basic Drugs Inc	5122	102
Basic Electronics Inc	3679	523
Basic Energy Services Inc	1389	8
Basic Fibres Inc	5093	77
Basic Grain Products Inc	2052	38
Basic Line Corp	7389	999
Basic Line Inc	3089	450
Basic Machinery Company Inc	5084	336
Basic Metals Inc	7389	2004
Basic Plastics Co	2673	62
Basic Rubber And Plastics Co	3053	29
Basic Software Systems	7372	1099
Basic Solutions	7372	4587
Basics Plus Inc	5049	125
Basile Construction Inc	1623	250
Basileia Investments Inc	2431	73
Basilius Inc	3544	419
Basiloid Products Corp	3537	93
Basin 2 Way Radio Inc	4899	235
Basin Broadcasting Co	4832	278
Basin Disposal Inc	4953	52
Basin Electric Power Coop	4911	576
Basin Pipeline Corp	4922	42
Basin Western Inc	4213	867
Basin-River Electrical Supply LLC	5063	645
BASIS International Ltd	7372	2571
Baskin Auto Truck And Tractor Inc	5511	1165
Baskin Robbins	2024	34
Basler Inc	3669	145
Basler Turbo Conversions LLC	3721	34
Basnight Construction Company Inc	1623	574
Basol Maintenance Service Inc	7349	153
BASON Company Inc	5045	264
Basque Plastics Corp	3089	1814
Bass and Associates Inc	7379	457
Bass Cabinets And Related Products Inc	2434	46
Bass' Electronics Inc	4841	165
Bass Farms Inc	2011	120
BASS Inc	2721	113
Bass Industries Inc	3993	134
Bass Pro Inc	5941	10
Bass Pro Shops Inc	5941	4
Bass Security Services Inc	5251	15
Bass Transportation Company Inc	4213	756
Bassamaire Sales LLC	3585	168
Bassco Foam Inc	3069	207
Bassco Incorporated Data Processing Consultants	7379	1410
Bassett and Bassett Inc	8743	198
Bassett Boat Co	5551	4
Bassett Dairy Products Inc	5143	16
Bassett Furniture Industries Inc	2511	9
Bassett Inc	1711	105
Bassett Industries Inc	3499	92
Bassett Law Firm	8111	513
Bassett Mechanical Contractors and Engineers Inc	1711	77
Bassett Transportation Inc	4213	2256
Bassette Printers LLC	2752	587
Bassetti Photo Inc	7335	17
Bassin Technical Sales Co	3643	103
Bass-Mollett Publishers Inc	2741	257
Basson Sound Equipment	1731	2431
Bass-United Fire and Security Systems Inc	5063	387
Bast Hatfield Inc	1541	58
Bastian Brothers and Co	2752	1315
Bastian Trucking Inc	4213	1202
Baswell Electrical Construction	1731	1598
Basys Inc	7372	1528
BAT Express Inc	4213	2085
Batampte Pickle Products Inc	2035	31
Batch Process Technologies Inc	7373	1132
Batchelor's Mechanical Contractors Inc	1711	25
Batching Systems Inc	3565	119
BatchMaster Software Inc	7372	2072
Bates Amusement Inc	7999	138
Bates Associates	8743	170
Bates Brothers Amusement Co	7999	141
Bates Container LLC	2653	22
Bates Electric Inc	1731	621
Bates Metal Products Inc	4783	17
Bates Technologies Inc	3545	132
Bates Utility Company Inc	1623	402
Batesville Casket Company Inc	3995	1
Batesville Guard Record	2711	539
Batesville Products Inc	3429	111
Batesville Tooling and Design Inc	3599	2351
Bath and Body Works Inc	5999	5
Bath Fitter Tennessee Inc	3443	108
Bath Iron Works Corp	3731	4
Bath-Tec Inc	3842	272
Batliner Paper Stock Co	5093	67
Baton Rouge Car Audio Inc	5731	29
Baton Rouge Developmental Centers Inc	8322	214
Baton Rouge Machine Works Inc	3599	463
Baton Rouge Printing Inc	2752	1090
Baton Rouge Tankwash	4213	1929
Baton Rouge Title Company Inc	6361	22
Baton Rouge Water Works Co	4941	54
Batrow Inc	7389	2126
Batson Mill LLC	2421	10
Batson Printing Inc	2752	474
Batson-Cook Co	1542	124
Battelini Transportation Systems	4213	2475
Battenfeld Management Inc	5172	118
Battenfeld-American Inc	2992	48
Batteries Direct Inc	5063	497
Batteries Plus LLC	5999	101
Battery Factory S/W Divn Inc	5531	69
Battery Handling Systems Inc	3536	24
Battery Products Inc	5063	1025
Battery Pros Inc	3691	47
Battery Specialties Inc	5063	788
Battery Studios	7389	625
Batterymarch Financial Management Inc	6282	476
Battle Creek Equipment Co	5091	67
Battle Creek Farmers Coop	5191	40
Battle Lumber Company Inc	2448	3
Battle Resource Management	8742	356
Bauch Quarry Products	5032	168
Baucom Press Inc	2752	1544
Baucom Truck Service Inc	4213	2991
Baudin's Sausage Kitchen Inc	2013	234
Baudville Inc	7372	1952
Bauer Built Inc	5014	8
Bauer Compressors Inc	3563	24
Bauer Construction Inc	1521	105
Bauer Electric Inc	1731	2252
Bauer Electrotech	3699	140
Bauer Financial Newsletters Inc	2741	465
Bauer Financial Reports Inc	6282	428
Bauer Inc	3829	123
Bauer Nike Hockey Inc	3949	23
Bauer Publishing Company LP	2721	77
Bauer Welding And Metal Fabricators Inc	3498	50
BauerFinancial Inc	8742	514
Baughman Tile Company Inc	3084	28
Bauhaus USA Inc	2512	11
Baukol-Noonan Inc	1221	18
Baum Control Systems Inc	7373	612
Baum Machine Inc	3599	644
Baum Precision Machining Inc	3599	1575
Bauman Machine Inc	3599	1516
Baumann Engineering Inc	3599	333
Baumann Paper Company Inc	5113	44
Baumark Accounting Software	7373	892
Baumbach Engineering Company Inc	3082	34
Baumer Foods Inc	2099	78
Baumgardner Imaging Inc	7384	30
Baumgartner Trucking Inc	4213	1894
Baumgartner's Electric Inc	1731	1805
Baums Castorine Company Inc	2992	62
Baune Dosen and Company LLP	8721	174
Bausch Advanced Technologies Inc	3599	1682
Bausch and Lomb Inc	3851	1
Bausch and Lomb Inc Eyewear Div	3827	2
Bausch and Lomb Pharmaceuticals Inc	2834	83
Bausman And Company Inc	2511	36
Bautech Inc	2591	18
Bauxite and Northern Railway Company Inc	4011	55
Bavaria Sausage Kitchen Inc	2013	235
Bavarian Computer Works Inc	7373	1098
Bavarian Motor Transport Inc	4213	167
Baw Plastics Inc	3083	17
Baxa Corp	3561	54
Baxstra Inc	2426	35
Baxter County Regional Hospital Inc	8062	197
Baxter County Regional Hospital	8099	35
Baxter Credit Union	6062	29
Baxter Financial Corp	6282	414
Baxter Healthcare Corp	3842	2
Baxter Healthcare Corp (Norwood Massachusetts)	8731	171
Baxter International Inc	3841	2
Baxter Machine and Tool Co	3544	432
Baxter Planning Systems Inc	5045	302
Baxter-Rutherford Inc	5074	73
Baxter's Asphalt And Concrete Inc	1611	209
Bay Air Conditioning Inc	5064	88
Bay Alarm Corp	7382	17
Bay Answerphone Inc	7389	2140
Bay Area Business Cards Inc	2759	338
Bay Area Circuits Inc	3672	222
Bay Area Data Supply Inc	7378	144
Bay Area Development Co	6153	32
Bay Area Eye Center	3827	125
Bay Area Industrial Contractors LP	7692	6
Bay Area Industrial Filtration Inc	3569	228
Bay Area Medical Exchange Of Florida Inc	7389	1728
Bay Area Oil Supply Inc	5084	749
Bay Area Systems And Solutions Inc	1731	222
Bay Bank and Trust Co	6022	366
Bay Beyond Inc	5149	202
Bay Bridge Enterprises LLC	5093	123
Bay Business Forms Inc	5112	92
Bay Carbon Inc	3624	26

Company Name	SIC	Rank
Bay Cast Inc	3325	36
Bay Cast Technologies Inc	3829	207
Bay Cities Paving and Grading Inc	1794	7
Bay City Crab Inc	2091	26
Bay City Motors Inc	5012	157
Bay City Shovels Inc	3599	1607
Bay City Television Inc	4833	140
Bay City Tribune	2711	720
Bay City Window Co	3089	1285
Bay Classifieds Inc	3555	107
Bay Coin Distributors Inc	5046	223
Bay Commercial Bank	6022	557
Bay Communications Inc	5065	178
Bay Container Repairs Of New Jersey Inc	7699	45
Bay Contract Maintenance	7349	431
Bay Controls LLC	3625	174
Bay Corrugated Container Inc	2653	44
Bay Country Enterprises Inc	1623	243
Bay Diesel Corp	7699	139
Bay Electric Company Inc	1731	68
Bay Electric Inc	1731	1492
Bay Electronic Support Tronics Inc	3672	117
Bay Electronics Inc	3625	223
Bay Fasteners and Components Inc	5085	468
Bay Finance Company Inc	6162	105
Bay Foods Inc	2041	48
Bay Guardian Co	2711	424
Bay Gulf Federal Credit Union	6061	90
Bay Harbour Electric Inc	1731	362
Bay Holdings Inc	6519	7
Bay Houston Towing Co	4492	7
Bay Microfilm Inc	7389	665
Bay Microsystems Inc	3674	341
Bay Motor Products Inc	3621	75
Bay Motor Transport Inc	4213	2476
Bay Network Funding	6162	86
Bay Ocean Seafood LLC	2092	74
Bay Oil Co	5541	42
Bay Polymer Corp	5162	13
Bay Precision Machining Inc	3599	2196
Bay Press Inc	2731	356
Bay Products Inc	3544	310
Bay Reprographics Inc	7334	27
Bay St Louis Newspapers Inc	2711	638
Bay Sales LLC	5049	170
Bay Security Company LLC	7381	169
Bay Ship and Yacht Co	3731	24
Bay Shipbuilding Co	3731	27
Bay Shore Systems Inc	3531	137
Bay State Associates Inc	3993	141
Bay State Cable Ties LLC	3496	73
Bay State Chowda Company Inc	6794	142
Bay State Computers Inc	7379	799
Bay State Elevator Company Inc	3534	16
Bay State Envelope Inc	2759	92
Bay State Milling Co	2041	20
Bay State Wire and Cable Company Inc	5063	446
Bay Tact Corp	2741	425
Bay Tech Industries Inc	3599	1517
Bay Technical Associates Inc	3661	65
Bay Technologies Consulting Group Inc	7371	1200
Bay Title and Abstract Inc	6361	36
Bay Verte Machinery Inc	5084	692
Bay View Dental Laboratory Inc	8072	19
Bay View Industries Inc	2541	19
Bay West Group	6552	119
Bay Zinc Company Inc	8748	459
Bayada Nurses Inc	8082	22
Baybutt Construction Corp	1542	367
BayCare Healh System Inc	6324	3
Baycare Health System Inc	8741	65
Bayer Bauserman and Co	7311	839
Bayer Built Woodworks	2431	28
Bayer Construction Company Inc	1623	75
Bayer Corp	2869	1
Bayern Company Inc	7372	3693
Bayfab Metals Inc	3599	1547
Bayfield Electric Cooperative Inc	4911	513
Bayhawk Ales Inc	2082	98
Bayhead Products Corp	3089	1508
Bayhill Capital Corp	4813	740
Baylake Bank	6022	242
Baylake Capital Trust I	6411	52
Baylake Corp	6712	300
Baylake Insurance Agency Inc	6331	128
Baylake Investments Inc	6159	27
Bayless Engineering and Manufacturing Inc	3599	117
Bayliss Machine and Welding Company LLC	5084	499
Bayloff Stamped Products Kinsman Inc	3469	173
Baylor Health Care System	3842	1
Baylor Health Enterprises Inc	2834	114
Baylor Hudson Corp	4953	23
Baylor Trucking Inc	4213	728
Baymark Inc	8748	430
Baymont Inns and Suites	7011	203
Bayonne Community Bank	6022	526
Bayou City Exploration Inc	1311	252
Bayou City Express Inc	4213	2809
Bayou City Pump Works 1 LP	5084	682
Bayou Electrical Services Inc	1731	1667
Bayou Gauging Services Inc	3829	386
Bayou Outdoor Equipment	3546	39
Bayou State Oil Corp	1311	205
Baypoint Components Inc	5065	868
Bays Company Inc	5063	1047
Bay's Southern Bread Inc	2051	175
Bayshore Electric Inc	1731	896
Bayshore Industrial Inc	3087	6
Bayshore Technologies Inc	7379	285
Bayside Business Solutions Inc	7372	2662
Bayside Controls Inc	3625	416
Bayside Printing Inc	2752	886
Baysouth Maintenance Service Inc	7349	485
BaySport Inc	8049	20
Baystate Health Systems Inc	8399	2
Bay-Tec Engineering	8711	470
Baytree Associates Inc	7379	691
Bay-Vanguard Federal Savings Bank	6035	199
Bayview Entertainment LLC	3651	182
Bayview Ford Lincoln-Mercury Inc	5511	1160
Bazaar Del Mundo Inc	5812	338
Bazon-Cox And Associates Inc	7373	675
Bazooka-Farmstar Inc	3523	144
BB and T Corp	6712	10
BB and T Correspondent Lending	6035	136
BB and T Insurance Services Inc	6321	70
BB and T Investment Services Inc	6211	175
BB Computer Concepts Inc	7371	1831
BB Kirkbride Bible Co	2731	255
BBA Aviation- Flight Support	3728	45
Bba Project Inc	5088	111
Bbb Industries LLC	3694	7
Bbc Biochemical Corp	3821	55
Bbc Corp	2752	1362
Bbc Industries Inc	3567	93
BBC Mass Inc	2082	8
Bbc Steel Corp	5051	300
BBC Worldwide America Inc	7822	1
BBCN Bank NA	6022	70
BBDO Worldwide Inc	7311	1
Bbf Custom Products Inc	3089	1583
Bbfm Inc	7311	551
BBG Management Group	5145	18
Bbg Technical Services Inc	8712	102
Bbgn Inc	3728	219
BBI BioSeq Inc	2835	28
BBI Biotech Research Laboratories Inc	2835	29
BBI Computer Systems Inc	7372	1991
Bbi Engineering Inc	7359	200
BBL Construction Services LLC	1541	52
Bbs Computing	5734	461
Bbs Enterprises Inc	3841	289
Bbsi Inc	7371	1663
BC Graphics Inc	2759	366
BC Laboratories Inc	8734	83
BC Marketing Concepts Inc	2082	53
Bc Pavers Inc	3531	192
BC Systems Inc	3679	359
BC Technologies	5734	243
BC Tire Service Inc	5014	46
Bc Underground LLC	1623	522
Bca Electric	1731	1828
BCB Bancorp Inc	6712	291
Bcb Group Inc	5063	595
BCBG Max Azria Group	5137	1
Bcbsm Inc	6321	64
Bcc Distribution Inc	3577	494
BCC Software Inc	7372	956
BCCUSA	8748	345
BCD Associates Inc	3577	655
Bcd Electro Inc	5065	717
B-C-D Metal Products Inc	3444	224
BCD Software Services Inc	7372	2923
BCH Mechanical Inc	1711	285
BCI Collet Inc	3545	305
BCJ Trucking Inc	4213	1708
Bck Inc	3625	313
BCL Electric Inc	1731	2296
Bcl Manufacturing Inc	3541	160
Bcl Technologies	7371	1076
Bcll Inc	3585	79
Bco Industries Of Western New York Inc	2759	324
Bcs Communications Systems Inc	1731	2271
Bcs Cuyahoga LLC	3316	27
BCS Industries LLC	3315	7
Bcs International Inc	3949	161
BCS Life Insurance Co	6311	158
Bcs Tech Center Inc	7379	1551
BCS*A	7373	637
BCSB Bancorp Inc	6035	103
BCSR Inc	5045	980
BCT International Inc	5111	30
BCW Transportation Inc	4213	2737
Bcwest LLC	2754	32
BD Biosciences	3651	14
BD Biosciences Systems and Reagents Inc	8731	8
BD Evans Construction Inc	1623	441
BD Fox Independent	7812	58
BD Medical Systems	3841	22
BD Pharmingen Inc	2835	11
BD Technologies	8731	243
BD Transportation Inc	4213	1330
BD Vacutainer Systems	3841	250
BDB Service and Supply Company Inc	5021	168
BDC Inc	3652	38
BDH and Young Space Design Inc	7389	647
Bdi Pharma Inc	5122	32
Bdisk Corp	3613	122
Bdk Group Of Northern Michigan Inc	1611	243
BDNA Corp	7373	208
BDO Seidman LLP	8721	68
Bdo USA LLP	8721	154
Bdops LLC	7389	834
Bdp Industries Inc	3523	148
BDP International Inc	4731	56
Bdr Management Inc	1731	1392
B-D-R Transport Inc	4213	706
Bds Marketing Inc	7311	127
Bds Systems Inc	3669	315
Bdz Developers Inc	1623	245
BE Aerospace Inc	2531	3
BE and K/Terranext LLC	8711	36
BE and K-Houston/MEI Consultants Inc	8711	276
Be Bilingual Inc	8299	77
Be Connected USA	7389	2021
B-E Hospital Equipment Company Inc	5999	233
BE Intellectual Property Inc	6794	4
BE Meyers and Company Inc	3827	24
Be Our Guest Inc	7359	69
BE Products Inc	2015	49
BE Wallace Products Corp	3536	52
BEA Inc	3679	217
BEA International Inc	8712	229
Beach Abstract and Guaranty Co	6541	13
Beach Banners Inc	7319	174
Beach Beacon	2711	748
Beach Brothers Printing Inc	2752	1539
Beach Business Bank	6022	413
Beach Cities Investigation and Protective Service Inc	7381	73
Beach City Software Inc	7372	4793
Beach Electric Co	1731	897
Beach Financial Corp	5734	464
Beach First National Bancshares Inc	6021	136
Beach Manufacturing Co	3714	292
Beach Media	7372	2193
Beach Products Inc	2834	93
Beach Sound Inc	7359	175
Beach Timber Company Inc	5099	126
Beachbody LLC	3652	17
Beachem Brothers Electric Inc	1731	432
Beachler Trucking Inc	4213	2968
Beach-Russ Co	3561	27
BeachWare Inc	7372	3981
Beacon Advanced Components	5063	1036
Beacon Brothers Development Corp	5084	625
Beacon Communications Inc	2711	512
Beacon Community Credit Union	6061	118
Beacon Container Corp	2653	51
Beacon Electrical Distributors Inc	5063	293
Beacon Enterprise Solutions Group Inc	4813	207
Beacon Fasteners And Components Inc	5072	134
Beacon Federal Bancorp Inc	6035	74
Beacon Financial Group Inc	6282	224
Beacon Group Inc	3724	40
Beacon Hill Software	7372	4663
Beacon Hill Staffing Group LLC	7361	65
Beacon Journal Publishing Co	2711	146
Beacon Looms Inc	2391	12
Beacon Metal Company Inc	5093	155
Beacon Metals Inc	5072	65
Beacon Piping Co	1623	155
Beacon Power Corp	4911	323
Beacon Press	2731	222
Beacon Printing Company Inc	2752	1318
Beacon Roofing Supply Inc	5033	3
Beacon Safety Products Inc	3965	29
Beacon Shoe Company Inc	5139	28
Beacon Technologies Inc (Nashville Tennessee)	4899	159
BeaconMedaes	3563	11
Beaconsfield Financial Services Inc	6211	294
Bead Industries Inc	3432	30
Beaden Screen Inc	3496	104
Beaird Agency Inc	7311	652
Beaird Inc	8742	625
Beakley Enterprises Inc	3564	112
Beal Bank	6211	184
Beal Cos	6531	160
Beal Group	6513	42
Bealine Service Company Inc	4213	908
Beall Concrete Enterprises Inc	3272	9
Beall Corp	3715	11
Beall Industries Inc	3272	10
Beall Investment Corporation Inc	3272	11
Beall Management Inc	3272	12
Beall Technologies Inc	3577	553
Beall Trailers Of Montana Inc	3443	58
Beall Transport Equipment Co	5511	1015
Beall's Department Stores Inc	5651	18
Beall's Inc	2331	1
Beals Lighting Gallery Inc	5063	740
Beam Brothers Trucking Inc	4213	407
Beam Construction Company Inc	1541	226
Beam Inc	2085	1

Company Name	SIC	Rank
Beam On Technology Corp	3569	204
Beam Radio Inc	5065	807
Beamaco LLC	3599	1812
Beamalloy Technologies LLC	3479	82
Beamco Inc	3829	329
Beamers Hells Canyon Tours and Excursions	4725	47
Beamin' Lasers Inc	3699	307
Beamon and Lassiter Inc	4213	3035
Bean Creative	7319	88
Bean Inc	1794	37
Bear Cartage and Intermodal	4213	2465
Bear Cat Manufacturing Inc	3531	133
Bear Computer Systems Inc	7372	4449
Bear Creek Smokehouse LLC	2013	154
Bear Graphics Inc	2782	36
Bear Lake Recreation Inc	6799	367
Bear River Associates Inc	7372	2613
Bear River Publishing Co	2711	698
Bear Stearns Companies Inc	6211	22
Bear Valley Mountain Resort	7999	108
Bearcom Operating LLC	5065	36
Beard Co	2819	136
Bearden Sandwich Company Inc	2099	177
Beardsley Farmers Elevator Co	5153	178
Bearing and Drives Inc	5085	23
Bearing Sales Corp	5085	335
Bearing Service Company of Pennsylvania	3562	21
Bearing Service Inc	5085	253
BearingPoint	8742	9
Bearse USA	2673	68
Bear-Stewart Corp	2033	77
Bearware Inc	7371	1776
Beasley Altoona Manufacturing Inc	3714	361
Beasley Broadcast Group Inc	4832	22
Beasley Broadcasting of Eastern North Carolina Inc	4832	75
Beatnik Inc	7371	203
Beatrice Concrete Co	3272	52
Beatrice Freight Line Inc	4213	2291
Beattie Farmers Union Cooperative Association	5191	68
Beatty Machine and Manufacturing Co	3599	704
Beaty Construction Inc	1622	35
Beauchamp Construction Co	1542	233
Beauchamp Distributing Co	5181	84
Beauchamp Enterprises Inc	6531	250
Beaudry Co	3842	227
Beaudry Electric Motors and Equipment Company Inc	5063	674
Beaufort Ems Inc	7389	2293
Beaufort Memorial Hospital	8062	115
Beaulieu of America LLC	2273	4
Beaumac Company Inc	3599	1578
Beaumont Birch Co	3535	189
Beaumont Concrete Co	3273	85
Beaumont Juice Inc	2033	62
Beaumont Products Inc	2844	78
Beaumont Rice Mills Inc	5153	180
Beauticontrol Inc	2844	48
Beauti-Vue Products Corp	2591	13
Beautopia Inc	2844	91
Beauty Alliance Inc	5087	9
Beauty Brands Inc	7231	3
Beauty Craft Supply and Equipment Co	5087	62
Beauty Fashion Inc	2731	301
Beauty Handbook Corp	2731	279
Beauty Towne Inc	5087	91
Beauvais Printing Inc	2752	1128
Beaver Builders Ltd	1522	45
Beaver Excavating Co	1794	14
Beaver Express	4213	596
Beaver Gravel Corp	1442	27
Beaver Manufacturing Company Inc	2295	18
Beaver Newspapers Inc	2711	872
Beaver Oil Company Inc	4953	115
Beaver State Plastics Inc	3089	1755
Beaver Street Fisheries Inc	5142	5
Beaverbrook Step Inc	8361	75
Beaverton Foods Inc	2035	17
Beazer Homes Holdings Inc	1521	81
Beazer Homes USA Inc	1531	26
Bebco Industries Inc	3448	40
Bebe Stores Inc	2339	5
beBetter Networks Inc	8099	50
BEC Electric Inc	1731	1359
BEC Systems Inc	3469	274
Beceem Communications Inc	3669	64
Becharas Brothers Coffee Co	5149	193
Bechdon Co	8711	458
Becher Engineering Inc	3089	1516
Bechert Brothers Manufacturing Company Inc	3545	240
Bechik Products Inc	2241	25
Bechtel Building Maintenance Corporation Of Columbus Inc	7349	281
Bechtel Group Inc	1541	1
Bechtel National Inc	8711	135
Bechtel Software Inc	7373	29
Beck and Masten Pontiac-Gmc Inc	5511	174
Beck and Son Incorporated Clayborne C	5031	260
Beck Associates Architects	8712	269

Company Name	SIC	Rank
Beck Building Services Inc	7349	445
Beck Computer Systems	7373	629
Beck Group	1542	39
Beck Imports Inc	5511	830
Beck Packaging Corp	5113	65
Beck Suppliers Inc	5171	30
Beck Tool Inc	3544	894
Beck Transportation Inc	4213	3031
Beckart Environmental Inc	3826	81
Beckenstein Men's Fabrics Inc	5131	28
Becker Capital Management Inc	6282	466
Becker Electric Company Inc	1731	1028
Becker Inc	3549	108
Becker Iron And Metal Inc	5051	472
Becker Machine Company Inc	7699	109
Becker Oregon Inc	3842	311
Becker Orthopedic Appliance Co	3842	127
Becker Transportation Inc	4213	1873
Beckerle Lumber Supply Company Inc	5211	148
Beckerman Public Relations	7311	358
Becker's Trucking Inc	4213	2154
Beckett Air Inc	3433	35
Beckett Corp	3561	9
Beckett Electrical Services LLC	1731	2514
Beckett Gas Inc	3433	27
Beckett Publications LP	2721	149
Beckley Water Co	4941	63
Beckman and Gast Company Inc	2032	19
Beckman Coulter Inc	3826	1
Beckman Machine Inc	3599	1822
Beckmann's Old World Bakery Ltd	2051	77
Becknell Wholesale Co	5072	89
Beck's North America Inc	5181	56
Beckson Manufacturing Inc	3561	112
Beckstrom Electric Co	1731	275
Beckwith Electric Company Inc	3675	8
Beckwith Lumber Company Inc	2421	121
Beckwith Machinery Company Inc	5082	11
Beckwith's Car Care	7538	15
Beckwood Services Inc	3625	77
Becmar Corp	3552	61
Beco Construction Power Co	7353	14
Beco Inc	4213	1370
Becon Inc	3829	213
Becotek Manufacturing Inc	3366	13
Becovic Management Group Inc	1731	2553
Becromal Of America Inc	3353	9
Becs Technology Inc	3625	133
Becton Dickinson and Co	3841	4
BeCubed Software Inc	7372	4664
Bed Bath and Beyond Inc	5719	1
Bed Rock Inc	4213	1927
Bedell-Kraus Flexographic And Pharmaceutical Rubber Inc	3069	126
Bedford Associates Inc	7372	3339
Bedford Communications Inc	2721	286
Bedford Crane LLC	3441	248
Bedford Entertainment Inc	7822	37
Bedford Fair Industries	5961	108
Bedford Falls Co	7812	89
Bedford Gazette LLC	2711	515
Bedford Granite Group Inc	7311	910
Bedford Industries Inc	2671	19
Bedford Motor Service Inc	4213	1712
Bedford Products Corp	3577	650
Bedford Reinforced Plastics	3089	100
Bedford Rural Electric Cooperative Inc	4911	521
Bedford Stuyvesant Early Childhood Development Center Inc	8351	22
Bedoukian Research Inc	2844	139
Bee Agricultural Co	5153	188
Bee Bee Que Inc	2038	71
Bee Berguall and Co	8721	57
Bee Electronics Inc	3161	13
Bee Publications Inc	2711	537
Bee Publishing Co	2711	455
Bee Trailers Inc	3523	278
Bee Window Inc	3089	209
Bee Zee Systems	7371	1852
Beebe Electric Inc	1731	1188
Beech Fork Processing Inc	1222	11
Beechcraft Products Inc	2431	133
Beechler's Printing Inc	2752	1507
Beechmont Investments Inc	5511	99
Beechmont Motors Inc	5511	885
Beechmont Press LLC	2752	186
Beech-Nut Nutrition Corp	2032	6
Beechwood Computing Ltd	7379	305
Beechwood Distributors Inc	5181	47
Beechwood Mountain LLC	5021	134
Beeco Inc	3625	289
Beeco Motors and Controls Inc	5063	321
Beef International Inc	2011	97
Beef Packers Inc	2011	41
Beehive Botanicals Inc	5122	96
Beekman Capital Management Ltd	6282	299
Beekman Co	1731	1918
Beeler Property Inc	6531	92
Beemak Plastics Inc	3089	1286
Beeman Jorgensen Inc	5192	41
Beemer Precision Inc	5085	172
Beemer Pricher Kuehnhackl and Heidbrink PA	8721	443
Beer And Slabaugh Inc	1794	41

Company Name	SIC	Rank
Beer Nuts Inc	2068	22
Beere Precision Products	3568	32
Beerntsen's Confectionery Inc	5441	11
Beers and Cutler PLLC	8721	55
Beetle Plastics LLC	3084	25
Beeville Publishing Co	2711	632
BEF Holding Company Inc	2013	1
Before and After	7336	238
Beginning Press	2731	195
Begley Enterprises Inc	1731	852
Begley Lumber Company Inc	2421	53
Begneaud Manufacturing Inc	3599	470
Behavior Tech Computer Corp	3651	26
Behavior Training Research Inc	8361	113
Behavioral Health Group	8051	50
Behavorial Technologies Corp	8331	140
Behemoth Corp	3575	26
Beheydt's Auto Wrecking	7542	3
Behler-Young Co	5075	11
Behlman Electronics Inc	3679	83
Behnke Inc	4213	1750
Behr Climate Systems Inc	3585	91
Behr Drilling Systems Inc	1623	637
Behr Heat Transfer Systems Inc	3714	136
Behr Iron and Steel Inc	5093	15
Behr Process Corp	2851	8
Behrends Feed and Fertilizer LP	2048	126
Behrmann Printing Company Inc	2752	1674
BEI Corp (Pasadena Texas)	8711	131
Bei Electronics LLC	3679	300
Bei International LLC	3523	203
Beidler's Implement Inc	5083	203
Beiersdorf Inc	2844	77
Beige Bag Software Inc	7371	1703
Beiner Inc	5063	647
Beis Moshiach Inc	2759	356
Beiswenger Hoch and Associates Inc	7371	104
Beitler Commercial Realty Services	6531	169
Beitler-Mckee Optical Co	3851	33
Bejed Inc	3661	211
Bek Systems Inc	3569	239
Bek Tronic Technology Inc	5045	1052
Bekaert Corp	3315	3
Bekemeier and Associates	7372	4665
Bekins Co	4214	7
Bekins Hawaiian Movers Inc	4213	1619
Bekins Van Lines LLC	4214	5
Bel Air Auto Auction Inc	7389	777
Bel Air Security Inc	7382	113
Bel Aire Foods Inc	2037	44
Bel Canto Design Ltd	3663	332
Bel Canto Foods Ltd	5141	198
Bel Fuse Inc	3677	1
Bel Mar Wire Products Inc	3496	109
Bel Stewart Connector	3678	27
Bel Thermal Units Inc	3567	107
Belair Road Supply Company Inc	5211	129
Bel-Air Turf Products LLC	3523	268
Belanger Inc	3589	40
Belar Electronics Laboratory Inc	3663	249
Belardi/Ostroy Alc LLC	7389	1843
Bel-Art Products Inc	6512	51
Belarus Tractor International Inc	5083	145
Belcan Engineering Group Inc	8711	39
Belcaro Group Inc	4813	420
Belco Industries Inc (Belding Michigan)	3563	29
Belco Manufacturing Company Inc	3089	476
Belco Technologies Corp	3569	134
Belco Works Inc	8331	200
Belcourt Corp	3053	78
Belden Inc	3357	5
Belden Plastics Inc	3448	53
Belden Tools Inc	3545	212
Belden Wire and Cable Co	3357	31
Belding Hausman Inc	2221	15
Belding Walridge LLC	1796	2
Belec Electrical Inc	1731	1114
Bel-Fab Co	3535	232
Belfonte Ice Cream Co	2024	37
Belfry Development Corp	6531	333
Belgioioso Cheese Inc	2022	31
Belgium Co	2021	3
Belhaven Cable T V Inc	4841	155
Believe Media	7336	24
Beljan Limited Inc	7374	384
Belk Brothers Co	5311	15
Belk Inc	5311	13
Belk Printing Inc	2791	7
Belk Stores Services Inc	7389	14
Belke Manufacturing Company Inc	3559	290
Belkin Corp	3577	34
Belkin International Inc	3643	5
Bel-Kur Inc	3544	335
Bell and Bates Inc	5731	195
Bell and Howell LLC	5045	14
Bell Building Maintenance Co	7349	177
Bell Buoy Crab Co	2092	28
Bell City Battery Manufacturing Inc	3691	41
Bell Component Sales Inc	5065	578
Bell Container Corp	2653	37
Bell County Iron and Recycling Company Inc	5093	158
Bell Electric Company of Penna Inc	5063	372
Bell Electrical Contractors Inc	1731	284

Company Name	SIC	Rank
Bell Electrical Contractors LLC	1731	1360
Bell Engineering Inc	3599	1686
Bell Equipment Co	3559	106
Bell Flavors And Fragrances Inc	2869	49
Bell Gas Inc	5171	4
Bell Hearing Instruments Inc	3842	295
Bell Honda	5511	504
Bell Inc	2657	17
Bell Industries Inc	5065	57
Bell Janitorial Supply LLC	5087	169
Bell Laboratories Inc	2879	13
Bell Litho Inc	2752	561
Bell Machine Company Inc	3599	1306
Bell Manufacturing Co	2241	27
Bell Mortgage Co	6162	25
Bell Nursery USA LLC	0181	5
Bell Performance Inc	2899	165
Bell Photographers Inc	2752	1255
Bell Pipe and Supply Co	5085	185
Bell Press Inc	2721	306
Bell Processing Inc	5051	238
Bell Sports Corp	3949	26
Bell Steel Co	3441	102
Bell Tool Inc	3544	732
Bell Trans Inc	4111	7
Bell Trucking Company Inc	4213	1713
Bella Books	2731	351
Bellagio LLC	7011	5
Bellair Expediting Service Inc	4513	11
Bellamax Inc	5045	310
Belland and Son's Edp and Network	5734	459
Bellatrix Systems Inc	3578	27
Bell-Carter Foods Inc	2033	39
Bellco Drug Corp	5122	20
Bellco Health Corp	5047	11
Bellcrest Homes	2451	5
Belle Haven Realty Co	6531	365
Belle Interiors	7389	1639
Belle Plaine Coop	5191	87
Belle Southern Frozen Foods Inc	2092	48
Belle-Aire Fragrances Inc	2869	85
Bellen Container Corp	3089	395
Bellerophon Publications Inc	2721	281
Belletech Corp	3231	38
Belleville Shoe Manufacturing Co	3143	9
Belleville Shoe South Inc	3143	14
Bellevue Radio Inc	4832	49
BellGroup Financial Services Inc	6163	16
Bellhawk Systems Inc	7375	246
Bell-Horn Inc (Carmel Indianapolis)	3842	289
Bellia Office Furniture Inc	5021	141
Bellingham Cold Storage Co	4222	6
Bellis Steel Company Inc	1791	20
Bellisio Foods Inc	2038	6
Bell-Mark Sales Company Inc	5084	151
Bells Advertising Inc	5199	129
Bell's Hardware Of Klamath Falls Inc	5072	144
Bell's Paging Inc	5065	586
Bellville Tube Company LP	3317	1
Bellwether Inc	3599	1899
Bellwether Software Corp	7372	2438
Bellwright Industries Inc	3599	221
Belmark Inc	2759	70
Belmarmi Inc	5032	118
Belmay Inc	2844	61
Belmet Products Inc	3469	254
Belmont Freight Corp	4213	506
Belmont Instrument Corp	3845	102
Belmont Plating Works Inc	3471	36
Belmont Springs Water Company Inc	5499	10
Belmont Textile Machinery Co	3552	26
Belmont Trading Company Inc	5065	249
Belmor Inc	3714	111
Belo Corp	4833	28
Belo Holdings Inc	4833	7
Belo Interactive	8999	5
Beloit Beverage Company Inc	5181	52
Beloit Special Machining Company Inc	3599	1401
Bel-Pro Products Inc	3599	2310
Belshaw Adamatic Group	3556	32
Belt Collins and Associates Ltd	8711	221
Belt Corporation Of America Inc	3052	20
Belt Line Railroad Co	4011	57
Belt Master Inc	3291	29
Belt Railway Company of Chicago	4013	3
Belt Technologies Inc	3568	56
Belterra Resort Indiana LLC	7993	11
Beltex Corp	2011	68
Belting Industries Company Inc	5085	173
Belton Foods Inc	2087	47
Belton Industries Inc	2299	13
Belton Metal Company Inc	5093	190
Beltrami Electric Cooperative Inc	4911	356
Beltrami Industrial Services Inc	5085	429
Beltran Associates Inc	3564	114
Beltran Electrical Contractor	1731	1241
Beltronics Inc	3845	111
Belt's Corp	4225	26
Beltsville Service Center	2759	342
Beltway International LLC	5511	1068
Belvac Production Machinery Inc	3569	68
Belvedere Capital Partners LLC	6712	724
Belvoir Publications Inc	2721	30
Belyea Company Inc	7629	13

Company Name	SIC	Rank
Belz Enterprises	6552	98
Belzon Inc	7379	439
BEM Services Inc	3339	23
Bema Film Systems Inc	3081	54
Bemci Electric Inc	1731	1321
Bemco Inc	3826	104
Bemcore Tool Inc	3544	574
Bemidji Cooperative Association	5191	150
Bemis Associates Inc	2891	13
Bemis Company Inc	2671	2
Bemis Manufacturing Company Inc	3089	79
Ben and Jerry's Homemade Inc	2024	12
Ben Bridge Jeweler Inc	5944	11
Ben Carter Properties Inc	6531	178
Ben E Keith Co	5141	33
Ben Franklin Design and Manufacturing Company Inc	3625	279
Ben Franklin Press and Label Co	2752	1423
Ben Franklin Press Inc	2752	1086
Ben Hill Griffin Inc	0174	2
Ben M Patterson Jr	1311	228
Ben M Radcliff Contractor Inc	1541	190
Ben Mar Inc	2252	23
Ben Meadows Company Inc	5082	114
Ben Porto and Sons Ltd	1741	19
Ben S Loeb Inc	5199	71
Ben Shives Truck Super Center Inc	5012	201
Ben Venue Laboratories Inc	2834	60
Benatec Associates Inc	8711	130
Bench and Fields Pet Foods LLC	2047	42
Benchcraft LLC	2512	13
Benchemark Printing Inc	2752	569
Bencher Inc	3861	115
Benchmade Knife Company Inc	3421	12
Benchmarc360 Inc	5045	79
Benchmark Bankshares Inc	6712	376
Benchmark Business Solutions	5044	150
Benchmark Communications Inc	4832	66
Benchmark Community Bank	6022	377
Benchmark Consulting International	8748	89
Benchmark Development Corp	1541	221
Benchmark Doors	3442	87
Benchmark Electronics Inc	3672	3
Benchmark Fixture Corp	2541	37
Benchmark Foam Inc	3086	95
Benchmark Graphics Inc	2759	179
Benchmark Group Inc	1541	118
Benchmark Hospitality International	7011	87
Benchmark Inc	2842	129
Benchmark Media Systems Inc	3663	313
Benchmark Network Solutions Inc	7373	754
Benchmark Products Inc	2899	196
Benchmark Sales Agency Inc	3442	112
Benchmark Software Inc	7372	2945
Benchmark Technologies	7372	582
Benchmark Thermal Corp	3567	57
BenchmarkQA Inc	7379	1401
Benchmark-Tech Corp	7389	690
Benco Industrial Supply Inc	5087	157
Benco Steel Inc	5051	360
Bencor LLC	3672	489
Bend Cable Communications LLC	4841	65
Bend Research Inc	8731	129
Bendan Technologies Inc	7372	4221
Bendco/Bending and Coiling Co	3317	58
Bendco Corp	3498	82
Bendco Machine and Tool Company Inc	3542	116
Bendek Cellulars And Accessories International Corp	5065	445
Bender Foundry Service Inc	3543	18
Bender/Helper Impact	8743	66
Bender Systems	5063	466
Bender Transportation Co	4213	2098
Benderson Development Company Inc	6512	49
Bendon Gear and Machine Inc	3599	1255
Bendtec Inc	3498	47
Benecom Computer Company Inc	5734	114
Benecon Group Inc	6324	106
Benedetto Gartland and Co	6211	290
Benedict Computer Co	3823	420
Benedict Enterprises Inc	7513	21
Benedict Group Inc	7372	3867
Benedict Refrigeration Service Inc	1711	229
Benedict-Miller LLC	5051	47
Beneficial Corp	6141	13
Beneficial Life Insurance Co	6311	103
Beneficial Mutual Bancorp Inc	6035	28
Beneficial Savings Bank (Burlington New Jersey)	6035	90
Benefit Concepts Incorporated of Rhode Island	7372	767
Benefit Cosmetics Inc	2844	84
Benefit Design Group	6411	287
Benefit Software Inc	7372	4169
BenefitMall	7389	235
Benefitnation Inc	4813	516
Benefits Resource Group LLC	8742	574
Benelogic LLC	7372	1470
Benesch Friedlander Coplan and Aronoff	8111	151
BeneSoft Inc	7372	2779
Beneteau USA Inc	3732	43
Benetech Inc	5169	45

Company Name	SIC	Rank
Benfield Electric Supply Inc	5063	87
Benicia Fabrication and Machine Inc	3443	97
Benihana Inc	5812	126
Benjamin Development Company Inc	1522	1
Benjamin E Sherman and Sons Inc	6531	346
Benjamin Hr Inc	1731	1749
Benjamin Media Inc	2721	327
Benjamin Moore and Co	2851	9
Benjamin Reporting Service	7338	34
Benjamin Sheridan Corp	3484	14
Benko Products Inc	3534	27
Benmarl Wine Company Ltd	2084	142
Benner Metals Corp	5051	425
Bennet and Sons Machine and Supply Company Inc	5085	320
Bennett and Curran Inc	2731	286
Bennett Brothers Inc	5099	26
Bennett Brothers Printing Company Inc	2752	654
Bennett Die and Tool Inc	3544	410
Bennett Electric And Industrial Contractors Inc	1731	1926
Bennett Electric Inc	1731	2449
Bennett Enterprises Inc	7011	140
Bennett Jacalyn ES And Co	5137	26
Bennett Kuhn Varner Inc	7311	166
Bennett Machine And Fabricating Inc	3599	897
Bennett Manufacturing Company Inc	3441	94
Bennett Marketing Group Inc	8742	689
Bennett Metal Products Inc	3544	263
Bennett Office Technologies Inc	5045	658
Bennett Packaging Of Kansas City Inc	2653	73
Bennett/Porter and Associates Inc	5045	754
Bennette Paint Manufacturing Company Inc	2851	109
Bennet-Tec Information Systems Inc	7372	4236
Bennett's Business Systems Inc	7334	22
Benni 5848 LP	8741	296
Bennington Iron Works Inc	3446	27
Benny Gage Inc	3545	207
Benny Lee Enterprises Inc	5064	134
Benny Machine Company Inc	3599	2448
Benny Whitehead Inc	4213	899
Benny's Inc	5531	32
Benoist Brothers Supply Co	5075	56
Benoit Machine Inc	5084	224
Benports Internetionel Inc	7373	1237
Benq Latin America Corp	5065	480
Benrich Service Company Inc	7389	1633
Ben's Auto Parts Corp	5013	369
Ben's Electric Co	1731	2162
Ben's Precision Instruments Inc	7699	79
Benson and McLaughlin PS	8721	411
Benson Electric Co	3648	44
Benson Hlavaty Architects Inc	8712	207
Benson Industries LLC	3231	2
Benson Marketing Group	8743	287
Benson Mineral Group Inc	1311	188
Benson Security Systems Inc	1731	322
Benson Sound Inc	1731	2414
Benson's Inc	2051	20
Bensussen Deutsch and Associates Inc	8748	17
Bent Electrical Contractors Inc	1731	702
Bent River Machine Inc	3599	1499
Bentek Corp	3679	250
Benteler Automotive Corp North American Div	3465	3
Bentley Associates LP	6211	356
Bentley Austin	8711	501
Bentley Co (Milwaukee Wisconsin)	8741	164
Bentley Instruments Inc	3523	162
Bentley Laboratories LLC	2844	79
Bentley Prince Street Inc	2273	3
Bentley Solutions Center	7372	4095
Bentley Systems Inc	7372	271
Bentley World-Packaging Ltd	4783	6
Bentley Yorba Linda	7372	1341
Benton Cooperative Telephone Co	4813	585
Benton Electronics Supply Inc	5065	973
Benton Foundry Inc	3321	26
Benton Offshore China Co	1311	130
Benton Offshore China Holding Co	6719	141
Benton Rural Electric Association	4911	426
Bentonville Casting Co	3321	60
Bentonville Plastics Inc	3089	1187
Bentwood Furniture Inc	2511	74
Benzel-Busch Motor Car Corp	5511	784
Benzsay and Harrison Inc	2819	135
BEO Bancorp	6712	591
Bepc Ltd	5137	11
Bepco Inc	3585	254
Ber Plastic Corp	3082	31
Beracah Homes Inc	2452	53
Beranek Inc	3728	145
Berardi's Fresh Roast Inc	5149	167
Berat Corp	5411	155
Berbee Information Networks Corp	7373	34
Berberian Nut Co	2068	4
Berbiglia Inc	5921	11
Berchtold Corp	3841	116
Berchtold Equipment Company Inc	5083	25
Berco Watch And Jewelers Supply Company Inc	5094	73
Berdon LLP	8721	215
Berea College Facilities Management	7349	420

Company Name	SIC	Rank	Company Name	SIC	Rank	Company Name	SIC	Rank
Berean Christian Stores	5942	12	Berlin Metals LLC	5051	108	Berwick Electric Co	1623	35
Berenergy Corp	1381	62	Berlin Packaging LLC	5085	14	Berwick Offray LLC	2396	3
Berenfield Containers Inc	3412	2	Berlin Transportation Inc	4213	925	Berwind Corp	2834	33
Beretta USA Corp	5091	56	Berline Group Inc	3993	147	Berwind Natural Resources Corp	6719	131
Berg Company LLC	3586	10	Berlinger Cohen	8111	268	Berwind Property Group Ltd	6552	124
Berg Equipment Corp	3523	142	Berlinsky Scrap Corp	5093	191	Beryl Cos	7389	220
Berg Grain and Produce Inc	4213	1098	Berlin-Wheeler Inc	7322	119	Besa Lighting Company Inc	3646	55
Berg Inc	1541	62	Berlitz International Inc	8299	6	Bescast Inc	3324	10
Berg Lacquer Inc	2851	48	Berman Center Inc	8049	28	BESCO Computer Centers	5734	41
Berg Steel Pipe Corp	3312	55	Berman Printing Co	2759	117	Besco Electic Supply Company of Florida Inc	5063	471
Berg Tool Inc	3541	201	Bermar Associates Inc	3089	1837	Besco Inc	7699	53
Berg Wholesale Inc	5072	132	Bermello Ajamil and Partners Inc	8712	78	Besco Steel Supply Of Georgia Inc	5051	419
Bergaila and Associates Inc	8999	57	Berner Tool and Die Inc	3544	184	Besco Supply Co	5075	87
Borgamot Brass Works Inc	3965	20	Bermil Industries Corp	5087	61	Besco Utilities Inc	1623	525
Bergauer Group Inc	3089	1626	Bermil Industries Corporation Wasco-mat of America	5087	23	Bescor Video Accessories Ltd	3861	110
Berg-Berry Associates Inc	6331	325	Bermo Inc	3469	80	Beshton Software Inc	7372	3982
Bergdorf Goodman Inc	5621	21	Bern Optics Inc	3827	124	Besicorp Development Company LLC	3443	19
Berge Ford Inc	5511	96	Bernal Inc	3544	258	Beskau Trucking Inc	4213	2852
Bergen Cable Technology LLC	3496	100	Bernard C Harris Publishing Company Inc	7373	24	Besler Industries Inc	3949	169
Bergen County Irrigation Inc	5087	168	Bernard Cap Company Inc	2353	8	Bespro Pattern Inc	3543	42
Bergen Protective Systems Inc	5063	1074	Bernard Controls Inc	3823	295	Bessemer Group Inc	6211	244
Berger/ABAM Engineers Inc	8711	151	Bernard D Harner and Son Inc	4213	2477	Bessemer Plywood Corp	2435	20
Berger and Company Recycling Inc	5093	70	Bernard Eckert	1731	1715	Bessemer Securities LLC	6211	152
Berger and Sons Inc	7538	36	Bernard Egan and Co	5148	54	Bessemer Trust Company NA	6021	366
Berger Brothers Co	3444	14	Bernard Hodes Group Inc	7311	38	Besser Co	3559	57
Berger Building Products Inc	3444	22	Bernard Johnson Young Inc	8712	86	Best Access Systems	3429	21
Berger Devine Yaeger Inc	7389	1729	Bernard Klein Inc	5113	55	Best and Donovan NA Inc	5084	636
Berger Lewis Accountancy Corp	8721	334	Bernard L Madoff Investment Securities LLC	6211	28	Best and Flanagan LLP	8111	410
Berge's Governor Service Inc	5084	564	Bernard Laboratories Inc	7389	2181	Best Battery Company Inc	5013	230
Bergey Windpower Company Inc	3621	96	Bernard Pavelka Trucking Inc	4213	2693	Best Best and Krieger LLP	8111	215
Bergh International Holdings Inc	4725	22	Bernard Weldcraft and Plazcraft Products	3548	10	Best Bilt Parts Company Inc	5013	318
Berghausen Corp	2843	14	Bernard Welding Equipment	3674	150	Best Bits and Bytes Inc	5092	48
Bergin Glass Impressions Inc	3231	63	Bernardino's Bakery Inc	2051	166	Best Brains Inc	7812	239
Berglin Corp	3599	1193	Bernardon Haber Holloway Architects PC	8712	154	Best Brands Corp	5149	9
Berglund Construction Co	1542	113	Bernardoni Electric Inc	1731	2128	Best Building and Supply Lumber Corp	5211	237
Bergquist Co	3679	76	Bernards Builders Management Services	1542	168	Best Building Components LLC	2439	39
Bergson Tire Company Inc	7534	6	Bernatello's Pizza Inc	2038	31	Best Built Inc	3442	84
Bergstrom Automotive	5511	453	Bernd Group Inc	7389	732	Best Bumper Supply Inc	5013	296
Bergstrom Company LP	3714	375	Berne Apparel Co	2326	16	Best Buy	5065	406
Bergstrom Inc	3714	117	Bernell Corp	3827	120	Best Buy Company Inc	5731	1
Bergstrom Taghert Film Productions Inc	7812	320	Bernell Hydraulics Inc	3594	23	Best Cab Co	4121	5
Bering Home Center Inc	5251	17	Berner Brothers Publishing Company Inc	2711	751	Best Carbide Cutting Tools Inc	3541	86
Bering Select Seafoods Co	2092	14	Berner Food and Beverage Inc	2022	18	Best Cartage Inc	4213	1360
Bering Technology Inc	3572	58	Berner Industries Inc	3559	457	Best Case Solutions Inc	7372	629
Beringea LLC	6211	187	Berner International Corp	3564	84	Best Computer Consulting Inc	7371	1434
Beringer Associates Inc	7379	1150	Berner Trucking Inc	4213	1598	Best Computer Supplies Inc	5961	147
Beringer Wine Estates Co	2084	6	Bernhard Woodwork Ltd	2541	49	Best Copy and Printing Inc	2752	1762
Berje Inc	5169	96	Bernhardt Furniture Company Inc	2511	2	Best Courier and Delivery Service	4213	2840
Berkebile Oil Company Inc	2992	46	Bernick Cos	2086	47	Best Cutting Die Co	3544	69
Berkeley Capital Management	6282	260	Bernier Cast Metals	3325	40	Best Data Products Inc	3669	55
Berkeley Design Automation Inc	3674	219	Bernina of America Inc	5064	33	Best Delivery Systems Inc	4213	2951
Berkeley Electric Cooperative Inc	4911	339	Berns Construction Company Inc	1611	140	Best Electric Contractors Inc	1731	2031
Berkeley Farms Inc	2026	21	Bernstein and Associates Inc (Houston Texas)	8743	245	Best Equipment Co	3594	5
Berkeley Forge and Tool Inc	3462	42	Bernstein-Rein	7311	46	Best Equipment Technologies Inc	3441	210
Berkeley International Capital Corp	6799	341	Bernthal Packing Inc	5421	23	Best Express Foods Inc	2051	98
Berkeley Lumber Co	5031	380	BernzOmatic	3548	19	Best Foam Fabricators Inc	2821	110
Berkeley Magnetics Inc	3612	100	Berran Industrial Group Inc	3599	1704	Best Foam Inc	3069	143
Berkeley Medevices	5047	180	Berrett Talega Corp	7342	63	Best Harvest LLC	2051	185
Berkeley Nutritional Manufacturing Corp	2834	351	Berrett-Koehler Publishers Inc	2731	300	Best Housekeeping Industries Inc	5064	144
Berkeley Telonic Inc	3679	789	Berridge Manufacturing Company Inc	3444	20	Best Image Systems Inc	5044	97
Berkely Group	6411	59	Berrodin Steel Inc	5013	360	Best Imaging Solutions Inc	7334	26
Berkery Noyes and Company LLC	6211	295	Berry Brothers General Contractors	1389	42	Best Impressions Inc	7372	2708
Berkley Group Inc	6552	102	Berry Companies Inc	5082	39	Best Kosher Foods Corp	2013	49
Berkley Insurance Co	6331	233	Berry Co	7319	8	Best Label Company Inc	5084	205
Berkley Integrated Audio Software Inc	7372	3517	Berry Holdings LP	1541	33	Best Life and Health Insurance Co	6324	92
Berkley Machine Works and Foundry Company Inc	3364	18	Berry Industrial Group Inc	2448	7	Best Medical International Inc	2834	235
Berkley Risk Administrators Company LLC	6411	128	Berry Metal Co	3433	41	Best Meridian Insurance Co	6311	200
Berkline/Benchcraft Holdings LLC	2512	8	Berry Network Inc	7319	9	Best Metal Products Company Inc	3599	219
Berks and Beyond Employment Services Inc	7361	214	Berry Petroleum Co	1311	43	Best Paging Inc	5065	736
Berks Electric Inc	1731	2016	Berry Plastics Corp	3089	8	Best Plumbing Supply Inc	5074	109
Berks Transportation Inc	4213	361	Berry Veal Corp	5147	70	Best Practice Systems Inc	8748	316
Berkshire Bank	6022	61	Berryman Products Inc	5169	43	Best Press Inc	2752	452
Berkshire Blanket Holdings Inc	2392	34	Bers Corp	3669	268	Best Printing And Duplicating Company Inc	2752	1825
Berkshire Corp	2269	8	Bert Hazekamp and Son Inc	2013	109	Best Provision Company Inc	2013	110
Berkshire Gas Co	4924	56	Bert Ogden Motors Inc	5511	1131	Best Rate Referrals LLC	7331	191
Berkshire Hathaway Homestate Insurance Co	6321	51	Bert Smith Oldsmobile Inc	5511	270	Best Signs Inc	7389	1698
Berkshire Hathaway Inc	6331	2	Bert Williams And Sons Inc	5531	36	Best Specialized and Logistics	4213	513
Berkshire Hills Bancorp Inc	6036	12	Bert Wolfe Ford Porsche Audi Toyota Inc	5511	269	Best Tool And Manufacturing Company Inc	3599	172
Berkshire Income Realty Inc	6798	160	Bertch Cabinet Manufacturing Inc	2434	13	Best Transportation Inc	4213	1970
Berkshire Industries Inc	3724	46	Bertech-Kelex Inc	5065	111	Best Value Inn	7011	180
Berkshire Investments LLC	3499	73	Bertelsmann Inc	2731	13	Best Value Technology Inc	7379	634
Berkshire Marketing Group Inc	8743	307	Berthel Fisher and Co	6163	14	Best Vinyl Inc	5162	5
Berkshire Partners LLC	6282	213	Berthold Farmers Elevator Co	5153	137	Best Way Express Inc (Vincennes Indiana)	4213	647
Berkshire Printing Inc	2752	1202	Berthold Gus Electric Co	3613	72	Best Way Transportation Inc	4213	1714
Berkshire Products Inc	3577	542	Bertis Carlson Trucking Inc	4213	2001	Best Western International Inc	7011	51
Berkshire Property Advisors LLC	6798	162	Bertlesmann Industry Services Inc	2732	6	Best Western Terrace Inn	7011	236
Berkshire Refrigerated Warehouse LLC	4222	17	Bertolotti's Ceres Disposal Inc	3639	18	Bestco Electric Inc	1731	369
Berkshire Systems Group Inc	5063	235	Bertram Dental Laboratory	8072	23	Bestco Group Inc	5045	688
Berkshire Travel Agency Inc	4724	140	Bertram Yacht Inc	3732	28	Bestec Inc	5063	814
Berland Printing Inc	2752	1185	Bertrand Products Inc	3728	180	Bestech Inc	3589	146
Berland Technologies Inc	7372	2450	Bert's Electric Supply Company Inc	5065	811	Bestech Tool Corp	3544	523
Berle Manufacturing Company Inc	2325	18	Bert's Truck Equipment Inc	5013	334	Bestek Manufacturing Inc	3577	371
Berlekamp Plastics Inc	3089	1784	Bertsche Engineering Corp	3541	239	Bestel Corp	5065	698
Berlin and Ocean City Ice	5999	240	Bertucci's Corp	5812	151	Bester Brothers Transfer and Storage	4213	2531
Berlin Building Supply	5031	107	Bertucci's Restaurant Corp	5812	182	Bestever Inc	3942	13
Berlin Food and Lab Equipment Co	1799	77				Bestforms Inc	2761	52
Berlin G Myers Lumber Corp	5211	284				Bestgen Typeworks Inc	7389	1134
Berlin Industries Inc	2752	20				Bestmark Inc	8742	413
						Bestop Inc	2394	1
						Bestsweet Inc	2064	13

Company Name	SIC	Rank	Company Name	SIC	Rank	Company Name	SIC	Rank
BesttransportCom Inc	7372	3089	Bevolo Gas and Electric Lights Inc	3648	27	Bickel and Brewer	8111	397
Best-Tronics Manufacturing Inc	3661	101	Bev-O-Matic Vending Co	3581	7	Bickel's Snack Foods	2096	5
Bestway Inc	7359	43	Bewick Publications Inc	2711	728	Bickers Metal Products Inc	3441	203
Bestway Rental Inc	7359	21	Bewley Allen Cadillac	5511	579	Bickford Motors Inc	5511	738
Bestway Systems Inc	4213	470	Bexar Concrete Works I Ltd	3272	65	Bickford's Family Restaurants	5812	261
Bestway Transport Co	4213	1772	Bexel Pharmaceuticals Inc	8731	261	Bickford's Holding Company Inc	5812	410
Bestweld Inc	3599	790	Bexil Corp	6799	297	Bickley Inc	3567	124
BET Holdings Inc	4841	41	Bext Inc	5065	828	Bico Inc (Burbank California)	3841	254
Bet Television Station	4833	168	Beyer Blinder Belle Architects And	8712	76	BICOM Inc	3661	153
Beta Control Systems Inc	3823	343	Planners LLP			Bicron Business Unit of Saint-Gobain	3841	138
BETA Design Group Inc	8712	217	Beyer Blinder Belle LLP	8712	62	Industrial Ceramics Inc		
Beta Electric Inc	1731	1022	Beyer Graphics Inc	2752	144	Bicron Electronics Co	3612	51
Beta Engineering Inc	3728	207	Beylik Drilling Inc	1781	1	Bid2win Software Inc	7371	969
Beta Fluid Systems Inc	2911	56	Beyond Commerce Inc	7375	284	BID2WIN Software Inc (Portsmouth	7372	5107
Beta Industries Corp	6719	189	Beyond Components Of Mas-	5063	250	New Hampshire)		
Beta Industries Inc	3599	965	sachusetts Inc			Biddeford and Saco Water Co	4941	53
Beta International Inc	3491	19	Beyond Email Inc	7373	819	Biddeford Internet Corp	4899	127
Beta Lasermike Inc	3823	79	Beyond Security Inc	5065	382	Biddle Consulting Group Inc	8748	232
Beta Raven Inc	3823	328	Beyond Words Publishing Inc	2731	244	Biddle Precision Components Inc	3599	220
BETA Systems Software of North	7372	450	Beyondcom Inc	7371	226	Bids Trading LP	6211	125
America Inc			BeyondTrust	7372	374	BidSync	7372	2329
Beta Technology Inc	3829	45	BEZ Systems Inc	7372	4187	Bid-Well Corp	3531	58
BetaData Systems Inc	7372	4903	Bezac Equipment Co	5046	152	Bidwell Industrial Group Inc	3824	35
BETAH Associates Inc	8742	376	Bezema Auto Body Inc	5511	1198	Bidwell Industrial Group Inc/Blu-Ray	3861	63
Betatech Inc	7361	253	BF Enterprises Inc	6552	304	Div		
Betatherm Corp	3822	59	BF Rich Company Inc	3089	291	Bidzcom Inc	7389	202
Betatron Electronics Inc	5065	294	B-F Sales Engineering Inc	5084	878	Biederlack Of America Corp	2221	20
Betatron Inc	3674	477	B-Fast Corp	4581	49	Biehl and Biehl Inc	7322	197
Betatronix LLC	3823	120	BFC Capital Trust	6022	701	Biehl International Corp	4499	5
Betco Inc	3448	30	BFC Financial Corp	6712	106	Bieker Electric Inc	1731	1546
Bete Fog Nozzle Inc	3499	70	Bfc Forms Service Inc	2752	231	Bielinski Brothers Builders Inc	1521	55
Betech Inc	3599	2247	BFI	7389	368	bieMedia LLC	7812	240
Betenbender Manufacturing Inc	3542	80	Bfi Print Communications Inc	2761	45	Bien Padre Foods Inc	2032	38
Beth Israel Deaconess Medical Center	8999	2	BFI Pump Inc	3561	121	Bieri Trucking Inc	4213	2902
Bethany Lowe Designs Inc	7336	116	Bfi Waste Systems Of North America	4953	38	Bierschbach Equipment and Supply	5032	19
Bethe Cohen Design Associates	7389	1237	Inc			Company Inc		
Bethel Food Market Inc	5411	248	BFL Inc	4213	1158	Biery Cheese Co	2022	27
Bethel Machine and Manufacturing Inc	3599	2332	BFI Marketing Communication Inc	7311	570	Biesanz Stone Co	1411	9
Bethel Park Printing Inc	2759	513	Bfmc LLC	3554	62	Big	7311	792
Bethel Plastics Inc	8999	99	Bfp Fire Protection Inc	1711	201	Big 10 Tire Co	5531	16
Bethesda Softworks LLC	2741	76	Bfs Business Printing Inc	7334	17	Big 3 Precision Mold Services LLC	3544	286
Bethlehem Apparatus International	2819	106	BFS Diversified Products LLC	2952	3	Big 3 Precision Products Inc	3544	60
Company Inc			BG Electronics Inc	5065	388	Big 5 Sporting Goods Corp	5941	9
Bethlehem Construction Inc	1541	74	BG Hoadley Quarries Inc	1411	14	Big A Drug Stores Inc	5912	30
Bethlehem Corp	3567	32	BG Industries Inc	3599	2308	Big Apple Circus	7999	77
Beth's Fine Desserts Inc	2052	7	BG Instruments Inc	3577	642	Big Apple Dairy Desserts	2024	17
Betmar Hats LLC	5137	32	B-G Machine Inc	7692	48	Big Apple Of New Hartford LLC	5731	134
Betsey Johnson Inc	5621	32	BG Medicine Inc	8071	59	Big B Manufacturing Inc	3599	996
Bett-A-Way Beverage Distributors	4213	1180	BG Products Inc	2911	54	Big Bang Idea Engineering Inc	7311	510
Bettcher Industries Inc	5084	931	BGBC Partners LLP	8721	21	Big Beam Emergency Systems Inc	3648	50
Bette and Cring LLC	1541	60	BGC Partners Inc	6211	65	Big Bear Fireworks Inc	5092	24
Better Baked Foods Inc	2099	88	BGE and C Inc	5065	181	Big Bear Mountain Resort	7011	184
Better Bank	6022	798	BGE Home Products and Services Inc	5722	10	Big Bear Oil Field Services Inc	3599	1344
Better Business Forms Inc	2761	2	BGF Industries Inc	2823	3	Big Blue Dot LLC	7812	274
Better Business Systems Inc	7363	76	BGI Contractors Inc	1541	92	Big Boulder Corp	7011	217
Better Cleaning Systems Inc	3635	7	BGI Inc	6519	29	Big Boy Restaurants International LLC	5812	300
Better Engineering Manufacturing Inc	3452	75	Bgrs Inc	3441	280	Big Boys Electronics And Entertain-	3651	178
Better Life Mobility Centers	7389	353	Bgs Industries LP	3599	702	ment Ltd		
Better Light Inc	3669	180	Bgsg Inc	5734	438	Big B'z Machine Shop	7699	180
Better Lists Inc	7331	279	Bgw Design Limited Inc	7922	41	Big C Lumber Company Inc	5211	23
Better Living Concepts Inc	2759	586	BH Aircraft Company Inc	3724	47	Big City Sales Inc	5063	845
Better Made Snack Foods Inc	2096	13	BH Bunn Co	3559	351	Big Communications	8742	296
Better Plastics Inc	3089	1844	BH Craig Construction Company Inc	1541	161	Big Country Electric Cooperative Inc	4911	527
Better Process Services	3559	344	Bh Electronics Inc	3677	21	Big Creek Lumber Co	5211	43
Better Programs Inc	7371	1824	BH G Inc	2752	109	Big D Bindery Inc	2789	62
Better Sleep Inc	2392	51	BH Holmes Construction Company Inc	1623	792	Big D Construction Corp	1542	56
Better Val-U Supermarkets Inc	5411	48	Bh North America Corp	3568	71	Big "d" Industries Inc	2842	132
Better Way Partners LLC	3089	388	B-H Transfer Co	4213	251	Big Deahl Productions Inc	7812	106
Betterbee-Meadery Inc	3523	187	BH Trucking Inc	4213	537	Big Dipper	2024	77
Better-Way Electric and Data Com-	1731	2253	BHA Group Holdings Inc	3564	9	Big Dog Satellite LLC	5731	103
munication Inc			Bhar Inc	3089	431	Big Dutchman Inc	3523	100
Bettis Electric Company Inc	1731	1735	Bharani Software Solutions Inc	7372	4666	Big Ear Inc	3661	210
Bettridge and Ryan Sales Inc	5065	925	Bharat Forge America Inc	3463	2	Big Film Design	7336	231
Betts Auto Campus	5511	298	Bharat H Barai Associates	7389	1621	Big Fish Films Inc	7812	75
Betts Industries Inc	3494	34	Bhatti Enterprises Inc	7389	1642	Big Fish Games Inc	3944	11
Betts Spring Co	3493	4	Bhb Solutions	7379	1034	Big Frog Mountain Corp	5063	1055
Betts USA Inc	3083	26	Bhirud Associates Inc	6282	572	Big Gain Inc	2048	51
Bettwy Electric Inc	1731	2238	BHM Express Inc	4213	1779	Big Gus Onion Rings Inc	2037	46
Betty A Jones Catering Inc	5812	389	B-House Security Consultants Inc	7381	157	Big Horn Cooperative Market Associa-	5191	91
Betty Jane Home Made Candies Inc	2064	118	BHS Design Group	7389	1374	tion Inc		
Betty Machine Company Inc	3541	63	B-H-W Sheet Metal Co	1761	24	Big Horn Radio Network	4832	28
Betz Cos	6531	179	BI (Minneapolis Minnesota)	8742	57	Big Horn Rural Electric Co	4911	573
Betz Industries Inc	3321	50	Bi Nutraceuticals Inc	2087	40	Big Huge Games Inc	5734	200
Betz/Mitchell Associates Inc	7322	56	Bi Ra Systems Inc	3577	487	Big I Trucking	4213	1539
Betz Transformers Inc	3612	89	Bi Rite Foodservice Distributors	5149	10	Big Island Scrap Metal LLC	5093	240
Beuerman Miller Fitzgerald	8743	113	BI Technologies	3679	196	Big J Milling and Elevator Company Inc	2041	59
Beus Gilbert PLLC	8111	452	Biad Chili Co	2033	98	Big Joe Lift Trucks Inc	5521	7
BevaccessCom Inc	7389	948	Bianchi and Sons Packing Co	0161	14	Big John Manufacturing Company Inc	5251	55
Bevans Oyster Co	2091	17	Bianchi Motors Inc	5511	317	Big John Tree Transplanter	3524	31
Bevcomm	4813	348	BIAS Corp	7373	363	Manufacturing Inc		
Beverage Capital Corp	2086	24	Biax-Fiberfilm Corp	3552	46	Big John's Electric Company Inc	1731	721
Beverage Control Inc	7699	91	Biazzo Dairy Products Inc	2022	51	Big John's Moving Inc	4213	2929
Beverage House Inc	2099	281	Blbb Collection Service Inc	7322	181	Big Johnsons Concrete Pumping	5032	71
Beverage Media Group Inc	2721	298	Bibbero Systems Inc	2752	289	Big L Corp	5211	66
Beverage South Inc	2086	87	Bibey Machine Company Inc	3599	1750	Big League Broadcasting LLC	4832	95
Beverage Transportation Inc	4213	1608	BiblioData	2731	361	Big Lots Inc	5331	7
Beverage-Air Corp	3585	21	Bibliographical Center For Research	8732	50	Big M Inc	5621	20
Beveridge and Diamond PC	8111	277	Rocky Mountain Region Inc			Big Monster Toys LLC	7389	2028
Beverly Clark Enterprises LLC	7389	2326	BIC America Inc	3651	176	Big Nickel	2741	239
Beverly Enterprises - Wisconsin Inc	8051	32	Bic Manufacturing Inc	3599	759	Big Night Entertainment Group Inc	5813	3
Beverly John Printers Inc	2752	1793	BICC Systems Inc	7372	4277	Big O Tires Inc (Englewood Colorado)	6794	36
Beverly Lumber Co	5211	159	Bicentennial Publishing Corp	2711	548	Big Ocean Corp	5063	480
Beverly Pacific Company Inc	3564	155	Bichelmeyer Meats A Corp	5421	25	Big Rapids Products Inc	3469	167
Beverly-Grant Inc	1542	279	Bicitis Group Inc	7379	642	Big Red LTL Transport Inc	4213	641

Company Name	SIC	Rank
Big River Industries Inc	1442	3
Big River Rubber And Gasket Company Inc	5085	267
Big River Zinc Corp	3356	27
Big Rivers Electric Corp	4911	276
Big Sandy Furniture Inc (South Point Ohio)	5712	34
Big Sandy Rural Electric Coop	4911	584
Big Sky Brewing Co	2082	79
Big Sky Insulations Inc	3086	102
Big Sky Irrigation Inc	5083	175
Big Sky Laser International Inc	3699	167
Big Sky Technologies Inc	7372	4201
Big Sky Travel Source Inc	4724	125
Big Sky Western Bank	6022	291
Big Spring Mill Inc	2041	50
Big Springs Inc	2086	63
Big State Electric Ltd	1731	193
Big State Logistics Inc	4213	2184
Big Tex Air Conditioning LP	1711	192
Big Thompson Watershed Forum	3823	473
Big Time Brewery Company Inc	2082	92
Big Top Party Shop Inc	5947	26
Big Tree Furniture and Industries Inc	2511	50
Big "v" Feeds Inc	2048	48
Big Valley Equipment LLC	5046	293
Big W Industries Inc	3545	300
Big West Oilfield Services	7353	96
Big Y Foods Inc	5411	75
Bigard and Huggard Drilling Inc	1381	20
BigBad Inc	7375	159
Bigbee Metal Manufacturing Company Inc	3523	168
Bigbee Steel And Tank Company Inc	3443	87
Bigbee Steel Buildings Inc	3448	39
Bigbee Transportation Inc	4213	1290
bigdoughcom Inc	7319	71
Bigelow Advertising	7311	407
Bigelow Group Inc	1521	122
Bigge Crane and Rigging Co	4213	2383
Bigger Faster Stronger Inc	7299	45
Biggs and Gilmore Communications	7319	33
Biggs Tool And Die Inc	3599	2217
Bigham Insulation And Supply Company Inc	3296	17
Bigink LLC	2752	1528
Biglari Holdings Inc	5812	77
Bigman Brothers Inc	1731	355
BigStage	7372	2663
Bigston Corp	3679	459
Bi-Jamar Inc	1731	679
Bijan Computers Inc	5734	364
Bijan Corp (Beverly Hills California)	5611	28
Bijan Fragrances Inc	2844	38
Bijoux Terner LP	8999	44
Bike Pedlar	5941	30
Bike Track Inc	3751	23
BilAmerica Inc	7322	4
Bilbo Transports Inc	4213	784
Bilco Tools Inc	3533	39
Bilingual Software Inc	7372	4079
Bi-Link Metal Specialties Inc	3469	86
Bil-Jac Foods Inc	2047	17
Bil-Jax Inc	3446	13
Bilken Industrial Fabricators Inc	3644	47
Bill And Amanda Hollibaugh	3674	495
Bill and George Gill Trucking Inc	4213	1933
Bill Anderson and Associates Inc	1731	1806
Bill Barrett Corp	4924	29
Bill Barrett Industries Inc	3599	2488
Bill Bartmann Enterprises	7389	886
Bill Benetreu Co	3069	177
Bill Black Chevrolet Cadillac	5511	505
Bill Black Electric Inc	1731	1146
Bill Bosse and Associates	7311	793
Bill Casey Electric Sales Inc	5063	404
Bill Currie Ford	5511	183
Bill Davis Trucking Inc	4213	1286
Bill Enyart and Sons Contracting Inc	1623	398
Bill H Battles	5065	936
Bill Hudson and Associates Inc	7311	536
Bill Jacobs of Joliet	5511	296
Bill Ledbetter's Dry Wall Sales Inc	5032	147
Bill Martin's Cee Bee Food Stores	5411	218
Bill Mcgowan Inc	1623	869
Bill Me Later Inc	8748	78
Bill Page Honda	5511	831
Bill Penney Toyota Company Inc	5511	659
Bill Perkins Automotive Group	5511	225
Bill Ray Nissan	5511	877
Bill Ross and Son Trucking Inc	4213	2984
Bill S Repair Shop Inc	5084	761
Bill Siler Contracting Inc	1623	614
Bill Sills Sportswear Inc	2339	46
Bill Sullivan Pontiac Inc	5511	475
Bill Ussery Motors Inc	5511	255
Bill Veazey's Party Store Inc	7359	189
Bill Voorhees Company Inc	5075	65
Bill Wahl Supply Inc	5033	50
Bill West Inc	7373	1160
Billboard Live	7312	28
Billco Manufacturing Inc	3559	121
Billco Motors Inc	5511	1202
Billet Industries Inc	3599	1465

Company Name	SIC	Rank
Billeting Fund	7349	502
Billie-Ann Plastics Packing Corp	3089	1451
Billig Trucking Inc	4213	2644
Billing Concepts Inc	8721	330
Billing Services Group Ltd	7374	49
Billingsley Precision Machining LLC	3599	2450
Billington Welding and Manufacturing Inc	3556	84
Billiou's	5083	112
Billmyr Enterprises Inc	7319	146
Billow Electric Supply Company Fe Inc	5063	426
Billows Electric Supply Co	5063	119
Bill's Electric Inc	1731	196
Bill's Electronics Inc	5063	711
Bill's Used Auto Parts Inc	5015	29
Billscom Inc	7374	52
Billtrust	8748	210
Billy Barnes Enterprises Inc	4213	284
Billy D Johnson Contractors Inc	1623	650
Billy Jack Hardware and Electronics	5731	199
Billy Joe Burrow Inc	4213	2802
Billy Penn Corp	3444	58
Billy Pugh Company Inc	3089	1278
BI-LO Holdings LLC	5411	51
Biloff Manufacturing Company Inc	3585	247
Bilsons Industries Inc	3479	98
Bilt Best Windows	2431	33
Biltmore Communications Inc	4813	543
Biltmore Construction Company Inc	1542	361
Biltmore Estate Wine Company Inc	2084	8
Biltmore Technologies Inc	7379	739
Biltrite Corp	3061	25
Biltrite Metal Products Inc	3444	278
Bimini Capital Management Inc	6798	187
Bin and Storage Authority	5085	436
Binaca Products Inc	5063	981
Binary Group	8748	96
Binary Research Inc	7372	3518
Binary Research International Inc	7372	2258
Binary Star Development Corp	7372	3340
BinaryLabs Inc	7372	2437
BinaryTreecom	7372	1093
Bind Rite Service Inc	2789	12
Bindagraphics Inc	2789	3
Bindery 1 Inc	2675	17
Bindery and Specialties Pressworks Inc	2789	42
Bindery Associates Inc	2789	70
Bindery Express Inc	2789	72
Binding Edge Inc	2789	106
Binding Site Inc	5047	132
Bindley Capital Partners	6282	226
Bind-Rite/Union Graphics LLC	2759	28
Bindtech Inc	2789	10
Bindview Corp	7371	150
Binford Electric LLC	1731	2382
Bingemann G Electric LLC	1731	2034
Binggeli Rock Products Inc	3273	50
Bingham and Taylor Corp	3089	655
Bingham Cooperative Inc	5191	71
Bingham Equipment Co	5084	59
Bingham McCutchen	8111	29
Bingham McHale LLP	8111	235
Bingham Trucking	4213	2257
Binghamton Simulator Company Inc	8999	87
Binghamton-Ithaca Express Inc	4213	2514
Bingo Cactus Supply Inc	3944	43
Binkelman Corp	5085	219
Binkowsky Inc	5087	49
BINOMIAL International Inc	7372	1683
Binsfeld Engineering Inc	3825	139
Binson's Home Health Care Centers	8082	43
Bintz Restaurant Supply Co	5046	51
Bio Compression Systems Inc	3841	316
Bio/Data Corp	2835	58
Bio Med Packaging Systems Inc	3842	246
Bio Online Inc	8731	398
Bio Plastics Co	2295	19
Bio Plus Inc	0723	30
BioAegean Corp	2836	95
Bioanalytical Systems Inc	3826	35
Bioautomation Corp	5049	104
Bio-Botanica Inc	2833	50
Bio-Brite Inc	3826	133
Biobubble Inc	3443	235
Biocentury Publications Inc	2711	655
Biochem Systems Inc	2842	128
Biochemical Diagnostics Inc	3841	313
Bioclimatic Inc	3564	124
BioClinica Inc	8734	17
Biocoat Inc	8731	367
Bio-Concepts Inc	3842	280
Biocontrol Systems Inc	8731	230
BioCryst Pharmaceuticals Inc	2836	36
Biodel Inc	2834	452
BioDelivery Sciences International Inc	2834	377
Biodesign Incorporated Of New York	3821	74
BIODESIGN International	2835	72
Bio-Detek Inc	3845	73
Biodex Medical Systems Inc	3842	93
BioElectronics Corp	2834	420
Bio-Energy Systems Inc	2869	110
Biofac Inc	2879	42
Biofield Corp	8731	311
Biofilm Inc	3841	219

Company Name	SIC	Rank
BioForce NanoSciences Holdings Inc	3826	140
BioForm Medical Inc	3841	73
BioFuel Energy Corp	2869	21
Biogen Idec Inc	2836	2
Biogenetics Corp	8099	109
Biogenex Laboratories	3841	172
Biohabitats Inc	8711	348
Bioheart Inc	2835	76
Biohorizons Implant Systems Inc	3843	24
BioImmune Inc	7389	2414
Bio-It World Inc	2721	1
Bioject Inc	3841	246
Bioject Medical Technologies Inc	3841	262
Bio-Key International Inc	3679	537
Biokyowa Inc	2048	119
BioLargo Inc	2899	248
Biolase Technology Inc	3843	15
Biolex Therapeutics Inc	2836	76
BioLife Solutions Inc	3841	360
Biolog Inc	2835	54
Biological Research Associates Inc	8731	294
Biomagnetic Research Inc	3577	482
BioMarin Holdings Inc	2834	418
BioMarin Pharmaceutical Inc	2834	70
Biomarine Inc	3823	211
BioMarker Pharmaceuticals Inc	8731	304
Bio-Matrix Scientific Group Inc	7389	2514
Bio-Med Devices Inc	3841	242
BioMed Realty Trust Inc	6798	57
Biomed Resource Inc	5047	232
BioMed Systems LLC	8731	371
Biomedic Data Systems Inc	3999	150
Biomedical Communications	4899	231
Biomedical Life Systems Inc	3699	135
Biomedical Polymers Inc	3069	169
Bio-Medical Products Corp	2835	73
Biomedical Research And Development Laboratories Inc	3841	317
Biomedical Systems Corp	8099	48
Biomedical Technology Solutions Holdings Inc	4959	28
Biomerica Inc	3843	51
Biomet Inc	3842	5
Biometric Applications and Technology Inc	7373	60
Biomimetic Solutions Plus Inc	5065	309
BioMimetic Therapeutics Inc	3841	378
Biomoda Inc	2834	468
Biomune Co	2836	31
Bion Enterprises Ltd	2835	35
Bion Environmental Technologies Inc	2879	56
Bionetics Corp	8711	94
Bionix Development Corp	3841	234
Bionostics Inc	2835	26
Bionovo Inc	2834	436
BioNumerik Pharmaceuticals Inc	2834	380
Bio-Oregon Inc	2077	17
Biopac Systems Inc	3577	274
BioPartners In Care Inc	8099	54
Biophan Technologies Inc	3841	398
BioPharm Systems	8742	236
BioPro Corp	2836	50
Biopro Inc	3842	209
Bioprogress Technology International Inc	8731	358
BIOQUAL Inc	8731	155
BIOQUANT Image Analysis Corp	7372	2946
Bio-Rad Laboratories Inc	3826	3
Bio-Reference Laboratories Inc	8071	5
Biosante Pharmaceuticals	2836	73
Bioscan Inc	3826	123
Bioscience Laboratories Inc	8071	48
Bioscreen Testing Services Inc	8734	86
Bioscrip Inc	5912	9
Biosensors International USA	5047	163
Biosonics Inc	8748	339
BioSpace Inc	8743	9
BioSpecifics Technologies Corp	2834	347
BioSphere Medical Inc	3841	97
Biospherical Instruments Inc	3812	187
Biospherix Ltd	3821	59
Biosynergy Inc	3829	353
Biotage Inc	3826	148
Biotec Inc	3843	50
Biotech Medical LLC	5047	90
Bio-Technical Resources LP	8731	363
Bio-Tek Instruments Inc	3845	58
Biothane Corp	8711	429
Biotics Building Partnership	2834	300
BioTime Inc	2836	67
Biotronic	8071	53
Biotronics Inc	7699	77
BioTrove Inc	8731	277
Biovail Technologies Ltd	2834	79
Biovest International Inc	2834	352
BioVex Group Inc	2834	237
Bioworks Inc	2879	40
Biozyme Inc	2048	53
Bipolarics Inc	3674	325
Birch Brothers Southern Inc	3552	37
Birch Communications	4813	87
Birch Equipment Company Inc	5082	100
Birch Grove Software Inc	7372	4794
Birchwood Best	2435	6

Company Name	SIC	Rank
Birchwood Farms Inc	7992	8
Birchwood Lighting Inc	3648	65
Birchwood Transport Inc	4213	1874
Birckhead Electric Inc	1731	316
Bird and Associates Inc	3625	409
Bird Blue Body Co	3713	8
Bird Brain Inc	3269	12
Bird Chevrolet Co	5511	1101
Bird Electronic Corp	3825	37
Bird Pretty International Inc	2048	131
Bird-Kultgen Inc	5511	725
Birdman Distribution Corp	5063	990
Birds Barbershop	7241	2
Birdsall Tool and Gage Co	3674	429
Birdsong Corp	5159	7
Bird-X Inc	3699	242
Birken Manufacturing Co	3724	48
Birkenstock Footprint Sandals Inc	5139	2
Birkenstock USA LP	5661	12
Birket Engineering Inc	8711	563
Birkett's International Inc	2041	14
Birkmire Trucking Co	4213	1875
Birko Corp	2819	82
Birlasoft Inc	7379	50
Birmingham Control Systems Inc	3699	255
Birmingham Data Systems Inc	7371	1416
Birmingham Fastener and Supply	3452	30
Birmingham Hot Metal Coatings Inc	5051	418
Birmingham Hydraulics Inc	3492	32
Birmingham Printing And Publishing Company Inc	2741	263
Birmingham Rail and Locomotive Company Inc	5088	32
Birmingham Rubber And Gasket Company Inc	3429	130
Birmingham Utilities Inc	4941	56
Birnbrey Minsk and Minsk	8721	113
Birner Dental Management Services Inc	8099	49
Biro Manufacturing Company Inc	3556	62
Birrell Bottling Co	2086	100
Birtcher Group	1522	36
BIS Computer Solutions Inc	7372	3478
Bisaga Inc	3599	2333
Bisco Dental Products Co	5047	238
Bisco Inc	3843	26
Bisco Industries Inc	5065	61
Bisco International Inc	3555	127
Biscom Inc	3661	66
Biscomerica Corp	2052	18
Bishamon Industries Corp	3559	307
Biship Electric Of Ocala Inc	1731	1935
Bishop Aviation Inc	3728	214
Bishop Construction Inc	1623	848
Bishop Distributing Co	5023	10
Bishop Electronics Corp	3675	36
Bishop Fixture And Millwork Inc	2541	22
Bishop-Wisecarver Corp	3499	46
Bisig Impact Group	7311	315
Bismarck-Mandan Security Inc	7381	144
Bison Building Materials LLC	5031	15
Bison Engineering Co	3599	746
Bison Federal Credit Union	6061	129
Bison Gear and Engineering Corp	3568	21
Bison Inc	3949	108
Bison Instruments Inc	3829	524
Bison Laboratories Inc	4783	26
Bison Printing Inc	2752	833
Bissell Homecare Inc	3589	13
Bissett Steel Co	5051	489
Bissinger And Stein Inc	3599	761
Bissman Company Inc	5181	74
Bisso Marine Company Inc	4499	6
Bisson Moving and Storage	4213	296
Bi-State Machinery Co	5999	244
Bi-State Rubber Inc	3069	255
Bistro Management Company Inc	5812	46
Bit By Bit Computing	7373	1186
Bit Computers Inc	7371	1525
BiT Group Inc	7379	657
Bit Shop Inc	3599	2466
Bitco Corp	6331	23
Bi-Tech Enterprises Inc	5734	351
Bitek Inc	7372	3479
Bitflow Inc	3672	448
bitMAX LLC	3695	70
Bitner Goodman	8743	304
BitPusher LLC	7379	748
Bitrage Inc	3679	145
Bitrode Corp	3829	70
Bitstream Inc	7371	318
Bittersweet Inc	8361	161
Bittner Industries Inc	3089	1834
Bittners Commerical Group	7389	805
Bituminous Casualty Corp	6331	87
Bituminous Fire and Marine Insurance Co	6331	280
Bitwise Inc	7373	445
Bitwise Software International Inc	7371	520
BitWise Solutions Inc	7372	3215
Bitzer Products Co	3599	1720
Bitzer Us Inc	3822	14
Bivar Inc	3679	419
Biven's Electric Inc	1731	546

Company Name	SIC	Rank
Bivio Networks Inc	8731	266
Biwal Manufacturing Company Inc	3599	1271
Bixby Energy Systems Inc	3567	109
Bixby International Corp	3083	21
Bixler Inc	7336	175
Biz Auction Corp	7389	2160
Biz Net Technologies	7376	30
Bizal Manufacturing Inc	3599	882
Bizbash Media	2741	81
Biz-comm Inc	7311	996
Bizerba Label Solutions	2759	255
Bizjet International Sales and Support Inc	3721	23
BizLand Inc	7379	502
Bizmate Consulting Inc	7373	933
Bizsellbrokers Inc	7389	1211
Bizzack Inc	1611	89
BJ Bindery	2789	36
BJ Cecil Trucking Inc	4213	1371
BJ Chemical Services	5169	116
BJ Communications Inc	8743	191
Bj Holdings Corp	5812	188
BJ McGlone and Company Inc	1742	12
BJ Services Co	1389	4
BJ Services Company USA LP	1389	12
BJ Terroni Company Inc	5074	193
BJ Transport Inc	4213	2049
Bjc Health Clincal Asset Management	8062	241
BJC Healthcare	8062	34
Bjc Management Inc	1711	190
Bjerke Forgings Inc	3312	61
BJJ Company Inc	4213	2622
Bjk Industries Inc	3081	32
Bjoin Limestone Inc	1411	10
BJ's Restaurants Inc	5812	83
BJ's Wholesale Club Inc	5411	12
Bjurman Berry and Associates	6282	580
BJW Berghorst and Sons Inc	5085	305
BK Associates International Inc	2095	54
BK Industries	2599	12
B-K Manufacturing Company Inc	3599	665
B-K Plumbing Supply Inc	5074	182
BK Signs Inc	1731	1796
BK Solutions Inc	7389	2421
BK Utility Contractors Inc	1623	598
BKF Asset Management Inc	6282	141
BKM Enterprises Inc	5712	28
Bkmfg Corp	3634	27
BKR Fordham Goodfellow LLP	8721	383
BKR Studio Inc	7336	166
Bkt Inc	3089	949
Bkv Inc	7311	505
Bkz Instruments Inc	3613	185
BL Companies Inc	8711	314
BL Cream Co	2026	73
BL Curry and Sons Inc	2435	22
BL Harroun And Son Inc	3498	63
BL Robinson Electric Supply Co	5063	657
BL Sizemore And Associates Inc	5046	328
Bl Trading LLC	5045	530
Blac Inc	3593	22
Blach Construction Co	1541	147
Blach Distributing Co	5181	95
Blachford Corp	2841	41
Black and Co	5085	39
Black and Decker Corp	3546	2
Black and Tan Corp	7311	943
Black and Veatch Holding Co	8711	15
Black and White Inc	2721	464
Black Ball Transport Inc	4482	3
Black Bayou Productions Inc	3861	50
Black Bear Bottling Group LLC	5145	23
Black Box Corp	3577	21
Black Box Network Services (Minnetonka Minnesota)	5065	8
Black Brothers Co	3553	28
Black Canyon Capital	6799	231
Black Chronicle Inc	2711	899
Black Clawson-Sano Inc	3559	184
Black Crow Media LLC	4832	79
Black Crow Media Of Valdosta LLC	4832	141
Black Diamond Inc	7372	232
Black Diamond Performance Reporting LLC	7372	1392
Black Dragon Resource Companies Inc	1381	57
Black Duck Software Inc	7372	1043
Black Electrical Supply Inc	5063	266
Black Enterprise Greenwich Street Corporate Growth Partners LP	6799	48
Black Entertainment Television LLC	4841	35
Black Gold Potato Sales Inc	5148	51
Black Helterline	8111	516
Black Hills Bentonite LLC	1459	2
Black Hills/Colorado Electric Utility Company LP	4911	208
Black Hills Corp	4911	62
Black Hills Exploration And Production Inc	1382	21
Black Hills Gold Jewelry By Coleman	3911	13
Black Hills Power Inc	4911	114
Black Hills Special Services Co-Operative	8361	29
Black Hills Trucking Inc	4213	788

Company Name	SIC	Rank
Black Hills Workshop and Training Center	3679	117
Black Hills Workshop And Training Center Inc	8249	11
Black Horse Carriers Inc	4213	891
Black Ice Security Services Inc	7381	253
Black Ice Software LLC	7372	4229
Black Marlin Pipeline Co	4613	13
Black Millwork Company Inc	2431	16
Black Mountain Community Bank	6022	644
Black Mountain Group	8748	282
Black Mountain Software Inc	7372	1793
Black Mountain Systems LLC	7372	2749
Black Oil Company Inc	5171	62
Black River Electric Coop (Fredericktown Missouri)	4911	172
Black River Electric Coop (Sumter South Carolina)	4911	294
Black River Industries Inc	8399	28
Black River Manufacturing Inc	3714	215
Black River Plastics Inc	3089	922
Black Star Publishing Company Inc	7335	31
Black Tie Hospitality Inc	7363	160
Black Tie Services LLP	5962	16
Blackball Inc	7372	858
Blackbaud Inc	7372	146
Blackbeard Communications Inc	3663	375
Blackbeard's Charters Inc	4725	68
Blackbird Technologies Inc	8748	47
Blackboard Inc	7372	121
Blackbourn Media Packaging	3999	24
Blackburn Building Services LLC	5087	140
Blackburn Manufacturing Co	2399	27
Blackburn-Russell Company Inc	5141	193
Blackey's Bakery Inc	2051	280
Blackfeet Head Start	8351	42
Blackfoot Electric Corp	1731	1839
Blackhawk Automatic Sprinklers Inc	3569	52
Blackhawk Bakery Ltd	2051	294
Blackhawk Bancorp Inc	6712	453
Blackhawk Bank and Trust	6022	523
Blackhawk Color	7371	1153
Blackhawk Inc	5045	393
Blackhawk Management Corp	8742	107
Blackhawk Molding Company Inc	3089	498
Blackhawk Steel Corp	5051	256
Blackhawk Transport Inc	4213	893
Blacklightning Publishing Inc	2731	373
BlackLine Systems	7371	611
Blackman and Holberton Move Planning Services	7389	1787
Blackman Kallick	8721	248
Blackmer Flow Technologies	3561	76
Blackmon Contracting Company Inc	1623	486
Blackmore Company Inc	3089	353
Blackrock Construction LLC	1751	10
BlackRock Income Opportunity Trust	6726	46
BlackRock Income Trust Inc	6726	21
BlackRock Inc	6211	12
BlackRock Insured Municipal Term Trust Inc	6726	95
Blackrock Kelso Capital Corp	6163	7
Blacks Electric	1731	2545
Blacksheep Inc	3842	97
Blackside Inc	7812	110
Blacksmith Inc	7372	2540
Blackstone and Cullen Inc	7373	432
Blackstone Business Enterprises Inc	3444	128
Blackstone Consulting Inc	8742	252
Blackstone Group Inc	8732	63
Blackstone Group LP	6282	23
Blackstone Technology Group	7389	215
Blackstone Ultrasonics Inc	3559	215
Blackstone Wood Products Inc	2426	43
Blackton Inc	5023	94
Blackwater Midstream Corp	5171	74
Blackwater Security Consulting LLC	7381	115
Blackwelder and Associates Electric Company Inc	1731	1936
Blackwell Baldwin Chevrolet Geo Oldsmobile Cadillac Inc	5511	125
Blackwell Global Consulting LLC	7372	1829
Blackwell Plastics LP	3089	989
Blackwell's Book Services	5192	14
Blackwell's Delaware Inc	5192	8
Blackwold Inc	3577	288
Blade Empire Publishing Company Inc	2711	716
Blade Runner Farms Inc	3523	239
Bladelogic Inc	7372	596
BlahUSA	7819	70
Blaine Jensen and Sons RV Centers of Utah	5561	16
Blaine Kern Artists Inc	7389	400
Blair Adhesive Products	2891	113
Blair and Associates Ltd	7819	46
Blair Cos	3993	14
Blair Dubilier and Associates Inc	7379	1113
Blair Inc	3993	114
Blair Machine and Tool Inc	3599	1186
Blair Milling and Elevator Company Inc	2048	122
Blair Packaging	2741	55
Blair Rubber Co	3069	151
Blair Strip Steel Co	3316	28
Blair-Fuehrer Inc	3599	2423

Company Name	SIC	Rank
Blake Brothers West Inc	5049	100
Blake Electric Contracting Company Inc	1731	529
Blake Utter Ford	5511	731
Blake Wire and Cable Corp	3357	78
Blake-Lamb Funeral Homes Inc	7261	5
Blakeman Industries Inc	3069	180
Blakeslee Prestress Inc	3272	60
Blakinger Byler and Thomas PC	8111	467
Blako Inc	3589	109
Blako Industries Inc	3081	137
Blanc and Otus	8743	99
Blanchard's Seafood Inc	5146	47
Blanchardville Cooperative Oil Association	5172	138
Bland Farms Inc	5148	10
Bland Garvey Eads Medlock and Deppe PC	8721	169
Blandford Machine and Tool Company Inc	3544	767
Blandin Paper Co	2621	34
Blank Rome LLP	8111	106
Blankenship And Associates Inc	5063	658
Blankenship Electric Inc	1731	1322
Blanket Security Inc	7382	163
Blankinship Distributors Inc	5122	118
Blanks Printing and Imaging Inc	2752	314
Blanton Studio Inc	7389	2194
Blaschke Trucking Co	4213	2903
Blase Manufacturing Co	3469	169
Blaser Die Casting Co	3429	82
Blasland Bouck and Lee Inc	8711	85
Blass Communications LLC	7311	366
Blass Employment Corp	7363	219
Blast Internet Services	7372	3177
Blast Radius	7371	92
Blasters Inc	1799	102
Blastgard International Inc	2892	9
Blastronix Inc	3577	571
Blatek Industries Inc	3829	199
Blatt and Myers Inc	1731	1069
Blauer Manufacturing Company Inc	2311	19
Blaw-Knox Construction Equipment	3531	31
Blaylock Robert Van LLC	6211	408
Blaylock Threet Engineers Inc	8711	445
Blaze Co	8743	138
Blaze Fireplace Of Northern California	5023	138
BLAZE SSI Corp	7372	3480
Blaze Systems Corp	7372	2443
Blaze Technical Services Inc	3829	327
Blazek Corp	1623	586
Blazent Inc	7372	2522
Blazer Industries Inc	2452	23
Blc International Inc	5063	649
BLD Products Ltd	3714	89
Bleacher Sales Co	3446	5
Blendco Inc	2099	287
Blended Waxes Inc	2999	4
Blender	2741	279
Blendex Company LLC	2041	34
Blendtec Inc	3634	3
Blenko Glass Company Inc	3211	17
Blentech Corp	3556	110
Bler Travel Inc	4724	130
Bless Precision Tool Inc	3599	1187
Blessing/White Inc	8331	22
Bleuchip International Inc	7331	85
Blevins Inc	5099	20
Blh Technologies Inc	7379	844
Blickman Casework and Design Corp	5999	232
Bliley Technologies Inc	5065	141
Blimp Photo and Video Co	7336	296
Blimpie International Inc	5812	320
Blind And Vision Rehabilitation Services Of Pittsburgh	8211	109
B-Line LLC	7389	950
Blink Electric Motors Inc	5063	1082
Blinker-Lite Safety Inc	7359	178
Blinkmind Inc	4813	469
Blinkx Inc	4813	265
Blish-Mize Co	5072	20
Bliss and Glennon Inc	6331	170
Bliss Brothers Dairy Inc	5143	29
Bliss House Inc	6794	160
Bliss Machine Inc	3599	2141
Bliss Murski Sales Inc	5091	139
Bliss Termite Control Div	7342	49
Blissfield Manufacturing Co	3498	25
Blistex Inc	2834	204
Blitz Manufacturing Company Inc	3471	90
Blitz Media Inc	7319	118
Blitz USA Inc	3085	16
Blizzard Digital Corp	5734	20
Blizzard Entertainment Inc	7372	314
Block And Company Inc	3469	20
Block Communications Inc	4841	27
Block Electrical Contracting Inc	1731	2304
Block Iron and Supply Company Inc	5031	311
Block Steel Corp	5051	111
Block Vision Holdings Corp	8011	126
Blockbuster LLC	7841	1
Blocksom and Co	3564	61
Bloemer Food Sales Co	2032	50
Blogher Inc	7373	542

Company Name	SIC	Rank
Blois Construction Inc	1623	101
Blomberg Building Materials Inc	3442	115
Blommer Chocolate Co	2066	7
Blond Lighting Fixture Supply Company Inc	5063	700
Blonder Tongue Laboratories Inc	3663	78
Blood Bank of Delmarva	8099	77
Blood Hound Inc	1623	651
Blood-Horse Inc	2721	174
Bloom Engineering Company Inc	3433	7
Bloom Hergott Diemer and Cook LLP	8111	432
Bloom Inc	3523	209
Bloom Industries Inc	3089	984
Bloomberg LP	7383	1
Bloomdale Plastics Co	3089	1068
Bloomer Candy Co	2066	27
Bloomer Plastics Inc	3081	29
Bloomfield Electric Company Inc	1731	1270
Bloomfield Electrical Supply Company Inc	5063	830
Bloomfield Foundry Inc	3321	64
Bloomfield Party Rental Corp	7359	181
Bloomingdale's Inc	5311	32
Bloomington Offset Process Inc	2752	410
Bloomington Subaru	5012	70
Bloomsburg Carpet Industries Inc	2273	23
Bloomsburg Mills Inc	2221	29
Bloomsburg Mills Inc (Bloomsburg Pennsylvania)	2211	14
Blossom Valley Foods	2087	72
Blossoms Inc	5992	14
Blough Inc	3471	71
Blount Farmers Coop	5191	123
Blount Inc	3523	4
Blount Inc Oregon Cutting Systems Div	3425	3
Blount International Inc	3489	6
Blount Memorial Hospital Inc	8062	205
Blount Parrish and Company Inc	6211	299
Blount Seafood Corp	2092	21
Blount Small Ship Adventures	4481	5
Blow Molded Specialties Inc	3089	136
Blower Application Company Inc	3589	177
Blowers Inc	3564	78
Blu Consulting Inc	7371	1544
Blue Ally	7371	478
Blue American Ice Co	2097	13
Blue and Gold Fleet	4489	4
Blue and Gold Sausage Inc	2013	251
Blue Angel Technologies Inc	7372	3171
Blue Atlas Interactive LLC	7371	131
Blue Bell Mattress CoInc	2515	11
Blue Blaze Coal Company and Capital Resource	1221	40
Blue Book Services Inc	7323	21
Blue Chair Advertising	7311	794
Blue Chip Casino LLC	7999	17
Blue Chip Group Inc	2673	67
Blue Chip Industries Inc	3599	2435
Blue Chip Inventory Service Inc	7389	820
Blue Chip Mailing Services Inc	7331	166
Blue Chip Stamps	6331	304
Blue City Digital	3695	170
Blue Coat Systems Inc	3572	11
Blue Cross and Blue Shield Association	6794	14
Blue Cross and Blue Shield of Alabama	6321	18
Blue Cross and Blue Shield of Arizona Inc	6321	57
Blue Cross and Blue Shield of Delaware Inc	6321	14
Blue Cross and Blue Shield of Georgia Inc	6321	7
Blue Cross and Blue Shield of Kansas	6321	10
Blue Cross and Blue Shield of Kansas City	6324	32
Blue Cross and Blue Shield of Michigan	6321	29
Blue Cross and Blue Shield of Minnesota	6321	38
Blue Cross and Blue Shield of North Carolina	6321	5
Blue Cross and Blue Shield of Rhode Island	6321	44
Blue Cross and Blue Shield Of Rochester	6324	68
Blue Cross and Blue Shield of South Carolina	6324	8
Blue Cross And Blue Shield Of Texas	6324	62
Blue Cross and Blue Shield of Vermont	6321	32
Blue Cross and Blue Shield of Western New York	6321	23
Blue Cross and Blue Shield United of Wisconsin	6321	48
Blue Cross Laboratories Inc	2841	19
Blue Desert International Inc	3589	103
Blue Dog Printing and Design	7336	140
Blue Dolphin Energy Co	1311	245
Blue Dolphin Pipe Line Co	4922	47
Blue Earth Pictures Inc	7812	282
Blue Feather Products Inc	3086	176
Blue Flame Credit Union	6062	103
Blue Flash Express Inc	4213	340
Blue Gem Inc	6798	139

Company Name	SIC	Rank
Blue Goose Productions Inc	7812	206
Blue Grass Chemical Specialties LLC	2899	220
Blue Grass Manufacturing Company Of Lexington Inc	3599	1321
Blue Grass Shows Inc	7999	100
Blue Heron Paper Co	2621	22
Blue Horse Inc	7311	428
Blue Island Citizens For Persons With Developmental D	8211	105
Blue Island Newspaper Printing Inc	2752	472
Blue Lance Inc	7372	686
Blue Light Images Company Inc	7312	32
Blue Lily Farms LLC	2048	146
Blue Marble Geographics	7372	3560
Blue Max Trucking Inc	4213	1086
Blue Moose Litigation Support Inc	7374	370
Blue Mt Express Inc	4213	2649
Blue Mountain Data Systems Inc	7372	2293
Blue Mountain Machine Inc	3599	399
Blue Mountain Meats Inc	5147	89
Blue Mountain Trucking Corp	4213	1212
Blue Nile Inc	5094	4
Blue Oasis Technologies Inc	7379	1072
Blue Ocean Press Inc	2752	715
Blue Origin LLC	3761	7
Blue Pearl Software Inc	7372	2664
Blue Print Data	5734	462
Blue Rhino Corp	5999	19
Blue Ribbon Business Products Co	5044	119
Blue Ribbon Transport Inc	4213	806
Blue Ridge Acquisition Company LLC	2273	19
Blue Ridge Arsenal Inc	7999	152
Blue Ridge Beverage Company Inc	5181	16
Blue Ridge/Clemson Orthopaedic ASC LLC	8011	57
Blue Ridge Communcation Tv 13	4841	117
Blue Ridge Construction Inc	1629	102
Blue Ridge Copiers Inc	5999	187
Blue Ridge Electric Membership Corp	4911	324
Blue Ridge Enterprizes Inc	5012	200
Blue Ridge Fabricators Inc	3053	100
Blue Ridge Group Inc	1382	13
Blue Ridge Holding Corp	2621	28
Blue Ridge Industries Inc	3089	1271
Blue Ridge Metals Corp	3316	14
Blue Ridge Networks	7373	241
Blue Ridge Printing Co	2759	260
Blue Ridge Products Company Inc	2515	31
Blue Ridge Quarries Inc	3281	55
Blue Ridge Real Estate Co	6531	411
Blue Ridge Tool and Machine Company Inc	3599	1518
Blue River Bancshares Inc	6712	584
Blue River Digital Inc	7374	390
Blue Rock Industries	1741	11
Blue Rock Products Co	2086	43
Blue Rock Technologies	7379	1411
Blue Runner Foods Inc	2033	91
Blue Sky Network LLC	4899	234
Blue Sky Productions	4833	139
Blue Sky Publishing	2771	27
Blue Sky Research Inc	7372	2947
Blue Star Computer Corp	5045	884
Blue Star Distributors Corp	5065	680
Blue Star Growers Inc	0723	16
Blue Star Jets Inc	4512	36
Blue Star Marketing Inc	3571	119
Blue Star Plastics Inc	3089	620
Blue Star Radios Inc	5065	685
Blue Streak Partners Inc	7361	217
Blue Sun Biodiesel LLC	2899	187
Blue Tangerine Solutions Inc	1521	92
Blue Tech Inc	7372	1315
Blue Tee Corp	5051	42
Blue Valley Ban Corp	6712	384
Blue Valley Machine And Manufacturing Co	3541	260
Blue Velvet Transport Inc	4213	2333
Blue Violet Networks	5065	74
Blue Water Finance and Insurance	7389	164
Blue Water Graphics Inc	7336	157
Blue Wave Micro	3577	342
Blue Wave Ultrasonics Inc	5169	163
Blue Wire Networks Inc	5045	1019
Bluebird Auto Rental Systems	7372	3115
Bluebird Inc	0723	9
Bluebonnet Communications Inc	4833	221
Bluebonnet Nutrition Corp	5122	54
Bluebook International Holding Co	7372	4959
Bluebox Communications Inc	7372	4407
Bluefield Gas Co	4922	44
Bluefish Wireless Management Inc	7379	366
Bluefly Inc	5961	86
Bluegate Corp	7389	2502
Bluegrass Business Services Inc	7331	74
Bluegrass Cellular Inc	8741	201
Bluegrass Tool Warehouse Inc	5072	110
Bluegrass Wire Harness Inc	3679	541
Bluegreen Corp	6531	90
Blueknight Energy Partners LP	4612	10
BlueLinx Holdings Inc	5031	6
Bluemedia	7336	26
Bluemountain Capital Management LLC	8742	502

Company Name	SIC	Rank
BluePay Processing LLC	6153	38
BluePoint Data Inc	7389	992
Blueprint Technologies Inc	4813	213
Blueradios Inc	3663	164
Bluerange Technology Corp	7379	1140
BlueRoads Corp	7372	1185
Blues Alley	5813	5
BlueScope Construction Inc	1541	72
Bluesky Capital Partners LLC	5045	852
Bluesocket Inc	3577	156
Bluespec Inc	5045	303
BlueStar Energy Services Inc	4911	214
Bluestar Silicones	2869	53
Bluestem Brands Inc	5961	122
Bluestem Farm and Ranch Supply Inc	5251	22
Blueteam Software Inc	7371	1879
Bluetech LLC	7371	1232
BlueTie Inc	7372	237
Bluewater Broadcasting Inc	3663	201
Bluewater Rubber and Gasket	5085	426
Bluewater Rubber and Gasket Co	5085	177
BlueWater Systems Inc	7372	4935
Blue-White Industries Ltd	3824	18
Bluewire Communications Inc	5065	677
Bluewolf Inc	7371	138
Bluff City Electronics	5065	50
Bluff Springs Paper Company Ltd	2675	7
Bluffton and Oyster Co	0913	4
Bluffton News Publishing and Printing Company Inc	2711	684
Blum Capital Partners	6211	266
Blum Inc	3429	68
Blum Investment Group Inc	7371	966
Blum Shapiro and Co	8721	48
Blumberg Excelsior Inc	2678	3
Blumberg Industries Ltd	3645	9
Blumcraft of Pittsburgh	3231	52
Blumenthal-Kahn Electric LP	1731	1840
Blumenthal-Lansing Company Inc	5131	46
Blumer USA Inc	5084	808
Blurton Banks and Associates	1623	571
BluWater Consulting Inc	7361	52
Bluzona	5065	363
Blyth Inc	3999	6
Blythe Construction Inc	1611	80
Bm Associates Inc	7371	1435
BM Kramer and Company Inc	5051	459
BM M Inc	5461	46
Bma Management Support Corp	7374	155
BMA Software Solutions Inc	7372	4033
BMB Munai Inc	1311	126
Bmc Holdings Inc	3433	6
Bmc Productions Inc	2759	380
BMC Software Inc	7372	21
BMC West Corp	2439	24
Bmci Inc	3549	50
Bmco Industries Inc	3535	225
Bmf Corp	5085	115
Bmg Metals Inc	5051	166
Bmg of Kansas Inc	3444	198
Bmi Associates Inc	5734	231
Bmi Automation Inc	3569	249
BMI Financial Group	6311	132
BMI Gaming Inc	5099	22
BMI Imaging Systems Inc	7389	719
BMIC Mortgage Inc	6162	81
BMO Capital Markets (Chicago Illinois)	6211	289
Bmp America Inc	3555	22
Bmp Industries LLC	3451	141
BMP Sunstone Corp	5122	34
BMS Enterprises Inc	7349	34
Bms Manufacturing Company Inc	3599	945
BMT Commodity Corp	5085	127
BMT Micro Inc	7372	1128
BMW Center	5511	188
BMW Constructors Inc	1541	49
BMW/Mini of Sterling	5511	338
BMW Northwest Inc	5511	645
BMW of Corpus Christi	5511	927
BMW Of Darien	5511	762
BMW Of North America LLC	3711	14
BMW of Sterling	5511	234
BMW of the Hudson Valley	5511	618
Bmw Precision Machining Inc	3599	1647
BMW South Atlanta	5511	732
Bmwc Group Inc	1629	30
BN Systems Inc	1731	1336
Bna Computing Inc	7379	1557
BNA Software	7372	309
Bnb Manufacturing Company Inc	3599	1504
BNC Bancorp	6021	59
BNC National Bank	6021	292
BNCCORP Inc	6712	349
BNI Solutions LLC	3669	225
Bnl Technologies Inc	5045	588
BNP US Funding LLC	6159	38
BNS Holdings Inc	6531	460
BNY Mellon Distributors Holdings Inc	7374	74
Bnz Materials Inc	3255	2
Bo Beuckman Ford Inc	5511	651
Bo/Gar Enterprises Inc	3599	390
Board Automotive Group Inc	5511	1002
Board Member Inc	2721	267

Company Name	SIC	Rank
Board Of Cooperative Educational Services	8249	4
Board Of Cooperative Educational Services Of Chautauqua County	8331	35
Board Of Education City Of Paterson	8211	45
Board Of Education Of Carroll County	8211	9
Board Of Education Of The City Of Trenton	8211	17
Board Of Water Supply	4941	29
Boarder To Boarder Trucking	4213	1102
Boardman Suhr Curry and Field	8111	360
Boardroom Communications Inc	8743	308
Boardwalk Pipeline Partners LP	4922	6
Boar's Head Provisions Company Inc	5147	1
Boart Longyear Co	1481	2
Boasso Construction LLC	1731	1816
Boat Center Inc	5551	5
Boater's World Marine Centers	5551	9
Boatright Company Inc	5078	15
Boatright Railroad Products Inc	2491	12
Boatswain's Locker I Inc	5088	57
Bob Biter Electrical Enterprises Inc	1731	325
Bob Brink Inc	4213	1391
Bob Brock Ford Inc	5511	1155
Bob Brooks Motor Co	3694	24
Bob Davidson Ford Lincoln Mercury Inc	5511	660
Bob Dunn Ford Inc	5511	661
Bob Evans Farms Inc	5812	34
Bob Evans Farms Inc (Rio Grande Ohio)	7999	1
Bob Evans Restaurants Inc	5812	2
Bob Fisher Chevrolet Geo	5511	569
Bob Frensley Chrysler Plymouth Isuzu Inc	5511	1134
Bob Gillingham Ford Inc	5511	1199
Bob Hall Chevrolet	5511	399
Bob Hall Inc	5181	34
Bob Harris Oil Co	5172	26
Bob Hill Enterprises Inc	5211	201
Bob Howard Chevrolet Inc	5511	470
Bob Hubbard Horse Transportation	4213	1821
Bob Hull Inc	1623	666
Bob Inc	3599	391
Bob Johnson Auto Group	5511	224
Bob Jones and Associates Inc	5063	991
Bob Maisano	1731	1654
Bob Mitchell Associates Inc	1796	36
Bob Moore Auto Group LLC	5511	162
Bob Moore Cadillac Inc	5511	337
Bob Paul Inc	0174	6
Bob Richards Chevrolet Company Inc	5511	521
Bob Rohrman Auto Group	7389	65
Bob Rohrman Indy Susuki Inc	5511	963
Bob Ross Buick Inc	5511	473
Bob Saks and Associates	8742	374
Bob Saks Motor Mall	5511	268
Bob Schmitt Homes Inc	1521	146
Bob Shelley's Special Effects International	7819	94
Bob Siemon Designs Inc	3961	12
Bob Thomas Cheverolet Cadillac Honda	5511	933
Bob Turner's Crane Service Inc	7353	64
Bob Vincent and Sons Wrecker Service Inc	7549	24
Bob Ward Electric	1731	1547
Bobak Sausage Co	5149	88
Bobalee Inc	3593	28
Bobb Corp	7389	1279
Bobby Davis Electric Company Inc	1731	1774
Bobby Dodd Institute Inc	8331	94
Bobby Fryar Trucking Company Inc	4213	1913
Bobby Henard Inc	5014	41
Bobby J Smith	5211	310
Bobby Layman Chevrolet-Geo	5511	621
Bobby Lehmann Inc	4213	2222
Bobby Murray Chevrolet Inc	5511	173
BobCAD-CAM Inc	7372	2352
Bobcat Co	3523	18
Bobcat Co/Apl	3531	210
Bobcat of Atlanta	5082	78
Bobcat Of New York Inc	7353	59
Bobcat Sports and Entertainment LLC	7941	19
Bobco Metal Co	5051	97
Bobco Metals LLC	5051	306
Bob-Leon Plastics Inc	3089	1675
Bobo Engineering Inc	3679	377
Bobo's Marketing Services LLC	7311	954
Bobrick Washroom Equipment Inc	3432	9
Bobs' Business Inc	5091	93
Bob's Pickup and Delivery Inc	4213	1746
Bob's Pool Service Inc	7389	2111
Bob's Space Racers Inc	3599	227
Bob's Stores Inc	5651	27
Bob's Transport and Storage Co	4213	760
Bobst Group North America Inc	5084	128
BOC Advertising Inc	7311	571
Boca Raton Community Hospital Physicians Group	8062	212
Boca Resorts Inc	7999	50
Boca Systems Inc	3577	247
Bocada Inc	5045	181
Boccard Pipe Fabricators Inc	3498	37

Company Name	SIC	Rank
Boccard Suddell Construction Corp	8712	230
Bochetto and Lentz PC	8111	528
Bock Electric Inc	1731	2021
Bock Industries Inc	3317	52
Bock Water Heaters Inc	3639	20
Bocra Industries Inc	3545	234
Bodacious Breads Inc	5149	152
Bodcaw Bank	6022	774
Boddie-Noell Enterprises Inc	5812	105
Bode Technology Group Inc	8734	39
Bodell Overcash Anderson and Company Inc	6211	243
Bodemuller The Printer Inc	5943	23
Boden Store Fixtures Inc	2541	11
Bodie Electrical Contractors Of Fla Inc	1731	1979
Bodies Dairy Markets Company Inc	5411	285
Bodiford Electric Inc	1731	1710
Bodine Aluminum Inc	3369	3
Bodine Inc	7389	644
Bodine Services Of Evansville LLC	1623	169
Bodine Tool and Machine Company Inc	3544	408
Bodman LLC	8111	351
Bodner Metal And Iron Corp	5093	217
Bodow Recycling Inc	5093	246
Body by Jake Enterprises LLC	7812	218
Body Central Corp	5621	24
Body Construction Personal Fitness Trainers	7999	110
Body Glove International LLC	2339	9
Body Shop Inc	5999	21
Body Shop (Wake Forest North Carolina)	2844	123
Bodycote Materials Testing Inc	8071	41
Bodycote Taussig Inc	8711	9
Bodypoint Designs Inc	7389	1699
Boe Farms Inc	0213	22
Boeckeler Instruments Inc	5064	113
Boehm Travel Cos	4724	55
Boehme-Filatex Inc	2869	64
Boehmer Transportation Corp	4213	2595
Boehm-Madisen Lumber Company Inc	5031	145
Boehm's Candies Inc	5441	9
Boehringer Ingelheim Corp	2834	47
Boehringer Ingelheim Pharmaceuticals Inc	2834	120
Boehringer Ingelheim Vetmedica Inc	2836	17
Boehringer Laboratories Inc	3841	285
Boeing Capital Corp	6159	17
Boeing Co	3721	1
Boeing Defense Space and Security	3721	3
Boeing Travel Management Co	4724	23
Boeing-SVS Inc	7379	140
Boekel Industries Inc	3826	82
Boelter and Lincoln	7311	341
Boelter Companies Inc	5046	22
Boelter Industries Inc	2657	28
Boenning and Scattergood Inc	6029	11
Boesl Packing Company Inc	5147	130
Boettcher Supply Inc	5063	206
Bofl Holding Inc	6099	9
Bogart and Brownell of Maryland Inc	6331	88
Bogdan Computer Services Inc	7373	1073
Bogen Communications Inc	3661	48
Bogen Communications International Inc	3661	57
Bogen Communications LLC	3661	49
Bogen Corp	3661	44
Boggs Electric Company Inc	1731	1149
Boggs Inc	3643	163
Boggs Natural Gas Co	1381	4
Boggus Ford	5511	680
Bogner of America Inc	2329	34
Bogue Machine Company Inc	3599	847
Bohannan-Huston Inc	8711	290
Bohl Equipment Co	5084	179
Bohl Machine and Tool Company Inc	3542	76
Bohler Uddeholm America Inc	5051	44
Bohler Well Service LLC	1623	708
Bohlmann and Co	8721	481
Bohn And Dawson Inc	3441	98
Bohn Brothers Inc	5511	624
Bohn Fiberglass Industries Inc	1799	138
Bohn Implement Co	5083	172
Bohnenstiehl Electric Co	5065	819
Bohning Company Ltd	3949	140
Bohr Precision Machining Inc	3599	1613
Bohren's Moving and Storage	4213	858
Boiling Springs Savings Bank	6036	34
Boiron Inc	2833	49
Boise Cascade Holdings LLC	5031	2
Boise Inc	2611	2
Boise Office Equipment Inc	7373	745
Boisset Family Estates	5181	101
Bojangles' Holdings Inc	5812	198
Bojangles' Restaurants Inc	5812	193
Bojangles Restaurants Inc	5812	195
Boja's Foods Inc	2092	92
BOK Financial Corp	6712	34
Bokan Brothers Inc	5013	263
Boker's Inc	3452	56
Bokler Software Corp	7372	4487
Bold Plastics Inc	3674	440
BOLData Technology Inc	7373	74
Boldt Group Inc	1542	78

Company Name	SIC	Rank	Company Name	SIC	Rank	Company Name	SIC	Rank
Boler Co	3714	18	Bongards' Creameries	2023	13	Borer Financial Communication LLC	7374	319
Bolero Industries Inc	3599	1614	Bonide Products Inc	2899	77	Borg Precision Inc	3599	2431
Boley Tool and Machine Works Inc	3599	207	Boniface Tool and Die Inc	3728	181	Borghese Inc	2844	65
Bolger and Associates	8721	273	Bonita Grande Mining LLC	1442	38	Borghesi Building and Engineering Co	1541	246
Bolger LLC	2752	99	Bonita Packaging Products Inc	2621	57	Borgwaldt Kc Inc	3823	224
Boliches AMF Inc	7933	2	Bonitron Inc	3699	163	BorgWarner Cooling Systems	3713	28
Bolind Inc	2754	50	Bonitz Contracting Co	1541	297	BorgWarner Inc	3714	11
Bolivar Farmers Exchange	5191	120	Bonjour Group Ltd	6794	152	Boride Products	3559	165
Bolke - Miller Co	7389	1873	Bonland Industries Inc	1711	82	Boring Machine Corp	3724	69
Boll Medical Inc	5999	144	Bonnamy and Associates LLC	7389	2279	Boring Transport Inc	4213	2645
Bollag International Corp	5093	57	Bonne Bell Inc	2844	28	Bor-It Manufacturing Inc	3541	216
Bolling Walter and Gawthrop	8111	535	Bonneau Production Services	7812	129	Bork Transportation of Illinois	4213	1081
Bollinger Capital Management Inc	6282	606	Bonnell Aluminum	3341	7	Borke Mold Specialist Inc	3544	793
Bollinger Electric Inc	1731	1158	Bonnell Industries Inc	3531	121	Borkholder Corp	2511	38
Bollinger Shipyards Inc	3731	9	Bonner and Associates	8743	214	Borlaug Systems Inc	3549	126
Bollman Hat Co	2353	4	Bonnette Page and Stone Corp	1541	176	Borneman and Peterson Inc	3451	154
Bollore Inc	2671	37	Bonneville Bancorp	6712	727	Bornhoft Group Inc	6282	624
Bolner's Fiesta Products Inc	2099	372	Bonneville Bank	6022	822	Bornquist Inc	5084	321
Bolon Hart and Buehler Inc	8721	482	Bonneville Communications	7311	412	Bornstein Seafood Inc	5146	29
Boloto Group Inc	7374	124	Bonneville International Corp	4832	16	Borough Park Computer Center Inc	5734	169
Bolt Media Inc	7375	61	Bonneville Transloaders Inc	4213	486	Borrego Solar Systems Inc	8999	71
BOLT Staffing Service Inc	7363	278	Bonney Forge Corp	3462	16	Borrego Springs Bank NA	6021	388
Bolt Technology Corp	3533	36	Bonney-Vehslage Tool Co	3544	907	Borrell Inc	1731	211
Bolton and Hay Inc	5046	104	Bonnie Be-Lo Markets Inc	5411	152	Borrmann Metal Center	5051	268
Bolton Corp	1711	129	Bonnier Corp	2721	26	Borroughs Corp	2541	1
Bolton Newspapers Inc	2711	682	Bonnot Co	3599	1216	Borsheim's Jewelry Company Inc	5944	17
Bolton Partners Inc	8742	314	Bonntech International Inc	3535	103	Borshoff Inc	8743	247
Bolton Smith Inc	5049	214	Bontempo Group Inc	7363	338	BOR-SON Cos	1542	187
Bolton-Emerson Americas Inc	3554	55	Bontex Inc	2824	12	Borton LC	1541	203
Boltswitch Inc	3613	83	Bon-Ton Department Stores Inc	5311	24	Borton Volvo Inc	5511	981
Boly-Welch Inc	7361	411	Bon-Ton National Corp	5311	37	Borwegen Trucking Inc	4213	1033
Bolzoni Auramo Inc	5084	418	Bon-Ton Stores Inc	5311	14	Bo's Hydraulic's Inc	5084	717
Bomac Inc	3679	369	Bonus Transportation Inc	4213	1723	Bos Machine Tool Services Inc	3541	258
Bomac Vets Plus Inc	2048	78	Book Systems Inc	7372	410	Bosak Motor Sales Inc	5511	755
Boman and Kemp Manufacturing Inc	3441	60	Book Tool Company Inc	3544	813	BOSaNOVA Inc	3577	465
Bomar Interconnect Products Inc	5065	104	Bookcliff Auto Parts Inc	5013	237	BOSC Agency Inc (Dallas Texas)	6211	359
Bomark Inc	2893	31	Bookcolor Bindery Services Inc	2789	135	Boscar Electric Inc	1731	2084
Bo-Mark Transport Inc	4213	390	Booker/Hancock and Associates LLC	8743	292	Bosch Communications Systems	3651	38
Bomarko Incorporated Delaware	2671	16	Booker T Washington Insurance Co	6311	138	Bosch Packaging Technology	3565	14
Bomat Ltd	3272	117	Booker Transportation Inc	4213	2056	Bosch Packaging Technology Inc	3565	7
Bomatic Inc	3089	682	Booklegger	5192	35	Bosch Rexroth Corp	3594	6
Bombard Society Inc	7999	116	Bookmasters Inc	7389	537	Bosch Rexroth Corp/Mobile Hydraulics	3594	4
Bombardier Capital	6159	23	BookPage	2721	103	Bosco Inc	5063	935
Bombardier Capital Rail Inc	6159	24	Books Inc	5942	19	Boscobel Marketing Communications Inc	7311	706
Bombardier Motor Corporation of America (Sturtevant Wisconsin)	3732	6	Books Of Love Inc	3999	163	Boscov's Department Stores Inc	5311	22
			Books-A-Million Inc	5942	7	Bose Corp	3651	11
Bombardier Motor Corporation of America (Waukegan Illinois)	3732	10	Booksource Inc	2789	9	Bose Electroforce Systems Group	3841	132
			Boomer Co	5032	66	Bose McKinney and Evans LLP	8111	217
Bo-Mer Plastics LLC	3089	934	Boomerang Software Inc	7371	822	Bosell Foods Inc	1541	307
Bomgar Inc	5045	406	BoomerangCom Inc	4822	19	BOSH Global Services Inc	8999	79
Bommarito Automotive Group	5511	64	Boomer's Inc	2752	733	Boshart Automotive Testing Services Inc	7389	1351
Bommer Industries Inc	5072	58	Boomtown Biloxi Casino	7948	7			
Bon Advertising Inc	7311	628	Boomtown Hotel and Casino Inc	7011	163	Bosley Construction Inc	1521	144
Bon Appetit Danish Inc	2051	96	Boomtown Inc	7999	44	Bosma Industries For The Blind Inc	8331	74
Bon Appetit Management Co	5812	25	Boon Edam Inc	3699	1	Boss Balloon Co	3069	29
Bon L Campo LP	3354	2	Boone and Darr Inc	1711	169	Boss Holdings Inc	2381	1
Bon L Holdings Corp	3354	3	Boone Bank and Trust Co	6022	14	Boss Inc	3577	622
Bon L Manufacturing Company of Virginia	3354	4	Boone Center Inc	8331	95	Boss Industries Inc	3563	34
			Boone County Bank Inc	6022	562	Boss Manufacturing Co	3842	99
Bon Secour Fisheries Inc	2092	53	Boone County Board Of Education	8211	60	Boss Tool and Manufacturing Inc	3599	2255
Bon Secours - Depaul Medical Center Inc	8062	180	Boone County National Bank	6021	132	Boss Unlimited	5932	19
			Boone County Rural Electric Membership Corp	4911	444	Bossier Newspaper Publishing Company Inc	2711	895
Bon Secours Health System Inc	8069	1				
Bon Secours - St Francis Medical Center Inc	8082	18	Boone Fetter Associates	6552	298	Bossier Parish Communications District 1 Inc	4813	596
			Boone News Republican	2711	846			
Bon Secours-Memorial Regional Medical Center Inc	8062	213	Boone Newspapers	2711	610	Bossong Hosiery Mills Inc	2251	3
			Boone Newspapers Inc	2711	901	Bossong's Commercial Delivery	4213	2341
Bon Tool Co	3423	47	Boone Rentals Inc	7359	157	Bost Harley-Davidson of Nashville	5571	8
Bon Venture Services Inc	2731	198	Boone's Abattoir Inc	5421	21	Bostik Inc(Wauwatosa Wisconsin)	2891	119
Bon Voyage Travel	4724	15	Boonton Electronics Corp	3825	30	Boston and Maine Corp	4011	25
Bonadio and Company LLP	8721	276	Boordy Vineyards Inc	0172	23	Boston Beer Company Inc	2082	3
Bonafide Management Systems Inc	7372	2665	Boos Products Inc	3599	2048	Boston Biomedical Research Institute Inc	8733	22
Bonal International Inc	3829	319	Boosey and Hawkes Inc	2741	280			
Bonal Technologies Inc	3599	1731	Boost Mobile LLC	4813	413	Boston Brace International Inc	3842	137
BonAmi Software Corp	7372	5011	Booster Inc	2711	832	Boston Brewing Company Inc	2082	5
Bonander Pontiac Inc	5511	572	Boosters Inc	2759	312	Boston Business Computing Ltd	7372	4488
Bonanza Beverage Co	5181	42	Booth Electrosystems Inc	3625	309	Boston Capital Ventures	6799	306
Bonanza Industries Inc	3281	20	Boothe Inc	3544	890	Boston Celtics Communications LP	4832	51
Boncosky Oil Co	5171	41	Boothroyd Dewhurst Inc	7372	1802	Boston Centerless Inc	3599	176
Bond Brothers Inc	1541	83	Boots and Coots International Well Control Inc	3533	23	Boston Community Access and Programing Foundation Inc	4841	121
Bond Drug Company of Illinois	5122	132				
Bond Equipment Company Inc	5012	90	Bootsector Industries Inc	5734	239	Boston Company Inc	6282	13
Bond International Software Inc	5045	681	Bootz Manufacturing Co	3431	4	Boston Consulting Group Inc	8742	15
Bond Optics LLC	3827	79	Booz Allen Hamilton Holding Corp	8742	4	Boston Dynamics Inc	3535	127
Bond Schoeneck and King PLLC	8111	150	Booz and Company Inc	8742	79	Boston Electric And Telephone Corp	1731	1630
Bondcote Corp	2295	12	Bopat Electric Company Inc	1731	292	Boston Financial Data Services Inc	7374	30
BondDesk Group LLC	7389	450	Bopp-Busch Manufacturing Co	3465	58	Boston Fruit Slice and Confectionery Corp	2064	95
Bonded Carriers Inc	4213	1282	Boral Material Technologies Inc	2899	48			
Bonded Credit Bureau Inc	7322	72	Bordelon Design Associates Inc	7389	1791	Boston Globe	2711	70
Bonded Electric Construction Inc	1731	877	Borden Office Equipment Co	5044	122	Boston Health Care Systems Inc	8361	73
Bonded Fiberloft Inc	2211	17	Bordenav's Marin Baking LLC	2051	160	Boston Lightning Rod Co	1521	165
Bonded Filter Co	7699	70	Border Apparel Laundry Ltd	2326	12	Boston Lumber and Builders Corp	5072	136
Bonded Rebuilders Inc	7538	31	Border City Tool And Manufacturing Co	3532	68	Boston Market Corp	5812	147
Bonded Services Inc	7389	749	Border Electric Inc	1731	533	Boston Matthews Inc	3559	339
Bondfire Co	3537	111	Border Foods Inc	2099	127	Boston Medical Center	8999	1
Bond-Tech Inc	6282	472	Border States Electric Supply	5063	14	Boston Microsystems Inc	8731	392
Bondurant Lumber Wholesale And Export Division Inc	5031	301	Border States Paving Inc	1771	14	Boston Mutual Life Insurance Co	6311	160
			Bordercomm Inc	7373	556	Boston Networking Group Inc	7361	289
Bone Frontier Co	3677	86	Borders Group Inc	5942	4	Boston Pipe and Fittings Company Inc	5085	297
Boneal Inc	3535	51	Borders Inc	5942	1	Boston Private Bank and Trust Co	6022	208
Bonell Manufacturing Co	3547	13	Borders Perrin and Norrander Inc	7311	255	Boston Private Financial Holdings Inc	6712	103
Bones Transportation Inc	4213	2437	Boreal Controls Inc	3599	2439	Boston Proper Inc	5961	32
Bonestroo Rosene Anderlik and Associates Inc	8711	266	Boren Explosives Company Inc	5169	141	Boston Properties Inc	6798	21
			Borenstein Group	7336	35			

Company Name	SIC	Rank
Boston Restaurant Associates Inc	5812	337
Boston Retail Products Inc	2542	35
Boston Safe Deposit and Trust Co	8721	19
Boston Sb Publishing Inc	2711	735
Boston Scientific Corp	3841	5
Boston Scientific (Glens Falls New York)	3842	44
Boston Scientific Scimed Inc	3845	8
Boston Trailer Manufacturing	3792	24
Boston Ventures Management Inc	6799	263
Boston Warehouse Trading Corp	5023	59
Boston Whaler Inc	3732	33
BostonCoach Inc	4729	7
Bostonian Shoe Co	5139	8
Boston-Power Inc	3691	17
Bostwick Laboratories Inc	8071	21
Bostwick-Braun Co	5072	25
Botanical Laboratories Inc	2834	253
Botello Lumber Company Inc	5211	186
Bothe Associates Inc	3599	830
Boton	3644	51
Bottcher America Corp	5084	156
Bottom Line Inc	8742	654
Bottomline Technologies Inc	7372	252
Bottrell Insurance Agency Inc	6411	157
Botts Welding and Truck Service Inc	5013	304
Bouchard Communications Group	8743	150
Bouchard Communications Inc	1623	434
Bouche Trucking Inc	4213	1431
Boucher Brothers Miami Beach LLC	8741	187
Boucher Company Inc	3599	2496
Boucher Family LP	7389	1493
Bouchette Electronics Inc	3625	383
Boulden Inc	5984	30
Boulder Beer Inc	2082	64
Boulder Blimp Co	3069	267
Boulder Canyon Natural Foods Inc	5099	10
Boulder Growth and Income Fund Inc	6726	65
Boulder Innovation Group	3577	388
Boulder Lumber Co	5211	216
Boulder Outdoor Center Inc	7999	164
Boulder Rural Fire Protection District	7389	1544
Boulder Valley Credit Union	6062	65
Bouldin Corp	5191	128
Boulevard Bank	6035	242
Boulevard Brewing Associates LP	2082	36
Boulevard Entertainment Inc	7389	1081
Boulevard Machine and Gear Inc	3599	1894
Boulton Machine Products Inc	3625	417
Bou-Matic LLC	3523	42
Boundary Bay Brewing Co	2082	20
Boundless Flight Inc	7371	991
Boundless Security Systems Inc	1731	2593
Boundless Technologies Inc	3571	31
Bountiful Bread	2051	292
Bountiful Psychiatric Hospital Inc	8063	12
Bourbon Limestone Co	1422	61
Bourbon Plastics Inc	3644	34
Bourdon Forge Company Inc	3429	152
Bourn and Koch Inc	3541	73
Bourne Industries Inc	2521	55
Bourne StenstromLent Asset Management Inc	6282	663
Bourns Inc	3679	321
Bourque Data Systems Inc	7372	2644
BoutellCom Inc	7372	3983
Bouten Construction Co	1541	248
Boutique Trims Inc	5094	63
Boutwell Owens and Company Inc	2752	249
Bovie Medical Corp	3841	119
Bovie Screen Process Printing Company Inc	2759	376
Bow Industries Of Virginia Inc	3577	591
Bow Management	5734	434
BOWA Builders Inc	1521	107
Bowdil Co	3532	55
Bowdoin Group Inc	7361	135
Bowe Machine Co	3599	1126
Bowen and Watson Inc	1542	319
Bowen Electric Service Inc	1731	2129
Bowen Engineering Corp	1629	58
Bowen Family Homes	1531	34
Bowen Machine Company Inc	3599	1568
Bowen Petroleum	5171	16
Bowen Property Management	6552	120
Bowen Real Estate Group	6531	118
Bowen Scarff Ford Sales Inc	5511	427
Bower Enterprises Inc	8748	143
Bowerman Associates Inc	5046	348
Bowers Fibers Inc	5093	99
Bowers Manufacturing Co	3471	10
Bowes Construction Inc	1611	185
Bowes Seal Fast LLC	5013	420
Bowie Industries Inc	3561	134
Bowie-Cass Electric Coop	4911	435
Bo-Witt Products Inc	3644	35
Bowl America Inc	7933	5
Bowler Petrophysics Inc	7372	3386
Bowles Fluidics Corp	3714	285
Bowles Rice McDavid Graff and Love LLP	8111	121
Bowlin Company Inc	8711	696
Bowlin Travel Centers Inc	5541	40
Bowling Green Winlectric Co	5063	1051

Company Name	SIC	Rank
Bowl-Tronics Enterprises Inc	3949	177
Bowlus Trucking Company Inc	4213	1961
Bowman and Brooke LLP	8111	352
Bowman and Company LLP	8721	297
Bowman Apple Products Company Inc	2035	10
Bowman Consulting Group Ltd	8711	300
Bowman Distillery Incorporated A Smith	2085	7
Bowman Group	7379	663
Bowman Tool and Machining Inc	3599	1484
Bowman-Hollis Manufacturing Company Inc	3552	21
Bowne Business Communications Inc	2752	24
Bowne Electric Inc	1731	1732
Bowne Financial Print	2752	131
Bowne Global Solutions Inc	7389	317
Bowne International Inc	2759	22
Bowne Management Systems Inc	7371	101
Bowne of Chicago Inc	2752	171
Bowne of Dallas LP	2752	300
Bowne Of Houston Inc	2759	72
Bowne of Los Angeles Inc	2752	96
Bowne of Phoenix Inc	2752	36
Bowsmith Inc	3089	1258
Bowstreet Inc	7372	896
Bowtie Inc	2721	125
Bowyer-Singleton and Associates Inc	8711	259
Box Dies Manufacturing Inc	3555	89
Boxco Incorporated Of Maryland	4841	104
Boxer Software	7371	1738
Boxes Of St Louis Inc	2653	38
Boxit Corp	2652	7
Boxlight Corp	5043	15
Boxnet Inc	4899	30
Boxsterview Inc	3577	289
Boyajian Inc	2091	7
Boyce Lumber Co	5211	219
Boyd and Associates	7381	39
Boyd and Co	1522	7
Boyd and Sons Inc	4213	2002
Boyd Brothers Inc	2752	232
Boyd Brothers Transportation Inc	4213	169
Boyd Chevrolet Of South Hill Va Inc	5012	188
Boyd Coffee Co	2095	11
Boyd Floatation/Royal Waterbeds Inc	2515	7
Boyd Gaming Corp	7999	6
Boyd Industries Inc	3843	35
Boyd Lighting Fixture Co	3645	36
Boyd Louisiana LLC	7999	31
Boyd Machine and Repair Company Inc	7699	215
Boyd Machine Company Inc	3599	2084
Boyd Tunica Inc	7999	7
Boyd Watterson Asset Management LLC	6282	178
Boyd-Bluford Company Inc	5194	23
Boyds Collection Ltd	5199	17
Boyds Operations Inc	3942	5
Boyer Automotive Center Inc	5731	131
Boyer Candy Company Inc	2064	48
Boyer Machine and Tool Company Inc	3599	906
Boyer's Sand and Rock Inc	1231	3
Boyertown Foundry Co	3433	36
Boyertown Furnace Co	3567	82
Boyertown Publishing Company Inc	2752	962
Boyett Enterprises LLC	7389	990
Boykin Hospitality	7011	226
Boyko Metal Finishing Company Inc	3479	57
Boyle Engineering Corp	8711	166
Boyle Inc	3544	798
Boyle Investment Co	6552	122
Boyle Meat Co	5147	55
Boyle Transportation Inc	4213	757
Boyne USA Resorts Inc	7032	1
Boynton Williams and Associates	8712	197
Boys and Girls Clubs Of Greater Fort Worth Inc	8322	127
Boys Club Of Mount Kisco Inc	7999	134
Boyt John Industrial Sewing Inc	7389	1692
Boyum and Barenscheer	8721	121
Boz Electrical Contractors Inc	1731	468
Bozeman Motors Inc	5511	913
Bozzuto Group	1521	73
Bozzuto's Inc	5141	26
BP Amoco Chemical Co	1311	3
BP Barber	8748	49
BP Chemicals Inc	2911	13
BP Design	7311	1039
BP Exploration Inc (Anchorage Alaska)	1381	34
Bp Industries Inc	5023	80
Bp Logix Inc	7371	1272
Bp Microsystems Management LLC	3577	303
BP Oil Co	5541	4
BP Oil Pipeline Co	4612	9
BP Prudhoe Bay Royalty Trust	2911	63
BP Solar International LLC	3674	129
Bp Solutions Group Inc	2752	464
B-P Supply Inc	5084	453
Bpc Acquisition Co	8742	499
BPC Corp	6712	401
BPD Inc	5211	217
Bpi Inc	2899	164
BPI Inc (Pittsburgh Pennsylvania)	3297	7
Bpi Media Group Inc	2752	686
BPI Transportation Inc	4213	2327

Company Name	SIC	Rank
Bpl Global Ltd	1731	2214
BPM Inc	2621	37
BPO Management Services Inc	7371	264
Bpr-Rico Manufacturing Inc	3537	45
Bps Inc	4783	11
Bps Printing and Graphics Inc	2752	1386
Bps Security LLC	7381	224
Bpx Films LP	2671	23
BPZ Resources Inc	1311	108
BQE Software Inc	7372	847
BR Amon and Sons Inc	1611	141
BR Associates Inc	5812	240
Br Direct Marketing	7311	944
BR Guest Inc	5812	390
BR Simpson Telephone Sales and Service Inc	5065	531
Br Technology LLC	5065	863
BR Williams Trucking Inc	4213	1103
Brabazon Pumpe Company Ltd	5084	544
Brabner And Hollon Inc	5072	129
Bracalente Manufacturing Co	3451	43
Bracewell and Giuliani LLP	8111	127
Bracken Technology Services Inc	5045	536
Brackett And Cochran Manufacturing Inc	3599	1974
Brackett Inc	3555	116
Brad Foote Gear Works Inc	3462	39
Brada Manufacturing Inc	3451	110
Bradbury and Stamm Construction Company Inc	1622	14
Bradbury Company Inc	3542	4
Bradco Rubber and Plastics Products Inc	3061	58
Bradco Supply Corp	5031	5
Braden Carco Gearmatic Winch Div	3531	40
Braden Construction Services Inc	3443	21
Braden-Sutphin Ink Co	2893	9
Bradenton Herald	2711	223
Bradford and Bigelow Inc	2752	247
Bradford Bank	6021	185
Bradford Built Inc	3523	244
Bradford Co	2653	35
Bradford County Telegraph Inc	2711	606
Bradford Electric Company Inc	1731	647
Bradford Industries Inc	2295	11
Bradford Neal Machinery Inc	3559	567
Bradford Publishing Co	2731	324
Bradford Realty Services Inc	6531	126
Bradford Technologies Inc	7372	2810
Bradford White Corp	3433	5
Bradford Yacht Limited Inc	3732	49
Bradington-Young LLC	2512	24
Bradken	3325	3
Bradken Inc	3325	9
Bradken Inc	3325	7
Bradlee Distributors USA Inc	5064	150
Bradley Arant Rose and White LLP	8111	225
Bradley Cleveland Services Inc	8322	84
Bradley Coatings Of Ga	2851	179
Bradley Communications Corp	2721	372
Bradley Co	7372	1684
Bradley Electric Inc	1731	1098
Bradley Excavating Inc	1794	40
Bradley Graphic Solutions Inc	2761	50
Bradley Images and Photography Inc	7384	59
Bradley Industries Inc	3999	171
Bradley Lifting Corp	3531	102
Bradley Pulverizer Co	3599	934
Bradley Reid Communications Inc	7311	905
Bradley S Shoen Inc	5074	119
Bradley Steffian Architects	8712	185
Bradley Sutton	1623	377
Bradley-Morris Inc	7361	223
Bradleys' Inc	7694	7
Bradley-Thompson Tool Co	3544	483
Bradmark Inc	7372	2541
Bradner Central Co	5111	9
Bradrock Molding Inc	3544	225
Brad's Electric Inc	1731	1255
Bradshaw Advertising	7311	600
Bradshaw International Inc	5023	25
Bradshaw Medical Inc	3841	184
Brady Corp	3999	5
Brady Distributing Co	5099	32
Brady Enterprises Inc	2099	76
Brady Farms Inc	2033	72
Brady Identification Solutions	2891	9
Brady International Co	2891	5
Brady International Sales Inc	2891	4
Brady Investment Co	6211	360
Brady Worldwide Inc	2891	14
Brae Burn Construction Co	1541	237
Bragg Companies Inc	1796	1
Bragg Crane and Rigging Co	1799	16
Bragg Crane Service LLC	7353	108
Braid Electric Company Inc	5063	36
Braid Sales And Marketing Inc	3553	34
Braided Matrix Inc	7372	2709
Brain Power Inc	3841	250
Brain Power International Inc	7379	1179
Brainard Rivet Co	3452	78
Brainer And Brown Plumbing Inc	1711	18
Brainerd Compressor Rebuilders Inc	3585	248
Brainerd Industries Inc	3469	231

Company Name	SIC	Rank
Brainerd International Raceway and Resort Inc	7948	23
Brainlink International Inc	7379	1149
Brains On Fire Inc	7311	814
Brainstorm Logistics LLC	8741	39
Brainstorm USA LLC	5045	464
Braintech Inc	7373	596
Braintree Inc	6153	46
Braintree Laboratories Inc	2834	283
Brainworks Software Inc	7372	612
BrainxCom Inc	7371	1558
Brake and Wheel Parts Industries	5013	164
Brake Parts Inc- Chowchilla	3714	141
Brake Roller Company Inc	3542	63
Brake Supply Company Inc	7699	15
Brake Systems Inc	4231	1
Brakebush Brothers Inc	2015	34
Brakes Express Inc	5013	301
Brakewell Steel Fabricators Inc	3411	18
Brakke Implements Inc	5083	41
Brakur Custom Cabinetry Inc	2541	24
Braley and Graham Buick Pontiac and GMC Truck	5511	536
Brama Inc	3563	49
Bramacint LLC	7389	2061
Braman Management Association	5511	51
Bramasol Inc	5045	735
Bramble Construction Company Inc	1623	786
Brambles USA Inc	7359	9
Bramkamp Printing Company Inc	2759	199
Brammall Inc	3429	105
Brammer Engineering Inc	1381	53
Bramson and Associates	7311	907
Bramson House Inc	2392	39
Brance-Krachy Company Inc	5063	177
Branch Banking and Trust Co	6021	5
Branch Banking and Trust Company of South Carolina	6022	38
Branch Group Inc	1522	2
Branch Manufacturing Co	3469	275
Branch Richards and Co	8721	479
Branchcomb Inc	3089	1743
Branch-Smith Resources	2752	293
Brand-Aromatics Inc	2087	42
Brand Connections LLC	7312	7
Brand Electric Inc	1731	667
Brand Energy and Infrastructure Services LLC	3446	2
Brand Energy Inc	1542	20
Brand Identity Inc	2752	1774
Brand Label Inc	2672	63
Brandeis Machinery and Supply Corp	5082	132
Brandenburg Electric Inc	1731	1060
Brandenburg Industrial Service Co	1795	3
Brandenburg Telephone Co	4813	130
Brandes Investment Partners Inc	6282	48
Brandir International Inc	8711	522
Brand-Nu Laboratories Inc	2899	175
Brandom Holdings LLC	2434	59
Brandon and Clark Inc	7694	1
Brandon Associates Inc	8743	216
Brandon Industries Inc	3645	67
Brandon Meats and Sausage Inc	5411	289
BrandsMart USA	5722	2
Brandstand Group Inc	7389	967
Brandsway International Inc	5734	183
Brandt and Hochman Literary Agents Inc	7389	2119
Brandt Consolidated Inc	2875	11
Brandt Construction Co	1623	799
Brandt Enterprises Inc	2752	740
Brandt Equipment LLC	2599	42
Brandt Information Services Inc	7371	368
Brandt Precision Machining Inc	3469	371
Brandt Technologies Inc	5169	52
Brandt Truck Line Inc	4213	1159
Brandtjen and Kluge Inc	3542	59
Brandtrust Inc	7311	357
Brand-Vaughan Lumber Company Inc	5031	181
Brandvia Alliance Inc	5199	72
Brandway Inc	5046	178
Brandywine Brokerage Services LLC	6211	19
Brandywine Cad Design Inc	7374	307
Brandywine Enterprises Inc	4953	146
Brandywine Fibre Products Company Inc	3089	1741
Brandywine Global Investment Management LLC	6282	360
Brandywine Investment Group Corp	3081	169
Brandywine Nursing and Rehabilitation Center Inc	8051	37
Brandywine Realty Trust	6798	55
Brandywine Recyclers Inc	5093	112
Brandywine Valley Fabricators Inc	3441	285
Braner USA Inc	3549	40
Branham Corp	5085	87
Branick Industries Inc	3545	85
Brankle Brothers Express Ltd	4213	2279
Branko Perforating Fwd Inc	3469	287
Brannan and Son Electric	1731	1497
Brannan Paving Company Inc	1611	28
Brannen Banks of Florida Inc	6712	459
Branner Printing Service Inc	2752	1395
Brannock Device Company Inc	3842	299

Company Name	SIC	Rank
Branscombe Cable Co	5063	399
Branscome Inc	2951	3
Branson Fowlkes/Russell Inc	6282	449
Branson Ultrasonics Corp	3541	14
Brantley Partners (Beachwood Ohio)	6799	354
Brantley Printing Company and Office Supplies	2752	1661
Brantley Telephone Company Inc	4813	288
Brantley Trucking Inc	4213	1633
Brasch Manufacturing Company Inc	3634	26
Braschler's Bakery Inc	5461	34
Brasfield and Gorrie LLC	1541	14
Brashe Advertising Inc	7311	801
Brasher Motor Company of Weimar Inc	5511	1126
Brasher's Cascade Auto Auction Inc	5012	88
Brasher's Northwest Auto Auction Inc	5012	96
Brasilians Press And Publications Inc	2711	549
Brass Alignment Inc	5013	374
Brass Aluminum Forging Ent	3463	6
Brass Valley LLC	7379	1422
Brass-Craft Manufacturing Co	3432	24
Brasseler Holdings Peter LP	5047	96
brassMEDIA Inc	2721	328
Brasure's Pest Control Inc	7342	95
Braswell Milling Co	2048	75
Braswell Precision Inc	3599	1365
Braswell Scale and Equipment Company Inc	5046	294
Brattleboro Savings and Loan Association FA	6035	224
Bratton Corp	3441	59
Braud Co	5085	264
Brauer Material Handling Systems Inc	5084	228
Brauer Supply Co	5051	70
Braun Electric Inc	5083	139
Braun Industries Inc	3711	54
Braun Intertec Corp	8711	103
Braun Northwest Inc	3711	63
Brauns International Inc	4213	3015
Brauntex Materials Inc	5032	80
Braverman and Associates	8111	567
Bravo Brio Restaurant Group Inc	5812	120
Bravo Communications Inc	3577	466
Bravo Electro Components Inc	5065	463
Bravo Health Insurance Company Inc	6321	50
Bravo Interactive Inc	7379	785
Bravo Networks	4841	60
Bravo Restaurants Inc	5812	344
Bravo Tech Inc	4812	52
Bra-Vor Tool and Die Company Inc	3544	743
BravoSolution US	7319	70
Brawley and Associates Inc	6531	353
Brawn Mixer Inc	3429	137
Braxton Culler Inc	5021	70
Braxton Manufacturing Company Inc	3965	13
Bray Manufacturing Company Inc	3199	15
Brayson Homes Inc	1531	65
BraytonHughes Design Studios	8712	195
Brazeway Inc	3354	11
Brazil Trucking Inc	4213	2365
Brazonics Inc	3599	206
Brazos Higher Education Authority Inc	6141	55
Brazos Private Equity Partners LLC	6719	162
Brazos Technology Corp	7379	868
BRB Contractors Inc	1541	155
BRC Imagination Arts	7922	26
Brd Printing Inc	2752	959
Brd Supply Inc	5013	376
BRE Properties Inc	6798	74
Bread Alone and Bakery Cafe	2051	192
Bread Factory LLC	2051	268
Bread Garden Ltd	2051	100
Bread Loaf Corp	1542	88
Breadeaux Pizza Inc	5812	404
Breads Of The World LLC	5812	208
Breadworks	2051	228
Breakdown Services Ltd	7389	1539
Breaker And Control Company Inc	5063	891
Breakers Mobile Electronics Inc	5731	164
Breakers Palm Beach Inc	7011	146
Breakthrough Computer Technology Inc	7379	1423
Breakthrough Productions	7372	1749
Breathing Color Inc	2672	54
Breaux Machine Works LP	3599	365
Breck Graphics Inc	2752	1223
Breck Media Inc	7374	381
Breck Operating Corp	1311	161
Breckenridge Brewery and Pub	2082	29
Brecon Knitting Mills Inc	2211	35
Breda Telephone Corp	4813	297
Brede Exposition Service	7389	319
Bredemus Hardware Company Inc	5072	167
Bredeweg and Zylstra PLC	8721	418
Breece Hill LLC	5045	240
Breedlove Dehydrated Food Inc	2034	26
Breen Systems Management Inc	7372	2409
Breene Kerr Productions	7812	283
Breene Lithograph Inc	2752	1830
Breese Publishing Company Inc	2752	428
Breeze Corp	2711	294
Breeze Hawaii Diving Adventures Corp	7999	150
Breeze Printing Co	2711	604
Breeze Reprographics Inc	2759	601

Company Name	SIC	Rank
Breeze-Eastern Corp	3728	38
Breezemaker Fan Company Inc	3564	151
Bregman and Company PC	8721	254
Brehm Communications Inc	2711	126
Brehob Corp	3621	49
Breidert Air Products Inc	3564	54
Breiner Company Inc	3053	139
Breitburn Energy Partners LP	1311	56
Breitinger Co	3441	132
Breland Building Supply Inc	5211	272
Bremen Castings Inc	3321	24
Bremen-Bowdon Investment Company Inc	2311	14
Bremer Financial Corp	6712	107
Bremner Inc	2052	10
Brenaman Electrical Service Inc	5063	627
Brencal Contractors Inc	1541	276
Brenco Inc	3562	3
Brenco Machine And Tool Inc	3599	2234
Brenda W Paul	1623	685
Brendan Vacations	4725	8
Brenholb Inc	2752	748
Brenmar Company Inc	5046	91
Brennan Beer Gorman/Architects	8712	82
Brennan Beer Gorman Monk/Interiors	7389	620
Brennan Electric Inc	1731	164
Brennan Equipment And Manufacturing Inc	3537	64
Brennan Machine Company Inc	3599	2212
Brennan's House Of Printing Inc	2752	1171
Brenneman Printing Inc	2752	534
Brennen Medical LLC	3842	262
Brennen Transportation Services	4213	1082
Brenner Group Inc	6282	119
Brenner Industries Inc	2796	73
Brenner Photo Productions	7335	23
Brenner Tank Services LLC	3715	18
Brenntag Great Lakes LLC	5169	1
Brenntag Latin America Inc	5169	35
Brenntag Mid-South Inc	5169	3
Brenntag North America Inc	5169	7
Brenny Specialized Inc	4213	2639
Brent Electric Inc	1731	1825
Brent G Theobald Construction	4213	2093
Brent Higgins Trucking Company Inc	4213	2952
Brent River Packaging Corp	3085	17
Brent Scarbrough and Company Inc	1623	74
Brent Woodward Inc	1623	629
Brentmark Software	7372	744
Brenton LLC	3565	39
Bren-Tronics Inc	3692	7
BRENTS Inc	2321	30
Brentwood Auto Parts Inc	5013	264
Brentwood Boulevard Hotel Development LLC	7011	196
Brentwood Communications Inc	7812	152
Brentwood Industries Inc	3089	233
Brentwood Originals Inc	2392	9
Brentwood Plastics Inc	3089	1417
Brentwood-Benson Music Publishing Inc	2741	60
Brera Capital Partners LLC	6799	201
Bresler and Reiner Inc	6513	22
Breslin Realty Development Corp	6552	126
Bresnan Communications Inc	4841	34
Bret Robinson Inc	7363	356
Bretford Manufacturing Inc	3651	157
Brethren Hillcrest Homes	8361	36
Brethren In Christ Media Ministries Inc	2731	323
Breton Industries Inc	2394	20
Breton Village Travel Services Inc	4724	60
Brett Aggregates Inc	1442	22
Brett Construction Co	1623	280
Breuer and Co	7371	1285
Brevan Electronics Inc	5065	343
Brevard Achievement Center Inc	8331	49
Brevard Electric Co	1731	1901
Brevard Robotics Inc	3599	1240
Brevard Water Conditioning Inc	7389	1566
Breveon Inc	7372	2871
Brewbaker Motors Inc	5511	682
Brewco Inc	3553	25
Brewer and Company of West Virginia Inc	1711	135
Brewer Corp	7353	46
Brewer Guard And Detective Service Inc	7381	95
Brewer Machine and Manufacturing Inc	3599	1331
Brewer Oil Co	5172	31
Brewer Science Inc	2851	42
Brewer-Cantelmo Company Inc	2782	73
Brewer-Garrett Co	1711	122
Brewery Credit Union	6062	86
Brewmatic Co	3556	71
Brewster Green Interval	7011	235
Brewster Home Fashions	5198	2
Brewster Panel Corp	2541	63
Brewster's Franchise Corp	6794	75
Brewton Express Inc	4213	2438
Brewton Iron Works Inc	3599	809
Breze Inc	7371	1244
BRH-Garver Construction LP	1799	22
Briad Main Street Inc	5812	185
Brian Cork Human Capital	7361	124

Company Name	SIC	Rank
Brian Electric Inc	1731	1937
Brian Kim	3663	280
Brian Moore Guitars Inc	3931	35
Brian Paul Inc	2752	730
Brian S Hickey Associates	8743	202
Brian Taylor International LLC	8999	181
Brian's Books Inc	5942	33
Brian's Toys	5961	135
Briartec Consulting Corp	5734	400
Briarwood Ford Inc	5511	167
Briarwood Printing Company Inc	2752	1766
Bri-Car Roofing and Sheet Metal Inc	1761	57
Brice Building Company Inc	1542	144
Brice Manufacturing Co	2531	18
Brice Vander Linden and Wernick PC	8111	290
Brick and Ballerstein Inc	2652	15
Brick Bodies Fitness Services Inc	7991	7
Brick Computer Co	3571	195
Brick Mill Studios	2771	14
Brick Street Software Inc	5734	259
Bricker and Eckler LLP	8111	186
Brickham Machining Company Inc	3599	1767
Brickhouse of NY Inc	7389	2364
BrickHouse Security	5063	220
Brickhouse Software Inc	7372	4278
Bricmont Inc	8711	414
Brico Electric Inc	1731	2546
Bricsnet America Inc	7372	1706
Bride Media International Inc	7819	74
Bridestone/Firestone Research	7549	2
Bridge Associates Inc	5045	885
Bridge Bancorp Inc	6712	312
Bridge Bank NA	6021	106
Bridge Business and Property Brokers Inc	8999	166
Bridge Capital Holdings	6021	102
Bridge City Publishing Inc	2711	833
Bridge Design Inc	8742	230
Bridge Family Center Of Atlanta Inc	8322	154
Bridge Industries Inc	5046	372
Bridge Integrated Communications	8742	212
Bridge Kitchenwares Corp	5046	358
Bridge Publications Inc	2731	94
Bridge Street Financial Inc	6021	323
Bridge Terminal Transport Inc	4213	122
Bridgecraft USA Inc	5072	170
Bridgefield Electrical Services Inc	1731	324
Bridgehampton National Bank	6021	99
BridgeHead Software	7372	2085
Bridgeline Digital Inc	7371	281
BridgeLux Inc	5065	56
Bridgeman Art Library International	7389	1451
Bridgeman Foods Inc	5812	248
Bridgemans Ice Cream	5812	457
Bridgemark LLC	7363	147
Bridgepoint Education Inc	8221	5
Bridgeport City School District	8211	16
Bridgeport Fittings Inc	3644	12
Bridgeport Insulated Wire Co	3357	66
Bridgeport Lumber	5211	327
Bridgeport National Bindery Inc	2789	26
Bridgeport Tool and Stamping Corp	3469	329
Bridgeport Truck Manufacturing Inc	3713	44
Bridgeport Wireless LLC	4812	115
Bridger Coal Co	1221	22
Bridger Scientific Inc	3823	462
Bridges Community Support Services Inc	8322	134
Bridges pbt	1542	217
Bridges USA Inc	8322	203
Bridges Young Matthews and Drake PLC	8111	523
Bridgestone Americas Holding Inc	3011	7
Bridgestone Americas Inc	3011	11
Bridgestone APM Co	2822	4
Bridgestone/Firestone Tire Sales Co	5014	13
Bridgestone Flowtech America	3052	26
Bridgestone Golf Inc	5091	9
BridgeStreet Worldwide	7021	1
Bridgetown Printing Co	2752	753
Bridgeview Bancorp	6712	476
Bridgevine Inc	5999	67
Bridgewater Associates Inc	8732	23
Bridgewater Interiors LLC	2399	5
Bridgewater Properties	6531	295
Bridgewater Raritan Board Of Education	8211	86
Bridgewater Savings Bank	6036	48
Bridgeway Capital Management Inc	6282	531
Bridgeway Systems Inc	5045	962
Bridgeways	3599	1199
Bridge-X Technologies Inc	7379	1355
Bridgford Food Processing Corp	2013	18
Bridgford Food Processing of Texas LP	2013	63
Bridgford Foods Corp	2013	30
Bridgford Marketing Co	2013	19
Bridon Cordage LLC	2298	3
Bridwell Oil Co	1311	169
Briefings Publishing Group	2741	64
Brigade Fire Protection Inc	1711	196
Brigade Quartermasters Ltd	5961	89
Brigandi And Associates Inc	7311	894
Briggs and Morgan PA	8111	157
Briggs and Stratton Corp	3511	4

Company Name	SIC	Rank
Briggs Equipment Inc	5082	44
Briggs Incorporated of Omaha	5074	33
Briggs Industries Inc	3543	30
Briggs Medical Service Co	2759	78
Brigham Exploration Co	1311	91
Brigham Oil and Gas LP	1311	97
Bright and Company Production Co	1382	4
Bright Computer Inc	7371	1749
Bright Enterprises Inc	3089	845
Bright Horizons Family Solutions Inc	8351	4
Bright Ideas in Broad Ripple Inc	7336	23
Bright Moments Inc	7311	775
Bright Now! Dental	8072	3
Bright Pharmaceutical Services Inc	8731	133
Bright Transportation Inc	4213	574
Brightdoor Systems Inc	7372	2118
Brighten Technologies LLC	5734	186
Brighton Agency Inc	7311	404
Brighton Bancorp	6712	624
Brighton Bank	6022	627
Brighton Brave Enterprises Inc	7349	528
Brighton Builders Inc	1531	47
Brighton-Best Socket Screw Manufacturing Inc	5072	34
Brightpoint Inc	5065	5
BrightStar Care	8082	30
BrightStar Consulting Inc	7373	796
Brightstar Corp	5063	3
BrightStar Credit Union	6062	119
Brightwork Advertising and Training Inc	7311	802
Brigittine Monks Gourmet Confections	2064	131
Brijot Imaging Systems Inc	3861	38
Bri-Lee Marketing Inc	2752	1256
Brilex Industries Inc	3441	123
Briley's Designs and Signs	2759	516
Brilliant Digital Entertainment Inc	7372	2496
Brilliant Jewelers/Mjj Inc	3911	25
Brilliant Store Inc	5731	183
Brilliant Technologies Corp	7372	5045
Brillion Iron Works Inc	3321	16
Brim Electronics Inc	3357	80
Brim Laundry Machinery Company Inc	5087	89
Brimad Enterprises Inc	7312	19
BriMar Wood Innovations Inc	5021	166
Brimberg and Co	6211	387
Brimhall Food Company Inc	2096	30
Brimrose Corporation Of America	3812	113
Brin Glass Co	5039	20
Brindle and Associates Inc	3629	124
Briner Electric Co	1731	381
Bringhurst Brothers Inc	5421	18
Bringing Up Baby Inc	5621	42
Brinker Industries	3993	142
Brinker International Inc	5812	18
Brinker's Fuels Inc	5983	18
Brinkman Products Inc	3541	34
Brinks B0662 PA Service Robin	7381	112
Brink's Co	4731	8
Brink's Inc	4213	7
BRIO Corp	5092	6
Brion Technologies Inc	3672	56
Brioschi Pharmaceutical International	2834	424
Brisar Industries Inc	3089	817
Brisk Rcr Coffee Company Inc	2095	52
Brisk Waterproofing Co	1799	5
Brisky Supply Company Inc	5032	119
Bristlecone Inc	7379	247
Bristol Bay Native Corp	6719	122
Bristol Capital Inc	7371	1750
Bristol Compressors International Inc	3563	5
Bristol Doors Corp	5031	268
Bristol Farms Inc	5411	185
Bristol Fiberlite Industries Inc	3089	600
Bristol Group Ltd	7372	2875
Bristol Hose and Fitting Inc	5074	211
Bristol Manufacturing Corp	7699	63
Bristol Metal Company Inc	5093	244
Bristol Metals LP	3312	27
Bristol Press Publishing Co	2711	327
Bristol Products Corp	2329	29
Bristol Publishing Enterprises Inc	2731	259
Bristol Seafood Inc	5146	30
Bristol Steel and Conveyor Corp	3441	180
Bristol Technology Inc	7372	1841
Bristol Tool and Die Inc	3599	2033
Bristol West Insurance Group	6331	172
Bristol-Myers Squibb Co	8731	1
Bristol-Myers Squibb Holding Pharma LLC	2834	117
Bristow Group Inc	4522	4
Bristow Optical	3851	79
Brita Litho Inc	2752	1321
Britannia Inc	7377	18
Britannia Press	2752	1619
Britcan Inc	5046	132
Brite Cleaning Service Inc	7349	128
Britek Consulting Inc	7379	1564
Briteline Extrusions Inc	3471	82
Brite-O-Matic Manufacturing Inc	3589	148
Brites Cartage Ltd	4213	1773
Brithinee Electric	5063	336
British American Publishing Ltd	2731	134
British Precision Inc	3545	223
Britstan Technology Inc	7361	183

Company Name	SIC	Rank
Britt Communications	2741	299
Britt Metal Processing Inc	3599	1958
Britt Trucking Co	4213	970
Brittain Industries Inc	3812	212
Brittain Trucking Inc	4213	2406
Brittany Dyeing And Printing Corp	2269	6
Brittany Maids Ltd	7349	463
Brittashan Enterprises Corp	1731	581
Britten Banners Inc	2399	11
Britten Media Inc	2759	59
Brittenford Systems	7372	2870
Britton and Koontz Capital Corp	6712	530
Britton and Koontz First National Bank	6021	128
Britton Lumber Company Inc	5033	23
Britz Store Equipment Inc	5046	240
Brix Group Inc	5065	26
BRJ Inc	2095	29
BRL Screening Inc	8731	93
Bro Tex Company Inc	2679	49
Broad and Cassel	8111	98
Broad River Electric Cooperative Inc	4911	446
Broad St Productions	7336	28
Broad Street Financial Co	6211	389
Broad Street Productions Inc	7812	99
Broadalbin Manufacturing Corp	3599	937
Broadax Systems Inc	3571	92
Broadband Communication Services Inc	8748	370
Broadband Specialists Inc	8742	442
BroadbandReportscom	7389	1802
Broadbent Co	1542	296
Broadbent Company Inc	6552	117
Broadbents Inc	7389	1409
Broadcast Electronics Inc	3663	101
Broadcast International Inc	7389	945
Broadcast Microwave Services Inc	3699	31
Broadcast Music Inc	6794	25
Broadcast News Networks Inc	7812	146
Broadcast Production Group Inc	7812	177
BroadCast Software International	7372	2119
Broadcast Supply Worldwide Inc	3663	149
Broadcast Technology Co	3663	191
Broadcast Tower Technologies Inc	1623	857
Broadcast Video Inc	7812	22
Broadcaster Press Inc	2752	6
Broadcasters General Store Inc	5049	32
Broadcom Corp	3674	6
Broadfoot Publishing Co	2731	352
Broadfoots Sand and Gravel Inc	1442	71
Broadford and Maloney Inc	7311	601
Broadhead Building Supplies Inc	5211	315
Broadlane Group Inc	5047	18
Broadlane Inc	7389	124
Broadleaf Group LLC	7379	479
Broadley-James Corp	3823	273
Broadlogic Network Technologies Inc	3674	212
Broadness LLC	7371	655
Broadnet	7389	906
Broadpoint Descap	6211	36
Broadreach Partners Inc	7389	1024
Broadridge Financial Solutions Inc	6282	34
Broadsoft Inc	7372	325
BroadSource Inc	8748	176
Broadspire Inc	7371	248
Broadspire LLC	6411	15
Broadspire Services Inc	8099	34
Broadstreet Inc	8742	351
Broadstripe	7376	4
Broadus Advertising and Public Relations	7311	408
Broadview Associates LLC	6211	85
Broadview Institute Inc	7812	96
Broadview Networks Inc	4813	42
Broadview Security Inc	7382	8
Broadvox LLC	4813	379
Broadway Bancshares Inc	6712	280
Broadway Bank	6021	278
Broadway Chevrolet Oldsmobile Inc	5511	295
Broadway Companies Inc	3544	169
Broadway Electric Service Corp	1731	84
Broadway Electrical Company Inc	1731	80
Broadway Federal Bank FSB	6035	139
Broadway Financial Corp	6712	469
Broadway Ford and Jeep	5511	176
Broadway Ford Truck Sales Inc	5511	820
Broadway Metal Works Inc	3441	204
Broadway National Bank	6021	103
Broadway Party and Tent Rental	8999	84
Broadway Service Corp	6162	40
Broadway Video Inc	7819	11
Broadwind Energy Inc	3369	2
Broan-Nutone LLC	3564	2
Broaster Co	6719	173
Brocade Communications Systems Inc	3577	9
Brock Cabinets and Appliances Inc	5031	419
Brock Enterprises Inc	1721	1
Brock Equipment Co	3594	22
Brock G And L Construction Company Inc	1623	282
Brock Grain Systems	3523	127
Brock Manufacturing	3523	6
Brock Schecter and Polakoff LLP	8721	43
Brock Supply Co	5013	116
Brock White Co	5084	169

Company Name	SIC	Rank
Brockette Davis Drake Inc	8711	378
Brockman Enterprises	3569	50
Brock-McVey Co	5078	22
Brockway Moran and Partners Inc	6799	75
Brockway-Smith Co (Andover Massachusetts)	5031	19
Broco Products Inc	3559	486
Brocomp Inc	5734	236
Broda Enterprises USA Inc	3842	48
Brodart Co	2531	10
Brodart Co- Books and Automation Div	7372	1840
Brode Management Group Ltd	6282	558
Broder Brothers Co	5136	2
Broderick Advertising	7311	518
Broderson Manufacturing Corp	3531	122
Brodeur Machine Company Business Trust	3469	199
Brodeur Partners	8743	34
Brodie Inc	5084	250
Brodnax Printing Company I LLC	2752	985
Brodock Press Inc	2752	331
Brody Chemical Company Inc	5169	62
Brody Transportation Company Inc	7513	17
Brody Weiss Zucarelli and Urbanek	8721	60
Broe Companies Inc	6552	6
Brogan Manufacturing Inc	3089	1790
Brogden Mills Of Smithfield Inc	7389	1710
Brogdon Tool and Die Inc	3544	236
Brokaw Inc	7311	685
Broken Arrow Electric Company Inc	1731	1159
Broken Arrow Productions Inc	2759	363
Brokers Logistics Genpar LLC	4225	30
Brolite Products Inc	5149	137
Broma Information Technology LLC	8748	424
Bromberg Holdings Inc	6719	166
Bromley Coats Inc	2337	8
Bromley Communications	7311	110
Bromley Engineering Inc	5734	385
Bromley Plastics Corp	2821	192
Bromley Printing Inc	2752	1365
Bromma Inc	3531	237
Bron Imaging Group	5043	11
Bronco Manufacturing Inc	3599	765
Broncorp Manufacturing Company Inc	3559	482
Broncus Technologies Inc	3842	109
Bronner Brothers Inc	2844	29
Bronner Display and Sign Advertising Inc	3699	17
Bronner Slosberg Humphrey Inc	7331	13
Bron-Shoe Co	7389	1993
Bronson and Bratton Inc	3544	72
Bronson Healthcare Group Inc	8069	4
Bronson Leigh Weeks	7311	546
Bront Machining Inc	3451	107
Bronto Software Inc	5045	425
Bronx Defenders	7389	785
Bronze Craft Corp	3365	30
Bronz-Glow Technologies Inc	2899	210
Brook Beech	8322	36
Brook Furniture Rental Inc	7359	17
Brook Hill Communications Inc	1623	634
Brook Ledge Inc	4213	2189
Brook Marketing Inc	5065	634
Brook Telephone Manufacturing and Supply Company Inc	3661	206
Brook Trout Technology Partners LLC	7373	1198
Brookdale Ford Inc	5511	757
Brookdale Living Communities Inc	6513	21
Brookdale Place of Fall Creek LLC	8051	53
Brookdale Plastics Inc	2621	61
Brookdale Senior Living Inc	8052	3
Brooke Distributors Inc	5064	57
Brooke Engineering and Photographic Equipment	3861	135
Brooke Industries Inc	7389	1670
Brooke Pottery Inc	5719	29
Brookfield and Co	6282	469
Brookfield Engineering Laboratories Inc	3826	39
Brookfield Office Properties Inc	6512	6
Brookfield Sand and Gravel Inc	1442	46
Brookfield Square JV	6531	227
Brookfield's Great Water Inc	5149	221
Brookhaven Instruments Corp	3826	119
Brookhaven Science Associates LLC	8733	24
Brookhurst Mill	2048	136
Brookings Radio	4832	238
Brooklace Inc	2679	36
Brookline Bancorp Inc	6712	166
Brookline Savings Bank	6036	38
Brooklyn Brewery Ltd	2082	24
Brooklyn Federal Bancorp Inc	6035	127
Brooklyn Fire and Ems Protection District	7389	1713
Brooklyn FSB	6035	120
Brooklyn Industries Corp	2329	28
Brooklyn Installations Inc	5031	376
Brooklyn Journal Publications Inc	2711	879
Brooklyn Printing and Advertising Inc	2752	1087
Brooklyn Resource Recovery Inc	5093	167
Brookman Auto Parts Inc	7389	844
Brookmeade Hardware and Supply Co	5064	111
Brookmeade Inc	7363	367
Brooks Automation Inc	3559	13
Brooks Beal Center	7389	1322
Brooks Brothers Inc	5611	2
Brooks CNC Services	3569	289
Brooks Courier Service Inc	4213	1833
Brooks Duplicator Co	5044	139
Brooks Food Group Inc	2038	21
Brooks Furniture Manufacturingrs Inc	2511	60
Brooks Group Inc	8742	525
Brooks Harris Film and Tape Inc	7372	3387
Brooks Instrument LLC	3824	4
Brooks Litho and Digital Group Inc	2752	1831
Brooks Lodden PC	8721	153
Brooks Logic LLC	7379	967
Brooks Machine Company Inc	3599	753
Brooks Manufacturing Co	2439	11
Brooks Montague and Associates Inc	6282	556
Brooks Precision Machining Inc	3469	376
Brooks Products Inc	3272	83
Brooks Reporting Inc	7338	43
Brooks Sports Inc	3149	25
Brooks Tactical Systems	2381	9
Brooks Technology Management Inc	7378	94
Brooks Tom Quitiquit and Cheewatts	8111	527
Brooks Tractor Inc	5999	58
Brooks Trucking Company Inc	4213	3003
Brookshire Brothers Ltd	5411	81
Brookshire Grocery Co	5411	62
Brookshire Publications Inc	2752	943
Brookside Associates LP	6513	7
Brookside Home Health Care	8082	79
Brookside Lumber and Supply Co	5211	122
Brookside Trucking Inc	4213	74
Brookstone Corp	1541	142
Brookstone Inc	5999	15
Brooktronics Engineering Corp	3471	127
Brooktrout Inc	3661	34
Brookville Locomotive Inc	3532	34
Brookville Wood Products Inc	2426	41
Brookwood Investments Inc	6799	311
Brookwood Media Arts	2741	242
Brookwoods Group Inc	8742	427
Broome Oldsmobile-Cadillac Inc	5511	763
Broome Welding Co	3441	229
Broomfield and Associates Inc	5065	958
Broomfield Laboratories Inc	3549	51
Bropfs Manufactured Homes Inc	5271	1
Brophy Engraving Company Inc	2796	40
Bross Trucking Inc	4213	736
B-R-O-T Inc	3444	246
Brotech Corp	2821	43
Brother Industries (USA) Inc	3579	11
Brother International Corporation USA	5044	4
Brother Wolf Inc	7372	4795
Brotherhood America's Oldest Winery Ltd	2084	74
Brotherhood Bancshares Inc	6712	527
Brotherhood Bank and Trust Co	6022	57
Brothers Air and Heat Inc	1731	269
Brothers and Company Of Oklahoma	8743	171
Brothers Baking Co	2051	183
Brothers Electric Co	1731	2393
Brothers Ii Business Machines Of LI Inc	7629	46
Brothers Optical Laboratory Inc	3851	38
Brothers Precision Tool Co	3545	433
Brothers Printing and Lithography Inc	2759	316
Brothers Supply Corp	5075	78
Brothers Trucking Company Inc	4213	909
Brotman Winter Fried Communications	8743	217
Broudy Precision Equipment Co	3825	73
Brougham Corp	3081	172
Brougher Inc	3449	10
Broughton Foods LLC	2026	44
Broughton International	7372	1685
Brouillard	7311	146
Broussard Iron Works and Welding Inc	3571	212
Brouwer and Janachowski	6282	362
Brouwer Relocation Inc	4213	2953
Broward Adjustment Services Inc	7322	102
Broward Bank of Commerce	6022	660
Brower Timing Systems	3625	404
Brown Advisory	6282	44
Brown and Associates LLC	6321	71
Brown and Bigelow Inc	2754	5
Brown and Brown Agency of Insurance Professionals Inc	6411	234
Brown and Brown Inc	6411	33
Brown and Brown Insurance of Arizona Inc	6411	156
Brown and Brown Insurance Services of El Paso Inc	6411	219
Brown and Brown Insurance Services of Texas Inc	6411	163
Brown and Brown Nissan	5511	556
Brown and Brown of Colorado Inc	6411	199
Brown and Brown of Lehigh Valley Inc	6411	175
Brown and Brown of Missouri Inc	6411	213
Brown and Brown of South Carolina Inc	6411	214
Brown and Brown of Washington Inc	6311	216
Brown and Caldwell	8711	67
Brown and Company Graphic Design Inc	7336	159
Brown and James PC	8111	240
Brown and Joseph Ltd	7322	54
Brown and Miller Advertising Inc	7311	653
Brown and Ross Of New Jersey Inc	5063	1086
Brown and Ruprecht	8111	510
Brown and Sharpe Manufacturing Co	3545	12
Brown and Watson Company Inc	1442	48
Brown Automotive Group Inc	5511	229
Brown Bear Corp	3537	114
Brown Bear Software	7372	5019
Brown Brothers Construction Co	1611	210
Brown Brothers Harriman and Co	6022	39
Brown Brothers Produce Co	5144	29
Brown Brothers Sand Co	1442	69
Brown Capital Management Inc	6282	272
Brown Co	3089	1899
Brown Construction Inc	1623	588
Brown Corrosion Services Inc	7389	1241
Brown County Cabinets Inc	2434	70
Brown County State Bank	6022	765
Brown Cow West Corp	2026	82
Brown Eassa and McLeod LLP	8111	433
Brown Electric Company Inc	1731	416
Brown Electric Construction Company Inc	1731	551
Brown Electric Inc	1731	1548
Brown Equipment Manufacturing Company Inc	3541	202
Brown Family Communities LLC	1531	71
Brown Food Service	5141	176
Brown Forman Cooperage Co	2449	3
Brown Gibbons Lang and Company LP	6211	269
Brown Industrial Inc	3713	56
Brown Industries Inc	3599	1434
Brown Innovations Inc	3669	146
Brown International Corp	3556	41
Brown Jordan Co	2514	3
Brown Jordan International Inc	2521	7
Brown Machine Works and Supply Inc	3554	59
Brown Machine Works Inc	3599	1991
Brown Manufacturing Corp	3523	134
Brown McCarroll LLP	8111	166
Brown Medical Industries Inc	3842	216
Brown Metals Co	5051	86
Brown Nelson Public Relations	8743	237
Brown Nissan Pontiac and Subaru Inc	5511	821
Brown Packing Company Inc	2011	43
Brown Palace Hotel Company Inc	7011	164
Brown Paper Goods Co	2674	15
Brown Precision Inc	3728	133
Brown Printers Of Troy Inc	2752	1720
Brown Printing Company Inc	2752	11
Brown Printing Inc	2752	1111
Brown Produce Inc	4213	2569
Brown Recycling and Manufacturing Inc	5015	20
Brown Rudnick Berlack Israels	8111	114
Brown Shoe Company Inc	3149	3
Brown Smith Wallace LLC	8721	278
Brown Stevens Elmore and Sparre	6531	309
Brown Street Furniture LLC	2511	90
Brown Traffic Products Inc	3669	162
Brown Transfer Co	4213	731
Brown Transport Inc	4213	172
Browne Lumber Inc	5031	251
Brownell Travel Inc	4724	42
Brownells Inc	5091	24
Brownfields Incorporated Of Boise	3842	281
Brown-Forman Corp	2085	2
Brown-Forman Employees Credit Union	6062	117
Brownies Marine Group Inc	3949	163
Browning Arms Co	3484	25
Browning Construction Co	1542	331
Browning Construction Inc	1541	73
Browning-Ferris Industries Inc	4953	3
Browning-Ferris Industries of Colorado (Commerce City Colorado)	4953	76
Browning's Welding Service Inc	1799	104
Brownlee Lighting Inc	3646	61
Brownlee Trucking Inc	4213	1025
Brownlie and Braden LLC	6282	518
Brownlow Publishing Co	2731	232
Brown-Rogers-Dixson Co	5072	116
Brown's Brewing Co	5812	442
Brown's Buick Inc	5511	986
Brown's Bun Baking Co	2051	187
Brown's Chicken and Pasta Inc	5812	216
Brown's Data Processing Service Center	7374	278
Browns Hill Engineering and Controls LLC	3829	381
Brown's Ice Cream Co	5143	32
Brown's Tool and Mold Company Inc	3544	844
Brown's Trucking	4213	379
Brownstein Group	7311	183
Brownstein Hyatt and Farber PC	8111	252
Brownstone Gallery Ltd	5023	51
Brownstone Research Group	7372	2632
Brownstown Electric Supply Company Inc	5063	264
Brownstown Quality Tool and Design Inc	3544	900
Brownsville Products Inc	3544	865
Browntech Inc	7372	3868
Brown-Wilbert Inc	3272	115

Company Name	SIC	Rank
Brownwood Acres Foods Inc	2037	39
Brownwood Furniture Inc	2511	82
Brox Industries Inc	2951	22
Broydrick and Associates	8743	126
Broyhill Asset Management	6282	72
Broyhill Furniture Industries Inc	2512	6
Broyhill Inc	3523	250
Broyhill Transport Inc	4213	1653
Brp Manufacturing Co	3069	147
BRRE Holdings Inc	6799	326
Brubacher Excavating Inc	1794	19
Brubaker Tool Inc	3541	16
Brucci Limited Inc	2844	173
Bruccoli Clark Layman Inc	2731	214
Bruce and Merrilees Electric Co	1731	172
Bruce Bell and Associates Inc	7372	3767
Bruce Diamond Corp	3545	165
Bruce Foods Corp	2032	5
Bruce Fox Inc	3914	6
Bruce Jones Design Inc	7372	3869
Bruce Kennedy Sand and Gravel Co	5211	287
Bruce Kreofsky and Sons Inc	1542	392
Bruce Lowrie Chevrolet Inc	5511	412
Bruce Oakley Inc	5153	6
Bruce Office Supply Inc	5044	78
Bruce Packing Company Inc	2011	29
Bruce Printing Inc	2752	623
Bruce Seed Farm	0139	4
Bruce Supply Corp	5074	104
Bruce W Eberle and Associates Inc	7331	66
Bruceton Farm Service Inc	5411	235
Brucken's Inc	5046	182
Bruckner Truck Sales Inc	5511	181
Bruckner Truck Sales - Tye	3519	33
Bruco Inc	5087	92
Bruder Inc	5211	279
Bruderer Machinery Inc	3542	43
Bruegger's Enterprises	2045	2
Brueton Industries Inc	2512	23
Bruewer Woodwork Manufacturing Co	3083	42
Brugg Wire Rope LLC	5051	207
Bruin Plastics Company Inc	2295	14
Brujan Inc	2752	1292
Bruker AXS Inc	3844	7
Bruker Corp	3826	6
Bruker Daltonics Corp	3826	14
Bruker Medical Inc	3826	37
Brulin and Company Inc	2842	42
Brumall Manufacturing Corp	3643	91
Brumley South Inc	3674	481
Brumlow Mills Inc	2273	18
Brundidge Electronics Corp	3672	248
Bruneel Tire Factory Inc	5014	31
Bruner Consulting Associates Inc	7379	836
Bruner-Cox LLP	8721	84
Bruning And Federle Manufacturing Co	3564	73
Brunk Industries Inc	3469	78
Brunner and Lay Inc	3532	11
Brunner Inc	3714	273
Brunner Manufacturing Company Inc	3965	7
Brunner-Hildebrand Lumber Dry Kiln Co	3559	78
Bruno and Tervalon	8721	370
Bruno Independent Living Aids Inc	3842	108
Bruno Scheidt Inc	5149	34
Bruno Specialty Foods Inc	5411	271
Bruno's Supermarkets Inc	5411	66
Brunozzi Transfer and Truck Rental	4213	949
Bruns Brothers Welding Inc	5084	400
Brunschwig and Fils Inc	5021	23
Brunsell Brothers Ltd	5211	113
Bruns-Gutzwiller Inc	1542	352
Brunsing Associates Inc	8711	574
Brunson Instrument Company Inc	3827	77
Brunstedt and Lambert Systems Inc	3625	255
Brunswick Bancorp	6712	658
Brunswick Corp	3732	2
Brunswick Corp US Marine Div	3732	8
Brunswick Electric Inc	1731	2267
Brunswick Electric Membership Corp	4911	166
Brunswick Instrument Inc	3545	432
Brunswick News Publishing Co	2711	471
Brunswick Press Inc	5112	62
Brunton Enterprises Inc	1791	10
Brunton Outdoor Inc	3829	109
Brush Contractors Inc	1731	537
Brush International Inc	3339	24
Brushfire Inc	7311	309
Bruss Co	2013	66
Bruster's Real Ice Cream Inc	2024	6
Brustman and Carrino Public Realations	8743	140
Brutocao Cellars	2084	85
Brutoco Engineering and Construction Inc	1622	25
Brw Tool Inc	3469	382
Bry-Air Inc	3585	161
Bryan and Bryan	4213	1928
Bryan and PatersonPC	8721	244
Bryan Baking Inc	5149	48
Bryan Bank and Trust	6029	18
Bryan Cave LP	8111	78
Bryan Chevrolet Inc	5511	250
Bryan Construction Co	1542	368

Company Name	SIC	Rank
Bryan Corp	3841	207
Bryan Enterprises Inc	2752	1529
Bryan Independent School District	8211	81
Bryan Pendleton Swats and Mcallister-Wells Fargo LLC	8999	148
Bryan Publishing Co	2711	480
Bryan Rock Products Inc	1422	42
Bryan Steam LLC	3443	114
Bryan Vincent Associates Inc	7379	1087
Bryant and Stratton Business Institute Inc	8244	2
Bryant Christie Inc	8748	277
Bryant Church Hardwoods Inc	5031	317
Bryant Control Inc	3613	171
Bryant Electric Repair and Construction Inc	1731	1517
Bryant Industrial Maintenance Inc	7692	25
Bryant Label Company Inc	2679	68
Bryant Motors Inc	5012	138
Bryant Rubber Corp	3053	36
Bryant W-D and Son Inc	5211	236
Bryant-Habegger Co	5075	17
Bryant's Precision M F G Corp	3469	299
Bryce Corp	2673	2
Bryce Johnson Inc	2671	53
Bryco Funding Inc	6162	66
Brydet Development	3532	41
Brydon Cleaning Co	7349	448
Bryit Group LLC	3672	391
Brylane Inc	5961	6
Brylski Co	8743	143
Bryn Mawr Bank Corp	6712	212
Bryn Mawr Brokerage Company Inc	6282	73
Bryn Mawr Trust Co	6022	406
Brynavon Group	6282	485
Brynwood Partners LP	6799	280
Brysan Utility Contractors Inc	1623	284
Bryson and Bryson Builders Inc	1623	735
Brystar Contracting Inc	1611	187
Bryton Technology Inc	3679	428
Bs Trading Co	5023	126
BS Xpress Inc	4213	2862
Bsa Industries Inc	3827	64
BSA Lifestructures	8712	116
Bsc Supply LLC	5734	174
BSD Medical Corp	3845	108
BSE Credit Union Inc	6062	96
Bse Industrial Contractors Inc	1541	209
BServ Inc	7389	837
Bsg Int'l LLC	6719	101
BSI Constructors Inc	1541	116
Bsi Corp	5047	230
Bsi Industries Inc	5084	775
BSI Scales Inc	5046	236
Bsk Associates	8711	319
Bsm Pump Corp	3561	164
BSML Inc	8072	5
BSN Inc	5122	35
Bsp Solutions Inc	7361	431
BSP Trans Inc	4213	1091
BSQUARE Corp	7389	240
B-Squared Designs Inc	7379	1471
BST Consultants Inc	7372	2333
BST Systems Inc	3692	8
BSV Transportation	4213	2425
BT Commercial Real Estate	6531	2
BT Infonet	7389	67
BT INS Inc	7379	11
BT Mancini Company Inc	1751	4
BT Operating Co	1381	47
BT Radianz	7376	3
BT S Inc	3661	200
BT Trucking Inc	4213	1053
BTA Oil Producers	1311	140
Btac Holding Corp	5192	10
BTB Inc	5045	601
BTC Electronic Components	3679	257
BTC Laboratories Inc	8734	170
BTC Wholesale Distributers Inc	5194	9
BTD Manufacturing Inc	3544	3
Btd Manufacturing Inc	3469	122
BTE Consulting Inc	7371	1499
B-Tec Solutions Inc	3599	372
Btec Turbines LP	3511	29
Bti Computers Inc	5045	576
Bti Environmental Services	7349	497
BTI Financial Group	6211	119
BTI Special Commodities Inc	4213	1160
Btl Machine	3812	97
BTLSR Toledo Inc	2821	109
BTM Industries Inc	3599	2392
Bto Servers Inc	5045	999
B-Tron Corp	3674	489
BTS Asset Management Inc	6282	126
Bts Consulting Group Ltd	7371	1787
BTU International Inc	3559	47
Btx Technologies Inc	3065	296
Buanno Transportation Company Inc	4213	2650
Bubba Foods LLC	2011	65
Bubba Gump Shrimp Company Restaurant and Market Inc	5812	179
Bubba Oustalet Ford Lincoln-Mercury Toyota	5511	588
Bublitz Machinery Co	8741	304

Company Name	SIC	Rank
Buca Inc	5812	146
Buccaneer Brokerage Inc	5046	166
BuchalterNemer LLC	8111	86
Buchan Trucking LLC	4213	1432
Buchanan Associates	7373	222
Buchanan Hardwoods Inc	2421	27
Buchanan Ingersoll PC	8111	75
Buchanan Lumber Birmingham Inc	2426	34
Buchart-Horn Inc	8711	156
Bucher Hydraulics Inc	3594	12
Bucher Willis and Ratliff Corp	8711	293
Buchheit Trucking Service	4213	1209
Buchmann Optical Inc	3851	74
Buchy Food Products Inc	5141	196
Buck Consultants Inc	8748	15
Buck Distributing Company Inc	5181	30
Buck Equipment Inc	3531	166
Buck Knives Inc	3421	11
Buck Kreihs Marine Repair LLC	3731	40
Buck Owens Production Company Inc	4832	52
Buck Research Instruments LLC	8731	418
Buck Scientific Inc	3823	262
Buck Wear Inc	2321	16
Buckardt Technologies Inc	7373	393
Buckell Plastic Company Inc	3089	1452
Buckeye Boxes Inc	2673	22
Buckeye Business Forms Inc	5112	98
Buckeye Business Products Inc	3579	29
Buckeye Excavating and Construction Inc	1623	736
Buckeye Exports	5049	138
Buckeye Fire Equipment Co	3999	55
Buckeye International Inc	2842	20
Buckeye Lumberton Corp	2611	5
Buckeye Machine and Fabricators Inc	3599	888
Buckeye Partners LP	4613	2
Buckeye Pipe Line Co	4613	10
Buckeye Pipe Line Company LP	2911	44
Buckeye Polymers Inc	2821	138
Buckeye Protective Service Inc	7381	63
Buckeye Ranch Inc	8361	14
Buckeye Rubber and Packing Co	5085	152
Buckeye Rural Electric Cooperative Inc	4911	231
Buckeye Stamping Co	3469	197
Buckeye Supply Co	5084	241
Buckeye Technologies Inc	2611	4
Buckeye Vacuum Cleaner Supply Co	3635	8
Buckhead Life Restaurant Group	5812	269
Buckhorn Inc	3089	72
Buckhorn Land Development Corp	1731	1427
Buckhorn Rubber Products Inc	3069	30
Buckingham Capital Partners	6719	66
Buckingham Doolittle and Burroughs LLP	8111	350
Buckingham Research Group Inc	6211	249
Buckland Security Services	7381	206
Buckle Down Publishing	2741	89
Buckle Inc	5651	14
Buckler Transport Inc	4213	1609
Buckley and Co	1611	142
Buckley Broadcasting Corp	4832	3
Buckley Co	2542	65
Buckley Graphics Inc	2672	76
Buckley Industries Inc	5033	31
Buckley Powder Co	2892	7
Bucklin Tractor and Implement	5083	15
Buckman Laboratories Inc	2869	18
Buckmaster Publishing	2741	138
Buckner News Alliance Inc	2711	352
Buck's Communication Co	1623	430
Bucks County Coffee Co	5499	15
Bucks County Fire Dispatch	8322	215
Buck's Sanitary Service Inc	7359	49
Buckshire Corp	8731	179
Buckskin Mining Co	1221	20
Buckstaff Company Inc	2531	15
Bucky Products Inc	2392	22
Bucolo Cold Storage Inc	4213	1077
Bucon Inc	1541	70
Bucyrus Blades Inc	3531	70
Bucyrus Precision Tech Inc	3714	274
Bud/Alan Plastics Inc	3089	1056
Bud Clary Chevrolet Oldsmobile Subaru Jeep Eagle Inc	5511	147
Bud Electronic Supply Co	5065	887
Bud Griffin Customer Support	5075	109
Bud Industries Inc	3469	126
Bud Red Industries Inc	3547	6
Bud Wil Inc	3086	97
Bud Wolf Chevrolet Inc	5511	832
Budd Built-In Vacuum Cleaners	3589	271
Budd Charles Corp	5072	82
Budd Chemical Company Inc	2821	145
Budd Group	7381	22
Budd Lake Machine And Tool Inc	3599	2256
Budd Van Lines	4213	495
Buddy Bar Casting Corp	3365	29
Buddy Lee Attractions Inc	7922	86
Buddy Moore Trucking Inc	4213	1147
Buddy Squirrel LLC	2066	11
Buddy's Carpet Inc	5713	3
Buddy's Kitchen Inc	2038	35
Buddy's Seafood Inc	5421	22
Buderic Inc	7331	121

Company Name	SIC	Rank
Budget Blinds Inc	6794	56
Budget Data Services Inc	3695	160
Budget Drug	5912	70
Budget Electrical Contractors Inc	1731	223
Budget Heating and Cooling LLC	5075	100
Budget Rent A Car System Inc	7514	4
Budget Restaurant Equipment Co	5046	324
Budney Industries Inc	3724	44
Budnick Converting Inc	2672	41
Budros Ruhlin and Roe Inc	6282	121
Bud's and Son Trucking Inc	4213	737
Bud's Best Cookies Inc	2052	36
Bud's Bulk Ice Service Inc	5199	124
Buds Cotton Inc	2844	157
Budway Enterprises Inc	4213	1506
Budwine Service Electric Company Inc	1731	1987
Budzar Industries Inc	3585	140
Buechel Stone Corp	3281	17
Buecomp Inc	3089	1448
Buedel Food Products Co	5147	34
Buehler Ltd	3821	14
Buehler Motor Inc	3621	61
Buel Inc	4213	1361
Buell Consulting Inc	7372	3870
Buell Manufacturing Co	3714	424
Buena Vista International Inc	7822	41
Buena Vista Pictures Distribution	7822	2
Buendia and Partners Inc	5032	151
Buenger Enterprises	3585	244
Buerg Software	7372	4366
Buesing Bulk Transport Inc	4213	1728
BUFC Financial Services Inc	6289	6
Buferd Company Inc	3469	133
Buffa Company Inc	5065	722
Buffalo Air Handling Co	3564	22
Buffalo Athletic Club Southtown LLC	7997	13
Buffalo Cardiology and Pulmonary Associates PC	8011	49
Buffalo Crushed Stone Inc	1423	3
Buffalo Dental Manufacturing Company Inc	3843	44
Buffalo Electric Inc	1731	2042
Buffalo Exchange	5932	4
Buffalo FSB	6022	460
Buffalo Games Inc	3944	21
Buffalo Gear Inc	3566	38
Buffalo Hotel Supply Company Inc	5046	33
Buffalo Industries Inc	2299	22
Buffalo Light and Supply Corp	5719	34
Buffalo Newspress Inc	2759	73
Buffalo Power Electronics Ctr	3714	189
Buffalo Printers Supply Inc	5043	38
Buffalo Pumps Inc	3561	24
Buffalo Savings Bank	6036	101
Buffalo Truck Center Inc	5012	52
Buffalo Wild Wings Inc	5812	72
Buffaloe Com Inc	5734	414
Buffamante Whipple Buttafaro PC	8721	27
Buffelen Woodworking Co	2431	121
Buffet Partners LP	5812	49
Buffets Holdings Inc	5812	43
Buffets Inc	5812	45
Buffkin Ceramic Tile Supply Inc	5032	126
Bufkor Inc	5199	55
Buflovak LLC	3556	109
Buford-Thompson Co	1542	27
Bug Busters Software Engineering Inc	7372	2948
Bug Off Exterminators Inc	7342	71
Bugbasher Inc	5012	174
Bugmobile Pest and Termite Control	7342	82
Bugs Burger Bug Killers Inc	7342	43
Buhl Press Inc	2752	430
Buhler Inc	3556	4
Buhler Sortex Inc	5049	89
Buhrke Industries LLC	3469	48
Buhrt Engineering and Construction Inc	3444	261
Build-A-Bear Workshop Inc	5945	6
Builder Investment Group Inc	6282	504
Builder Security Group Inc	7382	116
BuilderFusion Inc	7371	372
Builder's Concrete and Supply Company Inc	3273	57
Builders Fireplace and Supply Inc	5023	142
Builders FirstSource Inc	5031	14
Builders General Supply Co	5031	68
Builders Hardware And Hollow Metal Inc	5031	322
Builders Hardware and Supply Company Inc	5072	14
Builders Interior Designs Inc	7389	2064
Builder's Redi-Mix Inc	3272	13
Builder's Sales and Service Co	5064	190
Builders Service Company Of Fort Worth	5023	149
Builders Station Land LLC	5211	174
Builders Steel Co	3441	143
Builders Steel Company Inc	3441	209
Builders Supply Company Of Cookeville	5031	310
Builders Supply Inc	5072	146
Builders Support and Supply Inc	5031	274
Builders Transportation Company LLC	4213	233
Buildex Electronics Inc	3672	411
Building and Industrial Wholesale Co	5031	138
Building and Utility Contractors Inc	1623	513
Building Block Software Inc	7372	4489
Building Concepts Of America Inc	5039	46
Building Control Solutions LLC	3661	230
Building Control Technologies Inc	5084	538
Building Material Distributors Inc	5031	30
Building Materials Holding Corp	5211	11
Building Products Inc	5031	26
Building Service Company Inc	7349	376
Building Service Inc	1542	227
Building Services Co	7349	406
Building Services Inc	7349	261
Building Specialties Company Inc	5031	432
Building Supply Trading Corp	5031	318
Building Systems Design Inc	7372	3481
Building Systems Transportation Co	4213	1377
BuildingStars St Louis Inc	7349	100
Buildtopia Inc	7372	2120
Built-In-Systems Inc	1731	2579
Built-Rite Manufacturing Inc	3469	372
Buk Optics Inc	3827	146
Bulbman Inc	5063	92
Bulbrite Industries Inc	5063	453
BulbsCom Inc	7374	183
Bulbtronics Inc	5063	259
Bulbworks Inc	5063	912
Bulk Carrier Services Inc	4213	1688
Bulk Express Inc	4213	1307
Bulk Lift International Inc	3089	479
Bulk Molding Compounds Inc	2821	56
Bulk Transport Corp	4213	2132
Bulk Transportation	4213	667
Bulk TV and Internet	4841	82
Bulkmatic Transport Co	4213	196
Bulkregister LLC	7379	1293
Bull Data Systems Inc	3571	24
Bull Hn Information Systems Inc	5045	18
Bull HN Information Systems Inc (Billerica Massachusetts)	7379	26
Bull Metal Products Inc	2542	60
Bull Moose Tube Co	3317	30
Bull Publishing Co	2731	315
Bullard's Computer Solutions Inc	5045	632
Bulldog Battery Corp	3691	26
Bulldog Drummond Inc	7311	743
Bulldog Fire Apparatus Inc	7699	241
Bulldog Hiway Express	4213	937
Bulldog Multimedia	7336	325
Bulldog Solutions Inc	7319	108
Bullen Midwest Inc	2841	20
Bullet Electric Inc	1731	301
Bullet Guard Corp	3312	107
Bullet Line Inc	3993	41
Bulletin Board Inc	2721	436
Bulletin Net Inc	2711	834
Bulletin News LLC	2741	235
Bulletin News Network Inc	2741	284
BulletProof Corp	7372	1880
Bullfrog Films	2741	208
Bullhorn Inc	4813	234
Bullitt-Hutchins Inc	6531	393
Bullivant Houser Bailey PC	8111	214
Bulloch Fertilizer Company Inc	5191	124
Bullocks Express Transportation	4213	669
Bullrich Corp	5941	25
Bullseye Glass Co	3211	15
Bullseye Trucking LC	4212	74
BullseyeDisc	3695	145
Bully Dog Technologies LLC	3519	15
Bulman Products Inc	3586	6
Bulova Corp	5094	9
Bulova Technologies Group Inc	7372	5040
BUM International Inc	5136	10
Bumble Bee Seafoods LLC	2091	1
Bumper Bowling Inc	3949	171
Bumper Specialities Inc	3069	144
Bunch Transport Inc	4213	1272
Bundy Manufacturing Inc	3599	742
Bundy Typewriter Co	5734	193
Bunell and Associates Inc	5063	1012
Bunge Ltd	2099	1
Bunge North America Inc	2075	1
Bunker Corp	3714	255
Bunker Hill Cheese Company Inc	2022	59
Bunkie Trinite Trophies Inc	5999	283
Bunkley Electric Company Inc	1731	2239
Bunn Capitol Co	5141	139
Bunnell Electric Inc	1731	2436
Bunny Bread Inc	2051	61
Buntin Group Inc	7311	634
Bunting Bearings LLC	3566	9
Bunting Electric Inc	1731	1171
Bunting Inc	3953	8
Bunting Magnetics Co	3499	20
Bunting's Wholesale Market Inc	5147	79
Bunzl Distribution USA	5113	3
Bunzl Extrusion	3083	11
Bunzl Extrusion Philadelphia Inc	3089	960
Bunzl New Jersey Inc	5113	12
Bunzl Philadelphia	5162	6
Buono Brothers Bakery Inc	2051	258
Buquet and LeBlanc Inc	1542	374
Bur And Forman LLP	8111	230
Bur-Bak Plastics Corp	3089	745
Burbank Opthalmology ASC LP	8011	97
Burch and Cracchiolo PA	8111	447
Burch Food Services Inc	5962	13
Burch Porter and Johnson	8111	414
Burcham and McCune Inc	6719	148
Burco Molding Inc	3089	941
Burd and Fletcher Co	2657	14
Burd Ford Inc	5511	711
Burden's Machine and Welding Inc	1799	133
Burdick Packing Company Inc	5147	136
Burdorf-Kessler Inc	7389	1501
Bureau of Collection Recovery Inc	7322	28
Bureau Of National Affairs Inc	2731	10
Bureau Of Office Services Inc	7338	14
Bureau van Dijk Electronic Publishing Inc	7379	55
Bureau Veritas North America Inc	1521	150
Bureau Workers Compensation	7382	122
Burelbach Industries Corp	3553	17
Burford Corp	3556	61
Burger King Corp	5812	41
Burger King Holdings Inc	5812	21
Burger Maker Company Inc	5147	90
Burger Physical and Rehabilitation Agency Inc	8049	3
Burger Rehabilitation Systems Inc	8049	9
Burger's Ozark Country Cured Hams Inc	2013	85
Burgess and Niple Ltd	8711	165
Burgess Communications	7319	125
Burgess Computer Decisions Inc	7373	950
Burgess Construction Consultants Inc	7389	1108
Burgess Manufacturing Inc	3599	2257
Burgess Sales and Supply Inc	5072	159
Burgess Speciality Fabrication Inc	3599	459
Burgess Transportation LLC	4213	2727
Burgess Trucking Company Inc	4213	1845
Burgess-Manning Inc	3443	91
Burgess-Norton Manufacturing Co	3499	8
Burgett Inc	3931	17
Burggraf Tire Supply Inc	5014	15
Burghof Engineering and Manufacturing Co	3565	152
Burgiss Group Inc	7372	2096
Burgiss Group LLC	7379	608
Burglar Alarm And Security Company Inc	1731	2000
Burgon Tool Steel Company Inc	5051	138
Burgoon Co	5047	128
Burgreen Contracting Company Inc	1611	214
Burk Advertising and Marketing Inc	7311	855
Burk Consulting Inc	7379	1347
Burk Electronics	5731	271
Burk Royalty Co	1311	175
Burk Technology Inc	3663	239
Burke Beverages Inc	5181	66
Burke E Porter Machinery Co	3559	71
Burke Engineering Company Inc	5075	30
Burke Group Inc	6022	449
Burke Hosiery Mills Inc	2252	29
Burke International Tours Inc	4725	46
Burke Marketgrowth International Ltd	6282	480
Burke Products Inc	3674	346
Burke-Parsons-Bowlby Corp	2491	7
Burke-Parsons-Bowlby Corp Appalachian Div	2491	16
Burkert Contromatic Corp	3491	43
Burke's Bakery and Delicatessen Inc	5411	282
Burkett's Office Furnishings and Supplies	5021	66
Burkey Acquisition Inc	2096	44
Burkhalter Rigging Inc	7359	95
Burkhalter Travel Agency Inc	4724	28
Burkhart Dental Supply	5047	43
Burkhart Enterprises Inc	4213	1248
Burklund Distributors Inc	5145	2
Burkmann Feeds Of Glasgow LLC	2048	76
Burks Beverage	2086	106
Burks Tractor Company Inc	5083	82
Burlen Corp	2341	8
Burley Corp	3448	27
Burlingame Builder Inc	5085	469
Burlington A/V Recording Media Inc	5045	416
Burlington Aviation	4581	47
Burlington Broadcasting Inc	4832	202
Burlington Capital Group	6798	106
Burlington Chemical Company LLC	5169	182
Burlington Coat Factory Warehouse Corp	5651	5
Burlington Construction Company Inc	1541	199
Burlington Fabrics Inc	2211	11
Burlington Hawk Eye Co	2711	443
Burlington Healthcare Providers	7361	249
Burlington House Div	2261	1
Burlington House Upholstery	2221	45
Burlington Northern and Santa Fe Railway Co	4011	3
Burlington Northern Santa Fe LLC	4011	1
Burlington Rigid Box	2653	108
Burlington Times Inc	2711	300
Burmar Technical Corp	7336	286
Burndy LLC USA	3678	1
Burner Fire Control Inc	1731	642
Burnes of Boston	2782	8

Company Name	SIC	Rank
Burnes of Boston/Connoisseur Group	2499	8
Burnett and Son Meat Company Inc	2011	76
Burnett and Sons Planing Mill And Lumber Co	5211	185
Burnett Brothers Engineering Inc	5084	937
Burnett Companies Consolidated Inc	7361	41
Burnett Dairy Co-Operative Association	2022	17
Burnett Engraving Company Inc	2752	1849
Burney Co	6282	308
Burnham and Brown	8111	483
Burnham Holdings Inc	3443	16
Burnham Lumber Company Inc	1542	442
Burnham Polymeric Inc	3089	1883
Burnham Securities Inc	6211	216
Burnham Trucking Company Inc	4213	1161
Burningham Enterprises Inc	4213	2284
Burnley Workshop Of The Poconos Inc	8331	211
Burns and McDonnell	8711	45
Burns and Roe Enterprises Inc	1629	9
Burns and Wilcox Ltd	6411	58
Burns and Wilcox of San Francisco	6331	358
Burns Brothers Contractors	5051	32
Burns Data Control Inc	7371	1297
Burns Engineering Inc	3829	179
Burns Enterprises Inc	5411	252
Burns Janitor Service Inc	7349	201
Burns Publishing Company Inc	2759	309
Burnstead Construction Co	1521	62
Burnstein and Burnstein Inc	7322	150
Burnstein Von Seelen Precision Castings Corp	3366	6
Burr Engineering and Development Company Inc	3625	115
Burr Plumbing And Pumping Inc	1623	677
Burr Truck and Trailer Sales Inc	5511	1191
Burrell Communications Group Inc	7311	81
Burrell Printing Company Inc	2759	436
Burrell Professional Labs Inc	7384	27
Burrelle's/Luce	7383	11
Burrell's Information Services	2711	501
Burris Company Inc	3484	16
Burris Foods Inc	5142	4
Burris Logistics	4222	2
Burris Machine Company Inc	3545	352
Burris Photography Inc	7384	41
Burriss Electrical Inc	1731	741
Burroughs and Chapin Company Inc	6552	15
Burroughs Diesel Inc	5511	1213
Burroughs-Ross-Colville Company LLC	2421	132
Burrow Family Corp	2752	563
Burrows Paper Corp	2621	30
Burrows Tractor Inc	5083	170
Burrows Trucking Inc	4213	2641
Burrus Investment Group Inc	8741	247
Bursma Electronic Distributing Inc	5065	73
Burson-Marsteller	8743	2
Burst Communications Inc	7389	628
Burst Media Corp	7313	17
Burstabit Media Inc	7379	1289
BurstNET Technologies Inc	7379	1151
Burt and Associates	8741	116
Burt Automotive Network	5511	69
Burt Process Equipment Inc	5074	115
Burt Toyota Inc	5511	220
Burtech Pipeline Inc	1623	142
Burtner Electric Inc	1731	935
Burton and Associates Inc (Jacksonville Beach Florida)	8742	371
Burton and Mayer Inc	2752	270
Burton Auto Parts Inc	5531	53
Burton Building Products Inc	5033	16
Burton Holmes Associates Inc	7376	53
Burton Industries Inc	3679	242
Burton Industries Inc (Goodrich Michigan)	3559	118
Burton Livingstone and Kirk	7311	776
Burton Medical Products Corp	3845	103
Burton Systems Software Inc	7372	4667
Burtons Inc (Cumberland Maryland)	5611	24
Burtree Inc	3599	1505
Burtronics Business Systems Inc	5044	52
Buscemi's International Inc	5812	416
Busch Entertainment Corp	7996	2
Busch Industries Inc	3441	279
Busche Enterprise Division Inc	3599	113
Buschman Corp	3312	126
Busch's Valu Land	5411	132
BUSE Industries Inc	5065	1007
Buse Timber and Sales Inc	2421	42
Busey Bank	6022	240
Busey Group	6726	1
Bush Brothers and Co	2033	30
Bush Brothers Provision Co	2011	81
Bush Construction Corp	1522	39
Bush Industries Inc	2511	15
Bush Refrigeration	5064	213
Bush Refrigeration Inc	5064	128
Bush Wholesalers Inc	5075	107
Bushkill Group Inc	7033	4
Bushnell Illinois Tank Co	3523	119
Bushnell's Warehousing and Trucking	4213	2980
Bushwick Metals Inc	5051	6
Bushwick-Koons Steel	5051	112
Busin Valley Partners Inc	2752	1783
Business Aircraft Leasing Inc	7359	102
Business and Decision North America Inc (Wayne PA)	7372	274
Business and Legal Reports Inc	2741	72
Business Applications Performance Corp	7372	4588
Business Automation Inc	7372	2808
Business Automation Services Inc	8748	427
Business Bank (Vienna Virginia)	6022	662
Business Broadcast Systems	7312	21
Business Brokerage Group Inc	7389	1812
Business By Phone Inc	8331	237
Business Card Express	2791	36
Business Computer Associates LLC	7379	1299
Business Computer Design International Inc	7372	2451
Business Computing	5734	428
Business Connections	7361	284
Business Control Systems LP	7379	334
Business Couriers Inc	7389	1684
Business Design Studio	7336	319
Business Development Group (Wayzata Minnesota)	8748	74
Business Equipment Center Inc	5044	141
Business Equipment House Inc	7374	312
Business Equipment Unlimited	5044	32
Business Expansion Consulting Corp	8742	411
Business Exploration Inc	5084	405
Business Financial Publishing LLC	2741	266
Business Forecast Systems Inc	7372	4490
Business Furniture Corp	5021	5
Business Furniture Inc	5021	53
Business Images	2759	507
Business Imaging Systems Inc	5044	46
Business Industry and Environment Inc	7342	62
Business Information Graphics Inc	2741	411
Business Information Solutions Inc	7378	119
Business Integra Inc	7389	798
Business Integration Group	7379	1254
Business Interiors Northwest Inc	5021	27
Business Journal Of Portland Inc	2721	331
Business Journals Inc	2721	221
Business Logic Holding Corp	7371	1022
Business Machines Systems Inc	7372	5109
Business Management Systems Inc	7373	1099
Business Media Inc	5045	311
Business Microvar Inc	7379	621
Business Modeling Techniques Inc	7371	1704
Business Move Solutions Inc	7389	1384
Business Network International	7389	707
Business Network Technology Inc	3571	225
Business Office Systems Inc	5021	63
Business Only Broadband	4813	215
Business Phones Direct	5063	347
Business Press	2741	275
Business Printing Inc	2759	541
Business Publications Audit of Circulation Inc	8721	317
Business Publications Corp	2711	492
Business Publishers Inc	2721	389
Business Records Management Services Inc	7334	73
Business Recovery Services Inc	7374	331
Business Research Services Inc	2741	466
Business Resource Group	5021	2
Business Resource Software Inc	7372	3768
Business Security Software Inc	7379	1104
Business Services Network	7331	88
Business Software Inc (Norcross Georgia)	7372	206
Business Software Solutions	7372	1629
Business Software Systems Inc	7372	3811
Business Solution Providers	7374	254
Business Solutions Unlimited Inc	7379	1567
Business Stationery LLC	5112	40
Business Stationery Program	2752	188
Business Strategy Inc	8748	205
Business Success Center	7389	1803
Business Suppliers Inc	5734	343
Business Systems of America Inc	7372	720
Business Systems Processing Inc	7374	241
Business Technical Consulting LLC	7379	1058
Business Telecom Products Inc	5065	836
Business Telecommunication Systems Inc	5065	303
Business to Business Marketing Communications	7319	53
Business Transactions Technologies Inc	7371	1550
Business Travel Consultants	4724	89
Business Valuations Inc	6282	642
Business Video Productions Inc	7812	175
Business Voice Inc	7389	2036
Business West Mortgage Co	6162	146
Business Wire	7383	7
Business Word Inc	2721	289
Business World Inc (Little Rock Arkansas)	5044	56
Businessvn Inc	7375	207
BusinessWare Inc	7371	1308
Buske Lines Inc	4213	372
Busken Bakery Inc	5461	6
Busler Enterprises Inc	5812	378
Bus-Let Inc	7331	197
BusNet Inc	7372	5029
Bussco Inc	3643	133
Busse Brothers Inc	3565	55
Busse SJI Corp	3089	601
Bussen Quarries Inc	1422	13
Busseto Foods Inc	2013	148
Bustronic Corp	3672	177
Busware Inc	7372	2901
Busy Beaver Building Centers Inc	5211	40
Busy Bee Electric Inc	1731	1408
Busy Bee Janitorial Services LLC	7349	388
Busy Bee Tooling	3544	744
Busy Printing	2752	1237
BUT Inc	1623	351
Butch Oustalet Chevrolet Cadillac	5511	1102
Butcher Block Inc	2015	58
Butcher Boy Meats LLC	2013	230
Butler and Cook Inc	3599	988
Butler and Curless Associates Inc	7372	2633
Butler Automatic Inc	3555	35
Butler Capital Corp	6211	347
Butler Color Press Inc	2752	290
Butler Computer Systems	7371	1723
Butler County Motor Company Inc	5511	638
Butler County Publishing Company Inc	2711	393
Butler County Rural Electric Coop	4911	290
Butler Group Inc (Atlanta Georgia)	5023	71
Butler Mailing Service Inc	8999	197
Butler Manufacturing Co	3448	4
Butler Merchandising Solutions Inc	2675	8
Butler National Corp	3721	22
Butler National Services Inc	5084	806
Butler Paper Recycling Inc	5093	88
Butler Printing And Laminating Inc	2759	105
Butler Products Corp	3714	275
Butler Refrigerated Meats	4213	1697
Butler Rogers Baskett Architects PC	8712	209
Butler Rural Electric Cooperative Association Inc	4911	291
Butler Rural Electric Cooperative Inc	4911	367
Butler Shine and Stern	7311	126
Butler Technologies Inc	2759	304
Butler Tire Distributors Inc	5014	35
Butler Tool Inc	3599	354
Butler Transport Inc	4213	469
Butler Transport System	4213	2904
Butler Trucking Co	4213	808
Butler-Johnson Corp	5039	5
Butler's Office Equipment and Supply Inc	5943	33
Butterball Farms Inc	7389	688
Buttercup Farms Inc	4213	2872
Butterfield Foods Co	2015	51
Butters Construction and Development Inc	6552	155
Butterworth and Scheck Inc	1623	468
Button's Inventory Service Inc	7389	1393
Butts Ticket Company Inc	2752	1589
Buttweiler Environmental Inc	7349	240
Buty-Wave Products Co	2844	201
Buww Coverings Inc	3444	270
Buxbaum Group and Associates Inc	7389	1122
Buxton Acquisition Inc	5199	34
Buxton Co (Fort Worth Texas)	7389	272
Buxton Medical Equipment Corp	3841	286
Buy And Sell Press Inc	2741	453
Buy Direct Corp	5045	923
Buy Owner Inc	7311	738
buyCastings Inc	7389	1442
BUYCOM Inc	5961	36
BuyCostumescom	5122	15
Buyers Products Co	5013	109
Buyer's Resource Southeast Ltd	6531	417
Buy-Global Inc	5731	110
Buyonlinenowcom	5044	68
Buyseasons Inc	7389	1208
Buztronics Inc	3999	120
Buzz Oates Group of Cos	6552	52
Buzz Products Inc	5142	32
Buzzard Power Corp	4911	431
Buzzi Unicem Readymix LLC	3273	78
Buzzi Unicem USA Inc	3241	1
Buzzlogic Inc	7311	756
Buzzsaw Advertising and Design	7311	547
Buzztime Entertainment Inc	4833	25
Buzzword Inc	7371	1839
Buzzy's Recording	7311	728
BV Financial Inc	6035	210
BV Hedrick Gravel and Sand Co	1442	15
BV Unitron Manufacturing Inc	3679	356
Bvc Systems Inc	7373	980
BVJ Company Inc	1731	1974
BVK/McDonald Inc	7311	99
BVM Associates	3577	52
BW Clifford Inc	5145	37
BW D Inc	5084	678
BW Dyer and Co	5149	135
B-W Graphics Inc	2759	574
B-W Grinding Service Inc	3599	305
Bw Manufacturing Company Inc	3599	943
BW Norton Manufacturing Company Inc	3089	390
Bw Reprographics LLC	7336	137
Bw Resources LLC	8711	584

Company Name	SIC	Rank
BW Rogers Co	5085	94
Bw Technologies LLC	3829	368
BWAB Inc	1311	162
BWAY Holding Co	3411	5
BWB Inc	3272	14
BWBR Architects	8712	68
BWC Real Estate	6141	65
BWE Ltd	2671	71
Bwi Eagle Inc	3625	251
BWX Technologies Inc	2819	6
BXC Products Inc	7389	1630
BX-IR Corp	2992	69
By Design International Salon	7231	9
By Light Professional It Services	7375	119
Byallaccounts Inc	7371	1264
Byars Machine Company Inc	5084	522
Bybee Stone Company Inc	3281	22
Bycap Inc	3675	40
Byco Plastics Inc	3429	142
Byer California	2337	12
Byerly Ford Inc	5511	472
Byerly's Foods Of Illinois Inc	5411	245
Byers Engineering Co	7372	454
Byford Machine-Tool Inc	3599	2004
Bykowski Equipment Co	5084	502
Byles Janitorial Services	7349	322
Byles Welding And Tractor Company Inc	5082	211
By-Line Transit Inc	4213	2387
Byran Company Inc	3599	487
Byrd Cookie Co	2052	65
Byrd Operating Co	1382	67
Byrne Dairy Inc	2026	19
Byrne Electrical Specialists Inc	3679	189
Byrne Insurance Agency Inc	6411	221
Byrnes and Kiefer Company Inc	5461	5
Byron Folse Associates Inc	8999	195
Byron L Lang Inc	4213	1895
Byron Originals Inc	3089	1028
Byron Products Inc	7692	12
Byron Vineyard and Winery	0172	13
Byrtech Custom Machine Works Inc	3599	1098
Bystrom Brothers Inc	3451	92
Byte Brothers Inc	3577	503
Bytec Inc	2531	42
Bytemanagers Inc	7374	202
Bytemobile Inc	4899	100
Byteside Computer Services	5734	266
Bytespeed LLC	3571	59
Bytheway's Manufacturing Inc	5023	21
BYTWARE Inc	7372	3220
Bz Media LLC	2721	253
BZ/Rights and Permissions Inc	7389	2357
C and A Industries Inc	7361	242
C and A Machine And Repair Service Inc	3599	1210
C and A Tool Engineering Inc	3544	6
C and A Transducers Inc	3679	616
C and A Transportation Inc	4213	1729
C and A Trucking Inc	4213	2230
C and B Capital	6799	60
C and B Machinery Co	3541	92
C and B Piping Inc	5051	179
C and B Services	1711	183
C and C Acquisition Corp	3599	909
C and C Bindery Company Inc	2789	100
C and C Cast Polymers Inc	3281	46
C and C Communications	5731	257
C and C Concrete Pumping Inc	1771	28
C and C Duplicators Inc	3652	37
C and C Electrical Contractors	1731	1797
C and C Equipment Sales and Repairs Inc	1731	2422
C and C Fiberglass Inc	3089	414
C and C Laboratory Leasing Corp	7352	39
C and C Logistic Device Corporation Inc	5045	624
C and C Machine Inc	3599	1398
C and C Machinery Inc	5251	50
C and C Machining Inc	3599	413
C and C Paper Recycling	5093	212
C and C Partners Inc	5611	33
C and C Recycle	7389	573
C and C Studios	3695	117
C and C Trucking of Duncan Inc	4213	897
C and D Assembly Inc	3672	233
C and D Charter Holdings Inc	6719	82
C and D Electronics Inc	5065	270
C and D Enterprises Inc	2821	188
C and D Factory Direct Inc	5063	904
C and D Printing Co	2752	447
C and D Semiconductor Services Inc	3674	301
C and D Skilled Robotics Inc	3569	274
C and D Technologies Inc	3699	16
C and D Zodiac Inc	3728	17
C and E Plastics Inc	3089	1287
C and E Tooling Inc	3544	838
C and F Computers Inc	7373	1123
C and F Contracting And Rental LLC	1731	718
C and F Enterprises	5131	24
C and F Financial Corp	6022	186
C and F Forge Co	3312	112
C and F Machine Corp	3599	1789
C And F Machinery Corp	3599	1645

Company Name	SIC	Rank
C and F Packing Company Inc	2013	96
C and G Containers Inc	5113	51
C and G Electric Inc	1731	512
C and G Electronics Co	5065	667
C and G Feed and Supply Co	4213	2930
C and G Machine Tool Company Inc	3599	2174
C and G Systems Inc	3548	24
C and H Chemical Inc	2841	44
C and H Contact Lens Inc	3851	72
C and H Die Casting Inc	3363	20
C and H Distributors Inc	5084	65
C and H Distributors LLC	5084	329
C and H Electric Inc	1731	624
C and H Store Equipment Company Inc	5046	220
C and H Technology Inc	5065	442
C And H Tooling Inc	3599	1975
C and I Electrical Supply Corp	5063	574
C and I Management Corp	8741	262
C and J Computer Consulting Inc	7373	1067
C and J Forms and Label Inc	2752	781
C and J Gravel Products Inc	1442	87
C and J Industries Inc	3089	318
C and K Market Inc	5411	105
C and K Plastics Inc	3089	752
C and L Construction Inc	1623	276
C and L International Co	5023	169
C and L Manufacturing Enterprises Inc	3269	19
C and L Supply Co	5064	36
C and M Assets LLC	5085	351
C and M Building Materials Inc	5211	253
C and M Construction Inc	1623	251
C and M Conveyor Inc	3535	43
C and M Fine Pack Inc	3089	90
C and M Mills Inc	2252	27
C and M Press Corp	2732	38
C and N Electric Power and Line Construction Inc	1623	506
C and N Packaging Inc	3089	504
C and P Machine Company Inc	5599	24
C and P Oil Inc	5172	65
C and R Anderson Inc	7349	397
C and R Electric Inc	1731	1012
C and R Electrical Service Inc	1731	1636
C and R International Sales Inc	2047	45
C and R Mechanical Inc	1711	103
C and R Molds Inc	3089	1466
C and R Pipe And Steel Inc	5051	451
C and R Plating Corp	3471	100
C and R Security Inc	1731	2344
C and R Systems Inc	1731	338
C and S Associates LLC	7363	312
C and S Companies Inc	1623	189
C and S Companies Inc	8711	318
C and S Electronics Inc	3672	442
C and S Engineering Inc	3449	31
C And S Enterprises Inc	5999	178
C and S Inc	5171	72
C and S Machine and Manufacturing Corp	3599	1270
C and S Machine Products Inc	3599	469
C and S Press Inc	2752	547
C and S Products Inc	5065	448
C and S Research Corp	7372	3450
C And S Sales Inc	5199	51
C and S Wholesale Grocers Inc	5141	2
C and T Engineering Inc	3544	840
C and T Equipment Company Inc	5013	233
C and T Machining Inc	3599	1593
C And W Die Inc	3554	61
C and W Electric Company Inc	1731	1980
C and Z Enterprises LLC	1721	7
C B Developers Inc	1623	843
C Bamberger Molding Compounds Inc	5162	39
C Bean Transport Inc	4213	603
C Brewer and Company Ltd	0173	1
C Brewer Co	2389	9
C Construction Company Inc	1542	333
C Cowles and Co	3714	86
C D and N Manufacturing Inc	3599	496
C D Brown Const Inc	1623	241
C D Denison Orthopaedic Appliance Corp	3842	259
C D Sparling Co	3499	132
C Depot Ii	5731	242
C E Beckman Co	5063	473
C E Machine Company Inc	3599	831
C E Rogers Co	3556	80
C E Shepherd Company LP	3081	41
C E Toland and Son	1799	57
C F Burger Creamery Co	5143	33
C F Gollott And Son Seafood Inc	2092	55
C Forward Inc	7379	1324
C/G Electrodes LLC	3624	12
C H Babb Company Inc	3556	106
C H Guenther and Son Inc	2041	10
C H Guernsey and Co	8712	90
C H Martin Co	3842	170
C Hager and Sons Hinge Manufacturing Co	3429	47
C Herzog Supply Inc	5074	197
C Hoelzle Associates Inc	5045	265
C J Calamia Construction Company Inc	1623	526

Company Name	SIC	Rank
C J Foods Inc	2047	41
C Johnnie-On-The-Spot Portable Toilets Inc	7359	125
C J's Bus Supplies And Service Inc	4151	6
C L Downey Co	2679	58
C L Smith Co	5085	38
C L Smith Industrial Co	3479	77
C M Ambrose Co	3565	162
C M Media Inc	2711	201
C M R USA LLC	3679	704
C Machine Company Inc	3599	1757
C Management Solutions for Government	7372	1025
C/N Group Inc	6552	1
C N Robinson Lighting Supply Co	5063	273
C Nelson Manufacturing Co	3585	184
C O Christian and Sons Company Inc	1731	443
C Overaa and Co	1541	125
C P Bourg Inc	3579	20
C P Converters Inc	2759	77
C Products LLC	3484	23
C R J Enterprises Inc	5063	572
C R Newton Company Ltd	5999	188
C R Onsrud Inc	5084	444
C R V Electronics Corp	3679	344
C Roy Inc	2011	148
C S Osborne And Co	3423	40
C/S Solutions Inc	7379	903
C S Steen Syrup Mill Inc	2087	78
C Spirito Inc	1623	331
C Squared Communications Inc	2671	70
C Stegman Company Inc	7375	269
C Summers Inc	4213	3036
C Sys Labs Inc	3577	476
C Systems LLC	7372	4237
C T Electrical Corp	1731	1480
C Tech Corp	1731	2416
C Thorrez Industries Inc	3451	10
C W Brabender Instruments Inc	3829	230
C W Cole and Company Inc	3646	58
C W Fischer Elecfric Inc	1731	1079
C W Mill Equipment Company Inc	3523	163
C Williams Electrical Construction Inc	1731	1736
C Wright's Machine Tool Inc	3599	1157
C X and B United Corp	5199	136
C-2 Utility Contractors LLC	1623	55
C2C Outdoor	7312	14
C2C Systems Inc	7372	3424
C2p Group LLC	7361	235
C3 Design Innovations	3559	506
C3 Premedia Solutions Inc	7374	198
C3 Sales Inc	5045	805
C3D/Strata Software	7371	266
C3i Inc	7372	748
CA 2000	5734	81
CA Affinity Corp	4813	290
CA Botana International Inc	2844	180
CA D Electric Inc	1731	966
CA Foy Machine Co	3599	1482
CA Hull Company Inc	1622	28
CA International Inc	1799	141
CA Langford Company Inc	1422	43
CA Litzler Company Inc	3567	56
CA M Graphics Company Inc	3672	409
CA Mccourt and Associates Inc	5013	272
CA Muer Corp	5812	254
CA Murren and Sons Company Inc	1623	196
CA One Services Inc	5812	321
CA Perry and Son Inc	5159	22
CA Perry and Son Transit Inc	4213	2703
CA Properties Inc	1311	195
CA Rasmussen Inc	1611	75
CA Schroeder Inc	3296	13
CA T S Co	5045	505
CA Technologies	7372	8
CA Wilson Electric Service Inc	1711	251
Caap International Corp	5169	167
CAB International North American Office	2731	10
Caba Co	2621	67
Caballo Coal Co	1221	19
Cabco Inc	5063	594
Cabela's Inc	5941	3
Cabell County Community Services Organization Inc	8322	230
Cabinet And Bath Supply Inc	5031	266
Cabinet Distributors Of Georgia Inc	5031	227
Cabinet Press Inc	2711	625
Cabinetry By Karman Inc	2434	35
Cabinets Plus	2517	6
Cable Advertising of Metro Atlanta	7319	17
Cable Aml Inc	3663	298
Cable Assemblies Inc	3357	79
Cable Communications Inc	1731	481
Cable Concepts Inc	3625	163
Cable Corps Inc	4841	100
Cable Doctors Inc	7389	1263
Cable East Inc	1731	578
Cable Guyz Communications Inc	1731	2470
Cable Installers and Designers Inc	4841	123
Cable Line Installation Services Inc	4841	171
Cable Lock Inc	7389	995
Cable Manufacturing and Assembly Inc	3496	34
Cable Meat Center Inc	5147	127

Company Name	SIC	Rank
Cable News Network Inc	4841	12
Cable One Inc	4899	24
Cable Plus Inc	1542	438
Cable Services Company Inc	1799	34
Cable Services Group Inc	7374	31
Cable Systems Inc	1731	2556
Cable Systems Installations Inc	1731	1771
Cable Systems of North Haven Inc	8748	291
Cable Technologies Corp	4841	173
Cable Technologies Inc	3643	107
Cable Tv Construction And Installations Inc	1623	766
Cable Unlimited Inc	5731	145
Cable Utilities Inc	1731	717
Cable Ventures Inc	1623	164
Cable West Inc	3541	117
Cable World Technologies Inc	5065	658
Cablecom Corp	1731	1938
CableCom Inc	1623	12
Cablecom LLC	1731	813
Cablecon Inc	5065	704
Cableconn Industries Inc	3643	89
Cable-Dahmer Chevrolet Inc	5511	263
Cablelan Products Inc	5063	563
CableOrganizercom Inc	5963	24
Cables To Go Inc	3577	402
Cables Unlimited Inc	3679	432
Cablescan Inc	3825	241
CableSoft Inc	7373	1110
Cablesuite 541	4841	168
Cablesystem	4841	135
Cabletech Sling and Supply Co	5051	497
Cabletek Wiring Products Inc	3444	276
Cablevision Systems Corp	4841	6
CABLExpress Corp	3577	93
Cabling Services Corp	1731	1366
Cabling Systems Inc	4841	157
Cabot Corp	2895	1
Cabot Hosiery Mills Inc	5137	21
Cabot House Inc	5712	49
Cabot Microelectronics Corp	3674	56
Cabot Oil and Gas Corp	1311	39
Cabot Star Harold	2711	749
Cabot Supermetals	3339	12
Cabrun Ink Products Corp	2893	25
Cace Technologies Inc	7374	276
Cache Inc	5621	25
Cache Valley Bank	6022	507
Cache Valley Electric	1731	2277
Cache Valley Publishing LLC	2711	193
CACI Field Services Inc	8741	11
CACI Incorporated - COMMERCIAL	7373	16
CACI International Inc	7373	6
CACI Products Co	7372	1468
CACI Technologies Inc	7371	4
Cacique Distributors US	5143	19
Cacique USA Inc	2022	75
Cactus and Tropicals Inc	5992	2
Cactus Coatings Inc	3479	106
Cactus Computer Inc	3577	477
Cactus Custom Analog Design Inc	3825	233
Cactus Feeders Inc	0211	1
Cactus International Inc	4813	716
Cactus Sands Nursery and Garden Center	5261	20
Cactus Stone and Tile Inc	8999	52
CAD/CAM Consulting Services Inc	7372	694
CAD/CAM Integration Inc	3571	193
CAD/CAM Systems Inc	5045	895
CAD Consulting USA	7372	310
CAD Cut Inc	3599	2005
Cad Enterprises Inc	3599	248
CAD Systems Unlimited Inc	7373	912
CAD Technology Corp	7372	3984
Cadalog Inc	7372	648
Cadaret Grant and Company Inc	6211	257
Cadbury Corp	8051	65
Cadbury Schweppes Inc	2086	145
Cadco Program And Machine Inc	3577	492
CADD Microsystems Inc	7372	2841
Caddell Burns Manufacturing Company Inc	3677	82
Caddell Construction Company Inc	1541	17
Caddell Dry Dock and Repair Company Inc	3731	11
Caddo Connections Inc	3679	558
Caddock Electronics Inc	3676	4
Caddy Corporation Of America	3556	102
Cadec Global Inc	5045	408
Cadence Bank NA (Memphis Tennessee)	6021	279
Cadence Capital Management Corp	6282	14
Cadence Design Systems Inc	7372	53
Cadence Environmental Energy Inc	4953	81
CADENCE Management Corp	7372	1310
Cadence Mtc LLC	7349	132
Cadence Network Inc	8741	181
Cadence Pharmaceuticals Inc	2834	446
Cadence Technologies Inc	7373	496
Cadenza Group Inc	7374	379
Cadet Manufacturing Co	3634	20
Cadi Company Inc	3548	55
Cadient Group	5045	337
Cadillac Coffee Co	5149	93

Company Name	SIC	Rank
Cadillac Looseleaf Products Inc	2782	41
Cadillac Oil Co	2992	42
Cadillac Products Inc	3714	129
Cadillac Products Packaging Co	3081	38
CADint Inc	7372	3649
Cadiz Inc	4941	46
CADlink Technology Corp (Clinton Massachusetts)	7372	4668
CADMAN Corp	7372	4491
Cadman Inc	3273	103
Cadmax Corp	7372	4367
Cadmus Credit Union Inc	6062	124
Cadmus Micro Inc	3577	175
Cadnet Services	7373	1111
Cadnetics Inc	7373	761
Cadore-Miller Printing Inc	2752	1769
CadPlus Products Co	7372	4968
Cadre	5045	199
Cadri Company Inc	1731	2058
CadSoft Computer Inc	7372	2894
Cad-Tel Systems Inc	7371	893
Cadus Corp	2836	107
Cadwalader Wickersham and Taft	8111	62
Cadwell Laboratories Inc	3841	12
Cady Cheese Factory Inc	2022	55
Cadyville Firehouse	7389	2135
CAE Systems Inc	7373	1214
CAE-Link Corp (Albuquerque New Mexico)	7372	3812
Caelum Research Corp	7374	69
Caerus Oil and Gas LLC	1311	153
Caesars Entertainment Corp	7011	29
Caesars Entertainment Inc	7993	1
Cafaro Co	6552	32
Cafe Pacific Inc	7389	1556
Cafe Rio Inc	5812	305
CafepressCom Inc	2389	10
Caffco International	3999	37
Caffe Calabria Coffee Roasters LLC	2095	47
Caffe' D'amore Inc	2095	26
Cagle Lumber and Pallet	5211	257
Cagle's Farms Inc	5144	3
Cagle's Inc	2015	14
Cahall Brothers Inc	5083	157
Cahill Gordon and Reindel	8111	112
Cahoon Farms Inc	2033	102
CAI International Inc	7359	35
CAI/SIS Co	7373	638
Caid Industries Inc	3444	47
Caid Solutions LLP	7389	2406
Cain Brothers and Company LLC	6211	177
Cain Cellars Inc	2084	86
Cain Electrical Supply Corp	5063	75
Cain Food Industries Inc	2099	308
Cain Security Systems Inc	1731	1439
Cain Tree Inc	3663	417
Caine Farber and Gordon Inc	7372	630
Caine Transfer Inc	4213	1902
Caire Inc	3841	126
Cairns Helmets MSA	3842	72
Cairns Manufacturing Inc	3589	264
Cairo Banking Co	6022	699
Caitac Garment Processing Inc	2261	9
Caito and Klein Associates Inc	5065	625
Caito Fisheries Inc	2092	51
Cajoleben Inc	2051	35
Cajun Chef Products Inc	2035	29
Cajun Computers	5734	246
Cajun Cutters Inc	3541	74
Cajun Gold Catfish Processors Inc	2092	96
Cajun Sugar Co-Operative Inc	2061	12
Cakebread Cellars	2084	53
Cal Bind	2789	75
Cal Blen Electronic Industries Inc	3577	566
Cal Coil Magnetics Inc	3677	88
Cal Cover Products Inc	3999	158
Cal Events	4725	60
Cal Farley's Boys Ranch	8361	12
Cal Farleys Girlstown USA	8361	18
Cal Micro Inc	5045	378
Cal Partitions Inc	2542	70
Cal Testing Services Inc	8734	163
Cal Western Packaging Corp	7389	420
Calabash Animation Inc	7812	168
Calamos Asset Management Inc	6282	678
CalAmp Corp	3663	44
Calando Pharmaceuticals Inc	8731	326
Calandra Frank Inc	1241	5
Calandra Italian and French Bakery Inc	5461	19
Calarco Inc	5191	119
Calato J D Manufacturing Company Inc	3931	30
Calaveras Power Partners LP	1731	142
Calaveras-Standard Materials	3273	101
Calavo Growers Inc	0179	2
Calbag Metals Co	5093	55
Cal-Chip Electronics Inc	5065	297
Calco Controls Inc	3599	2402
Calco International Inc	2011	75
Calco Sprouts Inc	0182	9
Cal-Coast Dairy Systems Inc	3523	180
Calcomp Graphics LLC	5045	1020
Calcon Constructors Inc	1542	218
Calcot Ltd	5159	6
Calculated Industries Inc	3578	24

Company Name	SIC	Rank
Calder Brothers Corp	3531	117
Calder Race Course Inc	7948	17
Calder Testers Inc	3829	290
Calderon Brothers Vending Company Inc	5962	3
Caldwell and Orkin Funds Inc	6282	452
Caldwell Corp	7539	13
Caldwell Electrical Contractors	1731	1139
Caldwell Electronics Inc	7622	12
Caldwell Freight Lines Inc	4213	277
Caldwell Manufacturing Co	3495	7
Caldwell Milling Company Inc	2048	60
Caldwell Tanks Alliance LLC	1791	18
Caldwell Tanks Inc	3443	31
Caledonia Haulers Inc	4213	271
Calence Inc	7379	144
Calence / Insight Networking Solutions	7373	44
Calendar Club LLC	5947	8
Calendar Press Inc	2752	1129
Calera Capital	6722	149
Calevas Laboratories Inc	2087	81
Calex Express Inc	4213	1015
Calex Manufacturing Company Inc	3679	269
Calexico Freight Lines	4213	3043
Calgon Carbon Corp	2819	20
Calgon Carbon Investments Inc	6719	76
Calhoun Apparel Inc	2325	11
Calhoun Enterprises Inc	5411	214
Calhoun Plastics And Chemicals Inc	2869	89
Calibamboo LLC	5031	250
Caliber Advisors	6282	291
Caliber Collision Centers Inc	7538	7
Caliber Electronics Inc	3679	499
Caliber Holdings Corp	6719	97
Caliber Mold And Machine Inc	3544	352
Calibrated Forms Company Inc	2761	11
Calibrated Instruments Inc	3823	388
Calibrators Inc	3825	305
Calibre Door Closers Inc	1793	7
Calibre Inc	3479	37
CALIBRE Systems Inc	7373	138
Calibron Systems Inc	3823	375
Calico Corners	5714	4
Calico Cottage Inc	2066	21
Calico Precision Molding LLC	3089	1332
Caliendo-Savio Enterprises Inc	7389	536
Cali-Fame Of Los Angeles Inc	2353	9
Califone International Inc	5065	120
California Acrylic Industries Inc	5719	9
California Ammonia Co	5191	45
California Analytical Instruments Inc	3826	68
California Associated Power Inc	1731	1221
California Bank and Trust	6022	19
California Business Bank	6029	27
California Butcher Supply Inc	5046	125
California Capital Insurance Co	6331	295
California Carbon Company Inc	2819	123
California Cartage Co	4213	1574
California Cascade Industries	2491	13
California Casualty Management Co	8111	152
California Catalog and Technology Inc	4813	732
California Cedar Products Co	2499	12
California Chassis Inc	3444	97
California Citrus Producers Inc	2037	40
California Closet Company Inc	7389	896
California Closet Company Of Orange County/Long Beach Inc	5023	136
California Coastal Communities Inc	1531	80
California Combining Corp	2824	13
California Community Bank	6022	455
California Community News Corp	2711	120
California Computer Aided Design Solutions Inc	5734	433
California Computer Center Corp	5734	175
California Concentrate Co	2037	49
California Controlled Atmosphere	3585	198
California Credits Group LLC	7389	1394
California Culinary Academy Inc	8299	40
California Custom Fruits And Flavors Inc	2087	28
California Dairies Inc	2026	32
California Display Co	3993	63
California Dynamics Corp	3829	274
California Eastern Laboratories Inc	5065	47
California Economizer	3625	119
California Examiner	2711	284
California Expanded Metal Products Co	3444	24
California Feminist Federal Credit Union	6061	150
California First National Bancorp	7377	2
California Food Technology LLC	5084	716
California Friends Homes	8361	52
California Furniture Collections Inc	2519	10
California Gas Transport Inc	4213	2658
California Gasket And Rubber Corp	3069	214
California Glass Co	5085	145
California Hardware Co	5072	8
California Hydroforming Company Inc	3444	291
California Hydronics Corp	5075	39
California Industrial Fabrics	2394	31
California Industrial Rubber Company Inc	5085	78
California Instruments Corp	3651	101
California Integration Coordinators Inc	3672	270

Company Name	SIC	Rank
California Internet Inc	4813	671
California Kitchen Cabinet Door Corp	2434	39
California Lighting Sales Inc	5063	90
California Magnetics	3652	34
California Mailing Service Inc	7331	141
California Market Center	6519	11
California Marketing Enterprises Inc	3825	326
California Metal and Supply Inc	3499	108
California Micro Devices Corp	3679	122
California Millworks Corp	2431	140
California Minibridge Transportation	4213	2254
California Natural Products	2099	75
California Newspapers Partnership	2711	82
California Nuggets Inc	2068	29
California Office Maintenance	7349	413
California Offset Printers Inc	2721	68
California Olive Ranch Inc	2079	11
California On-Site Copying	7334	54
California Optical Corp	3089	663
California Panel and Veneer Co	5031	98
California Pellet Mill Co	3312	41
California Pharmaceutical Services Inc	8093	27
California Physicians' Service	6719	49
California Pizza Kitchen Inc	5812	80
California Portland Cement Co (Glendora California)	3241	8
California Precision Products Inc	3444	143
California Products Corp	2851	45
California Professional Manufacturing Inc	3841	391
California Quality Plastics Inc	3089	1133
California Radiographics Inc	5047	124
California Refrigerated Services Inc	4222	8
California Republic Bank	6022	405
California Retrofit Inc	1731	776
California Ribbon and Carbon Company Inc	3955	8
California Sales Co	3679	78
California Security Alarms Inc	7382	90
California Sensor Corp	3829	152
California Service Tool Inc	5082	155
California Shellfish Company Inc	2092	1
California Steel And Tube	3317	51
California Steel Industries	3312	16
California Steel Services Inc	5051	14
California Style Plant Service Inc	7389	1872
California Surveying and Drafting Supply Inc	5049	56
California Swiss Machine Inc	3452	91
California Tan Inc	2844	57
California Tank Lines Inc	4213	2243
California Tool and Welding Supply LLC	5084	307
California Traffic Safety Institute	8748	314
California Transport Enterprises	4212	40
California Truss Co	2439	12
California United Bank	6022	217
California Water Service Group	4941	4
California-American Water Co	4941	20
CaliforniaCom Inc	4813	223
Calion Lumber Company Inc	2426	25
Calip Dairies Operating Co	2024	28
Caliper Designs Inc	7371	1840
Calise and Sons Bakery Inc	2051	54
Calitoday Newspaper	2711	864
Calix Inc	3613	11
Calkins Electric Supply Company Inc	5063	733
Calko Steel Inc	5051	341
Calko Transport Company Inc	4213	1470
Call America Inc	7389	2307
Call Centers India Inc	7389	1092
Call Henry Inc	8744	8
Call Management Products Inc	3674	289
Call Newspapers Inc	2711	450
Call Now Inc	7948	36
Call One Inc	5065	62
Callaghan and Associates PCA	8721	399
Callahan Brothers Inc	4213	3046
Callahan Creek	7311	406
Callan Associates Inc	6282	98
Callaway Bank	6022	427
Callaway Carriers Inc	4213	1496
Callaway Companies Inc	3714	373
Callaway Contracting Inc	1623	267
Callaway Editions Inc	2731	320
Callaway Electric Coop	4911	300
Callaway Gardens Resort Inc	7011	172
Callaway Golf Co	3949	11
Callaway Graphicsoftware LLC	7372	4669
Call-Em-All LLC	7299	42
Callender Construction Company Inc	1422	35
CallerIDcom	3661	175
Caller-Times Publishing Co	2711	55
CallFire	8742	512
Callico Distributors Inc	5087	48
Callidus Software Inc	7372	557
Callidus Technologies LLC	3567	12
Callie's Candy Kitchens Inc	5441	16
Callison Architecture Inc	8712	25
CallMe Corp	7372	2666
Callon Petroleum Co	1311	119
Callon Petroleum Operating Co	1311	99
Callos Management Succession Team Inc	7363	233
Calloway's Nursery Inc	5261	2
Callstar Inc	7389	1890
CallWare Technologies Inc	7372	4222
CallWave Inc	4822	9
Cal-Maine Farms Inc	2015	10
Cal-Maine Foods Inc	0252	1
Cal-Maine Partnership Ltd	0252	4
Calmar Optcom Inc	3661	185
Calmark Inc	7331	22
Calmax Technology	3599	396
Cal-Mil Plastic Products Inc	3089	514
Cal-Mold Inc	3089	383
Calnet Inc	8742	232
Calo Corp	3613	118
Calogic LLC	3825	204
Cal-Ore Carbide Inc	5251	51
Cal-Ore Telephone Co	4813	410
Calorimetry Sciences Corp	3821	58
Calpian Inc	7372	5089
Calpico Inc	3643	124
Calpine Containers Inc	5113	13
Calpine Corp	4911	27
Cal-Quality Electronics Inc	3672	38
Calrad Electronics Inc	5065	564
Cal-Royal Products Inc	5072	133
CalsonicKansei North America Inc	6719	19
Calspan Corp	8731	387
Calstrip Steel Corp	3316	17
CAL-TEK Company Inc	5065	322
Cal-Temperature Services Inc	7363	345
Cal-Tex Lumber Company Inc	2421	33
Caltex Plastics Inc	2673	48
Calton Dental Lab	3842	233
Cal-Tron Corp	3089	1777
Caltron Industries Inc	3575	44
Cal-Tron Plating Inc	3471	105
Caltronix Inc	7629	40
Calty Design Research Inc	8711	277
Calumet Armature And Electric LLC	7694	18
Calumet Diversified Meats Inc	5147	36
Calumet Farm Inc	0272	3
Calumet Flexicore Corp	3272	114
Calumet Industries Inc (Calumet Oklahoma)	3499	116
Calumet Investment Corp	6211	240
Calumet Publishing Inc	2711	847
Calumet Specialty Products Partners LP	2911	25
Calutech Mobile Solutions Inc	3713	50
Calvary Design Team Inc	3599	84
Calvary Industries Inc	2819	84
Calvert Group	6211	9
Calvert Holdings Inc	8742	240
Calvert Lumber Company Inc	5031	409
Calvert Manufacturing Inc	3553	51
Calvert Preclinical Services Inc	8731	107
Calvert Wire and Cable Corp	5063	80
Calvert-McBride Printing Co	2752	510
Calvin B Taylor Banking Co	6022	371
Calvin Klein Inc	2329	1
Calwax LLC	2842	108
CalWeb Internet Services Inc	7372	4670
Cal-West Seeds Inc	5191	88
Cal-Western Paints	2851	143
Cal-Western Transport Inc	4213	1454
Calx Inc	3542	117
Calypso Technology Inc	5734	23
Calypte Biomedical Corp	3826	161
Calyptix Security Corp	7381	259
Calysto Communications Inc	8743	25
Calyx and Corolla Inc	5961	124
Calyx Software	7372	1479
Calzone Ltd	3161	7
CAM Audio Inc	5731	60
CAM Commerce Solutions Inc	7373	216
Cam Industries Inc	3599	1519
CAM Machine Inc	3599	1735
Cam Specialty Products Inc	3089	1058
CAMAC Group	5099	3
Camalloy Inc	5051	309
Camano Mold Inc	3599	2096
Camas Washougal Post Record	2711	908
Camatron Sewing Machine Inc	3639	31
Cambar Software Inc	7372	2542
Camber Corp	3699	14
Camberley Associates Inc	7011	128
Cambex Corp	3572	80
Cambex Foreign Sales Corp	3572	45
Cambex Securities Corp	6289	24
Cambiar Investors Inc	6282	258
Cambrex Charles City Inc	2899	61
Cambrex Corp	2834	92
Cambria Corp	3823	435
Cambria Tractor and Equipment Co	5082	174
Cambria Truck Center	5511	577
Cambrian Granite and Stone Inc	5032	169
Cambridge Bancorp	6712	285
Cambridge Brands Inc	2064	11
Cambridge Brewing Company Inc	2082	71
Cambridge Capital Management Corp	6282	603
Cambridge Chemists Inc	5912	76
Cambridge Credit Counseling Corp	7299	34
Cambridge Engineering Inc	3567	31
Cambridge Heart Inc	3845	114
Cambridge Holdings Ltd	6512	85
Cambridge Home Health Care Inc	8059	14
Cambridge Isotope Laboratories Inc	2869	63
Cambridge Machine and Supply Company Inc	3599	2290
Cambridge Ohio Production and Assembly Corp	3578	33
Cambridge Packing Company Inc	5147	53
Cambridge Research and Instrumentation Inc	3827	95
Cambridge Savings Bank	6036	16
Cambridge Scale Works Inc	3596	22
Cambridge Security Services Corp	7381	51
Cambridge SoundWorks Inc	3651	47
Cambridge Taxi Company Inc	7389	2161
Cambridge Technology Inc	3577	198
Cambridge Tool and Die Corp	3544	162
Cambridge Tool and Manufacturing Inc	3363	21
Cambridge Trust Co	6022	328
Cambridge Ventures LP	6799	242
Cambridge Viscosity Inc	3823	306
CambridgeSoft Corp	7372	1173
Cambrix Consulting Group LLC	2741	474
Cambro Manufacturing Company Inc	3089	146
Cambron Engineering Inc	3544	308
Cambyte Computer Services Inc	7378	85
Camcad Technologies Inc	7371	1664
Camcast Corp	8711	432
Camco Chemical Co	2992	31
Camco Financial Corp	6036	37
Camco Machining Inc	3599	2106
Camco Manufacturing Inc	2899	49
Camco Title Insurance Agency	6541	25
Camcor Inc	5731	56
Camdel Metals Corp	3357	86
Camden Flooring Co	5023	100
Camden Industries Inc	3089	1560
Camden National Bank	6021	72
Camden National Corp	6021	54
Camden Property Trust	6798	212
Camden-Clark Memorial Hospital Corp	8062	157
Cameca Instruments Inc	5049	10
Cameco Inc	5147	62
Camelback Community Bank	6022	586
Camelback Ford Lincoln	5511	348
Camelback Ski Corp	7011	166
Camellia Food Stores Inc	5411	114
Camellia General Provision Company Inc	2013	201
Camellia Home Health and Hospice	8082	73
Camelot Communications Inc	7319	34
Camelot Communications Ltd	7311	633
Camelot Corp	7372	5090
Camelot Entertainment Group Inc	7819	97
Camelot Lake Inc	8082	68
Camelot Limited Inc	7389	1923
Camelot Technologies Group LLC	7389	2365
Cameo Crafts	2759	370
Cameo Film Library Inc	7336	239
Cameo Inc	2844	152
Cameo Samples LLC	2789	39
Cameo Supply Company Inc	5087	66
Camera Bits	7372	1583
Camera House Inc	7359	206
Camera Tester Service Inc	5043	34
Cameron	3519	23
Cameron Alread Architects Inc	8712	282
Cameron Computers Inc	5065	395
Cameron Diversified Products Inc	3399	35
Cameron Drilling and Production Systems	3533	14
Cameron Electric Inc	1731	1266
Cameron Engineering and Associates LLP	8711	355
Cameron Health Inc	5047	102
Cameron Hughes Wine	5182	36
Cameron International Corp	3533	4
Cameron Machine Shop	3599	1089
Cameron Manufacturing and Design Inc	3441	67
Cameron Telephone Company Inc	4813	21
Cameron Tool Corp	3544	160
Cameron Valves and Measurement Group	3494	49
Cameron Welding Supply	5169	114
Cameron-Miller Inc	3841	340
Cametoid Technologies Inc	3479	107
Camfour Inc	5091	35
Camger Coatings Systems Inc	2851	115
Camie-Campbell Inc	2891	53
Camillus House Inc	8322	74
Camino Real Foods Inc	2038	29
Cammack Ranch Supply Inc	2048	124
Cammar Enterprises Inc	5065	784
Cammond Industries Inc	3531	212
Cammtech	7379	1633
Camo Construction Company Inc	1623	253
Camosy Inc	1542	53
Camp Bow Wow International Inc	8742	563
Camp Chevrolet	5511	108
Camp Courageous Of Iowa	7389	2442
Camp Curtin Transfer Inc	4213	2050
Camp Dresser and McKee Federal Programs Corp	8711	388

Company Name	SIC	Rank
Camp Dresser and McKee Inc	8711	14
Camp Systems International LLC	7371	537
Campaign Mail and Data Inc	7374	207
Campaigners Inc	7319	10
Campbell Alliance Group Inc	8742	222
Campbell Brothers Maintence Inc	5087	175
Campbell Coffee Roasting Co	2095	45
Campbell Concrete and Materials LP	3273	41
Campbell County School District 1	8211	82
Campbell Electric Inc	1731	705
Campbell Foundry Co	3321	61
Campbell Graphics Inc	2752	1371
Campbell Grinder Co	8711	464
Campbell Grinding and Machine Inc	3599	2111
Campbell Group Inc	6282	212
Campbell Incorporated Press Repair	7692	21
Campbell International Inc	3713	58
Campbell Manufacturing Inc	3494	64
Campbell Mithun Esty LLC	7311	36
Campbell Newman Asset Management Inc	6282	666
Campbell Oil Company Inc	5172	90
Campbell Printing Company Inc	2752	588
Campbell Scientific Inc	3823	46
Campbell Security Equipment Co	3829	355
Campbell Sorensen Company Inc	5084	108
Campbell Soup Co	2032	1
Campbell Supply Company Inc	5531	30
Campbell-Ewald Co	7311	17
Campbell-Randall Leather Machine Corp	3559	418
Campbells Floorcare Service	7349	334
Campbells Janitorial and Lawn Maintenance	7349	115
Campbellsville Industries Inc	3441	133
Camp-Hill Corp	3317	45
Campi Properties Inc	6531	216
Camping Companies Inc	7389	692
Camping World Inc	5561	1
Campmor Inc	5961	56
Campobello Foods	2038	91
Campus Apartment Inc	6513	4
Campus Communications Inc	2711	733
Campus Copy Partners Inc	7334	34
Campus Credit Union	6062	107
Campus Crest Communities Inc	6513	23
Campus Dimensions Inc	8742	290
Campus Federal Credit Union	6061	49
Campus Habitat Corp	6799	329
Campus Management Corp	7372	2029
Campus Party Inc	8742	675
Campus Works Inc	7379	911
Camrett Dedicated Logistics	4213	2223
Cams Inc	3545	263
Camshaft Machine Company LLC	3714	329
Camsight Company Inc	3843	43
Camstar International Inc	5072	122
Camstar Systems Inc	7372	1209
Cam-Tech Manufacturing LP	3724	64
Camtek USA Inc	5065	115
Can and Bottle Systems Inc	3559	272
Can Corporation Of America Inc	3411	13
Can Lines Engineering Inc	3535	82
Can Shed LLC	5093	160
Cana Inc	2431	85
Canaan Partners	6799	218
Canaan Printing Inc	2752	1247
Canaccord Adams Inc	6282	49
Canada Dry Bottling Company of Meriden Inc	2086	81
Canada Dry of Delaware Valley	5149	59
Canada Life Assurance Co	6311	18
Canadian Engineering and Tool Company Limited Inc	3544	301
Canadian Harvest-USA LP	2041	28
Canadian Pacific Railway (Minneapolis Minnesota)	4011	16
Canadian Valley Electric Coop	4911	310
Canadys Services Inc	7342	78
Canal Barge Company Inc	4412	11
Canal Capital Corp	6512	77
Canal Fulton Provision Inc	5147	117
Canal Insurance Co	6331	269
Canal Merchandise	5065	814
Canal Wood LLC	2411	5
Can-Am Express Inc	4213	951
Canam Technology Inc	3663	333
Canamer Intl LLC	2394	37
Canandaigua National Bank and Trust Co	6021	64
Canariis Corp	3561	122
Canary Communications Inc	3661	126
Canary Labs Inc	7372	3871
Canberra Corp	2842	24
Canby Builders Supply Co	5031	282
Canby Telephone Association	4813	98
Cancos Tile Corp	3281	2
Candela Controls Inc	7373	876
Candela Corp	3845	22
Candela Skin Care Centers of Boston Inc	3845	25
Candelis	3577	291
Candella Lighting Company Inc	3645	56
Candeltronics Corp	3679	880

Company Name	SIC	Rank
Candes Systems Inc	3825	225
Candid Color Photography Ltd	7335	28
Candid Litho Printing Ltd	2752	556
Candlelight Cabinetry Inc	2434	31
Candle-Lite Co	3999	107
Candor Electric Inc	1731	1639
Candy and Schonwald LLP	8721	466
Candy Basket Inc	2064	82
Candy Express Franchising Inc	5441	19
Candy Kitchen Shoppes Inc	5441	14
Candyman Ltd	5735	16
Candyrific LLC	5145	12
Cane Creek Cycling Components Inc	5091	129
CaneFire Software	7372	3813
Caney Fork Electric Cooperative Inc	4911	443
Caney Valley Cooperative Association Inc	4911	247
Canfield and Tack Inc	2752	257
Canfield Electronics Inc	3679	588
Canfield Machine and Tool LLC	3599	987
Canfield Systems Inc	5731	200
Canfield Technologies Inc	3341	21
Canfor USA Corp	2421	64
Cangelosi Co	5032	144
Cangene bioPharma Inc	2834	299
CANHELP LLC	7375	222
Caniff Electric Supply Company Inc	5063	391
Canine Caviar Pet Foods Inc	2048	127
Cannella Response Television	7379	548
Cannery	7336	19
Cannoli Factory	2051	153
Cannon and Wendt Electric Company Inc	1731	37
Cannon County Knitting Mills Inc	2231	3
Cannon Design	8712	24
Cannon Electric Co	1731	1907
Cannon Equipment Inc	3535	3
Cannon Equipment Southeast Inc	2542	17
Cannon Falls Beacon Inc	2711	494
Cannon Instrument Co	3823	94
Cannon Kevin Law Offices	7389	2141
Cannon Load Banks Inc	3825	228
Cannon Muskegon Corp	3341	16
Cannon Oil Corp	5541	43
Cannon Safe Inc	3499	27
Cannon Security Inc	5063	348
Cannon Sline Inc	1799	59
Cannon USA Inc	3559	116
Cannonball Express Transportation Co	4213	1621
Cannonball Trucking Inc	4213	2368
Cano and Co	6282	430
Cano Auto Electric Inc	5013	302
Cano Container Corp	2653	56
Cano Petroleum Inc	1311	158
Canoe Country Electric	1731	2077
Canoga Electric Supply Company Inc	5063	914
Canoga Perkins Corp	3661	70
Canon Business Solutions West	5044	1
Canon City Shopper Newspaper	2711	637
Canon Communications Inc	2721	57
Canon National Bank	6021	290
Canon USA Inc	3579	1
Canon Virginia Inc	3861	3
Canopies LLC	7359	123
Canopy Designs Ltd	5023	193
Canopy Group Inc	6719	115
Canson Inc	2679	39
Cantaloupe Systems Inc	5045	279
Cantare Foods Inc	2099	201
Cantata Technology Inc	3613	17
Canteen Service Co	5962	1
Cantel Medical Corp	3841	32
Canterbury Consulting Group Inc	8243	4
Canterbury Consulting Inc	6282	528
Canterbury Engineering Company Inc	3089	883
Canterbury Park Concessions Inc	5812	215
Canterbury Park Holding Corp	7948	20
Canterbury Press LLC	2741	329
Cantex Inc	3084	11
Canto Software Inc	7372	2363
Canto Tool Corp	3545	388
Canton Christian Home Inc	8361	85
Canton Drop Forge Inc	3462	18
Canton Mills Inc	2875	41
Canton Twp Public Works Inc	7389	1857
Cantor Fitzgerald LP	6211	99
Cantroll Motor Lines Inc	4213	2074
Cantu Electric Company Inc	1731	631
Canusa Corp	5113	46
Canvas and Upholstery Center Inc	3731	59
Canvas On Demand	5999	146
Canvas Systems LLC	7373	259
Canvys	3575	4
Canxpress Inc	4213	3061
Canyon Construction Corp	1541	287
Canyon Country Enterprises Inc	3273	92
Canyon Creek Cabinet Co	2434	9
Canyon Energy Inc	1311	243
Canyon Graphics Inc	7336	72
Canyon Materials Inc	3229	40
Canyon Plastics Inc	3089	1400
Canyon Ranch	7011	104
Canyon Ridge Contractors Inc	7359	126
Canzan Electric Inc	1731	2022

Company Name	SIC	Rank
Canzoniero Corp	5947	14
Cao Computer Technology	7373	583
Cap America Inc	2353	12
Cap and Seal Co	3469	315
Cap Collet and Tool Company Inc	3545	377
CAP Index Inc	8734	181
CAP Propane Plus Inc	5984	26
Cap Rock Winery	2084	141
Capacitec Inc	3829	299
Capacitor Sales and Engineering Inc	5065	917
Capacitor Supply Inc	5065	796
Capacitors Plus Inc	5065	338
Ca-Par Electric Inc	1731	1199
Capario	7374	78
Capax Technologies Inc	3629	89
Capco	7372	47
Capco Inc	3699	69
Capco Machinery Systems Inc	3555	57
Capco Plastics Inc	3089	688
Capco/Psa	3089	1522
Capcom Entertainment Inc	5099	24
Capcom USA Inc	7372	935
Capcon International Inc	3599	1391
Cape Bancorp	6022	162
Cape Care For Women LLC	7389	2174
Cape Clear Software Inc	7372	1252
Cape Cod Doormats Of Distinction Inc	3069	227
Cape Cod Express Inc	4213	365
Cape Cod Lumber Company Inc	5211	76
Cape Cod Potato Chip Co	2096	11
Cape Fear Chemicals Inc	2879	46
Cape Gazette Ltd	2711	804
Cape Haze Investments Ltd	3599	1865
Cape May Foods LLC	2091	9
Cape Notary Services	7374	326
Cape Publications Inc	2711	133
Cape Retirement Community Inc	8361	94
Cape Seafoods Inc	2092	90
Cape Setups LLC	3571	213
Cape Systems Group Inc	7372	3085
CAPE Systems Inc	7372	296
CapeCom Inc	7373	855
Capel Inc	5023	8
Capeletti Brothers Inc	6552	271
Capella Education Co	8221	7
Capella Healthcare Inc	8062	161
Capella Technologies LLC	7372	2876
Caperton Furnitureworks LLC	2511	72
Capgemini US LLC	8742	37
Capintec Inc	3829	97
Capistrano Toyota	5511	98
Capistrano's Bakery Inc	2051	172
Capital Access International	7372	4149
Capital Advanced Technologies Inc	3679	828
Capital Advantage Inc	6282	342
Capital Advisors Inc	6282	176
Capital Area Head Start	8351	25
Capital Auto and Truck Auction Inc	7389	733
Capital Automobile Co	5511	575
Capital Automotive REIT	6798	101
Capital Aviation Inc	3728	154
Capital Aviation Instrument Corp	5088	94
Capital Bancorp Ltd	6712	297
Capital Bank Corp	6712	231
Capital Bank NA	6021	356
Capital Bank (San Juan Capistrano California)	6029	29
Capital Beverage Corp	5181	109
Capital Blue Cross	6321	36
Capital Building Maintenance Services Inc	7349	415
Capital Bus Sales and Service Of Texas Inc	5012	189
Capital Business Credit LLC	6153	17
Capital Cargo International Airlines Inc	4512	17
Capital Chevrolet and Imports	5511	1176
Capital City Bank Group Inc	6712	170
Capital City Energy Group Inc	1311	240
Capital City International Trucks Inc	5511	899
Capital City Machine Shop Inc	3599	2107
Capital Cleaning Contractors Inc	7349	65
Capital Computer Associates Inc	7371	1389
Capital Computer Solutions Inc	7372	3872
Capital Confirmation Inc	7389	989
Capital Contracting Co	1623	603
Capital Crossing Bank	6091	15
Capital Development Co	6552	128
Capital Directions Inc	6712	504
Capital Educators Federal Credit Union	6061	88
Capital Electric Coop	4911	370
Capital Electric Wire And Cable	5063	677
Capital Electro-Circuits Inc	3672	317
Capital Engine Co	5084	756
Capital Fire Protection Co	1799	78
Capital Fitness Xsport Fitness	5091	88
Capital Foods Inc	2022	68
Capital For Business Inc	6799	294
Capital Ford Inc	5511	156
Capital Ford Lincoln Mercury	5511	983
Capital Gold Corp	1041	19
Capital Graphics Inc	7374	284
Capital Group Companies Inc	6722	42
Capital Growth Systems Inc	7389	422
Capital Guardian Trust Co	6091	13

Company Name	SIC	Rank
Capital H Group	8742	225
Capital Induction Inc	3567	117
Capital Industrial Supply Inc	5085	344
Capital Industries Inc	3469	120
Capital Institutional Services Inc	6211	69
Capital Inventory Inc	7389	1686
Capital Investment Counsel Inc	6282	499
Capital Investment Services of America Inc	6282	553
Capital Investment Strategies	6282	543
Capital Janitorial Supply and Service LLC	5087	102
Capital Legal Solutions	7372	578
Capital Lightning Protection Company Inc	3643	162
Capital Living and Rehabilitation Centres	8051	5
Capital Machine Company Inc	3559	224
Capital Mailing Services Inc	7331	163
Capital Management LLC	6282	412
Capital Market Risk Advisors Inc	6282	583
Capital Nephrology Medical Group	8011	162
Capital Offset Company Inc	2752	938
Capital One Bank	6022	8
Capital One Bank (Lynbrook New York)	6035	49
Capital One Financial Corp	6712	7
Capital Pacific Holdings Inc	1531	69
Capital Partners	6411	108
Capital Plastics Company Inc	2821	197
Capital Printing Co	2752	394
Capital Printing Corp	2752	350
Capital Quarries	5032	64
Capital Research and Management Co	6282	130
Capital Resin Corp	2821	69
Capital Resource Partners	6799	121
Capital Safety USA	5099	41
Capital Sand Company Inc	1442	31
Capital Senior Living Corp	8051	18
Capital Soap Products LLC	2842	149
Capital Southwest Corp	6799	85
Capital Stream Inc	7372	2348
Capital Structures Inc	2439	34
Capital Telecommunications Inc	4813	167
Capital Tire Inc	5014	7
Capital Tool Co	3544	322
Capital Trust Inc	6798	121
Capital Veneer Works Inc	2435	25
Capital Wholesale Lighting and Electric Supply Inc	5063	932
Capital X-Ray Inc	5047	166
Capital Z Investment Partners	6282	625
CapitalSource Bank	6022	31
CapitalSource Inc	6159	16
Capitol Aggregates Inc	3241	7
Capitol Aluminum and Glass Corp	3442	124
Capitol Auto Group	5511	90
Capitol Bancorp Ltd	6712	136
Capitol Beverage Packers	2086	95
Capitol Broadcasting Company Inc	4833	90
Capitol Cable and Technology Inc	5065	361
Capitol Cake Co	2051	196
Capitol Chevrolet Inc	5511	366
Capitol City Bancshares Inc	6712	639
Capitol City Bank and Trust Co	6022	521
Capitol City Container Corp	2653	118
Capitol City Fence Company Inc	1799	101
Capitol City Press Inc	2752	790
Capitol County Mutual Fire Insurance Co	6331	359
Capitol District Information Services Inc	7375	286
Capitol Electric Company Inc	1731	436
Capitol Express Inc	4213	984
Capitol Federal Financial	6712	79
Capitol Fiber Inc	7389	674
Capitol Filmworks Inc	7384	29
Capitol Foam Products Inc	5999	151
Capitol FSB	6035	33
Capitol Funds Inc	6035	258
Capitol Hill Building Maintenance Inc	7349	176
Capitol Light and Supply Co	5063	58
Capitol Lighting Plastics	3648	95
Capitol Litho Printing Corp	2752	1502
Capitol LLC	7389	521
Capitol Mazda	5511	704
Capitol Nashville Inc	6794	77
Capitol National Bank	6021	335
Capitol North American	4213	1250
Capitol Office Solutions Inc	5044	14
Capitol Paving of DC Inc	1611	117
Capitol Plywood Inc	5031	139
Capitol Projects Inc	8331	227
Capitol Records Inc	3652	6
Capitol Scientific Inc	5169	158
Capitol Services	7389	1452
Capitol Sign Company Inc	3993	79
Capitol Steel Corp	3441	168
Capitol Steps Productions Inc	7922	12
Capitol Technologies Inc	3542	111
Capitol Tool and Die LP	3544	508
Capitol Toyota	5511	420
Capitol Tunneling Inc	1622	44
Capitol Valley Bank	6022	737
Capitol Valley Electric Inc	1731	781
Capitol Warehousing Corp	4213	2931

Company Name	SIC	Rank
Capitol Welders Supply Company Inc	5084	487
Capitol Wood Works LLC	2542	41
Capitoline Tops Of Florida Inc	2541	27
CapLease Inc	6162	42
Capmark Bank	6029	1
Capmark Financial Group Inc	6163	1
Capodanno Electric Inc	1731	1289
Caporal Industries Ltd	3317	53
Caporale Engraving Company Inc	2796	68
Cappaert Manufactured Housing Inc	2451	29
Cappelli Development Corp	6552	220
Cappelli Miles spring	7311	512
Capps Manufacturing Inc	3728	99
Cappsco International Corp	5088	118
Capra Optical Inc	5049	145
Capra Press Inc	2731	357
Capri Foods Inc	5411	253
Capri Industries Inc	3231	67
Capri Optics Inc	3851	105
Caprica Internet Services	4813	323
Caprice Electronics Inc	5072	95
Capricon Enterprises Inc	5999	219
Capricorn Coffees Inc	5149	182
Capricorn Leisure Corp	4725	66
Capricorn Systems Inc	7379	244
Caprioni Sewerage Service Inc	4213	1937
Capris Furniture Industries Inc	2512	45
Caprius Inc	4959	27
Caprock Business Forms Inc	2761	69
CapRock Communications Corp	4813	116
Caprock Manufacturing Inc	3089	1269
Caprock Oil Tools Inc	3532	69
Caprock Pipe and Supply Inc	5051	154
Caprock Tractors Inc	5083	144
Caps and Tabs Inc	2023	30
CAPS Inc	3089	625
Capsalus Corp	2835	77
CAPISoftware	7372	2614
Capsonic Automotive Inc	3625	21
Capsonic Group LLC	3089	214
CapSource Financial Inc	4213	467
Capstan Inc	3625	367
Capstan Industries Inc	3399	13
Capstar Partners LLC	6799	168
Capstead Inc	6162	127
Capstead Mortgage Corp	6162	12
Capstone Corp	8711	139
Capstone Inc	7379	703
Capstone Information Technologies Inc	7379	1310
Capstone Partners LLC	6282	222
Capstone Press Inc	2731	181
Capstone Technology Inc	7372	4034
Capstone Therapeutics Corp	3841	415
Capstone Turbine Corp	3511	15
Capsule Communications Inc	4813	147
Capt Neill's Seafood Inc	2092	49
Captain D's LLC	5812	131
CapTech Ventures Inc	7372	2331
Captek Softgel International Inc	2077	3
Capterra Inc	7372	838
Captiva Group Inc	2752	535
Captiva Software Corp	7372	567
Captive Fasteners Corp	3452	8
Captive-Aire Systems Inc	3444	19
Captools Co	7372	3873
Captor Corp	3677	11
Captron Corp	3672	427
Capture 3d Inc	5734	188
Captured Live Productions LLC	7371	1724
Capway Systems Inc	3535	118
Capweld Inc	5084	555
Car Audio Specialist Inc	5731	175
Car - Mon Products Inc	3564	94
Car Parts Distributors Ltd	5013	343
Car Phone Factory Inc	5064	81
Car Tech Auction Inc	7389	1866
Car Toys Inc	5731	11
Car Wash Technologies	5087	127
Car Zone Auto Sales Inc	5012	183
Cara Group Inc	7379	678
Carabetta Companies	6552	54
Caracciolo Charles Steel And Metal Yard Inc	5093	222
Caraco Pharmaceutical Laboratories Ltd	2834	95
Caracol Broadcasting Inc	4832	104
Carahsoft Technology Corp	7379	24
Carando Machine Works Inc	3542	45
Carat North America	7311	12
Caraustar	2655	6
Caraustar Ashland Carton Plant	2657	3
Caraustar Industries Inc	2652	3
Caraustar Mill Group Inc	2631	5
Caraustar Recovered Fiber Group Inc	2631	12
Caraustar Saint Paris	2679	11
Caravan Bakery and Trading Co	2051	40
Caravan Bakery Inc	2051	245
Caravan International Corp	5065	715
Caravan Technologies Inc	2841	56
Caravan Trailer LLC	5511	1246
Carbaugh Tool Company Inc	3599	1569
Carbide Grinding Company Inc	3545	363
Carbide Grinding Inc	2819	131
Carbide Metals Inc	3291	30

Company Name	SIC	Rank
Carbide Probes Inc	3545	283
Carbide Processors Inc	3425	12
Carbide Products Inc	3545	341
Carbide Specialties Inc	5085	378
Carbide Technologies Inc	3356	34
Carbide Tools For Industry Inc	5085	241
Carbidie Corp	3544	43
Carbis Inc	3441	38
Carbit Paint Co	2851	107
Carbo Ceramics Inc	3299	2
Carboline Co	3479	19
Carbon Block Technology Inc	5074	87
Carbon Carbon Advanced Technologies Inc	3624	23
Carbon Express Inc	4213	2102
Carbon Healthcare	8742	164
Carbon Medical Technologies Inc	3841	361
Carbon Sales Inc	1231	2
Carbonator Rental Service Inc	7359	143
Carbonetworks Corp	7371	416
Carbonite Inc	7379	129
Carbro Corp	3545	171
Carbtrol Corp	2819	118
Carchex	8748	217
Carco International Inc	5399	18
Carcoustics USA Inc	3086	52
Card Pak Inc	2657	26
Card Palmer Sibbison and Co	8721	181
Card Technology Corp	3579	45
Card USA Inc	3999	139
Card Web	2721	123
Cardamation Company Inc	3861	107
Cardco Corp	2752	1792
Cardea Technology Inc	7371	1590
Cardello Electric Supply Co	5063	188
Carden Machine Shop Inc	3728	184
Carder Inc	5032	40
Cardiac Carr Co	7991	20
Cardiac Center LLC	3845	117
Cardiac Science Corp	8732	21
Cardica Inc	3841	176
Cardiff Software Inc	7372	951
Cardima Inc	3841	353
Cardinal Aluminum Co	3354	10
Cardinal Bancorp Inc	6712	412
Cardinal Bank	6022	90
Cardinal Bankshares Corp	6022	456
Cardinal Building Maintenance	7349	196
Cardinal Cartridge Inc	2865	12
Cardinal Color Group LLC	2752	397
Cardinal Comb and Brush Manufacturing Corp	3991	24
Cardinal Distribution LP	5122	3
Cardinal Engineering Inc	7372	2364
Cardinal Financial Corp	6712	194
Cardinal Freight Logistics Management	4213	110
Cardinal Health Inc	6719	4
Cardinal Homes Inc	2452	44
Cardinal Industrial Finishes Inc	2851	50
Cardinal Industrial Insulation Company Inc	1742	13
Cardinal Industries Inc	3679	790
Cardinal Laboratories Inc	3999	131
Cardinal Logistic Managment Inc	4213	45
Cardinal Machine Co	3549	81
Cardinal Mailing Services Ltd	7331	129
Cardinal Maintenance and Service Company Inc	7349	197
Cardinal Novelty Distributing Company Inc	5087	97
Cardinal Pharmaceuticals Inc	5122	63
Cardinal Pools Of Oklahoma Inc	5999	163
Cardinal Power Plant	4911	127
Cardinal Rubber and Seal Inc	5085	327
Cardinal Rubber Company Inc	3069	199
Cardinal Scale Manufacturing Co	3596	4
Cardinal Services Incorporated Of Indiana	8331	45
Cardinal Services Ltd	7331	183
Cardinal Sound and Communcations Corp	5065	875
Cardinal Steel Supply Inc	5051	424
Cardinal Technologies Inc (Bethesda Maryland)	7379	521
Cardinal Transport Inc	4213	458
Cardio Logic Inc	5045	1059
Cardiocommand Inc	5047	255
CardioDynamics International Corp	3841	118
CardioFocus Inc	3841	328
CardioGenesis Corp	3841	189
Cardiomedix Inc	7352	44
CardioMEMS Inc	3842	148
Cardionet Inc	3845	26
Cardiopulmonary Corp	7371	686
Cardiostaff Corp	8011	177
Cardiovascular Associates PSC	8011	77
Cardiovascular BioTherapeutics Inc	2834	457
Cardiovascular Systems Inc	3841	63
Cardish Machine Works Inc	3599	1100
Cardium Therapeutics Inc	8071	10
Cardlogix	3577	497
Card-Monroe Corp	3552	9
Cardolite Corp	2869	72
Cardona Manufacturing Corp	3728	194

Company Name	SIC	Rank
Cardone Industries Inc	3714	14
Cardoni Waddell LLC	8721	202
Cardservice International Inc (Simi Valley California)	6099	5
CardSystems Inc	7372	1816
CARDtools Systems Corp	7372	1768
Cardtronics Inc	7389	66
Cardwell Containers Inc	3085	32
Cardxx Inc	3089	1734
Care and Share Of Erie Count Inc	8322	221
Care Dynamix LLC	8049	16
Care Fusion	3845	45
Care Initiatives	8051	30
Care Investment Trust Inc	6798	185
Care Is 1 A California Corp	7371	999
Care Management International Inc	7371	70
Care Medical Of Athens Inc	7352	27
Care Rehab and Orthopaedic Products Inc	5047	147
Care Tv	4833	154
Care Wisconsin First Inc	8322	15
CareAdvantage Inc	6324	122
CareCall Inc	8999	33
Careen Inc	3621	57
Career Communications Group Inc	2721	333
Career Control Group Inc	7389	2358
Career Development	7389	2231
Career Education Corp	8249	1
Career Partners International LLC	8742	153
Career Press Inc	2731	175
Career Sports and Entertainment Inc	7941	38
Career TEAM LLC	8331	176
Career Transition Center	8331	164
CareerBuilder LLC	7389	64
CareerStaff Inc	7361	247
CareerStaff Unlimited Inc	7363	11
CareerTrack Inc	8299	10
CareerWise Inc	7389	2387
CareFirst BlueCross BlueShield	6321	7
Carefirst Of Fort Wayne Inc	5047	244
Carefree Distributing Inc	5013	340
Careful Courier Service	4215	10
CareFusion Corp	3841	7
Carefusion Solutions LLC	5047	22
CareGroup Inc	8062	221
Caremark Therapeutic Services	8082	54
CareMaster Inc	7374	362
Caremedic Systems Inc	7372	855
Carenbauer Wholesale Corp	5181	91
CareNet (San Antonio Texas)	8748	162
CareScience Inc	7379	383
CareStepscom Inc	7375	9
Carestia Trucking Co	4213	3072
Carestream Dental LLC	8742	59
Caretek Inc	5137	12
Caretree Systems Inc	3423	62
Carew Concrete and Supply Company Inc	3273	58
Carey International Inc	4119	6
Carey Manufacturing Company Inc	3699	160
Carey Services Inc	8361	56
Carey Systems Inc	7372	3874
Carey Transport Inc	4213	2661
CarFax Inc	7389	342
Car-Freshner Corp	2842	32
Cargill Cattle Feeders	0211	3
Cargill Corn Milling North America	2041	9
Cargill Cotton Inc	5159	9
Cargill Dry Corn Ingredients Inc	2041	33
Cargill Inc	2041	1
Cargill Kitchen Solutions	2062	6
Cargill Malt Co	2083	2
Cargill Pork	0213	13
Cargill Specialy Canola Oils	2046	7
Cargill Steel and Wire Div	3496	83
Cargille Laboratories Inc	2819	124
Cargille-Sacher Laboratories Inc	3826	86
Cargo Connection Logistics Holding Inc	4789	30
Cargo Express Inc	4213	1570
Cargo Helicopter Program Management Office	3721	36
Cargo Trac Inc	4213	2994
Cargo Transport Inc	4213	2670
Cargo Transporters Inc	4213	131
Cargocare Transportation Co	4213	673
Cargotec Solutions LLC	3537	36
Cargowise Inc	7373	681
Car-Graph Inc	3724	57
Carhart Lumber Co	5211	124
Carhartt Inc	2326	3
Caribbean Concepts	4725	62
Caribbean Intl Transportation and Consoli	4213	2954
Caribbean Products Ltd	2013	164
Caribbean Records Manufacturing Corp	3652	46
Caribbean Shipping Services Inc	4213	2466
Caribbean Whirlpools	5999	315
Caribou Coffee Company Inc	5812	136
Caridianbct Inc	8092	4
Carillon Properties	6552	229
Carimex International Trading Inc	5199	78
Carina Software	7372	4671
Caring Health Associate	5045	800
Caring Hrts Homecare Southeast Mo LLC	7363	349
Caris and Company Inc	6799	31
Carisch Inc	5812	256
Carithers-Wallace-Courtenay Inc	5021	25
Carizan Hospitality Inc	5064	183
Carl Beasley Ford Inc	5511	804
Carl Black Chevrolet	5511	431
Carl Black Of Orlando	5511	683
Carl Bolander and Sons Co	1629	67
Carl Buddig And Co	2013	51
Carl Burger Dodge	5511	353
Carl Cannon Chevrolet-Cadillac	5511	895
Carl F Ewig Inc	5088	120
Carl F Statz and Sons Inc	5083	66
Carl Fischer LLC	2741	153
Carl Group Inc	4899	64
Carl Hall	1731	1888
Carl Herrmann Associates	3559	210
Carl I Schaeffer Electric Co	1731	572
Carl Karcher Enterprises Inc	5812	42
Carl L Jonas Inc	4213	1433
Carl M Freeman Associates Inc	6552	153
Carl McCarty Trucking LLC	4213	2554
Carl Rittberger Sr Inc	2011	132
Carl Stahl Sava Industries Inc	3496	45
Carl Strutz and Company Inc	3559	241
Carl Waltzer Digital Services Inc	7336	240
Carl Zeiss Inc	5049	1
Carl Zeiss Industrial Metrology LLC	3545	1
Carl Zeiss Meditec	3845	36
Carla Corp	3911	31
Carlcin Restaurants	6794	30
Carlen Controls Inc	3829	453
Carlen Transport Inc	4213	358
Carleton Equipment Co	5084	416
Carleton Life Support Systems Inc	3728	48
Carleton Technologies Inc	3728	81
Carlevale John	2731	322
Carlex Glass Co	5013	170
Carlile Patchen and Murphy	8111	339
Carlile Transportation Systems	4213	211
Carlin America Inc	6794	144
Carlin Combustion Technology Inc	3433	44
Carlin Employment Services Inc	5047	254
Carlin Manufacturing Inc	2599	37
Car-Lin Offset Printing Company Inc	2752	1530
Carlin Systems Inc	5065	203
Carling Technologies Inc	3643	138
Carlisle And Finch Co	3648	43
Carlisle Carrier Corp	4213	477
Carlisle Coatings and Waterproofing Inc	2952	8
Carlisle Companies Inc	3069	2
Carlisle FoodService Products	3089	2
Carlisle Industrial Brake and Friction	3714	190
Carlisle Industrial Friction	3462	8
Carlisle Plastics Company Inc	3479	114
Carlisle Printing Of Walnut Creek Ltd	2752	994
Carlisle Road Associates Inc	1799	79
Carlisle Sanitary Maintenance Products Inc	3991	8
Carlisle SynTec Inc	2952	7
Carlisle Tire and Wheel Co	3011	3
Carlon Chimes Co	3699	28
Carlon Inc	5078	27
Carlon Meter Company Inc	3824	46
Carlos Printing Concepts Inc	2752	1446
Carl's Donuts Inc	5149	144
Carlsbad Bancorporation Inc	6712	374
Carlsberg Management Co	6531	188
Carlsmith Ball LLP	8111	282
Carlson Auction Service Inc	7389	1395
Carlson Companies Inc	7011	11
Carlson Company Inc	3568	53
Carlson Dimond and Wright	5084	705
Carlson Engineering and ManufacturingInc	3549	128
Carlson GMAC Real Estate	6531	190
Carlson Group Inc (Irvine California)	8712	283
Carlson Hospitality Worldwide Procurement Group Inc	6519	2
Carlson Hotels Worldwide	7011	40
Carlson Industries Inc	5083	196
Carlson JPM Store Fixtures Co	5046	100
Carlson Manufacturing Inc	3599	2432
Carlson Marketing	8742	62
Carlson Marketing Group	7311	24
Carlson Real Estate Co	6512	20
Carlson Restaurants Worldwide Inc	5812	26
Carlson Sign Co	7312	38
Carlson Testing Inc	7389	868
Carlson Tool and Machine Co	3559	449
Carlson Tool and Manufacturing Corp	3544	58
Carlson Wagonlit Travel Inc	4724	1
Carlson Wagonlit Travel (Tacoma Washington)	4724	52
Carlton Co	3425	7
Carlton Computor Support Service Inc	7374	357
Carlton Farms Inc	2011	49
Carlton Fields Ward Emmanuel Smith and Cutler	8111	43
Carlton Foods Corp	2013	52
Carlton Industries Corp	3672	201
Carlton Industries LP	2759	297
Carlton Property Group Ltd	7389	903
Carlton Staffing	7363	372
Carlton Transport Inc	4213	2662
Carlton-Bates Co	5065	49
Carlyle Group	6211	26
Carlyle Group Ltd	7361	70
Carlyle Johnson Machine Company LLC	3568	55
Carlyle Tower National Associates LP	6513	31
Carlyle Van Lines Inc	4213	426
Carma International Inc	8732	74
Carma Laboratories Inc	2834	206
Carman Inc	4213	1740
Carman Industries Inc	3535	69
Carman Productions Inc	7389	448
CarMax Inc	5511	4
Carme Cosmeceutical Services Inc	2844	197
Carmel Community Living Corp	8059	19
Carmel Contractors Inc	1541	302
Carmel Engineering Inc	1799	137
Carmel Food Group Inc	2099	263
Carmel Marina Corp	4953	36
Carmel Software Inc	7372	4589
Carmel Trader Publishing Inc	2721	147
Carmelita Provision Company Inc	2013	213
Carmen M Pariso Inc	4213	1422
Carmichael and Associates Inc	2721	350
Carmichael Honda	5511	463
Carmichael Lynch Inc	7311	72
Carmike Cinemas Inc	7832	8
Carm's Electric Company Inc	1731	1919
Carnation Software Inc	7372	4796
Carnegie Body Co	5013	71
Carnegie Hall Corp	7922	18
Carnegie Institution of Washington	8733	23
Carnegie Investment Counsel	6282	343
Carnegie Learning Inc	7372	1351
Carnegie Management Group LLC	5812	445
Carneiro Chumney and Company LC	8721	390
Carnes Trucking Company Inc	4213	1392
Carney Trucking Company Inc	4213	1258
Carnival Corp	4449	1
Caro Carbide Corp	3545	336
Caro Foods Inc	5141	166
Carol Franklin Associates Inc	7389	1453
Carol H Williams Advertising Agency	7311	57
Carol House Furniture Inc	5712	57
Carol Lighting and Supply Inc	5063	449
Carol Printing and Office Products Inc	2752	1776
Carol Reed Associates Inc	8743	206
Carol School Supply Company Inc	5049	159
Carol Tabor	3532	77
Carolane Propane Gas Inc	7389	010
Carole Fabrics Corp	2221	21
Carolina Apparel Group Inc	2341	6
Carolina Associates Inc	4131	8
Carolina Auto Auction Inc	5012	182
Carolina Bank Holdings Inc	6022	228
Carolina Base - Pac Corp	2448	39
Carolina Beer and Beverage LLC	2082	16
Carolina Beer Company Inc	5181	90
Carolina Beverage Corp	2087	44
Carolina Brace Manufacturers Inc	3842	305
Carolina Business Furniture Inc	2511	29
Carolina By-Products Co	8742	585
Carolina Cabinet Company Inc	2434	61
Carolina Canners Inc	2086	70
Carolina Cardiology Consultants	8011	84
Carolina Casualty Insurance Co	6331	256
Carolina Cellular Inc	4812	97
Carolina Classic Manufacturing Inc	3088	9
Carolina Classics Catfish Inc	2092	40
Carolina Coach Company Inc	4131	7
Carolina Color and Chemical Co	5085	455
Carolina Color Corp	3089	1120
Carolina Color Corporation Of Ohio	3089	1595
Carolina Communications and Fire Equipment Inc	5065	521
Carolina Container Co	2653	14
Carolina Cooperative Credit Union	6061	103
Carolina Cotton Works Inc	2258	11
Carolina Equipment and Supply Company Inc	5084	465
Carolina Express Delivery Inc	4213	1528
Carolina Federal Credit Union	6061	125
Carolina Filters Inc	5085	139
Carolina Fire Protection Inc	3569	205
Carolina Fluidair Inc	5084	371
Carolina Foam Inc	3086	82
Carolina Foods Inc	2051	58
Carolina Forge Company LLC	3562	19
Carolina Graphic Arts Inc	2752	1377
Carolina Hardwoods Inc	2431	108
Carolina Home Care Medical Equipment Center Inc	7352	24
Carolina Home Exteriors LLC	1521	138
Carolina Hosiery Mills Inc	2252	3
Carolina Kids Pediatric Associates	8011	169
Carolina Kneece's Cleaning Service Inc	7349	192
Carolina Koolers LLC	5999	287
Carolina Lantern Inc	3648	68
Carolina Laser Cutting Inc	3599	1721

Company Name	SIC	Rank
Carolina Loom Reed Company Inc	3552	52
Carolina Made Inc	5136	9
Carolina Manufacturer's Service	7389	367
Carolina Material Handling Services Inc	5084	318
Carolina Medical Products Co	2834	379
Carolina Metals Inc	3728	200
Carolina Mills Inc	2281	7
Carolina Model Home Corp	1521	161
Carolina Narrow Fabric Co	2241	14
Carolina North Granite Corp	3281	7
Carolina North Lumber Co	2426	15
Carolina Office Systems	5044	16
Carolina Opry	7922	11
Carolina Packers Inc	2013	117
Carolina Plastics Inc	3089	1233
Carolina Power Systems Of Sumter Inc	3613	79
Carolina Precision Components Inc	3599	1609
Carolina Precision Machining Inc	3599	2168
Carolina Prestress Corporation Of Lake City Inc	3272	118
Carolina Pride Foods Inc	2011	14
Carolina Print and Packaging Inc	5111	31
Carolina Public Warehouse Inc	4213	2525
Carolina Quarries Inc	1411	7
Carolina Rha/North Mr Inc	8744	10
Carolina Safety Sport International LLC	5099	70
Carolina Sand Inc	5032	93
Carolina Seafoods Inc	5146	71
Carolina Skiff LLC	5091	68
Carolina Stalite Company LP	3281	24
Carolina Steel Corp	3441	5
Carolina Sunrock LLC	1429	5
Carolina Swatching Inc	2789	107
Carolina Tank Lines Inc	4213	1100
Carolina Textile Sales Of Gastonia Inc	3599	2158
Carolina Time Equipment Company Inc	5063	402
Carolina Tractor and Equipment Company Inc	5082	12
Carolina Tractor/CAT	3599	39
Carolina Treet Inc	2033	119
Carolina Trust Bank	6021	248
Carolina Village Inc	8361	45
Carolina Visuals LLC	2399	24
Carolina Woman	7991	21
Carolinas HealthCare System	8062	11
Carolinas Telco Federal Credit Union	6061	78
Caroline Distribution	5099	19
Carolyn Adkinson	3829	511
Carolyn Collins Caviar Co	2091	20
Carolyn E Wylie Center For Children Youth and Families	8351	32
Caron Building Center Inc	5211	303
Caron Compactor Co	3531	60
Caron East Inc	5049	130
Caron Enterprises Inc	3679	525
Caron Pipe Jacking Inc	1623	822
Caron Products And Services Inc	3823	269
Carondelet Foundry Co	3325	20
Caroplast Inc	5074	194
Carotek Inc	5084	229
Carothers Construction Inc	1542	341
Carotron Inc	3625	220
Carousel Industries of North America Inc	7379	177
Carpathia Hosting Inc	7379	504
Carpel Video Inc	3695	75
Carpenter and Paterson Inc	3494	54
Carpenter Co	3086	2
Carpenter Contractors Of America Inc	1751	2
Carpenter Electric Inc	1731	557
Carpenter Engineering Inc	3613	175
Carpenter Group	3531	50
Carpenter Manufacturing CoInc	3549	96
Carpenter Melisa	7371	1910
Carpenter Steel Div	3312	22
Carpenter Technology Corp	3312	11
Carpenter's Motor Transport Inc	4213	2588
Carpenter's Time Center Inc	5944	38
Carpet Company Op	5023	198
Carpet King Inc	5713	9
Carpet Rentals Inc	2679	63
Carpet Services Inc	5087	77
Carpeteria Inc	5713	5
CARQUEST Corp	5013	12
Carr Business Systems Inc	5044	12
Carr Chevrolet Inc	5511	172
Carr Corp	3844	17
Carr Electric Company Inc	1731	2521
Carr Enterprises Inc	7699	171
Carr Lane Manufacturing Company Inc	3544	55
Carr Lane Roemheld Manufacturing Co	3429	146
Carr Machine and Tool Inc	3599	2236
Carr McClellan Ingersoll Thompson and Horn	8111	419
Carr Metal Products Inc	2542	33
Carr Supply Inc	5075	29
Carr Technologies Group Inc	1731	1150
Carr Tool Co	3532	49
Carrafiello Diehl and Associates Inc	7311	141
Carreker Corp	7374	51
Carrel Forwarding Inc	7389	1703
Carrera Casting Corp	3915	5
Carrera Investment Corp	5065	651
Carrera Systems and Service LLC	7372	1387

Company Name	SIC	Rank
Carriage Enterprises Ltd	5511	940
Carriage House Companies Inc	2035	1
Carriage House Foods Inc	5147	93
Carriage House Imports Ltd	5182	45
Carriage Inc	3792	11
Carriage Services Inc	7261	4
Carrier and Gable Inc	5063	439
Carrier Corp	3585	8
Carrier Johnson	8712	226
Carrier Refrigeration	3585	33
Carrier Transcold Of Maine	5078	38
Carrier Transicold AC Industries	3585	90
Carrier Vibrating Equipment Inc	3535	21
Carriker Ford Inc	5511	1135
Carringer Company Inc	5021	52
Carrington Foods Inc	2092	46
Carrio Cabling Corp	3679	441
Carris Reels Inc	3089	48
Carrizo Oil and Gas Inc	1311	100
Carrol Electric Inc	1731	840
Carroll Broadcasting Co	4832	266
Carroll Burdick and McDonough	8111	353
Carroll Coolers Inc	3585	145
Carroll Distributing Co	7389	1719
Carroll Electric Cooperative Corp	4911	151
Carroll Fulmer and Company Inc	4212	23
Carroll Guido and Groffman A LLP	8111	577
Carroll Industrial Molds Inc	3544	880
Carroll Publishing	2741	240
Carroll Seating Company Inc	5021	93
Carroll Service Co	5169	115
Carroll Tool And Die Co	3544	353
Carroll's Creek Fire Protection District	7389	1535
Carroll's Discount Office Furniture Co	5021	77
Carrollton Bancorp	6022	364
Carrollton Bank	6022	191
Carrollton Farmers Elevator Company Inc	5153	85
Carrollton Specialty Products Co	2675	13
Carrols Restaurant Group Inc	5812	73
Carrs/Safeway	5411	101
Carr-Trumbull Lumber Co	5211	280
Carrubba Inc	2869	98
Carruthers Equipment Co	3556	112
Carry All Trucking Inc	4213	3052
Carsan Engineering Inc	3629	102
CarsDirectcom Inc	5511	83
Carskadden Optical Company Inc	3851	68
Carson And Roberts Site Construction And Engineering Inc	1799	119
Carson Concrete and Decking Inc	1771	29
Carson Design Associates	7389	320
Carson Helicopters Inc	8713	1
Carson Industries Inc	3365	37
Carson Manufacturing Company Inc	3669	224
Carson Manufacturing Inc	3599	1615
Carson Nugget Inc	7999	63
Carson Oil Company Inc	5172	89
Carson Tredgett Serigraphics Inc	7336	321
Carson-Dellosa Publishing LLC	2731	30
Carsons Inc	2512	54
Carso's Pasta Company Inc	2098	26
CARSTAR Franchise Systems Inc	7539	4
Carstens Amaral	7311	935
Carstens Inc	3841	165
Carstens Industries Inc	3732	79
Carstens Publications Inc	2721	361
Carswell Distributing Company Inc	5065	94
Cartan Tours Inc	4725	65
CarteGraph Systems Inc	7372	3446
Carter and Associates LLC	6531	256
Carter and Crawley Inc	1731	538
Carter and Verplanck Inc	5085	81
Carter Associates Inc	8721	400
Carter Bank and Trust	6022	56
Carter Brothers LLC	7382	14
Carter Brothers Manufacturing Company Inc	3799	36
Carter Chambers LLC	5085	7
Carter Composition Corp	2791	8
Carter Distributing Co	5181	96
Carter Electric	1731	2043
Carter Electric Company Inc	1731	397
Carter Express Inc	4213	538
Carter Jones Lumber Company Inc	5211	20
Carter Ledyard and Milburn LLP	8111	275
Carter Lumber Co	5211	9
Carter Machine Company Inc	3593	27
Carter Manufacturing Company Inc	3469	318
Carter Paper and Packaging Inc	5112	51
Carter Printing and Graphics Inc	2752	1135
Carter Publishing Company Inc	2711	582
Carter Screen Inc	3555	123
Carter Street Corp	7389	1071
Carter Truck Lines Inc	4213	3116
Carteret Mortgage Corp	6162	102
Carteret Publishing Company Inc	2711	382
Carter-Hubbard Publishing Company Inc	2711	639
Carter-Pertaine Inc	7372	3256
Carter's Furniture Co	5712	63
Carter's Inc	2369	1
Carter's Shooting Center Inc	5941	40
Cartersville Newspaper Inc	2711	924

Company Name	SIC	Rank
Carter-Waters Corp	5039	21
Cartessa Corp	3672	429
Car-Tex Transport and Vacuum Service	4213	1649
Carthage Fabrics Corp	2221	22
Carton Craft Corp	2653	105
Carton Donofrio Partners Inc	7311	147
Carton Service Inc	2657	21
Cartoncraft Inc	2657	35
Cartoon Bank Inc	7375	253
Cartridge Actuated Devices Inc	2892	6
Cartridge Care Inc	5045	554
Cartruck Packaging Inc	7389	2195
Carts Of Colorado Inc	2599	43
Cartwright and Daughters Party Rentals	7359	78
Cartwright and Daughters Tent and Party Rentals Inc	7359	254
Cartwright Distributing Inc	5023	118
Cartwright International Van Lines Inc	4213	493
Cartwright School District 83	8211	77
Cartwright's Valley Meat Co	2011	91
Carty and Carty Inc	4213	1358
Carvel Corp	5143	12
Carver Bancorp Inc	6035	92
Carver Brewing Co	2082	19
Carver Federal Savings Bank	6035	93
Carver Financial Services Inc	6211	297
Carver Inc	3556	115
Carver Inc (Wabash Indiana)	3821	7
Carver Machine Works Inc	3441	172
Carver Pump Co	3561	96
Carver State Bank	6022	570
Carvin Corp	3931	13
Carwild Corp	3842	207
Cary Audio Design LLC	3651	128
Cary Health and Rehabilitation Center	8051	45
Cary Institute Of Ecosystem Studies Inc	8731	241
Cary Services Inc	1711	254
Caryl Communications Inc	8743	136
Carylon Corp	4952	1
CAS Corp	5046	210
Cas Enterprises Inc	5251	33
CAS Medical Systems Inc	3841	120
CAS Severn	7373	552
Cas Tech Inc	3543	35
Casa Di Bertacchi Corp	2013	75
Casa Herrera Inc	3556	39
Casa Pacifica Centers For Children And Families	8322	42
Casa Technology Systems LLC	1731	1668
Casa Valdez Inc	2099	332
Casa Vieja Contractors	1731	2215
Casafina Enterprises Ltd	5023	205
Casahl Technology Inc	7372	665
Casamba Inc	7371	1363
Casanova Pendrill Publicidad Inc	7311	116
CASAS International Brokerage Inc	4731	76
Cascade Ag Services Inc	2035	24
Cascade Bancorp	6712	216
Cascade Coffee Inc	2095	37
Cascade Communication Services Inc	4899	203
Cascade Computer Maintenance Inc	7378	45
Cascade Contracting Inc	1521	164
Cascade Controls Inc	7373	482
Cascade Corp	3537	7
Cascade Data Solutions	7372	3875
Cascade Designs	3949	56
Cascade Die Casting Group Inc	3363	27
Cascade Earth Sciences Ltd	4952	5
Cascade Engineering Inc	3089	55
Cascade Express	4213	1054
Cascade Federal Credit Union	6061	73
Cascade Forest Group LLC	5031	449
Cascade Gasket and Manufacturing Company Inc	3069	111
Cascade General Inc	3731	26
Cascade Hardwoods LLC	2421	43
Cascade Health Services	7361	46
Cascade Hydraulics And Machine Inc	7699	186
Cascade Laser Corp	5065	943
Cascade Lumber Co	5031	83
Cascade Machinery and Electric Inc	5084	70
Cascade Microtech Inc	3825	19
Cascade Ohio Inc	2431	32
Cascade Optical Coating Inc	3827	150
Cascade Orthopaedics Properties LLC	8011	160
Cascade Pattern Company Inc	3543	29
Cascade Precision Inc	3599	1671
Cascade Printing Co	2752	1651
Cascade Pump Co	3561	115
Cascade Rubber Products Inc	3069	138
Cascade Scientific Inc	5049	96
Cascade Specialties Inc	2034	18
Cascade Steel Rolling Mills Inc	3312	44
Cascade System Technology LLC	3674	354
Cascade Technical Sciences Inc	8734	195
Cascade Technologies Corp	3674	507
Cascade Timber Consulting Inc	0851	4
Cascade Western Representatives Inc	5063	772
Cascade Wholesale Hardware	5072	21
Cascade Wood Products Inc	2431	19
Cascaded Purchase Holdings Inc	3429	99
Cascades Sonoco Inc	2891	32

Company Name	SIC	Rank
Cascadia Corp	5064	75
Cascio Music Company Inc	5099	40
Casco Circuits Inc	3672	452
Casco Corp	8712	130
Casco Development Inc	7371	1096
CASCO International Inc	7389	441
Casco Manufacturing Inc	3679	546
Casco Products Corp	3714	119
Casco Services Inc	4213	878
CASD Inc	8721	421
Case Assembly Solutions Inc	3672	216
Case Boring Corp	1781	4
Case Consult Corp	7372	822
Case Design Corp	3161	12
Case Engineered Lumber Inc	5031	99
Case Enterprises Inc	4213	1980
Case Farms Of Ohio Inc	2015	17
Case Foundation Co	1771	10
Case Mason Filling Inc	4783	24
Case Partners Inc	7379	1100
Case Pork Roll Company Inc	2013	194
Case Princeton Company Inc	3089	1778
Case Systems Inc	2521	25
Case Technologies Inc	5045	669
CaseCentral Inc	7372	1331
Caseintel Corp	7371	1469
Casella Waste Systems Inc	4953	21
Caselle Inc	7372	2767
CASEMaker Inc	7372	2902
Casemer Tool and Machine Inc	3599	1722
CaseStack Inc	4213	339
CaseWare International Inc	7372	1782
Caseworks Industries Inc	2599	45
Casey Chevrolet Corp	5511	756
Casey Ciklin Lubitz Martens and O'Connell	8111	301
Casey Communications Inc	8743	271
Casey Construction Inc	1623	754
Casey Machine Company Inc	3599	273
Casey Peterson and Associates Ltd	8721	409
Casey Printing Inc	2752	360
Casey State Bank	6022	349
Casey Woodwyk Inc	5148	50
Casey's Color Center Inc	5211	273
Casey's General Stores Inc	5411	28
Caseys' Page Mill Ltd	2621	70
Casey's Seafood Inc	5146	24
Cash America Incorporated of Oklahoma	5932	16
Cash America International Inc	5999	7
Cash and Carry Building Supply Inc	5211	214
Cash and Go Management LLC	6141	52
Cash Construction Company Inc	1623	86
Cash Management Trust of America	6722	267
Cash Moulding Sales Of Alabama Inc	5023	52
Cash Register Sales Inc	5044	34
Cash Register Services Inc	5044	60
Cash Systems Inc	6153	37
Cash Technologies Inc	7389	2478
Cashco Inc	3491	20
Cashedge Inc	7372	384
Cashion Thermoplastics Inc	3089	1539
Cashway West Inc	5211	321
Casiano Communications Inc	2721	139
Casing Associates Inc	5147	61
Casing Inc	5045	842
Casino Party Masters	7359	165
Casio America Inc	3873	2
Casio Inc	5044	5
Cask LLC	8742	432
Casket Shells Inc	3995	5
Caskey Printing Inc	2752	754
Cason Engineering Inc	3599	1154
Cason Inc	4213	2570
Caspers Co	5812	383
Caspers Ice Cream Inc	2024	44
CASPR Library Systems Inc	7372	3814
Cass Commerce Bank	6022	753
Cass Communications Management Inc	4841	64
Cass County Electric Coop	4911	332
Cass Inc	5093	47
Cass Information Systems Inc	7389	241
Cass Polymers	2821	76
Cass Polymers Of Michigan Inc	2821	134
Cass Telephone Company Inc	4813	326
Cassano's Inc	5812	273
Cassavant Machining Inc	3599	1005
Casscom Media	3695	65
Cassel Farms	5153	70
Cassens and Sons Inc	5511	822
Cassens Corp	4213	164
Cassens Transport Co	4213	137
Cassette Works	3695	68
Cassidian Communications Inc	3661	88
Cassidy Turley	6531	388
Cassling Diagnostic Imaging Inc	5047	29
Cast Iron Systems Inc	3674	161
Cast Pac Inc	7389	1498
Cast Parts Inc	3324	6
Cast Products Corp	5074	39
Cast Products Inc	3364	16
Cast Products Inc (Athens Alabama)	3365	27
Cast Software Inc	7372	1015
Cast Technologies Inc	3365	8
CAST Transportation	4213	1274
Castalloy Corp	3321	39
Cast-Crete Corp	3999	45
Castec Inc	3559	493
Castellino Electric	1731	2305
Castello Cities Internet Network	7371	1465
Castells and Asociados Advertising	7311	861
Castillo Electric LLC	1731	2032
Castine Moving and Storage	4214	20
Casting Designs Inc	3275	7
Castino Corp	3089	1421
Castle Access	7376	29
Castle and Cooke Inc	6552	38
Castle and Cooke Properties Inc	6552	232
Castle BancGroup Inc	6712	445
Castle Bank NA	6022	764
Castle Brands Inc	2085	14
Castle Cheese Inc	2022	71
Castle Communications Inc	2752	1031
Castle Computers Inc	5734	324
Castle Concrete Co	1422	38
Castle Co-Packers LLC	2086	85
Castle Dental Centers Inc	8741	106
Castle Dental Centers of Florida Inc	8021	17
Castle Dental Centers of Tennessee Inc	8021	19
Castle Group (Honolulu Hawaii)	7011	38
Castle Group Inc	6282	318
Castle Harlan Inc	6282	107
Castle Hill Productions	7819	61
Castle Industries Inc	3699	261
Castle Industries Incorporated Of California	3444	205
Castle Industries LLC	2752	806
Castle Metals	5051	123
Castle Oil Corp	5983	4
Castle Park Amusement Co	7996	23
Castle Press Inc	2752	1781
Castle Resorts and Hotels Inc	7011	36
Castle Rock Computing Inc	7379	1077
Castle Rock Electric Inc	1731	2163
Castle Rock Entertainment Inc	7812	92
Castle Rock Innovations LLC	7371	1218
Castle Solutions Inc	7371	1883
Castleberry Office Furnishings	5021	51
Castlegarde Inc	7379	1358
Castle-Pierce Corp	2752	437
Castlereagh Printcraft Inc	3555	37
Castlerock Security Inc	7381	32
Castleview Hospital LLC	8062	231
Casto and Harris Inc	2732	55
Casto Travel Inc	4724	31
Castongia's Inc	5083	96
Castor Printing Company Inc	2752	1625
Castrejon Inc	1623	687
Castriota Chevrolet Inc	5511	1017
Cast-Rite Corp	3544	34
Castrol North America Holdings Inc	5172	2
Casual Driver Leasing Services Inc	7361	387
Casual Male Retail Group Inc	5651	17
Caswell Booe	0119	4
Cat I Manufacturing Inc	3229	17
CAT Inc	4213	2407
Cat Studios	7373	1163
Cataki International Inc	3843	72
Cataldi Public Relations Inc	8743	276
Catalent Pharma Solutions Inc	2834	35
Catalina Channel Express Inc	4482	4
Catalina Communications Inc	7336	195
Catalina Finer Food Corp	2032	30
Catalina Lighting Inc	3699	20
Catalina Marketing Corp	7311	48
Catalina Restaurant Group Inc	5812	124
Catalina Tool and Mold Inc	3544	244
Catalina Yachts Inc	3732	22
Catalis Inc	7371	787
Catalogcom Inc	7379	960
Catalogs By Design	2752	1009
Catalyst Computer Services Inc	7373	1079
Catalyst Corp	7372	4590
Catalyst Development Corp	7372	2615
Catalyst Health Solutions Inc	6411	12
Catalyst Inc	7311	835
Catalyst Learning Co	4841	98
Catalyst Pharmaceutical Partners Inc	2834	439
Catalyst Semiconductor Inc	3674	133
Catalyst Technology Group Inc	7379	1362
Catalytic Products IntnlInc	3567	99
Catalytic Solutions Inc	2819	13
Catamount Constructors Inc	1542	156
Catamount Energy Corp	4911	432
Catamount Glassware Company Inc	3229	34
Catamount Resources Corp	4911	430
Catamount Software	7372	4054
Catania-Spagna Corp	2079	9
Catapult Communications Inc	7311	671
Catapult Consultants LLC	7379	396
Catapult Systems Corp	7371	575
Catapult Technology Ltd	7373	171
Cataract Eye Center	8062	236
Cataract Travel Planners Inc	4724	146
Catasys Inc	8099	113
Catawba County Board Of Education	8211	50
Catawba Sox LLC	2252	17
Catbird Networks Inc	7375	212
Catbridge Machinery LLC	3552	28
Catch and Release Inc	7694	10
Catching Fluidpower Inc	5084	230
Catching Hydraulics Company Ltd	3593	57
Caterair Holdings Corp	5812	207
CaterMate	7372	3519
Caterpillar Financial Services Corp	6159	10
Caterpillar Inc	3537	1
Caterpillar Inc Engines Div	3519	2
Caterpillar Paving Products Inc	3531	20
Caterpillar Work Tools Inc	3532	10
Caterpillar World Trading Corp	7389	512
Catfish Wholesale Inc	5146	70
Catharon Software Corp	7372	2452
Cathay Bank	6022	30
Cathay Food Corp	2099	309
Cathay General Bancorp	6712	71
Cathedral Foundation Inc	2721	347
Cathedral Press Inc	2741	374
Catherines Inc	5621	27
Catherines Stores Corp	5621	9
Cathey Associates	7336	81
Cathie's Cartage Inc	4213	3057
Catholic Charities Foundation Of Northeast Kansas	8322	65
Catholic Charities Of Santa Clara County	8322	39
Catholic Charities Of The Diocese Of Worcester	8322	108
Catholic Comprehensive Services For Children Child Center-Marygrove	8322	116
Catholic Healthcare Partners	8062	21
Catholic Order Of Foresters Inc	6311	225
Catholic Printery Inc	2759	532
Cato and Newby Inc	8743	293
Cato Corp	5621	13
Cato Drilling Co	1794	46
Catocorpcom LLC	5621	3
Catoe's Welding and Fabrication Inc	3599	1995
Caton Connector Corp	3357	68
Cat's Pajamas LLC	7371	619
Catseye Pest Control Inc	7342	59
Catskill Delaware Publications Inc	2711	843
Catskill Hudson Bank	6022	631
Catspaw Inc	7372	2194
Cattaneo Brothers Inc	2013	247
Cattaneo Electric Co	1731	1242
Cattron-Theimeg Inc	3625	78
Catv Services Inc	3663	255
Caudell's Machine and Tooling Inc	3599	1972
Caughman's Meat Plant Inc	2011	122
Cauley Detective Agency Inc	7381	33
Caulfield Associates Inc	3089	1847
Causeway Lumber Company Inc	5211	156
Causey Demgen and Moore Inc	8721	406
Causey Machine Works Inc	3599	2142
Cauttrell Enterprises Inc	3441	39
Cavaform International LLC	3544	172
Cavalier Bolt and Nut Inc	5085	456
Cavalier Homes Inc	2451	8
Cavalier Maintenance Services Inc	7349	38
Cavalier Printing Ink Company Inc	2893	21
Cavalla Inc	3544	686
Cavallo and Cavallo Inc	3599	1555
Cavalry Security Gear and System	7922	59
Cavanagh Co	2052	53
Cavanagh Law Firm	8111	381
Cavanaugh and Associates Inc	7363	339
Cavanaugh Electrical Contracting Inc	1731	534
Cavanaugh Marketing Network Inc	7311	318
Cavanaugh Press Inc	2789	24
Cavanaugh Trucking Inc	4213	2399
Cavco Industries Inc	2451	7
Cave Manufacturing Inc	3599	1491
Cavender Buick Company Inc	5511	557
Cavender Cadillac	5511	662
Cavender's Boot City	5661	10
Cavendish Kinetics Inc	3674	196
Caveo Technology Inc	7379	1558
Cavico Corp	1771	8
Cavin S Business Solutions Inc	5999	173
Cavium Inc	3674	75
Cavotec USA Inc	5082	122
Cawley Gillespie and Associates Inc	8711	518
Cawood Auto Company Inc	5511	1103
Cawy Bottling Company Inc	2086	123
C-Axis Inc	3599	1475
Caxton Printers Ltd	5192	30
Caxton-Iseman Capital Inc	6726	4
Cay Industries Inc	5943	25
Cayce Mill Supply Co	5063	238
Cayenne Express Inc	4213	2186
Caylor Industrial Sales Inc	5074	190
Caylx Software Limited Inc	5045	482
Cayman Chemical Company Inc	2834	278
Cayman Graphics	7372	1729
Cayman Manufacturing Inc	2522	48
Caymus Vineyards	2084	17
Cayuga Crushed Stone Inc	1429	19
Cayuga Lake National Bank	6021	314
Caywood Electronics Inc	3679	894

Company Name	SIC	Rank
Cazayoux Commercial Investments LLC	4619	3
CB and I SERVICES Inc	3441	230
CB and K Supply Inc	5074	79
CB and T Bank of East Alabama	6022	675
CB and T Bank of Middle Georgia	6022	630
CB Caroon Crab Company Inc	2092	79
CB Financial Services Inc	6311	204
Cb Graduation Announcements LLC	2759	303
C-B Kenworth Inc	5012	94
Cb Ram Electronics Inc	3672	478
CB Richard Ellis Group Inc	6719	24
CB Richard Ellis Inc	6531	44
CB Richard Ellis Services Inc	6531	41
CB Software Systems Inc	7379	1389
CB Technology Inc	6022	628
Cbc Corporation Business Service	7389	1153
CBC Services Inc	1623	161
CBCInnovis	7323	7
CBE Technologies Inc	7373	247
Cbeyond Inc	4813	41
C-B-Gear and Machine Inc	3599	758
Cbi Communications	4813	612
CBI Corp	7389	1969
CBI Laboratories Inc	2844	63
CBIZ Actuarial and Benefit Consultants Inc	8748	360
CBIZ ATA of Topeka LLC	7291	9
CBIZ Beatty Satchell Business Services Inc	7291	8
CBIZ Benefits and Insurance Services Inc	8741	33
CBIZ Benefits and Insurance Services of Florida Inc	8741	130
CBIZ Benefits and Insurance Services of Maryland Inc	8741	49
CBIZ Colorado Inc	8741	100
Cbiz Duitch Franklin Parks Palmer	8721	341
CBIZ Financial Solutions Inc	6282	39
CBIZ Inc	7389	55
CBIZ McClain Accounting Tax and Advisory Inc	8721	31
CBIZ Southern California Inc	8721	66
CBL and Associates Properties Inc	6798	43
Cbm Inc	1542	407
Cbm Industries Inc	5065	532
Cbmc Inc	5063	434
CBOE Holdings Inc	6231	5
CBORD Group Inc	7372	1078
Cboss Inc	7374	325
CBRE Capital Markets	6162	115
CBRE Econometric Advisors	8732	107
Cbs Builders Supply Inc	5211	175
CBS Computers Inc	7378	63
CBS Corp	4833	4
Cbs Electric Inc	1731	2099
Cbs Interactive Inc	7319	23
Cbs Manufacturing Co	3724	65
Cbs Outdoor Inc	7312	6
CBS Television Distribution	7822	3
CBS Television Network - Div	4833	5
CBSInteractive	7374	63
Cbsj Financial Corp	7322	68
CBSL Transportation Services	4213	707
CBT Direct	7372	1258
Cbx Technologies Inc	7379	924
CC Caldwell Trucking Inc	4213	2493
CC Clark Inc	2086	31
Cc Coating and Machine Inc	3469	326
Cc Daman Products Company Inc	3492	18
CC Filson Co	2326	17
CC Foods Inc	2099	185
CC Graber Co	0179	5
CC Industries Inc	3537	4
CC Mangum Inc	1611	10
CC Media Holdings Inc	4832	1
CC Myers Inc	1611	56
CC Pollen Co	2099	53
CC Software Inc	7372	1584
CC Works Inc	5023	207
Cc1 Inc	3555	92
CCA Global Partners	5023	1
CCA Industries Inc	2844	51
CCB Corp	6712	305
Ccb Credit Services Incorporated	7322	44
Ccb Packaging Inc	7389	874
CCBB Inc	5084	823
CCC Group Inc	3441	10
CCC Information Services Group Inc	7372	243
CCC Information Services Inc	7372	145
CCC Steel Inc	5051	512
CCC Technologies Inc	1731	695
CCE	7372	484
Cce Services Inc	7389	929
CCF Holding Co	6712	501
CCFNB Bancorp Inc	6022	258
CCG Systems Inc	7372	2565
CCH Legal Information Services	7389	122
CCI Manufacturing	3799	23
Cci Manufacturing Illinois Corp	5169	143
CCI Mechanical Inc	1711	44
CCI (Milwaukee Wisconsin)	7379	633
CCI Spectrum Inc	1623	624
Cci Thermal Technologies Indiana Inc	3567	88

Company Name	SIC	Rank
Ccl Container Corp	3411	15
Ccl Insertco LLC	2752	135
CCL Label Inc	2759	582
Ccn International Inc	2521	37
CCRA International	7374	45
CCS and T Inc	7374	351
CCS Computer Systems Inc	7372	4279
Ccs Labs Inc	7322	159
CCS Presentation Systems Inc	5045	108
Ccs Stateline Scale Company LLC	5046	196
Ccs Stone Inc	5032	155
CCS-Inc	3571	33
CCT Laser Services Inc	3699	275
Cct Plastics Inc	3599	1687
CCT Telecommunications Inc	4899	123
Ccw Group Pacesetter Inc	4225	31
CCX Corp	3357	57
CD Group Inc	7372	1293
CD Haugen Inc	4213	717
Cd Holdings Inc	6719	187
CD Light LLC	7372	3985
CD Moody Construction Company Inc	1542	297
Cd Pro-Power Cords Inc	5063	807
CD Solutions Inc	3695	85
CD Stampley Enterprises Inc	5192	42
Cd Technologies LLC	5065	967
CD Universe Inc	5735	13
Cd Video Manufacturing Corp	3695	60
CD Warehouse Finance Co	5735	6
CD Works	3695	102
CDB Corp	3843	53
CDB Software Inc	7372	1783
Cdc Management Co	8741	205
Cdc Pool Specialties LLC	7389	2243
Cdc Security Corp	7381	155
CDC Small Business Finance Corp	6141	61
CDC Software	7372	75
Cde Electrical Contracting Inc	1731	1531
CDE Integrated Systems Inc	7373	709
CDE Software	7372	4408
Cdex Inc	3829	491
Cdf Corp	3089	571
Cdg Holding Co	7371	1103
CDHM Advertising Inc	7311	476
Cdi Electronics Inc	3519	24
CDI Management Corp	8071	4
Cdk Enterprises LLC	3599	1643
CDL Electric Company Inc	1731	444
CDL Technology Inc	3559	323
Cdm In Home Care Services	8322	190
Cdm Machine Co	3541	234
CDM Optics Inc	3861	119
Cdm Tool and Manufacturing Company Inc	3544	253
CDO Technologies Inc	7373	80
C-Double Web Development	7379	1486
Cdp Diamond Products Inc	3541	179
CDR Associates Inc	8721	8
CD-ROM Access	5045	540
Cd-Rom-Works LLC	3695	168
CDS Analytical Inc	3826	106
Cds Consulting LLC	7379	977
CDS Engineering Inc	3674	229
CDS Ensembles Inc	2392	12
CDS Global Inc	7372	65
CDS Graphics	3695	146
CDS Market Research	8732	96
Cds - Networks and Services Inc	7373	1043
Cds Telco Inc	5065	933
Cdsnet Soft Inc	7374	138
Cdt Micrographics Inc	7373	852
Cdt Resources LLC	4813	591
CDW Corp	5961	3
CDW LLC	7372	5
Cdw Service Center D and B Ltd	5051	427
Ce Acquisition LLC	1711	230
CE and W Enterprises Inc	4213	2784
Ce De Candy Inc	2064	17
CE Electronics Inc	3679	295
CE Fleming Corp	8712	232
C-E Minerals Inc	1099	3
CE Precision Assemblies Inc	3357	62
CE Walters and Associates Inc	6282	535
CEA Global Education	8299	59
Cea Technologies Inc	3845	74
Ceam Corp	5063	739
Ceasar and Smilow LLP	8721	473
Cebtt Inc	5045	916
CEC Consultants Inc	8711	548
CEC Controls Company Inc	3823	57
CEC Elevator Cab Corp	3534	18
CEC Entertainment Inc	5812	70
Cecil Bancorp Inc	6035	121
Cecil Construction Corp	1623	660
Cecil I Walker Machinery Co	7353	7
Cecil Service Corp	6035	130
Ceco Concrete Construction Inc	1611	55
Ceco Door Products	3442	118
CECO Environmental Corp	3564	12
CECO Filters Inc	3569	117
Cecol Inc	5065	362
Cedalion Corp	7372	4223
Cedar Bluff 24 Hour Towing Inc	7549	21
Cedar Brewing Co	5813	11

Company Name	SIC	Rank
Cedar Concepts Corp	2869	99
Cedar Document Technologies Inc	7372	1062
Cedar Fair LP	7996	5
Cedar Graphics Inc	2752	170
Cedar Graphics Inc (Ronkonkoma New York)	2752	103
Cedar Grove Cheese Inc	2022	41
Cedar Grove Composting Inc	2875	6
Cedar Hill Associates Inc	6282	337
Cedar Mountain Stone Corp	1429	14
Cedar Point Communications Inc	3669	43
Cedar Rapids and Iowa City Railway Co	4011	41
Cedar Rapids Bank and Trust Co	6022	280
Cedar Rapids Truck Center Inc	5012	132
Cedar Rapids Welding Supply Inc	5169	166
Cedar Recycling Inc	5021	119
Cedar Shopping Centers Inc	6798	110
Cedar Supply Inc	5031	253
Cedar Valley Cheese Inc	2022	62
Cedar Valley Corp	1611	78
Cedar Valley Services Inc	8331	65
Cedar Valley Supply Inc	5013	309
Cedarapids Inc	3531	41
Cedarberg Industries Inc	3545	428
Cedaredge Lumber Co	5211	307
Cedarlane Natural Foods Co	2099	44
Cedaron Medical Inc	5047	202
Cedarpoint Trucking Inc	4213	2704
Cedars Mediterranean Foods Inc	5149	119
Cedarwood Construction Company Inc	8741	252
Cedes Corporation Of America	5065	820
C-Edge Software Consultants LLC	7379	1116
Cedric Hartman Inc	3645	78
Cee Kay Supply Co	5084	273
Cee Sportswear	2339	58
Cee-Bee Aviation Products	2851	181
Cee-Kay Tires and Service	5013	189
Cefaratti Investigation and Process Services Inc	7381	248
CEG Technologies	7372	3986
Cei Electric Co	1731	1367
CEI Enterprises Inc	3443	13
Cei Group Inc	6411	99
CEI West Roofing Co	1761	35
Ceiba Technologies Inc	5065	238
Ceiling Pro Of San Antonio LLC	7349	149
Ceiling Solutions	1742	21
Ceitronics Inc	1731	17
Ceiva Logic Inc	3577	233
Cejka Search Inc	8742	394
Cel Corp	7372	4188
Celadon Group Inc	4213	56
Celadon Trucking Services Inc	4213	53
Celamark Corp	3823	316
Celanese Acetate	2824	5
Celanese Chemicals - Americas	2812	3
Celanese Corp	2821	4
Celantra Management Solutions	7372	3769
Celco Tool and Engineering Inc	3544	781
Celebrate Express	5947	12
Celebrate Express Inc	5999	31
Celebration Rentals Inc	7359	265
Celebrity Series Of Boston Inc	7922	53
Celebrity Service International Inc	2721	359
Celebrity Source Inc	7389	2352
Celebrity Suppliers	7929	9
Celefex Animation and Design	7812	284
Celerant Consulting Inc	8742	49
Celerant Technology Corp	7372	985
Celergo LLC	8721	304
Celergy Networks Inc	8748	422
Celeritas Group LLC	2675	2
Celerity Group Inc	3559	28
Celerity IT LLC	8748	87
Celestar Corp	7389	872
Celestial Seasonings Inc	2099	25
Celestial Software Inc	7373	909
Celestron Acquisition LLC	3827	48
Celetron USA	3679	200
Celgene Corp	2834	18
Celina Aluminum Precision Technology Inc	3592	4
Cell Biosciences	2835	34
Cell Division	2741	70
Cell Parts Manufacturing Co	3089	1853
Cell Signaling Technology Inc	8071	37
Cell Therapeutics Inc	2834	449
Cellcomm Inc	4812	44
CELL-CON Inc	5063	158
CellCyte Genetics Corp	2834	491
Celldex Therapeutics Inc	8731	98
Cellere LLC	4813	448
Celli Trucking Co	4213	2526
Celli-Flynn Brennan Architects and Planners	8712	261
Cellit LLC	7371	518
Cello Development Corp	7371	871
Cell-O-Core Co	3089	1046
Cello-Foil Products Inc	2671	8
Cellomics Inc	7372	731
Cellone Bakery Inc	2051	139
Cellotape Inc	2759	132
Cellport Systems Inc	8731	175

Company Name	SIC	Rank
Cellsys Inc	5734	465
Celltron Inc	3679	166
Cellu Tissue Holdings Inc	2679	76
Cellular Air Inc	5999	116
Cellular Concepts II Inc	5999	260
Cellular Products Distributors	5099	127
Cellular Sales Of Kentucky	4812	103
Cellular Specialties Inc	3663	64
Cellworks International Inc	5065	410
Cellxion LLC	4812	30
Cel-Net Communications Inc	5999	96
Cels Enterprises Inc	5139	14
CEL-SCI Corp	2836	80
Celsion Corp	2834	464
Celsis Laboratory Group	8734	110
Celsius Holdings Inc	2086	103
Celsius Joint Venture A California LP	5078	40
Celtech Corp	3812	106
Celtex Industries Inc	3625	201
CEM Corp	3821	5
Cemco Electric Inc	1731	2376
Cemec Inc	3677	73
Cemen Tech Inc	3531	62
Cement Test Equipment Inc	3829	468
Cemex	3241	20
Cemex Cement Inc	3241	21
Cemex Construction Materials Inc	5032	15
Cemex Construction Materials LP	3273	23
Cemex El Paso Inc	3273	33
Cemline Corp	3639	19
Cempro Inc	2674	20
Cen-Cal Wallboard Supply Co	5032	10
Cen-Clear Child Services Inc	8322	49
Cenco Inc (New Brighton Minnesota)	3812	118
Conoor Realty Services	6531	71
Cenergy Corp	7389	259
Cenergy LLC	8742	289
Ceng Plastic Inc	3089	1538
Cengage Learning Inc	7375	5
Cenicola-Helvin Enterprises	7389	849
Cenlar Capital Corp	6712	211
Cenlar FSB	6035	91
Cenneidigh Inc	8361	78
Cenpro Services Inc	1731	680
Censor Security Inc	7381	166
Centage Corp	7372	3048
Centaur Building Services Inc	7349	56
Centaur Systems Ltd	7372	4591
Centaur Technology Inc	3674	171
Centaur Tool and Die Inc	3544	811
Centauri Laboratories LLC	8734	114
CenTauri Solutions LLC	8748	127
Centech Inc	3714	423
Centech Plastics Inc	3089	572
Centella Consulting	7373	1184
Centene Corp	6324	13
Centenial Bank (Conway Arkansas)	6022	347
Centennial Bank	7374	91
Centennial Bank (Fountain Valley California)	6021	328
Centennial Bank of Mountain View Ar	6022	624
Centennial Bank of Omaha	6712	718
Centennial Bindery Inc	2789	29
Centennial Broadcasting Ii LLC	4832	112
Centennial HealthCare Corp	8051	15
Centennial Lending LLC	7389	2224
Centennial Plastics Inc	3084	26
Centennial Technologies Inc	3544	484
Centennial Ventures	6799	211
Centent Co	3571	176
Center Bancorp Inc	6712	271
Center Brothers Inc	1751	3
Center Capital Corp	6153	40
Center For Alternative Sentencing And Employment	8331	87
Center for Applied Sciences	8093	56
Center For Business Innovation Inc	5044	88
Center For Creative Leadership Inc	8299	19
Center For Disability Rights Inc	8322	35
Center For International Education Inc	7361	243
Center For Orthopedic And Research Excellence Inc	8011	124
Center For Science In The Public Interest	2741	122
Center For Tribology Inc	3577	500
Center Industries Corp	3469	71
Center Line Mold and Tool Inc	3544	887
Center Line Technologies Inc	1731	853
Center Line Tool Inc	7389	2430
Center Of Financial Technologies Inc	7371	900
Center Point Ambulance Services	5012	197
Center The Community Medical	8062	81
Centerbank (Milford Ohio)	6022	502
Centerbank of Jacksonville NA	6035	202
CenterBeam Inc	7379	127
Centercomm Corp	3571	122
Centerfield Technology Corp	7372	2121
Centerline Capital Group	6798	11
Centerline Holding Co	6719	95
Centerline Holdings LLC	7999	22
Centerline Manufacturing Ltd	3599	664
Centermark Technologies Inc	7371	1862
CenterOne Financial Services LLC	6141	22
Centerplate Inc	5812	75
CenterPoint Energy Inc	4911	24
Centerpoint ManufacturingColnc	3599	821
Centerpoint Marketing Inc	3993	47
CenterPoint Properties Corp	6798	151
Centerpointe Electric LLC	1731	2113
Centerprise Information Solutions Inc	7371	1028
Centerre Construction Inc	1542	416
CenterSoft Corp	7372	4346
CenterState Bank Central Florida NA (Winter Haven Florida)	6035	154
Centerstate Banks Inc	6021	66
Centerstone Software	7372	189
Centex Commercial Development LP	6552	91
Centex Corp	1531	3
Centex Development Company LP	6552	53
Centex Financial Services Inc	6162	13
Cen-Tex Fire Protection	5087	155
Centex Homes	1531	1
Centex Homes Realty Co	6531	361
Centex Multi-Family Development Co	6552	92
Centex Pipe and Equipment Inc	7359	117
Centex Television LP	4833	184
Centier Bank	6022	106
Centimark Corp	1761	1
Centime Industries Inc	5074	156
Centive Inc	7372	167
Cento Fine Foods	5141	81
Centoco Manufacturing Corp	3088	19
Centon Electronics Inc	3577	191
Centorr-Vacuum Industries Inc	3567	22
Centra Credit Union	6061	45
Centra Credit Union (New Albany Indiana)	6061	56
Centra Inc	4213	103
Centra Technology	7373	61
Centracare Clinic	8011	43
Central Air Conditioning Company Inc	1711	86
Central Air Freight Services	4213	2515
Central Airmotive Inc	5088	114
Central Alabama Electric Coop	4911	429
Central Alarm Signal Inc	7382	166
Central Aluminum Company LLC	3354	43
Central American Printing Inc	2759	300
Central American Transportation and Distribution	4213	489
Central Arizona Bank	6022	696
Central Arizona Farming Inc	6799	352
Central Arkansas Auto Auction Inc	5012	199
Central Armature Works Inc	7629	15
Central Atlantic Toyota Distributors Inc	5012	11
Central Audio Visual Equipment Inc	5043	44
Central Audio Visual Inc	5731	26
Central Bag Co	5113	42
Central Bancompany Inc	6712	45
Central Bancorp Inc	6712	468
Central Bancshares Inc (Golden Valley Minnesota)	6712	732
Central Bancshares Inc (Lexington Kentucky)	6712	372
Central Bank and Trust Co	6022	144
Central Bank and Trust (Lander Wyoming)	6022	684
Central Bank (Jefferson City Missouri)	6022	157
Central Baptist Breast Imaging	3671	19
Central Baptist Hospital Foundation Inc	8069	15
Central Beef Industry LLC	2011	72
Central Bindery and Looseleaf Co	2782	74
Central Bindery Co	2789	49
Central Blower Company Inc	3564	144
Central Blueprint Co	2752	1017
Central Boston Elder Services Inc	8322	28
Central Builder Supplies Of Gainesville Inc	5211	289
Central Building Maintenance Inc	7349	505
Central Building Supply Inc	5211	295
Central Business Communications Inc	1731	1692
Central Business Equipment Co	5021	78
Central California Container Manufacturing Inc	3089	1676
Central California Electronics Inc	5065	661
Central California Traction Co	4013	4
Central Carolina Hosiery Inc	2251	9
Central Carolina Products Inc	3089	408
Central Cass County Fire Protection District	7389	1836
Central Chevrolet Co (Jonesboro Arkansas)	5511	1076
Central Chevrolet Inc	5511	531
Central City Concern	8361	15
Central City Productions Inc	7812	88
Central City Scale Inc	5046	188
Central Coast Electronics Inc	1731	2512
Central Coast Wine Warehouse	2084	81
Central Coating Company Inc	1742	16
Central Command Inc	7372	115
Central Communications Corp	5731	225
Central Communications Credit Union	6062	54
Central Communications Installers Inc	1731	2216
Central Communications Systems Inc	5063	833
Central Concrete Corp	3272	15
Central Concrete Supply Company Inc	3273	47
Central Connecticut Co-Operative Farmers Association Inc	5191	133
Central Dairy Co	2026	61
Central Dakota Frontier Com	5171	83
Central Delivery Service of Wash	4213	674
Central Desktop Inc	7373	664
Central Dispatch Inc	4213	2777
Central Distributors Inc	5181	70
Central Dynamic Manufacturing Inc	3599	1054
Central Electric Company Of Tulsa Inc	1731	1071
Central Electric Coop	4911	394
Central Electric Cooperative Inc	4911	204
Central Electric LLC	1731	962
Central Electrical Service Corp	1731	1035
Central Electrical Systems Inc	1731	1440
Central Energy Partners LP	5172	147
Central Extrusion Die Company Inc	3544	52
Central Fabrication Inc	3842	197
Central Federal Corp	6712	581
Central Fire Protection Inc	1711	224
Central Florida Alarm Services Inc	1731	1950
Central Florida Educators' Federal Credit Union	6061	34
Central Florida Postal Credit Union	6061	132
Central Florida Publishing Inc	2711	790
Central Flying Service Inc	5599	13
Central Ford Center Inc	5511	525
Central Freight Lines Inc	4213	57
Central Garden and Pet Co	5199	2
Central Georgia Electric Membership Co-op	4911	174
Central Grain Co	5153	114
Central Grocers Co-op Inc	5141	27
Central Group Management Co	8741	208
Central Gulf Lines Inc	4412	24
Central Holidays	4724	49
Central House Technologies	5045	809
Central Illinois Manufacturing Co	3599	439
Central Illinois Steel Co	5051	131
Central Indiana Hardware Co	5072	57
Central Industrial Supply Inc	3599	1307
Central Industries Inc (Lafayette Louisiana)	1389	49
Central Ink Corp	2893	13
Central Investment LLC	2086	28
Central Iowa Power Coop	4911	278
Central Kentucky FSB	6035	229
Central Kentucky Savings and Loan Service Corp	6021	338
Central Ky Tool and Engineering Corp	3544	451
Central Leasing Inc	7353	57
Central Lock and Hardware Supply Company Inc	5072	166
Central/Long-Mcgehee Inc	1731	1687
Central Louisiana Communication	4813	627
Central Louisiana Electric Company Inc	4911	63
Central Machine Works Inc	3599	2258
Central Machining and Pump Repair Inc	3599	1308
Central Maine Cleaning Inc	7349	362
Central Maine Power Co	4911	107
Central Maintenance And Welding Inc	3443	84
Central Management Company Inc	8051	10
Central Management Inc	6531	149
Central Mass Auto Auction Inc	5012	123
Central Mechanical Systems Inc	1711	246
Central Medical Equipment Co	7352	30
Central Michigan Newspapers	2711	929
Central Milling LLC	2041	36
Central Mississippi Medical Center	8011	26
Central Missouri Agriservice LLC	2875	5
Central Missouri Electric Cooperative Inc	4911	514
Central Moloney Inc	3612	4
Central Motor Parts Corp	5013	250
Central Motors	5012	196
Central Moving and Storage	4213	3083
Central Moving Systems Inc	4213	1806
Central Mutual Insurance Co	6331	238
Central National Bank and Trust Co	6021	117
Central National-Gottesman Inc	5113	2
Central Natural Resources Inc	6792	10
Central Nebraska Auto Supply	5013	366
Central Nebraska Implement Inc	5083	178
Central Nebraska Packing Inc	2011	131
Central New York Business Systems Inc	5112	97
Central New York Regional Transportation Authority	4111	8
Central Newspapers Inc	2711	26
Central Office Systems Corp	5943	37
Central Ohio Graphics Inc	2752	788
Central Oil Company Inc	5172	123
Central Oil of Virginia Corp	5172	134
Central Optical Inc	3851	78
Central Optical Laboratories Inc	5049	127
Central Pacific Bank	6022	29
Central Pacific Financial Corp	6712	130
Central Paper Stock Company Inc	7389	1036
Central Parking Corp	7521	1
Central Parking System Inc	7521	12
Central Pattern Co	3543	49
Central Payment	7389	331
Central Peninsula General Hospital Inc	8062	199
Central Penn Transportation Inc	4213	576
Central Pennsylvania Transportation	4213	1156
Central Pet Supply	5199	4

Company Name	SIC	Rank
Central Power Electric Coop	4911	358
Central Precast Concrete Inc	3272	16
Central Pre-Mix Concrete Co	3273	30
Central Pre-Mix Prestress Co	3272	82
Central Printing Co	2752	1641
Central Printing Corp	2752	727
Central Products Inc	5087	151
Central Record Publications	2711	752
Central Refrigerated Service Inc	4213	954
Central Research Laboratories	3569	141
Central Resources Inc	1382	62
Central Rolled Thread Die Co	3545	51
Central Rubber and Plastics Inc	3069	248
Central Securities Corp	6211	94
Central Security Life Insurance Corp	6311	263
Central Security Systems Inc	5999	169
Central Service and Supply Inc	5084	768
Central Shippee Inc	5199	105
Central Sierra Electric Company Inc	1731	1463
Central Sierra Moldings Inc	3089	1829
Central Solutions Inc	2844	151
Central South Distribution Inc	5099	68
Central South Music Inc	5735	15
Central Sprinkler Corp	3569	26
Central State Electric Inc	1731	1122
Central State Enterprises Inc	3599	1047
Central States Coca-Cola (Springfield Illinois)	5149	61
Central States Electric Inc	1731	1640
Central States Fabricating Corp	3441	284
Central States Health and Life Company of Omaha	6311	238
Central States Non-Stock Coop	4212	67
Central Station Inc	5065	328
Central Steel and Wire Co	5051	28
Central Supply Company Inc	5031	176
Central Systems and Security Service	7382	168
Central Tape and Label Co	2752	1484
Central Technologies Inc	7372	2309
Central Texas Electric Cooperative Inc	4911	309
Central Texas Printing Inc	2752	1282
Central Textiles Inc	2261	12
Central Transit Inc	5032	194
Central Transport Co	4213	2349
Central Transportation Systems Inc	4214	11
Central Trucking Inc	4213	409
Central Trust Co	6712	512
Central Valley Bank	6035	232
Central Valley Bank NA	6021	385
Central Valley Builders Supply	5211	30
Central Valley Community Bancorp	6022	209
Central Valley Comunity Bank	6022	324
Central Valley Coop	5541	49
Central Valley Machine Inc	3599	462
Central Valley Meat Company Inc	2011	51
Central Valley Towing Inc	7549	16
Central Van Lines Inc	4213	2573
Central Vending Service Inc	5046	224
Central Vermont Public Service Corp	4911	122
Central Virginia Area Agency On Aging Inc	8322	195
Central Virginia Bank	6022	525
Central Virginia Bankshares Inc	6712	506
Central Virginia Maintenance Inc	1623	491
Central Washington Grain Growers Inc	0111	1
Central Welding and Industrial Supply Company Inc	5084	531
Central Wholesale Supply Corp	5039	8
Central Wisconsin Publications	2711	263
Central Woodwork Of Nashville Inc	5031	76
Centralia Ford Lincoln-Mercury Inc	5511	1162
Centraliant Inc	7371	1788
Centralite Systems Inc	3648	63
Centramark America Inc	5065	728
Centre Communications Inc	5731	102
Centre Partners Management LLC	6799	221
Centrelink Insurance and Financial Services	7389	1079
CentrePath Network Inc	7372	464
Centrex International LLC	3599	2155
Centrex Plastics LLC	3089	497
Centric Software Inc	7372	980
Centrifugal and Mechanical Industries	3567	43
Centrifugal Services Inc	3532	46
Centrifuge Systems Inc	7371	1398
Centrilift	3625	11
Centrix Inc	3843	25
Centro Inc	3089	77
Centro LLC	7311	152
Centro Watt	6531	116
Centroid Corp	3625	182
Centrome Inc	2087	62
Centron Data Services Inc	2759	261
Centron Industries Inc	3663	139
Centron International Inc	3089	366
Centron Software Technologies Inc	2741	271
Centrue Financial Corp	6021	95
Centrum Management LLC	8741	135
Centum Inc	7379	944
Centura Health at Home	8082	17
Centuria Corp	7379	261
Centurian Surplus Inc	5045	600
Centurion Alarm Services Inc	7382	185
Centurion Group Inc	7349	77
Centurion Non Destructive Testing Inc	3825	292
Centurion Products Inc	3272	53
Centurum Inc	8731	118
Century 21 Evans Realtors	6531	231
Century 21 Inc	5311	36
Century 21 Real Estate Corp	6794	1
Century Air Conditioning Supply Inc	5075	12
Century Aluminum Co	3334	6
Century Aluminum of West Virginia Inc	3339	7
Century Bancorp Inc	6712	164
Century Bank FSB	6035	163
Century Casinos Inc	7993	19
Century Companies Inc	1611	112
Century Consultants Ltd	7372	3482
Century Conveyor Service Inc	3535	81
Century Court Reporters Inc	7338	23
Century Design Inc	3559	353
Century Die Co	3544	131
Century Distribution Systems Inc	7372	1943
Century Drill and Tool Company Inc	3546	30
Century Employees' Savings Fund Credit Union	6061	157
Century Engineering Inc	8711	409
Century Equipment Inc	5084	97
Century Everglades LLC	5211	157
Century Fasteners Corp	5065	92
Century Flooring Company LLC	2426	7
Century Geophysical Corp	1382	61
Century Homebuilders LLC	1521	38
Century Industries Corp	2952	9
Century Kentucky Inc	3353	4
Century Lines Inc	4213	1251
Century LLC	5091	16
Century Manufacturing Inc	3089	357
century Marketing Solutions	2752	755
Century Metal Parts Corp	3663	207
Century Mold and Tool Co	7389	1983
Century Mold Company Inc	3089	331
Century Molded Plastics Inc	3089	1250
Century Mortgage	6162	98
Century National Bank (Zanesville Ohio)	6035	137
Century Park Capital Partners	6799	222
Century Park Pictures Corp	7819	6
Century Payments Inc	7389	524
Century Plastics And Engineering Inc	3089	1712
Century Publishing	2759	575
Century Service Systems Inc	7623	5
Century Services Inc	4213	2139
Century Software Inc (Salt Lake City Utah)	7372	2406
Century Sports Inc	5091	46
Century Stair Company Inc	1751	7
Century Steel LLC	5051	63
Century Steel Products Inc	3441	246
Century Theaters	7832	12
Century Tool And Design Inc	3545	353
Century Tool and Gage Co	3544	139
Century Tool Company Inc	3544	826
Century Tool Inc	3599	700
Century Travel Inc	4724	45
Century Tubes Inc	5051	436
Century Vintage Homes	1531	53
CenturyLink	4813	8
CenturyTel Interactive	7375	217
CenturyTel of Washington Inc	4813	31
Conveo Inc	2677	1
CEO Venture Fund	6799	266
Ceon Corp	7371	612
Cephalon Inc	2834	20
Cephas Holding Corp	7371	1911
Cepheid	3826	11
Ceprint Solutions Inc	2752	627
Cequent Performance Products	3799	9
Ceradyne Inc	3999	10
Ceramco Inc	3469	266
CeraMem Separations Inc	3569	261
Cerami and Associates	8711	392
Ceramic Color And Chemical Manufacturing Co	2816	13
Ceramic Industries Inc	1321	6
Ceramic Magnetics Inc	3264	18
Ceramic Tech Inc	3599	1378
Ceramic Technics Ltd	5032	128
Ceramic To Metal Seals Inc	3679	722
Ceramica Italiana Center Inc	5032	160
Ceramo Company Inc	3269	15
Ceram-Traz Corp	2851	85
Cerasis Inc	7372	821
Ceratizit - Michigan Corp	3545	130
Cerbaco Ltd	3599	2065
Cerberus Capital Management LP	6211	43
Ceregene Inc	8731	248
Cerenzia Foods Inc	5149	133
Cereplast Inc	2821	139
Ceres Solutions LLP	5191	15
Cereus Graphics Inc	2752	789
Cerex Advanced Fabrics Inc	2297	6
Cerexagri Inc	2879	6
Cerida Investment Corp	7389	1019
Ceridian Benefits Services Inc	6411	126
Ceridian Corp	7374	13
Ceridian Small Business Solutions Div	8721	73
Cerimon Pharmaceuticals Inc	8731	255
Cerious Software Inc	7372	4409
CERIS / NPIRS	7373	407
Cerner BeyondNow Inc	7372	2045
Cerner Corp	7373	11
Cernium Corp	7372	1280
Ceroni Piping Co	1623	162
Cerreta Candy Company Inc	2064	86
Cersosimo Lumber Company Inc	2421	35
Certain Software Inc	7372	898
CertainTeed Corp	2952	2
Certeon Inc	5045	234
Certified Ad Services	2752	128
Certified Alarm Company Of Alabama Inc	7382	127
Certified Alarm Technician	5063	498
Certified Associates Inc	7379	227
Certified Computer Service Inc	7379	1243
Certified Credit Reporting Inc	7323	34
Certified Cylinders Inc	5085	409
Certified Enameling Inc	3479	40
Certified Environmental Services Inc	1623	248
Certified Fabricators Inc	3769	11
Certified Fire Protection Inc	1711	231
Certified Freight Lines Inc	4213	844
Certified Grinding and Machine Inc	7389	2308
Certified Heat Treating Inc	3398	24
Certified Maintenance Services Inc	7349	317
Certified Management Software Inc	7372	2444
Certified Metals Services	3599	1520
Certified Safety Manufacturing Inc	3842	151
Certified Slings Inc	5084	334
Certified Stainless Service Inc	3443	74
Certified Temporary Services Inc	7363	57
Certified Testing Laboratories Inc	8734	59
Certified Thermoplastics Inc	3082	37
Certified Vacations Group Inc	4725	2
Certified Van Service Inc	4213	2116
CertiPay America LLC	8721	234
Certis USA LLC	5191	90
Certol International LLC	2841	37
Certpoint Systems Inc	2741	82
Certus Software Inc	7371	373
Cerulean Companies Inc	6321	31
Cerus Corp	3841	128
Cerylion Inc	7371	774
Ces Computers Inc	7378	34
Ces Industries Inc	3699	171
Ces Mail Communications Inc	7331	111
CES Security Inc	7381	56
CES Wireless Technologies Corp	3663	218
Cesar Castillo Inc	5122	33
Cesaroni Technology Inc	3483	6
Cesco Chemicals Inc	2819	137
Cessco Inc	5082	172
Cessna Aircraft Co	3721	5
CET Engineering Services	8711	428
Cetan Corp	7379	577
Cetc Inc	8331	239
Cetec Automation Inc	7372	3257
Cetek Inc	3299	14
Ceteris Inc	8748	242
Ceto and Associates	8742	379
Cetylite Industries Inc	2834	388
CEVA Inc	3674	151
Ceven Corp	5045	383
Cf and I Steel LP	3441	34
CF and S Tank And Equipment Co	1389	64
CF Haglin Sons	1541	275
CF Industries Holdings Inc	2873	2
CF Jameson and Company Inc	2851	174
CF Maier Composites Inc	2655	15
CF Martin and Company Inc	3931	6
Cf Metals LLC	3599	1737
CF Napa Design Inc	7336	123
CF Peters Corp	2741	340
CF Sauer Company Inc	2079	4
CF Schwartz Motor Company Inc	5511	1157
CF Systems Inc	5065	987
Cfan Co	3724	37
CFC Data Corp	7374	133
CFC International Inc	2891	18
CFC Transportation Inc	4213	1252
CFD Research Corp	7372	732
CFG Community Bank	6035	211
Cfhs Holdings Inc	6719	109
CFI Delivery Service	7389	1676
CFI Inc	5211	325
CFI Of Wisconsin Inc	2023	8
CFM Inc	7372	3987
Cfm International Inc	3724	56
CFM Strategic Communications Inc	8743	151
CFM/VR-Tesco Inc	1711	162
CFN Services Inc	4899	54
CFO Selections LLC	8742	576
CFOToday	8721	476
Cfpg Ltd	3261	4
CFS Bancorp Inc	6712	288
Cfs Forming Structure Company Inc	3272	105
Cfs Tax Software	7372	2502
cfSOFTWARE Inc	7372	3242
CG Automation And Fixture Inc	3544	596
CG Editorial	2721	92
Cg Electrical Services Inc	1731	1693
CG Power System USA Inc	3612	12

Company Name	SIC	Rank
CG Railway Inc	4011	12
CG Schmidt Inc	1541	69
CGA Associates Inc	6411	241
CGAP Software Inc	7372	1404
CGF Design	5063	738
Cgi Interactive Communication Inc	7336	160
Cgi International LLC	5085	261
CGI North America	2752	31
Cgmp Validation LLC	8731	223
Cgr Products Inc	3053	37
CGR/seven	7361	248
C-Graphic LLC	2752	295
CGS Industries Inc	2321	8
Cgs Machine and Tool Inc	3544	700
CGS Technology Associates Co	7372	3520
Cgt Enterprise Inc	7377	26
CGTech Inc	7372	1368
C-Gull Technologies Inc	7373	491
CH Attick Electric Inc	1731	1337
CH Briggs Hardware Co	5072	26
CH Dean and Associates Inc	6282	347
CH Electric Co	1731	1481
CH Energy Group Inc	4931	34
CH Grinding Inc	3599	1891
Ch Holdings USA Inc	1793	6
CH Morris Company Inc	5013	221
CH Products	3577	181
CH Robinson International Inc	4213	15
CH Robinson Worldwide Inc	4731	3
C-H Tool and Die	3423	85
CH2M Hill Companies Ltd	8711	6
CH2M Hill Inc (Bellevue Washington)	8711	79
CH2M Hill Industrial Design Corp	8741	23
CH2M HILL Managed Services	7375	80
Chaash Inc	7371	1456
Chace Productions Inc	7819	71
ChaCha Search Inc	7375	88
Chad Therapeutics Inc	3842	149
Chadbourne and Parke LLP	8111	108
Chadco Enterprises	3449	19
Chadderton Trucking Inc	4213	2642
Chaddock	8093	30
Chaddsford Winery Ltd	5921	17
Chadmar Group	6552	239
Chadrad Communications Inc	4832	289
Chadwick and Associates Management Systems Inc	7372	4174
Chadwick Electric Inc	1731	2407
Chadwick-BaRoss Inc	5082	20
Chadwick's of Boston	5961	15
Chaffe McCall LLP	8111	390
Chaffee and Partners	7311	862
Chaffey Joint Union High School District	8211	83
Chagrin Consulting Services Inc	8742	701
Chain Electric Co	1731	159
Chain Industries Inc	3324	20
Chain N Fantasia Inc	5094	38
Chain System Corparation	7371	1131
Chair Dancing International Inc	7812	225
Chair Place	5021	179
Chairmasters Inc	2521	39
Chalet Cheese Coop	2022	76
Challenge Dairy Products Inc	5143	7
Challenge Graphics Inc	2752	1466
Challenge Graphics Services Inc	2752	648
Challenge Industries Inc	8331	132
Challenge Machinery Co	3554	15
Challenge Manufacturing Co	3465	9
Challenge Park Xtreme LLC	7999	68
Challenge Printing Company Inc	2752	80
Challenge Publications Inc	2721	404
Challenge Tool and Manufacturing Incorporated	3631	12
Challenger Corp	7372	2836
Challenger Lifts Inc	3569	77
Challenger Minerals Inc	1381	31
Chalmers and Kubeck	7699	13
Chamber Data Systems Inc	7372	4450
Chamberlain Hrdlicka White Williams and Aughtry	8111	307
Chamberlain Machine Inc	3599	774
Chamberlin and Barclay Inc	2873	27
Chambers Communications Corp	4841	72
Chambers Gasket and Manufacturing Co	3053	70
Chambers Group	7311	840
Chambers Leasing Systems Inc	4213	1575
Chambersburg Waste Paper Company Inc	5093	130
Chambord Et Cie SARL	2085	27
Chameleon Color Cards Ltd	3993	119
Chamlian Enterprises Inc	5093	56
Chamness Relocation Services Inc	7389	1454
Champ Inc	5065	974
Champ Printing Company Inc	2752	763
CHAMP Software Inc	7372	2949
Champ Systems Inc	7372	2608
Champagne Metals LLC	5051	290
Champaign Landmark Inc	5153	21
Champaign Telephone Co	5999	92
Champion Air Compressors	3563	22
Champion Aluminum Corp	3442	73
Champion Awards Inc	2759	289

Company Name	SIC	Rank
Champion Bus Inc	3713	26
Champion Chemical CoOf Calif	5169	180
Champion Cleaning Systems Inc	7349	446
Champion Communication Services Inc	4899	240
Champion Computer Corp	5045	121
Champion Crane Rental Inc	7353	73
Champion Die Inc	3544	592
Champion Directories Inc	2741	382
Champion Enterprises Inc	2451	2
Champion Envelope Corporation-West	2677	3
Champion Fabricating And Supply Co	5039	28
Champion Fasteners Inc	3451	89
Champion Ford Katy	5511	833
Champion Ford Lincoln Mercury	5511	827
Champion Gasket and Rubber Inc	3053	135
Champion Hi-Tech Manufacturing Inc	3053	80
Champion Home Builders Inc	1521	46
Champion Industrial Contractors Inc	1711	164
Champion Industries Inc	2759	21
Champion Industries Inc (Winston-Salem North Carolina)	3632	5
Champion International Moving Ltd	7389	1382
Champion Lumber Co	5211	57
Champion Mortgage Co	6162	11
Champion Opco LLC	3089	92
Champion Optical Network Engineering LLC	5049	94
Champion Packaging and Distribution Inc	2842	28
Champion Publications Of Chino Inc	2711	822
Champion Solutions Group Inc	3577	208
Champion Steel Of Central Florida Corp	5051	270
Champion Systems	7371	1838
Champion Systems Corp	3577	297
Champion Technologies Inc	2819	3
Champion Toyota	5511	410
Champion Toyota of Corpus Christi	5511	164
Champion Visions World Inc	3695	118
Champion Window Company Of Kansas City Inc	3442	136
Champion Window Company Of Toledo	5211	227
Champion Window Inc	3442	34
Champions Life Insurance Co	6311	249
Champions Oncology Inc	2836	56
Champions Printing and Publishing Inc	2741	371
Championship Group Inc	7941	36
Champlain Beef Company Inc	5147	146
Champlain Cable Corp	3357	34
Champlain Chocolate Company Inc	2066	19
Champlain Software Inc	7372	3876
Champlin/Haupt Architects	8712	125
Champps Entertainment Inc	5812	163
CHAMPS Software Inc	7372	3521
Chan and Fung's Hardware Inc	5046	102
Chan SmartWare Inc	7336	176
Chance Rides Manufacturing Inc	3599	156
Chancery Resources Inc	1499	10
Chandler Construction Services Inc	1623	260
Chandler Ehrlich and Company Inc	7311	351
Chandler Electric Inc	1731	2044
Chandler Equipment Co	3713	49
Chandler Foods Inc	2013	156
Chandler Manufacturing Inc	3533	94
Chandler Materials Co	3271	19
Chandler Signs LP LLP	3993	34
Chandler Systems Inc	5074	116
Chanel Inc	2844	23
Chaney Enterprises LP	3273	48
Chaney Lumber Company Inc	5031	404
Change Parts Inc	3569	170
Change Point Inc	8093	40
Change Sciences Group Inc	7379	1560
Changemyratecom	6331	370
Changing World Technologies Inc	2999	8
ChangingOurWorldcom	7375	66
Channel 38 Christian Television	4833	255
Channel 8 Wpsj Tv	4833	252
Channel Electric Inc	1731	1379
Channel Fish Company Inc	2048	102
Channel Group Inc	5045	1040
Channel Industries Inc	3264	7
Channel Intelligence Inc	4813	193
Channel Manufacturing Inc	2499	61
Channel Marketing Corp	8742	220
Channel Methods Partners LLC	7389	1111
Channel Microwave Corp	3679	559
Channel Prime Alliance Inc	5162	47
Channel Products Inc	3822	24
Channel Publishing Ltd	2731	332
Channel Three Productions	4833	176
Channel Trend Inc	7372	4492
Channel Way Industries Inc	5063	454
ChannelinxCom Inc	7371	665
Channell Commercial Corp	3669	32
Channellock Inc	3423	20
Channel-Track and Tube-Way Industries Inc	5251	29
Channing Bete Company Inc	2731	103
Chansen Publishing Inc	2721	349
Chant Engineering Company Inc	3829	201
Chantilly Crushed Stone Inc	3281	27
Chantilly Printing and Graphics Inc	2752	1816
Chantland-Pvs Co	3535	46

Company Name	SIC	Rank
Chaparral City Water Co	4941	59
Chaparral Communications Inc	3663	48
Chaparral Distributing LLC	5078	26
Chaparral Technologies Inc	5084	236
Chapel Hill Residential Retirement Center Inc	8361	28
Chapin and Bangs Co	5051	206
Chapin Manufacturing Inc	3499	38
Chapin Watermatics Inc	3052	12
Chapman and Cutler	8111	94
Chapman Audio Systems	3651	242
Chapman Automotive Group LLC	5511	681
Chapman Chevrolet Isuzu	5511	63
Chapman Corp (Washington Pennsylvania)	8711	29
Chapman Ford Lincoln Mercury Nissan	5511	919
Chapman Ford of Lancaster	5511	743
Chapman Ford Sales Inc	5511	802
Chapman Grading and Concrete Company Inc	1611	223
Chapman Homes Inc	1521	64
Chapman Inc	5172	107
Chapman/Leonard Studio Equipment Inc	7819	31
Chapman Lumber Company Inc	5031	237
Chapman Williams International Inc	7361	324
Chapman's Las Vegas Dodge	5511	237
Chappell Graphics	7374	412
Chappell Steel Company Inc	5051	407
Chapter 13 Trustee	7389	1541
Chapter 2 Inc	3599	1085
Chapura Inc	7372	3504
Charco Inc	1389	50
Chardan Corp	3944	41
Chardon Tool and Supply Company Inc	3545	147
Charfen Institute	8742	407
Chargar Corp	5169	173
Chariot Cartage Inc	4213	3014
Chariot Eagle Inc	3792	18
Chariot Software Group	7372	4280
Charisma Brands LLC	3942	18
Charismac Engineering Inc	7371	1298
Charity Auction Services LLC	7389	1549
Charl Industries Inc	3599	1043
Charlene Palmer	4813	756
Charles A Gaetano Construction Corp	1541	185
Charles A Rogers Enterprises Inc	3469	238
Charles And Colvard Ltd	3911	38
Charles and Vinzant Construction Company LLC	1542	421
Charles Bailey Trucking Inc	4213	2295
Charles Blalock and Sons Inc	1611	113
Charles Bond Co	3566	44
Charles Brewer E D M Inc	3089	389
Charles C Brandt Construction Co	1542	224
Charles C Hart Seed Co	0181	20
Charles C Parks Company Inc	5141	159
Charles C Thomas Publisher	2731	303
Charles Costa Inc	3599	2399
Charles D Goodwin Inc	4213	1519
Charles D Owen Manufacturing Co	2221	19
Charles David Of California	5139	10
Charles Dolce Inc	7311	918
Charles Dunn Co	6531	55
Charles E Crowe and Son Inc	4213	1761
Charles E Groff and Sons Inc	4213	2499
Charles E Jarrell Contracting Company Inc	1711	98
Charles E Larson and Sons Inc	3462	46
Charles E Smith Residential Realty Inc	6531	87
Charles F Day and Associates LLC	8731	213
Charles F Evans Company Inc	1761	22
Charles F Shiels and Company Inc	5031	352
Charles G Lawson Trucking	4213	300
Charles Gabus Ford Inc	5511	340
Charles H Parks and Company Inc	2092	100
Charles Holston Inc	1311	137
Charles Inc	2512	57
Charles J Miller	1794	26
Charles Jacquin Et Cie Inc	2084	19
Charles Kessler and Associates	7371	1928
Charles Komar and Sons Inc	2341	3
Charles L Marvin and Company PC	8721	131
Charles Loomis Inc	3646	70
Charles M Shultz Creative Associates Inc	7336	234
Charles Machine Inc	3599	966
Charles McMurray Co	5072	50
Charles Meisner Inc	3544	735
Charles Norris	7389	2407
Charles P Blouin Inc	1711	120
Charles Pankow Builders Ltd	1542	123
Charles Ritter Company Inc	5712	104
Charles River Analytics Inc	7371	277
Charles River Associates Inc	8111	39
Charles River BRF Inc	5199	76
Charles River Broadcasting Inc	4832	72
Charles River Laboratories International Inc	2836	4
Charles River Malvern	8734	63
Charles River Systems Inc	7372	273
Charles Rose Architects	8712	286
Charles Ross and Son Co	3443	109
Charles Ryan Associates Inc	8743	38

Company Name	SIC	Rank
Charles S Pefley And Associates Realtors	6552	129
Charles Sadek Import Company Inc	5023	24
Charles Schwab Corp	6211	2
Charles Skinner Co	6552	281
Charles Stark Draper Laboratory Inc	8734	2
Charles Tombras Advertising	7311	196
Charles Town Races and Slots Inc	7948	12
Charles W Carter Co-Hawaii Inc	5013	159
Charles W Davidson Co	6552	74
Charles W Weaver Manufacturing Company Inc	3499	59
Charles Watkins Automobiles Inc	5012	131
Charlesbank Capital Partners LLC	6798	113
Charlesbridge Publishing Inc	2741	276
Charlesson LLC	2834	403
Charleston Area Senior Citizens Service Inc	8322	242
Charleston Lincoln Mercury Inc	5511	1168
Charleston Metal Products Inc	3451	22
Charleston Steel And Metal Co	3341	27
Charleston Stone Co	1422	32
Charlie Baucom Inc	4213	2370
Charlie Brown's Goodtime Travel	4724	109
Charlie Chan Printing Inc	2752	1784
Charlie Mann Electric Inc	1731	1118
Charlie Thomas Ford Ltd	5511	60
Charlie's RV and Camping Center Inc	5561	22
Charlies Specialties Inc	2052	47
Charloma Inc	3088	4
Charlotte Aircraft Corp	5088	110
Charlotte Broadcasting LLC	4832	38
Charlotte County Mining and Material Inc	1442	79
Charlotte Fire Department Credit Union	6062	102
Charlotte Instyle Inc	1423	6
Charlotte Pipe and Foundry Co	3084	5
Charlotte Postal Credit Union	6062	53
Charlotte Russe Holding Inc	5621	14
Charlotte Scott	7389	1362
Charlotte Sound and Visual Systems Inc	1731	2240
Charlotte Trimming Company Inc	2253	18
Charlotte Truck Center Inc	5012	66
Charlton Precision Products Inc	3643	159
Charlton Research Co	8732	127
Charm Sciences Inc	2899	95
Charmac Inc	3799	26
Charmant Inc	5048	6
Charmant USA	5048	1
Charmay Inc	7349	184
Charmer Sunbelt Group	6719	28
Charming Shoppes Inc	5621	4
Char-Nor Enterprises Inc	5084	697
Charon Planning Corp	7389	889
Chart Cryogenic Components	3559	105
Chart Cryogenic Systems	3829	139
Chart Heat Exchangers	3443	60
Chart Industries Inc	3443	8
Chart Software	7372	3877
Chart Tech Tool Inc	3541	207
Charter Advertising Saint Louis LLC	7313	4
Charter Automotive	3496	28
Charter Bank and Trust Co	6022	495
Charter Communications Inc	4841	7
Charter Communications VII LP	4841	25
Charter Distributing Co	5023	122
Charter Fabrics Inc	5131	26
Charter Financial Corp	6035	75
Charter Financial Inc	7389	2232
Charter Investment Advisors Inc	6282	515
Charter Manufacturing Company Inc	3312	15
Charter Medical Ltd	3845	46
Charter Oak Service Corp	7363	280
Charter Of Lynchburg Inc	2531	38
Charter One Bank NA	6035	12
Charter One Financial Inc	6712	13
Charter One Hotels and Resorts Inc	7011	70
Charter Services Inc	7359	150
Charter Software Inc	7372	2950
Charter Solutions Inc	7379	576
Charter Venture Capital	6799	269
Chartered Semi Conductors	3674	362
Charterhouse Group International Inc	6211	123
ChartLogic Inc	7372	1828
Chartrand Communications Group	8743	277
Chartscape LLC	7371	1369
Chartwell Care Givers Inc	8082	4
Chartwell Community Services Inc	8082	2
Chartwell Diversified Services Inc	8082	8
Chartwell Home Therapies LP	8082	3
Chartwell Inc	2711	410
Chartwell Metal Fabricating Inc	3547	19
Charys Holding Company Inc	6719	85
Chas G Allen Co	3541	182
Chas P Young Co	2752	277
Chas Wood and Son Moving Inc	4213	3089
Chase Agri Credit Systems Inc	7374	283
Chase Brass and Copper Company LLC	3351	12
Chase Candy Co	2064	105
Chase Com Corp	7373	1243
Chase Corp	3648	4
Chase Dan Taxidermy Supply Company Incorporated	3423	48
Chase Design Group	7389	910
Chase Enterprises	6552	164
Chase Enterprises Inc	5999	165
Chase Ergonomics Inc	3842	179
Chase Investigations Inc	7381	136
Chase Investment Counsel Corp	6282	446
Chase Lumber and Fuel Company Inc	5211	178
Chase Machine Company Inc	3599	1090
Chase Manufacturing	3469	268
Chase Office Supplies Ltd	5021	153
Chase Products Co	2813	22
Chaco Resorts Inc	7011	154
Chase Solutions Inc	7375	254
Chasecom LP	4813	152
Chase-Logeman Corp	5084	695
Chasing Fireflies LLC	2389	17
Chaska Chemical Company Inc	2869	116
Chassis Engineering Inc	5013	327
Chassis Plans	5045	465
Chastant Brothers Inc	2875	36
Chateau Grand Travers Ltd	2084	87
Chateau Montelena Winery	2084	22
Chateau Morrisette Inc	2084	103
Chateau Operations Ltd	0172	18
Chateau Potelle Inc	2084	116
Chateau St Jean	2084	16
Chatfield Electric Inc	1731	847
Chatham Components Inc	5063	1064
Chatham Corp	3625	29
Chatham Created Gems and Diamonds	5094	5
Chatham Imports Inc	5181	102
Chatham Lodging Trust	6798	178
Chatham News Publishing Co	2711	848
Chatham Steel Corp	5051	65
Chatmoss Cablevision Inc	4841	164
Chattanooga Bakery Inc	2052	39
Chattanooga Boiler and Tank Company Inc	3443	123
Chattanooga Labeling Systems Inc	7389	955
Chattem Chemicals Inc	2834	323
Chattem Inc	2834	71
Chaumette Inc	2084	93
Chauncey Wings Sons Inc	3579	72
Chauvin Arnoux Inc	3829	117
Chavers Gasket Corp	3053	101
Chaves Bakery Ii Inc	5461	10
Chaz Equipment Company Inc	1623	238
Chazak Value Corp	3577	453
CHC Inc	5713	20
CHC International Inc	7011	225
CHCA Conroe LP	8062	230
CHDT Corp	3648	51
CHE Consulting Inc	7378	28
Cheap Escape Company Inc	7331	76
Check Group LLC	2311	29
Check Into Cash Inc	6141	42
Check Point Software Technologies Inc	2731	8
Checkcare (Louisville Kentucky)	7389	1226
Checker Logistics Inc	4213	2371
Checkerboard Ltd	2759	596
Check-It Electronics Corp	3823	397
CheckMark Software Inc	7372	4281
Checkmate Boats Inc	3732	78
Checkmatic Recovery Systems	7389	2366
CheckOutStore Inc	5735	17
Checkpoint Security Group Inc	3669	25
Checkpoint Systems Inc	3669	10
CheckRite of Kansas City Inc	7375	250
CheckRite of Oklahoma Inc	7375	251
Checktech Financial Corp	8748	399
Checkvelocity Inc	7389	802
Checkworks Inc	2782	46
Checkwriter Associates International Inc	5049	207
Checon Corp	3643	56
Chedd-Angier Production Co	2741	187
Cheek Engineering and Stamping	3469	355
Cheer Ltd	7999	62
Cheesecake Factory Inc	5812	33
Cheesecake Factory Inc	5963	27
Cheeseman LLC	4213	177
Cheetah Chassis Corp	3711	50
Cheetah International	7372	3311
Cheetah Precision Inc	3599	1060
Chef America Inc	2038	5
Chef Francisco Inc	2038	20
Chef Jays Food Products	2051	225
Chef John Folse and Company Inc	2092	36
Chef Merito Inc	2099	173
Chef Solutions Inc	2099	12
Chef-Co Wholesale Distributors Inc	2038	82
Chef's Catalog Inc	5961	117
Chef's Catering Inc	2099	328
Chefs International Inc	5812	340
Chef's Requested Foods Inc	2011	61
Chegg Inc	5942	21
Chelar Tool and Die Inc	3544	97
Chellino Crane Inc	7353	76
Chelo Publishing Inc	2721	395
Chelsea Building Products Inc	3089	245
Chelsea Clock LLC	3873	18
Chelsea Green Publishing Company Inc	2731	298
Chelsea Investment Corp	6552	174
Chelsea Lumber Co	5211	65
Chelsea Milling Co	2041	23
Chelsea Moore Co	6531	320
Chelsea Pictures Inc	7812	213
Chelsea Piers Management Inc	6552	12
Chelsea Property Group Inc	6798	104
Chelsea Technologies Inc	7371	1564
Chelsea Therapeutics International Ltd	2836	93
Chelten House Products Inc	2035	9
Chelton Inc	3728	98
Chelton Microwave Corp	3663	136
Chem Aid Inc	2844	101
Chem Arrow Corporation Intl	2899	177
Chem Free Organic Pest Control Inc	7342	33
Chem Gro Of Houghton Inc	5153	60
Chem Service Inc	2865	27
Chemalloy Company Inc	3399	18
Chemart Co	3479	46
Chemat Technology Inc	8731	325
Chematics Inc	2835	71
Chem-Cast Ltd	3544	59
CHEMCENTRAL Corp	5169	11
Chemclean Corp	2842	133
Chemco Corp	2842	138
Chemco Manufacturing Company Inc	3569	164
Chemcoat Inc	2851	122
ChemConnect Inc	7389	294
Chemdaq Inc	3829	385
ChemDesign Corp	2834	196
Chem-Dyne Research Corp	3829	471
Chemed Corp	8082	7
Chemence Inc	2891	37
Chemequip Sales Inc	3519	27
Chemetrics Inc	3826	78
ChemFree Corp	2842	127
Chemglass Inc	3231	56
Chemglo USA	5099	137
Chemgro Fertilizer Company Inc	5191	135
Chemguard Inc	2843	7
Chemia Corp	2844	182
Chemical and Industrial Engineering Inc	8711	228
Chemical Associates Inc	5169	29
Chemical Automation Technologies Inc	3829	439
Chemical Bank and Trust Co	6022	55
Chemical Bank Key State	6022	318
Chemical Bank Shoreline	6712	251
Chemical Bank Shoreline (Marshall Michigan)	6022	754
Chemical Bank West	6022	409
Chemical Coatings Inc	2891	31
Chemical Corporation Of America Inc	2819	126
Chemical Design Service Company Inc	1629	109
Chemical Dynamics Inc	2875	27
Chemical Financial Corp	6712	111
Chemical Methods Associates Inc	3589	58
Chemical Research and Licensing Inc	8731	276
Chemical Safety Technology Inc	3559	328
Chemical Sanitizing Systems Ltd	5087	172
Chemical Solvents Inc	5169	66
Chemical Sources International Inc	2741	268
Chemical Specialists And Development Inc	2851	84
Chemical Specialties Manufacturing Corp	2842	29
Chemical Systems Inc	2842	171
Chemical Systems International Inc	7379	1456
Chemical Technology Inc	2891	114
Chemical Transfer Company Inc	4213	1019
Chemical Transportation Inc	4213	1331
Chemico Systems Inc	2869	42
Chemi-Graphic Inc	3479	68
Chemimage Filter Technologies LLC	3826	92
ChemIndustrycom Inc	7375	187
Chemineer Inc	3559	96
ChemInnovation Software Inc	7372	4672
Chemionics Corp	2869	86
Chemique Pharmaceuticals Inc	5912	68
Chemir Analytical Services Inc	8734	145
Chemistry Communications Inc	7311	379
Chemmasters Inc	2891	97
Chem-Met Co	2819	133
ChemoCentryx Inc	2834	316
Chemoil Corp	2911	38
Chemokine Pharmaceutical Inc	8731	330
Chemonics International Inc	8999	19
Chemotex Protective Coatings Corp	2899	230
Chemplex Industries Inc	3826	139
Chemprene Inc	3496	44
Chemring Energetic Devices Inc	3812	69
ChemShare Corp	7371	1665
Chemsol Inc	2899	173
ChemSol LLC	5169	71
Chemstar Products Co	8731	72
Chemstation International Inc	2842	45
Chemstations Inc	7372	3650
Chem-Tainer Industries Inc	3089	240
Chemtall Inc	2869	38
Chem-Tec Equipment Co	3823	233
Chem-Tech Finishers Inc	2273	30
Chem-Tech International Inc	2899	224

Company Name	SIC	Rank
Chemtech Plastics Inc	3089	627
Chemtex International Inc	8711	25
Chem-Tex Laboratories Inc	2899	207
Chemtex Print USA Inc	2759	373
Chemtrac Systems Inc	3823	292
Chemtrans	4213	2136
Chem-Trol Inc	2879	16
Chemtron Inc	2842	141
Chemtrusion Inc	3087	17
Chemtura Corp	2821	7
Chemung Canal Trust Co	6022	262
Chemung Financial Corp	6712	332
Chemwest Systems Inc	3674	319
Chen Instrument Design	3829	343
Chenal Heating and Air Inc	5064	146
Chenango Valley Pet Foods Inc	2047	33
Chenango Valley Technologies Inc	3544	433
Chenex Inc	5045	1048
Cheney Pulp And Paper Co	2611	10
Chenica Inc	3842	328
Cheniere Energy Inc	4924	12
Cheniere Energy Partners LP	4922	19
Chenoweth Ford Inc	5511	1244
Chep International Inc	7359	226
Chep USA	7359	12
Cherin Transportation Inc	4213	1365
Cheringal Associates Inc	2759	187
Cherith Valley Gardens Inc	2033	122
Cher-Make Sausage Co	2013	104
Chernay Printing Inc	2752	348
Chernoff Newman LLC	7311	586
Chernoff Sales Inc	5078	14
Cherokee Banking Co	6712	635
Cherokee Boys Club Inc	8399	18
Cherokee Brick and Tile Co	3251	7
Cherokee Chemical Company Inc	5169	118
Cherokee County Disabilities and Special Needs	8322	236
Cherokee Grading and Utility Contractors Inc	1623	714
Cherokee Hosiery Mills Inc	2252	16
Cherokee Inc	2321	11
Cherokee Industrial Tires Inc	5014	43
Cherokee Industries Inc	3715	45
Cherokee Information Services Inc	7373	150
Cherokee International Corp	3679	85
Cherokee Landing Corp	7033	6
Cherokee Nation Businesses LLC	6719	111
Cherokee Nation Industries LLC	7363	96
Cherokee National Life Insurance Co	6311	265
Cherokee Nitrogen Holdings Inc	2875	1
Cherokee Printing Inc	2752	1616
Cherokee Recreation and Parks Authority	7997	14
Cherokee Staffing LLC	7361	36
Cherry And Cherry Games Inc	5734	272
Cherry Avenue Auction Inc	7389	1365
Cherry Bekaert and Holland	8721	36
Cherry Brothers Inc	1623	800
Cherry Central Cooperative Inc	5148	17
Cherry Chukar Co	2034	34
Cherry Corp	3643	7
Cherry Creek Dodge Inc	5511	354
Cherry Creek Golf Course	7992	9
Cherry Creek Mortgage Company Inc	6162	96
Cherry Creek Woodcraft Inc	2499	31
Cherry Hill Construction Inc	1629	10
Cherry Hill Manor Nursing Ctr	8051	34
Cherry Lane Electrical Service Inc	1731	261
Cherry Lane Lithographing Corp	2752	1193
Cherry Lane Music Publishing Company Inc	6794	102
Cherry Meat Packers Inc	2013	152
Cherry Stix Ltd	5137	23
Cherrybark Flooring Inc	2426	40
Cherrydale Farms Inc	2064	12
Cherryfield Foods Inc	2033	82
Cherryland Electric Co-op	4911	497
Cheryl A Mangio Inc	7389	2225
Cheryl Andrews Marketing Communications Inc	8743	111
Chesapeake Bank Corp	6036	45
Chesapeake Bay Communications Inc	2721	428
Chesapeake Bay Packing LLC	2092	25
Chesapeake Bay Seafood House Associates LP	5812	296
Chesapeake Communications Inc	5065	624
Chesapeake Corp	2631	6
Chesapeake Document Services LLC	7374	208
Chesapeake Energy Corp	1311	12
Chesapeake Financial Shares Inc	6712	422
Chesapeake Fish Company Inc	2092	31
Chesapeake Grain Co	5153	80
Chesapeake Interlink Ltd	7372	613
Chesapeake Leather Works Inc	3544	786
Chesapeake Life Insurance Co	6321	30
Chesapeake Machine Co	3441	192
Chesapeake Network Installations Inc	4899	208
Chesapeake Operating Inc	1381	3
Chesapeake Publishing Corp	2711	216
Chesapeake Recycling Co	2631	24
Chesapeake Solar LLC	8999	193
Chesapeake System Solutions Inc	7372	140
Chesapeake Systems Inc	3577	442

Company Name	SIC	Rank
Chesapeake TechLabs Inc	7373	581
Chesapeake Treatment Company LLC	2086	119
Chesapeake Utilities Corp	4923	17
Cheshire Engineering Corp	7371	1693
Cheshire Medical Center	8062	149
Chesley Brown International Inc	8742	302
Chessco Industries Inc	3291	14
Chest LLC	5199	121
Chester Bancorp Inc	6712	683
Chester Bross Construction Service	1611	60
Chester County Independent Inc	2711	717
Chester Lancaster Disabilities Inc	7361	204
Chester National Bank of Missouri	6021	399
Chester Packaging LLC	2834	254
Chesterfeild County Treasurers	7389	1882
Chesterfield Yarn Mills Inc	2281	21
Chesterman Co	2086	42
Chester's Harley-Davidson Inc	5571	2
Chestnut Hill Local	2711	824
Chestnut Ridge Foam Inc	3069	67
Chet's Electric Inc	1731	1961
Cheviot Financial Corp	6021	213
Chevron Corp	2911	1
Chevron Phillips Chemical Company LLC	2911	24
Chevron Products Company Inc	2911	12
Chevron Real Estate Management Co	6552	9
Chevron Shipping Co	4412	23
ChevronTexaco Overseas Petroleum Inc	1382	3
Chevy Chase ASC LLC	8011	98
Chevy Chase Cars Inc	5511	566
Chevys Inc	5812	135
Chex Systems Inc	7389	172
Cheyenne Electric Inc	1731	1664
Cheyenne River Sioux Tribe Telephone Authority	4813	450
Chf Industries Inc	2391	1
CHF Solutions Inc	5047	51
CHG Healthcare Services Inc	7363	40
CHHJ Franchising LLC	4953	168
Chi Corp	3572	95
Chicago Art Production Services Inc	7336	61
Chicago Beef Co	5147	141
Chicago Board Options Exchange Inc	6231	11
Chicago Bridge and Iron Co	3443	7
Chicago Chain and Transmission Co	5085	225
Chicago Circuits Corp	3672	353
Chicago Citizen Newspaper Group	2711	519
Chicago City Limits	7929	7
Chicago Communications LLC	5999	56
Chicago Community Bank	6036	55
Chicago Consulting	8742	571
Chicago Cylinders Corp	3593	54
Chicago Deferred Exchange Corporation of California	6159	91
Chicago Dial Indicator Company Inc	3825	235
Chicago Dryer Co	3582	4
Chicago Electric Co	5084	563
Chicago Electric Sales Inc	5084	681
Chicago Envelope Inc	2752	552
Chicago Faucet Co	3432	23
Chicago Financial Technology Inc	7373	844
Chicago Freight Car Leasing Co	4741	5
Chicago Gear - D O James Corp	3566	19
Chicago Grinding and Machine Co	3599	646
Chicago Hardware and Fixture Co	3429	37
Chicago Heights Steel	3312	47
Chicago International Trucks (Joliet Illinois)	5511	1016
Chicago Laminating Inc	7336	156
Chicago Lighthouse For People Who Are Blind Or Visually Impaired	8331	127
Chicago Lighting Inc	5063	678
Chicago Manifold Products Company Inc	3069	31
Chicago Maroon	2711	780
Chicago Meat Authority Inc	2011	42
Chicago Metal Rolled Products Co	3441	135
Chicago Metallic Corp	3446	3
Chicago Metallic Products Inc	3497	7
Chicago Mold Engineering Company Inc	3544	201
Chicago Multilingua Graphics Inc	7389	2449
Chicago Pallet Service Inc	3537	99
Chicago Parts and Sound LLC	5013	254
Chicago Press Corp	2752	791
Chicago Producers Inc	3695	94
Chicago Rail Link LLC	4011	45
Chicago Recording Co	3695	33
Chicago Review Press Inc	5192	24
Chicago Rivet and Machine Co	3452	31
Chicago Roll Company Inc	3544	457
Chicago Scenic Studios Inc	3993	116
Chicago Soft Ltd	5045	223
Chicago SouthShore and Freight	4011	49
Chicago Stock Exchange Inc	6231	12
Chicago Story	7812	44
Chicago Studio City	7819	78
Chicago Suburban Express Inc	4213	1610
Chicago Sun-Times	2711	61
Chicago Switchboard Company Inc	3613	88
Chicago Textile Corp	2512	67
Chicago Tire Inc	5014	49

Company Name	SIC	Rank
Chicago Trust Company of California	6091	20
Chicago Turnrite Company Inc	3469	198
Chicago White Metal Casting Inc	3363	30
Chicagoland Cabling Solutions Inc	1731	1841
Chicagoland Christian Village Inc	8051	9
Chicagoland Quad Cities Express	4213	2955
ChicagoLand Television News Inc	4841	51
Chicagoland Transportation Solutions Inc	4119	20
Chicago-Soft Ltd	7372	876
Chick Lumber Inc	5031	216
Chick Machine Company Inc	3599	1272
Chick Master Incubator Co	3523	73
Chick N Portions Inc	2015	61
Chick Publications Inc	2731	253
Chick Workholding Solutions Inc	3545	105
Chick-A-Chop Electrical Contractor Inc	1731	1694
Chickasaw Container Co	2653	106
Chickasaw Distributors Inc	5084	377
Chickasha Manufacturing Company Inc	3441	273
Chick-fil-A Inc	5812	44
Chickies Club South Inc	5023	178
Chico Community Publishing Inc	2711	160
Chicopee Bancorp Inc	6712	437
Chicopee Electronics	1731	1913
Chicopee Provision Company Inc	2013	200
Chicopee Savings Bank	6036	47
Chico's FAS Inc	5621	7
Chicotec Inc	5734	405
Chief Automotive Systems Inc	3714	210
Chief Bauer Heating and Air Conditioning	5075	118
Chief Electric Co	1542	435
Chief Industries Inc	3448	42
Chief Manufacturing Co	2392	47
Chief Mining Inc	1481	6
Chief Supermarkets Inc	8741	129
Chiefland Crab Company Inc	2092	94
Child Abuse and Neglect	8322	217
Child and Family Center	8322	83
Child and Family Services Of Eastern Virginia Inc	8322	95
Child and Family Support Services Inc	8322	102
Child Care Resource and Referral Inc	8322	70
Child Development Center Inc	8361	69
Child Evangelism Fellowship Inc	2752	272
Child Guidance Center Inc	8322	106
Child Saving Institute Foundation Inc	8351	41
Childcare Network Inc	8351	2
Children and Families Inc	2721	339
Children's Book Press	2731	130
Children's Community Programs Of Ct Inc	8322	113
Children's Foundation Inc	8322	124
Childrens Home Inc	8361	115
Children's Home Of Easton Inc	8361	188
Children's Home Of Lubbock And Family Service Agency Inc	8361	159
Children's Home Of Stockton	8361	136
Childrens Home Of Wheeling Inc	8361	194
Children's Hospital and Medical Center	8062	72
Children's Hospital Pediatric Associates Inc	8011	20
Children's Medical Center of Dallas	8069	8
Children's Place LLC (Roanoke Virginia)	5641	5
Children's Place Retail Stores Inc	5651	9
Children's Progress Inc	7372	2822
Children's Technology Review	2721	245
Children's Village	8361	10
Childs/Dreyfus Group	7389	897
Childs Jw Equity Partners LP	6799	178
Chile Fund Inc	6726	74
Chiles Catering Inc	5812	455
Chilla Computer and Internet Services	7379	1487
Chiller City Corp	3825	247
Chillicothe Gazette	2711	489
Chillicothe Telephone Co	4813	159
Chima Inc	2281	26
Chimera Co	3641	34
Chimera Design LLC	7336	181
Chimera Investment Corp	6799	10
Chimes International Ltd	6719	103
Chimney Solutions Inc	7349	248
Chin Chin Inc	5812	104
China Direct Industries Inc	3331	2
China Fund Inc	6726	27
China Mist Tea Co	2099	337
China Pearl Inc	5094	23
China Products Inc	3679	406
China Times Printing Inc	2711	459
China Trust Bank USA	6022	136
China Voice Holding Corp	3661	155
Chindex International Inc	5047	26
Chino Hills Ford Sales Inc	5511	718
Chino Works America Inc	3823	260
Chin's Import Export Company Inc	5141	221
Chiodini Associates Inc	8712	221
Chip Estimate	7372	1870
Chip Inc	7378	55
Chip Steak and Provision Co	5147	143
Chip Supply Inc	3674	192
Chip Systems International	3535	226
ChipBLASTER Inc	3545	114

CHIPCHAT
Company Name Index

Company Name	SIC	Rank
ChipChat Technology Group	7372	1585
Chipco Computer Distributors Inc	5045	484
Chipman Moving and Storage (Spokane Washington)	4213	2231
Chipmatic Tool and Machine Inc	3599	539
Chipotle Mexican Grill Inc	5812	27
Chippenham and Johnston-Willis Hospitals Inc	8062	144
Chippewa Graphics Inc	2752	695
Chippewa Herald	2711	490
Chippewa Plastics Inc	3089	1351
Chippewa Systems Ltd	5084	928
Chippewa Valley Electric Coop	4911	453
Chippewa Valley Ethanol Company Lllp	2869	84
CHIPS Computer Consulting LLC	7373	483
Chiptec Inc	3469	324
Chipton-Ross Inc	7361	104
Chipwich Inc	5142	34
ChipWrights Inc	3674	310
Chiquita Brands International Inc	0179	1
Chiquita Fresh North America	5148	43
Chiral Technologies Inc	5049	34
Chirch Global Manufacturing LLC	3544	348
ChiroNET LLC	8721	353
Chiropractic USA Inc	6794	109
Chisesi Brothers Meat Packing Company Inc	2011	79
Chiswick Inc	2759	17
Chittenden Cider Mill	5947	30
Chiu Technical Corp	3661	191
Chiv Electrical	1731	1930
Chiyoda America Inc	2672	24
Chiyoda International Corp	8711	208
Chiyoda USA Corp	3465	49
Chizek Elevator and Transport	4213	752
Chlorinators Inc	3589	187
CHN Inc	8743	106
Choate Construction Co	1542	140
Choate Hall and Stewart LLP	8111	182
Choate Machine and Tool Company Inc	3489	20
Chocklett Press Inc	2752	250
Chockstone Inc	7375	99
Chocolate Delivery Systems Inc	3089	900
Chocolate In Topographic Co	2066	33
Choctaw Resort Development Enterprises	7011	107
Choctawhatchee Electric Cooperative Inc	4911	495
Choctaw-Kaul Distribution	2381	2
Choi Brothers Inc	2326	22
Choice Capital Corp	6794	57
Choice Cleaning Contractors	7349	456
Choice Communications	5065	966
Choice Communications LLC	4813	137
Choice Electric Corp	1731	1182
Choice Graphics Inc	4213	2768
Choice Homes Inc	1521	1
Choice Hotels International Inc	7011	55
Choice Media Satellite Systems Inc	4841	126
Choice Medical Management Services LLC	7389	508
Choice Mold Components Inc	3544	637
Choice Money Transfer Inc	7389	2309
Choice Parcel Service Inc	4215	17
Choice Precision Machine Inc	3599	727
Choice Products USA Inc	2038	46
Choice Products USA LLC	5199	47
Choice Systems Inc	6794	81
Choice Wireless LC	4812	66
ChoiceOne Financial Services Inc	6022	312
ChoicePoint Inc	7374	17
Choicestream Inc	7371	278
Chokio Equity Exchange Inc	5191	117
Cholestech Corp	3845	39
Chon Dal Inc	7299	8
Choo Choo Partners Ltd	7011	199
Chooljian Brothers Packing Company Inc	2034	21
Chopp and Company Inc	5031	154
Chopp Shop Productions Inc	7812	325
Choptank Electric Cooperative Inc	4911	293
Chordiant Software Inc	7372	524
Chordus Inc/Office Furniture USA	4213	1247
Chores Unlimited Inc	7349	208
Chore-Time/Brock International	3523	7
Chore-Time Egg Production Systems	3523	8
Chore-Time Poultry Production Systems	3523	9
Chou And Associates Inc	5046	360
Chow Time Foods Inc	2051	242
Chown Inc	5072	59
CHR Hansen Inc	2819	76
Chris Agee	1711	263
Chris Aire Corp	3599	805
Chris Candies Inc	2064	67
Chris Electric Company Inc	1731	1875
Chris Electronics Distributors Inc	5065	426
Chris J Alt Inc	4213	1327
Chris Stone and Associates	2269	2
Chris Supply Company Inc	5065	495
Chrislex Staffing Ltd	7363	145
Chris-Lin Construction Inc	1623	801
Chrisman Heavy Hauling Inc	4213	1124

Company Name	SIC	Rank
Chrisman Sales And Services Inc	3599	676
Christensen Computer Company Inc	7372	3166
Christensen Family Farms	0213	9
Christensen Shipyards Ltd	3731	44
Christenson Communication	1731	1603
Christian Brothers Employee Benefit Trust	6411	101
Christian Building Materials Inc	5031	290
Christian County Farmers Supply Co	5191	101
Christian Dior Inc	6794	74
Christian E Lewis	5046	370
Christian Financial Credit Union	6062	41
Christian Haven Inc	8361	101
Christian Light Publications Inc	2741	331
Christian Manufacturing Inc	3679	572
Christian Podlesko and van Musschenbroek Ltd	6282	598
Christian Schools International	8742	626
Christian Technologies Inc	7372	4673
Christian Wholesale Distributors Inc	5072	79
Christiana Bank and Trust Co	6022	532
Christiansen Amusements Inc	7999	155
Christiansen Aviation Inc	8299	58
Christiansen Construction Company LLC	1542	404
Christiansen Implement Of Burley Inc	5083	166
Christie Cookie Co	2052	58
Christie Digital Systems USA Inc	5043	12
Christie's Great Estates Inc	2721	93
Christman Co	8741	133
Christmas By Krebs Corp	3231	30
Christmas City Printing Company Inc	2752	897
Christmas Lumber Company Inc	5211	179
Christner Inc	8712	247
Christopher and Banks Corp	5621	19
Christopher Chadbourne And Associates Inc	7389	1160
Christopher Homes Development Co	1521	88
Christopher Tool and Manufacturing Co	3469	108
Christopherson and Co	7311	915
Christopherson John	7371	883
Christus Health Gulf Coast	8742	96
Christus Health Inc	8741	1
CHRISTUS Santa Rosa Healt Care	8062	71
Christy Communications Company Inc	4813	730
Christy Industries Inc	3669	214
Christy Industries Inc (Fraser Michigan)	3599	1976
Christy Metals Inc	5051	351
Christy Refractories Company LLC	5085	298
Christy Trucking Company Inc	4213	2105
Chroma Digital Corp	5065	507
Chroma Systems Solutions Inc	3825	180
Chroma Technology Corp	3827	33
Chromalab Inc	8734	116
Chromalloy Castings Tampa Corp	3511	17
Chromalloy Gas Turbine Corp	3728	31
Chromalloy Georgia	3724	13
Chromalox Inc	3567	4
Chromasource Inc	2752	223
Chromatech Printing Inc	2752	1799
Chromatic Incorporated Lithographers	2752	259
Chromatic Technologies Inc	3357	38
Chromatics Inc	2851	98
Chromatin Inc	8731	164
Chroma-Tone Inc	2752	1603
Chromcraft Revington Inc	2511	23
Chrome Electric LLC	1731	638
Chrome Machine	3599	1510
Chrome Systems Corp	7372	371
Chromium Industries Inc	3471	104
Chronicle	2711	753
Chronicle Books LLC	2731	90
Chronicle Guidance Publications Inc	7372	1069
Chronicle Inc	2711	860
Chronicle Of The Horse Inc	2721	385
Chronicle Printing Co	2711	402
Chronicle Publishing Co (San Francisco California)	2711	77
Chronister Oil Co	5172	135
Chronix International Inc	5065	699
Chrono-Log Corp	3841	346
Chronos LLC	7372	2648
Chronotype Publishing Co	2741	324
Chrysler Group LLC	3711	4
CHS Inc	2041	2
Cht R Beitlich Corp	2843	10
Chubb and Son Inc	8741	2
Chubb Corp	6331	19
Chubb Electric Service Inc	1731	1659
Chuck Bivens Services Inc	3559	509
Chuck Bohn and Associates Inc	7389	1757
Chuck Foster Trucking Inc	4213	1071
Chuck Levins Washington Music Sales Center Inc	5736	10
Chuckles Inc	2844	166
Chuck's Bakery	5149	217
Chuck's Electrical Service Inc	1731	1795
Chucks Stace-Allen Inc	3545	314
Chuckwalla Inc	7371	1327
Chudnow Manufacturing Company Inc	3585	171
Chugach Alaska Corp	2092	9
Chugach Electric Association Inc	4911	137
Chugach Industrials Inc	8744	45
Chugach Industries Inc	1542	112

Company Name	SIC	Rank
Chugach Management Services Inc	8744	12
Chugach World Services Inc	8744	9
Chugai Pharma USA LLC	8731	108
Chugai USA LLC	5063	319
Chugwater Chili Corp	2099	374
Chula Farmers Coop	5083	122
Chung's Products LP	2038	39
Church and Dwight Company Inc	2842	3
Church Art Works	7372	3562
Church Chair Industries Inc	2531	27
Church Hill Classics Ltd	2499	44
Church Home Of Hartford Inc	8361	33
Church Management Solutions	7372	4230
Church Mutual Insurance Co	6331	203
Church Offset Printing Inc	2789	97
Churchill Downs Inc	7948	4
Churchill Downs Management Co	7948	14
Churchill Transportation Inc	4213	557
Churchill's Super Markets Inc	5411	279
Churon Co	3462	53
Chyna Inc	3599	2353
Chyron Corp	3861	32
CI Castro and Co	2361	5
CI Mitchell and Best Inc	1521	23
CI Travel	4724	18
Ci2i Services Inc	8742	617
CIA LLC	7389	1677
Cianbro Corp	3444	186
Ciao Bella Gelato Company Inc	2024	57
Ciasons Industrial Inc	3053	94
CIB Marine Bancshares LLC	6712	551
CIBA Vision Corp	3851	3
Cibao Meat Products Inc	2013	151
Cibar Inc	7372	3576
CIBER Associates Inc	7379	19
Ciber Enterprise Solutions	7373	178
CIBER Inc	7371	12
CIBER International Inc	7379	103
CIC Associates Inc	7389	1305
CIC Group Inc	6719	40
CIC International Ltd	3484	3
Cic Mortgage Credit Inc	7323	32
Cicero Inc	7371	1062
Cicero Plastic Products Inc	3469	337
Cici's Enterprises Inc	5812	402
Cicogna Electric And Sign Co	3993	81
Cicoil LLC	3357	60
Cicon Engineering Inc	3679	221
Ci-Dell Plastics Inc	3089	1335
Cidra Corp	3823	87
Cieco Inc	3625	300
CIENA Corp	3669	3
Ciencia Inc	8731	282
CIF Inc	3089	827
CIFC Corp	6798	53
Cigas Machine Shop Inc	3599	1241
Cigital Inc	7372	532
CIGNA Corp	6311	26
CIGNA Dental Health	6324	59
CIGNA Group Insurance	6321	1
CIGNA Healthcare Mid-Atlantic Inc	6324	47
CIGNA HealthCare of Arizona Inc	6324	52
CIGNA Healthcare of Florida Inc	6324	77
CII Technologies Inc	3625	27
Cim Bar Code Technology Inc	3577	625
Cim Concepts Inc	7373	1010
CIM Tech Corp	7389	2008
Cima Labs Inc	2834	179
Cimarex Energy Co	1311	25
Cimarron Electric Cooperative Inc	4911	515
Cimarron Express Inc	4213	475
Cimarron Machine Service Inc	3599	2259
Cimarron Office Furniture Services Inc	7389	1768
Cimco Communications Inc	8742	108
Cimco Technologies LLC	3569	291
Cimcorp USA LLC	5734	199
Cimdata Inc	7379	539
Cimetrics Inc	3823	210
Cimetrix Inc	7372	2321
Cimmaron Software Inc	7372	3412
CIMNET Inc	7372	2381
Cimple Systems Inc	7372	2667
Cimpl's LLC	2011	19
CIMS Corp	5162	55
CIMS Lab Inc	7372	1923
Cimulus Inc	7372	1638
Cimx LLC	7372	3090
Cincinnati Air Filter Sales and Service Inc	5075	113
Cincinnati Asset Management Inc	6282	420
Cincinnati Bell Inc	4813	17
Cincinnati Bell Telephone Co	4813	26
Cincinnati Central Credit Union	6062	98
Cincinnati Children's Hospital Medical Center	8069	5
Cincinnati Color Press Inc	2752	604
Cincinnati Container Co	2759	53
Cincinnati Control Dynamics Inc	3625	337
Cincinnati Convertors Inc	2759	453
Cincinnati Enquirer	2711	182
Cincinnati Financial Corp	6331	50
Cincinnati Gasket Packing and Manufacturing Inc	3053	55

Company Name	SIC	Rank
Cincinnati Gilbert Machine Tool Company LLC	3541	149
Cincinnati Insurance Co	6331	113
Cincinnati Laser Cutting LLC	3699	116
Cincinnati Life Insurance Co	6311	131
Cincinnati Paperboard Corp	2631	17
Cincinnati Precision Plate Inc	3555	112
Cincinnati Preserving Co	2033	118
Cincinnati Printers Company Inc	2752	1842
Cincinnati Public Radio Inc	4832	73
Cincinnati Steel Products Co	5051	310
Cincinnati Stock Exchange	6231	13
Cincinnati Test Systems Inc	3823	84
Cincinnati Tool Steel Co	5051	215
Cincinnati United Contractors Inc	1541	154
Cincom Systems Inc	7372	321
Cindex Industries Inc	7699	204
Cine Corp	5094	68
Cine Magnetics Inc	7819	22
Cinecraft Productions Inc	7812	67
Cinedigm Digital Cinema Corp	7372	513
Cinedigm Digital Media Services Division	4833	191
Cinema Grill Systems Inc	7832	21
Cinema Tech Seating Inc	5021	177
Cinemark Holdings Inc	7832	4
Cinemills Corp	3648	97
Cinergi Productions Inc	7812	122
Cinesys Inc	5734	344
CineTel Films Inc	7812	139
Cinetic Landis Corp	3541	62
Cinetic Sorting Corp	3535	68
Cinex Inc	3599	524
Cinfab LLC	3444	100
CinFed Employees Federal Credit Union	6061	98
Cinnabar CA	3999	38
Cinnabon Inc	5461	1
Cinnamon Hills Inc	8361	46
Cinovation Inc	7372	5060
Cinram Inc	3652	11
Cintara	7311	429
Cintas Corp	2326	1
Cintas Document Management Imaging Div	7373	257
Cintech LLC	7372	2227
Cintel Corp	3674	501
Cintel Inc	3009	166
Cioffi Enterprises Inc	8361	192
Cip International Inc	7389	782
Cipher Corp	7373	1061
Cipher Systems	7372	1675
CipherMax	7373	205
Ciphersync	7379	1472
Ciphertechs Inc	7379	1161
Ciplex	7373	846
Ciproms Inc	8721	340
Cips Marketing Group Inc	7319	142
Cir	8731	224
Ciralsky and Associates Inc	5051	457
Ciraulo Brothers Building Co	5031	198
Circa Corp	8742	711
Circa Inc	5045	1049
CIRCA Information Technologies Inc	7372	2086
Circadence Corp	7372	631
Circle 4 Farms	0213	10
Circle A Electric Inc	1731	484
Circle Aviation Inc	5198	14
Circle B Enterprises Holding Company Inc	6719	106
Circle Bank	6022	475
Circle Bolt and Nut Company Inc	5072	83
Circle Boring and Machine Co	3599	1679
Circle Broach Company Inc	3545	399
Circle Chevrolet Co	5511	764
Circle City Security Systems Inc	1731	2050
Circle City Transport Inc	4213	1383
Circle Creations Inc	5199	111
Circle Entertainment Inc	6519	33
Circle Gear and Machine Company Inc	3566	33
Circle Inc	3577	330
Circle Industrial Manufacturing Corp	3567	94
Circle K Corp	5411	26
Circle K Stores Inc	5411	27
Circle Machine Rolls Inc	3547	14
Circle Mold Inc	3544	438
Circle Mortgage Corp	6162	56
Circle Noetic Services Inc	7372	1471
Circle Packaging Machinery Inc	3565	142
Circle Press Inc	2752	638
Circle Prime Manufacturing Inc	3672	275
Circle - Prosco Inc	2841	26
Circle Seal Controls Inc	3769	9
Circle Systems Inc	7372	4989
Circle U Foods Inc	2099	354
Circle V Specialized Inc	4213	2734
Circle W Trailers	3715	58
Circo Technology Corp	5045	1030
Circom Inc	3679	521
CIRCOR International Inc	3491	3
CIRCOR IP Holding Co	3494	19
Circosta Iron And Metal Inc	5093	139
Circuit Assembly Corp	3678	40
Circuit Automation Inc	3679	675

Company Name	SIC	Rank
Circuit Breaker Logic Inc	3613	176
Circuit Breaker Sales Company Inc	3613	86
Circuit Breakers Inc	5063	1045
Circuit Check Inc	3825	61
Circuit Components Inc	3675	21
Circuit Connect Inc	3672	221
Circuit Connections	3672	357
Circuit Engineering LLC	3672	191
Circuit Etching Technics Inc	3672	330
Circuit Express Inc	3672	107
Circuit Graphics Inc	3672	420
Circuit Interruption Technology Inc	3625	189
Circuit Manufacturing Inc	3679	347
Circuit Masters Inc	3672	371
Circuit Shop Electronic Systems Inc	1731	2130
Circuit Spectrum Inc	3577	565
Circuit World Inc	3672	253
Circuitcitycom Inc	5731	2
Circuitronics Corp	3672	393
Circuitronics LLC	3672	260
Circuits and Systems Inc	3596	20
Circuits West Inc	3672	329
Circuit-Tron Corp	1731	2059
Circular Advertising Company Inc	7331	100
Circulation Experti Ltd	7311	462
Cirexx International Inc	3672	137
Cirius Group Inc	7372	1881
Cirlot Agency Inc	7311	834
Cirqit Inc	7372	1979
Cirque Corp	3577	439
Cirrus Logic Inc	3674	62
Cirtec Medical Systems LLC	3841	153
Cirtech Inc	3672	140
CirTran Corp	3699	131
Cirtronics Corp	3672	84
Cisco Air Systems Inc	5084	370
Cisco Brothers Corp	2512	48
Cisco City Shop	7389	2132
Cisco Systems Inc	3577	1
Cisco-Linksys LLC	3577	36
Cision	2741	47
Cision US Inc	8743	208
Cissna Park Cooperative Inc	5153	149
Cistera Networks Inc	5045	759
Cisys Inc	7371	1169
CIT Group Inc	6159	4
Citadel Communications	2752	898
Citadel Comunications Ltd	4833	99
Citadel Security Inc	7381	99
Citadel Security Software Inc	5045	434
Citala Us Inc	3679	540
Citation Construction Co	1623	658
Citation Oil and Gas Corp	1311	143
Citation Solutions Inc	7378	141
Citation Technologies Inc	2741	56
CITCO Diamond and CBN Products	3545	36
Citect Inc	7372	1686
Citek Inc	3572	70
Citel America Inc	3699	41
Citel Technologies	4899	69
CITGO Petroleum Corp	2911	14
CITGO Pipeline Co	4612	6
CITGO Refining and Chemicals Inc	2911	30
Citi Lites Inc	1623	555
Citi Trends Inc	5699	4
Citibank NA	6021	2
Citibank Texas NA	6036	11
CitiCam Video Productions Inc	7819	88
Citicasters Co	4832	203
Citicorp Diners Club Inc	6141	12
Citie Sites	7374	315
Cities Electric Inc	1731	644
Cities West Publishing Inc	2721	239
Cities2Night Inc	7379	950
Citigroup Global Markets Holdings Inc	6211	7
Citigroup Inc	6331	1
Citihub Inc	7379	1257
Citinational Real Estate Inc	6798	140
Citipak Delivery System Inc	7389	1380
Citistreet Retirement Services LLC	6211	147
Citizen Bank Holding Inc	6712	557
Citizen Printing Co	2752	714
Citizen Telephone Corp	4813	648
Citizen Watch Company of America Inc	5094	10
Citizenhawk Inc	7371	590
Citizens and Northern Bank	6022	173
Citizens and Northern Corp	6712	258
Citizens Bancorp (Nevada City California)	6022	392
Citizens Bancorp(Corvalis Oregon)	6022	352
Citizens Bancshares Corp (Atlanta Georgia)	6712	522
Citizens Bank	6022	367
Citizens Bank and Trust Co (Springhill Louisiana)	6022	579
Citizens Bank (Flint Michigan)	6022	200
Citizens Bank (Kilgore Texas)	6022	382
Citizens Bank (Morehead Kentucky)	6022	558
Citizens Bank Mortgage Corp	6162	76
Citizens Bank of Clovis	6022	276
Citizens Bank of Cochran	6022	755
Citizens Bank Of Connecticut	6022	553
Citizens Bank of Farmington	6022	203
Citizens Bank of Florida	6022	667

Company Name	SIC	Rank
Citizens Bank of Massachusetts	6036	2
Citizens Bank of Michigan	6022	21
Citizens Bank of Mukwonago	6022	189
Citizens Bank of Northern California	6022	329
Citizens Bank of Pagosa Springs	6022	664
Citizens Bank of Rhode Island	6022	18
Citizens Banking Co (Sandusky Ohio)	6022	181
Citizens Business Bank	6022	36
Citizens Capital Inc	6799	320
Citizens Community Bancorp Inc	6035	114
Citizens Community Federal	6035	119
Citizens Deposit Bank and Trust Co	6022	361
Citizens Electric Co	4911	469
Citizens Electric Corp	4911	264
Citizens Federal Savings and Loan Association of Bellefontaine Ohio	6035	165
Citizens Financial Corp (Elkins West Virginia)	6712	578
Citizens Financial Group Inc	6712	354
Citizens First Bank Inc	6036	100
Citizens First Bank (Rome Georgia)	6022	546
Citizens First Corp	6712	541
Citizens First National Bank	6021	88
Citizens Holding Co	6022	202
Citizens Inc	6411	32
Citizens Independent Bank	6022	535
Citizens National Bank of Elkins West Virginia	6021	259
Citizens National Bank of Urbana	6035	157
Citizens Of Humanity LLC	2339	31
Citizens Publishing Company Inc	2711	890
Citizens Republic Bancorp Inc	6712	75
Citizens Savings Bank and Trust Co	6036	106
Citizens Savings Bank (Martins Ferry Ohio)	6036	70
Citizens Security Bank	6022	653
Citizens South Banking Corp	6712	308
Citizens Telephone Company Inc	4813	343
Citizens Transportation Company Inc	4213	2758
Citizens Trust Bank	6022	388
Citmed Corp	3842	241
Cito Products Inc	3825	201
Citra Trading Corp	5094	20
Citrin Cooperman	8721	414
Citrin Cooperman and Co	8721	283
Citrix	7371	7
Citrix Systems Inc	7372	31
Citrosuco North America Inc	5142	3
Citrus And Allied Essences Ltd	5109	00
Citrus County School District	8211	89
Citrus Publishing Inc	2711	301
Citrus Surgery and Endoscopy Center	8011	83
Citrus Systems Inc	2033	92
Citrus Valley Health Partners Inc	8062	77
Citrus Valley Publishing Co	2711	854
Citrus World Inc	2037	14
Cittio Inc	7371	239
City Alarm Co	5063	1097
City Aluminum Company Inc	2431	90
City Animation Co	5064	19
City Beach Films	7311	873
City Beverage	5181	93
City Blue Imaging Services Inc	7334	64
City Capital Corp (Metairie Louisiana)	6159	73
City Cartage Co	4213	2797
City Carton Company Inc	5093	76
City Cinemas	7832	22
City Computer Corp	5734	339
City County Data Center Commission	7374	367
City Dash Inc	4213	527
City Directory Inc	2741	495
City Electric Inc	1731	89
City Electric Of Plainview Inc	1731	1862
City Financial Corp	6141	9
City Foods Inc	2011	84
City Haul Inc	4213	2705
City Holding Capital Trust	6022	805
City Holding Capital Trust II	6022	806
City Holding Co	6712	160
City Ice Co	2097	24
City Industrial Tool and Die Inc	3312	134
City Lights and Supply Company Inc	5063	646
City Lights Electrical Company Inc	1731	56
City Machine Technologies Inc	3621	88
City Market Burleson Tx	5411	266
City Market Inc	5411	115
City Motor Company Inc	5511	934
City National Asset Management Inc	6022	723
City National Bancshares Corp	6712	310
City National Bancshares Inc	6712	172
City National Bank	6021	14
City National Bank (Mineral Wells Texas)	6022	659
City National Bank of Florida	6021	48
City National Bank of New Jersey	6021	261
City National Bank of West Virginia	6021	244
City National Corp	6712	37
City National Financial Services Inc	6021	379
City National Mortgage Co	6162	82
City National Securities Inc	6021	354
City Of Roses Newspaper Co	2711	584
City Of Tallahassee Electric Utilities	4911	442
City Optical Company Inc	5048	5
City Pipe And Supply Corp	5051	130

CITY

Company Name Index

Company Name	SIC	Rank
City Press Inc	2752	716
City Press Publishing Inc	2711	763
City Printing	2759	583
City Printing Company Inc	2752	1293
City Public Service Energy	4911	557
City Securities Corp	6211	320
City Store Gates Manufacturing Corp	3446	4
City Transfer Company Inc	4213	1214
City Wide General Cleaning and Maintenance Service Inc	7349	380
City Wide Maintenance Company Inc	7349	71
Cityblue Technologies LLC	2759	372
Cityon Systems Inc	7372	2753
Cityscapes International Inc	3631	160
CitySearch Inc	7375	122
Citytech Inc	7371	964
Citywide Bank of Aurora	6021	263
Citywide Banks of Colorado Inc	6712	255
CIVCO Medical Instruments Co	3541	47
Cives Steel Co	3441	6
Cives Steel Co Mid Atlantic Div	3441	79
Civic Recycling	4953	171
Civicorps Schools	8322	135
Civil Engineering Construction Inc	1623	723
Civil Solutions Inc	7335	26
Civilized Software Inc	7372	4261
Civils Associates Inc	5065	843
CJ Advertising LLC	7311	588
Cj and Associates Inc	5021	128
Cj Component Products LLC	3663	377
Cj Enterprises	3544	646
CJ Environmental Inc	5094	56
CJ Hughes Construction Co	1623	76
CJ Instruments Inc	3829	218
CJ Krehbiel Co	2732	12
CJ Link Lumber Co	5031	210
CJ Mabardy Inc	1794	38
CJ Mahan Construction Company Inc	1611	94
CJ Mailing and Fulfillment Inc	7331	213
Cj Model Home Maintenance Inc	7349	173
CJ Olson Market Research	8732	126
CJ Rogers Electronics Inc	3672	333
CJ Schlosser and Company LLC	8721	197
CJ Winter Machine Technologies Inc	3545	121
Cjj Inc	3559	297
Cjk Manufacturing LLC	3089	1756
Cjt Koolcarb Inc	3545	59
C-K Composites Inc	3089	837
CK Electric Inc	1731	2284
Ck Enterprises	3559	585
Ck Manufacturing Inc	3544	722
C-K Plastics Inc	3082	27
Ck Technologies Inc	3823	220
Ck Technologies LLC	3089	126
Ckb Inc	1731	2450
CKC Communications Inc	8743	95
CKC Industries Inc	3829	445
CKF Bancorp Inc	6712	674
Ckmt Associates Inc	2711	760
Ckot Inc	5045	973
CKR Transport Ltd	4213	2500
Cks Tool and Engineering Inc	3544	76
CKX Inc	7812	28
Cl and D Graphics Inc	2759	55
CL Boyd Company Inc	5082	76
CL Carson Inc	1522	46
CL Dews and Sons Foundry And Machinery Company Inc	3369	18
CL Frates and Co	6411	78
CL Graphics Inc	7336	210
CL King and Associates Inc	6282	232
CL Thomas Inc	5411	163
Cla Construction Diversified LLC	1623	611
Claas Concepts Corp	2542	6
Clabrook Farms Inc	7996	34
Clack Corp	3589	29
Clackamas County Bank	6712	405
Claddagh Commission Inc	8322	75
Claddah Corp	2051	188
Claffey Printing Co	2752	1437
Claiborne's Thriftway Supermarket	5411	254
Claim Jumper Restaurants	5812	369
Claims Resource Services Inc	7322	100
Clair Brothers Audio Enterprises Inc	7359	103
Clair Christo Corp	7379	880
Clair D Thompson and Sons Inc	2013	172
Claire/Alden Inc	7389	2343
Claire Manufacturing Company Inc	2842	14
Claire's Boutiques Inc	5632	6
Claire's Stores Inc	5632	2
Clairex Technologies Inc	3679	561
Clairmail Inc	4899	58
Clairmont Camera Inc	7359	91
Clairol Inc	2844	18
Clairon Metals Corp	3469	46
Clairsol Inc	7371	1016
Clairson Industries Corp	3089	602
Clairson Industries LLC	3089	418
Clamco Corp	3565	58
Clamp Swing Pricing Company Inc	3999	183
Clampco Products Inc	3429	100
Clampitt Paper Co	5111	21
Clamshell Structures Inc	2394	32
Clancy and Theys Construction Co	1542	48
Clancy Mance Communications Inc	4832	211
Clancy Moving Systems Inc	4213	1805
Clancy Systems International Inc	7372	2951
Clapper Publishing Company Inc	2721	242
Claraview Inc	8748	92
Clarcor Air Filtration Products Inc	3564	14
CLARCOR Inc	3714	31
CLARCOR International Inc	3714	32
Clare Computer Solutions	7373	969
Clare Inc	3674	266
Clare Rose Inc	5181	15
Clarence House Imports Ltd	5199	12
Clarence M Kelley and Associates Of Kansas City Inc	7381	119
Clarent Hospital Corp	8062	61
Clariant Corp	2869	26
Clarich Mold Corp	2821	198
Clarient Inc	3826	17
Clarins USA Inc	5122	27
Clarion Bathware Inc	3088	6
Clarion Capital Partners LLC	6282	251
Clarion Corporation Of America	5064	7
Clarion Sales Corp	7389	167
Clarion Sintered Metals Inc	3399	15
Clarion Technologies Inc	3714	109
Clarion Technology Center	3544	205
Claritas Inc	7389	108
Clarity Audio/Video Systems Inc	1731	1374
Clarity Coverdale Fury Advertising Inc	7311	256
Clarity Customer Management Inc	7389	1083
Clarity Visual Systems	3577	216
Clark and Koller CPA	8721	223
Clark and Reid Company Inc	4213	1407
Clark and Sullivan Constructors Inc	1541	182
Clark Appler and Optical	5995	18
Clark Brands LLC	6794	34
Clark Brothers Inc	1629	105
Clark Business Services Inc	7361	402
Clark Capital Management Group	6211	146
Clark Condon Associates Inc	0781	18
Clark Construction Company Inc	8741	36
Clark Construction Group LLC	1542	6
Clark Container Inc	2673	45
Clark County Indiana Teachers Federal Credit Union	6061	151
Clark DCC Builders LLC	1541	204
Clark Electric Coop	4911	487
Clark Energy Cooperative Corp	4911	245
Clark Enterprises Inc	6719	34
Clark Farms Trucking Inc	4213	1867
Clark Foam Products Corp	5169	107
Clark Foodservice Inc	5087	4
Clark Freight Lines Inc	4213	936
Clark Granco Inc	3542	23
Clark Graphics Inc	2752	879
Clark Grave Vault Co	3995	4
Clark Harry Plumbing and Heating	1711	238
Clark Hill PLC	8111	438
Clark Holdings Inc	6722	243
Clark Industries Inc	3599	1616
Clark/Kjos	8712	200
Clark Machine Corp	3443	171
Clark Machine Tool And Die Inc	3541	158
Clark Mailing Service Inc	7331	154
Clark Management Services Inc	5045	908
Clark Manufacturing Co	3599	479
Clark Metal Products Co	3444	131
Clark Nexsen PC	8712	249
Clark - Pacific Corp	3272	42
Clark Power Corp	1623	380
Clark Rubber Company Inc	3061	17
Clark Schaefer Hackett and Co	8721	266
Clark Seals LLC	3053	68
Clark Solutions	3829	254
Clark Specialty Company Inc	2542	66
Clark Sprinkler Fabrication Of In Inc	3569	199
Clark Testing Services LLC	8711	571
Clark Thomas and Winters PC	8111	218
Clark Tire and Auto Supply Company Inc	5531	18
Clark Trailer Service Inc	3715	54
Clark Transfer Inc	4213	514
Clark Transportation Inc	4213	1903
Clark Wholesale Inc	5064	98
Clarke County Democrat Inc	2711	888
Clarke County Publishing Inc	2711	861
Clarke County School District	8211	32
Clarke Distributors Inc	5181	75
Clarke Electric Company LLC	7382	186
Clarke Hess Communication Research	3825	263
Clarke Lanzen Skalla Investment Firm Inc	6282	12
Clarke Security Services Inc	7382	129
Clarklake Machine Inc	3599	1688
Clark-Mxr Inc	3826	124
Clark-Prout Insurance Agency Inc	6331	344
Clark-Reliance Corp	3494	35
Clark's Feed Mills Inc	0251	4
Clark's Guns And Ammo Inc	3599	871
Clark's Printing Service Inc	2752	1054
Clarksburg Publishing Co	2711	403
Clarkson Laboratory and Supply Inc	5049	178
Clarkston Financial Corp	6021	294
Clarkston State Bank	6022	541
Clarus Medical LLC	3841	407
Clarus Systems Inc	7371	688
Clarus Technologies LLC	3569	94
Clary Corp	3613	69
Clasen Quality Coatings Inc	2064	38
Class 1	3569	23
Class 1 Transport Inc	4213	1224
Class Act Federal Credit Union	6061	126
Class Encounters Co	7389	1769
Class Termite and Pest Control Inc	7342	56
Classen Manufacturing Inc	3523	210
Classic Album LLC	2782	26
Classic Automobiles Inc	5511	1231
Classic Balloon Corp	3069	92
Classic Carriers Inc	4213	1279
Classic City Beverages Inc	5181	78
Classic Coffee Concepts Inc	8999	104
Classic Coil Company Inc	3677	32
Classic Color Inc	2796	14
Classic Components Corp	5045	84
Classic Cosmetics Inc	2844	75
Classic Custom Vacations Inc	4725	61
Classic Delights Inc	5149	145
Classic Design Inc	8711	399
Classic Die Inc	3089	1581
Classic East Inc	5511	1223
Classic Egg Products Inc	2015	42
Classic Electric Inc	1731	2398
Classic Express Inc	4213	2608
Classic Ford Lincoln Mercury	5511	813
Classic Graphics Inc	2752	67
Classic Information Systems Inc	7372	2453
Classic Leather Inc	2512	37
Classic Lighting Corp	5063	411
Classic Lighting LP	5063	675
Classic Mold Company Inc	3089	648
Classic Moving and Storage Inc	4213	1553
Classic Optical Laboratories Inc	3851	42
Classic Packaging Co	3086	55
Classic Precision Inc	3599	1823
Classic Residence by Hyatt	6552	100
Classic Sheet Metal Inc	3444	145
Classic Software Inc	7372	4410
Classic Solutions	7372	4282
Classic Sport Companies Inc	3949	103
Classic Telephone Inc	4841	77
Classic Transport Inc	4213	93
Classic Transportation Services	4213	2041
Classic Turning Inc	3451	45
Classic Ventures Diversified Inc	5999	231
Classic Wire Cut Company Inc	3599	171
Classic X-Ray Ltd	5047	247
Classified Display	2711	611
Classified Ventures LLC	2741	28
Classmates Media Corp	7389	159
Classmates Online Inc	7389	754
Classroom Connect	2731	144
Classroom Inc	7372	3098
ClassroomDirectcom	7372	1342
Classy Closets Etc Inc	1799	38
Claud S Gordon Company Inc	3823	40
Claude Laval Corp	5084	272
Claude Perry Co	3523	190
Claudius Peters Americas Inc	8711	575
Clausen Supply Co	4214	16
Clausing Industrial Inc	5084	31
Claussen Pickle Co	2035	5
Claverack Rural Electric Cooperative Inc	4911	491
Clawson Communications Inc	1731	372
Clawson Tank Co	3443	176
Claxton Electric Inc	1731	2265
Clay And Bailey Manufacturing Co	3321	58
Clay Center Locker	2011	157
Clay County Rural Telephone Cooperative Inc	4813	195
Clay Endicott Products Co	3255	3
Clay Ingels Company Inc	5032	17
Clay Lacy Aviation	4512	40
Clay Laguna Co	3295	10
Clay Logan Products Co	3259	6
Clay Pipeline Inc	1623	464
Clayco Electric Co	1731	1750
Claydon's Hallmark Shops	2771	24
Clay-Groomer Machine Shop Inc	3599	2119
Claymore Sieck Co	5063	108
Claypool Electric Inc	1731	241
Clayton and McKervey PC	8721	20
Clayton Aquariums Inc	7389	2323
Clayton Corp	3586	12
Clayton Dubilier and Rice Inc	6799	153
Clayton H Landis Company Inc	3535	39
Clayton Holdings Inc	8748	106
Clayton Homes Inc	2451	1
Clayton Industries Inc	3441	289
Clayton L Scroggins Associates Inc	8742	393
Clayton Manufacturing Co	3569	46
Clayton Miller Hospitality Carpet	5023	185
Clayton Williams Energy Inc	1382	23
Clayton-Davis and Associates Inc	7311	329
Clayton's Crab Company Inc	5146	72
Claywell Electric Company Inc	1731	1466
Clc Cabling Service	1731	2342
CLC Construction Group Inc	8748	392

1438 Ward's Business Directory of U.S. Private and Public Companies, 55th Edition / Volume 5

Company Name	SIC	Rank
Clc Lubricants Co	2992	45
Cld Dynamics Inc	3829	475
Clean Air Products Co	3564	105
Clean Air Technology Inc	1542	412
Clean Coal Technologies Inc	8731	373
Clean Cuts Inc	3652	49
Clean Diesel Technologies Inc	2819	51
Clean Energy Fuels Corp	4932	7
Clean Foods Inc	2095	42
Clean Harbors Inc	4953	11
Clean Harbors of Braintree Inc	4953	7
Clean Harbors of Connecticut Inc	4953	105
Clean Innovation Corp	7349	140
Clean Line Inc	3589	203
Clean Machine Inc	3599	675
Clean Management Inc	7349	185
Clean Tech Systems Inc	7349	235
Clean Venture Inc	4959	8
Clean Yield Asset Management Inc	6282	548
Clean-Flo Laboratories Inc	3829	163
Cleaning Service Group Inc	7349	36
Cleaning Systems Inc	2841	18
Cleanlook Chemical Corp	2841	43
Cleanpack	7389	1678
Cleanscape Software International	7371	823
CleanScapes Inc	4953	83
Clean-Seal Inc	5085	231
Cleanserv Inc	7349	209
Clean-Tech Co	7349	63
Clear Align LLC	3699	189
Clear and Simple Inc	7372	4797
Clear Capital	6531	59
Clear Channel Broadcasting	4832	85
Clear Channel Communications Inc	7319	1
Clear Channel Metroplex Inc	4832	53
Clear Channel Outdoor Holdings Inc	7312	1
Clear Channel Spectacolor LLC	7311	266
Clear Choice Lien Service Inc	7389	1753
Clear Communications Inc	1731	2114
Clear Connection Corp	1731	167
Clear Creek Care Center	8051	80
Clear Creek Centers Inc	8051	64
Clear Creek Distillery Ltd	2084	135
Clear Creek Mutual Telephone Co	4813	362
Clear Creek National Bank	6021	376
Clear Edge Crosible Inc	2393	11
Clear Edge Filtration Inc	3569	30
Clear Fork Inc	1311	207
Clear Harbor LLC	7299	35
Clear Lake Press Inc	2752	946
Clear Lake Specialty Products Inc	2051	288
Clear Lam Packaging Inc	2671	11
Clear Mountain Spring Water	2086	107
Clear Pine Mouldings Inc	2431	55
Clear Staff	7363	97
Clear Technologies Inc	7372	362
Clear Technology Inc	7371	186
Clear Tone Hearing Center Inc	3842	244
Clear View Bag Company Inc	3081	52
Clear Vue Inc	3083	69
Clear Winds Technologies Inc	7379	1250
ClearAccess	7373	470
Clearance Unlimited Inc	8111	598
Clearant Inc	2836	78
clearAvenue LLC	7379	402
Clearbrook	8331	59
Clearbrook Elevator Association	5153	203
Clear-Com LLC	3669	148
Clearcomm Technologies LLC	3663	232
ClearCorrect Inc	3843	32
Clearcube Technology Inc	3571	63
CLEAResult Consulting Inc	8748	84
Clearfield Inc	3661	74
Clearfield Machine Company Inc	3321	66
ClearForest Corp	7372	2266
Clearing House Auction Galleries Inc	7389	1413
Clearlight Partners LLC	6799	246
Clearline Inc	5084	892
Clearlink	8999	167
Clearly H2o Inc	5074	218
ClearOne Communications Inc	3663	70
Clearpath Solutions Group	7373	267
Clearpoint LP	7389	1067
Clearsky Mobile Media Inc	7389	2245
Clearspan Components Inc	2431	100
Clearspeed Technology Ltd	5045	166
Clearspring Technologies	7372	785
Clearstream Wastewater Systems Inc	3589	192
Clearswift Ltd	5045	228
Clear-Tone Communications Incorporated LLC	4813	552
Clearview Software International Inc	7372	3596
Clear-Vu Products	5045	206
Clearwater Cable Vision Inc	4841	107
Clearwater Enterprises LLC	4924	49
Clearwater Packaging Inc	2752	1322
Clearwater Power Company Inc	4911	476
Clearwire Corp	4899	10
Cleary Building Corp	1541	110
Cleary Gottlieb Steen and Hamilton	8111	16
Cleary Millwork Company Inc	5031	182
Cleary Petroleum Corp	1382	24
Cleasby Manufacturing Company Inc	3531	176
Cleaver-Brooks Inc	3589	17
Cleburne Utility Construction Inc	1623	518
Cleco Evangeline LLC	4911	178
Cleco Generation Services LLC	4911	176
Cleco Marketing and Trading LLC	4911	179
Cleco Midstream Resources LLC	4911	180
Cleco Power LLC	4911	79
Cleco Support Group LLC	4911	181
Clem Lumber Distributing Company Inc	5031	115
Clemco Industries Corp	3549	16
Clemens Family Corp	2013	12
Clement Industries Inc	3713	53
Clement Lumber Company Inc	5211	258
Clement Pappas and Company Inc	2033	32
Clements Foods Co	2035	6
Clements Industries	3565	136
Clements International	6331	216
Clements National Co	3589	204
Clemons Inc	7371	1746
Clendenin Brothers Inc	3399	36
Cleo Inc	2679	7
CleoSci	7372	2195
Cleret Inc	5162	24
Clermont Communications Corp	5065	876
Clestra Hauserman Inc	3441	84
Cletronics Inc	3677	69
Cleveland BioLabs Inc	8731	181
Cleveland Brothers Equipment Company Inc	5082	32
Cleveland Cement Contractors Inc	1611	21
Cleveland Circuits Corp	3679	591
Cleveland Coca-Cola Bottling Company Inc	2086	58
Cleveland Corp	7389	505
Cleveland Die and Manufacturing Co	3469	119
Cleveland Dovington Partners Inc	7379	815
Cleveland Electric Co	1731	69
Cleveland Electric Inc	1731	45
Cleveland Enterprises LLC	1731	2100
Cleveland Express Trucking Company Inc	4213	2190
Cleveland Fp Inc	2865	8
Cleveland Gear Company Inc	3566	20
Cleveland Granite and Marble LLC	3281	34
Cleveland Hardware And Forging Co	3463	10
Cleveland Hoya Corp	3827	89
Cleveland Jsm Inc	3599	471
Cleveland Letter Service Inc	7331	282
Cleveland Medical Devices Inc	3842	282
Cleveland Menu Printing Inc	2759	422
Cleveland Plywood Co	5031	170
Cleveland Quarries Inc	1442	10
Cleveland Range Co	3632	4
Cleveland Ship LLC	3731	52
Cleveland Society For The Blind	8322	92
Cleveland Steel Specialty Company Inc	3443	192
Cleveland Steel Tool Co	3544	526
Cleveland Track Material Inc	3441	36
Cleveland Tubing Inc	3082	13
Cleveland Twist Drill Co	3545	10
Cleveland Unlimited Inc	4812	64
Cleveland Wheels	5088	61
Cleveland Wrecking Co	1795	4
Clevenger Ford	5511	1218
Clever Stone Company Inc	1422	62
Cleverbridge Inc	4813	425
Clf Warehouse Inc	5013	136
Cli Graphics Inc	7389	2162
CLI Transport LLP	4213	664
Click 3X Inc	7812	48
Click Industries Inc	3589	182
Click Trips Inc	4724	13
Click Wine Group	5182	28
Click4Care Inc	7372	1223
Clickability Inc	7372	1542
Clickable Enterprises Inc	5983	25
Clickfox Inc	7372	1817
Clickfuel Inc	7311	965
Clickiq Inc	4813	661
Clickshare Service Corp	7375	196
ClickSoftware Inc	7372	1452
ClickSpeed	7311	645
Client Marketing Systems Inc	7371	1177
Client Network Services Inc	8748	57
Client/Server Software Solutions Inc	7371	334
Client Services Inc	7322	9
Clients and Profits Inc	7372	3522
Clients First Inc	7336	251
Clif Bar and Co	2099	60
Cliff Buzick Inc	5211	202
Cliff Delsart Electric Inc	1731	1884
Cliff Hix Engineering Inc	3552	51
Cliff Reed Inc	4213	2568
Cliff Viessman Inc	4213	522
Cliff Weil Inc	5112	39
Cliffco Stands Inc	3544	638
Cliffdale Manufacturing Inc	3769	26
Clifford Associates Inc	6282	282
Clifford Chance LLP	8111	140
Clifford Gage	3546	49
Clifford H Jones Inc	3544	849
Clifford Hampton Construction Inc	3271	22
Clifford Manufacturing Company Inc	3599	1768
Clifford of Vermont Inc	5063	138
Clifford R Lathrop Inc	4213	3080
Clifford Thackson Inc	4813	613
Cliffs Mining Co	1011	2
Cliffs Mining Services Co	1011	3
Cliffs Natural Resources Inc	1011	1
Cliffstar Corp	2033	15
Cliflex Bellows Corp	3599	686
Clifton Adhesive Inc	2891	93
Clifton and Quigg Fertilizer Service Inc	5191	185
Clifton Equipment Rental Company Inc	7353	78
Clifton Group	6282	322
Clifton Gunderson LLC	8721	164
Clifton Moulding Corp	2431	72
Clifton Savings Bancorp Inc	6712	287
Clifton Savings Bank SLA	6035	88
Clifton Trucking Inc	4213	2837
Clifty Engineering And Tool Company Inc	3544	138
Climate Control Inc	3714	242
Climate Master Inc	3585	49
Climate Masters and Electrical Company Inc	1731	1953
Clim-A-Tech Industries Inc	3089	591
Climatemp Inc	1711	106
Climatic Corp	5064	13
Climatronics Corp	3829	247
Climax Metal Products Co	3568	40
Climax Packaging Inc	3993	85
Climax Portable Machine Tools Inc	3541	55
ClinAssure Inc	8734	119
Clinch Mountain Transport/CMT	4213	1830
Clinch River LLC	3441	149
Cline Acquisition Corp	3554	45
Cline Construction Inc	1623	584
Cline Davis and Mann Inc	7311	42
Cline Hose and Hydraulics LLC	3492	26
Cline Tool And Service Co	3545	81
Clines Corners Operating Co	5947	19
Clingan Steel Inc	3312	51
Clinical Chemistry Inc	2721	346
Clinical Innovations LLC	3841	195
Clinical Marketing Consortium	8742	244
Clinical Reference Laboratory Inc	8071	31
Clinical Research Laboratories Inc	8071	43
Clinical Research Management Inc	8732	43
Clinical Resource Network LLC	8099	68
Clinical Resources For Equipment Support Technology Services Inc	8742	215
Clinical Resources LLC	7361	239
Clinical Software Solutions	7372	3295
Clinical Specialties Inc	5047	48
Clinical Technology Inc	5047	199
Clinicomp International Inc	7373	341
Clinilabs Inc	8732	78
Clinipace Worldwide	8731	198
Clinkenbeard and Associates Inc	3599	1701
ClinLab Inc	7373	639
Clintex Laboratories Inc	2844	161
Clinton County Arc	8361	21
Clinton County Electric Cooperative Inc	4911	465
Clinton Fireworks Inc	2899	211
Clinton Group Inc	6282	230
Clinton Industries Inc	3841	307
Clinton Industries Inc	3559	349
Clinton Instrument Co	3823	270
Clinton Machine Inc	3535	111
Clinton Moving and Packaging Inc	4213	3119
Clinton Savings Bank	6022	309
Clintrak Clinical Labeling Services LLC	2754	16
Clio Inc	3829	243
Clipper Exxpress Co	4731	44
Clipper Magazine Inc	2721	70
Clipper Navigation Inc	4489	5
Clipper Publishing Co	2711	197
CLM Freight Lines Inc	4213	1401
Clobus Printing Inc	2752	1515
Clock Spring Co	3069	47
Clockwork Home Services Inc	6794	41
Clofine Dairy and Food Products Inc	5149	87
Clondalkin Pharma and Healthcare Inc	2752	33
Clontech Laboratories Inc	2836	24
Cloos Robotic Welding Inc	3542	46
Clopay Corp	3081	7
Clopay Plastic Products Co	3081	16
Clorox Co	2842	2
Clorox International Co	2842	10
Clos Du Val Wine Company Ltd	2084	60
Clos LaChance Wines Inc	2084	38
Clos Pegase Winery Inc	2084	49
Closet World Inc	1751	1
Closing the Gap Inc	2711	931
Closson's Co	7389	1022
Closure Medical Corp	3842	77
Closure Systems International	3469	5
Clothing Depot Inc	7389	869
Cloud 9 Living LLC	7999	132
Cloud Carpet and Draperies Inc	5713	13
Cloud Company Inc	3589	64
Cloud Creek Systems Inc	7379	420
Cloud Peak Energy Inc	1221	11
Cloudmark Inc	7372	819
Clough Harbour and Associates LLP	8711	125
Clougherty Packing LLC	2011	9
Clouse Trucking Inc	4213	1237
Clovelly Apartments LP	6513	8

Company Name	SIC	Rank
Clover Capital Management Inc	6282	267
Clover Club Bottling Co	5149	187
Clover Corporate Service LLC	8741	215
Clover Farms Dairy Company Inc	2026	46
Clover Garments Inc	2339	49
Clover Graphics Inc	7336	222
Clover Group Inc	5085	271
Clover Leaf Bank	6036	64
Clover Park School District 400	8211	67
Clover Systems	3669	39
Clover Technologies Group LLC	2865	2
Cloverdale Foods Co	2013	46
Cloverhill Pastry Vending Corp	2053	17
Cloverland Electric Coop	4911	353
Cloverleaf Cold Storage Co	7389	387
Cloverleaf Farms Distributors Inc	5149	69
Clover-Stornetta Farms Inc	2026	52
Clovis and Roche' Inc	7322	105
Clovis Bottlers Inc	2086	146
Clovis Group LLC	7361	264
Clow Stamping Co	3469	57
Cloyes Gear and Products Inc	3714	155
Cloyes Gear Co	3714	74
Clp Corp	5063	474
CLP Resources Inc	7361	31
CLS and Associates Incorporated Trucking	4213	1341
Cls Facilities Management Services Inc	5063	462
CLS Security Services Inc	7381	260
CLS Transportation Co	4213	2671
Club Billing Services Inc	7374	267
Club Europa	4724	139
Club One Inc	7997	9
ClubCorp Inc	7997	4
ClubMac Inc	3572	22
Cluen Corp	7379	1085
Clumeck Stern Schenkelberg and Get-zoff	8721	229
Clunette Elevator Company Inc	5191	131
Cluster Systems LLC	5045	892
Clutchco International Inc	3568	45
C-Lutions Inc	7371	1545
Clyde Bergemann EEC	3564	168
Clyde Bergemann Inc	3599	167
Clyde Cummings Candy Inc	2064	117
Clyde Electrical and Mechanical Construction Inc	1731	1047
Clyde Hardware Company Inc	5072	120
Clyde Jones Distributing Company Inc	5013	388
Clyde Machines Inc	3537	70
Cly-Del Manufacturing Co	3469	51
Clyde's Transfer Inc	4213	1203
ClydeUnion Pumps Co	3561	18
CM Automotive Systems Inc	3563	44
CM City Inc	5731	104
CM Furnaces Inc	3567	45
CM Holtzinger Fruit Company LLC	0175	2
CM Paula Co	5112	9
Cm Solutions Inc	3672	394
Cm Technologies Corp	3629	101
Cm3 Building Solutions Inc	5084	345
CMA Consulting Services Inc	7372	1529
Cmacm Technologies Inc	1731	2432
CMax LLC	6162	85
Cmb Printing Inc	2752	1590
CMC Americas Inc	7373	692
CMC Associates	8732	132
Cmc Corp	3599	2275
Cmc Group Inc	6719	147
CMC Howell Metal	3351	3
CMC Rebar Carolinas	3449	20
CMC Rebar Georgia	3441	169
CMC Rebarl Florida	3449	9
Cmc Rescue Inc	5999	82
Cmc Scaffolding Contractors Inc	7359	195
CMC Steel Group	3441	16
Cmc Steel Inc	3316	8
Cmc Trenching Inc	1623	652
Cmd Powersystems Inc	5063	831
Cme Arma Inc	3531	199
CME Group Inc	6231	3
Cme LLC	3621	14
Cmetrix Inc	3679	694
CMF of Kansas LLC	7699	4
CMG Holdings Inc	6798	218
CMG Inc	7372	4674
CMG Mortgage Insurance Co	6351	32
CMH Manufacturing Co	3369	25
CMH Software Inc	5734	415
CMH Sound And Video Inc	1731	2564
Cmi Champion LLC	3444	166
CMI Construction Inc	1541	241
CMI Equipment and Engineering Co	3556	142
Cmi Group	7322	45
CMI Inc	3829	287
Cmi Integrated Technologies Inc	3621	121
CMI Management Inc	8744	23
Cmi Technology Inc	3599	2120
CMI Terex Corp	3531	21
Cmi-Promex Inc	3312	118
Cmi-Schneible Co	3443	121
Cmj Information Technology Inc	7373	847
Cmmc Machine Inc	3599	1866
Cmn Inc	5013	397

Company Name	SIC	Rank
Cmn Plastics Inc	3089	1145
C-Mold Inc	3089	1428
C-Mor Co	2591	14
CMP Industries Inc	3843	19
Cmp Industries LLC	3843	31
CMR Construction and Roofing	1761	13
CMR Railroad Salvage Co	4789	26
Cmre Financial Services Inc	7322	48
CMS Associates Inc (Naperville Illinois)	7372	1395
CMS Bancorp Inc	6036	79
CMS Communications Inc	5099	12
CMS Companies Inc	6282	153
CMS Construction Software	7372	4238
CMS Consulting Inc	7379	559
Cms Development Group LLC	7382	159
Cms Duplication Inc	7379	1348
CMS Energy Corp	1311	7
CMS Generation Co	4911	130
CMS Gilbreth Packaging Systems	3081	27
CMS Peripherals Inc	3572	42
CMS Research Inc	7373	893
Cms Services Inc	5046	338
CMS Technologies	3577	332
Cms-Crane Manufacturing and Service	3536	48
Cmsolutions LLC	7376	50
Cmsp Corp	5043	33
CMT Ii Investments Inc	5461	41
Cmt Laboratories Inc	8734	143
CMT Partners	4812	42
CMV Sharper Finish	3582	10
Cmw And Associates Corp	7379	1032
CMW Inc	3643	35
CMX Group	7372	3178
CMX Systems Inc	7372	3770
Cmyk Corp	7379	1627
Cmyk Printing and Graphics Inc	2752	1642
Cn2	4841	139
CNA	6411	8
Cna Corp	8732	24
CNA Financial Corp	6331	18
CNA Insurance	6331	49
Cna Metals Ltd	5093	19
CNA National Warranty Corp	6399	7
CNA Surety Corp	6351	16
CNB Financial Corp (Clearfield Pennsylvania)	6712	227
CNB Financial Corp (Taylor Texas)	6712	391
CNC Industries Inc	3599	1806
CNC International LP	2843	17
Cnc Machine and Design Inc	3599	2278
CNC Machine Products Inc	3599	252
CNC Precision Machining Inc	3599	593
Cnc Prose Inc	3312	137
CNC Software Inc	7372	888
C-N-D Industries Inc	3441	189
CNET Networks Inc	7379	37
CNet Technology Inc	3674	130
CNG Internet Inc	4813	414
CNH Goodfield	3523	26
Cnh Welfare Benefit Trust	6733	7
CNL Financial Corp	6311	182
Cnn Electronics Inc	5063	942
CNO Financial Group Inc	6311	32
Cnp Solutions Inc	2752	620
Cnr Contractors Inc	1623	804
CNRG Apparel LLC	5651	25
CNS Communications LLC	1731	404
CNS Response Inc	8099	111
Cnw Limited LLC	2796	12
CNX Gas Corp	1311	49
CNY Medical Products Inc	5047	249
Co- Ax Technology Inc	3679	228
Coach Farm Inc	0241	2
Coach Inc	3172	1
Coach USA Inc	4111	1
Co-Advantage Resources Inc	8721	106
Coahoma Electric Power Association	4911	565
Coakley Company Inc	1623	755
Coakley Heagerty Companies Ltd	7311	367
Coal Country Industries Inc	5085	460
Coal Creek Construction Inc	1623	328
Coal Point Trading Co	2092	69
Coalfield Telephone Company Inc	4813	133
Coalition America Inc	8099	41
Co-Alliance LLP	5191	86
Coal-Mac Inc	1221	26
Coams Inc	7311	557
Coanda Intakes LLC	3441	288
Coast Air Inc	5063	548
Coast Aluminum And Architectural Inc	5051	85
Coast Cadillac Co	5511	355
Coast Central Credit Union	6062	38
Coast Controls Inc	3823	301
Coast Converters Inc	3081	15
Coast Counties Truck and Equipment Co	5084	84
Coast Crane Company Of Washington Inc	5082	101
Coast Dental Services Inc	8011	58
Coast Distribution System Inc	5013	46
Coast Electric Power Association	4911	308
Coast Electronic Manufacturing LLC	3679	887
Coast Engine and Equipment Corp	3743	23
Coast International Inc	4813	345

Company Name	SIC	Rank
Coast Machinery Movers	1796	17
Coast Packaging Inc	3086	156
Coast Resorts Inc	7999	37
Coast Satellite Inc	5731	98
Coast Seafoods Co	2091	8
Coast Sign Inc	3993	18
Coast Star	2711	680
Coast to Coast Business Equipment Inc	5044	9
Coast To Coast Carports Inc	3448	45
Coast to Coast Computer Products	5045	711
Coast to Coast Express Inc	4213	2905
Coast To Coast International	5013	135
Coast to Coast Resorts	7033	2
Coast To Coast Security Services Inc	5251	37
Coast to Coast Tickets LLC	7319	74
Coast To Coast Wireless Inc	4813	399
Coast Tool and Supply	5084	553
Coast United Bench Ad Co	7312	8
Coastal Bank and Trust	6022	282
Coastal Bank of Georgia	6022	538
Coastal Banking Company Inc	6021	192
Coastal Bend Tooling and Automation	3549	125
Coastal Beverage Company Inc	5181	50
Coastal Business Supplies Inc	5044	135
Coastal Cab Company Inc	4121	7
Coastal Chemical Company LLC	5169	39
Coastal Clinical And Management Services Inc	8049	11
Coastal Coatings Inc	3471	77
Coastal Contractors Inc	1623	536
Coastal Contractors Inc (Beaufort South Carolina)	1521	89
Coastal Courier Inc	4213	1639
Coastal Developmental Services Foundation	8322	14
Coastal Electric Construction Corp	5063	247
Coastal Electric Inc	1731	869
Coastal Engineering Corp	5084	469
Coastal Enterprises Of Jacksonville Inc	8331	44
Coastal Environmental Operations Inc	7699	168
Coastal Flow Measurement Inc	3823	153
Coastal Forest Resources Co	2436	14
Coastal Helicopters Inc	4522	34
Coastal Hotel Group Inc	7011	150
Coastal Industries Inc	3231	20
Coastal International Inc	5045	627
Coastal International Security Inc	7381	15
Coastal Lincoln	5511	765
Coastal Plain Ventures LLC	3442	116
Coastal Plains Pork LLC	0213	16
Coastal Plastic Molding Inc	3089	1835
Coastal Plastics Inc	2821	173
Coastal Plumbing Supply Company Inc	5074	173
Coastal Power Solutions LLC	1731	2537
Coastal Securities LP	6211	153
Coastal Software and Consulting Inc	7372	4961
Coastal Sound Shop Inc	5731	201
Coastal States Mortgage Corp	6162	79
Coastal Technologies	7371	1319
Coastal Tractor	5999	128
Coastal Traffic Systems Inc	5063	385
Coastal Transportation Inc	4424	11
Coastal Windows Inc	3089	1531
Coastcom Inc	3661	158
Coaster Company of America	5021	33
Coastline Distribution Inc	5075	21
Coastline Equipment Inc	3556	121
Coastline Utility Contractors Inc	1623	319
Coates International Ltd	3511	44
Coates Kokes	7311	456
Coates Screen Inc	2893	7
Coating Design Group Inc	3827	154
Coating Place Inc	2834	259
Coatings And Adhesives Corp	2851	81
Coats Electric Company Inc	1731	1641
Coaxial Components Corp	3679	581
Coaxis Inc	7372	3878
Cobalis Corp	2834	475
Cobalius Solutions PLLC	7375	264
Cobalt Blue LLC	7372	4055
Cobalt Electric Inc	1731	1817
Cobalt Group Inc	7372	409
Cobalt International Energy LP	1311	267
Cobalt Truck Equipment LLC	5013	290
CoBank ACB	6111	4
Cobatco Inc	3556	166
Cobb and Cole	8111	405
Cobb Carpet Supply Co	5084	674
Cobb Electric Membership Corp	4911	160
Cobb Hospital Inc	8062	93
Cobb Mechanical Contractors Inc	1711	52
Cobb Parkway Chevrolet	5511	527
Cobb Tool Inc	3544	803
Co-Been Electric Company LLC	1731	1607
Cobel Technologies Inc	3613	170
Cobey Inc	3498	44
Cobham Sensor Systems Inc	3679	50
Cobi Digital	7361	257
CoBiz Financial Inc	6021	53
CoBiz Insurance Inc	6021	107
Cobleskill Stone Products Inc	1422	8
Coborn's Inc	5411	111
Cobourn and Saleeby LLP	7389	1984

Company Name	SIC	Rank
Cobra Auto	7538	16
Cobra Electronics Corp	3663	46
Cobra Golf Inc	3949	28
Cobra Metal Works Inc	3444	35
Cobra Patterns and Models Inc	3543	19
Cobra Plastics Inc	3089	616
Cobra Systems Inc	3577	359
Cobra Technologies Corp	3663	243
Cobra Tool and Die Inc	3544	191
Cobra Transportation Services Inc	4213	2508
CoBuilder Inc	7319	175
Coburg Road Quarry LLC	1411	2
Coburn and Meredith Inc	6282	491
Coburn Electric Inc	1731	1456
Coburn Technologies Inc	3577	20
Coby Electronics Corp	5099	43
Coca Sales Inc	5085	382
Coca-Cola Aberdeen	5149	115
Coca-Cola Bottling Co	2086	101
Coca-Cola Bottling Company Consolidated	2086	4
Coca-Cola Bottling Company Of Cape Cod Inc	2086	108
Coca-Cola Bottling Company of Chicago	2086	8
Coca-Cola Bottling Company of Colorado	2086	50
Coca-Cola Bottling Company Of Hopkinsville Ky	2086	127
Coca-Cola Bottling Company Of Hot Springs	2086	110
Coca-Cola Bottling Company of Little Rock	2086	23
Coca-Cola Bottling Company Of Minot	2086	135
Coca-Cola Bottling Company of Mississippi	2086	40
Coca-Cola Bottling Company of New York	2086	20
Coca-Cola Bottling Company of Northern New England Inc	2086	9
Coca-Cola Bottling Company of Ohio	2086	18
Coca-Cola Bottling Company of St Louis	2086	14
Coca-Cola Bottling Company of West Point-LaGrange	2086	56
Coca-Cola Bottling Company of West Virginia	2086	22
Coca-Cola Bottling Company Rutland	2086	62
Coca-Cola Bottling Company Texarkana	2086	46
Coca-Cola Bottling Group Southwest	2086	78
Coca-Cola Bottling Works Of Tullahoma Inc	2086	69
Coca-Cola Co (Atlanta Georgia)	2087	1
Coca-Cola Enterprises	2086	92
Coca-Cola Enterprises Inc	2086	10
Coca-Cola Swire Pacific Holdings Inc	2086	17
Cocalico Biologicals Inc	2836	61
Cocco Brothers	3842	276
Cochecton Mills Inc	2048	128
Cochise Electric Inc	1731	1127
Cochlear Americas	3842	92
Cochran Electric Co	1731	1808
Cochran Electric Inc	1731	1441
Cochran Firm	8111	362
Cochran Inc	1731	59
Cochran Oil Mill and Ginnery	5191	113
Cochrane Technologies Inc	3812	84
Cockle Printing Company Inc	2752	1398
Cockrell Oil Corp	1311	104
Cockrell Printing Co	2752	353
CoConnect Inc	6799	343
Coconut Grove Bank	6022	801
Coconut Info	7372	1129
Coda Octopus Group Inc	3674	251
Coda Pharmaceuticals Inc	2834	356
Codale Electric Supply Inc	5063	86
Codan US Corp	3841	87
Code Blue Corp	3669	87
Code Consultants Inc	8742	188
Code Electric Inc	1731	2408
Code Hennessy and Simmons LLC	6799	219
Code Precast Products Inc	5039	67
Code Red Technologies LLC	7378	123
Code Shred Ltd	8999	187
Coded Systems LLC	7389	2240
Codefab Inc	7371	1445
CodeLab Technology Group	7371	1110
CodeSoft International Inc	7372	1454
CodeSource Software Corp	7372	4798
Codestreet LLC	7371	1147
Codeware Inc	7372	3483
Codex Inc	7379	1308
Codexis Inc	8731	63
Codina Group Inc	1542	282
Coding Products	3955	6
Coding Source LLC	8742	125
Codino's Foods Inc	2038	57
Codman and Shurtleff Inc	7372	1842
Codonics Inc	3663	49
Codorniu Napa Inc	2084	105
Codorus Valley Bancorp Inc	6712	317
Cody Company Inc	3444	60
Cody Laboratories	2834	138

Company Name	SIC	Rank
Coe Press Sales Corp	7359	119
Coeco Office Systems Greenville Inc	5045	525
Coefficient LLC	7373	1124
Coen Company Inc	3433	26
Coen Furniture Inc	2521	57
Coe-Truman Technologies Inc	7336	37
Coeur Bullion Corp	1011	4
Coeur D'alene Answering Service	7389	1837
Coeur D'alene Brewing Co	5812	463
Coeur D'alene Builders Supply Inc	3448	33
Coeur D'alene French Baking Co	2051	217
Coeur d'Alene Mines Corp	1041	2
Coeur Inc	3841	140
Co-Ex Pipe Co	3084	48
Co-Ex Plastic Tooling Inc	3544	666
Cofer Brothers Inc	5211	62
Cofer Pipe Construction LLC	1623	793
Coffee Beanery Ltd	5499	19
Coffee Holding Company Inc	2095	10
Coffee House Press	2731	347
Coffee Inns Of America LLC	3589	209
CoffeeCup Software Inc	7372	2107
Coffee-Serv Inc	7389	1905
Coffey Electric Inc	1731	1631
Coffeyville Resources Inc	1311	17
Coffeyville Sektam Inc	3599	281
Coffin Communications Group	8743	112
Coffin Turbo Pump Inc	3561	93
Coffin World Water Systems	3589	25
Coffman Computer Consultants	5734	146
Coffman Manufacturing Corp	3599	2218
Coffman Software Inc	7379	1511
Coffman Stairs LLC	2431	36
Coffman Truck Sales Inc	5511	379
Cofinity	6324	60
Cog Hill Second Inc	7992	6
Cogar Manufacturing Inc	5082	124
Cogdell Spencer Inc	6798	144
Cogency Software Inc	7372	1094
Cogenra Solar Inc	5074	216
Cogent Communications Group Inc	7372	193
Cogent Computer Systems Inc	3674	469
Cogentes Inc	7379	847
Cogentrix Energy LLC	4911	142
Cogentus Pharmaceuticals Inc	8731	283
Coggin and Fairchild Environmental Consultants Inc	0711	3
Coggin Automotive Corp	5511	30
Coggins-Welborn Machine Inc	3559	419
Coghill Composition Company Inc	2791	61
Coghlin Companies Inc	3613	36
Cogility Software Inc	7372	1882
Cogix Corp	7372	1883
Cognetics Corp	7372	3179
Cognex Corp	3571	17
Cognex Distribution Corp	3569	53
Cognex International Inc	3823	14
Cognex Technology and Investment Corp	3823	49
Cognis Corporation USA	2899	24
Cognitech Inc	7372	2122
Cognition Corp	7372	2823
Cognitive Enterprises	7371	1220
CognitiveDATA Inc	7331	60
Cognitronix (Poway California)	7371	1834
Cognizant Technology Solutions Corp	7371	2
Cognos Corp	7372	229
Cogsdill Tool Products Inc	3541	24
Coharie Farms Inc	0213	17
Coharie Hog Farm Inc	5154	3
Cohber Press Inc	2752	265
Cohen and Co	8721	291
Cohen and Company Creative Inc	7311	602
Cohen and Company LLC	6799	18
Cohen and Green Salvage Company Inc	5093	75
Cohen and Grigsby PC	8111	183
Cohen and Lombardo	8111	511
Cohen and Steers Inc	6719	87
Cohen and Wolf PC	8111	488
Cohen Brothers and Co	6799	17
Cohen Financial	6282	69
Cohen Klingenstein and Marks Inc	6282	352
Cohen Steel Supply Inc	5051	453
Cohen Technology Inc	5046	318
Cohen-Esrey Real Estate Services Inc	6531	25
Cohen's Bakery Inc	2045	10
Coherent Inc	3826	9
Cohesant Inc	1711	1
Cohesive Automation Inc	7373	502
Cohn and Gregory Inc	5085	182
Cohn and Wolfe	8743	12
Cohn Wolfe Read Poland and Associates	8743	3
Cohu Inc	3663	25
Cohutta Banking Co	6022	578
COI Telecom Inc	4841	114
Coil Clip Inc	3316	16
Coil Company Inc	3585	194
Coil Counts Ford and Cheney Inc	7373	568
Coil Manufacturing Inc	3621	73
Coil Slitting International LLC	5051	471
Coil Specialty Company Inc	3677	68
Coil Stamping Inc	3544	830

Company Name	SIC	Rank
Coil Tec Of Arizona Inc	3612	80
Coilform Co	3677	51
Coilhose Pneumatics Inc	3052	11
Coil-Q Corp	3677	122
Coils Inc	3677	8
Coils Unlimited Inc	3677	116
Coil-Tran Corp	3677	27
Coiltron Inc	3612	103
COIN Educational Products Inc	7372	3484
Coin Phones Inc	4813	630
Coinco Inc	3469	139
Coining Inc	3469	194
Coinmach Corp	7215	1
Coinmach Service Corp	7389	74
Coinstar Inc	7299	3
COKeM International Inc	5092	5
Coker Electric Company LLC	1731	1669
Cokeva Inc	7378	9
Colacino Industries Inc	5063	713
Colan Contracting Inc	1623	815
Colarelli Construction Inc	1542	259
Colarossi Associates	7991	19
Colbalt Holdings Group LLC	6798	153
Colbert Courier Journal Inc	2711	853
Colbert Packaging Corp	2657	12
Col-Bran Electric Inc	1731	1939
Colburn Communications Inc	1731	2306
Colby Furniture Company Inc	2511	79
Colby Instruments Inc	3829	432
Colby Metal Inc	3499	99
Colby Systems Inc	3663	354
Cold Heading Co	3452	45
Cold Hollow Cider Mill Inc	5149	207
Cold Jet LLC	2813	17
Cold Spring Bakery Inc	2051	147
Cold Spring Construction Co	1611	30
Cold Spring Cooperative Creamery	5191	139
Cold Spring Harbor Laboratory	8731	88
Cold Stone Creamery	2024	20
Coldcypress LLC	7379	783
Coldstream Press	2731	288
Coldvault LLC	3585	242
Coldwater Creek Inc	5621	11
Coldwater Lumber Co	5211	291
Coldwater Veneer Inc	2435	14
Coldwell and Company Inc	5085	306
Coldwell Banker Burnet	6162	21
Coldwell Banker Crossroads Realtors	6531	195
Coldwell Banker Gundaker	6531	65
Coldwell Banker Real Estate Corp	6531	3
Coldwell Banker Residential Brokerage	6531	52
Cole and Reed PC	8721	80
Cole and Weber United	7311	176
Cole Carbide Industries Inc	3545	11
Cole Chemical and Distributing Inc	5172	66
Cole Chevrolet-Cadillac Inc	5511	500
Cole Financial Service Inc	8741	299
Cole Hardwood Inc	5031	271
Cole Hersee Co	3613	27
Cole Instrument Corp	3621	81
Cole Martinez Curtis and Associates	7389	1424
Cole National Corp	5995	2
Cole Papers Inc	5111	10
Cole Screenprint Inc	2759	320
Cole Software LLC	7372	4368
Cole Sport Ski Shops	5941	39
Cole Taylor Bank	6022	81
Cole Tool and Die Co	3544	170
Cole Water Company LLC	2086	141
Cole-Haan Holdings Inc	3149	18
Cole-Layer-Trumble Co	6531	325
Coleman American Moving Services	4213	117
Coleman Assembly and Packaging Inc	7389	1540
Coleman Cable Systems Inc	3357	83
Coleman Machine Inc	3599	1296
Coleman Spohn Corp	1711	208
Coleman's Authentic Irish Pub	5812	387
Coleman's Lumber Yard Inc	5211	298
Colemans Mining And Electrical Equipment Inc	5065	837
Coleman's Towing and Recovery Inc	7549	14
Colerain Ford	5511	1036
Cole's Machine Service Inc	3544	823
Coles Media and Public Relations	8743	139
Coley Electric and Plumbing Supply Of Jesup Inc	5063	789
Coley Farm Services	5159	27
Colfax Corp	3561	23
Colfax International	5045	266
Colfor Manufacturing Inc	3462	4
Colfor Manufacturing Inc Forging Div	3462	7
Colfran Industrial Sales Inc	5169	175
Colgate Oral Pharmaceuticals Inc	2834	143
Colgate-Palmolive Co	2841	3
Coli Electric Contractors Inc	1731	1642
Colich and Sons	1623	42
Colimore Thoemke Architects Inc	8712	315
Colin Medical Instruments Corp	3841	205
CoLinear Systems Inc	7372	3879
Colite International Ltd	3993	88
Collabera	8742	63
Collaborative Consulting	7372	1174
Collaborative Fusion Inc	7371	914
Collaborative Strategies LLC	7379	856

Company Name	SIC	Rank
Collabraspace Inc	3571	55
Collection Consultants Of California Inc	7322	141
Collection Data Systems	7372	3659
Collective Brands Inc	5661	2
Collective Intellect Inc	8732	105
Collector	5944	27
Collectors Edition	2759	241
Collectors Universe Inc	7389	371
Colleen and Herb Enterprises Inc	3599	506
College Connections	8742	400
College Financial Aid Services	7389	473
College Hunks Hauling Junk Inc	8999	178
College Nannies and Tutors Inc	7361	148
College Of Charleston	8221	21
College Savings Bank	6036	83
College Station Electric Inc	1731	501
Collegedale Casework Inc	2531	30
Collegenet Inc	7371	567
Collegian Inc	2711	823
Collegiate Funding Services LLC	6163	4
Collegiate Licensing Co	7941	22
ColleMcVoy	8742	113
Collett Electric Inc	1731	880
Collexis Holdings Inc	7371	276
Colley Elevator Co	7699	162
Collier Communications Inc	7389	1246
Collier Enterprises	6531	139
Collier Well Equipment and Supply Inc	3533	42
Collier2way Communications Inc	5731	179
Collier-Keyworth Inc	3429	112
Colliers Arnold	6531	201
Colliers Arnold Management Inc	6531	69
Colliers Bennett and Kahnweiler Inc	6531	350
Colliers International USA	6531	81
Colliers Macaulay Nicolls International	6531	109
Colliers Meredith and Grew Inc	6531	370
Colliers Pinkard	6531	293
Colliers Reserve Gatehouse	7361	344
Colliflower Inc	5084	659
Collimated Holes Inc	3827	148
Collingwood Grain Inc	5153	17
Collins and Co	5031	267
Collins and Jewell Company Inc	1796	21
Collins Appliance Parts Inc	5064	58
Collins Building Services Corp	7349	395
Collins Bus Corp	3713	33
Collins Cashway Lumber Inc	5031	436
Collins Companies Inc	2426	1
Collins Computing Inc	7371	744
Collins Construction Of Saint George Island Inc	1623	811
Collins Consulting Inc	7379	311
Collins Corp	3599	2200
Collins Craft Corp	3559	554
Collins Crane and Rigging Service	4213	2706
Collins Digital Imaging	2752	1606
Collins Electric Company Inc	1731	141
Collins Entertainment Co	7359	71
Collins Industries	4213	1508
Collins Industries Inc	3711	34
Collins Instrument Company Inc	3599	933
Collins Machine and Manufacturing Inc	3599	1485
Collins Machine and Tool Company Inc	3312	132
Collins Pine Co	2421	50
Collin's Precision Manufacturing Inc	3599	2291
Collins Products LLC	2493	1
Collins Travers and Company Inc	7311	631
Collinsville Building and Loan Association	6036	99
Collinsville Printing Company Inc	2759	299
Collis Group	8011	168
Collis Toolholder Corp	3545	293
Collision King Inc	7538	13
Collman and Karsky Architects	8712	293
Collums Furniture Inc	2512	78
Collum's Lumber Products LLC	2421	47
Colma Drayage Inc	4213	2956
Colmac Coil Manufacturing Inc	3585	164
Colography Group Inc	8732	47
Coloma Frozen Foods Inc	2037	17
Colombo Sales and Engineering Inc	3535	218
Colonial Assembly and Design LLC	3672	274
Colonial Bag Company Inc	2674	9
Colonial Bag Corp	2673	30
Colonial Building Supply LLC	5031	211
Colonial Cadillac-Hyundai Inc	5511	584
Colonial Cartage Corp	4213	1312
Colonial Chevrolet	5511	293
Colonial Circuits Inc	3672	204
Colonial Claims Corp	6331	310
Colonial Coffee Roasters Inc	2095	40
Colonial Commercial Corp	5072	24
Colonial Construction Materials Inc	5032	99
Colonial Electronic Manufacturers Inc	3672	210
Colonial Engineering Inc	5085	379
Colonial Financial Services Inc	6021	151
Colonial Ford Truck Sales Inc	5511	620
Colonial Forest Products Inc	5031	378
Colonial Freight Systems Inc	4213	226
Colonial Full Service Car Wash Inc	7542	1
Colonial Hardware Corp	5085	146
Colonial Life and Accident Insurance Co	6311	68
Colonial Machine and Tool Company Inc	3599	733
Colonial Maintenance Contractors Inc	7349	477
Colonial Manufacturing LLC	3089	1854
Colonial Metal Products Inc	5051	150
Colonial Metals Co	3341	10
Colonial Mold Inc	3544	468
Colonial Oil Industries Inc	5171	12
Colonial Parking Inc	7521	9
Colonial Patterns Inc	3543	32
Colonial Pipeline Co	4613	8
Colonial Plumbing And Heating Supply Inc	5074	162
Colonial Press International Inc	2752	362
Colonial Processing Inc	3325	42
Colonial Properties Trust	6798	75
Colonial Rubber Co	3061	26
Colonial Savings FA	6035	85
Colonial Saw Inc	5251	41
Colonial Steel Corp	5051	434
Colonial Surgical Supply Inc	5047	251
Colonial Telephone Co	4813	561
Colonial Tin Works Inc	5063	588
Colonial Van and Storage Inc	4213	3140
ColonialWebb Contractors	1711	29
Colonie Plastics Corp	3089	548
Colonna's Shipyard Inc	3599	59
Colony Bankcorp Inc	6712	263
Colony Electric Company Inc	1731	891
Colony Financial Inc	6798	220
Colony Hardware Supply Company Inc	5251	32
Colony Insurance Co	6311	102
Colony Management Services Inc	6022	491
Coloplast Corp	3842	125
Color and Supply Company Inc	5231	9
Color By Deluxe	7336	3
Color Communications Inc (Naples Florida)	7812	246
Color Concepts Printing and Design Co	2752	1752
Color Craft Graphic Arts Inc	2752	349
Color Dreams Inc	7372	2877
Color Graphic Printing Inc	2752	1424
Color Graphics Inc	2759	498
Color House Company Ltd	2796	46
Color House Graphics Inc	2789	27
Color Imaging Inc	2865	15
Color Impressions Inc	2752	1503
Color Inc	2752	948
Color Ink Inc	2752	271
Color Me Beautiful Inc	5122	64
Color Me Mine Enterprises Inc	8299	49
Color Methods Inc	7359	154
Color Press Publishing Inc	2754	29
Color Process Inc	2759	387
Color Putty Company Inc	2851	142
Color Q LLC	2759	332
Color Reflections Inc	7384	33
Color Savvy Systems Ltd	7372	737
Color Science Inc	2865	28
Color Service Inc	2796	32
Color Spectrum Inc	2269	7
Color Spot Nurseries Inc	5193	1
Color Tek Inc	2796	35
Color West Inc	2752	373
Color Wheel Paint Manufacturing Company Inc	2851	39
Color World Of Montana Inc	2752	712
Colorado Access	8011	33
Colorado Accurate Inventory	7389	2408
Colorado Asphalt Services Inc	1771	24
Colorado Baggage Co	5948	2
Colorado Bluesky Enterprises	8331	42
Colorado Boxed Beef Co	5147	3
Colorado Boy's Ranch Foundation Inc	8063	19
Colorado Compressor Inc	5084	425
Colorado Consumer Credit Counseling Services of Greater Denver Inc	7389	667
Colorado Container Corp	2653	69
Colorado Counter-Tops Inc	2541	30
Colorado County Sand and Gravel Company LLC	1442	64
Colorado Crystal Corp	3679	500
Colorado Custom Electric Inc	1731	961
Colorado Digital Laboratories Inc	3823	347
Colorado Doorways Inc	5031	100
Colorado Fastners Inc	5063	723
Colorado Film and Television Studios Inc	7812	64
Colorado Industrial Construction Services Company Inc	1731	73
Colorado Interstate Gas Co	4923	15
Colorado Iron and Metal Inc	4953	153
Colorado Lime Co	1422	27
Colorado Lining International Inc	1799	67
Colorado Meat Packers Inc	2011	89
Colorado Molded Products Co	3069	262
Colorado Mountain Express Inc	4729	8
Colorado Paint Co	2851	60
Colorado PC Doctors Inc	7371	1476
Colorado Precision Machining Inc	3599	1158
Colorado Production Group	7812	59
Colorado Public Television Inc	4833	193
Colorado River Materials Inc	1623	176
Colorado Serum Co	2836	42
Colorado Springs Utilities	4931	44
Colorado State Bank and Trust	6712	319
Colorado Technical University Inc	8221	45
Colorado Telecommunications Center Inc	5065	479
Colorado Tortilla Company Inc	2099	299
Colorado Tower Work	1542	428
Colorado Video Inc	3829	193
Colorado WaterJet Co	3429	134
Colorado West Recovery Center	8322	99
Colorado Wire and Cable Company Inc	5063	801
Colorado Word Works Inc	2752	1571
Color-Box LLC	2653	18
COLORCOM	7389	2367
Colorcon Inc	2834	30
Colorcraft Of Virginia Inc	2752	352
Coloredge Visual LLC	2752	1612
Colorfast Of New York Inc	7335	10
Colorful Story Books Inc	2789	41
Colorlith Corp	2752	1059
Colormasters Gem Corporation of New York	5094	6
Colormasters LLC	2673	27
Colormetrix Technologies LLC	7379	1552
Colornet Printing And Graphics Inc	2752	313
Color-Ons Ltd	7323	39
Colors For Plastics Inc	2816	7
Colorsource Inc	2752	1287
Colortec Inc	5013	297
Colortech Graphics and Printing Inc	7334	76
Colortech Graphics Inc	2752	458
Colortech Inc	2752	1572
Colortech Of Wisconsin Inc	2759	345
Colortek	7384	36
Colortone Camera Inc	5999	217
Colortree Incorporated Of Virginia	2677	12
Colortyme Inc	6794	86
Colorvision International Inc	7335	14
ColorWare Inc	3571	131
COLOSSUS Inc	7373	151
Colossus Technology Inc	5734	96
Colotex Electric Supply Co	5063	359
Colour Concepts Inc	2752	158
Colour Matters International Inc	7372	4963
Colour Tech Marketing Inc	2759	482
Colourscape Inc	0781	25
Col-Pal Press Inc	2752	1574
Col-Pump Company Inc	3321	62
Colquitt Electric Membership	4911	153
Colsa Corp	8731	33
Colsky Media Inc	8999	153
Colson and Colson Construction Co	1522	19
Colt Contracting Co	1623	721
Colt Defense Inc	3484	12
Colt Inc	4953	139
Colt Tech LLC	7389	2454
Colt Temperature Control and Tube Inc	1796	27
Colt Truck Lines Inc	4213	1650
Col-Tab Inc	2679	72
Colton Truck Supply	5013	404
Coltrin and Associates	8743	152
Colt's Manufacturing Company LLC	3484	4
Colts Plastics Inc	3085	27
Colubris Networks Inc	5045	112
Colucci Sales Inc	5065	552
Columbia/Alleghany Regional Hospital Inc	8062	240
Columbia Analytical Services Inc	8734	24
Columbia ASC LLC	8011	154
Columbia ASC Northwest LLC	8011	156
Columbia Bank (Columbia Maryland)	6022	229
Columbia Bank (Tacoma Washington)	6022	182
Columbia Banking System Inc	6022	41
Columbia Basin Electric Cooperative Inc	4911	489
Columbia Basin Publishing Company Inc	2711	533
Columbia Beverage Co	6519	32
Columbia Books Inc	2731	101
Columbia Casualty Co	6331	247
Columbia Corrugated Box Company Inc	2653	28
Columbia Cosmetics Manufacturers Inc	2844	103
Columbia Data Products Inc	7372	2123
Columbia Data Systems Inc	5045	1021
Columbia Dentoform Corp	3843	40
Columbia Distributing Co	5181	17
Columbia Electric Inc	1731	777
Columbia Empire Farms Inc	0173	5
Columbia Empire Meat Company Inc	5147	77
Columbia Extrusion Corp	3442	88
Columbia Falls Aluminum Company LLC	3334	14
Columbia Forest Products Inc	2435	3
Columbia Gas of Maryland Inc	4924	60
Columbia Gas of Massachusetts	4924	37
Columbia Gas Of Ohio Inc	4924	5
Columbia Gas of Pennsylvania Inc	4924	31
Columbia Gas of Virginia Inc	4924	43
Columbia Gas Transmission Corp	4922	23
Columbia Gear Corp	3566	10
Columbia Glass and Windows	3442	99
Columbia Grinding Inc	3599	1521
Columbia Group Inc	8711	117

Company Name	SIC	Rank	Company Name	SIC	Rank	Company Name	SIC	Rank
Columbia Gulf Transmission Co	4922	27	Colvin Electric Inc	1731	411	Command Center Inc	7363	80
Columbia Health System Inc	8069	12	Colvin-Friedman LLC	3089	1615	Command Communications Inc	3577	326
Columbia Helicopters Inc	7699	19	Colwell Construction Company Inc	1611	212	Command Components Corp	3643	155
Columbia High Yield Municipal Fund	6722	158	Colwell Industries Inc	2752	32	Command Electronics Inc	3645	41
Columbia Hospital At Medical City Dallas Subsidiary LP	8062	82	Colwich Lumber and Supply Inc	5211	297	Command Medical Products Inc	3841	213
			Com Pac Filtration Inc	3589	211	Command Nutritionals LLC	2023	27
Columbia House Co	5961	24	Com Tec Printing and Graphics Inc	2752	1349	Command Plastic Corp	2671	52
Columbia Industries	8331	122	Comade Inc	5199	67	Command Security Corp	7381	14
Columbia Insurance Co	6331	73	Comair Holdings Inc	4512	32	Command Systems Inc	7379	251
Columbia Insurance Group Inc	6331	293	Comair Inc	4512	41	Command Tooling Systems LLC	3545	94
Columbia IT Solutions	3949	62	Comair Rotron Inc	3577	135	Command X	7371	1342
Columbia Laboratories Inc	2834	193	Comal Iron and Metals Inc	5093	205	Commander Premier Aircraft Corp	3721	33
Columbia Lighthouse For The Blind	8322	220	Comanche Bit Service Inc	3533	134	Commcare Pharmacy	5912	33
Columbia Lighting Inc	3646	7	Comanco Environmental Corp	4953	60	Commcorp Inc	1731	734
Columbia Lloyds Insurance Co	6331	354	Comar Inc	3089	313	Commdex Consulting LLC	8748	203
Columbia Machine Inc	3272	43	Comarco Inc	3663	80	Commeg Systems Inc	5065	850
Columbia Machine Works	3599	2485	Comarco Products Inc	5812	429	Commence Corp	7372	2595
Columbia Machine Works Inc	3599	431	COMARCO Wireless Technologies	3661	75	Commentator	2711	880
Columbia Management Co	6282	284	Comark Corp	3571	98	Commerce Bancorp (Seattle Washington)	6712	378
Columbia Manufacturing Corp	3442	55	Comau Pico Holdings Corp	3548	9			
Columbia Manufacturing Inc	2531	31	Comax Manufacturing Corp	2869	82	Commerce Bancshares Inc	6712	47
Columbia Manufacturing Inc	3724	50	ComAxis Technology	7372	1164	Commerce Bank	6035	193
Columbia Marking Tools Inc	3549	52	ComBase Communications	7379	1488	Commerce Bank and Trust Co (Worcester Massachusetts)	6022	250
Columbia Medical Inc	3841	363	Combest Inc	4813	254			
Columbia Metal Spinning Co	3469	239	CombiMatrix Corp	3826	107	Commerce Bank (Laredo Texas)	6022	33
Columbia Mid Cap Value A Fund	6722	117	Combine Systems Inc	1731	1616	Commerce Bank NA (Kansas City Missouri)	6021	41
Columbia National Group Inc	5093	8	Combined Computer Resources Inc	7372	3577			
Columbia/Okura LLC	3537	71	Combined Computer Technology Inc	7371	935	Commerce Bank NA (Omaha Nebraska)	6021	105
Columbia Packing Company Inc	5147	42	Combined Insurance Company of America	6321	26	Commerce Bank NA (St Louis Missouri)	6021	37
Columbia Paint Corp	2851	148	Combined Metals of Chicago LLC	5051	5			
Columbia Parcar Corp	3799	19	Combined National Systems Inc	7349	174	Commerce Bank NA (Wichita Kansas)	6021	15
Columbia Pipe and Supply	5051	83	Combined Properties Inc	6512	19	Commerce Bank of Hannibal NA	6021	372
Columbia Power and Water System	4911	237	Combined Systems Technology Inc	5045	563	Commerce Bank of Washington NA	6021	307
Columbia Printing and Graphics Inc	2752	1516	Combined Transport Inc	4213	405	Commerce Casino	7993	4
Columbia Recycling Corp	2299	12	Combinenet Inc	7372	200	Commerce Clearing House Inc	2731	16
Columbia Research Laboratories Inc	3825	193	Combotronics Inc	3531	236	Commerce Color Inc	2791	50
Columbia Restaurant Group Inc	5812	331	Combs and Co	7311	384	Commerce Construction Company Inc	1541	143
Columbia River Carbonates	1422	18	Combustion Associates Inc	3443	181	Commerce Controls Inc	7373	306
Columbia Rubber Mills Inc	3061	46	Combustion Research Corp	3585	223	Commerce CRG LLC	6531	327
Columbia Sales Inc	2679	62	Comca Systems Inc	7373	1161	Commerce Energy Group Inc	4911	262
Columbia Showcase and Cabinet Company Inc	2541	21	ComCables	3612	60	Commerce Financial Printers Corp	2752	995
			ComCam International	7389	845	Commerce First Bancorp Inc	6021	284
Columbia SLA (Milwaukee Wisconsin)	6036	105	Comcar Industries Inc	4213	69	Commerce Grinding Management Inc	3599	478
Columbia Southern Inc	5084	548	Comcast Cablevision of Detroit Inc	4841	61	Commerce Holdings Inc	6331	56
Columbia Sportswear Co	2329	2	Comcast Cablevision of Maryland Inc	4841	47	Commerce Insurance Co	6331	118
Columbia State Bank	6022	544	Comcast Corp	4841	1	Commerce Mortgage Corp	6162	49
Columbia Tool and Gage Co	3599	2334	Comco Inc	3559	273	Commerce National Bank	6021	168
Columbia Ultimate Business Systems Inc	7372	466	Comco Inc (Bettendorf Iowa)	5734	379	Commerce National Bank (Fullerton California)	6021	254
			Comco Plastics Inc	3081	141			
Columbia University Press	2731	136	ComCom Systems Inc	7372	2952	Commerce Printing Co	2752	773
Columbia Ventures Corp	5051	13	Comconnexion	7373	1040	Commerce Technologies Inc	7389	1383
Columbia Woodworking Inc	2431	70	ComCore Technologies Inc	3661	30	Commerce Velocity Inc	7372	387
Columbia-Csa/Hs Greater Canton Area Healthcare Systems LP	8062	132	Com-Corp Industries Inc	3469	202	Commerce Welding and Manufacturing Company Inc	3599	2219
			Comdaco Inc	3053	136			
Columbiaknit Inc	2253	22	Comdata Corp Merchant Services Div	3578	9	Commerce West Insurance Co	6331	176
Columbian Chemicals Co	2895	3	Comdel Inc	8711	490	CommerceBank Holding Corp	6712	129
Columbian Home Products LLC	3999	74	Comdie Inc	5065	759	CommerceNet	7389	971
Columbian Logistics Network	4225	22	Comdisco Holding Company Inc	7377	27	CommerceWest Bank NA	6021	214
Columbian Mutual Life Insurance Co	6311	155	ComDoc Inc	5943	5	Commercial And Coin Laundry Equipment Company Inc	7215	4
Columbine Federal Credit Union	6061	130	Comeau Computing	7372	3597			
Columbine Management Company Inc	6531	404	CoMed Communications Inc	8399	5	Commercial and Savings Bank of Millersburg Ohio	6022	402
Columbine Oxygen Service Inc	5047	228	Comedy Partners LP	4841	33			
Columbine Plastics Corp	3089	1306	Comelco Inc	1731	1586	Commercial Bancshares Inc (Upper Sandusky Ohio)	6712	565
Columbine Printing Co	2752	1338	Comentum Corp	7379	505			
Columbine Technology Inc	3679	765	Comer Electric Company Inc	1731	1814	Commercial Bank (Alma Michigan)	6021	230
Columbus Air Delivery	4213	2778	Comer Inc	5063	62	Commercial Bank and Trust Company of Troup County	6022	512
Columbus Bank and Trust Co	6022	99	Comer Packing Company Inc	5144	26			
Columbus Bride	2721	263	Comercial Communications Inc	2791	30	Commercial Bank and Trust of Pennsylvania	6021	169
Columbus Capital Partners LLC	7331	188	Comerica Inc	6712	24			
Columbus Chemical Industries Inc	5169	128	Comertec LLC	5045	937	Commercial Bank of Texas NA	6021	94
Columbus Coca-Cola Bottling Co	2086	52	Comet Automation Systems Inc	3599	395	Commercial Bank (Thomasville Georgia)	6022	424
Columbus Data Technologies Inc	7373	927	Comet Die and Engraving Co	3544	147			
Columbus Electric Cooperative Inc	4911	409	Comet Electric And Equipment LLC	1731	1315	Commercial Bank (West Liberty Kentucky)	6022	486
Columbus Engineering Inc	3599	1792	Comet Micro Systems Inc	7373	630			
Columbus Heating and Ventilating Co	1711	128	Comet Solutions Inc	7371	1612	Commercial Barge Line Co	4449	6
Columbus Hydraulics Co	3593	21	Comet Tool Company Inc	3089	1737	Commercial Blueprint Inc	5049	75
Columbus Industries Inc	3569	32	Comet Tool Inc	3545	106	Commercial Brick Corp	3255	5
Columbus Instruments International Corp	3826	73	Comet Way Inc	7372	2953	Commercial Building Maintenance Corp	7349	66
			COMETALS	3548	47			
Columbus It Partner USA Inc	7389	1082	Comey and Shepherd Realtors	6531	238	Commercial Building Services Inc	7349	253
Columbus Ledger Enquirer	2711	59	COMFORCE Corp	7363	29	Commercial Building Specialists Inc	1541	193
Columbus Marble Works Inc	2752	793	COMFORCE Telecom Inc	7363	44	Commercial Business Systems Inc	7372	4283
Columbus McKinnon Corp	3531	11	Comfort Engineers Inc	1711	123	Commercial Care Services Inc	1799	153
Columbus Messenger Co	2711	607	Comfort House Inc	7359	211	Commercial Carrier Corp	4213	212
Columbus Paper Company Inc	5085	95	Comfort Keyboard Company Inc	3577	589	Commercial Carving Co	2426	21
Columbus Pipe and Equipment Co	5051	252	Comfort Line Inc	3089	696	Commercial Cleaning Corp	7349	454
Columbus Qcb Inc	3412	6	Comfort Medical Supply LLC	5047	118	Commercial Clear Print Inc	2752	1800
Columbus Regional Hospital Inc	8062	193	Comfort Research LLC	2392	43	Commercial Collection Corporation Of New York	7322	99
Columbus Rubber and Gasket Co	3053	117	Comfort Supply Inc	5075	31			
Columbus Scrap Material Company Inc	5093	179	Comfort Systems USA	1711	63	Commercial Communications Inc	2752	57
Columbus Show Case Co	2541	13	Comfort Systems USA Inc	1731	5	Commercial Communications LLC	4899	217
Columbus Steel Castings Inc	3325	13	Comfort View Products LLC	5031	200	Commercial Corrugated Corp	2653	102
Columbus Technologies And Services Inc	8711	249	Comfortex Corp	2591	6	Commercial Creamery Co	2023	7
			ComFrame Software Corp	7372	1835	Commercial Crystal Laboratories Inc	3679	811
Columbus Truck and Equipment Company Inc	5511	1050	ComGlobal Systems Inc	7379	202	Commercial Data Systems Corp	7372	4675
			Comgraphics Inc	5946	10	Commercial Data Systems Inc	5734	9
Columbus Warehouse and Cartage	4213	2215	Com-Jan Inc	7349	217	Commercial Decal Of Ohio Inc	2759	433
Columbus Wireless Communications	5999	288	Comlink Information Systems Inc	7372	3341	Commercial Dispatch Publishing Company Inc	2711	472
Column Engineering LLC	7373	696	Comlink Wireless Technologies Inc	5065	877			
Column Technologies Inc	5045	88	Commack Union Free School District 10	8211	42	Commercial Distributing Co	5181	31
Colusa Elevator Company Inc	5153	58				Commercial Door Company Of Dallas Inc	5031	349
Colussy Chevrolet Inc	5511	987	CommAir Mechanical Services	1711	87			
Colvico Inc	1731	1112	Command Alkon Inc	7372	57			
Colville Tribal Services Corp	1542	194						

Company Name	SIC	Rank
Commercial Door Company Of Houston Inc	5031	272
Commercial Drywall Inc	7363	148
Commercial Electric Company Of Alexandria LLC	1731	1559
Commercial Electric Inc	1731	503
Commercial Electric Products Corp	5085	232
Commercial Enameling Co	3479	112
Commercial Energy LLC	4924	54
Commercial Energy Systems Inc	1731	846
Commercial Fire And Communications Inc	1731	608
Commercial Furniture Group	2599	3
Commercial Furniture Interiors Inc	5021	110
Commercial Furniture Services Inc	5021	65
Commercial Grinding Company Inc	7389	1947
Commercial Honing Company Inc	7699	183
Commercial Honing LLC	3599	170
Commercial Instruments and Alarm Systems Inc	7382	131
Commercial Interiors Of Jacksonville Inc	7389	1174
Commercial Janitor Service Corp	7349	427
Commercial Janitorial Maintenance	5085	451
Commercial Kitchens Inc	3469	211
Commercial Legal Software Inc	7371	16
Commercial Letter Inc	7331	75
Commercial Levin	7389	461
Commercial Lighting Industries Inc	5063	284
Commercial Lighting Sales	5063	413
Commercial Lithographing Company Inc	2752	167
Commercial Logic Inc	7372	2492
Commercial Machine Inc	3599	1951
Commercial Mail Service Inc	7331	133
Commercial Manufacturing	3556	105
Commercial Metal Fabricators Company Inc	3441	175
Commercial Metals Co	5051	3
Commercial Micro-Systems Inc	5045	940
Commercial Motor Co	5511	1039
Commercial Motors	5013	353
Commercial National Bank (Texarkana Arkansas)	6021	180
Commercial National Financial Corp (Ithaca Michigan)	6712	525
Commercial National Financial Corp (Latrobe Pennsylvania)	6712	539
Commercial Newspaper Service	2741	227
Commercial Office Furniture Co	5712	66
Commercial Office Interiors Inc	5021	74
Commercial Office Supply Inc	5112	67
Commercial Optical Manufacturing Inc	3229	42
Commercial Plastics Corp	3089	1782
Commercial Recovery Systems Inc	7322	57
Commercial Sand Company Inc	5032	174
Commercial Services Group Inc	7322	108
Commercial Sewing Inc	3161	6
Commercial Specialists Inc	5075	108
Commercial Steel Treating Corp	3479	22
Commercial Technology Group Inc	7382	170
Commercial Telephone Installations	4813	641
Commercial Timesharing Inc	7371	1282
Commercial Tire Co	5014	60
Commercial Tool and Die Inc	3544	53
Commercial Transfer Inc	4214	33
Commercial Transport Inc	4213	1699
Commercial Turf Products Ltd	3524	11
Commercial Vehicle Group Inc	3499	2
Commercial Warehouse and Cartage	4213	2873
Commercial Window Coverings Inc	5023	155
Commercial Wireless Solutions LP	4813	614
Commercial Wood Products Co	2521	30
Commercium Technology Inc	7382	56
Commerzbank Capital Markets Corp	6211	242
Commetrex Corp	7372	3598
Commex Corp	3081	140
Commint Inc	5961	179
Commission Junction Inc	7389	155
Commitment 2000 Inc	2051	191
Commitment Software Inc	7371	1679
Commitment To Keep	3679	754
Commline Inc	5731	233
Commnet Communications Network Inc	4813	618
Commodex	7375	216
Commodities Resource Corp	6221	15
Commodity Carriers Inc	4213	1332
Commodity Group LLP	3679	706
Commodity Specialists Co	5159	13
Commodity Systems Inc	7389	1415
Commodore Advanced Sciences Inc	4953	151
Commodore Applied Technologies Inc	4959	29
Commodore Builders	1541	146
Commodore Express Inc	4213	2625
Commodore Plastics LLC	3089	707
Commodore Transport LLC	4213	1968
Common Courage Press	2731	342
Common Sense Housing Inc	8361	176
Common Sense Solutions Inc	7372	2124
Common Sensing Inc	3823	475
CommonFund	6722	201
CommonPlaces e-Solutions LLC	7379	446

Company Name	SIC	Rank
Commonwealth Bancshares Inc (Shelbyville Kentucky)	6712	653
Commonwealth Bankshares Inc	6712	269
Commonwealth Biotechnologies Inc	8731	422
Commonwealth Business Bank	6022	385
Commonwealth Business Media	2741	437
Commonwealth Edison Co	4911	43
Commonwealth Electric Company of the Midwest	1731	118
Commonwealth Films Inc	7812	304
Commonwealth Financial Network	6211	141
Commonwealth Group Inc	6282	569
Commonwealth Industrial Services Inc	7389	1161
Commonwealth Machine Co	3599	2469
Commonwealth Mailing Services Inc	7331	214
Commonwealth Mailing Systems Inc	7331	148
Commonwealth Metal Corp	5051	53
Commonwealth Mutual Insurance Company of America	6331	350
Commonwealth National Bank	6021	285
Commonwealth Publishing Inc	2711	298
CommonWealth REIT	6798	39
Commonwealth Stone	1611	245
Commonwealth Supply Company Inc	5084	447
Commonwealth Technology Inc	3812	64
Commonwealth Tool And Machine Inc	3541	128
Commonwealth Trading Corp	5046	334
Commonwealth Warehouse and Storage	4213	309
Commonwealth Worldwide Chauffeured Transportation	7299	10
Commotion Promotions Ltd	7319	121
Comm-Pro Associates Inc	7372	3880
Commpro International	7311	672
CommScope Credit Union	6062	90
CommScope Inc	3663	4
Commstructures Inc	3663	127
Commsystems LLC	7373	803
Commtech 2000	3663	266
Commtech Inc	3674	379
Commtouch Inc	4822	16
Commtrak Corp	7322	169
Communication And Data System Consultants Inc	5734	316
Communication Automation Corp	3672	215
Communication Business Services Inc	7389	1751
Communication Cable Co	3496	102
Communication Centre Inc	7389	1377
Communication Coil Inc	3677	38
Communication Company Of South Bend Inc	5063	447
Communication Con Connectors Inc	3678	37
Communication Concepts Inc	5961	196
Communication Controls Inc	5065	847
Communication Corporation Of Connecticut	7311	895
Communication Devices Inc	3663	253
Communication Federal Credit Union	6061	71
Communication Graphics Inc	2759	168
Communication Graphics Inc (Glen Burnie Maryland)	2752	1359
Communication Intelligence Corp	3577	618
Communication Logistics Inc	7331	102
Communication Mailing Services Inc	7331	149
Communication Power Solutions Inc	1731	1382
Communication Products Corp Loudspeaker Component Div	3651	68
Communication Service Center Inc	7331	233
Communication Service Inc	5065	830
Communication Source Data Inc	5065	902
Communication Specialists Inc	5065	545
Communication Steel Inc	3441	176
Communication Systems Inc	7382	80
Communication Technologies Inc (Chantilly Virginia)	4899	49
Communication Technology For Business Inc	7379	792
Communications 21 Inc	8742	606
Communications and Power Engineering Inc	7371	179
Communications and Power Industries Inc	3671	11
Communications Cable And Wireless Inc	1731	2131
Communications Conveyor Company Inc	3535	137
Communications Corporation Of America	7331	27
Communications Corporation of Baton Rouge Inc	4833	88
Communications Creative Inc	8999	143
Communications Distributors Inc	5065	117
Communications Equity Associates	6799	64
Communications Etc	3663	265
Communications Group Inc (Little Rock Arkansas)	7311	430
Communications Manufacturing Co	3825	208
Communications Marketing And Distribution Services Inc	2759	80
Communications Marketing Southeast Inc	5099	65
Communications Of Fort Smith LLC	5999	162
Communications Plus Inc	1731	2357

Company Name	SIC	Rank
Communications Products and Services Inc	5063	123
Communications Products Inc	8711	327
Communications Resource Corp	5734	409
Communications Resource Inc	5045	327
Communications Solutions Inc	1731	2311
Communications Specialists Inc	2752	1789
Communications Specialties Inc	3577	256
Communications Supply Corp	5063	6
Communications Systems Inc	3661	27
Communications Technology Inc	1731	1409
Communications Televideo Ltd	5065	301
Communications Test Design Inc	7629	1
Communications Unlimited	1731	2164
Communications USA Inc	7359	212
Communications World of Dallas Inc	5065	597
Communications-Applied Technology Co	3663	199
Communications-Pacific Inc	8743	71
Communicators Group	8742	428
CommuniCreations Inc	7336	298
CommuniGate Systems Inc	7372	2058
COMMUNIQUE Inc (Jefferson City Missouri)	7311	795
Communispace Corp	7372	2530
Communispond	8742	335
Communitech Services Inc	5065	742
Community 1st Bank	6029	24
Community Access Inc	8322	171
Community Access Unlimited Inc	8361	17
Community Action Agency Of South Central Michigan	8322	52
Community Action Commission Of Belmont County	8322	133
Community Action Organization	8322	51
Community Action Project Of Tulsa County Inc	8322	22
Community Alert Network Inc	7382	157
Community Alternatives Nebraska Inc	8052	5
Community America Credit Union	6061	11
Community Answering Service Inc	7389	1927
Community Antenna Service Inc	4841	132
Community Asphalt Corp	1611	29
Community Bancorp	6021	172
Community Bank and Trust of Southeast Alabama	6022	623
Community Bank (Lancaster Ohio)	6022	465
Community Bank NA	6021	70
Community Bank of Florida	6022	272
Community Bank of the Bay	6022	661
Community Bank (Pasadena California)	6036	15
Community Bank Shares of Indiana Inc	6022	206
Community Bank System Inc	6712	101
Community Bankers Trust Corp	6712	289
Community Behavioral Health Inc	8322	1
Community Business Bancshares Inc	6712	666
Community Business Bank	6022	773
Community Business Bank (West Sacramento California)	6022	652
Community Capital Bancshares Inc	6021	273
Community Capital Corp	6021	137
Community Care Center Inc	8059	20
Community Care Services Inc	8049	17
Community Cash Management Corp	7322	131
Community Coffee Company LLC	2095	5
Community Communications Inc	4899	79
Community Coordinated Care For Children Inc	8322	13
Community Counselling Service Company Inc	8748	31
Community Development Institute Head Start	8351	8
Community Electric Coop	4911	420
Community Financial Corp (Staunton Virginia)	6035	115
Community Financial Members Federal Credit Union	6061	154
Community Financial Shares Inc	6035	146
Community First Bancorp	6022	298
Community First Credit Union	6062	81
Community First Credit Union of Florida	6062	33
Community Food Bank Of New Jersey Inc	8322	18
Community Health Systems Inc	8062	6
Community Hospital Of San Bernardino	8062	142
Community Hospitals	8062	17
Community Housing Options Integrated Community Emp Social Servs Inc	8322	237
Community Imaging Partners Inc	8093	21
Community Investors Bancorp Inc	6035	223
Community Isp Inc	4813	408
Community Light and Sound Inc	3651	94
Community Living Alliance Inc	8322	77
Community Media Corp	2711	428
Community Mobile Diagnostics LLC	8071	46
Community Mortgage Corp	6162	52
Community Motors Inc	5511	684
Community National Bancorp	6021	341
Community National Bank (Derby Vermont)	6022	230
Community Network Services Inc	4813	498
Community Newspaper Holdings Inc	2711	48
Community Newspapers Inc	2711	331

Company Name	SIC	Rank	Company Name	SIC	Rank	Company Name	SIC	Rank
Community of Science Inc	7375	89	Compeq International Corp	3672	62	Compressed Air Systems Inc	3563	16
Community Partners Bancorp	6022	232	Competence Software Inc	7372	3815	Compression Source Inc	5932	13
Community Premier Plus Inc	8011	37	Competenet Inc	7371	1230	Compressor Parts and Repair Inc	7623	13
Community Products LLC	3842	65	Competetive Carbide Inc	3541	206	Compressor Pump And Service Inc	5084	498
Community Rehabilitation Industries Inc	8331	212	Competition Cams Inc	3714	197	Compressor Sales Inc	5075	119
Community Residences Inc	8059	18	Competition Data Systems Inc	7371	1694	Compressor Systems Inc	7359	54
Community Resource Federal Credit Union	6061	120	Competition Electronics Inc	3625	364	Compressorworks Inc	3465	36
Community Resources Inc	8322	189	Competition Tv and Appliance	5064	151	Compri Consulting Inc	7379	483
Community Services Inc	8322	211	Competitive Computing Inc	7373	416	Compris Technologies Inc	7372	1836
Community Services Of Stark County Inc	8322	141	Competitive Engineering Inc	3769	19	COMPRO Consulting Group Inc	7379	272
Community Shoppers Inc	2741	162	Competitive Innovations LLC	7373	484	Comprobe Inc	3812	182
Community Shores Bank Corp	6022	467	Competitive Technologies Inc	6794	134	Comproducts Inc	5065	243
Community Support Resource	8742	554	Competitor Magazine	2721	378	Comprompter Inc	7372	3816
Community Support Services	8322	143	Compex Corp	3679	551	Comprose Inc	7372	3694
Community Surgical Supply Of Toms River Inc	5047	42	Compex Technologies Inc	3845	32	Compsat Technology Inc	7379	526
Community Techknowledge Inc	7371	810	Compiled Logic Corp	7371	551	Compsee Inc	3577	304
Community Television of Prince George's Inc	7812	297	Compix Inc	3829	428	Comptel Inc	7379	1162
Community Title and Escrow Inc	6541	17	Compix Media Inc	3577	30	Compton and Sons Inc	2752	1112
Community Trust Bancorp Inc	6021	43	Complete Care Medical Inc	6162	148	Compton Construction Company Inc	1623	306
Community Trust Bank Inc (Pikeville Kentucky)	6021	361	Complete Computer Inc	7379	1270	Comptrol Inc	3699	172
Community Unit School District 220	8211	96	Complete Computing Inc	5734	25	Comptron Data Inc	7372	2954
Community Valley Bancorp	6035	112	Complete Controls Inc	3823	441	Comptus Inc	5084	936
Community Valley Bank	6022	714	Complete Dewatering Pumps and Well-points Inc	7359	127	CompTutor-Computer Tutoring	8331	180
Community West Bancshares	6712	402	Complete Drives Inc	5085	223	Compu Graphics	3559	197
Community Workshop And Training Center Inc	8331	99	Complete Filtration Inc	3564	154	Compu-Aire Inc	3585	95
Community Workshop Inc	8331	39	Complete Genomics Inc	8731	222	CompuBridge Inc	7372	1730
Community Workshops Inc	8331	160	Complete Hand Assembly And Finishing Inc	2789	108	Comp-U-Build Computers Inc	3571	216
CommunityOne Bank	6021	101	Complete Healthcare Communications Inc	7311	158	Compucable Corp	3572	76
Commutair Inc	4512	34	Complete Inspection Systems Inc	5045	900	Compucharts Computer Products and Services Inc	7378	51
CommVault Systems Inc	7372	169	Complete Landscaping Systems Inc	0781	11	Compucolor Associates	2752	133
Commwise Inc	5065	1004	Complete Logistics Co	7389	2505	Compucolor Associates Inc	2752	745
Comm-Works Holdings LLC	1731	87	Complete Maintenance and Janitorial Inc	7349	234	Compucom Inc	3663	412
Commworld Of Cumberland LLC	1731	2534	Complete Medical Products Inc	5047	242	CompuCom Systems Inc	5045	12
Commworld Of Kern County Inc	1731	1902	Complete Office	5712	42	Compucon Corp	3823	266
Comnav Engineering Inc	3569	208	Complete Packaging Inc	2441	4	Compucorp Of South Florida	7374	232
Comnet Consulting Inc	7379	1489	Complete Production Services Inc	1389	11	Compucover Inc	3577	661
Comnet International Co	7379	287	Complete Property Maintenance Inc	7349	206	CompuCredit Corp	6141	27
Comnexia Corp	7379	962	Complete Robotics Inc	5099	110	CompuCredit Holdings Corp	6141	32
Como Industrial Equipment Inc	3569	244	Complete Rx Ltd	8742	112	Compucyte Corp	8731	343
Como Oil Company Inc	5984	18	Complete Tablet Solutions Ltd	5734	158	CompuData Inc	7373	448
Comor Inc	3089	1815	Complete Telecommunications Inc	7389	1247	Compudirect Holding Company Inc	5734	478
Comp America Inc	5045	917	Complete Water Services LLC	1629	117	CompuDyne Corp	3812	29
Comp Limited LLC	5045	730	Completecomm Telecommunications Inc	1731	1799	Compudyne Inc	3571	143
Comp Tech Sales	5065	869	Complex Fabricators Inc	3449	23	Compufox USA Corp	5045	871
Compac Corp	2679	12	Complex Litigation Integrators Inc	7374	174	Compugain Corp	7371	251
Compac Design Electronics Manufacturing Co	3679	717	Compliance Services International Inc	7389	2324	Compu-Gard Inc	3699	243
Compac Development Corp	3469	362	Compliance Worldwide Inc	8734	208	CompuGeek	7373	133
Compacker Systems LLC	3565	137	Compoint Inc	4813	704	CompuLaw LLC	7372	2073
Compact Cars Inc	5511	1233	Component Assembly Systems Inc	1522	27	Compulink Corp	3679	136
Compact Classics	2731	389	Component Construction Co	1542	396	CompuLink Electronic Inc	7371	519
Compact Disc Management Inc	5735	7	Component ControlCom Inc	7371	1133	Compulink Management Center Inc	7372	1172
Compact Industries Inc	7389	928	Component Engineering Inc	3599	1617	Compu-Lock Inc	7699	267
Compact Media Inc	7822	17	Component Engineers Inc	3469	70	Compumachino Inc	5084	816
Compact Mould East Inc	3089	1820	Component Enterprises Company Inc	5065	435	Compumail Information Services Inc	7389	1080
Compacting Tooling Inc	3544	549	Component Equipment CoInc	3678	35	Compumatics Group Inc	7372	4948
Compaction America Inc	3531	28	Component General Inc	3676	22	Compunet Consulting Group Inc	7379	1267
Companies Of Jj Young LLC	7363	173	Component Hardware Group Inc	3429	81	Compunet USA	5734	380
COMPanion Corp	7372	487	Component Machine Inc	3599	2494	Compunetics Inc	8711	618
Companion Life Insurance Co	6311	262	Component Manufacturing and Design Inc	3559	459	Compunetix Inc	3661	35
Companion Star Memorials	3221	12	Component Manufacturing Co	2452	26	Compunite Computers Inc	7373	1094
CompanionLink Software Inc	7371	656	Component Parts Machine Company Inc	3599	1564	Compunnel Software Group Inc	7372	1450
Company C Communications Inc	7311	577	Component Plastics Inc	3089	697	Compupack Inc	5045	909
Company of Dorosz and Drummer Inc	7389	1026	Component Sources International Inc	5065	713	Compupay Inc	8721	235
Company Seven Astro-Optics Div	5049	219	Component Specialty Inc	3599	352	Compu-Phone Inc	5999	182
Comparts Inc	5045	485	ComponentOne LLC	7372	2087	CompuQuilt	7372	4799
Compas Inc	7311	639	Components Company Inc	5051	384	Compurex Systems Corp	5045	168
Compass Aerospace Northwest Inc	3728	82	Components Corporation Of America	3679	138	CompUSA Inc	5734	2
COMPASS America Inc	8742	396	Components Electronic Systems	5065	940	Compusearch Software Systems Inc	7371	381
Compass Bancshares Inc	6712	28	Components Specialties Inc	5065	292	Compuserve	2741	25
Compass Bank Inc	6712	88	Componetics Inc	3677	112	Compushare Inc	7374	106
Compass Components Inc	5065	143	Componexx Corp	3663	361	Compusoft Integrated Solutions	7373	456
Compass Computer Group Inc (Twinsburg Ohio)	5045	356	Comporium Communications	4813	196	Compusource Systems Inc	7373	539
Compass Container Group Inc	5085	244	Composidie Inc	3544	19	Compusource Tech Inc	5045	799
Compass Diversified Holdings	7363	18	Composiflex Inc	3845	87	Computac Inc	7373	296
Compass Dodge Inc	5511	17	CompositAir	3624	16	ComputaLabel International Ltd	7372	4284
Compass Energy Services Inc	1311	118	Composite Engineering Inc	3089	371	Computational Applications and Systems Integrations Inc	7371	1447
Compass Group USA Inc	5812	8	Composite Image Systems	7389	407	Computational Engineering International Inc	7372	2842
Compass Intervention Center LLC	8069	21	Composite Modules Inc	3625	90	Computational Mechanics Inc	2731	345
Compass Knowledge Group Inc	7389	386	Composite Software Inc	5045	607	Compu-Teach Corp	7372	1130
Compass Lincoln-Mercury Inc	5511	18	Composite Technologies of America	3083	22	Compu-Teach Educational Software	2741	295
Compass Minerals International Inc	1479	1	Composites Horizons Inc	3089	124	Compu-Tech Inc	7371	1508
Compass Software Solutions	7372	3790	Compostar Inc	5065	941	Computech Inc	7379	377
Compass Solutions Corp	7379	567	Composting Toilet Systems Inc	3088	36	Comp-U-Tech Of America Inc	5045	1001
Compass Technology of Burlington Massachusetts	5065	14	Comprehensive Behavioral Care Inc	8063	15	Computech Support Services Inc	7379	1424
Compass Technology Partners Inc	6799	171	Comprehensive Care Corp	6324	109	COMPUtek Dental Systems	7373	361
Compass Water Solutions Inc	8734	64	Comprehensive Control Systems Inc	7699	225	Computel Communication Systems Inc	5065	529
CompassLearning	7372	789	Comprehensive Designers Inc	7363	20	Computel Systems Inc	7371	1343
Compasstools Inc	1731	865	Comprehensive Health Services Inc (Phoenix Arizona)	8049	32	Computer 1 Products Of America Inc	5734	55
Compatibility Plus Corp	7379	1453	Comprehensive Manufacturing Services LLC	3442	119	Computer Add-Ons Inc	5065	159
Compatible Manufacturing Inc	3599	971	Comprehensive Microsystems Inc	7372	3578	Computer Age Engineering Inc	8711	580
CompBenefits of Georgia Inc	6324	58	Comprehensive Systems Inc	8361	79	Computer Aid Inc	7372	133
Compco Inc	7372	3132	Comprehensive Video Group	5043	9	Computer Aided Business Solutions Inc	5045	790
Comped	3571	219	Compressed Air Concepts	3563	59	Computer Aided Products Inc	5045	755
Compendium Inc	8999	67				Computer Aided Solutions LLC	3823	261
						Computer Analytics Corp	7372	3221
						Computer and Communications Information Group Inc	2741	105
						Computer and Control Solutions Inc	3572	88
						Computer and Laser Services Inc	7378	92
						Computer and Network Services Inc	7379	1075
						Computer and Networking Services Inc	5045	619

Company Name	SIC	Rank
Computer Application Services Inc	7372	3258
Computer Applications Company Inc	7372	3660
Computer Arts Inc	7371	982
Computer Assets Inc	7373	562
Computer Assistance Company Inc	7331	230
Computer Assistance For Subsidized Housing	7379	1315
Computer Assistance Inc	7372	4800
Computer Assisted Manufacturing Technology Corp	3599	362
Computer Automation Systems Inc	7371	1061
Computer Brokers USA Inc	5045	771
Computer Business Solutions Inc	7372	4493
Computer Business Technologies Inc	7379	1258
Computer Cable Makers Inc	3496	124
Computer Cabling and Telephone Service	1731	1279
Computer Care Company Inc	7373	694
Computer Careers And Consulting Inc	7379	823
Computer Choices Inc	5045	894
Computer Chrome Inc	7336	202
Computer Circuit Inc	7373	992
Computer Circulation Center Inc	5045	753
Computer Color Corp	2796	61
Computer Company Inc	7373	806
Computer Components Inc	3625	283
Computer Composition Corp	2791	63
Computer Concern Inc	7379	749
Computer Condiments Inc	5734	331
Computer Consultants of America Inc	8748	116
Computer Consulting and Software Inc	7372	3881
Computer Consulting Services of WNY Inc	7379	1188
Computer Control Corp	3625	271
Computer Conversions Corp	3571	144
Computer Crafts Inc	3679	164
Computer Creations LLC	7373	1066
Computer Customware Inc	5734	278
Computer Data Forms Inc	2752	1163
Computer Data Inc	5734	93
Computer Decisions International LLC	7372	2543
Computer Design and Integration LLC	5045	535
Computer Designs Inc	3081	88
Computer Detailing Corp	7372	3695
Computer Direct Outlet LLC	5734	214
Computer Dynamics	7372	3259
Computer Dynamics Inc	7373	137
Computer Economics Inc	2741	269
Computer Embroidery Specialists Inc	7389	1938
Computer Employment Applications Inc	7372	2903
Computer Engineering Inc	7372	2621
Computer Engineering Operations Inc	7379	1196
Computer Enhancement Systems	5045	357
Computer Enterprise Inc	1731	2386
Computer Enterprises Inc	7373	186
Computer Evidence Specialists LLC	7379	704
Computer Express Inc	7379	128
Computer Facilities Service Corp	4841	124
Computer Forms Inc	2761	33
Computer Gallery Inc	7378	18
Computer Gate International	5734	162
Computer Generated Solutions Inc	7371	185
Computer Golf Software Inc	7372	2668
Computer Graphics Systems Development Corp	7372	3988
Computer Guidance Corp	7372	890
Computer Helper Publishing Inc	7372	1972
Computer Information Enterprises Inc	7373	1095
Computer Information Specialist Inc	7373	505
Computer Insights Inc	7373	640
Computer Instructors Corp	7379	1425
Computer Integrated Services Company Of New York LLC	7378	61
Computer Integrated Solutions Inc	7373	979
Computer Integration Technologies Inc	7389	344
Computer Intelligence Association Inc	5045	927
Computer Investment Advice Inc	7372	4347
Computer Keyes	7372	3312
Computer King Inc	5731	112
Computer Lab Inc	5045	883
Computer Lab International Inc	5045	360
Computer Language Company Inc	7372	4676
Computer Logic Group Inc	7373	417
Computer Mail Services Inc	7371	1077
Computer Management and Integraters Inc	7372	4096
Computer Management and Marketing Associates Inc	7372	2125
Computer Management and Support Services	7376	49
Computer Management Corp	5045	868
Computer Management Enterprises	7372	2955
Computer Management Services Inc	7361	314
Computer Manager Inc	7372	2419
Computer Marketing Group Inc	5734	431
Computer Marketplace Inc (Tewksbury Massaschusetts)	7371	824
Computer Media Technology	7372	2257
Computer Medic Center of North Palm Beach Inc	7378	103
Computer Metal Products Corp	3444	121
Computer Network Solutions Inc	4899	206
Computer Network Solutions LLC	7379	315
Computer Network Systems Inc	7373	951

Company Name	SIC	Rank
Computer Network Technology Group Inc	7373	1203
Computer Networks Inc	5045	718
Computer Office Solutions Inc	7373	776
Computer On Queue Inc	5045	700
Computer Operation Resource Group	7372	3989
Computer Optical Products Inc	3827	90
Computer Optics Inc	3827	151
Computer Organization System Inc	7371	1848
Computer Packages Inc	7372	936
Computer Performance Engineering Inc	7373	894
Computer Performance Inc	5734	140
Computer Peripheral Systems Inc	3661	133
Computer Physicians Inc	7379	750
Computer Plastics	3544	631
Computer Power Solutions of Illinois Inc	7372	1798
Computer Products Corp	5112	58
Computer Programmers Unlimited Inc	7371	941
Computer Programming and Systems Inc	7372	3428
Computer Programs and Systems Inc	7371	73
Computer Prompting and Captioning Co	7372	2956
Computer Pundits Corp	7372	2649
Computer Quick Corp	5045	849
Computer Renaissance Of Wisconsin LLC	5734	337
Computer Resources	7373	294
Computer Resources and Technology International Inc	7371	1758
Computer Resources LLC	7372	3451
Computer Revolution	5251	43
Computer Sales International Inc	5045	204
Computer Science Corporation Federal Sector	7373	2
Computer Sciences Corp	7373	1
Computer Sciences Parsons LLC	8711	308
Computer Security Consultants Inc	7372	2596
Computer Security Consulting Inc	7379	1612
Computer Security Products Inc	8748	394
Computer Service Professionals Inc	5045	487
Computer Service Technology Inc	3825	166
Computer Services And Consulting Inc	7373	801
Computer Services Co	7372	3990
Computer Services Group Inc	7373	464
Computer Services Inc	7374	40
Computer Services Industry	5734	338
Computer Shak Inc	5734	401
Computer SI Corp	5734	83
Computer Simulation and Analysis Inc	7371	1411
Computer Sites Inc	1542	371
Computer Software for Professionals Inc	7372	3696
Computer Software Innovations Inc	7373	152
Computer Software Plus Inc	5734	265
Computer Solution LLC	5734	357
Computer Solutions 2000	5045	738
Computer Solutions 911	7379	751
Computer Solutions Group Inc	5045	838
Computer Solutions Inc (Miami Florida)	7372	3206
Computer Solutions of Centerville	7372	4056
Computer Specialists Inc	7378	109
Computer Spectrum Inc	5734	389
Computer Staffing Services LLC	7361	381
Computer Supplies Inc	5045	886
Computer Supply Supermarket	5734	77
Computer Support Inc	7372	4202
Computer Sykes Inc	7379	626
Computer System Designers LLC	7373	351
Computer Systems And Services Inc	7371	1517
Computer Systems Approach Inc	7371	1820
Computer Systems Center Inc	7379	299
Computer Systems Design Co	7373	953
Computer Systems Engineering Inc	7373	584
Computer Systems Inc	5045	622
Computer Systems LLC	7374	230
Computer Systems Of Algona Inc	5734	413
Computer Task Group Inc	7371	28
Computer Tech	5734	13
Computer Technical Services Inc (Las Vegas Nevada)	7373	942
Computer Technology Associates Inc	8711	140
Computer Technology Link Corp	3571	94
Computer Telecommunications Company Inc	7389	811
Computer Telephone Inc	7379	1366
Computer Training Services	2731	358
Computer Tree Of Winston-Salem Inc	7373	932
Computer Trust Corp	7372	3661
Computer Upgrade Corp	7373	1074
Computer Van Lines USA	4213	504
Computer Visionaries	7371	1026
Computer Ware Inc	5734	373
Computer Warranty Services LLC	5734	150
Computer Wholesale Distributors	5045	539
Computer Works Of Arkansas Inc	5734	147
Computer Workstations Inc	7371	1618
Computer World Services Corp	7373	403
Computeran Systems Corp	7373	548
Computercraft Corp	2741	230
ComputerEase	7373	529
ComputerEase Construction Software	7372	2487

Company Name	SIC	Rank
ComputerGraphics/Atlanta	7379	1193
Computer-Integrated-Manufacturing America LLC	7372	4107
Computerised Business Systems Inc	7372	918
Computerized Fleet Analysis Inc	7372	4369
Computerized Imaging Reference Systems Inc	3841	305
Computerized Management	7363	293
Computerized Management of Vehicles Inc	7372	3817
Computerized Meter Corp	1731	2517
Computermart Medical Services Inc	7371	1309
ComputerPREP Inc	2741	144
Computers and Structures Inc	7372	1131
Computers and Telephones Inc	5734	352
Computers for Marketing	7372	548
Computers Unlimited Inc (Billings Montana)	7372	1202
Computershare Technolgy Sources Inc	7371	288
Computerware Inc	5045	466
ComputerWire Inc	2721	72
Computerwise Inc	3577	407
ComputerWorks Inc (Albany New York)	7372	2957
Computerworks Of Chicago Inc	7373	842
Computerworld Inc C W Database Div	2711	339
Computhink Inc	7372	1505
Computility Inc	7371	584
Computing Solutions Inc	5045	938
Computing Strategies Inc	7379	544
ComputorEdge Magazine Inc	2721	299
Computronics (Addison Illinois)	7372	4494
Compututor Inc	7372	4348
Computyme	7372	3697
Computype Inc	2672	4
Compuware Corp	7372	63
Compuwiz Enterprises Inc	5734	340
Compuzoo	3571	222
Comp-View Inc	5043	17
CompX International Inc	3429	17
ComQuest International	7361	303
Comroe Advance Power Inc	1731	1833
ComScore Inc	8732	9
comScore Media Metrix Inc	7389	254
Comsearch Holdings Inc	8711	65
Comsec LLC	7372	3698
Comsoft Corp	7371	985
Comsonics Inc	3663	91
Comsource Inc	5045	284
Comsources USA Inc	5734	451
Comspan Communications Inc	5099	112
ComSpec International Inc	7373	380
ComSquared Systems Inc	3572	56
Comstar Enterprises Inc	4213	1238
Comstar International Inc	2899	199
Comstar LLC	7373	1047
Comstock Dairy Enterprises Inc	2022	23
Comstock Homebuilding Companies Inc	1521	106
Comstock Homes Inc	1521	67
Comstock Inc	3826	134
Comstock Industries Inc	3599	1486
Comstock Records Ltd	7313	29
Comstock Resources Inc	1311	67
Comstor	7373	109
Comstor Corp	5045	454
Comstructure LLC	7373	698
COMSYS Information Technology Services Inc	7373	23
Comsys IT Partners Inc	7363	26
Comtech Antenna Systems Inc	3663	342
Com-Tech Construction Inc	1623	556
Comtech EF Data Corp	3663	31
Comtech International Inc	7373	1048
Comtech Micro System Inc	3571	178
Comtech Mobile Datacom Corp	4899	164
Comtech Network Systems Inc	7373	1183
Comtech PST Corp	3663	83
Comtech Systems Inc	3663	129
Comtech Telecommunications Corp	3663	24
Comtech Vipersat Networks Inc	5731	146
COMTEK	3663	188
Comtek Communications Technology Inc	3651	140
Comtek Services LLC	7372	3651
Comtel Corp	7389	841
Comtel Group Inc	5999	272
Comtel Systems Corp	5065	367
Comtel Systems Technology Inc	1731	560
Comten Industries	3829	214
COMTEX News Network Inc	7389	1001
Comtorgage Corp	3545	370
Comtran Associates Inc	5731	20
Comtrex Systems Corp	7373	509
Comtrol Corp	3674	189
Comtron Inc	3663	246
Comtronic Systems Inc	7372	444
Comtronics Inc	5065	831
Comus International Inc	3613	37
Comverse Inc	3669	22
Comverse Technology Inc	3661	1
ComVest Investment Partners	6799	57
Comvest Investment Partners Iii LP	6799	208
Comware International	7375	205
Con Cast Co	1623	437

Company Name Index CONSERVATEK

Company Name Index

Company Name	SIC	Rank
Con Rel Auto Electric Inc	3621	118
Conag Inc	1422	40
Conagra Dairy Foods Company Inc	2022	10
ConAgra Foods Inc	2048	2
ConAgra Frozen Foods	2015	8
ConAgra Grocery Products Co	2099	32
ConAgra Mills	5153	12
ConAgra Snack Foods Group	2099	27
Conair Corporate Office and Technology Centre	3565	18
Conair Group Inc	3559	36
Conarc Inc	7372	4102
Conard-Pyle Co	0181	12
Conart Precast LLC	3272	104
Conatser Construction I Inc	1623	71
Conatus Pharmaceuticals Inc	8731	286
Conax Technologies LLC	3823	101
Concentra Inc	8741	3
Concentra Network Services	6411	247
Concentra Operating Corp	8093	5
Concentrek Inc	4731	71
Concentric Industries Inc	3599	1544
Concentric Medical Inc	3841	192
Concentrix Corp	7372	636
Concep Machine Company Inc	3569	229
Concept Design Productions	7389	1577
Concept Development Inc	3672	292
Concept Electronics Inc	5072	179
Concept Freight Service Inc	4213	1187
Concept Group Inc	7311	890
Concept Group USA -Strategic Brand Consultants	8742	650
Concept Industries Inc	3086	34
Concept Molds Inc	3544	534
Concept One Accessories	7336	6
Concept Plastics Inc	3089	499
Concept Press Inc	2752	912
Concept Software Inc	7372	877
Concept Solutions LLC	7379	250
Concept Systems Inc	2731	292
Concept Technology Inc	3829	416
Concept Tool and Machine	3679	736
Conceptronic Inc	3567	46
Concepts And Controls Inc	3599	2499
Concepts And Designs Inc	3585	133
Concepts Inc	3993	160
Concepts Publishing Inc	2731	313
Concepts TV Productions Inc	7829	2
Conceptual Systems and Software Inc	7373	1015
Conceptual Systems International	7372	3882
Conceptus Inc	3841	50
Concern For Independent Living Inc	8361	60
Concerro Inc	7371	545
Concert Group Logistics LLC	4581	31
Concession Services Inc	5812	353
Concho Resources Inc	1311	41
Concho Supply Inc	5013	137
Concho Valley Electric Cooperative Inc	4911	199
Concierge Technologies Inc	7389	2415
Concise Industries Inc	3444	163
Concisesoft Inc	7379	1457
Conco Cement Co	1771	15
Conco Co's	5999	160
Conco Inc	3411	16
Con-Cor International Ltd	3944	44
Concord Asset Management LLC	6282	316
Concord Bank	6022	742
Concord Chemical Company Inc	2841	34
Concord EFS Inc	6099	6
Concord Electrical Contractors Inc	1731	2017
Concord Foods Inc	2099	85
Concord Hospitality Enterprises Co	7011	149
Concord Hospitality Inc	5812	177
Concord Inc (Philadelphia Pennsylvania)	8099	67
Concord Information Systems LLC	5734	365
Concord Litho Group	2752	68
Concord Payment Services Inc	7389	250
Concord Photo Engraving Company Inc	2796	70
Concord Printing Company Inc	2752	1148
Concord Road Equipment Manufacturing Inc	3531	182
Concord Securities Corp	6211	385
Concord Teacakes Etcetera Inc	5461	37
Concord Tool And Manufacturing Inc	3465	39
Concord USA Inc	7372	2843
Concorde Career Colleges Inc	8221	39
Concorde Construction Co	1541	262
Concorde Printing and Copying Inc	2752	1807
Concordia Coffee Systems	3634	13
Concordia Electric Co	4911	540
Concordia Publishing House	2731	98
Concorp Inc	1541	213
Concote Corp	3086	18
Concours Mold Alabama Inc	3544	411
Concours Motors Inc	5511	484
Concraft Restoration Services	1751	9
Concrete	7336	40
Concrete Controls Corp	3825	347
Concrete Coring Co (Denver Colorado)	2951	35
Concrete Delivery Company Inc	4213	2258
Concrete Express Inc	5032	41

Company Name	SIC	Rank
Concrete Formwork and Accessories Inc	5032	54
Concrete Materials Inc	3273	11
Concrete Mold Corp	3544	413
Concrete Safety Systems LLC	3272	47
Concrete Sealants Inc	3053	38
Concrete Structural Imaging Inc	5032	185
Concrete Tie Industries Inc	5032	53
Concur Technologies Inc	7372	150
Concurrent Computer Corp	3571	35
Concurrent Controls Inc	7371	486
Condat Corp	2992	52
Conde Nast Publications	2721	6
Conde Systems Inc	7389	1163
Condon Oil Company Inc	5172	92
Condon-Johnson and Associates Inc	1541	48
Condon's Auto Parts Inc	5015	32
CONDOR Computing Inc	7372	4495
Condor Corp	2052	35
Condor Earth Technologies Inc	8742	217
Condor Electronics Corp	3679	517
Condor Reliability Services Inc	3674	274
Condor Snack Co	2096	28
Condortech Services Inc	7373	514
Condotte America Inc	1542	190
Conduant Corp	3572	72
Conducive Corp	7371	721
Conducive Technology Corp	7372	2958
Conductive Circuits Inc	3672	443
Conductive Containers Inc	2671	55
Conductive Systems Inc	7629	45
Conductive Technologies Inc	3674	188
Conduit Systems Inc	7373	1075
Cone Construction Corporation Inc	1623	370
Cone Instruments Inc	5047	156
Conecuh Sausage Company Inc	2013	187
Conejo Industries Inc	3366	21
Conelec Of Florida LLC	3672	95
Conergy Inc	3561	17
Conery Manufacturing Inc	3822	82
Conestoga Bank	6022	527
Conetic Software Systems Inc	7372	3485
Conexant Spinco Inc	7379	20
Conexant Systems Inc	3674	81
Conexus Communication Systems Inc	7373	585
Conexx Staffing Services LLC	7363	260
Confer Plastics Inc	3089	529
Conference America Inc	8748	238
ConferenceCallcom Inc	4812	53
Conferencing Advisors Inc	3669	153
Confidential Background Investigations Inc	7381	122
Configuration Data Services Inc	7372	3599
Configuration Inc	8744	40
Configuration Management Inc	7374	94
Configuration Solutions Inc	7371	222
Confio Corp	7379	1260
Confirmit Inc	7371	745
Conforming Matrix Corp	3559	246
Confort and Company Inc	2752	84
Confortaire Inc	3086	113
Congleton Hacker Co	1541	97
Congoleum Corp	3089	89
Congress Asset Management Co	6282	285
Congressional Quarterly Inc	2732	13
Conklin Company Inc	2842	52
Conklin Equipment Company Inc	3549	127
Conkur Printing Company Inc	2752	1341
Conlan Co	1542	120
Conlan Corp	2752	1167
Conley Casting Supply Corp	3544	654
Conley Corp	3084	21
Conley Electric Inc	1731	2278
Conley Equipment LLC	5063	584
Conley Group	7381	203
Conley Transport II Inc	4213	866
Conlon and Collins Ford Jeep Eagle Inc	5511	878
Conlon Construction Co	1541	71
CONMED Corp	3845	7
ConMed Linvatec	3861	81
Connect Imaging Inc	7372	4084
Connect Inc (Lisle Illinois)	7372	1467
Connect Systems Inc	3663	277
Connect Tech International LLC	3577	572
Connect Technology Inc	1731	2483
Connect3 Systems Inc	7372	666
Connect-Air International Inc	5063	600
Connectec Company Inc	3643	65
Connecticut Bank and Trust Co	6022	439
Connecticut Coal Inc	5052	16
Connecticut Coining Inc	3599	872
Connecticut Computer Service Inc	7373	256
Connecticut Container Corp	2653	23
Connecticut Data Systems Inc	7372	2287
Connecticut Die Cutting Services Inc	3544	414
Connecticut Electric Equipment Company Inc	5063	339
Connecticut Hypodermics Inc	3841	182
Connecticut Industrial Gauging Inc	3823	476
Connecticut Laminating Company Inc	3089	849
Connecticut Light and Power Co	4911	55
Connecticut Limousine LLC	4111	5
Connecticut Limousine Service Inc	4111	10

Company Name	SIC	Rank
Connecticut Natural Gas Corp	4924	32
Connecticut Pest Elimination Inc	7342	98
Connecticut Public Broadcasting Inc	4833	142
Connecticut Radio Network	4832	45
Connecticut Rental Centers Inc	7359	249
Connecticut Society To Prevent Blindness Inc	8361	195
Connecticut Spring And Stamping Corp	3469	41
Connecticut Staffing Works Corp	7361	47
Connecticut Tool Company Inc	3089	1578
Connecticut Valley Biological Supply Company Inc	5961	176
Connecticut Water Co	4941	18
Connecticut Water Emergency Services Inc	4941	24
Connecticut Water Service Inc	4941	13
Connecting Point Computer Centers	5045	26
Connecting Point Computer Services	7379	393
Connecting Point Inc	5734	52
Connection Concepts Inc	2298	2
Connection Publishing Inc	2711	510
Connection Strategies Enterprises Inc	7379	432
Connections USA Inc	1731	2569
Connective Design Inc	3678	65
Connectlink Inc	4813	491
Connectlive Communications Inc	4813	359
Connectool Inc	3423	61
Connector Castings Inc	3629	43
Connector Concepts Inc	3644	30
Connector Manufacturing Co	3643	28
Connector Products Inc	3643	150
Connector Resources Unlimited Inc	3577	358
Connector Specialists Inc	5051	299
Connectors Unlimited Inc	5065	522
Connectronics Inc	3678	51
ConnectShip Inc	7373	705
ConnectU	7371	1863
Connectwise Inc	5734	149
Connell Brothers Company Ltd	5169	80
Connell Chevrolet	5511	209
Connell Communications Inc	2721	277
Connell Co	5153	8
Connell LP	3334	3
Connelly Machine Works	3599	1633
Connelly Skis Inc	3949	91
Conner Brothers Machine Company Inc	3599	381
Conner Development Co	1542	92
Conner Engineering Inc	3599	2006
Conner Partners	8741	94
Conner Steel Products Inc	3443	50
Conner Trucking Inc	4213	2707
Conners and Company Inc	6211	384
Connex Systems Inc	5044	75
Connexion Technologies Inc	5049	25
Connexis LLC	7378	59
Connexus Energy	4911	207
Connexus Technology LLC	7379	740
Connexxia LLC	7371	1418
Connie Maxwell Children's Home	8361	185
Conning and Co	6211	255
Connoisseurs Products Corp	2842	38
Connor and Company Inc	1521	118
Connor Formed Metal Products	3495	5
Connor Sport Court International Inc	3081	87
Connors Co	5065	693
Connors - Haas Inc	1731	433
Connors Investor Services Inc	6282	584
Connor-Winfield Corp	3625	43
Conn's Inc	5722	3
Conntrol International Inc	3625	307
Conn-Weld Industries Inc	3532	30
CONNX Solutions Inc	7372	2126
ConocoPhillips	2911	2
ConocoPhillips Pipeline Co	4612	15
Conolog Corp	7361	380
Conover John	7371	1192
Conquest Business Media Inc	2721	316
Conquest Systems Inc	7372	4451
ConQwest Inc	7376	37
Conrad Enterprises Inc	3713	63
Conrad Government Services	8721	355
Conrad Industries Inc	3731	13
Conrad Machine Inc	3533	114
Conrad Pharmaceutical Consultants Inc	8748	408
Conrad Phillips and Vutech	7311	431
Conrad-American Inc	3523	102
Conrad-Jarvis Corp	2241	16
Conrad-Johnson Design Inc	3663	278
Conrail Inc	4011	56
Conroe Plastics Molding Inc	3053	109
Conroe Welding Supply Inc	5084	509
Conroy's Inc	5992	6
Consarc Corp	3567	16
Conseco Annuity Assurance Co	6311	76
Conseco Medical Insurance Co	6321	68
Conseco Variable Insurance Co	6311	42
Consensus Orthopedics	3842	172
Consensus Research Group Inc	8742	450
Consensus Software Inc	7372	4801
Consero Global Solutions LLC	7389	1707
Conserv Inc	1731	1956
Conservatek Industries Inc	3441	145

Company Name	SIC	Rank
Conservation Technology Ltd	3646	71
Conserve Electrical Supply	5063	511
ConServit Integrated Teleservices	7389	421
Consign LLC	7996	39
Consigned Sales Inc	5092	36
Consignment Music	5736	20
Consist International Inc	7372	127
Consoer Townsend Envirodyne Engineers Inc	8711	92
ConSol Consulting and Solutions Corp	7379	108
CONSOL Energy Inc	1221	3
Consolidated Bank and Trust Co	6022	766
Consolidated Carbide Ltd	3545	344
Consolidated Cargo Carriers	4213	1038
Consolidated Casting Corp	3324	12
Consolidated Catfish Companies LLC	2092	4
Consolidated Communications	7379	234
Consolidated Communications Holdings Inc	4813	46
Consolidated Communications Inc	4813	91
Consolidated Communications Of Fort Bend Co	4813	187
Consolidated Companies Inc	5141	84
Consolidated Computer Services Inc	7378	65
Consolidated Container Company LLC	3085	4
Consolidated Container Co (Minneapolis Minnesota)	3412	4
Consolidated Crane And Rigging Ltd	7353	52
Consolidated Delivery and Logistics	4213	163
Consolidated Edison Inc	4931	2
Consolidated Electric Coop	4911	414
Consolidated Electric Cooperative Inc	4911	517
Consolidated Electrical and Mechanical Inc	1731	757
Consolidated Electrical Contractors And Engineers Inc	1731	482
Consolidated Electrical Distributors Inc	5063	729
Consolidated Electrical Distributors Inc	5063	4
Consolidated Electronic Wire and Cable Corp	3679	335
Consolidated Electronics Inc	5063	1019
Consolidated Engineering Company Inc	3567	38
Consolidated Fabrication And Constructors Inc	3325	15
Consolidated Fabricators Corp	3443	29
Consolidated Financial Investments Inc	6282	667
Consolidated Food Management Inc	8741	225
Consolidated Grain and Barge	5153	5
Consolidated Graphic Communications	2759	137
Consolidated Graphics Group Inc	2752	164
Consolidated Graphics Inc	2752	4
Consolidated Hinge And Manufactured Products	3599	1937
Consolidated Industries Inc	3364	6
Consolidated Insurance Co	6331	182
Consolidated Jet Printers Inc	2269	15
Consolidated Lab Service Inc	5049	115
Consolidated Mail Service Inc	7331	245
Consolidated Manufacturing Inc	3714	278
Consolidated Market Response Inc	7389	1012
Consolidated Metal Products Inc	3452	55
Consolidated Metal Services Inc	3532	66
Consolidated Models Inc	3089	1121
Consolidated Mutual Water Co	4941	51
Consolidated Personnel Services Inc	7363	324
Consolidated Pipe and Supply Company Inc	5074	7
Consolidated Plastic Products Corp	3089	1717
Consolidated Plastics Corp	5162	40
Consolidated Precision Products	3363	24
Consolidated Pressure Control LLLP	3533	109
Consolidated Printers Inc	2732	37
Consolidated Printing and Stationery Company Inc	2752	1008
Consolidated Printing Solutions	2752	501
Consolidated Productions Groups Inc	1623	812
Consolidated Publishing Company Inc	2711	266
Consolidated Purchasing Corp	5946	12
Consolidated Race Promoters Of Automobile Competition Inc	2711	592
Consolidated Rail Corp	4011	9
Consolidated Reprographics	2752	1591
Consolidated Restaurant Operations Inc	5812	38
Consolidated Software Services Inc	7334	83
Consolidated Steel Inc	5051	336
Consolidated Storage Companies Inc	2542	23
Consolidated Supply Company Inc	5031	192
Consolidated Systems Inc	3444	45
Consolidated Telephone Co	4813	97
Consolidated Transfer and Warehouse Co	4213	2688
Consolidated Transmission Parts Inc	5013	235
Consolidated Vending	5046	198
Consolidated-Tomoka Land Co	1531	86
Consona Corp	7372	184
Consonus Technologies Inc	7389	247
Consortium Book Sales and Distribution Inc	5192	32
Consortium Communications Inc	1623	861
Consortium For Worker Education Inc	8331	29
Conspec Controls Inc	3826	125
Constangy Brooks and Smith LLP	8111	238

Company Name	SIC	Rank
Constant Communications Answering Service Inc	7389	1694
Constant Contact Inc	7331	5
Constant Services Inc	2754	25
Constantine Engineering Labs Co	3577	583
Constar International LLC	3085	5
Constellation Brands Inc	2084	2
Constellation Energy Group Inc	4911	25
Constellation Energy Nuclear Group LLC	4911	209
Constellation Energy Partners LLC	1311	110
Constellation Mold Inc	3544	763
Constellation NewEnergy - Gas Div	4924	19
Constellation Technology Corp	8731	209
Constructech Inc	1542	433
Construction Aggregates Corporation Of Michigan	1442	83
Construction and Industrial Supply Company Inc	5084	869
Construction and Marine Equipment Company Inc	5082	200
Construction and Service Solutions Corp	1541	294
Construction Audio	5065	619
Construction BiddingCom LLC	4813	392
Construction By Camco Inc	1623	839
Construction Data Control Inc	7372	3454
Construction Dynamics Inc	3273	53
Construction Engineering Consultants Inc	8734	171
Construction Equipment Manufacturing Company Inc	3531	153
Construction Executive Online	8742	533
Construction Force Services Inc	7361	173
Construction Industry Solutions Corp	7372	2341
Construction Information Systems Inc	7372	4285
Construction Journal Ltd	2721	208
Construction Labor Services Inc	7361	320
Construction Ltd	1541	285
Construction Link Inc	5045	578
Construction Machinery Industrial LLC	5084	295
Construction Management Services Inc	1731	35
Construction Materials Inc	5211	138
Construction Monitor LLC	2741	491
Construction Partnership Inc	1799	83
Construction Planning and Management Inc	8741	123
Construction Resources Management Inc	7374	175
Construction Specialties Inc	5049	9
Construction Specialty	4213	2785
Construction Specialty Service Inc	1623	355
Construction Supervisors Inc	1541	283
Construction Supply	5211	115
Construction Systems Associates Inc	7372	382
Construction Trailer Specialists Inc	3715	42
Constructioncom	7389	658
Constructive Computing Company Inc	7372	4239
Constructors and Associates Inc	1542	170
Consul Tec Inc	7373	1133
Consulate Management Co	8069	2
Consulier Engineering Inc	7372	3072
Consulting Coop	7389	2327
Consulting Engineering And Development Services Inc	3599	349
Consulting Services Group LLC	6282	338
Consulting Services Inc (Oklahoma City Oklahoma)	7371	301
Consultis Inc	7363	95
Consultnet	7379	1107
ConsultNet LLC	8748	44
Consumer Adjustment Company Inc	7322	17
Consumer Capital Partners LLC	6799	20
Consumer Cooperative Oil Co	5172	37
Consumer Credit Counseling Service Of The Midwest Inc	7299	24
Consumer Credit Of Des Moines	7299	38
Consumer Discount Drug Store Inc	5912	71
Consumer Engineering Inc	3613	116
Consumer Home Mortgage Inc	6163	22
Consumer Oil and Supply Co	5541	59
Consumer Portfolio Services Inc	6153	34
Consumer Profiles Inc	7389	1902
Consumer Protection Services	7389	1883
Consumer Resource Network LLC	8742	291
Consumer Safety Technology Inc	5045	671
Consumer Source Inc	2741	103
Consumer Support Services Inc	8059	26
Consumerlink Inc	7389	1614
Consumers Bancorp Inc	6712	567
Consumers Concrete Corp	3273	44
Consumers Cooperative Oil Co	5171	80
Consumers Energy Co	4939	14
Consumers Inc	3441	274
Consumers National Bank	6022	215
Consumers Packing Company Inc	5147	50
Consumers Periodical Service Inc	7389	922
Consumers Pipe And Supply Co	5051	178
Consumers Produce Co	5148	34
Consun Food Industries Inc	5411	223
Con-Syst-Int Group Inc	3559	150
Conta-Clip Inc	3679	834
Contact Behavioral Health Services	8093	31
Contact Electric LLC	1731	1467

Company Name	SIC	Rank
Contact Industries Inc	3625	166
Contact Lumber Co	2431	23
Contact One Call Center Inc	7389	2018
Contact Rubber Corp	2822	20
Contact Systems Inc	3559	97
Contact Technologies Inc	3643	55
Contactpc Inc	7379	1372
Contactual Inc	7372	986
Container Freight EIT LLC	4213	934
Container Handling Systems Corp	3535	107
Container Machinery Incorporated - Versatile Machining Inc	3599	2049
Container Manufacturing Inc	3089	1180
Container Options Inc	3085	39
Container Products Corp	3411	19
Container Research Corp	3412	5
Container Store Inc	5719	6
Container Transfer Corp	4213	2346
Contaminant Control Inc	4213	1076
Contango Oil and Gas Co	1311	78
Contec	7622	1
Contec Inc	3829	52
Contec Microelectronics USA Inc	3571	106
CONTECH Bridge Solutions Inc	1622	7
Contech Construction Products Inc	3443	55
Contech Metal Forge	3363	6
CONTECH Stormwater Solutions Inc	3589	196
Contech Systems	7361	335
Contegra Systems Inc	7372	4411
Contek Design and Products Inc	7389	2498
Contek International Corp	3577	469
Contel Inc	1731	1208
Contempora Fabrics Inc	2253	9
Contemporary Computerwear Corp	2394	39
Contemporary Control Systems Inc	3577	367
Contemporary Cybernetics Group Inc	3572	38
Contemporary Design Plastics	3089	1704
Contemporary Electrical Services Inc	1731	232
Contemporary Galleries of Kentucky Inc	5712	99
Contemporary Galleries Of West Virginia Inc	5021	88
Contemporary Media Inc	2721	381
Contemporary Personnel Staffing Inc	7363	334
Contemporary Products Of Texas Inc	2519	8
Contemporary Software Concepts Inc	7371	712
Contemporary Sounds Of Oklahoma City Inc	5731	107
Contender Boats Inc	3732	37
Content Management Corp	2759	454
Contera Inc	7372	279
Contest America Publishers Inc	7331	119
Context Integration Inc	7379	239
Contextual Inc	7371	1397
Conti Enterprises Inc	8741	102
Conti Publishing Inc	2752	1417
Contico Manufacturing	3469	82
ContiGroup Companies Inc	2011	6
Contine Corp	3599	549
Continental A L 39404400	3728	144
Continental Aerial Surveys Inc	7389	1505
Continental Agra Grain Equipment Inc	5083	213
Continental Air Transport Co	4111	12
Continental Airlines Inc	4512	2
Continental Aluminum Corp	3341	33
Continental Aromatics	2844	183
Continental Auto Parts LLC	5013	172
Continental Automotive Corp	3714	26
Continental Baking Co	2051	248
Continental Binder And Specialty Corp	2782	22
Continental Bindery Corp	2789	28
Continental BMW of Darien	5511	844
Continental Broadband Inc	4899	53
Continental Building Maintenance Company Inc	7349	87
Continental Building Services Inc	7349	306
Continental Building Systems	1542	241
Continental Business Enterprises Inc	3469	356
Continental Carbon Co	2895	4
Continental Cast Stone South Inc	3271	14
Continental Casualty Co	6331	35
Continental Coatings Inc	2851	141
Continental Coin Corp	5999	103
Continental ColorCraft Inc	2796	34
Continental Computer Corp	7372	1561
Continental Connector Co	3678	54
Continental Contact and Supply Inc	5531	70
Continental Control Systems LLC	3825	321
Continental Controls Corp	3823	239
Continental Crane and Service	3535	211
Continental Datalabel Inc	2672	35
Continental Development Corp	6552	204
Continental Diamond Tool Corp	3545	163
Continental Diesel Inc	7538	39
Continental Dining and Refreshment Services	2068	16
Continental Disc Corp	3491	26
Continental Display and Store Fixtures Inc	2431	134
Continental Display Inc	5046	202
Continental Distilling Corp	3556	81
Continental Divide Electric Coop	4911	302
Continental Divide Fence Inc	5039	59
Continental Eagle Corp	3559	93

Company Name	SIC	Rank
Continental Electric	1623	207
Continental Energy Corp	1311	281
Continental Engines Inc	5084	167
Continental Equipment Company Inc	5049	131
Continental Equipment Corp	3589	246
Continental Express Inc	4213	777
Continental Fabricators Inc	3443	137
Continental Fan Manufacturing Inc	5075	66
Continental Federal Credit Union	6061	84
Continental Film and Video	7336	84
Continental Flooring Co (Scottsdale Arizona)	1752	9
Continental Forge Company Inc	3463	12
Continental General Insurance Co	6321	67
Continental Graphics Corp	7336	1
Continental Homes Inc	1521	7
Continental Industries Inc	3089	723
Continental Insurance Co	6331	123
Continental International	5085	48
Continental Jewelry	3911	12
Continental Laboratory Products Inc	5049	37
Continental Lighting Systems Inc	5063	690
Continental Loose Leaf Inc	2782	69
Continental Machine Tool Company Inc	3599	480
Continental Machinery Movers	4213	3092
Continental Machines Inc	3541	26
Continental Machining Co	3599	844
Continental Manufacturing	2842	49
Continental Manufacturing Chemist Inc	2833	65
Continental Materials Corp	3273	28
Continental Mechanical of the Pacific	1711	212
Continental Medical Labs Inc	5047	278
Continental Metal Products Company Inc	3842	205
Continental Mills Inc	2045	1
Continental Mortgage Bankers	6162	89
Continental National Bank of Miami	6021	258
Continental Nh3 Products Company Inc	3824	28
Continental Office Enviroments Inc	5021	10
Continental Packaging Corp	3089	1296
Continental Photo	5043	47
Continental Plastic Corp	3089	995
Continental Plastics Co	3052	4
Continental Pools Inc	7389	1146
Continental Precision Corp	3089	361
Continental Printing Services Inc	2752	1728
Continental Research Corp	2842	55
Continental Resources Inc	1311	44
Continental Resources Inc (Bedford Massachusetts)	3577	67
Continental Resources Of Illinois Inc	1311	223
Continental Sales and Marketing Inc	5063	337
Continental Steel And Conveyor Co	3535	102
Continental Structural Plastics Inc	3089	95
Continental Tire The Americas LLC	3011	1
Continental Van Lines Inc	4213	99
Continental Video Productions Inc	7819	86
Continental Web Press Inc	2752	42
Continental Western Insurance Co	6331	243
Continental Window and Glass Corp	3089	1047
Continental-Anchor Ltd	2754	21
Continental-Wirt Electronics Corp	3679	212
Continntal Screw Conveyor Corp	3535	96
Continuant	1731	153
Continucare Corp	8093	9
Continuent Inc	7372	477
Continuex Corp	7372	2127
Continuous Computing Corp	3577	48
Continuum Dynamics Inc	8731	215
Continuum International Publishing Group Inc	2731	190
Continuum Performance Systems Inc	7371	672
Continuum Technology Corp	7372	3397
Contitech Thermopol LLC	3052	8
Contour Design Inc	3577	307
Contour Hardening Inc	3567	67
Contour Inc	3695	40
Contour Pak Inc	3842	254
Contour Saws Inc	3425	8
Contour Tool Inc	3545	189
Contour360 Corp	7389	1109
Contours Express Inc	6794	131
Contra Costa Electric Inc	1731	6
Contra Costa Mosquito And Vector Control District	4959	21
Contra Costa Newspapers Inc	2711	95
ContrAcct Systems Corp	7372	2128
Contract Builders Hardware Inc	5072	164
Contract Data Services Inc	7373	783
Contract Design Group Inc	7389	1130
Contract Design Inc	3544	845
Contract Electric Co	1731	1167
Contract Environmental Services Inc	8748	64
Contract Filling Inc	7389	660
Contract Furniture Installations	7389	1758
Contract Industrial Tooling Inc	3599	353
Contract Labeling Services Inc	7389	1717
Contract Machining and Manufacturing Company Inc	3599	612
Contract Manufacturer LLC	3715	33
Contract Manufacturers Inc	3585	154
Contract Manufacturing Services Inc	3545	416
Contract Office Group	7389	1439

Company Name	SIC	Rank
Contract Packaging Associates Inc	7389	1564
Contract Packaging Resources Inc	7389	1353
Contract People Corp	7363	382
Contract Professionals Inc	7363	61
Contract Services Inc	7349	313
Contract Steel Sales Inc	3441	249
Contract Support Group	7389	2246
Contract Technologies International Inc	4841	113
Contract Wallcoverings Inc	5231	4
Contractor Express Inc	5031	367
Contractor Yard Inc	5211	90
Contractors Cargo Co	4213	1261
Contractors Heating and Supply Co	5075	52
Contractors Material Company Inc	5051	361
Contractors Roofing and Supply Company Inc	5033	43
Contractors Steel Co	5051	51
Contractors Supply Company Inc	5072	149
Contractual Carriers Inc	4213	2728
Contran Corp	6719	184
Contrarian Group	6282	395
Contravisory Research Corp	6282	544
Contrax Technologies Inc (Hanover Maryland)	3672	265
Contrex Inc	3625	217
Control 7 Inc	3613	120
Control Analytics Inc	5049	51
Control and Automation Inc	5084	934
Control and Equipment Company Of El Paso Inc	1731	1542
Control Associates/ Constantin Group LP	8742	322
Control Automation Technologies	8734	158
Control Cable Inc	3679	327
Control Chief Corp	3823	188
Control Chief Holdings Inc	3699	173
Control Components Inc	3491	12
Control Concepts And Technology Corp	3823	76
Control Concepts Inc	3674	389
Control Design and Manufacturing Inc	3537	112
Control Design Inc	3613	84
Control Dynamics Corp	3625	362
Control Electric Co	3625	210
Control Electronics Inc	3829	424
Control Engineering Group Inc	1731	2542
Control Flow Inc	3533	35
Control Gaging Inc	3823	171
Control Headquarters Inc	3823	416
Control Holding Corp	3625	68
Control House International Inc	5045	656
Control Instruments Corp	3823	134
Control Interface Inc	3613	179
Control Line Electric Inc	1731	2585
Control Logic Corp	3577	636
Control Logic Inc	3625	231
Control Manufacturing Company Inc	3679	710
Control Master Inc	7373	1223
Control Masters Inc	8711	636
Control Measurement Inc	3829	512
Control Micro Systems Inc	3699	165
Control Module Inc	3577	262
Control Products Corp	3648	28
Control Products Inc	3822	11
Control Resources Inc	3625	181
Control Sales Inc	5063	396
Control Services Co	3613	164
Control Signal Corp	3663	385
Control Source Inc	5063	529
Control Specialist Inc	1731	412
Control Specialists Inc	5084	803
Control Stuff Inc	3625	179
Control Switches International Inc	5065	386
Control System Innovators Inc	3625	334
Control Systemation Inc	3699	36
Control Systems International Inc	8742	268
Control Systems West Inc	3625	272
Control Technique Inc	3613	51
Control Technologies Of Centra	3669	275
Control Technology Corp	3625	164
Control Technology Inc	3577	473
Control Vision Corp	3577	406
Control Works Inc	3613	94
Control4	5045	60
Con-Trol-Cure Inc	3625	324
Controlled Access Inc	3829	382
Controlled Air Inc	1799	80
Controlled Automation Inc	3613	138
Controlled Magnetics Inc	3612	121
Controlled Molding Inc	3089	1025
Controlled Power Co	3679	52
Controlled Power Inc	3613	127
Controlled Release Technologies Inc	2842	159
Controlled Temperature Transit	4213	2071
Controllink Inc	7373	650
Controllix Corp	3625	287
Contrologic Environmental Inc	1731	1007
Controls Corporation Of America	3491	35
Controls Engineering Maintenance Corp	3732	83
Controls Southeast Inc	3498	30
ControlSoft Inc	7372	4231
Controlware Communications Systems Inc	3661	144
Contronic Devices Inc	2869	124

Company Name	SIC	Rank
Contrx Industries Inc	3536	34
CONUS Communications Company LP	7383	8
Conus Transportation Inc	4213	2738
Convaid Products Inc	3842	162
Conval Inc	3491	18
ConvaTec	3999	1
Convectronics Inc	3829	370
Convenience Electronics Inc	3577	507
Convenience Food Systems Inc	5084	36
Convenience Products Inc	3086	12
Convenience Retailers LLC	5411	156
Convenience Store Automation Inc	7372	3699
Convenient Food Mart Inc	6794	69
Convention Management Resources Inc	7389	924
Converge Inc	7389	69
Convergence Technology Consulting	8748	226
Convergent Audio Tech Inc	3651	170
Convergent Capital Management LLC	6282	304
Convergent Media Systems Corp	7373	169
Convergent Software Systems Inc	7372	1259
Convergent Technologies Inc	3669	194
Convergenz LLC	8742	203
Convergys Corp	7389	16
Convergys Corp (Odgen Utah)	7389	92
Convergys Information Management Group	7374	18
Conversa Language Center Inc	7389	2473
Conversational Computing Corp	7372	977
Converse All Steel Services Inc	5051	475
Converse Inc	3149	17
Conversion Devices Inc	3845	94
Conversion Services International Inc	7379	332
Conversion Technologies International Inc	7374	160
Conversion Technology Company Inc	3952	4
Converteam Inc	3629	6
Converted Organics Inc	2879	45
Converting Machines Inc	3554	42
Converting Technology Inc	3544	165
Converto Manufacturing Company Inc	3537	104
Convex Corp	3661	227
Convey Compliance Systems Inc	7336	12
Con-Vey/Keystone Inc	3535	109
Conveyant Systems Inc	3661	212
Conveying Industries Inc	3535	230
Conveyor Eng and Manufacturing Co	3535	79
Conveyor Handling Company Inc	5084	428
Conveyor Sales Co	7353	110
Conveyor Services Inc	1731	1454
Conveyor Technologies Of Sanford NC Inc	3535	74
Conviber Inc	5085	237
Convina LLC	7371	1742
Convio Inc	8742	156
Convivial Design Inc	2741	412
Con-Wal Inc	5083	95
Con-Wald Corp	2752	657
Conway Communications Company LLC	5063	406
Conway Data Inc	2721	67
Conway Detroit Corp	3341	39
Con-way Freight Inc	4212	24
Con-Way Freight-Western	4213	116
Conway Hospital Inc	8062	177
Con-Way Inc	4213	6
Conway Machine Inc	3541	208
Conway National Bank	6021	160
Conway Office Products Inc	5044	26
Conway Stores Inc	5611	11
Con-way Truckload	4213	98
Con-Wear Products Inc	1442	44
Conwed Corp	3089	833
Conwed Designscape	2493	15
Conwed Plastics Inc	3082	3
Conxall Corp	3678	17
Cook And Beals Inc	3556	186
Cook and Company Inc	7389	797
Cook and Franke SC	8111	429
Cook Brothers Automotive Inc	5013	132
Cook Brothers Insulation Inc	3086	108
Cook Children's Physician Network	8011	25
Cook Compression	3592	15
Cook County Lumber Co	5031	161
Cook County Photocopy Co	5044	130
Cook Group Inc	3841	18
Cook Industrial Electric Company Inc	1731	914
Cook Inlet Energy Supply	4922	36
Cook Iron Store Co	5085	334
Cook Moving Systems Inc	4213	1414
Cook Pump Co	3561	170
Cook Spring Company Inc	3495	23
Cook Systems International Inc	7371	425
Cook Technologies Inc	3496	61
Cook Telecom Inc	4812	95
Cook Tractor Company Inc	5083	97
Cook Trucking Company Inc	4213	1555
Cook Vascular Inc	3845	63
Cookbook Publishers Inc	2731	188
Cooke and Bieler Inc	6282	175
Cooke Manufacturing Company Inc	2512	69
Cooke Trucking Company Inc	4213	787
Cooke's Crating Inc	4213	1026
Cooke's Food Stores Inc	5411	226

Company Name	SIC	Rank
Cookie Kingdom Inc	2052	37
Cookie Specialties Inc	2052	84
Cookies Inc	2353	7
Cookietree Inc	2052	32
Cook's Communications Corp	5999	176
Cook's Pest Control Inc	7342	6
Cookshack Inc	3556	137
Cookson Co	3442	65
Cookson Door Sales Of Arizona Inc	5039	25
Cookson Electronics	3672	6
Cookson Electronics Assembly Materials Group	2842	19
Cookson Hills Publishers Inc	2711	379
Cookson Precious Metals Div	3264	3
Cookson-Hill Community Action Foundation Inc	8361	143
Cooktek Inc	3589	237
Cool Cargo Carriers Inc	4213	2018
Cool Transports Inc	4213	448
Coolearth Technologies Inc	7371	1591
Cooler Master USA Inc	3443	85
Cooley Godward Kronish LLP	8111	156
Cooley Inc	2295	2
Cooley Industries Inc	5031	38
Cooley Motors Corp	5511	1143
Cooley Transport Inc	4213	916
Coolibar	2353	10
Coolidge Electric LLC	1731	2594
Cooling and Applied Technology Inc	3585	97
Cooling Technology Inc	3585	202
Cool-Pak LLC	3089	671
Coolspring Stone Supply Inc	1411	11
Coolsystems Inc	3842	180
Coolware Company Inc	7371	1324
Coomes Inc	4213	2626
Coon Engineering Inc	8711	179
Coon Manufacturing Inc	3089	741
Cooney/Waters Group	8743	88
Coonrod Wrecker and Crane Service	7353	81
Co-Op Country Farmers Elevator	5153	156
Co-op Country Partners	5191	39
Co-op Services Credit Union	6062	80
Cooper Aerobics Enterprises	7991	5
Cooper and Clement Inc	2759	403
Cooper and Cooper Moving Inc	4213	544
Cooper and Dunham LLP	8111	318
Cooper and Kirk PLLC	8111	578
Cooper B-Line Inc	3629	5
Cooper Burdge	2754	14
Cooper Carry and Associates Inc	8712	104
Cooper Communities Inc	1521	59
Cooper Companies Inc	3851	2
Cooper Container Corp	2653	99
Cooper Corelite Inc	3646	40
Cooper Crouse-Hinds LLC	3531	17
Cooper Electric Supply Co	5063	29
Cooper Enterprises Inc	7384	32
Cooper Erving and Savage LLP	8111	477
Cooper Flexible Packaging Inc	2759	431
Cooper Health Care	8741	73
Cooper Hosiery Mills Inc	2252	4
Cooper Hotel Group Inc	7011	193
Cooper Industries Bussmann Div	3643	39
Cooper Industries PLC	3646	1
Cooper Leasing Inc	6159	96
Cooper Lighting Inc	3645	13
Cooper Machine Company Inc	3553	45
Cooper Microelectronics Inc	3674	317
Cooper Pest Solution Inc	7342	21
Cooper Power Systems LLC	3612	3
Cooper Products Inc	3053	45
Cooper Software Inc	7373	845
Cooper Tire and Rubber Co	3011	4
Cooper Tool and Machine Company Inc	3599	2296
Cooper Truck Line Inc	4213	1486
Cooper Turbocompressor Inc	3511	14
Co-Operations Inc	7389	486
Cooperative Bright Inc	3496	49
Cooperative Choice LLC	7382	43
Cooperative Country Farmer's Elevator	5153	77
Cooperative Development LLC	1623	339
Cooperative Educational Services	8733	21
Cooperative Farmer"s	5191	145
Cooperative Gas and Oil Company Inc	5171	66
Cooperative Grain and Supply (Hillsboro Kansas)	5191	73
Cooperative Health Services Inc	8071	14
Cooperative Home Care Associates Inc	8082	36
Cooperative Optical Services Inc	5995	16
Cooperative Plating Co	3471	63
Cooperative Printing Association	2752	538
Cooperative Reserve Supply Inc	5033	18
Cooperative Resources International	0751	1
Cooperative Resources International Inc	0751	3
Cooperative Sampo Corp	2048	68
Cooperative Transport	4213	2866
Cooperative Workshops Inc	2448	38
Cooperatives Computer Center Inc	5045	486
Cooper-Atkins Corp	3829	49
Cooper-General Corp	5065	626
Coopermatics Inc	3569	259
Cooper-Standard Automotive Inc	3714	16

Company Name	SIC	Rank
Cooper-Standard Holdings Inc	3061	1
Cooperstone Products Inc	1479	3
CooperSurgical Inc	3841	60
CooperVision Inc	3851	11
Cooper-Weymouth Peterson	3549	8
Co-Optics Of America Laboratory Inc	3851	101
Coordinate Machine Co	3545	320
Coordinated Designs and Controls Inc	3613	154
Coordinated Equipment Co	5084	195
Co-Ordinated Management Systems	7371	930
Coordinated Management Systems Inc	7374	119
Coors Ceramicon Designs Inc	3259	7
Coors Credit Union	6062	71
CoorsTek Inc	3679	46
Coos Bay Timber Operators Inc	1429	18
Coos Grange Supply Co	5261	21
Coosa Pines Federal Credit Union	6061	116
Coosa Steel Corp	5051	289
Coosa Valley Electric Cooperative Inc	4911	522
Coosa Valley Youth Services	8361	181
Coos-Curry Electric Coop	4911	272
Coots Materials Company Inc	1422	58
Copac Inc	2754	13
Copan Systems Inc	5045	255
Copano Energy LLC	4922	16
Copar Corp	3625	131
Copart Inc	5599	3
Copart Salvage Auto Auctions	5093	49
Copaz Packing Corp	2013	102
Copco Inc	3469	30
Cope Plastics Inc	5162	25
Cope-Bestway Express Inc	4213	1556
Copeland Electric Company Inc	1731	606
Copeland Paving Inc	1611	203
Copeland Truc-King Inc	4213	2107
Copen Associates Inc	2211	6
Copesetic Inc	3679	677
Copia International Ltd	7373	869
Copia Technologies Inc	7373	1029
Copier Fax Business Technologies Inc	5044	134
Copiers Northwest Inc	5044	33
Copiersnow Inc	5044	125
Copies Overnight Inc	2732	46
Copies Plus Printing Inc	7334	85
Copi-Mate Inc	3955	15
Co-Planar Inc	3469	321
Copland Industries Inc	5131	36
Copley Financial Services Corp	6282	643
Copley Press Inc	2711	36
Coplon's	5621	43
Copp Industrial Manufacturing Inc	3444	265
Coppel Corp	5021	8
Copper and Brass Sales Inc	5051	12
Copper Canyon Press	2731	334
Copper Clad Multilayer Products Inc	3672	318
Copper Mountain Electric LLC	1731	562
Copper River Seafoods Inc	2091	15
Copper State Rubber Of Arizona Inc	3052	25
Copper-Brite Inc	2879	55
Copperfield Publishing Inc	2759	271
CopperLogic Inc	3629	29
Copperweld BiMetallics LLC	3317	10
Coppinger Exhibits Inc	7389	2310
Copps Industries Inc	2891	94
Coprar Media Inc	2721	300
Coprintco Business Forms Inc	2752	1203
COPsync Inc	7372	3421
Coptech Inc	7379	1152
Copy and Camera Inc	5044	111
Copy Carriers Inc	4213	1066
Copy Cats	2752	1192
Copy Center Of Topeka Inc	2752	1420
Copy Craft Printers Inc	2752	332
Copy Express Inc	2752	1306
Copy Free Technology Inc	5044	109
Copy General Corp	7334	37
Copy Graphics Inc	5999	230
Copy Images Inc	5044	110
Copy King Inc	7334	62
Copy Link Inc	5044	113
Copy Masters Inc	2759	404
Copy Systems Inc	5044	36
Copy Vend Inc	5044	86
Copy Zone Ltd	7334	44
Copy-All Of Brevard Inc	5999	258
Copyfax Inc	5044	73
Copyright Clearance Center Inc	6794	28
CopyTele Inc	3577	584
Corad Technology Inc	3672	243
Coradiant Inc	7372	814
Coral Color Process Ltd	2752	857
Coral Graphic Services Inc	2752	123
Coral Group Inc	6799	323
Coral Industries Inc	3231	25
Coral Springs Moving and Storage	4213	3023
Coram Inc	8082	75
Coratolo Carrieri Associates LLC	6162	143
Cor-A-Vent Inc	3089	1570
Corbett Associates Inc	8743	278
Corbett Enterprises Inc	3589	242
Corbett Industries Inc	7699	223
Corbett Package Co.	2449	2
Corbett Steeves Pattern Works Inc	3365	47
Corbin Pacific Inc	3751	17

Company Name	SIC	Rank
Corbin Willits Systems Inc	7372	3600
Corbin-Hill Inc	2051	113
Corbis Corp	6794	12
Corbitt Manufacturing Inc	2421	28
Corbo Hotel Restaurant and Bar Supply Inc	5046	252
Corboy and Demetrio	8111	293
Corby Industries Inc	3625	375
Corby North Bridge Securities Inc	6211	304
Corcept Therapeutics Inc	2834	415
Corcoran Group Inc	6531	130
Corcoran Sawtelle and Rosprim Inc	3441	228
Cord Moving and Storage Co	4214	12
Cord Moving and Storage Inc	4213	2739
Cord Shattuc Specialties Inc	3643	145
Corda Corp	1311	248
Corder Associates Inc	7371	1310
Cordero Rojo Mining Co	1221	31
Cordia Corp	7389	374
Cordillera Asset Management Inc	6282	440
Cordin Co	3861	54
Cordis Corp	3841	33
Cordis Endovascular Systems Inc	3841	10
Cordis International Corp	2834	106
Cordmaster Engineering Company Inc	3643	125
Cordova Bolt Inc	5072	101
Cordova Electric Cooperative Inc	4911	433
Cordova Truck Company Inc	4213	2232
Cordova Ventures	6799	295
Cordset Designs Inc	3357	51
Core Assemblies Inc	3599	2050
Core BioTech Corp	2836	96
Core Bts Inc	7373	105
Core Communication Inc	1731	827
Core Communications	7374	268
Core Components Inc	3625	305
Core Education And Consulting Solutions Inc	7371	85
Core Furnace Systems Corp	3567	52
Core Health Care	8063	17
Core Laboratories Inc	8734	4
Core Labs LLC	3663	337
Core Logic Software Inc	7372	1884
Core Molding Technologies Inc	3089	4
Core Pipe Products Inc	3462	45
Core Products Company Inc	5087	164
Core Realty Holdings LLC	6531	129
Core Software Inc	7372	573
Core Software Technology	7372	3991
Core Technology Corp	7372	3180
Core2 Business Consulting Inc	7371	599
Core3 Inc	8721	94
Coreance Inc	8093	48
Corecare Associates	7311	997
Core-Create Inc	7311	333
Co-Rect Products Inc	3269	16
CoreHarbor Inc	7372	183
Corelis Inc	7372	3791
CoreLogic Inc	7389	277
Corelogic Marketlinx Inc	7372	4141
Core-Mark Holding Company Inc	5141	9
Core-Mark International Inc	5141	31
COREMedia Systems Inc	7372	2271
CoreMedical Group	7361	143
Corena USA Inc	7373	1185
Corente	7379	308
CoreObjects Software Inc	7372	3313
CorePartners Inc	7379	217
Corepoint Health LLC	7371	974
CORESense Inc	7372	1260
Coresite LLC	7376	21
CoreSite Realty Corp	6519	13
Coreslab Structures Inc	3272	71
Coreslab Structures Inc (Marshall Missouri)	3272	35
Coresoft Technologies Inc	7372	2959
CoreSource Inc	6411	17
Coresphere LLC	7379	1174
CORESTAFF Services	7361	15
CORESTAFF (Washington DC)	7363	58
Corestreet Ltd	5045	179
CoreTech Consulting Group Inc	7379	106
Coretrace Corp	7373	954
CoreTrans LLC	4213	723
Corey Associates Inc	3679	648
Corey Barton Homes	1531	68
Corey Steel Co	3316	18
Corfin Tinning Services Inc	3699	168
Corflex Inc	3842	214
Corfu Machine Inc	3511	41
Corgan Associates Inc	8712	60
Corgenix Inc	2835	44
Corgenix Medical Corp	2835	50
Coridian Technologies Inc	5045	429
Corinth Coca-Cola Bottling Works Inc	2086	73
Corinthian Colleges Inc	8221	3
Corinthian Communications Inc	7319	117
Corinthian Inc	2512	14
Corinthian Media Inc	7311	68
Coriolis Networks Inc	3661	168
Corizon Health Inc	8011	34
Corizon Inc	8099	13
Cork Industries Inc	2851	57
Corken Steel Products Co	5075	47

Company Name	SIC	Rank
Corkill Electric Service Co	1731	2186
Corky McMillin Cos	6552	29
Corky Wells Electric Inc	1731	281
Corky's Food Manufacturing LP	2013	155
Corlena Oil Co	1382	63
Corlett-Turner Co	3451	55
Corley Automotive Group	5511	485
Corley M L and Sons Sawmill Inc	2421	111
Corley Printing Company LLC	2752	677
Corliss Resources Inc	5032	22
Cormark Inc	3578	12
CorMedix Inc	2834	476
Cor-Met Inc	3496	93
Cormetech Inc	2819	29
Cormier Movers Inc	4213	3081
Cormier Rice Milling Company Inc	2044	14
Corn Belt Power Coop	4911	162
Corn Flour Producers LLC	2041	53
Corn Maiden Foods Inc	2032	23
Corn Plus	2869	90
Corn Products Development Inc	2046	6
Corn Products International Inc	2041	4
Cornbelt Beef Corp	5147	100
Cornelius IMI Inc	3585	1
Cornelius Nurseries Inc	5261	8
Cornelius Printed Products Inc	2761	62
Cornell and Associates Inc	6531	219
Cornell and Company Inc	1542	276
Cornell Brothers Inc	2041	46
Cornell Concepts Corp	3089	1255
Cornell Forge Co	3462	38
Cornell Harbison Excavating	1623	604
Cornell Iron Works Inc	3442	60
Cornell Oil Co	1382	70
Cornell Pump Co	3561	79
Cornell Surgical Co	5047	101
Cornell-Dubilier Electronics Inc	3675	10
Corner Electronics Inc	5065	643
Corner Homecare Inc	5912	51
Corner Products Co	3577	279
Cornerstone Accounting Group LLP	8721	92
Cornerstone Architects Inc	8712	303
Cornerstone Bancshares Inc	6021	186
Cornerstone Bank NA	6035	215
Cornerstone Bank NA	6712	529
Cornerstone Community Bank	6022	522
Cornerstone Community Federal Credit Union	6061	65
Cornerstone Community Financial	6061	99
Cornerstone Construction Services Inc	1771	34
Cornerstone Controls Inc	5085	77
Cornerstone Equity Investors LLC	6282	353
Cornerstone Financial Inc	6282	402
Cornerstone Information Systems Inc (Bloomington Indiana)	7372	306
Cornerstone Information Systems Inc (Hopkinsville Kentucky)	7372	4165
Cornerstone Materials Corp	5032	100
Cornerstone Medical Services - Midwest LLC	7352	38
Cornerstone Mortgage Co	6162	151
Cornerstone Ondemand Inc	8331	92
Cornerstone Press Inc	2752	1714
Cornerstone Software Inc	7372	1426
Cornerstone Solutions of Illinois Inc	5045	729
Cornerstone Strategic Value Fund Inc	6726	91
Cornerstone Studios Inc	7812	62
Cornerstone Telecommunications Inc	5063	394
Cornerstone Telephone Company LLC	4813	315
Cornerstone Therapeutics Inc	3829	24
Cornerstone Transportation Inc	4213	2501
Cornet Technology Inc	5065	155
Cornett Machine Shop Inc	3599	1618
Corney Transportation Inc	4213	1686
Cornfields Inc	2099	170
Cornhusker Motor Lines Inc	4213	519
Cornice	7378	149
Corning Cable Systems Credit Union	6062	79
Corning Cable Systems LLC	3669	9
Corning Inc	3357	1
Corning Natural Gas Corp	4923	30
Corning Publishing Co	2711	386
Corning Tropel Corp	3827	50
Cornish and Carey Commercial	6531	75
Cornucopia Software	7372	3883
Cornucopia Tool and Plastics Inc	3089	1346
Cornwell Data Services Inc	7374	306
Corona Clipper Inc	3423	15
Corona Magnetics Inc	3677	13
Corona Millworks Co	2434	65
Coronado Communications Inc	3679	177
Coronado Manufacturing Inc	3728	164
Coronado Paint	2851	27
Coronet Communications Inc	4833	202
Corpak MedSystems	3089	478
CorpComm Inc	8743	61
CorpisCom Inc	4813	672
Corporate Brokers LLC	7361	150
Corporate Building Systems Inc	7349	85
Corporate Business Cards Ltd	2759	394
Corporate Call Center Inc	7389	724
Corporate Central Credit Union Inc	6062	23
Corporate Claims Management Inc	7389	1336
Corporate Cleaning Systems Inc	7349	60

Company Name	SIC	Rank
Corporate Color	2752	846
Corporate Communications Center Inc	7331	159
Corporate Communications Inc	7311	603
Corporate Computer Systems Inc	3663	137
Corporate Consulting Service Instruments Inc	3829	440
Corporate Design Group	7389	655
Corporate Disk Co	7819	18
Corporate Document Solutions	2759	96
Corporate Electric Services	1731	577
Corporate Electronic Stationery Inc	2759	158
Corporate Executive Board Co	8742	47
Corporate Express USA Inc	5112	2
Corporate Fitness Works Inc	8742	320
Corporate Fleet Services	3721	28
Corporate Fulfillment Systems Inc	7331	116
Corporate Graphics Commercial	2759	3
Corporate ImageWorks	5199	46
Corporate Information Systems Inc	7361	392
Corporate Language Services	7389	1492
Corporate Mailing And Fulfillment Solutions Corp	7331	165
Corporate Marketing Inc	7331	177
Corporate Office Properties Trust Inc	6798	64
Corporate Performance Artists Corp	7379	1473
Corporate Press Inc	2752	149
Corporate Property Associates 14 Inc	6798	186
Corporate Psychology Resources Inc	8049	23
Corporate Realty	6531	220
Corporate Reports Inc	2721	87
Corporate Research International	8732	60
Corporate Resource Services Inc	7363	65
Corporate Resource Systems Inc	2759	224
Corporate Rotable and Supply Inc	5088	26
Corporate Safe Specialists Inc	5999	42
Corporate Services LLC	7379	835
Corporate Solutions Group Inc	7361	427
Corporate Source Group Inc	7361	378
Corporate Source Inc	8331	60
Corporate Sports Marketing Group Inc	2721	175
Corporate Sports Unlimited Inc	7991	10
Corporate Systems Engineering LLC	7379	563
Corporate Team Professionals	8742	329
Corporate Technologies Inc	7373	219
Corporate Technologies LLC	4841	42
Corporate VAT Management	8742	105
Corporate Visual Communications Inc	2752	1578
CorporateMagic	7922	72
Corporation Of Gonzaga University	8221	13
Corporex Companies Inc	6552	8
Corporex Development Services Inc	6552	4
Corprasoft Inc	7372	4104
CORPTAX LLC	7372	1204
Corpus Christi Gasket/Fastener Inc	3053	26
Corr Tech Inc	5162	29
Corr Wireless Communications LLC	4813	246
Correction Controls	3625	407
Correctional Health Services Inc	8093	6
Correctional Healthcare Solutions Inc	8082	56
Correctional Industries Georgia Administration	2311	23
Correctional Medical Associates Inc	8099	73
Corrections Corporation of America	8744	3
Corrections Products Company Ltd	5072	202
CorrectNet Global Information Solutions Inc	7372	1343
Correlated Products Inc	5169	152
Correll Porvin Associates	8721	182
Corridor Group Inc	8099	100
Corridor Recycling	5051	110
Corrigan Brothers Inc	1711	51
Corrigan Dispatch Co	4731	65
Corrigan Electric Company Inc	1731	686
Corrigent Systems Inc	3613	70
Corriher Trucking Inc	5032	75
Corriveau-Routhier Inc	5032	12
Corrosion Companies Inc	2821	184
Corrosion Engineering Inc	3069	133
Corrotec Inc	3559	284
Corrugated Container Corp	2653	68
Corrugated Replacements Inc	3554	23
Corrugated Services Corp	7372	2012
Corrugated Specialties Inc	2653	123
Corrugated Technologies Inc	7372	3083
Corry Contract Inc	3444	188
Corry Laser Technology Inc	7692	55
Corry Micronics Inc	3675	33
Corsair Components Inc	3577	61
Corsica Enterprises Ltd	7331	254
Corsican Table Co	2514	6
Corsicana Bedding Inc	2515	9
Corsicana Technologies Inc	2869	69
Corsoft Corp	7372	4099
Corstar Holdings Inc	5065	144
CORT Furniture Rental Corp	7359	28
Cortec Enterprises LLC	3621	151
Cortec Group Inc	2679	56
Cortek Engineering Inc	3825	322
Cortex Medical Management Systems Inc	7372	4175
Cortex Pharmaceuticals Inc	2834	310
Corti Brothers Market	5411	251
Cortina Tool and Molding Co	3089	569
Cortland Bancorp	6712	464

Company Name	SIC	Rank
Cortland Foundations LLC	5137	36
Cortland Line Company Inc	2298	8
Cortland Savings and Banking Co	6022	601
Cortland Standard Printing Company Inc	2711	526
Cortland Wood Products Inc	2421	76
Corum Real Estate Group Inc	6552	254
Corum USA LLC	5094	26
Corus Realty Holdings Inc	6531	167
Corval Group	1711	14
Corvalent Corp	3672	104
Corvallis Gazette-Times	2711	326
Corvallis MicroTechnology Inc	3571	90
CorVel Corp	6411	62
Corvin Inc	7371	1047
CorVu Corp	7372	1447
Corwil Technology Corp	3674	226
Corwin Toyota Inc	8742	310
Corwin-Churchill Motors Inc	5511	1040
Corydon Machine and Tool Company Inc	3544	524
Corzo Contracting Company Inc	1623	451
Co-Sales Co	5141	110
CosaTech Inc	7373	346
Cosaweb Technologies Inc	7379	291
Cosby-Carmichael Inc	1442	61
Cosco Agencies Los Angeles Inc	4412	28
Cosco Fire Protection Inc	1711	76
Cosec International Inc	7311	1018
Cosemi Technologies Inc	3674	460
Cosense Inc	3829	187
Cosentino Signature Wineries	2084	96
CoServ	4911	331
Cosgrove Associates Inc	7336	90
Cosgrove Enterprises Inc	5087	40
Coshocton Grain Co	5153	97
Coshocton Trucking Inc	4213	364
Cosi Inc	5812	230
Cosine Communications Inc	3577	672
Coskey Television and Radio Sales and Service Inc	7373	602
Cosmetic Imports International Corp	5122	99
Cosmetic Specialties International LLC	3089	912
Cosmetic Specialty Labs Inc	2844	94
Cosmic Computers Inc	5734	319
Cosmic Patterns	7372	3700
Cosmic Plastics Inc	3089	1188
Cosmic Software Inc	7372	2669
Cosmo Corp	3089	74
CosmoCom Inc	7372	2046
Cosmodyne LLC	3559	205
Cosmolab Inc	2844	34
Cosmopolitan and Associates Inc	7389	189
Cosmopolitan Chemical Co	2899	37
Cosmos Communications Inc	2752	284
Cosmos Electronic Machine Corp	3567	55
Cosmos Food Company Inc	2099	297
Cosmo's Food Products Inc	2035	52
Cosmos Partners LP	6282	460
Cosmotech Inc	7371	1104
Cospolich Inc	3585	190
Cossentino Contracting Company Inc	1623	228
Cost Management Services Inc	4924	68
Cost Management Services Inc (Lafayette Louisiana)	7389	426
Cost Plus Management Services Inc	5719	10
Cost Plus World Market Inc	5719	5
Costa Cruise Lines Inc	4481	9
Costa Fruit and Produce Co	5148	21
Costa Precision Manufacturing Corp	3599	1260
Costanza Contracting Co	1541	286
Costanzo's Bakery Inc	2051	222
CoStar Group Inc	7389	149
Costco Wholesale Corp	5331	2
Costello Electric Company Inc	1731	1044
CostFlex Systems Inc	7372	4496
Cost-U-Less Inc	5331	13
Costume Craze LLC	5699	15
Costume Specialists Inc	2389	37
CoSystems Inc	3672	124
Cote E T and Son Auto Exchange Inc	5015	27
Coteau Shopper Inc	2741	106
Cothern Computer Systems Inc	7371	1075
Cotner Electric Co	1731	1842
Cotner Wholesale Lighting and Electric Supply Inc	5063	562
Co-Tronics Inc	3089	1816
Cott Systems Inc	7373	357
Cotter Machine Company Inc	3469	281
Cottingham Paper Co	5113	36
Cottingham-Chalk and Associates Inc	6531	454
Cottman Transmission Systems Inc	8999	123
Cotton and Co	8721	328
Cotton Electric Cooperative Inc	4911	296
Cotton Foundation	8733	34
Cotton Goods Manufacturing Company Inc	3842	23
Cotton Hill Studios Inc	7389	1253
Cotton Inc	6794	40
Cotton States Life Insurance Co	6311	203
Cotton States Mutual Insurance Co	6331	190
Cotton Tails Inc	5641	8
Cotton Utility Constructors Inc	3643	131
CottonimagesCom Inc	7336	69

Company Name	SIC	Rank
Cottonwood Printing Company Inc	2752	1679
Cottonwood Software	7372	4802
Cottrell Inc	3713	29
Cottrell Paper Company Inc	2621	66
Coty Inc	2844	4
Cougaar Software Inc	7372	2129
Cougar Communication Services LLC	1731	1670
Cougar Electronics Corp	8731	391
Cougar Mountain Software Inc	7372	2221
Cougar Software Solutions Inc	7372	2960
Coughlan Products Corp	2844	141
Coughlin Stoia Geller Rudman Robbins LLP	8111	80
Cougle's Recycling Inc	4953	125
Coulter Cadillac Inc	5511	273
Coulter Companies Inc	4953	58
Council On Aging Silicon Valley Inc	8322	89
Councilor Buchanan and Mitchell PC	8721	378
Counsel For Secular Humanism	2721	355
Counsel on Call Inc	8999	118
Count Numbering Machine Inc	3555	103
Counter Attactics Inc	7999	123
Counter Culture Coffee Inc	2095	44
Counter Technology Inc	7363	127
Counterbalance Corp	3545	174
Counter-Fit Inc	2339	38
Counterpoint Systems	5734	207
Counterpoint Systems Ltd	7372	627
CounterSign Software Inc	7372	3884
Countess Gilbert Andrews	8111	443
Countri Corp	6712	709
Country Bank for Savings	6036	40
Country Classic Dairies Inc	2026	78
Country Club Bank (Leavenworth Kansas)	6712	392
Country Club Enterprises LLC	5091	39
Country Estate Products	6519	30
Country Financial	6311	110
Country Financial (Bloomington Illinois)	6311	105
Country Fresh Batter Inc	2052	42
Country Fresh LLC	2026	29
Country Fresh Mushroom Co	5148	60
Country Home Collection Co	5963	23
Country Home Creations Inc	2099	312
Country Home Products Inc	5961	140
Country Inns and Suites	7011	26
Country Investors Life Assurance Co	6311	67
Country Life Inc	2834	213
Country Mill Farms LLC	0175	11
Country Music Media Group	2721	417
Country Mutual Insurance Co	6331	79
Country Partners Co-Op Elevators	5153	170
Country Pride Coop	5172	101
Country Pride Services Coop	5541	47
Country Pure Foods Inc	2033	40
Country Saw And Knife Inc	7699	97
Country Snacks Manufacturing Inc	2013	220
Country Squire Florist	5992	17
Country Standard Time	2721	401
Country Systems	5734	374
Country Tonite Theatre	7922	66
Country Trust Bank	6035	99
Country Villa Service Corp	8051	2
Countryman Associates Inc	3651	194
Countrymark Cooperative Inc	5153	11
CountryPlace Mortgage Ltd	6162	46
Countryside Baking Inc	2051	122
Countryside Coop	5153	10
Countryside Foods LLC	5141	154
Countryside Nursery	5083	183
Countryside Publishing Company Inc	2741	197
Countrywide Financial Corp	6162	1
Countrywide Hardware Inc	3429	107
Countrywide Home Loans Inc	6162	18
Countrywide Tire And Rubber Inc	5014	28
Counts Sausage Company Inc	2013	225
County Bank Corp	6022	431
County Concrete Corp	3273	40
County Electric Inc	1731	2383
County Electrical Distributors Inc	5063	760
County Graphics Ltd	2752	1062
County Home Improvement Center Inc	5251	27
County Materials Corp	3271	7
County Of Fauquier	8322	6
County Of Macomb	8351	33
County Of Santa Rosa Board Of Public Instruction	8211	58
County Packaging Inc	7389	1185
County Property Appraisers Office	7389	2443
County TV and Appliance LOS Corp	5731	23
Countyline Co-Op Inc	5153	190
Coupa Software Inc	7372	1707
Coupons Inc	7372	873
Courier Corp	2732	4
Courier Div (Findlay Ohio)	2711	122
Courier E P I C	2752	41
Courier Graphics Corp	2752	479
Courier Herald Publishing Company Inc	2711	568
Courier Kendallville Inc	2732	3
Courier Printing And Lithography Inc	2752	1134
Courier Printing Company Inc	2752	500
Courier Printing Corp	2752	1438
Courier Publishing Co	2711	384

Company Name	SIC	Rank
Courier Systems Inc	4213	823
Courier Times Inc	2711	152
Courier-Herald	2711	809
Courier-Journal	2711	110
Courier-Journal and Times Credit Union Inc	6062	104
Courion Corp	7372	937
Courregas Pump Company Inc	5084	335
CourseAdvisor Inc	7375	123
Courser Inc	3599	1619
Court Reporter's Clearinghouse Inc	7389	1782
Court Reporters International Inc	7338	44
Court Square Capital Partners	6799	179
Court Square Data Group Inc	7379	579
Courterport Corp	3651	237
Courtesy Acura Isuzu	5511	35
Courtesy Associates Inc	7389	669
Courtesy Chevrolet	5511	1116
Courtesy Chevrolet Center	5511	423
Courtesy Chevrolet (Phoenix Arizona)	5511	138
Courtesy Chevrolet (San Jose California)	5511	191
Courtesy Cleaning Service Inc	7349	467
Courtesy Electric Co	1731	654
Courtesy Enterprises Inc	3713	46
Courtesy Ford	5511	936
Courtesy Ford Inc	5511	1052
Courtesy Ford Lincoln Mercury	5511	1006
Courtesy Ford-Lincoln-Mercury	5511	791
Courtesy Products Co	5963	22
Courtesy Sanitary Supply Inc	5169	168
CourtSmart Digital Systems Inc	3669	205
Couse and Bolten Co	3052	34
Cousins Metal Industries Inc	5093	221
Cousins Properties Inc	6798	123
Cousins Submarines Inc	5812	311
Coutts Brothers Inc	1623	688
Covance Inc	8731	5
Covance Periapproval Services Inc	8731	62
Covansys Corp	7371	25
Covanta Energy Corp	4939	4
Covanta Holding Corp	6331	96
Covario Inc	7371	204
Cove Electric Inc	1731	465
Cove Four-Slide and Stamping Corp	3496	50
Cove Marketing Inc	7929	2
Cove Of Lake Geneva	7011	222
Covega Corp	3231	33
Covenant Communications Inc	3652	35
Covenant House California	8361	88
Covenant Place Of Sumter Inc	8361	135
Covenant Transport Group Inc	4213	47
Covente Inc	8732	36
Coventor Inc	7372	2768
Coventry First LLC	6311	181
Coventry Health Care Inc	6324	10
Coventya Inc	2899	159
Coveo Software Inc	7372	803
Cover Sports USA	5091	94
Coverall Cleaning Concepts	6794	17
Cover-All Systems Inc	7372	291
Cover-All Technologies Inc	7372	1373
Covercraft Industries Inc	2394	11
Covered Wagon Train Inc	4213	2541
Coverlay Manufacturing Inc	3089	1473
Cover-Pools Inc	3999	109
Covestic Inc	7379	461
Covid Inc	3577	467
Covient Inc	7372	2296
Covigna Inc	5045	542
Covington and Burling LLP	8111	137
Covington Electric Cooperative Inc	4911	454
Covington Engineering Corp	3559	499
Covington Flooring Co	1752	8
Covington Machine And Welding Inc	3599	1366
Covington Virginian Inc	2711	840
Covisint LLC	7389	491
CoVision Inc	7379	658
Covista Communications Inc	4813	132
COW Industries Inc	3444	206
Cowan and Associates Inc	8742	593
Cowan Corp	5087	81
Cowan Plastics LLC	3089	1273
Cowan Systems LLC	4213	202
CoWare Inc	7372	1762
Cowart Electric and Industrial Contractors Inc	1731	902
Cowboy Charcoal LLC	2819	88
Cowboy Oil Co	5171	61
Cowen and Company LLC	6211	29
Cowen Group Inc	6211	158
Cowen Truck Line Inc	4213	417
Cowin and Company Inc	1622	36
Cowl Inc	2711	451
Cowles and Thompson	8111	263
Cowles Parkway Ford Inc	5511	801
Cowlitz Bancorp	6712	444
Cows Locomotive Manufacturing Co	3423	72
Cowtown Boot Co	5661	17
Cox 1 Inc	7331	223
Cox and Company Inc	3728	101
Cox and Powers Insurance Agency Inc	6712	726
Cox and Schepp Inc	1541	67
Cox and Smith Inc	8111	249

Company Name	SIC	Rank
Cox Castle and Nicholson LLP	8111	226
Cox Chevrolet Inc	5511	1250
Cox Construction Co	1542	343
Cox Control Systems	3625	410
Cox Die Casting Inc	5051	376
Cox Engineering Co	1711	12
Cox Enterprises Inc	2711	2
Cox Industries Inc	2491	3
Cox Interior Inc	2431	29
Cox Machine Company Inc	3559	451
Cox Manufacturing Co	3451	87
Cox Matthews and Associates Inc	7812	233
Cox Motor Express of Greensboro	4213	2141
Cox Paper and Printing Company Inc	5113	62
Cox Petroleum Transport	4213	935
Cox Radio Inc	4832	4
Cox Refrigerated Express Inc	4213	2313
Cox Richard Manufacturing Co	3523	253
Cox Transfer Inc	4213	1104
Cox Transportation Services Inc	4213	670
CoxCom Inc	4841	39
Coxe-Lewis Corp	2421	94
Coxline Inc	3553	22
Cox's Electrical Contracting And Engineering Inc	1731	1013
Coxwells Inc	3499	64
Coy Industries Inc	3444	156
Coy Trucking LLC	4213	2985
Coyle Business Products Inc	5044	147
Coyle Chevrolet Inc	5511	1144
Coyle Reproductions Inc	2752	224
Coyne Advertising and Public Relations Inc	7311	544
Coyne and Blanchard Inc	2721	216
Coyne Chemical Company Inc	5169	14
Coyne Graphic Finishing Inc	2672	73
Coyote Cabling LLC	1731	2217
Coyote Electronics Inc	3613	153
Coyote Gravel Products Inc	3273	60
Coyote Vision USA	5048	39
Coyotedata Security Limited Inc	7371	759
Coyotes Hockey LLC	7389	883
Cozen and O'Connor	8111	59
Cozy Harbor Seafood Inc	2092	72
Cozzoli Machine Co	3565	1
CP Auto Products Inc	3471	92
Cp Direct Inc	2752	473
CP Electronics Inc	5731	243
Cp Inc	2851	127
Cp Industries LLC	2899	197
Cp Manufacturing Inc	3559	122
CP Pistons LLC	3592	19
CP Software Group Inc	7372	681
CP Telecom	4813	298
CP Transporters Inc	4213	2841
CPA Global North America LLC	7372	2015
CPACinccom	5045	267
C-Pak Sea Foods Inc	2091	31
CPak Technology Solutions	7373	1080
CPAlead	8742	224
Cpc Aeroscience Inc	2842	65
CPC of Vermont Inc	3544	340
Cpd Industries Inc	3086	137
Cpe Peo Incorporated	7363	220
Cpeck Inc	5731	254
CPEX Pharmaceuticals Inc	2834	272
Cpf Inc	2086	99
Cpf Underground Utilities Inc	1623	156
CPI Aerostructures Inc	3728	47
Cpi Binani Inc	3089	892
Cpi Card Group - Colorado Inc	3089	412
Cpi Card Group - Indiana Inc	3089	413
Cpi Communications Inc	3825	287
CPI Contracting Inc	1623	851
CPI Corp	7221	5
CPI Econco Div	3671	12
CPI Engineering Services Inc	2992	24
CPI Group	7361	195
CPI International Inc	3663	21
CPI Malibu Div	3663	15
CPI Manufacturing Company Inc	5023	110
CPI Research and Development Inc	7221	3
Cpi Scranton Inc	3081	39
CPI Solutions Inc	7373	582
Cpi Technologies Inc	5045	1045
CPI Technology Corp	7221	4
Cpi Wirecloth and Screens Inc	3496	80
C-Plastics Inc	3089	1235
C-Plex Inc	3089	1857
Cpm Acquisition Corp	3523	39
CPM Construction Planning and Management Inc	1541	277
Cpm Inc	3861	126
CPO Commerce Inc	5999	61
CPO Inc	7311	286
C-Point Inc	2732	18
Cpp Inc	2741	127
Cpp International LLC	2678	7
Cppg Inc	7389	2013
Cpq Colorchrome Inc	7384	11
CPR Iii Inc	3825	270
CPR Inc	7363	267
CPR International	7372	4923
cPrime Inc	8741	266

Company Name	SIC	Rank
Cps Color Equipment Inc	3559	186
CPS Delivery System Inc	4212	30
CPS Distributors Inc	5083	71
CPS Express Inc	4213	1704
Cps Gumpert Inc	2752	355
Cps Of Ny Inc	7389	2163
Cps Printing	2752	423
Cps Products Inc	3585	195
CPS Technologies Corp	3269	6
CPU Medical Management Systems	7372	2373
Cpw Inc	2721	268
CPX Interactive	7311	174
CQ Communications Inc	2721	352
CQ Computer Communications Inc	7372	3523
CQ Inc	1241	9
CQ Products Inc	3679	866
Cqg Inc	7375	149
CQI Solutions Inc	5045	784
Cql Inc	7371	1211
Cqs Innovation Inc	8711	578
Cquest America Inc	7379	410
Cr Acquisition Corp	5044	81
CR Bard Inc	3841	8
Cr Cable Construction Inc	1623	240
Cr Contracting Ltd	1623	844
C-R Control Systems Inc	3812	213
CR Dispatch Service Inc	7381	88
Cr Electric Company LLC	1731	1719
CR Electronics Inc	5045	1056
CR England Inc	4213	24
CR International Inc	3661	148
CR Laurence Company Inc	3231	9
CR Machine Company Inc	3599	488
Cr Magnetics Inc	3825	190
CR Meyer and Sons Co	1521	61
CR Pittman Construction Company Inc	1542	108
Crab House Inc	5812	323
Crabbe Brown and James LLP	8111	319
Cracker Barrel Old Country Store Inc	5812	22
Craco Metal Supply Inc	5051	388
Craddock Finishing Corp	3479	78
Craft Brewer's Alliance Inc	2082	9
Craft Industrial Inc	3554	50
Craft Laboratories Inc	2819	128
Craft Machine Works Inc	3441	63
Craft Master Sign Corp	3993	176
Craft Mobile Tel	5999	285
Craft Pattern and Mold Inc	3543	36
Craft Press Inc	2752	1778
Craft Steel Products Inc	3568	67
Craft Wholesalers Inc	5092	20
Craftech Edm Corp	3089	285
Crafted Plastics Inc	3089	943
Crafted Smalltalk	7372	4994
Craftex Wholesale And Distributors Inc	5092	50
Craftique LLC	2511	78
Craftmaster Furniture Inc	2512	21
Crafts Electric Inc	1731	1889
Craftsman Book Co	2731	83
Craftsman Credit Union	6062	91
Craftsman Custom Metals LLC	3444	161
Craftsman Cutting Dies Inc	3423	65
Craftsman Electric Inc	1731	863
Craftsman Foam Fabricators Inc	3069	247
Craftsman Printers Inc	2759	223
Craftsman Printing Inc	2752	409
Craftsman Tool and Mold Co	5084	543
Craftsmen Photo Lithographers	2752	1559
Cragar Industries Inc	3714	426
Cragin Metals LLC	5051	442
Craig Allens	5087	189
Craig and Sons Termite and Pest Control Inc	7342	72
Craig Baker Marble Company Inc	3281	29
Craig Corey Travel Service	4724	152
Craig Envelope Corp	2752	826
Craig Industries Inc	2329	22
Craig Instruments Ltd	3599	1086
Craig J Phillips	3661	240
Craig Manufacturing Co	3714	184
Craig S Stevenson	7381	229
Craig Snair Security Inc	5063	330
Craig Systems Inc	7372	5002
Craig Technologies	7379	361
Craig Technologies Inc	3089	1399
Craig Tools Inc	3545	158
Craig Transportation Co	4213	761
Craig Van Lines Inc	4213	1434
Craig Welding And Manufacturing Inc	7692	18
Craig-Hallum Capital Group LLC	6211	113
Craighead Farmers Coop	5191	12
Craigslist Inc	7375	110
Crain Brothers Inc (Grand Chenier Louisiana)	1623	219
Crain Chemical Company Inc	2842	117
Crain Communications Inc	2721	31
Crain Cutter Company Inc	3429	103
Crain M-M Sales Inc	5012	57
Cram Communications LLC	4032	261
Cramco Inc	2511	42
Cramer Coil and Transformer Company Inc	3677	28
Cramer Fabrics Inc	2221	42
Cramer Inc	2522	46

Company Name	SIC	Rank
Cramer Motors Inc	5511	1147
Cramer Production Company Inc	7812	66
Cramer Rosenthal and McGlynn Inc	6282	218
Cramer-Krasselt Co	7311	25
Cranberry Hardwoods Inc	2421	12
CranBerry Sweets Co	2064	121
Crane Aerospace and Electronics	3812	38
Crane Aerospace Inc	3728	18
Crane and Company Inc	2621	25
Crane Co	3494	1
Crane Composites	5031	9
Crane Cost and Care Inc	7371	1825
Crane Dorray Corp	3625	382
Crane Engineering Sales Inc	5084	29
Crane Environmental	3569	61
Crane Equipment and Service Inc	3536	6
Crane Hill Machine Inc	3599	1522
Crane Interiors Inc	2392	35
Crane Johnson Company Inc	5211	25
Crane Manufacturing Inc	3823	302
Crane Materials International Limited Co	3082	6
Crane Plumbing LLC	3261	1
Crane Real Estate Group	6531	249
Crane Realty Services Inc	6531	296
Crane Rental Division Inc	7353	95
Crane Rental Service Inc	7353	51
Crane Research and Engineering Company Inc	3599	1000
Crane Technologies Group (Daytona Beach Florida)	3714	173
Cranel Inc	5045	271
Cranesville Block Company Inc	3271	13
Craneware Inc	7372	2514
Craneworks Inc	7353	24
Cranford Diagnostic Imaging	8071	55
Cranford Johnson Robinson Woods	7311	221
Cranford Woodcarving Inc/Plant 1	2499	27
Crank Works Inc	3559	454
Crankshaft Machine Co	3541	93
CrankyApecom	5012	59
Cranney Companies Inc	1731	727
Cranston Machinery Company Inc	3554	39
Cranston Print Works Co	2261	3
Cranston Textile Services	7389	1232
Cranston Trucking Co	4213	1266
Crapo Ltd	4213	2142
Crary Co	3523	29
Crary Industries	3523	16
Crash and Sue's	7819	40
CRAssociates Inc	8742	408
Crathern Machinery Group Inc	3554	16
Cravath Swaine and Moore	8111	148
Crave Foods Inc	2038	76
Cravey Green and Wahlen Inc	6159	56
Crawford and Co	6411	29
Crawford and Company HealthCare Management Inc	6411	160
Crawford Electric and Welding Inc	1731	1503
Crawford Electric Supply Co	3699	229
Crawford Furniture Manufacturing Corp	2511	33
Crawford Heating and Cooling Co	1711	178
Crawford Industries LLC	3089	480
Crawford International Theatrical Corp	5049	171
Crawford Knitting Company Inc	2252	24
Crawford Laboratories Inc	2851	119
Crawford Material Co	5032	76
Crawford Murphy and Tilly Inc	8711	254
Crawford Perspectives	2711	389
Crawford Pimentel and Company Inc	8721	137
Crawford Sales Inc	5031	373
Crawford Sausage Company Inc	2013	212
Crawford Sprinkler Co	3569	189
Crawford Steel Company Inc	5051	328
Craw-Kan Telephone Cooperative Inc	4813	99
Crawler Supply Company Inc	5082	117
Cray Federal Inc	3572	10
Cray Inc	3571	19
Crazy Computers Inc	5734	315
Crazy Shirts Inc	5699	9
Crazy Woman Creek Bancorp Inc	6712	651
CRC Design Inc	7372	1443
CRC Health Corp	8063	6
CRC Information Systems Inc	7372	1562
CRC Marketing Solutions	7311	311
CRC Press LLC	2731	77
Crc Print Inc	2752	1323
CRC-Evans Automatic Welding	1799	18
CRC-Evans Pipeline International Inc	3559	144
CRDaniels Inc	2394	2
CRE America Corp	7389	194
CRE Properties Inc	6519	8
Creamer Associates Inc	7336	229
Creamer Metal Products Inc	3523	211
Creamery Corp	2033	78
Creamland Dairies Inc	2026	63
Creare Inc	8711	20
Creata Vivendi Inc	7374	234
Creatas Footage	2721	32
Createhope Inc	7371	1006
Creating Results LLC	7311	844
Creation Group Inc	5013	16
Creations by Alan Stuart Inc	3942	15
Creative Aerosol Corp	2841	31

Company Name	SIC	Rank
Creative Age Publications Inc	2721	251
Creative Alliance Inc	7374	242
Creative Alliance Inc (Louisville Kentucky)	7311	153
Creative Analytics Inc	7379	1474
Creative and Response Research Services Inc	8732	32
Creative Apparel Associates LLC	2339	17
Creative Approaches Inc	7372	4592
Creative Artists Agency Inc	7922	15
Creative Associates International Inc	8742	119
Creative Audio Enterprises Inc	7389	850
Creative Automation Co	3559	252
Creative Automation Inc	3569	191
Creative Bath Products Inc	5074	84
Creative Book Manufacturing Inc	2782	65
Creative Business Concepts Inc	5734	29
Creative Cakes Inc	2051	181
Creative Capital Management Inc	6282	344
Creative Care Corp	8099	62
Creative Circle	7361	393
Creative Civilization	7311	342
Creative Coatings Of Carolina Inc	7389	1482
Creative Communication of America Inc	7311	660
Creative Communications Inc (Salt Lake City Utah)	4813	151
Creative Communications LLC	7331	104
Creative Communications Sales and Rentals Inc	5731	32
Creative Concept Unlimited	7389	2368
Creative Contractors Inc	1542	370
Creative Courseware Inc	7371	1705
Creative Data Concepts Limited Inc	4813	415
Creative Data Systems Inc	5734	435
Creative Design And Machine Inc	3469	322
Creative Design and Machining Inc	3599	1134
Creative Electronics And Software Inc	3672	162
Creative Embroidery Corp	2395	13
Creative Employment Opportunities Inc	7361	299
Creative Engineering Associates Inc	3625	285
Creative Engineering Inc	3999	210
Creative Entertainment Services Inc	7319	47
Creative Ergonomic Systems Inc	3535	147
Creative Events Enterprises	8742	388
Creative Fabrication Inc	3441	287
Creative Film Management Inc	7812	269
Creative Financial Group	6411	63
Creative Flooring Designs Inc	5023	154
Creative Foam Corp	3061	9
Creative Forming Inc	3083	9
Creative Graphics Group LLC	2759	42
Creative Graphics Inc	7336	95
Creative Group Inc	8742	150
Creative Impressions Inc	3081	126
Creative Imprints Inc	2752	874
Creative Infocity Ltd	7371	505
Creative Information Systems Co	7372	4286
Creative Information Technologies Inc	7379	263
Creative Label Inc	2796	24
Creative Laboratories Inc	2844	133
Creative Labs Inc	3571	12
Creative Licensing Corp	6794	149
Creative Light Source Inc	3646	77
Creative Logistics Solutions Inc	7373	929
Creative Machine Co	3599	1867
Creative Machining Systems Inc	3599	2235
Creative Machining Technologies LLC	3599	274
Creative Mailing Services Inc	7331	216
Creative Marketing Alliance Inc	7311	352
Creative Marketing Concepts Corp	5064	117
Creative Marketing Resource Inc	7311	974
Creative Marketing Sales Inc	7311	722
Creative Marketing Solutions LLC	7331	112
Creative Media Group	7371	1306
Creative Micro Designs Inc	3572	97
Creative Mold And Machine Inc	7692	33
Creative Mold Company LLC	3544	891
Creative Native Inc	7389	1669
Creative Networking Concepts Inc	7373	919
Creative Online Computer Services Inc	4813	466
Creative Packaging Inc	2653	103
Creative Paradise Inc	3544	851
Creative Planning Inc	6282	432
Creative Plastics International Inc	3089	1707
Creative Precision Inc	3544	723
Creative Presentations Inc	7359	63
Creative Print Group Inc	2752	1188
Creative Printing and Graphic Design Inc	2752	1063
Creative Printing Company Inc	2759	173
Creative Printing Services Inc	2752	403
Creative Research Systems Inc	7371	844
Creative Rock Concepts Inc	4832	284
Creative Screen Art Inc	2759	573
Creative Sign Services Inc	7312	33
Creative Socio-Medics Corp	7372	1198
Creative Solutions Editorial Inc	8999	221
Creative Stone Manufacturing Inc	3272	79
Creative Store Design Inc	5046	270
Creative Strategy Inc	7331	158
Creative Street Inc	7812	217
Creative Street Media Group Inc	5049	73
Creative Systems Inc	3535	231

Company Name	SIC	Rank
Creative Techniques Inc	3544	94
Creative Technology (Akron Ohio)	7812	42
Creative Technology Of Sarasota Inc	2731	333
Creative Technology Services Group LLC	5045	970
Creative Thinking Inc	7372	3571
Creative Tool and Machining Inc	3599	1785
Creative Urethanes Inc	3949	156
Creative Vision Technologies Inc	3571	126
Creative Waste Solutions Inc	3677	124
Creative Web Inc	7373	1031
Creative Wood Products Inc	2521	33
CreativeSoft Inc	7372	3792
Creativity Inc	7389	2120
Creatone Inc	8711	666
Creatron Services Inc	3861	112
Creaxion Corp	7372	1011
Credant Technologies	7371	328
Credence Speakers Inc	3651	100
Credentials Inc	7389	2087
Credit Acceptance Corp	6141	25
Credit Adjustment Board Inc	7322	183
Credit Adjustments Inc	7322	101
Credit Bureau Of Placer County Inc	7323	33
Credit Bureau Systems Inc	7323	26
Credit Bureau USA Inc	7323	35
Credit Card Processing USA Inc	7389	263
Credit Card Systems Inc	3083	83
Credit Central Inc	7323	42
Credit Clearing House Of America Inc	7322	187
Credit Data Idaho Inc	7323	30
Credit Data Resources Inc	7322	163
Credit Information Bureau Inc	7323	28
Credit One Bank	6712	89
Credit Service Inc	7322	115
Credit Solutions	7389	228
Credit Suisse Asset Management Ltd	6282	32
Credit Suisse First Boston Inc	6211	17
Credit Union of Denver	6062	47
Credit Union of Southern California	6061	82
Credit Union ONE	6062	13
Credit Union West (Sun City Arizona)	6061	134
Credit Unions Chartered In Sta	7389	1182
Credit Watch Services Ltd	7322	62
CreditCardscom Inc	7389	380
Creditex Inc	6211	101
Creditguard Of America Inc	6141	66
Creditlink Corp	7323	47
Creditors Collection Service Of Los Angeles	7322	113
Creditors Interchange Inc	7322	29
CreditRiskMonitorcom Inc	7322	58
Creditron Financial Corp	8742	207
CREDO Petroleum Corp	1311	180
Cree Employee Services Co	7991	2
Cree Inc	3674	39
Cree Lighting Co	3674	224
Cree Oil Ltd	1311	237
Creed-Monarch Inc	3599	119
Creek Diesel Services Inc	7538	41
Creekside Golf Dome	7999	159
Creekside Kitchen	2082	51
Creekstone Farms Premium Beef	2011	59
Creel Consulting LLC	7372	4370
Creel Printing and Publishing Company Inc	2752	113
Creel Printing Company Of California Inc	2759	189
CREF Money Market Fund	6722	28
Creftcon Industries Inc	3644	19
Crell Advertising Co	7331	194
Crematory Manufacturing and Service Inc	7699	184
Creme Curls Bakery Inc	2051	118
Crenlo LLC	2542	1
CreoScitex America Inc	7334	2
Crescend Technologies LLC	3663	250
Crescent Bay Software Corp	7372	4497
Crescent Cardboard Company LLC	2679	22
Crescent City Consultants	7389	555
Crescent City Security Inc	7382	27
Crescent Construction Co	1623	102
Crescent Decal Specialist Inc	7336	183
Crescent Design Inc	7371	1533
Crescent Duck Farm Inc	2015	65
Crescent Electric Supply Co	5063	13
Crescent Engineering Company Inc	1731	821
Crescent Equipment Company Inc	3523	217
Crescent Financial Corp	6712	328
Crescent Ford Inc	5511	356
Crescent Guardian Inc	7381	118
Crescent Inc	2252	7
Crescent Industries Inc	3089	516
Crescent Marketing Inc	2842	54
Crescent Metal Products Inc	3556	28
Crescent Paper Tube Co	2655	12
Crescent Printing Company Inc	2752	1447
Crescent Resources LLC	6552	13
Crescent Retail JV	5651	26
Crescent Solutions	8742	277
Crescent Sound and Light Inc	7359	77
Crescent State Bank	6035	70
Crescent Supply Of Penna Inc	5074	40
Crescent Systems LLC	7375	241

Company Name	SIC	Rank
Cresco Lines Inc	4213	299
Crescom Engineering Company Inc	5731	49
Cresent Enterprises Inc	2511	40
Cresline Plastic Pipe Company Inc	3084	18
Cresscare Medical Inc	5047	222
Cresset Chemical Company Inc	2899	225
Cressi-Sub USA Inc	5091	140
Cressler Trucking Inc	4213	219
Cressler's Marketplace	5411	181
Cresson Steel Co	5093	148
Cressona Knit Products Inc	2254	4
Crest Beverage LLC	5181	22
Crest Building Royal Maintenance	7349	341
Crest Cabinet Manufacturing Corp	2521	40
Crest Cadillac Inc	5511	850
Crest Coating Inc	3479	60
Crest Craft Co	2752	1499
Crest Electronics Inc	5065	217
Crest Foods Company Inc	2023	11
Crest Fruit Inc	0179	3
Crest/Good Manufacturing Company Inc	5074	167
Crest Manufacturing Company Inc	3677	72
Crest Meat Company Inc	5147	133
Crest National	3695	20
Crest Operations LLC	5063	122
Crest Rubber Company Inc	2822	17
Crest Software Corp	7372	3992
Crest Supply	5084	790
Crest Ultrasonics Inc	3589	24
Crestcom International Ltd	7389	770
Crestec Digital Inc	7336	275
Crestmark Bank	6029	25
Creston Publishing Co	2711	558
Crestron Electronics Inc	3571	27
Crestview Cadillac Corp	5511	920
Crestwood Inc	2434	42
Crestwood Midstream Partners LP	4922	22
Crete Carrier Corp	4213	12
Cretex Companies Inc	3089	5
Creve Coeur Camera and Video Inc	5731	30
Crevier Motors Inc	5511	555
Crew Connection Inc	7819	48
Crew Corp	8711	459
Crew Cuts Film and Tape Inc	7819	59
Crew Cuts Productions Inc	7336	191
Crexendo Inc	7373	135
CreXus Investment Corp	6798	134
CRF Inc	5045	97
CRFireline Inc	1711	249
Crg Management LLC	6531	419
CRH Transportation Inc	4213	427
Cri Advantage Inc	7371	460
Cricket Hosiery Inc	2252	10
Cricket Press Inc	2711	773
Cricket Technologies	7374	125
Crickett Staffing Services Inc	7361	317
Crider And Shockey Inc	3273	74
Crider Consulting Inc	7373	1134
Crider Inc	2099	59
Crilly Communication Co	1623	479
Crim Sales And Engineering Inc	3691	50
Crime Alert Alarm Co	1731	52
Crime Prevention Security Inc	7381	167
Crimestopper Millenium Enterpr	3699	202
Crimeye Inc	3663	390
Criminalistics Inc	3999	189
Crimson Cup Inc	7389	2188
Crimson Exploration Inc	1311	114
Crimson Fire Inc	3714	121
Crimson Insulations Company Inc	5033	40
Crimson Life Sciences	7389	2226
Crimson Semiconductor Inc	3674	336
Crippen Manufacturing Co	3523	198
Cripple Creek and Victor Gold Mining Co	1041	6
Crisafulli Consulting Inc	7379	1657
Crisci Food Equipment Company Inc	5169	169
Crisci Tool And Die Inc	3089	1061
Crisdel Construction Group Inc	1611	171
Cri-Sil LLC	2822	18
Crisis Computer Corp	7378	99
Crisis Intervention And Recovery Center Inc	8322	140
Crisnet Inc	7371	1002
Crisp Distribution Inc	5074	209
Crisp Enterprises Inc	7334	12
Crisp Fire Sprinklers Inc	1731	601
Crisp Manufacturing Company Inc	3532	78
Crispin Porter Bogusky	7311	43
Crisray Printing Corp	2759	333
Crissair Inc	3594	16
Crist Electrical Contractor Inc	1731	1153
Cristal Us Inc	5051	59
Cristek Interconnects Inc	3678	25
Cristi Cleaning Service Corp	7349	84
Cri-Tech Inc	3053	56
Criterion Bell and Specialty Inc	3499	122
Criterion Catalysts and Technologies LP	2819	54
Criterion Cellular	5063	667
Criterion Collection Inc	7812	97
Criterion Machine Works	3545	166
Criterion Machinery Inc	3559	577

Company Name	SIC	Rank
Criterion Technology Inc	3083	64
Criterion Tool And Die Co	3599	1589
Criterium-Liszkay Engineers	7389	1813
Critical Care Systems Inc	8093	10
Critical Care Systems Inc	8741	302
Critical Homecare Solutions Holdings Inc	8082	53
Critical Mass (Chicago Illinois)	7379	258
Critical Mention Inc	7389	893
Critical Path Software Inc	7371	1197
Critical Power Services Inc	5045	928
Critical Solutions International Inc	3812	168
Critical Thinking Co	2731	251
Critical Tools Inc	7372	4593
Crittenden Publishing Co	5943	15
Crittenton Womens Union	8322	100
CRJ Contracting Inc	1623	307
CRM Energy Inc	1311	238
CRM Learning	7812	174
Crm Solutions Inc	7372	5030
Crn Solutions Inc	5063	357
Crocker Crane Rentals LP	7353	91
Crocker Electrical Company Inc	1731	1102
Crocker Flanagan	8742	566
Crocker Technical Papers Inc	2621	64
Crockett Hospital LLC	8062	227
Crocs Inc	3021	3
Croft LLC	2431	7
Croft Lumber Co	5211	282
Croft Trailer Supply Inc	7539	11
Crofton and Sons Inc	2013	153
Crofton Construction Services Inc	1629	106
Croghan Bancshares Inc	6712	467
Croghan Colonial Bank	6022	179
Croissant Etc Corp	2053	22
Croll-Reynolds Engineering Company Inc	3569	284
Crom Corp	1629	63
Cromaglass Corp	3589	207
Cromers Inc	7359	236
Cromwell Architects Engineers Inc	8712	172
Cromwell Industries Inc	5085	458
Cromwell Printing Company Inc	2752	1510
Cronatron Welding Systems Inc	5085	104
Croney Enterprises Inc	3544	914
Cronin and Company Inc	7311	236
Cronin KIA	5511	1136
Cronkhite Industries Inc	3523	234
Crookston Welding Machine Co	5531	59
Croom Construction Co	1521	53
Crop Data Management Systems Inc	7371	967
Cropper Medical Inc	3842	190
Cropp-Metcalfe Inc	1711	37
Crosby Cadillac GMC Truck Inc	5511	1055
Crosby Electric Company Inc	1731	366
Crosby Export Specialties	5031	446
Crosby Group LLC	3429	1
Crosby Inc	7349	356
Crosby Marketing Communications Inc	7311	532
Crosby Trucking Service Inc	4213	575
Crosby's Drugs Inc	5912	63
Croscill Inc	2391	5
Crosman Corp	3484	17
Cross Access Corp	3695	96
Cross Brothers Company Inc	3535	161
Cross Check Inc	6099	19
Cross Chemical Company Inc	2899	235
Cross Co	5084	183
Cross Connection Communications Inc	4899	191
Cross Country Group Inc	7389	77
Cross Country Healthcare Inc	7363	32
Cross Country Local Inc	7363	36
Cross Country Travcorps Inc	7361	19
Cross Creek Apparel LLC	2321	7
Cross Creek Lincoln-Mercury Inc	5511	1037
Cross Creek Trading Co	4213	1088
Cross Industries Inc	3083	86
Cross Manufacturing Inc	3492	6
Cross Mark Southern California	5141	107
Cross Match Technologies Inc	3999	47
Cross Media Inc	2752	785
Cross Motors Corp	5511	810
Cross Oil Refining and Marketing Inc	2911	41
Cross River Publishing Consultants Inc	8742	691
Cross Services Inc	5084	590
Cross Sound Ferry Services Inc	4482	2
Cross Telephone Co	4813	454
Cross Tool and Manufacturing	3545	411
Cross Truck Equipment Company Inc	5084	610
Crossbeam Systems Inc	7372	1980
Crossbow Group LLC	7389	1759
Crossbow Technology Inc	3812	68
CrossCom National Inc	1731	86
CrossComm	7379	407
Cross-Country Courier Inc	4213	748
Crossfield Products Corp	2821	74
Crossfire Graphics Inc	2752	1151
Crossing Automation Inc	3559	17
Crosslake Sales Inc	5941	41
Crossley Economy Company Inc	3559	295
Crosslin Supply Company Inc	5211	89
Crosslink Technologies Inc	3674	480
Crossmark Graphics Inc	2752	494
CROSSMARK Inc	5141	5

Company Name	SIC	Rank
Crossridge Precision Inc	3549	87
Crossroad Services Inc	7389	538
Crossroads Bancorp Inc	6712	696
Crossroads Chevrolet Cadillac	5511	921
Crossroads Distributors Inc	5023	87
Crossroads Films Inc	7812	163
Crossroads For Youth	8322	191
Crossroads Ford Inc (Raleigh North Carolina)	5511	302
Crossroads Ford Truck Sales Inc	5511	969
Crossroads Systems Inc	3577	278
Crossroads Technologies Inc	7373	710
CrossTec Corp	7372	1700
Crosstech Systems Inc	7372	4677
Crosstex Energy Inc	5172	10
Crosstown Electrical and Data Inc	1731	1224
Crosstown Used Auto Parts	5015	19
Crossville Inc	3253	10
Crosswinds Communities Inc	1531	45
Crosswise Corp	7379	1647
Crouch Business Solutions Inc	7361	364
Crouch Industries Inc	3599	2479
Crouch Supply Company Inc	5084	288
Crounse Corp	4449	17
Crouse And Associates Insurance Brokers Inc	6411	104
Croushorn Equipment Company Inc	5082	125
Crow River Press	2752	1366
Crow Wing Cooperative Power and Light Co	4911	445
Crow Wing Transport Inc	4213	2272
Crowder Construction Co	1622	3
Crowder Industries Inc	8331	198
Crowder Mortgage Corp	6162	109
Crowdgather Inc	7375	260
Crowe and Dunlevy PC	8111	248
Crowe and Sons Electrical Corp	1731	1504
Crowe Chizek and Company LLP (Indianapolis Indiana)	8721	5
Crowe Paradis Services Corp	6331	357
Crowell and Moring LLP	8111	172
Crowell Corp	2672	45
Crowell Systems	7372	2130
Crower Cams and Equipment Co	3714	235
Crowley American Transport Inc	4424	4
Crowley Associates	5085	80
Crowley Maritime Corp	4492	1
Crowley Petroleum Services Inc	4412	18
Crowley Tool Co	3544	292
Crowley's Yacht Yard Lakeside LLC	4493	4
Crown Acquisition LLC	3585	177
Crown Asset Management LLC	7389	1013
Crown Automotive Co	5012	12
Crown Automotive Sales Company Inc	5013	123
Crown Battery Manufacturing Co	3691	7
Crown Beverage Co	5149	222
Crown Buick-GMC Truck Inc	5511	568
Crown Candy Corp	2064	65
Crown Castle International Corp	4899	3
Crown Castle South	7389	1138
Crown Central Petroleum Corp	2911	29
Crown Chrysler Jeep Inc	5511	483
Crown Clothing Co	2311	26
Crown Community Development	6552	295
Crown Cork and Seal Company Inc	3411	4
Crown Corr Inc	1761	10
Crown Crafts Inc	2211	10
Crown Delta Corp	2869	106
Crown Electrical Services and Automation Inc	3499	14
Crown Equipment Corp	3537	5
Crown Express LLC	4213	572
Crown Fence Co	1799	42
Crown Ford Inc	5511	226
Crown Group Inc	3479	3
Crown Hardware and Plumbing Supply Inc	5074	169
Crown Holdings Inc (Philadelphia Pennsylvania)	3411	2
Crown International	5045	581
Crown Iron Works	3556	13
Crown Machine Inc	3599	37
Crown Magnetics Inc	5064	120
CROWN Management Corp	6531	254
Crown Manufacturing Company Inc	3089	355
Crown Marking Equipment Co	3953	7
Crown Media Holdings Inc	4841	30
Crown Metal Manufacturing Co	3429	90
Crown Motors Inc	5511	715
Crown Moving and Storage Inc	4213	2853
Crown NorthCorp Inc	8741	177
Crown Packaging International Inc	5085	47
Crown Packaging LLC	7389	2196
Crown Paint Co	2851	123
Crown Partners LLC	7379	145
Crown Parts and Machine Inc	3599	275
Crown Plastics Co	2821	114
Crown Plastics Inc	5162	49
Crown Point Press	2759	579
Crown Pointe Div	6513	45
Crown Poly Inc	2673	19
Crown Power and Redevelopment Corp	6552	41
Crown Press Inc	2752	1267

Company Name	SIC	Rank
Crown Printing Inc	2759	418
Crown Processing Company Inc	2033	125
Crown Products Co	3993	55
Crown Products Company Inc	3441	107
Crown Products Inc	3444	257
Crown Relocations	4213	2276
CROWN Risdon	3089	82
Crown Roll Leaf Inc	3497	10
Crown Steel Sales Inc	5051	413
Crown Technology Inc	2899	161
Crown Technology LLC	2821	164
Crowne Plaza Downtown Columbus	7011	81
Crownlite Manufacturing Corp	3646	78
CrownNet Inc	7375	295
Crow's Truck Service Inc	5013	143
Crowson-Stone Printing Co	2759	192
Croyten LLC	7379	710
Crozer Keystone Health System	6324	38
Crozier Trucking	4213	2209
CRP Time Recording Systems Inc	5094	71
Crs Data Inc	7373	799
CRST Inc	4213	724
CRST International Inc	4213	49
CRT International Inc	7372	2670
CRT/tanaka	8743	91
CRU Price Risk Management	5051	335
Crucial Computers Inc	5045	964
Crucible Chemical Co	2842	160
Cruise America Inc	5561	4
CruiseCam International Inc	8748	457
Cruisers Inc	5049	141
Cruises Inc	4724	79
Cruises Only LLC	4724	32
Crum and Forster Holdings Inc	6331	68
Crum Electrical Supply Inc	5063	140
Crum Manufacturing Inc	3544	575
Crumb Rubber Technology Inc	3052	21
Crumbliss Manufacturing Company Inc	3825	311
Crumbs Bake Shop	5461	3
Crump Firm Inc	8712	114
Crump Group Inc	6411	42
Crump Insurance Services Inc	6411	167
Crumpler Plastic Pipe Inc	3084	31
Crumpler's Machine and Welding Service Inc	3599	1923
Crumpton Tv Audio and Video Center	5731	83
Crumpton Welding Supply And Equipment Inc	5084	406
Crumrine Manufacturing Jewelers	3965	26
Crusader Engines	3519	20
Crusader Insurance Co	6351	36
Crusader Staffing Associates LLC	4789	14
Crush Master Grinding Corp	3599	1793
Crushing Enterprises Inc	7319	59
Crushproof Tubing Co	3069	190
CrustBuster/Speed King Inc	3523	25
Crutchfield Corp	5961	91
Cruz Construction Corp	1623	148
Cruz Group Inc	5084	929
Cruz/Kravetz Ideas Inc	7311	359
Cruz Modular Inc	4214	22
Cruz Tec Inc	1623	653
Cruzio Internet	4813	224
Crv Lancaster	3545	371
CRW Graphics	2791	12
CRW Inc	4213	2348
Crw Systems Inc	7371	1492
Crydom Co	3679	114
Cryobanks International Inc	8099	104
Cryo-Cell International Inc	8999	90
Cryogenic Systems Equipment Inc	3559	305
CryoLife Inc	3841	53
Cryomagnetics Inc	3499	113
Cryomech Inc	3559	190
Cryoquip Inc	3585	52
Cryptek Inc	3669	156
CryptoMetrics Inc	7372	4678
Crystal Blanc Company Inc	5023	131
Crystal Blue Cleaning Service Inc	7349	344
Crystal Bomar Inc	3679	760
Crystal Bottling Company Inc	5149	28
Crystal Cal Lab Inc	3679	641
Crystal Canyon Interactive	2741	300
Crystal Ceres Industries Inc	1481	5
Crystal Clear Technologies LLC	7371	393
Crystal Communications LLC	5734	473
Crystal Computer Consulting Inc	7379	1431
Crystal Cream and Butter Co	2026	4
Crystal Creek Logistics LLC	4789	29
Crystal Deltronic Industries Inc	3674	383
Crystal Die And Mold Inc	3089	1048
Crystal Electric Inc	1731	1065
Crystal Employment Services LLC	7361	162
Crystal Farms Refrigerated Distribution Co	5144	6
Crystal Group Inc	3575	5
Crystal Incorporated - Pmc	2899	65
Crystal James Corp	3645	85
Crystal Lake Grindero	3599	490
Crystal Lake Manufacturing Inc	3991	15
Crystal Media Networks	7313	37
Crystal Metal Products Company Inc	3599	2195
Crystal Monitor Service	3663	418
Crystal Motor Express Inc	4213	551

Company Name	SIC	Rank
Crystal Point Inc	7372	3601
Crystal Print Inc	2759	124
Crystal Promotions Inc	5064	61
Crystal Rock Holdings Inc	5149	38
Crystal Smr Inc	5731	155
Crystal Software Inc	7372	3885
Crystal Specialties Inc	2819	93
Crystal Springs Print Works Inc	2261	13
Crystal Steel Corp	5051	221
Crystal Swarovski Components Ltd	5094	53
Crystal Technology LLC	3679	339
Crystal Welding Inc	3599	1924
Crystal Window and Door Systems Ltd	3442	42
CrystalGraphics Inc	7372	3524
Crystal-Like Plastics Co	3089	1891
Crystaltech Inc	3674	493
Crystek Crystals Corp	3679	183
Crystex Composites LLC	3299	12
CS and A Advertising Inc	7311	913
Cs and P Technologies LP	3561	78
CS Business Systems Inc	5045	506
CS Controls Inc	3823	195
CS Davidson Inc	8711	346
CS Hurd Electrical Contracting Inc	1731	1733
Cs Industries Inc	7699	99
Cs Manufacturing Inc	3089	570
CS Marketing Resources Inc	6311	256
CS McKee LP	6282	649
CS Precision Manufacturing Inc	3498	68
CS Tech-Fab Holding Inc	6719	12
Cs Tool Engineering Inc	3544	247
CS Wo and Sons Ltd	5712	58
CSA	3577	613
CSA Air Inc	4512	44
CSA Financial Corp	6159	62
CSA Group Inc	8712	20
Csam Marketing Inc	7376	42
CSB Bancorp Inc	6022	323
CSB Design	3672	488
CSC Business Services	7374	73
CSC Consulting Group	8742	51
CSC Credit Services Inc	7323	8
CSC Group Holding Co	7372	1205
Csc Inc	3449	30
Csc Publishing Inc	2721	314
CSC Scientific Company Inc	5049	99
Csc Technologies Group Inc	7371	1245
Csd Inc	7379	810
Csds LLC	3272	87
CSE Automation Engineering And Services Inc	3823	90
Cse Corp	5084	146
CSE Insurance Group	6311	232
CSF International Inc	7372	3652
CSG Direct Inc	3331	3
CSG Interactive Messaging	7372	1687
CSG Systems International Inc	7374	19
Csgi LLC	5045	589
Cshqa A PA	8712	233
Csi Acquisition Corp	3578	13
CSI Brokerage Services Inc	6311	206
Csi Holdings Inc	6411	257
Csi International	7371	1222
CSI International Inc	7349	250
CSI Keyboards Inc	3575	28
CSI Networks	7379	862
CSI Software Inc	7372	1261
Csi Technologies Inc	3675	37
Csic Corp	7373	605
CsitechnologyCom	5734	486
CSK Auto Corp	5531	6
CSM Corp	6552	10
Csm Instruments Inc	5049	195
Csm Manufacturing Inc	3599	1273
CSM Manufacturing Corp	3451	31
CSN Stores LLC	5531	14
CSO Schenkel Schultz	8712	109
Csoft Inc	7371	1534
Csols Inc	7379	715
Csp Enterprises	5734	302
CSP Inc	7373	127
CSP Securities Corp	7373	378
CSPS Pharmaceuticals Inc	7372	4803
Csr Electronics Inc	5065	75
Csr Interconnect LLC	3679	564
Csr Medical Inc	7363	253
CSS Alarms and Services Inc	5063	859
Css Antenna Inc	3663	195
CSS Distribution Group	2671	41
CSS Group Inc	7372	2253
CSS Industries Inc	2771	5
CSS International Corp	3535	205
CSS Laboratories Inc	3571	49
Css Publishing Company Inc	5192	37
CSSC Inc	7372	1246
CSSI Systems	3572	57
CST Environmental Inc	1799	13
CST Inc (Dallas Texas)	3829	194
Csw Inc	2796	9
CSX Corp	4011	5
CSX Intermodal Inc	4731	1
CSX Real Property Inc	6531	267
CSX Transportation Inc	4011	8
C-Systems Software Inc	7371	880

Company Name	SIC	Rank
CT Charlton and Associates Inc	7389	61
CT Corp	7371	17
CT Corporation System	8741	5
Ct Group LLC	5065	369
CT Holdings Inc (Los Angeles California)	7381	268
CT Hsu and Associates Inc	8712	279
Ct Investment Management Company LLC	7389	560
CT Lien Solutions	7375	145
CT Male Associates PC	7379	529
CT Realty Corp	6282	187
CT Wilson Construction Company Inc	1542	334
CT Wireless	4813	400
Cta Acoustics Inc	3714	134
CTB International Corp	3523	5
CTB/McGraw Hill LLC	2741	33
CTC Communications Corp	4813	75
Ctc Enterprises of New York LLC	3672	351
CTC Inc	4213	1930
Ctc International Inc	3565	126
CTC Parker Automation	3577	301
CTCE Federal Credit Union	6061	107
CTD Holdings Inc	2833	72
Cte California Tool and Engineering Inc	3599	1523
C-Tec Electric Corp	1731	2167
C-Tech Associates Inc	4899	200
C-Tech Tool and Molding Inc	3089	1643
CTG HealthCare Solutions Inc	7379	56
Ctg Inc	7389	2197
C-Thru Products Inc	3083	75
C-Thru Ruler Co	3089	818
CTI Communications	7372	2961
CTI Electronics Corp	3577	341
CTI Group Holdings Inc	7372	1449
CTI Industries Corp	3069	26
CTI Paper Company Inc	5111	22
Cti Products Inc	4813	747
CT-Innovations	3661	95
Cti-Ssi Food Services LLC	2013	58
CTL Distribution Inc	4213	334
CTL Electronics Inc	5731	255
Ctl Engineering Inc	8711	262
Ctl-Aerospace Inc	3728	52
CTLGroup	8731	168
Ctm Integration Inc	3565	111
Ctm Magnetics Inc	3677	26
CTM Media Holdings Inc	7319	41
Ctou Inc	7623	9
Ctp Carrera Inc	3089	266
CTPartners Executive Search Inc	8742	115
CTR Systems Inc	7372	1535
CTRL Systems Inc	3829	196
C-Tron Inc	3672	387
CTS Advantage Logistics	4213	175
CTS Automotive Products Inc	3694	9
CTS Corp	3679	38
CTS Corp Reeves Frequency Products Div	3679	367
CTS RF Integrated Modules	3679	69
CTS Services Inc	7378	91
CTS Technical Resources Inc	3555	104
CTSMarketing Inc	7311	919
Ctt Inc	3663	106
CTTS Information Services	4813	473
CTW Electrical Company Inc	5065	371
CTX Technologies Inc	3577	37
CTX-Lambie Inc	4213	1792
CTX-TL Inc	4213	2126
Cu Cooperative Systems Inc	6099	25
CU Cos	6719	104
CU Stoltzfus Manufacturing Inc	3523	231
Cuadra Associates Inc	7372	488
Cuadra Construction Inc	1731	1490
Cub Crafters Inc	3728	176
Cub Foods	5411	188
CUBE 3 Studio	8712	208
Cube Six Inc	7371	1518
Cubellis Inc	8711	75
Cubic Applications Inc	7389	88
Cubic Corp	3829	5
Cubic Simulation Systems Inc	3699	61
Cubic Wafer	3674	252
Cubic Worldwide Technical Services Inc	8744	28
Cubist Media Group Ltd	7812	140
Cubist Pharmaceuticals Inc	2834	49
Cubix Corp	3669	133
Cubix Latin America LLC	5045	132
Cubix Software Limited Inc	7372	4240
Cubrc Inc	8733	18
Cucoloris Films Inc	7812	200
Cudahy Lumber Co	5031	329
Cudner and O'Connor Co	2899	133
Cue and Case Sales Inc	5091	86
Cue Data Services Inc	7361	102
CUE Inc	3083	18
Cues Inc	3825	41
CUESOP Inc	5084	341
Cuesta Technologies LLC	7372	2962
Cuffs Planning and Models Ltd	7372	3602
CUI Global Inc	8999	66
Cuisine Solutions Inc	2099	46
Cuivre River Electric Cooperative Inc	4911	386

Company Name	SIC	Rank
Culberson Stowers Inc	5511	1158
Culinaire International Inc	5812	347
CulinArt Inc	5812	84
Culinarte Marketing Group LLC	2099	278
Culinary Ventures Vending	5812	309
Cullen/Frost Bankers Inc	6712	40
Culligan International Co	3589	2
Culligan of Greater Kansas City	2086	48
Culligan Water Conditioning Inc	5074	176
Cullimore and Ring Technologies Inc	7371	825
Cullinan Associates Inc	6282	385
Cullman Cabinet and Supply Company Inc	2434	54
Cullman Electric Coop	4911	346
Culmac Inc	3554	64
Cul-Mac Industries Inc	2841	32
Culmen International LLC	8742	478
Culp Construction Co	1541	186
Culp Inc	2211	5
Culpeper Farmers' Cooperative Inc	5191	69
Culpepper and Associates Security Services Inc	7382	178
Culver Company LLC	2741	372
Culver Duck Farms Inc	2015	44
Culver Franchising System Inc	5812	81
Culver Studios	7812	79
Culver Tool and Engineering Inc	7389	2178
Culvers Frozen Custard	2024	72
Culy Construction and Excavating Inc	1623	182
Cumberland Advisors	6282	615
Cumberland Container Corp	2653	91
Cumberland Dairy Inc	2026	58
Cumberland Electric Membership Corp	4911	155
Cumberland Electronics Inc	5065	268
Cumberland Farms Inc	5411	57
Cumberland Group	8742	340
Cumberland Machine Company Inc	7692	13
Cumberland Packing Corp	2869	30
Cumberland Pharmaceuticals Inc	2834	192
Cumberland Resources Corp	1222	8
Cumberland Services Group Inc	1731	1924
Cumberland Technologies Inc	6331	351
Cumberland Tool and Die Inc	3469	297
Cumberland Valley Cooperative Association	2048	92
Cumberland Valley Rural Electric Cooperative Corp	4911	314
Cumberland Valley Shows Inc	7999	79
Cumberland Wood Products Inc	2499	63
Cumbre Inc	6331	229
Cuming Corp	3533	135
Cuming County Public Power	4911	586
Cummings and Lockwood	8111	141
Cummings Group	7311	707
Cummings Holdings LLC	3499	105
Cummings Lighthouse Inc	5063	989
Cummings Moving Systems LLC	4213	2874
Cummings 'N' Good	7336	307
Cummings Transportation	4213	2320
Cummings-Moore Graphite Co	3624	27
Cummins and White LLP	8111	457
Cummins Bridgeway LLC	5084	75
Cummins Charles M Od And Elliot L Shack Od PA	5995	13
Cummins Electric Inc	1731	599
Cummins Engine Company Incorporated Engineering Test Services	3599	884
Cummins Faber PC	8721	247
Cummins Filtration	3714	61
Cummins Great Plains Inc	5084	32
Cummins Inc	3519	1
Cummins Intermountain Inc	5599	6
Cummins Label Co	2759	497
Cummins Manufacturing Inc	3599	1605
Cummins Npower	3621	11
Cummins Power Generation Inc	3621	21
Cummins Power Systems LLC	3519	7
Cummins Rocky Mountain LLC	5084	122
Cummins Southern Plains LLC	5013	56
Cummins West Inc	5084	166
Cummins-Allison Corp	3579	12
Cummins-Wagner Company Inc	5084	161
Cumpton Trucking Inc	4213	875
Cumulus Broadcasting Inc	4832	35
Cumulus Media Inc	4832	9
Cumulus Telecommunications Inc	4729	1
Cuna and Affiliates	6061	102
Cuna Mutual Business Services Inc	5112	10
CUNA Mutual Group	6311	58
CUNA Mutual Mortgage Corp	6162	93
Cunard Line	4481	6
Cunha International Inc	5051	480
Cunningham Childrens Home	8361	57
Cunningham Corp	5064	203
Cunningham Engineering Inc	3599	2040
Cunningham Manufacturing Co	3593	43
Cunningham Memorial Park Inc	6553	6
Cunningham Motors Inc	5511	677
Cunningham Pattern And Engineering Inc	3543	48
Cunningham Trey	3651	240
Cunningham Wholesale Company Inc	5181	77
Cupertino Electric Inc	1731	28

Company Name	SIC	Rank
Cupples' J and J Company Inc	3444	68
Cupp's Industrial Supply Inc	5085	310
Cura Group Inc	8742	337
Curb Records Inc	2782	48
Curbell Inc	5162	9
Curd Enterprises Inc	3089	1169
Curious Pictures Corp	7812	76
Curis Inc	2836	41
Curl Corp	7372	752
Curlee Manufacturing Co	3679	239
Curless Printing Co	2752	1557
Curley and Pynn Public Relations Management Inc	8743	199
Curosh Law Group PLLC	8721	243
Currahee Trailers Inc	3799	33
Curran and Connors Inc	7336	13
Curran Group Inc	1611	198
Curren Environmental Inc	1731	1540
Current Analysis Inc	7379	138
Current Computers LLC	3575	54
Current Controls Inc	3612	43
Current Electric Co	1731	733
Current Electric Of Battle Creek Inc	1731	1375
Current Electrical Contractors Inc	1731	2115
Current Media LLC	4841	59
Current Media LLC	4841	146
Current Publishing LLC	2711	569
Current River Die Sinking Inc	3599	2324
CurrentMarketing Inc	7311	594
Curriculum Advantage Inc	7372	1362
Curriculum Associates LLC	2731	133
Currie Peak and Frazier Inc	5045	430
Currier Plastics Inc	3089	590
Curries	3442	9
Curry Coastal Pilot	2711	835
Curry Control Company Inc	5084	327
Curry Corp (Scarsdale New York)	5511	55
Curry Ice and Coal-Carlinville	4213	1710
Curry Printing Ltd	2752	1224
Curt A Barad Audio-Video Inc	5731	120
Curt G Joa Inc	3554	3
Curtin-Hebert Company Inc	3559	472
Curtis Brown Ltd	7922	34
Curtis C Gunn Inc	5511	72
Curtis D Turner Company Inc	5023	173
Curtis Dyna-Fog Ltd	3559	188
Curtis Engine and Equipment Company Inc	5063	417
Curtis Instruments Inc	3825	20
Curtis Lumber Company Inc	5211	35
Curtis Mallet-Prevost Colt and Mosle LLP	8111	211
Curtis Manfredo Associates LLC	7389	2062
Curtis Packaging Corp	2657	20
Curtis Packing Co	2011	69
Curtis Packing Company Inc	2011	130
Curtis PMC Inc	3625	44
Curtis Products Inc	3498	32
Curtis Publishing Co	2721	58
Curtis Sallee and Co	8721	255
Curtis Screw Company LLC	3451	2
Curtis Specialized Moving and Storage	4213	2974
Curtis Steel Company Inc	5051	172
Curtis TradeGroup Inc	5093	248
Curtis Universal Joint Company Inc	3568	68
Curtis-Layer Construction Co	1541	265
Curtis-Maruyasu America Inc	3714	175
Curtis-Straus LLC	8734	65
Curtiss-Wright Accessory Services	4581	25
Curtiss-Wright Controls Embedded Computing (Dayton Ohio)	3823	127
Curtiss-Wright Corp	3599	5
Curtiss-Wright Flight Systems Inc	3728	60
Curtiss-Wright Flow Control Corp	3494	31
Curtis-Toledo Inc	3563	26
Curtition LLC	3089	1205
Curts Truck And Diesel Service	7538	40
Curwood Inc	3083	12
CUSA Technologies Inc	7372	448
Cushcraft Corp	3663	97
Cushing And Co	7334	13
Cushing Stone Company Inc	5032	192
Cushing Transportation Inc	4213	869
Cushing-Malloy Inc	2732	39
Cushioneer Inc	3086	93
Cushman/Amberg Communications Inc	8743	82
Cushman and Wakefield Inc	6531	36
Cushman and Wakefield of Arizona Inc	6531	412
Cushman and Wakefield of Colorado Inc	6531	426
Cushman and Wakefield of Florida Inc	6531	414
Cushman and Wakefield of Georgia Inc	6531	100
Cushman and Wakefield of Illinois Inc	6531	367
Cushman Winery Corp	5182	42
Custer Grain Company Inc	5153	196
Custodial Trust Co	6091	6
Cust-O-Fab Inc	3443	106
Custom Actuator Products Inc	3625	170
Custom Air Products and Services Inc	3599	128
Custom Alloy Corp	3498	41
Custom Alloy Sales Inc	5051	78
Custom Aluminum Products Inc	3354	18
Custom and Precision Products Inc	3444	298
Custom Applied Technology Corp	3589	245

Company Name	SIC	Rank
Custom Assemblies Inc	3089	1661
Custom Assembly Inc	3661	220
Custom Audio And Lighting Inc	1731	2586
Custom Automated Services Inc	3679	417
Custom Autosound Manufacturing Inc	5013	265
Custom Bilt Holdings LLC	5084	265
Custom Bindery	2789	141
Custom Biogenic Systems Inc	3443	182
Custom Biologicals Inc	1799	52
Custom Board Design Ltd	3575	42
Custom Bottle Inc	5085	90
Custom Building Products Inc	2891	10
Custom Business Forms Inc	2761	38
Custom Cabinet and Rack Inc	5046	199
Custom Cable Assemblies Inc	3679	740
Custom Cable Services Inc	1623	674
Custom Cables Inc	3679	600
Custom Capacitors Inc	3675	38
Custom Carbide Corp	3545	403
Custom Carbon Composite Creations Inc	3842	267
Custom Care Building Services Inc	7349	272
Custom Chemicals Corp	2899	106
Custom Chrome Manufacturing Inc	3751	10
Custom Clutch Joint and Hydraulics Inc	3714	384
Custom Coach International Inc	3711	68
Custom Coils Inc	3499	130
Custom Communications Inc	5063	369
Custom Companies Inc	4731	42
Custom Computer Cable Inc	1731	214
Custom Computer Designs Corp	4813	467
Custom Computer Inc	5734	99
Custom Computer Service Inc	7374	345
Custom Computer Solutions Inc	5045	865
Custom Computer Specialists Inc	7373	97
Custom Computers and Software Inc	3571	226
Custom Computing Inc	7372	3818
Custom Control Manufacturer Of Kansas Inc	3613	123
Custom Control Systems Inc	3625	399
Custom Controls Co	3585	229
Custom Controls Corp	1731	1565
Custom Conveyor Inc	3535	220
Custom Coolers LLC	3585	210
Custom Craft Controls Inc	3613	117
Custom Craft Plastics	3089	1323
Custom Culinary Inc	2099	153
Custom Cuts Fresh LLC	5148	45
Custom Cylinders International Inc	3443	229
Custom Data Products Inc	5112	29
Custom Design Inc	3544	514
Custom Drilling Technologies Inc	5065	969
Custom Electric and Design Inc	1731	2547
Custom Electric Inc	1731	1052
Custom Electric Manufacturing Co	3567	108
Custom Electronics Co	3672	334
Custom Electronics Inc	3675	24
Custom Electronics Systems Inc	3625	420
Custom Engineering Co	3069	65
Custom Engineering Inc	3599	558
Custom Equipment Design Inc	3565	145
Custom Faberkin Inc	7389	1730
Custom Fabrication Inc	3599	2330
Custom Feeder Company Of Rockford	3545	324
Custom Fiberglass Inc	3296	23
Custom Fiberglass Molding Inc	1799	114
Custom Fibreglass Manufacturing Co	3714	206
Custom Films Inc	2821	194
Custom Filter LLC	3564	67
Custom Flo Inc	3613	128
Custom Fold Doors Inc	3089	1803
Custom Food Group	3581	4
Custom Foods Inc	2035	56
Custom Glass Distributors Inc	5039	32
Custom Graphics And Plates Inc	7336	269
Custom HBC Corp	2844	146
Custom Hoists Inc	3593	2
Custom Honing Inc	3599	2440
Custom Hot Stamp Inc	3993	170
Custom Industries Inc	4213	3009
Custom Instrumentation Services Corp	3823	250
Custom Label and Decal LLC	2759	465
Custom Labels Inc	5131	43
Custom Labels Inc (Bossier City Louisiana)	2752	173
Custom Light And Sound Inc	5064	115
Custom Lithograph	2752	1448
Custom Loom's Rug Mills Inc	2273	41
Custom Machine and Design Inc	3549	101
Custom Machine and Tool Inc	3599	1410
Custom Machine Inc	3559	84
Custom Machine Manufacturer LLC	3531	159
Custom Machine Works Inc	3599	1896
Custom Machines Inc	3541	114
Custom Machining Inc	3599	2207
Custom Machining Services Inc	3599	712
Custom Magnetics Inc	3612	76
Custom Manufacturing Services Inc	3672	127
Custom Marketing Company Inc	5999	211
Custom Materials Inc	3644	18
Custom Meats Corp	2011	93
Custom Medical Services Inc	7322	139
Custom Medical Stock Photo/Media MDcom	7336	127

Company Name	SIC	Rank
Custom Metal Crafters Inc	3364	21
Custom Metal Designs Inc	3535	100
Custom Metal Fabricators Inc	3559	413
Custom Metal Inc	3441	258
Custom Metalcraft Inc	3556	31
Custom Micro Machining Inc	3599	1511
Custom Microwave Components Inc	3679	665
Custom Molded Products Of Georgia LLC	5033	58
Custom Molders Corp	3089	877
Custom Moulding and Accessories Ltd	7389	1329
Custom Pack Inc	3089	1796
Custom Packaging Inc	2653	58
Custom Pad And Partition Inc	2653	110
Custom Pak Illinois Inc	7389	1629
Custom Pipe Coating Inc	1799	127
Custom Plastic Card Co	3089	194
Custom Plastic Developments Inc	3089	894
Custom Plastics Inc	3089	284
Custom Powder Systems LLC	3556	76
Custom Power Ltd	3629	55
Custom Printers Inc	2752	696
Custom Product Development Corp	1761	43
Custom Production Grinding Inc	3599	955
Custom Profiles Inc	3083	61
Custom Resins Inc	3089	975
Custom Rollform Products Inc	3549	77
Custom Rollforming Corp	3449	24
Custom Rubber Corp	3069	122
Custom Sales and Service Inc	3713	43
Custom Sample Systems Inc	3826	149
Custom Scientific Instruments Inc	3829	476
Custom Seating Inc	3443	98
Custom Security	1731	2028
Custom Sensors and Technologies	3823	4
Custom Sensors Inc	3577	652
Custom Service Plastics Inc	3089	1442
Custom Service Printers Inc	2752	1553
Custom Shop Clothiers	5611	29
Custom Shoppe	2517	4
Custom Software Systems Inc	7372	4176
Custom Sound and Security Inc	7381	148
Custom Sound Of Athens Inc	5731	113
Custom Staffing Inc	7363	317
Custom Staffing Incorporated (Jacksonville Florida)	7361	164
Custom Systems Corp	7379	1259
Custom Systems Inc	3556	172
Custom Tapes Inc	2672	23
Custom Telephone Printing Inc	2752	1820
Custom Thermoelectric Inc	5065	956
Custom Tool and Design Inc	3544	472
Custom Tool And Die Co	3544	492
Custom Tool And Die Inc	3544	825
Custom Tool And Manufacturing Co	3544	116
Custom Tooling Systems Inc	3544	150
Custom Transfer Inc	4213	1623
Custom Transportation Service	4119	15
Custom Tree Care Inc	1799	131
Custom Truck Accessories Inc	5013	395
Custom Tv and Stereo Inc	5731	213
Custom Ultrasonics Inc	3699	154
Custom Video Design Inc	3663	281
Custom Welding And Metal Fabricating	3531	187
Custom Window Extrusions Inc	3089	481
Custom Window Systems Inc	3442	110
Custom Wire Industries Inc	3496	89
Custom Wiring Inc	3679	743
Custom Wood Products LLC	2434	45
Custom Words Inc	5734	442
Custom-Bilt Cabinet And Supply Inc	5072	81
Customer Communications Group Inc	8742	592
Customer Directory Inc	7371	1843
Customer Effective Inc	7379	711
Customer First Incorporated Of Naples	7336	203
Customer Metal Fabrication Inc	3599	853
Customer One Coop	5191	89
Customer Perspectives	7389	2335
Customer Potential Management Corp	7372	1390
Customer Research International Inc	8732	58
Customer Value Partners	8742	152
CustomerLink Systems Inc	7372	402
Customervision Inc	5734	412
Customink LLC	2752	106
Customized Energy Solutions Ltd	7389	723
Customized Support Services Inc	5063	420
Customnews Inc	2711	891
Customs Screens Inc	2262	5
Cutco Corp	5963	8
Cutera Inc	3845	49
Cutler/GMAC Inc	6531	166
Cutler Repaving Inc	1611	153
Cutler-Dickerson Co	5999	81
Cutler-Hammer De Puerto Rico Inc	3613	20
Cutter and Company Brokerage Inc	6211	394
Cutter Aviation Inc	5599	7
Cutter Communications Inc	5065	299
Cutter Information LLC	7379	957
Cutter Management Co	5511	41
Cutter Northern Refractories Inc	5085	349
Cutters Inc	7819	29
Cutters Production Inc	7812	65
Cutting Corp	7389	1154
Cutting Dynamics Inc	3599	257

Company Name	SIC	Rank
Cutting Edge Audio Group LLC	5065	160
Cutting Edge Bridgette Inc	3651	91
Cutting Edge Communications Inc	3651	186
Cutting Edge Design	5734	456
Cutting Edge (El Cajon California)	5045	363
Cutting Edge Machine And Tool Inc	3599	717
Cutting Edge Media Inc	2721	199
Cutting Edge Texstyles LLC	2261	21
Cutting Systems Inc	5271	5
Cutting Tool Innovations Inc	3541	251
Cutting Vision Co	7819	67
Cuttingedge Inc	7373	827
Cuyahoga Company Inc	8712	266
CV International Inc	8711	203
CV Perry and Co	6552	234
CV Source Inc	5013	396
CV Tool Company Inc	3599	653
CV Transport Inc	4213	2191
CVA Inc	1623	215
CVB Financial Corp	6712	100
Cvc Audio and Video Supply Inc	3695	142
Cvc Holding Company Inc	5984	9
CVD Equipment Corp	3559	123
CVF Technologies Corp	6799	360
CVI Melles Griot Inc	3827	26
CVK Corp	5995	17
Cvk Group Inc	5044	103
CVM Inc	8742	646
Cvp Systems Inc	3556	97
CVR Energy Inc	2911	18
CVR Partners LP	2873	6
CVRx Inc	8731	87
CVS Caremark Corp	5912	1
CVS Pharmacy Inc	5912	4
Cvs Systems Inc	5063	112
CW Campbell Electric Inc	1731	1561
CW Capital	6163	28
CW Capital Inc	6798	129
CW Harrelson Electric Co	1731	1829
CW Henderson Electric Inc	1731	233
CW Mars Inc	7374	215
CW Matthews Contracting Company Inc	1622	17
CW Network LLC	4833	23
CW Pond Contractors Inc	1731	1160
CW Silver Industrial Services Inc	3621	127
CW Wright Construction Company Inc	1623	16
CWA Manufacturing Company Inc	7389	1568
CWC Group Inc	5045	810
Cwc Industries Inc	5051	490
CWC Software Inc	7372	1231
CWC Textron	3714	96
CWCN Inc	8742	459
CWM Chemical Services LLC	4063	39
CWR Manufacturing Co	3452	15
CWS Corporate Leasing LLC	7021	3
CWT Farms International Inc	0252	8
CWT Inc	4213	708
Cxp Solutions LLC	4813	640
CXPress Trucking Inc	4213	1997
CXR Telcom Corp	3825	88
CYA Technologies Inc	7372	231
Cyan Worlds Inc	7372	2769
Cyanco LLC	2819	47
Cyanotech Corp	2833	46
Cyber F/X Inc	7379	673
Cyber Group Inc	7371	1428
Cyber Power Systems Inc	3577	115
Cyber Tv LLC	7371	1630
CyberAccess Inc	7372	3432
CyberAngel Security Solutions Inc	7372	2131
Cyber-Ark Software Inc	7372	1122
Cyberarts Licensing LLC	7371	960
CyberCrow Inc	7371	1725
CyberData Systems Inc	3651	175
CyberData Technologies Inc	7379	386
CyberDefender Corp	7372	746
Cyberdefenses Inc	7373	503
Cyberdyne Inc	3829	499
CyberEdge Informaton Services	7389	2344
Cyberex LLC	3629	21
Cyberforce Inc	7361	390
Cyberitas Enterprises LLC	7379	387
cyberLaptopscom	5734	129
CyberLink Communications	3669	252
CyberLink USA	7371	722
Cyberlogic Technologies Inc	7372	3094
Cybermetrics Corp	7372	3486
Cybernet Software Systems Inc	7372	27
Cybernet Systems Corp	7372	1311
Cybernetic Learning Systems Inc	7371	1864
Cybernetic Micro Systems Inc	3575	46
Cybernetic Solutions Company Inc	7372	4679
Cybernetics InfoTech Inc	7372	3235
Cyberonics Inc	3845	18
CyberOptics Corp	3827	17
Cyberpower Inc	5045	126
CyberResearch Inc	3571	107
CyberResources Corp	7373	1076
Cyberscience Corp	7371	1088
Cybersearch Ltd	7375	230
Cybershield of Texas	3674	118
CyberShift Inc	7372	610
Cyber-SIGN Inc	7372	695

Company Name	SIC	Rank
Cybersoft Co	7372	1285
CyberSoft Inc (Phoenix Arizona)	7372	4680
Cybersoft North America Inc	7371	1548
Cybersoft Solutions Inc	7372	1652
CyberSoft Technologies Inc	7372	4147
CyberSource Corp	7374	34
Cyberspace HQ LLC	7372	2963
CyberStaff America Ltd	8748	163
CyberStrategies Inc	7379	1197
Cybertech Inc	3577	515
cyberThink Inc	7371	192
CyberTools Inc	7372	1731
Cybertrol Engineering LLC	3625	103
Cyberware Inc	3571	194
CyberWarehouse	5734	100
Cyberwerx Inc	7371	777
Cyberwolf Inc	7371	1180
Cyber-World Solutions Inc	7373	374
CYBEX International Inc	3949	38
Cybortronics Inc	3826	89
Cybra Corp	7372	3701
Cybrdi Inc	2836	87
Cybrid Inc	7379	1083
Cybrix Group Inc	7374	99
Cycle Computer Consultants Inc	7371	1299
Cycle Country Accessories Corp	3714	319
Cycle INN Incorporated Engineered Software	7372	3579
Cycle News Inc	2711	577
Cycle Systems Inc	4953	96
Cycles Inc	3089	717
Cycle-Tex Inc	4953	118
Cyclics Corp	2821	42
Cyclo Manufacturing Co	3546	45
Cyclonaire Corp	3535	37
Cyclone Drilling Inc	1381	23
Cyclone Microsystems Inc	3571	127
Cyclone Steel Services Inc	5051	263
Cyclone Surface Cleaning Inc	7389	1123
Cyco Software Americas	7372	3603
CyDex Pharmaceuticals Inc	2834	281
Cydian Technology	4813	734
CygnaCom Solutions Inc	7372	1262
Cygnet Controls Inc	8748	382
Cygnus Automation Inc	3629	97
Cygnus Business Media Inc	2721	62
Cygnus Labs LLC	3571	172
Cyios Corp	7389	1875
Cylene Pharmaceuticals Inc	8731	176
Cylinder Heads International	5015	13
Cylix Corp	3661	172
Cylix Inc	3579	60
Cylogy Inc	4813	729
CYMA Systems Inc	7372	3181
Cymer Inc	3559	15
Cymfony Inc	7372	989
Cymphonix Corp	7379	824
Cymtec Systems Inc	7382	96
Cyn Environmental Services Inc	4953	41
Cynergies Consulting Inc	7379	587
Cynosure Inc	3845	37
Cynthia Rowley	2331	11
Cyoptics Inc	3827	12
Cyperceptions Inc	5045	982
Cypress Communications Holding Company Inc	4813	56
Cypress Creation Inc	3571	120
Cypress Dental Administrators	6324	120
Cypress Group LLC (New York New York)	6799	92
Cypress Hotel Management Company Inc	7011	114
Cypress Inland Corp	5045	946
Cypress Multigraphics LLC	3993	125
Cypress Pointe Resort LLC	7011	216
Cypress Provision Co	5147	102
Cypress Semiconductor Corp	3674	38
Cypress Semiconductor Inc (Round Rock Texas)	3674	116
Cypress Software Inc (Paradise Valley Arizona)	7372	4804
Cypress Technologies	7372	4805
Cypress Technology Inc	5045	778
Cypress Truck Lines Inc	4213	380
Cyracom International Inc	7389	1023
CYRANO Inc	7372	3683
Cyril Bath Co	3542	18
Cyrus Innovation Inc	7379	834
CyrusOne	7379	265
CYS Investments Inc	6798	28
CYSIP	8299	83
Cytec Fiberite Inc	2821	23
Cytec Industries Inc	2891	3
Cytex Plastics Inc	5162	31
Cyth Systems LLC	3827	68
CytoCore Inc	3841	405
CytoDyn Inc	2834	488
CytoGenix Inc	2836	104
Cytokinetics Inc	2834	392
Cyton Industries Inc	5013	89
Cytozyme Inc	2879	27
Cytozyme Laboratories Inc	2874	7
CytRx Corp	2836	100
Cyu Lithographics Inc	2752	649

Company Name	SIC	Rank
Cyveillance Inc	5045	461
Cyworld Inc	4813	372
D 3 Inc	7382	171
D A Blodgett For Children	8322	97
D A F Inc	5082	133
D/A Mid South Inc	5043	41
D and A Professional Resources Ltd	7361	429
D and A Truck Line Inc	4213	1751
D and B Holding Inc	5812	286
D and B Industrial Group	3089	255
D and B Machine Inc	3599	1159
D and B Machining Inc	3599	874
D and B Plastics Inc	3081	148
D and B Sales and Marketing Solutions	7372	829
D and B Trucking	4213	2813
D and D Commodities Ltd	2048	29
D and D Consulting Ltd	7373	530
D and D Display Group LLC	2789	40
D and D Equipment Company Inc	5083	104
D and D Equipment Rental LLC	7353	44
D and D Industrial Coatings Inc	3479	70
D and D Machine and Hydraulics Inc	3561	139
D and D Machinery And Sales Inc	3724	72
D And D Manufacturing LLC	3599	1634
D and D Marine Enterprises Inc	3677	123
D and D Printing Co	2752	1220
D and D Production Inc	3544	875
D and D Products Inc	3535	178
D and D Roland Enterprises LLC	7349	396
D and D Sexton Inc	4213	786
D And D Supply	5083	207
D and D Tooling And Manufacturing Inc	3469	93
D and D Transportation Services Inc	4213	1018
D and D Trucking and Services Inc	4213	2838
D and D Utility Contractors Inc	1623	425
D and E Builders Supply Inc	5072	172
D and E Electric Inc	1731	1876
D and E Livestock Transportation	4213	2623
D and E Machining Ltd	3599	419
D and E Manufacturing Inc	3531	195
D and F Liquidators Inc	5063	531
D and G Equipment Inc	5999	122
D and G Machine Company Inc	3599	1332
D and G Machine Products Inc	3599	423
D and G Manufacturing Inc	3599	1803
D and G Packaging Co	7389	2088
D and H Construction Company Inc	1623	261
D and H Distributing Co	5064	1
D and H Electronics Inc	5731	234
D and H Machine Service Inc	3599	1705
D and H Manufacturing Co	3599	190
D and I Trucking Inc	4213	2310
D and J Construction Company Inc	1442	17
D and J Enterprises Inc	1611	160
D and J Oil Co	1382	59
D and J Pallet Inc	7699	255
D and J Plastics Inc	3949	145
D and J Printing Inc	2752	118
D and J Quality Electric Inc	1731	1099
D and J Wholesale Tire LLC	5014	34
D and K Custom Machine Design Inc	3555	84
D and K Group Inc	2891	35
D and K Printing Inc	2752	1035
D and K Properties Inc	5045	373
D and K Truck Co	5012	155
D and K USA Inc	5064	217
D and L Foundry Inc	3321	46
D and L Machine Company Inc	3599	1417
D and L Manufacturing Inc	3533	91
D and L Technical Sales Inc	5065	999
D and L Tooling And Plastics Inc	3089	1094
D and L Trucking Company Inc	4213	2122
D and M Contracting Inc	1623	198
D and M Custom Injection Moldings Corp	3089	677
D and M Electrical Services Inc	1731	1119
D and M Enterprises Inc	5013	385
D and M Express Inc	4213	2019
D and M Instruments Inc	3823	481
D and M Water Service Inc	4213	2731
D and N Bending Corp	3465	47
D and N Electric Co	1731	112
D and N Precision Inc	3599	1594
D and P Custom Lights and Wiring Systems Inc	3646	50
D and R Autochuck Inc	3599	2452
D and R Boats Inc	5551	8
D and R Crane Inc	7353	25
D and R Machine Co	3599	1147
D and R Products Company Inc	3545	110
D and R Products Inc	5044	133
D and R Specialties Inc	3444	227
D and R Trucking	4213	2301
D and S Car Wash Equipment Co	3589	76
D and S Communications Inc	7629	20
D and S Creative Communications Inc	7311	580
D and S Electric Inc	1731	2307
D and S Exports Inc	5087	177
D and S Leasing Inc	7363	174
D and S Machine Service Inc	3599	129
D and S ManufacturingCoInc	3443	64
D and S Mobile Home Service	4213	3040
D and S Mold and Tool Co	3544	882
D and S Sign and Supply Inc	5046	264

Company Name	SIC	Rank
D and S Warehousing Inc	4225	35
D and T Fiberglass Inc	2221	43
D and T Trucking Company Inc	4213	840
D and V Trucking Inc	4213	688
D and W Awning And Window Co	3089	1036
D and W Diesel Inc	5013	96
D and W Electric Company Inc	1731	1325
D and W Enterprises	3356	25
D and W Food Centers Inc	5411	116
D and W Inc	3231	47
D and W Industries Inc	1541	290
D and W Truck Lines Inc	4213	447
D and W Wireline Inc	3533	130
D Audio Inc	3842	309
D/B Constructors	1542	411
D B Hess Co	2759	38
D Box Inc	7349	354
D C M Corp	8748	376
D C Systems Inc	3629	61
D C Tintle and Associates Inc	7311	863
D D Williamson and Company Inc	2087	46
D DeFranco and Sons Inc	0179	4
D/E Associates Inc	3621	135
D F Electronics Inc	3674	261
D Franklin Packaging Inc	5199	41
D G Yuengling And Son Inc	2082	14
D H Hutson Enterprises Inc	5091	127
D Hoover and Associates Investments Inc	6282	486
D/I Laser Products Of Dallas Inc	7378	35
D J Plastics Inc	3083	79
D L Cole and Associates Inc	5731	9
D L Electronics Inc	3679	640
D L Geary Brewing Company Inc	2082	89
D L Kellerman Company Inc	1623	700
D L Lee and Sons Inc	2013	47
D L Martin Co	3569	57
D Lariat D Enterprises Inc	7349	368
D Lawton Associates	7373	1197
D Litigation Support Services Inc	7334	68
D M and E Corp	5085	268
D M Merchandising Inc	5094	25
D Maldari and Sons Inc	3544	473
D Martone Industries Inc	3089	1407
D Mills Grinding and Machining Company Inc	3599	1739
D Myers and Sons Inc	5139	11
D Orser Inc	2752	1511
D P Electric Inc	1731	231
D P Tool and Machine Inc	3544	158
D Pierce Transportation Inc	4213	1023
D R Johnson Lumber Co	2421	61
D R Kincaid Chair Company Inc	2512	70
D R Sperry and Co	3589	136
D S Anthony and Sons Inc	3599	875
D S Manufacturing Inc	3751	21
D S Wilson Enterprises Inc	2752	1283
D Singer Engineering Inc	8711	667
D/V Technologies Inc	3661	145
D W Davies and Company Inc	5169	159
D W Dickey And Son Inc	5169	55
D W Evans Electric Inc	1731	614
D W Mack Company Inc	3089	1213
D W Ram Manufacturing Co	3663	261
D1 International Inc	5065	797
D2Audio Inc	3651	72
D2D LLC	3825	67
D2Hawkeye	7372	1421
D2K Inc	7372	1088
D3 Technologies Inc	8711	180
DA Collins Construction Co	1622	10
DA Consulting Group Inc	7389	519
D-A Lubricant Company Inc	2899	85
Da Neal Construction Inc	1623	865
DA Parrish and Sons Inc	1623	829
Da Publishing Inc	2711	527
Da Vinci Gourmet Ltd	2087	35
Da Vinci Systems Inc	3663	148
Daa Draexlmaier Automotive Of America LLC	3714	203
Dab Inc	3645	40
Dabko Industries Inc	3451	77
Dabmar Publishing Inc	3648	71
Dab-O-Matic Corp	3953	11
Dabora Inc	3199	11
Dac Inc	8361	123
Dac International Inc	3559	179
DAC International Inc (Austin Texas)	4581	32
Dac Systems Inc	3661	213
Daca Machine and Tool Company Inc	3599	605
DACCO/Detroit of Pennsylvania Inc	5013	310
Dacco Inc	3714	195
Daco Enterprises	7389	1647
Daco Inc	3599	177
Dacon Industries Co	3069	170
Dacor	3949	148
Dacor Inc	3639	9
Dacor Inc (Bowling Green Ohio)	7372	3314
Dacotah Bank (Rolla North Dakota)	6712	701
Dacotah Paper Co	5113	6
Dacra Glass Inc	3231	37
Dactek International Corp	3699	213
Dadant and Sons Inc	3999	89
Dadco Inc	3593	19

Company Name	SIC	Rank
D'addario and Company Inc	3931	4
D'Addario Industries Inc	1611	24
Daddy Ray's	2052	27
Daddy's Discount Stereo Inc	5731	70
Dade Bulb Inc	5063	1061
Dade Concrete Pumping Inc	5032	149
Dade County Federal Credit Union	6061	80
Dade Engineering Corp	3448	54
Dade Paper and Bag Co	5112	6
Dade Truss Company Inc	2439	28
Dae Advertising Inc	7311	459
DAE Trucking Inc	4213	2430
Daegis Inc	7372	730
Daewoo International (America) Corp	5131	3
Dafca Inc	7371	657
Daffin Mercantile	5141	184
Daffron and Associates Inc	7372	2344
DAG Online Inc	7379	596
Dagan Corp	3845	126
Dage Enterprises Inc	6552	308
Dage-Mti Of Michigan City Inc	3651	198
Dagen Trucking Inc	4213	3027
Daggett Truck Line Inc	4213	1285
D'Agostino and Associates	6531	374
D'Agostino Supermarkets Inc	5411	148
Da-Green Electronics Ltd	3679	565
Dahill Packaging Inc	7389	1171
Dahl Consulting Inc	7371	245
Dahl Robins and Associates Inc	5734	267
Dahlberg Light and Power Co	4911	585
Dahlgren and Company Inc	2064	7
Dahlinger Enterprises Inc	7349	411
Dahl-Morrow International	8999	127
Dahl's Foods Inc	5411	70
Dahlsten Truck Line Inc	4213	1378
Dahlstrom Display Inc	2752	413
Dahme Construction Company Inc	1623	269
Dahmes Stainless Inc	3556	93
Dahua Electronics Corp	3676	1
Dai Hing Fat Inc	5046	209
Dai Inc	7373	275
Dai Systems LLC	7371	1190
Daicel Safety Systems America LLC	3069	72
Daidone Electric Inc	1731	90
Daifuku America Corp	5084	294
Daigle and Houghton Inc	5511	978
Daigle Oil Co	1711	166
Dailey and Associates Inc	7311	80
Dailey And Wells Communications Inc	5065	162
Daily Atlanta World Inc	2711	812
Daily Beloit News	2711	376
Daily Bread Co	7389	2089
Daily Chinese News Inc	2711	313
Daily Electronics Inc	5065	980
Daily Ellensburg Record Inc	2711	615
Daily Express Inc	4213	497
Daily Foods Inc	2013	68
Daily Greenbrier Newspapers Inc	2711	798
Daily Item Publishing Co	2752	880
Daily Journal Corp	2711	178
Daily Lewiston Sun	2711	303
Daily Ludington News Inc	2711	415
Daily Midway Driller Inc	2711	856
Daily News LP	2711	103
Daily News Publishing Co	2711	521
Daily Newspaper	2711	640
Daily Newstribune Inc	2711	305
Daily Orange Corp	2711	914
Daily Planet Ltd	7819	35
Daily Press Inc	2711	155
Daily Printing Inc	2752	279
Daily Quill	2711	628
Daily Racing Form LLC	2711	86
Daily Sentinel Classified Advertising	2711	650
Daily Southtown Inc	2711	148
Daily Thermetrics Corp	3829	164
Daily Tryon Bulletin Inc	2711	817
Daily Union Inc	7313	22
Daily Variety Ltd	2721	118
Daily Wilson Times Inc	2711	444
Daily Woburn Times Inc	2711	359
Dailycandy Inc	2721	88
Dain Betty Creations Inc	3999	90
Dainippon Screen Engineering of America Inc	7372	2017
Dairy Conveyor Corp	3535	53
Dairy Farmers of America Inc	2021	2
Dairy Fresh Corp Cowarts Div	2026	7
Dairy Fresh Food Inc	5143	15
Dairy Fresh LLC	2026	42
Dairy Fresh Of Alabama LLC	5143	23
Dairy Fresh Of Louisiana Inc	2033	61
Dairy Fresh Products Co	5149	13
Dairy Maid Dairy Inc	2026	65
Dairy One Cooperative	8742	143
Dairy Queen Of Harrodsburg	7389	1917
Dairyfood USA Inc	5143	30
Dairyland Inc	5143	22
Dairyland Insurance Co	6311	29
Dairyland Midwest Inc	7372	3084
Dairyland Power Coop	4911	141
Dairyland Seed Company Inc	5191	74
Dairylea Cooperative Inc	5143	6
Dairyman's Supply Co	5039	19

Company Name	SIC	Rank
Dairy-Mix Inc	5143	41
Dairy-Tek Industries Inc	3556	154
Daisy Data Displays Inc	3571	48
Daisy Manufacturing Company Inc	3484	20
Daisy Publishing Company Inc	2721	181
Daitron Inc	3669	98
Daiwa Corp	5091	60
Daiwa Securities America Inc	6211	234
Daiwa Securities Trust Co	6726	84
Daja International LLC	8741	195
Dakat Inc	2531	40
Dakcoll Inc	5045	513
DAKCS Software Systems	7372	1492
Dakim Inc	3829	458
Dakota Aircraft Corp	3721	40
Dakota Alert Inc	5065	798
Dakota Brands International Inc	2051	215
Dakota Carriers Inc	4213	1827
Dakota Corrugated Box Co	2653	124
Dakota Country Cheese Company Inc	2023	18
Dakota Craft Inc	5031	180
Dakota Creek Industries Inc	3732	31
Dakota Electric Association	4911	136
Dakota Engineering Inc	3599	1476
Dakota Granite Co	3281	9
Dakota Growers Pasta Company Inc	2098	6
Dakota Kitchen and Bath Inc	5712	84
Dakota Line Contractors LLC	1623	773
Dakota Manufacturing Company Inc	3715	35
Dakota Micro Inc	3699	262
Dakota Minnesota and Eastern Railroad Corp	4011	13
Dakota News Network	4832	260
Dakota Pack Inc	2011	95
Dakota Plains Coop	5261	9
Dakota Prairie AG	5153	160
Dakota Roofing Supply Inc	5033	35
Dakota Security Systems Inc	1731	386
Dakota Software Corp	7372	2132
Dakota Specialty Milling Inc	2043	7
Dakota Style Inc	2096	58
Dakota Supply Group Inc	5063	42
Dakota Systems Inc	3312	72
Dakota Technologies Inc	3829	302
Dakota Tom's Sandwiches Inc	2099	307
Dakota Tube Inc	3599	141
Dakota Valley Electric Cooperative Inc	4911	371
Dakotah Inc	2392	49
Dakotaland Transportation Inc	4213	3133
DAKSOFT Inc	7371	414
Daktronics Inc	3993	1
Daktronix Computer Inc	5734	487
DAL Inc	8748	166
Dalanco Spry	7372	3260
Dalane Machining Inc	3599	1458
Dalb Inc	2759	113
Dalbar Financial Services Inc	6282	160
Dalbar Inc	8742	462
Dalbec Audio Lab	3651	126
Dalbo Inc	4213	943
Dalco Metals Inc	5051	357
Dalcon Technologies Inc	7372	4193
Dale and Maxey Inc	5031	206
Dale C Rossman Inc	1731	138
Dale Carnegie and Associates Inc	8244	4
Dale Corp	7389	425
Dale E Percy Inc	1442	88
Dale K Ehrhart Inc	6282	654
Dale L Quinn	5084	947
Dale Laboratories Inc	7384	57
Dale Medical Products Inc	3841	139
Dale Meyer Trucking Co	4213	1752
Dale Morris and Associates Inc	7922	27
Dale Pon Advertising Inc	7311	292
Dale Tile Co	5032	39
Dalec Electronics Inc	3629	121
Daleco Resources Corp	1311	260
Dalen Products Inc	3423	49
Daleo Inc	1623	249
Daleo Machining Inc	3599	982
Dalet Digital Media Systems USA Inc	5734	71
Daley Design Inc	3599	2178
Daley Tower Service Inc	1623	277
Dalhart R and R Machine Works Inc	7699	90
Daliah Plastics Corp	3081	100
Da-Lite Screen Company Inc	3861	16
Dalla Valle Vineyards	0172	22
Dallas A C Horn and Company Inc	3444	129
Dallas and Mavis Specialized Carrier Co	4213	197
Dallas Bias Fabrics Inc	2396	24
Dallas County Indigent Care Corp	8322	11
Dallas Data Processing Services Inc	7374	152
Dallas Digital Services LLC	7379	1439
Dallas Electronics Inc	3672	205
Dallas Fan Fares Inc	7389	506
Dalla's Machine Inc	3469	288
Dallas Market Center Company Ltd	5719	16
Dallas Metroplex Wiley College Alumni Association Inc	7389	1555
Dallas Morning News Inc	2711	57
Dallas Pest and Termite Services	7342	40
Dallas Plastics Corp	3081	93
Dallas Printing Company Inc	2752	1592

Company Name	SIC	Rank
Dallas Prompter and Captions Inc	4822	26
Dallas Security Systems Inc	7382	45
Dallas Tortillas Inc	2099	279
Dallas Wholesale Builders Supply Inc	5033	13
Dallastone System Solutions Inc	5045	814
Dallco Industries Inc	2392	38
Dalle Electronics Inc	3679	890
Dallis Brothers Inc	5149	174
Dalor Transit Inc	4213	3111
Dalo's Bakery Inc	2051	271
Dalrymple Gravel And Contracting Company Inc	1442	19
Daltech Inc	3599	2280
Dal-Tex Specialty and Manufacturing Co	3088	23
Dal-Tile International Inc	3253	1
Dalton Agency	7311	217
Dalton Bearing Service Inc	5085	205
Dalton Brothers Trucking	4213	2044
Dalton Corporation Kendallville Manufacturing Facility	3321	18
Dalton Electric Co	1731	2009
Dalton Electric Heating Company Inc	3567	69
Dalton Enterprises Inc	1611	205
Dalton Greiner Hartman Maher and Co	6282	349
Dalton Industries LLC	3547	12
Dalton Instrument Corp	5045	557
Dalton Trucking Inc	4213	699
Dalton Utilities	4939	9
Daly's Inc	5231	8
Daman Industrial Services Inc	3599	1148
Damar Group Ltd	8999	161
Damar Machine Co	3599	208
Damar Machinery Company Inc	3599	2276
Damar Natural Stone Imports Inc	5032	150
Damar Tool and Manufacturing Inc	3599	1010
Damasco Inc	5044	92
Damascus Equipment LLC	3532	40
Damascus Motor Company Inc	5511	1153
Damascus Peanut Co	5159	23
D'ambra Construction Company Inc	1611	207
Damen Carbide Tool Company Inc	3545	181
Dameron Alloy Foundries	3325	27
Dameron Hospital Association Inc	8062	137
Damerow Beaverton Ford	5511	85
Damick Enterprises	3599	2220
Damomics Computer Systems	7372	2964
Damon Company Of Salem Inc	3993	132
Damon G Douglas Co	8741	152
Damon's International Inc	6799	147
Damons Management Inc	5812	447
Dampney Company Inc	2851	131
Dampp-Chaser Electronics Corp	3634	35
Damron Corp	3089	1432
Damrow Co	8711	608
Dan A Hughes Co	1382	54
Dan Barclay Inc	4213	1780
Dan Carter Inc	8742	367
Dan Cooks Inc	5943	31
Dan Dipert Tours Inc	4725	48
Dan F Williamson and Company Inc	5084	458
Dan Gilbson Electric Company Inc	1731	1000
Dan Howard Industries Inc	5621	46
Dan Imig	3669	307
Dan Incorporated Oregon	5411	208
Dan Klores Communications	8743	36
Dan Lee Communications Inc	5065	573
Dan M Ogden and Sons Inc	4213	2969
Dan Pedone Inc	5734	196
Dan Perkins Group	5511	345
Dan River Inc	2299	2
Dan Ryan Builders	1531	63
Dan T Moore Co	8732	130
Dan Vaden Chevrolet Inc	5511	610
Dan Vos Construction Co	1541	144
Dana Chase Publications Inc	2721	326
Dana Communications Inc	7311	391
Dana Corporation Automotive Systems Group	3714	69
Dana Corp Plumley Div	3599	40
Dana Creath Designs Ltd	3645	42
Dana E Morrison Jr Co	2759	552
Dana Holding Corp	3714	6
Dana Innovations Inc	3651	111
Dana Kepner Co	5074	69
Dana Labels Inc	5131	53
Dana Sealing Products	3053	9
Dana Transport Inc	4213	3134
Danafilms Inc	3081	50
Danaher Controls	3625	56
Danaher Corp	3546	1
Danaher Industrial Controls	3824	1
Danaher Tool Group	3423	3
Dana-Saad Co	3089	1338
Danbar Equipment Company Inc	3751	22
Danbury Publishing Co	2711	261
Dance Brothers Inc	1771	25
Dancie Perugini Ware Public Relations	8743	153
Dancik International Ltd	7371	732
Dancker Sellew and Douglas Inc	5021	35
Dancor Inc	2752	899
Dancor Transit Inc	4213	1042
Dancraft Enterprises	3577	632
D'andrea Enterprises	1731	815

Company Name	SIC	Rank
Dandridge Equipment Inc	5999	166
Dandy Digger And Supply Inc	3531	228
Dandy Service Corp	4213	1050
Dane Falb Stone and Co	6282	609
Dane Systems LLC	3549	26
Danecraft Inc	3911	32
Danella Equipment Rentals Inc	7353	62
Danforth Wallace and Kupersmith Ltd	7311	885
Danforth-Gilman Grain Co	5153	186
Danfoss Chatleff LLC	3585	105
Danfoss Hago Inc	3432	28
Danfoss LLC	3585	60
Danhard Inc	3585	197
Daniel and Henry Co	6411	201
Daniel Company of Springfield	4213	2379
Daniel Cook And Associates	8712	176
Daniel Corp	6552	30
Daniel Electric Company Inc	1731	1309
Daniel F Young Inc	4731	34
Daniel G Schuster Inc	1771	16
Daniel H Wagner Associates Inc	7371	800
Daniel Industries Inc	3823	19
Daniel J Edelman Inc	7313	2
Daniel John Electric Inc	1731	2384
Daniel K Jackson	8731	412
Daniel L Ribbe Trucking Inc	4213	2516
Daniel Label Printing Inc	2759	343
Daniel Lamp Co	3645	71
Daniel Lampert Communications	7372	3431
Daniel Measurement and Control Inc	3824	5
Daniel Minzer Co	5021	174
Daniel (New York New York)	5812	281
Daniel O Scharf	3812	223
Daniel O'Connell's Sons Inc	8741	28
Daniel Smith Artist Materials	5999	65
Daniel Weaver Company Inc	2013	195
Daniele International Inc	2013	53
Daniella Koren Inc	2834	390
Danielle's DesignCom Web Site Services	7379	1490
Daniels and Roberts Latin America Inc	7311	425
Daniels Business Services Inc	2752	566
Daniels Cadillac BMW Inc	5511	974
Daniels Display Company Inc	5046	312
Daniel's Electrical Construction Company Inc	1731	448
Daniels Engraving Co	2796	71
Daniels Equipment Company Inc	5087	116
Daniels Long Chevrolet	5511	742
Daniels Manufacturing Corp	3423	39
Daniels Real Estate	1542	439
Danielson Tool and Die	3544	566
Danis Building Construction Co	1542	31
Danish Environment Inc	7349	349
Danken Inc	5193	17
Dankmeyer Inc	5999	118
Danko Arlington Inc	3544	152
Dankworth Packing Company Inc	2013	203
Danlin Industries Corp	3312	84
Danly Die Set Div	3544	9
Danly IEM	3544	769
Dan-Mar Components Inc	5065	520
Dan-Mar Inc	3674	397
Danmar Industries Inc	5251	54
Dannenbaum Engineering Corp	8711	234
Danning Gill Diamond and Kollitz LLP	8111	475
Dannon Company Inc	2026	12
Danny and Clyde's Food Store Inc	5411	162
Danny Herman Trucking Inc	4213	119
Danny Nicholson Inc	4213	1151
Danny's Glass Inc	3231	54
Danos and Curole Marine Contractors Inc	1389	25
Danpex Corp	3577	382
Danrik Construction Inc	1623	349
Dan's Fan City Inc	5722	6
Dan's Printing and Office Supplies Inc	5943	43
Dan's Prize Inc	5147	13
Dansko Inc	3143	7
Danson Inc	7381	93
Dantco Corp	3556	188
Dante Valve Co	5085	343
Dantel Inc	3661	120
Danter Company Inc	8748	231
Dantherm Air Handling Inc	3334	16
Dantona Industries Inc	3691	29
Dantronics Inc	8742	673
Dantz Development Corp	7372	1465
Danvers Farmers Elevator Co	5153	162
Danville Gasoline and Oil Company Inc	5172	145
Danville Manufacturing Inc	3843	61
Danville Metal Stamping Company Inc	3724	5
DAP Distributed Art Publishers	7822	13
DAPCO Software Engineering Inc	7372	2288
D'Appolonia	8711	615
Dapra Corp	5084	521
Daprex Inc	7372	2904
Da-Pro Rubber Inc	3069	59
Daptiv Inc	7372	711
Daq Electronics Inc	3823	142
DARA Biosciences Inc	2834	471
DaRan Inc	4213	2439
Darant Distributing Corp	5031	91
Darboy Stone Inc	5719	27

Company Name	SIC	Rank
Darby Group Companies Inc	5122	21
Darby Metalworks Inc	3444	230
Darco Enterprises Inc	7389	1334
Darco Products Inc	3599	2090
Darco Southern Inc	3053	122
Dard Products Inc	2759	120
Darden Restaurants Inc	5812	10
Dare Electronics Inc	3679	473
Dare Products Inc	3644	20
Darella Maintenance And Electric Corporation Inc	1731	2539
Daret Inc	2679	53
Dargan Construction Company Inc	1542	252
Darice Inc	5092	3
Darim Vision Corp	3674	218
Dark Hollow Farm	7311	984
Dark Horse Comics Inc	2721	185
Dark Moon Technologies	7379	1512
Darke Rural Electric Cooperative Inc	4911	564
Darko Precision Inc	3599	320
Darley at Jonabell Farm	0272	1
Darling Bolt Co	5072	64
Darling Industries Inc	3089	509
Darling International Inc	2079	1
Darlings	5511	113
Darlington County Water And Sewer Authority	1623	467
Darlington Fabrics Corp	2241	30
Darlington Veneer Company Inc	2426	11
Darly Custom Technology Inc	3599	2335
Darmark Corp	3825	81
Darnell and Dickson Construction Inc	1623	429
Darnell Group Inc	8732	119
Darnell-Rose	3069	38
Darocha's Outdoor Power Equipment	5083	177
Daroff Design Inc	8712	291
Darr Construction Inc	1731	620
Darr Equipment Company Inc	5084	38
Darrah Electric Co	3679	622
Dar-Ran Furniture Industries Inc	2521	24
Darrco Building Maintenance Inc	7349	255
Darrell Andrews Trucking Inc	4213	1139
D'Arrigo Brothers of Massachusetts Inc	5148	40
Dart America Inc	4212	26
DART Communications	7372	2965
Dart Container Corp	3086	1
Dart Services Inc	4212	32
Dart Transit Company Inc	4213	13
Dart Trucking Company Inc	4213	662
D'Artagnan Inc	5147	18
Darter Plastics Inc	3089	1049
Dartmouth Inc	2711	919
Dartmouth Motors Sales Inc	5511	1035
Dartmouth Power Associates Ltd	4911	437
Dartware LLC	7372	2671
Da-Rue Of California Inc	2339	47
Darvin Furniture and Appliances Inc	5712	47
Darwill Press Inc	2752	163
Darwin A Lewis Inc	2789	140
Darwin Professional Underwriters Inc	6351	24
Daryl Thomason Trucking Inc	4213	1280
Das Brot Inc	2099	371
DASCO Medical Properties Trust	6798	205
Dasco Systems Inc	2759	368
Dascoa Inc	5046	47
Da-Sh Components Inc	5065	553
Dash Designs Inc	2396	25
Dash In Food Stores Inc	5411	166
Dash Multi-Corp	2821	24
Dashe and Thomson Inc	7389	1438
Dashiell Corp	1629	51
Dasol Inc	3641	15
Dassault Falcon Jet Corp	3721	12
Dassault Systemes of America	7372	149
Dassault Systemes Simulia Corp	7371	38
DAT/EM Systems International	7389	2317
Dat Optic Inc	8742	629
Data 21	7371	1645
Data Access Corp	7371	214
Data Advantage Corp	2721	141
Data Associates Business Trust	2759	74
Data Base Architects Inc	5045	765
Data Base Systems International Inc	7376	27
Data Builders Inc	7371	1781
Data Cabling Solutions Inc	1731	1898
Data Center Inc	7374	237
Data Center Software Inc	7372	4594
Data Check Video Inc	3575	52
Data Code Inc (Bohemia New York)	7372	2454
Data Communication for Business Inc	3661	127
Data Company Inc	7389	572
Data Concepts Inc (Nashville Tennessee)	7372	4412
Data Concepts Inc (San Antonio Texas)	7372	2895
Data Connection	2741	223
Data Consultants Corp	7373	628
Data Consultants Inc (Fresno California)	7372	4155
Data Consulting Group Inc	8742	297
Data Control And Research Ltd	7371	1779
Data Conversion Laboratory	7374	219
Data Delay Devices Inc	3679	618
Data Description Inc	7372	3771
Data Design Corp	3699	257

Company Name	SIC	Rank
Data Design Group	7389	2476
Data Device Corp	3577	190
Data Directions	7371	998
Data Distributors Inc	7379	952
Data Domain Inc (Santa Clara California)	7371	46
Data Drive Thru Inc	3679	583
Data Electric Corp	1731	804
Data Electronic Devices Inc	3621	68
Data Enterprises Of The Northwest Inc	7372	4973
Data Entry Company Inc	7374	217
Data Exchange Corp	7372	460
Data Exchange Inc	7373	808
Data Financial Inc	7371	856
Data Flow Systems Inc	3825	95
Data Flute CNC Inc	3541	88
Data Fm Inc	8748	456
Data Forms Inc	5112	65
Data Foundry Inc	7375	84
Data Graphics Inc	3993	122
Data Guard Systems Inc	5045	659
Data Harmony Inc	7372	3208
Data I/O Corp	3825	63
Data I/O International Inc	3577	151
Data Image Corporation Of North America Inc	5065	786
Data Image Inc	7389	1317
Data Inc	7371	472
Data Information Services Systems	5045	791
Data Innovations Inc	7372	3580
Data Input Services Inc	7374	168
Data Integrity Inc (Newton Massachusetts)	7372	528
Data Intelligence Systems Corp	7372	4595
Data Label Inc	2754	12
Data Life Associates Inc	7372	3133
Data Limited Inc	3571	68
Data Linkage Software Inc	7372	2455
Data Machine Inc	3599	1751
Data Management Assistance Corp	7372	4287
Data Management Associates Inc	7372	2672
Data Management Associates Of Brevard Inc	7371	576
Data Management Inc	2752	697
Data Management Inc (San Angelo Texas)	7372	4288
Data Management Internationale Inc	3695	36
Data Management Solutions Corp	7371	1454
Data Matique Properties LP	3444	167
Data Media Products Inc	5065	542
Data Memory Systems Inc	5045	470
Data Miners Inc	7379	1600
Data Monster LLC	7379	1545
Data Optics International Inc	7372	2966
Data Path Inc	3663	228
Data Phone Wiring and Cable	1731	2200
Data Physics Corp	5045	523
Data Plus Inc	7372	3702
Data Point Systems Inc	7371	1203
Data Print Ltd	2782	52
Data Pro Accounting Software Inc	7372	1207
Data Pro Inc	7372	3993
Data Processing Consultants Inc	7372	2924
Data Processing Consultants Inc	5734	306
Data Processing Services Inc (Indianapolis Indiana)	7372	1337
Data Proof	3825	327
Data Publications	3695	175
Data Pure LLC	3577	483
Data Reproductions Corp	2732	26
Data Research and Applications Inc	3577	423
Data Retrieval Corp	5085	461
Data Robotics Inc	5045	400
Data Sciences Inc (Silver Spring Maryland)	7371	1710
Data Security Inc	3812	149
Data Seek	7373	738
Data Seek Corp	5734	215
Data Select Systems Inc	6163	45
Data Services Corp	7379	877
Data Shop Inc	7374	197
Data Source Inc	2752	174
Data Source Media Inc	5045	368
Data Source of Overland Park LLC	7374	313
Data Specialists Inc	7371	1751
Data Staff Inc	5734	209
Data Star Inc	7371	1478
Data Strategies Inc	7372	3455
Data Systems Analysts Inc	7371	282
Data Systems Group Of California	7371	666
Data Systems Hardware Inc	3577	378
Data Systems Of Texas Inc	7373	786
Data Systems Search Consultants	7361	78
Data Team Corp	7372	4596
Data Tech Communications Inc	7372	3819
Data Tech Computer Services Inc	5045	910
Data Technique Inc	7373	863
Data Techniques Inc (Burnsville North Carolina)	7372	4681
Data Technologies Inc	7372	4806
Data Technology Inc	3544	561
Data Tel US	1731	2493
Data Trace Chemistry Publishers Inc	2721	397
Data Tracking Systems Inc	7372	3379

Company Name	SIC	Rank
Data Translation Inc	3577	309
Data Transmission Network Corp	7375	29
Data Tree Incorporated Of Virginia	7371	872
Data Unlimited International Inc	7373	1174
Data Vista Inc	7378	83
Data West Corp	7372	1100
Data Workers	7372	3820
DATA2	2791	5
Data2logistics LLC	7374	57
DataArt Inc	7372	2521
Dataart Solutions Inc	7371	424
Databahn Inc	5063	885
Database Access Systems Inc	3661	193
Database Creations LLC	7372	3886
Database Inc	7372	3342
Database Management Technology Inc	7372	4452
Database Marketing Group Inc	7331	24
Database Publishing Software Inc	7372	3887
Database Services Inc	7372	4597
Database Solutions Inc (Cherry Hill New Jersey)	7371	144
Database Systems Corp (Phoenix Arizona)	7372	4241
Databit Inc	5961	142
Databranch	5734	49
DATACAD LLC	7372	3261
DataCal Enterprises LLC	7371	815
Datacap Systems Inc	3578	19
Datacard Group	3679	4
Datacenterinccom	7371	107
DataCert Inc	7373	210
Dataco DeRex Inc	3577	260
Datacolor Corporate Headquarters	3679	59
Datacom International Inc	7372	1132
Datacom Systems Inc	3571	128
Datacomm Management Sciences Inc	3825	215
Datacon Inc	3679	293
Datacor Inc	7372	1573
DataCore Software Corp	7372	1412
Data-Core Systems Inc	7372	4177
Datacore Web Publishing	7336	101
Datacut Inc	7372	3888
Datadesk Technologies Inc	3577	361
Datadirect Inc	7331	144
DataDirect Networks Inc	3572	20
DataDirect Technologies Ltd	7372	609
DataDisc Inc	3695	62
DataFaction	7372	2259
Dataflex Corp	5045	39
Dataflow Services	7374	235
Dataflow Systems Inc	7372	2289
Dataflow Systems LLC	7373	831
Dataforth Corp	3823	135
Datagraphic Computer Services Inc	7374	100
Datagroup Ltd	7373	1112
Dataguise Inc	7382	151
DataHand Systems Inc	3577	464
Datahouse Holdings Corp	7371	747
Datahouse Inc	7371	905
DataHouse Inc (Birmingham Alabama)	7372	2133
DATAIR Employee Benefit Systems Inc	7372	811
Datajet Services Inc	7373	1102
Datalex (USA) Inc	7379	907
Datalight Inc	7371	915
Dataline Verification Company LLC	7375	288
Datalink Corp	7373	43
Datalink Networks Inc	5065	492
DataLink Technologies Group Inc	7372	2134
Datalis Solutions Corp	7363	365
Datalogic Inc	3577	357
Datalogics Inc	7372	1563
Datalogistics Corp	7379	1412
dataLOK Co	7375	118
Datalux Corp	3577	143
Dataman Inc	3823	466
Datamann Inc	7372	2097
DatamanUSA LLC	7361	74
Datamark Graphics Inc	2759	456
DataMart Inc	7379	988
Datamasters Inc	7331	160
Datamate Inc	7371	1320
Datamatic Inc	7373	170
Datamatics Consultants Inc	7373	78
Datamatics Management Services Inc	7372	3525
Datamation Systems Inc	5999	141
Datamatrix Systems Inc	7373	1054
Datamax	7379	989
DataMax Corp (Winston-Salem North Carolina)	7322	46
Datamax Oneill	3577	109
Datamax Solutions Inc	7374	335
Datametrics Corp	3577	457
DataModes Inc	7372	4289
Datamonitor	8732	33
DataMotion	7372	1919
DataMotion Inc	7372	2967
Datanational Corp	7371	916
DataNOW LLC	7372	4371
Data Pac Mailing Systems Corp	3671	187
DataPath Inc	4899	17
Datapax Inc	7372	4290
Datapoint USA Inc	7373	1154
Dataprise Inc	7378	8
Datapro International Inc	3496	115
Dataprobe Inc	3661	125
Dataq Instruments	3577	501
Dataq Internet Equipment Corp	5065	93
Dataquick	7375	56
Dataradio Corp	3661	89
Dataram Corp	3572	28
Data-Rite Systems Group Inc	7379	1390
DaTARIUS Technologies Inc	3669	160
Datasafe	7379	618
Datascan Systems Inc	7373	604
DataScan Technologies LLC	7372	637
Datascape Inc	7371	1509
Datascension Inc	7389	656
Dataserv LLC	7379	639
Datasis Corp	2741	220
Datasite Northwest	7375	240
DataSoft Corp	7372	1364
DataSource Corp	7375	278
DataSource Inc	7371	180
Datasouth Computer Corp	3577	215
Dataspan Inc	3829	8
Datasplice LLC	5734	381
Datastick Systems Inc	7372	2456
DataStream Market Intelligence Inc	8732	120
Datastream Systems Inc	7372	417
Datasurge	7372	1924
DataSynapse Inc	5045	296
Datasystem Solutions Inc	7372	2135
Datatech Business Forms Inc	2761	68
Datatech Software Corp	7371	1132
DataTech Software Inc	7372	4291
Datatel Inc (Fairfax Virginia)	7372	327
Datatel Resources Corp	2761	36
Datatest Inc	3829	414
Datatex Media Dolls	7374	401
Datatex Textile Information Systems Inc	7372	1002
Datatrac Corp	7372	2544
Datatrac Information Services Inc	8742	101
Data-Trak Inc	7372	3703
DataTRAK International Inc	7372	2315
Datatrek Xtreme Inc	7378	90
Data-Tronics Corp	7374	83
Datatronics Romoland Inc	3612	55
DataVantage Corp	7372	728
DataViews Corp	7371	335
DataViz Inc	7372	208
DATAVOX Inc	5065	39
Dataware Inc	7373	1037
Datawatch Corp	7372	1370
Datawatch Systems Inc	1731	321
DataWave Technologies Corp	7371	1671
Dataway Inc	7379	506
Dataweb Inc	7373	917
Dataweld Inc	7372	4203
Dataworks Development Inc	7372	1578
Dataworld Service Inc	7334	101
Datco Manufacturing	3559	558
Dateapp Inc	5045	949
Datec Inc	7373	865
Da-Tech Corp	3672	79
Datech Solutions	7379	1153
Datel Systems Inc	5045	233
Datex Corp	5065	171
Datfax Services Corp	4899	207
Daticon Systems Inc	7379	376
Dativoci LLC	7379	1578
Datrex Inc	2099	266
Datron Dynamics Inc	3559	60
Datron Systems Inc (Vista California)	3663	56
Datron World Communications Inc	3663	42
Datrose Inc	7363	91
Dattner Dispoto and Associates	7922	56
Datum Dynamics USA LLC	3672	396
Datum Filing Systems Inc	2522	34
Datum Industries Inc	7389	2448
Datum Industries LLC	3544	223
Datum Software Inc	7371	573
Datumcom Corp	4813	426
Daubenspeck and Associates Ltd	7361	361
Dauber Company Inc	3674	368
Daubert Industries Inc	2671	15
Daubes Bakery Inc	5461	43
Dauenhauer Plumbing Inc	1711	115
Daugherty Systems	7371	120
Daugherty Tool And Die Inc	3542	33
Daum Trucking Inc	4213	1974
Dauntless Industries Inc	3544	528
Dauphin Electrical Supply Co	5063	149
DAVA Pharmaceuticals Inc	5122	52
Daval Technologies LLC	5065	557
Davalen LLC	7379	963
Davalor Mold Corp	3089	946
Davann Inc	5099	57
Davco Acquisition Holding Inc	5812	161
Davco Advertising Inc	5199	94
Davco Manufacturing Corp	3599	11
DavCo Restaurants Inc	5812	224
Dave and Buster's Holdings Inc	5812	90
Dave and Buster's of Georgia Inc	5812	287
Dave Bang Associates Inc	5091	58
Dave Clinard Truck Service	4213	2155
Dave Evans Transports	4213	2224
Dave Gill Trucks Inc	5012	162
Dave Grattan and Sons Inc	5072	97
Dave Hunter Company LLC	3599	1626
Dave Jones Design	3669	249
Dave Perkins Contracting Inc	1623	776
Dave Pybus Electric	1731	2106
Dave Schmidt Truck Service Inc	5013	408
Dave Shepard Enterprises Inc	2752	1165
Dave Sinclair Ford Inc	5511	1104
Dave Sinclair Mid Rivers Lincoln Mercury Inc	5511	1034
Dave Steel Company Inc	5051	149
Dave Syverson Inc	5511	469
Davel Communications Inc	4899	65
Daven Industries Inc	3599	1902
Davenport and Company LLC	6211	226
Davenport Auto Park	5511	1077
Davenport Community School District	8211	7
Davenport Electric Contract Co	1731	487
Dave's Construction Service Inc	1542	427
Dave's Custom Computers	7379	1513
Dave's Design Center Iii	5023	124
Dave's Emergency Roadside	5541	64
Dave's Web Dynamics	7379	1514
Davey Kent Inc	3532	60
Davey Tree Expert Co	0783	2
David A Bramble Inc	1629	11
David A Noyes and Co	6211	52
David A Smith Printing Inc	2752	900
David B Knight and Associates Inc	3631	16
David Briggs Enterprises Inc	5921	6
David Bruce Winery Inc	2084	119
David C Rowe	4813	610
David Cianciulli Electronics Supply Inc	3643	36
David Clark Company Inc	3663	85
DAVID Corp	7372	3487
David Crowell Electric Inc	1731	1513
David Distributing Company Inc	5087	173
David Dobbs Enterprises Inc	2789	14
David Evans and Associates Inc	7389	275
David Fee Is Magic Inc	7922	81
David Gingerela	3825	309
David Gomez and Associates Inc	7361	359
David Gooding Inc	8742	434
David Groth and Associates Inc	7372	3793
David H Fell and Company Inc	3341	9
David Hirschberg Co	5093	211
David Hocker and Associates Inc	6552	183
David Hoffman	7379	1581
David J Bailey and Company PC	8721	484
David J Thompson Mailing Corp	7331	288
David Judge	7389	1581
David K Burnap	7336	165
David K Burnap Advertising Inc	7311	396
David Kelkom Systems	3003	395
David Kopf Instruments	3841	302
David L Adams Associates Inc	8711	670
David L Addison Inc	7353	79
David L Aldridge Company Inc	7372	3237
David L Ellis Company Inc	3829	403
David M and Peter J Mancuso Inc	7389	1038
David Martin Inc	5044	57
David McDavid Honda of Irving	5511	97
David Michael Miller Associates	7389	2345
David Mitchell Inc	5144	31
David Morgan	3823	159
David Naylor and Associates Inc	7812	71
David New Drilling Company Inc	1381	36
David Photo Service Inc	7384	53
David Price Metal Service Inc	3599	265
David R Webb Company Inc	2435	7
David Santos Farming	7389	1311
David Saunders Inc	3845	112
David Self Ford Lincoln Mercury Inc	5511	897
David T Jennings	3625	405
David T Olson Inc	5084	747
David Taylor Cadillac Co	5521	4
David W Reed Co	5153	199
David W Taylor and Associates	5023	172
David Weber Company Inc	2653	64
David Weekley Homes	1522	8
David White and Associates Inc	6282	578
David Whitnack Distributing Inc	5063	579
David Wilson Ford of Orange	5511	771
Davidandgoliath	7311	189
Davidon Industries Inc	3585	239
Davidsohn Group	7372	1328
Davidson Brothers Inc	4213	1235
Davidson Cos	6282	228
Davidson County Board Of Education	8211	59
Davidson Hotel Company Inc	7011	19
Davidson Mike Sand and Gravel LLC	3291	23
Davidson Pipe Supply Company Inc	5074	59
Davidson Software Systems Inc	7372	1579
Davidson Technologies Inc	8711	241
Davidson Transfer and Storage	4213	2748
Davidson Trucking Inc	4213	2774
Davidson Trucking Inc	4213	2925
Davidson's Of Dundee	5145	21
Davies Molding Co	3089	118
Davies Precision Machining Inc	3599	2007
Davies Supply Co	5074	185
Davies-Imperial Coatings Inc	2851	110
Daviess County Metal Sales Inc	3444	49
Davila Electric Company Inc	1731	1786

Company Name	SIC	Rank	Company Name	SIC	Rank	Company Name	SIC	Rank
Davilyn Corp	5065	649	Dawson Dorothy Food Products Inc	2099	282	Dbnet Systems Inc	7379	892
DaVinci Technology Corp	7371	1711	Dawson Enterprises	3533	65	DBS Communications Inc	1731	2154
Davinci Virtual Office Solutions	4813	336	Dawson Geophysical Co	1382	22	Dbs Inc	3672	345
Davion Inc	2844	118	Dawson Heritage Furniture Company Inc	2511	86	DBS Systems Inc	7375	280
Davis Amusement Cascadia Inc	7999	89	Dawson Logistics	8999	46	dbSpectra Inc	3661	87
Davis and Kuelthau SC	8111	379	Dawson Metal Company Inc	3444	102	Dc and B Hot Shot And Trucking	1761	60
Davis and Pierce Die Service Inc	3544	629	Dawson Sales Co	5141	223	DC and R Construction Inc	1623	667
Davis Automotive Group Inc	5511	357	Dawson Subscription Service Inc	7389	264	DC Brands International Inc	2086	154
Davis Bacon Material Handling Inc	2542	57	Dawson Tarpaulins Inc	2394	29	DC Comics	2721	110
Davis Block Company Inc	5032	105	Dawson Welding Co	7349	162	Dc Communication LLC	4813	423
Davis Boat Works Inc	3599	437	Dawson's Printing Inc	2752	1436	Dc Consultants Inc	5734	88
Davis Brody Bond LLP	8712	184	Dax Systems Inc	3571	214	Dc Dental Supplies LLC	5047	78
Davis Brothers Oil Producers Inc	1311	191	Daxcon Engineering Inc	8711	316	DC Equipment Inc	5084	424
Davis Brothers Produce Boxes Inc	5031	451	Daxko LLC	4813	403	DC Express Inc	4213	2766
Davis Brothers Publishing Company Ltd	2721	271	Daxor Corp	3841	373	DC Group Inc	1731	266
Davis Carter Scott Ltd	7389	315	Day After Day Services	4213	2140	DC I Inc	3443	107
Davis Clark ButtCarithers and Taylor PLC	8111	568	Day and Night Printing Inc	2752	809	DC Industries Inc	3599	1367
Davis Computing Solutions Inc	7379	1491	Day and Zimmermann Group Inc	1541	9	DC Lites Co	3545	379
Davis Cookie Co	2052	50	Day and Zimmermann Inc Kansas Div	3483	2	DC Materials Inc	5032	62
Davis Core and Pad Company Inc	3086	104	Day and Zimmermann Inc Lone Star Div	3482	2	DC Micro Development Inc	7372	3889
Davis Cos	1311	176	Day and Zimmermann Information Solutions	7379	6	DC Morrison Company Inc	3545	333
Davis Cos	7363	136	Day and Zimmermann International Inc	8711	32	DC Pattern And Tooling Inc	3543	28
Davis Cowell and Bowe	8111	481	Day Carter International Inc	3569	108	DC Sales and Trucking Inc	4213	2787
Davis Crowley Research Inc	7372	4130	Day Deadrick and Marshall Inc	6311	250	DC Sales Company Inc	5074	92
Davis/Dinsmore Management Co	6282	409	Day Electrical Inc	1731	2132	DC Software Design Inc	7372	4904
Davis Electric Company Inc	7694	21	Day Music Co	5736	17	Dca Inc	5045	638
Davis Electrical Supply Company Inc	5063	159	Day Publishing Co	2711	269	Dca Manufacturing Corp	3672	208
Davis Elen Advertising Inc	7311	103	Day Runner Inc	2782	6	DCA Medical Services Inc	8092	10
Davis Entertainment Co	7812	149	Day Trucking Inc	4213	2749	DCA of Carlisle Inc	8092	5
Davis Excavation Inc	1623	782	Daybreak Express Inc	4213	1698	DCA of Chambersburg Inc	8092	8
Davis Flourescent	5063	886	Daybrook Holdings Inc	2077	1	DCA of Cincinnati LLC	8092	9
Davis Furniture Industries Inc	2522	30	Day-Glo Color Corp	2851	34	DCA of Mechanicsburg LLC	8092	7
Davis Graham and Stubbs LLP	8111	173	Daylay Egg Farm Inc	0252	7	DCA of Wellsboro Inc	8092	6
Davis Group Inc	7381	177	Daylight Corp	2045	15	Dca Services Inc	8721	385
Davis Group LLP	6531	187	Daymon Worldwide	8748	5	DCAP Management Corp	6411	121
Davis H Elliot Co	1731	106	Dayni Controls Manufacturing Co	3492	33	DCC Corp	6531	399
Davis Hospital and Medical Center Inc	8062	43	Day-N-Nite Transportation	4213	1984	Dcci LLC	1623	230
Davis Inotek Instruments LLC	5084	268	Daysequerra Corp	3663	300	Dcd Investments Inc	7389	1987
Davis Instruments Corp	3812	103	Daysol Inc	3993	109	Dcd Technologies Inc	3544	687
Davis Interiors Ltd	7389	1557	Daystar Computer Systems Inc	7372	2136	DCE Corp	5065	38
Davis Iron Works Inc	3441	137	Daystar Desserts LLC	5149	90	DCG Development Co	6552	157
Davis Lynch Glass Co	3229	27	Daystar Inc	3089	730	DCG Machine Inc	3599	648
Davis Machine Works Of Opelika Inc	3441	264	Daystar Software Inc	7372	4682	Dcg-Pmi Inc	3499	95
Davis Manufacturing Co	3599	1600	DayStar Technologies Inc	3999	215	DCI	3825	83
Davis Mining and Manufacturing Inc	2426	39	Day-Tec Tool and Manufacturing Inc	3559	401	Dci Food Equipment Inc	5046	216
Davis Muller Lighting	3646	87	Day-Timers Inc	3999	21	Dci Holdings Inc	3843	37
Davis Paint Co	2851	114	Dayton Andrews Inc	5511	772	Dci Marketing Inc	7389	10
Davis Partnership PC	8712	186	Dayton Bag and Burlap Co	2396	6	DCI Technical Inc	2731	261
Davis Petroleum Corp	1382	9	Dayton Bindery Service Inc	2789	128	DCL	7379	434
Davis Polk	8111	7	Dayton Board Of Education	8211	2	Dcl Inc	3535	101
Davis Printing And Business Forms	2752	1324	Dayton Containerized Freight	4213	2926	Dcm Computer Sales And Service	7378	174
Davis Printing Inc	2752	1393	Dayton Data Processing Inc	7372	2457	Dcm Tech Ii Inc	3541	134
Davis Rubber Company Inc	3069	277	Dayton Forging And Heat Treating Co	3462	28	DCM Transport Inc	4213	1497
Davis Staffing Inc	7361	328	Dayton Freight Lines Inc	4213	80	Dco Distribution Inc	5065	571
Davis Technologies Inc	8711	679	Dayton Industrial Corp	3663	388	DCP Midstream LLC	1311	16
Davis (Tempe Arizona)	8712	122	Dayton Mailing Services Inc	7331	175	DCP Midstream Partners LP	4922	17
Davis Tool and Die Company Inc	3544	119	Dayton Mall Venture LLC	6531	135	Dcpande Inc	5063	872
Davis Tool Inc	3089	491	Dayton Meat Co	2011	108	DCS Corp	8731	99
Davis Transfer Company Inc	4213	1043	Dayton Nut Specialties Inc	5145	30	Dcs Technologies	5734	482
Davis Transport Inc	4213	1040	Dayton Power and Light Co	4931	43	Dcsc Inc	7373	1024
Davis Trucking Company Inc	4213	2143	Dayton Progress Corp	3544	11	DCT Industrial Trust Inc	6798	83
Davis Tuttle Venture Partners LP	6799	200	Dayton Reliable Air-Filter Service Inc	5085	315	Dct Technologies Inc	4813	556
Davis Typewriter Company Inc	5044	89	Dayton Sand and Gravel Inc	3273	66	Dcx-Chol Enterprises Inc	3671	3
Davis Vision Inc	5995	3	Dayton Scientific Inc	7373	1208	DD and S Express Inc	4213	1721
Davis Wire Corp	3315	14	Dayton Steel Service Inc	5051	183	DD Jones Transfer and Warehouse Company Inc	4225	19
Davis Wright Tremaine LLP	8111	177	Dayton Superior Corp	3531	15	DD Wire Company Inc	3469	251
Davisco Foods International Inc	2023	9	Dayton Systems Group Inc	3565	79	DD Youells Machining Inc	3599	2062
Davis-Express Inc	4213	282	Dayton Utilities	3589	239	DDB Worldwide Communications Group Inc	7311	9
Davis-Frost Inc	2851	71	Dayton Water Systems	3589	23	DDC Advocacy	7379	321
Davis-Kidd Booksellers Inc	5942	11	Dayton Wheel Concepts Inc	3714	362	Ddc Electric Supply Inc	5063	575
Davis-Lynch Inc	3533	40	Daytona Aerospace Inc	5088	91	DDC-I Inc	7372	3526
Davison Electric Company Inc	1731	1410	Daytona Bolt And Nut Co	5072	104	Ddct Inc	2752	1748
Davison State Bank	6022	638	Dayton-Granger Inc	3812	52	Ddh Apple Valley Construction Inc	1623	724
Davison Transport Inc	4213	138	Dayton-Palmer Inc	3081	130	Ddh Enterprise Inc	3643	30
Davison-Rite Products Co	3451	109	Dayton-Phoenix Group Inc	3621	52	DDI Corp	3672	12
Davis-Stuart Inc	8361	166	Daytop Family Association	8322	199	Ddi Denver Corp	3672	69
Davis-Ulmer Sprinkler Company Inc	3432	8	Daz Systems	7372	757	DDI Enterprises Inc	8299	38
Davisville Travel	4724	122	Dazian LLC	2211	32	DDI Inc	7372	1732
DaVita Inc	8092	1	Db Access LLC	7379	573	Ddi North Jackson Inc	3672	44
Davka Corp	7372	2673	DB Consultants Inc	7372	1299	Ddi System LLC	7371	1004
Davlan Engineering Inc	3599	467	DB Kunz Inc	3231	73	DDL Systems Inc	7379	1440
Davlong Business Solutions LLC	7373	400	Db Marketing Technologies LLC	7371	1631	DDM Direct	7331	108
Davol Inc	3842	68	DB Plus Digital Services	3695	128	Dds Staffing Resources Inc	7361	184
Davric Plastic LLC	3089	1519	DB Professionals Inc	7373	376	De Am-Ron Building Systems LLC	3272	86
Davro Optical Systems Inc	3827	159	DB Sales Inc	5064	180	De An's Pork Products Inc	2013	197
DavTech Computer Center	5734	78	Dba Electric Inc	1731	1070	De Anza Land and Leisure Corp	7833	2
Davtron	3812	186	dbaDirect Inc	7376	15	De Anza Manufacturing Services Inc	3679	360
DAW TECH	1541	166	DBC Corp	2052	31	De Baufre Bakeries Inc	2052	79
Dawahares Inc	5651	22	Dbd Investors V LLC	6799	197	De Bruyn Produce Company Inc	0723	25
Dawar Technologies Inc	3577	347	Dbd Management Inc	8742	474	De Camp Medical Products Corp	3851	76
Dawkins Inc	2439	56	DBG Collection Inc	7322	134	De Carolis Truck Rental Inc	7513	19
Dawlen Corp	3451	24	Dbh Attachments Inc	3552	62	DE Enterprise Inc	2721	219
Dawn Communications Inc	5063	848	DBI Beverage Inc	5181	41	De Feo Transit Manufacturing Supply Inc	3714	382
Dawn Enterprises Inc	3714	178	DBI Services Inc	1623	287	DE Harvey Builders Inc	1542	145
Dawn Food Products Inc	2051	5	Dbisp LLC	4813	708	De Hoff Tool and Manufacturing Company Inc	3599	2268
Dawn Industries Inc	3089	1076	Dbk Concepts Inc	7629	8	DE Hokanson Inc	3841	364
Dawn Satellite Inc	5065	449	DBM Contractors Inc	1794	3	De Jong Manufacturing Inc	3443	179
Dawn Trucking Inc	4213	3055	DBM E Inc	7322	133	De La Cantera Ernesto	7349	439
Dawn Vme Products	3679	390	Dbm Optics Inc	3825	195	de La Garza Public Relations Inc	8743	326
Dawning Technologies Inc	7371	515	DBMS Inc	7372	3343	De La Rue North America Inc	2752	533
Dawn's Foods Inc	2099	267	DB-NET Inc	7372	4983			
Dawson Building Contractors Inc	1541	135						

Company Name	SIC	Rank	Company Name	SIC	Rank	Company Name	SIC	Rank
De La Torre Sheet Metal Manufacturing Company Inc	3444	275	deBoer Transportation Inc	4213	92	Dedicated Technologies Inc	8742	423
De Landsheer Sales Incorporated	5063	568	Debond Corp	3089	839	Dedicated Transport LLC	4213	285
De Lillo Chevrolet Co	5511	476	Deborah Edmonson	3651	253	Dedoes Industries Inc	3559	208
De Luca Liquor and Wine Ltd	5181	25	Deborah Malush	3613	145	Dee Brown Inc	1741	1
De Luxe Sales And Service Inc	5012	136	DeBow Communications Ltd	7311	926	Dee Cramer Inc	1711	38
de maximis Inc	4953	84	DeBragga and Spitler Inc	5147	22	Dee Paper Company Inc	2653	74
De Menno-Kerdoon	2992	8	Debrick Truck Line Co	4213	1993	Dee Pee Apparel Inc	5137	35
De Micco Brothers Inc	1623	188	Debron Industrial Electronics Inc	3679	475	Dee Sign Co	3993	67
De Mott Technologies Corp	3549	112	DeBruce Grain Inc	5153	2	Dee Zee Inc	3444	15
De Nooyer Chevrolet	5511	792	Debt Free Associates	7299	20	Dee-Blast Corp	3569	153
De Nooyer Leasing Inc	5511	558	Debt Resolve Inc	7389	2509	Deem LLC	1731	155
De Nora North America Inc	3479	97	Debtication Incorporated Corporate	7323	31	Deemsys Inc	8748	325
De Nora Tech Inc	2899	50	Debtmerica LLC	7299	22	Deen Meats and Cooked Foods	5147	46
De Novo Strategy Inc	8742	657	Dec Electrical Contractors Inc	1731	617	Deep Blue Sea Inc	7379	266
De Novo Ventures	6799	196	Dec Tool Corp	3544	593	Deep Creek Custom Packing Inc	5146	48
De Par Inc	8734	79	Deca Manufacturing Company Inc	3679	289	Deep East Texas Electric Coop	4911	385
De Paula Chevrolet Inc	5511	371	Decade Engineering	3679	849	Deep Foods Inc	2024	32
De Rossi and Son Company Inc	2311	24	Decal Information Systems	2752	1280	Deep River Fabricators Inc	3086	130
DE Shaw and Company LP	6211	11	Decal Source Inc	2752	1415	Deep Rock Water Co	2086	124
De Sousa Inc	7342	89	DeCarta Inc	7372	815	Deep South Products Inc	2033	29
De Toro Optical Inc	5049	74	Decatur Cooperative Association	5153	59	Deep Surplus	5961	139
De Wafelbakkers LLC	2038	24	Decatur County Rural Electric Membership Coop	4911	464	Deep Water Point LLC	8742	559
De Witt Products Co	2952	21	Decatur Electronics Inc	3812	81	DeepNines Inc	7372	481
Deacon Industrial Supply Company Inc	5074	70	Decatur Junction Railway Co	4011	27	Deepsea Power and Light Inc	3861	46
Dead River Co	5172	6	Decatur Mill Service Co	5032	132	Deepwater Chemicals Inc	2819	119
Deadwood Gulch Resort and Gaming Corp	7999	53	Decatur Mold Tool And Engineering Inc	3544	67	Deer Corp	3559	576
Deady Advertising	7311	985	Decatur Plastic Products Inc	3089	848	Deer Park Lumber Company Inc	5211	152
Deaf Inter-Link Inc	7389	1851	Decatur Wire Die LLC	3544	126	Deer Park Lumber Inc	5031	179
Deaf Link Inc	5047	186	Decaux J L USA	7312	25	Deer Valley Corp	2451	21
Deaf Services Inc	8999	202	Decc Company Inc	3479	66	Deer Valley Federal Credit Union	6061	152
Deal LLC	8748	154	Deccan Software Inc	7372	3994	Deere and Co	3523	1
Dealer Chemical	5169	184	Decco Graphics Inc	3469	255	Deere Electric Inc	1731	2499
Dealer Electronic Services Inc	5731	248	Deccofelt Corp	2299	20	Deere Power Systems Group	3519	6
Dealer Information Systems Corp	7372	1289	DeChants Fuglein and Johnson LLP	8721	214	Deere-Hitachi Construction Machinery Corp	3531	30
Dealer Management Agency Inc	5511	447	Dechert LLC	8111	41	Deerfield Auto Tag Agency Inc	5012	194
Dealer Operating Control Services Inc	5511	1238	Dechert LLP	8111	110	Deerfield Communications Inc	7372	411
Dealer Service Network Inc	5013	399	Decherts Machine Shop Inc	3599	1111	Deerfield Construction Company Inc	1542	206
Dealer Tire LLC	5014	30	DeciBel Research Inc	8711	278	Deery Brothers Inc	5511	461
Dealers Auto Auction Of Idaho LLC	5012	181	Decimal Inc	7389	1285	Dees Communication Inc	2721	463
Dealers Supply and Lumber Inc	5031	64	Decimet Sales Inc	3441	109	Deevan Inc	1623	838
Dealers Supply Co	5023	33	Decipher Inc	3944	32	Defelicecare Inc	5999	152
Dealers Truck Equipment Company Inc	5088	18	Decision Analyst Inc	8748	54	Defelsko Corp	3823	202
DealerTrack Holdings Inc	7373	36	Decision Distribution LLC	5063	130	Defender Direct Inc	5999	20
Dealnewscom Inc	7375	147	Decision Economics Inc	2721	297	Defender Security Company Inc	1731	279
Deal-Rite Feeds Inc	2048	98	Decision Graphics	5045	712	Defense Commissary Agency	5399	1
Deamco Corp	3535	176	Decision Strategies Inc	8748	213	Defense Solutions Group Inc	7374	371
Dean Ag Services	5082	37	Decision Support Systems LP	8732	41	DefenseWeb Technologies Inc	7371	243
Dean and Co	8742	155	Decision Support Technology Inc	7372	4453	Defenshield Inc	5699	17
Dean and DeLuca Inc	5411	196	Decision Systems Inc	3559	64	Defentect Group Inc	4813	717
Dean Brothers Inc	1731	973	Decision Systems Plus Inc	1731	1361	Deffenbaugh Industries Inc	4953	18
Dean Dairy Products Co	2026	34	Decision Technology Inc	7372	2137	Defi Global Inc	4813	718
Dean Dallas Inc	1623	454	DECISIONMARK Corp	7372	2390	Defiance Electric Inc	1731	1424
Dean Distributing LLC	5046	211	DecisionOne Corp	7378	3	Defiance Metal Products Co	3469	10
Dean Donald and Sons Inc	2511	59	DecisionOne Holdings Corp	7378	2	Defiance Precision Products	3451	8
Dean Dorton Ford PSC	8721	489	Decisionpoint Systems Inc	1081	1	Defiance Testing and Engineering Services Inc	8734	60
Dean Enterprises and Associates Inc	5065	230	Decisions and Advanced Technology Associates Inc	4731	89	Definiens Inc	5734	197
Dean Evans and Associates Inc	7372	3182	Decisive Analytics Corp	7373	200	Definition 6 LLC	7379	313
Dean Foods Co	2026	1	Decitek Corp	3577	630	Definity Health Corp	6321	25
Dean Investment Associates Div	6282	227	Deck And Fence Services LLC	2821	133	Deflecta-Shield Accessories Inc	3469	37
Dean Lawther Inc	5031	314	Decker and Bruce Electric Inc	1731	1330	DeFoe Corp	1622	11
Dean Machinery International Inc	5082	151	Decker Auto Supply Inc	5013	194	DeFouw Chevrolet-BMW Inc	5511	297
Dean Markley Strings Inc	3931	32	Decker Communications Inc	7812	138	Deft Inc	2851	32
Dean Mead Edgerton Bloodworth Capouano and Bozarth PA	8111	387	Decker Electric Company Inc	1731	302	Degen-Berglund Inc	5912	48
Dean Media Group	7311	503	Decker Jones McMackin McClane Hall and Bates PC	8111	479	Degenfelder John	3567	119
Dean Pump Div	3561	66	Decker Manufacturing Corp	3452	47	DeGol Organization	6719	167
Dean Research Corp	3535	196	Decker Precision Machining Inc	3541	127	Degood Dimensional Concepts Inc	3599	1788
Dean Sausage Company Inc	2013	74	Decker Steel and Supply Inc	5051	378	Degree Controls Inc	3822	38
Dean Sellers Ford Co	5511	507	Decker Supply Company Inc	3993	129	Dehler Manufacturing Company Inc	2514	9
Dean Steel Buildings Inc	3448	22	Decker Truck Line Inc	4213	187	DEI Holdings Inc	3651	23
Dean Technology Inc	3674	249	Deckers Outdoor Corp	3021	2	DEI Inc	8712	201
Dean Witter American Value Fund	6722	141	Decker's Plumbing Supply Inc	5074	174	Dei Services Corp	3629	48
Deanco Auction Company Of Mississippi Inc	7389	1005	Decker-Wright Corp	7373	1019	Deichman Excavating Company Inc	1623	373
Dean's RV Superstore Inc	5561	19	Decko Products Inc	2064	64	Deig Brothers Lumber and Construction Company Inc	1542	344
Dean's Water Service Inc	5963	26	Deco Productions Inc	7389	1366	Deimling/Jeliho Plastics Inc	3089	672
Dearborn Bancorp Inc	6712	341	Deco Products Co	3369	6	Deising's Bakery and Pastry Shop Inc	5461	16
Dearborn Crane And Engineering Co	7699	213	Deco TECHnology Group Inc	3669	208	Deister Electronics USA Inc	4911	533
Dearborn Electronics Inc	3675	20	Deco Tool Supply Co	5084	408	Deitsch Plastic Company Inc	2295	15
Dearborn Inc	3599	654	Deco Tools Inc	3563	47	Deitz Company Inc	3565	171
Dearborn Lithograph Inc	2752	1577	Deco West Inc	7389	1215	DeJarnette Research Systems	3845	80
Dearborn Precision Tubular Products Inc	3599	86	Dec-O-Art Inc	2759	202	Dekalb Feeds Inc	2048	34
Dearborn Wholesale Grocers LP	5141	100	DecoArt Inc	2851	66	Dekalb Molded Plastics Co	2821	96
Dearden's Inc	5712	15	DecoGard Products Inc	3089	215	DeKalb Office Environments	5712	48
Deardorff-Jackson Co	0161	9	DeConna Ice Cream Inc	5143	11	Dekalb Tool and Die Inc	3544	214
Dearinger Printing and Trophy Inc	7336	290	Decor Inc	3262	4	Deken Power Inc	5085	465
Dearth Motors Inc	5511	1137	Decor Moulding Ltd	5099	55	Dekker Ltd	7372	1224
Deaver Industries Inc	3648	33	Decor Products Inc	3354	46	Del and Wes Seapy Inc	3089	814
deb Construction Inc	1541	263	Decora Industries Inc	3645	37	Del Buono Bakery Inc	2051	257
Deb Of Findlay Inc	3089	895	Decorating Den Systems Inc	7389	982	Del Castillo Foods Inc	2099	257
Deb Shops Inc	5621	23	Decorating Supplies and Equipment Inc	5084	698	Del Ciotto Architects Inc	8712	31
Deb USA Inc	2844	50	Decorative Novelty Company Inc	2391	15	Del City Wire Company Inc	3357	20
Deban Enterprises Inc	3823	457	Decorator Industries Inc	2399	13	Del Frisco's Double Eagle Steak House	5812	352
De-Bar Contracting Company Inc	1623	816	DeCotiis Fitzpatrick and Cole LLP	8111	455	Del Frisco's Restaurant Group LLC	5812	197
Debarr Trucking Company Inc	4213	2643	Decoupage Supply Centre Inc	5943	44	Del Mar Avionics	3845	110
Debartolo Inc	7941	10	DeCrane Aerospace	3728	33	Del Mar Designs Inc	5719	13
Debco Electronics Inc	5734	230	Decurtis Corp	5045	024	Del Mar Food Products Corp	2033	34
Deb-El Foods Corp	2015	62	Decypher Technologies Ltd	7379	825	Del Mar Industries	3364	5
Deberry Electric Company Inc	1731	791	Dedeco International Sales Inc	3291	18	Del Mar Lighting LLC	5063	1032
Debevoise and Plimpton	8111	239	Dedicated Distribution Inc	5047	88	Del Medical Imaging Corp	3844	5
Debevoise and Plimpton LLP	8111	85	Dedicated Distribution Services	4213	490	Del Monte Electric Company Inc	1731	129
			Dedicated Media Inc	7311	744	Del Monte Foods Co	2033	4

Company Name	SIC	Rank
Del Monte Fresh Produce NA Inc	5148	63
Del Norte Technology Inc	3812	160
Del Ozone Holding Company Inc	6719	179
Del Packaging Ltd	3556	124
Del Pro Corp	5072	165
Del Rey Tortilleria Inc	2099	89
Del Rivero Messianu Advertising	7311	222
Del Sol Food Company Inc	2035	39
Del Technical Coatings Inc	2851	161
Del West Engineering Inc	3714	179
Dela Inc	2891	78
Delaco Steel Corp	5051	162
Delaco-Kasle LLC	5051	373
Delafield Corp	3599	60
Delafontaine Industries	3442	111
Delahaye Medialink	8732	117
Delair Group LLC	3949	117
Delan Associates Inc	8748	184
Deland Manufacturing Inc	3599	1824
Delaney Chevrolet Inc	5511	585
Delaney Group Inc	5032	5
Delano Growers Grape Products	2087	68
Delaplaine Creative	2741	296
Delasoft Inc	5734	304
Delavan Spray LLC	3499	58
Delavau LLC	2834	215
Delaware Corporate Bond R Fund	6726	101
Delaware County Daily Times Central States Publishing	2711	153
Delaware Diamond Knives Inc	3421	20
Delaware Electric Coop	4911	350
Delaware Gazette	2711	51
Delaware Investments	6282	127
Delaware Management Holdings Inc	6282	162
Delaware Motor Sales Inc	5511	574
Delaware North Companies Inc	5812	28
Delaware North Companies Travel Hospitality Services Inc	5812	187
Delaware Place Bank	6022	700
Delaware Public Auto Auction	5012	190
Delaware Ship Supply Oldco Inc	5088	99
Delaware Sunny Electrics Inc	7374	292
Delaware Technologies Inc	3821	81
Delaware Tool and Machine Company Inc	3599	2132
Delaware Valley Concrete Company Inc	3273	69
Delaware Valley Custom Marble Inc	1799	136
Delaware Valley Wholesale Florist	8999	172
Delay Line Distributors Inc	5065	870
Delcard Associates Inc	5075	32
Delcath Systems Inc	3841	411
Delco Corp	3544	311
Delcom Group LP	7378	52
Delcon Inc	1731	1151
Delconn Wireless LLC	5065	421
DelConte Hyde Annello and Schuch PC	8721	185
Delcor USA Inc	3441	64
Deleet Merchandising Corp	5084	271
Delek US Holdings Inc	2911	21
DeLeon and Stang CPA	8721	417
Delex Systems Inc	7389	552
Delfasco Inc	3483	5
Delfelice Corp	1623	796
Delfield Co	3632	3
Delfin Design and Manufacturing Inc	3089	1368
Delford Industries Inc	3061	22
Delgasco Inc	5172	21
Delgrosso Foods Inc	2033	80
Delhaize America Inc	6719	177
Delhomme Industries Inc	7699	195
Deli Food Manufacturing Inc	2032	32
Deli Management Inc	5812	419
Delia's Inc	5961	62
Delicato Vineyards	0172	2
Delicious Living	2721	119
Delicious Vinyl Inc	7922	71
Delight Grecian Foods Inc	2051	55
Delisle Inc	8734	104
Delivery Agent Inc	7379	288
Delivery Management Services Corp	7363	291
Delivery Solutions Inc	4215	13
DEL-JEN Inc	8744	6
Delk Inc	7379	1554
Dell and ASAP Software	5045	76
Dell Compellent	7372	356
Dell Inc	5961	1
Dell Marking Systems Inc	2899	240
Dell Perot Systems	7374	6
Della Femina Rothschild Jeary and Partners	7311	117
Della Systems Inc	3672	401
Dellas Graphics Inc	2752	719
Dellinger Enterprises Ltd	3569	219
Dellon Sales and Marketing Ltd	5074	136
Dell-Star Technologies Inc	3663	351
Delmar Bancorp	6712	266
Delmar Financial Co	6162	57
Delmar Office Products	7334	51
Delmar Products Inc	5162	45
Delmarva Collections Inc	7322	182
Delmarva Electric Motors and Machine Inc	7694	29
Delmarva Millwork Corp	5031	175
Delmarva Power and Light Co	4931	28
Delmarva Recycling Inc	5093	154
Delmarva2000	2834	409
Delmhorst Instrument Co	3824	38
Delmia Corp	7372	973
Delmo Inc	5063	1002
Delnetics Inc	3677	126
Deloitte and Touche LLP	8721	6
Deloitte Consulting (Chadds Ford Pennsylvania)	8742	110
Deloitte Touche Tohmatsu	8721	4
DeLong Company Inc	5191	36
Delong Equipment Company LLC	5084	452
Delong Manufacturing Company Inc	3599	2085
Delong Sportswear Inc	2329	8
DeLonghi America Inc	5064	31
Delongs Gizzard Supply Inc	5083	195
Delong's Inc	3441	49
Delori Products Inc	2099	265
DeLorme	2741	43
DeLorme Publishing Co	8999	62
Deloro Stellite Company Inc	3548	7
Delos Insurance Group	6399	19
Delp Printing and Mailing Inc	7331	235
Delphax Technologies Inc	3555	11
Delphi Automotive PLC	3714	3
Delphi Automotive Systems Corp	3694	8
Delphi Communications	7374	274
Delphi Control Systems Inc	3823	299
Delphi Financial Group Inc	6311	120
Delphi Healthcare Partners Inc	8011	70
Delphi Interior Systems	3714	12
Delphi International Software Inc	7379	664
Delphi Mechatronic Systems Inc	3625	53
Delphi Saginaw Steering Systems	5013	6
Delphi Systems Ltd	7379	1145
Delphi Technology Inc (Boston Massachusetts)	8999	35
Delphos Cooperative Association Inc	5153	163
Delphos Herald Inc	2711	97
Delphos Herald Of Indiana Inc	2711	641
Delray Lighting Inc	3648	26
Delray Sales Inc	5085	314
Delraye Investments Corp	3829	326
Del-Ren Associates Inc	5075	84
Delrio Tortilla Factory	2099	321
Delru Rigidflex Inc	3672	377
Del's Plating Industries Corp	3471	123
Delsen Testing Laboratories Inc	8734	175
Delson Properties Ltd	2752	273
Delta Air Lines Inc	4512	3
Delta Airgas Inc	2813	13
Delta Apparel Inc	5131	4
Delta Automation Inc	7378	121
Delta Bancshares	6712	458
Delta Brands Inc	3549	7
Delta California Contractors Inc	1731	521
Delta Carbona LP	2842	80
Delta Centrifugal Corp	5051	233
Delta Circuits Inc	3672	301
Delta Circuits Technology Inc	3672	378
Delta Community Credit Union	6062	10
Delta Computer Services Inc	5045	372
Delta Computer Systems Inc	3823	324
Delta Connection Academy Inc	8299	17
Delta Consolidated Industries Inc	3089	150
Delta Construction Corp	1623	97
Delta Consulting PA Inc	7379	1284
Delta Controls Company Inc	3823	379
Delta Controls Corp	3823	355
Delta Corrugated Paper Products Corp	2653	45
Delta Creative Inc	5092	11
Delta Data Software Inc	7372	2844
Delta Dental Plan of California	6324	21
Delta Dental Plan of Kentucky Inc	6324	85
Delta Design Inc	3679	106
Delta Disaster Services Inc	1799	92
Delta Diversified Enterprises Inc	1731	244
Delta Downs Racing Association Inc	7948	11
Delta Electric Company Inc	1731	917
Delta Electric Inc	5063	427
Delta Electric Services Inc	1731	1264
Delta Electrical Contractors Of Lansing Inc	1731	746
Delta Electronics Inc	3663	203
Delta Enterprises	2431	59
Delta Express Inc	4213	1085
Delta F Corp	3826	84
Delta Fabrication And Machine Inc	1541	184
Delta Fabricators Inc	3589	250
Delta Faucet Co	3432	13
Delta Flexible Products Inc	5085	443
Delta Foremost Chemical Corp	2842	40
Delta Forms Inc	2752	1504
Delta GearInc	3545	154
Delta Group Electronics Inc	3679	191
Delta Industrial Coatings Inc	2851	154
Delta Industrial Service Inc	3599	224
Delta Industries (East Granby Connecticut)	3724	27
Delta Information Systems Inc	8732	82
Delta Ironworks	3446	51
Delta Laboratories Inc	2851	103
Delta Land Developers	7352	28
Delta Machine and Tool Inc	3542	87
Delta Machining Inc	3599	500
Delta Management and Distribution Inc	5734	211
Delta Manufacturing Company Inc	3567	112
Delta Manufacturing Inc	3599	2319
Delta Marine Industries Inc	3732	20
Delta Marketing Group Inc	5045	958
Delta Materials Handling Inc	5084	81
Delta Media Inc	7312	35
Delta Metals Company Inc	5051	120
Delta Metals Incorporated	3444	178
Delta Mold Inc	3599	291
Delta Nameplate Company Inc	3613	82
Delta National Bancorp	6712	489
Delta National Bank	6021	188
Delta Natural Gas Company Inc	4923	20
Delta Network Services LLC	7373	1144
Delta Oil Company Inc	5171	79
Delta Oil Mill	2074	2
Delta Pacific Activewear Inc	2253	15
Delta Pacific Products Inc	3089	1053
Delta Petroleum Corp	1311	95
Delta Petroleum Products	5172	160
Delta Pi Inc	2752	1425
Delta Pipeline Inc	1623	659
Delta Plating Inc	3471	103
Delta Power Co	3492	9
Delta Precision Circuits Inc	3672	287
Delta Press Publishing Company Inc	2711	775
Delta Printing Company Inc	2759	353
Delta Process Equipment Inc	5084	351
Delta Products Corp (Beaverton Oregon)	3679	573
Delta Products Corp (Fremont California)	3577	96
Delta Publications Inc	2711	677
Delta Pure Filtration Corp	3569	200
Delta Research Corp	3714	315
Delta Research Inc	8731	279
Delta Rexam Inc	3089	290
Delta Rubber Co	3061	21
Delta Rubber Company Inc	5085	138
Delta Sales Corp	5051	331
Delta Sand and Gravel Co	1442	29
Delta Scientific Corp	3448	17
Delta Seaboard International Inc	6799	344
Delta Security Inc	7381	138
Delta Star Inc	3612	6
Delta T Corp	3564	40
Delta Tao Software Inc	7372	1396
Delta Tau Data Systems Incorporated Of California	3569	64
Delta Technical Systems Inc	5065	601
Delta Technologies Ltd	3674	410
Delta Technology Corp	3523	225
Delta Technology LLC	7373	68
Delta Terminal Services LLC	4225	6
Delta Testing and Inspection Inc	8734	96
Delta Tooling Co	3544	29
Delta V Electronics Inc	5065	615
Delta V Instruments Inc	3672	389
Deltacom Corp	1731	2415
Deltagen Inc	8731	349
Deltak LLC	3443	30
DeltaOne Software Inc	7372	3890
Deltapaper Corp	2679	42
Delta-T Group Inc	7363	59
DeltaTRAK Inc	3829	141
Delta-Unibus Corp	3629	30
Deltec	3825	312
Deltec Inc	3499	111
Deltec Inc (St Paul Minnesota)	3829	19
Del-Tec Packaging Associates Inc	3086	117
Deltech Corp	2899	114
DELTEK Inc	7371	44
Deltic Timber Corp	2421	19
Deltona Corp	6552	193
Deltona Marketing Corp	6531	292
Del-Tool Company Inc	3544	570
Deltran Corp	3612	26
Deltran PT	3625	101
Deltrol Controls	3613	80
Deltrol Corp	3625	32
Del-Tron Precision Inc	3562	37
Deltronic Corp	3827	61
Deltronic Labs Inc	3679	489
Deltyme Corp	7379	408
DeLuca Enterprises Inc	1541	211
DeLullo Trucking Corp	4213	3044
Delux Industries Inc	3544	633
Deluxe Building Systems Inc	1521	131
Deluxe Corp	2759	2
Deluxe Equipment Company Inc	3631	18
Deluxe Frame Company Inc	3089	1627
Deluxe International Trucks Inc	5012	117
Deluxe Marketing Inc	8742	419
Deluxe Motel	7011	120
Deluxe Plastics Inc	3089	712
Deluxe Printing Company Inc	2752	1204
Deluxe Stamping And Die Co	3465	69
Delva Tool and Machine	3599	889
Delzer Lithograph Co	2752	365
Demag Cranes and Components Corp	3536	1

Company Name Index DESIGN

Company Name Index

Company Name	SIC	Rank
Demand Communications Inc	1799	128
Demand Electric Inc	1731	1652
Demand Management Inc	7372	856
Demand Media Inc	7379	44
Demand Wave Solutions'	7372	4454
Demandforce Inc	7372	1448
DemandPoint	8748	448
DemandTec Inc	7372	496
Demandware Inc	7372	1068
Demar Direct Inc	7331	61
DeMaria Building Co	1541	85
DeMarini Sports Inc	3949	88
Demark Inc	8711	529
Demartino Fixture Company Inc	3585	155
DeMatteis Organizations	6552	63
DeMattia Group	1541	181
Demco Electronics Inc	3699	293
Demco Enterprises Inc	7342	20
Demco Group NA Inc	5065	816
Demco Inc	2631	16
Demco Manufacturing Inc	3599	1608
Demco New York Corp	1731	758
Demco Products Inc	3451	151
Demello and Sorli Enterprises Inc	2051	283
Dement Printing Co	2759	512
Demer IR Counsel Inc	6282	214
Demers Brothers Trucking Inc	4213	2970
Demert and Dougherty Inc	7389	2005
Demes Gourmet Corp	2013	223
Demeter Inc	5153	24
Demetrios Designs Ltd	2335	8
Deming Malone Livesay and Ostroff	8721	354
Demmer Engineering and Machine Co	6531	180
Demnent Construction Co	1611	123
Democrasoft Inc	7373	488
Democrat Printing and Lithographing Company Inc	2752	7
DeMontrond Auto Country Inc	5511	370
Demontrond Auto Group	5511	244
Demoteller Systems Inc	3578	30
DeMoulas Super Markets Inc	5411	52
Demoulin Brothers and Co	2389	24
Dempsey Industries Inc	3479	80
Dempster Industries Inc	3523	183
Demtech Services Inc	3089	1159
Den Hartog Industries Inc	3089	184
Denaka Partners LP	3061	37
Denali Advanced Integration Inc	7372	95
Denali Drilling Inc	1381	61
Denbury Resources Inc	1311	22
Denby Brandon Organizations Inc	6282	471
Denco Division Belcam	2844	55
Denco Electronics Inc	5731	168
Denco Manufacturing Inc	3599	182
Den-Col Supply Co	5051	236
Dencompany LLC	5531	43
Dendreon Corp	2834	188
Dendrite International Inc	7372	130
Dendritech Inc	2821	171
Deneau Construction Inc	1623	324
Deneb Inc	7372	2458
Deneen Powell Atelier Inc	7336	241
Denham Blythe Company Inc	8711	269
Denham Springs Publishing Company Inc	2711	737
Denim Group Ltd	7371	1041
Denim Processing Inc	2261	16
Denios Inc	3441	198
Denise Marcil Literary Agency Inc	7389	2369
Denison Bulletin and Review	2711	441
Denison Industries Inc	3365	13
Denlin Partners LLC	4813	715
Denmac Systems Inc	7372	2391
Denman and Davis	5051	36
Denmark Advertising and Public Relations	7311	519
Denmark Bancshares Inc	6712	307
Denmark Inc	5064	138
Denmark Sausage Company Inc	2013	181
Den-Mat Corp	2844	16
Dennen Steel Corp	5051	117
Denney Construction Co	1521	96
Denney Electric Supply Of Ambler Inc	5063	156
Dennis Belton	4812	73
Dennis Beverage Co	5141	183
Dennis C Gaughan	8111	562
Dennis Design and Manufacturing Inc	5084	732
Dennis Electric Incorporated	1731	441
Dennis Fehn Gravel and Excavating Inc	1442	41
Dennis Fink Trucking Inc	4212	78
Dennis Floyd Trucking Company Inc	4213	1676
Dennis Garberg And Associates Inc	7319	56
Dennis Green Ltd	3999	117
Dennis Millican and Associates Inc	8742	389
Dennis Myers Contracting Corp	1623	802
Dennis Publishing	2721	22
Dennis Sales Ltd	5141	156
Dennis Truck Lines Inc	4213	718
Denny Kincer Inc	5083	208
Denny Lamp Company Inc	5023	191
Denny Machine Company Inc	3599	484
Denny Menholt Frontier Chevrolet Inc	5511	218
Denny Transport Inc	4213	2025

Company Name	SIC	Rank
Denny's Copy Stop	4822	24
Denny's Corp	5812	89
DeNoisecom LLC	3695	119
Denoyer - Geppert Science Co	3999	180
Densitron Corp	3679	143
Denso Air Systems Michigan Inc	3714	245
DENSO International America Inc	3714	38
DENSO Manufacturing Tennessee Inc	3714	224
Dental Arts Laboratories and Supply Company Inc	8072	29
Dental Arts Laboratory Inc	8072	4
Dental Health Resources Inc	8021	2
Dental Network of America Inc	6324	98
Dental Professional Laboratories Inc	8072	34
Dental Prosthetic Services Inc	8072	18
Dental Prosthetics of Tucson Inc	3842	183
Dental Services Group	8072	30
Dental Solutions Inc	7361	274
Dental Technology Designs Inc	7373	632
Dente Trading Company Inc	5032	129
Dentech Inc	3544	140
Denton Cartage Company Inc	4213	1123
Denton Plastics Inc	4953	142
Denton Regional Medical Center Inc	8062	104
Dentrix Dental Systems Inc	7372	386
DENTSPLY International Inc	3843	2
DENTSPLY Rinn	3843	22
Dentt Inc	5092	18
Denver Bookbinding Company Inc	2782	72
Denver Business Journal	2711	574
Denver Children's Home	8361	153
Denver Commercial Builders Inc	1541	197
Denver Fire Department Federal Credit Union	6061	136
Denver Food System Inc	5812	428
Denver Health And Hospitals Authority Inc	8062	114
Denver jetCenter Inc	4581	36
Denver Merchandise Mart	5094	33
Denver Mining Finance Co	6282	416
Denver Newspaper Agency LLP	2711	50
Denver Publishing Co	2711	196
Denyo Manufacturing Corp	3621	158
Denzo Systems Inc	3679	850
Deodorant Stones of America	5122	95
DEP S Inc	7374	316
Department Of Media Studies	7319	171
Department of The Air Force	3663	134
DEPCO Inc	7372	1439
Depco Pump Company Inc	3561	3
Dependable Bagging Company Inc	3272	123
Dependable Cleaning Contractors Inc	7349	308
Dependable Food Corp	5141	201
Dependable Gage and Tool Co	3545	372
Dependable Highway Exp Inc	4213	90
Dependable Lithographers Inc	2752	1652
Dependable Logistics Services	4213	66
Dependable Machine Company Inc	3724	68
Dependable Medical Directory LLC	7389	1623
Dependable Pattern Works Inc	3543	22
Dependable Personnel Inc	7363	115
Dependable Plastics and Pattern Inc	3086	112
Dependon Inc	4213	1876
Deployment Solutions LLC	1731	844
DepoMed Inc	2834	149
Deposit Computer Services Inc	8743	13
Deposition Sciences Inc	3669	93
Depository Trust and Clearing Corp	6289	8
DePrince Race and Zollo Inc	6282	256
Depthography Inc	7336	308
DePuy DePuy Acromed and Codman	3841	43
DePuy Inc	3842	16
DePuy OrthoTech	3842	112
Depuy Spine	3841	287
De'ran Gear Inc	3566	27
Derby Associates International	7372	721
Derby Cellular Products Inc	3053	35
Derby Industries LLC	4225	16
Derby Molded Products Inc	3089	1584
Derco Aerospace Inc	5088	1
Derecktor Robert E Inc	3731	32
Derecktor-Gunnell Inc	3732	57
Derek And Constance Lee Corp	2013	114
Derek Consulting Group Inc	7372	2905
Derf Corp	8011	172
Derf Electronics Corp	5065	379
Dering Corp	3695	26
Deringer-Ney Inc	3643	32
Derita Precision Machine Company Inc	3469	369
Derma Sciences Inc	2834	178
Dermac Labs Inc	8011	176
Dermatology Associates of Atlanta	8011	61
Dern Moore Machine Company Inc	3599	2441
Dern Trophy Corp	3599	22
Dernis International Marketing Company Inc	5032	81
DeRosa Corp	5812	144
Derouen Electrical Service Incorporated	1731	2290
Derr and Gruenewald Construction Co	1791	4
Derr Flooring Co	5023	26
Derrick Corp	3533	30
Derrick Loadmaster and Equipment Inc	1791	17
Derrick Publishing Co	2711	333

Company Name	SIC	Rank
Derse Inc	3993	5
Dervey Distributing Co	5046	143
Des Architects Engineers Inc	8712	171
Des Champs Technologies Inc	3443	12
Des Inc	5063	526
Des Moines Register and Tribune Co	2711	46
Des Plaines Journal Inc	2711	452
DesAcc Inc	7372	2196
Desai Capital Management Inc	6282	589
Desaware Inc	7372	4242
Deschamps Printing Company Inc	2752	1064
Deschner Corp	3569	186
Deschutes Brewery Inc	2082	21
Desco Capital Partners	6799	232
Desco Corp	3442	57
Desco Electronics Corp	5731	115
Desco Equipment Corp	3555	86
Desco Inc	3559	358
DESCO Industries Inc	3629	33
dESCO LLC	7373	1096
Desco Manufacturing Company Inc	3599	1673
Desco U S A	5046	260
Dese Research Inc	8731	180
DeSears Appliances Inc	5722	14
Deseret Book Co	2731	60
Deseret Management Corp	6512	11
Desert Aire Corp	3634	19
Desert Coastal Transport Inc	4213	1354
Desert Commercial Bank	6022	596
Desert Community Bank	6022	797
Desert Cutting Tools Inc	3423	76
Desert Empire Transfer and Storage	4213	2606
Desert Equipment Company Inc	4212	52
Desert Extrusion Corp	3089	885
Desert Marketing Publications	7389	2065
Desert Microsystems Inc	3823	300
Desert Millwork Inc	2431	135
Desert Pepper Trading Co	2099	314
Desert Publications Inc	2721	196
Desert Schools Federal Credit Union	6061	5
Desert Sky Machining Inc	3599	1435
Desert Sky Software Inc	7372	4115
Desert Sun Publishing Co	2711	168
Desert Trailer Systems Inc	5012	180
Desert Truss Inc	2439	21
Deshazo Crane Company LLC	3536	17
Deshler Farmers Elevator Company Inc	5153	71
Desiato Sand and Gravel Corp	1794	44
Design 24 Inc	5714	7
Design 3000 Inc	7372	3891
Design 446 Inc	7311	501
Design 5 Creatives Inc	7336	135
Design Analysis Associates Inc	7373	360
Design and Molding Service Inc	3089	500
Design Assistance Corp	3699	248
Design At Work Corp	8743	264
Design Capital Planning Group Inc	6282	618
Design Carpet Company Inc	7217	6
Design Center Inc	7011	219
Design Central Inc	7389	1988
Design Collective Inc (Columbus Ohio)	7389	2303
Design Concepts and Associates Inc	7389	1814
Design Concepts Inc	2782	45
Design Consultants and Constructors	1731	1394
Design Continuum Inc	7389	2029
Design Controls LLC	5084	870
Design Craftsmen LLC	7389	879
Design Data Corp	7372	2740
Design Data Systems Inc	7373	682
Design Direct Sound LLC	3651	102
Design Distributors Inc	2759	89
Design Electric Inc	1731	493
Design Engineering Management Co	3541	153
Design Homes of Minnesota	2452	35
Design Image Group Inc	8743	62
Design Integrated Technology Inc	3443	236
Design Line Interiors Inc	7389	283
Design Lithographers Inc	2752	1613
Design Manufacturing Inc	5051	352
Design Material Inc	5023	82
Design Molded Plastics Inc	3089	598
Design Packaging Inc	2653	77
Design Partners Inc	7336	96
Design Partnership LLP	8712	155
Design Plastics Inc	3089	603
Design Point Inc	1623	615
Design Products Company Inc	5049	173
Design Ready Controls Inc	4953	158
Design Science Inc	7372	3604
Design Services Group	8711	438
Design Simulation Technologies Inc	7372	3821
Design Specialty Inc	3641	36
Design Standards Corp	3469	200
Design Strategy Corp	7379	309
Design/Systems Group Inc	5063	650
Design Systems Inc	3559	40
Design Teams Inc	8711	436
Design Technologies and Manufacturing Co	3549	110
Design Technology Inc	3825	224
Design Tool Inc	3549	106
Design Toscano Inc	5719	23
Design Video Communications	3695	54

Ward's Business Directory of U.S. Private and Public Companies, 55th Edition / Volume 5 1465

Company Name	SIC	Rank	Company Name	SIC	Rank	Company Name	SIC	Rank
Design Within Reach Inc	5712	20	Detroit News Inc	2711	176	Dexter and Chaney Inc	7372	1848
Design Wizards Inc	2741	356	Detroit Pistons Basketball Co	7941	24	Dexter Apache Holdings Inc	3321	10
Design Works By Dave And Mike Inc	7389	1197	Detroit Pump and Manufacturing Co	5084	275	Dexter Automatic Products Co	3592	11
Design Works Inc	7389	1455	Detroit Quality Brush Manufacturing Company Inc	3991	12	Dexter Axle	3537	9
Designatronics Inc	3824	6	Detroit Radiant Products Company Inc	3433	52	Dexter Fastener Technologies Inc	3452	17
DesignCraft Fabric Corp	2211	33	Detroit Recycling Center Inc	5064	108	Dexter Field Services	8999	149
Designed Business Interiors Of Topeka Inc	5021	131	Detroit Stoker Co	3433	19	Dexter Fortson Associates Inc	1731	623
Designed Conveyor Systems Inc	3535	64	Detroit Store Fixture Company Inc	5046	247	Dexter Hospitality Inc	2752	253
Designed Mobile Systems Industries Inc	1542	324	Detroit Testing Laboratory Inc	8734	68	Dexter Hospitality Inc	7389	632
Designed Stairs Inc	2431	58	Detroit Tool and Engineering Co	3545	28	Dexter Research Center Inc	3823	146
Designer Blinds Of Omaha Inc	2591	12	Detroit Tool Metal Products	3545	34	Dexterous Mold And Tool Inc	3089	1644
Designer Checks Inc	2782	4	Detroit Transmission Products Co	3714	243	Dexterra Inc	7372	299
Designer Diagnostics Inc	5122	120	Detronic Industries Inc	3444	189	Dextrys	7371	194
Designer Plastics Inc	2759	434	Dettinburn Transport Inc	4213	1072	Dey Appliance Parts Of Wisconsin Inc	5064	178
Designer Plumbing Outletcom	5251	34	Dettmer Mold Inc	3465	66	Dey Distributing Inc	5064	44
Designer Surfaces Unlimited Inc	1799	72	Detto Technologies Inc	7372	2750	Dey Pharma LP	2834	75
Designer's Choice Stainless Iv Inc	3556	101	Detwiler Fenton and Co	6211	55	DF Stauffer Biscuit Company Inc	2052	15
Designers' Press Inc	2759	167	Detwiler Fenton and Company Inc	6211	109	DFA Capital Management Inc	7371	463
DesigneRx Pharmaceuticals Inc	8731	253	Detyens Shipyards Inc	3731	6	Dfb Holdings Inc	3568	39
Designetics Inc	3559	213	Deublin Co	3498	23	DFCU Financial	6061	21
Designing Women Inc	7389	1456	Deuer Manufacturing Inc	3536	16	Dff Corp	3545	40
Designmark Building Services Inc	7349	148	Deutch and Weiss	8111	559	DFG Electric Inc	1731	1290
Designs and Prototype	3826	103	Deutsch Design Works Inc	7336	211	Dfg Inc	3851	51
Designs By FMC Inc	5094	35	Deutsch Engineered Connecting Devices Inc	3678	10	Dfi Technologies LLC	3571	42
Designs For Tomorrow Inc	3544	261	Deutsch Inc	7311	154	DFM Associates	5045	739
Designs For Vision Inc	3841	157	Deutsch Kase Haus Inc	2022	54	DFS Group	2761	9
Designs of Elegance	7389	1792	Deutsche Nickel America Inc	3351	13	Dfs Inc	2048	64
Designshop Display Communications Inc	7389	1860	Devan Lowe Inc	5511	1256	Dfw Business Telephones Inc	5065	407
DesignSoft Co	7372	4598	Devance Av Design Inc	3651	243	DFW Mobile Tech	7378	150
DesignTex Group Inc	5198	7	Devar Inc	3823	326	DG and G Electric Inc	1731	2274
DesignTex Inc	2211	7	Devco Corp	6719	159	DG Bancorp Inc	6712	429
DesignWare Inc (Watertown Massachusetts)	7372	3388	Devcon Construction Inc	1542	59	DG Beyer Inc	1542	274
Desjardins Bank	6035	237	Devcon Group Inc	1799	105	Dg Engineering Corp	3812	164
Desk Top Graphics Inc	2796	16	Devcon International Corp	7382	11	DG FastChannel Inc	7389	118
Desk Top Solutions Inc	2759	502	Devcon Ltd	2891	38	DG Industries	3541	261
Deskin Scale Company Inc	5046	281	Devcon Security Services Corp	7382	23	DG Nicholas Co	5013	185
Desks Inc	5021	60	Deveco Corp	5169	179	DG Printing Inc	7331	206
Desks Inc (Chicago Illinois)	5021	58	Developers Diversified Realty Corp	6798	38	DGF Stoess Inc	2899	228
Desktop Darkroom Inc	5734	44	Development Alternatives Inc	8748	9	Dgm 4 Parts Inc	5065	708
Desktop Graphic Services	7372	4807	Development Dimensions International Inc	8742	80	Dgm Electronics Inc	3825	334
Desktop Services Inc	5045	943	Development Homes Inc	8361	59	Dgp Inc	3296	19
Desktop Solutions Inc	5044	156	Development Through Self-Reliance Inc	5045	409	DGSE Companies Inc	5944	16
Desktop Solutions of Pennsylvania Inc	7372	5041	Development Workshop Inc	8331	123	DGT Holdings Corp	3679	107
Desktop Visual Products Inc	7359	170	Developmental Enterprises Corp	8361	116	DGWB Inc	7311	216
Desloge Oxygen and Medical Equipment	7372	3662	Developmental Industries Inc	3542	77	DH Blattner and Sons Inc	1611	146
Desmond Marcello and Amster Inc	7389	2121	Deven Resources Inc	1311	196	DH Campbell Inc	4213	2981
Desmond Virgulak Brown Commercial Realty Inc	6531	376	Dever Electric Inc	1731	1800	DH Melton Company Inc	3559	555
DeSoto Auto Mall Enterprise	5511	853	Devere Company Inc	5087	171	Dha Group Inc	7371	290
Desselle-Maggard Corp	5085	118	Devereaux Motor Sales Inc	5511	995	Dhap Digital Inc	7371	788
De-Sta-Co Industries	3429	14	Devers Group Inc	7373	1135	Dharma Systems Inc	7372	2059
Destefano And Partners Ltd	8712	187	Device Dynamics Inc	7389	1030	Dhc Inc	1731	2023
Destination Harley-Davidson	5571	4	Device Tech Inc	5045	686	Dhg Management Company LLC	8741	134
Destination Hotels and Resorts Inc	7011	61	DeviceAnywhere	7379	345	DHI Computing Service Inc	7372	437
Destination Ireland and Great Britain Inc	4725	56	Devicescape Software Inc	5045	192	Dhi Corp	5023	84
Destination Maternity Corp	5621	16	Devido Ranier Stone Co	3281	54	DHR International Inc	7361	24
Destination Outdoors Inc	3732	56	Devillier Communications Inc	8743	96	DHS Management Services Inc	8099	60
Destination South USA Inc	7389	1651	Devin Manufacturing Inc	3599	1554	DHT Transport	4213	791
Destination Television Inc	7812	328	Devine and Pearson Communications	7311	368	Di Camillo Baking Company Inc	5461	17
Destination Wedding Travel Inc	8999	69	Devine Brothers Inc	5211	205	Di Graphics	2752	454
Destiny Image Inc	2731	183	Devine Consulting Inc	4813	404	Di Renzo and Bomier	8111	462
Destiny Software Inc	7372	4940	Devine Systems Inc	7379	654	DI Y/Group Inc	7389	603
Destiny Transportation	4213	1410	Devington Technologies Corp	7372	4088	Di Zinno Thompson Integrated Marketing Solutions Inc	7311	432
Desu Machinery Corp	3556	75	Devlin Video International	3695	46	Diablo Country Magazine Inc	2721	186
DET Distributing Co	5181	24	Devon Bancorp	6712	206	Diablo Industries	3674	399
Det Norske Veritas Holding (USA) Inc	8711	81	Devon Energy Corp	1311	11	Diaco America Inc	5094	77
Detail Dynamics SC Inc	7349	468	Devon Health Services Inc	6324	84	Diacom Corp	3069	103
Detail Services Inc	7349	273	Devon Precision Industries Inc	3451	46	Diacritech Inc	7338	15
Detailed Machining Inc	3599	1571	Devon Self Storage LLC	7389	338	diaDexus Inc	8731	351
Detco Industries Inc	2842	98	Devor Tool and Die Inc	3599	2197	Diagnostic Clinic Medical Group PA	8011	56
Detcon Inc	3829	148	Devore Software and Consulting	7372	5013	Diagnostic Health Services Inc	8099	87
Detech Inc	1731	2002	Devries Bar Grinding Inc	7389	1760	Diagnostic Hybrids Inc	2835	22
Detectapro LLC	3669	284	Devries Instruments Inc	3599	2269	Diagnostic Imaging Associates	7374	167
Detector Electronics Corp	5049	222	Devro Inc	2013	45	Diagnostic Imaging Services Inc	8049	6
Detector Technology Inc	3671	14	DeVry Inc	6719	41	Diagnostic Instruments Inc	3827	107
Detention Electronic Consultants Inc	1731	786	DEW Graphics Inc	2759	328	Diagnostic Scanning	3841	265
Deters Dairy	5399	20	Dew Software Inc	7372	1885	Diagnostic Systems Laboratories Inc	3841	199
Dethmers Manufacturing Co	2752	69	Dewal Industries Inc	2672	39	Diagraph Corp	3953	4
Detmar Corp	3429	153	Dewar of Virginia Inc	7699	150	Diakonia Software Co	7372	3892
Detoronics Corp	3678	55	Dewberry Cos	8712	13	Dial A Nurse Of Fort Myers Inc	7361	176
Detrex Corp	2869	32	Deweese Enterprises Inc	5411	211	Dial Cos	8741	127
Detroit and Windsor Tunnel LLC	4785	2	Dewey and LeBoeufs	8111	435	Dial Global	4832	50
Detroit Chassis LLC	3711	26	Dewey Ballantine LLP	8111	58	Dial Global Inc	7922	5
Detroit Coil Co	3625	126	Dewey Electronics Corp	3489	17	Dial Machine Inc	3599	1283
Detroit Diesel Corp	3519	5	Dewey Ford Inc	5511	561	Dial Manufacturing Inc	3585	76
Detroit Diesel Overseas Distribution Corp	3519	4	Deweyl Tool Company Inc	3545	219	Dial One Security	7382	95
Detroit Div	5169	38	Dewied International Inc	2013	129	Dial One Telecommunications	1731	2475
Detroit Edison Co	4911	36	Dewig Brothers Packing Company Inc	5421	12	Dial Precision Inc	3599	279
Detroit Elevator Co	1796	22	DeWitt Brothers Inc	4213	2396	Dial Properties Co	6512	5
Detroit Engineered Products Inc	7373	711	Dewitt Company Inc	2221	23	Dial Realty Corp	6552	217
Detroit Free Press	2711	88	Dewitt Computer Technologies LLC	7373	1215	Dial Sound Data Systems	5734	171
Detroit Hoist and Crane Company LLC	3536	23	Dewolff Boberg and Associates Inc	8742	372	Dialect Technologies Inc	7379	1045
Detroit Legal News Publishing LLC	2711	136	Dews Research LLC	2834	372	Dialight Corp	3679	324
Detroit Media Partnership LP	2711	71	Dewys Manufacturing Inc	3444	112	Dialink Corp	5999	223
Detroit Medical Center	8062	41	Dex Media Inc	2741	4	Dialog Corp	7375	17
Detroit Metro Convention And Visitors Bureau Inc	7389	1682	Dex One Corp	2741	6	Dialogic Communications Corp	3661	105
			Dexas International Ltd	3089	748	Dialogue Marketing Inc	7389	439
			Dexco Company Inc	3599	1333	Dialup USA Inc	4813	587
			DexCom Inc	3841	64	Dial-X Automated Equipment Inc	3599	1044
			Dexstar Wheel Company Inc	3714	344	Diameters Inc	3599	2282
			Dexta Corp	3843	48	Diamond Antenna and Microwave Corp	3663	168
						Diamond Audio Technology Inc	3714	174
						Diamond Automations Inc	3523	60
						Diamond Bakery Company Ltd	2052	57

Company Name Index

Company Name	SIC	Rank	Company Name	SIC	Rank	Company Name	SIC	Rank
Diamond Bank	6035	189	Dick Dyer and Associates Inc	5511	251	Dig Safe System Inc	7389	1274
Diamond Black Blade Co	3531	136	Dick Farrell Industries Inc	7699	181	Digalog Systems Inc	3825	199
Diamond Blade Warehouse Inc	5085	150	Dick Gerharz Syrup Distributors	5046	81	Digco Utilities	1623	746
Diamond Blue Manufacturing Company Inc	3523	188	Dick Harris and Son Trucking Co	4213	860	Digerati Technologies Inc	4813	233
Diamond Builders Wholesale Inc	5031	363	Dick Huvaere's Richmond Chrysler/ Dodge/Jeep/Ram Inc	5511	428	Digest Publications Inc	4119	21
Diamond Business Graphics Inc	5112	80	Dick Irvin Inc	4213	1168	Digger Specialties Inc	3089	807
Diamond Casting And Machine Company Inc	3363	47	Dick Jones Trucking	4213	2259	Digi International Inc	3579	8
Diamond Castle Holdings LLC	6799	143	Dick Keffer Pontiac GMC Truck	5511	808	Digica Inc	7373	864
Diamond Cellophane Products Inc	2673	50	Dick Lavy Trucking Inc	4213	749	Digicert Inc	7379	694
Diamond Comic Distributors Inc	5092	4	Dick Masheter Ford Inc	5511	372	Digichrome Imaging Inc	7384	26
Diamond Construction Company Of Shattuck Inc	1389	41	Dick Norris Buick Pontiac GMC Inc	5511	287	Digiconcepts	5045	633
Diamond Creek Vineyards	0172	11	Dick Orkin's Creative Services Inc	7922	50	Digicorp Inc	5065	91
Diamond Crystal Brands Inc	2062	4	Dick Smith Automotive Group Inc	5511	883	Digi-Data Corp	3572	51
Diamond Danco Construction	1623	596	Dick Wildes Printing Company Inc	2752	1200	Digidesign	7372	500
Diamond Data Systems Inc	7372	1837	Dick Williams and Associates	7361	424	DigiEffects	7372	4413
Diamond Die And Mold Co	3544	888	Dickard Widder Industries Inc	2782	14	Digigraphics Inc	3695	29
Diamond Die Inc	3544	673	Dickerson Engineering Inc	7379	1180	Digi-Key Corp	5065	27
Diamond Discs International LLC	5082	189	Dickerson Group Inc	1611	125	DigiLog Inc	3825	187
Diamond Drinks Inc	2834	401	Dickerson Lumber Co	2421	118	Digimage Arts	7372	4683
Diamond Drugs Inc	5122	37	Dickerson Tool and Engineering LLC	3544	597	Digimarc Corp	7373	221
Diamond Electric Inc	1731	504	Dickey Manufacturing Co	7382	104	Digimatics Inc	2761	81
Diamond Electric Manufacturing Corp	3694	12	Dickey Transport	5172	136	Digimation Inc	7372	4292
Diamond Electrical Contractors Inc	1731	1338	Dickie McCamey and Chilcote PC	8111	199	Digineer Inc	7371	431
Diamond Energy Inc	4931	49	Dickinson Brands Inc (East Hampton Connecticut)	2844	86	Digioia/Suburban Excavating LLC	1623	171
Diamond Express Inc	4213	1829	Dickinson Equipment Company LLC	5084	612	Digiorgio Costantini Partnership	8712	262
Diamond Eze-Lap Products Inc	5085	454	Dickinson Financial Corp	6712	144	Digiray Corp	3844	34
Diamond Film and Video Inc	7812	298	Dickinson Wright PLLC	8111	122	DigiSpace Solutions LLC	7373	641
Diamond Foods Inc	2068	2	Dickirson Group Ltd	5012	146	Digi-Star LLC	3596	9
Diamond Graphics Inc	2796	65	Dick's Home Care Inc	5999	111	Digital Advertising LLC	7319	106
Diamond Hill Capital Management Inc	6282	165	Dick's Sporting Goods Inc	5941	1	Digital Angel Corp	3669	77
Diamond Hill Investment Group Inc	6211	252	Dickson Co	3822	33	Digital Audio Disc Corp	3695	21
Diamond Hill Plywood Company Inc	5031	28	Dickson Press Inc	2711	881	Digital Audio Labs Inc	3679	797
Diamond Hill Securities Inc	6211	372	Dickson Testing Company Inc	8734	84	Digital Authoring Solutions LLC	3695	161
Diamond Hoffman Products Inc	3425	10	Dickson's Inc	2759	218	Digital Broadcast Equipment Inc	5065	930
Diamond Images Inc (Miami Florida)	7336	320	Dickstein Shapiro LLP	8111	33	Digital Business Solutions Inc	7374	287
Diamond Lach Inc	3423	66	Dickten Masch Plastics LLC	3089	132	Digital Check Technologies Inc	3861	70
Diamond Lane	4813	575	Di-Coat Corp	3545	265	Digital Cheetah Solutions Inc	7371	986
Diamond Machine Werks Inc	3569	124	Dicom Corp	2732	34	Digital Chocolate Inc	7371	643
Diamond Manufacturing Co	3469	67	Dicom Inc	7319	163	Digital ChoreoGraphics	7372	4455
Diamond Manufacturing Inc	3531	158	Dicom Solutions	7372	2491	Digital Communications Technologies LLC	3577	600
Diamond Mind Business Services	8748	252	Dicon Connections Inc	3643	129	Digital Connection	3651	172
Diamond Mk Products Inc	3546	10	Dicon Fiberoptics Inc	3679	175	Digital Connection	3651	228
Diamond Motion Inc	3679	841	Dicon Technologies Inc	3651	223	Digital Connections Inc	5065	99
Diamond Offshore Drilling Inc	1381	5	Didicom Towers Inc	1623	668	Digital Connections Inc (Omaha Nebraska)	5063	488
Diamond P Enterprises Inc	5085	40	Didier Aaron Inc	5932	14	Digital Consulting and Software Services Inc	7379	821
Diamond Paper Box Co	7389	567	Didier Communications Tower Inc	1623	852	Digital Controls Corp	7372	1537
Diamond Parking Inc	7521	7	Diditcom LLC	7311	313	Digital Criterion Enterprises Inc	7379	1125
Diamond Phoenix Corp	7372	816	Didlake Inc	8331	20	Digital Cyclone Inc	7372	1469
Diamond Plastics Corp	3084	15	Die Cast Press Manufacturing Company Inc	5084	687	Digital DataVoice Corp	7372	461
Diamond Plastics Inc	3089	786	Die Cut Products Company Inc	3069	232	Digital Defense Inc	7382	103
Diamond Power International Inc	3443	17	Die Cut Technologies Inc	3053	104	Digital Design Inc	8711	565
Diamond Power Specialty Co	3443	52	Die-Boards Inc	5031	307	Digital Designs Inc	7372	3605
Diamond Resorts LLC	4724	67	Diebold Fire Services Virginia Inc	5063	414	Digital Destinations	7372	2306
Diamond Springs 2 Inc	5047	200	Diebold Inc	3578	2	Digital Dimensions Inc	5045	640
Diamond Systems Corp	3572	68	Diebolt Lumber and Supply Inc	5211	180	Digital Disc Manufacturing Inc	3565	185
Diamond Tech Inc	3546	47	Dieco Inc	3544	239	Digital Documents LLC	7379	956
Diamond Technologies Inc (New Castle Delaware)	7371	433	Dieco Manufacturing Inc	3544	199	Digital Domain Productions Inc	7372	436
Diamond Tool and Die Co	3544	275	Diecuts with a View	5943	7	Digital Dynamics Inc	3571	113
Diamond Tool And Die Inc	3599	519	Diedrich Coffee Inc	5499	7	Digital Dynamics Software Inc	7372	2138
Diamond Tool And Engineering	3544	601	Diedrich Drill Inc	3546	25	Digital Engraving Inc	2759	519
Diamond Tool Co	5031	351	Diego and Son Printing Inc	2752	1378	Digital Entertainment Systems Inc	5734	127
Diamond Tool Inc	3599	2336	Diehl Aerospace Inc	7699	48	Digital Envoy	7372	270
Diamond Transportation System	4213	1211	Diehl Machines Inc	3553	4	Digital Force Ltd	3695	86
Diamond Visionics LLC	7373	716	Diehl Steel Co	5051	438	Digital Foundry Inc	7372	2074
Diamond West Lumber Company LLC	5039	31	Diehl Woodworking Machinery Inc	5084	787	Digital Fountain Inc	7372	1886
Diamond Windows and Doors Manufacturing Inc	3442	120	Dielectric Communications	3651	30	Digital Fuel Technologies Inc	7372	1664
Diamond Z Trailer Inc	3546	16	Diem Digital Interiors LLC	3651	168	Digital Graphics Inc	7389	1545
Diamondback Steel Company Inc	3599	1334	Diemaster Machine and Tool LLC	3544	647	Digital Graphiti Inc	7371	1784
Diamondhead Casino Corp	7999	161	Diemasters Manufacturing Inc	2396	14	Digital Harbor	7372	1040
DiamondRock Hospitality Co	6798	95	Die-Matic Corp	3469	190	Digital Hearing Systems Corp	7372	3389
DiamondWare Ltd	7372	4999	Die-Matic LLC	3542	54	Digital Image Design Inc	3577	149
Dianal America Inc	2821	121	Die-Matic Tool Company Inc	3469	364	Digital Impressions Inc	2796	25
Diana's Mexican Food Products Inc	2099	116	Die-Mension Corp	3544	858	Digital Impressions Of Central Florida Inc	7335	21
Diane Adair Day Care Centers Inc	8351	28	Diemold Machine Company Inc	3089	1666			
Diane Electric Inc	1731	1411	Diemolding Corp	2655	7	Digital IMS Inc	7371	642
Diane Moser Properties Inc	6531	455	Dienes Apparatus Inc	3585	245	Digital Infuzion Inc	7379	586
Diane Von Furstenberg Studio	2361	9	Die-Quip Corp	3542	105	Digital Innovation Inc	5734	213
DIANON Systems Inc	8071	25	Dierbergs Markets Inc	5411	198	Digital Instruments Veeco Metrology Group	3829	32
Diaperscom	5999	29	Diesel Engine Parts Inc	5084	748			
Diapulse Corporation of America	3845	137	Diesel Equipment Co	5084	494	Digital Intelligence Systems Corp	7373	92
Diasorin Inc	3841	65	Diesel Exchange Inc	3519	21	Digital Interiors Inc	5731	169
Diaspark Inc	7379	456	Diesel Injection Service Inc	5084	103	Digital International Corp	7389	1101
DiaSys Corp	3826	136	Diesel Machinery Inc	5082	107	Digital Juice Inc	2741	102
Diaz Wholesale and Manufacturing Company Inc	5141	115	Diesel Power Equipment Co	5088	9	Digital Knowledge Inc	7379	1360
Dibok Inc	3827	87	Diesel Products Inc	3519	30	Digital Lagoon	2741	191
DiBona Bornstein and Random Inc	7311	843	Diesel Truck Sales Inc	5012	119	Digital Light LLC	3674	398
Dicar Inc	2822	8	Diesslin and Associates	6282	186	Digital Lightwave Inc	3663	131
Diccicco Battista Communications	7311	306	Die-Tech And Engineering Inc	3544	312	Digital Lynks LLC	7373	895
Dice Career Solutions Inc	7361	67	Die-Tech Inc	3544	130	Digital Machine	3599	2458
Dice Corp	3699	183	Die-Tech Industries Inc	3312	74	Digital Machine Company Inc	3599	1804
DICE Electronics LLC	5731	50	Dieterich Standard Inc	3823	82	Digital Machining Systems LLC	3599	1077
Dice Holdings Inc	7389	157	Dietert Foundry Testing Equipment Inc	3829	484	Digital Manga Inc	7372	4941
Dice Inc	7374	87	Dietrich and Associates Inc	6411	231	Digital Map Products Inc	4899	177
Dick Broadcasting Company Incorporated Of North Carolina	4832	199	Dietrich Industries Inc	3441	18	Digital Marketing Services Inc	8732	28
Dick Clark Productions Inc	7812	51	Dietrich's Milk Products LLC	2023	10	Digital Matrix Corp	3559	336
Dick Clark Restaurants Inc	5812	364	Dietrich's Specialty Processing LLC	2064	89	Digital Matrix Systems Inc	7372	1282
Dick Corp	1542	33	Dietsch Brothers Inc	2066	34	Digital Media Automation Inc	3565	163
			Dietz and Watson Inc	2011	28	Digital Media Graphix	2741	224
			Dietz-Nauman Inc	1731	1573	Digital Media Performance Labs Inc	7371	727
			Diffraction International Inc	7371	1328	Digital Minute	7336	94
			Dig Corp	3523	120	Digital Monitoring Products Inc	3669	127

Company Name	SIC	Rank	Company Name	SIC	Rank	Company Name	SIC	Rank
Digital Motorworks LP	7375	140	Dillman And Upton Inc	5211	153	Direct Data Corp	5045	467
Digital Movers LLC	7379	752	Dillon Bindery Inc	2789	121	Direct Dental Supply Co	5047	158
Digital Music Products Inc	7389	1793	Dillon Companies Inc	5411	29	Direct Digital Inc	2752	1579
Digital Music Systems Inc	7359	132	Dillon Manufacturing Inc	3545	385	Direct Electric Co	1731	2488
Digital Office Systems Inc	7359	115	Dillon Precision Inc	3599	1118	Direct Energy Marketing Ltd	4911	150
Digital One Networks Inc	7373	966	Dillon/Quality Plus Inc	5046	329	Direct Federal Credit Union	6061	81
Digital Outpost Inc	3577	496	Dillon Supply Co	5084	18	Direct General Corp	6331	177
Digital Peripheral Solutions Inc	3577	257	Dillon Works Inc	7389	1296	Direct Group	2759	6
Digital Pond	7374	190	Dilly Door Co	5211	238	Direct Images Interactive Inc	7336	102
Digital Power Corp	3679	560	Dilmar Oil Company Inc	5171	14	Direct Impressions Inc	2752	1575
Digital Press and Graphics LLC	2752	1707	Dilmar Oil Company Inc (Wilmington North Carolina)	5172	39	Direct Insite Corp	7373	429
Digital Printing Systems Inc	2752	442				Direct Insurance Co	6331	369
Digital Products International (St Louis Missouri)	5064	11	Dilo Company Inc	5084	328	Direct Line Inc	7389	1565
			Dilon Technologies Inc	3844	22	Direct Lines Inc	4213	1837
Digital Prototype Systems Inc	3629	72	Dilts Trucking Inc	4213	1825	Direct Mail Expertise Inc	7331	209
Digital Publishing Solutions	2721	332	Diluigi's Inc	2013	113	Direct Mail Express Inc	7331	12
Digital Pulp Inc	7311	701	Dimar Manufacturing Corp	3499	84	Direct Mail Lithographers Inc	2752	1146
Digital Pursuit Inc	7379	1515	Dimar Brothers Inc	5148	44	Direct Mail Managers	7375	233
Digital Realty Trust Inc	6798	47	DiMare Florida	5148	9	Direct Mail Of Maine Inc	7331	87
Digital Resources	7379	1475	DiMare Homestead Inc	5148	6	Direct Mail of Texas	7389	1773
Digital River Inc	5045	45	Dimares Italian Specialty Food	2098	18	Direct Mail Service Inc	2789	59
Digital Root Inc	7379	1533	Dimassimo Carr Brand Advertising	7311	321	Direct Mail Services Ltd	7331	180
Digital Security And Electronics Inc	1731	2144	Dimatic Die And Tool Co	3089	955	Direct Marketing Alliance Inc	7331	107
Digital Signage Inc	7336	163	Dimcogray Corp	3089	619	Direct Marketing Excellence Inc	7374	199
Digital Site Systems Inc	5084	859	Dime Bank	6022	285	Direct Marketing Solutions Inc	7331	63
Digital Society Computer Center Inc	5045	832	Dime Community Bancshares Inc	6035	31	Direct Pointe Inc	7379	292
Digital Solutions Inc	7371	640	Dime Savings Bank of Williamsburgh	6035	43	Direct Resources For Print Inc	7331	229
Digital Sound and Lighting LLC	3651	179	Dimeco Inc	6022	284	Direct Response Consulting Service	7331	33
Digital Sound And Satellite	3663	391	Dimeling Schreiber and Park	6211	346	Direct Response Holdings LLC	7331	190
Digital Spectrum Solutions	3651	44	Dimension 5 Solutions Inc	7372	4928	Direct Sales and Service Inc	2052	70
Digital Speech Systems Inc	5065	758	Dimension Enterprises Inc	3599	1590	Direct Service Transport Inc	4213	1529
Digital Storage Inc	5045	212	Dimension Graphics Inc	2752	326	Direct Services Miami Inc	7379	1274
Digital Systems Corp	3699	159	Dimension Health Inc	6324	103	Direct Source Inc	5046	17
Digital Systems Inc (Lenexa Kansas)	3663	157	Dimension Machine Tool Inc	3599	1149	Direct Systems Inc	7372	4204
Digital Techniques Inc	3651	98	Dimension Molding Corp	3089	325	Direct Tech Inc	7372	2185
Digital Technologies Inc	3823	464	Dimension Photo Engraving Company Inc	2752	1276	Direct Technologies Inc	8742	319
Digital Telecom Inc	5065	402				Direct Technology Group Inc	5734	249
Digital Telecommunications Corp	5999	109	Dimension Technologies Inc	3663	295	Direct Transport Ltd	4213	1854
Digital United Interactive Multimedia	2741	413	Dimension Technology Solutions Inc	7371	1283	Direct Utility Contractors LLC	1623	270
Digital Video Development Inc	3695	69	Dimensional Communications Inc	1731	575	Direct Way Personnel	7361	278
Digital Video Group Inc	5731	197	Dimensional Graphics Industries	2759	538	Directapps Inc	7379	953
Digital Vision (USA) Inc	3669	139	Dimensional Insight Inc	7372	1849	Directconnectgroup Ltd	7331	54
Digital Voice Corp	3661	167	Dimensional Merchandising Inc	7389	715	Directed Energy Solutions	3827	35
Digital VooDoo	7311	864	Dimensional Mold Engineering Inc	3089	1791	Directions Credit Union (Mansfield Ohio)	6062	52
Digital Wave Corp	5084	586	Dimensional Plastics Corp	3089	1718			
Digital Wave Technologies Inc	3565	186	Dimensional Validation Incorporated DVI	7389	2261	Directions in Design Inc	7389	1031
Digital Wireless Corp	3679	617				DirectNET Inc	5046	18
Digital Wisdom Inc	7372	4599	Dimensions Consulting Inc	8711	442	Directors Co	7922	75
Digital Wise Inc	7375	275	Dimensions International Inc	7373	123	Directors Holding Corp	6311	246
Digital Wizards Inc	7372	1660	Dimeo Construction Co	1541	66	Directory Advertising Specialists Inc	7311	877
Digital2Visual	2759	33	Dimex LLC	3089	307	Directory Distributing Associates Inc	7319	44
DigitalGlobe Inc	8999	20	Diminutive Network Solutions Inc	7379	807	Directpointe Inc	7379	187
Digital-Ink Inc	7389	819	Dimmick and Fornari	7311	731	DIRECTV Group Inc	4899	1
Digitalks Inc	5065	687	Dimmitt Chevrolet	5511	773	DIRECTV Holdings LLC	4841	83
DigitalNet Holdings Inc	7371	33	Dimock Gould and Co	5032	48	DIRECTV Inc	4841	20
DigitalPersona Inc	7372	1480	Dimon and Bacorn Company of Bing-hamton	4213	2729	Dirksen Transportation Inc	4213	1105
DigitalPost Interactive Inc	7375	263				Dirt Pros EVS	8999	165
DigitalTown Inc	7372	5021	Dimon and Sons Transportation Corp	4213	2086	Dirxion LLC	5045	507
DigitalWork Inc	7379	1396	Dimond Scrap Metals Inc	5093	197	Dis Pack Corp	7389	1102
Digitaria Interactive Inc	7336	141	Dimplex Thermal Solutions	3585	80	Disability Group Inc	8111	503
Digitas Inc	7389	71	Dinamica Inc	3572	81	Disaboom Inc	7389	54
Digite Inc	7372	2060	DineEquity Inc	6794	5	Disan Engineering Corp	3669	232
Digitec Inc	8731	324	Dinegy Inc	8711	450	Disaster Management Inc	8748	94
Digitec Office Solutions Inc	5999	205	Dinewise Inc	2038	93	Disaster Recovery Services Inc	7372	1286
Digitech Custom Audio and Video Inc	1731	1865	Dingley Press Inc	2752	95	Disc	2752	39
Digitech Publishing International Inc	7373	781	Dingman Data Systems Ltd	2621	65	Disc Makers (Pennsauken New Jersey)	3565	6
Digitek Computer Products Inc	5045	483	Diniz Design Inc	5032	116	DiscBurn	3577	362
Digitel Corp	5065	187	Dinn Brothers Inc	5999	140	Discerning Software Corp	8748	449
Digitiliti Inc	7371	1246	DI-NO Computers Inc	5734	76	DiscFarm Corp	3695	56
Digitize Inc	3669	258	Dino's Trucking Inc	4213	1552	Discflo Corp	3561	132
Digitool Inc	7372	4498	Dinosaur Electronics Inc	3679	686	Disco Machine and Manufacturing Inc	3599	1061
Digitran Div	3577	145	Dinsmore Manufacturing Company Inc	3559	324	Disconnect Reconnect LLC	7379	1105
Digitron Electronics	3575	18	Dinstuhl's Fine Candy Company Inc	5441	12	Discount Computer Services	7379	938
Digitron Electronics LLC	3823	340	Dinte Resources Inc	7361	44	Discount Drug Mart Inc	5912	14
Digitronics Software Inc	7372	3049	Diocesan Publications Incorporated Of Ohio	2759	170	Discount Drugs Wisconsin Inc	5912	40
Digium Inc	5045	86				Discount Fumigation Inc	7342	68
Dignus LLC	7371	1113	Diocese Of Camden New Jersey	2711	76	Discount Labels Inc	2672	11
DiHydro Services Inc	2899	107	Diodes Inc	3674	50	Discount Micro Sales	5045	801
Dihydro Services Inc Dihydro Analytical Services Div	8071	20	Diomex Inc	3545	229	Discount Office Items	2542	27
			Dionex Corp	3823	10	Discount Plumbing and Electrical Sup-ply	5063	629
Dii Computers Inc	5065	723	Dionics Inc	3674	484			
Dijet Inc	3545	205	Dioptics Medical Products Inc	3851	37	Discount Tire Co	5531	4
DiJulio Enter/Harbor Freightlines	4213	2172	Diotec Electronics Corp	5065	549	Discountcell Inc	5731	42
Dikar Tool Company Inc	3545	355	Dip Seal Plastics Inc	2821	207	Discover Bank	6022	7
Dikeman Laminating Corp	3083	62	Dipaco Incorporated L	5084	629	Discover Financial Services	6141	7
Dike-O-Seal Inc	3089	1824	Dipaolo Baking Company Inc	2051	151	Discover Marble and Granite Inc	5023	61
Dilbeck Realtors	6531	94	Dipasa USA Inc	5149	106	Discover Re Managers Inc	6331	132
Dilco Enterprises Inc	2064	108	DiPietro Trucking Co	4213	2003	Discovery Auto Parts Inc	5015	35
Dilco Industries Inc	3599	2159	DiPinto Brothers Transportation	4213	3069	Discovery Channel Retail Div	5947	7
DiLeonardo International Inc	8712	69	Diplomat Specialty Pharmacy	5912	21	Discovery Communications Inc	4841	9
Diligence Inc	5961	138	Diplomat Trading Inc	5064	94	Discovery Computing Inc	7389	2388
Dill and Norris Company Inc	1761	56	Diplomatic Language Services Inc	8299	35	Discovery House Publishers Inc	2741	335
Dill Brothers Inc	3599	2086	Dippin' Dots Inc	2024	25	Discovery Laboratories Inc	2836	92
Dill Construction Company Inc	1541	259	Diprima Marketing Services Inc	5014	62	Discovery Plastics LLC	3089	826
Dillard Department Stores Inc Fort Worth Div	5311	30	Direct Advertising Inc	7311	654	Discovery Research Group Of Utah Inc	7374	86
			Direct Affect Marketing	7372	109	Discovery Toys Inc	5092	9
Dillard Environmental Service	4213	2253	Direct Alliance Corp	7379	88	Discovision Associates	8111	376
Dillard Inc St Louis Div	5311	34	Direct Capital Corp	6153	3	Discraft Inc	3089	1540
Dillard Incorporated Southeast Div	5311	48	Direct Checks Unlimited LLC	2759	4	Disgraf Services Inc	7699	154
Dillard Travel Inc	4724	126	Direct Communications Corp	7389	1041	Dish Factory Inc	5087	67
Dillard's Inc	5311	8	Direct Communications Inc	1731	1721	Dish Network Corp	4841	4
Dillen Products	3089	152	Direct Communications Rockland Inc	4813	262	Dish Tv Inc	5731	100
Dilley Manufacturing Company Inc	2782	75	Direct Container Line Inc	4491	6	Disk Doctor Labs Inc	7378	138
Dillie And Kuhn Inc	1731	1981	Direct Data Capture (USA) Ltd	7379	21	Disk Software Inc	7372	3344

Company Name	SIC	Rank
Diskeeper Corp	7372	751
Diskette Duplication Mirror Images Inc	3695	147
Disk-o-Tape Inc	5045	304
Diskovery Educational Systems Corp	5045	51
Diskriter Inc	5045	374
Disney Educational Productions	7812	176
Disney Interactive Studios	2741	19
Disney Store Inc	5947	4
Disney-MGM Studios	7996	1
Disons Gems Inc	5094	15
Dispatch Consumer Services Inc	7319	89
Dispatch Printing Co	2711	39
Dispatch Software Inc	7372	4905
Dispatch Transportation Inc	4213	3038
Dispenser Services Inc	5046	133
Dispensers Optical Service Corp	3851	36
Dispersion Technology Inc	3829	348
Display Devices Inc	3861	65
Display Edge Technology Inc	3571	184
Display Group	7359	52
Display Options Inc	5046	300
Display Pack Inc	3089	188
Display Producers Inc	3993	33
Display Source Design and Factory Ltd	3496	26
Display Specialties Inc	5046	63
Displaymaker Productions Inc	3993	158
DisplayMate Technologies Corp	7372	3606
Displays by Rioux	2542	59
Displays Depot Inc	5046	146
DisplaySearch Inc	8731	327
Disposal Services	4953	69
Dispoz-O Products Inc	3089	204
Disston Precision Inc	3545	196
Distant Replays Inc	5941	44
Distek Inc	3826	67
Dister Inc	2759	362
Distillata Co	2899	121
Distinct Corp	7372	871
Distinctive Event Rentals Inc	7359	174
Distinctive Industries	3714	142
Distinctive Industries Of Texas Inc	2386	2
Distinctive Plastics Inc	3089	1112
Distinctive Properties Of Napa Valley	2721	380
Distinctive Roofing LLC	1761	7
Distinctive Solutions Corp	7372	3663
Distraction Media LLC	5045	1060
Distributed Energy Systems Corp	4911	417
Distributed Information Technologies Inc	7373	603
Distribution and Marking Services Inc	4225	3
Distribution Data Inc	8721	374
Distribution Management Systems Inc (Omaha Nebraska)	7372	874
Distribution Operations Center LLC	5047	21
Distribution Plus Inc (Wilmette Illinois)	5149	4
Distribution Postal Consultants Inc	8748	416
Distribution Services of America	4225	18
Distribution Support Service Inc	3531	88
Distribution Systems of America Inc	5192	19
Distribution Technologies Inc (Newbury Ohio)	4212	21
Distribution Transportation Services	4213	1469
Distribution Transportation Services Co	4731	59
Distribution Video and Audio Inc	7822	21
Distributor Sales Southwest Inc	5063	616
Distributors Processing Inc	2087	80
Distributors Warehouse Inc	5013	153
Distributors Warehouse Inc (Paducah Kentucky)	5013	75
District 5 Road and Public Works Commission Of St Landry Parish	3531	216
District Creative Printing Inc	2752	639
District Iii Governmental Coop	8322	246
District Lithograph Company Inc	2752	1729
District Petroleum Products Inc	5171	32
District Xi Human Resource Council	8399	30
Distron Corp	8711	340
Dita Inc	3851	111
Ditch Whitch	3531	32
Ditch Witch Iowa Inc	5082	192
Ditch Witch Of Illinois Inc	7699	100
Ditch Witch Of Maryland Inc	5082	173
Ditech Networks Inc	3663	100
ditechcom	6162	87
DIT-MCO International Corp	3825	86
Ditom Microwave	3679	794
Ditore Ruibal and Associates Inc	7322	172
Ditron Manufacturing Inc	8711	477
Ditta Meat Co	5147	51
Dittamore Implement Co	5083	188
Dittrich Specialties Inc	7389	1265
Divane Brothers Electric Co	1731	298
Divaris Real Estate Inc	6531	173
Divatex Home Fashion Inc	5023	17
DIVC O Inc	5084	688
Divcon LLC	7389	1594
Dive N' Surf Inc	2361	10
Dive Shop Inc	5941	36
Dive Station	5941	45
Divelbiss Corp	3625	160
Diventech Inc	3823	454
Diver Chevrolet Inc	5511	481
Diver Steel City Auto Crushers Inc	5093	188
Diver's Supply Company Inc	3949	128
Divers Supply Inc	5091	101
Diversatech Plastics Group LLC	7532	9
Diversco Inc	2759	142
Diverse Communications Solutions	1731	1599
Diverse Electrical Company Inc	1731	359
Diverse Logistics Inc	3572	62
Diverse Optics Inc	3827	118
Diverse Power Inc	4911	252
Diverse Staffing Inc	7361	89
Diverse Technology Solutions Inc	5045	947
Diversey Inc	2899	8
Diversified Account Systems Of Georgia Inc	7322	153
Diversified Alliances Inc	7372	3893
Diversified Business Communications	7389	279
Diversified Business Products and Sales LLC	5049	139
Diversified Business Solutions Inc	5999	84
Diversified Chemical Technologies Inc	2891	17
Diversified Communications Inc	4833	113
Diversified Companies Inc	3679	737
Diversified Computer Systems Inc	7372	2845
Diversified Concepts Inc	1731	2540
Diversified Conveyors Inc	3535	45
Diversified Cpc International Inc	2813	23
Diversified Credit Systems	7322	200
Diversified Creditors Service	7322	155
Diversified Design and Drafting Services Inc	7389	2037
Diversified Diagnostic Products Inc	3841	384
Diversified Dynamics Corp	3561	72
Diversified Electrical Products Inc	3643	149
Diversified Electrical Systems Inc	1731	1310
Diversified Executive Systems Inc	7361	238
Diversified Foam Inc	3086	116
Diversified Foods And Seasonings Inc	2099	83
Diversified Forest Products Inc	5031	371
Diversified Group Administrators Inc	6411	172
Diversified Heat Transfer Inc	3585	135
Diversified Imaging Supplies Inc	5734	155
Diversified Imports Division Co	5083	131
Diversified Inc	8331	136
Diversified Inspections-Independent Testing Laboratories	7389	424
Diversified International Sciences Corp	7371	536
Diversified Lighting Associates Inc	5063	301
Diversified Machine Milwaukee LLC	3363	10
Diversified Machining Inc	3599	947
Diversified Maintenance Systems LLC	7349	26
Diversified Manufacturing Corp	2844	97
Diversified Mercury Communications LLC	7319	100
Diversified Metals Inc	5051	285
Diversified Packaging Inc	3086	105
Diversified Pattern and Engineering Company Inc	3543	26
Diversified Personnel	7363	374
Diversified Pharmaceutical Services Inc	8742	109
Diversified Photo Supply Corp	5043	30
Diversified Plant Services LLC	3498	59
Diversified Precision Products Inc	3541	146
Diversified Printers Inc	2741	170
Diversified Printing Services Inc	2759	587
Diversified Private Equity Corp	6211	129
Diversified Restaurant Holdings Inc	8741	145
Diversified Scientific Services Inc	4953	77
Diversified Service Technologies Inc	3999	93
Diversified Suburban Newspapers Inc	2711	254
Diversified Supply Inc	3629	80
Diversified Systems Inc	3672	34
Diversified Technical Systems Inc	3679	354
Diversified Technology Group Inc	3577	162
Diversified Technology Inc	3674	239
Diversified Thermal Solutions Inc	3255	6
Diversified Traffic Products Inc	3679	287
Diversified Utility Services Inc	1623	64
Diversitech Inc (Cincinnati Ohio)	8711	384
Diversity Corp	7311	1020
Diversity Group International Inc	7389	2489
Divesco Inc	5084	875
Divihn Integration Inc	5045	405
Divine and Service Ltd	7322	77
Divine Brothers Co	3562	28
Divine Engineering Inc	3535	106
Diving Unlimited International Inc	3949	123
Division 10 Inc	5046	175
Division 16 Electrical Inc	1731	1843
Division Of Purchasing	4813	296
Division Ten Building Specialties Inc	5046	268
DiVosta and Company Inc	6552	19
DivX Inc	7371	142
Dix and Associates Pipeline Contractors Inc	1623	636
Dix and Eaton Inc	8743	54
Dix Metals Inc	5051	266
Dix Shipping Company Inc	4491	14
Dixie Art Supplies Inc	5112	84
Dixie Bedding Corp	2515	21
Dixie Box and Crating Inc	4783	18
Dixie Building Products Inc	5023	134
Dixie Chili Inc	5812	430
Dixie Cultured Marble Company Inc	3281	38
Dixie Cut Stone And Marble Inc	5032	9
Dixie Dental Inc	5047	152
Dixie Dew Products Inc	2099	329
Dixie Distributing Co	5013	280
Dixie Drayage Service Inc	4213	2651
Dixie Drilling Corp	1481	7
Dixie Electric Company Inc	1731	1059
Dixie Electric Membership Corp	4911	191
Dixie Electric Power Association	4911	413
Dixie Electrical Supply Company Inc	5063	936
Dixie Graphics Inc	2796	31
Dixie Group Inc	2273	6
Dixie Metal Products Inc	3446	24
Dixie Neon Supply Co	5046	226
Dixie Pipe Sales Inc	5051	74
Dixie Plywood Company Of Dallas Inc	5031	333
Dixie Poly-Drum Corp	3443	180
Dixie Precision Inc	3599	1392
Dixie Printing And Packaging LLC	2657	31
Dixie Printing Inc	2752	1680
Dixie Sales Company Inc	5083	34
Dixie Seal and Stamp Company Inc	3953	13
Dixie Southern Industrial Inc	1541	220
Dixie Store Fixtures and Sales Company Inc	5046	99
Dixie Tool and Die Company Inc	3544	207
Dixieline Lumber Co	5211	24
Dixien LLC	3089	409
Dixon Automatic Tool Inc	3599	930
Dixon Brothers Inc	4213	1222
Dixon Electric Inc	1731	396
Dixon Hughes PLLC	8721	155
Dixon Investments Inc	2813	24
Dixon Schwabl Advertising Inc	7311	448
Dixon Ticonderoga Co	3952	2
Dixon Tool and Die Inc	3544	873
Dj Acquisition Management Corp	3444	165
DJ Electrical Contractors Inc	1731	587
D-J Engineering Inc	3728	53
DJ Enterprises Incorporated Of Virginia	7382	106
DJ Franzen Inc	4213	1944
DJ Grey Company Inc	3679	745
DJ Orthopedics LLC	3842	26
DJ Pinciotti Construction Company Inc	1623	413
Dj Power International LLC	5045	1000
Dj Products Inc	3999	193
DJ Rose and Son Inc	1542	420
DJH Inc	5023	147
DJM Films Inc	7812	150
DJM Sales and Marketing Inc	7319	172
djmillernet Services	7379	147
DJO Inc	3842	25
DJO Surgical	3842	46
DJONT Operations LLC	7011	62
Djr Holding Corp	5014	68
DJW Inc	7372	4414
Dk/Amans Valve Inc	5085	300
DK Display Corp	5046	110
DK Manufacturing	3089	840
DK Publishing	2741	9
DK Realty Partners LLC	7389	972
D-Kal Engineering Inc	1623	830
Dks Enterprises Inc	1731	797
DL Adams Associates Ltd	8711	591
DL Belknap Trucking Inc	4213	494
DL Coates Transportation	4213	2213
DL Couch Wallcoverings Inc	5231	6
DL Evans Bank	6022	195
DL George and Sons Transportation	4213	2663
DL Heritage Transport Inc	4213	2898
DL Horton Enterprises Inc	3599	569
DL Instruments LLC	3829	358
DL Ryan Companies Ltd	8742	111
DL Williams Electric Company Inc	1731	1010
DL Withers Construction Inc	1542	69
DLD Grain and Feed Inc	4213	2971
Dlh Industries Inc	3089	447
D-Link Systems Inc	3577	74
Dlm Inc	3999	136
Dlo Enterprises Inc	7381	187
Dlp Enterprises Inc	7389	2296
dLs Consulting LLC	8721	384
DLS Electronic Systems Inc	8742	586
Dls Solutions Inc	7371	1303
DLT Solutions Inc	7373	39
Dlux Printing Inc	2752	1694
D-Lux Screen Printing Inc	2759	217
DLW Audio Consultants Inc	3651	246
DLZ Corp	8711	28
DM Bowman Inc	4213	118
DM Camp and Sons	0191	2
DM Manufacturing Inc	3443	178
DM Mattson Inc	5063	823
DM Stone Electrical Construction Inc	1731	2275
Dm Technology and Energy Inc	5065	474
DM Tool and Plastics Inc	3089	1572
D-Mac International Inc	5065	716
D-Mark Inc	3564	117
DMB Associates Inc	6552	131
DMB Consulting Services LLC	7379	392
DMB Group Inc	7379	541
DMC Consultants Inc	8748	357
DMC Financial Services	6211	110
Dmc Security Services Inc	5065	467
Dmd Data Systems Inc	5734	308
DMD Systems Recovery Inc	5045	965

Company Name	SIC	Rank	Company Name	SIC	Rank	Company Name	SIC	Rank
DMEInc	3429	104	Doddridge Controls Inc	3625	376	Domestic Securities Inc	7378	37
Dmg Corp	5075	55	Dodge and Cox Balanced Fund	6722	32	Domestic Violence Intervention Services Inc	8322	201
Dmg Equipment Company Ltd	1611	79	Dodge and Cox Income Fund	6722	22			
DMI Computer Technologies	7372	2411	Dodge and Cox Stock Fund	6722	11	Dometek Inc	5046	53
DMI Industries Inc	3441	7	Dodge Chemical Company Inc	2869	62	Dometic Corp	3714	122
DMI USA Inc	2759	227	Dodge City Cooperative Exchange	5251	8	Dom-Ex LLC	5082	65
DMIG Inc	2844	93	Dodge City Implement Inc	5083	93	Domin-8 Enterprise Solutions	7372	598
DMMI World Communications	7311	1026	Dodge City of McKinney	5511	787	Dominance Industries Inc	2493	5
Dmo Food Equipment Service Inc	7699	233	Dodgen Industries Inc	3792	21	Dominguez Family Enterprises Inc	2099	286
DMR Automotive Group LLC	5511	693	Dodson and Associates Inc	8711	662	Dominick and Dominick LLC	6211	155
DMS Architects Inc	8712	284	Dodson Brothers Exterminating Company Inc	7342	8	Dominick Terzuoli	2674	14
DMS Health Group	3844	6				Dominick's Finer Foods	5411	8
D-M-S Holdings Inc	3841	123	Dodson Group Inc	8742	325	Dominick's Supermarkets Inc	5411	54
DMS Imaging Inc	3844	8	Dodson Wholesale Lumber Company Inc	5031	146	Dominion Air and Machinery Co	5084	414
Dms Inc	3555	113				Dominion Appalachian Development Inc	1311	133
Dms Mail Management Inc	7331	83	Doe and Ingalls Inc	5169	105			
Dms/Sign Connection Inc	5046	158	Doe Run Resources Corp	1031	1	Dominion Building Products Inc	3442	140
DMS Systems Corp	7373	577	Doe-Anderson Advertising and Public Relations Inc	7311	92	Dominion Capital Inc	6162	103
Dms-Electric Inc	1731	1339				Dominion Care Home Health	7361	369
DMT Trucking Inc	4213	491	Doellken- Woodtape Inc	2431	71	Dominion Chemical Co	5169	155
Dmt Workholding Inc	3542	74	Doenges Ford Company Inc	5511	988	Dominion Clearinghouse	4911	185
Dmw Worldwide LLC	7331	68	Doeren Mayhew and Company PC	8721	487	Dominion Cove Point LNG LP	4922	34
DMX Music	7319	83	Doering Equipment Company Inc	5084	733	Dominion Electric Supply Co Inc	5063	84
DMX Transportation Inc	4213	879	Doerle Food Services LLC	5141	130	Dominion Enterprises	2721	11
Dna Productions LLC	7379	1636	Doerner Goldberg M Frannicola Inc	7338	25	Dominion Entertainment Inc	6794	127
Dna Search Inc	7361	434	Dof Holdings LLC	5021	137	Dominion Exploration and Production Inc	1311	8
Dna Specialty Inc	3714	322	Dog Lovers Central	0752	3			
DNASTAR Inc	7372	3456	DogBreath Software Inc	7372	2650	Dominion Homes Inc	1531	59
Dnb Engineering Inc	8734	138	Doggett Equipment Services Ltd	5084	304	Dominion Hope Inc	4924	53
DNB Financial Corp	6712	428	DogHouse Technologies	7336	8	Dominion Inc	1623	836
DND Inc	7372	4499	Dogleg Properties Inc	2064	54	Dominion Post Inc	3695	148
DNE Technologies Inc	3577	222	Dogswell LLC	2047	30	Dominion Repair Service Inc	7378	100
DNE World Fruit Sales Inc	5148	11	Doguet's Rice Milling Co	2044	13	Dominion Resources Black Warrior Trust	6733	16
Dnh Industries Inc	3625	384	Dogwood Industries LLC	1541	311			
DNI Corp	7374	286	Dogwood Pharmaceuticals	3826	55	Dominion Resources Inc	4911	9
Dnm Enterprises	7359	89	Dogwood Stable Inc	7948	30	Dominion Solutions Inc	5112	27
DNP IMS America Corp	7384	7	Doheny PC	5734	410	Dominion Technical Group Inc	7371	1849
DNP Select Income Fund Inc	6726	8	Doherty Employment Group Inc	7363	230	Dominion Ventures Inc	6799	241
Dnsllc Irmo SC Inc	5731	177	Doherty Giannini Reitz Construction Co	1623	477	Domino Engineering Corp	3429	157
Dnw Automotive And Detail Supply Inc	5013	284	Doherty Steel Inc	3441	141	Domino Holdings Inc	5084	177
Do It Best 3761	5072	198	Dohrn Transfer Co	4213	385	Domino's Pizza Inc	5812	35
Do It Best Corp	5251	1	Doings Newspapers Inc	2711	329	Domital Corp	5065	169
Doall Co	5085	45	Doka USA Ltd	5031	89	Domries Enterprises Inc	3523	169
Do-All Inc	8331	126	Dolan Capital Management	6282	607	Doms Inc	3569	295
Doane Agricultural Services Co	2731	172	Dolan Co	2711	58	Domus Inc	7311	741
Doane Pet Care Enterprises Inc	6719	72	Dolan Northwest LLC	5063	120	Don Allen Automotive Group	5511	227
Doar Communications Inc	3579	28	Dolan-Jenner Industries Inc	3625	55	Don Ayres Pontiac Inc	5511	769
Doba LLC	8999	115	Dolbey Systems Inc	7372	3173	Don Baker Inc	5065	443
Dobb Printing Inc	2752	865	Dolby Laboratories Inc	3663	12	Don Bell Inc	5084	722
Dobbs Inventory Services Inc	4813	576	Dold Foods Inc	2013	28	Don Blackburn and Co	5065	172
DOBBS RAM and Co	7371	316	Dole and Bailey Inc	5147	9	Don Brown Chevrolet Buick Inc	5511	509
Dobbs Tire and Auto Center Inc	7538	5	Dole Food Company Inc	2033	2	Don Bulluck Chevrolet Cadillac Inc	5511	449
Dobday Manufacturing Company Inc	3599	2371	Dole Fresh Vegetables Inc	2033	5	Don D Corp	7353	107
Dober Chemical Corp	2842	35	Dole Packaged Foods LLC	2037	16	Don Davis Auto Group	5511	221
Doble Engineering Co	3825	52	Dole Refrigerating Cos	3585	143	Don Davis Auto World Inc	5511	911
Doc Holiday Inc	7993	25	Dolik and Associates Inc	7373	793	Don Dennis And Associates Inc	5063	903
Doc Holliday Molds Inc	3275	9	Dolinger Electric Inc	1731	2321	Don Drennen Motor Company Inc	5511	903
Doceo Publishing Inc	7372	4906	Dolinka Van Noord and Co	8721	49	Don E Kelly Contractor Inc	1623	550
Dockins Graphics Inc	2752	820	Dollar Computer Corp	5045	312	Don Farr Moving Co	4213	1024
Doco Inc	3829	464	Dollar Financial Corp	6099	10	Don Frame Trucking Company Inc	4212	68
Doc's Drugs Ltd	5912	39	Dollar General Corp	5331	4	Don Gooley Cadillac Inc	5511	1041
Docs Etc Inc	7374	216	Dollar Rent A Car Systems Inc	6794	118	Don Gray Trucking Inc	4213	2319
Doctor Fume Inc	7342	47	Dollar Thrifty Automotive Group Inc	7514	3	Don Griffin	5063	1013
Doctor Inc	7379	1637	Dollar Tree Inc	5331	6	Don Grind Associates Inc	7389	2346
Dr Pepper/7-Up Bottling Company Of The West	2086	65	Dollard Enterprises LLC	1731	2339	Don Grubb	1731	2394
			DollarLink Software	7372	3262	Don Hagan and Sons Inc	4213	1695
Dr Pepper Snapple Group Inc	2086	2	Dolle's Candyland Inc	5441	18	Don Hubbard Contracting Co	1623	561
Dr Schenk of America LLC	3825	209	Dollins Pecan Company Inc	5159	21	Don Hummer Trucking Corp	4213	428
Dr Schneider Automotive Systems Inc	5013	176	Dollins Tool Inc	3544	420	Don Jerry X-Plo Inc	4213	3132
Dr Schueler's Health Informatics Inc	7372	2420	Dolly Madison Industries Inc	2511	14	Don Johns Inc	5087	79
Dr Seuss Enterprises LP	6792	5	Dollywood Co	7996	7	Don Johnson Electric Service	1731	1931
Dr Smoothie Enterprises	2087	77	Dolmar Gmbh	5072	11	Don Johnston Inc	7372	249
Dr Tattoff Inc	7299	48	Dolomite Inc	1422	24	Don King Productions Inc	7941	35
Dr Vinyl and Associates Ltd	6794	154	Dolores Robinson Ward Entertainment	7922	77	Don McGill Toyota Inc	5511	339
Doctors And Merchants Credit Bureau Inc	7322	87	Dolphin Cartage Inc	4213	511	Don Moorhead Construction Inc	1623	487
			Dolphin Inc	3365	28	Don Murphy Door Specialties Inc	5211	264
Doctors Co	6399	9	Dolphin Interconnect LLC	7372	4808	Don Pancho Authentic Mexican Foods Inc	2099	154
Doctor's Exchange Inc	7389	1848	Dolphin Line Inc	4213	1094			
Docu Mart Copy and Printing Inc	2752	940	Dolphin Machine Inc	7629	30	Don R Fruchey Inc	4213	1106
Docublue	7389	2247	Dolphin Manufacturing Inc	3714	383	Don Randon Real Estate Inc	6531	302
Docucon Imaging Services Inc	7812	197	Dolphin Marine Equipment Inc	1629	115	Don Rasmussen Co	5511	195
Docudata	7379	212	Dolphin Medical Inc	3829	18	Don Seelye Ford Inc	5511	336
Doculabs	7379	1061	Dolphin MultiMedia Inc	7389	979	Don Snow Trucking Inc	4213	1205
Doculynx Inc	7372	1818	Dolphin Shoe Company Inc	3144	6	Don Stockley Trucking LLC	4213	2502
Documation LLC	2759	135	Dolphin Spas Inc	3999	184	Don Sumpter Trucking Inc	4213	2542
Document Business Solutions LLC	5999	214	Doltronics LLC	8731	348	Don Wise and Co	7311	655
Document Capture Technologies Inc	7372	1512	DOMA Technologies LLC	7379	433	Don Young Company Inc	3442	90
Document Center Inc	7375	267	Domaille Engineering Inc	3599	26	Donahue Corp	3523	263
Document Imaging Dimensions Inc	5734	87	Domain Associates LLC	6799	106	Donahue Industries Inc	3421	21
Document Imaging Systems Corp	7374	184	Domain Group Inc	7311	467	Donahue Printing Company Inc	2752	520
Document Processing Solutions Inc	7374	146	Domain Inc	2048	73	Donahue Schriber	6552	172
Document Retention Systems Inc	7375	277	Domaine Carneros	0172	7	Donal Machine Inc	3599	929
Document Security Systems Inc	7373	338	Domaine Chandon Inc	2084	18	Donald B Cook and Associates	7372	4293
Document Solutions Inc	5044	65	DomainIt Inc	7379	597	Donald B Rice Tire Company Inc	5014	17
Document Solutions Of Dayton	5044	128	Domark International Inc	6719	199	Donald Blyler Offset Inc	2752	490
Documentation Services Group Inc	7338	20	Dombrovski Meats Co	2013	182	Donald Dean and Sons Inc	2434	69
Documentation Strategies Inc	7371	1286	Dome Publishing Company Inc	7372	2237	Donald E McNabb Co	5713	8
Docupak Inc	2782	38	Domenic Stangherlin	3625	396	Donald E Savard Company Inc	5084	904
Docusign Inc	7375	109	Domeny Tool and Stamping Co	3469	327	Donald Holland Trucking Inc	4213	2803
DocuSource LLC	5044	114	Domes International Inc	1521	132	Donald L Brown Trucking	4213	2536
Docustar Inc	2759	231	Domestic Casing Co	2013	240	Donald L Mooney Enterprises LLC	8331	232
DocuTech Corp	7373	184	Domestic Fabrics And Blankets Corp	2299	23	Donald Masi	5063	815
DocuTech Corp (Idaho Falls Idaho)	7372	830	Domestic Linen Supply and Laundry Co	7213	3	Donald R Frey and Company Inc	7372	4294
Dodd Camera and Video	5946	3				Donald R Husband Inc	3629	117

Company Name	SIC	Rank
Donaldson Company Inc	3564	1
Donaldson Electric Company Inc	1731	2595
Donaldson Group LLC	6531	433
Donamarc Water Systems Co	5084	846
Donatelle Properties	6512	66
Donatos Pizzeria Corp	5812	229
Doncar Inc	2711	764
Doncasters Inc New England Airfoil Products Div	3724	67
Donco and Sons Inc	1731	956
Done Right Building Services Inc	7349	175
Donegal Group Inc	6331	157
Donegan Optical Company Inc	3851	97
Don-Ell Corp	3674	288
Donell Inc	2834	426
Dongan Electric Manufacturing Co	3612	62
Dongieux's Inc	5087	51
Dongwon Autopart Technology Alabama LLC	3465	14
Donham Craft Inc	3599	1579
Donihe Graphics Inc	2752	751
Donlevy Lithograph Inc	2752	1019
Donley Technology	2721	452
Donley's Inc	1542	161
Don-Mar Creations Inc	5023	81
Donna Karan International Inc	2331	2
Donnally Vujcic Associates LLC	7389	1569
Donnar Inc	7349	513
Donnay Software Designs Inc	7372	4684
Donnell Systems Inc	7371	1141
Donnelly Custom Manufacturing Co	3089	375
Donnelly Mechanical Corp	1711	79
Donner Industries Inc	3496	86
D'Onofrio Inc	5411	192
Donohoe Companies Inc	6552	50
DonorWare LLC	7372	3183
Donoso Inc	1521	152
Donovan Auto and Truck Center	5511	1045
Donovan Controls LLC	3823	322
Donovan Electric Inc	1731	1243
Donovan Farmers Cooperative Elevator Inc	5153	140
Donovan Heat Treating Company Inc	3398	22
Don's Machine Shop Inc	3599	1825
Don's Truck Sales Inc	5012	86
Don's Trucking Inc	4213	1493
Don's Tv and Appliance Inc	5731	71
Donsco Inc	3398	4
Donson Machine Co	3599	347
Donver Inc	2421	131
Donwell Co	3479	67
Dony Electric Inc	1731	1273
Dooley Co	2759	441
Dooley Electric Company Inc	1731	217
Dooley Gasket And Seal Inc	5085	329
Dooley Oil Transport Inc	4213	3030
Doolim Corp	7311	958
Dooney and Bourke Inc	3171	2
Door Components Inc	3442	62
Door County Coffee and Tea Co	2095	55
Door County Cooperative Inc	5191	55
Door Store (Florence Kentucky)	7331	77
Door To Door Storage Inc	4225	27
Doorking Inc	3699	57
Door-Man Manufacturing Co	3699	187
Doosan Infracore America Corp	5084	91
Doozer Software Inc	7372	1186
Dopaco California Inc	2653	3
Dopaco Inc	2657	4
Dopar Support Systems Inc	5045	628
Doppler Systems	3993	192
Dora Dee's Products Inc	2013	205
Dorado Corp	7372	607
Dorado Network Systems Corp	7372	1371
Dorado Seafood Inc	3556	165
Dorado Software	7372	634
Doral Arrowwood	7011	135
Doral Bank	6035	13
Doral Bank (Catano Puerto Rico)	6162	9
Doral Bank FSB	6035	21
Doral Dental USA LLC	6324	100
Doral Financial Corp	6029	5
Doral Money Inc	6162	30
Doral Steel Inc	5051	201
Doran Precision Inc	3569	260
Doran Scales Inc	3596	12
Doranco Inc	3613	148
D'orazio Foods Inc	2098	13
Dorcas and Kalam Company Ltd	5013	393
Dorchester Minerals LP	1311	124
Dordan Manufacturing Co	3089	858
Doremi Cinema LLC	3861	57
Doremus and Co	7311	188
Dorf Feature Service Inc	7383	15
Dorfman Construction Company Inc	1623	541
Dorfman Museum Figures Inc	3999	204
Dorfman-Pacific Company Inc	5136	4
Dorian Ltd	7389	2072
Dorian Tool International Inc	3545	183
Dorignac's Food Center Inc	5411	146
Doris O Wong Associates Inc	7338	45
Dorling Kindersley Publishing Inc	2731	197
Dorman Products Div	5013	43
Dorman Products Inc	3714	66

Company Name	SIC	Rank
Dorn Equipment Corp	2891	117
Dornier Medtech	3845	31
Dorn's Delivery and Transfer Inc	4213	922
Dor-O-Matic Inc	3442	94
Dorothy C Thorpe LLC	3231	65
Dorothy Cox Candies Inc	2064	142
Dorothy's Candies	2064	143
Dorris Lumber And Moulding Co	2431	62
Dorrough Electronics Inc	3663	322
Dor-San Electric Washington Inc	1731	2191
Dorschel Automotive Group	5511	105
Dorsett Brothers Concrete Supply Inc	3273	68
Dorsett Industries LP	2273	34
Dorsey Alexander Inc	5063	1081
Dorsey and Whitney LLP	8111	161
DOS Transportation Inc	4213	1563
Dositec Inc	3829	492
Doskocil Manufacturing Company Inc	3089	109
Doss Electric Inc	1731	1671
Doster Construction Company Inc	1541	51
Doswell LP	4911	326
Dot Bananatree Com	7373	1207
Dot Blue Solutions Inc	7379	699
Dot C Software Inc	7371	1806
Dot Foods Inc	5141	17
Dot Genesis LLC	4813	748
Dot Hill Systems Corp	3572	15
Dot Hill Systems Inc (Longmont Colorado)	5045	291
Dot Line Corp	5043	13
Dot Passkey Com Inc	7389	1688
Dot Thermography Inc	2759	530
Dot VN Inc	7371	1605
Dotcom Distrubution Corp	7389	1489
Dotlich Inc	7353	104
Dot-Line Transportation	4213	1225
Dotomi Inc	7311	553
Dotson Company Inc	3322	1
Dotster Inc	7379	79
Doty Agency Inc	6311	215
Doty Computers	5734	172
Doty Scientific Inc	3845	121
Double A Trailer Sales Inc	5084	578
Double B Textiles Inc	2331	15
Double D Express Inc	4213	900
Double Diamond Construction Company Inc	1623	711
Double Diamond Inc	6552	99
Double E Auto Parts Corp	5013	356
Double E Company LLC	3545	52
Double Eagle Petroleum Co	1311	135
Double Eagle Services Inc	7378	151
Double Eagle Steel Coating Co	3479	34
Double E's Security Unlimited	7381	211
Double F Foods LLC	6794	107
Double G Coatings Company LP	3479	39
Double H Manufacturing Corporation Inc	3082	15
Double Helix Games	7372	128
Double J Trucking Co	4213	613
Double Life Corp	3533	92
Double M Trucking Inc	4212	42
Double "r" Electrical Contractors LP	1731	664
Double R Utilities Inc	1623	630
Double S Industries	8331	215
Double 'S' Truck Line Inc	4213	2113
Double VV Inc	4213	799
Double Z Broadcasting Inc	4832	168
DoubleClick Inc	7372	175
Double-E Inc	3533	67
DoubleStar Inc	7379	463
Double-Take Software Inc	7372	491
Doucette Industries Inc	3585	96
Doudell Trucking Co	4213	2286
Doug Bradley Trucking Inc	4213	1617
Doug Smith Production Consultants	7819	84
Dougherty and Company LLC	6211	100
Dougherty County School System	8211	54
Dougherty Lumber Co	5031	144
Dougherty's Pharmacy Inc	5912	50
Doughlety Equipment Company Inc	3537	95
Dough-To-Go Inc	5149	216
Douglas and Sons Inc	4213	2118
Douglas Autotech Corp	3714	135
Douglas Communications Corporation II	5963	15
Douglas Consulting and Computer Services Inc	8748	211
Douglas County Bottling Co	2086	138
Douglas Durand Inc	7331	181
Douglas Dynamics Inc	3524	3
Douglas Electrical Components Inc	3679	258
Douglas Electronics Inc	3674	461
Douglas Emmett Inc	6798	46
Douglas Furniture Of California LLC	2514	2
Douglas Hunter Fabrication Co	2591	9
Douglas Infiniti	5511	721
Douglas Machine And Engineering Company Inc	3544	699
Douglas Machine Inc	3565	8
Douglas Machines Corp	3589	161
Douglas Maddock Inc	7336	62
Douglas Manufacturing Company Inc	3535	125
Douglas Marine Corp	3732	82

Company Name	SIC	Rank
Douglas Patrick Inc	7361	415
Douglas Press Inc	2752	73
Douglas Printing Company Inc	2752	836
Douglas Publications LLC	2721	197
Douglas Quikut	3423	29
Douglas Steel Fabricating Corp	1791	11
Douglas T Ewing and Associates	5063	465
Douglas Tahoe Fire Protection	7389	1674
Douglass Fertilizer and Chemical Inc	2875	9
Douglass Screen Printers Inc	2759	326
Doug's Electrical Service Inc	1731	2145
Douloi Automation Inc	7372	3772
Doumak Inc	2064	27
Douron Inc	5021	37
Douthit Communications Inc	2711	290
Douthitt Corp	3861	78
Doutt Tool Inc	3544	745
Dove Building Services Inc	7349	315
Dove Electronic Components Inc	5065	236
Dove Enterprises	3565	92
Dove Lighting Systems Inc	3613	184
Dove Publications and Software Inc	2732	54
Dove Tree Canyon Software Inc	7372	3345
Dover Chemical Corp	2819	42
Dover Conveyor and Equipment Co	3535	224
Dover Corp	3559	1
Dover Diversified Inc	3351	5
Dover Dixon Horne PLLC	8111	507
Dover Downs Gaming and Entertainment Inc	7993	12
Dover Downs International Speedway Inc	7948	2
Dover Electric Supply Company Inc	5063	288
Dover Flexo Electronics Inc	3823	212
Dover Foods Inc	2045	13
Dover Highperformance Plastics Inc	3559	271
Dover Holding/Trust	7322	164
Dover Hydraulics Inc	7699	104
Dover Litho Printing Co	2752	1663
Dover Motorsports Inc	7948	15
Dover Opthalmology ASC LLC	8011	113
Dover Partners Inc	6282	450
Dover Post Company Inc	2711	362
Dover Resources Inc	3561	7
Dover Saddlery Inc	5941	23
Dover Sand And Gravel Inc	5032	179
Dover's Cylinder Head Service Inc	7538	35
Dovetail Construction Company Inc	1731	1092
Dovey Corp	3554	60
Dow Automotive	8731	11
Dow Chemical	2821	22
Dow Chemical Co	2819	1
Dow Chevrolet Oldsmobile Inc	5012	82
Dow Corning Corp	2869	4
Dow Cover Company Inc	2393	14
Dow Electronics Inc	5065	85
Dow Jones and Company Inc	2711	16
Dow Precision Hydraulics Inc	3599	526
Dow Screw Products Inc	3469	192
Dow Software Services Inc	7372	4907
Dow Theory Forecasts Inc	2741	362
Dowd - Witbeck Printing Corp	2752	1243
Dowdle Gas and Appliance Center	4925	3
Dow-Elco Inc	3612	113
Dowell Transport Inc	4213	1093
Dow-Key Microwave Corp	3643	60
Down East Machine and Engineering Inc	3542	96
Downeast Graphics and Printing Inc	2752	1772
Downey Brand LLP	8111	369
Downey Contracting LLC	1542	281
Downey Grinding Co	3541	104
Downey Investments Inc	3479	15
Downey Trucking Inc	4213	2614
Downhole Stabilization Inc	3533	68
Downhome Solutions	7371	1878
Downing Displays Inc	3993	87
Downing Wellhead Equipment Inc	3533	81
Downingtown Area School District	8211	75
Downingtown National Bank	6021	223
Down-Lite International Inc	2392	19
Downs Equipment Rentals Inc	7353	27
Downstream	7819	42
Downtown Denver News	2711	825
Downtown Emergency Service Center	8322	64
Downtown Ford Sales Inc	5511	238
Downtown Partnership of Baltimore Inc	8748	286
Dowslake Microsystems Corp	3663	99
Dox Electronics Inc	7373	443
Doyen Medipharm Inc	3565	112
Doyle Electric Company Inc	1731	2168
Doyle Equipment Co	5082	61
Doyle Equipment Manufacturing Co	3523	122
Doyle Group	2721	273
Doyle Group Inc	7382	31
Doyle Hartman Oil Producer	1311	211
Doyle Lumber Company Inc	5211	206
Doyle Printing And Offset Company Inc	2752	616
Doyle Security Systems	7382	34
Doyle's Electric Inc	1731	471
Dozier Crane and Machinery Inc	5082	182
DP Associates Inc	3721	29
DP Curtis Trucking Inc	4213	709
DP Directory Inc	7372	4809

Company Name	SIC	Rank	Company Name	SIC	Rank	Company Name	SIC	Rank
DP Equipment Marketing Inc	5045	537	Dreisilker Electric Motors Inc	5063	174	DRS Technologies Inc	3812	5
Dp Manufacturing Inc	3531	66	Dreison International Inc	3714	284	Drsdigital LLC	7379	524
DP Murphy Company Inc	2752	481	D-Rep Plastics Inc	3089	1262	Drt Manufacturing Co	3544	36
DP Software Inc	7372	3894	Dresco Reproduction Inc	5049	194	Drt Strategies Inc	7373	545
DP Solutions Inc	7372	2030	Dresdner RCM Global Investors LLC	6282	201	Drucker and Scaccetti	8721	371
Dp Systems Inc	7379	1569	Dresner Corporate Services Inc	8743	55	Drug Consultants Inc	7363	261
DP Technology Corp	7372	827	Dresser Inc	3494	4	Drug Delivery Technology LLC	2721	374
Dpa Labs Inc	3571	124	Dresser Piping Specialties	3494	36	Drug Package Inc	2752	316
DPC General Contractors Inc	1799	81	Dresser Wayne	3586	7	drugstorecom Inc	5912	19
Dpc Inc	3523	226	Dresser-Hull Co	5211	172	Drugstore-Direct Inc	3499	67
DPC Inc (Paris Tennessee)	7372	4124	Dresser-Rand Group Inc	3563	2	Druker Company Ltd	6552	46
Dpc Industries Inc	5169	73	Dresser-Rand LLC	3563	28	Drum Corp	5013	208
DPC Systems Inc	7372	2279	Dressler Consulting Engineers Inc	8711	623	Drum Mailing Inc	7331	224
Dpcc LLC	3535	200	Drew Child Development Corporation Inc	8322	40	Drumbeat Digital LLC	4813	266
DPD International Inc	7372	4243	Drew County Developmental Disability Council Inc	8082	71	Drummond American Corp	5085	52
DPE and Associates	7372	4995				Drummond Company Inc	1221	9
DPE Systems Inc	7379	547	Drew Foam Companies Inc	3086	46	Drummond Industries Inc	3089	1339
DPF Data Services Group Inc	7374	123	Drew Ford/Hyundai/Volkswagon	5511	77	Drummond Press Inc	2752	431
DPI Labs Inc	3728	150	Drew Hyundai	5511	744	Drummond Printing Inc	2679	60
Dpi LLC	1731	361	Drew Industries Inc	3442	5	Drury Design Dynamics Inc	7812	192
dPi Teleconnect LLC	3661	59	Drew Oil Corp	5172	47	Drury Development Corp	8741	57
DPL Enterprises Inc	3589	195	Drewco Corp	3545	235	Dry Coolers Inc	3443	213
DPL Inc	4931	26	Drews Trucking Inc	4213	1985	Dry Creek Vineyard No 1 LLC	2084	75
DPL Surveillance Equipment	5046	377	Drexel Bancshares Inc	6712	561	Dry Pocket Road Hotel Development LLC	7011	165
DPR Construction Inc	1542	17	Drexel Chemical Co	2879	11			
DPR Group	8743	114	Drexel Foods Inc	2013	188	Dry Soda Co	2086	118
Dps Infrastructure Monitoring Systems Inc	5734	141	Drexel Heritage Furnishings Inc	2511	5	Dry Storage Corp	4213	121
			Drexel Technologies Inc	2759	164	Dry Vac Environmental Inc	3826	76
DPS Laser	7378	155	Dreyco Inc	5013	166	DRYCO Construction Inc	1771	1
DPS Software Systems Inc	7372	3527	Dreyer Babich Buccola and Callaham and Wood LLP	8111	451	Drykef Inc	7389	1422
Dpt Laboratories Inc	2834	99				Drymalla Construction Company Inc	1542	117
Dr Dish Selective Systems Inc	4841	170	Dreyer Materials Management	5047	262	Drysdale Enterprises Inc	5049	188
DR Horton Inc	1531	4	Dreyer Wine LLC	2084	107	Dryvit Systems Inc	2851	29
DR Horton Incorporated - Torrey	6552	130	Dreyer's Grand Ice Cream Holdings Inc	2024	1	Drywall Distributors Inc	1742	19
DR Horton Schuler Div	1531	10	Dreyfus Corp	6282	104	DS Brown Company Inc	3061	20
DR Horton (Scottsdale Arizona)	1521	47	Dreyfus Discovery A Fund	6722	226	DS Distribution Inc	4213	410
Dr J Electric Inc	1731	2279	DrfirstCom Inc	7371	422	Ds Electronics Inc	3672	468
DR Joseph Inc	3822	36	DRG International Inc	5047	239	Ds Fibertech Corp	3567	60
Dr Joseph L Curtis Associates Builders and Contractors Inc	7389	1325	DRH Cambridge Homes Inc	1521	70	DS Graphics Inc	2752	156
			DRI Corp (Dallas Texas)	3663	52	DS Kennedy and Co	6211	380
Dr Mike's Ice Cream Inc	2024	83	DRI Operating Company Inc	1311	197	D-S Pipe and Supply Company Inc	5085	240
Dr Pepper/7-Up Bottling Co	2086	115	Dri-Air Industries Inc	3567	73	DS Simmons Inc	1542	270
Dr Pepper Bottling Company Of Dublin	2086	132	Dri-Eaz Products Inc	3589	69	DS Waters of America Inc	5499	3
DR Smith Trucking Inc	4213	2440	Driehaus Capital Management LLC	6282	202	DS Waters of America LP	5499	17
DR Systems Inc	8011	144	Driehaus Securities LLC	6282	539	DS3 Computing Solutions Inc	8748	114
Dr William Turner	7379	1318	Driessen Aircraft Interior Systems Inc	3728	50	DSC Integrated Logistics	4213	1075
DRA Strategic Communications	8743	141	Driftwood Hospitality Management LLC	7011	110	DSE Inc	2759	442
Draeger Safety Inc	5084	51	Driggs Corp	1611	36	Dse Inc	3489	13
Draeger's Supermarkets Inc	5411	182	Driggs Farms of Indiana Inc	2024	49	DSET Corp	7371	560
Draeving Machine Tool Inc	3544	739	Drillco Equipment Company Inc	3532	62	Dsi Document Solutions Inc	7334	25
Draftech Blueprinting Inc	5049	142	Drillco National Group Inc	3531	177	DSI (Englewood Colorado)	7372	1968
Drafting Graphics Inc	2752	1686	Drillers Service Inc	5084	129	Dsi Entertainment Systems Inc	7812	159
Drafto Corp	3596	10	Drilling Structures International Inc	3441	74	Dsi Of Hawaii Inc	7371	1752
DraftWorldwide Inc	7311	21	Drilling Supply And Manufacturing Inc	3532	51	DSL Extreme Inc	4813	321
Drago Supply Company Inc	5084	37	Drillmec Inc	3533	121	DSL Sound Inc	1731	2500
Dragonpoint Inc	7371	1541	Drillspotcom	5251	30	DSLi	4813	129
Draiswerke Inc	3555	94	Drilltec Technologies Inc	2655	9	DSLnet Inc	4813	136
Draka Cableteq USA Corp	3315	4	Dril-Quip Inc	3533	15	DSM and T Co	3679	169
Draka Cableteq USA Inc	3357	35	Drinker Biddle and Reath LLP	8111	40	Dsm Chemicals North America Inc	2819	23
Drake Alliance Corp	2653	70	Drinkmore Delivery Inc	2086	96	Dsm Desotech Inc	2821	35
Drake Beam Morin Inc	8742	44	Drinks Americas Holdings Ltd	2085	29	Dsm Dyneema LLC	2221	28
Drake Construction Co (Cleveland Ohio)	1542	155	Driscoll Electric Co	1731	994	Dsm Industries Inc	2841	51
			Driscoll Electric Company Inc	1731	1168	Dsm Neoresins Inc	2879	20
Drake Corp	3541	56	Driscoll Light and Power Inc	1731	1128	DSM NeoSol Inc	2821	86
Drake Enterprises Ltd	7372	337	Drive Line Service Of Portland Inc	5013	315	DSM Pharmaceuticals Products	2834	34
Drake Manufacturing Services	3541	89	Drive Source International Inc	3568	79	Dso Manufacturing Company Inc	3599	1466
Drake Petroleum Company Inc	5172	80	Drive Train Industries Inc	5013	74	dSoft Development Inc	7372	2710
Drakontas LLC	7372	3684	DriveCam Inc	5045	116	Dsoft Technology Co	7371	970
Dramatic Publishing Company Inc	2741	430	Drivecon Inc	3625	286	DSP Clinical Research LLC	8099	83
Dramco Tool Company Inc	3544	330	Drivekore Inc	5072	74	DSP Development Corp	7372	722
Dramm Corporation Of Manitowoc	3523	159	Driveline International Inc	4213	1308	Dsp Network Inc	1799	151
Dranetz	3825	48	Driver-Harris Co	3356	29	Dspc Co	3523	241
Draper and Kramer Inc	6531	57	Drives LLC	3462	34	Dspcon Inc	5045	218
Draper Communications Inc	4833	147	DriveSavers Inc	7378	23	DSS Funding Inc	8099	97
Draper Fisher Jurvetson	6799	40	Drivetech Inc	7378	147	DSS Networks Inc	5045	350
Draper Inc	3663	43	DriveTime Automotive Group Inc	5521	1	DSSI LLC	8741	172
Draper Valley Holdings LLC	0254	2	Dri-View Manufacturing Company Inc	4226	17	DST Inc	4213	2413
Draper's and Damon's	5621	29	Driving Momentum Inc	7363	223	DST International	7372	2527
Drawback Solutions Software Inc	7372	4908	Driv-Lok Inc	3429	92	DST Output	7372	50
Drawbase Software	7372	3563	Drl Services Inc	1731	2554	DST Systems Inc	7372	33
Draw-Tite Inc	3714	110	DRM Labs Inc	8748	283	DSU Peterbilt and GMC Truck Inc	5511	332
Draxler Transport Inc	4213	710	DRM Management Inc	2099	241	DSW Group Ltd	7379	472
Drayton Foods LLC	2045	7	Droege Computing Services Inc	7371	1672	DSW Inc	5661	3
DRB Systems Inc	7372	1148	Drogens Electric Supply	5063	341	DT Grantham Trucking Co	4213	1320
DRD Technology Corp	7371	1311	Droplet Measurement Technologies	3825	253	DT Sale Corp	3674	291
Dream Entertainment	7336	309	Drops and Props Inc	5043	32	DT Sari Company Inc	5051	493
Dream Home Source Inc	2741	222	DRP Trucking Co	4213	3109	dt Search Corp	7372	1887
Dream House Software Inc	7372	4810	DRS Architects	8712	219	DT Utility Contractors Inc	1623	737
Dream Pharmaceuticals Inc	2833	55	DRS C3 and Aviation Group	3812	13	DTC Communications Inc	3669	97
Dream Theater Inc	2741	94	DRS FPA Inc	3812	39	DTC Computer Supply	5045	336
DreamFactory Software Inc	7372	2109	Drs Industries Inc	2821	154	DTE Energy Co	4911	18
Dreamlight Inc	2741	475	DRS Infrared Technologies LP	7372	90	Dte Inc	7629	33
Dreamline Manufacturing Inc	2515	25	DRS Laurel Technologies	3694	14	D-TECH Inc	7372	1956
Dreamray	7311	856	DRS Optronics Inc	3827	11	Dtech Pos LLC	3578	46
Dreams Entertainment Inc	7941	21	DRS Photronics Inc	3812	57	D-Termination Wire Products Inc	3679	642
Dreams Inc	5945	11	DRS Sensors and Targeting Systems Inc	3812	14	Dth Publishing Inc	2711	744
Dreams Products Inc	3949	71				Dti Integrated Business Solutions Inc	5734	132
Dreamscape Online LLC	4813	664	DRS Surveillance Support System Inc	3812	40	Dtidatacom Inc	7378	70
Dreamsite Productions	7371	936	DRS Sustainment Systems Inc	7379	208	DTN Energy Services LLC	7372	186
DreamWorks Animation SKG Inc	7812	16	DRS Sustainment Systems Inc	3585	11	DTO Solutions Inc	7372	2968
DreamWorks LLC	7812	14	DRS Systems Inc	3812	41	DTS	4213	1269
Dreco Inc	3089	554	DRS Systems Management Corp	3812	42	DTS Inc	3651	37
Drees Co	1521	5	DRS Technical Services Inc	7378	13	Dtsystems Inc	3577	656
Drees Transportation	4213	2441				DTX Inc/Dart Container Corp	4213	831

Company Name	SIC	Rank	Company Name	SIC	Rank	Company Name	SIC	Rank
Du Fresne Manufacturing Company Inc	3441	139	Duke Energy Corp	4911	2	Duo-Fast Corp	3399	7
Dua Computer Resources Inc	7379	565	Duke Energy Group Inc	4911	187	Duo-Fast Northeast	5072	114
Dual Dynamics Inc	3592	29	Duke Energy Trading and Marketing LLC	8742	41	Duo-Fast Of Knoxville Inc	5084	467
Dual Printing Inc	2752	844				Duos Technologies Inc	8711	257
Dualcor Technologies Inc	3572	75	Duke Graphics Inc	2752	1015	Duo-Safety Ladder Corp	3499	114
Dualex Office Products Inc	5734	425	Duke Management Co	6282	149	Duo-Tec Tool Co	3544	449
Duall Div	3089	609	Duke Manufacturing Inc	3599	1274	Dupaco Community Credit Union	6062	72
Du-All Safety	8748	301	Duke Realty Corp	6798	41	Dupaco Inc	3841	267
Dual-Lite Inc	3648	5	DukeNet Communications Inc	4812	46	DuPage Machine Products Inc	3451	47
Duane Equipment Corp	7353	109	Dukes Electric Company Inc	1731	2035	Dupage Water Conditioning Company Inc	5074	213
Duane Livingston Trucking	4213	1730	Dukes Inc	3724	58			
Duane Morris LLP	8111	181	Dukes Titan Aviation LLC	3728	203	Duperon Corp	3569	194
Duane Reade Holdings Inc	5912	10	Dulce Systems Inc	3669	296	Duplainville Transport Inc	4213	411
Duane Whitlow and Company Inc	5045	543	Duley Press Inc	2752	1238	Duplantier Hrapmann Hogan and Ma- her	8721	388
Dubhouse	3565	127	Duluth Audio Distributing and Service	5731	166			
Dubin and Swieca Capital Manage- ment LLC	6282	229	Duluth Brass Manufacturing Inc	3366	20	Duplex Electrical Supply Corp	5063	591
			Duluth Superior Area Educational Tv Corp	4833	226	Duplex Mill and Manufacturing Co	3535	197
Dub-It Digital Media Services	3695	133				Dupli Graphics Corp	2759	60
Dublin Building Systems Inc	1542	358	Duluth/Superior Communications Inc	5999	158	Duplicating Products Inc	5044	54
Dublin Construction Company Inc	1542	203	Dumac Business Systems Inc	5044	66	Duplication Factory Inc	7819	32
Dublin Management Associates Of New Jersey Inc	3993	70	Dumas Candy Company Inc	2064	127	Duplication Specialists	7819	89
			Duma's Meats Inc	5421	27	Duplication Systems Inc	3577	631
DuBois Equipment Company Inc	3559	138	Dumont Company LLC	3545	269	Duplicator Sales And Service Inc	2752	155
Dubois Machine Company Inc	3553	26	Dumont Printing Incorporated	2752	1003	Duplin Wine Cellars Inc	2084	138
Dubois Production Services Inc	7692	44	Dumore Corp	3621	89	Dupli-Systems Inc	2759	128
Dubois Wood Products Inc	2511	46	Dumouchel Paper Company Of Con- necticut Inc	5087	121	DuPont	2821	1
Dubose National Energy Services Inc	5051	297				DuPont Automotive	8731	75
Dubric Industries Inc	3561	137	Dump Trucks Inc	4213	2517	DuPont Delaware Inc	2821	2
Dubuit of America Inc	3565	115	Dun and Bradstreet Corp	7323	4	DuPont EKC Technology Inc	2842	12
Dubuque Bank and Trust Co	6022	164	Dun Transportation and Stringing	4213	2941	DuPont Fabros Technology Inc	7373	9
Dubuque Stamping and Manufacturing Inc	3469	109	Dunamis Inc	3577	596	Dupont Performance Elastomers LLC	2822	3
			Dunavant Enterprises Inc	5159	2	DuPont Powder Coatings USA Inc	3479	9
Ducati North America Inc	5012	121	Dunaway Timber Co	2421	71	DuPont Protein Technologies International Inc	2075	2
DuCharme McMillen and Associates Inc	8748	110	Dunbar Bender and Zapf Inc	8999	114			
			Dunbar Cash Vault Services	7381	196	Dupont Publishing Inc	2721	176
Duchem Industries Inc	2842	103	Dunbar Cook and Shepard PC	8721	426	Dupont Tool and Machine Co	3599	1208
Duchossois Industries Inc	3625	3	Dunbar Machine Co	3599	2500	DuPont Vespel Parts and Shapes	3568	31
Duck	7812	178	Dunbar Mechanical Inc	1711	134	Dupre' Transport LLC	4213	280
Duck House Inc	3229	9	Dunbar Sales Company Inc	5141	182	Dupree and Phillips Enterprises Inc	3469	302
Duck Island Terminal Inc	5171	81	Dunbar Sales Company Inc	5198	9	Dupure International Inc	3589	179
Duck River Electric Membership Corp	4911	152	Dunbar Systems Inc	5046	167	Dura Automotive Systems Inc	3714	29
Duck Walk Vinyards	2084	117	Dunbarton Corp	3442	58	Dura Foam Inc	3086	134
Duckett Design Group Inc	8712	222	Dunbrooke Apparel Corp	7389	1150	Dura Plastic Products Inc	3089	585
Duckett Truck Center Inc	5012	61	Dunbrooke Sportswear Co	2329	9	Dura Sales Inc	5032	29
Duckor SpradlingMetzger and Wynne	8111	446	Duncan and Sons Building Maintenance Inc	7349	228	Dura Supreme Inc	2434	15
Ducktrap River Fish Farm LLC	2091	32				Dura Wax Co	2842	156
Ducky's Office Furniture	5712	111	Duncan Aviation Inc	4581	10	Durabag Company Inc	2673	37
Ducky's Office Furniture Inc	5712	108	Duncan Co	5085	137	Durabilt Industries Inc	3523	270
Du-Co Ceramics Co	3264	9	Duncan Energy Partners LP	4922	7	Durable Corp	3069	152
Ducommun AeroStructures Inc	3444	101	Duncan Enterprises	3269	5	Durable Inc	3497	4
Ducommun Inc	3728	16	Duncan Galvanizing Corp	3479	59	Durable Manufacturing Co	3559	281
Ducommun LaBarge Technologies	3812	18	Duncan Industrial Solutions Inc	5085	49	Durable Products Inc	3069	73
Ducommun Technologies	3728	14	Duncan Machinery Movers Inc	4212	36	Dura-Cast Inc	3364	22
Ducon Environmental Systems Inc	3823	182	Duncan Mcintosh Company Inc	2721	272	Dura-Cast Products Inc	3080	635
Ductilic Inc	3462	68	Duncan Oil Inc	1311	181	Duraclean International Inc	6794	145
Duct-O-Wire Co	3612	71	Duncan Parking Technologies Inc	3824	23	Duraco Inc	3069	34
Ducts Inc	1761	44	Duncan Smith Co	6211	390	Duraguard Products Inc	3648	55
Dudek and Bock Spring Manufacturing Co	3599	132	Duncan Valley Electric Coop	4911	482	Durakon Industries Inc	3713	19
			Duncker Streett and Company LLC	6282	500	Duralife Inc	3842	315
Dudek Foods Inc	2038	88	Dunco Enterprises Inc	5734	386	Dur-A-Lift Inc	3531	152
Dudick Inc	2851	93	Dundas Systems Inc	5087	130	Duraloy Technologies Inc	3325	28
Dudley C Jackson Inc	3569	135	Dundee Castings Co	3365	26	Duramaster Cylinders	3593	53
Dudley Martin Chevrolet Inc	5511	834	Dundick Corp	3545	172	Duramax Inc	3069	14
Dudley Perkins Co	5571	6	Dune Energy Inc	1389	30	Duramax Marine LLC	3069	93
Dudley Products Inc	2844	17	Dune Networks Inc	3674	175	Dura-Mill Inc	3545	197
Dudley's Bakery Inc	5461	22	Dunegan Engineering Company Inc	8711	688	Duran Freight Corp	4213	2564
Dudnyk Advertising and Public Rela- tions	7311	150	Dunes Properties Of Charleston Inc	6531	148	Durand Forms Inc	5084	33
			Dungarvin Group Inc	7389	1186	Durand Glass Manufacturing Company Inc	3229	4
Dudson Group USA Inc	5023	157	Dunham and Associates Investment Counsel Inc	6282	596			
Duecker Rubber Service Inc	3496	92				Durand Interstellar Inc	8711	626
Duerr Packaging Company Inc	3086	29	Dunham Express Corp	4213	859	Durand-Wayland Inc	3523	57
Duetche Bank	6021	384	Dunham Holdings Inc	6719	126	Duranet Inc	1731	1429
Duferco Steel Inc	5051	75	Dunham Machine Inc	3599	2403	Durango Herald Inc	2711	94
Duff and Phelps Corp	6211	124	Dunham's Athleisure Corp	5941	5	Durango Station Inc	7999	10
Duff and Phelps Management Co	6211	97	Dunk and Bright Furniture Company Inc	5712	70	Durant Iron and Metal Inc	5051	476
Duff and Phelps Utility and Corporate Bond Trust	6726	38				Durant's Tents And Events LLC	7359	167
			Dunkerton Cooperative Elevator	5153	53	Dura-Stress Inc	3272	34
Duff Electric Corp	1731	1072	Dunkin' Brands Group Inc	5812	109	Durasys Corp	3575	61
Duff Quarry Inc	1422	59	Dunkin' Donuts Inc	5812	343	Duratab Corp	3571	183
Duffek Sand and Gravel Inc	1611	196	Dunkin-Lewis Inc	5091	100	Duratech Industries Inc	2759	62
Duffel Financial and Construction Co	6552	301	Dunkley International Inc	3556	37	DuraTherm Inc	4953	80
Duffey Communications Inc	8743	97	Dunlap and Company Inc	1541	189	Durawood Products Inc	2431	84
Duffey Construction Company Inc	1541	236	Dunlap Oil Company Inc	5541	51	Duray Fluorescent Manufacturing Co	3645	19
Duffie Graphics Inc	2761	51	Dunlee Inc	3844	9	Durden Enterprises Ltd	3089	1232
Duffins-Langley Optical Company Inc	3851	48	Dunlop Tire	3011	12	Durden Outdoor Displays Inc	7359	86
Duffy and Associates Physical Therapy Corp	8099	5	Dunn and Company Inc	2732	30	DURECT Corp	2834	234
			Dunn County Electric Coop	4911	567	Durel Div	5065	114
Duffy and Shanley Inc	7331	192	Dunn Dataco Inc	7331	267	Durex Inc	3469	146
Duffy Brothers Inc	4213	2255	Dunn Edwards Corp	2851	16	Durex International Corp	3567	13
Duffy PC	7378	158	Dunn Investment Co	1541	299	Durex Products Inc	3532	20
Duffy's Electric Inc	1731	1870	Dunn Lumber Company Inc	5211	141	Durgin And Crowell Lumber Company Inc	2421	86
Dufour Pastry Kitchens	2038	40	Dunn Nutter and Morgan LLP	8111	552			
Dufrene Building Materials Inc	5211	241	Dunn Road Builders LLC	2951	24	Durham and Sons Inc	1731	1722
Dugan and Meyers Construction Co	1542	253	Dunn Solutions Group	7372	2041	Durham Co	3644	15
Dugan Construction Company Inc	1542	437	Dunnage Engineering Inc	3089	1007	Durham Ellis Pecan Co	2068	11
Dugan Kinetics LLC	8711	96	Dunning Photo Equipment Inc	3861	108	Durham Exchange Club Industries Inc	7389	144
Dugan Production Corp	1311	154	Dunn-Rite Glass Inc	1793	13	Durham Manufacturing Co	3469	100
Dugan Tool And Die Inc	7699	230	Dunn's Valve Testers Inc	3829	372	Durham Medical Office Building Inc	6798	223
Duggins Construction Inc	1541	291	Dunnwell LLC	7349	249	Durham Pump Inc	1629	91
Duhadaway Tool And Die Shop Inc	5049	33	Dun-Well Maintenance Inc	7349	346	Durham School Services	4151	1
Duhig and Company Inc	5051	278	Dunwody/Beeland Architects	8712	309	Durivage Pattern and Manufacturing Company Inc	3469	314
Duininck Cos	1611	119	Dunwody White and Landon PA	8111	514			
Dukane Corp	3669	80	Duo Building Maintenance Inc	7349	105	Durkee Testing Laboratories Inc	8734	147
Duke Capital Corp	4911	23	Duo-Corp	3089	1151	Durkee-Mower Inc	2099	165

Company Name	SIC	Rank
Durkopp Adler America Inc	5064	30
DURO Bag Manufacturing Co	2674	17
Duro Manufacturing Inc	3569	193
Duro Textiles LLC	2261	8
Duroc USA	5023	161
Duro-Last Inc	2295	1
Duro-Life Corp	3599	242
Duro-Sense Corp	3823	353
Durra Print Inc	2752	1325
Durrett Sheppard Steel Company Inc	5051	198
Durridge Company Inc	3825	271
Durst Image Technology Us LLC	7373	459
DUSA Pharmaceuticals Inc	2834	214
Dusouth Industries	3823	220
Dusson	5999	202
Dust Catchers Inc	7359	168
Dust Free LP	3564	93
Dustrol Inc	2951	16
Dutch Country Apple Dumplings Inc	2051	128
Dutch Gold Honey Inc	2099	40
Dutch Made Inc	2434	50
Dutch Miller Chevrolet-Hyundai Inc	5511	400
Dutch Prime Foods Inc	5147	66
Dutch Wonderland	7996	35
Dutchess Beer Distributors Inc	5181	54
Dutchess Quarry and Supply Company Inc	5032	113
Dutchland Inc	3272	70
Dutchland Plastics Corp	3089	269
Dutel Telecommunications Inc	7359	64
Dutelle Enterprises LLC	7389	1588
Dutile Glines and Higgins Inc	3823	381
Dutra Group	1629	23
Dutra Materials	1629	70
Dutt and Wagner of Virginia Inc	5144	10
Dutton Press Inc	2752	1178
Duty Free Americas Inc	5999	28
Duty Free Shoppers Group Ltd (San Francisco California)	5947	2
Duval Ford	5511	432
Dux Industries Inc	3843	42
Duxbury Systems Inc	7372	4194
Duyck Machine Inc	3599	2221
DV Die Cutting Inc	3053	91
DV Studio Technologies LLC	7372	3704
Dv Warehouse Inc	5734	95
Dv8 Enterprises Ltd	5065	282
DVC Company Inc	3669	124
DVC Inc	7819	44
Dvcc Inc	3492	1
DVD International	7379	1476
DVD Master	3695	151
DVD/Works	3565	129
DVDCITY Inc	5961	164
DVDPlay Inc	7841	7
DVDR4Less	5046	276
DVDTransfercom LLC	3695	129
DVE Manufacturing Inc	2353	22
D-Velco Manufacturing Of Arizona Inc	3599	91
Dvideo - Digital Productions Studio	3695	149
Dvirka and Bartilucci Consulting Engineers	8711	303
DVL	7359	186
Dvl Automation Inc	1731	452
DVL Inc	6798	196
DVO Enterprises Inc	7372	3822
Dvorak Kayak and Rafting Expeditions Inc	7999	148
DVS Digital Video Inc	3669	171
DVS InteleStream	3695	17
Dvs Shoe Company Inc	5139	17
Dvtel Inc	3699	47
Dw Direct Inc	7389	1282
DW Nicholson Corp	1796	6
Dw Practice LLC	7371	879
DW Smith Associates LLC	8711	520
D-W Tool Inc	3089	328
DW Tower Inc	1623	780
Dwain Johnson and Sons Trucking	4213	3022
Dwan and Company Inc	5181	94
DWD International LLC	3585	85
Dwfritz Automation Inc	8711	495
Dwight and Wilson Co	3743	28
Dwight Asset Management Co	6282	233
Dwight Darby and Co	8721	172
Dwight G Lewis Lumber Co	5031	316
DWJ Television	8743	255
Dworken Hillman LaMorte and Sterczala PC	8721	139
Dworkin Inc	4213	2278
DWS Inc	4832	92
Dws Inc	2066	17
DWW Software Inc	7372	4811
Dwyer Enterprises Inc	3599	1787
Dwyer Group Inc	6794	59
Dwyer Instruments Inc	3823	22
Dwyer Products Corp	2514	20
Dwyer-Curlett and Co	6162	78
Dx Electric Co	5065	530
Dx Service Co	7359	163
DXM Productions	7336	103
DXP Enterprises Inc	5084	11
Dy3 Productions Inc	3672	395
Dyad Constructors Inc	1541	215

Company Name	SIC	Rank
Dyadic International Inc	8731	298
Dyax Corp	8731	95
Dybrook Products Inc	3061	39
Dycam Service Company Inc	3669	108
Dyckman Electronics Center Inc	5731	92
Dyco Electronics Inc	3612	65
Dyco Inc	3565	65
Dyco Inc (Cave Creek Arizona)	3825	244
Dyco Paints Inc	5231	7
Dycom Industries Inc	1623	4
Dycos Services Inc	7349	150
Dydacomp Development Corp	7372	1957
Dye Candy Corp	2064	116
Dye Designs International Inc	0781	7
Dye Sheet Metal Products Inc	3444	282
Dyer Electric Co	1731	2451
Dyer Industries Inc	3312	130
Dyer Quarry Inc	1429	4
Dyer Tool and Die Inc	3544	674
Dyess-Peterson Testing Laboratory Inc	8734	166
Dyke Industries Inc	5031	8
Dykema Excavators Inc	1794	17
Dykema Gossett PLLC	8111	128
Dykes Dairyman Supplier Inc	5191	144
Dykes Lumber Company Inc	5211	70
Dylan's Candy Bar LLC	5441	7
Dylon Industries Inc	2992	41
Dymax Corp	2891	23
Dymax Inc	3531	179
Dymax Systems Inc	7372	3895
Dymo CardScan	7372	536
Dymo Corp	3577	321
Dyna Communication Corp	5045	740
Dyna Flex Of Missouri LP	3843	52
Dyna Group International Inc	3961	9
Dyna Veyor Inc	3535	229
Dynabrade Inc	3546	6
Dynacare Laboratories Inc	8071	15
Dynacast Inc	3544	15
Dynachem Inc	2821	129
Dynaco USA Inc	3089	1340
Dynacolor Graphics Inc	2752	799
Dynacomp Inc	7372	5014
Dynacon Inc	3531	68
Dynacq Healthcare Inc	8011	180
Dynacraft	3052	5
Dynacut Inc	3545	430
Dyna-Empire Inc	3724	51
Dyna-Fab Corp	3531	200
Dynaflux Inc	3548	50
Dynagraf Inc	2752	251
Dyna-Graphics Corp	3625	111
Dynak Inc	3599	2008
DynaLabs LLC	8748	356
Dynalco Controls	3625	86
Dynalectric Co	1731	39
Dynalink Systems Inc	4731	79
Dynalog Inc	7371	1123
Dynamac Corp	8748	41
Dynamax Corp	3792	17
Dynametal Technologies Inc	3399	23
Dynametric Inc	3661	222
Dynamex Corp	2298	14
Dynamex Inc	4215	1
Dynamex Operations West Inc	4213	950
Dynamic Air Engineering Inc	3564	89
Dynamic Air Inc	3535	23
Dynamic Animation Systems Inc	7371	541
Dynamic Bar Code Systems Inc	5063	816
Dynamic Cable Construction LP	1623	80
Dynamic Color Solutions Inc	2816	11
Dynamic Computer Corp	7373	815
Dynamic Computer Products Inc	5045	634
Dynamic Computer Resources Inc	8711	673
Dynamic Computer Solutions Of Topeka Inc	7373	759
Dynamic Concepts Inc (Aliso Viejo California)	7372	2890
Dynamic Concepts Inc (Washington DC)	7373	252
Dynamic Construction Inc	1541	282
Dynamic Consultants Inc	7389	1550
Dynamic Consulting	8742	674
Dynamic Corporate Solutions Inc	8742	368
Dynamic Corp	3743	18
Dynamic Details Inc	3672	19
Dynamic Engineering Inc (Houston Texas)	8711	523
Dynamic Enterprises Inc	3599	1101
Dynamic Equipment Corp	3542	106
Dynamic Flowform Corp	3599	647
Dynamic Healthcare Systems Inc	7371	1766
Dynamic Homes Inc	1521	120
Dynamic Hybirds Inc	3679	817
Dynamic Inc	1381	43
Dynamic Information Systems Corp	7372	1191
Dynamic Instruments Inc	3825	97
Dynamic Interface Systems Corp	7372	2081
Dynamic Isolation Systems Inc	3463	21
Dynamic Jig Grinding Corp	3599	1826
Dynamic Lighting Inc	3498	49
Dynamic Logic Systems Inc	7372	3184
Dynamic Machine and Fabrication Corp	3429	120

Company Name	SIC	Rank
Dynamic Management Company LLC	5812	304
Dynamic Manufacturing Co	3714	67
Dynamic Materials Corp	3399	5
Dynamic Metals Inc	5051	396
Dynamic Network Factory Inc	5045	590
Dynamic Office Systems Inc	7629	31
Dynamic Products Inc	3494	48
Dynamic Reprographics Inc	7334	97
Dynamic Sciences International Inc	3829	116
Dynamic Sealing Technologies Inc	3568	36
Dynamic Solutions Worldwide Inc	4813	534
Dynamic Systems Inc (Leicester North Carolina)	3842	155
Dynamic Systems Inc (Poestenkill New York)	3829	275
Dynamic Systems Integration Inc	5065	267
Dynamic Systems Resource Management Inc	7379	435
Dynamic Telecommunications Inc	5063	1007
Dynamic Tool and Design Inc	3544	200
Dynamic Tool Company Inc	3599	287
Dynamic Traders Group Inc	7372	3896
Dynamic Traffic Systems Inc	3669	297
Dynamic Transportation Co	4213	3102
DynamicLogic Inc	8748	99
Dynamics Direct Inc	7371	1535
Dynamics Research Corp	7373	48
Dynamics Research Corp Metrigraphics Div	3577	272
Dynamix Group Inc	7373	119
Dynamotors Inc	3694	53
Dynamp LLC	3825	191
Dynapac	3531	35
Dynapace Acquisition LLC	3535	158
Dynapar Corp	3823	39
DynaPath	3823	278
Dynapoint Technologies Inc	3599	2369
Dynapower Corp	3629	41
Dynasauer Corp	3089	1719
Dynascan Technology Inc	3679	624
Dynasil Corporation of America	3229	5
Dynasol Inc	2842	154
Dynasound Inc	3699	254
Dynasteel Corp	3443	47
Dynasty Consolidated Industries Inc	2515	17
Dynasty Electronic Corp	3679	538
Dynasty Hydraulic/Machine Ltd	3599	2059
Dynasty Technologies Inc	7372	3263
Dynasys Corp	3599	2095
Dynatabs LLC	2834	305
Dynatec Machine Inc	3599	2127
Dynatech International Corp	5088	53
Dynateck America Inc	5021	156
Dynatel Radio Access Inc	5999	237
Dynatem Inc	3571	134
Dynatex International	3674	377
Dynatorch Inc	3541	172
Dynatrace Software Inc	7371	1287
Dynatronics Corp	3845	55
Dynatronix Inc	3559	233
Dynavax Technologies Corp	2834	256
DynaVox Inc	7372	403
Dynawave Corp	3674	408
Dynawave Inc	3679	353
Dynaxys LLC	7371	195
DynCorp International Inc	7389	11
Dyne Duro Corp	3585	71
Dyne Systems Inc	3829	161
Dynecol Inc	4953	109
DynEd International Inc	7372	3488
Dynegy Energy Partners LP	1321	4
Dynegy Inc	1321	3
Dyneon Inc	2821	20
Dynetech Corp	8748	26
Dynetic Systems Co	3621	116
Dynetics Engineering Corp	3579	65
Dynetics Inc	8731	56
Dynex Capital Inc	6798	89
Dynics Inc	3575	33
Dyniverse Wireless Inc	4813	746
Dyno Nobel Transportation	4213	1171
Dyno One Inc	7699	145
Dynocom Industries Inc	3559	321
Dynomach Precision Inc	3599	2073
DynoTech Software	7372	4224
DynPort Vaccine Company LLC	2834	180
DynTek Inc	7389	207
Dyonyx LP	7379	277
Dyrsmith LLC	3679	298
Dyson-Kissner-Moran Corp	3448	5
Dystel and Goderich Literary Management	7389	1054
Dzsp 21 LLC	8744	22
E A Fischione Instruments Inc	3826	96
E A Pedersen Co	3613	40
E Aiudi And Sons Inc	1623	817
E and A Industries Inc	2899	73
E and A Information Inc	8299	69
E and A Materials Inc	5032	131
E and B Electric Supply Co	5063	491
E and B Paving Inc	1611	92
E and B Trucking Inc	4213	1483
E and C Manufacturing Company Inc	3559	396
E and C Olson Inc	2052	80

Company Name	SIC	Rank
E and E Aquisitions LLC	5031	249
E and E Lumber Inc	5211	323
E and G Classics Inc	3465	48
E and H Steel Corp	3441	110
E and J Gallo Winery	2084	3
E and J Trailer Sales and Service Inc	7519	5
E and J Transportation Inc	4213	443
E and J Trucking Inc	4213	1435
E and K Electric Inc	1731	2074
E and M Bindery Inc	2789	15
E and M Dissolution Corp	1761	39
E and M Electric And Machinery Inc	5084	202
E and M Engineers and Surveyors PC	8711	554
E and M International Inc	5099	123
E and M O'hara Inc	1731	1751
E and O Mari Inc	3931	26
E and O Tool and Plastics Inc	3089	540
E and P Electrical Contracting Company Inc	1731	1574
E and R Construction Inc	1623	519
E and R Electric	1731	1588
E and R Machine Inc	3599	1961
E and R Marine Electronics Inc	5065	947
E and R Powder Coatings Inc	3479	73
E and S Cabinets and Fixtures	5046	181
E and S Precision Machine Inc	3599	2113
E and W Enterprises Of Powell Inc	3465	55
E B Bronson and Company Inc	3599	1436
E B Stone and Son Inc	5191	108
E Benson Hood Laboratories Inc	3842	291
E C Schultz and Company Inc	2796	64
E C Styberg Engineering Co	3568	33
E Chabot Ltd	3911	46
E Commerce Group Inc	7372	684
E Commerce Group Products Inc	7372	902
E D Baker Company Ltd	1611	227
E D Supply Company Inc	5063	303
E Dillon and Co	1422	3
e/Doc Systems	5044	104
E! Entertainment Television Inc	4841	24
E Excel LLC	2833	58
E F Bavis and Associates Inc	5084	316
E F Belk and Son Inc	1731	672
E F E Laboratories Inc	3825	149
E/G Electro-Graph Inc	3674	223
E G L Company Inc	3641	17
E G Pump Controls Inc	3629	86
E Gluck Corp	3873	10
E Group Inc (Minneapolis Minnesota)	7319	91
E H Arbuckle Distributing Inc	5075	92
E H Inc	3567	95
E H Lynn Industries Inc	5084	551
E H Perkins Construction Inc	5032	63
E H Thompson Co	5046	346
E Haberli Electric LLC	1731	2312
E Ink Corp	3699	48
E J Bognar Inc	1459	7
E J Davis Co	3296	21
E J Enterprises Inc	5051	303
E J Stephens Co	5211	270
E J Victor Inc	2512	41
E Jordan Brookes Company Inc	5051	106
E Kinker and Co	6331	315
E L Pruitt Co	3569	43
E L Wagner Company Inc	1799	50
E M Hundley Hardware Co	5251	40
E Mac Transportation Company Inc	4213	1717
E McIlhenny and Sons Corp	2035	12
E - Micro Inc	5045	1053
E Morris Communications Inc	7311	328
E Noa Tours	4725	3
E O Wood Company Inc	5033	46
E P Heller Co	3545	237
E P Of Cleveland Inc	5084	623
E Plus Technology	7376	5
E Practical Solutions Inc	7363	358
E R Smith Associates Inc	3599	876
E Ritter and Co	4813	221
E Rowe Foundry and Machine Co	3596	6
E Sambol Corp	1623	79
E Scan Technologies Corp	7372	2744
E Solutions Corp	7376	26
E Street Cold Logistics LLC	4222	14
E/T Technologies Inc	3825	275
E Team Inc	7372	452
E Tech Inc	5084	342
E V M Inc	3429	147
E V Yeuell Inc	2752	1180
E Weinberg Supply Company Inc	5169	133
E Wynn	7349	453
E1 Entertainment US LP	5099	30
E1 Financial Credit Union	6062	60
E2 Acquisition Corp	3325	6
e2e Communications Inc	1731	2490
E2g Partners LLC	3663	221
E2v Aerospace And Defense Inc	3674	201
e2value Inc	7372	2634
E3 Consulting LLC	8742	328
E5 Systems Inc	7371	187
E-8 Publications Inc	7372	4600
Ea Consulting Inc	7379	624
EA Engineering Science and Technology Inc	8742	147
EA Hunter Transportation Inc	7379	1167

Company Name	SIC	Rank
EA Quirin Machine Shop Inc	3599	1135
EA Services Inc	1623	141
EA Sween Deli Express	2099	48
EA Technologies Inc	4899	44
Eac Electronics	3625	194
eAcceleration Corp	7379	306
EACO Corp	6519	17
EADS Barfield Inc	4581	20
Eads Co	5085	113
EADS North America	6719	26
Eagan Insurance Agency Inc	6411	31
e-Agency Inc	7372	1888
Eagle Air Freight Inc	4213	1634
Eagle Asset Management Inc	6282	120
Eagle Automation Corp	7373	1100
Eagle Automation Inc	3565	192
Eagle Bancorp Inc	6022	83
Eagle Bancorp Montana Inc	6712	556
Eagle Bank (Glenwood Minnesota)	6022	524
Eagle Bend Manufacturing Inc	3714	154
Eagle Boston Investment Management Inc	6282	368
Eagle Box Co	3089	434
Eagle Bridge Machine and Tool Inc	3599	1091
Eagle Bulk Shipping Inc	4412	16
Eagle Business Solutions LLC	7372	4121
Eagle Capital Growth Fund Inc	6726	98
Eagle Chemical Co	2819	113
Eagle Circuits Inc	3672	254
Eagle Collaborative Computing Services Inc	7379	1309
Eagle Compressors Inc	3563	42
Eagle Comtronics Inc	3663	68
Eagle Connector Corp	3613	156
Eagle Consulting and Development Corp	7379	720
Eagle Craft Inc	3792	28
Eagle Crusher Company Inc	3535	11
Eagle Data	7374	272
Eagle Delivery Systems Inc	7389	1685
Eagle Design and Technology Inc	7373	676
Eagle Design Group LLC	3678	39
Eagle Distributors Holding Company LLC	5064	64
Eagle Elastomer Inc	3069	160
Eagle Electric Inc	1731	1193
Eagle Electric Of Grand Forks Inc	1731	2241
Eagle Electronics Inc	3672	153
Eagle Engineering and Supply Co	5063	637
Eagle Engineering Inc	5084	427
Eagle Enterprises Ltd	7349	288
Eagle Environmental Technologies Ltd	4953	133
Eagle Fastners Inc	3089	1693
Eagle Financial Services Inc	6712	443
Eagle Fire Protection Inc	1711	239
Eagle Flo Pumps Inc	5084	791
Eagle Graphics Inc	2752	887
Eagle Group Ii Ltd	3523	208
Eagle Hospitality Properties Trust Inc	6798	157
Eagle Hurst Ranch	7389	2444
Eagle Industries LLC	2517	1
Eagle International Software	7389	2304
Eagle Investment Systems Corp	5045	47
Eagle Legacy Credit Union	6062	31
Eagle Lumber Inc	5211	222
Eagle Maintenance and Janitorial Services Inc	7349	230
Eagle Manufacturing Co	3411	12
Eagle Manufacturing Corp	3089	1655
Eagle Marketing Group Inc	5046	308
Eagle Materials Inc	3241	6
Eagle Media Partners LP	2711	412
Eagle Mountain Construction Company Inc	1623	145
Eagle Mountain-Saginaw Independent School District	8211	97
Eagle Movers Inc	4213	2051
Eagle National Holding Co	6712	662
Eagle Newspapers Inc	2711	208
Eagle Newspapers LLC	2711	792
Eagle One Logistics Inc	4215	21
Eagle Optical Inc	5048	42
Eagle Panel Systems Inc	4213	2753
Eagle Pass Independent School District	8211	78
Eagle Pneumatic Inc	3535	164
Eagle Point Software Corp	7372	2228
Eagle Power And Equipment Corp	5082	74
Eagle Precast Co	3273	34
Eagle Precision Products LLC	3469	361
Eagle Printing and Thermographing	2752	1172
Eagle Publications Inc	2711	439
Eagle Publishing Inc	2791	3
Eagle Ranch Pistachio Groves	2068	31
Eagle Rentals and Sales	7359	232
Eagle Research Corp	3823	168
Eagle Research Inc	7372	3222
Eagle Rock Energy Partners LP	1311	38
Eagle Sales and Service Inc	3559	404
Eagle Scaffolding Services Inc	1799	96
Eagle Software Inc	7372	3664
Eagle Support Services Corp	7363	142
Eagle Systems And Services Inc	8742	214

Company Name	SIC	Rank
Eagle Technology Inc (Mequon Wisconsin)	7372	4166
Eagle Technology Management Inc	7371	1510
Eagle Telephonics Inc	3661	201
Eagle Tool and Design Inc	3599	1003
Eagle Tool and Machine Company Inc	3728	128
Eagle Transport Corp	4213	316
Eagle Transportation LLC	4213	2192
Eagle Tribune Publishing Company Inc	2711	186
Eagle Valley Inc	4213	985
Eagle Ventures Inc	6211	404
Eagle Vision and Eye Clinic	8042	2
Eagle Vision International	5072	204
Eagle Web Press Co	2752	1780
Eagle West Insurance Co	6331	360
Eagle Window and Door Inc	3442	19
Eagle Wings Industries Inc	3714	236
Eagle Work Clothes Inc	2326	14
Eagle Xm LLC	2752	443
EagleBank	6022	98
Eagleburgmann Industries LP	3053	30
Eaglecom Real Estate LLC	6719	193
Eaglehead Manufacturing Company Inc	3965	25
Eagleherald Publishing LLC	2711	145
EaglePicher Corp	3691	3
Eaglepro Industries LLC	3679	555
EagleVision Inc	7812	219
Eai Acquisition Company LLC	7389	2311
Eais	3829	466
EAJ PHL Airport Inc	5812	427
Eakas Corp	3714	186
Eaker Construction LLC	1623	469
Eakin Press Sunbelt Media Inc	2731	206
Eamco Corp	3599	2300
Eam-Mosca Corp	5084	109
Eanytimo Corp	7373	463
Ear Ltd	7379	845
Earl D Arnold Printing Co	2752	924
Earl F Anderson Associates Inc	5046	105
Earl G Graves Ltd	2721	100
Earl G Graves Publishing Company Inc	2721	55
Earl Horne Inc	7349	390
Earl L Bonsack Inc	4213	1511
Earl L Henderson Trucking Co	4213	388
Earl Litho Printing Company Inc	2752	1770
Earl May Seed and Nursery LP	5261	3
Earl Owen Co	5013	220
Earl R Martin Inc	4213	1651
Earl Scheib Inc	7532	2
Earl Swensson Associates Inc	8712	48
Earle M Jorgensen Co	5051	9
Earle Press Inc	2752	1210
Earlex Inc	5064	214
Earley Tractor Inc	3523	243
Earl's Electrical Service Inc	5063	982
Earl's Manufacturing Company Inc	6512	82
Earlville Farmers Coop	5153	141
Early Childhood Alliance Inc	8351	27
Early Childhood Centers Of Greater Springfield Inc	8351	26
EarlyBirdCapitalcom Inc	6211	107
Earmold Design Inc	3089	1532
Earnest and Associates Inc	7371	227
Earnest Investments LLC	4213	2845
Earnest Machine Products Co	5072	60
Earnest Partners LLC	6282	85
Earnhardt Electric Service Inc	5063	542
Earnhardt Ford Sales Co	5511	48
Earnhardt Toyota	5511	286
Earnware Corp	7371	851
Earp Distribution	5147	8
Earth Brothers Ltd	5148	35
Earth Color Barton Press Inc	2752	77
Earth Energy Technology and Supply Inc	5075	103
Earth Exploration Inc	1799	29
Earth Resources Technology Inc	7379	253
Earth Search Sciences Inc	3829	520
Earth Sun Moon Trading Company Inc	3999	138
Earth Tech Inc	8711	7
Earth Tool Company LLC	3599	557
Earthbound Farm Inc	0161	10
Earthcam Inc	7371	763
EarthCom Inc	2389	14
Earth-Core Inc	7389	2137
EarthLink Inc	7371	9
Earthlinked Technologies Inc	3822	88
Earthmaster	3523	41
Earthquake Protection Systems Inc	3463	25
Earthquake Sound Corp	3651	132
Earthrise Nutritionals LLC	0191	5
Earthsearch Communications Inc	3663	311
Earthstone Energy Inc	1311	204
Earth-Tech Services Corp	1623	589
Earthway Products Inc	3523	137
Eas Contracting LP	1731	101
EAS Engineering Inc	8748	305
EAS Industries Inc	1731	2570
EASE Inc	7372	3346
Ease Technologies Inc	7373	615
EASI Computer Systems Inc	7372	4372
eAsic Corp	7373	525
Easom Automation Systems Inc	3544	198
East Alabama Electric Company Inc	1731	1482

Company Name	SIC	Rank
East Alabama Lumber Company Inc	2421	127
East Alabama Paving Company Inc	1611	191
East Arizona Good Luck Enterprises Inc	3825	328
East Balt Inc	2051	6
East Baltimore Development Inc	7389	926
East Baton Rouge Council On Aging Inc	8322	223
East Bay Clarklift Inc	5084	399
East Bay Ford Truck Sales Inc	5511	1184
East Bay Innovations	7389	1167
East Carolina Bank	6022	198
East Carolina Builders Inc	1623	715
East Carolina Supply Company Inc	5085	345
East Central Communications Co	2759	364
East Central Iowa Coop	5153	40
East Central Missouri Behavioral Health Services Inc	8052	13
East Central Oklahoma Electric Cooperative Inc	4911	266
East Central Planning and Development Inc	8748	202
East Chicago Machine Tool Sales Corp	3569	212
East Coast Computers	5734	247
East Coast Electrical Contractors Inc	1731	488
East Coast Electrical Equipment Company Inc	5063	679
East Coast Hoist Inc	3536	55
East Coast Investigative Services Inc	7381	250
East Coast Lightning Equipment Inc	3643	76
East Coast Lumber And Building Supply Company Inc	5211	118
East Coast Lumber and Supply Company Inc	5211	170
East Coast Machine and Design Inc	3599	2239
East Coast Microwave Sales and Distribution Inc	5065	295
East Coast Plastics Inc	3089	787
East Coast Publications Inc	2711	495
East Coast Seafood Inc	5146	14
East Coast Ship Supply LLC	5088	101
East Coast Sign Advertising Company Inc	3993	53
East County Urgent Care Industrial Medical Clinic Inc	8011	161
East Dubuque Bancshares Inc	6712	673
East Dubuque Savings Bank	6036	90
East End Lumber Co	5211	313
East End Plumbing Supply Inc	5074	141
East End Resources Inc	7371	1479
East End Welding Co	3599	222
East Greenwich Photo and Studio Inc	7384	48
East Group PA	8711	514
East Hampton Star Inc	2711	575
East Iowa Plastics Inc	3089	1836
East Kentucky Broadcasting Corp	4832	103
East Kentucky Power Cooperative Inc	4911	118
East Lake Tarpon Special Fire Control District	7389	1597
East Manufacturing Corp	3715	15
East Meets West Production Inc	7311	689
East Mississippi Electric Power Association	4911	397
East Muskegon Roofing and Sheet Metal Company Inc	1761	36
East Oregonian Publishing Co	2711	212
East Pasco Electric	1731	1772
East Pattern and Model Corp	3544	390
East Penn Manufacturing Company Inc	3699	10
East Penn Trucking Co	4213	704
East Perry Lumber Co	2421	110
East River Electric Power Coop	4911	171
East River Electric Power Cooperative Inc	4911	242
East River Lumber and Grain	4213	1741
East Shore Specialty Foods Inc	2099	302
East Shore Technologies Inc	7371	1619
East Side Beverage Co	5181	36
East Side Machine Inc	3545	228
East Side Plating Inc	3471	39
East Side Van and Storage Co	4213	2982
East Stroudsburg Area School District	8211	90
East Tech Inc	3559	489
East Tennessee Children's Hospital Association Inc	8069	13
East Tennessee Rent-Alls Inc	7359	141
East Texas Alarm Inc	1731	1777
East Texas Broadcasting Company Inc	4832	133
East Texas Electric Cooperative Inc	4939	11
East Texas Employment and Training	8331	129
East Texas Financial Corp	6712	335
East Texas Integrated Circuits	3674	485
East Texas Machine Works Inc	3599	363
East Texas Precast Co	3272	88
East Tulsa Dodge Inc	5511	735
East Valley Water District	4941	47
East West Bancorp Inc	6022	9
East West Bank	6022	40
East West Connection Inc	8742	346
East West Industrial Engineering Co	5085	74
East West Securities Co	6211	261
East West Trading Corp	5045	1057
East Wind Inc	4813	424
Eastbay Inc	5961	72
Eastbiz Corp	4789	24
Eastco Building Services Inc	7349	40
EastCoast Entertainment Inc	7829	1
Eastcoast Trading	7389	1838
Eastec Inc	1731	1672
Eastek Services LLC	7349	274
Easter Goodwill Seals Miami Valley	8331	24
Easter Seal New Hampshire Inc	8331	8
Easter Seal Society Inc	8361	156
Easter Seals Children's Development Center	8361	186
Eastern Adhesives Inc	2891	125
Eastern American Energy Corp	1311	63
Eastern American Natural Gas Trust	6792	4
Eastern Bank Corp	6035	26
Eastern Business Forms Inc	2761	39
Eastern Business Systems Inc	5044	157
Eastern Christian Children's Retreat Inc	8361	71
Eastern Colorado Publishing Co	2711	179
Eastern Co (Naugatuck Connecticut)	3429	19
Eastern Computer Exchange Inc	5734	105
Eastern Concrete Materials Inc	3272	17
Eastern Connection Operating Inc	4215	8
Eastern Consolidation and Distribution Services Inc	4213	2069
Eastern Controls Incorporated Of Pennsylvania	5084	426
Eastern Copy Products Inc	5044	30
Eastern Data Inc	5045	324
Eastern Data Of Virginia Inc	7373	813
Eastern Educational Television Network Inc	7922	38
Eastern Electric Supply Co	5063	478
Eastern Elevator Service and Sales	3534	22
Eastern Engineering Supply Inc	7334	43
Eastern Equipment Sales Inc	5082	82
Eastern Etching and Manufacturing Co	3479	31
Eastern Federal Corp	7832	16
Eastern Fisheries Inc	5146	20
Eastern Food Equipment Inc	5046	147
Eastern Horizons Inc	5511	1083
Eastern Illini Electric Coop	4911	381
Eastern Illinois University	8221	25
Eastern Industrial Automation	5063	35
Eastern Industrial Products Inc	3561	148
Eastern Industries Group Inc	5063	843
Eastern Industries Inc	5013	177
Eastern Instrument Laboratories Inc	7389	2102
Eastern Insurance Holdings Inc	6331	236
Eastern Investigational Services Inc	7381	192
Eastern James Inc	7389	2198
Eastern Kentucky University	8221	17
Eastern Kentucky University	8221	27
Eastern Life And Insurance Co	6311	153
Eastern Lift Truck Co	5084	74
Eastern Lift Truck Inc	5084	718
Eastern Logistics	4213	816
Eastern Los Angeles Regional C	8211	73
Eastern Los Angeles Regional Center	8211	71
Eastern Los Angeles Regional Center For The Developmentally Disabled Inc	8322	12
Eastern Machine and Conveyor Inc	3532	73
Eastern Metal Of Elmira Inc	3993	77
Eastern Michigan Bank	6022	568
Eastern Michigan Financial Corp	6712	325
Eastern Minerals Inc	2879	37
Eastern Molding International LLC	2821	186
Eastern Mountain Sports Inc	5941	22
Eastern National	5942	24
Eastern Oregon Telecom LLC	4813	272
Eastern Packaging Inc	2821	108
Eastern Plating Inc	3471	66
Eastern Region of Supervalu	5141	20
Eastern Sales and Marketing Co	7389	117
Eastern Science Company Inc	3599	1977
Eastern Sheet Metal Inc	3444	125
Eastern Shipbuilding Group Inc	3441	14
Eastern Shore Poultry Company Inc	2015	45
Eastern Shore Seafood Products LLC	2092	30
Eastern Sintered Alloys Inc	3399	37
Eastern Standard Productions Inc	3652	18
Eastern Technology Corp	3829	469
Eastern Telephone and Telecommunications Inc	4813	502
Eastern Time Designs Inc	3825	291
Eastern Tools and Equipment Inc	5049	18
Eastern Virginia Bankshares Inc	6022	149
Eastern Wholesale Fence Company Inc	5039	27
Easter-Owens Electric Co	3643	78
Eastex Laser Corp	5045	1043
Eastex Lumber and Supply Ltd	5031	147
Eastex Telephone Cooperative Inc	4813	185
Eastgate Systems Inc	2741	341
EastGroup-LNH Corp	6798	114
Eastlake Machine Products Inc	3599	985
Eastland Crane Service Inc	7353	85
Eastland Shoe Corp	5139	12
Eastlex Machine Corp	3552	44
Eastman Chemical Co	2821	5
Eastman Gelatine Corp	3861	23
Eastman Kodak Co	3861	2
Eastman-Booth Inc	3469	343
Easton Bancorp Inc	6022	590
Easton Controls Inc	3629	125
Easton Enterprises Inc	1731	1124
Easton Lakes Software	7372	3315
Easton Sports Inc	5091	10
Easton Spring Inc	5149	208
Easton Steel Service Inc	5051	1
Easton Technical Products Inc	3949	86
Easton Transportation Inc	4213	1983
Eastover Capital Management Inc	6282	631
Eastover Group of Cos	6282	124
Eastridge Group	7363	78
Eastside Commercial Bank NA	6021	321
Eastside Machine Company Inc	3599	1962
Eastside Wholesale Supply Co	5023	42
East-West Express Inc	4213	1838
East-West Inc	4213	1395
East-West Label Company Inc	2679	67
East-West Motor Freight Inc	4213	1576
Eastwood Carriers Inc	4213	1436
Eastwood Co	5961	120
Eastwood Construction Company Inc	1521	34
Eastwood Enterprises Inc	3599	652
Eastwood Litho Inc	2759	334
Easy Book Publishing Inc	2741	301
Easy Computer Systems	7373	924
Easy Gardener Products Ltd	2875	2
Easy Graphics Inc	2752	1721
Easy Lawn Inc	3524	34
Easy Print Inc	7334	87
Easy Reader Inc	2711	725
Easy Soft Inc	7372	3641
Easy Technology Inc	5045	564
Easy Way Leisure Corp	2392	16
EasyAsk Inc	7372	3564
Easyfine Asia Ltd	2369	6
EasyLink Services Corp	7375	54
Easylink Services International Corp	7372	288
Easyoffice Network Inc	7379	1458
EasyRun Inc	7372	3505
EasySeat	5999	263
Eat at Joe's Ltd	5812	449
Eatek	3679	827
Eatem Corp	2034	20
Eateries Inc	5812	60
Eaton Corp	3625	1
Eaton Corp Airflex Div	3568	15
Eaton Corp Golf Grip Div	3949	34
Eaton Fabricating Company Inc	3599	986
Eaton Forms Corp	5112	71
Eaton Manufacturing Company Inc	2759	554
Eaton Metal Products Company LLC	3312	38
Eaton Power Quality Group Inc	3629	7
Eaton Truck Components Div	3714	47
Eaton Vance California Municipals Fund	6722	189
Eaton Vance Connecticut Municipals Fund	6722	280
Eaton Vance Corp	6282	43
Eaton Vance Distributors Inc	6211	190
Eaton Vance Government Obligations R Fund	6722	278
Eaton Vance Greater India B	6722	224
Eaton Vance Income Fund of Boston	6722	115
Eaton Vance Limited Duration Income Fund	6722	90
Eaton Vance National Municipals Income B	6722	214
Eatonton Cooperative Feed Company Inc	5191	170
Eau Claire Cooperative Oil Co	8999	152
Eau Claire Press Co	2711	215
EB Bradley Co	5072	10
EB Lane and Associates Inc	7311	180
EB Morris Associates Inc	7389	265
Eb Pipe Coating Inc	3479	71
EB Trottnow Machine Specialties Inc	3599	2087
eB2B Commerce Inc	7372	3185
Ebaa Iron Inc	3321	28
Ebara International Corp	3561	56
eBay Inc	7389	5
Ebbtide Corp	3732	51
EBC Computers LLC	5734	35
Ebel Productions Inc	7812	275
Ebeling Associates Inc	7372	2186
Eberbach Corp	3821	51
Eberhard Architects LLC	8712	318
Eberhard Creamery Inc	2026	75
Eberhard Klemens Company Inc	7372	2674
Ebersole Electric Inc	1731	1964
Eberspaecher North America Inc	8711	252
Ebert Jacques Associates Inc	5065	669
Ebert Machine Company Inc	3599	1957
Ebg LLC	5065	981
EBI LP	3845	38
Ebisons Harounian Imports	5023	123
Ebix Inc	7372	426
eBizAutos	7371	196
Ebl Products Inc	3679	756
EBM-Papst Inc	5084	239
Ebner Furnaces Inc	3567	9
Ebo Group Inc	3568	62
E-Brain Solutions LLC	5045	649

Company Name	SIC	Rank	Company Name	SIC	Rank	Company Name	SIC	Rank
ebrary Inc	7375	100	Ecolab Inc	2841	6	Ed Hicks Imports	5511	535
eBridge Advertising	7311	305	Ecolab Inc Food and Beverage Div	5169	49	ED Industries Inc	3089	1509
Ebro Foods Inc	2032	16	Ecolab Inc Institutional Div	5169	5	Ed Kellum and Son Appliance Co	5731	25
Ebs Auto Electric Inc	7539	21	Ecolab Inc Professional Products Div	5169	27	Ed M Feld Equipment Company Inc	5999	171
EBS IT Solutions	7372	2878	Ecolab Inc Textile Care Div	5087	27	Ed Marling Stores Inc	5722	5
EBSCO Industries Inc	2721	7	Ecolite Manufacturing Co	3446	20	Ed Martin Nissan	5511	1000
EBSCO Publishing	7379	186	eCollegecom	8299	26	Ed - Medical Inc	7352	25
Ebtec Corp	7692	11	Ecologic Transportation Inc	7359	24	Ed Morse Automotive Group	5511	28
Ebtron Inc	3823	119	Ecological Fibers Inc	2679	14	Ed Morse Honda Inc	5511	904
e-Builder Inc	7372	1889	Ecological Laboratories Inc	2899	148	Ed Napleton Honda	5511	685
EBY Holding Co	3678	30	Ecological Linguistics	7372	4057	Ed Necco and Associates Inc	8099	69
Eby-Brown Company LLC	5194	1	Ecological Restoration and Manage-	1611	77	Ed Parker Inc	1542	432
EC Barton and Co	5211	19	ment Inc			Ed Phillips and Sons Co (Fargo North	5182	34
Ec/Edi Inc	4813	581	Ecological Services International Inc	3449	18	Dakota)		
Ec Electric Inc	1731	1256	Ecological Tanks Inc	3589	132	Ed Rinke Chevrolet Inc	5511	559
EC Ernst Inc	1731	303	Ecology and Environment Engnrng PC	8711	35	Ed Rocha Livestock Transportation	4213	1969
EC Kenyon Construction Company Inc	1542	335	Ecology and Environment Inc	8711	86	Ed Shults Chevrolet Inc	5511	489
EC Kitzel and Sons Inc	3545	291	Ecom Partners Inc	4813	709	Ed Stiglic	3599	2051
EC Machining Inc	3599	1758	Ecomass Technologies	3083	88	Ed Thayer Inc	4213	800
EC Morris Corp	2819	110	Ecommerce Inc	4813	245	Ed Voyles Chrysler Jeep Dodge	5511	488
EC Services Inc	4213	2906	Ecommercepartners	7374	213	Ed Voyles Honda	5511	56
EC Shaw Co	3555	76	eCompanyStore	5961	137	Edac Technologies Corp	3724	19
Ec Sourcing Group Inc	7371	1757	Econ-Abrasive Accessories Inc	5085	362	Edal Industries Inc	3679	619
eCaliper	7372	4415	Econo Machine Inc	3599	1996	Edan Naturals LLC	2834	365
eCardio Inc	5047	49	Econo Products Inc	5084	511	Edap Technomed Inc	5049	107
Ecast Inc	7372	1218	Econo' Scope	5065	1011	Edaq Inc	3825	338
ECB Bancorp Inc	6712	339	Econoclast Inc	6282	637	Edaron Inc	3944	28
ECC Capital Corp	6798	67	Econoco Corp	5046	68	Edart Truck Rental Corp	7513	18
Ecco Engineering And Construction	1731	1617	Econ-O-Copy Inc	5044	24	Edashop Inc	7372	2539
Company Inc			Econocorp Inc	3565	78	EDC Consulting LLC	8748	227
Ecco Inc	7322	117	Econocraft Worldwide Manufacturing	3589	263	EDCI Holdings Inc	3663	50
Ecco Select Corp	8742	412	Inc			Edco Inc	3544	281
Eccounting Solutions LLC	7371	1666	Econolite Control Products Inc	3669	81	Edco Supply Corp	3081	113
ECD Systems Inc	7371	658	Econometric Modeling and Computing	7372	4601	Edcor Data Services	7379	278
Ecenbarger Inc	3542	73	Corp			Edcor Electronics Corp	3651	153
ecfirstcom Inc	7372	2616	Econometric Modeling and Computing	6282	573	Edd Helms Group Inc	4911	490
Ecg Industrial Co	5063	753	Economic Analysis Associates Inc			EDD Inc	8711	393
Ecg Management Consultants	7389	1559	Economic Analysis Group Ltd	7372	2280	Eddie Bauer Holdings Inc	5611	6
Echelbarger Himebaugh Tamm and Co	8721	173	Economic Insight Inc	2741	390	Eddie Bauer LLC	5611	7
Echelon Corp	3577	106	Economic Modeling Specialists Inc	7371	910	Eddington Industries LLC	5074	208
Echelon Development LLC	6552	276	Economic Opportunity Committee Of St	8322	169	Eddington Thread Manufacturing	2284	3
Echo Appellate Press Inc	2752	1824	Clair County Inc			Company Inc		
Echo Commercial Printing Inc	2759	264	Economic Plastic Coating Inc	3479	90	Eddins Electric Company Inc	1611	134
Echo Communications Inc	2752	1545	Economic Research Institute Inc	7372	1543	Eddy Packing Company Inc	2011	32
Echo Design Group Inc	5137	10	Economic Research Services Inc	7389	251	Edelbrock Corp	3714	63
Echo Global Logistics Inc	8744	5	Economist Intelligence Unit	2741	52	Edelman	8743	7
Echo Imaging Inc	5045	981	Economos Properties Inc	8741	150	Edelman Financial Group Inc	6211	181
Echo Lake Foods Inc	2043	5	Economy Bar and Restaurant Supply	5046	359	Edelmann Scott Inc	7311	545
Echo Molding Inc	3089	1189	Inc			Edelson Technology Partners	6799	217
Echo Mountain Realty Inc	3663	185	Economy Cash and Carry Inc	5141	145	Edelweis Cheese Company Inc	2022	66
Echo Therapeutics Inc	3845	130	Economy Copier Service Inc	3661	231	Edelweiss Townhall Cheese	2022	84
EchoData Group	3695	30	Economy Folding Box Corp	2657	42	Edemco Dryers Inc	3634	33
Echolab Inc	3613	104	Economy Forms Corp	3441	22	Eden Cryogenics LLC	3559	251
EchoMail Inc	7372	739	Economy Locker Storage Company Inc	5147	95	Eden Oil Company Inc	5172	68
Echometer Co	3829	339	Economy Paper Company of	5111	26	Eden Processing Inc	2064	140
Echopass Corp	5045	154	Rochester			Eden Stone Company Inc	1411	3
Echostar Corp	3663	6	Economy Pencil Company Inc	3993	173	Edens Bank	6022	663
Eci Technology Inc	3826	113	Economy Printing Co	2761	59	Edens Distributing Company Inc	4213	711
Ecircuits LLC	3559	243	Economy Printing Company Inc	2752	1442	Edgar A Weber and Co	2087	73
Eck and Eck Machine Company Inc	3728	166	Economy Tank Co	3589	249	EDGAR Inc	7372	3705
Eck Enterprises Inc	5063	40	Economy Wiring Company Inc	1731	2088	Edgar Lomax Co	6282	394
Eck Industries Inc	3363	19	Econotek LLC	4813	509	EDGAR Online Inc	7389	568
Eck Plastic Arts Inc	3089	1541	EconRam Systems	5099	148	Edgar's Old Style Bakery	5461	28
Eck Supply Co	5063	89	Econtactlive Inc	7389	1141	Edge Access Inc	5045	226
Eckel Industries Inc	3296	14	E-Convergence Solutions LLC	5734	94	Edge Electronics Inc	5065	988
Eckel Manufacturing Company Inc	3533	52	Eco-Products Inc	2679	15	Edge Entertainment Distribution	5065	46
Eckert and Ziegler Isotope Products	3829	38	eCopy Inc	7372	703	Edge Films	7819	87
Inc			Ecoquest Manufacturing Inc	3634	12	Edge Industries Inc	3559	578
Eckert Enterprises Ltd	3599	2061	Ecora Corp	7372	1213	Edge Manufacturing Inc	3541	75
Eckert Trucking Inc	4213	1426	eCorp Inc	7379	368	Edge Mechanical Inc	3822	74
Eckhart and Associates	3559	131	Ecorse Machinery Sales and Rebuild-	3491	53	Edge Plastics Inc	3089	341
Eckhart and Company Inc	2782	33	ers Inc			Edge Products Inc (Ogden Utah)	3694	22
Ecklund-Harrison Technologies Inc	3829	456	Ecosea Adventure Inc	5045	769	EDGE Software Services Inc	7372	1890
Eckman Construction Inc	1542	346	EcoSphere Associates Ltd	8731	393	Edge Systems LLC	7372	2098
Eckroat Seed Co	5191	171	Ecosystem Inc	6531	457	Edge Technologies Inc	7372	994
Eck's Garage Inc	5012	92	Ecotality Inc	3621	104	Edge World	3571	67
Eclaro International Inc	7361	154	EcoTech Marine	5999	198	Edgecombe-Martin County Electric	4911	481
eClinicalWorks	7371	94	Ecova Inc (Spokane Washington)	7372	166	Membership Corp		
Eclinicalworks LLC	7371	79	Ecozone Inc	3559	319	Edgecraft Corp	3634	16
Eclipse Aerospace	3728	40	Ecp American Steel LLC	5051	235	Edgell Enterprises Inc	2721	218
Eclipse Capital Management Inc	6282	620	Ecp Corp	3469	242	Edgen Murray Ltd	3498	2
Eclipse Computing Inc	7372	4150	ECP Inc	2851	55	Edgeone LLC	3826	65
Eclipse Consulting Inc	7371	906	ECP Tech Services Inc	5063	467	Edge-Rite Tools Inc	3544	852
Eclipse Data Technologies	7372	3296	Ecr International Inc	3433	18	Edgerton Corp	5045	555
Eclipse Inc	3433	14	ECRI Institute	7372	1236	Edgerton/Irium Americas Inc	5734	320
Eclipse Lighting Inc	3646	67	ECRM Inc	3577	150	Edgetek Machine Corp	3541	72
Eclipse Manufacturing Co	3469	159	ECS Incorporated International	3679	23	Edgewater Manufacturing Company Inc	3451	116
Eclipse Marketing Group	3679	120	ECS International Inc	5063	897	Edgewater Networks Inc	5045	290
Eclipse Media	7379	1477	ECS Manufacturing Inc	3542	115	Edgewater Technology Inc	7373	110
Eclipse Messenger Service	7389	2025	ECS Prepaid LLC	6099	27	Edgewise Media Services Inc	5043	26
Eclipse Products Inc	3089	1720	ECT Inc	2842	74	Edgewood Fire Protection District	7389	1918
Ecliptek Inc	3679	426	Ect Technologies LLC	7371	1680	Edgewood Locker Inc	0751	13
Eclypse International Corp	3825	184	Ectaco Inc	5065	182	Edgil Associates Inc	7372	3665
Ecm Electronics	3357	77	Ector Drum Inc	5085	417	Edhard Corp	3599	1092
Ecm Enterprises Inc	1731	1369	Ectron Corp	3829	126	EDI Communications Corp	7372	4602
Ecm Photo Tooling Inc	3599	1868	Ecutel Systems Inc	5045	259	EDI Integration Corp	7372	4603
Ecm Plastics Inc	3089	522	Ed and Don's Of Hawaii Inc	2064	42	EDI Support Inc	7371	1078
ECM Publishers Forest Lake	2711	234	Ed Bertholet And Associates Inc	7389	1583	eDial Inc	5045	231
Ecm Publishers Inc	2711	199	Ed Braswell and Sons Inc	1623	418	e-Dialog	7319	25
Eco Safe Systems USA Inc	3589	256	Ed Bullard Co	3842	91	Edibar Systems Inc	7372	4225
ECO2 Plastics Inc	4959	20	Ed Cyber	3695	136	Edible Arrangements LLC	2038	11
ECOA Industrial Products Inc	3537	44	Ed Dang's Machine Works Inc	3599	1748	EDICT Systems Inc	7372	3445
Ecoair Corp	8731	262	ED Etnyre and Co	3531	18	eDietscom Inc	7299	21
Ecocion Inc	8748	280	Ed Fagan Inc	5051	392	eDigital Corp	7373	1021
			Ed Garvey And Co	2752	287			

Company Name	SIC	Rank
EDI-Health Group Inc	7372	1023
Edimax Computer Co	3577	126
Edinboro Molding Inc	3089	1886
Edinburg Fixture and Machine Inc	3599	2301
Edinger Engineering Inc	8711	627
Edison Chouest Offshore Inc	4499	2
Edison Control Corp	3531	63
Edison Controls Fci Inc	3625	352
Edison Design Group Inc	7372	3069
Edison Electric Inc	1731	1412
Edison Foard Inc	1541	242
Edison Industrial Systems Center	8711	516
Edison International	4911	7
Edison Mission Energy	4939	1
Edison Mission Group Inc	4931	46
Edison Mission Marketing and Trading Inc	4911	167
Edison Pharmaceuticals Inc	8731	331
Edison Price Lighting Inc	3646	28
Edison Schools Inc	8299	5
Edisto Electric Cooperative Inc	8999	47
Edit Point Video of Central New York Inc	7812	289
Editor and Publisher Company Inc	2711	340
Editorial Experts Inc	2721	379
Editorial Projects In Education Inc	2711	344
Editors Press Inc	2789	47
Edj Enterprises Inc	7371	1538
Edjean Technical Services Inc	3569	297
Ed-K Machine Inc	3444	240
EDL Packaging Engineers Inc	5084	459
Edlen Electrical Exhibition Services Inc	1731	720
EDLON Inc	3479	55
Edlong Corp	2087	38
EDM Supplies Inc	3624	22
Edman Corp	5093	23
Edmar Inc	5046	316
Edmar Manufacturing Inc	3469	216
Edmark Auto Inc	5511	358
Edmeades LLC	2084	122
Edmik Inc	3545	175
Edmond Public Schools	8211	15
Edmonds Dental Prosthetics Inc	8072	8
Edmondson Allen H Electrical Contractor	1731	1830
Edmore Tool and Grinding Inc	3599	1570
Edmund Jung and Associates Inc	7371	1448
Edmund Optical Manufacturing LLC	3827	60
Edmunds Manufacturing Co	3542	37
Edna Valley Vineyard	2084	44
Edna West Associates Ltd	1731	139
Edner Corp	2051	231
edocs Inc	7372	2330
Edom Laboratories Inc	5122	74
Edon Controls Inc	3625	368
Edon Corp	3089	670
eDoorways Corp	7389	2515
Edos Manufacturer's Representatives Inc	5074	199
EDP Computer Systems	5045	841
EDP System Services Inc	7372	4373
EDR Corp	7812	173
EDR Electronics Inc	3625	402
Edris Plastics Manufacturing Inc	3089	1459
Edro Corp	3582	17
Edro Engineering Inc	3544	87
Eds Corp	7374	277
Eds Enterprises Inc	7389	2045
EDS Manufacturing Inc	3679	84
Ed's Mower and Saw Shoppe Inc	5251	56
Ed's Supply Company Inc	5075	72
Edsal Manufacturing Company Inc	2599	4
Edstrom Industries Inc	3523	88
Education America Inc	8222	1
Education Center Inc	2721	209
Education Development Center Inc	8733	12
Education Lending Group Inc	6141	21
Education Management Corp	8221	2
Education Networks Of America Inc	4813	333
Education Realty Trust Inc	6798	138
Education Systems Inc	7372	878
Education World Inc	4813	651
Educational Activities Inc	7812	299
Educational Alliance Inc	8399	13
Educational Credit Business Inc	8721	219
Educational Data Systems Inc	7379	580
Educational Development Corp	5192	21
Educational Enhancements Inc	8748	440
Educational Equity Concepts Inc	8748	441
Educational Furnishings Of Arizona LLC	5021	172
Educational Insights Inc	3944	18
Educational Learning Systems Inc	5734	185
Educational Outfitters LP	6794	138
Educational Service Unit 9	8299	57
Educational Services Inc	8299	60
Educational Technology Consultants International	4899	202
Educational Technology Inc	3669	279
EducationDynamics LLC	7375	190
Educators Credit Union	6062	18
Educor International Inc	5046	342
EduSelf Multimedia Publishers Inc	2741	221
EduTrades Inc	8299	24

Company Name	SIC	Rank
Eduware Inc	5734	345
Edw C Levy Co	3273	19
Edward A Berg and Sons	5145	13
Edward A Sherman Publishing Co	2711	374
Edward C Smyers Co	5075	110
Edward Don and Co	5087	3
Edward Enterprises Inc	2752	862
Edward F Bauer	3599	2472
Edward Ferrell Lewis Mittman	2512	63
Edward Fields Inc	2273	31
Edward George Co	5039	23
Edward Hine Co	2752	1819
Edward Hines Lumber Co	5031	87
Edward Jones Ltd	6211	23
Edward Joy Co	1711	113
Edward Kraemer and Sons Inc	1611	184
Edward O Thorp and Associates LP	6282	391
Edward P Boutross Inc	5023	190
Edward Rose Building Enterprises	1522	10
Edward S Babcock and Sons Inc	8734	87
Edward Segal Inc	3559	364
Edward Speir Enterprises Inc	7372	1525
Edward Technology Group Inc	7378	113
Edward Tyler Nahem Fine Art	5999	44
Edward W Daniel Co	3452	24
Edward W Face Company Inc	8748	379
Edward White and Co	8721	61
Edwards and Associates Inc	3728	24
Edwards and Cromwell Manufacturing Inc	2891	127
Edwards and Kelcey Inc	8711	122
Edwards Answering Service Inc	7389	2400
Edwards Automotive Inc	5511	1172
Edwards Brothers Inc	2732	8
Edwards Chevrolet Company Inc	5511	245
Edwards Consulting	8721	350
Edwards Cos	6552	195
Edwards Creative Products Inc	2842	178
Edwards Creative Services LLC	7336	161
Edwards Engineering Corp	3594	19
Edwards Engineering Inc	1711	90
Edwards Equipment Sales Inc	5084	799
Edwards Federal Credit Union	6061	138
Edwards Fiberglass Inc	3089	1477
Edwards George D Electric Company Inc	1731	1673
Edwards Graphic Arts Inc	2752	395
Edwards Lifesciences Asset Management Corp	8731	25
Edwards Lifesciences Corp	3841	15
Edwards Lifesciences Financing LLC	8731	17
Edwards Lifesciences Japan Holdings Inc	8731	4
Edwards Lifesciences LLC	8731	18
Edwards Lifesciences US Inc	8731	19
Edwards Lifesciences World Trade Corp	8731	20
Edwards Ltd	3563	3
Edwards Lumber Company Inc	5031	433
Edwards Machining Inc	3599	1752
Edwards Major Electronics Supply Corp	5065	903
Edwards Manufacturing Co	3549	46
Edwards Moving and Rigging Inc	4213	2759
Edwards Scott Electronics Inc	3679	820
Edwards Subaru Hyundai	5511	774
Edwards Telecommunications Inc	1623	177
Edwards Transportation Co	4213	2014
Edwards/Wilmington Inc	1623	239
Edwards Wood Products Inc	2448	13
Edwin B Stimpson Company Inc	3452	39
Edwin F Kalmus Company Inc	2741	322
Edwin Hardy Trucking Inc	4213	2875
Edwin J Mckenica and Sons Inc	3599	1437
Edwin Schlossberg Inc	7389	1025
EE Forbes and Sons Piano Company Inc	5736	15
EE Newcomer Enterprises Inc	5031	34
EE Schenck Co	5131	13
EE Ward Moving and Storage Co	4214	8
EE Zimmerman Co	5169	89
Eei Global Inc	7389	832
EEI Holding Corp	1623	29
Eemax Inc	3639	17
Eemus Manufacturing Corp	3479	108
EES Companies Inc	7372	2675
Eezer Products Inc	2821	190
EF Britten and Company Inc	3443	239
EF Johnson Technologies Inc	4812	28
EF Precision Inc	3599	400
EF Technologies Inc	3548	67
EF Transit Inc	4213	910
EF Wall and Associates Inc	1541	117
EFA Technologies Inc	3599	76
Efacec Acs Inc	3571	84
eFashion Solutions LLC	2331	8
EFAX Corp	7372	3264
Effective Graphics Inc	2796	26
Effective UI Inc	8999	85
Efficiency Bindery Inc	2789	123
Efficiency Production Inc	3531	78
Efficient Machine Products Corp	3451	101
Effingham Automotive Warehouse Inc	5013	359

Company Name	SIC	Rank
Effingham Equity	2048	11
EFG Software Inc	7372	4685
EFI Electronics Corp	3679	255
EFI Georgia	3577	271
EFILM	7819	34
Efinger Sporting Goods Co	5091	62
Efird Chrysler Jeep Dodge Inc	5511	975
EFM Corp	3544	104
EFM Group Inc	2752	1257
eForce Inc	3577	82
Efp Corp	3086	24
Eft Corp	3679	604
Eftec NA LLC	2891	77
EFTEC North America LLC	8731	146
EG and G Defense Materials Inc	4953	53
EG Bowman Company Inc	6331	273
EG Plastics LLC	5093	124
EG Systems LLC	3559	69
EGads LLC	3993	27
eGAIN Communications Corp	7372	761
eGames Inc	7372	3099
Egan Co	1711	24
Egan Healthcare Services Inc	8082	55
Egan Mechanical Contractors Inc	1711	6
Egan-McKay Electrical Contractors Inc	1731	201
EGB Systems and Solutions Inc	7371	1288
Egc Enterprises Inc	2891	75
EGC Media Group Inc	7311	262
Egenera Inc	3571	39
Egenolf Machine Inc	1796	15
Eger Health Care and Rehabilitation Center	8051	49
Eger Products Inc	3089	550
Egerstrom Inc	5141	232
Egg Strategy	7389	612
Egge Machine Co	5013	247
Egger Steel Co	3441	158
Eggers Industries Inc	2431	11
Eggers Industries Inc Neenah Div	3442	26
Egging Co	3523	71
Eggland's Best Inc	0252	10
EgglestonWorks LLC	3651	142
Egide USA Inc	3679	314
Egizii Electric Inc	1731	53
Egli Machine Company Inc	3545	272
E-Glue USA Inc	5045	308
EGPI Firecreek Inc	1382	77
EGS Electrical Group LLC	3644	2
Egt Printing Solutions LLC	2752	193
Egypt Farms Inc	2875	39
Egypt Star Inc	2051	186
EH Hamilton Trkg and Wholesale Service	4213	397
EH Higgins and Son Inc	5812	450
EH Packing LLC	7389	680
EH SofSolutions Inc	7372	2625
EH Walker Supply Company Inc	5084	726
eHarmonycom Inc	8399	11
eHealth Inc	6411	76
Ehlert Publishing Group	2721	354
Ehlert Publishing Group Inc	2721	249
Ehm Holdings Inc	5093	120
Ehob Inc	3842	131
EHR3 and Associates Inc	7372	3995
Ehrenkrantz King Nussbaum Inc	6282	114
EI Associates	8712	83
EI du Pont de Nemours and Co	2819	2
EI du Pont de Nemours and Co Specialty Fibers Div	2824	1
EI Microcircuits	3069	33
EIA Inc	7373	364
Eic Solutions Inc	3585	183
EIC Systems Inc	3625	148
Eichelberger Construction Inc	1542	51
Eichenauer Inc	3634	32
Eichhorn Printing Inc	2752	1794
Eichleay Engineers Incorporated of California	8711	164
Eickman's Processing Company Inc	2011	140
Eid Passport Inc	7382	48
Eid-Co Buildings Inc	1521	142
Eide Bailly LLP	8721	9
Eide Industries Inc	2394	17
Eidelman Associates	7372	2879
Eidogen and Sertanty Inc	7371	1312
Eidos Interactive Inc	7372	360
Eidschun Engineering Inc	3559	302
Eidson and Ussery Inc	4213	2467
Eiffel Software	8711	390
Eifrid Systems Development	7372	2711
Eiger Machinery Inc	3541	266
Eight Crossings Inc	7389	1472
Eighth Floor Promotions LLC	3993	52
Eihab Human Services Inc	8322	79
Eii Inc	1731	70
Eikenberry and Associates Inc	3089	829
Eikenberrys Super Value Inc	5411	250
Eikenhout and Sons Inc	5033	10
Eiki International Inc	3861	27
Eileen West	2335	11
Eilen and Sons Trucking	4213	738
Eilenberger Baking Co	2051	135
Eilers Machine and Welding Inc	3441	202
Eimont Capital Group LLC	7389	650

Company Name	SIC	Rank
EIMS Ltd	5734	80
eInfochips Inc	7373	84
Einhorn Yaffee Prescott Architecture and Engineering PC	8712	35
Einstein Noah Restaurant Group Inc	5812	110
eInstruction Corp	2741	130
Eip Manufacturing LLC	3441	185
eIQnetworks Inc	7372	2334
Eire Ltd	5162	68
Eirich Machines Inc	3556	43
Eis Data Systems Inc	5045	577
Eisai Inc	2834	39
Eisbrenner Public Relations Inc	8743	179
Eisenhauer Nissan-Saab	5511	793
Eisenman Transportation Services	4213	2907
Eisenmann Corp	8711	500
Eisner and Lubin LLP	8721	138
Eisner Associates Inc	7372	3380
Eison Group Inc	5085	281
e-IT Professionals Corp	7361	180
Eitel Presses Inc	3542	118
EIZO Nanao Technologies Inc	5045	215
EJ Conrad and Sons Seafood Inc	2092	75
EJ Footwear Corp	3143	16
EJ Houle Inc	2048	37
Eja International	5063	921
Ejay Filtration Inc	3496	95
EJM Development Co	6552	133
Ejrex Inc	2752	502
EK Hydraulics Inc	5084	909
EK Machine Company Inc	3444	144
E-K Media Inc	3695	113
Ekagra Software Technologies Ltd	7372	3395
eKairecom Inc	7389	361
Ekato Corp	5084	299
EKCO Metals	5093	26
Ekk Inc	7371	1118
Eklips Enterprises Inc	1751	8
Eklund Appliance and TV	5731	90
Ekos Corp	3841	159
Ek-Ris Cable Company Inc	3643	88
Ekstrom Electric Inc	1731	2297
Ekstrom Industries Inc	3643	53
Ektelon	3949	57
Ektron Inc	7372	1063
Ekuber Ventures Inc	7379	1634
El Alteno Foods Inc	2032	41
El Burrito Market Inc	5411	261
El Burrito Mexican Food Products Inc	2099	247
El Cajon Ford	5511	359
El Camino Machine and Welding LLC	3599	1107
El Camino Resources International Inc	7377	1
El Camino Systems Inc	7379	791
El Campo Machine and Repair Inc	3599	1449
El Centro Foods Inc	6794	133
El Cerrito Lighting Inc	5063	1006
El Chico Restaurants Inc	5812	220
El Crepusculo Inc	2711	551
El Dorado Furniture Co	5712	37
El Dorado Paper Bag Manufacturing Company Inc	2674	11
El Dorado Printing and Stationery Company Inc	5943	35
El Dorado Savings Bank	6036	21
El Dorado Softworld	7372	5061
El Dorado Trading Group Inc	7378	120
El Encanto Inc	2038	32
EL Farmer and Co	4213	1589
El Gallo Giro Inc	5812	349
EL Hamm Associates Inc	8742	149
EL Harley Inc	3555	126
EL Harvey and Sons Inc	4953	88
EL Hollingsworth Group Inc	4213	419
El Jay Poultry Corp	8741	194
El Lago Tortillas Inc	2099	81
El Merendero Posas Inc	2041	60
El Mirasol Inc	2099	191
El Molino Winery	2084	108
El Monte Plastics Company Inc	3089	689
El Paso ARC Electric Inc	1731	837
El Paso ASC LP	8011	153
El Paso Communication Systems Inc	5065	275
El Paso Corp	4922	1
El Paso Electric Co	4911	83
El Paso Mailing Service Inc	7331	272
El Paso Natural Gas Co	4922	10
El Paso Press/Box Inc	2657	24
EL Payne Co	1711	216
El Pollo Loco Inc	5812	148
El Popocatapetl Industries Inc	2099	156
El Tapatio Market	2099	168
El Toro Meat Packing Corp	5147	104
El Tortillero LLC	2099	190
Elahi Enterprises Inc	7311	1012
Elaine Inc	3569	288
Elaine Lewis Ltd	7389	1794
Elam Sand and Gravel Corp	1442	39
Elan Chateau Resorts LLC	2084	20
Elan Chemical Co	2087	53
Elan Computer Group Inc	7372	3528
Elan Development LP	6552	218
Elan Gmk Inc	7371	1753
Elan Holdings Inc	2834	42
Elan Pharmaceuticals	8731	13
Elan Publishing Company Inc	2731	274
Elan Technology Inc	3231	46
Elan Trading Inc	5093	184
ELance Inc	7379	203
Elanders Seiz Inc	2752	475
Elandia International Inc	4813	84
Elan-Polo International	5139	5
Elasco Inc	2821	83
Elastic Creative	2741	113
Elastic Fabrics of America Inc	2258	3
Elastic Therapy LLC	3842	110
Elbe-Cesco Inc	2675	11
Elbeco Inc	2326	5
El-Bee Receivables Corp	5311	41
Elberta Crate and Box Co	2448	5
Elbex Corp	3061	23
Elbex Industrial Supplies LLC	3441	276
Elbit Systems of America LLC	3672	214
ELC Technologies	7371	464
Elcam Tool and Die Inc	3399	31
Elcan Optical Technologies	3861	35
Elco Corp	2869	67
Elco Electric	1731	1752
Elco Electric Service Corp	1731	2361
Elco Fastening Systems LLC	3452	11
Elco Laboratories Inc	2842	77
elcom Inc	7372	1435
Elcom Industries Inc	3699	270
Elcom International Inc	7371	1009
Elcom Services Group Inc	7379	33
Elcon Inc (San Jose California)	3599	393
Elcon Technologies Inc	8711	606
Elcor Inc	3694	46
Elcoteq Inc	3672	48
ELDEC Corp	3679	87
Elden Enterprises	5043	45
Elder Automotive Group	5511	58
Elder Care Services Inc	8361	4
Elder Construction Company Inc	1541	270
Elder Equipment Leasing Of Wyoming	5012	141
Elder Ford Inc	5511	607
Elder Ford of Tampa	5511	397
Elder Hosiery Mills Inc	2252	28
Elder Manufacturing Company Inc	2321	12
Elder Wood Preserving Company Inc	2491	11
Elder-Beerman Holdings Inc	5311	42
Elder-Beerman Indiana LP	5311	43
Elder-Beerman Operations LLC	5311	44
Elder-Beerman Operations LLC	5311	26
Elderlee Inc	3312	57
Elderly Home Health Care Inc	8082	94
Eldex Laboratories Inc	3826	152
Eldon	3089	107
Eldora Plastics Inc	3089	1243
Eldorado Artesian Springs Inc	5149	136
ElDorado National California Inc	3716	9
ElDorado National Kansas Inc	3716	8
Eldredge Lumber and Hardware Inc	5031	103
Eldridge Acrylics Inc	5023	208
Eldridge Electric and Son Inc	1731	1890
Eldridge Products Inc	3823	264
Eleanor Ettinger Inc	2731	318
Elearning Media Inc	4833	251
Eleccomm Corp	1623	414
Elecom Supply Co	5065	951
Elecsys Corp	3679	185
Elecsys International Corp	3625	69
Elect General Contractors Inc	1731	1244
Elec-Tec Inc	3679	337
Electec Norcal LLC	5065	459
Elec-Tech Electrical Services Inc	1731	1103
Election Data Direct Inc	3579	56
Election Systems and Software Inc	3577	206
Electra - Cord Inc	3699	136
Electramatic Inc	3679	366
Electrasem Corp	3822	81
Electraserve Inc	7382	128
ElectraSoft	7372	4604
Electra-Sound Inc	7622	2
Electrex Company Inc	1731	527
Electrex Inc	3694	23
Electric and Machine Services Inc	7692	53
Electric Apparatus Co	3621	106
Electric Battery Company LLC	5063	628
Electric Cable Compounds Inc	3087	16
Electric Car Company Inc	3621	152
Electric Contractors Inc	1731	668
Electric Control and Supply Inc	5063	825
Electric Controls And Systems Inc	1731	470
Electric Controls Co	3613	105
Electric Eel Manufacturing Company Inc	3423	59
Electric Equipment and Engineering Co	3613	101
Electric Factory Concerts Inc	7922	61
Electric Fixture and Supply Co	5063	216
Electric Furnace Co	3567	19
Electric Industries Corp	3647	19
Electric Lightwave Inc	4813	82
Electric Machinery Enterprises Inc	1731	62
Electric Maintenance And Construction Inc	1731	517
Electric Masters Service Inc	1731	2452
Electric Materials Co	3351	14
Electric Metal Fab Inc	3312	128
Electric Metering Corporation USA	3825	137
Electric Motor and Supply Inc	7694	9
Electric Motor Repair Co	7699	39
Electric Motor Rewind Inc	3621	136
Electric Motor Rewind Of Rupert Idaho Inc	5063	784
Electric Motor Sales And Supply Company Inc	5063	151
Electric Motor Sales Inc	5063	1020
Electric Motor Service Inc	5063	583
Electric Motors And Specialties Inc	3621	76
Electric Parts and Service Co	5063	967
Electric Picture Display Systems Inc	3651	160
Electric Power Equipment Co	3613	130
Electric Pump and Tool Service Inc	5063	212
Electric Resource Contractors Inc	1731	198
Electric Service Company Inc	7629	32
Electric Service Group Inc	1731	1023
Electric Service Of Clinton Inc	1731	675
Electric Speed Indicator Co	3829	454
Electric Supply and Equipment Co	5063	136
Electric Supply Company Inc	1731	889
Electric Supply Co (Raleigh North Carolina)	5063	661
Electric Supply Connection Inc	5063	559
Electric Switches Premier	5063	344
Electric Systems Of Duluth Inc	1731	2082
Electric Time Company Inc	3873	19
Electric Vine Inc	7371	1493
Electric Word Inc	7374	394
Electrical And Communications Services Inc	1731	2471
Electrical and Electronics Controls Inc	5065	383
Electrical And Instrumentation Unlimited Inc	1731	150
Electrical and Lighting Incorporated of Virginia A/K/A ELI Inc	1731	2495
Electrical and Mechanical Resources Inc	3621	134
Electrical and Mechanical Systems Inc	1731	1665
Electrical Construction Co	1731	42
Electrical Construction Management Inc	1731	1643
Electrical Contracting Services LLC	1731	1399
Electrical Contractors Inc	1731	1787
Electrical Controls And Maintenance Inc	1731	423
Electrical Controls Inc	3613	152
Electrical Design and Motor Control Inc	1731	1298
Electrical Distributing Inc	5064	26
Electrical Distribution Services Inc	5063	326
Electrical Distributors Co	5063	76
Electrical Dynamics Inc	1731	627
Electrical Engineering And Equipment Co	5063	49
Electrical Fasteners Company Inc	5085	216
Electrical Installations Inc	3613	71
Electrical Instrument Service Inc	3825	279
Electrical Insulation Suppliers Inc	5063	72
Electrical Line Services Inc	1623	612
Electrical Manufacturing and Distributors Inc	7371	1046
Electrical Power and Controls Inc	5065	440
Electrical Power Products Inc	3625	84
Electrical Power Products Of SC Inc	5063	371
Electrical Production Services Inc	1731	1214
Electrical Representatives West	5063	976
Electrical Sales Corp	1731	1589
Electrical Services Ltd	1731	1152
Electrical Solutions LLC	1731	1803
Electrical South Inc	7629	5
Electrical Supplies Unlimited Inc	5063	705
Electrical Systems and Solutions Inc	1731	1723
Electrical Systems Inc	1731	2313
Electrical Systems International LLC	5063	668
Electrical Technologies Inc	1731	2249
Electrical Technology Inc	1731	2409
Electrical Wholesale Supply Company Inc	5063	162
Electrical Work Inc	1731	2460
Electrical-Mechanical Drives Inc	5063	522
Electricians Inc	1731	218
Electricity and Lighting Inc	1731	802
Electrico Inc	1731	105
Electri-Cord Manufacturing Co	3699	72
Electrified Discounters Inc	5046	32
Electri-Flex Co	3644	8
Electri-Products Group Inc	5063	620
Electri-Tec Electrical Construction Inc	1731	555
Electri-Tec Investor Group Inc	3679	566
Electri-Tech Inc	1731	1520
Electrivert Inc	3643	83
Electrix Company Inc	1731	1788
Electrix Inc	3646	45
Electrnic Integration Inc	3629	78
Electro Acoustics and Video Inc	1731	903
Electro Adapter Inc	3643	51
Electro Arc Manufacturing Co	3541	148
Electro Assembly Source Inc	3674	503
Electro Brand Inc	5064	52
Electro Chemical Finishing Co	3471	24
Electro Circuits Corp	3672	271
Electro Circuits International LLC	3672	461
Electro Design Inc	1731	1260

Company Name	SIC	Rank
Electro Illumination and Design Inc	1731	709
Electro Impulse Laboratory Inc	3585	156
Electro Inc	3625	168
Electro Industries Inc	3822	22
Electro Lift Inc	3536	39
Electro Magnetic Products Inc	3544	380
Electro Maintenance Inc	1731	1303
Electro Management Inc	1731	21
Electro Mechanical Assembly Inc	3672	486
Electro Mechanical Engineering Corp	8711	647
Electro Mechanical Services Inc	3821	82
Electro Medical Equipment Co	3841	237
Electro National Corp	3672	239
Electro Optics Manufacturing Inc	3469	379
Electro Plate Circuitry Inc	3672	181
Electro Power Systems Of Utah	3679	632
Electro Products Inc	3823	242
Electro Rent Corp	7359	30
Electro Rent Corporation Data Rentals/ Sales Div	7377	4
Electro Sales Company Inc	3621	56
Electro Scientific Industries Inc	3699	18
Electro Seal Corp	3398	16
Electro Soft Inc	3672	291
Electro Standards Laboratory Inc	3661	137
Electro Steam Generator Corp	3569	224
Electro Surface Technologies	3672	236
Electro Switch Corp	3643	24
Electro Systems Electric Inc	1731	1903
Electro Technik Industries	3677	46
Electrocard Inc	3672	476
Electro-Ceramic Industries	3264	22
Electrochem Commercial Power	3692	6
Electro-Circuits Inc	3672	282
Electrocom Midwest Sales Inc	3643	158
Electro-Communications Co	1731	594
Electrocon International Inc	7372	3706
Electro-Connect Inc	3679	621
Electro-Core Inc	3679	364
ElectroCraft Arkansas	3621	41
Electrocraft New Hampshire Inc	3621	84
Electrocube Inc	3679	148
Electrodata Inc	3825	186
Electrodes Inc	5084	361
Electrodex Inc	3645	77
Electrodyn Choke Corp	3714	333
Electrodynamics Inc	3873	15
Electrofilm Manufacturing Company LLC	3699	125
Electro-Fix Inc	3825	217
Electro-Flex Heat Inc	3433	30
Electroglas Foreign Sales Corp	3559	38
Electroglas International Inc	3559	44
Electro-Hydraulic Automation Inc	3569	192
Electrol Specialties Co	3613	112
Electrol Systems Inc	5063	834
Electrol Wire Harness Company Inc	3679	286
Electrolab Inc	3625	202
Electroline Corp	3423	75
Electro-Line Inc	5065	192
Electrolux Home Products	3633	2
Electrolux International	5064	20
Electrolux Vacuum Cleaners and Polishers	5064	156
Electromatic Equipment Company Inc	5084	882
Electro-Matic Products Co	3625	295
Electro-Matic Products Inc	5063	93
Electromax Inc	3672	196
Electro-Mechanical Components Inc	3643	82
Electro-Mechanical Corp	3612	21
Electro-Mechanical Specialties Inc	3599	867
Electro-Mechanical Systems Group Inc	7694	31
Electro-Mechanisms Inc	3679	201
Electromed Inc	3845	65
Electro-Methods Inc	3724	33
Electro-Miniatures Corp	3621	80
Electro-Motive Diesel Inc	3519	3
Electromotive Inc	3679	831
Electron Beam Technologies Inc	3548	35
Electron Coil Inc	3621	93
Electron Factory Inc	7374	386
Elec-Tron Inc	3644	32
Electron Solar Energy	5074	215
Electron Technologies Corp	7389	1234
Electroneering Inc	3625	397
Electronic Arts Inc	7372	13
Electronic Assembly Services Inc	3672	400
Electronic Auto Systems Inc	3651	167
Electronic Billboard Technology Inc	3993	117
Electronic Cable Specialists Inc	3699	23
Electronic Cabling and Assembly Inc	3496	106
Electronic Cash Systems Inc	7389	185
Electronic Check Services	7389	676
Electronic Communications Inc	3672	467
Electronic Compliance Management Inc	7379	1114
Electronic Components and Equipment	5065	280
Electronic Components and Services Inc	3672	338
Electronic Components Inc	5065	755
Electronic Concepts And Engineering Inc	3672	405
Electronic Concepts Inc	3675	22
Electronic Connection Corp	3679	733

Company Name	SIC	Rank
Electronic Connector Service Inc	3643	96
Electronic Connectors Inc	3679	664
Electronic Consulting Services Inc	7373	446
Electronic Contract Assemblers Inc	3672	469
Electronic Control Security Inc	3669	204
Electronic Controlled Systems Inc	3679	373
Electronic Controls Co	3714	240
Electronic Controls Design Inc	3823	282
Electronic Corporate Pages Inc	7379	1492
Electronic Data Care	7373	471
Electronic Data Carriers Inc	4212	27
Electronic Data Collection Corp	7371	1313
Electronic Data Devices Co	3533	110
Electronic Data Magnetics Inc	2752	445
Electronic Decontamination Specialists	7374	265
Electronic Design and Manufacturing Co	3672	194
Electronic Design and Packaging Company Inc	3812	167
Electronic Design and Research Inc	3823	331
Electronic Design and Sales Inc	3677	31
Electronic Design Co	3669	102
Electronic Design Group Inc	5731	205
Electronic Development Laboratories Inc	3823	234
Electronic Devices Inc	3825	304
Electronic Directory Systems Inc	3663	373
Electronic Discount Sales Inc	5734	34
Electronic Displays Inc	3993	171
Electronic Electromechanical Equipment Assembly Inc	3829	265
Electronic Energy Control Inc	3577	665
Electronic Engineering and Manufacturing Inc	3651	121
Electronic Environments Corp	7376	18
Electronic Evidence Discovery Inc	7375	108
Electronic Evolution Technologies Inc	3672	71
Electronic Expeditors Inc	5065	461
Electronic Express Inc	5731	59
Electronic Fabrication Service	3679	536
Electronic Film Capacitors Inc	3675	26
Electronic Game Solutions Inc	5065	588
Electronic Hardware Ltd	5065	325
Electronic Healthcare Systems Inc	7372	3442
Electronic Home Inc	5731	246
Electronic Home Systems Inc	5731	157
Electronic Ink Inc	7374	140
Electronic Innovations Corp	3672	454
Electronic Installations Inc	3663	338
Electronic Instrumentation and Technology Inc	3672	47
Electronic Insurance Office Inc	6311	234
Electronic Interconnect Corp	3672	126
Electronic Maintenance Company Inc	5734	14
Electronic Manufacturing Technology Inc	3672	335
Electronic Marine Systems Inc	3669	199
Electronic Marketing Associates Inc	5065	821
Electronic Measuring Devices Inc	3823	394
Electronic Media International	3695	95
Electronic Micro Systems Inc	3534	5
Electronic Monitoring Systems	3575	21
Electronic Office Systems	5044	61
Electronic Online Systems International	7372	1708
Electronic Parts Specialists Inc	5065	803
Electronic Parts Unlimited Inc	5064	103
Electronic Payments Inc	7389	383
Electronic Plastics Co	3672	483
Electronic Power Design Inc	3621	114
Electronic Printing Solutions LLC	2759	371
Electronic Products Design Inc	3677	113
Electronic Prototype Development Inc	3679	666
Electronic Recordkeeping Services Inc	7372	3897
Electronic Registry Systems Inc	7371	1273
Electronic Resources Inc	5065	681
Electronic Response Inc	3672	372
Electronic Security Corporation Of America	1731	822
Electronic Security Protection LLC	5063	1034
Electronic Security Systems Inc	7382	91
Electronic Sensors Inc	3699	256
Electronic Service and Design Corp	3672	230
Electronic Service Products Corp	5065	655
Electronic Software Publishing Corp	7372	4812
Electronic Solutions	3672	75
Electronic Source Co	3672	160
Electronic Specialists Inc	3661	121
Electronic Storage Corp	7372	3212
Electronic Support Services Inc	3679	486
Electronic Surface Mounted Industries	3672	183
Electronic System Design Inc	3823	366
Electronic Systems Consultants Inc	1731	1505
Electronic Systems Design Inc	8711	687
Electronic Systems Engineering Company Inc	3861	29
Electronic Systems Inc	3679	18
Electronic Systems of Richmond Inc	5044	8
Electronic Systems Of Wisconsin Inc	3825	246
Electronic Systems Protection Inc	3612	78
Electronic Systems Services Inc	7378	20
Electronic Systems Southeast LLC	3629	111
Electronic Systems Technology Inc	3679	652
Electronic Technologies Corporation USA Inc	7382	21

Company Name	SIC	Rank
Electronic Technologies International Inc	3679	348
Electronic Technology Corp	3674	335
Electronic Tele-Communications Inc	3661	203
Electronic Test Equipment Manufacturing Co	3625	141
Electronic Theatre Controls Inc	3648	11
Electronic Tracking Systems LLC	5065	724
Electronic Training Solutions Inc	8741	132
Electronic Transaction Consultants Corp	7372	431
Electronic Transformer Corp	3677	50
Electronic Transmission Corp	8000	110
Electronic Trend Publications Inc	2741	460
Electronic Vision Access Solutions	7373	494
Electronic Warfare Associates Inc (Fort Huachuca Arizona)	3829	26
Electronic Waveform Lab Inc	3841	318
Electronics Aid Inc	3672	460
Electronics and Metals Industries Inc	3672	307
Electronics Assemblers Inc	3679	547
Electronics Boutique Holdings Corp	5734	3
Electronics Depot Inc	5731	218
Electronics Expo LLC	5731	73
Electronics For Imaging Inc	3577	33
Electronics Manufacturing Services	3672	459
Electronics Service Company Of Hamlet LLC	4812	116
Electronics Services Unlimited Inc	3679	768
Electronics Sonic	4813	710
Electronics Supply Company Inc	5065	197
Electronics Workbench	7372	1417
Electro-Numerics Inc	3823	332
Electro-Optical Industries Inc	3823	172
Electro-Optical Products Corp	3577	445
Electro-Optical Systems Inc	3559	527
Electro-Optics Technology Inc	3845	89
Electropac Company Inc	3672	226
Electro-Plasma Inc	3699	107
Electroprep Corp	3559	570
Electro-Pro Inc	3625	232
Electrorack Products Co	3444	118
Electrorep Inc	5063	441
Electrorep-Energy Products Inc	5063	514
Electrosem LLC	3679	649
Electro-Sense Of Pennsylvania Inc	5063	718
Electro-Sensors Inc	3823	185
Electrosonic Inc	8711	175
Electrosonics Inc	7372	3529
Electro-Space Fabricators Inc	3444	176
Electrospec Sales Inc	5065	772
Electrostatic Coating Technologies Corp	3479	109
Electro-Support Systems Corp	3679	633
Electroswitch Electronic Products	3643	8
Electrosynthesis Company Inc	3822	50
Electro-Tech Products Inc	3679	490
Electro-Tech Systems Inc	3825	213
Electro-Technic Products Inc	3812	189
Electrotechnics Corp	3679	596
Electrotek Corp	3672	73
Electro-Watchman Inc	7382	63
Electro-Wire Inc	5063	104
Elefunt Software	7371	1739
Elegant Fashions Inc	7389	1184
Elegant Illusions Inc	5944	26
Elegant Linens and Table Skirting	5023	186
Elegant Office Inc	4813	468
Elegant Surfaces	5032	35
Eleganza Tiles Inc	3253	6
Elektran Inc	5063	673
Elektromek Inc	2891	108
Elektron Components Corp	3613	167
Elemco Software Integration Group Ltd	7373	1081
Element K Corp	7379	46
Element LLC	7372	4965
Elementis Specialties	2869	20
Elements International Group LLC	5023	28
Elements (Tampa Florida)	7389	973
Elemica Inc	7379	8
Elena's Food Specialties Inc	2038	55
Elenbaas Company Inc	2048	49
Elenburg Exploration Inc	3532	39
Elenco Carbide Tool Corp	3545	278
Elenco Electronics Inc	3825	147
Eleni's Nyc Inc	2052	66
Elephant Group Inc	7389	90
Elesys Inc	3577	498
Elevation Partners	6799	97
Elevations Credit Union	6061	33
Elevations Inc	5046	206
Elevator Cable and Supply Co	3534	24
Elevator Components Company USA	3534	32
Elevator Enterances Of NY Inc	3534	30
Elevator Equipment Corp	3534	17
Elevator Modernization Company Inc	5084	435
Elevator Research and ManufacturingCo	3534	15
Elevator Systems Inc	3625	197
Elevator World	2721	383
Eleven Mile Truck Frame and Axle Inc	7538	23
Eleven West Inc	2759	527
Eleview International Inc	7379	1323
Elfring Soft Fonts Inc	7372	1733

Company Name	SIC	Rank
Elg Haniel Metals Corp	5093	59
ELG Metals	5093	14
Elge Inc	2834	333
Elgia Inc	7379	1319
Elgin Broadcasting Co	4832	157
Elgin Dairy Foods Inc	2023	21
Elgin Die Mold Co	3089	693
Elgin Milk Service Inc	4213	2372
Elgin Molded Plastics Inc	3089	624
Elgin National Industries Inc	8711	58
Elgin Super Auto Parts Inc	5015	14
Elgin Sweeper Co	3711	31
Eli Diamant	7349	310
Eli Lilly and Co	2834	6
Eli Lilly Federal Credit Union	6061	66
Elias Design Group Inc	7389	2328
Elias Fragrances Inc	2844	194
Elias Matz Tiernan and Herrick LLP	8111	533
Elias Spater	3661	239
Eliason Corp	3442	78
Eliason Inc	6531	122
Elie Tahari Ltd	2331	6
Elijah Electric	1731	1177
Eli's Cheesecake Co	2053	7
Elisco Advertising	7311	777
Elist Express LLC	4813	711
Elitch Gardens LP	7996	11
Elite Agency Inc	7381	96
Elite Cnc Machining Inc	3599	367
Elite Communications Inc	5731	180
Elite Component Service Inc	3629	62
Elite Computer Consultants LP	7371	341
Elite Es LLC	3613	125
Elite Exhibits LLC	7389	830
Elite Financial Group Inc	6163	25
Elite Flooring and Design Inc	5713	10
Elite Gold Products Corp	5094	65
Elite Impex	5122	127
Elite Laboratories Inc	8731	332
ELITE Landscaping Inc	0781	16
Elite Manufacturing Technologies Inc	3444	109
Elite Marketing Group	6399	31
Elite Model Management Corp	7922	13
Elite Mold and Engineering Inc	3544	648
Elite Pharmaceuticals Inc	2834	361
Elite Plastic Products Inc	3089	1292
Elite Production Inc	3089	1345
Elite Security Services Inc	7382	25
Elite Semi Conductor Products	3674	478
Elite Show Services Inc	7381	8
Elite Software Development Inc	7372	4456
Elite Solutions Inc	2821	199
Elite Spice Inc	2099	72
Elite Sportswear LP	2339	26
Elite Sweets Inc	5461	56
Elite Technology NY Inc	5044	70
E-Lite Tool and Manufacturing Co	3544	611
Elite Tool LLC	3599	1084
Elite Trade Show Sevices Inc	7389	1103
Elitegroup Computer Systems	3577	147
Elixir Industries	3469	3
Elixir Technologies Corp	7372	1530
Eliza Bryant Village	8322	72
Elizabeth Arden Inc	2844	10
Elizabeth Carbide Die Company Inc	3544	7
Elizabeth Locke Jewels	5944	37
Elizabeth Lucas Designs	2771	28
Elizabeth Ryan Floral Designs	5261	22
Elizabeth's Food Company Inc	2052	55
ElJet Aviation Services	8999	194
Eljobo Inc	3089	668
Elk Associates Funding Corp	6722	247
Elk Electric Inc	1731	494
Elk Environmental Services	4953	110
Elk Grove Milling Inc	2048	112
Elk Grove Pontiac Buick GMC	5511	794
Elk Grove Rubber and Plastic Company Inc	3061	65
Elk Lake Tool Co	3545	337
Elk Products Inc	7382	136
Elk River Machine Co	3599	426
Elk Supply Company Inc	5211	87
Elkay Manufacturing Co	3431	1
Elkay Plastics Company Inc	5113	26
Elkays Electronics	5065	914
Elkem Metals Inc	3313	2
Elkhart and Western Railroad Co	4011	28
Elkhart Cases Inc	3089	1297
Elkhart Community Schools Building Corp	8211	6
Elkhart Cooperative Equity Exchange	5153	65
Elkhart Farmers Co-Op Association Inc	5261	24
Elkhart Gamma Associate U	7389	1914
Elkhart Pattern Works Inc	3544	175
Elkhart Products Corp	3568	23
Elkhorn Rural Public Power	4911	277
Elkhorn Valley Packing Co	2011	114
Elki Corp	5149	68
Elkin Co	0252	11
Elkins Constructors Inc	1541	78
Elkins/McSherry LLC	6282	209
Elkins-Swyers Printing Co	2759	555
Elko Inc	5031	418
Elkton Gas	4924	59

Company Name	SIC	Rank
Elkus/Manfredi Architects Ltd	8712	103
Ellanef Manufacturing Corp	3728	76
Ellard Contracting Company Inc	1629	29
Ellcon-National Inc	3743	15
Ellendale Electric Co	1623	61
Ellendale Electric Company Inc	1731	391
Ellerbe Becket Construction Services Inc	1542	406
Ellermedia Group	7389	1679
Ellery Homestyles LLC	5023	20
Ellett Brothers Inc	5091	7
Ellicott Development Co	6552	143
Ellie Mae Inc	7372	642
Elliff Motors Inc	5521	5
Ellingson Inc	3599	2489
Ellington Financial LLC	6798	99
Ellington Industrial Supply Inc	3553	19
Elliot Amusement Co	7922	40
Elliot Tool Inc	3599	1120
Elliott Aviation Inc	5088	4
Elliott Bay Metal Fabricating Inc	3441	283
Elliott Bay Service Transfer	4213	2414
Elliott Brothers Truck Line Inc	4213	2156
Elliott Chevrolet Inc	5511	980
Elliott Co	3563	6
Elliott Company Of Indianapolis Inc	3086	91
Elliott Contracting Inc	1731	337
Elliott Control Company Ltd	3625	192
Elliott Controls Inc	1731	2453
Elliott Curson Advertising Ltd	7311	986
Elliott Electric Service Inc	1731	576
Elliott Equipment Co	3531	94
Elliott Foreign Sales Corp	6794	7
Elliott Homes Inc	1521	14
Elliott Industries Inc	3613	129
Elliott Kenneth Co	3593	35
Elliott Laboratories	8734	200
Elliott Machine Shop Inc	3599	440
Elliott Machine Works Inc	3713	52
Elliott Manufacturing Company Inc	3599	898
Elliott Mcgraw Broadcast	4832	217
Elliott Overseas Corp	3511	7
Elliott Precision Products Inc	3599	1706
Elliott Tool Technologies Ltd	7359	97
Elliott Transport Systems Inc	4213	1595
Elliott Truck Line Inc	4213	946
Elliott Wave International Inc	2741	232
Elliott/Wilson Capitol Trucks LLC	5599	9
Elliott/Wilson Trucks LLC	5012	101
Elliott-Lewis Corp	1711	40
Elliott's Ace Hardware	5251	19
Elliott's Air Conditioning And Electrical Inc	1731	1954
Elliott's Amazing Juices	2033	111
Elliott's Designs Inc	2514	19
Elliott's Evening Star Limousine	4119	19
Elliott's Hardware Inc	5251	23
Ellipso Inc	4812	56
Ellis and Watts International LLC	3585	119
Ellis Brooks Automotive	5511	498
Ellis Coffee Co	5149	84
Ellis Communications Kdoc LLC	4833	86
Ellis Corp	3582	9
Ellis Enterprises Inc	7372	996
Ellis Graphics Inc	3953	25
Ellis John	3823	490
Ellis Manufacturing Company Inc	3541	99
Ellis Popcorn Company Inc	2099	341
Ellis Stone Construction Company Inc	1541	200
Ellis Tool and Machine Inc	3599	1856
Ellis Trucking	4213	2876
Ellison Electric Supply Inc	5063	509
Ellison Graphics Corp	2752	835
Ellison Meat Co	2011	31
Ellison Systems Inc	7373	624
Ellis-Walker Builders Inc	1541	216
Ellora Energy Inc	1382	33
Ellstreet Corp	8712	9
Ellsworth Builders Supply Inc	5211	77
Ellsworth Coop	5153	151
Ellsworth Cooperative Creamery	2022	15
Ellsworth Corp	5169	69
Ellsworth Electric Of PA Inc	1731	809
Ellsworth Fund Ltd	6726	78
Ellwood Engineered Casting Co	3321	36
Ellwood Quality Steels Co	3312	68
Ellwood Texas Forge LP	3462	47
Elm Chevrolet Company Inc	5511	586
Elm City Rehabilitation Center Inc	8331	175
Elm Industries Inc	3089	1628
Elm Press Inc	2752	837
Elm Street Development Inc	6552	210
Elm Systems Inc	3825	265
Elma Electronic Inc	5065	79
El-Mar Plastics Inc	5162	61
Elmco Engineering Inc	3599	623
Elmech Inc	3679	759
Elmed Inc	3845	120
Elmer Buchta Trucking LLC	4213	255
Elmer Candy Corp	2066	16
Elmer Larson LLC	3273	59
Elmer Schultz Services Inc	5046	114
Elmer's Crane And Dozer Inc	1771	26
Elmer's Pancake and Steak Inc	5812	134

Company Name	SIC	Rank
Elmer's Restaurants Inc	5812	145
Elmet Technologies Corp	3641	7
Elmhirst Industries Inc	3545	145
Elmhult LP	5712	23
Elmhurst Dairy Inc	2026	48
Elmhurst-Chicago Stone Co	1422	17
El-Milagro Inc	2099	73
Elmira Quality Printers Inc	2752	1745
Elmira Savings Bank FSB	6035	142
Elmo Data Supply Inc	5045	762
Elmo Greer and Sons LLC	1611	151
Elmo Leather Inc	5199	3
Elna Ferrite Laboratories Inc	5065	256
Elna USA	5064	25
Elnorah Inc	4832	194
Elo TouchSystems Inc	3577	81
Elona Bio Technologies Inc	2834	238
Elontec	4899	193
Elopak Inc	3565	41
Eloquent Inc	7371	755
Elpac Electronics Inc	3629	42
Elpaco Coatings Corp	2851	139
Elpakco Inc	3678	67
El-Ranchero Food Products	2096	46
Elreha Printed Circuits Corp	3672	128
Elrod Electrical Service Inc	1731	540
ELS Productions	3695	152
Els Surveying and Mapping	7389	2073
Elsa Corp	3714	244
Elsevier Science Inc	2731	110
Elsevier Science Inc Secondary Publishing Div	7375	48
Elsinore Technologies Inc	7372	3186
Elsner Engineering Works Inc	3554	21
Elster Amco Water LLC	3824	7
Elstor Perfection Corp	3498	21
Elston-Richards Inc	4226	15
Eltec Instruments Inc	3812	120
Elton M Harvey Trucking Inc	4213	2532
Eltrex Industries Inc	4225	24
Eltron Research and Development Inc	8731	260
Elvish Consulting	7379	1658
ELVO Div	3559	177
Elwell Farms Inc	2015	71
Elwood Group Inc	3462	2
Elwood Publishing Company Inc	2711	411
Elwood Safety Company Inc	5084	734
Elwood Staffing Services Inc	7361	182
ELXSI Corp	5812	277
Ely Company Inc	3599	995
Ely Energy Inc	3625	198
Ely Services Inc	7389	1931
eLynx Ltd	5045	260
Elyon Inc	1731	2254
Elyria Manufacturing Corp	3451	49
Elysian Brewing Co	2082	76
EM Advertising	8742	425
EM Basile and Associates Inc	7389	2128
EM Design	3679	888
EM Duggan Inc	1711	153
Em Microelectronic Us Inc	7371	1584
Em Printing Inc	2752	815
EM Security Services Inc	7381	36
EM Smith and Co	3599	747
Em Technologies Inc	3663	343
EM Transcriptions Inc	7338	57
EM4 Inc	3674	172
EMA Corp	3621	26
EMA Services Inc	7389	477
Emabond Solutions LLC	3548	61
Emac Inc	7371	995
eMachines Inc	5961	23
Emag Technologies Inc	8732	123
Emagia Corp	7371	370
eMagin Corp	3674	186
emagination network LLC	7379	300
EMAK Worldwide Inc	7311	94
Emanoncom Inc	7373	1136
Emarketer Inc	8732	86
E-Markets Inc	7389	584
eMASON Inc	7372	1511
EM-Assist Inc	7372	2559
Emat Ultrasonics Inc	3829	477
E-Max Group Inc	5734	18
E-Max Instruments Inc	3625	199
EMAX Laboratories Inc	8711	320
Embarcadero Technologies Inc	7373	88
Embassy Industries Inc	3433	58
Embed Inc	7379	753
Embedded Communications Computing	3577	13
Embedded Planet Inc	7371	713
Embedded Plus Engineering LLC	7370	1374
Embedded Software Development Systems Inc	7372	3347
Embee Computer Design Group Inc	7373	606
Embee Inc	3471	20
Ember Corp	3679	93
Ember Industries Inc	3679	483
Emblaze Vcon Inc	1731	843
EmblemHealth Inc	6321	12
Embrex Inc	2836	22
Embrey Partners Ltd	1541	119
Embroidery Boulevard Inc	5699	21

Company Name	SIC	Rank
Embroidery Industries Inc	7389	1360
Embroidery Studio Inc	3823	483
EMC Capital Management Inc	6282	604
EMC Captiva	7372	1176
EMC Corp	3572	1
EMC Documentum Inc	7372	966
Emc Global Technologies Inc	3599	842
EMC Insurance Group Inc	6331	160
EMC Mortgage Corp	6163	3
EMC National Life Co	6311	80
EMC Schaffner Inc	5065	613
EMC Underwriters LLC	6331	72
EmCare Holdings Inc	8741	35
EmCare Inc	8741	270
Emcee Electronics Inc	3823	248
Emclaire Financial Corp	6021	175
EMCO Chemical Distributors Inc	5169	63
Emco Enterprises Inc	5031	109
Emco/Fgs LLC	2752	523
Emcor Construction Services	1731	19
Emcor Government Services	8711	143
Emcor Group Inc	1623	1
Emcore Corp	3559	26
Emd Chemicals Inc	2869	35
EMD Pharmaceuticals Inc	2834	184
Emdeon Business Services LLC	7389	39
e-MDs Inc	7372	531
Eme Technologies Inc	3599	877
Emeco Industries Inc	2522	51
Emeco USA	5082	190
E-Media Plus Inc	5045	498
EmeraChem LLC	2819	102
Emerald Carolina Chemical LLC	2899	162
Emerald City Graphics Inc	2752	54
Emerald Datacom Products Inc	5045	974
Emerald Forest Products Inc	2436	15
Emerald International Corp	5052	8
Emerald Pi Inc	7381	160
Emerald Produce Company Inc	7361	236
Emerald Resource Group Inc	7361	85
Emerald Services	4953	32
Emerald Tool Inc	7699	136
Emerald West Equipment Parts Inc	3714	316
Emerge Technologies	5065	751
Emergency 24 Inc	7382	59
Emergency Beacon Corp	3663	346
Emergency Computer Technician LLC	7378	101
Emergency Medical Services LP	4119	1
Emergency One Inc	3713	9
Emergency Physicians Dictation Services	8721	456
Emergency Power Controls Inc	1731	1039
Emergency Power Services Inc	7379	1146
Emergency Resources International Inc	5047	270
Emergency Systems Service Co	5063	318
Emergency World LLC	7812	322
Emergent BioSolutions Inc	2834	87
Emergin Inc	7373	570
Emerging Image Inc	7336	224
Emerging Technology Solutions LLC	7372	4295
Emerging Vision Inc	5995	10
Emergisoft Corp	7373	619
Emergitech Inc	5045	551
Emerick Construction Co	1541	157
Emeritus Corp	8059	2
Emerson Apparatus Inc	3821	73
Emerson Control Techniques	3625	7
Emerson Cooke Associates	7379	1615
Emerson Electric Co	3621	2
Emerson Electric Supply Co	5063	589
Emerson Hayes Advertising and Design	7311	649
Emerson Industries LLC	3544	853
Emerson Investment Management Inc	6289	18
Emerson Knives Inc	3421	13
Emerson Power Transmission	3562	9
Emerson Process Management Bettis Div	3593	6
Emerson Process Management Inc	3823	38
Emerson Process Management Power and Water Solutions	3625	15
Emerson Process Management Valve Actuation LLC	3823	74
Emerson Process Mangement	7372	2969
Emerson Radio Corp	3651	29
Emery Air Inc	4522	21
Emery Corp	3544	61
Emery Enterprises Inc	5251	45
Emery Trucking Inc	4213	2808
Emery Waterhouse Co	5072	15
Emeter Corp	7371	390
Emf Company Inc	3469	205
EMF Corp	3827	149
Emf Corp	3578	40
Emh Environmental Inc	1623	697
Emh Inc	3536	32
Emhart Glass Manufacturing Inc	3565	61
Emhart Teknologies Inc	3714	145
EMI Christian Music Group	6794	33
EMI Holding Corp Electro-Metrics Div	3823	275
Emi Inc	3556	153
Emi Industries LLC	3556	11
EMI Latin America Inc	7389	196
Emi Solutions Inc	3677	97

Company Name	SIC	Rank
EMI Strategic Marketing Inc	7311	231
Emi Technologies Inc	8711	512
Emids Technologies	7379	776
Emiex Corp	5065	633
Emigrant Savings Bank Executive Offices	6036	7
Emil A Schroth Inc	5093	164
Emil Pawuk and Associates Inc	7389	1042
Emiliani Enterprises Inc	5087	13
Emil's Pizza Inc	2038	69
Eminence Speaker LLC	3651	60
Eminent Technology Inc	3651	229
Emisphere Technologies Inc	2834	465
Emission Control Ltd	3679	769
Emission Methods Inc	3829	320
Emivest Aerospace Corp	3721	41
EMJ Corp	1542	122
Emjac Industries Inc	2542	31
Emkay Inc	6282	247
Emkay Inc	7371	1521
Eml Inc	7812	276
EMM Group Inc	7311	760
Emma Inc	2759	127
Emmanuel County Newspapers Inc	7692	43
Emmert Welding And Manufacturing Company Inc	5031	452
Emmet Vaughn Lumber Co	7812	308
Emmett/Furla Films Productions Corp	5812	440
Emmett's Tavern and Brewing Co	2022	19
Emmi Roth USA Inc	4832	11
Emmis Communications Corp	2721	5
Emmis Publishing Corp	1731	1468
Emms Electric Inc	2899	96
Emoral Inc	8062	5
Emory Healthcare	4213	2210
Emory Rothenbuhler and Sons	8331	89
Emory Valley Center	7379	775
EmoryDay LLC	8999	126
Emoto	3559	512
Emp Industries Inc	7372	2970
Empagio	7372	1383
Emphasys Software	7374	162
Emphusion	3841	47
Empi Inc	3559	469
Empire Abo Gas Plant	3569	102
Empire Abrasive Equipment Company LP	4513	14
Empire Airlines Inc	5013	149
Empire Auto Parts Supply Inc	6022	296
Empire Bank	3531	143
Empire Bucket Inc	2842	118
Empire Chemical Company Inc	1799	43
Empire City Iron Works	2095	48
Empire Coffee Company Inc	5031	16
Empire Company Inc	2752	944
Empire Corporation Kit Of America Inc	3911	21
Empire Diamond Corp	3363	18
Empire Die Casting Company Inc	4911	1
Empire District Electric Co	4911	510
Empire Electric Association Inc	1731	732
Empire Electric M and S Inc	3672	319
Empire Electronics Corp	1311	270
Empire Energy Corp	5031	94
Empire Enterprises Inc	4213	889
Empire Express Inc	5085	388
Empire Fasteners Inc	6411	186
Empire Financial Services Inc	5087	146
Empire Fire Prevention Company Inc	3471	12
Empire Hard Chrome Inc	8062	186
Empire Health Centers Group	1711	253
Empire Heating and Cooling Co	6799	212
Empire Investment Holdings LLC	3423	19
Empire Level Manufacturing Corp	3544	885
Empire Machine Co	7812	170
Empire Media Group Inc	3556	175
Empire Metal Manufacturing Inc	5099	141
Empire Music Group Inc	3851	62
Empire Optical Of California Inc	3442	40
Empire Pacific Windows Corp	2011	103
Empire Packing	5065	647
Empire Page Inc	1311	277
Empire Petroleum Corp	5074	153
Empire Plumbing Supply Inc	5084	104
Empire Power Systems	5093	42
Empire Recycling Inc	5812	253
Empire Resorts Inc	3577	43
Empire Resources Inc	2759	83
Empire Screen Printing Inc	5082	3
Empire Southwest LLC	7361	352
Empire Staffing Solutions Inc	2711	772
Empire State Weeklies Inc	5093	225
Empire Steel and Metals Corp	5083	117
Empire Stone Co	4813	*120
Empire Telephone Corp	3545	78
Empire Tool Company Inc	3444	294
Empire Ventilation Equipment Company Inc	3089	1502
Empire West Inc	7372	4457
Empirical Software	7372	392
Empirix Inc	7363	295
Employee Leasing Systems Inc	6411	105
Employee Welfare Benefit Plans Trust Of Fpl Group	7389	354
Employees Only Inc	7361	40
Employer Flexible		

Company Name	SIC	Rank
Employer Management Solutions Inc	7373	175
Employer Services Corp	7389	2525
Employers Holdings Inc	6321	20
Employers Mutual Casualty Co	6311	167
Employers Mutual Inc	7389	327
Employer's Relief Inc	7363	172
Employers Resource Management Company Inc	7363	43
Employer's Security Inc	7382	35
Employment and Employer Services Inc	7361	230
Employment and Training Association Inc	7361	293
Employment Atlanta	7361	304
Employment Connection	8331	197
Employment Contractor Services Inc	7363	202
Employment Horizons Inc	8331	111
Employment News LLC	2711	191
Employment Practices Solutions Inc	8748	418
Employment Source Inc	8742	553
Employment Trust Inc	7361	405
Employmentgroup Holdings Corp	7363	34
Emporium Specialties Company Inc	3541	242
Empower Mediamarketing Inc	7319	78
Empower Professionals Inc	7379	499
Empower RF Systems	3669	62
Empowerment Enterprises LLC	3669	312
Empress International Ltd	5146	4
Empress Of Ocean Springs Inc	5731	149
Empress Software Inc	7375	234
Emprise Bank	6021	65
Emprise Financial Corp	6712	188
Emprise Technologies LLC	7372	519
Empro Manufacturing Company Inc	3629	83
Emptoris	7372	468
Empyrean Services LLC	8748	95
Emrick And Hill Inc	5084	655
Emrick's Van and Storage Inc	4213	917
Emrise Corp	3679	152
Emrys Technologies Inc	7372	2260
Ems Aviation Inc	3577	231
EMS Consulting	7371	154
Ems Development Corp	3825	112
Ems Engineered Materials Solutions LLC	3351	11
Ems Industrial Inc	5063	221
Ems Innovations Inc	5047	145
Ems Laboratories Inc	8734	198
Ems LLC	5065	607
EMS Professional Shareware Libraries	7379	1598
EMS Professional Software	7371	1884
EMS Technologies Inc	3663	22
Ems Weeks Inc	5063	790
EMSAR Ventures Inc	3561	5
Emsco	5091	33
EMSCO Electric Supply Company Inc	5063	365
Em-Star Ambulance Service	4119	9
EMT Industries Inc	3061	38
EMT Ohio Knife and Grinding Co	3423	67
Emtec Inc	7389	143
Emtech Laboratories Inc	3842	263
Emteq Inc	8711	167
Emulation Technology Inc	3825	257
Emulex Corp	3577	46
Emulsicoat Inc	2952	24
EMusicquest	7379	1198
EMW Laser Inc	3679	693
Emx Controls Inc	3625	62
Emx Industries Inc	3699	184
EN Beard Hardwood Lumber Inc	5031	235
En Pointe Technologies Inc	5045	50
En Pointe Technologies Sales Inc	5045	29
En Pointe Technologies Ventures Inc	5045	30
En Technology Corp	7372	2139
En2go International Inc	7371	1902
Ena Meat Packing Inc	2011	88
Enable Holdings Inc	7389	378
Enablence Systems Inc	7372	1654
Enabling Technologies Co	3577	283
Enablx Inc	7389	1209
Enalasys Corp	7374	98
Enbridge Energy East Texas LLC	1311	52
Enbridge Energy Management LLC	4612	4
Enbridge Midcoast Energy Inc	4923	14
ENCAD Inc	3577	111
Encap Technologies Inc	3559	201
Encapsulite International Inc	3646	104
Encell Technology LLC	3691	31
Enceratec Inc	3714	398
Encinitas Natural Stone	5032	55
Encino Pool And SpA	7389	2302
Encirq Corp	7372	2971
Encite Inc	7372	2635
Encoder Products Co	3679	193
Encomium Data International Inc	7372	3243
Encompass Automation and Engineering Technolgies LLC	3823	403
Encompass Group Affiliates Inc	7389	258
Encompass Holdings Inc	8741	305
Encompass Tool and Machine Inc	3544	509
ENCOMPIX Software Inc	7372	2545
Encon Inc	3085	10
Encon Safety Products Inc	3842	166
Encore Bancshares Inc	6712	238

Company Name	SIC	Rank
Encore Bank (Houston Texas)	6035	62
Encore Broadcast Equipment Sales Inc	5065	129
Encore Capital Group Inc	6153	16
Encore Crown and Bridge Inc	8072	27
Encore Development Of North America Inc	7379	897
Encore Electronics Inc	3825	222
Encore Energy Partners LP	1311	85
Encore Image Group Inc	3993	25
Encore Imaging Systems Inc	7372	4416
Encore Insurance Group LLC	6331	153
Encore Leasing Group LLC	7377	29
Encore Manufacturing Company Inc	3524	33
Encore Marketing International Inc	7319	15
Encore Networks Inc	3577	396
Encore Productions Inc	7389	333
Encore Real Time Computing Inc	7373	236
Encore Software Inc	7372	1052
Encore Studios Inc	2754	18
Encore Wire Corp	3351	1
Encotech Inc	8742	705
End Ii End Communications Inc	7379	1547
End To End Inc	3679	494
End2End Inc	7372	1101
Endagraph Inc	3993	133
Endai Corp	7371	1178
Endeavor Capital Partners	6799	65
Endeavor Homes Inc	5082	160
Endeavour International Corp	1311	122
Endeca Technologies Inc	3571	29
EnDevCo Inc	1311	261
Endicott Coil Company Inc	3677	57
Endicott Machine and Tool CoInc	3444	141
Endicott Precision Inc	3444	84
Endicott Research Group Inc	3629	64
Endless Road Products Inc	2389	40
Endless Wireless Group Inc	5065	565
Endo Pharmaceuticals Holdings Inc	2834	21
Endo Pharmaceuticals Inc	2834	82
Endo Pharmaceuticals Solutions Inc	2834	151
Endocardial Solutions NV/SA	3841	92
Endocyte Inc	2834	450
Endodent Inc	3843	70
Endolite North America Ltd	5047	209
Endologix Inc	3841	71
Endoscopy Center of Centennial LP	8011	151
Endoscopy Center of Meridian	8011	147
Endoscopy Center of South Bay LP	8011	143
Endoscopy Center of Washington DC LP	8011	110
Endot Industries Inc	3084	24
Endres Manufacturing Co	3441	193
Endres Processing Ltd	2048	16
EndressHauser Inc	3823	27
Endura Plastics Inc	3089	721
Endurart Inc	3914	12
Enduris Extrusions Inc	3083	25
Enduro Industries LLC	3316	30
Enduro Products Inc	3519	37
Enduro Rubber Co	3069	274
Endyn Manufacturing Inc	3599	1179
Enequist Chemical Company Inc	5169	172
Ener1 Group Inc	3691	5
Ener1 Inc	3691	11
Enerac Inc	3823	371
Enerco Energy Services Inc	8711	576
Enerco Technical Products Inc	3433	53
Enercomp Inc	7372	4605
Enercon	3672	114
Enercon Engineering Inc	3625	59
Enercon Industries Corp	3679	263
Enercon Systems Inc	3433	61
EnerCorp Inc	6726	102
Enerdyne Technologies Inc	7371	398
Enerfab Inc	3443	28
Ener-G Foods Inc	2051	179
Energas Resources Inc	1382	74
Energen Corp	4924	22
Energenecs Inc	5084	611
Energenics Corp	3564	136
Energetic Systems Inc	7379	1638
Energetics Industrial Distributors Inc	5063	457
Energid Technologies	7372	2972
Energizer Battery Co	3692	1
Energizer Holdings Inc	3699	3
Energy Absorption Systems Inc	3089	71
Energy Alloys	5051	41
Energy Answers International Inc	5093	163
Energy Beam Sciences Inc	3826	130
Energy Composites Corp	3089	1241
Energy Conservation Techniques Ltd	1731	1442
Energy Consulting Service Inc	1731	2389
Energy Control Systems Inc	3825	264
Energy Conversion Devices Inc	3691	6
Energy Conversions Inc	3519	40
Energy Cooperative of Ohio	4911	161
Energy Corporation of America	1321	5
Energy Dispatch LLC	4213	832
Energy Economics Inc	1023	167
Energy Efficiency Systems Corp	7371	1189
Energy Efficient Motors and Controls Inc	5063	842
Energy Efficient Products Company Inc	5063	955
Energy Electric Company Inc	1731	936

Company Name	SIC	Rank
Energy Electric Inc	1731	1312
Energy Energy Design	7311	982
Energy Equipment Resources Inc	7359	172
Energy Exchanger Co	3443	101
Energy Federation Inc	5063	155
Energy Focus Inc	3645	11
Energy Future Holdings Corp	4911	8
Energy Group Inc	1623	150
Energy Independence of America Corp	8731	207
Energy Intelligence Group Inc	2741	181
Energy International Corp	5063	60
Energy Labs Inc	3585	54
Energy Machine Inc	3599	794
Energy Maintenance Services Group I LLC	1389	3
Energy Management Specialists Inc	1711	222
Energy Management Strategies	1731	2530
Energy Meter Systems Inc	3823	221
Energy NewsData Corp	2721	335
Energy Northwest	4911	49
Energy Options Inc	3822	55
Energy Partners Ltd	1311	74
Energy Plus Holdings LLC	4911	232
Energy Products and Design Inc	5074	219
Energy Publishing Inc	2721	465
Energy Recovery Inc	3559	67
Energy Research and Generation Inc	3769	29
Energy Saving Products And Sales Corp	3579	37
Energy Saving Technology Inc	5063	867
Energy Sciences Inc	3612	63
Energy Services Group International Inc	7363	88
Energy Services Providers Inc	4931	52
Energy Steel and Supply Co	5051	295
Energy Systems Group LLC	1731	104
Energy Tech LLC	3825	335
Energy Technologies Inc	3629	56
Energy Technology Solutions LLC	5045	891
Energy Transfer Equity LP	5999	1
Energy Transfer Partners LP	4922	4
Energy Transformation Systems Inc	3612	131
Energy USA - TPC	6719	137
Energy Ventures Analysis Inc	8731	220
Energy West Development Inc	4924	50
ENERGY WEST Mining Co	1222	10
Energy West Resources Inc	4924	52
Energy West Wyoming	4924	72
EnergyConnect Group Inc	1731	145
EnergynetCom Inc	1311	149
EnergyNorth Propane Inc	5172	23
Energy-Onix Broadcast Equipment Inc	3663	235
EnergySolutions Inc	2819	10
EnergySolutions LLC	8000	3
Enerjy Software	7371	215
Enerlume Energy Management Corp	1731	666
EnerNOC Inc	7379	48
Enerpro Inc	1731	1220
Enerstar Power Corp	4911	572
EnerSys Energy Products Inc	3691	14
EnerSys Inc	5063	7
Enertec Bas	3822	96
Enertech Corp	3679	763
Enertech Electrical Inc	1731	515
Ener-Tel Services Inc	7378	40
Enertia Software	7379	826
Enertron LLC	7376	43
Enesco Corp	3999	13
Enesco LLC	5199	5
Enetics Inc	3625	385
EnetstarsCom	3679	741
En-Fab Inc	3533	47
Enfield Federal Savings and Loan Assoc	6022	412
Enfield Technologies LLC	3492	36
Enflo Corp	3089	1850
EnFocus Software Inc	7372	1965
Enforcement Technology Group Inc	5049	150
ENfrastructure Technologies Inc	7373	339
Engage Communication Inc	7373	1063
Engage PR	8743	93
Engagement Marketing Experts LLC	7311	477
Engagent Inc	7371	1681
EnGarde Systems Inc	7372	4035
Engauge	7311	61
Engauge LLC	8742	422
Engberg Anderson Design Partnership Inc	8712	179
Engel Holdings Inc	1542	316
Engel Machinery Inc	3559	109
Engelbach Roberts and Co	8721	238
Engelberth Construction Inc	1542	42
Engelhardt Gear Co	3566	39
Engelhart Gourmet Foods Inc	2013	116
Engelkes Connor and Davis Ltd	8721	207
Engelmann-Becker Corp	8733	35
Engelsen Frame and Moulding Company Inc	5023	57
Engenium Corp	7371	1377
Engenius Technologies Inc	5065	166
Engenuity Financial	7389	1359
Engenuity Systems Inc	3822	75
Engeo Inc	8711	474
Engine Clean Technologies Inc	3599	2417

Company Name	SIC	Rank
Engine Components Inc	3728	102
Engine Distributors Inc	5084	347
Engine Lab Of Tampa Inc	3519	38
Engine Monitor Inc	3699	150
Engine Power Components Inc	3714	268
Engine Power Source Inc	5084	305
Engine Systems Inc	3621	74
Engine Textiles	2257	1
Engineered Abrasives Inc	3629	87
Engineered Arresting Systems Corp	3728	92
Engineered Automation of ME Inc	3699	264
Engineered Ceramics	3567	27
Engineered Communication Systems Inc	5999	227
Engineered Composites Inc	3089	1227
Engineered Controls International LLC	3491	7
Engineered Electronics Inc	3669	259
Engineered Fabrication Inc	3549	97
Engineered Fluid Inc	3561	77
Engineered Glass Products LLC	3211	10
Engineered Inserts and Systems Inc	3429	155
Engineered Inspection Services Inc	3825	339
Engineered Machined Products Inc	3519	9
Engineered Materials and Solutions Group Inc	3479	6
Engineered Medical Systems Inc	3841	196
Engineered Packaging Inc	3086	138
Engineered Plastic Components Inc	3089	270
Engineered Plastics Corp	3089	847
Engineered Plastics Inc	3544	44
Engineered Plastics Of Pickwick Inc	3089	1170
Engineered Polymer Products Div	3812	88
Engineered Polymer Solutions	2821	63
Engineered Precision Casting Co	3324	14
Engineered Production Equipment Inc	3559	294
Engineered Products and Services Inc	3479	69
Engineered Products Co	3699	138
Engineered Profiles LLC	3089	267
Engineered Sales Inc	3494	66
Engineered Services Inc	1731	1688
Engineered Software Inc	7372	2140
Engineered Specialty Textiles LLC	2211	23
Engineered Systems and Designs Inc	3823	474
Engineered Systems and Products Inc	3625	79
Engineered Systems Inc	1731	1988
Engineered Treatment Systems LLC	3559	458
Engineering Aggregates Corp	5032	117
Engineering Analysis Associates Inc	8999	121
Engineering and Equipment Co	5074	25
Engineering and Manufacturing Services Inc	1761	59
Engineering and Professional Services Inc	8711	150
Engineering Automation and Design Inc	1542	387
Engineering Center TEC	8742	602
Engineering Concepts (Fullerton California)	7379	1229
Engineering Concepts Unlimited Inc	3625	276
Engineering Consulting Services Ltd	8711	54
Engineering DataXpress Inc	7372	1102
Engineering Design and Development Inc	3599	1648
Engineering Design Industries Inc	3599	2130
Engineering Design Manufacturing Service Inc	5049	81
Engineering Design Systems Inc	5045	370
Engineering Diagnostics Inc	8711	621
Engineering Dynamics Corp (Beaverton Oregon)	7372	3898
Engineering Dynamics Inc (Kenner Louisiana)	7372	2626
Engineering Geometry Systems	7379	81
Engineering Industries Inc	3089	773
Engineering Laboratory Design Co	3821	68
Engineering Mechanics Research Corp	7372	2236
Engineering Model Associates Inc	3089	1659
Engineering Planning and Management Inc	7372	2354
Engineering/Remediation Resources Group Inc	8711	124
Engineering Solutions Inc (Tukwila Washington)	3577	478
Engineering Technology Inc	3533	105
Engineering Tube Specialties Inc	3498	61
Engineering Unlimited Inc	3613	109
Engineers and Constructors International Inc	8711	198
Engineers Tool Corp	3829	514
Engines Inc	3444	88
Engis Corp	3541	38
England and Corsair Upholstery	2512	17
England Audio Inc	5731	238
Engle Dental Systems Inc	3843	63
Engle Printing and Publishing Company Inc	2752	97
Englekirk and Sabol Inc	8711	499
Engler Electric Inc	1731	1644
Engler Engineering Corp	3843	74
Englert Inc	3444	29
Engles and Fahs Inc	1731	1834
Engles Trucking Services Inc	4213	550
Englewood Electric Inc	1731	1940
English Language Institute/China	7361	123

Company Name	SIC	Rank
English Motion Media Inc	7389	2389
English River Pellets Inc	2048	110
English Trucking Inc	4213	3007
English's All Wood Homes Inc	3089	1677
ENGlobal Constant Power Inc	8711	242
ENGlobal Construction Resources Inc	3823	20
ENGlobal Corp	8711	57
Englund Equipment Co	4213	1498
Englund Graphics Inc	2752	1012
Engrave Inc	3089	1827
Engstrom Design Group Inc	7389	727
Engstrom Inc	7363	269
Enhance A Colour Corp	7389	1191
Enhance America Inc	5046	200
Enhanced Laser Products	3861	42
Enhanced Network Solutions Group Inc	7373	762
Enhanced Recovery Company LLC	7322	27
Enhanced Telecommunications Inc	7371	691
Enhanced Tele-Services Inc	7389	1510
Enhanced Video Devices Inc	3844	28
Enhancers Inc	3613	99
EnHealth Environmental Inc	8734	205
enherent Corp	7371	524
ENI Products Group	3621	40
Enigma Inc	7372	1324
Enigma Software Group Inc	7372	332
Enjoy Life Natural Brands	2052	45
Enjoy Plastics USA Inc	3089	822
Enkei America Inc	3714	128
Enlightened Concepts LLC	7379	1543
Enlightened Inc	7379	224
ENM Co	3824	21
EnMark Gas Corp	1311	244
Enmark Systems Inc	7372	2873
Enmark Tool Co	3544	273
Ennis Electric Company Inc	1731	295
Ennis Inc	2761	4
Ennis Industries LLP	2851	52
Ennis Pellum and Associates PA	8721	41
Ennis Power Company LLC	4911	593
Ennis Tag and Label Co	2621	46
Ennis Traffic Safety Solutions	2851	49
Ennis Willie	2752	645
Enoch Manufacturing Co	3451	38
Enogex Inc	2911	36
Enogex Products Corp	2911	26
Enon Microwave Inc	3679	574
Enova Systems Inc	3679	341
Enovapremier Of Michigan LLC	5013	260
Enovation Graphic Systems Inc (Valhalla New York)	3695	13
ENPAC Corp	3089	140
Enpac LLC	3089	1064
Enpath Medical Inc	3841	89
Enphase Energy Inc	3621	72
Enpirion Inc	3674	159
Enplas USA Inc	3089	197
Enpro Inc	1311	167
EnPro Industries Inc	3053	3
Enprotech Corp	5046	3
Enprotech Mechanical Services Inc	3469	52
Enquatics Inc	3565	66
Enquip Inc	3823	230
ENR General Machining Co	3599	1723
Enrich IT Inc	7379	378
Enron Creditors Recovery Corp	4923	1
Enroute Networks Inc	7374	382
Ensales Inc	5063	1037
ENSCICON Corp	7379	492
ENSCO Inc	8731	66
Ensemble Business Software Inc	7372	3666
Ensemble Designs Inc	3663	291
Enseo Inc	3669	147
Ensequence Inc	4899	119
Enservco Corp	1311	174
Ensign Corp	3612	98
Ensign Emblem Ltd	2395	10
Ensign Equipment Inc	3559	387
Ensign Group Inc	8051	13
Ensign Power Systems Inc	3679	688
Ensign Systems Inc	7372	3134
Ensign United States Drilling Inc	1389	18
Ensign-Bickford Industries Inc	2892	2
Ensim Corp	5045	313
Ensinger Inc	2821	52
Enslin And Son Packing Co	2013	209
Enslow Publishers Inc	2731	192
Ensoco Inc	8748	435
Enspiria Solutions Inc	8748	173
Ensr International Corp	8748	27
ENSTAR Natural Gas Co	4924	48
Enstrom Helicopter Corp	3721	37
Ensure Technologies	7372	1352
Ensurity Group LLC	6399	29
Ensync Interactive Solutions Inc	7379	1376
Ensynch Inc	7371	332
Ensyte Energy Software International	7371	1424
Entact Inc	4953	65
Entact LLC	1629	34
Entec Composite Machines Inc	3549	67
Entec Systems Inc	1731	1891
Entech Data Systems Inc	7372	4296
Entech Environmental Systems Inc	3564	164
Entech Laboratory Automation Inc	3821	36
Entech Personnel Services Inc	7363	117
Entech Signs	5046	54
Entech Solar Inc	3433	65
ENTEGEE Inc	7361	111
Entegration Inc	7372	3899
Entegris Inc	3089	28
Entegrity Wind Systems Inc	3511	34
Entek Corp	3545	331
ENTEK International LLC	3089	19
Entelligence LLC	7361	109
Entera Inc	1799	71
Enterasys Networks Inc	3577	49
Entercom Communications Corp	4832	6
Entercom Kansas City Licensee LLC	4832	5
Entercom Norfolk LLC	4832	68
Entergy Arkansas Inc	4911	102
Entergy Corp	4911	11
Entergy Louisiana LLC	4911	116
Entergy Mississippi Inc	4911	148
Entergy Nuclear Generation Co	4911	226
Entergy Texas	4911	53
Enternet Solutions Inc	7371	1857
EnteroMedics Inc	3845	142
Enterprise Accounting Solution LLC	7379	1367
Enterprise Associates LLC	7374	120
Enterprise Bancorp Inc	6022	120
Enterprise Bank and Trust Co	6022	185
Enterprise Brass Works Corp	3491	38
Enterprise Communications Utility Contractors Of Florida Inc	1623	432
Enterprise Computing Solutions Inc	7373	266
Enterprise Courier Inc	7389	2199
Enterprise Data Concepts LLC	7379	1583
Enterprise Data Management	7371	382
Enterprise Electric Inc	1731	1332
Enterprise Electrical Contracting Inc	1731	870
Enterprise Events Group Inc	7389	836
Enterprise Financial Services Corp	6022	74
Enterprise Graphics Inc	2759	598
Enterprise Informatics Inc	7372	3123
Enterprise Information Management Inc	7379	388
Enterprise Infra Corp	7371	739
Enterprise Integration Group Inc	8731	216
Enterprise Integration Inc	7373	1058
Enterprise Management Technology LLC	7372	4686
Enterprise National Bank of Palm Beach	6021	242
Enterprise Newspaper Group Inc	2711	729
Enterprise Oil Co	5172	62
Enterprise Optical Inc	3851	99
Enterprise Partners Venture Capital	6799	122
Enterprise Products Inc	3496	24
Enterprise Products Operating LP	2911	62
Enterprise Products Partners LP	1321	1
Enterprise Protective Services Inc	7381	220
Enterprise Publishing Co	2711	594
Enterprise Rent-A-Car Co	7514	1
Enterprise Resource Procurement LLC	7379	972
Enterprise Sales Inc	3443	231
Enterprise Ship Company Inc	4412	5
Enterprise Software Solutions Inc	7372	276
Enterprise Solutions Inc	7372	3900
Enterprise Solutions Realized Inc	7379	649
Enterprise Staffing Agency LLC	7361	326
Enterprise Systems Consulting Inc	7379	779
Enterprise Technologies Inc	1731	1231
Enterprise Technology Servs LLC	7371	753
Enterprise Technology System Inc	7371	1358
Enterprise Tool and Die Company Inc	3544	897
Enterprise Tool and Die LLC	3544	216
Enterprise Transportation Co	4213	234
Enterprise Travel Inc	4724	127
Enterprise Truck Lines Inc	4213	2373
Enterprise Van Lines Inc	4213	3008
Enterprise Warehousing Solutions Inc	7379	723
Enterprises International Inc	3569	3
Enterprisewizard Inc	7372	2323
Enterpulse Inc	7371	111
Entersect Corp	5045	417
Enter-Space Inc	7812	141
Entertainment Arts Inc	1731	2098
Entertainment Brokers International	6411	150
Entertainment Gaming Asia Inc	3999	67
Entertainment Marketing and Communications International	8742	515
Entertainment Properties Trust	6798	85
Entertainment Solutions LLC	3825	214
Entertainment Systems Inc	5731	226
Entertron Industries Inc	3625	229
Enterworks Inc	7372	2224
Enthone-OMI Inc	2899	131
Entiera LLC	7371	717
Enting Water Conditioning Inc	3589	176
Entirenet LLC	7371	634
Entisoft	7372	3773
Entoleter LLC	3531	139
Entomo Inc	7372	3073
Entorian Technologies Inc	3674	121
Entrada Iron And Wood Doors LLC	5031	362
Entrade Inc	6719	134
Entratech Systems	3679	873
Entravision Communications Corp	4833	79
Entravision Communications Corp	7389	1335
Entravision Holdings LLC	4833	81
Entre Computer Center	5734	444
EntreMed Inc	2836	68
Entrepix	3674	142
Entrepreneur Consulting Group Inc	7371	664
Entrepreneur Media Inc	2721	156
Entrepreneur Venture Capital Inc	6799	299
Entrepreneurial Ventures Inc	5999	66
Entrinsik Inc	7372	4297
Entropic Communications Inc	3674	82
Entropy Ltd	7372	3607
Entrum Care Inc	8082	74
Entrust Bankcard LLC	6153	45
Entrust Inc	7371	102
Entrust One Facility Services Inc	7349	93
Entrust Technologies LLC	7372	416
Entrust Tool and Design Company Inc	3549	18
Entrx Corp	1742	10
Entuity Inc	7372	1493
Envelope 1 Inc	2677	10
Envelope Manager Software	7372	3530
Envelope Printery Inc	2677	17
Envelope Service Inc	2677	21
Envelopes and Forms Inc	2752	720
Envelopes Of Nevada Inc	2752	1704
Envelopes Only Inc	2752	384
Envelopes Unlimited Inc	2759	37
Envestnet Inc	6282	219
Envirco Corp	3564	113
Envirite Corp	4953	45
Enviro Sciences Inc	8731	397
Enviro Systems Inc	3585	41
Enviro Voraxial Technology Inc	8731	406
Envirochem Inc	2842	96
Enviro-Clean Services Inc	7349	42
Enviro-Clear Company Inc	3569	279
Enviro-Cote Inc	2672	62
Envirodyne Systems Inc	3589	150
Envirokare Tech Inc	3537	116
Envirologix Inc	3826	56
Enviromation Inc	1731	2501
Enviromental Systems Products Holdings Inc	8744	49
Envirometrics Inc	8734	189
Environeering Inc	8748	397
EnvironMax Inc	7372	1564
Environment One Corp	3561	53
Environmental Air Systems Inc	1711	53
Environmental Biotech Inc	6794	112
Environmental Business International Inc	2721	154
Environmental Capital Holdings Inc	6719	164
Environmental Capital Partners LLC	6733	14
Environmental Chemical Corp	5169	174
Environmental Co	8711	168
Environmental Consultants LLC	1623	520
Environmental Control Building Maintenance Co	7349	202
Environmental Control Systems Inc	5084	534
Environmental Control Systems Inc	8711	628
Environmental Controls Corp	1731	1056
Environmental Data Resources Inc	2741	67
Environmental Design and Construction LLC	1799	31
Environmental Dynamics Inc	3589	47
Environmental Energy Services Inc	5099	152
Environmental Engineering and Consulting Services	8748	113
Environmental Enterprises Inc	4953	116
Environmental Holdings Inc	3317	2
Environmental Inks and Coding	2893	14
Environmental Instruments Leasing Company Inc	3829	127
Environmental Lighting Concepts Inc	3641	23
Environmental Lighting For Architecture Inc	3646	49
Environmental Management Systems Consultants Inc	1731	146
Environmental Micro Analysis Inc	8734	180
Environmental Resource Center Inc	7372	602
Environmental Resources Management Group Inc	8748	11
Environmental Resources Management Inc	8748	28
Environmental Security Inc	7389	1605
Environmental Soil Management Inc	7389	914
Environmental Solutions International Inc	3823	284
Environmental Specialists Inc	4953	46
Environmental Stoneworks LLC	3281	15
Environmental Systems Corp	8711	283
Environmental Systems Products Inc	3825	49
Environmental Tectonics Corp	3699	34
Environmental Testing and Consulting Inc	8734	125
Environmental Transport Group	4213	2042
Environmental Treatment and Technology Inc	8734	90
Environments Group Company Inc	7389	414
Environments Inc (Beaufort South Carolina)	2511	98
Enviroplex Inc	2452	20
Enviro-Process System Inc	5085	295
EnviroStar Inc	3633	3

Company Name	SIC	Rank
Enviro-Systems Corp	3589	221
Envirotech Extrusion Inc	3061	34
Envirotech International Inc	5091	81
Envirotech Pumpsystems Inc	3561	4
Envirotech Remediation Services Inc	8744	39
Enviro-Tech Services Company Inc	5049	175
Enviro-Tech Services Inc	1629	90
Envirotronics Inc	3569	93
Envisage Information Systems	7371	1626
Envisage Technologies Corp	7371	1208
Envision Cmosxray LLC	3844	32
Envision Peripherals Inc	3575	7
Envision Pharmaceutical Services Inc	8721	78
Envision Products Inc	3842	217
Envision Tax and Accounting Services	8721	351
Envision Tech Inc	3599	2114
Envision Telephony Inc	7372	1329
Envision Wireless Inc	8711	668
Envisioning Business Inc	7336	297
Envisionink Co	2791	60
Envitec Inc	5075	121
EnVivo Pharmaceuticals Inc	8731	162
Envoy Data Corp	5734	79
Envoy Technologies Inc	7372	687
Envyr Corp	7372	1806
EnXnet Inc	7372	5072
Enzo Biochem Inc	8071	22
Enzo Clinical Labs Inc	8071	32
Enzo Therapeutics Inc	2835	31
Enzon Pharmaceuticals Inc	2836	15
Enzymatic Therapy Inc	2834	233
EO Habhegger Company Inc	5171	29
Eoff Electric Company Inc	5063	71
EOG Resources Inc	1311	14
Eoh Industries Inc	2844	156
EOI Inc	5712	109
Eoir Technologies Inc	7371	1128
EOL Inc	7371	624
eOn Communications Corp	4813	243
Eon Systems Inc	7371	1149
E-ON US LLC	4911	92
eonBusiness Corp	7373	489
E-ONE	3569	22
E-One Inc	3711	35
Eoriginal Inc	7371	1231
EOS Inc	7375	243
Eos International Inc	5963	13
EOS Power USA Inc	3679	15
Eos Private Equity	6722	164
Eos Systems Inc	7373	824
EP Global Communications Inc	2731	297
EP Graphics Inc	2752	217
EP Henry Corp	3271	2
Epac Software Technologies Inc	5045	859
E-Pak Machinery Inc	3565	90
Epam Systems Inc	7371	14
ePartners Inc	7379	65
EPC America LLC	5032	42
Epc Inc	3086	87
Epco Products Inc	3451	142
Epcon Industrial Systems Inc	3564	28
Epcon International Inc	8711	505
Ep-Direct Inc	2750	599
EPE Corp	1731	176
Epec LLC	3672	134
Eperformax Inc	7389	520
Epes Transport System Inc	4213	260
Epg Inc	3053	34
Ephraim Mcdowell Health Inc	8082	23
Epi 04 Inc	3089	1095
Epi Printers Inc	2752	43
Epi Systems Inc	5162	67
Epi Tech	3674	405
Epic Advisors Inc	6371	8
Epic Corp	2821	70
Epic Games Inc	7372	1153
Epic Machine Inc	3599	1827
Epic MedStaff Services	8059	11
Epic Metals Corp	3444	136
Epic Multimedia	7389	1131
Epic Systems Corp	7372	129
Epic Technologies LLC	3577	89
Epic Touch Company Inc	4813	370
Epicenter Network Inc	7319	51
EpiCept Corp	2834	423
Epicor Software Corp	7372	96
Epicurean Industries Inc	5046	265
Epicurean International Inc	5141	190
Epi-Hab Phoenix Inc	7389	2060
Epimed International Inc	3841	240
Epiphany Marketing Inc	8743	232
Epiphany Media LLC	7311	1021
Epiq Systems - Bankruptcy Solutions	8721	141
EPIQ Systems Inc	7371	41
Epiq Systems (Portland Oregon)	7374	64
Episcopal Church Clergy And Employees Benefit Trust	6733	12
Epistemic Corp	7379	1561
Epitomione	7373	702
Epiworks Inc	3674	280
Epix Films	7812	184
EPIX Inc	3577	516
EPL Inc	7372	3608
EPL Intermediate Inc	5812	139

Company Name	SIC	Rank
EPLAN Software and Services LLC	7372	415
Epley Enterprises Inc	3533	111
ePlus Content Services Inc	6794	47
ePlus Government Inc	7372	486
ePlus Group Inc	7377	9
ePlus Inc	5045	23
ePlus Systems Inc	6794	53
ePlus Technology of NC Inc	7372	893
EPM Inc	3823	289
ePM LLC	5045	472
Epnm Inc	3993	123
Epoch 5 Marketing Inc	8743	218
Epoch BioSciences Inc	2835	46
Epoch Corp	2452	36
Epoch Group LC	6411	187
Epoch Holding Corp	7999	66
Epoch Management Inc	1541	103
Epoch SL Vi Inc	8051	27
Epocrates Inc	7374	53
Epolin Holding Corp	3999	35
Epolin Inc	2821	177
ePolk	7371	625
Epoxies Etc	2891	60
Epoxy Technology Inc	2891	79
Epp Team Inc	3089	867
Eppic	8742	521
Eppley Laboratory Inc	3829	371
Epps Aviation Inc	4522	26
Eppstein Uhen Architects Inc	8712	77
Eprad Inc	3861	128
Eprize LLC	8743	44
EPS Evans Co	7349	352
Eps Printing Inc	2752	1215
Epsco International and Companies Inc	5085	212
Epsen Hillmer Graphics Co	2679	50
EPSIIA Corp	7372	577
Epsilon Data Management Inc	7372	182
Epsilon Data Management LLC	8742	204
Epsilon Lambda Electronics Corp	3679	851
Epsilon Products Co	3089	483
Epsilon Systems Solutions Inc	8741	140
ePsolutions Inc	7372	3399
Epson America Inc	3571	16
Epson Electronics America Inc	3674	273
Epson Portland Inc	3577	85
Epstein and Siebel Associates Inc	5065	558
Epstein Becker and Green PC	8111	130
Epstein Tabor and Schorr	8111	529
Ept Inc	5065	729
Eptam Plastics Ltd	3089	335
Epv Plastics Corp	3081	174
Epylon Corp	7372	1696
Eq Technologic Inc	7372	1759
EQ-The Environmental Quality Co	4953	35
Equalizer Industries Inc	5013	306
EqualLogic Inc	7379	121
Equal-Plus Inc	7371	1359
Equals Three Communications Inc	7311	160
e-Quantum Inc	7372	2267
EquaTerra Inc	8748	35
Equibase Company Inc	2741	364
Equifax Credit Information Services Inc	7323	5
Equifax Inc	7323	3
Equilibrium	7372	1866
Equine Network	2721	230
Equinix Inc	4813	20
Equinox Capital Management LLC	6282	497
Equinox Computer Systems Inc	5734	356
Equinox Corp	7373	870
Equinox Systems and Services Corp	5046	249
Equiom Inc	7371	1255
Equipex Ltd	5046	330
Equipment and Supply Inc	3728	177
Equipment Brokers Inc	3632	9
Equipment Concentration Site	5087	117
Equipment Data Associates LLC	7379	583
Equipment Depot	7359	6
Equipment Development Company Inc	3531	116
Equipment Development Services	7389	2501
Equipment Distributors International Co	3582	16
Equipment Fabricators Inc	3536	41
Equipment Finance Corp	6159	66
Equipment Merchants International Inc	3559	274
Equipment Parts Inc	3599	754
Equipment Preference Inc	5046	164
Equipment Rental Co	7353	93
Equipment Roundup and Manufacturing Inc	3441	216
Equipment Sales Inc	5075	26
Equipment Source Company Inc	5063	1093
Equipment Supply Company Inc	5045	568
Equipment Technologies Inc	5065	494
Equipment Technologies West LLC	5065	499
Equipment Technology Inc	3531	22
Equipment Valve and Supply Inc	5085	71
Equiptex Industrial Products Corp	5065	364
Equis International LLC	7372	2535
Equistar Chemicals LP	2873	1
Equlsys Inc	7371	1551
Equitable Bank SSB	6036	63
Equitable Energy LLC	1311	132
Equitable Financial Corp	6035	176
Equitable Financial Services LLC	7322	180
Equitable Gas Co	4923	13

Company Name	SIC	Rank
Equitable Life Assurance Society of the United States	6311	17
Equitable Production Group Div	7389	629
Equitable Resources Inc	4923	4
Equitrac Corp	7372	60
EQUITRANS LP	4922	41
Equity Elevator And Trading Co	5191	80
Equity Group Investments Inc	6799	78
Equity Lifestyle Properties Inc	6798	72
Equity Marketing Services Inc	7311	964
Equity Office	6512	72
Equity Office Properties Trust	6798	36
Equity One Inc	6722	86
Equity Protection Services Inc	8721	450
Equity Residential	6798	16
Equity Staffing Group Inc	7361	122
Equity Technologies Corp	7389	1985
Equity Title Co	6541	14
Equity Transportation Co	4213	700
Equivoice LLC	4813	607
eQuorum Corp	7372	2780
Equus Capital Corp	6282	142
Equus Capital Management Corp	6282	599
Equus Software LLC	7371	1526
Equus Total Return Inc	6799	275
Eqyss International Inc	2844	106
Er Equipment Inc	3531	23
ER Hitchcock Company Inc	2759	310
ER Jahna Industries Inc	1446	2
ER Lewis Transportation Inc	4213	3073
ER Moore Co	2389	15
E-R Productions LLC	5049	156
ER Wagner Manufacturing Company Inc	3469	39
ER Zeiler Excavating Inc	1623	616
Era Aviation Inc	4512	51
Era Industries Inc	3599	269
ERA Software Systems Inc	7372	2277
Erachem Comilog Inc	2819	56
ERAI Inc	7389	513
Eramet North America Inc	5051	423
Eran Engineering Inc	3599	1127
Erb and Roberts Inc	5083	179
Erb Electric Co	1731	195
Erb Equipment Company Of Illinois Inc	5082	153
Erb Industries Inc	3089	706
Erc Parts Inc	5065	176
ERCO Worldwide Inc	2819	31
Erd Specialty Graphics Inc	2759	545
ERDAS Inc	7372	1327
Erdco Engineering Corp	3823	174
Erdle Perforating Holdings Inc	3469	85
Erdman Anthony Associates Inc	8711	455
Erdmann Corp	5085	175
Erdner Brothers Inc	4213	619
Erect-A-Tube Inc	1542	408
Erell Manufacturing Co	3089	1696
ERepublic Inc	7389	828
eResearchTechnology Inc	8734	8
E-Resources LLC	7371	1051
ERF Wireless Inc	3669	182
Ergocraft Contract Solutions	5021	127
ErgoGenesis LLC	2522	14
Ergon Inc	2911	27
Ergon Trucking Inc	4213	63
Ergonomic Design Inc	7699	259
Ergonomic Solutions	7372	912
Ergonomics Inc	5084	932
ErgonomiXX Inc (Kensington Maryland)	3577	479
Ergotron Inc	2522	21
Ergytech Inc	5063	1056
Erhard and Gilcher Inc	2789	86
Erhard Motor Sales Inc	5511	499
Erhardt Construction Co	1541	240
ERHC Energy Inc	1311	271
Eric F Anderson Inc	1541	205
Eric Isaacson Software	7372	2712
Eric Mower and Associates Inc	7311	101
Eric Reiter	7379	1095
Eric Scott Leathers Ltd	3172	11
Eric Systems	7372	4298
Eric Trump Wine Manufacturing LLC	2084	120
Erica Garment Printing	7336	68
Erich Trucking	4213	1437
Erick's Lumber Company Inc	5031	382
Erickson Air-Crane Inc	4729	5
Erickson Corp	3599	1985
Erickson Electrical Contractors Inc	1731	1093
Erickson Living	6513	14
Erickson Transport Corp	4213	615
Erickson's Flooring and Supply Company Inc	5023	53
Erico International Corp	3441	62
Erico Products Inc	3644	3
Ericson Manufacturing Co	3643	57
Ericsson Inc	3663	30
Erie Bearings Co	5063	144
Erie Coke Corp	3312	79
Erie Engineered Products Inc	3443	156
Erie Enterprises Inc	4213	2602
Erie Family Life Insurance Co	6311	214
Erie Forge And Steel Inc	3462	36
Erie Growers Exchange Coop	5191	182
Erie Indemnity Co	6411	14

Company Name	SIC	Rank
Erie Industrial Supply Co	5084	439
Erie Industries Inc	3599	878
Erie Insurance Company of New York	6331	146
Erie Lake Graphics Inc	2752	1020
Erie M and P Company Inc	3542	81
Erie Manufacturing Inc	3535	221
Erie Plating Co	3471	88
Erie Press Systems Inc	3542	22
Erie Specialty Products	3679	403
Erie Strayer Co	3531	92
Erie-Austin Investors Inc	8062	127
Erieview Metal Treating Company Inc	3471	51
Erika Record LLC	3599	107
Erin Taylor Fine Art Inc	2741	431
ERisk Holdings Inc	7372	774
ERISS Corp	7379	729
Eritech International	5045	617
ERJ Insurance Group Inc	6351	45
Erl Properties Inc	6512	84
Erla's Inc	5147	54
Erler Industries Inc	3479	38
Erm Thermal Technologies Inc	3443	151
Erman Corporation Inc	5093	30
Ermco Inc	1731	182
ERM-Southwest Inc	8711	157
Ernest C Anderson Gravel and Ready Mixed Inc	1442	82
Ernest Communications Inc	4813	307
Ernest Packaging Solution	5113	20
Ernex Corporation Inc	2066	36
Ernie Ball Inc	3931	21
Ernie Elliott Inc	8711	538
Ernie Williams Ltd	5083	89
Ernst and Young LLP	8721	3
Ernst Flow Industries	3824	12
Ernst Timing Screw Co	3451	152
Ernst Van Praag Inc	7319	42
eRoom Technology Inc	7372	970
eRoomSystem Technologies Inc	3575	47
ERP Analysts Inc	7379	426
Error Free Software LLC	3695	97
Ers Industries Inc	5088	46
Ershigs Inc	3084	14
Erskine Attachments Inc	3524	25
ERT Inc	7371	177
eRT Investment Corp	6799	103
Eruston Corp	3679	832
Erva Tool and Die Co	3544	911
Ervin Electric Inc	1731	1174
Ervin Industries Inc	3325	8
Ervin Marketing Creative Communications Inc	8742	451
Ervin N Baker Inc	5511	1226
Erving Industries Inc	2621	36
Erving Paper Mills Inc	2621	58
Erwin Cole Enterprises Inc	3089	1775
ES Adkins and Co	5211	256
E-S Plastic Products Inc	3089	615
ES Ritchie and Sons Inc	3812	110
ES Robbins Corp	3081	57
ES Source Inc	5065	700
ES Sports Corp	2396	20
Esa Biosciences Inc	3826	52
ESA Technology Inc	5084	303
Esage Group LLC	7379	1176
Esaote North America	5047	45
ESB Bank FSB	6035	42
ESB Financial Corp	6712	199
ESB Financial Services Inc	6163	5
Esc Automation Inc	1731	807
Esc Control Electronics LLC	3559	345
Esc Inc	7374	145
Esc Products Corp	3823	477
ESC Select Inc	8999	76
Escada Inc (New York New York)	5621	40
Escalade Inc	3949	39
Escalate Inc	5045	67
Escalon Medical Corp	3845	56
Escalon Premier Brands Inc	2033	71
Escambia Molded Plastics Corp	3089	1564
Escape Enterprises Ltd	6794	95
Escape Technology Inc	7372	571
EscapeWire Solutions LLC	7373	996
Eschen Orthotic and Prosthetics Company Inc	3842	248
Esco Company LLC	2865	10
Esco Corp	3532	5
Esco Electric Supply Co	5063	489
Esco Industries Inc	5191	127
Esco Lighting Inc	3646	74
Esco Manufacturing Inc	3993	104
Esco Products	3827	97
ESCO Technologies Inc (St Louis Missouri)	3812	12
Esco Turbine Technologies - Syracuse Inc	3324	5
Escofab Inc	3523	242
Escort Inc	3812	65
eScreen Inc	7372	662
Escro Transport Ltd	4213	1530
Esd Waste 2 Water Inc	3589	149
Ese Inc	3625	258
eSecLendingcom LLC	6799	62
Esecuritytogo LLC	7379	1015

Company Name	SIC	Rank
E-Services Group Inc	7373	822
ESET LLC	7372	439
ESF Computer Services Inc	7372	3265
Esg Security Inc	7381	49
ESHA Research Inc	7372	3642
Esherick Homsey Dodge and Davis Architects Inc	8712	177
Esi Contracting	1731	1362
Esi Electronic Products Corp	3679	707
Esi Ergonomic Solutions LLC	2522	40
ESI Inc	1731	256
ESI Systems Inc	7372	1843
ESI/Technologies Inc	7372	1857
ESI Technology Corp	8748	433
eSignalcom Inc	7375	43
eSilicon Corp	3625	41
ESIS Inc	6411	146
Esker Inc	7372	2739
Eskridge Honda Co	5511	928
eSkye Solutions Inc	7379	241
Esma Inc	2819	127
Esmark Inc	3316	2
Eso Won Books	5942	36
eSoft Inc	7372	1844
E-SoftSys LLC	7372	3102
eSolar Inc	1711	95
eSolution Architects Inc	8748	328
ESolve Technologies Inc	7371	1821
ESOP Services Inc	6282	634
Esp Computers And Software Inc	5045	907
ESP Technologies LLC	7371	374
Esparza's Welding And Machine Shop Inc	3441	231
Esperanza Palms LLC	3061	59
Esperanzas Tortilleria Inc	2099	346
Espey Manufacturing and Electronics Corp	3679	157
Espo Engineering Corp	8711	452
Espo Engineering Corp	2095	20
Espresso Disposition Corporation 1	2095	20
Esprit Systems Inc	3575	29
ESQ Business Services Inc (Pleasanton California)	7372	1389
Esquire Deposition Services LLC	7338	1
Esrock Partners Advertising Inc	7311	826
Ess Group Inc	2835	42
ESS Inc	1731	1633
Ess Tec Inc	3089	1591
ESS Technology Inc	3674	177
Essa Bancorp Inc	6712	294
Essa Bank and Trust	6036	36
Essannay Show It Inc	3861	131
Esschem Inc	2821	84
Essco Geometric Inc	3086	133
Essco Inc	3554	34
Esselte	2782	1
Essen Nutrition Corp	2099	259
Essence Communications Partners	2721	49
Essential Baking Company Inc	5149	62
Essential Energy Services Inc	1731	871
Essential Industries Inc	2841	23
Essential Sealing Products Inc	3053	124
Essential Security Group	7381	195
Essential Technologies	7378	98
Essential Trading Systems Corp	3669	263
Essentiel Elements de la rue Verte	2844	163
Essex Brass Corp	3569	265
Essex County Welfare Board Inc	8322	23
Essex Crane Rental Corp	7353	8
Essex Cryogenics Of Missouri Inc	3728	118
Essex Electro Engineers Inc	3679	491
Essex Electronics Inc	3674	359
Essex Engineering Inc	3599	677
Essex Equipment	5046	154
Essex Grain Products Inc	5149	33
Essex Industries Inc	3559	68
Essex Investment Management Company LLC	6282	241
Essex Products Group Inc	3823	225
Essex Rental Corp	7353	13
Essex Technology Group Inc	5045	365
Essex West Graphics Inc	2796	29
Essexusa LLC	7373	989
Essick Air Products Inc	3534	7
Essie Cosmetics Ltd	2844	122
Essilor Of America Inc	3851	4
Essintal Enterprise Solutions	7373	202
Esslinger and Company Inc	5094	79
Essmueller Co	3535	91
Essroc Cement Corp	3241	15
ESSROC Italcementi Group	3241	14
Estate Assurance Systems Inc	8742	414
Estee Lauder Companies Inc	2844	2
Estee Lauder Inc	2844	5
Estee Mold and Die Inc	3544	474
Esterle Mold and Machine Company Inc	3498	60
Esterline and Sons Manufacturing Co	3599	1663
Esterline Korry Electronics Co	3728	21
Esterline Mason Controls	3643	11
Esterline Technologies Corp	3823	3
Estes Electric Inc	1731	742
Estes Express Lines Inc	4213	30
Estes Heating and Air Conditioning Inc	1711	142

Company Name	SIC	Rank
Estes Machine Co	3599	2108
Estes Park Brewery Inc	2082	94
Esteves-Dwd LLC	3544	242
Estex Manufacturing Company Inc	2394	3
Estey-Hoover Inc	7311	564
Estherville Foods Inc	2015	46
Estima	7372	3901
Estorian Inc	7372	2973
Estrada Hinojosa and Company Inc	6211	105
Estrela Marketing Solutions	8742	483
Estron Chemicals Inc	2821	122
Estwing Manufacturing Company Inc	3423	27
Esu Inc	5063	495
Esurance Inc	6411	277
E-Sync Networks Inc	4822	7
Esys Corp	8711	397
e-Systems Group LLC	2522	10
ET Browne Drug Company Inc	2844	52
ET Horn Co	5169	47
ET Lawson and Son	5172	99
ET Lowe Publishing Company Inc	2791	55
ET Oakes Corp	3556	152
ET Precision Optics Inc	3599	410
Et Wholesale Ltd	5014	12
Et Works LLC	3523	167
E-T-A Circuit Breakers	3613	13
Eta Engineering Consultants psc Inc	8711	465
E-Tactics Inc	2741	476
Etan Industries Inc	4841	49
ETCAI Products	7372	4813
Etched Images	7389	2175
Etching Industries Corp	7359	220
Etchomatic Inc	5065	323
ETCO Specialty Products Inc	3089	1449
Etec Inc	3825	167
Etec Systems Inc	3699	2
Etec-Durawear Inc	3069	269
Etech Micro Supply Inc	5045	896
EtechnologycorpCom	5045	760
Etek International Inc	7372	4262
E-Teknet Inc	3672	408
E-Tel Systems Corp	1731	1645
Etelos Inc	7371	1898
ETEMCO	3621	102
e-Tenants LLC	6519	28
eTERA Consulting LLC	8748	196
Eternal Image Inc	3995	11
Eternal Star Corp	2678	15
Etest It Inc	7371	907
Etex Ltd	3679	800
Etg Inc	3678	60
ETG Inc	8742	316
Ethan Allen Interiors Inc	2511	4
Ethan Interactive Inc	4813	462
Ethany Corp	7373	1148
EtherCom Corp	3661	150
Etheredge Manufacturing Company Inc	4212	58
Etheridge Electric Company Inc	1731	2107
Etheridge Printing Co	2752	468
Ethertronics Inc	3577	265
EtherWan Systems Inc USA	3679	53
Ethicalhax Inc	4813	750
Ethicon Endo-Surgery Inc	3842	33
Ethicon Inc	3842	21
Ethicspoint Inc	7375	82
Ethikos Inc	2721	467
Ethority Inc	3695	82
Ethostream	7371	1000
Ethyl Corp	2869	28
Ethylene Atlantic Corp	3599	1978
ETI	7372	924
Eti Engineering Inc	7373	1180
Eti Sound Systems Inc	3651	86
Etienne Aigner Inc	3111	3
Etko Machine Inc	3599	2442
E-T-M Enterprises I Inc	3544	31
Etm Studios Inc	7336	220
Etm—Electromatic Inc	3663	84
Etna Prestige Technology Inc	7349	222
Etna Products Inc	2992	53
Etna Tool and Die Corp	3599	2445
Eton Centers Co	6512	43
Eton Corp	5064	78
E-Town Computers	5734	411
E*Trade Bank	6035	46
E*Trade Business Solutions Group Inc	7372	1238
E*TRADE Financial Corp	6035	5
E*TRADE Securities Inc	6211	120
Etribeca LLC	5045	834
Etron Corp	3679	598
ETS Inc	5075	104
Etsy Inc	5961	69
Ettore Products Co	3061	10
Etymotic Research Inc	8732	99
Eubank Construction Company Inc	1623	756
Eubanks Engineering Co	3549	66
Euclid Chemical Co	2899	59
Euclid Discoveries LLC	7371	1552
Euclid Garment Manufacturing Co	2326	23
Euclid Machine and Manufacturing Company Inc	3545	427
Euclid Spiral Paper Tube Corp	5047	122
Euclid SR Partners Inc	6799	209
EUE/Screen Gems Ltd	7812	45

Company Name	SIC	Rank
Eufaula Manufacturing Company Inc	3949	125
Eufaula Pulpwood Company Inc	5099	59
Eugene Carter Enterprises Inc	7349	425
Eugene Sand and Gravel Inc	3295	12
Eugenio's Sheet Metal Inc	3469	342
EULER American Credit Indemnity	6351	40
Eunice News Inc	2711	350
Eunice Superette Inc	2011	156
Euphonix Inc	3621	70
Euphoria Chocolate Company Inc	2064	97
Euramax Holdings Inc	3355	1
Euramco Safety Inc	3564	127
Eurand Inc	2834	244
Eureka Chemical Co	2899	113
Eureka Electrical Products Inc	3366	19
Eureka Networks	7379	98
Eureka Stone Quarry Inc	2951	28
EurekaDIGITAL	7379	968
Eurekster Inc	7371	1114
Euro Brokers Inc	6099	20
Euro Brokers Investment Corp	6211	34
Euro Lloyd Travel Inc	4724	71
Euro RSCG 4D DRTV	7389	296
Euro RSCG Magnet	8743	28
Euro RSCG Middleberg	7311	145
Euro RSCG Tyee MCM	7812	56
Euro Tech Corp	3577	626
Eurohealth (USA) Inc	2834	116
Eurokera North America Inc	3269	4
Euromarket Designs Inc	5719	4
Euromed Inc	3842	133
Euromonitor International Inc	2731	218
Euronet Worldwide Inc	6099	12
Europ Assistance USA	4724	35
Europa Company Inc	5722	24
Europa Partners LLC	7389	1143
Europacific Parts International Inc	5013	118
Europackaging LLC	3081	89
Europe Through the Back Door Inc	4725	16
European and Pacific Stars And Stripes	2711	248
European Coffee Classics Inc	2095	61
European Equity Fund Inc	6726	81
European Mikrograph Corp	7372	3794
European Roasterie Inc	2095	36
Europlast Ltd	3089	1085
Europtec USA Inc	3231	51
EuroSoft Inc	7363	149
Eurosoft Inc (Cary North Carolina)	7372	1734
Eurostar Inc	5661	6
Eurotech Inc	3577	116
Eurotech Industries LLC	3823	251
Eurotek Inc	8742	708
Eurotextil Inc	5131	52
Eurotherm Inc	5084	277
Eurotherm International Inc	3823	31
Eurpac	7389	824
Eurton Electric Company Inc	7694	24
Eustis Company Inc	3829	203
Eutectic Engineering Company Inc	3341	36
Euthenics Inc	7389	2510
Eutsler Technical Products Inc	3069	137
Euvis	3674	487
EV Energy Partners LP	1311	70
EV Roberts	2821	118
ev3 Inc	3841	25
ev3 Neurovascular	3841	67
Evald Moulding Company Inc	5023	163
Evana Tool and Engineering Inc	3535	60
Evangelical Retirement Homes Of Greater Chicago Inc	8361	44
Evangeline Airmotive Inc	3724	25
Evangeline Farmers Coop	5191	165
Evanger Dog and Cat Food Company Inc	2047	46
Evanite Fiber Corp	3089	18
Evans Adhesive Corporation Ltd	2891	107
Evans Analytical Group	8731	96
Evans and Associates Enterprises Inc	1611	145
Evans and Company Inc	3829	361
Evans-and Sutherland Computer Corp	3699	53
Evans and Sutherland Graphics Corp	7372	77
Evans Bancorp Inc	6712	418
Evans Cabinet Corp	2434	36
Evans Components Inc	3674	388
Evans Construction Co	1542	385
Evans Data Corp	7371	942
Evans Dedicated Systems Inc	4213	582
Evans Delivery Company Inc	4213	349
Evans Drug Company Inc	5912	66
Evans East	8734	29
Evans Electric Co	5075	34
Evans Enterprises Inc	3625	31
Evans Environmental and Geosciences	8711	661
Evans Equipment Company Inc	4213	1219
Evans Griffiths and Hart Inc	7372	2278
Evans Hotels	7011	68
Evans Machinery Inc	3553	44
Evans Mactavish Agricraft Inc	3523	62
Evans Manufacturing Inc	3089	261
Evans Mechwart Hambleton and Tilton Inc	8711	280
Evans National Bank	6021	177
Evans Printing Co	2752	1804

Company Name	SIC	Rank
Evans Private Security Inc	7381	213
Evans Seafood Transport LLC	4213	851
Evans Services Inc	1731	378
Evans Steel Service Inc	3441	252
Evans Technology Inc	7373	433
Evans Tempcon Inc	3822	10
Evans Tool and Die Inc	3469	176
Evanston Northwestern Healthcare	8741	20
Evansville Arc Inc	8331	73
Evansville Association For The Blind Inc	7699	151
Evansville Auto Parts Inc	7389	1227
Evansville Corporate Design Inc	5021	118
Evansville Courier and Press	2711	169
Evansville Teachers Federal Credit Union	6061	54
Evansville Tool and Die Inc	3544	655
Evapco Inc	3443	23
Evax Systems Inc	3669	255
EVCI Career Colleges Holding Corp	8299	22
Evco	3089	1118
Evco Plastics	3089	57
EvCo Research LLC	2899	112
Evden Enterprises Inc	3599	1903
EVE USA Inc	8711	507
Eved Services Inc	7389	1745
Eveden Inc	5137	13
Evelec Corp	5063	747
Evelyn Baird Gentry Corp	1731	296
Evenheat Kiln Inc	3567	120
Evening Bulletin Inc	2711	873
Evening Post Publishing Co	2711	114
Evening Times	2711	930
Evenstar Inc	3672	247
Event Inc	7372	3417
Event Rentals Inc	7359	34
Event Streams LLC	7374	375
Eventide Inc	3669	123
Eventra Inc	7372	1123
Events Services Inc	7381	140
Eventz Extraordinaire Inc	8743	40
Ever Ready Pin and Manufacturing Inc	3544	174
Ever Ready Thermometer Company Inc	3823	213
Everbank	6035	22
Everbrite Electronics Inc	3612	77
Everbrite LLC	3993	10
Everburn Manufacturing Inc	3429	26
Evercare Co	3991	4
Evercase USA Inc	3571	205
Evercore Partners Inc	6159	50
Everdrive LLC	5013	205
Eveready Printing Inc	2752	1407
Eveready Products Corp	7389	2050
Everest Biomedical Instruments Company Inc	3841	368
Everest Software Corp	7372	2523
Everest Software Inc	7372	390
Everest Travel Inc	4724	106
Everett Charles Technologies Inc	3678	7
Everett Clay Associates Inc	8743	219
Everett Collection Inc	7336	60
Everett Dykes Grassing Company Inc	1611	126
Everett Hospital	8062	84
Everett Industries Inc	3291	27
Everett J Prescott Inc	5051	30
Everett Pattern and Manufacturing Inc	3544	251
Everett Quarries Company Inc	1422	28
Everett Smith Group Ltd	6719	77
Everfab Inc	2821	116
Everfast Inc	5949	2
Ever-Flex Inc	3842	234
Everfresh Food Corp	2099	315
Everge Group Inc	7379	348
Everglades Electric Supply Inc	5063	873
Everglades Steel Corp	5051	231
Evergreen Advertising and Marketing Inc	7311	927
Evergreen Alliance Golf Ltd	7992	2
Evergreen Avionics Inc	3674	407
Evergreen Center Inc	8361	40
Evergreen Country Shopper Inc	2741	252
Evergreen Data Continuity Inc	7379	1306
Evergreen Energy Inc	1221	43
Evergreen Engineering Inc	8711	233
Evergreen Express Lines Inc	4213	2610
Evergreen Homes Inc	8082	44
Evergreen House Health Center	8051	14
Evergreen Information Technology Services Inc	7378	44
Evergreen International Airlines Inc	4522	12
Evergreen International Aviation Inc	4512	12
Evergreen Mining Co	1241	6
Evergreen Oil Inc	2992	11
Evergreen Packaging Equipment	3565	5
Evergreen Professional Recoveries Inc	7322	109
Evergreen Publications Inc	2731	266
Evergreen Slate Company Inc	3281	25
Evergreen Solar Inc	3674	65
Evergreen Supply Co	5063	210
Evergreen Telecom Services LLC	4813	264
Everhard Products Inc	3423	41
Everhart Transportation Inc	4213	1562
Everhome Mortgage Co	6162	4

Company Name	SIC	Rank
Everlast Worldwide Inc	2339	18
Everlasting Images Inc	2752	1524
Evero Corp	7379	725
Everpoint Inc	7379	1007
Everpure LLC	3569	41
Ever-Ready Oil Co	5172	13
Evers and Whatley Electric Inc	1731	461
Eversan Inc	3625	291
Everseal Gasket Inc	3053	67
Everseal International Sales Company Inc	2851	167
Everson Spice Company Inc	2099	260
Eversun Technologies Inc	3661	124
Everwear Inc	3423	54
Every Supply Company Inc	5085	245
Everything Electric Inc	5063	892
Everything2gocom LLC	5712	78
EveryTicketcom	7999	128
eVestment Alliance	7372	1501
Evets Electric Inc	1731	447
Evga Corp	4813	398
EVH Manufacturing Company LLC	3523	85
Evident Software Inc	7372	2694
Eview Technology Inc	7372	3236
Evinco Professional Services Inc	7363	245
eVisibility	7389	301
Evision International Inc	6211	391
Evisions Inc	7371	794
Evite LLC	7299	25
EvO2 Inc	4812	82
Evogen Inc	3679	119
Evolution Benefits Inc	7374	85
Evolution Bureau	7311	369
Evolution Fuels Inc	1311	273
Evolution Impressions Inc	2752	876
Evolution Inc (Shawnee Mission Kansas)	7372	4374
Evolution Media Printing Inc	7313	41
Evolution Petroleum Corp	1311	210
Evolution Robotics Inc	7372	4299
Evolve Manufacturing Technologies Inc	3825	58
Evolving Systems Inc	7371	219
Evonik Rohmax USA Inc	2899	93
Evonik Stockhausen LLC	2869	47
eVox Productions	7379	581
Evvtex Company Inc	5094	84
EW Harmon Inc	1623	729
EW Howell Company Inc	1542	157
EW Scripps Co	2711	28
EW Thorpe Inc	1541	284
EW Wylie Corp	4213	755
Ewald Automotive Group Inc	5511	202
Ewald's Hartford Ford Lincoln Mercury	5511	1007
eWalk Software Inc	7372	4814
Ewart-Ohlson Machine Company Inc	3599	1500
EWC Controls Inc	3822	34
Ewh Spectrum Inc	3679	312
EWI Worldwide	7319	32
Ewing Asset Management Inc	6282	377
Ewing Brothers Inc	4213	1350
Ewing Electronics Inc	5065	670
EwingCole	8712	81
Ewitness LLC	7379	1530
Ewlz Express Corp	5734	30
EWM Electric Inc	1731	1209
eWorkplace Solutions	7373	145
Eworld Enterprise Solutions Inc	8742	511
Ewrc Inc	5051	499
Ex Libris Group	7372	697
Exa Corp	7372	1531
Exacom Inc	3661	180
Exacq Technologies Inc	3571	50
Exact	7372	943
Exact Cutting Service Inc	7389	2248
Exact Inc	3444	99
Exact Packaging Inc	3565	140
EXACT Sciences Corp	8731	272
Exact Software Co	7371	1625
Exact Software North America Inc	7371	54
Exacta Graphics Inc	2752	1065
Exacta Plastics Inc	3089	1892
ExacTax Inc	7372	3440
Exactbind West	3579	71
Exactech Inc (Gainesville Florida)	3842	39
Exact-Tool and Die Inc	3465	64
ExaGrid Systems Inc	5045	81
Exair Corp	3499	101
Exaktime Inc	7372	1393
Exal Corp	3411	14
Examination Management Services Inc	8099	32
Examiner Corp	7372	4417
ExamWorks Group Inc	8099	112
Exar Corp	3674	97
Exari Systems Inc	7372	3093
Excal Inc	3366	8
Excalibur Data Recovery Inc	7378	58
Excalibur Energy Services Inc	7359	98
Excalibur Films	5046	138
Excalibur Lab Specialists Inc	5047	155
Excalibur Machine And Sheet Metal Inc	3444	243
Excalibur Transportation Group	4213	880
Excel Business Partners	7361	197
Excel Communications Worldwide Inc	1731	2522
Excel Connection Inc	3679	446

Company Name	SIC	Rank
Excel Construction Inc	1623	740
Excel Courier Inc	4226	16
Excel Dryer Inc	3699	176
Excel Electric Inc	1731	1094
Excel Electro Assembly Inc	3672	447
Excel Electrocircuit Inc	3672	462
Excel Electronics Company Inc	5064	194
Excel Federal Credit Union	6061	100
Excel Health	6324	39
Excel Healthcare Receivable Management and Consulting Corp	7322	193
Excel Homes Inc	2452	3
Excel Injection Molding Inc	3089	1264
Excel Machine and Fabrication Inc	3444	220
Excel Manufacturing Inc	3599	957
Excel Meridian Data Inc	3572	47
Excel National Bank	6021	391
Excel Pattern Works Inc	3544	585
Excel Plating Technology Inc	3443	240
Excel Precision Corporation USA	3825	205
Excel Program Inventions	7379	1447
Excel Promotions Corp	2711	559
Excel Prosthetics and Orthotics Inc	3842	265
Excel Security Corp	1731	210
Excel Services	7361	323
Excel Software	7372	4815
Ex-Cel Solutions Inc	5045	490
Excel Specialty Corp	3679	629
Excel Technical Services Inc	7374	223
Excel Technology Inc	3699	22
Excel Technology International Corp	3679	818
Excel Tool And Manufacturing Inc	3544	378
Excel Tool Inc	3544	424
Excel Transport Inc	4213	1590
Excel Trust Inc	6798	141
EXCELCARE Inc	7372	3348
Excelco Developments Inc	3728	202
Excelda Manufacturing Co	2992	25
Excelics Semiconductor Inc	3674	318
Excelitas Technologies Holdings LLC	3648	3
Excelity	3369	24
Excell Color Graphics Inc	2759	283
Excell Data Corp	7379	59
Excell Electronics Corp	3672	296
Excell Global Services Inc	7389	178
Excell Hallmark Sweet Co	3915	1
Excell Machine Company Inc	3599	2320
Excell Management Corp	7349	483
Excell Technologies International Corp	3589	113
Excellance Inc	3711	66
Excellence in Motivation Inc	8748	43
Excellent Coffee Company Inc	2095	24
Exceller Software Corp	7372	4606
Excelligence Learning Corp	8299	12
Excello Circuits Manufacturing Corp	3672	257
Excello Tool Engineering and Manufacturing Co	3599	1524
Excellon Automation Co	3545	31
Excelltech Inc	7372	2974
eXcelon Corp	7372	585
Excelpro Inc	2022	38
Excelsior Blower Systems Inc	3564	123
Excelsior Inc	3053	23
Excelsior Manufacturing and Supply Corp	3444	59
Excelsior Packaging Group Inc	2673	14
Excelsior Plastics Industries Inc	3089	1138
Excelso Coffee Co	5149	104
Excelstor Technology Inc	7371	1225
Exceltech Inc	3672	397
Excent Corp	7371	795
Exceptional Persons Inc	8322	55
Exceptional Risk Advisors LLC	6311	273
Exceptional Sale Promotion Inc	2752	1580
Excess Technologies LLC	7389	156
Excess Trade LLC	5045	582
Exchange Bank	6022	114
Exchange Center Of California Inc	5131	49
Exchange Enterprises Inc	7389	1457
Exchange Network Inc	7389	2023
Excitron Corp	3625	366
Exclusive Beauty Supplies Inc	5087	107
Exclusive Transportation for Industry	4213	2193
Exclusively Expo Inc	5046	74
Exclusively Ours Inc	5048	34
Exco Extrusion Dies Inc	3544	125
EXCO Resources Inc	1311	53
Exec Search Inc	7371	577
Execu/Tech Systems Inc	7372	2846
Exec-U-Net Inc	7389	642
Execupharm Inc	8742	138
ExecuScribe Inc	7338	24
Execu-Search Inc	7361	234
ExecuStay LLC	7021	2
Executive Apparel Inc	2337	9
Executive Arts Inc	7336	289
Executive Business Media Inc	2721	83
Executive Business Services Inc	7371	888
Executive Car Leasing Co	7515	8
Executive Charge Inc	8721	277
Executive Cleaning Services Of Albany Inc	7349	311
Executive Coach Builders Inc	3711	41
Executive Coffee Service Co	2095	30

Company Name	SIC	Rank
Executive Coffee Service Inc	7389	1113
Executive Compumetrics Inc	7372	4036
Executive Consultants	7371	1578
Executive Consulting Group Inc	8742	178
Executive Data Systems Inc	7372	2459
Executive Direction Inc	7361	353
Executive Director Inc	8741	212
Executive Excellence Publishing LLC	2731	326
Executive Janitorial Service Inc	7349	294
Executive Jet Management	4522	29
Executive Media Communications Consultants Inc (Indianapolis Indiana)	8743	272
Executive Office Concepts	2521	54
Executive Printing	2759	263
Executive Printing and Mailing Inc	2741	444
Executive Recruiting Solutions	7361	426
Executive Reporting Service	8111	575
Executive Resources Group	7389	2271
Executive Security Specialists Inc	7381	75
Executive Security Systems Incorporated Of America	7381	79
Executive Suites	7372	4112
Executive Technologies Inc	7372	3707
Executive Telephony Solutions Inc	5999	274
Executive Trading Company Ltd	5199	70
Executive Visions Inc	8742	604
Executive Wine and Spirits Inc	2084	109
Executone/Rhode Island Inc	4813	429
Executone Systems Company Of Louisiana Inc	5065	312
Executone Telecommunications LLC	5065	227
ExecuTrain Corp	8243	2
ExecUtron Computers Inc	7373	485
ExecUtron Development Corp	7372	2975
Exedy Globalparts Corp	5013	72
Exel Direct Inc	4213	3
Exel Logistics Inc	4214	4
Exel Transportation Services Inc	4213	194
Exelixis Inc	8731	37
Exelixis Plant Sciences Inc	8731	78
Exelon Corp	4931	1
Exeltech Inc	3629	74
Exergen Corp	3826	38
Exergetic Systems Inc	7372	4418
Exeter Government Services LLC	7379	814
Exeter Machine Company Inc	3559	420
Exeter Software	7372	4996
Exhibit Express Air Freight	4213	2769
Exhibit Services Group Inc	7389	1624
Exhibit Works Inc	7389	576
Exhibitor Magazine Group	2721	243
Exhibits South Corp	5021	142
Exide Technologies	3691	2
Exigen Inc	7372	715
Exigen Services (USA) Inc	7371	1592
Exigo Office Inc	7372	4097
Exion Technology Inc	3821	53
Exiss Aluminum Trailers Inc	3799	7
Exit 76 Corp	5411	165
Exit41 Inc	7372	1494
Exley Mixon Inc	5065	324
ExLibris Inc USA	7372	442
Exline Inc	7699	30
ExlService Holdings Inc	7389	132
Exmark Manufacturing Company Inc	3524	7
Exobase Corp	7379	915
Exobox Technologies Corp	7372	5091
Exodus Inc	7389	1195
Exodus Integrity Service	7371	976
Exopack LLC	2674	1
Exostar LLC	7389	206
Exothermic Molding Inc	3089	1754
Exotic Electro-Optics Inc	3827	28
Exotic Metals Forming Company LLC	3728	84
Exotic Rubber and Plastics Corp	3089	199
Exovations Of Atlanta LLC	1522	58
ExOxEmis Inc	2836	77
EXP Computer Inc	3661	132
EXP Pharmaceutical Services Corp	4953	50
Expanco Inc	8331	188
Expand Networks Inc	3669	200
Expandable Software Inc	7372	1472
Expanded Rubber Products Inc	3069	189
eXpansys Inc	5961	134
Expedia Inc	4724	5
Expedited Fleet Systems Inc	5014	47
Expedition Networks Ltd	3575	17
Expeditors and Production Services Co	7363	240
Expeditors International of Washington Inc	4731	4
Expercom of Utah Inc	5734	366
ExperExchange Inc	7372	1001
Experian Information Solutions Inc	7323	1
Experian Marketing Services	7319	7
Experience In Software Inc	7372	4687
Experience Inc	7371	775
Experiencecom Inc	7361	108
Experienced Mail Transport Inc	4212	19
Experient Inc	8748	13
Experimental and Applied Sciences Inc	2834	115
Experimental Nylon Products Inc	3089	1348
Experi-Metal Inc	3469	95
Experior Corp	7372	2383

Company Name	SIC	Rank
Experis Technology Group Inc	7373	747
Expert Assembly Services Inc	3672	225
Expert Choice Inc	7379	1325
Expert Coating Company Inc	3312	136
Expert Comfort Solutions	1731	1383
Expert Communications Inc	7331	198
Expert Computer Technologies Inc	7371	1855
Expert Crane Inc	5084	727
Expert Electric Inc	1731	1695
Expert Forge and Machine Inc	3462	63
Expert Object Corp	7372	4349
Expert Satellite Inc	5731	270
Expert Semiconductor Technology Inc	3559	315
Expert Server Group	5045	7
Expert Services	7378	122
Expert Technology Group Inc	5045	971
Expertech LLC	5731	269
Expertez Inc	7371	1844
Experts In Home Health Management Inc	8082	80
Experts Inc	8999	191
ExperTune Inc	7372	3609
Exploration Resources Inc	7371	1682
Explus Inc	7389	451
Expo Group LP	7389	826
Expo Instruments	3823	455
Expo Promotions Inc	2752	964
Exponent Environmental Group Inc	8748	14
Exponent Inc	8742	65
Export Oil Field Supply Company Inc	5082	105
EXPORTech Company Inc	3599	2428
Exports of Washington Inc	8741	197
Exposure International Direct Marketing Systems Inc	7311	729
Express Business Resources LLC	7359	109
Express Business Service LLC	5999	76
Express Card And Label Company Inc	2759	248
Express Communications LLC	3663	111
Express Corde Enterprises LLC	2024	69
Express Employment Professionals	7361	8
Express Enterprises Inc	5211	247
Express Image Inc	2759	229
Express Inc	5621	6
Express Industries	5064	109
Express Maintenance Company Inc	7349	298
Express Manufacturing Inc	3672	9
Express Marine Inc	4424	10
Express Metal Fabricators Inc	3441	96
Express Metrix LLC	7372	2141
Express One International Inc	4512	43
Express Pest Control Company Inc	7342	99
Express Printing and Forms Inc	5112	78
Express Printing and Lithography Co	2752	1560
Express Publishing Inc	2711	800
Express Scale Parts Inc	3523	284
Express Scripts Inc	5912	6
Express Sixty Minute Delivery Service Inc	7389	2249
Express Solutions LLC	2732	48
Express Systems and Engineering Inc	3089	1670
Express Tax Service Inc	7291	11
Express Technologies Corp	7371	826
Express Tool and Die Co	3544	295
Express Visa Service Inc	7389	962
Express-1 Inc	4213	1049
ExpressJet Airlines Inc	4512	24
ExpressJet Holdings Inc	4512	28
ExpressoCom Corp	7371	912
ExpressPoint Technology Services Inc	7379	211
Expressway Lube Centers	7538	9
Expro Manufacturing Corp	2032	42
Exquisita Tortillas Inc	2099	115
Exsl/Ultra Labs Inc	2841	50
Exstar Financial Corp	6351	49
EXSYS Inc	7372	4244
Extech Building Materials Inc	5082	72
Extek Inc	7389	937
Extel Communications Corp	1731	1061
Extend America Inc	4813	273
Extend Health Inc	6324	96
Extend Inc	7372	1640
Extended Data Solutions Inc	7379	1255
Extended Enterprise Engineering and Design LLC	8711	557
Extended Software Solutions LLC	7372	3902
Extended Stay Hotels	7011	4
Extendicare Facilities Inc	8051	20
Extendicare Health Facilities Inc	8051	79
Extensis Products Group	7372	743
Exterior Performance Coatings Inc	5198	13
Exterior Wood Inc	2491	17
Exterran Holdings Inc	7359	2
Exterran Partners LP	4922	24
Extol Inc	7372	2770
Extol Of Ohio Inc	3296	20
Exton Inc	3089	1510
Extra Bilingual Publications Group	2711	671
Extra Clean Inc	7349	139
Extra Mile Transportation LLC	4731	67
Extra Packing Corp	2679	29
Extra Space Storage Inc	6798	93
Extrakare LLC	5047	187
Extrasensory Software	7372	4949
Extreme Carpets LLC	5023	158

Company Name	SIC	Rank
Extreme Connection	7389	2370
Extreme Molding LLC	3841	359
Extreme Networks Inc	3577	59
Extreme Precision Screw Products Inc	3599	1591
Extreme RV's LLC	3792	9
Extreme Technologies Inc	3661	94
Extron Electronics	3577	105
Extrude Hone Deburring Service Inc	3599	2289
Extruded Fibers Inc	2281	22
Extrudex LP	3089	1315
Extrusion Dies Industries LLC	3544	20
Extrusion Punch and Tool Inc	3599	1580
Extrusion Technology Corporation of America	3356	1
Extru-Tech Inc	3523	91
Exx Inc	3944	12
Exxcel Contract Management Inc	1542	261
Exxene Corp	3544	303
Exxon Mobil Corp	1311	1
Eye Care Centers of America Inc	5995	1
Eye Care Network Inc	6324	118
Eye Center Of Racine Ltd	8011	175
Eye/Communication Inc	7331	222
Eye Communication Systems Inc	5043	19
Eye Dialogue LLC	7812	300
Eye Health Services Inc	8011	125
Eye Kraft Optical Inc	3851	27
Eye Lighting International Of North America Inc	3641	12
Eye On Technology Inc	7371	1826
Eye Street Software Corp	7371	797
Eye Surgery Center of Paducah	8011	85
EyeCare Consultants Surgery Center LLC	8011	117
Eyekon Medical Inc	5048	20
Eyelematic Manufacturing Company Inc	3086	30
Eyelet Design Inc	3469	161
Eyemaginations Inc	7336	136
Eyemax Security LLC	1731	1778
EYEMG- Interactive Media Group	7336	242
Eyeonics	3827	37
Eyepvideo Systems LLC	3674	470
EyeTel Imaging Inc	3841	388
Eyewitness News At 5	4832	88
Eylander Electric Inc	3621	146
Ez Acceptance Inc	7359	74
E-Z Burr Tool Co	3545	424
E-Z Data Inc	7372	179
E-Z Do Inc	7299	14
EZ- Dumper	3537	77
EZ Hi-Tech Services Inc	7376	32
EZ Loader Boat Trailers Inc	3799	10
E-Z Mart Stores Inc	5411	10
EZ Nettools	4813	697
E-Z On Auto Tops Inc	2394	19
Ez Prints Inc	7384	20
EZ Sweep Corp	1611	247
E-Z Trail Inc	3523	170
EZ Way Inc	3799	21
eZangacom Inc	7311	592
EZCORP Inc	5932	1
Eze Castle Integration	7371	89
Eze Castle Software Inc	7372	1056
EZE Trucking Inc	4213	1923
Ezell-Key Grain Company Inc	2048	121
Ezenia! Inc	3575	36
EZ-Filing Inc	7372	3064
Ez-Flo International Inc	5074	88
E-Znet Inc	7336	299
E-Znet Inc	7375	236
EZPAWN Colorado Inc	5932	17
EZ-REF Courseware	8299	70
EZSolution Corp	7379	990
EZX Corp	7372	4075
Ezzell Trucking Inc	4213	1226
F and B Manufacturing Co	3469	53
F and D Oilfield Maintenance Inc	1623	374
F and E Aviation Holdings Inc	7699	47
F and F Consultants Inc	8711	694
F and G Tool And Die Co	3544	204
F and H Restaurant of Georgia Inc	5812	385
F and H Supply Inc	5032	109
F and K Delvotec Inc	5065	581
F and M Bank Corp	6712	454
F and M Financial Corp	6022	170
F and M Mafco Inc	5085	32
F and M Micro Products Inc	5045	829
F and N Enterprises Inc	1731	2322
F and P America Manufacturing Inc	3714	165
F and R Installers Corp	1751	16
F and S Carton Co	2657	38
F and S Distributing Inc	4213	1731
F and S Engraving Inc	3556	138
F and S Holdings Inc	2752	967
F and S Tool Inc	3544	83
F and T Trucking Company Inc	4213	2503
F and W Electrical Contractors Inc	1731	260
F and W Transportation Inc	4213	1615
F C L Graphics Inc	2752	162
F Cappiello Dairy Products Inc	2022	65
F D Hurka Co	5084	887
F Dohmen Co	5122	19

Company Name	SIC	Rank
F F and P Mobile Modular Technologies Inc	2451	26
F Gavina and Sons Inc	2095	17
F Gloss International	7361	360
F H Peterson Machine Corp	3599	527
F Henry Michell Co	5191	99
F Hoffmann-La Roche Ltd	2834	57
F J Remey Company Inc	2752	801
F K Everest Inc	1731	454
F L Motheral Co	2752	76
F M Howell and Co	2652	10
F M Machine Co	3599	728
F M Office Express Inc	5044	63
F Miller and Sons Inc	1611	172
F N Smith Corp	3599	826
F P Horak Co	2752	225
F P Rosback Co	3555	54
F R Blankenstein Co	5085	364
F Rizzo Construction Inc	1623	590
F Smith Cartage Co	4213	2344
F Tinker and Sons Company Inc	3545	297
F Triple Inc	2048	69
F1 Technologies	7372	4816
F4w Inc	4813	490
F5 Networks Inc	3577	19
FA Bartlett Tree Expert Co	8748	45
FA Davis Co	2731	171
FA Richard and Associates Inc	6411	122
FA Tech Corp	3599	1292
FA Technology Ventures Corp	6211	258
FA Wilhelm Construction Company Inc	1542	86
FAA Credit Union	6062	32
FAAC Inc	7371	165
Faast Pharmacy	5912	64
Faast Software	7372	4037
FAB Express Inc	4213	1220
Fab Fours Bumpers	3559	232
FAB Industries Corp	2258	5
Fab Masters Company Inc	3599	551
Fab Wright Inc	3589	133
Fabacraft Inc	3535	148
Fabarc Steel Supply Inc	3441	82
Fabbri Sausage Manufacturing	2013	177
Fabcad Inc	7379	1392
Fabco Equipment Company Inc	3556	50
FABCO Equipment Inc	5082	8
Fabco Inc	3531	69
Fabco-Air Inc	3491	30
Fabcon Inc	3272	57
Fab-Con Machinery Development Corp	5084	254
Fabcorp Inc	3443	63
Faber Enterprises Inc	3492	22
Fabergent Inc	7379	866
Fabian Enterprises Inc	5046	295
Fabick Cat	5082	5
Fabory USA Ltd	5072	84
Fabpro Oriented Polymers Inc	3081	92
Fabreeka International Inc	5085	112
Fabricast Inc	3679	592
Fabricated Components Corp	3672	86
Fabricated Metals Co	3599	249
Fabricated Metals LLC	3354	45
Fabricating and Production Machinery Inc	5084	619
Fabricating/Distributor Inc	1796	25
Fabrication Associates Inc	3443	169
Fabrication Concepts Corp	3444	34
Fabrication Services Inc	3444	210
Fabriclean Supply	5087	37
Fabricon Inc	3441	226
Fabricon Products Inc	2673	47
Fabricor Inc	2541	61
Fabricut Inc	2261	10
Fabriform Plastics Inc	3089	1496
Fabrik Industries Inc	3089	257
Fabri-Kal Corp	3089	53
Fabri-Quilt Inc	2395	2
Fabristeel Products Inc	3452	57
Fabritec Industries Inc	7389	1417
Fabritec International Corp	2842	130
Fabritek Company Inc	3599	959
Fabriweld Corp	3542	113
Fabsol LLC	3069	197
Fab-Tech Inc	3444	271
Fabtex Inc	5072	96
Fabtrol Systems Inc	7372	2374
Fabulous Furs	5961	143
Facchina Global Services LLC	8711	383
Face Electronics LC	3679	708
Facebook Inc	7389	12
Faceshot Inc	1731	2580
Facet Biotech Corp	2834	191
Facet Corp	7373	574
Facets Multimedia Inc	7822	20
Facey Medical Foundation	8099	26
Facilamatic Instrument Corp	3812	178
Facilitec Corp	3569	36
Facilitech Inc	1799	48
Facilities Consulting Group	7349	278
Facilities Services Group Inc	7349	350
Facilities Technology Group	7372	1103
Facility Engineering Associates PC	8748	353
Facility Group	8711	237
Facility Healthcare Services Inc	7363	376

Company Name	SIC	Rank
Facility Improvement Corp	1731	2169
Facility Innovations	7372	4038
Facility Services Partners LLC	7349	452
Facility Technology Services Inc	7376	41
Facility Wizard Software Inc	7371	1419
Factiva	7375	23
FACTOR	7372	1846
Factors Etc Inc	2752	792
Factory Card and Party Outlet Corp	5943	4
Factory Company International Inc	3532	36
Factory Direct Appliance Inc	5064	54
Factory Motor Parts Co	5013	30
Factory Systems LLC	3577	526
Facts and Comparisons Inc	2731	86
Facts Inc	7371	1430
Facts on File Inc	2731	173
FactSet Research Systems Inc	7375	11
Fada	3678	64
Fadal Machining Centers LLC	3541	18
Faegre Baker and Daniels	8111	120
FAF Inc	4213	208
FAFCO Inc	3433	38
Fag Bearings Corp	3562	24
Fagan Associates Inc	5063	752
Fagan Co	1711	65
Fagerdala USA - Lompoc Inc	3086	64
Fagerdala-Paclite Inc	3086	83
Fagor Automation Corp	5084	723
Fahlgren Inc	7311	95
Fai Industries Inc	2448	26
Fail Safe Testing Inc	7389	2074
Fair Grounds Race Course and Slots	7948	10
Fair Isaac Corp	7389	68
Fair Isaac International Corp	7389	139
Fair Isaac - San Diego	7372	329
Fair Manufacturing Inc	3524	41
Fair Oaks Farms LLC	2013	48
Fair Oil Ltd	1311	227
Fair Publishing House Inc	2759	405
Fair Wind Inc	4725	28
Fairbank Equipment Inc	5085	227
Fairbank Reconstruction Corp	2011	50
Fairbanks Co	3537	61
Fairbanks Morse Pump Corp	3561	58
Fairbanks Resource Agency Inc	8331	57
Fairbanks Sand and Gravel Inc	3273	95
Fairbanks Scales Inc	3596	3
Fairborn Equipment Company Mid-Atlantic LLC	5046	301
FairBrothers Inc	7372	4817
Fairchild Controls Corp	3724	24
Fairchild Corp	5699	6
Fairchild Equipment And Supply Co	3532	28
Fairchild Imaging Inc	3861	25
Fairchild Industrial Products Co	3823	64
Fairchild Semiconductor International Inc	3674	30
FairCom Corp	5734	228
Fairfax Glass Co	1793	4
Fairfax Imaging Inc	7372	3223
Fairfax Kitchen and Bath Inc	5722	21
Fairfax Management Group Ltd	8748	442
Fairfield Avenue Leasing Co	6531	449
Fairfield Chair Co	2512	27
Fairfield City Transit System	4111	13
Fairfield County Bank	6036	29
Fairfield Ford/Volkswagen/Hyundai/Mitsubishi Inc	5511	971
Fairfield Gourmet Food Corp	2052	41
Fairfield Homes Inc	1522	52
Fairfield Industries Inc	3829	21
Fairfield Laundry Machinery Corp	3582	18
Fairfield Lighting And Design Center Inc	5063	576
Fairfield Line Inc	2381	5
Fairfield Manufacturing Company Inc	3599	2068
Fairfield National Bank	6021	147
Fairfield Processing Corp	2824	11
Fairfield Publishing Co	2711	311
Fairfield Service Group Inc	8748	218
Fairfield Volkswagon Inc	5511	989
Fairhaven Software Products Inc	7372	723
Fairhill Cable Products Inc	3357	84
Fairlane Industries Inc	3053	129
Fairlawn Tool and Die Co	3599	302
Fairless Iron and Metal LLC	5093	216
Fairman Corp	1381	24
Fairmont Copley Plaza Hotel Corp	7011	75
Fairmont Hotel And Resorts US/Mexico Div	7011	90
Fairmont Sign Co	3993	57
Fairmount Capital Advisors Inc	6282	399
Fairmount Long Term Care	8741	153
Fairplay Inc	5411	171
FairPoint Communications Inc	4813	22
Fairport Asset Management LLC	6722	126
Fairport Yachts Ltd	3732	65
Fair-Rite Products Corp	3679	158
Fairview Capital Partners Inc	6799	38
Fairview Health Services	8062	35
Fairview Ministries Inc	8059	15
Fairway Building Products LP	3089	769
Fairway Chevrolet Co	5511	235
Fairway Ford Inc	5511	1178

Company Name	SIC	Rank
Fairway Ford Inc (Greenville South Carolina)	5511	456
Fairway Ford of Augusta Inc	5511	385
Fairway Ford Sales Inc (Placentia California)	5511	686
Fairway Injection Molding Systems Inc	3544	167
Fairway Packing Inc	5147	71
Fairwinds Credit Union	6061	18
Fairydust Lending and Investments Inc	6211	273
Faith Dairy Inc	0241	5
Faith Electric Service Inc	1731	605
Faith Enterprises Inc	1731	347
Faith For Today Inc	4833	237
Faith Hope And Charity Inc	8059	24
Faith Manufacturing Company Inc	3533	50
Faith Printing Company Inc	2752	1640
Faith Regional Health Services	8011	42
Faith Technologies Inc	1731	13
Fakespace Systems Inc	3577	470
Falcon Aerospace Inc	5088	85
Falcon Broadband Inc	4813	544
Falcon Communications Inc	1731	574
Falcon Communications Solutions Inc	4813	529
Falcon Companies International Inc	2599	27
Falcon Contracting Company Of Bartow	1623	638
Falcon Drilling and Blasting Inc	4213	2942
Falcon Electric Inc	3612	66
Falcon Electrical Contractors Inc	1731	1183
Falcon Equity Inc	2752	1699
Falcon Express Inc	4214	28
Falcon Fine Wire and Wire Products Inc	5064	18
Falcon Foam	3086	39
Falcon Foundry Co	3366	9
Falcon International Bank	6021	154
Falcon Lock	3429	30
Falcon Messenger Service	7389	1536
Falcon Northwest Computer Systems Inc	5961	181
Falcon Plastics Inc	3089	287
Falcon Precision Industries Inc	3599	1169
Falcon Printing Inc	2752	1449
Falcon Ridge Development Inc	6552	309
Falcon Ridge Technologies LLC	3571	220
Falcon Safety Products Inc	3861	45
Falcon Sales And Technology Inc	5065	769
Falcon Steel Inc	5051	428
Falcon Technologies Inc	5065	154
Falcon Tool Company Inc	3544	583
Falcon Transport Inc	4213	1591
Falconer Electronics Inc	3672	154
Falconer Printing and Design Inc	2752	1691
Falconer Street Group Home	8322	216
Falcone's Cookie Land Ltd	2052	60
Falconhead Capital LLC	6722	217
FalconStor Software Inc	7372	495
Falex Corp	8742	578
Falhgren Mortine	8743	130
Falk Corp	3566	4
Falken Industries LLC	7381	124
Falken Tire Corp	5014	32
Falkenberg Capital Corp	6211	274
Falkner Winery Inc	2084	48
Falkor Group LLC	7379	945
Fall Machine Company Inc	3545	155
Fall River Electrical Associates Inc	1731	885
Fall River Feedyard LLC	0211	13
Fall River Rural Electric Coop	4911	250
Fall River Tool and Die Company Inc	3364	31
Fallen Oak Packing LLC	4213	3032
Fallen Trucking	4213	712
Fallline Corp	3449	26
Fallon Visual Products Corp	3993	20
Fallon Worldwide LLC	7311	53
Falls Auto Parts and Supplies Inc	5013	68
Falls Church News Press	2711	922
Fallsnet LLC	5734	474
Fallsway Equipment Company Inc	5013	69
Falmouth Co-Operative Company Inc	5999	70
Falmouth Hospital Association Inc	8062	218
Falmouth Lumber Inc	5031	196
Falore Chrysler/Plymouth/Jeep and Eagle	5511	719
Falstrom Co	3469	156
Faltis Marketing Communications Inc	7311	673
Famarco Inc	2099	268
Famco Enterprises Inc	3599	1492
Famco Inc	1629	101
Fame Industries Inc	5084	613
Fame Tool and Manufacturing Company Inc	3544	716
Fame (USA) ProductsInc	5945	16
Fametech America Inc	3577	609
Family 1st of Texas Federal Credit Union	6061	146
Family Amusement Corp	3944	34
Family Brands International LLC	2011	52
Family Dollar Stores Inc	5331	5
Family Empowerment Council Inc	8322	87
Family First Federal Credit Union	6061	87
Family First Mortgage Corp	6162	120
Family Ford Sales Inc	5511	241
Family HomeCare Inc	8082	69

Company Name	SIC	Rank
Family Information Systems Inc	7371	1209
Family Life Communications Inc	4832	58
Family Life Insurance Co	6311	112
Family Loompya Corp	2099	357
Family Publishing Group Inc	2721	441
Family Resource Center	8322	151
Family Resources Community Action	8322	131
Family Room Entertainment Corp	7812	232
Family Service Agency	8322	243
Family Service Inc	8322	161
Family Service Organization Of Worcester Inc	8082	81
Family Sports Concepts Inc	5812	16
Family Stations Inc	4832	48
Family Trust Federal Credit Union	6061	101
FamilytravelCom	7375	294
Famlee Electronics Inc	5065	332
Famous Dave's of America Inc	5812	202
Famous Enterprises Inc	5085	15
Famous Footwear	5661	5
Famous Hospitality Inc	2761	16
Famous Lubricants Inc	2992	60
Famous Natchitoches Louisiana Meat Pie Co	2099	235
Famous Software LLC	7372	2349
Famous Supply Co	5075	3
Famous Supply Co	5075	111
Fan Equipment Company Inc	5084	437
Fan Group Inc	3564	70
Fanchiou Satellite Tv Corp	5063	1033
Fancort Industries Inc	3544	448
Fancy Fixtures OnlineCom	2499	59
Fancy Media Company Inc	3695	178
Fanelli Brothers Trucking Co	4213	1465
Fanelli's Windowpros Inc	5211	198
Fannie May Confections Inc	5441	3
Fannon Petroleum Services Inc	5172	36
Fanshawe Inc	1731	703
Fansonly Network	7375	133
Fansteel Inc	3463	5
Fanstel Corp	3661	118
Fanta Equipment Co	5084	792
Fantagraphics Books Inc	2721	344
Fantasia Industries Corp	2844	165
Fantastic Network Solutions Inc	7379	726
Fantastic Sams	6794	65
Fantasy Inc	3652	25
Fanuc Robotics America Corp	3559	18
Fapco Inc	4783	8
Fapp Brothers Petroleum Inc	5171	65
Far East Broadcasting Co	4832	267
Far East Energy Corp	1311	269
Far East National Bank	6021	71
Far International Corporation Of America	5065	983
Far Niente Winery Inc	2084	36
Far North Tours	4725	64
Far West Collection Services Inc	7322	130
Far West Rice Inc	2044	11
Far West Technology Inc	3829	366
Farason Corp	3565	95
Farber Specialty Vehicles Inc	3711	62
Farber Trucking Corp	3081	152
Farbest Foods Inc	2015	25
Farbest-Tallman Foods Corp	2023	23
Farella Braun and Martel LLP	8111	244
Fareway Stores Inc	5411	92
Fargo Assembly Co	3643	23
Fargo Assembly Of PA Inc	3679	133
Fargo Automation Inc	5084	385
Fargo Electronics Inc	3571	32
Fargo Freightliner Inc	5511	1075
Fargo Glass and Paint Co	5039	17
Fargo Tank And Steel Co	5031	158
Fargo Youth Commission Inc	8322	170
Faria Limited LLC	2844	74
Faribault Manufacturing Co	3089	1739
Farin and Associates Inc	7372	3187
Faris Mailing Inc	7331	93
Farley Group Inc	3589	61
Farley Printing Co	2752	1225
Farley's and Sathers Candy Company Inc	2064	4
Farleys Inc	3589	202
Farm And Home Publishers Limited Inc	2741	212
Farm Boy Meats Inc	5141	73
Farm Chemicals Inc	5153	146
Farm Country Co-Op	2875	7
Farm Credit Bank of Omaha	6111	6
Farm Credit Bank of Texas	6111	5
Farm Credit Leasing Services Corp	6159	35
Farm Credit Services of Mid-America	6159	25
Farm Depot	5191	116
Farm Equipment Center	5083	209
Farm Family Casualty Insurance Co	6331	94
Farm Family Holdings Inc	6331	144
Farm Fresh Foods Inc	5149	82
Farm Journal Inc	2721	131
Farm Progress Companies Inc	7389	686
Farmdale Creamery Inc	2026	68
Farmer Boy Ag Systems Inc	5083	77
Farmer Brothers Co	2095	7
Farmer Mold And Machine Works Inc	3599	1828
Farmers Alliance Mutual Insurance Co	6331	138

Company Name	SIC	Rank
Farmers and Merchants Bancorp	6712	205
Farmers and Merchants Bank (Granite Quarry North Carolina)	6022	445
Farmers and Merchants Bank of Central California	6022	161
Farmers and Merchants Bank of Long Beach	6022	47
Farmers and Merchants Bank of St Clair	6022	745
Farmers and Merchants Trust Co	6022	339
Farmers and Savings Bank	6022	442
Farmers Bank and Capital Trust Co	6022	146
Farmers Bank and Trust Co (Blytheville Arkansas)	6022	354
Farmers Bank (Frankfort Indiana)	6712	447
Farmers Bank of Gower	6022	815
Farmer's Building Supply Inc	5211	142
Farmers Capital Bank Corp	6021	96
Farmers Casualty Insurance Co	6331	239
Farmers Cellular Telephone Co	4812	124
Farmers Citizens Bank	6021	205
Farmers Commission Co	5191	95
Farmers Co-Op Association	5153	183
Farmers Coop (Carmen Oklahoma)	5153	139
Farmers Coop (Fort Smith Arkansas)	5191	166
Farmers Coop (Hanska Minnesota)	2875	19
Farmers Cooperative Association (Alva Oklahoma)	4221	7
Farmers Cooperative Association (Brule Nebraska)	5153	45
Farmers Cooperative Association (Gillette Wyoming)	5153	157
Farmers Cooperative Association (Jackson Minnesota)	5191	14
Farmers Cooperative Co (Dayton Iowa)	5153	9
Farmers Cooperative Co (Dows Iowa)	5153	112
Farmers Cooperative Co (New Hartford Iowa)	2048	45
Farmers Cooperative Co (Readlyn Iowa)	5153	101
Farmers Cooperative Compress	4221	1
Farmers Cooperative Creamery Of Mcminnville Oregon	2023	25
Farmers Cooperative Dairy Inc	5143	31
Farmers Cooperative Elevator Co (Echo Minnesota)	2048	25
Farmers Cooperative Elevator Co (Halstead Kansas)	5153	144
Farmer's Cooperative Elevator (Hudsonville Michigan)	2048	43
Farmers Cooperative Grain and Seed	5191	140
Farmers Cooperative Grain Co	5153	182
Farmers Cooperative Mill Elevator	5153	145
Farmers Cooperative of Pilger	5153	82
Farmers Cooperative Society	5153	22
Farmers Distributing	4213	2026
Farmers Electric Cooperative Corp	4911	439
Farmers Electric Cooperative Inc (Chillicothe Missouri)	4911	525
Farmers Electric Inc	1731	2010
Farmers Elevator and Exchange Inc	5191	167
Farmers Elevator and Supply Co	5153	120
Farmers Elevator Company Of Pelican Rapids	5153	201
Farmers Elevator Cooperative Of Rock Valley Iowa	5153	133
Farmers Elevator Grain And Supply	5153	198
Farmers Feed and Grain Co	5153	166
Farmers Gin Company Inc	5153	176
Farmers Grain Company of Chestnut	5153	130
Farmers Group Inc	6719	5
Farmers Holding Co	6712	582
Farmers Home Furniture	5712	2
Farmers Insurance Exchange	6331	7
Farmer's Mill and Elevator Company Inc	5153	169
Farmers Mutual Telephone Co	4813	456
Farmers National Banc Corp	6712	306
Farmers National Bank of Buhl	6021	264
Farmers National Bank of Canfield	6021	119
Farmers National Bank of Emlenton	6021	206
Farmers National Co	6531	366
Farmers New World Life Insurance Co	6311	87
Farmers Oil Company Inc	4213	948
Farmers Pride Inc	2015	23
Farmers Rice Coop	2044	9
Farmers Rice Milling Company Inc	2044	5
Farmers Rural Electric Cooperative Corp	4911	519
Farmers State Bank and Trust Co	6022	591
Farmers State Bank of Hamel	6022	781
Farmers State Bank of Western Illinois	6022	721
Farmers Supply Association Inc	5999	64
Farmers Telecommunications Coop	4813	220
Farmers Telephone Coop (Kingstree South Carolina)	4813	63
Farmers Union Cooperative Business Association Of St Marys Kan	5153	168
Farmers Union Industries LLC	2048	12
Farmers Union Oil Co (Devils Lake North Dakota)	5172	91
Farmers Union Oil Co (Ellendale North Dakota)	5541	45
Farmers Union Oil Company Inc	5191	94

Company Name	SIC	Rank
Farmers Union Oil Company of Kenmare	5541	52
Farmers Union Oil Co (Rolla North Dakota)	5172	157
Farmers Union Oil Coop	5171	45
Farmers Union Oil Coop (Watford City North Dakota)	5541	62
Farming Technology Inc	0721	2
Farmington Displays Inc	3993	124
Farmington Foods Inc	2013	91
Farmington State Bank	6022	813
Farmland Foods Inc	2013	4
Farmland Mutual Insurance Company Inc	6331	294
Farmour Security Service	5064	132
Farmstead Telephone Group Inc (Windsor Connecticut)	5065	60
Farnam Companies Inc	2834	131
Farnam Custom Products	3585	70
Farner-Bocken Co	8999	15
Farney's Incorporated Home And Building Center	5211	311
Farnham and Pfile Company Inc	1629	110
Farnham Electric Co	1731	828
Farnor Enterprises Inc	3621	149
Farnsworth Engineering	3599	2470
FarnumMorales Inc	7336	104
Faro Delaware Inc	3829	40
Faro Industries Inc	3089	1525
Faro Technologies Inc	3829	13
Faronics Corp	5045	141
Farouk Systems Inc	2844	21
FarPoint Technologies Inc	7372	1555
Farrar Corp	3599	169
Farrar Straus and Giroux LLC	2731	169
Farrell Brothers Holdings Inc	3599	2179
Farrell Duferco Corp	3356	19
Farrell-Calhoun Inc	2851	54
Farrington Design Group Ltd	7389	1239
Farris Fab and Machine Inc	3441	150
Farrow Amusement Company Inc	7999	101
Farrow Machine and Manufacturing Company Inc	3599	1707
Farruggio's Express	4213	2027
Farruggio's Express Inc	4213	1468
Farsight Technologies Inc	7371	876
FarStone Technology Inc	7372	1149
Farwest Aircraft Inc	3541	217
Farwest Corrosion Control Co	5169	17
Farwest Paint Manufacturing Co	2851	134
Farwest Steel Corp	5051	140
Farzati Manufacturing Corp	3599	1368
Fas Plastic Enterprises Inc	3089	1119
Fascinating Electronics Inc	3577	667
Fashion Graphics	7336	115
Fashion Inc	3444	213
Fashion Life Inc	2331	10
Fashionphile	5632	13
Fasig-Tipton Company Inc	7389	522
Fasson Roll North America	2621	3
Fast Action Alarms	5063	777
FAST and Fluid Management SRL	3561	1
Fast Appraisals Inc	6541	26
Fast Distributing Inc	3523	151
Fast Eddie's Bon Air	5812	339
Fast Electrical Contractors Inc	1731	985
Fast Fare Inc	5411	157
Fast Forward Video Inc	3651	203
Fast Foto Inc	7384	56
Fast Group Houston Inc	3053	24
Fast Heat Inc	3567	105
Fast Page Radio Inc	5999	184
Fast Semiconductor Inc	3679	803
Fast Track Communications Inc	5064	205
Fast Way Freight Systems Inc	4213	2460
FastBucks	6141	67
Fastcam Inc	5734	275
Fastcap LLC	3089	1645
Fastco Industries Inc	3452	36
Fastcut Tool Corp	3545	15
Fastek Products Inc	3544	54
Fastenal Co	5211	5
Fastenal Company Leasing	7513	6
Fastener Equipment Corp	5084	915
Fastener Industries Inc	3452	79
Fastener Specialty Inc	3678	73
Fasteners and Fire Equipment Inc	5072	194
Fasteners Inc	5072	61
Fasteners Inc	5072	29
Fastening Systems International Inc	5072	180
Fastforward Communications Inc	8743	322
Fastframe USA Inc	6794	91
Fastline Publications LLC	2721	71
Fastpulse Technology Inc	3699	265
Fastrack Healthcare Systems Inc	7372	2215
Fastrak Manufacturing Services Inc	3679	634
FastSpring	7372	2189
Fasttone Inc	4813	374
Fata Inc	7313	26
Fate Therapeutics Inc	8731	165
Fath Properties Inc	6513	10
Father and Son Moving and Storage	4213	3012
Fathom Five Divers Inc	7999	142
Fatigue Dynamics Inc	3829	508

Company Name	SIC	Rank
Fatigue Technology Inc	3728	69
Fatpipe Networks Inc	7373	277
Fatwire Corp	7372	770
Faulk and Foster Real Estate Inc	6531	345
Faulk and Winkler LLC	8721	159
Faulk Co	7349	35
Faulk Electric Corp	1731	1518
Faulkner Collision	5511	917
Faulkner Harrisburg Inc	5511	373
Faulkner Information Services Inc	2741	172
Faulkner USA Inc	1542	50
Faultless Starch/Bon Ami Co	2842	17
Faultline Brewing Company Inc	5812	421
Fauquier Bankshares Inc	6022	264
Fauquier County Public Schools	8211	93
Faurecia Automotive Seating	2531	26
Faust Goetz Schenker and Blee	7389	1891
Faust Printing Inc	2752	817
Faustel Inc	3599	301
Favorite Plastic Corp	3081	85
Fawkes Engineering LLC	3577	523
Fawn Industries Inc	3089	411
Fax Plastics Inc	3083	81
Fax Plus Inc	5999	89
FaxBack Inc	4822	21
Faxon Machining Inc	3541	29
FaxonGillis Homes Inc	1521	119
Fay Electric Wire Corp	5063	272
Fay Industries Inc	5051	258
Fay Spofford and Thorndike Inc	8711	285
Fayblock Materials Inc	3272	112
Fayette Community Hospital Inc	8062	125
Fayette Cos	8742	666
Fayette County Record Inc	2711	916
Fayette County Union Inc	2711	874
Fayette Electrical Service Inc	7382	47
Fayette Plaza LLC	6531	258
Fayette Publishing Inc	2759	474
Fayette Resources Inc	8322	48
Fayette Tool and Engineering Inc	3469	165
Fayette Tree And Trench Inc	1623	502
Fayetteville Publishing Company Inc	2711	221
Fayez Sarofim and Co	6282	131
Fazoli's Restaurants LLC	5812	176
Fazoli's System Management	5812	228
Fazzino Auto Parts Inc	5013	332
FB McFadden Wholesale Company Inc	5194	16
Fb Sale LLC	2051	89
FB Washburn Candy Corp	2064	84
FB Wright Co	5085	103
FBC Enterprises Inc	2789	52
FBC Industries Inc	2099	206
FBF Inc	5091	85
FBG Corp	7349	510
FBL Financial Group Inc	6311	72
FBProductions Inc	2752	278
FBR and Co	6211	157
FBR Investment Services Inc	6211	33
FBRD Company Inc	7311	828
FBS Corp	3592	28
FBS Systems Inc	7372	4375
FC Banc Corp	6712	614
FC Phillips Inc	3451	99
FC Witt Associates Ltd	3081	173
Fca Technologies LLC	7374	334
FCB Services Inc	6021	201
Fcc Acquisition LLC	2899	198
Fcc Commercial Furniture Inc	2599	16
FCC LLC	2796	47
FCCI Investment Group Inc	6282	88
FCCI Mutual Insurance Co	6331	142
FCG Inc	3672	106
F-Chart Software	7372	2310
Fci Americas Holding Inc	3643	10
FCI Electronics Inc	3679	124
FCKingston Co	3491	46
FCL Builders Inc	1541	175
FCM Investments	6282	406
FCS	3679	580
FCx Performance Inc	5084	64
Fcx Systems Inc	3621	64
Fd Johnson Co	5084	661
FD Lawrence Electric Co	5063	94
FD Stella Products Co	5046	189
FD Thompson and Company PLC	8721	249
Fda Enterprises Inc	1731	2170
FDC/aerofilter Inc	5088	39
F-D-C Corp	5049	60
Fdc Machine Repair Inc	3542	56
F-D-C Reports Inc	2721	213
Fdc Services Inc	7389	1004
FDI Consulting Inc	7372	865
Fds Infotech Inc	5045	508
FDS International Inc	7372	2597
FDS Manufacturing Co	2679	25
Fds USA Inc	7373	564
F-Dyne Electronics	3625	218
FE Hale Manufacturing Company Inc	2521	47
FE Wheaton Lumber Co (Wheaton Illinois)	5211	85
FE Wheaton Lumber Co (Yorkville Illinois)	5211	48
Fearey Group Inc	8743	127
Feather Larson and Synhorst	7389	1615

Company Name	SIC	Rank
Feather Larson and Synhorst	7389	1262
Feather Publishing Company Inc	2711	479
Featherlite Building Products	3271	6
Featherlite Inc	3715	6
Featherspring International Corp	5961	191
Feature Advertising and Creative Services	7311	604
Feature Marketing Inc	7359	60
February Fourteen Inc	4213	1599
FEC Electric Inc	1731	2148
FEC Highway Services Inc	4213	2708
FEC Inc	3569	232
Fec Technologies Inc	8711	510
FEC Technology Corp	5065	535
Fechheimer Brothers Company Inc	2326	6
Fed USA Inc	6794	29
Fedcap Rehabilitation Services Inc	8093	19
Fedco Electronics Inc	3691	23
Fedco Steel Corp	5051	79
Federal Agricultural Mortgage Corp	6111	13
Federal Alarm Inc	7382	144
Federal and State Inspectors Federal Credit Union	6061	159
Federal APD Inc	3823	50
Federal Assembly Inc	3569	293
Federal Bond And Collection Service Inc	7322	51
Federal Business Centers	6552	247
Federal Cartridge Co	3482	3
Federal Check Recovery Inc	7322	152
Federal Cleaning Contractors Inc	7349	320
Federal Communications Group Inc	4813	66
Federal Compress and Warehouse Company Inc	4221	2
Federal Deposit Insurance Corp	6399	1
Federal Eloctronics Inc	3679	161
Federal Equipment Co	5932	9
Federal Flavors Inc	2087	34
Federal Fruit and Produce Co	5148	48
Federal Home Loan Bank of Atlanta	6019	2
Federal Home Loan Bank of Boston	6019	8
Federal Home Loan Bank of Chicago	6019	4
Federal Home Loan Bank of Cincinnati	6019	3
Federal Home Loan Bank of Dallas	6019	12
Federal Home Loan Bank of Des Moines	6019	11
Federal Home Loan Bank of Indianapolis	6019	10
Federal Home Loan Bank of New York	6019	6
Federal Home Loan Bank of Pittsburgh	6019	7
Federal Home Loan Bank of San Francisco	6019	1
Federal Home Loan Bank of Seattle	6019	9
Federal Home Loan Bank of Topeka	6019	5
Federal Hose Manufacturing	3599	25
Federal Industries	3585	39
Federal Information and News Dispatch Inc	7374	358
Federal Insurance Co	6331	24
Federal International Inc	5093	79
Federal Letter Co	2752	1536
Federal Manufacturing Co	3523	109
Federal Medical Supplies Inc	5047	205
Federal Mogul Corp Sealing Systems Div	3714	75
Federal National Mortgage Association Fannie Mae	6111	1
Federal Pacific Credit	7322	190
Federal Package Network Inc	3089	1646
Federal Plastics Corp	3087	20
Federal Pump Corp	3561	129
Federal Realty Investment Trust	6798	70
Federal Research Service Inc	2731	353
Federal Reserve Bank of Boston	6011	8
Federal Reserve Bank of Chicago	6011	3
Federal Reserve Bank of Cleveland	6011	6
Federal Reserve Bank of Dallas	6011	7
Federal Reserve Bank of Kansas City	6011	9
Federal Reserve Bank of Minneapolis	6011	10
Federal Reserve Bank of New York	6011	1
Federal Reserve Bank of Philadelphia	6011	4
Federal Reserve Bank of Richmond	6011	2
Federal Reserve Bank of San Francisco	6011	5
Federal Sample Card Corp	2782	31
Federal Screw Works	3452	21
Federal Signal Corp	3711	21
Federal Telecommunications Inc	5046	31
Federal Tool and Engineering LLC	3544	296
Federal Trust Bank	6035	138
Federal Trust Corp	6712	435
Federal Warehouse Co	4225	4
Federal Wine and Liquor Co	5182	33
Federally Insured Savings Network	6211	277
Federal-Mogul Corp	3714	10
Federated Agency Group Inc	7291	3
Federated Co-Ops Inc	5989	3
Federated Foodservice	5141	170
Federated Funeral Directors Of America Inc	8742	321
Federated Group	5141	151
Federated Group Inc (Arlington Heights Illinois)	5141	91
Federated Investors Inc	6282	50

Company Name	SIC	Rank
Federated Life Insurance Co	6311	162
Federated Mutual Insurance Co	6331	107
Federated National Insurance Co	6331	234
Federated Paint Manufacturing Company Inc	2851	89
Federated Publications Inc	2711	260
Federated Rural Electric Association	4911	568
Federated Service Insurance Co	6331	34
Federated Telephone Co	4813	412
Federico Consulting Inc	7379	1369
FedEx Corp	4513	2
FedEx Custom Critical Inc	4213	39
FedEx Express Corp	4213	4
FedEx Freight East Inc	4213	16
Fedex Ground Package System Inc	4215	3
FedEx Office and Print Services Inc	7334	1
FedFirst Corp	6159	28
FedFirst Financial Corp	6712	544
Fedmet International Corp	5051	333
Fedresults Inc	8742	634
Fedstore Corporation Inc	7379	173
Fedvar Corporation Inc	7373	419
Fedway Associates Inc	5182	7
Feed Control Corp	5065	595
Feed Management Systems Inc	7372	222
Feedall Inc	3535	217
Feeding Concepts Inc	3559	440
Feeding Frenzy Inc	7389	1844
Feed-Lease Corp	3549	82
Feeger - Lucas - Wolfe Inc	5084	486
Feeley and Driscoll PC	8721	314
FeelGood for Life Inc	5961	146
Feesers Inc	5141	78
Fehr Brothers Industries Inc	5085	179
Fehr Foods Inc	2052	25
Fehrman Tool and Die Inc	3544	756
FEI Behavioral Health	8049	7
FEI Co	3559	11
Feinstein Kean Healthcare	8743	37
Feintool US Operations Inc	3469	81
Feith Systems and Software Inc	7372	1858
Feizy Import and Export Co	2273	24
Felbro Food Products Inc	2087	37
Felbro Inc	3993	49
Felco Industries Ltd	3535	222
FelCor Lodging Trust Inc	6798	96
Feld Entertainment Inc	7922	3
Feld Schumacher and Co	8721	435
Felder Communications Group Inc	7311	399
Feldman Mall Properties Inc	6798	219
Feldman Printing Inc	2759	510
Feldmann Engineering and Manufacturing Company Inc	3546	38
Feldmeier Equipment Inc	3443	15
Feldspar Trucking Company Inc	4213	2548
Felix Chevrolet	5511	384
Felix LLC	1623	190
Felix Manufacturing Company Inc	2511	62
Felix Roma and Sons Inc	2051	170
Felix Schoeller North America Inc	2672	53
Felix Thomson Co	3429	95
Felix's Caketeria	5461	4
Felker Brothers Corp	3317	26
Feller LLC	5063	586
Fellers Inc	3993	30
Fellowes Inc	3579	5
Felters Of South Carolina LLC	2299	18
Feltes Sand and Gravel Co	5032	38
Felton Inc	3991	14
Female Health Co	3069	71
Femco Inc	3523	108
Femto Tech Inc	8999	216
Fenbar Pricision Machinists Inc	3599	2034
Fenco Supply Company Inc	5078	25
Fencor Graphics Inc	2752	855
Fender Musical Instruments Corp	3651	24
Fenestra Winery	2084	57
Fenestrae Inc	7372	2421
Fenetech Inc	7371	1401
Fenguard Security Inc	7381	245
Fenico Precision Castings Inc	3369	21
Fenimore Asset Management Inc	6282	87
Fenimore Manufacturing Inc	3555	124
Fennemore Craig PC	8111	261
Fenner and Associates Inc	3829	413
Fenner Inc	2399	20
Fenner Presision Inc	3089	597
Fentech Inc	3442	127
Fenton and Lee Confections	2064	123
Fenton Art Glass Co	3229	13
Fenton Enterprises Inc	2064	55
Fentura Financial Inc	6712	500
Fenway Partners Inc	6799	149
Feole Technologies Inc	3829	356
Fepco Container Inc	4213	2672
Fepsco Inc	5046	201
Ferazzoli Imports Inc	5032	68
Ferber Sheet Metal Works Inc	1761	28
Ferche Millwork Inc	2435	13
Ferco Tech Corp	3728	97
Fergus Electric Cooperative Inc	4911	452
Fergus International Inc	5083	187
Ferguson Construction	1542	286

Company Name	SIC	Rank
Ferguson Construction Co (Sidney Ohio)	1542	175
Ferguson Consulting Inc	7371	532
Ferguson Enterprises Inc	5074	1
Ferguson Enterprises Inc (Newport News Virginia)	5074	2
Ferguson Equipment Inc	3542	107
Ferguson Fire and Fabrication Inc	5087	7
Ferguson Perforating and Wire Company Inc	3469	135
Ferguson Production Inc	3089	505
Ferguson Publishing Inc	2741	305
Ferguson Resources Inc	1382	71
Ferguson Supply And Box Manufacturing Co	2653	67
Ferguson Thrall Distribution	5085	180
Ferguson Tools Inc	3545	246
Feris Electric Co	1731	1021
Ferland Corp	6531	136
Ferman Automotive Group	5511	81
Fermer Precision Inc	3544	304
Fernandes Enterprises LLC	3699	193
Fernando Originals	5094	61
Fernco Inc	3432	25
Ferncrest Fashions Inc	2211	30
Ferndale Laboratories Inc	2834	177
Fernic Inc	7349	204
Ferno-Washington Inc	3842	87
Fernqvist Labeling Solutions	3577	460
Feroleto Steel Company Inc	3316	13
Ferotech Solution Services Inc	5045	1050
Ferox Microsystems Inc	7372	4500
Ferrante Manufacturing Co	2541	43
Ferrara Fire Apparatus Incorporated	3711	55
Ferrara Pan Candy Company Inc	2064	15
Ferrara Technology Partners Inc	7379	1582
Ferrari Importing Co	3949	137
Ferrari North America Inc	5012	56
Ferrari Technical Sales LLC	5063	1065
Ferrari-Carano Vineyards/Wine LLC	2084	28
Ferrario Ford Inc	5511	639
Ferrell Capital Management	6211	335
Ferrell Companies Inc	7371	1277
Ferrell Excavating Co	1429	9
Ferrell Industries Inc	5149	212
Ferrell Paving Inc	1611	114
Ferrellgas Inc	2911	31
Ferrellgas LP	5984	7
Ferrellgas Partners LP	5984	3
Ferrero U S A Inc	5145	1
Ferri Supermarkets Inc	5411	256
Ferrilli Information Group	8742	426
Ferring Pharmaceuticals Inc	2834	219
Ferriot Inc	3089	384
Ferris Chevrolet Inc	5511	1005
Ferris-Stahl-Meyer Packing Corp	5147	30
Ferro Corp	2851	5
Ferro Electronics Material Systems	3269	8
Ferro Magnetics Corp	3629	63
Ferronics Inc	3264	19
Ferrotherm Corp	3462	48
Ferrous Processing And Trading Co	5093	10
Ferry Electric Co	1731	332
Ferry Machine Corp	3599	1438
Ferry Morse Seed Co	3999	32
Ferry Transportation Inc	4213	2147
Ferson Optics Inc	3827	109
Fertility Solutions Inc	8099	106
Fertilizer Corporation of America	2873	21
Fertitta Enterprises	8741	290
Fertrell Co	2873	16
Fesco Inc	8711	56
Fess Parker Winery and Vineyard	2084	21
Fessenden Cooperative Association	5153	72
Fessenden Hall Inc	5031	55
Fessler Machine Co	3561	120
Festida Foods Ltd	2096	51
Festive Occasions	7359	255
Festo Corp	5085	105
Fet Engineering Inc	3089	1408
Fetch Logistics Inc	4213	794
Fette Ford and Imports	5511	264
Fetter Printing Co	2752	215
Fetterolf Corp	3491	47
Fettes Manufacturing Co	3451	90
Fetzer Vineyards	2084	12
Fetzers Inc	2431	49
Fey Publishing Co	2752	804
Feyenzylstra	5084	871
FFD Financial Corp	6712	611
FFE Software Inc	7372	4501
FFE Transportation and American Eagle Lines	4213	60
FFE Transportation Services Inc	4213	59
FFR-DSI Inc	5199	13
FFW Corp	6712	560
Fg Squared Multimedia Corp	8742	637
FGDI LLC	5153	123
FGI Research Inc	8741	165
FGM Inc	7371	122
Fgs-Wi LLC	2752	66
FGX International Holdings Ltd	3851	7
FH Ayer Manufacturing Co	3599	516
FH Bonn Co	5131	11

Company Name	SIC	Rank
FH Gaskins Company Inc	5088	98
FH Prince and Company Inc	6282	148
FH Uelner Precision Tools and Dies Inc	3544	189
FHC Health Systems Inc	8063	5
Fhc Holding Co	1711	152
Fiamingo Moving and Storage Inc	4213	2507
Fiamm Technologies	3714	100
Fiat USA Inc	5012	1
Fiber Bond Corporation Illinois	2297	5
Fiber Composites LLC	2899	41
Fiber Glass Industries Inc	3089	333
Fiber Glass Systems LP	3089	348
Fiber Innovation Technology Inc	2284	4
Fiber Instrument Sales Inc	3661	68
Fiber Logic Inc	1731	995
Fiber Materials Inc	3769	12
Fiber Optic Center Inc	5049	28
Fiber Optic Concepts And Lighting LLC	1623	376
Fiber Optic Supply Inc	5063	644
Fiber Pad Inc	3089	920
Fiber Resources Unlimited Inc	5093	177
Fiber Science Inc	2821	193
Fiber SenSys Inc	3827	99
Fiber Solutions Inc	5065	770
Fiber Tech Industries Inc	3083	35
Fiberall Corp	3661	179
Fibercor Div	3845	33
Fiberdome Inc	3443	93
Fiberesin Industries Inc	2493	7
Fiberglass Coatings Inc	3089	612
Fiberglass Engineering Co	3089	1678
Fiberglass Engineering Inc	3732	19
Fiberglass Fabricators Inc	5999	235
Fiberglass of Eatonton Inc	3088	28
Fiberglass Pool Resurfacing	1799	147
Fiberglass Structures Inc	5999	245
Fiberglass Technologies Inc	3089	1497
Fibergrate Composite Structures Inc	3089	103
Fiberguide Industries Inc	3229	24
Fiberlink Communications Corp	4899	63
Fiberlok Inc	3999	126
FiberMark DSI	2621	7
FiberMark Inc	2631	9
Fibernet Inc	4813	751
Fibernext LLC	1731	1696
Fiberod	3061	67
Fiberoptic Supply Inc	5065	844
Fiberoptic Systems Inc	3357	71
Fiberoptics Technology Inc	3229	18
FiberPlex Inc	3661	170
Fiberplus Federal Services Inc	7373	328
Fiberpro Inc	3089	869
Fiber-Tech Auto Parts Inc	5013	386
Fibertech Communications Inc	1731	2083
Fibertech Corp	3089	1409
Fiber-Tech Inc	3544	336
Fibertech Inc	1623	516
Fibertech Networks LLC	3661	20
Fiber-Tel Contractors Inc	1731	523
FiberTower Corp	4812	31
Fiber-Tron Corp	3716	13
Fiberweb Inc	2281	3
Fibre Converters Inc	2671	35
Fibre Materials Corp	3089	1366
Fibreflex Packing and Manufacturing Co	3053	119
Fibrek Recycling US Inc	4953	54
Fibrenetics Inc	7699	260
Fibrocell Science Inc	2836	81
Fic America Corp	3469	34
Fic Corp	3613	126
FiComm Inc	8743	327
Fidelifacts	7381	232
Fidelis Software Inc	7372	3433
Fidelity and Guaranty Life Insurance Co	6311	82
Fidelity Associates Inc	2731	263
Fidelity Bancorp Inc	6712	407
Fidelity BancShares NC Inc	6712	316
Fidelity Bank	6022	167
Fidelity Bankshares Mutual Holding Co	6712	84
Fidelity Bindery Co	2789	88
Fidelity Blue Chip Growth Fund	6722	40
Fidelity Building Services Industries LLC	7349	137
Fidelity Cablevision Inc	4841	93
Fidelity Communications Co (Sullivan Missouri)	4813	107
Fidelity Contrafund	6722	7
Fidelity Convertible Securities Fund	6722	91
Fidelity Creditor Services Inc	7322	142
Fidelity D and D Bancorp Inc	6712	441
Fidelity Deposit and Discount Bank	6022	270
Fidelity Federal Bancorp	6712	620
Fidelity Growth Strategies	6722	103
Fidelity Independence Fund	6722	71
Fidelity Industries Inc	3069	32
Fidelity Information Services Inc	7372	2515
Fidelity Inspection and Consulting Services	6794	137
Fidelity Inversters	6722	83
Fidelity Investments	6722	36
Fidelity Low-Priced Stock Fund	6722	21
Fidelity Magellan Fund	6722	24

Company Name	SIC	Rank
Fidelity National Capital Inc	6159	65
Fidelity National Financial Inc	6361	1
Fidelity National Information Services Inc	7389	9
Fidelity National Insurance Co (Omaha Nebraska)	6331	340
Fidelity National Title Company of Washington Inc	6361	38
Fidelity National Title Insurance Co	6361	3
Fidelity National Title Insurance Company of Dallas County	6361	21
Fidelity National Title Insurance Company of New York	6361	24
Fidelity Natural Gas Inc	4923	31
Fidelity Orthopedic Inc	3842	292
Fidelity OTC Fund	6722	63
Fidelity Overseas Fund	6722	53
Fidelity Paper Supply Inc	2679	64
Fidelity Properties Inc	7322	127
Fidelity Real Estate Investment	6722	77
Fidelity Select Automotive Fund	6722	219
Fidelity Select Brokerage and Investment Management Fund	6722	167
Fidelity Select Chemicals Fund	6722	181
Fidelity Select Computers Fund	6722	172
Fidelity Select Construction and Housing Fund	6722	235
Fidelity Select Defense and Aerospace Fund	6722	162
Fidelity Select Multimedia Portfolio	6722	241
Fidelity Southern Corp	6022	95
Fidelity Stock Selector	6722	160
Fidelity Technologies Corp	3663	72
Fidelity Telealarm LLC	7382	137
Fidelity Tool and Mold Ltd	3544	764
Fidelity Transfer Co	6280	34
Fidelity Trend Fund	6722	148
Fidelity Value Fund	6722	47
Fidelity Worldwide Fund	6722	132
Fidlar Printing Co	2752	419
Fiducial Century Small Business Solutions Inc	6794	124
Fiducial Triple Check Inc	7291	6
Fiduciary Capital Management Inc	6282	269
Fiduciary Management Associates Inc	6282	358
Fiduciary Management Inc	6282	172
Fiduciary Trust Company International	6211	18
Fiebing Company Inc	2843	11
Fiehrer Motors Inc	5511	722
Field Communications Inc	1731	1768
Field Controls LLC	3829	93
Field Environmental Instruments Inc	7359	144
Field Force Protective Services Corp	7381	135
Field Gymmy Inc	3523	285
Field Instruments And Controls Inc	5063	956
Field Investments Inc	1761	6
Field Packing Company LLC	2011	17
Field Solutions Inc	7379	527
Field System Machining Inc	7699	210
Fieldale Farms Corp	2015	13
Fieldbrook Foods Corp	2024	8
FieldCentrix Inc	7372	1059
Fieldcrest Fertilizer Co	5191	176
FieldGlass Inc	7372	1089
Fielding Manufacturing Inc	3089	1124
Fielding Manufacturing Zinc Diecasting Inc	3545	141
Fieldman Rolapp and Associates	6282	336
Fieldpoint Petroleum Corp	1311	218
Fields Company LLC	2952	12
Fields Equipment Company Inc	5083	72
Field's Fire Protection Inc	5087	45
Field's Inc	2053	21
Fieldstone Communities Inc	1531	39
Fieldstone Meats Of Alabama Inc	2011	135
Fieldtex Products Inc	3161	8
Fierst Distributing Co	5023	109
Fiesta Gas Grills LLC	3631	11
Fiesta Insurance Franchise Corp	6321	78
Fiesta Mart Inc	5411	102
Fiesta Mexican Foods Inc	2051	198
Fiesta Station Holdings LLC	7999	23
Fiesta Station Inc	7011	31
Fife Corp	3625	9
Fife Pearce Electric Co	7694	32
Fifteen Asset Management LLC	6513	24
Fifth Third Bancorp	6712	14
Fifth Third Bank (Cincinnati Ohio)	6022	10
Fifth Third Bank of Indiana	6022	130
Fifth Third Bank of Northern Kentucky Inc	6022	141
Fifth Third Bank of Northwestern Ohio NA	6021	62
Fifth Third Holdings LLC	6022	824
Fifth Wave	7372	4607
Fig Leaf Software Inc	7373	405
Figgins Transport Ltd	4213	2431
Figi's Inc	7389	188
Figtree Consulting Inc	7372	435
Figueroa International Inc	5149	132
Fiji Water LLC	2086	53
Fike and Fike Inc	7371	1660
Fike's Dairy Inc	2024	16
Fikes Truck Line Inc	4213	2169

Company Name	SIC	Rank
Fila USA Inc	5941	6
Filco Discount Center Inc	5065	260
Filconn Inc	3678	75
File On Q Inc	7372	2976
File Rite Inc	7389	1330
File-Ez Folder Inc	2678	20
FileMaker Inc	7372	160
Filemark Corp	7372	3531
Filene's Basement Corp	5311	33
FileNet Corp	7373	33
FileStream Inc	7372	4300
FileTek Inc	7372	1208
Fili Enterprises Inc	5812	293
Filing Source Inc	5044	120
Fill Rite Co	3629	126
Fillauer Inc	3842	88
Filler Specialties Inc	3565	156
Fillipone Enterprises Inc	5084	539
Fillmore Systems Inc	3625	290
FillPro Inc	3599	2404
Film and Video Stock Shots	7336	243
FILM Archives Inc	7336	128
FILM Archives Inc	7812	263
Film Finders Inc	7379	1189
Film Roman Inc	7812	60
Film Technologies International Inc	3999	75
Filmack Studios	7812	266
Filmcore Editorial San Francisco LLC	7819	73
Filmdex Inc	3861	106
Filmet Color Laboratories Incorporated A Close Corp	7384	18
Fil-Mor Express Inc	4213	607
Films Media Group of Cos	7372	1057
Filmtec Corp	3569	37
Filmtec Inc	3549	98
Filmtools Inc	5946	7
Filmtronics Inc	3674	373
Filnor Inc	3625	116
Filpro Corp	5085	410
Filtech Inc	3671	24
Filtek Inc	3679	842
Filter And Coating Technology Inc	5075	95
Filter Belts Inc	3569	128
Filter Concepts Inc	3677	63
Filter Fab	3569	237
Filter Fabrics Inc	3569	281
Filter Factory Inc	3569	220
Filter Fresh of Northern Virginia Inc	5046	70
Filter Research Corp	3677	81
Filter Services International	3564	157
Filter Systems Inc	3677	107
Filter Tech Inc	3569	142
Filter Technologies Inc	5085	472
Filters-NowCom Inc	3564	62
Filtertek Inc	3089	196
Filtran Aftermarket Products	3714	90
Filtra-Systems Manufacturing Co	3569	263
Filtration Specialties Inc	3569	286
Filtration Systems Inc	3569	167
Filtration Technology Corp	3533	129
Filtrine Manufacturing Co	3585	163
Filtrona Greensboro Inc	3999	84
Filtronetics Inc	3677	58
Fims Manufacturing Corp	3599	1038
Final Draft Inc	7372	1695
Finance and Thrift Co	6035	147
Finance Center Federal Credit Union	6061	51
Financial Accounting Systems Inc	7372	4458
Financial Center Credit Union	6062	17
Financial Computer Support Inc	7372	1549
Financial Courier Service Inc	7389	1625
Financial Database Services Inc	7372	2365
Financial Design Group Inc	8748	167
Financial Engineering Associates Inc	7372	2061
Financial Engines Inc	7372	318
Financial Equipment Company Inc	5065	491
Financial Federal Credit Inc	6159	39
Financial Graphic Services Inc	2759	86
Financial Guaranty Insurance Co	6351	11
Financial Industries Corp	6311	148
Financial Industry Computer Systems Inc	7372	2546
Financial Industry Technical Services Inc	8742	456
Financial Information Inc	2741	219
Financial Information Network Inc	7372	1550
Financial Information Systems Inc	7379	1413
Financial Institution Technologies Inc	7373	810
Financial Institutions Inc	6712	185
Financial Intelligence LLC	8721	323
Financial Management Control Inc	7322	170
Financial Management Solutions Inc	6282	626
Financial Modeling Specialists Inc	5045	756
Financial Navigator International	7372	3708
Financial Neural Computing	7372	957
Financial Pacific Co	6159	59
Financial Pacific Insurance Co	6321	73
Financial Profiles Inc	7372	1244
Financial Publishing Co	7372	1481
Financial Recovery Services Inc	7322	40
Financial Relations Board Inc	8743	4
Financial Security Assurance Inc	6351	5
Financial Service Corp	6211	166
Financial Services Inc	7374	71

Company Name	SIC	Rank
Financial Software Innovations Inc	7372	2651
Financial Software Systems	7372	1151
Financial Software Systems Inc	7371	1160
Financial Supermarkets Inc	6029	33
Financial Technology Laboratories Inc	7372	2977
Financial West Investment Group Inc	6211	352
Financo Inc	6799	136
Finca International Inc	8742	94
Fincannon and Associates Inc	7819	91
Finch Services Inc	5083	30
Finchers Inc	5731	263
Finck Cigar Co	2121	4
Fin-Con Assembly Group Inc	3643	94
Findaway World LLC	3663	96
Finder Relays Inc	3625	411
FindExcom Inc	7372	4076
Findingkings	5094	80
Findings Inc	3915	7
Findlay Automotive Inc	5511	386
Findlay Industries Inc	2396	1
Findlay Machine Tool Inc	3559	204
Findlay Publishing Co	2711	117
Findlay Refractories Co	3255	11
Findlay Truck Line Inc	4213	703
Findology Interactive Media Inc	7371	723
Findskills Inc	7379	1363
Fine Grinding Corp	2819	117
Fine Impressions Inc	2679	45
Fine Laboratories Inc	3663	237
Fine Line Circuits and Technology Inc	3672	288
Fine Line Graphics Corp	2752	159
Fine Line Graphics Inc	3555	33
Fine Line International	7372	4039
Fine Line Litho Inc	2752	1450
Fine Organics Corp	5085	366
Fine Print Graphics Inc	2752	1531
Fine Wine Brokers Inc	5182	32
Fineberg Management Inc	6552	287
Fineberg Publicity Inc	8743	323
Fineline Circuits Inc	3672	417
Fineline Graphics Inc	2752	416
Fineline Imprints Inc	5999	267
Fineman PR	8743	115
Fineman West and Company LLP	8721	194
Finesse Electric Inc	1731	950
Finest Engraving LLC	7389	2495
Finest Food Company Inc	2099	276
Finfrock Industries Inc	3272	50
Finger Food Products Inc	2038	64
Finger Lakes Chemicals Inc	2842	83
Finger Lakes Printing Company Inc	2711	430
Finger Office Furniture	5021	7
Fingerhut Companies Inc	5961	18
Fingerhut Powers and Associates	8743	134
Finial Company Inc	2591	16
Finial Investment Corp	6282	453
Finisar Corp	3669	8
Finish Line Ford Inc	5511	749
Finish Line Inc	5651	11
Finish Thompson Inc	3561	107
Finishes Unlimited Inc	2851	151
Finishing and Mailing Center LLC	2789	79
Finishing Equipment Inc	3559	479
Finishing Systems Corp	3582	21
Finishing Technologies Inc	5072	188
Finishing Touch Janitorial Service Inc	7349	384
FinishMaster Inc	5198	1
Finite Technologies Inc	5045	331
Finjan Software Inc	7372	2142
Finlay Enterprises Inc	5944	5
Finlay Printing LLC	2752	317
Finley and Cook PLLC	8721	54
Finley Colmer and Co	6282	570
Finley Design Services	3825	218
Finley Group Inc	6282	629
Finn Auto Parts	5531	66
Finn Enterprises Inc	7371	1885
Finn Graphics Inc	2752	838
Finn Industries Inc	2631	27
Finnegan Henderson Farabow Garrett and Dunner LLP	8111	135
Finney Company Inc	2842	146
Finney Impression Die Corporation Of Greenwood	3544	874
Finta Corp	5734	298
Fintel Inc	5065	891
FinTrack Systems Corp	7371	698
Finway Inc	1623	381
Finz and Finz PC	8111	498
Finzer Roller Inc	3069	75
Fionda LLC	4813	261
Fiore Di Pasta Inc	2099	261
Fios Inc	5045	77
Firaxis Games Inc	7372	1044
Fire 2 Wire	4813	416
Fire Alarm Control Systems Inc	5063	826
Fire and Flavor Grilling Co	2099	272
Fire Control Electrical Systems Inc	5063	638
Fire Detection Systems LLC	3669	234
Fire Extinguisher Sales and Service Of Asheboro Inc	5099	78
Fire Fox Technologies LLC	3651	214
Fire From Ice Ventures LLC	3585	243
Fire Insurance Exchange	6331	159

Company Name	SIC	Rank
Fire King International LLC	2522	5
Fire Management Associates Inc	1731	2218
Fire Master Fire Equipment Inc	5087	158
Fire Programs	7372	2880
Fire Protection Equipment Company Inc	5087	101
Fire Protection Systems Inc	1711	271
Fire Protection Testing Inc	1711	228
Fire Research Corp	7389	876
Fire Safety Inc	5087	80
Fire Sentry Corp	3669	164
Fireball Industries Inc	2759	327
Fireball Industry Inc	2759	100
Fireblast 451 Inc	3569	197
Firebrand Technologies	7372	2143
Firecom Inc	3669	131
Firecraft Of New York Inc	1731	915
Fired Up Inc	6794	19
Fire-End and Croker Corp	5087	86
Firefighters Community Credit Union Inc	6062	94
Firefly Millward Brown	8742	241
FireFold	5731	47
Firehook Bakers Ltd	5461	14
FirehouseCom	2721	442
Firelake Manufacturing LLC	3089	1376
Fireline Inc	3299	7
Fireman's Fund Insurance Co	6331	57
Firematic Supply Company Inc	5087	63
Firemen's Annuity Benefit Fund of Chicago	6371	6
Firemen's Insurance Company of Washington DC	6331	149
Firepower Inc	5063	623
Fireside Bank	6162	48
Firestar Software Inc	7371	1511
Firestone Associates	8743	314
Firestone Building Products Co	3069	6
Firestone Fibers and Textiles Co	2296	1
Firestone Metal Products LLC	5051	22
Firestone Polymers LLC	2822	6
Firestream Worldwide Inc	7379	610
Firetrace USA LLC	5063	416
Firetron Inc	5087	29
Firewall Forward Inc	7699	57
FirewiredirectCom Inc	3577	638
Fireworks By Grucci Inc	2899	191
Firkins Power Motive Inc	5084	873
Firley Moran Freer and Eassa	8721	135
Firm58 Inc	7371	1449
Firmin Printing and Office Equipment Co	5943	20
Firmlogic LLC	8748	121
FirmWorks	7372	4608
First Acceptance Corp	6331	241
First Acceptance Insurance Company Inc	6411	79
First Advantage Assessment Solutions	2741	175
First Advantage Corp	5045	27
First Advantage Recruiting Solutions	7389	1212
First Aid Only Inc	3842	96
First Alamogordo Bancorp of Nevada Inc	6712	548
First Albany Corp	6211	74
First Allied Securities Inc	6211	86
First Allmerica Financial Life Insurance Co	6311	85
First American Bank	6712	174
First American Bank and Trust (Vacherie Louisiana)	6022	584
First American Bank Group Ltd	6712	215
First American Bank (Naples Florida)	6021	190
First American Bank (Vincennes Indiana)	6022	490
First American CoreLogic Inc	2741	27
First American Equipment Finance	6159	32
First American Financial Corp	6361	5
First American Flood Data Services	7375	57
First American Home Buyers Protection Corp	6351	42
First American Printing And Direct Mail	2759	171
First American Real Estate Information Services Inc	7375	13
First American Title Company of Alaska Inc	6541	5
First American Title Insurance Agency Incorporated Utah	6361	13
First American Title Insurance Co	6361	6
First American Title Insurance Company of Oregon	6361	32
First Arkansas Bank and Trust Co	6022	355
First Assembly Of God	8351	21
First Atlantic Capital Ltd	6282	89
First Aviation Services Inc	7699	14
First Bancorp Inc (Damariscotta Maine)	6712	249
First Bancorp of Indiana Inc	6035	144
First Bancorp (Troy North Carolina)	6712	142
First BanCorp	6022	11
First Bancshares Inc (Hattiesburg Mississippi)	6021	170
First Bancshares Inc (Mountain Grove Missouri)	6712	615
First BancTrust Corp	6036	67
First Bank and Trust	6022	317
First Bank (Creve Coeur Missouri)	6022	24
First Bank (Florissant Missouri)	6022	429
First Bank Insurance Services Inc	6411	269
First Bank (McComb Mississippi)	6022	428
First Bank Muleshoe	6022	736
First Bank of Georgia	6022	166
First Bank of Missouri	6022	451
First Bank of San Luis Obispo	6022	425
First Bank Southwest (Perryton Texas)	6712	233
First Bank (Troy North Carolina)	6022	46
First Banking Center Inc	6712	434
First Banking Center-Burlington	6022	306
First Banking Services Of The South Inc	7374	228
First Banks Inc	6712	81
First Boaz Bancorp	6712	691
First Busey Corp	6712	140
First Business Financial Services Inc	6022	830
First Business Solutions Inc	7389	1986
First California Financial Group Inc	6712	207
First California Press Inc	2752	1581
First Call Heating And Cooling Co	5983	21
First Call Installation	3585	151
First Call Medical Staffing Inc	7361	237
First Call Personnel Services Inc	7361	432
First Capital Bancorp Inc (Glen Allen Virginia)	6022	287
First Capital Bancshares Inc	6712	720
First Capital Bank Holding Corp	6712	617
First Capital Equities Ltd	6211	336
First Capital International Inc	5045	1010
First Carolina Corporate Credit Union	6061	112
First Cash Financial Services Inc	5932	2
First CB Corp	6712	602
First Century Bank	6022	372
First Century Bankshares Inc	6712	509
First Chemical Corp	2869	31
First Cherokee Bancshares Inc	6712	627
First Cherokee State Bank	6021	371
First Chicago Bank and Trust	6029	12
First Choice Auto Auction Inc	5012	107
First Choice Food Service Inc	5962	20
First Choice Health Network Inc	6324	90
First Choice Logistics	4213	1001
First Choice Messenger Inc	7389	1746
First Citizens Banc Corp	6712	293
First Citizens Bancorporation Inc	6712	361
First Citizens Bancshares Inc (Dyersburg Tennessee)	6712	543
First Citizens BancShares Inc (Raleigh North Carolina)	6712	39
First Citizens Bank and Trust Co	6022	17
First Citizens National Bank	6021	92
First Citizens National Bank of Mansfield	6022	572
First Citizens National Bank of Upper Sandusky	6021	209
First City Bank of Fort Walton Beach	6022	632
First City Savings Federal Credit Union	6061	67
First Class American Credit Union	6062	111
First Class Credit Union	6062	59
First Class Direct Inc	7331	253
First Class Foods Inc	2011	71
First Class Inc (Atlanta Georgia)	8743	205
First Class Printing Inc	2752	1089
First Class Service Trucking Co	4213	2618
First Class Services Inc	4213	366
First Class Solutions Inc	8742	237
First Clover Leaf Financial Corp	6035	110
First Coast Intermodal Services	4213	1271
First Coast Lighting Inc	5063	493
First Coast Pallet Inc	7699	261
First Coast Security Services Inc	7382	28
First Coast Supply Inc	5064	60
First Colony Coffee And Tea Co	2095	32
First Commercial Bank (Birmingham Alabama)	6022	223
First Commercial Bank (Bloomington Minnesota)	6022	821
First Commercial Bank (Huntsville Alabama)	6022	518
First Commonwealth Bank	6022	86
First Commonwealth Financial Corp	6712	105
First Community Bancshares Inc	6712	190
First Community Bank Corporation of America	6035	124
First Community Bank FSB	6029	26
First Community Bank NA	6022	92
First Community Bank of Homer Glen and Lockport	6022	725
First Community Bank of Joliet	6022	289
First Community Bank of Mercer County Inc	6036	87
First Community Bank of Plainfield	6022	704
First Community Bank of Tifton	6022	464
First Community Corp	6712	431
First Community Credit Union	6062	8
First Community Financial Partners Inc	6022	180
First Community Services-Texas Inc	7374	101
First Computer Systems Inc	3679	303
First Connecticut Capital Corp	6159	90
First Consulting Inc	7379	619
First Continental Trading Inc	6211	142
First Cooperative Association	5191	82
First County Bank	6036	33
First Crawford State Bank	6022	482
First Data Corp	7374	1
First Data Merchant Services Corp	6099	4
First Data Resources Inc	7374	11
First DataBank Inc	7372	968
First Defense International	3482	5
First Defiance Financial Corp	6712	195
First Defiance Loan Servicing Co	6035	37
First Defiance Service Inc	6022	63
First Delta Bank	6022	793
First Detroit Corp	2741	502
First District Association	2023	2
First Eagle Federal Credit Union	6061	96
First Eastern Bankshares Corp	6712	313
First Eastern Mortgage Corp	6162	34
First Educators Credit Union	6062	97
First Electric Cooperative Corp	4911	145
First Electronics Corp	3679	271
First Electronics Inc	3672	200
First Equity Development Inc	6282	206
First e-Solutions LLC	6153	41
First Farmers Bank and Trust	6022	301
First Farmers Financial Corp	6712	625
First Federal Bancorp	6712	420
First Federal Bancshares of Arkansas Inc	6712	430
First Federal Bank	6035	36
First Federal Bank FSB (Kansas City Missouri)	6035	248
First Federal Bank of Arkansas FA	6035	78
First Federal Bank of Tuscaloosa	6035	68
First Federal Community Bank of Bucyrus	6035	226
First Federal Investments Inc	6035	251
First Federal of Charleston	6011	12
First Federal of Northern Michigan	6035	175
First Federal of Northern Michigan Bancorp Inc	6712	610
First Federal Savings and Loan Association Independence	6035	203
First Federal Savings and Loan Association of Bloomington	6035	243
First Federal Savings and Loan Association of Charleston	6035	29
First Federal Savings and Loan Association of Middletown	6035	219
First Federal Savings and Loan Association of Olathe	6035	252
First Federal Savings Bank of Boston	6035	234
First Federal Savings Bank of Champaign-Urbana	6035	212
First Federal Savings Bank of Dover	6035	208
First Federal Savings Bank of Elizabethtown	6035	66
First Federal Savings Bank of Frankfort	6035	216
First Federal Savings Bank of Iowa	6035	129
First Financial Bancorp	6712	98
First Financial Bancorp Service Corp	6211	48
First Financial Bank	6021	156
First Financial Bank (Celina Ohio)	6022	96
First Financial Bank NA	6021	42
First Financial Bank of Cleburne	6021	330
First Financial Bank (San Angelo Texas)	6022	790
First Financial Bank (Sweetwater Texas)	6021	348
First Financial Bankshares Inc	6712	126
First Financial Corp (Terre Haute Indiana)	6712	176
First Financial Credit Union	7389	1503
First Financial Federal Credit Union	6061	60
First Financial Holdings Inc	6712	146
First Financial Network Inc	6282	496
First Financial Northwest Inc	6036	26
First Financial Service Corp	6712	256
First Financial Services	6162	29
First Franklin Financial Corp	6162	17
First FSB (Huntington Indiana)	6035	257
First FSB (Monessen Pennsylvania)	6035	160
First Golf Corp	1629	87
First Grade Food Corp	2052	67
First Guaranty Bank	6022	295
First Harrison Financial Services Inc	6399	18
First Hawaiian Bank	6022	27
First Header Die Inc	3542	88
First Health Benefits Administrators Corp	7389	48
First Health Group Corp	6324	12
First Health Services Corp	7374	103
First Healthcare Products Inc	2782	37
First Holdrege Bancshares Inc	6712	562
First Home Builders of Florida Inc	1531	61
First Home Savings Bank (Mountain Grove Missouri)	6036	107
First Honolulu Securities Inc	6211	245
First Horizon National Corp	6712	31
First Impression Group Inc	2752	977
First Impressions Lithographic Company Inc	2752	919
First Impressions Printing	2752	1637
First Impressions Printing Inc	2752	1439
First Independence Corp	6712	633

Company Name	SIC	Rank
First Independence Corp (Detroit Michigan)	6712	679
First Independence National Bank	6022	540
First Independent Bank	6022	227
First Independent Group	6712	149
First Industrial Florida Finance Corp	6798	69
First Industrial Realty Trust Inc	6798	87
First Information Technology Services Inc	7373	631
First Insurance Company of Hawaii Ltd	6331	193
First Intermark Corp	8742	591
First International Computer of America Inc	3672	72
First Internet Bancorp	6022	269
First Internet Bank of Indiana	6022	299
First Interstate Bancsystem Inc	6712	92
First Interstate Bank	6022	43
First Interstate Bank of Alaska NA	6021	367
First Investors Financial Services Group Inc	6141	40
First Iowa Mortgage Inc	6035	239
First Iowa Title Services Inc	6035	240
First Ipswich Bancorp	6712	555
First Kansas Bank and Trust Co	6022	610
First Keystone Community Bank	6021	396
First Keystone Corp	6712	360
First Leasing and Rental Corp	4119	14
First Legacy Community Credit Union	6062	114
First Lenders Data Inc	7371	928
First Lexington Corp	3452	49
First Light Of New Orleans Inc	5063	986
First Line Communications Inc	5065	472
First Link Technology Inc	7371	1777
First M and F Corp	6712	225
First Manhattan Funding LLC	6162	84
First Marblehead Corp	6141	15
First Mariner Bancorp	6712	259
First Mariner Bank	6022	42
First Marketing Co	2721	108
First Marketing Group Int'l Inc	7311	736
First Merchants Bank NA	6021	31
First Merchants Bank of Central Indiana	6021	358
First Merchants Corp	6712	124
First Mercury Financial Corp	6331	231
First Metro Insurance Agency	6331	346
First Miami Bancorp Inc	6712	274
First Mid-Illinois Bancshares Inc	6712	240
First Mid-Illinois Bank and Trust	6021	81
First Midwest Bancorp Inc	6712	87
First Midwest Bank of Poplar Bluff	6022	645
First Midwest Securities Inc	6211	382
First Midwest Trust Company NA	6091	21
First Mortgage Corp	6162	28
First Mountain Bancorp	6712	665
First Mountain Bank	6022	576
First NA	6021	87
First National Bank	6712	600
First National Bank Alaska	6021	46
First National Bank (Ames Iowa)	6021	6
First National Bank Anchorage	6021	51
First National Bank and Trust (Atmore Alabama)	6712	355
First National Bank and Trust Co (Ardmore Oklahoma)	6021	315
First National Bank and Trust Company of McAlester	6021	187
First National Bank and Trust Company of Weatherford	6021	344
First National Bank (Antlers Oklahoma)	6021	343
First National Bank Eastland	6021	281
First National Bank (Fort Collins Colorado)	6021	49
First National Bank in Alamogordo	6021	217
First National Bank in Fairfield	6021	364
First National Bank in Mena	6021	360
First National Bank in Montevideo	6021	275
First National Bank in Tremont	6021	375
First National Bank (Independence Kansas)	6021	397
First National Bank (Midwest City Oklahoma)	6712	607
First National Bank of AltaVista	6021	222
First National Bank of Bar Harbor	6021	277
First National Bank of Barry	6021	249
First National Bank of Beardstown	6021	352
First National Bank of Berryville	6021	333
First National Bank of Brundidge	6021	362
First National Bank of Canadian	6021	346
First National Bank of Canton	6021	342
First National Bank of Central California	6021	67
First National Bank of Central Florida	6021	167
First National Bank of Chester County	6021	171
First National Bank of Colorado	6022	420
First National Bank of Damariscotta	6021	141
First National Bank of De Queen	6021	262
First National Bank of Durango	6021	129
First National Bank of Floydada	6021	387
First National Bank of Griffin	6021	158
First National Bank of Holdrege	6021	300
First National Bank of Huntsville	6021	301
First National Bank of Illinois	6021	193
First National Bank of Ipswich	6021	329
First National Bank of Izard County	6021	370
First National Bank of Jasper	6021	108
First National Bank of Jefferson	6021	401
First National Bank of Jeffersonville	6021	256
First National Bank of Long Island	6021	133
First National Bank of Marquette	6021	398
First National Bank of Midwest City	6021	274
First National Bank of Montana (Libby Montana)	6021	347
First National Bank of Muscatine	6021	239
First National Bank of North Platte	6021	200
First National Bank of Northern California	6021	93
First National Bank of Olathe	6021	112
First National Bank of Omaha	6021	30
First National Bank of Pasco	6035	180
First National Bank of Pennsylvania	6021	36
First National Bank of Polk County	6021	286
First National Bank of Pulaski	6021	260
First National Bank of St Louis	6021	125
First National Bank of Santa Fe	6021	189
First National Bank of South Georgia	6022	741
First National Bank of South Miami	6021	227
First National Bank of Southern California	6021	351
First National Bank of the Lakes	6021	389
First National Bank of Waverly	6712	554
First National Bank of Wynne	6021	179
First National Bank (Orrville Ohio)	6021	252
First National Bank (Paragould Arkansas)	6021	164
First National Bank (Ronceverte West Virginia)	6021	251
First National Bank (Sioux Falls South Dakota)	6712	486
First National Bank South Dakota	6022	641
First National Bank (Waverly Iowa)	6021	311
First National Community Bancorp Inc	6712	248
First National Corporation of Wynne	6712	449
First National Corp (Pulaski Tennesee)	6712	583
First National Corp (Strasburg Virginia)	6712	452
First National of Nebraska	6712	48
First National Panel Company Inc	3251	2
First National Security Co	6712	671
First Network Group Inc	5734	335
First New York Federal Credit Union	6061	91
First Niagara Financial Group Inc	6712	38
First Niles Financial Inc	6712	692
First NLC Financial Services Inc	6029	20
First Nonprofit Insurance Co	6321	55
First Northern Bank of Dixon	6022	362
First Northern Community Bancorp	6712	382
First of Long Island Corp	6712	217
First Olathe Bancshares	6712	463
First Option Inc	7373	1103
First Pacific Advisors LLC	6282	61
First PacTrust Bancorp Inc	6712	350
First Paragould Bankshares Inc	6712	406
First Parke State Bank	6022	468
First Performance Fabrics Inc	2299	9
First Physicians Capital Group Inc	8062	234
First Pioneer National Bank	6021	289
First Place Bank	6035	195
First Place Bank (Southfield Michigan)	6021	166
First Place Financial Corp (Warren Ohio)	6035	38
First Plastics Corp	3089	1831
First Potomac Realty Trust	6798	117
First Priority Inc	2834	266
First Pro Inc	7361	83
First Products Inc	3523	222
First Properties of The Carolinas Inc	6531	251
First Quadrant Corp	6282	527
First Quality Cleaning Service Inc	7349	330
First Quality Sausage	2013	243
First Real Estate Investment Trust of New Jersey	6798	175
First Realty Management Corp	6531	326
First Republic Bank	6036	3
First Republic Corporation of America	2092	15
First Republic Investment Management	6282	197
First Republic Preferred Capital Corp	6798	159
First Reserve Corp	6282	433
First Residential Mortgage Network Inc	6162	121
First Response Inc	7381	60
First Restoration Inc	1799	112
First Revenue Assurance LLC	7322	25
First Ridge Farm State Bank	6022	791
First Robinson Financial Corp	6712	619
First Robinson Saving Bank NA	6035	170
First Savings Bank	6035	186
First Savings Bank of Perkasie	6036	69
First Savings Bank of Renton	6036	39
First Savings Financial Group Inc	6035	113
First Security and Communications Sales Inc	5065	331
First Security Bancorp	6022	537
First Security Bancorp Inc (Searcy Arkansas)	6712	64
First Security Bank (Mountain Home Arkansas)	6022	73
First Security Bank of Clarksville	6022	650
First Security Bank of Missoula	6035	81
First Security Bank (Searcy Arkansas)	6022	35
First Security Group Inc	6021	90
First Security Mortgage Home Loans Inc	6162	92
First Service Credit Union	6062	92
First Service Pest Control	7342	83
First Solar Inc	3674	18
First Sound Inc	3651	254
First South Bancorp Inc (Spartanburg South Carolina)	6712	535
First South Bancorp Inc (Washington North Carolina)	6712	365
First South Bank Inc	6036	52
First South Bank (Spartanburg South Carolina)	6022	334
First South Bank (Washington North Carolina)	6022	528
First South Credit Union	6062	76
First South Production Credit Association	6159	41
First Southeast Fiduciary and Trust Services Inc	6099	28
First Southeast Insurance Services Inc	6351	47
First Southern Bancshares Inc	6712	688
First Southern Bank (Florence Alabama)	6022	434
First Southwest Asset Management Inc	6282	84
First Southwest Co	6211	236
First Southwest Corp	6712	629
First Spin Inc	3663	151
First State Bank and Trust Co	6022	437
First State Bank and Trust Company Inc	6022	438
First State Bank (Brazil Indiana)	6022	461
First State Bank (Kansas City Kansas)	6712	699
First State Bank of East Detroit	6022	244
First State Bank of Kansas City	6022	772
First State Bank of Rush City	6022	319
First State Bank of Winchester Illinois	6022	803
First State Bank (Tabor Iowa)	6022	777
First State Bank (Tell City Indiana)	6022	599
First State Bank (Waynesboro Mississippi)	6022	160
First State Community Bank	6022	66
First State Financial Corp	6712	175
First Step Internet LLC	7374	204
First Step Research Inc	7372	3457
First Stone Credit Consulting	7323	18
First String Enterprises Inc	2759	437
First Team Staffing Inc	7363	205
First Tek Technologies	7373	303
First Tenn Brokerage	6211	197
First Tennessee Bank NA	6021	16
First Tennessee Capital Assets Corp	6162	106
First Texas Bank	6022	692
First Texas Homes	1531	52
First Texas Products	3829	37
First Tool Corp	3542	42
First Toro Family LP	2051	117
First Trade Union Savings Bank FSB	6035	164
First Transit Inc	4151	2
First Trust of MidAmerica	6091	22
First Trust Portfolios LP	6211	230
First Tuskegee Bank	6022	733
First ULB Corp	6712	594
First United Bank and Trust	6021	50
First United Bank (San Diego California)	6022	636
First United Corp	6712	220
First United Security Bank (Thomasville Alabama)	6022	358
First US Community Credit Union	6061	115
First Utah Bancorp	6712	640
First Utah Bank	6022	738
First Victoria National Bank	6021	153
First Washington Realty Trust Inc	6798	147
First Watch Restaurants Inc	5812	94
First Wave Inc	5088	37
First Weatherford Bancshares Inc	6712	715
First West Capital Corp	6531	447
First West Virginia Bancorp Inc	6712	580
First Western Financial Inc	6712	728
First Wind Holdings Inc	4911	20
First Years Inc	3089	84
Firstbank Corp	6712	241
FirstBank Holding Company of Colorado	6712	86
Firstbank of Alma	6022	478
FirstBank of South Jeffco	6021	308
FirstBank of Tech Center	6021	368
FirstBank Southwest	6022	300
Firstbank-Lakeview	6022	682
Firstbank-Mount Pleasant	6022	399
Firstbank-West Branch	6022	331
FirstBase Software Inc	7372	3266
Firstborn Multimedia Corp	7371	646
Firstcare Nursing Services Inc	7361	321
FirstCity Financial Corp	6799	102
Firstcom Music Inc	2741	287
FirstComp Insurance Co	6399	6
FirstEnergy Corp	4911	12
FirstFed Bancorp Inc	6035	80
First-Knox National Bank of Mount Vernon	6021	145
Firstmark Corp	6726	100

Company Name	SIC	Rank
Firstmark Credit Union	6062	50
FirstMerit Bank NA	6029	2
FirstMerit Corp	6712	56
FirsTrust Mortgage	6162	129
Firstrust Savings Bank	6029	10
Fiscal Systems Inc	7372	3532
Fischer and Co	6531	158
Fischer and Frichtel Inc	1521	78
Fischer and Herron Inc	5963	30
Fischer and Hoehn Electric Inc	1731	2108
Fischer Custom Communications Inc	3825	173
Fischer Francis Trees and Watts Inc	6282	62
Fischer Homes Inc	1521	41
Fischer International Systems Corp	3577	252
Fischer Investment Group	6282	638
Fischer Medical Technologies Inc	5047	159
Fischer Mold Inc	3089	879
Fischer North America Inc	5085	442
Fischer Panda Generators Inc	5063	621
Fischer Sand and Aggregate LLP	1442	53
Fischer Solutions Inc	7371	1003
Fischer Tool and Die Corp	3544	63
Fischer-Watt Gold Company Inc	1041	29
Fisen Corp	3585	169
Fiserv	7371	45
Fiserv EFT Div	7374	84
Fiserv Imagesoft	7371	1148
Fiserv Inc	7374	5
Fiserv (Lincoln Nebraska)	7372	164
Fiserv (Stafford Texas)	7372	25
Fish and Crown Ltd	3161	4
Fish Brewing Co	2082	99
Fish Films Footage World	7336	252
Fish House Foods Inc	2092	24
Fish Processors Inc	2092	66
Fish Software Inc	7371	1480
Fishbelt Feeds Inc	2048	24
Fishbowl Inventory	7371	730
Fishel Co	1731	1660
Fisher and Arnold Inc	8712	175
Fisher and Associates Inc	8743	47
Fisher and Company Inc	3714	177
Fisher and Paykel Healthcare Inc	5047	162
Fisher Auction Company Inc	7389	742
Fisher Boyd Brown and Huguenard LLP	8111	517
Fisher Broadcasting Co	4832	17
Fisher Broadcasting - SE Idaho Tv LLC	4832	166
Fisher Brothers Steel Corp	5051	80
Fisher Clinical Services Inc	2834	136
Fisher Communications Inc	4833	82
Fisher Container Corp	2673	35
Fisher Controls International Inc	3494	14
Fisher Development Inc	1542	71
Fisher Graphic Industries A California Corp	3555	16
Fisher Hotel Group Inc	8741	222
Fisher Inc	2752	241
Fisher Industries Inc	5084	874
Fisher Manufacturing Company Inc	3432	33
Fisher Mortgage Company Inc	6162	145
Fisher Pierce	3699	24
Fisher Printers Inc	2752	1052
Fisher Printing Inc	2752	153
Fisher Products LLC	3599	1141
Fisher Radio Seattle	4832	62
Fisher Research Laboratory Inc	3829	31
Fisher Rushmer Werrenrath Keiner Wack and Dickson PA	8111	320
Fisher Systems Inc	5065	671
Fisher Tank Co	3443	118
Fisher Technical Services Rentals Inc	7374	411
Fisher Unitech Inc	7373	410
Fisher Vineyard	0172	16
Fisher Vista LLC	7389	851
Fisheries Supply Co	5088	14
Fisher-Klosterman Inc	3569	140
Fishermen's News Inc	2711	917
Fishero and Associates	7389	1410
Fisher-Price Inc	3944	8
Fishers Bakery And Sandwich Company Inc	2099	167
Fishers' Bakery Of Ellicott City	5461	57
Fisher's Document Systems Inc	5044	77
Fishhawk Fisheries Inc	5146	77
Fishing Holdings LLC	3732	24
Fishman and Tobin Inc	2329	3
Fishman Supply Co	5087	52
FishNet Security	8742	73
Fi-Shock Inc	3699	124
Fisk Alloy Wire Inc	3496	53
Fisk Corp	1731	8
Fiskars Royal Floor Mats	3069	116
Fiske Brothers Refining Company Inc	2992	22
Fiske Inc	1731	965
Fisker Automotive Inc	3711	47
Fisonic Corp	3561	152
Fisource Inc	1731	543
Fit Supply LLC	5091	136
FitCentric Technologies Inc	7372	3070
Fitch Dustdown Co	5087	55
Fitch Enterprises Inc	7389	1966
Fitch Ratings	6289	33
Fitco	3544	450

Company Name	SIC	Rank
Fitec International Inc	2298	15
Fitech Inc	3599	1869
Fitnesoft Inc	7372	3795
Fitness Club Warehouse Inc	5091	53
Fitness Firm	7991	17
Fitness Plus Equipment Services Inc	5999	261
Fitness Venture Group Inc	4813	657
FITT Highway Products Inc	2321	33
Fittings Inc	3089	978
Fittje Brothers Printing	2752	1055
Fitz Chem Corp	5169	70
Fitzco Inc	8734	141
Fitzgerald and Co	7311	108
Fitzgerald and Long Inc	7372	4688
Fitzgerald Auto Mall	5511	274
Fitzgerald Food Store Inc	5411	107
Fitzgerald Lumber Co	5031	300
Fitzgerald Snyder and Company PC	8721	465
Fitzgeralds Gaming Corp	7993	13
Fitzgeralds Tunica	7993	16
Fitzpak Inc	3086	120
Fitzpatrick And Weller Inc	2426	28
Fitzpatrick Dealership Group	5511	271
Fitzpatrick Industries Inc	3556	45
Fitz-Rite Products Inc	3625	234
Fiur Organization Inc	6531	405
Five D Newspapers	2711	893
Five Guys Enterprises LLC	5812	162
Five JAB Oilfield Construct	1623	463
Five JAB Rig Services LLC	7353	87
Five Nines Technology Group	8742	561
Five Peaks Technology LLC	3089	1506
Five Point Capital Inc	7389	417
Five Points Title Services Company Inc	6531	275
Five Rivers Hydraulics Inc	7699	226
Five Star Coop (Joice Iowa)	5153	155
Five Star Custom Foods Ltd	5141	212
Five Star Development Inc	7371	1029
Five Star Distributing Inc	5181	85
Five Star Electric Corp	1731	208
Five Star Foods Inc	2099	350
Five Star Ford	5511	464
Five Star Frozen Foods Inc	2038	54
Five Star Hydraulics	7699	159
Five Star Industries Inc	2511	92
Five Star International LLC	5511	419
Five Star Ltd	2741	499
Five Star Manufacturing Co	3585	176
Five Star Merchant's Service Inc	7374	337
Five Star Mining Inc	5052	10
Five Star Precision Printing Inc	2752	1667
Five Star Productions	3663	87
Five Star Products Inc	5072	16
Five Star Publishing Inc	2721	365
Five Star Quality Care Inc	8051	7
Five Star Speakers And Trainers LLC	7389	1037
Five Star Systems Inc	3599	517
Five Star Trucking Inc	4213	976
Five State Electric LLC	1731	1844
Five States Energy Company LLC	1311	92
Five9 Inc	7376	25
Five-M Apparel Inc	2326	29
Fives Bronx Inc	3547	9
Fives North American Combustion Inc	3433	23
Fixture Engineering Inc	3599	2467
Fixture Hardware Manufacturing Corp	3452	37
Fixture Plus Install Action Inc	5046	233
Fixture Resource Group Inc	5046	230
FJ Designs Inc	2499	42
FJ Krob and Co	5153	44
FJ Mahar Service Store Inc	5411	243
FJ Murphy and Son Inc	1711	218
FJ Weidner Inc	3544	913
FJD Trucking Company Inc	4213	2593
FJH Music Co	2741	133
Fjm Electric Inc	1731	2175
FJM Of Louisianna Inc	7363	378
Fjw Optical Systems Inc	3823	404
FK Bearings Inc	5085	424
FK Instrument Company Inc	3599	303
Fka Distributing Co	2393	5
Fki Logistex Automation Inc	3535	12
Fkn Systek Inc	3993	191
FKP Architects Inc	8712	105
FKQ Advertising Inc	7311	241
FL Haus Co	7389	1486
FL Roberts and Company Inc	5172	11
FL Smithe Machine Company Inc	3554	28
FL Viscosity Oil Co	8731	299
Fla Electric and Design	1731	1526
Fla Property Holdings Inc	2759	348
Flabeg Automotive Us Corp	3231	44
Flad and Associates	8712	32
Fladeboe Automotive Group	5511	542
Fladger and Associates Inc	7363	341
Flaggstaff Technology Group Inc	7379	417
Flagler Corp	3542	90
Flagler System Inc	7011	240
Flagship Automation Inc	5084	523
Flagship Bank and Trust Co	6022	356
Flagship Broadcasting LLC	4832	287
Flagship Converters Inc	3089	925
Flagship Group Inc (Norfolk Virginia)	6411	11
Flagship Maritime Adjusters Inc	6411	38

Company Name	SIC	Rank
Flagship Networks Inc	7379	777
Flagship Press Inc	2752	218
Flagship Ventures	6799	338
Flagstaff Publishing Co	2711	406
Flagstar Bancorp Inc	6035	14
Flagstar Bank FSB	6162	54
Flaherty and Crumine Preferred Income Opportunity Fund Inc	6726	79
Flaherty and Crumrine Inc	6282	658
Flaherty Sabol Carroll	7311	417
Flaherty Sabol Carroll Marketing Communications Inc	7311	896
Flair Communications Agency Inc	7311	605
Flair Data Systems	5045	606
Flair Molded Plastics Inc	3089	850
Flaire Print Communications Inc	2752	1522
Flambeau Corp	3089	61
Flame Engineering Inc	3728	174
Flame Treating Systems	3567	125
Flamemaster Corp	2899	192
Flameret Inc	2399	37
Flamex Sales Co	5046	335
Flamingo Discount Sales Inc	5122	97
Flamingo Surprise Inc	7389	565
Flamm Pickle And Packaging Company Inc	2035	55
Flanagan Brothers Inc	3728	121
Flanary and Sons Trucking Inc	4213	398
Flanco Gasket and Manufacturing Inc	3599	30
Flanders Corp	3564	6
Flanders Filters Inc	3564	5
Flanders Industries Inc	2519	4
Flanders Provision Co	2013	106
Flanigan Farms Inc	5149	197
Flanigan Plumbing Company Inc	1623	698
Flanigan's Enterprises Inc	5812	247
Flann Microwave Inc	5063	374
Flannery Enterprise Inc	4724	107
Flannigan Electric Co	5063	543
Flansburgh Associates Inc	8712	169
Flare Inc	3599	2443
Flare Multicopy Corp	2752	1542
Flash Appointments	7372	3996
Flash Electronics Inc	3672	22
Flash Networks Inc	7379	465
Flasher Ltd	1611	155
Flashes Publishers Inc	2752	233
Flashpoint Technology Inc	7371	506
Flat Rock Metal Inc	3471	7
Flat-Bed Services Inc	4213	689
Flatbush Moving Van Co	4213	3088
Flathead Electric Cooperative Inc	4911	143
Flatley Co	6531	225
Flatout Trucking Ltd	4213	2664
Flatt and Associates Ltd	8743	294
Flavor 1st Growers and Packers Inc	5148	33
Flavor Burst Inc	2087	9
Flavor Dynamics Inc	2087	74
Flavor House Inc	2087	64
Flavor Systems International Inc	2087	31
Flavorchem Corp	2087	29
FLAVORx Inc	3559	127
Flc Timber Inc	2421	98
Flecha Construction Inc	1623	645
Fleck Machine Company Inc	3599	923
Flecto Company Inc	2851	64
Fleenor Security Systems Inc	1731	875
Fleet Acquisitions LLC	5013	120
Fleet Car Carriers	4213	253
Fleet Computing International Inc	7372	3709
Fleet Electronics Inc	5065	964
Fleet Engineers Inc	3714	296
Fleet Equipment Corp	5012	80
Fleet Feet Inc	6794	120
Fleet Lease Disposal Inc	5012	135
Fleet Specialties Co	5013	83
FleetBoss Global Positioning Solutions Inc	7372	539
FleetCor Technologies Inc	6153	11
Fleet-Fisher Engineering Inc	8711	406
FleetNet America LLC	4789	10
Fleet-Net Corp	7372	1031
FleetPride Inc	5013	7
Fleetweather Inc	8748	352
Fleetwood Continental Inc	3366	11
Fleetwood Fibre Packaging and Graphics	2653	12
Fleetwood Forwarding	4213	2292
Fleetwood Homes of Florida	2451	19
Fleetwood Homes of Oregon	2452	25
Fleetwood Lock Company Inc	7699	256
Fleetwood Transportation Services	4213	363
Fleetwood Trucking Company Inc	4213	2995
Fleetwoodgoldcowyard Inc	3535	6
Fleischmann Office Interiors Inc	5712	95
Fleishman Hillard Inc (Cleveland Ohio)	8743	74
Fleishman-Hillard Inc	8743	6
Fleming Construction Company LLC	1623	136
Fleming Electric Inc	1731	1587
Fleming Hitchcock and Associates Inc	7311	558
Fleming Manufacturing Company Inc	3531	180
Fleming Metal Fabricators	3599	2027
Fleming-Babcock Inc	4213	1557
Fleming's Transportation Inc	4213	803

Company Name	SIC	Rank
Fleming-Shaw Transfer and Storage	4213	3087
Flemington Block and Supply Inc	3273	99
Flemington Fur Co	2371	1
Flemington Instrument Company Inc	8711	423
Flemish Master Weavers Inc	2273	27
Flesh Co	2761	6
Fletcher Asset Management Inc	6211	221
Fletcher Chicago Inc	5999	196
Fletcher Granite Company LLC	1411	4
Fletcher Granite Corp	1423	4
Fletcher Industries Inc	3552	41
Fletcher Jones Management Group	5511	45
Fletcher Machine Inc	3599	187
Fletcher Martin Ewing	7311	246
Fletcher Music Centers Inc	5736	7
Fletcher Terry Co	3423	34
Fletcher-Reinhardt Co	5063	96
Fletcher's Medical Supplies Inc	7352	15
Flex Products Inc	3081	30
Flex Products LLC	3083	29
Flex Resources Inc	7373	1150
Flexan Corp	3069	74
Flex-A-Seal Inc	5085	213
Flexaust Company Inc	3089	559
Flexco Inc	3728	190
Flexco Microwave Inc	3357	75
Flexcon Company Inc	3081	4
Flexfab Horizons International Inc	3599	52
Flexfab LLC	3052	7
Flex-Hose Company Inc	3599	1314
Flexial Corp	3053	50
Flexible Automation Inc	3569	161
Flexible Concepts Inc	3599	609
Flexible Controls Corp	3471	64
Flexible Materials Inc	2435	16
Flexible Metal Inc	3498	64
Flexible Plan Investments Ltd	6282	286
Flexible Resources Inc	7363	169
Flexible Whips Of Tennessee Inc	3643	62
Flexicell Inc	3565	34
Flexicon Corp	3565	35
Flexicore Of Texas	3272	73
FlexiInternational Software Inc	7372	3126
Flexi-Liner	3089	1533
Flex-Ing Inc	5085	353
Flexitallic Group Inc	3053	7
Flexi-Van Leasing Inc	7359	38
Flexmag Industries Inc	3499	71
Flexmaster USA Inc	3052	19
Flex-n-Gate Corp	3714	8
Flexo Tech Inc	3555	129
Flex-O-Glass Inc	3081	49
Flexo-Graphics LLC	2759	259
Flex-O-Lite Inc	3231	16
Flexopak Inc	7389	1648
Flexoplate Inc	3555	93
Flexoveyor Industries Inc	3535	175
FlexPrint Inc	7379	298
FLEXquarterscom Ltd	7371	1107
FlexSim Software Products Inc	7372	2460
FlexSoft Inc	7371	948
Flexstar Technology Inc	3825	104
Flexsteel Industries Inc	2519	1
Flex-Tech Hose and Tubing Inc	3083	56
Flextech Inc	3089	953
Flextech Packaging Ltd	2671	60
Flextron Inc	3599	2385
Flextron Industries Inc	3053	140
Flextronics America LLC	3679	3
Flexus International Corp	7372	4609
Flexway Trucking Inc	4213	322
Flex-Weld Inc	3599	2453
Flexwrap Corp	2673	59
Flickinger Industries Inc	3561	123
Flicks Software Inc	7372	4818
Fligg Holding Co	5033	36
Flight Express Inc	4513	9
Flight International Inc	4522	28
Flight Microwave Corp	3559	447
Flight One Software Inc	7371	1187
Flight Options	3721	8
Flight Structures Inc (Tulalip Washington)	3728	61
Flight Systems Inc	3571	154
Flight Systems Industrial Products Co	3625	109
Flightcom Corp	3663	212
Flightline Electronics Inc	3812	11
FlightSafety International	3699	21
FlightSafety International Inc	3699	19
Flik International Corp	8742	76
Flinchbaugh Engineering Inc	3499	43
Flink Co	3531	161
Flinn and Dreffein Engineering Co	3585	189
Flint Communications Inc	7311	638
Flint Energies	4911	218
Flint Energy Services Inc	4925	8
Flint Group North America Corp	2893	6
Flint Hills Resources LLC	5169	32
Flint Hills Resources LP	2911	43
Flint Hydrostatics Inc	3594	21
Flint Interactive LLC	7374	407
Flint Machine Tools Inc	5084	637
Flint Packaging Inc	4783	4
Flint River Mills Inc	2048	59

Company Name	SIC	Rank
Flint Telecom Group Inc	3669	71
Flintco LLC	1541	29
Flintec Inc	3679	503
Flippin Bruce and Porter Inc	6282	529
Flippo Construction Company Inc	1623	26
Flipside Inc	7372	685
Flipswap Inc	8999	105
FLIR Systems Boston	3823	51
FLIR Systems Inc	3812	8
Flite Line Acquisitions Corp	5088	74
Flitz International Ltd	2842	135
Flm Graphics Corp	2791	4
Floc	8322	241
Flodin Inc	3556	168
Flo-Gas Corp	4923	25
Flo-Kem Inc	2842	97
Flolo Corp	5063	239
Flood Testing Laboratories Inc	8734	137
FloodSource Corp	7379	113
Floor Covering Exchange Inc	7371	1436
Floor Productions LLC	2759	435
Floor Resources Inc	5023	148
Flooring America	5713	1
Flooring Design Associates Inc	5023	106
floppydiskcom	5961	180
Flo-Pro Systems Inc	3535	195
Flora Inc	2099	104
Flora Springs Wine Co	2084	113
Florage by Gayle Christie	7389	1795
Floral Supply Syndicate	5999	47
Floralsource International LLC	7389	864
Florence and Hutcheson	8711	89
Florence Crittenton Agency Inc	8322	162
Florence Crittenton Services Of Orange County Inc	8361	35
Florence Filter Corp	3564	148
Florence Macaroni Manufacturing Company Inc	2098	17
Flores Design Fine Furniture Inc	2512	82
Florham Park Endoscopy ASC LLC	8011	91
Floribbean Wholesale Inc	5146	8
Florida Bottling Inc	2037	37
Florida Bulb and Ballast Inc	5063	640
Florida Candy Factory Inc	2064	107
Florida Capital Partners Inc	6799	167
Florida Chemical Supply Inc	5169	176
Florida Clarklift Inc	5084	360
Florida Coast Lighting Inc	5063	972
Florida Coca-Cola Bottling Co	2086	25
Florida Commerce Credit Union	6061	83
Florida Community Bank	6036	88
Florida Community Services Corporation of Walton Count	4952	6
Florida Custom Mold Inc	3089	654
Florida Cypress Gardens Inc	8422	3
Florida Design Contractors Inc	1623	137
Florida Digital Inc	3577	458
Florida Direct Marketing Systems Inc	7331	273
Florida Distributing Source	8742	516
Florida East Coast Industries Inc	4011	17
Florida Electric Inc	1731	2515
Florida Electronic Business Resource Company Inc	5065	455
Florida Engineered Construction Products Corpora	3272	45
Florida Extruders International Inc	3354	23
Florida Family Insurance Services LLC	6331	249
Florida Farm Bureau Insurance Cos	6331	122
Florida Fertilizer Company Inc	5191	151
Florida Fire And Sound Inc	1731	971
Florida First Capital Finance Corp	6163	8
Florida Food Products Inc	2033	96
Florida Fruit Juices Inc	2033	107
Florida Funding Publications Inc	2731	176
Florida Gaming Corp	7999	113
Florida Gas Transmission Co	4922	30
Florida Graphic Printing Inc	2752	1788
Florida Infusion Services Inc	5122	49
Florida Logos Inc	3993	187
Florida Lumber Co	5211	96
Florida Magazine Administrators Inc	2721	292
Florida Medical Computers Inc	5734	191
Florida Medical Development Inc	7359	215
Florida Metal Services Inc	3469	170
Florida Metallizing Service Inc	3599	1211
Florida Micro Devices Inc	3674	482
Florida Natural Flavors Inc	2087	65
Florida Parishes Bank	6035	214
Florida Plating and Machining Inc	7699	167
Florida Plywoods Inc	2434	73
Florida Pneumatic Manufacturing Corp	3546	24
Florida Potting Soils Inc	2875	17
Florida Power and Light Co	4911	22
Florida Properties of Jacksonville Inc	7389	2390
Florida Public Utilities Co	4939	10
Florida Quality Truss Industries Inc	2439	52
Florida R S Technology	3679	774
Florida Radio Rental Inc	7999	115
Florida Radiology Imaging At Lake Mary LLC	3826	64
Florida Rental Solutions LLC	7359	169
Florida Reprographics Inc	7336	208
Florida Rock and Tank Lines Inc	4213	247
Florida Rock Industries Inc	3272	5

Company Name	SIC	Rank
Florida Rock Properties Inc	6552	255
Florida Seating Inc	5046	107
Florida Software and Data Systems Inc	7371	1402
Florida Software Inc	7372	3903
Florida Sound Engineering Company Inc	1731	2410
Florida Southeast Development Corp	6552	163
Florida SpA Covers and Vinyl Specialties Inc	2221	48
Florida State College At Jacksonville	8221	14
Florida Tel-Con Inc	1623	583
Florida Tile Industries Inc	3253	3
Florida Towers Service Inc	1731	1377
Florida Trade Graphics Inc	5111	32
Florida Veal Processors Inc	5142	42
Florida West Coast Public Broadcasting Inc	4833	166
Florig Equipment Company Inc	5013	119
Florig R and J Industrial Company Inc	3441	242
Florilli Transportation LLC	4213	648
Florim USA Inc	3253	5
Florissant Valley Sheltered	8331	222
Flortek Corp	2273	33
Flory Industries	3523	99
Floscan Instrument Company Inc	3824	32
Flotation Tech LLC	3089	546
Flotech Inc	3494	39
Flotek Industries Inc	2899	43
Floturn Inc	3599	80
Flour Power Inc	2045	18
Flow Automotive Cos	5511	38
Flow Dynamics Inc	8734	201
Flow International Corp	3569	13
Flow Management Technologies Inc	7372	1666
Flow Robotics (Jeffersonville Indiana)	3699	38
Flow Safe Inc	7389	2329
Flow Science Inc	7372	3710
Flow Systems	3699	4
Flow Systems Inc	8711	569
Flow Technology Inc	3823	117
Flower City Communications LLC	5731	227
Flower City Printing Inc	2657	10
Flowerfire	7372	2978
Flowers Baking Company Inc	2051	70
Flowers Baking Company of Birmingham LLC	2051	93
Flowers Baking Company Of Denton LLC	2051	169
Flowers Baking Company of Houston	2051	81
Flowers Baking Company of Texarkana LLC	2051	50
Flowers Foods Inc	2051	1
Flowerwood Garden Center Inc	5261	19
Flow-Eze Co	3993	172
Flowline Alaska Inc	1623	423
Flowmaster Inc	3714	207
Flowmaster USA Inc	7372	4376
Flowserve Corp	3561	8
Flowserve Fcd Corp	3491	9
Flowstar Corp	5063	765
Floyd and Beasley Transfer Company Inc	4213	1006
Floyd Blinsky Trucking Inc	4213	1055
Floyd Concrete Inc	3531	206
Floyd King and Sons Inc	1623	106
Floyd Thomas LLC	5045	749
Floyd V Wells Inc	5084	670
Floyd's Construction Inc	1623	448
Floyd's of South Carolina Inc	4213	3058
Floyd's Stores Inc	5399	19
Flp Group LLC	2752	1768
FLS Energy	1711	145
FLSmidth Inc	3559	50
Flsmidth Krebs Inc	3443	53
Flue-Cured Tobacco Cooperative Stabilization Corp	2141	1
Fluent Systems Inc	7373	926
Fluets Corp	3599	1369
Fluid Automation Inc	3561	155
Fluid Components International	3823	55
Fluid Conditioning Products Inc	7389	1414
Fluid Conservation Systems Corp	3599	2447
Fluid Dynamics Inc	3586	15
Fluid Energy Processing and Equipment Company Inc	3599	337
Fluid Handling Components Inc	3053	118
Fluid Line Products Inc	3492	20
Fluid Management Inc	3559	77
Fluid Management Operations LLC	3559	3
Fluid Management Systems Inc	3586	17
Fluid Power Equipment Inc	5084	663
Fluid Solutions Inc	7373	1218
Fluid System Components Inc	5084	349
Fluidics Inc	1711	22
Fluidigm Corp	3674	176
Fluidized Bed Technologies Inc	8711	524
Fluidmaster Inc	3494	12
Fluidthink	3823	421
Fluitec International LLC	3575	3
Fluke Metal Products Inc	3599	608
Fluke Networks	3825	23
Fluker Farms Inc	0279	1
Fluor Corp	8711	1
Fluor Employee Benefit Trust	6411	110

Company Name	SIC	Rank
Fluor Enterprises Inc	8711	2
Fluorescent Company Of America Inc	5063	957
Fluoresco Lighting-Sign Maintenance Corp	3993	12
Fluorochem Inc	8731	386
Fluorolite Plastics Inc	3089	1160
Fluoro-Plastics Inc	3089	1604
Fluortek Inc	3089	844
Flushing Financial Corp	6035	30
Flushing Savings Bank FSB	6035	63
Flutter Fetti Fun Factory	2679	80
Flying Bridge Technologies Inc	7379	1339
Flying Dutchman Management Inc	6552	269
Flying Spot Entertainment	2741	184
Flynn and Friends Advertising Inc	7311	606
Flynn Burner Corp	3567	71
Flynn Transport Inc	4213	2354
Flyte Tyme Productions Inc	7389	1124
Flytech Technology Inc (Fremont California)	3571	86
FM 107 W F M P Real Life Conversation	4832	59
FM Brown's Sons Inc	5191	53
FM Delaware Inc	3559	4
FM Facility Maintenance LLC	7349	27
FM Global	6331	52
FM Global Insurance Co	6331	67
Fm Industries Inc	3599	46
FM Resources	5112	20
Fm Structural Plastic Technology Inc	3089	330
Fm Systems Inc	3663	365
Fma Communicatons Inc	2721	246
FMA Enterprises Inc	7322	18
F-Matic Inc	5169	134
Fmaudit LLC	5045	845
FMC Corp	2879	2
FMC Food Technology	3556	67
FMC Foodtech Northfield	3585	121
FMC Technologies Inc	3533	5
FMC Technologies Measurement Solutions	3824	3
FMC Transport	4213	1869
FMC Wyoming Corp	2812	5
Fmf Racing	3751	14
FMG Design Inc	7311	848
FMG Enterprises	7699	101
FMH Corp	3599	250
FMI Express Corp	4213	906
Fmi Inc	3061	29
Fmmb LLC	2542	69
FMR LLC	6211	10
FMR Systems Inc	7371	1089
FMS Bonds Inc	6211	285
Fms/Magnacraft Inc	7331	113
Fn Manufacturing LLC	3484	15
Fna Ip Holdings Inc	5084	298
FNB Bancorp	6712	386
FNB Bank NA	6021	211
FNB Corp	6712	77
FNB United Corp	6712	202
FNC Realty Corp	6531	103
FNF Construction Inc	1611	12
FNS Bancshares Inc	6712	592
Foam Concepts Inc	3086	123
Foam Design Inc	3086	32
Foam Fabricators Inc	3086	20
Foam Factory and Upholstery Inc	5199	65
Foam Fair Industries Inc	3086	109
Foam Molders And Specialties	3086	44
Foam Plastic Specialties Inc	3086	159
Foam Products Inc	3069	249
Foam Products of San Antonio Inc	5199	33
Foam Seal Inc	3053	28
Foam Supplies Inc	3087	23
Foam Tec Products Inc	3086	140
Foamcraft Inc	3086	75
Foamtech Corp	2899	238
Foamworks Inc	3086	78
Focal Point LLC	3646	31
FocalPoint Partners LLC	6799	215
Focus 24 Inc	7373	1032
Focus Brands Inc	6719	53
Focus Camera Inc	5946	6
FOCUS Direct Inc	2752	40
Focus Electronics Inc	5731	65
FOCUS Enhancements Inc	3577	202
Focus Environmental Inc	8742	357
Focus Features	2741	90
Focus Group Inc	6513	19
Focus Industries Inc	3646	38
Focus On The Family Inc	8322	17
Focus Products Group LLC	5023	39
Focus Technology Group Inc	7372	2297
Focused Media	3695	134
Fodor's Travel Publications Inc	2741	111
Foerster Instruments Inc	3826	22
FOF Inc	5171	48
FOF Products Inc	2394	38
Fog City Software Inc	7372	1927
Fog Cutter Capital Group Inc	5812	285
Fogarty Homes Inc	1521	123
Fogarty Klein Monroe	8743	23
Fogarty Klein Monroe Agency	7311	322
Fogel-Anderson Construction Co	1541	206

Company Name	SIC	Rank
Fogle Computing Corp	5734	31
Fogle Manufacturing Services LP	3533	90
Fogmaster Corp	3523	277
FOI Services Inc	2741	157
Foit-Albert Associates Architects and Engineers PC	8712	80
Folder Factory Inc	2752	1460
Folding Shutter Corp	3442	36
Foley and Lardner LLP	8111	97
Foley and Wallace Associates Inc	5046	127
Foley Distributing Corp	5113	58
Foley Electric Inc	1731	1034
Foley Equipment Co	5082	50
Fuley Estates Vineyard and Winery	2084	125
Foley/Freisleben LLC	8743	279
Foley Hoag LLP	8111	103
Foley Mailing Services Inc	7331	62
Foley Material Handling Company Inc	3536	21
Foley Pattern Company Inc	3365	48
Foley Products Co	3272	48
Foley Supply LLC	7359	149
Foley-Belsaw Co	8331	133
Foley's Graphic Center Inc	7334	59
Foley's Pump Service Inc	3561	144
Folgergraphics Inc	2791	19
Foliage Enterprises Inc	2711	898
Foliage Software Systems	7372	401
FOLIOfn Inc	6282	158
Folks Creative Printers Inc	2752	1317
Folksamerica Holding Co	6311	146
Follett College Stores Co	5942	3
Follett Corp	3585	86
Follett Corp (River Grove Illinois)	5192	1
Follett Higher Education Group Inc	5942	6
Follett Software Co	7372	673
Follmer Development Inc	2813	25
Folsom Buick-Pontiac-GMC Inc	5511	518
Folsom Construction Co	1611	211
Folsom Corp	5091	14
Folsom Lake Ford	5511	91
Folsom Tool and Mold Corp	3599	639
Folsom Travel	4724	108
Foltz Machine Inc	3599	925
Foltz Trucking Inc	4213	1107
Fomo Products Inc	3086	62
Fona International Inc	2087	26
FONAR Corp	8093	26
Fonda Group Inc (Oshkosh Wisconsin)	2621	14
Foneco Business Systems Inc	5065	894
Fones West Digital Systems	5065	915
Fong Brothers Printing Inc	2752	115
Fong Huy Foods Inc	2033	112
Fongs Graphics and Printing Inc	2754	41
Fonix Corp	7373	1000
Fono Unlimited Inc	2024	64
Fonseca Citrus Harvesting LLC	7389	1646
Font Bureau Inc	3577	532
Fontaine International Inc	5039	10
Fontana Enterprises Inc	2752	1734
Fontana Lithograph Inc	2752	169
Fontana Rehabilitation Workshop Inc	8331	209
Fontanesi And Kann Co	5082	171
Fontarome Chemical Inc	2869	87
FontGear Inc	7372	4984
FontLab Ltd	7372	4689
Fontographics Inc	2741	477
Fonts and Software USA Inc	7372	2281
Food 4 Less of Southern California Inc	5411	30
Food Allergy and Anaphylaxis Network	8011	157
Food and Beverage International	8742	677
Food Automation - Service Techniques Inc	3823	71
Food Circus Super Markets Inc	5411	149
Food City USA Inc	2098	16
Food Concepts Inc (Middleton Wisconsin)	2541	36
Food Craft Inc	3556	77
Food Design Inc	3556	136
Food Employers Labor Rels Assoc & United Food & Comm Works H & W Fund	8743	8
Food Emporium	5411	291
Food Equipment Manufacturing Corp	3565	133
Food Equipment Technologies Co	3589	54
Food Express Inc	4213	833
Food Giant Super Markets Inc	5411	123
Food Instrument Corp	3556	185
Food Lion LLC	5411	17
Food Manufacturing	2754	11
Food Market Merchandising Inc	5199	96
Food Market Northwest Inc	5411	96
Food Maxx	5411	7
Food Process and Control Inc	5074	225
Food Sciences Corp	2023	17
Food Service Action Inc	5141	199
Food Services Inc	5962	17
Food Should Taste Good Inc	2041	21
Food Source Inc	5148	18
Food Technology And Design LLC	2064	88
Food Technology Corp	3826	132
Food Technology Service Inc	7389	1430
Food Warming Equipment Company Inc	3585	123
Foodbuy LLC	5141	90

Company Name	SIC	Rank
Foodco 6	7372	4419
Foodcomm International	5147	11
Foodcraft Inc	5149	94
Foodland Distributors	5141	47
Foodliner Inc	4213	259
Foodmaster Super Markets Inc	5411	170
FoodSalesWest Inc	5141	77
FoodScience Corp	5149	67
Foodservice Brokerage Company Ltd	5141	117
Foodsources Inc	5142	26
Foodswing Inc	2032	24
Foodtools Inc	3556	79
Foodtown International Inc	5411	280
FoodTrader International Inc	7389	435
Foot Locker Inc	5661	1
Foot Petals LLC	2389	23
Foote Cone and Belding	7311	8
Foothill Capital Corp	6141	33
Foothill Digital Inc	3695	130
Foothill Workshop For The Handicapped Inc	3479	83
Foothills Farmers Coop	5999	54
Foothills Machining Inc	3541	143
Foothills Mall Inc	6531	343
Foothills Trucking Company Inc	4213	1559
Footprint Retail Services	4789	13
Foot-So-Port (Oconomowoc Wisconsin)	3149	30
Footstar Inc	5661	21
Footsteps LLC	7311	393
Footwear Specialties International LLC	5139	27
For Bare Feet Inc	2252	18
For-A-Corporation of America	5046	5
Forage Genetics International	5191	103
Foram Management and Leasing Inc	6531	384
Foran Spice Company Inc	2099	138
Foranne Manufacturing Inc	3599	1036
Forbes Candies Inc	2064	81
Forbes Distributing Inc	5065	506
Forbes Inc	2721	28
Forbes Industries Div	2599	18
Forbes Technology Group	7379	598
Forbes Trinchera Ranch	6552	89
Forbo Industries Inc	3996	2
Force America Inc	5084	139
Force Control Industries Inc	3568	42
Force Electronics	4911	588
Force Electronics Inc	5065	58
Force Flow	3545	264
Force Industries Inc	2899	219
Force Manufacturing Inc	3579	59
Force Protection Inc	5012	24
Force Transportation Inc	4213	2415
Force10 Networks Inc	7379	90
Forced Exposure Inc	2721	373
Forcom Corp	5045	661
Ford and Harrison LLP	8111	142
Ford Bacon and Davis Inc	8711	115
Ford Boyer Trucks Inc	5013	231
Ford Construction Co	1611	147
Ford County Feed Yard Inc	0212	2
Ford Development Corp	1542	221
Ford Environmental Quality Office	3822	62
Ford Equity Research Inc	7372	4189
Ford Gum and Machine Company Inc	2067	2
Ford International Capital Corp	6159	7
Ford Lincoln Mercury of Bellevue	5511	990
Ford Lincoln of Cookville	5511	1235
Ford Models Inc	7363	102
Ford Motor Co	3711	2
Ford Motor Credit Company LLC	6141	4
Ford Motor Land Development Corp	6552	39
Ford Motor Service Co	5013	1
Ford Nassen and Baldwin PC	8111	472
Ford of Kirkland	5511	492
Ford of Montebello Inc	5511	1008
Ford of North Miami Beach	3711	25
Ford Powell and Carson Inc	8712	166
Ford Richmond LLC	5511	866
Ford Steel Co	5051	234
Ford Tool and Machining Inc	3544	106
Ford Tool Steels Inc	5051	448
Ford VAC Corp	3711	5
Ford World of Roselle Park	5511	1145
Fordyce Picture Frame Company Inc	2499	66
Fore Tool Co	3545	405
Forecast International Inc	2731	210
Forecast Product Development Corp	7389	1061
ForeclosuresDailycom	8748	358
Forecross Corp	7372	2804
Foreground Security	7379	452
Foreign Auto Preparation Services Inc	7538	11
Foreign Independent Tours	4725	45
Foreign Trade Corp	5065	233
Foreman Program and Construction Managers Inc	8712	210
Foreman Tool and Mold Corp	3089	809
Foremark Ltd	6531	446
Foremost Farms USA Coop	2026	6
Foremost Industries Inc	2452	29
Foremost Insurance Co	6331	169
Foremost Machine Builders Inc	3559	207
Foremost Manufacturing Company Inc	3471	74
Foremost Plastic Products Company Inc	3089	1186

Company Name	SIC	Rank
Foremost Pump and Well Services LLC	7699	95
Forensic Analytical Specialities Inc	8748	220
Forensic Fluids Laboratories	8071	49
Forensic Logic Inc	7372	5031
Forenta LP	3582	8
ForeRunner Corp	8741	178
ForeScout Technologies Inc	7372	1066
Foresight Consulting Inc	7379	1377
FORESIGHT Corp	7372	2572
Foresight Group Inc	2752	932
Foresight Imaging LLC	3577	350
Foresight Processing LLC	3674	458
Foresight Software Inc	7372	2979
Foresight Solutions Inc	7372	3533
Foresight Technologies Inc	3674	253
Foresight Technology Group Inc	7373	217
Forest City Commercial Group Inc	6512	12
Forest City Enterprises Inc	6512	7
Forest City Erectors Inc	1542	77
Forest City Management Inc	6512	16
Forest City Technologies Inc	3053	18
Forest City Trading Group LLC	5031	18
Forest Construction Company Inc	1623	318
Forest Corp	2752	310
Forest Cowee Products Inc	2499	62
Forest Dixieland Corp	1731	550
Forest Hambro Products Inc	2493	12
Forest Hill Communications Inc	1623	417
Forest Hills Hospital	8062	167
Forest Hunt Products Inc	2436	11
Forest Investment Associates	6798	130
Forest Laboratories Inc	2834	15
Forest Lawn Memorial Parks and Mortuaries	6553	2
Forest Oil Corp	1311	48
Forest Packing Co	2015	40
Forest Pharmaceuticals Inc	2834	45
Forest Plywood Sales	5031	129
Forest Post Productions Ltd	7371	932
Forest Products Inc	2421	79
Forest Products Northwest Inc	5031	312
Forest Products Sales Inc	2421	126
Forest Products Supply	6411	252
Forest Products Transports Inc	4213	1281
Forest Scientific Corp	5734	253
Forest Shaniko Products Inc	2421	113
Forest Silicon Electronics Inc	3672	81
Forest Siskiyou Products	2431	117
Forest Tmi Products Inc	2421	60
Forest Wellborn Products Inc	2434	33
Forest2Market Inc	7375	199
Forestar Group Inc	6552	96
Forestdale Inc	8322	69
Forestfarm	5961	109
Forestry Equipment Of Va Inc	3531	144
Forestry Suppliers Inc	5961	79
ForestWorld Inc	7372	2980
Forethought Financial Services Inc	6311	126
Forethought Life Insurance Co	6311	114
Foretravel Inc	3711	48
Forever 21 Inc	2361	1
Forever Broadcasting	4832	228
Forever Communications	4832	154
Forever Enterprises Inc	6311	209
Forever Living Products International Inc	5963	4
Forever Of PA Inc	4832	86
ForeverGreen IP LLC	2099	174
Forex Club LLC	6282	147
Forex International Trading Corp	7372	311
Forge Die and Tool Corp	3544	282
Forge Industries Inc	5085	4
Forge Precision Co	3599	1242
Forge Welkin LLC	3541	42
Forged Metals Inc	3462	15
Forget Me Knot Ltd	5199	133
Forgy Process Instruments Inc	5065	548
Fori Automation Inc	3545	25
Forklift of Minnesota Inc	5084	57
Forklifts Of St Louis Inc	5084	263
Forks Prairie Mart Inc	5411	130
Form Builders Inc	2752	1622
Form Centerless Grinding Inc	3599	854
Form Cut Industries Inc	3496	85
Form First Inc	5045	975
Form Grind Corp	3599	780
Form Plastics Co	3086	53
Form Roll Die Corp	3542	64
Form Services Inc	5082	95
Form Skillcraft Printers Inc	2759	350
Form Systems Inc	2759	103
Form/Tec Plastics Inc	3089	1443
Form Tool Technology Inc	3545	396
Form Tools Inc	3545	325
Form-A-Feed Inc	2048	50
Forma-Kool Manufacturing Inc	3585	227
Formall Inc	3081	124
Forman Inc	5113	32
Formatech Inc	2834	232
FORMation mg Inc	7372	3643
Formats Unlimited Inc	3695	49
Formax Technologies Inc	3699	200
Formcap Corp	7372	5092

Company Name	SIC	Rank
Form-Co Inc	7389	1958
Formco Metal Products Inc	3469	309
Formed Fiber Technologies LLC	2824	9
Formed Plastics Inc	3089	129
Formedic Communication Ltd	7311	444
Formetco Inc	3993	59
FormFactor Inc	3674	91
Formflex Inc	3081	20
Formica Corp	3083	3
Formosa Plastics Corporation USA	2821	27
Formosa USA Inc	5045	93
Formost Fuji Corp	3565	47
Formost Graphic Communications Inc	5112	50
Forms And Surfaces Inc	3446	8
Forms Management Inc	5943	16
Forms Resource Inc	5112	74
Formstore Inc	2761	35
Formtek Inc	7372	1175
Formtek Inc (Westfield Massachusetts)	3585	12
Formtek Metal Forming Inc	3547	4
Formula Consultants Inc	7372	2573
Formula Equipment Inc	5082	81
Formula Plastics Inc	3089	295
Fornance Physician Services Inc	8082	47
Fornax Corp	2721	165
Forney Corp	3823	28
Forney Holdings Inc	3829	239
Forney Industries Inc	3548	15
Forob Inc	7372	4690
Forona Technologies Inc	4813	621
Forproject Technology Inc	7372	2741
Forrer Business Interiors Inc	5021	57
Forrer Supply Company Inc	5074	125
Forrest Binkley and Brown	6799	123
Forrest Machining Inc	3728	70
Forrest S Chilton Iii Memorial Hosp	8062	150
Forrest Sherer Inc	6311	178
Forrester Research Inc	8999	26
Forsberg's Inc	3523	161
Forsch Corp	6799	21
For-Shor Co	5082	148
Forster Electrical Services Inc	1731	676
Forster Tool and Manufacturing Company Inc	3544	435
Forstmann Little and Co	6211	409
Forsyth Securities Inc	6211	224
Forsyth Water And Sewer Construction Inc	1623	654
Forsythe and Associates Inc	5045	954
Forsythe and Butler Advertising/Marketing	7311	669
Forsythe And Dowis Rides Inc	3599	328
Forsythe Solutions Group Inc	7373	20
Forsythe Technology	7379	1084
Fort Bragg Rent-All Inc	7359	274
Fort Dearborn Income Securities Inc	6726	16
Fort Dearborn Life Insurance Co	6311	96
Fort Edward Express Company Inc	4213	1864
Fort Fudge Shop Inc	5145	40
Fort Knox Federal Credit Union	6061	10
Fort Knox Security Products Inc	3499	82
Fort Lock Corp	3429	101
Fort Miller Service Corp	3272	77
Fort Myers Automotive And Industrial Supply Inc	5013	252
Ft Myers Digestive Health and Pain ASC LLC	8011	99
Fort Orange Press Inc	2752	830
Fort Recovery Equity Inc	2015	11
Fort Smith Railroad Co	4011	29
Fort Transfer	4213	814
Fort Walton Machining Inc	3599	121
Fort Washington Capital Partners	6799	26
Fort Wayne Foundry Corp	3365	1
Fort Wayne Metals Research Products Corp	3315	11
Fort Wayne Mold and Engineering Inc	3544	427
Fort Wayne Newspapers	2711	47
Fort Wayne Plastics Inc	3089	544
Fort Wayne Printing Company Inc	2752	1191
Fort William Henry Corp	7011	189
Fort Worth Bolt and Tool Company Ltd	5085	143
Fort Worth Carrier Corp	4213	750
Fort Worth City Credit Union	6062	101
Fort Worth Community Credit Union	6061	43
Fort Worth Lumber Co	5031	132
Fort Worth Tower Company Inc	3441	100
Fort Worth Weekly LP	2711	660
Forta Corp	2821	156
Forte and Tablada Incorporated Consulting Engineers	8711	306
Forte Automation Systems Inc	8742	528
Forte Internet Software Inc	7372	3297
Forte Product Solutions	3089	701
Forte Systems Inc	7371	487
Fortec Medical Inc	5047	168
Fortec Medical Lithotripsy LLC	3699	199
Fortegra Financial Corp	6411	72
Fortel DTV Inc	4833	91
Fortent Americas Inc	7373	232
Forteq North America Inc	3089	734
FORTH Inc	7371	926
Forth Technologies Inc	2869	92
ForTheFarm Inc	7389	762

Company Name	SIC	Rank
Forthmann Machines Inc	3554	47
Forticell Bioscience Inc	3841	416
Fortier and Fortier Inc	5083	114
Fortifiber Corp	2672	22
Fortinet Inc	7372	126
FORTIS Construction Inc	1541	63
Fortis Investment Management USA Inc	7389	1183
Fortitech Inc	2834	142
Fortner Aerospace Manufacturing Inc	3812	105
Fortney and Weygandt Inc	1542	172
Fortres Grand Corp	7372	3534
Fortress Forms	3496	58
Fortress Inc	2522	52
Fortress International Group Inc	8742	148
Fortress Investment Group LLC	6282	54
Fortress Protective Services Inc	7381	104
Fortress Security and Life Safety	7382	184
Fortress Technologies Inc	7372	894
Fortron Source Corp	3612	17
Forts Radio Group LLC	4832	189
Fortunately Yours	2052	83
Fortune Brands Home and Hardware Inc	3432	2
Fortune Champion Corp	3541	240
Fortune Group LLC	6211	367
Fortune Industries Inc (Indianapolis Indiana)	7389	298
Fortune International Realty	6531	56
Fortune Manufacturing Inc	3599	775
Fortune Metal Inc	5093	9
Fortune Tool and Machine Inc	7699	196
Fortune Transportation Company Inc	4213	1174
Fortune Valley Hotel and Casino	7011	80
FortuneBuilders Inc	8299	51
Fortunet Inc	3999	87
Fortunoff Fine Jewelry and Silverware Inc	5944	8
Fortville Feeders Inc	3599	1013
Forty Acres And A Mule Filmworks Inc	7812	180
Forty Plus of New York Inc	7361	144
Forum At The Woodlands Inc	8361	124
Forum Communication Systems Inc	7372	2636
Forum Communications Co	2711	52
Forum Communications International	3661	160
Forum Corp	8742	70
Forum Credit Union	6061	117
Forum Inc	3646	23
Forvus Research Inc	3577	534
Forward Air Corp	4731	22
Forward Association Inc	2711	409
Forward Corp	5983	11
Forward Design Inc	7336	253
Forward Edge Inc	7378	49
Forward Industries Inc	3089	336
Forward Newspaper LLC	2711	545
Forward Pay Systems Inc	3577	603
Forward Technology Industries Inc	3599	184
Forward Times Publishing Co	2711	826
Forward Ventures	6799	93
Fosda Inc	3599	2201
Foseco Inc	2899	123
Foshee Trucking Inc	4213	1581
Foss Co	5912	54
Foss Manufacturing Company Inc	2297	2
Foss Maritime Co	4492	2
Foss Nirsystems Inc	3826	47
Foss North America Inc	5049	44
Fossil Inc	3873	1
Fossil Industries Inc	3993	150
Fossil Stores II Inc	5999	32
Fossman Corp	5065	817
Fosta-Tek Optics Inc	3851	34
Foster Corp	2833	56
Foster Dairy Farms	2023	12
Foster F Wineland Inc	5084	366
Foster Family Farm	0161	19
Foster Management Inc	1521	85
Foster Manufacturing Company Inc	3498	71
Foster Pepper and Shefelman PLLC	8111	227
Foster Poultry Farms Inc	2015	9
Foster Printing Company Inc	2752	492
Foster Printing Co (Tustin California)	2752	565
Foster Printing Service Inc	2752	358
Foster Transformer Co	3612	116
Foster Wheeler Constructors Inc	1629	64
Foster Wheeler Energy Corp	3443	3
Foster Wheeler International Corp	8711	44
Foster Wheeler Martinez Inc	4911	470
Foster Wheeler Power Systems Inc	4911	100
Foster Wheeler Pyropower	1629	28
Fostermation Inc	3451	147
Fotel Inc	7335	11
Foth and Van Dyke and Associates Inc	8711	211
Foti Lazo Inc	7311	629
FotimaUSA Inc	5199	135
Foto Fantasy Inc	5043	21
Fotodyne Inc	5049	169
Fotofabrication Corp	3545	167
Fotofolio Inc	5199	49
Fought and Company Inc	1791	7
Foulds Inc	2099	218
Foundation Center Inc	2741	109
Foundation Constructors Inc	1629	72

Company Name	SIC	Rank
Foundation Savings Bank	6036	95
Foundation Software Inc	7372	289
Foundation Source Inc	8741	159
Foundation Systems Inc	7372	3667
Foundation Technologies Inc	7373	726
Foundation Workshop Inc	8331	234
Founders Equity Inc	6211	396
Founders Group	7389	829
Foundry Partners LLC	8742	421
Foundry Service Corp	4213	1801
Foundstone Inc	8748	8
Fountain American Soda Exchange Inc	5046	263
Fountain Building and Supply Company Inc	5211	312
Fountain Construction Company Inc	1711	96
Fountain Engineering Inc	1623	348
Fountain Industries Co	3559	229
Fountain Powerboat Industries Inc	3731	19
Fountain Powerboats Inc	3731	18
Fountain Rock Management Corp	2082	34
Fountainhead Group Inc	3563	25
Fountainhead Title Group Corp	6541	7
Four B Corp	5411	36
Four C Construction Inc	1731	881
Four Corners Financial Corp	6531	133
Four D Electric Inc	1731	1413
Four Daughters Inc	2051	278
Four Dimensions Inc	3825	251
Four Directions Inc	1731	1590
Four Flags Health Ventures Inc	8741	179
Four Guys Stainless Tank and Equipment Inc	7699	35
Four J's Development Tools Inc	5045	516
Four Oaks Bank and Trust Co	6022	459
Four Oaks Fincorp Inc	6022	176
Four Paws Products Ltd	3999	103
Four Peaks Brewing Co	2082	12
Four Queens Hotel and Casino Inc	7999	30
Four Rivers Software Systems Inc	7371	782
Four S Group Inc	5065	310
Four Seasons Coop	5399	11
Four Seasons Industries	3089	279
Four Seasons Messenger Service	4213	2996
Four Seasons Sales and Service Inc	5064	34
Four Seasons Services Inc	5087	137
Four Seasons Solar Products LLC	3448	11
Four Star Electric Inc	1731	1951
Four Star General Cleaning Corp	7349	299
Four Star Plastics LLC	3089	1721
Four Star Reproductions Inc	2752	1205
Four Star Tool Inc	3679	313
Four Truckers Inc	4213	666
Four Winds International Inc	3716	6
Four Winns Inc	3732	7
Fourb Technologies Inc	7373	1141
Fourmidable Group	6531	282
Fournier Rubber and Supply Co	5085	192
Fourroux Orthotics And Prosthetics Inc	5999	189
Foursome Inc	5651	24
Fourth Dimension Software	7372	2786
Fourth Generation Software Solutions Corp	7372	3298
Fourth World Media Corp	7372	4924
FourthWall Media	7372	1544
Fourway Machinery Sales Company Inc	5084	856
Four-Way Tool And Die Inc	3544	715
Fouts Electric Corp	1731	1340
Fowler Buick-GMC Inc	5511	360
Fowler Card Club Inc	5812	411
Fowler Electric Co	1731	524
Fowler Electrical Contractors Inc	1731	811
Fowler Equipment Company Inc	5087	36
Fowler Printing and Graphics Inc	2752	1207
Fowler Productions Inc	5065	218
Fowler Products Inc	3089	1748
Fowler White Boggs Banker	8111	131
Fowler's Tv Inc	5731	156
Fownes Brothers and Company Inc	3151	1
Fox 17 Studio Productions	4833	159
Fox 46	4833	208
Fox and Bubela Inc	6531	288
Fox and Hound of Fort Worth Ltd	5812	384
Fox and Hound of Houston Ltd	5812	372
Fox and Hound of Houston No 2 Ltd	5812	327
Fox and Hound of Indiana Inc	5812	361
Fox and Hound of Kansas Inc	5812	354
Fox and Hound of Lewisville Ltd	5812	357
Fox and Hound of Louisiana Inc	5812	367
Fox and Hound of Lubbock Ltd	5812	373
Fox and Hound of Michigan Inc	5812	313
Fox and Hound of Missouri Inc (Springfield Missouri)	5812	314
Fox and Hound of Nebraska Inc	5812	374
Fox and Hound of Ohio Inc	5812	381
Fox and Hound of Pennsylvania Inc	5812	334
Fox and Hound of Richardson Ltd	5812	335
Fox and Hound of San Antonio Ltd	5812	375
Fox and Hound of Tennessee Inc	5812	362
Fox and Hound of Virginia Inc	5812	328
Fox and Hound Restaurant Group	5812	165
Fox and James Inc	5511	1142
Fox Apparel Inc	2325	8
Fox Asset Management LLC	6282	135

Company Name	SIC	Rank
Fox Associates LLC	8741	30
Fox Bay Industries Inc	3842	325
Fox Bindery Inc	2789	13
Fox Broadcasting Co	4833	68
Fox Chapel Publishing Company Inc	2731	294
Fox Chase Bancorp Inc	6035	72
Fox Company Inc	2752	543
Fox Contractors Corp	1794	12
Fox Electric Ltd	1731	9
Fox Electric Limited Co	1731	1532
Fox Electrical Co	1731	1169
Fox Electronics	3679	25
Fox Entertainment Group Inc	7812	331
Fox Filmed Entertainment	7812	6
Fox Head Inc	2329	5
Fox Imports	7389	1925
Fox Inc	4833	83
Fox Industries Inc	2891	74
Fox Integrated Technologies Inc	5093	17
Fox International Limited Inc	8999	39
Fox Marine Service	4213	2081
Fox Network Center	4841	140
Fox Network Systems	3577	594
Fox Paine and Company LLC	7389	773
Fox Pool Of Lancaster Inc	3949	119
Fox Products Corp	3931	25
Fox Ridge Homes of Tennessee Inc	1531	81
Fox River Foods Inc	5149	32
Fox River Mills Inc	2252	13
Fox River Stone Inc	1411	5
Fox Rothschil LLP	8111	326
Fox Sports Networks	4841	148
Fox Sports Pittsburgh	4841	76
Fox Studios Inc	3211	23
Fox Technologies Inc	5045	105
Fox Trucking Inc	4213	2740
Fox Valley Fire and Safety Company Inc	1731	160
Fox Valley Machining Company Inc	3599	1870
Fox Valley Molding Inc	3089	492
Fox Valley Steel and Wire	3315	29
Fox Valley Tool and Die Inc	3544	80
Foxboro Co	3823	8
Foxboro Industries Inc	3599	1601
Foxconn Assembly LLC	3571	147
Foxfire Printing And Packaging Inc	2752	179
Foxhall Capital Management Inc	6282	579
Foxhill Press Inc	2731	319
FoxHollow Technologies Inc	3841	42
Foxit Corp	7373	434
Foxlink World Circuit Technology Inc	3672	281
Foxon Co	2671	66
Fox-Pitt Kelton Cochran Caronia Waller LLC	6211	228
Fox's Pizza Den Inc	6794	10
Foxsemicon Integrated Technology Inc	3674	316
Foxtronics Inc	3812	176
Foxtronix Inc	5065	948
Foxworth-Galbraith Lumber Co	5211	12
Fozzard Services Inc	7361	275
FP Developments Inc	3559	296
FP M LLC	3398	5
fP Technologies Inc	7372	3238
Fp Woll and Co	2299	24
FPA Capital Fund Inc	6722	119
FPA New Income	6722	68
FPA Paramount Fund Inc	6722	193
FPA Perennial Fund Inc	6722	194
FPB Bancorp Inc	6021	269
FPB Financial Corp	6035	190
Fpc Financial FSB	6035	196
Fpc Services Inc	1731	2590
Fpctechnology Group Inc	7378	143
FPEC Corporation A California Corp	3556	103
Fpi Electrical Inc	1731	424
FPIC Insurance Group Inc	6311	149
FPL Energy LLC	4911	84
Fpl Services	7374	205
FPMI Solutions Inc	8711	148
Fps Enterprises LP	8059	23
Fps Inc	5999	159
Fps Inc	7331	135
Fpt Cleveland LLC	4953	111
Fpt Schlafer	5093	143
FR Industries Inc	5063	659
Frabil Industries Inc	5063	941
Frac Tech Services LLC	3561	68
Fraen Corp	3469	66
Fraenkel Wholesale Furniture Company Inc	5021	32
Fragomen Del Rey Bernsen and Loewy PC	8111	164
Fragrance International Inc	5122	66
Fragrance Resources Inc	2844	85
FragranceNetcom Inc	5999	50
Frain Industries Inc	5084	462
Frakes Engineering Inc	7373	499
Fraley and Quattlebaum Inc	7623	14
Fraley and Schilling Inc	4213	663
Fralin and Waldron Inc	1521	16
Fralingers Inc	2066	31
Frame By Frame Productions	2741	400
Frame It And Company Inc	5023	197
Framerunner	7819	45

Company Name	SIC	Rank
Frames Data Inc	2741	291
Frame's Motor Freight Inc	4213	464
Framesource Manufacturing Corp	5023	184
Framework Technologies Corp	7372	3107
Frameworks Inc	3647	15
Framingham Welding and Engineering Corp	3599	624
Fran Corp	1731	365
Fran Wilson Creative Cosmetics	2844	107
France Compressor Products Div	3592	18
France Deco Trading Inc	5137	33
France/Scott Fetzer Co	3612	19
France Telecom North America Inc	4813	103
Franchelli Enterprises Inc	1623	210
Franchini Chevrolet Inc	5511	1065
Franchino Mold and Engineering Co	3544	318
Franchise Gator LLC	7375	193
Franchise Services Inc	6719	138
Franchise Solutions Inc	7389	1116
Franchise Times Corp	2759	499
Francis and Company PLLC	8721	230
Francis Bearsch	5065	763
Francis Brothers Sewer and Drainage	1623	605
Francis Emory Fitch Inc	2721	223
Francis Enterprises Inc	7699	65
Francis L Freas Glass Works Inc	3231	61
Francis Manufacturing Co	3369	16
Francis Marketing	7311	491
Francis O Day Company Inc	1611	156
Francis Powell Enterprises	4213	923
Franciscan Missonaries of Our Lady Health System Inc	8062	250
Franciscan Vineyards Inc	2084	34
Francisco Partners	6799	112
Francis-Mustoe and Co	5141	207
Franco Manufacturing Company Inc	2269	1
Franco Public Relations Group	8743	123
Franco-American Mezzaluna	2051	207
Frank Adams Jewelers Inc	5944	34
Frank And Jimmie's Propeller Shop Inc	5088	93
Frank B Fuhrer Wholesale Co	5181	48
Frank B Lesher Company Inc	1731	1575
Frank Betz Associates Inc	8712	275
Frank Chervan Inc	2511	44
Frank Condon Inc	3643	102
Frank Consolidated Enterprises	6719	47
Frank Cooney Company Inc	5021	130
Frank Edwards Co	5013	57
Frank Fletcher Companies Ltd	3231	22
Frank Freeman and Mathai	7311	857
Frank G Love Envelopes Inc	2677	13
Frank Horne Construction Inc	1623	332
Frank J Catanzaro Sons and Daughters Inc	5141	174
Frank Kent Motor Co	5511	143
Frank Korinek and Company Inc	2051	256
Frank Lill and Son Inc	7699	23
Frank Lowe Rubber and Gasket Company Inc	3053	65
Frank M Waters Inc	5046	292
Frank Mastoloni and Sons Inc	5094	14
Frank Mayborn Enterprises Inc	2711	314
Frank Mayer and Associates Inc	3993	13
Frank Mercede and Sons Inc	1541	162
Frank Messer and Sons Construction Co	1541	39
Frank Miller and Sons Inc	2819	98
Frank Miller Lumber Company Inc	2426	13
Frank Miller Lumber Company Incorporated Union City	2421	39
Frank Moran and Sons Inc	5092	43
Frank Motors Inc (National City California)	5511	294
Frank Parra Autoplex	5511	153
Frank Parsons Paper Co	5111	12
Frank Products Inc	3089	1758
Frank R Ring Transfer Inc	4213	2665
Frank Russell Co	6282	6
Frank Semeraro Construction Company Inc	1623	323
Frank Stubbs Company Inc	3842	201
Frank W Cawood and Associates Inc	2731	79
Frank Wardynski and Sons Inc	2013	173
Frank Wilson and Associates Inc	8743	159
Frank Z Chevrolet Company Inc	5511	702
Franke Con J Electric Inc	1731	187
Frankel and Anderson Inc	7311	998
Frankel Associates Inc	2299	26
Frankel Cadillac Land Rover	5511	785
Frankel Furniture Industries Inc	5021	170
Franke's Unlimited Inc	7389	1411
Frankford Candy and Chocolate Company Inc	2066	24
Frankfort First Bancorp Inc	6035	207
Frankfort Habilitation Inc	8331	226
Frankfort Manufacturing Inc	3544	494
Frankie Foundation	7389	1879
Frankl Electric Inc	1731	2003
Franklin Adjustable US Government Securities Fund	6722	111
Franklin Advisers Inc	6282	46
Franklin Alabama Tax-Free Income Fund	6722	197
Franklin Aluminum Company Inc	3354	14

Company Name	SIC	Rank
Franklin American Mortgage Co	6162	75
Franklin Arizona Tax-Free Income Fund	6722	134
Franklin Baking Company Inc	2051	45
Franklin California Insured Tax-Free Income Fund	6722	100
Franklin California Tax Free Income Fund Inc	6722	31
Franklin Collection Service Inc	7322	37
Franklin Colorado Tax-Free Income Fund	6722	168
Franklin Communications LLC	2752	238
Franklin Communications Services	7379	1516
Franklin Connecticut Tax-Free Income Fund	6722	174
Franklin Convertible Securities A	6722	163
Franklin Corp	2512	19
Franklin County Emergency Communications	3669	261
Franklin Covey Catalog Sales Inc	5099	8
Franklin Covey Client Sales Inc	7299	15
Franklin Covey Co	2789	2
Franklin Covey International Inc	2782	9
Franklin Covey Marketing Ltd	7389	255
Franklin Covey Mexico Inc	2789	1
Franklin Covey Product Sales Inc	5112	11
Franklin Covey Services LLC	7389	214
Franklin Covey Travel Inc	4789	6
Franklin Credit Holding Corp	6162	59
Franklin Designs Inc	7922	87
Franklin Display Group	3496	55
Franklin DynaTech A	6722	170
Franklin Electric Company Inc	3621	10
Franklin Electric Co (Philadelphia Pennsylvania)	5065	103
Franklin Electrofluid Company Inc	5084	397
Franklin Electronic Publishers Inc	3579	14
Franklin Estimating Systems	2731	338
Franklin Express Inc	4212	73
Franklin Feed and Supply Co	5999	68
Franklin Fibre-Lamitex Corp	3083	68
Franklin Financial Group Inc	6411	288
Franklin Financial Services Corp	6712	333
Franklin Florida Tax-Free Income Fund	6722	123
Franklin Foods Inc	2022	37
Franklin Fueling Systems	3561	104
Franklin Georgia Tax-Free Income Fund	6722	186
Franklin Global Health Care Fund	6722	232
Franklin Graphics Inc	2752	1712
Franklin Growth Fund A	6722	94
Franklin Heating Station	4931	54
Franklin High Yield Tax-Free Income Fund	6722	61
Franklin Homes Inc	2451	33
Franklin Income Fund A	6722	81
Franklin Instrument Company Inc	3873	23
Franklin Kentucky Tax-Free Income Fund	6722	212
Franklin Louisiana Tax-Free Income Fund	6722	190
Franklin Manufacturing Corp	3429	131
Franklin Maryland Tax-Free Income Fund	6722	171
Franklin Miller Inc	3559	187
Franklin Mint LLC	3942	10
Franklin Missouri Tax-Free Income Fund	6722	145
Franklin Money Fund A	6722	99
Franklin Mortgage Co	6162	100
Franklin New Jersey Tax-Free Income Fund	6722	120
Franklin North Carolina Tax-Free Income Fund	6722	136
Franklin NY Insured Tax-Free A Fund	6722	184
Franklin Oregon Tax-Free Income Fund	6722	135
Franklin Pennsylvania Tax-Free Income Fund	6722	131
Franklin Precision Industry Inc	3714	239
Franklin Press Inc	2789	38
Franklin Regional Hospital Association	8062	91
Franklin Registration	7379	1517
Franklin Resources Inc	6282	15
Franklin Sports Industries Inc	5091	28
Franklin Supply Inc	5194	21
Franklin Templeton Bank and Trust	6035	187
Franklin Templeton Distributors Inc	6211	270
Franklin Township Public School District Of Somerset	8211	80
Franklin Trucking Inc	4213	2830
Franklin US Government Secs A	6722	54
Franklin Utilities Fund	6722	102
Franklin Virginia Tax-Free Income Fund	6722	156
Franklin Web Printing Company Inc	2711	813
Franklin Wireless Corp	3661	56
FranklinCovey (Salt Lake City Utah)	6512	15
Franklite Corp	5063	791
Franklyn Ideas LLC	7311	823
Franks and Son Trucking LLC	4213	1210
Franks Cane and Rush Supply Inc	3429	156
Frank's Commercial and Home Services Inc	0781	12
Frank's International Inc	7353	17
Frank's Quality Services Inc	5078	32
Frank's Shoe Fitting and Sporting Goods Inc	5941	47
Franks Supply Company Inc	7359	58
Frank's Vacuum Truck Service	4213	1777
Frank's Welding Company Inc	3599	520
FranNet	8748	204
Fran's Chocolates Ltd	2064	50
Frantz Machine Products Inc	3599	1160
Franz Inc	7372	404
Franz Jeanes Lazo Cora Associates Inc	8712	220
Franzen Graphics Inc	2759	174
Franzen Graphics-Ohio LLC	2752	760
Frasca International Inc	3728	90
Frase Enterprises Inc	3644	37
Fraser Fab And Machine Inc	3599	1652
Fraser Grinding Co	3599	668
Fraser Manufacturing Corp	3489	19
Fraser Shipyards Inc	3731	21
Fraser/White Inc	7311	230
Frasernet Inc	2731	331
Fraser's Boiler Service Inc	7699	115
Fraser-Volpe Corp	3827	94
Frasinetti Winery	2084	55
Frate Service Inc	4213	1333
Fratelli Beretta USA Inc	2013	219
Fraternal Business Service Inc	5734	321
Fraternal Composite Service Inc	7335	2
Frazee Electric Inc	1731	2417
Frazee Industries Inc	2851	12
Frazer Frost LLP	8721	117
Frazer Lanier Company Inc	6211	378
Frazier and Frazier Industries Inc	3321	23
Frazier and Son LP	3535	188
Frazier Healthcare Ventures	6211	128
Frazier Industrial Company Inc	3441	17
Frazier Loudspeakers	3651	122
Frazier Machine and Supply Company Inc	5085	431
Frazier Precision Instrument Company Inc	3829	478
Frazier Quarry Inc	1422	30
Frazier-Simplex Machine Co	3599	1689
Frc Component Products Inc	3663	172
FRC Environmental Inc	3589	224
Frc Holding Corp	3069	11
FRCH Design Worldwide	8712	74
Freberg Environmental Inc	6351	37
Fred Alger and Company Inc	6282	525
Fred Alger Management Inc	6282	263
Fred Beans Holdings Inc	5511	126
Fred Beans Parts Inc	5013	174
Fred Burrows Trucking and Excavation	4213	849
Fred Christen and Sons Co	1761	32
Fred Clayton and Sons Inc	3523	229
Fred Cohen and Associates	8742	692
Fred D Pfening Co	3535	35
Fred Haar Company Inc	5083	103
Fred Harris and Assocs Inc	5099	122
Fred Harz and Son Inc	5014	52
Fred Hill and Son Co	5084	562
Fred Jones Enterprises LLC	3714	113
Fred Knapp Engraving Company Inc	3089	1174
Fred Martin and Associates	5021	169
Fred Martin Chevrolet	5511	562
Fred McGilvray Inc	1711	188
Fred Meyer Inc	5912	8
Fred Meyer Marketplace	5411	108
Fred Netterville Lumber Co	2421	84
Fred Radandt Sons Inc	1442	54
Fred Silver and Company Inc	3231	69
Fred Taylor Co	4213	160
Fred Usinger Inc	2013	90
Fred V Fowler Company Inc	5084	248
Fred Wilkinson Associates Inc	2391	13
Freda's Fancy Florist Antiques Inc	5992	16
Freddie Mac	6111	2
Frederic Fekkai Salons	7231	7
Frederic Printing Co	2752	140
Frederick and May Lumber Co	2431	118
Frederick Cowan and Company Inc	3612	123
Frederick Derr and Company Inc	1611	188
Frederick Engineering Inc	3679	178
Frederick Group Inc	7381	212
Frederick Hart Company Inc	2392	52
Frederick Industries Inc	4214	27
Frederick Mennonite Community	8361	41
Frederick Mutual Insurance Co	6331	342
Frederick Ross Co	6531	290
Fredericks Commercial	6531	311
Frederick's Machine and Tool Shop Inc	3533	51
Frederick's of Hollywood Inc	5632	7
Fredericksburg Farmers Coop	5153	51
Fredericksburg PC Users Group	7372	5106
Fredericksburg Publishing Co	2711	714
Fredericksburg Regional Telework Center	4813	535
Fredman Bag Co	3089	917
Fredman Brothers Furniture Company Inc	6512	46
Fredon Corp	3599	359
Fredricdorf John	5734	222
Fredrick Enterprises Inc	7331	156
Fredricks Design	7389	2142
Fredricks Electric Inc	1731	1591
Fredriksen and Sons Fire Equipment Company Inc	5099	140
Fredrikson and Byron PA	8111	188
Fred's Inc	5331	9
Fred's Micro Inc	7372	3904
Fred's Studio Tents and Canopies Inc	5091	112
Free Lance-Star Publishing Company Of Fredericksburg Va	2711	275
Free Play Productions	7372	4819
Free Press Publishing Co	2752	1066
Free Spirit Publishing Inc	2731	250
Free State Brewing Co	2082	88
Freebairn and Co	7311	362
Freeborn and Peters LLP	8111	234
Freed Advertising	7311	382
Freed Maxick Battaglia PC	8721	379
Freed Maxick Group	8721	37
Freedman Gibson and White Inc	7311	314
Freedman Seating Co	2531	25
Freedman's Bakery Inc	5149	24
Freedom Bank of Virginia	6022	500
Freedom Communications Inc	2711	33
Freedom Credit Union	6062	27
Freedom Electrical Company Inc	1731	1904
Freedom Ford Lincoln-Mercury Inc	5511	1012
Freedom Group Inc	3484	2
Freedom Health Inc	6371	10
Freedom Industries Inc (Tullahoma Tennessee)	2679	79
Freedom Lincoln Mercury	5511	401
Freedom Manufacturing Inc	3451	117
Freedom Marketing Corp	8742	473
Freedom Medical Inc	5047	114
Freedom Metals Inc	5093	89
Freedom Newspapers Of NM	2711	106
Freedom Oil	5541	32
Freedom Power Systems Inc	3629	60
Freedom Systems Corp	7372	4420
Freedom Technologies LLC	3661	174
Freedom Underground LLC	1623	808
Freedom USA Inc	3571	162
Freedom Wire Inc	3714	425
FreedomWare Software Products Inc	7372	2005
Freed's Bakery LLC	2051	150
Free-Flow Packaging International Inc	3086	10
Freehand Graphics Inc	7372	3267
Freehand Systems Inc	5045	53
Freeland Industries Inc	3523	258
Freeland Products Inc	7622	10
Freelin-Wade Co	3052	16
Freelite Inc	5063	748
Freeman Brothers Lumber Inc	2421	30
Freeman Contracting Inc	1611	241
Freeman Corp	2435	11
Freeman Cos	7389	17
Freeman Decorating Co	7389	32
Freeman Gas and Electric Company Inc	4925	5
Freeman Honda	5511	739
Freeman Manufacturing and Supply Co	5084	280
Freeman Metal Products Inc	3995	7
Freeman Pontiac Buick GMC	5511	361
Freeman Software	7379	1493
Freeman Spogli and Co	6159	30
Freeman White Inc	8712	63
Freemark Abbey Winery LP	2084	114
Freeport Center Associates	6531	206
Freeport Press Inc	2759	82
Freeport Roller Mills Inc	2048	101
Freeport Screen and Stamping Inc	3469	350
Freeport Technologies	4899	128
Freeport Transport Industries	4213	436
Freeport Welding And Fabricating Inc	3443	79
Freeport-McMoRan Copper and Gold Inc	1021	1
Freeport-McMoRan Sulphur Co	1479	2
FreeRun Technologies Inc	7375	215
Freescale Semiconductor Inc	3674	10
Freese and Nichols Inc	8711	162
Freestate Bookbinders Inc	2789	114
FreeTripcom Inc	7371	1632
Freewave Technologies Inc	3663	122
Freeway Ford Truck Sales Inc	5511	942
Freeway Motors Inc	5511	695
Freeze Frame Video Surveillance	1731	2526
Freezecom LLC	7379	327
Freiborne Industries Inc	2819	112
Freiday Construction Inc	1623	428
Freight All Kinds Inc	4213	2388
Freight Bay LLC	4813	601
Freight Expeditors Inc	4213	2859
Freight Lime and Sand Hauling	4213	3135
Freight Management LLC	4213	1558
Freight Systems Inc	4213	1616
FreightCar America Inc	3743	12
FreightDesk Technologies LLC	7389	801
Freightliner LLC	3711	11
Freightliner Of Hartford Inc	5511	1093
Freightliner Of San Antonio Ltd	5511	1163
Freightmaster Inc	4213	2403
Freightmasters Inc	4213	317
FreightMatrix North America Inc	7389	607
Freightquotecom Inc	7389	98

Company Name	SIC	Rank
Freirich Foods Inc	2011	80
Freitec Services	7349	371
Freixenet Sonoma Caves Inc	2084	65
Frelab Plastic Products Inc	5162	69
Fremantle Media North America Inc	7812	24
Fremar Industries Inc	3544	497
Fremarc Industries Inc	2519	7
Fremont Bancorp	6712	403
Fremont Bank	6022	152
Fremont Beef Co	2011	74
Fremont Co	2033	36
Fremont Contract Carriers Inc	4213	326
Fremont Flask Co	3559	470
Fremont Grain Inspection Department Inc	7389	617
Fremont Hotels Inc	7011	237
Fremont Industries Inc	2819	72
Fremont Plastic Products Inc	3089	312
French/Blitzer/Scott LLC	7311	928
French Corp	3643	116
French Market Foods Of Louisiana LLC	5421	1
French Oil Mill Machinery Co	3559	161
French Packaging Services Inc	2449	13
French Paper Co	2621	52
French Quarry Inc	5032	44
French Reflection Inc	3827	110
French Toast	5137	8
French Transit Ltd	5122	98
French Trucking Inc	4213	1953
Frenchman Valley Farmer's Cooperative Inc	5191	32
Frentzel Products Inc	3599	1384
Frenzelit Sealing Systems Inc	3053	4
Frequency Devices Inc	3825	273
Frequency Electronics Inc	3825	35
Frequency Selective Networks Inc	3677	105
Frequent Flyer Services	8742	682
Freres Lumber Company Inc	2436	13
Frerichs Freight Lines Inc	4213	2908
Fresca Mexican Foods LLC	2096	24
Fresch Electric Inc	1731	1989
Fres-Co Systems USA Inc	5084	255
Fresenius Medical Care North America	3845	2
Fresh Beginnings Inc	5199	31
Fresh Choice Inc	5812	290
Fresh Del Monte Produce Inc	0161	1
Fresh Enterprises Inc	5812	242
Fresh Express Inc	2099	17
Fresh International Corp	2099	14
Fresh Mark Corp	2879	50
Fresh Mark Inc	2013	11
Fresh Market Inc	5499	6
Fresh Meal Solutions Inc	2099	179
Fresh Music Library	7819	95
Fresh Point Inc	5148	14
Fresh Products Inc	2842	94
Fresh Squeezed Water Inc	3589	262
Fresh Start Bakeries Inc	2051	8
Freshco Ltd	2033	22
Fresher Then Fresh Inc	5146	60
Fresh-Pak Corp	3081	111
Freshpoint	4213	1672
FreshPoint Inc	5148	3
FreshPoint Southern California	5148	26
Freshway Foods Inc	5148	12
Fresno Distributing Co	5074	32
Fresno French Bread Bakery Inc	2051	235
Fresno Valves and Castings Inc	3494	9
Fretz Corp	5064	51
Freud America Inc	5072	73
Freudenberg Household Products LP	2392	24
Freudenberg-Nok GP	5085	1
Freund Baking Co	2051	48
Freund Container	5085	255
Frew Mill Die Crafts Inc	3544	828
Frey and Weiss Precision Machining Inc	3599	1275
Frey Media Inc	2741	367
Freyberg Hinkle Ashland Powers and Stowell SC	8721	195
Freyer Collaborative Architects	8712	257
Freymiller Inc	4213	958
Freysinger Pontiac Inc	5511	805
Fri Resins Corp	2891	98
Frick Transfer Inc	4213	3001
Fricke-Parks Press Inc	2752	514
Frick's Meat Products Inc	2013	93
Fried Frank Harris Shriver and Jacobson LLP	8111	48
Frieda's Inc	5148	47
Friedkin Companies Inc	5012	8
Friedlander M and R Supply Company Inc	5072	174
Friedman and Associates (Reisterstown Maryland)	7322	203
Friedman Corp	7372	1669
Friedman Fleischer and Lowe LLC	6799	39
Friedman Industries Inc	3312	59
Friedman LLP	8721	270
Friedrichs and Rath Inc	3089	776
Friend Tire Co	5014	11
Friendfinder Networks Inc	7372	716
Friendly Buick and Honda	5511	1098

Company Name	SIC	Rank
Friendly Consultants Inc	7379	1103
Friendly Ford	5511	127
Friendly Ford Inc (Springfield Missouri)	5511	544
Friendly Home Inc	8051	66
Friendly Ice Cream Corp	5812	91
Friendly Software Corp	7373	369
Friends And Family Inc	8361	175
Friends Enterprises	5541	44
Friends Lumber Inc	5211	281
Friends Retirement Concepts Inc	8361	31
Friendship Creative Printers Inc	2752	1226
Friendship Industries Inc	8331	170
Friendship Trap Company Inc	3496	94
Friendster Inc	7379	1082
Friesen's Inc	3531	118
Friess Associates	6282	271
Frigid Coil/Frick Inc	3585	83
Frigid Fluid Co	2869	117
Frigoscandia Inc	3533	19
Frimo Inc	3544	74
Fringe Benefits Management Co	8741	25
Frischhertz Electric Company Inc	1731	168
Frisch's Ohio Inc	5812	190
Frisch's Restaurants Inc	5812	130
Frisco Baking Company Inc	2051	108
Friskney Equipment Inc	5084	579
Frit Car Inc	4789	25
Frit Industries Inc	2875	8
Fritts Ford	5511	1141
Fritz Company Inc	5145	4
Fritz Industries Inc	2899	47
Fritz Ken Tooling and Design Inc	2679	74
FRIX Group	7311	661
Frizzelle and Parsons Die Sinking Co	3544	485
Frk/Jmk Investments Inc	2759	523
Frock Brothers Trucking Inc	4213	1175
Froedge Machine And Supply Company Inc	3553	29
Froehling and Robertson Inc	8734	21
frog design inc	7336	18
Frog Switch And Manufacturing Co	3325	23
Froley Revy Investment Company Inc	6282	551
From The Top Inc	8299	72
Fromm Family Foods LLC	2048	47
Front End Services	3663	245
Front Porch Digital Inc	7379	289
Front Range Custodial And Maintenance Inc	7349	457
Front Range Lumber Co	5031	345
Front Range Precast Concrete	3531	114
Front Range Tooling Inc	3544	675
Front Range Wireless Inc	1731	331
Front Row Systems	7372	3997
Front Royal Inc	6211	81
Frontenac Co	6799	46
Frontera Telecommunications Inc	4813	474
Frontier Adjusters of America Inc	6399	27
Frontier Airlines Holdings Inc	4512	23
Frontier Communications Corp	4813	11
Frontier Communications of Mondovi Inc	4813	687
Frontier Communications of the South Inc	4813	45
Frontier Communications of Viroqua Inc	4813	571
Frontier Cooperative Co	5153	25
Frontier Corp	4813	14
Frontier El Dorado Refining Co	1311	75
Frontier Electronic Systems Corp	3812	74
Frontier Electronics Corp	3677	98
Frontier Enterprises Inc	4724	9
Frontier Fabricating LLC	3532	67
Frontier Ford	5511	632
Frontier Ford Lincoln-Mercury Inc	5511	1150
Frontier FS Coop	5191	65
Frontier FS Coop	5191	60
Frontier Homes Inc	5271	6
Frontier Leasing Corp	7359	209
Frontier Natural Products Co-Op	5122	29
Frontier Pavement Specialists Inc	5032	106
Frontier Power Co	4911	408
Frontier Radio Inc	5064	173
Frontier Refining and Marketing Inc	2911	28
Frontier Technologies Corp	7372	3610
Frontier Transport Corp	4213	580
Frontier Transportation Inc	4213	1450
Frontier Travel and Tours Inc	4725	18
Frontier Vision Technologies Inc	7378	79
Frontier-Kemper Constructors Inc	1629	118
Frontline Communications	7371	938
Frontline Consulting Services Inc	7379	296
Frontline Data Inc	7389	1900
Frontline Data Solutions Inc	7371	1410
Frontline Manufacturing Inc	3088	6
Frontline Medical Associates Inc	7363	346
Frontline Mold Technology	3089	1605
Frontline Printing and Design Inc	2752	1786
Frontline Systems Inc	7372	3711
Frontline Test Equipment Inc	7372	2847
FrontRange Solutions Inc	7372	352
Frontrunner Network Systems Inc	3661	63
Frosch International Travel Inc	4724	47
Frost and Sullivan Inc	8742	168

Company Name	SIC	Rank
Frost Brown Todd LLC	8111	117
Frost Capital Group	6153	39
Frost Electric Company Inc	1731	1753
Frost Electric Supply Co	5063	63
Frost Engineering Inc	3556	151
Frost Inc	3536	22
Frost Insurance Agency	6311	188
Frost Magnetics Inc	3677	52
Frost Motors Inc	5331	15
Frost National Bank	6021	29
Frost PLLC	8721	296
Frothingham Electronics Corp	3825	325
Frozen Food Express Industries Inc	4213	77
Frozen Food Service Corp	5147	107
FrozencpuCom Inc	5734	90
Frpc Liquidating Inc	3086	26
FRS	7372	438
Fruhauf Uniforms Inc	2311	18
Fruit Dynamics LLC	2033	65
Fruit Growers Laboratory Inc	8734	95
Fruit Growers Supply Co	5191	29
Fruit Of The Earth Inc	5122	36
Fruit of the Loom Inc	2254	1
Fruitcrown Products Corp	2087	39
Fruitridge Printing and Lithograph Inc	2752	858
Fruitt Trucking	4213	1860
Frullati Cafe and Bakery Inc	5149	42
Frutarom Inc	2087	20
Fruth Pharmacy Inc	5912	34
Fry Equipment Company Inc	5083	94
Fry Foods Inc	2038	58
Frye Electronics Inc	3829	217
Frye Printing Company Inc	2752	1474
Frye-Williamson Press Inc	2759	336
Frymaster Corp	3569	304
Frymire Co	1542	381
Fry's Electronics Inc	5731	4
Fry-Wagner Moving and Storage	4213	1484
Fs Alarms Inc	1731	2549
FS Gateway Inc	5153	127
FS Repair Inc	7699	238
FS S Inc	2099	148
FS Van Hoose and Company Inc	5031	207
FS View and Florida Flambeau Newspaper	2711	810
FSA Association	8743	248
FSC Inc	3645	48
FSH Communications LLC	4813	71
Fsh Utility Services Inc	1623	777
FSI Automation Inc	7372	4301
FSI/Fork Standards Inc	3674	345
FSI International Inc	3559	39
FSI International Inc Microlithography Div	3559	488
FSI International Inc Surface Conditioning Div	3559	31
Fsi Label Co	2759	483
Fsr Construction Inc	7389	1948
FSR Inc	5012	127
FSR Inc	3663	114
Fssco Inc	5023	85
FSTW Inc	7372	3437
Fsu Computer Store	7378	136
Fsv Payment Systems Inc	7374	403
FT Group Inc	3555	109
FT Precision Inc	3714	131
FT Reynolds Company Inc	5411	237
FT Silfies Inc	4213	241
FTA Computer Consultants Inc	7373	1104
Ftc - Forward Threat Control	3669	288
FTD Group Inc	5992	4
FTDcom Inc	7389	200
Ften Inc	5045	131
Ftf Technologies Inc	7379	1619
Ftg Circuits Inc	3672	146
FTG Construction Materials Inc	5032	67
FTI/Bill Thompson Transport Inc	4213	498
FTI Consulting Inc	8742	18
Fti Inc	7379	1019
FTL Design Engineering Studio	8712	258
FTrans Corp	8748	387
Fts Inc	7389	1478
Fts Systems Inc	3821	23
Ftt Manufacturing Inc	3312	99
Fuchs Business Solutions Inc	5044	100
Fuchs Corp	2992	5
Fuchs Inc	4213	1471
Fuchs Machinery Inc	5084	235
Fuchs North America Inc	2099	55
Fuddruckers Inc	5812	239
Fuego World Wide Inc	7336	322
Fuel Data Systems Inc	7372	4502
Fuel Injection Sales And Service Inc	5013	317
Fuel Systems Solutions Inc	3714	70
Fuel Tech Inc	3564	19
FuelCell Energy Inc	3694	11
Fuellgraf Electric Co	1731	684
Fuelstream Inc	7389	2516
Fugent Inc	7371	488
Fugleberg Koch Architects Inc	8712	224
Fugle-Miller Laboratories Inc	3679	701
Fugro Geoconsulting Inc	5084	505
Fugro Geoservices Inc	8711	367
Fugro USA Inc	8711	174

Company Name	SIC	Rank
Fugro-Jason Inc	5045	785
Fuji American Advanced Sports Inc	5091	38
Fuji Component Parts USA Inc	5013	261
Fuji Foods US Inc	2011	77
Fuji Hi-Tech Inc	3577	196
Fuji Industries Corp	6799	293
Fuji Novel Batteries Inc	5065	428
Fuji Photo Film USA Inc	3695	2
Fuji Vegetable Oil Inc	2076	2
Fujifilm Diosynth Biotechnologies	2869	113
Fujifilm Hunt Chemicals USA Inc	3861	30
Fujifilm Medical Systems USA Inc	5047	76
Fujifilm Recording Media Manufacturing USA Inc	3577	187
Fujinon Inc	3843	10
Fujipoly America Corp	3678	36
Fujirebio Diagnostics Inc	2836	23
Fujitsu America Inc	7371	110
Fujitsu Computer Products of America Inc	5045	61
Fujitsu Frontech North America Inc	7373	83
Fujitsu Microelectronics Inc	3674	79
Fujitsu Network Communications Inc	3661	31
Fujitsu Semiconductor America Inc	8711	373
Fujitsu Systems Business of America Inc	7379	193
Fukken Wax	2842	90
Fukuvi USA Inc	3089	983
Fulbright and Jaworski LLP	8111	37
Fulcher S Point Pride Seafood Inc	2092	73
Fulcrum Analytics	7374	191
Fulcrum Design	3577	649
Fulcrum Incorporated Of Minneapolis	3085	35
Fulfillment America Inc	7319	98
Fulfillment Partners Inc	7331	172
Fulghum Industries Inc	3531	120
Full Circle Productions LLC	7311	820
Full Circle Studios LLC	7389	857
Full Court Press Inc (Indianapolis Indiana)	2752	1787
Full House Resorts Inc	7999	84
Full Information Software Inc	7372	3998
Full Power Enterprises Inc	5065	659
Full Range Security Protection Inc	1731	1845
Full Service Computing Corp	4813	300
Full Service Mailers Inc	7331	270
Full Vision Inc	3599	343
Full Web Inc	4899	132
FullArmor Corp	7372	2824
Fullbloom Baking Company Inc	2051	25
Fullenkamp Machine and Manufacturing Inc	3599	1922
Fuller Box Company Inc	2675	6
Fuller Brush Co	3991	3
Fuller Building Supply Company Inc	5211	207
Fuller Communications Ltd	7389	1327
Fuller Contracting Company LLC	1623	480
Fuller Dyal and Stamper Inc	7336	92
Fuller Engineering Company LLC	5065	473
Fuller Enterprises Inc	3625	418
Fuller Ford Inc	5511	213
Fuller Manufacturing Inc	3699	269
Fuller Marketing Inc	2541	33
Fullerton Mortgage and Escrow Co	6162	51
Fullerton Tool Company Inc	3545	53
Fullford Electric Inc	1731	287
FullNet Communications Inc	7374	302
FullNet Inc	7374	194
FULLnet Inc (Jasper Indiana)	4813	339
Fullone Trucking Inc	4213	2896
Fullstream DVD	7389	2391
FullTel Inc	4899	204
Fulmer Company LLC	3621	77
Fulmont Mutual Insurance Co	6331	367
Fulton Bank	6022	51
Fulton Bank NA	6021	19
Fulton Boiler Works Inc	3443	160
Fulton Breakefield Broenniman LLC	6282	520
Fulton Communications Inc	1731	1222
Fulton County Rehabilitation	8361	191
Fulton County Rural Electric Corp	4911	483
Fulton Financial Corp	6712	50
Fulton Homes Inc	1531	75
Fulton Industries Inc	3469	123
Fulton Lumber and Home Center Inc	5211	220
Fulton Packaging Inc	5021	139
Fulton Press Inc	2752	1147
Fulton Processors Inc	2015	47
Fulton Sun Gazette	2711	865
Fulton Tool Company Inc	3599	1813
Fulton-Marshall Coop	5153	79
Fultz and Associates Inc	7311	667
Fun Express Inc	5099	69
Fun Land Theatre and Swap Shop Inc	7389	2075
Fun Spot Trampolines	3949	168
Funai Corporation Inc	5064	2
Funambol Inc	7373	804
Function Junction Inc	5719	25
Functional Devices Inc	3625	102
Functional Industries Inc	8331	183
Functional Products Inc	2992	58
Fund Evaluation Group LLC	6282	123
FUND E-Z Development Corp	7372	3712
Fundamental Objects Inc	7372	4820

Company Name	SIC	Rank
Fundamental Software Inc	7372	2144
FundBalance	7372	2771
Fundcom Inc	8742	709
Fundcraft Publishing Inc	2732	35
Funder America Inc	2431	18
Fundis Co	4213	1702
FundQuest Inc	6282	378
FundsXpress Financial Network	6021	197
Funeral Directors Life Insurance Co	6311	208
Funk Luetke Skunda Marketing Inc	8743	124
Funk Manufacturing Co	3568	16
Funk Software Inc	7372	2881
Fun-Plex Inc	7996	33
Funrise Inc	5092	32
Funsource Partners	3069	205
Funtastic Factory Inc	3599	1021
Funtastic Shows Inc	3599	92
Fuqua Homes Inc	2451	22
Fuqua Ventures LLC	6282	644
Fur Breeders Agricultural Coop	2048	81
Furbay Electric Supply Co	5063	307
Furbush Roberts Printing Company Inc	2752	1790
Furman Foods Inc	2033	42
Furmanite America Inc	3599	131
Furmanite Corp	1799	9
Furmanite Worldwide Inc	5084	7
FURminator Inc	0752	1
Furnace Builders Inc	3567	84
Furnace Parts LLC	3823	218
Furnace Technologies Inc	3567	49
Furnari Furniture Corp	2512	84
Furnas County Farms	0213	19
Furness Trucking Inc	4213	1420
FurnishNet Inc	7389	482
Furniture Brands International Inc	2511	3
Furniture Consultants Inc	5021	11
Furniture Values International LLC	2511	35
FurnitureFIND Corp	5712	79
Furnlite Inc	3648	35
Furr's Restaurant Group Inc	5812	178
Furry Inc	3599	2288
Furst-Mcness Co	2048	10
Furukawa Information Technology Inc	7372	3415
Fuse Design Inc	2741	120
Fuse Science Inc	6799	368
FUSE3	2721	69
Fusebox Inc	7336	189
FuseboxWest	7311	929
Fused Kontacts Of Missouri Inc	3851	92
Fushan Enterprises	3577	456
Fusibond Piping Systems Inc	3084	49
Fusion Babbitting Company Inc	3568	83
Fusion Ceramics Inc	2899	193
Fusion Design	7373	1137
Fusion Electric LLC	1731	1773
Fusion Holdings LLC	5944	28
Fusion Imaging Inc	2759	159
Fusion Learning Systems Inc	7379	679
Fusion Media Inc	7336	292
Fusion Public Relations Inc	8743	173
Fusion Solutions	7361	26
Fusion Systems Inc	3599	927
Fusion Uv Systems Inc	3699	67
Fusionary Media	7319	96
Fusion-Io Inc	3572	30
fusionOne Inc	7372	1005
Fusionsoft LLC	7371	1139
Fusite	3679	89
Fuson Buick Cadillac and GMC Inc	5511	951
Futaba Corporation of America	3674	205
Futek Advanced Sensor Technology Inc	3823	93
Futron Corp	7379	307
Futronics Inc	5065	886
Futura Builders Group Inc	1522	56
Futura Circuits Corp	3672	220
Futura Corp (Boise Idaho)	3341	37
Futura Design Service Inc	8711	609
Futuramic Tool and Engineering Company Inc	3544	42
Future Advance Satellite Technology Inc	7379	1138
Future Brite	3679	858
Future Cellular Communications	5999	264
Future Computer Technologies Inc	5045	620
Future Controls Corp	3823	274
Future Cure Inc	3559	312
Future Designs Inc	7373	1051
Future Disc Systems Inc	3695	162
Future Dynamics Inc	5091	106
Future Estates Inc	6552	282
Future Foods	2099	209
Future Ford Inc	5511	179
Future Home Co	1731	1914
Future Home Technology Inc	2452	28
Future Information Design	5045	1016
Future Information Technology Inc	7373	292
Future Innovations Inc	7389	1655
Future Manufacturing Inc	3677	100
Future Metals Inc	5051	43
Future Mold Corp	3544	227
Future Network USA	2731	226
Future Now Group Inc	7389	1954
Future Pak Ltd	7389	1350

Company Name	SIC	Rank
Future Presence Inc	7361	86
Future Products Inc	3524	22
Future Reproductions Inc	2752	1451
Future Research Corp	8711	244
Future Solutions Inc	7373	784
Future Systems Solutions Inc	7372	1142
Future Tech Enterprise Inc	7373	149
Future Tech Procurement Solutions Inc	3577	628
Future Tech Systems Inc	7372	3668
Future Tek Inc	3674	459
Future Telecom Inc	1623	122
Future Unlimited Inc	7361	336
Future Us Inc	2721	105
FutureAds LLC	7311	130
Future-All Inc	3531	202
FutureBrand Company Inc	8742	530
Futurecom Inc	3625	363
Futuredontics Inc	8742	255
Futurefab Inc	3674	451
Futurelink Consulting Inc	7363	368
Futuremark Corp (Saratoga California)	7372	537
Futurenet Technologies Corp	7371	628
Futures Rehabilitation Center Inc	8331	220
Futures Unlimited Inc	8331	143
FutureSoft Engineering Inc	7372	1850
FutureSoft Inc	7372	540
Futuretech Consultants LLC	7379	631
FutureTrade Technologies	7372	1345
FutureWare Inc	7372	3905
Futurewei Technologies Inc	4813	154
Futureworld Technologies Inc	7379	1160
Futurex	7389	651
Futuristic Computers	5734	455
Fuzzy Systems Engineering and Actland Inc	7372	4821
FV Casno Electrical Contractor Inc	1731	1846
FV Martin Trucking Co	4213	484
FVNB Corp	6712	132
FW and T A Corp	3829	500
FW Davison and Company Inc	7372	2282
FW Kauphusman Inc	5063	761
FW Media Inc	2731	72
FW Webb Co	5074	5
FWA Group	8712	115
FWCC Inc	4213	795
Fwd Seagrave Holdings LP	3711	46
FX Alliance LLC	7389	330
Fx Digital Media Inc	2752	849
FX Energy Inc	1311	160
Fx Solutions Inc	6099	16
FXCM Inc	6221	5
Fxi Holdings Inc	3086	8
Fyda Freightliner Columbus Inc	5012	40
Fyda Freightliner Youngstown Inc	5012	104
Fydaq Company Inc	1623	325
Fyx Inc	7371	1068
FzioMed Inc	3842	128
G 3 Technology Group LLC	7336	284
G A Fleet Associates Inc	5084	559
G A W Inc	5084	390
G A Wright Marketing Inc	7331	95
G Amber Corp	7331	212
G and A StaffSourcing Inc	7361	63
G and B Electrical Co	1731	1390
G and B Liquidating Corp	3812	133
G and B Oil Company Inc	5171	50
G and B Specialties Inc	3599	162
G and C Building Maintenance Services Inc	7349	428
G and C Direct Mail Marketing Inc	7331	124
G and C Equipment Corp	7353	11
G and C Packing Co	2011	150
G and C Supply Company Inc	5074	71
G and D LLC	3315	21
G and D Transportation Inc	4213	425
G and E Delivery	7389	1371
G and E Machine Works Inc	3599	1606
G and E Systems Inc	7372	1641
G and F Industries Inc	3089	110
G and F Roof Supply Inc	5033	49
G and F Systems Inc	5084	679
G and F Tool Products	3544	589
G and F Trucking Leasing Inc	4213	2442
G and G Electric Inc	1731	2004
G and G Electric Service Company Inc	1731	726
G and G Electric Supply Company Inc	5063	183
G and G Grinding and Machine Inc	3599	1079
G and G Industrial Corp	3599	1198
G and G Instrument Corp	7371	1827
G and G Machine and Maintenance Inc	3599	1298
G and G Machine Technologies LLC	3599	1325
G and G Manufacturing Co	3599	561
G and G Manufacturing Co	3545	65
G and G Oil Company Of Indiana Inc	5541	53
G and G Organization Ltd	7363	139
G and G Products LLC	3599	2009
G and G Supermarket Inc	5411	136
G and G Technologies Inc	5065	965
G and H Computer Company Inc	5734	402
G and H Decoy Inc	3949	133
G And H Forty-Niners Inc	5144	28
G and H Industries Inc	3678	66
G and H Mail Service LLC	7331	260
G and H Motor Freight Lines Inc	4213	1808

Company Name	SIC	Rank
G and H Service Corp	5087	99
G and H Technology Inc	3643	49
G and H Telephone Answering Service Inc	7389	1194
G and J Import and Export Inc	5051	504
G and J Machine Shop Inc	3599	969
G and J Pepsi-Cola Bottlers Inc	2086	29
G and J Steel and Tubing	3498	72
G and K Services Inc	7218	2
G and L Precision Die Cutting	3599	31
G and L Realty Corp	6799	176
G and L Trucking Inc	4213	2128
G and M Company Inc	3469	313
G and M Die Casting Company Inc	3363	40
G and M Electric Sales Company Inc	5063	905
G and M Electrical Contractors Inc	1731	97
G and M Oil Company Inc	5171	39
G and N Aircraft Inc	5088	90
G and P Trucking Company Inc	4213	306
G and R Felpausch Co	5411	147
G and R Mineral Services Inc	7349	39
G and R Publishing Co	2731	227
G and R Trucking Company Inc	4213	2117
G and RG Inc	4213	1865
G and S Electric	1623	438
G and S Electrical Company LLC	1731	1905
G and S Foundry and Manufacturing Co	3363	39
G and S Packing Company Inc	5148	78
G and S Super Abrasives Inc	3291	32
G and T Air Expediting Service Inc	4213	2789
G and T Conveyor Company Inc	3535	8
G and T Electric Inc	1731	1847
G and T Industries Inc	3086	17
G and W Construction Company Inc	1623	258
G and W Enterprises Inc	2851	56
G and W Instruments Inc	3823	408
G and W Laboratories Inc	2834	169
G and W Piedmont Forklift Inc	5084	346
G and Z Industries Inc	3469	237
G and Z Systems Inc	7372	4503
G B Manufacturing Co	3444	209
G Bishop and Co	1731	1877
G Cole Davis and Associates	8743	295
G E M Litho-Print Inc	2752	1481
G F Cole Corp	3053	121
G Gasket and Supply Inc	3053	88
G H Leidenheimer Baking Company Ltd	2051	165
G H Meiser and Co	3824	39
G H Tool and Mold Inc	3544	85
G Hartzell and Son Inc	3843	68
G Helmer Construction Company Inc	1623	661
G I A Publications Inc	2741	282
G J Nikolas and Company Inc	2851	145
G J Olney Inc	3556	158
G Joannou Cycle Company Inc	5091	23
G K Construction Inc	1459	5
G K L Corp	3088	14
G L Frederick	1731	429
G L Mattress Inc	5021	175
G L Mezzetta Inc	2035	21
G Neil Direct Mail Inc	5961	101
G Q F Manufacturing Company Inc	3523	164
G R Helm Inc	7363	241
G R Manufacturing Inc	3599	255
G S and D Inc	5031	321
G S F Plastics Corp	3533	136
G/S Leasing Inc	7377	10
G S Precision Inc	3728	55
G T Michelli Company Inc	5046	94
G W Becker Inc	5084	843
G Williams and Associates Inc	7311	656
G1440 Holdings Inc	7389	106
G2 Communications Inc	7379	1624
G-2 Graphic Service Inc	2759	141
G2 Inc	8742	484
G2k Corp	3443	196
G3 Enterprises	4213	693
g4 Inc	7372	4504
GA Creative	8743	125
GA Food Services Of Pinellas County Inc	2038	13
GA Heaton Co	5094	87
Ga Janitorial Cleaning Services Inc	7349	464
GA Kraut Company Inc	8743	224
GA Telesis LLC	5088	13
GA Wright Sales Inc	7389	376
Gab Construction Inc	1731	1261
GAB Robins Inc	8734	3
Gabel Systems Inc	7372	2311
Gabelli Equity Trust Inc	6726	20
Gabelli Growth Fund	6722	169
Gabler Trucking Inc	4213	690
Gables Engineering Inc	3679	139
Gabriel Container Co	2653	42
Gabriele Macaroni Company Inc	2098	28
Gabron and Gabron Inc	5063	160
Gac Chemical Inc	2819	86
Gaco Western LLC	2822	13
Gadabout Vacations	4725	38
Gaddie Shamrock Inc	1771	33
Gadsden Coffee Company Inc	3089	263
Gadsden Tool Inc	3544	363

Company Name	SIC	Rank
Gae Trading LLC	3679	723
Gaertner Scientific Corp	3827	138
GAF Materials Corp	3292	1
Gaffney and Associates Inc	7311	999
Gaffney Ledger Inc	2711	740
Gaffney-Kroese Supply Corp	5063	131
Gage Applied Inc	3674	245
Gage Assembly Co	3545	119
Gage Bilt Inc	3452	81
Gage Brothers Concrete Products Inc	3272	63
Gage Marketing Group	7319	57
Gage Pattern and Model Inc	3599	594
Gage Products Co	2842	27
Cage Rite Products Inc	3545	404
Gagemaker LP	3829	166
Gaggenau USA Corp	5064	16
Gaging Technologies Inc	3544	841
Gagne Associates Inc	3089	1526
Gahr Line and Cable LLC	1623	546
GAI Consultants	8711	99
Gaiam Inc	7812	27
Gaiennie Lumber Company LLC	5031	245
Gail and Rice Productions Inc	7812	91
Gail Pittman Inc	5199	60
GAIM Plastics Inc	3089	1783
Gain Capital Group LLC	6091	1
GAIN Capital Holdings Inc	6099	18
GAIN Communications Inc	5065	754
Gain Industries Inc	3599	2028
Gain Securities	6211	151
Gaines Kriner Elliott LLP	8721	403
Gaines Motor Lines Inc	4213	195
Gainesville Printing Co	2752	1211
Gainesville Truck Center Inc	5012	128
Gainey Vineyard	0172	10
Gainey's Concrete Products Inc	5211	248
GAINSCO Inc	6331	260
Gainsville Ice	2097	18
GAINSystems	7372	2574
Gaither Tool Co	3559	442
GAI-Tronics Corp	3669	68
Gaits Inc	7376	19
Gaka Trading Inc	5064	168
GAL Construction Company Inc	1622	27
GAL Gage Co	3545	393
Gala Homes Ltd	1731	2026
Galamba Metals Group/Kaw River Shredding Inc	4953	149
Galamet Inc	5093	58
Galassi Gary Stone and Steel Inc	1411	18
Galasso Trucking Inc	4213	914
Galasso Trucking Service Inc	4213	2094
Galatea Associates LLC	7371	1512
Galaxie Corp (Jackson Mississippi)	2911	35
Galaxy Audio Inc	3651	151
Galaxy Circuits Inc	3672	379
Galaxy Design and Printing Inc	2752	1827
Galaxy Desserts	2053	9
Galaxy Die And Engineering Inc	3366	16
Galaxy Electronics Co	3643	112
Galaxy Energy Corp	1311	255
Galaxy Hotel Systems LLC	7372	1473
Galaxy Industries Inc	5084	581
Galaxy Manufacturing Inc	3469	370
Galaxy Nutritional Foods Inc	2022	35
Galaxy Scientific Corp	8731	158
Galaxy Tire and Wheel Inc	3011	5
Galaxy Tool Corp	3544	107
GalaxyHardware Publishers Inc	5045	583
Galca Mexican Food Inc	2099	338
Galco International Ltd	3199	9
Galderma Laboratories Inc	2834	118
Gale and Vallance	8111	574
Gale Associates Inc	8712	88
Gale Banks Engineering	3519	13
Gale Delivery Inc	4213	2819
Gale General Co	5251	39
Galectin Therapeutics Inc	2834	477
Galen Associates	6799	249
Galen Capital Group LLC	6029	15
Galen Healthcare Solutions	8099	96
Galena State Bank and Trust Co	6022	483
Gales and Associates	8721	259
Galesburg Manufacturing Co	3589	80
Galfab Inc	3537	110
Galgon Industries Inc	3451	56
Gali Corp	3728	197
Galichia Medical Group PA	8011	78
Galil Motion Control Inc	3577	267
Galil Moving and Storage Inc	4213	2788
Galilean Seafood Inc	2091	16
Galileo International Inc	7374	14
Galiso Inc	3829	197
Gallagher and Burk Inc	1611	192
Gallagher and Kennedy PA	8111	303
Gallagher Asphalt Corp	1611	222
Gallagher Bassett Services Inc	6411	119
Gallagher Benefit Services Inc	6411	189
Gallagher Benefit Services of Colorado Inc	6411	153
Gallagher Benefit Services of Kansas City Inc	6411	149
Gallagher Benefit Services of Michigan Inc	6411	181

Company Name	SIC	Rank
Gallagher Benefit Services of New York Inc	6411	174
Gallagher Benefit Services of the Carolinas Inc	6411	207
Gallagher Benefit Services of Washington DC	6411	180
Gallagher Captive Services Inc	6411	183
Gallagher Corp	2821	87
Gallagher Drilling Inc	1311	194
Gallagher Enterprises LLC	6799	74
Gallagher International	4213	2920
Gallagher-Kaiser Corp	3444	67
Gallahers Inc	7331	246
Galland Henning Nopak Inc	3542	30
Galland Kharasch Greenberg Fellman and Swirsky PC	8111	519
Gallant Graphices Limited Inc	2752	1319
Gallant Greetings Corp	2771	15
Gallatin Mortgage Co	6163	41
Galleano Winery Inc	2084	131
Gallegos Electric Inc	1731	1866
Galler Associates Inc	7373	826
Gallery Furniture Inc	5712	13
Gallery Graphics Inc	2499	51
Gallery of History Auctions Inc	7389	1132
Gallery of History Direct	5961	185
Gallery of History Inc	8999	220
Gallery Systems Inc	7372	3535
GalleryWatchcom Inc	7374	113
Galley Printing Company Inc	2752	1326
Galli Associates Inc	8743	203
Gallien Technology Inc	3651	108
Gallier and Wittenberg Inc	8743	243
Galliker Dairy Co	2026	53
Gallium Visual Systems	7372	1676
Gallo Displays Inc	3993	32
Gallo Salame	2013	24
Gallop Johnson and Neuman LC	8111	194
Gallopade International Inc	5192	39
Galloway-Chandler McKinney Insurance Agency Inc	6331	277
Gallup Inc	8732	70
Gallup Independent Co	2711	462
Gallus Inc	5084	198
Galpin Motors Inc	5511	27
Galt Alloys Inc	3341	15
Galto Trucking Inc	4213	2760
Galvan Industries Inc	3479	32
Galvanic Applied Sciences USA Inc	3827	111
Galvanic Printing and Plate Company Inc	2752	1288
Galveston Newspapers Inc	2711	37
Galvin Flying Service Inc	4581	23
Galvin Precision Machining Inc	3599	2180
Galvmet Inc	5051	345
Galvotec Alloys Inc	3365	5
Galy USA Inc	5046	221
GAM Electronics Inc	3679	881
GAM Information Systems Inc	7379	1354
Gama Aviation Inc	4522	5
Gamaliel Shooting Supply Inc	5091	70
Gamalski Building Specialties Inc	5072	184
Gamasutra CMP Media LLC	7379	1199
Gamay Foods Inc	5169	142
Gambit Communications	2721	304
Gambit Communications Inc	7371	1360
Gamble Electric Inc	1731	1104
Gamble Parts-Dart Inc	4213	2860
Gambrinus Co	5181	73
Gamco Investors Inc	6282	117
Gamco Products Co	3369	7
Game and Fish Publication Inc	2721	259
Game Country Inc	3949	175
Game Equipment LLC	3523	79
Game Source Inc	5092	39
Gameco Inc	3944	48
GameHouse	7372	1934
GameloftCom Inc	5092	34
Gamepal Inc	3944	36
GamePlan Financial Marketing LLC	6411	227
Gamer Packaging Inc	5085	304
Gamers Factory Inc	5092	13
Gamestop	5734	7
GameStop Corp	5734	1
Gamet Manufacturing Co	3523	280
GameTech International Inc	7999	81
Gametech Marketing Inc	5064	106
Gamfg Precision LLC	3714	222
Gaming Partners International Corp	3944	15
Gamma Construction Co	1541	121
Gamma Construction Company Inc	1542	128
Gamma High Voltage Research Inc	3699	240
Gamma Photo Labs	7384	3
Gamma Products Inc	3829	418
Gamma Scientific LLC	3829	147
Gamma Software Inc	7372	4505
Gamma Tech Computer Corp	3571	41
Gamma2 Inc	3089	947
Gammaflux LP	3823	177
Gammalux Systems Inc	3648	46
Gammerler US Corp	3535	29
Gammex RMI	3845	86
Gammill Quilting Machine Co	3639	27
Gammon Technical Products Inc	3823	124

Company Name	SIC	Rank
Gamry Instruments Inc	3829	281
GAMS Development Corp	7372	3713
Gamut Communications	5065	413
Ganahl Lumber Co	5211	28
Gancedo Lumber Company Inc	5031	247
Gand Music and Sound Inc	5736	16
Gander Mountain Co	5699	2
Gandy Co	3523	227
Gandy Printers Inc	2752	1646
Ganflec Architects and Engineers Inc	8712	11
Gangloff Industries Inc	4213	1904
Ganister Fasteners	5085	202
Ganley Chevrolet Inc	5511	845
Gann Car Crushing Inc	5093	146
Gannett Company Inc	2711	6
Gannett Company Inc Newspaper Div	2711	661
Gannett Fleming Inc	8711	21
Gannett Offset Marketing Services Group	2752	26
Gannett Welsh and Kotler Inc	6282	382
Gans Ink And Supply Company Inc	2893	16
Gantech Inc	7379	384
Ganucheau Capital Management	6282	590
Ganzcorp Investments Inc	3559	166
Gap Inc	5651	2
Gap Instrument Corp	7373	1226
G-A-P Supply Corp	5075	43
GapKids	5641	6
Gapvax Inc	3537	51
Gar Enterprises	5045	402
GAR International Corp	5082	150
Garabedian Brothers Inc	3599	1123
Garage Door Group Inc	3442	32
Garan Inc	2361	3
Garawco Inc	1711	283
Garber and Goodman Advertising Inc	7311	714
Garber Buick Co	5511	932
Garber Ice Cream Co	2024	67
Garber Management Group Inc	5511	929
Garber Scale Co	5046	187
Garber Travel Service Inc	4724	22
Garbo Motor Sales Inc	5511	1151
Garb-Oil and Power Corp	3559	559
Garcia And Sons Auto and Used Parts	5015	30
Garcia Hamilton and Associates	6282	600
Garcia Packaging Inc	7389	2445
Gar-Con Inc	1623	655
Gard Communications	7311	334
Gardan Inc	7389	1740
Gardei Industries LLC	2679	35
Garden City Co-Op Inc	5153	56
Garden City Group Inc	7389	140
Garden City Medical	3842	8
Garden City Western Railway Co	4011	30
Garden Confederate Point LP	6531	400
Garden Fresh Restaurant Corp	5812	154
Garden Fresh Salad Company Inc	5148	37
Garden Manor Extended Care Center Inc	8051	59
Garden of Life Inc	2834	76
Garden Properties Corp	6531	141
Garden Ridge	5023	187
Garden State Fireworks Inc	2899	226
Garden Street Iron and Metal Incorporated Of SW Florida	5093	80
Garden Valley Coop	5191	186
Garden Valley Retirement Village Inc	8361	146
Garden Valley Telephone Co	4813	197
Gardena Valley News Inc	2711	541
Gardenburger Inc	2038	26
Garden-Fresh Foods Inc	5148	56
Gardenia Software Systems Inc	7372	2676
Gardere Wynne Sewell LLP	8111	160
Gardes Energy Services Inc	1381	49
Gardner and Meredith Inc	5085	239
Gardner Asphalt Inc	3531	9
Gardner Auction Service Inc	7389	2076
Gardner Baking Company Inc	5461	25
Gardner Bender Inc	3629	8
Gardner Carton and Douglas	8111	71
Gardner Chevrolet Inc	7538	26
Gardner Cryogenics	3559	104
Gardner Denver Inc	3563	1
Gardner Denver Water Jetting Systems Inc	3589	111
Gardner Glass Products Inc	3231	29
Gardner Inc	5083	40
Gardner Machinery Corp	3535	223
Gardner Manufacturing Co	3444	98
Gardner News Inc	2711	622
Gardner Partnership Architects	8712	329
Gardner Products Co	3599	1925
Gardner Rich and Co	6211	313
Gardner Trucking	4213	3112
Gardner Trucking Inc	4213	1630
Gardner Zemke Co	1731	61
Gardner-Watson Inc	5999	174
Gare Inc	3269	13
Garelick Farms Inc	3999	22
Garelick Manufacturing Co	3429	87
Garey Construction Company Inc	1611	38
Garfield County Bancshares Inc	6712	707
Garfield Molding Company Inc	3089	1567
Gargiulo Inc	5148	52

Company Name	SIC	Rank
Garile Inc	2752	1426
Garkane Energy Cooperative Inc	4911	382
Garland C Norris Co	5113	30
Garland Converting	2741	164
Garland F Fulcher Seafood Company Inc	5146	36
Garland Farm Supply Inc	2048	46
Garland Heating and Air Conditioning Co	1711	232
Garland Industries Inc	3951	8
Garland Ventures Ltd	2038	66
Garlin Hotel Corp	8741	219
Garlinghouse Brothers Inc	3531	214
Garlock Helicoflex	3053	54
Garlock Printing And Converting Corp	2759	54
Garlock Sealing Technologies	3053	5
Garlock-East Equipment Co	5082	212
Garman Printing Company Inc	2789	125
Garman Routing Systems Inc	7372	4350
Garmin At Inc	3812	71
Garmin International Inc	3812	22
Garmin Ltd	3812	4
Garner Consulting Inc	8742	721
Garner Electric Inc	1731	618
Garner Industries Inc	3089	647
Garner Printing Co	2752	562
Garner Trucking Inc	4213	446
Garnet Logistics Inc	4225	17
Garnett and Helfrich Capital	6799	227
Garney Construction Co	1623	22
Garrand and Company Inc	7311	740
Garratt-Callahan Co	2899	64
Garrett Book Co	2731	336
Garrett Electric Company Inc	1731	835
Garrett Electronics Corp	5065	547
Garrett Electronics Inc	3812	90
Garrett Packing Co	2037	29
Garrett Trucking	4213	629
GarrettCom Inc	3577	280
Garrison Bradford Inc	6282	264
Garrison Brewer Co	2752	1079
Garrison Hauling Company Inc	4213	2248
Garrison Printing Co	2752	661
Garrison's Custom Cabinets Inc	5712	92
Garrity Printing LLC	2752	744
Garrod Hydraulics Inc	3593	42
Garroutte Inc	3556	183
Garsite TSR Inc	3537	48
Gartech Manufacturing Co	3423	69
Gartland Foundry Company Inc	3321	42
Gartner Inc	8741	13
Gartner Studios Inc	5111	23
Garton Tractor Inc	5083	20
Garver LLC	8711	214
Garvey Corp	3535	58
Garvey Schubert and Barer	8111	464
Garvey Transport Inc	4213	1764
Garvin Industries Inc	3643	81
Garwood Laboratories Inc	8734	91
Gary Bale Redi-Mix Concrete Inc	3273	62
Gary Bergman Associates Inc	7372	4459
Gary Community School Corp	8211	51
Gary Edmunds Inc	5063	773
Gary Foglio Trucking Inc	4213	2854
Gary Force Inc	5511	362
Gary Halgran	7363	203
Gary J Welch	3663	392
Gary Lyells Inc	3559	455
Gary Merlino Construction Co	1611	124
Gary Metal Manufacturing LLC	3444	94
Gary Nelson Inc	5013	146
Gary Plastic Packaging Corp	3089	213
Gary Pools Inc	1799	35
Gary R Olhoeft	7372	4058
Gary Transfer Company Inc	4212	60
Gary W Clem Inc	3523	101
Gary W Gray Trucking Inc	4213	861
Gary Yamamoto Custom Baits Inc	3949	106
Gary-Williams Co	1382	7
Gas America Services Inc	5541	10
Gas Control Technologies	1731	2476
Gas Equipment Co	5984	12
Gas Equipment Engineering Corp	3569	165
Gas Equipment Supply Co	5084	433
Gas Inc	5984	20
Gas Land Petroleum Inc	5172	64
Gas Natural Inc	4924	51
Gas Transmission Northwest Corp	4922	35
Gasbarre Products Inc	3542	12
Gasboy International Inc	3823	42
Gasco Energy Inc	1311	168
Gascosage Electric Coop	4911	541
Gasdorf Tool And Machine Company Inc	3599	1963
Gaska Tape Inc	3086	51
Gasket and Seal Fabricators Inc	3053	115
Gasket Engineering Company Inc	3053	43
Gasket Resources Inc	3053	75
Gaskets Inc	3053	142
Gasko Fabricated Products Co	3053	79
Gaslamp Hotel Management Inc	7011	210
Gasline Service Co	1623	764
Gasllc LLC	2092	37
Gasparilla Inn Inc	7011	100

Company Name	SIC	Rank
Gaspar's Inc	3443	161
Gasper Corp	7372	2048
Gasper T Puccio Jr Inc	7389	1735
Gasperetti's Distributing Inc	5099	100
Gasser and Sons Inc	3469	89
Gasser Chair Company Inc	2531	33
Gassett Metals Ltd	5051	369
Gast Manufacturing Inc	3561	52
Gastar Exploration Ltd	1311	144
Gaster Lumber and Hardware Inc	5211	58
Gaston Co	6519	26
Gaston Electronics LLC	3559	163
Gaston Gazette LLP	2711	238
Gaston LLC	7311	821
Gaston Security Inc	7382	92
Gaston Systems Inc	2672	81
Gastonia Sheet Metal Works Inc	1761	29
Gastonian	7389	2258
Gaston's White River Resort	7011	126
Gastrointestinal Associates PC	8011	71
Gastronomy Inc	5812	310
Gatco Inc	3549	99
Gate City Beverage Distributors	5181	23
Gate City Motor Company Inc	5511	710
Gate City Printing Company Inc	2752	1209
Gate Concrete Products Company Inc	3272	61
Gate Petroleum Co	5541	14
GatecraftersCom	3699	218
GateHouse Media Inc	2711	34
Gatekeepers Internet Marketing Inc	5734	355
Gately Communications Inc	5731	84
Gater Industries Inc	3429	108
Gates Automotive Group	5511	367
Gates Capital Corp	6211	376
Gates Machine and Fabrication Inc	3599	827
Gates McDonald and Co	6331	82
Gates That Open LLC	3699	106
Gateway Community Industries	8331	64
Gateway Co	6531	391
Gateway Concrete Forming Services Inc	1771	31
Gateway Co-Op	5153	93
Gateway Design Inc	7336	168
Gateway Energy Corp	4922	43
Gateway Funding Diversified Mortgage Services LP	6162	19
Gateway Group One	7381	17
Gateway Health Plan	6324	30
Gateway Homes Inc	1521	101
Gateway Inc	3571	9
Gateway Industrial Power Inc	3585	53
Gateway Insurance Comp	6331	257
Gateway International Holdings Inc	6719	165
Gateway Investment Advisors LP	6282	168
Gateway Manufacturing Inc	2511	91
Gateway Mastering Studios Inc	3695	87
Gateway Nursing Center	8051	41
Gateway Optical Company Inc	5048	37
Gateway Packaging Co	2679	21
Gateway Packaging Company Of Missouri	2674	12
Gateway Paint and Chemical Co	2851	112
Gateway Plastics Inc	3089	629
Gateway Press Inc (Louisville Kentucky)	2732	15
Gateway Printing and Graphics Inc	2752	1342
Gateway Printing Company Inc	2752	1394
Gateway Proclean	5169	138
Gateway Products Inc	2048	104
Gateway Software Corp	7372	3349
Gateway Supply Company Inc	5074	24
Gateway Supply Ltd	5085	449
Gateway Ticketing Systems Inc	7372	2764
Gateway Tire Company Inc	5014	18
Gatewaycdi Inc	5199	43
Gathright Services Inc	4213	2814
Gatlin Group Inc	3569	120
Gator Building Maintenance Inc	7349	440
Gator Glass Co	5039	68
Gator Metal Products Inc	5051	463
Gator Of Florida Inc	5137	17
Gator Security Inc	5065	846
Gator Supply Company LLC	5085	299
Gator Valve Inc	5085	254
Gatorade Co	2086	5
Gatorhyde Protective Coatings Inc	3089	1300
Gatorland	7996	32
GATR Technologies	3577	337
Gatti Medical Supply Inc	5047	103
Gatto Industrial Platers Inc	3471	73
GATX Corp	4729	2
GATX Financial Corp	4741	2
GATX Terminals Holding Corp	4226	4
Gaudet Associates Inc	8734	157
Gaudette Electric Inc	1731	1606
Gaudin Motor Co	5511	300
Gauging Systems Inc	3545	266
Gault Chevrolet Company Inc	5511	564
Gaum Inc	3599	781
Gauss Corp	3694	49
Gauss Interprise USA	7372	1241
Gauthier Biomedical Inc	3841	319
Gauthier Industries Inc	3444	114

Company Name	SIC	Rank
Gavan Graham Electrical Products Corp	3441	211
Gavial Engineering and Manufacturing Inc	3679	211
Gavson Inc	2389	38
Gay and Robinson Inc	2061	15
Gay Johnson's Inc	5541	46
Gayesco International LP	3823	107
Gayfer Montgomery Fair Co	5311	7
Gayla Industries Inc	3069	125
Gayle Manufacturing Company Inc	3441	40
Gaylor Electric	1731	25
Gaylor Inc	1731	41
Gaylord Brothers	2631	18
Gaylord Entertainment Co	7011	39
Gaylord Entertainment Co Entertainment Div	7011	47
Gaylord Industries Inc	3564	58
Gaymar Industries Inc	3841	107
Gayston Corp	3489	12
Gazelle	4899	115
Gazelle Transportation Inc	4213	675
Gazette	2711	882
Gazette Co	2711	127
Gazette Media Inc	2711	534
Gazette Newspapers Inc	2711	183
Gazette Press Inc	2759	458
Gazette Printing Company Inc	2752	254
Gazette Publishing Inc	2711	244
GB and G Construction	1623	497
GB 'Boots' Smith Corp	4213	1056
GB Embossing Inc	3479	110
Gb Foods Inc	2051	109
Gb Instruments Inc	5399	25
GB International Trading Company Ltd	3629	40
Gb Marketing Inc	3577	551
GB Products International Corp	2796	52
Gbc Metals LLC	3351	8
GBC Scientific Equipment Corp	3826	145
Gbf Inc	2835	47
G-Biz Unlimited	7336	310
Gbl Systems Corp	7373	537
Gbm Managment Group LP	1731	794
Gbn Machine and Engineering Corp	3553	50
GBR Systems Corp	3579	42
GBS Consultants Inc	7372	4506
Gbs Corp	5045	151
GBS Esecure LLC	7382	60
GBS Inc	7372	4351
Gbs Lumber Inc	5211	107
GBT Inc	3577	517
Gby Corp	3679	350
Gc Aero Inc	3433	62
GC Broach Co	3567	36
G-C Electric Company Inc	1731	694
GC Fabrication Inc	5065	287
GC Lables Inc	2759	395
GC Office Supply	5943	39
Gc Packaging LLC	2754	3
Gc Supply Inc	5088	75
GC/Waldom Electronics Inc	5065	71
GCAS Inc	7373	977
Gcfs Inc	7322	111
GCG Wealth Management Inc	6282	128
Gch Tool Group Inc	3546	33
GCI Communication Corp	4813	48
GCI Mobile	5064	202
Gci Technologies Corp	3651	85
Gcic LLC	5084	190
Gcm Medical	7539	5
Gcm North American Aerospace LLC	3728	112
GCOM Inc	7372	3581
Gcom Software Inc	7371	369
Gcp California Fund LP	5999	22
GCPS Inc	1623	842
GCT Semiconductor Inc	3674	111
Gd California Inc	3577	313
GD Mathews and Sons Inc	5149	126
GDA Technologies Inc	8711	76
Gdb International Inc	5093	41
Gdc Inc	3086	48
GDI Infotech Inc	7371	512
GDI LLC	7382	29
Gdm Electronic Assembly	3643	58
GDS Express Inc	4213	272
GDT Tek Inc	7379	1649
GE Aircraft Engines	3724	1
GE Analytical Instruments	3826	30
GE Aviation	3728	1
GE Capital	6159	3
Ge Capital Montgomery Ward	6141	57
GE Capital Rail Services	7629	2
GE Capital Real Estate	6798	6
GE Continental Controls Inc	7372	2347
GE Control Products	3625	13
GE Corporate Research and Development Center	8731	32
Ge Drives and Controls Inc	3612	23
GE Fanuc Automation Corp	3823	21
GE Fleet Services	4212	2
Ge Healthcare Holdings Inc	2835	14
GE Infrastructure Water and Process Technologies	3559	6
GE Investment Management Inc	6282	423
GE Ionics Inc	3559	22
GE Johnson Construction Company Inc	1541	88
GE Jones Electric Company Inc	1731	1354
GE Lighting	3641	1
GE Mathis Co	3599	507
GE Medical Systems	3841	3
GE Medical Systems Information Technologies	7372	2547
GE Mobile Water	3589	171
GE Nuclear Energy	8731	58
GE OEC Medical Systems Inc	3844	3
Go Oil and Gas Pressure Control LP	3491	11
GE Osmonics Inc	3569	14
GE Plastics	2672	2
GE Reuter-Stokes Inc	3829	68
GE SeaCo America LLC	5088	20
GE Security Inc	3669	11
GE Trailer Fleet Services	7519	1
GE Transportation Finance	7353	1
GE Transportation Systems	3743	6
Ge Transportation Systems Global Signaling LLC	3669	28
GE Tri-Remanufacturing Inc	3724	18
GE Water and Process Technologies	3599	6
Ge Wind Energy LLC	3511	13
GE Zenith Controls	3679	224
Gea Farm Technologies Inc	5083	2
Gea Fes Inc	3585	62
Gea Intec LLC	5083	128
Gea Westfalia Separator Inc	5083	1
Gear Holdings Inc	8999	171
Gear Products Inc	3568	59
Gear Works Seattle Inc	3566	18
Gearhost	3569	172
Gearn Industries Inc	3523	207
Gearworks Inc	7372	375
Geary Darling Lessee Inc	8741	190
Geary Pacific Corp	5075	23
Geater Machining And Manufacturing Co	3444	117
Gebauer Co	2834	362
GeBBS Healthcare Solutions	8999	112
Gebco Insurance Associates Inc	6411	230
Gecko Alliance	3561	161
Gecko Systems of Georgia Inc	7371	1761
Geckobytecom Inc	7371	1513
GECOM Corp	3714	104
Ged Integrated Solutions Inc	3559	107
Geddes Bakery Company Inc	2051	264
GEE Communications Inc	5999	129
Geek City Electronics Inc	5734	233
Geeknet Inc	7372	380
Geeks On Call Holdings Inc	7378	48
Geerpres Inc	3589	222
Geese Police Inc	7342	60
Geetingsville Telephone Company Inc	4813	574
Gefen Inc	7372	3796
Geffen Mesher and Company PC	8721	346
Gefran Isi Inc	3823	240
Gega Corp	3547	16
Gehan Homes Ltd	1531	74
Ge-Hitachi Nuclear Energy Americas LLC	2819	30
Gehl Electric Inc	1731	1483
Gehl Foods Inc	2022	11
Gehl Power Products Inc	3523	12
Gehr Industries Inc	3357	37
Gehring Corp	6512	70
Gehring Textiles Inc	2258	12
Gehry Technologies LLC	7372	2145
Geib Enterprises Ltd	3089	1184
Geib Industries Inc	5085	181
GEICO General Insurance Co	6331	20
Geico Indemnity Co	6331	37
Geier and Bluhm Inc	3625	151
Geifman Food Stores Inc	6552	280
Geiger and Peters Inc	3441	66
Geiger Manufacturing Inc	3599	2126
Geiger Tool and Manufacturing Company Inc	3565	160
Geile/Leon Marketing Communications	7311	607
Geis Building Products Inc	5211	116
Geis Construction Co	1541	247
Geisinger Health System	8741	18
Geist Plastics	3679	605
Geisz Agency	7311	865
Gekkeikan Sake USAInc	2085	23
Gel Electrophoresis Company Inc	5049	164
Gel Inc	1731	122
Gel Spice Company Inc	2099	49
Gelber Television	7812	155
Gelco Information Network Inc	7374	67
Gelia Wells and Mohr Inc	7311	157
Gelita USA Inc	2899	69
Geller Ragans James Oppenheimer and Creel	8721	150
Gelmart Industries Inc	2342	1
Gelson's Markets	5411	122
Gelstat Corp	2834	437
Gem Acquisition Company Inc	2761	78
Gem Companies Inc	7373	755
GEM Contractors Inc	1623	293
Gem Equipment Of Oregon Inc	3556	35
Gem Gravure Company Inc	3555	26
Gem Industries Inc	3429	8
Gem Instrument Co	3823	360
Gem Manufacturing Inc	3499	110
Gem Meat Packing Co	2011	70
Gem Of The Net LLC	7374	409
Gem Remotes Inc	3519	39
Gem Specialty Companies Inc	5199	86
Gem State Paper and Supply Co	5113	14
Gem State Transportation Inc	4213	2443
Gema Inc	3842	203
Gemalto Inc	5045	345
Gemco Manufacturing Company Inc	3493	12
Gemco Of Port Lavaca Inc	3544	667
Gemco Sales Inc	5063	749
Gemcor Ii LLC	3542	14
Gemcraft Homes Group Inc	1522	16
Gemeinhardt Company LLC	3931	31
Gemel Precision Tool Inc	3469	306
Gemfire Corp	3669	89
GemGroup	6411	-170
Gemi Trucking Inc	4213	1376
Gemini Building Systems LLC	7349	382
Gemini Circuits Inc	5063	759
Gemini Coatings Inc	2851	75
Gemini Controls LLC	3676	28
Gemini Corp	2721	270
Gemini Cosmetics	5122	128
Gemini Employee Leasing Inc	7363	326
Gemini Enterprises Inc	5084	809
Gemini Manufacturing LLC	2754	9
Gemini Mouldings Inc	2499	46
Gemini Partners Inc	6799	233
Gemini Pharmaceuticals Inc	2833	36
Gemini Plastic Enterprises Inc	3089	1380
Gemini Plastic Films Corp	2673	60
Gemini Tool and Manufacturing	3544	768
Gemini Transfer Sales Inc	4213	645
Gemline Frame Company Inc	2499	28
Gemma Power Systems LLC	1629	46
Gemstar Inc	3533	79
Gem-Top Manufacturing Inc	5531	31
Gemtrol Inc	3625	355
Gemtron Corp	3211	8
Gemu Valves Inc	3491	50
Gemvision Corporation LLC	3915	10
Gen Cap America Inc	6799	346
Genaissance Pharmaceuticals Inc	8731	160
GenAmerica Financial Corp	6311	24
Genband Inc	3577	86
Genca Corp	3544	122
Genco ATC	3714	27
Genco ATC Logistics and Electronics	3714	149
Genco Industries Inc	7389	1220
Genco Of Lebanon Inc	6512	24
Genco Shipping and Trading Ltd	4412	13
Genco Stamping And Manufacturing Co	3469	233
Gencom Technology LLC	7373	971
Gencor Industries Inc	3531	43
GenCorp Automotive	3089	35
GenCorp Inc	3764	1
Gendarme Fragrances	2844	176
Gene B Glick Company Inc	6531	24
Gene Beltz Shadeland Dodge	5511	1019
Gene Butman Ford Sales Inc	5511	843
Gene Hansen and Sons Trucking Inc	4213	1074
Gene Oswald Co	5063	901
Gene Rhodes Enterprises Inc	7349	241
Gene Schick Co	5064	68
Gene Stringfield Building Materials Co	5211	306
Geneca LLC	7371	563
Gene-IT USA	5045	950
GeneLink Inc	8071	45
Gen-El-Mec Associates Inc	3599	1627
Genemed Synthesis Inc	2835	64
Genencor International Inc	2835	7
Genentech Inc	2834	7
Generac Power Systems Inc	3621	24
General Air Corp	3559	548
General Air Products Inc	3563	39
General Air Service and Supply Company Inc	5084	286
General Aire Systems Inc	5084	558
General Aluminum Company Of Texas	3442	50
General Aluminum Manufacturing Co	3363	3
General American Investors Company Inc	6726	22
General Appliance and Electronic Distributors Inc	5064	104
General Asphalt Company Inc	3531	42
General Atomics	8731	45
General Atomics Aeronautical Systems Inc	3728	20
General Auto Repair Inc	5531	39
General Automatic Machine Products Company Inc	3451	81
General Automatic Transfer Co	3582	12
General Automation Inc	3451	36
General Aviation and Electronics Manufacturing Company Inc	3444	266
General Aviation Industries Inc	3537	78
General Aviation Manufacturing Inc	3724	71

Company Name	SIC	Rank
General Bearing Corp	3562	10
General Beverage Sales Co	5181	8
General Binding Corp Film Products Div	3083	4
General Broach Co	3541	257
General Building Maintenance Inc	7349	47
General Building Systems LLC	2439	29
General Business Envelope	2752	512
General Cable Corp	3357	2
General Cage LLC	3496	90
General Carbide Corp	3544	39
General Casualty	6331	36
General Casualty Cos	6411	22
General Casualty Insurance Cos	6331	92
General Chemical Corp	2819	19
General Chemical Industrial Products Inc	2812	6
General Chemical (Soda Ash) Inc	1474	3
General Clay Co	3993	135
General Coatings Technologies Inc	2851	51
General Cocoa Company Inc	6221	9
General Code LLC	8111	482
General Color and Chemical Company Inc	2816	8
General Communication Inc	4813	29
General Construction Co	1611	143
General Container	2653	101
General Converters And Assemblers Inc	7389	440
General Conveyor Inc	7699	124
General Council On Finance And Admin Of The United Methodist Church	7389	1367
General Crane And Hoist Inc	3536	50
General Cybernation Group Inc	7372	3906
General Data Company Inc	7371	57
General Data Systems Inc (St Louis Missouri)	7372	3582
General DataComm Industries Inc	3661	130
General Datatech LP	5045	297
General Delivery Inc	4213	2444
General Die And Die Cutting Inc	2653	111
General Die Casters Inc	3364	11
General Display Inc	3993	102
General Distributing Co	5084	363
General Distributing Co	5181	38
General Dynamics Armament and Technical Products Inc	3728	27
General Dynamics Corp	3732	1
General Dynamics Decision Systems	3663	5
General Dynamics Information Systems	3812	47
General Dynamics Land Systems Inc	3795	1
General Dynamics Network Systems/ International Telecom Group	3669	58
General Dynamics Ordnance And Tactical Systems Inc	3483	1
General Dynamics Robotic Systems Inc	3599	144
General Ecology Inc	3589	169
General Econopak Inc	3842	174
General Electric Capital Corp	6141	1
General Electric Capital Services Inc	6159	1
General Electric Co	3621	1
General Electric Company Power Systems	3511	1
General Electric Railcar Services Corp	4741	1
General Electrical Services Of Texas Inc	1731	872
General Electro Corp	3672	373
General Electrodynamics Corp	3596	11
General Electro-Mechanical Corp	3542	8
General Electronic Devices Inc	3679	781
General Employment Enterprises Inc	7361	73
General Engineering and Equipment Co	5063	582
General Engineering Company Of Virginia	3593	24
General Equipment Co	3531	83
General Extrusions Inc	3354	20
General Fabrications Corp	3559	245
General Factory Supplies Company Inc	5085	236
General Fibre Products Corp	2653	100
General Films Inc	3081	81
General Filters Inc	3585	120
General Finance Corp	5989	2
General Fire Protection Systems Inc	3669	289
General Foam Plastics Corp	3999	33
General Formulations Inc	2672	9
General Furniture Leasing Co	7359	47
General Glass Equipment Co	5084	715
General Gmc Truck Sales and Service Inc	5012	179
General Graphics	7336	326
General Graphics Corp	3953	15
General Grind and Machine Inc	3599	178
General Grinding Inc	3471	108
General Growth Properties Inc	6798	7
General Hearing Instruments Inc	3845	131
General Industries Inc	3443	177
General Investments Corp	2741	140
General Laboratory Supply Of Houston Inc	5049	121
General Loose Leaf Bindery Company Inc	2782	44

Company Name	SIC	Rank
General Machine CoOf New Jersey	3559	238
General Machine Corp	3433	46
General Machine Inc	3599	1807
General Machine Products Company Inc	3531	93
General Machine Service Inc	3599	1603
General Machine Shop Inc	3599	2029
General Machine Works Company Inc	3599	910
General Machine-Diecron Inc	3599	1664
General Machinery Corp	3556	180
General Magnaplate Corp	3479	45
General Manufacturing Inc	3648	38
General Maritime Corp	4412	14
General Material Co	3273	98
General Metal Finishing Company Inc	3471	53
General Metals Corp	7389	2517
General Micro Systems Inc	3577	163
General Microcircuits Inc	3672	116
General Microsystems Inc (Bellevue Washington)	5045	385
General Microsystems Inc (Chantilly Virginia)	3661	195
General Mills Inc	2041	3
General Moly Inc	1081	6
General Motors Co	3711	1
General Motors Financial Company Inc	6141	54
General Novelty Ltd	5947	16
General Novelty Ltd Coach House Gifts Div	5947	28
General Nuclear Corp	3829	158
General Nucleonics Inc	3829	261
General Nutrition Centers Inc	5499	4
General Oceanics Inc	8731	346
General Office Products Co	5112	28
General Oil Corp	5084	587
General Operating Corp	7334	96
General Optical Co	5995	22
General Packaging Corp	3086	15
General Packaging Equipment Co	3565	146
General Packaging Products Inc	2754	10
General Partitions Manufacturing Corp	2542	45
General Parts Inc	5013	9
General Pattern And Plastics Inc	3089	440
General Pattern Company Inc	3086	38
General Pencil Company Inc	3952	9
General Photonics Corp	3661	140
General Physics Corp	8249	8
General Plasma Inc	3565	67
General Plastex Inc	3452	86
General Plastics and Composites LP	3083	33
General Plastics Inc	3089	914
General Plastics Machines Inc	3559	566
General Plastics Manufacturing Co	3086	41
General Plug and Manufacturing Co	3325	33
General Plumbing Supply CoInc	5074	80
General Polymeric Corp	2821	104
General Pool and SpA Supply Inc	5091	15
General Porcelain Manufacturing Co	3269	14
General Press Colors Ltd	2865	21
General Press Corp	2752	573
General Printing and Design Inc	7389	2090
General Printing Co	2752	906
General Produce Company Ltd	5148	42
General Products	2782	28
General Products Delaware Corp	3599	63
General Pump and Equipment Co	3829	429
General Re Corp	6331	29
General Reliance Corp	3679	332
General Research Laboratories	2834	363
General Resource Corp	3564	15
General Rubber And Plastics Of Paducah Inc	5085	93
General Rubber Corp	3069	117
General Scientific Corp	3827	84
General Sealants Inc	2891	15
General Seating of America Inc	3714	158
General Security Service Inc	7381	71
General Services Inc	7349	236
General Sheet Metal Corp	1711	146
General Sound Co (Richardson Texas)	1731	81
General Sportwear Company Inc	2369	4
General Stair Corp	2431	104
General Standards Corp	3672	188
General Steamship Corporation Ltd	4491	8
General Steel Inc	5051	199
General Super Plating Company Inc	3471	32
General Supply And Metals Inc	5051	402
General Switchgear Inc	3613	98
General Technologies Inc	3089	1099
General Telcom Inc	5065	365
General Testing and Inspection Inc	8734	78
General Theming Contractors LLC	7389	578
General Thermodynamics	3433	10
General Tool and Supply Co	5072	36
General Tool Co	3599	93
General Tool Specialties Inc	3089	1817
General Tools and Instruments	3423	21
General Trading Company Inc (Carlstadt New Jersey)	5141	94
General Traffic Equipment Corp	3669	262
General Transervice Inc	3537	79
General Transport Inc	4213	2673
General Transworld Corp	5049	148
General Truck Parts and Equipment Co	5013	140

Company Name	SIC	Rank
General Truck Sales and Service Inc	5511	578
General Welding Works Inc	3443	111
General Weldments Inc	3599	1548
General Wholesale Co	5181	26
General Window Corp	3442	138
General Wire Products Inc	3357	64
General Wood Preserving Company Inc	2491	18
Generation Partners	6799	135
Generation Technologies Corp	7372	4507
Generation Tool Inc	3559	539
Generation21 Learning Systems Inc	7372	339
Generational Equity Co	8742	211
Generations Bank	6022	509
Generations Home Care LLC	7389	1388
Generator Power Systems	5063	963
Generic Distributors Inc	5122	107
Generic Systems Inc	7372	2422
Generics Group Inc	8731	410
Generra Co	2321	28
Gene's Plating Works Inc	3471	34
Genesco Inc	5661	4
Genesee and Wyoming Inc	4011	11
Genesee Packaging Inc	7389	602
Genesee Reserve Supply Inc	5031	106
Genesee Scientific Corp	5049	92
Genesee Survey Services Inc	7374	142
Genesis Consolidated Services Inc	7361	379
Genesis Corp	7379	58
Genesis Crude Oil LP	1311	64
Genesis Development Inc	3559	572
Genesis Electrical Systems Inc	1731	1818
Genesis Energy LP	5171	5
Genesis Financial Solutions Inc	6141	38
Genesis Fixtures Inc	2599	19
Genesis Group Software Developers Inc	7372	2981
Genesis HealthCare Corp	8051	3
Genesis Inc	3444	108
Genesis Lamp Corp	3646	102
Genesis Microchip Inc	3674	86
Genesis Molding Inc	3089	1900
Genesis One Technologies Inc	3695	177
Genesis Pipeline Texas LP	1311	37
Genesis Plastic Welding	8731	120
Genesis Plastics And Engineering LLC	3089	704
Genesis Plastics Technologies Inc	3089	1410
Genesis Telecom Inc	5065	536
Genesis Today Inc	2834	288
Genesis Total Solutions Inc	7371	1929
Genesis V Systems Ltd	7372	2423
GenesisFour Corp	7372	745
Genesistems Inc	7372	3774
Genessee Electric Inc	1731	1780
Genesta Partnership	7373	490
Genesys Conferencing Inc	4899	34
Genesys Software Systems Inc	7372	1661
Genesys Telecommunications Laboratories Inc	3577	56
Genetco Inc	5122	55
GeneThera Inc	2836	106
Genett Group Inc	7349	416
Geneva Construction Co	1611	248
Geneva Elevator Co	5153	115
Geneva Global Inc	8732	90
Geneva Group Inc	7373	881
Geneva Travel Inc	4724	148
Geneva Worldwide Inc	8743	145
Genevac Inc	3821	31
Geneve Corp	8999	4
Genex Cooperative Inc	0751	6
Genex Interactive	7379	427
GENEX Services Inc	6411	64
Genex Technologies Inc	3651	76
GeneXus Inc	7372	3756
Genexus USA Inc	7371	1565
GenFed Federal Credit Union	6061	85
Geniac Electric Inc	1731	1745
Genie Electronics Company Inc	1799	54
Genie Manufacturing Corp	7389	1519
Genie Manufacturing Inc	3531	27
Genie Repros Inc	2752	1427
Genie Trucking Line Inc	4213	2611
Genis Inc	5023	117
Genisco Filter Corp	3677	76
Genisys Credit Union	6061	41
Genisys Credit Union (Troy Michigan)	6061	86
Genius Inc	7379	248
Genius Products Inc	7819	5
Genlyte-Lightolier	5063	494
Genmar Michigan LLC	3732	12
Genmark Automation	3569	40
GenMark Diagnostics Inc	8099	103
Gennett Lumber Co	5211	326
GenNx360 Capital Partners	6799	100
Genoa Bank	6712	587
Genoa Banking Co	6022	605
Genoa Business Forms Inc	2752	691
Genome International Corp	7371	570
Genomic Health Inc	8071	12
Genomic Solutions Inc	7371	1069
GenOn Energy	4911	33
GenOn Mid-Atlantic LLC	4911	97
Genoptix Inc	8731	43

Company Name	SIC	Rank
GenoSpectra Inc	2836	28
GeNOsys Inc	2819	139
Genova Diagnostics	8734	16
Genova Partners	7311	550
Genova Products Inc	3089	211
Genova Technologies Inc	7371	1137
Genovation Inc	3577	408
Genovese and Massaro Inc	1731	498
Genoveva Chavez Community Center	7389	1530
Genpact	7374	44
Genpak Southwest LP	3089	338
Gen-Probe Gti Diagnostics Inc	2835	33
Gen-Probe Inc	3841	23
Genscape Inc	7389	693
Gensco Inc	5074	75
Gensia Sicor Inc	2834	111
Gensoft Systems Inc	8721	402
GenSource Corp	7371	1079
Genstar Capital LLC	6799	237
Gensym Corp	7372	1418
Genta Inc	2836	89
Gentec LLC	3621	143
GenTek Inc	3714	56
GENTEK Media Inc	3571	40
Gentex Corp	3714	34
Gentex Corp (Carbondale Pennsylvania)	3851	10
Genti Studios Inc	7384	23
Gentia Software Inc	7372	1035
Gentiva Health Services Inc	8082	6
Gentle Dental Service Corp	8741	54
Gentle Giant Moving Company Inc	4213	323
Gentle Touch Auto Wash	7542	4
Gent-L-Kleen Products Inc	2841	46
Gentner Inc	4213	1415
Gentran Div	3823	325
Gentry Development Co	6552	79
Gentry Ford Subaru Inc	5511	1119
Gentry Machine Works Inc	3599	760
Gentry Trucking LLC	4213	720
Gentrys Poultry Co	2015	18
Gentz Industries LLC	3769	13
Gentzler Tool and Die Corp	3469	335
Genuardi's Family Markets LP	5411	83
Genuine Machine Design Inc	3599	2451
Genuine Parts Co	5013	2
Genuine Sales Inc	5046	343
Genus Inc	3559	59
Genus Technologies LLC	8741	139
Genusys Group Inc	8748	334
Genusys Inc	7371	1580
Genvac Aerospace Corp	3827	156
GenVec Inc	2834	287
Genwal Resources Inc	1222	12
Genware Computer Systems	7379	1406
Genworth Financial Inc	6311	15
Genworth Financial Service	6311	81
Genworth Mortgage Insurance Corp	6162	45
Genzlinger Associates Inc	7372	4352
Genzyme Corp	2836	3
Genzyme General	2835	1
Genzyme Genetics Corp	8731	40
Geo Advertising and Marketing Inc	7311	511
Geo Byers and Sons Inc	5511	70
Geo Center Inc	7374	252
GEO Drilling Fluids Inc	5172	27
Geo F Alger Inc	4213	912
Geo Frontiers Corp	1382	30
Geo Graphics Inc	2752	274
GEO Group Inc	8744	4
Geo Heat Exchangers LLC	3443	223
Geo Knight and Company Inc	3443	190
Geo M Martin Co	3554	18
Geo Pfau's Sons Company Inc	2077	7
Geo Space LP	3577	90
Geo T Schmidt Inc	3542	28
Geo Vision Software Inc	3695	181
Geoanalytical Laboratories Inc	8734	196
GeoCapital Corp	6211	386
Geocel Corp	2891	55
Geocomp Corp	7372	2760
Geo-Con Inc	1794	24
Geocorp Industrial Controls Inc	3822	70
Geodesic Systems Inc	7372	2848
Geodesign Inc	7373	669
Geodigm Corp	8731	59
GeoEngineers Inc	8711	119
GeoEye Inc	4899	26
GeoFocus LLC	7372	2872
Geographic Expeditions	4725	32
Geokinetics Inc	1311	51
Geokinetics Processing Inc	7374	96
Geokinetics USA Inc	1382	2
Geokon Inc	3829	51
GeoLearning Inc	7372	710
Geologic Computer Systems Inc	5045	1022
GeoLogics Corp	7389	554
Geomation Inc	3823	243
Geomatrix Consultants Inc	8711	71
Geomatrix Productions	7812	135
GeoMet Inc	1311	151
GEOMET Technologies Inc	8734	53
Geometric Circuits Inc	3672	198
Geometric Technologies Inc	7372	3188
Geometrica Inc	1541	65
Geometrics Inc	3829	89
Geo-Microbial Technologies Inc	8731	365
Geonor Inc	5049	220
GeoPharma Inc	2833	20
Geophysical Research Company LLC	3823	103
Geophysical Survey Systems Inc	3812	95
Georator Corp	3621	138
GeoResources Inc	1311	109
Georetiary Networks Inc	7373	843
Georg Fischer LLC	3084	6
Georg Fischer Signet LLC	3823	89
George A Grant Inc	1542	269
George A Green Inc	1731	2314
George A Kint Inc	5087	128
George A Mitchell Co	3542	70
George and Lynch Inc	1622	23
George Apkin and Sons Inc	5093	108
George Benson Electric Inc	1731	2298
George Braun Oyster Company Inc	5146	46
George Butler Associates Inc	8711	313
George C Hopkins Construction Company Inc	1541	249
George C Matteson Company Inc	2759	45
George Coriaty	2752	772
George D L and Sons Transportation Inc	4212	43
George D Zamias Developer	6552	72
George Davidson and Son	7372	981
George Dolan	5461	54
George E Anderson Company Inc	5063	762
George E Kent Company Inc	5084	784
George E Runquist Enterprises Inc	8742	449
George Elkins Mortgage Banking Co	6162	132
George Eschbaugh Advertising Inc	3993	159
George Fischer Sloane Inc	3089	448
George Ford and Sons Inc	3545	326
George Foreman Enterprises Inc	3652	55
George G Ruppersberger and Sons Inc	5147	126
George G Sharp Inc	8711	70
George Gordon Associates Inc	3565	169
George H Buchanan	2752	1275
George H Dean Co	2752	335
George H Ratchford Inc	4213	2822
George Hansen and Company Inc	3544	776
George Harms Construction Co	1622	15
George Hildebrandt Inc	4213	1701
George Holden and Associates Inc	5075	88
George Husack Inc	4213	2909
George J Igel and Company Inc	1794	13
George Jue Manufacturing Company Inc	3546	20
George Junior Republic In Pennsylvania	8361	13
George K Baum and Co	6211	262
George K Baum Holdings Inc	6211	139
George Kessel Associates	6552	290
George Koch Sons LLC	3567	7
George Konik Associates Inc	7363	259
George Kun Travel Cruise Quarters	4724	84
George L Kovacs	3547	20
George L Wilson and Company Ltd	5032	18
George Mason Mortgage Corp	6162	104
George P Johnson Co	7319	14
George P Reintjes Company Inc	7389	52
George Putnam Fund of Boston A	6722	124
George R Gibson Chevrolet Inc	5511	886
George R Norris Inc	5511	42
George R Pierce Inc	5271	3
George R Ruhl and Son Inc	5046	92
George Risk Industries Inc	3669	161
George S Drummey Company Inc	1731	2334
George S May International Co	8742	120
George Sollitt Construction Co	1542	174
George Squires	5031	406
George Steel Fabricating Inc	3441	112
George W Banks Trucking	4213	2827
George W Burnett Inc	4213	2561
George W Park Seed Company Inc	5261	4
George W Warden Company Inc	5084	142
George W Weaver and Son Inc	4214	15
George Weintraub and Sons Inc	2311	11
George Weston Bakeries Inc	2051	19
George Yardley Company Inc	5085	166
Georges and Shapiro Lithograph Inc	2752	1307
George's Inc	2015	16
Georgeson Shareholder Communications Inc	6289	17
Georgetown Bancorp Inc	6036	85
Georgetown Newspapers Inc	2711	765
Georgetown Rail Equipment	4011	47
Georgia Bancshares Inc	6712	540
Georgia Bank and Trust Company of Augusta	6022	113
Georgia Baptist Health Care System Inc	8741	12
Georgia Boot LLC	3021	8
Georgia Cancer Specialists PC	8011	8
Georgia Carpet Finishers Inc	2273	22
Georgia Casualty and Surety	6331	158
Georgia Chair Co	2531	43
Georgia Crate and Basket Company Inc	2449	5
Georgia Crown Distributing Co	5181	6
Georgia Duplicating Products	5044	17
Georgia Electric Membership Corp	2721	178
Georgia Electric Supply Inc	5063	730
Georgia Florida United Methodist Federal Credit Union	6061	153
Georgia Foam Inc	2821	103
Georgia Gulf Corp	2812	1
Georgia Hardwoods Inc	5031	304
Georgia Hydraulic Cylinder Inc	3561	113
Georgia Lighting	5063	77
Georgia Logos LLC	3993	179
Georgia Messenger Service Inc	4215	15
Georgia National Forms Inc	2752	1094
Georgia Plastic Surgery PC	8011	179
Georgia Power Co	4911	577
Georgia Security Systems	7382	167
Georgia Southern University	8221	31
Georgia Steel and Chemical Co	5169	183
Georgia Tech Research Corp	7389	56
Georgia Timberlands Inc	0851	5
Georgia United Credit Union	6061	64
Georgia West Medical Center Inc	6324	72
Georgia-Carolina Bancshares Inc	6022	307
Georgia-Pacific Corp Building Products Div	2436	1
Georgia-Pacific Corp Professional Div	2676	9
Georgia-Pacific LLC	2421	3
Georgino Industrial Supply Inc	5085	283
Geos Communications Inc	4812	129
Geo-Solutions Inc	8742	416
Geosonics Inc	3829	142
Geospace Engineering Resources International LP	3829	11
GEOSPAN Corp	8731	217
Geospatial Holdings Inc	8711	678
Geotech Computer Systems Inc	7372	4421
Geotech Environmental Equipment Inc	3823	105
Geotechnical Group Inc	8711	589
Geotest Instrument Corp	5084	883
GEOTEST - Marvin Test Systems Inc	3825	162
Geotext Translations Inc	7389	711
GeoTrans Inc	8711	169
Geotronic Labs Inc	3721	44
GeoTrust Inc	7379	141
GeoVantage Inc	5045	351
GeoVax Labs Inc	8731	275
geoVue	7372	707
Gephart Electric Company Inc	1731	158
Gerace Construction Co	1542	247
Gerald A Teel Company Inc	6531	279
Gerald T Reilly and Co	8721	160
Gerald Welch	3571	235
Gerald Zakim Associates LLC	7389	1434
Gerali Custom Design Inc	2542	50
Gerard Thomas Company Inc	5013	324
Gerber Childrenswear LLC	2389	5
Gerber Metal Supply Co	5051	137
Gerber Products Co	2032	2
Gerber Radio Supply Co	5065	210
Gerber Scientific Inc	3559	16
Gerber Scientific Products Inc	3559	25
Gerber/Somma Associates Inc	6531	348
Gerber Technology Inc	3571	21
Gerdau AmeriSteel Corp	3312	8
Gerdau Ameristeel Perth Amboy Inc	3312	78
Gerdau Macsteel Atmosphere Annealing Inc	3398	17
Gerdes Electric Inc	1731	2439
Gerflor North America	5023	140
Gergel-Kellem Company Inc	2752	343
Gerhard's Inc	5722	12
Gerich Fiberglass Company Inc	3714	414
Gerland Corp	5411	178
Gerli and Co	0131	1
Gerlinger Foundry And Machine Works Inc	3441	170
German American Bancorp Inc	6712	204
German American Bank	6022	85
German Machine and Assembly Inc	3469	316
Germane Systems LC	7373	409
Germania Farm Mutual Insurance Association	6311	220
Germanow-Simon Corp	3089	1113
Germantown Bancorp	6712	413
Germantown Trust and Savings Bank	6036	97
Gerold Moving and Warehousing Co	4213	3103
Gerome Manufacturing Co	3444	82
Geron Corp	2834	373
Gerotech Inc	5084	201
Gerresheimer Glass Inc	3231	12
Gerretsen Building Supply Co	5031	199
Gerry Lane Enterprises Inc	5511	187
Gersh Agency Inc	7922	42
Gerson and Gerson Inc	2361	7
Gerson Company Inc	5094	3
Gerstman Harvey and Associates Inc	8742	266
Gerstner Electric Inc	1731	426
Gertler Industries Inc	3841	281
Gertrude Geddes Willis Life Insurance Co	6311	272
Gertrude Hawks Chocolate Inc	2064	14
GES Contractors LLC	7389	2200
GES Exposition Services Inc	7359	3
Gesco Inc	7389	2054

Company Name	SIC	Rank	Company Name	SIC	Rank	Company Name	SIC	Rank
Gesme Printing Inc	2752	1527	Gibbs Machine Company Inc	3599	1597	Gillespie Decals Inc	2759	258
Gessin Electrical Contractor Inc	1731	573	Gibbs Oil Co	5541	19	Gillespie Shorthand Reporting Corp	7338	39
Gessner Products Company Inc	3089	876	Gibbs Wire and Steel Company Inc	5051	48	Gillette Children's Specialty Healthcare	8069	18
Gesswein	5049	17	Gibco Motor Express LLC	4213	461	Gillette Co	3421	1
Gestamp South Carolina LLC	3465	42	Giberson Electric Inc	1731	1925	Gillette Machine and Tool Company Inc	3599	339
Get Control Inc	8711	659	Gibraltar Bank FSB	6035	65	Gilliam Communications Inc	4832	84
Get Engineering Corp	3823	252	Gibraltar Industries Inc	3312	17	Gilliam Electric Inc	1731	1549
Get Real Interactive	7374	257	Gibraltar Packaging Group Inc	2657	7	Gillies Coffee Co	2095	49
Get Well Network Inc	7371	430	Gibraltar Plastic Products Corp	3089	1462	Gillies Trucking Inc	4213	1137
Getchell Brothers Inc	5143	37	Gibraltar Trade Center Inc	6512	10	Gillig LLC	3713	13
Getco LLC	7389	1304	Gib's Classics Inc	2033	127	Gillin Jacobson Ellis and Larsen	8111	553
Getecha Inc	3669	111	Gibson Access Controls Inc	5031	390	Gillinder Brothers Inc	3229	20
GetFugu Inc	4899	238	Gibson Associates Inc	5049	88	Gillingham-Best Inc	3537	103
Gethmann Construction Company Inc	1542	375	Gibson Brokers Inc	6531	217	Gillis Electric Inc	1731	356
Getinge USA Inc	3842	40	Gibson County Area Rehabilitation Center Inc	8361	139	Gillis Gilkerson Inc	1522	18
GetMyHomesValuecom	6531	435	Gibson Dunn and Crutcher	8111	15	Gillispie and Ogilbee	8721	222
Getronics	7373	25	Gibson Dunn and Crutcher LLP	8111	100	Gillman Honda	5511	1056
Getsmart Solutions Inc	7379	1378	Gibson Electric Membership Corp	4911	391	Gilman Building Products LLC	2421	20
Gett Industries Ltd	3599	525	Gibson Enterprises Inc	5033	54	Gilman Cheese Corp	2022	89
Gettle Inc	1731	226	Gibson Farmers Coop	5191	42	Gilman Ciocia Inc	6211	268
Getty Images Inc	7389	46	Gibson Laboratories LLC	2899	194	Gilman Corp	3086	114
Getty Petroleum Marketing Inc	5172	22	Gibson Machine Co	3599	1361	Gilman Investment Co	2621	19
Getty Realty Corp	6531	198	Gibson Machinery LLC	5082	175	Gil-Men Electric Company Inc	1731	1499
Gettysburg and Northern Railroad Co	4011	31	Gibson McDonald Furniture Stores Inc	5712	86	Gilmore And Son Construction Corp	1623	347
Gettysburg Transformer Corp	3677	56	Gibson Products LP	3494	67	Gilmore Associates Inc	7331	278
Gevo Inc	2819	41	Gibson Wine Co	2084	90	Gilmore Diamond Tools Inc	3829	427
Gexpro	5023	2	Giddens Security Corp	7381	107	Gilmore Entertainment Group LLC	7922	20
Geysers International Inc	7372	2752	Giddings and Lewis Control Measurement and Sensing	3625	57	Gilpin Testing Service	8071	56
GF Goodman and Son Inc	3541	209	Giddings and Lewis Machine Tools LLC	3541	3	Gil's Distributing Service Inc	7319	113
GF Health Products Inc	5047	9	GIE Media Inc	2721	145	Gilson Machine and Tool Company Inc	3599	2010
GF Morin Co	5075	69	Gielow Pickles Inc	2035	14	Gilson Screen Inc	3829	178
Gfa Decorative Trade Services Inc	2675	16	Gierczyk Inc	1542	402	Gilster-Mary Lee Corp	2099	15
GFA Electronics Inc	7629	56	Glese Sheet Metal Company Inc	1711	180	Gilt Groupe Inc	5961	53
GFC Cartage LLC	4213	2921	Gieske Custom Metal Fabricators Inc	3444	262	Gilvin-Terrill Ltd	1611	128
GFC Inc	3053	90	Giffin Inc	3559	143	Gim Electronics Corp	3572	53
GFD Courier Corp	7389	1508	Giffin Interior and Fixture Inc	2541	40	Gima Pest Control Inc	7342	81
GFD Services Inc	2258	2	Gifford And Brown Inc	3643	127	Gimbal Brothers Inc	2064	87
Gfg Instrumentation Inc	3829	260	Gifford Fong Associates	6282	320	Gimpel Software	7372	4460
GFI America Inc	2011	15	Gifford Hillegass and Ingwersen	8721	16	Gindor Inc	3053	148
GFI Energy Ventures LLC	6799	277	Gifford Tv and Electronics Inc	5731	68	Giner Inc	8731	280
GFI Genfare	3581	6	Gifford's Dairy Inc	2024	76	Ginger Golden Products Inc	2035	51
GFI Group Inc	6211	63	Gift Box Corporation Of America	2674	10	Gingerbread Trim Company Inc	3086	160
GFI Mortgage Bankers Inc	6162	44	Gift Globally LLC	5999	203	Gingko Press Inc	2741	243
GFI Software USA Inc	7372	553	Giftcertificatescom	7379	142	Ginny's Printing Inc	2752	227
GFM Consulting Inc	7372	3350	GigaBeam Acquisition Corp	3663	216	Gino Morena Enterprises LLC	7241	1
GFV Associates Inc	3829	501	Gigacase Corp	7372	4974	Ginsan Industries Inc	3589	78
Gfx International Inc	7336	34	Giganews Inc	4813	383	Ginsburg and Co	7379	1494
GG Barnett Transport Inc	4213	499	Gigaram	3672	161	Ginsburg Bakery Inc	5149	77
GG C Inc	3554	31	Gigasoft Inc	7372	4691	Ginsey Industries Inc	2499	25
GG Premier Precision Inc	3599	1620	Gigatron Software Corp	7372	783	gINT Software Inc	7372	2147
GGB Industries Inc	3825	144	Giga-tronics Inc	3825	70	Gioffre Construction Inc	1542	359
GGNSC Holdings LLC	8052	1	Gigavac LLC	3625	288	Gioia P Ambrette Inc	4813	188
Ggp Publishing Inc	2731	335	Giggles N' Hugs Inc	5812	464	Giordano Construction Company Inc	1542	336
Ggs Information Services Inc	2796	7	Gigoptix LLC	3674	270	Giordano Inc	3599	1829
GH Bass and Co	3143	17	GII Solutions Inc	3559	503	Giovonni Foods Inc	5046	344
GH Bent Co	2052	85	G-III Apparel Group Ltd	2399	1	Gipe Automotive East Inc	5013	179
GH Miller and Sons Inc	4213	2624	G-III Brands Ltd	2399	8	Gipson Hoffman and Pancione	8111	366
GH Phipps Construction Companies	1542	106	G-III License Company LLC	2399	3	Giraffics	2759	147
Gh Printing Company Inc	2752	1343	Gil Acquisition LLC	3699	204	Girard Machine Sales	5084	907
GH Smith Construction Inc	1623	702	Gil Sewing Corp	7389	2143	Girard Motors Inc	5511	641
Ghafari Associates Inc	8712	21	Gila Electronics Of Yuma Inc	5065	656	Girard Video Inc	3695	63
GHB Radio Group	4832	55	Gila River Telecommunications Inc	4812	58	Girard Wood Products Inc	2448	24
Ghont Manufacturing Inc	2531	29	Gilbane Inc	1541	16	Girardi Distributors Corp	5181	89
Ghesquiere Plastic Testing Inc	7389	2280	Gilbert and Nash Company Inc	3554	67	Girardin Moulding Inc	3089	1785
GHG Corp	7372	492	Gilbert Architects	8712	180	Girtz Industries Inc	3444	126
GHH Engineering Inc	8711	404	Gilbert Foods Inc	5148	46	GIS Information Systems Inc	7372	293
Ghi Systems Inc	3577	577	Gilbert Group Inc	7819	68	Gischel Mechanical Service Company Inc	3599	1653
Ghilotti Brothers Inc	1795	1	Gilbert H Moen Co	1541	304	Giselle's Travel	4724	72
Ghirardelli Chocolate Co	2066	6	Gilbert Mechanical Contractors Inc	1731	88	Gish Biomedical Inc	3845	67
GHK Co	1311	183	Gilbert Motor Company Inc	5012	134	Gist and Herlin Press Inc	2752	228
GHM Industries Inc	3531	227	Gilbert Security Systems Inc	7381	62	Gitano Software	7372	1821
Ghn-Online Inc	4813	427	Gilco Trucking	4213	2511	Gits Manufacturing Co	3451	48
Gholson Electric Inc	1731	2362	Gilcrest/Jewett Lumber Co	5211	61	Giuffre Buick Inc	5511	795
Ghost Rider Pictures Inc	7812	321	Gilda Industries Inc	2052	43	Giuliani Partners LLC	8742	380
GHP Financial Group	8721	100	Gilderfluke and Co	3625	190	Giuliano-Pagano Corp	2051	112
GHR Advertising Inc	7311	778	Gilead Palo Alto Inc	2836	10	Giumarra Brothers Fruit Co	5148	27
GHR Systems Inc	7371	220	Gilead Sciences Inc	2836	1	Giumarra Vineyards Corp	0172	3
GHS International Inc	3931	12	Giles and Kendall Inc	2436	18	Giusto's Speciality Foods LLC	2041	47
GHS Property and Casualty Insurance Co	6331	373	Giles and Ransome Inc	3599	1954	Givaudan Flavors And Fragrances Inc	2869	25
Ghsp Inc	3714	140	Giles Chemical Corp	2819	99	Give Something Back Inc	5112	89
GHX Industrial LLC	3053	6	Giles Communications LLC	8743	160	GivenHansco Inc	7372	917
GI Endoscopy Center	8011	122	Giles Electric Co	1731	554	Givens Marine Survival Service Co	3069	281
G-I Holdings Corp	2952	1	Giles Enterprises Inc	3556	48	Givens Transportation Inc	4213	931
GI Plastek Wolfeboro	3089	162	Giles Industries Inc	2451	18	Gizmolab Inc	7371	1912
Giacona Container Co	5113	70	Gilford Securities Inc	6211	68	Gizmos-N-Gadjets	3629	122
Giannetti Contracting Corp	1623	488	Gilkey Window Company Inc	3089	437	GJ Chemical Company Inc	5169	87
Giannios Candy Company Inc	2066	30	Gill and Piette Inc	7372	4692	GJ Hopkins Inc	1711	262
Giant Auto Group of Ashland	5511	634	Gill Industres Inc	3469	25	GK and A Advertising Inc	7311	866
Giant Cement Co	3241	18	Gill Industries Inc	3465	10	GK Financing LLC	6153	43
Giant Cement Holding Inc	3241	11	Gill Insurance	6411	266	Gk Industrial	5084	735
Giant Communications Inc	4899	165	Gill Rock Drill Company Inc	3532	44	Gkc Total Solutions Inc	7378	81
Giant Eagle Inc	5411	16	Gill Services Inc	5084	354	Gki Inc	3599	1008
Giant Food Inc	5411	31	Gill Window Company Inc	5211	244	Gkn Aerospace Bandy Machining Inc	3728	111
Giant Food Stores Inc	5411	46	Gilland Electronics	5065	785	Gkn Aerospace Chem-Tronics Inc	3724	22
Giant Horse Printing Inc	2752	1700	Gillani Inc	7372	2146	Gkn Aerospace Transparency System	3089	382
Giant Industries Inc (Toledo Ohio)	3561	138	Gilleland Chevrolet Inc	5511	640	Gkn Armstrong Wheels Inc	3714	267
Giant Janitorial Service Inc	7349	142	Gillen Broadcasting Corp	4832	209	GKN Automotive Inc	3714	82
Gibbs and Associates	7372	3108	Gillespie and Powers Refractory and Engineering Inc	1711	211	Gkn Driveline North America Inc	3714	99
Gibbs College	8221	47	Gillespie Coatings Inc	2851	149	GKN Sinter Metals Inc	3316	4
Gibbs Die Casting Corp	3363	4	Gillespie Corp	8742	616	Gkn Sinter Metals-Germantown Inc	3312	10
Gibbs General Printing Inc	2752	1327				Gkn Westland Aerospace Inc	3728	37
Gibbs Landscape Co	0781	5				GKY and Associates Inc	8711	361
Gibbs M Smith Inc	2731	143				GL Barron Construction Inc	1542	264

Company Name	SIC	Rank
GL Communications Inc	3825	152
GL Engineering Company Inc	3625	303
GL Homes of Florida Corp	1521	8
GL Morris General Building Co	1541	126
GL Nemirow Inc	7311	350
Gl Roth Inc	2392	50
GL Tool and Manufacturing Company Inc	3599	1938
G-L Veneer Company Inc	2435	12
GL Wasko and Sons LLC	4213	3104
Glacier Bancorp Inc	6712	93
Glacier Bank FSB	6035	56
Glacier Bank of Whitefish	6022	125
Glacier Bay Technology	3569	96
Glacier Electric Cooperative Inc	4911	560
Glacier Garlock Bearings	3568	11
Glacier Water Services Inc	5962	2
Gladding Braided Products LLC	2298	9
Glade and Grove Supply Inc	5083	24
Glade Run Lutheran Services	8322	46
Glade's Taffy Town Inc	2064	25
Gladieux Lumber and Supply Company Inc	5211	275
Gladon Company Inc	3086	175
Gladstone Commercial Corp	6531	264
Gladstone Dodge Inc	5511	570
Gladstone International Inc	8743	256
Gladstone Investment Corp	6722	199
Glamos Wire Products Company Inc	3496	91
Glamour Shots Licensing Inc	7221	7
Glaro Inc	2542	54
Glaser Corp	2759	604
Glaser Gas Inc	5984	24
Glaser Weil Fink Jacobs Howard Archen and Shapiro LLP	8111	276
Glasfloss Industries Inc	3564	41
Glasgow Spray-Dry Inc	2023	19
Glasgow Trucking Inc	4213	1490
Glass City Black Brothers United	7389	1531
Glass Components Inc	3559	528
Glass Design Inc	1741	17
Glass Dynamics Inc	3231	50
Glass Expansion Inc	5049	158
Glass Jacobson PA	8721	170
Glass/McClure Inc	7311	310
Glass Menagerie	3229	41
Glass Merchants Inc	5231	11
Glass Technology Inc	3559	536
Glass Trucking Company Inc	4213	577
Glassautomatic Inc	5085	440
Glasscock Company Inc	4213	1352
Glasshouse Technologies Inc	7376	10
Glassline Corp	3545	49
Glassline Inc	2221	47
Glasslock Inc	1799	129
Glassman High Voltage Inc	3679	336
Glasstech Inc	3211	14
Glassworks Plus Inc	7536	3
Glastar Corp	3559	389
Glastender Inc	3589	50
Glastonbury Citizen Inc	2711	491
Glastonbury Press LLC	7389	2503
Glastron Inc	3732	21
Glatt Air Techniques Inc	5084	213
GlaxoSmithKline - USA	2834	3
Glaze Tool And Engineering Inc	3544	486
Glazers Distributers Of Iowa	2064	103
Glazer's Wholesale Drug Company Inc	5182	3
Glazier Foods Co	5141	80
Glazier Trucking Inc	4213	947
Glazing Rubber Products Of Ga Inc	3061	52
Glc Partners	7389	2422
Gleacher and Company Inc	6211	144
Gleacher Investment Corp	6726	5
Gleacher Partners LLC	6211	84
Gleason Corp	2393	3
Gleason Corporation and Precision Products	3069	5
Gleason Corp (Rochester New York)	3541	7
Gleason Cutting Tools Corp	3541	22
Gleason Printing Inc	2752	1647
Gleason Reel Corp	3499	31
Glebar Company Inc	3541	133
Gleco Plating Inc	3471	65
Gledhill Road Machinery Co	3531	129
Gleim Jewelers	3911	42
Gleim Publications Inc	2731	180
Glen Burnie Bancorp	6712	542
Glen Carbide Inc	3544	297
Glen H Womack	5084	267
Glen Magnetics Inc	3612	107
Glen Mauldon Construction	1623	834
Glen Oak Lumber and Milling Inc	2426	3
Glen Rock Building Supply Inc	5031	332
Glen Rose Meat Services Inc	5147	31
Glen Rose Petroleum Corp	1311	253
Glen Wayne Wholesale Bakery Inc	2051	149
Glenborough LLC	6512	58
Glenborough Realty Trust Inc	6798	116
Glenbrook Technologies Inc	3844	31
Glencairn Consulting Group Inc	7379	1639
Glencoe/McGraw-Hill	2731	67
Glencoe US Holdings Ltd	6331	217
Glencom Inc	3663	397
Glencore Ltd	6221	6
Glendale Opthalmology Inc	8011	60
Glendinning Marine Products	3825	106
Glen-Gery Corp	3251	4
Glenkirk	8361	48
Glenmeadow Inc	8361	97
Glenmede Trust Co	6091	2
Glenn and Wright Inc	1541	170
Glenn Associates Inc	7322	116
Glenn Computer	7372	667
Glenn E Thomas Co	5511	537
Glenn Electric Heater Corp	3634	28
Glenn Group	7311	282
Glenn Johnston Inc	1623	175
Glenn M Gelman and Associates	8721	427
Glenn Machine Works Inc	4213	192
Glenn O Hawbaker Inc	1422	9
Glenn Sound Company Inc	3663	378
Glenn Tool Inc	3599	837
Glenn Welt Studios Inc	7372	2111
Glenn-Lee Trucking Company Inc	4213	2038
Glenora Wine Cellars Inc	2084	88
Glenridge Machine Co	3599	708
Glenridge On Palmer Ranch Inc	8361	19
Glenro Inc	3567	68
Glenroy Inc	3081	22
Glens Falls National Bank and Trust	6021	194
Glenside Fire Protection District	7389	1849
Glentek Inc	3621	78
Glenture Group LLC	8742	365
Glenview State Bank	6022	183
Glenwood Financial Group Inc	7389	1672
Glenwood Hot Springs Lodge and Pool Inc	7011	99
Glenwood Manufacturing Co	3537	106
Glenwood Smoked Products Inc	5147	139
Glenwood State Bank	6022	751
Glesco Electric Inc	1731	526
Gless Brothers Inc	4213	1148
Glessner Protective Services Inc	7622	5
Glex Inc	8711	601
GLG Partners Inc	6282	113
Glick Associates Inc	7372	4822
Glick Textiles Inc	5131	39
Glickman Technology Inc	3695	179
Glickstein Laval Carris	8721	392
Gli-Dex Sales Corp	3599	1846
Glik Stores	5651	23
Glimcher Dayton Mall Inc	6519	14
Glimcher Lloyd Center LLC	6531	181
Glimcher Properties LP	6531	37
Glimcher Realty Trust	6798	107
Glimcher SuperMall Venture LLC	6531	274
Glimmerglass Networks Inc	5045	172
Glissen Chemical Company Inc	2841	25
Glit-Microtron	3291	9
Glitsch Technology Corp	8711	482
Glitterwrap Inc	2679	3
Glm Inc	7699	149
Glmnt Corp	3669	79
Global 360 Inc	7372	253
Global Access Communications Inc	4813	447
Global Advance Inc	5065	263
Global Advanced Products LLC	3465	28
Global Adventures LLC	5091	138
Global Aerosystems LLC	3812	46
Global Aircraft Solutions Inc	4581	26
Global American Sales Inc	7373	748
Global Automotive Alliance LLC	3714	84
Global Axcess Corp	7389	523
Global Bancorp	6712	669
Global Brass And Copper Holdings Inc	3351	9
Global Brass And Copper Inc	3351	7
Global Bridge Infotech Inc	7371	963
Global Business Consulting Services Inc	7379	440
Global Business Dimensions Inc	7372	1874
Global Cash Access Holdings Inc	6159	47
Global Cash Access Inc	7379	39
Global Casinos Inc	7993	23
Global CFS Inc	4212	64
Global Circuit Solutions	5065	304
Global CNC Industries Ltd	3545	169
Global Commerce Bank	6022	740
Global Communication	3663	406
Global Communication Semiconductors Inc	3674	126
Global Communications	5065	392
Global Computeronics Inc	5045	645
Global Conference Partners	4813	216
Global Consolidated Services USA Inc	7379	1050
Global Controls LLC	1623	798
Global Crossing Development Co	4813	95
Global Crossing North American Holdings Inc	4813	77
Global Crossing Telecommunications Inc	4813	85
Global Data Systems	7379	1495
Global Data Systems Inc	7373	155
Global Digital Datacomm Services Inc	4899	212
Global Directions Inc	2721	171
Global Distributors International LLC	5065	744
Global Document Solutions Inc	7331	11
Global Domains International Inc	7389	474
Global Ecology Corp	3812	222
Global Edge Software Inc	7373	79
Global EDM Supplies Inc	5084	609
Global Electric Inc	1731	1982
Global Electro-Communication International Inc	7371	1770
Global Electronic Music Marketplace Inc	7389	1043
Global Employment Solutions Inc	7363	126
Global Energy Inc (Cincinnati Ohio)	8742	444
Global Energy of Hutchinson	5541	58
Global Energy Services Inc	3533	33
Global Engineering Inc	3545	280
Global Enterprises Inc	4213	2337
Global Entertainment Corp	7999	107
Global Environmental Assurance Inc	7389	2112
Global Equipment Company Inc	3559	41
Global Equipment Marketing Inc	3569	56
Global eTelecom Inc	6099	23
Global Factory Inc	7372	330
Global Filtration Inc	5088	105
Global Financial Aid Services Inc	7389	631
Global Financial Services Inc	7379	105
Global Finishing Solutions LLC	3444	63
Global Fire and Safety	5063	519
Global Flow Technologies	5085	43
Global Foods Processing Inc	2013	88
Global Forestry Management Group	5099	28
Global Forex Trading Ltd	6211	220
Global Gateway Communications Inc	4813	623
Global Gauge Corp	3829	297
Global Geophysical Services Inc	1382	19
Global Gold Corp	1041	26
Global Graphics Software Inc	7372	706
Global Ground Support LLC	3537	34
Global Group Inc	2752	455
Global Harvest Foods Ltd	2048	9
Global Health Management Systems Inc	7389	1989
Global Healthcare Exchange LLC	7389	119
Global Home Video Inc	7812	226
Global Imaging Finance Co	5044	29
Global Imaging Systems Inc	5049	3
Global Impressions Inc	2752	1636
Global Inc	3599	1525
Global Industrial Components Inc	5085	165
Global Industrial Technologies Inc	3297	1
Global Industries Inc (Grand Island Nebraska)	3499	32
Global Industries Ltd	1389	14
Global Information Distribution Inc	3695	55
Global Insight Inc	8742	121
Global Intelligence Network LLC	8732	79
Global Intellisystems LLC	7319	170
Global Interactive Solutions LLC	5731	252
Global Internet Management Corp	7371	718
Global Investment Management Inc	3578	44
Global IP Solutions Inc	4899	140
Global It Solutions Usi Inc	7371	1399
Global Kitting Systems Co	3559	507
Global Knowledge Inc	7379	45
Global Knowledge Network Inc	8331	1
Global Link Language Services Inc	7389	852
Global Link Networking Solutio	5065	186
Global Link Solutions Inc	7379	899
Global Links Corp	7372	5053
Global Lion Group Inc	7389	2241
Global Machine Works Inc	3599	1072
Global Management Company LLC	8742	624
Global Management Systems Inc	7373	209
Global Management Technologies Corp	7372	1709
Global Manufacturing Inc	3535	171
Global Manufacturing Of Acadiana Inc	3599	1904
Global Manufacturing Services Inc	3672	263
Global Market Insite Inc	7371	75
Global Mechanical Inc	1623	494
Global Med Technologies Inc	8741	161
Global Medical Imaging LLC	5047	137
Global Micro Solutions Inc	7372	4132
Global Micro-Parts Depot Inc	5064	184
Global Midrange Technologies Inc	5045	866
Global Mine Service Inc	5063	346
Global Minerals Corp	5052	11
Global Netoptex Inc	1731	690
Global Networx Inc	3663	409
Global News Enterprises LLC	7299	32
Global Oil Tools Inc	3533	101
Global Optics San Antonio LP	1731	996
Global Packaging Inc	2759	104
Global Partners LP	5171	2
Global Parts Inc	5088	36
Global Payments Inc	7389	28
Global Performance	1541	198
Global Plastics Inc	3089	855
Global Polymer Industries Inc	3089	610
Global Power Equipment Group Inc	5084	6
Global Power Technology Inc	8711	446
Global Preferred Holdings Inc	6311	245
Global Print and Design	2752	1808
Global Procurement Solutions Inc	3559	362
Global Publishing Inc	3695	27
Global Real Estate Investors and Financial Services Inc	7389	2157
Global Relief Technologies LLC	7371	442

Company Name Index GOLDEN

Company Name	SIC	Rank
Global Satcom Technology Inc	3663	192
Global Scholar	7372	3116
Global Science and Technology Inc	7373	197
Global Security Inc	8742	436
Global Semisolutions Inc	5065	314
Global Service Solutions Inc	4813	72
Global Shop Solutions Inc	7372	2043
Global Soft Digital Solutions Inc	2752	390
Global Software Corp	7373	756
Global Software Inc	7372	1336
Global Software Resources Inc	7372	1263
Global Software Solutions	5734	488
Global Software Technologies Inc	7371	1837
Global Solar Energy Inc	3674	166
Global Solutions Network Inc	7371	789
Global Solutions Systems Inc	7371	1158
Global Sports Marketing Corp	4833	230
Global Strategic Solutions LLC	7379	1610
Global Supply Solutions LLC	4731	60
Global System Services Corp	7373	1082
Global Systems and Strategies	7373	381
Global Technologies Group Inc	3661	109
Global Technologies Inc	3357	52
Global Technologies Inc (Atlanta Georgia)	7371	724
Global Technology Associates Inc	7372	1977
Global Technology Associates Ltd	7363	132
Global Technology Group Ltd	5084	315
Global Technology Systems Consortium Inc	7371	546
Global Techpro LLC	7373	609
Global Telecom and Technology Inc	4813	113
Global Telecom Inc	4813	191
Global Textile Services LLC	2273	25
Global Tool and Manufacturing Co	3599	918
Global Tooling Systems Inc	3545	41
Global Trade Information Services Inc	7372	556
Global Trading And Sourcing Corp	5084	333
Global Traffic Network Inc	7389	216
Global Transportation Services Inc	4731	58
Global Trust Bank	6022	796
Global Tube Form Partners LLC	3498	42
Global Turbine Support LLC	7699	257
Global Turnkey Systems Inc	7372	420
Global Velocity Inc	4813	201
Global Vision Systems	3669	227
Global Water Group Inc	4952	9
Global Water Technologies Inc	8711	128
Global Weather Dynamics Inc	7372	1710
Global Wedge Inc	8999	100
Globalcynex Inc	7371	354
GlobalFluency	4899	21
GlobalHue	7311	41
GlobalLearningSystems Inc	2741	161
GlobalLogic	7372	2
GlobalMedia Group LLC	7375	87
GlobalOptions Group Inc	8742	716
Global-Pc Networks Inc	4813	446
Globalscape Inc	7372	1321
Globalscope Communications Corp	4813	665
GlobalSim Inc	8299	43
Globalstar Inc	4899	60
Globalstar LLC	4812	33
GlobalTec Solutions LLP	7372	168
GlobalTranz Inc	4731	53
Globalvision Inc	7812	301
Globalware Solutions	7372	418
Globe Bancorp Inc	6712	725
Globe Communications Inc	1731	297
Globe Contractors Inc	1623	449
Globe Dynamics International Inc	3599	2182
Globe Electric Supply Company Inc	5063	507
Globe Electronic Hardware Inc	3451	149
Globe Engineering Company Inc	3728	59
Globe Equipment Company Inc	5046	184
Globe Fire Sprinkler Corp	3569	112
Globe Life and Accident Insurance Co	6311	175
Globe Lithographing Company Inc	2752	1154
Globe Machine Company And Metal Fabricators Inc	3599	1080
Globe Machine Manufacturing Co	3553	6
Globe Mechanical and Electrical LLC	7539	16
Globe Mortgage America LLC	6162	111
Globe Motors	3621	9
Globe Newspaper Company Inc	2711	83
Globe Office Equipment And Supplies Inc	5021	113
Globe Petroleum Inc	5983	27
Globe Plastics Inc	3089	1606
Globe Products Inc	3599	1905
Globe Scientific Inc	5047	233
Globe Specialty Metals Inc	3313	4
Globe Storage and Moving Co	4213	1938
Globe Technologies Corp	3469	290
Globe Trailer Manufacturing Inc	5012	97
Globe Transport Inc	4213	145
Globe Turbocharger Specialties Inc	3714	402
Globe Union Group Inc	3261	2
Globecomm Systems Inc	3663	29
Globecot Inc	7375	167
Globexplorer LLC	4813	313
Globoforce Ltd	7372	589
Globtek Inc	3612	30
Globus Inc	1731	2477

Company Name	SIC	Rank
Glock Inc	3484	19
Glockner Chevrolet Company Inc	5511	203
GLoomis Inc	3949	151
Glo-Quartz Electric Heater Company Inc	3567	91
Glory (USA) Inc	5087	14
Glorybee Natural Sweeteners Inc	5149	129
Gloucester Associates Inc	3599	1112
Gloucester Dispatch Inc	4213	2084
Glouster Township	7389	1534
Glove House Inc	8322	117
Glover Oil Company Inc	5171	35
Glover Printing Inc	2752	856
Glover Wholesale Inc	5141	119
Glover's Transmission And Rear End Inc	5012	103
Glow Electric Co	1731	311
Glowa Manufacturing Inc	3577	395
Glowing Designs	7336	311
Glowpoint Inc	4813	165
GlowTouch Technologies	8748	253
Gls Co	2752	262
Glu Mobile Inc	7372	591
Gluefast Company Inc	2891	115
Glunt Industries Inc	3599	210
Glunz and Jensen K and F Inc	3555	27
Gluth Brothers Construction Inc	1623	492
GLW Inc	3651	114
Glw Specialty LLC	7373	763
GLY Construction Company Inc	1542	90
Glycomed Inc	8731	125
Glynn Trolz And Associates Inc	5013	200
GlynnDevins Inc	7311	199
Glynn-Johnson Corp	3429	34
Glyph Media Group Inc	2741	478
Glyph Systems LP	7372	3371
Glyph Technologies Inc	3572	50
Glyphix Studio Inc	7336	293
GM Allen and Son Inc	2037	50
GM Associates Inc	3679	351
Gm Cable Contractors Inc	1731	583
GM Offshore Inc	1382	1
GM Service Parts Operation	5013	4
GM Service Parts Operations	5013	5
GMA Electrical Corp	1731	305
Gma Tooling	3544	415
GMAC Commercial Credit LLC	6159	2
GMAC Financial Services LLC	6289	15
GMAC Global Relocation Services	8742	265
GMAC Insurance	6311	123
GMAC Insurance Holdings Inc	6331	62
GMAC Residential Holding Corp	6719	7
GMB Architects-Engineers	8712	110
Gmb Plastics Inc	2821	125
GMC Inc	3272	125
GMC Software Technology Inc	7372	1891
GMF Industries Inc	3449	14
Gmg Solutions LLC	7379	1418
GMH Engineering Inc	3825	313
Gmi Building Services Inc	7349	103
GMI Composites Inc	3089	1026
Gmi Group Inc	7349	329
Gmi Holdings Inc	3699	30
GMI Sound Corp	7389	2499
GMM Research Corp	3577	601
Gmmb Inc	8743	58
GMP Companies Inc	2834	24
Gmp Laboratories Of America Inc	2834	275
Gmp Manufacturing Inc	2099	316
Gmr Enterprises Inc	2771	21
GMR Marketing LLC	8742	60
GMR Technology Inc	3089	1429
Gms Electrical Contractors Corp	1731	2358
Gms Elevator Services Inc	3534	23
GMS Group LLC	6211	54
GMS International Inc	5045	847
Gmt Inc	3089	1234
GMX Resources Inc	1311	113
GN Inc	5063	887
GN Netcom Inc	3661	25
GN Resound North America	3842	66
Gnames Media Group Inc	7331	283
Gnb Corp	3541	80
GNB Management LLC	6022	827
GNC Franchising Inc	6794	21
GNC Holdings Inc	5499	5
Gnd Systems	5734	260
Gnome Digital Media	8331	238
Gnuco LLC	7371	339
GNW Machine Inc	3599	1155
GNW-Evergreen Insurance Services LLC	6411	120
Go Daddy Group Inc	7372	275
Go E BizCom	7374	294
Go Electronics Inc	5063	164
Go Inc	4833	234
Go Mini's	4789	28
Go Plastics LLC	3089	1015
Go The Travel Co	4724	123
Go West Presents	7922	62
Go Wireless Inc	5999	268
Goad Lumber Company Inc	5031	393
GoAhead Software Inc	7372	1859
Gobal Income Fund Inc	6726	97

Company Name	SIC	Rank
Gobble-Fite Lumber Company Inc	5211	139
Godbersen-Smith Construction Company Inc	3531	38
Goddard Valve Corp	3679	452
Godfrey and Kahn	8111	96
Godfrey Chevrolet-Buick Inc	5511	1084
Godfrey Design Consultants Inc	7389	1257
Godfrey Electric Inc	1731	1414
Godfrey Transport Inc	4213	310
Godfrey Trucking Inc	4213	1173
Godinger Silver Art Company Ltd (New York New York)	5094	7
Godiva Chocolatier Inc	2066	3
Godwin Corp	8021	8
Godwin Craig Inc	3533	89
Godwin Manufacturing Company Inc	3713	34
GodwinGroup	7311	149
Godwin-Sbo LP	3599	67
GOE Enterprises Ltd	4213	1664
Goebel Fixture Co	2521	13
Goeken Group Corp	3663	206
Goelzer Investment Management Inc	6211	150
Goeman Trucking Ltd	4213	1774
GoEngineer	7373	477
Goes Lithographing Company Inc	2752	599
Goetsch's Welding and Machine Inc	3599	767
Goettler Associates	7375	101
Goettsch International Inc	5084	603
Goettsch Partners	8712	194
Goetz Printing Co	2752	1041
Goetze's Candy Company Inc	2064	49
Goex Corp	3081	63
Goff Inc	3531	109
Goff Investment Group LLC	5113	68
Goffa International Corp	5092	29
Goglanian Bakeries Inc	5149	76
Go-Glass Corp	5039	33
Gogotech Inc	5731	48
Gohmann Asphalt And Construction Inc	1611	51
Gohrs Printing Service Inc	2752	617
GoIndustry Michael Fox International	7389	59
GoIndustry USA Inc	7389	652
Gojo Industries Inc	2842	15
Gokoh Corp	5085	59
Golan's Moving and Storage Inc	4213	2060
Gold and Associates PA	8111	399
Gold and Reiss Corp	5031	149
Gold and Siver Buyers	5094	32
Gold Arc Inc	5031	402
Gold Banc Corporation Inc	6712	125
Gold Bond Inc	3993	21
Gold Coast Beverage Distributors Inc	5181	9
Gold Coast Broadcasting LLC	4832	77
Gold Coast Freightways Inc	4213	450
Gold Coast Security Inc	1731	1618
Gold Crest Distributing LLC	5099	45
Gold Eagle Co	5013	81
Gold Effects Inc	3471	128
Gold Hill Inc	7372	3209
Gold Key Processing Inc	3069	68
Gold Line Connectors Inc	3825	87
Gold Medal Bakery Inc	2051	37
Gold Medal Hair Products Inc	5961	169
Gold Medal Packing Inc	2011	159
Gold Mills Inc	2258	8
Gold Nugget Publications Inc	2711	696
Gold Pure Food Products Company Inc	2035	22
Gold Reserve Inc	1041	20
Gold Seal Inc	3999	190
Gold Standard Baking Inc	2051	136
Gold Standard Enterprises Inc	5921	4
Gold Standard Inc (Tampa Florida)	7372	3109
Gold Star Chili Inc	2099	101
Gold Star Marble Corp	3281	56
Gold Star Mortgage Financial Group LLC	6162	123
Gold Star Sausage Co	2013	169
Gold Street Entertainment	3695	163
Gold Systems Inc	7372	354
Gold Type Business Machines Inc	5045	439
Goldak Inc	3812	154
Goldberg and Solovy Food Inc	5141	87
Goldberg Companies Inc	6552	240
Goldberg Fossa Seid Advertising	7311	538
Goldberg Katzman and Shipman PC	8111	458
Goldberger Company LLC	3942	17
Goldberg's Furniture	5712	30
Goldco Industries Inc	3537	41
Gold-Data	7372	1642
Gold-Eagle Coop	5153	20
Golden 1 Credit Union	6062	4
Golden Aluminum Company Inc	3355	3
Golden Artist Colors Inc	3952	6
Golden Banner Press Inc	2752	1124
Golden Bear Golf Inc	8741	214
Golden Belt Telephone Association Inc	4813	369
Golden Boy Pies Inc	2051	250
Golden Bridge Technology Inc	4813	522
Golden Brothers Inc	2512	44
Golden Business Forms Inc	2761	53
Golden Business Machines Inc	7359	105
Golden By-Products Inc	3559	202
Golden Chair Inc	2512	80
Golden Circle Printing Inc	2752	1194

Company Name	SIC	Rank
Golden Color Printing Inc	2752	1400
Golden Companies Inc	5065	37
Golden Corral Corp	5812	132
Golden Crust Bakeries Inc	5149	210
Golden Duck Inc	2015	73
Golden Eagle Insurance Co	6331	106
Golden Eagle Technologies LLC	7389	2392
Golden Enterprises Inc	2096	7
Golden Field Services Inc	8713	3
Golden Flake Snack Foods Inc	2096	8
Golden Fortune Semiconductor Inc	5063	906
Golden Franchising Corp	6794	121
Golden Furrow Fertilizer Inc	0711	2
Golden Gate Capital	6722	122
Golden Gate Glass and Mirror Company Inc	3231	62
Golden Gate Logistics LLC	4731	31
Golden Gate Service Inc	7349	96
Golden Gravel Co	1442	52
Golden Grove Trading Inc	5094	72
Golden Hawk Technology	7372	4823
Golden Isles Supply Company Inc	5063	1016
Golden Key Group LLC	7361	168
Golden Krust Caribbean Bakery Inc	2038	48
Golden Manufacturing Company Inc	2311	20
Golden Minerals Co	1041	16
Golden Neo-Life Diamite International LLC	5122	57
Golden Pacific Electronics Inc	3612	38
Golden Peanut Company LLC	2099	20
Golden Platter Foods Inc	2015	63
Golden Pond Resident Care Corp	8361	134
Golden Ribbon Corp	3955	10
Golden Ring Trucking Inc	4213	592
Golden River Fruit Company Inc	0723	23
Golden Road Industries Inc	5045	426
Golden Road Motor Inn Inc	7011	152
Golden Ross Industries Inc	3842	200
Golden Rule Financial Corp	6311	106
Golden Software Inc	7372	2982
Golden Southern Chicken Corp	6794	103
Golden Specialty Foods LLC	2032	35
Golden Star Holdings Ltd	1041	13
Golden Star Resources Ltd	1041	5
Golden Star Technology Inc	3571	43
Golden State Bank	6022	782
Golden State Boring and Pipe Jacking Inc	1623	338
Golden State Electrical Contractors Inc	1731	1355
Golden State Foods Corp	5199	1
Golden State Health Centers Inc	8059	3
Golden State Water Co	4941	11
Golden States Engineering Inc	3549	17
Golden Sun Feeds Inc	2048	20
Golden Sun Inc	2844	119
Golden Sunlight Mines Inc	1041	15
Golden Surplus	5045	447
Golden Transfer Co	4213	1259
Golden Valley Bank	6022	686
Golden Valley Electric Association	4911	156
Golden Valley Products Inc	2759	559
Golden West Homes	2451	13
Golden West Pipe and Supply Company Inc	5074	151
Golden West Technology	3672	234
Golden West Telecommunications Cooperative Inc	4813	70
Golden West Towing Equipment Inc	7549	23
Goldendale Aluminum Co	3334	8
Goldenrod	2064	36
GoldenRom Inc	3695	48
GoldenSource	7373	99
Goldentree Asset Management LP	6282	155
GoldenWest Lubricants Inc	2992	15
Golder Associates Inc (Atlanta Georgia)	8711	8
Golder Ranch Fire District	7389	1020
Goldfarb Electric Supply Company Inc	5063	464
Goldfield Corp	1731	137
Goldilocks Corporation Of California	2051	158
Goldin Associates LLC	6282	351
Goldin Metals Inc	3448	37
Golding Farms Foods Inc	2099	254
Golding Transport Inc	4213	2157
Goldline Controls Inc	3822	20
Goldman Sachs Group Inc	6211	5
Goldman Sachs Private Equity Group	6799	52
Goldner Associates Inc	5199	64
Goldner Hawn Johnson and Morrison Inc	6282	137
Goldon Windows and Mirrors Inc	5031	294
Gold's Gym International Inc	6794	93
Goldsboro Milling Company Inc	2048	3
Goldsmith Agio Helms and Co	6211	96
Goldsmith and Eggleton Inc	5169	51
Goldsmith and Hull A PC	7322	184
Goldsmith Associates Inc	1731	435
Goldstar Group Inc	6531	357
Goldstar Machine and Tool Limited Co	3599	843
GoldStar Products Company Ltd	5078	12
Goldstar U S A Inc	5021	159
Goldstein Schecter Price Lucas Horwitz and Co	8721	110
Goldstone Land Company LLC	2084	83
Goldtier Technologies LLC	7379	1294
GoldToeMoretz LLC	2251	2
Goldwell Of New York Inc	5087	46
Goleta Water District	4941	44
Golf Apparel Brands Inc	2339	42
Golf Associates Advertising Company Inc	2752	756
Golf Channel	4841	36
Golf Coast Products LLC	3829	374
Golf Diagnostic Imaging Center	8071	51
Golfsmith International Holdings Inc	3949	18
Golfview Developmental Center Inc	8361	120
Goli Enterprises Inc	5064	107
Golin/Harris International	8743	33
GoLive! Mobile	7819	26
Golling Pontiac Gmc Truck Inc	5511	1190
Gollust Management	6799	264
Golub Capital	6799	66
Golub Corp	5411	45
Golubitsky Corp	5734	452
Gomembers Inc	7372	2047
Gomez Inc	7372	921
Gone Wired Cafe	4813	719
Gonnella Baking Co	2051	52
Gonzales Boring and Tunneling Company Inc	1623	680
Gonzales Communications Inc	1731	1307
Gonzales Electric Service Inc	1731	2350
Gonzales Electrical Systems LLC	3613	111
Gonzales Industrial X Ray Inc	8734	194
Gonzalez Design and Engineering Inc	8711	31
Gonzalez Production Systems Inc	3544	22
Gooby Industries Corp	2657	29
Gooch and Housego LLC (Melbourne Florida)	3827	63
Good Advertising Inc	7311	495
Good Advice Press	2731	359
Good Chevrolet Inc	5511	783
Good Earth Organics Corp	5191	38
Good Earth Teas	2099	67
Good Earth Tools Inc	3531	81
Good Enterprises Ltd	2731	268
Good Harbor Fillet Company LLC	2092	57
Good Home Co	2844	164
Good L Corp	3089	1333
Good Life Broadcasting Inc	4833	239
Good News Broadcasting Association Inc	4832	71
Good News Publishing Company Inc	2721	318
Good Old Days Foods Inc	2024	41
Good Printers Inc	2752	637
Good Radio Tv LLC	4832	167
Good Samaritan Health System	8062	62
Good Samaritan Hospital Of Lebanon Pennsylvania	8062	147
Good Shepherd-Fairview Home Inc	8361	93
Good Times Drive Thru Inc	5812	326
Good Times Restaurants Inc	5812	346
Good Transport Services Inc	4213	1520
Good Will Publishers Inc	2731	151
Goodby Silverstein and Partners	7311	23
Goodbye Blue Monday Inc	2396	37
Goodcopy Printing Center Inc	7334	35
Goode Investment Management Inc	6722	234
Goode Motor Inc	5511	1216
Goodell DeVries Leech and Dann LLP	8111	291
Gooder-Henrichsen Company Inc	3441	173
Goodhart Sons Inc	3443	92
Goodheart-Willcox Company Inc	2731	120
Goodhue County Cooperative Electric Association	4911	72
Goodin Co	5074	50
Goodin Electric Inc	1731	1550
Gooding Company Inc	2754	28
Gooding Rubber Co	5085	169
Gooding Simpson and Mackes Inc	1761	23
Goodlander and Co	8721	289
Goodlin Systems Inc	5087	199
Goodluck Refrigeration Service	4213	1027
Goodman Ball Inc	3621	83
Goodman Consulting and Technology LLC	7373	614
Goodman Factors	7389	741
Goodman Food Products	2038	22
Goodman Global Inc	3585	10
Goodman Main Stopper Manufacturing Company Inc	3494	78
Goodman Networks Inc	7373	52
Goodman Tank Lines Inc	4213	2360
Goodman Truck and Tractor Company Inc	5511	1209
Goodman's Inc (Phoenix Arizona)	5712	29
Goodnature Products Inc	3556	156
Goodnight Brothers Produce Company Inc	5147	78
Goodrich Corp	2891	1
Goodrich Fuel and Utility Systems	3561	19
Goodrich Petroleum Corp	1311	79
Goodrich Petroleum Corporation Incorporated of Louisiana	1311	115
Goodrich Sensor Systems Div	3812	28
Goodson Electric Inc	1731	2566
Goodson Farms Inc	5148	41
Goodsx Ltd	7371	1224
Goodway Graphics Inc	2752	70
Goodway Graphics Of Virginia Inc	2752	175
Goodway Group Inc	2759	35
Good-West Rubber Corp	3069	79
Goodwill Industries Of Akron Ohio Inc	8331	54
Goodwill Industries Of Central Florida Inc	8331	31
Goodwill Industries of Greater Detroit	8331	41
Goodwill Industries Of Hawaii Inc	8331	33
Goodwill Industries Of Northern New England	8331	16
Goodwill Industries Of Rhode Island	8249	15
Goodwill Industries Of Southwestern Michigan	8331	88
Goodwill Industries Of Wayne And Holmes Counties Inc	8331	228
Goodwill Industries Rehabilitation Center Inc	8322	60
Goodwill Industries Vocational Enterprises Inc	8331	119
Goodwill Of Silicon Valley	7363	144
Goodwill Printing Co	2752	680
Goodwin Ammonia Co	2842	41
Goodwin Biotechnology Inc	2834	186
Goodwin Brothers Printing Co	2752	1258
Goodwin Graphics Inc	2752	794
Goodwin Procter LLP	8111	17
Goodyear Tire and Rubber Co	3011	2
Goody-Goody Liquor Store Inc	5921	20
Google Inc	7379	1
Goold Electric Inc	1731	1656
Goolsby Trucking Company Inc	4213	1786
Gooseneck Trailer Manufacturing Company Inc	3715	40
Gopher Electronics Co	5063	193
Gorant Chocolatier LLC	5441	2
Gorbel Inc	3536	12
Gordmans Stores Inc	5311	28
Gordon Advisors PC	8721	405
Gordon Aluminum Industries Inc	3354	27
Gordon and Zoerb Electrical Contractors Inc	1731	1245
Gordon Arata McCollam Duplantis Eagan LLP	8111	486
Gordon Bernard Company Inc	5199	84
Gordon Bernard Company LLC	2752	743
Gordon Biersch Brewery Restaurant Group Inc	5812	235
Gordon Brothers Corp	6799	115
Gordon Brothers Wholesale LLC	5137	5
Gordon Composites	3296	12
Gordon E And Betty I Moore Foundation	8748	33
Gordon Engineering Corp	3823	398
Gordon Feinblatt Rothman Hoffberger and Hollander LLC	8111	363
Gordon Food Company Inc	5143	43
Gordon Food Service Inc	5141	10
Gordon Haskett and Co	7389	2091
Gordon Haskett and Co	7372	2598
Gordon J Gow Technologies	5063	610
Gordon Laboratories Inc	2844	43
Gordon Paper Company Inc	2679	23
Gordon Rountree Motors Ltd	5511	1234
Gordon Rubber And Packing Company Inc	3069	233
Gordon Sevig Trucking Co	4213	267
Gordon Technical Consultants Inc	7389	956
Gordon Thomas Honeywell LLP	8111	403
Gordon Trucking Inc	4213	141
Gordon Waste Company Inc	5093	133
Gordon-Cross Inc	3669	209
Gordongraphics Inc	2752	1657
Gordon-Palmgren Inc	1623	369
Gordon's Div	5944	7
Gordons International Services Inc	5092	40
Gore Reporting Company Inc	7338	19
Gorecki Manufacturing Inc	3549	84
Gorell Enterprises Inc	3499	45
GoRemote Internet Communications Inc	7375	81
Gore's Inc	2026	37
Gores Technology Group	6799	132
Gorilla Graphics Inc	7334	94
Gorilla Polymedia	7336	164
Gorlitz Sewer and Drain Inc	3589	188
Gorm Inc	5087	143
Gorman Machine Corp	3549	109
Gorman Milling Company Inc	2048	23
Gorman Richardson Architects Inc	8712	259
Gorman-Redlich	3679	874
Gorman-Rupp Co	3561	30
Gorman-Rupp Industries	3561	75
Gorman's Inc	5712	64
Gortons	2092	3
Goshen Community Bank	6022	629
Goshen Hospital Association Inc	8062	118
Goshen Stamping Company Inc	3469	175
Gosiger Inc	5084	78
Gospel Advocate Co	5942	31
Gospel Light Publications	2731	142
Gosport Manufacturing Company Inc	2394	28
Goss Inc	3548	28
Goss International Corp	3555	2

Company Name	SIC	Rank
Gossen Corp	2431	26
Gossner Foods Inc	2022	30
Got Clicks	7389	2371
Gotham Direct	7319	64
Gotham Dream Cars LLC	5599	21
Gotham Inc	7311	104
Gotham Ink and Color Company Inc	2893	27
Gotham Sales Co	5064	14
Gotham Writers' Workshop	8331	151
Goto California Inc	3651	71
Gotoh Distribution Service	4213	1841
Gotta Have Dvd Inc	3695	88
Gottaplay Interactive Inc	7372	4693
Gottlieb Inc	5051	443
Gottschall Tool and Die Inc	3544	642
Goudy Honda Inc	5511	334
Gough Econ Inc	3535	133
Gougler Industries Inc	3533	34
Gould and Associates Global Services Inc	8742	580
Gould and Bass Company Inc	3825	169
Gould and Goodrich Inc	3199	12
Gould and Lamb LLC	6411	229
Gould Electronics Inc	3399	26
Gould Evans Affiliates	8712	65
Gould Paper Corp	5111	5
Gould Technology LLC	3229	33
Goulet Trucking Inc	4213	2061
Goulston Technologies Inc	2843	3
Gourmet Bakery Inc	2051	239
Gourmet Boutique LLC	2099	92
Gourmet Kitchens Inc	5149	124
Gourmet Mushrooms	0182	7
Gourmet Services Inc	8741	58
GourmetGiftBasketscom	5947	15
Gouverneur Bancorp Inc	6712	664
Gouverneur Savings and Loan Association	6035	181
GovConnection Inc	8299	16
GovDelivery Inc	7372	1222
Governair Corp	3585	77
Government Acquisitions Inc	5045	238
Government Contracting Resources Inc	8744	52
Government Data Publication	2731	270
Government Employees Credit Union	6061	47
Government Employees Insurance Co	6331	26
Government Intelligence and Proposal Resources Inc	7374	380
Government Network Solutions	5065	937
Government Properties Income Trust	6798	119
Government Scientific Source Inc	5049	14
Government Service Automation Inc	7373	625
Government Systems Inc	7371	1314
Government Systems Technologies Inc	8711	178
Government Technology Services Inc	5045	32
Governmentquotecom	7377	32
Governor's Distributing LLC	5194	22
Govolution Inc	7379	632
Gowan Company LLC	2879	12
Gowan Milling Company LLC	2879	19
GOW-MAC Instrument Co	3826	95
Goya Foods Inc	2032	7
Goyal Industries Inc	3441	261
Goyette Machine Associates Inc	3599	2501
Goyette Mechanical Company Inc	1711	91
GP Batteries Marketing (Latin America) Inc	5063	1039
Gp Companies Inc	5084	381
Gp Foam Fabricators Inc	2392	46
GP International Engineering and Simulation Inc	7373	575
GP Johnston Inc	5065	180
GP Manufacturing Inc	3599	2147
G-P Plastics Inc	3089	1697
Gp Solutions Inc	5045	684
GP Strategies Corp	8742	58
GP Systems Inc	5731	82
GPC Capital Corporation II	3089	25
Gpd Global Inc	3823	192
Gpd Optoelectronics Corp	3674	303
Gpk Products Inc	3089	254
G-Plex Inc	7331	176
GPS Holding LP	7374	21
Gps Information Guidance LLC	7371	1166
GPS Insight LLC	5049	57
Gps Networking Inc	3663	270
Gps Source Inc	3674	426
GPX Inc (Zelienople Pennsylvania)	7699	26
GR Daniels Trucking Inc	4213	2490
GR Leonard and Co	2741	185
GR Mccoy Inc	5999	215
Gr Spring and Stamping Inc	3496	13
GR Wood Inc	5031	366
GRA Inc	8732	118
Graa LP	5012	111
Gra-Bell Truck Line Inc	4213	654
Graber-Rogg Inc	3089	306
Graber's Kountry Korner	2051	296
Grabill Cabinet Company Inc	2431	51
Grabill Country Meat 1 Inc	5149	203
Grace and Wild Inc	7812	29
Grace Brothers Ltd	6211	222
Grace Communications Inc	2711	453
Grace Composites LLC	3432	37

Company Name	SIC	Rank
Grace Davison	2899	11
Grace Davison Discovery Sciences	3531	2
Grace Engineering Corp	3544	127
Grace Equity It Resource Corp	7379	1340
Grace Foods Inc	5411	232
Grace Holmes Inc	5611	13
Grace Manufacturing Inc	3577	299
Grace Pacific Corp	1611	17
Grace Technology Solutions	7371	1191
Graceland Fruit Inc	2034	19
Gracion Software	7372	4694
Graco Children's Products Inc	2514	1
Graco Children's Products Inc Century Products Div	2531	5
Graco Fertilizer Co	2875	25
Graco Inc	3586	4
Graco Minnesota Inc	3586	2
Gracy Woods Ii Nursing Center	8741	268
Gradall Co	3531	115
Gradall Industries Inc	3537	14
Gradick Communications Inc	4832	254
Gradient Corp	8748	134
Gradient Lens Corp	3827	144
Graduate Supply House Inc	7299	39
Grady Britton Advertising	7311	354
Grady Brothers Inc	1611	41
Grady Crawford Construction Company Incorporated Of Baton Rouge	1623	69
Grady Electric Membership Corp	4911	535
Grady Environmental Services Inc	1521	128
Grady Management Inc	6531	49
Grady R Jolley Electrical Contractors Inc	1731	1697
Graef Anhalt Schloemer and Associates Inc	8999	61
Graessle-Mercer Co	2752	1517
Graeter's Manufacturing Co	2024	24
Graetz Manufacturing Inc	3523	126
Graf Creamery Inc	2021	5
Graff California Wear Inc	2337	6
Graff Valve and Fittings Inc	5085	356
Grafica Inc	7311	289
Grafica Interactive	2741	298
Grafik Industries Ltd	2759	279
Grafika Commercial Printing Inc	2759	57
Graftech International Ltd	3624	1
Graftek Imaging	3577	389
Grafton Transit Inc	4213	2889
Grafx Systems	7372	3611
Graham Advertising Of Colorado Inc	7311	1013
Graham and Associates Inc	8732	29
Graham and Dunn PC	8111	259
Graham Cheese Corp	2022	85
Graham Companies Inc	3569	115
Graham Corp	3563	12
Graham Cos	1531	70
Graham County Electric Cooperative Inc	4911	257
Graham Critt Graphic Design Ltd	7336	268
Graham Engineering Corp	3569	38
Graham Ford L and M Inc	5511	1133
Graham Group Inc	6512	75
Graham Group (Lafayette Louisiana)	7311	413
Graham Group (York Pennsylvania)	6722	249
Graham Packaging Holdings Co	3085	1
Graham Research Inc	3599	808
Graham Security Police Inc	7381	174
Graham Ship By Truck Co	4213	2187
Graham Tech Inc	3544	912
Graham Trucking Company Inc	4213	2478
Graham-Field Bandage Inc	5047	121
Graham-Massey Analytical Laboratories Inc	8734	81
Graham-Michaelis Corp	1311	170
Graham-White Manufacturing Co	3743	20
Grain Belt Supply Company Inc	3441	90
Grain Dealers Mutual Insurance Co	6331	352
Grain Processing Corp	2046	2
Grain Store Elevators	5153	125
Grain Valley Tool and Manufacturing Company Inc	3599	1418
Grainger Solutions	7379	1341
Grainland Coop	5153	172
Grakon LLC	3714	250
GRALIN associates Inc	7372	4377
Gramco Inc	2048	39
Gramercy Capital Corp	6798	50
Gramercy Insurance Co	6331	332
GrammaTech Inc	7372	3172
Grammer Dempsey and Hudson Inc	5051	202
Grammer Industries Inc	4213	1152
GramTel LLC	7379	730
Granada Insurance Co	6331	244
Granahan Investment Management Inc	6282	585
Granard Pharmaceutical Sales and Marketing	8999	154
Granary Associates	8712	138
Granbury Contracting and Utilities Inc	1623	692
Grand Aire Inc	4522	22
Grand Blanc Printing Inc	2752	960
Grand Bluff Construction Services LLC	1623	191
Grand Canyon Education Inc	8221	8
Grand Cypress Florida Inc	7011	185

Company Name	SIC	Rank
Grand Electrical Equipment and Supply Corp	5063	663
Grand Entertainment Group Inc	7922	96
Grand Equipment Company LLC	7353	68
Grand Food Center	5411	220
Grand Forks Herald	2711	246
Grand Forms and Systems Inc	2759	593
Grand Furniture Discount Stores Corp	5712	16
Grand Harbor Yacht Sales And Service	3599	2474
Grand Havana Enterprises Inc	5812	397
Grand Haven Bank	6022	487
Grand Haven Gasket Co	3053	103
Grand Home Furnishings	5712	32
Grand Homes Inc	1521	75
Grand Hotel Co	7011	190
Grand Island Contract Carriers	4213	1742
Grand Island Express Inc	4213	558
Grand Products Inc	3999	72
Grand Rapids Chair Co	2511	56
Grand Rapids Controls Company LLC	3625	196
Grand Rapids Foam Technologies Inc	5199	24
Grand Rapids Gravel Co	3273	14
Grand Rapids Machine Repair Inc	7699	140
Grand Rapids Metaltek Inc	3599	1323
Grand Rapids Sash and Door Co	5031	79
Grand Rapids Scale Co	5046	72
Grand Rapids Transport Inc	4213	1244
Grand River Printing Inc	2752	305
Grand Slam Designs	7373	1224
Grand Stage Co	3648	73
Grand Stage Lighting Co	5999	236
Grand Strand Sandwich Co	5149	140
Grand Teton Lithography A Colorworld Printers Company Inc	2752	1743
Grand Teton Lodge Co	7011	133
Grand Transformers Inc	3499	89
Grand Transportation Inc	4213	1544
Grand Traverse Continuous Inc	2761	71
Grand Traverse Machine Co	3599	14
Grand Traverse Pie Co	5812	332
Grand Traverse Plastics Corp	3089	928
Grand Traverse Resort and SpA	7011	58
Grand Traverse Trucking Inc	4213	2015
Grand Valley LP	7011	200
Grand Valley Manufacturing Co	3599	719
Grand Valley Rural Power Lines Inc	4911	542
Grand View Hospital	8062	89
Grand X-Ray Supplies Co	5047	94
Grandbridge Real Estate Capital	6552	69
Grande Communications Holdings Inc	4812	22
Grande Hardware Company Inc	5251	53
Grande Truck Center Inc	5511	506
Grandeur Manufacturing Inc	3599	2069
Grandfather Mountain Inc	7999	140
Grandma LaMure's Spice'n Slice Inc	2099	369
Grandmother's Inc	5812	227
Grandoe Corp	3949	48
Grandview Enterprises Inc	4213	1600
Grandview Products Company Inc	2434	48
Grandview Window and Door Inc	5031	374
Grandville Printing Company Inc	2741	80
Grandy's Inc	5812	278
Grane Transportation Lines Ltd	4213	1242
Grange Cooperative Supply Association	5999	40
Grange Mutual Casualty Co	6411	26
Granger Construction Co	1542	230
Granger John	7373	920
Granger Telecom Corp	7373	654
Granger Trucking Inc	4213	1424
Grangers Cooperative Association	4213	2818
Granicus Inc	7375	152
Granite Bear Development	7372	5093
Granite Broadcasting Corp	4833	102
Granite Business Solutions Inc	5045	727
Granite Canyon Quarry A JV	1423	8
Granite City Electric Supply Co	5063	133
Granite City Electric Supply Co	5063	52
Granite City Food and Brewery Ltd	5812	237
Granite Construction Inc	1611	7
Granite Electronics Inc	5731	91
Granite Furniture Company Inc	5712	35
Granite Group Wholesalers LLC	5074	13
Granite Halmar Construction Company Inc	1611	9
Granite Hardwoods Inc	5031	295
Granite Industries of Vermont Inc	3281	18
Granite Knitwear Inc	2321	26
Granite Ledge Electrical Contractors Inc	1731	2133
Granite Microsystems Inc	3571	70
Granite Mountain Design Inc	3599	1794
Granite Rock Co	5032	4
Granite Savings Bank	6036	104
Granite State Credit Union	6062	24
Granite State Forest Products Inc	2421	138
Granite State Plastics Inc	3089	1224
Granite Telecommunications LLC	4813	49
Granitize Products Inc	2842	68
Granny B's Cookies LLC	2052	82
Granny's Kitchens LLC	2053	4
Granor Price Homes	1522	44
Grant Bennett Accountants	8721	208
Grant Contracting Inc	1731	477

Company Name	SIC	Rank
Grant Geophysical Inc	8711	231
Grant H Rockley	7311	838
Grant Harrison Advertising LLC	7311	769
Grant Industrial Controls Inc	5063	455
Grant Industries Inc	3465	46
Grant Industries Inc (Elmwood Park New Jersey)	2865	18
Grant Iron And Motors Inc	7538	25
Grant Leasing Inc	7359	224
Grant Park Packing Company Inc	5147	83
Grant Street Construction Inc	1623	639
Grant Street Group	7379	179
Grant Thornton International	8721	30
Grant Thornton LLP	8721	30
Grantco Manufacturing Inc	3086	152
Grantham Distributing Company Inc	5181	40
Grantham Mayo Van Otterloo and Co	6282	24
Grant-Pridco-Tube-Alloy	3599	2102
Granum Securities LLC	6211	210
Granutec Inc	3559	329
Granutech-Saturn Systems Corp	3559	136
Granville Bancshares Inc	6712	722
Granville Milling Co	5999	95
Granville Publications Software	7372	4610
Granville-Phillips	3823	170
Grapar Inc	3559	500
Grape Networks Inc	3829	221
Grapecity Inc	7371	1600
Grapevine Trading Inc	5149	134
Graphaids Inc	5049	62
Graphel Corp	5052	9
Graphic Applications Inc	7336	276
Graphic Art Productions Inc	2752	1607
Graphic Arts Ctr Publishing Co	2731	88
Graphic Arts Inc	2752	708
Graphic Binding Inc	2789	110
Graphic Chemical and Ink Company Inc	3952	17
Graphic Communication Specialists Inc	7336	185
Graphic Communications Corp	2752	665
Graphic Communications Inc	2752	1110
Graphic Composition Inc	2791	23
Graphic Composition Inc (Menasha Wisconsin)	2791	44
Graphic Computer Consultants	7379	1608
Graphic Concepts Group Inc	7311	409
Graphic Connections Group LLC	7336	215
Graphic Design Inc	2752	746
Graphic Design Services Inc	7336	33
Graphic Detail Inc	7371	1726
Graphic Developments Inc	2752	796
Graphic Display Systems Inc	3679	697
Graphic Engravers Inc	2796	57
Graphic Enterprises Inc	3861	18
Graphic Finishing Services Inc	2789	89
Graphic Forms and Labels Inc	2752	581
Graphic Globe	7336	273
Graphic Image Corp	2752	1737
Graphic Management Inc	2752	850
Graphic Packaging Holding Co	2657	1
Graphic Packaging Resources	3999	119
Graphic Partners Inc	2752	600
Graphic Printing Corp	2759	245
Graphic Prints Inc	2396	28
Graphic Process Inc	7336	218
Graphic Publications Inc	2711	590
Graphic Research Inc	3679	80
Graphic Research Unlimited Inc	2752	631
Graphic Resources Inc	2621	69
Graphic Response Inc	2752	1836
Graphic Sciences Inc	2893	20
Graphic Services LLC	2731	65
Graphic Solutions Group Inc	2789	22
Graphic Specialties Inc	3497	8
Graphic Systems Group Inc	7384	10
Graphic Systems Inc (Cambridge Massachusetts)	7379	754
Graphic Systems Inc (Memphis Tennessee)	5112	23
Graphic Systems Services Inc	7699	163
Graphic Tech Service LLC	7699	147
Graphic Tool Corp	3089	1493
Graphic Trade Bindery Inc	7331	50
Graphic Visions Group Inc	7336	89
Graphic World Inc	2791	24
Graphica LLC	7336	148
Graphical Dynamics Inc	7372	4695
GraphiCode	7372	2461
Graphics 55 Inc	7311	770
Graphics Arts Production Inc	7336	204
Graphics Development International Inc	7379	1590
Graphics East Inc	2732	40
Graphics Etc La	7336	198
Graphics Group Inc	2759	196
Graphics III Advertising Inc	2791	46
Graphics Microsystems Inc	2759	16
Graphics Plus Inc	2791	57
Graphics Systems Corp	7373	518
Graphics Type And Color Enterprises Inc	2759	415
Graphics Universal Inc	7335	8
Graphik Dimensions Ltd	3499	75
Graphisoft US Inc	7372	2849
Graphite Design International Inc	3949	155

Company Name	SIC	Rank
Graphite Die Mold Inc	3624	19
Graphite Electrodes Ltd	3599	2091
Graphite Sales Inc	3624	14
Graphix Products Inc	2759	140
Graphix Unlimited Inc	2759	298
Graphnet Inc	4813	171
GraphOn Corp	7372	2218
GraphPad Software Inc	7372	4508
Graphsim Entertainment	7372	3797
GraphTec Inc	2752	685
Graphx Inc	7372	4205
Graph-X Inc	7371	1814
Grason Inc	4953	128
Grason-Stadler Inc	3841	162
Grass Valley Group	3663	53
Grass Valley USA LLC	3663	150
Grassfed Livestock Alliance	8742	693
Grassi and Company CPAs PC	8721	76
Grassland Dairy Products Inc	2021	4
Grassland Equipment And Irrigation Corp	5083	22
Grasso Production Management	4522	7
Grassroots Enterprise Inc	7372	2795
Grate Signs Inc	3993	149
Gratis Internet LLC	7319	90
Gratry and Co	6282	467
Grattan Family Enterprises LLC	3714	360
Grattan Line Construction Corp	1623	847
Grav Company LLC	2842	166
Gravcom	7379	1230
Gravel Products Inc	1442	16
Graves and Associates Inc	1611	166
Graves Inc	1731	893
Graves Trucking Inc	4213	2555
Gravic Inc	7372	1565
Gravic Remark Products Group	7371	1613
Gravitate Design Studio	7373	1083
Gravity Payments Inc	7372	2781
GravityFree	7336	78
Gray and Associates LLP	8111	393
Gray and Walter Associates	7389	1258
Gray Audograph Agency Inc	1731	1941
Gray Construction	8711	52
Gray Daniels Auto Group	5012	28
Gray Engineering Laboratories Inc	3861	133
Gray Graphics Corp	2752	621
Gray Gray and Gray LLP	8721	395
Gray Kentucky Television Inc	4833	161
Gray Kirk/VanSant Advertising Inc	7311	151
Gray Lift Inc	5084	279
Gray Manufacturing Company Inc	3569	63
Gray Mold Company Inc	3365	49
Gray Oil Company Inc	5172	15
Gray Plant Mooty PA	8111	119
Gray Printing Co	2752	366
Gray Research Inc	7371	275
Gray Rider Truck Lines Inc	4213	2910
Gray Robinson PA	8111	143
Gray Rock Farms Inc	4213	2674
Gray Supply Corporation 70	5039	50
Gray Television Inc	4833	66
Gray Trucking	4213	2135
Graybar Electric Company Inc	5065	6
Graybill Bartz and Associates Ltd	6282	350
Graybill Electronics Inc	5731	184
Graybill's Tool and Die Inc	8711	633
Graycor Inc	1542	61
Graycor Industrial Constructors Inc	1541	191
Graydon Head and Ritchey LLP	8111	241
Grayhawk LLC	1742	8
Grayhill Inc	3613	22
Graying and Balding Inc	7812	186
Grayline Housewares Inc	3634	36
Grayline Inc	3082	24
Grayline of Seattle	4111	18
GrayMatter Corp	7372	4422
Graymills Corp	3561	111
Graymont Cooperative Association Inc	5153	110
Graymont Inc (Pleasant Gap Pennsylvania)	3274	1
Graymont Materials Inc (Plattsburgh New York)	1429	8
Gray's Ice Cream Inc	5812	461
Grays Petroleum Inc	5172	17
Grayson Armature Large Motor Division Inc	7694	15
Grayson Mitchell Inc	4213	347
Grayson Technologies Inc	7379	1587
Grayson Tool Co	3541	123
Grayson-Collin Electric Coop	4911	395
Graystone Tower Bank	6022	247
Graystone Tower Bank and Mortgage Co	6021	146
GrayTech Software Inc	7372	4423
Graytor Printing Company Inc	2752	632
Graywood Inc	2759	522
Graze Public Relations	8743	128
Graziano Krafft and Zale Inc	7336	270
Grb Holdings Inc	3295	8
Grc Enterprises Inc	2752	895
Grdg Holdings LLC	5945	9
Gre-America Inc	3575	10
Grease Monkey International Inc	7549	20
Great American Bancorp Inc	6712	650

Company Name	SIC	Rank
Great American Bank	6022	800
Great American Dessert Company LLC	2051	184
Great American Financial Resources Inc	6311	63
Great American Insurance Co	6331	95
Great American Lines Inc	4213	579
Great American Products Inc	3914	4
Great American Quilt Factory Inc	2731	238
Great American Tire and Auto Service Center	7538	17
Great American Title Agency	6541	4
Great American Transport Inc	4213	1263
Great American Wirebound Box Company Inc	2449	8
Great Atlantic and Pacific Tea Company Inc	5411	18
Great Atlantic Graphics Inc	2796	20
Great Basin Internet Services Inc	4813	225
Great Bay Services Inc	8331	192
Great Bend Cooperative Association	5153	98
Great Bend Feeding Inc	0211	6
Great Bend Industries	3593	25
Great Big Pictures Inc	7384	12
Great Central Insurance Co	6331	70
Great Central Steel Co	5051	319
Great Circle Ventures Holdings LLC	2339	50
Great Clips Inc	6794	46
Great Coastal Express Inc	4213	318
Great Dane Trailers Inc	5013	11
Great Eastern Color Lithographic Corp	2752	189
Great Florida Bank	6022	110
Great Gourmet Inc	5149	195
Great Harvest Franchising Inc	6794	136
Great Hill Partners LLC	6799	79
Great Lakes Advisors Inc	6282	386
Great Lakes Air Products Inc	3585	101
Great Lakes Automation Supply	5065	253
Great Lakes Aviation Ltd	4512	45
Great Lakes Bank NA	6022	82
Great Lakes Bankers Bank	6022	810
Great Lakes Boat Top Co	2394	5
Great Lakes Cable Communications Inc	1623	292
Great Lakes Calcium Corp	3295	18
Great Lakes Carbon Corp	2999	2
Great Lakes Cartage Co	4213	479
Great Lakes Castings Corp	3321	30
Great Lakes Cheese Company Inc	2022	5
Great Lakes Custom Tool Manufacturing Inc	5072	107
Great Lakes Die Cast Corp	3363	37
Great Lakes Dredge and Dock Co (Oak Brook Illinois)	1629	17
Great Lakes Educational Loan Services Inc	6111	12
Great Lakes Energy	4911	234
Great Lakes Energy Coop	4911	212
Great Lakes Gas Transmission LP	4922	25
Great Lakes Higher Education Corp	6111	11
Great Lakes Hydraulics Inc	3566	42
Great Lakes Industry Inc	3568	54
Great Lakes Integrated Inc	2752	252
Great Lakes International Inc	3589	153
Great Lakes LLC	3565	26
Great Lakes Maintenance and Security Corp	7381	129
Great Lakes Marketing Inc	5141	209
Great Lakes Media Technology Inc	7819	52
Great Lakes Mp	5065	419
Great Lakes Packaging Corp	2653	79
Great Lakes Packing Co	0723	26
Great Lakes Packing Company International Inc	2011	137
Great Lakes Paper Stock Corp	5093	92
Great Lakes Peterbilt Inc	5012	37
Great Lakes Plastics Company Inc	3082	36
Great Lakes Plastics Corp	3089	256
Great Lakes Plumbing and Heating Co	1711	57
Great Lakes Power and Lighting Inc	1731	1274
Great Lakes Pressed Steel Corp	3469	353
Great Lakes Production Support LLC	7389	2092
Great Lakes Publishing Co	2721	180
Great Lakes Publishing Inc	2741	489
Great Lakes Rubber Co	3069	140
Great Lakes Scrip Center Inc	7389	1338
Great Lakes Terminal and Transport	4213	1315
Great Lakes Tissue Company Inc	2621	62
Great Lakes Veneer Inc	5031	120
Great Lakes-Triad Plastic Packaging Corp	2653	95
Great Midwest Bank SSB	6036	58
Great Migrations LLC	7371	1712
Great Neck Saw Manufacturers Inc	5072	46
Great Northern Cabinetry Inc	2434	75
Great Northern Corp	2653	7
Great Northern Gas Co	1381	63
Great Northern Iron Ore Properties	6799	322
Great Northern Transportation Co	4213	2426
Great Northern Wheels Deals Inc	2711	659
Great Northwest Insurance Company Inc	6331	364
Great Pacific Enterprises (US) Inc	3089	105
Great Plains Energy Inc	4911	41
Great Plains Industries Inc	3586	9

Company Name	SIC	Rank
Great Plains Plastic Molding LLC	3089	1647
Great Plains Security Inc	7382	164
Great Plains Stainless	5051	337
Great Plains Trucking Inc	4213	220
Great Planes Model Distributors Co	5092	1
Great Point Investors LLC	6282	198
Great Promotions	5199	130
Great River Contractors LLC	1731	2559
Great River Energy	4911	123
Great Scott Enterprises Inc	7379	755
Great Scott! Productions	7812	194
Great Seats Inc	7922	84
Great South Metals Co	5051	338
Great South Texas Corp	7373	506
Great Southern Bancorp Inc	6712	139
Great Southern Bank	6035	102
Great Southern Bank One LLC	6162	8
Great Southern Capital Corp	6712	638
Great Southern Industries Inc	2653	76
Great Southern National Bank	6021	304
Great Southern Studios	7812	116
Great Southwest Tool Co	3544	668
Great Valley Auto	5511	433
Great Valley Industries Inc	5065	540
Great Valley Systems Corp	5063	714
Great Western Bancorporation Inc	6712	63
Great Western Bank (Watertown South Dakota)	6022	25
Great Western Beef Co	5147	72
Great Western Drilling Company Inc	1311	121
Great Western Electrical Inc	1731	1129
Great Western Inc	5046	349
Great Western Life Insurance Co	6411	21
Great Western Malting Co	2083	1
Great Western Manufacturing Company Inc	3556	58
Great Western Meats Inc	5141	152
Great Western Recycling Industries Inc	4491	12
Great Western Satellite Communications	4841	154
Great Western Securities Inc	6712	41
Great Western Supply Co	5085	130
Great Western Tortilla Co	2096	39
Great White Shark Enterprises Inc	7999	154
Great Wolf Resorts Inc	7011	85
Great Works Internet	4899	137
Greatbatch Inc	3692	2
GreatCall Inc	4899	32
Greater Data and Mailing Inc	7331	238
Greater Des Moines Convention And Visitors Bureau Inc	7389	1341
Greater Houston Group	6531	358
Greater Jersey Press Inc	2711	226
Greater Lafayette Health Services Inc	8062	194
Greater Lynn Senior Services Inc	8322	20
Greater Media Inc	2711	64
Greater Media Newspapers Inc	2711	338
Greater Missouri Builders Inc	1522	51
Greater Nebraska Television Inc	4833	186
Greater New Bedford Community Health Center Inc	8322	67
Greater Philadelphia Radio Group	4832	65
Greater Phoenix Electric Inc	1731	1551
Greater Richmond Transit Co	4131	9
Greater Rochester Advertiser Inc	2741	375
Greater Rochester Independent Practice Association Inc	8011	27
Greater Rockford Auto Auction Inc	5012	109
Greater Sacramento Bancorp	6712	511
Greater St Louis Agility	7389	1584
Greater Talent Network Inc	7389	509
Greater Texas Electric Inc	1731	2445
Greater Texas Federal Credit Union	6061	89
Greater Tri-Cities Services LLC	5962	18
GreaterValue	7389	2372
Greatland Corp	2761	19
Greatmark	5045	919
Great-West Life and Annuity Insurance Co	6311	52
Greatwide Logistics Services	4173	1
Greatwide Logistics Services LLC	4213	157
Greaves Company Inc	3823	244
Grebes' Bakeries Inc	2051	78
Grecian Imports	5064	167
Greco and Sons Inc	5149	51
Greco Brothers Inc	3559	383
Greco Sales Inc	5046	207
Greco Systems Inc	3571	148
Grecon Dimter Inc	5084	554
Grede Foundries Inc	3321	6
Grede Holdings LLC	3321	5
Grede Wisconsin Subsidiaries LLC	3321	19
Greek American Rehabilitation And Care Centre Inc	8051	62
Greeley and Hansen LLC	8711	90
Green Advertising Associates Inc	7311	349
Green And Son's Agency Inc	7322	132
Green Bankshares Inc	6022	76
Green Banner Publications Inc	2711	570
Green Bay Area Public Schools	8211	18
Green Bay Dressed Beef LLC	2011	25
Green Bay Packaging Inc	2653	5
Green Bay Packaging Kalamazoo Container Div	2653	25
Green Bay Pattern Inc	3543	41
Green Bay Plastics Inc	3089	1327
Green Beacon Solutions LLC	7372	1187
Green Beans Coffee Company Inc	5499	11
Green Bridge Technologies International Inc	3812	226
Green Bull Ladder	5084	72
Green Chevrolet Chrysler Inc	5511	545
Green Chevrolet Hummer Inc	5511	168
Green Chevrolet-Buick-Pontiac Inc	5511	1149
Green Circle Growers Inc	0181	13
Green Dot Corp	7389	91
Green Earth Technologies Inc	5169	136
Green Energy Corp	3663	282
Green Energy Industries	3621	85
Green Field Paper Co	2678	10
Green Garden Food Products Inc	2035	34
Green Gifford Motor Corp	5511	571
Green Globe International Inc	8742	704
Green Hasson and Janks LLP	8721	23
Green Hills Software Inc	7372	546
Green Lake Bank (Green Lake Wisconsin)	6022	666
Green Line Media Inc	2741	434
Green Machine and Tool Inc	3599	2393
Green Magic LLC	7342	34
Green Motor Lines Inc	4213	2615
Green Mountain Audio LLC	3651	207
Green Mountain Chocolate Company Inc	2066	37
Green Mountain Coffee Roasters Inc	2095	3
Green Mountain Power Corp	4911	192
Green Mountain Software Corp	7372	4824
Green Mountain Video Inc	7812	290
Green Nerd	5084	861
Green Plains Renewable Energy Inc	2869	8
Green Planet Group Inc	2911	6
Green Power Inc	5083	147
Green River Construction Company Inc	1623	562
Green Rubber-Kennedy Ag LP	5085	129
Green Solutions Inc	3695	89
Green Spot Packaging Inc	2086	102
Green Star Products Inc	5172	159
Green Team of San Jose	4953	86
Green Tokai Company Ltd	3714	102
Green Transfer and Storage Co	4213	2445
Green Tree Servicing LLC	6719	9
Green Valley Chemical Corp	2873	13
Green Valley Corp	1522	31
Green Valley Manufacturing Co	7389	2461
Green Valley Manufacturing Inc	3799	30
Green Valley Ranch Gaming LLC	7999	8
Green Valley Recreation Inc	7997	12
Green Valley Security	7389	1473
Green Valley Station Inc	7999	163
Greenbaum Interiors LLC	5712	83
Greenbaum Public Relations	8743	246
Greenbaum Rowe Smith Ravin Davis and Himmel LLT	8111	254
Greenberg and Traurig PA	8111	74
Greenberg Glusker Fields Claman Machtinger LLP	8111	196
Greenberg Grant and Richards Inc	7322	60
Greenberg Smoked Turkeys Inc	2015	72
Greenbriar Graphics LLC	7372	4611
Greenbriar Homes Co	6552	105
Greenbriar Scentex	3089	604
Greenbrier Companies Inc	3743	5
Greenbrier Rail Services	3462	1
Greenbrier Valley Memorial Vault Company Inc	3272	126
GreenChek Technology Inc	1041	27
Greenco Manufacturing Corp	3593	55
Greencore USA Inc	2099	52
Greendale Home Fashions LLC	3842	185
Greendata Inc	5045	839
Greendragon Creations Inc	7373	1041
Greene Bark Press Inc	2731	225
Greene Beverage Company Inc	5181	69
Greene Company Works Wastewater Treatment	4953	137
Greene County Bancorp Inc	6036	53
Greene Plastics Corp	3089	538
Greene Technologies Inc	3444	140
Greene Tweed and Co	3089	31
Greener Cleaner	7219	3
Greener Corp	3565	122
Greenerd Press and Machine Company Inc	3542	92
Greenery Unlimited	7359	201
Greeneville Publishing Company Inc	2711	432
Greeneway Enterprises Inc	2711	235
Greenfield Advertising Group Inc	7311	867
Greenfield Amermac Inc	3499	125
Greenfield Bancshares Inc	6712	729
Greenfield Banking Co	6022	492
Greenfield Builders Inc	1541	99
Greenfield Lumber Co	5031	217
Greenfield Research Inc	2396	17
Greenfield Wine Co	5182	39
Greenhaven Associates Inc	6282	501
Greenhaven Printing	2759	449
Greenhill and Company Inc	6211	108
Greenhorne and O'Mara Inc	8711	34
Greening Associates Inc	3825	183
Greenleaf Corp	3545	37
Greenleaf Industries Inc	3089	1503
Greenleaf Landscapes Inc	0781	9
Greenleaf Wholesale Florists	5193	12
Greenlee Textron Inc	3423	25
Greenlees Filter LLC	3564	79
Greenline Industries	3533	38
Greenline Service Corp	5083	81
Greenlite Lighting Corporation USA	5063	849
GreenLogic LLC	1711	214
GreenMan Technologies Inc	3089	1749
Greenman-Pedersen Inc	8711	30
Greenpages Inc	5045	159
Greenpoint Technologies Inc	2531	19
Greenprint Technologies LLC	5734	268
Greenray Industries Inc	3825	98
Green's Communications Inc	5064	182
Green's Moving and Storage Inc	4213	3084
Greensboro Auto Parts Company Inc	5013	402
Greensboro News and Record Inc	2711	174
Greensboro Plumbing Supply Co	5074	94
Greenscape Environmental Services	0782	11
Greensfelder Hemker and Gale PC	8111	174
Greenshift Corp	4959	15
Greenspring Energy LLC	4939	15
Greenspring Media Group Inc	2721	240
Greenstein Rogoff Olsen and Co LLP	8721	407
GreenStone Farm Credit Services	6061	1
Green-Tek Inc	5084	507
Greentree Packing Inc	5147	39
Greentree Systems Inc	7372	2424
Greentree Transportation Co	4213	466
Greenview Data Inc	7371	811
Greenview Manufacturing Company Inc	3999	211
Greenville Colorants Inc	2865	11
Greenville First Bancshares Inc	6712	380
Greenville Gravel Co	5032	121
Greenville Industrial Rubber and Gasket Company Inc	5085	437
Greenville Metal Works Inc	3548	42
Greenville Metals Inc	3452	23
Greenville Quarries Inc	1422	16
Greenville Ready Mix Concrete Inc	5032	52
Greenville Record Argus Inc	2711	699
Greenville Technology Inc	3714	115
Greenville Tool and Die Co	3544	57
Greenville Tractor Company Inc	5084	571
Greenville Transformer Co	3612	101
Greenville Tube Co	3312	29
Greenville Tv and Appliance Inc	5731	61
Greenwald Industries	3578	10
Greenwald Supply Inc	5032	182
Greenwald Surgical Company Inc	3841	355
Greenware Systems Inc	7371	1865
Greenway Co-Operative Service	5541	30
Greenway Equipment Inc	5083	138
Greenway Ford Inc	5511	1111
Greenway Home Services LLC	2517	5
Greenway Medical Technologies Inc	5999	74
Greenway Research Labs Inc	2759	365
Greenwell Interiors	5713	18
Greenwell-Chisholm Printing Company Inc	2752	971
Greenwich Alternative Investments	6282	448
Greenwich Associates	8742	185
Greenwich Capital Markets Inc	6211	112
Greenwich Software and Consulting Group Inc	7372	4424
Greenwich Studio Inc	7819	69
Greenwich Workshop Inc	5199	98
Greenwood County Financial Services Inc	6712	717
Greenwood Emergency Vehicles Inc	5087	75
Greenwood Ice Cream Company Limited Inc	2024	61
Greenwood Inc	3995	9
Greenwood Mills Inc	2211	12
Greenwood Products Inc	5211	215
Greer Electric Company Inc	1731	1014
Greer Laboratories Inc	2836	44
Greer Margolis Mitchell Burns Inc	7311	139
Greer Stop Nut Inc	3452	88
Greer's Inc	2011	161
Greeters of Hawaii Ltd	7999	87
Greetings and Readings Inc	5331	16
Greg A Vietri Inc	1731	462
Greg Foemmel Inc	5072	201
Greg-Co Piston Rings Inc	3592	27
Gregg Bruce Auto and Performance	7538	38
Gregg Electric Co	1731	648
Gregg Electric Corp	1731	1698
Gregg Electric Inc	1731	415
Gregg Express Inc	4213	1428
Greggo and Ferrara Inc	1611	127
Gregor Jonsson Associates Inc	3556	143
Gregory A Scott Inc	2395	17
Gregory and Appel Insurance Inc	6411	185
Gregory C Rigamer And Associates Inc	7379	290
Gregory Electric Company Inc	1731	2478
Gregory Electric Inc	1731	559
Gregory FCA Communications Inc	6282	96
Gregory Holdings Inc	3089	425
Gregory Industries Inc	3499	51

Company Name	SIC	Rank	Company Name	SIC	Rank	Company Name	SIC	Rank
Gregory L Seelenbinder and Associates	7372	3351	Griffon Steel Corp	5051	429	Group 1 Automotive Inc	5511	7
Gregory Logistics Inc	4213	1877	Grifols USA	5047	12	Group 3 Consultants Inc	7379	965
Gregory Manufacturing Inc	3841	221	Griggs and Browne Company Inc	7342	54	Group 42 Inc	7372	3714
Gregory Palmer and Sons	4213	3021	Griggs Productions Inc	7812	315	Group Delphi	3993	112
Gregory Poole Equipment Co	5082	13	Grigsby and Associates Inc	6211	321	Group Dynamic Inc	7374	330
Gregory Richard Media Group	7336	244	Grigsby Petroleum Inc	1382	68	Group Electric Company LLC	1731	1415
Gregory T Blair Inc	5015	26	Grijalva and Allen PC	8721	122	Group Enterprise Of North America Inc	8741	223
Gregory's Foods Inc	5149	156	Grillo's Home Of Bread Inc	2051	146	Group Health Cooperative of South Central Wisconsin	6411	1
Gregory's Wheat Shop Inc	2051	253	Grimes Oil Company Inc	5172	83	Group Health Credit Union	6062	82
Gregstrom Corp	3089	763	Grimes Publications of Georgia Inc	2721	392	Group Health Inc	6321	27
Greif Inc	2652	1	Grimley Financial Corp	7322	146	Group Industries Inc	3429	110
Greiner Extrusion Us Inc	3544	391	Grimm Industries Inc	3089	466	Group International Associates	7379	947
Greiner Motor Company Inc	5611	200	Grimm Mold and Die Company Inc	3599	1906	Group Logic Inc	7372	1353
Gremada Industries Inc	3599	198	Grimmway Farms Enterprises	0161	15	Group Loria LLC Joester	7311	763
Gremarco Industries Inc	3564	146	Grind Lap Services Inc	7389	1942	Group M Worldwide Inc	3993	3
Gremark Technologies Inc	7378	115	Grindal Co	3541	195	Group Management Services Inc	7363	10
Grenald Waldron Associates	7389	1228	Grind-All Corp	3541	111	Group Nine Marketing	7311	868
Greneker Inc	3999	78	Grindco Inc	3599	1142	Group One Capital Inc	5087	5
Greno Industries Inc	3599	293	Grinder Taber and Grinder Inc	1542	196	Group Publishing Inc	2731	135
Grenzebach Corp	3559	133	Grinding and Dicing Services Inc	3674	358	Group Three Systems LLC	7379	1078
Gresco Utility Supply Inc	5063	45	Grinding And Polishing Machinery Corp	3549	119	Group Voyagers Inc	4724	34
Gresham Driving Aids Inc	7549	27	Grinding Equipment And Machinery Company Inc	3547	23	Groupee Inc	7374	244
Gresham Enterprise Storage	7371	1059	Grinding Specialists Inc	3599	2011	Groupware Inc	7372	2238
Gresham Petroleum Co	5172	56	Grindley Manufacturing Inc	3599	1644	Groupware Technologies Inc	7372	3316
Gresham Smith and Partners	8712	8	Grindmaster Corp	3589	60	Grove Dale Corp	3556	129
Gresham Transfer Inc	4213	901	Grindstaff's Interior Inc	5712	87	Grove Gear	3566	17
Grey Direct Inc	7331	9	Griner Engineering Inc	3714	337	Grove Gill Electric Co	1731	751
Grey Eagle Distributors Inc	5181	45	Grinnell Mutual Reinsurance Co	6331	191	Grove Medical Inc	5047	143
Grey Electric Company Inc	1731	1469	Grins Sportspage Inc	7335	24	Grove Networks Inc	7373	1145
Grey Group Inc	7311	20	Grip Gear Inc	5065	791	Grove Solutions Inc	7378	156
Grey Healthcare Group Inc	7311	51	Grippe Machining And Manufacturing Co	3449	35	Grove Street Advisors LLC	6799	23
Grey House Publishing Inc	2741	99	Grippo Potato Chip Company Inc	2096	35	Grove Sun Newspaper Company Inc	2711	906
Grey Media Connections Inc	7311	35	Griptonite Games	7372	560	Grove Tools Inc	3599	2478
Greyfield Industries Inc	3661	152	Grisham Industries Inc	1796	30	Grove Worldwide LLC	3531	8
Greyhound Lines Inc	4131	1	Gristede's Foods Inc	5411	109	Grover Corp	5085	157
Greylawn Foods Inc	4213	2282	Griswold Industries	3492	14	Grover Gundrilling Inc	3599	435
Greylock Electrical Company Inc	1731	2285	Griswold Machine And Engineering Inc	3531	82	Grover Machine Co	3542	78
Greylock Management Corp	6799	181	Griswold Rubber Corp	3069	50	Grovesite Inc	4899	172
Grey's Inc	7382	65	Grivet Electric Inc	1731	1983	Grow Company Inc	2023	32
Greysmith Cos	7363	371	Grizzard Communications Group Inc	7331	17	Grow Electric Inc	1731	1443
Greyson International Inc	2844	54	Grizzly Designs	7379	1518	Grow Financial Federal Credit Union	6061	9
Greystar Corp	1389	34	GRMS Inc	7372	2148	Grow More Inc	2879	31
Greystar E I G LP	5039	41	Grob Inc	3541	81	Grower Shipper Potato Co	5148	81
Greystar Management Services LP	6531	171	Grob Systems Inc	3535	146	Growers Express LLC	0161	8
Greystar Realty Services	6531	257	Grobet File Company Of America Inc	3915	8	Growers Fertilizer Corp	2875	15
Greyston Bakery Inc	2051	103	Grocers Supply Company Inc	5141	23	Growers Ice Co	2097	7
Greystone Graphics Inc	2752	325	Grocery Outlets	5411	233	Growmark Fs LLC	2875	16
Greystone Logistics Inc	3559	102	Grocery Shopping Network Inc	7372	1636	GROWMARK Inc	5191	2
Greystone Of Lincoln Inc	3451	7	Grocery Supply Co	5141	92	Growth and Opportunity Inc	8331	244
GreyStone Power Corp	4911	135	Groco Paint Manufacturing Company Inc	2851	152	Growth Industries Inc	3728	134
Greystone Solutions Inc	7372	3612	Groen Brothers Aviation Inc	3721	46	Growth Properties	6531	369
Grg Construction Company Inc	1611	138	Groen Brothers Aviation USA Inc	3721	30	Grt Consulting Inc	7371	1880
Grgich Hills Cellar	2084	45	Groendyke Transport Inc	4213	41	GRT Corp	7379	443
GRH Electronics Inc	3823	399	Groff Meats Inc	5421	10	Grt Electronics LLC	3672	368
Gri Engineering and Development LLC	5013	391	Grogan Graffam PC	8111	402	Grt Utilicorp Inc	3541	196
Griban Technologies Inc	7374	378	Grogan's Farm Inc	2011	92	Grtw Corp	5013	357
Grid 4 Communications Inc	4813	314	Grogan's Healthcare Supply Inc	5047	36	Grubb and Ellis Affiliates Inc	6531	232
Grid One Solutions Inc	7363	194	Gromax Precision Die and Manufacturing Inc	3544	790	Grubb and Ellis Asset Services Co	6531	253
GridPoint Inc	7372	663	Groner Boyle and Quillin	8721	99	Grubb and Ellis Bissell Patrick	2721	148
Grieger Motor Sales Inc	5511	1100	Groom Law Group Chartered	8111	262	Grubb and Ellis Co	6531	74
Griesser Sales Company Inc	5063	795	Grooms Engines-Parts-Machining Inc	7538	19	Grubb and Ellis Consulting Services Co	6531	213
Grieve Corp	3567	29	Grooms Office Systems Inc	5021	125			
Griffin 88 Store Inc	5621	39	Groop	7311	845	Grubb and Ellis Institutional Properties Inc	6531	248
Griffin America	4724	68	Groove House Records	3565	167			
Griffin Analytical Technologies LLC	3826	83	Groove Networks Inc	7372	471	Grubb and Ellis Management Services Inc	6531	209
Griffin Automation Inc	3599	1181	Gro-Power Inc	2873	23			
Griffin Chase Oliver Inc	3669	287	Gropp Electric Inc	1731	1291	Grubb and Ellis Mortgage Group Inc	6531	339
Griffin Communications LLC	4833	136	Groschopp Inc	3621	47	Grubb and Ellis Mortgage Services Inc	6531	305
Griffin Consulting	7379	1496	Grosfillex Inc	3313	6	Grubb and Ellis New York Inc	6531	283
Griffin Contracting	1794	47	Gros-Ite Industries Div	3724	28	Grubb and Ellis of Michigan Inc	6531	347
Griffin Dewatering Corp	1799	47	Gross Brothers Printing Company Inc	2752	1540	Grubb and Ellis of Nevada Inc	6531	318
Griffin Food Co	2099	211	Gross Chandelier Co	3646	82	Grubb and Ellis of Oregon Inc	6531	340
Griffin Ford Inc	5511	626	Gross Electric Inc	5063	100	Grubb and Ellis Realty Advisers Inc	6531	186
Griffin Holdings Inc	2035	41	Gross Machine Inc	3545	412	Grubb and Ellis Utah Realty	6531	228
Griffin Inc	3713	42	Gross Mechanical Laboratories Inc	3599	620	Grubb Lumber Company Inc	2431	92
Griffin Industries Corp	3543	11	Gross Mortgage Finance Inc	6162	113	Grubbs Hoskyn Barton and Wyatt Inc	8711	235
Griffin Leggett Healey and Roth Inc	7261	12	Grossberg Company LLP	8721	396	Grubbs Infiniti	5511	1080
Griffin Leggett-Conway Inc	7261	16	Grosse Tool And Machine Co	3369	32	Gruber Industries Inc	4813	79
Griffin Lumber Co	2421	119	Grossel Tool Co	3548	48	Gruber Systems Inc	5162	4
Griffin Medical Products Inc	5047	172	Grossenburg Implement Inc	5083	19	Gruber Tool and Die Inc	3544	155
Griffin Motor Company Inc	5511	1079	Grossman and Associates Inc	7372	1192	GrubHubcom	7379	635
Griffin Pest Control Inc	7342	16	Grossman Iron and Steel Company Charitable Foundation	5093	24	Gruett's Inc	5083	99
Griffin Publishing Inc	2759	466				Gruma Corp	2096	2
Griffin Supply Inc	5085	224	Grossman's Kensington Home Furnishings Center	5713	6	Grunau Company Inc	1711	43
Griffin Technologies LLC	7372	1317				Grunau Corp	7623	1
Griffin Thermal Products Inc	3714	276	Grosso Jacobson Communications Corp	7812	214	Grunley Construction Co	1542	73
Griffin Tommy L Plumbing and Heating Co	1711	213	Grote and Weigel Inc	2011	23	Grunwald Printing Co	2791	39
Griffin Wood Company Inc	5031	51	Grote Industries Inc	3647	5	Grupe Co	1629	43
Griffin York and Krause	7311	251	Groth Brothers Oldsmobile Inc	5511	1095	Grupocomp LLC	5734	64
Griffin's Hub Chrysler Jeep Dodge	7514	9	Groth Corp	3491	44	Gruppo Levey and Co	6282	582
Griffith Electrical Control Systems Inc	3577	556	Grothe Industrial Coating	3479	81	GRW Advertising Inc	7311	497
Griffith Energy Services Inc	5983	2	Grotto Pizza Inc	5812	214	GRW Engineers Inc	8711	177
Griffith Inc	7389	618	Ground Hog Inc	3531	204	Grw Systems	7371	1886
Griffith Laboratories Inc	2099	11	Ground Swell Equity Partners	6799	216	Grw Technologies Inc	3544	287
Griffith Micro Science Inc	8099	59	Groundfloor Media Inc	8743	157	Grynberg Petroleum Co	1382	11
Griffith Rubber Mills	3061	15	Groundscare Ltd	7389	1994	Grynberg Production Corp	1311	159
Griffiths and Associates	7389	1229	Groundwork Open Source Solutions Inc	7371	284	Gryphon Corp	3559	540
Griffiths Holding Corp	3544	8				Gryphon Group Ltd	7378	54
Griffiths Inc	7381	116				Gryphon Technologies LC	7373	314
Griffith's Printing Co	2752	1586				GS and W Services Inc	7331	182
Griffiths Services Inc	2752	1067				GS Automation Builder Inc	7539	15
Griffon Corp	2671	4				GS Beckham Design Associates Inc	7389	1804
						GS Blodgett Corp	3556	9

Company Name	SIC	Rank
GS Costa Mesa Inc	3714	33
GS EnviroServices Inc	4953	173
Gs Industries Of Bassett Ltd	3089	1045
GS Schwartz and Company Inc	8743	212
GS1 US Inc	7372	353
GS5 LLC	8748	209
Gsa Design Inc	7389	833
GSC Associates Inc	7379	1200
GSC Enterprises Inc	5141	43
GSD and M	7311	186
GSE Construction Company Inc	1623	45
GSE Erudite Software Inc	7373	486
Gse Facility Services LLC	7349	316
GSE Lining Technology Inc (Houston Texas)	3081	6
GSE Power Systems Inc	7373	362
GSE Services Company LLC	7373	634
GSE Systems Inc	7373	168
GSF Safeway Inc	7349	4
GSF Safeway LLC	7349	102
GSG Builders Inc	1522	47
GSG LLC	2752	798
GSI Commerce Inc	7379	13
Gsi Engine Management Group Inc	3053	66
GSI Group Inc (Billerica Massachusetts)	3841	29
GSI Technology Inc	3674	107
Gsl Inc	5013	323
Gsm Systems Of New York Inc	8748	262
GSO Graphics Inc	7334	30
Gsp Marketing Technologies Inc	7336	30
GSP Precision Inc	3599	1635
GSS Communiqations Inc	7311	608
Gss Security Services Inc	7381	221
Gssc Inc	3563	18
Gst Inc	3572	64
Gstek Inc	8711	372
GSV Inc	1311	258
GSW Manufacturing Inc	3714	219
GT Advanced Technologies Inc	3674	42
GT Distributors Inc	5049	52
GT Industries Of Oklahoma Inc	5085	367
GT Manufacturing Inc	3523	254
Gt Micro Corp	7379	1332
GT Microwave Inc	3679	492
GT Nexus Inc	7372	909
Gt Plastics Inc	3089	1534
GT Sales and Manufacturing Inc	5085	68
GT Software Inc	7372	2548
GT Technologies	3351	6
Gt Technology Company Inc	5084	730
GT USA	4213	1179
GTC Biotherapeutics Inc	2836	71
GTC Falcon Inc	3829	419
GTC Group Inc	7371	1105
GTCO CalComp Inc	3577	102
GTCR Golder Rauner LLC	6799	91
GTE Airfone Inc	4812	23
GTE Federal Credit Union	6061	23
Gte Service Office	4813	582
GTECH Corp	7371	6
GTESS Corp	7372	1322
Gti Graphic Technology Inc	3648	75
GTL Transport Company Inc	4213	2640
Gtm Energy Partners LLC	3542	39
Gtp Acquisition Partners Ii LLC	4812	81
Gtp Greenville Inc	3552	4
Gtr Enterprises Inc	3599	1001
GTR Manufacturing Corp	3444	135
Gtran Inc	3679	206
GTT/FlexPoint	3999	166
GTX Corp	7373	848
GTX Corp (Los Angeles California)	3663	393
GTx Inc (Memphis Tennessee)	2834	167
G-U Hardware Inc	5072	185
Guadalupe Electric Inc	1731	2201
Guadalupe Valley Electric Cooperative Inc	4911	129
Guadalupe Valley Telephone Coop	4813	170
Guarantee Electrical Co	1731	67
Guarantee Specialties Inc	3469	143
Guaranteed Express Inc	7331	241
Guaranteed Foods Inc	5411	257
Guaranteed Solutions Inc	5045	815
Guaranteed Subpoena Service Inc	8111	540
Guaranty Abstract Co	6541	15
Guaranty Bancorp	6712	203
Guaranty Bancshares Inc	6712	723
Guaranty Bank and Trust Co (Denver Colorado)	6022	184
Guaranty Bank SSB	6036	50
Guaranty Bond Bank	6021	86
Guaranty Chevrolet Motors	5511	663
Guaranty Chevrolet-Pontiac-Oldsmobile	5511	80
Guaranty Corp (Baton Rouge Louisiana)	6311	127
Guaranty Federal Bancshares Inc	6712	397
Guaranty Federal Bank FSB (Dallas Texas)	6035	15
Guaranty Financial Group Inc	6712	49
Guaranty Home Equity Inc	6162	39
Guaranty Income Life Insurance	6311	195
Guaranty Savings Bank	6036	86
Guard Force Inc	7381	147

Company Name	SIC	Rank
Guard Publishing Company Inc	2711	99
Guard Services Inc	7381	180
Guard Tronic Inc	1731	754
Guardair Corp	3546	26
Guardco Security Services	7381	181
Guardian Asset Management Corp	6282	614
Guardian Automotive	3465	21
Guardian Companies Inc	1542	89
Guardian Corp	5812	160
Guardian Eagle Security Inc	7381	68
Guardian Electric Manufacturing Co	3679	315
Guardian Equipment Inc	3432	34
Guardian Glass Co (Westerville Ohio)	7536	5
Guardian Industries Corp	3211	1
Guardian Life Insurance Company of America	6311	31
Guardian Manufacturing Co	3069	206
Guardian Manufacturing Corp	3545	143
Guardian Metal Sales Inc	3549	41
Guardian Mortgage Documents Inc	5045	148
Guardian Moving and Storage Co	4213	155
Guardian Protection Services Inc	7382	4
Guardian Radon Mitigation and Electrical Services LLC	1731	1381
Guardian Savings Bank	6035	250
Guardian Security Inc	7381	216
Guardian Security Services Inc	7382	38
Guardian Systems Inc	1731	2134
Guardian-Ipco Inc	2899	217
Guard-Line Inc	3151	3
Guardsman Products Inc	2851	17
Guardsmark Inc	7381	5
Guckenheimer Enterprises Inc	5812	14
Gudebrod Inc	2824	10
Gudel Inc	3535	143
Gueldner Electric Co	1731	1543
Guelph Tool Sales Inc	3465	8
Guerlain Inc	2844	32
Guernsey Dairy Stores Inc	2024	46
Guernsey's	7389	2338
Guerrero Construction Corp	1623	575
Guess Electronics Company Inc	5065	133
Guess Freighways Inc	4213	2325
Guess Inc	2339	3
Guess Retail Inc	2339	1
Guesscom Inc	2339	2
Guest Communications Corp	2741	370
Guest Services Inc	5812	168
Guestclick Inc	5045	929
Guggenheim Funds Distribution Inc	6726	6
Guggisberg Cheese Inc	2022	61
Guhring Inc	3545	42
Guia International Corp	7372	2713
Guico Machine Works Inc	0599	817
Guidance Associates Inc	7812	211
Guidance Software Inc	7372	413
Guidance Solutions Inc	7379	267
Guidant Financial Group Inc	6282	463
Guidant's Cardiac Rhythm Management	3842	14
Guida's Milk and Ice Cream Co	2023	3
Guide Book Publishing	2741	358
Guide Corp	3647	2
Guide Engineering LLC	3599	1830
Guide Technologies LLC	7372	3420
Guide Technology Inc	3577	284
Guided Therapeutics Inc	3841	314
Guideline Inc	8732	37
GuideOne Mutual Insurance Co	6311	202
Guidesoft Inc	7379	359
Guidewire Software Inc	7372	1006
Guidry's Catfish Inc	5146	64
Guild Associates Inc	8731	281
Guild Mortgage Co	6162	67
Guild Technologies Ltd	3699	110
GuildMaster Inc	5021	89
Guilford Fabricators Inc	5999	252
Guilford Fibers	2221	14
Guilford Gas Service Inc	5984	15
Guilford Mills Inc	2258	1
Guilford Mills Michigan Inc	2258	6
Guilford Publications Inc	2741	225
Guill Tool and Engineering Company Inc	3544	228
Guitar Center Inc	5736	1
Guittard Chocolate Co	2066	12
Gulbrandsen Manufacturing Inc	2819	38
Gulbranson Excavating-West Inc	1623	244
Gulf Atlantic Electrical Constructors Inc	1731	1234
Gulf Business Forms Inc	2761	43
Gulf Chemical And Metallurgical Corp	3356	22
Gulf Coast American Blind Corp	5023	45
Gulf Coast Boring and Pipeline Inc	1623	246
Gulf Coast Building Products Inc	5033	52
Gulf Coast Chemical Inc	2842	86
Gulf Coast Downhole Technologies LLC	1731	2411
Gulf Coast Electric Co	1731	1612
Gulf Coast Galvanizing Inc	3479	87
Gulf Coast International LLC	5082	201
Gulf Coast Laundry Services Inc	7211	1
Gulf Coast Machine Services LLC	1389	57
Gulf Coast Pharmaceuticals Inc	5122	86
Gulf Coast Plastics Inc	3089	613

Company Name	SIC	Rank
Gulf Coast Power and Control Inc	3825	261
Gulf Coast Pre-Stress Inc	3272	49
Gulf Coast Regional Blood Center	8099	40
Gulf Coast Remediation LLC	1623	542
Gulf Coast Seal Ltd	5085	116
Gulf Coast Treatment Center Inc	8063	8
Gulf Coast Underground Inc	1623	301
Gulf Coast Ventures Inc	5094	40
Gulf Craft LLC	3732	69
Gulf Crane Services Inc	1799	60
Gulf Crown Seafood Company Inc	2092	58
Gulf Distributing Company Of Mobile LLC	2086	75
Gulf Eagle Supply Inc	5033	14
Gulf Electric Company Incorporated Of Mobile	1731	280
Gulf Electrical Wholesale Inc	5063	524
Gulf Electroquip Management LLC	5063	366
Gulf Enterprises	3677	65
Gulf Fleet Holdings Inc	4499	9
Gulf Island Fabrication Inc	3441	11
Gulf Machine Shop Inc	3599	904
Gulf Marine and Industrial Supplies	5141	175
Gulf Marine Repair Corp	3731	22
Gulf Oil LP	5172	5
Gulf Pacific Inc	5153	122
Gulf Pacific Rice Company Inc	5153	37
Gulf Packing Company LP	2011	110
Gulf Power Co	4911	76
Gulf Pride Enterprises Inc	5146	62
Gulf Publishing Co	2721	109
Gulf Sales And Supply Inc	5085	259
Gulf Services Industrial LLC	3629	79
Gulf South Infrasystems LLC	3612	97
Gulf South Machine Inc	3599	720
Gulf South Medical Supply Inc	5047	31
Gulf South Printing and Specialties Inc	2752	1659
Gulf States Asphalt Company LP	2891	51
Gulf States Canners Inc	2086	41
Gulf States Credit Union	6061	141
Gulf States Distributors Inc	5049	117
Gulf States Electric Inc	1731	1341
Gulf States Engineering Company Inc	5084	308
Gulf States Intermodal	4213	1561
Gulf States Marble Inc	2541	66
Gulf States Optical Laboratories Inc	5048	28
Gulf States Toyota Inc	5012	9
Gulf Stream Asset Management	6282	1
Gulf Stream Builders Supply Inc (Boynton Beach Florida)	5211	189
Gulf Stream Coach Inc	3716	4
Gulf Stream Media Group	2721	414
Gulf Tool Corp	3441	171
Gulfaccess Inc	5063	1098
Gulfcoast Telephone Company Inc	1731	1514
Gulfgate Dodge	5511	752
GulfMark Offshore Inc	1382	20
Gulfport Energy Corp	1311	76
Gulfshore Media LLC	2721	227
Gulfstar Group I Ltd	6211	137
Gulfstar Group II Ltd	6211	138
Gulfstream Aerospace Corp	3721	7
Gulfstream Community Bank	6035	241
Gulfstream Digital Solutions Inc	5734	372
Gulfstream International Airlines Inc	4512	48
Gulick Brothers House Of Sound	3651	163
Gulinello's Towne and Country Inc	5149	204
Gull Creek Center Inc	6513	16
Gull Industries Inc	5172	128
Gulley Computer Associates	7374	363
Gulton Inc	3577	489
Gum Log Movers Inc	4213	2795
Gumbiner Savett Inc	8721	336
Gund Company Inc	3644	22
Gund Inc	3942	6
Gunder and Associates LLC	5075	15
Gunderlin Limited Inc	3534	12
Gunderson Dettmer Stough Villeneuve Franklin and Hachigian	8111	265
Gundlach Equipment Corp	3531	110
Gundlach-Bundschu Winery	2084	46
Gundle/SLT Environmental Inc	3081	9
GUS Distributing Corp	5065	682
Gunkie Company Inc	7379	1659
Gunlocke Co	2522	3
Gunn Chevrolet Inc	5511	66
Gunn Oil Co	1382	60
Gunnar Electric Inc	1731	2219
Gunnebo Corporation U S A	3536	13
Gunning and Associates Marketing Inc	8748	378
Gunnoe Sausage Co	2013	165
Gunster Yoakley and Stewart PA	8111	204
Guntert and Zimmerman Const Division Inc	3531	127
Gunther Douglas Inc	7371	1289
Gunther International Ltd	3579	19
Gunton Corp	5031	215
Guntren Trucking	4213	2861
Gupta Permold Corp	3365	7
Gurecky Manufacturing Service Inc	3599	577
Gurley Precision Instruments Inc	3827	49
Gurney Brothers Construction Inc	1794	42
Gurney Seed and Nursery Corp	0181	7
Gurney Trucking Inc	4213	971

Company Name	SIC	Rank
Gurneys Inn Resort and SpA	7011	183
Guro Enterprises LLC	7373	830
Gurrola Reprographics Inc	7334	56
Gursey Schneider and Company LLP	8721	124
Gurtler Chemicals Inc	2841	27
Guru Inc	7379	1020
Gurus Information Technology Services LLC	7371	987
Gus Johnson ford Inc	5511	758
Gus Mayer	5611	31
Gus Pech Manufacturing Company Inc	3545	239
Gus Perdikakis Associates Inc	8711	473
Gushner Brothers Inc	5611	22
Gust Rosenfeld	8111	327
Gustafson Lighting	3645	25
Gustavson Associates Inc	8731	321
Gustman Chevrolet Sales Inc	5511	530
Gusto Brands Inc	5181	106
Gusto Packing Company Inc	2011	16
Gutchess International Inc	5031	377
Gutchess Lumber Company Inc	2421	44
Guth Laboratories Inc	3829	359
Guthrie Center Assembly LLC	7363	369
Guthrie Machine Works Inc	3451	102
Guthrie/Mayes and Associates Inc	8743	309
Guthy-Renker Corp	5963	19
Gutierrez Machine Corp	3599	2354
Guttenberg Industries Inc	3089	166
Guttenplan's Frozen Dough Inc	2041	17
Gutterman's Supply Corporation Of America	5051	239
Guy Bennett Lumber Co	2421	25
Guy Brown Fire and Safety Inc	7389	1542
Guy Brown Management LLC	3955	7
Guy Carpenter and Company Inc	6411	46
Guy Chemical Company Inc	7389	963
Guy E Temple Inc	5091	118
Guy F Atkinson Construction LLC	1622	4
Guy G Veralrud	3651	219
Guy Gray Supply Co	5063	538
Guy J Renzi and Associates	7338	28
Guy L Warden and Sons	5084	481
Guy M Turner Inc	4213	1037
Guy Shavender Trucking Inc	4213	1014
Guyan International Inc	3594	13
Guyan Machinery Company Inc	5082	158
Guyer Die Company Inc	3544	860
Guyer the Mover Inc	4212	70
Guyer's Superior Walls	3272	97
Guynes Printing Company of Texas Inc	2759	195
Guys Electric Service Of Westchester Inc	1731	2541
Guyson Corporation Of U S A	3569	125
Guzman's Machine Works Inc	3599	1327
Guzzler Manufacturing Inc	3564	34
GV Moore Lumber Company Inc	5031	136
GV Ranch Station Inc	7999	11
GVA Productions	7311	1000
GVI Inc	7812	202
GVI Security Solutions Inc	7372	727
Gvm Inc	3523	90
GVOX	7372	2425
Gvs Technologies LLC	3599	2035
Gw Electronics Ltd	5065	832
GW Hannaway and Associates	7372	4378
GW Instruments	7373	871
Gw Limited 40 LLC	7389	1858
GW Micro Inc	3571	121
Gw Plastics Arizona Inc	3089	135
GW Plastics Inc	3089	282
GW Steffen Bookbinders Inc	2789	51
GW Surfaces	3281	13
GW Van Keppel Co	5082	42
GW WebDesign	7379	552
Gwaltney Drilling Inc	1623	564
Gwaltney of Smithfield Ltd	2011	8
Gwartney Automotive Group Inc	5013	226
Gwatney Mazda of Germantown	5511	576
GWC Technology Inc	3577	80
Gwilliam Ivary Chiosso Cavalli and Brewer	8111	556
Gwillim Trucking Service	4213	2867
Gwin Dobson and Foreman Inc	8711	189
Gwinnett Health System Inc	8062	12
Gwin's Travel Planners	4724	57
Gwj Sourcenet Distribution Inc	5045	353
GWL Construction LLC	1522	33
GX Clarke and Co	6211	345
GX Technology Corp	7371	80
GXS Inc	7372	106
GyanSys Inc	8742	558
Gylan Building Services Inc	7349	275
Gym Source	5091	20
Gymboree Corp	2389	2
Gypsum Express Ltd	4213	269
Gyration Inc	3577	440
Gyro Inc	7311	219
Gyrocon Inc	7371	1171
Gyrodyne Company of America Inc	6512	67
Gyro-Trac Corp	3599	2355
Gyrus ACMI Inc	3841	121
Gyrus Systems Inc	7372	2149
GZA GeoEnvironmental Inc	4953	43
GZA GeoEnvironmental Technologies Inc	8711	212
H 2 Computers Inc	5734	119
H 4 Development LLC	7374	262
H A Dehart and Son	5012	114
H A Framburg and Co	3645	57
H/A Industries Inc	3569	151
H A Phillips and Co	3585	182
H and A Clarke Inc	5046	368
H and A Construction Co	1542	398
H and B Holdings Inc	5031	350
H and B Packing Company Inc	2011	87
H And B Products Inc	5075	93
H and B Tool and Engineering Co	3599	625
H and C Coffee Co	2095	31
H and D Steel Service Inc	5051	188
H and E Cutter Grinding Inc	3599	1136
H and E Equipment Services Inc	7359	10
H and F Manufacturing Company Inc	3444	150
H and G Industries International	3559	423
H and H Bindery Inc	2789	129
H and H Chief Sales Inc	5521	8
H and H Color Lab Inc	7384	5
H and H Computers	5045	951
H and H Diesel Service Inc	7538	32
H and H Engineering Company Inc	3443	244
H and H Farm Products Manufacturing Inc	3446	50
H and H Furniture Manufacturers Inc	2511	67
H and H Graphics Inc	7334	18
H and H Green LLC	5087	178
H and H Group Inc	1731	107
H and H Machine Company Inc	5074	166
H and H Machine Service LLC	3599	751
H and H Machine Shop of Akron Inc	3599	2372
H and H Mack Sales Inc	5012	152
H and H Manufacturing Company Inc	3599	674
H and H Meat Products Company Inc	5149	15
H and H Metal Source International Inc	5051	390
H and H Mold And Tooling Co	3544	670
H and H Overhead Door Company Inc	5031	281
H And H Pets And Waterproofing	7342	88
H and H Products Co	2087	60
H and H Publishing Company Inc	2731	309
H and H Servicco Corp	7372	4825
H and H Service Store Inc	5731	54
H and H Steel Fabricators Inc	3325	34
H and H Technologies Inc	3599	911
H and H Transformer Inc	5063	970
H and H Transportation Inc	4213	2638
H and H Utility Contractors Inc	1731	632
H and H Wood Recyclers Inc	2875	33
H and J Tool and Die Company Inc	3599	1243
H and K Dallas Inc	3589	46
H And K Tool And Machine Company Inc	3544	219
H and L Cartage Company Inc	4213	1128
H and L Electric Inc	1731	1123
H and L Electrical Inc	1731	1932
H and L Electrical of Raleigh Nc Inc	1731	1658
H and L Instruments LLC	3661	223
H and L Poultry Processing LLC	2015	53
H and L Tool Company Inc	3452	14
H and L Tooth Co	3531	36
H and M Bay Inc	4213	335
H and M Construction Company Inc	1541	82
H and M Constructors Co	1542	136
H and M Electric Co	1731	1206
H and M Lumber Company Inc	5211	296
H and M Machine Shop Inc	3599	2056
H and M Machining Inc	3544	757
H and M Metals LLC	3444	158
H and M Pipe Beveling Machine Co	3541	263
H and M Rubber Company Inc	3069	132
H and M Thread Rolling Company Inc	3599	2495
H and M Trucking Inc	4213	1004
H and M Ventures LLC	1731	1602
H and N Chevrolet-Buick Co	5511	930
H and N Manufacturing Inc	3089	1082
H and O Tool and Die Inc	3469	310
H and P Industries Inc	3842	145
H and P Tool Company Inc	3545	312
H and R Block Financial Advisors Inc	6282	99
H and R Block Inc	7291	1
H and R Block Tax Services Inc	7291	2
H and R Construction Parts and Equipment Inc	5082	129
H and R Enterprises Inc	5065	1014
H and R General Contractor And Custodian Services Inc	7389	1591
H and R Manufacturing And Supply Inc	3545	178
H and R Services Inc	8741	248
H and S Body Works and Towing	5093	178
H and S Chemical Company Inc	2865	29
H and S Company Inc	3533	127
H and S Enterprises Inc	4213	1951
H and S Hardware	5251	5
H and S Machine Company Inc	3599	2149
H and S Supply Inc	5074	186
H and S Swansons' Tool Co	3599	266
H and S Tool And Engineering Inc	3599	1353
H and S Valve Inc	7699	105
H and U Inc	2098	20
H and W Computer Systems Inc	7372	1495
H and W Contractors Inc	1623	510
H and W Products	5063	1089
H and W Transfer and Cartage Service	4213	1602
H and W Trucking Company Inc	4213	1057
H B Stubbs Holdings Inc	3993	48
H B Taylor Co	2087	70
H Betti Industries Inc	5064	8
H C Schau and Son Inc	5147	23
H CA S Of Florida Inc	7389	825
H D Industries Inc	3531	190
H David Pitzer Trucking Inc	4213	2911
H Dennert Distributing Corp	5181	59
H Dh Consulting	7378	172
H E Long Co	3545	422
H E Morse Co	3545	116
H E Williams Inc	3646	21
H Edwin Hauler	0172	17
H Enterprises International Inc	5047	56
H Fox and Company Inc	2087	66
H Fred Barefoot Trucking Inc	4213	2659
H G Roebuck and Son Inc	7389	2220
H G Steinmetz Machine Works Inc	3599	1907
H Galow Company Inc	3812	141
H Group Holding Inc	7011	14
H H Holmes Testing Laboratories Inc	8711	434
H Hoffman Co	5063	99
H Holcomb and Son Welding and Machine Works Inc	3537	91
H J Weber Carpet Co	5023	192
H Krevit And Company Inc	2869	130
H L Gage Sales Inc	5511	1140
H Lamm Industries Inc	1711	159
H Leff Electric Co	5063	103
H M Dunn Company LP	3599	202
H M-Electronics Inc	3669	99
H Meyer Dairy Co	2026	31
H Muehlstein and Company Inc	5162	1
H Nagel and Son Co	2041	40
H Neuman and Co	3429	148
H P Manufacturing Company Inc	3089	878
H P Neun Company Inc	2653	46
H P White Laboratory Inc	8731	344
H Pearce Real Estate Co	6531	125
H Putsch and Co	3556	160
H R S Fastener Inc	5085	342
H R Simon And Company Inc	3861	58
H Reisman Corp	2834	327
H Rockwell and Son Inc	2048	90
H Roslin Staffing Group LLC	7361	172
H S Crocker Company Inc	2671	31
H Sattler Plastics Company Inc	5162	26
H Schacht Electrical Supply Inc	5063	521
H Ski Corp	7999	46
H Smith Packing Corp	5148	22
H T Barnes Co	5023	168
H T Specialty Inc	3599	1921
H Wolf Edward And Sons Inc	5171	25
H2 Performance Consulting Inc	8748	369
H20 Associates LLC	7374	289
H2o Audio Inc	3651	169
H2o Ltd	2752	1773
H2O Plus LP	2844	20
H3 Freeway Tunnel Control	4785	3
H6 Systems Inc	3825	345
HA Campbell Supply Co	5074	191
HA Cumber Inc	1521	157
HA Gill and Son Inc	6531	268
HA Rider and Sons	2033	114
HA Steen Industries Inc	7312	29
HA Stiles Co	2499	65
Haagen-Dazs Company Inc	2024	3
Haaker Equipment Co	5012	83
Haakon Industries Inc	3585	150
Haartz Corp	2231	1
Haas and Wilkerson Inc	6411	162
Haas Automation Inc	3541	5
Haas Baking Company Inc	2051	130
Haas Cabinet Company Inc	2434	26
Haas Carriage Inc	4213	2244
Haas Door Co	3442	109
Haas Electric Inc	1731	1267
HAAS Factory Outlet	5084	890
Haas LewisDifiorey and Amos	8111	526
Haas Outdoors Inc/Mossy Oak	3949	73
Haas Printing Company Inc	2752	1485
Haas Wheat and Partner LP	6799	252
Hab Nab Transportation Inc	4213	2287
Habanero Computing Solutions Inc	7371	443
Habasit Holding USA Inc	3089	133
Habbersett Sausage Inc	5147	76
Habco Tool And Development Company Inc	3599	1479
Haber Group Inc	7379	1565
Haber Inc	3826	170
Haberer Registered Investment Advisor Inc	6282	581
Haberman Machine Inc	3599	1156
Habersham Bancorp	6712	482
Habersham Bank	6022	416
Habersham Bank (Canton Georgia)	6022	600
Habersham Electric Membership Corp	4911	173
Habersham Metal Products Company Inc	3442	86
Habersham Plantation Corp	2511	65

Company Name	SIC	Rank
Habilitation Inc	8331	193
Habitat Co	6531	32
Habitec Security Inc	7382	53
Habor Ucla Medical Center Inc	8062	136
HACH Ultra Analytics (Grants Pass Oregon)	3826	24
Hachette Filipacchi Holdings Inc	2721	54
Hacienda Escrow Corp	6531	403
Hacienda Lighting Inc	5063	305
Hacienda Mexican Foods LLC	2096	40
Hackett Group Inc	8742	72
Hackett Publishing Company Inc	2731	211
Hackworth Reprographics Inc	5999	153
Hadady Machining Company Inc	3594	25
Hadar Travel and Tours	4724	124
Hadassah Medical Relief Association Inc	8322	85
Hadco Inc	5064	12
Hadco International Appraisal Services	7389	1458
Haddad Brothers Inc	2321	23
Haddad International Transport	4213	1948
Haddam Volunteer Ambulance Service Inc	5012	205
Hader Industries Inc	3599	109
Hader-Seitz Inc	3593	38
Hades Manufacturing Corp	3823	382
Hadfield Communications Inc	7311	1015
Hadler Cos	6552	114
Hadley Farms Inc	2053	16
Hadley Gear Manufacturing Co	3566	41
Hadley Printing Company Inc	2752	1113
Hadley-Keeney Chipping Inc	3531	220
Hadley's Office Products Inc	5943	32
Hadlock Building Supply Inc	5211	209
Hadlock Plastics LLC	3089	720
Hadrian Corp	7389	2201
Hadron Systems Inc	7371	1179
Hadronics Inc	3471	91
Haeger Inc	3549	111
Haeger Industries Inc	3269	3
Haeger Potteries	3269	2
Haematologic Technologies Inc	2833	40
Haemonetics Corp	3841	20
Haemonics Enterprises Inc	3841	74
Haemotronic Ltd	5047	217
Haestad Methods Inc	7371	135
Haewa Corp	3499	134
Hafemeister Machine Corp	7692	41
Hagadone Directories Inc	2741	325
Hagadone Printing Company Inc	2752	207
Hagan Business Machines Of Butler Inc	3579	66
Hagan Electronics Inc	3523	275
Hagan Kennington Oil Company Inc	2992	13
Hagans Plastics Company Inc	3089	1475
Hagedorn Communications Inc	2711	369
Hagemeyer North America	5085	5
Hagemeyer Pps Ltd	5084	48
Hagen Kurth Perman and Company PS	8721	101
Hagen Pet Foods Inc	5149	75
Hager Sharp Inc	8743	75
Hagerman and Company Inc	7373	343
Hagerman Construction Corp	1542	32
Hagerty Insurance Agency	6331	116
Haggar Clothing Co	2325	4
Haggard and Stocking Associates Inc	5084	76
Haggard Hauling and Rigging Inc	4213	2062
Haggen Inc	5411	104
Haggin Marketing Inc	8742	68
Hagie Manufacturing Co	3523	51
Hagle Lumber Company Inc	5031	225
Hagopian and Sons Inc	5713	7
Hagopian Cleaning Services Inc	7217	3
Hagopian Fire and Flood Services Inc	1752	7
Hagopian Rug Outlet Inc	5713	21
Hagopian World of Rugs	5713	4
Hague Equipment Company Of Michigan Inc	5084	491
Hahl Inc	2821	78
Hahn and Clay	3443	82
Hahn Automotive Warehouse Inc	5013	45
Hahn Brothers Inc	5142	37
Hahn Equipment Company Inc	5084	389
Hahn Manufacturing Co	3549	35
Hahn Systems	5072	49
Hahn Transportation Inc	4213	972
Hahn's Old Fashioned Cake Company Inc	2051	300
Haidar Inc	3999	149
Haig Precision Manufacturing Corp	3599	468
Haig Press Inc	2752	724
Haigh Architects	7389	1815
Haigh-Farr Inc	3663	314
Haight Brown and Bonesteel	8111	391
Haights Cross Communications Inc	2731	26
Hail and Cotton Inc	5159	8
Hailwood Inc	6512	71
Hain Celestial Group Inc	2099	7
Haines and Company Inc	2741	101
Haines And Kibblehouse Inc	1794	25
Haines Equipment Inc	3523	160
Haip Inc	5099	49
Hair Club For Men Ltd	7231	6

Company Name	SIC	Rank
Hair Systems Inc	2844	71
Hair U Wear	5199	30
Haire Machine Corp	3554	51
Haitech LLC	7379	1295
Haitz Electric Company Inc	1731	1326
Hajoca	3494	51
Hajoca Corp	5074	6
Hake Head LLC	2064	98
Hakuba USA Inc	5043	28
Hal Copeland Company Inc	8743	333
Hal Leonard Corp	2741	29
Hal Mather and Sons Inc	2759	506
hal Systems Corp	7372	3572
Halabi Inc	3281	4
Halco (Mining) Inc	1099	2
Halcore Group Inc	3713	18
Halcyon Business Publications Inc	2721	426
Halcyon Marble Design Inc	3281	39
Halcyon Microelectronics Inc	3674	423
Halcyon Offshore Asset Management LLC	8741	258
Halcyon Underwriters Inc	6411	161
Haldeman Inc	5075	63
Haldeman-Homme Inc	5046	7
Haldex Brake Products Corp	3714	60
Haldor Topsoe Inc	2819	26
Hale Manufacturing Inc	3825	297
Hale Tj Co	2541	25
Hale Trailer Brake and Wheel Inc	5511	609
Haleiwa Supermarket Ltd	5411	203
Hale-Mills Construction Inc	1541	222
Haleo Corp	7372	4612
Halex Co	3369	17
Haley and Aldrich Inc	8711	204
Haley Brothers Inc	2431	25
Haley Paint Co	5231	5
Haley Technologies Inc	5734	313
Haleyville Drapery Manufacturing Company Inc	2391	6
Half Price Books Records Magazines Inc	5942	15
Halfcom	7371	261
Halff Associates Inc	8711	267
Hal-Hen Company Inc	3842	116
Halifax Gazette Publishing Company Inc	2711	827
Halifax Paving Inc	1611	137
Halifax Plastic Inc	2759	423
Halkey-Roberts Corp	3494	37
Hall Agency	7311	674
Hall and Associates Computing Inc	7378	170
Hall and Evans	8111	279
Hall Brothers Electrical Contractors Inc	1731	500
Hall Brothers Transportation Co	4213	907
Hall Chevrolet Company Inc	5511	318
Hall Chiropractic Inc	8041	6
Hall Community Bank	6022	820
Hall Dielectric Machinery Company Inc	3559	363
Hall Electric Co	1731	1724
Hall Electrical Contractor Incorporated John E	1731	278
Hall Letter Shop Inc	2752	1259
Hall Machine And Welding Company Inc	5085	291
Hall Management Corp	8741	162
Hall Manufacturing Corp	3089	1486
Hall of Fame Beverages Inc	2086	156
Hall Research Technologies	5045	274
Hall Signs Inc	3993	93
Hall Transfer and Storage Inc	4213	2400
Halladay Motors Inc	5511	510
Hallador Energy Co	1311	179
Hallador Petroleum LLP	1389	63
Hallagan Manufacturing Company Inc	2512	75
Hallamore Corp	4213	453
Hall-Erickson Inc	7389	510
Halliburton Co	1389	2
Halliburton WellDynamics Inc	5084	21
Halling Co	5141	218
Hallman/Lindsay Paints Inc	2851	63
Hallmark Air Conditioning Inc	1731	227
Hallmark Aviation Services LP	7363	130
Hallmark Building Supplies Inc	5039	14
Hallmark Cards Inc	2771	2
Hallmark Center-Fixture	2541	35
Hallmark Channel	7822	9
Hallmark Data Systems LLC	8748	168
Hallmark Energy Economics Inc	1731	475
Hallmark Entertainment Inc	7812	32
Hallmark Financial Services Inc	6399	8
Hallmark Global Technologies Inc	7379	519
Hallmark Insurance Co	6331	232
Hallmark Manufacturing Company Inc	3645	28
Hallmark Nameplate Inc	3613	56
Hallmark Refining Corp	5084	421
Hallmark Sweet	3915	2
Hallmarks Laser Imaging Inc	7378	128
Hallogram Publishing	5045	441
Halloran Software	7372	3907
Hallowell International LLC	3639	23
Hall's Arkansas Oilstones Inc	1499	9
Halls Merchandising Inc	5311	47
Halls of Cross Inc	4213	2342
Hall's Rental Service Inc	7359	85

Company Name	SIC	Rank
Hall's Warehouse Corp	4222	3
Hallsmith-Sysco Food Services	5141	62
Hallwood Group Inc	2221	8
Halm Industries Company Inc	3555	19
Halma Holdings Inc	3613	151
Halo Branded Solutions Inc	5199	10
Halo Burger	5812	241
Halo Custom Guitars Inc	3931	39
Halo Distributing Co	5181	29
Halo Optical Products Inc	3827	78
Halo Sheet Metal Company Inc	1711	124
Halo Technology Holdings Inc	7372	1074
Halox Technologies Inc	4941	68
Halozyme Therapeutics Inc	2834	315
Halpern's' Steak And Seafood Co	5147	14
Halpin Smith and Christian Real Estate Services Inc	6531	145
Halpin's Pharmacy Inc	5912	58
Halquist Stone Company Inc	1422	48
Halsen Enterprises Inc	5084	820
Halsey Myers Inc	5211	266
Halsey Street Inc	7379	1478
Halstad Elevator Co	5153	121
Halt Buzas and Powell LTD	8721	231
Hal-Tec Corp	8711	171
Halted Specialties Co	5065	537
Halter Capital Corp	7371	813
Halton Co	5082	48
Halvor Lines Inc	4213	496
Ham Honeybaked Co	5421	2
HAM Media Group	7313	1
Ham Stevison Co	2011	102
Ham Wayco Co	2013	227
Hamamatsu Corp	3671	10
Hamann Construction Co	1542	219
Hamar Laser Instruments Inc	5084	753
Hambolu Inc	3625	213
Hambrecht and Quist Capital Management LLC	6722	180
Hamburg Manufacturing Inc	3321	48
Hamburg Sud North America Inc	4412	12
Hamernik-Harrod Inc	3531	234
Hames Trucking Inc	4213	1787
Hamil Holding Company Inc	3568	91
Hamill Manufacturing Co	3599	108
Hamilton Advisors Inc	6282	431
Hamilton and Associates Inc	8721	446
Hamilton Animal Products LLC	3199	18
Hamilton Associates Inc	3829	124
Hamilton Automotive Warehouse Inc	5013	168
Hamilton Beach/Proctor-Silex Inc	3634	6
Hamilton Brothers Electric Inc	1731	1416
Hamilton Carter Smith and Company Inc	6162	112
Hamilton Chevrolet Inc	5511	548
Hamilton Communications Group	7311	276
Hamilton Cos	6211	278
Hamilton Equipment Inc	5083	26
Hamilton Exhibits LLC	3993	96
Hamilton Fixture Co	2541	7
Hamilton Form Company Ltd	3272	90
Hamilton Insurance Agency	6331	211
Hamilton Laboratories	7372	4909
Hamilton Laboratory Workstations	3821	3
Hamilton Lane Advisors Inc	6282	461
Hamilton Manufacturing Corp	3581	10
Hamilton Materials Inc	3259	4
Hamilton Miller Hudson and Fayne	4725	21
Hamilton Mold and Machine Company Inc	3544	326
Hamilton Plastics Inc	2671	29
Hamilton Precision Metals	3444	159
Hamilton Printing Company Inc	2732	24
Hamilton Robinson LLC	6799	355
Hamilton Safe Products Company Inc	5049	87
Hamilton Scrap Processors Inc	5093	169
Hamilton Software Inc	7372	3050
Hamilton Sundstrand Corp	3724	3
Hamker Enterprises Corp	1731	2117
Hamler State Bank	6022	775
Hamlin Electronics LP	3625	50
Hamlin Industries	3599	2493
Hamlin Steel Products LLC	3469	163
Hamlin Tool and Machine Company Inc	3714	308
Hamm and Phillips Service Co	4213	651
Hammacher Schlemmer and Company Inc	5961	73
Hammbros Inc	3639	29
Hammer and Wikan Inc	5399	13
Hammer Express Inc	4213	2012
Hammer Packaging Corp	2759	24
Hammer Plastics Inc	5162	57
Hammer Press Printers Inc	2752	336
Hammerhead Aviation LLC	5088	109
Hammerhead Distribution Inc	5031	259
Hammerlund Manufacturing Company Inc	3599	2394
Hammers Co	7372	2748
Hammersmith Manufacturing and Sales Inc	3443	115
Hammerton Inc	3646	47
Hammett Gravel Company Inc	1442	35
Hammill Manufacturing Co	3544	40
Hammond and Irving Inc	3463	16

Company Name	SIC	Rank
Hammond and Stephens Co	2741	104
Hammond Communications Group Inc	7812	234
Hammond Electronics Inc	5065	80
Hammond Group Inc	2819	48
Hammond Lumber Co	5211	38
Hammond Machinery Inc	3541	54
Hammond Press Inc	2752	904
Hammond Pretzel Bakery Inc	2052	81
Hammonds Technical Services Inc	3569	160
Hammonds Trkg Flatbed Div	4213	2633
Hammons Products Co	2068	21
Hamon-Custodis	1741	6
Hampden Bancorp	6712	438
Hampden Bank	0036	56
Hampden Engineering Corp	3679	297
Hampden Papers Inc	2671	34
Hampden Press Inc	2752	1080
Hampford Research Inc	2869	100
Hampshire Equity Partners	6799	24
Hampshire Group Ltd	2251	1
Hampstead Stage Co	7389	2472
Hampton Affiliates Inc	2421	8
Hampton Automotive Inc	5511	565
Hampton City School District	8211	10
Hampton Envelope Co	2677	18
Hampton Homes	1521	110
Hampton Inns Inc	7011	157
Hampton Machine Shop Inc	3599	899
Hampton Meat Processing Company Inc	2011	136
Hampton Roads Bancshares Inc	6021	45
Hampton Roads Crane and Rigging Co	4212	75
Hampton Roads Educational Telecommunications Association Inc	4833	149
Hampton Roads Sanitation District	4952	3
Hampton Technologies LLC	3699	198
Hampton Transfer Prints Inc	2752	61
Hamptons Luxury Homes Inc	1521	141
Hamrick Mills	2211	4
Hamrick's Inc	2339	8
Hamrock Inc	3315	16
Hamshaw Lumber Inc	5211	103
Han King Inc	3825	314
Hana Group Inc	7381	52
Hanagriff's Machine Shop Inc	3599	738
Hanan Products Company Inc	2026	85
Hanard Machine Inc	3599	322
Hanbury Evans Wright Vlattas and Co	8712	147
Hance Distributing Inc	5083	135
Hanchett Entry Systems Inc	3699	40
Hanchett Manufacturing	3599	1493
Hanchett Paper Co	5199	56
Hanco Inc	2599	28
Hancock Bank of Louisiana	6022	75
Hancock Fabrics Inc	5999	18
Hancock Holding Co	6712	43
Hancock Lumber Company Inc	5211	97
hancockfabricscom Inc	5949	7
Hancock-Wood Electric Cooperative Inc	4911	321
Hancor Inc	3084	7
Hand Family Beverage	5181	14
Hand Industries Inc	3471	122
Hand Piece Parts And Products Inc	3843	65
Handbill Printers LP	2752	195
Handgards Inc	3089	427
Handheld4me Inc	5734	254
Handi-Clean Products Inc	2842	125
Handicomp Inc	7372	2906
Handishop Industries Inc	8331	185
Handleman Co	5099	154
Handler Manufacturing Company Inc	3843	55
Handley Computer Corp	7372	2983
Handley Industries Inc	3089	1858
Handling and Storage Concepts Inc	5084	252
Handling Systems Inc	5084	765
Handmade Software Inc	7372	4696
Han-D-Pac Products Inc	5141	202
Hands Free America	3661	244
Handshake Software	7372	3908
Handshake Software Inc	5045	789
Handshake Solutions	7373	922
Handsome Dog Consulting Group	8742	603
Hands-on Mobile Inc	2741	16
Handy and Harman Ltd	3357	7
Handy and Harman Tube Company Inc	3317	11
Handy Andy Supermarkets	5411	142
Handy International Inc	2092	44
Handy Rents	7353	10
Handy Store Fixtures Inc	2542	42
Handy Truck Line Inc	4213	1472
Handyman's Inc	5072	193
Handysoft Global Corp	7371	417
Hane Security Safe Inc	5044	137
Hanefeld Brothers Inc	4213	1962
Hanel Corp	3451	83
Hanel Storage Systems LP	3599	1413
Hanes Erie Inc	3089	673
Hanesbrands Inc	5611	3
Haney Truck Line Inc	4213	553
Haney Trucking Inc	4213	1504
Hanford Bay Associates Ltd	7372	4461
Hanford Community Hospital	8062	176
Hanford Sentinel Inc	2711	104
Hanger Medical Center Brace Company Inc	3842	285
Hanger Orthopedic Group Inc	8093	7
Hangsterfers Laboratories Inc	2992	12
Hangtown Electric Inc	1731	1342
Hank Brandt Associates Inc	7311	987
Hank Graff Chevrolet	5511	490
Hank Thorn Co	5072	177
Hankamer Investments LP	3089	1672
Hankins Lumber Company Inc	5031	275
Hankison International	3569	34
Hank's Specialties Inc	5023	62
Hanley Industries Inc	2892	8
Hanley Lamont and Associates Inc	7322	84
Hanlo Gauges and Engineering Co	3545	395
Hanlund Phillips Corporate Design and Communications	2741	211
Hanmi Bank	6021	202
Hanmi Financial Corp	6712	155
Hanna and Morton LLP	8111	591
Hanna Andersson Corp	5961	125
Hanna Boys Center	8361	117
Hanna Brophy McLean McAleer and Jensen	8111	255
Hanna Instruments Inc	3825	101
Hanna Rubber Co	3069	52
Hanna Steel Corp	3317	23
Hanna Truck Line Inc	4213	1499
Hannaford Brothers Co	5411	125
Hannah Engineering Inc	3599	2284
Hannah International Foods Inc	2099	203
Hannan Products Corp	3565	118
Hannan Supply Co	5063	50
Hanna's Candle Co	3999	58
Hannay Reels Inc	3569	42
Hannibal Carbide Tool Inc	3545	76
Hannibal Industries Inc	3317	33
Hannig Construction Inc	1542	248
Hannis T Bourgeois LLP	8721	17
Hannmann Machinery Systems Inc	3561	168
Hanno Weber and Associates	8712	327
Hannon Co	3621	67
Hannon Hydraulics LP	7699	40
Hannover Fairs USA Inc	7389	1435
Hann's On Software Inc	7372	2925
Hanon-Mckendry Inc	7311	688
Hanora Spinning Inc	2281	20
Hanover Direct Inc	5961	41
Hanover Foods Corp	2033	13
Hanover Insurance Group Inc	6331	61
Hanover Juvenile Correctional Center	8361	183
Hanover-Adams Rehabilitation And Training Center Inc	8331	204
HanoverTrade Inc	7389	898
Hanovia Specialty Lighting LLC	3641	25
Hanrahan Meyers Architects	8712	287
Hans Hagen Homes Inc	6552	148
Hans Kissle Company Inc	2099	122
Hans Rothenbuhler and Son Inc	2022	56
Hans Rudolph Inc	3842	221
Hansan Group Inc	2711	209
Hansberger Global Investors Inc	6722	275
Hanscom Federal Credit Union	6061	42
Hansel Ford	5561	11
Hansel 'n Gretel Brand Inc	2013	94
Hansel Prestige Inc	5511	664
Hansen Beverage Co	2086	19
Hansen Corp	3625	25
Hansen Fabrication	3531	244
Hansen Fruit and Cold Storage Inc	2037	15
Hansen Information Technologies Inc	7372	1520
Hansen Manufacturing Corp	3535	84
Hansen Marketing Services Inc	5031	258
Hansen Medical Inc	3842	111
Hansen Natural Corp	2086	3
Hansen Plastics Corp	3089	825
Hansen Printing Company Inc	2752	1301
Hansen Quality Loan Services LLC	6289	19
Hansen Research Inc	3599	2514
Hansen Surfboards Inc	5941	38
Hansen Technologies Corp	3822	23
Hansen Trucking	4213	1853
Hansen's Cakes Inc	2051	204
Hanset Stainless Inc	1761	45
Hansome Energy Systems Inc	7629	16
Hanson and Company CPA/Consultant	8721	416
Hanson Building Materials America Inc	1442	1
Hanson Building Materials America-Hanson Brick and Tile	3271	9
Hanson Building Materials West	1442	12
Hanson Directory Service Inc	2741	259
Hanson Lab Furniture Inc	3821	46
Hanson North America Inc	2819	4
Hanson Pipe and Precast	3272	74
Hanson Porcelain Company Inc	3479	88
Hanson Pressure Pipe Inc	3272	58
Hanson Printing Company Inc	2752	1260
Hanson Production Co	1311	152
Hanson Research Corp	3826	57
Hanson Tire Service Inc	5014	48
Hanson Truss Inc	2439	27
Hantronix Inc	3559	94
Hanwha Machinery America Corp	3714	288
Han-Win Products Inc	3089	1357
Hapco Inc	2821	161
Happ Controls Inc	5065	147
Happel Excavating Inc	1623	533
Happijac Intellemax Co	3569	171
Happy Chef Systems Inc	5812	379
Happy Co	2499	49
Happy Harry's Inc	5912	26
Happy State Bank and Trust Co	6091	7
Happy Trucking Company Inc	4213	2732
Hara Electrical Contractors Inc	1731	1444
Harbar LLC	2099	364
Harben Inc	3589	235
Harber Industries Inc	2731	240
Harbin Ford Lincoln Mercury	5511	1227
Harbinger Communications Inc	1731	1257
Harbinger Group Inc	2077	10
Harbison-Fischer Inc	3533	37
Harbison-Mahony-Higgins Builders Inc	1542	262
Harbor Auto Liquidators	5015	12
Harbor Bank of Maryland	6022	450
Harbor Bankshares Corp	6712	622
Harbor BioSciences Inc	2834	470
Harbor Candy Shop Inc	2064	125
Harbor Capital Advisors Inc	6282	487
Harbor Capital Management Company Inc	6282	199
Harbor Castings Inc	3324	15
Harbor Chevrolet Corp	5511	311
Harbor Construction Company Inc	1731	1194
Harbor Diesel And Equipment Inc	5084	293
Harbor Duvall Graphics Inc	2752	1350
Harbor Electric Inc	1731	1802
Harbor Enterprises Inc	5172	19
Harbor Express Inc	4213	649
Harbor Freight Transport Corp	4213	1063
Harbor Industries Inc	2541	8
Harbor Island Machine Works Inc	3599	1939
Harbor Linen LLC	5023	58
Harbor Management Consultants Inc	4953	107
Harbor Marine Maintenance and Supply Inc	5088	100
Harbor Marketing Inc	5094	48
Harbor Metal Treating Co	3312	54
Harbor Packaging Inc	2653	43
Harbor Patterns	3544	910
Harbor Payments Inc	8748	46
Harbor Pipe And Steel Inc	5051	219
Harbor Steel And Supply Corp	5051	227
Harbor Sweets Inc	2064	58
Harbor Tool Manufacturing Inc	3599	358
Harbor Truck Sales And Service Inc	5012	81
Harbor Wholesale Electric Supply Inc	5063	294
Harbor Work Source Center	7361	386
HarborOne Credit Union	6062	49
Harborside Healthcare Corp	8051	17
Harbour Group	6799	4
Harbourvest	6799	25
Harco Brake Systems Inc	3714	328
Harco Industries Inc	3714	413
Harco Laboratories Inc	3829	69
Harco Manufacturing Co	3714	386
Harcourt Inc	5311	17
Harcourt Industries Inc	3952	10
Harcros Chemicals Inc	5169	25
Hard Chrome Plating Consultant Inc	8742	690
Hard Drive 911 LLC	7379	1629
Hard Drive Productions Inc	7379	1115
Hard Drives Northwest Inc	3571	44
Hard Manufacturing Company Inc	2514	17
Hard Rock Cafe International Inc	5812	55
Hardaway Concrete Company Inc	3273	61
Hardaway Construction Corp	1522	22
Hardcoat Inc	3471	116
Hardcore Computer Inc	3571	156
Hard-E Foods Inc	5148	87
Hardebeck Trucking	4213	1896
Hardee's Food Systems Inc	5812	51
Hardel Mutual Plywood Corp	2436	5
Harden Furniture Company Inc	2511	31
Harder Mechanical Contractors Inc	1711	67
Hardface Alloys Inc	5084	888
Hardie-Tynes Company Inc	3511	26
Hardin Computers	5734	244
Hardin Construction Company LLC	1542	54
Hardin County Publishing Company Inc	2711	612
Hardin Delivery Inc	4213	2137
Hardin Industries Inc	3621	147
Hardin Optical Co	3827	65
Hardin Tubular Sales Inc	5084	709
Harding Energy Inc	3691	35
Harding Metals Inc	5093	126
Hardinge Inc	3541	12
Hardinger Transfer Company Inc	4213	391
Hardin's-Sysco Food Services Inc	5141	60
Hardrives Inc	1611	64
Hardrives of Delray Inc	1611	13
Hardware Distribution Warehouses Inc	5072	23
Hardware Electric and Plumbing Supply Company Inc	5063	869
Hardware Specialty Company Inc	5072	54
Hardwick Clothes Inc	2311	9
Hardwick's Bar And Restaurant Supplies Inc	5046	190
Hardwire LLC	3795	3

Company Name	SIC	Rank	Company Name	SIC	Rank	Company Name	SIC	Rank
Hardwood Line Manufacturing Co	3559	379	Harold Johnson Optical Laboratories Inc	3827	106	Harris Environmental Systems Inc	3585	117
Hardwoods Of Michigan Inc	2421	49				Harris Farms Inc	0161	16
Hardwoods of Morganton Inc	5031	111	Harold K Scholz Co	3613	97	Harris Fire Protection Company Inc	7389	1321
Hardwoods Of Morristown Inc	2426	45	Harold L Keay and Son	5399	22	Harris Golf Management Inc	8741	206
Hardy Brothers Inc	4213	1233	Harold Lemay Enterprises Inc	4953	89	Harris Group Inc	8711	219
Hardy Corp	7349	516	Harold Levinson Associates Inc	5194	2	Harris Hardware Sales Corp	5072	125
Hardy Holzman Pfeiffer Associates LLP	8712	191	Harold Macquinn Inc	1541	271	Harris Holdings Inc (Manassas Virginia)	6411	191
Hardy Instruments Inc	3823	147	Harold R Clune Inc	1731	609			
Hardy Machine Inc	3599	1387	Harold Tymer Company Inc	5946	14	Harris Industrial Gases Inc	5084	121
Hardy Media	5047	72	Harold W Griffith Inc	5049	176	Harris Industries Inc	3321	57
Hare Pontiac Buick GMC	5511	922	Harold W Pelton Co	5411	275	Harris Information Technology Services	7371	37
Harford Bank	6021	243	Harold Warner Advertising Inc	7311	970	Harris Infosource International Inc	7323	15
Harford Systems Inc	3444	77	Harold's Photo Centers Inc	7384	17	Harris Instrument Corp	3825	289
Harger Inc	3643	74	Harold's Tire and Auto	5014	21	Harris Interactive Inc	8742	88
Hargis Industries LP	5085	100	Haroutunian Aramais	3825	308	Harris Interactive Media Inc	2752	890
Hargrove and Associates	1542	41	Harp Advertising Interactive	7319	137	Harris Lithographics Inc	2752	1428
Hargrove Design Group	7336	312	Harp Enterprises Inc	5087	135	Harris Machine Tools Inc	5084	657
Hargrove Electric Co	1731	509	Harpel's Inc	5112	99	Harris Manufacturing Company Inc	2385	2
Hargrove Inc	7389	322	Harper Air Tool Co	3531	155	Harris Manufacturing Inc	3646	33
Harich-Tahoe Developments	6552	244	Harper Brush Works Inc	3991	7	Harris Marketing Group Inc	7311	520
Harig Manufacturing Corp	3545	319	Harper Co	1611	148	Harris Massey and Herinckx	8743	57
Harig Products Inc	3531	231	Harper Contracting Inc	1794	9	Harris Material Exchange Inc	5093	127
Haringa Inc	7389	1009	Harper Corporation Of America	3555	18	Harris Metals Inc	5051	432
Hark Electronic Systems Inc	3661	237	Harper Electric Construction Company Inc	1731	795	Harris Miller Miller and Hanson Inc	8748	275
Harkcon Inc	8742	595				Harris MyCFO Inc	7372	48
Harkins Amusement Enterprises Inc	7832	17	Harper Engineering Co	3728	113	Harris Packaging Corp	2653	61
Harkins Builders Inc	1522	20	Harper Engraving and Printing Company Inc	2759	121	Harris Press Inc	2752	1162
Harkness Enterprises Inc	3089	708				Harris Publications Inc	2721	158
Harkness Industries Inc	3089	1517	Harper International Corp	3567	28	Harris/Ragan Management Group	8742	694
Harlan Bakeries-Avon LLC	5149	86	Harper Mullholland Co	3993	108	Harris Ranch Beef Co	2011	34
Harlan Electric Co	1731	44	Harper Oil Products Inc	5172	125	Harris Research Inc	6794	72
Harlan Graphic Arts Services Inc	2791	48	Harper Products Ltd	3951	5	Harris Restaurant Supply Inc	5113	61
Harlan Laws Corp	1799	62	Harper Shields and Co	5084	306	Harris Soup Co	2099	69
Harland Clarke	7389	93	Harper Trucks Inc	3537	31	Harris Steel Co	5051	217
Harland Clarke Holdings Corp	2759	5	HarperCollins Publishers Inc	2731	11	Harris Supply Solutions Inc	5051	61
Harland dataPRINT Inc	2782	2	Harper-Love Adhesives Corp	2891	54	Harris Technical Services Corp	1731	2
Harland Financial Solutions Inc	6211	145	Harperprints Inc	2819	87	Harris Teeter Inc	5411	39
Harlem Globetrotters International Inc	7941	23	Harper's Country Hams Inc	2011	78	Harris Transport Co	4213	1551
Harley Electric Company Inc	1731	1775	Harper's Magazine Foundation	2721	201	Harris Trust and Savings Bank	6022	6
Harley Ellis Devereaux Corp	8712	72	Harper's Model Home Maintenance Inc	7349	297	Harris Trust Bank of Arizona	6022	350
Harley Gray Stone Co	1411	20	Harper's Nurseries and Flower Shops	5992	15	Harrisburg Dairies Inc	2026	59
Harley Stanfield Inc	6798	200	Harper's Restaurants Inc	5812	140	HarrisData	5734	11
Harley Tool and Machine Inc	3599	2425	Harpo Inc	7822	4	Harrison and Harrison Inc	1623	670
Harley-Davidson Financial Services Inc	6141	41	Harpo Productions Inc	7822	5	Harrison and Lear Inc	6531	196
Harley-Davidson Inc	3751	2	Harpoon Technologies Inc	7379	1168	Harrison and Shriftman	8743	72
Harley-Davidson Motor Co	3751	1	Harp's Food Stores Inc	5411	118	Harrison and Star Business Group	7311	102
Harleysville Group Inc	6331	111	Harrah's Aviation Inc	7997	7	Harrison Associates PC	8721	115
Harleysville Insurance Company of New Jersey	6331	266	Harrah's Cherokee Casino and Hotel	7999	4	Harrison Bakery West	2051	237
			Harrah's Crescent City Investment Co	7999	73	Harrison Company Inc	5141	129
Harleysville Insurance Company of New York	6331	353	Harrah's Interactive Investment Co	7999	47	Harrison County Rural Electric Coop	4911	578
			Harrah's Kansas Casino Corp	7999	33	Harrison County Rural Electric Coop (Corydon Indiana)	4911	263
Harleysville Mutual Insurance Co	6311	113	Harrah's Laughlin Inc	7999	5			
Harleysville Savings Financial Corp	6712	356	Harrah's Michigan Corp	7999	67	Harrison Electrical Construction Inc	1731	1819
Harlingen Consolidated Independent School District	8211	25	Harrah's Operating Co	7011	32	Harrison Electro Mechanical Corp	3674	456
			Harrah's Operating Company Memphis Inc	7999	39	Harrison Falk Inc	7336	264
Harlis R Ellington Construction Inc	4212	49				Harrison Group (Ocean City Maryland)	7011	67
Harliss Specialties Corp	3443	184	Harrah's Phoenix Ak-Chin Casino	7999	34	Harrison Hose And Tubing Inc	3052	32
Harlo Corp	3537	40	Harrah's Wheeling Corp	7999	88	Harrison Industries Inc	2439	51
Harlo Products Corp	3537	53	Harrell Industries Inc	2899	116	Harrison Ironworks LLC	3321	41
Harlon's L A Fish LLC	5146	58	Harrell's Inc	2875	14	Harrison Leifer Dimarco Inc	7311	677
Harmac Medical Products Inc	3841	94	Harri Hoffmann Co	2842	113	Harrison Machine and Plastic Corp	3089	1310
Harman Consumer Products	3651	43	Harriet Walley Associates	7311	635	Harrison Manufacturing LLC	3089	1722
Harman Corp	3089	1146	Harrigan Lumber Company Inc	2421	120	Harrison Mullane Inc	3599	373
Harman International Industries Inc	3651	6	Harriman Associates	8712	89	Harrison Paint Co	2851	117
Harman Press Inc	2752	905	Harrington and Co	5033	34	Harrison Piping Supply Co	5051	148
Harman Professional Signal Processing	3651	35	Harrington Co	2086	72	Harrison Poultry Inc	0254	3
			Harrington Corp	3089	562	Harrison Seal Corp	3679	882
Harman-Management Corp	8741	82	Harrington Electric Co	1731	455	Harrison Specialty Company Inc	2844	149
Harmar Summit LLC	3534	13	Harrington Group Inc	7372	3135	Harrison Steel Castings Co	3325	11
Harmon Associates Corp	5093	43	Harrington Industrial Plastics Inc	5162	3	Harrison Trucking Inc	4213	1503
Harmon Auto Glass (Minneapolis Minnesota)	3231	5	Harrington Machine And Tool Company Inc	3599	1009	Harrison Western Construction Corp	1629	69
						Harrison-Nichols Company Ltd	4213	847
Harmon City Inc	5411	128	Harrington Services Corp	6411	30	Harrisonville Telephone Co	4813	83
Harmon Contract Asia Ltd	1793	3	Harrington Signal Inc	3669	136	Harriss and Covington International Inc	2252	8
Harmon Contract Inc	1793	2	Harrington Tool Co	3545	400	Harriston-Mayo LLC	3523	110
Harmonia Mundi USA Inc	7922	54	Harrington Tools Inc	3423	80	Harrold Ford	5511	522
Harmonic Inc	3663	19	Harrington Trucking Inc	4213	876	Harroun Enterprises Inc	3545	419
Harmonic Ranch	7819	80	Harrington's In Vermont Inc	2013	119	Harry and David Holdings Inc	5961	40
Harmonic Software Inc	7372	5119	Harris and Bruno Machine CoInc	3599	409	Harry C Johnson Co	3643	136
Harmonic Vision Inc	2741	348	Harris and Ford LLC	5169	26	Harry C Wenzel and Sons Inc	5143	44
Harmonium Inc	8351	13	Harris and Harris Group Inc	6799	202	Harry Davis and Co	7389	534
Harmony Agri Services Inc	5153	194	Harris/Arizona Rebar Inc	3449	17	Harry E Orkin Inc	5051	485
Harmony Computers and Electronics Inc	7373	368	Harris Associates LP	6282	180	Harry Fox Agency Inc	8742	134
			Harris Baio and Mccullough Inc	7311	632	Harry G Barr Co	3089	851
Harmony Country Coop	5191	125	Harris Bank	6091	8	Harry Green Chevrolet Inc	5511	696
Harmony Enterprises Inc	3569	121	Harris Bank Aurora - Branch	6021	299	Harry Grodsky and Company Inc	1711	112
Harmony Gold USA Inc	7812	54	Harris Bank Barrington NA	6021	150	Harry H Reich Company Inc	5051	508
Harmony Healthcare	8093	42	Harris Bank Hoffman-Schaumburg	6022	665	Harry Horn Inc	5063	1087
Harmony Hill School Inc	8361	89	Harris Bank of Oakbrook Terrace	6022	536	Harry J Bosworth Co	3843	47
Harmony Press Inc	2752	925	Harris Bank Palatine NA	6021	109	Harry J Lawall and Son Inc	3842	130
Harmony Sand and Gravel Inc	1442	57	Harris Bank Westchester	6022	471	Harry J Rashti and Company Inc	5137	25
Harmony Systems And Service Inc	3089	1011	Harris Bank Woodstock	6022	419	Harry Kahn Associates Inc	8231	1
Harmsco Inc	3589	85	Harris Bankcorp Inc	6712	26	Harry Kuhn W Inc	4212	47
Harnett County Board Of Education	8211	23	Harris Beach PLLC	8111	236	Harry L Laws and Co	2061	10
Harold A Burdette Dental Laboratories Inc	8072	10	Harris Chevrolet Inc	5511	281	Harry N Abrams Inc	2731	140
			Harris Corp	3579	3	Harry Ritchie's Jeweler Inc	5944	20
Harold Beck and Sons Inc	3625	82	Harris Corp Microwave Communications Div	3663	162	Harry Rock and Company Inc	5093	215
Harold Bibbs and Sons Trucking Inc	4213	1994				Harry Singh and Sons	0161	13
Harold C Brown and Company Inc	6211	106	Harris D Mckinney Inc	7311	880	Harry Walker Agency Inc	7389	697
Harold Dickey Transport Inc	4213	1117	Harris Design Associates Inc	8712	313	Harry Winston Inc	3911	9
Harold G Butzer Inc	1711	184	Harris Electric Inc	1731	32	Harry's Motor Service Inc	4213	1611
Harold Implement Company Inc	5083	60	Harris Enterprises Inc (Hutchinson Kansas)	2711	175	Harry's On The Hill	5511	319
Harold Import Company Inc	5023	36				Harsco Corp	3446	1

Company Name	SIC	Rank
Harsco Industrial Air-X-Changers	3443	37
Harsco Minerals	3291	3
Harsco Track Technologies	3743	17
Harsh International Inc	3536	4
Har-Son Manufacturing Inc	3599	1797
Hart and Cooley Inc	3446	6
Hart Associates Inc	7311	578
Hart Crowser Inc	8748	221
Hart Design and Manufacturing	3444	200
Hart Foundation	7389	2297
Hart Heat Transfer Products Inc	3443	152
Hart Hotels Inc	7011	48
Hart Intercivic Inc	5087	12
Hart Interior Design Ltd	7380	541
Hart Scientific Inc	3829	176
Hart Transportation Inc	4213	3090
Hartco Cable Inc	1623	400
Hartco Facilities Support Services Inc	7349	421
Hartcom Inc	5065	672
Harte-Hanks Data Services LLC	8742	353
Harte-Hanks Data Technologies LLC	7372	473
Harte-Hanks Direct Marketing/ Baltimore Inc	8742	127
Harte-Hanks Direct Marketing/Fullerton Inc	8742	26
Harte-Hanks Inc	2741	11
Harte-Hanks Shoppers Inc	2741	1
Hartel Industries Inc	7629	58
Harter Industries Inc	7699	114
Harter Secrest and Emery LLP	8111	136
Hartford Accident and Indemnity Co	6331	90
Hartford Aircraft Products Inc	3429	141
Hartford Auction Group Inc	7389	2298
Hartford Compressors Inc	3585	146
Hartford Courant Co	2711	105
Hartford Distributors Inc	5181	20
Hartford Electric Supply Co	5063	146
Hartford Financial Services Group Inc	6331	3
Hartford Fine Art and Framing Co	2499	58
Hartford Income Shares Fund Inc	6726	86
Hartford Insurance Company Of Illinois	6411	96
Hartford Life Inc	6311	261
Hartford Life Insurance Co	6311	59
Hartford School District	8211	27
Hartford Steam Boiler Inspection and Insurance Co	6331	16
Hartig Industries Inc	3599	1850
Hartin Paint and Filler Corp	2851	135
Harting Electronik Inc	3678	44
Harting Incorporated Of North America	5065	122
Harting's Bakery Inc	2051	102
Hartley Loudspeakers Inc	3651	184
Hartley Press Inc	2752	386
Hartline Supply Inc	1731	1878
Hartman Blitch and Gartside	8721	199
Hartman Enterprises Inc	3599	606
Hartman Plastics Inc	2679	71
Hartman Underhill and Brubaker	8111	456
Hartman-Fabco Inc	3532	47
Hartmann Controls Inc	3594	26
Hartmann Inc	3161	3
Hartmann Studios Inc	7389	751
Hartmann USA Inc	3842	102
Hartman-Walsh Painting Co	1721	11
Hartnack Engine Supply LLC	3714	146
Hartness Visy Automation LLC	3565	134
Harts Harbor Health Care	8051	46
Hartselle Utilities	4941	62
Hartson-Kennedy Cabinet Top Company Inc	3083	15
Hartstrings LLC	5641	4
Hartt Transportation Systems Inc	4213	556
Hartung Agalite Glass Co	3211	5
Hartville Group Inc	6321	76
Hartwell Corp	3585	206
Hartwell Industries Inc	5137	16
Hartwell Medical Corp	3842	319
Harty Press Inc	2752	299
Hartz Group Inc	6552	21
Hartz Truck Line Inc	4213	2550
Hartzell Hardwoods Inc	5031	269
Hartzell Machine Works Inc	3599	1831
Hartzell Manufacturing Company Inc	3599	36
Hartzell Propeller Inc	3728	88
Harvard Associates Inc	7372	3909
Harvard Bioscience Inc	3841	56
Harvard Business School Publishing Corp	2721	48
Harvard Clinical Technology Inc	3841	357
Harvard Coil Processing Inc	3312	123
Harvard Collection Services Inc	7322	86
Harvard Consulting Group Inc	7379	954
Harvard Drug Group LLC	5122	126
Harvard Folding Box Company Inc	2657	23
Harvard Health Publications	2741	435
Harvard House	7699	193
Harvard Magazine Inc	2721	369
Harvard Maintenance Inc	7349	18
Harvard Printing Group	2752	630
Harvard Steel Inc	5039	65
Harvel Plastics Inc	3089	131
Harvest Express Inc	4213	3067
Harvest Farms Inc	5142	29
Harvest Food Products Company Inc	2038	60

Company Name	SIC	Rank
Harvest Graphics LLC	7336	112
Harvest House Publishers Inc	2731	154
Harvest Investment Consultants LLC	6282	516
Harvest Land Coop	5153	28
Harvest Moon Hay LLC	3523	200
Harvest Moon Studio	2741	414
Harvest Natural Resources Inc	1311	198
Harvest Partners Inc	6799	350
Harvest Productions Ltd	2759	272
Harvest Solutions Inc	5734	273
Harvest Time International Inc	8322	8
Harvest Time Seafood Inc	2092	98
Harvey and Company Inc	4213	1947
Harvey Brothers Inc	7694	35
Harvey C Waters Inc	3651	123
Harvey Cadillac Co	5511	587
Harvey Chevrolet Corp	5511	1018
Harvey Construction Company Inc	1623	576
Harvey E Yates Co	1382	8
Harvey Fertilizer And Gas Co	5191	47
Harvey Industries Inc	5033	2
Harvey Instruments Inc	5049	101
Harvey Milling Company Inc	5999	194
Harvey Press Inc	2752	628
Harvey Preston Electric Co	1731	1754
Harvey S Freeman	3569	275
Harvey Software Inc	7371	1609
Harvey Spencer Associates Inc	7379	1466
Harvey Trucking Inc	4213	2148
Harvey Vogel Manufacturing Co	3469	31
Harvey Whitney Books Co	5045	24
Harveys Casino Resorts	7011	79
Harvin Choice Meats Inc	5147	110
Harwood Rubber Products Inc	3069	120
HAS Images Inc	7384	44
HAS Production Inc	3651	216
Hasbro Inc	3944	1
Hascall Steel Company Inc	5051	139
Hasco/Graphix Inc	5045	1007
Hasco Manufacturing Co	3533	100
Hasco Newspaper Inc	2711	884
Haselden Construction Inc	1542	67
Hasgo Power Equipment Sales Inc	8743	345
Hash Inc	7372	603
Haskel International Inc	3561	65
Haskell and White LLP	8721	345
Haskell Co	1541	25
Haskell Corp	1542	40
Haskell Lemon Construction Co	5032	13
Haskell Livestock Auction Company Inc	0211	16
Haskins Laboratories Inc	8733	27
Haskins Steel Company Inc	5051	301
Haskris Company Inc	3585	226
Hasselblad USA Inc	3861	86
Hassell and Hughes Lumber Company Inc	2421	66
Hassell Construction Company Inc	1623	65
Hassig and Sons Inc	5084	626
Hasslocher Enterprises Inc	5812	301
Hastie Mining and Trucking	1442	13
Hastings and Hastings Inc	7361	84
Hastings and Sons Publishing Co	2711	372
Hastings Bancorp Inc	6712	534
Hastings Cooperative Creamery Co	2026	45
Hastings Entertainment Inc	5735	2
Hastings Equity Grain Bin Manufacturing Co	3523	171
Hastings Fiber Glass Products Inc	3423	46
Hastings Hvac Inc	3433	56
Hastings Manufacturing Company LLC	3714	310
Hastings Mutual Insurance Co	6331	254
Hastings State Bank	6022	710
Hastings Tile and Bath Inc	5032	201
Hat World Corp	5136	11
Hatch And Bailey Co	5031	208
Hatch and Kirk Inc	5084	604
Hatch Milling Co	2048	32
Hatch Mott MacDonald Operating Services Inc	8999	177
Hatch Stamping Co	3465	16
Hatcher Center Inc	8331	219
Hatco Corp	3589	45
Hatfield and Company Inc	5084	172
Hatfield Enterprizes Inc	4213	1862
Hatfield Manufacturing Inc	3523	146
Hatfield Quality Meats	2013	10
Hathaway Agency Inc	6411	256
Hathaway Dinwiddie Construction Co	1542	44
Hathaway Electronics Inc	5065	895
Hathorne Enterprises	7331	215
Hatley and Associates Inc	5063	436
Hatley's Electrical Service	1731	2562
Hatteras Financial Corp	6798	14
Hatteras Inc	2752	870
Hatteras Networks Inc	5045	157
Hatteras Software Inc	7372	4379
Hattie Ide Chaffee Home	8051	81
Hatton Brown Publishers Inc	2721	312
Hatzel and Buehler Inc	1731	3
Haubrich Enterprises Inc	5181	98
Hauck Manufacturing Co	3564	42
Haugk Companies Inc	1711	276
Haugo Broadcasting Inc	4832	216
Haulette Manufacturing Inc	3599	1125

Company Name	SIC	Rank
Haumiller Engineering Co	3565	56
Haun Welding Supply Inc	5085	89
Hauppauge Computer Works Inc	3672	46
Hauppauge Digital Inc	3577	168
Hauptly Construction and Equipment Company Inc	1541	231
Hause Machines Inc	3559	168
Hauser Foundry Inc	3365	44
Hauser List Services Inc	7331	201
Hauser Printing Company Inc	2752	1367
Hauser Trucking Corp	4213	1445
Hausermann Controls Co	3625	268
Hausmann Industries Inc	2599	23
Hausmeister Inc	7349	441
Hautly Cheese Company Inc	5143	26
Havana Printing and Mailing	2752	1821
Havco Wood Products LLC	2426	9
Have Inc	7819	65
Have Trunk Will Travel	7999	143
Haveco Electric Inc	1731	2060
Haven Steel Products Inc	3493	8
Havens and Associates Inc	7373	856
Haverford Trust Co	6282	86
Haverly Systems Inc (Ventura California)	7372	2802
Haverstick-Borthwick Co	1542	332
Haverty Furniture Companies Inc	5712	6
Havertys Credit Services Inc	5712	77
Haviland Plastic Products Co	3089	1593
Haviland Products Co	5169	76
Haviland Telephone Co	4813	463
Havok Inc	7372	1993
Hawa Enterprises Inc	7379	1616
Hawaii Biotech Inc	8731	247
Hawaii Candy Inc	2064	109
Hawaii Coffee Co	2095	16
Hawaii Convention Center	7389	748
Hawaii Electric Light Company Inc	4911	138
Hawaii Electrical Export Co	5063	1067
Hawaii Engineering Services Inc	5049	116
Hawaii Forest and Trail Ltd	4725	25
Hawaii Hochi Ltd	2711	486
Hawaii Information Consortium	4813	673
Hawaii National Bancshares Inc	6712	552
Hawaii National Bank	6021	232
Hawaii Stage And Lighting Rentals Inc	7359	161
Hawaii Star Bakery Inc	2051	244
Hawaiian Beauty Products Ltd	5087	159
Hawaiian Commercial and Sugar Co	2062	5
Hawaiian Dredging Construction Co	1542	81
Hawaiian Electric Company Inc	4911	91
Hawaiian Electric Industries Inc	4911	39
Hawaiian Fruit Specialties LLC	2033	126
Hawaiian Holdings Inc	4512	20
Hawaiian Host Candies Of LA Inc	2064	76
Hawaiian Telcom Communications Inc	4813	38
Hawg-Ly Lure Co	3949	167
Hawk Associates Inc	8741	198
Hawk Corp	3728	29
Hawk Electric Inc	1731	864
Hawk Electronics	5065	16
Hawk Media Inc	7319	138
Hawk Of South Carolina Inc	3561	163
Hawk Quality Products Inc	3599	2302
Hawk Systems Inc	3577	668
Hawk Technologies Inc	7379	490
Hawk Tool And Machine Inc	3599	1759
Hawker Pacific Aerospace	3728	36
Hawkes Manufacturing Inc	3523	212
Hawkeye Alarm and Signal Co	1731	2518
Hawkeye Building Supply Co	5031	135
Hawkeye Communications	7311	47
Hawkeye Communications Of Clinton	4841	55
Hawkeye Inc	7389	2066
Hawkeye Information Systems	7372	3715
Hawkeye Molding Engineers Inc	3089	859
Hawkeye Of Iowa Ltd	3496	121
Hawk-Eye Picture Tube Manufacturing Inc	3671	28
Hawkeye Renewables LLC	2869	34
Hawkeye Security Services LP	7382	114
Hawkeye Tool And Die Inc	3599	1395
Hawkeye Truck Equipment Co	5013	193
Hawking Technologies	3577	122
Hawkins and Co	8721	267
Hawkins and E-Z Messenger Legal Support Providers LLC	8111	231
Hawkins Associates Inc	7363	66
Hawkins Company Inc	1711	284
Hawkins Electric Company Inc	1731	1233
Hawkins Electric Service Inc	1731	625
Hawkins Glass Wholesalers LLC	5039	37
Hawkins Hawkins Company Inc	5999	255
Hawkins Inc	6531	156
Hawkins Inc	5169	24
Hawkins Parnell Thackston and Young LLP	8111	474
Hawkins Service Co	1731	823
Hawkline Nevada LLC	3523	147
Hawks and Associates Inc	2759	302
Hawk's Cay Resort and Marina	7011	176
Hawks Electrics Inc	6512	80
Hawks Nest	5049	227
Hawks Sales Corp	5085	285

Company Name	SIC	Rank
Hawley Construction Inc	1623	452
Hawley Products Inc	3651	158
Haworth Inc	2521	2
Haworth Marketing and Media Co	7311	67
Haworth Press Inc	2731	84
Hawthorn Bancshares Inc	6712	272
Hawthorn Bank (Clinton Missouri)	6022	241
Hawthorn Bank (Jefferson City Missouri)	6022	131
Hawthorne Corp	4581	16
Hawthorne Credit Union	6062	42
hawthorne direct Inc	7319	35
Hawthorne Educational Services Inc	2731	306
Hawthorne Machinery Inc	5084	15
Hawthorne Race Course	7948	22
Hawthorne Rubber Manufacturing Inc	3069	171
Hay Group Inc	8721	119
Hay House Inc	2731	82
Hay Morrill Company Inc	0722	1
Hayden Electric Inc	7629	18
Hayden Electrical Systems Inc	3613	178
Hayden Homes Inc	1521	69
Hayden Manufacturing Company Inc	3523	283
Hayden - Mcneil LLC	2731	252
Hayden Products LLC	3443	139
Hayden-Murphy Equipment Co	5084	73
Hayden's Sport Center Inc	5091	52
Haydock Caster Co	3069	182
Haydon Construction Inc	1623	730
Haydon Corp	3449	12
Haydon Kerk Motion Solutions Inc	3452	65
Hayes And Associates Inc	4813	622
Hayes and Stolz Industrial Manufacturing	3556	78
Hayes Food Products Inc	5153	193
Hayes Holdings Inc	3089	794
Hayes Lemmerz International Inc	3714	20
Hayes Manufacturing Inc	3568	44
Hayes Marketing Communication Inc	7311	1001
Hayes Retail Services LLC	3446	15
Hayes School Publishing Co	2731	283
Hayes Seay Mattern and Mattern Inc	8712	55
Hayes Utley and Hedgspeth	6411	184
Hayes-Ivy Manufacturing Inc	3087	24
Hayfield Window and Door Co.	3442	117
Hayman Co	6531	176
Haymarket Group Ltd	2721	231
Hayneedle Inc	8999	21
Haynes and Boone LLP	8111	147
Haynes and Partners Communications Inc	7331	199
Haynes Building Service Inc	7349	129
Haynes Corp	3714	350
Haynes International Inc	3341	6
Haynes Manufacturing Co	2992	21
Haynes Motor Lines LLC	4213	850
Haynes Scaffolding and Supply Inc	7359	219
Haynes Trucking LLC	4213	1194
Haynsworth Sinkler Boyd PA	8111	272
Hays Fabricating and Welding Inc	3441	238
Hays Rental and Sales Company Inc	7359	191
Hayssen Inc	3565	11
Hayward Baker Inc	1799	6
Hayward Distributing Co	5083	46
Hayward Industrial Products Inc	3089	311
Hayward Lumber Company Inc	5211	22
Hayward Quartz Technology Inc	3674	181
Hayward Sister Hospital	8062	160
Hayward Tyler Inc	3561	106
Haywood Electric Membership Corp	4911	486
Haywood Printing Company Inc	2759	388
Haywood Vocational Opportunities Inc	8331	26
Hazel Heating and Air Conditioning Inc	1711	243
Hazel Trucking Company Inc	4213	1934
Hazelnut Growers Of Oregon Inc	2068	12
Hazeltine Advertising and Design	7311	624
Hazeltownship Fire Rescue Inc	7389	1693
Hazelwood Enterprises Inc	5947	11
Hazemag USA Inc	5084	893
Hazen and Sawyer PC	8711	72
Hazen Paper Co	2672	27
Hazen Research Inc	8731	79
Hazen Transport Inc	4213	1372
Hazle Park Packing Co	2011	121
Hazlehurst Lumber Company Inc	2421	100
Hazlitt 1852 Vineyards Inc	2084	67
Hazlow Electronics Inc	3679	548
Hazmat Environmental Group	4213	932
Haz-Mat Transportation and Disposal	4213	3004
HB and G Building Products Inc	2431	27
HB Communications	5046	2
HB Digital Arts and HB Blueprint	7336	232
HB Distributors	5065	447
HB Electronics Inc	5064	119
HB Frazer Co	1731	103
HB Fuller Co	2891	6
HB Hunter Co	2064	68
H-B Instrument Co	3823	216
Hb Molding Inc	3089	1266
HB Paulk Grocery Inc	5141	133
HB Phillips Inc	4212	53
HB Rouse and Co	3541	246
Hb Software Solutions	7371	1257
HBC Company Inc	1623	205

Company Name	SIC	Rank
HBC Insurance Group Inc	6022	100
HBD Construction Inc	1542	222
HBD Industries Inc	3429	18
HBE Acquisition Corp	4899	74
HBE Corp	1541	8
HBG Systems Inc	7372	4380
Hbh Enterprises	2048	95
Hbi Electric Inc	1731	1781
HBMG Inc	7371	1921
HBO Studio Productions	2741	115
Hbp Inc	2752	34
HBS Consulting	7371	1734
Hbw Insurance Services LLC	6411	109
HC Accents and Associates Inc	5199	7
Hc Composites LLC	3732	73
HC Contracting Inc	2339	54
HC Davis Sons' Manufacturing Company Inc	3531	233
HC Duke and Son Inc	3556	36
HC Gabler Inc	4214	14
Hc Holdings Inc	2752	633
HC Johnson Agencies Inc	5065	896
HC Lewis Oil Co	5171	56
HC Merchandisers Inc	1542	322
HC Miller Co	2752	396
HC Nutting Co	8734	18
Hca Health Services Of Tennessee Inc	8062	120
HCA Holdings Inc	8062	1
Hca Midwest Div	8741	74
HCAL Corp	7999	57
Hcap International LLC	7361	167
HCC Benefits	6324	61
Hcc Inc	3523	48
HCC Insurance Holdings Inc	6331	66
HCC Underwriters	6411	74
Hcf Management Inc	8051	24
Hci Direct Inc	2251	6
HCI Enterprises Inc	5999	276
HCItasca	8748	187
HCL America Inc	7379	12
Hcm and J Inc	1623	594
hcPro Inc	2721	75
Hcr Inc	3822	54
HCR ManorCare	8051	1
Hcs Electrical Supply LLC	5063	745
HCV Pacific Partners	6552	258
HD Chasen Company Inc	5084	785
Hd Electric Co	3825	124
HD Hudson Manufacturing Co	3523	58
Hd Pacific Inc	3674	395
HD Sheldon and Company Inc	5046	14
HD Smith Wholesale Drug Co	5122	18
HD Studios	3695	43
HD Supply Inc	5074	3
Hd Supply Waterworks Group Inc	5051	55
HD Vest Advisory Services Inc	6282	605
HD Vest Inc	6211	183
HD Vest Investment Securities Inc	6211	111
HD Vest Mortgage Services Inc	6163	6
Hdf Group	7371	1050
Hdi Instruments LLC	3533	128
HDI Solutions Inc	7372	831
HDM Furniture Industries	2511	47
HDMG Corp	3695	72
HDR Engineering Inc	8742	7
HDR Power Systems Inc	3679	511
Hdt Ep Inc	3585	75
Hdtv Electronic Assembly Inc	3999	207
Hdw Electronics Inc	5063	500
HE Anderson Company Inc	3586	18
HE Butt Grocery Co	5411	14
HE Installations	1799	123
HE McGonigals Inc	5511	814
H-E Tool and Manufacturing Company Inc	3544	416
HE Tyler Machine Tool Company Inc	5084	339
Head and Co	6799	312
Head Inc	1542	445
Headco Machine Works Inc (Keokukk Iowa)	3599	1940
Header Die And Tool Inc	3544	343
Header Products Inc	3452	60
Headington Oil Co	1311	125
Headrick Companies Inc	8741	200
Headroom Corp	3651	180
Heads and Threads International LLC	5072	33
Heads Up Technologies Inc	3647	22
Headset Zone	5961	159
Headsetscom Inc	5961	131
Headspring Systems	7372	2891
Headstrong Corp	7372	269
Headwall Photonics Inc	3829	335
Headwaters Inc	2999	1
Headway Research Inc	3674	432
Headwest Inc	3231	26
Heale Manufacturing Company Inc	3679	468
Healex Systems Ltd	7371	1437
Healey Fire Protection Inc	5063	386
Healey Railroad Corp	1629	71
Healing Staff Inc	7361	113
Health Advantage	6324	95
Health Alliance Plan of Michigan	6324	49
Health and Fitness Management Corp	7991	16
Health Business Systems Inc	7372	1665

Company Name	SIC	Rank
Health Care Communications Group	8743	149
Health Care Innovations Inc	7363	180
Health Care REIT Inc	6798	30
Health Care Resources Inc	7323	44
Health Care Service Corporation A Mutual Legal Reserve Co	6321	2
Health Care Software Inc	7372	1532
Health Care Suppliers Inc	5047	220
Health Care Systems Corp	7372	5054
Health Cost Solutions Inc	6411	275
Health Craft Inc	8731	177
Health Credit Union	6062	118
Health Data Services Inc	7372	4089
Health Decisions Inc	8731	195
Health Design Plus	8082	95
Health Design Plus Inc	6411	226
Health Diagnostics	8099	47
Health Dialog Services Corp	8099	43
Health Discovery Corp	4812	88
Health Facility Solutions Co	7389	1696
Health Financial Systems	7372	2490
Health First Health Plans Inc	6324	63
Health First Inc	8099	9
Health Fitness Corp	8099	46
Health Fitness Rehab Inc	8099	63
Health Grades Inc	7389	337
Health Hero Network Inc	7379	712
Health Insurance Plan of Greater New York Inc	6324	25
Health Labs Plus Inc	5064	201
Health Language Inc	7372	965
Health Management Associates Inc	8062	14
Health Management Corporation of America	8741	37
Health Management Services Inc	5047	44
Health Management Systems Inc	7373	214
Health Market Science Inc	7379	146
Health Mats Co	7213	9
Health Net Health Plan of Oregon	6324	82
Health Net Inc	6324	16
Health Net of California Inc	6324	18
Health Network Laboratories LP	8071	28
Health New England Inc	6324	81
Health One Pharmaceutical Inc	2834	301
Health Path Products LLC	7372	4101
Health Plus Pharmacy Inc	5122	111
Health Pro Inc	3999	82
Health Processes Inc	2891	111
Health Products Research Inc	8742	100
Health Promotion Management Inc	7389	853
Health Research Associates Corp	8748	429
Health Resources Inc	8099	45
Health Resources Of Glastonbury Inc	8361	129
Health Science Associates	7389	1425
Health Services District Of Northern Larimer County	8082	82
Health Software of Mt Pleasant	7372	4613
Health Solutions Plus Inc	5734	92
Health Systems Resources Inc	7372	2850
Health Systems Solutions Inc	7371	644
HealthAnswers Inc	7375	40
Healthanswerscom Inc	7375	117
HealthBlocks Inc	7389	1816
Healthcare Automation Inc	7372	2235
Healthcare Claims Management	7322	122
Healthcare Forecasting Inc	8742	605
Healthcare Management Inc	6324	113
Healthcare Management Systems Inc	7371	119
Healthcare Partners Inc	7361	165
Healthcare Programming and Management Services Inc	7372	4826
Healthcare Ratings Inc	8741	115
Healthcare Realty Trust Inc	6798	97
Healthcare Resource Network LLC	7361	158
Healthcare Services Group Inc	7349	9
Healthcare Shop Of North Central Indiana LLC	8741	235
Healthcare Strategies Inc	6371	15
Healthcare Ventures LLC	6799	118
Healthcare Waste Solutions Inc	4953	94
Healthcarecom Corp	7373	163
Healthcares Cooperative Credit Union	6062	3
HealthCo Information Systems Inc	8742	163
Healthcomm Interactive Inc	5065	1013
Healthcor Inc	8011	90
Healthdent of California Inc	6324	125
HealthDrive Medical and Dental Practices	8021	9
HealthE Goods	5499	22
HealthEos	6324	126
HealthForce Partners Inc	8099	56
Healthhelp LLC	8099	55
Healthient Inc	6163	46
Healthland	7372	319
Healthline Networks Inc	7375	113
HealthLine Systems Inc	7372	2338
HealthLink Inc	7379	62
Healthmarket Inc	6321	40
HealthMarkets Inc	6321	24
Healthpac Computer Systems Inc	7379	1074
HealthPlan Services Inc	6411	132
Healthplex Inc	6411	237
HealthPlus of Michigan Inc	6324	45
HealthPort Inc	8999	30

Company Name	SIC	Rank
HealthScope Benefits	6321	65
Healthserve LLC	7374	22
HEALTHSOUTH Corp	8093	3
HealthSport Inc	2834	393
HealthSpring Inc	6324	23
HealthStream Inc	7389	269
HealthTrans LLC	7372	357
HealthTrio Inc	7372	1580
HealthTronics Inc	8093	12
Healthware Corp	7371	1571
Healthware Solutions LLC	7371	1294
Healthwarehousecom Inc	5912	55
Healthways Communications Inc	7331	162
Healthways Inc	8099	10
Healthwise International LLC	7373	1002
Healthworks Alliance Inc	7372	1482
Healy News Store Inc	5994	1
Healy-Ruff Co	3823	83
Healy-Ruff Company LLC	3822	101
Heard Brothers Electrical Contractors Inc	1731	722
Heard Communications Inc	7312	23
Heard McElroy and Vestal LLP	8721	389
Hearlihy And Co	5961	184
Hearn Kirkwood	5148	38
Hearst Business Communications Inc	2721	79
Hearst Corp	2711	8
Hearst Interactive Media	2741	147
Hearst Television Inc	4833	27
Heart Graphics	7374	415
Heart Hospital IV LP	8062	223
Heart Hospital of BK LLC	8062	55
Heart Hospital of DTO LLC	8062	226
Heart of America Group	5812	164
Heart of Iowa Coop	5153	50
Heart Of Texas Controls LLC	1731	2202
Heart Truss and Engineering Corp	2439	36
Heartbeat Digital Inc	7372	1944
Heartfelt Inc	2499	45
Hearth and Home Technologies Inc	3429	10
Hearthbread LLC	2051	238
Hearthside Homes Inc	6552	115
HearthSong Inc	5961	162
Heartland Advisors Inc	6282	495
Heartland Bancshares Inc	6022	469
Heartland Bank	6022	616
Heartland Bank (Leawood Kansas)	6022	550
Heartland Behavioral Health Services Inc	8063	10
Heartland Brewery	5812	325
Heartland Building Center Inc	5211	133
Heartland Capital Management Inc	6282	330
Heartland Capital Trust I	6021	210
Heartland Communications Inc	4832	74
Heartland Co-Op	5153	15
Heartland Co-op (Trumbull Nebraska)	5153	83
Heartland Corn Products	2869	105
Heartland Enterprises Inc	6719	152
Heartland Enterprises Ltd	3563	36
Heartland Equipment Inc	3523	32
Heartland Express Inc	4213	58
Heartland Financial USA Inc	6022	52
Heartland Health	8011	1
Heartland Imaging Companies Inc	5043	6
Heartland Inc	1522	24
Heartland Industrial Partners LP	6799	247
Heartland Industries Inc	3949	44
Heartland ITS	7371	489
Heartland Label Printers Inc	5065	64
Heartland Manufacturing Group Inc	5039	60
Heartland Meat Company Inc	5147	48
Heartland Micorpayments	3577	242
Heartland Paper Co	5111	13
Heartland Payment Systems Inc	7374	10
Heartland Power Coop	4911	344
Heartland Properties Inc	6552	303
Heartland Pump Rental And Sales Inc	5084	216
Heartland Tank LLC	1791	21
Heartland USA Inc	2392	53
Heartland Video Systems Inc	5065	431
Heart-Smart Chicken Inc	3577	522
Heartwood Media Inc	2741	394
Heary Brothers Lightning Protection Company Inc	3643	119
Heat and Control Inc	3556	27
Heat Barrier Systems Inc	5065	719
Heat Controller Inc	3585	152
Heat Seal LLC	3565	46
Heat Sensor Technologie LLC	3567	113
Heat Tracing Specialties West Inc	5063	486
Heat Transfer Research Inc	7372	2759
Heatbath Corp	2819	62
Heatcon Composite Systems Inc	3625	113
Heatcraft Inc	3585	29
Heateflex Corp	3825	135
Heater Designs Inc	3567	96
Heater Specialists LLC	3255	7
Heath and Son Feed and Supply Inc	2048	137
Heath Consultants Inc	8711	222
Heath Press Inc	2752	1653
Heathco LLC	3699	73
Heathcott Associates Inc	7311	386
Heather Creek Foods LLC	2099	161
Heather Design Ltd	3829	502

Company Name	SIC	Rank
Heather Ridge Inc	6719	183
Heather Sound Amplification	3679	889
Heathkit Company Inc	3999	179
Heating and Cooling Supply Inc	5075	48
Heating and Plumbing Engineers	1711	62
Heating Inc	7379	1128
Heaton Adams and Co	8721	96
Heaton Brothers Construction Company Inc	1611	228
Heaton Electric Inc	1731	2067
Heaton Erecting Inc	7353	60
Heaton Pecan Farm	5961	182
Heaton Steel and Supply Inc	5051	441
Heatrex Inc	3567	61
Heatron Inc	3567	34
Heatscan Inc	7379	1497
Heat-Timer Corp	3822	46
Heatwave Interactive Inc	5045	751
Heaven Hill Distilleries Inc	2085	5
Heavy Construction Lumber Inc	5031	401
Heavy Construction Systems Specialists Inc	7372	1670
Heavy Duty Trux Ltd	4213	1955
Heavy Machines Inc	5084	148
Heavy Parts International	5013	204
Heb Manufacturing Company Inc	3469	319
Hebbard Electric Inc	1731	991
Hebco Products Inc	3714	161
Hebeler Corp	3599	103
Hebert Brothers Inc	4213	1129
Heberts Trucking and Equipment Service LLC	7359	204
HEC Reading Horizons	7372	2075
Hecht Spencer and Associates Inc	8743	269
Heck Enterprises Inc	3273	56
Heckethorn Manufacturing Co	3429	71
Heckler Associates	7311	1014
Heckman Bindery Inc	2789	5
Heckmann Corp	6719	75
Heco Inc	1731	997
Heco Industrial Service Groups Inc	5063	299
Heco-Pacific Manufacturing Inc	3535	170
Hector Communications Corp	4813	102
Hector Turf	5083	12
Hed International Inc	3567	110
Hedaya Home Fashions Inc	2392	33
Hedb Corp	3691	54
Hedberg Aggregates Inc	5032	58
Heddinger Brokerage Inc	5141	138
Hederman Brothers LLC	2752	408
Hedge and Herberg Inc	4213	327
Hedgewood Properties Inc	1521	93
Heding Truck Service Inc	4213	1753
Hedman Company Inc	3579	41
Hedrick's Hallowell Chevrolet Co	5511	487
Hedstrom Lumber Company Inc	2421	107
Hedtke Inc	5065	541
Hedwin Corp	3089	228
Heeby's Surplus Inc	5211	231
Heeco Associates And Equipment Company Inc	3541	183
Heel Inc	2833	45
Heel Quik Inc	6794	104
Heeley Creative Inc	7311	1002
Heelys Inc	3149	23
Heery International Inc	8712	6
Heetco Inc	5172	148
Heeter Printing Company Inc	2752	301
Heffelfinger's Meats Inc	2011	155
Hefner Stark and Marois	8111	522
Hefren-Tillotson Inc	6211	314
Heftee Industries LLC	7699	253
Hegedorns Inc	5411	200
Hegedus Aluminum Industries Inc	3365	38
Hegemony Inc	7371	937
Hegge Electrical Contractors Inc	1731	743
Hegwood Electric Service Inc	1796	37
Hehr International Inc	3442	7
HEI Diversified Inc	6712	735
Hei Inc	1731	796
HEI Investment Inc	6798	98
Heico Acquisitions Co	6799	309
HEICO Aerospace Holdings Corp	3724	14
Heico Companies LLC	6719	42
HEICO Corp	3724	7
Heico Holding Inc	3531	6
Heide and Cook Ltd	1711	141
Heide Wilson	7379	1432
Heidelberg/Baumfolder Corp	3579	25
Heidelberg Group Inc	2051	220
Heidelberg USA Inc	3555	3
Heiden and Garland Inc	6411	238
Heidenberger Construction Inc	1542	409
Heidenhain Corp	5084	186
Heidrick and Struggles International Inc	7361	17
Heidtman Steel Products Inc	3312	43
Heights Armature Works Inc	5063	633
Heights Electric Services Inc	1731	928
Heights-USA	3577	674
Heil Co	3713	4
Heil Environmental Industries Ltd	3441	186
Heil Sound Ltd	3663	327

Company Name	SIC	Rank
Heil Trailer International	3537	10
Heil-Brice Retail Advertising	7311	131
Heilind Electronics Inc	5065	119
Heim Trucking	4213	874
Hein and Associates LLP	8721	64
Hein Lighting And Electric Inc	1731	1576
Heineken USA Inc	5181	5
Heinen's Inc	5411	79
Heines Insulators Incorporated Of Jersey	5211	230
Heinhold Engineering and Machine Company Inc	3599	2151
Heinke Technology Inc	3089	539
Heinkel's Packing Company Inc	2011	142
Heinrich Ceramic Decal Inc	2759	204
Heinrich Marketing Inc	7311	587
Heins Balancing Systems Inc	3599	2426
Heinz Corp	8711	295
Heinz Frozen Food Co	2038	3
Heise Industries Inc	3544	186
Heiser Automobile Dealership Inc	5511	75
Heiser Chevrolet and Geo Inc	5511	1081
Heisler Industries Inc	3565	36
Heisler Tool Co	3599	2260
Heisler's Cloverleaf Dairy Inc	2024	38
Heitech Services Inc	7379	171
Heiter Electronics Inc	3679	427
Heiter Truck Line Inc	4213	2031
Heiting Tool And Die Inc	3599	2515
Heitman Advisory Corp	6531	76
Heitman Laboratories Inc	3829	400
Heitman LLC	6282	40
Heitmeyer Group LLC	7361	128
Heits Building Services Inc	7349	212
Heizer Aerospace Inc	3728	91
Hekman Furniture Co	2511	20
Helac Corp	3593	11
Held Properties	6552	189
Heldenfels Enterprises Inc	3241	19
Helders Motor Service Co	4213	2983
Held's Janitorial Service Inc	7349	109
Helen Dwight Reid Educational Foundation Inc	2731	215
Helen Gordon Interests Ltd	2711	297
Helen Inc	2851	104
Helen of Troy Ltd	5064	4
Helen of Troy Texas Corp	5064	17
Helena Chemical Co	5191	4
Helena Chemical Company Hughes	5191	155
Helena Industries Inc	8331	194
Helfer Tool Co	3544	183
Helfrich Brothers Boiler Works Inc	1711	220
Helga Designs Inc	2326	26
Helgesen Industries Inc	3443	78
Helical Products Company Inc	3568	38
Helicomb International Inc	7699	51
Helicopter Services Inc	4522	41
Helicos BioSciences Corp	2834	364
Helio Precision Products Inc	3592	12
Heliogramme America Inc	2752	1614
Helios and Matheson Information Technology Inc	7373	340
Helius Inc	7372	625
Helix BioMedix Inc	2834	431
Helix Electric Inc	1731	30
Helix Energy Solutions Group Inc	1389	7
Helix Medical LLC	3842	105
Hella North America Inc	3625	4
Hellebusch Tool and Die Inc	3544	344
Hellenbrand Inc	3589	123
Hellenic Times	2711	312
Heller Company Inc	1623	684
Heller Ehrman White and McAuliffe LLP	8111	126
Heller Industries Inc	3569	98
Heller Information Services Inc	4813	453
Heller Performance Polymers Inc	3087	12
Hellermanntyton Corp	3089	36
Hellman and Friedman LLC	6211	206
Hellman Electric Corp	1731	291
Hellmuth Obata and Kassabaum Inc	8712	14
Hellmuth Obata and Kassabaum Inc Sports Facilities Group	8712	119
Hello and Co	7812	35
Hello Direct Inc	5961	96
Hello Inc	5731	40
Hello World Communications	3695	25
HelloSoft Inc	7372	1758
Helm Corp	3544	550
Helm Inc	7389	416
Helm Instrument Company Inc	3829	273
Helm New York Inc	5122	112
Helm Precision Ltd	3599	682
Helm Tool Company Inc	3544	688
Helmark Steel Inc	3441	89
Helmel Engineering Products Inc	3829	277
Helmer Printing Inc	2711	419
Helmerich and Payne Inc	1381	8
Helmerich and Payne International Drilling Co	1381	40
Helmerich and Payne Properties Inc	6552	58
Helmholdt and Co	8721	44
Helmick Corp	3444	215
Helmitin Inc	2891	80

Company Name	SIC	Rank
Helmsley Enterprises Inc	6552	22
Helmsley-Spear Inc	6552	64
Help At Home Inc	8399	14
Help/Systems Inc	7372	1019
Helping Hand Of Goodwill Industries	8331	52
HelpSTARcom Inc	7372	1250
Helsel-Jepperson Electrical Inc	5063	338
Helsell Fetterman LLP	8111	371
Helser Brothers Transfer Co	4213	2416
Helser Industries Inc	3443	134
Heluva Good LLC	5143	13
Helwig Carbon Products Inc	3624	9
Helzberg's Diamond Shops Inc	5944	6
HEM Data Corp	7372	4425
Hem Inc	3541	59
HemaCare Corp	8099	57
Hemagen Diagnostics Inc	2835	56
Hemco Corp	3821	67
Hemcon Medical Technologies Inc	3842	139
Hemet Bancorp	6712	362
Hemingway Apparel Manufacturing Inc	2341	9
Hemisphere Communication Inc	4813	274
Hemispherx Biopharma Inc	2836	94
Hemlock Semiconductor Corp	3674	44
Hemming Morse Inc	8721	490
Hemocleanse Inc	3841	374
Hemphill and Son Inc	4213	2890
Hempstead Mazda Inc	5511	23
Hempt Brothers Inc	1611	105
Hench Brothers Inc	1542	369
Hencorp Becstone LC	6282	220
Hendee Enterprises Inc	2394	10
Hendela Systems Consultants Inc	7372	3716
Henderson Auctions Inc	5046	71
Henderson Automotive Family	5511	796
Henderson Coffee Corp	5149	186
Henderson Engineering Company Inc	3564	65
Henderson Glass Inc	7536	2
Henderson Gleaner	2752	199
Henderson Lumber Company Inc	5211	317
Henderson Products Inc	3537	21
Henderson Specialties Inc	4213	2533
Henderson Steel Corp	3441	113
Henderson Wheel and Warehouse Supply	5013	37
Henderson's Printing Inc	2752	263
Hendren Plastics Inc	3086	110
Hendrick Automotive Group	5511	10
Hendrick Inc	7389	626
Hendrix Batting Co	2299	14
Hendry Corp	3731	48
Henegan Construction Company Inc	1542	47
Henggeler Computer Consultants Inc	7371	184
Henkel Construction Co	1542	373
Henkel Corp Surface Technologies Div	2899	56
Henkel Loctite Corp	2891	22
Henkel-Harris Company Inc	2511	57
Henkels and McCoy East Region Headquarters	1623	25
Henkels and McCoy Inc	1623	8
Henkin Schultz Inc	7311	878
Henley Construction Inc	1623	813
Henley Group	1542	403
Henman Engineering And Machine Inc	3714	294
Hennepin Cooperative Seed Exchange	5191	160
Hennessey Capital Solutions Inc	7389	1859
Hennessy Funds Inc	6722	244
Hennessy Industries Inc	3559	115
Hennessy River View Ford Inc	5511	599
Hennigan Bennett and Dorman LLP	8111	385
Henniges Automotive North America Inc	5013	26
Hennigh's Warehouse Outlet	5064	215
Henniker Sand And Gravel Company Inc	5032	114
Henning Industrial Software Inc	7372	3299
Henninger Media Services Inc	7819	23
Henningsen Foods Inc	2015	28
Henningson Durham Richardson Inc	8711	22
Henri Bendel Inc	5621	30
Henri Studio Inc	3299	5
Henri's Bakery Inc	5461	15
Henrob Corp	5084	607
Henry A Bromelkamp and Co	7379	1433
Henry A Fox Sales Co	5181	82
Henry A Petter Supply Co	5085	20
Henry and Germann Public Affairs LLC	8743	324
Henry and Henry Inc	2033	60
Henry and Horne LLP	8721	316
Henry Brick Company Inc	3251	15
Henry Brothers Electronics Inc	4899	66
Henry Carlson Co	1541	133
Henry Co	2952	4
Henry County Rural Electric Membership Corp	4911	410
Henry Doneger Associates Inc	7389	947
Henry Electric Inc	1731	1699
Henry F Teichmann Inc	8711	481
Henry Gill Communications	7311	388
Henry H Ottens Manufacturing Company Inc	2087	30
Henry J Austin Health Center Inc	8011	108
Henry L Taylor Trucking LLC	4213	3063
Henry L Wolfers Inc	5063	313

Company Name	SIC	Rank
Henry Medical Center Inc	8062	97
Henry N Sawyer Company Inc	2752	1593
Henry Plastic Molding Inc	3089	461
Henry Pratt Co	3494	7
Henry Products Inc	3086	35
Henry Quentzel Plumbing Supply Company Inc	5074	135
Henry Radio Inc	3679	328
Henry Schein Inc	5047	2
Henry Schein Inc Dental Div	5047	7
Henry Servin and Sons Inc	5084	876
Henry Technologies Inc	3491	15
Henry Tools Inc	3541	272
Henry Troemner LLC	3821	13
Henry V Rabouin Inc	4213	2052
Henry Wurst Inc	2752	29
Henry-Lee and Company LLC	2339	56
Henry's Electric Inc	1731	1082
Henry's Hickory House Inc	2011	66
Henry's Tackle LLC	5091	12
Henschel Coating and Laminating Company Inc	7389	1574
Henschen and Associates Inc	7372	4206
Hensel Electric Co	1731	771
Hensel Phelps Construction Co	1542	3
Henshaw Electronics	5731	241
Henshaw Inc	8711	596
Hensley Attachments	3531	51
Hensley Fabricating and Equipment Company Inc	3443	189
Hensley Industries Inc	3325	17
Hensley Printing and Graphics	2752	1654
Henze Machine And Tool Company LLC	3544	490
Henzel Electric Company Inc	1731	2263
Heppner Hardwoods Inc	5031	222
Heppner Molds Inc	3089	1875
HER Realtors Inc	6531	35
Heraeus Electro-Nite Co	3823	53
Heraeus Kulzer LLC	3843	8
Heraeus Medical Components (St Paul Minnesota)	3643	21
Heraeus Metal Processing LLC	3341	20
Herakles LLC	4813	592
Herald And Banner Press	2721	457
Herald Association Inc	2711	328
Herald Durango Inc	2741	213
Herald Farmville Inc	2711	687
Herald Harrodsburg Inc	2711	836
Herald Media Inc	2711	66
Herald National Bank	6021	178
Herald Of Randolph	2711	907
Herald Of Truth Ministries Inc	4833	256
Herald Printing Co	2752	391
Herald Publishing Co	2711	323
Herald Publishing House	2721	254
Herald Reflector Inc	2711	484
Herald Sanford Inc	2711	805
Herald-Mail Co	2711	236
Herb Chambers Cos	5511	33
Herb Easley Motors Corp	5511	687
Herb Gordon Autoworld Inc	5511	625
Herbach and Rademan Co	5065	883
Herbalife International Inc	5963	5
Herbeau Creation Of America Inc	5074	161
Herbert Cooper Company Inc	3069	239
Herbert E Orr Company Inc	5013	142
Herbert H Landy Insurance Agency Inc	6411	217
Herbert L Flake Management Corp	5087	144
Herbert Machine Works Inc	3544	337
Herbert Malarkey Roofing Co	2952	13
Herbert Rowland and Grubic Inc	8711	209
Herbert S Hiller Corp	5099	62
Herbert Software Solutions Inc	7372	2984
Herbologics Ltd	5149	225
Herborium Group Inc	2834	443
Herb's Seafood LLC	2092	103
Herburger Publications Inc	2711	449
Hercky-Pasqua-Herman Inc	7311	609
Hercules Cement Company LP	3241	22
Hercules Chemical Company Inc	2899	40
Hercules Drawn Steel Corp	3316	24
Hercules Drilling LLC	8741	90
Hercules Engine Components LLC	3714	298
Hercules Glove Manfacturing Company Inc	2381	6
Hercules Offshore Inc	1381	15
Hercules Steel Company Inc	3441	81
Hercules Tire and Rubber Co	5014	3
Hercules Transport Inc	4213	1162
Herd Manufacturing Inc	3469	263
Hordell Printing and Lithography Inc	2752	1076
Herdeman Corp	3541	188
Here Media Inc	7389	494
Hereford Brand Inc	2711	866
Hereford Grain Corp	5153	128
Hereford State Bank	6022	690
hereUare Inc	7371	931
Hergert Milling Inc	2048	54
Herguth Laboratories Inc	8731	318
Herin Brothers Inc	4213	2805
Herion Co	1623	357
Heritage Bank (Longview Washington)	6022	255
Heritage Bank (Phoenix Arizona)	6022	779

Company Name	SIC	Rank
Heritage Bankshares Inc (Norfolk Virginia)	6022	440
Heritage Broadcasting Group	4833	152
Heritage Business Systems Inc	5044	87
Heritage Capital Corp	5961	29
Heritage Capital Management Inc	6282	481
Heritage Carbide Inc	3599	1348
Heritage Commerce Corp	6022	138
Heritage Community Bank	6022	480
Heritage Co	2741	283
Heritage Development Group Inc	6552	81
Heritage Electrical Corp	3625	311
Heritage Enterprise Inc	5712	102
Heritage Environmental Services Inc	4953	40
Heritage Equipment Co	5084	593
Heritage Family Specialty Foods Inc	2035	26
Heritage Financial Corp	6036	24
Heritage Financial Group Inc	6022	154
Heritage Food Services Of Georgia Inc	5087	149
Heritage FS Inc	5172	43
Heritage Group LLC	6162	147
Heritage Homecare Inc	7363	315
Heritage Homes Of Nebraska Inc	2452	40
Heritage Instant Printing Company Inc	2752	934
Heritage Laboratories International	7389	1405
Heritage Lace Inc	5023	31
Heritage Makers Inc	7371	603
Heritage Manufacturing Inc	3448	46
Heritage Marble Of Ohio Inc	3281	51
Heritage Microfilm Inc	7389	406
Heritage Oaks Bancorp	6712	324
Heritage Oaks Bank	6022	705
Heritage Operating LP	5984	6
Heritage Paper Company Inc	5113	10
Heritage Partners Inc	6159	94
Heritage Plastics South Inc	3084	34
Heritage Products Inc	3465	31
Heritage Recording Studio	3695	171
Heritage Savings Bank	6021	130
Heritage Store	2844	88
Heritage Texas Properties	6531	46
Heritage Trust Federal Credit Union	6061	46
Heritage web Solutions	7379	99
Heritage Wholesalers Inc	5033	47
Heritage Wire Harness LLC	3679	126
Heritage-Crystal Clean Inc	4953	56
Heritage's Dairy Stores Inc	5451	1
Herker Industries Inc	3451	18
Herkomi Inc	5013	333
Herkules Equipment Corp	5084	627
Herm Hughes and Sons Inc	1541	131
Hermac Inc	3679	498
Herman Associates Public Relations	8743	186
Herman Goldner Company Inc	5074	35
Herman Grant Company Inc	5082	127
Herman H Sticht Company Inc	3829	430
Herman Miller Greenhouse	2521	14
Herman Miller Inc	2521	3
Herman R Ewell Inc	4213	610
Herman Seekamp Inc	2051	84
Herman Strauss Inc	5093	96
Herman Street	5734	270
Hermann Associates Inc	5044	153
Hermann J Wiemer Vineyard Inc	2084	140
Hermann Oak Leather Co	3111	8
Hermann Services	4225	13
Hermanoff Public Relations	8743	225
Hermanson Co	1711	118
Hermell Products Inc	3842	215
Hermes Abrasives Limited A LP	3291	5
Hermes Architects Inc	8712	149
Hermes of Paris Inc	5651	15
Hermetic Coil Company Inc	3544	405
Hermetic Switch Inc	3679	247
Hermitage Group Inc	2741	149
Hermitage House Youth Services Inc	8361	167
Hermitage Press Inc	2752	1390
Hernandez and Solis Inc	5149	184
Hernandez Companies Inc	1522	55
Herndon Oil Corp	5541	26
Hernon Manufacturing Inc	2891	58
Hero Inc	7372	1643
Heroix Corp	7372	1332
Herold Salads Inc	2099	313
Herotek Inc	3663	180
Herr Foods Inc	2096	6
Herr Industrial Inc	3559	212
Herre Brothers Inc	1711	84
Herrera and Assoc	8742	695
Herrero and Sons Corp	5013	336
Herrick and Ashcraft Interiors and Furniture Co	5712	113
Herrick and White Ltd	2431	91
Herrick Company Inc	6512	42
Herrin Brothers Coal and Ice Co	5983	29
Herring Broadcasting Company Inc	4833	185
Herrin-Gear Chevrolet Inc	5511	1192
Herrmann Advertising Design	7311	475
Herrmann Printing and Litho Inc	2752	1099
Herr-Voss	3549	6
Hersam Publishing Co	2711	605
Herschap Backhoe and Ditching Inc	1623	354
Herschel-Adams Inc	3423	16
Herschend Family Entertainment Corp	7996	15

Company Name	SIC	Rank
Hersh Levitt Investments Corp	1521	176
Hershey Co	2066	2
Hershey Creamery Co	2024	10
Hershey-Philbin Associates Inc	8743	86
Herson's Inc	5511	101
Hertell Enterprises Inc	3571	75
Hertz Claim Management	7359	7
Hertz Corp	7515	1
Hertz Global Holdings Inc	4789	2
Hertz Truck and Van Rental	7359	8
Hertzberg Ernst and Sons	2752	839
Hertzberg-New Method Inc	5192	22
Hertzler Systems Inc	7372	3458
Herzfeld and Rubin PC	0111	200
Herzog Contracting Corp	1611	58
Herzum (North America) Inc	7379	1122
HES Electric Co	1731	2433
Hesco Inc	3089	1879
Hesco Parts LLC	3714	170
HESI	8711	391
Heska Corp	2836	19
Heska Des Moines	2834	174
heskethcom Inc	7371	715
Hesperia Resorter	2711	766
Hess Collection Winery	2084	30
Hess Corp	2911	5
Hess Engineering Inc	3544	117
Hess Marketing	7311	668
Hess Technologies Inc	3559	575
Hess Trucking Company Inc	4212	37
Hesse Inc	3713	65
Hesselbein Tire Company Inc	5531	19
Hessler's Inc	5713	12
Hetran Inc	3541	48
Hetrick Manufacturing Inc	3599	2316
Hetronic USA	3625	169
Hettich Instruments LP	5049	53
Heucotech Limited A New Jersey LP	2865	9
HEURIS	7371	864
Heuss Printing Inc	2752	1785
Hewes Marine Company Inc	3732	61
Hewes Yamaha Outboard Motors Export Inc	5091	132
Hewins/Carlson Wagonlit Travel	4724	64
Hewlett-Packard Co	3571	1
Hex Laboratory Systems	7372	1735
Hexagon Industries Inc	3452	73
Hexagon Metrology Services Inc	7389	1884
Hexatech Inc	5065	639
Hexco International	3559	113
Hexon Corp	2675	30
Hexpol Compounding Nc Inc	3069	108
Heyboer Transformers Inc	3612	114
Heyco Metals Inc	3469	26
Heyco Molded Products Inc	3089	506
Heyday Books	2731	339
Heyder Florida Inc	5023	128
Heydlauff's Inc	5731	125
Heying and Associates	8743	161
Heyl and Patterson Inc	3535	22
Heyl Truck Lines Inc	4213	179
Heyman Corp	5136	18
Heyrman Printing LLC	2759	349
Heyward-Charlotte Inc	5063	230
HF Anderson Engraving Co	2754	43
HF Campbell and Son Inc	4213	1176
HF Coors China Co	3262	5
HF Enterprises Inc	5949	6
HF Financial Corp	6712	273
Hf Group Inc	3861	53
HF Merchandising Inc	5949	4
HF Resources Inc	5949	5
Hf Rubber Machinery Inc	3542	35
HF Scientific Inc	3824	34
Hfa Inc	3497	1
HFB Financial Corp	6712	588
HFCS Transport Co	4213	1905
HFF Inc	6099	21
HFM Interiors LLC	5949	8
Hfw Industries Inc	7699	74
HG Fenton Co	6531	422
HG Hill Realty Group LLC	5411	195
HG Reynolds Company Inc	1541	238
Hgl Inc	2339	61
Hgr Industrial Surplus Inc	5084	472
HH Arnold Company Inc	3599	1740
HH Fluorescent Parts Inc	3641	10
HH Knoebels Sons Inc	7996	30
HH Omps Inc	4213	2468
hhgregg Inc	5722	1
HHHunt Corp	6531	12
Hi and Low Computers Inc	5734	60
Hi Country Snack Foods Inc	2013	186
Hi Delta Tech Inc	5047	282
HI Development Corp	7011	112
Hi Electronics Inc	3599	2325
Hi Fidelity of Lubbock Inc	5731	135
Hi Mountain Jerky Inc	2099	298
Hi Nabor Supermarket Inc	5411	228
Hi Plains Feed LLC	2048	87
Hi Pressure Inc	5084	601
Hi Rel Connectors Inc	3643	46
HI Solutions Inc	3625	183
Hi Tech Electronic Manufactoring Corp	3672	131

Company Name	SIC	Rank
Hi Tech Optical Inc	5048	41
Hi Tech Profiles Inc	3069	211
Hi Way Auto Inc	5015	28
HIA Inc	5084	181
Hialeah Hotel Inc	8741	251
Hialeah Meter Co	5063	969
Hias Inc	8322	63
Hiatt Enterprises Inc	7334	89
Hiawatha Communication	4813	205
Hi-Ball Trucking Inc	4213	2496
Hibbert Co	7331	15
Hibbert Group (Denver Colorado)	8742	173
Hibbett Sports Inc	5941	11
Hibbing Taconite Co	1011	5
Hibbs Electromechanical Inc	7694	16
Hibco Plastics Inc	3086	61
HIC Corp	2721	265
Hickenbottom and Sons Inc	5148	32
Hickey and Associates	5045	338
Hicklin Inc	3714	281
Hickman and Associates Inc	7311	335
Hickman Transport Company Inc	4213	561
Hickman Williams and Co	5052	2
Hickman-Fulton Counties RECC	4911	570
Hickman-Kenyon Systems Inc	7372	3459
Hickok Inc	3823	207
Hickory Brands Inc	2241	24
Hickory Business Furniture	2511	41
Hickory Construction Co	1541	178
Hickory Dyeing And Winding Company Inc	2282	5
Hickory Farms Inc	5499	18
Hickory Industries Inc	3589	214
Hickory Tech Corp	4813	73
Hickory White Co	2512	12
Hicks Acquisition Company II Inc	6289	35
Hicks And Associates Inc	8742	257
Hicks and Whittier Inc	7331	170
Hicks Convention Services Inc	7389	1892
Hicks Electric Inc	1731	2276
Hicks Electrical Company Inc	1731	958
Hicks Electronic Design Inc	8711	632
Hicks Inc	5091	44
Hicks Machine Inc	3599	1545
Hicks Trucking Company Inc	4213	2709
Hi-Class Business Systems Of America Inc	5045	522
Hico America	5063	710
Hi-Craft Engineering Inc	3544	177
HID Corp	3812	54
HID Global Corp	3577	18
Hidalgo County Appraisal District	7389	1155
Hidden Valley Electronics Inc	3577	293
Hideaway Restaurant Inc	5812	432
Hi-Desert Publishing Co	2711	291
HIDirect Inc	3641	9
Hidy Motors Inc	5511	503
HIE Contractors Inc	1623	753
HIG Capital Management Inc	6282	75
Higbee Inc	3053	58
Higdon and Hale CPA PC	8721	493
Higdon Furniture Co	2511	75
Higgenbotham Auctioneers International Limited Inc	7389	761
Higgerson-Buchanan Inc	1542	63
Higginbotham Brothers and Co	5211	101
Higginbotham-Bartlett Co	5211	67
Higgins Acquisition Inc	2353	19
Higgins Brick Co	3271	20
Higgins Supply Company Inc	3842	186
Higgs Fletcher and Mack LLP	8111	463
High Beam Resources LLC	7375	168
High Bridge Spring Water Company Inc	2086	136
High Brothers Inc	5211	183
High Concrete Group LLC	1791	6
High Country Bancorp Inc	6712	630
High Country Container Inc	2653	72
High Country Electric Construction Inc	1731	2089
High Country Tek Inc	3625	206
High Country Transportation	4213	870
High Desert Milk Inc	2026	71
High Falls Brewing Company Inc	2082	7
High Frequency Technology Company Inc	3559	483
High Grade Beverage	5149	11
High Grade Materials Co	3273	36
High Industries Inc	3441	4
High Liner Foods USA Inc	2092	10
High Mountain Transport LLC	4213	2063
High Performance Technologies Inc	7379	353
High Performance Test Inc	3825	318
High Performance Tube Inc	3498	76
High Plains Electric	1731	1984
High Plains Power Inc	4911	372
High Plains Services Inc	7353	50
High Point Control Systems Inc	3829	479
High Point Enterprise Inc	2711	270
High Point Furniture Industries Inc	2521	27
High Point Precision Products Inc	3541	197
High Point Printing LLC	2759	576
High Point Solutions Inc	5045	219
High Point Sprinkler Inc	1711	267
High Power Technical Services Inc	1731	320
High Precision Devices Inc	3829	383

Company Name	SIC	Rank
High Precision Grinding and Machining Inc	3599	1161
High Regard Software Inc	7372	4827
High Resolutions Inc	7374	339
High Rise Security Systems LLC	5063	592
High Rise Windows Inc	7349	495
High Sierra Sport Co	2253	14
High Society Magazine Inc	2721	447
High Street Partners Inc	7389	722
High Summit Distribution Inc	5421	11
High Tech Elastomers Inc	3479	93
High Tech Inc	3699	102
High Tech Research Inc	7371	1504
High Tech Resources Inc	7363	359
High Tech Samples Inc	2782	70
High Tech Systems Inc	5045	772
High Technology Corp	8731	377
High Technology Video Inc	7819	57
High Tide Seafoods	2092	77
High Top Products Corp	2013	128
High Valley Products Inc	5169	181
High View Inc	0241	3
High Voltage Components Inc	3675	43
High Voltage Maintenance Corp	1731	373
Highbeam Research Inc	7375	124
Highdata Software Corp	7379	811
Higher Octave Music Inc	7922	28
Higher One Holdings Inc	7389	160
Highfield Manufacturing	3699	151
Highfields Inc	8322	142
HighJump Software Inc	7372	1171
Highland Auto Parts Inc	5013	403
Highland Bancshares Inc	6712	693
Highland Bank	6021	265
Highland Campus Health Group LLC	6324	121
Highland Capital Management LP	6282	38
Highland Community Bank	6022	694
Highland Community Co	6712	690
Highland Computer Forms Inc	2761	14
Highland Consulting Group Inc	7372	2312
Highland Containers Inc	2653	13
Highland Engineering Inc	3535	38
Highland Graphics Inc	7336	58
Highland Homes Inc	1531	38
Highland Industries Inc	2221	16
Highland Laboratories Inc	2833	62
Highland Labs Inc	3999	108
Highland Machine and Screw Products Co	3599	188
Highland Machine Tool Inc	3599	1081
Highland Mills Inc	2251	10
Highland Park Ford Sales Inc	5511	1057
Highland Park Independent School District	8211	85
Highland Park Lincoln Mercury Sales Inc	5511	966
Highland Park Market Inc	5411	82
Highland Plastics Inc	3081	129
Highland Plating Co	3471	54
Highland Press Inc	2752	1626
Highland Propane Co	5984	23
Highland Tank And Manufacturing Co	3443	113
Highland Technology	3829	308
Highland Telephone Cooperative Inc	4813	141
Highland Tool Company Inc	3599	1844
Highlander Energy Products Inc	1623	252
Highlands Bankshares Inc	6712	517
Highlands Tractor Motorsports Inc	5083	161
Highlight Inc	3993	120
Highlight Industries Inc	3565	69
Highlights For Children Inc	2721	47
Highline Electric Association Inc	4911	493
Highline Portafab Inc	3599	1790
Highlite Printers Inc	2752	851
Highmark Blue Cross Blue Shield	6321	16
Highmark Inc	6324	7
HighNote Records Inc	7922	95
HighPoint Solutions	7336	44
HighReach Learning Inc	2731	68
Highrel Inc	3825	285
Highridge Partners	6552	134
Highroad Press LLC	2759	126
Highsmith Inc	5961	113
High-Speed Process Printing Corp	2752	1627
High-Tec Machining Center Inc	3369	34
High-Tech Industries Of Holland Inc	3369	31
High-Tech Machine and Tool Inc	3599	697
Hightechnique Inc	7379	1441
High-Technology Corp	8731	320
High-Tech-Tronics Inc	1731	730
Hightower Agency Inc	7311	893
Hightower Electric Company Inc	1731	2425
Hightower Oil and Petroleum Company Inc	5171	76
Hightowers Petroleum Co	5172	61
Highview Custom Fabricating Inc	3441	183
Highway Construction Company Ltd	1611	74
Highway Equipment Co	3531	89
Highway Handyman Products Inc	3993	195
Highway Machine Company Inc	3462	62
Highway Materials Inc	2951	42
Highway Safety Corp	3444	27
Highway Transport Chemical LLC	4213	144
Highwood Die and Engineering Inc	3469	285

Company Name	SIC	Rank
Highwoods Properties Inc (Raleigh North Carolina)	6531	20
Hi-Grade Meats Inc	2013	120
HIIFinance Corp	6799	348
Hiland Dairy Foods Company LLC	2026	11
Hiland Holdings GP LP	6719	71
Hiland Partners LP	1311	62
Hilb Rogal and Hobbs Company Pittsburgh LLC	6331	115
Hilbert Computing Inc	7372	4910
Hilco Appraisal Services LLC	7389	586
Hilco Capital LP	6163	20
Hilco Equity LLC	6799	125
Hilco Industrial LLC	7389	587
Hilco Merchant Resources LLC	7389	627
Hilco Plastics Products Company Inc	3089	918
Hilco Real Estate LLC	6552	149
Hilco Receivables LLC	7299	29
Hilco Trading Company Inc	6719	133
Hildebrandt Baker Robbins	8742	196
Hildy Licht Inc	3672	492
Hi-Lex Controls Inc	3714	234
Hi-Lex Corp	3679	92
Hilferty Gerard And Accociates Inc	7336	280
Hilgraeve Inc	7372	1711
Hi-Line Electric Co	5085	26
Hi-Line Plastics Inc	3086	84
Hi-Link Computer Corp	5045	675
Hilite International Inc	5013	130
Hi-Lite Machine Company Inc	3559	441
Hi-Lite Manufacturing Company Inc	3646	30
Hi-Lites Graphic Inc	2752	1385
Hill Aircraft And Leasing Corp	7359	153
Hill and Co (Bedford Texas)	7311	1022
Hill and Knowlton Inc	8743	10
Hill and Sons LLC	3556	60
Hill and Wilkinson Ltd	1542	110
Hill and Williams Brothers Inc	4213	2601
Hill Brothers Chemical Co	2899	45
Hill Country Publishing Company Inc	2711	862
Hill County Electric Coop	4911	407
Hill Dermaceuticals Inc	2834	374
Hill Engineering Inc	3599	341
Hill Farrer and Burrill LLP	8111	448
Hill Gilstrap PC	8111	501
Hill Grain Inc	4213	2471
Hill Holiday Connors Cosmopulos Inc	7311	33
Hill International Inc	8711	40
Hill Jerry Steady Cam Products	3663	419
Hill John M Machine Company Inc	7539	7
Hill Laboratories Co	3841	274
Hill Machinery Co	3544	371
Hill Manufacturing Co	3469	253
Hill Meat Co	2011	62
Hill Phoenix Inc	3585	22
Hill Specialty Company Inc	5084	766
Hill Wallack Attorneys at Law	8111	280
Hillandale-Gettysburg LP	0252	9
Hillard Bloom Packing Company Inc	2091	33
Hillard Heintze LLC	8742	548
Hillary Software Inc	7372	3910
Hillcrest Bancshares Inc	6712	388
Hillcrest Bank (Overland Park Kansas)	6022	94
Hillcrest Eggs and Cheese Co	5141	162
Hillcrest Enterprises Inc	5063	983
Hillcrest Foods Inc	5411	247
Hillcrest Labs Inc	4899	101
Hillcrest Precision Tool Company Inc	3599	2386
Hillcrest Terrace	8361	106
Hillcroft Services Inc	8322	86
Hilldrup Transfer and Storage	4213	142
Hiller Aircraft Corp	3721	26
Hillery Holding Co	6519	27
Hillestad Pharmaceuticals Inc	5122	125
Hillhouse Construction	1541	278
Hillhouse Naturals Farm Ltd	0115	3
Hilliard Corp	3564	21
Hilliard Lyons	6211	195
Hilliard's House Of Candy	2064	77
Hillis Printing Company Inc	2752	1610
Hillman Companies Inc (Cincinnati Ohio)	5085	13
Hillman Co	6799	291
Hillman Group Inc	5084	49
Hillman Shrimp and Oyster Co	2092	35
Hill-Rom Holdings Inc	3841	11
Hills Bank and Trust Co	6712	515
Hills Communities Inc	1531	56
Hills Inc	3552	18
Hills Materials Co	1611	122
Hills Newspaper Inc	2711	181
Hill's Pet Nutrition Inc	2047	2
Hill's Pool Service Inc	7389	712
Hillsboro Equipment Inc	5083	102
Hillsboro Industries Inc	3713	51
Hillsboro Journal Inc	2711	616
Hillsdale Automotive	3714	57
Hillsdale County National Bank	6021	326
Hillside Electronic Corp	7378	66
Hillside Hospital LLC	8062	220
Hillside Inc	8063	16
Hillside Plastics Corp	3081	82
Hillside Plastics Inc	3085	18
Hillside Recycling Equipment Corp	7532	13

Company Name	SIC	Rank
Hillsman Modular Molding Inc	3089	882
Hillson Group Inc	5731	111
Hillson Nut Co	5145	39
Hillstroms Aircraft Services	7389	1932
Hilltop Basic Resources Inc	1442	14
Hilltop Holdings Inc	6331	305
Hilltop Slate Inc	1411	19
Hilltop Steak House Inc	5812	298
Hilltop Transportation Inc	4213	1130
Hillwood Development Corp	6552	80
Hillyard Inc	2842	18
Hillyard Industries Inc	2842	36
Hilmar Cheese Company Inc	2022	6
Hilomast LLC	3663	386
Hilord Chemical Corp	3861	91
Hilscher Clarke Electric Co	1731	115
Hilsher Graphics	2759	565
HilSoft Inc	7375	273
Hiltech Inc	7373	1115
Hilton Audio Products Inc	3651	234
Hilton Capital Inc	6799	49
Hilton East Assisted Living	8361	128
Hilton Engineering Co	7389	2265
Hilton Hawaiian Village	7011	93
Hilton Head Exterminators Inc	7342	61
Hilton International Co	7011	10
Hilton Resort Palm Springs	7389	663
Hilton Scottsdale Resort and Villas	7011	209
Hilton Supply Management	5021	45
Hilton Tool Company Inc	3544	704
Hilton Worldwide	7011	2
Hima San Pablo Fajardo	8062	153
Himec Inc	1711	108
Hinchcliff Lumber Co	2448	31
Hinckley Allen and Snyder LLP	8111	212
Hinckley and Schmitt Inc	2086	30
Hinckley Co	3732	35
Hinda Incentives	8742	182
Hindle Power Inc	3612	70
Hindley Manufacturing Company Inc	3452	62
Hinds International Inc	3827	116
HindSight Ltd	7372	4509
Hiner Transport Inc	4213	599
Hines Flask Co	3559	428
Hines Horticulture Inc	0762	1
Hines Industries Inc	3829	241
Hines Interests LP	6552	42
Hines Interests Realty Advisers LP	6282	555
Hines Trucking Inc	4213	1149
Hinesburg Sand and Gravel Company Inc	5032	148
Hingham Institution for Savings	6036	31
Hingham Securities Corp	6036	49
Hinkle Chair Company Inc	2511	80
Hinkle Manufacturing LLC	3081	168
Hinkle Trucking Inc	4213	672
Hinkley Lighting Inc	3645	34
Hinkson Development Corp	6519	23
Hinman Associates	7379	1201
Hinsbrook Bank and Trust	5989	5
Hinsdale Nurseries Inc	5261	5
Hinshaw and Culbertson LLP	8111	190
Hinson Electric Inc	1731	677
Hinson Galleries Inc	5712	73
Hinton Lumber Products Inc	2449	7
Hinton Telephone Co	4813	457
Hinz Trucking Inc	4213	1995
Hipcricket	4899	39
HipLink Software	7389	2325
Hippo Studios Inc	7389	2179
Hippocrene Books Inc	2731	365
Hippopress LLC	2711	630
Hipro Manufacturing Inc	3523	240
Hipsher Tool and Die Inc	3544	846
Hi-Q Products Inc	6411	290
Hiram Electrical Contractors Inc	1731	48
Hirata Corporation Of America	8711	299
Hire Electric Inc	1731	1292
Hire Methods Inc	8331	150
Hire Priority	7361	145
Hire Solutions Inc	7389	2113
Hired Hands And Associates Inc	7361	430
Hi-Rel Capacitors Inc	3675	44
Hi-Rel Laboratories Inc	8734	115
Hi-Rel Products Inc	3674	385
HiRel Systems	3679	48
Hireright Inc	7379	120
Hirestrategy Inc	7361	114
Hiron's Memorial Works Inc	5999	317
Hirose Electric (USA) Inc	5065	88
Hirotec America Inc	3569	28
Hirsch/Bedner International Inc	7389	638
Hirsch International Corp	5084	153
Hirsch Machine Inc	3599	928
Hirsch Optical Corp	3851	54
Hirsch Sales Corp	5731	228
Hirschfeld Holdings LP	6719	86
Hirschfeld Steel Group LP	3441	15
Hirschmann Electronics Inc	3679	329
Hirschvogel Inc	3714	228
Hirsh Industries Inc	2522	11
Hirshfield's Inc	2851	25
Hirst Electric Company	1731	2061
Hirzel Canning Co	2033	69

Company Name	SIC	Rank
His House Inc	8322	139
His Manna Inc	8742	318
H-I-S Paint Manufacturing Company Inc	2851	96
His Vision Inc	3851	88
Hisco Pump Inc	5084	440
Hiscock and Barclay LLP	8111	197
Hi-Shear Technology Corp	3769	21
HiSoftware Inc	7372	3268
Hisonic Inc	3677	55
Hispanic Human Resources Council Inc	8322	226
Hispanic Print Media LLC	2711	904
Hissong Group Inc	6799	58
Hi-Standard Equipment and Supply Company Inc	5031	309
Hi-Stat Manufacturing Company Inc	3714	88
Historic Crags Lodge	7011	204
Historic Films Archive	7336	235
Historical Preservations of America	2731	304
HiT Software Inc	7372	1723
Hitachi America Ltd (Brisbane California)	5065	11
Hitachi America Ltd Computer Div	3572	21
Hitachi Automotive Products Inc USA	3694	4
Hitachi Cable Automotive Products USA Inc	3052	9
Hitachi Chemical Diagnostics Inc	2835	41
Hitachi Communication Technologies America Inc	3669	46
Hitachi Computer Products (USA) Inc	7373	86
Hitachi Construction Machinery Corp (Kernersville North Carolina)	3531	52
Hitachi Data Systems Corp	3572	4
Hitachi Electronic (USA) Devices Inc	3671	1
Hitachi Global Storage Technologies	3572	2
Hitachi Internetworking	8731	136
Hitachi Kokusai Electric America Ltd	5043	16
Hitachi Medical Systems America Inc	5047	23
Hitachi Metals America Ltd	3264	2
Hitachi Metals North Carolina Ltd	3264	11
Hitachi Software Engineering America Ltd	7372	2065
Hitcents Inc	7372	2765
Hitch Enterprises Inc	0211	2
Hitchcock Automotive Resources Inc	5599	4
Hitchcock Chair Company Ltd	2511	55
Hitchcock Fleming and Associates Inc	7311	202
Hitchcock Inc	3523	152
Hite Co	5063	95
Hite Parts Exchange Inc	5013	387
HITEC Group International Inc	5047	107
Hitec Integration Inc	7372	1736
Hi-Tec Machine Corp	3599	1402
Hitec Rcd LLC	5092	45
Hi-Tec Sports USA Inc	5139	3
Hi-Tec Systems Inc	7372	2907
Hi-Tech Advisers	7372	3798
Hi-Tech Applications LLC	3672	471
Hi-Tech Audio Systems Inc	5731	239
Hitech Circuits Inc	3672	466
Hi-Tech Color Inc	2893	36
Hitech Computers Of Ruston Inc	7373	1068
Hi-Tech Controls and Automation Inc	5063	750
Hi-Tech Distribution Inc	5045	932
Hi-Tech Electric Inc	1731	1066
Hi-Tech Electronic Displays	3993	37
Hi-Tech Express Inc	4213	1540
Hi-Tech Housing Inc	2452	48
Hi-Tech Inc	3469	374
Hi-Tech Machining and Engineering LLC	3769	28
Hi-Tech Machining LLC	3441	290
Hi-Tech Mold and Engineering Inc	3544	26
Hi-Tech Mold and Tool Inc	3089	621
Hi-Tech Mold And Tool LLC	3544	82
Hi-Tech Optics Cooperative Inc	3851	104
Hi-Tech Pharmacal Company Inc	2834	100
Hi-Tech Plastics Inc	3081	112
Hi-Tech Polymers Inc	3089	1793
Hi-Tech Pump and Crane Inc	5084	409
Hi-Tech Seating Products Inc	2396	7
Hitech Software Inc	7372	3352
Hitech Systems Inc	7372	3149
Hi-Tech Tool Industries Inc	3542	31
Hi-Tech Wire Inc	3312	101
Hi-Tek Data Corp	7379	819
Hi-Tek Manufacturing Inc	3599	164
Hi-Tek Professionals Inc	7363	107
Hi-Tek Rations Inc	2047	23
Hi-Temperature Graphics Inc	2759	491
Hi-Temperature Inc	3824	44
Hi-Temperature Insulation Inc	3296	4
Hi-Tide Sales Inc	3536	27
Hi-Touch Imaging Technologies Inc	5045	155
Hitran Corp	3612	41
Hitron International Inc	5064	199
Hi-Tron Semiconductor Corp	3674	400
Hitron Systems Inc	5045	811
HITT Contracting Inc	1521	13
Hitt Electric Company Inc	1731	563
Hitt Electric Corp	1731	514
Hittite Microwave Corp	3651	22
Hivelocity Ventures Corp	4813	615

Company Name	SIC	Rank
HiWAAY Internet Services	4813	157
Hix Corp	3567	50
Hixson Inc	8712	117
Hi-Z Technology Inc	3629	106
HJ Arnett Industries LLC	3825	223
HJ Baker and Bro Inc	2048	26
HJ Bergeron Pecan Shelling Plant Inc	5159	26
HJ Ford Associates Inc	8711	375
HJ Heinz Co	2033	1
HJ High Construction Co	1542	244
HJ Russell and Co	6552	85
HJ Stabile and Son Inc	1521	21
Hjd Capital Electric Inc	1731	344
HJG Trucking Inc	4212	82
Hjpc Corp	7379	430
Hjs Inc	7349	523
Hk Aerospace Kirkhill Aircraft Parts Co	5085	242
HK Canning Inc	2033	105
H-K Contractors Inc	1611	181
HK Graphics Inc	7336	230
HK Precision Parts Inc	3429	123
HK Research Corp	2821	105
HKK Machining Co	3599	1188
Hkm Direct Market Communications Inc	7331	44
HKN Inc	1311	189
HL Bennett Jr Inc	1623	853
HL Computer Inc	5734	281
HI Industries Inc	3543	16
HL Technologies LP	5049	54
HLC Hotels Inc	7011	89
HLH Inc	3444	226
HLI Operating Company Inc	3714	21
Hlk Construction Inc	1731	906
HLM Management Co	6282	323
Hlp Systems	3643	156
Hlpr Inc	3845	134
HLR Controls Inc	3492	35
Hlt Ltd	3799	31
HLW Fast Track Inc	5812	284
HLW International LLP	8712	29
Hlx Inc	5211	211
HM Cross and Sons Inc	5063	456
Hm Graphics Inc	2752	86
HM Kelly Inc	4213	1188
HM Patterson and Son Inc	7261	8
Hm Product Solutions Ltd	4731	82
HM Richards Inc	2512	20
HM Royal Inc	5052	5
HM White Holding Company Inc	3444	3
Hma Lab Supply Inc	5049	103
HMA Public Relations	8743	229
HMC Advertising LLC	7311	975
Hmc Corp	3553	30
HMC Electronics	5063	554
Hmc Industries Inc	2541	68
Hmc Instrument and Machine Works Ltd	3533	86
Hmc Int'l Division Inc	3829	503
HMC Products Inc	3599	678
HMC Shipping	5078	41
HMCM Inc	8741	38
Hmd Inc	3841	277
HME Providers Inc	6794	85
HMG/Courtland Properties Inc	6798	199
HMI Industries Inc	3635	4
Hmi Systems LLC	8731	202
HMK Enterprises Inc	3312	85
HMN Financial Inc	6712	345
Hmp Industries Inc	3451	54
HMR Architects Inc	8712	252
Hms Company Inc	8711	537
Hms Electronics Inc	3625	380
HMS Holding Company Inc	5051	433
HMS Holdings Corp	7389	110
HMS Inc (Arlington Virginia)	8742	263
Hms Industries Inc	3541	218
HMS Products Co	3549	25
HMS Technologies Inc	7379	214
HMSHost Corp	5812	4
Hmt Manufacturing Inc	3559	346
HMW Enterprises Inc	3571	165
HN Donahoo Contracting Company Inc	1623	139
HN Hinckley and Sons Inc	5211	223
HN Lockwood Inc	3089	1411
Hna Computers Systems Inc	7373	665
HNB Bank	6022	612
HNB Corp	6712	19
Hnedak Bobo Group Inc	8712	190
HNI Corp	2521	1
HNL Inc	3679	689
Ho Chien Electronic Group Inc	5065	534
Ho Ho Ho Express Inc	4213	1028
HO Penn Machinery Company Inc	5082	18
HO Trerice Co	3823	59
HO Wolding Inc	4213	500
HOAG Electronics Inc	8711	526
Hoagland Electric Inc	1731	2551
Hoak Capital Corp	6799	288
Hoar Construction LLC	1542	43
Hobart Corp	5084	8
Hobart Ground Power	3612	36
Hobart Sales and Service	5046	225
Hobart West Group Inc	7373	31

Company Name	SIC	Rank
Hobas Pipe USA Inc	3089	217
Hobbit Distributing Inc	3679	792
Hobbs and Black Associates Inc	8712	59
Hobbs Bonded Fibers Inc	2297	3
Hobbs Electric Inc	1731	1619
Hobbs Enterprises Inc	4213	2461
Hobbs/Herder Advertising	7311	506
Hobbs Iron and Metal Company Inc	5084	344
Hobbs Medical Inc	3841	356
Hobbs-Crump Inc	5065	993
Hobby Construction Company Inc	1623	192
Hobby Lobby Stores Inc	5945	3
Hobby Press Inc	2761	42
Hobby Products International Inc	5092	23
Hobby Publications Inc	2721	241
Hobby Town USA	6794	83
Hobbytroncom	5961	156
Hobes Country Hams Inc	2013	162
Hobet Mining Inc	1221	21
Hobgood Electric and Machinery Company Inc	7694	27
Hobson and Motzer Inc	3469	79
Hobsons	7372	483
Hochiki America Corp	3669	242
Ho-Chunk Inc	6719	113
Hockenberg Equipment Co	5046	11
Hockenbergs Equipment And Supply Company Inc	5046	45
Hocker Tool And Die Inc	3599	2222
Hocking Printing Company Inc	2741	253
Hockmeyer Equipment Corp	3559	158
Hocon Gas Inc	5984	13
Hodgdon Yachts Inc	3732	70
Hodge Co	5084	244
Hodge Electrical Contractors Inc	1731	1661
Hodge Foundry	3321	53
Hodge Hart and Schleifer Inc	6331	362
Hodge Tool Company Inc	3544	134
Hodges and Irvine Inc	2754	47
Hodges Transportation Inc	8711	281
Hodges Triad Electric LLC	1731	2291
Hodges Truck Company Inc	4212	29
Hodgins Engraving Company Inc	3555	41
Hodgins Printing Company Inc	2752	1815
Hodgson Mill Inc	2041	26
Hoefler Communications Inc	1731	1401
Hoefler Consulting Group	8999	53
Hoefner Corp	3599	1832
Hoenig and Company Inc	6719	120
Hoerbiger Automotive Comfort Systems Inc	3511	32
Hoerbiger Corporation Of America Inc	3491	27
Hoerler Milk Transport Inc	4213	2592
Hofer Machine and Tool Company Inc	3643	130
Hoffer Flow Controls Inc	3823	129
Hoffer Plastics Corp	3089	403
Hoffland Environmental Inc	3589	52
Hoffman Agency	8743	87
Hoffman and Hoffman Trenching Inc	1623	767
Hoffman Brothers Auto Electric Inc	5013	141
Hoffman Brothers Inc	2752	926
Hoffman California Fabrics	5131	23
Hoffman Commercial Group Inc	5441	10
Hoffman Construction Co	1542	197
Hoffman Enclosures Inc	3679	47
Hoffman Engineering Corp	8734	13
Hoffman International Inc	5082	98
Hoffman/Lewis	7311	129
Hoffman Management Co	7349	399
Hoffman Management LLC	6531	441
Hoffman McCann PC- Tofias New England Div	8721	62
Hoffman Media LLC	2721	45
Hoffman Precision Plastics Inc	3089	1711
Hoffman Supply Company Inc	5078	23
Hoffman Tool and Die Inc	3544	607
Hoffman Transport Inc	4213	1157
Hoffman-Cortes Contracting Co	1542	413
Hoffmann Die Cast Corp	3363	25
Hoffmann Filter Corp	3569	264
Hoffmann's Green Industries Inc	7389	2164
Hoffmaster Group Inc	2676	2
Hoffmeier Inc	4213	1185
HoffTek Inc	7373	913
Hofmann and Leavy Inc	2241	11
Hofmann Co	6552	107
Hofmann Industries Inc	3498	14
Hofmann Sausage Company Inc	2013	211
Hog Brothers Recycling LLC	4953	166
Hog Inc	5159	10
Hog Slat Inc	3523	22
Hogan and Sons Lumber Company Inc	5031	383
Hogan Flavors and Fragrances Inc	2844	200
Hogan Group Inc	6552	118
Hogan Lovells US LLP	8111	2
Hogan Manufacturing Inc	3999	56
Hogan Services Inc	8741	260
Hogan Steel Erectors Inc	7389	1867
Hogan Taylor LLP	8721	104
Hoge Lumber Co	2452	52
Hoge Motor Co	4213	2842
Hogentogler and Company Inc	3829	291
Hogg Construction Inc	1542	202
Hogil Pharmaceutical Corp	2834	416

Company Name	SIC	Rank
Hogland Transfer Co	4213	2004
Hogue Cellars Ltd	2084	13
Hogue Enterprises Inc	7359	235
Hogue Printing Inc	2752	351
H-O-H Water Technology Inc	3589	73
Hohl Machine And Conveyor Company Inc	3535	98
Hohner Inc	3931	10
Hoist Equipment Company Inc	3537	80
Hoist Fitness Systems Inc	3949	109
Hoist Liftruck Manufacturing Inc	3537	43
Hoke Inc (Spartanburg South Carolina)	3769	7
Hoku Corp	3679	522
Holaday Circuits Inc	3672	66
Holaday-Parks-Fabricators Inc	1711	70
Holahan Gumpper and Dowling	8111	580
Holbert Engineering Company Inc	7389	2069
Holbrook Manufacturing Inc	3444	217
Holbrook Tool and Molding Inc	3089	1248
Holcim Inc	3241	4
Holcim LP (Midlothian Texas)	2891	42
Holcomb Freightliner Inc	5012	58
Holcomb Fuel Company Inc	5983	24
Hold Brothers Inc	6221	3
Hold Brothers On-Line Investment Services Inc	6211	171
HoldCube	7319	144
Holden Landmark Corp	5963	32
Holden Machine and Fabrication Inc	5082	161
Holden Plastics Corp	3089	1474
Holder Construction Co	1541	53
Holdrege Irrigation Inc	5083	88
Holdren Brothers Inc	3599	2303
Hole Specialists Inc	3541	119
Holicong Locksmith's and Central Security Inc	1731	1477
Holiday Builders Inc	1521	9
Holiday Candy Corp	2066	32
Holiday Companies Inc	5411	76
Holiday Cruise Center	4725	69
Holiday Express Corp	4213	1058
Holiday Fenoglio and Fowler LP	6531	402
Holiday House Of Manitowoc County Inc	8331	157
Holiday Housewares Inc	3089	460
Holiday Ice Inc	3585	214
Holiday Inn Solomons	7011	241
Holiday Models Convention Services	7389	1433
Holiday Printing And Lithograph	2752	831
Holiday Retirement Corp	6513	11
Holiday Sewer And Construction Inc	1623	757
Holiday Statistics, Inc	7363	363
Holiday World of Dallas Ltd	5561	10
Holladay Construction Company Inc	1623	386
Hollaender Manufacturing Co	3498	62
Holland America Line Westours Inc	4481	7
Holland and Hart LLP	8111	246
Holland and Knight LLP	8111	10
Holland Awning Co	2394	12
Holland Capital Management LLC	6282	565
Holland Communications Inc	7311	463
Holland Computers Inc	5734	97
Holland Corporation Inc	1611	130
Holland Enterprises Inc	4213	1095
Holland Inc	5812	65
Holland Litho Service Inc	2759	162
Holland Manufacturing Co	2672	33
Holland Manufacturing Corp	3255	13
Holland Manufacturing Inc	3599	1908
Holland Pump Manufacturing Inc	3561	98
Holland Southwest International Inc	5031	193
Holland Special Delivery Inc	4213	1464
Holland Supply	5099	114
Holland Transfer Co	4213	1878
Holland Transplanter Company Inc	3523	238
Holland Transportation	4789	15
Hollar and Greene Produce Co	5148	39
Holler Chevrolet	5511	146
Hollerbach Equipment Company Inc	5082	163
Hollico Inc	1623	104
Hollingsead International Inc	3728	93
Hollingsworth and Vose Company Inc	2621	23
Hollingsworth Capital Partners LLC	6552	182
Hollingsworth Construction Co	1389	54
Hollingsworth John D On Wheels Inc	3552	5
Hollingsworth Mazda	5511	1232
Hollingsworth-Richards Inc	5511	546
Hollins Organic Products Inc	5083	215
Hollis Electronics Company LLC	8731	413
Hollis Graphics Inc	2796	48
Hollis Line Machine Company Inc	7692	15
Hollister Associates Inc	7361	209
Hollister Inc	3842	35
Hollister-Whitney Elevator Corp	3534	11
Holliston LLC	2211	13
Holliston Sand Company Inc	1446	8
Hollmann Manufacturing Technologies	5065	456
Holloman Energy Corp	1311	279
Holloway Equipment Company Inc	3599	2261
Holloway Shunts Inc	3825	348
Holloway Sportswear Inc	2329	6
Holloway-Houston Inc	5072	30
Holly Energy Partners LP	4613	9
Holly Hill Fruit Products Inc	2037	27

Company Name	SIC	Rank
Holly Label Company Inc	2672	77
Holly Pipe Corp	3545	423
Holly Sales and Service Inc	5046	331
Hollyer Brady Smith and Hines LLP	8111	542
Hollymatic Corp	5113	53
Holly's Custom Print Inc	2752	1351
Hollywood Builders Hardware Inc	5072	147
Hollywood Casino Corp	7999	40
Hollywood Edge	7822	29
Hollywood Entertainment Corp	7841	4
Hollywood Film Co	3861	51
Hollywood Media Corp	5999	156
Hollywood Park Casino	7993	8
Hollywood Records	3652	10
Hollywood Rental Company Inc	7819	37
Hollywood Ribbon Industries Inc	3089	121
Hollywood Sound International Corp	5064	209
Hollywood Sports Park LLC	7389	1002
Hollywood Vaults	7336	254
Hollywood Visual Productions	7812	337
Hollywood Woodwork Inc	2431	89
Holm Electric Inc	1731	1765
Holm Graphic Services Inc	2752	1726
Hol-Mac Corp	3593	5
Holman Boiler Works Inc	3443	89
Holman Cadillac Co	5511	858
Holman Distribution Center of OR	4213	1781
Holman Distribution Center of WA	4213	885
Holman Enterprises	5511	14
Holman United	4213	1648
Holman's Of Nevada Inc	7373	593
Holmatro Inc	3569	183
Holmberg Farms Inc	5193	13
Holme Roberts and Owen LLP	8111	13
Holmed Corp	3841	229
Holmes and Company Advertising	7311	796
Holmes Auto Group Inc	5511	1066
Holmes Automotive	5511	192
Holmes Brothers Inc	3829	231
Holmes By Products Co	2048	83
Holmes Cheese Co	2022	69
Holmes Co	2754	35
Holmes Drywall Supply Inc	5039	39
Holmes Equipment and Supply LLC	5046	261
Holmes Foods Inc	2015	38
Holmes Limestone Co	1221	42
Holmes Lumber and Building Center Inc	5031	77
Holmes Murphy and Associates Inc	6411	80
Holmes Oil Co	5172	155
Holmes Timber Company Inc	5099	36
Holmes Tool and Engineering Inc	3599	1690
Holmes Tuttle Ford Inc	5511	92
Holmes-Hally Industries Inc	3429	46
Holming Co	3564	97
Holmquist Lumber Inc	5031	437
Hol-N-One Donut Company Of Ark Inc	5046	197
Hologic Inc	3844	2
Holstein Association USA Inc	7372	646
Holston Gases Inc	5169	65
Holston Steel Services Inc	5051	484
Holsum Of Fort Wayne Inc	2051	64
Holt And Bugbee Co	5031	101
Holt Cat	5082	6
Holt Electrical Contractors Inc	1731	824
Holt Equipment Company Inc	5082	203
Holt McDougal	2731	48
Holt of California	5599	5
Holt Paper And Chemical Company Inc	5113	38
Holt Products Co	3451	82
Holt Tool and Machine Inc	3312	121
Holtco Inc	5087	57
Holten Meat Inc	2013	71
Holtkoetter International Inc	3645	43
Holton National Bank	6712	643
Holtz Rubenstein Reminick LLP	7291	10
Holy Caritas Family Hospital Inc	8062	189
Holy Cross Energy Inc	4911	170
Holy Name Medical Center Inc	8062	179
Holyoke Machine Co	3554	41
Holz Motors Inc	5511	303
Holz Rubber Company Inc	3069	97
Holzberg Communications Inc	5065	984
Holzmeyer Die And Mold Manufacturing Corp	3089	1244
Holzmueller Corp	5063	308
Holzschu Jordan Schiff and Associates	7379	1479
Homan Lumber Mart Inc	5031	243
Homark Company Inc	2451	38
Homasote Co	2493	9
Homasote International Sales Company Inc	2493	2
Home Access Health Corp	7389	588
Home Aide Home Care Inc	7361	410
Home And Away Inc	2721	188
Home and Garden Television	4841	175
Home and Hospital Medical Personnel Inc	7363	231
Home Automation Inc	3669	125
Home Bancorp Inc	6712	390
Home BancShares Inc	6022	54
Home Bank and Trust Co	6022	789
Home Bank (Seagoville Texas)	6022	716
Home Box Office	4841	11

Company Name	SIC	Rank
Home Building Savings Bank	6035	233
Home Buyer Publications Inc	2721	257
Home Buyers Warranty Corp	6351	15
Home Care Delivered Inc	5047	206
Home Care Equipment Inc	7352	23
Home Care Industries Inc	2674	7
Home Care Research Of Rochester Inc	8733	40
Home Care Services Of H R M C	7363	271
Home Care Specialists Inc	7352	14
Home Care Supply	7352	19
Home Care United Inc	5999	73
Home City Financial Corp	6712	660
Home City Ice Co	2097	1
Home Computer Support	3571	250
Home Debut Inc	7299	47
Home Diagnostics Corp	3845	66
Home Entertainment Systems Of Nj Inc	5064	137
Home Equity of America Inc	6211	82
Home Etc Inc	5099	50
Home Federal Bancorp Inc (Nampa Idaho)	6712	275
Home Federal Bancorp Incorporated of Louisiana	6712	631
Home Federal Bank Sioux Falls South Dakota	6035	4
Home Financial Bancorp	6712	702
Home For Aged Women-Minquadale Home Inc	8361	86
Home For Jewish Parents	8322	82
Home FSB	6035	82
Home FSB (Marshalltown Iowa)	6712	496
Home Guard Industries Inc	3442	105
Home Hardware	5072	189
Home Health Corporation of America Inc	8082	38
Home Health Outreach	8082	67
Home Healthcare Inc	7363	265
Home Instead Inc	8059	17
Home Integrity Service Financial Ltd	7322	189
Home Labor Associates Inc	7389	1893
Home Lighting Ltd	5063	1021
Home Link Of Nevada Inc	4813	517
Home Loan Financial Corp	6712	647
Home Lumber of New Haven Inc	5031	224
Home Market Foods Inc	2013	23
Home Media Stores LC	5731	192
Home Media Technologies Inc	7379	1617
Home Medical Care Inc	5047	271
Home Menders Inc	1731	2335
Home Of Fine Decorators LLC	7389	1348
Home Of The Hebert Candies Inc	5441	13
Home Office Solutions Inc	5719	32
Home Oil and Gas Company Inc	5172	115
Home Oil Co	6171	57
Home Oil Company of Sikeston Inc	5172	153
Home Place Inc	2451	37
Home Plan Software Inc	7372	2714
Home Port Seafood	2092	59
Home Products International Inc	3089	56
Home Properties Fentil Inc	6798	3
Home Properties Inc	6798	61
Home Properties Southern Meadows LLC	6798	8
Home Protection Center Inc	1731	1955
Home Raters Inc	7389	842
Home Recreation Center	5091	130
Home Run Inc	4213	245
Home Run Inn Inc	8742	417
Home Run Software Services Inc	7379	421
Home Safeguard Industries LLC	3829	253
Home Satellite Services Inc	4841	174
Home Savings and Loan Association of Oklahoma City	6036	108
Home Savings and Loan Company of Youngstown Ohio	6035	39
Home Savings Bank of Albemarle SSB	6036	84
Home Savings Bank (Salt Lake City Utah)	6022	776
Home Shopping Club Inc	4833	19
Home Style Foods Inc	5148	70
Home Tech Inc	5942	35
Home Town Bank	6035	191
Home Trust Bank	6036	25
Home Trust Co	6162	43
Home Video Library Electronics	5731	43
Home2us Communications Inc	4841	108
HomeAmerican Mortgage Corp	6162	37
Homeaway Inc	7375	36
HomeBanc Corp	6798	42
HomeBanc Mortgage Corp	6162	61
Homebuilders Financial Network Inc	6162	125
Homebuyers Guide Real Estate Inc	2721	375
HomeCall Inc	8082	51
HomeCall Incorporated McCulloh Home Health Agency	8082	32
Homecare Products Inc	3842	195
Homeclick LLC	5961	76
Homedeq Inc	7352	34
HomeFed Communities Inc	6519	20
Homefed Corp	6519	22
Homeguard Inc	1731	1246
Homeland HealthCare Inc	6411	193
Homeland Solutions Inc	1731	882
Homeland Stores Inc	5411	169

Company Name	SIC	Rank
Homeland Vinyl Products Inc	3081	170
HomeMed Channel Inc	5912	75
Homeowners Choice Inc	6331	301
HomePointe Property Management Inc	6531	444
Homeportfolio Inc	7372	1753
Homer Electric Association Inc	4911	248
Homer Optical Company Inc	3851	46
HomeReach Inc	5047	189
Homer's Ice Cream Inc	2024	74
Homes and Land Publishing Ltd	2721	106
Homes and Lifestyles Magazine Inc	2721	278
Homes Factory Dot Com	7371	1771
Homes Inc	2741	426
Homes Of Merit Inc	2451	12
Homescom Inc	7372	456
Homeshield	3442	18
Homesights By Design LLC	7389	1680
Homesphere Inc	7372	493
Homespun Tapes Ltd	7812	272
Homestead Baking Co	2051	138
Homestead Custom Computing	7379	1519
Homestead Electric Co	1731	2090
Homestead Lawn and Tractor Co	5083	159
Homestead Newspapers Inc	2711	730
Homestead Publishing Co	2711	308
Homestead Ravioli Company Inc	2032	43
Homestead Tool And Machine Inc	3544	389
HomeStreet Bank Inc	6712	60
Home-Style Industries Inc	2512	52
Hometelos LP	7372	3411
Hometime Video Publishing Inc	7812	181
Hometown America	6798	10
Hometown Bagel Inc	2051	140
Hometown Bancorp Inc	6712	655
Hometown Bancorp Ltd	6021	118
Hometown Bank	6021	295
Hometown Bank NA	6021	267
Hometown Broadcasting	4832	270
Hometown Insurors Inc	6035	255
Hometown Lumber And Hardware Inc	5211	269
Hometown News	2711	487
Hometown Oxygen Inc	5047	237
Hometown Publications Ii Inc	2711	562
Hometown Telecom	4822	12
Hometowne Energy Company Inc	5084	585
HomeVestors of America Inc	6531	312
Homewood Corp	1531	48
Homewood Press Inc	2752	840
HomeWorks Tri-County Electric Cooperative Inc	4911	484
Hom-Excel Inc	5023	90
Homeyer Tool and Die Co	3544	350
HOMISCO/VoiceNet	7372	1154
Hommel-Etamic America Corp	3829	58
Hommer Tool/Manufacturing Inc	3544	351
Homogeneous Metals Inc	3399	17
Homtex Inc	2211	25
Hon Blue Inc	7334	10
Hon Development Co	6552	207
Honda Electric Inc	1731	1210
Honda of America Manufacturing Inc	3711	9
Honda of Houston	5571	5
Honda of Tiffany Springs	5511	477
Hono Tree Company Inc	3599	806
Honee Bear Canning	2033	14
Honematic Machine Corp	3599	1315
Honest Tea Inc	2099	164
Honey Bear Ham	2013	241
Honey Creek Machine LLC	3559	371
Honey Silverbow Company Inc	2099	196
Honeybee Robotics Ltd	3769	23
Honeycutt Electric Inc	1731	1105
Honeycutt Machine Inc	3599	865
Honeyville Metal Inc	3523	116
Honeyware Inc	3089	637
Honeywell Access	7372	938
Honeywell Aerospace	3825	17
Honeywell Analytics	3829	61
Honeywell Enraf	3533	48
Honeywell Grimes Aerospace	3647	3
Honeywell Inc Micro Switch Div	3613	9
Honeywell International Commercial Electronic Systems Div	3812	6
Honeywell International Inc	3812	2
Honeywell International Specialty Materials	2819	5
Honeywell Scanning and Mobility	3577	39
Hong Hop Company Inc	2098	25
Hong Kong Noodle Company Inc	2098	22
Hong Yuan Industrial Company Ltd	2329	15
Honickman Affiliates	2086	6
Honigman Miller Schwartz and Cohn LLP	8111	92
Honiron Corp	3523	130
Honold and La Page Inc	5074	149
Honolulu Information Service	7389	1248
Honolulu Publishing Company Ltd	2721	362
Honomach Inc	3599	1646
Honor Hardware And Building Supply Inc	5211	166
Honor Truck and Transfer Inc	4213	2646
Honsa-Binder Printing Inc	2752	913
Hoober Inc	7699	24
Hood Corp	1623	123

Company Name	SIC	Rank
Hood Depot International Inc	3564	103
Hood Equipment Company Inc	5083	59
Hood Equipment Inc	3531	164
Hood Manufacturing Inc	3089	1131
Hood Marketing Solutions	7311	723
Hood Packaging Corp	2674	2
Hood River Cable Inc	3669	300
Hood River Distillers Inc	2085	20
Hood River Juice Company Inc	2099	238
Hook Industrial Sales Inc	3569	254
Hooker Ballew Printing Co	2752	1201
Hooker Creek Equipment and Supply	7359	250
Hooker Furniture Corp	2511	11
Hooley Inc	3312	119
Hooper Corporation	3444	18
Hooper Electric	1731	1920
Hooper Holmes Inc	8099	28
Hooper's Trailer Sales Inc	3715	52
Hoople Country Kitchens Inc	2099	342
Hoople Farmers Grain Co	5153	108
Hoosier Energy Rural Electric Cooperative Inc	4911	111
Hoosier Fiberglass Industries Inc	3089	1764
Hoosier Fire Equipment Inc	5087	152
Hoosier Gasket Corp	3053	33
Hoosier Plastic Fabrication Inc	3599	452
Hoosier Pride Plastics	3089	1607
Hoosier Racing Tire Corp	5014	39
Hoosier Spline Broach Corp	3545	238
Hoosier Tire Mid-Atlantic	4213	2087
Hoosier Tool and Die Company Inc	3544	309
Hoot Johnson Construction Inc	1623	411
Hootman Dental Laboratories Inc	8072	21
Hooven - Dayton Corp	2679	46
Hoover and Strong Inc	3341	26
Hoover and Wells Inc	1752	6
Hoover Business Systems LLC	3578	47
Hoover Color Corp	2865	24
Hoover Construction Company Inc	1611	173
Hoover Conveyor and Fabrication Corp	3535	154
Hoover Inc	1422	45
Hoover Industries Inc	3728	109
Hoover Instrument Service Inc	5063	832
Hoover Materials Handling Group Inc	3412	1
Hoover Precision Products Inc	3399	20
Hoover Transportation Services Inc	4212	71
Hoover Treated Wood Products Inc	2491	5
Hoover Universal Inc	2531	8
Hoover's Inc	2731	51
Hoover's Jewelers Inc	5944	31
Hop Industries Corp	2821	67
Hop Kee Inc	5148	71
Hope Communities Inc	6552	302
Hope Engineers Inc	8711	330
Hope Enterprises Inc	8331	14
Hope Network SE	8361	108
Hope Rehabilitation Services	8331	2
Hope Resource Center Inc	7361	382
Hopes Windows Inc	3442	92
Hopeton State Bank	6022	811
Hopewell Builders Supply Inc	5211	177
Hopewell Industries Inc	8331	249
Hopewell Publishing Company Inc	2711	681
Hopewell Valley Community Bank	6022	447
Hopf Equipment Inc	5083	39
HopFed Bancorp Inc	6712	302
Hopkins Agricultural Chemical Co	5191	30
Hopkins and Carley	8111	228
Hopkins and Company Inc	7361	301
Hopkins Carpet Co	5713	15
Hopkins Construction Inc	1623	329
Hopkins Distribution Co	4225	34
Hopkins Duley and Associates Inc	7374	305
Hopkins Financial Corp	6712	399
Hopkins Foodservice Specialists Inc	7389	1444
Hopkins Ford Inc	5511	349
Hopkins Furniture Inc	5712	101
Hopkins Illinois Elevator Company Inc	1796	10
Hopkins Manufacturing Corp	3714	166
Hopkins Technology LLC	7372	4828
Hopkins-Carter Company Inc	5088	38
Hopkins-Gowen Oil Company Inc	5171	33
Hopkinsville Elevator Co	5153	96
Hopkinsville Milling Co	2041	44
Hop-On Inc	3663	420
Hoppe Inc	6552	261
Hoppe Technologies Inc	3544	49
Hopper Development Inc	3089	1750
Hoppe's	3949	95
Hoppmann Communications Corp	7373	478
Hoppmann Printing Inc	2759	537
HOPS International Inc	7371	188
Hoquiam Plywood Company Inc	2436	19
Horace G Ilderton Inc	5511	1105
Horace Mann Educators Corp	6331	75
Horace Mann Insurance Co	6331	40
Horace Mann Life Insurance Co	6311	128
Horace Mann Lloyds	6331	39
Horace Mann Service Corp	6411	40
Horace Sullivan Inc	1731	1431
Horan Data Services Inc	7374	279
Horiba Instruments Inc	3826	40
Horiba/Stec Inc	3829	99
Horich Parks Lebow Advertising and Marketing Inc	7311	500
Horix Manufacturing Company Inc	5084	393
Horizon	5191	17
Horizon Air Industries Inc	4512	9
Horizon Air Services Inc	4213	2772
Horizon Bancorp	6712	246
Horizon Bank NA	6021	75
Horizon Behavioral Services Inc	8099	7
Horizon Bindery	2789	90
Horizon Cable TV Inc	4841	161
Horizon Carbide Tool Inc	3599	1062
Horizon Companies Inc	7371	317
Horizon Consulting Inc	7389	303
Horizon Credit Union	6062	84
Horizon Datacom Solutions Inc	5045	689
Horizon Die Company Inc	3544	567
Horizon Distribution Inc	5072	52
Horizon Educational Systems Inc	7371	1204
Horizon Electric Inc	1731	2085
Horizon Equipment Inc	5083	181
Horizon Food Service and Supply Ltd	5046	242
Horizon Freight Systems Inc	4213	293
Horizon Graphics	2752	650
Horizon Health Corp	8099	21
Horizon Healthcare Services Inc	6321	22
Horizon Holdings	6799	365
Horizon House Of Illinois Valley Inc	8322	247
Horizon International	5032	196
Horizon Lines Inc	4424	3
Horizon Machining and Manufacturing Inc	3599	2262
Horizon Media Inc	7319	19
Horizon Mortgage and Investment Co	6211	392
Horizon Moving Systems Inc	4213	1573
Horizon Music Inc	3357	26
Horizon Ohio Publications Inc	2711	525
Horizon Organic Farms Maryland Inc	2026	14
Horizon Organic Holding Corp	2026	20
Horizon Partners Ltd	6799	337
Horizon Payroll Services Inc	7371	271
Horizon Personnel Resources	7363	234
Horizon Plastics and Engineering Inc	3089	1467
Horizon Precision Assembly Co	3679	371
Horizon Publishing Co	2721	89
Horizon Services Corp	1731	855
Horizon Signal Technologies Inc	5046	204
Horizon Snack Foods Inc	2053	15
Horizon Software International LLC	5045	66
Horizon SpA and Pool Parts Inc	5074	145
Horizon Steel Treating Inc	3398	14
Horizon Tank Lines Inc	4213	1596
Horizon Technology Inc	5049	67
Horizon Technology Inc (Lake Forest California)	7372	2099
Horizon Telcom Inc	4813	93
Horizon Telephone Systems Inc	5065	662
Horizon Trust and Investment Management	6022	205
Horizon West Inc	8059	1
Horizon Wind Energy	5063	34
Horizon Wine and Spirits	5182	27
Horizon Worldwide	7389	1120
Horizontal Technology Inc	5084	772
Horlick Company Inc	3621	154
Hormann Flexon LLC	3442	129
Hormann LLC	3442	54
Hormel Foods Corp	2011	3
Horn Group Inc	8743	48
Horn International Packaging Inc	5085	217
Hornady Manufacturing Co	3482	4
Hornady Transportation	4213	404
Hornall Anderson Design Works LLC	7336	49
Hornbeck Offshore Services Inc	4449	7
Hornberger Management Co	7361	126
Hornblower Cruises and Events	4489	1
Hornblower Dining Yachts Inc	5812	167
Horne International Inc	8711	572
Horne Tipps Holding Company Inc	7313	18
Horner Electric Inc	3625	67
Horner Millwork Corp	5031	114
Hornerxpress Inc	5091	27
Hornerxpress Worldwide Inc	5091	123
Horning Brothers	6552	151
Hornish Brothers Inc	4213	1386
Hornwood Inc	2258	7
Horovitz Rudoy and Roteman	8721	312
Horrow Sports Ventures Inc	7941	43
Horry Electric Cooperative Inc	4911	159
Horry Telephone Cooperative Inc	4813	39
Horsburgh and Scott Co	3566	2
Horse FarmTours Inc	4725	53
Horsehead Holding Corp	3339	5
Horseless Carriage Carriers	4213	1342
Horsemen's Pride Inc	3089	1550
Horsepower Sales	5063	918
Horseshoe Casino and Hotel	7011	27
Horsley Co	5084	395
Horsley Company LLC	5084	392
Horst Construction Company Inc	1541	54
Horst Equipment Repair Inc	3599	1909
Horst Group Inc	1531	49
Horstmeier Lumber Company Inc	5031	359
Hortica Insurance and Employee Benefits	6331	338
Horton and Horton Printing Co	2752	1546
Horton Group	6411	56
Horton Homes Inc	2451	11
Horton Machine And Custom Design Inc	3599	1871
Horvick Inc	5083	124
Horween Leather Co	3111	5
Horwith Freightliner	4213	3093
Horwith Trucks Inc	4213	616
Hosales Inc	5065	1016
Hosch Company LP	3535	165
Hoschette Enterprises Inc	3089	1687
Hose and Fittings Etc	5074	150
Hose Assemblies Inc	3069	88
Hose Of South Texas Inc	5085	321
Hose Technology Inc	3599	2074
Hoselton Chevrolet Inc	5511	199
Hose-Mccann Telephone Company Inc	3661	147
Hoshino USA Inc	5099	14
Hoskins Chevrolet Inc	5511	402
Hoskins Electric Co	1731	622
Hosmer-Dorrance Corp	3842	118
Hosokawa Polymer Systems	3089	1470
Hosokawa Service Company Inc	7699	262
Hospice Of The Valley	8082	20
Hospira Inc	2834	16
Hospital Associates	5047	161
Hospital Bed Remanufacturing Company Inc	2599	40
Hospital Billing and Collection Service	7322	32
Hospital Disposables Inc	3089	1406
Hospital For Special Care	8069	14
Hospital Forms and Systems Corp	5112	37
Hospital Marketing Services Company Inc	3841	201
Hospital Service District	8062	129
Hospital Shared Services	7363	85
Hospital Solutions Inc	7389	483
Hospital Systems Inc	3845	42
Hospitality Automation Consultants Ltd	8742	223
Hospitality Control Solutions Of West Tennessee LLC	5045	827
Hospitality Depot LLC	5046	144
Hospitality Enterprise	7311	179
Hospitality Management Systems Inc	5045	766
Hospitality Mints LLC	2064	32
Hospitality Solutions International Inc	7372	765
Hospitality Unlimited Investments Co	8741	310
Hospi-Tel Manufacturing Co	2392	32
Host Depot Inc	4813	598
Host Engineering Inc	5734	282
Host Hotels and Resorts Inc	7011	12
Host Interface International Inc	7372	4697
Hostar International Inc	3535	150
HostdimeCom Inc	4813	308
Hostess Brands Inc	2051	2
Hostess Cake	2051	301
Hostess Cake Div	2051	17
HostingCom Inc	7379	137
HOSTINGCOM Inc	4813	148
Hostmann Steinberg Inc	2893	15
HostrocketCom Inc	4813	389
Hostway Corp	7375	92
Hot Action Sportswear Inc	2396	30
Hot Door Inc	7372	3372
Hot Food Boxes Inc	3556	144
HOT Graphic Services Inc	2791	42
Hot Graphics and Printing Inc	2791	35
Hot Melt Technologies Inc	3569	179
Hot Off the Press Inc	2731	137
Hot Shot Express Inc	4213	3136
Hot Springs Packing Company Inc	2011	149
Hot Supply Inc	5046	108
Hot Topic Inc	5632	3
Hotchkis and Wiley Capital Management	6282	246
Hotchkiss Inc	2752	1609
Hotel International Advisors	7011	230
Hotel Outsource Management International Inc	3581	3
Hotel Supplies-Online LLC	5046	215
Hotelicopter	7375	164
Hotelscom	7389	41
Hotflush Inc	5085	433
HotJobscom Ltd	7361	45
Hot-Line Freight System Inc	4213	896
Hotlines Inc	3663	352
Hotronic Inc	3661	183
Hotspot Fxi Inc	7374	130
Hottinger US Inc	6282	223
Hotubs Inc	7359	207
Hotwatt Inc	3822	26
Hotwire Communications LLC	4813	270
Houchen Bindery Ltd	2789	44
Houchens Industries Inc	5411	59
Houff's Feed And Fertilizer Company Inc	2873	17
Hougen Manufacturing Inc	5084	283
Houghton Chemical Corp	5169	91
Houghton International Inc	2869	24
Houghton Lake Resorter Inc	2711	849
Houghton Mifflin Co	2731	7

Company Name	SIC	Rank
Houles USA Inc	5131	47
Houlihan Lokey Howard and Zukin Inc	6211	174
Houlihan's Culinary Traditions Ltd	2099	330
Houlihan's Restaurant Group Inc	5812	11
Hour Electric Company Inc	1731	1030
Hour Media LLC	2721	237
Hour Publishing Co	2711	230
Hourglass Capital Management Inc	6282	655
Housatonic Curtain Company Inc	2391	3
House Electric Company Inc	1731	2323
House Foods America Corp	2075	9
House Industries Inc	7372	1072
House of Adjustments Inc	7322	36
House Of Blues Entertainment Inc	7922	8
House Of Cheatham Inc	2844	110
House Of Closets	1799	126
House Of Doolittle Ltd	2752	380
House Of Fans Inc	5064	174
House Of Flavors Inc	2024	14
House Of Graphics	2752	1227
House of Imports Inc	5511	217
House Of Packaging Inc	2652	17
House Of Plastics Unlimited Inc	3089	1779
House Of Ruth Maryland Inc	8322	172
House of Schwan Inc	5181	65
House Of Specialties Inc	5199	141
House of Telephones	3661	243
House Of Thaller Inc	2099	189
House Of White Birches Inc	2721	98
House Park and Dobratz PC	8721	189
House Party Inc	8732	42
House-Autry Mills Inc	2041	38
Housechem Inc	5162	32
House-Hasson Hardware Inc	5072	9
Household Bank NA	6021	26
Household Utilities Inc	3444	127
HouseMaster of America Inc	6794	98
Houser and Hennessee Advertising Corp	7311	293
Houser Transport Inc	4213	1685
Housing Devices Inc	3669	276
Houston 2-Way Radio	5731	64
Houston Advanced Research Center	8731	225
Houston Air Inc	1711	274
Houston American Energy Corp	1311	172
Houston Aquarium Inc	8422	2
Houston Area Services	7371	1150
Houston Bazz Co	3469	181
Houston Business Journals Inc	2711	560
Houston Casualty Co	6331	302
Houston Cement Company LP	3241	10
Houston City Temporaries	7363	182
Houston Communications Inc	5063	349
Houston County Public Works Dept	8711	291
Houston CPC Inc	7342	58
Houston Dataflow Inc	5045	773
Houston Dynamic Service Inc	3599	756
Houston Elbow and Nipple Company Inc	3498	86
Houston Eye Associates PC	8011	55
Houston Foam Fabricators Inc	3086	165
Houston Foam Plastics Inc	3086	16
Houston Grinding and Manufacturing Co	3561	117
Houston Hermetics Inc	7623	17
Houston Independent Maintenance	7349	305
Houston Manufacturing and Design Inc	7389	1894
Houston Manufacturing Specialty Company Inc	3053	113
Houston Marine Supply Inc	5091	113
Houston Motor and Control Inc	5063	642
Houston North Machine Inc	3599	1512
Houston Poly Bag I Ltd	2673	46
Houston Poultry and Egg Company Inc	5144	19
Houston Rsgrp Ltd	5033	8
Houston Sam State University	8221	35
Houston Title Co	6541	16
Houston Tomorrow	8733	28
Houston Transportation Inc	4213	2417
Houston Trust Co	6733	3
Houston Wire and Cable Co	5063	26
Houston's Inc	5046	25
HoustonStreet Inc	7389	2330
Hou-Tex Power Inc	1731	1807
Hovair Systems Inc	3535	213
Hoveround Corp	3842	29
Hovey Electric Inc	1731	1084
Hovnanian Enterprises Inc	1522	5
How It Works	7336	328
Howard and Howard Attorneys PC	8111	292
Howard Bancorp Inc	6712	559
Howard Berger Company Inc	5072	12
Howard Borress Enterprises Inc	1731	2575
Howard C Fletcher Company Inc	5074	159
Howard Company Inc	3993	73
Howard County Electric Company Inc	1731	2149
Howard Electric Inc	1731	1990
Howard Energy Company Inc	1311	136
Howard Fertilizer and Chemical Company Inc	2874	3
Howard Finishing LLC	3449	4
Howard Fischer Associates Inc	7361	388
Howard Foods Inc	2035	58
Howard G Hinz Company Inc	3548	54

Company Name	SIC	Rank
Howard Hanna Real Estate Services	6531	425
Howard Hughes Corp	6552	103
Howard Imprinting Machine Company Inc	3555	130
Howard Industries Inc	3612	2
Howard J Rubenstein Associates Inc	8743	14
Howard Leight Industries	3842	49
Howard M Schwartz Recording Inc	7389	530
Howard M Trerice Corp	3823	247
Howard Miller Co	3873	5
Howard Needles Tammen and Bergendoff	8712	2
Howard Payne Co	5064	155
Howard Precision Metals Inc	5051	242
Howard Price Turf Equipment Inc	3523	281
Howard Printing Company Inc	2752	1308
Howard Quinn Co	2752	949
Howard Rice Nemerovski Canady Falk and Rabkin	8111	205
Howard Sheppard Inc	4213	185
Howard Systems Voice Data And Video Wiring LLC	1731	1552
Howard Ternes Packaging Co	4783	1
Howard Tool Company Inc	3544	398
Howard Transportation Inc	4213	887
Howard Way and Associates	7372	2197
Howard Weil Inc	6211	172
Howard's Automotive Supply Inc	5013	415
HowardSoft	7372	1994
Howco Metals Management LP	5051	98
Howe and Rusling Inc	6282	387
Howe Barnes Hoefer and Arnett	6211	323
Howe Electric Construction Inc	1731	371
Howe Freightways Inc	4213	2032
Howe Printing Company Inc	2711	726
Howell and Howell Inc	5045	880
Howell Asphalt Co	2951	46
Howell Construction	1542	195
Howell D Buster	5199	142
Howell Engine Developments Inc	3714	420
Howell Laboratories Inc	5551	6
Howell Machine Products Inc	3599	2248
Howell Metal Corp	1541	308
Howell Mouldings LC	2899	174
Howell-Summers Engineering Inc	8711	588
Howes and Howes Trucking Inc	4213	1765
Howe's Standard Publishing Company Inc	2752	950
Howestemco Inc	3599	307
Howlan Inc	2759	542
Howland Capital Management Inc	6282	340
Howland Machine Corp	3469	340
Howl'n Dog Designs	2741	479
How-Mac Manufacturing Inc	3086	174
Howman Associates Inc	3625	370
Howman Electronics Inc	3625	284
Howmet TMP Corp	3544	27
Howmet Transport Services	4213	1541
Howse Implement Company Inc	3523	96
Hoya Corporation USA	3229	37
Hoya Largo	3851	94
Hoya Lens Of Chicago Inc	5048	27
Hoya Optical Inc	3851	40
Hoya Optical Laboratories	3851	58
Hoyleton Youth And Family Services	8351	17
Hoyt Brumm and Link Inc	1711	140
Hoyt Communications Inc	1731	1389
Hoyt Corp	3582	6
Hoyt Corp (Westport Massachusetts)	3821	79
Hoyt Electrical Instrument Works Inc	3825	123
Hoyt Inc	3949	76
Hoyt Stereo Inc	7622	11
HP Cummings Construction Co	1542	357
HP Electrical Designs Inc	1731	937
HP Hood LLC	2026	5
Hp Industries Inc	7389	907
HP Nemenz Food Stores Inc	5411	113
Hp Pelzer Automotive Systems Inc	3061	5
HP Products Corp	5087	6
HP Service Inc	7361	127
HPC Development LLC	8742	482
Hpc Foods Ltd	2099	99
HPC Foodservice	5141	103
Hpc Integrated Graphic Solutions LLC	2752	684
Hpc Of Pennsylvania Inc	2711	416
HPF LLC	5122	93
Hpi	3089	1877
Hpi Products Inc	7389	1349
Hpi Stampings Inc	3469	201
HPM Division Taylor's Industrial Services LLC	3542	19
Hpm Industries Inc	3399	27
HPMNC Inc	3444	37
HPN Inc	7311	708
Hppi LLC	7389	1965
HPS Office Systems	7359	44
HPS Simulations	7372	2985
Hq Group LLC	7361	290
HQ Inc	3845	132
HR Bookstrom Construction Inc	1623	690
HR Candee Construction Inc	1623	771
HR Distributors Inc	5065	926
HR Edgar Machining and Fabricating Inc	3599	537

Company Name	SIC	Rank
HR Industries Inc	2711	204
HR Kirkland Company Inc	3669	265
HR Staffing Solutions Inc	7361	178
HRD Corp	2999	6
Hrd Inc	7372	3429
HREF Tools Corp	7372	2986
HRH Construction Corp	8741	203
Hrh Door Corp	3442	3
HRH Financial Institutions Group Inc	6331	196
Hribar Trucking Inc	4213	1438
Hrm Recruitment Firm Inc	7389	1375
Hro Inc	2821	152
Hron Management LLC	2051	218
HRS/Erase Inc	7299	36
HRS Transport Inc	4213	1906
HRsmart Inc	7372	1377
HRT of Alabama Inc	6798	31
Hs International Inc	3841	370
HS3 Technologies Inc	4899	218
HSA Commercial Real Estate	6552	76
Hsa Construction Inc	1623	855
HSA Engineers and Scientists	8711	192
HSB Group Inc	6331	133
HSBC Bank USA NA	6022	5
HSBC Finance Corp	6141	5
HSBC USA Inc	6712	11
HSE Architects	8712	322
Hsi Accessories Inc	5023	199
HSI Corp	3593	14
HSI Fire And Safety Group	3829	495
HSN Inc	5961	10
hSoft Consulting	7372	4698
HSQ Technology Corp	7373	254
H-Square Corp	3674	323
HSR Interactive	7371	558
HSS Group	3053	17
HSTR Manufacturing Holdings Inc	2451	4
HSU Development Company Inc	1542	379
HSW International Inc	7374	153
HT And Associates Inc	7349	391
HT Electronics Inc	3651	51
HT Hackney Co	5141	22
HT Harvey and Associates	8748	138
HT Machine Company Inc	3599	1557
Ht Microanalytical Inc	3674	490
HTC Global Services Inc	7379	232
Hte Inc	5045	897
HTE Research Inc	3674	381
HTE/UCS Inc	7372	753
Htf Inc	3613	78
HTF Solutions Inc	7379	1520
HTI Voice Solutions Inc	4813	190
Htis Inc	1731	1789
Htm Concepts Inc	2396	36
Htmt Inc	7373	772
Htn Communications LLC	4899	216
Htp Inc	5084	116
Hts LLC	1731	1831
Htt Inc	3469	183
Hu Friedy Manufacturing Company LLC	3843	9
Huawei Technologies USA	7371	60
Hub City Ford Inc	5511	421
Hub City Inc	3566	8
Hub Construction Specialties Inc	5082	73
Hub Energy Services Inc	7699	143
Hub Folding Box Company Inc	2657	19
Hub Grain Company Inc	5153	187
Hub Group Inc	4731	10
Hub Group Kansas City LLC	4731	69
Hub International Ltd	6411	44
Hub Internationall Midwest Ltd	6411	2
Hub Kearney Publishing Company Inc	2711	397
Hub Labels Inc	2679	28
Hub Machine and Tool Inc	7692	36
Hub Manufacturing Company Inc	3469	348
Hub Of The Earth Inc	4813	735
Hub Plastics Inc	3089	766
Hub Supply Inc	5084	240
Hubacher Cadillac Inc	5511	775
Hubbard and Hoke Inc	5722	22
Hubbard Broadcasting Inc	4833	38
Hubbard Company Inc	2759	154
Hubbard Construction Co	1611	40
Hubbard Electric Inc	1731	2006
Hubbard Funeral Home Inc	7261	11
Hubbard Iron Doors Inc	5051	323
Hubbard Isa LLC	0254	4
Hubbard Peanut Company Inc	5441	17
Hubbard Publishing Co	2711	585
Hubbard Supply Co	5084	188
Hubbard Tool And Die Corp	3599	1708
Hubbard-Hall Inc	5169	83
Hubbardton Forge LLC	3645	14
Hubbell Electric Products Inc	1731	845
Hubbell Inc	3643	2
Hubbell Inc Kellems Wiring Device Div	8711	205
Hubbell Industrial Controls Inc	3823	43
Hubbell Killark	3699	35
Hubbell Mechanical Supply Co	5075	81
Hubbell Power Systems Inc	3643	29
Hubble Homes	1531	77
Hubbuch and Co	7389	1235

Company Name	SIC	Rank
Hub-City Blueprint and Supply Company Inc	5049	181
Huber Inc	3561	142
Huber Marketing Group Inc	7311	704
Huber Ring Helm and Company PC	8721	359
Hubert Co	5046	24
Hubert Distributors Inc	5181	51
Hubler Brothers Inc	5511	1230
Hubler Chevrolet Inc	5511	129
Hubspan Inc	7371	994
HubSpot Inc	7372	1445
Hubx Inc	4813	409
Huck International Inc	3452	6
Huck International Inc Aerospace Div	3452	19
Huckleberry Patch	5812	402
Huckleberry People	2064	85
Hucks Piggyback Service Inc	4213	2158
Hudalla Associates Inc	5091	102
Hudco Industrial Products Inc	3297	13
Hudd Steel Corp	5051	264
Huddle House Inc	5812	371
Hudson Access Group Ii	3651	192
Hudson And Marshall Inc	7389	1479
Hudson City Bancorp Inc	6712	21
Hudson City Preferred Funding Corp	6798	5
Hudson City Savings Bank	6036	5
Hudson Co	8721	386
Hudson Control Group Inc	7372	3536
Hudson Cos	5032	36
Hudson Extrusions Inc	3089	1147
Hudson Graphics Inc	2752	996
Hudson Highland Group Inc	7363	19
Hudson Lock LLC	3429	58
Hudson Microimaging Inc	7389	1495
Hudson News Co	5192	44
Hudson Oil Company of Texas	1311	199
Hudson Pacific Properties Inc	6798	133
Hudson Paper Co	5113	54
Hudson Paving Inc	1623	342
Hudson Physical Therapy Services Inc	8093	47
Hudson Printing Company Inc	2752	1261
Hudson Printing Inc	2752	935
Hudson Printing Incorporated Dba Hudson Digital Printing	2752	577
Hudson Products Corp	3443	18
Hudson Reporter Associates LP	2711	564
Hudson River Construction Company Inc	1611	193
Hudson Technologies Company Inc	5078	31
Hudson Technologies Inc	5078	9
Hudson Tire Exchange	5014	64
Hudson Transportation Inc	4213	2115
Hudson Valley Bank	6021	155
Hudson Valley Holding Corp	6712	167
Hudson Valley Homestead	2035	59
Hudson Valley Lighting Inc	3645	50
Hudson Valley Paper Co	5111	27
Hudson Valley Showcase LLC	5099	147
Hudson-Sharp Machine Co	3565	29
Hudspeth Motors Inc	5511	1166
Huebner and Son Trucking Inc	4213	2479
Huen New York Inc	1731	93
Huerta Design Associates	7336	190
Huestis Industrial	3599	138
Huff and Puff Trucking Inc	4213	2891
Huff Carbide Tool Inc	3541	247
Huff Floorcovering Inc	5023	99
Huff Grading and Pipeline Company Inc	1623	585
Huff Industries Inc	2842	177
Huff Technologies Inc	7379	1448
Huff United	5113	73
Huff United Paper Co	5113	39
Huffines Chevrolet Company Inc	5511	180
HuffingtonPostcom Inc	2741	200
Huffman Communications	8748	404
Huffman Corp	3699	158
Huffman Engineering Inc	1731	1700
Huffman Finishing Company Inc	2252	21
Huffman Security Company Inc	7382	118
Huffman Welding and Machine Inc	3599	709
Huffy Bicycle Co	3751	4
Huffy Corp	3949	14
Hufnagel Software	7372	4059
Hug Manufacturing Corp	3531	242
Hug-Condon Moving and Storage Co	4213	3016
Huggins Metal Finishing Inc	8734	108
Huggins Printing Co	2752	401
Hugh Duncan and Associates Inc	7311	97
Hugh Edward Sandefur Training Center Inc	2653	127
Hughes Brothers Aircrafters Inc	3544	221
Hughes Brothers Inc	3479	17
Hughes Capital Management Inc	6282	664
Hughes Christensen Co	3545	7
Hughes Company Incorporated Of Columbus	3556	116
Hughes Corp	5063	260
Hughes Electronics Products Corp	3672	354
Hughes Furniture Industries Inc	2512	38
Hughes Group Inc	1629	31
Hughes Hardwood International Inc	5031	190
Hughes Hubbard and Reed	8111	213
Hughes Integrated Inc	2796	51

Company Name	SIC	Rank
Hughes Law LLC	8111	592
Hughes Lumber and Building Supply Company Inc	5251	48
Hughes Lumber Co	5211	92
Hughes' Lumber Plus	5211	304
Hughes Network Systems Inc	3661	4
Hughes Plumbing and Utility Contractors Inc	1623	534
Hughes Rental And Sales Inc	7359	92
Hughes Supply Company of Thomasville Inc (Thomasville North Carolina)	3089	161
Hughes Systique Corp	7371	377
Hughes Telematics Inc	3812	62
Hughes Welch and Milligan CPA's Ltd	8721	183
Hughes Xerographic Equipment Agency Inc	5065	833
Hughes-Anderson Heat Exchangers Inc	3443	41
Hughes-Calihan Corp	7373	180
Hughes-Peters Inc	5063	223
Hughey and Associates	8743	280
Hughey Construction Company Inc	1623	527
Hugo Bosca Company Inc	3172	14
Hugo Boss USA Inc	2311	6
Hugo Neu-Proler Corp	5093	12
Hugo Vogelsang Machinenbau Gmbh	3561	174
Hugoton Royalty Trust	6792	1
Huhtamaki Inc	2656	1
Huitt-Zollars Inc	8711	389
Hukill Chemical Corp	7389	951
Hula Networks Inc	5045	504
Hula Software Inc	7372	2462
Hulbert Auto Park	5521	6
Hulbert Financial Digest	5192	36
Hulbert Holding Corp	5074	168
Hulick Metals Inc	5051	315
Hull Lift Truck Inc	5084	47
Hull Speed Data Products Inc	5065	978
Hull Supply Company Inc	5031	203
Hulman and Co	2099	110
HUM Music and Sound Design	7389	1775
Human Capital LLC	7363	75
Human Genome Sciences Inc	2835	13
Human Resource Development Press Inc	2741	338
Human Resource MicroSystems Inc	7372	3136
Human Resource Staffing LLC	7361	155
Human Resources Alternatives Inc	7363	318
Human Scale Inc	5045	757
Human Service Group Inc	8742	461
Human Software Company Inc	7372	1961
Human Synergistics Inc	2741	326
Human Technologies Corp	8331	63
Human Touch	3639	10
Humana/ChoiceCare	6324	97
Humana Inc	6324	6
Humancentric Technologies Inc	8732	112
HumanConcepts	7372	1300
Humanetics Corp	8731	284
Humberto Arguelles	3646	84
Humble Instruments and Services Inc	3823	138
Humboldt Group	5182	43
Humboldt Manufacturing Co	3829	150
Humboldt Petroleum Inc	5172	93
Humboldt Redwood Company LLC	5031	280
Humboldt Storage and Moving Co	4213	1195
HumCap	7361	81
Humco Holding Group Inc	5169	60
Humdinger Enterprises Inc	5046	345
Hume Specialties Inc	2032	39
Humedica	7372	1067
Humidial Corp	3823	238
Humidity Control Systems Inc (Carson City Nevada)	3822	90
HumiSeal	2821	77
Hummel Brothers Inc	2013	150
Hummel Croton Inc	2819	125
Hummel Distributing Corp	7331	243
Hummel Machine and Tool Co	3599	1526
Hummer Winblad Venture Partners	6799	248
Humphrey Electric Company Inc	1731	761
Humphrey Printing Company Inc	2752	968
Humphrey Products Co	3492	11
Humphrey Services	7379	1660
Humphrey's Enterprises Inc	1222	14
Humtown Pattern Co	3543	8
Hundman Lumber Do-it Center Inc	5031	29
Huneke Enterprises LLC	1731	765
Hung Thai Dental Corp	7389	2250
Hunger Hydraulics Cc Ltd	3593	56
Hungerford and Terry Inc	3589	125
Hungry Howie's Pizza and Subs Inc	6794	58
Hunington Properties Inc	6531	372
Hunkar Technologies Inc	3565	25
Hunley Exterminating Co	7342	74
Hunnicutt Software Inc	7372	3911
Hunt Adkins	7311	433
Hunt and Behrens Inc	5191	132
Hunt and Hunt Ltd	3599	253
Hunt Building Company Ltd	1522	11
Hunt Consolidated Inc	1382	6
Hunt Construction Group Inc	8741	16
Hunt Consulting	8999	140
Hunt Corp (Scottsdale Arizona)	8741	17

Company Name	SIC	Rank
Hunt Country Furniture Inc	2599	24
Hunt Design and Manufacturing Inc	3582	19
Hunt Electric Corp	1731	29
Hunt Global Resources Inc	4939	17
Hunt Howe Partners LLC	8742	401
Hunt Jack Coin Broker	5094	58
Hunt Jrt Inc	3599	735
Hunt Paving Corp	1611	236
Hunt Products Inc	7389	1731
Hunt Refining Co	2911	19
Hunt Technologies LLC	3825	60
Hunt Transportation Inc	4213	153
Hunt Valve Company Inc	3494	33
Huntair Inc	3585	88
HunTel Communications Inc	3663	209
Huntel Systems Inc	4813	721
Hunter Ambulette-Ambulance Inc	4119	12
Hunter Associates Inc	2721	310
Hunter Automated Machinery Corp	3559	141
Hunter Company Inc	3199	17
Hunter Contracting Co	1611	61
Hunter Digital Ltd	3577	195
Hunter Douglas Fabrication-Northern California	2591	7
Hunter Easterday Corp	7349	189
Hunter Engineering Co	3559	53
Hunter Grain Co	5153	142
Hunter Hamersmith and Associates Inc	7311	270
Hunter House Inc	2731	343
Hunter Manufacturing LLP	3269	10
Hunter Marine Corp	3732	44
Hunter Placement Inc	7361	215
Hunter Publishing Inc	2711	597
Hunter Publishing LP	2721	99
Hunter Service Group Inc	7349	282
Hunter Spice Inc	2099	216
Hunter Technology Corp	3672	99
Hunter Woods Nursing and Rehabilitation Center	8051	38
Hunterdon BMW	5511	1086
Hunterdon County Democrat Inc	2711	429
Hunterdon Transformer Company Inc	3612	79
Hunterspoint Steel LLC	5051	394
Huntford Printing	2752	1189
Hunting Innova Inc	3672	68
Hunting Oilfield Services	5082	169
Hunting Tubular Threading Inc	1389	52
Huntingdon Electric Motor Service Inc	7694	34
Huntington Bancshares Inc	6712	23
Huntington Bancshares Kentucky Inc	6712	456
Huntington Bancshares West Virginia Inc	6712	183
Huntington Beach Dodge	5511	665
Huntington Beach Ford	5511	776
Huntington Chevrolet Inc	5511	480
Huntington Electric Inc	3625	46
Huntington Holdings Inc	6211	102
Huntington Instruments Inc	3823	467
Huntington Mechanical Laboratories Inc	3559	137
Huntington National Bank	6021	11
Huntington National Bank of Indiana	6021	68
Huntington National Bank West Virginia	6021	241
Huntington National Bank-Private Financial Group	6091	3
Huntington Plating Inc	7699	211
Huntington Preferred Capital Inc	6712	128
Huntington Security Systems Inc	1731	1223
Huntington Testing and Technology Inc	7389	1929
Huntington Wholesale Furniture Co	5021	151
Huntleigh Securities Corp	6211	61
Hunton and Williams LLP	8111	111
Huntron Inc	3825	174
Huntsinger and Jeffer	7389	1117
Huntsman Chemicals Corp	2821	14
Huntsman Corp	2899	4
Huntsman International LLC	2865	1
Huntsman Polymers Corp	2821	3
Huntsville Dodge Inc	5511	495
Huntsville Electrical Services	1731	2557
Huntsville Radio Service Inc	5731	202
Huntsville Rehabilitation Foundation Inc	8331	37
Hunt-Wilde Corp	6512	87
Hunzicker Brothers Inc	5063	105
Hunzinger Construction Co	1541	168
Hupp Electric Motors Inc	5722	15
Hurckman Mechanical Industries Inc	1711	144
Hurco Companies Inc	3823	17
Hurco Design and Manufacturing	2541	60
Hurd Corp	3429	16
Hurletron Inc	3625	188
Hurley Chandler and Chaffer Advertising Inc	7311	572
Hurley Communications Inc	5065	774
Hurley Transportation Cos	4212	38
Huron Casting Inc	3325	19
Huron Consulting Group Inc	8748	12
Huron Inc	3451	6
Huron Machine Products Inc	3545	241
Huron Tool and Cutter Grinding Company Inc	3545	202
Huron Tool and Engineering Co	3541	102
Huron Valley Steel Corp	5093	27
Hurricane Electronics Lab Inc	3699	205

Company Name	SIC	Rank
Hurricane Express Inc	4213	2270
Hurricane Food Inc	5812	85
Hurricane Moving and Transfers	7389	2373
Hurricane Trucking Inc	4213	3065
Hurst Auto-Truck Electric Ltd	7539	20
Hurst Boiler and Welding Company Inc	3443	69
Hurst Chemical Co	2851	129
Hurst Electric LP	1731	340
Hurt Companies LLC	2752	1541
Hurt Electric Inc	1731	1284
Hurwitz and Associates Inc	7379	191
Hurwitz and Fine	8111	328
Hurwitz-Mintz Furniture Co	5712	60
Husa Accurate Machine Works Inc	3599	1057
HUSA Liquidating Corp	8051	35
Husch and Husch Inc	5191	134
Husch Blackwell LLP	8111	90
Husco International Inc	3492	3
HUSD Maintenance Operation	7349	335
Husdawg LLC	7372	4353
Huse Publishing Co	2711	447
Huselton and Morgan PC	8721	179
Hush-Hush Entertainment Inc	5045	685
Husite Engineering Company Inc	3543	44
Huskers Coop	5153	26
Huskey Truss and Building Supply Inc	3448	36
Husky Corp	3499	74
Husky Envelope Products Inc	2677	16
Husom and Rose Photographics	7372	4829
Husqvarna Professional Products Inc	5083	8
Huss Electric Company Inc	1731	1820
Hussey Seating Co	2531	22
Hussmann Corp	3585	4
Hussong Manufacturing Company Inc	3433	49
Huston Electric Inc	1731	124
Huston-Patterson Corp	2752	239
Hut Man Inc	4813	733
Hutchcraft Van Service Inc	4213	2088
Hutchens Industries Inc	3714	150
Hutcherson Metals Inc	5093	117
Hutcherson Tile Co	5032	61
Hutchins Trucking Co	4213	796
Hutchins Contracting Co	1711	107
Hutchinson Corp	3061	3
Hutchinson Leader	2711	896
Hutchinson Technology Inc	3679	54
Hutchinson-Mayrath	3423	8
Hutchison Hayes Separation Inc	3533	66
Hutchison Transportation	4213	1635
Hutchison-Allgood Printing Co	2752	548
Hutch-N-Son Construction	1611	238
Huth Manufacturing Corp	3498	81
Hutson Brothers Inc	3599	2154
Hutt Trucking Company Inc	4213	1050
Hutton Communications Inc	5065	108
Hutton Contracting Company Inc	5063	1071
Hutzel Hospital	8062	203
Huval Insurance Agency of Abbeville Inc	6411	137
Huval Insurance Agency of Arnaudville Inc	6411	138
Huval Insurance Agency of Church Point Inc	6411	139
Huval Insurance Agency of Grand Coteau-Sunset Inc	6411	140
Huval Insurance Agency of Lafayette Inc	6411	141
Huval Insurance Agency of Loreauville Inc	6411	142
Huval Insurance Agency of Opelousas Inc	6411	143
Hva LLC	3491	31
Hvac Distributors Inc	5075	28
Hvac Mechanical Services Of Texas Ltd	3599	56
HVAC Sales and Supply Company Inc	5075	61
HVH Transportation Inc	4213	539
Hvp Inc	5962	22
HVS Executive Search	7361	50
HVVi Semiconductors Inc	3674	209
HW Allen Co	6531	239
HW Culp Lumber Co	5031	48
HW Fairway International Inc	3991	22
HW Jencks Inc	3677	109
HW Jenkins Lumber Co	5211	31
HW Kaufman Financial Group Inc	6411	148
HW Nicholson Welding And Manufacturing Inc	3599	1093
HW Wilson Co	2741	23
HWA International Inc	7372	1441
Hwashin America Corp	5531	10
Hwd Acquisition Inc	2431	44
HWEckhardt Corp	5085	339
Hwh Corp	3714	260
HWS Energy Partners LLC	1731	2519
HY Connect	7311	1046
Hy LaBonne and Son Inc	5411	212
Hy Mark Wood Products Inc	5031	358
Hy Tech Forming Systems (USA) Inc	3089	1097
Hy Win Foods Inc	2047	43
Hyacinth Technology Inc	7389	1956
Hyatt Automotive LLC	5511	124
Hyatt Hotels Corp	7011	17
Hyatt Vacation Ownership Inc	6531	450

Company Name	SIC	Rank
Hyatt's Graphic Supply Company Inc	5999	94
Hybond Inc	5963	31
Hybrid Design Associates Inc	3674	256
Hybrid Electronics Inc	3674	169
Hybrid Sources Inc	3674	349
Hybrid Systems Limited Inc	7372	4699
Hybrinetics Inc	3634	23
Hy-Capacity Inc	3523	92
Hyco International Inc	3593	4
Hycomp LLC	3089	790
Hycon Corp	5065	298
Hycon Inc	3559	560
Hycor Biomedical Inc	2835	37
Hydac Rubber Manufacturing	3069	228
Hydac Technology Corp	3569	86
Hydaker-Wheatlake Co	1623	91
Hyde Company Inc	7372	2497
Hyde Electric Inc	1731	1161
Hyde Group Inc	3423	22
Hyde Park Bank	6022	676
Hyde Park Cooperative Society Inc	5411	221
Hyde Park Electronics LLC	3625	87
Hyden Citizens Bancorp Inc	6712	533
Hyder Construction Inc	1541	165
Hydes Business Services Inc	1731	2220
Hydra Group LLC	7313	14
Hydra LLC	7313	3
Hydra Plastics Inc	3088	20
Hydra Sponge Co	3999	156
Hydra Systems Inc	3661	197
Hydra Trucking Inc	4213	2829
Hydradyne Hydraulics LLC	5084	50
Hydra-Electric Co	3613	21
Hydraforce Inc	3492	8
Hydralift AmClyde Inc	3536	10
Hydra-Lock Corp	3545	156
Hydra-Matic Packing Company Inc	5033	32
Hydramedia LLC	7313	20
Hydranautics Inc	3589	6
Hydra-Rig Inc	3533	24
Hydratech LLC	3593	18
Hydration Technology Innovations LLC	3589	167
Hydraulic and Fabrication Services Inc	3731	30
Hydraulic Component Services Inc	3593	44
Hydraulic Controls Inc	5084	184
Hydraulic Power Technology-Texas Inc	3533	80
Hydraulic Press Brick Co	3295	13
Hydraulic Sales and Service Inc	7699	135
Hydraulic Service And Manufacturing Inc	7699	212
Hydraulic Service Company Inc	7699	86
Hydraulic Specialists Inc	3443	212
Hydraulic Specialty Company Inc	7699	234
Hydraulic Systems And Components Inc	5084	631
Hydraulic Systems Inc	3594	28
Hydraulic Technology Inc	3829	446
Hydril Co	3533	16
Hydril USA Distribution LLC	3533	25
Hydro Air Industries	3088	15
Hydro Aluminum North America	3354	40
Hydro Aluminum Rockledge Inc	3354	17
Hydro Dynamics Inc	5084	744
Hydro Electronic Devices Inc	3625	73
Hydro Engineering Inc	3523	83
Hydro Fitting Manufacturing Corp	3592	21
Hydro/Kirby Agri Services Inc	2875	18
Hydro Service and Supplies Inc	3589	124
Hydro Systems Inc	3431	7
Hydro Technology Inc	4213	2761
Hydro Tek Systems Inc	3589	98
Hydro - Temperature Corp	3585	173
Hydro Tube Enterprises Inc	3498	53
Hydroacoustics Inc	3594	31
Hydro-Aire Inc	3728	19
Hydro-Blast Inc	3589	180
Hydroblend Inc	2045	8
HydroCad Software Solutions LLC	7372	3823
Hydrocarbon Flow Specialist Inc	5085	249
Hydrocarbon Recovery Services Inc	5093	110
Hydrocomp Inc	7372	4510
Hydr-O-Dynamic Corp	3561	156
Hydrodyne-FPI Inc	3053	131
Hydrofarm Inc	3999	146
Hydrofera LLC	3086	155
Hydroform USA Inc	3728	77
Hydrogel Vision Corp	3851	49
Hydrogen Components Inc	3443	243
Hydrol Chemical Company Inc	2869	112
Hydrolec Limited Inc	3561	143
Hydro-Logic Inc	3625	172
Hydrolynx Systems Inc	3826	150
Hydromat Inc	5084	145
Hydromatic Pump	3561	13
Hydromer Inc	6794	125
Hydromotion Inc	3629	65
Hydron Technologies Inc	2844	207
Hydronic and Steam Equipment Company Inc	5074	82
Hydro-Pac Inc	3563	43
Hydropro Inc	3559	476
Hydroscience Technologies Inc	3812	67
Hydroseal Polymers Inc	2821	153
Hydrosol Inc	7389	821

Company Name	SIC	Rank
Hydro-Tech Fire Protection Inc	1711	259
Hydro-Test Products Inc	3563	57
Hydro-Thrift Corp	3585	200
Hydrox Chemical Company Inc	2844	108
Hygenic Corp	3069	56
Hygolet Inc	2499	60
Hygrade Business Group Inc	2761	44
Hygrade Precision Technologies Inc	3449	33
Hy-H Manufacturing Company Inc	3536	36
Hyland Co	2047	34
Hyland Enterprises Inc	4213	412
Hyland Software Inc	7372	364
Hylant of Indianapolis LLC	6331	187
Hyman Paper Company Inc	5113	59
Hyman Phelps and McNamara PC	8111	283
Hy-Meg Corp	3625	406
Hyndman Industrial Products	3699	49
Hynix Semiconductor America Inc	3571	22
Hyosung Inc (New York New York)	2297	7
Hypar Machine Co	7699	179
Hype Technology	5065	240
Hyper Alloys Inc	3499	96
Hyper Interactive Media LLC	7311	239
Hyper Tool Co	3541	238
Hyper/Word Services	8299	84
Hyperbaric Oxygen Therapy Systems Inc	3842	314
Hyperbaric Technologies Inc	3845	116
Hyperception Inc	7372	4302
Hypercom Corp	3578	3
Hypercomp Inc	7371	1183
Hypercube Inc	7372	1619
Hypercube LLC	7379	1070
Hyperdata	3577	23
Hyperdigm Research LLC	7379	1426
HyperDisk Marketing	7319	92
Hyperdynamics Corp	1311	208
Hyperflo LLC	3559	424
Hyperion Brookfield Asset Management Inc	6282	361
Hyperionics Technology LLC	7372	4060
HyperLogic Corp	7372	2150
Hypermedia Systems Inc	7379	574
Hypernet Communications Inc	4813	595
Hyperride Technologies Inc	7379	1202
Hypertech Inc	3714	348
Hypertension Diagnostics Inc	3841	381
Hypertherm Inc	3541	20
HyPex Inc	3599	7
Hyphen Solutions Ltd	7372	272
Hypneumat Inc	3541	198
Hy-Point Dairy Farms Inc	2026	69
Hy-Power Electric Co	1731	1015
Hypres Inc	3829	191
Hypro Corp	3561	14
Hypro Inc	3599	77
Hy-Production Inc	3519	16
Hyquip Inc	5085	309
Hysco America Co	5051	33
Hyseco Inc	7699	198
Hysen Technologies Inc	3663	269
Hyson Products	3495	4
Hyspan Precision Products Inc	3568	25
Hy-Tech Machining Systems LLC	3549	121
Hytech Tool and Design Co	3544	591
Hytek Finishes Co	3471	2
Hy-Tek Material Handling Inc	5084	258
Hytek Microsystems Inc	3674	267
Hytel Group Inc	3674	207
Hy-Ten Die and Development Corp	3089	1008
Hytrol Conveyor Company Inc	3535	13
Hytronics Corp	3677	6
Hyundai Electronics Pacific Inc	5065	213
Hyundai Information Service North America LLC	7378	132
Hyundai Motor America	5012	7
Hyundai Motor Finance Co	6159	22
Hyundai Translead	3715	16
Hyvair Corp	3594	24
Hyval Industries Inc	7699	203
Hy-Vee Inc	5411	23
Hy-Way Transit Inc	4213	2260
Hyway Trucking Co	4213	1011
HZS Inc	5045	998
I Am Smart Technologies LLC	5063	335
I and G Tool Company Inc	3545	302
I and I Sports Supply Co	5091	74
I and M Machine and Fabrication Corp	3312	103
I Auman Machine Co	3599	811
i Brands Corp	5045	1036
I Broomfield and Sons Inc	5093	247
I C E S Of Gaston County Inc	5084	815
I Cerco Inc	3567	8
I F Engineering Corp	3669	220
I H Schlezinger Inc	5093	85
I J Tri Cities Inc	5141	64
I Janvey and Sons Inc	5087	43
I/N Kote LLP	3479	11
I/NET Inc	7371	407
I Networld Marketing Group	7374	405
I/O Concepts Inc	3577	499
I/O Controls Corp	3625	88
I/O General LLC	3679	21
I/O Interconnect Inc	3679	325

Company Name	SIC	Rank
I/O Marine Systems Inc	3679	9
I/O Marine Systems Ltd	3679	13
I/O Nevada LLC	3679	10
I/O Texas LP	3679	11
I/OMagic Corp	3572	63
I Phase Electric Inc	1731	2367
I Schumann and Co	3339	15
I See Optical Laboratories Inc	3851	106
I Shalom and Company Inc	2389	21
I T Dealers Supply Inc	5031	276
I T Verdin Co	3931	23
I Technical Services LLC	3672	403
I Train Technologies Ltd	7379	1640
I Trust Motors	7311	966
I Understand	8299	78
I W Macfarlane Corp	1731	959
I Wanna Distribution Company Inc	5149	171
i2 Technologies Inc	7372	202
I24x7Com	4813	422
I2c Inc	5045	375
i2Gemini Inc	7372	4178
I2s Micro Implantable Systems LLC	3841	338
i3 Statprobe	8733	19
I360technologies Inc	7373	689
i365	7371	140
i365 Inc	7375	153
I3solutions Inc	7379	1009
I5 Wireless LLC	8711	549
I-74 Auto Truck Plaza	5541	56
IA Construction Corp	1611	20
IA Global Inc	7375	139
IAC/InterActiveCorp	4833	13
IAC Search and Media Inc	7375	24
IAC Securetech Inc	7379	1442
iambic Inc	7372	3051
Iameter Inc	7372	1483
Ian Ryan Interactive	2741	297
Ian-Conrad Bergan Inc	3823	219
Iandiorio Teska and Coleman	8111	571
iAnywhere Inc	7372	59
iAnywhere Solutions Inc	7372	920
Iap Inc	3564	64
Iap Research Inc	8731	268
Iap West Inc	5013	190
IAP Worldwide Services Inc	8744	2
Iaq Energy Solutions Inc	3674	502
IAR Systems Software Inc	7372	2987
IAS National Inc	3589	227
IASIS Healthcare LLC	8062	27
Iatric Systems Inc	5734	42
IB Dickinson and Sons Inc	7353	58
Ib Electric Inc	1731	1991
Iba America LLC	7373	1190
Iba Industrial Inc	3699	153
iBASEt	7372	1947
iBasis Inc	4813	19
Ibb Management Inc	7389	1700
Ibbotson Associates Inc	8748	72
IBC Advanced Technologies	2899	144
IBC Capital Corp	6211	15
IBC Southwest Inc	1542	289
IBC Subsidiary Corp	6712	96
IBC Trading Co	6111	3
Iberdrola Renewable Energies USA Ltd	3621	94
Iberdrola Renewables	4911	85
Iberiabank	6036	18
IBERIABANK Corp	6712	65
IBERIABANK fsb	6022	433
Ibew Local 441	1731	1057
IBEX Chemicals Inc	2899	178
Ibex Futurebilt JV	5039	52
Ibex Manufacturing Inc	3629	116
IBEX Systems	5045	544
Ibex Tech Corp	1731	1975
IBI Co	7372	2715
Ibid Power Inc	1731	2299
iBio Inc	2834	252
iBiquity Digital Corp	8731	85
Ibis Tek LLC	3699	58
Ibis USA Corp	7382	115
Ibj Corp	2711	473
Iblast Inc	4813	741
IBM Software Support	7372	153
IBM Support Systems	7371	383
iboats Inc	5961	133
Ibridge Group Inc	7371	1024
IBS America Inc	7372	2557
Ibs Electronic and Security Inc	7382	172
Ibs Electronics Inc	3672	186
Ibs Of America Corp	3554	66
IBS Of Central Mass Inc	5063	767
Ibs-Building Service Contractors Inc	7349	258
IBuyDigitalcom Inc	5961	102
IBW Financial Corp	6712	605
I-C Electrical Systems Inc	1731	2171
IC Engineering Inc	3577	527
IC Interactive Inc	8748	351
IC Interconnect LLC	4813	449
IC Security Printers Incorporated — Marketing	5111	33
IC System Inc	7374	28
ICA Auctions	5012	159
Ica Inc	3296	15
iCAD Inc	3841	103

Company Name	SIC	Rank
Icagen Inc	2834	307
Icahn Enterprises LP	6512	1
ICAP Energy LLC	6221	1
Icare Industries Inc	3851	17
Icas Computer Systems Inc	7372	3717
Icb LLC	3535	142
ICBA Securities Corp	6211	160
ICBC Broadcast Holdings Inc	4832	43
ICC Industries Inc	2819	11
ICC Insurance Agency Inc	6311	236
ICC Worldwide Inc	3577	659
Icd Publications Inc	2721	258
Ice Cold Products	4222	21
ICE Components Inc	5065	502
Ice Cream Club Inc	5812	443
Ice Industries Inc	3316	6
Ice Miller LLP	8111	50
Ice Products Inc	2097	8
IceCode LLC	3679	202
iCentera Corp	7372	334
Ice-O-Matic	3585	69
IceptsTechnology Group Inc	7373	101
Ices Production Hawaii	7389	2077
Iceskate Conditioning Equipment Co	3546	40
IceSolv Inc	7349	473
Icetech Inc	7378	126
IceWeb Inc	3572	77
IceWEB Storage Corp	3572	55
ICF International Inc	8742	34
ICF International (Sacramento California)	8748	6
ICF Kaiser Advanced Technology New Mexico	4953	6
Icf Macro Inc	8742	93
ICG Commerce Inc	7389	266
ICG Group Inc	8742	117
ICG Link Inc	7371	1646
Ichauway Inc	8733	25
Ichia USA Inc	3674	215
ICI Paints North America	2851	7
Icicle Seafoods Inc	2092	6
ICIMS Inc	7372	1291
Ickler Bearing and Machine Company Inc	3599	748
Icm Controls Corp	3625	26
ICM Holdings Inc	7389	218
ICM Inc	3559	492
Icms Holdings Inc	8741	237
ICN Corp	4813	342
Icn Integrated Communication Networks Inc	1731	2255
ICO Global Services Inc	3479	1
ICO Inc	3089	10
Icomm Corp	1731	421
Icomputerland LLC	5045	1064
Icomsys Inc	7373	944
Icon Enterprises International Inc	3663	247
Icon Fitness Corp	3949	17
ICON Health and Fitness Inc	3949	13
Icon Identity Solutions Inc	3993	6
Icon Information Consultants LP	7361	110
Icon International Inc	7389	136
Icon Mechanical Construction and Engineering LLC	8711	402
Icon Media Direct Inc	7319	102
Icon Metalcraft Inc	3444	116
ICON Resources Inc	3661	128
Icon Scientific Inc	5049	102
Icon Services Corp	7381	172
I-Con Systems Inc	8711	421
I-Concepts Inc	3577	363
Iconceptual	2741	158
Iconics Inc	7372	1538
Iconix Brand Group Inc	5139	4
ICONIX Software Engineering Inc	7372	3613
Iconixx Corp	7371	538
ICONMA LLC	7363	166
Iconologic LLC	7336	274
iContact Corp	7311	302
ICONTENT	7812	212
Icor Partners LLC	7389	469
Icore International Inc	3089	283
iCore Networks Inc	5734	36
ICOS Corp	2834	157
Icotech Inc	3625	301
ICR Inc	7389	260
iCrossing	8742	46
icruisecom	7375	144
ICS	8748	125
ICS Corp	2752	209
ICS Electronics	3577	528
Ics Inc	3471	115
ICS Inc (Jacksonville Florida)	7372	219
Ics Investment Inc-Gabreil Group	5963	25
Ics Service Of Miami Florida Corp	5734	198
ICS Software Inc	7372	5073
ICSN Inc	8711	431
Ict Inc	3911	51
ICT International Cellular Telephone Inc	5065	630
ICTC Group Inc	4812	91
ICTC USA	3679	657
ICU Medical Inc	3841	34
Icu Security LLC	7382	173

Company Name	SIC	Rank
iCue Corp	4822	14
ICUS Software Systems	7371	1904
ICV Capital Partners LLC	6799	228
ICX Global Inc	5063	172
ICX Photonics	3826	79
ICx Technologies Inc	3669	27
Icygen LLC	7373	473
ID Booth Inc	5074	81
ID Corp	1731	1655
ID Experts Corp	7373	430
ID Insight Inc	7372	3824
ID Label Inc	2759	61
ID Software Inc	7372	1442
ID Systems Inc	7389	488
ID TECH Inc (Fullerton California)	3577	114
ID Technology LLC	3579	27
ID8 Media	2741	148
IDACorp Inc	4911	57
Idaho Advantage Credit Union	6061	124
Idaho Beverages Inc	5149	128
Idaho Falls Foundry and Machine Company Inc	3325	41
Idaho Fresh-Pak Inc	2034	15
Idaho Independent Bank	6022	335
Idaho Information Consortium	4813	674
Idaho Laboratories Corp	3315	30
Idaho Law Review	2721	317
Idaho Milk Transport Inc	4213	429
Idaho Pacific Lumber Company Inc	5031	62
Idaho Power Co	4911	108
Idaho Press-Tribune Inc	2711	433
Idaho Sporting Goods Co	5091	107
Idaho Steel Products Inc	3556	38
Idaho Supreme Potatoes Inc	2034	11
Idaho Veneer Co	2436	6
Idaho Western Inc	5031	364
Idalica Corp	7373	778
Idant Laboratories Div	8099	108
IData Inc	8748	393
IdaTech Inc	3629	14
IDAutomationcom Inc	7372	2151
Ida-West Energy Co	1629	111
Idbs Inc	7371	741
IDC Corp	5063	515
IDC Framingham	2731	386
Idc Global Inc	7373	1006
Idc Research Inc	8732	18
Idd Aerospace Corp	3728	95
Iddings Trucking Inc	4213	1571
IDE Imaging Partners Inc	8093	23
Idea Art Inc	7372	1963
Idea Bank	7336	25
Idea Nuova Inc	5023	14
Idea Sciences Inc	7372	1506
Idea Tooling and Engineering Inc	3544	206
Idea Works Inc	7372	4830
Ideacom Healthcare Communications Of Florida Inc	5065	996
Ideacom Integrated Technologies Inc	5065	437
Ideàcom Mid-America Inc	1731	370
IdeaFisher Systems Inc	7372	5156
Ideaform Inc	7372	3825
Ideal Aerosmith Inc	3829	83
Ideal Automotive and Truck Accessories Corp	5013	126
Ideal Box Co	2653	29
Ideal Chemical and Supply Co	5169	77
Ideal Clamp Products Inc	3429	20
Ideal Door Co	2431	42
Ideal Electric Inc	1731	687
Ideal Fastener Corp	3965	6
Ideal Financial Solutions Inc	7371	654
Ideal Foam LLC	3086	86
Ideal Frame Company Inc	2511	81
Ideal Industries Inc (Sycamore Illinois)	3678	11
Ideal Innovations Inc	8999	55
Ideal Instruments Inc	3841	81
Ideal Jacobs Corp	2759	335
Ideal Lighting Inc	5063	802
Ideal Machine and Manufacturing Inc	3599	465
Ideal Manufacturing and Sales Corp	3559	386
Ideal Meats and Provision	5147	81
Ideal Medical Products Inc	3841	337
Ideal Precision Meter Inc	3825	117
Ideal Printing Co	2752	1286
Ideal Products Inc	3599	858
IDEAL Scanners and Systems Inc	5044	136
Ideal Snacks Corp	2096	19
Ideal Steel Inc	7389	789
Ideal Tape Company Inc	2672	34
Ideal Tool And Machine Company Inc	5084	924
Ideal Transportation Company Inc	4213	2675
Ideal Way Movers Inc	4213	2975
Idealab Capital Partners LP	6799	110
Idealease Services Inc	7513	12
Ideals Publications Inc	2721	189
Ideaman Inc	3993	144
IDEAMATICS Inc	3672	375
Ideas Incorporated Of Ohio	7373	1011
Ideas International	8732	61
Ideas International Inc	7373	404
Ideas Publishing Group	2721	137
Ideascape Inc	7336	300

Company Name	SIC	Rank
Ideasource Creative Marketng Services LLC	7374	408
Ideation Inc	2741	255
Ideation International Inc	7371	1425
IdeaWorks	7311	1028
IdeiaCom	4813	553
Ideker Inc	1622	39
Iden Industries Inc	3674	437
Idenix Pharmaceuticals Inc	2834	311
Identatronics Inc	7389	745
Identec Solutions Inc	7374	143
Identek Corp	8999	196
Identicomm LLC	7336	82
Identifax Of Greater Orlando Inc	7389	2450
Identification Technology Partners Inc	8748	261
Identigraphix Inc	7336	151
Identive Group Inc	3577	117
Identix Inc	7373	126
Identix Public Sector Inc	7373	188
IdenTrust DST	7371	306
Identrust Inc	7371	306
Identrust Services LLC	7374	255
IDEO Product Development Inc	8731	36
Ideographix Inc	7373	896
Idera Pharmaceuticals Inc	2836	40
Idesco Corp	5084	488
IDEX Corp	3561	16
IDEX Holdings Inc	6719	11
Idex Inc	7311	973
idEXEC Inc	8732	31
IDEXX Laboratories Inc	2835	3
Idg International Sales Corp	2721	405
IDG Manitowoc	5085	164
IDG World Expo Corp	7389	431
IDG York	5084	331
IDI Group Cos	1531	67
Idilus LLC	5045	676
iDine Restaurant Group Inc	7389	280
Idiom Communications LLC	4813	470
Idiom Press	2844	193
iDirect	3669	115
iDirect Marketing Inc	7311	724
Idlewood Electric Supply Inc	5063	113
IDM Trucking Inc	4213	1990
iDNA Inc	3669	121
IDP Companies Inc	7372	1092
IDP Inc	7374	129
Idq Operating Inc	2869	75
IDSC Holdings LLC	3829	111
IDSI Products Of Georgia Inc	3229	35
IDT Corp	4813	15
IDT Hospitality Group	7375	242
IDT Spectrum Inc	4899	195
IE and E Industries Inc	3544	659
IE Discovery	8742	420
IE Miller of Eunice Inc	4213	977
IEA Software Inc	7372	2988
IEC Corp	3621	156
IEC Electronics Corp	3672	20
IEH Corp	3678	28
IFI Barge Services Inc	4424	13
Iei Group Ltd	7389	2129
Iep Ltd	7382	111
IEP Publishers	7372	2716
IEPC Corp	7371	1035
Ieppert Machine Tool and Screw Products Inc	3541	226
Ier Fujikura Inc	3069	62
IES Interactive Training Inc	7372	1104
IES Texoma Inc	1731	1632
IESI Corp	4953	16
Iet Labs Inc	3825	154
iET Solutions LLC	7371	255
IEX Corp	7371	252
iExplore Inc	4725	36
If and P Foods Inc	5148	55
IF Software Inc	7372	5127
iFAX Solutions Inc	7379	675
Ifc Holdings Inc	8742	359
IFCO Systems North America	2448	1
IFCO Transport Inc	4213	589
IFI Claims Patent Services	2741	192
IFI/Plenum Data Corp	7379	470
Ifiber Optix Inc	3229	31
Ifinix Corp	7372	123
I-Flow Corp	3841	51
Ifm Efector Inc	3679	101
Iformata LLC	4813	526
Ifp Inc	6512	48
Ifpc Worldwide Inc	8721	325
IFS North America Inc	7371	8
Ifworld Inc	7371	1522
IFX Corp	7379	230
IG Brenner Inc	3559	518
ig Burton and Company Inc	5511	666
IGA Martins and Frozen Food Centers Inc	5411	242
IGA Worldwide	7371	725
iGate Corp	7371	43
IGC Inc	7372	2736
Igd Solutions Corp	4813	675
IGENE Biotechnology Inc	2879	44
Igenti	7361	296
IgG America Inc	8099	78

Company Name	SIC	Rank
Iggys House Inc	7375	290
Igh Enterprises Inc	2096	56
IGI Laboratories Inc	2836	59
Igi Printing Company Inc	2752	666
Igloo Products Corp	3089	81
Iglou Internet Services Inc	4813	128
IGN Entertainment Inc	7374	81
Ignify Inc	5734	47
Ignite Ltd	4939	7
Ignite Media Solutions	7311	451
Ignite Sales Inc	4813	676
Ignite Technologies Inc	7372	3269
Ignited Discovery LLC	7375	213
Ignited LLC	7311	118
Ignition Media	3577	669
iGo Inc	3577	167
iGoDigital LLC	7379	1123
Igraphics	2759	462
Igs Inc	3211	21
IguanaMed	2339	45
Igus Bearings Inc	5063	187
Ihc Inc	3471	43
IHF Capital Inc	3949	20
IHF Holdings Inc	3949	12
Ihly Industries Inc	3565	174
IHR Security LLC	7382	160
IHS Energy (Englewood Colorado)	7379	80
IHS Engineering	7372	391
IHS Inc	7379	14
IHT Health Products Inc	5912	32
Ii Stanley Company Inc	3647	6
Iic Technologies Inc	7371	895
Iicon Technology LLC	3575	62
Iidon Inc	7381	35
Iifotech International LLC	7371	1647
IIJ America Inc	7375	15
Iinchip Inc	5065	469
II-VI Inc	3827	4
IJ Co	5141	98
IJ Cos	5141	67
IJ Holdings Corp	3732	64
Ijet International Inc	4724	150
Ijkg Opco LLC	8741	166
IK Electric Co	1731	342
IK Systems Inc	5065	333
IKANO Communications Inc	7373	261
Ikanos Communications Inc	3674	87
Ikaria Inc	2834	88
Ika-Works Inc	3821	25
Ike Behar Apparel and Design Inc	5136	6
Ike Behar Inc	2321	9
Ike International Corp	5031	448
IKEA North America LLC	5712	14
IKEY Industrial Peripherals	3577	296
I-K-I Manufacturing Company Inc	7389	930
Ikon It Solutions Inc	7379	1443
IKON Office Solutions Inc	5045	4
Ikonics Corp	3861	44
Il Assembly Inc	3672	218
Il Fornaio America Corp	5812	225
Il Makiage Of 60th St Inc	2844	179
iLanguagecom Inc	7389	427
Ilapak Inc	5084	99
ILAR Systems Inc	7372	3059
Ilc Intelligent Lighting Controls Inc	3648	84
ILD Telecommunications Inc	4813	96
iLevel by Weyerhaeuser	2439	1
Ili Infodisk Inc	7373	566
Ilinc Communications Inc	7379	516
Ilis Inc	3571	182
Ilitch Holdings Inc	5812	40
Ilixco	3851	93
Illco Inc	5074	103
Illes Food Ingredients Ltd	2087	54
Illgen Simulation Technologies	8711	508
Illiana Machine and Manufacturing Corp	3599	556
Illiana Truck Parts Inc	5015	18
Illig Construction Co	1542	410
Illimite Inc	7372	4700
Illingworth Corp	1711	49
Illini Bank	6022	626
Illini Corp	6712	601
Illini FS Inc	5171	13
Illini Media Co	2711	589
Illinois Action For Children	8322	29
Illinois Agricultural Holding Co	6311	89
Illinois and Midland Inc	4011	23
Illinois Audio Productions Inc	7389	2496
Illinois Auto Electric Co	5084	58
Illinois Auto Truck Company Inc	5013	151
Illinois Blower Inc	3564	75
Illinois Blueprint Corp	5044	83
Illinois Bone And Joint Institute LLC	8011	40
Illinois Bottle Manufacturing Co	3089	841
Illinois Broaching Co	3541	199
Illinois Capacitor Inc	5065	384
Illinois Cement Co	3273	42
Illinois Collection Service Inc	7322	88
Illinois Educational and Training Center	7361	337
Illinois Electric Works Inc	7629	11
Illinois Fabricators Inc	3443	210
Illinois Farmers Insurance Co	6331	337
Illinois Fibre Specialty Company Inc	3429	140

Company Name	SIC	Rank
Illinois Glove Co	2381	7
Illinois Growth Enterprises Inc	8331	138
Illinois Industrial Tool Inc	5072	121
Illinois Instruments Inc	3826	126
Illinois Machine and Tool Works LLC	3599	146
Illinois Mold Builders Inc	3544	770
Illinois Municipal Electric Agency	4911	202
Illinois Mutual Life Insurance Co	6311	117
Illinois Office Supply Elect Printing Inc	2752	1429
Illinois Payphone Systems Inc	4813	549
Illinois Rack Enterprises Inc	2542	76
Illinois Security Services Inc	7381	94
Illinois Service Federal Savings and Loans Association	6035	221
Illinois Stock Transfer Co	6289	32
Illinois Switchboard Corp	3613	161
Illinois Tool Works Inc	3452	1
Illinois Underground Inc	1623	703
Illinois Valley Plastics Inc	3089	690
Illinois Wholesale Cash Register Inc	5044	38
Illumina Inc	3826	8
Illustration House Inc	5999	199
Ilmo Products Co	5084	257
Ilmor Engineering Inc	3714	221
ILOG CPlex Div	7372	3270
ILOG Inc	7372	1382
i-Logix Inc	7372	1055
Iloka Inc	5065	90
Ilona Financial Group Inc	6311	222
Iis International Launch Services Inc	3663	160
ILS Technology LLC	7373	115
ILX Bell Rock Inc	7011	162
Ilx Lightwave	3826	91
ILX Resorts Inc	6531	459
Ilyssa Manufacturing Corp	2099	237
IMA Technologies Inc	7374	4245
Imac Group LLC	7302	125
Image Access Inc	3577	258
Image Advantage	7372	3718
Image Api Inc	7374	117
Image Architects Inc	7372	3614
Image Asphalt Maintenance Inc	5032	72
Image Bank Getty Images	7336	5
Image Computer Products	5045	1017
Image Craft LLC	7335	4
Image Display Group Inc	7311	754
Image Entertainment Inc	7819	15
Image First Professional Apparel	5136	24
Image G Inc	7812	209
Image Generators	7389	974
Image Graphics Inc	3577	512
Image Group Inc	2752	1246
Image Information Inc	7373	648
Image Ink Ltd	7389	1406
Image Innovations Inc	8742	679
Image Iv Systems Inc	5044	55
Image Labs International	5043	25
Image Logic Corp	5099	124
Image Magazine Inc	2721	322
Image Management Systems Inc	5046	278
Image Matters Inc	3993	194
Image Metrics Inc	7371	652
Image Microsystems Inc	3571	95
Image Molding Inc	3842	206
Image Photo Services Inc	7335	15
Image Plant	2741	395
Image Process Design	7372	1090
Image Processing	7336	73
Image Processing Software Inc	7372	5120
Image Projections West Inc	3577	108
Image Recognition Integrated Systems Inc	7372	1519
Image Rotomolding Enterprises Inc	3089	1320
Image Sensing Systems Inc	3829	46
Image Software Services Inc	2759	571
Image Solutions Inc	2834	135
Image Stream Medical Inc	5047	141
Image Studios Inc	7335	22
Image Systems Inc	2752	1270
Image Technologies Corp	8748	315
Image Technology Laboratories Inc	7372	4990
Image Teleproducts Inc	7389	1524
Image Travel and Tours Inc	4724	69
Image Work Communications	2741	349
ImageMind Software Inc	7372	3912
Imagen USA Inc	1731	780
Imagenetix Inc	2834	337
ImageOne Inc	8742	315
Imagery State Wine Art Gallery	2084	80
Images On Metal Inc	2759	269
Images Productions	3695	164
Images USA Inc	7311	323
Imageseller LLC	7389	1656
Imagestat Corp	5045	389
Imagestream Internet Solutions Inc	7373	976
ImageTech Corp	7372	5121
Imagetech Inc	7373	767
Imagetek Inc	7379	876
Imagetek Partners LLC	5044	146
ImageTrak Software Inc	7372	4701
ImageWare Systems Inc	7372	2503
ImageWorks	3861	40
Imagex Inc	5044	117
ImageXpert Inc	7372	2677

Company Name	SIC	Rank
ImageXpres Corp	2759	487
Imaginant Inc	3829	211
Imaginary Forces	7812	37
Imaginary Universes	7371	1462
Imagination Inc	4813	481
Imagination Publishing	2721	94
Imagine Communications Inc	4899	51
Imagine Entertainment	7812	195
Imagine Fulfillment Services LLC	7389	710
Imagine IT!	7336	122
Imagine Nation Books Ltd	5192	15
Imagine Print Solutions Inc	2759	18
Imagine Products Inc	7372	2989
Imagine Schools Inc	8299	15
Imagine That Inc	7372	2239
Imagineering Machine Inc	3599	2270
Imaginethis	5961	187
Imaging 101 Inc	7371	1822
Imaging Alliance Group LLC	5044	59
Imaging and Microfilm Access Inc	7389	2130
Imaging and Sensing Technology Corp	3671	8
Imaging Business Machines LLC	3577	241
Imaging Diagnostic Systems Inc	3845	139
Imaging Resource Associates Inc	3572	106
Imaging Science and Services Inc	7375	142
Imaging Sciences International Inc	3843	30
Imaging Solutions Inc (Wallingford Connecticut)	7376	31
Imaging Supplies Depot Inc	5044	67
Imaging Systems LLC	3955	11
Imaginings 3 Inc	2064	96
Imaginova Inc	7379	369
Imagistic	7336	85
Imagistics International Inc	5044	6
Imagitek Ltd	7371	346
Imago Ltd	2329	38
Imaja	7372	5063
I-Many Inc	7372	801
IMAP Partners LLC	4813	249
iMapDatacom Inc	8742	383
Imation Corp	3695	4
Imbert International Inc	5084	560
Imbris Inc	4813	520
Imc Instruments Inc	3829	289
IMC Networks Corp	3572	41
iMC2	7319	29
ImClone Systems Inc	2836	6
Imco Carbide Tool Inc	3545	73
Imco Inc	3444	263
IMCO Inc (Moorestown New Jersey)	3599	1480
Imco Industrial Machine Corp	3599	1655
IMCO Recycling of Illinois Inc	7389	410
Imecom Group Inc	7372	2152
Imedia Inc	2752	1173
iMedia International Inc	2741	226
iMemories	7812	41
Imerge Consulting Group LLC	7371	827
Imerys USA Inc	1455	1
Imes Communications Of El Paso	2711	523
Imetal CE Minerals	2819	46
Imex Diamond Tools And Segments Inc	3545	151
Imi Fabi LLC	2869	102
Imi Inc	3672	286
IMI Norgren Inc	3569	39
Iml Inc	3677	49
Imlay City Molded Products Corp	3089	1638
Imlay Investments Inc	6282	503
IMM Interactive	7311	224
Imm Survivor Inc	3536	47
Immagetech Inc	3541	94
Immco Diagnostics Inc	3231	45
Immediate Connections Inc	7363	249
Immediate Mailing Services Inc	7331	58
Immediate Response Technologies Inc	3812	48
Immediatek Inc	7371	1236
Immersion Corp	3577	197
Immersion Media Inc	3695	153
Immersion Medical Inc	7812	73
Immersive Design Inc	7372	3583
Immersive Media Co	3651	62
Immix Technologies LLC CRI-SIL	2822	23
Immtech Pharmaceuticals Inc	2836	74
Immucell Corp	2835	60
Immucor Inc	2835	9
Immuno Laboratories Inc	8731	186
Immuno-Dynamics Inc	2836	82
ImmunoGen Inc	2834	269
Immunomedics Inc	2835	36
ImmunoVision Inc	2836	35
IMN Inc	7372	987
Imogen Corp	5045	1008
iMortgage Services LLC	6541	19
iMove Inc	7371	1056
Imp Holdings LLC	3694	33
Impac Lending Co	6162	15
Impac Mortgage Holdings Inc	6162	24
Impac Technologies Inc	3663	153
Impace Building Services Inc	7349	28
Impact Business Developers LLC	7379	1661
Impact Devices Inc	3579	67
Impact Fulfillment Services	3999	129
Impact Group	7389	341
Impact Information Inc	2741	277
Impact Instrumentation Inc	3845	57

Company Name	SIC	Rank
Impact Label Corp	2759	273
Impact LLC	3679	628
Impact Mailing of MN Inc	2789	25
Impact Plastics Inc	3089	698
Impact Precious Wood Inc	3442	131
Impact Printers and Lithographers Inc	2752	1122
Impact Solutions Inc	7372	4207
Impact Technology Inc	7374	187
Impact Telecom Inc	7389	2238
Impact Unlimited Inc	7389	350
Impairment Resources LLC	7389	289
Impaqt LLC	7371	566
Impax Laboratories Inc	2834	46
IMPCO Machine Tools	3541	25
Impedimed Inc	3841	300
Impediment Inc	5045	713
Impellimax Inc	3674	473
Imperia Software Solutions (USA) GmbH	7371	384
Imperial Capital Group LLC	6282	236
Imperial Capitol LLC	6211	60
Imperial Clinical Research Services Inc	2761	24
Imperial Commercial Cooking Equipment	3589	14
Imperial Commodities Corp	5149	31
Imperial Computer Corp	3571	199
Imperial Construction Group Inc	1542	138
Imperial Copy Products Inc	5999	301
Imperial Corporate Training and Development	8742	504
Imperial Counters Lllp	2542	64
Imperial Dax Co	2844	168
Imperial Design Group Inc	5032	134
Imperial Distributors Inc	5122	24
Imperial Electric and Lighting Supply Inc	5063	458
Imperial Electric Co	3621	44
Imperial Electric Inc	1731	633
Imperial Electronic Assembly Inc	3679	230
Imperial Fabricators Co	3644	39
Imperial Flooring Company Inc	5023	166
Imperial Foam and Insulation Manufacturing Co	3086	66
Imperial Graphic Communications Inc	2752	1271
Imperial Guard And Detective Services Inc	7381	27
Imperial Hardware Co	5251	18
Imperial Headwear Inc	2353	3
Imperial Holdings Inc	6141	56
Imperial Industries Inc	3299	3
Imperial Industries Inc (Pompano Beach Florida)	3291	15
Imperial Leasing Inc	7359	134
Imperial Lithographing Corp	2752	513
Imperial Machine and Tool Co	3825	136
Imperial Machine Company Inc	3599	1265
Imperial Manufacturing Ice Cold Coolers Inc	3585	111
Imperial Marble and Tile Company Inc	1743	2
Imperial Marble Corp	3281	8
Imperial Metal Products Co	3451	94
Imperial Palace Inc	7011	138
Imperial Paper Box Corp	2652	14
Imperial Parking (US) Inc	7521	4
Imperial Petroleum Inc	1381	52
Imperial Plastics Inc	3089	950
Imperial Pools Inc	3949	84
Imperial Printing Products Company Inc	2752	822
Imperial Punch and Manufacturing	3544	794
Imperial Realty Co	6531	218
Imperial Rubber Products Inc	3555	67
Imperial Software Technology Ltd	7372	2811
Imperial Stamping Corp	3469	193
Imperial Stone Corp	5032	158
Imperial Sugar Co	2062	2
Imperial Technical Services	3695	139
Imperial Tool and Plastics Corp	3544	886
Imperial Tool Inc	3544	605
Imperial Trading Co	5194	3
Imperial Wire Die Inc	3544	345
Imperial Woodworking Co	2541	12
Imperial Zinc Corp	3341	29
Imperium Renewables Inc	2869	56
Imperva Inc	7371	350
Impex International Group LP	3081	145
Impinj Inc	3674	168
Implant Sciences Corp	3841	241
Implantable Provider Group Inc	8099	72
Implement Dot Com LLC	7371	1161
Implement Sales LLC	5083	35
Implementation Specialists	8741	182
Impo International Inc	5139	15
Impolit Environmental Control	3823	296
Imported Interiors Inc	5023	200
Imports by Four Hands LP	5021	22
Impreso Inc	2761	10
Impression Point Inc	2759	585
Impression Technology	7371	1038
Impression Technology Inc	5045	976
Impressive Business Forms Inc	2761	67
Imprex Inc	3479	62
Imprima Management Services Inc	7389	1459
Imprimis Group Inc	7363	109

Company Name	SIC	Rank
Imprinted Sportswear Shop Inc	5611	32
Imprivata Inc	5045	70
Impromed LLC	5045	391
Improper Publications Inc	5192	38
ImproveNet Inc	7389	1396
Improving Enterprises	8748	161
Impulse Communications Inc	7389	2353
Impulse Manufacturing Inc	3444	83
Impulse Packaging Inc	3469	344
Impulse Point	7389	734
Imr Environmental Equipment Inc	5084	762
Imr Ltd	7373	167
Imrie-Gielow Inc	5085	347
Imron Corp	5065	001
IMS Co (Brea California)	8711	185
Ims Gear Holding Inc	3089	683
IMS Health Finance Ltd	7374	116
IMS Health Inc	7374	9
IMS Health Licensing Associates LP	7374	121
Ims Inc	7379	1251
IMS Inc (Sherman Oaks California)	7372	1688
IMS Products Inc	3751	26
IMS System Company Ltd (New York New York)	7372	1085
IMT Insurance Company Mutual	6331	327
IMT Precision Inc	3599	511
Imta Manufacturing Technology and Automation Company Inc	5084	155
Imtc	7363	327
Imtec Acculine Inc	3559	200
Imtech Corp	3823	63
Imtek Inc	7819	63
Imtra Corp	5091	47
Imtronics Industries Inc	5065	864
IMVU Inc	7379	167
In Control Inc	7373	857
In Demand LLC	4841	80
In Depth Leak Detection	7381	266
In House Media	3089	1033
In Mind Communications LLC	8742	717
In Private Inc	2321	24
In Publications Inc	2741	312
IN/QUEST LLC	7372	5128
In Terminal Services Corp	7389	634
In Touch Systems	3575	63
IN ZONE Brands Inc	3085	11
In2connect Inc	3714	393
Inalfa Road System Inc	3714	232
Inalfa/Ssi Roof Systems LLC	3465	54
INAMAR Insurance Underwriting Agency Inc	6411	83
Inamics Corp	7374	388
Inbit Inc	7372	1234
Inca Molded Products Inc	3089	1037
INCAT Systems Inc	7379	95
Ince Distributing Inc	5075	33
Incendia Partners	7361	149
Incentium LLC	5999	300
Incentive Concepts LLC	8742	200
Incentive Technology Group Inc	8748	178
Inchem Corp	2821	89
Inches-A-Weigh USA LLC	7991	22
In-Cide Technologies Inc	2819	85
Incineration Recycling Services Inc	7699	246
Incipio Technologies	3669	112
Incisent Technologies	7371	580
incjet Inc	3579	22
Inclinator Company Of America	3534	21
Inco Development Corp	2752	346
Inco United States Inc	3356	16
Incom Communications Corp	4812	123
Incom Inc	3229	8
Income Opportunity Realty Investors Inc	6798	191
Income Property Finance Corp	6282	627
Income Unlimited	5084	885
Incomm Holdings Inc	7374	43
Incomm Solutions Inc	7389	1314
Incommons Bank	6022	633
Incompass Inc	7372	5074
Incompass Solutions Inc	7372	2990
Incon Inc	3678	46
Incon Industries Inc	5063	428
Incon Processing LLC	8734	58
inContact Inc	4813	111
Incorporated Inc	7379	1604
Incorporated Research LLC	8731	53
Incorporatetimecom Inc	7374	193
Incredible Technologies Inc	7371	523
Incuity Software Inc	7371	498
Incyte Corp	8731	69
Indalex Aluminum Solutions	3354	16
Indalex Inc	3354	1
Indco Inc	3531	184
Inde Enterprises Inc	2711	793
Indeck Energy Services Inc	4911	124
Indeck Power Equipment Co	3443	67
Indel Inc	3567	3
Indelac Controls Inc	3625	282
Indemax Inc	3547	26
Indemnity Company of California	3555	68
Indepedent Telecommunications Systems Inc	4813	117
Independant Data Processing Corp	7372	4831

Company Name	SIC	Rank
Independence American Insurance Co	6311	184
Independence Blue Cross	6321	19
Independence Excavating Inc	1794	10
Independence FSB	6035	201
Independence Holding Co (Stamford Connecticut)	6311	136
Independence Lincoln Mercury Inc	5511	905
Independence Lumber Inc	2421	70
Independence Tube Corp	3317	34
Independent Agribusiness Professionals Cooperative Inc	5191	27
Independent Artists	7812	252
Independent Audio LLC	3669	250
Independent Bancshares Inc	6021	282
Independent Bank Corp (Ionia Michigan)	6712	173
Independent Bank Corp (Rockland Massachusetts)	6712	119
Independent Bank East Michigan	6022	555
Independent Bank of McKinney Texas	6022	140
Independent Bank South Michigan	6022	379
Independent Bank West Michigan	6022	670
Independent Bankers' Bank of Florida	6022	472
Independent Bankers of Colorado	6022	788
Independent Beverage Corp	2086	94
Independent Brewers United Inc	2082	6
Independent Can Co	3411	11
Independent Community Bankers of America	6211	116
Independent Components Corp	5084	557
Independent Dairy Inc	2024	51
Independent Divers Inc	7999	139
Independent Electric Supply Corp	5063	251
Independent Food Corp	2011	45
Independent Graphics Inc	2752	1036
Independent Grocers Association Inc	5141	168
Independent Industries Inc	3999	196
Independent Information Services Corp	2741	237
Independent Ink Inc	2899	79
Independent Insurance Associates Inc	6411	176
Independent Investors Inc	1731	460
Independent Living Inc	8322	231
Independent Machine Co	3569	234
Independent Mortgage Co-East Michigan	6162	77
Independent Mortgage Co-South Michigan	6162	65
Independent National Bank (Ocala Florida)	6021	403
Independent Nursing Services-New Inc	7361	156
Independent Operator Inc	4213	2932
Independent Opportunities Of Michigan Inc	8361	151
Independent Options	8322	206
Independent Packers Corp	2092	56
Independent Printing Company Inc	2752	1240
Independent Procurement Alliance Program LLC	5143	10
Independent Productions	7812	316
Independent Resources Inc	2752	1262
Independent School District 281	8211	20
Independent School District 833	8211	52
Independent School District No 271	8211	65
Independent Sheet Metal Company Inc	3444	191
Independent Stamping Inc	3469	332
Independent Stationers Inc	5112	8
Independent Stave Company Inc	2449	1
Independent Steel Company LLC	5051	121
Independent Systems and Programming Inc	7372	3615
Independent Technologies LLC	5045	977
Independent Technology Systems America Inc	7371	742
Independent Telephone Network Inc	5065	390
Independent Television Network Inc	7319	18
Independent Web Inc	7699	214
Independent Welding Co	2542	74
Independent's Service Co	2759	177
Inder Lali Color Lab Inc	7384	37
Indesign LLC	8711	493
Index 53 Optical Company Inc	3851	107
Index Engines Inc	7372	1630
Index Notion Company Inc	5947	13
Index Packaging Inc	2449	6
Index Publishing	2711	401
Indexing Research	7374	360
Index-Journal Co	2711	425
Indexx Inc	2752	266
India Abroad Publications Inc	2711	476
India Ink	2269	9
Indian Harvest Specialtifoods Inc	2044	10
Indian Head Industries Inc	3593	9
Indian Industries Inc	3949	165
Indian Motorcycle Corp	3519	18
Indian Rubber Company Inc	3069	188
Indian Springs Manufacturing Company Inc	2812	12
Indian Summer Coop	2033	41
Indian Valley Bulk Carriers Inc	4213	1810
Indian Valley Trucking Inc	4213	1500
Indiana Bond Bank	6211	370
Indiana Botanic Gardens Inc	5961	130
Indiana Bottle Company Inc	3089	1325
Indiana Bridge Midwest Steel Inc	3441	85

Company Name	SIC	Rank
Indiana Building Systems LLC	2451	16
Indiana Carton Company Inc	2657	32
Indiana Community Bancorp	6712	309
Indiana Concession Supply Inc	5141	188
Indiana Data Center LLC	4813	636
Indiana Farmers Mutual Insurance Co	6331	154
Indiana Harbor Belt Railroad Co	4013	2
Indiana Heat Transfer Corp	3433	40
Indiana Home Health Care Corp	7361	276
Indiana Insurance	6331	55
Indiana Knitwear Corp	2329	12
Indiana Limestone Company Inc	1411	6
Indiana Lumbermens Mutual Insurance Co	6331	307
Indiana Members Credit Union	6061	25
Indiana Michigan Power Co	4911	65
Indiana Nlmk Inc	3312	30
Indiana Packers Corp	2011	24
Indiana Paging Network Inc	4812	80
Indiana Plastics Inc	3089	1381
Indiana Pmg Corp	3714	180
Indiana Precision Grinding Inc	7389	1704
Indiana Printing And Publishing Co	2752	181
Indiana Southern Mold Corp	3544	557
Indiana Southwestern Railway Co	4011	32
Indiana Sports Corp	7941	25
Indiana Standards Laboratory	3829	303
Indiana Stone Works	1411	22
Indiana Supply Corp	5085	65
Indiana Tool and Manufacturing Company Inc	3545	43
Indiana Toyoshima Inc	3537	62
Indiana Transformer Inc	3677	37
Indiana Tube Corp	3498	17
Indiana United Methodist Childrens Home Inc	8361	147
Indiana University Health	8062	10
Indiana Vac-Form Inc	3089	1389
Indiana Veneers Corp	2435	21
Indiana Wood Products Inc	2426	30
Indiana-Kentucky Electric Corp	4911	101
Indiana-Kentucky Trucking Inc	4213	2770
Indianapolis Bakery	2051	28
Indianapolis Colts	7941	6
Indianapolis Economic Development Corp	6552	263
Indianapolis Electric Company Inc	1731	326
Indianapolis Power and Light Co	4911	98
Indianer Computer Corp	7371	1487
Indianhead Enterprises Of Menomonie Inc	8331	236
Indianola Pecan House Inc	2068	24
India-West Publications Inc	2711	672
Indi-Bel Inc	2048	62
Indicom Buildings Inc	2452	39
Indicom Electric Co	1731	763
Indicon Corp	3613	34
Indigo Development Inc	6552	289
Indigo Group Inc	6552	212
Indigo International Inc	6552	213
Indigo Office Inc	7371	1271
Indigo Pacific	7373	1164
Indigo Systems and Technology Inc	7371	1581
Indisoft LLC	7372	3669
Indital US Management LLC	5033	59
Individual Advocacy Group Inc	8322	66
Individual Software Inc	7372	1784
Indmar Products Company Inc	3519	26
Indon International LLC	5046	325
Indonesia Fund Inc	6726	94
Indovance	7389	452
Indrolect Co	1731	1470
IndSoft Inc	8742	503
Indspec Chemical Corp	2819	36
Indtool Inc	3599	1447
Inducomp Corp	3571	188
Inductel Inc	7372	4702
Induction Technology Corp	3567	101
Inductive Components Manufacturing Inc	3625	235
Inductive Solutions Inc	7371	1713
Induplate Inc	3471	19
Induron Coatings Inc	5198	10
Indus Corp	7372	397
INDUSA Technical Corp	7371	473
Indusol Inc	2821	172
Industrail Test Equipment Company Inc	3621	153
Industrial Accessories Company Inc	8711	502
Industrial Acoustics Company Inc	3448	23
Industrial Aid Inc	8331	152
Industrial Air and Hydraulics	5084	628
Industrial Alloy Fabricators LLC	3443	211
Industrial and Commercial Security Systems Inc	5999	299
Industrial and Financial Systems Inc	7372	1938
Industrial And Marine Engine Service Co	3613	172
Industrial Applications International Inc	3541	113
Industrial Appraisal Company Inc	7389	822
Industrial Arts Supply Co	5049	113
Industrial Automation Controls Inc	5063	681
Industrial Automation Specialists Corp	1796	34
Industrial Automation Supply Co	5065	404
Industrial Automation Supply Inc	5063	731

Company Name	SIC	Rank
Industrial Bancshares Inc	6712	440
Industrial Bank NA	6022	414
Industrial Battery Engineering Inc	3691	34
Industrial Battery Warehouse Inc	5063	605
Industrial Bearing and Supply Inc	5085	288
Industrial Bearing and Transmission Inc	5085	27
Industrial Brush Corp	3991	16
Industrial Carbide Saw and Tool Corp	5085	270
Industrial Cleanup Inc	4959	24
Industrial Coatings Contractors Inc	1799	45
Industrial Combustion Engineers Inc	3567	89
Industrial Commutator Corp	3621	125
Industrial Concepts Inc	3549	53
Industrial Construction Co (Cleveland Ohio)	1541	257
Industrial Container Inc	3443	208
Industrial Container Services LLC	3443	36
Industrial Contractors Inc (Bismarck North Dakota)	1711	33
Industrial Control and Design Inc	7373	993
Industrial Control Concepts Inc	3625	265
Industrial Control Engineering	3625	346
Industrial Control Service Inc	3599	2433
Industrial Control Systems Inc	3679	650
Industrial Controls Distributors Inc	3625	89
Industrial Converting Company Inc	3299	8
Industrial Custom Products Inc	3544	439
Industrial Data Entry Automation Systems Inc	5045	1035
Industrial Defender	7382	32
Industrial Design and Construction	1541	44
Industrial Design and Fabrication Inc	3559	317
Industrial Design Innovations Inc	7389	1576
Industrial Detection Systems	3829	515
Industrial Diamond Products Co	5085	405
Industrial Dielectrics Holdings Inc	3644	10
Industrial Distribution Group Inc	5085	9
Industrial Dynamics Company Ltd	3559	42
Industrial Economics Inc	8748	236
Industrial Electric Co	1731	513
Industrial Electric Inc	1731	1378
Industrial Electrical Sales Of Tulsa Inc	5063	577
Industrial Electrical Systems Inc	1731	842
Industrial Electronic Engineers Inc	3577	277
Industrial Electronic Service Ltd	3579	61
Industrial Electronic Supply Inc	5063	132
Industrial Electronics and Controls Inc	5065	812
Industrial Enclosure Corp	2542	55
Industrial Engineering Co	3599	1714
Industrial Engineering Inc	3599	375
Industrial Engineers Inc	4213	2747
Industrial Engraving and Manufacturing Corp	3554	19
Industrial Enterprises of America Inc	2813	16
Industrial Fabrics Corp	3089	679
Industrial Farm Tank Inc	3089	1573
Industrial Fiberglass Inc	3229	39
Industrial Fiberglass Specialties Inc	3084	37
Industrial Filter and Pump Manufacturing Co	3561	89
Industrial Filter Manufacturers Inc	3569	154
Industrial Finishing Products Inc	5198	12
Industrial Finishing Services Inc	7389	2176
Industrial Finishing Systems Ii LP	5085	262
Industrial Floor Corp	2891	83
Industrial Furnace Interiors Inc	3567	118
Industrial Gasket and Shim Company Inc	3499	61
Industrial Gasket And Supply Co	3053	74
Industrial Gasket Inc	3469	278
Industrial Graphics Service Inc	2752	1452
Industrial Handling Equipment Inc	5084	691
Industrial Hard Chrome Ltd	3471	42
Industrial Hardwood Products Inc	3715	49
Industrial Harness Company Inc	3714	370
Industrial Heater Corp	3567	40
Industrial Hydraulics Inc	7699	178
Industrial Indexing Systems Inc	3625	178
Industrial Instruments and Supplies Inc	5961	193
Industrial Insulation Group LLC	3296	2
Industrial Iron Works Inc	3523	68
Industrial Janitor Service Inc	7349	223
Industrial Lab Equipment Co	5049	179
Industrial Laboratories Company Inc	8734	165
Industrial Laminates/Norplex Inc	3089	339
Industrial Light and Magic Div	7812	33
Industrial Machine and Engineering Co	3599	919
Industrial Machine and Engineering Co	3451	131
Industrial Machine And Fabrication Inc	3599	1872
Industrial Machine and Hydraulics Inc	1799	154
Industrial Machine and Tool Company Inc	7699	144
Industrial Machine Manufacturing Inc	3559	366
Industrial Machine Repair Inc	3599	2379
Industrial Machine Service Inc	3544	506
Industrial Machine Work Inc	3599	1045
Industrial Machinery Corp	5084	941
Industrial Machining And Design Services Inc	3599	2405
Industrial Machining Services Inc	3544	406
Industrial Maintenance Welding and Machining Company Inc	3569	66
Industrial Maintenances and Engineering Corp	7694	20

Company Name	SIC	Rank
Industrial Management Inc	2599	33
Industrial Manufacturing Specialties Inc	3069	270
Industrial Market Place	2721	356
Industrial Measurement Systems Inc	3829	472
Industrial Metal Fabricators Inc	3441	201
Industrial Metal Products Company Inc	3444	137
Industrial Molded Plastics Inc	3083	80
Industrial Molding Corp (Lubbock Texas)	3089	274
Industrial Molds Inc	3544	75
Industrial Motion Control LLC	3545	14
Industrial Motor Service Inc	7694	23
Industrial Motor Supply Inc	5169	177
Industrial Nameplate Inc	3479	86
Industrial Nanotech Inc	2851	171
Industrial Netting Inc	3089	473
Industrial Network Systems Corp	7371	1010
Industrial Noise Control Inc	3625	173
Industrial Nut Corp	3452	58
Industrial Packaging Supply Inc	5084	699
Industrial Paper Shredders Inc	3589	265
Industrial Paper Tube Inc	3089	1688
Industrial Parts Depot LLC	3519	19
Industrial Parts Specialties	3561	130
Industrial Peer-To-Peer LLC	7372	406
Industrial Pipe And Supply Co	5085	215
Industrial Pipe Fittings Inc	3089	660
Industrial Piping Inc	3599	118
Industrial Plastic Products Inc	3089	1086
Industrial Plastic Systems Inc	3498	70
Industrial Plastics And Machine Inc	3089	1311
Industrial Plastics Of Minneapolis Inc	3089	1789
Industrial Plating and Grinding Inc	3599	1288
Industrial Polishing Services Inc	3471	5
Industrial Polymers and Chemicals Inc	2295	20
Industrial Polymers Inc	3089	1887
Industrial Power and Lighting Corp	1731	109
Industrial Power Generating Company LLC	3612	45
Industrial Power Systems Inc	3613	67
Industrial Precision Products Inc	3599	2198
Industrial Press Inc	2731	330
Industrial Printers Of California	2752	782
Industrial Products And Services Inc	3599	1423
Industrial Products Sales Inc	8742	651
Industrial Protection Devices LLC	3829	452
Industrial Pump Services Of North Carolina Inc	7699	69
Industrial Quartz Corp	3295	19
Industrial Recovery and Recycling Inc	4953	141
Industrial Recovery Service Inc	5084	742
Industrial Recycling Services Inc	5093	201
Industrial Representatives Inc	5065	286
Industrial Research and Engineering Inc	3553	58
Industrial Resin Recycling Inc	3089	1629
Industrial Resources Inc	1629	85
Industrial Rivet and Fastener Co	5072	142
Industrial Roller Co	3069	256
Industrial Rubber Company Inc	5085	252
Industrial Rubber Inc	3533	73
Industrial Rubber Products Inc	3069	23
Industrial Safety and Hygiene News	2731	381
Industrial Safety Sales Inc	3625	344
Industrial Safety Supply Co	5085	201
Industrial Sales and Manufacturing Inc	3599	330
Industrial Scale Service Inc	5046	313
Industrial Scales and Systems Inc	5046	134
Industrial Scientific Corp	3812	50
Industrial Screw Conveyors Inc	3535	114
Industrial Sensors and Instruments Inc	3679	829
Industrial Service And Installation Inc	3535	198
Industrial Service Technology	3672	374
Industrial Services Inc	7331	118
Industrial Services of America Inc	8742	54
Industrial Silosource Inc	7349	506
Industrial Soap Co	5087	18
Industrial Specialty Company Inc	3599	896
Industrial Stainless Supply Inc	5051	273
Industrial Standard Tooling Inc	3544	785
Industrial State Bank	6022	577
Industrial Steel and Wire Company Of Illinois LLC	5051	259
Industrial Steel Products LLC	5051	502
Industrial Steel Treating Co	3398	10
Industrial Stitchtech Inc	7389	778
Industrial Supply Company Inc (Salt Lake City Utah)	5085	56
Industrial Supply Solutions Inc	5085	37
Industrial Systems Inc	8711	649
Industrial Systems Laboratory	7372	5064
Industrial Systems Of Cape Girardeau Inc	5084	616
Industrial Technology Research	8731	187
Industrial Tectonics Inc	3562	25
Industrial Television Services Inc	7375	226
Industrial Terminal Systems Inc	7389	1354
Industrial Test Systems Inc	3826	105
Industrial Testing Laboratory	8734	160
Industrial Thermoform Inc	3089	1492
Industrial Tool and Die Corp	3544	730
Industrial Tool Die and Engineering Inc	3829	155
Industrial Tool Inc	3559	196
Industrial Tool Products Inc	5084	289

Company Name	SIC	Rank
Industrial Tool Services Inc	5084	847
Industrial Tooling Service Of Asheville Inc	3599	2482
Industrial Tools Inc	3559	211
Industrial Towel and Uniform Inc	7218	7
Industrial Transport Inc	4731	57
Industrial Tube Company LLC	3728	138
Industrial USA Inc	5099	142
Industrial Vehicles International Inc	3533	88
Industrial Ventilation Inc	3444	185
Industrial Video LLC	1799	65
Industrial Welders and Machinists Inc	3599	701
Industrial Welding and Supply Co	3599	458
Industrial Wire Products Inc	5099	116
Industrial Wood Fab and Packaging Co	2449	14
Industrial Woodworking Corp	2511	83
IndustrialValley Consultants Inc	7379	1296
Industriaplex Inc	5399	7
Industries Inc	8331	205
Industry Avenue LLC	7371	1762
Industry Color Printing Inc	2752	1582
Industry Entertainment Partners	7922	68
Industry Mortgage Associates LLC	6162	55
Industry Products Co	7692	2
Industry School Dist 621	8211	95
Industry Specific Software Inc	7372	3317
Industrybrains Inc	7371	453
Industrynext LLC	7379	1242
Industry-Railway Suppliers Inc	5088	50
Indusys Technology Inc	7373	534
Indy Indoor Sports Inc	7948	34
Indyme Solutions Inc	3663	116
InDyne Inc	7371	72
Inelec Corp	5063	966
Inelect Corp	7373	739
Ineoquest Technologies Inc	3571	34
Inergex Inc	7379	411
Inergy Automotive Systems (USA) LLC	3714	68
Inergy LP	5989	1
Inertia Dynamics LLC	3625	64
Inertial Airline Services Inc	3728	229
Inetcity Solutions Inc	4813	386
Inetsupport Inc	7373	974
Inetu Inc	7379	800
iNetWorks Corp	3674	248
Inetz Corp	7373	945
Inex Technologies LLC	5734	447
Infab Corp	3842	213
Infanti International	2599	38
Infassure	7373	858
Infax Inc	7379	1011
Inferno LLC	7311	812
Inferno Manufacturing Corp	3823	389
INFICON Holding AG	3823	13
INFICON Inc	3823	41
Infilco Degremont Inc	3589	1
Infimed Inc	3845	71
Infinata Inc	7372	2153
Infinera Corp	3661	11
InfiNetwork	7372	2896
Infinia Corp	8731	65
Infiniedge Software Inc	7371	1258
Infinigy Engineering	8711	504
Infinite Campus Inc	7371	458
Infinite Computer Solutions Inc	7375	60
Infinite Energy Construction Inc	1731	803
Infinite Graphics Inc	7372	2240
Infinite Group Inc	3699	126
Infinite Options Inc	7372	1586
Infinite Resource	7372	3913
Infinite Software Inc	7371	385
Infinite Software Solutions Inc	7371	1579
Infinite Solutions Group Inc	5045	273
Infinite Systems Services Inc	7378	80
Infinite Systems Support Inc	7375	289
Infinitec	7371	1223
Infinitec Inc	7389	1720
Infiniti Information Solutions	7371	1472
Infiniti Media Inc	3679	110
Infiniti of Chantilly	5511	797
Infiniti Systems Group Inc	7373	544
Infinity Box Inc	7372	2183
Infinity Contractors Inc	1711	195
Infinity Direct Inc	8742	307
Infinity Energy Resources Inc	1382	53
Infinity Information Inc	5065	904
Infinity Insurance Co	6331	44
Infinity Interactive Inc	7336	216
Infinity Management	7389	1249
Infinity National Insurance Co	6331	45
Infinity Packaging	3086	72
Infinity Pharmaceuticals Inc	2834	158
Infinity Products Inc	7389	2202
Infinity Property and Casualty Corp	6331	140
Infinity Quick Turn Material S	3679	742
Infinity Select Insurance Co	6331	30
Infinity Service Management LLC	7349	233
Infinity Software Development Inc	7372	1455
Infinity Solutions Group Inc	7379	1181
Infinity Watch Corp	3993	154
InfinityQS International Inc	7372	2154
Infinium LLC	7379	1326
In-Fisherman Inc	2731	145
Infitec Inc	3625	204

Company Name	SIC	Rank
Inflatable Technology Corp	3069	258
Inflation Systems Inc	3069	265
InfoAmerica Inc	7371	1648
InfoBase Holdings Inc	2731	184
Infocation	7379	1605
InfoCision Management Corp	7389	37
Infocon Corp	7374	259
InfoCrossing Inc	7374	419
InFocus Corp	3577	71
Infoexperience LLC	7379	584
InfoExpress Inc	7372	2991
Infoflex Inc	7372	3914
Infofusion LLC	7372	4087
Infogate Online Ltd	5045	8
Infogenic Systems	7372	4156
Infogix Inc	7372	1326
Infoglide Corp	7372	538
InfoGOLD Corp	3571	82
Infographics Inc	7336	79
Infogrip Inc (Ventura California)	3577	535
InfoGroup Inc	7331	4
InfoHarvest Inc	7372	2717
InfoHighway Communications Corp	4813	125
Infoimage Of California Inc	2759	118
Infolane Inc	7379	756
Infolink Information Services Inc	7376	40
Infologics Inc	7376	22
Infologix Inc	7389	256
Infomark Software Corp	7372	5075
INFOMART-Dallas LP	6512	22
Infomatics Inc	7379	886
Info-Matrix Corp	7379	959
Infomedia Service Corp	4813	637
Infomentis Inc	8331	46
Infometrix Inc	7372	3719
InfoNow Corp	5045	432
Infopeople Corp	7379	932
Infopoint Systems Inc	7372	4703
InfoPro Corp	7372	303
Infopro Group Inc	7389	1537
Infopro Inc	7372	1644
InfoPro Inc (McLean Virginia)	7372	1892
InfoPros	7389	589
InfoPros Drakeley-Smith Inc	7379	326
InfoQuest Inc	8399	26
InfoQuest Technologies Inc	7373	441
Infor (Alpharetta Georgia)	7372	527
Infor CRM Epiphany	7372	522
Infor Enterprise Solutions Holdings Inc	7372	26
Infor Global Solutions	7379	9
Infor Library and Information Solutions	7372	911
InfoRad Inc	4812	59
Inforeem Inc	7379	958
Inforeliance Corp	7371	90
Informa Investment Solutions Inc	7372	733
Informa Research Services Inc	8732	13
Informa Systems Inc	7371	1413
Informa USA Inc	2731	80
Informatica Corp	7372	83
Information 2 Extreme Inc	4813	677
Information Access Solutions Inc	7371	1393
Information Access Technologies Inc	4813	685
Information Advantage	7371	1740
Information Analysis Corp	7371	1887
Information Analysis Inc	7372	2317
Information Analytics Inc	7379	554
Information And Referral Network Inc	8322	240
Information Builders Inc	7372	198
Information Computer Inc	5734	416
Information Concepts Inc (Washington DC)	7371	268
Information Consultants Inc	7372	4303
Information Data Services Inc	7374	246
Information Development Consultants Inc	7372	2155
Information Dynamics LLC	7372	4911
Information Express	7379	555
Information Impact International Inc	7389	1817
Information Inc	7375	136
Information Innovators Inc	7379	172
Information International Associates Inc	8742	333
Information Label Inc	2759	561
Information Management Consultants and Associates Inc	7372	3318
Information Management Consultants Inc (McLean Virginia)	7372	885
Information Management Corp	7372	3489
Information Management Forum	7379	1030
Information Management Group	7379	256
Information Navigation Inc	7372	5032
Information Network Associates Inc	7381	126
Information Networks Inc	5734	109
Information On Demand	7334	19
Information Planning Associates Inc	7372	3616
Information Presentation Technologies Inc	7372	4246
Information Processing Corp	7371	1633
Information Processing Systems Of California Inc	3829	189
Information Processing Technology Inc	7375	237
Information Products Inc	7371	1607
Information Resources Inc	8732	5
Information Sales Associates Inc	7373	532
Information Sciences Corp	7371	988

Company Name Index INNOVATIVE

Company Name	SIC	Rank
Information Security Corp	7372	4247
Information Services Group Inc (Stamford Connecticut)	6722	223
Information Services International	7372	3670
Information Sources Inc	7375	244
Information Systems and Networks Corp	7373	1084
Information Systems and Services Inc	7372	2772
Information Systems Engineering Inc	8742	475
Information Systems Laboratories Inc	7373	1199
Information Systems of Florida	8999	54
Information Technologies International Inc	7371	873
Information Technology Architects Inc	7373	771
Information Technology Engineering Inc	7373	1020
Information Technology Partners	7379	165
Information Technology Resources Inc	7371	816
Information Technology Services Inc	7371	375
Information Technology Solutions Inc	7373	1176
Information Technology Trends Inc	8732	109
Information Television Network	7812	147
Information Today Inc	2721	182
Information Transformation Services	7372	4912
Information Transport Solutions Inc	7379	444
Information USA Inc	2731	243
Information Ventures Inc	8748	385
Information Works Inc	5734	483
Informative Graphics Corp	7372	280
Informative Technologies Limited Inc	7379	198
Informatix Inc	7372	523
Informed Systems Inc	7379	1566
Informedix Holdings Inc	3841	406
Informer Computer Systems Inc	3575	50
Inforom Inc	2731	372
Inforonics Inc	7372	2536
Infortrend Corp	5045	770
Infoscan	7374	359
Infoscitex Corp	8711	274
Infoserve Technology Corp (Glendale New York)	7379	1141
Infoshred LLC	7389	2122
Infosoft Technologies Inc	7373	832
InfoSolutions Inc	7373	387
Infosonics Corp	3661	36
InfoSource Inc	7372	1344
Infosources Publishing	2731	382
InfoSpace Inc	7374	36
InfoSpace Sales LLC	7375	175
Infospider Inc	7311	681
InfoSports	7389	2374
InfoStar Inc	7372	4614
InfoStreet Inc	7372	3506
Infosurv Inc	7371	1481
InfoSync Services	8721	290
Infosys International Inc	7372	1662
Infosystems Inc	7379	379
Infosystems Technology Inc	7372	3537
InfoTech Inc	7371	103
Infotech Management Inc	8742	607
InfoTech Marketing	7372	1807
InfoTech New York City	7373	618
Infotech Systems Inc	7372	1645
InfoTel Corp	7372	36
Infotext Systems Inc	7374	317
Infotility Inc	7371	1576
InfoTouch Corp	7372	1545
InfoTree Inc	7372	2908
Infotree Web Services	7372	1785
InfoTrends	8732	94
InfoUse	7372	3826
InfoValue Computing Inc	7372	4170
Infovision 21 Inc	7374	170
InfoVision Consultants Inc	7373	234
Infovision Software Inc	7372	3915
Infovision Technologies Inc	8748	191
Infovista Technology LLC	7371	874
Infoware Systems Inc	7371	1427
Infoway Software Inc	8742	627
InfoWest Global Internet Services Inc	4813	232
Infoworld Media Group Inc	2721	234
Infra Corp	3541	259
Infracell Inc	7373	555
Infragistics Corp	7371	88
Infrared Analysis Inc	3823	452
Infrared Associates Inc	3823	368
Infrared Components Corp	3812	184
Infrared Industries Inc	3826	144
Infrared Laboratories Inc	3826	116
Infrared Telemetrics Inc	3829	441
Infrared Testing Inc	7389	1666
Infrasafe Inc	7382	70
InfraSource Services Inc	1623	5
Infrastruct Security Inc	3669	61
Infrastructure Holdings Company LLC	1611	42
Infrastructure Management Systems LLC	7379	1541
Infrastructure Services Inc	1771	20
Infratrol Manufacturing Corp	3567	72
infraWise Inc (Chicago Illinois)	7372	2584
Infused Solutions LLC	7371	1221
Infusion Software Inc	7372	3104
Infusionsoft	7372	1456
InfuSystem Holdings Inc	7352	6
Infuturo Technologies LLC	7373	693

Company Name	SIC	Rank
ING America Insurance Holdings Inc	6311	84
ING America Life Corp	6311	77
ING Bank FSB	6035	6
ING Financial Advisers LLC	6324	27
ING Institutional Plan Services	6411	16
ING North America Insurance Corp	6311	92
Ingallina's Box Lunch Inc	2099	256
Ingalls and Snyder LLC	6211	176
Ingalls and Son Electrical Contr	1731	1533
Ingalls Conveyors Inc	3535	67
Ingalls Feed Yard	0211	8
Ingalls Health System	8062	63
Ingen Technologies Inc	8099	116
Ingenico Corp	3699	5
Ingenious Inc	7372	2537
Ingeniux Corp	7373	683
Ingenix	7372	423
Ingenuus Software Inc	7372	4704
Ingersoll Cutting Tool Co	3545	24
Ingersoll Machine Tools Inc	3542	1
Ingersoll Tractor Co	3524	32
Ingersoll-Rand Company Productivity Solutions	3546	9
Ingles Markets Inc	5411	44
Ingleside Homes Inc	8051	63
Ingleside Investments Inc	4832	135
Ingleside Machine Company Inc	7692	16
Inglett and Stubbs LLC	1731	451
Inglewood Unified School District	8211	94
Inglot Electronics Corp	3677	39
Ingomar Packing Company LLC	2033	38
Ingram and Associates LLC	8742	472
Ingram Barge Co	4449	4
Ingram Book Group Inc	5045	11
Ingram Content Group Inc	4449	2
Ingram J D "buck" Electric Company Inc	1731	1343
Ingram Micro Inc	5045	1
Ingram Trucking Inc	4213	530
Ingredient Resource Corp	5191	179
Inhand Electronics Inc	8731	347
InherentCom Inc	7371	798
Inhibitex Inc	2834	411
In-Home Supportive Services Consortium of San Francisco	8322	45
Inhouse Systems Inc	1731	1689
Ininet Inc	7373	934
Initial Contract Services USA	7349	10
Initials Interiors Inc	2392	37
Initiate Systems Inc	7372	185
Initiative Media North America	7319	3
Initiative (New York New York)	7311	16
Initio Corp	3577	281
Injection Works Inc	3089	870
Injectorall Electronics Corp	3672	493
Injectron Corp	3089	435
Injectronics Corp	3089	467
Injex Industries Inc	3714	209
Ink Cupsnow Corp	5084	750
Ink Impress USA Inc	7378	129
Ink Impressions Inc	8741	291
Ink Makers Inc	2893	40
Ink Solutions LLC	5734	240
Ink Spot Inc	7334	71
Ink Tech/Repeat-O-Type Manufacturing Corp	2893	38
Ink Technology Corp	2893	32
Inkcycle Inc	3955	5
InkjetsincCom Of Florida Inc	3955	17
Inkley's Inc	5946	4
Inkstone Inc	2752	1263
Inksure Technologies Inc	2899	215
Inland American Real Estate Trust Inc	6798	136
Inland Asphalt Co	1611	229
Inland Associates Inc	5045	247
Inland Bank and Trust	6022	422
Inland Desert Security And Communications	7389	2017
Inland Electric Inc	1731	1029
Inland Empire Components Inc	5065	416
Inland Empire Consultants	7389	2375
Inland Empire National Bank (Riverside California)	6021	357
Inland Empire Paper Company Inc	2621	41
Inland Fruit Co	0723	6
Inland Homebuilding Group Inc	6794	90
Inland Imaging Business Associates LLC	5047	113
Inland Inc	2891	87
Inland Industrial Tire North Inc	5014	50
Inland Industries Inc	6719	191
Inland Lakes Machine Inc	3599	599
Inland Mailing Services Inc	2752	544
Inland Management Corp	8741	238
Inland Marine Industries Inc	3499	63
Inland Northwest Dairies LLC	2026	62
Inland Press (Menomonee Falls Wisconsin)	2732	20
Inland Printing Company Inc	5084	686
Inland Productivity Solutions Inc	7371	1429
Inland Products Inc	2077	8
Inland Real Estate Corp	6512	8
Inland Sea Inc	4213	2834
Inland Seafood Corp	5146	1

Company Name	SIC	Rank
Inland Showcase and Fixture Company Inc	5046	176
Inland Star Distribution Cente	3559	378
Inland Tool Co	3469	213
Inland Transporters LLC	4213	3105
Inland Valley Engineering Inc	1623	858
Inland Waters Pollution Control Inc	4953	63
Inlandesign Group Inc	7311	1029
Inlet Technologies	3629	24
Inline Digital Image LP	2752	1628
In-Line Labeling Equipment Inc	3555	111
Inline Plastics Corp	3089	223
Inline Plastics Inc	3089	1268
Inlink International Inc	7379	1275
Inlite Corp	3645	76
Inlite Research Inc	7373	526
Inlustra Technologies Inc	3559	531
InMage Systems Inc	7372	2332
Inmagic Inc	7372	2773
Inman Associates Inc	7371	1280
Inman Construction Corp	1541	102
Inman Electric Company Inc	1731	2324
Inman Mills	2281	8
Inman Trucking Management	4213	1612
Inmar Inc	8744	7
Inmedius Inc	7372	508
Inncom International Inc	3643	26
Inner City Electrical Contractors Inc	1731	744
Inner Media Inc	7372	3720
Inner Parish Security Corp	7381	50
Inner Space Design Inc	7389	2376
Inner-City Underwriting Agency Inc	6331	365
Innergy Power Corp	3691	13
Innermountain Distributing Co	2086	155
Innerpac LLC	2653	20
Innersound LLC	3651	232
Innerspec Technologies Inc	8742	641
Inner-Tite Corp	3699	95
Innerwireless Inc	5063	228
InnerWorkings Inc	2759	7
Innex Industries Inc	3545	243
Innkeepers Hospitality Florida Inc	8741	275
Innkeepers USA Trust	6798	128
InnLink LLC	7011	116
InnoCentive LLC	7379	367
Innocomp	3679	843
Innodata Isogen Inc	7374	66
Inno-Flex Corp	3625	52
InnoMed Technologies Inc	5047	14
Innomedia Inc	7371	911
Innominata	2835	65
Innominds Software Inc	7372	432
Innonet LLC	7374	290
Innopath Software	5045	73
Innophos Holdings Inc	2819	18
Innospec Active Chemicals LLC	2869	43
Innospec Inc	2869	12
Innospire Systems Corp	7379	400
InnoSys Inc	7371	924
Innotek Corp	3569	130
Innotrac Corp	7389	273
In-N-Out Burgers	5812	407
Innova Communications LLC	4813	341
Innova Electronics Corp	3661	91
Innova Ideas and Services	7336	265
Innova Industries Inc	3699	142
Innova Pure Water Inc	3599	2490
Innovair Corp	5075	94
Innovak International Inc	7372	3827
Innovance Inc	3599	54
Innovaro Inc	6211	332
InnovaSafe Inc	7379	1182
Innovasic Inc	5065	370
Innovate E-Commerce Inc	7371	399
Innovated Machine and Tool Company Inc	3441	184
Innovatek Microsystems Inc	7373	1244
Innovation Associates Inc	8711	376
Innovation Data Processing Inc	7372	758
Innovation First Notice	7371	257
Innovation Group (New Orleans Louisiana)	8742	354
Innovation Industries Inc	1731	1826
Innovation Management Group Inc	7372	2637
Innovation Marine Corp	3764	4
Innovation Products Inc	3669	24
Innovation Silicon Inc	3674	115
Innovation Specialties Inc	5094	36
Innovation Sports Inc	3842	115
Innovation USA Trading Inc	5731	58
Innovative Alternatives Inc	7371	671
Innovative Analytics Inc	7379	955
Innovative Cabling Systems Inc	1623	591
Innovative Candy Concepts LLC	2064	63
Innovative Card Technologies Inc	3679	493
Innovative Certified Technical Plating LLC	3471	22
Innovative Circuits Arizona Inc	3672	180
Innovative Circuits Engineering Inc	3825	181
Innovative Circuits Inc	3699	237
Innovative Coatings Inc	3479	103
Innovative Communication Concepts Inc	5065	293
Innovative Communication Corp	4813	44

Ward's Business Directory of U.S. Private and Public Companies, 55th Edition / Volume 5 1539

Company Name	SIC	Rank
Innovative Components Inc	3089	996
Innovative Composite Engineering Inc	3624	20
Innovative Computer Concepts and Services Inc	7373	764
Innovative Computer Services Inc	7331	110
Innovative Computing Corp	7372	2044
Innovative Control Solutions Inc	8711	494
Innovative Control Systems Inc	5065	884
Innovative Controls Corp	3613	96
Innovative Decisions Inc	7371	917
Innovative Designs Inc (Pittsburg Pennsylvania)	2394	36
Innovative Direct Response LLC	7311	1035
Innovative Electrical Components Limited Inc	3621	162
Innovative Electronic Designs	3651	81
Innovative Employee Solutions Inc	8721	118
Innovative Energy Systems	5063	796
Innovative Exhibits Ltd	3823	400
Innovative Foods Inc	8748	240
Innovative Handling and Metalfab LLC	3535	192
Innovative Health Care Concepts Inc	8741	289
Innovative Inc	5045	914
Innovative Industries Inc	8331	241
Innovative Instrumentation Inc	3825	341
Innovative Integration	3674	343
Innovative Interfaces Inc	7372	430
Innovative Kitchens and Baths LLC	5047	243
Innovative Leisure Inc	7389	1796
Innovative Lighting Inc	3647	13
Innovative Logistics Techniques Inc	7373	102
Innovative Machine Corp	3599	1006
Innovative Machine Specialists Inc	3599	812
Innovative Managed Care Systems Ltd	7372	515
Innovative Management and Technology Services LLC	7373	352
Innovative Marketing Consultants	5199	92
Innovative Marketing Services Inc	5064	191
Innovative Medical Device Solutions	2836	34
Innovative Micro Technology Inc	3674	250
Innovative Micro Technology Inc	3572	26
Innovative Mold Inc	3544	444
Innovative Molding	3089	392
Innovative Peening Systems Inc	3629	99
Innovative Plastech Inc	3089	674
Innovative Plastic Machinery	3559	484
Innovative Plastic Solutions Inc	3089	1073
Innovative Plastics Corp	3089	277
Innovative Plastics South Corp	3081	110
Innovative Postal Services Inc	4212	66
Innovative Products and Services of Boston	7372	2851
Innovative Programming Associates Inc	7372	2638
Innovative Research Inc	7372	5009
Innovative Routines International	7371	1274
Innovative Routines International Inc	7372	1893
Innovative Security Systems Inc	7371	1265
Innovative Software/Firmware Products Inc	7372	4832
Innovative Software Products Inc	7371	1620
Innovative Software Technologies Inc	7389	2477
Innovative Solutions and Support Inc	7371	287
Innovative Supply Inc	5051	500
Innovative System Solutions Corp	7379	670
Innovative Systems Inc	7372	2787
Innovative Systems LLC	7373	315
Innovative Technologies Corp	8742	466
Innovative Technologies Group And Co	8711	680
Innovative Technologies Inc	4813	149
Innovative Technology International Inc	3841	372
Innovative Technology Ltd	5045	918
Innovative Test Systems Inc	3829	509
Innovative Utility Products Corp	8742	631
Innoveda Inc	7372	459
Innovend LLC	3089	788
Innovene Inc	2899	2
Innoventions Inc	3825	259
Innovex Inc (Maple Plain Minnesota)	3679	105
Innovex Ltd	3499	22
INNOViON Corp	3674	153
Innovision Design Inc	7371	1463
Innovonics Inc	3578	32
Innov-X Systems	3429	41
Inns By The Sea	7011	220
Inns of America	7011	88
InnSuites Hospitality Trust	6798	202
Inntechnology Inc	5065	970
Innuity Inc	7372	2322
Innvision Hospitality Supply Inc	5021	76
Inoac Packaging Group Inc	3089	519
Inolex Chemical Co	5169	92
Inone Technology LLC	7379	1327
Inotek Pharmaceuticals Corp	8731	297
iNOVA Corp	7372	1536
INOVA Diagnostics Inc	2835	25
Inova Health System	8062	31
Inova Technology Inc	7372	1167
In-O-Vate Inc	2952	22
Inovative Transport System	4213	1784
Inovent Engineering Inc	8711	683
Inovio Pharmaceuticals Inc	3841	245
Inovis Inc (Alpharetta Georgia)	7372	181
Inovo Inc	3841	273
INOW Inc	7379	757

Company Name	SIC	Rank
Inphi Corp	3679	103
Inphinet Interactive Communications Inc	7372	5129
InphonexCom LLC	4813	699
In-Place Machining Company Inc	3599	258
Inplex Custom Extruders LLC	3089	1126
In-Print Graphics Inc	2752	626
Inpro Corp	3081	19
INPRO International Inc	7372	4705
Inpro/Seal LLC	5085	99
Input 1 LLC	7374	88
Input Automation Inc	5045	812
Input Center	3695	57
Input Inc	8732	45
Input/Output Technology Inc	3577	490
Input Technology Inc	7389	709
InQuira	7372	638
INR Beatty Lumber Co	5211	93
In-Roads Creative Programs Inc	8322	37
Insaco Inc	3827	58
Inscape Inc (Falconer New York)	2542	30
Inscerco Manufacturing Inc	3579	46
Inscitek Microsystems Inc	7379	1054
Insco Corp	7389	1089
InScope International Inc	7379	158
Inscribe Inc	7371	737
Inserra Supermarkets Inc	5411	90
Inserts East Inc	5043	18
Inserts USA Inc	2789	16
Inservco Inc	3679	227
Inside Communications Inc	2731	217
Inside Council	2721	433
Inside Mortgage Finance Publications Inc	2721	390
Inside Out Networks	3577	331
Inside Source	5021	81
Insider Software Inc	7372	4511
Insideview Inc	7372	1631
Insideview Technologies Inc	5045	741
Insight Capital Inc	6722	82
Insight Capital Research and Management Inc	6282	317
Insight Communications Company Inc	4841	15
Insight Distributing Inc	5046	156
Insight Enterprises Inc	5961	7
Insight Equity Holdings LLC	6722	216
Insight For Living	4832	56
Insight Global	7361	16
InSight Health Services Corp	8071	9
Insight Inc	5045	346
Insight Investments LLC	7377	6
Insight Lighting Inc	3645	24
Insight Manufacturing Software Inc	7372	4970
Insight Media Advertising	7311	824
InSight Medical Management Systems Inc	7372	1133
Insight Midwest LP	4841	19
Insight Realty Group Inc	6531	362
Insight Resource Group Inc	8748	245
Insight Satellite	5731	127
Insight Software Solutions Inc	7372	4615
Insight Sourcing Group Inc	7389	1224
Insight Vacations Inc	4725	41
Insignia/Esg Hotel Partners Inc	6512	25
Insignia Systems Inc	3999	53
Insignia Technology Services LLC	8748	229
Insignis Inc	7375	177
Insinc Corp	7379	1102
Insinger Machine Co	3589	119
In-Sink-Erator	3639	7
Insite Group Inc	7372	2093
Insite Group LP	2721	296
Insite One Inc	5045	222
InSite Vision Inc	2834	302
In-Situ Inc	3822	30
Insituform Of New England Inc	1623	385
Insituform Technologies Inc	1623	6
Insmark Inc	7372	2488
Insmed Inc	2834	338
Insound LLC	7379	917
InSource Inc	7363	247
Insource Tech Inc	3585	149
Inspection Services Inc	8734	148
Inspection Specialists Inc	8734	202
Insperity Inc	8742	14
Inspira Inc	7371	1054
Inspiration Software Inc	7372	1484
Inspiration Technology Inc	7372	2518
Inspirational Network Inc	4841	45
Inspiromedia Corp	7336	313
Inspironix Inc	7372	3052
instaCare Corp	7371	361
Insta-Copy Printing Office Supply Inc	5943	34
INSTALLS Inc	3629	18
InstallShield Software Corp	7372	749
Instant Print King Inc	2752	1668
Instant Products Inc	3944	42
Instant Recall Inc	7372	4833
Instant Shade Trees Inc	2752	1555
Instant Tax Service	7291	7
Instantiations Inc	7379	152
Instantwhip Foods Inc	2026	10
Instantwhip-Dayton Inc	2026	86
Insta-Print Inc	2752	1143

Company Name	SIC	Rank
Instaset Corp	3089	951
In-Stat Inc	8732	100
Instead Sciences	3841	334
Instec Inc	3823	412
Insteel Industries Inc	3399	3
Insteel Wire Products Co	3496	10
InStep Software LLC	7372	1615
Instinet Inc	6211	67
Institech Inc	7361	423
Institute For Independent Information Technology Professionals LLC	7371	1193
Institution Food House Inc	5141	125
Institutional Casework Inc	3821	24
Institutional Equipment Inc	5046	115
Institutional Financial Markets Inc	6798	168
Institutional Investor Inc	7389	639
Institutional Sales Associates	5141	105
Institutional Venture Partners	6799	205
Institutional Wholesale Co	5141	164
In-Store Opportunities Inc	7389	604
Instromedix Inc	3845	77
Instron Corp	3829	17
Instructional Systems Div	8249	9
Instructional Technology Inc	7371	754
Instructive Visiting Nurse Association	8082	96
Instructivision Inc	8299	81
Instrumedical Technologies Inc	3842	176
Instrument And Control Systems Inc	7629	59
Instrument Associates Inc	3663	103
Instrument Control Company LLC	7629	60
Instrument Control Systems Inc	3823	181
Instrument Development Corp	3599	530
Instrument Engineers	5063	810
Instrument Personnel Inc	3829	497
Instrument Specialists Inc	5085	467
Instrument Technical Services Inc	1731	685
Instrument Technology Inc	3827	81
Instrumental Inc	7371	585
Instrumentalists Inc	2721	415
Instrumentation and Control Systems Inc	3625	330
Instrumentation And Controls Inc	7389	1500
Instrumentation Industries Inc	3841	194
Instrumentation Laboratory Co	8731	26
Instrumentation Northwest Inc	7359	183
Instrumentation Technology Systems	3577	563
Instrumented Sensor Technology Inc	3829	352
Instrumentors Inc	3829	473
Instruments And Control Inc	3824	49
Instruments and Equipment Co	5045	593
Instruments For Industry Inc	3663	140
In-Style Software Inc	7371	462
Insua Graphics Inc	2752	927
Insulation Corporation Of America	3086	111
Insulation Specialties Of America Inc	3299	11
Insulation Technology Corp	3564	133
Insul-Bead Corp	3086	142
Insul-Board Inc	3086	131
Insulectro Corp	5063	53
Insulet Corp	3841	46
Insultab Inc	3082	11
Insultech LLC	2899	138
Insurance and Risk Management	6411	248
Insurance Auto Auctions Inc	5013	25
Insurance Company of the West	6331	194
Insurance Counsellors of Bryn Mawr Inc	6411	54
Insurance Data Services Inc	8721	327
Insurance Exchange Inc	6399	20
Insurance Information Institute Inc	6411	262
Insurance Information Technologies Inc	7372	2037
Insurance Network	6311	275
Insurance Programs Inc	6411	144
Insurance Publishing Plus Corp	2731	282
Insurance Resources Group Cos	8748	331
Insurance Services Office Inc	6411	9
Insurance Systems Group	7373	1125
Insurance Technologies Corp	7372	2524
Insurance Technology Consultants Inc	7372	837
Insurance Temporary Services Inc	7363	281
InsuranceAgentscom	7375	146
InsurMark Inc	6411	249
InsWeb Corp	7389	384
InsWeb Insurance Services Inc	7389	418
Insyght Interactive Inc	7389	814
Insync Corp (Woods Cross Utah)	5045	545
Insync Inc	7372	4067
InSync Software Inc (San Jose California)	7372	1894
In-Synch Systems LLC	5045	690
Insynq Inc	7379	1359
In-Sys Solutions Inc	7373	1091
Insys Therapeutics Inc	2836	99
Insyst Inc	7379	806
Int Technologies	7379	118
Intag Inc	1623	867
Intalco Aluminum Corp	3334	10
Intalio Inc	5045	275
Intarcia Therapeutics Inc	2834	248
Intarome Fragrance Corp	2844	124
Intat Precision Inc	3321	27
Intcomex Inc	5045	19
Intec Group Inc	3089	259
Intech Bearing Inc	5085	464

Company Name	SIC	Rank
Intech EDM	3823	125
Intech Enterprises Inc	8742	632
InTech Group Inc	8748	306
Intech Inc (Chattanooga Tennessee)	8713	4
Intechra Group LLC	5932	3
INTECK Corp	7372	4354
Intecom	3661	40
Intecon Inc	7373	1036
Intecon LLC	7379	397
INTEDATA Systems	7372	4616
Integbusiness Services Inc	7389	2413
Integer Group	7311	26
Intego	7323	45
Intego Systems Inc	3669	198
Integon Corp	6331	155
Integra Bank Corp	6712	179
Integra Business Systems Inc	7372	1712
Integra Computing	7372	5076
Integra Consulting and Computer Services Inc	5734	181
Integra Information Inc	7372	4304
Integra LifeSciences Holdings Corp	2836	5
Integra Management Systems	7378	152
Integra NeuroSupplies Inc	5999	155
Integra Plastics Inc	3081	127
Integra Realty Resources Inc	6531	461
Integra Sales Inc	5063	951
Integra Systems Corp	3663	371
Integra Technologies	8734	45
Integra Technology Consulting Corp	7379	617
Integra Telecom Inc	4813	60
IntegraClick Inc	7311	132
Integracolor Ltd	2752	92
Integracore LLC	7379	436
Integral 7 Inc	7371	1044
Integral Automation Inc	3599	72
Integral Development Corp	7372	599
Integral Protection Inc	7381	254
Integral Systems Inc	7373	62
Integral Vision Inc	3823	365
IntegraMed America Inc	8011	13
Integraphx Inc	2752	931
Integratas Maintenance Corp	7349	101
Integrated Alliance LP	7389	873
Integrated Archive Systems Inc	7379	245
Integrated Book Technology Inc	2732	27
Integrated Business and Industrial Systems Inc	3571	200
Integrated Business Group Inc	7371	1683
Integrated Business Systems and Services Inc	7372	3470
Integrated Business Systems Inc (Cedar Grove New Jersey)	7373	835
Integrated Cable Solutions Inc	3357	76
Integrated Circuit Packaging Corp	3672	199
Integrated Communication Services Inc	5065	610
Integrated Communications Inc	4822	13
Integrated Communications Services Inc	1731	1262
Integrated Components Source	5065	582
Integrated Computer Concepts Inc	7373	391
Integrated Computer Solutions Inc	7372	2852
Integrated Comtel Inc	4813	510
Integrated Control Corp	3625	136
Integrated Controls Inc	3829	393
Integrated Custom Software Inc	7373	1085
Integrated Data Corp	4812	43
Integrated Decision Support Corp	7371	405
Integrated Decisions and Systems Inc	7372	155
Integrated Defense Technologies Inc	3812	17
Integrated Design Engineering Systems Corp	7373	565
Integrated Design Inc	7372	4208
Integrated Development and Manufacturing Co	3822	32
Integrated Device Technology Inc	3674	51
Integrated Digital Systems/ Scanamerica Inc	7373	449
Integrated Display Company LLC	5046	298
Integrated DNA Technologies Inc	8731	244
Integrated Electrical Services Inc	1731	12
Integrated Electronics Corp	5065	97
Integrated Electronics Inc	5731	101
Integrated Environmental Restoration Services Inc	8999	204
Integrated Environmental Solutions Inc	8748	246
Integrated Financial Group	7389	1618
Integrated Grain and Milling Inc	2048	42
Integrated Health Ideas Inc	2834	97
Integrated Healthcare Holdings Inc	8062	57
Integrated Healthcare Strategies	8742	264
Integrated Housekeeping Management Inc	1799	99
Integrated Information Solutions Inc	7373	1022
Integrated IT Solutions Inc	7373	249
Integrated Management Concepts	7372	1895
Integrated Management Services PA	8711	394
Integrated Marketing Technologies Inc	7374	135
Integrated Media Systems Inc	1731	1403
Integrated Medical Solutions LLC	8742	402
Integrated Medical Systems Inc	5047	95
Integrated Metering Systems Inc	3825	258
Integrated Micro Systems Inc	7373	833
Integrated Microelectronics (USA) Inc	3672	308

Company Name	SIC	Rank
Integrated Microwave Corp	3679	355
Integrated Microwave Technologies LLC	3663	341
Integrated Mobile Inc	7371	217
Integrated Molding Solutions Inc	3089	1527
Integrated Mortgage Solutions	7389	813
Integrated Office Solutions	7378	104
Integrated Packaging and Fastener Inc	7389	2223
Integrated Packaging Corporation Inc	2653	52
Integrated Paper Services Inc	8734	126
Integrated Pos Inc	5045	764
Integrated Power Corp	1796	7
Integrated Power Designs Inc	3679	278
Integrated Power Solutions Inc	7389	728
Integrated Power Sources Of Virginia Inc	5063	615
Integrated Precision Systems Inc	7373	691
Integrated Print and Graphics Inc	2752	138
Integrated Procurement Technologies Inc	5088	21
Integrated Production Systems Inc	3599	1715
Integrated Productivity Systems Inc	7372	3916
Integrated Resources Inc	8331	148
Integrated Science Solutions Inc	8711	479
Integrated Secure LLC	8748	298
Integrated Security Corp	3699	238
Integrated Security Systems Inc	3669	185
Integrated Security Technologies Inc	7382	94
Integrated Sensing Systems Inc	3829	232
Integrated Silicon Solution Inc	3674	72
Integrated Software Design Inc	7372	3490
Integrated Software Specialists Inc	7371	241
Integrated Software Systems	7371	1930
Integrated Software Technologies Inc	7372	5130
Integrated Solutions and Systems LLC	7373	897
Integrated Supply Network LLC	5013	73
Integrated Support Systems Inc	7373	780
Integrated Surveying Solutions Inc	5049	146
Integrated Systems Analysts Inc	7373	143
Integrated Systems and Contraols of NY Inc	7371	593
Integrated Systems Corp	3651	127
Integrated Systems Management Inc	7371	631
Integrated Systems Technology Inc	7372	2156
Integrated Technologies Inc (Danville Vermont)	8711	555
Integrated Technology Solutions Inc	7373	746
Integrated Textile Solutions Inc	2394	16
Integrated Time Systems Inc	3823	446
Integrated Trade Systems Inc	7389	1445
Integrated Wave Technologies Inc	8999	119
Integrated Wireless Communications	4813	555
Integration and Automation Solutions Inc	7373	1166
Integration Computers Inc	5045	934
Integration Services Inc	7371	1566
Integration Systems LLC	5734	221
Integration Technolgy Partners	7373	797
Integrative Health Technologies Inc	7352	53
Integrator Services Inc	3829	435
Integrex	8711	310
IntegriChain Inc	7379	828
Integrien Corp	7371	269
Integris (Billerica Massachusetts)	7371	253
Integris Federal Credit Union	6061	147
Integris Rural Health Inc	8062	217
Integrity Asset Management LLC	6799	332
Integrity Building Services	7349	500
Integrity Capital Partners LLC	6411	253
Integrity Communications Ltd	4813	678
Integrity Credit Services	7323	41
Integrity Electric Inc	1731	799
Integrity First Inc	7338	37
Integrity Graphics Inc	2752	342
Integrity Iron and Metal	5093	206
Integrity Life Insurance Co	6371	4
Integrity Management Consulting Inc	8742	535
Integrity Manufacturing Corp	3451	129
Integrity Media Inc	3652	9
Integrity Mold and Die Ltd	3089	1621
Integrity Music	3652	12
Integrity Office Solutions Inc	5734	395
Integrity Recovery Inc	7389	2203
Integrity Recycling Inc	5093	174
Integrity Saw and Tool Inc	3599	1860
Integrity Security Systems	3699	272
Integrity Staffing Solutions Inc	7363	93
Integrity Steel Co	5051	422
Integrity Technology Corp	3679	612
Integrity Tower Inc	1623	621
IntegrityWare Inc	7372	4706
Integrium LLC	8734	38
Integro LLC	3648	47
Integrys Consults LLC	7372	1776
Integrys Energy Group Inc	4931	14
Intek Inc	3823	222
Intek Integration Technologies Inc	7372	805
Intek Plastics Inc	3089	276
INTEKnet LLC	7373	910
Intekras Inc	7373	427
Intel Corp	3674	1
Intelect Technologies Inc	3661	215
Intelectric Inc	1731	1137
InteleTravel 2000	4724	50

Company Name	SIC	Rank
InteLex Corp	2741	388
Intelicoat Products	3089	99
Inteliport Inc	4813	694
Intelisyn Inc	8741	137
Intelius Inc	7379	135
Intelix LLC	3651	165
Intelk Inc	5065	985
Intella Interventional Systems Inc	3841	224
Intellectual Property Enterprises LLC	7371	1802
Intellectual Ventures LLC	7379	221
Intellex Consulting Services Inc	7379	431
Intellica Corp	7371	1025
Intellicell Biosciences Inc	7372	5004
Intelli-Check Mobilisa Inc	7372	1655
Intellicode Software Inc	7373	911
Intellicom Inc	7373	557
Intellicom Technologies	1731	2531
IntelliCorp Inc	7372	654
Intellidot Corp	5049	27
Intellidyn Corp	7375	298
Intellidyn Inc	7375	285
INTELLIGENCE	7389	2393
Intelligence Support Group Ltd	3699	263
Intelligencer Printing Co	2752	59
Intelligent Automation Inc	8731	91
Intelligent Beauty Inc	7311	316
Intelligent Computer Solutions Inc (Chatsworth California)	3577	437
Intelligent Decisions Inc	7379	92
Intelligent Enterprise Inc	7379	1364
Intelligent Information Systems Inc	7371	543
Intelligent Instrumentation Inc	3577	253
Intelligent Integration Systems Inc	7375	141
Intelligent Logistics LLC	4731	75
Intelligent Machine Control Inc	7373	1113
Intelligent Micro Systems Inc	7371	1649
Intelligent Mobile Solutions Inc	7374	139
Intelligent Products Company Inc	5063	797
Intelligent Security Systems International Inc	7371	525
Intelligent Solutions and Technologies LLC	7378	107
Intelligent Staffing Solutions	8742	713
Intelligent Systems Corp	7372	1446
Intelligent Systems Software Inc	3577	161
Intelligent Systems Technology Inc	7372	2283
Intelligraphics Inc	7371	765
Intelligroup Inc	7373	82
Intellikey Corp	3699	283
Intellilink Services Inc	7371	1798
Intellimagic Inc	5045	893
Intellimar Inc	5065	173
Intellimed International Inc	8731	219
Intelli-Mine Inc	7373	1033
IntelliNet Corp (Atlanta Georgia)	7379	184
IntelliNet Technologies Inc	7371	358
Intellinetics Inc	5734	322
Intellinex	7372	73
Intellione Technologies Corp	7371	769
Intelliphone Inc	5065	546
IntelliPower Inc	3612	118
Intellipro Inc	7371	1527
Intelliquest Systems Inc	7379	1018
Intelliquis	2741	96
Intellisense Software Corp	7372	2272
Intellisight LLC	7373	712
Intellisoft Inc	7372	3189
Intellisource Consulting Services Inc	7373	1151
Intelliswift Software Inc	7379	275
Intellisys Group	5065	70
Intellitax	7372	645
Intellitec Security Services LLC	1731	1095
IntelliTools Inc	3577	209
Intellitrack Inc	5045	347
Intelliworks Inc	7372	1264
Intellix Media	7311	911
Intelsat Global Service Corp	4899	15
Intelution Inc	7373	818
Intensive Maintenance Care Inc	7349	69
Intensus Engineering Incorporated LLC	1629	89
Inteq Group Inc	8748	82
Inter Basic Resources Inc	3829	143
Inter City Press Inc	2759	473
Inter Coastal Electronics Inc	8731	197
Inter County Energy Cooperative Corp	4911	461
Inter Electronics Corp	3651	236
Inter Mountain Company Inc	2711	538
Inter Packing Inc	3086	166
Inter Parfums Inc	2844	11
Inter Parfums USA LLC	2844	60
Inter Plan Design Group Inc	7389	1770
Interact Holdings Group Inc	6141	69
Interaction Research Institute Inc	7372	3828
Interaction Systems Inc	3577	558
Interactive Brokers Group Inc	6211	73
Interactive Business Information Systems Inc	5045	403
Interactive Business Systems Inc	7379	41
Interactive Business Technologies Inc	7379	1379
Interactive CAD Systems	7372	4305
Interactive Data Corp	6282	63
Interactive Data Visualization Inc	7371	1466
Interactive Design and Development Inc	7372	2100

Company Name	SIC	Rank
Interactive Effects Inc	7372	806
Interactive Factory Inc	2741	188
Interactive Games And Creations Inc	7389	1631
Interactive Graphics Inc	7374	352
Interactive Health Systems Inc	7372	4617
Interactive Intelligence Inc	7372	286
Interactive Knowledge Inc	2741	306
Interactive Management Systems Corp	7371	1233
Interactive Marketing Technologies	7379	589
Interactive Media Communications Inc	2741	244
Interactive Multimedia Artists	2741	401
Interactive Network Technologies Inc	7372	2392
Interactive Payer Network LLC	7376	38
Interactive Planet Inc	7379	936
Interactive Sales Solutions Inc	7372	3353
Interactive Sites Inc	7371	1162
Interactive Solutions Inc (Hasbrouck Heights New Jersey)	7372	1962
Interactive Solutions Inc (Memphis Tennessee)	5065	250
Interactive Solutions Inc (Pleasanton California)	7372	3917
Interactive Systems Inc (North Billerica Massachusetts)	7372	4192
Interactive Systems Worldwide Inc	7373	1187
Interactive Technologies Group Inc	7371	958
Interactive Technologies Inc (Missoula Montana)	7372	2463
Interactive Technology Inc	7371	1727
Interactive Technology Solutions LLC	7379	110
Interactive Telesis Inc	7371	1023
Interactive Training Inc	2741	343
Interad Limited LLC	3812	195
Inter-American Investment Corp	6159	54
Interamerican Motor Corp	5013	49
Interamerican Zinc Inc	3341	24
Interaudi Bank	6022	148
Interbank FX LLC	6211	275
InterBank (Oklahoma City Oklahoma)	6022	320
InterBase Corp	5045	256
interbiznet	7379	997
Interboro Mutual Indemnity Insurance Co	6331	186
Interbrand	7389	467
Intercage Inc	4813	652
Intercall Systems Inc	3669	239
Intercard Inc	3577	346
InterCare DX Inc	7372	1091
Intercasting Corp	7374	196
Intercat Inc	2819	73
Intercept Inc	7374	37
Interceramic Inc	5032	3
Interchange Bank	6022	794
Interchange Equipment Inc	5084	410
Interchange Inc	2741	503
Interchange Technologies Inc	7379	922
Interchem Corp	2833	25
Intercim LLC	7372	2241
Intercit Inc	2899	78
Intercities Electric Company Inc	1731	841
Intercity Inc	3679	844
Intercity Maintenance Inc	7349	307
Inter-City Printing Company Inc	2752	1105
Interclick Ad Network	7389	525
Interclick Inc	7389	232
Intercoastal Diving Inc	7389	2301
InterCom	2741	155
Intercom of Norfolk Inc	4832	102
Inter-Commercial Business Systems Inc	5065	377
Inter-Community Telephone Co	4813	172
Inter-Community Telephone Company II LLC	4899	148
Inter-Community Telephone Company LLC	4899	133
Intercomp Co	3596	8
Intercomp Design Inc	7379	973
Intercon 1	3679	690
Intercon Associates Inc	7372	2853
Intercon Chemical Co	2842	53
Intercon Inc	3679	331
Intercon Industries Inc	5065	523
Intercon Solutions Inc	5093	140
Intercon Truck Equipment Inc	5531	46
Interconnect Computer Cabling Services Inc	1731	1111
Interconnect Devices Inc	3679	173
Interconnect Systems Inc	3674	230
Interconnect Technology Inc	3613	158
Interconnect West	5961	188
Interconnect Wiring Harnesses Inc	3694	25
Interconsal Associates Inc	5065	307
Intercontinental Asset Management Group Ltd	6282	613
Intercontinental Auto Parts Inc	5013	338
Inter-Continental Corp	2653	107
Intercontinental Energy Group LLC	4911	571
InterContinental Life Corp	6311	133
Intercontinental Lubricants Corp	2992	44
InterContinental National Bank	6021	390
Intercontinental Television Group Inc	6799	81
IntercontinentalExchange Inc	6719	56
Inter-County Co-Op Publishing Association Inc	2711	436

Company Name	SIC	Rank
Intercounty Engineering Inc	1623	335
Inter-County title Company of El Dorado	6361	28
InterDent Inc	8072	1
InterDigital Inc	6794	11
Interdyn	7379	53
Interdyn AKA	7379	54
Interdyne Inc	3069	254
Interep Associates Inc	5065	283
Intereum Inc	5021	21
Interface and Control Systems Inc	7371	206
Interface Cable Assemblies And Services Corp	1731	384
Interface Consulting Solutions Inc	7379	1142
Interface Displays and Controls Inc	3812	116
Interface Electronics Inc	3577	413
Interface Inc	2273	5
Interface Logic Systems Inc	7629	54
Interface Media Group	7819	53
Interface Multimedia Inc	7336	51
Interface Technologies Inc (Raleigh North Carolina)	7379	758
InterfaceFLOR LLC	2273	16
Inter-Faith Food Shuttle	7389	744
Interfaith Older Adult Programs Inc	8322	129
Interferometrics Inc	8731	312
Interfilm Holdings Inc	3081	10
Interflight Services Inc	8742	253
Interfoods Of America Inc	5812	196
Interform Commercial Interiors Inc	5021	92
Inter-Global Inc	3648	32
Interglobal Partners LLC	8742	684
Intergolf Vacations	4725	52
Intergraph Corp	7373	21
Intergrated Industrial Systems Inc	3547	5
Intergrated Networking Technologies LLC	1731	1271
Intergroup Corp	6513	18
InterGroup International Ltd	3339	21
Interhealth Nutraceuticals Inc	2834	282
Interim Healthcare Inc	7363	92
Interim Pastor Ministries Inc	7389	193
Interim Solutions for Government LLC	8748	181
Interimage Inc	7371	848
Interior Architects Inc	7389	645
Interior Concepts Inc	5712	82
Interior Design Associates Inc	7389	806
Interior Design Force Inc	7389	2339
Interior Investments LLC	5712	22
Interior Office Solutions Inc	5712	74
Interior Plant Design Inc	7389	1657
Interior Space Design Inc	7389	1460
Interior Space Management of Michigan Inc	7389	2354
Interior Supply Inc	5031	162
Interior Systems Contract Group Inc	7389	585
Interior Systems Design Inc	7372	3271
Interkal LLC	2531	32
Interlab Inc	3559	343
Interlaken Technology Corp	3829	314
Interlatin Inc	5084	281
Interlectric Corp	3641	18
Interleukin Genetics Inc	2835	67
Interlex Communications	7311	320
Interline Brands Inc	5211	7
Interline Insurance Services Inc	6411	28
Interlink Communication Systems Inc	5045	244
Interlink Computers Inc	5734	307
Interlink Electronics Inc	3577	348
Interlink Global Corp	4813	293
Interlink Networks Inc	7372	1318
Interlink Technologies	7371	710
Interlink Us Network Ltd	4899	241
interlinkONE Inc	7372	2645
Interlock Industries Inc	2952	6
Intermap Technologies Inc	7389	755
Intermarine LLC	1381	27
Intermark Communications Inc	7311	191
Intermark Design Group Inc	7389	1995
Intermatic Inc	3612	18
Intermdia Cable Advertising Dept	7313	31
Intermec Inc	3577	24
Intermec Technologies Corp	3577	25
InterMed Holdings Inc	3842	293
Intermedia Group Inc	7373	153
Intermedia Interactive Software Inc	7371	571
Intermedia Print Communications	7311	1003
IntermediaNET Inc	7379	155
IntermediaNet Inc	4813	251
Intermessage Communications Inc	5999	213
Intermet Corp	3325	2
Intermet Metals Services Inc	5051	466
Intermet Stevensville	3363	34
Intermetra Corp	5065	193
InterMetro Communications Inc	4899	139
Intermex Wire Transfers Inc	4822	10
Intermodal Cartage Company Inc	4214	13
Intermountain Air LLC	5088	51
Intermountain Business Forms Inc	5112	79
Intermountain Color Inc	2759	52
Intermountain Community Bancorp	6712	320
Intermountain Concrete Co	4213	2261
Intermountain Design Inc	2823	6
Intermountain Electric Inc	1731	152

Company Name	SIC	Rank
Intermountain Health Care Inc	8062	23
Intermountain Industries Inc	4924	39
Intermountain Rural Electric Association	4911	182
Intermountain Technology Group	5045	175
Intermountain Traffic Safety Inc	3669	277
Intermountain Voice Messaging Systems Inc	7389	1461
Intermountain West Civil Constructors Inc	1623	209
Intermountain Wood Products Inc	5031	151
Intermune Inc	2834	251
Intern Inc	7371	1585
Internal Data Resources Inc	7379	620
Internal Telecommunication Systems Inc	1731	2325
Internap Network Services Corp	7379	49
Internatational Point Of Sale	3578	37
International A I	3523	286
International Abrasive Manufacturing Co	2844	204
International Access Inc	4813	511
International Advanced Materials Inc	8731	383
International Airmotive Holding Company Inc	7699	1
International Architectural Group LLC	3442	11
International Assemblers Inc	3679	282
International Automotive Components	3714	5
International Bag Applications Corp	5084	696
International Bakers Services Inc	2087	75
International Baler Corp	3569	116
International Bancorp of Miami Inc	6712	366
International Bancshares Corp	6712	66
International Bank of Commerce	6022	245
International Bank of Commerce Zapata	6022	762
International Bank of Miami NA	6021	173
International Banking Technologies LLC	8748	384
International Bar Code Systems Inc	3577	639
International Battery Inc	3691	18
International Beauty Products LLC	2844	147
International Bicycle Tours Inc	4725	59
International Biomedical Ltd	3842	136
International Bridge and Iron Co	3441	166
International Building Services	7349	178
International Building Technologies Group	2439	59
International Business Communications Inc	3086	23
International Business Machines Corp	3571	3
International Business Systems-United States Inc	7372	1832
International Car Parts Of New Hampshire LLC	5013	389
International Carbide Corp	3545	429
International Carbonic Inc	3581	9
International Casings Group Inc	2013	98
International Cellulose Corp	2621	60
International C-Food Marketing	5146	37
International Checkout Inc	7379	471
International Chemical Co	2842	161
International Chimney Corp	1741	7
International Cigar Bar of Tampa	5993	1
International Coatings Company Inc	2891	69
International Coil Inc	3612	91
International Cold Storage Co	3585	37
International Color Posters Inc	2759	181
International Color Stock Inc	7336	167
International Comfort Products	3585	20
International Commodity Distributors Inc	5145	28
International Communications and Marketing Inc	8743	310
International Communications Research Inc	8732	68
International Computer Marketing Corp	5045	558
International Computer Negotiations Inc	7379	310
International Computer Systems Inc	7322	49
International Construction Equipment Inc	7353	54
International Consulting Group Inc	7379	1012
International Consulting Resources Group	7361	338
International Contact Inc	4899	149
International Contact Technologies Inc	3825	230
International Container Systems	3089	262
International Contract Furnishings Inc	5021	28
International Control Services Inc	3672	27
International Convention And Event Services	7389	1546
International Converter Inc	3497	3
International Crankshaft Inc	3714	139
International Creative Data Industries Inc	3679	610
International Cryogenics Inc	3559	444
International Crystal Laboratories	3827	127
International Crystal Manufacturing Co	3679	661
International Cutting Die Inc	3544	458
International Daily News	2711	535
International Dairy Queen Inc	6794	18
International Data Collection Inc	8732	54
International Data Corp	8742	43

Company Name	SIC	Rank
International Data Group Inc	2741	2
International Decision Systems	7372	529
International Decoratives Company Inc	5193	19
International Dehydrated Foods Inc	2038	45
International Diagnostic Systems Corp	3829	250
International Dispensing Corp	3069	284
International Electric	1731	2182
International Electric Supply Corp	5065	9
International Electro Magnetic Inc	3825	330
International Electronic Machines Corp	3829	103
International Electronic Research Corp	3679	408
International Electronics Inc	3669	122
International Engineering and Manufacturing Inc	3429	88
International Environmental Corp	3585	92
International Equipment Distributors	3533	131
International Executive Service Corp	8748	295
International Expert Systems Inc	7372	3829
International Extrusion Corp	3442	43
International Fidelity Insurance Co	6351	43
International Film and Video Center Inc	7841	9
International Filter Manufacturing Corp	3569	216
International Financial Group Inc	6331	288
International Flavors and Fragrances Inc	2869	6
International Flora Technologies Ltd	2844	155
International Foam Products Inc	2396	23
International Food Bakeries Inc	2051	233
International Food Group Inc	5142	16
International Food Solutions	2099	45
International Forest Products Corp	5113	7
International Fruit Inc	2087	59
International Gamco Inc	2754	36
International Game Technology Inc	3999	3
International Generating Co	1629	36
International Global Metals Inc	5051	397
International Graphics Inc	2761	27
International Group Inc	2911	40
International Healthcare Services Inc	6324	91
International Historic Films Inc	7822	32
International Housing Div	1521	129
International Hydraulics Inc	3089	1168
International Hydronics Corp	8734	136
International Imaging Materials Inc	3955	4
International Immunology Corp	2835	55
International Industries Inc	5031	23
International Information Services	7372	3830
International Information Technology Team	7379	820
International Inspirations	3961	8
International Inventory Management LLC	3559	310
International Isotopes Inc	3823	187
International Laminating Corp	3083	73
International Language Services Inc	7389	2451
International Laser Group Inc	3861	26
International Launch Services Inc	3812	10
International Lease Finance Corp	7359	13
International Leisure Hosts Ltd	7011	224
International Lottery and Totalizator Systems Inc	3578	22
International Lubrication and Fuel Consultants Inc	8731	238
International Machine and Tool Inc	3599	1411
International Machine and Welding Inc	7353	29
International Machine Technology Inc	3559	399
International Machinery Sales Inc	3499	94
International Machining Inc	3599	989
International Managed Care Strategies Inc	6324	115
International Management Group	7922	1
International Manufacturing Services Inc	3676	14
International Marketing Specialists Inc	5084	879
International Marketing Strategies Inc	2721	446
International Masters Publishers Inc	7331	18
International Material Handling Equipment Ltd	3535	191
International Meat Company Inc	5147	118
International Mechanical Design Inc	8711	681
International Medcom Inc	3829	399
International Medical Group Inc	6411	71
International Medical Industries Inc	3841	294
International Meeting Planners Ltd	7389	2359
International Merchant Services	5044	35
International Metals and Chemicals Group	3471	3
International Metals Reclamation Company Inc	3341	18
International Microwave Corp	3669	174
International Millennium Consultants Inc	7363	319
International Minerals Corp	1041	11
International Molding Machine Co	3559	501
International Monetary Systems Ltd	7389	682
International Moving Service	4213	2799
International Muffler Co	3714	397
International Museum Corp	7389	504
International Packaging Corp	3499	39
International Packaging Inc	7389	1200
International Paper Co	2631	1
International Paper Co Land and Timber Div	0831	2

Company Name	SIC	Rank
International Paper Foodservice Business	2656	2
International Parallel Machines Inc	3625	171
International Patterns Inc	3993	31
International Playthings LLC	5092	12
International Polymers Corp	4953	95
International Power Dc Power Supplies Inc	3679	589
International Precision Components Corp	3089	212
International Precision Inc	3599	1808
International Precision Machining	3599	739
International Precision Parts Corp	5013	354
International Process Equipment Company Inc	3532	81
International Protection Group LLC	5065	348
International Protection Systems Inc	7381	219
International Purchase Systems Inc	5045	43
International Purchasing and Supply Inc	5045	1058
International Quality and Productivity Center	8244	1
International Quality Consultants Inc	8742	358
International Radiation Detectors Inc	3674	452
International Rags Ltd	5093	101
International Recovery Associates Inc	7322	112
International Rectifier Corp	3674	32
International Rectifier HiRel Products LLC	3612	20
International Refining and Manufacturing Co	2992	16
International Registries Inc	8742	500
International Remote Imaging Systems Inc	3826	16
International Renaissance Festivals Ltd	7922	90
International Resistive Company Inc	3676	3
International Resources Group Ltd	8742	285
International Respiratory Systems Inc	5047	281
International Restaurant Equipment and Supplies	5046	363
International Restaurant Equipment Company Inc	5046	355
International Roll-Call Corp	3579	50
International Safe Manufacturing Inc	5044	149
International Science and Technology Associates Inc	2741	480
International Securities Exchange Holdings Inc	6231	6
International Security Inc	5065	596
International Semiconductor Engineering Laboratories	8734	33
International Sensor Systems Inc	3674	416
International Sensor Technology Inc	3829	246
International Services Inc	8741	59
International Shell Inc	5146	28
International Shipholding Corp	4412	15
International Shipping Partners Inc	5088	80
International Smart Tan Network Inc	2721	386
International Software Engineering	7372	4512
International Software Integration Services Inc	8243	15
International Software Products	7371	1900
International Software Systems Inc (Greenbelt Maryland)	7371	699
International Solar Electric Technology Inc	8731	396
International Solutions Group Inc	7379	1252
International Space Enterprises Inc	3714	290
International Specialty Products	3643	120
International Specialty Products Inc	2869	11
International Speedway Corp	7948	3
International Sports Broadcasting LLC	4832	297
International Spring Co	3495	20
International Staple and Machine Co	3496	19
International Star Corp	3053	62
International Steel Services Inc	8711	251
International Stem Cell Corp	2834	413
International Strategy and Investment Group Inc	8732	72
International Sulphur Inc	2819	28
International Supplies And Construction LLC	5046	165
International System Strategies Inc	7373	928
International Systems and Controls Corp	3823	60
International Systems Management Inc	5734	283
International Systems Marketing Inc	7372	3617
International Systems Of America LLC	7629	9
International TechneGroup Inc	7373	353
International Technidyne Corp	3841	99
International Technology Concepts Inc	7371	1034
International Teknologies LLC	7379	1562
International Tela-Com Inc	1731	2135
International Telecommunications Components Inc	3679	806
International Telematics Corp	7373	1007
International Temperature Control	3823	433
International Textile Group Inc	3714	55
International Theatres Corp	5812	158
International Thermal Systems LLC	3567	21
International Thermocast Corp	2541	28
International Thermoproducts	5084	633
International Tool Inc	3599	1549

Company Name	SIC	Rank
International Tool Machines Of Florida Inc	3541	168
International Totalizing Systems Corp	3661	178
International Towers Inc	1623	460
International Trade Consultants Inc	3281	47
International Trade Information Inc	7389	1818
International Transcription	7389	1970
International Transducer Corp	3825	54
International Transmissionn Co	4911	255
International Transport Solutions Inc	8999	48
International Transportation Service Inc	2047	6
International Travel and Resorts Inc	4724	103
International Travel Specialists Inc (Irvine California)	4724	59
International Tray Pads and Packaging Inc	2671	57
International Truck Sales Of Richmond Inc	5511	479
International Typeface Corp	7372	1808
International Valve and Instrument Corp	7699	221
International Veneer Company Inc	2435	5
International Wafer Service Inc	5065	732
International Waterjet Parts Inc	3589	232
International Wholesale Supply Inc	5099	53
International Window Corp	3442	51
International Window Corp (Hayward California)	3442	29
International Window-Arizona Inc	3442	53
International Wire Group Inc	3357	6
International Wireless Corp	4812	119
International Wood Industries Inc	2436	4
Internet 123 Inc	5045	972
Internet Advancement Inc	7374	131
Internet Advertising Group Inc	7371	418
Internet Alliance Inc	5043	36
Internet America Inc	7372	2316
Internet At Cyber Mesa	4813	417
Internet Brands Inc	7389	236
Internet Broadcasting Systems Inc	7375	94
Internet Business Enterprises And Marketing Inc	5734	417
Internet Business Systems Inc	7375	223
Internet Concepts Inc	7336	65
Internet Connections Inc	7374	391
Internet Corporation for Assigned Names and Numbers	7371	479
Internet Customer Solutions	7389	1797
Internet Data Technology	7372	3053
Internet Development Company LLC	4813	506
Internet Development Inc	7372	2599
Internet Doctors Dba DockNet	4813	703
Internet Effective	7379	1521
Internet Express Inc	4813	421
Internet Ideas Work LLC	7374	328
Internet Infinity Inc	5099	155
Internet Junction Corp	4813	384
Internet Montana	7379	174
Internet Nebraska	4899	95
Internet Pipeline Inc	7372	714
Internet Professionals Inc	7375	268
Internet Programming and Consulting Inc	7372	4513
Internet Resource Center Inc	7374	392
Internet Security Advisors	7379	1169
Internet Specialties West Inc	7375	154
Internet Texoma Inc	7374	273
Internet Transaction Solutions Inc	8741	188
Internet World Media Inc	7375	44
Internetwork Services Inc	7379	623
InterNetworking Technologies Inc	7373	279
InterNetworX Systems Inc	7372	4248
Interni Design Inc	7389	476
Internodal International Inc	7372	3491
InterNoded Inc	7372	3460
Interocean Industries Inc	3812	142
Interop JV	8711	297
Inter-Pacific Corp	5139	18
Inter-Pacific Inc	5065	497
Interpacific Investors Services Inc	6211	284
Interpak Inc	3089	1179
Interpark Inc	7521	3
Interphase Corp	3577	250
Interphase Technologies Inc	3812	179
Interplast Inc	2824	15
Interplastic Corp	5169	18
Interplay Entertainment Corp	7372	4111
Interplay Productions	7372	702
Interplex Engineered Products Inc	3469	195
Interplex Industries Inc	3469	22
Interplex International LLC	7373	986
Interplex Nas Inc	3544	84
Interpoint Corp	3629	11
Interpolymer Corp	2821	92
Interpool Inc	7359	25
Interpower Corp	5063	236
Interpretive Software Inc	7372	3319
Interprint Inc	2752	411
Interprise Inc	7389	1216
Interpro Inc	7371	661
Interprose Inc (Reston Virginia)	8743	158
Interpublic Group of Companies Inc	7311	7
INTERROLL Corp	3535	24
Interscan Corp	3826	75

Company Name	SIC	Rank
Interscope Manufacturing Inc	3599	595
InterSearch Group Inc	7372	1073
InterSec Research Corp	6282	341
Intersections Inc	7374	29
Intersense Inc	3643	115
Intersight	5734	436
Intersil Corp	3674	47
Intersoft Corp	7371	783
InterSoft Group	8999	93
Intersoft Inc	7371	197
Intersoft Systems Inc (Beaverton Oregon)	7372	3538
Intersol Inc	7389	2453
Intersol Industries Inc	3625	331
Intersource Recovery Systems Inc	3569	196
Interspace Battery Inc	3356	36
Interspace Office Furniture Inc	5021	98
Intersphere Communications Ltd	2741	229
Interstaff Inc	7363	257
Interstate Battery System of America Inc	5063	9
Interstate Battery System of Dallas Inc	5013	24
Interstate Bearing Systems	5085	153
Interstate Bearing Technology Inc	3519	14
Interstate Cablevision Co	4841	153
Interstate Carrier Xpress	4213	352
Interstate Cash Register Inc	7699	107
Interstate Chemical Company Inc	5169	95
Interstate Cleaning Corp	7349	46
Interstate Commodities Inc	5153	16
Interstate Companies Inc	5063	30
Interstate Concrete And Asphalt Co	1611	186
Interstate Diesel Service Inc	5013	82
Interstate Distributor Co	4213	97
Interstate Distributors Of Dunn Inc	5072	72
Interstate Edp and Direct Mail Center Inc	7331	47
Interstate Electric Company Inc	5046	29
Interstate Electronics Corp	3812	34
Interstate Equipment Corp	3441	282
Interstate Foam and Supply Inc	3069	70
Interstate Food Processing Corp	2037	30
Interstate General Company LP	4953	164
Inter-State Hardwoods Company Inc	2426	19
Interstate Highway Construction Inc	1611	31
Interstate Highway Sign Corp	3993	43
Interstate Hotels and Resorts Inc	7011	46
Interstate Industrial Technology Inc	3625	386
Interstate Industries Of Mississippi LLC	3694	27
Interstate Intermodal Inc	4213	1859
Interstate Lift Trucks Inc	5084	131
Interstate Logos LLC	3993	164
Interstate Meat Distributors Inc	5147	40
Interstate National Dealer Services Inc	7549	9
Interstate NationaLease Inc	7513	14
Interstate Paper Supply Company Inc	2679	40
Interstate Plastic Inc	3084	30
Interstate Power and Light Co	4931	24
Interstate Printing Co	2752	516
Interstate Resources Inc	2631	14
Interstate Screw Corp	5072	109
Interstate Security	7382	165
Interstate Service Of Fergus Fls	5083	107
Interstate Supply Co	5023	49
Interstate Tool Corp	5084	880
Interstate Treating Inc	7353	32
Interstate Truck Equipment Inc	7538	28
Interstate Truckers Inc	7549	28
Interstate Van Lines Inc	4213	124
Interstate Waste Technologies Inc	6552	230
Interstate Window Corp	3442	98
Interstate Wood Products Inc	4213	2652
Interstates Construction Services Inc	1731	72
Interstates Control Systems Inc	3829	79
Intersystem Concepts Inc	7372	2157
InterSystems Corp	7371	108
Intersystems USA Inc	3575	8
Intertape Polymer Group (Columbia South Carolina)	2672	3
Intertec Corp	3559	126
InterTech Computer Products Inc	7378	21
Inter-Tech Corp	3572	98
Intertech Development Co	3569	123
Intertech Digital Entertainment Inc	7622	3
InterTech Group Inc	2821	6
Intertech Inc	7371	690
InterTech Information Management Inc	7371	705
Intertech Plastics Inc	3089	649
Intertech Software Consulting Inc	7379	951
Intertech Trading Corp	5045	744
Intertech Training and Consulting Inc	7379	901
Intertech USA Inc	7371	1482
Intertek CM-USA-Deer Park Lab	8731	185
Intertek Laboratories Inc	3812	143
Intertrade International Inc	5064	157
Intertrade Ltd	5065	52
InterTrade Systems Corp	7372	1860
Intertrend Communications Inc	7311	682
InterTrust Technologies Corp	7372	4157
Interval International Inc	7389	177
Interval Leisure Group Inc	8999	17
Inter-Valley Health Plan Inc	6324	74
InterVascular Inc	3845	72
Intervest Bancshares Corp	6021	60

Company Name	SIC	Rank
Intervest Construction Inc	1521	28
intervest Mortgage Investment Com	6162	63
Intervest National Bank	6022	683
Intervet Inc	2836	13
Intervid Inc	7382	69
Intervideo Duplication Services	7336	331
InterVISTAS Consulting Group	8249	17
Intervoice Services Inc	8748	51
Interweave Press LLC	2731	152
Interwest Construction Company Inc	1541	212
Interwest Construction Inc	1623	129
Interwest Medical Corp	8051	29
InterWest Partners LLC	6799	117
Interwest Safety Supply Inc	3993	153
Inter-Wire Products Inc	5051	223
InterWorking Labs Inc	7379	848
InterWorld Communications Inc (Torrance California)	4899	104
Intesel Inc	7372	2464
Intesource Inc	7371	659
inTEST Corp	3825	40
Intetics Co	7372	756
Intetnational Marking Group	8742	545
Intevac Inc	3559	46
Intex Corp	2295	3
Intex Solutions Inc	7372	892
Inthinc Technology Solutions Inc	3812	92
Intier Automotive Inc (Novi Michigan)	2211	2
INTL FCStone Inc	6719	73
Intometal Inc	3469	186
InTouch Inc	8999	179
Intouch Solutions Inc	8742	239
Intown Holding Company LLC	6712	663
InTown Suites Management Inc	7011	124
Intoximeters Inc	3829	145
Intra Action Corp	3827	101
Intra Computer Inc	3823	406
Intra Corp	3545	60
Intrabay Automation Inc	3674	479
Intrac Systems Inc	7372	4306
Intracel Corp	8731	356
Intracellular Imaging Inc	7371	1706
Intraco Corp	7389	152
Intraco Inc	3523	271
Intracoastal City Drydock And Shipbuilding Inc	3731	56
Intracoastal Liquid Mud Inc	4214	26
Intra-Coastal Packing Inc	5144	22
Intracorp Real Estate LLC	6552	233
Intrado Inc	7389	138
Intradyn Inc	3577	554
Intrahome Technologies Inc	4813	599
Intraline Inc	5063	774
IntraLinks Holdings Inc	7372	263
Intralox LLC	3535	18
Intranet Communications Group Inc	1731	2403
Intrans Book Service	2731	363
Intransa Inc	5045	213
Intraop Medical Corp	3844	19
Intrapack Corp	3679	412
Intrasonics Inc	3599	2491
Intrasphere Technologies Inc	7373	304
Intratek Computer Inc	7378	22
InTrec Software Inc	7372	4514
Intren Inc	1623	46
Intrend International Inc	3679	896
Intrepid Capital Corp	6282	193
Intrepid Capital Management Inc	6282	164
Intrepid Detective Agency Inc	7381	162
Intrepid Enterprises Inc	1741	14
Intrepid Group Inc	7331	161
Intrepid Machine Inc	3469	296
Intrepid Molding Inc	3089	1382
Intrepid Potash Inc	1481	1
Intrepid Potash - Moab LLC	2812	11
Intrepid Systems	7372	4707
IntrexNet	4899	61
Intricate Grinding And Machine Specialties Inc	3449	36
Intricon Corp	3669	53
Intrinsix Corp	7371	343
Intri-Plex Technologies Inc	3469	116
Intrix Systems Group Inc	7372	1855
Intruder Inc	3999	168
Intrusion Inc	3577	397
INTRUST Bank NA	6021	27
INTRUST Financial Corp	6712	169
Intsel Steel West	5051	37
Intt America	7389	2144
Intuit Construction Business Solutions	7372	1951
Intuit Financial Services	7389	142
Intuit Inc	7372	10
Intuit Inc Personal Finance Div	7372	4135
Intuitive Business Solutions Inc	7373	1069
Intuitive Computers Inc	5734	271
Intuitive Manufacturing Systems Inc	7372	2220
Intuitive Research and Technology Corp	7373	425
Intuitive Solutions	7379	1231
Intuitive Surgical Inc	3842	10
Intuitive Technology Group LLC	7379	380
Intusoft	7372	3671
Inuvo Inc	7319	39
Invacare Corp	3842	9

Company Name	SIC	Rank
Invacare Technologies Corp	3842	30
Invecom Inc	5065	989
Invemed Associates Inc	6211	211
Inventec Manufacturing (North America) Corp	2259	1
Invention Cos	8999	31
Invention Machine Corp	7372	142
inVentiv Health Inc	8742	25
Inventive Systems Inc	3823	422
Inventix Manufacturing LLC	3364	19
Inventory Conversion Inc	5045	701
Inventory Locator Service LLC	7379	188
Inventrix Inc	7371	1778
Inventure Foods Inc	2099	34
Inventure Group Inc	7336	197
Inverness Capital Partners LP	6799	114
Inverness Corp	3999	77
Inverselogic LLC	4813	619
Invesco Distributors Inc	6722	203
INVESCO Mortgage Capital Inc	6798	2
Invesco Utilities Fund	6722	268
Invesco Van Kampen Municipal Trust	6726	25
INVEST Financial Corp	6211	131
Investcorp International Inc	6211	24
Investec	6552	181
Investech Research	2741	497
Investment Centers of America Inc	6799	194
Investment Counsel Co	6282	297
Investment Counselors of Maryland LLC	6282	195
Investment Directions Inc	6798	211
Investment Enterprises Inc	2759	102
Investment Property Exchange Service Inc	6289	25
Investment Scorecard Inc	7372	2340
Investment Support Systems Inc	7372	1871
Investment Systems Co	7379	1467
Investment Technologies	7372	4040
Investment Technology Group Inc	6719	65
Investment Trust Co	6282	468
INVESTools Inc	8299	7
Investor Force Inc	7375	105
Investor Relations International Inc	8742	448
Investorplace Media LLC	2741	165
Investors Advisory Services Inc	6282	574
Investors Bancorp Inc	6712	70
Investors Capital Holdings Ltd	6799	327
Investors Capital Management Group	8741	191
Investors FastTrak	7372	2882
Investors Heritage Capital Corp	6311	187
Investors Heritage Life Insurance Co	6311	144
Investors Life Insurance Company of North America	6311	141
Investors Management Corp	6719	17
Investors Real Estate Trust	6798	111
Investors Savings Bank	6029	4
Investors Title Accommodation Corp	6361	11
Investors Title Co	6361	20
Investors Title Co (Glendale California)	6361	37
Investors Title Insurance Co (Columbia South Carolina)	6361	41
Investors Title management Services Inc	6361	12
InvestorsBancorp Inc	6035	205
InvestorsBank	6022	739
Invidi Technologies Corp	7371	1210
Inviro Medical	3841	214
Invisa Inc	3823	491
InvisibleHand Networks Inc	7372	1397
Invision Power Services Inc	7374	304
Invision Research Corp	7372	3137
InVision Software Inc	7372	2926
Invivo Corp	3845	48
Invizion Inc	8748	98
Invo Spline Inc	3545	72
Invodo Inc	7372	1437
Invoke Solutions Inc	5045	182
Involta Inc	7371	614
Involve Test And Control Inc	1731	2506
Invue Security Products Inc	3089	342
Inwesco Inc	3315	26
Inwood Laboratories Inc	2834	86
Inwood Office Furniture Inc	2521	34
INX Inc	5045	52
Inx International Ink Co	2893	3
Inyo Register	2711	841
I-O Corp	3674	237
Iobjectsolutions Inc	7374	353
Iochem Corp	2819	74
IOGEAR	3577	152
iolo technologies LLC	7372	5157
Ion Alloy Wheels	5013	156
Ion Beam Milling Of New Hampshire Inc	3674	424
Ion Corp	3699	148
Ion Exhibits LLC	5046	150
ION Geophysical Corp	1382	18
ion interactive Inc	7379	1154
Ion Laboratories Inc	2834	328
Ion Media Network - Houston	4833	18
ION Media Networks Inc	4833	73
Ion Media Networks - Knoxville	4833	8
Ion Metrics Inc	3812	227
Ion Physics Co	3621	103

Company Name	SIC	Rank	Company Name	SIC	Rank	Company Name	SIC	Rank
Ion Technologies Corp	5084	788	IR Industries Inc	5049	123	Irwin Enterprises Inc	2752	1264
ION Television	4833	9	Ir Mueller Corp	7381	179	Irwin Financial Corp	6712	116
Ion Television Denver	4833	10	Ira E Clark Detective Agency Inc	7381	54	Irwin Industries Inc	1629	19
IONA Technologies	7371	776	Ira Green Inc	3999	62	Irwin International Inc	5088	31
iOne Technology Inc	7379	63	Ira Higdon Grocery Company Inc	5149	47	Irwin Manufacturing Corp	2341	10
Ionglyph Inc	7371	1905	Ira Middleswarth and Son Inc	2096	37	Irwin P Sharpe and Associates Business Research and Surveys Div	7372	4515
Ionic Marketing	7331	38	Irama Corp	7311	479			
Ionidea Inc	7371	1040	Iran Times Inc	2711	572	Irwin Printing Company Inc	2759	389
IOP Inc	3841	367	Irathane Systems Co	3089	457	Irwin Seating Co	2531	13
iOR Consulting and Design	7336	260	Irby Construction Co	1623	34	Irwin-Hodson Co	2752	417
IOR Technologies Inc	7389	1819	Irdata Corp	3699	306	IS Motorsport Inc	5065	982
Iota Consulting Services Inc	5049	137	Iredell Memorial Hospital Inc	8062	164	IS Parts International Inc	3443	167
Iota Holding Co	3648	22	Ireland Bancorp Ltd	6712	336	ISA Consulting	7373	253
Iovation Inc	7371	262	Ireland Bank	6022	479	ISA Internationale Inc	7322	206
Iowa E P S Products Inc	2821	128	Ireland Stapleton Pryor and Pascoe PC	8111	406	Isaac Fair Corp	7371	77
Iowa Engineered Processes Corp	3559	403	Ireland Technologies Inc	5734	235	Isaacson Miller Inc	7361	54
Iowa First Bancshares Corp	6712	503	Irell and Manella LLP	8111	198	Isabel Bloom LLC	3272	68
Iowa Information Inc	2711	511	Ire-Tex Corp	3089	1558	Isabella Bank and Trust	6022	786
Iowa Interstate Railroad Ltd	4011	42	Irex Corp	5033	4	Isabelle's Kitchen Inc	2099	163
Iowa Lamb Buyers	2011	138	Irgens Development Partners	6552	142	Isc Datacom Inc	3663	364
Iowa Lamb Corp	2011	85	Irides LLC	4813	616	Isc Engineering LLC	3629	76
Iowa Laser Technology Inc	3499	62	Irides Web Hosting	7372	2494	Isc Inc	2013	146
Iowa Machinery and Supply Company Inc	7699	66	IRIDEX Corp	3845	51	Isc Instrument Service Co	3829	461
			Iridio Inc	2796	10	Isco Inc	3599	2436
Iowa Mold and Engineering Inc	3089	1291	Iris Creative Group LLC	7311	715	ISCO Inc (Lincoln Nebraska)	3823	35
Iowa Mold Tooling Company Inc	3536	5	Iris Medical Inc	7372	2101	ISCO Industries LLC	3084	32
Iowa National Properties LLC	6512	65	Iris Software Inc	7371	67	ISCO International Inc	3825	116
Iowa Network Services Inc	4813	78	Iris Technlogies Inc	8731	366	Isd Audio Video Inc	1731	2270
Iowa Newspapers Inc	2711	45	Iris USA Inc	3089	406	ISDN*tek	3669	246
Iowa One Call	1731	1308	Iris Window Coverings	1799	33	ISE America Inc	2015	52
Iowa Pacific Processors Inc	2011	94	Irish Construction	1623	54	ISE Inc	7371	828
Iowa Physicians Clinic Medical Foundation	8011	38	Irish Homes Inc	2452	1	iSeatzcom	7379	236
			Irm Group Inc	3829	395	iSECUREtrac Corp	3669	149
Iowa Realty Company Inc	6531	453	IRM Inc	7322	173	Isee Systems Inc	7372	4307
Iowa Rotocast Plastics Inc	3089	699	Irmo Equipment Rental Inc	7359	227	Iselann Moss Industries Inc	7699	206
Iowa Select Farms LP	0213	11	Irmscher Inc	1542	293	Iseli Co	3451	3
Iowa State Bank and Trust Co	6022	310	Irmscher Suppliers Inc	5031	288	Isemoto Contracting Company Ltd	1629	54
Iowa State Daily	5994	2	iRobot Inc	3569	9	Iserv Co	7375	64
Iowa Steel and Wire Co	3315	24	Iron and Metals Inc	5093	63	Iserve Technologies Inc	4813	692
Iowa-American Water Co	4941	35	Iron Brick Associates LLC	7373	322	iSeva Inc	7389	82
IP Commerce Inc	7372	1255	Iron City Distributing Company Inc	5181	81	Isf Trading Inc	5146	11
Ip Elements LLC	7379	1311	Iron Data LLC	7372	254	ISG Novasoft	7373	215
Ip Fabrics Inc	7371	1598	Iron Data Solutions LLC Transportation Sector	7389	1104	Isg Solutions	5045	683
IP Video Networks Inc	3669	278				ISH Industries Inc	7371	231
IP5280 Communications Inc	4899	146	Iron Design	7336	236	Ishihara Corporation USA	2879	43
Ipaco Inc	5085	350	Iron Eagle Group Inc	1541	312	Isi Inc	5199	131
i-Pak DVD NA	7379	351	Iron Horse	5812	245	Isi Inspection Services Inc	7389	1142
IPALCO Enterprises Inc	4911	93	Iron Mountain Confidential Destruction LLC	4226	8	Isi/Pss Group JV	7373	955
iParty Corp	5947	10				Isi Telemanagement Solutions Inc	8748	201
Ipas	8399	12	Iron Mountain Inc	4226	1	ISI Telemanagement Systems	7371	224
iPass Inc	7374	41	Iron Mountain Information Management Inc	7389	544	ISI-Biz Inc	7372	4077
iPay Technologies LLC	7372	451				Isilon Systems Inc	5045	114
iPayment Inc	7389	57	Iron Mountain Off-Site Data Protection Inc	7379	107	ISIS Banner Personnel Service	7361	259
IPC Acquisition Corp	3661	15				Isis Corp	8748	234
Ipc Cal Flex Inc	3672	297	Iron Works Enterprises Inc	3715	57	Isis Pharmaceuticals Inc	2834	137
IPC Communication Services Inc	3695	6	Iron-A-Way Inc	3633	6	Isis Supply and Service Co	5051	495
IPC Inc	7699	123	IronCAD	7373	329	Isis Surface Mounting	3699	76
Ipc Power Resistors International Inc	3625	156	Ironclad Performance Wear Corp	5099	46	iSite Design Inc	7379	385
IPC Print Services Inc	2721	65	IronPlanet Inc	7389	325	Iskra Computers USA Inc	5045	794
Ipc Printing Inc	2752	1532	IronPort	7372	967	iSky Inc	7379	28
IPC Systems Holdings Corp	3661	13	Ironrock Capital Inc	3253	7	Island Air	4512	55
IPC Technologies Inc (Richmond Virginia)	7379	362	Ironsoft Ltd	7371	1329	Island Computer Products Inc	7372	559
			Ironstone Bank	6022	79	Island Def Jam Music Group	7389	561
IPC the Hospitaist Company Inc	8099	15	Irontite By Kwik-Way	2891	91	Island Dehy Inc	2048	134
iPCS Inc (Schaumburg Illinois)	4812	12	Ironton Publications Inc	2711	258	Island Dental Supply Co	5047	167
IPD Printing	2752	172	Ironware Technologies LLC	7372	2825	Island Electric Maui Inc	1731	1646
IPEC	3089	278	Ironwood Communications	3669	215	Island Hospitality Management Inc	8742	83
Ipeco Holdings Inc	5088	92	Ironwood Electronics Inc	3679	425	Island Lighting and Power Systems	1731	1684
IPExtreme Inc	7372	2184	Ironwood Industries Inc	3089	775	Island Lincoln-Mercury Inc	5511	596
Ipg Holdings Inc (Bradenton Florida)	2672	7	Ironwood Lithographers Inc	2752	291	Island One Resorts Management Co	7041	3
IPG Photonics Corp	3679	42	Ironwood Pharmaceuticals Inc	2834	165	Island Press-Center For Resource Economics	2731	236
iPhotonix	3629	54	Ironwood Plastics Inc	3089	374			
iPhrase Technologies Inc	7372	1214	Ironwood Software Inc	7371	1866	Island Ready-Mix Concrete Inc	3273	35
Ipitek Photonic Technology	3669	72	Ironworks Consulting LLC	7379	330	Island Tech Services LLC	7379	1177
IPKeys Technologies LLC	7371	597	Iroquois Gas Transmission Company LP	4922	33	Island Transportation Corp	4213	520
iplacement Inc	7361	213				Island Water Sports Inc	5941	32
IPM Lithographics	2752	1806	Iroquois Industries Inc	3465	41	Isle of Capri Casinos Inc	7999	18
IPM Precision Inc	5084	919	Irotas Manufacturing Company Inc	3555	30	Isler and Co	8721	58
IPOP Management Inc	3829	9	Irotas Manufacturing Company LLC	3555	55	Islero Inc	5065	454
Ipower Distribution Group LLC	7389	229	Irrc Solutions	7372	4068	Ism Services Inc	7376	45
Ipr Systems Inc	3679	815	Irrigation Machine and Supply Inc	3561	171	Ismeca USA Inc	5084	532
Ipremise Inc	4813	492	Irrigation Supply Inc	5087	191	Iso Group Inc	5088	49
Ipressroom Inc	7372	3405	Irrigators Inc	5083	155	ISO Industries Inc	5172	54
IPRO Tech	7372	875	Irrometer Company Inc	3829	144	Iso Plastics Corp	3089	896
iProspect	8999	43	Irv Seaver Motorcycles	5012	71	Iso Services Inc	7375	30
I-Prospect Inc	7371	647	Irvco Asphalt and Gravel Inc	1442	75	Isochem Colors Inc	2865	26
IPS of Boston	7371	933	Irvine Access Floors Inc	1752	3	ISODISC/Software Services Group	3695	51
Ipso Facto Consulting Inc	7371	1835	Irvine Company Inc	6552	34	Isodyne Inc	3663	400
Ipsos-ASI Inc	7389	324	Irvine Compiler Corp	7372	3539	iSoft Integration Systems Inc	7371	444
Ipsos-Vantis	7389	563	Irvine Electronics Inc	3672	113	I-Solutions Global Ltd	7371	770
IPS-Sendero	7372	1080	Irvine Scientific Sales Company Inc	2836	37	Isom Industrial Metals Inc	3599	2183
Ipswich Shellfish Company Inc	5146	19	Irvine Sensors Corp	3674	242	Isomedix Inc	8099	51
Ipswitch Inc	7372	1245	Irving Gravel Co	1442	33	Isomet Corp	3641	29
Ipt Northwest LLC	5045	780	Irving Langbaum Associates Inc	5065	612	Isonas Inc	3669	36
IPV Inc	3732	86	Irving Materials Inc	3273	25	IsongCom Inc	7372	4116
Iq Products Co	5169	79	Irving Oil Corp	5983	9	Isopur Fluid Technologies Inc	5085	413
IQ Software Services	7372	1124	Irving Press Inc	2752	1181	Isoray Medical Inc	3841	271
IQ Stored Inc	7371	697	Irving Tool and Manufacturing Company Inc	3444	134	Isotec International Inc	2821	150
IQ Systems Inc (Reno Nevada)	5045	376				Isotek Corp	3676	29
Iqe Inc	3674	255	Irvin's Country Tinware	3645	31	Isotemp Research Inc	3677	61
IQMS	7372	1265	Irvin's Inc	5063	423	Iso-Tex Diagnsotics Inc	2834	277
IQor Inc	7372	152	Irwin Automation Inc	3599	1393	Isothermal Systems Research	8711	386
IQS Inc	7372	2699	Irwin Car and Equipment Inc	3535	83	Iso-Trude Inc	3089	856
IQue Inc	7372	2082	Irwin Electric Membership Corp	4911	327	Isovac Engineering Inc	7389	2165

Company Name	SIC	Rank
Isovolta Inc	3644	23
Isp Associates Inc	7375	261
ISP Chemical Products Inc	2869	16
ISP Chemicals Inc	2869	17
ISP Sutton Laboratories	2844	132
ISPcom	4899	28
iSqFt	7389	1098
ISR Group Inc	7389	449
ISRA Surface Vision Inc	7373	882
Israel Discount Bank of New York	6022	59
Israel Katcher	7378	76
Israeloff Trattner and Company CPA's PC	8721	15
Isram World of Travel	4725	12
Isramco Inc	1311	145
ISS Inc	3823	333
ISS Solutions	8741	50
ISS (USA) Inc	5049	70
Iss/Wai LLC	7381	202
Issaquah Dental Lab Inc	3843	28
Issgr Inc	2752	961
Isspro Inc	3714	306
Issues and Answers Network Inc	8742	254
Issues Management Inc	7389	1264
IssueTrak	7372	1553
Ista Pharmaceuticals Inc	2835	10
iStar Financial Inc	6798	37
i-STAT Corp	3845	43
Istech Inc	7373	812
Isthmus Engineering and Manufacturing Coop	3599	315
Isthmus Publishing	2721	308
Istonish Inc	7379	604
Istor Networks Inc	7379	784
ISTS Worldwide Inc	7374	114
ISU Insurance Services of Colorado Inc	6331	282
iSuppli Corp	7379	136
Isupportisp LLC	4813	507
ISYS/Biovation	7372	2108
Isys Business Systems	7372	5022
Isys Inc	7379	342
Isys Search Software (Englewood Colorado)	7372	1462
IT Crown Services Inc	7379	1480
It Partshouse	7373	883
IT Pathworx Ltd	7373	898
It People Corp	7379	462
It Professional Recruiting LLC	7379	928
IT Remarketing Inc	7373	787
IT Services Marketing Association	8732	51
It Services Of Utah Inc	5734	342
IT Source Corp	7371	600
IT Staff Inc	7371	1415
It Strategies International Corp	7377	20
IT Support Guys	7379	759
It Takes Two Inc	2771	25
It Trailblazers LLC	7389	1147
It Wizard Inc	7373	1200
It Works Inc	7371	1505
IT4LA	7379	268
ITA Inc	4213	945
ITA International LLC	8742	363
ITA Software Inc	7371	82
ITAAS Inc	7371	307
ITAC Systems Inc	3577	292
Ital Sales Inc	5065	673
Italia Foods Inc	2038	74
Italia Moda Inc	5094	69
Italian Bakery Inc	5461	45
Italian French Baking Co	5149	180
Italian Peoples Bakery Inc	2051	32
Italian Rose Garlic Products Inc	2099	105
Italianni's	5812	322
Italk Global Communications Inc	4813	493
iTalk LLC	7372	118
Italk Telecontracting Inc	1731	2203
Itasca Construction Associates Inc (Itasca Illinois)	1542	114
Itasca Fire Protection District 1	7389	2155
Itasca-Bemidji Inc	3679	318
Itasca-Mantrap Co-op Electrical Association	4911	368
ITC Holdings Corp	4911	58
ITC Inc (Hunt Valley Maryland)	3255	15
ITC Integrated Systems Inc	7372	2927
Itc Systems	3577	298
ITCN Inc	7371	298
ITCS Inc	7389	1250
Itcube LLC	7371	638
ITD California Inc	5014	29
ITE Distributing	5044	116
Ite LLC	3537	87
ITEC Attractions Inc	7832	23
I-Tech Automation Inc	7372	2678
Itech Retail Inc	7372	4131
iTech US	7379	68
ITEDO Software LLC	7372	3721
Itek Graphics LLC	2752	787
Item House Inc	2337	10
Iten Chevrolet Co	5511	314
Iten Industries Inc	3089	347
Iteq Integrated Technologies Inc	7373	273
Iteris Inc	3663	59
ITEX Corp (Bellevue Washington)	7389	616
Itfusion Inc	7379	1117
ITG Inc	6289	13
Itg - International Technology Group LLC	3841	394
ITG Software Inc	7371	21
ITG-MEDEV Inc	5122	56
Ithacan Publishing Company Inc	2711	400
Ithaco Space Systems Inc	3812	111
ITM Associates Inc	7372	2646
ITM Electronics Inc	1731	2561
Itmedica Inc	7338	55
Ito En (USA) Inc	2086	67
Ito Industrics Inc	3672	187
ITOCHU International Inc	5082	33
ITOCHU Technology Inc	3577	220
Itoh Denki USA Inc	3535	55
iTok LLC	7372	1225
Itouchless Housewares and Products Inc	3089	1105
Itox LLC	5045	565
ITP Business Communications Inc	7372	3775
Itr Concession Company Holdings LLC	4785	1
iTrendz Inc	7373	504
Itron Inc	3825	3
Itronics Inc	8731	345
Itronics Metallurgical Inc	5093	134
It's Academic of Illinois Inc	3089	1031
ITS Barcode Solutions	5045	1009
Its Engineered Systems Inc	3589	93
ITS Global Relocation Services	4213	2877
ITS Instrument Corp	3679	532
Its Telecommunications Systems Inc	1731	1421
Itscinc	7379	1287
ItsHotcom	5094	67
ITSM Academy Inc	8243	9
ITT Corp	3825	1
ITT Educational Services Inc	8249	2
ITT Federal Services Corp	3679	2
ITT Gilfillan Inc	3812	35
ITT - Goulds Pumps	3561	11
ITT Industries Inc Aerospace Controls Div	3592	3
ITT Industries Inc Bell and Gossett Div	3561	41
ITT Industries Inc Cannon Div	3678	9
ITT Industries Inc Conoflow Div	3679	241
ITT Industries Inc Engineered Valves Div	3494	18
ITT Industries Inc Flojet Div	3594	11
ITT Industries Inc Fluid Technology Div	3594	2
ITT Power Solutions Inc	3679	22
ITT Technical Institutes	8221	37
ITT Water and Wastewater USA Inc	3559	85
Ittner Bean and Grain Inc	5153	164
I-Tul Design and Software Inc	7379	1498
ITW American Safety Technologies	2851	59
ITW Angleboard	2631	10
ITW Ark-Les Corp	3643	15
ITW Bee Leitzke	3429	25
ITW BGK Finishing Systems	3433	31
ITW Chemtronics Inc	2899	87
ITW Deltar Tekfast	3089	122
ITW DeVilbiss	3589	35
ITW Drawform	3469	32
ITW Dymon	2899	81
ITW Dynatec	3569	81
ITW Electronic Component Packaging Systems	2671	39
ITW Fastex	3452	34
ITW Food Equipment Group LLC	3556	1
ITW Hi-Cone Div	3089	458
ITW Highland	3469	27
ITW Impro	3089	202
ITW Linx	3643	17
ITW Paktron Inc	3675	29
ITW Philadelphia Resins	2821	57
ITW Plastiglide Manufacturing Corp	3089	281
ITW Plexus	2891	36
ITW Poly Craft Systems	3563	50
ITW Ramset/Red Head	2891	25
ITW Ransburg Electrostatic Systems	3569	168
ITW Sexton	3411	8
ITW Shakeproof Assembly Components	3999	110
ITW Southland	3053	12
ITW Space Bag	3089	300
ITW Switches	3643	70
ITW Thielex	3089	731
ITW Waterbury Buckle Co	3965	18
ITW Workholding Group	3545	54
ItworldCom	4813	418
Itx Corp	7371	979
Itz Electric Inc	1731	1081
iUniverse Inc	2741	509
IV S LLC	7371	1815
Ivan Allen Furniture Co	2521	10
Ivan Allen Workspace LLC	5712	67
Ivan Extruders Company Inc	3452	93
Ivan Leonard Chevrolet Inc	5511	611
Ivanhoe Broadcast News Inc	7812	262
Ivar's Inc	5812	88
Ivarson Inc	3599	729
Ivascu Consulting LLC	7379	1449
IVAX Diagnostics Inc	2834	324
IVC Industrial Coatings Inc	2851	65
IVC Ti-Kromatic Industrial Coatings	2851	155
IVCi LLC	7373	129
Ivedha Inc	7363	298
Ivek Corp	3561	126
Iverify Inc	5065	222
Iverson Language Associates Inc	7389	1939
Ives Business Forms Inc	5943	24
Ives Corporation E H	1731	456
Ivey Construction Inc	1422	54
Ivey Sound Lighting and Multimedia	5065	962
Ivey's Construction Inc	1542	389
IVI Communications Inc	7389	2488
IVI Corp	3567	121
IVID Communications	2741	350
iVillage Inc	7379	122
iVillage International Holding Corp	2721	61
iVision Technology Services	8742	446
Iviz Group Inc	7371	1473
Ivoclar Vivadent Inc	3843	5
iVoice Inc	7373	1227
Ivory Homes A Utah LP	1531	42
Ivory Systems Inc	7371	435
ivpcare Inc	5122	48
Ivs 3d Inc	7371	1304
Ivs Computer Technology Inc	7373	607
Ivy Biomedical Systems Inc	3845	95
Ivy Steel and Wire	3496	2
IW Group Inc	8742	30
Iwaki America Inc	3561	110
Iwaki Walchem Corp	3561	70
IWC Resources Corp	4941	7
Iwen Tool Supply Co	5085	328
Iwerks Entertainment Inc	7832	20
Iwerks Touring Technologies Inc	8999	94
Iwi Inc	5084	638
Iwired Inc	1731	1506
IWX Motor Freight	4213	3126
IX Systems	3577	428
Ixia	3825	9
Ixmation Inc	3599	154
iXP Corp	7373	237
Ixpalia Inc	2096	50
IXYS Corp	3674	63
iYogi Inc	7378	177
IZ Technologies Inc	8748	276
Izzo And Sons	1731	759
Izzo Electric and Sons Inc	1731	713
Izzy Dot Net Inc	7375	281
Izzy's Franchise Systems Inc	5812	358
J A English Ii Inc	3544	553
J A Woollam Company Inc	3826	80
J Adams Electrical Contractor Inc	1731	1737
J Alexander's Corp	5812	201
J Alexander's Restaurants Inc	5812	76
J Alexander's Restaurants of Kansas Inc	5812	316
J and A Grinding Inc	7699	235
J and A Industries Inc	3743	27
J and A Manufacturing Inc	3599	685
J and A Printing Inc	2752	230
J and AK Inc	3625	107
J and B Fast Freight	4213	2850
J and B Fasteners LP	5085	63
J and B Manufacturing Corp	3231	36
J and B Meats Corp	2011	27
J and B Medical Supply Company Inc	5047	64
J and B Sausage Company Inc	2013	41
J and B Software Inc	7372	812
J and B Technologies Ltd	5734	284
J and C Co	3672	446
J and C Industries Inc	3599	1037
J and C Meador Inc	1623	635
J and C Stringer Trucking Inc	4213	2159
J and C Trucking of Forest Lake Inc	4213	1439
J And C Water Inc	7359	253
J and D Auto Electric	5013	401
J and D Burgess Inc	4213	590
J and D Construction	1623	498
J and D Enterprises	7319	164
J and D Equipment Inc	5012	170
J and D Hauling Inc	4213	1186
J and D P/M Diversified Inc	8741	156
J and D Printing Inc	2752	1344
J and D Sales Incorporated Of Eau Claire Wisconsin	3523	112
J and D Trucking Inc	4213	2326
J and D Trucking Inc	4213	2957
J and E Associates	7349	48
J and G Steel Corp	3441	83
J and H Aluminum	1761	46
J And H Carpets Inc	2273	40
J and H Oil Co	5541	29
J and H Trucking Inc	4213	1374
J and J Air Parts Inc	5088	108
J and J Amusements Incorporated An Oregon Corp	5531	54
J and J - Bmar Joint Venture LLP	7349	43
J and J Carbide and Tool Inc	3545	128
J and J Delivery Inc	4213	3029
J and J Drive-Away Inc	4213	3096
J and J Electric Inc	1731	1515
J and J Electronics Inc	3646	75

Company Name	SIC	Rank
J and J Exterminating Company Of Lake Charles Inc	7342	65
J and J Machine Products Company Inc	3451	139
J and J Manufacturing Co	3569	65
J and J Packaging Inc	2657	27
J and J Plastics Inc	3089	1735
J and J Snack Foods Corp	2052	6
J and J Snack Foods Corp Bakery Div	2052	13
J and J Snack Foods Corp/Mia	2024	2
J and J Snack Foods Corporation of California	2052	4
J And J Wall Baking Company Inc	5142	31
J and J Welding Inc	7692	56
J and K Ingredients Inc	2099	255
J and K Pipeline Inc	1794	45
J and K Resources Inc	2752	1408
J and L Custom Plastic Extrusions Inc	3089	1358
J and L Fasteners And General Maintenance Supplies Inc	5072	138
J and L Fiber Services Inc	3554	12
J and L Honing Company Inc	7699	244
J and L Industrial Supply Co	5085	19
J and L Manufacturing Company Inc	3498	75
J and L Marketing Inc	7331	220
J and L Microfilm Service Inc	7389	2467
J and L Motor X-Press Inc	4213	2897
J and L Precision Machine Company Inc	3599	1170
J and L Press Inc	2752	1248
J and L Tool Company Inc	3544	576
J and L Turning Inc	3599	2437
J and L Utility Service Co	1623	197
J and L Welding and Machine Company Inc	7692	39
J and L Wire Cloth LLC	3496	79
J and M Associates	3559	537
J and M Electric Inc	1731	2315
J and M Electrical Service	1731	1484
J and M Industries Inc	2393	7
J and M Laboratories Inc	2869	118
J and M Leasing Co	4213	2676
J and M Machine Inc	3599	2043
J and M Machine Products Inc	3599	421
J and M Manufacturing Company Inc	3523	23
J and M Printing Inc	2752	942
J and M Reproductions Corp	2752	593
J and M Sales Inc	5651	19
J and M Service Inc	5211	324
J and N Computer Services Inc	3571	161
J and N Trucking Company Inc	4213	918
J and P Enterprises Of The Carolinas Inc	3552	49
J and P Investments Inc	2752	1611
J and R Automotive Inc	5013	239
J and R Construction Co	1623	389
J and R Electronics Inc	5999	279
J and R Engineering Company Inc	3569	209
J and R Express Inc	4213	2826
J and R Machine Works	3599	1910
J and R Moviola	3861	49
J and R Schugel Trucking Inc	4213	753
J and R Slaw Inc	3272	100
J and R World Trading Group Inc	5046	231
J and S Electric Inc	1731	1040
J and S Industrial Machine Products Inc	3559	160
J and S Machine and Valve Inc	3491	55
J and S Supply Corp	5033	20
J and S Ventures Inc	5084	720
J and W Counter Tops Inc	5031	417
J and W Instruments Inc	5084	471
J and W Seligman and Company Inc	6282	93
J Arthur Trudeau Memorial Center	8361	25
J B Feed Fertilizer and Farm Service Inc	5191	161
J B Gury Manufacturing Co	3552	42
J B Kreider Company Inc	2752	810
J B Manufacturing Inc	3599	1212
J B Nottingham and Company Inc	3612	94
J B Vending Company Inc	5962	10
J Bar B Foods	4213	354
J Barbour Inc	5112	73
J Bauer Trucking Inc	4213	455
J Baxter Brinkmann International Corp	3648	10
J Brach and Sons Trucking Inc	4213	1655
J Brisbois Tool Sales and Service Inc	3599	1814
J Brooks Potter Marketing	8742	722
J Brown/LMC Group	8742	128
J C Ford Co	3556	55
J C Manufacturing Inc	2672	79
J C Newman Cigar Co	2121	3
J C Steele And Sons Inc	3559	95
J Caldarera and Company Inc	1542	454
J Calnan and Associates Inc	1542	148
J Coleman Alvin and Son Inc	1542	277
J Co	3089	451
J Corliss Electric Inc	1731	1008
J Crew Group Inc	5961	17
J C's United Building Maintenance Inc	7217	2
J D Cousins Inc	3599	1388
J D Graphic Company Inc	2752	891
J D Lincoln Inc	2295	5
J D Ott Company Inc	3728	107
J D Parrella Electric Inc	1731	564
J D Products Inc	3089	1185
J D Streett and Company Inc	5171	18
J D Young Company Inc	5999	93
J De Sigio Construction Inc	1623	450
J Dedoes Enterprises Inc	5084	866
J Diamond Group Inc	7381	24
J Diamond Inc	3812	155
J F Burns Machine Company Inc	3599	1459
J F Duncan Industries Inc	3589	87
J F Fredericks Tool Company Inc	3724	61
J F Schroeder Company Inc	3544	676
J Frank Blakely Co	1731	812
J G Edelen Company Inc	5072	105
J G Kern Enterprises Inc	3714	340
J Gibson McIlvain Co	5031	153
J Grady Randolph Inc	4213	228
J Grothe Electric Inc	1731	1496
J H and H Management Inc	3599	1656
J H Benedict Company Inc	3544	235
J H Benedict-Volusia Inc	7311	563
J H Craver And Son Inc	2511	76
J H Fletcher and Co	5082	64
J Harris and Sons Co	3999	96
J Hellman Frozen Foods Inc	2037	33
J Hellman Produce Inc	5148	30
J Horst Manufacturing Co	3599	587
J Ii Inc	3589	108
J J and H Ltd	7361	93
J J Ferguson Sand and Gravel Inc	1622	33
J J Nichting Company Inc	5083	108
J J Plank Corp	3554	13
J J Ryan Corp	3312	75
J Jill Direct Inc	5961	11
J Jill Group Inc	5961	38
J K Pulley Company Inc	3429	53
J Kinderman and Sons Inc	3999	71
J Kings Food Service Professionals Inc	5142	6
J L Davis Electrical Contractor Inc	1731	2250
J L Fisher Inc	3861	64
J L French LLC	3363	1
J L Haley Enterprises	3599	98
J L Shepherd And Associates	3829	154
J Lee Hackett Co	5084	811
J Lee Milligan Inc	2951	33
J Letterman and Associates Inc	1623	340
J Loew and Associates Inc	6552	196
J M Fabrication Company LLC	3599	2263
J M Martinac Shipbuilding Corp	3731	36
J M T Machine Co	3599	2202
J Mac Electric Inc	1731	1041
J Magnum Products Inc	5045	787
J Marion Bryan and Sons Inc	1799	68
J Meyer and Sons Inc	3087	10
J Milano Company Inc	5072	160
J N White Associates Inc	2759	98
J Newell Corp	3599	655
J O Spice And Cure Company Inc	2099	318
J P Finley and Son Mortuary Inc	7261	10
J P Pattern Inc	3543	38
J Palazzolo Son Inc	2844	187
J Paul Horst and Associates Inc	7372	4072
J Paul Levesque and Sons Inc	2421	6
J Pollard Staley	3559	390
J R Carlson Laboratories Inc	5122	68
J R Clancy Inc	1799	85
J R Hoe and Sons	3441	160
J R Peters Inc	2875	34
J R Schneider Company Inc	3569	271
J Ray McDermott Holdings Inc	1622	1
J Ray McDermott SA	1622	2
J Ray Patterson Inc	7353	75
J Rayl Transport Inc	4213	1560
J Richards Industries	3535	7
J River Inc	7372	1226
J Robert Scott Inc	5131	32
J Robert Scott Textiles Inc	2221	46
J Rubin and Co	5051	49
J Scott International Inc	8748	365
J Sosnick and Son Inc	5149	50
J Stadler Machine Inc	3599	1345
J Stephen Scherer Inc	2844	145
J Stokes and Associates	8743	103
J Strickland And Co	2844	112
J Supor Trucking and Rigging Co	4213	1318
J T Cullen Company Inc	3443	143
J T D Stamping Company Inc	3452	80
J - T E C H	3678	24
J T V Inc	1623	758
J T White Hardware And Lumber Company LLC	5211	285
J T Yates Electric Service Inc	1731	1544
J Trans Inc	4213	2150
J Tropeano Inc	1623	371
J Vilkaitis Consultants	7372	2718
J W Boarman Company Inc	2789	91
J W Holdings Inc	3548	49
J W Peters Inc	3272	64
J W Treuth and Sons Inc	5421	7
J W Winco Inc	5085	266
J Walter Miller Co	3369	27
J Walter Thompson Co	7311	11
J Waters Inc	7381	218
J Weil and Co	5149	183
J Weston Walch Publisher	2731	150
J Wine Co	2084	14
J W's Image Printing Inc	2752	1632
J-2 Contracting Co	1623	290
j2 Global Communications Inc	4822	4
J2 International Inc	3577	623
J2a Systems LLC	7379	561
JA Becker Co	5063	78
JA Carman Trucking Company Inc	4213	2247
JA Cunningham Equipment Inc	5084	353
JA Frate Inc	4213	1754
JA Glynn and Co	6211	369
JA Johnson Paving Co	1611	174
JA Jones Inc	8741	7
JA Jones Management Services Inc	8741	105
Ja Max Machine Company Inc	3578	38
Ja Oilfield Manufacturing Inc	7353	33
Ja Ri Machining Company Inc	3599	2292
JA Riggs Tractor Co	5082	24
JA Snyder and Associates Inc	7361	254
JA Tiberti Construction Inc	1542	104
JA Trucking Inc	4213	1872
JA Vassilaros and Sons Inc	5149	40
Jaarsma Bakery	2051	210
Ja-Bar Silicone Corp	2822	11
Jabara Ventures Group	6799	319
Jabat Inc	3082	19
Jabber Inc	7372	4158
Jabil Circuit Inc	3672	1
Jabo Supply Corp	5051	94
JAC Custom Pouches Inc	2393	19
J-A-C Electric Cooperative Inc	4911	546
Jac Manufacturing Inc	3613	177
Jac Vandenberg Inc	5148	24
Jacam Chemicals LLC	2899	147
Jace Pharmaceutical Inc	5122	110
Jacer Corp	7379	322
Jacer International Inc	7371	913
Jaciva's Inc	2051	223
Jack A Farrior Inc	3444	175
Jack B Kelley Inc	4213	151
Jack B Wooten Co	4213	2149
Jack Boyd's Atlas Security Inc	7381	227
Jack Brown Produce Inc	5148	76
Jack C Drees Grinding Company Inc	3599	2012
Jack Christenson Inc	6531	123
Jack Conway and Company Inc	6531	30
Jack Cooper Transport	4213	337
Jack Cooper Transport Co	4213	128
Jack Daniel Distillery	2085	6
Jack Doheny Supplies Inc	5012	108
Jack Engle and Co	5093	32
Jack Farrelly Co	5074	142
Jack Fm	4832	171
Jack Garner and Sons Inc	7692	59
Jack Gray Transport Inc	4213	804
Jack Griffin Ford Inc	5511	859
Jack Henry and Associates Inc	7373	18
Jack Hood Transportation Inc	4213	1367
Jack in the Box Inc	5812	29
Jack Ingram Motors Inc	5511	123
Jack Jennings and Sons Inc	1541	208
Jack Jones Trucking Inc	4213	1020
Jack Kent Cooke Inc	4841	86
Jack Key Auto Transportation	4213	2245
Jack Lawton Inc	1382	57
Jack Loeks Theaters Inc	7832	18
Jack Lyon and Jones PA	8111	512
Jack Lyons Truck Parts Inc	5531	50
Jack M Berry Inc	0174	3
Jack M Zufelt	7389	1798
Jack Moorman Electrical Contractors Inc	1731	752
Jack Morris Ford Lincoln Mercury Inc	5511	1206
Jack Morton Inc	7389	111
Jack of All Games	7822	12
Jack Onofrio Dog Shows LLC	7389	988
Jack Parker Corp	6552	154
Jack Peirce Electric	1731	1528
Jack Rice Insurance Inc	6311	252
Jack Rouse Associates	8712	196
Jack Rubin and Sons Inc	5051	163
Jack Schwartz Shoes Inc	3021	6
Jack T Hill Electric Co	1731	407
Jack Treier Moving and Storage Inc	4213	691
Jack Tyler Engineering Of Arkansas Inc	5084	501
Jack Tyrrell and Co	6531	356
Jack Walters and Sons Corp	3448	25
Jack Williams Tire Company Inc	5531	11
Jack Young Company Inc	5013	112
Jack Young Super Market Inc	5411	238
Jackburn Manufacturing Inc	3496	99
Jackel Inc	3089	1017
Jackie B Lovett Trucking Co	4213	2033
Jackie Evans Trucking Inc	4213	2068
Jacklin Steel Supply Co	5051	346
Jackmont Hospitality Inc	5812	170
Jackpine Press Inc	5943	28
Jack-Post Corp	2514	22
Jack's Diving Locker Inc	7999	131
Jack's Maintenance Service Inc	7349	135
Jack's Truck And Equipment	5082	96
Jackson Acura	5511	608
Jackson and Blanc Inc	1711	116

Company Name	SIC	Rank
Jackson and Dial Inc	5063	1028
Jackson and Ryan Architects	8712	212
Jackson Automotive Inc	5511	759
Jackson Bates Engraving Company Inc	2759	284
Jackson Brace and Limb Co	3842	250
Jackson Builders Inc	1541	243
Jackson Coca-Cola Bottling Co	5149	55
Jackson County Bank (Seymour Indiana)	6022	332
Jackson County Developmental Center Inc	8331	231
Jackson County Rural Electric Membership Corp	4911	475
Jackson Digital Imaging Corp	7373	1062
Jackson Electric Coop	4911	563
Jackson Engineering Co	3677	110
Jackson Farms Dairy	0241	7
Jackson Flexible Products Inc	3061	55
Jackson Healthcare Solutions	7363	53
Jackson Hewitt Tax Services Inc	6794	23
Jackson Hole Magazine	2711	859
Jackson Hole Mountain Resort	7011	125
Jackson Kearney Group	4491	3
Jackson Laboratory	8731	74
Jackson Lumber And Millwork Company Inc	5211	60
Jackson Machinery Inc	3559	421
Jackson MSC Inc	3589	12
Jackson National Life Insurance Co	6311	16
Jackson Opthalmology ASC LLC	8011	106
Jackson Paper Company Inc	5111	15
Jackson Paper Manufacturing Co	2631	23
Jackson Pottery Inc	5023	56
Jackson Precision Industries Inc	3469	261
Jackson Produce Co	5148	89
Jackson Purchase Energy Corp	4911	402
Jackson Purchase Medical Center	8062	70
Jackson Securities	7375	210
Jackson Securities LLC	6799	86
Jackson Spah Dental Studio Inc	8072	22
Jackson - Terral Inc	7311	622
Jackson Truck Center Inc	5083	153
Jackson Tube Service Inc	3317	44
Jackson Walker LLP	8111	51
Jackson Wheeler Metals Service Inc	3568	51
Jackson-Cook LC	1629	99
Jackson-Jennings Farm Bureau Coop	5191	79
Jackson-Lee-Pearson Inc	5999	62
Jackson-Mitchell Inc	2023	26
Jackson's Cleaning Service Inc	7349	459
Jackson's Hardware Inc	5072	205
Jacksonville Auto Auction Inc	5012	115
Jacksonville Bancorp Inc	6712	414
Jacksonville Electric Authority	4911	95
Jacksonville Holdings Inc	6512	50
Jacksonville Savings Bank	6036	75
Jacksonville Specialty Advertising Inc	2759	492
Jacksonville Urban League Inc	8322	56
Jaclyn Inc	3199	2
Jacmar Food Service Distribution	2099	39
Jaco Electronics Inc	5065	41
Jaco Engineering	3599	1203
Jaco Inc	3674	257
Jaco Manufacturing Co	3089	525
Jaco Oil Co	5541	25
Jaco Racing Products Inc	3559	374
Jacob Group Ltd	2096	15
Jacob Licht Inc	1799	98
Jacob Medinger and Finnegan LLP	8111	364
Jacob North and Co	2759	27
Jacob North Printing Company Inc	2752	234
Jacob Stern and Sons Inc	5199	19
Jacobi Sales Inc	5083	45
Jaco-Bryant Printers Inc	2752	784
Jacobs Applied Technology Inc	3559	63
Jacobs Boiler and Mechanical Industries Inc	7699	207
Jacobs Company Inc	6331	348
Jacobs Constructors Inc	8748	22
Jacobs Creek Stone Company Inc	1411	25
Jacobs Engineering Group Inc	1629	1
Jacobs Engineering Group Medical Plan Trust	8711	101
Jacobs Entertainment Inc	7999	43
Jacobs Financial Group Inc	1381	54
Jacobs Levy Equity Management Inc	6282	306
Jacobs Management Corp	2099	193
Jacobs Manufacturing Co	3321	63
Jacobs Mechanical Co	1711	136
Jacobs Trading Co	5023	66
Jacobs Vehicle Systems	3714	130
Jacobsen Construction Company Inc	1542	83
Jacobsen Division of Textron Inc	3799	3
Jacobsen Industries Inc	2675	22
Jacobsen Manufacturing Inc	2451	15
Jacobson and Company Inc	1742	7
Jacobson Capital Services Inc	5131	10
Jacobson Computer Inc	8243	10
Jacobson Consulting Applications Inc	7379	883
Jacobson Hat Company Inc	2679	32
Jacobson Plastics Inc	3089	767
Jacobson Southwest Storage and Distribution Co	4213	713
Jacobson Transport Inc	4213	1755
Jacobson Warehouse Company Inc	4225	15
Jacobs-Sirrine Engineers Inc	8711	41
Jacobus Energy Inc	5171	23
Jacoby and Meyers Law Offices LLP	8111	178
Jacon Aircraft Supply Company Inc	5085	176
Jacon Fasteners and Electronics Inc	5085	276
Jacor LLC	7361	152
Jacoway Financial Corp	6282	415
Jacques Moret Inc	2253	17
Jacuzzi Brands Inc	3432	5
J-Ad Graphics Inc	2741	166
Jad LLC	3823	223
Jadco Manufacturing Inc	5051	311
Jade Alarm Co	7382	84
Jade Associates Inc	5065	501
Jade Communications Inc	1731	800
Jade Engineered Plastic Inc	3053	63
Jade Food Products Inc	2034	17
Jade Restoration Corp	7353	101
Jade Tool Inc	3545	306
Jademar Corp	5063	208
Jadent Inc	2721	138
Jado Sewing Machines Inc	3639	28
Jador International Corp	1731	1042
Jadra Inc	3089	944
Jadtec Computer Group	7371	484
Jae Electronics Inc	5065	63
Jaeger Construction Inc	1623	436
Jaeger Lumber Co	5211	82
Jaf Converters Inc	3993	127
Jaffe Associates Inc	8743	108
Jaffe/Braunstein Films Ltd	7812	104
Jaffe Raitt Heuer and Weiss PC	8111	295
J-A-G Construction Co	1542	330
JaGee Holdings LLP	5153	48
Jagemann Plating Co	3471	79
Jagemann Stamping Co	3469	74
Jagged Peak Inc	7372	1166
JAGI Cleveland - Independence LLC	7011	213
Jagr Holdings LLC	7379	1192
Jaguar Consulting Inc	7372	1632
Jaguar Industries Inc	3679	724
Jaguar Land Rover North America LLC	5012	45
Jaguar Mining Inc	1041	8
Jaguar of Novi	5511	430
Jahabow Industries Inc	2541	14
JAI Pulnix	3669	109
Jailcraft Inc	5049	177
Jain Irrigation Inc	3089	134
Jain Malkin Inc	7389	2281
Jaindl's Farms LLC	0253	2
Jake Sweeney Auto Leasing Inc	7515	9
Jakeel Consulting Inc	7372	3425
Jake's Equipment and Repair Inc	5046	116
Jakes Machining and Rebuilding Service Inc	3599	931
Jake's Pizza Enterprises	5812	399
JAKKS Pacific Inc	3942	2
Jakob Metzger	7379	1680
Jakob Mueller Of America Inc	5084	848
Jakubson Telecommunications Inc	7389	2394
Jalate Ltd	2361	6
Jam Industries Inc	3542	79
Jam Plastics Inc	3089	1265
Jam Software Inc	7372	5077
Jamaica Lamp Corp	3999	182
Jamal's Enterprises Inc	2024	59
Jamco America Inc	3728	43
Jamcracker Inc	7373	204
Jameco Electronics Inc	5961	116
James A Cummings Inc	1542	167
James A Hahn Inc	1623	592
James A Kiley Co	3713	55
James A Smith	5731	136
James A Smith Transportation	4213	1690
James Alexander Corp	7389	1172
James Associates	7372	4834
James B Nutter and Co	6162	122
James Babcock Inc	1731	1073
James Banyon Photo Engraving Inc	2796	67
James C White Co	6512	76
James Cable LLC	4841	67
James Calvetti Meats Inc	5147	56
James Candy Company Inc	5441	6
James Conolly Printing Company Inc	2752	1401
James Corlew Chevrolet Inc	5511	335
James D Collier and Company Inc	6411	179
James D Gilliam Electric Inc	1731	1809
James D Morrissey Inc	1622	20
James D Nall Company Inc	3585	240
James D Young Company Inc	2752	1601
James Digeorgia and Associates Inc	2711	620
James E Headley Oyster Co	5146	52
James E Owen Trucking Inc	4213	2280
James Eagen Sons Co	3535	152
James F Pedersen Company Inc	1623	415
James F Rigell	7373	981
James Garner and Sons Screen Printing Inc	2759	547
James Gath Trucking Inc	4213	1834
James Group	7311	1004
James Group International Inc	4213	287
James H Clark and Son Inc	4213	573
James H Cone Inc	1542	418
James H Drew Corp	1611	199
James Halstead and Associates PC	7372	2992
James Harb Architects	8712	264
James Hardie Transition Company Inc	3275	1
James Helwig and Son Inc	4213	536
James Hoyer and Newcomer PA	8111	494
James Imaging Systems Inc	5044	71
James Injection Molding Co	3089	1662
James Ippolito and Company Of Connecticut Inc	3429	118
James J Boyle and Co	4731	51
James J Flanagan Shipping Corp	4731	28
James J Tuzzi Jr	5461	35
James Jones Co	3492	17
James L Taylor Manufacturing Co	3553	40
James Luterbach Construction Company Inc	1541	298
James Lynah Electric Company Inc	1731	2150
James M Davidson and Co	6282	366
James M Depaul	5023	204
James Machine Works Inc	3443	125
James Manufacturing Inc	7699	194
James McCullagh Company Inc	1711	175
James McHugh Construction Co	1611	57
James Morris	3559	332
James Mulligan Printing Co	2752	426
James Newspapers Inc	2711	711
James Oil Co	5171	82
James Original Coney Island Inc	5812	180
James Pappas Investment Counsel	6282	677
James Printing Inc	2752	612
James R Glidewell Dental Ceramics Inc	8072	2
James R Moder Crystal Chandelier Inc	3645	46
James R Poshard and Son Inc	4213	2241
James R Smith Trucking Company Inc	4213	1348
James Ray International	2731	102
James Reynolds Transport Inc	4213	1907
James Rilott Enterprises Inc	8734	167
James River Mechanical Inc	1623	570
James River Technical Inc	7371	617
James Scanlon	7379	1427
James Skinner Co	2053	13
James Steele Construction Co	1541	230
James Thompson and Company Inc	2299	4
James Tool Machine and Engineering Inc	3545	67
James Truss Co A Nevada Corp	2439	10
James Varley and Sons LLC	2879	26
James W Bell Company Inc	5082	104
James W Bunger and Associates Inc	8711	506
James W Knight Electric Inc	1731	898
James W Mcclellan and Associates Inc	3569	185
James W Smith Printing Co	2752	721
James Walker Manufacturing Co	3053	81
James Young Green Inc	4213	2653
Jameson Inns Inc	6798	182
Jamestown Advanced Products Corp	3444	197
Jamestown Implement Inc	5083	27
Jamestown Plastics Inc	3089	665
Jamesville Office Furnishing	5021	122
Jamesway Tool And Die Inc	3544	495
Jami Enterprises Inc	8748	415
Jami Inc	2522	53
Jamieson Manufacturing Company Inc	3541	268
Jamieson-Hill A General Partnership	5541	21
Jamik Associates Inc	2791	31
JAMIS Software Corp	7372	2102
Jamison Bedding Inc	2515	13
Jamison Door Co	3442	81
Jamison McKay LLP	7311	247
Jamison Steel Rule Die Inc	3544	243
Jamo Inc	3273	75
Jampole Communications Inc	8743	167
Jampro Antennas Inc	3663	141
JamSync	3695	131
Jan Britton and Associates Inc	7338	46
JAN Services Inc	7349	111
Jan-Air Inc	3564	134
Janalent Corp	7373	655
Janco Inc	3672	174
Jancyn	8742	298
Janda Company Inc	3548	53
Jane Carter Solution	2844	190
Janel Glass Company Inc	3231	53
Janel World Trade Ltd	7389	237
Jane's Information Group USA	2731	75
Janesco Inc	3451	108
Janesville Sand and Gravel Co	3273	76
Janesville Tool and Manufacturing Inc	3544	804
Janesway Electronic Corp	5065	109
Janet Diederichs and Associates Inc	8743	348
Janet McAfee Inc	6531	84
Janet Pomeroy Center	8322	164
Jani Serv Inc	7349	486
Janice W Lake and Associates CPA	8721	212
Janie's Cookie Co	5461	12
Jani-King International Inc	7349	131
Jani-King of Fort Worth	7349	57
Janis Plastics Inc	3993	76
Janis Research Company LLC	3821	35
Janitorial Services Inc	7349	130
Janitorialex Building Services Inc	7349	318
Janklow and Nesbit Associates	7389	1520

Company Name	SIC	Rank
Janko Rasic Associates Architects	8712	297
Janler Corp	3544	354
Janlynn Corp	2395	14
Jannette Hughes	2389	30
Janney Montgomery Scott LLC (Philadelphia Pennsylvania)	6211	148
Jano Justice Systems Inc	7371	1384
Janon Printing Corp	2752	704
Janovic Plaza Inc	5719	11
Janson Industries	1799	63
JanSport Inc	2389	19
Jantec Inc	3535	215
Jantek Electronics Inc	3577	414
Jantek Industries LLC	5031	238
Jantran Inc	4492	8
Jantzen LLC	2339	62
Jantz's Yard 4 Automotive Inc	5015	9
January Co	2013	174
Janus Balanced Fund	6722	69
Janus Capital Group Inc	6282	47
Janus Cleveland - Independence Inc	7011	214
Janus Elevator Products Inc	3534	6
Janus Enterprise Fund	6722	108
Janus Flexible Income Fund	6722	72
Janus Growth and Income Fund	6722	67
Janus Hotels and Resorts Inc	7999	78
Janus International Corp	3442	61
Janus Pharmaceuticals Inc	8731	401
Janus Research Fund	6722	78
Janus Short-Term Bond Fund	6722	113
Janus T Fund	6722	44
Janus Twenty Fund	6722	43
Janus Worldwide Fund	6722	92
Janway Company USA Inc	5111	34
JAO Meat Packing Company Inc	5147	2
Japan Electronic Manufacturers	5065	799
Japan Engine Inc	5013	286
Japan Graphics Corp	2752	1512
Japan Network Group Inc	4841	87
Japan Travel Bureau USA Inc	4724	17
Japanese Weekend Inc	2339	48
Japer Electronics Inc	5064	131
Japs-Olson Co	2752	35
Jaquith Industries Inc	3312	95
JaRay Software Inc	7371	420
Jarb Broadcasting Co	4832	156
Jarden Consumer Solutions	3634	2
Jarden Corp	3089	7
Jarden Plastic Solutions	3089	298
Jarden Zinc Products Inc	3356	21
Jardine Fleming China Region Fund Inc	6726	82
Jardine Foods Inc	2033	97
Jardine Hawaii Motor Holdings Ltd	5511	175
Jaro Transportation Services	4213	413
Jaroth Inc	1731	314
Jarp Industries Inc	3593	13
Jarrard Seibert Pollard and Co	8721	445
Jarrdd Inc	5065	990
Jarrell Distributors Inc	5064	46
Jarrett Electric Inc	1731	1879
Jarrett Machine Co	3599	1293
Jarrett Welding Company Inc	3441	254
Jarritos Inc	5149	19
Jarvis	2084	110
Jarvis Caster Co	3714	225
Jarvis Cutting Tools Inc	3541	49
Jarvis Downing and Emch Inc	1541	227
Jarvis Manufacturing Inc	3599	2121
Jarvis Press Inc	2752	72
Jarvis Products Corp	3556	49
Jarvis Steel and Lumber Company Inc	5031	189
Jas Steel Co	5051	464
Jasco Tools Inc	3544	50
Jasco Window Corp	1751	15
Jasinski Dental Lab Inc	3843	82
Jasmine Bakery Inc	2051	297
Jason Inc	3511	3
Jason Industries Inc	3792	20
Jason Office Products Inc	5943	30
Jason Pharmaceuticals Inc	2833	5
Jasper Chair Co	2521	36
Jasper County Rural Electric Membership Inc	4911	412
Jasper Desk Company Inc	2521	18
Jasper Electric Motors Inc	7694	17
Jasper Electronics	3679	504
Jasper Engineering and Equipment Company Inc	5082	113
Jasper Engines And Transmissions Exchange Inc	5013	203
Jasper Ford Lincoln Mercury	5511	1182
Jasper Lightning Protection Inc	1731	1106
Jasper Lumber Company Inc	2421	90
Jasper Penske Engines	3519	25
Jasper Seating Company Inc	2521	21
Jasper Wyman and Son	2033	79
Jasper-Newton Electric Cooperative Inc	4911	574
Jassin O'Rourke	8742	341
Jasteck Inc	7372	4835
Jat Computer Consulting Inc	7379	640
JAT of Fort Wayne Inc	4213	1227
Jatal Inc	3089	1478
Jatco Inc	3089	376

Company Name	SIC	Rank
Jatco Machine and Tool Company Inc	3544	705
Jathco Inc	5734	439
Jaton Corp	3672	67
Java City	2095	1
Javanni Inc	3695	99
Javatec Inc	3625	412
Javelina Corp	3694	52
Javin Machine Corp	3599	2184
Javo Beverage Company Inc	2095	21
Jawonio Inc	8361	190
Jax Asphalt Company Inc	1731	2256
Jax Inco	5172	85
Jax Industries	7379	1662
Jaxx Manufacturing Inc	3679	438
Jay Advertising Inc	7311	275
Jay and Associates Inc	3672	348
Jay C Food Stores	5411	61
Jay County Rural Electric Membership	4911	552
Jay Dee Contractors Inc	1794	30
Jay Enn Corp	3543	6
Jay Franco and Sons Inc	2392	6
Jay Management LLC	1311	81
Jay Packaging Group Inc	2752	114
Jay Petroleum LLC	1311	82
Jay R King	2064	119
Jay R Smith Manufacturing Co	3432	18
Jay Silverman Productions	7812	109
Jaya Apparel Group LLC	2339	13
Jayborl Inc	5063	888
Jayco Inc	3792	2
Jayco Interface Technology Inc	3679	496
Jay-Em Aerospace Corp	3728	187
Jaygo Inc	3559	276
Jayhawk Millwright and Erectors Company Inc	3535	180
Jayhawk Pipeline Corp	4612	14
Jay-Kay Independent Lumber Corp	5031	156
Jaymor Electric Inc	1731	1344
Jayna Inc	3599	401
Jaynes Corp	1542	46
Jaypar Inc	7389	1683
JayRay	7311	573
Jaysell Inc	2752	1268
Jazz Basketball Investors Inc	7941	16
Jazz Inc	3651	141
Jazz Pharmaceuticals Inc	2834	90
Jazz Review	7374	288
Jazz Semiconductor Inc	6799	145
Jazz Times Inc	2721	424
Jazzercise Inc	6794	44
Jazzy Electronics Corp	6512	68
JB Booth And Co	3452	90
JB Clark Services Inc	7349	353
JB Computer Consulting	7373	1238
JB Construction Inc	1623	728
JB Equipment Specialists Inc	5999	190
JB Goodwin Residential Corp	6531	336
JB Hanauer and Co	6211	238
JB Hunt Transport Services Inc	4212	5
JB Industries Inc	3585	44
JB Lee Transportation Inc	4213	1334
JB Miller Electric Company Inc	1731	2326
JB Moving Services Inc	4213	2972
JB Poindexter and Company Inc	3711	28
JB Prince Company Inc	5046	174
JB Sullivan Inc	5411	78
JB Tool and Die Company Inc	3599	1968
JB Tool Die and Engineering Company Inc	3544	77
Jba International LLC	7379	1089
jBase Software Inc	7372	3167
JBAT Inc	3599	1709
JBC Safety	5099	144
JBCStyle	8999	109
JBG Cos	6552	146
JBI Inc (Long Beach California)	2599	10
Jbi Technologies Inc	7371	989
Jbk Manufacturing LLC	3599	1217
JBL Consumer Products	3651	15
JBL Hawaii Ltd	5072	92
JBL International Inc	3443	155
JBL Professional Inc	5065	31
JBM Builders Inc	1542	363
JBM DataCom	2522	56
Jbm Fibers Inc	3552	32
JBN Telephone Company Inc	4813	181
JBoss Inc	5045	170
Jbp International Inc	5713	19
Jbr Engineering	5065	994
JBS Associates Inc	5099	73
Jbs Packerland Inc	2011	20
JBS USA Holdings Inc	2011	10
JBS USA LLC	2013	2
JBT FoodTech	2819	7
Jc Bowling and Company LLC	7361	161
Jc Brown Inc	7342	75
JC Carter Company Inc	3728	57
JC Compton Contractor	1442	6
JC Doyle Inc	7371	1763
JC Duggan Inc	4213	2273
JC Duncan Company Inc	4953	92
JC Ehrlich Company Inc	7342	94
JC Electric	1731	1716
JC Gibbons Manufacturing Inc	3451	123

Company Name	SIC	Rank
JC Hauling Co	4213	3139
JC Industrial Manufacturing Corp	3599	651
JC Licht Company Inc	5198	5
JC Malone Associates	7361	99
JC Milling Company Inc	3599	2347
JC Nabity Lithography Systems	3559	508
JC Parry and Sons Company Inc	2671	56
JC Penney Company Inc	5311	6
JC Penney Mexico Inc	5311	35
Jc Plastics Inc	3089	1806
JC Potter Sausage Co	2013	40
JC Research	2741	83
JC Smith Inc	5082	135
JC Snavely and Sons Inc	2439	17
JC Viramontes Inc	2261	23
JC Watson Company Inc	0191	3
JC White Office Furniture and Interiors	5712	62
JC Whitney and Co	5531	8
JC Wright Sales Co	5141	150
Jca Electron Co	7373	501
Jca Ventures Inc	5014	45
JCarrington Group	7311	657
JCB Inc	3531	12
JCB Precision Tool And Mold Inc	3089	1723
JCC Homes	6552	214
JCCConnectnet	3575	40
Jcd Manufacturing Inc	3643	141
Jcdecaux San Francisco LLC	7312	31
JCH Enterprises Inc	5063	516
JCI Jones Chemicals Inc	2812	7
JCL Company Ltd	5045	546
JCM Engineering Corp	3599	380
JCM Industries Inc	3537	11
Jcomp Technologies Inc	5045	747
J-Con Reprographics Inc	2752	1754
J-C-R Tech Inc	3541	243
JCS Tool and Manufacturing Company Inc	3544	613
Jcv Investment Systems	7379	1459
JD Abrams LP	1611	5
JD Color Lab	7384	28
JD Donovan Inc	4213	2160
JD Dye	1623	455
JD Heiskell and Co	0119	1
JD Heiskell and Holdings LLC	2048	13
JD Hudson Company Inc	5063	996
JD Lumber Inc	2421	65
JD Martin and Co	6282	459
Jd Norman Industries Inc	3469	107
JD Posillico Inc	1611	102
JD Power and Associates	8732	6
Jd Research Inc	5045	988
JD Rush Company Inc	5084	234
JD Taylor Construction	1541	279
JD Tool and Machine Company Inc	3544	771
Jda Lithographic Group LLC	2759	205
JDA Software Group Inc	7372	99
Jdc Enterprises Inc	2741	432
Jdc Power Systems Inc	5063	775
JDD Enterprises	7379	1407
JDF Enterprises Inc	3672	412
JDI Communications Inc	8743	281
Jdi Contracts Inc	8742	680
Jdi Mold And Tool LLC	3089	1822
JDK Electrical Inc	1731	1942
JDL Technologies Inc	7373	246
JDM Systems Consultants Inc	7379	398
Jdr Cable Systems Inc	5051	412
Jdr Engineering Consultants Inc	3089	639
JDR Enterprises Inc	3069	99
JDR Franchises LLC	7514	11
JDR Holdings Corp	7322	5
JDR Microdevices Inc	5045	298
JDS Refrigerated Transportation	4213	1638
JDS Uniphase Corp	3825	7
JDS Uniphase Corp	3674	26
Jdwi	8331	202
JE Abercrombie Inc	1541	122
JE Berkowitz LP	3231	24
JE Dunn Construction	1541	11
JE Dunn Construction Co	1542	9
JE Dunn Construction Group Inc	1541	10
JE Grote Company Inc	3589	66
JE Higgins Lumber Co	5031	42
JE Hoffman and Co	3599	939
JE Morgan Knitting Mill Inc	2322	2
JE Myles Inc	5085	407
JE Phillips and Sons Inc	4213	2347
JE Reedy Inc	1731	1275
JE Shekell Inc	1711	147
Je Systems Inc	7382	50
JE Williams Trucking Inc	4213	1521
JE Wood Co	3545	421
Jead Auto Supply Inc	5013	91
Jean Mart Inc	5137	18
Jean-Georges Enterprises LLC	5812	282
Jeanne D'Arc Credit Union	6062	125
Jeannette Shade And Novelty Co	3229	19
Jeannine's Baking Company Of Santa Barbara	2051	274
Jean's Used Auto Parts	5015	31
Jeb Florida Enterprises Inc	3599	2281
Jebco Inc	3499	76
Jeco Plastic Products LLC	3089	1671

Company Name	SIC	Rank
Jedco Inc	3724	45
Jedi Communications	3663	225
Jedlick Molding Corp	3089	219
Jedtco Corp	3069	245
Jeff Davis Electric Cooperative Inc	4911	357
Jeff Dudley LLC	5049	72
Jeff Foster Trucking Inc	4213	1217
Jeff Kagan	8748	450
Jeff Kelley Cne	3825	349
Jeff Rowland Design Group Inc	3651	217
Jeff Schmitt Auto Group	5511	716
Jeff Wyler Dealer Group	5511	31
Jeffboat LLC	3731	17
Jeffco Electric Inc	1731	2502
Jeffco Fibres Inc	5087	33
Jeffco Leasing Company Inc	4213	399
Jeffco Publishing Company Inc	2711	651
Jeffco Subcontracting Inc	8331	242
Jeffer Mangels Butler and Mitchell LLP	8111	256
Jefferds Corp	5084	119
Jefferies Advisers Inc	6282	9
Jefferies and Company Inc	7372	1896
Jefferies Fixed Income	6211	79
Jefferies Group Inc	6211	37
Jefferies Quarterdeck LLC	6211	186
Jeffers Handbell Supply Inc	5736	5
Jefferson Associates Inc	7361	412
Jefferson Bancshares Inc	6035	111
Jefferson Bank and Trust Co (St Louis Missouri)	6022	221
Jefferson Beach Marina Inc	5551	3
Jefferson City Coca-Cola Bottling Company Inc	2086	120
Jefferson City Oil Company Inc	5171	51
Jefferson City Tool Co	3546	11
Jefferson County Federal Credit Union	6061	92
Jefferson County Publications Inc	2711	217
Jefferson Current Electric Inc	1731	1798
Jefferson Federal Bank	6035	132
Jefferson Fiberglass Company Inc	3089	1574
Jefferson Fire and Safety Inc	5099	96
Jefferson Homebuilders Inc	2491	6
Jefferson Ice Co	2097	25
Jefferson Industries Corp	3711	27
Jefferson Partners LP	4131	6
Jefferson Rehabilitation Center Inc	8322	26
Jefferson Rubber Works Inc	3069	107
Jefferson Security Bank	6022	444
Jefferson State Bank (San Antonio Texas)	6022	268
Jefferson Trucking Co	4213	1084
Jefferson Waterman International LLC	8743	268
Jeffersonville Bancorp	6712	497
Jeffrey Alec Communications	7319	115
Jeffrey and Foster Inc	2759	321
Jeffrey Chain LP	3568	9
Jeffrey Dombach	3829	519
Jeffrey Elevator Company Inc	1796	33
Jeffrey Group Inc	8743	300
Jeffrey M Brown Associates Inc	8741	29
Jeffrey Parker Architects	8712	304
Jeffrey Phillips Mosley and Scott PA	8721	123
Jeffrey/Scott Advertising Inc	7311	242
JeffreyM Consulting Inc	8748	251
Jeff's Movers Inc	4213	2958
JEI	3663	293
Jel Sert Co	2024	18
JELD-WEN Inc	2431	1
Jelec USA Inc	1731	597
Jelight Company Inc	3641	21
Jellico Chemical Company Inc	2851	170
Jelly Belly Candy Co	2064	148
Jem America Corp	3825	145
Jem Automatics And Tooling Inc	5084	849
Jem Electronics Inc	3679	238
Jem Engineering and Manufacturing Company Inc	3441	227
JEM Sales Inc	2752	908
Jem Systems Inc	5045	1061
Jem Tool and Manufacturing Co	3599	2129
Jemco Electrical Contractors Inc	1731	1957
Jemez Mountain Electric Coop	4911	379
Jemison Investment Company Inc	2421	14
Jemison-Demsey LLC	5051	54
Jemm Inc	3714	428
Jemm Wholesale Meat Company Inc	5147	64
Jena Band Of Choctaw Indians	3571	223
Jenard Co	3089	860
Jenark Business Systems Inc	7372	900
Jenco Metal Products Inc	3544	883
Jenco Productions Inc	7389	492
Jendoco Construction Corp	1542	347
Jeneil Biotech Inc	8731	315
Jeneric/Pentron Inc	3843	14
Jenesse Center Inc	7363	286
Jenfab Inc	3444	260
Jenkins and Associates Inc	5063	703
Jenkins Brick and Tile Company LLC	3251	9
Jenkins Construction Inc	8742	339
Jenkins Farms Inc	4213	2480
Jenkins Foods Inc	2013	180
Jenkins Gas Company Inc	5984	14
Jenkins Hyundia Of Leesburg	5012	185
Jenkins-Lara Corp	7376	44

Company Name	SIC	Rank
Jenks Public Works Authority	4941	55
Jenlor Ltd	3679	812
Jenner and Block	8111	88
Jennerjahn Machine Inc	3554	30
Jennie-O Turkey Store Inc	2015	12
Jennifer Convertibles Inc	5712	36
Jennings Premium Meats Inc	2013	236
Jennings Strouss and Salmon PLC	8111	317
Jennings Technology Company LLC	3679	68
Jennings Trucking Service Inc	4213	1329
Jennison Precision Machine Inc	3545	217
Jenny Craig Inc	7299	6
Jenny Craig Weight Loss Centers Inc	7299	7
Jenny Products Inc	3589	160
Jenny Pruitt and Associates Inc	6531	237
Jensen and Koerner Crane Service Inc	7353	41
Jensen and Walker Inc	8743	334
Jensen Cabinet Inc	2541	57
Jensen Construction Co	1622	6
Jensen Distribution Services	5072	37
Jensen Electric Co	1731	1553
Jensen Enterprises Inc	3272	59
Jensen Fabricating Engineers Inc	3559	247
Jensen Industries Slc Inc	3843	20
Jensen International Inc	3321	29
Jensen Meat Company Inc	5147	33
Jensen Mixers International Inc	3531	148
Jensen Scientific Products Inc	3221	9
Jensen Transport Inc	4213	2357
Jensen Tuna Inc	2092	91
Jensen's Inc	2844	196
Jensen's Inc (Southington Connecticut)	1531	87
Jentec Inc	8711	672
Jentree Inc	5047	112
Jenzabar (Knoxville Tennessee)	7372	2355
Jenzano Inc	3569	278
Jenzbar Inc	7372	2216
Jeol USA Inc	5049	12
JEPICO America Inc	5065	405
Jeppesen DataPlan Inc	7375	131
Jeppesen Sanderson Inc	2741	48
Jepson Precision Tool Inc	3545	414
JER Investors Trust Inc	6798	179
Jerald Inc	3799	34
Jerames Industries Inc	3728	206
Jer-Co Industries Inc	3441	165
Jeremiah Pick Coffee Co	2095	33
Jeremy Hiltz Excavating Inc	1623	337
Jergens Inc	3544	10
Jerhel Plastics Inc	3089	1301
Jerhen Industries Inc	3545	107
Jerico Products Inc	2048	84
Jerith Manufacturing Company Inc	3446	14
Jerl Machine Inc	7692	20
Jer-Mac Industries Inc	3596	21
Jero Manufacturing Inc	3589	175
Jerome Group Inc	3842	157
Jerome Industries Corp	3679	342
Jerome Remien Corp	3499	136
Jerome's Furniture Warehouse	5712	38
Jeron Electronic Systems Inc	3669	159
Jerpbak-Bayless Company Inc	3599	1244
Jerr-Dan Corp	3713	17
Jerrik Inc	3629	9
Jerry Barnes Electric Inc	1731	2494
Jerry Berman Enterprises Inc	2752	922
Jerry Biggers Chevrolet Inc	5511	633
Jerry F Hawkins	3559	586
Jerry Gleason Chevrolet Inc	5511	459
Jerry Hamm Chevrolet Inc	5511	1001
Jerry Holliday Construction Inc	4213	676
Jerry Jackson Associates Ltd	7372	4913
Jerry James Trailers Inc	3523	189
Jerry Lee Chemical Company Inc	7389	997
Jerry Lee's Grocery Inc	5411	151
Jerry Lipps Inc	4213	1569
Jerry Pybus Electric Inc	1731	417
Jerry Roberts Machine Co	3599	1194
Jerry Scott Drilling Company Inc	1311	247
Jerry Seiner Chevrolet	5511	116
Jerry Van Dierendonck Inc	3674	427
Jerry W Bailey Trucking Inc	4213	1245
Jerry Williams and Son Inc	2421	106
Jerry Zabel Electric Company Inc	1731	1538
Jerry's Chevrolet/Buick Inc	5511	594
Jerry's Famous Deli Inc	5812	249
Jerry's Iron Works Inc	3589	241
Jerry's Sport Center Inc	5091	8
Jerry's Transmission Service Inc	5012	186
Jersey Central Power and Light Co	4911	71
Jersey Cow Software Company Inc	2741	351
Jersey Mike's Franchise Systems Inc	6794	87
Jersey Plastic Molders Inc	3089	542
Jersey Precast Corp	1771	12
Jersey Printing Associates Inc	2752	888
Jersey Shore State Bank	6022	231
Jersey Shore Steel Co	3312	40
Jervis B Webb Co	3535	1
JES Hardware Solutions Inc	7373	982
Jes Publishing Corporation Management	2721	285
Jesco Electric Inc	1731	1400
JESCO Industrial Services Inc	7349	79
Jesco Injection Molding Inc	3089	1851

Company Name	SIC	Rank
Jesco Lighting Group LLC	5063	289
Jescorp Inc	3565	59
Jesre Inc	5734	387
Jess Diaz Trucking Inc	4213	1579
Jess Howard Electric Co	1731	23
Jesse Baro Inc	4213	1762
Jesse C Stewart Co	5153	131
Jesse Engineering Co	3441	88
Jesse Ford Trucking	4213	2432
Jessee Brothers Machine Shop Inc	3599	2233
Jessen Manufacturing Company Inc	3451	65
Jesses Enterprise Electric	1731	1085
Jesse's Fine Meats Inc	2013	244
Jessica Cosmetics International Inc	2844	130
Jessico	5085	381
Jessup Engineering Inc	2899	128
Jessup Manufacturing Company Inc	3089	512
Jessup Transportation Inc	4213	1945
Jester Company Inc	2731	260
JestMaster Productions Inc	7922	74
Jesup and Lamont Inc	6211	279
Jesup and Lamont Securities Corp	6231	8
Jet Asphalt and Rock Co	1611	226
Jet Aviation Holdings Inc	4522	2
Jet Avion Corp	3724	9
Jet Brew Inc	7389	2204
Jet Centers Inc	4581	42
JET Delivery Systems Inc	4213	1375
Jet Engineering Inc	3369	12
Jet Express Inc	4213	1578
Jet Fuel Oil Co	5983	31
Jet Grinding and Manufacturing	3599	2406
Jet Inc	4213	1143
Jet Industries Inc	3441	207
JET Intermodal Inc	4213	593
Jet Lithocolor Inc	2752	64
Jet Machine Works Inc	3599	963
Jet Pay LLC	7389	1596
Jet Plastica Industries Inc	3089	155
Jet Plastics	3089	680
Jet Process Corp	3559	529
Jet Pulverizer Company Inc	3541	122
Jet Resource Inc	4522	36
Jet Rubber Co	3069	176
Jet Software	5045	569
Jet Technologies Inc	3672	370
JetAir Technologies LLC	3564	119
JetBlue Airways Corp	4512	10
Jetco Delivery Inc	4213	2293
Jetcommerce	7374	229
JetCorp	4522	10
Jeter Cook and Jepson Architects Inc	8712	50
Jet-Lube Inc	2992	7
Jetram Sales Inc	3086	163
Jetrion LLC	5046	383
Jetsoft Development Co	7372	3776
JetStream Federal Credit Union	6061	110
Jetstream of Houston Inc	3669	41
Jetstream of Houston LLP	3669	38
Jetstream Software Inc	7372	340
Jett Racing And Sales Inc	5947	27
Jetta Corp	3088	17
Jetta International Inc	3571	64
Jettron Products Inc	3498	80
Jeunique International Inc	2833	15
Jevco International Inc	5065	465
Jewel Case Corp	3499	55
Jewel Electric Supply Co	5063	403
Jewel Swiss Co	5049	191
Jewel Vallorbs Co	3451	63
Jewell Electric Inc	1731	1848
Jewell Hudgens Inc	3531	225
Jewell Instruments LLC	3679	130
Jewell Tool Technology	3541	71
Jewelry Corner Inc	5094	46
Jewels Connection Inc	5094	44
Jewett Automation Inc	3599	951
Jewett Machine Manufacturing Company Incorporated Bryce D	3599	604
Jewett Publications Inc	2752	1216
Jewett-Cameron Seed Co	0119	3
Jewett-Cameron Trading Company Ltd	5211	71
Jewish Community Center Of Richmond	8322	152
Jewish Community Center Of The Greater Palm Beaches Inc	8322	88
Jewish Community Centers Of South Broward Inc	8322	166
Jewish Community Federation Of Louisville Inc	8399	23
Jewish Exponent Inc	2711	408
Jewish Home and Hospital For Aged	8361	7
Jewish Press Inc	2711	306
Jewish Vocational Services	8331	93
Jewish Week Inc	2711	573
JF Allen Co	3271	12
JF Barton Contracting Co	1611	249
JF Braun and Sons	5149	58
JF Daley International Ltd	2841	15
JF Electric Inc	1731	43
Jf Electrical Contractors Inc	1731	2078
JF Good Co	5085	50
JF Johnson Holdings Inc	5211	105
JF Lazartigue Inc	5122	116

Company Name	SIC	Rank
JF Lomma Inc	4213	1582
JF Morrow and Sons Inc	5049	140
JF Shea Company Inc	3273	4
JF Stouffer Co	3088	33
JF White Contracting Co	1622	21
JF Wilkerson Contracting Company Inc	1623	334
Jf2 LLC	1623	94
JFC International Inc	5149	17
Jfh Technologies LLC	3679	516
JFilippi Vintage Co	5921	19
JFK Machine Inc	3599	1979
JFShea CoInc	3273	21
Jfw Industries Inc	3825	74
JG Boswell Tomato Company - Kern LLC	2033	100
JG Machine Inc	3599	2513
JG Plastics Group LLC	3089	1009
JG Studio HD	3695	76
JG Townsend Jr and Company Inc	2037	41
JG Van Holten And Son Inc	2035	25
JGB Bank	6021	331
JGB Enterprises Inc (Liverpool New York)	5074	42
Jgb Industries Inc	7538	27
JGS Precision Tool Manufacturing LLC	3541	214
JH Baxter and Co	2491	4
JH Bender Equipment Co	3559	359
JH Castro Designs Corp	5063	902
JH Chapman Group LLC	6211	377
JH Cohn LLP	8721	144
JH Electric Of New York Inc	1731	480
JH Findorff and Son Inc	1542	165
JH Global Services Inc	5561	18
Jh Industries Inc	3599	588
JH Larson Co	5063	44
JH Lynch and Sons Inc	1611	68
JH Miles Company Inc	0913	2
JH Robotics Inc	3494	68
JH Service Company Inc	5063	523
JH Sims Trucking Company Inc	4213	1456
JH Smith Company Inc	3499	103
JH Strain and Sons Inc	1611	183
JH Technology Inc	3625	345
JH Williams Oil Company Inc	5171	22
Jhawar Industries Inc	3567	24
Jhc Inc	5065	490
Jhci Acquisition Inc	4225	8
JHG-Townsend	7311	561
Jhj Investments Inc	3089	501
JHL Mail Marketing Inc	7331	171
JHM Engineering	3841	369
JHM Hotels Inc	7011	59
Jhn Inc	7349	203
JHR Inc	3441	217
JI Garcia Construction Inc	1521	77
Jian Tools For Sales Inc	7372	3419
JibJab Media Inc	8999	75
Jiffy Air Tool Inc	3546	29
Jiffy Fastening Systems Inc	5085	204
Jiffy Lube International Inc	6794	8
Jiffy-Jr Products	2842	120
Jifram Extrusions Inc	3089	1319
Jiku	7373	1216
JIL Design Group Inc	7389	1783
Jilco Equipment Leasing Company Inc	5012	75
Jilco Industries Inc	5088	69
Jim Barnard Chevrolet Geo Inc	5511	1022
Jim Beam Brands Co	2085	3
Jim Bender Inc	4213	2306
Jim Bilton Ford Inc	5511	1174
Jim Bradley Pontiac Buick GMC Inc	5511	583
Jim Buckley Offsetting Services Inc	2759	500
Jim Burke Automotive	5511	171
Jim Click Ford Inc	5511	109
Jim Click Inc	5511	150
Jim Coleman Cadillac	5511	388
Jim Coleman Co	3559	86
Jim Culligan's Inc	5511	491
Jim Dressler Inc	3544	612
Jim Ellis Auto Dealership Inc	5511	854
Jim Ellis Chevrolet Inc	5511	984
Jim Fresard GMC-Oldsmobile	5511	375
Jim Henson Company Inc	2731	45
Jim Keeler Enterprises Inc	4213	2064
Jim Keim Ford Inc	5511	511
Jim Keras Chevrolet Memphis	5511	89
Jim Koons Management Co	5511	25
Jim L Shetakis Distributing Co	5149	44
Jim Luca Electrical Contractor Inc	1731	440
Jim McKay Chevrolet Inc	5511	688
Jim Murphy Pontiac Buick GMC	5511	1203
Jim Myers and Sons Inc	3589	121
Jim Myers Drug Inc	5912	47
Jim Palmer Trucking Inc	4213	422
Jim Perry	2789	116
Jim Price Automotive	5511	1030
Jim Reed Chevrolet Co	5511	305
Jim Ressler Trucking Inc	4213	1601
Jim Riehls Friendly Automotive Group	5511	1220
Jim Sloan Inc	7372	1030
Jim Smith Contracting Company LLC	1611	157
Jim Smith Electric Service Inc	1731	405
Jim Taylor Chevrolet Olds Pontiac Gmc Truck Inc	5012	202

Company Name	SIC	Rank
Jim Thompson Silk Co	5131	34
Jim Walter Resources Inc	1222	2
JIMachine Company Inc	3599	1873
Jimco Lamp and Manufacturing Co	3645	23
Jimdi Plastics Inc	3544	463
Jimenez Manuel Dba Telemetrics	5065	559
Jimlar Corp	5139	6
Jimmie Tucker Trucking Inc	4213	1981
Jimmy Closner and Sons Construction Company Inc	1623	193
Jimmy D Hill Inc	5063	684
Jimmy Dean Foods	2013	16
Jimmy Harris Trucking Inc	4213	2175
Jimmy John's Inc	5812	368
Jimmy Sanders Inc	5191	84
Jimmy T Wood Inc	4213	1897
Jimmy Walker Auto Group	5511	614
Jimmy Whittington Lumber Co	5211	117
Jim's Electric Inc	1731	1519
Jim's Formal Wear Co	5136	14
Jim's Lumber and Building Supply Inc	5211	250
Jim's Supply Company Inc	5051	170
Jim's Travel Link Inc	4724	111
Jim's Water Service Inc	4213	526
Jimson Inc	5046	191
Jimson Manufacturing Company Inc	2511	52
Jin Electric Inc	1731	1058
Jindal Pipes USA Inc	3443	127
Jinpan International Ltd	3612	8
JinTek LLC	7372	5122
Jist Publishing	2731	57
J-I-T Distributing Inc	3569	146
Jit Industries Inc	3593	34
JIT Packaging LLC	2842	145
JIT Reshippables	2674	18
JIT Tool and Die Inc	3599	1964
Jiva Infotech Inc	7371	1254
Jive Software	7372	525
JJ Bender LLC	5044	95
JJ Collins Sons Inc	2678	1
JJ Gumberg Co	6552	90
JJ Keller and Associates Inc	2731	34
JJ Sedelmaier Productions Inc	7922	97
Jjc Group Inc	5045	992
JJR Enterprises Inc	5731	28
JJ's and Associates Inc	4213	3076
Jjw Interests Inc	3533	78
JK Adams Company Inc	2499	37
JK Auto Parts Inc	5013	184
JK Chevrolet Isuzu	5511	753
Jk Communications and Construction Inc	1623	125
Jk Electric Inc	1731	1976
JK Group Inc	7373	128
JK Manufacturing Co	3599	42
JK Miller Corp	3679	772
Jk Packing Co	5148	90
Jk Products and Services Inc	3949	94
J-K Prosthetics and Orthotics Inc	3842	271
JK Tool and Die Inc	3544	381
J-K Tool Company Inc	3599	1769
JK Williams LLC	4213	2735
Jka Technologies Inc	7372	2319
JKC Trucking Inc	4213	953
JKG Group Inc	2752	100
JKH Holding Company LLC	7291	4
Jkh Services Inc	3564	160
Jkl Components Corp	3647	12
JKM Manufacturing	3679	658
JKP Enterprises Inc	7389	1578
JL Analytical Services Inc	8731	316
Jl Audio Inc	5065	106
JL Bainbridge and Company Inc	6282	524
JL Enterprises Inc	7336	285
JL Freed and Sons Inc	5511	861
JL Henderson and Co	5141	228
JL Honberger Company Inc	7389	2205
JL Houston Company Inc	3312	96
JL Maupin Enterprises Inc	1731	399
JL Rothrock Inc	4213	1583
JL Rushing Machine Shop Inc	3599	1034
JL Schroth Company Inc	3069	263
JL Shandy Transportation	4213	3113
JI Special Investigations LLC	7381	178
JL Systems Inc	7372	649
JL Wilson Co	5087	94
JL Wingert Co	3589	127
Jlab Audio	3651	143
Jlb Plastics Inc	3089	1901
JLCooper Electronics	3663	74
J-Lenco Inc	3545	96
Jlg Enterprises Inc	7538	33
JLG Industries Inc	3531	3
JLG Manufacturing LLC	3531	49
JLG Medical Inc	7338	4
Jlh Coastal Fumigators Inc	7342	44
Jli Electronics Inc	3571	231
J-Line Pump Co	5084	212
JLL Partners Inc	6722	147
JLM Couture Inc	2335	3
JLM Industries Inc	5169	21
JLM Wholesale Inc	5072	91
Jlr Enterprises Inc	5031	279
Jls Building Services LLC	3585	178

Company Name	SIC	Rank
JLT Mobile Computers Inc	3571	102
JM Ahle Company Inc	3462	20
Jm Associates Inc	7922	80
JM Bozeman Enterprises Inc	4213	677
Jm Consolidated Industries LLC	3469	83
JM Corporation and Son Inc	1731	768
JM Die Co	3599	743
JM Eagle Company Inc	3084	1
JM Electronics	5065	991
JM Family Enterprises Inc	5012	6
J-M Farms Inc	0182	6
Jm Fittings LLC	3494	60
J-M Foods Inc	5431	2
JM Fry Co	2893	17
JM Gaske Inc	2754	48
JM Hartwell LP	6282	509
JM Huber Corp	1311	29
JM Hutton and Company Inc	3995	6
JM Jayson and Company Inc	6531	337
JM Kusch Inc	3544	639
JM Mold Inc	3544	808
JM Mold South Inc	3544	455
JM Murray Center Inc	2673	31
JM Originals Inc	2361	11
JM Schmidt Precision Tool Company Inc	3599	1541
JM Smith Corp	5122	22
JM Smucker Co	2033	3
JM Smucker LLC	2033	25
JM Smucker Pennsylvania Inc	2033	6
'jm' Temporary Services and Affiliates Inc	7361	362
J-M Transports Inc	4213	855
JM Walters and Son Inc	1731	1143
JM Wechter and Associates Inc	5199	113
JMA Solutions LLC	4581	43
JMA Trucking Inc	4213	2815
JMAC Inc	3714	50
J-Mar Enterprises Inc	4213	2878
J-Mar Metal Fabricating Company Inc	3559	530
JMAR Precision Systems Inc	3829	125
JMAR/SAL NanoLithography Inc	3829	65
JMAR Technologies Inc	3829	438
JMark Business Solutions Inc	7373	406
Jmb Construction Inc	1623	126
JMB Properties Co	6552	47
JMB Realty Corp	6282	55
JMBZ Inc	7389	1548
JMC Financial Corp	6282	334
JMC Insurance Services Corp	6282	335
JME of Monticello Inc	4213	1868
Jmg Security Systems Inc	1731	766
JMH Printing Co	2752	823
Jmj Corporation Warehouse	5712	107
JMJ Projects Inc	4213	2605
Jmk Inc	3677	45
JMK International Inc	2822	2
JML Optical Industries Inc	3827	59
Jml Quarries Inc	1422	53
Jmm Type Inc	7338	9
JMP Group Inc	6211	200
JMP Securities LLC	6159	34
Jmpb Inc	7361	224
Jmr Electronics Inc	3572	83
Jmr Holdings Inc	3625	100
JM-RM Mack Corp	7812	94
Jms Berkshire Resources Inc	5047	246
Jms Construction LLC	1623	528
Jms Electronics Inc	5065	764
JMS Enterprises Inc	2052	86
Jms Graphics Inc	2752	766
Jms Ices Inc	2024	55
Jms Industries Inc	2821	200
Jms Manufacturing Inc	3089	1766
Jms Southeast Inc	3822	43
JMSD Telecommunications Inc	4813	204
JMSI Inc	7372	3565
JMT Consulting Group Inc	7372	700
Jmw Industries	7389	1971
JMW Trucking Services Inc	4213	2540
JN Electric Of Tampa Bay Inc	1731	530
JN Moser Trucking Inc	4213	1034
JNetDirect Inc	7372	2652
JNJ Computer Inc	7373	1030
JNJ Industries Inc	3699	214
Jnt Lighting Inc	5063	606
Jo/Don Farms Inc	7999	137
Jo El Electric Supply Co	5063	639
JO Emmerich and Associates Inc	2711	550
JO Galloup Co	5039	16
Jo Gunn Enterprises LLC	3679	852
Joachim Machinery Company Inc	5084	526
Joan Fabrics Corp	2211	3
Joan M Cables La Femmina Beauty Salons Inc	7231	11
Joan Smith Enterprises Inc	1799	75
Jo-Ann Stores Inc	5949	1
Joao And Bradley Construction Company Inc	1623	577
JO'B Consultants	7371	626
Job Dave's Shop Inc	3599	1581
Job Finders Employment Service Co	7361	282
Job Squad Inc	8322	210
Job Store Inc	7363	186

Company Name	SIC	Rank
Jobbers Inc	3211	19
Jobdango Inc	7313	24
Jobingcom LLC	7361	29
Jobs2web Inc	7379	481
Jobscope Corp	7372	1948
Jobsoft Design and Development Inc	7379	760
Jobson Medical Information LLC	2721	46
JobTime Systems Inc	7372	3831
Jochim Chrome Laboratory Inc	8072	36
Jockey International Inc	2254	2
Jodi Kristopher Inc	2335	4
Jodon Engineering Associates Inc	3826	138
Jody Maroni's Sausage Kingdom	5812	403
Joe Basil Chevrolet Inc	5511	206
Joe Christensen Inc	2791	16
Joe Chronister Construction Co	1521	116
Joe Claud Electric Inc	1731	1074
Joe Corbi's Wholesale Pizza Inc	2099	77
Joe Costa Trucking Inc	4213	1455
Joe Dieter and Sons Inc	4213	2233
Joe Fazio Bakery Inc	2051	176
Joe Fox Wholesale Electric and Lighting Inc	5063	835
Joe Hall Ford	5511	873
Joe Hill Company Inc	5084	736
Joe Holland Chevrolet Inc	5511	248
Joe Hotze Ford Inc	5511	1129
Joe Kane Productions Inc	8999	164
Joe Kirwan Company Inc	5046	302
Joe L Smith Jr Inc	2752	929
Joe Lombardo Plumbing and Heating of Rockland Inc	1711	273
Joe Lunghamer Chevrolet Inc	5511	451
Joe Money Machinery Co	5082	115
Joe Myers Automotive Inc	5521	2
Joe Myers Ford Inc	5511	94
Joe N Guy Company Inc	1542	249
Joe Pietryka Inc	3089	791
Joe Pippin Auctioneers	7389	2419
Joe Pizik Electric Inc	1731	2387
Joe Self Chevrolet Inc	5511	667
Joe Van Horn Chevrolet Geo Inc	5511	1179
Joedy Sharpe Construction Company Inc	1521	172
Joel A Trimm Construction Company Inc	1623	446
Joel Isaacson and Company Inc	6282	280
Joel Olson Trucking Inc	4213	2194
Joel Wasserman Associates Inc	5065	403
Joelle's Salon Day SpA	7359	194
Joeris Inc	1542	205
Joe's Jeans Inc	2399	7
Joe's Refrigeration Inc	5083	167
Joey Records Inc	3652	40
Jofco Inc	2521	23
Joffe Lumber and Supply Company Inc	5031	178
Jofran Sales Inc	5021	85
Jogler Inc	3823	344
Johanna Foods Inc	2033	35
Johanson and Yau Accountancy Corp	8721	180
Johanson Dielectrics Inc	3675	12
Johanson Manufacturing Corp	3675	14
John A Belanger Associates Inc	5046	136
John A Earl Inc	5087	111
John A Eberly Inc	5072	203
John A Hilt Enterprises Inc	7349	412
John A Keane and Associates	7372	5158
John A Martin and Associates Inc	8711	698
John A Van Den Bosch Co	2048	67
John A Vassilaros and Son Inc	2095	34
John Adams Associates Inc	8743	120
John Akridge Co	6552	97
John and Low And Company Inc	7311	815
John and Sandra Inc	4213	2694
John B Long Co	3829	396
John B Sanfilippo and Son Inc	2068	3
John Boyd Inc	1623	768
John Buck Co	6552	184
John Bunning Transfer Co	4213	1215
John Burns Construction Company Of Texas Inc	1623	144
John C Dolph Co	2851	126
John C Grimberg Company Inc	1542	137
John C Hipp Inc	4213	2262
John C Lincoln Health Network	8062	73
John C Myres Jr Inc	1731	2095
John C Otto Company Inc	2752	892
John C Proctor Endowment Home	8361	157
John Chezik Holding Company Inc	5511	512
John Christian Company Inc	3579	30
John Christner Trucking Inc	4213	72
John Conti Coffee Co	7389	871
John Coyne Electrical Contracting Inc	1731	1892
John Crane Inc	3053	11
John Crane Sealol	3053	2
John Crosland Co	1531	88
John D Brush and Company Inc	3089	206
John Day Co	5083	49
John Deere Capital Corp	6159	9
John Deere Credit Co	6159	13
John Deere/Des Moines Works	3523	14
John Deere Landscapes	5193	3
John Deere Landscapes Inc	5063	41
John Deere Parts Distribution Center	3541	185
John Deere Reman - Springfield LLC	3523	24
John Deere Southeast Engineering Center	3524	17
John Deery Motor Co	5511	1120
John DeGrand and Son Inc	4213	2504
John Deklewa and Sons Inc	1542	176
John E Andrus Memorial Inc	8361	38
John E Fox Inc	5084	639
John E Green Co	1711	26
John E Jones Oil Company Inc	5172	119
John E Kelly and Sons Electrical Construction Inc	1731	189
John E Koerner and Company Inc	5149	127
John E Quarles Co	5031	230
John Eppler Machine Works Inc	3554	53
John Eramo and Sons Inc	1794	33
John F Blair Publisher Inc	2731	366
John F Mahaney Co	5072	171
John F Otto Inc	1542	163
John F Trompeter Co	5145	17
John Ferris Trucking Inc	4213	2892
John G Phillips and Associates	8111	367
John G Rubino Inc	3621	129
John G Shelley Company Inc	5085	279
John G Ullman and Associates Inc	6282	577
John Gallin and Son Inc	1542	188
John Garner Meats Inc	5147	113
John Gerlach and Co	8721	224
John Grady Inc	7372	4708
John H Burrows Inc	5148	20
John H Daniel Company Inc	2311	3
John H Dekker and Sons Inc	2789	17
John H Kooy Trucking Inc	4213	2848
John H Urban Inc	2759	603
John Hall Motors Inc	5511	1248
John Hamm and Associates	7336	66
John Hancock Financial Services Inc	6311	75
John Hancock Funds LLC	6211	115
John Hancock Investors Trust	6726	62
John Hancock Patriot Premium Div Fund II	6726	30
John Hancock Subsidiaries Inc	6282	7
John Hassall Inc	3452	61
John Hayes and Sons	8999	158
John Henry Foster Co (St Louis Missouri)	5084	80
John Hine Pontiac Mazda Dodge	5511	567
John Hoadley And Sons Inc	5074	172
John Hofmeister and Son Inc	2013	81
John Hogan Interests Inc	2087	57
John Hope Settlement House	8322	208
John Hsu Capital Group Inc	6211	118
John I Haas Inc	0119	2
John J Adams Die Corp	3544	608
John J Hoober Inc	5191	147
John J Steuby Co	3451	27
John Johnson Co	2394	13
John Juliano Computer Services Co	7372	4061
John Kaldor Fabricmaker USA Ltd	5131	50
John Kautz Farms	0172	5
John Keeler and Company Inc	0913	1
John Knox Village Inc	6513	12
John Krizay Inc	3229	30
John L Adams and Company Inc	8748	401
John L Armitage and Co	2851	130
John L Conley Inc	3448	38
John L Perry Studio Inc	3089	1318
John L Scott Real Estate	6531	1
John L Sullivan Chevrolet	5511	130
John L Ulmer and Son Builders	1521	168
John L Wortham and Sons LLP	6411	164
John Leonard Employment Services Inc	7363	305
John Lincoln Co	2842	174
John M Allen Co	5084	706
John M Baxter Sales Company Inc	5087	112
John M Floyd and Associates	8748	93
John M Hartel and Company Inc	5074	55
John Maneely Co	3317	7
John Marovskis Audio System Inc	3651	259
John Michael's Photography and Video-FX	7812	227
John Morrell and Co	2011	47
John Mourier Construction Inc	1521	26
John Mullen and Company Inc	6411	263
John Muller and Company Inc	7311	745
John N John Truck Line	4213	678
John Neri Construction Company Inc	1623	656
John Newcombe Tennis Ranch Inc	7011	232
John Nolan Auto Service	5511	496
John P Nissen Jr Co	2851	160
John Patrick Publishing LLC	2741	256
John Patsey Sales Inc	5063	400
John Paul Mitchell Systems	2844	53
John Plott Company Inc	1623	302
John Portman and Associates	8712	193
John Prosock Machine Inc	3599	1848
John Pryor Company Inc	2873	12
John Q Hammons Hotels Inc	7011	52
John R Hess and Company Inc	5169	46
John R Lawson Rock and Oil Inc	4213	529
John R Loomis Inc	4213	2263
John R Lyman Co	2392	13
John R Morreale Inc	2011	38
John R Nalbach Engineering Company Inc	3565	114
John R Robinson Inc	3443	224
John R Seiberlich Inc	5075	40
John R Trucking Company Inc	4213	2358
John R Walker Inc	1623	625
John R White Company Inc	5143	27
John Ray Enterprises	4213	1200
John Rogin Buick Inc	5511	1047
John Roth and Son Inc	2048	141
John Ryan Performance Inc	7319	162
John S Clark Company Inc	1542	93
John S Connor Inc	4731	30
John S Frey Enterprises	3441	9
John S Milam Optical Co	5048	40
John S Swift Company Inc	2752	507
John Sakash Company Inc	5082	126
John Sandy Productions Inc	7812	327
John Schmidt and Sons Inc	5083	121
John Scoggins Company Inc	5169	148
John Snow Inc	8742	42
John Soules Foods Inc	2013	70
John Sterling Corp	3429	102
John Stuckey Ford Inc	5511	879
John Sullivan Dealerships	5511	111
John T Fields and Associates LLC	8111	583
John T Jones Construction Co	1541	273
John T Wilson	7349	386
John Taylor Fertilizers Co	5191	76
John Tillman and Co	3199	6
John Tse Computers	3571	171
John Tyler Enterprises Inc	7371	357
John Volpi and Company Inc	2013	105
John W Danforth Co	1711	85
John W Heaton Inc	3599	1381
John W Kennedy Company Inc	3559	244
John W Lucas Specialty Manufacturers Inc	3089	365
John Wagner Associates Inc	3452	9
John Watson Chevrolet Inc	5511	972
John Wieland Homes and Neighborhoods Inc	1521	20
John Wiley and Sons Inc	2731	5
Johncox Trucking Inc	4213	2518
Johnnie Ryan Company Inc	2086	152
Johnny B Electric Inc	1731	545
Johnny Cat Inc	1623	107
Johnny Cupcakes	2389	35
Johnny Londoff Chevrolet	5511	482
Johnny Ravioli Cigars	5993	3
Johnny Rockets Group Inc	5812	279
Johnny's Fine Foods Inc	2099	245
Johnny's Pizza House Inc	5812	118
Johnny's Super Market Inc	5411	270
Johns Brothers Inc	1711	204
Johns Computer Depot Inc	5961	144
Johns Manville Corp	2621	8
Johns-Byrne Co	2752	210
Johnson and Bell Ltd	8111	304
Johnson and Galyon Contractors	1542	234
Johnson and Johnson	2833	1
Johnson and Johnson Consumer Products Co	2844	26
Johnson and Johnson Medical Inc	3842	41
Johnson and Johnson Merck Consumer Pharmaceutical Co	2834	164
Johnson and Murphy Advertising LLC	7311	897
Johnson and Towers Inc	5084	175
Johnson and Walee Inc	5731	186
Johnson/Anderson and Associates Inc	5112	38
Johnson Automotive Group Inc	5511	78
Johnson B W Manufacturing Company Inc	3555	102
Johnson Bank	6712	426
Johnson Brass and Machine Foundry Inc	3366	7
Johnson Brothers Co (St Paul Minnesota)	5182	6
Johnson Brothers Construction Company Inc	1623	360
Johnson Brothers Corp	1611	96
Johnson Brothers Rubber Company Inc	5199	53
Johnson Bryce Inc	2759	25
Johnson Caldraul Inc	3728	196
Johnson Capital Group Inc	6282	150
Johnson Carbide Products Inc	3545	200
Johnson Carlier Inc	1542	189
Johnson City Publishing Company Inc	2796	74
Johnson Clark Associates Inc	7311	610
Johnson Communications	4813	441
Johnson Communications Inc	4812	112
Johnson Company Of Rochester Minnesota	2752	975
Johnson Concentrates Inc	2037	47
Johnson Contracting Company Inc	1761	33
Johnson Controls Building Automation Systems LLC	3822	39
Johnson Controls Inc	2531	1
Johnson Controls Interiors	3429	4
Johnson County Aggregates	1429	15
Johnson County Egg Farm	5144	23
Johnson Cox Company Inc	2732	52
Johnson Crane Service Inc	7353	88

Company Name	SIC	Rank
Johnson Crushers International Inc	3531	71
Johnson - Davis Inc	1623	100
Johnson Electric Coil Company Inc	3612	57
Johnson Electric Co	1731	1849
Johnson Electric Company Inc	1731	34
Johnson Electric Inc	1731	273
Johnson Electric Motors Inc	1731	2208
Johnson Electric Supply Co	5063	254
Johnson Electric Supply Inc	5063	590
Johnson Electric USA	3621	42
Johnson Equipment Sales and Service Inc	5013	215
Johnson Farm Machinery Company Inc	3523	262
Johnson Foods Inc	5148	59
Johnson Forging Equipment	3544	649
Johnson Gage Co	3545	186
Johnson Gas Appliance Co	3567	6
Johnson Graphics Inc	2752	1360
Johnson Group Inc	1731	878
Johnson Harris and Goff PLLC	8721	209
Johnson Hosiery Mills Inc	2252	12
Johnson Implement Company Of Belzoni	5999	87
Johnson Industrial Sheet Metal Inc	3444	297
Johnson Industries	5013	31
Johnson International Inc	6712	99
Johnson International Inc	5031	410
Johnson Level and Tool Manufacturing Company Inc	3423	32
Johnson Litho Graphics Of Eau Claire Ltd	2752	545
Johnson Machine And Fibre Products Company Inc	3599	2185
Johnson Mackowiak and Associates LLP	8721	228
Johnson Manufacturing Company Inc	2899	206
Johnson Manufacturing Inc	3599	2133
Johnson Matthey Inc Precious Metals Div	3339	13
Johnson Motor Co	5511	1127
Johnson Motor Sales Inc	5511	846
Johnson Motors Inc	5511	896
Johnson Oil Company of Gaylord	5171	44
Johnson Outdoors Inc	3949	16
Johnson Pattern and Machine Works Inc	3599	1874
Johnson Power Ltd	3714	287
Johnson Press Of America Inc	2721	283
Johnson Printing And Packaging Corp	2657	36
Johnson Publishing Company LLC	2721	15
Johnson Richard A Cedar Products Inc	5031	239
Johnson Screens	3569	17
Johnson Steel and Wire Corp	3315	1
Johnson Storage and Moving Company Inc	4213	201
Johnson Supply and Equipment Corp	5075	9
Johnson System Inc	3441	194
Johnson Technology Inc	3728	35
Johnson Telephone Co	4813	525
Johnson Tool and Manufacturing Inc	3599	1621
Johnson Truck Bodies Inc	3585	57
Johnson Welded Products Inc	3714	254
Johnson Wholesale Floors Inc	5023	54
Johnson-Nash Metal Products Inc	3444	258
Johnson-Rast and Hays Company Inc	6531	334
Johnson's Bakery Inc	2051	270
Johnson's Office Solutions Inc	2752	1309
Johnson's Restaurant And Hotel Supply Company Inc	5046	373
Johnson's Tire Service Inc	5531	25
Johnsonville Sausage LLC	2013	27
Johnsrud Transport Inc	4213	841
Johnstech International Corp	3678	32
Johnston Applegate Inc	1542	301
Johnston Bank	6022	32
Johnston Boiler Co	3443	149
Johnston Casuals Furniture Inc	2514	15
Johnston Construction Co	1629	75
Johnston Dandy Co	3554	32
Johnston Enterprises Inc	5153	36
Johnston Gremaux and Rossi LLP	8721	381
Johnston Lithograph Inc	2752	596
Johnston Printing Inc	2752	1299
Johnston Technical Services Inc	3669	137
Johnston-Morehouse-Dickey Company Inc	2299	19
Johnston's Trading Post Inc	2449	12
Johnstown Welding And Fabrication Inc	7692	4
Johnstown Wire Technologies Inc	3312	39
Johnthan Leasing Corp	2782	55
Joint Commission Resources Inc	8748	83
Joint Production Technology Inc	3545	236
Joint Purchasing Corp	7389	470
Joint Technologies Ltd	3571	192
Joint Venture Marketing	8742	608
Jointa Galusha LLC	5032	91
Joka Industries Inc	3599	1546
Jokake Construction Co	1541	171
Jokari/US Inc	3089	1152
Jolico/J-B Tool Inc	3544	315
Joliet Metallurgical Laboratories Inc	8734	176
Joliet Sand And Gravel Company Inc	1411	8
Joliet Technologies LLC	3625	302
Jolt Technology Inc	3679	112

Company Name	SIC	Rank
Joma Machine Company Inc	3599	998
Jomar Corp	3559	206
Jon B Jolly Inc	5065	995
Jonaco Machine Inc	3599	179
Jonal Laboratories Inc	8711	527
Jonas Equities Inc	6513	34
Jonathan Cohen and Associates	8712	270
Jonathan Engineered Solutions Corp	3429	64
Jonathan Helfand Music	8999	209
Jonathan Neil and Associates Inc	7322	107
Jonathan Paul Eyewear Limited LLP	5099	145
Jonathan's Landing Inc	6552	37
Jonco Die Co	3544	230
Jonco Industries Inc	7389	681
Jonel Engineering	3596	17
Jones and Brown Company Inc	3441	187
Jones and Carpenter 2051 Inc	2752	361
Jones and Roth PC	8721	107
Jones and Son Pest Control	7342	97
Jones And Sons Inc	3273	54
Jones Apparel Group Holdings Inc	2339	12
Jones Automatic Sprinkler Inc	1711	194
Jones Automotive Engine Inc	7538	24
Jones Boat Yard Inc	4493	2
Jones Brewing Company Inc	2082	77
Jones Brothers Transport Inc	4213	975
Jones Brothers Trucking Inc	4213	1631
Jones Chevrolet Inc	5511	860
Jones Companies Limited LP	2281	16
Jones Co	1531	41
Jones Dairy Farm	2013	76
Jones Day	8111	12
Jones Digital Century Inc	7372	1301
Jones Education Co	4833	121
Jones Financial Companies LLLP	6719	14
Jones Ford Inc	5511	424
Jones Gregg Creehan and Gerace LLP	8111	515
Jones Heavy Equipment Products Inc	3531	207
Jones Holt Enterprises Inc	3086	128
Jones Interactive Systems Inc	4841	52
Jones International Ltd	4841	68
Jones International Networks Ltd	4832	27
Jones Knowledge Group Inc	8221	44
Jones Lang LaSalle Inc	6531	17
Jones Lumber Company Inc	2653	63
Jones Machine and Tool Inc	3089	1439
Jones Medical Instrument Co	3841	344
Jones Metal Products Inc	3444	90
Jones Motor Group Inc	4213	376
Jones Paint And Glass Inc	3442	82
Jones Photo Inc	7384	19
Jones Plastic And Engineering Company LLC	3089	123
Jones Popcorn Inc	2099	183
Jones Potato Chip Co	2096	41
Jones Printing Service Inc	2752	710
Jones Professional Services Corp	7371	1845
Jones Publishing Inc	2721	294
Jones Soda Co	2086	83
Jones Waldo Holbrook and McDonough	8111	337
Jones Worley Design Inc	7336	129
Jones Zylon Co	3089	159
Jonesboro Coca-Cola Bottling Co	5149	99
Jonesboro Sun	2711	115
Jones-Campbell Co	5021	162
Jones-Hamilton Co	2819	67
Jones-Onslow Electric Membership Corp	4911	258
Jonesreport Inc	2721	461
Jonesville Tool and Manufacturing LLC	3469	235
Jonick and Company Inc	4213	2013
Joongang USA	2711	255
Joplin Globe Publishing Company Inc	2711	262
Joplin Workshops Inc	8331	147
Jorban-Riscoe Associates Inc	5075	71
Jordan Acquisition Group LLC	3822	47
Jordan Associates (Oklahoma City Oklahoma)	7311	836
Jordan Auto Aftermarket Inc	3714	43
Jordan Auto Parts Inc	5015	16
Jordan Automotive Group	5511	642
Jordan Azzam Inc	7311	901
Jordan Carriers Inc	4213	239
Jordan Edmiston Group	8742	378
Jordan Equipment Supply Corp	3559	471
Jordan Group	5999	292
Jordan High Voltage Inc	1731	1024
Jordan Industries Inc	2752	10
Jordan Klein Productions	7812	309
Jordan Lumber and Supply Inc	2421	63
Jordan Machinery Corp	3599	840
Jordan Manufacturing Co	3469	345
Jordan Reses Supply Company LLC	5047	38
Jordan Technologies Inc	3564	138
Jordan Tool Corp	3544	531
Jordan Valley Electric Inc	1731	2136
Jordan Vineyard and Winery	0172	8
Jordan-Kitt Music Inc	5736	6
Jordano Electric Company Inc	1731	367
Jordanos Inc	5181	13
Jordan's Furniture Inc	5712	18
Jore Corp	3546	14
Jorge Vasquez Labor Contractor	1731	945

Company Name	SIC	Rank
Jorgensen Conveyors Inc	3535	112
Jorgensen Ford Sales Inc	5511	1058
Jorgensen Laboratories Inc	5047	69
Jorgensen Machining Corp	3599	1911
Jorgensen Tool and Stamping Inc	3599	1113
Jorge's Pharmacy	5912	73
Jorway Corp	3571	244
Jos A Bank Clothiers Inc	5699	3
Jo's Candies	2064	80
Jos L Muscarelle Inc	1541	288
JOS Projection Systems Inc	5043	31
Josam Co	3431	11
Jose Carlos Cigars	2111	10
Joseph A Gilosa Bindery Inc	2789	122
Joseph Abboud Manufacturing Corp	2311	13
Joseph and Sammel Inc	5063	1022
Joseph Antognoli and Co	5141	194
Joseph Barton Inc	4213	2933
Joseph Berning Printing Co	2752	914
Joseph C Woodard Printing Company Inc	2752	1537
Joseph Canova and Son Inc	1623	294
Joseph Co	2721	410
Joseph Co (St Louis Missouri)	7379	599
Joseph D Fail Engineering Company Inc	8711	279
Joseph Davis Inc	1711	80
Joseph Enterprises Inc	2875	22
Joseph F Sexton Co	6552	44
Joseph Ford and Associates Inc	7379	1641
Joseph Freedman Company Inc	3355	7
Joseph G Pollard Company Inc	5039	36
Joseph Galliani	7373	825
Joseph H Smith	1731	2484
Joseph Industries Inc	3714	341
Joseph J Duffy Co	1542	153
Joseph J Henderson and Son Inc	1542	76
Joseph J Sheeran Inc	7331	122
Joseph Kavanagh Co	3599	2419
Joseph Khabbaz and Co	5021	150
Joseph L Balkan Inc	1623	606
Joseph L Ertl Inc	3089	583
Joseph M Zimmer Inc	1799	36
Joseph Machine Company Inc	3549	45
Joseph Mccormick Construction Company Inc	1611	217
Joseph Merritt and Company Inc	3861	72
Joseph Oat Corp	3443	145
Joseph P Mazzeo Associates Inc	5065	860
Joseph Pedott Advertising Inc	7311	434
Joseph Schmitt and Sons Construction Company Inc	1541	258
Joseph Seviroli Inc	2038	18
Joseph Systems Inc	7373	589
Joseph T Fewkes and Co	5063	564
Joseph T Hardy and Son Inc	1623	312
Joseph T Ryerson and Son Inc	1791	1
Joseph Trenk and Sons	5144	27
Joseph W Small Associates Inc	2752	1655
Joseph Weil and Sons Inc	5113	15
Joseph Weinstein Electric Corp	1731	258
Josephine Chaus	2339	16
Joseph's Lite Cookies Inc	5149	30
Josephson's Smokehouse and Dock	5421	26
Joshua LLC	3542	71
Josie Accessories Inc	2392	28
Joslyn Electronic Systems Company LLC	3643	20
Joslyn Manufacturing Co	3089	1479
Jossart Brothers Inc	1623	265
Jossey-Bass Inc	2731	85
Jost and Kiefer Printing Co	2752	1056
Jost Chemical Co	2834	264
Jost International Corp	3714	249
Jos-Tech Inc	3089	1528
Jostens Inc	3911	5
Joule Inc	8744	18
Joule Power Inc	3679	859
Joule Yacht Transport Inc	4213	3137
Jourdan Technologies Inc	3661	163
Journal Broadcast Group	4832	18
Journal Communications Inc	2711	49
Journal Graphics	2711	232
Journal Of Bone And Joint Surgery Inc	2721	183
Journal of Commerce Group	2711	364
Journal Printing Co	2761	72
Journal Publications Inc	2721	202
Journal Register Co	2711	44
Journal Times	2711	295
Journal-Chronicle Co	2752	603
Journal-News Publishing Company Inc	2711	532
Journey Electronics Corp	3672	484
Journeyman Machine and Supply Company Inc	3599	2209
Journeyman Press Inc	2752	722
Journyx Inc	7372	1485
Jouve Data Management Inc	7379	537
Jova/Daniels/Busby Inc	8712	218
Jove LLC	7372	1803
Jovil Manufacturing Company Inc	3549	78
Jovon Broadcasting Inc	4833	228
Jowa USA Inc	3823	291
Jowett Garments Factory Inc	2339	52
Jowin Express Inc	4213	2161

Company Name	SIC	Rank
Joy Cone Co	2052	14
Joy Frn	4832	159
Joy Global Inc	3532	1
Joy Mining Machinery	3532	3
Joy Signal Technology LLC	3643	95
Joy Truck Lines Inc	4213	2317
Joyce Agency Inc	5074	140
Joyce Brothers Inc	5141	214
Joyce Buick GMC	5511	1221
Joyce/Dayton Corp	3569	80
Joyce Food LLC	2034	14
Joyce Iron and Metal Co	5093	186
Joyce Janitorial Services	7349	423
Joyce Telectronics Corp	3679	840
Joyce Van Lines Inc	4213	1636
Joy-Mark Inc	3297	10
Joyner and Associates	3663	204
Joyner Cable Telecommunications Inc	1731	1738
Joyner Electric Inc	1731	1016
Joyner Lumber and Supply Co	5031	297
Joyva Corp	2064	62
JP Cullen and Sons Inc	1542	208
JP Donmoyer Inc	4212	33
JP Electronics Import and Export Inc	5065	604
JP Everhart and Co	6351	55
JP Graphics Inc	2752	1782
JP Hogan and Company Inc	7311	534
JP Jenkins Inc	5731	88
JP Manufacturing Inc	3827	135
JP McHale Management Co	7342	35
JP Mchale Pest Management Inc	7342	13
JP Morgan Invest LLC	6282	593
JP Morgan Securities LLC	6211	8
JP Noonan Transportation	4213	126
JP Oil Company Inc	1311	117
JP Rainey and Company Inc	1731	368
JP Software Inc	7372	4516
Jp Telecom Inc	3669	294
J-Pac LLC	2671	44
JPC Architects LLC	8712	211
Jpc Pasta Company LLC	2099	114
J-Peam LLC	2752	1077
JPI	6552	18
JPI Investments Inc	1522	15
Jpm Global Services Inc	8748	264
Jpm Inc	7336	74
JPM Marketing Communications	7311	803
Jpm Of Mississippi Inc	3562	36
JPM Productions Inc	7812	39
JPMA Inc	7372	4179
Jpmc Inc	5045	851
JPMorgan Chase and Co	6712	1
JPMorgan Chase Bank NA (New York New York)	6021	318
Jpmorgan Chase Veba Trust For Retiree	6733	9
JPS Industries Inc	3089	69
Jps Labs LLC	3651	225
Jps Technologies Inc	5084	794
JR Abbott Construction Inc	1542	263
JR Automation Technologies LLC	3549	10
Jr Bakery	2051	241
JR Custom Metal Products Inc	3535	77
JR Filanc Construction Company Inc	1629	37
JR Finishers Inc	2789	46
JR Higgins Associates LLC	3599	1912
JR Jones Fixture Co	2541	42
JR Lambert Enterprises Inc	5087	162
JR Linn Electric Inc	1731	2187
JR Lukeman and Associates Inc	3441	291
JR Machine Company LLC	3599	1563
JR Mailing Services Inc	7331	277
JR Metal Frames Manufacturing Inc	5031	439
JR O'dwyer Company Inc	2741	504
JR Resources	1311	201
JR Roberts Enterprises Inc	1521	130
JR Rowell Printing Company Inc	2759	551
JR Simplot Company Inc	2037	1
JR Simplot Minerals and Chemicals Group	2873	5
Jr3 Inc	3823	424
Jrb Company Inc	5032	135
Jrc Inc	7331	237
Jrcruz Corp	1623	98
JRD Electric Company Inc	1731	911
Jrd Electric Corp	1731	1043
JRD Trading Inc	5051	354
Jre Inc	3672	266
JRH GoldenState Software Inc	7372	2993
Jri Holdings Inc	3589	151
J-Rie Inc	3645	69
Jrl Ventures Inc	3429	94
Jrlon Inc	2821	91
Jrm Industries Inc	2241	26
J-Rod Inc	3799	29
J-Ron Inc	3089	1344
JR's Trucking Inc	4213	881
Js Alternator and Starter Supply Inc	5013	410
JS Paluch Company Inc	7372	778
JS Technologies Inc	7372	2653
Js Trade Bindery Services Inc	2789	48
JS West Milling Company Inc	2048	111
JSA Healthcare Corp	8011	14
Jsb Holdings Inc	3812	124

Company Name	SIC	Rank
Jsb Orthotics and Medical Supply Inc	3842	279
JSB Research and Analysis Company Inc	6282	645
Jsc Global Solutions Inc	5734	263
JSG Trucking Company Inc	4213	2397
Jsi Research And Training Institute Inc	8742	89
Jsj Corp	3465	5
Jsj Seating Company Texas LP	2521	31
JSM Music Inc	7389	899
JSMN International Inc	7379	215
JSN Industries Inc	3089	792
JSR Microelectronics Inc	2899	71
JSS Electric Inc	1731	1516
JST Corp	3678	5
Jst Enterprises	8741	173
JST Sales America Inc	3643	106
JSW Security Inc	7382	39
JSW Steel (USA) Inc	3312	69
JSymmetric Inc	8742	633
JT Adams Company Inc	8734	149
JT Automotive Warehouse Inc	5013	232
JT Communications	3663	410
JT Davenport and Sons Inc	5141	95
JT Fennell Company Inc	3599	715
JT Holding Co	6719	194
JT Lumber	5211	74
JT Marketing Ltd	3523	273
JT Nakaoka Associates Architects	8712	296
Jt Oilfield Manufacturing Company Inc	3533	106
JT Sands Corp	4213	1564
JT Sports	5999	27
JT Wein Inc	4213	2366
Jt3 LLC	8711	97
JTA Leasing Company LLC	7377	28
Jtc Inc	2791	58
Jtd Health Systems Inc	8741	107
Jth Lighting Alliance Inc	5063	598
JTI Inc	3651	65
Jtl Technical Services LLC	7379	1382
Jtm Foods Inc	2051	131
JTM Materials Inc	4213	1036
JTM Products Inc	2992	37
Jtm Provisions Company Inc	2013	54
Jtm Technologies Inc	3674	421
JTS Communities Inc	1531	33
JTS Enterprises Inc	5169	178
JTW Air Express Inc	4213	2324
Juan Don Foods Inc	5411	277
Juan Mendoza	1623	517
Juan Montoya Design Corp	7389	2347
Juanita's Foods	2032	13
Jubilant Hollisterstier LLC	2834	182
Jubilee Embroidery Company Inc	7389	933
Jubilee Enterprises Inc	7349	494
Jubilee Foods Inc	2092	97
Jubitz Corp	5541	35
Judah Manufacturing Corp	2033	116
Judd Brown Designs Inc	8712	239
Judd Thomas Smith and Company Inc	8721	425
Judge Group Inc	7379	52
Judge Manning Horse Transportation	4213	3106
Judge's Inc	3582	11
Judicial Arbiter Group Inc	7389	957
Judith Leiber LLC	3171	5
Judson Rosebush Co	7372	4618
Judson Studios	3231	64
Judson-Atkinson Candies Inc	2064	41
Judy Diamond Associates Inc	2741	281
Judy Jeong	5045	664
Judy Jones Trucking Inc	4213	2446
Judy's Candy Co	2066	28
Juergens Produce and Feed Co	5153	126
Jug Shop Inc	2084	111
Jugs Inc	3949	142
Juice Manufacturing Inc	3559	561
Juice Tyme Inc	2033	53
Juicy Couture Inc	5632	5
Jujamcyn Theaters Corp	6512	54
Juki Automation Systems Inc	5084	479
Jule-Art Inc	3089	1018
Jules and Associates Inc	6159	77
Jules Seltzer and Associates	5021	109
Julia Dyckman Andrus Memorial Inc	8211	102
Julian A Mcdermott Corp	3648	67
Julian Freirich Food Products Inc	5147	28
Julian W Perkins Inc	5171	36
Juliana Co	5065	745
Julie Fund Inc	7389	2446
Julien Chateau Inc	5182	44
Julien LLC	7361	325
Julin Printing Company Inc	2752	1123
Julius Koch USA Inc	2221	25
July Systems Inc	7371	205
Jumbo Plastics Inc	3089	1592
Jumbobag Corp	2673	69
Jumby Bay Studios LLC	7812	247
Jump Jump Music	7822	8
Jump River Electric Coop	4911	506
JUMP Technology Services	7372	2600
Jumpstart Inc	8743	79
Jumpstart Point Of Arrival LLC	7379	1652
Junction City Wire Harness Inc	3641	27
Junction Solutions	7372	754
Junction Solutions Inc	5045	283

Company Name	SIC	Rank
June Roesslein Interiors Inc	7389	2340
Juneau Electric Co	1731	2221
Jung Brothers Trucking	4213	2078
Junge Control Inc	3823	294
Jungle Lasers LLC	4813	483
Juniata Fabrics Inc	2221	32
Juniata Valley Bank	6022	207
Juniata Valley Financial Corp	6712	491
Junior's Building Materials Inc	5211	130
Juniper Elbow Company Inc	3444	57
Juniper Group Inc	1731	1657
Juniper Networks Inc	3669	1
Junkin Safety Appliance Company Inc	3842	236
Juno Inc	3089	430
Juno Lighting Inc	3648	2
Juno Online Services	7375	49
Jupe Feeds Inc	2048	63
Jupe Mills Inc	2048	79
Jupiter Aluminum Corp	3353	7
Jupiter Communications LLC	2752	1174
Jupiter Electric Inc	1731	1215
Jupiter Marine International Holdings Inc	3732	58
Jupiter Medical Center Inc	8062	98
Jupiternet Inc	7378	164
Jurado Inc	2035	33
Juran Institute Inc	7389	311
Juris Inc	7372	1772
JuriSearchcom LLC	7375	204
Jus Rite Engineering Inc	3544	603
Just Bagels Manufacturing Inc	5149	113
Just Born Inc	2064	16
Just Cruisin Plus	4724	151
Just Desserts Inc	5461	7
Just For Wraps Inc	2339	34
Just Manufacturing Company Inc	3431	9
Just Marketing International	7311	303
Just Mobile Inc	5999	248
Just My Carlaz Thing	5932	6
Just Packaging Inc	7389	882
Just PC Inc	5021	165
Just Plastics Inc	3089	1317
JUST TOMATOES Co	2034	32
Just Us Books Inc	2731	312
Just Voices Inc	7922	103
Justa Truck Trucking Inc	4213	2472
Justand Plastics Inc	3089	1561
Justcom Tech Inc	3613	65
JustConnect Corp	7372	724
Justice 900 Inc	8111	30
Justice Brothers Dist Company Inc	2843	13
Justice Electronics Training Services Inc	7389	2341
Justice Network Inc	7375	184
Justin Brands	3149	13
Justin Electronics Corp	5065	134
Justin Industries Inc	3143	8
Justin Tanks LLC	3089	1412
Justin Vineyards and Winery	2084	104
Justiss Oil Company Inc	1381	35
Justrite Manufacturing Company LLC	3412	11
JustSystems Evans Research Inc	7372	3190
Just-Us Printers Inc	2752	1242
Juvenile Justice Center Of Philadelphia	8322	91
JV Equipment Co	5084	245
JV Hii/Ske	5065	787
JV Industrial Companies Ltd	7692	1
JV Int'l Trading Corp	5063	785
JV Manufacturing Inc	3589	30
JV Northwest Inc	2834	314
JV Packaging Inc	3089	1762
JV Precision Machine Co	3599	1245
JV Products Co	3714	416
JV Rigging Inc	4213	2934
JV Rockwell Publishing Inc	2721	204
JVB Electronics Inc	3672	272
Jvb Enterprises Inc	1731	2440
JVB Financial Group LLC	6282	305
JVC Professional Products Co	5065	22
Jvi Inc	3069	246
JW Aluminum Co	3353	5
JW Appley And Son Inc	3599	2067
JW Bailey Construction Co	1541	292
JW Brett Inc	5032	143
JW Childs Associates LP	6726	7
JW Costello Beverage and SW Vending Service	5182	29
JW Custom Cabinets and Countertops	5031	391
JW Davis and Co	3663	176
JW Electric Inc	1731	290
JW Fishers Manufacturing Inc	3812	206
JW Jung Seed Company Inc	5961	50
J-W Labs Inc	7374	329
JW Manufacturing Inc	3533	98
JW Marriott Ihilani Resort and SpA	7011	53
JW Mays Inc	6512	59
JW Messner Inc	7311	474
JW Miller Magnetics	3677	89
JW Molding Inc	3544	831
J-W Operating Co	3533	20
JW Pepper and Son Inc	5736	8
JW Performance Transmission Inc	3714	388
JW Pierson Co	5983	14
JW Terrill Inc	6351	35

Company Name	SIC	Rank
JW Werntz and Son Inc	5031	334
Jwb Manufacturing Inc	3531	142
JWD Machine Inc	3599	338
J-West Oilfield Services Transportation	4213	2793
Jwf Industries Inc	3599	1035
Jwj Electronics Inc	5734	396
JWJ Inc	1623	259
JWP Gowan Inc	1711	45
JWS Corp	7372	2796
JWS Health Consultants Inc	7361	133
JWT Action	7311	135
JWT Specialized Communications Inc	7311	86
Jwwtew LLC	1623	225
JX Crystals Inc	3674	467
JY Legner Associates Inc	7389	975
JYACC Inc	7371	303
JZ Allied International Holdings Inc	5072	39
K 2 W Group Inc	5065	793
K A Steel Chemicals Inc	5169	88
K and A Machine And Tool Inc	3599	672
K and A Precision Machine Inc	3599	636
K And B Company Inc	5149	162
K and B Machine Works LLC	3599	58
K and C LLC	8059	9
K and C Machine Company Inc	3599	2213
K And C Plastics Inc	3089	1038
K and D Co	3599	79
K and D Graphics	2752	449
K and E Manufacturing Co	3469	351
K and E Plastics Inc	3089	1730
K and F Electronic Inc	3672	347
K and G Manufacturing Co	3545	93
K and G Men's Center Inc	5611	9
K and H Corp	1731	1850
K and H Industries Inc	3641	28
K and H Printers-Lithographers Inc	2752	489
K and J Machine Inc	7699	231
K and J Trucking Inc	4213	1898
K and K Inc	3544	862
K and K Industries Inc	2439	38
K and K Iron Works Inc	3441	164
K and K Langham Ltd	3281	10
K and K Material Handling Inc	5084	584
K and K Mine Products Inc	3535	128
K and K Service	2752	1847
K and K Sound Systems Inc	5065	953
K and K Stamping Co	3465	59
K and K Supply Inc	3317	59
K and K Trucking	4213	2695
K and K Trucking Inc	4213	1292
K and L Gates	8111	38
K and L Gates LLC	8111	35
K and L Looseleaf Products Inc	2782	29
K and L Microwave Inc	3679	24
K and L Wholesale Inc	5063	913
K and M Distributing LLC	5065	747
K and M Engineering and Consulting Corp	8711	193
K and M Machine-Fabricating Inc	3599	94
K and M Newspaper Services Inc	5084	350
K and M/Nordic Company Inc	2759	307
K and M Printing Company Inc	2752	296
K and M Satellite Inc	5731	196
K And N Electric Inc	5063	343
K and N Electric Motors Inc	5063	175
K and N Engineering Inc	3751	8
K and P Pattern Company Inc	3543	54
K and P Trucking LLC	4213	2005
K and R Custom Software Inc	7372	3777
K and R Enterprises I Inc	7692	14
K and R Industries Inc	5131	35
K and R Products Inc	3089	1134
K and R Transportation Inc	4213	828
K and S Machine Manufacturing Inc	3599	1913
K and S Management Supply Inc	7349	180
K and S Tank Lines Inc	4213	2825
K and S Tool Die and Manufacturing Inc	3544	108
K and T Electrical Contractors Inc	1731	731
K and Us Equipment Inc	3674	496
K and W and Fathers Inc	4812	125
K and W Manufacturing Company Inc	3599	2326
K and W Underground Inc	1623	256
K Bar Texas Electric Inc	1731	1685
K C Envelope Company Inc	2677	25
K Carrender Construction Company Inc	1521	154
K G Moats and Sons LLC	3625	225
K Heeps Inc	5147	19
K Hein Machines Inc	3599	2481
K Herron Construction Co	1622	41
K Hovnanian at Washington LLC	1531	31
K Hovnanian Forecast LLC	1531	32
K Hovnanian Windward Homes LLC	1531	72
K L Steven Company Inc	3728	170
K Mac Inc	4911	598
K/Micro Inc	7373	240
K MI It Consulting Inc	7379	1576
K Mold And Engineering Inc	3544	871
K/P Corp	2752	8
K Rieger Company Inc	1731	1887
K Tek Systems Inc	7371	1772
K Triple L	4832	269
K Truck Lines Inc	4213	1879
K - W Electric Inc	1731	735
K W Griffen Co	3842	196
K Weilbaecher Enterprises Inc	7389	1072
K Yamada Distributors Ltd	5113	17
K12 Inc	7379	29
K-12 MicroMedia Publishing Inc	2741	342
K2 Energy Solutions	3691	33
K-2 Engineering Group LLC	7373	1034
K2 Network Inc	5734	51
K2 Sports	3949	50
K4 Solutions Inc	7379	572
Ka Custom Design Inc	7389	2006
Ka Inc	8712	128
Kaat's Water Conditioning Inc	5999	121
Kaba Benzing America Inc	7372	2050
Kaba Ilco Corp	3429	36
Kaba Mas LLC	3429	129
Kaban Optical Inc	3851	114
Kabana Inc	3911	29
Kabar Manufacturing Corp	3565	88
Kabat Textile Corp	5131	40
KABB Licensee LLC	4833	35
Kabelin Hardware Company Inc	5251	16
Kabelschlepp America Inc	3545	224
Kabel-X USA LLC	1731	2532
Kabira Technologies Inc	7372	131
Kable Distribution Services Inc	5192	18
Kable Media Services Inc	5192	7
Kable News Export Ltd	5192	3
Kable News International Inc	5192	4
Kacal and FreehanPC	8111	340
Kadant AES	2679	33
Kadant GranTek Inc	3554	69
Kadant Inc	3554	1
Kadant Solutions	3554	8
Kadco Ceramics	3674	471
Kadel Engineering Corp	3679	527
Kadence Healthcare Inc	5047	215
Kadence (USA) Inc	8732	113
Kadon Precision Machining Inc	3451	57
Kaechele Publications Inc	2711	767
Kaegan Corp	7379	373
Kaelbel Wholesale Inc	5142	20
Kaelber Co	1711	177
Kafco Sales Co	5084	669
Kaf-Tech Inc	3644	28
Kaga (USA) Inc	3469	259
Kagan Realty Investors	6531	389
Kage Poly Products LLC	2673	77
Kagmo Electric Motor Co	3621	124
Kagome Inc	2033	17
Kahala-Cold Stone Corp	5812	315
Kahant Electrical Supply Co	5063	557
Kahiki Foods Inc	2038	36
Kahl Scientific Instrument Corp	3829	347
Kahlenberg Industries Inc	3599	449
Kahler Automation Corp	3829	159
Kahn and Company Inc	3823	486
Kahn Tractor and Equipment Inc	5999	161
Kahny Printing Inc	2752	1186
Kahului Trucking and Storage Inc	4111	14
Kahunaville Management Inc	5812	271
Kai Paalaa Market Inc	5411	276
KAI Pharmaceuticals Inc	8731	189
Kai USA Ltd	3421	9
Kaidara Software Inc	7372	824
Kaikor Construction Company Inc	1611	179
Kairak Innovation Inc	3585	93
Kaiser Aluminum and Chemical Corp	3353	2
Kaiser Aluminum Corp	3334	4
Kaiser Associates	8743	335
Kaiser Electric Inc	1731	206
Kaiser Electrical Contractors Inc	1731	1867
Kaiser Federal Financial Group Inc	6712	352
Kaiser Foundation Health Plan of Colorado	6324	35
Kaiser Foundation Health Plan of Georgia Inc	6324	41
Kaiser Foundation Health Plan of the Northwest	6324	17
Kaiser Group Holdings Inc	4953	174
Kaiser Marketing	7311	426
Kaiser Systems Inc	3679	184
Kaiser Transport Inc	4213	2281
Kaiser Ventures LLC	6552	173
Kaiser Wholesale Inc	5194	11
Kaizen Direct Inc	7389	1708
Kajun Kettle Foods Inc	2035	28
Kal Kan Foods Inc	2047	14
Kal Tool And Die Company Inc	3444	171
Kalama Telephone Co	4812	122
Kalamar Industries USA Inc	3537	58
Kalamazoo Packaging Systems Inc	3559	543
Kalamazoo Steel Processing Inc	3441	255
Kalamazoo X-Ray Sales Inc	5047	219
Kalan LP	2771	19
Kalas Manufacturing Inc	3357	42
Kalb Corp	5063	1066
Kalba International Inc	8748	333
Kalco Machine and Manufacturing Co	3531	147
Kalcor Coatings Company Inc	2851	125
Kale Companies Inc	1731	919
Kaleidescape Inc	5731	22
Kalencom Corp	3171	7
Kalglo Electronics Company Inc	3577	480
Kalian Cos	1531	55
Kalido	7372	226
Kalil Bottling Co	2086	44
Kalil Printing Inc	2752	1109
Kalinda Software	7372	3154
Kalish Communications	7812	156
Kalkreuth Roofing and Sheet Metal Inc	1761	17
Kallies Electric Inc	1731	2118
Kallir Philips Ross Inc	7311	111
Kallman Associates Inc	7389	1784
Kallmeyer Brothers Enterprises	4213	2382
Kalman Floor Company Inc	1752	4
Kalmbach Feeds Inc	2048	14
Kalnin Graphics Inc	2752	1182
KaloBios Pharmaceuticals Inc	8731	154
Kalorama Information	8732	53
Kalsec Inc	2099	70
Kalt Manufacturing Co	3549	61
Kalt Rosen and Company LLC	8743	315
Kaltec Of Minnesota Inc	8711	682
Kaltec Scientific Inc	3823	442
Kaltech Int Corp	7379	1172
Kaltenbach Inc	5084	759
Kalwall Corp	3089	175
Kalyn/Siebert	3537	113
Kam Companies Inc	7379	1589
KAM Tool and Die Inc	3544	658
Kamakura Corporation Dba Delaware Kamakura	7371	1129
Kaman Aerospace Corp	3721	16
Kaman Aerospace Group Inc	5085	16
Kaman Corp	3721	11
Kaman Industrial Technologies Inc	5085	8
Kamatics Corp	3562	13
Kamax LP	3452	32
Kambara USA Inc	2782	25
Kamcor Ltd	5064	149
KameddataCom Inc	8748	235
Kamel Peripherals Inc	3577	400
Kamel Software Inc	7372	3320
Kamen Entertainment Group Inc	7389	1242
Kamish Food Products	2034	33
Kammann Machines Inc	8999	14
Kammer Furniture Inc	5712	106
Kamminga and Roodvoets Inc	1611	88
KAMO Electric Cooperative Inc	4911	227
Kamo Manufacturing Company Inc	5087	136
Kamp Implement Co	5599	19
Kamper Fabrication Inc	3523	204
Kamper Inc	8243	13
Kampgrounds of America Inc	7033	3
Kampi Components Company Inc	5088	28
Kamps Inc	2448	21
Kamp-Synergy LLC	3625	335
Kamtel Inc	3679	478
Kan Build Inc	3716	7
Kana Pipeline Inc	1623	127
Kanabec Publications Inc	2711	885
Kanaflex Corp	5085	260
Kanawha Manufacturing Co	3443	144
Kanawha Scales and Systems	5046	6
Kanawha Stone Co	1794	11
Kanbay International Inc	7372	173
Kandar Enterprises Inc	7379	1048
Kandey Company Inc	1623	133
Kandi Kountry Express Ltd	3537	46
Kandiyohi Cooperative Electric Power Association	4911	601
Kandu Software Corp	7372	4836
Kane And Associates Incorporated Anthony	7331	99
Kane and Finkel LLC	7311	422
Kane Engineering Group Inc	8748	458
Kane Industries Corp	5399	21
Kane is Able Inc	4225	12
Kane Manufacturing Company Inc	3199	16
Kane Manufacturing Corp	3569	87
Kane McKenna and Associates Inc	6282	562
Kane Transport Inc	4213	321
Kaneb Pipe Line Company LLC	4613	7
Kanecal Inc	7371	1782
Kaneka High-Tech Materials Inc	3081	36
Kaneka Pharma America LLC	5047	160
Kaneland Publications Inc	2711	902
Kanematsu USA Inc	5051	20
Kane-Miller Corp	2077	4
Kanet Chambless and Baker	7311	488
Kahet Pol Bridges Inc	2752	705
Kang and Lee Advertising Inc	7311	148
Kangaroo Brands Inc	2051	90
Kankakee Scrap	5093	243
Kankakee Terrace Operator LLC	8059	25
Kankakee Valley Construction Co	1611	152
Kankakee Valley Publishing Co	2711	390
Kankakee Valley Rural Electric Co	4911	369
Kann Manufacturing Corp	3713	45
Kanoodlecom Inc	7371	223
Kanouse-Harper And Associates	5063	380
Kan Pak LLC	2026	54
Kansa Technology LLC	2731	262
Kansas Bank Note Company Inc	2752	611
Kansas Bankers Surety Co	6399	23
Kansas Blue Print Company Inc	5049	85
Kansas City Auto Auction Inc	5012	206

Company Name	SIC	Rank
Kansas City Aviation Center Inc	8299	36
Kansas City Aviation Center Inc Optica USA Div	5088	6
Kansas City Bindery and Mailing	2789	133
Kansas City Call	2711	905
Kansas City Hardwood Corp	5031	370
Kansas City Life Insurance Co	6311	94
Kansas City Power and Light Co	4911	96
Kansas City Sausage Company LLC	2013	138
Kansas City Southern	4011	10
Kansas City Southern Railway Co	4011	15
Kansas City Star Co	2711	72
Kansas City Telecom	1731	2390
Kansas Elks Training Center For The Handicapped Inc	8331	72
Kansas Forklift Inc	5084	801
Kansas Grain Inspection Service Inc	7389	993
Kansas Logos Inc	3993	180
Kansas Medical Mutual Insurance Co	6321	74
Kansas Mutual Insurance Co	6331	368
Kansas Public Telecommunications Service Inc	4833	223
Kansas University Physicians Inc	8011	19
Kansas Venture Capital Inc	6799	303
Kansmackers Manufacturing Co	3559	452
Kanson Electronics Inc	3625	261
Kantar Group	8748	2
Kantek Inc	3577	404
Kanter International LLC	7311	819
Kantola Productions LLC	7812	235
Kantronics Company Inc	3663	362
Kanuga Conferences Inc	7389	334
Kanzaki Specialty Papers Inc	2672	6
Kao Brands Co	2844	37
Kaon Interactive Inc	7372	2609
Kap Contracting Company Inc	1731	1769
Kap Graphics Inc	2752	983
Kap Tag and Label	2759	460
Kapak Company LLC	2673	36
Kapalua Land Company Ltd	7011	159
Kaplan and Zubrin	2035	36
Kaplan Co	5961	115
Kaplan Cos	1542	210
Kaplan Inc	8299	61
Kaplan Interactive	2741	506
Kaplan Lumber Company Inc	5031	160
Kaplan/McLaughlin/Diaz	8712	53
Kaplan Professional	8299	1
Kaplan Thaler Group Ltd	7319	116
Kaplan Trucking Co	4213	278
Kapowsin Water District	7389	1963
Kapp Advertising Services Inc	2741	145
Kapp Construction Co	1542	169
Kapp Surgical Instrument Co	3841	371
Kapp Technologies LP	3291	20
Kappa Graphics LP	2759	79
Kappa Publishing Group Inc	2721	206
Kappes Miller Management	6531	191
Kappler Safety Group Inc	3842	56
Kappler USA Inc	3842	103
Kappus Plastic Company Inc	3081	116
Kaps-All Packaging Systems Inc	3565	193
Kapstone Paper and Packaging Corp	2621	17
Kaptein Dykstra and Company PC	8721	420
Kar Auction Services Inc	5012	15
Kar Ice Service Inc	2097	26
Kar Nut Products Co	5145	7
Karaoke Kandy Store Inc	5731	170
Karaoke Now Inc	5064	158
Karavan Trailers Inc	3799	11
Karbra Co	3915	6
Kard Inc	7389	2475
Karder Machine Co	3599	295
Kardex Production USA Inc	5084	899
Kardex Remstar LLC	5084	270
Kardex Systems Inc	2542	38
Kardia Health Systems Inc	7372	2465
Kardmaster Graphics	2741	448
Kardol Quality Products LLC	2679	59
Kardon Communications Inc	7361	271
Kardon Industries Inc	6552	252
Karem Inc	2047	20
Karen Bakula and Company Inc	8743	238
Karen Kane Inc	2339	27
Karen Weiner Escalera Associates Inc	8743	162
Karg Corp	3552	45
Karges Furniture Company Inc	2511	68
Kar-Gor Inc	5064	90
Kari and Associates	7389	2395
Karibe Inc	2396	29
Karisma Enterprises Inc	7373	1228
Karl Albrecht International	7372	3384
Karl Ehmer Inc	2013	161
Karl Lambrecht Corp	3827	134
Karl Malone Toyota	5511	392
Karl Schmidt Unisia Inc	3592	8
Karlee Co	3599	133
Karlitz and Co	8743	76
Karl's Transport Inc	4213	414
Karlsberger Cos	8712	137
Karma Inc	3585	188
Karmak Inc	7372	1451
Karman Inc	2321	21
Karman Rubber Co	3069	86

Company Name	SIC	Rank
Karn Meats Inc	2011	99
Karnak Corp	2952	18
Karner Blue Marketing	7319	109
Karnes Electric Cooperative Inc	4911	415
Karol Western Corp	5199	93
Karona Inc	2431	69
Karp Associates Inc	3442	91
Karr Graphics Corp	2754	26
Karr Tuttle Campbell	8111	415
Karsen Co	5023	201
Karsten Co	2452	7
Karsten Equipment Co	1623	551
Karsten Homes LLC	2452	24
Karsten Manufacturing Corp	3949	25
Kart Marketing Group Inc	2721	453
Kartagener Associates	7311	869
Kar-Tech Inc	3625	215
Kartemquin Films Ltd	7812	77
Karwoski and Courage	8743	184
KAS Trucking Inc	4213	2297
Kasa Companies Inc	3613	43
Kasbar National Industries Inc	2299	15
Kasc Inc	1731	1464
Kasco Manufacturing Company Inc	3553	42
Kase Equipment Corp	3555	25
Kaseman LLC	8741	142
Kasgro Rail Corp	7699	155
Kash n' Karry Food Stores Inc	5411	77
Kasha Industries Inc	2816	12
Kashi Co	2043	6
Kasi Demos/Kirby Demos and Merchandising	8742	659
Kaskaskia Tool And Machine Inc	3599	1592
Kaskaskia Workshop Inc	8331	110
Kasle Steel Corp	5051	186
Kaslen Textiles	5131	16
Kasp Inc	5012	150
Kaspar Broadcasting Company Of Missouri Inc	4832	256
Kaspar Ranch Hand Equipment LP	5013	158
Kaspar Scale Inc	5046	376
Kasper Industries Inc	3599	1691
Kasper Machine Co	3541	227
Kasper Trucking Inc	4213	1265
Kasper's Meat Market Inc	5421	17
Kaspersky Lab Inc	7372	2211
Kass Brothers Inc	1794	31
Kass Products Inc	2047	19
Kassbohrer All Terrain Vehicles Inc	5012	130
Kassik Milling Company Inc	2048	72
Kassis Superior Sign Company Inc	5039	58
Kasson and Keller Inc	3442	37
Kastalon Inc	3089	768
Kastle Systems Inc	7382	58
Kastler and Reichlin Inc	3544	396
Kaswell and Company Inc	3069	224
Katalyst Network Group	7373	455
Kataman Metals Inc	5051	62
Katana Summit LLC	3511	21
Katcef Sales Inc	5087	181
Katech Inc	8734	140
Katecho Inc	3841	98
Katena Products Inc	5047	224
Kater-Crafts Inc	2789	73
Kate's Klean Company Inc	7349	469
Katherine's Collections At Silver Lake Inc	5199	69
Kathleen D Crane A Law Corp	8111	595
Kathom Manufacturing Company Inc	3089	1642
Kathrein Holding USA Inc	3663	147
Kathy Andrews Interiors Inc	7389	916
Kathy Barnum Public Relations	8743	336
Kathy Casey Food Studios Inc	8748	332
Katina Productions LLC	7819	81
Kato Engineering Inc	3621	31
Kato Kagaku Company Ltd	6512	27
Katron Technologies Inc	3661	62
Katun Corp	5112	15
Katy Industries Inc	3559	33
Katz and Klein Inc	3851	57
Katz Dochtermann and Epstein Inc	7311	336
Katz Media Corp	7319	6
Katz Properties Inc	6531	310
Katz Sapper and Miller LLP	8721	39
Katzson Brothers Inc	5087	44
Kauai Medical Clinic	8011	65
Kaufer Miller Communications Inc	8743	187
Kaufer's Religious Supplies Inc	5049	128
Kauffman Engineering Inc	3679	153
Kaufman and Broad Mortgage Co	6162	99
Kaufman and Co	6211	397
Kaufman Company Inc	5085	368
Kaufman Container Co	5085	85
Kaufman Engineered Systems Inc	3567	39
Kaufman Films and Television Inc	7812	277
Kaufman Manufacturing Co	3541	79
Kaufman Partnership Ltd	7389	2355
Kaufman Stairs Inc	2431	93
Kaufmann Window and Door Corp	3442	126
Kaufmann's Streamborn Inc	5961	183
Kaupulehu Developments Inc	6552	288
Kautex Textron North America	3714	53
Kavanaugh's Restaurant Supplies Inc	5046	97
Kaw Valley Electric Coop	4911	322

Company Name	SIC	Rank
Kawai America Corp	3931	11
Kawasaki Construction	3537	56
Kawasaki Heavy Industries (USA) Inc	3531	154
Kawasaki Microelectronics America	3674	53
Kawasaki Motors Corporation USA	5012	22
Kawasaki Motors Corp USA Engine Div	5084	132
Kawasaki Motors Manufacturing Corporation USA	3799	5
Kawasaki Rail Car Inc	3743	11
Kawasaki Robotics Inc (Wixom Michigan)	3569	88
Kawneer Company Inc	3442	46
Ka-Wood Gear and Machino Co	3599	615
Kay and Associates Inc	4581	4
Kay and Kay Contracting Inc	1623	95
Kay Automotive Distributors Inc	5013	121
Kay Electric Supply Company Inc	5063	624
Kay Forbes-Smith and Associates Inc	7311	898
Kay Green Design and Merchandising Inc	7389	648
Kay Green Design Inc	7389	867
Kay Home Products Inc	3499	97
Kay Manufacturing Co	3599	214
Kay Screen Printing Inc	2752	44
Kay Toledo Tag Inc	2752	306
Kayakcom	4724	61
Kayco Leasing	3993	65
Kay-Dee Feed Co	2048	57
Kaydon Corp	3562	5
Kaydon Custom Filtration Corp (LaGrange Georgia)	3569	71
Kaydon Group LLC	4911	447
Kaydon Ring and Seal Inc	3369	8
Kaye Corp	5083	85
Kaye Personnel Inc	7363	217
Kaye Public Relations Inc	8743	116
Kaye Sandy Enterprises Inc	3732	77
Kayem Foods Inc	2011	21
Kayes Inc	2752	248
Kaye-Smith Enterprises Inc	2761	18
Kayex	3674	134
Kaylim Supplies Inc	5072	153
Kayline Processing Inc	3081	106
Kayne Anderson Rudnick Investment Management LLC	6282	194
Kays Engineering Inc	3541	97
Kayser-Roth Corp	2252	2
Kaysun Corp	3089	360
Kaytek	5065	1006
Kayton International Inc	5083	48
KAZI Austin Community Radio	4832	293
Kazoo Software Inc	7372	5078
Kb Concrete Inc	5032	83
Kb Electronics Inc	3621	45
KB Holdings LLC	5945	4
KB Home	1522	4
KB Home Colorado Inc	1521	18
KB Home Nevada Inc	1521	3
KB Home South Bay Inc	1521	24
K-B Lighting Manufacturing Co	3645	63
KB Offset Printing Inc	2752	651
KB Publishing Inc	2752	367
Kb Systems Inc	3556	119
KB Tooling and Manufacturing Co	3599	600
KBA Engineering LLC	3533	27
Kba North America Inc	5084	126
KBC Advanced Technologies Inc	7372	1767
KBC of America Inc	2211	38
Kbc Tools Inc	5084	215
kbd/Technic Inc	8711	675
Kbew Inc	4832	195
KBG Advertising	7311	858
Kbh Corp	3523	65
K-Bin Inc	2821	162
KBJ Architects Inc	8712	38
KBJX Hot 106	7313	35
Kbk Industries LLC	3443	147
Kbr Inc	3624	28
KBR Inc	8711	3
KBR Inc (Birmingham Alabama)	1542	24
KBS Computer Services Inc	7373	938
KBS Inc	4212	31
KBSI Licensee LP	4833	74
KBT Inc	4213	2408
Kbtt	4832	109
KBW Inc	6211	149
Kc Book Manufacturing LLC	2732	44
Kc Cleaning Solutions	7349	283
KC Company Inc	5031	134
KC Electric Association Coop	4911	549
Kc Hilites Inc	3647	21
KC Mini Storage	1731	2280
KC Photo Engraving Co	3555	78
KC Productions Inc	7922	83
Kc Publications Inc	2731	364
K-C Refrigeration Transport Co	4213	3059
KC Transportation Inc	4213	512
Kca Financial Services Inc	7322	59
KCBX Terminals Co	4432	2
Kcc Corrosion Control Company Ltd	2899	221
KCE Electric Inc	1731	1011
Kcen Operating Company LLC	4833	194
Kcft 20 Christian Family Tv Inc	4833	249
KCG Communications Inc	5065	882

Company Name	SIC	Rank
Kch Services Inc	3564	122
Kci Communications Inc	2721	313
KCI Computing Inc	7372	2466
KCI Technologies Inc	8711	102
Kck Utility Construction Inc	1623	214
KCM Holdings Corp	7389	2429
Kcm Marketing Inc	5063	249
K-Com	3569	298
Kcomm Inc	5065	822
Kcs International Inc	3732	23
KCS International Inc (Leola Pennsylvania)	7311	930
Kcts Television	4833	134
KD Consulting Group Inc	7371	1673
Kd Electric Inc	1731	2036
KD Johnson Inc	5063	973
KD Marketing Inc	4813	452
KDC Systems/Dynalectric	1731	46
KDG InterActive	7319	69
Kdi Technologies Inc	3544	232
Kdindustries Inc	3585	180
Kdl Precision Molding Corp	3061	36
Kdm Construction LLC	1623	507
Kdm Signs Inc	2759	90
Kds Holding LLC	3823	176
KDS Software and Consulting Inc	7372	5131
Kdv Label Company Inc	2672	32
Keadle Lumber Enterprises Inc	2421	104
Kealy Trucking Co	4213	3075
Kean Development Co	1521	49
Kean University	8221	19
Keane Federal Systems Inc	7373	136
Keane Fire and Safety Equipment Company Inc	5099	88
Keane Inc	7379	38
Keane Inc Healthcare Solutions Div	7371	1
Keane Thummel Trucking Inc	4213	1584
Kearflex Engineering Company Inc	3812	151
Kearney Commercial Bank	6021	324
Kearney Electric Inc	1731	94
Kearney Publishing Corp	7319	156
Kearney Winlectric Inc	5063	997
Kearney's Aluminum Foundry Inc	3363	50
Kearns-Tribune Corp	2711	280
Kearny County Feeders Inc	0211	11
Kearny Financial Corp	6712	156
Kearny Smelting and Refining Corp	3356	37
Keary Advertising Company Inc	7331	244
Keas Stainless Steel Fabricators Inc	1761	51
Keasling's Drug Store	5912	67
Keating Muething and Klekamp	8111	219
Keating Of Chicago Inc	5046	59
Keats Manufacturing Co	3496	56
Keb America Inc	3625	127
Kebalo Electric Company Inc	1731	2300
Keco Inc	3089	753
Keco R and D Inc	3829	304
Keds Corp	3149	20
Kee Electrical Contractors Inc	1731	2014
Kee Trans Inc	4213	468
Keeble Cavaco and Duka	8743	107
Keebler Foods Co	2052	3
Keebler USA Inc	2052	33
Keefe McCullough and Company LLP	8721	29
Keefer Printing Company Inc	2759	406
Keeler Instruments Inc	3827	114
Keeler Motor Car Co	5511	185
Keeley Asset Management Corp	6282	434
Keen Impressions Inc	2752	1701
Keen Inc	5139	19
Keen Infotek Inc	8748	324
Keen Transport Inc	4213	174
Keenan Supply	5074	214
Keenan Transit Co	4213	1972
Keene Construction Company of Central Florida Inc	1542	193
Keene Engineering Company Inc	3532	19
Keene Publishing Corp	2711	346
Keene Technology Inc	3554	24
Keener Oil and Gas Co	1311	142
Keener Printing Inc	2752	1828
Keener Rubber Co	3069	234
Keene's Transfer Inc	4213	2133
Keeney Manufacturing Company Inc	3432	17
Keeney Truck Lines Inc	4213	877
Keenline Conveyor Systems Inc	3535	185
Keenline Inc	5084	677
KEEP Co	8999	144
Keeper Corp	5131	29
Keepers Inc	7361	174
Keepers International	5136	12
Keesal Young and Logan	8111	296
Keesing's Worldwide LLC	2741	415
Keesler Federal Credit Union	6061	35
Kegel Company Inc	3589	41
Kegler Brown Hill and Ritter Company LPA	8111	354
Kehe Food Distributors Inc	5141	75
Kehl-Kolor Inc	2752	1095
Kehoe Electronic and Electrical Products Co	5063	937
Kei Advisors LLC	8742	485
Kei Trading Company Inc	5064	127
Keidel Supply Co	5074	77

Company Name	SIC	Rank
Keihin Indiana Precision Technology Inc	3714	36
Keiler and Co	7311	272
Keilson-Dayton Co	5194	15
Keim TS Inc	4213	776
Keinath Leasing Co	7359	244
Keiro Services	8741	158
Keith and Miller PC	7338	47
Keith and Schnars PA	8711	301
Keith Const Custom Metal	5051	501
Keith L Fontana	7381	158
Keith M Merrick Company Inc	2759	188
Keith Manufacturing Co	8731	167
Keithco Inc	3663	413
Keithley Instruments Inc	3825	16
Keithley International Investment Corp	3825	15
Keithly Electric Co	1731	1345
Kejr Inc	3523	93
Keker and Van Nest LLP	8111	401
Kekst and Co	8743	56
Kelar Corp	7371	801
Kelatron Corp	2834	331
Kelburn Engineering Co	5063	865
Kelch Corp	3089	454
Kelco Contracting LLC	1623	234
Kelco Inc	7363	332
Kelco Industries Inc	3599	1
Kelcourt Plastics Inc	3082	5
Kelderman Manufacturing Inc	3523	181
Kele Inc	5075	27
Kelgun Enterprises Ltd	7373	1013
Kelkris Associates Inc	7322	166
Kell Communications	7311	988
Kell Holdings Corp	2653	47
Kell Munoz Architects Inc	8712	153
Kellaway Terminal Inc	4424	8
Kellco Services Inc	8734	132
Keller and Heckman LLP	8111	206
Keller Engineering Inc	3599	1379
Keller Enterprises Inc	6289	20
Keller Foundations Inc	1799	11
Keller Group Inc	3462	14
Keller International Publishing LLC	2721	264
Keller Oil Inc	5172	158
Keller Products Inc	2435	24
Keller Rohrback LLP	8111	484
Keller Stonebraker Insurance Inc	6411	159
Keller Supply Co	5074	17
Keller Technology Corp	3599	44
Keller Transfer Lines Inc	4214	2
Keller Transport Inc	4213	2831
Keller Trucking Company Inc	4213	1659
Keller Williams Realty Inc	6531	54
Kellerhaus Inc	2024	79
Kellermeyer Co	5087	15
Kelles Inc	3599	2138
Kelley Automotive Group Inc	7549	1
Kelley Bean Company Inc	5153	87
Kelley Blue Book Company Inc	2721	107
Kelley Communications Inc	3663	347
Kelley Drye and Warren LLP	8111	55
Kelley Manufacturing Co (Tifton Georgia)	2068	9
Kelley Manufacturing Inc	3531	185
Kelley Pagels Enterprises LLC	2752	916
Kelley Swofford Roy Inc	7311	370
Kelley Technical Coatings Inc	2851	99
Kelley's Personal Communications Inc	7389	595
Kelliher/Samets/Volk Marketing Communications Inc	7311	184
Kellmark Corp	2752	859
Kellner DiLeo Cohen and Co	6211	357
Kellogg Brown and Root Inc	3317	25
Kellogg Co	2038	1
Kellogg Crankshaft Co	3714	325
Kellstrom Aerospace LLC	5088	7
Kellstrom Commercial Aerospace Inc	5088	8
Kellwood Co	2335	1
Kelly Aerospace Power Systems Inc	3694	15
Kelly Cadillac Inc	5511	1154
Kelly Chevrolet-Cadillac Inc	5511	320
Kelly Communications Systems Inc	5065	757
Kelly Company Inc	3089	1329
Kelly Computer Supply Company LLC	5045	837
Kelly Computer Systems Inc	3577	320
Kelly Corned Beef Company Of Chicago	5147	97
Kelly Electric LLC	1731	247
Kelly Everwear Brush Company Inc	5087	139
Kelly Fabricators Corp	3444	193
Kelly Generator and Equipment Inc	5063	503
Kelly Hart and Hallman LLP	8111	299
Kelly It Engineering Resources	7363	270
Kelly Km Inc	1731	285
Kelly Manufacturing Co	3812	78
Kelly Mitchell Group Inc	7372	395
Kelly Paper Group	5111	8
Kelly Pipe Company LLC	5051	40
Kelly Press Inc	2752	79
Kelly Protection	7382	152
Kelly Restaurant Group LLC	8322	98
Kelly Run Sanitation Inc	4953	150
Kelly Services Inc	7363	4
Kelly Staff Leasing Inc	7363	68

Company Name	SIC	Rank
Kelly Supply Company of Iowa	5074	107
Kelly Tractor Co	5084	40
Kelly Trucking	4213	826
Kelly-Moore Paint Company Inc	2851	15
Kelly's Directional Inc	3531	235
Kelly's Pipe and Supply Co	5074	52
Kelly's Professional Cleaning Service Inc	7349	369
Kelly's Sports Ltd	5091	50
Kelly's Super Market	5411	281
Kelman-Lazarov Inc	6282	656
Kelmar Systems Inc	3861	109
Kelmax Equipment	3589	141
Kelsch Machine Corp	3599	687
Kelsey Vel Lumber And Supply Co	5211	224
Kelsho Communications LP	4832	96
Kelso and Company LP	6799	44
Kelso-Burnett Co	1731	149
Keltec Inc	3569	110
Kel-Tech Plastics Inc	3089	1488
Keltner and Associates Inc	5199	73
Keltner Enterprises Inc	5172	109
Keltner Research Inc	3633	7
Keltron Corp	3669	183
Keltron Electronics Corp	3679	735
Kelvyn Press Inc	2752	116
Kelworth Trucking Company Inc	4213	1460
Kelyniam Global Inc	8711	697
Kem Equipment Inc	8711	641
KEMA Consulting Inc	7299	16
Kemba Cincinnati Credit Union	6062	93
Kemble Interiors Inc	7389	771
Kembric Manufacturing Corp	3089	1453
Kemco Systems Inc	3582	5
KEMET Corp	3675	3
KEMET Electronics Corp	3675	4
Kemira Chemicals Inc	2869	48
Kemira Water Solutions Inc	2899	1
Kemkraft Engineering Inc	3829	486
Kemlon Products and Development Company Inc	3678	33
Kemmons Wilson Inc	7011	191
Kemp and Smith LLP	8111	297
Kemp Instruments Inc	5065	957
Kemp Manufacturing Co	3599	296
Kemp Stone Inc	1429	13
Kemper Corp	6311	73
Kemper Insurance Cos	6331	69
Kemper Investors Life Insurance Co	6311	79
Kemper Lesnik Integrated Communications	7941	26
Kemper Sports Management Inc	7992	4
Kempsmith Machine Company Inc	3599	1385
Kemron Environmental Services Inc	8748	171
Kemske Paper Co	5112	82
Kemtah Group Inc	7379	371
Kem-Tron Technologies Inc	3533	59
Ken Ag Inc	2621	71
Ken Akins	5734	469
Ken Blanchard Co	8743	16
Ken Boudreau Inc	2521	48
Ken Bratney Co	1542	235
Ken Cal Ltd	7699	133
Ken Cook Co	2741	234
Ken Curran Electric Inc	1731	2172
Ken Die Cutting Supplies Inc	3544	724
Ken Duncan Co	3089	1893
Ken Elliott Company Inc	3462	78
Ken Forging Inc	3462	43
Ken Garff Motors	5511	723
Ken Griffin Landscaping Contractors Inc	5083	119
Ken Leiner Associates	7361	117
Ken Luneack Construction Inc	2439	22
Ken Mar Machine Manufacturing Corp	3842	257
Ken Martin School Supply Inc	5049	119
Ken Morgan Enterprises Inc	7389	1853
Ken Nix and Associates Inc	1731	975
Ken Slauf and Associates Inc	7311	920
Ken Smith Inc	5065	481
Ken Thompson Inc	8711	401
Ken Wilson Chevrolet Inc	5511	1071
Kenai Peninsula Borough School District	8211	79
Kenalloy Foundry Manufacturing Company Inc	3364	27
Kenan Advantage Group Inc	4213	79
Kenan Advantage Group West	4213	315
Kenan Transport Co	4213	33
Ken-A-Vision Manufacturing Company Inc	3861	95
Ken-Bar Tool and Engineering I	3544	563
Kenclaire Electrical Agencies Inc	5063	295
Kenco Electric Inc	1731	1251
Kenco Engineering Inc	3531	183
Kenco Enterprises Inc	1731	710
Kenco Group Inc	4225	5
Kenco Logistic Services Inc	4225	9
Kencoil Inc	3621	87
Kencraft Inc	2064	29
Kendall Electric Inc	5063	46
Kendall Healthcare Properties Inc	8059	12
Kendall/Hunt Publishing Co	2731	125
Kendall Sign Company Inc	5046	314

Company Name	SIC	Rank
Kendallville Terminal Railway Co	4011	33
Ken-Dec Inc	3369	30
Kendell Doors and Hardware Inc	5072	98
Kendle International LLC	8731	29
Kendon Candies Inc	2064	128
Kendor Steel Rule Die Inc	7389	1695
Keneal Industries Inc	2759	569
Kenergy Corp	4911	190
Kenesis Corporate and Information Consulting LLC	8742	270
Kenexa Corp	7372	247
Kenexa (Philadelphia Pennsylvania)	7372	1500
Kenix Global Technologies LLC	5065	694
Kenlee Precision Corp	3599	280
Kenmode Tool And Engineering Inc	3469	105
Kenmore Air Harbor Inc	7359	59
Kenmore Construction Company Inc	1611	70
Kenmore Development and Machine Company Inc	3599	2362
Kennametal Inc	3545	35
Kennametal Inc (Latrobe Pennsylvania)	3541	1
Kennco Manufacturing Inc	3523	255
Kennebec Technologies	3544	332
Kennecott Exploration Co	1081	4
Kennecott Greens Creek Mining A JV	1031	4
Kennecott Utah Copper Corp	1021	5
Kennedy and Bowden Machine Company Inc	3544	847
Kennedy Associates/Architects Inc	8712	113
Kennedy Associates Inc	6282	81
Kennedy Capital Management Inc	6282	132
Kennedy Childs PC	8111	420
Kennedy Communications Inc	8742	452
Kennedy Diversified Inc	5015	25
Kennedy Engine Company Inc	5084	394
Kennedy Glass Inc	1793	11
Kennedy Group Inc	2671	43
Kennedy Gustafson And Cole Inc	3564	121
Kennedy Homes LP	8742	387
Kennedy Industries Inc	3491	29
Kennedy Ink Company Inc	2893	39
Kennedy/Jenks Consultants Inc	8711	100
Kennedy Machine and Manufacturing Inc	3599	1665
Kennedy Machine and Tool Inc	3599	342
Kennedy Oil Company Inc	5172	150
Kennedy Tank and Manufacturing Company Inc	3443	105
Kennedy Wholesale Inc	5145	16
Kennedy-Wilson Holdings Inc	6531	243
Kennerley-Spratling Inc	3089	294
Kennesaw Transportation Inc	4213	642
Kenneth Bordewick Interior Designs Inc	7389	1347
Kenneth Cole Productions Inc	3149	14
Kenneth Fox Supply Co	2393	12
Kenneth J Gerbino and Co	6282	610
Kenneth L Kurz and Associates	7379	1297
Kenneth M Weinstein CPA	8721	352
Kenneth Nieman	5511	261
Kenneth R Brand	5063	743
Kenneth S Jarrell Inc	2899	239
Kenneth West Inc	1623	392
Kennewick Industrial and Electrical Supply Inc	5063	345
Kenney and Company Staffing Inc	7361	226
Kenney Communications Inc	2721	295
Kenney Machinery Corp	5083	43
Kenney Manufacturing Co	2591	5
Kennickell Printing Co	2752	546
Kennihan and Company Inc	5045	704
Kennley Corp	3469	386
Kenny Industrial Services LLC	8744	38
Kenny's Candy Company Inc	2064	22
Kennys Home Plaza	5039	53
Kennywood Entertainment Co	7996	28
Kenoff and Machtinger LLP	8111	584
Kenona Industries Inc	3543	12
Kenosha Achievement Center Inc	8331	82
Kenosha Beef International Ltd	4213	2781
Kenra Ltd	2844	116
Kenro Inc	3089	128
Kens Electronics	3677	129
Ken's Stereo-Video Junction Inc	5731	69
Kensen Tool and Die Inc	3544	809
Kensey Nash Corp	3841	68
Kensey Nash Holding Co	8731	134
Kensib Inc	7311	691
Kensington Community Corporation For Individual Dignity	8361	137
Kensington Design and Build LLC	7389	2267
Kensington Group Inc	2741	361
Kensington Realty Advisors Inc	6282	207
Kenson Plastics Inc	3089	1551
Kent Adhesive Products Co	2679	43
Kent Corp	2542	18
Kent Cos	5541	34
Kent Demolition Tool	3545	394
Kent Electric Co	1731	380
Kent Financial Services Inc	6211	406
Kent Foundry Co	3321	52
Kent G Smith	3089	1640
Kent Homeopathic Associates Inc	7372	4462
Kent International Holdings Inc	2834	485
Kent Investment Corp	7359	196

Company Name	SIC	Rank
Kent Machine Inc	3544	577
Kent Marine Inc	3089	1566
Kent Mold And Manufacturing Co	3544	365
Kent Quality Foods Inc	2011	60
Kent Security Services	7381	20
Kent Sign Company Inc	5046	361
Kent Sporting Goods Company Inc	3949	75
Kent Tool And Die Inc	3544	680
Kent Warehouse And Labeling LLC	7389	1158
Kentec Inc	5072	38
Kentec Medical Inc	5047	100
Ken-Tech Products Corp	3826	167
Kentek Corp	3993	29
Kentmaster Manufacturing Company Inc	5084	221
Ken-Tron Manufacturing Inc	3469	150
Ken-Tronics Inc	3544	746
Kentronics Inc	3669	304
Kentrox LLC	3663	41
Kent's Tire Service Inc	5014	61
Kentuckiana Curb Company Inc	3444	182
Kentuckiana Trucking Inc	4213	2162
Kentucky Bancshares Inc	6022	238
Kentucky Bank	6035	69
Kentucky Bourbon Distillers Ltd	2085	28
Kentucky Container Service	4213	1640
Kentucky Electronics Inc	3544	146
Kentucky Employees Retirement System	6371	3
Kentucky Fertilizer LLC	5191	142
Kentucky First Federal Bancorp	6035	168
Kentucky Logos LLC	3993	184
Kentucky Lottery Corp	7389	58
Kentucky Machine and Engineering Inc	3599	617
Kentucky Machine and Tool Co	3599	2285
Kentucky Motor Service South Inc	5013	248
Kentucky Oil And Refining Co	5171	49
Kentucky Power Co	4911	128
Kentucky Textiles Inc	2339	21
Kentucky Utilities Co	4911	285
Kentucky West Virginia Gas Co	4923	22
Kentucky-Tennessee Clay Co	1455	4
Kentwood Manufacturing Co	2426	44
Kentwool Co	2281	12
Kenwal Pickling LLC	3471	94
Kenwal Steel Corp	5051	90
Kenway Corp	3089	732
Kenway Distributors Inc	5087	24
Kenwel Printers Inc	2752	933
Kenwell Corp	3599	622
Kenwood Service Inc	5013	412
Kenwood Silver Company Inc	3421	2
Kenwood USA Corp	5064	15
Kenworth Northwest Inc	5511	478
Kenworth Of Cincinnati Inc	5012	91
Kenworth of Indianapolis Inc	5511	991
Kenworth of Mid-Iowa Inc	5511	1121
Kenworth of Tennessee Inc	5012	54
Kenworth Sales Company Inc	5012	26
Kenworth Truck Co	3713	15
Kenyon Dodge Inc	5511	726
Kenyon International Inc	3631	14
Kenyon Press Inc	2752	860
Kenyon-Peck Inc	5511	1114
Keo Cutters Inc	3541	70
Keokuk Junction Railway Co	4011	34
Keokuk Savings Bank and Trust Co	6022	717
Kep Electric Inc	1731	2204
Kepco Inc	3612	32
Kephart Trucking Co	4213	108
Kepner Plastics Fabricators Inc	3089	1523
Kepner-Tregoe Inc	8742	169
Keppel Amfels Inc	1629	21
Keppler Speakers	7922	29
Ker and Downey Inc	4725	51
Kerasotes ShowPlace Theaters LLC	7832	11
Kerber Milling Co	2048	77
Kercher Machine Works Inc	3599	1162
Keri Systems Inc	3699	90
Kerkhoff Associates Inc	2439	47
Kerley and Sears Inc	5084	721
KERM Transportation Inc	4213	2584
Kerma Medical Products Inc	3842	164
Kermit K Kistler Inc	5599	16
Kermitool Inc	3545	407
Kern County Tractor Parts Inc	5082	194
Kern Electronics and Lasers Inc	3699	266
Kern Maintenance and Construction Corp	1731	2281
Kern Meat Company Inc	5147	140
Kern Oil and Refining Co	2911	39
Kern Regional Center	8322	16
Kern-Liebers USA Inc	3495	18
Kerns Group Architects PC	8712	294
Kerns Manufacturing Corp	3469	99
Kerns Trucking Inc	4213	1411
Kerr Concentrates Inc	2087	48
Kerr Corp	3843	12
Kerr Drug Inc	5912	15
Kerr Group Inc	3085	23
Kerr Machine Co	3561	150
Kerr Russell and Weber	8111	342
Kerrington Health Systems Inc	8741	233
Kerry Co	2099	222

Company Name	SIC	Rank
Kerry Company Inc	3593	45
Kerry Ford Inc	5511	622
Kerry Ingedients and Flavors	2038	10
Kerry Transport Inc	4213	2447
Kersey and Kersey Inc	8712	289
Kershner and Moreno	8111	572
Kervick Enterprises Inc	3462	29
Kerwin Communications Inc	7311	768
Keryx Biopharmaceuticals Inc	2834	456
Kes Science and Technology	5083	123
Kesclo Financial Inc	3446	47
Kesio Inc	4911	596
Kesler and Rust	8111	543
Keson Industries Inc	3953	14
Kessel Lumber Supply Inc	5031	450
Kesseli Morse Company Inc	5039	18
Kessler and Associates Inc	8721	285
Kessler Containers Ltd	3089	820
Kessler Industries Inc (Paterson New Jersey)	5074	120
Kessler International Corp	5088	89
Kessler-Ellis Products Co	3829	101
Kesslers Inc	2013	145
Kester Solder Div	3341	3
Kestrel Consulting Ltd	7361	302
Kesu System and Services Inc	3825	200
Ketcham Lumber Company Inc	5031	270
Ketcham Pump Company Inc	3561	172
Ketchie-Houston Inc	3462	73
Ketchikan Indian Corp	8322	101
Ketchum Directory Advertising Inc	7319	28
Ketchum Inc	8743	1
Ketera Technologies Inc	7372	2223
Kett Engineering Corp	8734	54
Kettelhut Construction Inc	1542	179
Kettle Cuisine Inc	2032	15
Kettle-Lakes Coop	5191	61
Kettler Forlines Homes Inc	1522	37
Kettler Janitorial Services Inc	7349	424
Kettley Publishing Co	7372	2393
Keurig Inc	3631	6
Keusch Glass Inc	5039	44
Kevil Tool and Die Inc	3541	241
Kevin F Donohoe Company Inc	6531	242
Kevin Inc	5941	28
Kevin P Carey and Associates Inc	7381	230
Kevko Race And Manufacturing Inc	3559	564
Kevlin Corp	3679	229
Kevro Chemical Co	3089	1270
Kewanee Burner Supply and Sales	5074	220
Kewaskum Frozen Foods Inc	5147	138
Kewaunee County Banc-Shares Inc	6022	151
Kewaunee Fabrications LLC	3531	74
Kewaunee Scientific Corp	3821	4
Kewill Electronic Commerce	7372	849
Key Bank USA NA	6021	8
Key Blue Prints Inc	5049	36
Key Boston Inc	5064	50
Key Broadcasting Inc	4832	248
Key Cadillac Oldsmobile	5511	615
Key Chemical and Equipment Company Inc	3825	350
Key City Furniture Company Inc	2512	71
Key Construction Inc	1542	85
Key Construction Inc (Gilbert Arizona)	1521	39
Key Consulting Group Inc	7379	837
Key Container Company Inc	2653	17
Key Container Corp	2653	40
Key Controls Of Tampa Inc	5084	530
Key Curriculum Press Inc	2731	33
Key Energy Services Inc	1381	7
Key Enterprises LLC	2721	207
Key Equipment Finance	6153	1
Key Fire Hose Corp	3052	14
Key Food Stores Cooperative Inc	5141	120
Key Handlings System Inc	3535	14
Key High Vacuum Products Inc	3589	190
Key Industries Inc	5136	23
Key Information Systems Inc	7373	283
Key Life Network Inc	5065	712
Key Logistics	4213	1302
Key Machine Tool Inc	5084	646
Key Oil Co	5541	63
Key Opportunities Inc	8331	247
Key Packaging Company Inc	3086	89
Key Plastics	3089	37
Key Plastics LLC	7389	187
Key Polymer Corp	2899	169
Key Principal Partners LLC	6799	99
Key Print Shop Inc	5044	155
Key Safety Systems Inc	3714	35
Key Tech Corp	2891	95
Key Tech Inc	2865	31
Key Technology Inc	3556	5
Key Tronic Corp	3577	72
Key Trucking Inc	4213	714
Key West Boats Inc	3732	71
KeyBanc Capital Markets Inc	6211	135
KeyBank NA	6021	4
KeyCorp Insurance Agency USA Inc	6311	164
KeyCorp	6712	15
Keydata International Inc	3571	61
Keyes Asset Management Inc	6531	8
Keyes Company Realtors	6531	5

Company Name	SIC	Rank
KeyImpact Sales and Systems Inc	5141	24
Keyin Inc	3695	140
Key-James Brick and Supply Inc	5032	56
Keyline Corp	2752	589
Keylogic Systems Inc	7379	441
Keymark Corp	3354	13
Keymark Enterprises LLC	7372	3112
KeyMark Inc	7371	653
Keymarket Communications LLC	4832	63
Keynes Brothers Inc	2041	16
Keynote Systems Inc	7389	230
Keynoter Publishing Co	2711	666
KeyOn Communications Holdings Inc	4812	74
KeyPoint Credit Union	6062	51
Keypoint Services International Inc	1731	1701
Keyport Life Insurance Co	6311	49
KeyResults Solutions	7372	2679
Keys Complete Inc	7389	2166
Keys Fitness Products Inc	5091	22
Keys Printing Co	2752	503
Keyser Brother's Inc	5146	75
Keyston Brothers	2221	6
Keystone Acquisition Company Inc	7694	19
Keystone Adjustable Cap Company Inc	2676	10
Keystone Aggregate Products Co	5032	30
Keystone Aniline Corp	5169	86
Keystone Automotive	7389	391
Keystone Automotive Industries Inc	5013	20
Keystone Battery	3691	46
Keystone Building Products Inc	5031	118
Keystone Cable Corp	3694	48
Keystone Carriers Inc	4213	2082
Keystone Cement Co	3241	16
Keystone Computer Associates Inc	7372	3443
Keystone Consolidated Industries Inc	3312	23
Keystone Consultants Inc	7379	1026
Keystone Consulting	7371	1774
Keystone Containers LLC	3085	41
Keystone Custom Fabricators Inc	3444	229
Keystone Electrical Manufacturing Co	3613	54
Keystone Electrical Supply Company Inc	5063	545
Keystone Electronics Corp	3678	26
Keystone Engineering and Manufacturing Corp	3531	208
Keystone Filler and Manufacturing Co	3295	15
Keystone Food Products Inc	2096	23
Keystone Foods LLC	2013	5
Keystone Freight Corp	4213	203
Keystone Friction Hinge Co	3469	178
Keystone Health Plan Central	6324	42
Keystone Information Systems Inc	7372	2356
Keystone Laboratories Inc	2844	184
Keystone Leasing Services LLC	7353	19
Keystone Lime Co	1611	246
Keystone Mills	5191	104
Keystone North Inc	3562	43
Keystone Pharmaceuticals Inc	5122	94
Keystone Plastics Inc	3082	12
Keystone Powdered Metal Co	3399	10
Keystone Press Inc	2752	1328
Keystone Printing Ink Co	2893	24
Keystone Property Group	6531	241
Keystone RV Co	3792	5
Keystone Screw Corp	3452	77
Keystone Steel and Wire Co	3496	1
Keystone Systems Inc	7372	862
Keystone Wire And Cable	5063	626
Keystops LLC	5172	38
Keystrokes Transcription Inc	7338	21
KEYTEC Inc	3577	508
Keytronics Inc	3612	67
KEYW Holding Corp	8711	123
Keyware Technologies Inc	7372	1000
Keyways Inc	5045	978
Keywest Technology Inc	3651	154
Kf Controls LLC	3625	341
Kf Fiberglass Inc	3714	395
Kf Foods Inc	2099	129
KF Industries Inc	3494	10
KF Sales Corp	3494	13
K-Fab Inc	3544	103
KFC Corp	5812	467
Kfia Radio	4832	173
K-Five Construction Corp	4213	230
Kforce Inc	7363	15
K-Form Inc	7373	660
Kfox-Tv Inc	4833	173
Kfp Corp	3088	32
KFPX TV-Des Moines	4833	57
KFT Inc	3535	85
Kfyr Radio	4832	213
KG Construction Co	1389	55
Kg Solutions Inc	1623	840
KGAN Licensee LLC	4833	52
kgb	7389	86
Kgb Texas Marketing / Public Relations Inc	7311	748
kgb USA	4899	55
Kgf Associates Inc	7371	1474
Kgns Laredo Inc	4833	181
Kgp Group Inc	3555	28
KGP Telecommunications Inc	5049	2
KH Smith Communications Inc	1623	83

Company Name	SIC	Rank
Kha Kenney Products Inc	3541	186
Khameleon Software	7372	1847
Khan Enterprises Inc	7389	1152
Khj Integrated Marketing Inc	7311	576
KHM Plastics Inc	3089	1216
Khojna Technologies	7389	2423
Khs Corp	3599	782
Khs USA Inc	3556	15
KHS-Bartelt	3565	3
Khush Multimedia	2741	402
Khuu's Inc	3599	445
Ki Industries Inc	3089	982
Ki (USA) Corp	3465	25
Kia Motors America Inc	5012	29
Kiamichi Electric Coop	4911	282
Kiawah Resort Associates	6552	40
KIB Enterprises Corp	3613	63
Kibble and Prentice Holding Co	6282	680
Kibler Construction Company Inc	1611	218
KIC Enterprises	7349	337
Kice Industries Inc	3444	52
Kickapoo Valley Cheese Corp	5143	25
Kickapps Corp	7372	982
Kickerillo Building Co	6552	161
Kiczan Manufacturing Inc	3441	213
Kid Brands Inc	3942	4
Kid Glove Inc	4214	29
Kid Glove Service Inc	4213	2710
Kid Stuff Marketing Inc	5199	99
KIDASA Software Inc	7372	2854
Kidd and Company LLC	6799	310
Kidd Pipeline and Specialties Inc	3492	38
Kidde Fire Trainers Inc	3699	100
Kidder and Associates Inc	7371	1695
Kidder Mathews Inc	6531	40
Kideney Architects/Laping Jaeger Associates PC	8712	163
Kidkusion Inc	3086	167
Kidron Electric Inc	1731	774
Kids Ii Inc	3944	22
Kids Stuff Inc	5961	165
Kidspeace National Centers For Kids In Crisis Inc	8322	4
Kidspeace National Centers For Kids In Crisis Of New England	8361	42
Kidtech Inc	3577	543
Kid-U-Not Inc	2396	26
Kidwell Inc	1731	393
Kiefel Inc	3559	111
Kiefer Bonfanti and Company LLP	8721	393
Kiefer Built LLC	3715	46
Kiemle and Hagood Co	6531	95
Kiemle-Hankins Co	7694	6
Kiene Diesel Accessories Inc	3541	189
Kiernan Consulting Inc	5734	217
Kiesub Corp	5063	194
Kiewit Construction Group Inc	1611	6
Kiewit Corp	3273	2
Kiewit Southern Co (Atlanta Georgia)	1622	32
Kiewit Western Co	1611	14
Kig Healthcare Solutions	7379	1079
Kiger Brothers Machine Tool and Die Works Inc	3544	706
Kigre Inc	3699	230
Kiix Sports Radio 1410 Am	4832	177
Kik Custom Products Inc	2841	9
Kikiaola Land Company Ltd	6552	199
Kikkoman Foods Inc	2035	4
Kikkoman Sales USA Inc	5149	117
Kiko Foods Inc	2099	226
Kiku Obata and Co	7336	158
Kilby E D Manufacturing and Farming Inc	3523	213
Kilby Steel Company Inc	3599	2109
Kilder Corp	3082	26
Kildrummy Inc	7371	1275
Kilgannon	7311	319
Kilgore and Kilgore PLLC	8111	536
Kilgore Ford	5511	880
Kilgore Machine Company Inc	3728	210
Kilgore Manufacturing Company Inc	3841	247
Kilgore Pavement and Maintenance	7349	432
Killbuck Bancshares Inc	6712	513
Killbuck Savings Bank	6022	417
Killdeer Mountain Manufacturing Inc	3679	58
Killearn Properties Inc	6552	236
Killen Contractors Inc	1731	1025
Killen Group Inc	6282	418
Killer Beads And Everything Else You Need Inc	5094	89
Killer Tracks	2741	85
Killian Branding	7311	514
Killingsworth Enviromental Inc	7342	53
Killingsworth Pest Control	7342	55
Killington Ltd	7011	169
Kilmer Wagner And Wise Paper Company Inc	3086	127
Kiln Drying Systems and Components Inc	3559	375
Kilo Ampere Switch Corp	3613	186
Kilohana Corp	8711	141
Kilopass Technology Inc	3674	127
Kilowatt Electric Co	1731	1200
Kilowatts Electric Supply Corp	5063	352

Company Name	SIC	Rank
Kilpatrick Equipment Co	5044	159
Kilpatrick Stockton LLP	8111	23
Kilroy Co	3544	124
Kilroy Metal Products Inc	5031	166
Kilroy Structural Steel Co	3441	232
Kilroy's Wonder Market Inc	5411	265
Kim Celano	4813	759
Kim Evans and Associates	7372	3999
Kim Zeder	7389	1649
Kimal Lumber Co	5211	136
Kimastle Corp	3599	317
Kimball Electronics Inc	2521	6
Kimball Hill Inc	1531	15
Kimball International Inc	2521	4
Kimball Medical Center	8062	183
Kimball Physics Inc	3821	45
Kimball Sand Company Inc	5032	94
Kimbel Publication Inc	2711	819
Kimber Petroleum Corp	5172	74
Kimberley Manufacturing Co	3089	1010
Kimberly Machine Inc	3599	1537
Kimberly-Clark Corp	2621	1
Kimble Machines Inc	3599	2327
Kimbrell Electric Inc	1731	186
Kimbrell's Furniture Distributors Inc	5712	43
Kimchuk Inc	3625	58
Kimco Development Corp	6552	132
Kimco Realty Corp	6798	27
Kimco Staffing Services Inc	7361	68
Kim-Kraft Inc	2754	19
Kimley-Horn and Associates Inc	8711	69
Kimlor Mills Inc	2392	27
Kimmel Center Inc	7922	19
Kimmey Plumbing Co	5047	179
Kimmins Contracting Corp	1541	41
Kimmins Corp	1623	62
Kimnach Ford Inc	5511	321
Kimoto Tech Inc	3081	91
Kimray Inc	3829	35
Kimre Inc	3585	148
Kimro Manufacturing Inc	5699	18
Kimwood Corp	3553	37
Kimzey Welding Works Inc	3599	2388
Kinamor Inc	3089	1500
Kinaneco Inc	2752	1453
Kinard Trucking Inc	4213	223
Kincaid and Decker Inc	5023	72
Kincaid Auction Service House Inc	7389	1579
Kincaid Construction Inc	1623	495
Kincaid Furniture Company Inc	2511	22
Kinder Electric Company Inc	1731	382
Kinder Group Inc	3993	90
Kinder Guard LLC	5731	194
Kinder Lydenberg Domini and Company Inc	6282	97
Kinder Morgan Bulk Terminals Inc	4789	17
Kinder Morgan Energy Partners LP	4613	1
Kinder Morgan Kansas Inc	4923	2
KinderCare Learning Centers Inc	8351	5
Kinder-Harris Inc	5023	105
Kindred Healthcare Inc	8052	2
Kindred Operating Incorporated Benefit Trust	6351	41
Kindsvater Inc	4213	637
Kinecta Federal Credit Union	6061	16
Kinedyne Corp	3714	77
Kinematic Automation Inc	3841	238
Kinematics And Controls Corp	3625	356
KineMed Inc	8731	139
Kinemetrics Inc	3829	121
Kinemotive Corp	3492	23
Kinergy Corp	3535	186
Kinesis Corp	3577	529
Kinesix Corp	7372	2794
Kinetek Corp	7373	774
Kinetic Ceramics Inc	3674	406
Kinetic Concepts Inc	2599	1
Kinetic Instruments Inc	3843	75
Kinetic Presentations Inc	7372	2774
Kinetic Software Inc	7371	521
Kinetic Systems Inc	1799	10
Kinetic Technology Agency	7372	3110
Kinetic Ventures LLC	6799	270
Kinetico Quality Water Systems	3589	243
Kinetics Industries Inc	3679	433
Kinetics Systems Inc	2899	53
KineticSystems Company LLC	3823	24
Kinetik Information Technology	7371	1627
Kinetronics Corp	5043	43
Kinfine USA Inc	5021	30
King and Associates	7311	1027
King and Ballow	8111	466
King And Company Inc	3086	169
King and Company Inc (New Orleans Louisiana)	1742	4
King and Spalding	8111	34
King and Spalding LLP	8111	116
King Antenna Inc	5731	266
King Arthur Flour Inc	2041	11
King Associates Ltd	3643	42
King Auto Mall	5511	102
KING Broadcasting Co	4833	95
King Brothers Electric Company Inc	1731	619
King Business Forms Corp	2752	945

Company Name	SIC	Rank
King Business Interiors Inc	5021	71
King Centerless Grinding Company Inc	7389	2485
King Circuit	3672	356
King Communications Inc	7389	2093
King Communications USA Inc	5065	823
King Computer Services Inc	7372	1928
King Construction Inc	1611	240
King Electric LLC	1731	711
King Electric Of Ocaloosa Inc	1731	2292
King Electrical Manufacturing Co	3634	21
King Engineering Corp	3829	391
King Estate Winery Inc	2084	35
King Filler Co	2439	49
King Fisher Company Inc	3669	222
King Fisher Marine Service Inc	1629	14
King Fuels Inc	5172	57
King Group Inc (Cleveland Ohio)	6531	230
King Group Inc (Dallas Texas)	7311	466
King Hershey PC	8111	576
King Hickory Furniture Co	2512	46
King Industrial Corp	3544	254
King Instrument Company Inc	3823	155
King International Corp	2752	1197
King Junk	5093	241
King Kitchens Inc	1799	26
King Kold Inc	2038	84
King Kullen Grocery Company Inc	5411	98
King Kutter Inc	3523	94
King Limestone Inc	1422	55
King Lithographers Inc	2752	333
King Load Manufacturing Co	2542	16
King Luminaire Company Inc	3646	54
King Machine And Tool Co	3544	765
King Media Enterprises Inc	2711	563
King Milling Co	2041	19
King Model Co	3999	160
King Nut Co	2068	10
King Nutronics Corp	3823	298
King Of Pita Bakery Inc	5461	24
King Pharmaceuticals Inc	2834	32
King Pipeline And Utility Company Inc	1623	132
King Plastic Corp	3081	67
King Plastics Inc	3089	503
King Printing Company Inc	2732	29
King Provision Corp	5142	19
King Ranch Inc	0212	1
King Research Inc	2842	150
King Soopers Inc	5411	64
King Soopers Inc Bakery Div	2051	26
King Supply Company LLC	5039	9
King Systems Corp	3841	72
King Technologies Inc	7379	698
King Tester Corp	3829	420
King Tool and Die Inc	3599	1558
King Tool Co	3541	211
King Tool Co	3599	150
King Tortilla Inc	2099	142
King Trucking Inc	4213	1131
Kingbright Corp	3674	357
Kingdom Express Inc	4213	2053
Kingdom Tapes and Electronics	5735	3
Kingery Printing Co	2752	111
Kingfisher Systems Inc	8742	238
Kingland Companies Ltd	7371	260
Kingland Systems Corp	7372	2031
Kingman Dedicated Service Inc	4213	2145
KingMax Micro Technology Inc	3577	62
Kings Bay Communications Inc	4841	129
Kings Command Foods Inc	2013	97
King's Credit Services	7322	110
King's Custom Builders Inc	2451	32
Kings Express	4213	2138
Kings Family Restaurants	5812	263
Kings Film and Sheet Inc	3081	159
Kings Liquor Inc	5921	13
King's Medical Group	7352	5
Kings Mountain Software Engineering	7372	4837
Kings Nissan of Cincinatti	5511	1214
Kings Plush Inc	2221	26
King's Prosperity Industries LLC	3089	1359
Kings Road Entertainment Inc	7812	324
Kings Tire Service Inc	5014	57
Kings Welding And Fabricating Inc	3599	1041
Kingsbridge Holdings LLC	7377	19
Kingsbury Corp	3541	61
Kingsbury Inc	3568	20
Kingsdown Inc	2515	14
Kingsford Broach and Tool Inc	3545	195
Kingsland Entertainment Agency	7922	91
Kingsley Kranzler Communications Ltd	8742	623
Kingsley ManufacturingCo	3842	288
Kingsolver Inc	3991	21
Kingspan Insulated Panels North America Inc	3448	1
Kingsport Livestock Auction Corp	5154	7
Kingsport Publishing Corp	2711	277
Kingston Anesthesia LLC	8049	19
Kingston Contracting Inc	1731	1457
Kingston Machine Tool Inc	3541	231
Kingston Oil Supply Corp	5172	82
Kingston Technology Company Inc	3674	7
Kingstone companies Inc	6411	222
Kingsville Publishing Company Inc	2711	830
Kingsway Amigo Insurance Co	6331	355

Company Name	SIC	Rank
Kingsway Exterminating Company Inc	7342	42
Kini Information Technologies Inc	7379	912
Kinnan Engineering Inc	1623	741
Kinnetic Laboratories Inc	8731	274
Kinney Agency Inc	6411	190
Kinney Drugs Inc	5122	14
Kinney Electrical Manufacturing Co	3613	49
Kinney Industries Inc	8711	496
Kinney Office Systems	5044	151
Kinney Tool And Die Inc	3469	115
Kinnser Software Inc	7372	2785
Kino International Corp	7812	95
Kinop Sports Complex	4832	113
Kinpak Inc	2899	109
Kinray Inc	5122	5
Kinsel Ford Inc	5511	11
Kinsel Motors Inc	5511	387
Kinsey's Outdoors Inc	5091	90
Kinship Venture Management LLP	6799	334
Kinsley Construction Inc (York Pennsylvania)	1542	70
Kinswood Electronics Corp	3679	179
Kintec LLC	2439	57
Kintek Corp	5049	200
Kin-Tek Laboratories Inc	3821	61
Kinter Electric Inc	1731	1952
Kintetsu International Express	4724	51
Kintock Group Of New Jersey Inc	8322	33
Kinton Carbide Inc	3398	23
Kintronic Laboratories Inc	3663	198
Kintronics Inc	3572	69
Kinyo Company Inc	3651	55
Kinzua Environmental Inc	2842	144
KIO Kables Inc	3496	113
Kiolbassa Provision Co	2013	95
Kiosk Information Systems	3577	133
Kiowa Line Builders Inc	1623	461
KIP America Inc	3577	180
Kipany Productions Ltd	7389	224
Kipe Molds Inc	3544	832
Kipp Brothers Inc	5092	19
Kipper Tool Co	5085	18
KIRA Inc	8744	16
Kirby and Holloway Provisions Company Inc	2013	166
Kirby Co	3635	2
Kirby Corp	4449	3
Kirby Engine Systems Inc	3599	461
Kirby Inland Marine LP	4491	5
Kirby Lester LLC	3559	227
Kirby Manufacturing Inc	3523	104
Kirby Oil Co	5172	121
Kirby Pines Estates	8741	27
Kirby Risk Electrical Supply	3699	127
Kirby - Smith Machinery Inc	7353	6
Kirchner Block And Brick Inc	3271	16
Kirco Manix	1541	180
Kirin Pharma USA Inc	6794	159
Kirk and Blum Manufacturing Company Inc	1711	8
Kirk Horse Insurance Inc	6399	30
Kirk Root Designs	5944	36
Kirk Trucking Service Inc	4213	2965
Kirk Williams Company Inc	1711	176
Kirkbride Bible and Technology Inc	7372	3224
Kirkegaard and Perry Labs Inc	2836	54
Kirker Kubala Inc	5063	926
Kirkey Products Group	7371	807
Kirkham Michael and Associates Inc	8711	411
Kirkhill-TA Co	3061	7
Kirkland and Ellis LLP	8111	8
Kirkland's Inc	5999	16
Kirkpatrick Pettis Inc	6211	328
Kirk-Rudy Inc	3554	17
Kirksey and Partners Architects Inc	8712	84
Kirkwood Commutator Co	3621	51
Kirkwood Electric Inc	1731	315
Kirkwood Motors Inc	5511	516
Kirkwood Printing Company Inc	2752	286
Kirlins Hallmark Inc	5947	3
Kirmin Die and Tool Inc	3465	65
Kirr Marbach and Co	6282	601
Kirsan Engineering Inc	3541	96
Kirsch Kohn and Bridge LLP	8721	461
Kirschbaum-Krupp Metal Recycling LLC	5093	48
Kirsh Foundry Inc	3321	44
Kirshenbaum Bond Senecao and Partners	7311	54
Kirtas Technologies Inc	3577	248
Kirtland Capital Corp	6799	244
Kirtland Inc	1731	2165
KIS Information Systems Inc	7372	4619
Kisco Information Systems	7372	3832
Kishwaukee Community Hospital	8062	112
Kiska Construction Corp	1522	43
KiSKA Construction Corporation - USA	6552	116
Kismet Rubber Products Corp	3061	42
Kiss My Face Corp	2844	105
Kissel Brothers Shows Inc	7999	121
Kissler and Company Inc	7629	43
Kisters Kayat Inc	3565	62
Kistler Ford Inc	5511	343
Kistler Instrument Corp	3829	114

Company Name	SIC	Rank
Kistler-Morse Corp	3829	108
Kistler-O'brien Fire Protection	5063	198
Kit Carson Electric Coop	4911	360
Kit Contractors Inc	1521	169
Kit Home Builders West LLC	3792	8
Kitamura Machinery of USA Inc	3541	100
Kitch Drutchas Wagner Valitutti and Sherbrook	8111	195
Kitch Engineering Inc	3599	1171
Kitch N Cook D Potato Chip Company Inc	2096	59
Kitchell CEM	8741	93
Kitchell Corp	1542	36
Kitchell Development Co	6552	246
Kitchen Collection Inc	5719	38
Kitchen Cooked Inc	2096	47
Kitchen Creations Inc	5031	420
Kitchen Guild	5211	154
Kitchen Kompact Inc	2434	10
Kitchen-Quip Inc	3363	49
Kitchens Brothers Manufacturing Co	2421	22
Kitchens by Krengel Inc	8712	288
Kitco Inc	5088	70
Kitcor Corp	3469	267
Kite Realty Group Trust	6798	126
Kiti 1420 Am	4832	198
Kitko Wood Products Inc	2426	24
Kitsap Bank	6022	111
Kitsap Credit Union	6061	61
Kittatinny Manufacturing Services Inc	3599	603
Kittle's Home Furnishings	5712	81
Kittredge Equipment Company Inc	5046	131
Kittyhawk Molding Company Inc	3089	1457
Kiva Container Corp	3086	173
Kiva Designs Inc	5091	144
Kiva Inc	1623	744
Kiva North America Inc	7373	1146
Kivort Steel Inc	5051	129
Kiwa Bio-Tech Products Group Corp	2041	67
Kiwash Electric Cooperative Inc	4911	422
Kiwi Tek LLC	5734	255
Kiwiboxcom Inc	7372	5050
Kiwiplan Inc	7372	1546
Kix Kutzler Express Inc	4213	437
Kizmet Interactive	7319	124
KJ Bradley Inc	4213	1253
KJ Electric Inc	5063	176
KJ International Inc	2087	71
KJ Quinn and Company Inc	3479	36
K-Jack Aero Industries LLC	3728	211
Kjb Security Products Inc	5065	412
Kjb Supply Company Inc	5023	89
Kjel Radio	4832	205
Kjellstrom and Lee Inc	1541	235
Kjjr Am 880 Newstalk	4832	229
Kjm Enterprises Inc	2759	235
Kjolhede Inc	5049	135
KK Custom Improvements Inc	7349	377
KK Stevens Publishing Co	2711	438
K-K Tool And Design Inc	3544	788
Kkaj 957 Fm	4832	162
Kke Architects Inc	8712	157
Kki Corp	5734	314
KKR Financial Holdings LLC	6798	32
Kkt Inc	3334	15
Kktu Television	4833	232
KKW Trucking Inc	4213	568
KL Bradley Electric Inc	1731	938
KL Electronics Inc	3672	376
Kl Fenix Corp	5045	776
KL Harring Transportation and Warehousing	4213	692
KL House Construction Company Inc	1542	348
K-L Manufacturing Company Inc	2339	39
Klamath Publishing Co	2711	113
Klapec Trucking Co	4213	1239
Klarity Multimedia Inc	7389	2011
Klarmann Rulings Inc	3231	68
KLAS Enterprises LLC	7375	296
Klasek Letter Company Inc	2752	498
Klasky Csupo Inc	7379	205
Klassen Business Computer	5045	782
KLAS-TV Inc	4833	110
KLA-Tencor Corp	3827	1
Klauber Brothers Inc	2258	9
Klauer Manufacturing Company Inc	3444	55
Klaussner Casegoods Div	2511	93
Klaussner Corporate Services Inc	2512	62
Klaussner Furniture Industries Inc	2512	5
Klc Consulting Inc	7379	625
KLC Enterprises	7372	4914
Klc Holdings Ltd	3089	468
Kld Labs Inc	3829	184
Klear-Vu Corp	2392	20
Kleber and Associates Advertising	7311	294
Kleen Maid Inc	2392	25
Kleen Polymers Inc	3061	64
Kleen Supply Co	5141	222
Kleenair Products Co	3567	81
Kleenco Corp	7349	123
Kleenco Maintenance and Construction Inc	7349	166
Kleenmark Services Corp	7349	92
Kleen-Rite Building Maintenance Inc	7349	517

Company Name	SIC	Rank
Kleer-Fax Inc	2678	9
Kleet Lumber Company Inc	5211	114
Kleier Communications Inc	7311	418
Klein Associates Inc	3812	119
Klein Bank (Waconia Minnesota)	6021	199
Klein Bicycle Corporation Of Washington	3751	19
Klein Brothers Holdings Ltd	2068	27
Klein Financial Inc	6712	228
Klein Foods Inc	2084	29
Klein National Bank of Madison	6021	386
Klein Optical Instruments Inc	3829	504
Klein Plastics Company LLC	3089	667
Klein Products Of Kansas Inc	3443	186
Klein Smoked Meats LLC	5149	211
Klein Steel Service Inc	5051	152
Klein Tools Inc	3423	11
Kleinberg Electric Inc	1731	240
Kleiner Perkins Caufield and Byers	6799	262
Kleinfelder Inc	8741	103
Kleinknecht Electric Company Inc	1731	151
Kleinpeter Farms Dairy LLC	2026	50
Kleinschmidt Inc	7374	75
Klemp Corp (Chicago Illinois)	3446	17
Klepper Oil	4212	44
Klever Marketing Inc	7372	5012
Klh Industries Inc	3541	156
Kliegel Machine Company LLC	3599	2516
Kliewer Knife Co	3579	52
Klik Technologies Corp	7374	134
Klikwood Corp	3565	17
Klimaire Products Inc	3585	216
K-Line Industries Inc	8711	491
Kline Keppel and Koryak PC	8111	537
Kline Process Systems Inc	7373	320
Klines Auto Inc	5013	160
Kline's Construction Company Inc	1623	227
Kling	8712	39
Klingberg Family Centers Inc	8361	196
Klinge Corp	3585	191
Klingensmith Inc	5999	71
Klinger Constructors LLC	1541	90
Klinger Educational Products Corp	5049	189
Klingler Electric Corp	1731	16
Klingspor Abrasives Inc	3291	7
Klink Trucking Inc	4213	1228
Klinke Brothers Ice Cream Co	2024	33
Klipp Colussy Jenks DuBois Architects PC	8712	156
Klise Manufacturing Co	2431	116
Klitzner Industries Inc	3911	41
KLLM Transport Services Inc	4213	28
Kln Steel Products Company LLC	2514	4
Klocke Of America Inc	7389	1270
Klode Co	5063	719
Kloeckner Pentaplast of America Inc	3083	8
Kloehn Company Ltd	3841	62
Klondike Cheese Co	2022	24
Klopp International Inc	3578	36
Klos Technologies Inc	7372	4838
Klosterman Baking Co	2051	24
Klote International Corp	2512	42
Klt Associates Inc	7371	1483
KLT Gas Inc	4612	16
KLT Inc	4911	341
Klukwan Inc	2411	4
Klundt Hosmer Design Assoc Inc	7336	288
Klure and Harris Inc	5051	447
Klute Communications	8743	288
Klutts Property Management	1521	125
Klutz Press	2731	52
Klynas Engineering	3732	4463
K-M Concessions Inc	5812	159
Km Group LLC	5021	117
K-M Machine Company Inc	3599	703
Kma Broadcasting LP	4832	249
K-Mac Enterprises Inc	5812	37
Kmart Corp	5331	3
K-MAX Corp	5085	17
KMC Corp	5181	87
Kmc Inc	3568	63
Kmc Systems Inc	3812	102
Kmco LP	2899	126
KMG Chemicals Inc	2899	35
KMHL Broadcasting Corp	4832	99
Kmi Systems Inc	3569	76
KMJ Commuications Inc	7372	4000
KMJ/Corbin and Co	8721	191
Kmk Consulting Inc	7379	1266
Kmmc LLC	1241	8
KMMX Mix 1003	4832	178
KmpartsCom Inc	5065	775
KMS 2000 Inc	2752	1104
Kms Consulting Services Inc	7379	1368
K-M-S Industries Inc	3599	1276
Kms Machine Works Inc	3599	2030
Kmt International Inc	3533	55
KMT Management Inc	2082	31
Kmt Robotic Solutions Inc	3569	110
KMT Waterjet Systems	5084	56
Kmw Ltd	3523	74
KN Kaminaka Inc	5531	42
Knape and Vogt Manufacturing Co	2541	3
Knape Industries Inc	3599	2230

Company Name	SIC	Rank
Knapp Chevrolet	5511	322
Knapp Engineering PC	3823	190
Knapp Manufacturing Inc	2842	137
Knappe and Koester Inc	3599	329
Knappen Milling Co	2041	42
Knepper Press Corp	2752	285
Knestrick Contractor Inc	1521	121
KNF and T Staffing Resources	7363	167
Knf Clean Room Products Corp	3699	155
KNF Corp	2821	85
Knf Neuberger Inc	3821	27
Kng Inc	2752	441
Knickerbocker Baking Inc	2051	266
Knickerbocker Construction LLC	7389	1397
Knickerbocker Partition Corp	2653	84
Knife Company Inc	5719	28
Knife River Construction	1629	27
Knife River Corp	1222	15
Knight and Carver Yachtcenter Inc	3732	47
Knight BondPoint Inc	7372	1867
Knight Capital Group Inc	6211	59
Knight Carbide Corp	3545	134
Knight Communications Inc	7379	447
Knight Distributing Company Inc	5122	30
Knight Electrical Services Corp	1731	179
Knight Execution and Clearing Services LLC	6211	196
Knight Images	7319	50
Knight Inc (Lake Forest California)	3639	11
Knight Industries and Associates Inc	3537	19
Knight LLC	3559	5
Knight Management Services Inc	8742	13
Knight Marketing Corporation Of New York	5087	47
Knight Media Inc	2759	424
Knight Piesold and Co	8711	543
Knight Point Systems	8748	193
Knight Printing Co	7389	827
Knight Protect Inc	5063	984
Knight Technologies Inc	7389	1906
Knight Tool Works Inc	3544	850
Knight Transportation Inc	4213	44
Knight Trucking Inc	4213	3142
Knighten Machine And Service Inc	3599	813
Knighton's Automotive Machine Shop Inc	3599	1628
Knight's Fabrication and Welding Inc	1799	134
Knights of Columbus	8999	6
Knightsbridge Advisers Inc	6282	563
Knightsbridge Plastics Inc	3089	1181
Knik Construction Co	1629	77
Knipes-Cohen Associates Inc	7338	8
Knipp Equipment Inc	5075	68
Knise and Krick Inc	3544	725
Knitcraft Corp	2253	6
Knitec Inc	5731	274
Knit-Rite Inc	3842	117
Knitting Factory Entertainment	7922	23
Knk Apparel Inc	2326	15
Kno Inc	3699	111
Knoa Software Inc	7371	980
Knobby Krafters Inc	3089	1374
Knock On Wood	5021	160
Knogo North America Inc	3669	113
Knoll Inc	2521	5
Knology	4813	458
Knology Holdings Inc	4841	70
Knology Inc	4812	14
Knology of Augusta Inc	4812	35
Knology of Columbus Inc	4812	36
Knology of Huntsville Inc	4812	27
Knology of Knoxville Inc	4812	37
Knology of Montgomery Inc	4812	38
Knology of Panama City Inc	4812	39
Knology (Sioux Falls South Dakota)	4841	38
Knopf and Sons Bindery Inc	2789	71
Knopf Publishing Group	2731	24
Knorr and Associates PC	8721	295
Knorr Associates Inc	7372	668
Knot Inc	5999	26
Knott Floyd Land Company Inc	1221	38
Knott Partners LP	6282	401
Knott's Berry Farm Foods Inc	7996	8
Knott's Wholesale Foods Inc	5141	163
Knouse Foods Cooperative Inc	2033	20
Knova Software Inc	7371	1871
Knovalent Inc	7379	590
Knovel Corp	7375	114
Knowland Group Inc	7372	2013
Knowledge Adventure Inc	7372	475
Knowledge Ag Inc	7371	1325
Knowledge Computers Inc	5045	723
Knowledge Development Centers	8249	16
Knowledge Factor Inc	7371	1063
Knowledge in a Nutshell	8743	337
Knowledge Learning Corp	8351	3
Knowledge Marketing	7372	3091
Knowledge Mosaic Inc	7379	1037
Knowledge Networks Inc	8999	8
Knowledge Quest	7372	2719
Knowledge Systems and Research Inc	8742	198
Knowledge Systems Corp	7379	761
Knowledge Tek	8331	134
Knowledge Unlimited Inc	2741	319

Company Name	SIC	Rank
KnowledgeBroker Inc	3571	108
KnowledgeStorm Inc	7379	325
KnowledgeSum Inc	7372	2158
Knowles Electronics Holdings Inc	3651	32
Knowles Publishing Inc	2731	191
Knowles-McNiff	7372	4232
Knowlogy Corp	8331	21
Knowlton Enterprises Inc	2097	5
Knowlton Machine Co	3599	832
Knowtions Inc	5734	279
Know-Ware Consulting Inc	7371	1198
Knox and Co	6211	231
Knox Associates Inc	5065	183
Knox County ARC	8331	61
Knox Enterprises Inc	3315	17
Knox Fertilizer Company Inc	0782	15
Knox Industries Inc	1761	16
Knox Machine Company Inc	3599	684
Knox New Hope Industries Inc	8331	223
Knox Nursery Inc	5199	6
Knoxville Bolt and Screw Inc	5072	190
Knoxville Milling Co	2041	7
Knoxville Stamping And Assembly LLC	3549	102
Knozall Software Inc	7372	2994
Knucklestrutz Toys LLC	5092	53
Knudsen Gardner and Howe Advertising Inc	7311	804
Knudsen Trucking Inc	4213	1482
Knudson Lumber Co	5031	285
Knudson Manufacturing Inc	3542	60
Knust-Sbo Ltd	3599	53
KNW Public Finance	6282	348
KO Enterprises	7389	1570
KO Manufacturing Inc	2841	28
KOA Holdings Inc	7033	8
KOA Speer Electronics Inc	5065	44
Koa Trading Co	5141	189
Koala Corp	2599	7
Koambra Inc	5065	274
Koba Corp	3089	908
Kobal Collection	7336	130
KOBC Radio Station	4832	257
Kobelco Compressors (America) Inc	3563	32
Kobelco Stewart Bolling Inc	3559	82
Kobey Corporation Inc	7389	1280
Kobo Utility Construction Corp	1731	1566
Kobold Instruments Inc	3492	31
Kobold Watch Company LLC	5944	13
Kobrin Builders Supply Inc	5039	13
Kobrin Builders Supply Of Sarasota Inc	5032	104
Kob-Tv LLC	4833	120
KOCB Inc	4833	29
KOCB Licensee LLC	4833	33
Koch and Company Inc	2434	23
KOCH Enterprises Inc	3714	58
Koch Eye Associates	8011	95
Koch Filter Corp	3585	89
Koch Heat Transfer Co	3443	32
Koch Industries Inc	4612	1
Koch Meat Company Inc	0251	1
Koch Membrane Systems Inc	3569	47
Koch-Glitsch LP	3443	22
Kocolene Marketing LLC	5541	23
Kocolene Oil Corp	5541	12
Kocour Co	3829	262
Kocsis Brothers Machine Co	3599	229
Kodak Colorado Div	3861	8
Kodak Professional Photography Div	3861	17
Kodiak Cartoners Inc	3565	80
Kodiak Electric Association Inc	4911	392
Kodiak Fishmeal Co	2077	5
Kodiak Machining Company Inc	3599	2122
Kodiak Networks Inc	4899	82
Kodiak Northwest Inc	3711	69
Kodiak Oil and Gas Corp	1382	35
Koegel Meats Inc	2013	79
Koehl Brothers Inc	5084	767
Koehler Instrument Company Inc	3823	143
Koehler-Bright Star Inc	3648	21
Koehlke Components Inc	5065	340
Koellmann Gear Corp	3566	12
Koenig Advertising and Public Relations	8742	660
Koenig and Strey Incorporated Realtors	6531	91
Koenig-Pretempco Inc	3625	338
Koeppel Companies LLC	6531	184
Koerner Distributors Inc	5182	25
Koester Corp	3599	428
Koester Metals Inc	3469	214
Koetter and Smith Inc	5099	84
Koetter Woodworking Inc	2431	57
Koeze Co	5441	5
Kofax Image Products Inc	3577	88
Koffee Kup Bakery Inc	2051	86
Kogap Electrical Division Inc	1731	375
Koger/Air Corp	1796	18
Koger Inc	7379	319
Kngok Corp	3444	30
Kohel Interstate Transport Corp	4213	1379
Koh-I-Noor Inc	3952	3
Kohl and Madden Inc	2893	2
Kohl And Vick Machine Works Inc	3599	2471
Kohlberg and Co	6211	143

Company Name	SIC	Rank
Kohlberg Capital Corp	6159	57
Kohlberg Kravis Roberts and Co	6211	89
Kohler Co	3432	3
Kohler Mix Specialties LLC	2023	4
Kohler Oil and Propane Co	5171	70
Kohlhase Electric Inc	1731	723
Kohlman Systems Research Inc	3829	288
Kohl's Corp	5311	5
Kohl's Department Stores Inc	5311	10
Kohner Properties Inc	6531	70
KOI Siferd-Hossellman Co	5013	67
Kojo Worldwide Corp	2599	9
Koke Inc	3637	06
Koke New Century Inc	2752	1021
Koken Manufacturing Company Inc	3999	116
Kokomo Gas and Fuel Co	4924	57
Kokosing Construction Company Inc	1541	23
Kokua Nurses	7363	215
Kol Bio-Medical Instruments Inc	5047	197
Kolano and Saha Engineers Inc	8731	263
Kolb Boyette and Assoc Inc	2752	1057
KolbCo	8721	13
Kolbe and Kolbe Millwork Company Inc	2431	14
Kolbe Cycle Sales	5571	1
Kolcraft Enterprises Inc	2515	10
Kolda Corp	5085	450
Kold-Ban International Ltd	3694	39
Koldkiss LLC	5078	42
KOLEASECO Inc	4213	868
Kolene Corp	2899	183
Kolenick Corp	5736	21
Kolga U S A	5063	971
Kolias and Co	3571	246
Koller Craft Plastic Prouducts Div	3089	130
Koller Enterprises Inc	3089	253
Koller Industries Inc	3471	117
Kollmorgen Corp	3621	53
Kollmorgen Corp Electro-Optical Div	3851	20
Kollmorgen Industrial/Commercl	3621	32
Kollsut Scientific Corp	3841	220
Kolmar Technologies Inc	3812	218
Kolnik Trucking Inc	4213	3019
Kolonaki	5137	19
Kolor View Press Div	2752	142
Kolorcure Corp	2893	28
Kolorfusion International Inc	2759	548
Kolpak Inc	3585	63
Kolpin Outdoors Inc	3949	87
Kolstad Company Inc	3713	40
KOM NETWORKS Inc	7372	2407
Komar Industries Inc	3589	70
Komarnicki Tool and Die Co	3544	133
Komatsu America International Co	3531	7
Komatsu Equipment Co	5082	9
Komax Corp	3599	460
Komax Systems Rockford Inc	3569	155
Komech Corp	3823	430
Komfort Corp	3792	12
Kominiarek Presler Harvick and Gudmundson LLC	8111	347
Komodo Enterprises Inc	1711	244
Komori America Corp	5084	69
Komp Equipment Company Inc	5169	149
Kompany Com	7371	1553
Komtech Cable Services	1623	157
Komtek Corp	3669	319
Komtek Inc	3462	30
Kona Brewing Co	2082	101
Kona Grill Inc	5812	238
Kona Pacific Farmers Coop	5149	219
Kona Printing And Graphics	2752	1845
Konami Computer Entertainment Of America Inc	7371	773
Konarka Technologies Inc	3691	37
Kondex Corp	3523	66
Kone Inc	7699	6
Konecranes Americas Inc	3536	7
Koneta/LRV	3069	44
Kongsberg Defense Corp	3812	107
Kongsberg Maritime	3812	162
Kongsberg Power Product Systems I Inc	3569	75
Kongsberg Underwater Technology Inc	3812	75
Konica Copiers	5044	126
Konica Minolta Business Solutions	5999	8
Konica Minolta Photo Imaging USA Inc	5043	1
Konica Minolta Sensing Americas Inc	5084	666
Konigsberg Instruments Inc	3841	225
Konner Harbus and Schwartz PC	8721	483
Konnerth Sales Associates LLC	5063	536
Konnext Inc	3643	161
Konoike-Pacific California Inc	4222	11
Konop Companies Inc	5962	12
Konover and Associates Inc	6512	13
Konrad Corp	3547	18
Konrad Marine Inc	3547	25
Konsep Co	5085	375
Kon-Suit Inc	3545	356
Konsyl Pharmaceuticals Inc	2833	61
Kontrol Automation Inc	3823	390
KOO Construction Inc	1542	294
Kooima Co	3599	543
Kool 107 9 Inc	4832	138

Company Name	SIC	Rank
Kool Ice And Seafood Company Inc	2091	28
Kooltronic Inc	3585	110
Koonce Securities Inc	6211	296
Koons Ford Annapolis Inc	5511	434
Koontz-Wagner Holdings LLC	3491	21
Kootenai Electric Cooperative Inc	4911	366
Kopco Inc	2752	700
Kop-Coat Company Inc	2861	2
Kopf Builders Inc	1522	17
Kopf Trucking Inc	4213	1108
Kopf Zimmermann Schultheis Advertising Inc	7311	620
Kop-Flex Inc	3568	10
Kopioo Inc	2752	1533
Kopin Corp	3674	102
Kopis Machine Company Inc	3599	1736
Kopp Investment Advisors Inc	6282	300
Kopper's Chocolate Specialty Company Inc	2064	72
Koppers Holdings Inc	2499	3
Koppers Inc	2491	1
Kopp's Frozen Custard	2024	45
Kopy Kat Copier	5045	802
Kopy Kween Inc	2752	312
Kopykake Enterprises Inc	3469	249
Kor Electronics	3812	70
KOR N/ K Q R N Radio	4832	262
Koral Industries Inc	3089	1437
Kor-Chem Inc	2842	89
Kord Information Systems	7372	2298
Kord Technologies Inc	8742	661
Kore Federal Inc	8748	361
Korean Channel Inc	4841	151
Kore-Linq Co	7373	1149
Korem Corp	7372	2751
Koret Inc (New York New York)	3171	1
Koret Of California Inc	2339	7
Korey Kay and Partners Inc	7311	556
Korff Holdings LLC	3325	32
Korg USA Inc	7389	362
Korman Residential	6552	144
Korn/Ferry International	7361	6
Kornick Lindsay Inc	7389	858
Kornitzer Capital Management Inc	6282	279
Kornylak Corp	3535	202
Koro Industries Inc	3541	264
Korral Kool Inc	1711	250
Korte Co	1542	149
Kortenhaus Communications Inc	8743	301
Korth Transfer Inc	4213	715
Kortzendorf Machine and Tool Inc	3599	2139
Korum Motors Inc	5511	713
Korvan Industries Inc	3523	113
Kosakura and Associates Inc	2541	41
Kosciusko County Rural Electric Membership Corp	4911	494
Koski Construction Co	1611	178
Kosmos Tool Inc	3613	160
Koss Construction Company Inc	1611	72
Koss Corp	3651	45
Kossuth Fabricators Inc	3556	92
Kostelac Grease Service Inc	2077	16
Koster Construction Company Inc	2521	56
Koster Keunen Manufacturing Inc	2842	46
Kosto Food Products Co	2087	83
Koszegi Industries Inc	3172	7
Kott Koatings Inc	2851	158
Kountry Kraft Kitchens Inc	2434	52
Kountry Wood Products LLC	2434	47
Koustas Realty Inc	6552	264
Koutech Systems Inc	3571	99
Kova Fertilizer Inc	5191	112
Kovacs Machine And Tool Company Inc	3599	1048
Kovair Inc	7372	1689
Koval Marketing Inc	5023	18
Kovalchick Salvage Co	5088	67
Kovatch Castings Inc	3324	11
Kovatch Corp	3711	67
Kovel/Fuller Advertising and Marketing	7311	244
Kowalski Companies Inc	2013	86
Koyo Machinery USA Inc	3541	222
Koyosha Graphics of America Inc	7372	366
Koza Inc	2759	233
Kozacko Enterprises Inc	7389	1820
Kozik Brothers Inc	1623	607
Kozlin Associates Inc	7361	219
Kozlowski Farms A Corp	5149	199
Kozyak Tropin and Throckmorton PA	8111	445
KP Carriers Inc	4213	1335
KPA LLC	7372	848
Kpaul Properties LLC	5112	36
K-Paul's Louisiana Enterprises Inc	5812	276
Kpc Media Group Inc	2711	318
KpekNet Inc	5734	489
KPFF Consulting Engineers Inc	8711	42
Kpg Global Enterprises LLC	7373	699
Kpgr Radio Station	4832	190
KPI Consulting	7379	1118
Kpi Ultrasound Inc	5047	89
Kpk Technologies Inc	7379	1245
Kpmg LLP Health Plans Trust	6733	6
KPMG LP	8721	18
KPS Group Inc	7389	453

Company Name	SIC	Rank
Kpua 670 Am	4832	263
KPXM TV-Minneapolis	4833	98
KPXO TV- Honolulu	4833	11
KPXR TV-Cedar Rapids	4833	145
Kqed Inc	4833	103
Kqmx	4832	176
Kqtv	4833	209
KQV Newsradio	4832	223
KR Electronics Inc	3679	149
KR Komarek Inc	3531	107
KR Tools Inc	5072	157
KRA Corp	7371	71
Krack Corp	3585	31
Krackeler Scientific Inc	5049	63
Kraco Enterprises LLC	3069	22
Kracor Inc	3089	1199
Krad Inc	4832	140
Kraemer Brothers LLC	1541	104
Kraemer Company LLC	1442	42
Kraemer Textiles Inc	2281	18
Kraft and Kennedy Inc	7373	415
Kraft Brothers Funeral Directors Inc	7261	15
Kraft Chemical Co	5169	37
Kraft Construction Company Inc	1522	13
Kraft Fluid Systems Inc	5084	480
Kraft Food Ingredients Corp	8731	101
Kraft Foods Inc	2022	1
Kraft Foods North America Inc	2022	2
Kraft Group LLC	8748	284
Kraft Hardware Inc	3432	35
Kraft Pizza Company Inc	2038	9
Kraft Power Corp	5084	96
Kraft Tool Co	3423	36
Kraftmaid Cabinetry Inc	2434	3
Kraftube Inc	3498	43
Kraftware Corp	3499	119
Kragnes Farmers Elevator	5153	205
K-Rain Manufacturing Corp	3432	32
Kraissl Company Inc	3494	75
Kramer Beverage Company Inc	5181	53
Kramer Consulting Inc	7379	1573
Kramer Entertainment Agency Inc	7999	122
Kramer Graphics Inc	2796	28
Kramer Levin Naftalis and Frankel LLP	8111	154
Kramer Lighting	3646	8
Kramer-Wilson Company Inc	6331	284
Krames Communications Inc	2731	159
Kramis And Associates LLC	7379	1679
KRAnderson Colnc	5169	104
Kranz Automotive Body Co	7539	10
Kranz Inc	5087	31
Krasdale Foods Inc	5141	68
Kraton Polymers LLC	2821	15
Kratos Defense and Security Solutions Inc	7389	102
Kratzenberg and Associates Inc	7389	859
Kraus and Naimer Inc	5063	328
Kraus/Sound	5023	41
Kraus-Anderson Capital LLC	6552	26
Kraus-Anderson Inc	1541	31
Krause Gentle Corp	5411	292
Kravco Simon Co	6552	106
Kravet Fabrics Inc	5099	2
Krayer Detective Agency Inc	7381	188
Kraytec Business Solutions Inc	5734	479
Krazan and Associates	8748	104
Krb Music Companies Inc	5099	117
Krcb Radio	4832	151
Krcs Hot 931 Fm	4832	30
Kre Inc	3452	89
Kreamer Feed Inc	2048	27
Kreative Kamaaina Enterprises LLC	5023	97
Krebbs Inc	3564	86
Kreco Antennas	3663	401
Kreg Electric Inc	1731	1432
Kreg Information Systems	7372	3472
Kregel Inc	2731	148
Kregel Publications Inc	2731	219
Kreider Corp	3469	208
Kreider Services Inc	8331	47
Kreilkamp Trucking Inc	4213	452
Kreis Tool and Manufacturing Company Inc	3544	475
Kreisler Industrial Corp	3769	14
Kreisler Manufacturing Corp	3724	35
Krell Development	8733	31
Kreller Business Information Group Inc	7323	29
Krementz and Co	3911	23
Kremin Inc	3599	2304
Krempp Lumber Co	5211	68
Krendl Machine Company Inc	3599	580
Krenz and Company Inc	3564	137
Krenzen Cadillac Pontiac Inc	5511	450
Kress Corp	3531	72
Krest Products Corp	3089	1498
Kretchmar Bakery Inc	5461	49
Kretz Lumber Company Inc	2421	77
KRG Capital Partners LLC	6719	132
Krieg DeVault LLP	8111	305
Krieg - Taylor Lithograph Company Inc	2752	1702
Krieger Electric Inc	1731	986
Krieger Motor Company Inc	5511	600
Krieger Publishing Company Inc	2731	296
Kringstad Ironworks Inc	3523	173

Company Name	SIC	Rank
Kris Kandy Inc	5441	21
Kris Mechanical Inc	1623	316
Krisalis Inc	3599	1833
Krisken Electronics Corp	8712	260
Krisp Pak Company Inc	5148	80
Krispy Kreme Doughnuts Inc	5812	116
Krist Krenz Machine Inc	3451	74
Kristal Auto Mall Inc	5511	1067
Kristel LP	3575	13
Kristel Marketing Ltd	8742	468
Kritech Corp	3679	644
Kriti Holdings Inc	1382	47
Kritzer Industries Inc	3699	215
Kroehler Furniture Manufacturing Company Inc	2512	36
Krofam Inc	3542	62
Kroger Co	5411	1
Kroger Co Atlanta Div	5411	213
Krohn-Hite Corp	3825	128
Krohns Coverings Inc	5023	115
Kroll Becker and Wing LLC	7361	246
Kroll Factual Data Inc	7374	68
Kroll Inc	7381	72
Kroll Ontrack Inc	7373	106
Kroll Photography	7335	33
Kroll Zolfo Cooper Inc	8721	246
Krome Communications Inc	7311	464
Kronenberger Manufacturing Corp	3599	856
Kroner Publications Inc	2711	147
Krones Inc	3565	2
Kronheim Company Inc	5182	15
Kronick Moskovitz Tiedemann and Girard	8111	294
Kronos Foods Corp	2013	56
Kronos Inc	7372	98
Kronoc Inc (Beaverton Oregon)	7372	137
Kronos Inc (Cranbury New Jersey)	2816	6
Kronos Worldwide Inc	2899	14
Kronospan LLC	2493	10
Kronoswiss Of America LLC	5023	194
Kroot Corp	5093	121
Kropf/Chs LLC	2048	109
Kropp Equipment Inc	7353	42
Kropp Holdings Inc	6141	53
Krown Manufacturing Inc	3661	209
Kroy Industries Inc	3353	10
Kroy LLC	3579	33
Kroy Sign Systems LLC	3993	113
Krozak Information Technologies Inc	7371	808
KRPL Inc	4832	192
KRQE	4833	200
Krueger Bearings Inc	3599	508
Krueger Enterprises	2869	126
Krueger Excavating Inc	1623	520
Krueger Inc	5046	205
Krueger International Inc	2522	2
Kruepke Trucking Inc	4213	1818
Krug Associates Inc	1731	474
Kruger Foods Inc	2035	18
Krumor Inc	3829	404
Kruse And Son Inc	2013	218
Kruse Asset Management	7389	2526
Kruse International	5521	3
Kruse Meat Products Inc	5147	145
Krusinski John	5147	116
Kruts Electric Inc	1731	1965
Krxi	4833	210
Kryptiq Corp	7371	530
Krystal Co	5812	231
Krystal Gravel Company Inc	5211	203
Krytar Inc	3679	512
KS and Company Inc	4213	1479
KS and D Rentals Inc	4213	2741
KS Bancorp Inc	6712	553
KS Bank Inc	6036	71
KS Fashion	7389	1972
KS North America Salt Holdings LLC	2899	38
KS Of West Virginia Company Ltd	3469	228
KSA Inc	8712	323
KSA Industries Inc	7941	5
kSaria Corp	3699	84
Ksb Consulting	7379	1345
Ksc Industries Inc	3651	79
Kscoam 1080 Red Hot News Talk Radio	4812	109
KSDInc	3599	1724
K-Sea Transportation Partners LP	4449	8
KSI Computer Centers	5734	98
Ksi Professional LLC	3651	191
Ksi Trading Corp	5013	326
KSJ and Associates Inc	8742	269
KSJ Associates LLC	5031	173
KSK Studios	2741	416
KSM Associates Inc	7371	852
Ksm Electronics Inc	5065	228
Ksmeg Cable Marketing And Installation Company Inc	1731	946
KSN News	7812	36
Ksrv Inc	4832	184
Kst Electric Ltd	1731	143
KSW Inc	5075	18
KSW Mechanical Inc	1711	155
K-Swiss Inc	3143	4
K-T Enterprises Inc	5731	150

Company Name	SIC	Rank
Kta-Tator Inc	8711	258
K-TEC Inc	3634	14
Ktech Corp	8731	55
K-Tech International Inc	3534	29
K-Ter Imagineering Inc	3531	198
Kt-Grant Inc	7353	23
Ktgy Group Inc	8712	170
Kth Parts Industries Inc	3714	147
Ktlm Tv	4833	195
Ktlr Gospel 890 Inc	4832	117
KTRETV Station	4833	190
K-Tron America Inc	3823	30
K-Tron International Inc	3823	15
K-Tronics Inc	3676	21
KTS Network Solutions Inc	5065	72
KTSM-TV	4833	171
KTU Worldwide Inc	5211	318
K-Tube Corp	3317	56
Kubala Washatko Architects Inc	8712	276
Kubat Equipment and Service Co	5084	474
Kubera Software Inc	7372	4839
Kubic Marketing Inc	5091	41
Kubik Inc	3593	49
Kubik Maltbie Inc	3993	40
Kubota Tractor Corp	5083	16
Kubotek USA Inc	5045	189
Kubricky Construction Corp	1622	38
Kucera Electric Inc	1731	2340
Kuechle Underground Inc	1623	296
Kuehn Motor Inc	5511	553
Kuei Tyan LLC	5093	214
Kuert Concrete Inc	3273	63
Kuester Tool and Die Inc	3469	262
Kugler Oil Co	2875	12
Kuhar Metallizing Company Inc	7699	117
Kuhl Corp	3556	87
Kuhlman Companies Inc	7812	330
Kuhlman Corp (Toledo Ohio)	3273	37
Kuhlman Instrument Co	3823	447
Kuhlmann Design Group Inc	8712	131
Kuhn and Sons Inc	2842	139
Kuhn and Wittenborn Inc	7311	644
Kuhn Industries Inc	3599	535
Kuhn North America Inc	3523	20
Kuhn Tool and Die Co	3544	772
Kuhnle Brothers Inc	4213	1724
Kuka Assembly And Test Corp	3829	56
Kuka Welding Systems and Robot Corp	3535	4
Kukurin Contracting Inc	1623	153
Kulak Electric Inc	1731	907
Kuleto Villa LLC	2084	115
Kulicke and Soffa Industries Inc	3674	46
Kulite Semiconductor Products Inc	3829	10
Kullman Industries Inc	1521	43
KULR Corp	4833	132
Kultur International Films Ltd	7812	118
Kum and Go LLC	5411	63
Kumho Tires USA Inc	5014	9
Kunath Karren Rinne and Atkin Inc	6282	243
Kunde Enterprises Inc	2084	82
Kuni Enterprises Inc	5511	189
Kuni Honda on Arapahoe	5511	694
Kunkel Services Co	5013	98
Kuntz Lesher Capital LLC	8721	492
Kuntz Manufacturing Company Inc	3599	1246
Kunzler and Company Inc	2011	40
KUPN Licensee LLC	4833	75
Kurani Interactive Inc	7379	857
Kurdex Corp	3577	555
Kurisu and Fergus	6798	149
KURM Radio	4832	31
Kuroi International Corp	5065	606
Kurt J Lesker Co	5049	20
Kurt Manufacturing Company Inc	3499	13
Kurt S Adler Inc	5199	16
Kurt Salmon Associates Inc	8742	86
Kurtosys Systems Inc	7372	913
Kurtus Technologies	8243	16
Kurtz and Friends Animation	7812	133
Kurtz Brothers	2621	54
Kurtz Brothers Inc	7389	221
Kurtzman Carson Consultants LLC	8111	400
Kurz Electric Solutions Inc	5063	596
Kurz Instruments Inc	3823	158
Kurzweil Educational Systems Inc	5045	109
Kusel Equipment Co	3556	100
Kushner La Graize	8721	347
Kushner Smith Joanou and Gregson LLP	8721	397
Kushner-Locke Co	7812	130
Kushwood Chair Inc	2511	37
Kussmaul Electronics Company Inc	3629	57
Kusters Corp	3552	7
Kustom Blending LLC	2899	151
Kustom Machine Inc	3444	256
Kutak Rock	8111	155
Kutastha Software Solutions Inc	7372	5132
Kutol Products Company Inc	7389	991
Kutrubes Travel Inc	4724	154
Kutter Products Inc	7389	2433
Kutzner Manufacturing Company Inc	3599	1582
Kuvo/Denver Educational Broadcasting Inc	4832	259

Company Name	SIC	Rank
KV F-Quad Corp	3599	20
KV Pharmaceutical Co	2834	246
Kvaerner North American Construction Inc	1542	102
Kval Inc	3553	10
K-Va-T Food Stores Inc	5411	65
KVFX 945	4832	142
KVH Industries Inc	3663	45
KVM Switches Online LLC	5961	118
Kvr Communication	4812	90
KVS Information Systems Inc	7372	2803
KVSF Talk	4832	139
KVSO Request Line	4832	251
Kvt Koenig LLC	8742	582
KW Brock Directories Inc	2741	107
Kw Inc	3544	316
Kw Industries Inc	3648	17
K-W Manufacturing Co	3524	38
Kw Plastics	3081	46
Kw Products Inc	3559	147
KW Thompson Tool Company Inc	3484	22
Kwatros Corp	7338	18
Kwbb	4833	175
Kween Industries Inc	1731	1189
Kwik Kopy Printing	2752	402
Kwik Shop Inc	5411	263
Kwik Tech Inc	3544	677
Kwik Trip Inc	5411	20
Kwik-File LLC	2522	28
Kwik-Kopy Corp	5999	108
Kwikprint Manufacturing Company Inc	3469	377
Kwik-Sew Pattern Company Inc	2741	321
Kwik-Way Inc	5411	138
KWJ Wholesale	5094	85
KWMI Manufacturing	3523	111
Kwoz Arkansas 103	4832	193
Kws Manufacturing Company Ltd	3535	54
Kxbz B 104 7 Fm	4832	187
Kx-TdCom Inc	5065	622
KY-3 Inc	4833	54
Kyb America LLC	5013	108
Kycon Cable and Connector Inc	3678	53
Kyle Electric Inc	1731	957
Kyle Jones Enterprise Inc	7389	1391
Kymco USA Inc	5063	697
Kyne and Son Electric Co	1731	1790
Kyocera America Inc	3674	113
Kyocera Industrial Ceramics Corp (Mountain Home North Carolina)	3299	4
Kyocera International Inc	3674	25
Kyocera Mita America Inc	3577	8
Kyocera Solar Inc	3433	22
Kyocera Tycom North America	3545	8
Kyoho Manufacturing California	3465	37
Kyowa America Corp	5162	20
Kyo-Ya Company Ltd	7011	72
Kyphon Inc	3841	28
Kypipe LLC	5045	1027
Kyra Communications	2721	120
Kyran Research Associates Inc	7371	1441
Kyrene School District 28	8211	57
Kysor Panel Inc	3556	63
Kysor Panel Systems Inc	3585	65
Kysor Warren Corp	3585	13
KyTek Inc	7372	4840
Kyzen Corp	2842	82
KZ Store Fixtures	5932	21
Kzrv LP	3792	16
L A Benson Company Inc	5072	69
L A Commercial Group Inc	7322	75
L A Martin Co	3451	140
L and A Trucking Company Inc	4213	2855
L and B Cartage Inc	4213	1816
L and B Pipe And Supply Co	5074	170
L and B Realty Advisors Inc	6512	37
L and B Realty Advisors LLP	6282	215
L and B Transport LLC	4213	291
L and C Meat Inc	5147	80
L and D Drivers Service Inc	7363	170
L and D Scrap And Salvage Inc	5093	156
L and E Associates Inc	7373	465
L and E Bottling Company Inc	5149	25
L and E Cleaning Service LLC	7217	7
L and H Construction Inc	1623	543
L and H Industrial Inc	3599	55
L and H Manufacturing Co	5561	15
L and H Mechanical	1711	215
L and H Mold and Engineering Inc	3544	338
L and H Trucking Company Inc	4213	242
L and J Of New England Inc	3471	107
L and J Sharp Graphics	7336	287
L and J Technologies Inc	3494	44
L and JG Stickley Inc	2511	7
L and L Albuquerque Electronics Inc	3672	362
L and L Assemblies Inc	3672	428
L and L Custom Shutters Inc	2431	78
L and L Electrical Inc	1731	836
L and L Engineering and Manufacturing Inc	3559	478
L and L Industries Inc	3444	242
L and L Machine Tool Inc	3541	151
L and L Machinery Inc	3553	41
L and L Nursery Supply Inc	5193	8
L and L Products Inc	3053	10

Company Name	SIC	Rank
L and L Special Furnace Company Inc	3567	104
L and L Transportation LLC	4213	1462
L and L Utilities Inc	1623	699
L and M Construction Chemical Inc	2899	181
L and M Drywall LLC	5031	440
L and M Electric Inc	1731	1647
L and M Fabrication And Machine Inc	3443	132
L and M Food Service Inc	5087	82
L and M Laminates And Marble Inc	3088	3
L and M Machine Inc	3599	1875
L and M Machining Corp	3678	49
L and M Merchandising Corp	5065	725
L and M Publications Inc	2711	724
L and M Steel Company Inc	3441	161
L and N Corp	3679	770
L and N Metallurgical Products Co	3829	53
L and N Transport Inc	4213	1494
L And O Electric Inc	1731	383
L and P Machine Co	3599	2502
L and P Machine Inc	3599	2456
L and P Media	7812	162
L and R Distributors Inc	5131	8
L and R Manufacturing Co	3841	186
L and R Security Services Inc	7381	66
L and S Electric Inc	1731	55
L and S Langco Properties LLC	3089	1195
L and S Trucking	4213	2935
L and S Trucking Inc	4213	2527
L and W Engineering Inc	3714	331
L and W Equipment Inc	3556	159
L and W Machine Corp	7692	58
L And W Quarries Inc	1422	56
L and W Stone Corp	5032	47
L and W Supply Corp	8999	7
L and Z Tool And Engineering Inc	3544	487
L B Limited Inc	7389	677
L B Plastics Inc	3089	694
L B White Company Inc	3433	37
L Bogdanow Partners Architects PC	8712	316
L Bornstein and Company Inc	5023	78
L Brown And Sons Printing Inc	2752	1060
L Cotton Thomas and Co	8721	236
L D Willcox and Son Inc	5531	64
L D'agostini and Sons Inc	1623	48
L Double Inc	3523	124
L E Jones Co	3592	9
L E Phillips Career Development Center Inc	8331	145
L E Sauer Machine Co	3554	27
L F M Enterprises Inc	3599	1247
L F Manufacturing Inc	3089	422
L Foppiano Wine Co	2084	101
L/G Research	6282	617
L Hardy Company Inc	3545	126
L Harper Everett And Son Inc	1623	617
L L Pelling Company Inc	1611	43
L Lavery and Co	7311	732
L M Barnes Co	5039	43
L Merrill Michael and Associates Inc	5065	188
L N D Inc	3829	182
L R Borelli Inc	1799	88
L R Falk Construction Co	1422	25
L Rivas Enterprises Inc	5065	976
L Robert Kimball and Associates	8711	55
L Siracusa and Associates Inc	7381	85
L Suzio Concrete Company Inc	3273	88
L Sweet Lumber Company Inc	5211	233
L T C Roll and Engineering Co	3355	5
L T Hampel Corp	3089	317
L W Connelly and Son Inc	7353	38
L W Fritts Construction Company Inc	1623	763
L W Schneider Inc	3599	795
L Walker Marvin and Associates Inc	5021	95
L1 Corp	3955	14
L-1 Identity Solutions Inc	7373	32
L2 Consulting Services Inc	3812	94
L3 Advertising Inc	7311	779
L-3 Aeromet Communications	8748	4
L-3 AMI Instruments Inc	3699	8
L-3 Aviation Recorders	3812	56
L-3 Communications AeroTech LLC	7699	5
L-3 Communications Global Network Solutions	3571	81
L-3 Communications Henschel Inc	3625	19
L-3 Communications Holdings Inc	3663	2
L-3 Communications Systems and Imagery Div	3577	182
L-3 Communications Titan Corp	7372	22
L-3 Display Systems	3728	10
L-3 ESSCO	3663	108
L-3 Ocean Systems	3812	44
L-3 Power Paragon	3612	137
L-3 Satellite Networks	4899	2
L-3 Telemetry-East	3663	93
L-3 Telemetry-West Conic	3812	51
L3 Telemetry-West Telemetry and Instrumentation	3825	27
La Agencia de Orci and Asociados	7311	124
La Baguette Bakery Inc	5812	434
La Barca Tortilleria Inc	2099	215
La Barge Inc (Holland Michigan)	2511	28
La Belle Exchange	7389	2078
La Bonita Inc	2099	285
La Brisa Ice Cream Company LLC	2024	60

Company Name	SIC	Rank
LA Burdick Chocolates	2064	53
La Canasta Mexican Food Products Inc	2099	102
La Capitol Federal Credit Union	6061	164
La Caze Development Co	6552	278
LA Communications Inc	7331	257
LA Computer Center	5734	123
La Criolla Inc	5149	190
La Cro Products Inc	3679	714
La Crosse Graphics Inc	2752	212
La Crosse Truck Center Inc	7538	12
LA Data Systems LLC	5734	219
LA Destination Inc	5023	133
La Dow and Spohn Inc	2752	1525
La Esperanza Baking	2051	224
La Espiga De Oro Inc	2099	108
La Fama Foods Inc	2099	227
La Favorite Industries Inc	3069	243
La Force Inc	5072	75
La Fortaleza Inc	2099	169
LA Gauge Company Inc	3599	1128
LA Gear Inc	3149	21
La Gloria Foods Corp	5461	9
La Grange Electrical Assemblies Co	3679	749
La Grange Products Inc	3443	110
La Grange Troup County Hospital Authority	8062	80
LA Hair Inc	7361	228
LA Hearne Co	0723	10
La Indiana Tamales Inc	2032	34
La Jalisciense Inc	2099	363
La Jolla Endoscopy Center LP	8011	166
La Jolla Pharmaceutical Co	2836	105
LA Lakers	7941	13
LA M Incorporated De	3826	128
La Mar Lighting Company Inc	3646	44
La Marche Manufacturing Co	3629	53
La Mesa RV Center Inc	5561	9
La Mesa-Spring Valley School District	8211	92
La Mexicana Inc	2099	186
La Mexicana Tortilleria Inc	2099	233
La Motte Chemical Products Company Inc	3826	48
La Mousse	2038	61
La Nair Company Inc	3842	187
La Parent Magazine	2721	419
La Pash Inc	8742	672
La Petite Academy Inc	8351	6
La Pine Scientific Co	3826	146
La Pine Truck Sales Inc	5599	17
La Plata Electric Association Inc	4911	243
La Porte Publishing LLC	2711	161
La Prairie Inc	2844	188
LA Prep Inc	7319	130
La Princesita Tortilleria Inc	2099	275
La Reina Inc	2099	47
La Ronga Bakery and Delicatessen	5149	121
La Rosa del Monte Express Inc	4214	6
La Rosa Refrigeration and Equipment	3585	116
La Salle Copy Service	7334	91
La Salle International Inc	5047	37
LA Sax Co	3931	37
La Superior Food Products Inc	2099	283
La Tapatia Inc	2099	351
La Tapatia Tortilleria Inc	2099	107
La Tempesta Bakery Confections Inc	2064	71
La Tolteca Foods Inc	2099	305
La Tribuna Publication Inc	2711	692
La Vie Parisienne Corp	5094	81
LA Weaver Company Inc	3553	59
LA Wireless Inc	4812	127
Lab Depot Inc	5049	124
LAB Equipment Inc	3599	1316
Lab Gaynes Engineering Co	7389	1355
Lab Medical Manufacturing Inc	3841	211
Lab Safety Supply Inc	5961	75
Lab Support Inc	7363	105
Labatt Institutional Supply Company Inc	5141	72
Labatt USA Inc	5181	11
Labatt USA LLC	2082	57
Labchem Inc	2899	167
Labcon North America	3089	315
Label Aid Systems Inc	2672	57
Label Art	2672	15
Label Art-Home Of Eas-E Stik Labels Inc	2759	360
Label Maker Inc	2759	390
Label Printing Systems Inc	2679	69
Label Source Inc	2759	426
Label Specialties Inc	2759	470
Label Systems Inc	2672	37
Label Tech Inc	2754	15
Label Technologies Inc	2675	27
Label Vision Systems Inc	3577	573
Labelcraft USA Inc	2679	73
Labella Electric Inc	1731	2045
Labeltape Inc	2759	521
Labeltex Mills Inc	2241	8
Labor Health and Wel Trust Fndne CA	8099	25
Labor Remedy Inc	7363	343
Laboratory Control Systems Inc	3679	731
Laboratory Corporation of America Holdings	6719	25

Company Name	SIC	Rank
Laboratory Supply Company Inc	5047	47
Laboratory Systems Group Inc	7372	3354
Laborde Diagnostics Inc	8071	54
Laborers-Employers Benefit Plan Collection Trust	6411	91
LaborLawCenter Inc	7389	1190
Labovitz Enterprises Inc	8741	62
Labrada Nutritional Systems Inc	2834	274
Labrador Technology Inc	7379	1163
LaBreche LLC	8743	303
Labree's	2053	8
Labsoft Inc	7371	1684
Labsphere Inc	3827	66
LabVantage Solutions Inc	7373	286
Labware Holdings Inc	7371	133
LabWare Inc	7372	1096
Labwerks Inc	7371	1356
Labworks Inc	3679	762
Labyrinth Software Solutions Inc	7372	5133
Lac Qui Parle Broadcasting Company Inc	4832	290
Lacamas Laboratories Inc	2869	101
Lacascia's Bakery Inc	5461	33
Lace Foodservice Corp	5046	333
Lace Lastics Company Inc	2258	10
Lace Technologies Inc	3679	728
Lacek Group	8742	118
Lacerta Group Inc	3565	44
Lacerte Software Corp	7372	558
Lacey-Champion Inc	2273	42
Lachappelle Electric Co	1731	1541
Lachut Electrical Sales Inc	5063	977
LaCie USA Ltd	3572	18
Lacityweb Inc	4813	597
Lack Valley Stores Ltd	5712	8
Lackawanna Products Corp	2048	36
Lackey's Electrical Inc	1731	1495
Lackmann Culinary Services	5812	62
Lackner Group Inc	7371	1315
Lacks Enterprises Inc	3089	73
Lacks Enterprises Inc Plastic Plate Div	3089	224
Lacks Stores Inc	5712	25
Laclede Chain Manufacturing Co	3462	9
Laclede Gas Co	4924	36
Laclede Group Inc	4924	20
Laclede Inc	3843	57
Laconia Magnetics Inc	3677	62
Lacorte Companies Inc	1731	212
Lacosta Facility Support Services	7349	31
LaCrosse Footwear Inc	3021	5
Lacrosse Furniture Co	2515	26
Lactalis American Group Inc	2022	9
Lacy Diversified Industries	5013	19
Lacy Street Production Center	7812	157
Lad Technology Inc	3672	324
LAD Truck Lines Inc	4213	2234
Ladco Inc	5021	104
Ladder Capital Finance LLC	6798	137
Ladenburg Thalmann and Company Inc	6211	232
Ladenburg Thalmann Financial Services Inc	6211	170
Ladorn Systems Corp	7374	354
Ladove Industries Inc	2844	95
Laducer And Associates Inc	7374	137
Lady Bugs Transportation Inc	4213	2992
Lady Grace Stores Inc	5621	38
Lady Little Foods Inc	2038	7
Lady Luck Casino (Caruthersville Missouri)	7993	17
Laer Pearce and Associates	8743	168
Laetitia Vineyards and Winery Inc	2084	52
Lafarge Aggregates Southeast Inc	1423	2
Lafarge Construction Materials (Albuquerque New Mexico)	3273	10
Lafarge North America Inc	3241	5
Lafata Cabinet Shop	5211	86
Lafayette Ambassador Bank	6022	357
Lafayette Bank and Trust Co (Lafayette Indiana)	6022	277
Lafayette Community Bancorp	6712	700
Lafayette Development Corp	7389	2396
Lafayette Electronic Supply Inc	5065	878
Lafayette Grinding LLC	7389	1756
Lafayette Instrument Company Inc	3829	140
Lafayette Life Insurance Co	6311	221
Lafayette Motor Company Inc	5511	803
Lafayette Printing Co	2752	1289
Lafayette Quality Products Inc	3444	268
Lafayette Savings Bank FSB	6035	148
Lafayette Utility Construction Company Inc	1629	93
Lafayette Utility System	1623	121
Lafayette Venetian Blind Inc	2591	4
Lafayette Wire Products Inc	3496	75
Lafayette Work Center Inc	8331	187
Lafferty Chevrolet Inc	5511	1029
Lafitte Frozen Foods Corp	2092	17
Lafond Express Inc	4213	2997
LaForgia Fuel Oil Co	5983	6
Lafourche Parish School Board Inc	8211	39
Lafourche Sugars LLC	2061	11
Lafourche Telephone Company Inc	4813	209
LaFrance Corp	2796	1

Company Name	SIC	Rank
Lafromboise Newspapers	2711	343
Lagasse Works Inc	7692	61
Lages and Associates Inc	8743	215
Lagoe-Oswego Corp	3599	1403
Lagonda Machine Inc	3599	1666
Lagoon Corp	7996	12
LaGrou Distribution Systems Inc	7389	336
Lagunitas Brewing Co	2082	85
Lagus Applied Technology Inc	3823	427
Laharco Inc	3699	177
Lahlouh Inc	2752	125
Lahm-Trosper Inc	3541	203
LAI International	3599	123
Laibe Electric Co	1731	439
Laiben Holdings Inc	7389	2167
Laidig Inc	3523	128
Laika	7336	4
Lainiere De Picardie Inc	5162	30
Laird Manufacturing LLC	3523	131
Laird Norton Tyee	6091	4
Laird Plastics Inc	5162	15
Laird Technologies	3469	64
Laird Telemedia	7371	175
Laitram Machinery Inc	7359	93
Lake Air Metal Stamping LLC	3469	223
Lake Beaver Transport Inc	5082	181
Lake Beverage Corp	5181	76
Lake Book Manufacturing Inc	2732	22
Lake Business Products Inc	5044	19
Lake Capital	6799	363
Lake Charles Electric Company LLC	1731	603
Lake Charles Instruments Inc	7699	248
Lake Charles Rubber and Gasket Company LLC	5085	307
Lake City Bank	6022	165
Lake City Printing Inc	2752	1175
Lake City Trucking	4213	919
Lake Companies Inc	5045	610
Lake Co	3441	262
Lake Consumer Products Inc	2834	284
Lake Country Cnc Machining Inc	3599	1026
Lake Country Corp	5162	46
Lake Country Foods Inc	2066	20
Lake County Business Bureau Inc	7322	103
Lake County Parts Warehouse Inc	5013	238
Lake County Power	4911	205
Lake County Press Inc	2752	127
Lake County Record Bee	2711	132
Lake Cumberland Regional Hospital LLC	8062	51
Lake Cumberland Stone Inc	5032	197
Lake Data Center Inc	7374	177
Lake Elbow Co-Op Grain	5153	104
Lake Electronic Service Inc	5064	121
Lake Engineering Inc	3599	521
Lake Erie Construction Co	1531	76
Lake Erie Electric Inc	1731	123
Lake Forest Bank and Trust Co	6022	517
Lake Forest Sportscars Ltd	5511	1194
Lake Kezar Computer	7379	1663
Lake Lad Inc	8361	66
Lake Lithograph Co	2752	675
Lake Mead Station Holdings LLC	7999	12
Lake Mead Station Inc	7999	19
Lake Michigan Mailers Inc	7331	114
Lake Mountain Co	7011	179
Lake Nona Corp	6552	75
Lake Norman Tractor Co	5083	68
Lake Powell Resorts and Marinas	7011	178
Lake Printing Company Inc	2752	818
Lake Products Company Inc	8999	162
Lake Road Welding Co	3441	260
Lake Shore Bancorp Inc	6712	470
Lake Shore Cryotronics Inc	3812	96
Lake Shore Electric Corp	3625	135
Lake Shore Weekly News	2711	842
Lake State Transport Inc	4213	1971
Lake States Lumber Inc	5031	47
Lake Steel Ltd	5051	187
Lake Sunapee Bank FSB	6035	86
Lake Superior Software Inc	7371	391
Lake Valley Seed Company Inc	5191	187
Lake Weiss Egg Company Inc	0252	6
Lakefield Telephone Co	4813	531
Lakefront Brewery Inc	2082	97
Lakehead Constructors Inc	1542	229
Lakehead Trucking Inc	4213	2546
Lakeland Bancorp Inc	6712	159
Lakeland Bank	6022	582
Lakeland Electric Inc	1731	499
Lakeland Engineer Equipment Co	5063	469
Lakeland Financial Corp	6712	168
Lakeland Finishing Corp	3714	300
Lakeland Graphics Inc	2759	416
Lakeland Industries Inc	3842	52
Lakeland Mold Co	3365	31
Lakeland Plastics Inc	3089	1027
Lakeland Sand and Gravel Inc	1442	62
Lakeland Shopping Guide Green	2711	609
Lakeland Tool And Engineering Inc	3089	398
Lakeman Inc	7349	267
Lakes Area Advertiser Inc	2741	196
Lakes Enterprises Inc	3715	44
Lakes Entertainment Inc	7999	90

Company Name	SIC	Rank
Lakes Mall LLC	6531	197
Lakes Pipe and Supply Corp	5074	155
Lakeshirts Inc	2395	8
Lakeshore Coal Handling Corp	5052	15
Lakeshore Display Company Inc	3993	107
Lakeshore Document Services	7389	2282
Lakeshore Fittings Inc	3451	88
Lakeshore Group Ltd	7372	3799
Lakeshore Roller World Inc	7389	2483
Lakeshore Staffing Group Inc	7361	107
Lakeshore Utility Trailer Inc	5511	1122
Lakeshore Vault Inc	5087	154
Lakeside Contracting Inc	1623	568
Lakeside Curative Services Inc	8331	153
Lakeside Industries Inc	1611	73
Lakeside Manufacturing Co	3599	1294
Lakeside Mills Inc	2041	49
Lakeside Oil Company Inc	5171	63
Lakeside Park Co	7996	36
Lakeside Plastics Inc	2821	75
Lakeside Specialized Transportation	4213	2188
Lakeside Supply Co	5085	117
Lakeside Systems Inc	5083	109
Lakeside Toyota	5511	486
Lakeview Center Inc	8069	17
Lakeview Company Inc	3663	402
Lakeview Dirt Company Inc	1429	16
Lakeview Farms Inc	2026	47
Lakeview Industries Inc	3069	163
Lakeview Light and Power	4911	396
Lakeview Packing Company Inc	2011	145
Lakeview Precision Machining Inc	3451	145
Lakeview Rock Products Inc	1442	78
Lakeville Lumber	5211	50
Lakeville Motor Express Inc	4213	42
Lakeville Winlectric Co	5063	855
Lakeway Center For The Handicapped Inc	8361	152
Lakeway Container Inc	2653	93
Lakeway Manufacturing Inc	3567	79
Lakewood Electric Company Inc	1731	1045
Lakewood Fordland	5511	393
Lakewood Homes Inc	1531	79
Lakewood Manufacturing Company Inc	2511	53
Lakey Electric Company Inc	1731	457
Lakim Industries Inc	3991	20
Lakin Milling Company Inc	2048	138
Lakone Co	3089	749
Lallie Inc	2759	472
Lally-Pak Inc	3081	107
Lam Research Corp	3559	2
Lamar Advertising of Colorado Springs Inc	7312	4
Lamar Advertising of Kentucky Inc	7312	39
Lamar Advertising of Michigan Inc	7312	18
Lamar Advertising of Oklahoma Inc	7312	12
Lamar Advertising of Youngstown Inc	7312	16
Lamar Company LLC	3993	51
Lamar Enterprises Inc	3612	122
Lamar International Inc	2221	37
Lamar of Birmingham	7312	15
Lamar Oklahoma Holding Company Inc	7312	13
Lamar Outdoor Advertising Co	3993	71
Lamar Software Inc	7372	1398
Lamar Texas LP	7312	3
Lamar Wholesale Supply Inc	5063	1008
La-Mar-Ka Inc	2819	100
LaMarque Dodge Inc	5511	259
Lamarque Motor Co	5511	454
Lamart Corp	2672	38
Lamartek Inc	3949	150
Lamaute Capital Inc	6211	398
Lamb and Assoc	5047	276
Lamb County Electric Cooperative Inc	4911	354
Lambda Optical Systems	8731	228
Lambda Physik USA Inc	3699	78
Lambda Publications Inc	2721	460
Lambda Research Corp	7371	663
Lambda Research Inc	8734	153
Lambda Research Optics Inc	3826	66
Lambda Tech International	2759	200
Lambda Technologies Inc	3567	100
Lamberson Koster and Co	6351	28
Lambert Coal Company Inc	1221	32
Lambert Corporation Florida	3272	111
Lambert Moving and Storage Inc	4213	2529
Lambert Vet Supply LLC	5047	40
Lambert's Cable Splicing Company LLC	1623	39
Lambert's Orthotics And Prosthetics Inc	3842	275
Lambert's Point Docks Inc	4491	15
Lambretta South Inc	5571	7
Lambro Industries Inc	3444	85
Lambs Farm Inc	8331	58
Lamb's Machine Works Inc	3599	1805
Lamb-Weston Inc	2099	3
Lamco Machine Tool Inc	3559	453
Lamco Slings and Rigging Inc	5084	662
Lamcraft Inc	7389	1908
Laminall Inc	2672	78
Laminar Flow Inc	3822	48
Laminate Technologies Inc	2439	7
Laminated Industries Inc	2679	61
Laminated Products Inc	2542	49

Company Name	SIC	Rank
Laminating Services Inc	2295	13
Lamination Specialties Corp	3469	179
Laminet Cover Co	2673	71
Lamit Industries Inc	7389	2259
Lamm Rubenstone Totaro and David LLC	8111	550
Lammes Candies Since 1885 Inc	2064	52
Lamm's Machine Inc	3599	1649
Lamont Ltd	5131	44
Lamp Recyclers Of Louisiana Inc	4953	156
Lamp Technology Inc	5063	691
Lampasas Builder's Mart Inc	5031	375
Lampin Corp	3462	72
Lampire Biological Labs Inc	3841	174
Lamplight Farms Inc	3648	9
Lamps Plus Inc	5719	7
Lampson Tractor and Equipment Company Inc	5083	78
Lampton Welding Supply Company Inc	5084	200
Lamptronix Company Ltd	5063	410
Lamsco West Inc	3083	23
Lamson and Cutner PC	8111	585
Lamson and Goodnow Manufacturing Co	3421	15
Lamson and Sessions Co	3699	13
Lamson Home Products	3084	12
Lan Lab Communications	7373	817
Lan Solutions Inc	7378	77
Lan Systems Inc	7379	1303
Lan Utilities Electric Inc	7373	538
LANA MARKS Boutique	3171	6
LAN-ACES Inc	7372	2995
Lanard Toys Inc	7389	2108
Lancaster Automobile Spring Company Inc	3713	60
Lancaster Brewing Co	5812	451
Lancaster Colony Corp	2099	8
Lancaster Fine Foods Inc	2035	44
Lancaster Knives Inc	3423	52
Lancaster Metal Products Inc	3544	791
Lancaster Metals Science Corp	3599	1716
Lance Camper Manufacturing Corp	3792	15
Lance Private Brands	2052	12
Lance Trucking Corp	4213	630
Lance Wire and Cable Inc	5063	656
Lancer Corp	3585	36
Lancer Inc	2512	73
Lancer Label Inc	2672	43
Lancer Orthodontics Inc	3843	46
Lancesoft Inc	7379	139
Lanco Assembly Systems Inc	3559	139
Lancope Inc	7372	1298
Land Air Express Inc	4213	535
Land Air Express of New England	4213	381
Land Air Water Environmental Services Inc	4953	127
Land And Sea Forest Products Of Pennsylvania Corp	2491	21
Land And Sky Inc	2511	66
Land and Water Resources Inc	0781	26
Land N Sea Inc (New York New York)	2331	3
Land O'Lakes Inc	2021	1
Land Records of Texas Inc	6541	6
Land Span Inc	4213	83
Land Title Services Inc	6361	33
Land Trucking Co	4213	2660
Landacorp Inc	7389	464
Landair Transport Inc	4213	35
LandAirSea Systems Inc	3577	431
Landar Corp	6552	257
Landau and Heyman Inc	6512	62
Landau Building Co	1542	317
Landau Public Relations	8743	311
Landau Uniforms Inc	2326	8
Landauer Hospitality International Inc	6531	313
Landauer Inc	8734	12
Landauer Securities Inc	6531	306
LandDesign Inc	8748	56
Landec Corp	2821	29
Landeck Group LLC	7371	1572
Lander Bookbinding Corp	2789	58
Lander International LLC	8748	437
Landers Auto Sales Inc	5511	474
Landers McLarty Dodge Chrysler Jeep Ram	5511	1173
Landes Audio and Video LLC	1731	2574
Landes Trucking Inc	4213	438
LandisGyr Inc	3825	38
Landmark Bancorp Inc	6712	442
Landmark Communication Inc	8743	239
Landmark Credit Union	6062	37
Landmark Data Systems Inc	7372	4426
Landmark Document Services-Chicago LLC	7334	78
Landmark Electric Inc	1731	1620
Landmark Engineering Ltd	8713	10
Landmark Entertainment Group	8711	304
Landmark Financial Corp (Englewood Colorado)	7359	107
Landmark Ford Inc	5511	275
Landmark Industries Inc	4783	23
Landmark International Trucks Inc	5012	87
Landmark Lincoln Mercury Inc	5511	1042
Landmark Manufacturing Corp	3444	89

Company Name	SIC	Rank
Landmark Media Enterprises	2711	30
Landmark Media Inc	7812	93
Landmark Partners Inc	6282	108
Landmark Plastic Corp	3089	309
Landmark Print Inc	2752	459
Landmark Protection Inc	7381	120
Landmark Signs and Electrical Maintenance Corp	7539	9
Landmark Staffing Resources Inc	7361	279
Landmark Systems Inc	7378	97
Landmark Technology Inc	3679	410
Landmark Theatre Corp	7832	19
Landmark Trailers Parts and Services Inc	5013	358
Landoll Corp	3537	20
Landor Associates	8742	142
Landreth Inc	5063	672
Land-Ron Inc	1721	8
Landrum Professional Employer Services Inc	7363	35
Landrum Software Inc	7372	4841
Landry Group	5812	36
Landry's Restaurants Inc	5812	58
Landry's Seafood House (Birmingham Alabama)	5812	324
Lands' End Inc	5961	5
Lands Plus Centennial Inc	5063	707
LandSafe Inc	6531	152
Landscape Masterpiece	0781	19
Landscape Structures Inc	3949	82
Landscapes Unlimited LLC	1629	26
Landshire Inc	2099	80
Landslide Technologies Inc	7372	1574
Landstar Development Corp	1531	54
Landstar Development Corp Central Florida Div	1521	76
Landstar Express America Inc	4213	288
Landstar Gemini Inc	4213	805
Landstar Inc	7349	438
Landstar Inway Inc	4213	162
Landstar Ligon Inc	4213	40
Landstar Logistics Inc	4731	2
Landstar Ranger Inc	4213	73
Landstar System Holdings Inc	4213	113
Landstar System Inc	4213	17
LANDTECH Data Corp	7372	3757
LandUse USA LLC	7379	1664
LandWare Inc	7372	2639
Lane and Coady Inc	8743	265
Lane and Lane Inc	5063	383
Lane and Sons Inc	3523	233
Lane and Waterman	8111	313
Lane Bryant Inc	5621	12
Lane Construction Corp	2951	4
Lane Conveyors and Drives Inc	5085	193
Lane Electric Cooperative Inc	4911	501
Lane Equipment Co	5078	21
Lane Furniture Industries Inc	2512	7
Lane Gorman Trubitt PLLC	8721	67
Lane Guide	2741	392
Lane Hospitality Inc	7011	123
Lane Industries Inc	1611	1
Lane Industries Inc	3761	9
Lane Industries Inc (Northbrook Illinois)	7011	41
Lane Labs - USA Inc	2833	32
Lane Marketing Communications Inc	8743	181
Lane Powell Spears Lubersky LLP	8111	165
Lane Press Inc	2759	84
Lane Punch Corp	3544	115
Lane Steel Company Inc	5051	99
Lane Supply Inc	3446	23
Lane Telecommunications Inc	7372	3492
Lane Telecommunications Incorporated - Little Rock	3577	544
Lane Tool and Manufacturing Company Inc	3599	2013
Lane Winpak Inc	3565	60
Laneko Roll Form Inc	3547	17
Lane's Equipment Rental Inc	4213	2922
Lane-Scott Electric Cooperative Inc	4911	544
Laney Machine Inc	3533	133
Laney's Inc	1731	162
Lanford Equipment Company Inc	5082	178
Lanford Manufacturing Corporation Inc	3571	203
Lang Asset Management Inc	6282	396
Lang Chevrolet Co	5511	751
Lang Dental Manufacturing Company Inc	3843	54
Lang Exterior Inc	3442	101
Lang Ligon and Company Inc	3552	54
Langa Tool and Machine Inc	3599	2014
Langan Products Inc	3577	606
Langboard Inc	2493	6
Langdale Chevrolet-Pontiac	5511	1208
Langdon Place Of Dover Inc	8051	69
Langdon Wilson Architects	8712	66
Lange Electric Company Inc	7694	33
Lange Financial Corp	7389	1398
Lange Grinding Inc	7389	2109
Lange Precision Inc	3599	1258
Langenfelder Marine Inc	7389	1363
Langer Construction Co	1542	377
Langer Juice Company Inc	2037	8
Langers Juice Company Inc	2033	21

Company Name	SIC	Rank
Langham	4731	54
Langham Creek Machine Works Inc	3599	503
Langie Audio Visual Systems Company Inc	5065	652
Langley/Empire Candle LLC	3999	148
Langley Recycling Inc	5093	97
Langlinais Baking Company Inc	2051	199
Langlois Co	2045	9
Lang-Mekra North America LLC	3231	15
Langston Companies Inc	2674	8
Langston Co	5311	51
Langton Cherubino Group Ltd	7336	131
Language Computer Corp	7371	1567
Language Connection	7389	783
Language Intelligence Ltd	8299	80
Language Line Services Inc	8999	22
Language Quest Software Co	7372	2720
Language Solutions	7389	2424
Language Weaver Inc	7371	466
Lanhold Investments Inc	6798	146
Lanier Clothes Co	2311	12
Lanier Publishing International	2731	305
Lanier Worldwide Inc	5044	2
Lank Oil Co	5172	28
Lankfer Diversified Industries Inc	3647	9
Lankford and Associates Inc	6552	270
Lan-Leasing Inc	3585	23
Lanlyn Instrument Company Inc	3599	2492
Lanman Transportation Inc	4213	2846
Lanmark Circuits Inc	3672	470
Lanner Group Inc	7372	2255
Lannett Company Inc	2834	132
Lanphere Enterprises Inc	5511	142
Lanport Chassis Pool	2448	40
Lans Of Texas Inc	3699	301
Lansa Inc	7371	95
Lansa USA Inc	5045	68
Lanscape Inc	5734	359
Lansco Colors	5198	8
Lansco Die Casting Inc	3364	13
Lansdale Semiconductor Inc	3825	28
Lansdowne Security Inc	5812	465
Lansing Building Products Inc	5031	124
Lansmont Corp	3829	100
Lansolutions LLC	7373	678
LANspeed Systems Inc	7373	733
Lans-R-Us	7373	1239
Lantal Textiles Inc	2231	7
LantechCom LLC	3565	12
Lan-Tel Communications Services Inc	1731	422
Lantelligence Inc	1731	1577
Lanter Co	4213	311
Lanter Co Transportation Div	4213	625
Lantier Construction Company Inc	1623	421
Lantis Eyewear Corp	3851	21
Lantronix Inc	3577	157
Lantz Security Systems Inc	7381	65
Lanyon Inc	7372	2440
Lanz Cabinet Shop Inc	2434	24
Lapcad Engineering	7372	1134
Lapco Manufacturing Inc	3199	14
Lapeer County Bank and Trust Co	6022	814
Lapeer Industries Inc	3728	103
Lapel Software Inc	7372	5134
Lapham-Hickey Steel Corp	5051	192
Lapidary Journal	2721	85
Lapin Sheet Metal Co	3444	164
Laplume and Sons Printing Inc	2754	38
Lapmaster International LLC	3549	36
Lapoint-Blase Industries Inc	3812	209
Lapointe Hudson Broach Company Inc	3545	210
LaPolla Industries Inc	2851	30
LaPorte Bancorp Inc	6035	131
LaPorte Sehrt Romig and Hand	8721	422
Lapp Insulators LLC	3264	8
Lappert's Ice Cream and Coffee	2024	36
Laptalo Enterprises Inc	3444	132
Laptop and Desktop Repair LLC	7378	95
Laptop Co-Op	7379	1320
Laptop Service Center LLC	7378	60
Laptops and Bags Matter Inc	5734	466
Laptops Plus Inc	5734	241
Laramie Enterprises Inc	4213	1533
Laramie Newspaper Inc	2711	140
Larcan-TTC Inc	3651	202
Larcor	3629	119
Laredo Paving Inc	1611	99
Lares Research	3843	36
Largo Circuit Design Inc	3672	474
Largo Vista Group Ltd	5172	161
Largus Speedy Print Corp	2752	1454
LaRich Chevrolet Cadillac	5511	550
Larimore Associates Inc	7371	729
Lario Oil and Gas Co	1311	138
Lark Builders Inc	3448	41
Lark Enterprises Inc	8331	173
LARK Industries Inc	7389	615
Larkin Center	8361	76
Larkin Enterprises Inc	7363	63
Larkin Newco LLC	3679	807
Larkin Products LLC	3561	92
Larmco Windows Inc	3089	1251
Laron Inc	3443	54
Laros Equipment Company Inc	3535	172

Company Name	SIC	Rank
Lar-Par Inc	5149	70
Larrabee Sound Inc	7389	839
Larrett Inc	1623	163
Larriva's Corp	5064	124
Larry Baker Contracting	1623	716
Larry Causey Inc	1731	252
Larry Clark Construction Inc	1623	863
Larry De George	1731	2192
Larry H Miller Group	5511	13
Larry H Miller Honda	5511	741
Larry Jones Trucking	4213	2783
Larry Lubenow and Associates Inc	8743	328
Larry Mcgee Co	3663	360
Larry Methvin Installations Inc	3231	17
Larry Morris	7812	326
Larry Moxon	5045	984
Larry Oswalt Trucking Inc	4213	1766
Larry S Sausage Co	2013	163
Larry Schefus Trucking Inc	4213	2006
Larry Schlussler	3632	10
Larry Smith and Associates Inc	7311	874
Larry Smith Contractor's Inc	1623	262
Larry's Cartage Company Inc	4213	1759
Larry's Northern Electronics Inc	5731	214
Larry's Window Service Inc	7349	360
Larsen and Toubro Infotech Ltd	7379	61
Larsen Associates Inc	5045	813
Larsen Bakery Inc	5461	51
Larsen Chevrolet Oldsmobile Aurora Inc	5511	1107
Larsen Cooperative Company Inc	5983	12
Larsen Design and Interactive	7336	16
Larsen Design Office Inc	7336	45
Larsen Graphics Inc	2759	509
Larsen's Manufacturing Co	3569	152
Larson Al Boat Shop	3731	47
Larson Allen Weishair and Co	8721	157
Larson Automation Inc	7371	1457
Larson Crane Service Inc	1623	868
Larson Design Group Inc	8711	260
Larson Distributing Company Inc	5023	43
Larson Manufacturing Company Of South Dakota Inc	3442	25
Larson Meter-Craft Inc	5084	837
Larson Plumbing And Utility Co	1623	358
Larson Products Inc	0291	1
Larson Publishing Inc	2711	598
Larson Software Technology Inc	7372	4308
Larson Systems Inc	3599	2015
Larson Themed Construction Company Inc	1799	40
LarsonO'BrienAcumen	8742	647
Larter and Sons	3911	33
Las Cruces Machine Manufacturing And Engineering Inc	3449	22
Las Savell Jewelry Inc	5944	30
Las Vegas Ad-Ventures	7011	202
Las Vegas America Corp	5812	439
Las Vegas Dissemination Inc	4812	84
Las Vegas Golf and Tennis Inc	5091	69
Las Vegas Opthalmology ASC LLC	8011	111
Las Vegas Sands Corp	7011	7
Las Vegas Sports Consultants Inc	7374	46
Las Vegas Sun Inc	2711	398
Las Vegas Valley Water District	4941	9
Lasalle Bristol LP	5023	4
LaSalle Business Credit Inc	7323	14
LaSalle Hotel Properties	6798	84
LaSalle National Bank Broker-Dealer Services	6211	214
Lasalle Systems Leasing I	7359	156
Laschober Construction Inc	1542	448
LASCO Fittings Inc	3494	8
Lasco Foods Inc	2099	258
Lasensky Paper Stock Inc	5093	116
Laser Action Plus Inc	5045	763
Laser Atlanta LLC	3826	169
Laser Automation Inc	3699	276
Laser Cladding Services Ltd	7692	26
Laser Concepts Inc	5113	66
Laser Connection LLC	3861	96
Laser Design Inc	3825	113
Laser Devices Inc	3699	46
Laser Diode Array Inc	3699	302
Laser Electric Supply Inc	5063	850
Laser Energetics Inc	3699	227
Laser Fabrication and Machine Company Inc	3599	786
Laser Fare Inc	3699	55
Laser Graphic Systems Inc	2796	5
Laser Image Inc	2759	215
Laser Ink Corp	2759	475
Laser Law Firm	8111	524
Laser Life Inc	5044	31
Laser Light Technologies Inc	2759	397
Laser Line Inc	5112	90
Laser Materials Corp	3679	623
Laser Mechanisms Inc	3699	103
Laser Photo Tooling Services Inc	7373	972
Laser Print Plus Inc	2759	290
Laser Printer Services Co	7334	98
Laser Printing Technologies Inc	5734	32
Laser Products Inc	5084	632
Laser Pros International	7379	363

Company Name	SIC	Rank
Laser Recharge Inc	3555	75
Laser Reference Inc	3821	47
Laser Resource	5045	1065
Laser Saver Inc	5045	692
Laser Scan Inc	8713	9
Laser Sensor Technology Inc	3829	229
Laser Shot Inc	3699	74
Laser Solutions International LLC	5044	144
Laser Systems Inc (Kaysville Utah)	7372	4151
Laser Technology Inc	3824	20
Laser Technology Inc (Norristown Pennsylvania)	3829	90
Laser Tool Company Inc	3541	250
Laser Tool Inc	3544	539
Laser Vision Centers Inc	8011	53
Laserage Technology Corp	3699	117
Lasercam LLC	3544	268
LaserCard Corp	3572	25
Lasercard Systems Corp	3577	99
Lasercharge Holdings LLC	5734	346
Lasercutting Services Inc	3544	758
Lasereliance Technologies	3699	259
Laserequipment Inc	3555	64
Laserfab Inc	3699	217
LaserFiche Document Imaging	7372	1826
LaserGifts	5947	18
Lasergraphics Inc	3577	65
LaserInkJetLablescom	2759	400
Laserland Inc	5045	1002
Laserlink International Inc	5734	360
Lasermax Inc	3699	182
Lasermax Roll Systems Inc	3554	10
Laser-Pacific Media Corp	7819	10
Laserplus Inc	7371	1450
Laserquipt Inc	3955	16
Lasers Etc	3829	434
Laser's Resource Inc	3861	99
Laserscope Inc	3845	23
LaserSight Inc	3845	92
Lasertec Inc	2759	193
Laserwords Maine	2791	49
Lashore Press Inc	2791	56
Lasiter Utility Backhoe Inc	1623	765
Lasko Products Inc	4789	11
Lasonic Electronics Corp	3577	390
La'spec Industries Inc	3648	90
Lassus Brothers Oil Co	5541	33
Last Mile Inc	4813	226
Last Word	7331	151
Lasting First Impressions Inc	2752	1683
Lasting Impressions Event and Party Rentals Inc	7359	145
Laszlo Systems Inc	7372	1266
Latanick Equipment Inc	8711	619
Latco Inc	1542	298
Latent Lettering Company Inc	2752	1467
Latenzero Inc	7371	1400
Latex Equipment Sales and Service Inc	3559	236
Latex Foam International LLC	2392	23
Latham and Watkins LLP	8111	3
Latham Motors Inc	5511	1115
Latham-Hall Corp	3599	2016
Lathem Time Corp	3579	31
Lathrop and Gage LC	8111	95
Lathrop Company Inc	1542	100
Lathrop Engineering Inc	8711	568
Latina Inc	5149	147
Latina Media Ventures LLC	2721	73
Latina Niagara Importing Co	5948	3
Latina Style Inc	2721	244
Latino Enterprises Inc	2099	130
Latis Technologies LLC	7371	1412
Latitudes Inc	3069	215
Latoff Wainer and Co	5044	80
Latorra Paul and McCann Inc	7311	377
Latour Construction Inc	1623	110
Latour Management Inc	5812	194
Latrobe Associates Inc	3089	1100
Latrobe Foundry Machine and Supply Co	3363	51
Latrobe Pattern Co	3543	46
Latrobe Specialty Steel Co	3312	34
Latshaw Enterprises Inc	6719	74
Latta Graphics Inc	2752	1068
Lattavo Brothers Inc	4212	79
Lattice Engines	7372	2076
Lattice Inc	3661	111
Lattice Inc (Wheaton Illinois)	7372	2855
Lattice Materials LLC	3827	92
Lattice Semiconductor Corp	3674	70
Lattimore Black Morgan and Cain PC	8721	263
Latva Machine Inc	3599	285
Lau Industries Inc	3564	16
Lau Lau Plant	2099	353
Laub Engineering Corp	3565	175
Laube Technology Inc	5065	190
Lauber CFOs	6211	316
Lauderbach Builders Supply Company Inc	5031	302
Lauderdale Electric Inc	1731	1173
Lauderdale Graphics Corp	2752	1278
Laudermilch Meats Inc	5421	5
Lauer-Manguso and Associates Architects	8712	198
Lauers Supermarket Inc	5411	71
Laufers Pastries Inc	5461	32
Laughlin/Constable Inc	7311	207
Laughlin Electric Co	1731	2437
Laughlin International USA	8742	398
Laughlin Marinaccio and Owens Inc	7311	585
Laughlin Trucking Inc	4213	1915
Laughlin-Sutton Construction Co	1541	281
Launch Media Inc	2741	386
Launch Technologies Of Georgia LLC	7371	1537
Launchability	8322	219
Laundry and Cleaners Supply Inc	5087	84
Laundry By Shelli Segal	2339	37
Laun-Dry Supply Company Inc	5087	126
Laura Chenel's Chevre Inc	2022	77
Laura Waller Advisors Inc	6282	505
Lauraine Murphy Jericho Inc	5812	274
Laura's French Baking Company Inc	2051	269
Laureate Education Inc	8299	3
Laureate Learning Systems Inc	7371	1080
Laurel Adjustment Bureau Inc	7389	1551
Laurel Aggregates Inc	5191	157
Laurel Cable LP	4841	176
Laurel Computer Systems Inc	7376	48
Laurel Electronics Inc	3679	695
Laurel Farms	5149	172
Laurel Ford Lincoln Mercury Inc	5511	924
Laurel Grocery Company Inc	5141	76
Laurel Highlands River Tours Inc	7999	54
Laurel Holdings Inc	4941	26
Laurel Industries Inc	3827	85
Laurel Machine And Foundry Co	3441	99
Laurel Machine Inc	3599	417
Laurel Mercedes-Benz	5511	1070
Laurel Sand and Gravel Inc	1422	4
Laurel Valley Farms Inc	0139	2
Laurell Technologies Corp	3674	422
Lauren Corp	8099	76
Lauren Engineers and Constructors Inc	1541	50
Lauricella Public Relations Co	8743	329
Laurin Publishing Company Inc	2721	195
Laurinburg Milling Co	2048	133
Laurus Technologies Inc	7379	123
Laury Group Agency Inc	7363	188
Lausell Aluminum Jalousies Inc	3442	47
Lauster Radu Architects	8712	299
Lauth Property Group Inc	6552	137
Lautman Maska Neill and Co	7331	109
Lautrec Aquisition Co	6531	61
Laux Sporting Goods Inc	5091	77
Lava Lite LLC	3645	38
Lavaca Telephone Company Inc	4813	163
Lavallee And Ide Inc	3541	269
Lavalley Building Supply Inc	5211	69
Lavalley Transportation Inc	4213	1343
Lavandera Electric Co	1731	1992
Lavastorm Inc	7371	861
Lavatec Inc	3582	13
LavaTurtle Software Inc	7372	4051
Lavelle Industries Inc	3069	51
Lavelle Machine and Tool Company Inc	3545	115
Lavezzi Precision Inc	3861	55
Lavi Industries	3446	30
Lavigne Manufacturing Inc	3599	232
Lavin Candy Company Inc	5145	19
Lavoi Corp	2045	5
Law Actors Inc	7922	57
Law Bulletin Publishing Company Inc	2741	79
Law Company Inc	1541	112
Law Enforcement Associates Corp	3663	196
Law Enforcement Supply Inc	3496	122
Law Forum LLC	8748	412
Law Offices of Bernard P Wolfsdorf	8111	396
Law Offices of David A Carter PA	6211	308
Law Offices of George G Braunstein Co	8111	596
Law Offices of Pat Maloney PC	8111	557
Law Offices of William W Price PA	8111	564
Law Snakard and Gambill PC	8111	489
Law Weathers PC	8111	377
LawCrossing	7389	170
Lawes Coal Company Inc	5983	22
LawFinance Group Inc	6153	25
Lawgic Publishing Co	2741	190
LawInfocom	7375	112
Lawler and Stanz Inc	1623	818
Lawler Ballard Van Durand	7311	484
Lawler Foods Inc	2051	38
Lawler Manufacturing Corp	3829	192
Lawley Service Insurance	6331	46
LawLogix Group	7371	371
Lawn Fire Co	1731	2587
Lawnview Industries Inc	3999	219
Lawrence and Schiller Inc	7311	339
Lawrence Brothers Inc	3532	63
Lawrence Cable Service Inc	1731	1370
Lawrence County Exchange	5153	100
Lawrence D Oliver Seed Company Inc	5191	138
Lawrence Enterprises Inc	5199	117
Lawrence Equipment Inc	3556	21
Lawrence Foods Inc	2033	43
Lawrence Gravel Inc	5211	246
Lawrence Group Inc	8712	135
Lawrence Journal-World Co	2711	78
Lawrence Leasing Ii LLC	7359	51
Lawrence Metal Products Inc	3446	26
Lawrence Mold And Tool Corp	3544	307
Lawrence Paper Co	2653	26
Lawrence Photo and Video	5043	39
Lawrence Plastics Inc	3089	793
Lawrence Printing	2752	1594
Lawrence Printing Co	2752	979
Lawrence Productions Inc	7372	2467
Lawrence Pumps Inc	3561	46
Lawrence R Mccoy and Company Inc	5031	43
Lawrence Ragan Communications Inc	2741	202
Lawrence Ripak Company Inc	8734	73
Lawrence Street Industry LLC	5064	95
Lawrence Street Publications	2721	342
Lawrence Tool and Molding Co	3089	515
Lawrence Transportation Systems Inc	4214	18
Lawrenceville Brick Inc	3251	16
Lawruk Machine and Tool Company Inc	3599	936
Lawson Cattle and Equipment Inc	5083	184
Lawson Chevrolet	5511	1177
Lawson Hawks Insurance Associates	6411	240
Lawson Labs Inc	3577	597
Lawson M Whiting Inc	3532	74
Lawson Mardon Thermaplate Corp	3083	16
Lawson Printers Inc	2752	1114
Lawson Products Inc	5085	12
Lawson Software Inc	7372	85
Lawson-Hemphill Inc	3552	23
Lawton Brothers Inc	5087	73
Lawton Printers Inc	2752	1118
Lawton Public School District I-008	8211	84
Lawton Publishing Company Inc	2711	351
LAWTRAC Development Corp	7372	2826
Lawyers and Judges Publishing Co	2731	354
Lawyers Title Insurance Corp	6361	4
Lawyers Title of Arizona Inc	6361	31
LAX Wheel Refinishing Inc	5013	178
Laxmi Group Inc	7371	738
Laydon Enterprises Inc	3545	149
Layfield Environmental Systems Corp	3081	74
Layke Inc	3599	1150
Layke Tool and Manufacturing Company Inc	3545	307
Layman Plastics Corp	3082	33
Laymon Candy Company Inc	5145	32
Layne Christensen Co	1799	2
Layton Construction Co	1542	37
Layton Manufacturing Co	3531	138
Layton Manufacturing Corp	3585	241
Lazare Kaplan International Inc	5094	2
Lazarus Group Inc	1623	805
La-Z-Boy Inc	2512	1
Lazer Telecommunications Inc	5063	569
Lazo Technologies Ltd	7374	269
Laz-Trans Inc	4213	3005
Lazydays	5561	2
Lazzati Construction Company Inc	1623	567
LB Capital Inc	6282	345
LB Carpenter PA	8721	145
LB Electric Supply Company Inc	5063	302
LB Foster Co	3312	21
LB Foster Co Allegheny Rail Products Div	3743	25
Lb Fragrance LLC	2386	1
LB Industries Inc	7359	128
LB Transport Inc	4213	2020
LBA Group Inc	3679	678
Lbi Us LLC	7379	364
LBM Construction Company Inc	1542	318
LBM Products Inc	3089	1855
LBM Systems LLC	7372	3355
LBU Inc	3172	13
LC Bullfrog International	3999	85
LC Colormark	2752	398
LC Doane Co	3646	43
LC Dumac	2752	1294
LC Elite Marketing	7372	3155
LC I-Connect	7371	903
LC Liftpak	5084	683
LC Miller Co	3398	21
LC Products LLC	3089	801
LC Radise International	7371	1460
LC Smith Co	3545	431
LC Technologies Inc	8731	227
LC Trucking Inc	4213	1029
LC Whitford Company Inc	1611	23
LC Williams and Associates	8743	213
LCA-Vision Inc	8093	16
LCC International Inc	4812	21
LCD Systems Corp	3679	243
Lcf Systems Inc	5088	106
LCG Associates Inc	6282	356
Lcg Systems LLC	7379	454
Lci Corporation International	3559	154
LCI Ltd	5169	58
Lcl Electronics Inc	3679	725
LCL Transit Co	4213	243
LCNB Corp	6712	369
LCNB National Bank	6021	140
L-com Inc	3577	302
LCOR Inc	6552	152
LCR-M Corp	5074	14

Company Name	SIC	Rank
Lcs Precision Molding Inc	3089	1504
LCS Site Services LLC	1799	100
LCT Transportation Services	4213	456
LD Amory and Company Inc	5146	31
LD Astorino Companies	8748	59
LD Kichler Co	3645	8
LD O'Mire Inc	6411	208
LD Plastics Inc	3089	1454
Ld Products Inc	5045	196
LDB Corp	5812	393
Ldc Industries Inc	3537	117
Ldg Electronics Inc	3571	190
LDG Management Company Inc	6321	59
Ldh Electrical Contractor Inc	1731	067
Ldi Industries Inc	3569	67
LDI Ltd	5013	8
LDJ Inc	2711	921
Lds Vacuum Products Inc	3589	164
Ldt Ltd	1731	2428
Ldw Inc	5032	198
Le Beouf Brothers Towing LLC	4492	6
Le Clair Industries Inc	3086	49
Le Claire Manufacturing Co	3365	11
Le Colonial Corp	5812	345
Le Creuset of America Inc	5046	8
Le Fiell Co	3535	99
Le Jeune Steel Co	3441	28
LE Johnson Products Inc	3429	78
LE Myers Co	1731	83
Le Pafe Inc	2051	59
LE Schwartz and Son Inc	3444	69
LE Seitz Associates Inc	7389	769
LE Smith Co	2431	74
LE Sommer and Sons Inc	5999	157
Le Streghe	5812	426
Le Sueur Cheese Co	2022	12
Le Sueur Inc	3363	14
Le Sueur Manufacturing Co	3625	392
LE Warren Inc	3599	2348
Lea Albert Electric Co	1731	886
Lea County Electric Cooperative Inc	4911	267
Lea County State Bank	6022	539
Lea Electric LLC	1731	336
Lea Elliott Inc	8711	190
Lea Industries Inc	2511	99
LEA International Inc	3612	127
Lea Williams Inc	8741	81
Leach and Garner Co	3356	23
Leach Enterprises Inc	5013	196
Leach Farms Inc	0161	21
Leach Grain and Milling Company Inc	2048	125
Leach's Industrial Service Inc	3599	1914
Lead Research Group	7311	526
Lead Screws International Inc	7699	121
LEAD Technologies Inc	7372	3138
Leadcom Integrated Solutions USA Inc	4899	150
Leader Business System's Inc	7629	42
Leader Communications Inc	7379	71
Leader Engineering-Fabrication Inc	3599	589
Leader Instruments Corp	5063	261
Leader Publications Inc	2711	474
Leader Publishing Co (Pontiac Illinois)	2711	667
Leader Publishing Group Inc	2721	367
Leader Publishing Inc	2711	497
Leader Tech Inc	3469	229
Leader Technologies Inc	7371	1650
Leader Tool Company Inc	3544	233
Leaders Manufacturing Inc	3291	25
Leadership Companies Inc	7372	2426
Leadership Directories Inc	2741	171
Leadership Software Corp	6719	198
LeadersLife Insurance Co	6311	226
Leadertech Systems Of Chicago Inc	5045	453
LeadFlashcom	6163	29
Leading Edge Design and Systems Inc	7371	1528
Leading Edge Distribution Ltd	5065	161
Leading Edge Systems Richmond Inc	7371	849
Leading Market Technologies Inc	7372	672
Leading The Way With Dr Michael Youssef Inc	7922	36
Leadman Electronics	5961	127
Leadmaster Operating Co	7389	1032
Leadnomics	8742	524
LeadQual LLC	7374	132
Leadsoft Inc	7371	1497
Leadstream	7371	3
Leadswell Inc	4813	578
Leadtrack Software	7372	4842
Leaf Financial Corp	6153	10
Leaf River Ag Service	5191	162
Leaf Terminator	3089	1807
Leahy-Wolf Co	2992	64
Leak Meter Services Inc	7629	38
Leake and Watts Services Inc	8322	19
Leaman Building Materials LP	5211	36
Leamar Industries Inc	5032	95
Leancor LLC	8742	599
Leander Trucking Company Inc	4213	1189
Leandro M and E Inc	7349	443
Leanin Tree Inc	2771	11
Leaning Post Productions	7371	1728
Leanlogistics	7372	1302
Leap Partnership Inc	7311	584
Leap Software Inc	7372	3225

Company Name	SIC	Rank
Leap Wireless International Inc	4812	8
LeapFrog Enterprises Inc	3944	4
Leapley Construction Group of Atlanta LLC	1542	239
Lear Corp	2531	2
Lear Engineering Corp	3827	139
Lear Siegler Services Inc	4581	3
Learfield Communications Inc	4832	40
Learjet Inc	3721	43
Learning Annex LP	8221	9
Learning Care Group Inc	8351	7
Learning Communications LLC	8741	300
Learning Design	2741	482
Learning Disabilities Association Of The Genesee Valley Inc	8322	118
Learning Labs Inc	5999	186
Learning Multi-Systems Inc	7372	4309
Learning Resources Inc	3999	92
Learning Tools International	7372	3618
Learning Tree International Inc	8299	11
Learning Tree International USA Inc	8243	1
Learning Voyage Inc	8299	45
Learningcom Inc	7373	181
LearningstationCom Inc	7372	4083
LearningWare Inc	7372	850
LearnKey Inc	7812	38
LearnSomething Inc	2741	116
Learnwright Inc	8331	246
Lease Crutcher Lewis Builds	1542	66
Lease Management Inc	1389	60
Lease Midwest Inc	7359	214
LeasePlan USA	7359	14
LeaseTeam Inc	7372	2549
Leasing Associates Inc	7513	16
Leason Ellis LLP	8111	546
Least Cost Formulations Ltd	7372	2498
Leatex Chemical Co	2843	16
Leatherback Publishing Inc	2752	1137
Leathercraft Inc	2512	65
Leathers Oil Co	5541	36
Leatherwood Construction Inc	1623	678
Leatherwood Manufacturing Inc	3441	191
Leavins Seafood Inc	2092	34
Leavitt Corp	2099	132
Leavitt Machine Co	3541	270
Leavitt Tube Company LLC	3317	37
Leavitt's Freight Service	4213	1304
Lea-Wayne Knitting Mills Inc	2252	9
LEB Electric Ltd	1731	1969
Lebanon Apparel Corp	2339	44
Lebanon Building Systems Inc	1542	378
Lebanon Citizens National Bank	6022	218
Lebanon Machine and Manufacturing Company Inc	3599	1309
Lebanon Publishing Company Inc	2759	277
Lebanon Tool Company Inc	3599	218
Lebanon Valley Engraving Inc	3953	17
Lebco Graphics Inc	2752	1389
Lebhar-Friedman Inc	2721	63
Leblanc and Associates Inc	5084	446
LeBlanc and Schuster Public Relations Inc	8743	220
Lebon Press Inc	2752	1155
Lec Inc	3823	149
Lecere Corp	7372	5094
LeCesse Construction Co	1542	183
LeChase Construction Services LLC	1542	96
Lechler Laboratories Inc	2844	181
Lechner Realty Group Inc	6531	307
LeCordon Bleu Colledge of culinary Arts in Portland	8221	49
LECORP Inc	8711	552
Lectorum Publications Inc	5192	28
Lectra Circuit Inc	3672	300
Lectra North America	7372	100
Lectro Communications Inc	5065	792
Lectro Engineering Co	3559	348
Lectro Tek Services Inc	3596	23
Lectrodryer LLC	3569	157
Lectroetch Co	3953	26
Lectrosonics Inc	3651	58
LED Lumina USA LLC	3641	16
Leda Corp	3651	162
Leddy Electric Inc	1731	1893
Lederle Machine Co	3555	29
Ledford Engineering Company Inc	3544	623
LEDIC Management Group	6531	31
Ledoux and Company Inc	8734	172
Ledow Company Inc	3535	233
Ledtronics Inc	3674	241
Ledwell and Son Enterprises Inc	3715	24
Ledyard Financial Group Inc	6712	519
Lee Air Inc	3728	218
Lee and Eastes Tank Lines Inc	4213	2401
Lee Apparel Company Inc	2325	3
Lee Baxter Enterprises Inc	5063	924
Lee Brass Co	3366	4
Lee Brick and Tile Co	3251	13
Lee Brothers Inc	2035	20
Lee Builder Mart Inc	5211	242
Lee Butter and Associates Inc	5063	811
Lee Co	3823	29
Lee Controls Inc	3312	105
Lee Corp	2752	1615

Company Name	SIC	Rank
Lee County Electric Cooperative Inc	4911	117
Lee Davis Electric Inc	1731	1837
Lee Dopkin	5074	195
Lee E Norris Construction and Grain Company Inc	3523	123
Lee Electric Inc	3669	264
Lee Electric Supply Company Inc	5063	549
Lee Enterprises Inc	2711	29
Lee Group Inc	7389	725
Lee Haimowitz	5065	977
Lee Hartman and Son Inc	5046	10
Lee Hecht Harrison Inc	7361	43
Lee Industries Inc	3443	75
Lee Jennings Enterprises Inc	4213	1406
Lee Jensen Sales Company Inc	3496	103
Lee Kum Kee Foods Inc (City of Industry California)	2099	144
Lee Kum Kee USA Inc	5149	66
Lee Lumber and Building Materials Corp	5211	79
Lee Masonry Products Inc	3271	15
Lee Metals Inc	3341	40
Lee Pharmaceuticals Inc	2844	125
Lee Plastics Inc	3089	1182
Lee Precision Inc	3423	51
Lee Precision Machine Shop Inc	3599	663
Lee Publications Inc	2711	373
Lee Publishing Co	2711	668
Lee Ray-Tarantino Company Inc	5148	29
Lee Reger Builds Inc	1542	430
Lee Rj Group Inc	8731	116
Lee Roy Jordan Redwood Lumber Co	5031	102
Lee Smart PS Inc	8111	426
Lee Sperling Hisamune A/C	8721	471
Lee Sperling Hisamune Accountancy Corp	8721	239
Lee Spring Co	3495	12
Lee Supply Corp	5074	37
Lee Technologies Group Inc	5075	6
Lee Tilford Agency Inc	7311	886
Lee Tractor Company Inc	5084	365
Lee Transport Equipment Inc	5013	187
Lee Traynham Trucking Inc	4213	2764
Lee Williams Meats Inc	5421	9
Leeann Plastics Inc	3089	1765
Leebaw Manufacturing Company Inc	3537	102
Leech Carbide	2819	92
Leech Industries Inc	8711	426
Leeco	5084	862
Leeco Steel Products Inc	5051	69
Leed Corporate Services Inc	7363	84
Leed Electric Inc	1731	1141
Leed Selling Tools Corp	2789	6
Leede Operating Company LLC	1381	48
Leedo Manufacturing Company Inc	2434	38
Leeds Equity Partners	6799	195
Leeds Seitel and Associates Inc	7373	595
Leedy Manufacturing Company LLC	3714	339
Leefson Tool and Die Co	3469	277
Leelanau Fruit Co	5142	35
Leelanau Industries Inc	3599	1363
Lee-Lynn Machining Inc	3599	1932
Lee-Perfect Transcribing Company Inc	7338	6
Leepfrog Technologies Inc	7371	1560
Leer Electric Inc	1731	1075
Leer Inc	3585	28
Leer Inc	3713	24
Leerink Swann and Company Inc	6722	270
Lee's Grinding Inc	3599	1218
Lee's Imperial Welding Inc	3441	95
Lee's Sausage Company Inc	5147	128
Lees Supermarket	5411	174
Lee's Trucking Inc	4213	474
Leese and Company Inc	3599	972
Leeser TX Inc	4213	1986
Lee-Smith Inc	5511	291
Leesville Lumber Company Inc	2421	114
Leevac Industries LLC	3731	28
Leever's Foods Inc	5411	93
Leeway Inc	3523	247
Leeway Transportation Inc	4213	2539
Lefco Environmental Technology	4953	82
LeFebvre and Sons Inc	4213	1978
Leffler Agency	7311	435
LeFiell Manufacturing Co	3317	41
Lefrak Organization Inc	6552	7
Left Behind Games Inc	7372	4086
Left Hand and Tabernash Brewing	2082	80
Legacy Audio Inc	3651	144
Legacy Automotive Inc (McDonough Georgia)	5511	617
Legacy Bank of Texas	6022	101
Legacy Bank (Wiley Colorado)	6022	608
Legacy Cabinets LLC	2511	34
Legacy Capital Equipment LLC	3674	363
Legacy Capital Management Inc	6099	30
Legacy Financial Group Inc	6162	118
Legacy Ford	5511	1112
Legacy Health System	8399	1
Legacy Holdings LLC	5045	733
Legacy Housing Ltd	2451	20
Legacy Inc	5045	458
Legacy Laboratory Services	8071	34
Legacy Meridian Park Hospital	8062	187

Company Name	SIC	Rank
Legacy Photographics Inc	7221	13
Legacy Publishing Co (Westbrook Maine)	2741	507
Legacy Reserves LP	1311	66
Legacy Stone Products Inc	5032	96
Legacy Wealth Management Inc	6282	451
Legal Aid Bureau Of Buffalo Inc	8111	531
Legal Applications Holding Corp	7371	771
Legal Club of America Corp	8111	586
Legal Computer Solutions Inc	7379	744
Legal Courier LCL	7389	514
Legal Directories Publishing Company Inc	2741	215
Legal Files Software Inc	7372	2812
Legal News Publishing Co	2791	29
Legal Plus Software Group Inc	7372	4975
Legal Research Center Inc	8111	491
Legal Rights Defenders	7311	817
Legal Technology Inc	7373	991
LegalEdge Software	7372	2103
LegalShield	7299	5
Legato A Vanguard California Corp	5021	108
Legend Advisory Services Inc	6282	144
Legend Brewing Co	2082	78
Legend Engraving Company Inc	5065	731
Legend Group	6282	379
Legend Home Corp	1531	60
Legend Industries Inc	3555	80
Legend Merchant Group Inc	7389	1681
Legend Silicon Corp	3674	154
Legend Technical Services Of Arizona Inc	8742	587
Legend Valve and Fitting Inc	3494	57
Legend Wireless Group Us Inc	3663	107
Legendary Holdings Inc	2353	11
Legendary Lighting LLC	3648	76
Legere Group Ltd	2431	43
Legg Mason Inc	6282	27
Leggat McCall Properties LLC	6552	216
Leggett and Platt Inc	2515	1
Leggett and Platt Office Components	3363	8
Leggett-Southwest Carpet	3086	33
Leghart Associates Inc	8711	695
Legion Lighting Company Inc	3646	62
Legislative Demographic Services Inc	7373	523
Legler Systems Co	8742	663
LeGlue and Company CPA's	8721	444
LEGO Systems Inc	3944	3
LeGrand Hart	8743	73
Legrand Holding Inc	6719	108
Legrand Software Inc	7372	1267
Legris Inc	3491	39
Lehigh Acres Concrete Supply Company Inc	5064	135
Lehigh Cement Company LLC	3241	9
Lehigh Electric Products Co	3648	56
Lehigh Equipment Company Inc	5046	386
Lehigh Fluid Power Inc	3593	47
Lehigh Precision Company Inc	7699	264
Lehigh Valley Health Network	8011	178
Lehigh Valley Public Telecommunica-tions Corp	4833	192
Lehman Brothers Bank FSB	6211	208
Lehman Brothers Holdings Inc	6211	3
Lehman Foods Inc	2099	293
Lehman Millet Inc	7311	201
Lehman Pipe And Plumbing Supply Inc	5084	191
Lehman Sugarfree Confections Inc	2064	69
Lehman-Roberts Co	1611	27
Lehman's Egg Service Inc	5144	17
Lehman's Pipe and Steel Inc	5051	359
Lehman-Smith and McLeish PLLC	8712	250
Lehrkind's Inc	2086	60
Lei Companies Inc	1731	394
Leibold Communications Inc	1731	2155
Leica Camera Inc	3861	80
Leica Geosystems Hds LLC	3577	344
Leicht Transfer and Storage Co	4213	1966
Leico Industries Inc	5051	496
Leidy's Inc	2011	30
Leif Johnson Ford Inc	5511	240
Leifer Construction Inc	1623	443
Leigh Custom Homes Inc	1521	145
Leigh Fibers Inc	2299	8
Leight Sales Company Inc	5072	55
Leightner Electronics Inc	3677	80
Leighton Broadcasting	4832	114
Leighton Consulting Inc	1542	429
Leimkuehler Inc	5999	241
Leinenkugel Jacob Brewing Co	2082	30
Leiss Tool and Die Co	3599	271
Leister Productions Inc	7372	3918
Leisure Associates Inc	5065	734
Leisure Deck Inc	7349	476
Leisure Life Ltd	3732	59
Leisure Properties LLC	3732	32
Leisure Publishing Company Inc	2721	215
Leisure Time Products Inc	3952	16
Leisure Vision Of Nevada City	3851	53
Leisure World Health Clubs	7991	13
Leitelt Iron Works	7699	222
Leitner Electric Co	1731	2555
Leitner-Poma Of America Inc	3799	20
LEK Pharmaceutical Inc	5122	84

Company Name	SIC	Rank
Lektro Inc	4581	34
Lektron Inc	3577	491
Leland Manufacturing LLC	2599	14
Lelanite Corp	3086	85
Lelia Industries Inc	5023	164
Lello Appliances Corp	5064	166
Lely USA Inc	3635	11
LEM Products Inc	5099	58
Lemac Corp	3531	215
Lemac Mine Service	7699	161
Lemac Packaging Inc	5085	84
LeMaitre Vascular Inc	2672	17
Leman Machine Co	3441	259
LeMans Corp	5013	44
LeMaster and Daniels PLLC	8721	281
Lematic Inc	3556	74
Lemco Mills Inc	2251	7
Lemco Tool Corp	3546	34
Lemica Corp	2431	136
Lemke Industrial Machine Inc	3599	1770
Lemle and Kelleher LLP	8111	300
LemmonTree Enterprises Inc	8748	285
Lemo USA Inc	5065	69
Lemoine Company LLC	1542	125
Lemoine Multinational Technologies Inc	3577	518
Lemon Creek Winery Ltd	2084	99
Lemon-X Corp	2087	21
Lemore Transportation Inc	4213	604
Lempco Industries Inc	3544	2
Len Industries Inc	3599	270
Len Libby's Inc	2064	126
Len Lyall Chevrolet Company Inc	5511	806
Lenac Warford Stone Inc	7311	400
Lenape Resources Inc	1311	157
Lenard Tool and Machine Inc	3544	736
Lenaro Paper Company Inc	5111	29
Lenawee Stamping Corp	3465	33
Lenco Electronics Inc	3612	82
Lenco Incorporated - Pmc	3089	299
Len-Co Lumber Corp	5211	121
Lenco Marine Inc	3699	166
Lenco Mobile Inc	4899	157
Lend Lease	1799	1
Lend Lease Inc (New York New York)	6799	207
Lender Processing Services Inc	7389	19
Lender Support Systems Inc	7372	3117
Lenderlive Network Inc	7389	313
Lender's Service Inc	6159	18
Lending Trimming Company Inc	2396	22
LendingTree Inc	6159	80
Lendio Inc	6163	43
Lenel Systems International Inc	7372	939
Lengner and Sons Produce Express	4213	1732
Lenhardt Tool And Die Co	3544	190
Lenk Broadcasting Company Inc	4832	123
Lenmar Chemical Corp	2843	4
Lennar Corp	1531	5
Lennar Homes of California Inc	6552	180
Lennertson Sample Co	2782	43
Lenni Electric Corp	1731	699
Lennox Industries Inc (Richardson Texas)	3433	1
Lennox Industries Inc (Stuttgart Arkansas)	3585	42
Lennox International Inc	3585	9
Lenoir Mirror Co	3231	41
Lenovo Group Ltd	3571	5
Lenox Corp	3269	1
Lenox Instrument Company Inc	3827	119
Lenox Laser Corp	3829	276
Lenox Wealth Management Inc	6712	516
Lenox-Martell Inc	5149	139
Lenric Corp	8748	228
Lens Express Inc	5963	9
Lens Masters Inc	5048	22
Lensco Inc	5063	798
LensCom Inc	3827	152
LensCrafters Inc	5048	43
Lenser Filtration Inc	5085	470
Lensvector Inc	3851	45
Lenthor Engineering	3672	136
Lentros Engineering Inc	3599	859
Lenz Inc	3451	113
Lenzart Inc	7384	55
Leo A Daly Co	8712	22
Leo and Sons Inc	1389	53
Leo Burnett USA	7311	50
Leo Burnett Worldwide Inc (Chicago Illinois)	7311	18
Leo F Maciver Company Inc	3131	2
Leo Hoffman Chevrolet Inc	5511	541
Leo Journagan Construction Co	1611	97
Leo Lam Inc	2752	1004
Leo Prager Inc	2542	46
Leo Wolleman Inc	5094	24
Leoleo International Inc	5045	860
Leon County School District	8211	21
Leon E Wintermyer Inc	1611	255
Leon Hand-Crafted Speakers Inc	5065	616
Leon Henry Inc	7331	280
Leon Jones Feed and Grain Inc	4213	631
Leon Korol Co	5113	29
Leon Max Inc	2337	4
Leon Plastics Inc	3714	162

Company Name	SIC	Rank
Leona Group LLC	8211	100
Leonard Aluminum Utility Buildings Inc	5531	29
Leonard and Mayer Advertising Inc	7311	595
Leonard B Hebert Jr and Company Inc	1629	41
Leonard Fountain Specialties Inc	7359	80
Leonard Green and Partners LP	6211	334
Leonard Hudson Drilling Company Inc	1381	44
Leonard Machine Tool Systems Inc	3549	94
Leonard Mountain Inc	2033	106
Leonard Peterson and Company Inc	3821	26
Leonard Rue Video Productions Inc	7336	314
Leonard S Stern Plumbing	5074	122
Leonard Transport Inc	4213	3077
Leonard Transportation Corp	4213	2534
Leonardi Manufacturing Company Inc	3462	75
Leonardo Studio Inc	7336	255
Leonard's Bakery Ltd	5461	40
Leonard's Express Inc	4213	744
Leonard's Hardware Inc	5072	99
Leone Industries	3221	6
Leonetti Frozen Foods Inc	2038	56
Leonhardt Group Inc	7336	91
Leonhardt Manufacturing Company Inc	3498	46
Leoni Motor Express Inc	4213	2352
Leoni Wiring Systems Inc	3679	72
Leon's Fine Foods Inc	2099	141
Leon's Frozen Custard	2024	66
Leopard Communications Inc	8742	385
Leopard Enterprises Inc	5734	361
Leopardo Companies Inc	1542	82
Leo's Exterminating Company Inc	7342	64
Leo's Professional Audio Inc	5999	130
Lepage Bakeries Inc	2051	31
Lepel Corp	3565	170
Leppo Eqjipment Inc	5082	112
Leprino Foods Co	2022	4
Lerner Publishing Group	2731	165
Leros Associates Inc	6794	70
Leroy Cooperative Association Inc	5153	68
Leroy Haynes Center For Children And Family Services Inc	8361	70
Leroy Hill Coffee Company Inc	2095	19
Leroy Plastics Inc	3498	78
Leroy Smith Inc	5148	57
Leroy's Food Service Equipment Inc	5046	303
Leroy's Horse and Sports Place	7999	93
Lerro Products Inc	2841	53
Les Boulangers Associes Inc	2053	20
Les Chateaux De France Inc	2038	73
Les Faerber	3575	32
Les Schwab Tire Co	5531	5
Les Wallen USA Inc	5731	77
Les Wilson Inc	1381	58
Lesaffre Yeast Corp	2099	29
Lesaint Logistics Transportation	4213	2072
Lescarden Inc	8731	409
LESCO Inc	2879	4
LeSEA Broadcasting Corp	4833	129
LeSEA Inc	4833	44
Lesher Printers Inc	2759	384
Lesko Enterprises Inc	3089	744
Lesley Roy Designs LLC	7389	1754
Lesley Thomas Schwarz and Postma	8721	415
Leslie Company Inc	2782	23
Leslie Controls Inc	3494	28
Leslie Davis	7311	892
Leslie Electric Services Inc	1731	2446
Leslie Fournberg	5045	788
Leslie's Poolmart Inc	5999	43
Lesnau Printing Co	2752	1570
Leson Chevrolet	5511	875
L'esprit De Campagne Inc	2034	37
LesserEvil Brand Snack Co	2099	197
Lessman Electric Supply Company Inc	5063	484
Lessors Inc	4213	1177
Lester Brothers Excavation Inc	1794	43
Lester Building Systems LLC	2452	4
Lester Coggins Trucking Inc	4213	276
Lester Detterbeck Enterprises Ltd	3541	109
Lester Lithograph Inc	2752	757
Lester M Prange Inc	4213	2202
Lester R Summers Inc	4213	1017
Lester Sales Company Inc	5063	388
Lester Schwab Katz and Dwyer LLP	8111	257
Lester's Machine Company Inc	3599	2203
Lesueur-Richmond Slate Corp	1429	7
LET Corp	7349	402
Letellier Material Handling Equipment Inc	3536	37
Letherer Truss Inc	2439	50
Letica Corp	2656	4
LeTip International Inc	7389	454
LeTourneau Inc	3532	7
Letourneau Plastics Inc	3089	1472
LeTourneau Sales and Service Co	3531	90
Let's Go Aero	3716	15
Let's Go Inc	2741	69
Let's Talk Cellular and Wireless Inc	5731	16
Let's TalkCom Inc	4812	75
Letsch Manufacturing Inc	3544	876
Letsgolearn Inc	7371	1546
Letsos Co	1711	46
Letter Systems Inc	2752	196
Lettercomm Type Inc	2752	528

Company Name	SIC	Rank	Company Name	SIC	Rank	Company Name	SIC	Rank
Lettergraphics - PFS	2759	503	Lewis Truck Lines Inc	4213	2418	Libbey Inc	3229	1
Letton Gooch Printers Inc	2752	848	Lewisburg Container Co	2653	27	Libbey-Owens-Ford Co	3211	3
Letts Industries Inc	3462	21	Lewisburg Printing Inc	2752	211	Libby Hill Seafood Restaurants Inc	5812	336
Lettuce Entertain You Too Inc	5812	174	Lewis-Clark Recyclers Inc	5093	187	Libby Laboratories Inc	2844	186
Leucadia Financial Corp	6211	207	Lewis-Goetz And Company Inc	5085	35	Libco Industries Inc	3829	394
Leucadia National Corp	2499	1	Lewiston Hardware And Lumber Inc	5251	49	Liberman Broadcasting Corp	4832	23
Leucadia Properties Inc	6331	258	Lewiston Trucking Company Inc	4213	1814	Libert Machine Inc	3541	249
Leucos USA Inc	3229	21	Lewtan Industries Corp	3993	105	Liberty ALL-STAR Equity Fund	6726	32
Leupold and Stevens Inc	3827	19	Lewus Electric Company Inc	3625	421	Liberty Appliances Trading Corp	5064	211
Lev Software	7372	4843	Lex Products Corp	5065	156	Liberty Associated Inc	4841	8
Levan Enterprises Inc	3541	150	Lexan Industries Inc	3679	702	Liberty Auto Salvage	5015	11
Levan Machine Company Inc	3599	1422	Lexar Media Inc	3861	4	Liberty Bancorp Inc (Liberty Missouri)	6712	481
Levangie Electric Company Inc	1731	328	Lexecon LLC	8748	36	Liberty Bank and Trust Co	6022	279
Levas Inc	2721	387	Lexel Imaging Systems Inc	3671	15	Liberty Bank (Middletown Connecticut)	6035	262
Levco Communication	5065	942	Lexica Inc	3823	470	Liberty Bank of Arkansas	6022	719
Levcor International Inc	5131	33	Lexico Publishing Group LLC	7375	188	Liberty Bell	7389	511
Level 3 Communications Inc	7379	3	LexiCode Corp	7389	248	Liberty Bell Bank	6022	543
Level Brand Inc	7311	825	Lexicom Computer Systems Inc	7373	642	Liberty Bell Steak Co	5147	114
Level II Inc	7372	3191	Lexicom Computer Systems LLC	5734	382	Liberty Book And Bible Manufactures Inc	3111	10
Level One Consulting Inc	7371	1696	Lexi-Comp Inc	2731	178	Liberty Building Systems Inc	1541	217
Level One LLC	7379	721	Lexicon Branding Inc	8748	279	Liberty Business Forms	2759	203
Level Sensor Technology	3643	167	Lexicon Consulting Inc	8748	174	Liberty Business Systems Inc	5044	62
LevelfieldCom Inc	7372	4137	Lexicon Inc	3651	53	Liberty Cab Company Inc	4121	4
LevelTen Interactive	8741	169	Lexicon Pharmaceuticals Inc	2834	358	Liberty Capital Group	7389	787
Levenger Co	5961	94	Lexington Abrasives Inc	3291	17	Liberty Capital Inc	6712	247
Levenson and Hill Inc	7311	140	Lexington B and L Financial Corp	6712	687	Liberty Communication Software Solutions Inc	7371	1152
Levernier Construction Inc	1541	134	Lexington Building and Supply Company Inc	5031	240	Liberty Construction Corp	8741	112
Leverwood Machine Works Inc	3545	415	Lexington Corporate Enterprises Inc	5075	7	Liberty Container Co	2653	88
Levex Engineering Co	3625	413	Lexington Corp	2531	46	Liberty Dairy Co	2026	36
Levi Ray and Shoup Inc	7372	414	Lexington Cutter Inc	3541	152	Liberty Distributors Inc	5064	125
Levi Strauss and Co	2325	2	Lexington Furniture Industries Inc	2512	9	Liberty Diversified International Inc	2653	1
Leviathan Corp	6159	69	Lexington Insurance Co	6331	114	Liberty Electric Company Corp	1731	2209
Levic Plastics Inc	3089	1480	Lexington Nursing Home Inc	8052	7	Liberty Electric Sales Inc	5063	893
Levin Enterprises Inc	4491	10	Lexington Partners	6799	107	Liberty Electrical Supply Company Inc	5063	353
Levin Furniture	5712	7	Lexington Plastic Molding Co	3089	1127	Liberty Embroidery Inc	2395	7
Levin Public Relations and Marketing Inc	8743	346	Lexington Precision Corp	3069	17	Liberty Energy Corp	1389	65
Levine Leichtman Capital Partners	6799	47	Lexington Press Inc	2752	1829	Liberty Envelope Corp	2677	19
Levinge Transportation LLC	4213	1892	Lexington Realty Trust	6798	78	Liberty Express Inc	4213	2754
Levins Auto Supply LLC	5013	113	Lexington Rubber Group Inc	3061	4	Liberty Financial Services Inc (New Orleans Louisiana)	6712	682
Levinson and Santoro Electric Corp	1731	528	Lexington Steel Corp	5051	180	Liberty Geneva Steel Ltd	8741	131
Levis Chevrolet Cadillac	5511	1053	Lexington Technology Inc	7372	3722	Liberty Global Inc	4841	5
Leviton Manufacturing Company Inc	3643	6	Lexington Telephone Long Distance Co	4813	131	Liberty Gold Fruit Co	5141	217
Levitz Furniture (New York New York)	5712	85	Lexis Nexis	2731	49	Liberty Group (Houston Texas)	7361	87
Levlad Inc	2844	62	Lexis Nexis InterAction	7372	1413	Liberty Group Publishing	2711	781
Levolor/Kirsh	2591	3	LexisNexis Group	7379	7	Liberty Homes Inc	2452	10
Levon Graphics Corp	2752	344	LexisNexis Publishing	2731	31	Liberty Inc	3523	121
Levy Group Inc	2337	3	LexisNexisCourtLink Corp	7375	93	Liberty Industries LC	3441	219
Levy Home Entertainment LLC	5192	6	Lexitech Inc	7371	1243	Liberty Information Management Systems	7372	1419
Lew A Cummings Company Inc	2752	216	Lexiteria Corp	7375	224	Liberty Interactive Group	7389	3
Lew Electric Fittings Co	3644	31	LexJet Corp	5961	126	Liberty Laboratories Inc	8734	150
Lew Horton Distributing Co	5091	42	Lexmark Carpet Mills Inc	2273	20	Liberty Life Insurance Co	6311	152
Lew Horton Distributing Company Inc	5091	121	Lexmark International Inc	3577	4	Liberty Lithographers Inc	2752	641
Lewan and Associates Inc	5044	15	Lexnet Consulting Group Inc	7371	1321	Liberty Manufacturing	3559	568
Lewco Inc	3535	62	LEXON Technologies Inc	3291	21	Liberty Maritime Corp	4412	25
Lewcott Corp	2821	31	Lexseco LLC	3825	336	Liberty Media Corp	7812	3
Lewin Group Inc	8742	64	Lextek International Inc	7371	1743	Liberty Media For Women LLC	2721	412
Lewis Advertising Company Inc	2752	1069	Lextel Manufacturing LLC	3674	442	Liberty Moving and Storage Co	4213	254
Lewis and Lambert LLLP	1711	89	Lexus	5012	14	Liberty Mutual Fire Insurance Co	6331	126
Lewis and Michael Inc	4213	1127	Lexus of Dayton Inc	5511	733	Liberty Mutual Group Inc	6719	3
Lewis and Robey Inc	4213	2620	Lexus of Huntsville	5511	754	Liberty Mutual Insurance Co	6331	10
Lewis and Roca LLP	8111	242	Lexus of Memphis Inc	5511	265	Liberty National Life Insurance Co	6311	109
Lewis Barricade Inc	7353	74	Lexus of Mishawaka	5511	631	Liberty Oil Company Inc	5172	141
Lewis Brisbois Bisgaard and Smith LLP	8111	191	Lexus Santa Monica Inc	5511	215	Liberty Opportunities	7389	2336
Lewis Brothers Land and Timber Inc	2421	95	Leylegian Investment Management Inc	6282	676	Liberty Orchards Company Inc	2064	61
Lewis Brothers Stages	4725	57	Leyman Manufacturing Corp	3713	41	Liberty Packaging and Extruding Inc	3089	1293
Lewis Color Lithographers Inc	2752	1251	Lezza Spumoni And Desserts Inc	2024	71	Liberty Partners	6211	248
Lewis Communications Inc (Birmingham Alabama)	7311	162	Lezzer Lumber Inc	5211	42	Liberty Parts Team Inc	5045	301
Lewis Computer Services Inc	7371	645	LF and P Inc	2671	54	Liberty Personnel Services Inc	7361	291
Lewis Construction Of Virginia Inc	1623	803	LF Driscoll Company LLC	8741	108	Liberty Playing Cards LP	2752	1088
Lewis Contractors	1542	204	LFD Home Furnishings	5712	59	Liberty Printing Inc	2752	1561
Lewis Contractors Inc	1623	134	Lfg and E International Inc	1623	263	Liberty Publishing Company Inc	7372	4976
Lewis Controls Inc	3823	358	LFP Inc	2721	168	Liberty Pumps Inc	3561	105
Lewis County Dairy Corp	2022	49	LG Almony and Sons Inc	4213	2893	Liberty Reed Company Inc	3552	56
Lewis County Electric Rural Cooperative Association	4911	440	LG and E Energy Systems Inc	4911	66	Liberty Research Company Inc	3451	97
Lewis County Senior Citizens Center Inc	8322	224	Lg Associates Inc	7379	1064	Liberty Savings Bank (Wilmington Ohio)	6035	32
Lewis Drug Inc	5912	18	Lg Chem Michigan Inc	5013	52	Liberty Steel Products Inc	5051	50
Lewis Electric LLC	1731	1162	Lg Electronics Mobilecomm USA Inc	5065	150	Liberty Tax Service	7291	5
Lewis Energy Group LP	1311	89	LG Everist Inc	1442	5	Liberty Technologies	3599	601
Lewis Entertainment Group	5541	55	LG Hetager Drilling Inc	1799	111	Liberty Theaters Inc	7832	25
Lewis Environmental Services Inc	4959	9	Lg Inc	2395	9	Liberty Threads NA Inc	2284	6
Lewis Fire Protection Inc	1711	281	LG Seeds Inc	0181	4	Liberty Tool Company Inc	5084	573
Lewis Furniture Company Inc	5064	91	Lgar Health and Rehabilitation	8322	198	Liberty Tool Inc	3541	180
Lewis Hollingsworth LP	6211	338	L'Garde Inc	3761	4	Liberty Travel Inc	4724	4
Lewis Label Products Corp	2759	57	Lgc Scientific Supply Inc	5049	82	Liberty Underground Inc	1623	503
Lewis Lee Inc	1623	297	LGC Wireless Inc	3357	30	Liberty Vegetable Oil Co	2079	10
Lewis Lumber And Supply LLC	5211	274	LGE (Old Co) Inc	8711	66	Liberty-Pittsburgh Systems Inc	3999	101
Lewis Machine and Tool Co	3599	414	Lginternational Inc	2672	64	Libertyville Bank and Trust Co	6022	303
Lewis Machine And Tool Company Inc	3599	2208	LGL Group Inc	3679	128	Libertyville Chevrolet	5511	513
Lewis Marine Supply Inc	5088	44	Lgs Technologies LP	3469	162	Libertyville Lincoln Mercury Sales Inc	5511	582
Lewis Motor Repair Inc	5063	680	LH Carbide Corp	3469	129	Libla Industries Inc	2448	23
Lewis Printing Co	2752	1272	LH Chaney Materials Inc	4213	1568	Libman Business Forms Inc	2759	294
Lewis Publishing Company Inc	2711	855	LH Corp	3556	184	Libman Co	3991	6
Lewis Realty Advisors	6531	371	LH Flaherty Company Inc	5084	412	Libra Inc	5199	97
Lewis Rice and Fingersh LC	8111	341	LH Lacy Company Inc	1611	90	Libra Industries Inc	3672	87
Lewis Sausage Company Inc	2013	226	LH Network Inc	7371	1295	Libra Systems Corp	3625	327
Lewis Spring and Manufacturing	3495	11	LH Stamping Corp	3469	62	Librandi Machine Shop Inc	3471	60
Lewis Steel Works Inc	3443	124	LHC Group Inc	8082	9	Libraries Of Middlesex Automation Consortium	7376	47
Lewis Supply Company Inc (Memphis Tennessee)	5085	109	Lhv Power Corp	3679	773	Libraries Online Inc	7375	8
Lewis Transport Inc	4213	1880	Li Cor Inc	3826	29			
			Li Hao	5731	272			
			Liaison International Inc	7371	669			
			Liaison Software Company LLC	7372	3833			
			Liam Services Inc	7378	111			

Company Name	SIC	Rank	Company Name	SIC	Rank	Company Name	SIC	Rank
Library Automation Technologies	3581	18	Lifeware TEK	7372	5111	Lightspeed Technologies Inc	3651	80
Library Bindery Company Of PA Inc	2789	84	LifeWatch Corp	3845	53	Lightspeed Trading LLC	7372	1156
Library Binding Service Inc	2789	8	LifeWay Christian Resources	2731	21	Lightsquared	7379	201
Library Corp	7372	932	Lifeway Foods Inc	2099	56	Lightstone Group LLC	6519	3
Library of Natural Sounds	7389	243	Lifewise Assurance Co	6311	199	Lightwave Logic Inc	3089	1902
Library Publications Inc	2731	156	LifeWise Health Plan of Oregon Inc	6321	58	Lightway Industries Inc	3646	79
Library Systems and Services LLC	2741	193	Lifoam Industries LLC	3086	4	Lightwedge LLC	5063	276
Library Technologies Inc	7374	293	Lift Moore Inc	3537	66	Lightworks Optics Inc	3827	45
Library Video Co	7822	27	Lift Truck Service Center Inc	5084	383	Lightyear Capital LLC	6799	144
Libredigital Inc	2741	49	Lift-All Company Inc	3496	35	Ligi Tool and Engineering Inc	3545	281
Libscorp LLC	7323	40	Liftech Handling Inc	5084	214	Ligna Machinery Inc	3553	60
LIC Screen Printing Inc	2759	514	Lifting Gear Hire Corp	7359	50	Ligon Electric Supply Co	5063	115
Licco Inc	8331	248	Liftruck Service Company Inc	5084	373	Ligon Industries LLC	3593	15
Lico Chemicals	5087	109	Ligand Pharmaceuticals Inc	2834	240	Ligos Corp	7372	359
Liconix Industries Inc	5045	952	LIGATT Security International	7379	422	Liguori Publications	2731	199
LICT Corp	6719	124	Ligature	2759	253	Liguria Foods Inc	2013	60
Lida Advertising Co	7311	921	Ligature Software Inc	7372	102	Li-Ion Motors Corp	3621	131
Liddell Trailers LLC	5012	166	Liggett Corp	2329	32	LIK Inc	3679	805
Liddy's Machine Shop Inc	3599	2017	Liggett-Stashower Inc	7311	187	Likom Caseworks USA Inc	3575	23
Lidestri Foods Inc	2033	27	Light and Ink Corp	2759	595	Lil' Thrift Food Marts Inc	5411	202
LIDP Consulting Services Inc	7379	487	Light Brite Distributing Inc	5063	401	Lile International Cos	4213	295
Liebenow and Torok Inc	7991	9	Light Bulbs Etc Inc	5063	688	Lilienthal Southeastern Inc	2752	1595
Lieberman and Associates	7372	708	Light Corporation Inc	3646	29	Liliha Bakery Ltd	2051	205
Lieberman Group LLC	7379	1316	Light Craft Manufacturing Inc	3646	105	Lille Corp	7374	368
Lieberman Research Worldwide Inc	8732	12	Light Engineering Corp	3621	139	Lillenas Publishing Co	2731	161
Lieberman Technologies	7372	4310	Light Enterprises Inc	5051	305	Lillian Vernon Corp	5961	67
Liebert Corp	3613	8	Light Express Inc	4213	2203	Lillian Vernon Fulfillment Services Inc	5961	59
Liebherr Construction Equipment Co	5082	139	Light Fabrications Inc	2672	26	Lillian Vernon International Ltd	5961	25
Liebherr Mining Equipment Co	3532	9	Light Lines Inc	5063	836	Lillie Suburban Newspapers Inc	2711	342
Liebherr-America Inc	5082	28	Light Logic Inc	3645	66	Lilly Machinery Inc	3441	263
Liebmann Optical Company Inc	3827	98	Light Metals Coloring Company Inc	3471	50	Lily Transportation Corp	7513	15
Liebovich Brothers Inc	5051	35	Light Metals Corp	3354	21	Lima Elevator Company Inc	5999	289
Liechty Farm Equipment Inc	5083	11	Light Milling Co	5191	163	Lima Head Start	8322	181
Liedtka Trucking Inc	4213	210	Light Process Co	3641	8	Lima Plastics Inc	3089	1349
Lieff Cabraser Heimann and Bernstein LLP	8111	412	Light Sciences Corp	8731	218	Lima Sheet Metal Machine and Manufacturing Inc	3589	189
			Light Sciences Oncology Inc	8731	204			
Lie-Nielsen Toolworks Inc	3425	9	Light Source	5063	715	Limbach Facility Services LLC	1711	185
Lif Industries Inc	3442	89	Light Sources Inc	3641	11	Limco-Piedmont Inc	4581	17
LIF Publishing Corp	2721	236	Light Speed Networks LLC	7373	1086	Lime Energy Co	3641	5
Lifco Hydraulics Inc	5084	615	Light Vision	2064	147	Lime Engineering Inc	3444	277
Life and Health Underwriters Inc	6311	254	LightbarsCom LLC	5084	842	Limelight Networks Inc	7389	154
Life Care Centers of America Inc	8052	4	LightBound	4813	206	Limerick Machine Company Inc	3599	1063
Life Care Ponte Vedra Inc	8361	32	Lightbridge Corp	1481	4	Limerick Studios-DVD	7319	77
LIFE Corp	3841	332	Lightech Fiberoptic Inc	3679	466	Limerock Industries Inc	1422	57
Life Cycle Engineering Inc	7372	281	Lightech Inc	1731	1779	Limited Brands Inc	5651	3
Life Enterprise USA Inc	5065	691	Lightedge Solutions Inc	5045	177	Limited Industries Inc	3599	1453
Life Fitness	5091	6	Lightfleet Corp	3571	109	LimitLess International Inc	4731	80
Life Fitness Consumer Div	3949	27	Lighthorse Technologies Inc	3577	383	Limitorque Corp	3452	20
Life Insurance Company of the Southwest	6311	189	Lighthouse Communications	5999	249	Limoneira Co	0174	4
			Lighthouse Computer Services Inc	7373	211	Limra International Inc	2721	23
Life Line Communications Of Long Island Inc	1731	2469	Lighthouse Electric Controls Co	3613	181	LIN TV Corp	4833	55
			Lighthouse Electrical Suppliers Inc	5063	544	Linak US Inc	5065	232
Life Line Packaging Inc	2671	72	Lighthouse For The Blind Inc	8331	15	Linatex Corporation Of America	5084	356
Life Of The Party LLC	3089	1236	Lighthouse Medical Staffing Inc	8082	88	Linbeck Construction Corp	1542	80
Life Partners Holdings Inc	6311	247	Lighting Accents Inc	3648	74	Linc Logistics Co	8742	77
Life Quest Inc	7363	252	Lighting and Design Inc	5063	929	Linc Technology Corp	3669	216
Life Quotes Inc	7374	89	Lighting and Electronic Design Inc	3646	93	Lincare Holdings Inc	8099	1
Life Re Corp	6311	36	Lighting and Electronics Inc	3648	72	Lincare Inc	8082	41
Life Saver Pool Fence Systems Inc	3496	112	Lighting Components and Design Inc	3648	14	Lincare New York Inc	8082	85
Life Science Associates	7372	1054	Lighting Control Systems Inc	1731	2583	Linco Construcion Company Inc	1623	195
Life Sciences Research Inc	8731	39	Lighting Depot Inc	5063	381	Linco Equipment Inc	5083	158
Life Style Furniture Company Inc	2512	32	Lighting Dynamics Inc	5063	894	Lincoln and Co	7371	1651
Life Style Staffing	7363	183	Lighting Gallery LLC	5063	907	Lincoln And Lancaster County Child Guidance Center Inc	8322	184
Life Technologies Corp	3826	2	Lighting Innovations Inc	3648	42			
Life Time Fitness Inc	7997	3	Lighting Maintenance Inc	1731	518	Lincoln Benefit Life Co	6311	139
Life Win Inc	8748	179	Lighting Oil Co	1311	215	Lincoln Builders Inc	1542	191
Life-Assist Inc	5047	174	Lighting Sales and Service	5063	585	Lincoln Child Center	8361	50
Lifecare Technologies Inc	7371	746	Lighting Science Group Corp	8051	42	Lincoln Construction Inc	1542	337
LifeCell Corp	8731	49	Lighting Sciences Inc	3648	83	Lincoln Contractors Supply Inc	5211	199
Lifecodes Corp	8734	37	Lighting Services Inc	3646	39	Lincoln Data	7372	948
Lifeguard Consulting LLC	7379	1403	Lighting Showroom Inc	5063	987	Lincoln Educational Services Corp	8249	3
Lifeline Amplification Systems Inc	1731	2327	Lighting Solutions Of Illinois Inc	5063	933	Lincoln Electric Co	3548	68
Lifeline BioTechnologies Inc	3829	521	Lighting Technology Services Inc	3612	75	Lincoln Electric Holdings Inc	3549	1
Lifeline Food Company Inc	2022	88	Lighting Trends Inc	5063	1014	Lincoln Electric Products Company Inc	3613	85
Lifeline Products Inc	3841	257	Lighting Virginia LLC	5063	876	Lincoln Equipment Inc	5091	64
Lifeline Systems Securities Corp	3663	40	Lighting World Inc	3646	51	Lincoln Food Service Products	3589	36
LifeLock Inc	7299	9	Lightlab Imaging LLC	3845	59	Lincoln General Insurance Co	6331	313
Lifemark Corp	8741	85	Lightmaker USA Inc	7371	1259	Lincoln Heritage Life Insurance Co	6311	260
LifeMatters USA	8082	72	Lightmore Electric Associates Inc	1731	1674	Lincoln Industrial Corp	3569	12
Lifemed Of California	3841	350	Lightmotive Inc	7812	270	Lincoln Industries Inc	3471	18
LifePlans Inc	6282	289	Lightning Bolt Entertainment Co	2741	436	Lincoln Journal Star	2711	159
LifePoint Hospitals Inc	8062	24	Lightning Diversion Systems Inc	3643	147	Lincoln Laser Co	3826	63
Lifequest	8331	96	Lightning Group Northwest	5063	652	Lincoln Logs Ltd	2452	21
Life's Work Of Western PA	8331	115	Lightning Master Corp	3629	91	Lincoln Machine Inc	3599	783
LifeScan Inc	2835	4	Lightning Media Inc	3695	23	Lincoln Manufacturing Inc	5082	162
Lifesize Communications Inc	4812	29	Lightning Phase II Inc	7372	688	Lincoln Mold and Die Corp	3544	208
Lifespace Communities Inc	8059	6	Lightning Rv Supply Inc	5531	62	Lincoln National Corp	6311	5
Lifespan Corp	8741	19	Lightning Source Inc	2732	16	Lincoln National Life Insurance Co	6311	41
LifeStore Financial Group	6712	566	Lightolier/A Genlyte Co	3646	17	Lincoln Office Supply Company Inc	5021	31
Lifestream Services Inc	8322	107	Lightolier Inc	3645	21	Lincoln Packing Co	2013	206
LifeStreet Corp	7319	43	LightPath Technologies Inc	3674	265	Lincoln Paper And Tissue LLC	2621	29
Lifestyle Foods Inc	3556	118	Lightpoint Colocation and Hosting LLC	7374	395	Lincoln Park Boring Co	3599	1550
Lifestyle Industries Inc	5047	257	LightPointe Communications Inc	3577	234	Lincoln Pharmacy	5912	62
Lifetec Inc	5047	257	Lightriver Technologies Inc	4899	189	Lincoln Poultry and Egg Co	5144	2
Life-Tech Inc	3841	163	Lightronics Inc	3648	62	Lincoln Precision Machining Co	3536	43
Lifetime Brands Inc	3421	4	Lights Of America Inc	3645	6	Lincoln Press Company Inc	2759	484
Lifetime Entertainment Services	4841	18	Lightsense Corp	8999	185	Lincoln Property Co	1542	13
Lifetime Industries Inc	3564	56	Lightship Group	7319	95	Lincoln Provision Inc	5142	24
Lifetime Memory Products Inc	3672	251	Lightspec Inc	5063	407	Lincoln Service LLC	5063	889
Lifetime Products Inc	3949	35	Lightspeed Aviation Inc	5088	96	Lincoln Technical Institute Inc	8249	6
Lifetouch Inc	7221	1	Lightspeed Data Solutions Inc	7371	1768	Lincoln Tool and Die Inc	3544	643
Lifetouch Portrait Studios Inc	7221	8	Lightspeed Networks LLC	1799	150	Lincoln Tool and Machine Corp	3599	851
Lifetouch Portrait Studios Inc (Mobile Alabama)	7221	12	Lightspeed Research Inc	8742	85	Lincoln Training Center and Rehabilitation Workshop	8331	77
Lifevantage Corp	2834	211	Lightspeed Systems	7372	489			

Company Name	SIC	Rank
Lincoln Trust Co	6091	5
Lincoln Winlectric Company Inc	5063	701
Lincoln Wood Products Inc	2431	47
Lincoln-Way Electronics	5731	162
Linda Christas	8244	5
Linda Sue Sandidge	5734	299
Linda Tool and Die Corp	3599	1542
Linda Viviani Touring Company Inc	7389	1526
Linda Weston Personnel Inc	7361	151
Lindal Cedar Homes Inc	2452	15
Lindar Corp	3545	124
Lindau Chemicals Inc	2869	61
Lindberg Enterprises Inc	5065	264
Lindbergh Liquidating Inc	5013	84
Lindblad Expeditions	4725	37
Linde Enterprises Inc	1629	116
Linde Group	7379	448
Linde Material Handling North America Corp	3537	12
Linde Process Plants Inc	3444	110
Linde Rss LLC	7352	40
Linde-Griffith Construction Co	1541	228
Lindeman Moving Company Inc	4212	45
Linden Alschuler and Kaplan Inc	8743	154
Linden Bulk Transportation Co	4213	528
Linden Cookies Inc	2052	56
Linden Group Corp	7379	1129
Linden Industries Inc	3559	242
Linden Lab	7371	1897
Linden Mold And Tool Corp	3544	305
Linden Nut Company Inc	2099	228
Linden Resources	8331	79
Lindenmeyr Munroe	5112	16
Linder Group Inc	6512	40
Linder Industrial Machinery Co	5082	75
Linderlake Corp	4899	35
Lindgren RF Enclosures Inc	3621	13
Lindgren RF Enclosures Inc (Glendale Heights Illinois)	3569	21
Lindi Skin	2834	343
Lindley Food Services	5812	246
Lindley Laboratories Inc	2843	18
Lindo Systems Inc	7372	4381
Lindquist Investment Co	6719	201
Lindquist Machine Corp	3599	311
Lind-Remsen Printing Company Inc	2752	986
Lindsay Automotive Group	5511	236
Lindsay Concrete Products Company Inc	3272	93
Lindsay Corp	3523	11
Lindsay Foods Inc	5147	119
Lindsay Ford of Wheaton	5511	310
Lindsay Manufacturing Inc	3635	9
Lindsay Sash Inc	2431	130
Lindsay Stone and Briggs Inc	7311	330
Lindsay Transportation Inc	4213	2959
Lindsey Manufacturing Co	3644	9
Lindsey Office Furnishings Inc	5712	105
Lindsey Transport Service Inc	4213	1444
Lindstrom Cleaning and Construction Inc	1521	149
Lindt and Sprungli (USA) Inc	2066	8
Line 6 Inc	3931	7
Line 9 Productions Inc	7812	291
Line Construction Inc	1623	298
Line Contracting Company Inc	1623	530
Line Craft Tool Co	3599	68
Line - Load Electrical Contractor's Inc	1731	1404
Line Precision Inc	3599	1230
Line4 Inc	7372	1786
Linear Air	4522	24
Linear and Metric Co	3599	1915
Linear Corp	3669	96
Linear Industries Ltd	5085	151
Linear Integrated Systems Inc	3674	402
Linear Lighting Corp	3646	24
Linear Logic Computers Inc	7371	1754
Linear Measurement Instruments Corp	3599	1861
Linear Rubber Products Inc	3069	221
Linear Technology Corp	3674	33
Linebarger Goggan Blair and Sampson LLP	8111	82
Linedata Services Inc	7372	462
Linemark Printing Inc	2752	288
Linemaster Switch Corp	3625	45
Linens of the Week	7213	5
Linergroup Inc	7379	1546
Liners Direct Inc	3431	6
Linetec Co	3471	6
Linett and Harrison Inc	7311	348
Linett Company Inc	3499	54
Linette James P Inc	2066	15
Lingate Financial Group Inc	6719	175
Lingle Brothers Coffee Inc	2095	53
Lingner Group Productions Inc	7812	166
Lingo Manufacturing Company Inc	2542	53
Lingo Sand Company Inc	1442	86
Lingua Science Corp	7389	2283
Linguatech International Inc	7371	1873
Linguistic Products Inc	7372	4709
Linguistic Systems Inc	4899	120
Linguist's Software Inc	7372	4844
Linguisystems Inc	2721	275
Linhart Corp	5511	170
Linium LLC	8742	271
Link Aka Communications Corp	4813	537
Link America Inc	8742	181
Link and Associates Inc	5072	175
Link Computer Corp	7372	1296
Link Computer Graphics Inc	3577	629
Link Control Systems Inc	3613	157
Link Depot Corp	3571	204
Link Electric and Safety Control Company Inc	3822	71
Link Electronics Inc	3651	190
Link Manufacturing Inc	3829	41
Link Medical Computing Inc	7373	792
Link Neighborhood Inc	7373	996
Link Simulation and Training	3699	15
Link Snacks Inc	2099	43
Link Solutions Inc	7379	701
Link Staffing Services	7363	134
Link Testing Laboratories Inc	8734	109
Link Truck Service Inc	4213	1652
Link Trucking Inc	4213	2111
Link2consult Inc	7372	4122
Linkage Inc	8742	162
Link_A_Media Devices Corp	7379	235
Link-Belt Construction Equipment Company LP Lllp	3531	10
Linked Software	7372	2721
Linked Technologies Inc	7379	1548
Linkedge Technologies Inc	7379	1060
Linkedin Corp	4813	36
Linker Systems Inc	7372	4517
Linkmont Technologies Inc	1731	740
Linkous Construction Company Inc	1542	199
LinkPro Technologies Inc	7372	4969
Linkpro Technologies Inc	7371	1554
Links Medical Products Inc	3559	198
LinkShare Corp	7389	286
Linkspace LLC	5045	1037
Linktek Corp	5045	989
Linkus Enterprises Inc	1623	60
Linmark Machine Products Inc	3599	1488
Linn Building Maintenance Inc	7349	231
Linn County Rural Electric Coop	4911	164
Linn Energy LLC	1311	36
Linn Gear Co	3568	35
Linn Software Inc	7372	3919
Linn Star Transfer Inc	4213	1982
Linn West Paper Co	2621	44
Linographics Inc	7372	1897
Linoma Software Inc	8742	523
Linowes and Blocher LLP	8111	315
Linrose Electronics Inc	5065	730
Linsalata Capital Partners Inc	6799	169
Linsco/Private Ledger Corp	6211	39
Linseis Inc	3825	277
Linspire Inc (San Diego California)	7372	4162
Linstar Inc	7382	141
Lintech	3625	117
Lintech Components Company Inc	5065	326
Lintern Corp	3585	139
Linton Shafer Computer Services Inc	7371	1201
Linux Labs International Inc	7371	1621
LinuxCertified Inc	8243	6
LinuxForce Inc	7371	1931
Linvatec Corp	3842	36
Linwood Tool Company Inc	3544	634
Linx Data Terminals Inc	3575	11
Linzer Products Corp	5199	54
Liochem Inc	2899	100
LION and FOX Recording	3695	77
Lion Brewery Inc	2082	15
Lion Raisins Inc	2034	9
Lion Recording Services Inc	7334	100
Lion Tool and Die Co	3544	759
Lionakis Design Group	8712	51
Lionbridge Technologies Inc	7389	104
Lionel Harris Oil Company Inc	5013	65
Lionetti Associates LLC	5093	105
Lionfish Solutions Inc	7374	416
Lionheart Technologies Inc	3823	32
Lion's Den Software	5045	1067
Lions Gate Entertainment Corp	7812	10
Lion's Share Credit Union	6062	2
Lions Volunteer Blind Industries Inc	2515	32
Lionshead Specialty Tire and Wheel LLC	5014	55
Lionudakis Firewood	5999	78
Lionzden Inc	5045	828
Lipari's Sausage Inc	2013	216
Liphart Steel Company Inc	3441	54
Lipman Hearne Inc	7336	27
Lipo Chemicals Inc	2869	68
Lipo Technologies Inc	2869	104
Lipomics Technologies Inc	8071	26
LipoScience Inc	8071	24
Lippert Brothers Inc	1541	163
Lippert Components Inc	3792	13
Lippert/Heilshorn and Associates Inc	8743	100
Lippert Inc	5046	88
Lippes Mathias Wexler Friedman LLP	8111	508
Lippi and Company Advertising	7311	859
Lippincott	8742	183
Lippincott Williams and Wilkins	2731	61
Lippo Binding Inc	2789	92
Lippolis Electric Inc	1731	1285
Lipsey Mountain Spring Water	2086	134
Lipsey Youngren Means Ogren and Sandberg LLP	8721	53
Lipsitz Management Company Inc	5093	54
Liquent Inc	7372	1113
Liquent Ltd	7373	124
Liquid 8 Technologies Inc	7371	1367
Liquid Blue Inc	2261	19
Liquid Cargo Inc	4213	2304
Liquid Controls Corp	3824	10
Liquid Controls LLC	3586	1
Liquid Crystal Resources LLC	3829	149
Liquid Crystal Technologies LLC	3679	875
Liquid Development Co	2899	242
Liquid Engineering Corp	7389	1516
Liquid Machines Inc	5045	174
Liquid Molding Systems Inc	2822	9
Liquid Motors Inc	7379	1155
Liquid Soap Products	2841	59
Liquid Solids Control Inc	7699	208
Liquid Transport Corp	4213	238
Liquidation Station Inc	5731	117
Liquidhub Inc	8748	109
Liquidity Services Inc	7389	150
Liquidmetal Technologies Inc	2899	86
Liquidnet Holdings Inc	6211	104
Liquinox Co	2873	24
Liquipak Corp	4783	28
Liquitrol Co	5084	933
Lisa Adelle Design Inc	7311	378
Lisa Express Inc	4213	1738
Lisa Frank Inc	2759	47
Lisa Motor Lines Inc	4213	213
Lisbon Cleaning Inc	7349	251
Lisbon Sausage Company Inc	2013	239
Lisk Trucking Inc	4213	758
Liska and Associates	7389	735
Liska Imaging Inc	5946	13
Lisle Corp	3423	31
List Industries Inc	2542	9
Lista International Corp	2599	15
Listen Inc	5065	838
Listen Up Espanol Inc	7389	776
Listencom Inc	7389	757
Listerhill Credit Union	6062	77
Lister-Petter Americas Inc	5084	209
Listingbook LLC	7372	2511
Liston Manufacturing Inc	3568	60
Litchfield Bancorp	6036	93
Litco International Inc	2448	11
Lite Line Illuminations Inc	5063	1072
Lite Machines Corp	3944	45
Lite Source Inc	5064	56
Lite Touch Inc	3648	34
Lite-Check	3825	207
Lite-Form Technologies LLC	3086	161
Litehouse Custom Printing Inc	2759	412
Litek Inc	3829	506
Litelab Corp	3646	34
Lite-Makers Inc	3646	86
Lite-Minder Co	3647	25
Lite-On Trading USA Inc	5045	567
Literary Classics Of The Us	2731	216
Liter's Inc	1422	33
Litescape Technologies Inc	7371	857
Litetronics International Inc	5063	219
Litex Industries Ltd	5064	55
Lithgow Agency	5063	968
Lithgow Industries Inc	5611	21
Lithia Ford Lincoln Mercury of Grand Forks	5511	312
Lithia Motors Inc	5511	12
Lithia Of Sioux Falls	5511	103
Lithibar Matik Inc	3536	44
Lithium Corp	4899	242
Lithium Technology Corp	3691	32
Litho - Flexo Grafics Inc	2759	91
Litho Graphics Print Communications Inc	2752	1441
Litho Press Inc	2752	1156
Litho Tech Inc	3555	53
Litho-Craft Company Inc	2752	1538
Lithocraft Inc	2752	893
Lithographic Communications LLC	2759	280
Lithographic Industries Inc	2752	670
Lithographic Services Inc	7389	2012
Lithographics Of Wisconsin Inc	2796	56
Lithonia Lighting Inc	3645	4
Lithoprint Company Inc	2752	1334
Lith-O-Roll Corp	3555	52
Lithotone Inc	2752	320
Lithotype Company Inc	2752	532
Litigation Risk Analysis Inc	7379	1687
Litigation Solution Inc	7334	29
Litmor Publishing Corp	2711	811
Litmus Concepts Inc	2835	49
Litra Manufacturing Inc	3661	164
Littelfuse Inc	3613	2
Littell International Inc	3542	44
Litter Quality Propane	5984	21
Little America Hotels and Resorts	7011	16
Little and Company Inc	5085	447
Little Bank Inc	6022	418

Company Name	SIC	Rank
Little Bay Lobster Co	0913	3
Little Brown and Co	2731	12
Little Caesar Enterprises Inc	5812	53
Little Cleaning Services Inc	7349	527
Little Company Of Mary Hospital Of Indiana Inc	8062	196
Little Crow Foods	2043	8
Little Diversified Architectural Consulting Inc	8712	91
Little Enterprises Inc	3599	397
Little Giant Pump Co	3561	45
Little Kentucky Smokehouse LLC	3556	24
Little Kids Inc	3944	38
Little Ocmulgee Electric Membership Corp	4911	318
Little Printing Co	2761	58
Little Professor Book Center	5942	22
Little River Seafood Inc	5146	27
Little Rock Back Yard Burgers Inc	5812	420
Little Rock Tool Service Inc	3599	382
Little Sisters Of The Poor Of Saint Paul	8051	72
Little Six Inc	7993	9
Little Tikes	3944	2
Little Wing Productions Inc	7389	1833
Little Woodrows	2097	23
Littlecrest Machine Shop Inc	3599	2223
Littlefield Corp	7999	112
Littlefield Marketing and Advertising Inc	7311	288
Littlejohn and Company LLC	6799	345
Littler Diecast Corp	3365	22
Littlestone LLC	6513	47
Littleton And Sons Sand And Supply Inc	5032	73
Littleton Coin Company Inc	5999	30
Littman Dental Laboratory Inc	8072	37
Litton Engineering Laboratories	3559	519
Litton Loan Servicing LP	6099	11
LitWatch Inc	2711	857
Litz Manufacturing Inc	5087	197
Live Bait Boat The	5941	48
Live Oak Gottesman LLC	6552	145
Live Oak Multimedia Inc	7371	1330
LiveBridge	7389	25
LiveDeal Inc	7371	934
Lively Cadillac-GMC	5511	938
Lively Exploration Co	1382	39
Livengood Feeds Inc	5191	121
Livengood Trucking Inc	4213	2986
LiveOffice LLC	7372	889
LiveOnTheNet	7371	1652
LivePerson Inc	7389	201
Liveprocess Corp	7373	773
Livernois Engineering Co	3714	258
Livers Bronze Co	3446	31
LiveWire Mobile Inc	3661	116
Livewire Printing Company Inc	2711	578
Liveworld Inc	7389	946
Livhome Corp	8361	162
Livin' Lite Recreational Vehicles	3792	26
Living Water Funding	6163	47
Living Ways Inc	8322	245
Livingston Chocolate Company Inc	2026	84
Livingston Oakland Human Service Agency	8399	15
Livingston Parish School District	8211	55
Livingston Pipe and Tube Inc	5051	294
Livingston Regional Hospital LLC	8062	135
Livingston Wilson and Associates Inc	8748	409
Livingston-Wyoming County Chapter Nysarc	8331	38
Li-Way Transfer and Storage Inc	4213	2427
Liz Claiborne Accessories	2389	3
Liz Claiborne Inc	2339	4
Liz Claiborne Incorporated Special Markets	2339	14
LizardTech Inc	7372	3100
Lizton Financial Corp	6712	597
LJ Altfest and Company Inc	6282	151
LJ Construction Inc	1731	913
LJ Cos	7353	35
LJ Gonzer Associates	7363	69
LJ Lubin Inc	2741	456
LJ Machine Works Inc	3533	122
LJ Rogers Jr Trucking Inc	4213	2689
LJ Star Inc	3823	293
Lja Engineering and Surveying Inc	8711	240
LJC Investments Inc	6799	89
Ljl Truck Center Inc	5012	156
Ljm Packaging Company Inc	2449	11
LJO Inc	5139	21
LJR Recapture Services Inc	6211	219
L-K Industries Inc	3533	112
L-K Industry Inc	2821	185
LK Wood Realty Inc	6531	210
Lka Computer Consultants Inc	7378	131
LKC Technologies Inc	3841	382
LKG Industries Inc	5065	234
Lkm Industries Inc	3511	36
LKQ Corp	5015	1
Lkrg Consulting Group Inc	7379	731
LKT Laboratories Inc	8731	333
LL and E Royalty Trust	6792	12
LL and T Inc	5719	31
LL Bean Inc	5961	21

Company Name	SIC	Rank
LL Brown Inc	3599	1335
LI Building Products Inc	3444	17
LI Cultured Marble Inc	2493	16
LL Smith Trucking	4213	1440
Llamagraphics Inc	7372	4845
Llamas Plastics Inc	3728	127
LLC Shield Pack	3081	69
LLC Whitaker Brothers	7359	155
Llebroc Industries	2531	34
LLL Transport Inc	4213	1667
LIII Construction Company Inc	1623	669
Lloyd And Bouvier Inc	5063	597
Lloyd Center	6512	31
Lloyd Controls Inc	3625	138
Lloyd E Hennessey Jr	3599	868
Lloyd F McKinney Associates Inc	5065	663
Lloyd Group Inc	7379	269
Lloyd Inc	2834	236
Lloyd Industries Inc	3679	855
Lloyd Lamont Design Inc	7379	112
Lloyd's Barbecue Co	2013	36
Lloyd's Florist	5992	8
Lloyd's Refrigeration Inc	1542	394
Lloyd-Silber Prosthetics Inc	8049	24
Llrien Inc	8361	169
Llsco LLC	5719	33
LM Capital Management Inc	6282	653
LM Communications Inc	4832	126
LM Gill Welding and Manufacturing LLC	7692	42
LM Henderson and Company PC	8721	382
LM Scofield Co	2899	104
Lm Technologies Corp	7371	1247
LM Wind Power (USA) Inc	3511	16
LMI Advertising	7311	797
LMI Aerospace Inc	3728	22
LMI Finishing Inc	2851	14
LMI Manufacturing	3599	2160
Lmi Safety Inc	5049	210
LMS International	7549	5
LMS Marketing	5065	968
LMT Trucking Company Inc	4213	1998
Lmt USA Inc	5084	376
LMZ Soluble Coffee Inc	2099	370
LN Curtis and Sons	5099	17
LN White and Company Inc	5146	69
LNB Bancorp Inc	6712	283
Lns Software Solutions LLC	7371	1913
Lns Technologies Inc	7373	1157
Load Rite Trailers Inc	3799	15
Load Technology Inc	3825	153
Loadcraft Industries Ltd	3533	22
Loader Services and Equipment Inc	5082	105
Loadstar Sensors Inc	3677	127
Loaf 'N Jug Inc	2051	7
Loan Administration Network Inc	7361	421
Loan Management Services Inc	7322	97
Loan Protector Insurance Services	7372	842
Loan Toolbox	7389	846
LoanPerformance	7375	137
Lobel Chemical Corp	2879	30
Lobiondo Brothers Motor Express	4213	2114
Lobob Laboratories Inc	2834	349
Lobright Manufacturing Company Inc	5064	140
LOC Federal Credit Union	6061	94
Loc Performance Products Inc	3541	19
Local Baking Products Inc	2052	62
Local Biz U S A Inc	7373	758
Local Insight Regatta Holdings Inc	2741	14
Local Matters Inc	7372	2022
Local Splash	7379	612
Localcom Corp	7375	51
LocalNet Corp	4899	126
Localtel Communications	4813	431
LocatePLUS Holdings Corp	7374	144
Locating Inc	1623	31
Location Labs Inc	7379	337
Loch Sand And Construction Co	1611	216
Lochmead Dairy Inc	2026	80
Lock Inspection Systems Inc	3565	86
Lock Joint Tube LLC	3317	39
Lockamy Scrap Metal Inc	5093	223
Locke Insulators Inc	3264	10
Locke Lord Bissell and Liddell LLP	8111	163
Locke Lord LLP	8111	138
Locke Technical Services Inc	7363	306
Locke Wern-Rausch Advertising Inc	7311	813
Lockhart Cadillac Inc	5511	547
Lockheed Federal Credit Union	6061	93
Lockheed Martin Aeronautics Co	3721	6
Lockheed Martin Aspen Systems	7379	96
Lockheed Martin Astronautics	3761	2
Lockheed Martin Corp	3812	1
Lockheed Martin Corp Tactical Defense Systems Div	3679	88
Lockheed Martin Enterprise Information Systems	3699	6
Lockheed Martin Government Services Inc	8741	78
Lockheed Martin Information Technology	7379	47
Lockheed Martin Logistic Services Inc	4581	12

Company Name	SIC	Rank
Lockheed Martin Management	7372	176
Lockheed Martin Michoud Operations	3769	3
Lockheed Martin Missiles and Fire Control	3489	10
Lockheed Martin Missiles/Space Co	3761	1
Lockheed Martin Space Operations	4581	5
Lockheed Martin Technology Services	8742	8
Lockheed Window Corp	3442	103
Locklear Contracting Inc	1623	508
Locks Co	5072	141
Lockton Cos	6411	35
Lockwood Andrews and Newnam Inc	8712	27
Lockwood Company Inc	2752	1058
Lock-Wood Electric Inc	1731	940
Lockwood Financial Group Inc	8742	467
Lockwood Inc	6512	81
Lockwood Kessler and Bartlett Inc	8711	270
Lockwood Technology Corp	7379	1156
Lockwood Trade Journal Company Inc	2721	363
Locus Inc	3663	163
Locus Telecommunications Inc	4813	110
Locust Valley Electric Inc	1731	1445
Lodal Inc	3713	48
Lodan Electronics Inc	3496	39
Lode Data Corp	7372	4929
Lode Data Systems Inc	7372	4355
Lodestar Consulting LLC	7373	323
Lodge Manufacturing Co	3429	22
LodgeNet Interactive Corp	4899	22
Lodgian Inc	7011	94
Lodging and Gaming Systems Inc	7373	558
Lodging By Liberty	2512	55
Lodging Resources Inc	7011	233
Lodi Canning Company Inc	2033	109
Lodner Printing Inc	2631	30
Loeb and Loeb LLP	8111	115
Loeb Electric Co	5063	27
Loebl Schlossman and Hackl Inc	8712	126
Loecy Precision Manufacturing Inc	3599	2309
Loehmann-Blasius Chevrolet Inc	5511	377
Loehmann's Holdings Inc	5621	22
Loersch Corporation Of PA	3861	124
Loews Corp	6331	14
Loews Hotels Holding Corp	7011	118
Loews Hotels Holdings Corp	7041	2
Loews Ventana Canyon Resort	7011	60
Loftin and Company Inc	2752	1839
Loftis Construction Corp	1623	166
Loftness Specialized Farm Equipment Inc	3523	67
Lofton and Jennings	8111	603
Lofton Label Inc	2672	47
Loftus Electric Inc	1731	2308
Loftware Inc	7372	843
Log Cabin Democrat LLC	2711	421
Log House Foods Inc	5149	164
Log On Computer and Mailing Services Inc	7331	59
Logan	3861	102
Logan Brothers Printing Inc	2752	1650
Logan Business Machines Inc	5044	142
Logan Clutch Corp	3568	70
Logan Community Resources Inc	8361	61
Logan Corp	5084	174
Logan County Bank	6022	761
Logan County Cooperative Power Light Association Inc	4911	474
Logan Enterprises Inc (West Liberty Ohio)	3812	207
Logan Graphic Products Inc	3545	111
Logan Industries Inc	3679	349
Logan Industries Inc (Palm Bay Florida)	7372	5135
Logan Machine Co	3599	360
Logan Marketing and Communications Inc	7311	1036
Logan Memorial Hospital LLC	8062	225
Logan Regional Medical Center	8062	122
Logan Trucking Inc	4213	1068
Logan's Roadhouse Inc	5812	297
Logansport Financial Corp	6712	659
Logansport Machine Company Inc	3545	349
Logansport Savings Bank FSB	6035	200
Logantex Inc	5131	38
Logemann Brothers Co	3542	36
LogEtronics Corp	3861	87
Logex/Logistics Express Inc	4213	570
Logghe Stamping Co	3465	32
Logi Graphics Inc	3672	419
Logic Controls Inc	3578	28
Logic Devices Inc	3674	441
Logic eXtension Resources	7372	3778
Logic Factory	2741	265
Logic Group Inc	7372	4620
Logic Planet Inc	7379	485
Logic Product Development	5045	129
Logic Systems Corp	3672	435
Logic Systems Sound And Lighting Inc	1731	2087
Logic Trends Inc	7379	458
Logic20/20 Inc	7379	838
Logica Advantage KBS Inc	7379	948
Logical Choice Technologies Inc	5045	225
Logical Data Solutions Inc	7372	4311
Logical Decisions	7372	5136

Company Name	SIC	Rank
Logical Design Solutions Inc	7372	2234
Logical Devices Inc	3823	417
Logical Information Machines Inc	7372	1388
Logical Innovations Inc	8748	258
Logical Net Corp	4899	161
Logical Products Inc	3672	173
Logical Resources Inc	7371	1375
Logical Software Solutions Inc	7372	4915
Logical Solutions Inc	7372	3723
Logical Source Microfilming Inc	7389	2083
Logical Technical Services Corp	7375	38
LogicalsolutionsNet Inc	5734	70
LOGICARE Corp	7372	1898
Logico Response Corp	7359	233
Logicom Sales Inc	5064	197
Logicom Systems	3577	662
Logik	8741	284
Logility Inc	7372	792
Login Consulting Services Inc	7379	562
LogiSolve LLC	8748	158
Logistechs Inc	8742	403
Logistic Dynamics Inc	8748	188
Logistic Services International Inc	7699	22
Logistic Specialties Inc	7389	227
Logisticare Inc	4213	71
Logistics 2020 Inc	8744	36
Logistics and Environmental Support Services Corp	8742	91
Logistics Company Inc	7379	252
Logistics Concepts Inc	5043	40
Logistics Engineering and Environmental Support Services Inc	7389	278
Logistics Inc	7389	938
Logistics Insight Corp	8742	90
Logistics Management Solutions	7389	329
Logistics One	4213	2380
Logistics Resources Inc	7373	438
Logistics Supply Corp	5065	963
Logistix Inc	3571	149
Logitech Inc	3577	29
Logitech Product Group	3577	210
Logitek Electronic Systems Inc	3663	244
Logitek Inc	3825	31
Logix Communications Enterprises Inc	4813	89
Logix Development Corp	7371	210
Logix Inc	7373	731
Logix Transportation Inc	4213	2299
Logixml Inc	3571	73
Loglogic Inc	5045	57
Logmatix Inc	2759	291
LogMeIn Inc	7372	379
Log-Net Inc	5045	35
Logobranders Inc	7389	1732
LOGOS Communications Inc	7375	134
Logos Research Systems Inc	2741	50
Logos Systems International	7374	364
Logosol Inc	7371	711
Logoworks	7379	156
Logue Industries Inc	3672	223
Logus Manufacturing Corp	3679	422
Lohmiller and Co	5075	58
Lohr Design Inc	7389	1446
LOI Inc	3559	223
Lois A Valeskie	3829	426
Lois Paul and Partners	8743	29
LoJack Corp	3669	30
LoJack of California Corp	5013	347
LoJack of New Jersey Corp	5013	63
Lokota Woods International	2435	30
Loleta Cheese Factory	2022	90
LoLyn Financial Corp	6712	609
Loma Automation Technologies Inc	3559	407
Loma Scientific International	3663	304
Lomanco Inc	3444	66
Lomar Machine and Tool Co	3549	30
Lomas Santa Fe Group	6552	262
Lomax Companies LP	8011	52
Lombard Enterprises Inc	2752	1352
Lombard Inc	6799	257
Lombardi Software Inc	7372	586
Lombart Instruments US	5995	6
Lomont Holdings Company Inc	2394	27
Londen Insurance Group Inc	6311	185
London Church Furniture Inc	2531	48
London Computer Systems Inc	7379	1531
London Farm Service Inc	5083	163
London Financial Capital LLC	6163	44
London Litho Services Inc	2752	585
Lone Eagle Systems Inc	7371	1906
Lone Elm Sales Inc	5143	36
Lone Star Bakery Inc	2053	6
Lone Star Beef Processors LP	2011	58
Lone Star Company Inc	5171	69
Lone Star Compressor Corp	3563	52
Lone Star Corrugated Container Corp	2653	65
Lone Star Exhibits Inc	7389	2236
Lone Star Food Service Co	5147	75
Lone Star Fork Lift Inc	5084	475
Lone Star Industrial Corporation Of Texas	3495	27
Lone Star Industries Inc	3241	3
Lone Star Logistics Inc	3317	3
Lone Star Materials Inc	5032	115
Lone Star Medical Products Inc	3841	256

Company Name	SIC	Rank
Lone Star Printing And Office Supply LP	2752	1763
Lone Star Siding and Windows	1521	170
Lone Star Software Corp	7372	825
Lone Star Software Engineering Services Inc	7371	1932
Lone Star Steakhouse and Saloon Inc	5812	79
Lone Star Steel Co	3498	4
Lone Star Steel International LP	3317	4
Lone Star Transportation LLC	4213	149
Lone Star Trucking Inc	4213	1284
Lone Star Utilities LLC	1623	447
Lone Star Wheel Components Inc	3011	21
Lone Wolf Software Inc	7372	3249
Lonero Engineering Company Inc	3544	440
Lonestar Transportation Inc	4213	232
Long and Foster Real Estate Inc	6531	6
Long and Levit LLP	8111	459
Long Barn Inc	5211	259
Long Beach Enterprise Inc	2092	82
Long Beach Redwood Shavings Company Inc	2421	134
Long Cabinet Co	5072	161
Long Distance Partnership LLP	4813	428
Long Electric Co	1731	801
Long Electric Company Inc	1731	173
Long Elevator And Machine Company Inc	3534	14
Long Island Cauliflower Association	7389	2049
Long Island Educational TV Council Inc	4833	151
Long Island Materials Testing Labs Inc	7389	2233
Long Island Power Authority	4931	12
Long Island Rail Road Co	4013	1
Long Island Sound Services Inc	5731	207
Long Island Water Corp	4941	28
Long John Silver's Inc	5812	92
Long Lewis Hardware Co	5072	7
Long Lines Ltd	7011	195
Long Motor Corp	5961	61
Long Painting Co	1721	5
Long Point Capital	6799	364
Long Trail Brewing Co	2082	61
Long Utility Corp	1623	115
Long Wave Inc	7372	1819
Long Wholesale Distributors Inc	5141	116
Longaberger Co	2499	4
Longacre's Modern Dairy Inc	2026	87
Longboard Inc	7371	465
Longford Group	1521	95
Longhorn Barbecue Production Center	2013	210
Longhorn Construction Inc	1623	693
Longhorn Inc	5083	56
Longhorn Packaging Inc	2671	61
Longhorn Pool Service Inc	7389	1996
Longhorn Produce Co	4213	635
Longhorn Trucking Company Inc	4213	2073
Longleaf Partners Fund	6722	37
Long-McArthur Inc	5511	700
Longo Electrical-Mechanical Inc	7629	10
Longo Sewer Construction Co	1623	837
Longport Inc	3845	124
Long's Amusement Co	5941	50
Longs Distributing Inc	5031	415
Long's Jewelers Ltd	5947	9
Longstreth Sporting Goods LLC	5091	65
Longview Capital Corp	6712	714
Longview Fibre Co Central Container Div	2653	32
Longview Fibre Paper and Packaging Inc	2653	4
Longwood Industries	8331	240
Longwood Industries LLC	3069	9
Longwood Manufacturing Corp	3599	2249
Longwood Systems Inc	7371	1461
Lonza Inc (Allendale New Jersey)	3353	1
Lonza Viral	2834	487
Looking Glass Microproducts Inc	7372	4846
LookNet LLC	4899	196
Lookout Leasing Co	7359	100
Lookout Security Systems Inc	5065	808
Lookout Valley Tool and Machine Inc	3469	264
LookSmart Ltd	7374	77
Loomcraft Textile and Supply Co	5131	27
Loomis	7381	40
Loomis Industries Inc	3825	234
Loomis Products Co	3542	103
Loomis Sayles and Company LP	6282	20
Loon Mountain Recreation Corp	7999	96
Looney Ricks Kiss Architects Inc	8712	71
Loop Capital Markets LLC	6159	37
Loop LLC	3695	66
Loop Tech International Ltd	3585	209
LoopNet Inc	7375	58
Loos and Company Inc	3315	8
Loos and Dilworth Inc	5169	34
Loos Machine Shop Inc	3441	270
Loosbrock Digging Service Inc	4841	136
Loose Plastics Inc	3089	937
Lootens Distributing Inc	5099	102
Lopes Picture Company Inc	7812	143
Lopez Chaff and Wiesman Associates Inc	7389	2007
Lopez Foods Inc	2013	14
Lopez Negrete Communications Inc	7311	234

Company Name	SIC	Rank
Lopez Printing Inc	2752	1489
Lopez Scrap Metal Inc	5093	61
Lopezgarcia Group	8711	309
Lor Manufacturing Company Inc	3625	350
Lorain County Automotive Systems Inc	3714	157
Lorain County Stationery and Office Equipment Company Inc	5044	79
Lorain National Bank	6021	163
Lor-AL Products Inc	3523	36
Loral Skynet	4899	155
Loral Space and Communications Inc	4812	11
Loram Maintenance Of Way Inc	3743	10
Loramar Technologies Inc	1731	2454
Loran International Sales Inc	5064	129
Loranger International Corp	3825	100
Lorann Oils Inc	5149	158
Loras Industries Inc	5065	589
Lord and Taylor	5311	19
Lord Ga'y Foundry Enterprises Inc	3559	380
Lord Publishing Inc	7372	4847
Lord's Computer Group Partners Inc	5045	276
Lords Electric Inc	1731	2388
Lord's Sausage and Country Ham Inc	2013	199
L'Oreal USA Inc	2844	3
Loren Company Industries Inc	2759	580
Loren Cook Co	3564	20
Lorentson Manufacturing Company Inc	3089	657
Lorenz Corp	2741	214
Lorenz Manufacturing Co	3531	211
Lorenz Publishing Co	2731	241
Lorenzi Dodds and Gunnill Inc	8712	167
Lori Holding Co	5147	103
Lorie Line Music Inc	6794	161
Lorik Tool Inc	3541	219
Lorillard Inc	2111	6
Lorillard Tobacco Co	2111	7
Lorin Industries Inc	3471	29
Loring Ward Advisor Services	6211	202
Lorlin Test Systems	3825	293
Lormac Plastics Inc	3089	1797
Lorton Data Inc	7374	245
Lortone Inc	3541	228
Lortz Manufacturing Co	3312	65
Lorusso Corp	2951	31
Los Alamitos Ornamental Castings Inc	5051	454
Los Alamos Technical Associates Inc	8742	67
Los Altos Food Products Inc	5143	28
Los Altos PC Inc	5734	179
Los Altos Technologies Inc	7371	829
Los Altos Trophy Company Inc	5094	55
Los Amigos Tortilla Manufacturing Inc	2099	192
Los Angeles Cold Storage Co	4222	13
Los Angeles Conservation Corps	7363	124
Los Angeles Dodgers Inc	7941	7
Los Angeles Federal Credit Union	6061	32
Los Angeles Jewish Publications Inc	2711	505
Los Angeles Lighting Co	3641	14
Los Angeles National Bank	6021	305
Los Angeles Nut House	5145	3
Los Angeles Paper Box and Board Mills Inc	2657	11
Los Angeles Police Federal Credit Union	6061	38
Los Angeles Salad Company Inc	2099	181
Los Angeles Scientific Instruments Company Inc	3823	329
Los Angeles Sentinel Inc	2711	504
Los Angeles Turf Club Inc	7948	9
Los Angles Hwc	1731	1718
Los Bagels Inc	5461	42
Los Gatos Brewing Co	2082	28
Los Gatos Telephone Answering Service	5065	720
Los Potros Distribution Center LLC Dist Of Mexican and American Products	2032	44
Loss Mitigation Services Inc	7699	29
Lost Arrow Corp	5699	22
Lost Planet Inc	7819	58
Losurdo Inc	5046	168
Lot	7812	52
Lotec Inc	3545	170
LOTH	5021	56
Loth Mbi Inc	5021	47
Lotridge Enterprises LLC	3069	209
Lott Enterprises Inc	3564	62
Lott Industries Inc	8331	27
Lotte USA Inc	2067	3
Lotus Broadcasting Corp	4832	69
Lotus Cars USA Inc	5012	73
Lotus Consulting Group	7372	3272
Lotus Development Corp	7372	82
Lotus Fixture LLC	5932	11
Lotus Light Inc	5122	87
Lotz Trucking Inc	4213	679
Lou Bachrodt Auto Mall	5511	890
Lou Beres and Associates Inc	7311	346
Lou Bo Inc	5063	513
Lou Fusz Automotive Network Inc	5511	32
Lou LaRiche Chevrolet Inc	5511	637
Lou Malnati's Pizzeria	5812	291
Lou Marks and Sons Inc	5063	1042
Loubat Equipment Company Inc	5046	183
LOUD Technologies Inc	3651	28
Loudon Steel Inc	3441	152

Company Name	SIC	Rank
Loudoun Healthcare Inc	8062	29
Loudoun Milk Transportation	4213	2604
Loudoun Stairs Inc	2431	82
Loudspeaker Components LLC	3651	115
Loughlin Manufacturing Corp	3599	2093
Loughlin Meghji and Co	8748	147
Loughmiller Machine Tool and Design	3545	311
Louie's Finer Meats Inc	2013	84
Louies Home Center Inc	5211	184
Louis A Jammer Company Inc	5211	292
Louis Allis Co	3621	101
Louis Berger Group Inc	8711	18
Louic Berkman Co	3444	1
Louis C Eitzen Co	3823	423
Louis Diamond Glick Corp	5094	13
Louis Foehrkolb Inc	5146	10
Louis J Grasmick Lumber Company Inc	5031	86
Louis J Kennedy Trucking Co	4213	661
Louis J Rheb Candy Company Inc	2064	112
Louis Lakis Ford Inc	5511	514
Louis M Gerson Company Inc	3842	67
Louis Marsch Inc	2951	47
Louis Maull Co	2033	113
Louis Neibauer Company Inc	2731	276
Louis P Batson Co	3552	38
Louis P Canuso Inc	5085	195
Louis P Cote Inc	4213	1778
Louis Padnos Iron and Metal Co	3339	9
Louis Perry and Associates Inc	8711	334
Louis Saint Brewery Inc	2082	39
Louis Systems and Products Inc	3663	379
Louis Vuitton NA Inc	5632	9
Louisa Food Products Inc	2038	47
Louisa Publishing Company Ltd	2711	768
Louisburg Cider Mill	2099	208
Louisiana Bancorp	6036	72
Louisiana Baptist Convention	4841	78
Louisiana Binding Service Inc	2731	228
Louisiana Chemical Equipment Co	6531	177
Louisiana Chemical Pipe Valve and Fitting Inc	5085	340
Louisiana Coca-Cola Bottling Co	2086	66
Louisiana Coca-Cola Bottling Company Ltd	2086	26
Louisiana Container Company Inc	2655	16
Louisiana Cos	6411	270
Louisiana Federal Credit Union	6061	121
Louisiana Health Service and Indemnity Co	6321	54
Louisiana Lottery Corp	8741	42
Louisiana Millwork LLC	5031	447
Louisiana Mobility Of Central La Inc	5047	280
Louisiana Moulding and Supply	5999	273
Louisiana Nesco Ltd	1731	688
Louisiana Office Products	5112	30
Louisiana Plastic Converting Corp	4953	108
Louisiana Plastic Industries Inc	3081	83
Louisiana Press Journal	2752	1552
Louisiana Publishing	2711	440
Louisiana Safety Systems Inc	5085	174
Louisiana Sewn Products Inc	7389	1086
Louisiana Staffing Unlimited Inc	7361	347
Louisiana Sugar Cane Cooperative Inc	2061	13
Louisiana Tank Inc	4213	1824
Louisiana Valves and Machine Works Inc	3491	57
Louisiana Workers' Compensation Corp	6331	298
Louisiana-Pacific Corp	2421	7
Louisiana-Pacific Corporation Division Office	2421	13
Louisville and Jefferson County Metropolitan Sewer District	4952	2
Louisville Auto Spring and Brake Company Inc	5013	361
Louisville Baseball Club Inc	7941	39
Louisville Bedding Company Inc	2392	11
Louisville Cartage Company Inc	4213	639
Louisville Cooler Manufacturing Co	3585	175
Louisville Corporate Services Inc	7389	1761
Louisville Endoscopy Center	8011	100
Louisville Federal Credit Union	6062	106
Louisville Gas and Electric Co	4931	21
Louisville Gas and Electric Company Credit Union	6062	74
Louisville Ladder Group LLC	3499	19
Louisville Lamp Co	3641	35
Louisville Magazine Inc	2721	422
Louisville Medical Center Federal Credit Union	6061	135
Louisville Metro Police Officer Credit Union	6062	123
Louisville Paving Company Inc	1611	154
Louisville Pecan Company Inc	5159	32
Louisville Tile Distributors Inc	5032	1
Louisville Tin and Stove Co	3444	62
Louisville Water Co	4941	39
Lounora Industries Inc	2511	69
Loup Power District	4911	390
Loupe Video Productions	7812	310
Lourdes At Home	5047	216
Lourdes Industries Inc	3795	7
Lou's Sausage Ltd	2013	242
Lo-Vac Inc	4213	762
Love Advertising Inc	7311	411
Love and Quiches Ltd	2053	5
Love Bottling Co	2086	82
Love Communications LLC	7311	423
Love Machine Company Inc	5084	702
Love Scherle and Bauer	8111	558
Lovee Doll and Toy Company Inc	3942	16
Lovegreen Industrial Services Inc	1796	11
Lovejoy Chaplet Corp	3545	284
Lovejoy Controls Corp	3613	132
Lovejoy Inc	3568	19
Lovejoy Surgicenter Inc	8062	243
Lovejoy Tool Company Inc	3545	148
Loveland Screw Machine Ltd	3599	2092
Lovell Minnick Partners LLC	6722	165
Loveman Steel Corp	3341	25
Loveridge Machine and Tool Inc	3599	713
Love's Bakery Inc	2051	62
Love's Travel Stops and Country Stores Inc	5541	8
Loveshaw Corp	3565	9
Lovett Miller and Co	6799	273
Loving and Campos Architects Inc	8712	183
Loving Care Agency Inc	8082	26
Lovitt and Touche Inc	6411	61
Low Country National Bank	6021	257
Low Temperature Industries Inc	3589	53
Low Voltage Wiring Ltd	1731	783
Lowder Construction Co	1542	450
Lowe	7311	52
Lowe and Partners Worldwide (New York New York)	7311	13
Lowe Enterprises Inc	6552	16
Lowo Industries Inc	3556	170
Lowe Leasing Co	7353	72
Lowe Manufacturing Company Inc	3531	105
Lowe Oil/Champion Brands	2992	29
Lowe Products Company Inc	2499	33
Lowe Trucking Co	4213	2079
Lowell Engineering Corp	3999	18
Lowell Inc	3599	404
Lowell Manufacturing Co	3679	283
Lowell Packing Co	2011	109
Lowell Paper Box Company Inc	2631	25
Lowen Corp	2759	93
Lowe-North Construction Inc	1623	366
Lowenstein Sandler PC	8111	70
Lower Shore Enterprises Inc	8331	177
Lower Valley Energy	4911	471
Lowe's Companies Inc	5211	2
Lowe's Food Stores Inc	5411	85
Lowe's Home Centers Inc	5211	3
Lowes Pellets And Grain Inc	5153	67
Lowe's Printing Inc	2752	1706
Lowestfarecom	4729	6
Lowrance Electronics Inc	3812	53
Lowrance Machine Shop Inc	3599	1370
Lowrey Powell and Stevens	8721	338
Lowry Computer Products Inc	7373	248
Lowry Manufacturing Co	3523	195
Lowry Mechanical Inc	1711	236
Lowry Telephone Company LLC	4841	152
Lowry Tool and Die Inc	3544	854
Loxcreen Company Inc	3354	15
Loyal Manufacturing Corp	3444	274
Loyalty Nursing Service	7361	307
LoyaltyExpress Inc	7379	722
Loyd Armature Works Inc	5063	952
Loyd-Paxton Inc	7389	2356
Loyola Enterprises Inc	8711	296
Loyola University Physician Foundation	8721	152
Lozano Enterprises Inc	2711	79
Lozier Corp	2541	2
LP Aero Plastics Inc	3089	1171
LP Building Products	5031	7
LP Cox Co	1542	254
LP Glassblowing Inc	3679	518
LP Macadams Company Inc	2759	133
LP Safford Inc	5511	429
LP Shanks Co	5141	235
LP Systems	7371	1833
LPA Holding Corp	8351	1
LPA Inc	8712	93
Lpb Communications Inc	3663	366
Lpc Technology Inc	5045	936
Lpg Industries Inc	3829	334
LPI Corp	3769	15
LPI Information Systems	7372	3054
Lpi Printing And Graphic Inc	2741	378
Lpkf Distribution Inc	5049	111
LPL Financial Retirement	8999	82
LPL Holdings Inc	6719	58
LPL Investment Holdings Inc	7379	4
LPS Industries Inc	3089	332
LPS Laboratories Inc	2992	20
LQ Management LLC	7011	56
LR Baggs Co	3651	106
LR Environmental Equip Company Inc	5084	713
LR Horn Capital Concepts Inc	6282	421
LR Lipps Impressive Printing Inc	2754	46
LR Marketing	5084	918
LR Powder Coats Div	3479	104
LRAD Corp	3651	57
L-Ray	3829	493
LRG Capital Group LLC	6282	372
LRG Corp	3599	1598
Lrm Industries Inc	3273	67
LS Industries Inc	3559	267
LS Investigations	7381	269
LS Men's Clothing Co	2321	29
Ls Research LLC	8711	533
LS Starrett Co	3429	12
Lsa United Inc	3469	153
LSB Financial Corp	6712	532
LSB Holdings Inc	6719	31
LSB Industries Inc	2819	17
LSEC	7363	303
Lsf5 Cavalier Investments LLC	5411	172
LSG Sky Chefs Inc	2099	35
LSI Adapt Inc	8711	486
Lsi Computer Systems Internat'l Ltd	3674	337
Lsi Computers Inc	5734	422
LSI Controls Inc	3823	448
LSI Corp	3674	22
Lsi Corporation Of America Inc	2434	43
LSI Greenlee Lighting	3646	2
LSI Industries Inc	3646	5
Lsi International Inc	3844	18
LSI Kentucky LLC	3646	6
LSI Lightron Inc	3646	16
LSI Logic Broadband Entertainment Div	3577	68
LSI Logic Storage Systems Inc	3572	12
LSI Marcole Inc	3679	6
LSI Midwest Lighting Inc	3646	12
LSI Staffing Solutions	7361	22
LSK Enterprises Inc	5078	44
Lsoft International Inc	7372	1227
Lsp Products Group Inc	3089	442
Lsq Ii LLC	7379	1010
LSSD Inc	4213	986
Lssi Data	5045	169
LT Industries Inc	3823	334
LT Litho and Printing Co	2752	1617
Lt Moses Willard Inc	3645	80
LT Services Inc	7349	244
Lta/D-Cemco Inc	3643	126
LTC Corp	8741	218
LTC Properties Inc	6798	143
Lti Flexible Products Inc	3053	60
LTI Optics LLC	7372	2468
Lti Power Systems	3612	117
Ltl Management Inc	7389	2145
Ltl Supply Inc	5063	756
LTM Inc (Havelock North Carolina)	7371	259
Ltpc Inc	2392	44
Lts Lohmann Therapy Systems Corp	2834	128
Lts Scale Corp	3596	25
LTX-Credence Corp	3825	10
Lubbock Audio Visual Inc	5065	359
Lubbock Electric Co	5063	364
Lubbock Radio Paging Service Inc	7389	981
Lube Stop Inc	7549	6
Lubeco Inc	2992	50
LubePro's International Inc	6794	130
Lubicom Marketing Consulting	7311	976
Lubricating Specialties Co	2992	23
Lubrication Engineers Inc	2992	35
Lubrication Technology Inc	2992	19
Lubrizol Corp	2869	2
Lubromation Inc	5084	828
Lubron Bearing Systems	5085	322
Luby Publishing Inc	2721	399
Luby's Inc	5812	119
Lucas And Greer Inc	5065	566
Lucas Associates Inc	7361	33
Lucas Digital Limited LLC	7819	8
Lucas Ford Inc	5511	627
Lucas Horsfall Murphy and Pindroh LLP	8721	177
Lucas Industrial	5063	1052
Lucas Precision LP	7699	187
Lucas Precision Machine Tool Group	3541	91
Lucas Products Corp	2891	89
Lucas Systems Inc	7373	657
Lucas Underground Utilities	1731	1306
Lucasfilm Ltd	7812	12
Lucas-Milhaupt Inc	3559	56
Lucchese Boot Company Inc	3143	6
Lucchese Inc	3143	12
Luce Forward Hamilton and Scripps	8111	66
Luce Schwab and Kase Inc	5075	62
Lucent Polymers Inc	3081	28
Lucerne Textiles Inc	5131	9
Lucero Cables Inc	3679	274
Lucero Research Corp	7371	1760
Lucey Boiler Co	1791	24
Lucia Specialized Hauling Inc	4213	1782
Lucias Pizza Co	2038	72
Lucid Audio Video Inc	5731	224
Lucidyne Technologies Inc	8711	531
Lucifer Furnaces Inc	3567	103
Lucifer Lighting Co	3646	42
Lucille Roberts Health Spas	7991	6
Lucinda Hall Public Relations	8743	282
Luck Stone Corp	1429	2

Company Name	SIC	Rank
Luckett and Farley Architects Engineers And Construction Managers Inc	8712	192
Luckett Holdings Inc	5159	31
Luckie and Company Ltd	7311	178
Luckinbill Inc	1711	93
Luckmarr Plastics Inc	3089	905
Lucks Co	2051	65
Lucky Country Inc	2064	92
Lucky Duck Productions Inc	7812	111
Lucky Eagle Casino	7993	18
Lucky Farmers Inc	5191	44
Lucky Foods LLC	2038	90
Lucky Heart Cosmetics Inc	2844	203
Lucky Line Products Inc	3089	1153
Lucky Sand and Gravel Company Inc	1442	73
Lucky Star Industries Inc	5064	114
Lucor Inc	7538	1
LUCRUM Inc	7379	189
Lucta USA Inc	2048	96
Lucy Activewear Inc	5137	7
Lucy's Tire Inc	5014	20
Ludl Electronic Products Ltd	3825	161
Ludlow Composites Corp	3069	61
Ludlow Cooperative Elevator Company Inc	5153	55
Ludlum Measurements Inc	3829	43
Ludtke-Pacific Trucking Inc	4213	2163
Ludvik Electric Co	1731	60
Ludwig Inc	3086	146
Luecke's Hauling Inc	4213	1441
Luedemann and Associates	6531	406
Luedtke Engineering Co	1629	68
Luetzow Industries LLP	3089	906
Luffland Industries Inc	3523	248
Lufkin Industries Inc	3561	20
Lufkin Industries Inc Automation Div	1389	32
Lufkin Industries Inc Oil Field Div	3532	82
Luhr Brothers Inc	1629	74
Luick Quality Gage and Tool Inc	3544	787
Luige's Pizza Factory Ltd	2038	87
Luitpold Pharmaceuticals Inc	2834	66
Luitporia Software Consultancy Inc	7373	1245
LuJack Auto Plaza	5511	79
Lujack's Northpark Auto Plaza	5511	144
Luk Clutch Systems LLC	3714	151
Lukas Machine Inc	3599	657
Lukas Microscope Service Inc	5049	192
Lukas Nace Gutierrez and Sachs	8111	525
Luke and Associates Inc	6324	86
Lula Westfield LLC	2061	9
Lumark Technologies Inc	7379	1328
Lumatronix Manufacturing Inc	3629	100
Lumbee River Electric Membership Corp	4911	336
Lumber And Things Industries Inc	2448	15
Lumber Liquidators Holdings Inc	5211	13
Lumber Products Inc	5031	252
Lumber Specialties Ltd	2439	16
Lumber Transport Inc	4213	963
Lumberjack Building Center Inc	5211	120
Lumberjack's Lll Inc	5031	422
Lumberman's Wholesale Distributors Inc	5031	337
Lumbermen's Inc	5031	45
Lumbermen's Merchandising Corp	5031	431
Lumbermen's of Indiana	5031	209
Lumberyard Suppliers Inc	5033	28
Lumco Manufacturing Co	3545	357
Lumedx Corp	7372	910
Lumen Legal LLC	7361	191
Lumen Power Sources West Inc	5063	696
Lumen Systems Inc	7372	3139
Lumension Security Inc	7372	104
Lumenton Inc	3648	70
Lumenyte International Corp	3559	303
Lumeon Software Corp	7379	849
Lumidigm Inc	3577	259
Lumigent Technologies Inc	7372	1215
Lumi-Lite Candle Co	3999	112
Lumina Decisions Systems Inc	7372	3920
Lumina Foundation For Education Inc	6111	10
Luminair Film Productions Inc	2741	302
Luminaire Service Inc	7349	471
Luminant Generation Company LLC	4925	7
Luminator Aircraft Products	3728	63
Luminator Holding LP	3646	11
Luminer Converting Group Inc	2672	70
Luminescent Systems Inc	3646	14
Luminex Corp	8731	48
Luminex Software Inc	7372	1955
Luminite Products Corp	2796	21
Lumintel Corp	7373	878
Luminus Devices Inc	3648	20
Lumitex Inc	3646	26
Lummus Corp	3559	80
Lummus Supply Co	5211	51
Lumos and Associates Inc	8711	447
Lumsden and McCormick LLP	8721	86
Lumtron Technologies Inc	7372	3226
Luna Imaging Inc	3572	96
Luna Innovations Inc	8731	123
Luna Labs	3571	236
Luna Tech Inc	3679	395

Company Name	SIC	Rank
Luna Vineyards	0172	9
Lunan Corp	5812	184
Lunar Cow Design Inc	7374	179
Lunar Tool and Mold Inc	3544	800
Lunar Tool LLC	3599	1506
Lunardi's Super Market Inc	5411	204
Lunchtime Solutions Inc	8322	93
Lund Equipment Company Inc	3444	287
Lund Industries Inc	3669	170
Lund International Holdings Inc	3714	39
Lund Martin Construction	1542	401
Lund Performance Solutions	7372	2797
Lunda Construction Co	1622	13
Lunday-Thagard Co	2952	11
Lundbeck Research USA Inc	8731	68
Lundberg Survey Inc	2721	302
Lundell Enterprises Inc	3559	460
Lundell Manufacturing Corp	3069	104
Lundquist Associates Ltd	1731	2455
Lund's Fisheries Inc	5146	17
Lunquist Manufacturing Corp	3599	1355
Lupaul Industries Inc	3544	226
Lupe Rubio Construction Company Inc	1623	410
Lupient Automotive Group	5511	52
Lupin Pharmaceuticals Inc	5122	26
Luquire George Andrews Inc	7311	261
Lurgan Leasing	4213	2249
Lurgi PSI Inc	8711	239
Lurn Inc	8331	107
Lusitania Savings Bank	6061	104
Lusive Decor	3646	52
Lusk Metals and Plastic	5051	147
Luskey's/Ryons Inc	5651	31
Luster Products Inc	2844	49
Luster-On Products Inc	2899	190
Lustre-Cal Nameplate Corp	3471	72
Lutamar Electrical Assemblies Inc	3644	42
Lutco Bearings Inc	3451	40
Luther Brookdale Chrysler Jeep Dodge Inc	5511	788
Luther P Miller Inc	5172	100
Lutheran Care Center	8351	23
Lutheran Home-Hickory Inc	8361	2
Lutheran Housing Of Erie Inc	8361	122
Lutrel Trucking Inc	4213	1204
Lutron Electronics Company Inc	3625	8
Luttmann Precision Mold Inc	3089	1260
Lutz Frey Corp	1711	92
Lutz Sales Company Inc	5085	196
Luv N' Care Ltd	3085	9
Luvata Buffalo Inc	3351	20
Luvel Dairy Products Inc	2024	26
Luverne Truck Equipment Inc	3714	237
Lux Products Corp	3823	140
Luxco Inc	2085	15
Luxfer Inc	3728	71
Luxo Corp	3646	99
Luxology LLC	7371	1502
Luxon Printing Inc	2752	1735
Luxor (Waukegan Illinois)	2522	29
Luxottica USA Inc	3851	14
LuxSpan International Inc	8748	327
Luxtera Inc	3674	155
Luxury Bath Liners Inc	3088	25
Luxury Delivery Service Inc	4213	1666
Luxury Link LLC	7375	115
Luzenac America Inc	3295	2
Luzerne Optical Laboratories Ltd	3851	41
Luzier Personalized Cosmetics Inc	2844	167
Luzo Maxi Market	5141	210
LVC Retail Corp	5961	60
Lvc Window Blinds Inc	5023	86
LVI Services Inc	1799	3
Lvm Systems Inc	7371	1146
LVMH-Moet Hennessy Louis Vuitton	2084	1
LVO Manufacturing Inc	3589	210
LVR Inc (Hannacroix New York)	1799	82
LW Bills Co	3669	240
LW French Inc	5063	769
LW Miller Transportation Inc	4213	1062
LW Ramsey Advertising Agency	7311	1030
LW Reinhold Plastics Inc	3089	863
LWB Corp	7384	49
LWO Corp	2431	106
LWPB Architects and Planners PC	8712	152
Lwr Time Ltd	5063	1029
Lxd LLC	3679	699
LXE Inc	3663	47
LXI Corp	7372	2357
Lycatel LLC	3661	129
Lycos Inc	7375	22
Lycro Products Company Inc	3599	869
Lydall Distribution Services Inc	4789	20
Lydall Inc	2824	2
Lydall Industrial Thermal Sales/Service LLC	5085	28
Lydall Thermal/Acoustical Inc	2297	1
Lydall Transport Ltd	4213	1276
Lydian Trust Co	6722	142
LYDIG Construction Inc	1541	111
Lyford Gin Association	0724	3
Lykes Agriculture	0174	1
Lykes Brothers Inc	2873	8
Lykins Contracting Inc	1623	819

Company Name	SIC	Rank
Lyle Industries Inc	3714	309
Lyle Printing and Publishing Company Inc	2721	222
Lyles Diversified Inc	1629	52
Lyman Farm Inc	0175	7
Lyman Lumber Co	2431	15
Lyman Parts Depot Inc	5083	198
Lyman Products Corp	3559	125
Lyman-Richey Corp	3273	1
Lyme Computer Systems Inc	5045	193
Lymtal International Inc	2851	80
Lynbrook Glass and Architectural Metals Corp	1793	5
Lynch Brothers Manufacturing Co	3769	24
Lynch Investment Co	6282	457
Lynch Metals Inc	5051	177
Lynch Telephone Corporation III	4813	51
Lynchburg Foundry Co	3363	2
Lynchburg Presort Service	7331	139
Lynchburg Sheltered Industries Inc	8093	49
Lynchburg Steel and Specialty Company Inc	3441	51
Lynco Electric Company Inc	1731	582
Lynco Grinding Company Inc	3599	2279
Lyncole Grounding Solutions LLC	3643	114
Lynde Co	5169	109
Lyndee Press Inc	2752	549
Lynden Air Freight Inc	4522	1
Lynden Door Inc	2431	110
Lynden Inc	6719	89
Lynden Transport Inc	4213	338
Lynde-Ordway Company Inc	3579	47
Lyndon Steel LP	3441	68
Lyne Laboratories Inc	2834	339
Lynfred Winery Inc	2084	76
Lynn Electric Inc	1731	1048
Lynn Electronics Corp	3315	28
Lynn Elliott Company Kc Inc	5063	398
Lynn H Scott Inc	4213	2211
Lynn Investment Corp	7389	499
Lynn Ladder And Scaffolding Company Inc	5082	58
Lynn Learning Labs	2741	272
Lynn Products Co	3823	160
Lynn Products Inc	3577	125
Lynn Protein Inc	2023	29
Lynnfield Drug Inc	5912	29
LynnSoft Inc	7372	4710
Lynnway Auto Auction Inc	5012	151
Lynswell Technologies Inc	7374	374
Lyntegar Electric Cooperative Inc	4911	268
Lyn-Tron Inc	3452	68
LynuxWorks Inc	7372	1516
Lyn-Weld Company Inc	3599	1980
Lynwood Unified School District	8211	26
Lynx Group Inc	2752	570
Lynx Media Inc	7372	2996
Lynx Network Services Inc	7373	701
Lynx System Developers Inc	3625	221
Lynxtron Connections	5045	913
Lyon and Associates Realtors	6531	105
Lyon and Billard Co	5211	72
Lyon and Healy Holding Corp	3931	22
Lyon Capital Ventures	6513	37
Lyon Conklin and Company Inc	5051	38
Lyon Shipyard Inc	3731	31
Lyon Technologies Inc	3523	154
Lyon Video Inc	7812	84
Lyon Workspace Products LLC	2542	4
LyonHeart	7311	172
Lyon-Lincoln Electric Cooperative Inc	4911	507
Lyons Company Inc	1711	203
Lyons Direct Inc	7371	957
Lyons Equipment Company Inc	5082	47
Lyons Industries Inc	3088	12
Lyons Machine Tool Company Inc	3599	1497
Lyons Parts Distributors Inc	5013	308
Lyons Tool and Die Co	3469	265
Lyons Tool and Engineering Inc	3544	884
Lyons-Magnus Inc	2066	4
Lyric Opera of Kansas City	7922	37
Lyris Inc	7372	810
Lyris Technologies Inc	7372	1690
Lyrix Design Inc	8999	192
Lyssy and Eckel LP	2048	74
Lytle Electric Co	1731	408
M 2 V P Inc	7379	1398
M/A/R/C Research	3429	31
M/A-COM Inc	3674	64
M/A-COM Sigint Products	3812	104
M and A Electronics Inc	5731	160
M and A Plastics Inc	3089	1312
M and A Technology Inc	5045	295
M and B Carriers Inc	4213	2711
M and B Hangers Co	3496	20
M and B Headwear Company Inc	2353	14
M and B Products Inc	2033	75
M and C Trucking Company Inc	4213	892
M and D Transport Inc	4213	2894
M and E Manufacturing Company Inc	3556	111
M and F Bancorp Inc	6022	408
M and F Development LLC	7361	428
M and F Gauge and Specialty Company Inc	3599	1450

Company Name	SIC	Rank
M and F Machine and Tool Inc	3599	1513
M and F Reporting	7338	38
M and F Worldwide Corp	2087	10
M and G Building Materials Corp	5211	88
M and G Distributors Inc	5531	41
M and G Electronics Corp	3613	28
M and G Graphics Inc	2759	322
M and H Crates Inc	2448	28
M and H Engineering Company Inc	3599	801
M and H Enterprises Inc	5137	28
M and H Plastics Inc	3085	44
M and H Vincotte Partnership	8711	186
M and I Bank South Central	6022	511
M and J Frank Inc	5046	282
M and J Materials Inc	1761	40
M and J Transportation	4213	992
M and J Wilkow Ltd	6798	73
M and K Engineering Inc	3599	1053
M and K Industrial Sewing	3559	562
M and K Industries Inc	3672	341
M and L Electric Inc	1731	1621
M and L Engine LLC	5084	754
M and L Enterprises Inc	5063	860
M and L Industries Inc	5084	231
M and L Jewelry Manufacturing Inc	3911	3
M and L Pharmaceutical Inc	8731	237
M and L Trucking Inc	4213	605
M and M Associates Inc	7331	137
M and M Bakery Products Inc	2051	124
M and M Bumper Service Inc	3069	259
M and M Cartage Inc	4213	771
M and M Chemical and Equipment Company Inc	4953	123
M and M Computers Inc	5045	596
M and M Designs Inc	2759	185
M and M Displays Inc	7319	99
M and M Electric Inc	1731	772
M and M Electric Of N W Florida Inc	1731	2053
M and M Harrison Electric Company Inc	1731	1130
M and M Industries Inc	3089	502
M and M Interiors Inc	5032	165
M and M Lighting LP	5063	333
M and M Lighting Sales Inc	5063	946
M and M Manufacturing Inc	2851	146
M and M Metals International Inc	5093	181
M and M Power LLC	1731	1978
M and M Printed Bag Inc	2673	54
M and M Reporting Inc	7338	36
M and M Representatives Inc	5064	153
M and M Sales Inc	5063	510
M and M Supply Co (Duncan Oklahoma)	5084	285
M and M Technology Inc	3679	716
M and M Tile Co	5023	145
M and M Transport Inc	4213	1842
M and M Trucking Company Inc	4213	465
M and N Alloy Cast Products Inc	3462	57
M and N Equipment LLC	7353	37
M and O Perry Industries Inc	3565	101
M and P Industries Inc	5169	137
M and P Quality Goods Inc	5065	608
M and P Transport Company Inc	4212	51
M and P Transportation Inc / Skyway	4213	1275
M and Q Plastics Products Inc	3089	63
M and R Consulting Services Inc	8733	39
M and R International Inc	5113	37
M and R Precision Machining Inc	3599	1172
M and R Technologies Inc (Dayton Ohio)	3572	74
M and R Technologies Inc (Palm Bay Florida)	7372	4848
M and S Automated Feeding Systems Inc	3565	155
M and S Computer Products Inc	3571	227
M and S Industrial Metal Fabricators Inc	3444	133
M and S Precision Machine Inc	3545	97
M and T Bank Corp	6712	20
M and T Bank NA	6021	395
M and T Mortgage Corp	6162	108
M and T Trucking Inc	4213	518
M and V Wholesale Distributors Inc	5064	147
M and W Engineering Inc	3599	1941
M and W Equipment Company Inc	5251	46
M and W Manufacturing Company Inc	3599	798
M and W Manufacturing Inc	3599	2210
M and W Sales Inc	5021	161
M and W Transportation Company Inc	4213	1943
M and Y Trading Corp	5092	25
M Arthur Gensler Jr and Associates Inc	8712	16
M Bar D Rail Car Tech Inc	4213	1839
M Barrington Corp	6411	265
M Belmont Verstandig Inc	4832	221
M Bloch and Company Inc	5093	93
M Braun Inc	3826	50
M Bruenger and Company Inc	4213	964
M Dryce and Associates	7372	3071
M/C/C Inc	7319	60
M C I Foods Inc	2038	42
M C Steel Inc	5051	374
M Company Ltd	3533	123
M Conley Co	5113	8

Company Name	SIC	Rank
M Constantino Inc	7231	4
M Cubed Technologies Inc	3599	147
M Curry Corp	3544	644
M/D Control Systems Inc	3625	342
M D Henry Company Inc	3612	85
M E Baker Co	3559	148
M E Dey and Company Inc	4731	81
M Ecker and Company Inc	1721	3
M F S E Inc	5046	387
M Farris and Associates	5045	257
M Foster Associates Inc	5137	22
M/G Transport Services LLC	4449	23
M Geller Ltd	5094	74
M Gervich and Sons Inc	5051	391
M Gitlin Company Inc	1731	1755
M Gottlieb Associates Inc	5065	631
M H Detrick Co	3567	53
M Hidary and Company Inc	2321	14
M Hiller and Son Inc	5093	141
M/I Homes Inc	1531	29
M J Brunner Inc	7311	192
M J Hoffmann Services LLC	7349	429
M/K Huron Steel	5051	368
M K Products Inc	3548	25
M Kamenstein Corp	3421	5
M L Bath Company Ltd	5021	107
M L Rongo Inc	2599	36
M Lange Inc	4213	3028
M Lavine Design Workshop Inc	2542	71
M Lazy Inc	3645	82
M Lee Smith Publishers LLC	2752	240
M Little and Company Inc	7336	154
M Logic Inc	7361	401
M M C Inc	1623	78
M M Weaver And Sons Inc	5083	42
M Marlon Ivy and Associates Inc	1623	608
M Mauritzon and Company Inc	5085	206
M N Gumbert Corp	5085	402
M Network Television Inc	4833	206
M P and A Fibers Inc	7389	1376
M P Industries Inc	3061	48
M P N Inc	3714	187
M PT International Corp	5085	371
M - R Electronics Inc	3829	236
M/Rad Corp	3699	250
M Rivenburg Inc	1731	2273
M Robert Goldman and Company Inc	6162	72
M Robzen Inc	2011	151
M Rodrigue and Son Inc	3599	1266
M Rogers Design Inc	7389	1267
M Rosenthal Co	2759	296
M Rubin and Sons Inc	2321	17
M S —Action Machining Corp	3599	736
M S Co	3911	37
M S Plastics And Packaging Company Inc	5199	120
M S Walker Inc	5182	24
M Sakuma Electric Inc	1731	1327
M Schwam Inc	7336	147
M Shanken Communications Inc	2721	157
M Soft Inc	7373	946
M Spiegel and Sons Oil Corp	5172	122
M Squared Electronics Inc	3829	447
M Systems International Inc	7371	1639
M T Deason Company Inc	4924	73
M Trudeau Electric Inc	1731	2205
M Trumbull A R S Inc	3069	251
M Tucker Company Inc	5046	41
M W Bevins Co	3423	73
M W Waldrop Co	3556	150
M Works Inc	3695	92
M-1 Tool Works Inc	3544	259
M2 Antenna Systems Inc	3679	679
M2 Global Technology Ltd	3549	42
M2 Media Group LLC	7311	562
M2 Software Inc (Santa Monica California)	7372	4849
M2m Data Corp	7389	2251
M2S	7373	250
M7 Aerospace LLC	4581	29
M-80 Films	7812	241
M9 Defense Inc	2655	11
MA and Sons	2034	28
MA Architecture LLC	8712	298
MA Bongiovanni Inc	1623	70
MA Brands Inc	3911	11
MA Deatley Construction Inc	5082	21
MA Gedney Co	2033	57
MA Harrison Manufacturing Company Inc	3365	35
MA LABS Inc	3571	13
MA Mortenson Co	1542	5
MA Patout and Son Ltd	2061	8
MA Silva Corks USA LLC	5099	108
MA Walker Company LLC	1422	52
Maac Machinery Company Inc	3559	235
Maas-Hansen Steel Corp	5051	72
Maass Flanges Corp	3463	14
Maass Midwest Manufacturing Inc	3533	75
Maax Hydro Swirl Manufacturing Co	3088	13
MAAX SpA Industries Corp	3431	2
Mab Enterprises Inc	3829	377
Mabe Trucking Company Inc	4213	941
Mabis DMI Healthcare Inc	5047	41

Company Name	SIC	Rank
Mabry Foundry Company Inc	3321	68
Mabry Software Inc	7372	4312
Mabuchi Motor America Corp	5063	66
Mabus Brothers Construction Company Inc	1623	199
MAC Aviation Services LLC	3728	162
Mac Brothers Electric	1731	2597
Mac Cal Co	3444	138
Mac Const Inc	1622	45
Mac Donald and Evans Inc	2752	671
Mac Engineering And Equipment Company Inc	3559	195
MAC Equipment Inc	3535	16
Mac Fadden Holdings Inc	2721	233
Mac Fawn Enterprises Inc	7349	442
Mac General Inc	1731	1927
Mac Gregor Smith Blueprinters Inc	3861	92
MAC Group	5043	22
Mac Guys	5734	168
Mac Haik Chevrolet Inc	5511	148
Mac Haik Ford Inc	5511	117
Mac Haik Realty Corp	6531	18
MAC II LLC	7389	960
Mac Innes Enterprises Inc	2741	123
Mac Machine and Metal Works Inc	3544	434
Mac Machine Company Inc	3599	276
Mac Molding Company Inc	3089	1383
Mac Naughton Lithograph Company Inc	2752	107
Mac Panel Co	3823	180
Mac Pro Systems and Software	5734	264
Mac Productions Inc	7359	152
Mac Products Inc	3643	52
Mac Stripers Inc	3531	229
Mac Technology Inc	3679	755
Mac Tools Inc	3423	13
Mac Trailer Manufacturing Inc	3715	20
Mac Valves Inc	3492	39
Maca Plastics Inc	3694	34
MacAlaster Bicknell Company Inc (New Haven Connecticut)	5049	42
MacAlaster Bicknell Company of New Jersey Inc	3821	50
MacAllister Pitfield MacKay Inc	6211	388
MacAllister Machinery Company Inc	5082	7
Macaluso Group	6211	324
MacAndrews and Forbes Holdings Inc	2087	2
MacArthur Associated Consultants LLC	8711	468
MacArtney Offshore Inc	8999	110
Macase Industrial Corp	3577	51
Macatawa Bank Corp	6022	107
Macaulay-Brown Inc	8711	61
Macawber Engineering Inc	3535	177
MacBeath Hardwood Company Inc	2435	4
MACC Private Equities Inc	6722	276
Maccourt Products Inc	3083	27
Macdaddy Computers	5045	903
MacDermid Graphic Arts Inc	3555	4
MacDermid Inc	2899	23
Macdermid-Canning Ltd	2992	43
Macdivitt Rubber Company LLC	3061	63
Macdonald Carbide Co	3544	718
Macdonald Consulting Group Inc	7379	889
Macduff Underwriters Inc	6311	239
Mace Adhesives And Coatings Company Inc	2891	102
Mace Metal Sales Inc	5051	405
Mace Security International Inc	2899	120
Macera and Martini Trans Inc	4213	987
Macerich Co	6798	34
Macey's Inc	5411	126
MacFarms of Hawaii	0173	3
MacGraphics Services	7336	80
Mac-Gray Corp	7219	2
MacGregor Publishing Co	2741	142
Macgregor Yacht Corp	3732	74
MacGuffin Films Ltd	7812	85
MacGurus	5045	714
Mach I Packaging Inc	7389	1839
Mach Mold Inc	3544	333
Machado Environmental Corp	7349	359
Machen Inc	3728	216
Machida Inc	3845	78
Machine and Environmental Products Inc	3559	468
Machine And Fabrication Industries LLC	3599	883
Machine And Process Design Inc	8711	594
Machine and Welding Supply Co	5169	68
Machine Applications Corp	3823	465
Machine Builders and Design Inc	3991	1046
Machine Building Specialties Inc	3556	145
Machine Center Inc	3599	2036
Machine Components Corp	3568	76
Machine Craft Company Inc	3599	2264
Machine Craft Of San Diego Inc	3599	1114
Machine Diagnostics Inc	3829	455
Machine Experience and Design Inc	3599	1638
Machine Head	3652	31
Machine Power Inc	3599	1667
Machine Products Co	3599	1049
Machine Products Company Inc	3599	1760
Machine Rebuilders and Service Inc	3599	2356
Machine Sciences Corp	3545	160

Company Name	SIC	Rank
Machine Service Inc	3714	171
Machine Specialties Inc	3599	130
Machine Tek Systems Inc	3544	533
Machine Tool and Gear Inc	3462	40
Machine Tool and Supply Corp	5084	504
Machine Tool Engineering Inc	3599	1650
Machine Transportation Co	4213	1052
Machine Vision Products Inc	3827	43
Machine World Inc	3559	513
Machined Metals Company Inc	3552	30
Machined Metals Manufacturing Inc	3599	2152
Machined Products Co	3541	132
Machinery Maintenance Inc	7699	98
Machinery Sales Co	5084	194
Machinery Systems Inc	5084	110
Machinewell Inc	3599	1109
Machining and Fabricating Inc	3545	176
Machining Center Inc	3599	1027
Machining Concepts Inc	3599	990
Machining Corporation of America	3599	124
Machining Programming Manufacturing Inc	3599	534
Machining Solutions LLC	3599	2075
Machinists Inc	3599	122
Machintek Co	3599	626
Macho Products Inc	3949	141
Machollywood Inc	5734	429
MachroTech LLC	7372	1899
Machtronic Products Company Inc	3555	83
Mack and Rosa Inc	5013	198
Mack Boring And Parts Co	5084	296
Mack Energy Corporation Welding Shop	7692	19
Mack Hils Inc	3444	180
Mack Housby Inc	5511	1138
Mack Iron Works Company Inc	3446	45
Mack L Victoria LC	5012	165
Mack Manufacturing Inc	3531	134
Mack Massey Motors Inc	5511	766
Mack Mid-Hudson Inc	5012	158
Mack Pontiac Buick GMC (Hicksville New York)	5511	943
Mack Prototype Corp	3089	1413
Mack Technologies Inc	3577	134
Mack Tidewater Inc	5511	1210
Mack Transport Inc	4213	2381
MacKay and Somps Civil Engineers Inc	8711	454
Mackay Communications Inc	3663	60
Mackay Manufacturing Inc	3599	355
Mackay Mitchell Envelope Company LLC	2677	6
Mackay Telephone Systems Inc	1731	2548
Mack-Cali Realty Corp	6798	60
Macke Brothers Inc	2789	32
Macken Instruments Inc	3825	359
Mackenzie Laboratories Inc	3674	366
Mackenzie-Childs LLC	3263	2
MacKichan Software Inc	7372	3619
Mackin Engineering Co	8711	382
Mackinac Financial Corp	6712	471
MacKinney Systems Inc	7372	3250
Macklowe Properties Inc	6531	98
Mack's Liver Mush Inc	2013	248
MacLaughlin and Co	6531	285
MacLean Maynard LLC	3452	51
Maclean Power Systems	3644	24
Maclean Precision Machine Company Inc	3599	1110
Maclean Vehicle Systems	3452	41
MacLean-Fogg Co	3452	7
MacLean-Fogg Power Systems	3229	3
Maclee Virtual Systems LLC	4813	589
Macleod Pharmaceuticals Inc	8731	249
MacMastery	7379	151
MacMedics	7378	57
Macmillan/McGraw-Hill	2731	58
Mac-Mold Base Inc	3544	503
MacMulkin Chevrolet Geo Inc	5511	601
Macneill Engineering Company Inc	3089	1039
Macnichol Electric Inc	1731	1885
Maco Bag Corp	3081	72
Maco Tool and Engineering Inc	3544	547
Macomb Pipe and Supply Company Inc	5085	24
Macomb Printing Inc	2752	954
Macomb Steel Inc	5051	479
Macon Machine Inc	3599	1371
Macon Resources Inc	8093	29
Macon Systems Inc	7372	4850
Macon Telegraph	2711	84
Maconomy Inc	7372	570
Macoser Inc	5084	894
Macoy Publishing and Masonic Supply Company Inc	2389	33
Macpherson Inc	3651	239
Macpro Inc	3599	2407
Macquarie Airfinance Ltd	7359	133
Macquarie Equipment Finance LLC	7377	12
Macquarie Infrastructure Company LLC	7389	49
MacQueen Equipment Inc	5084	951
Macro 4 Inc	7372	449
Macro Enter Corp	7372	4070
Macro Industries Inc	7372	4711

Company Name	SIC	Rank
Macro Plastics Inc	3089	545
Macro Tool and Machine Company Inc	3599	2380
Macrodyne Inc	3825	282
Macrogenics Inc	8731	70
Macrolink Inc	3823	152
Macromatic Controls LLC	3625	262
Macronix America Inc	5065	168
Macrosearch Inc	7379	695
Macrosoft Inc	7371	392
Macrotron Systems Inc	3571	135
Macrovision Inc (Doylestown Pennsylvania)	7311	780
MacSema Inc	3578	26
MacServices	5045	715
MacSolutions Inc	7372	344
Macsports Inc	5091	83
MACSTEEL	3312	5
Macsteel International USA Corp	5051	355
Macsteel Service Centers USA	5051	10
Mactavish Machine Manufacturing Co	3559	515
Mactivity Inc	7389	1440
Macton Corp	3599	1151
Mactronix	3674	271
Macuch Steel Products Inc	5051	261
MacUpdate LLC	7371	843
Macwest Associates Inc	5734	101
Macy Movers Inc	4213	3079
Macy's Florida Welfare Benefits Trust	5311	38
Macys Inc	5311	21
Macy's Inc	5311	3
Macy's Systems and Technology	7374	26
Macy's West Inc	5311	12
Macyscom Inc	5311	9
Mad 4 Marketing Inc	7336	76
Mad Anthony's Inc	5812	156
Mad Butcher Inc	5411	191
Mad Catz Inc	7372	784
Mad Catz Interactive Inc	3944	7
Mad Dad Inc	7379	1579
Mad Engine Inc	2759	123
Mad River Post Inc	7812	63
Mad River Transportation Inc	4213	920
Mad Scientist Software	7372	2997
Mada Medical Products Inc	5047	79
Madaba Enterprises Inc	7379	1499
Madan Plastics Inc	3089	664
Madana Manufacturing	5031	423
Maddak Inc	3999	65
Madden Communications Inc	2752	14
Madden Contracting Company Inc	1611	253
Madden Ltd	4213	1673
Madden Sales and Services Inc	5084	518
Madden Systems Inc	1382	25
Maddenco Inc	7372	4113
Maddox Foundry and Machine Works Inc	3321	13
Maddox Industries Inc	3544	726
Maddox Marketing Group Inc	7311	625
Maddox Metal Works Inc	3556	69
Maddux Publishing Inc	2721	155
Made Rite Sandwich Company Of Chattanooga Inc	2099	135
Madelaine Chocolate Novelties Inc	2066	9
Madell Technology Corp	5065	834
Maden Tech Consulting Inc	7371	181
Mader Construction Corp	1542	372
Madera Component Systems Inc	2439	37
Madera Private Security Patrol	7381	175
MadeToOrder	3999	167
Madewell and Madewell Inc	5093	165
Madgar Genis Corp	3565	191
Madgetech Inc	3699	194
Madico Inc	3081	58
Madill Carbide Inc	3545	382
Madison Ave Media Inc	7375	293
Madison Avenue Family Life Center	8331	203
Madison Bohemian Savings Bank	6022	410
Madison Bottling Co	5181	104
Madison Cable Corp	3357	47
Madison Capital Partners Corp	6799	8
Madison Co	3643	92
Madison Company Inc	2387	5
Madison Computer Corp	5734	210
Madison County Coop	5191	177
Madison Courier	2711	715
Madison Cutting Tools Inc	3541	175
Madison Dearborn Partners LLC	6799	3
Madison Direct Marketing Ltd	7331	275
Madison Electric Co	5064	23
Madison Electronics Inc	3672	413
Madison Farmers Elevator Co	5153	38
Madison Fire Protection LLC	3569	231
Madison Gas and Electric Co	4931	36
Madison Group Inc	4899	107
Madison Hobbs Inc	7379	585
Madison Hotel Inc	7011	168
Madison Industries Inc	2392	15
Madison Investment Advisors Inc	6282	221
Madison Lighting Ltd	5063	520
Madison Magazine Inc	2721	440
Madison Management Corp	6282	390
Madison Medical LLC	3841	308
Madison Mill Inc	2499	24
Madison National Bank	6021	235

Company Name	SIC	Rank
Madison National Life Insurance Company Inc	6311	192
Madison Oil Co	5983	13
Madison Pharmacy Associates/Bajamar Women's HealthCare	5912	53
Madison Polymeric Engineering Inc	3086	92
Madison Research Corp	7372	584
Madison River Communications Corp	4813	65
Madison Sand and Gravel Company Inc	1442	47
Madison Service Co	5153	181
Madison Square Garden Inc	6512	9
Madison Technical Software Inc	7372	4851
Madison Tool And Die Inc	3544	161
Madison-Kipp Corp	3363	15
MadmodcomputingCom	7378	175
Madonna's Bail Bonds	7389	2229
Mad*Pow	7311	909
Madruga Electric Inc	1731	1851
Madsen and Howell Inc	5085	218
MaeDae Enterprises LLC	7372	4712
Maersk Inc	4412	1
Maes Tool and Die Company Inc	3544	866
MAF Developments Inc	6552	108
Maf Industries Inc	3565	50
Mafco Electrical Contractors Inc	1731	569
Mafco Holdings Inc	2087	15
Mafco Inc	3599	1456
MAFInc	5023	111
Mag Aerospace Industries Inc	3431	3
Mag Flux Corp	3677	41
Mag Inc	2721	425
MAG Industrial Automation Systems	3541	2
Mag Instrument Inc	3648	6
MAG Trucks	3713	61
Magary Construction Inc	5085	325
Magavern Magavern and Grimm LLP	8111	499
Magazine Group Inc	2721	152
Magazine I Spectrum E	2721	337
Magdesian Brothers Inc	3144	5
Magee Enterprises Inc	7372	798
Magee Machine And Manufacturing Inc	3599	1876
Magee Marketing Group Inc	7311	541
Magee Plastics Co	3083	41
Magee Rieter Automotive Systems	2273	10
Magellan Behavioral Health Inc	8063	4
Magellan Health Services Inc	8063	2
Magellan Medical Technology Consultants Inc	3841	125
Magellan Midstream Partners LP	4613	4
Magellan Navigation Inc	3812	128
Magellan NGL LLC	4613	5
Magellan Petroleum Corp	1382	51
Magellan Publishing	2721	458
Magellan Terminals Holdings LP	6719	63
Magenic Technologies Inc	7379	284
Magento Inc (Culver City California)	7372	518
Magex Corp	7379	480
Maggio Data Forms Printing Ltd	2761	40
Maggiore Public Salt Co	5182	48
Maggy London International Ltd	2335	2
Magi Realty Inc	6552	194
Magic 16 Weup	4832	185
Magic Aire	3433	13
Magic American Corp	2842	31
Magic Circle Corp	3524	8
Magic City Implement Inc	5083	132
Magic City Sprinkler Inc	1711	237
Magic Design/Visual Dynamics Inc	7336	294
Magic Embedments Inc	2821	176
Magic Exterminating Company Inc	7342	39
Magic Hat Brewing Company and Performing Arts Center Inc	2082	55
Magic Industries Inc	7359	84
Magic Kids and Co	5137	3
Magic Logix	7336	56
Magic Maintenance Inc	7349	481
Magic Makers Inc	3944	47
Magic Metals Inc	7692	7
Magic Moments Inc	5045	550
Magic Mouse Productions	7372	4713
Magic Novelty Company Inc	3961	10
Magic Plastics Inc	3089	781
Magic Seasoning Blends Inc	2099	175
Magic Software Enterprises Inc	7372	3461
Magic Teleprompting Inc	7372	3921
Magic Valley Bank	6022	688
Magic Valley Electric Coop	4911	206
MagicBox Inc	3669	282
MagicHour Films Inc	7812	285
MagicRAM Inc	3577	338
Magid Glove and Safety Manufacturing Company LLC	3151	2
Magik Technology Solutions	7373	914
Magill Construction Company Inc	1541	256
Magiq Technologies Inc	3699	273
Magister Corp	3842	302
Magix Entertainment Corp	7372	978
Magixsoft Technical Servi	7379	1653
Magla Products LLC	5137	2
Maglebys Custom Cabinets	5031	218
Magline Inc	3537	50
Magma Design Automation Inc	7372	322
Magma Engineering Co	3542	109

Company Name	SIC	Rank	Company Name	SIC	Rank	Company Name	SIC	Rank
Magna Chek Inc	8734	47	Magparts	3365	17	Mainline Printing Inc	2752	485
Magna Electric Supply Company Inc	5063	776	Magra Inc	4213	1613	Mainline Supply of Jonesboro Inc	1623	559
Magna Industrial Tools Div	3423	23	Magruder Limestone Company Inc	1422	29	Mainsail Marketing Information Inc	7379	1481
Magna Machine and Tool Company Inc	3599	946	Magsoft Corp	7372	3356	Mainship Corp	3732	54
Magna Machine Co	3556	46	Mag-Tec Casting Corp	3364	30	MainSoft Corp	7372	1575
Magna Manufacturing Inc	3086	132	Magtech and Power Conversion Inc	3677	108	MainSource Bank	6022	395
Magna Mirrors North America LLC	3231	13	Mag-Tran Equipment Corp	3612	102	Mainsource Bank of Illinois	6021	380
Magna Mirrors Of America Inc	3231	1	Mag-Trol Associates Inc	5065	858	MainSource Financial Group Inc	6712	161
Magna Publications Inc	2721	384	Magtrol Inc	3829	146	Mainstay	7372	2427
Magna Services of America Inc	3711	38	Magtrol Inc (Tucson Arizona)	5065	242	Mainstay Software Corp	7372	2998
Magna Tool Inc	3599	1877	Maguire Electrical Construction LLC	1731	2567	Mainstream Commercial Divers Inc	7389	1504
Magna Visual Inc	3089	1059	Maguire Group Inc	8711	136	Mainstream Data Inc	7373	399
Magnacare LLC	8742	274	Maguire Oil Co	1311	173	Mainstream Engineering Corp	3585	207
MagnaDrive Corp	3714	408	Maguire Products Inc	3824	26	Mainstream Software Inc	7371	1366
Magna-Lab Inc	8731	432	Magyar Bancorp Inc	6035	117	Mainstreet Communications LLC	4813	662
Magna-lastic Devices Inc	8731	399	Mah Machine Co	7692	10	Mainstreet Integration Services and	7379	875
Magnatech Engineering Inc	3569	55	Maha USA LLC	7353	28	Consulting Inc		
Magnatech LLC	3548	32	Mahan Packing Company Inc	2011	139	Mainstreet Property Group LLC	6798	209
Magna-Tel Inc	3993	110	Mahar Tool Supply Company Inc	5084	34	MainStreet Software Corp	7372	879
Magna-Tex Inc	3061	45	Mahaska Bottling Co	2086	104	MainStreet Solutions Inc	7379	1203
Magnat-Fairview Inc	3599	494	Mahomed Sales and Warehousing LLC	4225	14	Mainstreet Systems and Software Inc	7372	1646
Magnatone Hearing Aid Corp	3842	140	Mahoney Environmental Inc	2079	6	Mainstreet Technologies Inc	7378	47
Magnatron Inc	7372	3213	Mahoney Express Inc	4213	2583	Maintain Systems Inc	7371	1901
Magnebit Holding Corp	3825	212	Mahoney Group	6331	137	Maintech	7378	4
Magneco/Metrel Inc	3297	5	Mahoney's Rocky Ledge Farm Nursery	5261	10	Maintenance Alternatives Inc	7378	139
MagneComp Inc	3677	93	Mahoning Landfill Inc	4953	134	Maintenance Builders Supply Inc	5099	64
MagneLab Div	3612	115	Mahopac National Bank	6022	730	Maintenance Connection Inc	7372	1556
Magnelink Inc	3625	371	Mahr Federal Inc	5084	105	Maintenance Division City Shops	1623	384
Magnepan Inc	3651	136	Mahrenholtz Inc	5734	202	Maintenance Engineering Corp	5169	150
Magnesium Elektron North America Inc	3356	28	Mahzel Metals Inc	5093	209	Maintenance Management Company	7349	269
Magnesium Products Of America Inc	3364	7	MAI Systems Corp	7372	1406	Inc		
Magnet LLC	3499	41	Maico Diagnostics Inc	3842	150	Maintenance Mart Inc	7349	205
Magnet Sales and Manufacturing	3499	53	Maicon LLC	7349	470	MaintSmart Software Inc	7372	4852
Company Inc			Maida Development Co	3559	117	Mainxchange Inc	7374	327
Magnet Works Ltd	3999	162	Maidenform Brands Inc	5311	27	Maisons Marques and Domaines USA	5182	30
Magnetech Industrial Services Inc	7623	3	Maid-Rite Corp	5812	302	Inc		
Magnetek Inc	3679	90	Maid-Rite Steak Company Inc	2013	35	Maita Automotive Group	5511	122
Magneti Marelli Powertrain USA LLC	3714	194	Maids International Inc	6794	79	Maita Toyota	5511	543
Magnetic Analysis Corp	3829	87	Maier Electronics Inc	3674	488	Maitland Engineering Inc	3842	193
Magnetic Automation Corp	3829	315	Maiers Transport and Warehousing	4213	2462	Maitlen and Benson Inc	3548	44
Magnetic Circuit Elements Inc	3679	444	Mail Bag Inc	7331	78	Majac Inc	3312	97
Magnetic Coil Manufacturing Co	3677	101	Mail Boxes Etc Inc	7389	209	Majesco Entertainment Co	7372	355
Magnetic Component Engineering Inc	3499	66	Mail Co	2752	319	Majestic Cleaning Service Inc	7349	392
Magnetic Design Labs Inc	3679	746	Mail Computer Services Inc	7331	69	Majestic Construction Co	1522	40
Magnetic Inspection Laboratory Inc	8734	99	Mail Handling Inc	2752	245	Majestic Distilling Company Inc	2085	12
Magnetic Instrumentation Inc	3613	30	Mail Marketing Systems Inc	7331	25	Majestic Electric Company Inc	1731	1675
Magnetic Instruments Corp	3599	96	Mail Print Inc	2752	456	Majestic Homes Inc	2451	25
Magnetic Metals Corp	3542	10	Mail Tech Enterprises Inc	7331	96	Majestic Jewelry Inc	3089	46
Magnetic Power Systems Inc	3568	17	Mail Tribune Co	2711	279	Majestic Manufacturing Inc	3599	900
Magnetic Products and Services Inc	5045	143	Mailcentro Inc	4813	532	Majestic Marine Inc	4213	1939
Magnetic Seal Corp	3728	167	MailCoups Inc	7331	200	Majestic Mold and Tool Inc	2821	191
Magnetic Sensors Corp	3679	416	Mailing Advantages Inc	7331	202	Majestic Properties	6531	363
Magnetic Springs Water Co	5149	107	Mailing House Inc	7374	122	Majestic Steel USA Inc	5051	144
Magnetic Technology Inc	3677	102	Mailings Unlimited	7331	210	Majestic Tool And Machine Inc	3599	1734
Magnetic Windings Company Inc	3612	96	Maillis Strapping Systems USA Inc	3089	1225	Majesty Maintenance Company Inc	7349	302
Magnetico Inc	3679	443	Mailpro Inc	7331	284	Majesty Music Inc	2741	445
Magnetics Intl Inc	2816	9	Mailrite Inc	7331	142	Majilite Corp	2295	16
Magnetics Test Lab	5063	866	Mailtrust	4812	77	Major Acquisition Corp	6719	44
Magnetika Inc	5063	279	Mailways Enterprises Inc	7389	765	Major Automotive Companies Inc	5511	59
Magnetix Corp	3652	21	Maiman Co	2431	115	Major Automotive Group Inc	5511	16
Magneto-Inductive Systems Ltd	3663	158	Maimin Technology Group Inc	3531	197	Major Automotive of New Jersey Inc	5511	1249
Magnetrol International Inc	3823	56	Main Amundson and Assoc	8721	232	Major Automotive Realty Corp	6512	2
Magnevolt Inc	3691	49	Main Electric Ltd	1731	263	Major Brands Inc	5182	13
Magni Group Inc	2899	82	Main Events Inc	7941	32	Major Brands-Columbia	5182	37
Mag-Nif Inc	3944	27	Main Industries Inc	4499	7	Major Chevrolet Inc	5511	19
Magnifique Parfumes and Cosmetics	2844	15	Main Iron Works LLC	3731	39	Major Chrysler Jeep Dodge of Long	5511	20
Inc			Main Point Productions	7389	1788	Island City Inc		
Magni-Flood Inc	3646	88	Main Resource Inc	8748	374	Major Commercial Cleaning Inc	7349	279
Magnify Inc	7372	851	Main Robert A and Sons Holding	3496	70	Major Custom Cable Inc	3679	357
Magno Sound and Video	3695	22	Company Inc			Major Die and Engineering Co	3599	43
Magnode Corp	3354	22	Main Station Advertising Inc	7311	1005	Major Electronix Corp	5065	470
Magno-Humphries Labs Inc	2834	222	Main Store Display and Fixtures	5046	229	Major Fleet and Leasing Corp	7515	6
Magnolia Audio Video	5731	15	Main Street Capital Corp	6159	48	Major Inc	7376	35
Magnolia Coca-Cola Bottling Co	2086	45	Main Street Checks Inc	2782	30	Major Kia Inc	5511	21
Magnolia Forest Products Inc	5031	93	Main Street Gourmet LLC	2053	10	Major League Baseball	7941	8
Magnolia Metal Corp	3366	5	Main Street Lighting Standards Inc	3648	66	Major League Electronics LLC	3678	45
Magnolia Plastics Inc	2891	90	Main Street Management Co	6211	133	Major Media Inc	3695	114
Magnolia Processing Inc	2092	39	Main Street Music Hall Inc	7922	99	Major Micro Systems Inc	7372	2198
Magnolia Shrewsbury	8322	212	Main Street Produce Inc	4222	10	Major Orange Properties LLC	5511	22
Magnolia Steel Company Inc	3441	42	Main Street Technologies	5045	994	Major Products Company Inc	2034	23
Magnolia Tool and Manufacturing	3469	365	Main Street Trading Company Inc	5731	208	Major Properties Realtors Corp	6531	301
Company Inc			Main Tool and Manufacturing Co	3599	41	Major Sewer and Water Contractors	1623	820
Magnolia Trailers Inc	3715	61	Mainconcept LLC	7372	944	Inc		
Magnum Communications Ltd	7372	2055	Maine and Maritimes Corp	4911	260	Major Theatre Equipment Corp	5049	97
Magnum Construction Services Inc	3441	196	Maine Antique Digest Inc	2721	403	Major Tool And Machine Inc	7692	5
Magnum D'Or Resources Inc	7389	2508	Maine Biotechnology Services Inc	2836	63	Major World Wide Ltd	5199	126
Magnum Electric Service Inc	1731	1299	Maine Machine Products Co	3999	102	Majors Plastics Inc	3089	296
Magnum Fabrications Inc	3569	245	Maine Market Refrigeration LLC	3585	160	Majr Products Corp	3679	747
Magnum Hunter Resources Corp	1311	103	Maine Metal Recycling Inc	5093	200	MAK Technologies Inc	7372	509
Magnum International and Inc	8711	684	Maine Oxy-Acetylene Supply Co	5169	82	Make It Or Break It Videos	7359	223
Magnum Magnetics Corp	3499	42	Maine Potato Growers Inc	5191	83	MakeBuzz LLC	7379	665
Magnum Marine Corp	3732	84	Maine Recycling Corp	4953	130	MakeMusic Inc	7372	1375
Magnum Mud Equipment Company Inc	7353	70	Maine Securities Corp	6211	339	Maker's Mark Distillery Inc	2085	18
Magnum Opus Inc	8711	699	Maine Woods Company LLC	2421	130	Makino Inc	3541	11
Magnum Semiconductor Inc	3674	140	Mainely Trusses Inc	2439	55	Makita USA Inc	5072	3
Magnum Steel and Trading Inc	5093	51	Maines Paper and Food Service Inc	5111	4	Makjohn LLC	3599	1317
Magnum Technologies Inc	7379	149	Maines Paper and Food Service Inc	5046	4	Makkos Of Brooklyn Ltd	2052	46
Magnum Tool Company Inc	3599	262	Equipment and Supply Div			Mako Compressors LLC	3563	41
Magnus Group Inc	2791	21	MaineStreet Communications Inc	4899	173	Mako Rentals Inc	7359	282
Magnus Inc	1731	2461	Maingate Inc	2339	43	MAKO Surgical Corp	3842	76
Mago Construction Co	1623	481	Mainjoy Unlimited Inc	5083	186	Makovsky and Company Inc	8743	59
Magone Marine Service Inc	7699	71	Mainline Contracting Inc	1623	295	Makowski's Real Sausage Co	2013	184
Magor Mold Inc	3544	279	Mainline Information Systems Inc	7373	55	Makray Manufacturing Company Inc	3089	634
Magotteaux Inc	3369	10	Mainline National Bank	6021	174	Makro Janitorial Services	7349	276

Company Name	SIC	Rank
Mak-System Corp	3695	141
Malachi Mattress America Inc	5021	143
Malaco Records Inc	6799	325
Malaga Bank SSB	6036	46
Malaga Financial Corp	6712	363
Malcap Mortgage LLC	6162	141
Malco Products Inc	3423	30
Malco Theatres Inc	7832	15
Malcolite Corp	3641	22
Malcolm Cunningham Automotive Group Inc	5511	623
Malcolm Eaton Enterprises	8322	163
Malcolm M Dienes and Co	8721	419
Malcolm T Gilliland Inc	5084	671
Malcolm's Meat Service Inc	5147	121
Malcon Inc	3823	183
Malden International Designs Inc	2499	41
Male LLC	3579	48
Malema Engineering Corp	3823	36
Malenke Barnhart LLC	7311	891
Maleport's Sault Printing Company Inc	5112	95
Malhame and Company Publishers and Importers Inc	2731	281
Malibu Boats LLC	3732	29
Malibu Entertainment Worldwide Inc	7996	24
Malibu News Enterprises Inc	7313	39
Malibu Software Group Inc	7372	4518
Malibu's	7389	1919
Malikco LLC	8742	527
Malin Space Science Systems Inc	3728	140
Malish Corp	3991	10
Malko Electric Company Inc	1731	419
Mall Delivery Service	4213	2206
Mall of America Co	6531	78
Mall Telecommunications	5065	519
Mallard Frame Inc	3999	213
Mallen and Friends Advertising Arts	7311	980
Mallett and Sons Trucking Company Inc	4213	2879
Malley's Candies Inc	5441	4
Mallinckrodt Inc	3845	4
Mallory and Evans Inc	1711	130
Mallory Propane	5172	75
Malloy Inc	2732	21
Malloy Montague Karnowski Radosevich and Company PA	8721	440
Malloy North Carolina Inc	5084	546
Malmberg Engineering Inc	3599	518
Malmberg Travel Cos	4724	114
Malnove Inc	2657	2
Malnove Incorporated Of Utah	2391	4
Malolo Beverages and Supplies Ltd	2087	61
Maloney and Bell General Contractors Incorporated of California	1542	325
Maloney Tool and Mold Inc	3544	320
Maloney's Custom Ocular Prosthetics Inc	3842	322
Maloof Distributing LLC	5181	19
Malott's Honda and Yamaha	5571	12
Malt Products Corporation Of Nj	2083	3
Maltby Electric Supply Company Inc	5063	178
Malt-O-Meal Co	2043	2
Malvern Federal Bancorp Inc	6036	41
Malvese Equipment Company Inc	5082	116
Malwin Electronics Corp	3699	249
Maly Companies LLC	5031	342
Mama Rosie's Company Inc	2038	70
Mamac Systems Inc	3823	86
Mama's Garden Design Studio	7389	2348
Mamco Corp	3621	38
Mamma Ilardo's Corp	6794	88
Mammobase LLC	3695	173
Mammography Reporting System Inc	7371	1124
Mammoth Inc	3585	26
Mammoth Medical Inc	5047	54
Mammoth Mountain Ski Area	7011	161
Man Data Inc	7322	143
Man Investments Div	6282	30
Man Maven Medical Manufacturing Inc	3841	304
MAN Roland Inc	3555	7
Man Turbo Incorporated USA	5084	168
Mana Products Inc	2844	30
Manac Trailers USA Inc	3715	37
Manage Operations	7372	4313
Managed Business Services Inc	8721	337
Managed Business Solutions	8742	683
Managed Care Consultants Inc	6324	119
Managed Care Network Inc	7389	1389
Managed Care On-Line Inc	7379	741
Managed Care Professionals Inc	7389	729
Managed Care Systems Inc	7374	280
Managed Communications Services LLC	3663	309
Managed HealthCare Northwest Inc	8011	64
Managed Objects Solutions Inc	7372	216
Managed Security Solutions Group	7382	30
Management 360	7922	82
Management and Engineering Technologies International Inc	7379	162
Management by Innovation Inc	7331	34
Management Cleaning Controls LLC	7349	5
Management Computer Controls Inc	7372	2575
Management Concepts Inc	8299	27

Company Name	SIC	Rank
Management Consulting and Research LLC	8742	249
Management Controls Inc	7372	2747
Management Data Inc	7371	1394
Management Decisions Inc	7363	94
Management Dynamics Inc	7372	125
Management Financial Group	6311	180
Management Industrial Solutions SA de CV	8742	439
Management Industries Inc	2341	4
Management Information Consulting Inc	7379	468
Management Information Control Systems Inc	7372	3834
Management Information Systems Co	7373	975
Management Network Group Inc	8742	160
Management Planning Systems	7372	4041
Management Potentials Inc	8742	397
Management Recruiters International Inc	7361	13
Management Recruiters Of North Oakland County Inc	7361	357
Management Recruiters of Portland Inc	7361	59
Management Science Associates Inc (Pittsburgh Pennsylvania)	8732	39
Management Sciences Inc	7372	4382
Management Software Inc	7372	3672
Management Software Systems Inc	7379	1285
Management Systems Consulting LLC	7379	1618
Management Systems Inc (Fort Collins Colorado)	7372	2305
Management Systems Services Inc	7379	1076
Management Technology Inc	8742	32
Management Training Scientific Support Services Inc	8741	97
Managementf Paper Company LLC	2711	468
Managers Funds LP	6722	271
ManageSoft Corporation Inc	7372	1667
Managing Editor Inc	7372	1268
Manan Tool and Manufacturing Inc	3541	15
Manassa Stock Building Supply	2431	39
Manatee Fruit Co	5193	5
Manatee River Laboratories Inc	8733	41
Manatron Inc	7373	185
Manatron ProVal Corp	7372	755
Manatt Phelps and Phillips	8111	27
Manchester Corp	8711	599
Manchester Creamery LLC	5812	400
Manchester Memorial Hospital Inc	8062	95
Manchester Metals LLC	3321	45
Manchester Molding And Manufacturing Co	3089	1229
Manchester Motor Freight Inc	4213	2677
Manchester Packaging Co	3081	123
Manchester Packing Company Inc	2011	101
Manchester Tank and Equipment Company Inc	3443	25
Mancine Optical Company Inc	5048	26
Mancini Packing Co	2032	25
Mancon Empire Industrial Products	5085	132
Man-Con Inc	1623	560
Manconix Inc	3699	104
Mancor-Sc Inc	8741	95
Mancuso Cheese Co	2022	74
Manda Packing Company LLC	2013	17
Mandala Communications Inc	7311	436
Mandalay Entertainment	7812	332
Mandaree Enterprise Corp	3672	97
Mandarin Soy Sauce Inc	2035	54
Mandel Co	2752	1228
Mandex Inc	7372	2366
Mane Inc	2099	98
Mane USA Inc	2869	51
Mane-California	2087	76
Manekin LLC	6552	95
Maner Builders Supply Company LLC	5031	82
Manetek Inc	3559	368
Manfredi and Associates Inc	8742	304
Manfredi Mushroom Inc	4213	2235
Manga Entertainment LLC	7812	74
Mangan Holcomb Rainwater Culpepper Inc	7311	452
Manganaro MidatlanticLLC	1742	6
Mangar Medical Inc	3841	124
Mangelsen's	5099	6
Manger Packing Corp	5147	98
Mangia Pasta LLC	5411	287
Mangia Pizza and Pasta Inc	5812	406
Mango Capital Inc	7373	1233
Mangrove Employer Services Inc	7371	889
Man-Grove Industries Inc	2752	470
Manhattan Associates Inc	7372	161
Manhattan Bancorp	6712	656
Manhattan Beer Distributors LLC	5181	7
Manhattan Brass and Copper Company Inc	5052	4
Manhattan Bridge Capital Inc	2741	194
Manhattan Community Access Corp	4841	105
Manhattan Construction Co	1541	30
Manhattan Drug Company Inc	2834	218
Manhattan Group LLC	3942	11
Manhattan Information Systems Inc	5044	58
Manhattan Mortgage Co	6163	12
Manhattan Pharmaceuticals Inc	2834	480

Company Name	SIC	Rank
Manhattan Scientifics Inc	7379	1279
Manhattan Telecommunications Corp	4813	182
Manhattan Transfer Edit Co	7819	50
Manhattan Wire Products	5251	42
Manheim	5012	2
Manheim Indianapolis Auto Auction	5012	193
Manheim Specialty Machine Inc	3599	2175
Manhole Builders Inc	1623	663
Manifold Capital Corp	6411	200
Manildra Group USA	2046	5
Manischewitz Co	2052	19
Manischewitz Co	5149	5
Manistique Papers Inc	2621	50
Manitex International Inc (Bridgeview Illinois)	3829	27
Manitou North America Inc	3523	45
Manitowoc Company Inc	3531	1
Manitowoc Cranes Inc	3536	56
Manitowoc Foodservice	3585	257
Manitowoc Ice Inc	3585	50
Manitowoc Pattern And Manufacturing Co	3543	50
Manitowoc Public Utilities	4911	165
Manix Manufacturing Inc	5065	635
Mankato Free Press Co	2711	317
Mankato Motors	5511	1031
Mankato Rehabilitation Center Inc	8331	18
Manke Lumber Company Inc	2421	24
Manley Architecture Group	8712	305
Manley Laboratories Inc	3663	138
Manley Meats Inc	5421	20
Manley Performance Products Inc	3714	261
Mann and Hummel Advanced Filtration Concepts Inc	3569	101
Mann and Parker Lumber Co	5031	248
Mann Consulting	8742	342
Mann Consulting Multimedia	2741	137
Mann Corp	3679	676
Mann Group	7371	1188
Mann Health Services Inc	8052	14
Mann Properties	6552	208
Mann Travel and Cruises	4724	27
Manna Inc	5087	165
Manna Inc (Louisville Kentucky)	5812	127
Mannatech Inc	2833	12
Mannhardt Inc	3559	182
Mann-Hummel Automotive	3089	205
Manning and Napier Information Services	7389	590
Manning Electric Inc	5063	636
Manning Equipment Inc	5012	43
Manning Lighting Inc	3646	66
Manning NavComp Inc	7372	3724
Manning Selvage and Lee Inc	8743	5
Manning's Beef LLC	2011	86
Mannington Mills Inc	3996	1
Mannino Electric Inc	1731	2018
MannKind Corp	2834	445
Mann's Bait Company Inc	3949	147
Mannsville Chemical Products Corp	8732	89
Manny's Music	5736	9
Manor Electric Supply Corp	3699	180
Manor Tool And Manufacturing Company Inc	3469	155
Manown Engineering Company Inc	3433	63
Manpower Inc	7363	1
Mansai Corp	7372	3413
Mansell Group Inc	7372	2290
Mansfield Brass and Aluminum Corp	3365	32
Mansfield Electric Supply Inc	5063	134
Mansfield Oil Company of Gainesville Inc	5172	110
Mansfield Paper Company Inc	5113	43
Mansfield Plumbing Products LLC	3261	3
Mansfield Software Group Inc	7372	5065
Mansfield Structural And Erecting Co	3441	247
Mansfield Truck Sales and Service Inc	5511	398
Mansfield-King Inc	2841	36
Mansion on Turtle Creek	5812	386
Manson Construction Co	1629	61
Manson Meads Complex	3589	194
Mansur and Co	6799	187
Manta Media Inc	7375	120
Manta Technologies Inc	7372	3800
Manta-Ray Inc	5999	275
Man-Tech Associates Inc	5049	180
ManTech International Corp	8741	8
ManTech Systems Engineering Corp	7373	172
ManTech Test Systems Inc	3825	46
Mantel Machine Products Inc	3451	66
Manternach Development Co	2452	45
Mantex Corp	3089	772
Manth-Brownell Inc	3451	15
Manthei Inc	2435	29
Manti Resources Inc	1382	48
Mantissa Corp	7372	2394
Mantrose-Hauser Company Inc	2064	9
Mantz Automation Inc	3544	109
Manu Tec Inc	3679	601
Manual Labour Inc	7372	4001
Manual Woodworkers and Weavers Inc	2511	19
Manuel Huerta Trucking Inc	4213	1061
Manuels Mexican American Fine Foods Inc	2099	236

Company Name	SIC	Rank	Company Name	SIC	Rank	Company Name	SIC	Rank
Manufab Inc	3446	32	Marathon Ashland Petroleum LLC	2911	9	Mardone Inc	7349	99
Manufacture Resource Products Inc	2298	13	Marathon Bindery Services Inc	2789	98	Mardrian Group Inc	1542	295
Manufactured Component Parts Ltd	3312	110	Marathon Cheese Corp	7389	35	Mared Mechanical Contractors Corp	1731	204
Manufactured Concrete Ltd	3272	110	Marathon Coach Inc	3716	10	Marek Brothers Co	1799	61
Manufactured Duct and Supply	5075	117	Marathon Co	3911	35	Marek Group Inc	2752	194
Manufactured Housing Enterprises Inc	1521	140	Marathon Consulting	8748	343	Marel Seattle Inc	3556	47
Manufactured Rubber Products Co	3053	144	Marathon Electric Manufacturing Corp	3621	15	Marel Stork Poultry Processing Inc	3556	17
Manufacturers Alliance Insurance Co	6351	31	Marathon Electrical Contractors Inc	1731	136	Marelco Power Systems Inc	3677	33
Manufacturers Bank (Los Angeles California)	6022	134	MARATHON Engineers/Architects/ Planners LLC (Appleton Wisconsin)	8712	205	Maren Engineering Corp	3559	262
Manufacturers Chemicals LP	2819	24	Marathon Equipment Co	3589	20	Marena Industries Inc	3545	381
Manufacturers Community Development Corp	6159	40	Marathon Heater LLC	3433	25	Marena Systems Corp	3825	229
Manufacturers Industrial Group LLC	3449	1	Marathon Industries Inc	3011	26	Marentco Inc	7353	47
Manufacturers Leasing Services Corp	6159	76	Marathon Infants And Toddlers Inc	8322	121	Marfield Inc	2752	1534
Manufacturers' News Inc	2741	168	Marathon Management Inc	8741	136	Marfo Co	3911	15
Manufacturer's Products Inc	5075	82	Marathon Manufacturing Inc	3442	132	Marfred Industries	2653	30
Manufacturers Reserve Supply Inc	5031	119	Marathon Media	4832	24	Marge Carson Inc	2512	64
Manufacturers Resources Inc	2891	126	Marathon Monitors Inc	3823	272	Margo Caribe Inc	0181	18
Manufacturers Service Inc	3469	331	Marathon Norco Aerospace Co	3679	144	Margolin Winer and Evens LLP	8721	287
Manufacturing Action Group Inc	7372	2159	Marathon Oil Corp	1311	2	Marguerite Rodgers Ltd	7389	2312
Manufacturing and Consulting Services Inc	7372	1183	Marathon Pipe Line LLC	4612	8	Margulies Perruzzi Architects	8712	150
Manufacturing And Design Technology Inc	8712	311	Marathon Press Inc	2752	525	Margus Automotive Electric Exchange Inc	3714	367
Manufacturing and Engineering Excellence Inc	8711	544	Marathon Redevelopment Corp	3694	1	Maria Terra Corp	7379	942
Manufacturing and Research Inc	3841	96	Marathon Technology Corp	3829	365	Mariah Industries Inc	3714	330
Manufacturing Automation Software and Systems Group Inc	7372	3540	Marauder Corp	7322	151	Mariah Media Inc	2721	136
Manufacturing Data Systems Inc	7373	836	Maravia Corporation Of Idaho	3949	166	Mariak Industries Inc	5023	44
Manufacturing Industries Inc	3672	482	Mar-Bal Inc	3089	470	Marian Graphics Inc	2759	381
Manufacturing Information System Inc	7372	2291	Marberry Machine Inc	3589	135	Marian Heath Greeting Cards Inc	2771	16
Manufacturing Resource Group Inc	3625	97	MARBLE Computer Inc	7372	2722	Marian Heath Greeting LLC	2771	8
Manufacturing Sciences Corp	3341	34	Marble Designs Inc	3281	49	Marian Inc	3679	195
Manufacturing Solutions And Technologies LLC	3549	104	Marble Emporium Inc	5032	108	Marianna Sunland Facility	8361	26
Manufacturing System Services Inc	7372	3321	Marble Granite Tiles Inc	5032	70	Mariano Construction Inc	1731	1017
Manufacturing Systems and Equipment Inc	5063	611	Marble Knits Inc	2253	23	Marich Confectionery Company Inc	2064	75
Manufacturing Technology Inc	3548	16	Marble Lite Products Corp	3088	31	Maricom Systems Inc	7371	242
Manufacturing Trade Inc	4813	712	Marble Machine Inc	3599	1602	Marie Anna Designs Inc	2331	12
ManufacturingCom Inc	7389	1499	Marble Products Inc	3281	19	Mariemont Insurance Co	6331	361
Manugraph Dgm Inc	3555	24	Marble Slab Creamery Inc	5812	425	Marietta Corp	5122	10
Manus-Products-Minnesota Inc	2891	70	Marburg Technology Inc	3577	189	Marietta Design Group Inc	7372	3922
Manutech Assemble Inc	3612	31	Marc Climatic Controls Inc	3585	115	Marietta Drapery and Window Coverings Company Inc	5023	12
Manutronics Co	3571	129	Marc Ecko Enterprises Inc	2321	4	Marietta Industrial Enterprises Inc	4491	13
Manville Rubber Products Inc	3069	198	Marc Glassman Inc	5912	11	Marietta Systems Inc	7372	4979
Manzana Products Company Inc	2033	94	Marc Miller Pontiac GMC Inc	5511	154	Mariette Systems International	7373	1116
Manziel Interests	1311	155	Marc Nichols Associates Inc	7361	322	Marigold Mining Company	1041	9
Maola Milk And Ice Cream Company LLC	2026	25	Marc Paul Inc	5251	12	Marilyn Magder	7336	263
MAP Mobile Communications Inc	4812	17	Marc Refrigeration Manufacturing Inc	3585	213	Marilyn Miglin LP	2844	104
MAP Pharmaceuticals Inc	2834	448	Marc Truant and Associates Inc	7389	596	Marimon Business Systems Inc	5044	39
Map Supply Inc	5199	110	Marc USA	7311	91	Marin Acura Inc	5511	1059
Mapa Professionel	3069	64	MARC USA Inc	7311	73	Marin Baking LLC	2051	203
Mapal Inc	3545	79	Marc Woodworking Inc	2521	43	Marin Brewing Company Inc	5812	422
Mapes and Sprowl Steel Ltd	5051	101	Marca Hispanic LLC	7311	908	Marin Digital	3695	154
Mapes Piano String Co	3495	8	Marcanti Electric Inc	1731	851	Marin French Cheese Company Inc	2022	87
Mapframe Corp	7372	1552	Marcel S Garrigues Co	7389	2094	Marina Associates Ltd	7011	105
Maple City Ice Co	5181	68	Marcello Distributors/Thibaut Oil Co	5172	102	Marina Biotech Inc	2834	394
Maple City Rubber Co	3069	131	Marcellus Construction Company Inc	1623	419	Marina Cartage Inc	4213	341
Maple Companies of Texas	1382	42	March Analytical	5049	167	Marina LP	6552	235
Maple Donuts Inc	2051	33	March Furniture Manufacturing Inc	2512	34	Marina Medical Instruments Inc	5047	223
Maple Grove Farms Of Vermont Inc	2099	157	March Johnson Systems Inc	3564	77	Marina Power Company Inc	3612	136
Maple Hill Farms Inc	2026	74	March Manufacturing Inc	3561	94	Marina Shores Beauty Supply	5087	124
Maple Island Inc	2023	20	March Plasma Systems Inc	3559	209	Marinco	3429	69
Maple Leaf Foods USA Inc	2051	23	Marchel Industries Inc	3965	24	Marine and Industrial Hydraulics Inc	3625	273
Maple Leaf Inc	0259	1	MarChem Coated Fabrics Inc	2821	58	Marine Animals Productions Inc	0752	2
Maple Press Co	2732	10	MarChem Pacific Inc	3089	369	Marine Bank	6020	351
Maple Systems Inc	3625	147	Marchetti Robertson Brickell Insurance Inc	6411	242	Marine Bank FSB	6036	96
Maple Valley Plastics LLC	3089	1083	Marchex Inc	7389	238	Marine Bank Springfield	6022	404
Maplehurst Bakeries LLC	2051	15	Marchon Eyewear Inc	3851	6	Marine Construction and Design Company Inc	3949	157
Maplehurst Farms Inc (Rochelle Illinois)	5191	21	March-Westin Company Inc	1542	184	Marine Container Services Inc	4213	1890
Maples Industries Inc	2273	12	Marcia Davis and Associates Inc	7389	2360	Marine Cross Country Inc	4213	2229
Mapleton Communications	4832	224	Marcive Inc	7372	3192	Marine Electric Company Inc	1731	497
Maplewood Beverage Packers LLC	2086	74	Marc-Michaels Interior Design Inc	7389	890	Marine Electric Systems Inc	3825	165
Maplewood Ice Company Inc	2097	14	Marco Book Company Inc	5192	31	Marine Engineering Systems Company Inc	7389	503
Maplewood Imports	5511	1156	Marco Consulting Group	6282	488	Marine Exchange of Los Angeles-Long Beach Harbor Inc	3625	122
Maplewood Machine Company Inc	3599	2449	Marco Display Specialists Gp LC	2521	12	Marine Hydraulics International Inc	3731	8
Maplewood Packing Inc	5421	16	Marco Fine Arts Galleries Inc	2759	402	Marine Industrial Fabrication Inc	3731	41
Mapp Construction LLC	1542	134	Marco Machine and Design Inc	3599	2214	Marine Medical Inc	5047	169
MapQuest Inc	7389	535	Marco Manufacturing Company Inc	3469	280	Marine Mooring Inc	2394	26
MarcomNordic	2675	5	Marco Molding Inc	3089	1553	Marine Muffler Corp	3089	940
Mapresources	2741	245	Marco Ophthalmic Inc	5048	14	Marine Pollution Control Corp	4213	343
Mapscom	7379	1147	Marco Supply Company Inc	5063	179	Marine Products Corp	3732	14
Maq Investments Group Inc	3544	554	Marco Supply Inc	5013	191	Marine Propulsion Systems Inc	5088	112
MAQ Software	7372	1269	Marcoa Publishing Inc	2741	128	Marine Research Specialists	8731	239
Maquoketa Newspapers Inc	2711	464	MarCole Enterprises Inc	2741	294	Marine Sonic Technology Ltd	3812	177
Maquoketa Valley Rural Electric Coop	4911	457	Marcom LLC	7361	348	Marine Steel Painting Corp	1799	116
Mar Graphics	2752	371	Marcon Marketing Concepts Inc	3089	1200	Marine Systems Technology Inc	8742	718
Mar Leen Inc	7389	1840	Mar-Con Services LLC	1623	300	Marine Technical Services Inc	7699	96
Mar Tek Electronics Inc	3672	364	Marconi Society Inc	4812	131	Marine Technologies Inc	3669	236
Mara Transport Inc	4213	2849	Marco's Inc	5812	157	Marine Terminals of Arkansas Inc	4449	14
Maracay Homes Arizona I LLC	1521	84	Marcum Denver Inc	3827	807	Marine Transport Inc	4213	1146
Maracle Industrial Finishing Company Inc	3471	113	Marcum Electric Inc	1731	348	Marine Travelift Inc	3536	18
Maracom Corp	2752	540	Marcus and Associates Inc	7311	781	Marine Trust Company of Carthage	6022	685
Maracor Software and Engineering Inc	8742	590	Marcus and Millichap Real Estate Investment Brokerage Co	6531	229	MarineMax Inc	5551	2
Maramont Corp	2099	71	Marcus Corp	7011	73	Mariner Software Inc	7372	3835
Maranatha Industries Inc	3663	284	Marcus Paint Co	2891	76	Mariner Software Inc(Minneapolis Minnesota)	7372	3923
Marange Printing Company Inc	2752	742	Marcus Productions Inc	7812	248	Mariner Trading Company Inc	5021	140
Marani Brands Inc	5122	130	Marcus Restaurants Inc	5812	272	Marino Enterprises Inc	3728	171
Marantz America LLC	3651	112	Marcus Thomas LLC	7311	143	Mario Industries Of Virginia Inc	3645	27
			Marcy Design Group Inc	7311	922	Mario Sinacola and Sons Excavating Inc	1794	6
			Mardel Trucking Company Inc	4213	2164			
			Marden Discount Store Inc	5399	3	Marion Computer Technologies LLC	4899	174
			Marden-Kane Inc	8742	299	Marion County Bancshares Inc	6712	383
			Mardinly Enterprises LLC	3599	1878			
			Mardon Manufacturing Co	3541	275			

Company Name	SIC	Rank
Marion County Implement Company Inc	5083	192
Marion Engineering and Technology Inc	5085	330
Marion Ford Tractor Inc	5083	87
Marion Industrial Electric Supply Inc	5063	856
Marion Leigh Corp	7381	87
Marion Metal Products Inc	3441	257
Marion Mixers Inc	3531	169
Marion Mold and Tool Inc	3544	210
Marion Montgomery Inc	7311	240
Marion Plywood Corp	2435	9
Marion Tool and Die Inc	3545	190
Mario's Express Service Inc	4213	2236
Mariotti Building Products Inc	5031	141
Mariplast North America Inc	3089	1732
Mariposa Corp	3053	110
Mariscal Weeks McIntyre and Friedlander	8111	404
Marisco Ltd	3731	38
Marisol Federal Credit Union	6061	149
Maritec Corp	3599	1986
Maritime and Seafood Industry Museum	7389	2026
Maritime Beach Club	6531	448
Maritime Communication Services Inc	3669	91
Maritime Management Services	8741	246
Maritime Pacific Brewing Company Inc	2082	90
Maritz Inc	8742	24
Maritz Performance Improvement Co	7389	31
Maritz Research Inc	8732	14
Maritz Travel Co	4724	3
Marja Corp	3672	425
Marjac Holdings LLC	2015	15
Marjon Specialty Foods Inc	2035	23
Mark - 10 Corp	3823	280
Mark Anderson And Associates Inc	5113	50
Mark Bolles	5734	204
Mark Boyar and Co	6211	330
Mark Bric Display Corp	2541	58
Mark Bst-Pro Inc	3555	40
Mark Chevrolet Inc	5511	952
Mark Corp	2789	61
Mark Custom Recording Service	3695	132
Mark David A Divison Of Baker Knapp and Tubbs	5021	145
Mark Debiase Inc	5047	195
Mark Design Associates	7389	2500
Mark Doman	7374	203
Mark Dri Products Inc	3951	3
Mark Electronics Inc	5065	327
Mark Feldstein and Associates Inc	5044	160
Mark Gordon Co	7384	52
Mark Herlinger Productions	3695	155
Mark I Publications Inc	2711	571
Mark III Systems Inc	7372	2445
Mark Industries Inc	3061	61
Mark Iv Enterprises Inc	7389	1997
Mark IV Graphics Inc	2759	592
Mark IV Industries Inc	3714	30
Mark Line Industries Of Pennsylvania Inc	2451	31
Mark Lithography Inc	2752	811
Mark Maker Company Inc	3953	16
Mark of Fitness Inc	3841	251
Mark of the Unicorn Inc	7372	3140
Mark Olson Electric Inc	1731	1524
Mark One Corp	3549	56
Mark Optics Inc	3827	136
Mark Precision Inc	3599	2135
Mark Ronald Associates Inc	3081	60
Mark Ross and Company International	5141	158
Mark/Ryan Associates Ltd	7361	292
Mark Shale Co	5611	19
Mark/Space Inc	7372	3924
Mark Steel Corp	3443	99
Mark Technology Services	7379	881
Mark Thomas and Company Inc	8711	343
Mark Tool and Die Company Inc	3545	298
Mark Travel Corp	4725	1
Mark/Trece Inc	3555	14
Mark V Systems Ltd	7372	3725
Markal Finishing Company Inc	2672	69
Mar-Kal Products Corp	3999	176
Markco Machine Works Inc	3533	117
Mark-Costello Co	5046	38
Markel Corp	6331	63
Marken Communications Inc	8743	325
Marker Group Inc	7389	875
Marker Security Inc	7382	161
Market America Inc	7389	148
Market Antiques and Homefurnishings Inc	5719	19
Market Builder Inc	7389	1342
Market Channels Inc	7389	1521
Market Dimensions Inc	7372	1399
Market First Inc	7311	539
Market Force Information Inc	8732	62
Market Forge Industries Inc	3469	96
Market Leader Inc	6531	330
Market Line Associates Inc	7371	660
Market Line Computers	7372	3239
Market Logic Inc	7331	92
Market Northwest Inc	5046	253
Market Pathways Financial Relations Inc	8743	226
Market Planning Solutions Inc	7372	2057
Market Profile Theorems Inc	6289	30
Market Resource Partners	7311	155
Market Scan Information Systems Inc	7372	400
Market Strategies Inc	8732	40
Market Strategies International	8732	2
Market Technologies LLC	7372	1677
Market Transport Ltd	4213	248
MarketAxess Holdings Inc	7379	43
Market-Based Solutions Inc	8742	546
MarkeTech Group	8742	542
Marketech International Inc	3441	256
MarketerNet LLC	8742	311
Marketex Computer Corp	5045	541
Marketfare Foods Inc	5142	21
Marketing Affiliates Inc	5074	205
Marketing Alliance Group Inc	2752	63
Marketing Alliance Inc (St Louis Missouri)	6411	223
Marketing Analysts Inc	7389	591
Marketing and Planning Systems	8748	111
Marketing and Research Resources	8732	52
Marketing Art Science	7311	385
Marketing Assistance Inc	7311	847
Marketing Associates Inc	5065	927
Marketing Company Inc	7331	285
Marketing Decision Support Systems Inc	7372	5123
Marketing Design Group	7311	489
Marketing Developments Inc	7311	1047
Marketing Direct Inc	7373	461
Marketing Displays International	3993	24
Marketing Drive Worldwide Inc	7319	21
Marketing Informatics	8999	70
Marketing Management Analytics Inc	7372	250
Marketing Management Services LLC	7311	805
Marketing Products Inc	5731	95
Marketing Research Services Inc	7389	190
Marketing Response Solutions	4813	691
Marketing Services By Vectra Inc	2752	81
Marketing Services Inc	6799	140
Marketing Software Company A California Corp	7374	107
Marketing Support Inc	7311	120
Marketing Team Alpha Inc	2752	1303
Marketing Technology Concepts Inc	7319	52
MarketingSherpa Inc	7389	701
MarketLab Inc	5047	127
MarketLive Inc	7372	1761
MarketMAX Inc	7372	740
Marketplace Direct Inc	7331	147
Marketplace Investors Inc	3674	393
Marketplace Productions LLC	7389	1469
Marketron Broadcast Solutions	7372	97
Marketry Inc	7331	252
MarketSense LLC	7311	194
Marketshare Partners Inc	8742	639
MarketStar Corp	8742	27
MarketTools Inc	7372	3111
Marketware Inc	5734	48
MarketWatch Inc	7375	86
Marketwizz Internet Solutions	7379	1681
Markey's Rental and Staging	5731	33
Markham Broadcasting Inc	4832	264
Markham Machine Company Inc	3599	2115
Markham Vineyards	2084	41
Marki Microwave Inc	3679	484
Markin Tubing LP	3317	42
Marking Services Inc	2679	30
Markland Industries Inc	3751	12
Markley Enterprise Inc	3993	83
Markload Systems Inc	3625	298
Markon Computer Science Inc	7378	159
Markov Processes International LLC	7371	802
Markovitz Enterprises Inc	3462	12
Marks and Salley Inc	7389	1821
Marks Design Group Inc	7389	1822
Mark's Electric Inc	1731	2210
Mark's Machine Company Inc	3599	553
Marks Products Inc	3829	425
Mark's Transportation Inc	4213	763
Markstein Beverage Co	5181	61
Markstein Beverage Company of Sacramento	5181	27
Markwell Manufacturing Company Inc	5072	200
MarkWest Energy Partners LP	1311	30
Markzware Software	7372	2410
Marlabs Inc	7371	68
Marlac Electronics Inc	5065	427
Marlan Tool Inc	3544	727
Marland Mold Inc	3549	38
Marlboro Publishing Co	2711	777
Marlee Manufacturing Inc	3841	231
Marlen International Inc	3556	54
Marley Cooling Technologies	3089	41
Marley-Wylain Co	3585	6
Marlin Blue Systems Inc	7372	2762
Marlin Business Services Corp	7359	20
Marlin Co	8999	120
Marlin Controls Inc	3829	421
Marlin Equity Partners	6282	359
Marlin Holdings Co	5611	30
Marlin Manufacturing Corp	3823	112
Marlin Technologies Inc	3625	176
Marling and Associates Inc	5084	552
Marling Lumber Company Inc	5211	108
Marlite Inc	2542	3
Marlo Electronics Inc	3672	169
Marlo Furniture Company Inc	5712	40
Marlo Incorporated Of Racine Wisconsin	3589	74
Marlo Manufacturing Company Inc	2599	32
Marlo Plastic Products Inc	3089	1589
Marlow Industries Inc	3585	72
Marlow Printing Company Inc	2759	420
Marlow Trucking Company Inc	4213	2895
Marlowe-Van Loan Corp	2869	120
Marmac Co	3569	266
Mar-Mac Manufacturing Company Inc	2389	25
Marmon Group LLC	6722	60
Marnap Industries Inc	2869	121
Maro Display Inc	2542	52
Maro Electronics Inc	3679	620
Maro Precision Tool Co	3545	364
Marocchi Trucking Company Inc	4213	2097
Marocco Construction Company Inc	1623	572
Maroon Development Inc	6552	265
Maroone Chevrolet Inc	5511	160
Marposs Corp	5084	211
Marq Packaging Systems Inc	3565	120
Marquardt Printing Co	2752	1455
Marquardt Switches Inc	3625	28
Marque Dental Laboratory Inc	3843	77
Marque Foods Inc	5143	45
Marquest Financial Inc	6162	71
Marquette Commercial Finance Inc	6141	59
Marquette Grain Systems Inc	5083	211
Marquette National Bank	6021	196
Marquette National Corp	6712	292
Marquette Public Service Garage	5511	736
Marquette Savings Bank (Erie Pennsylvania)	6036	76
Marquette Tool And Die Co	3544	129
Marquette Venture Partners	6799	336
Marquis Corp	3999	70
Marquis Industries Inc	5023	119
Marquis Software Solutions Inc	7379	259
Marquis Yachts LLC	3732	85
Marr Equipment Corp	7353	55
Marr Printing	2752	1107
Marr Scaffolding Co	7353	26
Marr Scaffolding Company Inc	7359	62
Marra Corp	1622	42
Marrakech Housing Options Inc	8361	39
Marra's Pharmacy Inc	5912	43
Marriott International Inc	7011	1
Marriott Worldwide Sales And Marketing Inc	8741	92
Marrlin Transit Inc	4213	445
Marrone and Company Inc	5064	101
Marrs Printing Inc	2752	1846
Mars 2000 Inc	3089	195
Mars Advertising Company Inc	7311	71
Mars Electrical LLC	1731	1648
Mars Inc	2064	1
Mars International Inc	5045	901
Mars Labs LLC	3823	449
Mars National Bank	6021	220
Mars Retail Group Inc	2066	14
Marsden Company Inc	5045	371
Marsden Inc	3567	92
Marsh and McLennan Companies Inc	6411	7
Marsh Aviation Co	3541	166
Marsh C W Co	3053	114
Marsh Creek	1731	2423
Marsh Electronics Inc	5065	101
Marsh Inc	6411	4
Marsh Plating Corp	3471	86
Marsh Pottery LLC	5719	15
Marsh Software Systems Inc	7372	3925
Marsh Supermarkets Inc	5411	84
Marshall and Bruce Co	2752	483
Marshall and Ilsley Bank	6712	446
Marshall and Ilsley Corp	6712	22
Marshall and Ilsley Trust Co	6091	18
Marshall and Stevens Inc	6531	387
Marshall and Sullivan Inc	6282	659
Marshall and Swift/Boeckh	7372	1045
Marshall Cavendish Corp	2731	170
Marshall Communications Inc	8743	155
Marshall Egg Products Inc	2015	74
Marshall Elevator Co	1796	14
Marshall Ford Lincoln Mercury	5511	1091
Marshall Graphics Systems	7372	3273
Marshall Instruments Inc	3823	456
Marshall L H Co	3823	338
Marshall Long Acoustics	7389	2377
Marshall Manufacturing Co	3496	111
Marshall Manufacturing Co (Minneapolis Minnesota)	3599	1965
Marshall Network Services	7379	762
Marshall News Messenger Inc	7383	18
Marshall Optical Systems Inc	3651	41
Marshall Pottery Inc	3269	9
Marshall Publishing Company LLC	2711	782
Marshall Ruby and Sons Inc	3599	2238

Company Name	SIC	Rank	Company Name	SIC	Rank	Company Name	SIC	Rank
Marshall Sample Laboratories Inc	3291	28	Martin Universal Design Inc	5199	115	Marymount Hospital Inc	8062	108
Marshall Steel Inc	3715	53	Martin W Cohen and Company PC	8721	451	Mary's Salads And Produce LLC	5148	85
Marshall-DeKalb Electric Coop	4911	220	Martin Werbelow LLP	8721	47	Marysville Auto Parts Inc	5013	244
Marshall's Electric Inc	1731	857	Martin Wheel Company Inc	3714	303	Marysville Marine Distributors Inc	5088	60
Marshall's Express Inc	4213	2587	Martin Williams	7389	349	Marysville Mutual Insurance Co	6331	363
Marshall's Industrial Hardware Inc	5072	178	Martin Wine's Ltd	5921	9	Marysville Newspaper Inc	2711	631
MarshallSoft Computing Inc	7372	4714	Martinez And Turek Inc	3599	165	Maryvale Day Care Center	8351	15
Marshall-Starke Development Center Inc	8331	137	Martinez Corp	7389	1747	Maryville Technologies Inc	7373	118
Marshalltown Broadcasting Inc	4832	174	Martinez Electronics	3571	210	Marzik Inc	7373	964
Marshalltown Newspaper Inc	2711	399	Martinez Manufacturing Inc	3679	244	Marzuco Electric Inc	1731	1534
Marshalltown Ymca-Ywca	8322	200	Martingale and Co	2731	239	Mas Air Systems Inc	8711	635
Marshallville Packing Company Inc	5421	13	Martin-Harris Construction Enterprises Inc	1541	89	MAS Consulting Inc	7379	850
Marsh-Armfield Of Newton Inc	5169	127	Martinic Engineering Inc	3599	1725	Mas Electrical Services Inc	1731	1756
Marshfield Associates	6282	545	Martin-Marks Minerals LLC	1382	64	MAS Sales Ltd	2099	273
Marshfield Broadcasting Company Inc	4832	180	Martino Industries Inc	3312	129	MAS Systems	3577	547
Marshfield Clinic Inc	8999	9	Martinovich Trucking Inc	4213	1542	Masada Bakery Inc	5149	120
Marshfield Doorsystems Inc	2431	30	Martinrea Metal Industries Inc	5013	414	Masami Foods Inc	2011	64
Marsh-Mcbirney Inc	3823	197	Martin's Bulk Milk Service	4213	439	Masar-Johnston Advertising and Design Inc	7311	716
Marsilli North America Inc	5065	512	Martin's Caterers Inc	5812	330	Mascal Electric Inc	1731	511
Marsoft Inc	7372	2160	Martins Elevators Inc	2048	99	Mascari and Mascari Services Inc	2789	53
Marson and Marson Lumber Inc	5211	126	Martin's Potato Chips Inc	2096	18	Maschhoffs Inc	0213	2
Marspec-Abernaqui-America Corp	3571	181	Martin's Pretzel Bakery	2052	71	Masco Corp	3432	1
Marta Cooperative of America	5064	65	Martin's Specialty Sausage Co	5147	131	Mascoma Corp	8731	89
Martco Inc	5065	226	Martin's Super Markets Inc	5411	50	Mascot Pecan Shelling Company Inc	5148	91
Martco LP	2493	3	Martin-Schaffer Inc	7311	542	Masda Corp	5074	160
Martec International Trading	5088	48	Martin-Smith Publishing Inc	2731	200	Masergy	4899	38
Martec USA LLC	5122	129	Martinson-Nicholls	5099	47	Mashell Telecom Inc	4813	244
Martech Computers	3575	39	Martinsound Inc	8731	382	MASI Ltd	6211	395
Martech Medical Products Inc	3069	57	Martinsville Bulletin Inc	2711	417	Masino Maintenance Corp	7349	451
Martek Biosciences Boulder Corp	8731	170	Martrex Inc	5191	51	Mask Technology Inc	3679	549
Martek Biosciences Corp	2836	7	Martronic Engineering Inc	3699	251	Mask-Off Company Inc	2891	106
Martek Power Inc	3679	121	Martronix Inc	7373	1167	Masland Carpets Inc	2273	13
Martek Power Laser Drive LLC	3679	333	Marts and Lundy Inc	7389	558	Maslon Edelman Borman and Brand LLP	8111	408
Martel Construction Inc	1521	100	Martz and Associates Inc	7311	355	Maslow Media Group Inc	7812	100
Martel Electronics Corp	3825	160	Martz Group	4141	2	Mason and Dixon Truck Lines	4213	261
MarTel International Inc	7389	2313	Marubeni America Corp	5051	4	Mason and Hanger Corp	7349	7
Martel Laboratories JDS Inc	8734	134	Marubeni Disc Systems Inc	3669	251	Mason Box Co	2652	13
Martel Tool Corp	3545	276	Marubeni Specialty Chemicals Inc	5169	33	Mason Companies Inc	5961	97
Martele	5065	1015	Maruchan Inc	2098	4	Mason Corp	3441	93
Marten Models and Molds Inc	3544	606	Maruhide Marine Products Inc	2092	61	Mason County Forest Products LLC	2421	34
Marten Transport Ltd	4213	52	Maruva Technologies Inc	7379	1290	Mason Dental Midwest Inc	8072	11
Martens Cars of Washington Inc	5511	1152	Marvac Scientific Manufacturing Inc	3821	43	Mason Distributors	5122	42
Mar-Test Inc	8734	100	Marval Industries Inc	2869	70	Mason Dixon Farms Inc	2026	70
Martex Software Inc	7373	1181	Marvel Aero International Inc	5063	669	Mason Inc	7311	209
Martexport Inc	5199	108	Marvel Communications Company Inc	3663	194	Mason Industries Inc	3625	54
Martha Pullen Company Inc	5131	51	Marvel Engineering Co	3569	126	Mason Machinings Inc	3541	162
Martha Stewart Living Omnimedia Inc	2721	36	Marvel Entertainment Group Inc	2731	20	Mason State Bank	6022	411
Martha Weems Ltd	7389	1805	Marvel Entertainment LLC	6794	13	Mason Transparent Package Company Inc	2671	64
Martha's Vineyard Mortgage Company LLC	6163	23	Marvel Group Inc	2522	16	Mason Wells	6799	260
			Marvel Manufacturing Company Inc	3425	5	Masonic Home For Children At Oxford Inc	8361	96
Martignetti Cos	5181	10	Marvel Photo Inc	3559	504	Masonry Center Inc	5032	31
Martin Ac Partners Inc	8712	160	Marvel Screw Machine Products Inc	3451	118	Masonry Equipment and Supply Co	5082	167
Martin Advertising Inc	7311	59	Mar-Vel Tool Company Inc	3544	650	Masonry Reinforcing Corporation Of America	3496	29
Martin Agency Inc	7311	44	Marvell Semiconductor Inc	3674	173	Masotta Variety and Deli	5331	17
Martin Aircraft Tool Co	3541	274	Marvell Technology Group Ltd	3674	11	Maspeth Federal Savings	6035	100
Martin and Bayley Inc	5411	19	Marvelous Market Inc	5411	112	Masque Publishing	7371	758
Martin Apparatus Inc	5012	124	Marvin and Palmer Associates Inc	6282	257	Mass Bay Brewing Company Inc	2082	50
Martin Archery Inc	3949	107	Marvin Bill Electric Inc	1731	1333	Mass Computer Systems Inc	5734	287
Martin Automatic Inc	3565	31	Marvin Group	3599	4	Mass Design Inc	3672	192
Martin Automotive Group Inc	5511	82	Marvin K Brown Auto Center Inc	5511	524	Mass Electric Construction Co	1731	22
Martin Bircher, Buller and Flynn PC	8721	216	Marvin Land Systems	5013	47	Mass Mailing Inc	7331	225
Martin Brinkerhoff Associates Inc	7812	142	Marvin Ward Trucking Inc	4213	2204	Mass Web Printing Company Inc	2732	36
Martin Broadcasting Corp	2711	722	Marvin Windows Of Tennessee Inc	2431	31	Massa Products Corp	3679	343
Martin Brothers Distributing Co	5141	34	Marvins Inc	5211	15	Massachusetts Audio Visual Equipment Corp	7359	82
Martin Cadillac Company Inc	5511	118	Marvol USA Corp	5065	476	Massachusetts Capital Resource Co	6799	289
Martin Calibration	5084	226	MarWare	7372	5033	Massachusetts Community Develop-ment Finance Corp	6159	81
Martin Chevrolet Chrysler	5511	549	Marwas Steel Co	3315	22	Massachusetts Continuing Legal Education Inc	8299	67
Martin Chevrolet Inc	5511	1204	Marwell Corp	3613	142	Massachusetts Envelope Company Inc	2759	119
Martin Chevrolet Inc (Torrance California)	5511	1123	Marwest LLC	5088	43	Massachusetts Financial Services Co	6282	91
Martin Electric Company Inc	7694	28	Marwit Capital	6799	236	Massachusetts General Hospital	8062	148
Martin Engineering Co	3829	36	Marx Brothers Inc	2099	311	Massachusetts Lumber Co	6211	363
Martin Fish Company Inc	5146	74	Marx Communications Studios	7812	164	Massachusetts Mutual Life Insurance Co	6311	9
Martin Franchises Inc	6792	3	Marx Layne and Co	8742	343	Massachusetts Technology Develop-ment Corp	6799	331
Martin Francis International Associates Inc	7363	250	MARX Software Security	7372	3407	Massapequa Post	2711	844
Martin George M Co	3554	5	Mary Ann's Chocolate Factory Inc	2066	41	Massaro Electric Corp	1731	2343
Martin Glenn Scott Inc	2759	467	Mary Elizabeth Bourne	2741	487	Massasoit/Tackband Inc	2241	29
Martin Graphics and Printing Services	2741	131	Mary Greeley Medical Center	8062	185	Massey Automotive Group	5511	798
Martin Greenfield Clothiers Ltd	2311	27	Mary Kate Foods	5142	44	Massey Burch Capital Corp	6799	318
Martin Interactive	7311	397	Mary Kay Inc	5963	3	Massey Energy Co	1221	5
Martin K Eby Construction Company Inc	1542	250	Mary Lawrence Corp	5411	225	Massey Hauling Company Inc	4213	739
			Mary Maxim Inc	5199	37	Massey Services Inc	7342	9
Martin Lithograph Inc	2752	614	Mary Of Puddin Hill Inc	2051	299	Massey Wood and West Inc	5172	113
Martin Luther King Jr Community Health Center	8011	115	Mary Spencer Company Inc	5021	180	Massie Manufacturing Inc	3443	225
Martin Marietta Aggregates	1442	2	Mary Thureson	5734	113	Massillon Cable TV Inc	4841	69
Martin Marietta Composites LLC	1499	3	Maryanov Madsen Gordon and Camp-bell PC	8721	71	Massillon-Cleveland-Akronsign Co	3993	61
Martin Marietta Materials Inc	1411	1	Maryhurst Inc	8322	94	Massini Group Inc	7319	134
Martin/Martin Inc	8711	302	Maryl Group Inc	1521	117	Massive Inc	5045	42
Martin Midstream Partners LP	5171	11	Maryland And Virginia Milk Producers Cooperative Association Inc	5143	2	Massive Telecom Inc	4812	60
Martin Oil Co	5171	7	Maryland Ceramics And Steatite Company Inc	3679	477	Massively Parallel Technologies Inc	3679	125
Martin Printing Company Inc	2752	329	Maryland Glass and Mirror Co	5039	45	Massman Automation Designs LLC	3565	93
Martin Publishing Company Inc	2711	738	Maryland Hotel Supply Company Inc	5142	25	Massman Construction Co	1629	53
Martin Resource Management Corp	4924	21	Maryland Industrial Trucks Inc	5084	483	Massman Enterprises Inc	3443	218
Martin Rosol's Inc	2013	238	Maryland Lava Co	3264	20	Mass-Marketing Inc	2741	154
Martin S Abattoir And Wholesale Meats Inc	2011	56	Maryland Marketing Source Inc	8732	83			
Martin Screen Prints Inc	3552	34	Maryland Meggitt Inc	3829	119			
Martin Supply Company Inc	5084	398	Maryland Midland Railway Inc	4011	58			
Martin Thomas Inc	8743	21	Maryland Paper Company LP	2621	49			
Martin Transportation Systems	4213	403	Maryland Plastics Inc	3089	235			
Martin Trucking Inc	4213	1478	Maryland Seafood Inc	2092	43			
			Maryland Thermoform Corp	3089	916			

Company Name	SIC	Rank
MassMutual Premier International Bond S	6722	263
Masson Cheese Corp	2022	46
Massop Electric Inc	5521	9
Massoud Furniture Manufacturing Co	2512	74
Mast Drug Company Inc	5912	35
Mast Trucking Inc	4213	2106
Mastagni Holstedt and Chiurazzi	8111	355
MasTec Inc	1623	2
Mastel Precision Surgical Instruments Inc	3841	362
Masten-Wright Inc	8741	282
Master Appliance Corp	3699	156
Master Automatic Machine Company Inc	3451	26
Master Bond Inc	2891	92
Master Chemical Corp	2992	9
Master Clean Inc	7349	498
Master Communications Inc	7822	15
Master Containers Inc	3086	58
Master Control Inc	7372	2233
Master Control Systems Inc	3629	82
Master Dynamics Of Vacaville	2822	26
Master Electrical Contractors Inc	3648	48
Master Engineering Inc	3537	68
Master Fibers Inc	5093	86
Master Finish Co	3471	46
Master Graphics	2752	1229
Master International Corp	3679	115
Master Key Consulting	8748	157
Master Key Industrial Inc	5065	992
Master Klean Janitorial Inc	7349	75
Master Level Controls Co	3823	413
Master Lock Co	3429	29
Master Machining Inc	3599	1834
Master Maintenance Inc	7349	125
Master Media Systems Inc	5731	137
Master Metal Machining Inc	3599	415
Master Metal Products Co	3444	292
Master Meter Inc	3824	8
Master Mix Co	2891	116
Master Model Makers Inc	3999	199
Master Molded Products Corp	3089	578
Master Plastics Inc	3089	1463
Master Pneumatic-Detroit Inc	3569	136
Master Pontiac Buick GMC Inc	5511	635
Master Precision Machining Inc	3599	1372
Master Precision Products Inc	3544	368
Master Precision Tool Corp	3544	801
Master Print Inc	2752	154
Master Printing Co	2752	1273
Master Recording Supply Inc	3577	391
Master Security Company LLC	7381	38
Master Service Mid-Atlantic Inc	1731	1371
Master Signal Inc	3679	867
Master Solutions Inc	3535	138
Master Solutions LLC	7371	1070
Master Swaging Inc	3728	227
Master Teacher Inc	2741	182
Master Technology Group Inc	1731	874
Master Tool and Die Inc	3544	681
Master Tow Inc	3715	56
Master Translating Services Inc	7389	129
Master Window Systems Inc	3089	1016
Master Workholding Inc	3544	737
Masterbilt Inc	3599	2363
Masterbuilt Manufacturing Inc	3631	4
MasterCard Inc	7389	8
Mastercard International Inc	7389	180
Mastercom Inc	3669	299
Mastercraft Engineering Inc	3469	317
Mastercraft Flooring Distributors Inc	5023	76
Mastercraft Inc	2512	29
Mastercraft Industries Inc	2434	37
Mastercraft Mold Inc	3544	180
Mastercraft Tool and Machine Co	3599	38
Master-Cut Tool Co	3545	350
Mastercut Tool Corp	3545	117
MasterDigital Corp	3695	156
MasterFoods USA Inc	2044	1
Masterform Tool Co	1791	28
Masterline Design and Manufacturing	3568	78
Masterlink Corp	5065	184
Mastermind Marketing Inc	7389	763
Mastermolding Inc	3089	1256
Masterpiece Studios Inc	5112	3
Masterpieces Of Central Florida Inc	7389	2206
Masterplan	7389	389
MasterPlan Financial Software	7372	1135
MasterPlans	8748	294
Masterpress Inc	3679	421
Masterprint Inc	2752	1710
Masters Company Inc	2819	109
Masters Electrical Contractors Association	1731	866
Masters Electrical Services Ltd	1731	271
Masters Machine Co	3541	53
Masters Supply Inc	5085	101
Masterson Company Inc	2087	24
Masterson's Manufacturing Corp	3599	2364
Masterspas Inc	3999	49
Masterstaff Ii Inc	7363	310
Mastertech Security Services Inc	1731	1933
MasterVision Inc	7812	201

Company Name	SIC	Rank
Masterwork Electronics Inc	3672	141
Masterwork Recording Inc	3695	45
Masterworks International Inc	5045	183
Mastery Technologies Inc	7372	520
Mast-Lepley Silo Inc	5083	173
Mastor Telecom Equipment Inc	5999	222
Mastro Graphic Arts Inc	2759	285
Mat Cactus Manufacturing Co	2273	38
Mat Nuwood LLC	2631	34
Mataco	3541	271
Matador Processors Inc	2099	334
Matador Records Inc	7922	35
Matanuska Electric Association Inc	4911	169
Matanzas Creek Winery	2084	79
Matchcom LP	8999	27
Matchless Machine and Tool Company Inc	3544	469
Matchless Metal Polish	2842	43
Matchless Metal Polish Co	2842	76
Matchmaker International	7299	44
Matchmaster Dyeing and Finishing Inc	2269	5
Mat-Co Business Forms Inc	2752	703
MATCO Group Inc	3577	6
Matco Tools Corp	3423	5
MATCOR Inc	3471	118
Mate Co	5045	277
Mate Inc	3715	59
Mate Precision Tooling Inc	3542	13
Matec Instrument Companies Inc	3825	120
Matejcek Implement Co	5083	79
Mater Manufacturing Inc	3669	248
Material Delivery Service	4213	834
Material Fabricators Inc	3053	147
Material Handling Supply Inc	5084	157
Material Handling Systems Inc	5084	460
Material In Motion Inc	8748	259
Material Packaging Corp	3241	12
Material Sand and Stone Corp	5032	183
Material Sciences Corp	3479	8
Material Service Corp	1442	7
Material Testing Technology Co	3829	251
Material Transfer And Storage Inc	3599	1879
Materials and Electrochemical Research Corp	8731	259
Materials and Energy Corp	4953	75
Materials Handling Systems Inc	8711	561
Materials Management Group Inc	7389	479
Materials Research Furnaces Inc	3821	54
Materials Software System Inc	7371	445
Materials Transportation Co	3559	91
Materion Corp	3469	4
Materion Microelectronics and Services	3679	29
Materion Natural Resources Inc	1099	4
Materion Technical Materials Inc	3559	54
Matfer Bourgeat Inc	3556	68
Math Corp	7372	4519
Math Mechanical Inc	1711	279
Mathemaesthetics Inc	7372	4916
Mathematica Inc	8732	17
Matheny Motor Truck Co	5012	46
Mather Hamilton and Co	8721	394
Mathes Electric Supply Company Inc	5063	360
Mathes Of Alabama Electric Supply Company Inc	5063	186
Matheson Fast Freight Inc	4213	546
Matheson Higgins Congress Press Inc	3544	604
Matheson Tri-Gas Inc	2813	4
Matheus Lumber Company Inc	5031	52
Mathew Hall Lumber Co	5211	106
Mathews Associates Inc	3691	21
Mathews Brothers Co	2431	60
Mathews Co	3523	97
Mathews Inc	3949	104
Mathews Ready-Mix Inc	3273	102
Mathews Wire Inc	3496	97
Mathey Dearman Inc	3533	95
Mathias Die Company Inc	3544	262
Mathias Electric and Plumbing Inc	1731	2222
Mathieu Electric Company Inc	1731	1107
Mathiowetz Construction Co	1629	62
Mathis Earnest and Vandeventer	8743	101
MathTensor Inc	7372	2723
MathWorks Inc	7372	112
Mathy Machine Inc	3542	58
Matich Corp	1611	139
MATISSE Software Inc	7372	345
Matlab Inc	2851	67
Matlinpatterson Ata Holdings LLC	4581	13
Matlock and Associates Inc	8743	32
Matlock Electric Company Inc	5063	445
Matous Construction Ii Ltd	1629	78
Matov Industries Inc	3645	83
Matresspro	5021	132
Matrex Mold And Tool Inc	3544	707
Matrix 20 Inc	2752	1664
Matrix Asset Advisors Inc	6282	309
Matrix Automation Inc	5046	95
Matrix Communications Group Corp	1731	117
Matrix Composites Inc	2821	136
Matrix Computers	5734	490
Matrix Controls Company Inc	3823	350
Matrix Drilling Products Co	3532	52
Matrix Essentials Inc	2844	19
Matrix Group International Inc	7374	270

Company Name	SIC	Rank
Matrix Information Consulting Inc	8748	79
Matrix Integration	5045	1070
Matrix Iv Inc	3089	997
Matrix Label Systems Inc	2759	293
Matrix Logic Corp	7372	1070
Matrix Machine And Repair Inc	7699	129
Matrix Mailing LLC	4731	88
Matrix Management Corp	6799	73
Matrix Packaging Machinery Inc	3565	77
Matrix Packaging of Florida Inc	2655	1
Matrix Plus Inc	7372	2724
MATRIX Resources Inc	7363	14
Matrix Separation LLC	3569	198
Matrix Service Co	1799	4
Matrix Service Mid-Continent Inc	3443	200
Matrix Settles	7389	529
Matrix Stream Technologies Inc	3651	201
Matrix Systems Inc	3669	48
Matrix Tool and Machine Inc	3599	1699
Matrix Tooling Inc	3544	256
Matrix Visual Solutions	4899	105
Matrixx Group Inc	5162	37
Matrixx Initiatives Inc	2834	162
Matsch Financial Systems Ltd	7372	4427
Matson Integrated Logistics	4731	32
Matson Lumber Co	2426	14
Matson Navigation Company Inc	4424	5
Matt Construction Corp	8742	348
Matt Construction Services Inc	1541	207
Matt Prentice Restaurant Group	5812	459
Matt Umanov Guitars	5736	19
Mattel Inc	3942	1
Matter Communications Inc	8743	233
Matter of Fax	5731	53
Mattersight Corp	8742	140
Matthew Bender and Company Inc	2731	17
Matthews Automotive Group	5511	1252
Matthews Cremation Div	3567	18
Matthews Four Seasons	2499	19
Matthews Homes	1531	36
Matthews International Corp	3364	1
Matthews International Corp Bronze Div	3364	2
Matthews International Corp (Searcy Arkansas)	3479	115
Matthews Marine Systems Inc	3594	33
Matthews Marks	7311	307
Matthews Paint Co	2851	70
Matthews Printing Company Inc	2752	1363
Matthews Redwood Inc	2499	30
Matthews-Hargreaves Chevrolet Co	5511	703
Matthey Johnson Inc	3341	8
Mattocks Five Inc	5191	181
Mattoon Precision Manufacturing Inc	3714	223
Mattress Firm Holding Corp	2515	24
Mattress Giant Corp	5712	19
Matt's Cash and Carry Building Materials	5211	80
Mattsco Supply Co	5051	382
Mattson Technology Inc	3559	29
Mattson Thermal Products Inc	3674	66
Matuszko Trucking Inc	4213	2007
Matzen Construction Services LLC	1542	60
Matzinger Electric	1731	1562
Matz-Traktman Inc	7338	17
m-Audio	3672	23
Maudlin and Son Manufacturing Inc	3469	346
Maui Condominium and Home Realty Inc	6531	287
Maui Divers Of Hawaii Ltd	3911	4
Maui Electric Company Ltd	4911	119
Maui Land and Pineapple Company Inc	2033	76
Maui Soda and Ice Works Ltd	2086	79
Maui Wowi Inc	6794	139
Mauk Design	7336	245
Maule Air Inc	3721	42
Maumee Pattern Company Inc	3543	33
Maumee Plumbing and Heating Supply Inc	5074	164
Mauna Lani Resort Inc	6552	59
Maupintour LLC	4725	27
Maurer Electric Inc	1731	708
Maurey Instrument Corp	3676	25
Maurice and Maurice Engineering Inc	3334	17
Maurice Lacroix USA	5094	62
Maurice Landstrass	3825	245
Maurice Pincoffs Company Inc	3316	23
Maurice S Dessau Company Inc	3545	182
Maurice Vaughan Inc	5712	112
Maurices Inc	5621	17
Mauro Electric Inc	1731	1634
Maury Boyd and Associates Inc	7389	1668
Maury Microwave Inc	3679	245
Maury Office Systems Inc	2521	52
Mauston Farmers Cooperative Association	5191	49
Mauston Tool Corp	3544	358
Mautino Distributing Company Inc	5181	99
Mavco Inc	5065	341
Mave Enterprises Inc	2064	93
Maven Companies Inc	7379	1606
Mavenspire Inc	7379	1047
Maverick Boat Company Inc	3732	63

Company Name	SIC	Rank	Company Name	SIC	Rank	Company Name	SIC	Rank
Maverick Business Forms Inc	2759	246	Maxxis Corp	5014	24	Mb-F Inc	7331	73
Maverick Communications Inc	1731	858	Maxxon Corporation	5032	89	Mbh Engineering Systems	5084	938
Maverick Construction Corp	1623	140	Maxygen Inc	8731	117	Mbi Associates Inc	7322	167
Maverick Design Inc	3275	8	Maxymillian Technologies Inc	4959	12	Mbi Communications Inc	5064	206
Maverick Industries Inc	3699	130	May and Co	8721	126	MBI Gluckshaw Group	8743	92
Maverick International Inc	3577	429	May Center For Adult Services	8322	160	Mbi Holding Inc	4212	17
Maverick Machine Tool	3599	1942	May Construction Inc	1623	862	MBI Inc	3262	2
Maverick Machinery Company Inc	5932	20	May Exterminating Co	7342	69	MBI International	7372	2375
Maverick Media Holdings LLC	4832	46	May Foundry and Machine Co	3599	422	MBI Publishing Co	2731	93
Maverick Precision Manufacturing Ltd	3599	1209	May Gruhn Inc	1623	732	MBIA Inc	6351	1
Maverick Publications Inc	2731	370	May Star Corp	5072	192	MBIA Insurance Corp	6351	4
Maverick Ranch Natural Meats	5147	4	May Tool And Mold Company Inc	3544	71	MBK Real Estate Ltd	6552	188
Maverick Services Inc	7349	478	May Trucking Co	4213	827	Mbl Associates Inc	7363	311
Maverick Technical Systems Inc	3613	173	May Ventures LLC	5045	643	mBlox Ltd	5045	125
Maverick Technologies	7373	164	Maya Design Inc	7371	894	MBM Corp	5149	3
Maverick Tool Company Inc	3545	359	Maya Gage Co	3544	818	Mbm Engineering Inc	5065	944
Maverick Transportation LLC	4213	183	Maya Group Inc	5092	56	Mbm Industries Inc	2678	17
Maverick USA Inc	4213	161	Mayab Happy Tacos Inc	2041	51	Mbm Logistech LLC	7389	2103
Maverig Freight Inc	4213	2089	Mayacamas Vineyards	2084	129	Mbms Inc	7371	1036
Maverik Country Stores Inc	5541	16	Maybelline New York	2844	6	Mbna Consumer Services Inc	6211	192
Mawson and Mawson Inc	4213	462	Maybrook Corp	5064	195	Mbo Binder and Company Of America	5084	133
Max and Erma's Restaurants Inc	5812	175	Maydao Corp	7389	2521	MBO Precast Inc	3272	107
Max Daetwyler Corp	3599	181	Mayday Communications Inc	5065	617	Mbp Company LLC	2023	33
Max Endura Inc	3589	234	Mayday Manufacturing Co	3728	96	MBR Industries Inc	5065	196
Max Express (Carson California)	4213	2362	Mayer Berkshire Corp	2341	5	MBS Associates Inc	7379	328
Max Foote Construction Company Inc	1623	68	Mayer Brown LLP	8111	5	MBS Dev Inc	8748	244
Max Glide Inc	5734	257	Mayer Cherbonnier and Associates Inc	7371	702	MBS Textbook Exchange Inc	5192	5
Max Group Corp	7372	1152	Mayer Electric Supply Co	5063	33	Mbsiinet Inc	7372	4140
Max Home LLC	2512	39	Mayer Hoffman McCann PC	8721	264	MBSIINet LLC	7372	3274
Max J Derbes Inc	6531	260	Mayer Homes Inc	1521	79	MBT Financial Corp	6712	265
Max J Kuney Co	1542	240	Mayer Tool and Engineering Inc	3544	284	Mbtm Limited Inc	3524	23
Max Machinery Inc	3824	43	Mayer Truck Line Inc	4213	1881	M-B-W Inc	3531	141
Max Media LLC	4833	131	Mayer Wildman Industries Inc	3552	17	Mbw Inc	2679	34
Max Media Of Kentucky	4833	246	Mayers Electric Company Inc	1731	177	Mc Afee Tool and Die Inc	3544	407
Max Optical LLC	5731	253	Mayes Printing Co	5112	47	Mc Allister Industries Inc	2754	37
Max Revenue Solutions Ltd	7322	91	Mayes Testing Engineers	8734	80	Mc Brady Engineering Inc	3556	164
Max Rouse and Sons Inc	7389	904	Mayfair Lumber Co	5211	234	Mc Dride's Research and Machine Inc	3599	1943
Max System Inc	3663	387	Mayfair Window and Door Company LP	3442	100	Mc Clean-Anderson Inc	3559	248
Max Welders Inc	1389	47	Mayfare Software Solutions LLC	7371	1121	Mc Cleary Jp Offshore Construction Inc	1623	664
Maxam Vending Services Inc	7359	197	Mayfield Dairy Farms LLC	2026	17	Mc Com Inc	1731	1739
Maxant Technologies Inc	3829	206	Mayfield Fund	6799	98	MC Communications LLC	8331	12
Maxcam Corp	8748	396	Mayfield Machine and Tool Inc	3599	2112	Mc Cord Crane Service Inc	7353	97
Maxco Inc	5199	29	Mayfield Printing Company Inc	2752	980	Mc Cormack Manufacturing Company Inc	3585	172
Maxco Supply Inc	5113	23	Mayfield Transfer Company Inc	4213	1512	Mc Cormick Motors Inc	5012	140
Maxcor Inc	6719	37	Mayflower Bancorp Inc	6022	458	Mc Cormick's Bindery Inc	2789	64
Maxcy Design	7389	2361	Mayflower Software Inc	7372	1053	Mc Court Manufacturing Inc	2531	44
MaxCyte Inc	2836	55	Mayflower Splint Co	3842	283	Mc Crary Electric Co	1731	747
Maxfield Candy Co	2064	37	Mayflower Tours Inc	4725	11	Mc Cully Mac M Corp	3621	119
Maxi Aids Inc	3841	188	Mayflower Transit LLC	4213	96	Mc Daniel Metals Inc	3444	79
Maxijet Inc	3523	179	Mayfran International Inc	3535	20	MC Davis Company LLC	3677	35
Maxil Technology Solutions Inc	8748	322	May-Han Electric Inc	1731	579	Mc Donald Metal and Roofing Supply Corp	5033	56
Maxim Crane Works	7353	2	Mayhew Breen Productions Inc	7812	278	Mc Donald's Amusements Inc	7993	26
Maxim Douglas	5032	161	Mayhew Steel Products Inc	3423	45	Mc Elwee Electric Inc	1731	2137
Maxim Global Inc	3711	78	Mayhill Publications Inc	2711	395	Mc Equipment Inc	5012	142
Maxim Holding Company Inc	3524	27	Mayline Group	6719	186	M-C Fabrication Inc	3441	156
Maxim Integrated Products Inc	3674	19	Maynard Cooper and Gale PC	8111	338	Mc Gee Pest Control Inc	7342	80
Maxima Group LLC	8742	707	Maynard Group Inc	4813	464	Mc Gervey Electric Inc	1731	2119
Maxima Technologies and Systems LLC	3825	42	Maynard Inc	3469	137	MC Gill Corp	3728	230
Maximation Inc	8742	369	Maynard Precision Inc	3599	49	Mc Grath Press And Graphic Services Inc	2752	1490
Maximized Software Inc	7372	3300	Maynard Software Solutions Inc	7372	5007	Mc Kenney Supply Inc	5063	964
Maximum Communication Inc	1731	1821	Maynard Steel Casting Company Inc	3325	22	Mc Kenzie Brewing Co	2082	75
Maximum Exposure Public Relations	8743	240	Maynard Supply Company Inc	5063	958	MC L Inc	3663	77
Maximum Inc	3829	409	Mayne-Mc Kenney Inc	5013	337	Mc Lelland Tv Inc	5731	176
Maximum Media	7311	596	Mayo Knitting Mill Inc	2252	22	Mc Leod Electric Company Inc	1731	1507
Maximum Technology Corp	7373	821	Mayo Manufacturing Company Inc	7699	240	MC Machinery Systems Inc	3541	32
Maximum Ventures Corp	2731	388	Mayo Manufacturing Corp	2512	53	MC Mieth Manufacturing Inc	3579	64
Maximus Inc	7389	43	Mayon Plastics Inc	3083	87	Mc Millen Inc	7389	1949
Maxis	7372	1247	Mays Byrd and Associates	8111	565	MC Miller Company Inc	3825	177
MaxisIT Inc	8748	208	Mays Chemical Company Inc	5169	30	Mc Minnville Molding Company Inc	3089	1274
MaxIT Corp	7372	2999	May's Drug Stores Inc	5912	20	MC Molds Inc	3089	1203
Maxitrol Co	3612	11	Mays Meats Inc	5149	74	Mc Neal Industries Inc	5085	312
Maxium Performance LLC	5091	105	Mays-Shedd Sales Co	5084	656	MC Pack Inc	7389	1203
MaxLinear Inc	3669	44	Maysteel LLC	3444	2	MC Parcel Delivery Inc	4213	2090
Maxmar Controls Inc	3699	260	Maytag Aircraft Corp	5172	116	Mc Pherson Industrial Corp	3545	144
Maxmedia Of Pennsylvania LLC	4832	196	Maytag Dairy Farms Inc	2022	58	Mc Pherson Plastics Inc	3089	811
MaxMpact	5044	152	Mayville Die and Tool Inc	3544	460	MC Systems Inc	3674	443
MAXON Computer Inc	7372	689	Mayville Engineering Company Inc	3469	15	MC Tank Transport Inc	4213	2448
Maxon Furniture Inc	2521	17	Maywood Printing Company Inc	2752	1676	MC Test Service Inc	3672	17
Maxon Industries Inc	3531	178	Mazak Corp	3541	6	MC Van Kampen Trucking Inc	4213	444
Maxon Lift Corp	5084	237	Mazda Research And Development Of North America Inc	8711	433	MC Ward Inc	3544	313
Maxons Restorations Inc	1751	6	Mazer's Discount Home Centers Inc	5211	125	Mc2 Security Inc	7381	31
Maxson Automatic Machinery Co	3554	33	Mazon Associates Inc	6153	29	MC2 Studios Inc	7371	557
Maxstream Inc	4812	65	Mazza Electric Corp	1731	1852	MCA Communications Inc	1731	289
Maxtek Components Corp	3674	167	Mazzarelli's Bakery Inc	5149	205	MCA Computer Corp	5045	716
Maxton Motors Inc	5511	1195	Mazzetta Co	5146	9	MCA Inc (Mountain View California)	8743	249
MaxTorque LLC	3599	1196	Mazzio's Corp	6794	6	MCA Solutions Inc	7371	292
Maxtrol Corp	3625	224	M-B Companies Inc	3531	47	Mcabee Construction Inc	1541	75
Maxum Development Corp	7372	4002	Mb Dynamics Inc	3829	234	McAdams Graphics Inc	2752	132
Maxus Energy Corp	1311	47	MB Financial Bank NA	6035	19	McAdams Wright Ragen Inc	6211	91
MaxVision Corp	3571	152	MB Financial Inc	6712	73	McAfee Inc	7372	23
Maxwell Bakery Inc	2051	291	Mb Holdings Inc	3562	42	Mcalister Design Inc	7371	1488
Maxwell Electrical Services Inc	1731	235	MB Kahn Construction Company Inc	1541	46	Mcallen Medical Center LP	8062	103
Maxwell Hardwood Inc	2426	16	MB Productions Inc	7359	171	McAllister	1711	189
Maxwell Resources Inc	7372	4383	M-B Products Inc	3442	123	McAllister Equipment Co	5082	97
Maxwell Systems Inc	7372	1771	MB Real Estate	6552	158	Mcallister Machine Inc	3599	2110
Maxwell Technologies Inc	3671	4	MB Software and Consulting Inc	7372	4314	McAllister Towing and Transportation Company Inc	4492	9
Maxwell Technologies Systems Division Inc	8731	67	MB Visnic Custom Homes	1521	134	McAndrews Held and Malloy Ltd	8111	579
Maxwell Welding And Machine Inc	3441	220	MBA Holdings Inc	6411	274	McArthur Business Systems Inc	7372	4715
MAXXAM Inc	3334	11	MBA Software and Consulting	7372	4520	Mcb Collection Services Inc	7322	125
MAXXAM Property Inc	2411	3	MBC Applied Environmental Sciences	8731	354	MCBA Inc	7372	563
Maxxar Corp	3577	325	MBE Electric Inc	1731	1459			
Maxxess Systems Inc	5045	642	MBE Inc	4212	56			

Company Name	SIC	Rank
McBain Systems	5047	81
Mcbc Holdings Inc	3732	27
Mcbee Supply Corp	5013	154
McBride and Associates Inc	7373	366
McBride and Shoff Inc	3599	1173
McBride and Son Enterprises Inc	1531	40
McBride and Son Homes Inc	1531	27
McBride Construction Resources Inc	1542	87
McBride Distributing Co	5181	58
Mcbride Quality Care Services Inc	8361	95
Mcbride Stone Company Inc	3281	57
Mcbroom Electric Company Inc	7694	8
MCC Aviation Services Inc	6159	85
MCC Broadcasting Company Inc	4832	201
MCC Group LLC	1711	41
Mcc Inc	3273	49
McCabe and Associates Inc	7372	1210
McCadam Cheese Company Inc	2022	20
McCaddon Cadillac Buick GMC Truck	5511	1117
Mccaffery and Ratner Inc	7311	559
McCahan Helfrick Thiercof and Butera Accountancy Corp	8721	205
Mccain Inc	3669	83
Mccain Printing Company Inc	2752	861
Mccall Farms Inc	2033	67
Mccall Of The Wild Inc	2452	38
McCall Oil and Chemical Co	5171	19
Mccall Service Inc	0782	9
McCallie Associates Inc	7372	1773
Mccall's Incorporated Of Johnsonville SC	5075	16
Mccallum and Associates Inc	7338	58
Mccallum Print Group Inc	2759	110
McCallum Transfer Inc	4213	2363
McCamish Systems LLC	6311	154
McCammon Trucking Inc	4213	2419
McCann Electronics	7699	94
McCann Industries Inc	5082	54
Mccann Plastics Inc	3087	11
McCann-Erickson Inc	7311	22
McCann-Erickson Worldwide Inc	7311	2
Mccann-Southworth Printing Co	2752	1329
McCaren Designs Inc	0781	23
Mccarley Electric Inc	1731	1225
Mccartan	7389	2314
McCarter and English	8111	69
McCarthy Building Companies Inc	1541	3
McCarthy Improvement Co	1611	107
McCarthy Morse Chevrolet Inc	5511	425
McCarthy Tire Service Co	7538	6
Mccarthy's Shops Inc	5085	355
Mccartney's Inc	5021	94
Mccarty Printing Corp	2791	11
McCaskey Co	5063	297
Mccauley Brothers Inc	2048	120
McCauley Propeller Systems	3728	67
Mccauley Sound Inc	3651	139
McCauley Trucking Co	4213	1399
Mccizer Pipeline Inc	1623	499
Mcclafferty Printing Co	2752	634
Mcclain Printing Co	2752	1562
Mcclain S Stone Company Inc	5999	195
McClain's RV Inc	5561	6
McClatchy Brothers Inc	4213	1715
McClatchy Co	2711	22
McCleary/German Associates Inc	8712	290
Mccleary Inc	2096	22
McClellan Truck Lines	4213	2315
McClendon Corp	7363	62
Mcclendon Electrical Services	1731	883
McClesky Mills Inc	5159	11
McClinton Chevrolet Company Inc	5511	729
McClinton-Anchor Div	2951	13
Mcclung Printing Inc	2752	993
Mcclung-Logan Equipment Company Inc	5082	71
McClure Co	1711	31
McCluskey Chevrolet-Geo Inc	5511	292
McClymonds Supply and Transit Company Inc	4213	134
McCollister's Transportation Systems	4213	218
Mccomb Electric Supply Company Inc	5063	874
McCombs Enterprises Inc	7538	2
McConnell Budd and Romano Inc	6282	354
Mcconnell Grading And Utilities and Co	1623	704
McConnell Heavy Hauling Inc	4213	1254
McConway and Torley Group	3325	43
McCook Public Power District	4911	505
Mccorkle Reporting Co	7338	32
McCormick Advertising Agency	7311	283
McCormick and Company Inc	2099	4
Mccormick and Schmick Holding Corp	5812	191
McCormick and Schmick Holdings LLC	5812	117
McCormick Computer Resale	5045	299
Mccormick Computer Resale Inc	5045	571
McCormick Construction Management Co	8741	117
Mccormick Distilling Company Inc	2085	16
Mccormick International USA Inc	5083	90
McCormick Paints	7549	4
Mccormick Place Convention Center	7389	579
McCormick Systems Inc	7372	2084
Mccormick-Armstrong Company Inc	2752	435
McCormick's Enterprises Inc	5139	16

Company Name	SIC	Rank
McCorriston Miller Mukai MacKinnon	8111	392
Mccorvey Sheet Metal Works LP	3444	32
Mccoun and Associates Inc	6531	440
Mccourt Label Cabinet Co	2752	497
Mccowat-Mercer Packaging Inc	2657	37
Mccoy Associates Inc	5063	1099
McCoy Corp	5211	16
McCoy Group Inc (Shullsburg Wisconsin)	4213	270
Mccoy Investments Inc	5082	142
McCoy Transport Inc	4213	2936
McCoy-Mills Ford Inc	5511	580
McCracken Financial Solutions Corp	7372	2558
McCracken Motor Freight Inc	4213	1851
McCracken Oil and Propane Co	5171	64
Mccraken Electric Inc	1731	1423
Mccray Press	3089	1776
McCrea Equipment Company Inc	1711	60
Mccreary Modern Inc	2512	22
McCrone Inc	8711	498
Mccrorie Group LLC	2499	34
McCrory Construction Company LLC	1541	115
McCue Corp	3599	158
Mccullers Investments Inc	7349	172
McCulley Cuppan LLC	8748	307
Mccullough Creative Inc	7336	266
Mccullough Crushing Inc	1423	5
Mccullough Electric Company LLC	1731	2101
Mccullough Industries Inc	3537	88
Mccurdy Tool and Machining Co	3544	290
Mccusker-Gill Inc	1761	25
Mccutcheon Apple Products Inc	2099	326
MCD International Inc	1731	1313
Mcdal Corp	1796	29
Mcdaniel Electric Corp	1731	888
McDaniel Fire Systems Inc	1731	343
McDaniel Motor Co	5511	602
Mcdavid Knee-Guard Inc	3842	135
Mcdermott Associates Inc	5599	25
McDermott International Inc	3443	1
McDermott Will and Emery	8111	68
McDevitt and Andreason	8721	485
Mcdiarmid Controls Inc	1731	1226
McDonald and Eudy Printers Inc	2752	433
McDonald Automotive Group	5511	110
Mcdonald Electric Service Inc	1731	2005
McDonald Lumber Company Inc	5031	286
McDonald Sanders PC	8111	425
Mcdonald Steel Corp	3312	77
Mcdonald Technologies International Inc	3672	37
McDonald Toole and Wiggins PA	8111	473
McDonald's Corp	5812	1
Mcdonald's Meats Inc	5147	120
Mcdonald's Restaurants Of Florida Inc	5812	186
Mcdonald's Restaurants Of Michigan Inc	5812	172
McDonnell Douglas Helicopter Co	3721	14
Mcdonough Associates Inc	8711	357
Mcdonough Democrat Inc	2752	1695
Mcdonough Holdings Inc	2431	24
McDonough Power Coop	4911	330
McDowell and Craig Manufacturing Co	2522	22
McDowell Rice Smith and Buchanan PC	8111	383
Mcdowell Valley Vineyards Inc	0172	21
Mcduff Designs Inc	7336	323
Mcduffie County Newspapers Inc	2711	837
McElroy Deutsch Mulvaney and Carpenter LLP	8111	333
Mcelroy Manufacturing Inc	3559	66
Mcelroy Metal Mill Inc	3448	7
Mcenroe Voice and Data Corp	5045	553
Mcentee Broadcasting Of Florida Inc	4832	153
McEwen Trucking Inc	4213	2613
Mcf Services Inc	1731	458
MCF Software LLC	7372	5159
Mcfadden Farm	0112	1
Mcfadden Lighting Company Inc	3646	65
Mcfadden Machine and Manufacturing Co	3569	240
McFarland and Company Incorporated Publishers	2731	63
McFarland Cascade	2491	2
McFarland Hanson Inc	8742	430
McFarland Truck Lines	4213	1118
Mcfarlands Inc	7699	265
Mcfarling Foods Inc	5147	26
McFeely's Co	5961	123
MCG Capital Corp	6799	53
Mcg Electronics Inc	3674	302
MCG Global LLC	6799	274
MCG Inc	3621	28
MCG LLC	8748	380
Mcgaha Electric Company Inc	1731	1181
Mcgard LLC	5072	78
McGaw Graphics	2754	4
McGean Inc	2899	66
McGeary Organics Inc	5153	111
Mcgee Corp	3448	34
McGee Group Inc	5048	17
Mcgill Corp	3564	39
McGill Smith Punshon Inc	8711	288
Mcginnis Brothers Inc	7699	116

Company Name	SIC	Rank
Mcginnis Inc	4491	11
McGinnis Lochridge and Kilgore LLP	8111	427
McGinnis Lumber Company Inc	5031	292
Mcginnis Protective Services Inc	7381	251
McGladrey and Pullen LLP	8721	2
McGlinchey and Associates Inc	7311	717
McGlinn Capital Management Inc	6282	211
McGoodwin Williams and Yates Inc	8711	321
McGough Construction Co	1542	68
McGowan Electric Supply Inc	5063	109
McGranahan Carlson and Co	6552	272
McGrath Electric Inc	1731	1211
McGrath/Power Public Relations Inc	8743	257
McGrath Rentcorp	7359	26
Mcgraw Communications Inc	4813	162
McGraw Group Of Affiliated Cos	6411	25
McGraw/Kokosing Inc	1541	313
McGraw-Hill Companies Inc	2731	1
McGraw-Hill Construction	2731	22
McGraw-Hill Contemporary Learning Series	2731	160
McGraw-Hill Education	2731	6
McGraw-Hill Higher Education	2731	18
McGraw-Hill/Osborne Media	2731	128
Mcgreevy's Midwest Meat Co	5142	36
Mcgregor-Surmount Corp	3629	35
Mcgriff Industries Inc	7534	3
McGriff Transportation Inc	4213	727
Mcgrory Inc	2541	38
Mcguire Furniture Company Inc	2519	6
Mcguire Industries Inc	7353	111
McGuire Transportation Inc	4213	1950
McGuire-Nicholas Company Inc	3199	7
McGuireWoods LLP	8111	76
McGuyer Homebuilders Inc	1531	30
Mchal Corp	3542	110
McHenry Metals Golf Inc	3949	173
McHone Industries Inc	3312	120
McHone Trucking Inc	4213	2999
McHugh Enterprises Inc	1611	18
MCI Sales and Service Center	6719	62
MCI Service Parts Inc	5013	10
Mcilvaine Co	2741	383
McIlvaine Trucking Inc	4213	1622
McIlvaine Trucking International	4213	938
McInnis Brothers Construction Inc	1542	246
Mcinnis Consulting Services Corp	7379	685
McIntosh Controls Corp	3823	287
McIntosh Farm Service Co	2041	56
Mcintyre Softwater Service	3589	225
Mcjak Candy Company LLC	2064	113
McJunkin Red Man Holding Corp	5085	2
MCK Communications Inc	7372	1514
Mckamish Inc	1711	119
Mckay Acquisition Inc	3462	49
Mckay Auto Parts Inc	5013	117
McKay Press Inc	2752	244
McKean Defense Group LLC	8748	73
McKeany-Flavell Company Inc	6221	12
Mckee Communitions Inc	3663	339
McKee Foods Corp	2051	4
McKee Group	6552	179
McKee Network Inc	8748	462
Mckee Wallwork Cleveland LLC	7311	297
McKeever Services Corp	7389	2318
McKelvey Homes LLC	1521	102
McKelvey Trucking Co	4213	521
Mckenna Professional Imaging	7384	9
McKenna Storer Rowe White and Farrug	8111	602
Mckenzie and Associates Electrical LLC	1731	982
Mckenzie Compressed Air Solutions Inc	5075	44
Mckenzie Handling Systems Inc	5084	804
McKenzie of Vermont	2013	140
Mckenzie River Broadcasting Inc	4832	129
Mckenzie Sports Products LLC	3949	72
Mckenzie Tank Lines Inc	4213	330
Mckeon Products Inc	3842	219
McKeough Land Company Inc	6552	170
McKesson Corp	5122	1
McKesson Health Solutions	7389	351
McKesson Medical-Surgical	3841	19
Mckesson Packaging Services	7389	1509
Mckey Perforating Company Inc	3469	160
McKim and Creed PA	8711	374
McKinley Communications Inc	7311	465
Mckinley Equipment Corp	5084	320
McKinley Trucking Company Inc	4213	585
Mckinney and Mckinney Technical Services Inc	7371	961
Mckinney Drilling Co	1794	1
McKinney Partnership Architects	8712	240
McKinnon and Mooney Inc	6411	215
McKinnon Associates	0781	24
Mckinnon Enterprises	2721	364
McKinsey and Company Inc	8742	5
Mckinsey Steel and Supply Of Florida Inc	5051	514

Company Name	SIC	Rank
Mckinstry Company LLC	1711	50
McKissick Trucking of Ohio Inc	4213	3042
McKlim Milk Transit Inc	4213	640
McKonly and Asbury	8721	89
Mckowski's Maintnce Systems Inc	7349	154
MCL Cafeterias Inc	5812	138
McL Cos	6552	109
Mcl Industries Inc	8748	338
Mclain Electric Company Inc	1731	2062
Mclanahan Corp	3532	17
McLane Advanced Technologies LLC	8741	126
McLane Company Inc	5141	6
McLane Foodservice Distribution	5141	19
McLane Foodservice Inc	5141	8
McLane Livestock Transport Inc	4213	1316
McLane Manufacturing Inc	3524	15
Mclarand Vasquez Emsiek and Partners Inc	8712	173
Mclaren Industries Inc	3011	20
McLaren Performance Technologies Inc	8711	359
McLarty Auto Mall	5511	790
McLaughlin and Moran Inc	5181	28
McLaughlin Associates Corp	7389	1044
Mclaughlin Body Co	3713	27
McLaughlin Delvecchio and Casey Inc	7311	962
Mclaughlin Gormley King Co	2879	23
Mclaughlin Group Inc	3545	75
Mclean and Mclean Security and Intercom Inc	5065	765
McLean Contracting Co	1629	59
McLean County Truck Company Inc	5012	49
Mclean Implement Inc	5083	14
Mclean Industries Inc	2752	1138
McLean Koehler Sparks and Hammond	8721	376
McLean Media	2741	481
Mclean Packaging Corp	2652	8
Mclellan Equipment Inc	3713	57
Mclellan Temporaries Inc	7363	323
McLemore Building and Maintenance Inc	7349	15
McLendon Co	5149	170
McLendon Hardware Inc	5251	9
Mcleod Belting Company Inc	2399	30
McLeod Express LLC	4213	725
McLeod Inc	4213	2125
Mcleod Machine Works Inc	3599	2215
Mcloone Metal Graphics Inc	2759	148
Mcm Composites LLC	3089	777
MCM Construction Inc	1622	16
Mcm Corporation Of Oneida	3599	1012
MCM Environmental Technologies Inc	3999	141
Mcm Integrated Systems Inc	7382	88
Mcm Systems Inc	3625	357
McMahon Associates Inc	8711	159
McMahon Ford Inc	5511	1212
McMahon Group	8711	182
McManus Microwave	3679	798
McMaster-Carr Supply Co	5961	42
Mcmenamins Inc	5813	2
Mcmichael Mills Inc	2241	22
Mcmillan Brothers Electric Inc	1731	108
Mcmillan Electric Co	3621	65
Mcmillan Fiberglass Stocks Inc	3089	1106
Mcmillan Study Guides Inc	1731	2379
McMillan Transport Inc	4213	3013
Mcmillan's Mechanical and Machine Company Inc	3599	824
McMillin Commercial	1541	37
McMillin Homes	1521	11
McMillin Mortgage	6162	41
Mcminnville Manufacturing Co	2426	31
Mcminnville Tool and Die Inc	3469	286
McMoran Exploration Co	1311	60
McMullen Air Conditioning and Refrigeration Service	1711	223
Mcmunn Associates	2721	376
McMurray Fabrics Inc	2257	2
Mcmurry Publishing Inc	2721	130
McMurry Ready Mix Co	1611	71
McMurtrey/Whitaker and Associates Inc	7372	2928
Mcnab Inc	3812	157
McNally Industries Inc	3599	272
McNally Temple Associates Inc	7311	493
Mcnamed Inc	7352	46
Mcnaughton and Gunn Inc	2732	17
Mcnaughton Newspapers	2711	413
McNaughton-McKay Electric Company Inc	5063	32
McNay Truck Line	4213	863
Mcnc	8731	258
McNeal Enterprises Inc	3599	590
McNees Wallace and Nurick	8111	334
Mcneil and Nrm Intl Inc	3559	90
Mcneil Industries Inc	3366	15
McNeil Technologies Inc	7389	372
Mcneill Sound and Security Systems	1731	1993
McNeilus Companies Inc	3531	14
McNell-Wilson Communications Inc	8743	26
Mcnichols Co	5051	71
McNish Corp	6719	149
M-Co Construction Inc	1623	388
MCO Transport Inc	4213	1283
Mcot Inc	7322	174

Company Name	SIC	Rank
Mcp Company Inc	2796	37
Mcp Computer Products Inc	5045	731
Mcp Industries Inc	3069	55
McPhail Fuel Co	5064	83
Mcpherson Inc	3826	108
Mcpherson Manufacturing Corp	3053	76
McQ Productions	7372	4716
McQuay International	3585	17
McQuay of Georgia LLP	3585	147
McQueeny-Lock Co	5251	25
McQuerter Group Inc	8743	178
McQuiddy Printing Co	2752	255
Mcr Technologies Inc	5734	148
McRae Agency	8743	283
McRae Industries Inc	3149	15
McRae Software International Inc	7372	5095
McRee Ford Inc	5511	182
Mcrobert's Protective Agency Inc	7382	110
McRyan Hauling Inc	4213	871
MCS Group Inc	7389	101
MCS Management Corp	7372	3416
Mcs Of Tampa Inc	1731	92
McShane Enterprises Inc	5087	30
Mcshares Inc	2041	31
Mcshelle National Inc	7373	1126
McStain Neighborhoods	1522	34
Mcsweeney's Inc	3532	32
Mct Industries Inc	3715	22
MCT Worldwide Inc	3825	84
McTyre Trucking	4213	1624
McVay Brothers Siding and Windows	3089	174
McVay Drilling Co	1381	46
Mcwilliams Fluid Connectors Inc	5085	399
Mcx Inc	3544	532
MCZ Development	6552	93
MD Anderson Cancer Center	8069	20
M-D Building Material Company Of Illinois Inc	5031	226
M-D Building Products Inc	3442	38
MD Buyline Inc	8748	461
Md Electric Co	1731	788
MD Holdings LLC	3556	189
MD Miller Trucking Inc	4213	2937
MD Moody and Sons Inc	5082	140
MD On-Line Inc	7372	3156
MD Solutions Inc	7372	4125
MD Stetson Company Inc	2841	33
MD Systems/Clair Brothers	7389	343
Md7 LLC	7389	996
MDA Leadership Consulting	8049	25
Mdb Group Inc	2759	421
MDC Holdings Inc	1531	23
Mdci	3699	219
Mdco Inc	3670	761
Mde Corp	5084	391
Mde International Inc	8734	42
Mdf Tool Corp	3544	795
MDG Computer Services Inc	7371	623
Mdg Studio Inc	5045	1028
Mdh Acquisition LLC	3363	38
MDI Achieve Inc	7372	328
MDI Electrical Construction Inc	4899	116
MDI Entertainment Inc	7999	92
Mdi Imaging and Mail LLC	8742	497
MDI Inc	3861	41
Mdi Products LLC	3089	633
MDI Security Systems	3699	62
MDJ Inc	7379	1173
MDK Inc	7699	202
MDM Inc	3552	63
Mdm Scaffolding Services Inc	1799	148
Mdp Contracting Inc	7353	102
MDR Equipment Transportation	4213	2976
MDS Disk Service	7379	991
MDS Manufacturing Inc	3523	155
Mds Pharma Services Us Inc	8731	102
MDSS Inc	7372	506
MDU Communication International Inc	4899	99
MDU Resources Group Inc	4932	6
MDVip Inc	8011	4
ME C Inc	1731	778
ME Companies Inc	1611	116
Me Global Inc	3325	18
ME Neuber Industrial Diamonds Company Inc	3545	351
ME Pfahler Construction Inc	1731	1033
ME Productions	7389	1533
ME Thompson Inc	2099	57
ME Wilson Company Inc	6331	322
Mead Industries Inc	3599	2486
Mead Johnson Nutrition Co	2833	2
Mead Metals Inc	5051	279
Mead Technologies Inc	2869	125
Meade And Shepherd Coal Company Inc	1522	50
Meade County Rural Electric	4911	423
Meade Electric Company Inc	1731	64
Meade Group Inc	5511	184
Meade Instruments Corp	3827	27
Meaden Precision Machined Products Co	3451	50
Meador Staffing Services Inc	7361	69
Meadow Brook Dairy Co	2026	43
Meadow Creek Truck Supply Inc	5013	319

Company Name	SIC	Rank
Meadow Park Land Co	6552	277
Meadow Valley Corp	1623	14
Meadowbrook Furniture Inc	2512	72
Meadowbrook Golf Group Inc	8742	98
Meadowbrook Insurance Group Inc	6331	134
Meadowbrook Inventions Inc	3952	15
Meadowbrook Machine and Tool Inc	3531	174
Meadowbrook Orchards Inc	0175	8
Meadow-Farms Sausage Co	2013	158
Meadowland Farmers Coop	5153	116
Meadowlands Bindery Inc	2789	68
Meadows Holdings LP	8062	238
Meadows Mills Inc	3553	47
Meadows Office Furniture Co	5712	54
Meadows Publishing Solutions Inc	7372	4944
Meadowvale Inc	2023	34
Meadville Forging Co	3462	13
Meadville New Products Inc	3089	1825
MeadWestvaco Containerboard	2631	11
MeadWestvaco Corp	2621	2
Mean Machine Computers	3571	247
Mears Transportation Group	4111	6
Mearthane Products Corp	3089	630
Measurement and Control Systems Inc	7371	1685
Measurement Computing Corp	3577	356
Measurement Inc	2752	27
Measurement Research Inc	3577	663
Measurement Specialties Inc	3829	12
Measurement Systems Intl Inc	3596	7
Measurement Systems Technology	3825	363
Measurement Techniques Inc	7372	4315
Measurement Technology Northwest Inc	3823	276
Measurementation	3823	354
Measurements International Inc	3829	516
Measurements Technology Inc	3571	237
Meat Handler Co	7372	4521
Meat-O-Mat Corp	2013	245
Meats Plus Inc	2011	63
MEC Analytical Systems Inc	8734	43
M-E-C Co	3441	61
MEC Technologies Inc	3674	295
Mec Water Resources Inc	8711	655
Meca Electronics Inc	3679	304
Mecco Partners LLC	3953	24
Meccon Industries Inc	1711	68
Meccor Industries Ltd	1622	37
Mechanical Control Systems	3829	462
Mechanical Designs Of Virginia Inc	3599	1268
Mechanical Development Company Inc	3545	77
Mechanical Device Co	3599	1551
Mechanical Engineering Controls Automation Corp	8711	654
Mechanical Equipment Company Inc	3589	68
Mechanical Products Manufacturing Company LLC	3441	46
Mechanical Rubber Products Co	3053	133
Mechanical Safety Equipment Corp	3842	253
Mechanical Servants Inc	5122	69
Mechanical Supply Co	5074	132
Mechanical Technology Inc	3829	172
Mechanical Tool and Engineering Company Inc	3594	10
Mechanical Transplanter Company LLC	3523	196
Mechanics and Farmers Bank	6022	508
Mechanized Enterprises Inc	3559	494
Mechanized Science Seals Inc	3829	278
Mechdyne Corp	3577	230
Mechling Computers and Communications Networking	3571	248
Mech-Tronics Corp	3444	149
Mecklenburg Electric Coop	4911	406
Meckley's Limestone Products Inc	1422	21
Meco Corp	3631	10
Mecosta Osceola Area Rehabilitation Center	8322	137
Mecpro Inc	3599	1514
MECS Global	1541	80
Mectron Engineering Company Inc	3826	90
Med Air Inc	5088	103
Med Associates Inc	3826	62
Med Bus Inc	7389	1742
Med Com Inc	7389	1973
Med Evolve Inc	8742	583
Med Services Inc	3845	21
Med Share Inc	5047	123
Med Supply Cabinet Inc	5047	258
Med1Online Inc	5047	208
Med3000	8099	36
Med7 Urgent Care Center Medical Group	8011	137
MedAdvantage Inc	6321	52
MedAiro Inc	8059	16
Medalcraft Mint Inc	3469	157
Medallia Inc	7371	249
Medallion Cabinetry Inc	2434	29
Medallion Financial Corp	6726	36
Medallion Homes Inc	1521	160
Medallion Instrumentation Systems LLC	3714	265
Medallion Lighting Corp	3645	62
Medaptus Inc	7379	898
Medart Inc	3089	1238
Medart Inc (Fenton Missouri)	5013	39

Company Name	SIC	Rank
MedAssets Inc	7372	139
MedAssurant Inc	7372	67
Medax International Inc	5049	95
MedBillsAssist	6411	294
MedCath Corp	8062	116
MedcenterdirectCom Inc	4813	253
Medco Health Solutions Inc	5912	3
Medcom Inc	7812	81
Medcom Information Systems Inc	7372	2680
MedCom USA Inc	7372	3394
Medcomsoft	7371	10
Medcor Inc	8099	53
Medcost LLC	8011	74
Med-Craft Inc	5088	71
MedData	7379	160
Medeanalytics	7389	162
MED-E-CELL	3842	318
Medecins Sans Frontieres USA Inc	8399	9
MEDecision Inc	7372	750
Medeco Security Locks Inc	3499	25
MedeFinance Inc	7372	940
Medela Inc	5047	108
Medelco Inc	3559	392
Medelez Inc	4213	1423
Medennium Inc	3851	70
Medex Assistance Corp	8099	75
MEDEX Global Group Inc	6324	93
Medflow Inc	7371	756
Medfone Nationwide Inc	7363	163
Medforce Inc	7363	218
Medford Cooperative Inc	5191	33
MEDformatics Inc	7372	4980
Medgyn Products Inc	5047	151
Medi Group Ltd	7372	4249
Medi Manufacturing Inc	3842	188
Media 100 Inc	3577	246
Media Blast and Abrasive Inc	3589	248
Media Breakaway LLC	7331	36
Media Captioning Services Inc	7379	1055
Media Circus Inc	3695	183
Media City Teleproduction Center	7819	60
Media Communication Inc	7812	119
Media Computing Inc	7372	2654
Media Crew	7311	739
Media Cybernetics Inc	7372	2585
Media Design Inc	1731	1175
Media Entertainment Inc	7812	245
Media Etc	7379	1665
Media Event Concepts Inc	7389	1118
Media Evolved LLC	3695	31
Media Flex Inc	7372	3244
Media Fx Technologies Inc	7371	1170
Media General Broadcasting of South Carolina Holdings Inc	4833	2
Media General Communications Inc	4833	1
Media General Inc	2711	31
Media General Operations Inc	7375	3
Media Group Inc	7373	1117
Media Images Inc	7812	136
Media Index Publishing Inc	2721	439
Media Information Services	7389	419
Media Lab Inc	7372	3157
Media Logic	7311	195
Media Management And Magnetics Inc	5112	93
Media Management Services	3695	157
Media Management Systems Inc	7372	3779
Media Net Link	7379	978
Media Networks Inc	7311	107
Media Northstar Inc	2752	636
Media Palmer Inc	2711	700
Media Planning Group	7319	2
Media Print Inc	2759	361
Media Quarry Company Inc	1411	21
Media Relations Inc	8743	147
Media Sciences Inc	3577	17
Media Sciences International Inc	2893	43
Media Services Group Ltd	7372	2761
Media Services Inc	7389	1940
Media Services Solution Center Inc	8721	148
Media Shoppe Sdn Bhd	7372	1064
Media Spree Marketing	7313	42
Media Storm LLC	7311	161
Media Supply Inc	5045	25
Media Systems Inc	7379	793
Media Tech Inc	7371	1714
Media That Deelivers Inc	2721	315
Media Theatrical Services Inc	7922	49
Media Transcripts Inc	2741	442
Media Two Interactive	8743	85
Media Ventures Inc	2741	379
Media West Communications Inc	8743	284
Mediabridge Infosystems	7372	4717
Mediacentrix Inc	7383	13
Mediacom Communications Corp	4841	16
Media-Com Inc	4832	111
Mediacom USA	7311	1045
MediaCom Worldwide	7311	58
Mediacross Inc	7311	751
Mediafour Corp	7372	1105
mediaHYPERIUM	3695	158
Mediajoe Inc	4899	232
MediaLinx	7378	178
Medialynx Group	7389	653
MediaMind Technologies Inc	7372	503

Company Name	SIC	Rank
MediaMorphosis	2741	471
MediaNet Inc	7372	1929
MediaNews Group Inc	2711	21
Mediaone International Holding Inc	4841	150
Mediaplatform Inc	7372	445
Mediaplex Inc	7372	455
MediaRingcom Inc	7372	1115
Mediasouth Computer Supplies Inc	5734	184
Mediaspace Solutions	8748	151
MediaSpan Group Inc	7372	132
MediaSpan Media Software	7372	122
Mediaspectrum Inc	7372	914
Mediastar Inc	7812	86
Mediatech Inc	2836	39
Mediatechnics Corp	7371	1532
Mediatechnics Systems Inc	3669	230
MediaTrust	7372	624
Mediawave Inc	5045	911
Mediawhiz Holdings LLC	4899	41
Medica	6324	26
Medica Inc	3841	396
Medical Action Industries Inc	3842	31
Medical Administrators Inc	7322	156
Medical Advantage Group	6324	110
Medical Artificial Intelligence	7372	1157
Medical Assurance	6351	33
Medical Business Systems Inc	7389	518
Medical Center At Princeton New Jersey	8062	92
Medical Chemical Corp	2869	129
Medical Clinic of Houston	8011	31
Medical Clinic of North Texas	8011	11
Medical Coaches Inc	3711	65
Medical Communication Systems Inc	7372	593
Medical Communications Systems Inc	1731	1921
Medical Connections Holdings Inc	8742	463
Medical Couriers Inc	7389	2207
Medical Credit Bureau Inc	7322	168
Medical Data Information Services Inc	5734	161
Medical Device Technologies Inc	8731	166
Medical Documenting Systems Inc	7371	1808
Medical Elastomer Development Inc	2822	19
Medical Energy Inc	3845	129
Medical Equipment Distributors Inc	2741	293
Medical Health Care Solutions Inc	8721	333
Medical Imaging Systems Inc	5047	225
Medical Industries America Inc	3841	298
Medical Information Technology Inc	7372	171
Medical Knowledge Systems Inc	7372	4621
Medical Laser Rental and Service Co	7352	49
Medical Liability Mutual Insurance Co	6399	13
Medical Makeover Corporation of America	7389	2522
Medical Marketing Associates Inc	5047	236
Medical Media Television Inc	4841	167
Medical Mutual Group	8099	64
Medical Mutual Liability Insurance Society of Maryland	6351	23
Medical Mutual of Ohio	6321	28
Medical Nutrition USA Inc	2833	47
Medical Office Software Inc	7372	3141
Medical Park Family Care	8011	145
Medical Present Value Inc	7371	218
Medical Professionals On Call Inc	7361	367
Medical Properties Trust Inc	6798	122
Medical Resources Home Health Corp	8082	34
Medical Resources Inc	8071	16
Medical Screening Laboratories Inc	3841	354
Medical Security Card Company Inc	7389	478
Medical Services Of Northwest Florida Inc	8082	77
Medical Solutions	7361	82
Medical Specialties Distributors Inc	5047	35
Medical Staffing Network Holdings Inc	7363	37
Medical Store Of Palm Beach County Inc	5047	287
Medical Supply Corp	5047	181
Medical Systems Development Corp	7373	1070
Medical Systems Inc	8082	50
Medical Systems Support Inc	7372	2161
Medical Team Inc	8082	65
Medical Technology Industries Inc	2599	35
Medical Transcription Corp	8011	129
Medical-Dental Bureau Inc	8099	81
Medicalodges Inc	8051	43
Medicap Pharmacies Inc	5912	22
Medicia Holdings LLC	2844	41
Medicine Shop	5912	72
Medicine Shoppe International Inc	6794	63
Medicines Co	2834	72
MediciNova Inc	2834	462
Medicis Pharmaceutical Corp	2834	51
Medico Industries Inc	3483	3
Medico Insurance Co	6321	56
Medico-Mart Inc	5047	191
Medicomp Systems Inc	7372	2299
Mediconnect Global Inc	7372	864
Medicore Inc	3679	134
Medicus Group International	7311	30
Medidata Solutions Inc	7372	285
MediData Solutions Worldwide (Conshohocken Pennsylvaina)	7372	1625
Medifast Inc	2099	21
Medifax Inc	7363	299

Company Name	SIC	Rank
MediGain Inc	8748	383
Medi-Globe Corp	3841	420
Mediil News Service	7383	16
Medikmark Inc	5047	85
MedImmune Vaccines Inc	2836	11
Medin Corp	3841	135
Medina County Sheltered Industries Inc	8331	214
Medina Electric	5063	922
Medina Farmers Exchange Co	5199	114
Medina Plating Corp	3471	101
Medina Recycling Inc	4953	138
Medina Robert and Sons Concrete And Sand Inc	5032	138
Medina Software Inc	7372	2725
Medina Supply Co	3273	55
MedInformatix Inc	7372	1566
MediNiche Inc	3599	942
Medinitiatives	8999	141
Medio Systems Inc	7372	958
MedioStream Inc	7371	256
MediQual Systems Inc	7372	180
Medi-Quip Inc	7352	50
MediQuip International	5047	110
Medi-Rents and Sales Inc	7352	18
Medis Technologies Ltd	3845	141
Medisca Inc	5122	90
Mediscan Diagnostic Services Inc	8099	80
Mediserve Medical Equipment Of Kingsport Inc	7352	21
Medispec Management Services	8721	457
Medisyn Technologies Inc	7371	552
Medi-Tech International Corp	3842	222
Meditech Solutions Group	7372	190
Mediterra Gatehouse	6552	285
Mediterranean Gyros Products Inc	5149	130
Meditext Inc	7389	2315
MEDIVAN Inc	8099	91
Medivance Inc	3841	178
Medivation Inc	2834	108
Mediware Information Systems Inc	7373	146
Med-Kas Hydraulics Inc	3714	410
Med-Lab Supply Company Inc	5047	46
Medley Electric Company Inc	1731	1554
Medley Steel And Supply Inc	5051	318
Medliant	7361	373
Med-Lift and Mobility Inc	2512	55
Medlin and Son Engineering Service Inc	3599	1448
Medlin Equipment Company Of Mississippi County Inc	5083	194
Medline Industries Inc	3842	7
Medlink International Inc	7372	2517
Medlink Management Services Inc	8099	6
Mednax Inc	8062	42
Mednik Wiping Materials Company Inc	5093	192
Medovations Inc	3841	83
Medplast West Berlin Inc	3599	166
MedPlus Inc	7372	931
MedQuist	7373	8
MedQuist Inc	7374	27
Medrad Inc	3841	26
Medreco Inc	2599	44
Medrx Inc	3841	299
Med-Scribe Transcription Service Inc	7338	48
MedSeek Inc	5045	113
Medsite Inc	7375	83
Medsorb Dominicana SA	3842	101
MedSource Consulting Inc	8731	306
Medsphere Systems Corp	7372	832
Medstaff Contract Nursing Inc	7361	136
Med-Staff Inc	8093	55
Medstar Health	8062	36
Med-Stat Health Care Inc	7361	398
Medsupply Corporation Inc	5047	260
Medsynergies Inc	8741	154
MedTeams	7363	74
Medtech Automation LLC	3569	243
Medtech Inc	5734	176
Medtech Insight LLC	8742	355
Med-Tech Resource Inc	7389	1168
Med-Techna Inc	3842	284
Medtek Devices Inc	3841	222
MEDTOX Diagnostics Inc	2834	223
Medtox Laboratories Inc	8071	27
MEDTOX Scientific Inc	8071	23
MEDTRON Software Intelligence Corp	7372	4160
Medtronic Inc	3845	1
Medtronic MiniMed Inc	3842	34
Medtronic PS Medical Inc	3841	75
Medtronic Puerto Rico Inc	3841	45
Medtronic Sofamor Danek Inc	3842	24
Medtronic Xomed Inc	3841	40
Medtuity Inc	7372	3322
Meduri Farms Inc	2035	13
Medusind Solutions Inc	7389	717
MedValue Offshore Solutions Inc	8748	377
Med-Vantage Inc	8742	228
MedVantx Inc	7372	594
Medved Brutyn Ford Lincoln and Mercury Inc	5511	517
MedVentive LLC	7371	308
Med-Vision LLC	8742	486
MedWare Inc	8099	38
Medway Plastics Corp	3089	626

Company Name	SIC	Rank
Medway Tool Corp	3599	1749
Medweb Inc	7372	2883
Medx Inc	3844	10
Mee Enterprises Inc	5084	206
Mee Industries Inc	3585	128
MEE Productions Inc	7812	161
Meeco Inc	3823	204
MEECO Inc (Warrington Pennsylvania)	3829	292
Meegan Tool Sales Co	5049	187
Meehan Corp	5999	224
Meehan Electronics Corp	3679	744
Meeks Building Centers	5211	14
Meek's Inc	5211	267
Meeks Lithographing Co	2752	741
Meek's - The Builder's Choice	5211	21
Meem Technologies Inc	7379	1370
MEEMIC Holdings Inc	6331	148
Meenan Oil Company Inc	5948	1
Meer Electrical Contractors Inc	1731	1615
Meese Inc	3089	323
Meeting Expectations Inc	8741	309
Meeting Maker Inc	7372	1995
Meeting Management Associates Inc	8742	645
Meetingmatrix International Inc	7372	2326
Meetings and Incentives in Latin America	4724	87
Mefcor Inc	3532	80
Mefiag Div	3569	225
Meg and Michael Weddings	7221	14
MEG Restaurant Enterprises Ltd	5812	355
Mega Circuit Inc	3672	152
Mega Circuits Inc	3672	365
Mega Communication Technologies Inc	3577	519
Mega Computer Corp	5045	786
Mega Corp	3089	1744
Mega Industries LLC	3003	214
Mega International Corp	7372	399
Mega International Inc	7353	34
Mega Manufacturing Inc	3421	14
Mega Rentals Inc	3669	280
Mega Sand Enterprises Inc	1442	37
Mega Solutions Of Massachusetts	7361	258
Mega Staffing Services	7361	272
Mega Star Media Inc	7379	763
Mega Sun Inc	5099	150
Mega Systems Inc	3651	213
Mega Tech Express Inc	5045	625
Mega Tool and Manufacturing Corp	3599	1798
Megabyte International Corp	7372	1701
Megadyne Information Systems	7371	1634
MegaDyne Medical Products Inc	3841	136
MegaForce LLC	7373	643
Megagate Broadband Inc	7374	249
MegageM Digital Media	7372	4062
Meg-Alert Inc	3629	113
Megalodon CD/DVD Manufacturing	3695	120
Megamedia Inc	7336	169
Megapath Networks Inc	7375	95
Megaphase LLC	3678	43
Mega-Pro International Inc	2833	66
Megapulse Inc	3812	126
Megaputer Intelligence Inc	7372	1486
Megasoft Ltd	7371	878
Megasource Hospitality Resources Inc	5046	121
Megasys Hospitality Systems Inc	7371	1395
Megatech Corp	2741	327
Megatel Industries Corp	4899	227
Megatex World Inc	5084	782
Megatrux Transportation Inc	4213	2338
Megen Construction Company Inc	1629	57
Megger Group Ltd	3825	33
Meggitt Inc (Londonderry New Hampshire)	3728	74
Meggitt Inc (North Hollywood California)	3491	28
Meggitt Safety Systems	3812	37
Meggitt Thermal Systems Inc	3728	141
Meggitt-USA Inc	3812	32
Megown Test and Measurement Inc	3629	69
MEGTEC Systems Inc	3555	9
Mehdi Dilmaghani and Company Inc	5023	143
Meherrin Agricultural and Chemical Co	5169	22
Mehigan Bellone and Associates Inc	7336	187
Mehler And Hagestrom Inc	7338	22
Mehron Inc	2844	153
Mehta Tech Inc	3625	227
Mei Equipment Inc	5046	326
Mei Inc	3578	11
Mei LLC	3559	108
MEI Solutions	7372	2601
Mei Technologies Inc	8711	106
Meier Clinics	8093	62
Meier Supply Company Inc	5075	42
Meier Transmission Inc	5063	560
Meijer Employee Benifits Plan and Trust	6733	8
Meijer Inc	5411	9
Meiko America Inc	4213	2112
Meinecke-Johnson Company Inc	1542	166
Meineke Car Care Centers Inc	6794	51
Meisei Inc	3651	137
Meisner Electric Incorporated Of Florida	1731	100
Meissner Filtration Products Inc	3569	287
Meister Media Worldwide Inc	2721	179
Meitler Consulting Inc	3823	419
Mekatronics Inc	3679	630
Mekong Printing Inc	2752	1345
Mekorma Enterprises Inc	7371	1404
Mekos Corp	7379	1444
Mekus Studios Ltd	7389	532
Mel Bay Publications Inc	2731	47
Mel Bernie And Company Inc	3961	7
Mel Chemicals Inc	5169	44
Mel Cottons Sporting Goods	5941	35
Mel Printing Company Inc	2752	1183
Mel Quale's Electronics Inc	5731	223
Mel Rapton Honda	5511	288
Mela Sciences Inc	3841	412
Melaleuca Inc	2834	64
Melange Computer Services Inc	7371	885
Melanie Machine Co	3559	313
Melanson Company Inc	3444	38
Melaphyre Inc	7373	1004
Melching Machine Inc	3599	1231
Melco Group International Inc	7372	3926
Melcor Corp	3674	114
Mele Companies Inc	5199	62
Meletio Electrical Supply	5063	201
Melfred Borzall Inc	3599	2459
Melhinch Inc	5063	163
Melillo Consulting Inc	7372	771
Melin Tool Company Inc	3545	101
Melissa Data Corp	7372	1953
Melissa Lighting Inc	3645	58
Melissa's/World Variety Produce Inc	5148	5
Melita Corp	5149	123
Melitta North America Inc	2095	23
Mel-Kay Electric Company Inc	1731	219
Melkes Machine Inc	3599	627
Melland Gear and Instrument Of Hauppauge Inc	3824	36
Mellanox Technologies Inc	3674	76
Mellen Company Inc	3821	48
Mellies Products Inc	3441	278
Melling Tool Co	3451	5
Mellon 1st Business Corp	6022	145
Mellon Capital Management	6282	301
Mellon Financial Markets LLC	6211	201
Mellon Security and Sound Systems Inc	7382	124
Melloy Brothers Enterprises Inc	5511	889
Melmarc Products Inc	2329	19
Melodeo Inc	7371	336
Melody House Inc	3652	53
Melrose Baking Co	2051	127
Melrose Farm Service Inc	5191	158
Melrose Nameplate and Label Co	3469	204
Melrose Supply and Sales Corp	5083	101
Melrose Transport Systems	4213	2762
Mel's Auto Specialists Inc	5012	187
Melstrom Manufacturing Corp	3679	460
Melt Inc	5441	20
Melting Pot Restaurants Inc	6794	60
Melton Franchise Systems Inc	7349	120
Melton Machine and Control Co	3548	30
Melton Sales and Service	7699	85
Melton Truck Lines Inc	4213	384
Meltzer Lippe Goldstein and Breitstone LLP	8111	460
Melvin Bush Construction Inc	1623	456
Melyx Corp	7372	2428
Member Home Lending Services Inc	7389	1864
Member Services Inc	7311	449
Membrane System Specialists Inc	3599	2060
Membrane Technology And Research Inc	8731	122
MEMC Electronic Materials Inc	3674	16
MEMC Pasadena Inc	3674	202
Memeco Sales and Service Corp	5063	919
Memex Books Inc	2678	21
Memorial Estates Inc	6553	4
Memorial Health Services Inc	8062	45
Memorial Hermann Katy Hospital	8062	210
Memories and More Inc	5945	13
Memory Gardens Management Corp	6553	5
Memory Man Inc	5045	717
Memory Storage Devices	3572	102
MemoryTen Inc	5045	195
Memosun Inc	5045	1031
Memphis Chemical Janitorial Supply Inc	5169	40
Memphis Communications Corp	5999	139
Memphis Folding Stairs Inc	2431	103
Memphis Funeral Home Inc	7261	6
Memphis Hardwood Flooring Company Inc	2421	68
Memphis International Motorsports Corp	7948	35
Memphis Material Handling Inc	5084	630
Memphis New Holland Inc	5261	18
Memphis Publishing Co	2711	118
Memphis Sash and Door Co	2431	87
Memphis Wire and Iron Works Inc	3441	221
Memry Corp	3841	88
Mems Optical Inc	3827	117
Memsic Inc	3674	165
Memtec Corp	3572	67
Memtech SSD Corp	3674	131
Memtron Technologies Inc	3679	45
Menage Automation Inc	5063	890
Menard Electric Coop	4911	600
Menard Electronics Inc	5065	504
Menard Inc	5211	4
Menasha Corp	2656	3
Menasha Corp Thermotech Div	3089	40
Menches Tool and Die Inc	3812	169
Mendell Machine And Manufacturing Inc	3599	562
Mendelsohn/Zien Advertising LLC	7311	83
Mendenhall Motor Co	5013	367
Mendocino Brewing Company Inc	2082	27
Mendocino Sea Vegetable Co	5146	61
Mendon Leasing Corp	7513	10
Mendota Agri-Products Inc	2077	11
Mendota Insurance Co	6331	235
Mendoza Tool	3544	820
Menendez-Donnell and Associates	1521	151
Menezes Brothers Inc	2048	145
Menges Roller Company Inc	5084	648
Menke And Associates Inc	7389	1331
Menlo Acquisition Corp	6719	169
Menlo Business Systems Inc	7372	3541
Menlo Innovations	7379	423
Menlo Tool Company Inc	3545	100
Menlo Ventures	6799	220
Menlo Worldwide Logistics Inc	4789	1
Mennen Medical Corp	3841	86
Mennie Machine Co	3599	145
Menno Travel Service	4724	121
Mennonite General Hospital Inc	8062	184
Mennonite Press Inc	2752	1164
Menominee Tribal Enterprises	2421	80
Menomonie Farmers Union Coop	5172	84
Men's Wearhouse Inc	5611	5
Mensor Corp	3823	123
MensRedTagcom	2389	36
Mental Automation Inc	7372	1809
Mental Health Assoc	7363	375
Mental Health Management Inc	8063	9
Mental Health Network Inc	8093	24
Mental Health Outcomes Inc	8099	94
Mentalix Inc	7372	3620
Mentat Inc	7371	553
Mentholatum Co	2834	200
Mentor Corp	3842	28
Mentor Dynamics Limited Inc	3089	1767
Mentor Family Foods	5411	273
Mentor Graphics Corp	7373	19
Mentor Lumber and Supply Company Inc	5031	96
Mentor Software Inc	7372	4853
Mentor Technologies Inc	8732	125
MentorU	2741	176
Mentus Inc	7336	77
Mentzer Electronics	3672	328
Menu Printers Inc	2752	1081
Menusoft Systems Corp	7372	628
Menzner Lumber And Supply Co	2431	40
Meow Mix Co	2047	18
Mep Acquisition Corp	3679	222
Mequoda Group LLC	7379	1450
Mera Pharmaceuticals Inc	8731	416
Meramec Electrical Products Inc	3612	34
Meramec Group Inc	3021	7
Meramec Valley Bank	6022	792
MERANT Inc	7372	259
Merastar Insurance Co	6331	131
Mer-Cal Electric Inc	1731	1247
Mercantec Inc	7372	2681
Mercantil Commercebank NA	6021	33
Mercantile Bancorp Inc (Quincy Illinois)	6712	338
Mercantile Bank Corp	6022	104
Mercantile Bank of Boca Raton	6022	618
Mercantile Capital Corp	6159	55
Mercantile International NA Inc	5065	779
Mercantile Press Inc	2752	1217
Mercantile Printing	2752	619
Mercantile Trust and Savings Bank	6022	288
Mercator Asset Management Inc	6282	381
Mercatus Energy Advisors LLC	8742	614
Merced Systems Inc	7372	1197
Mercedes Benz of Austin	5511	363
Mercedes Benz of Sacramento	5511	462
Mercedes Electric Supply Inc	5063	152
Mercedes Homes Inc	1531	21
Mercedes Medical Inc	5047	61
Mercedes-Benz of Buckhead	5511	186
Mercedes-Benz of Calabasas	5511	533
Mercedes-Benz Of Cincinnati	5511	595
Mercedes-Benz of Encino	5511	727
Mercedes-Benz of Ft Pierce	5511	190
Mercedes-Benz of Houston Greenway	5511	165
Mercedes-Benz of Pompano	5511	112
Mercer and Ussery Inc	1623	549
Mercer Capital Management Inc	6282	287
Mercer Companies Inc	6552	147
Mercer Construction Co	1623	120
Mercer County Surgery Center LLC	8011	135
Mercer Forge Corp	3462	25
Mercer Gasket And Shim	3053	92
Mercer Group Ltd/Baby Blanket	2844	202

Company Name	SIC	Rank	Company Name	SIC	Rank	Company Name	SIC	Rank
Mercer Human Resource Consulting Inc	8742	55	Mercy Health Partners	8062	215	Mer-Kote Products Inc	2899	214
Mercer Inc	6282	646	Mercy Hospital Of Scranton PA	8062	159	Merle Norman Cosmetics Inc	5999	33
Mercer Insurance Group Inc	6331	202	Mercy Memorial Hospital Foundation	8741	76	Merlin International Inc	7379	228
Mercer Landmark Inc	5153	86	Mercy Special Care Hospital	7363	143	Merlin Management Company Inc	8741	224
Mercer Machine Company Inc	3599	2389	Merdan Group Inc	7372	4718	Merlin Petroleum Company Inc	5171	68
Mercer Tool Corp	5072	131	Merdian M R I	7374	310	Merlin Printing Inc	2759	292
Mercer Transportation Company Inc	4213	95	Meredith and Hall Inc	8743	296	Merlon International	1311	264
Mercer Trucking Company Inc	4213	2023	Meredith Corp	2721	9	Mermaid Manufacturing Of Southwest Florida Inc	3585	222
Mercer-Zimmerman Inc	5063	268	Meredith Enterprises Inc	7389	1525	Mer-Mar Inc	3672	258
MercFuel Inc	5172	49	Meredith Industries Inc	3949	160	Merrell Brothers Inc	8999	125
Merchant and Gould PC	8111	407	Meredith Software Inc	7372	5079	Merriam-Webster Inc	2731	114
Merchant Data Service Inc	7389	985	Meredith - Webb Printing Company Inc	7331	80	Merrick and Co	8711	64
Merchant du Vin Corp	5181	105	Meredith-Springfield Associates Inc	8731	317	Merrick Engineering Inc	3089	116
Merchant Expo LLC	5734	481	Mereen-Johnson Machine Co	3553	23	Merrick Machine Co	3546	21
Merchant Factors Corp	6153	24	Meretek Inc	8071	52	Merrick Printing Company Inc	2752	315
Merchant One Inc	7389	582	Merex Corp (Tempe Arizona)	8299	39	Merrick Utility Associates Inc	1623	725
Merchant Processing Services Inc	7322	43	Merfish Pipe and Supply LP	5051	332	Merrick's Inc	2048	30
Merchant Solutions USA Inc	1522	54	Merge eClinical	7372	1408	Merrick's Of Nebraska LLC	2011	154
Merchant Technologies	7372	2395	Merge Healthcare Inc	7372	220	Merrill and Ring Inc.	0811	5
Merchants and Farmers Bank	6022	748	Mergent International Inc	7372	1668	Merrill Consultants	7372	4854
Merchants and Farmers Bank of Kosciusko	6022	119	Meri Meri Inc	2771	23	Merrill Corp	2752	5
Merchants and Manufacturers Bancorp	6712	599	Meriam Process Technologies	3823	61	Merrill Equipment Co	3441	199
Merchants Bancshares Inc	6712	237	Merical Inc	7389	551	Merrill Farms Inc	0161	6
Merchants Bank (Cannon Falls Minnesota)	6021	383	Merichem Co	5169	23	Merrill Fine Arts Engraving Inc	2759	160
Merchants Bank of California	6021	250	Mericle Commercial Real Estate Group Inc	6512	14	Merrill Iron and Steel Inc	3441	32
Merchants Co	5141	99	Mericle Commercial Real Estate Group Inc - Logistics Div	6552	33	Merrill Lynch and Company Inc	6211	407
Merchants Coupon Exchange Inc	2741	330	Meriden Cooper Corp	5085	414	Merrill Lynch Credit Corp	6162	32
Merchants Credit Corp	7322	79	Meriden Machine Shop Inc	3861	116	Merrill Lynch Video Network Co	7812	1
Merchants' Credit Guide Co	7322	76	Meriden Manufacturing Inc	3469	147	Merrill Manufacturing Corp	3496	69
Merchants Delivery Moving and Storage	4213	1665	Meridian Aerospace Group Ltd	5088	72	Merrill/May Inc	2752	16
Merchants Distributors Inc	5141	40	Meridian America Inc	3651	82	Merrill Research and Associates LLC	8732	84
Merchants Financial Group Inc	6712	477	Meridian Auto Wrecking	5015	23	Merrill Tool and Machine Inc	3549	15
Merchants Forwarding Co	4213	2343	Meridian Bank	6022	220	Merrill Y Landis Ltd	2391	14
Merchants Grocery Co	5141	51	Meridian Bioscience Inc	2835	12	Merrill-Stevens Dry Dock Co	3732	62
Merchants Group Inc	6331	265	Meridian Broadcasting Inc	4832	57	Merrimac Industries Inc	3679	159
Merchant's Inc	5014	6	Meridian Capital Group LLC	6163	9	Merrimac Textile	5131	41
Merchants Insurance Company of New Hampshire Inc	6331	262	Meridian Capital LLC	6211	267	Merrimack Valley Business Machines Inc	7629	35
Merchants National Bank of Winona	6021	208	Meridian Corp	2759	546	Merrimack Valley Distributing Company Inc	5181	62
Merchants Paper Co	5063	683	Meridian Electrical Associates Inc	1731	1195	Merrimack Valley Federal Credit Union	6061	57
Merchants Security Service Of Dayton Oh Inc	7381	80	Meridian Graphics Inc	2752	427	Merriman Curhan Ford and Co	6211	56
Merchants Solutions	5044	94	Meridian Healthcare Group Inc	7363	161	Merriman Holdings Inc	6211	292
Merchants Terminal Corp	4222	7	Meridian Holdings Inc	7376	51	Merrit Press Inc	2752	1230
Merchantwired LLC	4813	350	Meridian Homes Inc (Houston Texas)	1521	127	Merritt and Pardini	8712	133
Mercier Electric and Communications Inc	1731	2538	Meridian Industries Inc	2269	4	Merritt and Son Equipment Inc	4213	2607
Mercier Tool and Die Company Inc	3599	952	Meridian Interstate Bancorp Inc	6036	20	Merritt Brothers Lumber Company Inc	2421	99
Merck and Company Inc	2834	2	Meridian Investments	6211	213	Merritt Company Inc	5169	121
Merck Holdings Inc	2834	110	Meridian IT	7378	6	Merritt Contracting Inc	1623	178
Merck Millipore	3826	5	Meridian Jet Prop Inc	5599	23	Merritt Equipment Co	3715	19
Merck Research Laboratories	8731	242	Meridian Laboratory Inc	3621	140	Merritt Machinery LLC	3553	49
Merck Technical Consulting Inc	7379	1666	Meridian Mall Company Inc	6531	234	Merritt Mosby Advertising Inc	7311	936
Merco Inc	1622	40	Meridian Medical Associates	8011	89	Merritt Properties LLC	6531	163
Merco Manufacturing Co	3728	201	Meridian Medical Technologies Inc	3841	61	Merriwether and Williams Insurance Service Inc	6411	48
Merco/Savory Inc	3589	39	Meridian Moulding Inc	5099	75	Mer-Roc FS Inc	5191	102
Mercom Corp	4899	90	Meridian Partners	7371	616	Merry Maid Inc	4225	36
Mercom Systems Inc	7372	1228	Meridian Precision Inc	3089	1582	Merry Maids LP	6794	3
Mercotac Inc	3643	84	Meridian Printing Inc	2752	495	Merry Maids Of Oklahoma Inc	7349	378
Mercury Adjustment Bureau Investigations Ltd	6411	280	Meridian Products Inc	2434	66	Merry Mechanization Inc	7371	446
Mercury Air Group Inc	5172	29	Meridian Service Group Inc	7373	1155	Merryman Company Excavation	1623	273
Mercury BE LLC	5064	185	Meridian Services Inc	5064	186	Merryvale Vineyards LLC	2084	71
Mercury Companies Inc	6162	3	Meridian Star Inc	2711	142	MerryWeather Foam Inc	3089	737
Mercury Computer System Inc	3571	145	Meridian Systems	7372	1824	Merschman Seeds Inc	5191	149
Mercury Computer Systems Inc	3679	63	Meridian Technologies Inc	3679	587	Mersen USA Bn Corp	3624	2
Mercury Data Systems Inc	7373	116	Meridian Technology Group Inc	7371	366	Mersen USA Greenville-Mi Corp	3624	15
Mercury Displacement Industries Inc	3625	94	Meridian Venture Partners	6159	78	Mersen USA Newburyport-Ma LLC	5063	54
Mercury Equipment Finance Group	6163	32	Meridian World Travel	4724	80	Mershon Concrete LLC	3272	122
Mercury General Corp	6331	101	Meridianlink Inc	7371	805	Mersoft International LLC	7372	2489
Mercury Group LLC	7373	703	Meridium Inc	7372	1004	Merten Co	2752	662
Mercury Insurance Co	6331	25	Meriliz Inc	2752	124	Mertz Enterprises Inc	3599	1425
Mercury Insurance Services LLC	7372	747	Merillat Industries Inc	2434	2	Mertz Inc	3441	78
Mercury International Technology Inc	7372	3836	Merin Hunter Codman Inc	6531	86	Meru Networks Inc	5045	140
Mercury Iron and Steel	8711	651	Mering and Associates Inc	7311	693	Meruelo Maddux Properties Inc	6552	197
Mercury Lighting Products Company Inc	3646	27	MeringCarson	7311	590	Mervin Manufacturing Inc	3949	101
Mercury Luggage Manufacturing Co	3161	9	Merion Lower School District Inc	8211	3	Mervis Industries Inc	3341	13
Mercury Machining Company Inc	3599	1795	Merion Publications Inc	2721	132	Merz Inc	2834	273
Mercury Mambo	7311	591	Merisant Worldwide Inc	2869	23	Mesa Air Group Inc	4512	22
Mercury Manufacturing Co	3451	37	Merisel Inc	7389	288	Mesa Bank	6022	496
Mercury Marine Group	3519	8	Merit Electric Company Inc	1731	1958	Mesa/Boogie Ltd	3651	93
Mercury Media Holdings	7372	959	Merit Electrical Inc	1731	120	Mesa Brothers Inc	1731	1393
Mercury Partners 90 Bi Inc	5074	111	Merit Electronic Design Company Inc	3679	216	Mesa Consolidated Water District	4941	34
Mercury Plastics Corp	3089	1724	Merit Ends Inc	3444	251	Mesa Fully Formed Inc	3083	19
Mercury Plastics Inc	3089	576	Merit Energy Co	5172	162	Mesa Industries Inc	2865	17
Mercury Print Productions Inc	2752	91	Merit Fasteners Corp	5072	45	Mesa Laboratories Inc	3823	52
Mercury Printing Company Inc	2752	368	Merit Medical Systems Inc	3841	30	Mesa Royalty Trust	6792	6
Mercury Publishing Services Inc	2721	307	Merit Network Inc	7373	270	Mesa Systems Inc	4213	845
Mercury Solar Systems Inc	1796	4	Merit Paper Co	5162	44	Mesa Systems Inc	5045	526
Mercury Tool And Engineering Co	3544	898	Merit Printing Inc	2752	571	Mesaba Aviation Inc	4512	35
Mercury Tool And Machine Inc	3599	1040	Merit Sensor Systems	3674	347	MESBIC Ventures Holding Co	6799	68
Mercury Transportation Inc	4213	2334	Meritage Homes Corp	1531	22	Mesco Building Solutions	3441	72
Mercury United Electronics Inc	3679	575	Meritage Hospitality Group Inc	5812	250	Mesco Inc	3825	219
Mercury Waste Solutions LLC	4953	101	Meritage Private Equity Funds	6799	101	Mescon Technologies Inc	5065	1001
Mercy Air Service Inc	4522	18	MeritCare Health System	8062	50	Mese Hsin Tung Yang Foods Company Inc	2013	168
Mercy Anderson Hospital Inc	8062	87	Meritek Electronics Corp	5065	216	Meshberger Brothers Stone Corp	1422	15
Mercy Care Management Inc	8011	44	Meritool LLC	3546	35	Mesher Shing and Associates	8712	319
Mercy Center At Madison	7389	2234	Meritor Inc	3714	13	Meshkani Company Inc	5012	167
Mercy Health Partners	8062	192	Meriwest Credit Union	6062	43	Mesick Precision Co	3544	906
			Meriwether Lewis Electric Coop	4911	450	Mesirow Financial Holdings Inc	6153	21
			Merizon Group Inc	7379	523	Mesirow Financial Inc	6211	31
			Merkle Direct Marketing Inc	7374	50	Mesirow Stein Real Estate Inc	6531	212
			Merkle Inc	5045	209	Mesker Door Inc	3442	77
			Merkle-Korff Industries Inc	3621	33			
			Merkley and Sons Inc	5421	4			

Company Name	SIC	Rank
Mesonic America Inc	7372	773
Mesorah Publications Ltd	2731	231
Mesoscale Environmental Simulation and Operations Inc	8999	206
Mesquite Software Inc	7372	1810
Message Center Communication Inc	7389	1619
Message Technologies Inc	4813	312
MessageLabs Inc	5045	160
Messaging Solutions LLC	7373	1055
Messe Dusseldorf North America	7389	1230
Messe Frankfurt Inc	7389	471
Messenger Corp	7389	1701
Messenger Molding Inc	3089	1450
Messenger Post Newspapers	2711	109
Messenger Publication Inc	2711	648
Messer Cutting Systems Inc	3545	16
Messier Services America Inc	3728	51
Messina Hof Wine Cellars Inc	2084	61
Messner and Smith	6282	635
Messner Vetere Berger McNamee Schmetterer/Euro RSCG	7311	32
Mesta Electronics Inc	3674	403
Mestek Inc	3585	24
Met One Instruments Inc	3829	88
Met Photo Inc	7334	47
Met Pro Supply Inc	5084	703
Meta Financial Group Inc	6712	264
Meta Health Technology Inc	7372	671
Meta Information Services	7379	979
Meta Manufacturing Corp	3599	33
Meta Software Corp	7372	2469
Meta Tec Development Inc	7699	243
MetaBank	6035	230
MetaBank	6035	206
Metabloc Inc	3669	305
Metabo Corp	5072	106
Metabolic Maintenance Products Inc	2834	370
Metabollx Inc	3089	1889
Metachem Resins Corp	2891	99
MetaCommunications Inc	7372	734
Metadata Co	7371	1686
Metafile Information Systems Inc	7372	2576
Metagenics Inc	2833	8
Metagraphics Software Corp	7372	4522
Metairie Opthalmology ASC LLC	8011	101
Metal Art Of California Inc	3993	62
Metal Building Compnents Inc	3499	6
Metal Building Supply Inc	5039	34
Metal Cladding Inc	3479	50
Metal Classics Inc	2514	16
Metal Coaters	3479	35
Metal Coatings Corp	3479	51
Metal Coatings International Inc	2899	119
Metal Components LLC	2522	37
Metal Craft Machine and Engineering Inc	3841	164
Metal Cutting Corp	3679	386
Metal Cutting Service Inc	3599	890
Metal Detectors Inc	3829	411
Metal Essence Inc	3599	1129
Metal Fabricating Corp	2542	37
Metal Fabrications	1761	58
Metal Finishing Equipment Company Inc	3471	129
Metal Finishing Supply Company Inc	5085	438
Metal Flow Corp	3469	55
Metal Forming and Coining Corp	3462	23
Metal Forming Industries Inc	3351	24
Metal Forms Corp	3444	252
Metal Fusion Incorporated	3631	20
Metal Goods Manufacturing Company Inc	3821	71
Metal Improvement Company Inc	3398	3
Metal Improvement Company LLC	3398	2
Met-Al Inc	3355	11
Metal Mafia	3911	48
Metal Masters Food Service Equipment Company Inc	3589	37
Metal Masters Foodservice Equipment Co	3694	43
Metal Mechanics Inc	3599	2328
Metal Prep	3398	19
Metal Processing Company Inc	3679	816
Metal Processing Corp	7389	1598
Metal Products Inc	3544	111
Metal Recycling Services LLC	5093	91
Metal Research Inc	3599	1460
Metal Resource Solutions	3315	35
Metal Rubber Corp	3599	2446
Metal Sales Manufacturing Corp	3448	15
Metal Seal and Products Inc	3451	23
Metal Services Group	3599	2044
Metal Storm Inc	8999	28
Metal Suppliers Online LLC	7389	736
Metal Surfaces Inc	3471	30
Metal Technologies Of Murfreesboro Inc	3599	792
Metal Technology Of Indiana Inc	3449	38
Metal Toad Media	7379	742
Metal Traders Inc	5051	23
Metal Trades Inc	3444	56
Metal Ware Corp	3634	15
Metal Works Inc	3444	139
METALAST International LLC	8731	188

Company Name	SIC	Rank
Metalclad Insulation Corp	1799	74
Metalcraft Enterprises Inc	3444	177
Metalcraft Mining Equipment Rebuilders Inc	3599	572
Metalcraft Of Mayville Se Inc	3599	189
Metalcraft Technologies Inc	3444	122
Metalcut Products Inc	3599	267
Metaldyne Corp	3356	12
Metalex Manufacturing Inc	3599	89
Metalfab Inc	3444	183
Metal-Fab Inc	3444	26
Metal-Flex Hosing Inc	3661	229
Metal-Flex Welded Bellows Inc	3599	1022
Metalforms Manufacturing Inc	3443	119
Metalico Inc	3341	5
Metalife Resources Inc	4953	165
Metalink Corp	3559	544
Metalink Technologies Inc	7375	227
Metalist International Inc	5084	867
Metalite Corp	3645	39
Metallic Products Corp	3446	37
Metallics Inc	3479	26
Metal-Line Corp	3599	1799
Metallized Carbon Corp	3624	13
Metallized Products Inc	3089	758
Metallizing Service Company Inc	3479	72
Metallurg Inc	3313	1
Metallurgical Products Co	3364	26
Metalmark Inc	5051	212
Metalmart Co	5051	452
MetalMart International Inc	5051	210
Metal-Matic Inc	3317	27
Metal-Mation Inc	8748	419
Metalmite Corp	3599	2116
Metaloptics Inc	3646	41
Metalor USA Refining Corp	3341	19
Metalore Inc	3599	1219
Metals And Additives Corp	2819	77
Metals Fabrication Company Inc	3599	512
Metals Recycling LLC	5093	98
Metals Technology Corp	3398	8
Metals USA Building Products South-East Inc	3354	29
Metals USA Holdings Inc	5051	15
Metals USA Plates And Shapes South-central Inc	5051	66
Metals USA Plates and Shapes-Philadelphia	5051	81
Metals USA Plates and Shapes-Shreveport Div	5051	156
Metals USA Specialty Flat Rolled - Kansas City	5051	82
Metals USA Specialty Flat Rolled-Northbrk	5051	31
Metals USA (Wilmington North Carolina)	3441	57
Metalsco Inc	5093	11
Metal-Tech Controls Corp	3625	322
Metal-Tech Inc	3599	1356
Metaltech Industries Inc	3444	146
Metaltech Investments Inc	6719	171
Metal-Tech Manufacturing Inc	3599	1028
Metal-Tech Partners	3661	106
MetalTek International	3366	10
Metalworking Group	3444	76
Metalworking Lubricants Co	5172	44
Metalworks Inc	3499	44
Metamora Grain	5153	84
Metaphase Technologies Inc	3827	155
Metaplus Inc	3669	316
Metapo Inc	3577	536
Metapoint Partners LP	3089	1866
Metara Inc	3825	358
Metastable Instruments Inc	5049	216
Metastorm Inc	7372	615
MetaSwitch	4899	109
Metasys Technologies Inc	7371	406
Metasystems Inc	7372	3644
Metavac Inc	3827	67
Metavideo Inc	3679	825
MetaWare Inc	7372	2813
Metaweb Technologies Inc	7379	246
Metcalf and Eddy Inc	4953	33
Metcalf Bank	6022	376
Metcalf Davis	8721	428
Metco Manufacturing Company Inc	3544	192
Metco Treating And Development Co	3471	55
Metcom Inc	3469	221
Met-Con Inc	3441	53
Metem Corp	3599	137
Metem International Corp	3599	848
Meteor Express Inc	4213	2131
Meteor Graphics LLC	7336	228
Meteor Supply Inc	3599	1389
Meteorcomm LLC	3663	123
Meteorological Products Inc	5049	221
Meter Devices Company Inc	3625	12
MeterNet Corp	7319	105
Motorc Inc	3586	22
Metex Corp	3496	36
Method Home Products	5963	18
Method Studios	3695	12
Methode Development Co	3672	8
Methode Electronics Inc	3678	6

Company Name	SIC	Rank
Methodist Childrens Home	8322	234
Methodist Healthcare	8062	49
Methodist Home Medical Equipment LLC	7352	51
Methodist Medical Center	8011	17
Methodist Medical Center Of Oak Ridge	8062	171
Methods and Solutions Inc	7372	3726
Methods Tooling and Manufacturing Inc	3545	201
Metier	7371	1622
Metier Ltd	7372	2052
Metlife Bank NA	6021	224
MetLife Inc	6719	1
MetLife Insurance Co	6311	210
MetLife Insurance Company of Connecticut	6311	170
MetLife Investors Insurance Co	6311	150
Metlsaw Systems Inc	3541	190
Met-L-Tec LLC	3544	462
Meto Corp	3537	89
Meto-Grafics Inc	2759	557
Metokote Corp	3479	2
Metompkin Bay Oyster Company Inc	5146	42
Metpar Corp	3446	18
Metplas Inc	3083	48
Met-Pro Corp	3564	18
Met-Pro Corp Keystone Filter Div	3564	126
Met-Pro Corp Systems Div	3564	25
Metra Electronics Corp	3651	49
MetraTech Corp	7372	1060
Metreo Inc	7372	1567
Metric Design and Manufacturing Inc	3544	859
Metric Halo Laboratories Inc	5734	448
Metric Manufacturing Company Inc	3599	434
Metric Products Inc	2342	3
Metric Systems Corp	3663	334
Metricon Corp	3826	157
Metrics Inc	8731	110
MotrioStream Inc	7372	742
Metriguard Inc	3825	164
Metritech Inc	8999	190
Metrix Co	3841	177
Metrix Inc	7372	1243
Metrix Instrument Company LP	3823	48
Metro Air Services Inc	4213	3049
Metro Alloys Inc	5093	90
Metro Audio Dynamics Inc	5731	181
Metro Automation Inc	3535	119
Metro Bancorp Inc	6712	184
Metro Bank	6021	148
Metro Bay Associates Inc	7389	2362
Metro Business Systems Inc	5734	53
Metro Cleaners Of Knoxville Inc	7349	503
Metro Communication Systems Inc	7382	139
Metro Construction Inc	1623	691
Metro Containers Inc	2653	98
Metro Copier Service	3579	70
Metro Corp	2721	193
Metro Creative Graphics Inc	7336	31
METRO Credit Union	6062	83
Metro Custom Plastics Inc	3089	1622
Metro Drugs Inc	5912	36
Metro Education and Entertainment Inc	7389	1343
Metro Electric Company Inc	1731	294
Metro Environmental Inc	5093	195
Metro Equipment Service Inc	1623	362
Metro Express Inc	4213	2609
Metro Financial Services	6153	18
Metro Fire Detection LLC	5063	820
Metro Fire Equipment Inc	5099	87
Metro Fire Protection Inc	5087	113
Metro Fire Safety Guards Inc	7389	779
Metro Ford Truck Sales Inc	5511	1082
Metro Group Inc (Long Island City New York)	2899	39
Metro Group Inc (Salt Lake City Utah)	5051	102
Metro Ice Inc	5199	134
Metro Industries Inc	3053	120
Metro Lifts and Equipment LLC	5046	381
Metro Machine and Engineering Corp	3549	31
Metro Machine Corp	3731	14
Metro Machine Works Inc	3599	2331
Metro Materials Inc	3273	79
Metro Meadows Associates Inc	7922	43
Metro Metal and Design Inc	3599	669
Metro Metals Corp	5093	25
Metro Metals Northwest	5093	16
Metro Moulded Parts Inc	3069	164
Metro Music Production	7389	2378
Metro Networks Inc	8999	12
Metro Newspaper Advertising Services Inc	7313	10
Metro North Newspapers Inc	2711	743
Metro Office Solutions Inc	5021	158
Metro One Lpsg	7381	208
Metro Optics Inc	3851	113
Metro Park Warehouses Inc	4225	28
Metro Plastics Technologies Inc	3089	761
Metro Print Center Inc	2752	1822
Metro Printers Guild Inc	2752	1563
Metro Printing and Publishing Inc	2752	1738
Metro Products And Construction Inc	3273	72
Metro Ready Mix Concrete LLC	3273	45
Metro Recycling Company Inc	5093	72

Company Name	SIC	Rank
Metro - Sales Inc	5044	22
Metro Stairs Inc	5211	195
Metro Technologies Ltd	3543	10
Metro Therapy Inc	8093	35
Metro Times Inc	2711	858
Metro Trailer Repair Company Inc	7539	12
Metro Transport Inc	4212	48
Metro Travel and Tours Inc	4724	70
Metro Video Systems Inc	5731	75
Metro Web Corp	2752	517
Metro Weighing and Automation Inc	3565	157
Metro Xpress	4213	1393
MetroBank NA (Houston Texas)	6022	253
MetroCast Cablevision of New Hampshire LLC	4841	57
Metrocities Mortgage LLC	6162	149
Metroclean Express Corp	1611	232
Metrocorp Bancshares Inc	6712	235
Metrocorp Inc	6712	502
Metrodial Corp	7382	133
Metro-Fabricating LLC	3444	194
Metrofuser LLC	3577	434
Metro-Goldwyn-Mayer Inc	7812	9
Metrohm-Peak LLC	5047	198
Metroland	5192	40
Metrolaser Inc	3826	88
Metrolina Greenhouses Inc	5193	6
Metrolina Plastics Inc	3089	1013
Metrolina Steel Inc	5051	283
Metrologic Instruments Inc	3577	78
Metrolpolis Mastering LP	3652	44
Metromedia International Group Inc	4812	49
Metromont Corp	3272	37
Metron Home Care	5047	274
Metron Optics Inc	3827	100
Metron Time Clock Co	7372	4855
Metron-Athene Inc	7371	977
Metronet-Telecom Inc	4813	512
Metronic Engineering Company Inc	3599	2293
Metronics Inc	3829	228
Metronome Inc	5045	496
Metropark Communications Inc	5064	66
Metropark USA Inc	5611	15
MetroPCS Communications Inc	4899	3
Metro-Plex Bindery Inc	2789	142
Metroplex Inc	1731	1757
Metroplex Printing And Finishing Inc	7389	1722
Metropole Products Inc	3663	259
Metropolitan Advertising Company Inc	7312	27
Metropolitan Alloys Corp	5051	467
Metropolitan Audio Visual Company LLC	5065	800
Metropolitan Baking Co	2051	116
Metropolitan Bank Group	6712	327
Metropolitan Cadillac Inc	5511	1087
Metropolitan Communication Services Inc	7389	737
Metropolitan Edison Co	4911	86
Metropolitan Fire Extinguisher Co	5099	129
Metropolitan Graphic Arts Inc	2752	734
Metropolitan Health Networks Inc	8011	10
Metropolitan Hospital Center Inc	8062	172
Metropolitan Industries Inc	3561	182
Metropolitan Inter-Faith Association	8322	96
Metropolitan Mechanical Contractors Inc	1711	286
Metropolitan New York Coordinating Council On Jewish Poverty Inc	8322	62
Metropolitan Poultry and Seafood Company Inc	5144	11
Metropolitan Presort Inc	7389	696
Metropolitan Properties of America	6531	88
Metropolitan Rolling Door Inc	5031	324
Metropolitan School District Wayne Township	8211	87
Metropolitan Theatres Corp	7832	13
Metropolitan Tickets Inc	7922	21
Metropolitan Transit Authority	7312	20
Metropolitan Vacuum Cleaner Company Inc	3635	5
Metro-Republic Commercial Service Inc	7322	106
Metrosoft Inc	7373	610
MetroSpec Technology LLC	3674	370
Metrotech Chemicals Inc	2842	95
Metrotech Corp	3812	101
Met-Rx USA Inc	2834	159
Metsch Refractories Inc	3264	16
Metso Automation USA Inc	3494	29
Metso Minerals Inc	3532	2
Metso Minerals Industries Inc	3321	9
Metso Paper USA Inc	3061	18
Metso Power	3554	4
Metso Wyesco Service Center Inc	7699	92
Mette Evans and Woodside	8111	423
Metters Industries Inc	7373	281
Mettiki Coal LLC (Oakland Maryland)	1222	5
Mettler Electronics Corp	3841	269
Mettler-Toledo Inc	3596	2
Mettler-Toledo Safeline Inc	3844	12
Metts Brothers Inc	3643	110
Metuchen Capacitors Inc	3675	28
Metwood Inc	3441	271
Metz Beverage Company Inc	5181	80

Company Name	SIC	Rank
Metz Communication Corp	3663	403
Metz Electronics Corp	3672	289
Metzgar Conveyor Company Inc	3535	134
Metzger Associates Inc	8743	250
Meunier Electronics Supply Inc	5065	194
Meurer Research Inc	3589	56
Mexamerica Foods Inc	2099	274
Mexco Energy Corp	1311	241
Mexican Restaurants Inc	5812	257
Mexicanal LLC	4833	188
Mexichem America Inc	5162	8
Mexico Fund Inc	6726	45
Mexico Independent Inc	2711	693
Mexico Plastic Co	2673	17
Mexi-Snax Corp	2099	335
Mextel Inc	3577	176
Meyer and Associates Inc	7389	1254
Meyer and Lundahl Manufacturing Co	2431	94
Meyer and Wallis Inc	7311	264
Meyer Associates Inc (Ardmore Pennsylvania)	7389	445
Meyer Broadcasting Co	4833	143
Meyer Co	3556	25
Meyer Corp	3469	1
Meyer Darragh Buckler Bebenek and Eck PLLC	8111	465
Meyer Design Inc	7389	1599
Meyer Equipment Company Inc	4214	24
Meyer Gage Company Inc	3545	386
Meyer Global Security Inc	1731	755
Meyer Handelman Co	6282	156
Meyer Industries Inc	3535	78
Meyer Laboratory Inc	2899	140
Meyer LLC	5148	61
Meyer Manufacturing Corp	3523	81
Meyer Plastics Inc	3089	367
Meyer Sales Company Inc	5511	1229
Meyer Scherer and Rockcastle Ltd	8712	215
Meyer Sound Laboratories Inc	3651	64
Meyer Tool Inc	3724	21
Meyer Unkovic and Scott LLP	8111	266
Meyercord Revenue Inc	2752	404
Meyer-Manz Real Estate Inc	6531	373
Meyers Associates LP	6211	344
Meyers Co	2752	83
Meyer's Sausage Co	2013	246
Meyers Sheet Metal Box Inc	3444	296
Meyer's Western Import Parts Inc	5013	212
Meyocks Group	7311	360
MeziMedia	4899	57
MF Global Ltd	6211	4
MFA Atelier Inc	2752	1310
MFA Financial Inc	6798	24
Mfj Enterprises Inc	3663	115
MFM Industries Inc	1459	4
MFried Store Fixtures Inc	5046	82
MFS Charter Income Trust	6726	34
MFS Government Markets Income Trust	6726	59
MFS High Yield Municipal Trust	6726	55
MFS Intermediate High Income Fund	6726	88
MFS Intermediate Income Trust	6726	26
MFS Investment Management	6798	1
MFS Special Value Trust	6726	96
MFS Supply Inc	5531	26
Mft Construction Inc	1611	237
Mg Concepts Inc	5046	44
MG Design Associates Corp	7389	297
MG Digital Rentals	7359	270
Mg International Inc	2821	44
MG Machine Inc	3599	1428
MG Machining	3545	233
MG Midwest Inc	7841	5
MG Newell Company Inc	5084	120
M-G Novelty Co	5947	24
MG West Co	8744	46
MGA Investment Company Inc	2741	422
MGB Engineering Company Inc	3559	226
MGE Energy Inc	4939	5
MGE Inc	2741	354
MGE Power LLC	6541	8
Mge Underground Inc	1623	303
mGen Inc	5045	281
Mgh Advertising Inc	7311	554
Mgh Enterprises Inc	1731	983
MGI Electronics LLC	3559	255
MGI Inc	1731	2109
MGIC Investment Corp	6351	18
Mgk Industries Inc	1629	98
Mgl Americas Inc	7379	74
Mgl International Inc	3565	190
M-G-M Co	5031	191
MgM Gold Communications Ltd	7311	989
MGM Instruments Inc	3841	309
MGM Interactive Inc	7372	4523
MGM Networks Latin America LLC	4841	85
MGM Resorts International	7011	6
MGM Service Co	7349	430
Mgm Transformer Co	3612	49
MGM Transport Corp	4212	8
MGM-UA Inc	7812	31
MGP Direct Inc	7331	286
Mgq Inc	5032	79
Mgr Equipment Corp	3585	208

Company Name	SIC	Rank
MGR HOMECARE Inc	8082	70
MGR Molds Inc	3544	833
Mgs Inc	3443	120
Mgs Machine Corp	3565	45
MGS Manufacturing Inc	3549	29
MGW Group Inc	6794	158
Mh Inc	2038	68
MH Software Inc	7373	578
MH Stallman Company Inc	3086	106
Mhart Express Inc	4213	2481
MHC Kenworth	5012	31
MHC Services Inc	7219	4
MHF Express Inc	4213	600
MHF Logistical Solutions Inc	4214	30
MHI Hospitality Corp	6798	180
MHM Correctional Services Inc	8063	3
MHO Networks	4899	205
Mhr Inc	7699	258
Mhrh Facilities	7349	284
MI 2009 Inc	3559	12
MI Inc	3599	1944
M-I LLC	2992	3
Mi Mama's Tortillas Inc	2099	210
Mi Ranchito Food Inc	2032	45
Mi Rancho Tortilla Factory	2099	375
Mi Rancho Tortilla Incorporated	2099	213
MI Windows And Doors	3442	24
Mi16 Inc	7373	918
Mi8 Corp	7376	17
Miami Air Mechanical Inc	4961	6
Miami ASC LP	8011	123
Miami Beef Company Inc	5142	33
Miami Cass County Rural Electric Membership Corp	4911	405
Miami Computer Distributors Inc	5734	325
Miami County Publishing Company Inc	2711	678
Miami Herald Publishing Co	2711	19
Miami Industrial Supply And Manufacturing Inc	3549	100
Miami Machine Corp	3554	58
Miami Micro Export Inc	5045	1054
Miami Purveyors Inc	5147	69
Miami River Stone Co	1422	39
Miami Subs Corp	5812	200
Miami Systems Corp	2761	12
Miami Tape Inc	3652	50
Miami Thread	2284	7
Miami Valley Christian Broadcasting Association Inc	4832	271
Miami Valley Gasket Company Inc	3053	111
Miami Valley Punch and Manufacturing Inc	3544	708
Miami Valley Steel Service Inc	5051	218
Miami Wall Systems Inc	3442	107
Miami Waste Paper Company Inc	5093	147
Miamibras Inc	5045	1044
Miami-Dade Housing Agency	7389	1179
Miami-Luken Inc	5122	47
Miarer Transportation Inc	4213	1427
Miat Inc	5047	184
Mib Industries Inc	2752	511
MiBAC Music Software Inc	7372	4856
Mibar Marketing Corp	5065	271
MIC Industries Inc	3531	86
MIC Systems and Software Inc	7373	750
Mica Information Systems	7371	1451
Mica Tool and Manufacturing Inc	3599	1595
Micafil Inc	3559	194
Micah Group LLC	4959	23
MicahTek Inc	7372	463
Micalline Products Inc	3089	1563
Miceli Dairy Products Co	2022	14
Miceli Homes	1522	59
Michael A Burns and Associates Inc	8743	109
Michael A Long Construction Inc	1623	726
Michael A Yedinak	3829	324
Michael and Morris Enterprises Inc	5064	102
Michael and Sons Real Estate Inc	6531	401
Michael Anthony Jewelers Inc	3911	14
Michael Baker Corp	8741	31
Michael Baker International Inc	8741	307
Michael Best and Friedrich LLP	8111	193
Michael Bolchalk Marketing Inc	7311	971
Michael Brothers Inc	3089	998
Michael B's LLC	2032	36
Michael Business Machines	5084	62
Michael Diehl Design	2741	344
Michael Dunn Center	8331	70
Michael Edmond Gray	2731	383
Michael Flicker	4813	728
Michael Foods Group Inc	0252	2
Michael Foods Inc	2015	6
Michael Foods Investors LLC	0252	3
Michael G Kessler and Associates Ltd	7381	58
Michael Graphics Inc	2752	1330
Michael Gray and Associates Inc	7379	812
Michael J Arnold and Co	3069	283
Michael J Collins Inc	4213	1507
Michael J Manfredi	1731	1396
Michael Levine Music Inc	7389	2397
Michael Lewis Co	5113	19
Michael Nash Interiors Inc	7389	1721
Michael O'connor	1731	2193
Michael Pace Interactive	3565	148

Company Name Index MICROPAC

Company Name Index

Company Name	SIC	Rank
Michael R Panter and Associates	8111	560
Michael Simon Inc	2253	21
Michael Stapleton Associates Ltd	7382	176
Michael Stevens Interests Inc	6531	375
Michael Termondt	4841	125
Michael Thomas Furniture Inc	2512	59
Michael Weinig Inc	5084	269
Michael's Arts and Crafts	5092	54
Michaels' Lighting Inc	3646	69
Michaels of Oregon Co	3484	10
Michael's Printing Inc	2752	1491
Michaels Ross and Cole Ltd	7372	3727
Michaels Stores Inc	5945	2
Michaelson Connor and Boul	8742	272
Michaud Cooley Erickson and Associates Inc	8711	356
Michele Audio Corporation of America	3695	19
Micheletti Inc	6411	210
Michelin North America Inc	3011	6
Michelman Inc	2869	41
Michelman-Cancelliere Iron Works Inc	3441	122
Michels and Wilde Inc	3711	73
Michel's Bakery Inc	2051	79
Michelson Laboratories Inc	8734	123
Michgian Seamless Tube LLC	3316	7
Michiana Accounting Solutions Inc	5734	294
Michiana Plastics Inc	3544	453
Michigan Agricultural Commodities	5153	81
Michigan Automotive Compressor Inc	3585	25
Michigan Bottling and Custom Pack Co	2086	113
Michigan Carbonic Of Saginaw Inc	7359	218
Michigan Celery Promotion Co-Operative Inc	5148	75
Michigan Chronicle Publishing	2711	213
Michigan Commerce Bank	6022	680
Michigan Commerce Bank (Grand Rapids Michigan)	6022	646
Michigan Community Bancorp Ltd	6022	732
Michigan Composites Inc	2822	25
Michigan Contractor and Builder	2721	370
Michigan Dessert Corp	2099	194
Michigan Development Corp	8732	48
Michigan Drill Corp	3545	57
Michigan Educational Credit Union	6062	115
Michigan Electric LLC	1731	2395
Michigan First Credit Union	6062	69
Michigan Fluid Power Inc	5084	256
Michigan Foundation Company Inc	3273	64
Michigan Government Television Inc	4833	257
Michigan Hand Rehabilitation Center Inc	8093	60
Michigan Industrial Finishes Corp	2851	166
Michigan Instruments Inc	3845	127
Michigan Logos LLC	0990	180
Michigan Maple Block Company Inc	2541	46
Michigan Mechanical Services Inc	8711	517
Michigan Message Ctr Inc	7389	1386
Michigan Metal Transporters	4213	1039
Michigan Millers Mutual Insurance Co	6331	156
Michigan Mold Inc	3471	114
Michigan Pipe Supply LLC	5074	224
Michigan Produce Haulers Inc	4213	430
Michigan Production Machining Inc	3599	136
Michigan Rebuild And Automation Inc	3599	1039
Michigan Rod Products	3496	41
Michigan Satellite	3663	200
Michigan Services Credit Union	6062	121
Michigan Software Services Inc	7371	1687
Michigan Southern Railroad Co	4011	35
Michigan Spline Gage Company Inc	3545	309
Michigan Sporting Goods Distributors Inc	5941	17
Michigan State Afl-Cio Human Resources Development Inc	7361	121
Michigan Transport Inc	4213	2612
Michigan Tube Swagers And Fabricators Inc	2522	17
Michigan Turkey Producers Cooperative Inc	2015	43
Michigan Valley Irrigation Co	5083	176
Michigan Web Press Inc	2752	646
Michigan Wheel Corp	3365	6
Mici Inc	1542	299
Mickelberry Communications Inc	2752	17
Mickey Truck Bodies Inc	3713	16
Mickle Wagner Coleman Inc	8711	305
Micom Corp	3672	77
Micom Systems	5734	418
MI-Comply	8748	366
Micon Computer Co	3571	58
MICON Consulting	7379	846
Micon Systems LLC	3823	458
MIControls Inc	5063	182
Miconvi Properties Inc	3565	117
Micor Inc	3089	1074
MICR Automation Inc	7372	5137
Micrel Inc	3674	77
Micrgraphics Printing Inc	2752	1583
Micro 100 Tool Corp	3545	90
Micro 2000 Inc	7372	2798
Micro Accessories Inc	3577	285
Micro Alarm Systems Inc	5063	242
Micro Analysis and Design Inc	7372	1827
Micro Analytics Of Virginia Inc	7372	3501

Company Name	SIC	Rank
Micro Basics Co	3571	224
Micro Brew I Inc	7389	1476
Micro Burn-In and Technology Inc	3825	242
Micro Centric Corp	3545	157
Micro Circuit Inc	3672	404
Micro Computer Analysts Inc	3571	174
Micro Computer Cable Company Inc	3357	73
Micro Computer Systems Of South West Florida Inc	3679	180
Micro Connectors Inc	3577	504
Micro Contacts Inc	3469	222
Micro Control Co	3825	65
Micro Cooling Concepts Inc	3823	438
Micro Craft Inc	3694	20
Micro Craft Inc (Huntsville Alabama)	7372	3728
Micro Crystal	3825	243
Micro Data Systems Inc	7378	130
Micro Decisions Corp	3625	379
Micro Depot Inc	7373	571
Micro Design Engineering Corp	7379	1414
Micro Design International Inc	3572	48
Micro Design International (USA) Inc	3999	98
Micro Design Services LLC	7371	875
Micro Development Services Inc	5045	691
Micro Digital Inc	7372	4316
Micro Dynamics Corp	3672	21
Micro Electronics Corp	5065	959
Micro Electronics Inc	5734	4
Micro Encoder Inc	8731	208
Micro Engineering Inc	3674	331
Micro Estimating Systems Inc	7372	3357
Micro Express Inc	3571	60
Micro Focus Group PLC	7371	389
Micro Gage Inc	3674	340
Micro Generation Technologies Inc	1731	2527
Micro Identification Technologies Inc	6794	163
Micro Industries Corp	8711	449
Micro Industries Inc	3364	24
Micro Innovations Inc	7371	1792
Micro Instrument Corp	3599	163
Micro J Systems Inc	7372	1900
Micro Lambda Wireless Inc	3679	423
Micro Lapping and Grinding Company Inc	3599	1360
Micro Lithography Inc	3823	54
Micro Logic Corp	7372	3275
Micro Machine Company LLC	3599	466
Micro Madness Ltd	7373	1162
Micro Magic Inc	7373	1194
Micro Manufacturing Inc	3599	1439
Micro Map and CAD	7371	1894
Micro Matic USA Inc	3585	58
Micro Medics Computer/Printer Service Inc	7378	41
Micro Metals Inc	3399	21
Micro Methods	7372	457
Micro Metl Corp	3444	54
Micro Mini Hydraulics	5084	886
Micro Mo Electronics Inc	5063	227
Micro Mold Company Inc	3089	1360
Micro Mold Plastics Inc	3089	1812
Micro Motion Inc	3823	23
Micro Net Associates Inc	7379	1281
Micro Parts and Supplies Inc	5045	1023
Micro Performance Inc	7371	1495
Micro Planning International Inc	7372	3409
Micro Plastics Inc (Chatsworth California)	3089	1667
Micro Pneumatic Logic Inc	3492	16
Micro Power Electronics Inc	3691	20
Micro Power Systems Inc	3674	101
Micro Precision Corp	3599	583
Micro Precision Of Texas Inc	3599	1890
Micro Probe Inc	3826	147
Micro Quality Calibration Inc	7699	217
Micro Quality Semiconductor Inc	3674	411
Micro Ray Electronics Inc	5065	913
Micro Sales Inc	5065	749
Micro Seven Inc	3661	161
Micro Solutions Enterprises Inc	3577	136
Micro Solutions Plus Inc	5045	556
Micro Specialties Inc	7372	4464
Micro Stamping Corp	3841	84
Micro Star Software Inc	5045	100
Micro Steel Inc	3769	25
Micro Strategies Inc	7371	468
Micro Surface Engineer Inc	3399	29
Micro Symplex Inc	3571	93
Micro Systems Engineering Inc	3674	106
Micro Tech Computer Service Inc	7379	884
Micro Technology Consultants Inc	7373	684
Micro Technology Groupe Inc	7379	801
Micro Technology Unlimited	3651	205
Micro Tool Engineering Inc	3599	2349
Micro Tool Service Inc	3545	345
Micro Tracers Inc	8734	186
Micro Visions Inc	7379	1537
Micro Wire Forms Inc	3496	123
MicroAge Inc	7373	53
Microagility Inc	7379	1134
Micro-Aide Inc	3629	114
Micro-Aire Surgical Instruments Inc	3841	106
MicroAnalytics Inc	7372	3502
Microanalytics Instrumentation Corp	3829	92

Company Name	SIC	Rank
MicroAutomation Inc	7372	3542
Microbac's Wilson Division	8734	49
Microban Products Co	2842	73
Microbes Inc	8711	530
Microbest Inc	3451	32
MicroBilt Corp	7373	198
Microbiologics Inc	2835	68
Microbiz Security Co	5065	515
Microboard Processing Inc	3672	52
Microboards Technology Inc	3571	53
Microboards Technology LLC	3577	235
Microcal LLC	3821	41
Microchem Corp	2899	153
Microchip Technology Inc	3674	31
Microchip Technology Incorporated Analog and Interface Products Div	3674	174
Micro-Coax Inc	3679	32
Microcom Corp	3577	335
MicrocomNet Inc	1731	2223
MicroComputer Specialists	7372	4925
Microcomputer Systems Inc	3823	471
MicroControls International	7372	4428
Microcosm Inc	8711	207
Microdata Group Inc	7373	1097
Micro-Design Inc	3823	392
Microdesk Inc	7372	5043
Microdrive Corp	3572	90
Microdry Inc	3567	115
Microdynamics Corp	7374	109
Microdyne Outsourcing Inc	3661	46
Microdyne Plastics Inc	3089	532
MicroEdge LLC (New York New York)	7372	1411
Microenergy Systems Inc	3823	443
Microfab Inc	3679	753
Microfibres Inc	2221	11
Microfilm Products Co	3579	53
Micro-Filtration Inc	3569	277
MicroFinancial Inc	6159	68
Microfinish International Technologies	7371	1922
Microflex Inc	3494	27
Microfluidics International Corp	3821	18
Microforms Inc	2752	536
Microframe Corp	3663	296
Micro-G Lacoste Inc	3829	242
Microgear	5045	396
Microglobe Networkz Inc	4813	626
MicroGlyph Systems	7372	4524
Micrograms Software	7372	3276
MicroGroup Inc	3317	17
Micro-Hybrid Dimensions Inc	3674	387
Microlab-FXR	8999	138
Micro-Labs Inc	3672	456
Microland Electronics Corp	5045	424
Microlap Technologies Inc	3915	11
Microlaw Inc	7373	1204
MicroLeague Multimedia Inc	7372	2507
Microline Surgical Inc	3841	109
Microlink Enterprises Inc	5045	286
Microlite Corp	7372	4931
Microlog Corp	3661	162
Micrologic Business Systems Inc	5045	599
Micrologic Inc (Westboro Massachusetts)	3669	110
MicroMass Communications Inc	7372	1333
MicroMat Computer Service	7378	148
Micromat Inc	7372	4384
Micromatic Electronic Distribution Inc	7373	1005
Micromatic Screw Products Inc	3451	143
Micro-Mechanical Inc	3599	771
Micromedia Studios	7373	727
Micromedics Inc	3841	141
MicroMega Systems Inc	7379	732
Micromet Corp	3812	220
Micromet Inc	2836	27
Micrometals Inc	3679	160
Micromex Inc	3679	883
Micromint Inc	3577	561
Micromod Automation Inc	3625	244
Micro-Mode Products Inc	3663	118
Micromold Products Inc	3494	73
Micron Business Products Inc	3861	122
Micron Corp	3672	398
Micron Electrical Contracting Inc	1731	2462
Micron Enviro Systems Inc	3599	2518
Micron Inc	8734	204
Micron Machine Co	3599	1668
Micron Manufacturing Inc	3451	69
Micron Molding Inc	3089	1062
Micron Optics Inc	8732	81
Micron Products Inc	3965	21
Micron Research Corp	3624	32
Micron Systems Corp	7372	2550
Micron Systems Inc	7371	1156
Micron Technology Inc	3674	5
Micronas USA Inc	3651	90
Micronet Systems Inc	7372	4429
MicroNet Technology Inc	3572	35
Micronetics Inc	3679	140
Micronetics Incorporated Information Management Systems	7372	2077
Micronics Inc	3599	34
Micronics Technologies Inc	3672	455
Micro-Ohm Corp	3676	27
Micropac Industries Inc	3674	216

MICROPACT

Company Name Index

Company Name	SIC	Rank
MicroPact Engineering Inc	7372	2376
Micropatent LLC	2741	163
Micropen Technologies Corp	3676	11
Microphase Corp	3663	125
Microphor Inc	3089	729
Microphoto Inc	3569	236
Microporous Products LP	3061	16
Microprecision Inc	3469	127
Micro-Precision Inc	3559	397
Micro-Precision Technologies Inc	3674	448
MicroPress Inc	7372	3685
Micro-Processor Services Inc	7372	5015
Micropulse Inc	3841	130
Micropump Inc	3561	180
MicroQuill Software Publishing Inc	5734	242
Microridge Systems Inc	3625	387
MICROS Systems Inc	7373	17
Microscale Industries Inc	2752	1730
Microscan Systems Inc	3577	112
Microscope Store LLC	5049	114
Microscreen LLC	3999	164
Microsearch Corp	7372	3000
MicroSearch Inc	5045	418
MicroSECONDS International Inc	7372	1136
Microsemi Corp	3674	45
Microsemi Integrated Products	3674	147
Microsemi-RFIS	3669	118
Microsensor Systems Inc	3812	159
Microserv Computer Technologies Inc	4813	385
Micro-Serv Corp	7379	389
MicroServ Inc	7372	3055
MICROS-Fidelio Southeast Inc	5044	105
MICROS-Fidelio Southwest Inc	7373	451
Micro-Smart Systems Inc	3571	166
Microsoft Corp	7372	1
Microsonic Inc	3089	1316
Microsource Inc	3679	64
Microspace Communications Corp	4812	45
Microsphere Inc	5734	388
Microspy	7378	157
MICROS-Retail	7372	1116
Micro-Star Computer Services Inc	5734	317
Microstar Laboratories Inc	3577	375
Microstore Inc	3577	557
MicroStrategy Inc	7372	105
Microsun Technologies LLC	3699	92
Micro-Surgical Technology Inc	3841	203
Microsys Information Systems Inc	7373	766
Microsystems Development Technologies Inc	7372	4977
Microsystems Technology Inc	5045	792
Microtab Inc	7372	4525
MicroTech	7379	216
Microtech Computers Inc	5045	524
Micro-Tech Designs Inc	3823	401
Microtech Electronics Inc	5063	1094
Microtech Inc	3643	104
Microtech Systems	3577	203
Microtechnologies Inc	3674	462
Microtechnologies LLC	7379	192
Microtek Inc	3634	29
MicroTek Inc (Oakbrook Terrace Illinois)	7377	11
Microtek Lab Inc	3577	121
Micro-Tek Laboratories Inc	3823	304
Microtek Medical Inc	3842	71
Microtel Computer Systems Inc	7379	630
Micro-Tel Inc	7372	2396
Microtel Inns and Suites	6794	115
Microtelecom Systems LLC	7371	1582
Microtex Inc	5023	146
Microtherm Inc	5064	171
Microtool And Instrument Inc	3545	161
Micro-Trap Corp	3669	310
Micro-Tronics	3679	783
Micro-Tronics Inc	3599	192
Microtronics Inc	3625	266
MicroUnity Systems Engineering Inc	7371	1090
MicroVision Development Inc	7372	2429
Microvision Inc	3679	464
Microvisions Computer Systems Inc	7371	1383
Micro-Vu Corporation Of California	3827	46
Microwave Applications Group	3679	571
Microwave Circuit Technology Inc	3679	533
Microwave Communications Laboratories Inc	3679	597
Microwave Data Systems Inc	3669	65
Microwave Devices Inc	3679	823
Microwave Dynamics	3663	294
Microwave Engineering Corp	3679	290
Microwave Filter Company Inc	3679	447
Microwave Instrumentation Technologies LLC	3825	85
Microwave Technology Inc	3679	358
Microwave Transmission Systems Inc	3663	51
Microweld Engineering Inc	3369	29
MicroWest Software Systems Inc	7372	3227
MicroWorks Inc	7372	2162
Microworks Pos Solutions Inc	5734	152
Micrus Endovascular Corp	3841	58
Mictron Inc	3599	2204
Mid America Computer Corporation Inc	7373	995
Mid America Frame Inc	2499	38
Mid America Machine Inc	3599	1408
Mid America Motorworks	5961	104
Mid America Publishers	2711	702
Mid America Steel Inc	3441	27
Mid America Telephone Systems	5999	286
Mid American Growers	5193	15
Mid Atlantic Health Management Inc	8741	261
Mid Atlantic Medical Services Inc	6324	36
Mid Atlantic Sports LLC	3949	115
Mid Atlantic Xpress Inc	4213	2043
Mid Cities Motor Freight Inc	4213	377
Mid City Bank Inc	6021	271
Mid Columbia Children's Council Inc	8351	19
Mid Continent Controls Inc	3812	137
Mid Continent Marketing Services	5074	171
Mid Continent Van Service	4213	2109
Mid Eastern Builders	1622	43
Mid Florida Electrical and Controls Inc	1731	1676
Mid Florida Steel Corp	3449	28
Mid Iowa Coop	5153	31
Mid Island Die Cutting Corp	2675	4
Mid Island Y Jewish Community Center Inc	8322	128
Mid Kansas Machine Inc	3599	1426
Mid Missouri Telephone Co	4813	451
Mid Oklahoma Coop	5084	769
Mid Penn Bancorp Inc	6022	248
Mid Penn Bank	6022	302
Mid Rockland Imaging Partners Inc	8093	20
Mid Seven Transportation Co	4213	632
Mid South Extrusion Inc	3081	71
Mid South Machine Inc	3599	1137
Mid South Transport	4213	1002
Mid State Machine Products	3545	17
Mid States Electric Co	1731	1196
Mid States Paper/Notion Co	5122	103
Mid Valley Dairy Company-Turlock	5143	9
Mid Valley Equipment	5084	796
Mid Valley Industries LLC	3599	268
Mid West Co	5063	496
MIDAC Corp	3829	177
Midaco Corp	3599	849
Mid-AM Building Supply Inc	5031	24
Midamar Corp	5147	17
Mid-America Apartment Communities Inc	6798	92
Mid-America Auto Auction Inc	5012	106
Mid-America Business Systems And Equipment Inc	8742	550
Mid-America Cabinets Inc	2434	49
Mid-America Cardiology Associates PC	8011	79
Mid-America Door Co	3442	72
Mid-America Festivals Inc	7999	130
Mid-America Hardwoods Inc	2431	50
Mid-America Health Centers	8059	22
Midamerica Holdings Corp	3354	42
Midamerica Hotels Corp	7011	129
Mid-America Lumber Inc	5211	277
Mid-America Machining Inc	3599	405
Mid-America Manufacturing Corp	3531	181
Mid-America Manufacturing Inc	3599	2365
Mid-America Packaging	2674	3
Mid-America Plastic Co	3089	1390
Mid-America Plastics Inc	3089	1263
Midamerica Printing	7389	1933
Mid-America Services Inc	7349	414
Mid-America Steel Corp	5051	288
Mid-America Taping and Reeling Inc	7694	13
Mid-America Telephone Systems Inc	5065	561
Mid-American Elevator Company Inc	1796	8
MidAmerican Energy Co	4911	19
MidAmerican Energy Holdings Co	4911	26
Mid-American Precision Products LLC	3499	17
Midamerican Printing Systems Inc	2752	607
Mid-American Products Inc	3089	377
Mid-American Water and Plumbing Inc	5074	146
Midas Foods International	2099	184
Midas Inc	5013	36
Midas International Corp	3714	181
Midas Special Equities Fund Inc	6722	101
Mid-Atlantic Computers Inc	7373	707
Mid-Atlantic Control Systems LLC	1731	2079
Mid-Atlantic Corporate Federal Credit Union	6061	77
Mid-Atlantic Data System Inc	7379	851
Mid-Atlantic Manufacturing And Hydraulics Inc	3492	28
Mid-Atlantic Packaging	2653	49
Mid-Atlantic Transportation Services LL	4213	2288
Midbrook Inc	3559	129
MidCap Business Credit	6159	74
Mid-Carolina Electric Coop	4911	194
Mid-Carolina Steel and Recycling Company Inc	3341	22
Mid-Central Manufacturing Inc	3728	172
MidCenturyJewelrycom	5632	12
Mid-City Foundry Co	3543	3
Mid-City Iron and Metal Corp	5093	65
Mid-City Precision Inc	3599	1726
Midco Fabricators Inc	3533	93
Mid-Co Implement Inc	5083	200
Mid-Coast Electric Supply Inc	5063	263
Midcoe Transportation Co	4213	2195
Midcon Cables Co	3679	36
Midcon Cables Company Inc	3679	203
Mid-Continent Aircraft Corp	5599	15
Mid-Continent Capital LLP	6282	595
Mid-Continent Casualty Co	6331	199
Midcontinent Communications	4841	21
Midcontinent Communications Inc	4841	32
Mid-Continent Engineering Inc	3599	316
Midcontinent Media Inc	4832	13
Mid-Continent Tool and Molding Inc	3089	1630
Mid-Counties Electric Inc	1731	1873
Mid-County Coop	5191	23
Middco Tool and Equipment Inc	3469	357
Middle Atlantic Products Inc	3441	8
Middle Atlantic Warehouse Distributor Inc	5013	35
Middle Bay Consulting Inc	7371	1895
Middle East Bakery Inc	2051	141
Middle East Baking Co	2051	287
Middle Tennessee Electric Membership Corp	4911	133
Middle Tennessee Lumber Company Inc	2421	108
Middle Tennessee Natural Gas Utility District	4924	63
Middle Tyger Times	2711	721
Middleberg Riddle and Gianna	8111	416
Middlebrook Group Inc	7311	471
Middleburg Financial Corp	6021	104
Middlebury Electric Inc	1731	1791
Middlebury Hardwood Products Inc	2431	56
Middlebury National Corp	6712	526
Middleby Corp	3585	18
Middleby Marshall Inc	3556	3
Middlecreek Corp	1623	640
Middlefield Original Cheese Coop	2022	81
Middlefield Plastics Inc	3089	1107
Middlesboro Coca-Cola Bottling Works Inc	2086	68
Middlesex Hospital Inc	8741	192
Middlesex Water Co	4941	12
Middleton Aerospace Corp	3724	29
Middleton Doll Co	6798	207
Middleton Holdings LLC	5999	293
Middleton Machining and Welding Inc	3599	1050
Middleton Motors Inc	5511	1060
Middleton Printing Company Inc	2752	1803
Middletown Adolescent Leaders Achieve	7389	2431
Middletown Ford Inc	5511	964
Middletown Press Publishing Co	2711	396
Middletown Tube Works Inc	3312	90
Middleville Tool and Die Company Inc	3469	196
Middough Associates Inc	8711	218
Mide Technology Corp	3625	121
Mid-Eastern Industries Div	3679	362
Mideo Systems Inc	7373	734
Midern Computer Inc	3571	111
Midessa Television LP	4833	180
MidFirst Bank	6035	25
Mid-Florida Forklift Inc	5084	651
Mid-Florida Publications Inc	2741	490
Midgard Inc	3089	552
Mid-Georgia Courier Inc	4215	6
Mid-Hudson Communications Inc	8748	375
Midi Music Center Inc	3931	24
Midian Electronics Inc	3663	273
MIDIator Systems	3577	676
Mid-Island Electrical Sales Corp	5063	117
Mid-Kansas Cooperative Association	2048	18
Midlab Inc	2842	56
Mid-Lakes Distributing Co	3444	53
Midland 66 Oil Company Inc	5171	26
Midland Asphalt Materials Inc	1611	165
Midland Bioproducts Corp	2835	59
Midland Capital Holdings Corp	6035	222
Midland Cogeneration Venture LP	4931	42
Midland Communications Inc	4812	110
Midland Community Center Inc	8322	126
Midland Computer Inc	5045	460
Midland Consumer Radio Inc	3679	505
Midland Cut Stone Company Inc	3281	42
Midland Electric Co	1731	669
Midland Electric Supply Inc	5063	915
Midland Engineering Company Inc	1761	15
Midland Financial Co	6035	27
Midland Forge	3462	35
Midland Industries Inc	3356	33
Midland Information Systems Inc	5045	538
Midland Loan Services Inc	6798	183
Midland Manufacturing Company Inc	3085	29
Midland Medical Supply Co	5047	57
Midland Metal Products Co	2542	40
Midland National Bank	6021	363
Midland National Life Insurance Co	6311	101
Midland Plastics Inc	5162	23
Midland Precision Machining Inc	3545	398
Midland Press Corp	2759	109
Midland Radio Corp	5065	66
Midland Railway Supply Inc	5088	54
Midland States Bancorp Inc	6712	32
Midland Steel Warehouse Corp	5051	313
Midland Technologies Inc	3089	1867
Midland Wellhead Inc	3599	1087
Midlands Millroom Supply Inc	5084	618
Midlands Packaging Corp	2657	22

Company Name	SIC	Rank
Midlothian Laboratories	5122	88
MidMark Capital LLC	6799	243
Midmark Corp	3648	8
Mid-Michigan Industries Inc	8331	55
Midnet Media (Columbus Ohio)	7319	122
Midnight Media Group	7819	36
Midnite Express	4513	12
Midnite Express Inc	4213	1240
Mido Printing Company Inc	2752	903
MidOcean Capital	6799	67
Mid-Ohio Electric Co	7694	26
Mid-Ohio Forklifts Inc	5084	640
Mid-Ohio Pipeline Company Inc	1623	105
Mid-Ohio Products Inc	3544	202
Midor- Ltd	2023	31
Midori America Corp	5065	780
Mid-Park Inc	3444	75
Midpoint International Corp	8711	492
Midpoint National Inc	7331	261
Midrange Performance Group Inc	7372	2929
Midrange Software Inc	7372	1284
Midrange Support and Service Inc	7371	1661
Midrex Corp	8711	379
Mid-Rivers Telephone Cooperative Inc	4813	119
Mid-Ship Logistics	7389	900
Mid-Ship Marine Inc	7389	547
Mid-Shore Electronics Inc	5731	116
MidSouth Bancorp Inc	6712	321
MidSouth Bank NA	6021	191
Mid-South Builders Inc	1623	221
Mid-South Building Supply of Maryland Inc	5033	22
Mid-South Conveying Inc	3535	203
Mid-South Electric Contractors Inc	1731	792
Mid-South Electronics Inc	3824	9
Mid-South Engine Systems Inc	7699	148
Mid-South Express Delivery	4213	2100
Mid-South Extrusion Die Company Inc	3544	28
MidSouth Geothermal LLC	5075	80
Mid-South Industries Inc	3585	98
Mid-South Industries Inc	3999	11
Mid-South Machine and Welding Company Inc	3599	1710
Midsouth Media Group	2721	459
Mid-South Milling Company Inc	2048	71
Mid-South Publishing Company Inc	2752	970
Mid-South Sewing Machine Sales Inc	5722	23
Mid-South Synergy	4911	183
Mid-South Telecommunications Co	4813	356
Mid-South Wire Company Inc	3315	20
Mid-Southern Savings Bank FSB	6035	183
Mid-State Automotive Parts Rebuilders Inc	3714	390
Mid-State Bolt and Nut Company Inc	5072	88
Mid-State Chemical and Supply Corp	2992	39
Mid-State Communications and Electronics Inc	5065	273
Midstate Construction Corp	1542	280
Mid-State Contracting LLC	1711	181
Midstate Electronics Co	5065	174
Midstate Environmental Services LP	5093	250
Mid-State Group Inc	5083	143
Mid-State Industries Operating Inc	3316	29
Mid-State Machine and Fabricating Corp	3443	34
Midstate Manufacturing Company Inc	3599	174
Mid-State Mechanical Inc	1731	706
Midstate Medical Supply and Equipment Rental Inc	5047	193
Midstate Mills Inc	2041	30
Midstate Mold and Engineering	3089	1679
Mid-State Printing Inc	2752	1759
Mid-State Sand and Gravel Company Inc	2951	40
Midstate Security Company LLC	7382	77
Midstate Steel Inc	3441	134
Mid-States Controls Corp	3625	388
Mid-States Corp	3535	155
Midstates Engineering Corp	3823	459
Mid-States Express Inc	4213	509
Midstates Industrial Group Inc	7373	715
Mid-States Millwright and Builders Inc	1796	23
Mid-States Paint and Chemical Co	2851	150
Midstates Printing Inc	2752	185
Mid-States Supply Company Inc	5085	42
Midstates Tool and Die And Engineering Inc	3541	193
Mid-Step Services Inc	8361	51
Mid-Tenn Ford Truck Sales Inc	5511	493
Midtown Computer Services	4899	197
Midtown Partners and Company LLC	6153	23
Midtown Printing Co	2752	974
Midtown Printing Inc	7336	150
Midtronics Inc	3825	72
Midvale Industries Inc	5084	219
Midvale Paper Box Company Inc	2657	45
Mid-Valley Grain Coop	5172	112
Mid-Valley Labor Services Inc	7361	90
Midvalley Publishing Inc	2711	783
Mid-Valley Services Inc	6162	90
Mid-Valley Supply LLC	5085	369
Midway Auto Parts Inc	5015	7
Midway Building Supply Inc	5211	196
Midway Collections Inc	7322	160

Company Name	SIC	Rank
Midway Ford Truck Center Inc	5511	115
Midway Grinding Inc	3599	870
Midway Interactive Inc	7372	218
Midway Machine and Instrument Company Inc	3599	2098
Midway Manufacturing Inc	3593	48
Midway Motors Inc	5511	494
Midway Motors Supercenter	5511	906
Midway Muffler Inc	7538	18
Midway Oil Co	5171	46
Midway Products Group Inc	8741	199
Midway Rotary Die Solutions	2754	34
Mid-Way Supply Inc	5075	51
Midway Winnelson Co	5063	499
Midweek Inc	2741	366
Midwesco Filter Resources Inc	3564	7
Midwest Accounting Services Inc	7291	18
Midwest Acoust-A-Fiber Inc	5531	24
Midwest Air Group Inc	4512	29
Midwest Air Products Company Inc	3564	141
Midwest Aircraft Products Company Inc	3728	223
Midwest Appliance Parts Co	5064	163
Midwest Asphalt Corp	1611	195
Midwest Auto Clubs LLC	4724	134
Midwest B R D Inc	3556	169
Midwest Brake Bond Co	3714	389
Midwest Bus Corp	7532	3
Midwest Byline	2711	676
Midwest Cabinet and Counter Inc	5031	385
Midwest Can Company and Container Specialties Inc	3089	803
Midwest Canvas Corp	3081	48
Midwest Cargo Systems Inc	4213	2544
Midwest Coast Transport	4213	503
Midwest Coca-Cola Bottling Co	2086	27
Midwest Collaborative for Library Services	5045	263
Midwest Commercial Interiors	5943	11
Midwest Computer Register Corp	3999	188
Midwest Container And Industrial Supply Co	3085	37
Midwest Continental Inc	4213	548
Midwest Control Corp	3613	143
Midwest Cooperatives	5153	49
Midwest Copier Exchange LLC	5044	76
Midwest Cortland Inc	2631	33
Midwest Curtainwalls Inc	3449	16
Midwest Cutting Tools Inc	3545	288
Midwest Detection Systems Inc	1731	1611
Midwest Distributing Corp	5046	319
Midwest Drywall Company Inc	1521	35
Midwest Editions Inc	2789	81
Midwest Elastomers Inc	2822	14
Midwest Electric	1731	132
Midwest Electric Inc	4911	556
Midwest Electric Products Inc	3699	118
Midwest Electrical Appliance Service Center Inc	5046	243
Mid-West Electrical Supply Inc	5063	916
Midwest Energy Emissions Corp	7311	1044
Midwest Energy Inc	4931	50
Midwest Energy Management Inc	3823	436
Midwest Express Corp	4213	2225
Mid-West Fabricating Co	3714	205
Midwest Family Broadcasting Inc	4832	136
Midwest Farm Service Co	5083	169
Mid-West Feeder Inc	3545	322
Midwest Fibre Sales Corp	2611	9
Midwest Filtration Co	3569	106
Midwest Flex Systems Inc	3825	294
Midwest Floor Coverings Inc	5023	68
Midwest Fluid Power LLC	5084	891
Midwest Food Service Equipment Inc	5046	266
Mid-West Forge Corp	3462	31
Midwest Gasket Corp	3053	134
Midwest Grain Products Inc	3999	16
Midwest Graphics Inc	3555	60
Midwest Graphite Company Inc	3297	14
Midwest Health Services Inc	8361	132
Midwest Imaging and Roller Services Inc	2796	66
Midwest Independent Bancshares Inc	6712	457
Midwest Independent Bank	6022	783
Mid-West Industrial Chemical Co	2891	101
Midwest Industrial Metals Corp	5093	161
Midwest Industrial Supply Incorporated	2899	122
Midwest Industrial Tools Inc	5084	569
Midwest Industries and Development Ltd	3599	502
Midwest Industries Inc	3799	8
Midwest Ink Co	2893	26
Midwest Insert Composite Moulding and Assembly Corp	3089	1252
Midwest Instrument Company Inc	3469	58
Midwest International Standard Products Incorporated Intermidwest Ltd	3531	65
Midwest Interstate Electrical Construction Co	1731	604
Midwest Janitorial Services	8331	83
Midwest Laboratories Inc	8734	61
Midwest Laser Systems Inc	3599	1421
Midwest Machining Inc	3544	635
Midwest Maintenance Company Inc	7349	88

Company Name	SIC	Rank
Midwest Maintenance Inc	7349	327
Midwest Marble Co	3281	44
Mid-West Materials Inc	5051	114
Midwest Media Group Inc	5045	335
Midwest Medical Copy Service Inc	7375	201
Midwest Medical Management Inc	8741	239
Midwest Metal Products Co	3441	105
Midwest Metals Inc	5051	372
Midwest Mixing Inc	3559	524
Midwest Modelmakers Inc	3999	185
Midwest Mold and Texture Corp	3544	113
Midwest Mole Inc	1623	235
Midwest Motor Express Inc	4213	67
Midwest Natural Gas Corp	4924	69
Midwest Oil Co	5171	17
Midwest Outdoors Ltd	2721	305
Midwest Paralegal Services Inc	7389	2272
Midwest Patterns Inc	3543	5
Midwest Plastic Engineering Inc	3089	796
Midwest Plastics Company Inc	3085	49
Midwest Precision Tool and Die Inc	3599	776
Midwest Prefinishing Inc	2431	125
Midwest Press Brake Dies Inc	3544	697
Midwest Products And Engineering Inc	3444	78
Midwest Promac Inc	3643	140
Midwest Publishing Inc	2721	112
Midwest Quality Gloves Inc	5199	39
Midwest Recreational Clearinghouse LLC	5599	12
Midwest Recycling Co	4953	152
Midwest Regional Credit Union	6062	109
Midwest Roll Forming and Manufacturing Inc	3449	8
Midwest Rubber Service and Supply Co	5085	229
Midwest Sales and Service Inc	5064	72
Midwest Scientific Inc	5047	119
Midwest Screw Products Inc	3599	799
Midwest Sealing Products Inc	3053	83
Midwest Service Center LLC	7629	22
Midwest Service Warehouse Inc	4226	13
Midwest Siding Distributors	5033	61
Midwest Special Services Inc	8331	85
Midwest Specialized Transportation	4213	415
Mid-West Spring and Stamping	3495	2
Midwest Stainless Technologies LLC	1751	12
Midwest Stamping Inc	3469	14
Mid-West Steel Building Co	3448	2
Midwest Super Store	5511	745
Midwest Supply and Distributing	5191	126
Midwest Systems	4213	106
Midwest Technology Connection Inc	5734	37
Midwest Timer Service Inc	3823	194
Midwest Tool and Cutlery Co	3421	16
Midwest Tool and Die Corp	3544	417
Midwest Tool and Engineering Co	3544	543
Midwest Tool Distributors	5072	67
Midwest Tool Inc	3542	68
Midwest Towers Inc	2499	10
Midwest Trading Co	5013	352
Midwest Tropical Inc	3231	66
Midwest Urethane Inc	3081	171
Midwest Utility Trenching Service	1623	785
Midwest Vending Inc	3581	14
Midwest Veterinary Supply Inc	5047	15
Midwest Viking Inc	4213	3002
Midwest Walnut Company Iowa	5031	244
Midwest Web Inc	2752	309
Mid-West Wholesale Lighting Corp	5063	300
Mid-West Wire Products Inc	3496	66
Midwest Wire Products LLC	3496	77
Midwest Wrecking Co	5015	3
Midwestern Audit Services Inc	8721	436
Midwestern Broadcasting Co	4832	94
Mid-Western Car Carriers Inc	4213	1625
Midwestern Contractors	1623	181
Midwestern Industries Inc	3559	55
Mid-Western Machinery Company Inc	3532	64
Midwestern University	8221	22
Midwest-Northern Inc	5145	29
MidWestOne Financial Group Inc	6712	232
Mid-Willamette Lumber Products Inc	2421	78
Mid-Wisconsin Financial Services Inc	6022	297
Mid-Wood Inc	5399	17
Midwood Quarry and Construction Inc	5211	293
Mid-York Press Inc	2679	47
MiE America Inc	3829	301
MIE Corp	5084	380
Mies Equipment Inc	5083	100
Miesfeld's Triangle Market Inc	5421	6
MIG and Co	7379	644
MIG Inc	7319	152
Migatron Corp	3829	325
Migatron Precision Products Inc	3541	178
Mighty Distributing System of America Inc	5013	28
Mighty Mat Inc	2299	27
Migration Specialties International Inc	7379	926
Migu Press Inc	2752	1157
Miguel Tejera Enterprises	8742	712
Miicor Inc	7371	1083
Miille Applied Research Co	8731	381
Mija Industries Inc	3823	198
Mi-Jack Promotions LLC	7948	39

Company Name	SIC	Rank
Mi-Jenn Ventures Inc	7349	259
Mika Co	6552	190
Mika International Inc	3231	75
Mika Meyers Beckett and Jones PLC	8111	449
Mikab Corp	1623	485
Mikara Corp	5087	11
Mikart Inc	2834	230
Mikasa Inc	3262	1
Mikawaya	2051	178
Mike Alexander Dies Inc	3544	385
Mike and Jerry's Paint and Supply	5013	329
Mike Balter Mallets	3931	36
Mike Brooks Inc	4213	1041
Mike Bubalo Construction Company Inc	1623	146
Mike Campbell and Associates Ltd	4213	695
Mike Castrucci Ford Sales Inc	5511	276
Mike Collins and Associates Inc	5734	84
Mike Crivello's Camera Centers Inc	5946	15
Mike Daugherty Chevrolet Inc	5511	368
Mike Garcia Merchant Security LLC	7381	74
Mike Gibson Electric Inc	1731	2242
Mike Hage Distinctive Concrete and Masonry	1771	6
Mike Haggarty Pontiac GMC Truck and Volkswagen Inc	5511	907
Mike Horall	5087	76
Mike Hudson Distributing Inc	5147	49
Mike Jensen Farms	0175	6
Mike Kenney Tool Inc	3599	956
Mike McGrath Auto Center	5511	668
Mike McMahan Desk Inc	5021	176
Mike Murach and Associates Inc	2731	108
Mike Posey Photography and Video Inc	7812	293
Mike Pruitt Honda	5511	692
Mike Riehl's Chrysler Plymouth Jeep	5511	306
Mike Shad Ford at the Avenues	5511	435
Mike Shaw Automotive	5511	198
Mike Shaw Texas Motors Inc	5012	65
Mike Smith Auto Plaza	5511	282
Mike Young Motor Co	5511	1106
Mikel Machine Inc	3599	2018
Mikels Construction Co	1623	593
Mikelson Machine Shop Inc	3812	173
Miken Specialties	7353	61
Mike's Electric Inc	1731	1305
Mike's Hard Lemonade Co	2082	17
Mike's Loading Service Inc	4731	47
Mike's Micro Parts Inc	3599	1064
Mike-Sell's Potato Chip Co	2096	12
Mikim Industries Inc	3599	879
Mikon Systems	7372	1507
Mikron Corp (Denver Colorado)	3569	78
Mikron Infrared Inc / E2T	3823	288
Mikros Engineering Inc	3089	642
Mikros Systems Corp	3663	217
Mil Electronics Inc	3679	864
Mil Ltd	3441	80
Mila Kofman	5149	223
Milacron Resin Abrasives Inc	3291	2
Milady Bridals Inc	2335	5
Milagro Systems Inc	7372	4985
Milan Express Company Inc	4213	105
Milan Properties	6531	194
Milan Supply Co	5082	136
Milan Tool Corp	3728	159
Milano Brothers International Corp	5065	208
Milan's Machine Shop and Welding Service Inc	3599	1454
Milan's Machining and Manufacturing Company Inc	3599	546
Milara Inc	3555	59
Milastar Corp	3398	9
Milazzo Industries Inc	2842	78
Milbank Manufacturing Co	3825	25
Milberg Factors Inc	6153	48
Milbert Corp	3651	221
Milco Industries Inc	2258	4
Milco Utilities Inc	1623	717
Milco Waterjet LLC	3599	2420
Milco Wire Edm Inc	3599	2123
Milcom Corporation Inc	7373	1118
Mil-Com Distributors Inc	5065	776
Milcom Services Inc	3199	19
Mile Hi Frozen Food Co	5142	15
Mile High Beverages Inc	2086	126
Mile High Food Equipment Inc	5046	371
Milo High Greyhound Racing at Wombly Park	7948	24
Mile High Racing and Entertainment	7948	19
Mile Marker International Inc	3714	305
Milea Hudson Valley Truck Center Corp	5012	139
Mile-Hi Machine Inc	3599	1786
MilePost Credit Union	6062	40
Miles 33 International Ltd	7372	587
Miles Capital	6282	561
Miles Consulting Corp	7373	622
Miles Electric Vehicles	3799	22
Miles Farm Supply LLC	5261	11
Miles Fiberglass and Composites Inc	3089	316
Miles Kimball Co	5961	20
Miles Media Group Inc	2721	164

Company Name	SIC	Rank
Miles Rubber and Packing Co	3053	89
Miles Treaster and Associates	5021	29
Milesbrand Inc	7311	753
Miles-McClellan Construction Company Inc	1542	119
MilesTek Corp	3669	177
Milestone Cleaning LLC	7349	525
Milestone Construction Services Inc	1541	232
Milestone Contractors LP	1611	34
Milestone Field and Post Inc	7812	228
Milestone Growth Fund Inc	6799	356
MileStone Healthcare	8069	22
Milestone Internet Marketing	7374	393
Milestone Merchant Partners LLC	6029	17
Milestone Metals Inc	3365	4
Milestone Properties Inc	6512	47
Milestone Scientific Inc	3842	159
Milestone Venture Partners LLC	6799	127
Mile-X Equipment Inc	5085	425
Milfoam Corp	3089	1537
Milford Bank	6036	43
Milford Enterprises Inc	2541	26
Milford Manufacturing Services LLC	3672	120
Milford National Bank and Trust Co (Milford Massachusetts)	6021	139
Milford Printers	2752	1413
Milford Regional Healthcare Foundation Inc	8062	154
Milford Supply Co	5074	163
Milhous Control Co	3559	461
Mili Pharmaceuticals Inc	8731	287
Milici Valenti Ng Pack Advertising	7311	177
Military/Aerospace Division of Pulse	3679	457
Military Car Sales Inc	8741	210
Military Marketing Services Inc	2731	307
Military Personnel Services Corp	8999	11
Military Sales and Service Co	7389	636
Militec Inc	2899	188
Miljavac Electric Corp	1731	2316
Miljoco Corp	3823	165
Milk Products LLC	2023	14
Milk Products LLC	2024	82
Milk Specialties Co	2048	15
Milk Transport Inc	4213	1956
Milkco Inc	2026	24
Milko Tool and Die Inc	3599	1927
Milky-Way Transport Company Inc	4213	2176
Mill and Mine Supply Co	5084	763
Mill and Motion Inc	3599	2124
Mill Assist Services Inc	3547	22
Mill Cove Lobster Pound Co	5146	65
Mill Creek Entertainment LLC	5735	18
Mill Creek Lumber and Supply Co	5031	44
Mill Hardware and Food Service Inc	5046	250
Mill Masters Inc	3543	14
Mill Pond Press Inc	2752	847
Mill Power Inc	3535	206
Mill Sprocket and Machinery Corp	3568	75
Mill Steel Co	5051	181
Mill Tool And Manufacturing Corp	3544	689
Mill Valley Molding Inc	3089	915
Millard Lumber Inc	5211	56
Millard Public Schools	8211	34
Millat Industries Corp	3714	279
Millbrook Distribution Services Inc	5141	122
Millbrook Printing Co	2752	795
Millbrook Travel Consultants Inc	4724	144
Millburn Peat Company Inc	1499	6
Mille Fabricators	2499	57
Mille Lacs Gourmet Foods	5149	111
Millenium Cable and Wireless LLC	7373	802
Millenium Computer Solutions LLC	5734	390
Millenium Technologies	7371	1396
Millennia Corp	7372	4622
Millennia Technology Inc	3679	181
Millennial Media	7373	166
Millennial Net Inc	5045	547
Millennium Bank NA	6021	183
Millennium Bankshares Corp	6021	270
Millennium Business Solutions Group Inc	7371	1215
Millennium Carpet Mills Inc	2273	28
Millennium Commercial Cleaning Services Inc	7349	286
Millennium Die Group Inc	3544	690
Millennium Digital Media Holdings LLC	4841	44
Millennium Electronics Inc	3679	265
Millennium Enterprises Unlimited Inc	1731	714
Millennium Films Inc	7336	142
Millennium Ford Inc	5511	902
Millennium Group Of Delaware Inc	8744	27
Millennium Iii Inc	3679	891
Millennium India Acquisition Company Inc	6799	315
Millennium Industries Corp	3469	60
Millennium Machining LLC	3599	673
Millennium Marketing Solutions Inc	2752	1518
Millennium Marking Co	3953	12
Millennium Microwave Corp	3663	319
Millennium Partners	6552	48
Millennium Pharmaceuticals Inc	2834	62
Millennium Pharmacy Systems Inc	7372	429
Millennium Plastics Technologies LLC	7539	2
Millennium Press Inc	2752	1402

Company Name	SIC	Rank
Millennium Steel Services LLC	3449	5
Millennium Technology Partners LLC	5065	269
Millennium Three LLC	3599	1919
Millennium Transit Services LLC	3711	74
Miller Agency Inc	7311	473
Miller and Chevalier	8111	223
Miller and Company Inc	5031	53
Miller And Company Portable Toilet Services Inc	7359	176
Miller and Holmes Inc	5541	28
Miller and Jedrziewski Associates	7389	1468
Miller and Long Company Inc	1771	11
Miller and Norford Inc	1542	419
Miller and Schroeder Financial Inc	6211	309
Miller and Smith Inc	1521	52
Miller and Weber Inc	3829	317
Miller Auto Company Inc	5511	119
Miller Automotive Group Inc	5511	155
Miller Bakery Inc	2051	174
Miller Bearing Company Inc	3562	41
Miller Bearings Inc	5085	25
Miller Bonded Inc	1731	192
Miller Broach Inc	3545	203
Miller Brooks Inc	7311	533
Miller Brothers Chevrolet Inc	5511	953
Miller Brothers Express LC	4213	1044
Miller Building Systems Inc	3448	13
Miller Canfield Paddock and Stone PLC	8111	53
Miller Carbonic Inc	3625	381
Miller Castings Inc	3324	7
Miller Communications Inc	1731	519
Miller Co	3444	86
Miller Construction Co	1521	65
Miller Container Corp	2653	36
Miller Cooper and Company Ltd	8721	282
Miller Curber Company LLC	3531	224
Miller Curtain Company Inc	2391	2
Miller/Davis Co	7372	4180
Miller Design and Equipment LLC	3674	454
Miller Dial Corp	2796	4
Miller Distributing Inc	5194	7
Miller Edge Inc	3699	105
Miller Electric and Technology Inc	1731	700
Miller Electric Co (Jacksonville Florida)	1731	49
Miller Electric Company Of Indiana Inc	1731	1131
Miller Electric Co (Omaha Nebraska)	1731	126
Miller Electric Manufacturing	3548	40
Miller Electric Manufacturing Co	3548	8
Miller Energy Resources Inc	1311	164
Miller Engineering Co	1711	168
Miller Equipment Company Inc	7359	108
Miller Excavating Inc	1442	77
Miller Felpax Corp	3743	26
Miller Formless Company Inc	3531	189
Miller Funeral Home	7261	14
Miller Group Advertising	7311	662
Miller Hardware Co (Harrison Arkansas)	5251	13
Miller Heiman Inc	8748	88
Miller Industrial Products Inc	3369	23
Miller Industries Inc (Ooltewah Tennessee)	3713	6
Miller Isaacson Inc	7361	106
Miller Johnson Snell and Cummiskey	8111	210
Miller Jones Corp	7389	1319
Miller Kaplan Arase and Company LLP	8721	59
Miller Legg and Associates Inc	8711	337
Miller Machine and Tool Company Inc	3599	2161
Miller Machine and Welding LLC	1799	107
Miller Machine Inc	3599	1527
Miller Magazines Inc	2721	262
Miller Manufacturing Company Inc	5199	50
Miller Manufacturing Co (South Saint Paul Minnesota)	3523	31
Miller Manufacturing Inc	3599	2322
Miller Metals Service Corp	5051	220
Miller Microcomputer Services	7372	4719
Miller Mining And Engineering Technologies // Oregon LLC	7389	1506
Miller Mold Co	3559	259
Miller Nash LLP	8111	162
Miller O'connell Corp	2752	965
Miller Oil Co	5172	60
Miller Packing Co	2013	159
Miller Paint Company Inc	2851	20
Miller Plant Farms Inc	0181	11
Miller Printing Company Inc	2752	1771
Miller Real Estate Investments	6552	176
Miller/Russell and Associates Inc	6282	184
Miller St Nazianz Inc	3523	44
Miller Sales and Engineering Inc	5082	119
Miller Shingle Company Inc	2411	7
Miller Stuart Inc	3679	424
Miller Studio Inc	3299	9
Miller Systems Inc (Boston Massachusetts)	7372	712
Miller Technologies International	2671	42
Miller Tool and Die Co	3542	29
Miller Tool and Die Company Inc	3544	388
Miller Transporters Inc	4213	781
Miller Travel Services Inc	4724	65
Miller Truck Lines Inc	4213	809
Miller Veneers Inc	2435	17

Company Name Index

MIRACLE

Company Name	SIC	Rank
Miller Veterinary Supply Company Inc	5047	148
Miller Wagner and Company PLLC	8721	81
Miller Waste Mills Inc	3087	5
Miller Welding And Machine Co	7692	3
Miller Weldmaster Corp	3548	43
Miller Wire Works Inc	3496	64
Miller Zell Inc	8742	132
Miller-Brands-Milwaukee LLC	5181	44
MillerCoors LLC	2082	4
Miller-Davis Co (Kalamazoo Michigan)	1541	145
Miller-Eads Company Inc	1731	82
Miller-Holzwarth Inc	3827	70
Miller-Jackson Co	3661	177
Miller-Marek Inc	7389	1180
Miller's American Honey Inc	2099	109
Miller's Carpet One	5712	93
Miller's Country Hams Inc	2013	224
Miller's Dodge	5511	1197
Miller's Feeding Solutions Inc	3559	436
Miller's Health Systems Inc	8052	8
Miller's Interiors Inc	5713	11
Miller's Shady Oaks Inc	5812	441
Millersburg Ice Co	2097	22
Millersburg Tire Service Inc	5014	19
Miller-Valentine Group	6519	10
Millgard Corp	1794	36
Millie and Severson Inc	1542	338
Milligan Workshops Inc	3061	57
Milliken and Co	2211	1
Milliken Chemical	3999	2
Milliken Investments Inc	5063	438
Milliman Inc	8742	40
Millington Telephone Company Inc	4813	754
Millinocket Fabrication And Machine Inc	3312	124
Millionair Club Charity Inc	8322	238
Millionaire Corp	5399	12
Millipart Inc	3599	1692
Millis Transfer Inc	4213	331
Mill-Log Equipment Company Inc	5084	203
Millman Lumber Co	5031	37
Mill-Max Manufacturing Corp	3678	15
Millrite Machine Inc	3599	1094
Mill-Rose Co	3841	137
Mills and Partners Inc	6282	668
Mills Co	2522	44
Mills Distributing	4213	3039
Mills Heating and Air Conditioning Inc	5075	59
Mills Machine Company Inc	3533	103
Mills Manufacturing Corp	2399	14
Mills-James Inc	7812	114
Millstadt Rendering Co	5159	28
Millstein Industries	6531	421
Millstone Bangert Inc	1611	190
Millstone Enterprises Inc	5084	825
Millstone Medical Outsourcing LLC	7389	1068
Milltech Manufacturing Co	3599	807
Millward Brown Inc	8732	3
Millwood Inc	2448	2
Millwood Industries LLC	5211	210
Millwood Trucking Inc	4213	586
Millwork Distributors Inc	5031	184
Millwork Sales Georgia LLC	5031	168
Millwork Sales of Valdosta LLC	5031	340
Milmar Food Group Ii LLC	2038	34
Milne Fruit Products Inc	0723	8
Milner Milling Inc	5149	92
Milo Gordon Auto Mall	5511	1124
Milo Stallcop	5065	748
Mil-Pac Technology Inc	7372	2884
Milpitas Materials Co	5032	156
Milplex Circuits Inc	3672	130
Milport Enterprises Inc	5169	113
Milprint Inc	2759	75
Milsco Manufacturing Co	2531	17
Milspec Industries Inc	5072	111
Mil-Specialties Magnetics Inc	3677	91
Miltec Corp	8734	23
Miltimore Sales Inc	5065	583
Milton Bradley Co	3944	6
Milton Electric Company Inc	1731	616
Milton J Wood Co	1542	97
Milton Newspapers Inc	2711	900
Milton Roy Co	3561	59
Milton Samuels Advertising Agency Inc	7311	437
Milton Terry Associates Inc	5021	102
Milton Transportation Inc	4213	1059
Milton Vermont Sheet Metal Inc	3599	505
Miltons Inc	5611	26
Miltope Group Inc	3577	160
Miltronics Manufacturing Services Inc	3679	481
Milvets Systems Technology Inc	7373	444
Milwaukee Bearing and Machining Inc	3568	58
Milwaukee Broach Company Inc	3541	110
Milwaukee Catholic Press Apostolate Inc	2711	673
Milwaukee Chaplet Inc	5085	401
Milwaukee Cylinder	3593	17
Milwaukee Electronics Corp	3625	61
Milwaukee Endoscopy Center	8011	174
Milwaukee Gear Company Inc	3566	7
Milwaukee International Inc	3536	49
Milwaukee Job Center North	7361	181
Milwaukee Machinetool Corp	3545	225
Milwaukee PC Incorporated A Wisconsin Corp	3575	12
Milwaukee Public Theatre	7922	100
Milwaukee Punch Corp	3544	600
Milwaukee Resistor Corp	3625	108
Milwaukee Sign Company LLC	3993	78
Milwaukee Sprayer Manufacturing Company Inc	3563	48
Milwaukee Stove and Furnace Supply Company Inc	5074	91
Milwaukee Valve Company Inc	3494	32
Milwaukee Waterworks	1623	286
Milwhite Inc	1459	6
Milwright Co	3089	804
Mimeo Inc	7334	8
MimeoCom Inc	2759	31
MIMICS Inc	7372	4250
Mimi's Cafe	5812	17
Minardi Baking Company Inc	5149	159
Minarik Corp	3625	17
Minatronics Corp	7382	181
Minco Manufacturing LLC	3861	114
Minco Technology Labs LLC	5065	258
Mincon Rockdrills USA Inc	3545	216
Mincron SBC Corp	7372	1671
Mind Design Systems	7372	4042
Mind Media Inc	7372	5023
Mind Over Media	7812	123
Mind Path Technologies Inc	3577	675
Mind Software Inc	7372	2512
Mindbank Consulting Group Inc	7379	82
Mindbank Consulting Group Of Denver LLC	7379	796
Mindbody Inc	7372	2025
Mindbridge Systems Inc Realtrac Div	7372	1400
Mindemann Trucking Inc	4213	2786
Minden Exchange Bank and Trust Co	6022	668
MindFire Inc	7372	1503
MindGate Technologies Inc	7372	2892
MindIQ Corp	8299	46
Mindjet Corp	7372	741
MindLeaders	2741	66
MindLeaf Technologies	7373	474
Mindmatters Technologies Inc	7371	1205
Mindpix Corp	7371	764
Mindrum Precision Products Inc	3824	25
Mindshift Technologies	7373	190
Mindshift Technologies Inc	7371	130
MindSmack Inc	7379	1017
Mindsource Inc	7363	272
Mindspeed Technologies Inc	7372	290
MindTouch Inc	5045	1075
MindVision Software Inc	7371	1260
Mindwave Research Inc	8748	175
Mindwrap Technologies Inc	7372	3584
Mine and Mill Supply Company Inc	5082	68
Mine Safety Appliances Co	3842	13
Mine Supply Co	5085	135
Min-E-Con LLC	3678	47
Mineola Packing Co	5147	85
Miner and Miner Consulting Engineers	7372	1177
Miner Enterprises Inc	3743	19
Mineral Daily News Tribune	2711	691
Mineral Labs Inc	8734	51
Mineral Research and Development	2819	79
Mineral Resources International Inc	2834	375
Minerallac Co	3644	17
Minerallac Electric Co	3644	11
Minerals Technologies Inc	2819	14
Minerva Cheese Factory Inc	2022	13
Minerva Networks Inc	7373	397
Mines Management Inc	1081	5
Mines Press Inc	2752	178
Mine-Safe Electronics Inc	7699	200
MINEsoft Ltd	7372	4857
Minetta Live LLC	7832	26
Ming Pao Inc (Long Island City New York)	2711	345
Minges Bottling Group	5149	29
Mingledorffs Inc	5075	10
Mingo Manufacturing Inc	3533	63
Mini Computer Exchange Inc	5045	448
Mini Computer Services Inc	5045	881
Mini Fibers Inc	2282	2
Mini Graphics Inc	2759	524
Mini Melts	2024	23
Miniature Plastic Molding LLC	3559	556
Miniature Precision Components Inc	3089	97
Miniature Precision Inc	3599	2346
Minicom Advanced Systems Limited - US Office	3674	135
Minier Cooperative Grain Co	5153	92
Minigrip/Zip-Pak	3089	286
Minimatics Inc	3599	567
Mini-Max Marble and Composites LLC	3281	36
Mini-Mcro Supply Inc (New York New York)	5045	474
Mining Controls Inc	3612	24
Miningham and Oellerich Inc	7371	1020
MiniSoft Inc	7372	1983
Mini-Systems Inc	3676	7
Minit Print It	2752	1456
Minitab Inc	7372	1517
Minka Lighting Inc	5063	121
Min-Max Machine Ltd	3728	168
Minmetals Inc	5052	12
Minn-Dak Co	7538	20
Minn-Dak Farmers Cooperative Inc	2099	24
Minn-Dak Growers Ltd	2048	58
Minn-Dak Yeast Company Inc	2099	340
Minneapolis Grain Exchange	6231	9
Minnesota Air Inc	5074	43
Minnesota Architectural Alliance Inc	8712	223
Minnesota Chemical Co	5087	70
Minnesota Computers Corp	5045	491
Minnesota Corrugated Box Inc	2653	83
Minnesota Dehydrated Vegetables Inc	2034	22
Minnesota Diversified Industries Inc	3089	703
Minnesota Diversified Products Inc	3086	47
Minnesota Electric Technology Inc	3621	123
Minnesota Elevator Inc	3534	10
Minnesota Energy Ethanol LP	2869	44
Minnesota Fabrication and Machine Inc	3599	2162
Minnesota Financial Development Corp	6552	283
Minnesota Flexible Corp	5085	211
Minnesota Insty-Prints Inc	2752	1573
Minnesota Life Insurance Co	6311	37
Minnesota Logos Inc	3993	181
Minnesota Mining and Manufacturing Co Electronics Markets Materials Div	2671	9
Minnesota Mining and Manufacturing Company Industrial Mineral	3295	7
Minnesota Petroleum Service Inc	5078	30
Minnesota Pipeline Co	4612	13
Minnesota Produce Inc	5148	74
Minnesota Professional Nursing Services	7363	264
Minnesota Rusco Inc	5211	288
Minnesota Shredding LLC	5093	166
Minnesota Southern Wireless Inc	4813	81
Minnesota Spokesman-Recorder	2711	330
Minnesota Suburban Publications LLC	2711	347
Minnesota Supply Co	5084	232
Minnesota Tool and Die Works Inc	3312	115
Minnesota Twist Drill Inc	3545	30
Minnesota Valley Testing Laboratories Inc	8734	85
Minnesota Valley Transport	4213	2214
Minnesota Wire	3643	31
Minnetonka Audio Software	7371	661
Minnich Manufacturing Company Inc	3531	193
Minnick Supply Company Inc	5063	780
Minn-Kota Ag Products Inc	4221	4
Minnkota Power Cooperative Inc	4911	265
Minnotte Contracting Corp	1799	23
Minnow Bear Computers	7372	5138
Minntech Corp	3842	61
Minolta Corporation Business Products Group	3861	11
Minolta-QMS Inc	3577	95
Minooka Grain Lumber and Supply Co	5153	165
Minor Rubber Company Inc	3061	31
Minority Auto Handling Specialists Inc	4731	64
Minot Restaurant Supply Company Inc	5046	286
Minowitz Manufacturing Co	3069	229
Minson Corp	2512	26
Minster Machine Co	3542	3
Mint Systems Corp	3825	302
Mintec Inc	7372	1378
Minteq International Inc	3297	9
Minterbrook Oyster Co	2091	6
Mintie Corp	7389	323
Minto Research and Development Inc	3842	317
Minton Door Co	5031	355
Minton-Jones Co	5021	87
Mintronix Inc	3578	21
Mintz and Hoke Inc	7311	198
Mintz Levin Cohn Ferris Glovsky and Popeo PC	8111	125
Minuta Architecture PLLC	8712	245
Minuteman Controls Company Inc	5085	318
Minuteman Electric LLC	1731	2489
Minuteman International Inc	3589	38
Minuteman Laboratories Inc	3827	112
Minuteman Press International Inc	6794	108
Minuteman Security Inc	7381	185
Minuteman Trucks Inc	5012	89
Minuteman UPS	3629	84
Minutemen Precision Machining and Tool Corp	3728	165
Minyard Food Stores Inc	5411	88
Mio Publication Inc	2721	445
Miox Corp	3589	130
MIPS Technologies Inc	3674	117
Mir3 Inc	4813	189
Mir3Com Inc	4813	334
MIRA Digital Publishing	7372	3168
Mira Inc	3841	301
Mira Lighting and Electrical Service Inc	7349	433
Mirabilis Design Inc	5734	195
Mirac Inc	7371	1529
Miracle Auto Painting Inc	7532	4
Miracle Exclusives Inc	5064	218
Miracle International Corp	5084	450
Miracle Place International Church	7389	2230
Miracle Recreation Equipment Company Inc	3949	30
Miracle Software Systems Inc	7379	89

Ward's Business Directory of U.S. Private and Public Companies, 55th Edition / Volume 5

1597

Company Name	SIC	Rank
Miracle Tools America LLC	3546	23
Miracle Tv Corp	5045	864
Miraco	3523	117
Miraco Inc	3315	34
Miracon Wireless LLC	4812	128
Mirage Enterprises Inc	3799	35
Mirage Resorts Inc	7011	66
Mirage Studios	8999	210
Mirak Chevrolet Inc	5511	347
MiraLink Corp	7372	3543
Miramar Dielectric Laboratory	3679	884
Miramar Federal Credit Union	6061	119
Miramar Securities Inc	6211	271
Miramax Film Corp	7812	57
Mirapoint Inc	7372	110
Mirart Inc	2824	14
Mirenco Inc	3714	427
Miriello Grafico	7336	329
Mirion Technologies Inc	5063	43
Miro Consulting Inc	8748	248
Miroglio Textiles USA Inc	5131	42
Mirro/Calphalon	3365	2
Mirror Image Internet Inc	7371	207
Mirror Image Media Solutions Inc	5045	629
Mirwec Film Inc	3081	164
MIS Construction Software Inc	7372	4932
Misa Metals Inc	5051	8
Miscellaneous Metals Inc	3446	28
Misco/Minneapolis Speaker Company Inc	3651	120
Misco Products Corp	2842	51
MISCOR Group Ltd	7623	2
Misha Consulting Group Inc	7379	677
Mishler Packing Company Inc	5147	144
Miskelly Furniture	5712	31
Miskin Scraper Works Inc	3523	95
Misonix Inc	3821	20
Miss Daisy's Home Care LLC	8082	87
Miss Eaton Inc	2512	77
Miss Elaine Inc	2341	12
Miss Paige Ltd	7361	95
Missco Corporation of Jackson	5021	24
Mission Announcement Co	2759	488
Mission Clay Products Corp	3259	2
Mission Community Bancorp	6021	287
Mission Controls Company Inc	3625	351
Mission Data LLC	7372	4127
Mission E Commerce LLC	7379	449
Mission Essential Personnel LLC	7361	11
Mission Federal Credit Union	6061	27
Mission Foods Corp	2099	36
Mission Health System	8062	244
Mission Hills Mortgage Bankers	6162	68
Mission Laboratories	2842	87
Mission Microsystems Inc	3625	325
Mission Mortgage of Texas Inc	6162	58
Mission Mountain Enterprises Inc	8331	158
Mission Mountain Winery	2084	136
Mission National Bank	6021	293
Mission Oaks Bancorp	6712	654
Mission Oaks National Bank	6021	63
Mission Of Mercy	7389	659
Mission Petroleum Carriers	4213	298
Mission Produce Inc	5148	49
Mission Rubber Co	3069	13
Mission Solutions Engineering LLC	7371	50
Mission Support Corp	7379	1667
Mission Technology Group Inc	3577	427
Mission Tool and ManufacturingCoInc	3599	991
Mission Trail Waste Systems Inc	4953	113
Mission Valley Ford Trucks Sales Inc	5012	33
Mission West Properties Inc	6512	33
Mississippi Central Railroad Co	4011	36
Mississippi Coast Coliseum Commission	7389	1736
Mississippi Home Corp	6162	50
Mississippi Insurance Services Inc	6411	260
Mississippi Limestone Corp	1422	5
Mississippi Logos LLC	3993	185
Mississippi One Call System	7389	1952
Mississippi Phosphates Corp	2819	40
Mississippi Police Supply Co	5049	208
Mississippi Power	4911	69
Mississippi River Transmission Corp	4922	20
Mississippi Safety Services Inc	5192	25
Mississippi Tank Company Inc	3443	86
Mississippi Valley Equipment Co	5082	110
Mississippi Welders Supply Company Inc	5084	111
Missoula Area Education Coop	7361	354
Missoula Federal Credit Union	6061	58
Missouri Baking Co	2051	289
Missouri Equipment Co	3444	211
Missouri Forge Inc	3462	56
Missouri Higher Education Loan Authority	6111	9
Missouri Logos LLC	3993	182
Missouri Machinery and Engineering Co	7699	59
Missouri Petroleum Products Company LLC	5033	11
Missouri Poster And Banner Company Inc	2759	549
Missouri Pressed Metals Inc	3568	57

Company Name	SIC	Rank
Missouri Rural Electric Coop	4911	438
Missouri-American Water Co	4941	23
Missourian Publishing Co	2711	368
Mistequay Group Ltd	3544	35
Mister Bee Potato Chip Co	2096	42
Mister Ralph's Inc	5023	152
Mister Sparky Inc	1731	535
Mistick Construction	1542	255
Mistral Inc	3812	66
MISTRAS Group Inc	8711	50
Misty Mate Inc	3999	133
Misys International Banking Systems	7372	1303
MIT Group Inc	7372	4385
MIT International Inc	2392	5
MIT Lincoln Laboratory	8731	41
Mitann Inc	2899	139
Mitas Group Inc	7372	4181
Mitch Murch's Maintenance Management Co	7349	13
Mitcham Industries Inc	7359	36
Mitchel and Scott Machine Company Inc	3451	9
Mitchell A Fink Associates Inc	7372	3358
Mitchell Aircraft Spares Inc	5088	68
Mitchell and Mccormick Inc	7373	713
Mitchell and Son Inc	3599	1320
Mitchell and Titus LLP	8721	52
Mitchell Associates Inc	7389	1627
Mitchell Carlson Stone Inc	8712	267
Mitchell Company Inc	1531	57
Mitchell Container Services Inc	5085	269
Mitchell Electric Membership Corp	4911	256
Mitchell Electronics Corp	3677	78
Mitchell Electronics Inc	3679	853
Mitchell Enterprises Inc	1542	321
Mitchell Gold Plus Bob Williams Co	2512	58
Mitchell Golf Equipment Co	3949	136
Mitchell Graphics Inc	2752	1051
Mitchell Group	6282	445
Mitchell Humphrey and Co	7372	2799
Mitchell Instruments Company Inc	5084	829
Mitchell International	2741	10
Mitchell Lewis and Staver Co	5084	326
Mitchell Machine Inc	3559	318
Mitchell Manufacturing LLC	3599	983
Mitchel/Martin Inc	7361	38
Mitchell Metal Products Inc	3444	195
Mitchell Rubber Products Inc	3061	11
Mitchell Rubber Products Inc	3069	15
Mitchell Selling Dynamics Inc	7375	271
Mitchell Signs Inc	3993	121
Mitchell Silberberg and Knupp	8111	247
Mitchell Supreme Fuel Co	5172	12
Mitchell Temporary Services Inc	7363	287
Mitchell Williams Selig Gates and Woodyard PLLC	8111	274
Mitchellace Inc	2241	15
Mitchell-Carroll Homes Inc	1521	91
Mitchell's Management Corp	7299	18
Mitchell's Salon and Day SpA Inc	7231	10
Mitchum Inc	2096	48
Mitchum-Schaefer Inc	3599	407
Mitco Industries Inc	3533	116
Mi-Te Fast Printers Inc	2752	1013
Mi-Tech Inc	3511	33
Mi-Tech Steel Inc	5051	52
Mitek Systems Inc	3577	318
Mitek Worldwide	3842	64
Mitem Corp	7372	1856
Mitenergy Upstream LLC	1382	29
Mithun Partners Inc	8712	162
Mi-T-M Corp	3569	45
Mitographers Inc	2752	999
Mitos Pharmaceuticals Inc	8731	334
Mitratech Holdings Inc	7372	979
Mits LLC	3812	214
Mitsuba Bardstown Inc	3714	138
Mitsubishi Caterpillar Forklift America Inc	3537	16
Mitsubishi Chemicals America Inc	2833	11
Mitsubishi Electric and Electronics USA	3651	12
Mitsubishi Electric and Electronics USA Inc - Semiconductor Div	3674	95
Mitsubishi Electric Automotive America Inc	3694	13
Mitsubishi Electric Power Products	3613	45
Mitsubishi Electric Power Products Inc	3613	7
Mitsubishi Electric Research Laboratories	7371	211
Mitsubishi Elevator Co	3534	26
Mitsubishi Gas Chemical America Inc	3674	119
Mitsubishi Heavy Industries America Inc	3728	12
Mitsubishi Heavy Industries Climate Control Inc	3563	17
Mitsubishi International Corp	5141	89
Mitsubishi Motor Sales of America Inc	5012	3
Mitsubishi Motors North America Inc	3711	18
Mitsubishi Polycrystalline Silicon America Corp	3339	17
Mitsubishi Rayon America Inc	3081	37
Mitsubishi UFJ Financial Group Inc	6029	9
Mitsui and Co USA Inc	5051	24
Mitsui Foods Inc	5149	26

Company Name	SIC	Rank
Mitsui Plastics Inc	5162	7
Mitsui Seiki (USA) Inc	5084	210
Mitsui Sumitomo Marine Management (USA) Inc	8741	163
Mitsushiba International Inc	3949	131
Mitten Software Inc	7372	3927
Mitternight Boiler Works Inc	3443	62
Mittler Corp	3599	948
Mitutoyo America Corp	5084	77
Mity Enterprises Inc	2522	8
Mitzel's American Kitchen Inc	5812	219
Miu LLC	3089	1219
Miva Corp	7372	3462
Mix 102 5	4832	80
Mix Printing Company Inc	2752	1274
MIX Software Inc	7372	4526
Mixed Logic LLC	3699	299
Mixer Systems Inc	3531	76
Mixman Technologies Inc	2741	267
Mixmor Inc	3531	222
Mixon Fruit Farms Inc	5148	79
Miyachi Unitek Corp	3548	12
Miyagi Tscuchida Inc	8111	561
Miyama USA Inc	3585	122
Miyano Machinery USA Inc	5084	352
Mize Houser and Company PA	8721	120
Mizpah Healthcare Inc	8361	168
Mizpah Precision Manufacturing	3592	30
Mizuho OSI	3842	62
Mizuho Securities USA Inc	6211	343
Mizuno USA Inc	3949	68
MJ Allen Inc	5082	145
MJ Daly and Sons Inc	1711	125
MJ Halgard Construction	1623	470
MJ Harden Associates Inc	7389	641
MJ Losito Electrical Contractors Inc	1731	715
Mj Manufacturing Co	3714	359
MJ Metal Inc	5093	71
Mj Optical Inc	5048	13
MJ Peterson Real Estate Inc	6552	185
MJ Soffe Company Inc	2339	6
Mj Technologies of Nj Inc	7379	1135
MJ Whitman Holding Corp	6211	92
MJ Whitman Inc	6211	93
MJB Manufacturing Company Inc	2323	3
MJC Cos	1531	50
Mjc Engineering And Technology Inc	3542	94
Mjl Sales and Marketing Inc	5065	918
Mjm Industries Inc	3643	75
Mjm Manufacturing Inc	3444	181
MJM Programming Consultants	5734	485
MJM Software Design	7372	4720
Mjo Services LLC	7389	2218
Mjs Cleaning Services Inc	7349	518
Mjs Designs Inc	8711	600
Mjw Inc	3561	108
MK and Associates Inc	7379	1101
MK Chambers Co	3451	93
M-K Express Co	4213	478
MK Hansen Co	3822	100
Mk Management Inc	5045	646
MK Morse Co	3425	4
MK Smith Chevrolet Inc	5511	329
MK Technical Services Inc	7363	226
Mkm Machine Tool Company Inc	3451	19
MKP Transport Inc	4213	1620
Mks Inc	3646	92
MKS Inc (Wayne Pennsylvania)	7372	4527
MKS Industries Inc	5031	143
MKS Instruments Inc	3823	6
MKS Instruments Inc Spectra Products Div	3674	210
Mks Pipe and Valve Co	5085	198
Mks Services Inc	7349	343
MKS Software Inc	7372	800
Mkt Innovations	3599	482
Mktc Telenet USA Inc	4813	605
MKTG Inc	7319	27
ML Holdings Inc	6719	188
ML Macadamia Orchards LP	0139	3
ML McDonald Sales Company Inc	1721	2
ML Pace Computer Consulting	7371	1914
ML Pfeffer Associates	7379	1630
Mlaskoch Utility Construction Inc	1623	618
MLB Advanced Media LP	7999	35
MLB Industries Inc	1542	271
MLG Commercial	6531	83
Mlh Services LLC	7375	287
MLJ and Associates	7379	1334
MLK Delivery Service Inc	4213	3121
MLM Software Solutions Inc	7372	4721
Mlogica Inc	7371	1013
MLP Seating Corp	2522	50
MM Industries Inc	3559	320
MM Reif Ltd	2394	25
MM Smith Storage Warehouse Inc	4213	3017
MM Systems Corp	3446	29
MM Temps Inc	7361	285
MMA Creative	7319	55
MMC and P Retirement Benefit Services Inc	8742	537
MMC Communications	8743	318
Mmc Materials Inc	3273	43
MMC Metrology Lab Inc	5065	353

Company Name	SIC	Rank
MMC Systems Inc	8748	321
Mmcomm Inc	3663	262
Mmd Mountain Mold And Die Inc	3544	834
MMD Stone LLC	1422	60
MMedia Research Corp	7372	5096
MMG Corp	3499	21
MMG Corp (St Louis Missouri)	2323	2
Mmi Engineered Solutions Inc	3089	520
MMI of Mississippi Inc	2541	51
MMI Products Inc	3496	4
Mmk Trading Inc	5045	750
MML Bay State Life Insurance Co	6311	213
Mml Diagnostics Packaging Inc	2836	72
MML Pension Insurance Co	6311	137
Mmlj Inc	3569	173
MMM Carpets Unlimited Inc	5713	14
MMO Music Group Inc	3652	47
MMR Group Inc	1731	2485
MMR Technologies Inc	3679	123
MMRGlobal Inc	2834	472
MMS A Medical Supply Co	5047	19
Mms Inc	5734	318
Mmt Technology Inc	3679	567
Mmyb Inc	3556	173
MN Badeaux Construction Services Inc	1731	2224
Mnemonics Inc	8711	345
Mnemonics Inc (Mount Laurel New Jersey)	7372	4043
MngnExcel Business Supplies Inc	5021	116
Mnm Group Inc	5063	232
Mnp Corp	3452	16
Mnsg Acquisition Company LLC	7373	795
Mnstar Technologies Inc	3714	421
MO Dion and Sons Inc	5172	73
MO Nelson and Sons Inc	4213	2008
Moai Technologies Inc	7371	254
Mo-Ark Communications And Electronics Inc	5731	151
Mobel Inc	2511	49
Moberg Electric Inc	5063	992
Mobi	7372	1504
Mobile 365	4812	16
Mobile Air Transport Inc	4213	1954
Mobile Concrete Inc	5032	124
Mobile Equipment Co	3536	45
Mobile Fixture And Equipment Company Inc	5046	43
Mobile Home Stuff Store Inc	5039	57
Mobile Homes Central	5271	4
Mobile Line Communications Corp	5065	200
Mobile Manufacturing Co	3553	57
Mobile Mex-Media Group	8742	81
Mobile Mini Inc	7519	3
Mobilo Office Machines Inc	7378	137
Mobile Paint Manufacturing Company of Delaware Inc	2851	43
Mobile Press Register Inc	2711	200
Mobile Productivity Inc	7375	26
Mobile Rosin Oil Co	2861	4
Mobile Satellite Connection LLC	3663	317
Mobile Software Inc	7379	1381
Mobile Solutions Inc	7372	3758
Mobile Technology Inc	3663	130
Mobile Telesystems Inc	4899	121
MobileDemand	3571	136
MobilePro Corp	3661	77
Mobilerobots Inc	8711	417
Mobile's Answer Service Inc	7389	2095
Mobiletec International Inc	7373	959
Mobility Services International LLC	7389	365
Mobilogic Inc	7372	4858
Mobious Microsystems Inc	3674	233
MobiTV	4833	58
Mobium Corp	7336	38
Mobius Communications Co	8748	388
Mobius Venture Capital	6799	226
Mobo USA Corp	3663	283
Moc Acquisition Corp	3851	26
Mocap LLC	3089	145
Mocaro Dyeing and Finishing Inc	2257	9
Mocaro Industries Inc	2257	10
Moco Inc	7311	887
Moco Transportation Company Inc	4213	2678
MOCON Inc	3829	47
Moctec Enterprises Inc	5141	211
Mod Electronics Inc	3873	21
Mod I Set Plastics Inc	3089	1878
Mod Tech Industries Inc	3599	573
Mod-Ad Agency Inc	5092	30
Modafferi and Maether	5065	195
Modagrafics Inc	2759	161
Modar Inc	2541	39
ModCloth Inc	5137	20
Modco Inc	3669	266
Modco Inc	4213	127
MODCOMP Inc	7372	974
Modea Corp	7336	86
Modec Inc	3564	156
Model Die and Mold Inc	3544	148
Model Electric Inc	1731	1170
Model Imperial Fine Fragrances Inc	5122	50
Model Machine Company Inc	3599	2080
Model Master LLC	7372	3390
Model Optics Inc	3827	83

Company Name	SIC	Rank
Model Pattern Company Inc	3543	27
Model Rectifier Corp	3612	95
Model Technology Inc	7372	4085
ModelOffice Inc	7372	5051
Modelwerks Inc	8711	350
Modem Express Inc	3577	40
Modena Software Inc	7371	943
Modern Alpha Plastics Inc	3089	1845
Modern Aluminum Fabricators Inc	3471	97
Modern Art Photograph	7221	15
Modern Auto Company Inc	5511	1125
Modern Banking Systems Inc	5045	797
Modern Bindery Inc	2789	120
Modern Blending Technologies Inc	3829	384
Modern Builders Supply Company Inc	5211	271
Modern Builders Supply Inc	5032	14
Modern Building Systems Inc	2452	31
Modern Business Machines Inc	5112	24
Modern Cable Technology Inc	1623	482
Modern Chevrolet Co	5511	737
Modern Concrete Inc	1771	32
Modern Continental Companies Inc	1522	6
Modern Creative Services Inc	7374	399
Modern Custom Fabrication Inc	3312	109
Modern Densifying Inc	4953	161
Modern Die Systems Inc	3544	747
Modern Digital Inc	7819	54
Modern Dispersions Inc	3087	14
Modern Drop Forge Co	3462	64
Modern Drummer Publications Inc	2721	411
Modern Electric Of F M Inc	1731	2225
Modern Electric Water Company Inc	4931	58
Modern Equipment Company Inc	3599	716
Modern Equipment Company Inc (Port Washington Wisconsin)	3334	13
Modern Exploration Inc	1382	16
Modern Exterminating and Termite Control Inc	7342	48
Modern Home Products Corp	3631	17
Modern Industries Inc	3599	1657
Modern Italian Bakery Of West Babylon Inc	2051	63
Modern Litho-Print Co	2752	338
Modern Machine And Tool Company Inc	3829	212
Modern Machine Co	3599	1429
Modern Machine Shop Inc	3599	721
Modern Machine Tool Co	3541	159
Modern Machinery Of Beaverton Inc	3559	288
Modern Mailers Inc	7389	2252
Modern Masonry Products Inc	5032	170
Modern Media Inc	2752	1007
Modern Metalcraft Inc	3444	293
Modern Metals Industries Inc	3841	272
Modern Mold and Tool Inc	3089	957
Modern Molding Inc	3089	932
Modern Mushroom Farms Inc	0182	4
Modern Muzzleloading Inc	3484	1
Modern Of Marshfield Inc	2512	68
Modern Options Inc	7922	89
Modern Packaging Inc	3599	456
Modern Piping Inc	1711	138
Modern Plastic Inc	3089	230
Modern Plastics Corp	3089	1208
Modern Plastics Inc	5162	12
Modern Plating Corp	3471	67
Modern Polymers Inc	3086	119
Modern Printing Co	2752	774
Modern Products Inc	2045	12
Modern Reproductions Inc	2752	969
Modern School Supplies Inc	5049	71
Modern Sewer Service	1623	791
Modern Silicone Technologies Inc	3053	40
Modern Solution Inc	7331	19
Modern Store Fixtures Manufacturing Company Inc	5046	337
Modern System Concepts Inc	1731	2138
Modern Tool Inc	3444	51
Modern Tools Inc	3544	62
Modern Videofilm Inc	7819	14
Modern Welding Company Of Texas Inc	3443	220
Modern Woodcrafts LLC	2541	18
Modernfold/Styles Inc	1799	56
Modernistic Inc	2759	94
Moderns	7389	920
Moderntech SL	7371	1057
Modesto and Empire Traction Co	4011	52
Modified Plastics Inc	3089	992
Modified Technologies Inc	3544	291
Modine Climate Systems Inc	3585	68
Modine Manufacturing Co	3714	28
Modjeski and Mastes Inc	8712	1
MOD-PAC Corp	2657	9
Modtech Holdings Inc	2452	9
Modular Building Sales Inc	7389	2425
Modular Communications Systems	3663	275
Modular Components National Inc	3672	157
Modular Devices Inc	3621	82
Modular Industrial Solutions Inc	3577	514
Modular Information Systems	3571	115
Modular International Inc	3646	76
Modular Medical Corp	3841	327
Modular Process Technology Corp	3559	352

Company Name	SIC	Rank
Modular Structures of PA Inc	2452	32
Modular Systems Inc	3452	92
Modular Transportation Co/MTC	4213	1363
Modulus Data Systems Inc	7373	1195
Modulus Financial Engineering Inc	7379	1317
Modus Associates LLC	7373	943
Modus Technology Inc	7379	1119
ModusLink Global Solutions Inc	7389	45
Modutek Corp	3823	258
Modyne Machining and Manufacturing Inc	3599	920
Moebius Design	2796	54
Moebs Services Inc	8999	146
Moed de Armas and Shannon Architects PC	8712	285
Moehrle Inc	3545	375
Moelis and Co	6029	34
Moeller Aerospace Technology Inc	3724	52
Moeller Electric Corp	3625	34
Moeller Electric Inc	1731	1578
Moeller Products Company Inc	3714	347
Moeller Trucking Inc	4213	314
Moen Industries	3554	36
Moews Seed Co	0115	2
Mofab Inc	3441	240
Moffatt and Nichol Engineers	8711	80
Moffatt Products Inc	3646	100
Moffett Precision Products Inc	3579	73
Moffitt Cancer Center	8011	41
Moffly Publications Inc	2721	256
Mofield Brothers Construction Co	1623	789
Mofoco Enterprises Inc	5013	349
Moftware LLC	4899	190
Mogas Industries Inc	3491	8
Mogility Technology Inc	7371	1688
Mohave County Miner Inc	2711	293
Mohave Electric Cooperative Inc	4911	280
Mohawk Dental Supply Company Inc	5999	175
Mohawk Electrical Systems Inc	3699	216
Mohawk Electro Techniques Inc	3677	24
Mohawk Fine Papers Inc	2672	13
Mohawk Finishing Products Inc	2851	35
Mohawk Flush Doors Inc	2431	38
Mohawk Hospital Equipment Inc	5047	50
Mohawk Industries Inc	2273	1
Mohawk Manufacturing and Supply Co	5013	201
Mohawk Valley Knitting Machinery	3552	55
Mohawk Western Plastics Inc	2673	57
Mohegan It Group LLC	1731	586
Mohegan Tribal Gaming Authority	7011	34
Mohican Mills Inc	2257	4
Mohler Nixon and Williams	8721	45
Mohler Nixon and Williams Accountancy Corp	8721	308
Mohr Davidow Ventures	6799	339
Mohr Engineering Inc	3089	1433
Moises G Duenas	7389	1748
Moison Investment Co	6531	185
Mojave Foods Corp	2099	128
Mojave Water Agency	4941	52
Mojo Interactive Corp	7371	1248
Mok Industries LLC	3674	382
MoKan Container Services Inc	4213	1518
Mol Belting Systems Inc	3052	13
Molalla Communications Co	4813	173
Molalla Telephone Co	4813	284
MOLAM International Inc	5093	44
Mold Craft Inc	3544	461
Mold Masters Intl Inc	3544	41
Mold-A-Matic Corp	3549	68
Mold-Base Industries Inc	3544	176
Moldcraft Inc	3544	691
Molded Devices Inc	3089	1562
Molded Dimensions Inc	3069	145
Molded Plastic Industries Inc	3537	63
Molded Products Inc	3069	220
Molded Rubber and Plastic Corp	3069	115
Moldex Tool and Design Corp	3544	156
Moldex-Metric Inc	3842	79
Moldieco Plastic Products Inc	3089	1090
Mold-In Graphics Systems Inc	3999	113
Molding Box	4226	14
Molding Corporation of America	3089	250
Molding International And Engineering Inc	3089	567
Moldmaster Engineering Inc	3089	1222
Mold-Rite Inc	3089	980
Mold-Rite Plastics LLC	3089	362
Molds And Plastic Machinery Inc	3089	1881
Moldtronics Inc	3089	1102
Molectrics	3471	126
Molecular	7336	10
Molecular Bio-Products Inc	3089	225
Molecular Insight Pharmaceuticals Inc	2834	348
Mole-Richardson Co	3861	31
Molex Inc	3678	2
Molex Inc Industrial Div	3678	16
Molex Industrial Div	3643	12
Molex Premise Networks	3661	102
Molina Healthcare Inc	8011	3
Molinari Supply Inc	5087	64
Moline Dispatch Publishing Co	2711	74
Moline Forge Inc	3462	58
Moline Machinery Ltd	3556	64

Company Name	SIC	Rank
Moline Postal Service	7389	1289
Molino Co	2752	359
Moll Industries Inc	3089	151
Mollenberg-Betz Inc	1711	99
Moller International	3721	47
Molloy Corp	2752	1249
Molly Maid Inc	7349	37
Molnar Engineering Inc	3599	823
Molokai Mule Ride Inc	4725	63
Molsoft LLC	7372	4317
Molson Coors Brewing Co	2082	2
Mol-Son Inc	3544	99
Molter Corp	5085	359
Molycorp Inc	1061	1
Momar Inc	2842	33
Momeni Inc	5023	23
Momenta Pharmaceuticals Inc	2836	47
Momentive Performance Materials Inc	3339	1
Momentive Specialty Chemicals Inc	2899	5
Momentum Data Systems Inc	7372	3673
Momentum India Private Ltd	7371	1888
Momentum Industries Inc	3544	709
Momentum Information Technology Inc	8742	526
Momentum Market Intelligence	8748	112
Momentum- NA Inc	7941	29
Momentum Systems Ltd	7372	3493
Mom's Apple Pie Co	2051	302
Mon Valley Technologies LLC	7373	679
Mona Electric Group Inc	1731	63
Mona Lisa Chocolates and Confection Company LLC/Mona Lisa Chocolatier	2064	145
Mona Slide Fasteners Inc	3965	14
Monacacy Valley Electric Inc	1731	600
Monaco Air Duluth LLC	7359	158
Monaco Enterprises Inc	3669	76
Monaco RV LLC	3716	1
Monadnock Developmental Services Inc	8322	38
Monadnock Paper Mills Inc	2621	43
Monaghan and Associates Inc	3545	346
Monaghan Medical Corp	3842	168
Monahan Brothers Inc	2752	736
Monahan Co	1542	310
Monarch Analytical Laboratories Inc	8734	142
Monarch Art Plastics LLC	2759	163
Monarch Bay Software Inc	7372	3928
Monarch Beverage Co	2087	50
Monarch Casino and Resort Inc	7011	106
Monarch Cement Co	3273	27
Monarch Cement of Iowa Inc	3273	31
Monarch Coin And Security Inc	3581	19
Monarch Color Corp	2893	19
Monarch Community Bancorp Inc	6712	589
Monarch Dental Corp	8099	11
Monarch Electric Company Inc	5063	129
Monarch Financial Holdings Inc	6022	201
Monarch International Inc	3824	29
Monarch Knitting Machinery Corp	3552	15
Monarch Lathes LP	3541	139
Monarch Life Insurance Co	6311	173
Monarch Litho Inc	2752	60
Monarch Manufacturing Inc	3599	2373
Monarch Nutritional Laboratories Inc	2833	37
Monarch Products Co	3544	669
Monarch Toilet Partition Inc	5046	311
Monarch Tool and Die Co	3544	222
Monark Equipment Technologies Co	3559	410
Monash Research Services	7379	1500
MonaVie LLC	2834	68
Monco Products Inc	3559	234
Mon-Cre Telephone Cooperative Inc	4813	387
Moncrief Heating and Air Conditioning Inc	1711	154
Mondavi Marc and Peter Jr Enterprises	2084	10
Monday Morning America Inc	6794	110
Monderacom Inc	7379	764
Mondz Distribution	7379	1559
Monessen Hearth Systems Co	3433	32
Monet International Inc	3961	3
Moneta Group LLC	6282	66
Monetta Financial Services Inc	6282	292
Money Centers of America Inc	6099	33
Money Mailer LLC	7331	21
Money Management International	7322	52
Money Systems Technology	3578	45
Money Tree Software	7372	1137
Moneygram International Inc	7389	36
Moneygram Payment Systems Inc	6099	22
MoneyLine Lending Services Inc	7389	369
Moneynet Inc	7379	593
MoneySoft Inc	7372	4623
Monfox LLC	7372	3001
Monico Alloys Inc	5051	195
Monico LLC	7372	4386
Monier Lifetile LLC	3272	40
Monin Inc	2087	19
Monis Software Inc	7372	4624
Monitor Clipper Partners	6799	137
Monitor Instruments Inc	3826	165
Monitor Medical Inc	7352	20
Monitor Products Inc	5075	74
Monitor Technologies LLC	3823	199

Company Name	SIC	Rank
Monitor Technologies LLC (Elburn Illinois)	3625	134
Monitronics International Inc	7382	7
Monks Associates Inc	7379	1253
Monks Manufacturing Company Inc	3599	1815
Monmouth Internet Corp	7379	696
Monmouth Rubber Corp	3061	33
Monmouth University	8221	33
Mono Engineering Corp	3599	640
Monoflo International Inc	3089	399
Monogram Aerospace Fasteners Inc	3452	26
Monogram Biosciences Inc	2835	19
Monogram Credit Card Bank Of Georgia	6022	554
Monogram Food Solutions LLC	5142	9
Monogram International	3089	802
Monolith Productions Inc	7372	655
Monolithic Power Systems Inc	3674	84
Monolithic Sound Inc	3651	211
Monoprice Inc	5045	201
Monosphere Inc	5045	380
Monotype Imaging Holdings Inc	7372	408
Monro Muffler Brake Inc	7533	1
Monroe 2-Orleans BOCES	8249	7
Monroe and Associates Inc	5141	224
Monroe And Meadows Systems Inc	1731	634
Monroe Cable Company Inc	3357	40
Monroe Communications Inc	5064	67
Monroe County Publishers Inc	2752	1744
Monroe Engineering Products Inc	3714	286
Monroe Enterprises Inc	5013	157
Monroe Environmental Corp	3569	79
Monroe Fluid Technology Inc	2992	59
Monroe Graphics Inc	2752	1468
Monroe Hardware Co	5072	27
Monroe Iko Inc	2952	20
Monroe Litho	2752	202
Monroe Publishing Co	2759	180
Monroe Rubber and Gasket Company Inc	5085	380
Monroe Sweeris and Tromp PC	8721	192
Monroe Systems for Business Inc	3661	97
Monroe Table Co	3537	115
Monroe Title Insurance Corp	6361	15
Monroe Tool And Manufacturing Co	3599	2186
Monroe Tractor and Implement Company Inc	5082	63
Monroe Truck Equipment Inc	5013	105
Monroe-Tufline Manufacturing Company Inc	3523	174
Monroeville Municipal Authority	4941	64
Monsanto Co	2879	1
Monson Companies Inc	5169	119
Monsoon Inc	8748	466
Monster Cable Products Inc	3357	29
Monster Offers	7389	2439
Monster Scooter Parts	5571	10
Monster Trendz Inc	5094	90
Monster Worldwide Inc	7363	17
MonsterCom	7311	114
Monsterslayer Inc	5094	92
Montagar Software Concepts Inc	7379	1501
Montage Media Corp	2721	232
Montage Software Systems Inc	7372	4981
Montague Co	3589	75
Montague Industries Inc	3554	29
Montague Partners	6211	405
Montague Tool And Manufacturing Co	3599	486
Montajz Magazine Inc	7319	168
Montalbano Group	7311	658
Montalvo Corp	3599	1163
Montana Banana	7379	745
Montana Brand Produce Co	4213	1495
Montana Cancer Consortium Inc	7374	421
Montana Coffee Traders Inc	2095	2
Montana Community Banks Inc	6712	704
Montana Construction Corporation Inc	1623	93
Montana Limestone Co	2869	103
Montana Lines Inc	1799	108
Montana Metal Products LLC	3444	73
Montana Mills Bread Company Inc	2051	119
Montana Peterbilt (BillingsMT)	5012	67
Montana Resources LLP	1061	2
Montana State University Inc	8221	11
Montana Sulphur and Chemical Co	2819	94
Montana Transfer Co	4213	2987
Montano Cigarettes Candy and Tobacco Inc	5194	17
MontaVista Software Inc	5045	82
Montco Silicon Technologies	3674	298
Monte Shelton Motor Co	5511	1013
Monte Vista Cooperative Inc	5541	37
Montebello Brands Inc	2085	21
Montebello Plastics LLC	3081	102
Montechristo Trade Corp	5094	54
Montello Inc	2899	179
Montena/Taranto Foods Inc	2022	72
Monterey Auto Supply Inc	5531	49
Monterey Bay Restaurant Equipment Inc	5046	227
Monterey Carpets Inc	2273	29
Monterey Chemical Company Inc	5191	85
Monterey Consultants Inc	8748	341
Monterey Gourmet Foods Inc	2098	3

Company Name	SIC	Rank
Monterey Insurance Co	6331	290
Monterey Learning Systems Inc	2731	233
Monterey Mechanical Co	1629	35
Monterey Mushrooms Inc	0182	1
Monterey Peninsula Artists Inc	7922	33
Monterrey Iron and Metal Ltd	5093	150
Monterrey Tile Co	5023	135
Montessori Home Inc	8748	460
Montevideo Publishing Co	2741	58
Montgomery Air Freight	4213	2559
Montgomery Bank	6021	124
Montgomery Barnett Brown Read Hammond and Mintz LLP	8111	440
Montgomery Chevrolet	5511	242
Montgomery Communications Inc	2711	877
Montgomery Community Action Committee and Cdc Inc	8351	12
Montgomery County Of Public Service Authority P S A	1623	609
Montgomery Data Services Inc	7374	275
Montgomery Eye Surgery Center LLC	8011	102
Montgomery Industries International Inc	3532	72
Montgomery Inn	5812	103
Montgomery Investment Technology Inc	7371	1667
Montgomery Little Soran and Murray PC	8111	421
Montgomery Machine and Fabrication Inc	3599	1204
Montgomery Machine Company Inc	7692	23
Montgomery McCracken Walker and Rhoads LLP	8111	123
Montgomery Media	2711	5
Montgomery Products Ltd	2653	121
Montgomery Stire and Partners	7311	663
Montgomery Technology Inc	3699	203
Montgomery Trucking Co	4213	1882
Montgomery Truss and Panel Inc	2439	40
Montgomery Zukerman Davis Inc	7311	200
Monti Inc	3644	14
Monticel Inc	2759	508
Monticello Flooring and Lumber Company Inc	2426	23
Monticello Times Inc	2741	454
Monticello Tool And Die Inc	3544	510
Montinore Vineyard Limited Inc	2084	84
Montour Industrial Supply Inc	5074	128
Montoya Electric Service Inc	1731	2463
Montrenes Financial Services Inc	7323	20
Montrose Fire Protection District	7389	2242
Montrose Publishing Company Inc	2791	62
Montrose Travel	4724	33
Montville Plastics and Rubber Inc	3089	1108
Montzingo and Associates	7311	990
Monument Farms Inc	0241	4
Monument Industries Inc	2673	74
Monumental Investment Corp	1711	7
Monumental Life Insurance Co	6311	50
Monumental Supply Company Inc	5085	64
Moo and Oink Inc	5411	197
Moody Aldrich Partners LLC	6282	400
Moody and Phillips Electric Company Inc	1731	1346
Moody Construction Company Inc	1542	443
Moody Corp	3599	2224
Moody Creek Produce Inc	5148	66
Moody Dunbar Inc	2033	47
Moody Electric Inc	1731	2054
Moody International Inc	7389	307
Moody Rambin Interests	6531	113
Moody-Nolan Inc	8712	136
Moody-Nolan Limited Inc	8712	43
Moody's Analytics Inc	7323	11
Moody's Corp	7323	2
Moody's Electric Inc	1731	283
Moody's Investors Service Inc	2741	7
Moody's KMV Co (Walnut Creek California)	7372	86
Moog Component Group	3621	30
Moog Inc	3599	3
Moog Schaeffer Magnetics Div	3823	66
Moomers Homemade Ice Cream LLC	2024	78
Moon Cutter Company Inc	3541	115
Moon Distributors Inc	5181	63
Moon Kochis Productions Inc	7812	311
Moon Lake Electric Association Inc	4911	355
Moon Security Services Inc	1731	476
Moon Shine Trading Co	2099	367
Mooney Aerospace Group Ltd	3721	39
Mooney Airplane Company Inc	3721	15
Mooney Farms	0723	11
Mooney General Paper Co	5113	22
Mooney Industrials Inc	7389	1436
Moonstruck Chocolate Co	2064	40
Moore and Son Site Contractors Inc	1623	283
Moore and Van Allen	8111	101
Moore Brothers Inc	4213	2562
Moore Cadillac Company Inc	5511	777
Moore Capital Management LP	6282	125
Moore Coal Company Inc	7389	1418
Moore Companies Inc	7331	228
Moore Co	5084	827
Moore Computing LLP	7379	1248
Moore Control Systems Inc	8711	457

Company Name	SIC	Rank
Moore Electric Company Inc	1731	767
Moore Electrical Contracting Inc	1731	253
Moore Electrical Contractors Inc	1731	1717
Moore Fabrication Inc	3089	1290
Moore J B Electrical Contractor Inc	1731	941
Moore Land Company Inc	3541	33
Moore Material Handling Group Inc	5084	364
Moore Medical LLC	5047	24
Moore Partners Inc	7336	57
Moore Production Tool Specialties Inc	3541	163
Moore Protection	5063	1078
Moore Sales Company Inc	5065	707
Moore Stephens Lovelace PA	8721	85
Moore Stephens Tiller LLC	8721	63
Moore Twining Associates Inc	8734	62
Moore Wallace Andrews-Connecticut	2752	120
Moore-Addison Co	3599	1256
Moore-Langen Printing Company Inc	2752	297
Moore's Pump and Services Inc	3441	234
Moorhead Electric Inc	7379	93
Moorhead Machinery and Boiler Co	3567	48
Moorman Farms Inc	4213	614
Moors and Cabot Inc	6211	32
Moose River Lumber Company Inc	2421	46
Moosylvania Marketing	7336	9
Mo-Pa Enterprise Inc	6512	89
Moped Mafia	5012	203
Morabito Baking Company Inc	2051	85
Morad Electronics Corp	3663	380
Moraine Materials Co	3273	38
Moralmar Kitchen Cabinets Inc	2434	51
Moral's Precision Machine Manufacturing Company Inc	3599	1897
Moran Art Pontiac-GMC Inc	5511	436
Moran Printing	2752	184
Moran Tools	3542	91
Moran Towing and Transportation Company Inc	4492	3
Moran Towing Corp	4492	5
Morasch Meats Inc	5411	262
Moravia It Inc	7389	860
Moravits and Mazurek Inc	7378	160
Morbark Inc	3599	57
Morbelli Russo and Partners Advertising	7311	782
More Bakery Inc	2051	284
More Media Direct Inc	7311	884
More Than Bikes Inc	5091	133
More Than Bread Inc	3556	157
MoreDirect Inc	7389	335
Morehouse Foods Inc	2035	37
Morehouse Instrument Co	3825	206
Moreland Altobelli Associates Inc	8711	155
Moret Advertising Inc	7311	521
Moretrench American Corp	1522	30
Morette Company Inc	1542	16
MoreVisibility	8742	509
MorevisibilityCom Inc	7379	1065
Morey Enterprises Inc	4213	1396
Morey Evans Advertising Inc	7311	611
Morey's Piers	7996	21
Morgal Machine Tool Co	3469	124
Morgan Adhesives Co	2672	5
Morgan Advanced Materials And Technology Inc	3624	5
Morgan and Burt Electric Company Inc	1731	1268
Morgan and Myers Inc	8743	175
Morgan and Sampson USA	5122	115
Morgan Borszcz Consulting	8742	250
Morgan Bronze Products Inc	3599	321
Morgan Brothers Inc	7342	32
Morgan Brothers Millwork Inc	2431	53
Morgan Buildings and Spas Inc	5211	78
Morgan Clock Co	5944	39
Morgan Communications Inc	5731	261
Morgan Corp	3713	5
Morgan Creek Music Group	7812	46
Morgan Foods Inc	2032	10
Morgan Gallacher Inc	2842	62
Morgan Hill Plastics Inc	3089	1708
Morgan Industries Inc	3559	526
Morgan Investments Inc	6282	254
Morgan Joseph and Co	8748	81
Morgan Keegan and Company Inc	6211	71
Morgan Lewis and Bockius LLP	8111	6
Morgan Newton Company LP	3672	163
Morgan Optical Inc	3851	86
Morgan Precision Instruments LLC	3545	426
Morgan Printers Inc	2752	1421
Morgan Printing Co	2759	515
Morgan Stanley	6159	8
Morgan Stanley and Company Inc	6211	42
Morgan Stanley Capital International Inc	6211	83
Morgan Stanley Real Estate Fund	6531	208
Morgan Street Brewery and Tavern Inc	2082	42
Morgan Tire and Auto Inc	5531	7
Morgan Trucking Co	4213	3053
Morgan Trucking Inc	4213	2679
MorganFranklin Corp	8711	111
Morgan's Foods Inc	5812	236
Morgans Hotel Group Co	7011	92
Morganti Group	1541	96
Morgantown Machine and Hydraulics Inc	3561	62
Morgan-Wightman Supply Company Inc	5031	73
Morgen and Oswood Construction Company Inc	1541	264
Morgen Evan and Company Inc	6211	300
Morgenthaler Ventures	6799	213
Morgood Tools Inc	3545	108
Mor-Gran-Sou Electric Cooperative Inc	4911	345
Morgro Inc	2899	149
Moria Inc	5048	24
Morinda Inc	2033	10
Moritani America Inc	5084	262
Moritz Aerospace Inc	3728	89
Morkes Inc	2064	133
Morlandt Electric Company LLC	1731	947
Morlang Flooring	1752	15
Morley Candy Makers Inc	2064	30
Morley Financial Services Inc	6282	530
Morley Group Inc	7361	329
Morley Sales Company Inc	5146	18
Morley-Murphy Co	5065	207
Mormax Inc	7389	2480
Mormil Corp	5093	135
Morneau Sobeco	7372	148
Morning Star Packing Co	2033	12
Morningstar Inc	6282	71
Moro Corp	3462	17
Morocco Electric Inc	1731	1147
Moroch and Associates	7311	225
Moroni Feed Co	2015	7
Moroso Performance Products Inc	3714	226
Morpac Industries Inc	3531	131
MORPACE International Inc	8732	38
MorphiusDisc Manufacturing	3565	22
Morphix Technologies Inc	3829	209
Morphotrak Inc	7373	231
Morrell Inc	5084	300
Morrell Instrument Company Inc	5049	68
Morrie's Cadillac/Saab	5511	954
Morrilton Packing Company Inc	2011	113
Morris Advertising and Design Inc	7311	565
Morris and Associates	7389	1582
Morris And Lee Inc	3821	57
Morris Bank	6022	620
Morris Bean and Co	3365	10
Morris Communications Company LLC	2711	35
Morris Construction Inc	1623	581
Morris County Duplicating Corp	2752	434
Morris Coupling Co	3568	30
Morris Heating and Cooling Inc	1731	884
Morris Industrial Corp	3553	9
Morris J Golombeck Inc	5140	116
Morris Kimmel Corp	7379	705
Morris Kreitz and Sons Inc	1796	24
Morris Kurtzon Inc	3646	83
Morris Mailing Inc	7334	77
Morris Manning and Martin LLP	8111	284
Morris Manufacturing And Sales Corp	3714	291
Morris Material Handling Inc	3536	2
Morris Merchants Inc	5074	158
Morris Multimedia Inc	2711	11
Morris Murdock Travel	4724	20
Morris Newspaper Corporation Of Kansas	2711	581
Morris Oil Inc	5171	78
Morris Polich and Purdy	8111	386
Morris Printing Group Inc	2752	146
Morris Products Inc	3625	321
Morris Publications	2711	600
Morris Rose Auto Parts Inc	5013	279
Morris Sheet Metal Corp	3444	157
Morris Transparent Box Co	3089	1575
Morris Trucking Corp	4213	659
Morrisette Paper Company Inc	5113	33
Morrison Agency Inc	7311	267
Morrison and Foerster LLP	8111	31
Morrison Berkshire Inc	3552	22
Morrison Brothers Co	3559	81
Morrison Brown Argiz and Farra LLP	8721	343
Morrison Cohen LLP	8111	329
Morrison Construction Co	1711	73
Morrison County Record	2711	644
Morrison Freight Company Inc	4213	3068
Morrison Industrial Equipment Co	5084	94
Morrison Industries Inc	5084	22
Morrison Kattman Menze Inc	8712	244
Morrison Mahoney LLP	8111	118
Morrison Management Specialists Inc	5812	9
Morrison Medical	3841	323
Morrison Milling Co	2041	27
Morrison Supply Company Inc	5072	195
Morrison Textile Machinery Co	3552	10
Morrison Timing Screw Company Inc	3535	123
Morrison Weighing Systems Inc	3596	26
Morrison's Home Center Inc	5072	140
Morrisonville Farmers Coop	5153	150
Morrissey Brothers Printers Inc	2759	480
Morrissey Electric Company Inc	1731	2159
Morristown Driver's Service Inc	4213	460
Morrow and Sons Inc	1794	48
Morrow Equipment Company LLC	7353	9
Morrow Technologies Corp	3993	128
Morrow-Meadows Corp	1731	31
Morrow-Meadows Corporation Northern California	1731	379
Morse Automotive Corp	3714	80
Morse Communications Inc	5999	75
Morse Data Corp	7372	1713
Morse Distribution Inc	5085	144
Morse Industries Inc	5051	158
Morse Laboratories LLC	8734	162
Morse Micro Solutions Inc	5734	163
Morse Richard Weisenmiller and Associates Inc	8742	567
Morse Watchmans Inc	3699	161
Mortara Instrument Inc	8731	141
Mor-Tech Design Inc	3542	82
Mortech Manufacturing Company Inc	5087	50
Morter HealthSystem	8731	359
Mortex Manufacturing Co	3089	1680
Mortgage Builder Software Inc	7372	1032
Mortgage Cadence Inc	7371	189
Mortgage Computer Applications Inc	7372	2163
Mortgage Fax Inc	7323	23
Mortgage Guaranty Insurance Corp	6351	7
Mortgage Guaranty Investment Corp	6351	9
Mortgage Press Ltd	2711	731
Mortgage Research Center	6163	36
Mortgage Resources Inc	6163	31
Mortgage Source LLC	6162	88
MortgageAmerica Inc	6162	114
Mortgagebot LLC	7379	324
MortgageFlex Systems Inc	7372	833
MortgageIT Holdings Inc	6163	2
Morton and Associates Ltd	7291	16
Morton and Company Inc	3599	1267
Morton Automatic Electric Co	3613	169
Morton Bassett LLC	2099	248
Morton Consulting	8748	270
Morton G Thalhimer Inc	6531	80
Morton Grinding Inc	3965	17
Morton Grove Medical Imaging LLC	3826	111
Morton Industrial Group Inc	3089	59
Morton Industries LLC	3498	18
Morton Machining LLC	3599	1727
Morton Manufacturing Co	3446	25
Morton Salt	2899	26
Morton's of Chicago Inc	5812	226
Morton's Restaurant Group Inc	5812	133
Mortuary Associates Co	5099	132
Morway Corp	2893	10
Mos International Inc	3596	18
Mosaic Advertising and Marketing	7311	664
Mosaic Co	2874	1
Mosaic Phosphates MP Inc	2874	4
Mosaica Education Inc	8211	99
Mosbacher Energy Co	1311	139
Mosby and Moore Inc	5083	217
Mosby Packing Company Inc	2013	222
Mosebach Manufacturing Co	3634	18
Moseley Associates Inc	3663	95
Moser and Marsalek PC	8111	504
Moser Corp	5712	89
Moses Anshell Inc	8732	73
Moses Lake Industries Inc	2869	65
Moses Lake Steel Supply Inc	5051	507
Mosey Manufacturing Company Inc	3541	31
Mosier Automation Inc	5065	373
Mosites Construction Co	1542	146
Mosites Rubber Company Inc	3069	78
Mosler Auto Care Center Inc	3711	75
Mosley Electronics Inc	3699	308
Mosley Tractor And Supply Inc	5085	423
Mosquito Abatement District	4959	26
Mosquito Fire Protection District	7389	2168
Moss Adams LLP	8721	241
Moss Brothers Dodge	5511	369
Moss Peoples Gin Company Inc	5153	174
Moss Point Marine Inc	3732	55
Moss Supply Co	3442	67
Mossberg and Company Inc	2752	182
Mossberg Industries Inc	2499	43
Mosser Construction Inc	1542	22
Mossimo Inc	2321	10
Mossor Computers	5045	1038
Mosso's Medical Supply Company Inc	5047	109
Mosstype Holding Corp	3555	47
Mossy Motors Inc	5511	1054
Mossy Nissan Houston	5511	689
MOST Brand Development and Advertising	7311	233
Mostad and Christensen Inc	8742	517
Mostly Memories Inc	3999	122
Mosys Inc	3672	101
Motek-Team Industries Inc	3444	21
Motel Development Inc	1522	28
Mother Lode Printing and Publishing Company Inc	2711	467
Mother Nature Inc	5912	59
Mothers Polishes Waxes Cleaners Inc	5169	171
Motif Designs Inc	7389	1580
Motif Industries Inc	3851	87
Motion City Films	3695	121
Motion Control Engineering Inc	3534	9
Motion Control Systems Inc	3625	145
Motion Controls	3561	179

Company Name	SIC	Rank
Motion Devices Technology Inc	3621	159
Motion Engineering Company Inc	5065	434
Motion Holdings Inc	3613	15
Motion Industries Inc	5085	3
Motion Machine Co	3599	2057
Motion Over Time Inc	2741	210
Motion Picture Laboratories Inc	7819	49
Motion Systems Corp	3593	30
MotionMasters Inc	7812	273
MotionPoint Corp	8999	92
Motion-Tronix Inc	7629	57
Motiva Enterprises LLC	2911	51
Motivation Excellence Inc	8742	424
Motivation Marketing and Communica-tions Inc	8742	491
Motivation Through Incentives Inc	7389	1045
Motivatit Seafoods LLC	0273	1
Motive Energy Inc	5063	67
Motive Energy Telecommunication Group Inc	1731	127
Motive Parts Company Of St Louis	5013	124
Motive Power Inc (Boise Idaho)	3743	8
Motley Fool Inc	6282	302
Motor Capacitors Inc	3629	105
Motor Cargo Inc	4213	146
Motor Carrier Service Inc	4213	1163
Motor City Fastener Inc	5072	103
Motor City Plastics Co	3089	1019
Motor City Services Inc	5065	376
Motor City Stampings Inc	3465	34
Motor Club of America Insurance Co	6331	339
Motor Coach Industries International Inc	3713	3
Motor Inn Co	5511	1061
Motor Magnetics Inc	3621	130
Motor Martco LLC	3554	25
Motor Parts and Equipment Inc	5013	344
Motor Parts Distributors Inc	5013	267
Motor Power Equipment Co	5012	105
Motor Products	3621	25
Motor Protection Electronics Inc	3625	332
Motor Services Hugo Stamp Inc	5084	164
Motor Specialty Inc	3621	92
Motor Technology Inc	3625	74
Motor Ways Inc	6331	356
Motor Week	4833	245
Motor West Inc	4213	764
Motor Works Inc	5015	22
Motorcar Parts America Inc	3694	6
Motorcasting Inc	3321	31
Motorcycle Stuff Inc	5013	41
Motorists Mutual Insurance Co	6331	145
Motorola Broadband Communications Sector	3663	27
Motorola Inc AIEG Div	3714	48
Motorola Inc Communications Div	3663	7
Motorola Incorporated Energy Systems Group	3691	4
Motorola Sales And Services Inc	5065	48
Motorola Solutions Inc	3663	1
Motors and Controls International Inc	3545	193
Motors And Drives LLC	5063	965
Motors Insurance Corp	6331	102
Motorsports Designs Inc	2759	225
MotorVac Technologies Inc	3599	225
Motown Record Company LP	3652	15
Motricity Inc	7372	335
Mo-Trim Inc	3524	37
Motson Graphics Inc	2759	529
Mott Corp	3564	38
Mottes Materials Inc	1442	67
Mott's Inc	2037	2
Mouldagraph Corp	3599	420
Moultrie Feeders LLC	3949	139
Mound Laser and Photonics Center Inc	3699	42
Mt Bachelor Inc	7011	44
Mt Carmel Health and Rehabilitation Center	8051	57
Mt Carmel Stabilization Group Inc	1611	93
Mount Everest Contract Sewing	2399	32
Mount Fury Company Inc	3823	478
Mt Hawley Insurance Co	6331	206
Mt Hood Beverage Co	5181	21
Mt Hood Solutions Co	2841	21
Mount Joy Wire Corp	3496	37
Mount Lucas Management Corp	6282	154
Mt Mansfield Co	7011	137
Mount Palomar Winery Inc	2084	72
Mount Pleasant Seafood Co	5146	68
Mount Pleasant Transfer Inc	4213	1817
Mount Sinai Medical Center	8062	16
Mount Snow Ltd	7011	95
Mount St Helena Brewing Co	2082	40
Mount Taylor Programs	7372	3359
Mount Vernon Plastics Corp	3089	1702
Mount Vernon Printing Co	2752	337
Mount Victory State Bank	6712	730
Mount Washington Resort	7011	208
Mount Zion First Baptist Federal Credit Union	6061	139
Mountain Advocate Media Inc	5112	81
Mountain Air Cargo Inc	3728	64
Mountain Alloys Corp	5051	435
Mountain Broadcasting Corp	4833	218

Company Name	SIC	Rank
Mountain Cascade Inc	1623	41
Mountain City Electric Inc	1731	1101
Mountain City Meat Co	2013	26
Mountain Co	1761	3
Mountain Creek	7996	29
Mountain Creek Entertainment LLC	7371	1370
Mountain Development Corp	6552	83
Mountain Dog Media Inc	4832	212
Mountain Electric Cooperative Inc	4911	193
Mountain Fuel Supply Co	4924	74
Mountain Glacier LLC	7389	633
Mountain Hardwear Inc	3949	64
Mountain Hawk Corp	7379	154
Mountain Lako Broadcasting Corp	4832	210
Mountain Lake Corp	6531	396
Mountain Machine Works	5084	689
Mountain Man Nut and Fruit Co	2068	8
Mountain Management Inc	7389	2136
Mountain Marketing Inc	8743	338
Mountain Materials Inc	5032	130
Mountain Molding Ltd	3089	1063
Mountain Network Systems Inc	7371	309
Mountain - Pacific Quality Health Foundation - Wyoming	8011	21
Mountain Parks Electric Inc	4911	419
Mountain Precision Tool Company Inc	3599	2052
Mountain Printing Company Inc	2752	1000
Mountain Products LP	2759	136
Mountain Properties Preservation Corp	7011	206
Mountain Rural Telephone Cooperative Inc	4813	258
Mountain Scales Inc	5046	350
Mountain Services Inc	8742	276
Mountain State Information Systems Inc	7373	1071
Mountain States Airgas Inc	2813	18
Mountain States Automation	3569	51
Mountain States Electric	1731	2287
Mountain States Lithographing Co	2752	1660
Mountain States Motors Co	5511	955
Mountain States Pipe and Supply Co	5074	57
Mountain Systems Inc	7372	4430
Mountain Tarp And Awning Inc	2394	18
Mountain Tech Sales and Assembly	3672	278
Mountain Travel-Sobek	4725	20
Mountain Valley Contracting Inc	1623	580
Mountain Valley Express Co	4213	838
Mountain Valley Spring Company Inc	5084	41
Mountain View Bancshares Inc	6712	675
Mountain View Coop	5191	62
Mountain View Equipment Company Inc	5083	47
Mountain View Ford Inc	5511	327
Mountain View Telephone Co	4813	583
Mountain Vista Development Inc	1731	1304
Mountain West Distributors Inc (Coeur d'Alene Idaho)	6022	143
Mountain West Distributors Inc	5064	82
Mountain West Endoscopy Center	8011	75
Mountain West Research Center	8732	76
Mountain Wireless Construction Inc	4812	69
Mountaineer Gas Co	4922	39
Mountaineer Inc	2759	337
Mountaineer Manufacturing Inc	3599	1933
Mountainland Business Systems Inc	5044	129
Mountainland Supply Co	5074	51
Mountaire Corp	2048	1
Mountanos Brothers Coffee Co	2095	14
Mounted Memories Inc	3089	1464
Mountville Mills Inc	2273	7
Mountz Inc	3823	148
Mouser Electronics Inc	5065	20
Mo-Vac Service Company Inc	4213	1206
Movado Group Inc	3873	3
Move Inc	6531	127
Move Networks Inc	4841	58
Moveable Cubicle Inc	5085	250
Movers Specialty Service Inc	4212	41
Movers Unlimited Inc	4213	2144
Movex Inc	4212	46
Movie Exchange Inc	7841	8
Movie Gallery Inc	7841	2
Movies Unlimited Inc	5961	58
Moving Pictures Video and Film Inc	7812	102
Moving Right Along Service Inc	4213	3047
Moviola Inc	5065	432
Moweaqua Farmers Cooperative Grain Co	5153	171
Mowrey Elevator Company Inc	7699	176
Moxa Americas Inc	3577	403
MoxiE Inductor Corp	3677	92
Moxie Interactive Inc	7336	14
Moxie Java International Inc	6794	157
Moxie Media Inc	7812	108
Moxie Pictures	7812	279
Moxtek Inc	3827	30
Moxy Trucks Of America LLC	5082	180
Moya Terra Aqua Inc	3511	45
Moye Electric Company Inc	1731	1138
Moyer and Son Inc	5191	56
Moyer and Sons Inc	4213	1416
Moyer Electronics Supply Co	5065	666
Moyer Group	5045	348
Mozel Inc	5169	61

Company Name	SIC	Rank
Mozgomedia	2741	403
Mozian and Associates Inc	3695	165
Mozzarella Co	2022	86
Mozzicato Pastry and Bake Shop Inc	5461	13
MP Baker Electric Inc	1731	1758
Mp Biomedicals LLC	5047	39
MP Consulting Inc	7379	1628
MP Environmental Services Inc	4213	628
MP Husky Corp	3443	140
MP Jackson LLC	3625	254
MP Productions Co	5063	540
MP Pumps Inc	3561	97
MP Tapes Inc	3572	86
Mp Technologies Inc	8711	587
Mp Tool and Engineering Company Inc	3545	204
M-Pact Corp	3444	264
Mpak Technologies Inc	5734	291
Mpb Group LLC	7389	691
Mpb Industries Inc	3599	2367
MPC Plating Inc	3471	56
Mpc Promotions LLC	5199	59
Mpd Inc	3671	7
MPE Business Forms Inc	2752	1519
MPEG LA	8111	554
Mpell Solutions LLC	7311	381
Mpex Pharmaceuticals Inc	8731	140
Mpf Acquisitions Inc	3081	103
MPG Office Trust Inc	6512	18
MPG Services and Sales Inc	3559	408
Mph Entertainment Inc	4833	216
mPhase Technologies Inc	3699	309
MPI International Inc	3469	16
MPI Investment Management Inc	6282	669
MPI Label Systems	2754	2
MPI Media Group	7822	22
MPI Tech Inc	3577	154
MPI Technologies Inc	3661	23
MPK Enterprises	1731	1053
MPL Systems Inc	7373	418
MPLC Holdings LLC	7389	398
MPM Technologies Inc	1099	7
MPO Videotronics Inc	3651	36
MPPW Consultants Information Systems LLC	6282	462
MPR Associates Inc	8711	326
Mpr Plastics Inc	3089	1361
MPR Services Inc	2899	117
MPS Group Inc (Detroit Michigan)	7389	249
MPS Multimedia Inc	5045	574
M-Pulse Microwave Inc	3674	386
MPW Industrial Services Group Inc	7349	23
MQ Associates Inc	8071	8
Mq Operating Co	5084	913
MQSoftware Inc	7372	1657
MR Beal and Co	6282	112
Mr Bs Fun Foods Inc	2064	110
Mr B's Of Abbotsford Inc	2015	67
Mr Christmas Inc	3699	141
MR Danielson Advertising	7336	170
Mr Dell Foods Inc	2037	32
M-R Electric and Security Alarms Inc	1731	2104
Mr Foamy Southwest FI LLC	2431	137
Mr Gatti's Inc	5812	292
MR Glenn Electric Inc	7694	25
Mr Golf Carts Inc	5088	64
Mr Goodcents Franchise Systems Inc	5812	377
MR Home Care Inc	8322	156
Mr Ink Jet Inc	5734	354
MR Lee Building Materials Inc	5211	299
Mr Long-Arm Inc	3423	38
MR Mold and Engineering Corp	3544	423
Mr Quick Print Inc	2752	1475
Mr Sign Inc	3571	238
Mr Software of East Coast Inc	7372	2682
Mr Tubs Inc	3088	11
Mr Window Tinting	5065	788
Mr Wire	1731	1835
Mr Youth	7311	405
MRA Technologies	7373	973
MRB Public Relations Inc	8743	195
MRC Bearings	3562	4
Mrc Polymers Inc	2821	45
Mrc Technology Inc	3629	98
MrchocolateCom LLC	2064	136
MRE Consulting Ltd	7372	1386
MRG Document Technologies	7375	50
MRG Software Inc	7371	1933
Mrg Tool And Die Corp	3469	245
Mri Flexible Packaging Co	2759	138
MRI Interventions	3841	330
MRJ Technology Solutions Inc	7373	91
MRK Technologies Ltd	5045	314
MRL Equipment Company Inc	5082	120
Mrl Manufacturing Inc	3599	1373
Mrm Holdings LLC	3273	22
Mrm Inc	3081	131
Mrm Industries Inc	2821	203
MRM Worldwide	7319	16
MRO Software Inc	7372	241
Mrp Inc	5085	393
Mrpc Inc	7384	50
Mrr Dr Inc	7349	224
Mrs Baird's Bakeries Inc	2051	9
Mrs Cubbison's Foods Inc	2051	123

Company Name	SIC	Rank
Mrs Field's Original Cookies Inc	2052	9
MRS Foods Inc	2099	221
Mrs Gerry's Kitchen Inc	2099	172
Mrs Grissom's Salads Inc	2099	204
Mrs Grossman's Paper Co	2678	11
Mrs Homecare Inc	7359	88
MRS Machining Company Inc	3599	1143
Mrs Smith's Bakeries of Spartanburg LLC	2051	76
Mrs Stratton's Salads Inc	2035	16
Mrsw Management LLC	4899	209
MRV Communications Inc	3674	74
MRW Communications LLC	7311	612
MS Aerospace Inc	3452	25
MS Berkoff Company Inc	5072	162
MS Consultants Inc	8711	216
Ms Data Service Corp	7374	236
MS Engineering Inc	3571	56
MS Howells and Co	6211	317
MS Ii Graphics Inc	2752	1633
Ms Inet LLC	7373	201
MS Intertrade Inc	2092	54
MS Management Associates Inc (Indianapolis Indiana)	6531	151
Ms Precision Components LLC	5084	545
MS Rubber Co	5085	392
MS Willett Inc	3544	120
MSA Professional Services Inc	8711	91
MSB Financial Corp	6035	145
Msb Inc	7331	89
MSC Industrial Direct Company Inc	5084	2
MSC Industrial Supply Co	3545	3
MSC Software Corp	7372	203
MSCI Barra Inc	7372	94
MSCO Inc	6719	69
MSD Capital LP	6799	56
Msdsonline Inc	7389	781
MSDSpro LLC	7372	1283
MSE Inc	8711	173
Mse Media Solutions	3695	112
MSE Technology Applications	8731	350
MSGI Security Solutions Inc	7389	2511
MSHI Inc	7373	573
MShift	7371	1106
MSI Barnes and Associates	8721	50
MSI Data Systems Inc	7372	3566
MSI General Corp	1542	308
MSI International East Inc	8742	189
MSI International Inc	7363	87
Msi Marketing Inc	7311	340
Msi Mold Builders Southeast Inc	3544	96
Msi Security Systems Inc	5999	298
MSI Systems Integrators Inc	7373	42
MSI-PRO Co	5211	140
MSJ Trucking Inc	4213	1096
Msmb2b Inc	4813	713
MSN Communications Inc	7373	227
Msn Corp	2013	115
MSNBC Cable LLC	4841	46
Msp Corp	3829	102
mSpot Inc	7389	666
Mss Inc	3559	431
MSS Technologies Inc	7372	2242
Mssc Inc	3714	107
MST Express Inc	4213	1109
Mst Steel Corp	5051	176
MSTI Holdings Inc	4841	118
MSX International Inc	7363	22
Mt Acquisitions LLC	3544	73
Mt Top Auto Supply	5013	365
MTA Systems Inc	7372	3426
Mtc Direct Inc	5045	104
MTC Kenworth Inc	5511	1175
MTCI	8331	10
MTCSC Inc	7371	87
MTD Products Inc	3524	2
Mtd Southwest Inc	3524	4
Mth Information Solutions LLC	7379	1093
MTI Corporation (Paramus New Jersey)	5049	6
MTI Electronics Inc	3672	96
MTI Home Video Inc	7812	107
MTI Instruments Inc	3829	30
MTI Precision Products LLC	3841	342
MTI Systems Inc	7372	1138
Mti Tech Products Inc	5045	819
MTI-Milliren Technologies	3825	93
Mtm Communications Inc	7389	2123
MTM Molded Products Co	3089	1434
Mtm Recognition Corp	3911	18
MTM Technologies Inc	7373	64
Mtm Wireless Inc	5065	627
Mtone Wireless Corp	4899	111
MTP Inc	3082	16
MTR Gaming Group Inc	7948	6
MTR Western	4142	2
M-Tron Components Inc	5063	476
M-Tron Manufacturing	3769	27
MtronicsCom Inc	3679	326
MtronPTI	3679	41
MTS Medication Technologies Inc	3569	31
Mts Services Inc	1731	406
MTS Systems Corp	3829	7
MTS Technologies Inc	8711	268

Company Name	SIC	Rank
MTS Telecommunications Management Inc	5065	81
MTS Travel Inc	4724	24
Mtu Onsite Energy Corp	3621	58
MTV Networks Inc	4841	159
MTVi Group Inc	7389	881
MTW Solutions LLC	7372	3729
MTX Audio	3651	13
Mu Sigma Inc	7379	170
Muckleshoot Indian Casino	7993	5
Mud Control Equipment Corp	7353	86
Mud Lake Tele Co-Op Association Inc	4813	620
Mu-Del Electronics Inc	3663	307
Mudlogging Company USA LP	1389	45
Muecke's Shrimp Boiler LLP	3812	221
Mueller Art Cover and Binding Co	2782	42
Mueller Brass Co	3498	12
Mueller Copper Tube Company Inc	3351	2
Mueller Corp	3471	31
Mueller Gages Co	3545	402
Mueller Gas Products	3714	336
Mueller Inc	3448	28
Mueller Industries Inc	3356	4
Mueller Machine and Tool Company LLC	3544	132
Mueller Optical Co	5049	69
Mueller Plastics Corp	3089	1872
Mueller Sports Medicine Inc	2834	286
Mueller Water Products Inc	3491	1
Mueske Electric Inc	1731	1784
Muhlenkamp and Company Inc	6282	161
Muhler Company Inc	5031	164
Muir Enterprises	5148	36
Muirhead Canning Co	2033	124
Mukai Greenlee and Co	8721	467
Mulberry Metal Products Inc	3644	13
Mulcrone and Associates Inc	5063	527
Mule-Durel Inc	5112	85
Muleshoe Valley Inc	1731	1915
MuleSoft Inc	7371	310
Mulholland Brothers	3161	10
Mulholland Positioning Systems Inc	3841	179
Mull Drilling Company Inc	1311	226
Mull Machine Co	3599	944
Mullahey Fullerton Chevrolet	5511	1096
Mullen Advertising and Public Relations Inc	7311	888
Mullen Advertising Inc	7311	40
Mullen Circle Brand Inc	2992	66
Mullen Publications Inc	2711	774
Mullen Testers	3559	547
Muller Erosion Control Inc	0711	4
Muller Inc	5181	49
Muller Media Conversions Inc	7372	3567
Muller Muller Richmond Harms and Myers PC	8111	538
Mulligan Printing Corp	2741	368
Mullinax Ford North Canton	5511	252
Mulliniks Recycling Inc	7389	1600
Mullinix Packages Inc	3089	358
Mullins Buildings Products Inc	5072	62
Mullins Food Products Inc	2033	23
Mullins Max B Auto Parts Salvage Inc	5093	208
Mullins Rubber Products Inc	3069	174
Mulrooney and Sporer Inc	1731	925
Multatech-Freese and Nichols JV	8712	94
Multax Corp	3599	555
Multi AG Media Company LLC	2721	90
Multi Corp	4581	22
Multi Distributing LLC	5046	367
Multi Image Productions Inc	7812	125
Multi Lab Inc	3672	294
Multi Metrics Inc	5045	1062
Multi Services Inc	1731	1725
Multi Tool Inc	3544	493
Multi Two Electric Inc	1731	1934
MultiAd Inc	7372	905
Multiband Corp	4813	55
Multibeam Systems Inc	3829	402
Multicase Inc	7371	1858
Multicitycom Inc	7372	2164
Multi-Color Corp	2759	10
Multicom Inc	5063	405
Multicom Inc (Phoenix Arizona)	5063	141
Multicomm Inc	5731	212
Multicomp Inc	2752	1805
Multicon Construction Inc	1542	390
Multi-Con Inc	1731	2180
Multi-Conveyor LLC	3535	66
Multi-Craft Litho Inc	2752	557
Multidata Computer Systems Inc	7372	4318
Multifab Inc	5085	61
Multifilm Packaging Corp	3081	56
Multi-Fineline Electronix Inc	3672	7
Multi-Flow Dispensers LP	3585	84
Multigrains Inc	2051	51
Multi-Health Systems Inc	7372	255
Multilayer Prototypes Inc	3672	388
MultiLing Corp	4899	31
Multilingual Communications Corp	7389	2468
Multi-Link Communications Products	5045	449
Multi-Link Inc	3661	199
Multilink Inc	5063	199
Multilink Security Inc	7382	150

Company Name	SIC	Rank
Multi-Machining Company Inc	3599	1791
Multimedia Abacus Corp	7371	1252
Multimedia Broadcast Investment Corp	6799	328
MultiMedia Communications LLC	3841	131
Multimedia Data Storage LLC	7379	1613
Multi-Media Duplication Inc	3565	150
Multimedia Express Inc	5045	1003
Multimedia Games Holding Company Inc	7372	351
Multimedia Graphic Network	7372	4465
Multimedia Ink Designs	7379	1682
Multimedia Integrated Technology Inc	5065	387
Multimedia Production Services	7336	105
Multimedia Research Group Inc	2741	385
Multi-Media Solutions Inc	5044	106
Multimek Inc	3672	380
Multimetal Products Corp	3444	236
Multinational Technologies Inc	5045	732
Multi-Pak Corp	3589	215
Multipath Corp	5045	955
Multiplan Inc	6324	37
Multi-Plastics of New Mexico Inc	3089	1804
Multi-Plate Circuits Inc	3672	316
Multiple Systems Inc	3559	257
Multi-Plex Inc	3357	43
Multiplex Technologies Inc	3672	490
Multipli Machinery Corp	5084	898
Multi-Precision Detail Inc	3544	276
Multiprens USA Inc	3812	165
Multiprocess Computer Corporation Inc	7373	769
Multipurpose Cleaning Services Inc	7349	170
Multiquip Inc	5082	67
Multiscope Inc	2752	706
Multiseal Inc	2891	43
Multi-Shifter Inc	3537	92
Multisoft Inc	4813	278
Multisorb Technologies Inc	3295	3
Multisupport Computer Systems	3695	81
Multi-Swatch Corp	2782	21
Multisystems Inc	7372	1295
Multi-Tech Industries Inc	3644	49
Multi-Tech Systems Inc	3577	141
Multivariate Software Inc	7372	4003
Multiview Corp	7372	1470
Multivision Inc (Fairfax Virginia)	8748	126
Multiware Inc	7372	3065
Multi-Wing America Inc	3564	107
Multix Inc	7371	1697
Mulvaney Homes Inc	1531	83
Mulzer Crushed Stone Inc	1422	10
MumboJumbo	7372	4100
Mumford Micro Systems	7372	4528
Munchkin Inc (North Hills California)	3999	137
Muncie Aviation Co	4581	33
Muncie Casting Corp	3543	25
Muncie Novelty Company Inc	2791	10
Muncie Power Products Inc	3714	97
Muncie Reclamation And Supply Company	7699	102
Muncy Homes Inc	2452	8
Munder Capital Management	6282	143
Mundi Corporate Inc	7381	127
Mundi-Westport Corp	3172	2
Mundorff Graphics	2752	1457
Munger Tolles and Olson LLP	8111	180
Munich Reinsurance America Inc	6331	71
Munich Welding Company Inc	3441	151
Munich-American Holding Corp	6331	287
Municipal Code Corp	2721	160
Municipal Employees Credit Union of Oklahoma City	6062	88
Municipal Energy Agency Of Nebraska	4911	240
Municipal Mortgage and Equity LLC	6162	36
Municipal Utilities Inc	1623	783
Munics Informations Systems Inc	7372	4190
Munimetrix System Corp	7372	1737
MuniServices LLC	6211	78
Munivest Financial Group LLC	7389	2253
Muniz Plastics Inc	2519	11
Munn Rabot LLC	7311	438
Munnell and Sherrill Inc	5085	33
Munot Plastics Inc	3089	1511
Munro and Company Inc	3143	3
Munro Electric Company Inc	1731	1622
MUNROKids - Perfection Div	3149	19
Munsch Hardt Kopf Harr PC	8111	428
Munsee Meats Inc	5147	134
Munson Machinery Company Inc	3532	42
Munson's Candy Kitchen Inc	2064	78
Munster Donut	2051	286
Munters Moisture Control Services	7349	200
Muntz Industries Inc	3677	67
Murakami Farms Inc	0723	22
Murakami Produce Co	2034	7
Muralo Company Inc	2851	13
Murano Software Inc	7371	830
Murata Machinery USA Inc	5084	92
Murcal Inc	3625	237
Mur-Ci Homes Inc	8361	141
Murdock Companies Inc	5063	255
Murdock Electric Inc	1731	2102
Murdock Holding Co	6719	15
Murdock Webbing Company Inc	2241	9
Muriel Siebert and Company Inc	6211	325

Company Name	SIC	Rank
Murko Machinery and Die A Ykk USA Inc	3559	340
Murko Machinery and Die Corp	3599	1152
MurkWorks Inc	7372	2199
Murnane Building Contractors Inc	1542	177
Murnane Packaging Corp	2675	14
Murphy And Nolan Inc	5051	146
Murphy and Partners	6282	674
Murphy Capital Management Inc	6282	510
Murphy Co	2435	8
Murphy Co (Columbus Ohio)	5043	20
Murphy Consolidated Industries Inc	1541	293
Murphy Electric Company Inc	1731	1555
Murphy Equipment Co	5083	216
Murphy Exploration and Production Co	1311	46
Murphy Industries Inc	3315	33
Murphy Oil Corp	2911	8
Murphy Rigging and Erecting Inc	4213	2712
Murphy S Mother Laboratories Inc	2087	17
Murphy Software Co	7372	4991
Murphy Transportation Inc	4213	978
Murphy W E Special Events Management	7389	2104
Murphy Wall Products International Inc	3272	113
Murphy Warehouse Co	4213	836
Murphy-Brown LLC	0213	1
Murphy-Jahn Inc	8712	132
Murphy-Rodgers Inc	5084	594
Murphy's Electric Supply Co	5063	702
Murphy's Waste Oil Service Inc	4959	5
Murray and Heister Inc	5112	77
Murray and MacDonald Insurance Services Inc	6411	195
Murray Associates Architects PC	8712	231
Murray Building and Crane Industries Inc	2452	50
Murray Cabinet and Fixtures Inc	2521	42
Murray Chevrolet Co	5511	835
Murray Controls Inc	3613	114
Murray Corp	3452	50
Murray Feiss Import LLC	5063	47
Murray Feiss Industries	3645	74
Murray Lighting Inc	5063	662
Murray Newspapers Inc	2711	629
Murray Ridge Production Center Inc	8331	217
Murray Transfer and Storage Company Inc	4214	3
Murray's Ford-Lincoln-Mercury Inc	5511	315
Murray's Sheet Metal Company Inc	3444	155
Murray's Transfer and Storage Inc	4213	2634
Murrietta Circuits	3672	165
Murrow's Transfer Inc	4213	1216
Mursix Corp	3469	92
MurTech Consulting LLC	7361	139
Murzan Inc	3561	140
Musashi Auto Parts Michigan Inc	3714	253
Muscatine Foods Corp	2869	27
Musco Corp	7359	55
Muse Communications Inc	7311	159
Muse Research Inc	7372	4356
Muselli Commercial Realtors	6531	344
Museum Arts Inc	7389	2260
Musgrave Pencil Co	3952	5
Mushield Company Inc	3559	350
Mushkin Inc	7379	469
Music A La Carte	4899	188
Music and Arts Center Inc	5736	4
Music Bakery	7379	591
Music Carter Chevrolet Buick	5511	1148
Music Caterer	7999	146
Music Center Operating Co	8741	46
Music City Optical Media Inc	3652	4
Music City Record Distributors Inc	5099	48
Music Express Broadcasting Corp	4832	273
Music Millenium Inc	5735	10
Music on the Move Plus Inc	7929	3
Music People Inc	5065	164
Music Theatre International	6794	64
Music Video Distributors Inc	7822	23
Musick International Inc	7372	4431
MusicMatch Inc	7379	262
Musicol Inc	7389	2469
Musicol Recording	3695	122
Musimatic Electronics Inc	3651	124
Muskegon Construction Co	1541	219
Muskegon Development Co	1311	233
Musson Theatrical Inc	7922	39
Musson-Patout Automotive Group Inc	5511	669
Mustang Electric Supply LLC	5063	226
Mustang Engineering Inc	8711	5
Mustang Expediting Inc	4213	1429
Mustang Industries Inc	5063	1009
Mustang Manufacturing Company Inc	3537	28
Mustang Marketing and Advertising	8742	518
Mustang Publishing Co	2731	384
Mustang Sportswear Inc	2339	55
Mustang Survival Manufacturing Inc	3069	136
Mustang Tractor and Equipment Co	5082	19
Mustek Inc	3577	100
Muster Associates Inc	5012	143
Muth Lumber Company Inc	5031	407
Muthig Industries Inc	3544	748
Mutt and Jeff Enterprises Inc	2096	55

Company Name	SIC	Rank
Mutual Assignment and Indemnification Co	7322	93
Mutual Assurance Agency of Ohio Inc	6331	328
Mutual Bank (MuncieIndiana)	6022	117
Mutual Central Alarm Services Inc	7382	64
Mutual Collection Company Inc	7322	158
Mutual Engraving Company Inc	2754	17
Mutual Industries North Inc	3842	107
Mutual Insurance Company of Arizona	6399	11
Mutual Library Bindery Inc	2789	118
Mutual Liquid Gas and Equipment Company Inc	5984	19
Mutual Management Services Inc	7322	171
Mutual of America Life Insurance Co	6311	62
Mutual of Omaha Insurance Co	6331	28
Mutual of Omaha Investor Services Inc	6211	205
Mutual Savings Life Insurance Co	6311	211
Mutual Trading Company Inc	5141	226
Mutual Trust Life Insurance Co	6311	156
Mutual Wheel Co	5084	113
MutualFirst Financial Inc	6712	245
Mutual-Target LLC	3241	25
Muza Metal Products LLC	3469	73
Muzak Holdings LLC	6719	88
Muzak LLC	3652	7
Muze Inc	7379	150
Mv Corporation Inc	2311	25
MV Mason Electronics Inc	3677	125
MV Oil Trust	1389	35
MV Transportation Inc	4111	2
mValent Inc	5045	232
MVC Corp	7379	716
Mvd Communications LLC	4813	238
Mverify Corp	7373	1049
MVI Administrators Inc	6411	216
MVM Inc	7381	11
Mvoc LLC	6799	362
MVP Communications Inc	7812	68
Mvp Consulting Plus Inc	7379	249
Mvp Laboratories Inc	2834	334
Mvs Fulfillment Services Inc	3086	96
MW Builders Inc	1541	107
MW Industries Inc	3429	7
MW Leahy Company Inc	4213	2988
MW McWong International Inc	5063	139
MW Periscope Inc	2759	286
Mw Studios Inc	7336	143
Mwa Speaker Parts Inc	5731	275
MWC Management Corp	7389	2316
MWH	8711	206
MWH Global Inc	8711	19
Mwi Corp	3561	61
Mwi Inc	3624	6
MWI Veterinary Supply Inc	5047	8
Mwm Acoustics LLC	5065	509
Mwmpc Corp	1731	74
Mwp LLC	5191	111
MWS Enterprises Inc	5411	144
MWSausse and Company Inc	3625	99
Mwt Materials Inc	3812	208
MWW Group	8743	64
Mx Consulting Services Inc	7378	89
MX Logic Inc	7372	1453
MXL Industries Inc	2821	41
Mxros Inc	3651	156
My 1063 Fm Klmy	7313	32
My Channellock Tools	2796	11
My Own Meals Inc	2099	159
My Own Place Inc	8361	99
My Pony Party Inc	7999	124
My Therapy Net Inc	4813	569
Myat Inc	3663	193
MyBizOffice Inc	7372	2104
Myco Industries Inc	3841	403
Mycogen Corp	2879	9
Mycogen Seeds	0181	10
My-Con Inc	1623	682
Mycone Dental Supply Company Inc	5047	34
Mydax Inc	3585	233
Myer Show Print Inc	3842	306
Myerberg and Company LP	6282	217
Myer-Emco Inc	5731	13
Myers and Crow Company Ltd	1541	309
Myers Brothers Of Kansas City Inc	5085	294
Myers Controlled Power LLC	3613	53
Myers Electric Of Eastern New Mexico Inc	1731	729
Myers Engineering Inc	3559	220
Myers F E Co	3561	39
Myers Group Inc	7361	189
Myers Houghton and Partners Inc	8711	331
Myers Industries Inc	3089	29
Myers Industries International Inc	3089	22
Myers International Midways Inc	7999	95
Myers Power Products Inc	3629	46
Myers Quality Machine Company Inc	3552	47
Myers Recording Studio	8331	4
Myers Tire Supply International Inc	2821	34
Myers-Holum Inc	8742	165
Mylan Inc (Canonsburg Pennsylvania)	2834	12
Mylan Pharmaceuticals Inc	2834	29
Mylan Technologies Inc	2833	30
MyLifecom Inc	7389	455
Myllykoski North America Inc	6719	182

Company Name	SIC	Rank
Mymic LLC	8731	201
Myogen Inc	2836	57
Myotronics Noromed Inc	3843	79
MyPointscom Inc	7319	37
MyPRGenie Inc	7371	311
Myprint Corp	7372	1047
MYR Group Inc	1623	9
Myriad Development	8999	102
Myriad Entertainment and Resorts Inc	7999	162
Myriad Genetic Laboratories Inc	8731	34
Myriad Genetics Inc	2835	8
Myriad Restaurant Group Inc	5812	171
Myrick Computer Services Inc	7372	5124
Myricom Inc	3577	179
Myrmo and Sons Inc	5531	37
Myron Corp	5199	32
Myron L Co	3823	236
Myron Toback Inc	5094	50
Myron Zucker Inc	1731	2380
Myron's Dental Laboratories Inc	8072	15
MYS Designs Inc	2759	463
MySQL AB	5045	341
Mystateusa	4813	495
Mystery Electronics	5065	1008
Mystic Assembly and Decorating Company Inc	7389	1502
Mystic Lake Casino Hotel	7993	10
Mystic Ltd	2653	81
Mystic Management Systems Inc	7372	3780
Mystikal Solutions LLC	8748	323
Mytee Products Inc	3589	152
Mytex Polymers Us Corp	3089	1321
Mythic Entertainment Inc	7372	907
MyWeather LLC	7372	511
Myweddingcom	8999	116
MZ Carpet Inc	5023	181
Mza Associates Corp	7371	1019
MZI Group Inc	8741	234
N and D Technical Services Inc	1731	1810
N and K Enterprises Inc	7349	158
N and L Instruments Inc	3571	175
N and N Machine Inc	3599	1376
N and N Manufacturing Inc	3679	545
N and N Transport Inc	4213	2560
N and P Engineers and Land Surveyor PLLC	8711	368
N and S Tractor Co	5083	61
N and S Used Foreign Car Parts	5015	33
N and T Digmore Inc	1623	206
N And W Printing Associates Inc	2761	75
N B West Contracting Co	2951	18
N C Industries Inc	3545	20
N/C Servo Technology Corp	7629	36
N C Tax Service	7291	17
N Chasen and Son Inc	1721	9
N E Tech-Air Inc	1761	34
N Gil Electric Company Inc	1731	1323
N I C Group	7373	988
N J D Wiring and Electric Inc	1731	163
N J Shaum and Son Incorporated Electrical Contractors	1731	593
N Jonas and Company Inc	5169	101
N Merfish Plumbing Supply Co	5074	63
N Pandelena Construction Company Inc	1623	681
N Penn Comprehensive Health Services	8322	34
N/S Corp	3589	114
N S Farrington and Co	5087	54
N Siperstein Inc	5231	2
/n software Inc	7372	3323
N Stuart Design	7336	278
N Systems Inc	3679	766
N Wasserstrom and Sons Inc	3556	10
NA Bar Inc	3556	174
NA Degerstrom Inc	1041	10
NA Elmos Inc	7373	289
Na Hoku Inc	3911	50
NA Petroflex Ltd	3084	22
NAADM Inc	7363	357
Nab Construction Corp	1541	87
Nabco Entrances Inc	3699	99
Nabholz Construction Corp	1542	55
Nabi Biopharmaceuticals	2836	84
Nabisco Biscuit Co	2052	2
Nabisco Inc	2068	1
Nabors Alaska Drilling Inc	1381	60
Nabors Drilling International Ltd	1381	38
Nabors Drilling USA Inc	1381	17
Nabors Inc	5511	968
Nabors International Inc	1381	33
Nabors Offshore Corp	1381	32
Nabors Offshore Corp Inland Div	1389	17
Nabors Well Services Ltd	1389	19
Nac Carbon Products Inc	3624	25
Nacci Printing Inc	2752	1379
NACCO Industries Inc	3537	2
NACCO Materials Handling Group	3537	22
Nachi America Inc	5084	93
Nachi Robotic Systems Inc	3559	76
NACM Credit Services Inc	7323	37
Nacm Tampa Inc	7323	27
Naco Express	4213	2832
NACO Industries Inc	3089	200

Company Name	SIC	Rank
Nadel Architects Inc	8712	108
Nadolife Inc	2024	47
Nadrich Corp	5734	445
Nady Systems Inc	3651	92
Naegle's Industrial Leather Machinery Co	3559	485
Nagakura Engineering Works Company Inc	3714	318
Nagarro Inc	7372	383
Nagase America Corp	3679	118
Nagel Precision Inc	3541	66
Nagelbush Mechanical Inc	1711	9
Nagele Manufacturing Company Inc	2541	53
Nagle Toledo Inc	4213	1270
Naglee Moving and Storage Inc	4213	2519
Nagle's Veal Inc	2011	125
Nahan Printing Inc	2759	49
Nahuel Trading Corp	3663	238
Nai Cranes LLC	3536	25
NAI Partners Commercial	6531	112
NAI Southern Real Estate Inc	6531	203
Naiad Of New Hampshire Inc	3559	429
Nail Emporium	5087	87
Nailor Industries	3822	6
Nailor Industries Of Texas Inc	3822	12
Naimco Inc	3841	235
Naked Optics Corp	3679	95
Nakra Labs Inc	5734	376
NAL Worldwide Inc	7371	40
Nalco Holding Co	2899	6
Nalge Nunc International Corp	3089	26
Nallatech Inc	5045	162
Nalley Automotive Group	5511	34
Nalley Nissan	5511	437
Nally and Hamilton Enterprises Inc	1221	30
Nalpac Enterprises Ltd	5199	58
Nam LLC	7349	333
Namaste Solar Electric Inc	1731	239
Nambe LLC	2514	13
Namco Controls Corp	3625	48
NAME-IT	7389	2331
NameMedia Inc	7375	63
Nameplates For Industry Inc	2759	267
Names In The News California Inc	7331	250
Namias Of Arizona Inc	2038	83
Namifiers Lanyards and Name Tags	2261	2
Nammo Talley	3569	19
Namsco Plastics Industries Inc	3089	718
Namtra Business Solutions Inc	7379	428
Nana/Colt Engineering LLC	8711	261
Nana Development Corp	4911	73
Nana Dynatec Mining LLC	1081	3
Nana Regional Corporation Inc	1389	27
Nanas Stern Biers Neinstein and Co	8721	356
Nance International Inc	3585	165
Nancy A Palermo	7331	271
Nancy Bailey and Associates Inc	6794	117
Nancy Brownstein	5063	409
Nancy Leffingwell Enterprises	7379	1522
Nancy Sales Company Inc	5099	54
Nancy Scott Jones and Associates	8743	142
Nancy's Homemade Fudge Inc	2064	111
Nanka Seimen Co	2098	23
Nanlee Industries	3663	263
Nanlee Tooling Inc	3544	397
Nanmac Corp	3829	293
Nanney and Son Inc	3545	188
Nano Electronics Inc	5065	330
Nano-C LLC	1499	4
NanoChem Solutions Inc	2899	141
Nanometrics Inc	3829	15
NanoOpto Corp	3679	97
NanoPac Inc	7372	4529
Nanophase Technologies Corp	3399	25
Nanosphere Inc	3841	348
Nanostring Technologies Inc	8099	71
Nanosys Inc	3674	374
Nanotek Machines LLC	5999	284
Nanshing America Inc	5023	113
Nantero Inc	3674	238
Nanticoke Memorial Hospital Inc	8062	224
Nantucket Allserve Inc	2033	31
Nantucket Bake Shop Inc	2051	305
Nantucket Bank	6036	80
Nao Inc	3823	203
NAP of the Americas Inc	4813	753
Napa Group LLC	7372	2284
NAPA Transportation Inc	4213	240
Napa Valley Aloft Inc	4522	38
Napa Valley Balloon Inc	7999	149
Napa Wine Company LLC	2084	77
Napco Inc	2782	27
Napco Inc (Sparta North Carolina)	2782	17
NAPCO Marketing Corp	5199	21
Napco Security Systems Inc	3669	42
Napersoft Inc	7372	1875
Naperville Electrical Contractors Inc	1731	2139
Naperville Psychiatric Ventures	8063	14
Naples Endoscopy Anesthesia LLC	8049	22
Naples Endoscopy ASC LP	8011	87
Naples Graphics and Printing Inc	2752	812
Naples Lumber and Supply Company Inc	5211	218
Naples Pool Service Inc	7389	1626
Naples Registry Resort	7011	69
Napleton Auto Group	5511	87
Napleton Cadillac Saab	5511	1020
Napo Associates Inc	5082	202
Napo Pharmaceuticals Inc	8731	415
Napoleon Bakery Inc	2051	145
Napoleon Inc	2711	688
Napoleon Videographics	7336	36
NAPP Systems Inc	2796	8
Napp Technologies Inc	2834	318
Napp-Grecco Co	1623	92
Nappi Trucking Corp	4213	2767
Naprotek Inc	3672	142
Napster Inc	7371	81
Narco Avionics Inc	3812	156
Nardo Group International LLC	3669	207
Narragansett Business Forms Inc	2752	1564
Narragansett Improvement Co	6552	177
Narragasett Jewelry Inc	3961	6
Narrow Fabric Industries Corp	2241	10
Narrow Fabrics of America Corp	2241	2
Nartron Corp	3679	30
Narup Engraving Company Inc	2796	60
Narus Inc	7373	206
NAS Recruitment Communications	7311	85
NASB Financial Inc	6712	267
Nasby Agri Systems Co	5083	204
Nascentric Inc	3674	194
NASCO International Inc NASCO West Div	5961	90
Nascote Industries	3714	71
Nasdaq OMX Group Inc	6231	1
Nasdaq OMX PHLX Inc	6231	7
Naselle Rock and Asphalt Co	1429	6
Nash Brothers Construction Company Inc	1623	223
Nash Engineering Company Inc	6719	81
Nash Finch Co	5141	13
Nash Johnson and Sons' Farms Inc	0254	1
Nash Manufacturing Inc	3949	113
Nashau School District	8211	37
Nashbar and Associates Inc	5961	136
Nash-Rocky Mount Schools	8211	61
Nashua Circuits Inc	3672	232
Nashua Corp	2679	5
Nashua Homes Of Idaho Inc	2451	27
Nashua Label Products	2672	12
Nashville Bank and Trust Co	6022	594
Nashville Broadcasting LP	4833	183
Nashville Chemical and Equipment Company Inc	5169	157
Nashville Electric Service Co	4911	40
Nashville Gas Co	4923	24
Nashville Machine	8711	362
Nashville Plywood Inc	5031	357
Nashville Rubber And Gasket Company Inc	5085	183
Nashville Sash and Door Company Inc	5031	186
Nashville Steel Corp	5051	173
Nashville Welding and Machine Works Inc	7692	34
Nasin Electric LLC	1731	2051
Naso Industries Corp	3679	434
Nasoft USA Inc	7371	884
Nason Company Inc	3822	28
Nasoya Foods Inc	2099	134
Nassau Broadcasting Maine	4832	119
Nassau Broadcasting Partners LP (Princeton New Jersey)	4832	12
Nassau Lens Company Inc	3851	25
Nassau Pools Construction Inc	1799	86
Nassau Suffolk Lumber and Supply Corp	5211	84
Nassau Tool Works Inc	3728	149
Nassi Group LLC	7389	1462
Nassor Electrical Supply Company Inc	5063	482
Nas-Tra Automotive Industries Inc	3714	282
Nasuni Corp	7374	281
Natalia Marketing Corp	5094	60
Natchez Coca-Cola Bottling Co	2086	80
Natchez Group Inc	7379	335
Natchez Trace Electric Power Association	4911	230
Natchitoches Ford Lincoln Mercury Inc	5511	996
Natchitoches Times Inc	2711	712
NATCO/Carlton	3541	276
Natco Products Corp	3996	3
NatCom Marketing Communications Inc	8742	538
Natel Engineering Company Inc	3679	34
Nath Minnesota Franchise Group Inc	5812	189
Nathan Alterman Electric Company Inc	1731	213
Nathan Segal and Company Inc	5153	129
Nathaniel Group Inc	3679	635
Nathan's Famous Inc	5812	267
Nation Company LP	2721	252
Nation Magazine Co	2721	170
Nation Pizza Products LP	2033	18
Nation Safe Drivers	7373	192
Nationair Insurance	6411	211
National Able Network Inc	8322	41
National Academies Press	2731	230
National Air Vibrator Co	3612	112
National Aircraft Service Inc	3728	222
National American Insurance Co	6321	33
National American University Holdings Inc	8221	38
National Ammonia Co	5169	123
National Amusements Inc	7832	1
National Aperture Inc	3827	141
National Applied Computer Technologies Inc	3661	76
National Arbitration Forum Inc	7389	793
National Asset Recovery Services Inc	8748	23
National Auction Co	7389	1259
National Auction Group Inc	7389	184
National Auto Parts	5531	34
National Automatic Sprinkler Co	1711	226
National Bakery Inc	5461	18
National Bancshares Corp	6712	531
National Band Saw Co	3546	42
National Bank and Trust Co	6022	387
National Bank and Trust Co (Norwich New York)	6021	400
National Bank of Arizona	6021	44
National Bank of Arkansas	6021	283
National Bank of Blacksburg	6021	195
National Bank of California	6021	221
National Bank of Indianapolis	6021	123
National Bank of Middlebury	6021	297
National Bank of Sallisaw	6712	536
National Bank of Texas at Fort Worth	6021	255
National Bankcard Systems Inc	5046	37
National Banking Corp	6712	521
National Bankshares Inc	6712	315
National Banner Company Inc	2399	18
National Barricade Company LLC	7359	142
National Bearings Inc	3562	29
National Beverage Corp	2086	12
National Beverage Screen Printers Inc	3993	131
National Bias Fabric Co	2396	34
National Biological Corp	3841	243
National Boston Video Center	7336	39
National Braille Press Inc	2721	290
National Breaker Services LLC	5063	698
National Builders Hardware Co	5072	135
National Bulk Equipment Inc	3599	497
National Bus Sales And Leasing Inc	5012	147
National Business Data Systems Inc	7372	3929
National Business Forms Inc	2761	54
National Business Furniture Inc	5021	17
National Business Media Inc	2721	198
National Business Services Inc	2521	53
National Cabinet Lock	3429	48
National Cancer Coalition LLC	8099	31
National Capital Bank of Washington	6021	253
National Capital Industries Inc	5082	121
National Car Mart Inc	5012	72
National Car Rental System Inc	7514	7
National Carriers Inc	4213	85
National Carton and Coating Co	2631	26
National Casein Co	2891	39
National Cash Processors Inc	6099	32
National Cash Register Co	3578	1
National Catastrophe Adjusters	6411	209
National Catholic Reporter Publishing Co	2711	493
National Center For Dispute Settlement LLC	7389	2332
National Chemicals Inc	2841	57
National Church Residences Of Denver	8361	145
National Church Supply Company Incorporated Envelope Service	2677	15
National Cigar Corp	0132	1
National CineMedia Inc	7319	11
National Coatings Inc	2851	100
National Color Corp	7334	42
National Communication Service	5065	255
National Community Development Services Inc	7389	1125
National Computer Print Inc	2782	7
National Coney Island Chili Co	2032	47
National Contracting Group Ltd	6512	79
National Conveyor Corp	3535	173
National Conveyors Company Inc	3535	162
National Cooperative Bank	6021	73
National Copper and Smelting Company Inc	3351	16
National Corporate Research Ltd	8732	44
National Council On Family Violence	8322	229
National Credit Center Inc	7323	22
National Creditors Connection Inc	7322	144
National Cycle Inc	3714	324
National Datacast Inc	4899	187
National Datacomputer Inc	3571	207
National Dentex Corp	8071	13
National Design Group Inc	1731	1028
National Detective Agency	7381	243
National Detroit Inc	3546	31
National Diagnostics Inc	2835	48
National Direct Dataflow	3555	125
National Distributing Company Inc (Atlanta Georgia)	5182	8
National Distribution Systems Inc	5084	751
National Distribution Warehouse Inc	5063	267
National Distributor Systems Inc	7372	3653
National Distributors Inc	5149	64
National Distributors Leasing Inc	4213	487

Company Name	SIC	Rank
National Diversified Co	6719	196
National Diversified Sales Inc	3089	114
National Economic Research Associates Inc	8732	30
National Educational Acceptance Corp	7322	16
National Electric Coil Inc	7694	2
National Electric Company Inc	1731	1132
National Electric Manufacturing Corp	3646	89
National Electrical Co	1731	1083
National Electro-Coatings Inc	2522	39
National Electronics Warranty Corp	6411	24
National Electrostatics Corp	3822	49
National Element Inc	3567	78
National Elevator Cab and Door Corp	3534	20
National Emblem Inc	2395	6
National Envelope Corp	2677	2
National Enzyme Company Inc	2869	76
National Equipment Company Inc	5046	141
National Everclean Services Inc	8734	102
National Exchange Bank and Trust	6021	135
National Fab And Machine Inc	3532	70
National Fabrication Inc	3842	142
National Fidelity Mortgage Inc	6162	124
National Filter Media Corp	3569	59
National Financial Corp	7389	2079
National Financial Services Corp	6211	88
National Fire and Marine Insurance Co	6331	97
National Fire Services LLC	7389	953
National Flange and Fitting Co	3463	18
National Flavors Inc	2087	82
National Foundation Life Insurance Co	6311	219
National Freight	4213	100
National Freightways Inc	4213	2912
National Frozen Foods Corp	2037	6
National Fruit Vegetable Technology Corp	2037	38
National Fuel Gas Co	4924	17
National Fuel Gas Supply Corp (Williamsville New York)	4924	27
National Fuel Resources Inc	4924	64
National Furniture Liquidators I LLC	5021	101
National Fuse Products Inc	5063	1003
National Geographic Film Library	7336	20
National Geographic Society Inc	2721	21
National Golf Properties Inc	6798	45
National Government Services Inc	8099	19
National Grange Mutual Insurance Co	6331	207
National Grid Holdings Inc	4931	9
National Grid USA	4911	82
National Guard Products Inc	3442	59
National Guardian Life Insurance Co	6311	122
National Gym Supply Inc	7389	958
National Handicapped Workshop	7389	1529
National Hanger Company Inc	3089	510
National Healing Corp	7372	1474
National Health Data Syst Inc	7379	1532
National Health Insurance Agency Inc	6411	258
National Health Investors Inc	6798	148
National Health Management Inc	8052	9
National HealthCare Corp	8051	12
National Herald Inc	2711	593
National Heritage Academies Inc	8211	98
National Highway Express Inc	4213	658
National Holdings Corp	6211	203
National Home Health Care Corp	8082	29
National Home Products Inc	3633	4
National Horse Transfer Inc	4213	2264
National Hybrid Inc	3674	264
National Hydraulics Inc	7699	61
National Indemnity Co	6331	11
National Indemnity Company of Mid-America	6331	270
National Indemnity Company of the South	6331	324
National Indexing Systems Inc	2678	14
National Industrial Lumber Co	5031	61
National Information Services Corp	2741	391
National Information Solutions Cooperative Inc	7372	46
National Instrument LLC	3565	89
National Instruments Corp	7372	55
National Insurance Law Service	2741	124
National Interstate Corp	6331	150
National Jet Company Inc	3541	184
National Journal Group Inc	2731	118
National Knife Company Inc	3423	74
National Label Co	2672	16
National Laboratory Specialists Inc	5049	41
National Lampoon Inc	7812	137
National Las Vegas Inc	2759	567
National Law Enforcement Telecommunications System Inc	4813	353
National Law Library Inc	7372	1838
National Liability and Fire Insurance Co	6331	218
National Library Bindery Company Of Georgia Inc	2789	74
National Life Group	6311	48
National Lift Truck Inc	7359	81
National Limestone Quarry Inc	1422	23
National Live Trap Corp	5091	45
National Logistics Management Inc	4213	424
National Lumber (Berlin Massachusetts)	5211	167
National Lumber Co (Mansfield Massachusetts)	5211	17
National Lumber Co (Warren Michigan)	5211	45
National Machine Co	3599	70
National Machinery Exchange Inc	5084	485
National Machinery LLC	3542	5
National Magnetic Sensors Inc	3625	377
National Magnetics Group Inc	3264	13
National Mail Advertising Inc	7331	71
National Mail Graphics Corp	2752	187
National Maintenance Inc	1799	89
National Manufacturing Company Inc	3469	98
National Marine Consultants Inc	7389	1412
National Medical Supply Company Inc	5047	126
National Meeting Company Inc	7389	1702
National Metal Fabricators LLC	1761	47
National Multiple Listing Inc	2721	293
National Nail Corp	5051	164
National Nonwovens Inc	2231	5
National Oilwell Varco Inc	3533	2
National Online Registries LLC	7389	1046
National Out Of Home Message Inc	7312	22
National Packaging Company Inc	7389	580
National Paper and Envelope Corp	2752	1195
National Partitions Inc	2541	15
National Parts Depot Inc	5045	562
National Parts LLC	5015	2
National Patent Analytical System Inc	3829	226
National Patent Development Corp	3999	216
National Patient Services	7311	125
National Pattern Inc	3543	31
National Payment Corp	6099	31
National Penn Bancshares Inc	6712	80
National Penn Bank	6021	58
National Penn Investment Co	6798	208
National Penn Investors Trust Co	6798	94
National Penn Life Insurance Co	6311	69
National Pharmaceutical Returns Inc	7389	545
National Pipe and Plastics Inc	3084	4
National Plastek Inc	3081	146
National Plastering Industries Joint Apprenticeship Trust Fund	8331	190
National Plastics Color Inc	2865	13
National Positions USA	7311	525
National Posters Inc	2752	28
National Power Equipment Inc	5063	1023
National Powersport Auctions	5561	3
National Precast Inc	3272	85
National Presto Industries Inc	3489	7
National Print Group Inc	2752	3
National Printing Co	2759	505
National Printing Converters Inc	2759	69
National Product Sales Inc	5961	51
National Products LLC	2842	64
National Prosource	7379	418
National Protective Services Inc	7381	198
National Publishers Marketing Center Inc	7389	1643
National Purity Inc	2841	49
National Quality Care Inc	8099	117
National Raisin Co	0172	4
National Readerboard Supply Company Inc	3993	163
National Realty and Development Corp	6552	123
National Recovery Systems Inc	4953	19
National Recovery Technologies Inc	7699	122
National Refrigerants Inc	5169	85
National Refrigeration Co	3639	13
National Relocation Services Inc	7389	1358
National Renal Alliance	8092	3
National Reprographics Inc	7334	7
National Research Corp	8731	80
National Research Labs Inc	3672	449
National Research LLC	8732	69
National Response Corp	4959	18
National Retail Properties	6798	88
National Retail Transportation	4213	257
National Review Inc	2721	255
National Risk Services Inc	7389	1785
National Rural Utilities Cooperative Finance Corp	6159	11
National Safety Commission	8299	44
National Scent Co	2834	490
National Seating and Mobility Inc	5999	117
National Securities Corp	6211	260
National Security Agency Inc	7381	182
National Security Alliance Consultants LLC	1731	2467
National Security Group Inc	6311	229
National Security Technologies LLC	8711	95
National Service Contract Insurance Company Risk Retention Group Inc	6411	177
National Service Industries Inc	3646	3
National Sheet Metal Machines Inc	3542	86
National Shipping Company of Saudi Arabia (America) Inc	4731	73
National Shopping Service	8748	1
National Sign and Signal Co	3669	188
National Specialty Alloys LLC	5051	100
National Spinning Company Inc	2281	6
National Spirit Group Ltd	2339	29
National Staffing Associates Inc	7363	235
National Steel and Shipbuilding Co	3731	3
National Strategy Group Inc	7389	1841
National Subscription Fulfillment Service	7372	4071
National Surgical Care	8052	6
National Tech Design Inc	7361	395
National Technical Systems Inc	8734	11
National Technology Inc	3672	103
National Telecoin Corp	7349	491
National Telecommunications Services Inc	7389	2529
National Temporary Personnel Service	7363	302
National Tenant Network Inc	7323	24
National Ticket Co	2752	235
National Time Recording Equipment Company Inc	3579	62
National Toner and Ink	5045	635
National Tool Supply Inc	5072	113
National Trade Supply LLC	5963	20
National Trailer Center Of Michigan Inc	7519	4
National Transportation Corp	4213	2339
National Transportation Exchange Inc	7372	211
National Truck and Trailer Service LLC	4213	2998
National Tube Supply Co	5051	169
National Turf Inc	1711	266
National Ultrasound Inc	3829	272
National Underwriter Co	2731	139
National Union Fire Insurance Company of Pittsburgh Pennsylvania	6331	320
National Van Lines Inc	4213	789
National Vinegar Company Inc	2099	113
National Vinegar Co (St Louis Missouri)	2099	126
National Vision Inc	5999	14
National Vitamin Company Inc	2834	228
National Waste Services Inc	5084	443
National Water Purifiers Inc	5074	180
National Waterworks Inc	5085	11
National Western Life Insurance Co	6311	70
National Wine and Spirits Inc	5182	4
National Wire and Cable Corp	3357	44
National Wire and Metal Technologies Inc	3469	328
National Wire Fabric Inc	3496	65
National Wiretec Communications Inc	1731	2226
National Wood Products Inc	5031	121
National Wood Products Of Maine	5031	442
National Wrecking Co	1795	2
Nationalease Of Maine Inc	7389	2491
National-Standard Co	3315	6
Nation-Ruskin Inc	3089	935
Nations Best Delicatessen Company Inc	2011	107
Nations Express Inc	4731	43
NationsBuilders Insurance Services	6399	21
Nationshealth Inc	5047	33
NationStar Mortgage	6162	150
Nationwide Advertising Specialty Inc	5199	61
Nationwide Agribusiness	6331	59
Nationwide Autoworld Infiniti	5511	307
Nationwide Bank	6035	52
Nationwide Beauty and Barber LLC	5087	119
Nationwide Biweekly Administration Inc	7389	786
Nationwide Children's Hospital	8069	7
Nationwide Circuits Inc	3672	302
Nationwide Collection Agencies Inc	7322	120
Nationwide Corp	6311	130
Nationwide Credit Service LLC	7322	126
Nationwide Custom Homes Inc	2452	11
Nationwide Electrical Testing Inc	1731	1966
Nationwide Electronics Inc	5734	216
Nationwide Entertainment Services Inc	7922	78
Nationwide Equipment Company Inc	7353	16
Nationwide Exchange Services Inc	8999	50
Nationwide Financial Services Inc	6311	12
Nationwide Graphics	2752	25
Nationwide Healthplan	6324	80
Nationwide Homes Network Inc	7389	1755
Nationwide Housing Properties LP	6531	22
Nationwide Housing Systems LP	1522	35
Nationwide Industries Inc	2431	67
Nationwide Insurance Company Of Florida	6411	87
Nationwide Life Insurance Co	6311	11
Nationwide Lift Trucks Inc	5511	1014
Nationwide Magazine/Book Distrib	4213	1458
Nationwide Mutual Fire Insurance Co	6331	108
Nationwide Mutual Insurance Co	6331	6
Nationwide Paging Inc	4812	121
Nationwide Precision Products	3599	104
Nationwide Security	7381	131
Nationwide Sports and Injury Inc	8049	18
Nationwide Theatres Corp	7833	1
Nationwide Transport LLC	4731	41
Nationwide Transportation	4213	1229
Nationwide Truck Brokers Inc	4213	571
Nationwide Trucking Inc	4111	11
Nationwide Value Computers Inc	7373	1143
Nationwide Vision Center PC	5995	11
Nationwide-Southeast Inc	4213	1296
Native American Bank NA	6021	359
Native American Energy Group Inc	5983	32
Native New Yorker Inc	5812	318
Native Tele-Data Solutions Inc	1731	992
Natixis Global Asset Management	6799	55
Natoli Engineering Company Inc	3559	88

Company Name	SIC	Rank
Natori Company Inc	2384	1
Natrel Communications Inc	7311	702
Natrol Inc	2833	10
Natural Aggregates Corp	1442	74
Natural Alternatives International Inc	2833	21
Natural Blue Resources Inc	4899	239
Natural Chemistry Inc	2842	104
Natural Data Inc	7361	49
Natural Essentials Inc	2844	159
Natural Fruit Corp	2024	35
Natural Fuels Company LLC	3586	14
Natural Gas Odorizing Inc	2842	60
Natural Gas Processing Corp	4924	61
Natural Gas Services Group Inc	1389	38
Natural Grocers by Vitamin Cottage Inc	5499	9
Natural Habitat Adventures	4725	29
Natural Health Trends Corp	5199	52
Natural Illuminating Technologies Inc	3645	84
Natural Light Inc	3645	52
Natural Lighting Co	3648	82
Natural Materials LLC	1475	2
Natural Meat Specialties	5147	132
Natural Nutrition Group Inc	2099	26
Natural Power Inc	4911	594
Natural Resource Partners LP	1221	16
Natural Resources USA Corp	1499	5
Natural Selection Inc	7371	1635
Natural Soda Inc	2812	9
Natural Stone Care Inc	7349	447
Natural Wireless LLC	7374	231
NaturaLawn of America Inc	0782	14
NaturalInsight	7372	1996
Naturally Fresh Inc	2035	7
Nature America Inc	2721	52
Nature Scapes Inc	0782	7
NatureForm Hatchery Systems Inc	3523	80
Natureform Inc	3523	216
Nature's Blend Wood Products Inc	2434	62
Nature's Cure Inc	2844	135
Nature's Envy Inc	3999	115
Nature's Formula Inc	2844	120
Nature's Recipe Pet Foods	2047	36
Nature's Sunshine Products Inc	2834	78
Natureworks LLC	3089	420
Naturex Inc	2833	24
Naturipe Farms	0171	1
Natus Medical Inc	3845	15
Naugatuck Glass Co	3231	14
Naugatuck Valley Financial Corp	6712	439
Naugatuck Valley Savings and Loan SB	6035	97
Naugler Mold and Engineering Inc	3544	879
Naumann Equipment Company Inc	5032	189
Naumes Concentrates Inc	2037	42
Nautic Partners LLC	6799	95
Nautica Apparel Inc	6794	16
Nautica Enterprises Inc	6794	15
Nautica International Inc	5136	3
Nautica Jeans Co	2389	6
Nautilus Inc	3949	29
Nautilus Insurance Co	6331	267
Navagate Inc	7372	1487
Navajo Express Inc	4213	193
Navajo Express Inc (Denver Colorado)	4213	249
Navajo Refining Co	2911	34
Navajo Shippers Inc	4213	65
NavalTees LLC	7336	301
Navarre Corp	5045	38
Navarro County Electric Cooperative Inc	4911	463
Navarro Discount Pharmacies Inc	5912	23
Navarro Research and Engineering Inc	8711	194
Navarro Winery	2084	51
Navasota Odessa Energy Partners LP	1623	646
Navasota Valley Electric Cooperative Inc	4911	436
Navatek Ltd	3731	33
Navcom Defense Electronics Inc	3812	86
Navcor	7377	25
Nave Communications Co	5065	351
Navellier and Associates Inc	6282	94
Naverus Inc	7372	1049
Naviant	7372	1188
Navico Inc	5087	192
Navigant Consulting Inc	8742	33
Navigation Laboratories Inc	3812	211
Navigational Construction Inc	7389	1762
Navigators Group Inc	6331	104
Navigators Insurance Co	6331	252
Navigators Insurance Services of Texas Inc	6331	314
Navigators Insurance Services of Washington Inc	6331	333
Navillus Tile Inc	1741	2
NaviMedix Inc	7372	147
NaviSite Inc	7389	205
Navistar Financial Corp	6159	31
Navistar International Corp	3713	1
Navitaire	7372	3096
Navitaire Inc	7372	569
Navitar Inc	3699	66
Navman Wireless	3577	614
Navone Engineering Inc	3651	224
Navopache Electric Coop	4911	223

Company Name	SIC	Rank
Navrat's Inc	2752	1458
Navrat's Office Products	2752	915
Navsys Corp	3812	122
Navtec Inc	3731	51
NAVTEQ Corp	7389	47
Navy Federal Credit Union	6061	3
Nax Products Inc	3496	116
Nayak Aviation Corp	2869	97
Naylor Capital Corp	6799	290
Naylor Inc	2752	143
Naylor Pipe Co	3317	32
Nazarene Publishing House	2731	123
Nazdar Co	2893	5
Nazem and Co	6799	271
NB and T Financial Group Inc	6712	394
NB Coatings Inc	2821	33
Nb Finishing Inc	7389	1776
NBA Entertainment	7812	18
NBA Inc	7941	12
NBBJ	8712	23
NBBJ Design	8712	7
NBC 10	4833	94
Nbc Holdings Corp	5192	13
NBC Internet Inc	4833	119
NBC News Archives	7336	111
NBC Universal Inc	4833	3
NBC Universal Network Television	6794	38
Nbo Systems Inc	7999	106
Nbs Corp	5085	400
Nbs Design Inc	3672	182
NBS Systems Inc	7371	1674
NBT Bancorp Inc	6712	110
NBTY Inc	2834	19
Nc Auto Parts LLC	5013	90
NC Carpet Binding and Equipment Corp	3559	433
Nc Dynamics Inc	3599	260
NC Frozen Foods Inc	2097	27
Nc Iv Inc	4841	160
NC Mach C0 E Wenatchee	5082	206
NC Machinery Co (Seattle Washington)	5084	19
Nc4 Public Sector LLC	7371	1266
Nca Inc	2298	17
NCAL Bancorp	6712	528
Ncal Computer Source Inc	5734	102
Ncb Management Services Inc	6162	117
NCC Acquisition Corp	3825	360
NCC Automated Systems Inc	3535	71
Ncd Acquisition Inc	3081	109
Ncdr LLC	8741	180
Ncds Medical	5045	719
NCE Computer Group	7371	411
NCE Storage Solutions	3577	243
NCEY Holding LLC	1311	214
NCG Porter Novelli	8743	148
NCH Corp	2842	5
Nci Affiliates Inc	8331	159
NCI Building Systems Inc	3448	3
NCI Holding Corp	6719	16
NCI Inc (Reston Virginia)	7379	25
NCI Information Systems Inc	7373	50
NCIA Insurance Agency Delaware	6311	276
nCipher Inc (Milpitas California)	7379	302
NCL Corporation Ltd	4481	2
Ncl Graphic Specialties Inc	2752	105
Ncl Of Wisconsin Inc	5049	90
NCM Capital Management Group Inc	6722	204
Ncme Holding Corp	8299	73
Ncmi-Brueggemann Inc	3599	2381
NCO Financial Systems Inc	7322	1
NCO Financial Systems Inc Health Services Div	7322	64
NCO Group Inc	7322	3
Ncp Coatings Inc	2851	82
Ncri Inc	3255	9
NCS	7389	1323
Ncsplus Inc	7322	114
NCSS	7372	5139
NCTC Internet	4813	628
Nd Industries Inc	3452	38
Nda Distributors LLC	5064	112
NDC LLC	6531	4
NDE Inc	3672	331
Nde Quality Systems Inc	8742	490
Ndev Technology	5045	1011
NDR Energy Group LLC	8999	59
NDS Americas Inc	7371	116
NDS Media Solutions Inc	3695	52
NDS Products Inc	3829	373
Nds Surgical Imaging LLC	5047	28
NDS Systems LC	7372	1270
NDT International Inc	3829	357
NDT Systems and Services (America) Inc	7389	295
Ne Computing Corp	5045	745
NE Finch Co	4212	39
NE Hospitality Management Services Inc	7373	721
Ne Inc	1731	1677
NE Jones Oil Company Inc	5541	50
NE Penna Salvage Company Inc	5012	184
NE Technologies Inc	7371	419
Nea Electronics Inc	3678	62
Nea Manufacturing Inc	3672	314

Company Name	SIC	Rank
NEAC Compressor Service USA Inc	3563	58
Neace Lukens	6411	89
Neah Power Systems Inc	3691	51
Neal And Associates Inc	7381	149
Neal Auction Company Inc	5099	105
Neal Electric Corp	1731	171
Neal Gerber and Eisenberg	8111	267
Neal Nelson and Associates	7372	4530
Neal Perschke	3599	1711
Nealon Transportation Inc	4213	2298
Neapco Components LLC	3568	5
Near North Insurance Brokerage Inc	6411	47
Nearfield Systems Inc	3669	175
Nearhoof Machine Inc	7699	197
Neas Inc	1711	121
Neasi-Weber International	7372	2397
Neat Co	7371	118
NEATOCOM	7372	2165
Neaton Auto Products Manufacturing Inc	3714	98
NEB Corp	6712	311
Nebraska Beef Ltd	2011	7
Nebraska Boiler Co	3443	61
Nebraska Book Company Inc	5192	9
Nebraska Coast Inc	4213	2389
Nebraska Digital	7374	414
Nebraska Educational Telecommunications	8999	24
Nebraska Electronic Transfer Systems Inc	7371	919
Nebraska Electronics Inc	3672	185
Nebraska Furniture Mart Inc	5712	11
Nebraska Logos Inc	3993	168
Nebraska Machine Products Inc	3451	134
Nebraska Machinery Co	5082	34
Nebraska Pork Partners LLC	0213	3
Nebraska Printing Cener	2711	233
Nebraska Printing Inc	2752	304
Nebraska Public Power District	4911	60
Nebraska Transport Company Inc	4213	524
Nebraska Welding Ltd	3599	1862
Nebulatronics Inc	3825	202
NEC Corporation of America	7372	5105
NEC Display Solutions of America Inc	3674	108
NEC Laboratories Inc	8733	16
Nec Service Co	1731	691
NEC Sphere Communications Inc	7372	1271
NEC Transmission Systems Inc	3661	32
Necco Coffee Company Inc	7359	198
Necessary Objects Ltd	2335	7
Neco LLC	1731	701
NECS Inc	7372	2683
Nectar Pharmaceuticals Inc	5122	121
Ned Bard and Son Co	4213	1718
Ned R Healy And Company Inc	5013	192
Nederlander Producing Company of America Inc	7922	25
NedGraphics Inc	7372	1997
Nedland Industries Inc	3589	140
Nedlog Co	2087	85
Nedmac Inc	3599	1430
Neeco-Tron Inc	3672	217
NeedacellCom Inc	5065	420
Needelman Asset Management Inc	6282	477
Needham and Company LLC	6211	51
Needham Inc	2011	119
Neelco Industries Inc	3523	249
Neeltran Inc	3612	48
Neely Coble Company Inc	5511	135
Neemar Inc	1731	2412
Neenah Foundry Co	3321	1
Neenah Paper Inc	2621	18
Neese Country Sausage Inc	2013	193
Neese Industries Inc	2385	1
Nefcom Inc	4813	363
Nefertiti Protective Services	7382	73
Neff Corp	7359	29
Neff Electric Company Inc	1731	2184
Neff Instrument Corp	3825	286
Neff Power Inc	5084	650
Nefra Communication Center Inc	7389	1705
Nehalem Valley Care Center	8051	21
Nehmen-Kodner Inc	7311	783
Nehring Electrical Works Co	3351	22
Nehrwess Company Inc	3644	50
Nei Software Inc	7373	667
Neidiger Tucker Bruner Inc	6211	353
Neie Construction Services LLC	1623	689
Neighborhood Baking Co	2051	246
Neighborhood Credit Union	6062	14
Neighborhood Development Co	6552	171
Neighborhood Service Resource Center	8322	205
Neighbors Organized For Adequate Housing	8322	194
Neil A Kjos Music Co	2741	98
Neil Enterprises Inc	3089	513
Neil F Lampson Inc	7353	22
Neil Huffman Automotive Group	5511	654
Neil Huffman VW Inc	5511	589
Neill Aircraft Co	3728	75
Neiman Brothers Company Inc	5149	181
Neiman Enterprises Inc	2421	62
Neiman Group Inc	7311	529

Company Name	SIC	Rank
Neiman Marcus Co	5311	4
Neiman Marcus Inc	5311	11
Nek Advanced Securities Group Inc	8748	40
Nekoosa Corp	3599	661
Nektar Therapeutics	2834	156
Nel Frequency Controls Inc	3679	296
Nelco Electric Inc	1731	1248
Nelco (Green Bay Wisconsin)	3679	147
Nelco Products Inc	3083	14
Nelgo Industries Inc	3599	2037
NELiX Inc	7371	944
Nella Oil Co	5541	11
Nel-Logiplex Co	3669	295
Nellymoser Inc	4822	8
Nelnet Inc	6141	11
Nelsen Steel And Wire LP	3316	22
Nelson	8712	263
Nelson Air Device Corp	3444	46
Nelson and Associates Inc	7389	840
Nelson and Gilmore	7311	326
Nelson and Schmidt Inc	7311	237
Nelson B Cooney And Sons Inc	1731	1062
Nelson Capital Management Inc	6282	566
Nelson Case Corp	2449	15
Nelson Communications	6799	13
Nelson Co	2448	25
Nelson Company Inc (Baltimore Maryland)	2448	35
Nelson Container Corp	2653	122
Nelson Crab Inc	2092	86
Nelson Electric Supply Company Inc	5063	240
Nelson Ford-Lincoln-Mercury Inc	5511	863
Nelson Global Products Inc	3714	112
Nelson Inc	4213	2549
Nelson Industries Inc	3714	103
Nelson Irrigation Corp	3494	43
Nelson Laboratories Inc	8734	28
Nelson Laboratories LP	5047	82
Nelson Leasing Inc	5012	78
Nelson Lewis Inc	1623	321
Nelson Machine and Welding Corp	7699	76
Nelson Metal Technology Inc	3599	2244
Nelson Mullins Riley and Scarborough	8111	93
Nelson Name Plate Co	2759	85
Nelson Numeric Inc	3599	722
Nelson Paint Company Of Oregon Inc	2851	176
Nelson Paper Recycling Inc	4953	154
Nelson Petroleum Inc	5172	81
Nelson Pipeline Constructors Inc	1623	151
Nelson Services Systems Inc	7349	226
Nelson Sports Inc	3149	27
Nelson Stud Welding Inc	3452	40
Nelson Tool Corp	3544	868
Nelson Tractor And Equipment Of Sikeston Inc	5083	133
Nelson Truck Equipment Company Inc	5013	199
Nelson Trucking Company Inc	4213	1760
Nelson Westerberg Inc	4213	374
Nelson White Systems Inc	5999	107
Nelson Wholesale Corp	5046	40
Nelson-Jameson Inc	5083	50
Nelson-Ricks Creamery Co	2022	21
Nelson-Rose Inc	3599	379
Nelson's Bus Service Inc	4151	5
Nelson's Vegetable Storage Systems Inc	3572	100
Nel-Tech Labs Inc	3669	221
NEMA Inc	4213	2127
Nemadji Research Corp	7379	804
Nemak USA Inc	3714	126
Nemanco Inc	1542	283
Nematron	3571	103
Nemco Electronics Corp	3675	13
Nemer Fieger and Associates Inc	7311	364
Nemertes Research Group Inc	7379	1342
Nemeth Engineering Associates Inc	8711	586
Nemetschek North America Inc	7371	117
Nemetschek Vectorworks Inc	7372	1830
Nemi Publishing Inc	2752	709
Nemonix Engineering Inc	3577	647
Nemont Telephone Cooperative Inc	4813	67
Ne-Mo's Bakery Inc	2051	80
NEO Corp	1799	24
Neo Pacific Holdings Inc	3089	1051
Neo Technologies Inc	5734	353
NeoAccel Inc	7372	945
Neoc Inc	4214	35
Neocomp Systems Inc	5734	58
Neodesha Plastics Inc	3089	865
Neogen Corp	2834	109
Neogen Corp- Animal Safety Div and Life Sciences Div	2835	24
Neohapsis Inc	7376	14
Neologic International Inc	8711	644
NeoMagic Corp	3674	455
Neomark Inc	5063	1083
NeoMedia Technologies Inc	7373	970
Neomonde Baking Co	2051	111
NeoMPS Inc	2836	62
Neon and Beyond Inc	5046	374
NEON Communications Group Inc	7375	59
Neon Engineering Inc	5063	512
Neon Enterprise Software Inc	5045	142
Neo-Pet LLC	7363	238

Company Name	SIC	Rank
NeoPhotonics Corp	3827	9
Neopost USA	3579	10
Neoprint Inc	2752	707
Neoprobe Corp	3841	197
Neoris DFW	7379	459
Neos Therapeutics Inc	2834	291
NeoSan Pharmaceutical Inc	8731	92
Neoscape Inc	7374	148
Neosho Construction Company Inc	1542	8
Neosho Trompler Inc	3599	528
NEOSOFT Corp	7372	4859
Neosong USA Inc	5065	618
Neostem Inc	3845	40
NeoSurg Technologies Inc	3841	335
Neotec Graphic International Inc	3577	365
Neovest Inc	7372	2342
NEP Broadcasting LLC	4833	20
NEP Inc	3253	9
NEPA Venture Fund LP	6799	335
Nephew Lewis Company LLC	5031	412
Nephi Rubber Products Corp	3052	15
Nephron Pharmaceuticals Corp	2834	175
Nephros Inc	3841	339
NEPSK	4841	109
Neptco Inc	3496	22
Neptune Communications LLC	3229	14
Neptune Machine Inc	3599	1945
Neptune Tech Services Inc	3083	53
Neptune Underwater Services (USA) LLC	7389	497
Neptune-Benson Inc	3589	191
NER Data Products Inc	3955	1
Nercon Eng and Manufacturing Inc	3565	32
Nereus Pharmaceuticals Inc	8731	183
Neri's Bakery Products Inc	5149	60
Nerk Enterprises LLP	5063	324
Nerland Agency Inc	8743	67
Nerone and Sons Inc	1623	341
Nes Of Commerce	5063	608
NES Rentals Holdings Inc	7359	15
NES Traffic Safety LP	3669	4
Nesbit Systems Inc	7372	2602
Nesbitt Contracting Company Inc	1611	110
Nesbitt Services Inc	7349	72
Nesco Electrical Distributors Inc	5063	287
Nesco Inc (Mayfield Heights Ohio)	7361	14
Nesco Manufacturing Inc	2851	177
Neshaminy Abstract Co	6361	40
Neshaminy Electrical Contractors Inc	1731	313
Nesko Electric Co	1731	565
Ness Energy International Inc	1311	259
Nessen Lighting Inc	3645	32
Nessinger Inc	7353	63
Nest Collective	2032	12
Nest Family LLC	7812	61
Nest Group Inc	5122	124
Nestech Machine Systems Inc	3565	189
Nestle Purina PetCare Co	2047	1
Nestle USA - Beverages Division Inc	2095	4
Nestle USA Inc	2066	1
Nestle USA - Prepared Foods Division Inc	2038	4
Nestor and Sons LLC	4213	2713
Nestor Inc	7372	2345
Nestor Sales Company LLC	5084	173
NET and Die Inc	3599	1020
Net Dot Stuff	7336	53
Net Engineers Inc	5734	383
NET Federal Inc	3661	51
Net Forge Inc	3462	51
Net Friends Inc	7373	677
Net Matrix Solutions	8742	295
Net Nanny Software Inc	7372	927
Net Optics Inc	7372	1272
Net Source	3695	39
Net Systems	5734	59
Net Tech Inc	7379	1269
Net World America Inc	4813	375
Net2phone Inc	4813	118
NetAcquire Corp	7372	1901
Netafim Irrigation Inc	3523	61
NetApp Inc	3572	5
NetAppl Inc	7379	1434
netASPx Inc	7373	355
NetBank Payment Systems Inc	5046	26
NetBotz Inc	7372	1428
Netbrain Technologies Inc	7372	2745
Netcast Media Corp	7373	1222
NETcellent System Inc	7372	1724
Netcentra Inc	4813	706
Netchemistry Inc	7374	376
Netco Extruded Plastics Inc	3089	1585
Netcom Inc	3679	219
Netcomm Solutions Inc	7373	788
Netcommerce LLC	7374	396
netCOMPONENTS Inc	7372	507
Netcon Enterprises Inc	3679	775
NETCONN Solutions	7379	109
NetCracker Technology Corp	7372	116
NetCreations Inc	7389	549
Netcube Systems Inc	7372	895
NetDIVE Inc	7372	4319
Neteam Systems LLC	5065	229
Netease Inc	4813	376

Company Name	SIC	Rank
NETEC International Inc	7372	1106
Neteffect Technologies LLC	7379	1365
Neteffects Inc	7371	522
NetEffects Inc	7371	1735
Netegories	4813	698
Netellink Inc	3679	854
NeteSolutions Corp	8742	562
Netezza Corp	5045	78
Netfast Communications Inc	7373	321
Netflix Inc	7841	3
Netforensics Inc	7371	529
NetFormx Ltd	7372	3101
Netgain Information Systems Co	7373	686
Netgear Inc	3661	5
NetHere Inc	7372	5140
Netherland Rubber Company Inc	5085	154
Netherland Typewriter Inc	4813	434
Nethosting Corp	7379	508
NETiMAGE Inc	7373	899
Netinfo Inc	7371	1881
Netinlink	3575	57
netINS Inc	4813	227
Netiq Corp	7372	633
Netis Technology Inc	7373	572
NetJumper Software LLC	7372	4722
Netkey Inc	7372	2531
Netkomp	5045	887
Netline Corp	7371	347
Netlink (Madison Heights Michigan)	8748	137
Netlogic Inc	7372	4531
NetLogic Microsystems Inc	3669	16
Netmagic Systems Inc	7371	620
NetMap Analytics	5045	315
Netmar Inc	7379	1482
NetMasters Inc	8243	11
NetMedia Inc	7372	377
Netmethods LLC	7379	1409
NetMotion Inc	5084	227
NetMotion Wireless Inc	7372	953
Netnames USA Inc	4813	292
Netniques Corp	7374	271
NetObjective LLC	7373	728
NetOps Information Solutions	8748	66
NetPlanner Systems Inc	1731	98
NetPro Computing Inc	7372	1334
NetQuest Corp	3661	190
Netrate Systems Inc	7373	872
NetReach Inc	7371	167
Netreflector Inc	7379	233
NetRep	7372	5141
NetResults Corp	7372	3730
Netrics Inc	7372	3621
Netriver Inc	4813	649
Netro City Design and Information Systems Inc	4813	477
Netscada Inc	5734	194
Netscaler Inc	7379	464
Netscope Inc	7313	40
NetScout Systems Inc	7373	45
Netserve365 LLC	7373	685
Netservices Inc	7378	108
NETsilicon Inc	3577	153
Netsmart New York Inc	7371	129
Netsmart Public Health Inc	7372	3193
Netsmart Technologies Inc	7374	62
Netsol Technologies Inc	7372	863
Netsolace Inc	5734	33
Netsolutions Group Inc	7374	295
Netsource Inc	3496	110
Netsource One Inc	7371	1489
NetSpan Corp	3577	644
NetSpend Holdings Inc	7374	33
Netsphere Inc	7373	452
Netstal Machinery Inc	3544	569
NetSteps Inc	7372	2327
Netstream Communications LLC	4813	593
NetSuccess Inc	7319	110
NetSuite Inc	7372	213
NetTech Inc	7372	5055
NetTechs Inc	7379	1683
NetTempo Inc	7379	1502
Netting and Pace CPA	8721	472
Netuno USA Inc	2092	26
NeTV Networks LLC	7336	246
Netversant - Northern California Inc	1731	353
NetVersant Solutions - Chesapeake	5065	139
NetVersant Solutions Inc	7371	5
Netvia Group LLC	3672	252
NETView Communications Inc	7379	1219
Netvigilance Inc	7371	1775
NetVision Inc	7372	1787
netViz Corp	7372	2398
Netwar Defense Corp	7373	941
Netwest Inc	7371	1698
NetWolves Corp	7373	295
Netwolves Resicom Corp	4813	138
NetWolves Technologies Corp	7373	258
Netwood Design Centre	7336	177
Network 1 Financial Group	3089	1641
Network 1 Financial Securities Inc	6211	188
Network 2000 LLC	7373	541
Network Access Corp	5065	525
Network Access Corp (Pittsburgh Pennsylvania)	5045	959

Company Name	SIC	Rank
Network Access Products Inc	7373	652
Network America	4813	471
Network Analysis Inc	3826	143
Network Automation Inc	7372	1998
Network Cabling Infrastructures Inc	1731	395
Network Cabling Systems Inc	1731	467
Network Central	7373	1229
Network Communications Group Inc	7373	1191
Network Communications Installation Inc	1731	2317
Network Connections USA Inc	1731	1922
Network Consulting Solutions Inc	7379	1183
Network Controls International Inc	7372	2268
Network Cybernetics Corp	7371	1924
Network Data Systems Inc	7373	428
Network Designs Inc	7373	372
Network Dynamics Inc	7373	213
Network Electric Inc	1731	696
Network Electronic Marketing Inc	5065	897
Network Engineering Inc (Indianapolis Indiana)	7373	453
Network Engines Inc	7372	187
Network Equipment Technologies Inc	3577	142
Network Global Logistics	8741	53
Network Hardware Resale LLC	5045	33
Network Installation Services Inc	7373	706
Network Instruments LLC	7372	424
Network Integration Company Partners Inc	7373	251
Network Interpreting Service Inc	7389	1870
Network Management Corp	4899	117
Network Management Inc	7373	1092
Network Management Resources Inc	7378	42
Network Media Partners Inc	7313	30
Network Multifamily Corp	7382	6
Network News Service LLC	7383	14
Network Operator Services Inc	4813	179
Network Outfitters Inc	5045	250
Network Outsource Inc	7373	623
Network Pcb Inc	3672	322
Network Presence LLC	7373	877
Network Recovery Services Inc	7322	41
Network Resource Technologies Corp	7373	1093
Network Services Group Inc	1623	809
Network Shipping Ltd	4731	48
Network Solutions Inc	7379	42
Network Solutions International Inc	7379	1684
Network South Inc	4813	548
Network Spectrum Inc	5045	983
Network Suppliers	5045	510
Network Support Group	7373	900
Network Synergy Corp	7373	561
Network Tallahassee Inc	4813	679
Network Telephone Services Inc	4822	3
Network-1 Security Solutions Inc	7372	930
Networkd Corp	7373	511
Networkers Inc	7371	1699
NetworkFloss	7373	717
Networkguys Inc	7373	935
Networking Dynamics Corp	7372	4320
Networking Technologies and Support Inc	7378	17
Networks Electronic Corp	3562	12
Networks in Motion Inc	7372	1796
Networks Inmocean Inc	7373	1039
Networks International Corp	3679	445
Networld Solutions Inc	7379	1184
Netwurx	4813	263
Netxperts Inc	7373	752
Netzsch Inc	3569	74
NETZSCH Instruments Inc	3825	129
Neu Dynamics Corp	3544	792
Neuberger and Berman Focus Fund	6722	129
Neuberger and Berman Genesis Fund Inc	6722	191
Neuberger and Berman Government Money Fund	6722	205
Neuberger and Berman Municipal Securities Trust	6722	253
Neuberger and Berman Partners Fund Inc	6722	116
Neuberger Berman Cash Reserves	6722	137
Neuberger Berman Inc	6282	67
Neuberger Berman Short Duration Bond Fund	6722	238
Neubus Inc	7375	182
NeuCo Inc	7372	1354
Neudecker Manufacturing Of Indiana Inc	3544	877
Neudesic LLC	7379	206
Neuenhauser Inc	5084	261
Neuens Fredonia Lumber Company Inc	5031	379
Neuenschwander Asset Management LLC	6282	311
Neuhaus Investment Company Inc	7335	9
Neumade Products Corp	3861	62
Neuman Bakery Specialties Inc	2051	161
Neumann Enterprises Inc	1521	115
Neumann/Smith and Associates	8712	127
NeuMedia Inc (Los Angeles California)	6794	97
Neumeier Engineering Inc	3599	1284
NeuralWare Inc	7372	3127
Neuralynx Inc	5049	132
Neurion Pharmaceuticals Inc	8731	226

Company Name	SIC	Rank
Neuro Kinetics Inc	3841	377
Neuro Logic Systems Inc	3669	126
Neurobiologics Inc	2834	357
Neurocrine Biosciences Inc	2836	26
NeuroDimension Inc	7372	3324
NeurogesX Inc	2834	434
Neurologix Inc	2834	467
NeuroMetrix Inc	3841	169
Neuron Electronics Inc	3577	446
NeuroPace Inc	3999	214
Neuroscape Communications Resources	7379	1685
Neu's Building Center Inc	5072	93
NeuStar Inc	7389	80
Neusys Inc	7372	3930
Neutral Posture Ergonomics Inc	2522	36
Neutral Posture Inc	2522	45
Neutral Tandem Inc	4813	62
Neutron Interactive	7379	486
Neutron Products Inc	2899	158
Neutronics Enterprises Inc	3679	576
Nevada Barricade and Sign Company Inc	1611	208
Nevada Beverage Co	5181	33
Nevada Business Management Inc	7389	2114
Nevada Byproducts Inc	2077	14
Nevada County Publishing Co	2711	167
Nevada Gold and Casinos Inc	7999	75
Nevada Land and Resource Company LLC	6519	19
Nevada Nile Ranch Inc	0291	2
Nevada Power Co	4911	110
Nevada Publishing Inc	2731	89
Nevada Railroad Materials Inc	5088	52
Nevada State Bank	6022	336
Nevalon Technologies LLC	7373	1007
Nevco Inc	3993	86
Neverfail Inc	7372	1029
Neversoft Entertainment Inc	7372	134
Nevion USA	3663	289
Nevis Group LLC	3695	180
Nevron Plastics Inc	3679	750
Nevrona Designs	7372	3731
New 9 Inc	3569	147
New Age Digital	7378	73
New Age Electronics	5734	167
New Age Electronics Inc	5045	118
New Age Industrial Corporation Inc	3556	40
New Age Software Services Corp	7363	314
New Albion Records Inc	6794	162
New Aqua LLC	3589	72
New Aspects of Software Inc	7371	1344
New Avenues Lease Ownership LLC	7359	94
New Bakery Company Of Ohio Inc	2051	56
New Balance Athletic Shoe Inc	3149	7
New Bedford Panoramex Corp	3669	191
New Belgium Brewing Company Inc	2082	25
New Berlin Plastics Inc	3089	543
New Best Packers Inc	2013	167
New Boston Rtm Inc	2821	178
New BoundaryTechnologies Inc	7372	1788
New Bremen Machine and Tool Co	3469	312
New Brunswick Industries Inc	3672	261
New Buck Corp	3433	45
New Buffalo Shirt Factory Inc	2395	11
New Can Company Inc	3469	171
New Canaan Alarm Company Inc	1731	1458
New Canaan Community Ymca Inc	8322	110
New Car Test Drive Inc	2721	443
New Carbon Company Inc	5149	175
New Castle Company Inc	3535	228
New Center Stamping Inc	3465	52
New Century Bancorp Inc	6022	251
New Century Education Corp	7372	533
New Century Enterprises Inc	2759	305
New Century Marketing Concepts	7389	2398
New Century Metals Southeast Inc	3356	7
New Chapter Inc	2834	195
New City Communications	2752	1412
New City Packing Company Inc	5147	101
New Community Corp	6552	23
New Concept Energy Inc	1311	232
New Consolidated International Corp	5084	895
New Cooperative Inc	5153	90
New Country Motor Car Group Inc	5511	62
New Country Pontiac GMC Buick and Oldsmobile	5511	812
New Country Volkswagon Of Greenwich	5511	283
NEW Curative Rehabilitation Inc	8322	71
New Data Systems Inc	7372	4004
New Dimensions Precision Machining Inc	3599	193
New Dimensions Research Corp	3993	68
New Directions Publishing Corp	2731	368
New Edge Network Inc	7375	34
New Energy Corp	2869	57
New England Alloys	3313	8
New England Art Publishers Inc	2771	12
New England Bancshares Inc	6712	398
New England Brace Company Inc	3842	238
New England Brewing Co	2082	100
New England Building Materials LLC	5211	144
New England Business Media LLC	2711	732

Company Name	SIC	Rank
New England Business Service Inc	2761	5
New England Cable News	4841	73
New England Center For Children Inc	8361	11
New England Communications Corp	1731	2091
New England Communications Inc	5999	123
New England Computer Remarketing Inc	5045	941
New England Computer Resources Inc	5045	783
New England Confectionery Co	2064	19
New England Controls Inc	5085	98
New England Country Pies Inc	2051	259
New England Development	6512	61
New England Die Cutting Inc	3423	63
New England Electric Motor Service Corp	5063	517
New England Electronics and Technology Corp	5734	280
New England Extrusion Inc	3081	73
New England Financial	6311	64
New England Finishing Inc	2675	19
New England Foam Products LLC	3069	179
New England Health And Maintenance Corp	7349	160
New England Homes Inc	2452	41
New England Industrial Truck Inc	5084	330
New England Keyboard Inc	3575	22
New England Machinery Inc	3565	103
New England Manufacturing Group Inc	3469	136
New England Mold Sterling Inc	3544	369
New England Motor Freight	4213	152
New England Newspaper Supply Company Inc	5085	60
New England Newspapers Inc	2711	274
New England Organics Inc	4953	120
New England Paper Tube Company Inc	2655	4
New England Pension Consultants Inc	6282	152
New England Pest Control Company Inc	7342	22
New England Photoconductor Corp	3812	199
New England Plastics Corp	3089	192
New England Pottery Co	5193	11
New England Realty Associates LP	6513	30
New England Satellite Systems Inc	4899	147
New England Security Inc	7382	180
New England Sheet Metal Works	1711	133
New England Sterling Inc	3499	69
New England Tap Corp	3545	420
New England Tea and Coffee Inc	2095	18
New England Television Corp	4833	17
New England Transcription Inc	7338	54
New England Typographic Service Inc	2791	25
New England Union Company Inc	3498	69
New England Wire Technologies Corp	3357	26
New England Woodcraft Inc	2512	40
New England Wooden Ware Corp	3993	16
New Enterprise Associates	6799	180
New Enterprise Stone and Lime Company Inc	1611	52
New Era Builders Inc	1542	356
New Era Canning Co	2033	45
New Era Cap Company Inc	2353	2
New Era Converting Machinery Inc	3599	791
New ERA Life Insurance Co	6311	135
New Era of Networks Inc	7372	257
New Era Ohio LLC	3561	64
New Era Optical Co	3851	19
New Era Portfolio	2741	218
New Era Production	3651	264
New Era Publications	2731	362
New Era Publishing Inc	2741	315
New Era Technologies Co	3691	43
New Fashion Pork Inc	0213	7
New Focus Inc	3827	29
New French Bakery	2051	273
New Frontier Bank	6022	637
New Frontier Energy Inc	1311	262
New Frontier Media Inc	7822	14
New Frontiers Software Inc	7373	888
New Gencoat Inc	3559	264
New Generation Biofuels Holdings Inc	2869	122
New Generation Technologies Inc	7372	2640
New Germany Fund Inc	6726	51
New Glarus Brewing Co	2082	93
New Global Telecom Inc	4899	77
New Hampshire Bindery Inc	2789	115
New Hampshire Electric Cooperative Inc	4911	157
New Hampshire Insurance Co	6331	174
New Hampshire Odd Fellows Home	8361	84
New Hampshire Optical Company Inc	5048	10
New Hampshire Plastics Inc	2821	82
New Hampshire Thrift Bancshares Inc	6712	322
New Hankey Company Inc	5091	91
New Hartford Medical Supply	7352	26
New Haven Terminal Inc	4491	9
New Henley Holdings Inc	6719	139
New Hippodrome Hardware Inc	5063	827
New Holland Construction	5082	56
New Holland North America Inc	3523	3
New Hong Kong Noodle Company Inc	2098	14
New Hope Crushed Stone And Lime Co	1422	49
New Hope Natural Media	2721	111

Company Name	SIC	Rank	Company Name	SIC	Rank	Company Name	SIC	Rank
New Hope Telephone Coop	4813	310	New Orleans Paddlewheels Inc	7999	94	New York Thermal Systems LLC	3823	191
New Hope Village Inc	8361	55	New Orleans Tourism Marketing Corp	7999	111	New York Times Co	2711	12
New Horizon Computer Learning Center (Miami Florida)	8244	6	New Partners Inc	8082	25	New York Times Syndication Sales Corp	7383	9
New Horizon Enterprises Inc	8351	34	New Penn Motor Express Inc	4213	68	New York Twist Drill Inc	3541	23
New Horizon Graphics Inc	2752	702	New Process Fibre Co	3089	1084	New Yorker Boiler Company Inc	3433	64
New Horizon Kids Quest Inc	8351	10	New Process Steel LP	5051	25	New York-New York Hotel and Casino LLC	7011	86
New Horizon Publishers	2711	909	New Products International Inc	5199	101	New York's Little Elves Inc	7349	245
New Horizons AG Services	5153	102	New Pros Communications Inc	7331	98	NewAge Industries Inc	3089	485
New Horizons Baking Company Inc	2051	67	New Radio Star Inc	7375	252	NewAgeSys Inc	7376	34
New Horizons Communications Inc	5065	516	New Republic Inc	2721	229	Newall Electronics Inc	5065	153
New Horizons Computer Learning Centers Inc	8244	3	New Resource Bank	6022	547	NewAlliance Bank	6021	21
New Horizons Corp	8331	156	New Richmond Industries Inc	3429	125	Newark Endoscopy ASC LLC	8011	131
New Horizons Diagnostics Corp	3841	389	New River Electrical Corp	1623	18	Newark Fibers Inc	2299	11
New Horizons Of Northwest Florida	8361	171	New Riverside Ochre Company Inc	1479	7	Newark Group Inc	2631	8
New Horizons Rehabilitation Inc	8331	162	New Season Foods Inc	2034	31	Newark InOne	5065	881
New Horizons Supply Coop	5191	11	New Seasons Market	5411	231	Newark Morning Ledger Co	2711	124
New Horizons Telecom Inc	4813	106	New Skies Networks Inc	4899	210	Newark Paperboard Products	2655	2
New Horizons Worldwide Inc	8299	32	New South Agency Inc	6399	26	Newark Trade Typographers	2791	59
New Idea Inc	3569	280	New South Bancshares Inc	6035	59	Newart Miami	7819	56
New Image Auto Glass LLC	5013	225	New South Companies Inc	2421	1	Neways Inc	2833	22
New Image Building Services Inc	7349	90	New South Construction Co	1542	28	Newbern Fabricating Inc	1542	441
New Image Computers	5734	484	New South Construction Company Inc	1541	64	Newberry Electric Cooperative Inc	4911	401
New Image Press Inc	2752	1115	New South Network Services	7379	1220	Newberry Group Inc	7379	416
New Image Technology Corp	7379	316	New Star Lasers Inc	3845	85	Newbold Corp	3579	21
NEW Industries Inc	3599	126	New Stockton Poultry Inc	5144	20	NewBridge Bancorp	6712	208
New Innovations Inc	3577	660	New Stuff Company Inc	2721	134	NewBridge Bank	6022	84
New Instruction LLC	7379	1435	New Target Inc	7371	945	Newbridge Communications Inc	5961	129
New Jernberg Sales Inc	5051	56	New Tech Industries Inc	3544	441	Newbrook Machine Corp	3728	125
New Jersey Community Publishing Inc	7319	169	New Tech Machinery Corp	3547	2	Newbury Comics Inc	5735	5
New Jersey Headwear Corp	2353	17	New Tech Systems Inc	3533	76	Newbury Consulting Group Inc	7379	466
New Jersey Institute Of Technology	8221	32	New Tech Texas Inc	3571	189	Newby Rubber Inc	3069	217
New Jersey Logos LLC	3993	183	New Technologies and Associates Inc	7379	522	Newcastle Construction Inc	1771	22
New Jersey Manufacturers Insurance Co	6331	86	New Thermo-Serv Ltd	3089	363	Newcastle Industries Inc	3674	497
New Jersey Meter Co	3492	37	New Times Media Group	2711	703	Newcastle Investment Corp	6798	71
New Jersey Micro Electronic Testing Inc	8734	103	New Trend	5063	1073	Newchem Inc	2819	130
New Jersey Mirror And Bath Accessories Inc	1799	110	New Ulm Precision Tool Inc	3544	656	Newco Fibre Co	2823	5
New Jersey Natural Gas Co	1382	27	New Ulm Telecom Inc	4813	156	Newco Inc	2679	54
New Jersey Property Liability Insurance Guaranty Association	6411	103	New Unison Corp	3541	137	Newco Metals Inc	5093	175
New Jersey Public Broadcasting Authority	4833	133	New United Inc	1731	673	Newcogen Group Inc	8742	588
New Jersey Resources Corp	4924	11	New Vad LLC	3861	36	Newcomb and Boyd	8711	145
New Jersey Tool And Die Co	3544	501	New Valley LLC	6512	52	Newcomb Oil Co	5411	94
New Jersey Transit Corp	4131	2	New Vavin Inc	0172	12	Newcomb Print Communications Inc	8742	594
New Jersey-American Water Co	4941	10	New View Gifts and Accessories Ltd	5099	33	Newcor Inc	3714	116
New Leaf Brands Inc	2086	121	New Vision Coop	5153	32	Newcor Rubber and Plastic Group	3714	277
New Leaf Press Inc	2731	223	New Vista Corp	3559	563	Newcut Inc	3479	84
New Lexington Clinic PSC	8011	47	New Washington State Bank	6022	281	Newdata Solutions Inc	7373	1050
New Life Discovery Schools Inc	8351	39	New Water Street Corp	6531	162	NewDominion Bank	6022	426
New Life Electronics Inc	3651	255	New Wave Converting Inc	2673	43	Newedge USA LLC	6289	23
New Light Industries Ltd	7372	3837	New Wave Electronic Services Inc	3672	441	Newegg Inc	3577	10
New Line Cinema Corp	7812	13	New Wave Systems Inc	5063	483	Newell Machinery Company Inc	1796	12
New Line Home Video Inc	7922	6	New Way Electric Inc	1731	990	Newell Novelty Company Inc	7389	708
New Line USA Inc	3699	289	New West Physicians	8011	92	Newell Paper Co	5111	25
New Logic Research Inc	3559	128	New World Environmental Inc	7389	1487	Newell Recycling Of San Antonio LP	3341	28
New London Press Inc	2752	869	New World Graphics Inc	7372	3002	Newell Rubbermaid Inc	2591	1
New Market Plastics Inc	3089	1694	New World Library	2731	129	NewEra Software Inc	7371	454
New Market Poultry Products Inc	0751	8	New World Machining Inc	3599	1741	Newfield Exploration Co	1311	23
New Maryland Clothing Manufacturing Inc	2311	28	New World Manufacturing Co	3081	167	Newgate LLC	6726	35
New Mather Metals Inc	3714	377	New World Network USA Inc	4899	75	Newgen Advanced Orthotics Laboratory	3842	270
New Media Communications	7379	509	New World Pasta Co	2098	1	NewGeneration Software Inc	7372	2577
New Media Printing	2752	1469	New World Van Lines Inc	4213	70	Newgistics Inc	8999	37
New Media Strategies Inc	8743	180	New WPI LLC	5021	19	NewGround	8712	47
New Metal Crafts Inc	3646	64	New Year Tech Inc	7373	688	Newhall Land and Farming Co	6552	43
New Mexican Inc	2711	287	New York and Company Inc	5621	10	Newhaven Distribution Services	4213	1546
New Mexico Banquest Corp	6712	417	New York Bagel Baking Co	5461	38	Newhouse Dental Supply	5047	259
New Mexico Business Weekly Inc	2711	784	New York Bakeries Inc	5149	185	Newhouse Manufacturing Company Inc	3523	235
New Mexico Chili Products Inc	2034	35	New York Brite Inc	7363	351	Newins Bay Shore Ford Inc	5511	697
New Mexico Communications Inc	7389	2418	New York Brunch Basket	7299	49	Newkirk Electric Associates Inc	1731	76
New Mexico Food Distributors Inc	2032	20	New York Bus Sales LLC	5012	122	Newkirk Products Inc	2731	107
New Mexico Metal Systems LLC	3444	216	New York Business Development Corp	6159	67	Newland Communities	6282	42
New Mexico Mexican Foods	2099	250	New York Camera and Video Inc	5731	87	Newleads Inc	5734	190
New Mexico Technet Inc	7375	218	New York Carolina Express	4213	190	NewlineNoosh Inc	7389	261
New Mexico Travertine Inc	3281	37	New York City Design Co	7389	1419	Newman and Company Inc	2631	19
New Mexico Underground Contractors Inc	1623	288	New York Commercial Bank	6022	787	Newman Associates Inc	5074	139
New Mexico Utilities Inc	4971	2	New York Community Bancorp Inc	6036	1	Newman Lumber Co	5031	88
New Mexico Water Service Co	4941	60	New York Components Inc	5065	562	Newman Machine Company Inc	3553	5
New Mexico-American Water Co	4941	32	New York Computer Help LLC	7378	116	Newman Printing Company Inc	2752	1026
New Millenium Directories Inc	2741	439	New York Daily Challenge Inc	2711	867	Newman Sanitary Gasket Company Inc	3053	73
New Millennium Building Systems	3441	73	New York Entertainment Corp	2721	163	Newman Signs Inc	7312	24
New Millennium Communications Inc	8748	405	New York Health and Racquet Club Inc	7991	4	Newman Technology Inc	3714	123
New Moon Noodle Inc	5149	209	New York Health Care Inc	8082	42	Newman-Burrows Co	2752	378
New Mount Pleasant Bakery	2051	214	New York Interactive Inc	7374	299	Newman's Own Inc	2033	87
New NGC Inc	3275	3	New York Internet Company Inc	4813	513	Newmar Corp	3716	5
New Office Temps Ltd	7363	380	New York Legal Publishing Corp	2741	455	Newmark Knight Frank	8748	3
New Options Inc	3842	228	New York Life Insurance Co	6311	47	Newmark Rug Co	2273	14
New Orleans Bourbon French Perfume Co	5999	314	New York Life Investment Management LLC	6282	10	NewMarket Corp	2869	7
New Orleans Cold Storage and Warehouse Company Ltd	4222	20	New York Mortgage Trust Inc	6798	166	Newmarket International Inc	7372	788
New Orleans East Chiropractic Clinics Inc	8041	2	New York National Bank	6021	350	NewMarket Technology Inc	4813	90
New Orleans Firemen's Federal Credit Union	6061	50	New York Post	2711	119	Newmast Marketing and Communications Inc	7336	205
New Orleans Flooring Supply Inc	5023	40	New York - Presbyterian Hospital	8062	37	Newmerix Inc	7372	315
New Orleans Hearst-Argyle Television Inc	4833	156	New York Press Inc	2711	528	Newmik International Corp	5065	997
			New York Public Interest Research Group Fund Inc	8732	64	Newmont Gold Co	1041	3
			New York Skyline Inc	7999	59	Newmont Mining Corp	1041	1
			New York Staffing Services Inc	7361	207	NewNet Inc	4813	545
			New York State Energy Research And Development Authority	8731	124	Newnex Technology Corp	3577	569
			New York State Industries For The Disabled Inc	8322	7	Newocean Micro LLC	5734	419
			New York State Theatre For Opera and Ballet/Subscription	7389	2182	Newood Display Fixture Manufacturing Co	2541	47
			New York Susquehanna and Western Railway Corp	4011	43	NewPage Corp	2621	5
			New York Technology Partners Inc	7379	530	NewPage Holding Corp	2621	4

Company Name	SIC	Rank	Company Name	SIC	Rank	Company Name	SIC	Rank
Newpark Environmental Management Company LLC	4953	106	Nexgen Technologies LLC	3674	328	NGK-Locke Polymer Insulators Inc	3644	7
Newpark Environmental Services LLC	4953	48	NexHorizon Communications Inc	7812	296	NGP Capital Resources Co	6799	133
Newpark Resources Inc	3533	12	Nexia Holdings Inc	6411	282	nGroup Inc	7361	190
Newpoint Technologies Inc	7372	4251	Nexiant	5045	127	Ngs Printing Inc	2759	238
Newpoint Thermal	3433	42	Nexic Inc	7371	1810	NGTS LLC	7389	62
Newport Adhesives And Composites Inc	5169	93	Nexidia Inc	7372	80	Ngtv	4841	111
Newport Bancorp Inc	6712	484	Nexity Bank	6022	278	NH Bragg and Sons	5085	66
Newport Corp	3821	2	Nexlink Communications LLC	5065	854	NH Kelman Inc	5093	180
Newport Creamery LLC	2024	30	Nexon Technology Distribution LLC	5045	806	NH Research Inc	3825	110
Newport Creative Communications Inc	7331	53	Nexpak Corp	3089	1330	NHC Inc	5172	124
Newport Cutter Grinding Company Inc	3549	105	NeXplore Corp	7372	4957	NHCOP LP	8051	31
Newport Federal Bank	6035	174	Nexsan Technologies Inc	3572	54	NHL Enterprises Inc	7941	28
Newport FSB	6035	104	Nexstar Broadcasting Group Inc	4833	62	Nhrc LLC	3663	367
Newport Graphics Inc	2752	1196	Nexsys Electronics Corp	3577	506	NHS Inc	3949	97
Newport Group	6411	34	Next Communications Inc	7311	940	NHT Global Inc	7389	766
Newport Laminates Inc	3089	1402	Next Day Blinds Corp	5023	63	NI Acquisition Corp	6331	271
Newport Medical Instruments Inc	3841	122	Next Day Gormet and Superior Cataloge Outlet	5078	1	Ni Autowindow Systems Inc	5013	269
Newport News Industrial	3561	80	Next Electronic Systems Inc	5065	629	NIA Group LLC	6311	99
Newport Plastics Corp	3089	1821	Next Events Meeting Productions Inc	5049	182	Niagara Blower Co	3585	118
Newport Publishing Company Inc	2711	754	Next Generation Energy Corp	7331	289	Niagara Bottling LLC	2086	57
Newport Stationers Inc	5943	12	Next Generation Enrollment Inc	6371	16	Niagara Falls City School District	8211	68
NewportWave Inc	7372	4321	Next Inc (Chattanooga Tennessee)	7299	26	Niagara Falls Water Board	7389	495
Newport-West Data Services Inc	7372	3003	Next Level Data and Telephone Systems Inc	1731	1216	Niagara Fiberglass Inc	3089	1588
Newprint Offset Inc	2752	1677	Next Level Solutions LLC	8243	5	Niagara Manufacturing Co	3599	2337
News America Inc	7812	8	Next Pharmaceuticals	5122	131	Niagara Mohawk Power Corp	4931	10
News America Marketing Interactive Inc	7319	4	Next Specialty Resins Inc	3087	22	Niagara Precision Inc	3599	1629
News and Observer Publishing Co	2711	101	Next Star Broadcasting Group LLC	4833	153	Niagara Transformer Corp	3612	25
News Banner Publications Inc	2711	653	Next Step Computer Training LLC	7379	1642	Niagara Tying Service Inc	2013	178
News Chronicle Company Inc	2711	750	Next Step Technologies Inc	7372	3931	Niagara Water	5149	8
News Communications Inc	2711	320	Next Technology Consulting Inc	7379	1361	Niakwa Inc	7372	2856
News Corp	2711	1	Next View Software Inc	7373	737	Nibbles and Bits Computer Technologies Corp	7379	1043
News Daily Paper	2711	636	NextAce Corp	7372	3077	NIBCO Inc	3498	6
News Data Corp	2741	449	Nextag Inc	2741	180	NIC Inc	8742	75
News Eagle	2711	755	Nextance Inc	5045	532	Nica Corp	3089	1848
News Gazette Printing Co	2759	570	Nextar Broadcasting	4833	227	Nicassio Enterprises Inc	1623	806
News India Times	2711	283	Nextconstruct Inc	7371	1602	Nicca USA Inc	2843	5
News Media Corp	2711	247	Nextcorp Ltd	7374	182	Nice N Easy Grocery Shoppes Inc	5411	154
News Printing Co	2711	241	NextDocs Corp	7379	482	Nice People Home Care and Staffing	7363	325
News Radio Corp	4832	281	NexTec Group Inc	7372	1229	Nice-Pak Products Inc	2621	31
News Reporter Company Inc	2711	514	Nex-Tech Aerospace Inc	3599	85	Niche Electronics Technologies Inc	3672	305
News Tribune Co	0272	2	Nex-Tech Processing Inc	3471	41	Niche Retail	5999	49
News USA Inc	8743	210	Nextech Solutions Inc	7389	2416	Nichelson Rentals	7359	231
News World Communications Inc	2711	185	Nextech Solutions LLC	7363	283	Nichimen Graphics Inc	7372	2243
Newsbank Inc	7375	55	NexTech Systems Corp	7372	3245	Nichirei Foods Inc	2092	88
Newscale Inc	7372	611	Nextek Inc	3812	79	Nicholas Bredice	2759	591
Newschannel 11s New Media Sales	4833	130	Nextengine Inc	7373	559	Nicholas Coffee and Tea Co	2095	59
Newsday Inc	2711	10	NextEra Energy Inc	4911	4	Nicholas Data Services Inc	7372	656
News-Gazette Inc	2711	268	Nextera Enterprises Inc	2844	134	Nicholas Financial Inc	6153	28
Newsgraphics Of Delmar Inc	2721	351	Nextest Systems Corp	3674	132	Nicholas Financial Inc (Clearwater Florida)	6153	8
News-Journal Corp	2711	157	NextG Networks Inc	4812	61	Nicholas Limited Edition Inc	6722	273
Newsletters Ink Corp	2721	368	NextGen Healthcare Information Systems Inc	7372	224	Nicholas Turkey Breeding Farms	0253	1
NewsMax Media Inc	7375	67	NexTier Bank	6021	120	Nicholas-Applegate Capital Management	6282	26
NewSoft America Inc	7372	3325	NextIO Inc	3674	197	Nichols Aluminum	3353	6
Newsom Oil Company Inc	5172	117	Nextlabs Inc	7371	863	Nichols and Company Inc	7371	490
Newspaper Agency Corp	2759	46	Nextlinx Corp	7371	508	Nichols Electric Supply Inc	5063	550
Newspaper Electronics Corp	7373	1064	NextNine Inc	7378	31	Nichols Foodservice Inc	5141	177
Newspapers First Inc	7311	175	NextPage Inc	7372	1086	Nichols Ford Inc	5511	277
Newspapers Of New England Inc	2711	14	Nextpharma Technologies USA Inc	2834	290	Nichols Graphics Inc	7336	212
News-Press and Gazette Company Inc	2711	192	Nextran Industries Inc	3578	23	Nichols Oxygen Service Inc	5087	194
NewStar Financial Inc	6719	48	NextRidge Inc	7363	82	Nichols Tillage Tools Inc	3523	77
Newstar Fresh Food LLC	4783	3	Nextron Medical Technologies	5047	130	Nicholson Construction Co	1629	56
News-Telegraph Publishing Corp	2711	802	Nextround Inc	5734	45	Nicholson Inc	5251	35
Newsweb Corp	2752	622	Nextus Inc	3577	385	Nicholson Kovac Inc	7311	133
Newsweek Inc	2721	41	Nextwarehouse Inc	5045	874	Nicholson Manufacturing Company Inc	3553	8
Newt Red Cellars Inc	2084	112	NextWave Pharmaceuticals Inc	8731	143	Nick Crivelli Ford LLC	5511	1025
Newtech Imaging Inc	2759	533	Nextwave Wireless Inc	4812	41	Nick Jorae Excavating Inc	1623	442
Newtech Infosystems Inc	7373	278	NextWeb Inc	4899	179	Nick Sciabica and Sons A Corp	2079	12
New-Tech Packaging Inc	2653	71	Nexum	5734	22	Nick Strimbu Inc	4213	1473
Newtek Business Services Inc	7389	219	Nexus Consortium Inc	5045	499	Nickel Ads Newspaper Inc	2741	177
Newtek Inc	7372	2775	Nexus Custom Electronics Inc	3679	220	Nickel Technologies Inc	5045	419
NewTek Partners	3669	47	Nexus Group	4899	113	Nickell Moulding Company Inc	2431	68
Newtex Industries Inc	2241	18	Nexus Office Systems Inc	5065	320	Nickels and Dimes Inc	7996	22
Newton Associates Inc	7311	784	Nexus Plastics Inc	3081	40	Nickerson Company Inc	5084	576
Newton C R Company Ltd	3842	184	Nexus Recovery Center Inc	8361	133	Nickerson Lumber Co	5211	73
Newton Crouch Inc	3523	191	Nexvisionix Inc	7372	729	Nickerson Machinery Company Inc	3559	376
Newton Manufacturing Co	3511	42	Nexx Systems Inc	3674	198	Nickles Bakery Inc	2051	92
Newton Vineyard LLC	2084	27	Nexxio Group Ltd	8742	620	Nick's Transport Inc	4213	1852
Newton-Wellesley Health Care System Inc	8741	70	Nexxtworks Inc	5046	42	Nickson's Machine Shop Inc	3599	1473
Newtown Manufacturing And Building Supply Corp	3089	653	Nexxus Lighting Inc	3357	67	NICO Machine Inc	3599	1257
Newtron Group Inc	1731	541	Nexxus Marketing Group LLC	7374	55	Nico Products Inc	3471	44
New-Tronics Ltd	3663	178	Neyenesch Printers Inc	2752	377	Nicole and Aron Pharmaceutical Inc	5122	104
NewView Technologies Inc	7372	2105	NF Smith and Associates LP	5065	30	Nicolet Plastics Inc	3089	956
NewVision Systems Corp	7371	618	Nfc Castings Inc	3321	4	Nicoletti Hornig and Sweeney	7389	1401
Newwave Communications	4841	53	nFinanSe Inc	7375	202	Nicor Gas	1311	20
NewWave Technologies Inc	7379	260	Nfinity Products and Services Inc	3149	29	NICOR Inc	4924	4
NewWest Mezzanine	6799	229	NFJ Investment Group	6282	205	Nicosia Creative Expresso Ltd	7336	227
Nexans Berk-Tek Electronics Cable	3357	11	NFL Films	7819	9	Nicotri Electric Inc	1731	1347
Nexcel Synthetics	2299	6	Nflexion Consulting Service LLC	7379	1371	Nicra Inc	3625	353
Nexcelom Bioscience LLC	3841	270	Nfm/Welding Engineers Inc	3599	134	Nida Corp	3825	50
Nexcore Healthcare Capital Corp	6531	413	NFO Migliara/Kaplan	8732	35	Nidatoch Inc	5049	228
NexCycle Inc	5093	4	nFrame Inc	8741	99	Nidec America Corp	3621	37
Nexen Petroleum USA Inc	1311	84	NFS-Radiation Protection Systems Inc	7372	2827	Nidec-Shimpo America Corp	5085	203
Nexeon International Corp	8742	435	nFusion Group LLC	8748	108	Nidek Inc	5048	18
Nexergy Inc	3679	197	Ngc Inc	5146	38	Nidek Medical Products Inc	3841	239
Nexgen Constructors Inc	1623	633	Ngen LLC	5045	734	Nieco Corp	3589	104
Nexgen Enterprises Inc	5032	43	NGH Enterprises LLC	7374	165	Niedwick Corp	3599	730
NexGen Fueling Inc	3443	102	Ngi Electronics LLC	3679	542	Niedwick Machine Co	3599	245
Nexgen Pharma Inc	2834	170	NGK Ceramics USA Inc	3264	4	Niehaus Home Center	5031	56
NexGen Software Technologies Inc	2721	114	NGK Spark Plugs Inc USA	3694	3	Niello Co	5511	166
			NGK Spark Plugs USA Inc	3694	17	Niels Fugal Sons Co	1623	37
			NGK-Locke Inc (Baltimore Maryland)	3644	1	Nielsen and Bainbridge	2675	1

Company Name	SIC	Rank	Company Name	SIC	Rank	Company Name	SIC	Rank
Nielsen Business Media Inc	2721	20	Nitco Materials Handling Solutions	5084	178	Noblestar Systems Corp	7373	85
Nielsen BuzzMetrics	7372	3113	Nite Ize Inc	3648	31	Nobleworks Inc	2771	26
Nielsen Co	2721	12	Nite-Bright Sign Company Inc	3993	155	Noblis Inc	8733	6
Nielsen Engineering and Research Inc	8731	390	Nitech Inc	5063	754	Noblitt Electric Inc	1731	1348
Nielsen Media Research	8732	4	Nitel Inc	5046	35	Noblitt PC Inc	7378	153
Nielsen//NetRatings	7389	271	Niterider Technical Lighting and Video	3648	41	Nochar Inc	2899	243
Nielsen Sessions	3469	271	Systems Inc			NOCO Energy Corp	5172	59
Nielsons Inc	1611	16	Nitram Energy Inc	3443	173	Nocopi Technologies Inc	8999	217
Nieman Printing	2752	161	Nitro Pdf Inc	7371	908	Nodland Construction Co	1623	254
Niemann Foods Inc	5411	131	NitroMed Inc	2834	292	Noel Burt	3592	25
Niepraschk Enterprises Inc	5039	56	Nitronex Corp	3674	290	Noel Communications Inc	4813	241
Niester Sausage Co	2013	232	NitroSecurity Inc	7372	820	Noel Corp	2086	55
Nieto Computer Services LLC	5734	91	NitroSteel Div	3317	60	Noel Systems Inc	3444	249
Nifco LLC	3089	68	Nitsa's Custom Draperies Inc	5714	6	Noelle Couture	7389	1420
Nifty-Bar Inc	3312	122	Nitta Casings Inc	2013	73	Noel's Inc	5085	374
Night Kitchen Interactive	7379	660	Nittany Bank	6035	151	Noel-Smyser Engineering Corp	3694	37
Night Optics USA Inc	3669	154	Nittany Financial Corp	6712	569	Noetic Software Inc	7372	2930
NightHawk Radiology Holdings Inc	8099	29	Nittany Oil Co	5171	42	Noetix Corp	7372	1294
Nighthawk Total Control Inc	4899	192	Nitterhouse Concrete Products Inc	3272	81	Noevir Inc	2844	131
Nightingale Metals Inc	5051	339	Nitto Denko America Inc	2671	36	NOFFS/Atlantic Relocation Systems	4213	2810
Nightingale Services Inc	7363	383	Nitty Gritty Record Care	3699	297	Noffsinger Manufacturing Company Inc	3523	72
Nightlight Electric Company Inc	1731	2188	Nitv LLC	3829	451	NoFire Technologies Inc	2899	244
Nihilistic Software Inc	7372	1160	Nitze-Stagen and Company Inc	6531	204	Nofziger Door Sales Inc	3442	66
Nihon Kohden America Inc	5047	97	Nivek Industries Inc	3643	80	Nogginlabs Inc	7371	1610
NII Brokerage LLC	6411	276	Nivis LLC	7373	310	No-Go International	5063	197
NII Holdings Inc	4812	5	Niwot Networks Inc	7372	1647	Noguska Industries	7372	2857
Niitakaya USA Inc	5149	150	Nix and Company Inc	7349	232	Nohl Corp	3644	33
NIKA Technologies	8711	471	Nixon Cabinet Company Inc	2434	82	Noise Inc	7311	613
Nike Inc	3149	1	Nixon Peabody LLP	8111	175	Noise Suppression Technologies Inc	3625	333
Nikken and Associates Inc	1731	224	Nixon Power Services Co	5063	1104	Nokia Inc	3577	69
Nikken International Inc	5199	8	Nixon Software Group Inc	7372	3360	Nokia Mobile Phones	8731	73
Nikko America Inc	5092	31	Nixon Software Solutions Inc	7371	1111	Nokia Siemens Networks Us LLC	3663	105
Nikles Design Corp	7319	159	Nixon Tool Company Inc	3599	2497	Nolan Amusement Co	7999	69
Niknejad Inc	2752	797	Nixon Uniform Service Inc	2389	13	Nolan H Brunson Inc	4213	1783
Nikolas Management Group Inc	4899	230	Nixsol Inc	7379	495	Noland Co	5074	4
Nikolic Industries Inc	3599	1880	NJ Industrial Research Center Inc	7378	168	Nolato Contour	3089	340
Nikon Americas Inc	3572	84	NJ Precision Technologies Inc	3599	1115	Nolatron Inc	3679	845
Nikon Inc	5043	4	NJ Protocall Inc	7363	52	Nolen and Associates Inc	7311	806
Nikon Precision Inc	3559	52	Nj Transportation Bd Mst	3531	167	Noll Inc	7361	368
NIKSUN Inc	3577	137	Njb Security Services Inc	7381	67	Nollenberger Capital Partners Inc	6211	75
Nile Inc	3822	53	NJR Corp	5065	98	Nolmar Corp	5169	124
Nile Therapeutics Inc	2834	17	NJS Systems Inc	7349	254	Nolocom Inc	2731	166
NileNet Ltd	4899	175	NJVC LLC	7376	2	Nol-Tec Systems Inc	3535	65
Niles Audio Corp	5065	116	Nk Technologies Inc	7373	998	Nolting Manufacturing Inc	3639	24
Niles Barton and Wilmer	8111	411	Nkc Of America Inc	3535	9	Nomaco Inc	3089	144
Niles Bolton Associates Inc	8712	203	Nkk Switches Of America Inc	5063	378	Nomad Designs and Services LLC	7336	206
Niles Inc	5013	255	NKS Distributors Inc	5182	19	NOMADICS ICX	3577	169
Niles Manufacturing and Finishing Inc	3469	148	Nl and A Collections Inc	5023	98	Nomadix Inc	7379	350
Niles Precision Co	3724	42	NL C Inc	3548	52	Nomura America Corp	5084	13
Nilodor Inc	2842	121	NL Industries Inc	2819	33	Nomura and Company Inc	5153	103
Nilpeter USA Inc	3555	20	NLB Leasing LLC	7359	79	Nomura Capital Management Inc	6282	314
Nilson Farms Inc	2041	64	Nllj Holdings Inc	7376	46	Nomura Pacific Basin Fund Inc	6722	13
Nilson Van and Storage	4213	611	NLS Group	6552	156	Nomura Securities International Inc	6211	134
Nilsson Electrical Laboratory Inc	3612	134	NLX Corp	3699	27	Non Literal Inc	5045	1072
Niltronix Circuits Inc	3672	406	NM Direct	5961	48	Non Metallic Machining Assembly Inc	3599	2305
Nimbus Water Systems	3589	219	NM Knight Company Inc	3823	201	Non Metallic Resources Inc	3084	19
Nimco Corp	3556	107	NMB Inc (Chatsworth California)	3577	35	Nonagon Technology Corp	5045	677
Nim-Cor Inc	3568	49	NMB Technologies Corp	3577	38	Non-Ferrous Extrusion and Scrap Met-	3463	15
Nimlok Co	3993	80	Nmc Group Inc	5085	148	als Inc		
Nimnicht Chevrolet Co	5511	233	Nmc/Wollard Inc	3537	52	Nonin Medical Inc	3841	110
Nims and Associates	8748	133	Nmedia Systems Inc	5734	248	Non-Invasive Monitoring Systems Inc	3845	138
Nimsoft	7371	137	Nmp Inc	3599	768	Non-Linear Systems	3825	295
Nina Enterprises	3469	118	Nms Imaging Inc	7373	543	Non-Metallic Components Inc	3089	823
Nina Footwear Inc	3144	4	NMT Corp	7372	2560	Nonpareil Corp	2034	8
Nina Plastic Bags Inc	2821	66	NMT Innovasive Systems Inc	3841	149	Non-Profit Services Inc	7389	1601
Nina's Mexican Foods Inc	2099	240	NMT Medical Inc	3841	175	Non-Stop Productions LLC	7812	257
Nine Eleven Software Inc	7372	5142	NN Inc	3562	7	Noodles and Company Inc	5812	183
Ninfa's Inc	5812	108	Nnncc Ranch	7389	1058	Noodles By Leonardo Inc	2098	10
Ninja Jump Inc	3949	122	NNT Enterprises Inc	5084	510	Nook Industries Inc	3451	29
Nintendo of America Inc	3944	10	No Brainer Inc	5714	2	Noonday Pictures Inc	7812	185
Nintex USA LLC	5734	220	No Bull Sim Racing	3644	52	Nooter Corp	3443	6
NIP Group Inc	6411	81	No Fear Inc	2329	10	Nor Cal Marine Service LLC	7699	250
Nippon America Inc	5065	760	No Red Tape Mortgage	6159	29	Nor Pak Services Inc	4783	27
Nippon Express Travel USA Inc	4724	43	No Soap Productions	8999	211	Nor Service Inc	3599	2477
Nippon Express USA Inc	4512	18	No Time Delay Electronics Inc	5065	644	Nor Tec Electric Inc	1731	1994
Nippon Paper Industries USA	2621	42	No Time Inc	1731	20	Norac Inc	2834	226
Company Ltd			Noah Precision LLC	3559	216	Noralph Inc	5731	74
Nippon Steel USA Inc	5051	515	Noah Technologies Corp	2819	66	Noram Capital Holdings Inc	7389	657
Nipro Diagnostics Inc	3845	24	Noah's Ark Processors Corp	2011	115	NorAm International Partners	5942	17
Nipro Medical Corp	5047	17	Nobel Biocare USA LLC	3843	1	Noramar Company Inc	3823	445
Niron Inc	3544	393	Nobel Learning Communities Inc	8211	1	Noramco Inc	2834	224
Nirvana Systems Inc	7372	3544	Nobel Limited Co	4813	161	Norampac New York City Inc	2675	3
Nirvanix Inc	4813	501	Nobel Systems Inc	7379	178	Noran Engineering Inc	7372	4005
Nis Inc	7371	1876	Nobelmen Group LLC	6799	150	Noranda Aluminum Holding Corp	3334	5
Niscayah (Kansas City Missouri)	7373	450	Nobeltec Inc	7372	3130	Norandex Building Materials Distribu-	3089	32
Nisen and Elliott LLC	8111	450	Nobility Homes Inc	2451	28	tion		
Nisene Technology Group Inc	3825	232	Noble Americas Corp	5149	52	Noran-Land Engineering Corp	7371	1091
Nishikawa Standard Co	3442	20	Noble Automotive Group	5511	698	Noraxon USA Inc	3845	81
NiSource Energy Partners LP	4923	16	Noble BioMaterials	2299	10	Norbert E Mitchell Company Inc	5983	10
NiSource Inc	4932	1	Noble Drilling Services Inc	1381	10	Norbert Industries Inc	3599	344
Nissan Forklift Trucks	5084	854	Noble Energy Inc	1311	18	Norbest Inc	5144	30
Nissan Industrial Engine Manufacturing	3519	34	Noble Environmental Power Inc	4911	99	Norbet Trucking Corporation Inc	4213	1870
Nissan North America Inc	3711	17	Noble House Funding Corp	7373	1059	Norbord Alabama Inc	2493	11
Nissan of San Bernardino	5511	323	Noble Investment Group LLC	7011	83	Norbord Minnesota Inc	2493	8
Nissan Technical Center North America	8711	230	Noble Marketing Group	7319	136	Norca Corp	5051	375
Inc			Noble Properties Inc	1381	45	NorCal Community Bancorp	6712	590
Nissan-Mitsubishi-Kia of Lake Charles	5511	811	Noble Roman's Inc	5812	395	Nor-Cal Distribution Services	4213	3048
Nissin Brake Ohio Inc	3714	163	Noble Rural Electric Membership Coop	4911	498	Norcal Mutual Insurance Co	6411	69
Nissin Foods Company Inc (Gardena	2098	2	Noble Systems Corp	3661	71	Norcal Printing Inc	2752	1409
California)			Noble Tool Corp	3599	1236	Nor-Cal Produce Inc	5148	28
Nissin International Transport Inc	4731	13	Noble USA Inc	5065	191	Nor-Cal Products Inc	3494	45
Nissin Precision North America Inc	3663	117	Noble Wholesale Inc	5031	387	Norcia Bakery	2051	279
Nisus Software Inc	7371	1284	Noble-Met LLC	3317	31	Norcimbus F Crawford Iv Inc	3559	330
Nisus Technology Corp	7371	1470	Nobles Cooperative Electric	4911	335	Norco Inc	2813	10

Company Name	SIC	Rank
Norco Injection Molding Inc	3089	477
Norco Printing Inc	2791	51
Norco Technologies	7379	1643
Norcold Inc	3632	8
Norcom Systems Inc	7389	2284
Norcomp Inc	5065	358
Norcon Electronics Inc	5065	653
Norcostco Inc	5049	55
Norcraft Companies LP	2434	5
Norcross Corp	3823	285
Nord Gear Corp	3566	13
Nord Resources Corp	1455	3
Nordaas American Homes	1521	83
Nordam Group Inc	3728	25
Nordby Electric Inc	1731	2146
Nordcast Inc	3559	535
Nordco Inc	3531	54
Nordco Rail Services and Inspection Technologies	3577	438
Nordec Inc	2759	190
Nordenia USA Inc	2671	21
Nordent Manufacturing Inc	3843	49
Nordic Co	5162	66
Nordic Construction Ltd	1522	42
Nordic Fiberglass Inc	2221	34
Nordic Foods Inc	2011	111
Nordic Group of Companies Ltd	3089	12
Nordic Interior Inc	2431	63
Nordic Refrigerated Services	4222	5
Nordic Software Inc	7372	4357
Nordick Electric and Sheet Metal Inc	1731	924
NordicTrack Inc	3949	24
Nordique Tours	4725	50
Nordis Direct	8748	48
Nordix Computer Corp	5045	292
Nordon Inc	5046	140
Nordonia Computer Services Inc	7379	737
Nord's Electric Supply Company Inc	5063	694
Nordson Asymtek	3586	8
Nordson Corp	3569	6
Nordson EFD	3586	3
Nordstrom Automotive Inc	5015	8
Nordstrom Inc	5611	1
Nordt Company Incorporated John C	3911	39
Nordyne Inc	3567	1
Nor'eastern Trawl Systems Inc	2399	16
Noreen Seabrook Marketing Inc	2273	39
Noremac Enterprises LLC	7322	129
Noremac Manufacturing Corp	3599	810
Noren Products Inc	3823	164
NORESCO LLC	3822	5
NOREX Inc	7379	946
Norfolk Corp	2851	169
Norfolk Dredging Co	1629	66
Norfolk Machine And Welding Inc	3599	1916
Norfolk Southern Corp	4011	6
Norfolk Southern Railway Co	4011	7
Norforge And Machining Inc	3462	52
Norgaard Trucking Inc	4213	2331
Norgren Automation Solutions Inc	3625	65
Norit Americas Inc	2819	120
Noritsu America Corp	5043	24
Norka Futon	2515	27
Norkol Converting Corp	2621	38
Nor-Lake Inc	3585	61
Norlake Manufacturing Co	3677	15
Norland Group	7379	1031
Norland International Inc	5074	183
Norland Products Inc	2891	109
Norlen Inc	3469	61
Norlite Corp	3295	20
Norm and Doe Electrical Supply Inc	5063	1057
Norm Marshall and Associates Inc	7311	837
Norm Reeves Honda Superstore Inc	5511	104
Norm Thompson Outfitters Inc	5961	82
Normac Inc	3541	95
Norman Archery Inc	5091	124
Norman Brothers Produce	5431	1
Norman Data Defense Systems Inc	7372	4432
Norman Frede Chevrolet Co	5511	717
Norman Horowitz Co	2741	483
Norman Jones Enlow and Co	8721	102
Norman Noble Inc	3599	95
Norman Paper And Foam Company Inc	2671	69
Norman Scott Company Inc	3599	734
Norman Supply Co	5074	133
Norman Tool Inc	3545	383
Normandeau Associates Inc	8748	192
Normandeau Communications Inc	1731	2479
Normandin Chrysler-Plymouth-Jeep-Eagle	5511	855
Normandy Industries Inc	3089	182
Normandy Machine Company Inc	3599	619
Normangee Tractor and Implement Company Inc	5083	165
Normans Inc	5141	191
Normark Corp	5091	61
Normco Supply Company Inc	7389	1637
Norment Security Group	3669	15
Norms' Refrigeration And Ice Equipment Inc	5078	24
Noroestana De Exportaciones Cxa	5031	369
Norotos Inc	3599	217

Company Name	SIC	Rank
Norpac Food Sales	5142	14
Norpac Foods Inc	2037	3
Norpak Corp	2671	58
Norplex Inc	3089	1093
Norquay Technology Inc	2869	115
Norquest Seafoods Inc	2092	45
Norrenberns Foods Inc	5411	124
Norris and Cotes	7311	931
Norris Perne and French LLP	6282	621
Norris Precision Manufacturing Inc	3724	59
Norris Satellite Communications Inc	4899	214
Norris Screen And Manufacturing LLC	3532	35
Norris Systems LLC	5045	122
Norriseal	3491	42
Norscot Group Inc	3944	31
Norseland Inc	5143	8
Norsemen Trucking Inc	4213	431
Norsk Hydro Americas Inc	3334	7
Nor-South Corporation Ltd	5099	31
Norstam Veneers Inc	2421	87
Norstan Inc (Minnetonka Minnesota)	7389	134
Norstan Inc (Waukegan Illinois)	3643	77
Norstar Aluminum Molds Inc	3544	105
Norstar Office Products Inc	2522	13
NorStates Bank	6022	235
Nortech Engineering Inc	3571	105
Nortech Systems Inc	3679	94
Nortek Inc	2431	3
Nortex Corp	1311	235
North America Title Co	6361	27
North American Acquisition Corp	3714	198
North American Autonet Inc	5012	116
North American Bullet Proof Inc	3211	20
North American Bus Industries Inc	3711	30
North American Capital Management Co	6282	538
North American Carbide Of Missouri Inc	3545	360
North American Cerutti Corp	3555	36
North American Clutch Corp	3568	48
North American Coal Corp	1221	12
North American Color Inc	2796	49
North American Company for Life and Health Insurance	6311	111
North American Connection	3661	181
North American Container Corp	2441	2
North American Electronics Components LLC	3643	73
North American Filter Corp	3564	82
North American Filtration Inc	6719	174
North American Fire Hose Corp	3052	18
North American Fly Ltd	3151	4
North American Forest Products Inc	2421	51
North American Graphics Inc	2791	52
North American Halal Food Industries Inc	5147	142
North American Hoganas Holdings Inc	5169	112
North American Hydraulics Inc	5084	719
North American Latex Corp	3069	139
North American Lighting Inc	3647	1
North American Marine Jet Inc	3519	32
North American Medical Management-Desert Region Inc	8741	269
North American Membership Group Inc	2721	37
North American Plastics Ltd	3089	1554
North American Plywood Corp	5031	234
North American Rescue LLC	3842	208
North American Roofing Services Inc	1761	4
North American Safety Valve Industries Inc	5085	317
North American Savings Bank FSB	6035	64
North American Science Associates Inc	8731	132
North American Seal and Supply Inc	5085	363
North American Shipbuilding LLC	3731	25
North American Signal Co	3648	36
North American Software Inc	7372	4358
North American Stainless General Partnership	3316	10
North American Steel Co	5051	487
North American Technology Exchange Inc	5065	487
North American Theatrix Ltd	7922	45
North American Title Group Inc	6541	2
North American Tool Corp	3545	39
North American Trade Corp	5082	83
North American Video And Sound Company Inc	5065	517
North Anoka Control Systems Inc	3625	130
North Arkansas Electric Cooperative Inc	4911	351
North Atlantic Fish Company Inc	2092	83
North Atlantic Inc	5065	511
North Atlantic Industries Inc	3825	79
North Atlantic Networks LLC	7379	1261
North Atlantic Operating Co	2131	3
North Atlantic Publishing Systems Inc	7372	1925
North Atlantic Telecom Inc	5065	743
North Atlantic Utilities Inc	4924	65
North Bay Construction Inc	7389	939
North Bay Developmental Disabilities Services Inc	8331	3
North Bay Networks Inc	5734	367
North Canton Plastics Inc	3089	1246
North Canton Transfer Co	4213	1092

Company Name	SIC	Rank
North Carolina Electric Membership Corp	4911	106
North Carolina Insurance Underwriting Association	6331	285
North Carolina Manufacturing Inc	3599	1835
North Carolina Mutual Life Insurance Co	6311	231
North Carolina Mutual Wholesale Drug Co	5122	38
North Carolina State Employees' Credit Union	6062	1
North Castle Partners LLC	6799	162
North Central Bancshares Inc	6712	485
North Central Cooperative Inc	5172	46
North Central Electric Coop	4911	340
North Central Excavating Trucking and Masonry Inc	1623	665
North Central Grain Coop	5153	69
North Central Industries Inc	5092	46
North Central Life Insurance Co	6311	240
North Central Mississippi Electric Power Association	4911	418
North Central Missouri Electric Cooperative Inc	4911	561
North Coast Bearings LLC	5085	190
North Coast Brewing Company Inc	2082	54
North Coast Communications	7812	182
North Coast Consultants Inc	7335	27
North Coast Credit Union	6062	25
North Coast Energy Inc	1311	141
North Coast Medical Inc	5049	23
North Coast Nissan Inc	5511	1228
North Coast Patrol Inc	7381	247
North Coast Sea-Foods Corp	2092	22
North Coast Software Inc (Oswego New York)	7372	3932
North Coast Technical Sales Inc	5065	862
North Coast Web Design	7371	1850
North Community Bank	6022	214
North Country Engineering Inc	3599	2066
North Country Harley-Davidson Inc	5571	3
North Country Internet Access Inc	4813	658
North Country Publishing Co	2711	814
North Country This Week	2711	876
North County Advertising	7311	747
North Dallas Bank and Trust Co	6022	169
North Dallas Warehouse Equipment Inc	5046	195
North East Cutting Die Corp	3599	1881
North East Knitting Inc	2241	17
North East Machine and Tool Co	3599	340
North East Placement Service Inc	8331	154
North East Precision Inc	3599	618
North East Transfer Inc	4213	1069
North East Welding And Fabrication Inc	7692	40
North Electric Supply Inc	5063	322
North End Composites LLC	3732	75
North European Oil Royalty Trust	6792	7
North Face Inc	3949	9
North Florida Lincoln-Mercury Inc	5511	872
North Florida Lumber Company Inc	2421	101
North Florida Shipyards Inc	3731	23
North Florida Web Press Inc	2752	1047
North Fulton Medical Center Volunteer Services Organization Inc	8062	198
North Hartland Tool Corp	3544	314
North Highland Co	8742	194
North Hills Lincoln-Mercury Sales Inc	5511	501
North Hollywood Carburetor and Ignition Inc	5013	209
North Houston Pole Line Corp	1623	20
North Industries Inc	3444	302
North Iowa Cooperative Elevator	5153	200
North Jersey Bobcat Inc	7359	66
North Jersey Community Bank	6022	368
North Jersey Media Group Inc	2711	69
North Lake Tahoe Bonanza	2711	282
North Landing Limited LLC	5146	32
North Light Color Inc	5084	529
North Metro Community Services Incorporated	8322	31
North Milwaukee State Bank	6022	695
North Mississippi Conveyor Company Inc	3535	126
North Of Boston Library Exchange Inc	7375	256
North Pacific Crane Company LLC	3536	54
North Pacific Group Inc	5031	10
North Park Lincoln-Mercury Inc	5511	106
North Park Transportation Co	4213	332
North Penn Bancorp Inc	6712	649
North Penn Telephone Company Inc	4813	373
North Plains Electric Cooperative Inc	4911	543
North Ridge Software Inc	7372	4387
North Shore Bank FSB	6035	40
North Shore Bottling Company Inc	5181	79
North Shore Gas Co	4924	44
North Shore Laboratories Corp	3714	419
North Shore Long Island Jewish Health System	8062	15
North Shore Office Machine Company Inc	5044	115
North Shore Printers Inc	2752	1658
North Shore Rental Inc	7359	269
North Shore Strapping Inc	3081	98

Company Name	SIC	Rank
North Shore Supply Company Inc	5051	34
North Side Bank and Trust Co	6022	485
North Slope Telecom Inc	1623	330
North South Foods Group Inc	5144	4
North - South Machinery Company Inc	5084	524
North Star Agency Inc	6411	267
North Star Auto Electric Inc	7539	18
North Star Beverage Company Inc	2086	128
North Star Bluescope Steel LLC	3312	71
North Star Cold Storage	2092	84
North Star Communications Inc	5065	922
North Star Delivery Inc	4213	2989
North Star Electric Cooperative Inc	4911	520
North Star General Insurance Co	6411	102
North Star Glass Industries Inc	1793	14
North Star Glove Co	2381	4
North Star Lighting Inc	3646	35
North Star Mutual Insurance Company Inc	6331	299
North Star Nameplate Inc	2759	531
North Star Orthodontics Inc	3843	33
North Star Publishing LLC	2752	598
North Star Ranch Inc	4213	1626
North Star Refrigeration Heating and Cooling	5078	39
North Star Scientific Corp	8711	536
North State Communications	4813	174
North State Flexibles	3089	320
North Tool And Manufacturing Co	3544	733
North Town Electric Company Inc	1731	1995
North Valley Bancorp	6712	344
North Valley Bank	6022	193
North West Rural Electric Coop	4911	458
North Wind Student Newspaper	2711	723
Northbend Pattern Works Inc	3543	34
NorthCenter Foodservice Corp	5141	135
Northeast Acura Inc	5511	898
Northeast Air Solutions Inc	5051	398
Northeast Analytical Inc	8731	295
Northeast Arkansas Federal Credit Union	6061	69
Northeast Bancorp	6712	432
Northeast Bank	6022	273
Northeast Building Products Corp	3442	63
Northeast Capital and Advisory Inc	6211	239
Northeast Carbide Inc	3544	881
Northeast Community Bancorp Inc	6035	126
Northeast Community Bank	6035	133
Northeast Computer Systems Inc	5734	347
Northeast Controls Inc	5084	382
Northeast Coop	5153	99
Northeast Copier Systems Inc	5044	50
Northeast Electronics Corp	3679	317
Northeast Engineering Inc	5084	276
Northeast Equipment Inc	3561	151
Northeast Express Transportation Inc	4213	303
Northeast Indiana Bancorp Inc	6712	586
Northeast Innovations Inc	3661	234
Northeast Land Co	6531	438
Northeast Laser and Electropolish Inc	7389	1522
Northeast Laser Image Of New England Inc	5734	250
Northeast Lens Corp	3851	77
Northeast Machine And Motor Supply Inc	7538	29
Northeast Manufacturing Company Inc	3599	1380
Northeast Metal Traders Inc	5093	128
Northeast Metrology Corp	3825	283
Northeast Mississippi Coca-Cola Bottling Co	2086	39
Northeast Missouri Electric Power Coop	4911	342
Northeast Nebraska Media Inc	2711	920
Northeast Nebraska Public Power District	4911	566
Northeast Offset Inc	2752	1028
Northeast Ohio Regional Sewer District	4959	6
Northeast Oklahoma Electric Coop	4911	168
Northeast Photocopy Company Inc	5999	179
Northeast Plastic Supply Company Inc	5162	41
Northeast Plastics Inc	3089	1653
Northeast Printing and Distribution Company Inc	2752	737
Northeast Quality Services LLC	3599	688
Northeast Scene Inc	2721	400
Northeast Securities Corp	6712	644
Northeast Security Systems Inc	1731	1662
Northeast Services Inc	1623	759
Northeast Telecom LLC	4813	366
Northeast Temperature Controls Inc	1731	1894
Northeast Texas Electric Cooperative Inc	4911	215
Northeast Texas Farmers Co-Op	5191	110
Northeast Texas Online Inc	7372	4433
Northeast Tire Molds Inc	3544	403
Northeast Utilities	4911	30
Northeast Utilities Inc	4911	524
Northeast Utilities Service Company Inc	1623	23
Northeast Wholesale Lumber Inc	5031	397
Northeast Wisconsin Printing Company Inc	2752	1265
Northeastern Import Export Inc	5023	167

Company Name	SIC	Rank
Northeastern Michigan Rehabilitation And Opportunity Center	8331	199
Northeastern Rural Electric Membership Coop	4911	269
Northeastern Sheet Metal Company Inc	1761	52
Northeastern Water Jet Inc	3545	215
Northeastern Wisconsin Results LLC	7379	1523
Northeimer Manufacturing Inc	3679	453
Northern Air Inc	4581	19
Northern and Nye Printing Inc	2752	1368
Northern Apex Corp	3672	311
Northern Arizona Regional Behavioral Health Authority Inc	8093	14
Northern Bottling Co	2086	98
Northern Building Products Inc	3442	97
Northern Business Machines Inc	5999	99
Northern California Collection Service Inc	7322	73
Northern California Graphics Inc	2752	1130
Northern Cap And Glove Manufacturing LLC	2353	20
Northern Catv Sales Inc	5065	53
Northern Chemical Co	5087	68
Northern Coating and Chemical	2851	128
Northern Computing Consultants	7372	4532
Northern Concrete Pipe Inc	3272	98
Northern Contours Inc	3083	13
Northern Cooperative Services (Lake Mills Iowa)	5171	71
Northern Counties Secretarial Service Inc	7338	12
Northern Eagle Beverages Inc	5181	97
Northern Electric Cooperative Inc	4911	555
Northern Electric Inc	1731	99
Northern Electric Of Durham Inc	1731	2037
Northern Engraving Corp	3469	24
Northern Extrusion Tooling	3542	57
Northern Factory Sales Inc	5013	95
Northern Filter Media Inc	1446	9
Northern Illinois Health Plan	8741	144
Northern Illinois Mold Corp	3544	773
Northern Illinois Steel Supply Co	5051	312
Northern Improvement Co	1629	40
Northern Indiana Fuel and Light Company Inc	4932	9
Northern Indiana Manufacturing Inc	3451	85
Northern Indiana Public Service Co	4939	3
Northern Industrial Electric	1731	1594
Northern Industrial Services Inc	8711	475
Northern Lakes Co-op Inc	5311	52
Northern Leasing Systems Inc	8999	25
Northern Light Technology LLC	7379	219
Northern Lights Inc	4911	338
Northern Lights Post Inc	7819	72
Northern Lights Software	7372	2726
Northern Machine Tool Co	3544	271
Northern Metal Products	3479	12
Northern Motor Co	5511	1159
Northern Natural Gas Co	4922	26
Northern Neck Coca-Cola Bottling Company Inc	2086	147
Northern Neck Electric Coop	4911	516
Northern Neck Transfer Inc	4213	1889
Northern Nevada Equipment LLC	5046	151
Northern Oak Capital Management	6282	670
Northern Pines Inc	7011	228
Northern Pipe Products Inc	3089	115
Northern Plains Construction	1771	35
Northern Plains Electric Coop	4911	328
Northern Plains Electric Coop (Carrington North Dakota)	4911	526
Northern Prairie Polymers LLC	3069	225
Northern Precision Casting Co	3324	2
Northern Precision Inc	3544	701
Northern Precision Plastics Inc	3089	1352
Northern Precision Products Inc	3599	1229
Northern Pride Inc	2015	37
Northern Products Co	3086	80
Northern Software Inc	7372	4533
Northern Software Tools Inc	7372	4936
Northern Stamping Co	3465	4
Northern Star Bank	6022	769
Northern Star Co	2099	51
Northern Star Financial Inc	6712	719
Northern States Financial Corp	6712	479
Northern States Power Co	4931	6
Northern States Power Co	4931	40
Northern States Supply Inc	5085	141
Northern Stationers Inc	5044	47
Northern Steel Castings Inc	5051	326
Northern Tool and Equipment Catalog Co	5961	33
Northern Tool Manufacturing Company Inc	3089	1781
Northern Transitions Inc	8331	196
Northern Trust Bank/DuPage	6022	585
Northern Trust Bank/Lake Forest NA	6021	181
Northern Trust Bank of California NA	6021	231
Northern Trust Bank of Florida NA	6021	40
Northern Trust Corp	6712	18
Northern Trust Global Advisors Inc	6282	576
Northern Trust International Banking Corp	6091	14

Company Name	SIC	Rank
Northern Trust Securities Inc	6211	193
Northern Trust Services Inc	8742	17
Northern Virginia Electric Coop	4911	139
Northern Virginia Transportation Commission	4111	4
Northern Wholesale Supply Inc	5091	51
Northern Wire LLC	3496	54
Northfield Bancorp	6712	181
Northfield Bank	6035	57
Northfield News Publishing Co	2711	442
Northfield Savings Bank	6036	51
Northfield Tractor and Equipment Inc	5083	13
Northgate Electric Corp	1731	220
Northgate Lincoln Mercury Inc	5511	253
Northlake Engineering Inc	3612	69
Northlake Shipyard Inc	3731	54
Northlake Software Inc	7372	4723
Northlake Steel Corp	3398	12
Northland Aluminum Products Inc	3089	378
Northland Communications (Utica New York)	4812	120
Northland Corrosion Services Ltd	1731	2025
Northland Group Inc	7322	61
Northland Industries Inc	3949	100
Northland Insurance Cos	6331	246
Northland Machine Inc	3469	294
Northland Motor Technologies (Watertown New York)	3621	60
Northland Plastics Inc	3089	1101
Northland Process Piping Inc	3312	76
Northland Royalty Co	1311	250
Northland Systems Inc	5045	761
Northland Technology Inc	1623	705
Northland Telephone Systems Ltd	4813	121
Northland Television Inc	4833	163
Northland Tool and Die Inc	3544	529
Northlich Stolley LaWarre	7311	165
Northlight Web Site Design Group Inc	7379	864
Northpark Dental Group LLC	8021	20
Northpoint-Pioneer Inc	8093	36
Northport Corporation Of StCloud	3732	67
Northridge Laboratories Inc	2833	59
Northrim BanCorp Inc	6712	318
Northrim Bank	6022	726
Northrop Grumman Corp	3721	2
Northrop Grumman Information Technology	7372	5104
Northrop Grumman Information Technology - Computing Systems Div	7373	5
Northrop Grumman Norden Systems	3812	36
Northrop Grumman Shipbuilding Inc	3731	50
Northrop Grumman Space Technology	8731	15
Northrop Grumman Systems Corp	3731	1
North's Bakery California Inc	2051	208
Northshore Manufacturing Inc	3531	106
Northshore Mining Co	1011	7
Northside Gastroenteroloty Endoscopy Center LLC	8011	171
Northside Physical Therapy Inc	8093	54
Northside Transportation LLC	4213	2600
Northstar Access	4813	455
Northstar Automotive Glass Inc	5013	214
NorthStar Business and Property Brokers	7389	1636
Northstar Computer Forms Inc	2761	8
Northstar Controls Inc	3613	187
Northstar Counselors Inc	8743	227
Northstar Electric Co	1731	1236
Northstar Electrical Service LLC	1731	1600
Northstar Equipment Inc	3559	464
Northstar Exterminators Inc	7342	37
Northstar Fabrication And Machine Inc	3599	2343
NorthStar Healthcare Investors Inc	8052	10
NorthStar Industries Inc (Wayzata Minnesota)	6799	300
Northstar Machine and Tool Company Inc	3728	151
NorthStar Realty Finance Corp	6798	68
Northstar Steel and Aluminum Inc	5051	277
Northstar Studios	7812	43
Northstar Systems Inc	3577	11
NorthStar Systems International Inc	7371	649
Northstar Travel Media LLC	2741	68
Northstate Recycling Inc	5093	149
Northtown Capital Strategies	6211	379
Northtown Sounds	2741	303
Northville Cider Mill Inc	5431	3
Northville Industries Corp	5172	70
Northway Bank	6021	345
Northway Financial Inc	6712	416
Northway Industries Inc	2542	34
Northway State Bank	6022	770
Northwest Administrators Inc	7363	114
Northwest Aluminum Specialties Inc	5051	275
Northwest Analytical Inc	7372	4161
Northwest Arkansas Certified Development Co	7361	263
Northwest Automated Machining Inc	3432	29
Northwest Bancshares Inc (Warren Pennsylvania)	6712	85
Northwest Bank and Trust Co	6712	623
Northwest Bank (Lake Oswego Oregon)	6022	702

Company Name	SIC	Rank
Northwest Bank (Spencer Iowa)	6035	118
Northwest Biotherapeutics Inc	2834	478
Northwest Cable Construction Inc	1623	407
Northwest Cad Services Inc	8711	607
Northwest Capital Corp	6799	6
Northwest Coatings Corp	2891	40
Northwest Community Bank (Winsted Connecticut)	6036	61
Northwest Co	2211	29
Northwest Composites Inc	3089	345
Northwest Containers Services Inc	4212	35
Northwest Corporate Real Estate Inc	6531	408
Northwest Cosmetic Labs LLC	2844	45
Northwest Dairy Association	2026	22
Northwest Dairy Forwarding Co	4213	1726
Northwest Direct Teleservices Inc	7389	1006
Northwest Distribution Tools for Schools Inc	5149	95
Northwest Door And Supply Inc	5031	347
Northwest Electric Inc	1731	464
Northwest Electric Motor Co	5063	1015
Northwest Electronics Distributing Co	5065	533
Northwest EMC	8734	88
Northwest Equipment Inc	5046	340
Northwest Essex Community Health Care Network Inc	8331	141
Northwest Evaluation Association	8299	23
Northwest Florida Facility Management Inc	5812	391
Northwest Foam Products Inc	3086	139
Northwest Friction Distributors	5013	311
Northwest Fuel Systems Inc	5084	582
Northwest Gel Inc	2097	29
Northwest Geophysical Associates Inc	7372	4724
Northwoct Graphics Inc	2752	1731
Northwest Hardwoods Div	2426	20
Northwest Hills Pharmacy and Florist Corp	5912	49
Northwest Indiana Bancorp	6712	415
Northwest Information Systems Inc	7372	3251
Northwest Installations Inc	1796	31
Northwest Iowa Power Coop	4911	383
Northwest Machining and Manufacturing Inc	3599	563
Northwest Mack Parts And Service Co	5013	258
Northwest Mailing Service Inc	7331	82
Northwest Mannequin	5046	382
Northwest Manufacturing and Distribution Inc	5082	209
Northwest Manufacturing Company Inc	3599	1232
Northwest Marketing Team LLC	5065	555
Northwest Media Washington LP	2711	286
Nortliwest Millwork Co	5031	325
Northwest Missouri Cellular LP	4812	100
Northwest Multiple Listing Service Inc	6531	424
Northwest Natural Gas Co	4924	14
Northwest Naturals Corp	2033	89
Northwest Network Inc	7373	948
Northwest Nevada Telco Inc	4813	354
Northwest Ohio Endoscopy Center	8011	119
Northwest Pallet Supply	2448	8
Northwest Paper Box Manufacturerss Inc	2653	90
Northwest Pea and Bean Co	5153	179
Northwest Pet Products Inc	2047	16
Northwest Pipe Co	3317	14
Northwest Pipeline Corp	4923	18
Northwest Print Strategies Inc	5943	40
Northwest Professional Color Inc	7384	15
Northwest Protective Service Inc	7381	19
Northwest Pump and Equipment Co	5084	259
Northwest Regulator Supply Inc	3315	31
Northwest Research Associates Inc	8731	200
Northwest Rock	1442	30
Northwest Rubber Extruders Inc	3081	138
Northwest Savings Bank	6036	6
Northwest Scale Systems Inc	5046	128
Northwest Staffing Resources Inc	7363	54
Northwest Steel and Pipe Inc	5051	281
Northwest Swiss-Matic Inc	3451	71
Northwest Tiller's Inc	3524	40
Northwest Tire Factory LLC	5014	59
Northwest Tool and Die Company Inc	3544	178
Northwest Tool and Machine Inc	3544	624
Northwest Tool And Manufacturing Company Inc	3544	470
Northwest Traffic Control Inc	7389	1385
Northwest Transformer Company Inc	7629	29
Northwest Wholesale Inc	5191	58
Northwestern Corp	3581	11
NorthWestern Corp (Sioux Falls South Dakota)	4931	29
Northwestern Inc	2431	77
Northwestern Indiana Telephone Company Inc	4813	230
Northwestern Industries Inc	3211	18
Northwestern Mutual Financial Network	6311	142
Northwestern Mutual Life Insurance Co	6311	6
Northwestern Plastics Ltd	3523	87
Northwestern Publishing House	5999	124
Northwestern Savings Bank and Trust	6036	57
Northwind Financial Inc	4813	465
Northwind Industries Inc	3599	1796
Northwinds Of Wyoming Inc	1623	382

Company Name	SIC	Rank
Northwood Industrial Machinery Inc	3553	24
Northwood Manufacturing Inc	3792	7
Northwoods Evergreen	0811	7
Northwoods Software Development Inc	7372	2561
Northwrite Inc	7371	1081
Nortia Capital Partners Inc	6159	93
Norton and Norton Electric Company Ltd	5063	363
Norton Brothers Inc	4213	2449
Norton Ditto Inc	5611	25
Norton Healthcare Inc	8062	40
Norton Press Inc	2711	506
Norton-Lambert Corp	7371	962
Nortra Cables Inc	3679	280
Nortrax Inc	5084	4
Nortridge Software Inc	7372	3216
Norva Plastics Inc	3083	67
Norvanco International Inc	4731	27
Norvax Inc	7379	209
Norvell Company Inc	3556	163
Norvell Electronics Inc	5063	241
Norwalk Precast Molds Inc	3544	710
Norwalk Rehabilitation Services Inc	8361	72
Norwalk Wastewater Equipment Co	3589	137
Norway Bancorp Inc	6712	192
Norwe Inc	3082	38
Norwell Manufacturing Company Inc	3645	49
Norwest Venture Capital Management Inc	6282	134
Norwood Financial Corp	6022	286
Norwood Hardware and Supply Company Inc	5072	80
Norwood Marketing Systems	3549	32
Norwood Marking Systems	3469	220
Norwood Promotional Products Inc	5085	6
Norwood Sash and Door Manufacturing Company Inc	5211	95
Norwood Transportation Inc	4213	3101
Noshok Inc	3823	186
Nosler Inc	3482	6
Nostalgia Products Group LLC	3639	12
Nostalgic Whimsy	7319	165
Nota Bene	7372	4466
Notations Inc	2331	5
Notebook Computers Inc	5045	905
NotePage Inc	7372	583
Noteworthy Industries Inc	3993	19
Noteworthy Medical Systems Inc	7371	355
Nothing But NET	5734	124
Nothum Manufacturing Co	3556	146
Notify Md	7389	1689
Notify Technology Corp	3661	136
Notlob Inc	7349	511
Nott Ltd	1799	152
Notthoff Engineering L A Inc	3728	152
Nottingham Advisors	6282	411
NOVA American Group Inc	6331	242
Nova Audio Inc	3651	215
Nova Biomedical Corp	2833	17
Nova Blue Inc (Chantilly Virginia)	2752	659
NOVA Casualty Co	6331	220
Nova Cellular West Inc	5999	226
NOVA Chemicals Inc (Pittsburgh Pennsylvania)	2821	28
Nova Cor Ltd	4213	2520
Nova CTI Inc	7372	2269
Nova Datacom LLC	7379	517
Nova Drilling Services Inc	3672	285
Nova Electric	3679	51
Nova Electronics Data Inc	3648	59
Nova Financial Holdings Inc	6712	574
Nova Fire Protection Inc	3569	162
Nova Graphics Inc	2752	1755
Nova Magnetics Inc	3677	25
Nova Marketing Inc	7311	683
Nova Marketing Ltd	5065	394
Nova Polymers Inc	2821	130
Nova Solutions Inc	2522	35
Nova Technology Corp	3841	275
Nova USA Wood Products LLC	5031	108
Novacap Inc	3675	9
Novacare	8049	30
NovaCare Outpatient Rehabilitation (Indianapolis Indiana)	8049	12
NovaCentrix	2899	103
NovaCopy Inc	5044	40
Novae Corp	3524	26
Novaflex Hose Inc	5085	122
Novak Electronics Inc	3663	181
Novak Trucking Service LLC	4213	1822
Novalar Pharmaceuticals Inc	8731	137
NovaLogic Inc	7372	1414
NovaLynx Corp	3829	300
NovaMed Inc	8741	80
Novapointe LLC	7374	256
Novar Controls Corp	3625	10
Novariant Inc	5045	272
Novarra Inc	4813	282
Novartis Pharmaceuticals Corp	2834	4
NovaSol	3827	54
NovaStar Financial Inc	6798	201
Novastar Technologies Inc	3548	64
NovaStor Corp	7372	446
Novatech Inc	3545	315

Company Name	SIC	Rank
Novatech LLC	3822	9
Novatech Process Solutions LLC	3823	37
NovaTek Corp	7372	4534
Novatel Ltd	4813	500
Novatel Wireless Inc	3577	57
Novatron Corp	3829	75
Novavax Inc	2836	86
Novco Inc	4213	2165
Novel Iron Works Inc	3441	115
Novelis Inc	3411	1
Novelix Pharmaceuticals Inc	8731	307
Novell Inc	7372	76
Novellus Systems Inc	3559	7
Novelty Cone Company Inc	2052	73
Noven Pharmaceuticals Inc	2834	127
Noventri	3993	138
Noveon International Inc	2899	18
Novi Die and Engineering Co	3544	684
Novi Precision Products Inc	3549	88
Novint Technologies Inc	3577	651
NOVO 1	7375	19
Novo Innovations Inc	5045	305
Novo Nordisk Inc	5122	6
Novocol Inc	3843	29
Novodynamics Inc	7371	1484
Novogradac and Company LLP	8721	213
Novologix	7372	941
Novostent Corp	3841	297
Novotechnik Us Inc	3825	170
Novozymes Inc	8732	59
Novum Pharmaceutical Research Services	8731	178
Novurania Of America Inc	3732	72
Novus Inc	2842	126
Novus International Inc	2833	16
Novus Marketing Inc	7331	106
Novus Media Services Inc	3695	123
Novus Print Media Inc	7319	5
Novus Technic Inc	7379	1301
Novus Technologies Inc	2298	11
Now and Zen Inc	3873	16
Now Disc	3565	75
Now Foods	5122	72
Now Impressions Inc	2761	76
NOW Micro Inc	5045	224
Now Solutions LLC	7372	2504
Now Technology Group	7372	3933
Nowak Associates Inc	7311	363
Nowak Products Inc	3469	383
Nowata Nursing Center Inc	8051	19
Nowell Steel and Supply Company Inc	5051	377
Nowmy Net Works LLC	7379	1143
Nox-Crete Manufacturing Inc	2899	201
Nuxubee County Producers Inc	2092	50
Noyes Fiber Systems Inc	3825	118
Nozone Inc	7374	291
Np Sterling Labs Inc	7389	1332
NP Systems Inc	7372	4535
Npa Coatings Inc	2851	41
Npc Inc	2752	48
NPC International Inc	5812	66
Npc Processing Inc	2015	70
NPD Group Inc	8732	25
NPE LLC	8748	340
Npi Solutions Inc	3315	27
Npk Construction Equipment Inc	5082	85
NPO Solutions Inc	7372	2814
NPS Pharmaceuticals Inc	2836	14
nQativ	7372	2603
Nqueue Inc	7379	1025
Nr Electronics LLC	5065	928
NR Hamm Quarry Inc	1422	7
Nr Systems Inc	8748	454
Nrai Corporate Services Inc	7389	2044
Nrg El Segundo Operations Inc	4911	416
NRG Energy Inc	4911	17
Nrg Power Inc	1731	1063
Nri Data And Business Products Inc	5045	693
Nri Electronics Inc	3672	108
NRI Staffing Resources	7363	113
Nrk Inc	1731	979
Nrl and Associates Inc	3541	103
NRS Appliance Brokers Ltd	5064	179
NRT LLC	6531	72
Nrv Inc	2048	113
NS Bienstock Inc	7922	69
Ns Controls Inc	3625	93
NS Troutman and Sons Inc	2011	147
Nsa Industries LLC	3444	50
NSA International Inc	2833	41
Nsb Electronics Inc	5065	458
NSB Public Finance	6282	536
NSC Inc	7372	4434
Nse Consulting	7379	1312
Nsg Corp	2329	18
NSGDatacom Inc	3669	70
NSI Communications Inc	5065	355
Nsi Industries LLC	3643	44
NSI Tork Inc	3822	21
Nsi-Systems Inc	1731	2052
Nsk Steering Systems America Inc	3714	176
Nsoro	3669	31
NSP Ventures	6512	63
Nspire Health Inc	3841	142

Company Name	SIC	Rank
Nsrw Inc	5084	712
NSS Corp	7372	2604
Nss Enterprises Inc	3589	26
Nstar	4911	44
nStreams Technologies Inc	7375	90
NSU Corp	3714	289
NT International Inc	3824	22
Nt Window Inc	5031	232
Nta Graphics Inc	2752	246
NTA Ltd	4213	1949
NTC Group Inc	6799	357
NTD Architecture	8712	58
NTE Electronics Inc	5065	55
N-Tech Inc	5084	420
N-Tech Solutions Inc	8748	344
N-Telligent LLC	7379	1620
NTELOS Holdings Corp	4813	33
NTELOS Inc	4813	35
Nth Degree Global LLC	8999	40
nth Generation Computing Inc	7372	1050
Nth Inc	3523	266
Nti LLC	1623	314
NTK Holdings Inc	3639	2
Ntm Consulting Services Inc	7379	1356
Ntm Properties Inc	6519	31
NTN Bearing Corporation of America	3562	17
NTN Buzztime Inc	4833	123
Ntn Driveshaft Inc	3568	13
Ntn-Bower Corp	3562	16
Ntp/Republic Clear Thru Corp	3089	1690
NTP Software Inc	7372	2532
N-trig Inc	3577	392
NTS Corp	6552	61
Nts Data Service Inc	7371	891
NTS Development Co	7992	5
Nts Inc	1623	77
NTS Inc (Culver City California)	7379	240
NTS Realty Holdings LP	6799	124
NTS Test Systems Engineering	7373	367
NTT Electronics Corp	3679	61
Ntt Enterprises Inc	7819	85
NTT Multimedia Communications Laboratories Inc	4812	54
NTW	5013	92
Ntw Inc	3672	168
Nu Aire Inc	3821	10
Nu Horizons Electronics Corp	5065	19
Nu Info Systems Inc	7371	263
Nu Life Restorations Of L I Inc	3843	41
Nu Skin Enterprises Inc	5122	12
Nu Skin International Inc	5122	11
Nu Steel Supply Inc	5032	32
Nu Tech Inc	3646	98
Nuair Filter Company LLC	5085	246
Nuance Communications Inc	7372	44
Nuance Industries Inc	2261	24
Nuance9	7379	1524
Nubiola	5169	41
Nu-Cast Inc	3365	24
Nucero Electrical Construction Company Inc	1731	542
Nucity Publications Inc	2711	745
Nuclear Imaging Ltd	3845	68
Nucleic Assays Corp	8731	240
Nucleus LLC	7372	2018
NuCo2 Inc	5169	36
Nucomm Data Inc	7372	3373
Nucon Inc	3449	40
Nucon International Inc	5199	103
Nucor Corp	3312	2
Nucor Fastener Div	3429	39
Nucor-Yamato Steel Co	3441	23
Nu-Court Electrical Construction Inc	1731	1996
Nucraft Furniture Co	2521	19
Nu-Dell Manufacturing Company Inc	3999	76
Nu-Di Products Company Inc	3825	82
Nuell Inc	7699	118
Nuera Communications Inc	3661	45
Nu-Era Holdings Inc	3569	182
Nuffer Smith Tucker Inc	8743	131
Nu-Foam Products Inc	3086	6
Nu-Fone Secretarial Service Inc	7389	1737
NuGen Technologies Inc	8731	206
Nugent Organization Inc	2752	1596
Nugent Sand Co	1442	20
Nugent Sand Company Inc	1446	7
Nugget Markets	5411	119
Nuhart and Company Inc	3081	95
Nu-Hope Laboratories Inc	3842	229
Nukote Inc	3955	2
Nulaid Foods Inc	5144	12
Nulco Manufacturing Corp	3645	12
Nuline Technologies Inc	1731	270
Null's Machine and Manufacturing Inc	3532	61
Nullstone Corp	7372	4006
Nu-Look Fashions Inc	2311	22
Nu-Lustre Finishing Corp	3471	85
Numa Tool Co	3532	24
Numaco Packaging LLC	3172	8
Numara Software Inc	7372	516
Numark Industries LP	5736	3
Numark Laboratories Inc	2834	353
Numark Office Interiors	5021	34
Numax Inc	5049	46

Company Name	SIC	Rank
Numberall Stamp and Tool Company Inc	3953	23
Numbers Only Inc	7379	381
Nu-Meat Technology Inc	5084	798
Numerex Corp	3669	54
Numeric Computer Systems Inc	7372	3128
Numerica Credit Union	6061	48
Numerical Algorithms Group	7372	1945
Numerical Concepts Inc	3555	32
Numerical Control Computer Sciences Inc	7372	1429
Numerical Control Support Inc	3599	777
Numerical Precision Inc	3599	1319
Numerical Productions Inc	3599	633
Numerics Unlimited Inc	3544	361
Numeridex Inc	5045	614
Numina Group	7372	3240
Numonics Corp	3577	193
Nunes Company Inc	0161	17
Nunley Trucking Company Inc	4213	2960
Nunn and Associates	7311	937
Nunn Constructors Ltd	1629	108
Nunnery-Freeman Inc	3589	251
Nuova Distribution USA LLC	5046	244
Nu-Pak Solutions Inc	3086	172
Nuparadigm Government Systems Inc	7371	1420
NuParadigm Systems Inc	7372	3448
NuPathe Inc	2834	435
Nupla Corp	3089	533
Nu-Puttie Corp	2851	118
Nuralnet Inc	7373	1240
Nuritech Inc	5734	432
Nurse Bank Inc	7361	225
Nursecore Management Services LLC	8741	75
Nursefinders Inc	7363	7
Nurses Prn Staffing Inc	7361	327
Nursestat LLC	7361	384
Nursing Corporation Of America Inc	7361	394
Nursing Home and Hospital Consultant Corp	8742	275
Nurstat	7361	203
Nurture Inc	2032	18
NUS Consulting Group	8748	18
Nu-Sash Of Indianapolis Inc	5211	161
Nushagak Electric and Telephone Cooperative Inc	4813	235
Nussbaum Trucking Inc	4213	646
Nussmeier Engraving Co	2754	45
NuStar Energy LP	4612	5
Nu-Star Inc	3599	1457
Nustone Industry Inc	7389	1763
Nut Bar Co	5145	33
Nut Factory Inc	2068	30
Nutcracker Brands Inc	2068	19
Nutech Fire And Security Inc	7382	66
Nutech Industries Inc	3612	108
Nu-Tel Communications Of New Jersey Inc	4899	222
Nutel Electronics Corp	3663	355
Nutfield Technology Inc	3577	520
Nuthatch Information Technologies Inc	8299	85
Nutherm International Inc	3613	103
Nutis Press Inc	2752	321
Nutley Heating and Cooling Supply Company Inc	5074	48
Nutmeg Recycling LLC	5099	79
Nutmeg Securities Ltd	6211	291
Nutmeg Utility Products Inc	3825	134
Nutone Inc	3931	2
Nutra Pharma Corp	2833	69
NutraCea Inc	2041	22
Nutraceutical International Corp	2833	13
Nutra-Flo Co	2873	11
NutraSweet Co	2099	19
NutraSweet Kelco Co	2869	9
Nutriad Inc	2048	139
Nutricap Labs	2833	38
NutriCology Inc	5149	36
NutriSystem Inc	5961	35
Nutrition 21 Inc	2836	18
Nutrition Co	7372	4044
Nutrition Inc	5812	258
Nutrition International Inc	5122	114
Nutrition Management Services Co	5812	350
Nutrition Now Inc	2834	185
Nutrition Services Inc	0213	20
Nutritional Laboratories International	2833	48
Nutro Corp	3569	138
Nutter Corp	1623	119
Nutter McClennen and Fish LLP	8111	159
Nuun and Company Inc	2834	405
NuVasive Inc	3842	20
Nuveen California Investment Quality Municipal Fund Inc	6726	52
Nuveen California Municipal Marketing Opportunity Fund Inc	6726	75
Nuveen California Municipal Value Fund Inc	6726	60
Nuveen California Performance Plus Municipal Fund Inc	6726	53
Nuveen California Premium Income Municipal Fund	6726	87
Nuveen Florida Quality Income Municipal Fund	6726	77

Company Name	SIC	Rank
Nuveen Insured California Premium Income Municipal Fund 2 Inc	6726	56
Nuveen Insured Municipal Opportunity Fund	6726	11
Nuveen Investment Quality Municipal Fund Inc	6726	31
Nuveen Investments Inc	6282	59
Nuveen Investments LLC	6211	16
Nuveen Maryland Premium Income Municipal Fund	6726	67
Nuveen Massachusetts Premium Income Municipal Fund	6726	80
Nuveen Michigan Quality Income Municipal Fund Inc	6726	68
Nuveen Municipal Income Fund Inc	6726	85
Nuveen Municipal Market Opportunity Fund Inc	6726	23
Nuveen Municipal Value Fund Inc	6726	12
Nuveen New Jersey Investment Quality Municipal Fund	6726	43
Nuveen New Jersey Premium Income Municipal Fund Inc	6726	54
Nuveen New York Municipal Value Fund Inc	6726	69
Nuveen New York Performance Plus Municipal Fund Inc	6726	48
Nuveen New York Select Quality Municipal Fund Inc	6726	37
Nuveen Ohio Quality Income Municipal Fund Inc (Chicago Illinois)	6726	61
Nuveen Pennsylvania Investment Quality Municipal Fund	6726	49
Nuveen Performance Plus Municipal Fund Inc	6726	17
Nuveen Premier Insured Municipal Income Fund Inc	6726	42
Nuveen Premier Municipal Income Fund	6726	47
Nuveen Premium Income Municipal Fund Inc	6726	18
Nuveen Select Tax-Free Income Portfolio	6726	58
Nuveen Texas Quality Income Municipal Fund Inc	6726	64
Nuveen Virginia Premium Income Municipal Fund	6726	72
Nuvek LLC	7371	1438
Nuvell Credit Corp	6159	14
Nuventix Inc	3564	101
Nuvera Fuel Cells Inc	3629	20
NuVidia	3695	38
Nuvidia LLC	3695	138
Nuvilex Inc	2833	73
NuVim Inc	2033	128
Nuvite Chemical Compounds Corp	2842	168
Nuvo Inc	2711	685
Nuvo Network Management	7373	305
NuVox Inc	7373	27
Nu-Wa Industries Inc	3792	10
NuWare Technology Corporation Inc	7373	262
Nu-Way Auto Parts	5531	33
Nu-Way Concrete Forms Inc	5039	15
Nu-Way Concrete Forms Southeast LLC	5032	69
Nu-Way Printing and Envelope Co	2752	1208
Nu-Way Products Company Inc	5087	160
Nu-Way Supply Company Inc	5074	28
Nu-Way Transportation Services	4213	225
Nu-Way Trucking Inc	4213	2494
NuZoo Media Inc	7371	1331
Nuzzolese Brothers Ice Corp	5199	132
NV Energy	4931	35
NV Energy Inc	4931	13
NVE Corp	3674	183
Nveg Inc	7379	874
NVIDIA Corp	3577	5
N-Viro International Corp	6794	143
NVIS Inc	3679	579
Nvoq Inc	7371	892
NVP Hospitality Design Inc	5087	129
NVR Inc	1531	6
NVR Mortgage Finance Inc	6162	110
Nvt Savannah LLC	4833	169
NW Electric Power Coop	4911	233
NW Financial Group	6211	303
NW Metal Fabricators Inc	1799	117
NW Priority Credit Union	6062	28
Nw Works Inc	8331	174
Nwa Heart and Vascular Center	3845	125
NWD Investment Management Inc	6722	93
NWinds Inc	7372	4322
NWL Transformers Inc	3612	22
Nwp Manufacturing Inc	2842	155
NWP Services Corp	5045	83
NWS Corp	5045	477
NxStage Medical Inc	3845	16
Nxtbook Media	8999	151
NY One Corporate Car Inc	7359	251
NY Orthopedic USA Inc	3842	163
Nyacol Nano Technologies Inc	2819	111
Nyc Media Group	4833	178
NYCO Products Co	2842	57
Nycom Networks Corp	1731	1726
Nyconn Horse Transportation Corp	4213	3086

Company Name	SIC	Rank
Nyden Corp	3679	411
NYFIX Inc	7373	90
Nygala Corp	5199	26
NYK Logistics Inc	4731	7
Nykon Inc	3651	212
Nylacarb Corp	3089	1469
NYLIFE Inc	8999	222
Nylon Corporation Of America Inc	2821	95
Nyloncraft Inc	3083	7
Nylube Products Company LLC	3646	85
NYMEX Holdings Inc	6231	4
NYMOX Corp	2834	297
Nyne Equipment Inc	5084	577
Nypro Inc	3089	3
Nyrev Inc	2721	303
Nysarc Incorporated Ontario County Chapter	8331	40
Nysco Products LLC	2653	96
NYSE Euronext	6211	21
Nysernet Inc	7375	247
Nytex LLC	5734	443
Nytone Inc	3629	107
Nyx Inc	3089	65
O A Newton and Son Co	5084	515
O Alpine Pressed Metals Inc	3399	24
O and A Manufacturing Inc	3444	222
O and F Machine Products Co	3599	318
O and G Industries Inc	1542	180
O And G Spring And Wire Form Specialty Co	3469	212
O and I Transport Inc	4213	2880
O and K American Corp	3312	92
O and R Precision Grinding Inc	3544	409
O and S Research Inc	3827	103
O and S Trucking Inc	4213	333
O B Macaroni Co	2098	27
O Berk Company LLC	5085	123
O C Keckley Co	3625	120
O C White Co	3646	91
O Chilli Frozen Foods Inc	2038	78
O Design Group	7336	67
O E M Controls Inc	3625	47
O Grayson Co	2844	136
O H Burg Corp	1731	1822
O K Co-Operative Grain and Mercantile Co	5191	175
O/K Machinery Corp	3496	108
O Keller Tool Engineering Co	3544	255
O Weaver Hosea And Sons Inc	1629	65
O1 Communications Inc	4899	87
O2 Ideas Inc	7311	254
O2 Micro Inc	7373	347
OAG Worldwide Ltd	2721	140
Oai Electronics Inc	3663	142
Oak Bay Technologies Inc	3663	394
Oak Burr Tool Inc	3544	370
Oak Cliff Family Healthcare PA	7389	2033
Oak Contracting Corp	1542	220
Oak Council Investment Corp	6159	63
Oak Creek Homes LP	2451	17
Oak Creek Housing Properties LP	6531	328
Oak Crest Homes Inc	8322	81
Oak Electric Company Inc	1731	1535
Oak Enterprises Data Services Inc	7371	1503
Oak Furniture West LLC	5021	136
Oak Group	7372	3194
Oak Group Inc	7372	3277
Oak Grove Institute Foundation Inc	8011	128
Oak Grove Technologies	8748	156
Oak Hall Industries LP	5699	14
Oak Harbor Freight Lines Inc	4213	265
Oak Hill Capital Partners	6799	34
Oak Investment Partners Inc	6799	333
Oak Knoll Winery Inc	2084	58
Oak Manufacturing Company Inc	3581	17
Oak Printing Co	2759	240
Oak Ridge Associated Universities Inc	8733	11
Oak Ridge Capital Group Inc	6021	272
Oak Ridge Financial Services Inc	6021	219
Oak Ridge Foundation Inc	7389	1159
Oak Ridge Micro-Energy Inc	3691	52
Oak Ridge Products	3089	805
Oak Ridge Tool - Engineering Inc	3599	705
Oak Software Inc	7372	5056
Oak State Products Inc	2051	69
Oak Steel Supply Co	5051	393
Oak Tiger Publications Inc	2721	260
Oak-Bark Corp	2869	74
Oakdale Cotton Mills	2281	27
Oakdale Engineering	7372	1738
Oakdale Industrial Electronics Corp	3679	726
Oakdale Precision Inc	3599	1310
Oakdale Printing Company Inc	2752	1037
Oaken Barrel Brewing Company Inc	5813	7
Oakes Equipment Company Inc	3535	212
Oakgrove Construction Inc	1611	170
Oakhouse Farm Inc	2051	193
Oakhurst Apartments LP	6513	48
Oakland Corp (Story City Iowa)	7372	3210
Oakland Management Services Inc	7379	1399
Oakland Printing Services Inc	2752	652
Oakland Raiders	7941	14
Oakland Software Inc	7372	5143
Oakland Stamping LLC	3469	75

Company Name	SIC	Rank
Oakland Tribune Inc	2711	170
Oaklawn Jockey Club Inc	7948	29
Oakleaf Waste Management LLC	4959	2
Oaklee International Inc	2672	56
Oakley Die and Mold Company Inc	3544	454
Oakley Inc	3851	5
Oakley Industries Inc	3312	82
Oakley Transport Inc	4213	418
Oakmark Fund	6722	1
Oakmark International Fund I	6722	66
Oakridge Energy Inc	1311	254
Oakstone Publishing LLC	2741	179
Oaktree Capital Management LP	6722	39
Oaktree Systems Inc	7372	5110
Oakwell Farms LP	6513	25
Oakwood Bindery	2789	99
Oakwood Fruit Farm Inc	0175	9
Oakwood Healthcare System Inc	8062	20
Oakwood Industries Inc	3341	30
Oakwood Metal Fabricating Co	3465	30
Oakwood Products Inc	8731	341
Oakwood Solutions LLC	7372	3004
Oakwood Systems Group Inc	7373	388
OAM Avatar LLC	6282	266
OAP Inc	5731	44
OAS Software Corp	7372	3732
Oasis Car Wash Systems Inc	5084	821
Oasis CD Manufacturing	3695	42
Oasis Coffee Corp	2095	62
Oasis Communications LLC	4841	90
Oasis Corp	3634	10
Oasis Disc Manufacturing	3695	61
Oasis Foods Inc	2033	93
Oasis Mediterranean Cuisine	2099	252
Oasis Petroleum Inc	1311	68
Oasis Pipe Line Company Texas LP	4922	38
Oasis Publishing Inc	2741	498
Oasis Supply and Trade Inc	1799	109
OASIS Technology Inc	7372	1691
Oasis Telecommunications Data and Records Inc	1731	2486
Oasis Trading Company Inc	2079	5
Oasys Mobile Inc	7389	865
O-At-Ka Milk Products Cooperative Inc	2023	6
Oatsystems Inc	7372	1158
OB Hill Trucking and Rigging Co	4213	2110
OBA Federal Savings and Loan	6035	152
Obagi Medical Products Inc	2834	129
O'bannon Publishing Company Inc	2711	618
Obars Machine And Tool Co	3451	98
Obayashi Construction Inc	1542	391
OBBCO Consolidated Industries Inc	3463	23
Obbi LLC	2341	11
OBC Northwest Inc	2393	16
Oberbeck Grain Co	5153	119
Oberg Freight Co	4213	1585
Oberg Industries Inc	3469	19
Oberlander Communication Systems Inc	5999	297
Oberle and Associates Inc	1542	354
Oberthur Card Systems USA	3089	179
Oberto Sausage Co	2011	22
Oberweis Asset Management Inc	6282	166
Oberweis Emerging Growth Fund	6722	228
Obie Media Corp	7312	9
Object Frontier Inc	7371	1256
Object Innovation Inc	7371	1163
Object Nirvana Inc	5045	1073
Objectcrafters Inc	7379	879
ObjectFX Corp	7372	1339
Objectif Lune LLC	7372	3436
Objective Interface Systems Inc	7372	3142
Objective Solutions Inc	7361	399
Objective Systems Integrators Inc	7372	576
Objective Technologies Inc	7372	5097
Objectivity Inc	7372	1613
Objects Worldwide Inc	7371	1012
Objectsoft Inc	7372	5160
ObjectVideo	5045	111
Objectwave Corp	7379	686
Objecutive Inc	7372	2742
Oblicore Inc	7372	1460
Oblivion Events	5051	494
OBN Holdings Inc	4833	172
O'brien and Company Inc	2013	133
O'Brien and Gere Engineers Inc	8711	701
O'Brien and Gere Laboratories Inc	8734	173
O'Brien and Gere Ltd	6512	35
O'Brien and Gere Manufacturing	3567	102
O'Brien and Gere Technical Services Inc	8741	9
O'Brien Auto Park	5511	95
O'brien Cut Stone Co	1741	21
O'brien Installation Inc	5021	126
Obs Inc	5012	144
Observer Daily and Sunday Newspaper	2752	387
Observer Group Inc	2711	518
Observer News Enterprise Inc	2711	871
Observer Publishing Co	2711	304
Obsidian Software Inc	7372	2837
OC McDonald Company Inc	1711	148
OC Systems Inc	7372	3195
OC Tanner Recognition Co	3911	10

Company Name	SIC	Rank
Ocala Endoscropy ASC LP	8011	73
Ocariz Gitlin and Zomerfeld LLP	8721	161
OCC Technology LLC	3679	830
Occam Networks Inc	3577	119
Occidental Chemical Corp	2812	4
Occidental Fire and Casualty Company of North Carolina	6331	312
Occidental Oil and Gas Corp	1311	4
Occidental Petroleum Corp	1311	6
Occunomix International LLC	3842	199
Occupational Health Research	7372	2551
Occupational Services Inc	8331	216
Oce Business Services	8741	21
Oce Printing Systems USA Inc	3577	44
Ocean - 7 Development Inc	7336	124
Ocean Answer	7389	2441
Ocean Applied Research Corp	3669	223
Ocean Beauty Seafoods LLC	2092	7
Ocean Bio-Chem Inc	2842	39
Ocean Blue Inc	3086	90
Ocean Breeze Respiratory Service	7352	31
Ocean Cable Group Inc	4841	128
Ocean City Home Bank	6035	98
Ocean Corp	7389	1119
Ocean Crest Seafoods Inc	5146	66
Ocean Divers Inc	7999	151
Ocean Gold Seafoods Inc	2092	32
Ocean Interface Company Inc	5045	397
Ocean Mist Farms	0723	7
Ocean National Bank	6022	87
Ocean Optics Inc	3826	32
Ocean Pacific Apparel Corp	5136	17
Ocean Park Pictures Inc	7812	169
Ocean Power Technologies Inc	3621	35
Ocean Quest Dive Center	7999	144
Ocean Shore Holding Co	6035	77
Ocean Spray Cranberries Inc	2033	8
Ocean Spray Pool Services Inc	7389	1953
Ocean State Jewelry Inc	3089	47
Ocean State Signal Co	5063	993
Ocean Tomo LLC	7389	654
Ocean Trading Inc	5045	452
Ocean Waves Inc	3851	103
Ocean Way Recording	7389	1165
Ocean Yachts Inc	3732	41
Oceana Therapeutics Inc	5122	51
Oceana's Herald-Journal Inc	2711	887
Oceaneering International Inc	1389	5
OceanFirst Bank	6035	94
OceanFirst Financial Corp	6712	180
Oceanic Bank Holding Inc	6712	706
Oceanic Cablevision Inc	4841	23
Oceanic Exploration Co	1311	256
Oceanit Laboratories Inc	8731	245
Oceanos Marketing	7389	1126
Oceanside Knish Factory Inc	2051	295
Oceanside Unified School District	8211	43
Oceco Inc	3494	76
Ocenture LLC	5049	30
Oce-USA Inc	3579	4
OCH International Inc	6794	49
O'Charley's Inc	5812	69
O'Charley's Sports Bar Inc	5812	329
Och-Ziff Capital Management Group LLC	6282	74
Oci Chemical Corp	1474	1
OCI Construction Company Inc	1623	483
Ockham Development Group Inc	7379	111
Oclaro (Acton Massachusetts)	5045	184
Oclaro Inc	5063	20
Oclc Online Computer Library Center Incorporate	7375	25
OCO Inc	7372	919
Ocoee River Transport Inc	4213	2420
Oconee Electric Membership Corp	4911	316
Oconee Publishing Inc	2711	434
O'Connell Companies Inc	8741	32
O'connell Electric	4911	534
O'Connell Electric Company Inc	1731	77
O'Connell Landscape Maintenance Inc	0782	2
O'Connell Oil Associates Inc	5541	41
O'Connor and Partners Inc	8742	648
O'Connor Chevrolet Inc	5511	946
O'Connor Constructors Inc	1541	267
O'Connor Davies Munns and Dobbins LLP	8721	286
O'connor Sales Inc	5074	212
O'connor Technologies LLC	1731	2178
O'Connor's Express Inc	4213	2881
Oconomowoc Developmental Training Center Of Wisconsin LLC	8361	49
Oconomowoc Manufacturing Corp	3562	35
Oconto County Lumber Inc	5211	286
Oconto Electric Coop	4911	374
Ocp Group Inc	3575	37
Ocp Inc	3084	38
OCT Equipment Inc	5082	86
Octa Inc	3599	960
Octagon Systems Corp	3672	219
Octamer Inc	8731	394
Octameron Associates	2731	207
Octave Software Group Inc	7371	1332
Octavo Corp	2741	246
Octel America Inc	2911	52

Company Name	SIC	Rank
Octel Starreon LLC	5169	185
Octet Corp	7373	1230
Octo Consulting Group	8742	273
October Company Inc	3499	57
Ocular Instruments Inc	3827	75
Oculus Innovative Sciences Inc	3841	208
Ocwen Federal Bank FSB	6035	24
Ocwen Financial Corp	6712	118
OCZ Technology Inc	3674	88
OD Miller Electric Company Inc	1731	1663
O'Daniel Designs	7379	510
Odat Machine Inc	3599	1002
Odawara Automation Inc	3599	1326
O'Day Equipment Inc	3586	13
Odee Co	5112	49
Odeen Hibbs Trucking Co	4213	2123
Odell Associates Inc	8712	141
Odell Electronics Cleaning Stations	5999	318
O'dell Printing Company Inc	2752	676
Odell Simms and Associates	7331	131
Oden and Associates Inc	7336	138
Oden Corp	3565	121
Oden Industries Inc	7371	1021
Oden Marketing and Design	7311	337
Odenberg Inc	3556	140
ODesk Corp	7375	65
Odessa Regional Hospital LP	8069	10
Odessa Trading Company Inc	5153	136
Odesus Inc	7379	467
Odhner Holographics	3679	876
Odimo Inc	5944	40
Odin Technologies Inc	7379	1022
Odl Inc	2431	46
Odm Tool and Manufacturing Company Inc	3469	151
Odom Industries Inc	2819	65
O'donnell Line Construction Company Inc	1623	835
O'donnell Manufacturing Inc	3663	329
Odorite Company Of Baltimore Inc	5087	115
ODS Health Plan Inc	6324	44
ODS-Petrodata Inc	2741	135
ODT Inc	8742	539
Odu-Usa Inc	5065	231
ODV Inc	3829	128
Odwalla Inc	2033	86
Odyssey America Reinsurance Corp	6331	143
Odyssey Communication Group Inc	7374	387
Odyssey Communications Inc	4832	161
Odyssey Computing Inc	7372	2166
Odyssey Digital Printing Inc	2752	555
Odyssey Golf Inc	3949	77
Odyssey Group Of Cos	7373	104
Odyssey House Inc	8361	127
Odyssey Industries Inc	3721	31
Odyssey Investment Partners LLC	6719	145
Odyssey Logistics and Technology Corp	4731	19
Odyssey Marine Exploration Inc	7389	540
Odyssey Medical Inc	3841	315
Odyssey Press Inc	2752	883
Odyssey Re Holdings Corp	6331	64
Odyssey Reinsurance Corp	6331	316
Odyssey Systems Consulting Group Ltd	7379	207
Oe Enterprises Inc	8361	109
OEA International Inc	7372	3934
OEC Graphics Inc	2791	1
Oechsle International Advisers LP	6282	234
OEConnection LLC	7389	213
Oehme Carrier Corp	4213	852
Oelwein Publishing Company Inc	2711	543
Oem Components Inc	3533	57
Oem Corp	3564	142
OEM Inc	3695	14
OEM Industries Inc	3462	77
Oem Parts Outlet	5075	120
Oem Press Systems Inc	3599	1596
OEM Sales Inc	3444	219
Oem Worldwide LLC	3672	54
Oemmcco Inc	3599	772
Oerlikon Optics USA Inc	3083	31
Oerlikon USA Holding Inc	3563	15
Oester Trucking Inc	4213	1632
Oetiker Inc	3429	66
Oeuf Inc	7374	336
OF Mossberg and Sons Inc	3484	13
O'fallon Electric Co	1731	1500
Ofb Industries LLC	2051	307
Off Duty Services Inc	7381	61
Off The Wall Company Inc	7336	52
Offenhauser Co	3443	163
Office and Commercial Cleaning-Wv LLC	7349	295
Office Automation	5045	443
Office Automation Consultants Inc	7372	4725
Office Buildings of Houston Inc	6531	431
Office Connection Inc	5044	108
Office Depot Inc	5943	2
Office Depot Inc Business Services Div	5021	9
Office Dynamics Inc	2752	1620
Office Environments of New England LLC	2522	55
Office Furniture USA	5021	13

Company Name	SIC	Rank
Office Machine Mart	5045	742
Office Movers Inc	4213	375
Office Paper Systems Inc	5113	40
Office Pavilion Inc (Houston Texas)	5712	53
Office Peeps	5999	69
Office Planning Group Inc	5021	97
Office/Pro Technologies Inc	7373	853
Office Resources Inc	5712	21
Office Star Products	2522	19
Office Supply Services Incorporated Of Charlotte	2752	955
Office Systems Inc	3579	44
Office World Inc	5045	492
OfficeCare Corp	7378	26
Officemate International Corp	5112	34
Officemate Software Solutions Inc	7371	1048
OfficeMax Inc	5111	1
Offices Limited Inc	5021	73
OfficeScapes Business Furniture	5021	12
OfficeTiger	7373	125
Official Offset Corp	2752	1190
Official Payments Corp	7389	433
Offis Corp	5045	930
Offiserve Inc	5999	55
Offitbank Investment Group	6722	76
Offset Impressions Inc	2752	460
Offset Paperback Manufacturers Inc	2732	1
Offshore Cleaning Systems LLC	1799	53
Offshore Energy Services Inc	1389	37
Offshore Inland Services Of Alabama Inc	7699	58
Offshore Press Inc	2721	471
Offtech Inc	5044	13
Offutt Securities Inc	6282	374
OFIS by Powell	5021	84
Ofm Distributors Inc	7373	873
Ofs Brands Holdings Inc	2521	8
Ofs Brightwave LLC	3357	16
OFT Construction Inc	1623	719
O'gallerie Inc	5999	193
Ogando Associates Inc	8742	664
O'Gara Group	3842	80
O'gara Satellite Systems Inc	5065	551
OGAS	7372	3278
Ogburn Truck Parts LP	5013	171
Ogburns Truck Parts Inc	5013	316
Ogden Brothers Inc	5943	21
Ogden City Utilities	1623	399
Ogden Forklifts LLC	5084	668
Ogden Newspapers Inc	2711	62
Ogden Publications Inc	2721	167
Ogden Publishing Corp	2711	259
Ogden Welding Systems Inc	5084	343
OGE Energy Corp	4931	17
Ogemaw County Herald Inc	2711	756
Ogihara America Corp	3465	13
Ogilvy and Mather Worldwide Inc	7311	3
Ogilvy CommonHealth Worldwide LLC	7311	29
Ogilvy Public Relations Worldwide	8743	24
OgilvyOne Worldwide	7331	2
Ogio International Inc	2389	16
Oglethorpe Power Corp	4911	52
Oglio Entertainment Group	7929	8
Ogre Partners Ltd	7373	468
O'Guinn Corp	8072	38
Ogura Corp	3714	301
Ohana Wireless Inc	3669	301
O'hara Corp	0912	1
O'Hare Auto Group	5511	324
O'hare Systems Corp	5045	412
O'Harrow Construction	1541	192
Ohc Group Inc	5045	56
O'Herron and Co	6282	611
OHI Co	3556	95
Ohigro Inc	5191	77
Ohio Aluminum Industries Inc	3365	18
Ohio Art Co	3944	20
Ohio Auto Delivery Inc	4213	2913
Ohio Automotive Supply Company Inc	5013	275
Ohio Baking Company Inc	2041	62
Ohio Beverage Systems Inc	2086	150
Ohio Blow Pipe Co	3535	108
Ohio Broach and Machine Co	3541	205
Ohio Calculating Inc	5044	11
Ohio Camshaft Inc	3599	1346
Ohio Casualty Corp	6331	84
Ohio Casualty Insurance Co	6331	27
Ohio County Coal Co	1222	9
Ohio Crankshaft Co	3714	407
Ohio Decorative Products Inc	3086	11
Ohio Distinctive Enterprises Inc	7372	3545
Ohio Distribution Warehouse Corp	4226	6
Ohio Drill and Tool Co	5085	233
Ohio Eastern Express Inc	4213	1661
Ohio Electric Motors Inc	3621	100
Ohio Fresh Eggs LLC	5144	13
Ohio Gas and Appliance Co	5948	4
Ohio Gasket And Shim Company Inc	3053	53
Ohio Gear and Transmission Inc	5085	430
Ohio Grain Co	5153	204
Ohio Graphco Inc	5084	731
Ohio Gratings Inc	3446	16
Ohio Health	8741	14

Company Name	SIC	Rank
Ohio Hickory Harvest Brand Products Inc	5145	15
Ohio Hydraulics Inc	3492	29
Ohio Indemnity Co	6331	259
Ohio Laminating and Binding Inc	7389	1602
Ohio Legacy Corp	6021	317
Ohio Logos Inc	3993	165
Ohio Machine and Manufacturing Company Inc	3599	1174
Ohio Magnetics Inc	3499	102
Ohio Metal Technologies Inc	3462	50
Ohio Metal Working Products Company Inc	3545	231
Ohio National Financial Services	6311	44
Ohio Nut and Bolt Co	3452	12
Ohio Pacific Express Inc	4213	563
Ohio Packing Co	2011	54
Ohio Pet Foods Inc	2048	94
Ohio Precision Molding Inc	3089	1215
Ohio Presbyterian Retirement Services	8361	5
Ohio River Bank	6022	698
Ohio River Metal Services Inc	3316	21
Ohio Roll Grinding Inc	3599	1431
Ohio Security Insurance Co	6331	366
Ohio Semitronics Inc	3674	281
Ohio Stamping and Machine LLC	3465	53
Ohio State Bank Inc	6022	598
Ohio Steel Slitters Inc	7389	1998
Ohio Supercomputer Center	7375	130
Ohio Transmission and Pump Co	5084	114
Ohio Transport Corp	4213	894
Ohio Valley 2-Way Radio Inc	5065	804
Ohio Valley Banc Corp	6712	353
Ohio Valley Bistro's Inc	8741	253
Ohio Valley Cable Services	4841	92
Ohio Valley Cartons Inc	2657	43
Ohio Valley Coal Co	1241	7
Ohio Valley Communications Inc	1731	1349
Ohio Valley Electric Corp	4911	134
Ohio Valley Gas Corp	4924	66
Ohio Valley Goodwill Industries Rehabilitation Center Inc	5932	7
Ohio Valley Industrial Services Inc	5085	360
Ohio Valley Plastics Inc	5162	51
Ohio Valley Reload Inc	4213	2714
Ohio Valley Supply Co	5162	21
Ohio Willow Wood Co	3842	104
Ohio-American Water Co	4941	43
Ohio-Kentucky Steel Corp	7389	1423
Ohl LLC	4225	7
Ohlin Sales Inc	5063	393
Ohline Corp	2431	96
Ohlinger Industries Inc	3599	324
Ohm International Inc	5032	59
OHM Laboratories Inc	2834	271
OHM Systems Inc	7372	69
Ohmega Technologies Inc	3699	244
Ohmstede Inc	3443	27
Ohnward Bancshares Inc	6712	520
Ohsman and Sons Co	5159	15
OHSN Inc	2011	118
OI Analytical	3823	34
OI Corp	3826	46
OIA Global Logistics	4731	66
Oil and Gas Consultants International Inc	7371	762
Oil and Gas Information Systems Inc	7372	1902
Oil Capital Valve Co	3599	425
Oil Center Manufacturing Inc	2992	36
Oil Chem Inc	5172	151
Oil Chem Technologies	2899	150
Oil Data Inc	8999	124
Oil Equipment Company Inc	5084	264
Oil Equipment Sales And Service Company Inc	5084	660
Oil Equipment Supply Corp	5084	290
Oil Express National Inc	6794	119
Oil Process Systems Inc	3569	175
Oil Purification Systems Inc	3519	35
Oil Recovery Corp	4213	2521
Oil Skimmers Inc	3569	238
Oil States Industries Inc	3533	13
Oil States International Inc	3533	7
Oil Well Service Co	1389	39
Oil Well Survey Instrument Company Inc	3823	268
Oil-Air Products LLC	5084	375
Oilco Machine Shop Inc	3599	1852
Oil-Dri Corporation of America	3999	20
Oil-Dri Corporation Of Georgia	2842	13
Oil-Dri Production Co	2842	37
Oiles America Corp	3562	34
Oilfield Electric Inc	1731	485
Oilfield Motor and Control Inc	5065	399
Oilfield Publications Inc	2741	352
Oilgear Co	3594	1
Oil-Rite Corp	3569	122
Oiltanking Holding USA Inc	4226	9
Oiltanking Houston LP	4226	7
OIX Inc	4213	1705
O'jacks Inc	5147	84
Ojai Valley Newspapers LLC	2711	194
Ok 1 Manufacturing Co	3842	134
OK Electric Supply Co	5063	309

Company Name	SIC	Rank
OK Industries Inc	2048	7
Ok Machine and Manufacturing Inc	3599	1095
Ok Manufacturing	3581	15
OK Moving and Storage Company Inc	4213	3026
Okaloosa Publishing Company Inc	2711	710
Okaw Truss Inc	2439	18
Okaya Infocom Private Ltd	7371	733
Okaya USA Inc	5051	254
Okc Electrical Contractors Inc	1731	1282
Okeelanta Corp	2061	1
Oki Data Americas Inc	3577	15
OKI Semiconductor	5065	35
OKI Systems Ltd	5084	101
Okk USA Corp	5084	238
OKL Can Line Inc	3565	87
Oklahoma City National Memorial Foundation	7389	1609
Oklahoma City Thrift Federal Credit Union	6061	137
Oklahoma Educators Credit Union	6062	126
Oklahoma Electric Co-Operative Inc	4911	270
Oklahoma Employees Credit Union	6062	87
Oklahoma Federal Credit Union	6061	140
Oklahoma Gas and Electric Co	4931	20
Oklahoma Heart Hospital LLC	8069	16
Oklahoma Logos LLC	3993	188
Oklahoma Medical Research Foundation	8733	13
Oklahoma Municipal Power Authority	4911	236
Oklahoma Natural Gas Co	4924	30
Oklahoma Office Systems Inc	5044	69
Oklahoma Offset Inc	2752	412
Oklahoma Publishing Co	2711	112
Oklahoma RE and T Employees Credit Union	6062	70
Oklahoma Respiratory Care Inc	7352	52
Oklahoma Steel and Wire Company Inc	3496	51
Okland Construction Company Inc	1541	28
Okolona Pest Control Inc	7342	50
Okon Metals Inc	5093	172
Okonite Company Inc	3357	21
O'Krent Floor Covering Co	5713	17
OKS-Ameridial Inc	7389	70
Okt/Colson Company Inc	3993	97
Oktex Baking LP	2052	64
Okuhara Foods Inc	2092	63
Okura Hardware and Lumber Inc	5072	102
Olairos Investments Inc	5999	269
Olan Mills Inc	7221	6
Olan Plastics Inc	3089	1201
Olathe Aggregate Inc	5032	162
Olathe Glass Company Inc	5039	64
Olathe Millwork Co	5031	263
Olcott Plastics Inc	3089	577
Olcr Inc	5065	637
Old 97 Co	2844	36
Old American Insurance Co	6311	171
Old Bridge Chemicals Inc	2819	114
Old Castle Apg Northeast Inc	3271	4
Old Dominion Brush Company Inc	3991	9
Old Dominion Electric Coop	4911	94
Old Dominion Enterprises Corp	7379	1204
Old Dominion Floor Company Inc	5023	127
Old Dominion Freight Line Inc	4213	23
Old Dominion Grain Corp	5153	153
Old Dominion Peanut Corp	2099	223
Old Dutch International Ltd	3639	25
Old Dutch Mustard Company Inc	2099	50
Old Europe Cheese Inc	2026	67
Old Fashioned Foods Inc	2022	43
Old Fashioned Kitchen Inc	2038	44
Old Fashioned Meat Company Inc	5147	147
Old Hickory Mall Venture	6531	214
Old Hickory Tool and Die LP	3544	559
Old Kent Mortgage Services Inc	6351	30
Old Kentucky Insurance Inc	6411	271
Old Line Bancshares Inc	6712	514
Old Mansion Inc	2099	269
Old Marietta Printers Inc	2791	47
Old Medina Winery	2084	56
Old Mill Winery	2084	32
Old Mutual Investment Partners Inc	7311	98
Old National Bancorp	6712	78
Old National Bank	6712	36
Old Navy Inc	5621	1
Old Point Financial Corp	6712	343
Old Republic International Corp	6331	47
Old Republic National Title Insurance Co	6361	26
Old Republic Title Co	6361	19
Old Republic Title Company of Conroe	6361	39
Old Republic Title Company of St Louis	6541	18
Old Republic Title Insurance Group Inc	6361	16
Old Second Bancorp Inc	6712	178
Old Second Bank-Yorkville	6021	353
Old Second National Bank	6021	310
Old Second National Bank of Aurora	6021	184
Old South Service Inc	4213	1046
Old Spaghetti Factory	5812	102
Old Sturbridge Inc	2099	16
Old Town Canoe Co	3732	18
Old Trapper Smoked Products Inc	2013	214
Old Virginia Brick Company Inc	3251	11

Company Name	SIC	Rank
Old World Specialties Inc	2099	345
Oldaker Manufacturing Corp	3699	287
Oldcastle Apg South Inc	3272	76
Oldcastle Apg Texas Inc	5032	45
Oldcastle Buildingenvelope Inc	3211	12
Oldcastle Glass Group	3211	7
Oldcastle Inc	3272	2
Oldcastle Materials	3273	105
Oldcastle Materials Inc	2951	1
Oldcastle Precast Group	3272	3
Oldcastle Sw Group Inc	1611	115
Olde Town Brokers Inc	6531	137
Oldenburg Group Inc	3532	4
Older Adults Care Management	8082	76
Oldfield Davis Inc	7311	670
Oldham Associates Inc (Springvillo Utah)	2711	123
Oldland Distributing Inc	4213	2177
Olds-Olympic Inc	2911	57
Ole' Mexican Foods Inc	2099	63
Ole South Properties Inc	1531	82
Olean Wholesale Grocery Cooperative Inc	5141	118
O'leary Brothers Signs and Awnings Inc	3089	904
Oleco Inc	3699	152
Oles Envelope Corp	2677	7
Oleson's Food Stores	5411	206
Olhausen Billiard Manufacturing Inc	3949	80
Oli Systems Inc	7372	3422
Oliby Inc	4813	707
Olin Corp	2812	2
Oliner Fibre Company Inc	5113	67
Olinger Distributing Co	5182	18
Oliphant Tool Co	3544	479
Olive Garden Restaurants Div	5812	24
Olive Musco Products Inc	2033	54
Olive Software Inc	7372	1554
Oliveira-Lucas Enterprises Inc	1731	805
Oliver Construction Co	1542	326
Oliver Electric Construction Inc	1731	922
Oliver Equipment Co	5084	649
Oliver Gear Inc	3462	70
Oliver Group LLC	7374	243
Oliver H Van Horn Company Inc	5085	92
Oliver M Dean Inc	5083	126
Oliver Of Adrian Inc	3541	265
Oliver Peoples Inc	5048	8
Oliver Printing Company Inc	2752	699
Oliver Productions Inc	7812	153
Oliver Rubber Co	3069	10
Oliver Russell and Associates Inc	7311	401
Oliver Steel Plate Co	5051	125
Oliver Stores Inc	5082	137
Oliver Technologies Inc	2451	36
Oliver Trucking Company Inc	4213	3118
Oliver Wine Company Inc	5921	12
Oliver Worldclass Labs Inc	5045	517
Oliver Wyman Co	8742	92
Oliverio's Italian Style Peppers Inc	2032	37
Oliver-Tolas Healthcare Packaging Inc	2671	48
Oliver-Tolas Healthcare Packaging LLC	2672	20
Olivia Cruises and Resorts	8999	68
Olivia Machine and Tool Inc	3599	2169
Olla Beauty Supply Inc	5087	41
Ollie Steele Burden Manor Inc	8051	67
Ollila Industries Inc	3625	248
Olm LLC	4813	257
Olmec Systems Inc	7373	994
Olmsted Medical Center	8062	195
Olmsted Office Systems	7372	4726
Olmsted Transportation Co	4213	2482
Ologie LLC	8742	464
Olr America Inc	7379	902
Ols Trading Inc	5021	100
Olsen and Fielding Moving Services	4213	1952
Olsen Audio Group Inc	3651	159
Olsen Distributing Co	5083	171
Olsen Tool And Plastics Inc	3089	750
Olshan Lumber Co	5211	131
OLSolutions	5045	293
Olson And Olson Inc	3599	628
Olson Carriers Inc	4213	1255
Olson Communications Inc	7311	490
Olson Co	1531	44
Olson Floor Covering Inc	5023	159
Olson Industries Inc	3599	151
Olson Irrigation Systems	3523	230
Olson Machining Inc	3599	740
Olson Neaves and Co	8721	260
Olson Research Associates Inc	6282	364
Olson Technologies Inc	3491	45
Olson Technology Inc	3663	222
Olsonite Inc	3089	249
Olsten Staffing Services	7363	6
Olsun Electrics Corp	3612	44
Oltmans Construction Co	1542	131
Olton Grain Cooperative Inc	5153	66
Olum'c of Binghamton Inc	5712	56
Olympia Candy Kitchen	5812	444
Olympia Computing Company Inc	7372	549
Olympia Federal SLA	6035	143
Olympia Lighting Center Inc	5063	824
Olympia Sports Center	5941	18

Company Name	SIC	Rank
Olympia TradingCom Inc	5065	316
Olympian Co	5541	15
Olympian Tool LLC	3544	636
Olympic Adhesives Inc	2891	64
Olympic Awards Inc	3999	118
Olympic Bindery Inc	2789	30
Olympic Controls Corp	3625	159
Olympic Electrical Wiring Corp	1731	610
Olympic Fiberglass Industries Inc	3089	1044
Olympic Ice Cream Company Inc	2024	40
Olympic Instruments Inc	3829	397
Olympic Janitorial	7349	504
Olympic Manufacturing Group Inc	3357	13
Olympic Metals Inc	7389	1974
Olympic Pipe Line Co	4613	12
Olympic Software	5045	925
Olympic Steel Inc	5051	16
Olympic Steel Inc (Schaumburg Illinois)	5051	126
Olympic View Publishing LLC	2711	198
Olympus America Inc	8734	6
Olympus Managed Health Care Inc	6324	87
Olympus Partners	6719	144
Olympus Press Inc	2752	1070
Olympus Real Estate Corp	6552	200
Olympus Surgical and Industrial America Inc	3845	17
OM Group Inc	2819	12
OM Jones Inc	3674	157
Omagine Inc	5046	380
Omaha Bedding Co	2515	22
Omaha Beef Company Inc	5147	43
Omaha Compound Co	2842	101
Omaha Graphics Inc	2752	1687
Omaha Hardwood Lumber Co	5031	125
Omaha Meat Processors Inc	2013	157
Omaha Printing Co	2752	275
Omaha Sprinkler Co	1711	278
Omaha Standard Inc	3713	32
Omaha Steaks International	5147	5
Omaha Steel Castings Co	3325	30
Omaha Wholesale Hardware Co	5072	123
Omaha World-Herald Co	2711	90
Omanhene Cocoa Bean Co	2066	29
Omar Coffee Co	2095	41
Omar Mc Call and Associates Inc	7379	1291
Omco Group Ltd	3559	557
OMD Corp	7372	2346
Omega 7 Inc	2721	450
Omega Advisors Inc	6282	324
Omega Alpha Plastics Co	3089	986
Omega Automation Inc	3549	74
Omega Cabinets Ltd	2434	6
Omega Circuit And Engineering Corp	3672	337
Omega Communications Inc	4841	162
Omega Consolidated Corp	3541	200
Omega Design Corp	3565	70
Omega Electronic Instrument Inc	7378	166
Omega Engineering Inc	3822	7
Omega Entertainment Ltd	7822	31
Omega Extruding Co	2673	9
Omega Flex Inc	3599	62
Omega Healthcare Investors Inc	6798	90
Omega Heater Company Inc	3567	37
Omega Laboratories Inc	3825	331
Omega Leads Inc	3679	638
Omega Legal Systems Inc	7372	2578
Omega Medical Imaging Inc	3844	29
Omega Optical Inc	3827	53
Omega Performance Corp	8742	199
Omega Plastic Corp	2673	3
Omega Plastics Inc	3089	1841
Omega Precision	3599	1742
Omega Printing Inc	2752	420
Omega Protein Corp	2077	2
Omega Qse Inc	1542	384
Omega Research and Development	3669	94
Omega Securities Inc	6211	399
Omega Technologies Inc	7373	668
Omega Tool Inc	3544	220
Omega World Travel Inc	4724	46
Omegatype Typography Inc	2791	28
O'Melveny and Myers LLP	8111	49
Omen Technology Inc	7372	5098
Omeros Corp	2834	398
OMG Americas Inc	2899	33
OMG Electronic Chemicals Inc	2899	74
Omg Midwest Inc	1611	85
Omi Crane Systems Inc	3536	29
Omico Inc	3089	469
Omicron Nanotechnology USA LLC	5049	61
Omitron Inc	8711	200
OMJC Signal Inc	5063	786
Omneon Video Networks Inc	7372	568
Omnesys Technologies Inc	7371	1593
Omnetics Connector Corp	3678	20
Omni Cable Corp	5063	425
Omni Care Health Plan Inc	6324	48
Omni Components Corp	3999	124
Omni Connection International Inc	3679	172
Omni Consulting Group Inc	7371	1281
Omni Control Technology Inc	3625	317
Omni Crown Trucking Inc	4213	618
Omni Custom Meats Inc	5147	105
Omni Data LLC	7379	1166

Company Name	SIC	Rank	Company Name	SIC	Rank	Company Name	SIC	Rank
Omni Data Systems Limited LLP	5045	552	On-Board Media Inc	2721	121	OnForce Solar Inc	1711	197
Omni Electrical and Constructors Inc	1731	1536	On-Board Services Inc	7363	328	Ongoing Care Solutions Inc	3842	245
Omni Environmental LLC	4953	114	Onbrand 24 Inc	7389	1490	ONGroup	7372	2399
Omni Flow Computers Inc	3571	196	Oncall Interactive Inc	7371	1213	Ongweoweh Corp	2448	19
Omni Group Inc	7372	2254	Oncogene Science of Siemens Health-care Diagnostics Inc	2835	61	Onicon Inc	3823	179
Omni Information Systems Inc	7373	807				Onion Mountain Technology Inc	7379	1550
Omni International Inc	2531	41	OncoGenex Pharmaceuticals Inc	2835	38	Onity	3499	26
Omni Materials Inc	1422	19	Oncologix Tech Inc	3841	421	Onix Networking Corp	5045	428
Omni Media Group	7311	347	Oncology Services International Inc	5047	106	ONIX Systems Inc	3674	96
Omni Optical Lab	6794	111	Oncontact Software Corp	7372	1355	Onkyo USA Corp	5064	87
Omni Rail Products Inc	3531	98	On-Cor Frozen Foods LLC	2038	53	Onlc Consulting	7379	719
Omni Seals Inc	3061	27	Oncothyreon Inc	2836	88	Online Commerce Group LLC	5021	173
Omni Services Of New York Inc	5084	482	OncoVista Innovative Therapies Inc	2834	481	Online Computers Inc	7372	3733
Omni Systems Inc	3825	353	Onctek LLC	7379	1451	On-Line Computing Inc	5045	898
Omni Telecommunications Inc (Greenville South Carolina)	4899	151	OnCURE Medical Corp	8741	167	On-Line Copy Corp	7334	81
			Onda Corp	3629	52	Online Electronics Inc	3672	315
Omni Tool Inc	3544	861	OnDemand Resources LLC	7361	220	On-Line Electronics Inc	5065	570
Omni Vision Inc	3663	219	On-Demand Software Consultants Inc	7379	161	Online Expansions	7371	1500
Omnia Italian Design Inc	5021	48	One Call Medical Inc	8099	20	Online Insight Inc	7372	2273
OmniAmerican Federal Credit Union	6061	24	One Call Now	4899	181	On-Line Instrument Systems Inc	7372	2187
Omnibus Advertising and Marketing	7319	45	ONE Color Communications LLC	2796	23	Online Marketing and Public Relations	7319	176
Omnica Corp	5047	150	One Communications Corp	4813	40	On-Line Power Corp	3613	16
Omnicare Clinical Research Inc	8731	24	One Equity Partners	6799	77	Online Resources Corp	7379	73
Omnicare Inc	5122	4	One Lambda Inc	2833	34	OnLine ToolWorks Corp	7372	3838
Omnicell Inc	3571	20	One Liberty Properties Inc	6798	161	Online Training Solutions Inc	2731	208
Omnicia Inc	7371	1555	One Mile Up Inc	7372	3935	Online Transport Inc	4213	1078
Omnicom Group Inc	7311	4	One National Bank	6021	138	OnlineMetalscom Inc	7389	1039
Omnicom Tower Ltd	4832	234	One Organization For The Needs For Elderly	8361	158	Ono Industries Inc	3089	1242
Omnicor	5063	218				OnPoint Community Credit Union	6062	9
OmniData Corp	7378	74	One Planet Corp	7389	976	onProject Inc	7371	1345
Omnidyne Corp	3571	242	One Point Inc	5943	18	OnRequest Images Inc	7335	1
Omnifics Inc	5021	72	One Point Solutions Inc	5734	118	Onset Computer Corp	3572	52
OmniGene Bioproducts Inc	8731	368	One Reel	7922	24	Onset Marketing LLC	8742	487
Omnigraphics Inc	2731	168	One Right Business Printing Inc	5112	57	OnSet Technology Inc	7372	2068
Omnikron Systems Inc	7372	1673	One Source Facility Services Inc	7349	188	onShore Inc	7336	21
Omnilife Health Care Systems Inc	8059	28	One Source Industries LLC	8742	305	On-Shore Technology Inc	3678	76
Omni-Means Ltd	8711	322	One Source Internatiol Maintenance Inc	7349	194	Onsite Energy Corp	8711	416
Omnimedia Group	2741	307				On-Site Financial Inc	8721	391
Omnion Inc	3826	153	One Source Management Inc	7349	1	On-Site Fuel Service Inc	5172	18
Omniphone Inc	3661	151	One Source Networks	7371	421	On-Site LaserMedic Corp	7629	26
Omniplex World Services Corp	7381	10	One Source Plus Inc	5961	172	On-Site Solutions Inc	7379	1205
Omnipod Inc	7372	396	One Source Printer Service and Supply	5045	319	On-Site Sourcing Inc	7334	5
Omnipro Systems Inc	5045	605	One Stop Brake Supply Santa Ana Inc	5013	186	OnStaff	7361	10
Omnipure Filter Company Inc	3589	57	One Stop Facilties Maintenance Corp	7349	95	Onstott and Associates	8721	245
Omnis Health LLC	5047	272	One Stop Media Shop	3577	165	Onstott Group	8748	362
Omnisil	3674	367	One Stop Permits Inc	7389	1135	Onstream Media Corp	7373	290
OmniSoft Inc	7373	901	One Stop Shop	5112	46	On-Target Supplies and Logistics Ltd	7389	300
OmniSource Corp	5093	5	One System Inc	7373	849	Ontarget Technologies LLC	3577	635
OmniSource Transport LLC	4213	583	One Technologies	7311	208	Ontario Corp	5045	1074
Omnisyn Corp	3699	292	One Touch Inc	4813	617	Ontario Die Company Of America	3544	37
Omnitec Precision Manufacturing Inc	3599	1328	One Touch Systems Inc	7372	1488	Ontario Plastics Inc	3082	21
Omni-Tech Corp	7371	1542	One Way Products Inc	5087	122	Ontario Recycling Inc	4953	172
Omnitech Robotics Inc	8731	374	One Way Service Corp	1799	146	Ontario Stone Corp	5032	27
Omnithruster Inc	3643	139	One Way Shopping LLC	5399	15	Ontario Systems Corp	7372	505
OmniTI Computer Consulting Inc	7371	388	One Wish LLC	5063	551	Ontel Products Corp	5023	13
OmniTranslations	7389	2379	One Workplace L Ferrari	5021	39	OneAero	7389	738
OmniTrax Inc	4011	19	OneAero	7389	738	Ontel Security Services Inc	7382	89
Omnitrend Software Inc	7372	4536	O'neal Electirc Co	1731	2359	Ontelaunee Orchards Inc	0175	1
Omnitrol Networks Inc	7373	587	O'Neal Melton and Sons Inc	4213	2824	OnTimeSuppliescom	5021	123
Omnitron Systems Technology Inc	3661	82	O'Neal Steel Inc	5051	11	Ontonagon County Telephone Co	4813	74
Omnitronics LLC	3357	74	O'neal's Feeders Supply Inc	5191	109	Onvia Inc	7389	468
Omnitronix Corp	3679	510	OneAmerica Financial Partners Inc	6712	33	Ony Inc	2834	340
OmniVision Technologies Inc	3674	40	OneCap	6162	130	Onyx Acceptance Corp	6141	39
Omni-X USA Inc	3545	129	OneCoast Network Corp	7389	211	Onyx Collection Inc	3088	7
Omniyig Inc	3679	543	OneCommand	7372	1034	Onyx Computing Inc	7371	842
Omnova Solutions Inc	3069	3	Onedia Ltd	3914	1	Onyx Graphics Inc	7372	154
OMNOVA Wallcovering Inc	2679	13	OnediscCom Inc	7371	1238	Onyx Industries Inc	3451	17
Omntec Manufacturing Inc	3625	180	Oneida Communications Inc	1731	662	Onyx Pharmaceuticals Inc	8731	38
Omron Electronics LLC	3674	67	Oneida Financial Corp	6036	42	Onyx Soft Inc	5045	644
Omron Healthcare Inc	5047	10	Oneida Foundries Inc	3321	70	Onyx Water Products Inc	3561	160
Omron Systems LLC	3571	51	Oneida Publications Inc	2711	617	OOC Inc	5812	408
Omsac Inc	3559	450	Oneida Research Services Inc	8734	155	Ookla	7379	693
Omtool Ltd	7372	1405	Oneida Savings Bank	6036	78	Oompa Enterprises Inc	5945	15
On A Roll Sales Inc	5812	307	Oneida Tool Corp	3599	964	OP Schuman and Sons Inc	3599	891
On Assignment Inc	7363	33	O'neil and Associates Inc	2741	73	Op Shop Inc	8331	144
On Call Communications Inc	3663	325	O'neil Awning And Tent Inc	7359	122	OPA Inc	7372	5144
On Center Software Inc	7371	992	O'neil Data Systems LLC	2754	7	Opamp Labs Inc	3651	226
On Demand Printing	2759	504	O'Neil Industries Inc	1541	36	Opc Packaging Corp	2672	75
On Demand Technologies Inc	7372	2067	O'neil Printing Inc	2752	340	Opco Inc	2821	179
On Letterhead	7389	2401	O'Neil Software Inc	7372	1459	Opco Laboratory Inc	3827	133
On Line Inc	1731	1422	O'Neill Automotive Plaza	5511	528	Opelco Inc	3861	132
ON Semiconductor Corp	3674	12	O'neill Industrial Corp	3625	296	Open Book Systems	7336	134
On Site Service	7379	1585	Oneill Industries Inc	2841	58	Open Computer Systems	7379	1668
On Smooth Inc	2821	93	O'neill Wetsuits LLC	3069	27	Open Door Center	8322	104
On Stage Entertainment Inc	7922	22	O'Neil's Markets Inc (St Louis Missouri)	5411	229	Open Door Networks Inc	7372	4045
On Target Marketing	5085	287	Onelife Digital Inc	7379	603	Open Doors Inc	8322	138
On Target Marketing LLC	7331	168	OneNeck IT Services Corp	7376	9	Open Field Software Inc	7372	5080
On Target Promotions	5137	34	Onenet USA Inc	8741	288	Open Link Financial Inc	7372	323
ON Technology Corp	7372	887	ONEOK Energy Resources Co	1381	55	Open Mind Technologies USA Inc	7372	2516
On The Border Corp	5812	192	ONEOK Inc	4923	3	Open Options Systems Inc	1731	1067
On The Go Magazines Inc	2721	406	ONEOK Leasing Co	6512	83	Open Software Technologies Inc	7372	923
On The Move Technology Inc	7373	1038	OneOk Partners LP	4922	5	Open Solutions FiTECH Systems	7372	1203
On the Scene Productions Inc	7812	128	Oneonta Trading Corp	5148	67	Open Solutions Inc	7372	209
On The Web Marketing Group Inc	5021	135	OnePath Networks Inc	3661	84	Open Systems Inc (Shakopee Minnesota)	7372	1117
On Time Delivery Inc	4213	531	Onesolution Light And Control	3648	78			
On Time Electric and Air	1711	240	OneSource Inc	2759	314	Open Systems Integrators Inc	7371	1049
On Time Promotions Inc	3993	152	OneSource Information Services Inc	7375	69	Open Systems International Inc	7371	273
On Time Systems Inc	7371	1316	OneSource Software Solutions	7372	995	Open Systems Management Inc	7372	1926
On2 Technologies Inc	7373	300	OnesourceCom Inc	7389	2169	Open Systems of Cleveland Inc	5045	344
Onamac Industries Inc	3599	186	Onestop Wireless Inc	4813	570	Open Systems Technologies Inc	1731	130
Onancock Building Supply Inc	5211	245	OneUnited Bank	6021	162	Open Terra Inc	3663	382
Onanon Inc	3672	229	OneWayFurniturecom	5712	80	Open Text Digital Media Group	7372	485
Onate Feed Company LLC	5191	152	OneWest Bank FSB	6035	8	Open Window	7372	4860
ONB Finance Inc	6099	13	One-Write Co	2752	446	OpenBase International Ltd	7372	3005

Company Name	SIC	Rank
OrderMotion Inc	7371	320
Ordnance Unlimited Inc	5065	579
Ore Pharmaceutical Holdings Inc	2835	78
Ore-Cal Corp	5146	5
Oreck Corp	3589	11
Oreco Duct Systems Inc	3444	103
Oregon Aero Inc	3469	188
Oregon Asphaltic Paving Co	2951	41
Oregon Blue Print Co	2759	501
Oregon Cabaret Theatre Inc	7922	98
Oregon Cherry Growers Inc	2033	24
Oregon Credit Systems Inc	7322	175
Oregon Cutting Systems Group	3423	4
Oregon Dental Service Inc	6324	40
Oregon Electro-Mec Inc	3823	479
Oregon Entertainment Corp	7841	6
Oregon Freeze Dry Inc	2013	33
Oregon Fruit Products Co	2037	35
Oregon Glass Co	3231	34
Oregon Industrial Repair Inc	3599	1285
Oregon Iron Works Inc	3441	26
Oregon Lox Co	2091	12
Oregon Mint Co	2131	6
Oregon Newspaper Publishers Association Inc	7313	13
Oregon Pacific Bancorp	6021	322
Oregon Pacific Banking Co	6022	713
Oregon Potato Co	2034	10
Oregon Precision Industries Inc	3089	911
Oregon Scientific Inc	5064	100
Oregon Select Inc	5084	470
Oregon Steel Mills Inc	3312	9
Oregon Transfer Co	4213	1172
Oregonian Publishing Company LLC	2711	913
O'Reilly and Associates Inc	2731	78
O'Reilly Automotive Inc	5531	2
O'Reilly Ozark Automotive	5013	27
Ore-Lube Corp	2992	61
Oren Elliott Products Inc	3675	27
Orena Development Corp	7371	1490
Orepac Holding Co	6719	142
Orevox USA Corp	5065	539
Orexigen Therapeutics Inc	2834	419
Orf Construction Inc	1623	845
Orffeo Printing Company Inc	2759	445
Orfid Corp	3825	210
Orfila Vineyards Inc	2084	102
Orgain Bell and Tucker LLP	8111	394
Orgain Building Supply Co	5211	104
Organic Dyestuffs Corp	8743	118
Organic Inc	7371	170
Organic People Inc	7379	940
Organic to Go Food Corp	5812	363
Organicare Inc	7389	1622
Organization Resources Counselors Inc	8742	440
Organogenesis Inc	3841	191
Organon Pharmaceuticals USA Inc	2834	105
Orgill Inc	5072	4
ORI Services Corp	7376	16
Orian Rugs Inc	2273	26
Orica USA Inc	2892	1
Orick Tool And Die Inc	3469	240
O'Rielly Chevrolet Inc	5511	403
Orient Bancorp	6712	499
Orient Lines	4481	4
Orient Machining and Welding Inc	3599	433
Orient Overseas Container Line USA Inc	4412	10
Orient Travel Inc	4724	149
Oriental Financial Group Inc	6022	26
Oriental Financial Services Corp	6282	25
Oriental Lumber Land Inc	5031	434
Oriental Motor U S A Corp	5063	91
Origen Financial Inc	6141	34
Origen Financial LLC	6141	28
Original Bradford Soap Works Inc	2841	14
Original California Magic Car Duster Co	3714	343
Original Greek Specialties Inc	2013	221
Original Herkimer County Cheese Company Inc	2022	53
Original Impressions LLC	2752	180
Original Pete's Pizza Pasta Grill Inc	5812	342
Original Sixteen to One Mine Inc	1041	23
Original Smith Printing Inc	2752	121
Original Sound Records Company Inc	3652	32
Originalpower Inc	3674	353
OriginLab Corp	7372	1697
Origio Inc	5047	135
O-Rings Inc	5085	457
Orion America Inc	5064	39
Orion Associates Inc	1629	96
Orion Behavioral Healthcare Services	7372	3404
Orion Construction Company Inc	1623	327
Orion Corp	3366	2
Orion Energy Services Inc	3629	17
Orion Engineering and Service Inc	5065	378
Orion Group Software Engineers Inc	7371	920
Orion HealthCorp Inc	8011	86
Orion Industries	3444	290
Orion Integration Group	1731	707
Orion International Technologies Inc	8731	131
ORION Law Management Systems Inc	7372	2430

Company Name	SIC	Rank
Orion Machinery Company Ltd	3563	53
Orion Marine Group	1629	12
Orion Marketing Group Inc	7389	1096
Orion Mobility Solutions LLC	7372	1620
Orion Pacific Inc	2671	38
Orion Payment Systems Inc	7389	2034
Orion Press Inc	2752	813
Orion Publishing Co	2731	291
Orion Real Estate Services Inc	6531	146
Orion Safety Products Corp	2899	99
Orion South Inc	5084	135
Orion Systems Inc	3669	201
Orion Tech	3663	323
Orion Tool Die and Machine Co	3599	1354
Orionsoft	7371	1853
Oritani Financial Corp	6022	72
Orix USA Corp	6282	647
Orizon Industries Inc	3441	33
Orkin Inc	7342	2
Orlandi Gear Company Inc	3568	72
Orlandi Inc	3999	73
Orlando Auto Auction Inc	5012	112
Orlando Baking Co	2051	49
Orlando Diaz-Azcuy Designs Inc	7389	854
Orlando Dodge Inc	5511	1069
Orlando Health	8062	2
Orlando Jai Alai	7999	58
Orlando Mitts Moore and Company	8721	184
Orlando Predators Entertainment Inc	7941	34
Orlando Products Inc	3086	81
Orlando Regional Healthcare System Inc	8062	47
Orlando Resort Development Group Inc	7389	2096
Orlando Rock and Sealing Corp	1799	39
Orlando Sentinel Communications Co	2711	23
Orlando Spring Corp	3495	24
Orlando Waste Paper Company Inc	7359	87
Orleans Capital Management Corp	6282	439
Orleans Furniture Inc	2511	51
Orleans Homebuilders Inc	1531	28
Orlotronics Corp	3452	83
Orly International Inc	2844	56
Ormandy Inc	7372	3546
Orman's Welding and Fab Inc	1799	144
Ormat Technologies Inc	4911	90
Ormco Corp	3843	11
Ormec Systems Corp	3672	249
Ormet Corp	3334	9
Ormsby Trucking Inc	4213	1154
Ormsby's Computer Store Inc	5734	430
Ornamental Products Inc	2431	97
Ornelas Enterprises Inc	3679	463
ORODAY Inc	5045	185
Orograin Bakeries Manufacturing Inc	2051	14
Orono Financial Inc	6712	721
O'rourke and Sons Inc	5051	358
O'Rourke Brothers Incorporated of Atlanta	5021	138
Oroville Hospital	8062	165
Orphagen Pharmaceuticals	8731	308
Orpine Inc	7379	682
Orr Cadillac-Pontiac Inc	5511	1170
ORR Chevrolet Searcy	5511	809
Orr Felt Co	2231	10
Orr Safety Corp	5099	9
Orrell's Food Service Inc	5141	160
Orrick Herrington and Sutcliffe LLP	8111	170
Orrstown Bank	6022	109
Orrstown Financial Services Inc	6022	115
Orscheln Products LLC	3496	48
Orsus Solutions	7371	726
Orsus Solutions Ltd	7372	793
ORSYP Software Inc	7372	1978
Ort Tool and Die Corp	8711	335
Ortco Inc	3533	104
Ortec Inc	2869	59
Ortec International USA Inc	7371	157
Ortek Data Systems Inc	3571	241
Ortho Arch Co	3843	85
Ortho Arch Laboratory Inc	3843	71
Ortho Clinical Diagnostics (Raritan New Jersey)	3845	5
Ortho Computer Systems Inc	7372	1340
Ortho Development Corp	3842	113
Ortho Rite Inc	3842	239
Orthodontic Supply Corporation and Research Inc	3843	87
Orthodontic Technologies Inc	3843	69
Orthofix Inc	7352	3
Orthogen Corp	3843	86
Orthometrix Inc	3826	127
Orthopedic Service Company Of Raleigh Inc	5999	238
Orthpli Corp	3843	59
Orthoscan Inc	3844	24
OrthoSynetics Inc	8021	3
Ortho-Tex Inc	5047	71
Orthotic And Prosthetic Specialties Inc	3842	310
Orthotic and Prosthetic Lab Inc	3842	158
Ortloff Engineers Ltd	3491	24
Ortronics Inc	3357	36
Orval Kent Food	2099	38
O'ryan Group Inc	7389	621

Company Name	SIC	Rank
O'ryan Industries Inc	3646	96
Orycon Control Technology Inc	3544	620
Os Employee Leasing Services Inc	7363	354
OS Hill and Company Inc	5012	62
Os Hood County News Inc	2711	831
O-S Inc	3599	402
Os Stephenson Millwork Company Inc	2431	83
OS Walker Company Inc	3545	50
Osage Bancshares Inc	6035	197
Osage Cooperative Elevator	5153	57
Osage Valley Electric Coop	4911	311
Osam Document Solutions Inc	5044	91
Osborn and Barr Communications	7311	136
Osborn Brothers Inc	5141	141
Osborn Engineering Co	8711	412
Osborn Jim Reproductions Inc	7336	277
Osborn Maledon PA	8111	520
Osborn Products Inc	3545	254
Osborn Transportation Inc	4213	3127
Osborne Brothers LLC	1731	2363
Osborne Construction Co	1542	79
Osborne Distributing Company Inc	5191	43
Osborne Industries Inc	3523	55
Osborne Transformer Corp	3612	110
Osborne-McCann Cadillac Inc	5511	973
Oscar and Associates Inc	7336	47
Oscar De La Renta LLC	2335	6
Oscar J Boldt Construction Div	1541	35
Oscar L Foster Inc	5084	835
Oscar Mayer Foods Corp	2013	8
Oscar Renda Contracting Inc	1623	28
Oscar T Smith Co	2752	1106
Oscar Wilson Engines and Parts Inc	5084	193
Oscarware Inc	3631	15
Osco Inc	5084	549
Osco Industries Inc	3321	20
Oscoda Plastics Inc	3089	563
Oscor Inc	3841	143
Osda Contract Services Inc	3679	524
OSE USA Inc	3674	348
Osec Robotics Inc	3571	252
Osemi Inc	3674	475
Oser Press Inc	2752	1479
Osf International Inc	5812	203
OSG America LP	4424	6
Osg Tap and Die Inc	5084	225
Osgood Industries Inc	3565	53
Osha Industrial Products Inc	5085	243
Oshkosh Architectural Door Co	2431	86
OshKosh B'Gosh Inc	2369	2
OshKosh B'Gosh Retail Inc	5641	3
Oshkosh Corp	3711	8
Oshkosh FeedYard Corp	0211	9
OSI Collection Services Inc	7322	11
OSI Financial Technologies	7372	79
OSI Group	6719	13
OSI Optoelectronics	3674	278
OSI Pharmaceuticals Inc	2835	5
OSI Restaurant Partners LLC	5812	15
OSI Systems Inc	3674	48
Osiris Therapeutics Inc	8731	104
Oskaloosa Food Products Corp	2015	55
Oskaloosa Manufacturing Inc	3599	1269
OSL Holdings Inc	7819	98
Osmose Inc	2491	14
Osmosis Partners Ltd	7991	18
Osmosis Technology Inc	3589	223
Osp Sling Inc	2399	28
Ospey The SAP Division of NIIT Technologies	8748	117
Osprey Technologies Inc	3661	47
Osram Sylvania Inc	3645	3
OSS Corp	7371	1485
OSS Nokalva Inc	7372	1568
Ossid LLC	3565	63
Ossur Americas Inc	3842	78
Ost Inc	7371	299
OST Trucking Company Inc	4213	783
O'steen Meat Specialties Inc	5147	65
Osteen Publishing Co	2711	337
Osteometer MediTech Inc	3841	54
Oster and Associates Inc	7311	923
Oster Sand And Gravel Inc	1442	80
Osterkamp Trucking Inc	4213	820
Ostex International Inc	2835	57
Ostrander Implement and Farm Center Inc	5063	1100
Ostrem Tool Company Inc	3545	173
Ostroff Electrical Contractors Inc	1731	590
Ostrowski and Co	6211	348
Osu Surgery LLC	8721	261
O-Sun Company Inc	7359	277
Oswego Industries Inc	8331	76
OT Hall And Sons Inc	5063	770
OT Printing Co	2752	236
O'tasty Foods Inc	2038	52
Otb Machinery Inc	3553	62
Otc Holdings Corp	5945	8
Otec Inc	3561	67
Oteco Inc	3561	73
Otek Corp	3625	233
Otelco Inc	4812	25
Oteri's Italian Pastries Co	2051	114
Otey White and Associates	7311	1019

Company Name	SIC	Rank
Othy Inc	3841	69
Oticon Inc	3842	114
Otis Elevator Co	3534	2
Otis Warren Real Estate Services Inc	6531	428
Otix Global Inc	3842	54
Otsego County Chapter Association For Retarded Children	8322	44
Otsuka America Pharmaceutical Inc	8733	15
Ott Communications Inc	7311	699
Ott Inc	5072	119
Ott Packagings Inc	2657	41
Ottawa Cooperative Association Inc	5191	115
Ottawa Dental Labs Inc	8072	7
Ottawa Publishing Company Inc	2711	377
Ottawa Savings Bancorp Inc	6035	182
Otten Johnson Robinson Neff and Ragonetti	8111	441
Ottenweller Company Inc	3443	103
Otter Computer Inc	5045	207
Otter Creek Brewing Inc	2082	83
Otter Products LLC	3577	159
Otter Tail Corp	4911	103
Otter Tail Energy Services Company Inc	4924	13
Otterbein's Bakery	2051	137
OtterBox	3999	23
OtterStream Multimedia Inc	2741	247
Otto Baum Company Inc	1741	3
Otto Electric Inc	1731	1087
Otto Enviornmental Systems Az LLC	3089	1341
Otto Industries North America Inc	3537	30
Otto Printing And Entertainment Graphics	2752	1643
Otto/Walker Architects Inc	8712	324
Ottumwa Courier	2711	190
Ottumwa Media Holding LLC	4833	162
Ouachita Coca-Cola Bottling Co	2086	34
Ouachita Electric Cooperative Corp	4911	424
Ouachita Machine Works Inc	3554	43
Ouellette Machinery Systems Inc	3565	135
Ounce of Prevention Systems	7379	1483
Our Lady Bellefonte Hospital Inc	8062	138
Our Lady Of Lourdes Health Care Services Inc	8741	89
Our Lady Of Victory Homes Of Charity Inc	8399	21
Our365	7221	9
Ourisman Chevrolet Company Inc	5511	49
OurPet's Co	3089	452
Ourtech Solutions Inc	7373	1028
Out of Your Mindand Into the Marketplace	7372	4728
Out Today	5074	221
Outdoor Adventure River Specialists Inc	4725	14
Outdoor Adventures Unlimited Inc	5941	37
Outdoor Channel Holdings Inc	4833	97
Outdoor Channel Inc	4841	62
Outdoor Connection Inc	3949	146
Outdoor Outfitters of Wisconsin Inc	5065	690
Outdoor Products Inc	5091	135
Outdoor Recreation Group Inc	2393	8
Outdoor Recreation Group Incorporated Outdoor Products	2393	2
Outdoor Research Inc	2393	4
Outdoor Resorts of America Inc	6515	2
Outdoor Sports Headquarters Inc	5091	11
Outdoor Venture Corp	2394	7
Outer Edge Software	2731	209
OuterLink Corp	4899	72
Outernet Inc	4813	365
Outhink Inc	7372	4951
Outlaw Trucking and Logistics Inc	4213	3143
Outlook Computing Inc	7372	4862
Outlook Group Corp	2759	26
Outlook Label Systems Inc	3086	13
Outlook Technologies Inc	7372	2909
Outokumpu Stainless Pipe Inc	3317	28
Output Exploration LLC	1311	150
Output Technology	3669	134
Outrigger Enterprises Inc	7011	64
Outrigger Lodging Services	7011	173
Outside Rms Inc	5084	814
Outside The Box Interactive LLC	2741	393
Outsource Manufacturing Inc	3679	225
Outsource Partners International Inc	7363	30
Outsource Technologies Inc	3089	1705
Outsourcing Solutions Inc	8721	98
Outstart Inc	7372	159
Outten Chevrolet Inc	5511	819
Outwater Plastics Inc	5072	53
Ouzerne County Correctional Facility	8744	24
Ovadia Corp	3089	1166
Ovako North America Inc	3312	56
Ovation Health and Life Services Inc	6411	289
Ovation Instore	3993	28
Ovation Instruments	3931	28
Ovation Marketing Inc	7311	211
Ovation Travel	4724	53
Ovation Travel Group (Harrison New York)	4724	36
Oven Fresh Baking Company Inc	2051	88
Oven Industries Inc	3822	60
Over and Back Inc	5023	70
Over And Under General Contractors Inc	1623	535
Over the Road Trucking Inc	4213	2171
Overbeck Machine	3599	2136
Overbilt Trailer Co	3441	265
Overbuilt Paving and Mining Inc	3531	241
OverByte Computer Systems	7379	1235
Overcoffee Productions LLC	7374	348
OverDrive Inc	7372	769
Overhead Conveyor Co	3535	26
Overhead Door Company Of Beaumont Inc	5031	298
Overhead Door Company Of Jacksonville	5031	365
Overhead Door Company Of Madison Inc	5031	305
Overhead Door Company Of Roswell Inc	5031	424
Overhead Door Corp	3442	1
Overhead Material Handling Inc	3536	38
Overhill Farms Inc	2038	8
Overland Bancorp Inc	6712	575
Overland Park Jeep Inc	5511	330
Overland Services Inc	4213	2745
Overland Storage Inc	3577	130
Overland Tank Inc	3537	76
Overlook Vineyards LLC	2084	63
Overly Manufacturing Co	3446	46
Overman Mark and Richard Bean	5046	375
Overnite Software Inc	7372	3087
Overpeck Gas Co	5984	29
Oversea Casing Company LLC	2013	189
Overseas Connection Inc	5731	38
Overseas Freight Inc	4213	2374
Overseas Military Sales Corp Ltd	5511	1110
Overseas Packing LLC	2449	4
Overseas Shipholding Group Inc	4412	8
Overseenet	7372	196
Overseer Inc	7379	1654
Overstockcom Inc	7389	38
Overt Press Inc	2759	306
Overton and Sons Tool and Die Co	3599	12
Overton Gear and Tool Corp	3566	16
Overtone Inc	7379	301
Overture Networks Inc	7379	220
Overture Technologies Inc	7379	816
Overwatch Systems Ltd	7371	64
Ovid Healthcare Center	8051	39
Ovidon Manufacturing LLC	3544	224
OvisLink Technologies Corp	7379	1648
Ovivo USA LLC	3589	131
Ovo Studios LLC	7371	1599
Owen and Thorp Inc	8721	274
Owen Community Bank SB	6036	94
Owen Electric Inc	1731	2368
Owen G Dunn Company Inc	2752	75
Owen Industries Inc	3441	24
Owen Manufacturing Inc	2431	113
Owen Mumford USA Inc	3826	31
Owen Oil Tools Inc	3533	18
Owen Trucking LLC	4213	1064
Owen-Ames-Kimball Co	1542	91
Owens and Dove Inc	1623	232
Owens and Hurst Lumber Co	2421	123
Owens and Minor Inc	5047	1
Owens Audio Video Design Inc	3651	174
Owen's CFS Inc	4213	2522
Owens Companies Inc	1711	71
Owens Corning	3296	1
Owens Corning Fabricating Solutions	3444	5
Owens Corning Solutions Group	2221	12
Owens Design Inc	3599	698
Owens Industries Inc	3599	641
Owens Precision Inc	3599	575
Owens Services Corp	1711	174
Owens Steel and Machine Works Inc	3599	2019
Owensboro Brick and Tile Co	3255	14
Owensboro Federal Credit Union	6061	122
Owensboro Grain Co	2075	5
Owensboro Messenger-Inquirer Inc	2711	278
Owens-Illinois Inc	3221	1
Owera Inc	7373	838
OWI Inc	5064	176
Owl Cos	8742	74
Owl Wire Logistics Inc	4213	2578
Ownbey Enterprises Inc	5172	48
Owners' Resorts And Exchange Inc	6531	395
Owosso Automation Inc	3545	417
Owosso Graphic Arts Inc	2796	30
OWP/P	8712	10
Owt Industries Inc	5251	31
Owyhee Construction Inc	1623	504
Ox Bodies Inc	3713	35
Oxarc Inc	2813	8
Oxberry LLC	3861	129
Oxbo International Corp	3523	52
Oxbow Corp	5171	3
Oxbow Machine Products Inc	3544	110
Oxbridge Communications Inc	2741	492
Oxegen Generating Systems Intl	3569	158
Oxendine Publishing Inc	2721	434
Oxford Alarm And Communications	1731	2588
Oxford Alfalfa Inc	2048	147
Oxford Bank and Trust (Addison Illinois)	6022	210
Oxford Bank Corp	6036	66
Oxford Consulting Group Inc	7379	22
Oxford Eagle Inc	2711	785
Oxford Financial Corp	6712	448
Oxford General Industries Inc	3499	129
Oxford Health Plans LLC	6324	19
Oxford Hills Typesetting	2791	53
Oxford Industries Inc	2311	2
Oxford Industries Of Connecticut Inc	2821	165
Oxford Life Insurance Co	6311	172
Oxford Management Services	7299	11
Oxford Mining Company Inc	1221	28
Oxford Obg-Waterton Skokie Hotel Property Co	7389	1193
Oxford Realty Services Corp	6282	33
Oxford Resource Partners LP	1221	14
Oxford Semiconductor Ltd	3674	146
Oxford University Press Electronic Publishing Div	2741	31
Oxford University Press Inc	2731	53
Oxford Wire and Cable Services Inc	3679	461
OXiGENE Inc	2836	97
OXIS International Inc	8731	429
Oxlife Of Nc LLC	3842	303
Oxmoor Corporation LLC	3651	189
Oxmoor House Inc	2731	111
Oxnard Lemon Co	0723	13
Oxxford Clothes Xx Inc	2325	10
Oxxford Information Technologies Ltd	6282	376
Oxy-Dry Corp	3563	13
Oxygen Electronics LLC	5065	493
Oxymoron Unlimited	7371	1915
Oxysense Inc	3823	425
Oyo Corporation USA	3829	29
OYO Geospace Corp	3829	16
OYO Instruments LP	3825	11
Oz Arc/Gas Equipment and Supply Inc	5084	466
Oz Architecture	8712	112
O-Z/GEDNEY	3644	4
Oz Technology Inc	3585	253
Ozanne Construction Company Inc	1541	124
Ozark Delight Candy Co	2064	90
Ozark Empire Distributors Inc	2051	83
Ozark Mailing Service Inc	7331	195
Ozark Motor Lines Inc	4213	222
Ozark Mountain Bank	6022	593
Ozark Steel Fabricators Inc	3441	162
Ozarka Spring Water Co	2086	35
Ozarks Coca-Cola/Dr Pepper Bottling Co	2086	129
Ozarks Electric Cooperative Corp	4911	186
Ozarks Electric Inc	1731	2110
Ozarks Methodist Manor	8741	250
Ozarks Optical Laboratories Inc	3851	84
Ozburn-Hessey Transportation LLC	4213	1351
Ozeki Sake U S A Inc	2084	94
Ozinga Illinois RMC Inc	3273	46
Ozone Company Inc	3559	571
Ozone Inc	7372	2200
Ozonia North America Inc	3559	167
Ozotech Inc	3589	252
Oztec Business Machines Inc	3589	269
Oztec Industries Inc	3531	157
Ozzie's Pipeline Padder Inc	3569	73
P 2 P Technologies Inc	1731	2391
P/A Industries Inc	3549	23
P and A Administrative Services	7363	244
P and B Capital Group LLC	7322	78
P And B Services Inc	3625	269
P and B Transportation Inc	4213	981
P and C Construction Co	1541	280
P and C Insurance Systems Inc	7372	2885
P and C Trucking Enterprises Inc	4213	1402
P and D Curtis Enterprises Inc	4213	1916
P and E Construction Inc	1623	671
P and E Machine Company Inc	3541	253
P and E Rubber Processing Inc	3069	266
P and F Industries Inc	3546	7
P and F Machine	3599	2408
P and F Machining Inc	3568	69
P and G Auto Inc	5013	314
P and G Steel Products Company Inc	3469	215
P and G Trading Company Inc	5146	56
P And H Auto Electric Inc	7538	21
P and H Graphic Communications Inc	2752	1108
P and H LP	5992	5
P and H Manufacturing Co	3599	99
P and H Mining Equipment Inc	3532	8
P and H Transportation Inc	4213	2547
P and I Supply Co	5085	108
P and J Computers Inc	7378	84
P and J Machining Inc	3728	137
P and K Condo Management Inc	0782	13
P and K Steel Service Inc	5051	403
P and L Development Of New York Corp	7389	714
P and L Machine Company Inc	3599	1771
P and M Communications Contractors Inc	1629	103
P and M Exhaust Systems Warehouse Inc	5013	328
P and M Technical Sales Co	3089	1703

Company Name	SIC	Rank
P and N Holdings Inc	2711	296
P and N Machine Company Inc	3599	481
P and N Packing Inc	5147	125
P and N Technologies	7373	527
P and P Agrilabor	7361	269
P and P Industries Inc	3089	988
P and P Manufacturing Company Inc	3545	366
P and P Press Inc	2752	713
P and R Associates International	7311	771
P and R Industries Inc	3544	346
P and R Specialty Inc	2499	54
P and S Diesel Service Inc	3519	28
P and S Electric Supply Company Inc	5063	635
P and S Enterprises Inc	4213	1446
P and S Machining And Fabrication Inc	7692	30
P and S Molded Products Inc	3089	1613
P and S Products Inc	3089	830
P and S Ravioli Co	5499	20
P and T Metals Inc	5093	210
P and T Technologies	7379	1540
P and W Quality Machines Inc	3599	529
P D Circuits Inc	5065	151
P D Q Tooling Inc	3544	889
P E Barnes and Sons Ltd	2421	124
P F Laboratories Inc	2834	203
P Feiner and Sons Inc	3564	106
P Flanigan And Sons Inc	1611	76
P G Molinari and Sons Inc	2013	207
P Gioioso and Sons Inc	1623	67
P H I Group Inc	2759	244
P J Ellis Electric Company Inc	1731	1569
P Judge and Sons Inc	4213	1819
P K Guido Inc	1442	66
P Kaufman Inc	5131	7
P Kay Metal Inc	5051	406
P Kay Metal Supply	3356	30
P L Custom Body And Equipment Company Inc	7359	68
P O Mcintire Co	3469	307
P R Machine Works Inc	3599	659
P/R Mortgage and Investment Corp	6163	34
P S Greetings Inc	2771	13
P SC Industrial Outsourcing Inc	1731	401
P T M Corp	3714	321
P Tool and Die Company Inc	3544	498
P Value Communications LLC	4899	169
P1 Group Inc	1711	23
P2 Electric Inc	1731	2038
P2 Energy Solutions Inc	7372	41
P22 Type Foundry Inc	7372	5117
P3S Corp	8742	301
P4 Corp	5087	10
P4c Global Inc	5065	381
PA C Publishing Inc	2721	334
PA Hicks and Sons Inc	5031	330
PA Hutchison Co	2732	31
PA J Inc	5094	31
PA Landers Inc	1611	100
PA Menard Inc	5812	317
PAA Natural Gas Storage LLC	1311	65
Paarlo Plastics Inc	3089	866
Paasche Airbrush Co	3952	11
PAB Bankshares Inc	6712	260
PAB Moving and Storage Co	4213	3114
Pabco Roofing Products	2952	14
Pabst Enterprises Equipment Co	3441	272
Pabst Farms	0723	28
PABTEX GP LLC	4226	10
Pac Group	7389	2058
PAC Software Inc	7372	3936
Pac Strapping Products Inc	3089	1114
PACA Body Armor Inc	3842	121
PACA Foods LLC	2045	14
Pacal LLC	3531	57
PACCAR Financial Services Corp	6153	30
PACCAR Inc	3711	7
PACCAR Inc Parts Div	5013	34
Paccomm Packet Radio Systems Inc	3661	235
Pace Advertising	7311	271
Pace American Enterprises Inc	3715	7
Pace and Partners Inc	8742	636
PACE Applied Technology Inc	7372	3169
Pace Communications Inc	2721	166
Pace Dairy Foods Co	2022	91
Pace Deis Corp	7336	144
Pace Electric Inc	1731	1811
PACE Electrical Construction Inc	1731	704
Pace Inc	3699	93
Pace Industries Inc	3585	14
Pace International LLC	2875	10
Pace Learning Systems Inc	2731	325
Pace Machine and Tool Inc	3544	814
Pace Machine Tool Inc	3599	1836
Pace Micro Technology	3577	53
Pace Packaging Corp	3565	102
Pace Polyethylene Manufacturing Company Inc	3081	96
Pace Products Inc (Overland Park Kansas)	2899	186
Pace Punches Inc	3544	234
PACE Resources Inc	8711	133
Pace Scientific Inc	3651	185
Pace Software Systems Inc	7372	4937
Pace Tech Inc	3841	249
Pace Window And Door Corp	3089	909
Pacemaker Press Pp and S Inc	2752	653
Pacemaker Steel And Piping Company Inc	5085	140
Pacer Corp	8062	237
Pacer Furniture Manufacturing Inc	2512	83
Pacer International Inc	4731	12
Pacer Stacktrain	4213	78
Pacesetter Electronics Inc	3651	197
Pacesetter Steel Service Inc	5051	45
PaceWorks Inc	7372	4134
Pacfas	5072	108
Pacific Aerospace and Electronics Inc	3679	12
Pacific Air Switch Corp	3613	55
Pacific Alliance Bank	6022	655
Pacific Allied Products Ltd	3086	77
Pacific American Commercial Co	5082	92
Pacific Bay Homes LLC	1521	32
Pacific Beverage Company Inc	5181	46
Pacific Biomarkers Inc	8731	209
Pacific Biosciences Inc	8731	52
Pacific Biosciences of California Inc	3826	34
Pacific Blue Micro Inc	7373	287
Pacific Building Services Inc	7349	144
Pacific Bulk Transportation Co	4213	2265
Pacific Capital Bancorp	6712	104
Pacific Capital Bank NA	6021	34
Pacific Century Group Inc	7373	915
Pacific City Bank	6022	832
Pacific Clay Products Inc	3259	1
Pacific Cleaning Service Inc	7349	342
Pacific Coast Air Tool and Supply Inc	3599	2382
Pacific Coast Bankers Bancshares	6712	162
Pacific Coast Bankers Bank	6022	103
Pacific Coast Building Products Inc	5031	12
Pacific Coast Electric	1731	2399
Pacific Coast Feather Co	2392	10
Pacific Coast Installations Inc	1799	103
Pacific Coast National Bancorp	6021	337
Pacific Coast Optics	3827	129
Pacific Coast Recycling LLC	5093	28
Pacific Coast Restaurants Inc	5812	137
Pacific Coast Seafoods Co	2092	12
Pacific Coast Steel	1541	57
Pacific Codeworks Inc	7372	3374
Pacific Color Inc	7384	39
Pacific Columns Inc	3999	54
Pacific Commerce Bank NA	6021	302
Pacific Compensation Insurance Co	6331	151
Pacific Consolidated Industries LLC	3569	89
Pacific Construction Services Inc	1542	424
Pacific Continental Bank	6022	97
Pacific Continental Corp	6712	270
Pacific Conveyor Systems Inc	3535	179
Pacific Cookie Company Inc	5461	36
Pacific Cornetta Inc	5088	41
Pacific Corporate Group Inc	6282	384
Pacific Credit Exchange	7322	137
Pacific Crest Securities Inc	6211	287
Pacific Crest Software Inc	2731	367
Pacific Cycle Inc	3751	9
Pacific Data Management Inc	7371	1333
Pacific Dental Services Inc	7389	217
Pacific Design and Construction Corp	1731	463
Pacific Design Center LLC	5021	50
Pacific Dimensions Inc	7389	1667
Pacific Domes Inc	1542	444
Pacific Dunlop Investments (USA) Inc	3069	12
Pacific Eagle USA Inc	3069	213
Pacific Echo Inc	5085	54
Pacific Electronic Enterprises Inc	7629	47
Pacific Electronic International Corp	3679	691
Pacific Embroidery LLC	7389	1945
Pacific Energy Construction Corp	1731	2116
Pacific Enterprises Ltd	4213	2565
Pacific Ethanol Inc	2899	30
Pacific Event Productions Inc	7389	308
Pacific Exchange Parts Rebuilders Inc	3694	50
Pacific Facility Service Inc	7349	242
Pacific Fibre Products Inc	2421	45
Pacific Film Laboratories	7819	17
Pacific Financial Corp	6712	419
Pacific Fixture Company Inc	2541	6
Pacific Fluid Systems LLC	5084	536
Pacific Forge Inc	3462	19
Pacific Gas and Electric Co	4931	22
Pacific Grain Products Intl	2044	7
Pacific Grip and Lighting Inc	7819	90
Pacific Growth Equities Inc	6211	329
Pacific Guardian Life Insurance Company Ltd	6311	258
Pacific Health Alliance	6324	124
Pacific Home Products Inc	2541	67
Pacific Image Electronics Inc	3577	372
Pacific Industries Inc	3081	47
Pacific Instruments Inc	3825	227
Pacific Insulation Co	5033	41
Pacific International Equities Inc	6552	201
Pacific International Rice Mills Inc	2044	4
Pacific Internet	7375	52
Pacific Investment Management Co	6282	60
Pacific Jobbers Warehouse Inc	5013	213
Pacific Lamp and Supply Co	5063	384
Pacific Life Insurance Co	6311	13
Pacific Lighting and Standards Co	3646	68
Pacific Lighting Sales Inc	3648	92
Pacific Macadamia Nuts Corp	3523	221
Pacific Machinery and Tool Steel Co	5051	104
Pacific Maintenance Co	7349	74
Pacific Management Inc	8741	279
Pacific Manufacturing Ohio Inc	3714	204
Pacific Marine and Supply Co	3731	46
Pacific Market Research	8732	103
Pacific Mat and Commercial Flooring LLC	5023	120
Pacific Materials Handling Solutions Inc	5012	69
Pacific Mdf Products Inc	2431	88
Pacific Mechanical Supply	5085	191
Pacific Media Associates	8732	129
Pacific Media Center Inc	7812	305
Pacific Medical Center Clinic	8011	18
Pacific Medical Clinics	6324	83
Pacific Medical Inc	7389	569
Pacific Mercantile Bancorp	6712	314
Pacific Molding Inc	3069	242
Pacific Multiforms Company Inc	2761	73
Pacific Mutual Door Co	5031	40
Pacific National Auto Parts Inc	5013	341
Pacific Northwest Baking Co	2051	110
Pacific Northwest Ballet Foundation	7922	30
Pacific Northwest Federal Credit Union	6061	55
Pacific Northwest Generating Coop	4911	224
Pacific Northwest Gigapop	7379	690
Pacific NorthWest National Laboratory	8731	16
Pacific Northwest Telco Inc	1731	2257
Pacific Nutritional Inc	5122	79
Pacific Office Furnishings	5112	33
Pacific Office Properties Trust Inc	6726	41
Pacific Packaging Products Inc	5113	18
Pacific Paper Box Company Inc	2675	25
Pacific Pavingstone	1741	15
Pacific Perforating Inc	3599	1065
Pacific Pier Inc	2673	7
Pacific Piston Ring Company Inc	3592	17
Pacific Plastic Technology Inc	3083	45
Pacific Plastics Design Inc	2821	189
Pacific Power and Engineering Inc	3613	137
Pacific Power Products	5084	17
Pacific Power Source	3612	83
Pacific Power Systems Integration Inc	7373	1219
Pacific Power Tech LLC	3594	7
Pacific Power Testing Inc	1731	2563
Pacific Premier Bancorp Inc	6712	358
Pacific Premier Bank FSB	6035	135
Pacific Premier Financial Insurance Services Inc	6411	125
Pacific Press Technologies Inc	3542	47
Pacific Pride Seafoods Inc	5146	16
Pacific Printing and Fulfillment Inc	2752	711
Pacific Property Assets	6798	210
Pacific Publishing Co (Seattle Washington)	2711	165
Pacific Pure-Aid Co	2034	27
Pacific Quartz Inc	3827	108
Pacific Radio Electronics Inc	5063	168
Pacific Radomes Inc	3663	231
Pacific Rim Capital Inc	7359	42
Pacific Rim Printers/Mailers	7331	248
Pacific Rim Resources Search Agency	7361	206
Pacific River LLC	7381	222
Pacific Roller Die Company Inc	3599	2148
Pacific Rubber and Packing Inc	5085	316
Pacific Sands Inc	2819	132
Pacific Saw And Knife Co	3425	6
Pacific Scientific Energetic Materials Co	3489	11
Pacific Scientific HTL/Kin-Tech	3812	55
Pacific Scientific Oeco Corp	8711	202
Pacific Service Federal Credit Union	6062	19
Pacific Ship Repair and Fabrication Inc	3731	29
Pacific Shredco LLC	7389	1217
Pacific Smoking Co	2091	11
Pacific Software Publishing Inc	7372	3471
Pacific Southwest Container LLC	2671	10
Pacific Southwest Sales Company Inc	5039	35
Pacific Specialty Insurance Co	6331	125
Pacific Spice Company Inc	5149	102
Pacific Sports Medicine	8093	33
Pacific Star Seafoods Inc	2092	104
Pacific States Felt and Manufacturing Company Inc	3053	137
Pacific Steel Casting Co	3369	4
Pacific Stock	7389	1447
Pacific Storage Co	4213	440
Pacific Sunwear of California Inc	5611	8
Pacific Sunwear Stores Corp	5611	16
Pacific Supply Co	5013	61
Pacific Systems Group	7372	5099
Pacific Talent Inc	7922	58
Pacific Tank and Pipeline	1623	854
Pacific Terminals Ltd	4231	3
Pacific Theatres Corp	7832	10
Pacific Timesheet	7372	772
Pacific Tool and Gauge	3545	327
Pacific Tool Inc	3544	437
Pacific Topsoils Inc	2421	58
Pacific Trade International Inc	3999	51
Pacific Transformer Corp	3612	47

Company Name	SIC	Rank	Company Name	SIC	Rank	Company Name	SIC	Rank
Pacific Union Bank	6036	28	Paddock Masonry Inc	1741	18	Palco Telecom Service Inc	3661	79
Pacific Utility Construction	1623	489	Paddock Pool Equipment Company Inc	3589	99	Palermo Bakery Inc	2051	255
Pacific Valves	3494	30	Paddock Productions Inc	7812	317	Palermo Villa Inc	5149	80
Pacific Vascular Inc	8731	278	Paddock Publications Inc/Daily Herald	2711	125	Palisade Corp	7372	3147
Pacific Veneer Ltd	2436	7	Paddycake Bakery	5461	23	Palisades Media Group Inc	7389	413
Pacific WebWorks Inc	7372	2019	Padgett Machine Tool Company Inc	3599	2099	Palisades Research	7372	2209
Pacific West Bank	6029	32	Padgett Manufacturing Inc	3535	90	Pall Aeropower Corp	3599	15
Pacific West Coast Dies Inc	3544	197	Padgett Strateman and Company LLP	8721	56	Pall Corp	3569	2
Pacific West Litho Inc	2752	438	Padgett-Swann Machinery Company Inc	7699	127	Pall Life Sciences Div	3589	9
Pacific Western Bank	6021	32				Palladian Partners Inc	7389	721
Pacific Western Bank (San Diego California)	6021	82	Padilla Speer Beardsley Inc	8743	35	Palladium Equity Partners Iii LP	6211	182
Pacific Wireless Communications LLC	4812	57	Padre Island Brewing Company Inc	5084	664	Pallas International Corp	7372	1811
Pacific Wood Laminates Inc	2436	8	Paducah and Louisville Railway Inc	4011	20	Pallet Central Enterprises Inc	5031	221
Pacific World Corp	2844	44	Paducah Printing Corp	2752	1665	Pallet Consultants Of Georgia Inc	7699	64
Pacifica Chemical Inc	5169	144	Padus Inc	7372	4538	Pallet Express Inc	4213	505
Pacifica Contracting Inc	1623	814	Pae and Associates Inc	1629	97	Pallet Factory Inc	2448	10
Pacifica Electrical Contractors	1731	1678	PAE Inc	7372	4539	Pallet Masters Inc	2448	34
PacifiCare Health Systems Inc	6324	5	Paetec Communications Inc	4899	14	Pallet Repair Systems Inc	3537	108
PacificHealth Laboratories Inc	2833	60	PAETEC Holding Corp	4899	6	Pallet Resource Of NC Inc	2448	29
Pacifico Group	5511	88	Paez-Fletcher Co	5065	905	Palletone Inc	2448	4
PacifiCorp	4911	29	Pagasus Claims Service Inc	6162	139	Pallets-R-Us Ii	5031	429
PacifiCorp Group Holdings Co	4813	9	Page Automated Telecommunications Systems Inc	3661	154	Pallflex Products Co	2672	58
PacifiCorp Holdings Inc	4911	37				Palm Beach Habilitation Center Inc	8331	125
Paciolan Systems Inc	7372	1833	Page Electrical Corp	1731	591	Palm Beach Iron Works Inc	3599	2199
Pacira Pharmaceuticals Inc	2834	293	Page ETC Inc	4213	1883	Palm Beach Jewelry and Antiques	7389	977
Pacitto and Forest Construction Co	1623	626	Page Litho Inc	2789	93	Palm Beach Maintenance Inc	7349	357
Pack Air Inc	3535	95	Page Mill Properties	6531	341	Palm Beach Media Group Inc	2721	284
Pack and Process Inc	7389	1014	Page One Inc	2711	662	Palm Beach Tan Inc	7299	17
Package Design and Manufacturing Inc	2621	63	Page One Inc (Albuquerque New Mexico)	5942	30	Palm Express Inc	4213	1167
Package Development Industries Inc	3081	65				Palm Freight Systems Inc	4213	3064
Package Machinery Company Inc	3565	183	Page One Printers Inc	2752	1470	Palm Harbor Manufacturing LP	2452	22
Package Printing Company Inc	2671	63	Page Properties Corp	6552	250	Palm Harbor Marketing Inc	6531	138
Packaged Business Solutions Inc	7371	1084	Page Southerland Page	8712	64	Palm International Inc	2819	53
Packageworks Inc	7372	5034	Page Studio Graphics	7372	4863	Palm Management Corp	5812	223
Packaging and Shipping Center Inc	4783	16	Page Technology Marketing Inc	7372	4540	Palm Optical Company Inc	5049	47
Packaging Automation Corp	3565	104	Pageflex Inc	7372	302	Palm Peterbilt-Gmc Trucks Inc	5084	247
Packaging Concepts and Design	5085	167	Pageland Screen Printers Inc	2262	2	Palm Springs Mirror And Glass Inc	5039	49
Packaging Concepts Inc	5113	21	PagePath Technologies Inc	7372	2471	Palm Springs Printing Inc	2752	1513
Packaging Concepts Ltd	2542	7	PagePoint	7379	980	Palm Springs Unified School Dist	8211	5
Packaging Corporation of America	2652	2	Page's Produce Co	2032	22	Palm Station LLC	7999	20
Packaging Distribution Services Inc	5113	64	PageTek	3669	181	Palma Tool and Die Company Inc	3544	456
Packaging Dynamics Corp	6719	100	Pagetek Printing and Design Inc	2759	239	Palman Electric Inc	1731	1567
Packaging Graphics Inc	3555	97	Pagliaro Brothers Stone Company Inc	1741	16	Palmborg Associates	5065	845
Packaging Materials Inc	3069	195	Pagnotti Enterprises Inc	6411	232	Palmentere Brothers Cartage Services	4213	1048
Packaging Personified Inc	2671	13	Pagoda Electric Inc	1731	520	Palmer and Co	2064	39
Packaging Pioneers Inc	5113	71	Pahl Tool Service	3599	2153	Palmer and Dodge	8111	229
Packaging Plus LLC	3089	142	PAI Corp	8711	541	Palmer And Sicard Inc	1711	182
Packaging Service Company Inc	7389	601	Pai Industries Inc	3714	256	Palmer Auto Group	5511	523
Packaging Services Inc (Ivyland Pennsylvania)	7389	1764	Paid Inc	7389	949	Palmer Company Inc	5087	83
			Paielli's Bakery Inc	2051	154	Palmer Computer Services Inc	7372	1587
Packaging Services Inc (Weyers Cave Virginia)	7389	257	Paige Electric Company LLC	1731	948	Palmer Distributors Inc	3089	605
			Paige Electric Company LP	5063	55	Palmer Electronics Inc	3829	465
Packaging Services Of Maryland Inc	2653	80	Paige Hendricks Public Relations Inc	8743	222	Palmer Engineered Products Inc	3365	51
Packaging Specialists Incorporated Southwest	3086	98	Pailet Meunier and LeBlanc LLP	8721	477	Palmer Envelope Co	2759	485
			Pain D'avignon 11 Inc	2051	202	Palmer Instruments Inc	3823	178
Packaging Specialties Of Georgia Inc	2759	23	Pain Enterprises Inc	2813	14	Palmer International Inc	3499	52
Packaging Strategies Inc	3086	150	Pain Therapeutics Inc	2834	304	Palmer Machine Company Inc	3599	1498
Packaging Systems International Inc	3565	130	Paine Electronics LLC	3823	111	Palmer Manufacturing Company LLC	3724	23
Packaging Technologies Inc	3565	23	Paint Supply Co (Hampton Virginai)	5231	12	Palmer Moving and Storage Co	4213	328
Packaging Technology Inc	2448	37	Paintball Dave's Inc	7999	98	Palmer Paint Products Inc	2851	74
Packard Shutter Co	3861	125	Painted Feather Precision LLC	3599	1105	Palmer Paving Corp	1611	82
Packard Truck Lines Inc	4213	1190	Painters Supply Company Inc	5013	278	Palmer Printing Inc	2752	767
Packer Metal Works Inc	3599	1641	Pair Gain Communications Inc	5065	288	Palmer Products Inc	3599	2421
Packer Transportation Company Inc	4213	2746	Pair Networks Inc	7379	1207	Palmer Steel Supplies Inc	3441	97
Packerland Holdings Inc	6719	50	Paisano Publications LLC	2721	212	Palmer Transport Corp	4213	1645
Packers Manufacturing Inc	3556	149	Paisley Consulting Inc	7372	2553	Palmer Vineyards Inc	0172	19
Packerware LLC	3089	198	Paisley Trucking Inc	4213	2558	Palmer Wahl Instrumentation Group	3823	126
Packet Design Inc	7371	674	Paitson Brothers Ace Hardware	5251	44	Palmetco Inc	5051	421
Packet Design LLC	5045	158	Paiute Trailers	3537	90	Palmetto ASC LP	8011	148
Packet Digital LLC	7373	718	Pajukale Inc	7359	179	Palmetto Automatic Sprinkler Company Inc	1711	172
Packet Video Technologies	7372	17	Pak Mail Centers of America Inc	4731	72			
Packet360 Inc	7373	235	Pak Mail Crating and Freight Service Inc	4731	70	Palmetto Canning Co	2033	120
Packetmotion Inc	7371	1007				Palmetto Electric Cooperative Inc	4911	261
PacketVideo Corp	7372	1522	Pak Technologies Holding Company Inc	8741	244	Palmetto Ford Inc	5511	649
Packing Inc	3577	319				Palmetto Loom Reed Co	3552	25
Packiq LLC	8742	635	Pakedge Device and Software Inc	3577	548	Palmetto Oil Equipment Company Inc	5084	495
Packless Metal Hose Inc	3585	112	Pak-It Inc	4783	29	Palmetto Pigeon Plant	0259	2
Packnet Ltd	3089	396	Pako Inc	3728	72	Palmetto Scale Services	5046	248
Pack-Rite Machines	3565	181	Pak-Rite Industries Inc	4783	7	Palmetto Shelters Inc	3663	315
Packwell Inc	5085	29	Paksense	3829	110	Palmetto State Transportation	4213	680
Pacmoore Products Inc	7389	1356	Pal Graphics Inc	2791	15	Palmetto Synthetics LC	2281	19
Paco Plastics and Engineering Inc	3089	1846	Pal International Corp	3679	654	Palmor Products Inc	3524	30
Paco Steel and Engineering Corp	5051	247	Pal Manufacturing Inc	3442	134	Palms of Pasadena Hospital LP	8069	9
Paco Winders Manufacturing Inc	3554	54	Pala International Inc	5944	24	Palmyra Bologna Co	2013	147
Pacon Corp	2679	16	Palace Construction Company Inc	1521	97	Palo Alto Networks Inc	7371	201
Pacon Inc	3089	644	Palace Electrical Contractors Inc	1731	838	Palo Alto Research Center Inc	8732	26
Pacon Manufacturing Corp	2389	22	Palace Packaging Machines Inc	3565	108	Palo Alto Software Inc	7372	2062
Pacor Inc	5033	38	Palace Production Center	3695	35	Paloma Systems Inc	7373	395
PacOrd Inc	3731	45	Palace Sports and Entertainment	6512	30	Palomár Medical Products Inc	3845	34
Pac-Paper Inc	2621	55	Palace Theater	7922	48	Palomar Medical Technologies Inc	3795	2
Pacs Industries Inc	3613	44	Paladin Capital Group	6799	164	Palomar Mountain Premium Spring Water LLC	2086	148
Pactiv Corp	2653	2	Paladin Consulting Inc	8748	86			
Pactolus Communications Software Corp	5045	44	Paladin Data Systems Corp	7371	694	Palomar Technologies Inc	3549	2
			Paladin Enterprises Inc	2752	1139	Palomino Euro Bistro	5812	129
Pac-Van Inc	5084	39	Paladin Holdings Inc	3751	20	PALOS Software	7372	4435
Pacware Software Development Inc	7372	3327	Paladin Industry Inc	2599	34	Palpac Industries Inc	3089	1808
PacWest Bancorp	6712	109	Paladin Software Inc	7372	4007	Pals Inc	5083	63
Pacwest Scale	5046	290	Paladyne Corp	4899	168	Palstar Inc	3825	278
Pac-West Telecomm Inc	7375	47	Paladyne Systems Inc	7372	597	Palumbo Sand and Gravel Company Inc	1442	36
Pad And Publication Assembly Corp	2754	39	Palagonia Bakery Company Inc	2051	107			
Padd Electrical Inc	1731	2528	Palatine Builders Supply Inc	5031	389	PAM Dedicated Services Inc	4213	552
Paddock Chevrolet Inc	5511	867	Palatine Welding Co	5084	641	Pam Printers And Publishers Inc	2721	438
Paddock Laboratories Inc	2834	209	Palazzo Creative	7319	126	PAM Transport Inc	4213	94
						PAM Transportation Services Inc	4213	91

Company Name	SIC	Rank
Pamarco Technologies Inc	3953	2
Pamco Inc	3523	176
Pamco Machine Works Inc	3599	1220
Pamek Trading Corp	3651	187
Pamela A Keene Public Relations Inc	8743	299
Pamela Stavroff Design Associates Inc	7389	1786
Pamida Inc	5399	4
Pamlico Capital	6799	45
Pamlico Home Builder and Supply Company Inc	5211	239
Pamlico Packing Company Inc	2092	52
Pampa Machine and Supply Inc	5084	850
Pampered Chef Ltd	5023	65
Pan Am Railways	4011	21
Pan American Bank	6022	567
Pan American Express Inc	4213	702
Pan American Tool Corp	3545	87
Pan Communications Inc	8743	129
Pan De Vida Inc	5092	35
Pan Pacific Enterprises Inc	5084	800
Pan Western Corp	4213	1051
Panache Designs	2512	49
Panache Resources and Systems Corp	7379	484
PanAgora Asset Management Inc	6282	167
Panama Jack Inc	2844	199
Panama Transfer Inc	4213	1287
Panamax	3679	55
Pan-American Life Insurance Co	6311	119
Panarama Inc	2053	11
Panasas Inc	7376	12
Panashield Inc	3825	185
Panasoft Software	7372	3937
Panasonic Avc American Laboratories Inc	7313	19
Panasonic Consumer Electronics Co	5065	15
Panasonic Disc Services Corp	3695	15
Panasonic Electric Works Corporation of America	3679	7
Panasonic Personal Computer Co	3571	79
Panattoni Development Co	6552	11
Panavision Inc	3861	12
Panavision International LP	3861	14
Pancho's Management Inc	5147	16
Pancho's Mexican Buffet Inc	5812	262
Panda Software	7372	1999
Pandel Inc	3069	53
Pandigital	5399	8
Pandisc Music Corp	7389	1233
Pandjiris Inc	3548	39
Pandora Manufacturing LLC	7389	1378
Pandora Media Inc	7375	31
Panduit Corp	3643	4
Pandya Computers Inc	7378	145
Panef Corp	7389	2055
Panek Precision Products Co	3599	240
Panel Center Inc	5031	425
Panel Monster Inc	3613	139
Panel Prints Inc	2752	41
Panel Shop Inc	3613	102
Panel-Fab Inc	3613	50
Panelfold Inc	2679	27
Panelgraphic Corp	3083	54
Panella Trucking Inc	4213	244
Panelmatic Inc	3613	89
Panel-Oven Engineering Company Inc	3613	174
Panel-Tec Inc	3823	391
Paneltronics Inc	3613	57
Panera Bread Co	5812	31
Panera LLC	5812	275
Pangborn Corp	3564	76
Pangborn Design Ltd	7336	291
Pangea Inc	1542	307
Pangea3 LLC	8748	148
PANGEATWO	7361	211
Pangenex Corp	2833	74
Pangere Corp	1761	9
PanGo Networks Inc	7372	1273
Panhandle Buyers Guide	2711	701
Panhandle Oil and Gas Inc	1311	107
Panhandle Packing and Gasket Inc	5085	274
Panhandle State Bank	6022	156
Panhandle Telecasting LP	4833	150
Panhandle Telephone Cooperative Inc	4813	101
Panini America Inc	2752	152
Pan-International Electronics Inc	5045	777
Panish Controls Inc	3625	398
Pankl Aerospace Systems	3369	20
Panko Electrical and Maintenance Inc	1731	1446
Pankratz Lumber Co	0811	6
Pannell Kerr Forster of Texas PC	8721	108
Pannier Corp	3953	10
Pano Logic Inc	7372	796
Panoff Publishing Inc	2721	225
Pan-O-Gold Baking Co	5149	18
Panola Pepper Corp	2099	270
Panolam Industries International Inc	3083	34
Panoptic Communications Inc	7336	247
Panoptic Corp	7379	765
Panoptic Media	7336	315
Panorama City Corp	6513	33
Panoramic Images	7336	106
Panoramic Press Inc	2752	1022
Pan-Oston Co	2542	8
Pantagraph Printing And Stationery Co	2752	357

Company Name	SIC	Rank
Pantagraph Publishing Co	2711	53
PanTerra Networks Inc	7379	865
Pantheon Inc	7371	325
Panther Expedited Services Inc	4789	7
Panther Graphics Inc	2752	1715
Panther Products Corp	3531	95
Panther Technologies Inc	4959	17
Panthera Inc	5085	444
Panthera Interactive LLC	7319	104
Pantograms Manufacturing Co	3559	98
Pantone Inc	2741	132
Pantrol Inc	3823	141
Pantronix Corp	3674	227
Pantropic Power Products Inc	5083	7
Pantry Inc	5499	2
Panzica Construction Co	1542	182
Paoli Inc	2521	11
PAP Security Printing Inc	2759	43
Papa Cantella's Inc	2013	141
Papa Charlie's Inc	2013	208
Papa Gino's Holdings Corp	5812	166
Papa Gino's Inc	5812	93
Papa John's International Inc	5812	50
Papa John's USA Inc	5812	376
Papa Murphy's Pizza	6794	43
Papa Romanos Inc	5812	409
Papachinos Franchise Corp	5812	382
Papadatos Partnership LLP	8712	271
Papagalos and Associates Inc	7311	733
Papas Bakery Inc	5461	29
Papec LLC	3823	480
Pape-Dawson Consulting Engineers Inc	8711	292
Paper Coating Co	2672	44
Paper Handling Solutions Inc	5084	438
Paper House Productions Inc	2771	18
Paper Machinery Corp	3554	6
Paper Magic Group Inc	2771	6
Paper Mart	5113	27
Paper Mill Graphix Inc	7334	74
Paper Place	5943	27
Paper Products Company Inc	5113	24
Paper Publishing Company Inc	2721	203
Paper Research Materials Inc	3829	510
Paper Systems Inc	2679	19
Paper Transport of Green Bay	4213	1277
Paper Valley Corp	1521	36
Paperboard Packaging Corp	2671	28
Papercone Corp	2677	11
Papercraft Inc	2759	578
Paperfold/Graphic Finishers Inc	2789	45
Papers Inc	2752	110
PaperWise Inc	7372	3114
Paperwork Co	2752	1801
Paperworks Inc	5112	7
Pape's Pecan House	0173	4
PAPP Clinic PC	8011	66
Pappa's Bar-B-Que	5812	264
Pappas Telecasting Of Centralne-braska LP	4833	170
Pappy's Enterprises Inc	2041	54
Pappy's Meat Company Inc	2099	323
Pap-R Products Co	2679	44
Papy's Foods Inc	2099	300
Par 4 Inc	5046	339
Par 4 Plastics Inc	3089	725
PAR Environmental Services Inc	8731	256
Par Forms Corp	2752	1764
Par Mar Oil Co	5411	153
PAR Marketing Inc	8711	629
Par Nuclear Inc	3569	230
Par Pharmaceutical Companies Inc	2834	43
Par Pharmaceutical Inc	2834	53
Par Springer Miller Systems Inc	7372	476
PAR Technology Corp	3578	4
Para Plate and Plastics Company Inc	3555	96
Para Research Inc	7372	3158
Para Systems Inc	3679	556
Para Tech Coating Inc	3479	61
Para Technologies	7372	4541
Paraben Corp	7371	921
Parabit Systems Inc	3699	212
ParAccel Inc	7371	1604
Paraclipse Inc	3699	208
Paraco Gas Corp	5172	9
ParaComp Inc	7372	3839
Par-A-Dice Gaming Corp	7993	7
Paradies Shops Inc	5947	5
Paradigm Alliance Inc	7389	1975
Paradigm Asset Management Company LLC	6726	13
Paradigm Energy Inc	1731	1906
Paradigm Health Corp	8011	48
Paradigm Holdings Inc	7371	229
Paradigm Infotech Inc	7372	177
Paradigm Interiors Inc	7389	1789
Paradigm Learning Inc	8742	251
Paradigm/Lord Lasker	7311	235
Paradigm Medical Industries Inc	3841	397
Paradigm Packaging	3089	651
Paradigm Packaging East LLC	3089	397
Paradigm Printing Inc	2752	981
Paradigm Services Inc	7371	993
Paradigm Solutions Corp	7372	652

Company Name	SIC	Rank
Paradigm System Solutions Inc	5045	743
Paradigm Systems Inc	7372	2910
Paradigm Systems Integration Inc	7379	1023
Paradigm Tax Group	7389	1714
Paradis Inc	4212	55
Paradise Ford Inc	5511	636
Paradise Inc	2099	123
Paradise Music and Entertainment Inc	7812	259
Paradise Printing Inc	2752	1369
Paradise Tomato Kitchens Inc	2033	70
Paradise Video Inc	3695	107
Paradysz Matera Company Inc	7331	6
Parafin Corp	1311	280
Parago Inc	7372	517
Paragon Advertising Inc	7311	540
Paragon Airheater Technologies	3433	54
Paragon Asset Management	6282	592
Paragon Automation Inc	3599	2231
Paragon Bank and Trust	6022	529
Paragon Book Reprint Corp	2731	138
Paragon Capital Corp	7377	15
Paragon Communications Inc	5064	37
Paragon Computer Professionals Inc	7379	91
Paragon Controls Inc	3822	79
Paragon Custom Plastics Inc	3086	145
Paragon Development Systems Inc	7373	194
Paragon Die and Engineering Co	3544	47
Paragon Films Inc	3081	51
Paragon Firstronic Of NA Corp	3625	114
Paragon Forms Inc	2752	461
Paragon Furniture LP	2522	43
Paragon Hotel Corp	7011	211
Paragon Household Products Inc	2842	151
Paragon International Inc	3589	173
Paragon Investment Management Inc	6282	410
Paragon Media Inc	3695	32
Paragon Medical Inc	3089	176
Paragon Metals Inc	3321	35
Paragon Molds Corp	3544	824
Paragon Music Center Inc	5736	18
Paragon Optical Company Inc	3211	22
Paragon Packaging Inc	2759	210
Paragon Pattern And Manufacturing Co	3543	45
Paragon Pipe and Steel Inc	5039	54
Paragon Plastic Sheet Inc	3081	25
Paragon Plastics Inc	3089	153
Paragon Precision Inc	3728	169
Paragon Products Inc	2752	1565
Paragon Real Estate Equity and Investment Trust	6798	221
Paragon Software Inc	7371	1334
Paragon Solutions and Technologies Inc	7379	1321
Paragon Solutions Group Inc	7379	242
Paragon Sporting Goods Corp	5941	29
Paragon Supply Co	2752	294
Paragon Supply Inc	5032	102
Paragon Technologies Inc	3599	522
Paragon Technologies Inc (Warren Michigan)	7699	119
Paragon Tours Inc	4725	23
Paragon Towers Inc	3663	11
Paragon Travel Agency Inc	4724	86
Paragon Vision Sciences Inc	3851	71
Paragon Water Systems Inc	3589	168
Paragon Wholesale Foods Corp	5148	53
Paralan Corp	3679	98
Parallax Capital Partners LLC	6719	161
Parallax Design Group Inc	2741	404
Parallax Inc	3571	77
Parallel Petroleum LLC	1311	86
Parallel Quantum Solutions LLC	7371	1799
Parallel Systems Corp	3577	564
Parallel Technologies Inc	7373	317
Paramax Productions	7336	64
Parameter Developments Inc	7371	1916
Parameter Generation And Control Inc	3822	66
Parameters Industries Inc	3599	1259
Parametric Portfolio Associates Inc	6282	492
Parametric Technology Corp	7372	52
Paramit Corp	3672	36
Paramont Machine Company Inc	3599	1565
Paramount Apparel International Inc	2353	5
Paramount Bakeries Inc	2051	156
Paramount Can Company Inc	5085	235
Paramount Chemical Specialties Inc	2842	123
Paramount Computer Corp	7373	408
Paramount Convention Services Inc	7389	911
Paramount Die Company Inc	3544	188
Paramount Export Co	5148	23
Paramount Farms Inc	0723	4
Paramount Feed and Supply Inc	5191	168
Paramount Fitness Corp	3949	89
Paramount Games Inc	2759	143
Paramount Industrial Companies Inc	2515	15
Paramount Industries Inc	3679	396
Paramount Miller Graphics Inc	2752	842
Paramount Molded Products Inc	3089	1020
Paramount Pictures Corp	7812	20
Paramount Plastics Inc	3089	1304
Paramount Precision Products Inc	3599	427
Paramount Pumps and Supplies Inc	3533	108
Paramount Restaurant Supply Corp	5087	19
Paramount Security Bureau Inc	7381	153

Company Name	SIC	Rank
Paramount Software Associates Inc	7371	1519
Paramount Software Associations Inc	7371	272
Paramount Stone Company Inc	5032	78
Paramount Technologies Inc	5065	851
Paramount Termite Control Of Fresno Inc	7342	84
Paramount Tool LLC	3469	325
Paramount Unified School District	8211	91
Paramount Wire Company Inc	5051	455
Paramus Building Supply Company Inc	5211	260
Parasense Inc	5063	947
Parasoft Corp	7372	2032
Parasound Products Inc	3651	195
Parata Systems APS	7352	7
Paratech Inc	3569	95
Paratek Microwave Inc	5063	116
Paravis Industries Inc	3544	617
Parc Presentations Inc	6512	36
PARC Technical Services Inc	8734	66
Parco Inc	3053	20
Pardee Construction Co	1522	9
Pardoe's Perky Peanuts Inc	2068	23
Pardon Inc	3714	379
Parent and Child Together For West Central Illinois	8322	173
ParenteBeard LLC	8721	251
Parenti and Raffaelli Ltd	2431	45
Parenting Press Inc	2731	346
ParentWatch Inc	7379	445
PAREXEL International Corp	8731	12
Parfums de Coeur Ltd	5122	39
Parfums Givenchy Inc	2844	90
Pargraphics Inc	2752	923
Pari Innovative Manufacturers Inc	5047	264
Paric Corp	1542	132
Parijat Controlware Inc	7372	3006
Paris Accessories Inc	2253	8
Paris Art Label Company Inc	2672	50
Paris Beacon News	2711	762
Paris Blues LLC	2339	41
Paris Corp	2761	13
Paris Foods Corp	2037	34
Paris Metal Products LLC	3469	177
Paris Printing	2752	655
Paris Publishing Co	2711	704
Paris Transport Inc	4213	798
Pariser Industries Inc	2843	9
Parish Chemical Company Inc	8731	379
Parish Data Systems Inc	7372	421
Parish Manufacturing Inc	2673	49
ParishSOFT	7372	1312
Parisi Associates Inc	3679	703
Parisi Inc	2599	21
Parity Computing Inc	7371	1032
Pariveda Solutions Inc	8748	131
Park 100 Foods Inc	2013	31
Park Air Corp	3565	141
Park at Countryside LP	6513	39
Park at Fifty Eight LP	6513	41
Park Avenue Bank (Valdosta Georgia)	6022	462
Park B Smith Inc	2392	18
Park Bancorp Inc	6712	613
Park Chemical Co	2819	89
Park Circle Motor Co	5511	678
Park City Group Inc	7374	128
Park City Group Inc (Park City Utah)	7373	356
Park City Packaging Inc	4783	25
Park Community Federal Credit Union	6061	72
Park Corp (Cleveland Ohio)	3325	4
Park Electrochemical Corp	3672	15
Park Engineering And Manufacturing Co	3599	1248
Park Engineering Inc	3561	178
Park Enterprises Of Rochester Inc	3545	409
Park Federal Credit Union	6061	44
Park FSB	6035	171
Park Hill School District	8211	38
Park Hyde Partners Inc	5084	171
Park Industrial Foams Inc	7336	162
Park Lane Litho Plate	2796	44
Park Madison Group Inc	2771	20
Park Manufacturing Corp	3496	63
Park Nameplate Company Inc	3471	38
Park National Bank	6021	83
Park National Corp	6712	94
Park Place Dealerships	5511	1171
Park Place International	5045	110
Park Place Motor Cars	5511	344
Park Place West Inc	7381	176
Park Press Quality Printing Inc	2752	1505
Park Printing House Ltd	2752	484
Park Printing Inc	2752	374
Park Region Mutual Telephone Co	4813	349
Park Shirt Co	2253	19
Park Speedway	3644	45
Park Sterling Bank Inc	6035	105
Park Towne Ltd	7521	6
Park Trace Apartments LP	6513	38
Park Translations LLC	7389	2097
Park View FSB	6035	84
Park View Manufacturing Corp	3949	118
Park Water Co	4941	41
Park West Development Co	1522	49
Par-Kan Co	3443	158
Parkdale America LLC	2281	5
Parkdale Mall Associates	6531	277
Parkdale Mills Inc	2281	2
Parke Bancorp Inc	6022	216
Parke-Bell Limited Inc	5961	151
Parkell Products Inc	3843	23
Parkeon Inc	3824	24
Parker and Cowing Electric Inc	1731	1054
Parker and James Communications	7311	734
Parker and Lancaster Corp	1521	42
Parker and Sons Stone LLC	1422	51
Parker Auto Collection	5511	1187
Parker Boiler Co	3433	47
Parker Carlson and Johnson Inc	6282	435
Parker Compound Bows Inc	3949	60
Parker Drilling Co	1381	14
Parker Drilling Company North America Inc	1381	18
Parker Electric Co	1731	1253
Parker Group Inc	7336	271
Parker Hannifin Corp	3593	1
Parker Hannifin Corp Airborne Div	3728	78
Parker Hannifin Corp Aircraft Wheel and Brake Div	3728	108
Parker Hannifin Corp Brass Products Div	3432	7
Parker Hannifin Corp Chomerics Div	3444	11
Parker Hannifin Corp Cylinder Div	3593	16
Parker Hannifin Corp Daedel Div	3812	61
Parker Hannifin Corp Electronic Systems Div	3728	41
Parker Hannifin Corp Hose Products Div	3492	7
Parker Hannifin Corp Instrumentation Valve Div	3494	40
Parker Hannifin Corp Pneumatic Div	3593	7
Parker Hannifin Corp Racor Div	3599	50
Parker Hannifin Corporation Refrigerating Specialties	3494	25
Parker Hannifin Corp Skinner Valve Div	3494	6
Parker Hannifin Corp Tube Fittings Div	3492	2
Parker Hannifin Hydraulic Pump Div	3569	33
Parker Hannifin Techseal Div	3069	45
Parker Hosiery Company Inc	2252	15
Parker House Manufacturing Co	2517	2
Parker House Sausage Co	2013	190
Parker/Hunter	6211	354
Parker Industries Inc	3089	1435
Parker Industries Inc (Bohemia New York)	3561	81
Parker Industries Inc (Connelly Springs North Carolina)	3599	1989
Parker K Bailey and Sons Inc	4213	1322
Parker Marine Enterprises Inc	3732	48
Parker Milliken Clark O'Hara and Samuelian	8111	332
Parker North America Operations Inc	1381	19
Parker Paint Manufacturing Company Inc	2851	19
Parker Pest Control Inc	7342	93
Parker Power Systems Inc	5063	877
Parker Powis Inc	3579	24
Parker Precision Products	3544	842
Parker Research Corp	3829	406
Parker Services LLC	6311	235
Parker Smith and Feek Inc	6411	67
Parker Station Inc	2084	124
Parker Steel Co	5051	253
Parker Stevenson Brokerage Co	6531	409
Parker Systems Inc	3999	165
Parker Tooling and Design Inc	3354	47
Parker Towing Co	4449	21
Parker-Hannifin Corp Fluid Control Div	3492	13
Parker-Mccrory Manufacturing Co	3699	88
Parker's Express Inc	4213	2421
Parkervision Inc	3663	416
Parkhill Furniture Company Inc	2512	18
Parkhill Smith and Cooper Inc	8711	134
Parking Products Inc	3559	538
Parkland Plastics Inc	5162	35
Parklawn Inc	6553	7
Park-Ohio Holdings Corp	3462	3
Park-Olson Lumber Co	5031	299
Parks Capital Management Inc	6282	639
Parks Chevrolet Inc	5511	690
Parks Corp	2851	26
Parks Electric and Quality Controls Inc	1731	2194
Parks Metal Products Inc	3444	247
Parks Moving and Storage Inc	4213	516
Parkside Candy Company Inc	2066	38
Parkside Management Services LLC	6552	221
Parksite Group	5039	3
Parkvale Financial Corp	6712	209
Parkvale Savings Bank	6036	19
Parkview Home Health and Hospice	8082	1
Parkview Metal Products Inc	3469	28
Parkway Bank and Trust Co	6022	64
Parkway Chevrolet	5511	836
Parkway Drugs Inc	5912	38
Parkway Place Inc	6531	271
Parkway Plastics Inc	3089	1065
Parkway Steel Rule Cutting Dies Inc	3544	778
Parkway-Kew Corp	3599	1981
Parlano Inc	7371	491
Parlex Corp	3672	24
Parlex Dynaflex Corp	3672	178
Parlux Fragrances Inc	2844	27
Parma International Inc	3944	39
Parmatech Corp	3544	68
ParMed Pharmaceuticals Inc	5122	43
Parmelee Industries Inc	3851	16
Parnassus Investments	6282	586
Parnassus Software	7372	4864
Parnell Pharmaceuticals Inc	5122	109
Parnell-Martin Co	5074	47
Paro Services Co	7349	19
Par-Pak Inc	3089	1226
Parr Instrument Co	3821	9
Parreco Equipment Company Inc	7353	66
Parr-Green Mold and Machine Co	3544	594
Parris Manufacturing Co	3944	37
Parris Tool and Die Co	3544	749
Parrish Consulting	7379	894
Parrish McDonald's Restaurants Ltd	5812	217
Parron-Hall Corp	5021	43
Parrot Press Inc	2759	287
Parrot-Ice Drink Products of America Inc	2037	25
Parrten Products Inc	3324	24
Parry Center For Children	8361	43
Parry Romani DeConcini and Symms	8743	221
Pars Industries Inc	2434	83
Pars Publishing Corp	7336	63
PARSEC Group	7379	1402
Parsoft International	7372	422
Parson And Sanderson Inc	5084	599
Parson Group LLC	8742	154
Parsons and Whittemore Inc	2611	3
Parsons Brinckerhoff Construction Services Inc	8741	77
Parsons Brinckerhoff Inc	0711	16
Parsons Buick Co	5511	1072
Parsons Company Inc	3599	112
Parsons Corp	1541	6
Parsons Electric Inc	1731	442
Parsons Engineering Science Inc	8711	83
Parsons Infrastructure and Technology Group Inc	8711	10
Parsons Manufacturing Corp	3089	1501
Parsons Publishing Company Inc	2711	828
Parsons Sales Company Inc	5075	115
Parsons Steel Rule Dies Inc	2631	32
Parsons Transportation Inc	8711	63
Parsons Worley International	8742	82
Partco Inc	3599	1205
Partec Inc	3581	8
ParTech Inc	3578	6
Partee Flooring Mill LLP	2426	36
Partek Inc	7372	5024
Parter Medical Products Inc	3821	11
Partex Marking Systems Inc	5063	720
Parthenon Metal Works Inc	3312	35
Parti Line International	2679	65
Particle Drilling Technologies Inc	1389	51
Particle Measuring Systems Inc	7389	687
Particle Size Technology Inc	3399	32
Parties Plus Tucson LLC	7359	202
Partin Management Inc	3441	267
PartMiner Worldwide Inc	7389	84
Partner Pak Inc	3565	164
PartnerRe USA	6321	41
Partners 4 Design	7389	2349
Partners Data Systems Inc	3661	194
Partners Electrical Services LLC	1731	357
Partners Financial Services Inc	7322	138
Partners for Growth	7372	4729
Partners HealthCare System Inc	8062	13
Partners Human Resources Co	7363	131
Partners of Progress Inc (Troy Michigan)	7629	52
Partnership Capital Growth Advisors	6282	559
Partnerships In Community Living Inc	8361	30
Partnersolve LLC	7379	727
Parton Lumber Company Inc	2421	75
Parts And Machinery Company Inc	3498	67
Parts Central Inc	5012	74
Parts Expediting And Distribution Co	3714	371
Parts Fit Industry Co	5013	320
Parts Now! Inc	5045	133
Parts Now LLC	5045	147
Parts Plus Of New Mexico Inc	5013	133
Parts Port Inc	5045	979
Parts Specialists Inc	5084	906
Parts Tool And Die Inc	3728	153
Parts Unlimited Inc	3429	109
Parts Warehouse Distributors Inc	5013	148
PartsBase Inc	7389	392
Partsmax Inc	5013	381
Party By Design Inc	7389	1429
Party City Corp	5999	12
Party Fair Inc	5999	250
Party Maxx Inc	7359	234
Party Planners West Inc	7389	702
Party Planning By Stephanie LLC	7359	260
Party Rentals	7359	208
Party Rentals By Lisa Inc	7359	272
Party Time Manufacturing Co	2679	81
Parvin-Clauss Sign Company Inc	7389	1518

Company Name	SIC	Rank
Parvus Corp	3823	217
Parwan Electronics Corp	3577	461
Par-Way Tryson Co	3556	30
Parx Group Of New York Inc	7379	638
PAS U Inc	3444	96
Pasa Services Inc	2752	1353
Pasadena Center Operating Co	8741	207
Pasadena Computer Works	7379	766
Pasadena Tank Corp	3443	104
Pascack Bancorp Inc	6021	234
Pascack Community Bank	6022	359
Pascal Company Inc	3843	73
Pascap Company Inc	5093	109
Paschall Truck Lines Inc	4213	135
Pasco Auto Wrecking Inc	5093	229
Pasco Corporation Of America	2038	49
Pasco Products Inc	4213	3056
Pas-Com Inc	3663	414
Pascual J And L Of Santa Fe Inc	5731	185
Pasha Group Co	5013	422
Pashupati Ltd	5734	40
Paslin Co	3548	14
Paso Del Norte Publishing Inc	2711	465
Paso Sound Products Inc	3663	267
PASport Software Programs Inc	7372	3007
Pasquale Trucking Company Inc	4213	2627
Pasquariello Electric Corp	1731	760
Pasquinelli Construction Co	1521	19
Pass and Seymour Inc	3643	13
Pass Consulting Corp	7371	1794
Pass Word Inc	7389	891
Passageways LLC	7372	3473
Passageways Travelcom	4724	90
Passaic Metal Building Supply	5075	116
Passaic Rubber Co	3061	40
Passport Brands Inc	2253	5
Passport Carpets Inc	3069	141
Passport Corp	7372	3143
Passport Health Communications Inc	8748	65
Passport Software Inc	7373	382
Passport Systems Inc	5045	300
Passur Aerospace Inc	3575	16
Pasta Montana LLC	2098	11
Pasternack Enterprises Inc	3357	61
Pastoral Solutions Inc	2731	153
Pastorelli Food Products Inc	2032	27
Pastries By Edie Inc	2051	209
Pat and Wes Productions	4832	237
PAT Auto Transport Inc	4213	1181
Pat Clark Pontiac GMC	5511	612
Pat Kuleto Restaurant Development and Management Co	7389	1806
Pat McGrath Chevrolet Inc	5511	945
Pat Meier Associates PR	7319	93
Pat Milliken Ford Inc	5511	852
Pat Paton Public Relations	8743	298
Pat Patterson Motor Sales Inc	5511	679
Patagonia Inc	5961	12
Patapsco Bancorp Inc	6712	585
Patapsco Bank	6035	161
Patch Rubber Co	3069	18
Patchogue Advance Inc	2711	586
Patel International Inc	7379	1090
Patelco Credit Union	6062	11
Patent Construction Systems	3446	7
Patented Acquisition Corp	7389	1091
Patented Systems Inc	7699	191
Patents Pending Inc	3089	1725
Path Master Inc	5063	190
Pathcom Inc	1731	2094
Pathcomm LLC	1623	772
Pathfinder Cell Therapy Inc	3842	329
Pathfinder Industries Inc	3444	272
Pathfinder LLC	8741	230
Pathfinder Services Inc	8331	53
Pathfinder Systems Inc	7371	1636
Pathfinders Inc	7361	305
Pathfinders Software	7372	4730
PathGuide Technologies Inc	7372	3279
Pathmark Stores Inc	5411	41
Pathology Associates International Corp	8734	71
Pathway Computing Inc	4813	642
Pathway Homes Inc	8361	92
Pathway Lighting Products Inc	3646	37
Pathway Press	2721	169
Pathways To Housing Inc	8322	43
Pathwayz Communications Inc	4812	107
Pati Petite Butter Cookies Inc	2052	75
Patient Care Inc	8082	84
Patient Care Technology Systems	7372	1569
Patient Equipment Rebuild Inc	7699	182
Patient Safety Technologies Inc	3842	138
Patientkeeper Inc	7371	342
Patio Living Concepts	3645	73
Patisserie Poupon Inc	2051	281
Patnick Inc	1623	514
Patotech Software Inc	7371	1115
Patricia Seybold Group	2721	391
Patrick Cudahy Inc	2013	15
Patrick Custom Vinyl Industries	3083	70
Patrick Electric Service Inc	1731	1142
Patrick Energy Services Inc	8711	381
Patrick Henry Broadcasting Corp	4832	288
Patrick Henry Creative Promotions	7389	670
Patrick Industries Inc	2431	10
Patrick Industries Inc Patrick Metals Div	3354	30
Patrick Lumber Company Inc	5031	35
Patrick Redmond Design	7336	302
Patrick Townsend and Associates Inc	7372	3328
Patrina Corp	7374	301
Patriot 3 Inc	3812	152
Patriot Alarm Systems Inc	7382	154
Patriot Bancshares Inc	6712	734
Patriot Buick GMC	5511	670
Patriot Coal Company LP	1221	7
Patriot Communications LLC	7373	96
Patriot Courier Service Inc	4213	2621
Patriot Engineering and Environmental Inc	8734	70
Patriot Engineering Co	8711	691
Patriot Machining and Maintenance Services Inc	3545	230
Patriot Memory LLC	5045	322
Patriot Metals Inc	5093	95
Patriot National Bancorp Inc	6712	373
Patriot National Bank (Stamford Connecticut)	6021	111
Patriot Paint LLC	2851	133
Patriot Premium Dividend Fund I	6726	40
Patriot Rail Corp	4789	3
Patriot Risk Management Inc	6321	62
Patriot Scientific Corp	3669	135
Patriot Services Inc	7361	345
Patriot Technologies Inc	7372	317
Patriot Transportation Holding Inc	4215	4
Patriot-News Co	2711	189
Pat's Electric Inc	1731	1929
Patson Inc	5511	597
Patsons Press	2752	388
Pattco Priority Printer Solutions Inc	5045	651
Patten Enterprises Inc	7372	5025
Patten Industries Inc	5082	17
Patten Tool And Engineering Inc	8711	646
Pattern Associates Inc	7371	1530
Patterson and Dewar Engineers Inc	8711	284
Patterson and Murphy Public Relations	8743	290
Patterson and Wilder Construction Company Inc	1623	213
Patterson Bancshares Inc	6712	626
Patterson Bank	6022	551
Patterson Belknap Webb and Tyler LLP	8111	146
Patterson Brothers Meat Co	5147	25
Patterson Capital Corp	6282	270
Patterson Chevrolet Inc	5511	1128
Patterson Companies Inc	5047	5
Patterson Dental Supply Inc	5047	27
Patterson Fan Company Inc	3564	83
Patterson Frozen Foods Inc	2037	48
Patterson Office Supplies	2759	606
Patterson Oil Co	5984	8
Patterson Pump Co	3561	43
Patterson Storage Warehouse Co	4213	3018
Patterson Warehouses Inc	4225	21
Patterson-Erie Corp	6513	27
Patterson-Kelley Employees Federal Credit Union	6061	163
Patterson-Schwartz and Associates Inc	6531	281
Patterson-UTI Energy Inc	1381	6
Patti Joe Seafood Co	5421	8
Pattison Koskey Howe and Bucci CPA's PC	8721	404
Pattison Precision Products Inc	3599	1106
Patton and Patton Software Corp	7372	4008
Patton Electronics Co	3661	117
Patton Harris Rust and Associates PC	8711	47
Patton Kiehl Group Inc	7331	120
Patton Music Company Inc	5962	14
Patton Tool And Die Inc	3089	1876
Patty Girardi	7373	586
Patuxent Materials Inc	5032	28
Patuxent Publishing Co	2711	149
Patuxent River Park	5091	134
Patwin Plastics Inc	3089	1077
Patz Corp	3599	97
Patz Sales Inc	3523	76
Paul Arpin Van Lines	4214	10
Paul Baker Printing Inc	2752	976
Paul C Buff Inc	3648	49
Paul C Emery Co	4213	2943
Paul Capital Partners	6799	70
Paul D Sheriff and Associates Inc	7372	2472
Paul D Taylor CPA	8721	401
Paul Davis Automation Inc	5065	746
Paul Davis Restoration Inc	1521	30
Paul De Lima Company Inc	2095	27
Paul E Smith Company Inc	1731	185
Paul Feed and Supply Co	5211	243
Paul Ferrante Inc	3999	177
Paul Garnsey and Son Inc	4213	2715
Paul Guggenheim and Associates Inc	7372	2201
Paul H Rohe Company Inc	2951	50
Paul Harvey Ford Sales Inc	5511	554
Paul Hastings Janofsky and Walker LLP	8111	14
Paul Hemmer Cos	1542	256
Paul Heuring Motors Inc	5511	884
Paul King Co	5084	917
Paul L Henry	5441	22
Paul Machine Corp	3599	1636
Paul Marshall Produce Inc	4213	1975
Paul McInnis Inc	7389	1463
Paul Miller Ford-Mazda Inc	5511	178
Paul Moak Pontiac Inc	5511	892
Paul Mueller Co	3443	20
Paul O Young Co	5084	776
Paul Patrick Electric Inc	1731	2544
Paul Piazza and Son Inc	5146	44
Paul Reed Smith Guitars LP	3931	19
Paul Revere Corp	6321	53
Paul Risk Associates Inc	1521	87
Paul S Amidon and Associates Inc	2752	405
Paul Scherer and Company LLP	8721	324
Paul Schurman Machine Inc	3599	2125
Paul Snider Enterprises	5511	1239
Paul Stuart Inc	5611	17
Paul Taylor	5046	357
Paul W Marino Gages Inc	3441	225
Paul Wales Inc	2759	413
Paul Watts Trucking Inc	4213	2483
Paul Weiss Rifkind Wharton and Garrison LLP	8111	64
Paul Werth Associates Inc	8743	77
Paul Wiley Electrical Contractors Inc	1731	1899
Paula Black and Associates	7336	248
Paulding-Putnam Electric Cooperative Inc	4911	477
Pauli Systems Inc	3599	1357
Paulk's Moving and Storage Inc	4213	2966
Paul-Munroe Enertech	3594	3
Paulo Products Co	3471	27
Paul's Run Inc	8361	22
Paul's TV - King Of The Big Screen	5731	12
Paulsen Inc	1611	98
Paulsen Printing Co	2752	852
Paulson Capital Corp	6211	319
Paulson Investment Company Inc	6211	283
Paulson Manufacturing Corp	3089	351
Paulson Press Inc	2752	1102
Paulstra Crc Corp	3069	25
Pauluhn Electric Manufacturing Co	3629	49
Pauly Rogers and Co	8721	412
Paumanok Vineyards Ltd	0721	3
Pavan and Kievit Enterprises Inc	3823	305
Pavarini Construction Company Inc	1542	121
Pavco Inc	2899	75
Pavco Industries Inc	2435	18
PAVE Technology Co	3678	31
Pavement Tool Manufacturing Inc	3953	22
Pavilion Furniture Inc	2514	12
Pavilion Technologies Inc	7372	1463
Pavlik Electric Company Inc	1731	2092
Pavone	7311	197
Pavsner Press Inc	2752	878
Pavyer Printing Machine Works Inc	7699	201
Pawlik Supply Company Inc	5211	308
Pawling Corp	3061	13
PawnMart Inc	5999	39
Pawtucket Auto Supply Inc	5013	413
Pawtucket Times	2711	89
Pax LLC	3443	71
Pax Machine Works Inc	3469	38
Pax World Balanced Fund Inc	6722	104
Pax World Management Corp	6282	182
Paxcell Group Inc	5045	702
Paxson Communications of Birmingham-44 Inc	4833	262
Paxton Company Inc	5088	27
Paxton Media Group LLC	2711	225
Paxton Van Lines Inc	4213	759
Paxton-Mitchell Co	3322	2
Pay and Save Inc	5411	127
Paychest Inc	8742	714
Paychex Business Solutions Inc	8721	293
Paychex Inc	8721	24
PayChoice	7374	346
Paycor Inc	8721	320
Paydata Inc	3559	334
Payden and Rygel	6282	58
Payette Associates Inc	8712	67
Payformance Corp	3577	213
PayLease LLC	7379	787
Payler Corp	2731	328
Payless Car Rental System Inc	6794	66
Pay-Less Office Products Inc	5112	31
Paylocity Corp	8721	322
Paymaster Technologies Inc	3579	38
Payment Data Systems Inc	6099	34
Payment Software Corp	7372	3008
Payment Systems for Credit Unions Inc	7389	151
PaymentMax	7389	775
Paymentone Corp	4813	439
Payments Resource One	6099	29
Payne and Cambron Inc	2273	37
Payne and Morrison Florists	5992	11
Payne Electric Co	1731	2046
Payne Engineering Company Inc	3625	263
Payne Inc	4213	408
Payne Lynch and Associates Inc	4731	83
Payne Magnetics Corp	3677	29

Company Name	SIC	Rank
Payne Printery Inc	2759	197
Payne Publishers Inc	2741	169
Payne Todd Sulak and Co	8721	454
Pay-O-Matic Corp	6099	2
PayPal Inc	7389	158
Payplus Inc	7363	340
Payroll 1 Inc	8721	331
Payroll Associates Inc	7372	1797
Payroll Consulting Services Inc	7363	352
Payscape Advisors	7374	188
Payson Casters Inc	3429	49
Paytel Communications Inc	7389	1337
Pb Car Movers	7389	1477
PB Express Inc	4213	1474
PB Farradyne Inc	7372	1239
Pb Holdings Inc	3545	27
PB Leiner USA	2099	368
PB Systems Inc	7373	476
PBC Sound Technologies	1731	2591
PBD Inc	5192	20
PBE Jobbers Warehouse Inc	5013	70
PBI Bank	6021	225
Pbi-Gordon Corp	2879	18
PBM Inc	3494	53
PBN Co	8743	42
PBS Control	3829	309
PBS Enterprises Inc	4899	25
PBS Supply Company Inc	3952	12
PC Accountant Inc	7371	1119
PC Assistance Inc	7379	1329
PC Audio Labs	7373	1088
PC Campana Inc	3498	35
PC City	3575	60
PC Connection Inc	5961	14
PC Depot Inc	7378	125
PC Distributors LLC	5045	1046
PC Dynamics Inc	7372	3840
PC Electric Inc	1731	1623
PC Electrocraft Inc	5063	861
PC Enterprises Inc	5734	192
PC Export House Corp	5045	665
PC Fling	4813	497
PC Group Inc	3842	75
PC Helpers Inc	7379	1331
PC I Paper Conversions Inc	2679	48
PC Mac Connections	7822	40
PC Mall Gov Inc	3571	18
PC Mall Inc	5961	22
PC MAX	5045	820
PC McKenzie Co	5074	196
PC Menu Inc	5734	397
PC Netrix	3825	354
PC One Professional Systems Inc	7373	1077
PC Open Inc	3699	64
PC Outlet LLC	7378	134
PC Parts Inc	5961	100
PC People Inc	5734	423
PC Power and Cooling Inc	3577	273
PC Pricer Inc	1731	1364
PC Products and Services Inc	5734	143
PC Professional Incorporation	7378	62
PC Pros Inc	4813	684
PC Rc Products LLC	3829	517
PC Richard and Son	5722	4
PC Scale Inc	7372	4436
PC Solutions Inc	5734	327
PC Supply Co	5734	398
PC Transformer Corp	3677	111
PC Transport Inc	4213	2543
PC Treasures Inc	5734	67
PC Workshop Inc	8742	706
Pca Electronics Inc	3677	53
PCB Solutions Inc	3672	366
PCC Airfoils Inc	3728	11
PCC Chemax Inc	2899	91
PCC Natural Markets	5411	194
Pccp Studio City Los Angeles Tcs Acquisition LLC	7812	172
Pccw Global Inc	4813	24
Pcd	1731	2156
PC-Doctor Inc	7372	1845
Pcf Inc	3823	411
Pcfs 2000 Inc	5734	137
PCG Software Inc	7372	3009
Pci Energy Services Inc	1799	44
PCI Geomatics	7372	2337
Pci Inc	2842	136
PCI Manufacturing Division Inc	3663	330
Pci Micro Corp	5045	873
Pci Procal Inc	3571	163
PCI Roads Inc	1611	83
Pci Services Inc	7349	138
PCI Transportation Inc	4213	1243
Pciroads LLC	1611	50
Pcl Construction Inc	1542	101
PClaptops LLC	5734	17
PCLendercom	7372	1313
Pclt Corp	5719	36
Pcm Products Inc	3479	102
Pcmechanic	7379	966
PCN Strategies	8748	346
PCnet Inc	7373	264
Pcnet LP	7373	616
Pc-N-U Inc	5734	289

Company Name	SIC	Rank
PCP Inc	3085	47
Pcps Inc	5734	453
Pcretro Inc	5734	261
PCS Edventures!com Inc	8299	2
Pcs Power and Communications Solutions Inc	1731	1166
Pcs Telecorp Inc	4812	20
PCS Wireless Inc	5045	55
Pcs-Phone Inc	1731	663
PCT International	3663	189
Pct Systems Inc	3674	355
PCTEL Inc	3663	55
PCTV Inc	7812	154
P-Cube Inc	7373	183
PCW Computer	5734	234
Pcy Enterprises Inc	1761	55
Pda Panache Corp	3577	633
Pdc Facilities Inc	1542	323
Pdc Glass And Metal Services Inc	5031	85
Pdc International Corp	3565	85
Pdc Machines Inc	3545	249
Pddc A R C	8322	248
PDF Solutions Inc	7371	156
PDG Environmental Inc	4959	13
Pdi Communications Inc	5065	121
PDI/Dreamworks Inc	7812	11
PDI Inc (Upper Saddle River New Jersey)	7389	192
PDL BioPharma Inc	2836	8
PDM Bridge LLC	3441	13
PDM Steel Service Centers Inc	5051	84
PDMA Corp	3825	125
PDME Inc	5044	28
Pdns LLC	4813	361
Pdp Enterprises Inc	7381	123
PDQ Food Stores Inc	5411	175
PDQ Manufacturing Inc	2842	122
Pdq PC Design Inc	7373	1236
PDQ Plastics Inc	3089	1608
Pdq Print Center	3823	279
Pdq Printing Of Las Vegas Inc	7334	36
Pdq South Injection Technologies Inc	3089	1673
Pdq Supply Inc	5064	141
PDQ Tool and Stamping Co	3544	464
Pdr Inc	5734	454
PDS Agent Inc	4213	2914
PDS Gaming Corp	6159	53
PDS Services	7363	246
Pdu Lad Corp	3914	11
PDV America Inc	2911	11
PDVSA Services Inc	2911	47
PE Kramme Inc	4213	1733
Pea River Electric Coop	4911	315
Peabody Energy Corp	1221	2
Peabody Hotel Group	6531	155
Peabody Office Furniture Corp	5021	82
Peabody Recreational Lands LLC	7033	7
Peace City International Inc	4899	220
Peace Design	7389	1807
Peace Flooring Company Inc	2421	133
Peace River Citrus Products Inc	0174	7
Peace Security Inc	7381	193
Peace Technology Inc	7379	1097
Peace Textile America Inc	2262	3
PeaceHealth	8062	54
Peach Chevrolet	5012	175
Peach County Holdings Inc	3713	11
PEACH DVD	2741	44
Peach Net Communications Inc	5999	208
Peach State Integrated Technologies Inc	5084	359
Peach State Truck Centers	5511	816
Peach Street Properties Inc	5074	201
Peach Systems	5734	457
Peachin Schwartz and Weingardt PC	8721	198
Peachtree Business Products LLC	2761	20
Peachtree Capital Corp	6282	262
Peachtree Data Inc	7374	338
Peachtree Doors and Windows Inc	3442	28
Peachtree Electric Lighting Inc	1731	980
Peachtree Fabrics Inc	5131	12
Peachtree Ford	5511	508
Peachtree Lighting Inc	3646	95
Peachtree Packaging Inc	2653	59
Peachtree Planning Corp	6311	147
Peachtree Publishers Ltd	2731	321
Peachtree Residential Properties	1521	44
Peachtree Settlement Funding	6799	27
Peachtree Special Risk Brokers LLC	6411	225
Peachtree Tooling Corp	3545	150
Peacock and Lewis Architects and Planners Inc	8712	295
Peacock Engineering Co	4783	2
Peacock Industries Inc	3599	1990
Peacock Press Inc	2752	1535
Peacock Products Inc	2759	313
Peacock Sales Company Inc	5074	123
Peak 10 Inc	7373	148
Peak 10 (Richmond Virginia)	7372	787
Peak Biety Inc	7311	709
Peak Body Systems Inc	3949	121
Peak Communication Systems Inc	5065	650
Peak Computer Services Inc	3575	49
Peak Computer Solutions	5045	956

Company Name	SIC	Rank
Peak Contract Manufacturing LLC	3643	87
Peak Creative Media	7336	182
Peak Horizons Inc	7372	4625
Peak Industries Company Inc	3544	245
Peak Minerals-Azomite Inc	2873	18
Peak Oilfield Services Co	1389	29
Peak Service Corp	7389	1861
Peak Technical Services Inc	7363	98
PEAK Technologies Inc	5065	33
Peak Uplink Inc	4841	147
Peak6 Investments LP	6282	196
Peaker Services Inc	3559	169
Peanut Processors Inc	5145	9
Peapack-Gladstone Bank	6022	122
Peapack-Gladstone Financial Corp	6712	254
Peapod LLC	5961	68
Pearce Bevill Leesburg and Moore PC	8721	88
Pearce Foundry Inc	3561	153
Pearce Industries Inc	5084	118
Pearce Plastics Inc	3089	1282
Pearl Brewing Co	2082	13
Pearl Buck Center Inc	8331	25
Pearl Buck Production Services	8331	13
Pearl Computer Services Inc	7379	733
Pearl Law Group	8111	505
Pearl Pressman Liberty Communications Group	2752	198
Pearl River Communications Inc	4832	186
Pearl River Pastries LLC	2064	104
Pearl River Valley Electric Power Association	4911	378
Pearl Technology Corp	5045	586
Pearl Valley Cheese Inc	2022	79
Pearland Independent School District	8211	36
Pearlstine Distributors Inc	5181	35
Pearpoint Inc	3663	220
Pearson Assessments	3577	7
Pearson Candy Co	2064	33
Pearson Electronics Inc	3612	128
Pearson Engineering Corp	3479	105
Pearson McMahon Fletcher England	7311	317
Pearson Scott Foresman	2741	18
Pearson Technologies Inc	1382	43
Pearson's Inc	3523	260
Pease and Curren Inc	3341	14
Pease Industies Inc	3442	70
Peavey Corp	6719	156
Peavey Electronics Corp	3651	21
Peavy and Son Construction Company Inc	1611	182
Pebble Beach Co	7011	158
Pebblebrook Hotel Trust	6798	217
PEC Systems Inc	3625	274
Pecan Point Food Products Inc	5142	43
Pech Optical Corp	5048	4
Pechter's Baking Group LLC	2051	43
Peck Madigan Jones and Stewart Inc	8743	132
Peck Precision Machine and Tool	3599	2512
Peck Road Gravel Pit	1442	56
Peck Sosa Inc	7349	529
Peck Spring Corp	3495	19
Peck Water Systems Inc	5999	281
Peckham Guyton Albers and Viets Inc	8712	87
Peckham Industries Inc	2951	21
PECO Energy Co	4931	31
Peco Fasteners Inc	5085	257
PECO Inc	3524	19
PECO Manufacturing Company Inc	3822	13
PECO Manufacturing Inc	3714	399
Pecos Valley Pump Inc	1711	270
Pedagogue Solutions	7372	1969
Pedavena Mould And Die Company Inc	3544	660
Pedcor Cos	1521	56
Peddinghaus Corp	3541	17
Pedernales Electric Cooperative Inc	4911	87
Pedersen Media Group Inc	7812	302
Pederson Kolb and Associates Inc	7361	196
Pederson Tool and Design Inc	3544	783
Pediatric Home Nursing Services Inc	8082	11
Pediatric Prosthetics Inc	3842	320
Pediatric Services Holding Corp	8082	24
Pediatric Services of America Inc	8082	28
Pediatrix Medical Group of Florida Inc	8011	5
Pedifix Footcare Co	2844	175
Pedigo Products Inc	2522	20
Pedigree Technologies LLC	5065	346
Pedmic Converting Inc	3086	168
Pedro's Tamales	2038	63
Ped-Stuart Corp	3999	206
Pee Wee Workout Inc	7991	23
Peebles Corp	6552	67
Peebles Inc	5311	31
Peek 'N Peak Recreation Inc	7011	181
Peek Traffic Inc	3812	77
Peek Traffic Signal Maintenance Inc	7629	7
Peelle Co	3442	93
Peeples Industries Inc	4491	2
Peeq Media LLC	7384	2
Peer Bearing Co	3568	8
Peer Chain Co	5005	248
Peer Media Technologies	7372	1009
Peerless Chain Co	3496	16
Peerless Coffee And Tea	2095	35
Peerless Coffee Co	2095	13

Company Name	SIC	Rank
Peerless Electronic Equipment Company Inc	5065	462
Peerless Electronics Inc	5065	65
Peerless Heater Co	3443	76
Peerless Industries Inc	3429	55
Peerless Insurance Co	6331	77
Peerless Lighting	3646	48
Peerless Machine and Tool Corp	3554	26
Peerless Machinery Corp	3556	56
Peerless Manufacturing Co	3569	29
Peerless Materials Co	2842	110
Peerless Pattern Works Inc	3565	176
Peerless Plastics Inc	3089	890
Peerless Pottery Inc	3261	6
Peerless Printing Co	2752	1739
Peerless Products Inc	3442	52
Peerless Pumps Sales and Service	5084	844
Peerless Steel Co	5051	184
Peerless Supply Inc	5084	204
Peerless Trucking Co	4213	1132
Peerless Tyre Co	5531	17
Peerless Umbrella Company Inc	3999	97
Peerless-Premier Appliance Co	3631	7
Peerless-Winsmith Inc	3621	34
Peerlis Inc	7373	644
Peet Brothers Co	5999	256
Peet Frate Line Inc	4213	2944
Peet's Coffee and Tea Inc	2095	8
Peg Perego USA Inc	5099	56
Pegasus Business Intelligence LP	7375	41
Pegasus Capital Advisors LP	6722	139
Pegasus Cleaning Corp	7349	126
Pegasus Communications Inc	2741	493
Pegasus Disk Technologies Inc	7372	4252
Pegasus Laboratories Inc	2834	229
Pegasus Manufacturing Inc (Middletown Connecticut)	3498	27
Pegasus Scientific Inc	5049	163
Pegasus Software Systems Inc	7372	3624
Pegasus Solutions Inc	7374	39
Pegasus Steel LLC	7389	1281
Pegasus Transportation Group	4213	911
Pegasus Transportation Inc	4213	180
Pegasystems Inc	7372	157
Peggs Company Inc	7699	44
Peggy Nye and Lodin Inc	7389	1055
Pehler and Sons Inc	4213	1964
Pei Cobb Freed and Partners	8712	107
Pei Cobb Freed and Partners LLP	8712	158
PEI Genesis	3674	141
Pei/ Genesis Inc	3678	8
Pei Liquidation Co	3231	31
Peirce Park Group	6282	546
Peirce Software Inc	7371	1350
Peirce-Phelps Inc	7373	87
Peju Province Winery Ltd	5921	18
Pekay Machine and Engineering Company Inc	3559	445
Pekin Life Insurance Co	6311	90
Peking Noodle Company Inc	2099	125
Pelco Industries Inc	7349	20
Pelco Press Inc	2752	1635
Pelco Tool and Mold Inc	3544	499
PeleSoft	7372	4542
Pel-Freez Arkansas LLC	2836	60
Pelham Machine and Tool Inc	3599	1233
Pelican Equipment Company Inc	5082	204
Pelican Financial Inc	6021	296
Pelican Ice and Cold Storage Inc	2097	16
Pelican Optical Labs Inc	5048	33
Pelican Pictures Inc	7812	334
Pelican Products Company Inc	3951	7
Pelican Products Inc	3648	12
Pelican Publishing Company Inc	2731	271
Pelican Real Estate Corp	7381	132
Pelican Reef Inc	5021	99
Pell Artifex Co	3648	89
Pell Communications Inc	7311	718
Pella Corp	2431	5
Pella Window and Door LLC	5031	323
Pelland Advertising	7379	1650
Pellerin Laundry Machinery Sales Company Inc	5087	69
Pellerin Milnor Corp	3582	3
Pellet America Corp	2999	7
Pelletizer Knives Inc	3423	79
Pelletreau and Pelletreau	8111	582
Pelletrox Inc	7538	22
Pellettieri Rabstein and Altman	8111	431
Pelli Clarke Pelli Architects	8712	79
Pelmor Laboratories Inc	3061	28
Peloton Manufacturing Corp	3625	150
Pelron Corp	2833	63
Pelton Company Inc	3625	423
Pem Systems Inc	3999	121
Pemaco Inc	3843	78
Pemberton Fabricators Inc	3444	168
Pemberton Inc	3531	135
Pemberton Truck Lines Inc	4213	653
Pembroke's Inc	5734	164
Pemco Corp	3699	60
Pemco Dental Corp	5047	173
Pemco Inc	3841	383
Pemco World Air Services	3724	17

Company Name	SIC	Rank
Pemco-Naval Engineering Works Inc	3441	243
Pemcor Printing Company LLC	2759	34
Pemer Packing Company Inc	7361	101
Pemiscot Dunklin Electric Coop	4911	421
Pemko Manufacturing Co	3442	44
Pen And Incorporated Of Milwaukee Inc	3861	77
Pen Publishing Interactive Inc	4813	518
Pen Ro Mold And Tool Inc	3544	540
Pence Company J H	5049	83
Pen-Cell Plastics Inc	3089	1021
Penco Graphic Supply Inc	5999	320
Penco Precision	3599	523
Penco Tool LLC	3544	609
Pencom Systems Inc	7372	217
Pencor Services Inc	4841	110
Pencraft Corp	2752	1399
Penda Corp	5013	87
Pender Adult Services Inc	8322	213
Pender Packing Company Inc	2013	192
Pending Inc	3599	2250
Pendleton Corp	5735	19
Pendleton Creek Farms Construction Inc	1731	1227
Pendleton Flour Mills LLC	2041	32
Pendleton Grain Growers Inc	5153	18
Pendleton Woolen Mills Inc	2337	5
Pendock Mallorn Ltd	7372	4865
Pendragon Software Corp	7372	3938
Pendrell Corp	4813	755
Pendu Manufacturing Inc	3553	18
Pendulab Ltd	7372	3361
Pendulum Instruments Inc	3825	299
Penegon West Inc	7389	1634
Penetone Corp	2842	44
Penetradar Corp	3812	132
PenFact Inc	7372	834
Pen-Fern Oil Co	5172	126
Penflex Corp	3599	564
Penford Corp	2046	3
Penford Food Ingredients Co	8731	112
Penford Products Co	2046	4
Peng Engineering	7372	2202
Penguin Group Inc (New York New York)	2731	32
Penguin Group (USA) Inc	2731	42
Penguin Point Franchise Systems Inc	5046	119
Penhall Co	1771	2
Penick Corp	2834	387
Peninsula Airways Inc	4512	52
Peninsula Asset Management Inc	6282	139
Peninsula Battery Inc	5063	806
Peninsula Bottling Company Inc	5149	71
Peninsula Building Materials Company Inc	5031	430
Peninsula Concrete And Steel Inc	5051	437
Peninsula Control Panels Inc	3613	162
Peninsula Copper Industries Inc	2819	60
Peninsula Fruit Exchange Inc	5148	84
Peninsula Gaming Company LLC	7999	60
Peninsula Group Inc	1752	2
Peninsula Iron Works	3599	1007
Peninsula Laboratories Inc	2833	68
Peninsula Mobil Wash	7349	336
Peninsula Software Of Virginia Inc	7371	1290
Peninsula Truck Lines Inc	4213	600
Peninsular Electric Distributors Inc	5063	101
Peninsular Inc	3443	175
Peninsular Printing of Daytona Beach Inc	2752	1669
Peninsular Securities Co	6211	318
Pen-Link Ltd	7371	1237
Penmac Personnel Services Inc	7361	75
Penmor Lithographers Inc	2752	673
Penn and Sons Inc	7349	198
Penn Bottle and Supply Co	3221	7
Penn Cigar Machines Inc	3599	1206
Penn Color Inc	2865	4
Penn Computer Corp	7373	1158
Penn Detroit Diesel Allison LLC	3519	12
Penn Diagnostic Center Inc	8011	170
Penn Emblem Co	2395	12
Penn Energy	2741	78
Penn Engineering and Manufacturing Corp	3452	10
Penn Engineering Components	3679	700
Penn Foam Corp	3069	146
Penn Independent Corp	6331	297
Penn Industries Inc	2791	2
Penn Iron Works Inc	3443	183
Penn Line Service Inc	1623	51
Penn Lyon Homes Corp	2452	34
Penn Machine Inc	3533	119
Penn Manufacturing Industries Inc	3599	498
Penn Mutual Life Insurance Co	6311	60
Penn National Gaming Inc	7948	1
Penn National Insurance	6331	74
Penn North Technology Inc	3674	308
Penn Panel and Box Co	3613	87
Penn Plastics Inc	3089	1210
Penn Racquet Sports	3949	58
Penn Refrigeration Service Corp	3585	136
Penn Security Bank and Trust Co	6022	348
Penn Separator Corp	3823	281

Company Name	SIC	Rank
Penn Shadecrafters Inc	3999	202
Penn Staffing Services LLC	7361	240
Penn State Industries Inc	5092	8
Penn Street Inc	7336	196
Penn Systems Group Inc	5734	288
Penn Traffic Co	5411	91
Penn Treaty American Corp	6321	34
Penn Treaty Network America Life Insurance Co	6311	115
Penn United Technologies Inc	3544	4
Penn Virginia Corp	1311	71
Penn Virginia GP Holdings LP	1241	2
Penn Virginia Resource Partners LP	1241	1
Penn Warehousing and Distribution	4491	7
Penn West Industrial Trucks LLC	5084	413
Penn Wood Products Inc	5031	212
Penn Yan Plumbing And Heating Inc	5063	920
Penna Powers Brian And Haynes Inc	7311	881
Pennaco Energy Inc	1311	231
Penn-America Group Inc	6351	14
Penn-America Insurance Co	6331	308
Pennant Moldings Inc	3469	77
PennantPark Investment Corp	6141	31
Pennatronics Corp	3678	21
Penncat Corp	5063	763
Pennco Containers Ltd	5085	188
Pennco Tool and Die Inc	3544	682
PennComp Inc	7372	2911
Pennfield Corp	5144	7
Pennfield Oil Co	5191	143
Pennfield Transport Co	4213	1678
PennFirst Capital Trust I	6091	12
PennFirst Financial Services Inc	6099	14
Pennichuck Corp	4941	21
Pennichuck Water Works Inc	4941	42
Penniman and Browne Inc	8734	117
Pennington Partners	6799	296
Pennock Co	5193	7
Pennoyer-Dodge Co	3545	177
Penn's Best Inc	4213	283
Penns Woods Bancorp Inc	6712	393
Pennsbury School District	8211	24
Pennsy Supply Inc	3273	17
Pennsylvania Brewing Co	5813	10
Pennsylvania Brine Treatment Inc	2899	145
Pennsylvania Drilling Co	1623	158
Pennsylvania Electric Co	4911	77
Pennsylvania Electric Motor Service Inc	7694	14
Pennsylvania Industrial Heat Treaters Inc	3312	49
Pennsylvania Life Insurance Co	6311	278
Pennsylvania Machine Works Inc	3462	26
Pennsylvania Manufacturers' Association Insurance Co	6331	240
Pennsylvania Manufacturers Indemnity Co	6351	13
Pennsylvania Mutual Fund Inc	6722	118
Pennsylvania Networks Inc	1731	1046
Pennsylvania Power Co	4911	105
Pennsylvania Precision Cast Parts Inc	3324	13
Pennsylvania Real Estate Investment Trust	6798	77
Pennsylvania Sewing Machine Co	5084	419
Pennsylvania State Bank	6022	520
Pennsylvania Steel Corp	5051	503
Pennsylvania Tool And Gages Inc	3545	252
Pennsylvania Transformer Technology Inc	3612	33
Pennsylvania Trust Co	6091	10
Pennsylvania-American Water Co	4941	49
Penn-Tech International Inc	1799	139
Penntech Machinery Corp	3559	432
Penntecq Inc	3714	312
Penn-Union Corp	3643	37
Pennway Express Inc	4213	819
Penny Marketing LP	2721	323
Penny Newman Milling LLC	2048	22
Penny Ohlmann Neiman Inc	7311	325
Penny Publications LLC	2721	159
PennyMac Mortgage Investment Trust	6799	361
Pennysaver Publications Inc	2721	82
Pennyweb Inc	7319	61
Penobscot Mccrum LLC	2037	23
Penobscot Shoe Co	3144	3
Penrod Co	5031	92
Penrose Machining Inc	3469	269
Penrose Press	2741	417
Penseco Financial Services Corp	6712	340
Penser Transportation Inc	4213	1021
Pension Associates Inc	6722	179
Penske Automotive Group Inc	5511	2
Penske Corp	7513	1
Penske Logistic Inc	4213	38
Penske Truck Leasing Company LP	7513	3
Penson Worldwide Inc	8999	23
Pent Plastics Inc	3089	426
Penta Corp	7373	757
Penta International Corp	5149	114
Penta Technologies Inc	7372	2063
Pentadyne Power Corp	3499	35
Pentaflex Inc	3469	185
Pentagon 2000 Software Inc	7371	345
Pentagon Federal Credit Union	6061	6

Company Name	SIC	Rank
Pentagraphix Offset Printing Inc	2752	978
Pentair Inc	2621	6
Pentair Pool Products	3589	22
Pentana Inc	7371	1816
Pentas Controls Inc	3679	846
Pentax of America Inc	3827	7
Pentech Pharmaceuticals Inc	2834	382
Pentek Inc	5084	743
Pentel Of America Ltd	5112	21
Penthouse Manufacturing Company Inc	3172	6
Pentland USA	2321	18
Penton Internet Inc	7375	28
Penton Media Inc	2721	42
Penton Overseas Inc	2731	193
PenTrust Real Estate Advisory Services Inc	6282	513
Pentwater Wire Products Inc	3496	68
Penzeys Spices Inc	2099	28
People Care Inc	7363	101
People Electric Coop	4911	325
people for people	7372	4997
People Lease Inc	8721	468
People Network Inc	8741	254
People Sciences Inc	7372	3781
People Sentinel	2711	757
People Signs	5045	844
People To My Site	7319	149
PeopleAdmin Inc	7379	536
Peopleclick Authoria Inc	7372	866
Peoplelink Staffing Solutions	7361	53
PeopleMedCom Inc	7372	1346
Peoplequest Inc	8711	634
Peoples Bancorp (Auburn Indiana)	6712	475
Peoples Bancorp Inc	6712	210
Peoples Bancorp (Lynden Washington)	6712	577
Peoples Bancorp of North Carolina Inc	6712	304
Peoples Bancorporation Inc	6712	450
Peoples Bank and Trust of Lincoln County	6022	340
Peoples Bank (Lynden Washington)	6022	795
Peoples Bank (Mount Washington Kentucky)	6022	534
Peoples Bank NA	6022	760
Peoples Bank (Newton North Carolina)	6022	316
Peoples Bank of Commerce	6022	679
People's Benefit Life Insurance Co	6311	57
Peoples Cartage Inc	4213	933
Peoples Community Bank	6022	407
People's Community Bank	6022	581
People's Community Credit Union	6061	113
People's Computer Company Inc	7372	3463
Peoples Credit Union	6062	110
Peoples Education Holdings Inc	8299	33
People's Electric Coop	4911	235
Peoples Electrical Contractors Inc	1731	184
Peoples Energy Corp	4924	8
Peoples Exchange Bancorp	6712	593
Peoples Exchange Bank of Beattyville Kentucky	6022	476
People's Express Inc	7363	331
Peoples Federal Savings Bank of De-Kalb County	6035	107
Peoples Federal SLA	6035	177
Peoples Financial Corp (Biloxi Missis-sippi)	6022	199
Peoples Financial Services Inc	6282	242
Peoples First Properties Inc	6552	14
Peoples Foreign Exchange Corp	7389	817
Peoples Gas Light and Coke Co	4923	11
People's Graphics Inc	2752	1756
Peoples Insurance Agency Inc	6411	291
Peoples Jewelry Company Inc	7631	1
Peoples Liberation Inc	2331	7
People's Pharmacy Inc	5912	45
Peoples Rural Telephone Cooperative Corporation Inc	4813	236
Peoples Savings Bank (Rhineland Mis-souri)	6036	102
Peoples Southern Bank	6022	621
People's United Bank (Burlington Vermont)	6022	45
People's United Bank (Portland Maine)	6022	192
People's United Equipment Finance Corp	6159	33
People's United Financial Inc	6035	7
PeopleServe Inc	7361	79
PeopleShare	7361	115
Peoples-Sidney Financial Corp	6712	667
Peopletree Staffing Solutions	7363	162
Peopleware Technical Resources Inc	7361	273
Peoria Area Convention And Visitors Bureau	7389	1999
Peoria Disposal Co	4953	91
Peoria Packing Ltd	2011	96
Peoria Tube Forming Corp	3498	54
Pep Boys-Manny Moe and Jack	5531	3
Pep Direct Inc	2771	9
Pepco Holdings Inc	4911	31
Pepco Manufacturing Co	3444	87
PepCom Inc	7389	917
Peperkins Toolworks	7372	3391
Pepe's Inc	6794	78
Pepe's Wholesale Pizza Co	5149	78
Pepin Manufacturing Inc	3841	279

Company Name	SIC	Rank
Pepin-Ireco Inc	5169	162
PEPP Unlimited	8748	439
Pepper Construction Companies LLC	1541	22
Pepper Construction Company of Indiana	1542	257
Pepper Dining Inc	5812	205
Pepper Hamilton LLP	8111	20
Pepper Lawson Construction Inc	1542	243
Pepper Patch	2033	121
PepperCom Inc	8743	46
Pepperidge Farm Inc	2051	3
Pepperite Thermographers Inc	2759	358
Pepperjam Network	7375	208
Pepperl and Fuchs Inc	3625	33
Pepper-Lawson Construction LP	1542	109
Pepperman Emboulas Schwartz and Todaro	8721	452
Peppermill Casinos Inc	7011	119
Peppers and Rogers Group / Marketing 1to1	8742	11
Pepperweed Consulting LLC	7373	331
Peppy's Foods Inc	2038	80
Pepro Enterprises Inc	3089	165
Pepsi Bottling Ventures LLC	5149	85
Pepsi Bottling Ventures Of Idaho Inc	2086	51
Pepsi Midamerica Co	2086	32
PepsiCo Inc	2086	1
Pepsi-Cola Bottling Company Incorporated Of Norton Va	2086	88
Pepsi-Cola Bottling Co (Nashville Ten-nessee)	2086	37
Pepsi-Cola Bottling Company of Rochester	5149	22
Pepsi-Cola Bottling Company of Yakima	2086	36
Pepsi-Cola Bottling Of Aroostook	2086	117
Pepsi-Cola Champaign Urbana Bottler Company Inc	2086	109
Pepsi-Cola Memphis Bottling Co	2086	140
Pepsi-Cola of Siouxland	5149	96
Pepsi-Cola Ogdensburg Inc	2086	116
Pequot Capital Management	6799	30
Per Annum Inc	2741	248
Per Diem Inc	7361	346
Per Mar Security and Research Corp	7382	16
Perazzi Apparel Co	2339	57
Perbix Machine Company Inc	3599	571
Percepta LLC	7389	163
Perceptics LLC	3572	43
Perceptionist Inc	7389	2084
Perceptions Inc	7812	190
Perceptis LLC	7379	356
Perceptive Informatics Inc	7389	581
Perceptive Software Inc	7372	225
Perceptron Inc	3827	10
Percival Scientific Inc	3821	32
Percussion Software Inc	7372	1457
Percussionaire Corp	3845	136
Perdido Trucking Service Inc	4213	367
Perdue Inc	2015	4
Perdues Inc	2511	71
Peregrin Technologies Inc	3578	42
Peregrine Industries Inc	3569	302
Peregrine Pharmaceuticals Inc	2835	39
Peregrine Semiconductor Corp	3674	232
Peregrine Surgical Ltd	3841	268
Pereles Brothers Inc	3089	631
Perelson Weiner LLP	8721	344
Perennial Inc	7372	3734
Perera Construction and Design Inc	1542	192
Perers Enterprises Inc	5712	96
Perey Turnstiles Inc	3829	263
Perez Interboro Asphalt Company Inc	1611	129
Perez Trading Company Inc	5111	14
Perfecseal Inc	3089	191
Perfect Circle Solutions Inc	7372	1739
Perfect Commerce Inc	7372	561
Perfect Cut-Off Inc	7389	1658
Perfect Equipment Company LLC	3714	369
Perfect Fitness	5941	24
Perfect Image Inc	2752	1749
Perfect Patterns Inc	3543	20
Perfect Performance Products LLC	3694	35
Perfect Plastic Printing Corp	2752	78
Perfect Software (Arcadia California)	7371	1653
Perfect Software Inc	7372	2088
Perfect Web Technologies Inc	7371	1875
Perfecta USA	3555	91
Perfect-Climate Heating And Air Conditioning Inc	5075	112
Perfection Bakeries Inc	2051	12
Perfection Equipment Inc	3585	215
Perfection Learning Corp	2731	109
Perfection Machine And Tool Works A California Corp	3599	976
Perfection Mold and Machine Co	3544	895
Perfection Printing	2759	558
Perfection Products Inc	3674	364
Perfection Spring and Stamping Corp	3465	50
Perfection Tool Co	3544	750
Perfecto Industries Inc	3547	8
Perfecto Tool and Engineering Company Inc	3599	1014
Perfectserve Inc	4813	396

Company Name	SIC	Rank
PerfectSoftware (Norwalk Connecticut)	7372	3674
Perfekta Inc	3599	111
Perfetti Trucking Inc	4213	532
Perfetti Van Melle USA Inc	5145	6
Perficient Inc	7371	58
Perficient Meritage Inc	7373	239
Per-Fil Industries Inc	3565	105
Perfman	7372	2579
Perforce Software Inc	7372	1356
Perform Air International Inc	7699	32
Performa Entertainment Real Estate Inc	6531	245
Performance Assessment Network Inc	8742	259
Performance Associates International Inc	7372	2800
Performance Automotive Inc	5013	256
Performance Bindery Inc	2789	136
Performance Capital Management LLC	6211	351
Performance Chevrolet	5511	131
Performance Chrysler Jeep and Dodge LLC	5511	308
Performance Clean LLC	7349	98
Performance Coatings Inc	2851	147
Performance Communications Group Ltd	8743	172
Performance Composites Inc	3229	28
Performance Contracting Group Inc	1742	2
Performance Contractors Inc	3498	13
Performance Designs Inc	2399	21
Performance Electric Inc	1731	1916
Performance Engineered Products Inc	3089	779
Performance Fabricating LLC	3441	218
Performance Films Distributing Inc	5031	361
Performance Food Equipment Group Inc	5046	332
Performance Food Group Inc	5141	7
Performance Imaging Corp	3571	215
Performance Imaging LLC	1731	859
Performance Inc	5941	16
Performance Industries Manufacturing Inc	5013	259
Performance Machine Inc	3751	11
Performance Management Inc	7373	383
Performance Mechanical Inc	1541	79
Performance Metal Works Inc	3799	24
Performance Methods Inc	8742	723
Performance Motors	5511	1003
Performance Motorsports Inc	3592	10
Performance Oriented Solutions Inc	7371	1573
Performance Pattern and Machine Inc	3599	1185
Performance Pipe Div	3494	62
Performance Plastics Ltd	3089	952
Performance Plus Tire and Auto	5014	36
Performance Polymer Technologies LLC	3069	101
Performance Printing (Dallas Texas)	7389	191
Performance Resource Press Inc	2731	340
Performance Sample Inc	2782	64
Performance Software Corp	7371	613
Performance Software Group	7372	3939
Performance Solutions Technology LLC	7372	4731
Performance Sound and Light Inc	3648	57
Performance Strategies Inc	8742	536
Performance Support Inc	8748	336
Performance Systematix Inc	3089	611
Performance Technologies Inc (Rochester New York)	3577	214
Performance Technology Partners LLC	7379	1096
Performance Tradeshow Group Inc	7389	1585
Performance Trends Inc	7372	5035
Performance Warehouse Co	5013	100
Performance Woodworking Inc	5031	384
Performanceit Inc	7378	124
Performex Machining Co	3599	1882
Performix Inc (Houston Texas)	7372	1627
Performix Technologies	2899	163
PerformTech Inc	7371	337
Perfumania Holdings Inc	5912	16
Pergolis-Swartz Associates Inc	6162	70
Peri Software Solutions Inc	7379	453
Perich and Partners Ltd	7311	371
Pericom Semiconductor Corp	3674	93
PerifiTech of Ohio Inc	3571	57
Perigon PA	8711	250
Perillo Tours	4725	55
Perimeter Digital Imaging and Supply	7389	818
Perimeter Internetworking	7376	7
Perimeter Technology Inc	7372	2069
Perimeter Transportation Company LLC	4213	1987
Perini Building Company Inc	1541	38
Perini Land and Development Co	6552	110
Period Lighting Fixtures Inc	3645	86
Periodical Management Group Inc	5192	26
Periodico El Vida	2711	747
Peripheral Computer Support Inc	7378	5
Peripheral Dynamics Inc	3577	16
Peripheral Manufacturing Inc	3577	602
Peripheral Resources Inc	5045	442
Peripheral Sciences Inc	7371	1755
Peris Companies Inc	1541	223
Periscope Inc	7311	84
Perkasie Industries Corp	3089	929
Perket Technologies Inc	7379	1383

Company Name	SIC	Rank
PerkinElmer Inc	3826	4
Perkin-Elmer Instruments	3826	12
PerkinElmer Life and Analytical Sciences Inc	2899	46
Perkins	5141	161
Perkins and Company PC	8748	103
Perkins and Will Inc	8712	70
Perkins Coie LLP	8111	104
Perkins Eastman Architects PC	8712	44
Perkins Family Restaurants LP	5812	68
Perkins Investment Management LLC	6211	373
Perkins Scale Corp	5046	130
Perkins Specialized Transportation	4213	1404
Perko Inc	3429	56
Perlectric Inc	1731	225
Perlo McCormack Pacific	1542	228
Perm Industries Inc	3544	625
Perma Glas-Mesh Inc	2295	7
Perma Plastics Inc	3672	304
Perma Pure LLC	3821	38
Permabit Inc	7372	1496
Permabond International Corp	2891	34
Perma-Cal Industries Inc	3823	327
Permacor Inc	3264	21
Permadur Industries Inc	5084	223
Perma-Fix Environmental Services Inc	4953	44
Perma-Fix of Florida Inc	4953	51
Perma-Fix of Fort Lauderdale Inc	4953	104
Perma-Fix of South Georgia Inc	4953	67
Perma-Glaze Inc	5198	15
Perma-Graphics Inc	3089	1353
Permagreen Products Co	2875	38
Perma-Greetings Inc	2771	22
Permalith Plastics LLC	3089	1003
Permaloc Security Devices Inc	1731	2424
Permanent Concrete Solutions Inc	1799	106
Permark Inc	5047	284
Permasteelisa North America Corp	1793	1
Permatype Company Inc	5047	252
Permay Protypes and Composites Inc	3089	1768
Permedion	8742	312
Permessa Corp	7372	4167
Permian Electronics Inc	3825	351
Permian Plastics Inc	3089	1191
Permian Supply and Manufacturing	3599	2503
Permian Tank and Manufacturing Inc	3443	57
Permlight Products Inc	3674	338
Permobil Inc	5047	32
Pernix Group Inc	1521	104
Perona Langer BeckSerbin and Mendoza	8111	302
Perot Group	6552	168
Perot Systems Healthcare Solutions Inc	5045	242
Perra and O'toole Inc	7384	58
Perram Electric Inc	1731	398
Perretta Graphics Corp	3555	72
Perrier Group of America Inc	5149	2
Perrier Party Rentals Inc	7359	216
Perrigo Co	2834	25
Perrigo Company Of South Carolina	2833	9
Perrigo Iowa Inc	2834	249
Perris Valley Aviation Services Inc	7363	336
Perritt Capital Management Inc	6282	671
Perry and Young Inc	8072	14
Perry Ballard Inc	7311	646
Perry Bancshares Inc	6712	546
Perry Broadcasting Company Inc	4832	60
Perry Brothers Inc (Lufkin Texas)	6512	17
Perry Buick Co	5511	893
Perry Contract Services Inc	7349	372
Perry Dell Farms	0241	6
Perry Ellis International Inc	2321	3
Perry Engineering Company Inc	1794	28
Perry Foam Products Inc	3086	74
Perry Homes - A Joint Venture Inc	1521	12
Perry Johnson Inc	7372	526
Perry Slingsby Systems Inc	3537	29
Perry Supply Company Inc	5074	54
Perry Technology Corp	3545	74
Perry Videx LLC	5084	233
Perry's Ice Cream Company Inc	2024	11
Perrysburg Machine And Tool Inc	3469	282
Perryton Equity Exchange	5153	39
PerSeptive Biosystems Inc	3845	30
Pershing LLC	6289	1
Persinger Supply Co	5064	40
Persis Corp	2711	129
Persistent Construction Inc	1623	220
Person and Covey Inc	2844	115
Persona Inc	3993	58
Personal Communications Center Inc	5065	339
Personal Composer Inc	7372	4866
Personal Data Systems Inc	7372	5003
Personal Mail International Inc	7389	1523
Personal Marketing Company Inc	7331	189
Personal Selling Power Inc	2721	329
Personal Support Medical Suppliers Inc	5047	170
Personal Systems Plus Inc	7373	1053
Personal TeX Inc	7372	5115
Personal Touch Cleaning and Maintenance Inc	7349	221
Personalized Communications Inc	7389	1361
Personna American Safety Razor Co	3421	6

Company Name	SIC	Rank
Personnel Data Systems Inc	7373	334
Personnel Decisions International Inc	8742	280
Personnel Inc	7361	210
Personnel One (Dallas Texas)	7361	39
Personnel One Inc	7363	129
Personnel Preference Inc	7363	255
Personnel Resource Corp	7361	146
Persons-Majestic Manufacturing Co	3751	13
Perspective Network	4813	602
Perstorp Compounds Inc	2821	62
Perstorp Polyols Inc	2869	58
Persystent Software	7372	1903
Per-Tech Inc	3679	636
Pertech Resources Inc	3577	238
Pertronix Inc	3822	31
Peruno USA	5065	247
Pervasip Corp	4813	633
Pervasive Software Inc	7372	713
Pervigil Inc	7379	1555
Pesce Baking Company Ltd	2051	285
Pesch Publishing Company Inc	2711	674
Pesch Redi Mix Inc	5032	98
Pestana Pacific Ltd	1623	631
Pestco Inc	2819	101
Pestcon Systems Inc	5191	105
Pestmaster Services Inc	7342	23
Pet DRx Corp	0742	2
Pet Ecology Brands Inc	2048	151
Pet Factory Inc	2047	28
Pet Food Services Inc	2013	202
Pet Poultry Products Inc	5144	25
Pet Safety Systems Inc	1731	1228
Petada Company LLC	5084	701
Petaluma Acquistion LLC	2015	32
Petco Animal Supplies Inc	5999	6
Pete Keiger Printing Company Inc	2752	1091
Pete Mathieu and Associates Inc	7311	494
Pete Store	5012	76
Peter A Mayer Advertising Inc	7311	115
Peter Arnold Inc	7336	330
Peter Baker and Son Co	2951	23
Peter Basso Associates Inc	8711	370
Peter Brown Associates	8741	242
Peter F Sheridan Inc	5063	437
Peter Garafano and Son Inc	5012	164
Peter Hantz Company Inc	2844	198
Peter Hughes Diving Inc	7999	120
Peter J Phethean	5045	437
Peter Kiewit Sons' Inc	1611	2
Peter Lang Publishing Inc	2731	146
Peter Meier Incorporated LLC	5031	335
Peter Michael Winery Inc	2084	42
Peter Pan Bus Lines Inc	4131	5
Peter Pan Seafoods Inc	2092	23
Peter Parts Electronics Inc	5065	422
Peter Paul Electronics Company Inc	3491	32
Peter Piper Inc	5812	57
Peter R Brown Construction Inc	1542	339
Peter Schwabe Inc	8712	181
Peterbilt Motors Co	3537	85
Peterbilt of Las Vegas Inc	5012	53
Peterbilt Of Louisville Inc	5511	799
Peterbilt Of Utah Inc	5012	64
Peterbrooke Chocolatier Inc	5441	15
Peter-Lisand Machine Corp	3651	248
Peters and Chandler PC	8721	318
Peters Equipment Inc	3532	57
Petersen Inc	3441	43
Petersen Machine Company Inc	3599	912
Petersen Precision Engineering LLC	3599	216
Petersen Trucking Inc	4213	3094
Peterson American Co	3495	3
Peterson and Co	3451	132
Peterson Autoplex	5511	260
Peterson CAT	5082	27
Peterson Companies LC	6552	94
Peterson Construction Co	1542	209
Peterson Contractors Inc	1611	69
Peterson Industries Inc	3792	19
Peterson Jig and Fixture Inc	3544	349
Peterson Milla Hooks	7311	372
Peterson Pacific Inc	2411	8
Peterson Steel Corp	5051	417
Peterson Systems International Inc	2822	24
Peterson Tool Company Inc	3545	55
Peterson Tractor Co	5082	15
Peterson's North Branch Mill Inc	5191	114
Pete-Za-Ria Pizza Inc	2041	58
Pet-Friendly Publications Inc	2741	505
Petitto Mine Equipment Inc	3532	37
PetMed Express Inc	5912	25
Petoskey Plastics Inc	3081	55
PetPlacecom	7379	1016
Petra Electronic Manufacturing Inc	3672	418
Petra Geotechnical Inc	8748	105
Petra Manufacturing Co	2396	19
PetRays	0752	4
Petrelli Electric Inc	1731	2015
Petrex Inc	3533	72
Petri Baking Products Inc	2052	23
Petricca Industries Inc	1611	109
Petrie Heating and Cooling	1711	202
Petrik Laboratories Inc	2873	28
Petrinovich Pugh and Company LLP	8721	424

Company Name	SIC	Rank
Petro Chem Industries Inc	5084	540
Petro Extrusion Technology Corp	3089	1115
Petro Holdings Inc	5983	1
Petro Hunt LLC	2819	43
Petro Packaging Company Inc	2821	135
Petro Plastics Company Inc	3089	884
Petro Probe Investigations Inc	8731	335
Petro Stopping Centers Holdings LP	5541	9
Petro Stopping Centers LP	5541	5
PetroAlgae Inc	2869	128
Petrobras America Inc	1311	129
Petrobyte	7372	5100
Petro-Canada America Lubricant Inc	7389	2254
Petro-Chem Development Company Inc	3567	2
Petrochem Field Services Inc	1389	33
PetroChem Insulation Inc	1799	27
Petro-Hunt Corp	1382	34
PetroHunter Energy Corp	1311	278
Petroleum and Resources Corp	6726	29
Petroleum Data Specialists Inc	5045	721
Petroleum Development Corp	1381	22
Petroleum Elastomers Inc	3533	84
Petroleum Helicopters Inc	4522	9
Petroleum Helicopters International Inc	4522	20
Petroleum Inc	1311	251
Petroleum Marketers Inc	5171	28
Petroleum Pipe and Supply Company Inc	5051	431
Petroleum Place Inc	7389	412
Petroleum Service Co	5172	32
Petroleum Transport Company Inc	4213	890
Petron Automation Inc	3541	191
Petron Inc	4213	297
Petron Industries Inc	3679	218
Petron Pacific Inc	1011	6
Petroquest Energy Inc	1311	88
PetroSkills	8742	364
Petrospec Technologies	7372	1812
Petrotechnics USA Inc	7371	990
Petroway Inc	7372	2727
Petrusha Enterprises Inc	1731	1579
Petry Media Corp	7311	28
Petry Television Inc	7311	49
PETsMART Inc	5999	2
PETsMARTcom Inc	5999	13
Petters Group Worldwide	4822	1
Pettey Machine Works Inc	3599	1883
Pettibone LLC	3531	24
Pettibone/Traverse Lift LLC	3537	47
Pettisville Grain Co	5153	189
Pettit and Company PC	7372	4467
Pettit and Pettit Consulting Engineering Inc	8711	430
Pettit Machinery Inc	5999	110
Pettit's Pastry Inc	2051	251
Petty Machine and Tool Inc	3541	144
Petty Machine Company Inc	3565	153
Petz Enterprises Inc	7372	2562
Petzl America Inc	5091	98
Peugeot Citroen Engines	5013	107
Pevarnik Brothers Inc	8748	60
Pevco Systems International Inc	3535	41
Pew Corp	1542	447
Pexco Packaging Corp	2673	58
Pexx Inc	7389	1464
Peyronnin Construction Company Inc	1542	345
Pez Candy Inc	5145	27
Pez Manufacturing Corp	2064	46
PF Chang's China Bistro Inc	5812	48
PF Moon And Company Inc	1629	48
Pf Technologies Inc	3089	816
Pfaff Manufacturing	3861	73
Pfaffco Inc	2759	577
Pfaudler Inc	3443	45
Pfc Inc	3732	30
Pfc Inc	2512	61
Pfeiffer Electric Company Inc	1731	505
Pfeiffer Foods Inc	2035	11
Pfeiffer Vacuum Inc	3559	217
Pfeiffer's California Custom Packing Inc	2033	101
Pfenyan Kappa International Inc	5045	779
Pferd Milwaukee Brush Company Inc	3991	13
Pffj Inc	0213	21
PFG Lester Company Inc	5046	9
PFG Milton's	5141	82
Pfingsten Partners LLC	6799	206
Pfister Energy	4939	18
Pfizer Animal Health Group	2833	3
Pfizer Inc	2834	1
PFM Asset Management LLC	6282	31
Pfm Inc	3564	88
Pfpc Enterprises Inc	5023	91
Pfr Acquistons LLC	5031	63
PFR Engineering Systems Inc	7372	929
PFSweb Inc	7389	126
PFSweb Retail Connect Inc	5961	64
Pfw Industries Corp	5082	214
PG and E Corp	4931	11
PG Calc Inc	7371	1381
Pg Computers	5734	460
Pg Drives Technology Inc	3842	301
Pgba LLC	8322	2

Company Name	SIC	Rank
Pgc Acquisition LLC	3229	38
Pgf Technology Group Inc	3679	568
Pgi Fulfillment Inc	2759	169
Pgi Group Inc	1731	1465
Pgi Inc	2326	28
PGK Inc	3822	99
PGP Corp (Palo Alto California)	7379	94
PGR Media	7311	214
PGS Data Processing Inc	1311	87
PGS Enterprises	1731	2070
PGT Inc	3442	16
Pgt Industries Inc	3442	12
Ph Cellular Inc	5065	809
PH Chadbourne and Co	2421	93
PH Glatfelter Co	2621	10
Ph Tool	3312	133
Phacil Inc	7379	72
Phadia Us Inc	5047	55
Phamatech Inc	3845	61
Phantom Reality Inc	7371	1689
Phaostron Instrument and Electronic Co	3613	62
Pharaoh Information Services Inc	7372	3841
Pharmacal Research Labs Inc	2841	38
Pharma-Care Inc	8099	99
Pharmaceutical Corporation Of America	5122	113
Pharmaceutical Innovations Inc	2834	399
Pharmaceutical Product Development Inc	8731	10
Pharmaceutical Research Plus	7389	954
Pharmaco-Kinesis Corp	3841	349
Pharmacy Computer Services Inc	7372	1777
Pharmacyclics Inc	2834	432
Pharmalinkfhi	8731	97
Pharmalucence Inc	5047	116
PharmaNet Development Group Inc	8731	27
Pharmasol Corp	2834	216
Pharmasset Inc	2834	430
Pharmavite Corp	2833	14
PharmChem Inc	8071	29
PharMerica Corp	5122	8
PharMetrics Inc	7372	261
PharMingen	2836	20
Pharmos Corp	2834	483
Pharos Capital Group LLC	6799	72
Pharos Science and Applications Inc	5065	342
Pharr Brothers Inc	4213	2091
Pharr Yarns LLC	2281	1
Phase 1 Technology Corp	5065	503
Phase 2 Medical Manufacturing Inc	5047	111
Phase Dynamics Inc	3825	99
Phase Iv Engineering Inc	8731	380
Phase Masters Inc	1731	2080
Phase Matrix Inc	3825	78
Phase One Consulting Group	8748	142
Phase One Graphic Resources Inc	5199	102
Phase One Inc (Northport New York)	3577	585
Phase Technology Corp	5065	132
Phase Three Logic Inc	7372	5001
Phased Logic Microsystems	7371	1917
Phasetek Inc	3663	301
Phasetronics/Motortronics Inc	3625	20
PHAZAR Corp	3663	155
Phaztech Inc	3599	2345
Phb Inc	3363	48
PHC Inc	8082	37
PHC of Michigan Inc	8093	37
PHC of Utah Inc	8093	38
PHC of Virginia Inc	8093	39
PHD Inc	3593	3
Phd Michigan LLC	7319	132
PHE Inc	5961	98
Phelps and Associates Inc	7311	252
Phelps County Bancshares Inc	6712	641
Phelps County Bank	6022	515
Phelps County Regional Medical Center	8062	139
Phelps Dodge International	3496	7
Phelps Dunbar LLP	8111	83
Phelps Implement Corp	5083	32
Phelps Industrial Products Inc	3053	106
Phelps Industries Inc	3537	67
Phelps Security Inc	7381	76
Phelps Tire Company Inc	5014	25
Phenix Food Service Inc	5141	208
Phenix Label Company Inc	2679	38
Phenix Solutions Inc	7311	833
Phenix Supply Co	5087	17
Phenix Technologies Inc	3825	109
Phenome Technologies Inc	3841	404
Phenomenex Inc	3826	20
Pherin Pharmaceuticals Inc	8731	336
PHH Corp	8741	4
PHH Vehicle Management Services LLC	7513	11
PHI Group Inc (Huntington Beach California)	8741	280
PHI Service Agency Inc	7389	1723
Phibro Animal Health Corp	2819	35
Phibro Energy Production Inc	1382	41
Phibro LLC	5171	47
Phifer Inc	3496	11
Phihong USA Corp	5045	89

Company Name	SIC	Rank
Phil Hall Electric Inc	1731	2019
Phil Long Automotive Group Inc	5511	15
Phil Matic Screw Products Inc	3599	2271
Phil Reome Inc	1623	393
Phil Smart Inc	5511	650
Phil Waterfords Manteca Ford Mercury	5511	847
Philadelphia Agustawestland Corp	3721	25
Philadelphia American Life Insurance	6321	46
Philadelphia Bourse Inc	3728	231
Philadelphia Candies Inc	2066	40
Philadelphia Coca-Cola Bottling Co	2086	13
Philadelphia Consolidated Holding Corp	6719	29
Philadelphia Contributionship Insurance Co	6331	192
Philadelphia Developmental Disabilities Corp	8322	146
Philadelphia Fund Inc	6722	236
Philadelphia Gas Works Co	4923	7
Philadelphia Instruments and Controls Inc	3823	349
Philadelphia Insurance Cos	6331	141
Philadelphia Media Holdings LLC	2711	75
Philadelphia Newspapers Inc	2711	73
Philadelphia Protection Bureau Inc	7382	37
Philadelphia Reserve Supply Co	5033	30
Philadelphia Scientific Int'l Inc	8711	637
Philadelphia Sign Co	2452	14
Philadelphia Style Magazine LLC	2721	421
Philadelphia Suburban Water Co	4941	8
Philadelphia Tire Service Inc	5014	54
Philadelphia Toboggan Coaster Inc	3599	2341
Philadelphia Tramrail Enterprises Inc	3523	49
Philadelphia Tribune Co	2711	420
Philbin Manufacturing Co	7699	266
Philcord Packaging Inc	7389	2255
Phil-Good Products Inc	3089	861
Philip E Sikora and Sons Inc	5049	93
Philip Holzer And Associates LLC	2752	863
Philip Industrial Services Group Inc	4953	2
Philip Johnson/Alan Ritchie Architects	8712	253
Philip Livestock Auction	5154	6
Philip Morris Capital Corp	6159	42
Philip Morris International Inc	2111	1
Philip Morris USA Inc	2111	3
Philip Morse	7371	1889
Philip R Friedman and Associates LLP	8721	51
Philip Reinisch Company LLC	2511	63
Philip Services Corp	5093	1
Philip Vogel and Company PC	8721	348
Philipp Lithographing Co	2752	219
Philipps Brothers Supply Inc	5082	177
Philips and Co	5063	487
Philips Consumer Electronics Co	3651	8
Philips Electronics North America Corp	3651	4
Philips Healthcare Communications Inc	7311	785
Philips Lighting Co	3641	2
Philips Medical Systems Hsg	3675	7
Philip's Plastics	3089	1843
Philips Products Inc	3442	14
Philips Research USA	8731	193
Philips Semiconductors Embedded Processor Div	3674	136
Philips Semiconductors (Sunnyvale California)	3674	17
Phillip Townsend Associates Inc	8742	300
Phillips and Johnston Inc	3841	152
Phillips and Jordan Inc	1629	7
Phillips and Temro Industries Inc	3714	156
Phillips Brothers Plastics Inc	3083	78
Phillips Communication and Equipment Co	5065	305
Phillips Components Inc (Laguna Hills California)	3679	801
Phillips Contracting Co	1611	169
Phillips Corp	3599	8
Phillips Corp Federal Div	5084	180
Phillips Crab House Inc	5812	121
Phillips Distributing Corp	5182	35
Phillips Diversified Manufacturing Inc	3089	622
Phillips Electric Inc	1731	1328
Phillips Foods Inc	5812	63
Phillips Graphic Finishing Inc	2675	10
Phillips lighting	3612	1
Phillips LLC	3679	562
Phillips Lytle LLP	8111	77
Phillip's Machine And Welding Company Inc	7373	469
Phillips Machine Service Inc	7699	21
Phillips Manufacturing And Tower Co	3312	63
Phillips Mushroom Farms LP	0182	5
Phillips Oppenheim Group Inc	7361	212
Phillips Plating Corp	2891	56
Phillips Precision Inc	3841	117
Phillips Productions Inc	7812	237
Phillips Property Management Inc	6552	162
Phillips Real Estate LLC	6531	45
Phillips Service Industries Inc	7699	16
Phillips-Smith-Machens Venture Partners	6799	298
Philly's Famous Water Ice Inc	2024	29
Philmat Inc	8322	148
Philosophy Communication Inc	8743	230
Philosophy Inc	5122	78

Company Name	SIC	Rank
Philpotts and Associates Inc	7389	672
Philtek Power Corp	5063	1030
Philway Products Inc	3672	35
Phineas Corp	8361	8
Phinney/Bischoff Design House	7336	55
Phinney Tool and Die Company Inc	3544	135
Phipps and Bird Inc	3829	423
Phld Inc	5734	449
Phoenician Properties Realty	6531	377
Phoenician Stone	5932	8
Phoenix Advisory Partners LLC	7389	436
Phoenix Aerial Tow Operations	7359	114
Phoenix Aerospace Inc	3724	63
Phoenix Air Group Inc	4522	14
Phoenix America Inc	3824	41
Phoenix American Inc	6159	86
Phoenix Biomedical Corp	3842	249
Phoenix Cable Inc	3357	81
Phoenix Capital Management Inc	5065	126
Phoenix Casting and Machining Inc	3365	45
Phoenix Coca-Cola Bottling Co	3411	6
Phoenix Commercial Electric Inc	1731	1714
Phoenix Companies Inc	6719	10
Phoenix Composite Solutions LLC	3728	146
Phoenix Contact Services Inc	5063	248
Phoenix Container Inc	3411	17
Phoenix Controls Corp	3823	67
Phoenix Creative Co	7311	248
Phoenix Data Inc	2761	30
Phoenix Data Systems Inc	7372	1637
Phoenix Digital Corp	3661	192
Phoenix Down Corp	2392	21
Phoenix East Aviation Inc	8299	48
Phoenix Electric Corp	3629	71
Phoenix Electric Manufacturing Co	3089	1220
Phoenix Engineering Company Inc	7363	216
Phoenix Enterprise Inc	5099	153
Phoenix Fabricators and Erectors Inc	3443	68
Phoenix Films Inc	3089	1871
Phoenix Foods Inc	2015	60
Phoenix Forging Company Inc	3462	54
Phoenix Gold International Inc	3651	50
Phoenix Graphics Inc	2752	1241
Phoenix Group	5045	481
Phoenix Imports Ltd	5181	103
Phoenix Inc	3541	140
Phoenix Installation and Management Co	5084	614
Phoenix Instruments Inc	7699	249
Phoenix Instruments Inc (Naperville Illinois)	5047	240
Phoenix International	3823	11
Phoenix International Freight Services Ltd	7389	34
Phoenix Investment Partners Ltd	6282	116
Phoenix Kiosk LLC	3571	197
Phoenix Language Services Inc	7389	1876
Phoenix Legal LLC	7374	220
Phoenix Lithographing Corp	2752	104
Phoenix LLC	7389	1926
Phoenix Logistics Inc	3678	50
Phoenix Loss Prevention Inc	6411	281
Phoenix Marketing Group Inc	7311	548
Phoenix Medical Management Inc	8011	69
Phoenix Metals Co	5051	39
Phoenix Motorcars Inc	5012	77
Phoenix Newspapers Inc	2711	54
Phoenix Pest Control Inc	7342	26
Phoenix Petroleum Co	5172	96
Phoenix Pharmaceuticals Inc	2834	359
Phoenix Phive Software Corp	7372	2006
Phoenix Press Inc	2752	469
Phoenix Printing Companies Inc	2732	47
Phoenix Process Equipment Company Inc	3542	34
Phoenix Products Co	5169	72
Phoenix Promotions Inc	7389	2426
Phoenix Publishing Inc	2731	212
Phoenix Rehabilitation and Health Services Inc	8049	10
Phoenix Rep Sales Inc	5065	733
Phoenix Rising Industries Inc	7389	1302
Phoenix Scale Company Inc	5046	369
Phoenix Small Tool Inc	3829	496
Phoenix Software International Inc	7372	1502
Phoenix Systems Inc (Atlanta Georgia)	7372	2782
Phoenix Technologies Ltd	7372	575
Phoenix Technology Ltd	3089	1154
Phoenix Testing Inspection LLC	7389	2146
Phoenix Textile Corp	5023	27
Phoenix Transportation Services	4213	857
Phoenix Tube Company Inc	3317	50
Phoenix Vanguard Inc	7371	952
Phoenix Wheel Company Inc	5013	245
Phoenix Wire And Cable LLC	5063	1058
Phoenix-Lamar Corp	3679	594
Phoenix-PDQ Inc	4213	2178
Phokus Inc	2741	418
Phone Acce Enterprise Inc	7371	1433
Phone Bank Systems Inc	7380	1007
Phone Directories Company Inc	2741	75
Phone Labs Technology Company Inc	5065	212
Phone Masters Ltd	1731	626
Phone Power	4813	327

Company Name	SIC	Rank
PhoneAmerica Corp	5065	664
Phonefactor Inc	7373	588
Phones Plus Inc	5065	471
Phonex Broadband Corp	3661	123
Phong Le Co	5064	160
Phonic Ear Inc	3679	28
Phonon Corp	3679	451
Phonoscope Ltd	4899	97
Phosphate Holdings Inc	5191	19
Photikon Corp	3861	117
Photo Ad Inc	7384	34
Photo Agora	7372	3392
Photo Emblem Inc	2399	33
Photo Fabricators Inc	3672	167
Photo Medic Equipment Inc	3844	16
Photo Protective Technologies Inc	2821	196
Photo Research Inc	3825	75
Photo Researchers Inc	7336	32
Photo Sciences Inc	3577	435
Photo Specialty Shop Inc	1731	2507
Photo Stencil LLC	3679	285
Photo Systems Inc	3861	47
PhotoBooks Inc	2741	289
Photodex Corp	7372	2473
Photoengraving Inc	3861	76
Photographic Works Inc	7384	31
Photolibrary Index Stock	7389	377
Photomation	7384	16
Photon Inc	3823	352
Photon Technology International Inc	3827	74
Photonic Products Group Inc	3679	284
Photo-Scan Of Los Angeles Inc	1731	2301
Photosense LLC	3674	413
Photoshot	7336	178
PhotoSpin Inc	7375	245
PhotoThera	8731	172
Photo-Tron Corp	3679	857
PhotoWorks Inc	7384	8
Photronics Inc	3674	52
PHR Design	7389	1474
Phs Industries Inc	3498	48
PHT Corp	7372	170
Phyco/Jm Inc	5065	923
Physic Systems Inc	5734	368
Physical Electronics USA Inc	3826	26
Physical Optics Corp	3577	120
Physical Sciences Inc	8731	130
Physical Testing Equipment Services Inc	3829	485
Physical Weekly	2741	433
Physicans Services Corporation Of Southern II	8741	267
Physicians Billing Management Inc	7374	324
Physicians Eyecare Network LLC	5049	211
Physicians Formula Holdings Inc	2844	35
Physicians Health Plan Of Northern Indiana Inc	8011	45
Physicians Insurance Company of Ohio	6311	259
Physicians Mutual Insurance Co	6321	21
Physicians' Pharmaceutical Corp	2834	308
Physicians Postgraduate Press Inc	2721	266
Physicians Practice Group	8721	176
Physicians Programs Inc	8721	455
Physicians' Reciprocal Insurers	6351	19
Physicians Record Company Inc	2752	1300
Physicians Reference Laboratory	8071	58
Physicians' Service Center Inc	8721	362
Physicians Services	3841	351
Physician's Weekly Inc	7375	157
Physicians Weight Loss Centers of America Inc	6794	84
Physicians World	7375	102
Physimetrics Inc	5045	478
Physique 57	7991	8
Physmark Inc	7372	191
Phytec America LLC	3571	118
Phytel Inc	7372	901
PI and I Motor Express Inc	4213	114
PI Components Corp	3053	44
Pi Edit	7819	79
PI Engineering Inc	3577	329
PI Inc	3089	158
PI Manufacturing Corp	5065	105
Pi Mechanical Inc	1711	200
PI Roof Maintenance Inc	1761	18
Pi Sigma Inc	7379	1393
Pi Tape Corp	3544	855
PI Technology	7372	1147
Piacere International Inc	2095	51
Piad Precision Casting Corp	3369	14
Piano and Organ Distributors Inc	5736	12
PianoDisc	3931	9
Piantedosi Baking Company Inc	2051	39
Piasecki Aircraft Corp	8731	273
Pibly Residential Programs Inc	8361	82
PIC Business Systems Inc	7372	2641
Pic Corp	2879	32
PIC Maintenance Inc	7349	112
Pic Manufacturing Inc	3555	118
Picanol of America Inc	5084	147
Picasso Travel	4725	43
Picatti Brothers Inc	1731	317
Piccadilly Restaurants LLC	5812	142
Picerne Construction/Fm LLC	7389	1266

Company Name	SIC	Rank
Picis Inc (Wakefield Massachusetts)	7372	1082
Pick and Pull Auto Wrecking	5093	238
Pick Electric Inc	1731	849
Pick Instrument Products Company Inc	3599	2286
Pick Professionals Inc	7371	1675
Pickard Artistic Blasting Inc	5084	948
Pickarski Inc	1623	720
Pickering Inc	8712	49
Pickett Hosiery Mills Inc	2252	20
Pickus Construction and Equipment Company Inc	1541	245
Pickwick Co	3444	104
Pickwick Electric Coop	4911	274
Pic-Mount Imaging Corp	3861	60
Pico Electrical Equipment Inc	3281	60
PICO Holdings Inc	6719	64
Pico Macom Inc	3663	121
Pico Metal Products Inc	3444	273
Pico Publishing	7372	4938
Pico Systems	5065	1017
Pico Wholesale Electric and Lighting Supplies Inc	1731	2348
PICOM Claims Services Corp	6331	263
Piconics Inc	3674	327
Picor Corp	3629	36
Picosecond Pulse Labs Inc	3629	39
Pics Inc	8099	114
Pics Telecom International Corp	5065	100
Pictographics International Corp	7372	4437
Picton Corp	2731	375
Pictorial Offset Corp	2752	56
Pictsweet Co	2037	12
Picture Galleries Inc	5023	55
Picture People	7221	2
Picture Vision Inc	2741	461
PicturePhone Direct	5065	674
Pictures And More Inc	5023	101
PictureTel Securities Corp	3669	21
Picut Manufacturing Co	3541	60
Piece of Work Corporation of Boynton Beach	1731	1838
Pieceworks Inc	5023	209
Pied Piper Mills Inc	2048	105
Piedmont Airlines Inc	4581	1
Piedmont Business Forms Inc	2752	1547
Piedmont Candy Co	2064	66
Piedmont Chemical Industries Inc	2841	13
Piedmont Community Bank	6022	493
Piedmont Dielectrics Corp	3613	48
Piedmont Electric Membership Corp	4911	228
Piedmont Express Inc	4213	2266
Piedmont Foam Inc	3086	126
Piedmont Graphics Inc	2752	749
Piedmont Hospital Inc	8062	235
Piedmont Investment Advisors LLC	6799	159
Piedmont Lumber and Mill Co	2421	21
Piedmont Mechanical Inc	1711	158
Piedmont Mining Company Inc	1041	30
Piedmont National Corp	5113	11
Piedmont Natural Gas Company Inc	4924	10
Piedmont Office Realty Trust	6798	56
Piedmont Precision Machine Company Inc	3599	432
Piedmont Systems Inc	7372	4468
Piedmont Telecommunications Inc	1731	810
Piedmont Telephone Membership Corp	4813	568
Piedmont Transportation Inc	4213	3100
Piedmont Transportation of Vale NC	4213	2422
Piedmont Triad Computer Consulting Inc	7371	1640
Piehler Buick GMC	5511	728
Piemonte Bakery Company Inc	5149	201
Pieper Electric Inc	1731	334
Piepho Moving and Storage Inc	4213	2355
Pier 1 Imports Inc	5712	4
Pier 19 Inc	5072	199
PIER 39 LP	6512	32
Pier Foundry and Pattern Shop Inc	3321	55
Pier 'n Port Travel Inc	4724	129
Pier Transportation Inc	4213	2716
Pieratt's Inc	5722	7
Pierce Aluminum Company Inc	5051	118
Pierce Arrow Inc	3711	77
Pierce Communications Inc	7311	798
Pierce Co	2752	524
Pierce Company Inc	3714	127
Pierce Corp	3523	59
Pierce Enterprises	4213	1797
Pierce Foam And Supply Inc	3086	151
Pierce Goodwin Alexander and Linville	8712	73
Pierce Inc	3541	252
Pierce Manufacturing Inc (Bradenton Florida)	3715	38
Pierce Packaging Co	4783	5
Pierce Riesbeck and Associates LLP	8721	253
Piercefield Corporation Inc	2439	41
Pierceton Trucking Company Inc	4213	2290
Piercey Toyota	5511	780
Piercing Pagoda Inc	5944	14
Pieri Creations LLC	3645	55
Pierini Clark	8721	302
Pierino Frozen Foods Inc	2038	67
Pier-Mac Plastics Inc	3089	1375
Pierpont Communications Inc	8743	177

Company Name	SIC	Rank
Pierre Country Bakery Inc	2051	243
Pierre M Sprey Inc	3651	206
Pierre Part Store Inc	5399	16
Pierre's French Ice Cream Inc	2024	68
Pierre's Ice Cream Co	5143	4
Pierry Manufacturing Inc	3823	369
Pierson Building Center Inc	5211	135
Pierson Chevrolet Inc	5511	956
Pierson Construction Corp	8711	371
Pierson Products Inc	3599	2400
Pietragallo Gordon Alfano Bosick and Raspanti LLP	8111	331
Piezo Systems Inc	3679	835
Piezo-Metrics Inc	3674	334
Pifers Airmotive Inc	3728	228
Pig Improvement Company USA	0751	2
Pig Pen Studios Inc	7336	179
Pigeon Creek Hardwoods Inc	5031	427
Pigeon Productions	7812	205
Piggie Park Enterprises Inc	2035	8
Piggly Wiggly Alabama Distributing Company Inc	5141	109
Piggly Wiggly Carolina Company Inc	5141	50
Piggly Wiggly Co	5411	99
Piggly Wiggly Midwest	5411	110
Pigott Inc	5021	64
Pii Inc	6719	110
Pii North America Inc	4613	14
Pik Rite Inc	3523	136
Pike and Fischer Inc	2721	248
Pike Creek Turf Farms Inc	0139	1
Pike Electric Corp	1731	10
Pike Industries Inc	2951	2
Pike Online Inc	7379	1336
Pikes Peak Boces	8211	104
Pikes Peak Plastics Inc	3089	1586
Pikewerks Corp	7371	404
Pile Dynamics Inc	3825	159
Pileated Pictures LLC	7373	1142
Pilgrim Badge and Label Corp	3083	43
Pilgrim Communications Inc	1623	849
Pilgrim Manor Inc	8361	111
Pilgrim's Corp	2015	2
Pilkington Holdings Inc	3211	6
Pilko and Associates LP	8742	480
Pillar Data Systems Inc	3572	31
Pillar Of Fire Corp	4832	148
Pillar Technologies Inc	3559	218
Pillar Technology Group LLC	7371	471
Piller Plastics Inc	3089	968
Piller USA Inc	3699	39
Pillsbury Co	2053	2
Pilosoft Inc	4813	608
Pilot Air Freight Corp	4731	17
Pilot Chemical Corp	2843	2
Pilot Corp	5541	3
Pilot Corporation Of America	5112	17
Pilot Flying J	5541	1
Pilot Freight Services	4522	11
Pilot LLC	2711	498
PIMCO Commercial Mortgage Securities Trust Inc	6798	174
Pina John Jr and Sons	2084	70
Pinamar LLC	7359	111
Pinch-A-Penny	5999	48
Pinckney Molded Plastics Inc	3089	886
Pincus Group	7389	978
Pindar Systems Inc	7372	2339
Pinder Instruments Company Inc	3672	295
Pine Bluff Cotton Belt Federal Credit Union	6061	127
Pine Bluff Sand And Gravel Co	2951	19
Pine Bluffs Gravel and Excavating	4213	2059
Pine Branch Coal Sales Inc	1221	35
Pine Cone Lumber Company Inc	5031	69
Pine Glow Products Inc	2842	115
Pine Grove Manufactured Homes Inc	2451	30
Pine Hall Brick Company Inc	3251	8
Pine Hill Plastics Inc	3089	1194
Pine Instrument Co	3625	83
Pine Island Sportswear Ltd	2321	32
Pine Lesser and Sons Inc	5194	14
Pine Manor Inc	2048	35
Pine Ridge Farms LLC	2011	12
Pine River Healthcare Center	8051	47
Pine Street Chinese Benevolent Association	8049	35
Pine Timber Wood Production Inc	2411	10
Pine Tree Building Materials	5031	306
Pine Tree Lumber Co	5211	64
Pine Tree Telephone and Telegraph Co	4813	109
Pine Valley Electric Inc	1731	1679
Pinebreeze Technologies Inc	7379	1073
Pinehurst Co	7011	33
Pinellas Provision Corp	2013	139
Pines Manufacturing Inc	5084	319
Pinewood Care Center	8051	44
Pinewood Plumbing Supply Inc	5074	83
Piney Mountain Press Inc	7372	3842
Ping Identity Corp	7371	285
Pingtone Communications Inc	4813	200
Pink OTC Inc	6289	29
Pinkard Construction Co	1541	137
Pinkerton and Laws of Georgia Inc	1542	328

Company Name Index

PLAN

Company Name Index

Company Name	SIC	Rank
Pinkerton Consulting and Investigations	7381	1
Pinkerton Government Services Inc	7381	270
Pinmax Corp	5063	768
Pinnacle Airlines Corp	4512	26
Pinnacle Bancshares Inc	6712	621
Pinnacle Bank (Gilroy California)	6029	23
Pinnacle Bank (Jasper Alabama)	6022	481
Pinnacle Bankshares Corp	6712	550
Pinnacle Building Services Inc	7349	301
Pinnacle Cable South Inc	1623	752
Pinnacle Computer Services Inc	7373	937
Pinnacle Converting Equipment Inc	3599	1467
Pinnacle Credit Union	6062	68
Pinnacle Data Systems Inc	7371	258
Pinnacle Electronic Systems Inc	1731	473
Pinnacle Entertainment Inc	7999	16
Pinnacle Financial Group Inc	7322	19
Pinnacle Financial Partners Inc	6712	117
Pinnacle Foods Group LLC	2099	6
Pinnacle Gas Resources Inc	1389	44
Pinnacle Industrial Enterprises Inc	3089	573
Pinnacle Management Group Inc	8742	495
Pinnacle Manufacturing Company Inc	3599	1494
Pinnacle Materials Inc	1442	43
Pinnacle Petroleum Inc	5172	94
Pinnacle Plastics Inc	3089	659
Pinnacle Precision Sheet Metal Corp	3469	87
Pinnacle Services Inc	1731	670
Pinnacle Software Inc	7373	420
Pinnacle Solutions Inc	8742	669
Pinnacle Staffing Inc	7363	38
Pinnacle Stanrick Inc	4783	15
Pinnacle Systems Inc	3861	10
Pinnacle Technical Resources Inc	8742	48
Pinnacle Truck and Trailer Sales LLC	5012	125
Pinnacle West	6799	369
Pinnacle West Capital Corp	4911	32
Pinnacom Solutions Inc	7371	1536
Pinneastcom Inc	7371	492
Pinnell/Busch Inc	8741	301
Pinner Wire and Cable Inc	3679	277
Pinny Food Center and HWI Hardware	5411	236
Pinpoint Laser Systems Inc	3821	64
Pinpoint Systems Inc	7371	1700
Pinpoint Systems International Inc	3699	43
Pinta Foamtec Inc	3086	60
Pinta's Cultured Marble	3281	41
Pinwheel Software Inc	7372	3329
Pinzar Technology Inc	7371	1597
Pion Inc	5049	129
Pioneer Aerospace Corp	2399	10
Pioneer Air Systems Inc	3585	204
Pioneer Althetics	5091	72
Pioneer America Income Trust Fund	6371	2
Pioneer Announcements Inc	2759	539
Pioneer Auto Parts and Service Company Inc	5013	375
Pioneer Automotive Technologies Inc	3714	227
Pioneer Balloon Co	3999	43
Pioneer Bankshares Inc	6021	320
Pioneer Broach Co	3545	109
Pioneer Cabinetry Inc	2434	68
Pioneer Center For Human Services	8361	67
Pioneer Circuits Inc	3672	39
Pioneer Companies Inc	2899	25
Pioneer Consulting LLC	8732	97
Pioneer Contract Services Inc	1542	300
Pioneer Credit Recovery Inc	7322	7
Pioneer Custom Molding Inc	3089	1596
Pioneer Data Systems Inc	7371	434
Pioneer Design Inc	7389	2436
Pioneer Directories	4813	186
Pioneer Drilling Co	1381	13
Pioneer Drilling Services Ltd	1381	1
Pioneer/Eclipse Corp	3589	97
Pioneer Electric Cooperative Inc (Greenville Alabama)	4911	246
Pioneer Electric Inc	5063	142
Pioneer Electronics Inc	2741	39
Pioneer Equipment Rental LLC	5046	67
Pioneer Europe Select Equity Fund	6722	215
Pioneer Fasteners and Tool Inc	5085	187
Pioneer Freight Systems Inc	4213	1940
Pioneer Funds Distributor Inc	6211	114
Pioneer Group Inc	6282	238
Pioneer Growers Co-Op	5159	16
Pioneer Health Services Inc	8742	213
Pioneer Hi-Bred International Inc	0115	1
Pioneer Hotel and Gambling Hall	7011	63
Pioneer Industrial Corp	5085	53
Pioneer Industrial Railway Co	4011	37
Pioneer Industries LLC	5031	205
Pioneer Investment Management USA Inc	2844	13
Pioneer Janitorial Services Inc	7349	291
Pioneer Machine and Tooling Co	3599	2251
Pioneer Management Possibilities Inc	8742	655
Pioneer Manufacturing Co	3531	101
Pioneer Manufacturing Inc	3537	75
Pioneer Marketing Research Inc	7374	166
Pioneer Materials Inc	3670	102
Pioneer Medical Inc	7352	41
Pioneer Metal Finishing LLC	3471	4
Pioneer Mutual Life Insurance Co	6399	14
Pioneer National Latex Inc	3069	37
Pioneer Natural Resources Co	1311	19
Pioneer Natural Resources USA Inc	1311	54
Pioneer North America Inc	3651	56
Pioneer Oil and Gas	1311	202
Pioneer Oilfield Services Inc	7353	105
Pioneer Optics Company Inc	3845	109
Pioneer Packaging and Printing Inc	2759	56
Pioneer Photo Albums Inc	2782	19
Pioneer Pipe Inc	3498	9
Pioneer Plastics Corp	3089	574
Pioneer Plastics Corp (Auburn Maine)	3083	10
Pioneer Plumbing Inc	1711	257
Pioneer Point Corp	3554	65
Pioneer Precision Products Inc	3599	1853
Pioneer Printing and Stationery Inc	2752	885
Pioneer Printing Company Inc	2711	697
Pioneer Products Inc	3599	106
Pioneer Railcorp	4011	48
Pioneer Railroad Equipment Company Ltd	4741	4
Pioneer Resources Inc	6517	1
Pioneer Rural Electric Cooperative Inc	4911	287
Pioneer Service Inc	7389	1369
Pioneer Southwest Energy Partners LP	1311	77
Pioneer Speakers Inc	3679	60
Pioneer Steel Corp	5051	255
Pioneer Super Market	5411	186
Pioneer Supply Company Inc	5085	158
Pioneer Surgical Orthobiologics Inc	3841	341
Pioneer Surgical Technology Inc	3842	126
Pioneer Telephone Association Inc	4813	150
Pioneer Telephone Coop (Philomath Oregon)	4813	146
Pioneer Telephone Cooperative Inc	4813	124
Pioneer Telephone Directories Corp	2741	373
Pioneer Teletechnologies LLC	7375	255
Pioneer Transportation Ltd	4213	1803
Pioneer Valley Hospital Inc	8062	78
Pipco Transportation Inc	4213	2654
Pipe and Steel Industrial Fabricators Inc	5051	404
Pipe and Tube Supply Inc	7389	546
Pipe Distributors Inc	5051	136
Pipe Inc	1623	742
Pipe Transportation Company Inc	4213	2882
Pipelayers Inc	1623	208
Pipelife Jet Stream Inc	3084	8
Pipeline Contractors Inc	8742	638
Pipeline Data Inc	7389	363
Pipeline Equipment Inc	3533	125
Pipeline Interactive Inc	7374	260
Pipeline Software Inc	7371	190
Pipeline Video Inspection LLC	7389	1765
Pipemasters Inc	1623	466
Piper Impact Inc	3356	17
Piper Jaffray Companies Inc	6211	117
Piper Media Services Inc	7819	76
Piper Plastics Inc	3599	180
Piper Products Inc	3556	83
Pipestone Publishing Company Inc	2711	588
Pipestone Veterinary Clinic	0741	1
Pipevision Products Inc	1623	762
Piping and Equipment Company Inc	1623	89
Piping Supply Company Inc	5051	265
PipingSolutions Inc	7372	696
Pipkins Inc	7372	1789
Piqua Technologies Inc	3296	5
Piqua Transfer and Storage Co	4213	1855
Piracle Inc	7372	2805
Piragis Northwoods Co	5961	107
Piramal Glass - USA Inc	3221	5
Piramide Imports	5136	25
Pirelli Tire Corp	3011	16
Pirelli Tire North America	3011	9
Pirkle Electric Company Inc	1731	808
Pirolli Printing Company Inc	2752	1629
Pirollo Transport Company Inc	4213	2586
Pisani Enterprises Inc	5094	57
Pisarkiewicz Mazur Co	7311	710
Pisces Fish Machinery Inc	3556	147
Pisenti and Brinker LLP	8721	373
Pisgah Yarn And Dyeing Company Inc	2261	7
Piston Automotive LLC	3999	26
Pistorius Machine Company Inc	3553	27
Pitcairn Trust Co	6282	397
Pitco Frialator Inc	3556	14
Pitman Co	5043	3
Pitney Bowes Business Insight	7372	381
Pitney Bowes Inc	3579	2
Pitney Bowes Inc Mailing Systems Div	8742	69
Pitney Bowes Management Services Inc	2752	406
Pitney Bowes Software Systems	7372	1763
Pitt and Greene Electric Membership Corp	4911	550
Pitt Ohio Inc	4213	279
Pittcraft Printing Inc	2752	777
Pittman Construction Co	1611	162
Pittman Inc	3621	48
Pitts Engine And Transmission Inc	5082	208
Pittsburg Tank and Tower Company Inc	3443	48
Pittsburgh Associates	7941	4
Pittsburgh Brewing Co	2082	22
Pittsburgh City Paper Inc	2759	440
Pittsburgh Crankshaft Service Inc	3714	368
Pittsburgh Design Services Inc	5084	781
Pittsburgh Embossing Services Inc	5049	190
Pittsburgh Logistics Systems Inc	4731	33
Pittsburgh Mack Sales and Service Inc	5012	113
Pittsburgh Paints San Bernardino	2851	88
Pittsburgh Plumbing and Heating Supply Corp	5074	16
Pittsburgh Recycling Services LLC	4953	160
Pittsburgh Technologies Inc	3089	1745
Pittsburgh Tube Co	3317	16
Pittsburgh Tubular Shafting Inc	3498	79
Pittsburgh Water and Sewer Authority	4941	31
Pittsburgh Wire And Cable Inc	5063	704
Pittsburgh-Fayette Express	4213	817
Pittsfield Plastics Engineering Inc	3089	930
Pittsfield Products Inc	3569	54
Pittsfield Weaving Co	2241	19
Pittston Coal Co	1221	41
Pivot Corp	3441	138
Pivot Inc	7372	78
Pivot Interiors	5021	15
Pivot Power Inc	5083	201
Pivot Punch Corp	3544	342
Pivot3 Inc	3577	178
Pivotal Group Inc	6719	153
Pivotel LLC	5065	703
Pix Video Film and Multimedia Inc	7812	144
Pixar Animation Studios	7812	26
Pixe International Corp	3829	487
Pixel Creative	7336	171
Pixel USA	7373	874
Pixel USA Computer LLC	5734	475
Pixelan Software	7372	5026
Pixelligent Technologies LLC	3674	445
PixelTools Corp	7371	493
Pixelworks Inc	3674	125
Pixfusion LLC	2741	139
Pixion Inc	7372	4209
Pixley Richards Holding Inc	3089	400
Pixxures Inc	7335	6
Pizer Inc	7372	4469
Pizza Brothers East Ii Inc	8748	237
Pizza Corner Inc	2038	65
Pizza Hut Inc	5812	13
Pizza Inn Inc	6794	61
Pizzaco Inc	5812	341
Pizzagalli Construction Co	1542	75
Pizzuti Cos	6552	141
Pizzuti Inc	6552	166
Pj Doland Web Design Inc	7373	1179
PJ Electronics Inc	3829	480
PJ Marketing Services Inc	5199	137
Pj Systems Inc	5734	38
PJ United	5812	30
PJAX Inc	4213	184
PJM Interconnection LLC	4911	184
Pjrs Technology	3571	185
Pjs Electric Inc	1731	390
Pjs Of Texas Inc	7349	113
PK Controls Inc	8999	223
PK Neuses Inc	3825	323
P-K Tool and Manufacturing Co	3469	140
Pk USA Inc	3465	11
Pk3 Group Inc	3599	949
Pka Technologies Inc	7371	1165
PKC Corp	7372	2528
PKD Inc	1623	578
PKD Professional Systems Inc	1731	2442
PKG Equipment Inc	3559	291
Pkgingcom	5113	49
PKM Electric Cooperative Inc	4911	387
Pkm Steel Service Inc	3441	118
Pkmm Inc	7371	736
PKWARE Inc	7372	1778
PL and E Sales Inc	5063	699
Pl Enterprises Inc	5087	125
PL Rohrer and Brother Inc	5191	146
Place Motor Inc	5511	1167
Placemark Investments Inc	6371	7
Placerville Hardware	5251	20
Plaid Enterprises Inc	3952	1
Plaid Pantries Inc	5411	141
Plain Dealer Publishing Co	2711	107
Plain 'N Fancy Kitchens Inc	2434	22
Plainfield Lumber and Hardware Co	5211	111
Plainfield Molding Inc	3089	632
Plainfield Trucking Inc	4213	441
Plains All American Pipeline LP	4612	2
Plains Capital Corp	6712	54
Plains Equipment Group	5083	62
Plains Equity Exchange	5153	109
Plains Exploration and Production Co	1311	27
Plains Grain and Agronomy LLC	5153	88
Plains Meat Company Ltd	5147	112
Plains Power and Equip Inc	5083	116
Plains Transportation Inc	4213	1164
PlainsCapital Bank Corp	6021	35
Plainview Batteries Inc	3692	10
Plainville Machine Works Inc	3599	1069
Plainville Stock Co	3911	45
Plaisted Companies Inc	4213	2121
Plan and Print Systems Inc	7334	67

Ward's Business Directory of U.S. Private and Public Companies, 55th Edition / Volume 5

1635

Company Name	SIC	Rank
Plan Consulting Group LLC	8748	139
Plan Tech Inc	3089	1549
Planalytics	8742	505
Planar Systems Inc	3679	71
Plancorp Inc	6282	367
Planes Moving and Storage Inc	4213	345
Planet Antares Inc	5087	16
Planet Associates Inc	7373	336
Planet Beach Franchising Corp	6794	135
Planet Blue	7379	998
Planet Com Internet Services Inc	4813	217
Planet Dj Inc	5065	768
Planet Fitness Inc	7991	3
Planet Ford	5511	46
Planet Hollywood International Inc	5812	283
Planet Studio LLC	7371	1899
Planet Tool and Gear Inc	3544	241
Planetweb Inc	7371	832
Planit Advertising Inc	7311	642
Planit Solutions Inc	7371	363
PlanItMichigan	4725	70
Planned Residential Communities Inc	6531	111
Planned Systems International Inc	7372	566
Planning and Development Services Inc	7389	2189
Planning Design Research Corp	7389	462
Plansee USA LLC	3463	9
Plansmith Corp	7372	4210
Plant Enterprises Inc	3643	61
Plant Equipment Company Inc	3429	138
Plant Foods Inc	2875	40
Plant Health Care Inc	5169	140
Plant Improvement Co	1771	5
Plant Machine Works Inc	3599	710
Plant Maintenance Service Corp	7699	33
Plant Reclamation	1795	7
Plant Sitters Inc	7359	273
Plant Span Inc	7389	2183
Plant Two G A	5051	488
Plant Wind Turbine Group	3511	40
Plantain Products Co	2099	284
Plantation Pecan and Gift Inc	5441	23
Plantation Pipe Line Co	4613	11
Plantation Products LLC	2873	14
Plante and Moran LLP	8721	146
Planter Inc	3499	78
Planters Cotton Oil Mill Inc	2074	4
Planters Equipment Company Inc	5083	110
Plantmobile Inc	7389	1470
Plant-N-Power Services LLP	7389	794
Plantronics e-Commerce Inc	8999	13
Plantronics Inc	3661	9
Plantscape Inc	3999	105
Plantscapes Inc	7389	1188
PlanView Inc	7372	1084
Plasco Inc	3089	1487
Plasfinco Inc	3479	92
Plasidyne Engineering and Manufacturing Inc	3089	1599
Plaskolite Inc	2821	50
Plas-Labs Inc	3821	60
Plasma Etch Inc	3841	185
Plas-Mac Corp	3543	7
Plasma-Tec Inc	3599	1349
Plasmetex Industries	3089	1798
Plaspack USA Inc	2673	38
Plaspros Inc	3089	432
Plasser American Corp	3531	59
Plas-Tanks Industries Inc	3089	186
Plas-Tech Molding And Design Inc	3089	1769
Plasteco Inc	3648	77
Plasteel Corp	3086	164
Plastek Group	3089	17
Plaster Development Company Inc	1531	73
Plastex Extruders Incorporated USA	2821	72
Plastex Industries Inc	3089	1362
Plasti Dip International Inc	3479	95
Plasti Fab Inc	3089	1681
Plastic and Metal Center Inc	3069	134
Plastic Assembly Corp	3089	1874
Plastic Card Systems Inc	3555	49
Plastic Components Inc	3089	999
Plastic Compounders Inc	2821	147
Plastic Concept Inc	3089	1426
Plastic Concepts Inc	3089	1682
Plastic Container Corp	3085	2
Plastic Craft Inc	3089	1631
Plastic Depot Inc	5085	453
Plastic Design Inc	2821	148
Plastic Design International Inc	3089	784
Plastic Designs Inc	3089	1336
Plastic Development Co	3999	169
Plastic Development Inc	3081	94
Plastic Dip Moldings Inc	3089	1436
Plastic Distributors and Fabricators Inc	3599	967
Plastic Dress-Up Co	3089	293
Plastic Engineering and Technical Services Inc	3544	299
Plastic Enterprises Company Inc	3089	303
Plastic Enterprises Inc	3089	785
Plastic Extruded Products Co	3089	938
Plastic Extrusion Technologies Ltd	3089	1648
Plastic Forming Company Inc	3089	976
Plastic Industries Inc	3085	22

Company Name	SIC	Rank
Plastic Ingenuity Inc	3089	111
Plastic Injection Molders Of Arizona Inc	3089	1716
Plastic Line Manufacturing Inc	2542	67
Plastic Manufacturers Inc	2673	76
Plastic Mart Inc	2821	160
Plastic Mold Technologies Inc	3544	265
Plastic Molded Concepts Inc	3089	555
Plastic Molded Technologies Inc	3559	437
Plastic Molding Development Inc	3089	1894
Plastic Molding Technology Inc	3089	821
Plastic Moldings Company LLC	3089	275
Plastic Monofil Company Ltd	3089	1367
Plastic Packaging Corp	3089	628
Plastic Packaging Inc	3089	292
Plastic Packaging Technologies LLC	2673	26
Plastic Processors Inc	3089	1813
Plastic Products Company Inc	3089	94
Plastic Products Inc	5162	42
Plastic Products Manufacturing Corp	3599	2454
Plastic Recycling Inc	4953	131
Plastic Reel Corporation Of America	3089	1167
Plastic Sales and Service Inc	7692	45
Plastic Sales Southern Inc	5162	63
Plastic Services Inc	3082	22
Plastic Specialties And Technologies Inc	3052	1
Plastic Specialties Inc	2821	151
Plastic Suppliers Inc	3081	3
Plastic Surgery Center	8011	68
Plastic Techniques Inc	3089	1569
Plastic Technologies Inc	3648	79
Plastic Technologies Inc	8734	82
Plastic Technologies Of Vermont Inc	3085	21
Plastic Tubing Industries Inc	2679	66
Plastican Inc	3089	210
Plasticards Inc	3089	1175
Plastic-Craft Products Corp	3089	1355
Plastico Industries Inc	3089	1736
Plasti-Coat Corp	2821	183
Plasticoid Company Inc	3069	167
Plasticoid Manufacturing Inc	3829	266
Plasticolor Molded Products Inc	3714	259
Plasticorp	3089	650
Plasticos Arco Iris Of San Antonio	3089	1869
Plasticos Arco Iris Of San Antonio Inc	3085	43
Plasticraft Manufacturing Company Inc	3089	592
Plasticrest Products Inc	3469	380
Plastics Advanced Research Technology Inc	5031	339
Plastics Design And Manufacturing Inc	3089	1000
Plastics Dynamics Inc	3089	1414
Plastics Engineering Company Inc	2821	64
Plastics Extrusion Machinery Inc	3559	435
Plastics Management Corp	3086	3
Plastics Molding Co	3089	517
Plastics R Unique Inc	2673	64
Plastics Research Corp	3083	30
Plastics Resources Inc	3084	45
Plastics Unlimited Inc	3089	1499
Plasti-Fab Inc	3089	1587
Plastifab Inc	3083	65
Plastiflex Company Inc	7389	605
Plastikoil Of Pennsylvania Inc	2789	56
Plastikoil Plus Inc	2789	127
Plastikon Industries Inc	3089	234
Plastikos Corp	3089	1624
Plastikos Inc	3089	1369
Plasti-Kote Company Inc	2851	24
Plastilam Inc	7389	2124
Plastimayd Corp	3081	14
Plastinetics Inc	3089	931
Plastipak Holdings Inc	6719	90
Plastipak Packaging Inc	3085	3
Plastirunn Corp	2656	5
PlastiVac Inc	3559	254
Plastival Inc	5039	6
Plas-Tix USA Inc	3089	1709
Plastixs LLC	3559	545
Plasto Tech International Inc	3089	1632
Plast-O-Foam LLC	3089	608
Plast-O-Matic Valves Inc	3089	853
Plastomer Corp	3053	41
Plas-Tool Co	8742	547
Plastore Inc	5084	922
Plastrglas Inc	3299	6
Plastronics Interconnections Inc	3089	1231
Plastronics Socket Company Inc	3825	43
Plastruct Inc	3089	1055
Plateau Systems Ltd	7372	1595
Plateco Inc	3471	81
Plateronics Processing Inc	3471	109
Platform Solutions Inc	5045	682
Plating Engineering	3559	587
Plating Technology Inc	3471	15
Platinum Builders LLC	1521	175
Platinum Db Consulting Inc	7379	1027
Platinum Equity LLC	6799	14
Platinum Maintenance Services Corp	7349	211
Platinum Mortgage Inc	6162	91
Platinum Realty	6531	429
Platinum Solutions Inc	7372	530
PLATO Inc	7372	320
PLATO Learning Inc	6719	130
Plato Woodwork Inc	2434	53

Company Name	SIC	Rank
Platt Brothers and Co	3356	26
Platt Electric Supply Inc	5063	37
Platt Luggage Inc	3161	14
Platte Canyon Multimedia Software Corp	7372	4732
Platte River Power Authority	4911	203
Platte Valley State Bank and Trust Co	6022	257
Platte-Clay Electric Coop	4911	352
Plattform Holdings Inc	7371	1601
Plattner Automotive Group	5511	628
Platts Global Energy	2741	199
Platt's Mill Inc	5191	184
Plattsburgh Quarry	3281	59
Platypus Inc	5719	26
Plaudit Design	7379	981
Play Time Toys Inc	7359	118
Playback Technologies Inc	7819	51
Playbill Inc	2721	172
Playboy Enterprises Inc	2721	34
Playboy Entertainment Group Inc	7812	50
Playcore Inc	3949	36
Playdom Inc	2741	91
Player Wire Wheels Ltd	5014	10
Players Computer Inc	7372	606
Play-it Productions Inc	7334	99
Playmates Toys Inc	3942	7
Playmobil USA Inc	5092	22
Play'mor Trailers Inc	3792	27
Playnetwork Inc	7999	56
PlayPower LT Farmington Inc	3949	54
Playworld Systems Inc	3949	93
Plaza Bank	6022	326
Plaza Construction Corp	1542	23
Plaza Fleet Parts	5013	163
Plaza Ford Inc (Bel Air Maryland)	5511	823
Plaza Ford-Lincoln-Mercury Inc	5511	1108
Plaza Home Mortgage Corp	6162	20
Plaza Imports International Inc	5064	181
Plaza Information Technologies Inc	7379	1120
Plaza Motors Co	5511	76
Plaza Motors Inc	5511	671
Plaza Packaging Corp	2652	11
Plaza-Ford-Ideal Laundry And Dry Cleaners Inc	5087	28
PLC Enterprises Inc	2672	10
PLC Medical Systems Inc	3841	206
PLC Systems Inc	3845	105
Plc-Multipoint Inc	3672	450
Plcs Inc	2891	104
Plcs Plus International Inc	7371	602
Plea Inc	8351	18
Pleasant Excavating Co	1794	4
Pleasant Gardens Machine Inc	3599	2076
Pleasant Holidays LLC	4725	4
Pleasant Living Healthcare Inc	8361	121
Pleasant Living Inc	8361	187
Pleasant Trucking	4213	394
Pleasant View Dairy Corp	5143	40
Pleasanton Garbage Service Inc	4953	126
Pleasanton Tool and Manufacturing Inc	3599	1182
Pleasantville Ford Inc	5511	992
Pleasurecraft Marine Engine Co	3519	22
Pleatco LLC	3589	162
Pleating Plus Ltd	2395	18
Pleiger Plastics Company LP	2821	143
Plenum Publishing Corp	2721	126
Pletronics Inc	5065	319
Plex Systems Inc	7372	1058
Plexent LP	7379	1144
Plexon Inc	3577	485
Plexsys Interface Products Inc	7373	350
Plextor LLC	3572	17
Plexus Co	5046	61
Plexus Corp	3672	4
Plexus Installations Inc	7373	424
Plexus M/2 Holdings LLC	4813	503
Plexus Publishing Inc	2721	448
Plexus Services Corp	8711	11
Plexus Web Creations	7379	858
Pliant Corp	2671	7
Pliant Plastics Corp	3089	979
Pliant Solutions Corp	2671	5
Plibrico Sales And Service	5085	432
Pliner Solutions Inc	7372	2912
Plitek LLC	3083	39
Plochman Inc	2035	35
Plot Multimedia Developers LLC	7374	238
Plote Inc	1794	20
Plotter Pros Inc	7373	1196
Plotworks Inc	7372	1740
Plourde Sand and Gravel Company Inc	5032	82
Plouse Machine Shop Inc	3599	504
Plow and Hearth Inc	5961	26
Plow and Hearth LLC	5961	70
PLS Logistics Services	4212	13
Plug Power Inc	3621	63
Plugged In LLC	7372	4927
Plug-In Storage Systems Inc	5734	348
Plugout LLC	3699	298
Pluim Publishing Inc	2711	791
Plum Creek MDF Inc	5031	11
Plum Creek Northwest Plywood Inc	5031	13
Plum Creek South Central Timberlands LLC	0851	2

Company Name	SIC	Rank
Plum Creek Southern Timber LLC	0851	1
Plum Creek Timber Company Inc	6798	125
Plum Grove Printers Inc	2752	1140
Plum Hall Inc	7372	3010
Plum Healthcare Group LLC	7389	1309
Plumas Bancorp	6153	20
Plumas Bank	6022	393
Plumb Supply Co	5074	26
Plumber's Supply Co	5074	27
Plumbing Planning Corp	1623	457
Plumb-It Inc	3423	83
PlumChoice Inc	7371	36
Plumrose USA Inc	2013	160
Plunkett Raysich Architects LLP	8712	145
Plus 2 Recording Studio	7389	1880
Plus Communications Inc	2731	132
Plus One Corp	3599	2344
Plus One Engineering	3651	247
Plus One Holdings Inc	8049	4
Plus Relocation Services Inc	7389	1373
Plus Three LP	7371	719
PLUS Vision Corporation of America	3861	15
Plus1 Media LLC	7311	899
Plush Appeal LLC	5092	49
Plush Pippin Corp	2053	12
Pluskota Electric Manufacturing Co	3694	45
Plustar Inc	5084	710
Pluswood	5031	236
Plx Inc	3827	52
PLX Technology Inc	3674	103
Ply Gem Holdings Inc	2431	6
Plycon Van Lines Inc	4213	1120
Plyler Construction	1711	66
Plymkraft Inc	2282	4
Plymold Furnishing Solutions	2599	6
Plymouth Foam Inc	3086	28
Plymouth Foundry Inc	3321	65
Plymouth Printing Company Inc	2752	256
Plymouth Publishing Inc	2741	427
Plymouth Rubber Company Inc	3069	20
Plymouth Steel Corp	3312	93
Plymouth Tube Co	3317	24
Plywood Supply Inc	5031	97
PM Armor Inc	3599	1213
Pm Fasteners Inc	5085	278
Pm Graphics Inc	2752	728
PM Liquidating Corp	7374	65
PM Realty Group LP	6531	154
PM Testing Laboratory Inc	3471	102
PMA Companies Inc	6331	127
PMA Literary and Film Management Inc	8741	204
PMB Securities Corp	6211	264
PMC - Colinet Inc	3541	36
PMC Commercial Trust	6798	177
PMC Funding Corp	6163	18
Pmc Liquiflo Equipment Company Inc	3594	27
PMcD Design	7812	318
Pmco LLC	2679	20
PMC-Sierra Inc	3674	49
PMFG Inc	3569	20
Pmg Digital Inc	3823	385
PMG Mentors	7389	983
PMH Enterprises Inc	7379	615
Pmhcc Inc	8741	143
Pmi	3824	37
Pmi Cartoning Inc	3565	38
Pmi Computer Supplies Inc	5045	613
PMI Group Inc	6351	10
PMI Mortgage Insurance Co	6351	26
PMI Phoenix Metallurgical Inc	3545	304
PML Exploration Services LLC	7372	294
PML Inc	2834	255
PML Microbiologicals Inc	2836	21
Pmm Electric Inc	1731	2183
Pmp Composites Corp	3089	1430
Pmr Precision Manufacturing and Rubber Company Inc	3069	216
PMS Instrument Co	3826	168
PMSD Inc	3599	241
PMSI Inc	5122	53
Pmt Forklift Corp	5084	595
Pmt Group Inc	3541	45
Pmw Products Inc	3089	972
Pmx Industries Inc	3366	1
PN Hoffman Inc	1522	14
PNC Bank Delaware	6022	48
PNC Bank NA	6021	3
PNC Equity Management Corp	6799	225
PNC Financial Services Group Inc	6712	5
PNC Inc	3672	93
PNC National Bank of Delaware	6022	566
Pneu Fast Inc	3315	36
Pneudralic Power Inc	5084	758
Pneumatic Products Corp	3564	31
Pneumatic Scale Corp	3565	15
Pneumatic Systems Company Inc	3599	2055
Pneumech Systems Manufacturing LLC	3564	81
Pneumercator Company Inc	3823	226
Pneutek Inc	3546	48
PNG Telecommunications Inc	4813	92
Pni Sensor Corp	5088	76
PNI Transportation Inc	4213	2669

Company Name	SIC	Rank
Pnl Publications Inc	2741	236
PNM Resources Inc	4923	6
PNT Marketing Services Inc	7371	376
PNY Technologies Inc	3674	59
Pobco Inc	3089	1555
Pocahontas Foods USA Inc	5141	180
Pocahontas Land Corp	6519	18
Pocasset Machine Corp	3469	303
Pocatello Railroad Federal Credit Union	6061	111
Pocino Foods Co	2013	59
Pocket Soft Inc	7372	3196
Pocky Inc	2752	521
Poclain Hydraulics Inc	5084	89
Pocono Mountain School District	8211	31
Pocono Springs Co	5149	141
Podesta Group	8743	69
Podnar Plastics Inc	3089	1535
Podolsky Northstar Realty Partners LLC	6552	175
Poet Nutrition Inc	5191	141
Poeton Max Power Inc	3471	112
Poggi Press Inc	2752	1100
Pogo Linux Corp	5734	46
Pohang Steel America Corp	5051	292
Pohl Transportation Inc	4213	386
Pohlad Cos	8742	219
Pohlman Inc	3451	84
Poinciana Vacation Villas	6531	451
Point 4 Data Corp	7373	902
Point B	8742	139
Point Blank Solutions Inc	3842	43
Point Dedicated Services	4213	726
Point Eight Power Inc	3613	29
Point Financial Inc	7377	31
Point Group Inc	7311	507
Point Loma Rehabilitation Center LLC	8322	136
Point of Sale System Services Inc	5044	138
Point Pleasant Plumsteadville Ems	5012	204
Point Six Inc	8741	287
Point To Point Technology (USA) Inc	5045	748
Point West Insurance Associates	6311	242
Point360	7819	27
Pointandship Software Inc	7372	425
PointB Communications Inc	5045	349
Pointclear LLC	8743	43
Pointcross Inc	7372	3843
Pointe Hilton Resorts Inc	7011	50
Pointe Precision Inc	3724	55
Pointe Scientific Inc	3841	295
Pointe Technology Group Inc	7373	173
Pointe Vista Development LLC	6552	292
Pointing Color Inc	2087	3
PointRoll Inc	5045	150
Pointsmith Point-Of-Purchase Management Services LP	2396	15
Pointwise Inc	7372	2684
Pok Of North America Inc	5087	170
PokerTek Inc	3999	127
Poklar Power And Motion Inc	5063	934
Pola USA Inc	5122	60
Polack Printing Inc	2741	198
Polar Air Cargo Inc	4512	33
Polar Communications Mutual Aid Corp	4813	337
Polar Electro Inc	5047	60
Polar Industries Inc	3086	100
Polar Plastics Inc	3089	183
Polar Semiconductor Inc	3674	178
Polar Tech Industries Inc	3089	280
Polaris Direct LLC	7334	6
Polaris Electronics Corp	3548	58
Polaris Engineering Inc	3599	2194
Polaris Industries	3651	125
Polaris Industries Inc	3799	1
Polaris Manufacturing Inc	3444	254
Polaris Pool Holdings Corp	3589	33
Polaris Sales Company Inc	3643	97
Polaris Software Inc	7372	4146
Polarity Electric Inc	1731	1368
Polarity Post Productions	7389	1127
Polaroid Consumer Electronics International LLC	3861	6
Polaroid Holding Co	3861	7
Polar-Ply Corp	3644	46
Polartec LLC	2211	16
Polatis Inc	3613	121
Polatis Photonics Inc	5049	49
Polco Metal Finishing Inc	3471	124
Polcraft Inc	3599	1461
Pole Line Contractors Inc	1623	343
Polebridge Press Inc	2731	355
Poleset Inc	1623	787
Polhemus Inc	3577	463
Polibrid Coatings Inc	2851	95
Police and Fire Federal Credit Union	6061	19
Police Equipment Worldwide Inc	5999	147
Police Shield Corp	2731	316
Policy Administration Solutions Inc	7371	909
Policy Studies Inc	8741	121
Polinger Shannon and Luchs Inc	6531	39
Polish American Radio Program	4832	222
Polish and Slavic Federal Credit Union	6061	29
Polish Daily News	2711	547
Polish National Alliance	8399	8

Company Name	SIC	Rank
Polishing Corporation Of America	3674	372
Polk Audio Inc	3999	36
Polk County Farmers Coop	5541	39
Polk County Publishing Co	2711	499
Polk County Youth Services Inc	8322	209
Polk Mechanical	1731	58
Polk-Burnett Electric Coop	4911	238
Polk's Meat Products Inc	2011	83
Pollacks-Belz Broadcasting CoLlc	4833	182
Pollard Games Inc	2752	85
Pollard Group Inc	2752	698
Pollard-Swain Inc	5172	144
Poller and Jordan Advertising Agency	7311	799
Polley Inc	3569	233
Pollington Machine Tool Inc	3544	277
Pollo Tropical	5812	153
Pollock Corp	5093	46
Pollock Investments Inc	5113	31
Pollock Printing Inc	2752	735
Pollstar	2721	235
Polly Knapp Pig Inc	3086	136
Polman Transfer Inc	4213	1719
Polo Electric Corp	1731	544
Polonia Bancorp	6035	155
Polonia Bank	6035	185
Poloplaz	2842	63
Polu Kai Services LLC	1541	183
Poly Craft Industries Corp	2673	44
Poly Enterprises	3081	134
Poly Fabricators Inc	3089	1780
Poly Films Inc	3081	162
Poly Flex Products Inc	3089	681
Poly Pak America Inc	2673	8
Poly Plastics Inc	3089	1794
Poly Plate Inc	3555	108
Poly Portables Inc	3431	8
Poly Print Ino	2671	59
Poly Processing Company LLC	2821	54
Poly Products Inc	3559	541
Poly Profiles Technology Corp	3312	127
Poly Sat Inc	2899	189
Poly Software International Inc	7372	3844
Poly Tech Industries Inc	3089	1747
Poly USA Inc	5093	83
Polycon Industries Inc	3089	246
Poly Vinyl Company Inc	3089	484
Poly-America LP	3081	13
Polycel Structural Foam Inc	3089	961
Polychem Alloy Inc	2821	167
Polychem Dispersions Inc	2869	93
Polychem Systems	3089	104
Polychromix Inc	3577	339
Polyclutch	3531	64
Polycom Inc	3661	2
Polycon Industries Inc	3089	246
Polycraft Inc	2759	517
Polycraft Products Inc	3061	53
Polydeck Screen Corp	3532	27
Polydyne Inc	3559	521
PolyDyne Software Inc	8748	434
Polyfab Corp	3089	1692
Polyfab Display Co	3089	1805
Polyfab Plastics And Supply Inc	3089	1460
Polyfet Rf Devices Inc	3674	311
Polyfil Corp	2821	159
Poly-Flex Circuits Inc	3625	5
Poly-Flex Inc	3089	852
Polyflon Co	3679	113
Polyfoam Corp	3086	59
Poly-Foam Inc	3089	1343
Polyform Inc	3089	1576
Polyform US Ltd	3089	910
Polyfusion Electronics Inc	8711	562
Polygon Co	3452	44
Polygon Industries Inc	7372	859
Polygon Network Inc	7375	185
Polygon Northwest Company Inc	1521	33
Polyguard Products Inc	2295	17
Poly-Ject Inc	3089	1714
Polyjohn Enterprises Corp	3089	640
Polyline Corp	3651	96
Polymask Corp	3081	101
Polymath Inc	5045	935
PolyMedica Corp	2834	52
PolyMedica Healthcare Inc	3842	129
PolyMedica Pharmaceuticals Inc USA	3841	223
Polymer Concentrates Inc	2821	141
Polymer Conversions Inc	3089	798
Polymer Corp	3089	459
Polymer Corp (Rockland Massachusetts)	3089	352
Polymer Dynamics Inc	2823	4
Polymer Enterprises Inc	3069	42
Polymer Group Inc	2221	1
Polymer Holdings LLC	2821	204
Polymer Industries LLC	3089	401
Polymer Instrumentation And Consulting Services Ltd	3089	1155
Polymer Machinery Company Inc	5084	840
Polymer Molding Inc	3089	1276
Polymer Process Development LLC	3080	757
Polymer Products Company Inc	3676	13
Polymer Products LP	3089	1838
Polymer Recovery Systems Inc	3559	522
Polymer Technology Corp	3851	80

Company Name	SIC	Rank
Polymerex Medical Corp	3082	35
Polymeric Imaging Inc	2893	23
Polymeric Resources Corp	2821	49
Polymeric Systems Inc	2891	61
Polymeric Technology Inc	3069	158
Polymerics Inc	3069	121
Polymicro Technologies LLC	3827	42
Polynesian Adventure Tours Inc	4725	15
PolyOne Corp	2821	10
Polypack Inc	3565	81
Poly-Pak Industries Inc	2221	10
Polyply Composites LLC	3083	50
Polypore International Inc	2899	22
Polyrock Equipment Company Inc	5085	411
Polysciences Inc	2800	08
Polyscientific Research And Development Corp	2869	94
Poly-Seal Corp	3089	271
Polyset Company Inc	2819	107
Polyshot Corp	3442	135
Polysi Technologies Inc	7389	1538
Polysort Inc	7379	1300
Polystyrene Products Company Inc	2821	170
PolySystems Inc	7372	2335
Poly-Tainer Inc	3085	13
Polytank Inc	3443	204
Polytec Plastics Inc	3082	20
Polytec Products Corp	3599	778
Poly-Tec Products Inc	3053	145
Polytech Industries Inc	3089	1512
Polytech Molding Inc	3089	1810
Polytechs Software Development Group Inc	7371	1701
Polytek Development Corp	2822	22
Polytex Environmental Inks Ltd	3952	7
Polytex Fibers Corp	2393	9
Polytop Corp	3089	248
Polytron Corp	3625	142
Polytronix Inc	3679	319
Polytype America Corp	2752	258
Polyumac Inc	3559	172
Polyurethane Engineering Techniques Company Inc	3555	34
Polyurethane Molding Industries Inc	3544	630
Polyurethane Products Corp	2851	138
Poly-Vac Inc	3842	84
Polyvinyl Films Inc	3081	70
PolyVision Corp	3679	79
Polyvulc USA Inc	3069	161
Polywell Computers Inc	3571	78
Polyzen Inc	3841	209
Pom Inc	3824	33
Pomalee Electric Company Inc	1731	566
Pomare Ltd	2329	13
Pomco LLC	2752	750
Pomeroy Electric Inc	1731	128
Pomeroy IT Solutions Inc	5045	36
Pomeroy Tool Inc	3599	2480
Pomona College	8221	29
Pomona Textile Inc	5714	5
Pomona Wholesale Electric Inc	5063	643
Pompano Honda	5511	413
Pompano Precision Products Inc	3545	211
Pompanoosuc Mills Corp	5712	91
Ponam Limited Inc	3829	387
Pond Branch Telephone Company Inc	4813	199
Pond-Ekberg Co	2752	558
PondelWilkinson Inc	8743	258
Ponderosa Homes Inc	6552	169
Ponderosa Industries Inc	3599	1104
Ponderosa Telephone Co	4813	160
Ponders Inc	2759	382
Ponds and Sons Construction Company Inc	1521	156
Poniard Pharmaceuticals Inc	2834	473
Ponica Industrial Company Ltd	3577	379
Pontchartrain Fresh Foods LLC	5046	341
Ponte Vedra Corp	7997	5
Pontem Software	7372	3675
Pontiac Electric Motor Works Inc	5063	1026
Pontiflex	7375	121
Pontrelli and Laricchia Limited A California LP	5147	109
Pony Corp	2759	493
Poof Slinky Inc	3944	17
Pool and Electrical Products Inc	5091	29
Pool Corp	5091	2
Pool Cover Corp	3089	356
Pool Water Products	5091	3
Pool World Supplies	5091	49
Poole and Kent Company Of Florida	1611	48
Poole Chemical Company Inc	2875	24
Poolmaster Inc	3944	24
PoolPak Inc	3585	100
Poolpak International	3585	125
Pools Press Inc	2752	1775
Poor and Co	3559	326
Pop Displays USA LLC	3993	7
Pop Labs Inc	7311	761
Pop N Go Inc	3581	20
Popcorn County USA Inc	2099	344
Popcorn Factory Inc	2099	195
Popcorn Movies LLC	3861	134
Popcorn Parlor Inc	2819	134

Company Name	SIC	Rank
Popcorn Press Inc	2752	1295
Pope And Associates	7389	1832
Pope and Talbot Inc	2421	9
Pope and Talbot Lumber Sales Inc	5031	3
Pope and Talbot Pulp Sales USA Inc	5031	4
Pope Resources LP	0811	3
Pope Transport Co	4213	1223
Pope Transport Inc	4213	2092
Popeyes Inc	5812	107
Poplar Bluff Internet Inc	4813	433
Poplar Bluff Regional Medical Center Inc	8062	152
Popp Cement Tile Products Inc	3084	36
Popp Machine and Tool Inc	7699	131
Poppoo's Popcorn Inc	5145	25
Pop's Bakery Inc	2099	322
Popular Front Studio Inc	4813	550
Popular Inc	6712	29
Popular Mattress Factory Inc	2515	28
Porath Business Services Inc	2752	1692
Porcaro Communications Inc	8743	104
Porcelain Products Co	3264	6
Porchdog Software Inc	7372	5145
PorchLight Entertainment	7812	179
Porcini Software Inc	7371	1934
Porex Technologies Corp	3089	167
Pori and Rowe Associates Inc	3845	144
Pork King Packing Inc	2011	55
Porkie Company Of Wisconsin Inc	2096	54
Porky Products Inc	5147	6
Porous Materials Inc	3826	114
Porsche Cars North America Inc	5012	27
Port Authority Of San Antonio	8741	243
Port City Cabinet Works Inc	3083	72
Port City Communication Inc	4812	89
Port City Development Center	8322	235
Port City Metal Products Inc	3364	17
Port City Trucking Inc	4213	2009
Port Computers	5734	406
Port Electric Supply Corp	5063	481
Port Erie Plastics Inc	3089	156
Port Industries Inc	3531	162
Port Iron Ltd	5093	204
Port Jersey Transportation	4213	1491
Port Jervis Electric Inc	1731	2008
Port Plastics Inc	5162	18
Port Townsend Publishing Company Inc	2711	718
Port80 Software Inc	7372	2167
Porta Phone Company Inc	3679	528
Portable Church Industries	8744	47
Portable Computer Systems LLC	3575	59
Portable Machine Works Inc	3599	1374
Portable One Inc	5045	966
Portable Systems Solutions Inc	3577	452
Portable Warehouse Corp	3575	25
Portables Unlimited Inc	4813	212
Porta-Fab Corp	3448	44
Portage Area Regional Transportation Authority	8742	618
Portage Casting and Mold Inc	3365	36
Portage Commerce Bank	6022	443
Portage Communications Inc	7372	3381
Portage Electric Products Inc	3822	15
Portage Inc (Idaho Falls Idaho)	8711	184
Portage Industries Inc	8331	142
Portage Plastics Corp	3089	705
Portage Wire Systems Inc	3694	40
Portal Blocks	4813	744
Portal Industries Inc	8331	168
Portal Service Co	5211	165
Portal Solutions LLC	7379	1108
Portales National BancShares Inc	6712	359
PortBridge Internet Services LLC	4813	324
Portco Packaging Corp	2673	32
Portec Rail Products Inc	3743	14
Portellus Inc	7371	193
Porter Athletic Equipment Co	3949	85
Porter Auto Group	5511	74
Porter Bancorp Inc	6712	214
Porter Corp	3448	32
Porter Engineered Systems Inc	3714	231
Porter-Henderson Implement Co	5083	137
Porter Le Vay and Rose Inc	8743	188
Porter Lee Corp	5734	116
Porter Of Racine	5712	27
Porter Oil Company Inc	5171	59
Porter Pipe and Supply Co	5074	78
Porter Precision Products Co	3544	64
Porter Valley Software Inc	7372	3940
Porter White and Company Inc	6211	375
Porter Wright Morris and Arthur LLP	8111	105
Porter's Building Center Inc	5211	109
Porter's Electric Motor Service Inc	5063	617
Portersville Valve Co	3491	52
Porter-Trustin-Carlson Co	5032	145
Porterville Recorder Co	2711	446
Portesi's Italian Foods Inc	2038	85
Portfolio Associates Inc	7311	705
Portfolio Capital Management Inc	6282	346
Portfolio Creative Inc	7361	250
Portfolio Media Inc	2741	260
Portfolio Recovery Associates Inc	7322	6
Portfolio Recovery Associates LLC	7322	24

Company Name	SIC	Rank
Portier Fine Foods Inc	5421	24
Portillo's Food Service Inc	5147	68
Portionables Inc	2038	28
Portland Bindery Inc	2789	96
Portland Bolt and Manufacturing Company Inc	3452	76
Portland Bottling Co	2086	93
Portland Electrical Construction Inc	1731	887
Portland Forge	3462	22
Portland General Electric Co	4911	50
Portland Implement Inc	5083	168
Portland Patrol Inc	7381	191
Portland Pattern Inc	3544	738
Portland Plastics Co	3087	25
Portland Pottery Supply	5084	830
Portland Precision Manufacturing	3599	1528
Portland Saturday Market	5999	113
Portland Specialty Baking LLC	5149	89
Portland Valve and Fitting Company Inc	5074	148
Portland Willamette	3429	43
Portman Holdings LP	6552	35
Port-of-Subs Inc	5812	233
Portola Group Inc	6282	173
Portola Packaging Inc	3089	52
Portola Pharmaceuticals Inc	8731	114
Portrait Displays Inc	7372	3159
Portraits International of The Southwest Inc	7384	24
Portsmouth City School Board	8211	53
Portsmouth Square Inc	6531	278
Portsmouth Tool and Die Corp	3544	581
Port-To-Print Inc	2741	496
Portu-Sunberg and Associates Inc	5023	107
Pos America Inc	5045	595
POS International Inc	7372	3362
Pos Plus Inc	5046	213
POS World Inc	5063	127
Posa-Cut Corp	3541	181
POSDATA Inc	7373	207
Poseidon Computer Systems Inc	5734	468
Poseidon Design Systems Inc	7371	1603
Posera USA Inc	5044	43
Posey County Farm Bureau Cooperative Association Inc	5191	41
Posiflex Business Machines Inc	3575	30
Posillico Civil Inc	1611	49
Positech Corp	3593	32
Positive Business Solutions Inc	7378	46
POSitive Concepts	2893	34
Positive Networks Inc	7371	295
Positive Power LLC	1731	2328
Positive Promotions Inc	8743	20
Positive Safety Manufacturers Co	3625	319
POSitive Software Co	5045	388
Positive Source Inc	5045	816
PositiveID Corp	3669	308
Positran Manufacturing Inc	3672	172
Positrol Inc	3545	213
Positron Corp	3845	99
Posner Advertising	7311	274
Possehl Connector Services	3471	80
Possiblenow Inc	7372	2021
Possidento Electric LLC	1731	2572
Post and Schell	8111	273
Post Apartment Homes LP	6531	120
Post Apple Scientific Inc	5049	151
Post Asylum	2741	126
Post Buckley Schuh and Jernigan Inc	8748	10
Post Citizen Media	2711	587
Post Gazette Publishing Co	2711	96
Post Group Inc	7812	82
Post Literate Productions	2741	484
Post Oak Mall	6531	272
Post Oak Oil Co	1311	216
Post Precision Castings Inc	3324	8
Post Printing Co	2759	129
Post Properties Inc	6798	102
Postal Instant Press	2752	145
Postal Mail Sort Inc	7331	193
Postal Presort Inc	7331	101
Postal Systems Examiner	2711	652
Post-Bulletin Company LLC	2711	273
Postcraft Co	2392	48
Postec Inc	5044	64
Postini Inc	7372	498
Postive Feed Inc	2048	108
Postlethwaite and Netterville	8721	342
Postmark Ink Inc	7331	255
PostMaster Software Inc	7372	502
Poston Packing Company Of Florence Inc	5147	67
Postpress Services Inc	2759	237
PostScript Inc	7311	623
Post-Up Stand Inc	7336	193
Pos-T-Vac Inc	3842	232
Potash Corporation Of Saskatchewan Sales	1479	5
Potbelly Sandwich Works LLC	5812	143
Potdevin Machine Co	3565	143
Poteat Motor Lines Inc	4213	1884
Potemkin Industries Inc	3563	45
Poten and Partners Inc	8731	109
Potential Design Inc	3556	133

Company Name	SIC	Rank
Potential Industries Inc	5093	36
Potentials	8742	609
Potentials Management Corp	5734	178
Potlatch Corp	6798	154
Potlatch Corp Pulp and Paperboard Market Services Div	2621	21
Potlatch Corp Wood Products Western Div	2421	23
Potocnie Enterprises Inc	5031	320
Potomac Bancshares Inc	6022	415
Potomac Basin Group Associates Inc	6411	168
Potomac Electric Power Co	4911	54
Potomac Fusion Inc	7372	1162
Potomac Hills Fire Station	7389	1715
Potomac Hospital Foundation	8741	66
Potomac Management Group Inc	7371	126
Potomac News Service	4832	282
Potomac Photonics Inc	8731	364
Potomac Services LLC	7349	44
Potomac Supply Corp	2491	15
Potomac Valley Brick and Supply Co	3251	19
Potter and Associates Inc	2752	1795
Potter Distributing Inc	5064	45
Potter Drilling Inc	8731	288
Potter Electric Signal Company LLC	3669	95
Potter Roemer LLC	5031	105
Potter Transport Inc	4213	773
Potters Industries Inc	3231	23
Potter-Taylor and Co	6531	246
Pottery Barn Inc	5719	3
Pottle's Transportation Inc	4213	250
Potts Welding and Boiler Repair	3443	141
Pottsville Republican Inc	2711	319
Poudre Tech Aggregates Inc	1442	58
Poudre Valley Rural Electric Association Inc	4911	289
Pouliot and Corriveau Inc	4213	2484
Poulsbo RV Inc	5561	5
Poultry Plus Corp	5251	52
Poultry Products Company Inc	5144	14
Pound International Corp	5122	77
Pounding Mill Quarry Corp	1422	22
Pouw and Associates Inc	8712	330
Powder Cote Ii Inc	3479	28
Powder River Energy Corp	4911	149
Powder River Livestock Handling	3523	50
POWDR Corp	6719	155
Powel Inc	5734	226
Powell Building Group	1542	237
Powell Chevrolet Oldsmobile Inc	5511	539
Powell Co	5023	19
Powell Construction Company Inc	1541	47
Powell Electrical Manufacturing Co	3613	18
Powell Electrical Manufacturing Co North Canton Div	3612	73
Powell Electro Systems LLC	3052	27
Powell Electronics Inc	3678	12
Powell Energy Systems Inc	3613	5
Powell Fabrication and Manufacturing Inc	3559	287
Powell Group	0811	2
Powell Industries Inc	3613	6
Powell Relocation Group	4213	2075
Powell Tate	8743	65
Powell Transportation Company Inc	4213	1988
Powell Valley Assisted Living And Alsheimer's Community	8361	189
Powell-ESCO Manufacturing Co	3612	50
Powell-Process Systems Inc	3613	4
Powell's Books Inc	5942	20
Powells Inhome Services Inc	7349	450
Power Advocate Inc	7363	150
Power Analytics Inc	7372	1715
Power And Composite Technologies LLC	2899	84
Power And Control Distributors Inc	5063	985
Power and Industrial Services Corp	3291	19
Power and Telephone Supply Company Inc	5065	25
Power Battery Company Inc	3691	10
Power Brands	4813	720
Power City Electric Inc	1731	14
Power Clean 2000 Inc	5084	600
Power Construction and Maintenance Inc	7699	88
Power Construction Co	1542	118
Power Container Corp	3589	178
Power Control Systems Inc	3612	126
Power Controls Inc	3679	748
Power Cooling Inc	1711	160
Power Country Inc	4832	272
Power Distribution Inc	3677	20
Power Drive Enterprises Inc	5063	1043
Power Dynamics Inc	3629	45
Power Efficiency Corp	3625	372
Power Electric Co	1731	1425
Power Electronic Systems	3621	90
Power Electronics International Inc	3674	314
Power Engineering and Manufacturing Ltd	3499	109
Power Engineering Co	3471	99
Power Engineers Inc	8711	147
Power Equipment Company Inc	3621	120

Company Name	SIC	Rank
Power Equipment Co (Knoxville Tennessee)	5082	66
Power Equipment Co (Rochester New York)	5063	653
Power Film Systems Inc	3676	26
Power Financial Credit Union	6061	53
Power Flame Inc	3433	17
Power Gear	3594	15
Power Glass Co	3612	119
Power Great Lakes Inc	5084	309
Power Home Technologies	5063	270
Power House Electrical Supply	5063	974
Power Images	2741	359
Power Integrations Inc	3674	69
Power Integrity Corp	3629	95
Power Io LLC	3625	158
Power Line Hardware LLC	5063	534
Power Line Services Inc	1623	21
Power Magne-Tech Corp	3612	120
Power Magnetics Inc	3621	145
Power Mate Technology Inc	3677	103
Power/mation Inc	5063	81
Power Motive Corp	5082	57
Power Nissan South Bay	5511	415
Power Now LLC	5063	781
Power Pallet Inc	7699	49
Power Partners Inc	3612	10
Power Parts International Inc	5085	466
Power Plant Service Inc	7699	125
Power Plus Controls Inc	3679	892
Power Plus Sound and Lighting Inc	5064	161
Power Port Products Inc	3699	220
Power Print Digital Fabric Construction	3577	604
Power Products And Services Company Inc	5085	251
Power Pro-Tech Services Inc	8999	128
Power Quality Equipment Inc	5063	899
Power Quality Inc	3825	239
Power Repair Service Inc	3599	256
Power Resources Inc	7379	1333
Power Sales And Advertising Inc	5199	88
Power Select Inc	7389	2263
Power Service Concepts Inc	1731	641
Power Service Products Inc	2899	168
Power Shift Computer Services Inc	4813	656
Power Solutions Electrical Contractors Inc	1731	2055
Power Sources Unlimited Inc	5065	929
Power Systems and Controls Inc	3577	225
Power Tech Electrical Sales Inc	5063	975
Power Technical Services Inc	1731	2552
Power Technology Southeast Inc	3621	112
Power Test Inc	3829	167
Power Tools and Supply Inc	5085	280
Power Train Components Inc	5013	216
Power Train Service Company Inc	5531	28
Power3 Medical Products Inc	8731	430
Powerain Systems Inc	3589	42
Powerbar Inc	2064	34
PowerBASIC Inc	7372	3547
Powerboss Inc	3589	96
Powerbridge Inc	4931	59
Powerco Federal Credit Union	6061	105
Powercom America Inc	3679	20
Powercom Electrical Services Inc	4899	142
Powercomm Construction Inc	1623	268
PowerComm Engineering Inc	8711	362
Powercon Corp	3613	31
PowerData Corp	5045	706
Powered Inc	7372	1024
Powerex Inc	3674	112
Powerfields	5063	618
Powergenix	3692	5
Powerhold Inc	3545	289
Powerhouse Battery Inc	5063	900
Powerhouse Diesel Services Inc	5084	737
Powerhouse Electric Of Nc Inc	1731	1471
Powerhouse Electrical Services Inc	1731	1117
Powerhouse Systems LLC	5065	934
Powerline Freight Systems	4213	1756
Powerlink Environmental Services LLC	7349	78
Powermaster Inc	3694	42
PowerMate Software LLC	7372	3056
Powermetal Technologies Inc	7379	1056
Powermotion Inc	5084	693
Powernail Co	5084	401
Powerohm Resistors Inc	3676	12
PowerON Services Inc	5734	75
Power-One Inc	3679	27
Powerpact LLC	7311	480
PowerProduction Software Inc	7372	2685
PowerQuest Corp	7372	301
Powers and Associates Inc	7311	280
Powers and Sons Construction Company Inc	1542	215
Powers Candy And Nut Co	5145	24
Powers Construction	1623	493
Powers Distributing Company Inc	5181	18
Powers Equipment Company Inc	3585	185
Powers Generator Service LLC	5063	692
Powers News Inc	5731	171
PowerScan Inc	7373	735
Powerscreen Mid-Atlantic Inc	5082	99
Powerscreen Of Florida Inc	5084	572

Company Name	SIC	Rank
PowerSecure Inc	7389	730
Powersecure International Inc	7389	239
Powersim Solutions Inc	7372	4093
PowerSource Online Inc	7372	3548
Powerspan Corp	8711	539
Powerspeak	8299	68
Powersports Network Inc	7371	228
PowerSpring Inc	7389	2527
Powers-Swain Chevrolet Inc	5511	789
Powerteam Inc	7379	1044
Powertec Inc	1731	1263
Powertech Equipment Inc	3559	579
PowerTech Inc	3674	375
Powertek Corp	7374	108
Powertest Software Sales Inc	7379	557
Powertex Inc	3089	1337
Powertrain Product and Chassis LLC	3714	304
Powertrain Recycling Inc	5015	10
Powertran Corp	3677	79
Powertronic Systems Inc	3613	100
Powertronics Inc	5063	1095
Powervar Inc	3629	27
PowerVerde Inc	4911	599
Power-Volt Inc	3677	83
Powerware Corp	3629	13
Powerwave Technologies Inc	3663	16
Powill Manufacturing and Engineering Inc	3599	284
Powis Corp	3625	339
Powr-Ups Corp	3625	205
Poynting Products Inc	7371	1786
Poyry Management Consulting	0851	6
Pozas Brothers Trucking Co	4213	2318
POZEN Inc	2834	160
PP M Inc	3825	284
Pp System International Inc	5049	185
Ppc Industries Inc	3081	62
PPD Development	8731	3
PPD Informatics	7379	303
PPG Industries Inc	2851	1
Ppi/Time Zero Inc	3672	109
PPL Corp	4911	14
PPL Electric Utilities Corp	4911	51
PPL Energy Supply LLC	4911	28
PPL Gas Utilities Corp	4924	45
PPL Global LLC	6159	5
PPM America Capital Partners LLC	6722	30
PPM Consultants Inc	8711	246
ppoONE Inc	7372	2168
Ppp LLC	3089	1096
Pps Plus Software	5045	853
Ppsb Warehouse	7389	2020
PPT VISION Inc	3823	214
P-Q Controls Inc	3625	137
PQ Corp	3231	8
P-R Farms Inc	0175	4
PR Faulk Electrical Corp	1731	1163
PR Hoffman Machine Products Inc	3541	4
PR Newswire Association Inc	7383	6
PR Nutrition Inc	2099	171
Pr Trading Company Inc	5099	139
Pr1mus Printing Inc	2752	951
Pr3 Systems Inc	7379	1277
PRA Co	3089	711
Pra Inc	3823	330
PRA International	7389	112
PRAB Inc	3559	146
Practec LLC	3825	352
Practical Applied Computer Technology Inc	3674	444
Practical Automation Inc	3555	50
Practical Components Inc	5065	475
Practical Computer Solutions Inc	7372	4733
Practical Engineering Inc	7371	1459
Practical Software Solutions Inc	7371	1249
Practical Systems Inc	5049	48
Practical Technologies Inc	3672	195
Practical Vision LLC	5734	237
Practicare Medical Management Inc	8721	319
Practice Management Group LLC (Murrells Inlet South Carolina)	8742	344
Practice Manager Group LLC	7372	1936
Practice Partner	7372	2776
Practicelink Ltd	7374	282
Practicewares Dental Supply Inc	5047	65
PracticeWorks Inc	8742	141
Pradeep K Gupta Inc	7372	2008
Pradon Construction and Trucking	4213	1767
Praedea Solutions Inc	7372	4926
Praendex Inc	8742	513
Praet Tool and Engineering Inc	3544	544
Pragma Systems Corp	7379	1208
Pragma Systems Inc	7372	4323
Pragmatek Consulting Group Ltd	8742	338
Pragmatic Marketing Inc	8299	75
Pragmatics Inc	7371	105
Praim Inc	3571	150
Prairie Capital	6799	141
Prairie Central Cooperative Company Inc	4221	6
Prairie Company LLC	5734	480
Prairie Farms Dairy Inc	2026	3
Prairie Farms Dairy Inc Ice Cream Specialties Div	5143	17

Company Name	SIC	Rank
Prairie Grain Partners LLC	5153	91
Prairie Group Inc	7372	4438
Prairie Lakes Coop	5153	34
Prairie Lines Inc	4213	2717
Prairie Livestock LLC	5154	1
Prairie Material Sales Inc	3273	20
Prairie Mountain Publishing Company LLC	2711	143
Prairie Plastics Inc	3089	1859
Prairie Pride Coop	5171	60
Prairie Products Inc	3851	115
Prairie Ready Mix Inc	3273	94
Prairie Sand and Gravel	1442	84
Prairie Technologies Incorporated Of Minnesota	1731	753
Prairie View Inc	8063	13
Prajin 1 Stop Distributors Inc	5099	60
Pralay Advanced Supply Chain Solutions LLC	5099	134
Prana Inc	7389	1552
Prangley Marks LLP	8721	449
Prate Installations Inc	1761	27
Prater Enterprises Inc	1389	48
Pratham Software Inc	7371	145
Prather Engineering Inc	3599	2422
Prather Wellness Center	8049	31
Pratt and Buehl	7311	522
Pratt and Whitney	3724	2
Pratt and Whitney Auto-Air Inc	3728	34
Pratt and Whitney Power Systems	3519	11
Pratt and Whitney PSD	3714	435
Pratt and Whitney Rocketdyne Inc	3769	8
Pratt Communications Inc	1731	207
Pratt Feed and Supply Co	5191	188
Pratt Industries Inc	2611	6
Prattville Machine And Tool Company Inc	3599	230
Pratzel Bakery Company Inc	2051	177
Praxair Inc	2813	2
Praxair Services Inc	8734	118
Praxair Surface Technologies Inc	3251	5
Praxinet Inc	7379	1040
Praxis Bookbindery	2789	143
Praxis Bookstore Group LLC	5942	14
Praxis Engineering Products LLC	5045	843
Praxis Film Works Inc	7812	319
Praxis Technology Group	7389	2147
Pray Trucking Inc	4213	988
PRC Corp	3674	137
PRC Digital Media	7371	494
Prc Liquidating Corp	8731	246
PRC-DeSoto International Inc	2891	8
PRD Inc	3089	242
Prebon Yamane Inc USA	6099	15
Pre-Cast Specialties Inc	3272	84
Precept Financial Solutions	7389	1659
Precept Ministries Of Reach Out Inc	2731	234
Precheck Inc	7323	17
Precious Plate Inc	3471	78
Precipart Corp	3566	15
Precipitator Services Group Inc	3564	60
Precis Corp	8744	48
Precise Aerospace Manufacturing	3089	1446
Precise Cables Inc	3679	709
Precise Circuit Company Inc	3672	325
Precise Connections Inc	3672	298
Precise Corp	3841	232
Precise Die and Coating Inc	2675	20
Precise Engineering Corp	8711	521
Precise Industries Inc	3444	92
Precise Machine and Manufacturing Inc	3599	1189
Precise Machine Co	3728	6
Precise Machine Partners LLP	3728	7
Precise Medical Transcription	7338	49
Precise Networks Inc	7379	1644
Precise Plastics Inc	3089	873
Precise Power Corp	3621	91
Precise Products Corp	3599	234
Precise Rotary Die Inc	3544	355
Precise Time And Frequency Inc	3825	288
Precise Tool and Die Company Inc	3599	921
Precise Tool and Die Inc	3544	535
Precise Tool and Manufacturing Inc	3541	43
Precision Aerospace Corp	3625	66
Precision Aerospace Inc	3545	19
Precision Aerospace LLC	3511	28
Precision Airmotive LLC	3724	54
Precision Assembly Inc	3672	145
Precision Automation Company Inc	3569	127
Precision Bearing and Machine Inc	3599	1658
Precision Blasting Inc	8748	406
Precision Blasting Services	8711	613
Precision Body and Frame	7532	14
Precision Boring Co	3544	288
Precision Boring Technology Inc	1623	810
Precision Brake and Wheel	5013	339
Precision Cable Assemblies LLC	3679	232
Precision Cable Inc	3671	27
Precision Cable Of Tennessee Inc	3699	228
Precision Cartographics Inc	7389	2380
Precision Castparts Corp	3324	1
Precision Castparts Corp Structurals Div	3324	3

Company Name	SIC	Rank
Precision Circuits West Inc	3672	434
Precision Coating Rods	3823	346
Precision Coatings Inc	2821	59
Precision Communication Services Inc	3661	7
Precision Component and Machine Inc	3069	219
Precision Component Industries LLC	3599	1221
Precision Computer Methods Inc	7372	4867
Precision Computer Service Inc	7372	1741
Precision Computer Services Inc (Shelton Connecticut)	5045	156
Precision Computer Solutions Inc	7371	1531
Precision Concepts Inc	3469	373
Precision Concrete Construction Company Inc	1771	23
Precision Consulting Inc	7379	1538
Precision Contacts Inc	3663	226
Precision Contract Manufacturing Inc	3672	85
Precision Countertops Inc	5031	148
Precision Cryogenic Systems Inc	3443	232
Precision Custom Components LLC	3443	44
Precision Custom Products Inc	3089	1130
Precision Cutter and Tool Co	3545	376
Precision Data Products Inc	5045	245
Precision Data Systems Inc	7372	4543
Precision Defense Services Inc	3599	213
Precision Devices Inc	3625	80
Precision Die- Cutting Inc	3599	2088
Precision Die Technologies Inc	3544	382
Precision Digital Corp	3613	92
Precision Disc Grinding Corp	3599	2383
Precision Display Technologies Corp	3577	580
Precision Document Solutions Inc	3861	34
Precision Dynamics Corp	3089	168
Precision Electric Contractors LLC	1731	826
Precision Electronic Glass Inc	3231	49
Precision Electronics Company Inc	3678	79
Precision Fabricating and Cleaning Company Inc	3823	122
Precision Feedscrews Inc	3451	127
Precision Fiberglass Products	3644	44
Precision Filters Inc	3825	158
Precision Finishing Inc	3471	59
Precision Fitting and Gauge Co	5085	91
Precision Flooring Solutions Inc	3469	17
Precision Flow Technologies Inc	3825	32
Precision Fluorocarbon Inc	3089	936
Precision Foods Inc	2034	13
Precision Forms Inc	3599	1462
Precision Gage and Tool Co	3545	267
Precision Gage Inc	3714	352
Precision Gasket Co	3053	57
Precision Governors LLC	3714	405
Precision Graphic Services Inc	7336	186
Precision Graphics Of Oregon Inc	2752	1380
Precision Grinding and Manufacturing Corp	3544	38
Precision Grinding Inc	3443	228
Precision Hermetic Technology Inc	3679	291
Precision Husky Corp	3553	11
Precision Inc	3677	10
Precision Inc (Minneapolis Minnesota)	3612	61
Precision Industries Corp	3542	84
Precision Industries Inc	3316	20
Precision Industries Inc (Flint Michigan)	3544	774
Precision Industries Inc (Omaha Nebraska)	5085	22
Precision Innovations Inc	3599	361
Precision Inspection Company Inc	7389	1151
Precision Instrumentation Co	3559	355
Precision Interface Electronics Inc	5064	136
Precision International Automotive Products Inc	5013	125
Precision Intricast Inc	3842	312
Precision Laboratories Inc	2879	34
Precision Lighting Company Inc	5063	782
Precision Lighting Systems Inc	5063	803
Precision Litho	2752	602
Precision Litho Service Inc	2752	508
Precision Machine And Manufacturing Company LLC	3441	56
Precision Machine and Metal Fabrication Inc	3444	214
Precision Machine And Supply Inc	3599	236
Precision Machine and Welding Inc	3599	1583
Precision Machine Company Inc	3599	2462
Precision Machine Controls Inc	3625	177
Precision Machine Inc	3599	536
Precision Machine Of Savannah Inc	3469	154
Precision Machine Products Inc	3552	19
Precision Machine Works Inc	3728	39
Precision Machined Products Div	3599	1487
Precision Machining Services Inc	3599	1121
Precision Machining Sheet Metal Inc	3599	1837
Precision Management and Construction Inc	1623	622
Precision Manifold Systems Inc	3714	374
Precision Manufacturing And Assembly LLC	3089	1612
Precision Manufacturing And Engineering Company Inc	3599	1584
Precision Manufacturing Company Inc	3679	316
Precision Manufacturing Group LLC	3599	345
Precision Marble Inc	3089	1392
Precision Marketing	5044	112

Company Name	SIC	Rank
Precision Masking Inc	3544	661
Precision Masters Inc	3545	279
Precision Measurement Company Inc	3823	414
Precision Measurements Inc	7629	17
Precision Measurements Inc (Atlanta Georgia)	3829	249
Precision Mechanisms Corp	3679	508
Precision Medical Products Inc	3841	148
Precision Metal Crafters Ltd	7692	27
Precision Metal Form Div	3499	126
Precision Metal Industries Inc	3444	190
Precision Metal Products Inc	3841	133
Precision Metal Works Inc	3599	1175
Precision Metalcrafters Inc	3599	1622
Precision Metals And Hardware Inc	5031	303
Precision Metalsmiths Inc	3364	4
Precision Mold and Engineering Inc	3544	678
Precision Mold Base Corp	3544	293
Precision Mold Technologies Inc	3089	1862
Precision Molding Inc	3089	521
Precision Motion Controls	3679	847
Precision Offset Inc	2752	928
Precision Optical Company Inc	3851	67
Precision Optical Group Inc	8071	42
Precision Optical Laboratory Inc	3851	82
Precision Optics Corporation Inc	3845	119
Precision Packaging Products Inc	3089	1123
Precision Packing Corp	2891	85
Precision Paper Tube Co	2655	3
Precision Part Systems Of Winston-Salem Inc	3423	70
Precision Parts International LLC	3499	3
Precision Pattern Inc (Tacoma Washington)	3544	445
Precision Pcb Services Inc	7378	171
Precision Personnel Inc	7361	417
Precision Photo-Fab Inc	3469	256
Precision Photonics Corp	3827	93
Precision Piping And Mechanical Inc	1711	78
Precision Plastic And Die Co	3089	1542
Precision Plastics Inc	3089	1800
Precision Plus Inc	3451	105
Precision Plus Vacuum Parts Inc	3563	38
Precision Polymer Manufacturing Inc- Man	3089	1183
Precision Polymer Products Inc	3069	113
Precision Powerhouse	3565	72
Precision Prefinishing Inc	2421	128
Precision Press Inc	2752	1703
Precision Printing Group Inc	2752	762
Precision Printing Inc	2796	42
Precision Process Corp	3544	504
Precision Products Company Inc	3672	463
Precision Products Inc	3524	16
Precision Products Machine and Fab Inc	3444	231
Precision Products Of Asheville Inc	3599	880
Precision Pump and Valve Service Inc	5084	325
Precision Punch Corp	3544	266
Precision Quincy Corp	3448	49
Precision Rebuilders Inc	3714	354
Precision Resistive Products Inc	3676	19
Precision Resistor Company Inc	3676	20
Precision Response Corp	7389	123
Precision Results Manufacturing Inc	3599	1857
Precision Roll Grinders Inc	3471	14
Precision Rubber Plate Company Inc	3555	43
Precision Samplers Inc	3829	294
Precision Screw Machine Products Inc	3599	1585
Precision Seating LLC	5021	171
Precision Service Motor Inc	3542	102
Precision Shapes Inc	3599	961
Precision Sharpening Devices Inc	5084	940
Precision Small Engine Co	3524	39
Precision Southeast Inc	3089	343
Precision Specialists Inc	3599	1772
Precision Specialty Metals Inc	3312	14
Precision Speed Equipment Inc	3822	27
Precision Speed Instruments Inc	3829	306
Precision Spring and Stamping Corp	3545	185
Precision Steel Services Inc	5051	204
Precision Strip Inc	5051	77
Precision Sure-Lock	3531	56
Precision Switch Design Inc	3625	414
Precision Switching Inc	3613	144
Precision Systems Concepts Inc	7372	844
Precision Systems Inc	3841	343
Precision Tech Electric Inc	1731	2195
Precision Technologies Inc	3599	1164
Precision Technology And Manufacturing Inc	3643	93
Precision Technology Corp	3369	33
Precision Therapeutics Inc	3841	385
Precision Thermoplastic Components Inc	3089	531
Precision Timer Company Inc	3625	320
Precision Tool and Die of Ponca City Inc	3544	446
Precision Tool and Engineering Of Gainesville Inc	3549	107
Precision Tool And Machine Co	3599	1674
Precision Tool and Stamping Inc	3469	250
Precision Tool Company Inc	3545	367

Company Name Index PRESTIGE

Company Name	SIC	Rank
Precision Tool Die And Machine Company Inc	3469	50
Precision Tool Inc	3545	361
Precision Tool Work Inc	3599	2077
Precision Trim Inc	3083	71
Precision Tube Co	3498	19
Precision Tube Inc	3312	100
Precision Turned Components Corp	3451	73
Precision Valley Communications	1623	124
Precision Waveguide Components Inc	3679	877
Precision West Engineered Products Inc	3599	2163
Precision Wire Components	3315	39
Precision Wire Products Inc	3496	60
Precisionform Inc	3451	52
Precisionmatics Company Inc	3599	755
Precix Inc	3053	14
Precoat Metals	3479	5
Precor Inc	3949	15
Precyse Solutions LLC	8999	16
Predator Software Inc	7372	4128
Predator Systems Inc	3594	20
Predictive Maintenance Inspection Inc	7382	182
Predix Pharmaceuticals Inc	2834	422
Preeminent Protective Services	7381	244
Pre-EmployCom Inc	7381	186
preEmptive Solutions Inc	7379	767
Prefab Software Inc	7372	4253
Preferred Bank	6035	198
Preferred Bank (Los Angeles California)	6022	135
Preferred Billing Management Services Inc	8721	265
Preferred Care Partners Inc	6324	51
Preferred Community Services	7389	1308
Preferred Data Systems LLC	7372	880
Preferred Employers Group Inc	6331	237
Preferred Foods Martin LP	5142	27
Preferred Homecare	8082	49
Preferred Inc	1761	14
Preferred Industries Inc	3544	182
Preferred Labor Corp	7363	263
Preferred Legal Services Inc	7338	40
Preferred Machine and Tool Products Corp	3599	886
Preferred Manufacturing Associates LLC	5065	815
Preferred Meal Systems Inc	5812	333
Preferred Medical Marketing Corp	7372	1557
Preferred Medical Products Inc	3841	282
Preferred Plastics and Packaging Company Inc	5084	537
Preferred Pump and Equipment LP	5084	143
Preferred Quality Services Inc	7389	2038
Preferred Rubber Compounding Corp	2822	5
Preferred Sales Agency Ltd	5065	400
Preferred Security Components Incorporated Of PA	3699	279
Preferred Systems Solutions Inc	7373	243
Preferred Technology Inc	3669	243
Preferred Tool and Die Company Inc	3544	521
Preferred Tool and Die Inc	3469	166
Preferred Tool Inc	3544	560
Preferred Transportation Corp	4213	2275
Preferred Unlimited Inc	6799	19
Preferred Utilities Manufacturing Corp	3829	84
Preferred Warranties Inc	6399	28
Preferred Yield Inc	6282	473
PreferredOne Administrative Services Inc	6321	61
Preh Electronics Inc	3577	226
Preimer Atms Inc	3578	41
Preit-Rubin Inc	6552	198
Prejean Winery Inc	2084	133
Pre-Mach Inc	3599	763
Premarc Corp	3272	44
Premcom Corp	7373	493
Premera Blue Cross	6324	29
Premier America Credit Union	6061	30
Premier Amusements Inc	7993	24
Premier and Carriage Trade Inc	5812	306
Premier Bank	6022	446
Premier Bank and Trust	6021	325
Premier Bank (Maplewood Minnesota)	6022	369
Premier Brands Of America Inc	3842	175
Premier Builder Supply Inc	5211	235
Premier Business Products Inc	5044	98
Premier Cleaning Service Inc	7349	400
Premier Color Graphics Inc	2752	1339
Premier Colors Inc	2899	231
Premier Commercial Bancorp	6712	493
Premier Commercial Bank NA	6021	336
Premier Companies LLC	7389	1943
Premier Consulting Group Inc	7379	616
Premier Control Systems LLC	1731	1372
Premier Cooperative	5153	23
Premier Design Systems Inc	7372	823
Premier Die Casting Co	3363	44
Premier Electric Inc	1731	692
Premier Electric Supply Inc	5063	490
Premier Electrical Corp	1799	55
Premier Engineering And Manufacturing Inc	3728	122
Premier Environmental Services Inc	8742	233

Company Name	SIC	Rank
Premier Equipment Inc	7389	465
Premier Events	7299	37
Premier Events and Design	7389	1823
Premier Exhibitions Inc	7999	76
Premier Fabrication Inc	3599	566
Premier Facility Group Inc	7389	2417
Premier Feeds LLC	2048	44
Premier Finance Co	6159	71
Premier Financial Bancorp Inc	6022	147
Premier Forest Products Inc	5031	392
Premier Furniture Manufacturing Inc	3553	56
Premier Gear and Machine Works Inc	3462	67
Premier Gear and Machining Inc	3599	1440
Premier Global Services Inc	7389	120
Premier/GMAC Real Estate	6531	354
Premier Graphics Inc	2752	1459
Premier Home Improvements Inc	5021	155
Premier Ims Inc	7331	55
Premier Inc	8742	122
Premier Inc (Charlotte North Carolina)	8741	113
Premier Ink Systems Inc	2851	31
Premier Integrity Solutions Inc	8748	129
Premier Internet Inc	7379	1186
Premier It Solutions	7371	1138
Premier Lighting	5999	303
Premier Manufacturing Corporation	3496	71
Premier Marine Inc	3732	15
Premier Medical Supplies Inc	5047	176
Premier Members Federal Credit Union	6061	79
Premier Mortgage Co	6162	101
Premier Network Solutions Inc	7373	823
Premier Office Solutions Inc	5021	129
Premier Packaging Corp	3565	48
Premier Pan Company Inc	3469	191
Premier Payment Systems	7389	346
Premier Pipe LLC	3498	10
Premier Pneumatics Inc	3535	34
Premier Power Renewable Energy Inc	5074	23
Premier Practice Management	8011	63
Premier Prints Inc	2752	1508
Premier Prototype Inc	3469	232
Premier Pyrotechnics Inc	5092	55
Premier Quilting Corp	2221	41
Premier Rental Center	7353	106
Premier Resorts Inc	7011	170
Premier Roofing and Construction	1761	48
Premier Sash and Door Ltd	5031	291
Premier Service Bank	6022	571
Premier Software Associates Inc	7371	1251
Premier Software Ventures Inc	7371	559
Premier Southern Ticket Company Inc	2759	249
Premier Technical Plastics Inc (Minden Louisiana)	3089	475
Premier Technical Sales Inc	5065	51
Premier Technologies Inc	3669	158
Premier Technology Inc	5046	21
Premier Technology Solutions Inc	7379	1066
Premier Tool and Die Cast Corp	3364	9
Premier Tooling and Manufacturing Inc	3364	10
Premier Transportation and Warehousing	4213	681
Premier Truck Centers Inc	5012	48
Premier Truck Sales and Rental Inc	5012	207
Premier Trust of Nevada	6282	191
Premier Valley Bank	6022	290
Premier World Marketing Inc	7389	1033
Premier Yarn Dyers Inc	2231	11
Premiere Builders Supply Inc	5031	398
Premiere Communications Inc	4813	112
Premiere Computer Systems Inc	5045	986
Premiere Conferencing Networks Inc	4813	140
Premiere Copier Inc	7359	261
Premiere Credit of North America LLC	7322	30
Premiere Global Services Inc	4899	23
Premiere Hardwoods LLC	5099	98
Premiere Lock Company LLC	5099	128
Premiere Medical	5047	277
Premiere Music And Film Systems Inc	1731	1585
Premiere Packaging Inc	2842	67
Premiere Plastics Inc	3088	24
Premiere Properties Inc	7375	257
Premiere Radio Networks Inc	4832	29
Premiere Sales	5074	226
PremierGarage Systems LLC	2514	11
PremierWest Bancorp	6021	77
PremierWest Bank	6021	113
PremierWest Bank (Elk Grove California)	6022	370
PremierWest Investment Services Inc	6159	72
Premio Foods Inc	2013	83
Premise Maid Candies Inc	2066	39
Premium Allied Tool Inc	3469	84
Premium Color Graphics Inc	7335	12
Premium Distributors of Washington DC LLC	5181	57
Premium Financing Specialists Inc	6153	7
Premium Iowa Pork LLC	2013	125
Premium Lift Inc	5084	927
Premium Marketing Systems Inc	7389	1315
Premium Meats Inc	2011	158
Premium Metals Inc	5051	468
Premium Oil Co	5541	27
Premium Payment Plan	6153	31
Premium Poultry Co	2015	69

Company Name	SIC	Rank
Premium Protein Products LLC	2013	112
Premium Retail Services Inc	8742	38
Premium Seating Products Inc	5046	245
Premium Technology Inc	7371	540
PremiumWear Inc	2329	11
Premix Inc	3089	385
Premtec Inc	3552	27
Prent Corp	3089	149
Prentice Machine Works JR	3599	1934
Prentiss LLC	2879	36
Prentke Romich Co	3822	19
Prep Sportswear	2389	29
Preparatory Magazine Group Inc	2721	358
Preparatory Rehabilitation For Individual and Emp Inc	8211	108
PrepaYd Inc	6141	71
PrePlayed Entertainment	5735	8
Pres Air Trol Corp	3643	105
Presbyterian Medical Care Corp	8062	211
Presbyterian Publishing Corp	2731	203
Presbyterian Special Services Inc	8059	21
Prescient Development Inc	7379	568
Prescient Software jrd Inc	7372	4917
Prescient Worldwide	4813	536
Presco Inc	3699	271
Presco Polymers LP	3829	55
Presco Telecommunications Inc	1731	1556
Prescolite Inc	3646	4
Prescotech Industries Inc	4783	9
Prescott Aerospace Inc	3599	973
Prescott Newspapers Inc	2711	218
Prescott Precision Die Inc	3599	1277
Prescott's Limbs and Braces	5999	167
Prescription Optical Inc	5995	20
Prescription Software Inc	7371	1594
Presence From Innovation LLC	2542	28
Presence Incorporated Corporate	5199	44
Presentation Folder Inc	2675	15
Presentation Group Inc	7389	1181
Presentation Media Inc	5065	756
Presentation Services - Long Beach CA	7389	30
Presentation Strategies Inc	7336	29
Preserva-Products Inc	2851	106
Preservation Resources	7822	6
Preserver Group Inc	6331	311
Preserver Insurance Co	6331	345
President Container Inc	2653	15
President Enterprise Inc	2759	262
President Global Corp	2052	51
President Titanium Company Inc	5051	116
Presidential Life Corp	6311	98
Presidential Life Insurance Co	6311	107
Presidential Realty Corp	6798	203
Presidential Service Industries Inc	7349	437
Presidio Bank	6022	622
Presidio Components Inc	3675	15
Presidio Inc	7379	27
Presidium Inc	8299	52
Pres-On Tape and Gasket Corp	3053	61
Presort Plus Inc	7389	1733
Presque Isle Electric and Gas Coop	4931	53
Presrite Corp	3462	27
Press A Light Corp	3648	86
Press America Inc	2752	1038
Press And Journal Inc	2711	601
Press and News in Osseo	2711	166
Press Brake Tooling Corp	3544	892
Press Holding Corp	2711	349
Press Media Corp	2752	660
Press Of Ohio Inc	2732	7
Press Printing Enterprises Inc	2752	689
Press Repair Engineering Sales And Services Inc	7699	120
Press Seal Gasket Corp	3053	51
Press Sentinel Newspapers Inc	2711	177
Press-A-Print International LLC	3555	62
Pressco Technology Inc	3829	86
Presscom Electronics LLC	3672	440
Presscraft Papers Inc	2752	1245
Presscut Industries Inc	3053	85
Press-Enterprise Inc	2711	219
Presses Inc	3542	48
Pressline Ink And Supply Company Inc	2796	50
PressOK Entertainment Inc	3577	393
Presstek Inc	3555	8
Presstime Graphics Inc	2752	1584
Pressure BioSciences Inc	3829	392
Pressure Chemical Co	2899	160
Pressure Concrete Inc	1622	34
Pressure Products Company Inc	3231	72
Pressure Switches Inc	3823	468
Pressure Systems Inc (Hampton Virginia)	3625	71
Pressure Vessel Service Inc	5169	19
Pressure-Tech Inc	3443	238
Presswerx Inc	5084	897
Prestage Farms Inc	0213	8
Presti Rubber Products Inc	3011	25
Prestige Audio Visual Inc	7359	104
Prestige Auto Corp	5511	1092
Prestige Automotive Group	5511	39
Prestige Brands Holdings Inc	2834	81
Prestige Brands Inc	2834	84

Company Name Index

Company Name	SIC	Rank
Prestige Bread Company Of Jersey City Inc	2051	167
Prestige Care Inc	8051	40
Prestige Color Inc	2752	739
Prestige Display And Packaging LLC	2653	126
Prestige Envelope and Lithographic Corp	2752	1740
Prestige Flag and Banner Company Inc	2399	25
Prestige Ford	5511	1099
Prestige Home Centers Inc	2451	39
Prestige Insurance Services Inc	6411	202
Prestige International Inc	5045	673
Prestige Lens Lab Inc	5049	168
Prestige Lumber and Supplies Inc	5211	100
Prestige Maintenance Inc	7349	118
Prestige Management Services Inc	8741	257
Prestige Mold Inc	3544	171
Prestige Party Rental Inc	7359	177
Prestige Properties and Development Company Inc	6552	279
Prestige Security	7381	82
Prestige Software Inc	7371	833
Prestige Stamping Inc	3452	53
Prestigeline Inc	3645	29
Presto Delivery Inc	5149	118
Prestolite Electric LLC	3621	22
Prestolite Wire LLC	3694	5
Preston Casteel Electric Company Inc	1731	682
Preston Citizen	2711	799
Preston Glass Industries Inc	3641	32
Preston Hood Chevrolet Inc	5511	1038
Preston Industries Inc	3821	16
Preston Wynne SpA	7231	8
Preston-Eastin Inc	3548	56
Prestonwood Eye Care	3851	112
Prestressed Casting Co	3272	120
Pretec	3577	416
Pretech Corp	3272	119
Pretium Packaging LLC	3085	7
Pretty Products LLC	3089	180
Prettyman Broadcasting Corp	4832	181
Pretzels Inc	2052	20
Prevail Credit Union	6062	78
Prevaro Marketing Solutions LLC	2789	87
Prevention Research Inc	8731	211
Prezenta Presentation Products	7336	267
Prg Systems	7372	3079
PRGX Global Inc	8721	140
PRI Research and Development Corp	8731	395
Pri Systems Inc	7371	1240
Priasoft Inc	7372	3280
Price Brothers Realty Co	6531	329
Price Communications Corp	4833	135
Price Compressor Company Inc	3563	55
Price Electric Company Inc	1731	1727
Price Heneveld Cooper DeWitt and Litton	8111	469
Price LogPro	3553	16
Price Milling Company Inc	0723	29
Price Modern LLC	5021	40
Price Pfister Inc	3432	10
Price Products Inc	3599	1070
Price Pump Manufacturing Co	3561	125
Price Telecommunications Inc	5065	906
Price Truck Line Inc	4213	1487
Price Trucking Inc	4213	1914
Price Weber Marketing Communications Inc	7311	478
Priceless Resource Inc	5064	35
Pricelinecom Inc	7373	7
PriceSmart Inc	5331	11
PriceSpective LLC	8748	194
PricewaterhouseCoopers LLP	8721	1
Pride Air Conditioning and Appliance Inc	7623	7
Pride Cast Metals Inc	3365	21
Pride Container Corp	2653	55
Pride Conveyance Systems Inc	3535	88
Pride Enterprises	4213	2990
Pride Environmental Construction Inc	1623	440
Pride Equipment Corp	5084	154
Pride Family Brands Inc	5021	36
PRIDE Head Start	8351	35
Pride In Graphics Inc	2752	1741
Pride Industries	7349	6
Pride Manufacturing Company LLC	2411	6
Pride Printing Company Inc	2752	1520
Pride Printing LLC	2752	372
Pride Products Distributor LLC	5112	68
Pride Utility Construction Co	1623	271
Pridgeon and Clay Inc	3465	6
Priebe Security Services	7382	175
Priefert Manufacturing Company Inc	3523	38
Pries Enterprises Inc	3354	35
Priester Aviation Inc	4512	58
Priester Pecan Company Inc	2068	13
Prikos and Becker Tool Co	3469	260
Prillaman and Pace Inc	1623	305
Prim Hall Enterprises Inc	3555	115
Prim Industrial Contractors Inc	1731	1050
Prima Lighting Corp	3645	64
Prima North America Inc	3699	85
Prima Technologies Inc	3999	181
Prima Yerba Inc	2834	400
Primadonna Company LLC	7011	96
Primal Media Corp	2741	345
Primalyn Enterprises Inc	5046	235
Primary Care Partners	7389	2098
Primary Electrical Contracting And Design Inc	1731	2346
Primary Energy Recycling Corp	8748	61
Primary Eyecare Associates	8042	1
Primary Instruments Inc	8734	168
Primary Pictures	7812	229
Primary Security Services Inc	7381	109
Primary Services LP	7363	176
Primary Source Media	2741	178
Primavera Systems Inc	7372	441
Primax Software Corp	7371	1729
Prime Access Inc	7311	277
Prime Advisors Inc	6282	140
Prime Buchholz and Associates Inc	6282	250
Prime Cable	6799	109
Prime Cabling Services Inc	1731	2039
Prime Choice Foods West	2096	49
Prime Cleaning Services Inc	7349	152
Prime Colorants Inc	2851	111
Prime Computer Systems Inc	7373	952
Prime Controls LP	5065	138
Prime Conveyor Inc	3535	130
Prime Deli Corp	2099	180
Prime Enterprises Inc	2844	109
Prime Factors Inc	7371	1196
Prime Financial Corp	6799	7
Prime Food Processing Corp	2013	123
Prime Group Realty Trust	6552	25
Prime Healthcare Services Inc	8741	67
Prime Heat Inc	3567	98
Prime Holdings Corp	6719	32
Prime Home Entertainment Inc	4899	211
Prime Image Inc	5065	396
Prime Inc	4213	55
Prime Industries LLP	3085	34
Prime Instruments Inc	3825	102
Prime Investments Inc	2752	1410
Prime Label Consultants Inc	7372	3735
Prime Leather Finishes Co	2851	101
Prime Lending Inc	6163	10
Prime Machine and Tool Inc	3599	2415
Prime Market Targeting Inc	7311	686
Prime Materials Corp	5999	247
Prime Materials Recovery Inc	5093	62
Prime Medical Supply Corp	5047	149
Prime National Publishing Corp	2721	437
Prime Office Products Inc	5112	14
Prime Packaging Corp	5199	82
Prime Printing Inc	2752	936
Prime Products Inc	3599	670
Prime Property Investors Ltd	6513	29
Prime Protective Services Inc	7381	164
Prime PVC Inc	3087	9
Prime Recognition Corp	7371	1112
Prime Retail LP	6531	104
Prime Retail Services Inc	8741	211
Prime Service Center	5999	142
Prime Smoked Meats Inc	5147	123
Prime Solutions Inc	3674	404
Prime Star Group Inc	2086	158
Prime Supply Co	5074	217
Prime Systems	5045	117
Prime Systems Inc	3648	40
Prime Technological Services LLC	3679	261
Prime Technology Group Inc	7371	161
Prime Technology LLC	3676	5
Prime Tempus Inc	6411	261
Prime Time Manufacturing Inc	3911	20
Prime Time Thermographics Inc	2752	425
Prime Time Transportation	4213	2450
Prime Wire and Cable Inc	3357	63
Primearray Systems Inc	3572	103
Primedge Inc	3556	20
Primedia Enthusiast Publication Inc	2721	135
Primedia Enthusiast Publications Inc	2721	127
PRIMEDIA Inc	2721	35
PrimeEnergy Corp	1311	105
Prime-Line Products Co	3429	23
PrimeNet Marketing Services Inc	8742	284
Primeon Inc	5045	176
Prime-Pak Foods Inc	2013	108
Primepoint LLC	7372	3401
PrimeQ Solutions Inc	7372	1633
Primera Foods Corp	2015	22
Primera Plastics Inc	3089	534
Primera Technology Inc	3577	224
Primerica Financial Services Inc	6282	21
Primerica Inc	6311	66
Primero Systems Inc	7371	1690
Primescape Solutions Inc	7299	41
PrimeSource Food Service Equipment Inc	5049	11
PrimeSouth Bank	6022	292
Primestaff Inc	7363	256
Primestream Corp	7379	971
PrimeTech Inc	3999	44
Primetime Publicity and Media Inc	8743	259
Primewood Inc	2434	17
Primex Plastics Corp	3081	18
Primm Valley Resort And Casino	7011	111
Primo Microphones Inc	3651	110
Primo Water Corp	5149	57
Primore Inc	3491	40
Primoris Service Corp	6719	59
Primrose Candy Co	2064	31
Primrose Oil Co	2992	17
Primus Builders Inc	1799	17
Primus Capital Funds	6799	340
Primus Global Services Inc	7373	319
Primus Knowledge Solutions Inc	7372	623
Primus Software Corp	7371	146
Primus Technologies Corp	3625	22
Primus Telecommunications Group Inc	4813	28
Prince and Sons Contractors LLC	1623	738
Prince Black Distillery Inc	2085	25
Prince Corp	5031	65
Prince George Electric Coop	4911	400
Prince Industries Inc	3545	18
Prince International Corp	5094	75
Prince Minerals Inc	2816	3
Prince of Peace Enterprises Inc	5149	91
Prince Of The Sea Ltd	2092	76
Prince Perelson and Associates LLC	7361	409
Prince Rubber and Plastics Company Inc	3069	172
Prince Security Services Inc	7389	1922
Prince Sports Group Inc	3949	61
Prince Transport	4213	2833
Prince Ventures LLC	1623	352
Prince-Bush Management Co	7011	215
Princess House Inc	5719	17
Princeton Book Company Publishers	2731	348
Princeton Case West Inc	3089	1759
Princeton Data Source LLC	8732	111
Princeton Delivery System	3537	49
Princeton Disc Corp	3565	91
Princeton Display Technologies Inc	5045	1004
Princeton Financial Corp	6162	135
Princeton Financial Systems Inc	7372	766
Princeton Gamma-Tech Inc	3812	93
Princeton Industrial Products Inc	3451	155
Princeton Instruments Acton	2821	73
Princeton Insurance Co	6719	105
Princeton Machinery Service Inc	7699	165
Princeton Measurements Corp	3829	323
Princeton National Bancorp Inc	6712	295
Princeton Packet Inc	2711	267
Princeton Partners Inc	7311	298
Princeton Polymer Laboratories	8742	610
Princeton Profit Associates Inc	4731	90
Princeton Resource Associates Inc	7379	1588
Princeton Review Inc	2731	28
Princeton Technology Inc	3577	426
Princeton University Press	2731	119
Princeton Upholstery Company Inc	2521	32
Principal Decision Systems International	7372	2400
Principal Financial Advisors Inc	6282	64
Principal Financial Group Inc	6311	7
Principal Financial Services Inc	6035	53
Principal Global Investors LLC	6282	231
Principal Life Insurance Co	6311	270
Principal Manufacturing Corp	3469	42
Principia Partners LLC	7371	447
Principle Business Enterprises Inc	2676	7
Principle Plastics	3021	11
Principle Solutions Group	8748	115
PrinciplesGroup LLC	7379	923
Prine Systems Inc	5734	82
Print Box Inc (New York New York)	2759	581
Print Communications Inc	2752	165
Print Direction Inc	2752	269
Print Inc	5734	12
Print King Inc	2752	1716
Print Management Corp	2752	987
Print Mount Company Inc	5084	925
Print Pad Ltd	2752	222
Print Perfect Inc	2752	1644
Print Resource Inc	7389	1448
Print Rite Inc	2752	1125
Print Shop	2752	354
Print Shop Inc	2752	1316
Print Source Inc	2752	635
Print South Corp	2752	58
Print Tech LLC	2752	541
Print Tech Of Western Pennsylvania	2752	783
Print Tek	3674	498
Print Turnaround Inc	2752	1711
Print Wrap Corp	2752	1670
Printco Inc	2752	853
Printcraft Press Inc	2752	1558
Printcraft Printing Inc	2752	1693
Printcrafters Inc	2791	41
Printech Enterprises Inc	7378	154
Printech/Instant Ads Inc	2759	346
Printed Circuits Assembly Corp	3672	57
Printed Circuits Inc	3672	224
Printed Specialties Inc	2752	550
Printedd Products and Services Ltd	2759	157
Printek Inc	3577	173
Printelligent Corp	7379	375
Printelogy Inc	7378	117
Printer Friends Inc	3577	420

Company Name	SIC	Rank
Printer Inc	2752	205
Printer Solutions	5734	471
Printer Wizard	7629	39
Printer Works Inc	3577	471
Printer Zink Inc	2791	13
Printerm Datascribe Inc	3577	530
Printers and Stationers Inc	5112	44
Printers Bindery Service Co	2789	137
Printer's Bindery Services Inc	2789	43
Printers Computers and Lans Inc	7373	916
Printers Finishing Touch Inc	2789	134
Printer's Repair Parts Inc	3555	87
Printers Software Inc	7372	3801
Printers Trade Inc	2752	1206
Printers' Unlimited Inc	2752	1717
PrintersEdge	3541	173
Printery	2752	407
Printex Inc	3555	44
Printex Packaging Corp	3089	799
Printhead Specialists	7378	173
Printing and Packaging Inc	2631	31
Printing Arts Center Inc	2752	1812
Printing Arts Inc	2752	1817
Printing Associates Inc	2754	23
Printing Center Inc	2752	866
Printing Communications Associates Inc	7372	4868
Printing Concepts Inc	2752	1044
Printing Corporation Of The Americas Inc	2752	1071
Printing Enterprises Inc	2759	236
Printing Ideas By Me Inc	2752	1688
Printing Images Corp	8742	621
Printing Images Inc	2752	592
Printing Incorporated Of Louisville Kentucky	2752	1370
Printing Inc (Wichita Kansas)	2752	52
Printing Island Corp	2752	1482
Printing Mart Inc	2752	1638
Printing Palace Inc	2752	1604
Printing Port Inc	2752	1335
Printing Research Corp	3555	38
Printing Resource Inc	2752	803
Printing Services Of Greensboro Inc	2752	1336
Printing Station Corp	2752	1648
Printing Technology Inc	2893	8
PrintingForLesscom Inc	2759	87
printLEADER Software	7372	1140
Printmail Inc	2752	1837
Printmailers Inc	2752	531
Printmanagement LLC	2752	988
Printmark Industries Inc	8743	144
Printmasters Professional Printers Inc	2759	391
Print-O-Stat Inc	2752	160
Print-O-Tape Inc	2759	97
Printpack Inc	2671	6
PrintPlacecom	2759	40
PrintPoint Inc	7372	1033
Printron Engravers Inc	7389	888
Printronix Inc	3577	101
Printswell Inc	2754	27
Print-Tech Inc	2752	1119
Printwell Acquisition Company Inc	2789	18
Printworks South LP	2759	99
Printworx Inc	3577	575
PrintXcel	2761	31
Prinz Grain and Feed Inc	5153	184
Prinzing Enterprises Inc	2396	33
Prior Lake Aggregates Inc	1442	85
Priority Components LLC	5065	898
Priority Designs Inc	8731	148
Priority Dispatch Inc	4213	780
Priority Electric Inc	1731	2011
Priority Envelope Inc	2759	116
Priority Express Courier Inc	4215	7
Priority Express Inc	4213	1208
Priority Fulfillment Services Inc	7379	31
Priority Health Government Programs Inc	8099	27
Priority Health Managed Benefits Inc	6324	56
Priority Leasing	6159	43
Priority One Services Inc	8731	115
Priority Press Inc	2759	251
Priority Publications Inc	2741	316
Priority Services Inc	4213	2938
Priority Systems Inc	5999	309
Prism Color Corp	2752	393
Prism Pointe Technologies LLC	7378	15
Prism Software Corp	3577	576
Prism Software Solutions Inc	7372	3625
Prism Technology Group Inc	1731	1853
Prism Visual Software Inc	7372	3330
Prisma Graphic Corp	2752	221
PrismNet Ltd	4813	228
Prison Health Services Inc	8093	8
Pristine Water Solutions Inc	2899	204
Pritchard Electric Company Inc	1731	95
Pritchard Industries Inc	7349	21
Pritchett and Hull Associates Inc	2731	341
Pritchett Trucking Inc	4213	569
Prithvi Information Solutions International LLC	7379	578
Pritzlaff Wholesale Meats Inc	5147	73
Privacy Inc	7372	3494

Company Name	SIC	Rank
Private Bank of California	6022	265
Private Brand Merchandising Corp	2335	14
Private Capital Management Inc	6282	95
Private Duty Registry Services Inc	7361	330
Private Export Funding Corp	6159	19
Private Eyes Inc	7389	885
Private Label Foods Of Rochester Inc	2033	104
Private Medical-Care Inc	6324	73
Private Secretary Inc	8099	88
PrivateBancorp Inc	6022	15
PrivateBank	6022	365
PrivateBank and Trust Co	6022	809
Privilege International Inc	5021	96
Privo Inc	7379	1601
Prize Performance Inc	8743	251
PRL Inc	3399	22
PRM Realty Group LLC	6531	280
PRN Corp	4833	24
Prn Health Solutions Inc	7389	1277
PRN Medical Software	7372	701
Prn Resources Inc	7361	422
Pro Action Of Steuben And Yates Inc	8322	61
Pro Active Therapy of Ahoskie Inc	8093	50
Pro Audio Services Inc	5731	193
Pro Bar Inc	7373	1217
Pro Brand International Inc	5063	367
Pro Cellular Wireless Communication Inc	4812	47
Pro Clean Janitorial Service Inc	7349	499
Pro Collect Inc	7322	178
Pro Company Sound Inc	3643	79
Pro Controls Inc	3625	318
Pro Design and Vending Technologies Inc	5046	228
Pro Dive	2329	39
Pro Document Solutions Inc	2752	192
Pro Electric Inc	1731	1472
Pro Em LLC	8741	175
Pro Equipment Company Inc	3589	236
Pro Fleet Transport Corp	4213	801
Pro Golf Discount Inc	5941	31
Pro Golf International Inc	3949	143
Pro Golf of America Inc	3949	144
Pro Graphics LLC	7336	200
Pro Industrial Welding Inc	1791	22
Pro Line Headwear Inc	2353	16
Pro Logic Computer Systems Inc	7371	1385
Pro Look Sports Inc	2329	16
Pro Mark Graphics	2759	584
Pro Med Center	5047	279
Pro Media Inc	7319	133
Pro Met Steel Inc	5051	115
Pro Orthopedic Devices Inc	3842	230
Pro Pac Labs Inc	2834	322
Pro Plastics Inc (Linden New Jersey)	3089	1860
Pro Pools Management Inc	7389	788
Pro Precision Inc	3541	262
Pro Printing and Graphics Inc	2752	1746
Pro Products LLC	5169	42
Pro Quest Security Inc	7381	137
Pro Quip Inc	3559	189
Pro Sales Inc	3556	86
Pro Security Group Inc	7381	264
Pro Softnet Corp	7379	496
Pro Surg Inc	3841	352
Pro Systems Fabricators Inc	3699	258
Pro Systems Inc (Charlotte North Carolina)	5734	375
Pro Tech Computer Supply Inc	3577	368
Pro Tech Inc	3672	139
Pro Tech Search Inc	7361	400
Pro Tech Technologies Inc	4813	680
Pro Techmation Inc	3569	294
Pro Transport and Leasing Inc	4213	1403
Pro Unlimited Inc	7371	139
Pro Window and Door Company Inc	3089	1177
Proact Inc	8331	56
PRO*ACT LLC	5141	195
Pro-Active Communications Inc	7389	2170
Proactive Technology LLC	7371	1568
Pro-Active Technology Marketing Inc	3571	217
ProactiveNet Inc	7372	192
ProAir LLC	3585	109
Pro-Am Safety Inc	5084	362
Pro-Am Software (Warrendale Pennsylvania)	7372	1681
Pro-Arc Electrical Construction Company Inc	1731	1280
ProAssurance Casualty Co	6331	204
ProAssurance Corp	6331	89
Probablistic Software Inc	7389	812
Probaris Technologies Inc	7371	1378
Pro-Bell and Snell and Wilcox	3669	143
Probe-Logic Inc	3571	110
Probing Solutions Inc	3825	333
Probo Data Group Inc	7373	956
Pro-Boll Chemical and Fertilizer Company Inc	2874	6
Probst Electric Inc	1623	82
Probst Supply Company Inc	5074	207
Prob-Test Inc	3699	267
Probuild Company LLC	5211	34
Pro-Build Holdings Inc	2499	2
ProBusiness Services Inc	7374	82

Company Name	SIC	Rank
Proby and Associates Inc	8743	339
Procaccianti Az Ii LP	7011	121
Procam Controls Inc	5085	422
ProCard Inc	7372	640
ProCare One Nurses LLC	8099	82
Procedyne Corp	3567	62
Proceed Technical Resources Inc	7379	808
Process Automation Technologies Inc	3535	219
Process Control and Instrumentation LLC	7373	512
Process Control Systems International	3825	77
Process Control Technology Inc	7372	726
Process Development Corp	3559	316
Process Displays Co	2752	204
Process Engineered Equipment Co	3589	255
Process Engineering and Equipment Co	5084	369
Process Equipment and Service Company Inc	3443	43
Process Equipment Company Of Tipp City	3599	75
Process Equipment Inc	3531	34
Process Fab Inc	3599	102
Process Graphics Corp	2759	340
Process Industries Consortium Inc	3566	32
Process Innovations Inc	3569	292
Process Level Technology Ltd	3823	395
Process Manufacturing Company Inc	3599	223
Process Measurement and Controls Inc	3825	189
Process Mechanical Piping And Erection Inc	1796	16
Process Networks Plus Inc	7371	1467
Process Physics Inc	5065	695
Process Plus LLC	8711	196
Process Pressure Vessels	3569	250
Process Products and Service Co	3822	95
Process Research Products	2899	129
Process Screw Products Inc	3451	106
Process Sensors Corp	3823	255
Process Software Corp	7372	2828
Process Solutions and Integration Inc	5084	436
Process Solutions Inc	3625	104
Process Specialties Inc	3496	76
Process Systems and Components Inc	7699	113
Process Technologies Group Inc	3625	401
Process Thermal Dynamics Inc	3823	380
Processed Foods Corp	2038	16
Processing And Packaging Supplies Co	3082	17
Processing Technologies Inc	3559	173
Processmodel Inc	7371	1707
Processors Mailing Inc	2752	1072
Prochem Analytical Inc	8731	153
Prochem Inc	8731	147
Prochnow Transport Inc	4213	1234
Pro-Clean Of Arizona Inc	2842	59
Proclivity Systems	7372	2474
Proco Products Inc	3069	90
Procon Products	3561	25
Proconex Inc	8711	187
Procopio Cory Hargreaves and Savitch LP	8111	356
Pro-Copy Inc	7334	45
Procor Inc	7322	201
Procore Solutions LLC	7361	433
Procter and Gamble Co	2841	1
Procter and Gamble Cosmetics	2844	14
Procter/Gamble Pharmaceutical	2834	73
Proctor International Inc	3661	157
ProcureStaff Technologies Ltd	7372	543
Pro-Cut International Limited LLC	5013	165
Procyon Corp	2834	484
PRODATA Computer Services Inc	7372	3645
Prodata Systems Inc	7378	140
Prodecom International Corp	5045	869
Prodege LLC	7371	474
Prodenco Group Inc	3843	39
Prodesco Inc	2299	16
Prodeva Inc	3599	2395
Pro-Dex Inc	5047	66
ProdEx Technologies Inc	7372	2509
Prodo-Pak Corp	3565	151
ProDPI	7384	40
Produce Alliance LLC	5148	16
Produce Packaging Inc	3053	32
Produce World Inc	2099	200
Producers Dairy Food Inc	2026	30
Producers Grain Co	5153	158
Producers Library Service	7336	172
Producers Peanut Company Inc	2099	343
Producers Rice Mill Inc	2044	3
Product Design And Development Inc	3545	194
Product Development Technologies Inc	8711	341
Product Distribution Co	4213	1145
Product Dynamics Ltd	3999	194
Product Information Network	4841	84
Product Line Inc	7389	276
Product Manufacturing Inc	3599	2045
Product Marketing Group Inc	7311	924
Product Miniature Company Inc	3993	66
Product Packaging West Inc	4783	20
Product Reports Inc	7374	218
Product Resources Inc	3625	162

PRODUCT

Company Name Index

Company Name	SIC	Rank
Product Support Solutions Inc	7379	498
Product Ventures Ltd	7389	1573
PRODUCT4 Inc	5045	72
Productigear Inc	3566	30
Production Castings Inc	3364	15
Production Control Units Inc	3829	185
Production Craft Inc	7812	286
Production Design Services Inc	3569	113
Production Engineering Corp	3479	49
Production Engineering Inc	3599	159
Production Equipment Co	3536	40
Production Facilities Equipment Company Inc	3533	99
Production Fenceworks Inc	1799	41
Production Machine and Tool Co	7692	28
Production Machine Tool Co	3599	2311
Production Machining Inc	3599	2020
Production Machining Of Alma Inc	3599	1318
Production Management Industries LLC	3533	28
Production Mold Inc	3544	619
Production Pattern	3543	21
Production Plastics Corp	3089	958
Production Plating Inc	3471	83
Production Ready Programming Inc	7371	1756
Production Resource Group LLC	3651	107
Production Saw and Machine Co	3599	489
Production Service Too LLC	7389	637
Production Supply Company Of Florida Inc	5051	410
Production Systems Automation Inc	8711	604
Production Systems Inc	3535	227
Production Technologies Inc	3679	606
Production Technology Inc	3599	2225
Production Threaded Parts Co	3541	244
Production Tool and Grinding Inc	3541	229
Production Tool and Manufacturing Co	3599	1468
Production Tool Companies LLC	3599	699
Production Tool Supply	5085	21
Productioneered Products Co	3533	107
Productions Unlimited Inc	1731	1038
Productive Alternatives Inc	8331	101
Productive Automated Systems Corp	5084	517
Productive Data Commercial Solutions Inc	7363	137
Productive Data Management Inc	7372	2446
Productive Data Systems	7374	54
Productive Electric Inc	1731	2419
Productive Plastics Inc	3089	783
Productive Products Inc	5084	348
Productive Solutions Inc	3545	226
Productive Systems Inc (Auburn Hills Michigan)	7372	3281
Productive Tool Products Inc	5085	308
Productivity Center Inc	7372	3363
Productivity Inc	8742	158
Productivity Innovations Inc	7371	1846
Productivity Quality Systems	7372	2244
Producto Dieco Corp	3544	375
Producto Electric Corp	3644	38
Products Engineering Corp	3423	60
Products for Automation	3593	58
Products Plus Inc	5065	657
Products Resources Inc	2673	55
Prodyne Enterprises Inc	2499	56
Proex Inc	7371	1262
Profab Electronics Inc	3672	299
Pro-Fab Inc (Bosque Farms New Mexico)	3355	9
Pro-Fab Metals Inc	3444	289
Pro-Fac Cooperative Inc	5141	229
Profacture Corp	5065	880
Profed Mortgage Inc	6035	238
Professional Accounting Solutions Inc	7373	790
Professional Aircraft Accessories Inc	4581	24
Professional Automation Services Inc	7372	4992
Professional Aviation Associates Inc	5088	77
Professional Basketball Club LLC	7941	18
Professional Bull Riders Inc	8999	42
Professional Business Bank	6022	531
Professional Business Computer Systems Inc	7372	5116
Professional Business Systems Inc	5044	99
Professional Color Service Inc	7384	42
Professional Communication Services	7389	2409
Professional Communications Network LP	7389	1204
Professional Component Sales Inc	5065	580
Professional Compounding Centers of America Inc	2834	341
Professional Computer Solutions Inc	5045	861
Professional Computer Systems Co	7372	1861
Professional Computing Resources Inc	7372	3464
Professional Control Corp	7372	1672
Professional Credential Verification Services Inc	6324	114
Professional Cutlery Direct LLC	5961	114
Professional Data Dimensions Inc	7374	154
Professional Data Systems Inc	7373	794
Professional Designers and Engineers Inc	7372	5146
Professional Duplicating Inc	2752	723
Professional Electrical Services Inc	1731	2227

Company Name	SIC	Rank
Professional Electronic Components Assembly Inc	3663	370
Professional Electronics Company Inc	8711	545
Professional Employment Group Inc	7361	339
Professional Engineering Consultants Inc	8711	407
Professional Garage Door Systems Inc	5211	187
Professional Gem Sciences Inc	1499	8
Professional Graphic Communications Inc	5112	61
Professional Graphics Inc	2752	1753
Professional Graphics Printing Co	2752	1250
Professional Graphics Systems And Services Inc	5045	384
Professional Health Sales Inc	5047	212
Professional Image Inc	2752	574
Professional Image Inc (Newport Beach California)	7311	870
Professional Image Printing and Packaging	2741	59
Professional Janitorial Service of Houston Inc	7349	30
Professional Life Underwriters Services Inc	6311	223
Professional Lighting and Supply Inc	5063	732
Professional Litho-Art Company Inc	7335	7
Professional Maintenance Of Michigan Inc	7349	179
Professional Maintenance Of New Orleans La Inc	7349	169
Professional Management Recruiters Inc	7361	267
Professional Medical Staffing Corp	7361	331
Professional Meters Inc	1796	9
Professional Network Services Inc	5045	591
Professional Office Services Inc	2761	21
Professional Ophthalmic Laboratories Inc	5048	29
Professional Photographers Of America Inc	8249	12
Professional Pipeline Contractors Inc	1623	179
Professional Placement Inc	7361	64
Professional Placement Resources Inc	7361	80
Professional Planning Group	7389	1166
Professional Plating Inc	3471	49
Professional Polish Inc	7349	532
Professional Power Products Inc	3613	38
Professional Practice Insurance Brokers Inc	6331	309
Professional Printing Center Inc	2752	729
Professional Products Inc	3842	123
Professional Project Services Inc	7363	123
Professional Protection Inc	7381	204
Professional Registry Of Nursing Inc	8299	76
Professional Reproductions Inc	7334	50
Professional Research Consultants Inc	8742	294
Professional Resource Associates Inc	8331	221
Professional Resource Management Inc	7372	3011
Professional Resources In Information Systems Management Inc	7363	157
Professional Respiratory Care Service Inc	7363	229
Professional Roofing and Exteriors	1761	42
Professional Security Corp	3999	159
Professional Security Inc	7381	91
Professional Service Industries Inc	8711	13
Professional Services Transportation	4213	1856
Professional Software Associates Inc	7372	4626
Professional Software Development Corp	7372	4052
Professional Software Engineering Inc	7371	113
Professional Software Solutions Ne Inc	7379	798
Professional Sports Authenticator	7389	1137
Professional Sports Planning Inc	7922	51
Professional Staffing Group Inc	7361	131
Professional Stylist Resource	5087	156
Professional System Associates Inc	7372	2285
Professional Systems Associates Inc	7371	1052
Professional Systems Corp	7372	4009
Professional Systems Corp (Valley Forge Pennsylvania)	7373	187
Professional Systems Engineering Inc	3651	260
Professional Systems Maintenance Corp	7349	292
Professional Technical Systems Inc	4813	686
Professional Technology Services Inc	7379	614
Professional Telecommunication Services Inc	5065	302
Professional Tool Grinding Company Inc	3541	135
Professional Transcriptions Of Northwest Florida	7363	350
Professional Video and Sound	1731	2349
Professional Video Supply Inc	5065	374
Professional Water Services Inc	7389	1606
Professionalized Products And Services Inc	3823	254
Professionals Advocate Insurance Co	6351	21
Professionals LLC	7382	85
Proffesional Resource Group Inc	8748	411
Proficient Computing Solutions Corp	7372	2618
Proficient Machining Co	3599	1677
Profile Digital Printing LLC	7334	60

Company Name	SIC	Rank
Profile Grinding Inc	3451	138
Profile Manufacturing Inc	3714	356
Profile Of Santa Cruz	7361	309
Profile Plastics Inc	3089	722
Profile Plastics Inc	3082	4
Profile Rubber Corp	3069	272
Profile Technologies Inc	3559	581
Profileright Inc	7371	896
Profiling Solutions Inc	7371	1595
Profit Concepts International Inc	7373	498
Profit Investment Management LLC	6722	178
Profit Technologies Corp	7371	244
Profitec Business Services Inc	4813	229
Profitfuel Inc	7389	1017
ProfitKey International Inc	7372	2566
ProfitLine Inc	8721	298
Profitool Inc	7372	3549
ProfitPoint Inc	8999	150
PROFITsystems Inc	7372	2567
Proflex Manufacturing Inc	2298	16
Proflow Inc	3823	161
Profold Inc	3554	52
Pro-Football Inc	7941	3
Proforma Corp	7372	2384
Progas Service Inc	5169	48
Progeni Corp	7372	1193
Progenics Pharmaceuticals Inc	2834	325
Progeny Inc	3844	20
ProGolfcom Inc	3949	132
Program Automation Inc	7373	1192
Program Planning Professionals Inc	8742	229
Program Productions	3695	108
Program Workshop Inc	7372	4544
Programmable Control Service Inc	3569	282
Programmable Devices Inc	7371	1668
Programmable Orienting Systems Inc	5084	944
Programmable Products Div	3612	7
Programmed Products Corp	3993	100
Programmed Test Sources Inc	3825	172
Programmers' Consortium Inc	7379	357
Programmers Investment Corp	7331	72
Programming Resources Inc	7371	1809
Prographics Inc	2752	843
Progreen Properties Inc	8734	199
Progress Container Corp	2653	85
Progress Energy Inc	4911	13
Progress Fuels Corp	5052	1
Progress Industries	8361	62
Progress Instruments Inc	3672	92
Progress Investment Management Co	6282	443
Progress Lighting Inc	3645	5
Progress Machine and Tool Inc	3545	184
Progress Machine Inc	3599	1529
Progress Printers Inc	2752	1758
Progress Printing Co	2796	3
Progress Printing Company Inc (Lynchburg Virginia)	2752	53
Progress Printing Corp	2759	409
Progress Rail Services Corp	3743	4
Progress Sharing Co	6321	81
Progress Software Corp	7372	108
Progress Tool and Stamping Inc	3544	447
Progressive Ag Center LLC	5153	138
Progressive Ag Cooperative	5153	41
Progressive Balloons Inc	5092	14
Progressive Bank NA	6021	159
Progressive Bank NA (Bellaire Ohio)	6021	291
Progressive Beauty Systems Inc	5087	118
Progressive Business Equipment Inc	5112	86
Progressive Casualty Insurance Co	6331	93
Progressive Chevrolet Co	5511	331
Progressive Communications	2711	458
Progressive Companies Inc	5146	7
Progressive Computer Service Inc	5734	218
Progressive Computer Services Inc	5045	609
Progressive Computing Inc	7379	1539
Progressive Computing LLC	7371	596
Progressive Concepts Inc	5065	59
Progressive Converting Inc	2679	17
Progressive Corp	6331	33
Progressive Design and Machine	3559	409
Progressive Die and Stamping Inc	3469	366
Progressive Dynamics Inc	3679	270
Progressive Electric Inc	1731	719
Progressive Employer Services Inc	8744	34
Progressive Foundry Inc	3321	71
Progressive Furniture Inc	2511	30
Progressive Graphics Inc	2752	1284
Progressive Group Alliance	6719	121
Progressive Group Inc	7372	2627
Progressive Inc	3812	91
Progressive Information Technology	7363	254
Progressive Lighting Inc	5719	24
Progressive Machine Die Inc	3429	127
Progressive Machine Inc	3441	268
Progressive Machine Works Inc	3599	2409
Progressive Maintenance	7349	385
Progressive Medical Inc	7352	4
Progressive Microtechnology Inc	7372	3012
Progressive Molding Of Bolivar Inc	3544	86
Progressive Nursing Staffers	7361	318
Progressive Partners Inc	2752	1621
Progressive Plastics Inc	3089	208
Progressive Produce Co	5148	31

Company Name	SIC	Rank
Progressive Publishing Co	2711	370
Progressive Recovery Inc	3569	133
Progressive Resources LLC	7371	1575
Progressive Services Inc	1731	773
Progressive Software Computing Inc	7373	144
Progressive Solutions Inc (Brea California)	7372	3941
Progressive Specialty Glass Company Inc	5023	108
Progressive Surface Inc	3569	90
Progressive Swine Technologies	0213	4
Progressive Systems Network Inc	5111	36
Progressive Technology Inc	3253	8
Progressive Telephone Systems and Communications Inc	1731	2228
Progressive Tool and Industries Co/ Wisne Design	3548	4
Progressive Tool And Manufacturing Co	3444	235
Progressive Tool Co	3544	586
Progressive Tool Company Inc	3599	1207
Progressive Travel Promotions Inc	7319	147
Pro-Grind Inc	7389	1632
Prohealth Physicians Inc	8741	185
Pro-Health Systems Inc	7374	80
ProHelp Systems Inc	7371	1335
Pro-Inspect Inc	8711	282
PROIV Technology Inc	7372	19
Project Assistants Inc	7379	829
Project Austin Inc	4813	482
Project E	2253	20
Project Enterprises	7379	1594
Project HOME Community Development Corp	8322	196
Project Horizon Inc	7359	65
Project Leadership Associates Inc	8999	34
Project Management Inc	6531	355
Project Management Solutions Inc	8742	282
Project Open Hand	8322	103
Project Packaging Inc	7389	1644
Project Partners LLC	7379	818
Project Planning and Support Inc	7373	1119
Project Resources Inc	8742	584
Project Services Group Inc	3589	82
Projected Sound Inc	3699	209
Projectline Services Inc	8999	113
Project-One-Services Inc	7349	490
Projector People	5064	6
Projects Inc	3829	98
projekt202 LP	7371	348
ProKarma Inc	8741	147
Pro-Kennex	3949	120
Pro-Kold Corp	3842	321
Prolab Nutrition Inc	2099	54
Prolease Of America Inc	7359	148
Prolexys Pharmaceuticals Inc	8731	94
ProLiance Energy LLC	4923	28
Proliant Inc	2099	86
Pro-Line Boats Inc	3732	26
ProLinks Services Inc	4213	1586
Proliteracy Worldwide	8299	53
Prologic Engineering Inc	3577	502
ProLogis	6798	18
ProLogis First GP LLC	6798	26
Prom Krog Altstiel Inc	7311	415
P-Rom Software Inc	3679	826
Proma Inc	3843	56
Promag Ltd	3823	370
Promar International	8748	402
Promark Co/OI Partners Inc	7389	1772
Promark International Inc	3861	52
Promark Research Corp	7371	954
Promark Technology	5045	229
Pro-Mart Industries Inc	2392	45
ProMax Systems Inc (Irvine California)	3577	228
Promaxima Manufacturing Ltd	5941	34
Promed Molded Products Inc	3061	68
Pro-Med Pharmacies Inc	5912	61
Promedia Digital	3695	50
Promedica Health System Inc	8062	247
Promedica Inc	3841	236
Promedica International	8742	381
PromedixCom Inc	5047	165
Promega Biosciences LLC	2833	57
Promega Corp	8734	10
Promerica Bank	6022	654
Promesa Behavioral Health	8361	110
Promet Energy Partners LLC	4932	8
Promet International Inc	3827	157
Pro-Met Machining Inc	3599	2046
Promet Processing Corp	5051	498
Prometco Inc	3441	286
Prometheus Books Inc	2731	264
Prometheus Laboratories Inc	2834	89
Prometheus Real Estate Group Inc	6513	3
Prometheus Research LLC	7371	1362
Prometric Inc	7373	700
Promex Industries Inc	3674	204
Promex International Plastics Inc	3089	1196
Promextecnoligies LLC	3841	322
Prominent Title Insurance Agency Inc	6361	34
ProminicNet Inc	7372	4010
Promise Regional Medical Center - Hutchinson Inc	8051	22

Company Name	SIC	Rank
Promise Technology Inc	3572	14
Promix Electrotec	3669	107
Promo Works LLC	8742	292
PROMODEL Solutions	7372	2815
Pro-Mold Inc	3544	384
PromoMedia Concepts Inc	2656	6
Promopeddler Inc	8999	129
Promotek Inc	5065	380
Promotion Associates Inc	2782	59
Promotion Company Inc	7941	42
Promotion Execution Partners LLC	7331	179
Promotional Arts LLC	3999	195
Promotional Development Inc	3999	123
Promotional Graphics Inc	7336	201
Promotions By Design Inc	3999	125
Promotions On Campus Inc	7331	138
Promotionscom Inc	7319	86
Pro-Motor Engines Inc	5013	419
Prompt Mailers Inc	7331	86
Prompton Tool Inc	3599	796
Promptu Systems Corp	7371	953
Promptus Electronic Hardware Inc	3699	201
Promusic Inc	7389	1047
Pronto Post Inc	7331	103
Pronto Products Co	3589	126
Pronto Tool and Die Company Inc	3544	476
Pronto Travel Service	4724	113
Proof Advertising LLC	7311	447
Proofpoint Inc	7371	326
Pro-Pac Inc	8742	678
Propac Marketing Inc	7389	643
ProPacific Fresh	5148	7
Pro-Pack Testing Laboratory Inc	8734	190
Propane Equipment Corp	5084	863
Propane Resources Transportation	4213	2699
Propel Marketing LLC	7319	173
Propel Software Corp	7372	1942
Proper Polymers-Anderson Inc	3544	48
Property and Casualty Insurance Guaranty Corp	6351	48
Property Automation Software Corp	7372	1904
Property Insight LLC	8741	22
Property Inventory Auditor	7389	1842
Property Management Systems Corp	7372	4324
Property Markets Group	6799	148
Property One Inc	6512	38
Property Solutions International Inc	6519	25
Property Tax Consultants Inc	7291	15
Property Title Inc	6541	20
PropertyMaps Inc	7375	116
Pro-Pet LLC	2047	37
Propet USA Inc	3149	26
Propex Inc	2221	9
ProPhase Labs Inc	2834	294
Prophecy Technology LLC	3577	451
Prophesy Transportation Solutions Inc	7372	2789
ProPhotonix Ltd	3827	40
Propix	7335	25
Proplanner Inc	7371	1628
Proposal Technologies Network Inc	7371	1747
Proprietary Controls Systems Corp	3829	180
Proprietary Software Systems Inc	7372	4325
Pro-Print Inc	2759	266
PropSys Real Estate Management Inc	6531	207
ProQuest LLC	2741	26
Prorail Manufacturing Inc	3669	311
PROS Holdings Inc	7372	440
Pro's Market Inc	5411	168
Prosero Inc	7389	1015
Proserv Crane and Equipment Inc	3536	11
Pro-Serve Of Memphis Inc	2879	29
Proset Systems Inc	3088	18
ProSidian Consulting	8742	715
Prosig USA Inc	7372	2245
ProSight Inc	7372	1949
Proskauer Rose LLP	8111	61
Proske Plastic Products Inc	3083	66
Prosoco Inc	2899	125
Prosoft Engineering Inc	7372	2605
Prosoft Inc	7372	4211
ProSoft Technology Group Inc	7373	421
ProSoft Technology Inc	3823	9
ProSolutions Inc	7372	1621
Prosource Industries LP	3643	64
Prosource International Inc	5099	94
Prosource Management Inc	5023	162
Prosource One	5191	37
Prospect Capital Corp	6799	35
Prospect Concrete Inc	3273	100
Prospect Foundry Inc	3321	47
Prospect Products Inc	3674	292
Prospect Waterproofing Co	1799	37
Prosper Business Development Corp	8742	454
Prospera Financial Services	6211	333
Prosperity Bancshares Inc	6022	20
Prosperity Bank	6022	28
Prosperity Holdings Inc	6719	52
Prospx Inc	7372	2000
Prosser Construction Co	1611	251
Prost Mueller PC	8721	366
ProStar Computer Inc	3571	74
Prostar Staffing Services Inc	7363	337
Prostat Corp	3825	319
Prosthodontics Intermedica	8021	7

Company Name	SIC	Rank
Prostor Systems Inc	5045	202
Prostrollo Motor Co	5511	947
Prosum Inc	7379	115
Pro-Sweep LLC	7349	264
Prosys Information Systems Inc	5045	20
Protameen Chemicals Inc	2819	78
Protano and Sons Inc	5149	105
Protatek International Inc	2836	65
Proteam Inc	3589	88
Protean Instrument Corp	3829	407
Protec Association Services	7349	195
ProTec Building Services Inc	1522	53
Pro-Tec Equipment Inc	3531	108
ProTech Associates Inc	7373	333
Pro-Tech Auction Inc	7389	1268
Pro-Tech Controls Company Inc	7373	1221
Pro-Tech Design and Manufacturing Inc	7389	1297
Protech E2 Inc	5731	99
Pro-Tech Interconnect Solutions LLC	3672	129
Pro-Tech International Security Systems Inc	1731	1460
Pro-Tech Machine Inc	3549	85
Pro-Tech Manufacturing and Distribution Inc	3531	171
Protech Service Company LLC	5087	138
Protech Solutions Inc	7371	232
Pro-Tech Systems Inc	7373	723
ProTechnics International Inc	1389	24
Protect All Inc	2842	91
Pro-Tect Computer Products Inc	3083	82
Protect Controls Inc	3448	21
Protect-All Inc	2671	49
Protected Cargo Transport	4213	997
Protection Controls Inc	3613	115
Protection One Inc	7382	2
Protection Services Inc	3531	73
Protection Source LLC	7382	174
Protection Systems Technologies Inc	5063	909
Protection Technologies Inc	3679	655
Protective Capital Structures Corp	6159	83
Protective Group Inc	3699	87
Protective Insurance Co	6331	120
Protective Life Corp	6311	25
Protective Life Insurance Co	6311	91
Protective Lining Corp	2673	42
Protective Technologies International Ut LC	3699	274
Protecto Wrap Co	3069	94
Protectoseal Co	3795	6
Protectowire Company Inc	3669	217
Protegga LLC	8734	207
Protegrity Inc	7372	234
Protegrity USA Inc	7382	75
Protein Inc	1380	20
Protein Polymer Technologies Inc	8731	419
Protein Technologies Inc	5049	79
Protek Devices LP	3674	304
Protel Communications Inc	4813	478
Protel Inc	5065	175
Pro-Telligent LLC	7371	164
Protemps Health Services Inc	7363	224
Proteus Electronics Inc	3629	112
Proteus Industries Inc	3823	136
Protex Inc	3083	84
Protex International Corp	3699	112
ProText Mobility Inc	7372	5057
Protherics Inc	2834	367
Protide Pharmaceuticals Inc	2836	83
Protis Executive Innovations Inc	7361	295
Proto Circuits Manufacturing	3672	472
Proto Corp	3292	3
Proto Plastics Inc	3089	1111
Proto - Plastics Inc	3089	1190
Proto Quick Inc	3672	491
Proto Space Engineering Inc	3599	1278
Protocall Communications Inc	7389	792
ProtoCAM	3679	456
Proto-Cast Inc	3364	28
Proto-Cast LLC	3089	1350
Protoco Enterprises LLC	3089	1795
Protocol Ii Inc	5961	160
Protocol Integrated Direct Marketing	7311	78
Protocol Marketing Group	8748	7
Protocol Recovery Service Inc	7322	74
Protocol Telecommunications Inc	7359	281
Proto-Cutter Inc	3545	365
Protoline Inc	3672	414
Protomatic Inc	3841	331
Protomold Company Inc	3089	101
Proto-Mold Products Company Inc	3089	1481
Proton Corp	5064	84
Proton Electric LLC	1731	908
Proton OnSite	3629	12
ProtoNet	7372	4734
Protonmedia Inc	7371	495
Protopac Inc	3496	120
ProtoQwik	3672	453
Protostar Ltd	3663	320
Prototek Corp	3669	274
ProtoTest LLC	7379	949
Prototron Circuits Southwest Inc	3672	143
Prototype and Plastic Mold Company Inc	3089	1135

Company Name	SIC	Rank
Prototype and Production Co	3541	220
Prototype Equipment Corp	3565	68
Prototype Plastic Extrusion Company Inc	3089	1633
Prototype Products Inc	3545	208
Pro-Touch Nurses Inc	7363	248
Proto-Vest Inc	3589	244
Protrans International Inc	4731	39
Protronics Computer Systems	7372	3282
Protronics Inc	3672	465
Protronix Inc	7373	673
Protune Corp	3829	522
Proturn Inc	3599	894
Proudfoot Consulting	8742	180
Proulx Manufacturing Inc	3089	1078
Prous Science	7372	4918
Provar Industrial Corp	3823	317
Provect Technologies Inc	7371	1764
Provectus Pharmaceuticals Inc	2834	479
Provectus Technology Inc	7379	969
Provell Inc	5961	37
Proven Direct Inc	7331	123
Proven Method Inc	7372	660
Proven Partners Group LLC	2099	131
Proven Software Inc	7372	5008
Provena Health	7374	126
Provenance Vineyard	2084	59
Provenir	7372	1042
Provest LLC	7389	73
Provico Inc	5153	27
Provide Commerce Inc	7389	131
Providence and Worcester Railroad Co	4011	44
Providence Business News Inc	2711	758
Providence Equity Partners LLC	6722	84
Providence Homes Inc	1521	71
Providence Lacquer and Supply Centre Inc	5085	159
Providence Metallizing Company Inc	3471	119
Providence Saint John Foundation Inc	8399	10
Providence Service Corp	8399	3
Providence Software Solutions Inc	7372	3561
Providenet Communications Corp	7372	3398
Provident Bank	6036	74
Provident Central Credit Union	6061	31
Provident Community Bancshares Inc	6712	508
Provident Financial Corp	6035	225
Provident Financial Holdings Inc	6712	257
Provident Financial Services Inc (Jersey City New Jersey)	6712	95
Provident Life and Casualty Insurance Co	6311	1
Provident New York Bancorp	6036	9
Provident Savings Bank	6036	13
Provident Savings Bank FSB	6035	140
Provideo Management Inc	8742	433
Provider Gateway Inc	7372	2325
Provider HealthNet Services Inc	7371	65
Providge Consulting LLC	7371	709
Providus	7361	129
Provimi Foods Inc	2011	57
Provimi North America Inc	2048	5
Provine School Pictures LLC	7221	11
Provion LLC	7379	1126
ProVision Technologies Inc	5074	229
Provista Life Sciences LLC	2834	344
Provista Software International	7371	1641
Provisur Technologies Inc	3999	4
ProVue Development Corp	7372	4869
Pro-Ware	7372	3782
ProWorks LLC	7372	4326
Proxim Wireless Corp	3663	79
Proxima Corp	3861	20
Proximex Corp	7372	2169
Proxy Manufacturing Inc	3672	267
Proxy Networks Inc	7371	1583
Proxycare Inc	5122	70
ProZyme	2833	35
PRR	8743	60
Pruco Life Insurance Co	6311	121
Prudent Publishing Company Inc	5961	150
Prudent Technologies Inc	8731	212
Prudential Annuities	6211	263
Prudential Bancorp Incorporated of Pennsylvania	6712	466
Prudential Blake Atlantic Realtors	6531	132
Prudential Builders Center	5064	92
Prudential Capital Group	6799	69
Prudential Carruthers Realtors	6531	82
Prudential Connecticut Realty	6531	14
Prudential Financial Inc	6311	2
Prudential Fox and Roach Inc	6531	43
Prudential Gardner Realtors	6531	16
Prudential Kansas City Realty	6531	47
Prudential Lighting Corp	3646	18
Prudential Mortgage Capital Co	6162	16
Prudential New Jersey Properties Inc	6531	34
Prudential Overall Supply Inc	7218	4
Prudential Preferred Properties (Lynnwood Washington)	6531	434
Prudential Real Estate Affiliates Inc	6794	32
Prudential Savings Bank (Philadelphia Pennsylvania)	6036	59
Prudential Slater James River Realtors	6531	168
Pruet Oil Co	1382	15

Company Name	SIC	Rank
Pruett Medical Ltd	5047	171
PruGen Inc	2834	335
Pruitt Company Of Ada Inc	5085	434
Prunty Construction Company Inc	1623	523
PRWT Services Inc	7374	72
PRx Inc	8743	252
Pryba Tobin and Company PC	8721	462
Pryer Machine and Tool Co	3812	85
Prym Dritz Corp	3965	16
Pryntcomm Ltd	2752	1161
Pryor Johnson Montoya Carney and Karr PC	8111	521
Pryor Products	3841	228
Pryor Stone Inc	1422	26
PS Acquisition Company Corp	3585	181
PS Development Corp	1731	351
PS Energy Group Inc	5172	86
PS Marcato Elevator Inc	7699	36
PS Marston Associates Inc	4213	1405
Ps Solutions Inc	3572	104
PSA Airlines Inc	4512	37
PSA Insurance and Financial Services	6311	279
PSA Professional Liability Inc	6411	115
PSAV Presentation Services	7389	212
Psb	7311	816
PSB Bancshares Inc	6712	483
PSB Group Inc	6712	480
PSB Holdings Inc	6022	254
Psb Industries Inc	3569	91
PSC Fabricating Corp	3089	221
PSC Metals Inc	5093	7
Pscomm LLC	7379	927
PSCU Financial Services Inc	7374	24
PSCU Service Centers Inc	7389	97
Psd Solutions Inc	7371	1379
Pseg Energy Holdngs LLC	6153	33
PSEG Global LLC	4939	12
PSEG Nuclear LLC	4911	592
PSEG Power LLC	4911	75
Psf Industries Inc	3443	90
Psf Management	5812	448
Psg Controls Inc	3822	42
PSG International Inc	7372	1958
PSI Corp	6719	190
Psi/Eye-Ko Inc	3842	298
Psi Fire	7371	898
PSI Industries (Rosemead California)	3714	409
PSI International Inc	7371	61
Psi Long Island LLC	8742	649
PSi Printer Systems International	3577	158
Psi Sales Inc	5082	118
PSI Software Inc	7371	881
Psiber Data Systems Inc	3825	188
Psinapse Technology Ltd	7361	177
Psitech Inc	3571	191
Psj Enterprises Inc	7374	332
Psk Steel Corp	3544	325
PSM Fastener Corp	5085	435
PSM Holdings Inc	6162	144
Psm Industries Inc	3499	68
Psomas	8711	127
Psp Industries Inc	3533	6
PSS World Medical Inc	5047	6
Pssc Labs	5045	767
PSS-Product Support Solutions	7379	543
PST Computers Inc	3571	186
Pst Technologies Inc	7372	3802
P-Stat Inc	7372	2858
PSX Inc	7922	64
Psyche Systems Corp	7372	2564
Psychemedics Corp	8071	30
Psychiatric Solutions Inc	8093	4
Psychological Software Solutions Inc	7372	736
PT Ferro Construction Co	1794	15
PT Freeport Indonesia Co	1021	4
PT Systems Inc	8711	560
Ptc Enterprises Inc	3089	1087
Ptc-In-Liquidation Inc	3544	467
Ptek LLC	3825	274
Ptg International Inc	7372	3430
Pti Engineered Plastics Inc	3089	462
Ptm and W Industries Inc	3083	63
Ptm Inc	3089	1507
PTO Today Inc	2721	301
Ptr Manufacturing Inc	3599	881
Ptrl West Inc	8731	290
PTS Inc (Las Vegas Nevada)	3845	128
PTV America Inc	7372	1813
Pubco Corp	3531	44
Public Abstract Corp	6541	1
Public Access Networks Corp	7379	511
Public Affairs Associates Inc	8743	305
Public Auto Auction Inc	7389	1316
Public Broadcasting Of Colorado Inc	4832	61
Public Broadcasting of Northwest Pennsylvania	4833	220
Public Citizen Inc	8733	30
Public Communications Worldwide	7319	62
Public Currency Inc	6099	7
Public Employees Credit Union	6062	122
Public Employees' Retirement System of Mississippi	6371	5
Public Financial Management Inc	6282	100
Public Interest Data Inc	7375	203

Company Name	SIC	Rank
Public Investment Corp	6531	66
Public Priority Systems Inc	8732	95
Public Relations Advertising Co	7311	312
Public Safety Center Inc	5999	112
Public Sector Solutions Inc	7372	3151
Public Service Audience Planners	7331	269
Public Service Company of Colorado	4931	15
Public Service Company of New Hampshire	4911	81
Public Service Company of New Mexico	4931	27
Public Service Company of North Carolina Inc	4924	41
Public Service Company of Oklahoma	4911	70
Public Service Electric and Gas Co	4931	19
Public Service Enterprise Group Inc	4931	3
Public Storage	6798	29
Public Strategies Inc	8743	18
Public Supply Co	3442	71
Public Systems Associates Inc	7371	680
Public Utilities Board	4931	47
Public Utilities Reports Inc	2731	242
Publication Printers Corp	2752	168
Publication Services Inc	2731	249
Publications and Communications LP	2721	228
Publications Expediting Inc	7331	105
Publications International Ltd	2731	117
Publications Printing Of Nebraska Inc	2752	1296
Publicidad Siboney Corp	7311	811
Publicis and Hal Riney	7311	119
Publicis Dallas TX	7311	79
Publicis Dialog Chicago	8743	176
Publicis Meetings USA	7389	411
Publicis Modem	7389	326
Publicis New York New York	7311	27
Publicity Matters	8743	342
Publicker Gasohol Inc	2899	134
Publicker Inc	2899	135
Publicom Inc	8743	263
Publishers Clearing House	5961	45
Publishers Consulting Corp	2741	452
Publishers Group West Inc	5192	17
Publisher's Guild Inc	2741	195
Publisher's Mail Service Inc	7331	247
Publishers Printing Company LLC	2752	18
Publisher's Renewal Service Co	7331	115
Publishers Software Systems Inc	7372	5027
Publishing Concepts LP	2741	143
Publishing Forest LLC	2711	669
Publishing Group of America Inc	2721	129
Publitek Inc	5045	21
Publix Super Markets Inc	5411	5
Pucci International Ltd	5046	148
Puck Implement Co	5083	92
Puckett Machinery Co	5082	22
Pueblo Bank and Trust Co	6022	423
Pueblo Diversified Industries Inc	8331	112
Pueblo Publishers Inc	2711	815
Pueblo School District No 60	8211	66
Puffin Electric Inc	1731	1384
Puget Bindery Inc	2789	111
Puget Energy Inc	4911	35
Puget Press Multiple Inc	2761	57
Puget Sound Alarm Company Inc	1731	2309
Puget Sound Bank	6022	484
Puget Sound Blood Center and Program	8071	18
Puget Sound Energy Inc	4911	34
Puget Sound Pipe And Supply Co	5074	74
Puget Sound Truck Lines Inc	4213	523
Pugh Capital Management Inc	6282	413
Pugleasa Company Inc	5087	98
Pugmire Lincoln Mercury Inc	5511	746
Pugsley's Sandwiches Inc	2099	217
Pulaski Bank	6022	124
Pulaski Financial Corp	6035	60
Pulaski Furniture Corp	2511	10
Pulaski Meat Products Co	2013	204
Pulaski Publishing Inc	2752	480
Pulaski Service Corp	6022	69
Pulaski Web Inc	2754	42
Pulau Electronics Corp	7378	11
Pulcir Inc	5049	212
PULIC Insurance Services Inc	6411	116
Pulice Construction Inc	1611	103
Pulizzi Engineering Inc	3679	91
Pullen Brothers Inc	4213	1213
Pulliam Motor Co	5511	137
Pulliam Trucking Company Inc	4213	2863
Pullman Manufacturing Corp	3495	28
Pull'r Holding Company LLC	3423	44
Pulpdent Corp	3843	38
Pulsafeeder Inc	3561	48
Pulsar Inc	3672	399
Pulsar Microwave Corp	5065	510
Pulsar Systems Inc	7372	3759
Pulse Communications Inc	3823	81
Pulse EFT Association	7373	120
Pulse Electronics Corp	3679	44
Pulse Engineering Inc	3679	174
Pulse Inc	7373	729
Pulse Instruments	3825	192
Pulse Medical Inc	3842	255
Pulse Metric Inc	7372	4735

Company Name	SIC	Rank
Pulse Plastics Products Inc	3089	1773
Pulse Sciences Inc	8731	300
Pulse Systems Inc	3699	305
Pulse Technologies Inc	3841	150
Pulseworks LLC	3651	119
Pulsonics Inc	3569	299
Pulte Diversified Companies Inc	1521	174
Pulte Financial Companies Inc	6799	16
Pulte Homes of New Mexico Inc	1531	58
Pulte Mortgage LLC	6162	10
PulteGroup Inc	1531	2
Pulva Corp	3531	146
Puma Industries Inc	7699	2
Pummill Business Forms Inc	2761	46
Pump Arts Inc	3599	1753
Pump Engineering Inc	3561	135
Pump It Up	7999	119
Pump Pro's Inc	5084	484
Pump Star Inc	3561	33
Pumpernick's Restaurant and Delicatessen	5812	458
Pumpkin Networks Inc	4813	604
Pumps Parts and Service Inc	5084	386
Punch Networks Corp	7379	734
Punch Tech	3541	204
Punchgini Inc	7389	2208
Pundmann Ford Inc	5511	230
Pungo Machine Shop Inc	7699	242
Puradyn Filter Technologies Inc	3533	113
Purakal Cylinders Inc	3593	37
Puratos Corp	2099	65
Purcell Co	3599	1165
Purcell Enterprises Inc	2721	336
Purcell Tire and Rubber Company Inc	7534	5
Purcell-Murray Company Inc	5074	101
Purcell's Seafood Inc	5146	73
Purcelltel Inc	5065	871
PurchaseSoft Inc	7372	5017
Purchasing Management International LP	7389	1895
Purchasing Services Limited Inc	3565	188
PurchasingNet Inc	7372	453
Purco Fleet Services Inc	7322	121
Purdue Pharma LP	2834	65
Purdue Student Publishing Foundation	2711	694
PurduePharma LP	2834	44
Purdy Brothers Trucking Company Inc	4213	471
Purdyco Ltd	2064	47
Pure Advertising LLC	7311	1006
Pure Beverage Inc	5149	54
PURE Bioscience Inc	3599	935
Pure Cycle Corp	3589	10
Pure Foods Inc	2099	355
Pure Humidifier Co	3585	193
Pure Octane Inc	7311	537
Pure Resources Inc	1311	55
Pure Touch LLC	7389	2237
Pure World Inc	2833	23
PureChoice Inc	3564	102
Pure's Food Specialties Inc	2052	54
PureSafe Water Systems Inc	3589	272
PureSafety	8331	9
Pure-Seed Testing Inc	8731	157
Puretek Corp	2844	42
Purewater Dynamics Inc	7359	228
Purina Mills LLC	2048	4
Puritan Bakery Inc	2051	47
Puritan Clothing Company of Cape Cod Inc	5651	30
Puritan Industries Inc	3559	391
Puritan Maintenance Company Inc	7349	465
Puritan Press Inc	2752	590
Puritan Products Inc	2899	156
Puritan Systems Inc	3999	186
Puritan-Bennett Corp	3841	31
Purity Ice Cream Company Inc	2024	80
Purity Software Inc	7372	4627
Purity Wholesale Grocers Inc	5141	41
Purkey's Fleet Electric Inc	5063	440
Puroflux Corp	3677	60
Purolator Air Filtration	3564	3
Purolator Facet Inc	3492	15
Puronics Inc	3561	26
Pur-O-Zone Inc	5169	120
Purple Communications Inc	4812	24
Pursell Construction Inc	1731	2456
Pursuant Group Inc	8748	80
Pursuit of Excellence Inc	8742	386
Purvis Ford Inc	5511	396
Puryear Tank Lines Inc	4212	72
Puryear Trucking Inc	4213	1196
Pusan Pipe America Inc	5051	142
Push Media Group Inc	7374	222
Pushman Manufacturing Company Inc	3599	1693
Puskar Precision Machining Co	3599	1559
Putco Inc	3714	345
Putman Media Inc	2721	187
Putnam American Government Income Fund	6722	154
Putnam California Tax Exempt Money Market Fund	6722	277
Putnam Classic Equity Fund	6722	161
Putnam Community Medical Center LLC	8062	59

Company Name	SIC	Rank
Putnam Convertible Income-Growth Y	6722	240
Putnam County Comprehensive Services Inc	8331	131
Putnam Diversified Income Trust	6722	9
Putnam Electrical Contractors LLC	1731	829
Putnam Global Income Trust	6722	225
Putnam High Income Securities Fund	6726	76
Putnam High Yield Y	6722	251
Putnam Hospital Center Foundation Inc	8062	170
Putnam Imaging Corp	7384	54
Putnam International Value A	6722	195
Putnam Investment Management Inc	6282	4
Putnam Investments Inc	6282	78
Putnam Investments LLC	6289	14
Putnam Machine Products Inc	3599	1145
Putnam Managed Municipal Income Trust	6726	39
Putnam New Opportunities Fund	6722	80
Putnam NY Tax Exempt Income A	6722	127
Putnam OTC Emerging Growth Fund	6722	96
Putnam Pennsylvania Tax Exempt Income Fund	6722	274
Putnam Precision Molding Inc	3089	846
Putnam Premier Income Trust	6726	24
Putnam Reinsurance Co	6331	200
Putnam Rf Components Inc	5063	676
Putnam Tax Exempt Income Fund	6722	125
Putnam Tax-Free Income Insured Fund	6722	187
Putnam US Government Income M	6722	261
Putnam Utilities Growth and Income Fund	6722	166
Putnam Voyager Fund	6722	26
Putney Paper Company Inc	2621	56
Putney Pasta Company Inc	2038	77
Putnum Stainless Tubes Inc	5023	160
Putterman Scharck and Associates Inc	5063	537
Putzmeister America Inc	3561	63
Puzzle Systems Corp	7372	3626
PV Tool Company Inc	3599	2058
Pva Tepla America Inc	3599	1441
Pvc Industries Inc	3089	1898
Pvf Acquisitions LLC	2015	39
PVF Capital Corp	6712	370
PVH Corp	2321	1
Pvp Contracting Company Inc	7363	209
PVT	4213	1999
PW Minor and Sons Inc	3143	11
PW Stephens Inc	1799	64
PW Trucking Inc	4213	2010
Pwi Inc	3647	17
Pwl/Bpc Joint Venture LLC	7374	365
PWS Inc	6531	300
PXL8R	7336	333
Pyco Inc	3823	208
Pyco Industries	2074	3
Pycon Inc	3672	14
Pygmy Computer Systems Inc	7372	2412
Pyle Joe R Complete Auction Service	7389	808
Pyle Machine Company Inc	3599	1311
Pylman Power Inc	1731	998
Pylon Manufacturing Corp	3714	247
Pynco Inc	3728	212
Pyne Sand and Stone Company Inc	5032	152
Pyne-Davidson Co	2752	1045
Pyott-Boone Electronics Inc	3661	64
Pyper Tool and Engineering Inc	3544	366
Pyramid Audio and Video Ltd	5064	152
Pyramid Breweries Inc	2082	18
Pyramid Building Systems Inc	1541	300
Pyramid Consulting Inc	7372	103
Pyramid Digital Solutions LLC	7372	1674
Pyramid Electric Inc	1731	410
Pyramid Films Corp	7822	35
Pyramid Healthcare Solutions Inc	8721	32
Pyramid Inc	3568	87
Pyramid Life Insurance Co	6311	228
Pyramid Mountain Lumber Inc	2421	59
Pyramid Oil Co	1311	230
Pyramid Paper Products Inc	2653	120
Pyramid Plastics Inc	3087	26
Pyramid Precision Machine Inc	3599	247
Pyramid Printing And Advertising Inc	2752	1444
Pyramid Solutions Inc	7371	595
Pyramid Sound and Light Inc	1731	1527
Pyramid Systems Inc	8711	387
Pyramid Technologies LLC	3579	36
Pyramid Tubular Products LP	5082	164
Pyraponic Industries Incorporated II	3231	74
Pyratech Security Systems Inc	7381	239
Pyrenees French Bakery Inc	2051	254
Pyro Industrial Services Inc	1741	20
Pyro Shows Inc	7999	114
Pyro-Communication Systems Inc	1731	197
Pyro-Matic Inc	5063	708
Pyromatics Corp	3221	11
Pyromation Inc	3823	62
Pyrometric Company Inc	1731	2503
Pyron Technologies Inc	7374	296
Pyrosignal and Suppression Inc	5999	125
Pyrotechnic Specialties Inc	3489	18
Pyrotection Specialists Inc	1731	2012
Pyrotek Inc	3399	4
Pyrotex Inc	7999	102
Pyxis Solutions LLC	8748	182

Company Name	SIC	Rank
Pzena Investment Management Inc	6282	244
Q A Technologies Inc	7379	778
Q and A Recruitting LLP	7361	7
Q B Johnson Manufacturing Inc	3533	56
Q Carriers Inc	4213	258
Q Circuits Inc	3672	363
Q Com Inc	3625	228
Q Communication International Inc	7389	359
Q Comp Technologies Inc	8711	559
Q Hot Line	4832	225
Q Interactive Inc	7389	409
Q Power Inc	3651	113
Q Research Solutions Inc	8732	56
Q Sea Specialty Services Qss LLC	2092	64
Q Source Inc	5065	524
Q Trucking Inc	4213	1430
Q Up Arts Sample Collections	7822	34
Q1 Labs Inc	5045	145
Q2 Software Inc	7372	1757
QAD Eastern United States	7372	120
QAD Inc	7372	228
QAI Inc	4813	317
Qantel Technologies Inc	7372	2586
Qatalys Inc	7371	630
QATechnology CoInc	3825	108
Qbos Inc	4813	381
QC A Inc	3652	48
QC and G Financial Inc	6099	8
Qc Communications Inc	1623	315
Qc Electronics Inc	3565	177
QC Holdings Inc	6163	24
Qc Inc	8734	36
QC Industries LLC	3535	234
QC Laboratories Inc	8734	144
Qc Manufacturing Co	3549	114
Qc Plus Computer Inc	5734	297
Qc Tv Corp	4899	183
Q-Cast Inc	3089	1597
QCE USA	3679	458
Qcera Inc	7373	1089
QCH Inc	3089	564
QCI Asset Management Inc	6282	405
QCM Inc	3699	285
Qcm Inc	3679	804
QCOnics Ventures LP	3714	83
QCR Holdings Inc	6022	533
Qcsystems Inc	5065	907
Qdea Inc	7371	1730
Qdoba Restaurant Corp	5812	125
Q-E Manufacturing Company Inc	3599	509
QED Environmental Systems Inc	3561	91
QED Inc	3812	139
QED Information Systems	7373	528
QED Press	2731	224
Qei Inc	3823	121
Qems Inc	3679	470
QEP Company Inc	3423	7
QEP Resources Inc	1382	5
Qestrel Claims Management Inc	6411	284
Q-Fab Inc	3672	475
Qfc Plastics Inc	3089	566
Qflow Systems LLC	7371	877
Qi Consulting LLC	7379	813
Qioptiq Imaging Solutions	3827	82
QK Healthcare Inc	5122	59
Qk4	7389	316
Q-Lab Corp	3823	130
Qlik Technologies Inc	7372	165
Qlog Corp	8748	398
QLogic Corp	3577	32
QLT USA Inc	2834	187
Qlvs Inc	5734	139
Qmagiq LLC	3674	453
Q-Mark	5063	492
Q-Mark Manufacturing Inc	3823	321
Q-Matic Corp	7372	405
QME Inc	3544	426
Qmf Metal and Electronic Solutions Inc	3444	203
Qmp Inc	3589	138
Qn Electric Inc	1731	1491
QNB Corp	6712	364
Qortex LLC	7379	1157
Qorval Integrated Solutions Inc	7371	344
Qos Telesys	5065	855
Qosina Corp	3842	144
Qpay Inc	4813	184
QPC Lasers Inc	3674	145
Q-Peak Inc	7389	2216
QPI Multipress Inc	3542	20
QPR Software Inc (Alameda California)	7372	1161
Qps LLC	8748	177
Qqc Printing LC	2752	1430
Qqest Software Systems Inc	7372	1403
QQQ Software Inc	7372	1648
QR Energy LP	1381	26
Qrp Inc	3069	226
QRS Inc	5093	38
QRS Music Technologies Inc	3931	16
QS/1 Data Systems	7372	903
QS I Inc	2752	1046
QSC Audio Products Inc	3651	27
Qsc Of Northfield Inc	7349	407
Qse Inc	3677	18
QSGI Inc	7389	1528

Company Name	SIC	Rank
Qsi Automation Inc	3599	1055
QSI Systems Inc	5065	527
Q'so Inc	2891	66
Qsoft Solutions Corp	7372	1814
QSR Automations Inc	5045	190
QSS Group Inc	7371	53
QSS International Inc	1629	113
QST Inc	2821	157
QST Industries Inc	2396	5
QStar Technologies Inc	7372	1497
Qt Technologies LLC	7373	687
Qtechnology International Inc	7389	2209
Qtm Inc	3599	1851
Quabaug Corp	3069	36
Quabbin Wire and Cable Company Inc	3357	50
Quad 4 Plastics Inc	3089	1513
Quad Cast Inc	3363	28
Quad City Bank and Trust Co	6022	128
Quad City Engineering Company Inc	3544	671
Quad City Equipment	5046	208
Quad City Hose	3492	30
Quad City Safety Inc	5099	83
Quad City Salvage Auction Inc	7389	2035
Quad City Satellite	5065	567
Quad/Graphics Inc	2759	1
Quad Group Inc	3829	349
Quad Plus LLC	3566	24
Quadbase Systems Inc	7372	4327
Quad-City Brick and Stone Inc	5032	110
Quadco Printing Inc	2752	1630
Quadco Rehabilitation Center Inc	8331	186
Quadel Industries	3089	1298
Quadion Corp	6719	118
Quadlogic Controls Corp	3825	103
Quadra Manufacturing Inc	3799	32
Quadralay Corp	7372	3465
QuadraMed Corp	7371	74
Quadrangle Capital Partners	6799	214
Quadrangle Group LLC	6799	96
Quadrangle Press Inc	2752	1029
Quadrant Chemical Corp	2821	131
Quadrant Components Inc	3674	220
Quadrant Corp (Bellevue Washington)	6552	139
Quadrant Epp USA Inc	2824	4
Quadrant Software Inc	7371	1365
Quadrant Solutions Inc	3499	81
Quadrant Tool And Manufacturing Co	3599	1442
Quadrants Inc	1541	310
Quadratic Systems Inc	7371	1539
Quadrel Inc	3565	94
Quadrivius Inc	4731	35
Quadro Corp	2394	35
Quadron Corp	7372	5081
Quadros Systems Inc	7372	3495
Quady Winery Inc	2084	92
Quadzilla Performance Technologies Inc	7373	961
Quaero Corp	5045	138
Quail Electronics Inc	5063	421
Quaint Oak Bancorp Inc	6712	689
Quaint Oak Bank	6036	98
Quake City Casuals Inc	2253	13
Quaker Chemical Corp	2992	4
Quaker City Plating and Silversmith A California LP	3471	16
Quaker Furniture Inc	2521	49
Quaker Maid Meats Inc	2013	42
Quaker Manufacturing Corp	3469	94
Quaker Oats Co	2043	1
Quaker Plastic Corp	3089	549
Quaker Window Products Co	3442	56
Quakertown National Bank	6021	204
Quala Die Inc	3544	168
Qualastat Electronics Inc	3643	118
QualChoice Health Plan Inc	6324	94
QUALCOMM Inc	3663	3
QualCore Logic Inc	3674	193
Qualedi Inc	7372	4109
Qualex Consulting Services Inc	7379	651
Qualex Inc	7384	4
Qualex Manufacturing LC	3444	95
Qualfax Inc	7389	1299
Qualicaps Inc	2899	89
Qualico Steel Company Inc	3441	52
Qualified Presort Service LLC	7389	880
Qualified Printers Inc	2752	1765
Qualigen Inc	3821	33
Qualis International Inc	5113	48
Qualitas Inc	7372	4545
Qualitau Inc	3825	130
Qualitech Computer Systems	7373	1138
Qualitech Solutions Inc	7372	3627
Qualitek Engineering and Manufacturing Inc	3544	782
Qualitek International Inc	2899	97
Qualitel Corp	3679	198
Qualitest Pharmaceuticals Inc	5122	17
Qualitex Co	2842	162
Qualiton Imports Ltd	5065	306
Qualitor Inc	5013	13
Qualitrol Company LLC	3625	96
Qualiturn Inc	3599	1446
Quality Accents Inc	5092	51
Quality Accessories Inc	3851	83

Company Name	SIC	Rank
Quality Aircraft Tooling Inc	3599	1801
Quality America Inc	7372	4254
Quality Associates Inc	7389	661
Quality Associates Inc (Columbia Maryland)	7334	11
Quality Assurance Institute Inc	7372	3301
Quality Assurance International Corp	3545	338
Quality Assured Enterprises Inc	2752	761
Quality Assured Label Inc	2759	201
Quality Assured Plastics Inc	3089	1403
Quality Assured Services Inc	5047	117
Quality Automotive Company Inc	3714	164
Quality Aviation Inc	5088	66
Quality Beauty Supply Company Inc	5087	131
Quality Beverage Inc	5181	1
Quality Bindery Service Inc	2789	82
Quality Biological Inc	2836	48
Quality Bioresources Inc	2834	317
Quality Boat Lifts Inc	3536	35
Quality Bolt and Screw Corp	5072	47
Quality Boneless Beef Company Inc	5147	45
Quality Books Inc	5192	27
Quality Brands of Omaha Inc	4213	2045
Quality Building Stone Inc	5032	163
Quality Bumper Service Of Dallas/Fort Worth Inc	5013	350
Quality Business Solutions Inc	7371	112
Quality Cabinet And Fixture Co	2431	120
Quality Cable and Components	3679	626
Quality Carbide Tool Inc	3545	64
Quality Carriers Inc	4213	50
Quality Cartage Inc	4213	2538
Quality Castings Co	3321	32
Quality Cctv Systems Inc	1731	1895
Quality Chemical Co	5087	132
Quality Circle Products Inc	2679	52
Quality Circuit Assembly Inc	3672	156
Quality Circuits Inc	3672	61
Quality Coast Inc	7361	385
Quality Coils Inc	3677	12
Quality Communications of Florida Inc	1731	507
Quality Companies Inc	7389	1291
Quality Concepts Manufacturing Inc	3699	178
Quality Concepts Telecommunications Ltd	3825	231
Quality Containment Solutions Inc	7389	1344
Quality Contour Inc	3599	1838
Quality Contract Assemblies Inc	3679	767
Quality Contract Manufacturing LLC	3672	155
Quality Control Corp	3451	13
Quality Control Inspection Inc	7389	986
Quality Controls Inc	3491	51
Quality Corp	3537	69
Quality Crab Company Inc	5146	33
Quality Craft Inc	2511	77
Quality Croutons Inc	2051	216
Quality Cryogenics Of Atlanta LLC	3312	98
Quality Custom Cabinetry Inc	2434	27
Quality Custom Molding LLC	3089	1305
Quality Cylinder Head Repair Corp	7538	34
Quality Demonstration Services Inc	7389	127
Quality Die Set Corp	3469	347
Quality Dining Inc	5812	20
Quality Electric And Controls Inc	1731	1767
Quality Electric Company Inc	1731	1207
Quality Electric Of Douglas County Inc	1731	1508
Quality Electric Of Valdosta Inc	1731	1018
Quality Electric Service Company LLC	1731	1997
Quality Electrical Service Inc	1731	1437
Quality Electrodynamics LLC	3826	49
Quality Electronics Inc	3679	469
Quality Elevator Products Inc	3534	19
Quality Engineering And Tool Co	3599	2465
Quality Engineering Associates Inc	3829	378
Quality Engineering Services Inc	8711	566
Quality Extrusion Inc	3081	160
Quality Fab and Mechanical LLC	3441	181
Quality Fabrication	3444	119
Quality Fabrication and Design Inc	3444	174
Quality Fabrication and Machine Works Inc	3443	162
Quality Fabrication Inc	3599	1809
Quality Fabricator's Inc	3444	113
Quality Facility Specialists Inc	7349	460
Quality Fencing and Supply	3089	1307
Quality Filters Inc	3569	300
Quality First Systems Inc	3829	328
Quality Foam Packaging Inc	3086	70
Quality Food Centers Inc	5411	80
Quality Foods From The Sea Inc	2091	18
Quality Forming LLC	3728	126
Quality Formulation Laboratories Inc	2834	369
Quality Formulations Inc	2099	120
Quality Gage Inc	3829	318
Quality Graphics and Forms Inc	2752	1747
Quality Grinding Company Inc	3545	380
Quality Home Staffing Inc	7363	330
Quality Housing Supply LLC	2451	34
Quality Hydraulics and Pneumatics Inc	5084	324
Quality Industrial Products Inc	3053	143
Quality Industrial Solutions	7372	3942
Quality Industrial Supplies Inc	3613	163
Quality Industries LLC	3089	1206
Quality Ingredients Corp	2041	52

Company Name	SIC	Rank
Quality Inks Inc	2893	22
Quality Inspection and Containment Company Inc	7389	2479
Quality Interconnect Cabling LLC	4822	25
Quality International Packaging Ltd	5046	98
Quality Inventory Services Inc	7389	1690
Quality King Distributors Inc	5122	10
Quality Label Inc	3999	114
Quality Lime Co	1422	36
Quality Litho Inc	2752	1742
Quality Litigation Services Inc	7334	49
Quality Logistics Inc	4213	1680
Quality Logistics Systems Inc	4225	29
Quality Lumber Building Wholesalers Inc	5031	326
Quality Lumber Company LLC	5031	400
Quality Machine and Tool Works Inc	3599	541
Quality Machine And Welding Company Inc	3441	131
Quality Machine Co	3599	857
Quality Machine Engineering Inc	3599	833
Quality Machine Inc	3545	389
Quality Machine Works Inc	3599	1138
Quality Machining And Manufacturing Inc	3492	34
Quality Mail Marketing Inc	7331	234
Quality Mailing Services Inc	7331	239
Quality Manufacturing Company Inc	3599	173
Quality Manufacturing Corp	3441	120
Quality Match Plate Co	3365	50
Quality Meat Inc	5421	14
Quality Mechanical Inc	1711	56
Quality Media Resources Inc	7812	292
Quality Medical Publishing Inc	2731	295
Quality Metal Finishing Co	3364	14
Quality Metal Products Inc	3541	142
Quality Metalcraft Inc	3544	16
Quality Metals Inc	5051	141
Quality Mill Supply Company Inc	5085	82
Quality Mobile Communications LLC	5064	71
Quality Model and Pattern Co	3543	39
Quality Mold Inc (Akron Ohio)	3544	12
Quality Mold Shop Inc	3544	511
Quality Mould Inc	3544	734
Quality Musical Systems Inc	3651	135
Quality Name Plate Inc	3625	76
Quality Oil Company LLC	5983	3
Quality One Woodwork LLC	2541	23
Quality Packaging Inc	2068	28
Quality Park Products	2677	4
Quality Pattern Corp	2335	9
Quality Perforating Inc	3469	90
Quality Photographic Imaging	7372	4736
Quality Pipe Products Inc	3498	65
Quality Plastics And Engineering Inc	3089	1331
Quality Plywood Company Inc	2435	23
Quality Pool Supply Co	5091	36
Quality Pork International Inc	2011	48
Quality Precision Inc	3599	1694
Quality Press Inc	2752	1639
Quality Printing and Supply Inc	5943	17
Quality Printing Group Corp	2759	590
Quality Printing Inc	2759	250
Quality Printing Service Inc	2752	1414
Quality Production Ltd	3672	197
Quality Products and Machine LLC	3599	1015
Quality Products Inc	3069	58
Quality Profile Services Inc	3089	1324
Quality Protection Services Inc	7381	102
Quality Quartz Engineering Inc	3679	506
Quality Quartz Of America Inc	3679	885
Quality Quick Print Inc	2752	1277
Quality Rock Inc	5191	180
Quality Rolling And Deburring Company Inc	3471	70
Quality Rubber Manufacturing Company Inc	3544	211
Quality Sample Company Incorporated Of High Point NC	2782	56
Quality Samples Inc	2789	109
Quality Sausage Company Inc	2013	55
Quality Shipyards LLC	3732	50
Quality Software Systems Inc	7372	2089
Quality Solutions Group LLC	7389	1724
Quality Spring/Togo Inc	3493	11
Quality Sprinkler Company Inc	1711	167
Quality Staffing Services	7361	370
Quality Staffing Solutions Inc	7363	200
Quality Standby Services LLC	1731	1462
Quality Steels Corp	5051	380
Quality Stone and Ready Mix Inc	3281	35
Quality Supply Co	5046	90
Quality Surface Mount Inc	3672	336
Quality Switch Inc	3679	539
Quality Systems Inc	7373	35
Quality Systems Integrated Corp	3672	53
Quality Systems International Corp	7372	2003
Quality Systems Laboratories Inc	7372	1347
Quality Team Associates Inc	7371	1458
Quality Tech Services Inc	3841	288
Quality Tech Tool Inc	3545	146
Quality Telecommunications Services Inc	7389	2276
Quality Thermistor Inc	3823	137

Company Name	SIC	Rank
Quality Thermoforming Inc	3089	1404
Quality Time Components	3873	24
Quality Tool and Stamping Company Inc	3469	152
Quality Trailer Products LP	3714	185
Quality Transformer and Electronics Inc	3612	42
Quality Transmission Components	5085	46
Quality Transparent Bag Inc	2673	39
Quality Transport Co	4213	2054
Quality Transport Inc	4213	562
Quality Transport Inc	4213	1771
Quality Transportation Inc	4213	1587
Quality Transportation Services	4213	2512
Quality Truck Tires Inc	5014	67
Quality Ultra Print Inc	2752	1597
Quality Underground Inc	1623	706
Quality Unlimited LLC	7389	2481
Quality Warehouse and Distrib Co	4213	2939
Quality Wholesale and Supply Inc	7349	207
Quality Wiring Inc	1731	2413
Quality Wood Products Inc	2434	71
Quality Wood Products Ltd	5031	155
QualityLogic Inc	7372	2053
QualMark Corp	3821	19
Qual-Pro Corp	3672	89
Qualsoft Group LLC	7379	569
Qual-Tron Inc	3679	418
Qualtronic Devices Inc	3571	173
Qualtronics LLC	3694	41
Qualution Systems Inc	7371	1346
Quam-Nichols Co	3651	88
Quandel LLC	1542	173
Quandis Inc	7371	1390
Quandt Transport Service Inc	4213	2915
Quanex Building Products Corp	3442	2
Quanex Corporation Chatsworth Group	3353	11
Quanta Services Inc	1731	1
Quanta Systems Corp QDI Div	3999	15
Quanta Systems LLC	8711	225
Quantachrome Corp	3829	94
Quantapoint Inc	8713	2
Quantech Machining Inc	3599	515
Quantech Services Inc	8742	209
Quantem Corp	3825	194
Quantex Industries Inc	7378	112
Quantex Instrument Co	3599	980
Quantier Inc	7379	1404
Quantimetrix Corp	2835	40
Quantitative Financial Strategies Inc	6282	325
Quantitative Micro Software	7372	3013
Quantitative Software Management Inc	7372	3550
Quantity Photos	7384	38
Quantrell Inc	5511	438
Quantronic Corp	3672	228
Quantronix Inc	3577	488
Quantum Color Inc	2752	864
Quantum Compliance Systems Inc	7372	113
Quantum Controls Inc	1731	860
Quantum Corp	3572	9
Quantum Data Inc	3621	97
Quantum Electric Inc	1731	1686
Quantum Engineered Products Inc	3559	258
Quantum Films Software	7372	4737
QUANTUM Fuel Systems Technologies Worldwide Inc	3679	199
Quantum Group Inc	3829	118
Quantum Inc	5122	105
Quantum Instruments Inc	3861	43
Quantum Leap Innovations Inc	7371	1278
Quantum Leap Productions Inc	7389	1824
Quantum Loyalty Systems	7319	68
Quantum Materials Corp	1011	9
Quantum Medical Imaging LLC	3845	50
Quantum Mold and Engineering LLC	3559	473
Quantum Research Services Inc	8732	93
Quantum Resources	7363	146
Quantum Retail Technology Inc	7371	312
Quantum Systems International Corp	5045	906
Quantum Windows and Doors Inc	2431	95
Quantum3D Inc	3695	7
Quantumdirect	7331	32
QuantumWorks Corp	7372	4546
Quanturo Publishing Inc	2721	466
Quardev Inc	7371	890
Quark Inc	7372	101
Quarles and Brady LLP (Chicago Illinois)	8111	52
Quarles and Brady LLP (Milwaukee Wisconsin)	8111	144
Quarles Building Maintenance Inc	7349	141
Quarry Electric Inc	1731	2196
Quartech Corp	3577	657
Quarterly Review Of Wines	2721	360
Quarterwave Corp	8740	438
Quartz Scientific Inc	3295	14
Quartzdyne Inc	3829	525
Quartztech Engineering Inc	3679	757
Quasar Aerospace Industries Inc	6411	293
Quasar Engineering Inc	8711	263
Quasar Power and Technologies Inc	3629	32
Quashnick Tool Corp	3089	1091
Quasius Construction Inc	1542	272
Quatech Inc	3577	376
Quatrix Inc	7372	5082

Company Name	SIC	Rank
QuatRx Pharmaceuticals Co	2834	220
Quattro Investments Inc	5021	157
Qube Connections Inc	7372	4547
Qube Corp	3089	1823
Qube Software Inc	7372	1576
Quebecor World Infiniti	2752	327
Quebrada Bakery Co	2051	232
Queen Anne Window and Door Inc	5211	147
Queen Capital Group LLC	1731	2261
Queen City Audio Video and Appliances	5731	19
Queen City Barrel Co	3412	7
Queen City Electrical Supply Company Inc	5063	304
Queen City Federal Bancorp Inc	6712	731
Queen City FSB	6035	156
Queen City Paper Co	5113	47
Queen City Plastics Inc	3644	29
Queen City Polymers Inc	3089	970
Queen City Printers Inc	2752	889
Queen City Sausage and Provision Inc	2013	171
Queen City Wholesale Inc	5145	14
Queen Cutlery Co	3421	17
Queen Enterprises Inc	5063	573
Queen's Bakery Inc	2051	272
Queens Industrial Electric Corp	5063	603
Queen's Parent Resource Center Inc	8322	149
Queenstowne Realty Inc	6531	221
Quench Press Specialists Inc	3567	42
Quenneville Enterprises Inc	3599	2021
Quepasa Corp	7375	180
Quermback Electric Inc	5063	356
Querrey and Harrow Ltd	8111	589
Quest America Inc	7379	805
Quest Analytics LLC	7372	5046
Quest Business Agency Inc	7311	260
Quest Business Systems Inc	7373	1234
Quest Business Systems Inc (Oakland California)	7372	4738
Quest Construction Engineering and Management Inc	1542	414
Quest Continuing Education Solutions	8299	47
Quest Controls Inc	3829	204
Quest Corp	3559	314
Quest Diagnostics Inc	8071	1
Quest Diagnostics Inc (San Juan Capistrano California)	2835	6
Quest Fabrication Corp	3599	1728
Quest Graphics LLC	2752	422
Quest Group	7361	28
Quest Integrated Inc	8731	360
Quest International Fragrance	2844	39
Quest International Inc (Irvine California)	5045	146
Quest - Iv Inc	7372	4108
Quest Lithographers Ltd	2752	594
Quest Manufacturing Inc	3443	227
Quest Microwave Inc	3629	104
Quest Personnel Resources Inc	7363	276
Quest Plastics Inc	3089	1713
Quest Securities Inc	6211	383
Quest Software Inc	7372	70
Quest Solutions Inc	5045	316
Questa Corp (New York New York)	7372	4098
Questar Assessment Inc	8299	29
Questar Capital Corp	6211	282
Questar Corp	1311	35
Questar Corp (New Hope Pennsylvania)	3229	26
Questar Duluth Inc	8093	57
Questar Exploration and Production Co	4922	32
Questar Inc	5065	289
Questar Inc (Chicago Illinois)	7822	26
Questar InfoComm Inc	7374	58
Questar Los Alamitos Inc	8093	58
Questar Victorville Inc	8093	59
QuestaWeb Inc	7372	1716
Questcor Pharmaceuticals Inc	2834	126
Questech Services Corp	3599	1329
Questek Manufacturing Corp	3625	98
Questinghound Technology Partners LLC	7379	1384
Question Mark Corp	7372	2622
Questmark Information Management Inc	7331	56
Questor Management Company LLC	6722	196
Questor Systems Inc	7372	3943
QuestSoft	7372	675
Queststar Medical Inc	3841	393
Questvapco Corp	2842	61
Questys-Solutions	7372	2606
Quetzal Info Systems	7372	5118
Queue Inc	7372	3736
Queues Enforth Development Inc	3695	111
Quick America Corp	7372	4548
Quick Auto Parts Distributors Inc	5013	321
Quick Cable Corp	3643	48
Quick Caption	7389	2474
Quick Charge Corp	3629	93
Quick Check	7009	640
Quick Chek Food Stores Inc	5411	145
Quick Communications Inc	4813	438
Quick Connect Communications Inc	5065	429
Quick Courier Service Inc	4213	1140

Company Name	SIC	Rank
Quick Delivery Service Inc	4213	1711
Quick Electronics Inc	5734	166
Quick Lease Inc	7363	165
Quick Link Information Service LLC	4822	23
Quick Point Inc	3993	56
Quick Print	2752	1011
Quick Printing Plus	2752	1811
Quick Solutions Inc	7361	105
Quick Tab Ii Inc	2752	465
Quick Tech Graphics Inc	2761	48
Quick Test Inc	7375	27
Quick Tick International Inc	2752	997
QuickArrow Inc	7372	1220
Quicken Loans Arena	7941	31
Quickie Manufacturing Corp	2392	17
QuickLogic Corp	3674	195
Quick-Med Technologies Inc	3841	392
Quickoffice Inc	7372	1922
Quickpartscom Inc	3499	80
QuickSet International Inc	3861	79
Quickshot Technology Inc	5045	410
Quicksilver Analytics Inc	3826	115
Quicksilver Express Courier of MN	4213	660
Quicksilver Interactive Group Inc	7374	340
Quicksilver Resources Inc	1311	42
Quicksilver Software Inc	7371	1142
QuickStart Intelligence Inc	7372	1600
Quickutz Inc	2782	34
Quick-Way Inc	4213	3033
Quidel Corp	2835	15
Quidsi	5912	27
Quik Flex Circuit Inc	3672	457
Quik Manufacturing Co	3531	191
Quik Mart Inc	5411	227
Quik Stop Markets Inc	5411	207
Quikcut Inc	3443	198
Quikey Computer Systems Inc	7373	1105
Quikey Manufacturing Company Inc	3993	60
Quikrete Companies Inc	3272	1
Quiksilver Inc	2321	2
Quiksoft Corp	7372	676
Quikteks LLC	7379	1282
QuikTrip Corp	5411	21
Quill Computer Div	5734	5
Quill Corp	5044	7
Quiller and Blake Advertising	7311	614
Quillin's Inc	5411	187
Quilogy Inc	7379	117
Quilt In A Day Inc	5961	168
Quimbik Inc	5045	875
Quinault Pride Seafoods	2091	23
Quincy Compressor Div	3563	20
Quincy Joist	3441	108
Quincy Street Inc	2013	69
Quinn Andersen Inc	5063	948
Quinn/Brein Public Relations	8743	196
Quinn Broadcasting Inc	4833	254
Quinn Communication LLC	7372	2913
Quinn Data Corp	5045	548
Quinn Electric Corp	1731	1886
Quinn Emanuel Urquhart Oliver and Hedges LLP	8111	25
Quinn Fable Advertising Inc	7311	343
Quinn-Curtis Inc	7372	4628
Quinnox Inc	7379	213
Quinoa Corp	2041	43
Quinsig Ave Overflow Treatment	5074	131
Quinstar Corp	7372	3438
Quinstar Technology Inc	3679	311
QuinStreet Inc	7319	12
Quint Measuring Systems Inc	3829	340
Quintas Marketing LLC	7389	1090
Quintech Electronics and Communications Inc	3663	156
Quintech Security Consultants Inc	3679	683
Quintessential School Systems	7372	2286
Quintex Corp	3089	923
Quintiles Transnational Corp	8731	6
Quinton Manor	8051	23
Quintron Systems Inc	3661	100
Quintum Technologies Inc	7379	592
Quintus Inc	3841	303
Quinzani's Bakery Inc	2051	132
Quip Laboratories Inc	2842	153
Quipcon Inc	5046	277
QuipNet Inc	7375	225
Quirk and Quirk	8111	509
Quirk Auto Park	5511	246
QuirkWorks	7336	332
Quist International Inc	3577	511
Quixave Technologies Inc	5084	831
Quixote Corp	3089	119
Quizno's Corp	5812	351
Qumas Inc	7371	565
Quon Yick Noodle Company Inc	2098	19
Quoizel Inc	3645	7
Quogue Sinclair Fuel Inc	5172	129
Quorum Architects Inc	8712	241
Quorum Business Solutions Inc	7371	127
Quorum Business Solutions (USA) Inc	7372	658
Quorum Federal Credit Union	6061	70
Quorum Health Resources LLC	8742	23
Quorum Hotels and Resorts	7011	42
Quorum Radio Partners Of Virginia Inc	4832	206

Company Name	SIC	Rank
Quorum Technical Sales	5065	825
Quotable Cards Inc	2678	12
QuoteMedia Inc	7375	231
QuoteWizard	6411	228
QVC Inc	5961	4
QVS Inc	3699	68
Qw Memphis Corp	2752	1159
Qwik Print and Bindery Of Florida Inc	2752	1176
QwikQuote Development	7372	2686
Qxest Holdings LLC	7379	1262
Qxq Inc	3825	179
R A Adams Enterprises Inc	5599	20
R A Cullinan and Son Inc	2951	14
R A Designs Inc	1521	153
R A Industries LLC	3599	1249
R A Jones and Company Inc	3565	21
R A Kerley Ink Engineers Inc	2893	33
R A Lesso Seafood Inc	2092	70
R A Miller Industries Inc	3669	84
R A Wood Associates	7372	2687
R and A Associates	7311	948
R and A Equipment Corp	7352	16
R and A Tool and Engineering Co	3545	214
R and B Collections Inc	7322	66
R and B Electric Inc	1731	2243
R and B Electronics Inc	3728	183
R and B Films Ltd	8999	183
R and B Grinding Company Inc	3451	33
R and B Machinery Corp	3559	388
R and B Mold And Die Inc	3599	2504
R and B Plastics Machinery LLC	3559	159
R and B Wholesale Distributors Inc	5064	59
R and C Electronics	4822	27
R and D Batteries Inc	3691	25
R and D Circuits Inc	3672	135
R and D Custom Machine and Tool Inc	3599	1183
R and D Dynamics Corp	3511	30
R and D Electronics Inc	3679	215
R and D Engineering Incorporated Of Earlham	3312	111
R and D Industries Inc	5045	318
R and D Manufacturing Company Inc	3556	70
R and D Manufacturing Inc	3544	329
R and D Medical Staffing Inc	7363	309
R and D Molders Inc	3089	871
R and D Plastics Inc	3089	1288
R and D Precision Inc	3444	280
R and D Sleeves LLC	2679	55
R and D Tool and Engineering Co	3544	17
R And D Tool Inc	3549	59
R and D Transport Inc	4213	1861
R and E Tooling and Plastics Inc	3089	1770
R And G Enterprises Of Ohio Inc	5092	47
R and H Construction Co	1541	94
R and H Manufacturing Inc	3429	116
R and H Motor Cars Ltd	5511	712
R and H Solutions Inc	2353	15
R and H Systems Inc	1799	135
R and J Components Corp	5065	372
R and J Cylinder and Machine Inc	3593	41
R and J Homes LLC	1521	94
R and J Manufacturing Co	3053	116
R and J Randall Enterprises Inc	7377	33
R and K Building Supplies Inc	5031	113
R and L Carriers	4212	12
R and L Development Company Inc	1629	79
R and L Electric Inc	1731	652
R and L Engineering Inc	8711	652
R and L Enterprises Inc	3599	1463
R And L Machine Shop Inc	3599	1926
R and L Smith Trucking Inc	4213	1991
R and L Spring Co	3495	17
R and M Associates	5084	860
R and M Deese Inc	3993	151
R and M Equipment Rentals Inc	7353	56
R and M Fluid Power Inc	3593	46
R and M Leasing Corp	4213	1682
R and M Welding Products Inc	5085	389
R and N Hydraulics Inc	7699	199
R and N Knitted Headwear Inc	5136	26
R and N Leasing Inc	5045	855
R and O Transportation LLC	4213	624
R and R Advertising	7311	651
R and R Bindery Service Inc	2789	11
R and R Electric Of Southwest Florida Inc	1731	1728
R and R Erectors Inc	3441	178
R and R Inc	5511	747
R and R Loopers Inc	3559	495
R and R Machine Industries Inc	3599	1443
R and R Machine Products Inc	3679	778
R and R Marketing LLC	5182	16
R and R Partners Inc	7311	63
R and R Products Inc	3469	40
R and R Provision Co	5147	63
R and R Rubber Molding Inc	3061	60
R and R Security Inc	7381	225
R and R Technologies LLC	3089	370
R and R Tool Manufacturing Inc	3599	1960
R and R Transportation Inc	4213	734
R and R Truck Sales Inc	5511	1243
R and R Trucking Inc	4213	451
R and R Trucking LLC	4213	543
R and S Carpet Service Inc	5023	121

Company Name	SIC	Rank
R And S Computers Inc	7373	611
R and S Digital Media	2796	63
R and S Lines Inc	4213	2696
R and S Mexican Food Products Inc	2099	212
R and S Processing Company Inc	3069	118
R and S Roberts Enterprises Inc	2064	146
R and S Steel Co	5051	17
R and S Transportation Inc	4213	2733
R and S Welding and Fabricating	1799	155
R and S-Godwin Truck Body Company LLC	3713	20
R and T Electric Inc	1731	2105
R and T Electric LLC	1731	2229
R and V Industries Inc	3089	843
R and W Engineering Inc	7379	1137
R and Z Ventures Inc	2033	81
R Associates Inc	5045	746
R B Allen Company Inc	5063	415
R:Base Technologies Inc	7372	4328
R Brooks Associates Inc	7389	1283
R Buse Printing and Advertising	2759	106
R/C Machining Company Inc	3451	153
R C Tway Co	3715	29
R C Williams Enterprises Inc	7349	229
R Conley Inc	4213	1900
R D Bowman and Sons Inc	0723	20
R D Braswell Construction Co	1623	401
R D Crumley and Sons Inc	1623	152
R D Niven and Associates Ltd	3993	115
R E Darling Company Inc	3069	81
R E Erickson Company Inc	4941	65
R E Phelon Company Inc	3694	16
R E Prescott Company Inc	5084	684
R E W Group Inc	1731	552
R F Berkheimer And Sons Inc	5013	115
R F Higginbotham Inc	3444	283
R F Ltd	5731	143
R Freedman and Son Inc	5093	20
R G Hansen and Associates	3823	357
R G Management Inc	2752	1269
R G Ray Corp	3429	42
R/GA	7311	122
R/GA Digital Studios Inc	4833	22
R Graphics Inc	2759	411
R H Barden Inc	3677	99
R H Bolick and Company Inc	3599	2483
R H Scales Company Inc	5014	42
R Ibarra's Inc	2041	39
R J Lillis Enterprises Inc	5999	191
R J Mcglennon Company Inc	2851	137
R J Skelding Company Inc	1731	899
R J Zappen Printers and Designers Inc	2752	819
R J Zeman Tool and Manufacturing Company Inc	3544	173
R/K Belting Specialties Inc	3535	63
R Kern Engineering and Manufacturing Corp	3678	41
R L Best Co	3599	554
R L Bryan Co	2752	280
R L Coward Construction Inc	1623	679
R L Jones Company Inc	1623	217
R L Lewis Industries Inc	3599	1131
R L Perlow Corp	5051	182
R L Ryerson Company Inc	5083	148
R M Industries Inc	3599	757
R M Wright Company Inc	5085	302
R M Young Co	3829	115
R Mar Coat	3479	75
R Michael Donovan and Company Inc	7372	1905
R Miller Sales Company Inc	2791	38
R P Fedder Corp	3564	69
R P Industries Inc	3089	795
R P N Inc	3599	1970
R Palmieri Electrical Contractor Inc	1731	1473
R R Street and Company Inc	2842	30
R R Templeton Corp	3444	921
R Roese Contracting Company Inc	1623	165
R S Corcoran Co	3561	159
R/S Development Co	1521	159
R S Stover Co	5084	159
R Square Products Inc	2841	40
R- Squared Aluminium LLC	3714	295
R Stahl Inc	5063	351
R Stresau Laboratory Inc	3489	15
R Systems Inc	7371	39
R Tech Laboratories	8733	26
R Tech Systems	3571	251
R Torre and Company Inc	2087	32
R W Armstrong and Assoc Inc	8712	33
R/W Bowman Corp	5712	97
R W Garcia Company Inc	5145	10
R W Lyall and Company Inc	3088	5
R W Patterson Printing Co	2752	642
R W Thompson Company Inc	5082	170
R Wales and Son LLC	3069	154
R West	7311	956
R Zoppo Corp	1622	30
R4 Technical Center North Carolina LLC	7699	55
RA Bright Construction Inc	1794	16
Ra Company Amo Inc	3672	421
RA Heller Co	3471	125
RA Mercer and Co	8721	40
RA Pearson Company Inc	3565	33

Company Name	SIC	Rank
RA Rapaport Publishing	2721	357
RA Reed Productions Inc	7922	44
RA Reynolds Appraisal Service Inc	6531	418
RA Scott Construction Co	1623	211
RA Serafini Inc	3544	555
RA Zweig Inc	3599	501
Raac Technologies Inc	3577	637
Raani Corp	2844	89
Raapnet Inc	7373	800
Rab Lighting Inc	3625	75
RABA Technologies LLC	7372	617
Raba-Kistner Consultants Inc	8748	183
Rabb Brothers Trucking Inc	4213	481
Rabbit Creek Products Inc	2034	36
Rabbitsoft	7372	3014
Rabco Systems Inc	3089	1896
Rabe Environmental Systems Inc	1711	163
Raber Packing Co	2011	35
Rabe's Quality Meat Inc	2011	33
Rabideaux's Sausage Kitchen Inc	2013	237
Rable Machine Inc	3599	579
Rabo AgriFinance	5191	16
Rabobank (El Centro California)	6712	278
Rabobank NA	6021	18
Raborne Electric Corp	1731	2230
Rabuck Stranger	7311	786
RAC Enterprise LLC	5399	26
RAC Solutions	7377	23
Rac Tek Inc	7377	30
RAC Transport Company Inc	4213	722
Race On Motor Sports	7389	2456
Race Street Foods Inc	5146	26
Race Telecommunications Inc	7379	600
RaceCom Inc	7371	1351
RaceTrac Petroleum Inc	5541	6
Racette Ford of Oshkosh	5511	1004
Rachel Carter PR	7389	2381
Rachel Perry Inc	2844	154
Racine Federated Inc	3542	114
Racine Metal-Fab Ltd	3599	637
Racine Plastic Inc	3089	1002
Racine Unified School District	8211	70
Rackemann Sawyer and Brewster	8111	314
Racket Merchandise Co	3262	6
Rackmaster Systems Inc	3571	167
Rackow Polymers Corp	3089	1384
Rack-Rite Inc	5063	709
Racks Inc	2542	5
Rackspace Hosting Inc	7379	18
RACO General Contractors Inc	1541	195
Raco Inc	1623	84
Raco International LP	5084	802
Raco Manufacturing Engineering Co	3699	221
Raco Steel Company Inc	5051	205
Racoe Inc	2329	36
Racoh Products Inc	3599	1289
RACOM Products Inc	3669	228
Racore Technology Corp	3577	300
Racquet Club of Columbus Ltd	7991	15
RAD Data Communications Inc	3577	60
Rad Electric Inc	3826	155
RAD Game Tools Inc	7372	3241
RAD Printng LLC	2752	1736
RAD Transport Inc	4213	2129
Rad Video Inc	4813	650
Rada Manufacturing Co	3914	9
Radant Technologies Inc	8731	221
Radar Industries Inc	3469	106
Radar Pictures Inc	7812	112
Radar Technology Inc	3812	150
Radcal Partners la California LP	3829	170
Radcliffe and Associates Inc	8743	340
Radco Exteriors Inc	3442	122
RADCO Media Inc	2741	346
RADCOM Equipment Inc	3825	211
Radebaugh-Fetzer Co	5047	188
RaDec Construction Company Inc	1542	426
Rademann Stone and Landscape Company Inc	0781	22
Radeum Inc	3663	286
Radford Co	5031	20
Radford Manufacturing Inc	3569	290
Radford Tech Services Inc	1731	1380
Radiac Abrasives Inc	3291	4
Radiad Manufacturing Inc	3544	362
Radial Industries Inc	3089	508
Radiall America Inc	3678	13
Radian Audio Engineering Inc	3663	240
Radian Group Inc	6351	8
Radian Precision Inc	3544	421
Radian Research Inc	3825	90
Radiance Technologies Inc	7371	168
Radianse Inc	3679	99
Radiant Aviation Services Inc	8731	199
Radiant Energy Systems Inc	3567	77
Radiant Logic Inc	7373	308
Radiant Power Corp	3728	30
Radiant Research Inc	8731	119
Radiant Systems Inc (South Plainfield New Jersey)	7372	1515
Radiant Technologies Inc	7372	3331
Radiant Thermal Products Co	3823	256
Radiation Management Associates LLC	7363	159
Radiation Monitoring Devices Inc	3829	122

Company Name	SIC	Rank	Company Name	SIC	Rank	Company Name	SIC	Rank
Radiation Power Systems Inc	3679	860	Rail Bearing Service Inc	3568	1	Ralph Lauren Corp	5136	1
Radiation Services Of Indiana Inc	5047	218	Rail Co	3721	27	Ralph Lauren Home	6794	128
Radiation Technical Services Co	4953	121	Rail Delivery Services Inc	4213	1288	Ralph M Parsons Co	8711	37
Radiation Therapy Services Inc	8734	5	Rail Europe Group Ltd	4724	29	Ralph Martinez Trucking Inc	4213	2473
Radiator Express Warehouse	5013	122	Rail Europe Holding	4724	21	Ralph Moyle Inc	4213	286
Radiator Specialty Company Inc	2899	44	Rail Management Corp	4011	54	Ralph Pill Electric Supply Co	5063	98
Radiaulics Inc	3679	637	Rail Systems Inc	7699	25	Ralph Schomp Automotive Inc	5511	1251
Radicom Inc	5065	179	RailAmerica Inc	4011	14	Ralph W Cook	3556	171
Radicom Research Inc	3661	217	Railcrew Xpress LLC	4131	4	Ralph Walker Inc	4213	2718
Radient Pharmaceuticals Corp	2834	444	Railroad Construction Company Inc	1629	73	Ralph White Electric Company Inc	1731	963
Radio Adventures Corp	5734	120	Railroad Yard Inc	5211	305	Ralph Williams and Associates	7011	139
Radio Cap Company Inc	3231	21	Railway and Industrial Services Inc	3743	21	Ralph's Foods	5411	230
Radio Central Coast	4832	243	RailWorks Corp	4731	20	Ralphs Grocery Co	5411	25
Radio Component Corp	3429	126	Rain Bird Sprinkler Manufacturing Corp	3523	19	Ralph's Industrial Sewing Machine Company Inc	5084	745
Radio Data Group Inc	7371	1623	Rain Cal-West Inc	5083	57	Ralphs Of Lafayette Inc	5065	205
Radio Flyer Inc	3944	29	Rain For Rent	1623	359	Ralph's Packing Co	2011	134
Radio Frequency Intertronics Corp	3675	16	Rainbo Record Manufacturing Corp	3652	22	Ralphs-Pugh Company Inc	3535	86
Radio Frequency Systems	3577	170	Rainbow Casino	7993	20	Ralston Drug Stores Inc	5912	52
Radio Group	4832	105	Rainbow Computer Services Inc	7379	982	Ralston Foods Inc	2052	11
Radio Hendersonville Inc	4832	250	Rainbow Cotton Candy LLC	2064	114	Ralston Instruments LLC	3829	219
Radio Holland USA	5063	10	Rainbow Cultured Marble	3281	53	Ralston Trucking Co	4213	2883
Radio Oem Inc	3651	233	Rainbow Data Systems Inc	7379	794	RAM Aircraft Corp	3599	149
Radio One Inc	4832	8	Rainbow Enterprises Inc	3545	180	Ram Communication Inc	7373	782
Radio One of Boston Inc	4832	41	Rainbow Glacier Inc	2024	53	RAM Consolidated Industries Inc	5085	446
Radio One of Boston Licenses LLC	4832	42	Rainbow Graphics Inc	2752	450	Ram Construction General Contractors Inc	1623	184
Radio One of Charlotte LLC	4832	34	Rainbow Holding Company Inc	4724	96	Ram Custom Services Inc	7349	345
Radio One of North Carolina LLC	4832	39	Rainbow Hotel Casino	7011	84	Ram Electric Inc	5013	417
Radio Research Instrument Company Inc	3812	190	Rainbow Inc (Pearl City Hawaii)	5142	13	Ram Electronic Industries Inc	3679	309
Radio Satellite Integrators Corp	3663	10	Rainbow Lighting Inc	3645	70	RAM Energy Resources Inc	1311	106
Radio Service Company Inc	5731	106	Rainbow Linens Inc	5023	79	Ram Enterprises Inc	7372	4164
Radio Shop Inc	5731	158	Rainbow Maintenance and Cleaning Corp	7349	215	Ram Freezers And Coolers	1711	277
Radio Sound Inc	3751	18	Rainbow Networking	7374	264	RAM Inc	3599	429
Radio Systems Design Inc	3663	274	Rainbow Packaging Inc	3565	187	RAM Inc (Cisco Texas)	3089	1444
Radio Waves Inc	3663	133	Rainbow Play Systems Inc	3949	63	Ram Informatics Ltd	7372	5005
Radiodetection	3661	169	Rainbow Samples Inc	2782	71	Ram Information System Inc	7371	1227
RadioFilms Inc	7311	1024	Rainbow Satellite Communications Inc	3663	389	Ram International Ltd	5812	101
Radiological Associates of Sacramento Medical Group Inc	8011	7	Rainbow Studios	7372	1357	Ram Machine Tooling Inc	3599	2226
Radiology Alliance	8011	114	Rainbow Technology Corp	5169	139	Ram Meter Inc	5065	389
Radiology Resource Inc	7363	196	Rainbow Technology Inc	7371	1241	RAM Nationwide Inc	4213	848
Radiology Support Devices Inc	3841	306	Rainbow Tool And Machine Company Inc	3544	562	Ram Offset Lithographers LLC	2752	1177
Radionic Industries Inc	3612	54	Rainbow Travel Corp	4724	141	Ram Optical Instrumentation Inc	3625	14
RadioShack Corp	5731	3	Rainbow Travel Service Inc	4724	135	Ram Printing Inc	2752	717
Radiotronics Inc	3663	335	Rainbow Trucking LLC	4213	1531	Ram Publications Inc	2752	779
Radisphere National Radiology Group	8734	40	Rainbow Westbank	5511	958	Ram Sensors Inc	3823	290
Radisson Hotels and Resorts	7011	3	Raincastle Communications Inc	7336	199	Ram Software Systems Inc	7371	1654
RadiSys Communications Platform Div	3571	25	Raindrop Advertising and Specialties Inc	7311	946	RAM Technologies Inc (Fort Washington Pennsylvania)	7372	3435
RadiSys Corp	7373	40	Rainer Investment Management Inc	6282	255	Ram Tool and Supply Co	5072	44
Radium	7819	25	Raines and Fischer	8721	469	Ram Tool Company Inc	3544	867
Radius Corp	3991	23	Rainforest Cafe Inc	5812	150	Ram Tool Inc	3544	137
Radius LLC	3625	393	Rainforest Cafe Inc (Overland Park Kansas)	5812	265	RAM Trucking Inc	4213	765
Radix Corp	3571	30	Rainforest Industry	3577	640	Rama Corp	3567	35
Radix Ii Inc	4813	488	Rainhart Co	3829	269	Rama Fabrication Inc	3533	126
Radix Laboratories Inc	2834	312	Rainier Cold Storage Inc	4222	12	Rama Food Manufacture Corp	2099	246
Radix Organizations	4731	77	Rainier Industries Ltd	2394	4	Ramann Enterprises Inc	5084	492
Radix Wire Co	3357	46	Rainier Plastics Inc	4953	144	Ramapo Information Systems Inc	7372	510
RadixNet Inc	7375	299	Rainier Plywood Co	2672	65	Ramapo Lighting and Electric Supplies Inc	5063	875
Radixx Solutions International Inc	7372	1163	Rainier Stained Glass Inc	5039	61	Ramar-Hall Inc	3728	185
Radke Machine and Tool Inc	3599	1810	RainMaker Software Inc	7372	1221	Rambow Enterprises	7372	4739
RadNet Inc	8071	6	Rainmaker Systems Inc	8741	149	Rambus Inc	3674	68
Radoil Inc	3533	77	Rains Electrical Sales Inc	5063	1017	Ramcar Batteries Inc	3691	28
Radon Inc	2231	12	Rainsville Technology Inc	3089	337	Ramcel Engineering Co	3469	217
Rados Co	1622	24	Rainsweet	2037	18	Ramco Construction Tools Inc	3532	50
RADVA Corp	3086	69	Rainwater Gas and Oil Company Inc	5411	215	Ramco Enterprises LP	0723	5
RADvision Inc	3661	50	Rainwater Inc	6799	51	Ramco Industries Inc	3647	18
Radware Inc (Mahwah New Jersey)	3661	72	Rainwise Inc	3829	336	Ramco Systems Corp	7372	1169
Rae Corp	3585	55	Rairdon's Chrysler Jeep of Kirkland	5511	705	Ramco-Gershenson Properties LP	6512	29
Rae' Launo Corp	2095	57	RAIT Financial Trust	6798	82	Ramcomm Inc	1731	1624
RAE Systems Inc (Sunnyvale California)	3829	28	Raith USA Inc	5065	829	Ramdy Corp	3541	118
Raeco Inc	5084	565	Raj India Autoparts Outsourcing	8999	145	Ramec Engineering	3721	45
Raf Acquisition Co	3471	121	Raj Manufacturing Inc	2339	60	Rame-Hart Inc	3826	135
RAF Industries Inc	6211	198	Rajbhog Foods Inc	2064	79	Ramer Products Inc	3829	498
Raf Tabtronics LLC	3612	39	Rajor Inc	4213	1567	Ramey and Kampf PA	8111	492
Rafael Orozco	7379	1631	Rajpootana Holdings Ltd	5023	176	Ramey Chevrolet Inc	5511	374
Rafael Ruiz	3691	53	Rak Corrosion Control Inc	1799	118	Ramey Contractor Engineers Inc	1623	587
Raff Printing Inc	2752	318	Rakar Inc	3089	733	Rami E Geffner MD PA	8011	155
Rafferty Aluminum and Steel Company Inc	5031	127	Rake Publishing Inc	2741	440	Ramirez and Company Inc	6211	217
Raffield Fisheries Inc	5146	54	Rakoz Electric Inc	1731	1580	Ramona's Mexican Food Products Inc	2099	93
Rafi Systems Inc	3851	110	Ral Supply Group Inc	5074	86	Ramos and Associates Inc	1623	367
Raflex	7379	1669	Ralco Industries Inc	2821	144	Ramos Oil Company Inc	1381	51
Rafn Co	1542	306	Ralco Nutrition Inc	2048	55	Rampage Systems Inc	7372	1906
Rafte and Co	8742	488	Ralcorp Holdings Inc	2052	1	Rampart Capital Corp	6531	420
Rafter Equipment Corp	3542	53	Raleigh America Inc	5091	57	Rampart Group	6411	134
Rafu Shimpo	2711	794	Raleigh Mine And Industrial Supply Inc	5085	76	Rampart Investment Management Company Inc	6799	42
RAG Tooling Co	3559	491	Raleigh Precision Products Inc	3089	1294	Rampart Systems Inc	7379	1670
Rage Corp	3089	581	Raleigh TV and Film Studios	7819	33	Ramparts Inc	7011	103
Ragland Mills Inc	2048	70	Raley's Inc	5411	47	Rampell and Rampell PA	8721	70
Ragnar Benson Inc	1541	109	Ralls County Electric Coop	4911	411	Rampp Co	3533	60
Rago and Son Inc	3469	112	Rally Software Development Corp	7379	185	RampRate LLC	8742	541
Ragozzino Foods Inc	2038	41	Raloid Corp	3599	499	Ramrod Enterprises LLC	2499	36
Ragsdale Industries Inc	3599	1920	Raloid Tool Company Inc	3544	760	Ramrod Industries LLC	3593	20
Rahco Rubber Inc	3069	95	Ralph A Hiller Co	5085	208	Ramrod Trucking Inc	4213	2884
Rahn Bahia Mar Ltd	7011	102	Ralph Clayton and Sons LLC	5032	11	Ramsay Fabrics Inc	2241	31
Rahn's Trucking Inc	4213	2119	Ralph E Ames Machine Works	3599	591	Ramsbottom Printing Inc	2752	917
Rahway Steel Drum	5085	319	Ralph Good Inc	2096	38	Ramsey Electronics Inc	3825	131
RAI Technology Inc	5944	32	Ralph H Burns and Son Inc	4213	3095	Ramsey Popcorn Company Inc	5145	22
Ralch Ende Malter and Co LLP	8721	284	Ralph Hamel Forest Products Inc	2421	48	Ramsey Products Corp	3499	88
Raider Express Inc	4213	754	Ralph Hodge	1522	57	Ramsey Property Management Inc	1382	65
Raider Manufacturing Ltd	5085	220	Ralph Hodge Construction Co	1623	289	Ramsey Ward Electric Co	1731	1329
Raider Trucking Inc	4213	1513	Ralph L Wadsworth Construction Company Inc	1611	163	Ramstar Mills Inc	2321	31
Raiford Printing Company Inc	3089	1852						

Company Name	SIC	Rank
Ramtec Associates Inc	3089	1440
Ramtech Building Systems Inc	1542	309
Ramtel Corp	3661	187
Ramtron International Corp	3674	123
Ran Technologies Inc	3613	73
Ranac Computer Corp	7373	931
Ranac Corp	7372	4168
Ra-Nav Laboratories Inc	8711	676
Rance Industries Inc	3441	277
Ranch Fiberglass Inc	3792	25
Ranchers Tractor Company Inc	5083	142
Rancho Carlsbad	6515	1
Rancho Mesa Properties	7389	678
Rancho Mission Viejo	6552	260
Rancho Santa Fe National Bank	6021	218
Rancho Security Services LLC	7381	154
Rancho Station LLC	7999	2
Rancho Technology Inc	3577	472
Ranch-Way Inc	2048	56
Ranco Fertiservice Inc	3523	129
Ranco Sand and Stone Corp	4212	57
Ranco Security Inc	7381	133
Rancocas Metals Corp	5051	314
Rancon Financial Corp	6552	167
Rand Capital Corp	6722	256
Rand Construction Co	1541	174
RAND Corp	8732	19
Rand Financial Services Inc	6221	4
Rand International Leisure Products Ltd	5091	34
Rand Logistics Inc	4449	13
Rand Machine Products Inc	3544	88
Rand McNally and Co	2731	36
Rand McNally-TDM Inc	7372	1464
Rand Whitney Packaging Corp	7389	1198
Rand Worldwide Inc	7372	799
Randa Accessories Leather Goods LLC	5136	20
Randa Solutions	7379	839
Randal Optimal Nutrients LLC	2834	368
Randall Bearings Inc	3562	31
Randall Brothers Inc	5031	150
Randall Cloud	7389	1920
Randall Davis Co	6552	237
Randall's Food Markets Inc	5411	56
Randall-Story State Bank	6022	22
Randcastle Extrusion Systems Inc	3559	425
Randel Electric Inc	1731	2068
Randers Engineers and Constructors	8731	434
Randles Sand and Gravel Inc	1442	23
Randolph and Baldwin Inc	3679	646
Randolph and Hale Inc	5065	856
Randolph and Son Builders Inc	1542	376
Randolph Bank and Trust Co	6022	559
Randolph Capital Management	6722	284
Randolph Co	3829	74
Randolph Electric Membership Corp	4911	259
Randolph Engineering Inc	3851	73
Randolph Jewelers	5944	33
Randolph Packing Co	2013	111
Randolph Tool Company Inc	3599	2338
Randolph Trucking Inc	4213	1908
Randolph-Brooks Federal Credit Union	6061	28
Random Access Inc	7336	249
Random House Inc	2731	3
Rand's Camera And Hi-Fi Inc	5731	161
Rand's Trucking Inc	4213	1394
Rand-Scot Inc	3841	375
Randstad USA	7363	13
Rand-Whitney Container LLC	2653	33
Randy Curnow Buick/GMC	5511	1169
Randy Martin Inc	3599	2187
Randy Reed Nissan	5511	515
Randy Rowe Trucking Inc	4213	1260
Randy's High Country Towing Inc	7549	11
Ranew's Truck and Equipment Company LLC	3714	251
Raney Recording Studio and Print Inc	7389	2068
Ranfac Corp	3841	190
Range Cooperatives Inc	5984	25
Range Online Media	8742	191
Range Resources Corp	1311	33
Range Television Cable Company Inc	4841	145
Rangel Distributing Co	5064	164
Rangeland Exploration Co	1382	66
Ranger Aerospace LLC	6719	117
Ranger All-Season Corp	5088	115
Ranger Automation Systems Inc	3559	260
Ranger Communications Inc	5065	165
Ranger Construction Industries Inc	1611	39
Ranger Conveying and Supply Company Inc	3535	157
Ranger Insurance Co	6331	221
Ranger Joe's International	5999	192
Ranger Land Systems Inc	7389	1094
Ranger Pipelines Inc	1623	47
Ranger Riverton Inc	2711	542
Ranger Security Detectors Inc	3812	138
Ranger Tool and Die Co	3544	536
Rangers Die Casting Co.	3363	46
Ranieri and Company Inc	6799	245
Rank Industries Inc	3589	266
Rank Technology Corp	3572	71
Rankin Automation Company LLC	5084	714

Company Name	SIC	Rank
Rankin Communication Systems Inc	5065	568
Rankin County School District	8211	44
Rankin Fitness Group Ltd	7389	1587
Rankin Group Ltd	7311	389
Rankin-Delux Inc	3589	247
Rankin's Inc	5211	261
Ranon Construction	1531	89
Ran-Shel Inc	3599	714
Ransom International Corp	3829	459
Ransome Engine Inc	5082	184
Rantec Microwave Systems Corp	3679	554
Rantec Microwave Systems Inc	3812	89
Rantec Power Systems Inc	3679	281
Rao Design International Inc	3559	171
Raosoft Inc	7372	899
Rapac Liquidating Company Inc	2821	81
Rapat Corp	3535	56
Rapco Distributing Co	4213	2351
Rapco International Inc	3679	252
Rapid	2791	68
Rapid Air Systems	2515	30
Rapid Armored Corp	4213	1743
Rapid Bind Inc	2789	77
Rapid Chevrolet-Cadillac	5511	395
Rapid Circuits Inc	3672	284
Rapid Circular Press Inc	2752	1760
Rapid City Journal	2711	353
Rapid Die and Engineering Inc	3544	89
Rapid Electroplating Process Inc	3559	546
Rapid Engineering LLC	3585	127
Rapid Finishing Corp	3479	100
Rapid Granulator Inc	3559	304
Rapid Industries Inc	3535	116
Rapid Manufacturing A California LP	3496	21
Rapid Mold Solutions Inc	3544	541
Rapid Output Co	7372	4629
Rapid Print Inc	2752	1844
Rapid Printers Of Monterey	2752	1492
Rapid Processing LLC	2611	8
Rapid Product Solutions Inc	3599	1336
Rapid Rack Inc	2542	19
Rapid Rack Industries Inc	2542	43
Rapid Rater Co	2752	896
Rapid Reporting Co	7375	128
Rapid Response Monitoring Services Inc	7382	22
Rapid Service Inc	4213	2283
Rapid Systems Inc	7373	751
Rapid Transport Ltd	4213	2719
Rapides Station LLC	1731	1509
Rapidprint	3579	32
RapidStream Inc	7379	60
Rapidware Inc	7371	1903
Rapier Electric Inc	1731	584
Rapit Printing Inc	2752	292
Rapp Collins Worldwide	7331	3
Rapp Industries Inc	7372	2313
Rapp Systems Corp	8742	710
Rappahannock Electric Coop	4911	140
Rappahannock Goodwill Industries Inc	8331	30
Rappahannock Record	2711	886
Rapport Inc	5065	352
Rapport Inc (Redwood City California)	3674	222
Rapt Inc	7372	1297
Raptor Pharmaceutical Corp	2834	469
Rapture Technologies Inc	7371	676
Raque Food Systems LLC	3565	54
RAR Electric Inc	1731	1812
Rare Hospitality International Inc	5812	61
Rarin Federal Credit Union	6061	155
Raritan Computer Inc	5045	71
Raritan Valley Broadcasting Company Inc	4832	64
Raritan Valley Technology Group Inc	7372	3628
Ras Industries Inc	3089	305
Rasch Graphic Services Corp	2789	76
Raser Technologies Inc	4911	582
Rasirc Inc	3559	280
Raskin Jerry Needle Doctor Inc	5731	140
Rasky Baerlein Strategic Communications Inc	8743	52
Rasmussen Group Inc	1622	22
Rasmussen Software Inc	7372	4740
Rason Asphalt Inc	2951	39
Rasp Inc	3625	281
Rassey Industries Inc	3599	2022
Rast Construction Inc	1623	180
RATA Associates LLC	7371	1300
Ratchet	7372	2583
Ra-Tech Industries Inc	7389	2148
Ratepoint Inc	7372	3060
Ratheon Solipsys	7372	922
Rathje Enterprises Inc	1731	190
Ratigan Motor Center Inc	5511	699
Ratio Architects Inc	8712	225
Ratner Cos	7231	1
Rattikin Title Co	6361	25
Rattlesnake Mountain Brewing Co	5813	9
Rauch Inc	8331	120
Rauch Milliken International Inc	7322	162
Rauch Weaver Norfleet Kurtz and Co	6531	443
Rausch Brothers Trucking of Ionia	4212	69
Rauxa Direct LLC	7331	16
Ravago Manufacturing Americas LLC	3087	8

Company Name	SIC	Rank
Rave Computer Association Inc	5046	62
Rave Inc	7389	1494
Rave Wireless Inc	4899	84
Raven Electric Inc	1731	1002
Raven Electronics Corp	3661	205
Raven Industries Inc	3672	11
Raven Maps and Images	2741	462
Raven Printing Inc	2752	1675
Raven Rock Workwear Inc	2326	21
Raven Software Corp	7372	1678
Raven Transport Company Inc	4213	346
Ravenna Pattern and Manufacturing Inc	3543	23
Ravenswood Studio Inc	3999	31
Ravenswood Winery Inc	2084	25
Raving Brands Inc	6794	48
Raw Bandwidth Communications Inc	7372	4741
Raw Skate Parks Inc	7641	1
Rawcar Group LLC	3069	66
Rawhide Inc	8361	68
Rawhide Trucking Inc	4213	2170
Rawle and Henderson LLP	8111	323
Rawle-Murdy Associates Inc	7311	257
Rawlings Manufacturing Inc	3553	63
Rawlings Sporting Goods Company Inc	3949	40
Rawls and Winstead Inc	4813	562
Rawson and Company Inc	5065	29
Raxco Software Inc	7372	2385
Raxon Fabrics Corp	2262	1
Ray Anderson Company Inc	5031	257
Ray Bellew and Sons Inc	4213	1775
Ray Brothers and Noble Canning Company Inc	2033	103
Ray Cammack Shows Inc	7999	80
Ray Electric Co	1731	1113
Ray Envelope Company Inc	2677	23
Ray Flaig	7331	173
Ray Fogg Building Methods Inc	1542	115
Ray Group Inc	8712	242
Ray Jones Trucking Inc	4213	638
Ray L Hellwig Plumbing and Heating Inc	1711	94
Ray Lee Equipment	5083	205
Ray Machine Inc	3599	584
Ray Moses Co	7379	1671
Ray Moving and Storage Inc	4213	1643
Ray Ontko and Co	7372	4470
Ray S Pantel Inc	1731	309
Ray Sauers Associates Inc	7371	1731
Ray Schumann and Associates Inc	2796	58
Ray Skillman Auto Center	5511	672
Ray Sorrell Travel Co	4724	131
Ray Walker Trucking Company Inc	4213	1566
Ray White Lumber Company Inc	2421	102
Raybar Inc	3599	1702
Rayben Enterprises Inc	7349	16
Raybestos Powertrain LLC	5013	405
Ray-Block Stationery Company Inc	5943	22
Rayburn Country Electric Cooperative Inc	4911	388
Rayburn Electric Company Inc	1731	1187
Raycap Inc	3643	59
Raycar Tool and Machine Co	3566	37
Ray-Carroll County Grain Growers Inc	4221	3
Rayco Burial Products Inc	3444	241
Rayco Electronic ManufacturingInc	3677	43
Rayco Inc	3677	16
Rayco Industries Inc	3553	36
Rayco International	5045	423
Rayco Supply Inc	5734	377
Raycom Electronics Inc	3699	122
Raycom Media Inc	4833	60
Raycom Sports	7922	10
Raycon Technology Inc	3678	77
Raydar and Associates Inc	8711	354
Raydar Incorporated Of Ohio	3069	253
Raydon Exploration Inc	1382	28
Raydot Systems LLC	3564	118
Rayken Inc	7389	2219
Rayle Electric Membership Corp	4911	313
Rayloc	3714	191
Raymar Information Technology	5065	550
Raymarine Inc	3429	32
Raymath Co	3541	77
Raymond and Lae Engineering Inc	3599	2188
Raymond Building Supply Corp	5211	81
Raymond Corcoran Trucking Inc	4213	1353
Raymond Corp (Greene New York)	3537	13
Raymond Engineering Operations	3643	45
Raymond James and Associates Inc	6211	27
Raymond James Financial Inc	6719	33
Raymond James Financial Services	6211	401
Raymond James Trust Company West	6091	16
Raymond Oil Co	5171	84
Raymond Oil Company Inc	1311	221
Raymond Software Inc	2741	421
Raymond Vineyard and Cellar Inc	0172	15
Raymour and Flanigan Furniture Co	5712	17
Raymow Construction Company Inc	1623	422
Rayner Associates Inc	6282	660
Rayogram	7336	132
Rayonier Distribution Corp	2823	2
Rayonier Inc	2823	1
Raypress Corp	2754	20

Company Name	SIC	Rank
Ray's Brand Products Inc	2032	49
Ray's Electric Inc	1731	1510
Ray's Ice Cream Company Inc	2024	73
Ray's Transportation Inc	4213	2828
Ray's Wholesale Meats Inc	5147	59
RaySat Inc	4899	40
Rayside Truck and Trailer Inc	5531	38
Raytech Corp	3499	7
Raytek Corp	3823	157
Raytex Fabrics Inc	5131	19
Raytheon Aircraft Co	3721	13
Raytheon Aircraft Holdings Inc	6719	46
Raytheon Co	3812	3
Raytheon Electronic Systems	3812	20
Raytheon Technical Services Company LLC	8741	15
Raytown-Lee's Summit Community Credit Union	6062	73
Rayven Inc	3081	128
Rayvern Lighting Supply Company Inc	5063	350
Raywen Enterprises Inc	5072	151
Rayzist Photomask Inc	3955	12
Razorback Bumper Service Inc	5013	300
Raztech Lighting LLC	5063	949
Razvi Inc	7374	210
Razzi Corp	3089	1029
RB and W Manufacturing LLC	3547	1
Rb Balch And Associates Inc	7379	1549
Rb Design Inc	3672	358
RB Everett and Co	5082	108
RB Howell Co	5092	15
RB Humphreys Inc	4213	1671
RB Iii Associates Inc	2329	20
R-B Industries Inc	5072	148
Rb Machine Works Inc	3599	800
RB Management Inc	3714	54
RB Manufacturing Inc	3672	481
RB Matheson Trucking Inc	5013	17
RB Pamplin Corp	2221	4
Rb Publishing Inc	2721	408
RB Recycling Inc	3069	16
R-B Rubber Products Inc	3069	100
RB Watkins Inc	3825	272
RB Zack and Associates Inc	7371	1291
RBA Consulting	8748	136
RBB Architects Inc	8712	236
RBB Corp	3646	46
Rbb Systems Inc	3625	110
RBC Bank	6712	30
RBC Bearings Inc	3562	8
RBC Capital Markets	6211	209
RBC Dain Rauscher Inc	8742	12
RBC Enterprise S Fund	6722	230
RBC Exploration Co	1311	165
RBC Inc	7379	320
Rbc Industries Inc	2821	101
RBC Life Sciences Inc	5199	45
RBC Small Cap Core S	6722	254
RBC Ventures Inc	6799	321
Rbe Electronics Inc	3822	85
RBF Consulting	8711	172
RBI Corp	5013	77
Rbi Manufacturing Inc	3545	187
RBJ Inc	2051	221
RBKTool and Die	3544	711
Rbm Conveyor Systems Inc	3556	104
RBM LLP	8721	441
Rbm Services Inc	7349	312
R-Bo Company Inc	3469	304
Rbo Printlogistix Inc	5112	32
Rbp Chemical Technology Inc	2899	152
RBR Meat Company Inc	2011	90
RBR Trucking Inc	4213	2505
Rbs Fab Inc	3599	2375
Rbs Family Corp	5051	474
RBS Global Inc	3568	2
RBS Lynk	7374	35
Rbt Services Inc	3535	113
RBX Inc	4213	608
RC and Jt Inc	7373	753
RC Bigelow Inc	2099	96
RC Electronics Inc	3829	337
RC Electronics International Inc	5734	107
RC Fine Foods Inc	2099	178
Rc Industries Inc	2033	117
RC Merchant and Company Inc	5065	675
Rc Microsystems Inc	4813	736
RC Moore Inc	4213	903
RC Productions Inc	7311	810
RC Smith Co	2541	4
RC Systems Inc	3577	616
RC Tronics Inc	3672	392
RC Willey Home Furnishings	5712	12
RC2 Corp	5092	2
RCA Home Theater Showcase Inc	5731	41
RCA Rubber Co	3069	21
RCBS Operations	3559	119
Rcc Inc	4812	106
Rcd Components Inc	3676	2
RCD Trucking Inc	4213	2506
Rcf Technologies Inc	5085	439
RCG Information Technology Inc	7379	32
RCG Technology Systems of North Carolina Inc	1731	1055

Company Name	SIC	Rank
Rch Associates Inc	3559	463
Rcm and Associates	5065	574
RCM Design Inc	2337	11
RCM Industries Inc (Franklin Park Illinois)	3363	12
RCM Technologies Inc	7363	60
RCMS Group LLC	7379	390
RCN Corp	4813	30
Rco Sales Inc	5065	632
Rco Systems Inc	7373	936
R-Cold Inc	3585	130
R-Computer	7373	719
Rcp Block and Brick Inc	3271	8
RCR Wireless News	2741	264
RCV Industries	5162	72
RD Blue Construction Inc	1623	552
RD Dane Corp	3599	2517
RD Offutt Co	5148	1
RD Olson Construction LP	1542	111
RD Rubber Technology Corp	3061	47
RDA Container Corp	2653	112
Rda Corp	3594	29
RDA Inc	7373	672
RDA International LLC	7336	22
RDD Enterprises Inc	5099	92
Rdf Corp	3822	40
RDI Group	3569	48
RDI Trading Inc	5094	27
Rdk Corp	5149	163
Rdl Group Inc	7379	1272
Rdm Electric Company Inc	1731	1229
Rdm Industrial Electronics Inc	3699	139
Rdm Technologies Inc	5963	28
Rdn Manufacturing Company Inc	3559	265
RDO Agriculture Equipment Co	5083	3
RDO Equipment Co	5083	5
RDO Equipment Co Minnesota Construction Equipment Div	5082	89
RDO Truck Center Co	5012	42
RDR Inc (Portland Oregon)	7372	4549
Rds Manufacturing Inc	3599	308
Rds Manufacturing Inc	3443	138
Rdss and Company LLC	7359	61
Rdw Group Inc	7311	93
RE Adams	4213	2277
RE Barber Ford Inc (Holland Michigan)	5511	573
RE Barber Ford Inc (Ventura California)	5511	817
Re Community Holdings Ii Inc	4953	37
RE Garrison Trucking	4213	307
RE Lee and Son Inc	1542	207
RE Lee Electric Company Inc	1731	1133
RE Mason Company Of The Carolinas	5085	358
Re Max Elite Properties Inc	8742	522
Re/Max International Inc	6531	48
Re/Max North Realtors	6531	235
RE May Inc	2796	69
RE Michel Company Inc	5074	15
RE Newcomb Electric Inc	1731	1269
RE Purcell Construction Co	1542	65
RE Services LLC	5962	8
RE Systems Group Inc	7372	2754
RE Uptegraff Manufacturing Co	3612	81
RE West Inc	4213	1080
RE Yates Electric Inc	1731	595
re2g	1711	193
REA Energy Cooperative Inc	4911	462
Reach Media Inc	4832	100
Reach Publishing Systems Inc	2721	348
Reach Sports Marketing Group Inc	7319	141
Reach Technology Inc	3577	447
ReachLocal Inc	7311	60
Reactel Inc	3679	454
Reaction Design Inc	7371	400
Reaction Technology Inc	3674	378
Reactive NanoTechnologies Inc	8731	14
Reactive Resin Products Co	3565	113
Reactive Systems Inc	7372	3283
Read and Stevens Inc	1311	182
Read Technologies Inc	5045	699
Readco Inc	5084	779
Readco Kurimoto LLC	3549	92
Reade Advanced Materials	3399	14
Reade Manufacturing Co	2819	91
Reader's Digest Association Inc	2721	8
Reading Anthracite Coal Co	1231	1
Reading Body Works Inc	3713	23
Reading Crane and Engineering Co	5084	123
Reading Eagle Co	2711	229
Reading Federal Credit Union	6061	156
Reading International Inc	6513	15
Reading Pretzel Systems	3556	53
Reading School District	8211	48
readMedia	7375	270
ReadSoft North America	7372	813
Readwood Inc	3553	52
Ready Electric Company Inc	1731	264
Ready Industries Inc	2752	1673
Ready Metal Manufacturing Co	2542	22
Ready Mix Concrete Company of Knoxville	3272	18
Ready Mixed Concrete Co	3273	51
Ready Molds Inc	3544	339
Ready Pac Produce Inc	2099	9

Company Name	SIC	Rank
Ready Trucking Inc	4213	1009
ReadyCom Inc	3661	219
Ready-Mix Concrete Co (Rochester Minnesota)	3273	39
ReadyServe Computer Center	7374	361
Ready-to-Run Software Inc	7372	4359
Real Capital Solutions	6512	26
Real D Scientifics	7372	1217
Real Estate Data X-Change Inc	5045	570
Real Estate Image Inc	5961	154
Real Estate Magazines Ltd	2721	462
Real Estate Mart of Tennessee Inc	6531	165
Real Estate One Inc	6531	9
Real Estate Video Educational Institute Inc	7372	4962
Real Good Food Store Inc	5411	268
Real Goods Solar Inc	5961	92
Real Intent Inc	3674	234
Real Kosher Sausage Company Inc	2013	250
Real Mechanical Inc	1711	205
Real Mex Foods Inc	5141	97
Real Mex Restaurants Inc	5812	96
Real Pro-Jections Inc	7372	4870
Real Property Management LLC	6531	437
REAL Seal Company Inc	3053	99
Real Soft Inc	7379	237
REAL Software Systems LLC	7372	1774
Real Time Computer Services Inc	7372	4630
Real Time Consultants Inc	5045	326
Real Time Data	7372	3015
Real Time Enterprises Inc	7373	479
Real Vision Software Inc	7371	1159
Real World Enterprises Inc	2752	1297
Realage Inc	5734	62
Realco Recycling Company Inc	4953	119
RealD Inc	7819	7
RealData Inc	7372	4550
RealFoundations Inc	7379	181
Reality Digital Inc	5734	223
Reality Publishing Co	8999	203
Reality Systems LLC	7374	180
Realitybuy Inc	4813	351
RealLegal	7372	1679
Realm Technologies Corp	3577	619
Really Innovations LLC	3559	120
Really Strategies Inc	7379	661
Realm Communications Group Inc	5065	334
Realmed Corp	7374	112
RealNet Equities LLC	6531	439
RealNetworks Inc	7371	34
RealPage Inc	7372	197
Realtech Inc	7379	802
Real-Time Data Management Services Inc	3578	14
Realtime Enterprise Networks Communications LLC	1731	2404
Real-Time Innovations Inc	7372	305
Real-Time Laboratories LLC	3823	200
Realtime Software Corp	7373	645
Realtime Solutions Group LLC	7371	1793
Realtimepublisherscom Inc	7375	169
Realtimetraderscom	2711	683
Realtrac	7372	3944
Realty and Relocation Services of GA	7323	38
Realty Asset Advisors LLC	6531	247
Realty Computer Solutions Inc	7375	239
Realty Executives International Inc	6794	39
Realty Finance Corp	6798	115
Realty Income Corp	6798	58
Realty Investment Company Ltd	6552	222
Realty One Group Inc	6531	304
Realty Trac Inc	6531	252
RealtyU Group	8299	50
Ream Printing Company Inc	2759	417
Reamco Inc	3533	64
Reams Computer Corp	7372	2475
Ream's Food Stores	5411	97
Reardon Machine Company Inc	3599	1362
Rears Manufacturing Co	3523	86
Reason Computer Inc	3571	96
Reasoning LLC	7372	1779
Reavis Respiratory and Medical Equipment	5047	268
Reaxion Corp	7372	1430
Reb Steel Equipment Corp	5046	83
Reba Software and Services Inc	7371	1172
Rebar Engineering Inc	1791	8
Re-Bath LLC	3088	21
Rebb Industries Inc	3599	977
Rebco Inc	3399	30
Rebecca's Commissary Inc	5812	113
Rebel Electric Heating and Air Conditioning Inc	1731	2047
Rebel Lumber Company Inc	2421	56
Rebel Oil Company Inc	5171	24
Reber Corp	4213	1328
Reber Machine and Tool Company Inc	3544	373
Rebman Properties Inc	6531	364
Reborn Cabinets	2434	64
Rebsco Inc	3535	174
Rebuilders Enterprises Inc	3714	429
Rebus Inc	2731	254
Rebus Inc (Aston Pennsylvania)	2816	10
Rec Advanced Silicon Materials LLC	3339	6

Company Name	SIC	Rank
Rec Protective Systems Inc	5063	1004
REC Solar Inc	8999	63
Rec World Advertising	7311	762
Recall Systems Inc	3695	169
Receivable Management Inc	7322	147
Receivables Control Corp	7322	95
Receivables Incorporated Corporate	7322	70
Receivables Outsourcing Inc	7322	42
Receivables Recovery	7322	194
ReCellular Inc	5049	22
Reciprocal Inc	7371	429
Recital Corporation Inc	7372	3737
Reckart Equipment Co	5082	149
Reckitt Benckiser LLC	2842	9
Reckitt Benckiser Pharmaceutical Inc	2834	80
Reclamation Technologies Inc	2869	88
Recoating-West Inc	3444	201
Recognition Research Inc	7372	2343
Recognition Systems Inc	5043	5
Recology	4953	14
Recom Group Inc	7319	135
Recom Technologies Inc	7374	169
Recommind Inc	7371	380
Re-Con Co	1731	674
Recon/Optical Inc	3861	9
Reconditioned Systems Inc	2522	38
Reconserve of Colorado	2047	7
ReConserve of Illinois	2047	3
Reconserve of Maryland	2047	8
Reconserve of Texas	2047	9
ReCor Corp	7372	2431
Record A Phone Corp	5065	266
Record Herald	2711	354
Record Plant Inc	7389	1426
Record Play Tek Inc	3651	145
Record Press Inc	6022	828
Record Products Of America Inc	5084	855
Record Publishing Company Inc	2711	520
Record Searchlight Co	2711	100
Record Technology Inc	3652	41
Recorder Publishing Co	2711	309
Recordex Manufacturing Inc	3651	193
Recording Workshop	7389	630
Record-Journal Real Estate Co	2711	288
Recordpressingcom	3695	53
Recore Electrical Contractors Inc	1731	445
Recortec Inc	3571	168
Recover Care	7352	12
Recover Inc	4213	2801
Recovered Capital Corp	7389	1777
Recovery Direct Inc	5065	726
Recreational Enterprises Inc	7011	122
Recreational Equipment Inc	5941	7
Recreational Marketing Inc	7389	1734
Recreational Vehicle Products Inc	3585	107
Recruitment Group	7361	42
Recto Molded Products Inc	3089	893
Rector Motor Car Co	5511	590
Rector Phillips Morse Inc	1521	58
Rector-Duncan and Associates	7311	460
Rectorseal Corp	2891	29
Recursion Software Inc	7372	860
Recycle to Conserve Inc	2047	4
Recycle to Conserve TX Inc	2047	5
RecycleBank LLC	4953	49
Recycled Baseball Items	7389	1617
Recycled Micro Inc	5734	467
Recycled Systems Furniture Inc	5712	98
Recycled Wood Products	5199	57
Recycling Center Inc	5093	111
Recycling Works Inc	5093	251
Red Alert Group Inc	7381	89
Red And Black Publishing Company Inc	2711	734
Red Apple Group Inc	2911	22
Red Arrow Products Company LLC	2087	14
Red Ball Oxygen Company Inc	5084	196
Red Bend Software Inc	5045	420
Red Bird Farms Distribution Co	5147	52
Red Book Credit Services	2789	105
Red Bricks Media	7311	684
Red Canoe Credit Union	6062	63
Red Canyon Software Inc	7371	1405
Red Castle Bakeries	2011	53
Red Deer Ventures Inc	7379	1607
Red Devil Inc	2891	30
Red Diamond Capital Inc	6799	157
Red Dragon Imports Inc	5021	147
Red Eagle Enterprises Inc	2099	214
Red Earth Software Inc	7372	2300
Red Ewald Inc	3089	326
Red Gold Inc	2033	9
Red Hat Inc	7372	66
Red Hawk Industries	7382	3
Red Holman Pontiac Co	5511	1254
Red House Records Inc	3652	51
Red Jacket Pumps	3561	12
Red Lake County Cooperative Inc	5191	122
Red Line Research Laboratories Inc	3691	48
Red Lion Group A Cintas Co	7382	62
Red Lion Hotels Corp	7011	108
Red Lion Television Inc	4833	213
Red Lobster Div	5812	19
Red McCombs Automotive Center Inc	5511	540
Red Mile Inc	7948	37
Red Moon Marketing LLC	7311	439
Red Peacock International Inc	5063	258
Red Rib Inc	3089	1247
Red River Implement Company Inc	5083	130
Red River Motor Co	5511	376
Red River Rural Telephone Association	4813	328
Red River Shipping Corp	4412	30
Red River Valley Cooperative Power Association	4911	575
Red River Valley Rural Electric Association	4911	329
Red Robin Gourmet Burgers Inc	5812	64
Red Rock Computer	5734	491
Red Rock Distributing Co	5172	67
Red Rock Gravel LLC	5032	178
Red Roof Inns Inc	7011	74
Red Rose Mailing Services Inc	7331	226
Red Rover Trading Company LLC	7389	2039
Red Sail Sports Inc	4725	40
Red Sea Shipping Co	4731	87
Red Seal Electric Co	3644	25
Red Spot Paint and Varnish Company Inc	2851	28
Red Spot Westland Inc	2851	68
RED Stamp Inc	3565	83
Red Star Fertilizer Co	2873	15
Red Star Oil Co	2911	50
Red Star Restaurant Equipment Inc	5046	241
Red Stick Armature Works Inc	7694	22
Red Streak Corp	5072	28
Red Studio Design	7374	417
Red Top Rentals Inc	7699	108
Red Truck Films	7313	38
Red Valve Company Inc	3491	13
Red Ventures LLC	8742	116
Red Wing Publishing Co	2711	272
Red Wing Software Inc	7372	2569
Red7e Inc	7311	373
REDA Pumping Systems	3561	118
RedBack Networks Inc	7389	181
Redbank Transport Inc	4213	432
Redbarn Pet Products Inc	2047	39
Redbuilt LLC	2439	9
Redburn Tire	5014	5
Redcats USA Inc	5961	30
Redco Audio Inc	3496	119
Redco Communications Inc	5731	189
Redco Foods Inc	2099	103
Redco Machine Shop Inc	3599	932
Redcom Laboratories Inc	8731	106
Reddaway Manufacturing Company Inc	3069	276
Redden Electrical Contractors Inc	1731	2360
Reddick Equipment Company Inc	3523	220
Reddico Construction Company Inc	1623	149
Redding Bancorp	6712	612
Redding Bank of Commerce	6022	403
Redding City Electric Utility	1623	496
Redding Lumber Transport	4213	967
Redding Machine Shop Inc	3599	2306
Redding Printing Company Inc	2752	1098
Redding-Hunter Inc	3484	24
Reddog Industries Inc	3544	128
Reddwerks Corp	7372	915
Reddy Construction Company Inc	1623	694
Reddy Ice Corp	2097	3
Reddy Ice Holdings Inc	2097	2
Rede	8742	501
Redemtech Inc	7379	273
Redfern Integrated Optics Inc	3827	137
Redfield and Company Inc	2752	522
Redgwick Construction Co	1611	62
Redhead Cos	7311	719
Redi Controls Inc	3585	218
Redi-Direct Marketing Inc	6719	55
Redi-Floors Inc	5023	83
Redi-Gro Corp	5191	130
Rediker Software Inc	7372	2049
Redington Counters Inc	3825	141
Redington Inc (Westport Connecticut)	8743	241
Redi-Tag Corp	3089	1668
Redix International Inc	7371	1556
Red-Kap Sales Inc	5172	77
Redken Laboratories Inc	2844	33
Redland Brick Inc	3251	3
Redlands Centennial Bank	6022	363
Redlee Inc	7349	52
Redline Services LLC	4813	340
Redlon and Johnson Inc	5074	20
Redman Communications Inc	7311	991
Redman Energy Corp	1311	222
Redman Homes Inc	2451	14
Redman Industries Inc	2451	3
RedMax Komatsu Zenoah America Inc	5084	291
Redmond Bcms Inc	2752	491
Redmond Cable Corp	3679	577
Redmond Minerals Inc	2899	62
Redmond Technology Partners LLC	7371	790
Redner's Markets Inc	5411	106
Redoc Inc	7372	3945
Redondo's LLC	2013	170
Redpeg Marketing	7311	481
Redpepper LLC	7311	1011
Redpoint Bio Corp	8731	384
RedPrairie Holding Inc	7372	136
Redseal Systems Inc	7372	2688
Redsis Corp	5045	931
Redsky Technologies Inc	5045	241
Redstar Inc	7372	4133
Redstar Yeast and Products	2099	205
Redstick Internet Services LLC	4813	731
Redstone Aerospace Corp	3663	316
RedVision Systems Inc	7379	168
Redw Technologies LLC	8721	306
Redwold Inc	3577	290
Redwood Bank	6022	510
Redwood Capital Bank	6022	494
Redwood County Telephone Co	4813	757
Redwood Empire Inc	5031	59
Redwood Empire Public Television Inc	4833	248
Redwood Empire Stereocasters	4832	160
Redwood Health Services	7371	1064
Redwood Instrument Co	3829	34
Redwood Software Inc	7371	527
Redwood Trust Inc	6798	49
Redwoods A Community Of Seniors	8361	58
RedyRef Division-Dawnex Industries Inc	3444	259
Redzone Robotics Inc	8711	460
Reebok International Ltd	3149	2
Reece and Nichols	6531	7
Reece Electric Inc	1731	1702
Reece Oil Co	5171	73
Reece Supply Company Of Dallas	5085	131
Reed And Barton Corp	3914	5
Reed and Perrine Inc	2873	22
Reed and Thomas Electrical Contractors Inc	1731	724
Reed and Witting Co	2752	802
Reed Business Information	2721	13
Reed Construction Data	2721	53
Reed Electric Company Inc	1731	2369
Reed Elsevier Inc	2721	4
Reed Exhibition Cos	7389	306
Reed Group Ltd	8099	58
Reed Instrument Company Inc	3599	1495
Reed International	3532	56
Reed Lallier Chevrolet Inc	5511	404
Reed Manufacturing and Services	3571	158
Reed Motors Inc	5511	957
Reed Oven Co	3556	141
Reed Presentations Inc	2782	39
Reed Print Inc	2711	460
Reed Smith LLP	8111	187
Reed Tool and Die Inc	3545	316
Reed Trucking Co	4213	2226
Reed Union Corp	2842	79
Reed Westlake Leskosky Ltd	8712	100
Reeder Chevrolet Co	5511	868
Reeder Distributors Inc	5171	21
Reeder Management Inc	6531	96
Reedex Inc	3679	437
Reed-Hann Litho Co	2752	601
Reedholm Instruments Co	3679	552
Reedman Toll Auto World	5511	68
Reed-Rite Inc	2759	396
Reed's Cleaning Service Inc	7349	266
Reed's Dairy Inc	2026	81
Reed's Fuel and Trucking	4213	1709
Reed's Inc	2086	77
Reeds Jewelers Inc	5944	15
Reed's Precision Machine Inc	3599	1078
Reedy Industries Inc	1711	27
Reedy International Corp	5099	52
Reedy Manufacturing and Repair Service Inc	7699	216
Reef Industries Inc	3081	53
Reef Tool and Gage Co	3544	835
Reel Grobman and Associates	7389	901
Reel Picture LLC	3695	16
Reel Security Corp	7381	257
Reel-Core Inc	3089	1431
Reelcraft Industries Inc	3499	47
Reell Precision Manufacturing Corp	3462	32
ReelPlaycom Inc	7379	473
Reelworks Animation Studio Inc	7812	287
Rees Companies Inc	1796	19
Rees Electric Company Inc	3621	160
Rees Inc	3625	242
Rees Scientific Corp	3822	45
Rees Trucking Company Inc	4213	1603
Reese Enterprises Inc	3089	391
Reese Kitchens Inc	5031	262
Reese Lower Patrick and Scott Ltd	8712	143
Reese Pharmaceutical Co	5122	122
Reese Trucking Co	4212	63
Reesman's Excavating and Grading Inc	1623	118
Rees-Memphis Inc	3535	131
Reeve Cattle Co	0211	12
Reeve Store Equipment Co	2542	32
Reeve Trucking Co	4213	368
Reeves Brothers Trucking Inc	4213	1218
Reeves Business Forms	2741	472
Reeves Coinc	3089	1616
Reeves Exploration and Technologies	8999	111
Reeves Extruded Products Inc	3082	10
Reeves Import Motorcars Inc	5511	136

Company Name	SIC	Rank
Reeves Plastics LLC	3089	1482
Reeves-Wiedeman Co	5074	106
REFAC Optical Group	7389	1799
RefCheck Information Services Inc	7375	219
Ref-Chem Construction Corp	8711	138
Ref-Chem LP (Odessa Texas)	1629	39
Reference Systems Inc	7373	521
Refinishing Material Specialties Inc	5013	400
Reflect Scientific Inc	4822	18
Reflection Sound Productions Inc	7389	1825
Reflector Publishing/Printing	2711	646
Re-Flek Corp	3648	16
Reflexis Systems Inc	5045	41
Reflexite Corp	3081	17
Refly Of Miami Inc	3572	91
Reform LLC	7991	24
Refraction Technology Inc	3829	72
Refractory Maintenance Corp	1711	247
Refractory Specialties Inc	3297	11
Refreshments Inc	5962	15
Refrigerated Delivery Service	4213	636
Refrigerated Food Express Inc	4213	1885
Refrigerated Transport Inc	4213	1670
Refrigeration and Electric Supply Co	5078	13
Refrigeration Engineered Systems Inc	3585	235
Refrigeration Research Inc	3433	55
Refrigeration Sales Corp	5075	19
Refrigeration Specialties Inc	5046	304
Refrigeration Supplies Distributor	5078	4
Refrigeration Supply Inc	5031	123
Refrigiwear Inc	2329	17
Refri-Parts Inc	5075	53
Refron Inc	5989	4
REG Inc	3579	57
Regal Art Press Inc	2752	1840
Regal Business Machines Inc	7629	41
Regal Chemical Co	2879	41
Regal Cinemas Corp	7832	5
Regal Cutting Tools Inc	3545	26
Regal Electronics Inc	3679	210
Regal Employment Inc	7361	413
Regal Entertainment Group	7832	2
Regal Finishing Co	3089	1373
Regal Ford Inc	5511	871
Regal Health Foods International Inc	2068	26
Regal Home Collections Inc	5023	22
Regal Kitchens LLC	2434	32
Regal Machine and Engineering Inc	3599	1971
Regal Marine Industries Inc	3732	17
Regal Mold and Die	3544	387
Regal Office Services Inc	7349	404
Regal Originals Inc	2395	16
Regal Plastic Supply Co	5162	27
Regal Plastic Supply Co	5162	10
Regal Press Inc	2759	125
Regal Printing Co	2752	718
Regal Research And Manufacturing Company LLC	3679	167
Regal Ware Inc	3469	9
Regal-Beloit Corp	3621	6
Regal-Beloit Corp Durst Div	3568	28
Regal-Beloit Flight Services Inc	3545	6
Reganis Auto Center Inc	5511	931
Regberg and Associates Inc	7311	983
Regence Group	6324	14
Regency Affiliates Inc	3714	433
Regency Cap and Gown Co	2389	27
Regency Centers Corp	6798	62
Regency Cosmetics Inc	2844	92
Regency Credit LLC	7322	149
Regency Elevator Products Corp	3534	28
Regency Energy Partners LP	1311	31
Regency Finance Co	6163	30
Regency House Pictures And Frames Inc	5199	122
Regency Investment Advisors Inc	6282	636
Regency Janitorial Service	7349	165
Regency Plastics - Ubly Inc	3089	372
Regency Realty Corp	6798	158
Regency Telecommunications Corp	5999	270
Regency Transportation Inc	4213	1373
Regency Travel and International Market	4724	100
Regency Typographic Services Inc	2741	459
Regency-Superior Ltd	7389	768
Regeneration Press Inc	2741	323
Regeneron Pharmaceuticals Inc	2834	69
Regenex Corp	3089	831
Regent Aerospace Corp	1799	25
Regent Broadcasting of El Paso Inc	7313	5
Regent Broadcasting of Evansville/ Owensboro Inc	7313	6
Regent Broadcasting of Flint Inc	7313	7
Regent Broadcasting of Ft Collins Inc	7313	9
Regent Broadcasting of Grand Rapids Inc	4832	32
Regent Broadcasting of Lexington Inc	7313	12
Regent Broadcasting Of Utica/Rome Inc	4832	81
Regent Care Center Of Laredo LP	8741	256
Regent Circle LLC	6513	36
Regent Education Inc	7372	2432
Regent Pacific Management Corp	8741	220
Regent Sports Corp	5091	25
Reggio's Pizza Inc	5812	401
Regin HVAC Products Inc	3829	436
Regina Behar Enterprises	2321	13
Reginas Bay Bakery	2051	162
Region Broadcasting Of El Paso	4832	120
Region Oil	5172	95
Regional Adjustment Bureau Inc	7322	38
Regional Associates Inc	4213	2469
Regional Automotive Warehouse Corp	5013	251
Regional Communications Inc	4813	371
Regional Data Services Inc	7371	1523
Regional Economic Models Inc	7371	1092
Regional Educational Technology Network	4833	258
Regional Emergency Dispatch Center	3669	269
Regional Enterprises Inc	4213	1525
Regional Integrated Logistics	4213	1480
Regional International Corp	5013	58
Regional Medical Center Of Orange-burg and Calhoun Counties	8062	88
Regional Medical Rental and Sales	5047	144
Regional Technology Strategies Inc	7379	736
Regional West Medical Center	8062	134
Regions Bank Marion	6022	530
Regions Bank Nashville Tn	6021	100
Regions Bank (New Orleans Louisiana)	6712	549
Regions Financial Corp	6712	12
Regions Interstate Billing Services Inc	7322	34
Regis Belt Maintenance Inc	1796	13
Regis Corp	7231	2
Regis Delta Tools Inc	3546	44
Regis Milk Company Inc	2026	76
Regis Technologies Inc	3826	71
Register Company Inc	2711	24
Register Graphics Inc	2752	1372
Register Lakota Printing Inc	2754	49
Register Lithographers Ltd	2752	953
Register Publishing Co	2711	741
Register Tapes Unlimited Inc	7311	238
RegisterCom Inc	7389	233
Registration Control Systems Inc	7389	1173
RegNow Digital River Inc	7373	636
RegScan Inc	7372	349
Regulus Integrated Solutions LLC	2752	51
RehabCare Group Inc	8069	6
Rehabilitation Associates Ltd	8322	204
Rehabilitation Opportunities Inc	8331	161
Rehagen Jack Municipal Swimming Pool	5091	116
Rehau Inc	3089	170
Reheis Inc	2899	63
Rehkemper Invention and Design Inc	7389	2010
REI Adventures	4724	58
REI Systems Inc	7373	268
Reich Tool and Design Inc	3544	356
Reichard Buick Inc	5511	655
Reichard Software Corp	7372	4742
Reichel Foods Inc	2011	44
Reichert Chevrolet and Buick Sales Inc	5511	1062
Reichhold Inc	8731	21
Reichman Crosby Hays Inc	5085	119
Reichs Ford Trailer Rentals LLC	4213	3115
Reico Distributors Inc	5031	21
Reico Technology	3829	488
Reid and Clark Screen Arts Co	2262	6
Reid Products Inc	3599	797
Reid Supply Co	5085	86
Reid-Ashman Manufacturing Inc	3825	92
Reidco Inc	2099	347
Reidler Decal Corp	2752	608
Reid-O'donahue and Associates	7311	953
Reif Carbide Tool Company Inc	3545	406
Reifer Consultants Inc	7379	1209
Reiff and Nestor Co	3545	131
Reil and Associates Inc	5064	93
Reil Rock Products Inc	3089	1760
Reilly Construction Company Inc	1611	106
Reilly Dairy and Food Co	5143	24
Reilly Foam Corp	3069	89
Reilly Penner and Benton LLP	8721	167
Reilly Worldwide Inc	2431	79
Reiman Corp	1541	55
Reimann and Georger Corp	3536	30
Reimbursement Concepts LLC	7363	192
Rein Nomm and Associates Inc	7389	2382
Reinauer Petroleum Co	5172	152
Reinberger Printwerks	2752	381
Reinco Inc	3531	223
Reindl Printing Inc	2752	385
Reines RV Center Inc	5561	12
Reinforced Structures For Electronics Inc	2821	181
Reinhart Boerner Van Deuren SC	8111	207
Reinhart Institutional Foods Inc	5141	38
Reinhart Institutional Foods Inc Milwaukee Div	5141	69
Reinhausen Manufacturing Inc	3643	19
Reinhold Ice Cream Co	2024	39
Reinhold Industries Inc	3728	62
Reinke Manufacturing Company Inc	3711	52
Reinsurance Group of America Inc	6321	4
Reis Environmental Inc	5099	13
Reis Inc (New York New York)	7389	463
Reis Services LLC	7375	68
Reis Trucking Inc	4213	1073
Reisen Lumber and Millwork Co	5031	283
Reiser Group	7389	767
Reiss Industries LLC	3089	405
Reisterstown Lumber Co	5211	150
Reitech Corp	3625	297
Reiter Dairy LLC	2026	23
Rekcut Photographic Inc	7384	13
REL Communication Inc	4813	443
Rel Corp	3949	134
Rel Inc	1731	2336
Related Companies LP	6513	1
Related Components Inc	5063	851
Relational Architects International Inc	7372	2833
Relational Funding Corp	7377	3
Relational Security Corp	7372	3078
Relativity Inc	7371	1790
Relativity Technologies Inc	7372	768
Relavis Corp	7372	2377
Relay House Inc	4899	129
Relay Service Co	3625	326
Relay Specialties Inc	5065	78
Relco LLC	3556	12
Relevant Automation Corp	7379	1574
Relevant Business Systems Inc	7372	2353
Relevante Inc	8999	106
Relex Software Corp	7372	4263
Reliability Center Inc	7372	2859
Reliability Inc	3825	362
Reliable Automatic Sprinkler Company Inc	3569	24
Reliable Business Concerns Inc	1731	2262
Reliable Cable Co	3661	171
Reliable Caps LLC	3089	1253
Reliable Chevrolet Inc (Springfield Missouri)	5511	205
Reliable Cleaning Service Inc	7349	181
Reliable Communications Inc	3577	574
Reliable Contracting Company Inc	1611	86
Reliable Copy Service Inc	7334	9
Reliable Elections Systems Inc	7374	181
Reliable Electronics Of Mt Vernon Inc	3577	486
Reliable Envelope and Graphics Inc	2759	301
Reliable Environmental Transport Inc	5093	171
Reliable Fire Equipment Co	5063	107
Reliable Health Systems Inc	7372	3551
Reliable Life Insurance Co (Monroe Louisiana)	6311	269
Reliable Life Insurance Company of Missouri	6311	165
Reliable Liquid Transport	4213	1744
Reliable Manufacturing Company Inc	3724	60
Reliable Manufacturing Inc	3599	2265
Reliable Of Milwaukee	2253	11
Reliable Plastic Seals Inc	3089	1691
Reliable Plating and Polishing Company Inc	3471	110
Reliable Production Service Inc	1389	31
Reliable Products Inc	3053	132
Reliable Review Services	7361	194
Reliable Runners Courier Service Inc	7389	1603
Reliable Sites LLC	7379	1484
Reliable Tank Line LLC	4213	1294
Reliable Tool and Die Inc	3599	1382
Reliable Tool and Machine Company Inc	3714	346
Reliable Trailer Systems Inc	5012	163
Reliable Transportation Specialists	4213	400
Reliable Trucking Inc	4213	623
Reliable Voice and Data Systems Inc	1731	1854
Reliable Water Services LLC	3624	33
Reliable Welding and Machine Work Inc	3559	338
Reliable Wholesale Lumber Inc	5031	67
ReliableRemodelercom Inc	8999	135
Reliance Connects	4813	301
Reliance Controls Corp	3613	68
Reliance Electric Inc	1731	1759
Reliance Fire Protection Inc	7389	2294
Reliance Gear Corp	3566	29
Reliance Inc	6162	142
Reliance Industries Inc	3599	1075
Reliance It Inc	7379	1121
Reliance Machine Company Inc	3599	1640
Reliance Machine Products Inc	3674	307
Reliance Medical Products Inc	3841	183
Reliance Sheet and Strip CoInc	5051	465
Reliance Standard Life Insurance Co	6311	97
Reliance Steel and Aluminum Co	5051	2
Reliance Steel Co	5051	113
Reliance Technical Services Inc	3672	310
Reliance Tool and Engineering LLC	3544	836
Reliance Tool and Manufacturing	3544	123
Reliance Trailer Manufacturing Inc	3715	27
Reliance Upholstery Supply Company	2392	29
Reliant Enterprise LLC	7379	840
Reliant Inventory Services Inc	7389	1077
Reliant Molding Inc	3089	1363
Reliant Recovery Services Inc	7322	157
Reliant Worldwide Plastics LLC	2821	79
Relief Enterprise Inc	7361	175
Relief Nursing Services Inc	7361	349
Relios Inc	3911	26
Reliv' International Inc	5122	45

Company Name	SIC	Rank
Reliv' World Corp	5149	12
Relli Technology Inc	5072	42
RELM Wireless Corp	3669	86
Relocation Center	7389	2410
Relocation Systems LLP	4213	2305
Rel-Tech Electronics Inc	3679	266
Rel-Tek Corp	3829	415
Relton Corp	2899	154
Relume Corp	3669	303
Relume Technologies Inc	3674	293
Rem Products Inc	3429	150
REM Sales Inc	5084	162
Remac Information Corp	7389	2133
Remanage Inc	7371	1071
Remarque Manufacturing Corp	3599	1992
Rembert Company Inc	5046	254
Rembrandt Commercial Cleaning Inc	7349	262
Remcal Products Corp	3812	188
Remco Inc	3679	808
Remco Industries International Inc	3556	82
Remco Software Inc	7371	901
Remcon Plastics Inc	3089	656
Remcon-North Corp	3679	415
Remcor Technical Industries Inc	3812	171
Remcraft Lighting Products Inc	3645	79
ReMed Recovery Care Centers	8069	11
Remedi Senior Care	8082	52
REMedia Inc	7372	4986
Remedios Siembieda Inc	7389	1865
Remedy Intelligent Staffing	7363	31
Remedy Roofing Inc	5033	24
RemedyMD Inc	7372	2170
Remel Sims Inc	4213	1463
Remelt Sources Inc	5051	245
Remer Inc	7311	968
Reminder Media Inc	2711	249
Reminger and Reminger Company LPA	8111	378
Remington and Vernick Engineers	8711	410
Remington Arms Company LLC	3484	8
Remington Employers Corp	8741	193
Remington Group Inc	8748	71
Remington Industries Inc	5013	175
Remington Products Company LLC	3634	11
Remington Steel Inc	5051	282
Remington Support Services Inc	7389	1934
Remit Corp	7322	204
Remitdata Inc	7372	2695
Remitstream Solution LLC	6153	44
Remke Industries Inc	3643	72
Remke Markets Inc	5411	193
Remlinger Manufacturing Company Inc	3523	133
Remlitho Inc	2752	1416
Remmele Engineering Inc	3599	45
Remote Connections Inc	5063	837
Remote Control Systems Inc	8711	639
Remote Medical International	8099	84
Remote Ocean Systems Inc	3648	30
Remote Processing Corp	3674	491
Remotescan Corp	7372	4123
Removable Media Solutions Inc	3572	94
Rempac LLC	3086	27
Rempco Inc	3542	98
Remtec Engineering	3569	156
Remtec Inc	3671	17
Rem-Tech Inc	3599	1279
REMTECH Inc	3829	305
Remtron Inc	3625	129
Rem-Tronics Inc	3679	394
Remy Cointreau USA Inc	5182	11
Remy International Inc	3694	2
REMY Investors and Consultants Inc	6282	511
Ren Potterfield Trucking Inc	4213	2451
REN Testing Corp	7373	646
Rena Systems Inc	3577	421
Rena Ware Int'l	5963	14
Renae Telecom LLC	3663	167
Renaissance At South Shore	8742	279
Renaissance Capital Alliance	7359	72
Renaissance Capital Group Inc	6282	454
Renaissance Capital LLC	6282	171
Renaissance Chicago Downtown Hotel	7011	141
Renaissance Corporate Services	7372	338
Renaissance Creative Services Inc	7311	945
Renaissance Electronics Corp	3679	346
Renaissance Financial Corp	7389	1063
Renaissance French Doors and Sash Inc	2431	105
Renaissance House International	8743	234
Renaissance Investment Management	6282	138
Renaissance Learning Inc	7372	347
Renaissance Medical Management Co	8741	151
Renaissance Restaurant Group LLC	2099	320
Renaissance Services Inc	7379	1408
Renaissance Woodworking Company Inc	1542	135
Renasant Bank	6022	477
Renasant Corp	6712	123
Renault Winery Inc	5812	435
Renco Group Inc	3711	10
Renco Machine Company Inc	3599	246
Ren-Cris Litho Inc	2752	1623
Rendas Tool and Die Inc	3599	1982
Rendercore Inc	7379	1591

Company Name	SIC	Rank
Rendigs Fry Kiely and Dennis LLP	8111	436
Rendition Networks	4813	484
Rene Bates Auctioneers Inc	7389	921
Rene Swiss Corp	5084	930
Renee Sacks Associates Inc	8743	163
Renegade Publishing Inc	2721	430
Renesan Software	7372	2476
Renet Financial Corp	6162	140
Renew Life Formulas Inc	2834	279
Renew Resources Inc	3069	135
Renew Valve and Machine Company Inc	7699	130
Renewable Corp	8731	431
Renewable Energy Group Inc	2999	3
Renewaire LLC	3564	59
Renewal Unlimited Inc	8331	104
RenewData Corp	7389	408
Renfro Corp	5949	3
Renfro Foods Inc	2035	50
Renfrow and Company Inc	2761	61
Renfrow Brothers Inc	1541	250
Renier Construction Corp	1542	171
Renishaw Inc	5084	208
Renite Co- Lubrication Engineers	2992	68
Renkim Corp	7374	149
Renkus-Heinz Inc	3651	48
RENN Global Entrepreneurs Fund Inc	6726	89
Rennco Automation Systems Inc	3569	184
Rennen International	2396	13
Renner Architects LLC	8712	332
Renner Trucking	4213	620
Rennhack Marketing Services Inc	8748	198
Rennoc Corp	2389	1
Reno Agriculture and Electronics	3812	115
Reno Forklift Inc	5084	441
Reno Information Services	7375	262
Reno Machine Company Inc	3599	444
Renold Inc	3568	37
Renova Lighting Systems Inc	3646	90
Renovator's Supply Inc	3429	73
Renquist Associates Inc	8748	423
RENS Metal Detectors	3829	162
Rensen House Of Lights Inc	5722	18
Rent A Mom Inc	3635	12
Rent A Tech Inc	1623	462
Rent and Rave Inc	7359	237
Rent Rite Equipment Co	7359	238
Rent-A-Bit Inc	7377	16
Rent-A-Center Inc	7359	1
Rental Car Finance Corp	6159	36
Rental Management Inc	7372	1907
Rental World Of Osceola County Inc	7359	258
Rentalscom Inc	6531	359
Rent-A-Wreck of America Inc	6794	141
Rentbitscom	7375	214
Rentech Boiler Services Inc	3443	112
Rentech Development Corp	2851	37
Rentech Inc	2851	18
Rentech Services Corp	2851	38
Rentenbach Constructors Inc	1542	211
Rentgrow Inc	7379	873
Renton School District 403	8211	19
Rentrak Corp	7822	10
RentRight Inc	7372	2261
Rents and Sales	5021	167
Reny and Company Inc	3089	1610
Renz America Company Inc	3555	74
Renze Display Co	2759	308
Reo Allegiance Inc	7389	635
Reo Hydraulic and Manufacturing Inc	5084	822
Reo Plastics Inc	3089	444
Reol Services LLC	7374	311
Reorganized School District No 4 Of Jackson County Mo	8211	22
Rep Associates Inc	3053	141
REP Profit Management System	7372	2696
Repair Industries Of Michigan Inc	3412	8
Repair Processes Inc	5084	950
Repair Technology Inc	7699	236
Repco Printers and Lithographers Inc	2752	624
Repco Replacement Parts Inc	3822	91
Repcolite Paints Inc	2851	102
Repcor	3571	157
Repete Corp	3625	186
Replacement Parts Industries Inc	3843	67
Replacements Ltd	5961	81
Replas Of Texas Inc	2821	175
Replex Mirror Co	2821	166
Replica Technology	7372	4743
Replication Unlimited LLC	3089	1514
Repligen Corp	2836	29
Replogle Enterprises	2421	85
Replogle Globes Inc	3999	81
Reply! Inc	7375	91
Reporter	2711	383
Reporter Company Inc	2752	1166
Reporter Publishing Company Inc	2711	705
Reportmill Software Inc	7372	4871
Reprint! Inc	2752	1848
Reprise Media Inc	7375	166
Repro Acquisition Company LLC	2752	854
Reproducta Company Inc	2678	16
Reproductions Inc	7334	20
Reproductive Genetics In Vitro Inc	8011	103

Company Name	SIC	Rank
Repro-Graphics Inc	2752	400
Reprographics One Inc	5099	18
Reprographics Specialists Inc	7334	79
ReproMax Inc	7373	1120
Repros Therapeutics Inc	2836	101
ReproSource Inc	8731	149
Repsco Inc	3083	51
Repssouth Inc	5046	317
Reptel Inc	4813	590
Reptron Electronics Inc	5065	17
Reptron Manufacturing Services	3672	16
Republic Airways Holdings Inc	4512	15
Republic Bancorp Inc (Louisville Kentucky)	6712	134
Republic Bancorp (Oak Brook Illinois)	6712	473
Republic Bank and Trust Co	6022	681
Republic Bank and Trust Co (Louisville Kentucky)	6022	127
Republic Capital Trust	6022	711
Republic Companies Group Inc	6331	195
Republic Data Products Inc	4899	237
Republic Die and Tool Co	3544	306
Republic Drill/Apt Corp	3541	37
Republic Electric Co	5063	145
Republic Engineered Products Inc	3312	26
Republic Enterprise Systems	7349	436
Republic Express Inc	4213	2359
Republic Financial Corp	6722	138
Republic Financial Services	6022	785
Republic First Bancorp Inc	6712	347
Republic Foil-Garmco USA	3353	12
Republic Ford Lincoln Inc	5511	467
Republic Indemnity Company of America	6331	161
Republic Industries Inc	2434	16
Republic Mills Inc	2048	140
Republic Mortgage Home Loans LLC	6162	47
Republic National Distributing Co	5182	2
Republic National Distributing Co (Louisville Kentucky)	5182	9
Republic Newspapers Inc	2711	795
Republic Packaging Corp	3089	49
Republic Paperboard Co	2631	13
Republic Plastics LP	3081	86
Republic Powdered Metals Inc	2952	17
Republic Properties Corp	6552	228
Republic Roller Corp	3069	230
Republic Services Inc	4953	1
Republic State Mortgage Co	6162	133
Republic Textile Equipment Company Of South Carolina Inc	5084	839
Republic Tobacco LP	5194	20
Republic Underwriters Insurance Co	6331	91
Republic Valve Service Inc	7699	229
Republic Waste Services	4213	1959
Republican Co	2711	171
Republic-Lagun Machine Tool Co	3599	226
Request Foods Inc	2038	33
ReQuest Inc (Ballston Spa New York)	3651	97
Require LLC	7371	1157
Requirement Experts	7372	2886
Res Exhibit Services LLC	7389	1062
Rescar Inc	4789	8
Res-Care Inc	8361	1
Res-Care Inc Persons with Disabilities Div	8361	3
Resco Products Inc	3255	10
ResCom Mortgage Corp	7372	2336
Rescot Systems Group Inc	7371	236
Research and Advanced Methods Industries Inc	3089	1424
Research and Diagnostic Systems Inc	3841	57
Research Applications Inc	3823	359
Research Associates Inc (New York New York)	8748	342
Research Automation Inc	3549	73
Research Corporation Technologies Inc	2869	55
Research Data Design Inc	8732	8
Research Design Resources Inc	7372	1017
Research Dimensions Inc	8732	98
Research Electronics International LLC	3699	157
Research Electro-Optics Inc	3827	36
Research Enhanced Design	7374	350
Research Frontiers Inc	8731	404
Research Inc	3599	741
Research International USA Inc	8732	15
Research Network Inc	8732	122
Research on Demand Inc	7375	282
Research Organics Inc	2899	51
ReSearch Pharmaceutical Services Inc	8731	127
Research Planning Inc	8733	33
Research Products International Corp	5047	192
Research Seeds Inc	5191	64
Research Service and Engineering	5063	1084
Research Software Consulting Group Inc	7372	3364
Research Software Design	7372	5125
Research Technologies Inc	3821	77
Research Technologies International Div	8731	361
Research Technology International Co	3861	74
Research Triangle Software	7372	1717
Reser's Fine Foods Inc	2099	23
Reservation Center Inc	7374	97

Company Name	SIC	Rank
Reservation Connection Inc	8742	404
Reservation Telephone Coop	4813	299
Reserve Group	6719	185
Reserve Industries Corp	1446	11
Reserve Petroleum Co	1382	56
Reserve Silica Corp	1446	4
Reserve Supply of Central New York Inc	5033	63
Reserve Warehouse Corp	5031	327
Reserves Network Inc	8741	168
Residential Care Services Inc	8399	22
Residential Cleaning Co	7349	514
Residential Computing	4813	395
Residential Control Systems Inc	3822	76
Residential Development Group Inc	6552	238
Residential Electric Inc	1731	1276
Residential Plaza At Blue Lagoon Inc	6513	43
Residential Properties Management Inc	6531	262
Residential Systems Inc	5731	105
Residual Technologies LP	4953	28
Resilience Corp	3571	62
Resillo Press Pad Co	3582	14
Resilux America LLC	3085	15
Resin Systems Corp	3089	994
Resin Systems Inc	3084	42
Resinall Corp	2851	21
Resinart Corp	3089	1245
Resistance Technology Inc	3672	29
Resistance Welding Solutions Inc	3548	62
ResMed Inc	3841	17
Res-Net Microwave Inc	3679	379
Resnick Supermarket Equipment Corp	5046	76
ReSoft International LLC	7372	4744
Resolute Energy Corp	1311	90
Resolute Forest Products Augusta Newsprint Co	2621	32
Resolute Solutions Corp	7371	162
Resolute Systems Inc	7389	23
Resolution Consulting	7372	3103
Resolution Inc	7812	19
Resolution Technology Inc	7373	1170
Resolutions Multimedia Group Inc	2741	308
Resonance Inc	3651	148
Resonance Technologies Inc	3678	48
Resonate Inc	7372	1822
Resort at Squaw Creek	7011	160
Resort at the Mountain	7011	201
Resort Data Processing Inc	7372	3474
Resort Golf Group LLC	7999	127
Resort Television Cable Company Inc	4841	40
ResortQuest International Inc	7011	98
Resotech Inc	3679	878
Resource America Inc	6799	111
Resource Assistance Inc	8742	510
Resource Capital Corp	6798	105
Resource Capital Trust I	6035	179
Resource Data Inc	7374	413
Resource Data Management	3577	643
Resource Data Services Inc	5045	793
Resource Design	7389	2235
Resource Electronics LLC	5065	924
Resource International Inc	7371	535
Resource International Publishing Inc	7371	1606
Resource Investments Advisory Inc	6282	455
Resource Management Systems Inc	8742	600
Resource Management Systems Inc	7363	360
Resource One Computer Systems Inc	5734	19
Resource One Inc	5169	84
Resource One Inc (Commerce Georgia)	7372	3302
Resource One International LLC	7389	1298
Resource Optimization Inc	7372	4119
Resource Options Inc (Needham Massachusetts)	7361	142
ReSource Pro LLC	8748	159
Resource Production Co	3533	74
Resource Properties Inc	6531	423
Resource Recovery Corp	4213	1323
Resource Services Inc	6282	408
Resource Technology Corp	3829	330
Resource Transportation of America	4213	993
Resource Ventures Ltd	8742	323
Resources Connection Inc	7389	76
Resources For Child Caring Inc	8322	111
Resources For You Inc	7361	374
Resourcesoft Inc	7371	526
RESPEC	8748	62
Respect Your Universe Inc	2389	42
Respironics Inc	3842	12
Respironics - New Jersey	3829	181
Respitek Inc	5047	63
Respond 2-U Inc	7372	4103
Respond2 Inc	7311	156
Response Advertising and Marketing Corp	7311	807
Response Electric Inc	1731	1868
Response Genetics Inc	3841	129
Response Media Products Inc	7331	40
Response Technology Inc	7372	4551
Responsive Information Management Systems and Service Inc	5065	513
Responsive Software	7372	5066
Responsive Solutions Inc	7373	884
Responsive Systems Co	7372	3738

Company Name	SIC	Rank
Responsive Trucking Inc	4213	1747
Responsys Inc	7372	389
RES-Q Healthcare Systems Inc	7372	2171
Resqsoft Inc	7379	1008
Restaurant Associates Corp	5812	67
Restaurant Data Concepts Inc	5045	587
Restaurant Equipment Marketing Co	5046	232
Restaurant Equipment Paradise Inc	5046	172
Restaurant Partners Inc	8742	556
Restaurant Services Inc	7389	987
Restaurant Technology Inc	7372	2538
Restaurant Warehouse Inc	5087	100
Restaurantcom Inc	7389	1387
Restaurants Unlimited Inc	5812	218
ResTech Inc	1389	62
Restek Corp	3821	6
ReStockItcom	5999	90
Reston Hospital Center LLC	8062	38
Restoration Hardware Inc	5712	5
Restoration Preservation Conservation	5199	118
Restoration Resources Inc	7349	449
Restorative Care Of America Inc	3842	154
Restore Inc	2911	49
Restore Therapy Services Ltd	8361	16
Results Marketing Communications LLC	7311	1007
Results Technologies Inc	7389	285
Results Technology	5045	135
Resultz Staffing LLC	7379	1268
Resumes On-Line Inc	7361	199
Resurgence Financial LLC	6282	490
Resys Inc	3589	261
Retail Anywhere	7372	2860
Retail Concepts Inc	5941	13
Retail Design Group Inc	7389	2487
Retail Design Services LLC	5046	194
Retail Information Systems	7371	1267
Retail Navigator	7379	1385
Retail Reporting Corp	2721	407
Retail Service Company Inc	5046	305
Retail Solutions Inc	7379	329
Retail Technologies Corp	7371	1072
Retail Technology Group Inc	7378	27
Retail Ventures Inc	5331	10
Retama Entertainment Group Inc	7948	31
Retco Tool Company Inc	3545	191
Retcomp Inc	3672	464
Retech Systems LLC	3567	23
Retek Retail Systems	7372	158
Retherford Holdings Inc	2711	336
Rethink Group Inc	7311	746
Retif Oil and Fuel Inc	5172	79
Retina Systems Inc	3827	123
Retirement Living Tv LLC	4833	197
Retirement Plan Company LLC	7372	1935
Retirement Planning Associates Inc	6411	273
Retirement System Consultants Inc	6411	218
Retlaw Industries Inc	3089	1117
Retlif Testing Laboratories	8734	127
Retractable Technologies Inc	3841	91
Retrieval Systems Corp	7371	1382
Retrieval-Masters Creditors Bureau Inc	7322	31
Retrievex Holdings Corp	8741	171
Retro Lightng and Cnsv LC	3648	69
Retro-Fit Technologies Inc	5045	462
Retrotech Inc	1541	266
Retterbush Injection Molded Fiberglass Corp	3089	1299
Rettew Associates Inc	8711	78
Rettig Machine Shop Inc	7692	47
Return Path Inc	7379	274
Returnable Services Inc	4213	1534
Retzlaff Inc	3625	400
Reub Williams and Sons Inc	2711	556
Reube's Plastics Company Inc	3089	1623
Reuel Inc	3264	15
Reuland Electric Co	3621	59
Reulet Electric Supplies Inc	5063	257
Reunion Industries Inc	3089	154
Reunited Inc	7389	1465
Reuseitcom	8999	160
Reuser Inc	2421	135
Reuter Recycling of Florida Inc	4953	78
Reuters America LLC	7383	2
Reuters Information Technology LLC	7372	954
Reuters Loan Pricing Corp	7375	106
Reuther Engineering	3599	2117
Reuther Mold and Manufacturing Company Inc	3544	164
Reva Systems Corp	3663	109
REVAC Inc	6531	303
Revak Turbomachinery Services	3511	11
Rev-A-Shelf Company LLC	3429	27
REVCO Technologies Inc	3826	21
Revcor Inc	3564	30
Reve Medical Tourism LLC	4724	145
Revel Companies Inc	6531	121
Revel Consulting Inc	8742	309
Revel Technology Inc	3669	320
Revelar Corp	7372	4745
Revelation Design Inc	7371	1890
Revelation Industries Inc	3679	593
Revelation Software	7372	2689
Revelation Technologies Inc	7372	2292

Company Name	SIC	Rank
Revelex Corp	7373	435
Revell Communications	8743	133
Revels Tractor Company Inc	5261	12
Revelwood Inc	7372	2001
Revent Inc	3556	65
Revention Inc	7371	1008
Revenue Enhancement Group	7389	515
Revenue Group	7322	196
Revenue Markets Inc	5084	519
Revenue Production Management Inc	8742	260
Reveo Inc	3699	77
Revere Control Systems Inc	3625	60
Revere Data LLC	7389	1571
Revere Electric Supply Co	5063	24
Revere Electric Supply Co (Rockford Illinois)	5063	167
Revere Graphics Inc	7374	206
Revere Group Ltd	7379	126
Revere Inc	7372	1769
Revere Independent	2711	868
Revere Industries LLC	3497	5
Revere Mills Inc	5023	50
Revering Group Inc	4813	494
Review	2711	623
Reviva Inc	5013	106
Reviva Labs Inc	5122	101
Revlon Holdings LLC	2844	7
Revlon Inc	2844	9
Revolabs Inc	3651	109
Revolution Tea LLC	2099	239
Revonah Pretzel LLC	5145	34
Revonate Manufacturing LLC	3571	117
Revonet Inc	5045	120
Rew Material Inc	5031	60
Rewald Electric Company Inc	1731	716
Rewards Network Inc	7389	223
Rewardsnow Inc	7389	1567
Rex American Resources Corp	5731	10
Rex Auto Parts	5013	147
Rex Chemical Corp	5087	72
Rex Cut Products Inc	3291	16
Rex Energy Corp	1389	28
Rex Fine Foods	6794	151
Rex Heat Treat	3398	11
Rex Lumber Co	2421	15
Rex Moore Electrical Contractors and Engineers	1731	50
Rex Nichols Architect International PA	8712	328
Rex Oil Company Inc (Thomasville North Carolina)	5172	71
Rex Pipe and Supply Co	5074	117
Rex Plastics Inc	3089	1543
Rex Production Services Inc	7819	75
Rex Realty Co	3452	71
Rex Sales Company Inc	5013	331
Rex Supply Co	5084	71
Rex Systems Inc	3812	123
Rex Three Inc	2796	6
Rexall Sundown Inc	5122	23
Rexam Closures and Containers	3089	201
Rexam Inc	3081	80
Rexarc International Inc	3498	73
Rexcon Inc	3613	135
Rexcon LLC	3531	112
Rexel Inc (Dallas Texas)	5065	12
Rexel Norcal Valley	5063	370
Rexford - Albany Municipal Supply Company Inc	5074	127
Rexford Rand Corp	2842	148
Rexhall Industries Inc	3716	12
Rex-Hide Inc	3061	2
Rexnord Holdings Inc	3714	23
Rexnord Industries Inc	3562	27
Rexnord Technical Services	8742	226
REYcomp Inc	3577	415
Reyes Holdings LLC	5149	1
Reyes Industries Inc	2394	8
Reyhan Pgf	3861	75
Reymond Products International Inc	3599	1884
Reyna Capital Corp	6159	87
Reynard Corp	3827	102
Reynen and Bardis Development LLC	1531	43
Reynolds American Inc	2111	4
Reynolds and Company Inc	3599	2070
Reynolds and Reynolds Co	7373	12
Reynolds Bone and Griesbeck PLC	8721	372
Reynolds Brothers Ltd	7334	57
Reynolds Communications Inc	4832	232
Reynolds Co	2891	45
Reynolds Cycling LLC	3498	39
Reynolds Dewalt Corp	8742	507
Reynolds Electric Inc	1731	2288
Reynolds Inc (Orleans Indiana)	1623	17
Reynolds Machine Company Inc	3599	822
Reynolds Nationwide	4213	540
Reynolds Polymer Technology	2821	97
Reynolds Road Ira	8361	180
Reynolds Smith and Hills Inc	8711	110
Reynolds Tech Fabricators Inc	3559	268
Reynolds Transport Co	4959	16
Reynolds Trucking Company Inc	4213	1142
Reynolds Vehicle Registration Inc	7373	10
Rezex Corp	2269	13
RF Applications Inc	5731	264

Company Name	SIC	Rank
RF Chamberland Inc	4213	766
RF Code Inc	7372	1570
Rf Communications	4812	85
RF Connectors	3678	29
Rf Ideas Inc	3699	121
RF Industries Ltd	3678	22
RF Kimball Company Inc	5065	865
RF Micro Devices Inc	3674	37
RF Monolithics Inc	3663	75
RF Products Inc	3663	179
RF Suering Company Inc	5084	902
Rf Tec Manufacturing Inc	3678	78
RF Technologies Inc	3845	64
Rfb Electric Inc	1731	2352
Rfe Ri Inc	4832	150
RFF Electronics	7372	4872
RFI Communications and Security Systems	7382	12
Rfid Inc	3825	280
RFIP Inc	7379	645
Rfps Management Company Ii LP	1389	23
RFX Inc	7372	2203
Rg Acquisitions Inc	2752	1152
RG Barry Corp	3142	1
RG Egan Equipment Inc	5084	912
RG Group Inc	5085	34
RG Hanson Company Inc	3599	2410
RG Hawkes Trucking Inc	4213	3085
RG Research Inc	8711	648
RG Shakour Inc	5122	92
Rg Technology	5045	920
RG Transport Inc	4213	952
RGA Reinsurance Co	6311	35
RGB Display Corp	3575	45
Rgb Networks Inc	3669	106
RGB Productions Inc	3565	165
RGB Spectrum	3577	323
RGB Technology Inc	7373	859
RGC Resources Inc	4923	23
RGF Environmental Group	3564	49
Rggd Inc	5099	21
Rgi Publications Inc	2741	381
RGIS Inventory Specialists	7389	1
Rgm Constructors Of Texas LLC	1542	388
Rgm Industries Inc	4911	583
RGP Orthopedic Appliance Inc	5999	295
RGR Inc	2048	114
RGS Communications Inc	5065	935
RGS Energy Group Inc	4931	32
R-G-T Plastics Co	3089	1372
RH Barringer Distributing Company Inc	5181	43
RH Bauman and Company Inc	2087	84
RH Blake Inc	7311	615
RH Boelk Truck Lines Inc	4213	2655
RH Enterprises	5045	889
RH Hoover Inc	1542	451
RH Keenan Co	0172	24
RH Kuhn Co	5712	46
RH Murphy Company Inc	3089	1888
RH Positive Computer Systems	7372	3629
RH Power and Associates Inc	7311	787
RH Products Company Inc	2891	123
RH Rosenfield and Company Inc	2752	1521
RH Sheppard Company Inc	3321	15
RH Tinney Inc	1711	282
Rha Community Services Of Utah	8361	125
Rhamdec Inc	2522	54
Rhba Acquisitions LLC	3569	139
Rhc Holdings LP	6719	99
Rhe Hatco Inc	2353	1
Rheaco Inc	3599	552
Rheaume's House Of Lettering Inc	2759	476
Rheem Manufacturing Co	3585	15
Rhein Tech Laboratories Inc	8734	203
Rhetech Inc	3559	99
Rhg Group Inc	8742	441
Rhi Monofrax Ltd	3297	6
Rhi Refractories Holding Co	3297	3
Rhiel Supply Company Inc	5087	105
Rhimco Industries Inc	3643	143
Rhina International Direct Inc	7311	952
Rhinehart Development Corp	3523	232
Rhinestahl Corp	3544	327
Rhino Building Services Inc	7349	190
Rhino Energy LLC	1222	7
Rhino Equipment Corp	5046	217
Rhino Foods Inc	2024	42
Rhino Inc	3089	709
Rhino Linings USA Inc	3679	205
Rhino Performance Products LLC	2893	42
Rhino Records Inc	7922	16
Rhino Resource Partners LP	1221	15
Rhino Systems Inc	7379	1041
Rhinoceros Times	2711	708
RhinoCorps Limited Co	7372	1498
Rhintek Inc	7372	3016
Rhizome Internet LLC	7379	768
RHK Technology Inc	3826	100
RHM Fluid Power Inc	3593	10
Rhn Splicing Inc	4841	143
Rhoades McKee	8111	409
Rhoads and Sinon	8111	345
RHO-Chem Div	4953	74
Rhoda Lee Inc	2331	13

Company Name	SIC	Rank
Rhode Island Joint Reinsurance Assoc	6331	283
Rhode Island Public Radio	4832	131
Rhode Island Resource Recovery Corp	4953	55
Rhode Island Soft Systems Inc	7372	4966
Rhode Island State Employees Credit Union	6062	21
Rhode Island Telephone Inc	1731	2373
Rhodes Associates Executive Search Inc	7361	71
Rhodes Supply Company Inc	5031	90
Rhodia Inc USA	2899	28
Rhombus Industries Inc	3679	163
RHR International LLP	8742	145
Rhr Technologies Inc	3672	367
Rhs Corp	8741	55
Rhs Enterprises Inc	2752	1649
RHS Inc	3523	153
Rhumbline Advisers Corp	6722	281
Rhycom Advertising Inc	7311	871
Rhythm Engineering	7372	2214
Rhythm NewMedia	7311	331
RI Carbide Tool Co	3545	220
RI Lampus Co	3271	11
Ria Connect Inc	5065	221
Riada Corp	7373	1189
Riata Technologies Inc	7379	538
Riba Foods Inc	2032	21
Riback Supply Company Inc	5074	93
Ribapharm Inc	2834	91
Ribbon Webbing Corp	2241	13
Ribco Manufacturing Inc	3965	22
Ribelin Sales Inc	5162	16
Ribit Productions Inc	2741	396
Ric Electrical Services LLC	1731	2197
Ricart Automotive	5511	114
Ricart Chrysler Plymouth	5511	3
Ricavision International Inc	3571	234
Riccar America Inc	5064	122
Ricci Brothers Sand Company Inc	1442	49
Rice and Brouillard Electric Inc	1731	1792
Rice Belt Warehouse Inc	0723	21
Rice Epicurean Markets	5411	177
Rice Financial Products Co	6799	126
Rice Fruit Co	0175	5
Rice Hall James and Associates	6282	192
Rice Hydro Inc	7389	2434
Rice Integration LLC	3575	35
Rice Nuclear Diagnostics LP	3829	470
Rice Packaging Inc	2657	33
Rice Planters Mill LLC	2044	6
Rice Village Animal Hospital	7389	2285
Riceland Foods Inc	2044	2
Riceland Foods Inc Lecithin Div	2075	8
Ricerca Bioscience LLC	8731	128
Rice's Market Inc	7389	2210
Ricetec Inc	2044	8
Rich Ice Cream Co	2024	27
Rich Media Technologies	7372	4746
Rich Millwork	2431	48
Rich Mount Inc	3714	262
Rich Products Corp	2023	1
Rich Thompson Trucking Inc	4213	601
Richa Inc	7374	258
Richard A Alaimo Associates	8711	395
Richard A Heaps Electrical Contractor Inc	1731	446
Richard B Rudy Inc	4213	1501
Richard Bellerud Trucking	4213	3097
Richard Bertram Inc	7389	501
Richard Bowers and Co	6531	170
Richard Carrier Trucking Inc	4213	442
Richard D Schafer Company Inc	1623	784
Richard Desberg and Associates Inc	7311	445
Richard Diercks Company Inc	2741	249
Richard Dudgeon Inc	3569	262
Richard E Jacobs Group LLC	6552	249
Richard Enterprises Inc	5063	1048
Richard F Kline Inc	1611	133
Richard Fujikura Manufacturing Inc	3599	2460
Richard G Mirarchi	2789	80
Richard Greene Co	5063	245
Richard H Bird and Company Inc	3451	79
Richard Hall	7381	108
Richard Heiman Advertising Inc	7311	720
Richard Henshaw Group	8111	599
Richard I Green Inc	4213	2166
Richard J Cassidy Inc	5015	36
Richard J Curley Inc	1731	1729
Richard J Wolk and Associates	7319	111
Richard Keldsen	5099	77
Richard L Aronson Inc	7363	177
Richard L Hodges Inc	4213	1325
Richard Lewis Communications Inc	7311	938
Richard M Middleton LLC	3672	359
Richard Manufacturing Co	3674	296
Richard Nestor Inc	4213	1522
Richard O'brien Companies Inc	1771	27
Richard Scott Salon and Day SpA	5091	104
Richard W Blatt Pattern Shop Inc	3543	53
Richard Wayne and Roberts	7361	61
Richard Wolf Medical Instruments Corp	5047	73
Richards and Richards	4226	11
Richards and Southern Inc	8742	531
Richards Apex Inc	2992	40

Company Name	SIC	Rank
Richards Arklay S Company Inc	3823	312
Richards Brick Co	5032	50
Richards Brothers Supermarket Inc	5399	14
Richards Cajun Foods Corp	2013	57
Richards Carlberg	7311	134
Richards Community Pool	5091	142
Richards Corp	3861	66
Richards Electric Motor Co	5063	315
Richards Graphic Communications Inc	2752	1356
Richards Group Inc	7311	31
Richards Industries Inc	3491	33
Richards Layton and Finger	8111	271
Richards Lighting Distributors Inc	5063	451
Richards Machine Tool Company Inc	3599	1703
Richards Manufacturing Company Sales Inc	5063	59
Richards Paint Manufacturing Company Inc	2851	78
Richards Products Inc	5122	40
Richard's Publishing Company Inc	2711	850
Richards Sheet Metal Works Inc	3441	136
Richards-Klein Sheet Metal Fabricators Inc	3449	34
Richardson and Edwards Inc	2752	867
Richardson and Partners	5511	47
Richardson Electrical Company Inc	1731	1909
Richardson Electronics Ltd	5065	45
Richardson Enterprises	1521	155
Richardson Industries Inc	7389	1671
Richardson Logic Control Inc	1731	1703
Richardson Manufacturing Co	3599	348
Richardson Munson and Weir	7389	1826
Richardson Place LLC	3599	845
Richardson Printing Corp	2752	1048
Richardson Printing Inc	2759	213
Richardson Researches Inc	8748	444
Richardson Seeds Inc	5191	92
Richardson Technology Systems Inc	5065	163
Richardson Trident Co	5051	213
Richardson Trucking Inc	4213	1788
Richardson Trucking Inc	4213	1891
Richco Janitor Service Inc	7349	97
Richdel Inc	2048	144
Richemont North America Inc	5944	23
Richers Trucking Inc	4213	682
Richey Capacitor Inc	3675	18
Richfield Holdings Inc	7011	23
Richfield Hospitality Services Inc	8741	292
Richies Delivery Inc	4213	2434
Richie's Pharmacy And Medical Supply Inc	5047	104
Richland Gordon and Co	6211	305
Richland Industrial Inc	5049	223
Richland Ltd	3714	394
Richland Market	5411	190
Richland Partners LLC	5171	20
Richland Research Corp	2869	78
Richland Trust Co	6022	353
Richlands Piggly Wiggly	7389	1554
Richloom Fabrics Corp	2391	10
Richmar Controls and Service Company Inc	1731	1293
Rich-Mar Corp	3845	123
Richmark Company Inc	2672	51
Richmond American Homes Inc	1521	6
Richmond American Homes of Colorado Inc	6552	82
Richmond American Homes of Maryland Inc	1521	103
Richmond American Homes of Nevada Inc	6552	206
Richmond Baking Co	2052	30
Richmond Bumper Service Inc	5013	362
Richmond Ceramic Tile Distributors Inc	5032	86
Richmond Commercial Services Inc	7389	1517
Richmond Communications Group Inc	1731	2251
Richmond Farm and Lawn Inc	5083	182
Richmond Industries Inc	3469	257
Richmond Instruments And Systems Inc	3829	379
Richmond Machine Co	3599	1515
Richmond Machinery And Equipment Company Inc	5082	123
Richmond Motor Company Inc	5511	471
Richmond Optical Company Inc	3851	90
Richmond Printing LLC	2752	518
Richmond Security Service Inc	7381	134
Richmond Sprinkler Corp	7382	117
Richmond Supply Co	5085	214
Richmond Yarns Inc	2281	14
Richmor Aviation Inc	4522	25
Richner Communications Inc	2711	325
Richter Productions Inc	7812	158
Richter7	7311	356
Richton Farms	3511	25
Richway Industries Ltd	3523	182
Richwood Meat Co	2011	13
Rick Doyle Action Photography	2741	419
Rick Hendrick Toyota Jeep Eagle	5511	267
Rick Johnson and Company Inc	7311	643
Rick Warner and Associates Inc	7311	659
Rickabaugh Pentecost Development LLC	1623	266
Rickard Circular Folding Co	2789	35

Company Name	SIC	Rank
Rickenbaugh Building Supply Inc	5031	354
Rickenbaugh Cadillac/Volvo	5511	197
Rickly Hydrological Co	3823	265
Rickman Machine Company Inc	3728	209
Rickreall Farms Supply Inc	5083	180
Rick's Cabaret International Inc	5813	1
Rick's Computers Inc	5734	440
Rick's Gate Works Inc	1731	1436
Rick's Quick Printing Inc	2759	428
Ric-Lo Productions Ltd	3648	45
Ric-Man Construction Inc	8741	245
Rico Motor Company Inc	5511	325
Rico Puerto Telephone Company Inc	4813	69
Ricoh Americas Corp	3555	5
RICOH Business Systems Inc	5044	45
Ricoh Electronics Inc	3579	6
Ricoh Printing Solutions	3577	84
Ricom Inc	5065	485
Ricomm Systems Inc	7372	1960
Ricon Colors Inc	3089	1832
Ricon Corp	3534	4
Riconda Data Systems LLC	7371	981
Rico's Pizza Inc	6794	105
RICS Software	7372	3845
Ridco Casting Co	3369	19
Riddell Inc	3949	79
Riddick Engineering Corp	8711	625
Riddio Construction Company Inc	5031	84
Riddle Machine Co	3599	1849
Riddles Group Inc	3873	9
Ride and Show Engineering Co	8711	503
Ride Inc	3999	50
Ride Manufacturing Inc	3949	45
Rider Dickerson Inc	2752	440
RideSafelycom	7319	87
Ridewell Corp	3714	264
Ridex Integral Inc	5065	908
Ridge Associates Inc	3672	175
Ridge Engineering Inc	3812	59
Ridge Recyclers Inc	4953	155
Ridge Tool Co	3545	9
Ridgefield Acquisition Corp	3577	617
Ridgeland Chetek Coop	5191	97
Ridgeleys	7334	102
Ridgestone Financial Services Inc	6712	733
Ridgeview Manufacturing Inc	7389	1976
Ridgeway Electric	1731	2206
Ridgewood Corp	5074	121
Ridgewood Savings Bank	6036	22
Ridg-U-Rak Inc	2542	14
Ridgway Mailing And Fulfilment Company Inc	7331	264
Ridgway Roof Truss Co	2439	45
Ridley's Book Bindery Inc	2789	144
Ridout Lumber Cos	5211	18
Ridout Plastics Co	3081	125
Rieches Baird Advertising	7311	284
Riechmann Transport Inc	4213	942
Rieck's Letter Service Inc	2752	1718
Riedell Shoes Inc	3949	126
Riedon Inc	3676	6
Riegel By-Products Company Inc	2077	6
Riegel Transportation Inc	4213	329
Riegle Press Inc	2752	871
Riegner and Associates Inc	7336	219
Riegseckers Inc	5947	25
Rieke Office Interiors Inc	2521	46
Riekes Equipment Co	5084	27
Riekes International LP	7389	1572
Rieman and Arszman Custom Distributors Inc	5064	97
Riemann Family Funeral Homes	7261	9
Riemer and Braunstein LLP	8111	316
Riemer Reporting Service Inc	7323	36
Ries Graphics Ltd	2752	311
Riesbeck Food Markets Inc	5411	180
Riester Corp	7311	173
Rietech Global LLC	3545	410
Rieter Automotive North America Inc	3714	148
Rietta Flea Market	7389	2149
Rife Hydraulic Engine Manufacturing Co	3561	165
Rifenburg Construction Inc	1611	19
Rigaku Americas Corp	3844	11
Rigaku Innovative Technologies Inc	3827	69
Rig-A-Lite Ltd	5063	283
Rigden Inc	7372	3017
Rigdon Marine LLC	3731	53
Rigel Pharmaceuticals Inc	2834	123
Riggers Inc	4213	2916
Riggins Engineering Inc	3599	762
Riggins Inc	5172	108
Riggs Company Incorporated A	7389	1738
Riggs Counselman Micheals and Downes Inc	6411	93
Riggs Distler and Company Inc	1711	36
Riggs Industries Inc	3441	12
Riggs Supply Corp	5039	12
Riggsbee Hardware Company Inc	5072	158
Right Ascension Inc	5734	74
Right Connection Electronics Inc	5065	393
Right Cooperative Association	5153	76
Right Honda	5012	35
Right Management Consultants Inc	8742	50

Company Name	SIC	Rank
Right Networks LLC	7374	322
Right On Programs	7372	3568
Right Solutions Inc	5734	476
Righter Group Inc	5031	403
Rightline Equipment Inc	3537	73
RightNow Technologies Inc	7372	260
Rights International Group	7389	2531
Rightstar Inc	7373	161
RightStartcom Inc	5945	10
Rightway Fasteners Inc	3965	11
Rigid Products	3423	33
Rigidply Rafters Inc	5031	264
Rigiflex Technology Inc	3672	360
RigNet Inc	4899	52
Rigo International	2329	33
Rigos Sheet Metal	3535	204
Rigsby Hull	7389	1255
Rih Inc	3651	59
Rihm Kenworth	5084	176
RIJ Pharmaceutical Corp	2834	396
Rika Denshi America Inc	3825	143
Riker Danzig Scherer Hyland and Perretti LLP	8111	72
Riker Products Inc	3498	33
Rilea Group Inc	6552	291
Riley CA Electric Construction Corp	1731	2504
Riley Creek Lumber Co	2421	103
Riley Equipment Inc	3535	187
Riley Gear Corp	3462	55
Riley Industrial Services Inc	3563	21
Riley Industries International LLC	7373	947
Riley Power Inc	3569	25
Riley's Ready Pack Inc	7389	1558
Rilo Electric and Communication Construction LLC	1623	710
Rim and Wheel Service Inc	5013	85
Rim Manufacturing LLC	3089	1490
Rima Manufacturing Company Inc	3451	58
Rimage Corp	3577	113
Rimco Plastics Corp	3089	1617
Rimex Metals (USA) Inc	5051	327
Rimm Kaufman Group LLC	8748	348
Rimnetics Inc	3089	1075
Rimpull Corp	3532	22
Rimrock Cadillac GMC	5511	520
Rimrock Corp	3569	103
Rimtec Corp	2821	80
Rina Systems Inc	7371	1373
Rinchem Company Inc	4213	273
Rincon Engineering Corp	3599	1959
Rincon Research Corp	8711	181
Rinda Technologies Inc	7372	3803
Rinderer's Drug Stores Inc	5912	46
Rinehart's Meat Processing Inc	5147	86
Rinehart's Trucking Corp	4213	1886
Rines Market Inc	5411	272
Rinestock Studios LLC	4813	752
Ring and Pinion Service Inc	5013	99
Ring Communications Inc	5065	899
Ring Container Technologies Inc	3085	12
Ring Power Corp	5084	3
Ring Power Lift Trucks	5084	448
RingCentral Inc	7372	4153
Ringdale Inc	3661	85
Ringfeder Corp	3568	22
Ringgold Management Systems Inc	7372	853
Ringler Associates Inc	6411	154
Ringling Brothers and Barnum and Bailey Circus and Combined Shows Inc	7999	41
Rings Battery and Forklift Service Inc	5084	868
Ringside Creative LLC	2741	62
Ringside Inc	3949	67
Ringwood Co	3531	123
Rink Printing Co	2752	529
Rinker Boat Company LLC	3732	34
Rinker Materials Corp	3273	8
Rio Algom Mining LLC	1094	1
Rio Grande Co	5032	25
Rio Grande Plumbing Supply Inc	5074	175
Rio Grande Service Center	4213	2250
Rio Grande Valley Dme	8741	264
Rio Grande Valley Sugar Growers Inc	2061	3
Rio Holdings Inc	4813	80
Rio Hotel and Casino Inc	7011	71
Rio Rico Realty Inc	6531	131
Rio Rico Utilities Inc	4941	67
Rio Tinto Procurement	1021	7
Rio Valley Chili Inc	2034	24
Rio Vista Media	7819	82
Riot Games Inc	7371	734
Rip Off Press Inc	2721	470
Ripley Co	3357	53
Ripley Entertainment Inc	7999	83
Ripley Industries Inc	3492	21
Ripley Precision Inc	3599	649
Ripon Award Jackets Inc	2329	23
Ripon Electric Inc	1731	2464
Ripon Manufacturing Co	3556	161
Ripple Technologies Inc	7372	2433
Ripplewood Holdings LLC	6719	125
Rippy Cadillac Oldsmobile Inc	5511	534
Riptide Software Inc	7371	481
RIS Electrical Contractors Inc	1731	655

Company Name	SIC	Rank
Ris Paper Company Inc	5111	6
Risdall Marketing Group LLC	7311	96
Rise Interactive	7319	120
Risenheart Consulting	5045	1041
Rish Equipment Co	5082	10
RISI Inc	2721	39
Rising Dough Bakery	5149	194
Rising Edge Technologies Inc	3572	79
Rising Medical Solutions Inc	7374	102
Rising Sun Express Inc	4213	1706
Rising Sun Solar Electric LLC	3612	87
Risinger Brothers Transfer Inc	4213	740
Risk Enterprise Management Ltd	6331	54
Risk Management Association	7372	239
Risk Management Services Corp	7389	559
Risk Management Solutions Inc	7372	308
Risk Services Corp	6399	15
Risk Technologies Inc	7379	1280
RiskWatch International	7372	677
RISO Inc	3577	3
Rist Transport Ltd	4213	1045
Ristow Trucking Inc	4213	1922
Risvold's Inc	2099	234
RiT Technologies Inc	7372	4255
Rita Blanca Electric Cooperative Inc	4911	523
RITA Corp	2833	44
Ritchey Produce Company Inc	5148	83
Ritchey's Dairy	5451	4
Ritchie Construction Company Inc	1623	769
Rite Aid Corp	5912	7
Rite Aid Pharmacy Atlanta	5912	57
Rite Engineering Co	3599	818
Rite Mark Stamp Co	3953	21
Rite Stuff Foods Inc	4225	32
Rite Systems Inc	2865	20
Rite Time Pharmaceuticals Inc	5912	69
Rite Way Electric Inc	1731	2151
Rite Way Industries Inc	3545	227
Rite Way Oil and Gas Company Inc	5172	78
RITEC Corp	2759	430
Ritec Inc	3699	277
Ritedose Corp	2834	217
Rite-Hite Company LLC	5084	35
Riten Industries Inc	3545	122
Rite-Style Optical Co	3851	29
Rite-Temperature Associates Inc	5078	28
Riteway Brake Dies Inc	3542	95
Ritrama Inc	2672	25
Ritron Inc	3663	120
Rittal Corp	3469	11
Ritter Disposables Inc	5093	224
Ritter Feeds Inc	4213	1535
Ritter Manufacturing Inc	5084	780
Ritter Technology LLC	5085	55
Ritus Corp	3069	87
Ritz Camera Centers Inc	5946	1
Ritz Carlton Hotel Company LLC	6552	2
Ritz Holman Butala Fine LLP	8721	437
Ritz Interactive Inc	5946	5
Ritz-Craft Corporation of Penna Inc	2451	10
Ritzville Warehouse Co	5153	43
Riva Jewelry Manufacturing Inc	3911	36
Riva Marble and Granite	5032	199
Riva Networks Inc	5065	543
Rival Technologies Inc	3569	303
Rivard's Quality Seeds Inc	5191	156
Rivco Products Inc	3599	2357
Rivendell Media Inc	7313	23
River Bank Laboratories Inc	3841	376
River Bend Sand and Gravel Co	1442	18
River Birch Homes Inc	2451	24
River Capital Inc (Atlanta Georgia)	6799	302
River City Bank	6022	343
River City Bank (Sacramento California)	6712	371
River City Brewery Inc	5813	8
River City Communications Corp	4813	316
River City Communications Inc	5065	852
River City Fire Equipment Company Inc	7389	2046
River City Newspapers LLC	2711	357
River City Petroleum Inc	5172	72
River City Products Inc	3089	1313
River City Publishing	2731	311
River City Security Services Inc	7381	92
River City Software Development Inc	7372	4873
River City Software LLC	7372	5018
River City Sound Productions	7389	2383
River City Steel and Recycling Inc	4953	163
River City Valve Service Inc	7699	219
River Country Coop	5191	72
River Drive LP	6513	9
River Falls Machinery Sales Inc	5082	188
River Hawk Aviation Inc	7359	120
River Hill Coal Company Inc	1221	39
River Mills Outfitters	7389	2040
River Oaks Chrysler Dodge Jeep Ram	5511	807
River Port Truck Stop LLC	8741	241
River Publishers Inc	2711	838
River Recycling Industries Inc	2821	71
River Run Computers Inc	3571	80
River Valley Bancorp	6712	523
River Valley Community Bank	6022	607
River Valley Financial Bank	6035	153

Company Name	SIC	Rank	Company Name	SIC	Rank	Company Name	SIC	Rank
River Valley Machine Inc	3312	125	Rjr Circuits Inc	3672	269	RN Rouse and Company Inc	1542	223
River Valley Manufacturing Inc	3523	145	RJS and Associates	8748	363	Rn Specialties Inc	7363	227
River Valley Plastics Inc	3089	1458	RJS Racing Equipment Inc	2399	26	Rna Corp	2844	68
River Valley Telecommunications Coop	4813	485	RJS Software Systems	7379	1222	Rnb Enterprises Inc	3679	595
River View Solutions Corp	4899	158	RJS Systems International	3577	474	RNC Genter Capital Managment	6282	101
Riverbay Corp	6531	27	RJS Tool and Gage Co	3545	257	RNC Industries Inc	3086	99
Riverbed Technology Inc	3577	26	Rjt Industries Inc	3089	1393	Rnj Electronics Inc	5065	921
Riverbend Express LLC	4213	1485	RJW Manufacturing Inc	3544	698	Rnr Enterprises Inc	7349	124
Riverdale Mills Corp	3496	59	Rk Cable Contractors Partnership Ltd	1623	379	RNS International Inc	5013	277
Riverdale Window And Door Corp	2431	64	RK Electric Inc	1731	191	RO Wetz Transportation Co	4213	2885
Riverdale Ym-Ywha	8351	16	R-K Electronics Inc	3625	292	Roach Brown McCarthy and Gruver	8111	493
Riverfront Times	2711	502	Rk Inc	3559	514	Roach Manufacturing Corp	3535	48
Rivergreen Bank	6022	677	RK Manufacturing Corporation Of Connecticut	3599	319	Road 9 Inc	4813	479
Riverhead Building Supply Corp	5211	46				Road America Inc	2752	1818
Riverhill Publications and Printing Inc	2759	600	RK Miles Inc	5211	164	Road Constructors Inc	1611	25
Riverlake Partners LLC	6799	259	RK Music Production	7812	216	Road Machinery Co	5082	23
Riverland Energy Coop	4911	275	RK Sales Inc	5046	321	Road Runner Holdco LLC	4813	61
RiverLift Trucking	4213	1183	RK Software and Hardware Inc	5045	268	Road Runr Maintenance Inc	7349	339
Rivermine Software Inc	7372	795	RKA Petroleum Companies Inc	5171	10	Road Scholar Transport Inc	4213	846
Riverrun Press	2752	1212	RKC Instrument	3825	316	Road Systems Inc	3715	17
River's Edge Energy Inc	3621	142	Rkf Engineering Solutions LLC	8711	638	Roadhole Utility Systems Inc	1623	733
Rivers Metal Products Inc	3499	87	Rki Inc	3713	31	Roadlink USA	4213	779
Rivers West Apparel Inc	2211	34	Rki Instruments Inc	5084	403	Roadmap Technologies Inc	7372	1508
Riverside Bancshares Inc	6712	680	Rkknb Inc	1731	2111	Roadmaster Transportation Inc	4213	1857
Riverside Clay Company Inc	3255	1	RKO Pictures	2741	150	Roadmasters Transport Co	4213	955
Riverside Community Bank	6029	19	Rkon Inc	7373	594	Roadrunner Dawes Freight Systems Inc	4213	188
Riverside Co	6799	186	RKR Corp	5051	132			
Riverside Electric Inc	1731	1218	RKS Design Inc	7389	1223	Roadrunner Manufacturing Company Inc	3523	272
Riverside Electronics Ltd	3672	28	RKS Electric Corp	1731	1148			
Riverside Engineering	3462	10	RL Bolin	1381	50	Roadrunner Transportation Services Holdings Inc	4731	24
Riverside Foods Inc	2038	50	RL Coolsaet Construction Co	1623	317			
Riverside Furniture Corp	2511	26	RL Deppmann Co	7389	502	Roadrunner-Dawes Transport Inc	4213	84
Riverside Imagesetters	7336	107	RL Drake Co	3663	86	Roadshow Services Inc	4213	2636
Riverside Machine and Automation Inc	3599	835	RL Holdings Inc	3089	789	Roadside Auto and Truck Transport	4213	2581
Riverside Machine Company Inc	3599	922	RL Leek Industries Inc	4213	1835	Roadside Lumber and Hardware Inc	5031	228
Riverside Machine Works Inc	3599	2272	RL Morrissey and Associates Inc	5085	168	Roadtec Inc	3531	19
Riverside Manufacturing Company Inc	2789	19	RL Polk and Co	2741	22	Roadway Express Inc	4213	19
Riverside Paper Corp	2672	14	RL Rider and Co	1611	175	Roanoke Cement Company LLC	3241	13
Riverside Partners LLC	6799	165	RL Russ and Associates Inc	7372	3946	Roanoke Companies Inc	6351	20
Riverside Physician Services Inc	8999	32	RL Schmitt Company Inc	3545	295	Roanoke County Public Schools	8211	41
Riverside Plastics Inc	3089	726	RL Schreiber Inc	2099	151	Roanoke Electric Membership Corp	4911	468
Riverside Publishing	2741	86	RL Turner Corp	1541	108	Roanoke Electric Zupply Inc	5063	908
Riverside Scrap Iron	7389	892	RL Utilities Inc	1623	770	Roanoke Electronic Controls Inc	3625	216
Riverside Scrap Iron and Metal Corp	5093	118	Rlc Electronic Systems Inc	3825	221	Roanoke Gas Co	4924	58
Riverside Spline and Gear Inc	3462	65	RLC Electronics Inc	3679	363	Roanoke Times	2711	163
Riverside Transport Inc	4213	1207	Rlc Holding Company Inc	2951	25	Roar Industries Inc	3444	285
Riverstar Inc	1541	177	RLC Industries Co	2435	1	Roaring Spring Blank Book Co	2678	4
Riverstone Holdings LLC	6211	126	Rlcb Inc	8331	163	Roark Capital Group	6799	120
Riverton Motors Inc	5511	740	Rle Industries LLC	3646	57	Roark Group Inc	2752	515
Rivertree Productions Inc	3651	241	RLE International	8711	255	Rob Geoffroy	3679	868
Riverview Bancorp Inc	6712	351	Rlh Industries Inc	3661	165	Rob S Computer Services	7379	1621
Riverview Community Bank	6035	58	RLI Corp	6331	175	Rob Salamida Company Inc	2035	48
Riverview Health And Rehabilitation Center Inc	8741	216	RLI Insurance Co	6331	198	Robalo Acquisition Company LLC	3732	4
			RLJ Lodging Trust	7011	97	Ro-Banks Tool and Manufacturing Co	3469	248
Riverview Systems Group Inc	7359	113	RLM Industries Inc	3324	19	Robberson Ford Sales Inc	5511	416
Riverway Personnel	7363	277	RLRA Inc	7379	1419	Robbie D Wood Inc	4213	968
RiverWood Bank	6022	724	RLW Inc (Las Vegas Nevada)	5812	280	Robbie Manufacturing Inc	3081	61
Riverwood Home Appliances Inc	5064	73	Rm Business Solutions Inc	5734	441	Robbins and Myers Inc	3561	21
Rivet Software	7372	2020	Rm Educational Software Inc	7372	2011	Robbins Auto Top LLC	7549	19
Riviana Foods Inc	2099	18	RM Electric Inc	8748	381	Robbins Co (Solon Ohio)	3541	35
Riviera Holdings Corp	7011	127	RM Hiner Construction Company Inc	1623	613	Robbins Hardwood Flooring Inc	2426	10
Riviera Operating Corp	7011	115	Rm International Inc	3999	173	Robbins Inc	2426	5
Riviera Ravioli Co	2098	29	RM King Co	3523	54	Robbins Lightning Inc	3643	121
Riviera Tool LLC	3544	143	RM Precision Of Neveda Inc	3451	60	Robbins LLC	3069	91
Rivkin Radler LLP	8111	224	RM Reutlinger Inc	3089	1698	Robbins Lumber Inc	2421	88
Rivkind Associates Inc	2752	1422	RM Shoemaker Co	1541	91	Robbins Manufacturing Company Inc	2491	9
Rizen LLC	5461	30	RM Towill Corp	8742	159	Robbins-Gioia Inc	8741	119
Rizo-Lopez Foods Inc	2022	45	RM Wade and Co	3523	56	Robb-Jack Corp	2819	80
Rizzo and Sons Industrial Service Company Inc	1731	1625	RMA Electronics Inc	5045	707	Robb's Electric Inc	1731	2596
			Rma Land Construction Inc	0782	5	Robby Len Fashions	2339	23
Rizzo Consulting Inc	4899	171	RMA Road Yard 2	4959	25	Robeck Fluid Power Inc	5084	310
Rizzo Packaging Inc	7389	799	Rmb Inc	7322	71	Robeco Investment Managemnet	6282	190
RJ Allen Inc	7353	49	Rmc Group Inc	5049	174	Roberson Advertising Service LLC	2711	529
RJ Chevrolet Inc	5511	993	RMC Property Trust Inc	7389	485	Robert A Denton Inc	1731	262
Rj Controls Inc	5063	1085	RMC Research Corp	8732	22	Robert A Siegel Auction Galleries Inc	7389	2350
RJ Corbus Inc	3599	1773	RMC South Florida Inc	3272	32	Robert Abbey Inc	3645	15
RJ Dale Advertising and Public Relations Inc	7311	232	RMCN Credit Services Inc	7322	80	Robert Allen Fabrics Inc	5131	2
			Rmd Holdings Ltd	1799	21	Robert Anderson Electrical Contracting Inc	1731	1823
RJ Gibson Advertising Inc	7311	725	Rmd Manufacturing Ltd	2452	51			
RJ Gordon and Co	8742	350	Rme Filters Inc	3677	120	Robert B Aikens and Associates	6552	241
RJ Graphics Inc	7336	184	Rmf Inc	1731	2573	Robert Bailey Electric Inc	1731	650
RJ Hanlon Company Inc	2394	24	Rmf Printing Technologies Inc	2761	37	Robert Bearden Inc	4213	515
R-J Intn'l Inc	5083	128	RMF Products Inc	3823	487	Robert Berning Productions Inc	7812	260
RJ O'Brien and Associates Inc	6289	12	Rmf Steel Products Co	3325	31	Robert Bosch Corp	3714	9
RJ Pavlik Inc	7389	480	RMG Consultants Inc	7379	1460	Robert Bosch Tool Corp	3425	1
RJ Reynolds Tobacco Co	2111	5	Rmg Direct Inc	4822	285	Robert Brogden Pontiac Buick	5511	1009
Rj Stuckel Company Inc	3469	341	Rmg International LLC	5014	69	Robert Busse and Company Inc	3842	90
Rj Technologies Group LLC	5063	726	RMH Associates Inc	6282	159	Robert C Rhein Interests Inc	6552	256
Rj Torching Inc	7389	1743	Rmh Enterprises Inc	5084	533	Robert C Weisheit Company Inc	3599	596
RJ Van Drunen and Sons Inc	2099	61	RMI Advertising	7311	461	Robert Childs Inc	5084	528
Rjd Computers Inc	5045	737	RMI Nutron Plastics	3089	1092	Robert Colburn Electric Inc	1731	839
RJD Machine Products Inc	3544	812	Rml Electric Inc	1731	459	Robert Coleman and Partners	7389	611
Rje Interiors Inc	5021	115	Rmo Inc	3843	84	Robert Crist and Company RV	5561	7
RJE Telecom Inc	8742	19	RMR and Associates Inc	7311	440	Robert Derector PE PC	8711	347
Rjf - Keiser Industries LLC	2452	18	Rmr Inc	2099	356	Robert E Derecktor Inc	3732	68
Rjg Technologies Inc	3823	91	RMS Communications Group Inc	4899	29	Robert E Lee and Associates	8711	213
Rjglobal Wika LLC	3441	190	Rms Co	3599	110	Robert E Mason and Associates Inc	5084	853
Rjlg Ventures Inc	8734	26	Rms Precision Inc	7699	232	Robert E Nolan Company Inc	8742	395
Rjm Enterprises Of Minnesota Inc	7389	1095	RMS Purchases Inc	5063	1088	Robert F Henry Tile Company Inc	5032	49
Rjm Manufacturing Inc	2672	48	RMT Electric Corp	1731	929	Robert F Wiseman and Assoc Inc	2875	30
RJM Systems Inc	7372	4631	RMT Inc (Madison Wisconsin)	8711	158	Robert Ferrilli LLC	7379	1352
Rjms Corp	5084	125	RMW Architecture and Interiors	8712	204	Robert Green Chevrolet Oldsmobile Inc	5511	908
RJN Group Inc	8711	358	RMX Holdings Inc	3272	66	Robert Guzzo	4812	130
Rjp Electric LLC	1731	306	RN Fink Manufacturing Co	3085	40	Robert H Ham Associates Ltd	5046	93

Company Name	SIC	Rank
Robert Half International Inc	7363	5
Robert Harrell Inc	6282	532
Robert Heath Trucking Inc	4213	463
Robert J Devereaux Corp	1623	111
Robert J Hanafin Inc	6411	192
Robert J Jenkins Co	8711	592
Robert J Matthews Co	5122	71
Robert L Bradley and Associates Inc	6531	291
Robert Latorre Productions Inc	7812	113
Robert Lloyd Electric Co	1731	1164
Robert Lloyd Sheet Metal Inc	1711	139
Robert Long	7389	2471
Robert Lundquist	5013	411
Robert M Consulting Inc	7379	1028
Robert M Goff and Associates	7011	182
Robert M Hadley Company Inc	3677	30
Robert Mcclure Trenching Inc	1623	557
Robert Mcdorman	5012	191
Robert Mckeown Company Inc	5065	245
Robert McNeel and Associates Inc	7372	2264
Robert Mitchell Company Inc	1761	38
Robert Mondavi Corp	2085	4
Robert P Davis Architects	8712	333
Robert P Lepley Electrical Contractor	1731	1078
Robert P Powell	5065	1009
Robert R Bogaczyk	5084	841
Robert R Wix Inc	2759	278
Robert Ramey Software Development	7372	4063
Robert Reiser and Company Inc	5084	61
Robert Rothschild Farms LLC	0171	2
Robert Saylers Artistry	7336	282
Robert Shields and Associates	7361	103
Robert Skeels and Co	5072	186
Robert T Winzinger Inc	1611	135
Robert Talbott Carmel	2323	1
Robert W Baird and Company Inc	6282	92
Robert W Hunt Co	7389	790
Robert W Johnson Inc	5944	25
Robert Warren LLC	3679	264
Robert Weed Plywood Corp	5031	187
Robert Weiler Co	6552	294
Robert Wholey and Company Inc	5146	6
Robert Winner Sons Inc	0213	18
Robert Yick Company Inc	3589	197
Robertet Fragrances Inc	2844	102
Robertet Inc	2087	45
Robert-James Sales Inc	5051	27
Roberts American Gourmet Food LLC	2096	60
Roberts and Dybdahl Inc	5031	25
Roberts and Schaefer Co	8711	108
Roberts and Sons Aluminum Inc	5051	334
Roberts Automatic Products Inc	3451	86
Roberts Broadcasting Co	4833	112
Roberts Communications and Marketing Inc	8742	596
Roberts Company Inc	3443	10
Roberts Consolidated Industries Inc	2851	73
Roberts Dairy Co	2024	5
Roberts Electric Company Inc	1731	1863
Roberts Fire Protection Inc	3569	235
Roberts Group (San Antonio Texas)	7311	566
Roberts Motor Co	5084	98
Roberts Motor Sales Inc	5511	1185
Roberts Motors Inc	5511	937
Roberts Polypro Inc	3565	76
Robert's Precision Engineering Inc	3728	204
Roberts Quality Printing Inc	2752	597
Roberts Realty Investors Inc	6798	198
Roberts Security And Investigations Inc	7381	238
Roberts Sysco Foods Inc	5142	12
Roberts Tool and Die Co	3469	230
Roberts Tool and Supply Company Inc	5072	137
Roberts Tool Co	3552	36
Roberts Tower Co	4833	16
Roberts Trucking Inc	4213	2513
Roberts Webforge Inc	4813	758
Robert's Wood Products Inc	2499	40
Roberts-Gordon LLC	3433	3
Robertshaw Uni-Line North America	5075	13
Robertson Airtech International Inc	5722	17
Robertson Controls Inc	3613	159
Robertson Electric Company Inc	1731	657
Robertson Equipment Company Inc	3555	48
Robertson Furniture Company Inc	2512	79
Robertson Heating Supply Co	5074	34
Robertson Optical Labratories Inc	5048	19
Robertson Precision Inc	3674	332
Robertson Supply Inc	5074	102
Robertson Transformer Co	3531	84
Robertson-Ceco Corp	3442	10
Robertson-Ceco Ii Corp	3448	10
Robertson's Hams Inc	2011	146
Robertson's Ready Mix	3272	4
Robeson Electric Company Inc	1731	2063
Robetex Inc	3089	1259
Robin Enterprises Co	2752	243
Robin Hood Container Express	4213	2666
Robin Hood Supplies Inc	5084	711
Robin Lynn Mills Inc	2252	11
Robina Inc	5023	156
Robina Wood Inc	5023	202
Robindale Energy Services Inc	5052	3
Robinett Business Systems Inc	5044	127
Robinette Co	2759	50

Company Name	SIC	Rank
Robinette Inc	3743	29
Robin's Food Distribution Inc	5141	187
Robinson and Cole	8111	167
Robinson and Maites Inc	7319	49
Robinson Bradshaw and Hinson PA	8111	287
Robinson Brick Co	3251	6
Robinson Brothers Construction Inc	1623	174
Robinson Builders-Mart Of Newton Inc	5211	320
Robinson Corp	4832	146
Robinson Dairy LLC	2026	40
Robinson Electric Inc	1731	1428
Robinson Electric Supply Company Inc	5063	229
Robinson Engineering Company Inc	3625	236
Robinson Fans Inc	3564	24
Robinson Farms Feed Co	2048	135
Robinson Fin Machines Inc	3714	366
Robinson Graphics Inc	7336	194
Robinson Helicopter Co	3721	18
Robinson Home Products Inc	5023	73
Robinson Hosiery Mill Inc	2252	30
Robinson Industries Inc	3089	407
Robinson Knife Manufacturing Co	3421	10
Robinson Manufacturing Co	2322	1
Robinson Radio Inc	7311	906
Robinson Steel Company Inc	3312	31
Robinson Tower Inc	1623	712
Robinson Transport Inc	4213	929
Robinson Transport Inc	4213	998
Robinson-Latva Company LLP	3599	1802
Robinson's Marketing Division Inc	5087	103
Robison Oil Corp	5983	16
Robison Tire Company Inc	5014	40
Robix America Inc	2891	27
Robles Brothers Inc	2099	264
Robmar Precision Manufacturing Inc	3599	1414
Robocom Systems International Inc	7373	1242
Robocom Us LLC	0741	259
Robodock and Door	5039	66
Robot-Coupe Incorporated USA	3556	19
Robotics Technologies Inc	3861	97
Robrad Tool and Engineering Inc	3599	693
Robson Communities Inc	1531	17
Robt Morgan Inc	2048	97
Robus Leather Corp	3111	4
ROC EasySpooler	7372	2829
Roc Industries Inc	3624	29
ROC Software LP	5045	306
Rocal Corp	3089	1419
Rocal Inc	3993	50
Rocco Altobelli Inc	7231	5
Rocco J Russo Ltd	1731	2523
Roche Brothers Supermarkets	5411	129
Roche Colorado Corp	2834	121
Roche Diagnostics Corp	3841	38
Roche Manufacturing Company Inc	0724	1
Roche NimbleGen Inc	3826	25
Rocheleau Tool And Die Company Inc	3559	249
Rochelle Communications Inc	3661	134
Rochelle Printing Company Inc	2752	559
Rochester 100 Inc	2677	14
Rochester Armored Car Co	4213	694
Rochester Big and Tall Clothing Corp	5611	14
Rochester Business Journal	2711	706
Rochester Corp	3496	25
Rochester Electronics LLC	3674	504
Rochester Gas and Electric Corp	4931	25
Rochester Gear Inc	3599	195
Rochester Industrial Control Inc	3625	167
Rochester Machine Corp	3599	1337
Rochester Meat Co	5147	27
Rochester Medical Corp	3841	80
Rochester Orthopedic Laboratories Inc	3842	194
Rochester Precision Optics LLC	3827	47
Rochester Rotational Molding Inc	3089	1763
Rochester Shoe Tree Company Inc	2499	32
Rochester Software Associates Inc	7371	296
Rochester Stampings Inc	3544	806
Rochester Syracuse Auto Auction LP	5012	126
Rochester Telemessaging Center	7389	1960
Rochester Visual Horizons Inc	5064	198
Rochlin Settleman and Dobres PA	8111	563
Rochling Engineering Plastics LP	3082	2
Rochling Glastic Composites LP	3089	87
Rochling Machined Plastics	3644	40
Rochon Corp	1542	305
Rock Bancshares Inc	6712	451
Rock Bottom Restaurants Inc	5812	152
Rock Capital Management	6282	521
Rock Communications Ltd	2752	122
Rock Financial Corp	6162	2
Rock Hill Industrial Piping and Fabrication Inc	1541	295
Rock Hill Mechanical Corp	1711	100
Rock Hill School District 3	8211	30
Rock Island Express	4213	3024
Rock of Ages Corp	3281	1
Rock River Cartage Inc	4213	2575
Rock River Lumber and Grain Co	5153	47
Rock River Tool And Die Inc	3542	93
Rock River Tool Inc	3545	221
Rock Solid Janitorial Inc	7349	193
Rock Springs Winlectric Co	5063	340
Rock Tool and Machine Company Inc	3541	129
Rock Transport Inc	4213	2585

Company Name	SIC	Rank
Rock Valley Oil and Chemical Company Inc	2992	34
Rock Valley Publishing LLC	2711	481
Rock Valley Tool LLC	3545	261
Rock Wool Manufacturing Co	3296	16
RockBottomGolfCom	5941	33
Rockbridge Farmers Coop	5191	136
Rock-Built Inc	3537	100
Rockdale Pipeline Inc	1623	7
Rockefeller Financial	6722	20
Rockefeller Group Inc	6512	28
Rockefeller University Faculty And Sudents Club Inc	8733	3
Rockefeller's Cleaning And Restoration Co	7349	257
Rocker Solenoid Co	3679	308
Rocket Aldon	7372	1061
Rocket Ball Ltd	7941	11
Rocket City Broadcasting LLC	4832	204
Rocket Jewelry Box Inc	5199	81
Rocket Oil Inc	5983	23
Rocket Software Inc	7372	49
Rocket Software Inc	7371	198
Rocket Software OSS Unit	7371	1655
Rockett Inc	3443	135
Rockett Interactive Inc	7311	851
Rockey Company Inc	8743	182
Rockfield Painting And Graphic	7336	149
Rockfish Interactive	7319	76
Rockford Blacktop Construction Co	1611	180
Rockford Burrall Machine Company Inc	3599	866
Rockford Co	3469	298
Rockford Corp	3651	42
Rockford Drill Head Inc	3541	235
Rockford Gkn Inc	3714	208
Rockford Homes Inc	1521	113
Rockford Industrial Welding Supply Inc	5084	30
Rockford Manufacturing Group Inc	3549	37
Rockford Map Publishers Inc	2741	457
Rockford Metals	5052	7
Rockford Packaging Systems Inc	3565	131
Rockford Process Control Inc	3429	67
Rockford Rigging Inc	3643	101
Rockford SalesCom Inc	3651	20
Rockford Systems Inc	3545	112
Rockford Toolcraft Inc	3469	72
Rockford-Ettco Procunier	3541	90
Rockhill Holding Co	6331	147
Rockhurst College Continuing Education Center Inc	7389	496
Rockies Fund Inc	6799	351
Rocking C Truck Lines Inc	4213	2028
Rockingham Cooperative Inc	5191	8
Rockingham Corp	5731	57
Rockingham Electrical Supply Company Inc	5063	166
Rockingham Publishing Company Inc	2711	361
Rocking-T Transportation	4213	818
Rock-it Cargo USA Inc	4731	49
Rockland Bakery Inc	2051	44
Rockland Corp (Tulsa Oklahoma)	2842	88
Rockland Electric Co	4911	307
Rockland Federal Credit Union	6061	62
Rockland Immunochemicals Inc	2869	45
Rockland Inc	3531	97
Rockland Industries Inc	2261	11
Rockland Products Inc	3715	30
Rockland Standard Gear Inc	7537	2
Rockland Trust Co	6022	274
Rockledge Hma LLC	8062	151
Rockler Companies Inc	5251	21
Rockliffe Inc	7372	807
Rocklin Manufacturing Co	3471	106
Rockmor Group Inc	7363	153
Rockmore International Inc	3532	25
Rockmount Research and Alloys Inc	5085	383
Rocko Meats	5147	135
Rockrose Development Corp	6552	49
RockShox Inc	3751	7
Rocksteady Networks LLC	7372	1012
Rockstedt Tool and Die Inc	3544	856
Rock-Tenn Co	2631	2
Rock-Tenn Converting Co	3993	4
Rock-Tred Corp	3272	96
Rockview Dairies Inc	5143	5
Rockville Financial Inc	6021	69
Rockville Fuel And Feed Company Inc	3273	65
Rockwall Economic Development Corp	8732	110
Rockware Inc	7372	881
Rockwell Automation Inc	3829	2
Rockwell Collins Inc	3728	3
Rockwell Medical Technologies Inc	3845	44
Rockwell Publishing Co	2731	205
Rockwell Software Inc	7372	605
Rockwest Training Company Inc	8399	29
Rockwood Casualty Insurance Co	6331	181
Rockwood Holdings Inc	2899	7
Rockwood Manufacturing Co	3429	98
Rockwood Quarry LLC	3281	16
Rockwood Service Corp	6799	192
Rockwood Specialties Group Inc	2819	21
Rocky Brands Inc	3149	16
Rocky Duron and Associates Inc	5046	123
Rocky Kohl Excavating Inc	1623	416

Company Name	SIC	Rank
Rocky Mount Cord Co	2298	7
Rocky Mountain Air And Lubrication Inc	7699	220
Rocky Mountain Baking Co	2051	129
Rocky Mountain Bank	6022	313
Rocky Mountain Business Systems Inc	5999	148
Rocky Mountain Chocolate Factory Inc	2099	100
Rocky Mountain Colby Pipe Co	3084	29
Rocky Mountain Fabrication Inc	3443	95
Rocky Mountain Fiber Plus Inc	1623	734
Rocky Mountain Food Factory Inc	2032	33
Rocky Mountain Foods Inc	5141	219
Rocky Mountain Health Plans	6324	53
Rocky Mountain Lasers and Instruments Inc	5049	133
Rocky Mountain Power Generation Inc	5063	838
Rocky Mountain Prostate Thermotherapy LLC	8099	90
Rocky Mountain Ram LLC	3674	286
Rocky Mountain Recorders	7389	1251
Rocky Mountain Recycling Inc	5093	125
Rocky Mountain Sunscreen Co	2844	178
Rocky Mountain Technologies LLC	1731	2508
Rocky Mountain Tool Manufacturing Inc	7699	157
Rocky Mountain Transit and Laser Inc	5049	98
Rocky Mountain Welding and Fabricating Inc	3443	128
Rocky Peanut Company Inc	5145	26
Rocky River Brewing Co	2082	73
Rocky River Resort Inc	7011	234
Rockydale Quarries Corp	3274	3
RockySoft Corp	7372	1165
Rocmond Area Youth Services	8399	25
Rocom Corp	3568	81
Rocon Manufacturing Corp	3599	436
Roconex Corp	3555	121
Rod And Staff Publishers Inc	2731	317
Rod Baker Ford Inc	5511	1043
Rod Fraser Enterprises	5812	74
Rod Golden Corp	5084	461
Rod L Electronics Inc	3825	198
Rodac USA Corp	3648	81
Rodale Inc	2721	40
Rodale Wireless Inc	3699	147
Rodarte Construction Inc	1623	274
RoData Inc	5065	321
Rodbard and Associates	5734	170
Rodda Electric Inc	1731	698
Rodda Paint Co	2851	40
Roddan Co	7311	694
Roden Electrical Supply Co	5063	126
Roderick Arms And Tool Corp	3541	164
Rodey Dickason Sloan Akin and Robb PA	8111	288
Rodgers Broadcasting Corp	4832	91
Rodgers Instruments Corp	3931	20
Rodgers Travel Inc	4724	99
Rodgers Trucking Co	4213	1155
Rodheim Marketing Group Inc	8743	316
Rodico Inc	5084	620
Rodman and Renshaw Capital Group Inc	6211	227
Rodman Publishing Corp	2721	250
Rodney Hunt Company Inc	3491	14
Rodney Rohrbaugh Trucking Inc	4213	2680
Rodney Square Management Corp	6282	507
Rodney Strong Vineyards	2084	11
Rodon Products Inc	3677	95
Rodriguez and Quiroga Architects Chartered	8712	214
Rodriguez Company Inc	2099	294
Rod's Pawz LLC	5947	21
Roe Dental Laboratory Inc	8072	17
Roe Machine Inc	3599	1507
Roebbelen Contracting Inc	8711	112
Roebic Laboratories Inc	2842	84
Roebling Financial Corporation Inc	6712	645
Roebuck Printing Inc	2752	1032
Roeder Cartage Company Inc	4213	1642
Roehl Transport Inc	4213	136
ROEL Construction Inc	1542	84
Roepnack Corp	1541	260
Roe's Of San Antonio LLC	2011	124
Roesch Inc	3469	117
Roese Pipeline Company Inc	1623	500
Roettele Industries	3053	127
Roffe Container Inc	3085	42
Roffman Miller Associates Inc	6282	146
Rofin-Baasel Inc	3699	37
Rofin-Sinar Inc	3699	29
Rofin-Sinar Technologies Inc	3699	11
Rogan Building Services Inc	7349	183
Rogar International Inc	3599	2128
Roger Bouchard Insurance Inc	6411	239
Roger Electric Inc	1731	1568
Roger H Silverberg Advertising	7336	303
Roger Industry	3672	410
Roger Michael Press Inc	2782	77
Roger Richman Agency Inc	7922	76
Roger Shaw and Associates	5734	301
Roger Williams Hospital	8062	117
Roger Williams Medical Center	8062	130
Roger Wood Foods Inc	2013	64
Rogers and Company Cpas PC	7373	1023
Rogers and Cowan Inc	8743	70
Rogers Burgun Shahine and Deschler Inc	8712	213
Rogers Cartage Co	4213	665
Rogers Construction Company Ltd	1611	201
Rogers Construction Inc	1611	189
Rogers Corp	2821	21
Rogers Corporation Advanced Circuit Materials	3672	30
Rogers Electric Supplies Co	5065	261
Rogers Electro-Matics Inc	3625	280
Rogers Engineering And Manufacturing Company Inc	3567	41
Rogers Family Co	2095	12
Rogers Foam Corp	3086	14
Rogers Gourmet Coffee and Tea Market	2005	25
Rogers Group	8743	207
Rogers Group Inc	1611	22
Rogers Holding Company Inc	3812	129
Rogers Industrial Products Inc	3542	52
Rogers Iron and Metal Corp	5051	506
Rogers L-K Corp	2821	17
Rogers Loose Leaf Company Inc	2782	62
Rogers Lovelock and Fritz Inc	8712	95
Rogers Manufacturing Co	3089	614
Rogers Manufacturing Company Inc	3713	47
Rogers Manufacturing Inc	3541	256
Rogers Printing Company Inc	2752	957
Rogers Printing Inc	2752	214
Rogers Software Development Inc	5734	157
Rogers Specialty Materials Corp	2821	18
Rogers Stereo Inc	5064	76
Rogers-O'Brien Construction Co	1541	127
Rogersol Inc	5087	196
Rogerson Aircraft Corp	3728	54
Rogerson Kratos	3812	72
Rogue Valley Door Inc	2431	52
Rogue Valley Firewood	5099	135
Rogue Valley Manor	6512	3
Rogue Wave Software Inc	7372	779
Rohde and Schwarz Inc	3825	34
Roher Public Relations Inc	8743	200
Rohm and Haas Co	2821	209
Rohr Steel Inc	5051	409
Rohr Systems Inc	5045	967
Rohrback Cosasco Systems Inc	3829	171
Rohrer Corp	3089	143
Rohrer Trucking Inc	4213	2452
Rohrich Cadillac Inc	5511	394
Roi Eligibility Services Corp	7322	90
Rojan Electronics Inc	3699	169
Roku Inc	3651	39
Rol Manufacturing Of America Inc	3053	42
Ro-Lab American Rubber Company Inc	3061	32
Roland Corporation US	5099	5
Roland Digital Group America	5045	258
Roland J Robert Distributors Inc	5171	8
Roland Machinery Co	5082	43
Rolands and Associates Corp	7371	887
Roland's Electric Inc	1731	170
Rolco Inc	3089	933
Rolenn Manufacturing Inc	3089	1022
Rolf Koerner LLC	3569	226
Rolf Stone Inc	3272	127
Rol-Flo Engineering Inc	3544	712
Rolf's Patisserie Inc	2051	148
Rolin Graphics Inc	7336	281
Roll Coater Inc	3471	23
Roll Former Corp	3542	66
Roll Forming Corp	3499	11
Roll Global LLC	5961	13
Roll Master Corp	3562	39
Rolla Farmers Exchange	5191	153
Rollac Shutter Of Texas Inc	5039	30
Rolladen Inc	3442	74
Rolled Alloys Inc	5051	153
Rolled Steel Products Corp	5051	124
Rolled Threads Unlimited LLC	3599	597
Rolleigh Inc	3544	827
Roller Derby Skate Corp	5091	37
Roller Equipment Manufacturing Company Inc	3547	21
Roller Service Corp	3555	66
Rollercoat Industries Inc	3991	18
Rollerz	5812	388
Rollex Corp	3444	40
Rollform Of Jamestown Inc	3449	39
Rollie's Sales and Service Inc	1799	120
Rolligon Corp	3799	16
Rolling Hills Progress Center	8331	43
Rolling Thunder Software Inc	7371	834
Rollins Inc	7349	8
Rollins-PCI Construction	1542	245
Roll-Offs Of America Inc	3469	121
Rollout Express Inc	4213	1461
Rolloversystems LLC	7371	766
Rolls Battery Of New England	3691	45
Rolls Corp	3651	138
Rolls Technology Inc	3321	40
Rolls-Royce Energy Systems Inc	3511	5
Rolls-Royce Inc	3724	76
Rolls-Royce Naval Marine	3429	38
Rolls-Royce North America Inc	3724	32
Roll-Tech LLC	3011	23
Rollway Bearing International Ltd	3545	29
Rolsafe International LLC	3089	393
Rolta Tusc Inc	7379	382
Rol-Tec Inc	3069	196
Rolyn Inc	3911	47
Rom Acquisition Corp	3448	29
Roma Bakery and Imported Foods	2052	78
Roma Bakery Inc	2051	143
Roma Financial Corp	6035	44
Roma Food Enterprises Inc	5149	7
Roma Tool and Plastics Inc	3089	1054
Romac Electric Inc	1731	1690
Romac Industries Inc	3494	38
Ro-Mac Lumber and Supply Inc	5211	37
Romac Supply Company Inc	3613	64
Romacorp Inc	5812	268
Roman Catholic Diocese Of Paterson	8211	62
Roman Electric Inc	1731	1557
Roman Inc	5199	11
Roman Meal Co	2051	82
Roman Research Inc	5961	161
Roman Sentry Security Systems Inc	7381	141
Romanelli and Son Inc	5172	50
Romanoff Electric Inc	1731	194
Romar Cabinet and Top Company Inc	2434	57
Romar Machine and Tool Co	3599	2023
Romar Transportation Systems Inc	4212	16
Romark Industries Inc	5084	812
Romart Inc	2311	30
Romatic Manufacturing Co	2396	9
Romco Inc	2491	20
ROME Corp	7379	535
Rome Electric Motor Works Inc	5063	331
Rome Ltd	7699	93
Rome Machine and Foundry Co	3552	50
Rome Packing Company Inc	5146	53
Rome Plow Co	3523	27
Rome Savings Bank	6022	252
Rome Street Apparel Inc	5136	22
Rome Tool and Die Company Inc	3469	88
Rome Truck Parts and Repair Inc	3713	64
Romeo Engineering Inc	8711	405
Romeo Observer Inc	2711	851
Romeo Packing Co	2875	26
Romeo RIM Inc	3714	143
Romeo Technologies Inc	3544	151
Romer/Cimcore Inc	3812	130
Romero Foods Inc	2099	37
Romero's Food Products Inc	2099	150
Romo Inc	2759	150
Romtec Utilities Inc	1623	794
Ron Burge Trucking Inc	4213	1691
Ron Callis CPA	7372	2314
Ron Carter Automotive Group	5511	278
Ron Jon Surf Shop	5941	21
Ron Pair Enterprises Inc	3564	120
Ron Pfaff Electric Inc	1731	1595
Ron Scott Photography Inc	7372	4064
Ron Sherman Advertising Inc	7311	446
Ron Thomas Advertising Inc	7311	949
Ron Tonkin Chevrolet Co	5511	71
Ron Turley Associates Inc	7372	3496
Ronald A Kawahara and Company CPA's Inc	8721	442
Ronald L Jordan Co	3599	2024
Ronald Levitt Public Relations Associates Inc	8743	312
Ronald Trahan Associates Inc	8743	164
Ronald Wetherell Inc	3523	256
Ronan Engineering Co	3825	69
Ronard Industries Inc	3499	133
Roncelli Plastics Inc	2821	106
Ronco Communications and Electronics Inc	5065	76
Ronco Industries Inc	5087	108
Ronco Inventions LLC	3634	7
Rondy Inc	3069	112
Roni Casting Inc	5094	70
Ronile Inc	2269	3
Ronk Electrical Industries Inc	3621	99
Ronken Industries Inc	3629	75
Ronkin Construction Inc	1623	420
Ronlo Engineering Ltd	3599	1222
Ronnie Bledsoe Trucking Inc	4213	926
Ronnie Gale Personnel Corp	7361	371
Ronnie Mullins and Sons Inc	1623	790
Ronnie Sharp Trucking Inc	4213	1931
Ronny Turner Construction Company Inc	1623	281
Ronpak Inc	2759	65
Ron's Cabinets Inc	2431	122
Ron's Electric Inc	1731	2160
Ron's Tv	4841	172
Ronsco Electric Inc	1731	2302
Ronshare Inc	3541	223
Ronsil Rubber Div	3069	286
Ronsley Inc	5992	12
Ronson Aviation Inc	4789	16
Ronson Machine and Manufacturing	3599	19
Ron-Vik Inc	3089	881
Ronwal Transportation Inc	4213	2780
Rooc Inc	8331	233
Roodhouse Envelope Co	2677	22
Roofing Supply Of Charlotte LLC	5211	300

Company Name	SIC	Rank
Roofing Wholesale Company Inc	5033	7
Roofline Inc	5033	42
Roofmaster Inc	5082	141
Room and Board Inc	5712	44
RoomLinX Inc	4841	106
Roommate Express	7389	2333
Rooms To Go Inc	5712	3
Rooney Contracting Company Inc	7353	92
Rooney Holdings Inc	1522	3
Rooney Optical Inc	3851	44
Roos Instruments Inc	3825	127
Roosevelt Capital LLC	7319	67
Roosters 25th St Brewing Co	2082	26
Roosters Bar and Grill	5812	460
Root Consulting Inc	7371	1085
Root Group Inc	3571	36
Root Learning Inc	8748	273
Root Neal and Company Inc	5063	290
Root Spring Scraper Co	3531	213
Root-Lowell Manufacturing Co	3523	82
Rooto Corp	2842	170
RootsMagic Inc	7372	4747
Roover's Inc	3579	69
Ropak Corp	3089	6
Ropak Manufacturing Company Inc	3565	97
Roper Industries Inc	3823	2
Roper Pump Co	3561	55
Roper Scientific	3861	22
Roper Whitney Of Rockford Inc	3542	15
Ropers Majeski Kohn and Bentley	8111	336
Ropir Industries Inc	4841	95
Roplast Industries Inc	2673	28
Roppel Industries Inc	5013	86
Rorke Data Inc	3572	36
Rory Properties Inc	7349	435
Rosa Brothers Inc	5421	19
Rosa West Inc	2844	58
Rosalind Candy Castle Inc	2064	139
Rosati Windows LLC	3442	102
Rosauers Supermarkets Inc	5411	159
Rosauer's Supermarkets Inc	5411	11
Rosboro LLC	2436	12
Rosco Laboratories Inc	3861	89
Roscoe Moss Manufacturing Co	3317	54
Roscoe Steel And Culvert Co	3441	37
Roscoe Tool and Manufacturing Inc	3544	728
Rose Acre Farms Inc	5144	8
Rose America Corp	2221	24
Rose and Walker Supply Inc	5211	240
Rose Associates Inc	6552	71
Rose Brick and Materials Inc	5211	262
Rose Business Solutions	7379	558
Rose Corp	5075	46
Rose Dental Associates	8021	12
Rose Electric Inc	1731	2231
Rose Electronic Components Inc	5065	262
Rose Electronics	3577	239
Rose Hills Co	7261	3
Rose Ice and Coal Company Inc	2097	21
Rose Industries Inc	5091	95
Rose International Inc	7361	91
Rose Law Firm	8111	359
Rose Machine and Tool LLC	3599	1214
Rose Machinery Inc	3553	64
Rose Management Services	8742	95
Rose Metal Processing Ltd	5093	131
Rose Packaging and Design	3565	172
Rose Printing Company Inc	2732	23
Rose Products And Services Inc	5087	42
Rose Solomon Co	2389	39
Rose Systems Corp	5734	258
Ro-Search Inc	3559	230
Rosebriar Holdings Corp	6798	195
Rosebud Electric Cooperative Inc	4911	531
Rosebud Farmers Union Cooperative Associates Inc	5172	149
Rosebud Manufacturing Company Inc	2434	79
Roseburg Forest Products Co	2435	2
Roseburrough Tool Inc	5072	128
Rosedale Products Inc	3569	129
Rosedale Transport Inc	4213	501
Roselle Paper Company Inc	2678	6
Roselm Industries Inc	3663	268
Rosemark Bakery Inc	2051	277
Rosemont Center Inc	8361	112
Rosemont Exposition Services Inc	7389	310
Rosemount Analytical Inc	3829	54
Rosemount Inc	3545	2
Rosemount-Apple Valley And Eagan	7389	166
Rosen Group Inc	8748	90
Rosen Group Inc	7389	1896
Rosen Mandell and Immerman Inc	2789	21
Rosen Publishing Group Inc	2731	149
Rosen Seymour Shapss Martin and Company LLP	8721	268
Rosenau Equipment Company Inc	5083	73
Rosenberg Communications	8743	105
Rosenberg Kolb Architects PC	8712	268
Rosenberger Cds LLC	3577	353
Rosenberry Consulting Ltd	4931	56
Rosenblatt And Associates Inc	5063	1044
Rosenbloom and Associates CPAs PC	8721	453
Rosenblum-Silverman-Sutton SF Inc	6282	427
Rosendin Electric Inc	1731	18

Company Name	SIC	Rank
Rosenfeld Concrete Corp	3273	90
Rosenfeld Meyer and Susman LLP	8111	490
Rosenman's Inc	5093	249
Rosenmund Inc	3569	267
Rosen's Diversified Inc	5169	12
Rosen's Inc	5191	34
Rosenthal and Kaplin	8721	480
Rosenthal and Rosenthal Inc	6153	9
Rosenthal Automotive Group	5511	40
Rosenthal Collins Group LP	6221	2
Rosenthal Jewelers Supply Corp	5094	59
Rosenthal Manufacturing Company Inc	3554	44
Rosenthal Siegel Muenkel and Maloney LLP	8111	500
Rose's Oil Service Inc	5172	137
Rose's Quality Paints Inc	2851	178
Rose's Southwest Papers Inc	2676	6
Rosetta Inpharmatics LLC	7372	835
Rosetta LLC	8742	84
Rosetta Marketing Group LLC	8748	63
Rosetta Stone Consulting Group	7379	1672
Rosetta Stone Ltd	7372	565
Rosetta Technologies Corp	5045	497
Roseview Heights Mutual Water Company Inc	7389	1560
Rosewood Hotels and Resorts Inc	7011	153
Rosewood Property Co	7011	197
Roshell Electric Inc	1731	1277
Rosher Electric Company Inc	1731	1026
Rosholt Farmers Cooperative Elevator Co	5153	161
Rosin Eyecare	5995	8
Rosina Food Products Inc	2013	77
Rosito And Bisani Imports Inc	5046	214
Roskam Automatic Machinery Inc	3555	61
Roskam Baking Co	2051	13
Rosle U S A Corp	5023	189
Roslovic and Partners Inc	1542	422
Ross Aluminum Castings LLC	3365	14
Ross and Associates Environmental Consulting Ltd	8748	185
Ross and Associates Inc	7311	721
Ross And Son Utility Contractor Inc	1623	458
Ross And Wallace Paper Products Inc	2674	16
Ross Aviation Inc	4512	59
Ross Barney Architects	8712	182
Ross Bicycles USA Ltd	5091	48
Ross Brothers and Company Inc	1542	285
Ross Buehler Falk and Co	8721	256
Ross Capital Finance LLC	5734	16
Ross Caves and Son Inc	4213	2945
Ross Computer Systems Inc	7372	1358
Ross Electric Inc	1731	1815
Ross Express Inc	4213	1408
Ross Laboratories Inc	3812	204
Ross Lane and Co	8721	439
Ross Machine Company Inc	3599	310
Ross Manufacturing Company Inc	3523	264
Ross Marine LLC	7389	145
Ross Mould Inc	3544	24
Ross Name Plate Co	3993	146
Ross Neely Systems Inc	4213	507
Ross Network Inc	2752	93
Ross Optical Industries Inc	3827	143
Ross Printing Co	2752	770
Ross Printing Inc	2752	690
Ross Publications Inc	2741	429
Ross Publishing LLC	2741	485
Ross Racing Pistons	3592	23
Ross Realty Investments Inc	6531	189
Ross Reporting Service Inc	7338	29
Ross Rigby and Patten LLP	8721	474
Ross Schonder Sterzinger Cupcheck PC	8712	255
Ross Stores Inc	5651	4
Ross Training Center Inc	8331	191
Ross-Campbell Inc	8743	347
Rosser International Inc	8712	124
Rosset Electric Co	1731	848
Rossfelder Corp	3812	224
Ross-Gage Inc	2675	23
Rossi and Company Incorporated SC	1623	595
Rossi Building Materials Inc	5211	182
Rossi Contractors Inc	1623	224
Rossi Pasta Factory Inc	2098	15
Rossignol Ski Co	3949	52
Rossmann MacDonald and Benetti Inc	8721	475
Ross-Simons Jewelers Inc	5961	65
Rostra Precision Controls Inc	3714	270
Rostra Tool Co	3423	56
Roswell Bookbinding Co	2789	4
Roswell Daily Record Inc	2711	477
Roswell Lumber Co	5031	265
Rosy Brothers Inc	5083	190
Rota File Corp	3545	347
Rotary Airlock LLC	3443	222
Rotary Corp	5083	10
Rotary Forms Press Inc	2761	82
Rotary Offset Press Inc	2752	206
Rotary Pen Corp	3951	4
Rotary Printing Company Inc	2761	63
Rotary-Graphics Corp	2759	528
Rotating Engineered Products Inc	3524	28
Rotating Precision Mechanisms Inc	3663	171

Company Name	SIC	Rank
Rotation Dynamics Corp	3069	8
Rotational Molding Of Utah Inc	3089	1394
Rotational Molding Technologies Inc	3089	985
Rotec Industries Inc	3535	47
Rotech Healthcare Inc	7359	19
Rotek Inc	3562	22
Rotek Instrument Corp	3825	226
Rotella's Italian Bakery Inc	2051	27
Rotex Global Lcc	3826	41
Rotex Industries LLC	3829	505
Rotex Punch Company Inc	3542	112
Roth Bookstein and Zaslow LLP	8721	387
Roth Brothers Inc	1711	42
Roth Capital Partners LLC	6211	253
Roth Cash Register Company Inc	5999	253
Roth Corp	5064	22
Roth Distributing Co	5064	5
Roth Manufacturing Corp	3599	424
Roth Property Maintenance LLC	7349	216
Roth Pump Co	3561	116
Roth Staffing Companies LP	7363	64
Roth Trucking	4213	2742
Rothco	5091	17
Rothe Development Inc	7371	510
Rothenberg Sawasy Architects Inc	8712	228
Rothenberger Construction Inc	1623	641
Rothman Furniture Stores Inc	5712	55
Rothrock Motor Sales Inc	5511	519
Rothschild/Pell Rudman Inc	6282	200
Rothschild Realty Inc	6799	28
Rothschild Strategies Unlimited LLC	7372	3804
Rothstein Kass	8721	7
Rothtec Engraving Corp	7371	572
Roth-Williams Industries Inc	3544	515
Rotman Collectibles Inc	7389	703
Rotman's	5712	24
Roto Form Corp	3679	861
Roto Graphic Printing Inc	2752	827
Roto Lincoln-Mercury and Subaru Leasing Inc	5511	591
Roto Manufacturing Company Inc	3648	96
Roto Salt Company Inc	2899	185
Rotoblock Corp	3621	163
Rotocast Technologies Inc	3365	41
Roto-Die Company Inc	3544	21
Rotometals Inc	3341	41
Rotomotion LLC	3812	191
Rotonics Manufacturing Inc	3089	185
Roto-Plastics Corp	3086	179
Rotor Clip Company Inc	3429	74
Rotor Electric Co	1731	1581
Rotork Process Controls	3625	70
Roto-Rooter Inc	7699	8
Rotronic Instruments Corp	3823	318
Rotterdam Ventures Inc	6552	73
Rott-Keller Supply Co	5014	27
Rottler Manufacturing Co	3541	87
Rottlund Company Inc	1531	64
Rotuba Extruders Inc	3083	20
Rotwein and Blake Associated Architects PA	8712	300
Rough and Ready Lumber Co	2421	112
Rough Notes Company Inc	2761	66
Roughneck Systems Inc	7372	3739
Roughrider Electric Cooperative Inc	4911	425
Round Ground Inc	5051	298
Round Hill Cellars	2084	68
Round Rock Auto Group	5511	673
Round Table Franchise Corp	6794	123
Round Table Group Inc	8742	565
Round Two Inc	2759	219
Round2 Technologies Inc	7379	414
Roundarch Inc	7372	641
Roundbank	6022	818
Rounder Records Corp	6794	71
Roundtable Press Inc	2732	32
Roundtree Automotive Group LLC	5511	93
Roundtree Ford Lincoln Mercury	5511	767
Roundtree Materials Inc	1442	50
Roundy's Supermarkets Inc	5141	16
Rountree Group Inc	8743	291
Roussey Associates Inc	8711	614
Route Brokers Inc	7389	1466
Route Electronics 22 Inc	5065	569
Routematch Software Inc	4813	269
Routercad Inc	7371	1708
Roux Associates Inc	8742	262
Rouzer Sales Company Inc	5063	792
ROV Technologies Inc	8711	476
Rovanco Piping Systems Inc	3498	45
Rovi Corp	2721	17
Ro-Vic Inc	5087	25
Roving Networks Inc	3669	231
Roving Software Inc	7372	4939
Rovinter Inc	5043	29
Rovisys Co	8711	307
Row Electrical Equipment Inc	5063	938
ROW Window Co	2431	141
Rowan Business Forms Inc	2761	64
Rowan Companies Inc	1381	12
Rowan Inc	1731	536
Rowan University	8221	24
Rowe Cos	2519	2
Rowe Diversified Inc (McLean Virginia)	2512	2

Company Name	SIC	Rank
Rowe Furniture Inc	2512	10
Rowe Machinery and Manufacturing Co	3549	24
Rowe Machinery Inc	4213	924
Rowe Pottery Works Inc	3269	11
Rowe Properties Inc	2512	3
Rowe Worldwide Inc	2512	4
Rowell Chemical Corp	5169	111
Rowell Laboratories Inc	2834	320
Rowenta Inc	5064	29
Rowerdink Inc	5013	102
Rowland Associates Inc	7389	1402
Rowland Technologies Inc	3081	90
Rowland Worldwide Inc	8743	83
Rowley Building Products Corp	5211	63
Rowley Tool Corp	3544	796
Rowmark Inc	3089	394
Rowpar Pharmaceuticals Inc	2844	195
Rowse Hydraulic Rakes Company Inc	3523	139
Rox Trucking Inc	7359	239
Roxar Inc	3824	31
Roxburgh Agency Inc	7311	515
Roxcoal Inc	1222	13
Roxio Inc	7372	618
Roy Anderson Corp	1542	141
Roy Brake and Associates LLC	5064	208
Roy Brothers Inc	4213	2237
Roy Coggins	7389	2457
Roy E Hanson Jr Manufacturing	3443	146
Roy E Lay Trucking Inc	4213	685
Roy E Roth Co	3561	31
Roy E Wilson Co	5063	327
Roy Houff and Co	5193	9
Roy I Kaufman Inc	3496	117
Roy Johnson Inc	3069	106
Roy Johnston	3651	244
Roy Kirby and Sons Inc	1542	355
Roy M Mcdougal	3559	588
Roy Miller Freight Lines Inc	4213	1380
Roy Motors Inc	5541	54
Roy N Carlson Inc	4213	2185
Roy N Dailey Inc	7372	3947
Roy Price Car Crushing Inc	5093	226
Roy Robinson Chevrolet Subaru	5511	342
Roy Spittle Associates Inc	1731	1294
Royal 4 Systems Inc	7372	1634
Royal Alliance Associates Inc	6211	179
Royal and SunAlliance USA	6331	110
Royal Appliance Manufacturing Co	3635	1
Royal Audio Video Supply Inc	7359	37
Royal Automotive	5511	619
Royal Bancshares of Pennsylvania Inc	6712	326
Royal Bank of Pennsylvania	6022	516
Royal Baths Manufacturing Company Ltd	3842	81
Royal Battery Distributors Inc	5531	45
Royal Business Forms Inc	2761	29
Royal Buying Group Inc	7389	671
Royal Cabinets Inc	2434	18
Royal Canin USA Inc	2047	21
Royal Caribbean Cruises Ltd	4481	1
Royal Concrete Pipe Inc	3272	108
Royal Consumer Information Products Inc	5044	48
Royal Contracting Company Ltd	1611	66
Royal Crest Dairy Inc	5451	3
Royal Crown Bottling Corp	2086	33
Royal Cup Inc	2095	15
Royal Custom Designs Inc	2512	51
Royal Dental Manufacturing Inc	3843	34
Royal Design and Manufacturing Inc	3559	203
Royal Die and Stamping Company Inc	3469	128
Royal Diversified Products Inc	3544	379
Royal Eagle Services LLC	8748	216
Royal Electric Company Of Central Florida Inc	1731	1051
Royal Electrical Services Inc	1731	1252
Royal Electronics	7822	11
Royal Enterprise America Inc	3272	103
Royal Enterprise Cleaning System	7349	303
Royal Express Inc	4213	862
Royal Filter Manufacturing Co	3569	207
Royal Furniture Co	5712	65
Royal Gate Dodge Chrysler	5511	350
Royal Gold Inc	6799	163
Royal Gorge Bridge Co	7999	118
Royal Haeger Lamp Co	3645	75
Royal Hand Equity Corp	3564	125
Royal Ice Cream Co	2024	22
Royal Label Company Inc	2759	520
Royal Lock Corp	3429	113
Royal Machine And Tool Corp	3545	127
Royal Manufacturing Company Inc	5046	287
Royal Master Grinders Inc	3541	82
Royal Meats Inc	5147	122
Royal Mercantile Trust Corporation Of America Inc	7322	195
Royal Metal Building Component LLP	5051	482
Royal Metal Industries Inc	5051	320
Royal Metal Products Inc	3444	81
Royal Mortgage Corp	6163	40
Royal Oak Boring	3544	51
Royal Oak Ford Sales Inc	5511	346
Royal Oak Industries Inc	3443	49

Company Name	SIC	Rank
Royal Outdoor Products Inc	3089	810
Royal Packing Co	0161	11
Royal Paper Box Company Of California	2657	18
Royal Paper Stock Company Inc	5093	69
Royal Park Uniforms Inc	2389	26
Royal Personnel Services	7363	279
Royal Plastics Corp	3081	166
Royal Plastics Inc	3089	302
Royal Premium Budget Inc	6141	70
Royal Reservation Inc	8742	405
Royal Riders	5999	114
Royal Sales Inc	5013	363
Royal Sausage Company Inc	5141	178
Royal Securities Co	6211	225
Royal Services Inc	7349	29
Royal Sovereign Corp	5075	37
Royal SpA Corp	3088	10
Royal Ten Cate USA Inc	2299	3
Royal Textile Mills Inc	2322	3
Royal Tractor Company Inc	3537	65
Royal Vendors Inc	3581	1
Royal Window Coverings (USA) LP	3089	719
Royal Wire Products Inc	3496	67
Royale Cheesecake Inc	2051	227
Royale Comfort Seating Inc	2392	36
Royale Energy Inc	1311	193
Royale International Beverage Company Inc	5182	41
Royall-Matthiessen Equipment And Supply Co	7353	83
Royals Inc	5712	52
Royalston Foods LLC	2024	48
Royalton Manufacturing Inc	3599	1783
Royalty Carpet Mills Inc	2273	15
Royalty Investments LLC	3599	1394
Royberg Inc	3541	105
Royce and Associates LLC	6282	5
Royce Campbell and Sons	4213	2864
Royce Designs Inc	7374	366
Royce Hosiery Mills Inc	2252	1
Royce Instruments Inc	3825	155
Royce International Eyeware	5049	172
Royce Rolls Ringer Company Inc	3589	220
ROYDAN Enterprises Ltd	7372	2887
Royell Manufacturing Inc	3728	100
Royer Corp	3999	9
Royer Group Inc	2759	451
Royersford Foundry And Machine Company Inc	3599	1444
Royle Printing Co	3565	106
Roys and Associates LLC	7361	297
Roy's Electric Motor Service Inc	5063	717
Roy's Transfer Inc	4213	2765
Royson's Corp	3083	37
Royster Enterprises Inc	4213	492
Royster's Machine Shop LLC	3599	441
Royston Laboratories	3479	63
Roytec Industries Inc	3496	52
Roytex Inc	2329	25
Roytman Information Services Inc	7361	57
Rozal Industries Inc	3599	1287
Rozelle Inc	2844	172
Rozendal Associates Inc	3812	194
Rozier Mercantile Co	5411	255
Rozum Motor Co	5511	1196
Rozzi Window Manufacturing Inc (Reading Pennsylvania)	3089	864
Rp Fletcher Machine Company Inc	3553	15
RP Gatta Inc	3559	438
RP Johnson and Son Inc	5211	221
RP Lumber Company Inc	5211	39
Rp Schroeder Construction Inc	1623	484
R-P Screw Machine Products Inc	3599	1469
RPC Inc	1389	10
RPD Inc	7372	3740
Rpg Diffusor Systems Inc	3663	187
Rpg Inc	4953	148
RPGA Design Group Inc	8712	280
Rph Recruiter Inc	7361	315
Rpi Color Service Inc	2752	436
RPI Of Indiana Inc	3443	209
RPL Supplies Inc	5045	343
Rpm Carbide Die Inc	3544	357
Rpm Industrial Sales LLC	5063	812
RPM Industries Inc	3089	1139
RPM Industries LLC	3625	187
RPM International Inc	2851	4
RPM Pizza Inc	5812	95
RPM Transportation Inc	4213	1357
Rpp Corp	3069	114
Rpr Graphics Inc	3663	170
RPR Industries Inc	3069	285
RPR Wyatt Inc	7371	1789
Rps Construction Services Inc	3089	1140
Rps Corp	3589	106
RPS Engineering Inc	3444	279
Rps Inc	5047	138
RPS Products Inc	2842	66
Rps Shenandoah Inc	3498	85
RPTS Express Inc	4213	3045
RPV Business Systems	7372	2204
RR Bowker LLC	2731	9
RR Donnelley	2761	1

Company Name	SIC	Rank
RR Donnelley and Sons Co	2754	1
RR Donnelley and Sons Company Digital Media Center	2741	258
RR Plumbing Services Corp	5169	2
RR Software Inc	7372	4632
RRD Direct	2759	14
RRE Ventures LLC	6282	333
RRJ Company Inc	3672	273
RRR Transportation Inc	4213	369
RS Andrews Enterprises Inc	1711	35
RS Audley Inc	1611	65
RS Communication	1731	2189
RS Electrical Contractors Inc	1731	1184
RS Electronics Inc	5065	82
RS Felder Enterprises Inc	7349	145
RS Graphic Services Inc	2796	33
Rs Industries Inc	3089	1863
Rs Interest Inc	7379	566
RS Investments	6211	156
RS Knapp Company Inc	5045	333
RS Microwave Company Inc	3679	430
RS Mowery and Sons Inc	1541	138
RS Pressman and Associates Inc	7372	4748
RS Roofing and Sheet Metal Company Inc	1761	49
RS Technical Services Inc	3826	53
RSA Corp	2869	108
RSA Data Security Inc	7372	704
Rsa Industries Inc	8734	178
RSA Netwitness	7371	352
RSA Security Inc	3577	63
Rsb Transmissions NA Inc	3599	197
RSC Equipment Rental	7353	3
RSC Holdings Inc	7359	4
RSD America Inc	7372	1466
RSD Systems Inc	7389	2171
Rsdc Of Michigan LLC	7389	753
RSE Grading Company Inc	1611	220
Rsg/Aames Security Inc	3669	237
Rsg Forest Products Inc	2421	29
Rsgrp Dallas-Fort Worth Inc	5033	33
RSI Bank	6035	116
RSI Co	3559	301
RSI Home Products Inc	2434	1
Rsig Security Inc	7381	18
Rsk Tool Inc	3544	400
RSL Woodworking Products Co	2431	65
Rsm Electron Power Inc	3674	214
RSM McGladrey Inc	8721	147
RSMeans	2731	40
RSP Architects Ltd	8712	120
RSR Corp	3341	4
RSR Electronics Inc	3999	134
RSR Goup Inc	5091	13
RST Engineering	5961	197
RSVP Party Rentals Inc	7359	106
RT and T Machining Inc	3451	126
Rt Associates Inc	2752	488
RT Dooley Construction Co	1541	179
Rt Electric Inc	1731	469
RT Engineering Service Corp	5065	735
RT Machine Co	5084	833
RT Milord Co	1541	224
RT Nelson and Associates Ltd	6411	236
RT Plastics Inc	3089	1023
RT Systems Inc	7372	4329
RT Vanderbilt Company Inc	2833	6
Rta Inc	7338	11
R-Tas Systems Inc	3579	39
RTC Group LLC	7373	651
RTC Inc	3089	456
RTC Industries Inc	3993	11
RTC Relationship Marketing	7311	215
RTD Embedded Technologies Inc	3577	312
R-Tech Feeders Inc	3523	237
R-Tech Inc	3672	164
RTG Data Systems	7372	1742
RTI Biologics Inc	3842	42
RTI CT	3356	6
RTI Energy Systems Inc Business Offices	3356	8
RTi Energy Systems Inc Manufacturing Facility	3356	2
RTI Energy Systems Manufacturing Facility	3356	9
RTI Fabrication and Distribution Inc	3356	10
RTI Fabrications LP	3356	3
RTI Insurance Services of Florida Inc	6411	283
RTI International Metals Inc	3356	13
RTI Niles	3356	5
RTI Pierce-Spafford	5051	211
Rti Recycled Technology Inc	3069	244
RTI St Louis Inc	3356	11
RTI Software	7372	3160
Rti Technologies Inc	3559	283
RTI Tradco Inc	3444	18
RTI Transport Inc	4213	2390
RTI Visual Communications Inc	7812	295
RTI-DFD	7389	609
RTKL Associates Inc	8712	5
RTKL International Ltd	8712	3
RTL Networks Inc	7376	24
RTMX Inc	7372	3284
Rto Software Inc	7371	1817

Company Name	SIC	Rank
Rtp Corp	3672	209
RTP Group Inc	7372	4471
Rtp LLC	7371	423
RTR Business Products Inc	5044	90
RTR Inc	3089	939
Rtr Industries LLC	3592	22
Rtr Packaging Corp	2674	19
Rtron Management Inc	3679	886
R-Tronics LLC	3496	118
Rts Cutting Tools Inc	3545	179
RTS Packaging LLC	2631	21
Rts Realtime Systems Inc	5045	457
Rts Transformers Inc	5063	601
Rtt Associates Inc	7379	1375
Rtw Janitorial LLC	7349	519
RTX Systems Inc	3812	217
RTZ Software	7372	3018
Ruach Day Camp	8351	30
Ruan Transport Corp	4213	82
Ruan Transportation Management Systems	6159	49
Ruane Cunniff and Company Inc	6282	290
Rubatex International LLC	3069	203
Rubber and Accessories Inc	5085	226
Rubber and Gasket Company Of America Inc	5085	97
Rubber and Plastic Applicators Inc	3069	250
Rubber and Silicone Products Company Inc	3069	241
Rubber Applications Inc	1799	84
Rubber City Machinery Corp	3559	286
Rubber Developments Inc	3069	268
Rubber Engineering And Development Company Inc	3069	192
Rubber Enterprises Inc	3069	49
Rubber Industries Inc	3069	130
Rubber Specialties Inc	3060	231
Rubberball Productions	7372	3303
Rubbercraft Corporation Of California Ltd	3061	14
Rubberfab Gasket And Molding Inc	3494	72
Rubberlite Inc	5085	58
Rubbermaid Home Products Div	3069	7
RubberNetworkcom LLC	7389	284
Rubel Machine and Tool Inc	3714	400
Rubens and Marble Inc	2254	5
Rubenstein Associates Inc	8743	19
Rubenstein Brothers Inc	5611	27
Rubicon Enterprises Inc	7349	187
Rubicon Express	3559	292
Rubicon Financial Inc	6282	18
Rubicon Technology Inc	3674	122
Rubigo Cosmetics	2844	205
Rubin Brothers Inc	2326	18
Rubin Manufacturing Inc	2211	20
Rubin Postaer and Associates	7311	45
RubinBrown LLP	8721	46
Rubio's Restaurants Inc	5812	169
Rubloff Inc	6531	107
Rubschlager Baking Corp	2051	308
Ruby and Quiri Leasing Corp	5021	124
Ruby Tuesday Inc	5812	47
Ruby's Diner Inc	5812	71
Ruch Carbide Burs Inc	7699	174
Rucker and Kolls Inc	3559	369
Rucker Fuller Co	5021	20
Ruckus Wireless Inc	5045	87
Rudco Products Inc	3443	136
Rudd Company Inc	2851	87
Rudd Container Corp	2653	117
Rudd Equipment Co	5082	29
Ruddick Corp	5411	40
Ruddock Manufacturing Company Inc	2321	22
Ruden McClosky Smith Schuster and Russell PA	8111	203
Ruder Electric Inc	1731	1212
Ruder Finn Inc	8743	22
Rudig Olympic Award Company Inc	5094	64
Rudisill Enterprises Inc	5181	88
Rudolph and Sletten Inc	1541	26
Rudolph Chevrolet Inc	5511	1028
Rudolph Foods Company Inc	2096	16
Rudolph Instruments Inc	3826	160
Rudolph International Inc	2844	143
Rudolph/Libbe Companies Inc	1542	94
Rudolph/Libbe Inc	1542	19
Rudolph Technologies Inc	3823	16
Rudolph Transfer and Storage Co	4213	3110
Rudox Engine And Equipment Co	5084	464
Rudy Luther Imports Inc	5511	837
Rudy Mantel and Associates Inc	7379	1503
Rudy Salem Staffing Services	7363	387
Rudy's Dad Inc	3571	239
rue21 Inc	5632	4
Rueckert Advertising and Public Relations LLC	7311	726
Rueff Lighting Co	5063	291
Ruemelin Manufacturing Company Inc	3569	269
Rueschhoff Corp	5999	265
Ruf Strategic Solutions	7372	2401
Ruff Bond Cobb Wade and McNair LLP	8111	573
Ruffin and Payne Inc	5031	177
Ruffin Building Systems Inc	3448	31
Ruffin Cos	6531	53

Company Name	SIC	Rank
Ruffin Enterprises Inc	4841	120
Rugby Farmers Union Elevator Co	5153	177
Ruger Investment Castings Div	3324	23
Rugg Manufacturing Company Inc	3531	219
RuggedNotebookscom	3571	201
Ruggedtronics Inc	3577	87
Ruggieri Brothers Inc	1752	11
Ruggiero Seafood Inc	5146	12
Rugid Computer Inc	3571	228
Ruhle Companies Inc	3679	383
Ruhlin Co	1541	132
Ruiz Enterprises LLC	7389	2067
Ruiz Food Products Inc	2038	94
Ruiz Mexican Foods Inc	2099	95
Ruland Associates Inc	7376	36
Ruland's Used Office Furnishings	5021	148
Rulersmith Inc	3083	76
Rules-Based Medicine Inc	2835	30
RuleSpace Inc	7379	1394
Rulon Electric Illuminations Company Inc	3648	53
Rumar Manufacturing Corp	3443	116
Rumbletree	7311	852
Rumbold and Kuhn Inc	5153	185
Rume Corp	1731	678
Rummel Industries Inc	5162	58
Rumpke Consolidated Companies Inc	4953	10
Rumpke Consolidated Inc	4953	24
Rumpke Container Services Inc	4953	4
Rumsey Electric Inc	5063	38
Rumson Capital LP	6411	235
Rundle-Spence Manufacturing Co	5074	76
Ru-Nell Inc	2673	75
Runestone Electric Association	4911	361
Runge Paper Company Inc	5113	45
Runge Trucking Inc	4213	2391
Runners Diversified Inc	3842	95
Run-PCcom	5046	86
Run-R-Way Express Company Inc	4213	3107
RunTex Inc	5661	19
Runtime Design Automation Inc	7373	649
RunTime Technologies	7379	769
Runway Inc	8748	302
Runyon Saltzman and Einhorn Inc	7311	182
Ruoff and Sons Inc	3599	1250
Rupari Food Services Inc	2011	82
Rupert Gibbon and Spider Inc	3952	14
Rupp Air Management	3567	126
Rupp Construction Company Inc	1611	206
Rupp Construction Inc	1442	89
Ruppert Nurseries Inc	0181	1
Ruprecht Schroeder Hoffman Architects	8712	101
Rurak and Associates Inc	7361	363
Rural Electric Coop (Lindsay Oklahoma)	4911	554
Rural/Metro Corp	4119	3
Rural/Metro of Indiana Inc	4119	10
Rural Mutual Insurance Cos	6331	330
Rural Telephone Service Company Inc	4813	135
Rurban Financial Corp	6712	408
Rurban Mortgage Co	6162	26
Rus Industries Inc	3443	199
Rusach International Inc	3545	358
Rusch Inc	3841	145
Ruscilli Construction Company Inc	1541	56
Ruscoe Co	2891	65
Rush Communications of New York Inc	7812	25
Rush Electric Company Inc	1731	1238
Rush Enterprises Inc	5599	1
Rush Gold Inc	3537	84
Rush Graphics Inc	2752	1023
Rush Index Tabs Inc	7389	1075
Rush Sales Co	3533	46
Rush Transportation and Logistics	4215	9
Rush Truck Center Whittier	5012	50
Rushent Sales Inc	5012	169
Rusher Loscavio and LoPresto	7361	147
Rusken Packaging Inc	2652	6
Ruskin Co	3444	130
Rusmar Inc	2899	232
Ruspak Corp	7389	1483
Russ Bassett Corp	2522	27
Russ Darrow Group Inc	5511	36
Russ Kiko Associates Inc	7389	964
Russ Lyon Realty Co	6531	314
Russ Reid Co	7311	88
Russco Inc	2789	138
Russelectric Inc	3613	19
Russell	3585	35
Russell and Miller Inc	7331	29
Russell Belden Electric Co	5063	196
Russell Chevrolet-Geo-Honda Inc	5511	140
Russell Corp	2253	1
Russell Crosby	3559	582
Russell Development Company Inc	6552	306
Russell Electric Incorporated Of Rocky Mount	1731	2072
Russell Financial Services Inc	2253	2
Russell Investment Management Co	0282	380
Russell Investments	6282	169
Russell James Engineering Works Inc	3443	188
Russell Johns Associates LLC	7313	28
Russell Knickerbocker Company Inc	5082	93

Company Name	SIC	Rank
Russell Lands Inc	6552	205
Russell Martin and Associates	7379	1190
Russell Petroleum Corp	5172	33
Russell Pipe and Foundry Co	3321	43
Russell Plastics Technology Company Inc	3089	589
Russell Publications	2711	796
Russell Reynolds Associates Inc	7361	23
Russell Servicing Company Inc	2253	24
Russell Standard Corp	1611	164
Russell Stover Candies Inc	2064	5
Russell T Bundy Associates Inc	5046	15
Russell-Moore Lumber Inc	5211	225
Russell-Newman Inc	2341	7
Russells Crane Service Inc	7353	94
Russell's Exterminating Company Inc	7342	66
Russell's Guides Inc	2741	494
Russell's Technical Products Inc	3569	177
Russellville Hospital LLC	8062	232
Russellville Newspapers Inc	2759	216
Russellville Steel Company Inc	5051	196
Russin and Vecchi LLP	8111	593
Russo Company Inc	5087	166
Russo Farms Inc	0161	12
Russos' Inc	2064	144
Russound/Fmp Inc	3651	70
Rust Communications Inc	2711	265
RUST Constructors Inc	1542	266
Rust Publication Company Inc	2711	807
Rust-Oleum Corp	2821	61
Rust-Oleum Corp (Hagerstown Maryland)	2899	60
Rust-Oleum Corp (Tulsa Oklahoma)	3479	111
Ruston Aviation Inc	5088	65
Rusty Inc	3949	83
Rusty's Weigh Scales and Service Inc	5084	547
Ruszel Woodworks Inc	2441	3
Rutan and Tucker LLP	8111	149
Rutgers Pressure Forming Company Inc	5162	56
Ruth Meric Catering	5812	394
Rutherford and Associates Inc	7372	3497
Rutherford County Adult Activity Center	8322	179
Rutherford Electric Membership Corp	4911	389
Rutherford Farmers Coop	5191	174
Rutherford The Tennessean	2711	613
Ruth's Chris Steak House Inc	5812	122
Ruth's Hospitality Group Inc	5812	115
Rutland Dickson Asset Management Inc	6282	571
Rutland Industries Inc	7389	2494
Rutland Lumber Company Inc	2426	38
Rutland Plastic Technologies Inc	3087	15
Rutland Plywood Corp	2435	10
Rutledge Company Inc	5084	149
Rutter Networking Technologies Inc	7373	454
R-V Industries Inc	3589	67
Rvf Investments Group Inc	5734	285
RVI Guaranty Company Ltd	6351	44
RVI Services Company Inc	6351	39
RVL Packaging Inc	2241	20
Rvs and Co	3364	33
rVue Inc	7311	361
rVueInc	4833	71
RW Hartnett Co	3555	69
RW Jones Trucking Co	4213	1644
RW Lynch Company Inc	8742	187
RW Machine and Tool Inc	3599	968
RW Machine Inc	3599	1858
RW Publications Division Of Waterhouse Publication Inc	2711	513
RW Raddatz Inc	3599	306
RW Sanders Trucking Inc	4213	1935
RW Sauder Inc	2015	30
RW Scott Construction Inc	1623	707
RW Setterlin Building Co	1541	172
RW Sowers and Associates Inc	1791	477
RW Wilson Inc	3089	1489
RW3 Technologies Inc	7372	1571
RWA Financial Services Inc	6221	16
Rwc Inc	3549	13
RWD Technologies Inc	7389	60
RWE Inc	3444	301
RWI Group	6799	210
Rwi Manufacturing Inc	2542	10
RWI Transportation LLC	4213	792
RWK Tool Inc	3599	1929
Rwl Construction Inc	1623	333
RWTUV USA	8734	128
RxAmerica LLC	5912	24
RXi Pharmaceuticals Corp	2834	454
RxUSA Inc	5961	54
RY Timber Inc	2421	83
Ryan Beck and Company Inc	6211	281
Ryan Building Group Inc	1531	51
Ryan Chevrolet Inc	5511	874
Ryan Coffee Co	2095	63
Ryan Companies US Inc	6552	27
Ryan Direct	7331	10
Ryan Electric Inc	1731	2075
Ryan Health Centers	8051	77
Ryan Herco Products Corp	5162	11
Ryan Homes	1521	37
Ryan Incorporated Central	1794	2

Company Name	SIC	Rank
Ryan Iron Works Inc	3446	41
Ryan Labs Inc	6282	185
Ryan LLC	8748	20
Ryan Machine Inc	3599	2498
Ryan Management Group	8742	126
Ryan Manufacturing Inc	3599	356
Ryan Olsen Development	1521	124
Ryan Partnership Promotion Agency	7311	82
Ryan Peters LLC	2752	663
Ryan Trucking Company Inc	4213	3070
Rybovich Spencer	3732	42
Rycoline Products LLC	2842	11
Rycom Instruments Inc	3829	283
Rycon Construction Inc	1542	349
Rydalch Electric Inc	1731	236
Rydell Automotive Group Inc	5511	857
Rydell Chevrolet Mitsubishi Inc	5511	439
Rydell Chevrolet Olds Cad Inc	5511	411
Ryder Communications Inc	5065	801
Ryder Election Services LLC	2752	1645
Ryder Integrated Logistics	4213	27
Ryder System Inc	7513	2
Ryder-Heil Bronze Inc	3364	25
Rydex SGI	6722	45
Rydin Sign and Decal Inc	2752	505
Rye Gentry Trucking Inc	4213	1847
Rye Hospital Center	8063	7
Rye Printing Inc	2759	392
Rye Telephone Co	4813	320
Ryeco Inc	3599	1424
Ryerson Holding Corp	5051	7
Ryerson Procurement Corp	5051	57
Rykel Global Inc	5731	122
Ryko Manufacturing Co	3589	27
Rykodisc Inc	3652	14
Ryland Group Inc	1531	18
Ryland Mortgage Co	6162	53
Ryle Manufacturing Co	3568	90
Ryley Carlock and Applewhite PA	8111	310
Rynone Manufacturing Corp	3281	3
Ryobi Die Casting (USA) Inc	3714	168
Ryobi Technologies Inc	3546	15
Ryss Laboratory Inc	2833	43
Rytan Inc	3541	224
Rytech International Inc	7379	1461
Ryt-Way Industries LLC	7389	175
Ryzex Group	7374	59
RZ Trucking	4213	3054
RZO Productions LLC	8741	293
S 2 Yachts Inc	3732	80
S A Day Manufacturing Company Inc	5085	273
S Abraham and Sons Inc	5194	4
S and A Distributing Corp	5013	145
S and B Electric Supply Corp	5063	840
S and B Engineers and Constructors Ltd	8711	27
S and B Machine Inc	3599	1639
S and B Tool And Die Company Inc	3599	2297
S and C Electric Co	3613	12
S and D Coffee Inc	2095	6
S and D Machine and Tool Inc	3599	1816
S and E Consulting Inc	7379	1673
S and G Enterprises Inc	3821	80
S and G Manufacturing Group LLC	3441	87
S and G Tool Aid Corp	3546	22
S and G Waldrop Electric Inc	1731	1880
S and H Computer Systems Inc	7372	4942
S and H Electric Company Inc	1731	1068
S and H Engineering Inc	3549	91
S and H Express	4213	581
S and H Lone Star Electric Inc	1731	392
S and H Metal Works and Manufacturing Inc	3559	132
S and H Products Inc	3365	39
S And H Rubber Company Inc	3069	271
S and H Steel Company Inc	3441	70
S and H Tool Inc	3599	2505
S and H Trucking Inc	4213	2196
S and J Diamond Corp	5094	47
S and J Industrial Supply Corp	5085	390
S and J Lighting/Lense Supply Inc	5063	998
S and J Precision Inc	3599	744
S and K Acquisition Corp	5084	100
S and K Electronics Inc	3679	240
S and K Industries Inc	2099	244
S and L Computer Services Inc	5045	758
S and L Electric Inc	1731	277
S and L Mailing Service Inc	7331	185
S and L Materials Inc	5031	414
S and L Services Inc	4213	2794
S and L Warshawsky Inc	5013	406
S and M Bikes Inc	5091	109
S and M Brands Inc	2111	9
S and M Food Service Inc	5148	77
S and M Lumber Co	5031	220
S and M Moving Systems	4213	360
S and M Sakamoto Inc	1541	218
S and N Manufacturing Inc	3625	214
S and P Architectural Products Inc	5031	152
S and P Co	6719	61
S and P Solutions Inc	7379	394
S and R Transport Inc	4213	2212
S and S Acrylic Inc	2499	64
S and S Auction Inc	7389	1901
S and S Automotive Inc	5013	23
S and S Bakery Inc	2051	168
S and S Buying Service Inc	5731	45
S and S Cartage Ltd	4213	2267
S and S Communication Services Inc	1623	308
S and S Electric Inc	1731	1760
S and S Engineering LLC	3599	1280
S and S Farm Center	5153	202
S and S Foods LLC	2013	25
S and S Machinery Corp	3541	65
S and S Meat Company Inc	5147	88
S and S Metal And Plastics Inc	3644	41
S and S Programming Inc	7372	4749
S and S Promotional Group Inc	7389	1276
S and S Promotions Inc	2759	318
S and S Quality Meats LLC	2011	106
S and S Refrigeration Corp	3585	170
S and S Research Inc	3679	397
S and S Rock Inc	5032	180
S and S Screw Machine Company LLC	3451	76
S and S Seeds Inc	5083	174
S and S Specialty Systems Inc	3599	2078
S and S Steel Services Inc	5051	244
S and S Tool And Machine Co	3545	83
S and S Tool Inc	3599	2227
S and S Transport Inc	4213	584
S and S Transportation Inc	4213	2617
S and S Trucking Inc	4213	2720
S and S Welding Company Inc	3599	1893
S and S Welding Inc	3446	44
S and S Wholesale Tire Of Knoxville Inc	5014	58
S and S Worldwide Inc (Colchester Connecticut)	5945	12
S and S X-Press LLC	4213	2485
S and S X-Ray Products Inc	3844	13
S and T Bancorp Inc	6712	127
S and T Bank	6022	80
S and T Welding Inc	7692	52
S and W Contracting Company Inc	1731	339
S and W Industries Inc	4213	2798
S And W Lumber Co	5211	228
S and W Manufacturing Company Inc	3469	218
S and W Plastics LLC	3089	1148
S and W Utility Contractors Inc	1623	563
S and Y Industries	3672	123
S and Z Enterprises Inc	5734	290
S B Machining Inc	5961	167
S B Phillips Company Inc	7361	232
S Beckman Print and Graphic Solutions Inc	2752	1382
S Corporation Inc	7374	397
S D Ireland Concrete Construction Corp	1771	19
S Diamond Co	1623	183
S Dulek Enterprises Inc	7363	335
S E Macmillan Company Inc	1623	403
S Freedman and Sons Inc	5113	25
S/G Industries Inc	5065	415
S G Torrice Company Inc	5075	50
S Gager Industries Inc	3089	1792
S Group Inc	7389	1431
S Himmelstein And Co	3825	133
S Holland Company Inc	1623	427
S Howes Inc	3559	361
S I Jacobson Manufacturing Co	2211	22
S J Electric Inc	1731	2081
S J Mccullagh Inc	2095	39
S J Smith Company Inc	5169	78
S Joseph and Sons Inc	5944	21
S Kivett Inc	1799	73
S/L/A/M Collaborative Architects	8712	75
S M Lorusso and Sons Inc	1442	21
S Martinelli and Co	2033	26
S Moranz Inc	3589	170
S/N Precision Enterprises Inc	3562	40
S N S South Inc	4226	12
S Parker Hardware Manufacturing Corp	3429	119
S R Holding Company Inc	7359	264
S Randall Electric Inc	1731	1090
S Ruppe Inc	5112	53
S S Kemp and Co	5046	56
S S Logan Packing Co	5147	35
S S S Lumber Company Inc	1422	50
S S Steele and Company Inc	2452	55
S Tech Corp	3812	63
S W Anderson Co	5072	94
S W H Supply Co	5078	17
S Woods Enterprises Inc	5511	65
S1 Community and Regional eFinance Solutions Group	7379	182
S1 Corp	7372	236
S2 Security Corp	7382	97
S2F Engineering Inc	3535	208
S3 Integration LLC	7373	621
S3 Investments Company Inc	5141	233
S4 Inc	7379	340
S4i Systems	7372	4330
S4Software Inc	7372	4360
SA Communications Services	7311	616
SA Extended Medical Inc	3841	35
SA Kitsinian Inc	5094	51
SA Piazza And Associates LLC	2038	51
SA Technology	3999	48
Saab Aircraft of America Inc	5088	19
Saatchi and Saatchi	7311	39
Saatchi and Saatchi X Inc	7311	420
Saati Americas Corp	5131	31
Saaya Inc	5049	196
Saba Software Inc	7372	388
Sabadell United Bank	6021	157
Sabah International Inc	1731	323
Saba's Western Stores	5651	29
SABC Realty Inc	6512	4
Sabel Industries Inc	5051	128
Saber Industries Inc	3552	13
Saber Partners LLC	6282	293
Sabert Corp	3089	265
Sabic Polymershapes	3081	5
Sabin Robbins Paper Co	2621	35
Sabine Inc	3699	134
Sabine Royalty Trust	6792	8
Sabine State Bank and Trust Co	6021	276
Sabino Crystal Co	3231	71
Sabino Electric Inc	1731	775
Sable Systems International Inc	3821	69
Sabol and Rice Inc	5075	54
Sabre Communications Corp	3663	37
Sabre Holdings Corp	6719	36
Sabre International Inc	7359	278
Sabre Realty Management Inc	6552	191
Sabroso Co	2037	7
Sabroso Foods	5149	191
Sabry Lee Inc	5013	242
Sabtech Industries	3672	212
SAC - Sulamerica Corp	5064	212
Saccucci Lincoln-Mercury-Honda Inc	5511	630
Sachem Central School District At Holbrook	8211	8
Sachem Inc	2869	52
Sachs Electric Co	1731	26
Sachs Investment Group	6282	456
Sachs North America	3714	125
Sachs Properties Inc	6552	159
Sacoma International Inc	3469	59
Sacon Inc	1731	2370
Sacramento Baking Company Inc	2051	163
Sacramento Computer Power Inc	5063	978
Sacramento Credit Union	6062	64
Sacramento District Postal Employees Credit Union Co	6062	113
Sacramento Employment and Training Agency	8331	7
Sacramento Envelope Company Inc	2759	589
Sacramento Municipal Utility District	4911	59
Sacramento Regional Waste Water Treatment Plant	4952	4
Sacred Heart University Inc	8221	16
SACS Trucking Inc	4213	2353
Sadaka Technology Consultants LLC	7371	340
Saddington Shusko LLP	8721	438
Saddle Barn Tack Distributors	5191	183
Saddle Brook Controls	5065	391
Saddle Creek Corp	4225	11
Saddlebrook Resorts Inc	7011	175
Sadelco Inc	3825	122
Sadisco of Florence	5012	63
Sadler Brothers Inc	3827	142
Sadler Brothers Trucking and Leasing Inc	4213	701
Sadler Electric Inc	1731	1003
Sadler Materials Corp	3273	91
Sadler-Necamp Financial Services Inc	7371	681
Sadler's Smokehouse Ltd	2013	43
Sadoff's Investment Management LLC	6282	373
SAE Circuits Colorado Inc	3672	102
SAE Group Inc	7372	3507
SAE Magnetics	3679	182
SAE Mastering	3695	124
SAE Materials Inc	3672	133
SAE Power	3679	204
Saeco USA Inc	5046	79
Saeger Machine Inc	3599	2312
Saehan Bancorp	6712	409
Saehan Bank	6022	197
Saehan Electronics America Inc	3672	121
Saenz Utility Contractors Ltd	1623	453
SAES Getters USA Inc	3561	131
SAES Pure Gas Inc	3559	74
Saf T Cart Inc	3589	145
Safari Software Inc	7372	4874
Safco Corp	3714	372
Safe Auto Insurance Group Inc	6331	253
SAFE Credit Union	6061	15
Safe Deposit Company Inc	7375	165
Safe Flight Instrument Corp	3812	87
Safe Harbor Water Power Corp	4911	244
Safe Passage International Inc	8299	64
Safe Passage International LLC	6351	52
Safe Reflections Inc	2389	18
Safe Security Inc	7381	100
Safe Systems Inc	3589	254
Safe Systems Inc (Alpharetta Georgia)	7379	774
Safe T Lighting LLC	1731	1385
Safe-Air Of Illinois Inc	3444	152
Safeco Alarm Systems Inc	7382	138
SAFECO Corp	6331	60

Company Name	SIC	Rank
SAFECO Financial Institution Solutions Inc	6411	92
SAFECO Properties Inc	6531	108
Safeguard Alarm Systems Inc	1731	1489
Safeguard Business Systems Inc	2782	3
Safeguard Chemical Corp	2842	58
Safeguard Health Enterprises Inc	6324	89
Safeguard Products Inc	3496	78
Safeguard Properties Inc	8741	157
Safeguard Protection Systems Inc	8748	390
Safeguard Scientifics Inc	7389	114
Safeguard Security Holdings Inc	7381	57
Safeguard Security Services	7381	48
Safeguards Technology LLC	7382	100
SafeHarbor Technology Corp	5045	124
Safehome Security Inc	7382	26
Safelite Glass Corp	7536	1
Safenet Consulting Inc	7371	408
SafeNet Holding Corp	3663	20
Safe-N-Sound Security Inc	7382	87
Safepak Corp	3669	281
Safer Textile Processing Corp	7389	613
SafeRent Inc	7389	6
Saferock Retail	7371	925
Safespan Inc	3446	39
SafeStitch Medical Inc	7373	1232
SafeStone Technologies Ltd	7372	759
SafeSurf	7372	1680
Safetec of America Inc	2819	55
Safetouch Security Systems Inc	7382	55
Safetran Traffic Systems Inc	3669	163
Safe-T-Shore	3531	151
Safety 1st Inc	3089	76
Safety Guys LLC	5099	67
Safety House of Southwest Louisiana LLC	5063	813
Safety Insurance Group Inc	6331	165
Safety Light Corp	5046	169
Safety National Casualty Corp	6321	39
Safety Net Corp	1731	2341
Safety Short Production Inc	7812	312
Safety Steel Service Inc	3441	30
Safety Systems Specialist Inc	5063	870
Safety Today	5087	22
Safety Training Systems Inc	3699	164
Safety Vision Inc	3699	51
SafetyForumcom	8999	130
Safety-Kleen Holdco Inc	4953	20
Safety-Kleen Services Inc	4953	17
Safeware Inc (Columbus Ohio)	6399	25
Safeware Inc (Landover Maryland)	5049	15
Safeway Inc	5411	2
Safeway Moving Systems Inc	4213	370
Safeway Pet Food Plant	2047	22
Safeway Transportation Co	4213	348
Saffron Supply Co	5072	187
Safian Communications Services Inc	7311	1037
Safian Investment Research Inc	6282	628
Safilo USA	5048	3
Safra Asset Management Corp	6282	294
Safra National Bank of New York	6035	67
Safran	3679	14
Saf-T-Co Supply	3644	27
Saf-Tee Siping and Grooving Inc	3559	180
Saf-T-Lok International Corp	2891	105
Sag Harbor	2337	2
Sag Harbor Industries Inc	3621	79
Saga Communications Inc	4832	21
Saga Communications Of Illinois LLC	4832	19
Sagamore Health Network Inc	6324	105
Sagara Trucking Inc	4213	1815
Sage Accpac	7371	123
Sage Action Inc	5049	215
Sage BusinessVision	7372	2369
Sage Group Consulting Inc	8742	493
Sage Instruments	3825	138
Sage Laboratories Inc	3829	42
Sage Management Enterprise LLC	8742	443
Sage Products Inc	3842	38
Sage Publications USA	2731	15
Sage Telecom Inc	4813	252
Sage Telecommunications Corp (Denver Colorado)	1731	1037
Sage Timeslips	7372	1605
Sage V Foods LLC	2044	12
Sagemark Companies Ltd	8093	61
Sagent Advisors Inc	6029	7
Sager Electronics Inc	5063	28
Sager Metal Strip Company LLC	3535	149
Sageworks Inc	7372	1946
Sagicor Life Insurance Co	6311	248
Sagient Research Systems Inc	6282	594
Saginaw Bay Plastics Inc	3089	897
Saginaw Control and Engineering Inc	3699	80
Saginaw Machine Systems Inc	3541	52
Saginaw Products Corp	3535	42
Saginaw Valley Ford Lincoln - Mercury	5511	1078
Sagrocry Inc	2899	136
Sahaj Management Corp	8741	263
Sahara Air Conditioning and Heating Inc	7623	16
Sahara Nevada Corp	7011	143
Sahlman Seafoods Inc	2092	89
Sahni Enterprises	3639	16

Company Name	SIC	Rank
Sai Hydraulics Inc	3241	24
Sai Inc	5063	612
Sai People Solutions Inc	7363	73
Sai Systems International Inc	7379	276
Saia Inc	4213	36
Saia Motor Freight Line Inc	4213	37
Saia (Waunakee Wisconsin)	4213	1046
Saia-Burgess Automotive Actuators Inc	3625	38
SAIC Inc	7373	3
Saicomm Inc	7372	3332
Saicon Consultants Inc	7361	342
SAIF Corp	6331	222
Sail Electric Inc	5063	764
Sail Inc	4899	233
Sailboats Inc	7999	70
Sailfish Communications Inc	1731	2120
Sailing Specialties Inc	3089	1491
Sailor Equipment Inc	3089	1710
Sain Construction Co	1542	287
Sainberg and Company Inc	3199	13
St Aemilian-Lakeside Inc	8361	24
Saint Andrews Hall Inc	6512	74
St Ann Transportation Inc	4213	1197
St Anne's Credit Union	6062	22
St Anne's Maternity Home	8361	65
Saint Ann's Infant And Maternity Home	8361	160
Saint Arnold Brewing Co	2082	48
St Bernard Software Inc	7372	1248
St Casimirs Savings Bank	6036	89
St Charles Consulting Group LLC	8748	75
St Charles Hospital And Rehabilitation Center	8062	99
St Charles Hospital Port Jefferson New York	8071	17
St Charles Sports and Physical Therapy Inc	8049	21
St Clair Foods Inc	2099	139
St Claire Inc	8741	298
St Clare Hospital	8062	204
St Cloud Industrial Products Inc	5084	107
St Cloud Mining Co	1031	3
St Coletta's Of Illinois Inc	8211	103
St Croix Valley Hardwoods Inc	2426	8
St Elizabeth Hospital Inc	8062	146
Saint Francis Hospital	8062	123
St Francis' Hospital Poughkeepsie New York	8062	190
Saint Francis Memorial Hospital	8062	110
St Francis Mercantile Equity Exchange	5153	159
St Gabriel Valve Service LLC	7699	209
Saint Gobain Container LLC	3221	2
St Hart Container	2653	60
St James Winery Inc	2084	66
St Joe Towns and Resorts LP	1531	13
St John and Partners Advertising And Public Relations	7311	121
St John Knits International Inc	2331	4
St Johnland Nursing Center Inc	8322	25
St Johns Bank and Trust Co	6022	338
Saint Johns County School Board	8211	29
St Johns Investment Management Co	6282	259
St Joseph Health System LLC	8062	68
St Joseph Hospital	8062	119
St Joseph's Children's Home	8361	119
Saint Joseph's Home For The Elderly Of The Little Sisters Of The Poor	8361	105
St Jude Medical Cardiac Rhythm Management Div	3845	3
St Jude Medical Daig	3842	47
St Jude Medical Inc	3842	3
St Jude Shop Inc	5049	58
St Julian Wine Company Inc	2033	83
St Laurent Brothers Inc	2099	295
St Lawrence Explosives Corp	5169	106
St Lawrence Gas Company Inc	4924	62
St Lawrence Steel Corp	5051	260
St Lawrence-Troy LLC	7629	50
St Louis Conveyor Co	1799	115
St Louis Electric Supply Inc	5063	161
St Louis Gear Company Inc	3566	28
St Louis Helicopter LLC	4522	40
St Louis Lithographing Co	2752	1002
St Louis Paper and Box Co	5113	57
St Louis Post-Dispatch	2711	93
St Louis Post-Dispatch LLC	2711	15
St Louis Testing Laboratories Inc	8734	124
St Luke's Cornwall Hospital	8062	86
Saint Luke's Health System Inc	8062	76
St Martin Oil and Gas Inc	5171	34
St Martin's Press LLC	2731	95
St Mary Minerals Inc	1311	96
St Mary Sugar Shipping Company Inc	2061	4
St Mary's Bank La Caisse Populaire Ste-Marie	6062	36
St Marys Carbon Company Inc	3399	16
St Marys Foundry Inc	3321	69
Saint Mary's Health Care Corp	8062	156
St Mary's Health Care System Inc	8062	102
St Mary's Manor	8361	53
Saint Marys Press Of Minnesota	2731	278
St Mary's Tool and Die Inc	3544	360
Saint Media Inc	3565	166
St Meinrad Archabbey	8221	48

Company Name	SIC	Rank
St Monica/St Martin Federal Credit Union	6061	160
St Moritz Building Services Inc	7349	45
St Nick Decorators	3645	65
St Paul Fire and Marine Insurance Co	6331	5
Saint Paul Pioneer Press	2711	41
Saint Peter Counseling Center	8322	225
St Rose Dominican Hospital	8062	181
St Tours	4724	112
St Vincent Press Inc	2752	1608
Saint Vincent's Home	8322	122
St Vincent's Medical Center	8062	166
Saint Wire and Cable Company Inc	3679	578
Sainte Partners	4833	240
Saint-Gobain BTI	3296	6
Saint-Gobain Performance Plastics	3089	30
Saitech Inc	7373	466
Saja Bankcard Services Inc	7389	1087
Sajan Inc (River Falls Wisconsin)	3674	236
Sajar Plastics Inc	3089	465
Sajasa Construction Inc	1623	394
Sajiun Electric Inc	1731	1474
Sakaiya Company Of America Ltd	3465	62
Sakata Seed America Inc	3999	42
Sakeone Corp	2085	26
Saker Aviation Services Inc	4581	35
Saker Shoprites Inc	5411	74
Sakonnet Vineyards LP	0172	20
Sakor Technologies Inc	3577	598
Sakrete Inc	3273	93
Saks Holdings Inc	5651	8
Saks Inc	5311	16
Saks Jandel	5632	11
Sakura Finetek USA Inc	3999	41
Sal Electric Company Inc	1731	1704
Sal Johnson and Associates Inc	7371	581
Saladino Furniture Inc	5021	164
Salamander Technologies Inc	7371	1082
Salamonie Mills Inc	5191	172
Salarycom Inc	7372	738
Salco Inc	3599	1130
Salco Industries Inc	3699	233
Salco Machine Inc	3599	2342
Sale Line Inc	7331	204
Saleen Special Vehicles Inc	3711	43
Sale-In-A-Box Inc	5092	41
Salem '66' Auto Sales	4213	3123
Salem Baking Co	2051	104
Salem Communications Corp	4832	14
Salem Electric	4911	254
Salem Equipment Inc	3553	12
Salem Five Cents Savings Bank	6036	14
Salem Leasing Corp	7513	13
Salem Media Of Colorado	4832	230
Salem Packing Co	2011	152
Salem Plastics Inc	3089	1520
Salem Plumbing Supply Company Inc	5074	129
Salem Press Inc	2731	62
Salem Senior Housing	6513	44
Salem Technologies Inc	3089	1657
Salem Times-Commoner Publishing Company Inc	2711	381
Salem Tool Inc	3532	79
Salem Trucking Co	4213	1236
Salem Tube Inc	3317	38
Salem Ventilating International Inc	5013	283
Salem Village Craftsmen Inc	5712	103
Salem-Republic Rubber Co	3052	24
SalePoint Inc	5045	235
Sales Corporation of Alaska	5141	148
Sales Graphics Corp	7371	1239
Sales Opportunity Services Inc	7389	2528
Sales Partnerships Inc	8999	155
Sales Record Publishing Company Inc	7371	1867
Sales Unlimited Inc	5049	225
Salesforcecom Inc	7375	6
Saleslogic LLC	5045	96
SalesPage Technologies Inc	7371	707
SalesQuest LLC	8748	347
Salestream Software Inc	7372	3948
Salford Systems	7372	550
Salient Mobility LLC	7319	151
Salient Surgical Technologies Inc	3841	101
Saliga Machine Company Inc	3599	860
Salima Technologies	5045	1068
Salina Concrete Products Inc	3271	1
Salina Journal Inc	2711	184
Salinas Valley Ford Sales Inc	5511	417
Salinger Electric Co	5063	787
Salinon Corp	7372	4875
Salisbury Bancorp Inc	6035	109
Salisbury Bank and Trust Co	6035	235
Salisbury by Honeywell	3052	2
Salk International Travel Premiums Inc	2731	360
Sallee Horse Vans Inc	4213	1592
Sallisaw Lumber Company Inc	5211	194
Sally Beauty Holdings Inc (Denton Texas)	5087	1
Sally Corp	7999	74
Sally White and Associates Inc	7389	1333
Sallys Home Service	7381	261
Salmen Tech Company Inc	5045	708
Salmolux Inc	2091	14
Salmon Legacy Creek Hospital	8062	131

Company Name	SIC	Rank
Salo LLC	8999	45
Salof Refrigeration Company Inc	3585	162
Salomon North America Inc	5091	21
Salon Interiors Inc	1542	434
Salon Media Group Inc	7319	129
Salsbury Industries Mailboxes	3444	71
Salt Lake Brewing Company LC	5813	6
Salt Lake Mailing and Printing Inc	7331	127
Salt Lake Physical Therapy Associates Inc	8099	92
Salt Lake Regional Medical Center Inc	8062	69
Salt Lake Sand And Gravel Inc	1611	225
Salt Palace Convention Center	7389	1057
Salt River Project	4911	80
Salta's Tire Company Inc	7538	30
Saltchuk Resources Inc	4424	12
Saltec Systems	7371	835
Salter Labs	3841	90
Saltire Software Inc	7372	882
Saltmarsh Cleaveland and Gund	8721	11
Saltmine Inc	7372	534
SaltWorks Inc	5199	42
Saltzburg Ray and Bergman LLP	8111	437
Saltzman Hamma Nelson Massaro LLP	8721	162
Saltzman Printers Inc	2796	38
Salvadorini Consulting LLC	5047	289
Salvajor Co	3589	129
Salvation Army	8322	167
Salvatore Polizzi	5023	144
Salvo Tool and Engineering Company Inc	3542	108
Salzman Electric Company Inc	1731	1730
Sam Ash Megastores LLC	5099	97
Sam Ash Music Corp	5736	2
Sam Broussard Trucking Company Inc	4213	1457
Sam Flax Inc	5021	16
Sam Freitas Trucking Inc	4213	2843
Sam Johnson Cross Creek Lincoln	5511	691
Sam Kane Beef Processors Inc	2011	11
Sam Levitz Furniture Co	5712	39
Sam Moore Furniture Industries Inc	2512	28
Sam Nichols Electrical Inc	1731	2364
Sam O Hirota Inc	8711	456
Sam Rodgers Enterprises Inc	6552	223
Sam S Accursio and Sons Packing and Produce Inc	2033	90
Sam Swope Automotive Group Inc	5511	43
Sam Tell And Son Inc	5046	36
Samar Company Inc	3052	28
Samaritan Medical Center	8062	107
Samaritan Pharmaceuticals Inc	8731	293
Samaritan Wholesale Tire Company Inc	5014	23
Samas Telecom	5065	841
Samax Precision Inc	3599	913
Sambazon Inc	8999	136
Samco Antennas Inc	3663	396
Samcotime Inc	7373	722
Same Day Inc	4213	2667
SAME Inc	3679	288
Samepage LLC	7379	1247
SamePage Solutions LLC	7372	2172
Saminco Inc	3625	165
Samluk Communications Inc	8743	320
Samm Enterprises Inc	1731	1740
Sammamish DataSystems Inc	7372	4472
Sammarco Electric Company Inc	1731	1943
Sammons Enterprises Inc	6311	39
Sammy's Woodfired Pizza	5812	199
Samorlana LLC	2752	554
Sample Barn	2653	119
Sample Concepts Inc	2789	78
Sample Machining Inc	3599	850
Sample Media Inc	2752	1145
Samples Inc	2782	58
Sampoerna Holdings USA Inc	7371	562
Sampson Coatings Inc	2851	121
Sampson Construction Company Inc	1542	35
Sampson Lumber Company Inc	5211	193
Sampson Resources	2741	369
Sampson Steel Corp	5051	168
SAM'S Club	5912	5
Sam's Electrical Contractors Inc	1731	1537
Sam's Wine and Spirits	5921	7
Samsill Corp	2782	10
Samson Electronics Inc	5064	130
Samson Investment Co	2911	33
Samson Metal And Machine Inc	3443	203
Samson Moving and Storage Company Inc	4213	3060
Samson Oil and Gas LLC	1311	224
Samson Plastic Pipe Inc	3084	44
Samson Products Inc	2542	12
Samson Resources Co	1311	185
Samson Rope Technologies Inc	2298	4
Samson Security Services	7381	143
Samson Technologies Inc	3651	33
Samsonite Corp	3199	1
Samsung Electro-Mechanics America Inc	5045	325
Samsung Electronics America Inc	5064	3
Samsung Networks America Inc	4813	208
Samsung Semiconductor Inc	3674	36

Company Name	SIC	Rank
Samsung Telecommunications America Inc	7373	59
Samuel Aaron Inc	3911	27
Samuel Cabot Inc	2851	33
Samuel Clark	3444	269
Samuel French Inc	2731	201
Samuel Specialty Metal	5051	89
Samuel Stamping Technologies LLC	3544	651
Samuel Strapping Systems Inc	3499	40
Samuels Glass Co	3442	121
Samuels Jewelers Inc	5944	4
Samuels Products Inc	2759	276
Samwha USA Inc	5065	411
Samy's Camera Inc	5946	8
San Andreas Regional Center	8322	3
San Angelo Security Service Inc	7382	153
San Antonio Board Of Realtors Inc	7375	179
San Antonio Constructors Inc	1541	202
San Antonio Current Co	2711	553
San Antonio Extended Medical Care Inc	7352	22
San Antonio Federal Credit Union	6061	17
San Antonio Independent School District Network Div	3825	150
San Antonio Informer Publishing	2711	554
San Antonio Lighthouse For The Blind	8331	78
San Antonio Observer	2711	878
San Antonio Spurs LLC	7941	15
San Antonio Telephone Co	1731	1521
San Antonio Thermo King Inc	5078	33
San Antonio Winery Inc	2084	26
San Benito Bank	6021	212
San Bernard Electric Cooperative Inc	4911	216
San Bernardino County School District	8211	72
San Diego Brewery Co	2082	11
San Diego Convention Center Corp	7389	183
San Diego County Office Of Education	8299	20
San Diego Gas and Electric Co	4911	45
San Diego Magazine Publishing Co	2721	190
San Diego Metropolitan Business Magazine	2721	449
San Diego Padres Baseball Club LP	7941	1
San Diego Precision Machining Inc	3444	196
San Diego Stage and Lighting Supply Inc	5999	278
San Diego Transit Corp	4131	3
San Diego Travel Group	4724	12
San Diego Trolley Inc	4111	9
San Diego Trust Bank	6022	506
San Dieguito Printers Inc	2752	282
San Esters Corp	5169	74
San Fernando Metals Inc	5099	133
San Fernando Swap Meet and Flea Market	7389	1845
San Francisco Bay Brand Inc	2048	85
San Francisco Design Center	6531	315
San Francisco Ford Lincoln Mercury	5511	228
San Francisco Foundation	7389	173
San Francisco Gravel Company Inc	5032	101
San Francisco Stereo Inc	5731	72
San Gabriel/Pomona Valleys Developmental Services Inc	8322	5
San Gabriel Valley Water Co	4941	16
San Joaquin General Hospital	8011	32
San Joaquin Helicopters	3799	2
San Joaquin Refining Company Inc	2911	61
San Joaquin Valley A PC D	8748	249
San Joaquin Valley Dairy Equipment	5083	164
San Jose Business Journal	2711	552
San Jose Group	7311	299
San Jose Mailing Inc	7331	217
San Jose Mercury News Inc	2711	111
San Jose Scientific Company Inc	5049	80
San Juan Brewing Company Inc	2082	91
San Luis Obisbo Eye Associates A Me	5995	19
San Luis Sourdough	2051	125
San Luis Valley HMO Inc	6324	107
San Miguel Produce Inc	0721	1
San Patricio Publishing Company Inc	2711	801
San Ramon Valley Times	2711	250
San-Aid Company Inc	5087	148
SANBlaze Technology Inc	5045	695
Sanborn Chevrolet Inc	5511	724
Sanborn Plastics Corp	3089	828
Sancap Liner Technology Inc	3081	64
Sancliff Inc	3544	878
Sanco Industries Inc	3599	1153
Sancoa International Company LP	2759	81
Sancor Lighting Inc	5063	917
Sanctum Inc	7372	1021
Sand Creek Energy LLC	2861	3
Sand Creek Post and Beam	2499	48
Sand Seed Service Inc	5153	167
Sand Trap Service Company Inc	4953	169
Sand Video Inc	3674	24
Sandar Industries Inc	3545	290
Sandata Technologies Inc	7374	115
Sandbagger Corp	3599	2427
Sandberg Enterprises Inc	3599	1983
Sandberg Furniture Manufacturing	2511	24
Sandberg Industries Inc	3679	374
Sandco Industries	8331	229
Sandee Manufacturing Co	3089	618
Sandee Plastic Extrusions	3089	487

Company Name	SIC	Rank
Sanden Of America Inc	3585	38
Sanderling Ventures	6799	265
Sanders and Parks PC	8111	442
Sanders Ford Inc	5511	881
Sanders Gallery	5999	242
Sanders General Construction LLC	1623	807
Sanders Industries Co	3363	32
Sanders Lead Company Inc	3339	3
Sanders Manufacturing Company Inc	3694	38
Sanders Pipeline Construction Co	1623	547
Sanders Sanders and Block PC	7389	1293
Sanders Satellite Systems	5731	235
Sanders Security Inc	7382	155
Sanders Truck Transportation	4213	1442
Sanders Wingo	7311	128
Sanders Wingo Galvin and Morton Advertising Inc	7311	144
Sanders Wood Products Inc	2421	73
Sanderson Farms Inc	2015	5
Sanderson Farms Inc (Jackson Mississippi)	2038	17
Sanderson Ford Inc	5511	54
Sanderson Pipe Corp	3084	27
Sanderson Plumbing Products Inc	2499	11
Sanderson Safety Supply Co	5087	39
Sanderson-Macleod Inc	3991	11
Sandglass Systems	7375	291
Sandhill Scientific Inc	3841	276
Sandhill Telephone Coop	4813	302
Sandhills Contractors Inc	1623	751
Sandhills Publishing Co	2721	50
Sandifer Engineering and Control	5075	105
SanDisk Corp	3572	6
Sandler Capital Management	6799	76
Sandler O'Neill and Partners LP	6211	53
Sandler Travis and Rosenberg PA	8111	237
Sandmeyer Steel Co	3312	87
Sandoval Brothers Inc	7361	265
Sandra K Easley Trucking/DET Co	4213	2486
Sandra K Schmitz	7381	194
Sandray Precision Grinding Co	3599	394
SandRidge Energy Inc	1311	32
Sandridge Food Corp	2099	74
Sands Chevrolet	5511	301
Sandsport Data Services Inc	7374	92
Sandusky Electric Inc	5063	137
Sandusky Fabricating and Sales Inc	3535	166
Sandusky International Inc	3325	21
Sandusky Newspapers Inc	4832	44
Sandvik Mining and Construction USA LLC	3532	14
Sandvik Process Systems Inc	3823	166
Sandvik Tamrock USA Inc	3532	18
Sandwich Isles Communications Inc	4813	352
Sandwich Isles Termite and Pest Control	7342	19
Sandy Beach Resort	7011	136
Sandy Spring Bancorp Inc	6712	137
Sandy Spring Bank	6021	47
Sandy-Alexander Inc	2752	119
Sanese Services Inc	5962	4
Sanford and Hawley Inc	5211	128
Sanford Coca-Cola Bottling Co	2086	90
Sanford Cohen and Associates	8748	212
Sanford Electric Company Inc	1731	1649
Sanford Health	8062	242
Sanford Holshouser Economic Development Consulting	8111	569
Sanford L Alderfer Auction Company Inc	7389	1295
Sanford LP	3951	1
Sanford Rose Associates (Akron Ohio)	6794	132
Sanford Studios Inc	7335	13
Sanford-Lussier Inc	5031	277
Sangamo BioSciences Inc	8731	210
Sangean America Inc	5064	200
Sani-Co Products	2841	22
Sani-Hut Company Inc	7359	229
Sani-Matic Inc	3499	79
San-I-Pak Pacific Inc	3443	172
Sanitary Process Systems Inc	1799	87
Sanitary Supply and Chemical Company Inc	5087	179
Sanitary Tortilla Manufacturing Company Inc	2099	310
Sanitek Products Inc	2842	163
Sanitors Southwest Of San Antonio Inc	7349	73
San-J International Inc	2035	46
San-Mar Laboratories Inc	2844	73
Sanmina-SCI Corp	3672	2
Sanmina-SCI PCB	3672	13
Sanna Mattson MacLeod Inc	7311	455
Sanofi Pasteur Biologics Co	8731	57
Sanofi Pharmaceuticals Inc	2834	27
Sanolite Corp	5169	122
Sanrad North America	5045	197
Sanrise Inc	7374	105
Sans Consulting Services Inc	7379	257
Sans Pareil Inc	5048	36
Sansegal Sportswear Inc	2395	4
Sansei Showa Company Ltd	3823	377
Sansing Electric	1731	2268
Sanson Co	5148	13
SanSpot	5045	364

Company Name	SIC	Rank
Sanstrom Scale Company Inc	5046	364
Sansum Clinic	8011	28
Santa Barbara Applied Research Inc	7389	720
Santa Barbara Bank and Trust	6022	53
Santa Barbara Brewing Company LLC	2082	45
Santa Barbara Engineering Inc	3695	103
Santa Barbara Infrared Inc	3823	114
Santa Barbara Instrument Gp Inc	3861	100
Santa Barbara Olive Co	2033	88
Santa Barbara Software Products Inc	7372	4750
Santa Clara Convention Center	7389	1846
Santa Clara Nut Co	5145	20
Santa Clara Transfer Service	4213	2495
Santa Clara Valley Bank NA	6021	339
Santa Clarita Studio Corp	7819	55
Santa Cruz Biotechnology Inc	2836	38
Santa Cruz Guitar Corp	3931	33
Santa Cruz Sentinel Publishers	2711	80
Santa Fe Beauty Salon	5087	185
Santa Fe Financial Corp	6799	256
Santa Fe Ole Inc	2099	376
Santa Fe Reporter Inc	2711	829
Santa Fe Rubber Products Inc	3069	162
Santa Fe Systems Inc	3577	484
Santa Fuel Inc	5983	7
Santa Maria Electric Inc	1731	833
Santa Maria Ford	5511	925
Santa Maria Software Inc	7372	4633
Santa Maria Times Inc	2711	310
Santa Monica Bay Physicians Health Services Inc	8011	94
Santa Monica Homeopathic Pharmacy Inc	5912	56
Santa Monica Partners	6211	259
Santal Corp	7336	279
Santana Property Group Inc	6531	392
Santander Holdings USA Inc	6712	17
Santander BanCorp	6712	97
Santander International Bank	6029	6
Santaniello Electric LLC	4911	589
Santarus Inc	2834	122
Santa's Best	3999	46
Santa's Enchanted Forest Inc	7996	37
Santee Electric Cooperative Inc	4911	295
Santee Print Works	2261	4
Santee Redi-Mix Corp	5032	181
Santeen Supply Co	2842	180
Santeon Group Inc	7374	389
Santora CPA Group	8721	175
Santos Precision Inc	3728	173
Santoso Associates	7379	803
San-Tron Inc	3678	38
Santronics Software	7372	4331
Santur Corp	4899	86
Sanwa USA Inc	3442	17
SANYO Customs Brokerage Inc	4789	21
Sanyo Fisher Corp	3651	75
Sanyo Foods Corporation Of America	7997	15
SANYO Logistics Corp	4789	22
Sanyo Sales and Supply Corp (Wood Dale Illinois)	5064	27
SANYO Semiconductor Corp	3674	180
Sanyo Transportation Co	4213	621
SAP Americas Inc	7372	9
SAP Labs Inc	7372	107
Sapa Extrusions	3354	5
Sapa Profiles Inc	3354	12
Sapiens Americas Inc	7372	458
Sapient Corp	7373	15
Sapient Securities Corp	7371	93
Sapona Manufacturing Company Inc	2282	1
Sapphire Envelope and Graphics Inc	2759	468
Sappi Fine Paper North America	2621	11
Saputo Cheese And Protein LLC	2022	34
Saqqara Systems Inc	7372	1908
Sar Inc	7371	1409
Sara Lee Bakery	2013	3
Sara Lee Foods	2013	6
Sara Lee Refrigerated Foods Foodservice	2015	21
Sara Mana Business Products Inc	7699	172
Sara Sales Co	5065	554
Sara Weems Home Interiors	7389	2057
Sarach Systems Inc	7363	154
Sarah Spencer Solutions LLC	7379	1504
Saraide Inc	7375	176
Saranac Brand Foods Inc	2099	280
Saranac Glove Co	3151	5
Sarasota Brewing Co	2082	95
Sarasota Endoscopy ASC LLC	8011	120
Sarasota Opthalmology ASC LLC	8011	107
Saratoga County Chapter Nysarc Inc	8361	20
Saratoga Eagle	5181	60
Saratoga Food Specialties	2087	23
Saratoga Industries Div	3679	135
Saratoga Investment Corp	6211	122
Saratoga National Bank and Trust Co	6021	236
Saratoga Partners III LP	6719	151
Saratoga Security Guard Service	7381	86
Saratoga Spring Water Co	2086	139
Saratoga Systems Inc	7372	1046
Saratogian LLC	2711	92
Saratogo On Line Systems Inc	7371	847
SARCOM	7376	13
SARCOM Inc	7373	26
Sarcon Microsystems Inc	3812	192
Sard Verbinnen and Co	8743	63
Sardee Corporation Of California	3535	139
Sardello Inc	5088	58
Sare Electric Inc	1731	1201
Sare Plastics Inc	3089	1649
Sares-Regis Group	6552	45
Sarga Solutions Inc	5734	262
Sargent and Lundy LLC	8711	60
Sargent Controls and Aerospace	3568	26
Sargent Corp	1629	13
Sargent Electric Co	1731	85
Sargent Manufacturing Co	3429	44
Sargent Metal Fabricators Inc	3441	146
Sargent Pipe Company Inc	3533	71
Sargent-Sowell Co	3993	82
Sargent-Welch Scientific Co	5049	40
Sargon Consulting LLC	7379	1343
Sarlo Power Mowers Inc	3524	35
Sarnia Corp	6512	73
Sarnoff Corp	3651	25
Sarofim Realty Advisors	8748	223
Sarolo Bagel Restaurant Corp	5149	196
Sarott Construction Co	3531	194
Sarraff and Son Inc	5046	219
Sarris Candies Inc	5812	405
SARS Corp	7372	4226
SARS Software Products Inc	7371	836
Sarstedt Inc	5047	59
Sartek Industries Inc	3663	348
Sartell Group Inc	7373	1056
Sartomer Company Inc	3087	4
Sartori Food Corp	2022	28
Sartorius North America Inc	3821	1
Sartorius Stedim Systems Inc	3559	92
Sartorius Tcc Co	3821	30
SAS Institute Inc	7372	20
SAS Manufacturing Inc	3679	448
SAS Safety Corp	3842	86
Sasaki Associates Inc	8711	104
SASCO	1731	1
Sasco Electric	1731	4
Sashco Inc	2891	44
Sasker Repair	7699	18
Sasol North America Inc	2869	3
Sasquatch Books Inc	2731	91
Sass and Associates	7311	567
Sass J and J Electric Inc	1731	1185
Sassafras Software Inc	7372	4388
SAT Corp	7372	482
SAT Corp (Sunnyvale California)	7372	883
Sat Pak Communications Inc	5063	862
Sat Suma Valve and Controls LLC	5085	352
Satake (USA) Inc	5084	284
Satcher Motor Co	5511	1118
Satco Inc	1741	10
Satco Products Inc	5063	200
Satcom Global Inc	4813	268
Satcom Resources LLC	3663	124
SatCon Technology Corp	3674	90
Satec Inc	3825	107
Sate-Lite Manufacturing Co	3647	11
Satellink Communications Inc	4812	18
Satellink Inc	3663	182
Satellite 2000 Systems International Corp	5063	334
Satellite Communication Systems Inc	4899	92
Satellite Dish Communications	4841	97
Satellite Industries Inc	3448	14
Satellite Link Corp	3679	795
Satellite Receivers Ltd	5063	362
Satellite Solutions LLC	5731	55
Satellite Tool and Machine Company Inc	3728	195
Satellite TV Supermarket	5731	240
Satellites Unlimited Inc	5731	165
Satiety Inc	8731	163
Satilla Health Services Inc	8062	169
Satin American Corp	3613	91
Satisloh North America Inc	5049	16
Satmetrix Systems Inc	7372	1251
Satnam Data Systems Inc	7379	1263
SATO America Inc	3577	188
Satori Chiropractic Software Inc	7372	4876
Satori Group Inc	5045	282
Satori Software Inc	7372	2580
Satpro Network Inc	3679	607
Sattell Johnson Appel and Co	8721	142
Sattler Companies Inc	3599	1946
Sattler Homes Inc	1521	147
Saturday Audio Exchange Inc	5731	148
Saturday Knight Ltd	2392	41
Saturn Business Systems Inc	7373	457
Saturn Electronics and Engineering Inc	3672	10
Saturn Electronics Corp	3672	49
Saturn Enterprises Inc	5065	576
Saturn Fasteners Inc	3429	97
Saturn Freight Systems Inc	4213	482
Saturn Industries Inc	3624	24
Saturn LLC	3711	6
Saturn Machine And Welding Company Inc	3567	75
Saturn Machine Inc	3599	485
Saturn Network Services	4813	436
Saturn of Memphis Inc	5511	1023
Saturn of Orlando South	5511	457
Saturn Overhead Equipment LLC	3537	105
Saturn Systems Inc	7371	1027
Saturn Tool and Die Co	3544	901
Sauber Manufacturing Co	3531	99
Saucony Inc	5941	19
Sauder Custom Fabrication Inc	3443	148
Sauder Feeds Inc	5191	164
Sauder Manufacturing Co	2531	23
Sauder Woodworking Co	2511	6
Sauer Inc (Pittsburgh Pennsylvania)	1799	7
Sauer-Danfoss Co USA	3568	3
Sauer-Danfoss Inc	3592	1
Sauereisen Inc	3297	12
Sauers Group Inc	2752	526
Saugatuck Capital Company LP	6799	234
Saul Centers Inc	6798	132
Saul Ewing LLP	8111	102
Saul Ewing LLP	8111	134
Saul QRS Inc	6798	100
Saul Zaentz Co	7812	53
Sault Sainte Marie Tribe Of Chippewa Indians	8748	32
Saum Enterprises Inc	3564	167
Sauna Warehouse Inc	5961	171
Saunders Dental Laboratory LLC	8072	35
Saunders Engine And Equipment Company Inc	7699	103
Saunders Hotels Group	8741	10
Saunders Manufacturing Company Inc	3499	86
Saurer Holding Inc	3552	1
Saurer Textile Systems Charlotte Inc	5084	322
Sau-Sea Foods Inc	5146	76
Saussy Burbank	1521	82
Sava Transportation Inc	4213	3141
Savage Arms Inc	3484	11
Savage Brothers Co	3556	122
Savage Design Group Inc	7336	41
Savage Engineering Inc	3542	83
Savage Equipment Inc	3523	228
Savage Industries Inc (Salt Lake City Utah)	4212	3
Savage Sports Corp	3484	9
Savage Universal Corp	5043	23
Savage Ventures Inc	3544	436
Savage Wholesale Building Materials Inc	5031	261
Savala Construction Co	1623	537
Savala Equipment Company Inc	7353	39
Savamco Manufacturing Inc	3581	12
Savane International Corp	2325	6
Savannah Bancorp Inc	6021	90
Savannah Blueprint Co	7334	38
Savannah Distributing Company Inc	5181	83
Savannah Foods and Industries Inc	2062	3
Savannah Recycling LLC	5051	411
Savannah Transport Inc	4213	2637
SAVANT Audiovisuals Inc	7812	183
Savant Inc	8734	161
Savant Software Sciences Inc	1731	2174
Savard Software	7372	5147
SavaSeniorCare	8051	51
SavaSeniorCare LLC	8051	8
Save Mart Supermarkets	5411	49
Save The World Air Inc	5072	207
Save-A-Lot Ltd	5411	89
SaveOnResortscom LLC	4724	147
Savers Inc	5311	29
Savers Marketing Corp	6311	257
Savers Property and Casualty Insurance Co	6351	50
Save-U-Rental Center Inc	7359	252
Savex Manufacturing Company Inc	3841	402
Savi Technology Inc	3669	67
SaviCorp	6794	164
Savient Pharmaceuticals Inc	2833	53
Savignano Food Corp	2038	62
Savin Corp	5044	3
Savings Bank Life Insurance Co	6311	163
Savings Bank of Maine	6035	71
Savings Bank (Wakefield Massachusetts)	6036	60
Savings Institute Bank and Trust	6036	27
Savings Institute Bank and Trust Co	6036	65
Savingsbondscom Inc	7372	3019
SavingsCom Inc	7319	63
Savmart Pharmaceutical Services Inc	5122	85
Savoie's Sausage And Food Products Inc	2013	134
Savol Bleach Co	5169	64
Savory Creations International	2048	150
Savoy Corp	6552	226
Savoy Medical Supply Company Inc	5047	183
Savr Communications Inc	3663	303
Savvion Inc	7372	698
Savvis Inc	7372	62
Savvy Rest Inc	2515	29
Saw Daily Service Inc	5085	184
Saw Menominee And Supply Company Inc	7699	158
Saw Misenheimer and Tool Inc	3545	118
Saw Systems Inc	5084	384

SAW Company Name Index

Company Name	SIC	Rank
Saw Textiles Inc	2339	59
Sawbrook Steel Castings Co	3365	9
Sawgrass Technologies Inc	7373	370
Sawmill Hydraulics	3553	53
Sawtooth Group Inc	7311	421
Sawtooth Software	7372	4212
Sawyer Products Inc	2879	21
Sawyer Technical Materials LLC	3679	268
Sax Software Corp	7372	3741
Saxon Capital Inc	6162	22
Saxon Global Inc	7373	467
Saxon Group Inc	1541	100
Saxon Industries Inc	3533	102
Saxon John Printing Inc	2752	1464
Saxon Mortgage Services Inc	6162	33
Saxon Shoes Inc	5661	14
Saxony Ice Co	2097	12
Saxton Falls Sand and Gravel Co	1442	70
Saxton Inc	6552	251
Saxton Pierce Restaurant Corp	5812	155
Saybrook Capital LLC	6211	127
Sayco Container Inc	2653	11
Sayco Enterprises Inc	2759	427
Sayers Group LLC	5045	130
Saylent Technologies Inc	7379	666
Saylor Electric Products Corp	5531	47
Saylor-Beall Manufacturing Co	3563	19
Saylors Dental Laboratory Inc	8072	25
Sayre Electric	1731	1944
Sb Capital Group LLC	7389	340
SB Foot Tanning Co	3111	2
SB International Inc	5013	234
SB Liquidating Co	2789	50
Sb Midwest Holding Corp	5013	128
SBA Communications Corp	8711	26
SBA Network Services Inc	8711	380
SBA Properties Inc	8711	363
SBA Sites Inc	8711	364
SBA Towers Inc	8711	365
Sbarro America Inc	5812	173
Sbarro Inc	5812	123
SBC Systems Company Inc	7372	2816
Sbc Yellow Pages	2741	251
Sbd Holding Company LLC	5531	44
SBG Technology Solutions Inc	8748	128
SBI Razorfish	7372	1775
SBK Brooks Investment Corp	6211	199
Sbm Site Services	7349	147
Sbmc Solutions LLC	3545	86
Sbpi Inc	2752	1231
SBS	7349	293
Sbs Industries Inc	3451	30
Sbs Investments Of Dade County Inc	7359	203
SBT Bancorp Inc	6162	73
SBT Business Technologies Inc	7372	2477
SC and B Owners Inc	3625	203
SC Direct	5961	112
SC Electronics Inc	3612	86
SC Industrial Resource Group Inc	5084	770
SC Johnson and Son Inc	2842	1
SC Manufacturing Inc	3599	387
SC Valley Engineering Inc	1623	396
SCA Enterprises Inc	7389	574
SCA Schucker Company LP	3586	20
Scadaware Inc	7371	996
Scafa-Tornabene Art Publishing Company Inc	5199	91
Scaffold Erections Inc	7361	396
Scaffolding Solutions LLC	7359	99
Scai Inc	7389	1352
Scala Inc	7372	2554
Scalable Software Inc	7372	1048
Scale Electronics Corp	3823	434
Scale Watcher North America Inc	3589	267
Scales Industrial Technologies Inc	7699	34
Scales Unlimited Inc	3596	14
Scaletron Industries Ltd	3596	27
Scaletta Moloney Armoring Corp	3799	17
Scalfo Electric Inc	1731	237
Scalzo Realty Inc	6531	114
Scamardo Metal Fabricators Inc	3444	284
Scan Group Inc	2796	18
Scan Inc	8322	105
Scan Technology Inc	3577	570
Scan Tool and Mold Inc	3089	1420
Scan/US Inc	7372	1107
SCANA Corp	4931	8
Scanart	7336	213
Scanco Inc	7372	4213
ScanData Systems Inc	7372	3452
Scandia Amusement Park	7996	38
Scandia Manufacturing Company Inc	3599	1754
Scandia Packaging Machinery Co	3565	107
Scandia Plastics Inc	2821	117
Scandic Electronics Inc	5065	683
Scandinavian Formulas Inc	2099	303
Scanivalve Corp	3823	162
Scanlan International Inc	3841	266
ScanlanKemperBard Companies Inc	6552	150
Scanner Applications Inc	8732	104
Scanner Graphics Inc	7336	153
Scanner Technologies Corp	3559	467
Scanning Electron Analysis Laboratories Inc	8748	417
Scan-Optics LLC	3577	207
Scanport Inc	3577	12
Scans Group Corp	3829	483
ScanSource Inc	5045	9
Scantech Color Systems Inc	7335	20
Scantek Inc	5065	688
Scantibodies Laboratory Inc	2835	20
Scantland Broadcasting Ltd	4832	215
Scantron Corp	3577	79
Scanvec Amiable Ltd	7372	1539
Scapa Tapes North America Inc	2672	19
Scarborough Group Inc	6211	366
Scarborough Specialties Inc	5199	77
Scardina Refrigeration Company Inc	5046	129
Scariano Brothers LLC	5141	143
Scarponi Electric LLC	1731	2040
Scarr Moving and Storage Inc	4213	2755
Scavolini USA Inc	5031	405
SCB Bancorp Inc	6712	537
SCBT Financial Corp	6712	135
Scbt NA	6021	319
Scearce Satcher and Jung PA	8721	178
Scene Three Inc	7812	132
Scenic Airlines Inc	4522	31
Scenic Fruit Co	2037	26
Scenic Rivers Energy Coop	4911	298
Scentations Inc	3999	172
Scentsy Inc	5999	17
Scepter Hardwoods Inc	2426	37
Sceptre Technologies Inc	3571	38
SCF Partners	6799	204
Schaake Corp	0211	15
Schaben and Westling Inc	4213	3011
Schaedler Yesco Distribution Inc	5063	61
Schaefer Enterprises Of Deposit Inc	1422	46
Schaefer Homes	1521	135
Schaefer Mold Inc	3089	380
Schaefer Ventilation Equipment	3564	29
Schaeferrolls Inc	3069	238
Schaefers Enterprise Of Wolf Lake Inc	3599	24
Schaefers Market	2011	117
Schaefer's TV and Appliance Center Inc	5731	27
Schaeffer Marketing Group Inc	5063	994
Schaeffler Group USA Inc	3562	1
Schaeperkoetter Sales and Service	5399	6
Schaerer Mayfield USA Inc	5047	273
Schafer Condon Carter	7311	218
Schafer Gear Works Inc	3499	56
Schafer International	5065	702
Schafer's Fisheries Inc	4213	856
Schaffer Partners Inc	8741	183
Schaffner Manufacturing Company Inc	3291	6
Schagby Inc	5731	124
Schaller Anderson Inc	8099	24
Schaller Corp	3469	102
Schaller Manufacturing Corp	2013	126
Schaller Tool and Die Co	3544	578
Schaller's Bakery Inc	2051	189
Schamas Manufacturing CoInc	3531	232
Schap Specialty Machine Inc	3829	295
Schapira's Coffee and Tea Company Inc	2095	38
Scharch Manufacturing Inc	3559	465
Scharff Weisberg Inc	7359	75
Schat Dot Net	5734	310
Schatz Bearing Corp	3562	32
Schaumburg Toyota Inc	5511	132
Schawbel Corp	5064	69
Schawk Inc	2752	9
Schawk Inc (Minneapolis Minnesota)	2796	15
Schawk Retail Marketing	7336	11
Schawk USA Inc	2759	152
Schechter Dokken Kanter	8721	491
Schechter Dokken Kanter Andrews and Selcer Ltd	8721	136
Scheck Mechanical Corp	1623	426
ScheduAll Software	7372	960
Scheels All Sports Inc	5941	15
Scheer Bay LP	3541	215
Scheffel and Co	8721	65
Scheffer Inc	3555	21
Scheid Vineyards Inc	0172	6
Scheirer Machine Company Inc	3532	76
Schell and Kampeter Inc	2047	25
Schell Electronics Inc	3679	836
Schellenbach and Associates Inc	7372	4634
Schema Inc	7372	245
Schema Research Corp	7372	4877
Schematic Inc	7373	212
Schemers Inc	7373	384
Schenck Accurate Inc	3823	77
Schenck Foods Company Inc	5141	126
Schenck Rotec Corp	3549	19
Schenck Trebel Corp	3545	92
Schenectady Steel Company Inc	3441	106
Schenk Hampton Advertising	7311	788
Schenkel and Shultz Inc	8712	142
Schenkelberg Implement Co	5083	86
Schenkel's All-Star Dairy LLC	2026	35
Schenone Specialty Foods Inc	2066	43
Scherer Brothers Lumber Co	5211	33
Schering Berlin Inc	2834	9
Schermerhorn Brothers Co	5085	96
Scherping Electric Inc	1731	2472
Scherping Systems Inc	3499	24
Scherr Furniture Rentals Inc	7359	230
Scherrer Resources Inc	7372	4182
Scherzer International Corp	7389	784
Scherzinger Corp	7342	17
Schetky Northwest Sales Inc	5012	51
Schetter Electric Inc	1731	413
Scheu Manufacturing Co	3433	39
Scheu Steel Supply Co	5051	287
Schewel Furniture Company Inc	5712	33
Schibley Chemicals Company Inc	5169	125
Schick Wilkinson Sword	3421	8
Schiele Graphics Inc	2752	471
Schiele Group	2752	90
Schienke Electric and Machine Services Inc	3541	267
Schiff Food Products Company Inc	2099	121
Schiff Nutrition International Inc	5149	14
Schiffer Publishing Ltd	2731	220
Schiffmayer Plastics Corp	3089	919
Schifino/Lee Inc	7311	687
Schildberg Construction Company Inc	5032	16
Schilli Corp	4213	139
Schilli Transportation Services Inc	4213	154
Schilling Enterprises	5511	380
Schiltz Foods Inc	2015	64
Schimatic Cash Transactions Network-com Inc	7389	2513
Schippers and Crew Inc	3672	170
Schirf Brewing Co	5812	418
Schirm USA Inc	2879	24
Schlage Lock Co	3429	9
Schlagel Inc	3523	106
Schlessman Seed Co	5191	159
Schleuniger Inc	3569	144
Schlichting and Sons Excavating Inc	1794	39
Schlitter Tool Inc	3545	317
Schlossmann's Honda City	5511	133
Schlotter Precision Products Inc	3089	1395
Schlotterbeck and Foss Company Inc	2035	42
Schlotzsky's Inc	5812	270
Schlueter Co	3589	77
Schlumberger/EMR	1389	43
Schlumberger Ltd	1389	1
Schlumberger Omnes	4813	5
Schmald Tool and Die Inc	3544	507
Schmell And Azman Bakery	2051	262
Schmelzer Industries Inc	1799	125
Schmid and Son Packaging Inc	7389	1066
Schmid Tool and Engineering Corp	3599	1530
Schmidt Associates Inc	8712	159
Schmidt Baking Company Inc	2051	22
Schmidt Cabinet Company Inc	2434	80
Schmidt Construction Company Inc	1623	509
Schmidt Electric Company LP	1731	113
Schmidt Electric Inc	1731	1301
Schmidt Electric LLC	1731	2347
Schmidt Equipment and Supply Inc	5046	238
Schmidt Feintechnik Corp	3549	79
Schmidt Insurance Agency Inc	6411	272
Schmidt Kaplan Electric Inc	1731	363
Schmidt Machine Co	5083	53
Schmidt N Graphic Design Group	7336	283
Schmidt Printing Company Inc	2752	1075
Schmidt Printing Inc	2752	38
Schmidt Sign Service Inc	7389	1725
Schmidt Westergard and Company PLLC	8721	429
Schmidtlein Electric Inc	1731	1782
Schmidt's Restaurants and Catering	5812	380
Schmidt's Wholesale Inc	5074	112
Schmiede Corp	3542	26
Schmit Ford Mercury Corp	5511	1181
Schmit Laboratories Inc	3999	157
Schmitmeyer Inc	3599	2416
Schmitt Industrial Marketing Corp	5065	810
Schmitt Industries Inc	3823	118
Schmitt Measurement Systems	3569	190
Schmitt Music Co	5735	4
Schmitt Telecom Partners Inc	1731	2447
SchmolzBickenbach USA	3312	42
Schmuck Lumber Co	5211	160
Schmuckal Oil Co	5411	137
Schnabel Engineering Associates Inc	8748	120
Schnabel Foundation Co	1794	5
Schnader Harrison Segal and Lewis LLP	8111	57
Schnadig Corp	2512	35
Schneeberger Inc	3829	78
Schnee's Inc	5661	18
Schneider and Associates Inc	8743	253
Schneider and Marquard Inc	3544	662
Schneider Electric Buildings Americas Inc	3822	1
Schneider Electrical Inc	1731	2400
Schneider Graphic's Inc	7532	12
Schneider Kleinick Weitz and Dam-ashek	8111	374
Schneider Logistics Inc	4789	5
Schneider National Bulk Carriers Inc	4212	20
Schneider National Inc	4212	6
Schneider Specialized Carriers Inc	4213	304
Schneidereith and Sons Inc	2752	1463

1670 Ward's Business Directory of U.S. Private and Public Companies, 55th Edition / Volume 5

Company Name	SIC	Rank
Schneider's Manufacturing Inc	3599	1312
Schneider's Trucking Inc	1623	378
Schneller LLC	2295	8
Schneps Publications Inc	2711	727
Schnitzer Investment Corp	6798	13
Schnitzer Steel Industries Inc	5093	2
Schnuck Markets Inc	5411	58
Schoeller Arca Systems Inc	3089	1228
Schoeller-Bleckmann Energy Services LLC	3532	38
Schoeneck Containers Inc	3085	19
Schoeneman Brothers Co	5211	127
Schoettler Research And Engineering Corp	5064	159
Schoffman's Inc	5083	199
Schofield Enterprises Inc	3694	32
Schofield Media Ltd	2721	144
Schofield Printing Inc	2759	479
Schoitz Engineering Inc	3544	428
Scholar Craft Commercial Furniture	2521	50
Scholars Inn Bakehouse	2051	290
Scholastic Inc	2731	4
Schold Machine Corp	3559	275
Scholfield Pontiac GMC	5511	674
Scholl Electric Inc	1731	2266
Scholl Forest Inc	5031	117
Scholle Corp	3081	12
Scholle Custom Packaging Inc	6512	60
Scholz Design Inc	8712	272
Schonstedt Instrument Company Inc	3812	112
Schonwetter Enterprises Inc	2013	191
School Annual Publishing Co	2741	117
School District 5 Of Lexington and Richland Counties	8211	11
School District Of Indian River County	8211	4
School Health Corp	5047	105
School Innovations And Advocacy Inc	8742	331
School Specialty Inc	5112	4
School Systems Federal Credit Union	6061	142
Schoolcraft Auto Auction Inc	5012	95
Schooldude Com Inc	7389	1021
Schoolhouse Software Inc	7372	1864
Schoollink Inc	7373	480
Schoolman Transportation Group	4119	17
Schoolnet Inc	7371	396
Schoolwires Inc	8299	41
Schoon Construction Inc	1623	313
Schooner Information Technology Inc	3577	204
Schooner Petroleum Services Inc	7353	21
Schooner Retirement Community Inc	8322	157
Schoonover Electric Co	1731	202
Schostak Brothers and Company Inc	6552	57
Schott International Inc	5131	17
Schott Magnetics	3677	94
Schott Metal Products Co	3469	203
Schott North America Inc	3231	19
Schottenstein Stores Corp	5311	20
Schott-Fostec LLC	3827	25
Schowalter and Jabouri PC	8721	42
Schrader Bridgeport International Inc	3714	137
Schram Enterprises Inc	3599	1029
Schramm Inc	3533	44
Schreiber Foods Inc	2022	3
Schreiber Incorporated R G	2752	1548
Schreiber LLC	3589	86
Schreiber Specialties Inc	2759	247
Schrey and Sons Mold Company Inc	3544	334
Schrillo Realty Inc	3728	163
Schrodinger LLC	7372	304
Schroeder Construction Company Ltd	1623	515
Schroeder Industries LLC	3569	97
Schroeder Publishing Company Inc	2731	189
Schroeder Tool and Die Corp	3599	1139
Schroedl's Brothers Inc	5147	124
Schroer Manufacturing Co	3821	17
Schrupp Industries Inc	3441	250
Schu Industries Inc	2521	44
Schuck Component Systems	2439	8
Schuco USA LP	2431	80
Schuette Manufacturing And Steel Sales Inc	3523	158
Schuff International Inc	1791	3
Schuff Steel Co	1791	2
Schuff Steel Management	3441	235
Schukei Chevrolet Inc	5511	1132
Schulenburg Printing and Office Supplies Inc	2752	1311
Schuler Bauer Real Estate Services	6531	97
Schuler Engineering Corp	1623	831
Schuler Inc	3714	314
Schuler Manufacturing	3441	197
Schulmerich Carillons Inc	3931	29
Schult Engineering	3599	1478
Schult Homes Corp	3448	8
Schult Industries LLC	3993	130
Schulte Corp	3496	32
Schulte Roth and Zabel LLP	8111	179
Schultz Communications	7311	925
Schultz Controls Inc	3613	168
Schultz Engineering Services Inc	8711	616
Schultz Machine Company Inc	3594	30
Schultz Supply Co	5046	66
Schultz-Bernstein and Associates Inc	7379	1462
Schulz Clearwater Sanitation Inc	7359	162
Schulz Electric Co	3621	86
Schulz Transportation Service	4213	342
Schulze And Burch Biscuit Co	2051	21
Schulze Manufacturing Inc	3621	155
Schulze Tool Co	3544	568
Schumacher Electric Corp	3629	10
Schumacher Elevator Co	7699	28
Schumacher European Ltd	5511	216
Schumacher Manufacturing Inc	3531	218
Schumaker Technical Assembly	3679	791
Schumann Printers Inc	2752	130
Schunk Graphite Technology LLC	3624	8
Schunk Inex Corporation Inc	3369	26
Schuon Manufacturing Company Inc	3553	39
Schuppann Corp	5072	169
Schur Success Auction Services	7389	564
Schurz Communications Inc	2711	27
Schuster Company Inc	4213	525
Schutt Sports Inc	3949	33
Schutte Lithography Inc	2752	1116
Schutte Lumber Company Inc	5031	81
Schutte Msa LLC	5084	503
Schutte Pulverizer Company Inc	3531	209
Schutz Container Systems Inc	2655	5
Schuyler Roche and Zwirner PC	8111	601
Schuyler Rubber Company Inc	3069	235
Schuylkill Capital Management Ltd	6282	429
Schuylkill Haven Casket Company Inc	3995	10
Schwaab Inc	3953	9
Schwab Capital Markets LP	6211	164
Schwab Government Money Fund	6722	27
Schwab Holdings Inc	6211	25
Schwabe Williamson and Wyatt	8111	439
Schwabel Fabricating Company Inc	3443	206
Schwan Cosmetics USA Inc	2844	59
Schwan Electric Inc	1731	1363
Schwan Food Co	2038	2
Schwann Electric Company Inc	1731	1855
Schwan's Consumer Brands North America Inc	5142	10
Schwan's Sales Inc	2024	65
Schwan's Technology Group Inc	7373	458
Schwartz and Company LLC	7389	998
Schwartz Boring Company Inc	3599	2079
Schwartz Communications Inc	8743	27
Schwartz Farms Inc	0213	6
Schwartz Industries Inc	3599	1030
Schwartz Industries Inc (Huntsville Alabama)	3711	45
Schwartz Investment Counsel Inc	6282	681
Schwartz Iron And Metal Co	5093	119
Schwartz Machine Co	3599	779
Schwartz Manes and Ruby	8111	541
Schwartz Manufacturing Co	2675	29
Schwartz Steel Service Inc	5051	363
Schwartzman Company Inc	5093	81
Schwarz Paper Co	5113	35
Schwarzschild Jewelers Inc	5944	22
Schweiger Construction Company Inc	1542	160
Schweitzer E O Manufacturing Company Inc	3825	94
Schweitzer Real Estate Inc	6531	265
Schweitzer-Mauduit International Inc	2621	16
Schwend Inc	4213	578
Schwerdtle Stamp Co	3953	18
Schwerman Trucking Co	4212	1
Schwing America Inc	3531	16
SCI Corp	5072	152
SCI Engineered Materials Inc	3629	66
SCI Floor Covering Inc	5023	130
SCI Real Estate Investments LLC	6798	76
SCI Solutions	7372	367
SCI Tronics Inc	3669	292
Sciaky Inc	3699	146
Sciambra-Passini French Bakery Inc	2051	226
SciClone Pharmaceuticals Inc	2834	146
Scicom Data Services Ltd	7331	39
Scicom Inc	5045	876
Scidyne	3571	206
Science and Technology International Inc	8732	121
Science Applications International Corp (Linthicum Maryland)	8748	21
Science Horizons Inc	7371	1219
Science Management Company LLC	8741	110
Science Management Corp	8711	77
Science Pump Corp	3829	312
Science Regulatory Services International Corp	8999	207
Science Service Inc	2721	153
Science Systems And Applications Inc	8731	83
Sciencebased Health	2833	31
SciencelabCom Inc	5049	184
ScienceLogic LLC	8748	297
Scientech Inc	3821	76
Scientech Inc (Milford Connecticut)	8742	174
Scientemp Corp	3585	232
Scientific Adsorbents Inc	3826	156
Scientific Alloys Corp	3443	237
Scientific American Inc	2721	122
Scientific and Commercial Systems Corp	8744	43
Scientific Certification Systems Inc	8742	326
Scientific Coating Labs	3479	113
Scientific Components Systems Inc	3646	107
Scientific Computing Associates Corp	7372	4552
Scientific Computing Associates Inc	7372	3552
Scientific Cutting Tools Inc	5084	496
Scientific Device Laboratory Inc	5047	250
Scientific Endeavors Corp	7372	5148
Scientific Engineering Instruments Inc	3823	409
Scientific Exterminating Services	7342	91
Scientific Fabrication Service Inc	3312	117
Scientific Games Corp	7999	29
Scientific Games Holdings Corp	7373	56
Scientific Games International Inc	2759	15
Scientific Games Management Corp	7373	297
Scientific Games Royalty Corp	7373	58
Scientific Industries Inc	3826	87
Scientific Learning Corp	8299	28
Scientific Machine and Supply Company Inc	3821	75
Scientific Marketing Services Inc	8742	564
Scientific Materials Corp	3699	197
Scientific Microscopes Inc	3827	51
Scientific Molding Corporation Ltd	3089	314
Scientific Monitoring Inc	7371	359
Scientific Motion LLC	3569	268
Scientific Plastics Corp	3089	1556
Scientific Plastics Ltd	3089	1861
Scientific Process and Research	3559	481
Scientific Process and Research Inc	3829	331
Scientific Protein Laboratories Inc	2834	181
Scientific Research Corp	8731	54
Scientific Research Products Inc	2844	177
Scientific Software Tools Inc	7372	4256
Scientific Solutions Inc	3577	132
Scientific Systems and Software International Corp	5045	261
Scientific Systems Company Inc	7372	1489
Scientific Systems Inc	3826	94
Scientific Technologies Corp	7372	4154
Scientific Test Inc	3825	306
Scientific Therapeutics Information Inc	2731	290
Scientific Tool Inc	3599	1096
Scientifics	5961	16
Scientronix Inc	3829	431
Sciforma Corp	7372	763
Scimage Inc	7371	501
SciMetrika	8748	214
Scio Consulting International LLC	7373	1173
Scion Corp	3577	475
Scion Inc	5051	353
Scios Inc	2834	133
Scioto County Counseling Center Inc	8322	112
Scioto Downs Inc	7948	18
Scioto Services LLC	7349	114
SciQuest Inc	7372	679
Scivanta Medical Corp	3841	418
SciVantage Inc	5045	359
Scj Associates Inc	3825	142
SCK Inc	7379	671
Sclm Enterprises Inc	2752	1566
Scm Container Machinery Inc	3554	57
SCM Group USA Inc	3553	1
SCM Microsystems	3577	118
Scm Products Inc	7373	1171
SCO Inc	1731	1031
Scobell Company Inc	1711	149
Scolari's Food and Drug Co	5411	22
SCOLR Pharma Inc	2835	74
S-Con Services Inc	1731	1447
Sconnix Broadcasting LLC	4832	97
Sconza Candy Co	2064	24
SCOOTER Store Inc	5963	7
Scope Energy Resources Inc	2047	10
Scope Imports Inc	5136	5
Scope Industries Inc	2047	15
Scope Orthotics and Prosthetics Inc	5999	115
Scope Products Inc	2047	11
Scope Properties Inc	2047	12
Scope Shoppe Inc	5049	205
SCOR Reinsurance Co	6331	197
Score Acquisitions Corp	5145	5
Scorelogix LLC	7371	1432
Scores Holding Company Inc	7999	160
Scori Mold And Engineering Inc	3544	602
ScoringAgcom	7379	1210
Scorpio Tankers Inc	4412	26
Scorpion Sports Inc	5091	97
Scosche Industries Inc	3651	63
Scot Forge Co	3462	11
Scotch Corp	2819	95
Scotch Paint Corp	2851	162
Scotch Plywood Company Inc	2436	9
Scotsco Inc	5084	217
Scotsman Ice Systems	3585	48
Scott and Baldwin CPAs PC	8721	470
Scott and Daughters Publishing Inc	2741	129
Scott and Stringfellow Financial Inc	6211	178
Scott and Stringfellow Inc	6211	64
Scott Banks Trucking Inc	4213	2179
Scott Boatner Construction Inc	1731	1391
Scott Bolt and Screw Company Inc	5085	419
Scott Clark's Toyota City	5511	440
Scott Construction Inc	1611	120
Scott Electronic Services	3625	389
Scott Electronics Inc	3679	306

Company Name	SIC	Rank
Scott Engineering Inc	3629	70
Scott Equipment Co	3559	145
Scott Equipment Inc	5082	144
Scott Fetzer Co	3589	4
Scott G Williams LLC	2879	52
Scott Incorporated Of Milwaukee	7311	678
Scott Industrial Systems Inc	5084	88
Scott Industries Inc	3296	3
Scott Industries Of Kentucky LLC	3089	887
Scott Lamp Company Inc	3646	32
Scott Lithographing Company Inc	2789	83
Scott Machine Inc	3728	155
Scott Machinery Co	5082	41
Scott Melvin Transportation Inc	4213	2590
Scott Molders Inc	3089	872
Scott Motors Inc	5511	1048
Scott Office Systems LLC	3559	434
Scott Paint Company Inc	2851	180
Scott Paper Co	2676	11
Scott Partnership Architecture Inc	8712	227
Scott Pet Products Inc	5199	35
Scott Pipitone Design Ltd	7311	904
Scott Powerline Utility and Equipment LLC	7353	15
Scott Process Systems Inc	3498	24
Scott Resources Inc	3944	40
Scott Rice Co	2522	15
Scott Rice of Kansas City Inc	5712	51
Scott Richard Aviation Services Inc	4512	56
Scott Sabolich Prosthetics and Research Center LLC	3842	268
Scott Sheldon LLC	7373	775
Scott Specialties Inc	3842	120
Scott Stephens and Associates Inc	6531	322
Scott Transportation Inc	4213	2524
Scott Transportation Inc	4213	979
Scott Truck and Tractor Company Inc	5083	6
Scott Van Keppel LLC	5082	109
Scott Yaw Associates LLC	8742	687
Scottdel Cushion LLC	3086	147
Scotti Graphics Inc	2759	206
Scotti Research Inc	8732	128
Scottish Re (US) Inc	6311	224
Scott-McRae Automotive Group	5511	44
Scottrade Bank	6035	35
Scottrade Inc	8742	22
Scott-Randall Systems Inc	5084	838
Scott's Bakeries Inc	5461	26
Scott's Co	3524	10
Scott's Feed Inc	2048	103
Scott's Inc	5143	46
Scott's Liquid Gold Inc	2844	98
Scotts Miracle-Gro Co	2873	3
Scotts Valley Magnetics Inc	3677	85
Scottsbluff Motor Company Inc	5511	1063
Scottsdale Healthcare Family Practice	8011	35
Scottsdale House Inc	7349	479
Scottsdale Pool Service Inc	7389	2041
Scottsdale Villa Mirage	7389	1099
ScottWorld	7379	1505
Scotty's Construction Company LLC	1731	1945
Scotty's Contracting And Stone LLC	1629	88
Scotty's Fashions Company Inc	2339	24
Scougal Rubber Corp	3069	119
Scoular Co	5153	3
Scout Bond	6722	222
Scout Electric Inc	1731	2166
Scout Risk Management Inc	7381	246
Scovill Fasteners Inc	3965	5
Scp Control Inc	3823	345
SCP Private Equity Partners	6719	92
SCR Inc	5999	294
SCR Molding Inc	3089	1656
Scranton Times LP	2711	173
ScreamDVD	7371	1108
Screen America Inc	2759	414
Screen Graphics Of Florida Inc	2759	268
Screen Machine Industries Inc	3532	21
Screen Specialty Shop Inc	2759	540
Screen Tech Incorporated Of New Jersey Inc	2759	178
Screen (USA) Inc	3577	306
Screening Room LLC	5731	222
Screening Systems Inc	3826	101
Screenprint/Dow	2759	108
Screenscape Studios	7812	208
Screenworks USA Inc	2261	17
Screenwriters Inc	2759	443
Screw Conveyor Corp	3535	44
Screw Products Inc	5072	173
Screwmatic Inc	3599	455
Screwmatics Of South Carolina Inc	3451	78
Scribner Cohen and Co	8721	430
Scribner Engineering Inc	3089	1422
ScripNet Inc	7379	391
Scripps Laboratories Inc	2836	69
Scripps Networks Interactive Inc	4841	13
Scripps Treasure Coast Publishing	2711	385
Script to Screen Inc	7812	117
Scriptfleet	4213	913
ScriptLogic Corp	7372	72
Scroll Technologies	3563	9
Scrollmotion Inc	7372	670

Company Name	SIC	Rank
Scrub Inc	7349	83
Scrubair Systems Inc	3564	140
Scrufari Construction Company Inc	1541	128
Scruggs Poultry Inc	5144	21
Scrutiny Inc	7372	4878
SCS Engineering Inc	7372	3846
Scs Machine and Fabricating Inc	3599	1351
Scsi Inc	7378	127
Scsistuff LLC	5045	549
SCT Cable Corp	4841	99
SCT Inc	7373	402
Scubapro/Uwatec	3949	130
Sculli Brothers Inc	5147	137
Scullin Oil Co	5172	34
Scully Distribution Services	4213	319
Scully Metal Fabrication	3441	269
Scully Signal Co	3823	110
Sculpt Image Studio	7379	1211
Scurlock Electric LLC	5063	184
SCV Systems	7379	983
SCW Corp	3645	60
SD Deacon Corp	1542	105
SD Deacon Corp of California	1542	178
SD Enterprises Inc	5149	198
SD Myers Inc	8734	55
SD Richman Sons Inc	5093	129
SDB Inc	1541	164
SDC Coatings Inc	3291	10
Sdc Inc	3364	32
SDCR Business Systems	7372	1609
SDD Inc	7372	2173
SDG Corp	7379	1678
SDGblue LLC	7373	515
Sdi Industries Inc	3535	32
SDI Media	7389	89
SDI Networks Inc	7373	176
Sdi Technologies Inc	3651	66
SDL Waltham	7372	348
SDN Global	4899	102
Sdn Technologies LLC	5045	436
SDP Manufacturing Inc	3589	218
Sdr Plastics Inc	5093	45
Sds Financial Technologies Inc	5045	512
SDS International Inc	4813	105
SDS Lumber Co	2421	52
SDV Inc (Houston Texas)	4731	52
SDV Solutions Inc	7379	405
SDV Telecommunications Inc (Grass Valley California)	4899	59
SE Arnold And Company Inc	5023	150
SE Blueprint Inc	7334	70
SE C Inc	3556	139
SE Cline Construction Inc	1611	215
SE Financial Corp	6712	564
SE International Inc	3829	296
SE Technologies Inc	8711	154
SE Technologies Inc (Stamford Connecticut)	7372	1939
Sea Best Express Inc	4213	2782
Sea Breeze Fruit Flavors Inc	2087	56
Sea Change Systems Inc	7372	1984
SEA CON/Brantner and Associates	3643	18
Sea Converting Inc	3353	15
Sea Fox Boat Company Inc	3732	13
Sea Gardens Beach And Tennis Resort Inc	7011	218
Sea Gardens Seafoods Inc	2097	28
Sea Harvest Packing Co	2092	62
SEA Inc	3663	345
Sea Island Bank	6022	498
Sea Lane Express Inc	4213	888
Sea Lion Inc	2869	83
Sea Pearl Seafood Company Inc	5146	35
Sea Ranch Properties Inc	6552	284
Sea Ray Boats Corp	3732	3
Sea Safari Ltd	2092	102
Sea Sense Inc	7999	145
Sea Snack Foods Inc	2092	60
Sea Star Seafood Corp	2092	87
Sea Transfer Corp	4213	994
Sea Truck Inc	4213	2392
Sea View Technologies Inc	5065	189
Sea Vision USA	3851	65
Sea Watch International Ltd	2092	2
Sea West Products Inc	3728	220
Sea World of Florida Inc	7996	19
Seaberg Company Inc	3842	251
Seaberg Industries Inc	3531	125
Seaberg Rice and Co-op	2044	15
Seaboard Asphalt Products Co	2851	92
Seaboard Bindery Inc	2789	101
Seaboard Construction Group	1541	43
Seaboard Corp	2011	4
Seaboard Folding Box Corp	2657	16
Seaboard International Inc	3533	49
Seaboard Marine Ltd	4731	25
Seaboard Security Inc	7381	240
Seaboard Service Inc	5983	26
Seabourn Cruise Line	4481	3
SeaBright Insurance Holdings Inc	6331	168
Seabright Laboratories	2879	54
Seabring Marine Industries Inc	5091	31
Seabrook Brothers and Sons Inc	2037	13
Seabrook International LLC	3599	278

Company Name	SIC	Rank
Seabrook Plastics Inc	3544	657
Seabrook Seafood Inc	2092	65
Seabrook Wallcoverings Inc	5231	3
Seabulk International Inc	4412	9
Seabury and Smith Inc	6411	77
SeaChange International Inc	3663	32
Seacoast Asphalt Services Inc	4213	2598
Seacoast Banking Corporation of Florida	6712	196
Seacoast Commerce Bank	6022	625
Seacoast Imprint	5199	144
Seacoast Medical LLC	5122	62
Seacoast National Bank	6021	97
Seacoast Seafoods Sales Inc	5142	38
Seacoast Telecommunication Service Bureau Inc	4813	459
Seacon Advanced Products LLC	3678	42
Seacon Phoenix LLC	3643	9
SEACOR Holdings Inc	4412	4
SEACOR Marine LLC	4412	6
SeaCube Container Leasing Ltd	4731	37
Seaena Inc	5999	183
Seafari Marine Group	5088	116
Seafax Inc	7389	430
Seafood International Distributor Inc	2092	80
Seafood Producers Coop	2092	105
Seaford Retirement and Rehabilitation Center	8051	78
Seaforth Mineral and Ore Company Inc	5169	28
Seafreeze Ltd	2092	81
Seafreeze LP	2092	41
Seagate Hospitality Group	7011	167
Seagate Plastics Co	3089	899
Seagate Transportation Services	4213	2685
Seagil Software Co	5734	341
Seagull Operating Company Inc	1311	190
Seagull Printing Services Inc	2752	1523
Seagull Scientific Inc	7372	3498
Seagull Software Systems Inc	5045	366
Seahawk Drilling	1382	32
Seahorse Transportation Inc	4213	1087
Seakr Engineering Inc	3674	179
Seal and Co	5621	37
Seal Company Enterprises Inc	5085	263
Seal Consulting Inc	7379	294
SEAL Laboratories	8734	179
Seal Master Corp	3069	84
Seal Methods Inc	2672	40
Seal Reinforced Fiberglass Inc	3089	1455
Seal Science Inc	3053	47
Seal Tite LLC	3498	58
Sealant Equipment and Engineering Inc	3823	144
Sealaska Corp	2411	2
Seal-A-Tron Corp	3565	178
Sealco Commercial Vehicle Products Inc	3714	230
Sealcon LLC	5063	277
Seald-Sweet Growers Inc	5148	92
Sealed Air Corp	2671	1
Sealed Unit Parts Company Inc	3585	94
Sealevel Systems Inc	3577	249
Sealing Devices Inc	5085	57
Sealing Systems Inc	2821	205
Sea-Logix LLC	4213	747
Seals Communications Corp	7812	70
Seals Unlimited Inc	3053	71
Seals-Eastern Inc	3053	46
Sealtec	3053	123
Seal-Tite Plastic Packaging Company Inc	2673	40
Sealy Corp	2515	3
Sealy Mattress Company Of New Jersey Inc	2515	19
Seam	6221	7
Seam LLC	8742	644
Seaman and Associates Inc	8732	77
Seaman Corp	2221	18
Seamark International LLC	3577	493
Seamast Inc	7379	360
Seamen's Society For Children and Families	8322	57
Seamless Peer To Peer LLC	7371	845
Seamless Sensations Inc	2391	8
Seamlessweb Professional Solutions Inc	7389	345
Seamtek Inc	3559	583
Sean John Clothing Inc	5136	27
Sea-Net Holdings Inc	7319	112
Seanet Technologies Inc	7371	1426
Seapac Of Idaho Inc	5146	40
Seapass Solutions Inc	7372	1314
Seapine Software Inc	7372	817
Seaport Group LLC	6211	165
Seaport Meat Co	2013	103
Seaport Software Inc	7372	2700
Seaquest Software Inc	7372	4954
Seaquist Closures LLC	3561	6
Search Cactus LLC	7379	1534
Search Wizards Inc	7363	156
Search123com Inc	7389	379
SearchKing Inc	7379	662
Searchtec Inc	7375	200
SearchWare Inc	7372	1305

Company Name	SIC	Rank
Searcy Newspapers Inc	2759	401
SeaRiver Maritime Inc	4412	27
Searle Blatt Ltd	2337	7
Searles Graphics Inc	2752	984
Searles Valley Minerals	1474	2
Sea-Ro Inc	3559	574
Sears Holdings Corp	6719	6
Sears Home Improvement Products Inc	1521	51
Sears Imported Autos Inc	5511	441
Sears Roebuck Acceptance Corp	6153	2
Sears Roebuck and Co	5311	2
Sease Gerig and Associates	8743	165
Seashore Insurance And Associates Inc	6411	90
Seaside Buick Inc	5511	1074
Seaside Printing CoInc	2752	989
SeaSolve Software Incorporated	7372	961
Seasons' Enterprises Ltd	2051	211
Seasons Harvest Inc	2035	61
Seasons-4 Inc	3585	87
Seastone LLC	3999	83
Seastrom Manufacturing Company Inc	3469	172
Sea-Tac Electric Inc	1731	728
Seatech Consulting Group Inc	7379	910
Seatek Company Inc	3423	77
Seaton Publishing Co	2711	544
Seaton Publishing Company Inc	2711	435
Seatorque Control Systems LLC	3625	245
Seatrade International Company Inc	2092	13
Seatronics Inc	5087	183
Seattle Aero LLC	5088	73
Seattle Business Journal Inc	2711	418
Seattle Children's Home Inc	8361	140
Seattle Chinese Post Inc	2759	481
Seattle Chocolate Company LLC	2066	22
Seattle Genetics Inc	2836	12
Seattle Goon Squad	7381	256
Seattle Gym	7991	12
Seattle Institute For Biomedical And Clinical Research	8733	20
Seattle Iron and Metals Corp	5093	73
Seattle Lab Inc	7372	2801
Seattle Lighting Fixtures Co	5719	20
Seattle Metropolitan Credit Union	6061	68
Seattle Mortgage Co	6162	23
Seattle Office Furniture LLC	5712	76
Seattle Pacific Industries Inc	2321	6
Seattle Service Bureau Inc	7322	69
Seattle Sound and Vibration Inc	7371	1805
Seattle Support Group	2741	405
Seattle Times Co	2711	211
Seattle-Northwest Securities Corp	6211	162
Seaver Co	5099	74
Seavin Inc	2084	69
Seawall Specialty Company Inc	5199	125
Seaward Management Corp	6282	357
Seaward Products Corp	3585	157
Seawave Corp	2711	736
Seaway Bancshares Inc	6712	460
Seaway Bank and Trust Co	6021	203
Seaway Manufacturing Corp	3089	553
Seaway Pattern Manufacturing Inc	3543	37
Seaway Plastics Corp	3089	1518
Seaway Plastics Engineering Inc	3544	166
Seaway Valley Capital Corp	7389	274
Seawolf Design Inc	3559	426
Seaworld Parks and Entertainment Inc	7996	20
SeaWorld San Diego	7996	17
Seaworthy Systems Inc	8711	577
Seawright Holdings Inc	2086	157
Sebastian International Inc	2844	31
Sebastiani Vineyards Inc	2084	47
Sebewaing Tool And Engineering Co	3429	115
Sebotek Hearing Systems LLC	3842	189
Sebright Products Inc	3559	176
Sebring Transport Inc	4213	2591
Sec Electrical Inc	5063	622
Secant Technology Inc	7373	903
Sechlers Pickles Inc	2035	47
Sechrist Industries Inc	3841	93
Secnap Network Security Corp	7371	313
Seco Warwick Corp	3567	11
Secoa Inc	1799	30
Seco-Larm USA Inc	5063	619
Secom Group Inc	1731	712
Secom International	7373	392
Second Circuits Corp	3679	613
Second City	7812	23
Second City Communications	7812	34
Second Foundation Consulting	5045	163
Second National Bank	6035	209
Second Nature Software Inc	7372	3783
Second Source Inc	8711	598
Second Systems Inc	5021	152
Second Wind Systems Inc	3829	130
Secondary Operations Inc	3599	2411
SecondMarket Holdings Inc	6289	21
Secord Contracting Corp	1623	760
Secs Inc	3462	59
Sector 7 - USA Inc	7379	343
Sector Micro Computer Inc	7372	3285
Securance LLC	8742	667
Secur-Com Inc	1731	567
Secure Care Products Inc	5047	140
Secure Collateral LLC	6531	462
Secure Communication Systems Inc	3663	71
Secure Computing Systems Inc	7372	3020
Secure Data Solutions Inc	7373	1016
Secure Family Records	4813	551
Secure First Credit Union	6062	100
Secure Mission Solutions LLC	7382	46
Secure System Inc	7382	93
Secure Tech Peripherals Inc	5065	960
Secure Wrap Of Miami Inc	8742	460
Secure-24 Inc	7379	575
Secure64 Software Corp	7371	1269
Securecorn Inc	1731	430
Secured Data Inc	7372	709
Secured Digital Applications Inc	7374	76
Secured Fibres	7389	1654
Secured Services Inc	7371	1053
SecureInfo Corp	7372	908
Secure-It Inc	3577	531
SecureLogix Corp	7379	175
SecureNet Technologies Inc	7372	1108
Secureone Inc	7381	142
SecurePay Inc	7373	635
SecureUSA Inc	5087	32
Securewebs Inc	4813	722
Secureworks Inc	4813	256
Securian Financial Group Inc	6231	2
Securitas Security Services USA Inc (Parsippany New Jersey)	7381	28
Securities Industry Software	7372	1381
Securities Management and Research Inc	6282	392
Securities Research Inc	6211	215
Securities Service Network Inc	6211	250
Security Alarm Financing Enterprises Inc	7382	57
Security Alliance Of Florida LLC	7381	42
Security And Fire Electronics Inc	3699	234
Security Arts Corp	7381	235
Security Associates International Ltd	7381	214
Security Ballew Inc	6282	464
Security Bancorp Inc (McMinnville Tennessee)	6712	648
Security Bank of California	6022	513
Security Bank of Kansas City	6021	240
Security Benefit Group of Companies Inc	6311	161
Security Bindery Inc	2789	112
Security Business Bank of San Diego	6021	268
Security by Design	7379	647
Security California Bancorp	6712	505
Security Claims Consultants	7382	158
Security Concepts Inc	7381	197
Security Consulting Services Inc	5063	895
Security Couriers Inc	7389	2222
Security Credit Services LLC	7322	13
Security Credit Systems Inc	7322	67
Security Data and Cable Hq Ltd	5065	879
Security Defense Systems Corp	3844	33
Security Engineered Machinery Company Inc	3554	20
Security Engineering Company Inc	5063	561
Security Equipment Inc	1731	250
Security Federal Bank	6035	264
Security Federal Corp	6712	337
Security Federal Savings Bank (McMinnville Tennessee)	6022	583
Security FSB (Elizabethton Tennessee)	6035	246
Security Gold Exchange Inc	5094	83
Security Instrument Corporation Of Delaware	1731	341
Security Integrators And Consulting Inc	5065	584
Security Intelligence Technologies Inc	3999	187
Security Lab Inc	5045	1005
Security Life Insurance Company of America	6311	218
Security Management Of South Carolina LLC	7381	44
Security Management Services Inc	7381	183
Security Mutual Life Insurance Company of New York	6311	116
Security National Automotive Acceptance Corp	6141	51
Security National Bank (Enid Oklahoma)	6712	547
Security National Bank of Enid	6021	288
Security National Bank of Sioux City Iowa	6021	198
Security National Bank Springfield Ohio	6021	165
Security National Corp	6712	187
Security National Financial Corp	6311	183
Security One Inc	7381	41
Security One Systems	7382	24
Security Operations and Solutions Inc	7381	201
Security Personnel Inc	7363	103
Security Plus USA	7381	173
Security Properties Inc	6552	187
Security Recovery Inc	7389	2105
Security Sentry Inc	5999	138
Security Service Northwest Inc	7382	61
Security Signals Inc	3451	14
Security Source Inc	7372	350
Security Steelcraft Corp	3821	70
Security Supply Corp	5074	19
Security Systems Techniques Inc	3669	273
Security Telecommunications of Porterville Inc	5063	395
Security Union Title Insurance Co	6361	30
Security Van Lines Inc	4213	655
SecurityMetrics Inc	7379	318
SecurTech Co	3577	607
Securus Enterprises	3674	401
SECURUS Technologies Inc	7372	316
SED International Holdings Inc	5045	34
Sedaghat and Associates Engineers	1623	859
SEDALCO Inc	1541	187
Sedalia Steel Supply Inc	5051	307
Sedenquist-Fraser Enterprises Inc	3714	406
Sedgwick Claims Management Services Inc	6411	97
Sedgwick County Electrical Cooperative Association Inc	4911	545
Sedgwick Detert Moran and Arnold LLP	8111	208
Sedona Corp	7372	4120
Sedona GeoServices Inc	3577	586
Sedona Group	7361	134
Sedona Resort Management Inc	7011	131
See Corp	7372	4389
See First Technology Inc	7373	741
See Kai Run	5641	7
See The Matrix Inc	7379	1436
Seeburger Inc	7371	1194
SEEC Inc	7372	2324
SEECO Inc	1311	80
Seed Corn Advertising Inc	4813	668
Seed Factory Northwest Inc	2048	118
Seed Intellectual Property Law Group PLLC	8111	270
Seed Resource Inc	5191	107
Seed Resources LLC	2048	88
Seed Wireless and Accessories Co	4812	132
Seedburo Equipment Co	3523	186
Seedorf Construction	1623	823
Seedorff Masonry Inc	1741	4
Seedway	5191	66
Seegers Truck Line Inc	4213	1858
SEEK Inc	7361	97
Seek Systems Inc	3572	61
SeekingSitters	8351	29
Seekirk Inc	3823	336
Seekonk Local Cable Studio	4833	211
Seekonk Manufacturing Company Inc	3423	71
Seeley Machine Inc	3599	1586
Seely Mullins and Associates PC	8721	203
Seelye Plastics Inc	5074	113
Seemann Composites Inc	3089	756
Seen On Tv Inc	5064	49
See's Candy Shops Inc	2064	2
SeeSaw Networks Inc	7371	837
See-Technology Inc	7373	1003
Seewhy Inc	7372	2174
Sef Inc	2761	74
SEF Stainless Steel Inc	1791	26
Sefton Resources Inc	1311	239
Segal and Morel Inc	1521	66
Segal Co	8748	97
Segall Bryant and Hamill Investment Counsel	6282	444
SegaSoft Networks Inc	7372	68
Segebarth General Contracting Inc	5012	172
Seger Communications Inc	1623	599
Segerdahl Corp	2752	13
Segerdahl Graphics Inc	2752	141
Seger-Elvekrog Inc	6282	661
Seghesio Wineries Inc	2084	91
Segnet Technologies Inc	8748	389
Segtel Inc	7389	1660
Segue Electronics Inc	3669	140
Segue Software Inc	7373	196
Segue Technologies Inc	7371	779
Seh Enterprises Inc	7371	633
Sehgal Sons Inc	1622	12
Sehrer Holding Co	2521	45
SEI Aaron's Inc	7359	27
SEI Capacitors Inc	5065	500
SEI Group Inc	8711	286
SEI Information Technology	7379	336
SEI Investments Co	6211	80
Sei Manufacturing Inc	3599	1419
Seibels Bruce and Co	6331	227
Seibels Bruce Group Inc	6331	292
Seibold Security Inc	5065	484
Seidel Inc	3471	47
Seidio Inc	5065	706
Seidle Enterprises Inc	5511	157
Seidler Companies Inc	6211	311
Seidl's Bindery Inc	2789	20
Seidman Brothers Inc	5046	180
Seifert and Group Inc	8748	292
Seifert Electric Inc	1731	2371
Seiffert Office Products	5112	54
Seigle's Home and Building Centers Inc	5211	26
Seika Machinery Inc	5046	273
Seiko Corporation of America	3873	6
Seiko Instruments USA Inc Business and Home Office Products Div	3577	294

Company Name	SIC	Rank
Seikoh Giken USA Inc	5063	358
Seiler and Company LLP	8721	299
Seiler Instrument And Manufacturing Company Inc	3827	18
Seiler Plastics Corp	3089	1611
Seiler Tank Truck Service Inc	4212	22
Seimac Inc	5065	842
Seismic Energy Products LP	3441	147
Seismic Micro-Technology Inc	7372	1823
Seitel Inc	1382	36
Seiter and Miller Advertising Inc	7311	223
Seitlin and Co	6411	68
Seitz Corp	5084	199
Seitz Technical Products Inc	3861	130
SEI-US Employees Credit Union	0001	158
Sejersen Dps Inc	4822	22
Sejin America Inc	5045	28
Sejong Alabama LLC	3714	101
Sekan Printing Company Inc	2752	884
Sekidenko Inc	3823	100
Sekisui Jushi America Inc	2821	126
Sekisui Voltek LLC	3086	21
Sekon Enterprise Inc	7379	641
Se-Kure Controls Inc	3577	310
Sela USA Inc	3827	131
Selane Products Inc	3843	27
Selas Fluid Processing Corp	3567	25
Selco Custom Time Corp	5094	49
Selco Inc	7389	1612
Selco Products Co (Buena Park California)	3822	52
Select Benefits Group Inc	6324	116
Select Circuits	3672	473
Select Comfort Corp	2515	5
Select Communications Inc	5731	217
Select Drink Inc	5145	35
Select Electronics Corp	5045	817
Select Energy Services Inc	8711	287
Select Engineered Systems Inc	3699	223
Select Engineering Inc	8711	542
Select Equipment Company Inc	5063	999
Select Fabricators Inc	3812	193
Select Group	7361	132
Select International Corp	3465	1
Select Janitorial Services Inc	7349	444
Select Marketing Solutions	2542	61
Select Medical Holdings Corp	8093	2
Select Office Solutions	5044	25
Select Personnel Investig	7381	231
Select Plastics LLC	3089	1342
Select Portfolio Servicing Inc	6162	6
Select Properties Ltd	6531	319
Select Publishing Inc	7331	150
Select Sales	5045	361
Select Sires Inc	0751	7
Select Solutions Group LLC	7379	895
Select Staffing Services	7363	133
Select StaffingSM	7363	46
Select Steel Inc	5051	356
Select-A-Form Inc	2759	212
SelectCare Inc	6324	128
Selectech Inc	3089	1699
SelectForce Inc	7389	1238
Selectica Inc	7373	326
Selective Enterprises Inc	2591	11
Selective Insurance Company of America	6331	152
Selective Insurance Company of South Carolina	6411	147
Selective Insurance Group Inc	6331	83
Selective Marketing Communications Inc	7311	860
Selective Med Components Inc	3823	257
Selective Petfood Services Inc	2047	40
Selective Way Insurance Co	6331	224
Selectleaders LLC	7363	386
Selecto Inc	3589	83
Selecto-Flash Inc	2759	130
Select-O-Hits Inc	5099	37
Selectouch Corp	3625	247
Selectric LLC	1731	2509
Selectron Technologies Inc	7371	868
Selectronics Corp	4841	74
Selectronix Inc	3823	484
Selecttech Services Corp	8744	35
Selee Corp	3269	7
Selektro Power Inc	5045	603
Self Industries Inc	3469	47
Self-Help Credit Union	6062	85
Selfix Inc	3089	321
Selflock Screw Products Company Inc	3451	111
Selig Chemical Industries	2841	12
Selig Enterprises Inc	6552	138
Seligman Friedman and Company PC	8721	72
Seljan Tool Company Inc	3469	236
Selkey Manufacturing Co	3441	188
Sell My DVDscom	7822	18
Selland Auto Transport Inc	4213	459
Sellars Absorbent Materials Inc	2297	4
Sellars Nonwovens	2297	8
sellcom Inc	7389	1048
Sellen Construction Company Inc	1542	143
Sellenriek Construction Inc	1623	135
Sellers Equipment Inc	5082	52

Company Name	SIC	Rank
Sellers Optical Inc	3827	73
Sellers Richardson Holman and West LLP	8721	91
Selling Precision Inc	3498	74
Selling Source LLC	7311	113
Sellmark Corp	3949	152
Sellmore Industries Inc	5033	26
Sellner Corp	3714	172
Sellner Manufacturing Co	3599	1892
SellPoint Inc	7319	40
Sellstrom Manufacturing Co	3842	152
Selma Communications Service	5731	203
Selman Chevrolet	5511	351
Selmax Corp	3089	1371
Selmet Inc	3369	11
Sel-Mor Distributing Co	5044	101
Selsi Company Inc	5049	193
Selzer-Ornst Company Inc	1542	258
Sem Products Inc	2851	79
Semanchin and Wetter	8721	210
Semantic Research Inc	7373	791
Semaphore Corp (Seattle Washington)	7372	2628
Se-Mar Electric Company Inc	3613	106
Semarca Corp	7372	5149
Sematco Inc	3599	1116
Sembler Co	6552	84
Semblex Corp	3452	33
Sembol Systems Inc	3599	1451
Semco	3829	332
Semco Color Press Inc	2752	1198
Semco Duct And Acoustical Products Inc	3444	39
SEMCO Energy Gas Co	4923	12
SEMCO Energy Inc	4924	25
Semco Enterprises Inc	3339	16
Semco Machine Corp	3599	1630
Semco Plastic Co	3089	251
Seme and Son Automotive Inc	3599	2506
Semele Group Inc	6798	194
SemGroup LP	4924	3
Semi Conductor Manufacturing Corp	3674	339
Semi Logic Entertainments Inc	7372	3403
Semi-Automations and Technologies Inc	3674	350
Semico Research Corp	8748	308
Semicon Associates	3671	5
Semicon Products Manufacturing Inc	3599	650
Semiconductor Circuits Inc	3629	37
Semiconductor Components Inc	3674	417
Semiconductor Components Industries LLC	3674	13
Semiconductor Equipment Corp	3559	411
Semiconductor Hybrid Assembly Inc	3672	432
Semiconductor Technology Inc	3674	365
Semiconductor Test Inc	5065	1002
Semiconix Corp	3674	392
Semicore Equipment Inc	5065	575
Semi-Express Inc	4213	2796
Semifab Inc	3444	179
Semifreddi's Inc	5149	108
Semi-Kinetics Inc	3672	112
Semikron Inc	5065	87
Semilab Sdi LLC	3699	170
Seminex Corp	3674	396
Seminis Inc	0181	2
Seminis Vegetable Seeds Inc	8734	1
Seminole Electric Cooperative Inc	4911	104
Seminole Express	4213	1674
Seminole Precast Manufacturing Inc	3272	92
Seminole Tribe Of Florida Inc	5194	6
Semitool Inc	3559	35
Semitronics Corp	3674	294
Semix Inc	5063	430
SEMO Electric Coop	4911	343
Semonin Realtors	6552	31
Semper Truck Lines Inc	4213	2509
Sempra Energy	4932	2
Semprex Corp	3825	266
Semrock Inc	3827	15
Semtech Corp	3674	55
Semtorq Inc	3549	44
Semtronic Associates Inc	5065	177
SemWare Corp	5961	149
SEMX Corp	3469	138
Sena Systems Inc	7379	882
Senasys Inc	3625	230
Sencer Inc	3674	468
Senco Products Inc	3546	3
Sencommunications Inc	5065	77
Sencore Inc	3823	75
SencorpWhite Inc	3599	9
Send Out Cards LLC	2771	7
Sendec Corp	3679	192
Sendio Inc	5045	381
Sendmail Inc	7372	1144
Sendouts LLC	5734	159
Sendside Networks Inc	7372	1909
Sendthisfile Inc	7379	1625
Seneca Beverage Corp	4213	815
Seneca Consolidated Industries Corp	3564	130
Seneca Energy Ii LLC	1731	2524
Seneca Falls Machine Tool Company Inc	3541	167
Seneca Foods Corp	2033	7

Company Name	SIC	Rank
Seneca Foods International Ltd	2037	5
Seneca Gaming Corp	7993	6
Seneca Insurance Inc	6331	347
Seneca Resources Corp	1311	93
Seneca Sawmill Co	2421	54
Senecio Software Inc	7372	1649
Senesac Inc	2873	10
Senesco Technologies Inc	8731	428
Senez Roofing LLC	1542	440
Senga Engineering Inc	3599	725
Senica Security South Inc	7381	242
Senior Aerospace Composites	3728	65
Senior Aerospace Jet Products Corp	3724	20
Senior Flexonics Inc	3441	44
Senior Housing Properties Trust	6790	59
Senior Industries Inc	3643	98
Senior Life	7313	33
Senior Market Sales Inc	7375	77
Senior Network Inc	2741	313
Senior Operations LLC	3599	16
Senior Residential Care Inc	8361	47
Senior Services Inc	8322	90
Senior Solutions for South Florida Inc	8082	93
Senior Systems Inc	7372	1974
Senior Systems Technology Inc	3674	243
Senior Whole Health LLC	6324	70
Seniors First Inc	8322	109
Senix Corp	3823	407
Senomyx Inc	8731	135
Senoret Chemical Co	2842	102
SensAble Technologies Inc	3577	192
Sense Technologies Inc	3714	431
Sensenig Trucking	4213	2619
Sensiba San Filippo LLP	8721	332
Sensible Micro Corp	5065	130
Sensible Software Inc	7372	3646
Sensical Inc	2759	184
Sensidyne LP	3823	88
Sensient Colors Inc	2087	13
Sensient Dehydrated Flavors LLC	2034	5
Sensient Flavors Inc	2087	11
Sensient Flavors International Inc	2087	4
Sensient Flavors LLC	2087	12
Sensient Food Colors LP	2087	5
Sensient Health Care Management Co	2087	6
Sensient Holding Inc	2087	7
Sensient Imaging Technologies Inc	2087	8
Sensient Technologies Corp	2869	10
Sensing Devices Inc	3823	374
Sensing Systems Corp	3586	21
Sensis	7311	703
Sensis Corp	3812	43
Sensitech Inc	7375	126
Sensitron Associates Inc	3823	482
Sensitron Inc	5045	253
Senske and Son Transfer Co	4213	2453
Senso-Metrics Inc	3829	412
Sensor Developments Inc	3829	376
Sensor Electronics Corp	3823	116
Sensor Manufacturing Co	3679	738
Sensor Scientific Inc	3829	245
Sensor Switch Inc	3812	73
Sensor Systems Inc	3663	92
Sensor Systems LLC	3825	96
Sensor Technologies Inc	7371	202
Sensorlink Corp	3825	156
Sensormatic Electronics Corp	3669	6
Sensormatic Hawaii Inc	7382	130
Sensorphysics Inc	3674	300
Sensors For Medicine And Science Inc	8733	42
Sensors Unlimited Inc	3357	12
Sensortags Inc	5063	570
SensorTec Inc (Fort Wayne Indiana)	3823	405
Sensortech Systems Inc	3823	372
SensorTran	3829	222
Sensory Computer Systems LLC	7372	4879
Sensory Effects Powder Systems Inc	2099	182
Sensotec Inc	3829	48
Sensus Precision Die Casting Inc	3714	65
Sensys Networks	7379	401
Sentara Healthcare	8062	246
Sentec Automation Components	5063	1000
Sentech Corp	3826	154
Sentech Inc	3825	255
Sentech Medical Systems Inc	5047	131
Sentek Consulting Inc	7371	651
SENTEL Corp	8711	201
Senterra Real Estate Group LLC	6552	127
Sentex Corp	5063	818
Sentigy Inc	8742	245
Sentinel Benefits Group Inc	8744	20
Sentinel Corp	2711	776
Sentinel Group Inc	7381	146
Sentinel Integrity Solutions - USA LP	2711	457
Sentinel Lubricants Inc	2992	32
Sentinel Power Inc	3674	500
Sentinel Printing Company Inc	2752	478
Sentinel Real Estate Corp	6798	192
Sentinel Service Inc	7349	383
Sentinel Services Inc	7382	79
Sentinel Silent Alarm Company Inc	7382	72
Sentinel Standard Inc	2711	341
Sentinel Systems Corp	3699	211
Sentinel Technologies Inc	7371	265

Company Name	SIC	Rank
Sentinel Transportation/DuPont-ConocoPhilips	4213	107
Sentor Technologies Inc	7389	2268
Sentral Assemblies and Components Inc	3679	262
Sentri Inc	7379	1029
Sentrigo Inc	7372	1918
Sentrol	3669	56
Sentry Electric and Controls Inc	1731	1475
Sentry Electric Incorporated Of Central Florida	1731	420
Sentry Equipment Corp	3443	73
Sentry Equipment Erectors Inc	3535	31
Sentry Industries Inc	5169	145
Sentry Insurance Group	6331	65
Sentry Life Insurance Co	6311	129
Sentry Medical Products Inc	5047	177
Sentry Products Inc	3669	19
Sentry Recovery Company Inc	7322	165
Sentry Refrigeration Inc	5143	47
Sentry Security Systems Inc	5063	1024
Sentry Surveillance Inc	7382	71
Sentry Technology Corp	3669	155
Sentry Watch Inc	1731	1179
Sentury Raider Pattern Shop	3543	15
SEOmoz	8742	246
Separation Technologies LLC	8731	250
SEPE Inc	3661	98
Sephardic Yellow Pages	2759	560
Sepracor Inc	2834	38
Sepracor Securities Corp	2834	40
Septagon Industries Inc	1542	201
Septronics International Inc	5065	591
Seqgen Inc	5049	183
Sequa Corp	3511	6
Sequachee Valley Electric Coop	4911	365
Sequan Software	7372	4919
Sequel Special Products LLC	3841	329
Sequel Studio LLC	7336	152
Sequenom Inc	3829	33
Sequent Inc	7363	122
Sequential Software Inc	7372	4880
Sequoia Capital	6799	193
Sequoia Concepts Inc	7322	33
Sequoia Equipment Company Inc	5082	131
Sequoia Grove Winery Partnership	2084	24
Sequoia Insurance Co	6331	164
Sequoia System International	8299	62
Sequoia Voting Systems	3577	104
Sequoyah Software And Consulting Inc	7371	1847
Ser Construction Inc	1611	131
SER Solutions Inc	3661	55
SERA Architects and Interiors	8712	97
SeraCare Life Sciences Inc	2835	23
Serafine Inc	7389	1252
Seraphein Beyn Inc	7311	597
Seravalli Inc	1731	310
Serb Systems Inc	7359	180
Serban's Background Music Inc	1731	943
Serbin Printing Inc	2791	37
Serco Management Services Inc	4173	2
Sercombe Trucking Company Inc	4213	2316
Seren Industrial Power Systems Inc	3679	582
Serena Software	7372	4920
Serena Software Inc	7372	427
Serendipity Systems Inc	7372	4046
Serengeti Systems Inc	7372	3949
Serenic Corp	7372	1937
Serenity Electronics Inc	5065	740
Serenity Information Tech Inc	7372	1921
Serfilco Ltd	3589	142
Sergeant's Pet Care Products Inc	5199	14
Sergi Construction Inc	1623	824
Serial Scene Inc	7629	49
Series 1 Support Services Inc	7371	1569
Serif Inc	7372	542
Serigraphic Arts Inc	2759	543
Serino Coyne Inc	7311	142
Serious Accounting Software Inc	7372	4881
Serious Energy Inc	2531	35
Ser-Jobs For Progress Of The Texas Gulf Coast Inc	8331	130
Sermatech International Inc	2891	16
Sermatech-Lehr	3724	36
Serotta Maddocks Evans and Co	8721	459
Serpentix Conveyor Corp	3535	210
Serra Automotive Inc	5511	24
Serra Manufacturing Corp	3053	64
Serra Stone Corp	5032	136
Serralta Rebull Serig Inc	8711	617
Serrano Industries Inc	3599	1071
Serta Inc	2515	6
Serta Restokraft Mattress Company Inc	2515	20
Sertco Industries Inc	3728	148
Sertec Corp	8742	303
Sertoma Center Inc	8361	155
Sertoma Centre Inc	8331	68
Serus Corp	7372	1423
SerVaas Factories Inc	8742	445
Servaas Laboratories Inc	2842	81
Servaas Manufacturing Corp	2819	138
Servants Inc	2653	97
Servco Pacific Inc	6719	83
Serveco Inc	1711	275

Company Name	SIC	Rank
SerVend/ Multiplex	3581	2
Server Products Inc	3589	89
Server Racks Online LLC	5046	19
Server Technology Inc	5045	211
Serverbeach Ltd	4813	519
ServerLogic Corp	7372	1095
Serveron Corp	3829	104
Serverplus LLC	4813	486
ServerSide Inc	7379	859
Servervault Corp	7375	161
Serverware Corp	5045	722
ServerWorks Corp	3674	190
Servex Electronic Distributing Inc	5731	121
Service 800 Inc (Minneapolis Minnesota)	7389	312
Service Assurance Corp	7378	36
Service Bindery Enterprises Inc	2789	113
Service Bureau LLC	7323	46
Service By Air Inc	4731	46
Service Care Of America Inc	8741	278
Service Center Ltd	7331	42
Service Center LLC	3829	367
Service Center Metals LLC	3316	15
Service Champ Ii LP	5013	110
Service Chevrolet Inc	5511	426
Service Construction LLC	1623	795
Service Construction Supply Inc	5031	112
Service Corporation International	7261	1
Service Electric Cable Television Inc	4841	88
Service Electric Corporation Of Va	1731	999
Service Electric Inc	1731	1522
Service Electric Supply Company Inc	5063	799
Service Electric Supply Inc	5063	256
Service Electrical Supply Company Inc	5063	475
Service Engineering Inc	3559	175
Service Experts Inc	1711	4
Service Experts LLC	1711	260
Service Financial LLC	6799	324
Service First Inc	7349	265
Service Foods Inc	2099	66
Service Force USA LLC	7349	67
Service Graphics Inc	7389	1196
Service Group Inc	5065	689
Service Guide Inc	3599	239
Service Hydraulic and Supply	5084	621
Service Intelligence Inc	7389	498
Service Link LP	6541	11
Service Litho-Print Inc	2752	692
Service Machine and Supply Inc	3599	984
Service Machine And Welding Company Inc	3443	159
Service Machine Company Inc	3599	2089
Service Machine Specialties Inc	3599	901
Service Manufacturing Corp (Aurora Illinois)	2394	9
Service Master Of Springfield Inc	7349	408
Service Metal Fabricators Inc	3444	147
Service Motors Inc	5511	912
Service Office Supply and Printing Inc	5112	88
Service Oil Inc	5171	27
Service One	4924	71
Service Pak Inc	7336	70
Service Photo Copy Inc	7334	84
Service Plus Lawn and Tree Care	7217	5
Service Power Inc	7371	695
Service Printers Of Duluth Inc	2752	800
Service Printing Company Inc	2759	339
Service Publication Inc	2711	789
Service Smoked Fish Corp	5146	55
Service Station Computer Systems Inc	7372	3124
Service Steel Aerospace Corp	5051	241
Service Steel Inc	5051	145
Service Storage International Inc	3572	93
Service Tectonics Sales Inc	3569	276
Service Tire Truck Center Inc	7534	4
Service Trade Corp	5063	625
Service Transport Co	4213	101
Service Trucking Inc	4213	902
Service Works Inc	7382	107
ServiceBenchcom Inc	7372	551
ServiceCentral Technologies Inc	7372	2861
ServicechannelCom Inc	4813	377
ServiceMagic Inc	7389	244
ServiceMaster Co	8741	6
ServiceMaster Consumer Services LP	7342	1
Servicemaster Of Central North Dakota Inc	7349	237
Service-Nowcom Inc	7371	153
Services For Plastics Inc	5085	394
Services Group of America Inc	5141	29
Services Transport	4213	1397
Service-Vision Consulting Inc	7379	1081
Servico Building Maintenance Company Inc	7349	289
Servient Inc	7371	693
Servigistics Inc	5045	342
Serving by Irving Inc	7389	1236
Servint Corp	4813	523
Servitech Industries Inc	3479	65
Servi-Tek LLC	7349	151
Servo Corporation of America	3812	121
Servo Instrument Corp	3676	16
Servo Systems Co	5065	505
Servolift LLC	5084	832

Company Name	SIC	Rank
Servos and Simulation Inc	3625	424
Servpro (Bear Deleware)	1799	66
Servpro Intellectual Property Inc	7349	25
Servpro Of Hanover Inc	7349	487
Serv-Rite Meat Company Inc	2013	149
Servtronics Inc	5072	183
Serv-U Pharmacies	5912	44
Ses America Inc	5063	1018
SES Industries Inc	3589	240
SESAC Inc	6794	45
Sesame Software Inc	7372	3021
Sesco Products Group Inc	3545	102
Sescoi USA Inc	7372	2408
Sessa Sheet Metal Contractors Inc	1761	21
Session Fixture Company Inc	5046	173
Sessions Company Inc	0723	18
Sessoms Construction Company Inc	1542	417
SET Enterprises Inc	7372	3022
SET Enterprises Inc (Warren Michigan)	3356	32
SET Laboratories Inc	7372	5067
Set Liquidation Inc	3842	167
Seta Corp	5961	95
Setco Inc	3089	157
Setco Sales Co	3545	62
Setex Inc	2531	9
Sethness Products Co	2087	43
Sethness-Greenleaf Inc	2087	69
Seth's Lighting and Accessories Inc	5063	685
Set-N-Me-Free Aloe Vera Co	2844	100
Seton Company of Michigan	3111	12
Seton Health System Inc	8062	182
Setpoint Systems Inc	8711	440
SETS LLC	4213	2589
Setter Leach and Lindstrom Inc	8712	161
Setterstix Corp	2679	51
Settimo Group Inc	7379	1335
Settlement Funding LLC	8742	429
Setton Pistachio Of Terra Bella Inc	5149	81
Setton's International Foods Inc	2034	12
Setzers and Company Inc	5064	80
Seubert Excavators Inc	3295	9
SEV/Sherwin-Greenberg Productions	7812	307
Sev-Cal Tool Inc	3545	328
Sevcon Inc	3679	404
Seven Bridges Radio LLC	4832	214
Seven Corners Printing	2759	165
Seven D Wholesale	5031	22
Seven Hills Womens Health Centers	8011	142
Seven J Stock Farm Inc	1311	184
Seven Networks Inc	7372	2230
Seven O's Inc	5561	20
Seven Resorts Inc	4493	1
Seven Seas Technology Inc	7379	531
Seven Springs Mountain Resort	7011	37
Seven-O-Electric Inc	1731	2103
Seven's Paint and Wallpaper Co	5198	4
Sevenson Environmental Services Inc	4953	57
Seventh Wave Technology Inc	7379	1069
Seventy Five State Street	8361	144
Seventy-Three Manufacturing Company Inc	3823	313
Seven-Up Bottling Co (Watertown Wisconsin)	5149	125
Severance Foods Inc	2096	31
Severance Tool Industries Inc	3545	140
Severance Trucking Company Inc	4213	1110
Severn Bancorp Inc	6712	331
Severn Engineering Company Inc	3824	47
Severn Peanut Company Inc	5159	18
Severn Savings Bank FSB	6035	167
Severn Trent Envirotest	7389	1673
Severson and Werson Inc	8111	324
Severt Trucking Inc	4213	1514
Seville Central Mix Corp	3273	77
Seville Flexpack Corp	3089	684
Seville Sand and Gravel Inc	1442	76
Seville Temporary Services Inc	7363	207
Sevin Rosen Funds	6799	138
Sew Cal Logo Inc	2353	21
SEW Friel LLP	2033	52
Sew Team No 3	7389	1957
Seward Motor Freight Inc	4213	839
Seward Sales Corporation LLC	5169	53
Seward Sand and Gravel Inc	4213	2961
Sewell Industrial Electronics Inc	3625	226
Sewell Printing Service Inc	2752	1131
Sewer Equipment Company Of America	3589	91
SEW-Eurodrive Inc	3566	6
Sewing Source Inc	5023	48
Sextant Search Partners LLC	8748	195
Sexton and Sexton School Supply Inc	5049	152
Sexton Chevrolet Co	5511	1011
Sexton Pest Control Inc	7342	14
Seyfarth Shaw	8111	89
Seymour Manufacturing Company Inc	3423	28
Seymour Of Sycamore Inc	2851	58
Seymour Tubing Inc	3312	62
Sf Alternator Starter Exchange Inc	5013	292
SF Holdings Group Inc	6719	54
SF Research Corp	7373	777
SFB Bancorp Inc	6035	244
SFB Plastics Inc	3089	511
Sfbc LLC	2657	25

Company Name	SIC	Rank
Sfc Graphics Cleveland Ltd	2752	786
Sferra Brothers Ltd	5023	93
Sfi Acquisition Inc	3537	59
Sfi Gray Steel Ltd	3325	39
Sfi Of Tennessee LLC	3465	17
SFI-Delaware LLC	2752	12
Sfm Services Inc	7349	530
SFN Group Inc	7363	9
SFP Pipeline Holdings Inc	4011	18
SFRT Inc	5063	852
Sftc LLC	2041	35
SG and D Communications and Design	7336	173
SG Schoggen and Co	7372	4882
SG Supply Co	5074	29
SG Wholesale Roofing Supply Inc	5033	21
SG Wilson Truck and Equipment Co	4213	2779
SGA Business Systems Inc	7374	400
Sgb Enterprises Inc	3575	31
Sgc World Inc	3663	306
SGD Holdings Ltd	2611	11
SGE Inc	3559	27
Sgf Holdings Inc	6719	170
SGI	8748	100
SGI Integrated Graphic Systems	2671	26
Sgjb Business Holdings Inc	3469	338
SGL Technic Inc/Polycarbon Div	3624	4
Sgm Company Inc	3433	57
Sgm Corp	3674	297
SGPA/Architecture and Planning	8712	134
SGS International Inc	2759	11
Sgs Life Science Services	8734	92
Sgs North America Inc	6531	153
SGS Northview Laboratories Inc	8734	57
Sgs USTesting Company Inc	8732	55
SGT Enterprises	5046	379
SH Lee Corp	7389	2411
SH Leggitt Co	3491	22
SH Pierce and Co	7372	3784
SH Trading Inc	5072	145
Shaan Seet Inc	2411	11
Shaant Industries Inc	3081	133
Shable and Associates	7311	932
Shachihata Incorporated USA	3953	1
Shackelford Machine Shop	3599	1538
Shadin LP	3829	156
Shadow Box Theatre Inc	5999	319
Shadow Broadcast Services Inc	4833	122
Shadow Fax Inc	3861	94
Shadow Plastics Inc	2673	63
Shadow Productions	7319	153
Shadow Trucking Inc	4213	2690
Shadowfax Inc	3827	147
Shadyside Honda	5511	675
Shafer Commercial Seating Inc	2599	26
Shafer Kline and Warren Inc	8711	170
Shafer Magnetic Components	3679	234
Shaffer Communication Services Inc	4899	106
Shaffer Manufacturing Corp	3556	98
Shaffer Trucking Inc	4213	86
Shaffstall Corp	3577	381
Shahinian Acoustics Ltd	3651	249
Shaker Advertising Agency Inc	7311	203
Shakertown 1992 Inc	2429	1
Shakespeare and Co	5942	13
Shakespeare Company LLC	2824	8
Shakespeare Fishing Tackle	3949	47
Shakespeare Machine Stamping Of Wisconsin Inc	3291	31
Shakespeare Squared LLC	8299	74
Shakey's Inc	6794	99
Shakour Publishers Inc	2711	869
Shallco Inc	3613	124
Shallis' Services Inc	7349	484
Shambhala Publications Inc	2731	277
Shamrock Building Materials Inc	5031	36
Shamrock Cabinet and Fixture Corp	2434	41
Shamrock Chevrolet Geo Inc	5511	100
Shamrock Companies Inc	8744	25
Shamrock Companies Inc	1731	1856
Shamrock Die Cutting Company Inc	2675	18
Shamrock Engineering Inc	3569	213
Shamrock Farms Dairy Div	5141	111
Shamrock Foods Co	5141	35
Shamrock Industrial Fastener Corp	6512	34
Shamrock Pipe Tools Inc	3589	185
Shamrock Plastics Inc	3089	1456
Shamrock Printing Inc	2752	872
Shamrock Scientific Specialty Systems Inc	2759	182
Shams Group Inc	7372	1606
Shanachie Entertainment Corp	6794	96
Shanafelt Manufacturing Co	3537	60
Shane Group Inc	3949	65
Shanghai Company Inc	0182	10
Shanin Co	2752	939
Shank Public Relations Counselors Inc	8743	201
Shanks and Wright Inc	5065	1012
Shanley Pump and Equipment Inc	5084	675
Shannahan Crane and Hoist Inc	7699	110
Shannon and Wilson Inc	8742	243
Shannon Brothers Company Inc	4213	1134
Shannon Gracey Ratliff and Miller LLP	8111	285
Shannon Lumber Co	5211	263
Shannon Precision LLC	3544	653

Company Name	SIC	Rank
Shan-Rod Inc	3491	54
Shapco Printing Inc	2752	200
Shape Products	2899	229
ShapedWire	3312	64
Shapell Industries Inc	1531	37
Shape-Master Tool Co	3545	253
Shapes Of Plastic Inc	3085	46
Shapiro Salvage and Supply Co	5093	235
Shapolsky Publishers	2731	284
Shar Systems Inc	3559	309
Sharcar Enterprises Inc	3281	23
Shar-Craft Inc	5085	333
Share Corp	2842	69
Share One Inc	7371	761
Shared Financial Services	7389	2080
Shared Mail Aquisitions LLC	2752	687
Shared Service Systems Inc	5047	53
Sharefax Credit Union Inc	6061	95
ShareFile	7379	564
Shareholdercom	5045	167
Shares Inc	7389	878
Sharestaff Inc	7363	384
Sharevis Inc	5045	968
Shareway Industries Inc	3599	892
Shari Neff	5046	347
Sharif Designs Ltd	3172	4
Shari's Management Corp	5812	204
Shark Holdings Inc	7375	12
Shark Lines Inc	4213	1447
Shark Technology Inc	7371	767
Sharkey Howes and Javer Inc	6282	651
Sharkey Transportation Inc	4213	125
Sharn Veterinary Inc	5154	5
Sharon Baptist Board Of Directors Inc	8351	20
Sharon Brooks and Associates Inc	7311	527
Sharon Coating LLC	3479	14
Sharon Manufacturing Inc	3443	230
Sharon Merrill Associates Inc	8743	98
Sharon Packing Company Inc	5147	106
Sharp Attitude Corp	5731	276
Sharp Bancsystems Inc	7371	1455
Sharp Chevrolet Inc	5511	603
Sharp Communication Services Inc	5065	424
Sharp Corp (Conshohocken Pennsylvania)	2752	21
Sharp Electronics Corp	3651	263
Sharp Electronics Satellite	7372	3423
Sharp Energy Inc	5984	16
Sharp Health Plan	6324	66
Sharp Healthcare	8062	32
Sharp Honda	5511	1088
Sharp International Corp	3873	7
Sharp Laboratories of America Inc	8731	44
Sharp Manufacturing Co of America	3639	3
Sharp Microelectronics Group	3572	39
Sharp Model Co	3544	217
Sharp Technologies Inc	3469	387
Sharp Tool Service Inc	3545	287
Sharp Transport Inc	4213	930
Sharp Transportation Inc	4213	1295
Sharp Water Inc	1382	12
Sharpco Inc	5082	205
Sharpe and Preszler Construction Company Inc	1623	375
Sharpe Buick and BMW Inc	5511	748
Sharpe Business Systems Corp	5999	37
Sharpe Dry Goods Co	5611	18
Sharpe Images Properties Inc	5999	135
Sharpe Mixers Inc	3561	158
Sharpening Specialists LC	7699	228
SharpeSoft Inc	7372	2175
Sharpline Converting Inc	2396	11
Sharps Compliance Corp	3842	122
Sharron Group Inc	5012	153
Shartsis Friese LLP	8111	269
Shasta Industries Inc	1799	8
Shatila Food Products Inc	5149	97
Shaudra Company Inc	3911	49
Shaum Electric Company Inc	1731	1417
Shavel Home Products	2211	21
Shaver Construction Inc	1542	364
Shaver Specialty CoInc	3556	177
Shaver Transportation Co	4492	10
Shavers Inc	5411	249
Shaw Alloy Piping Products Co	3494	16
Shaw and Slavsky Inc	2542	51
Shaw and Todd Inc	7311	485
Shaw Construction LLC	1522	23
Shaw Contract Flooring	1752	1
Shaw Development LLC	3069	149
Shaw Electric Co	1731	304
Shaw Electric Company Inc	1731	110
Shaw Environmental and Infrastructure Inc	4953	13
Shaw Environmental and Infrastructure Inc (Trenton New Jersey)	4959	10
Shaw Group Inc	3498	1
Shaw Industries Group Inc	2273	2
Shaw Lumber Company Inc	5211	229
Shaw Management	6282	641
Shaw Mudge and Co	2844	114
Shaw Newspapers	2711	137
Shaw Solid Waste Management	8711	114
Shaw SSS Fabricators Inc	3441	111

Company Name	SIC	Rank
Shaw Steel Inc	7389	1868
Shaw Systems Associates Inc	7372	925
Shaw Trucking Inc	4212	34
Shaw-Clayton Corp	3089	1868
Shawcor Pipe Protection LLC	3479	13
Shaw-Lundquist Associates Inc	1542	151
Shawmark Group	6799	134
Shawmut Advertising Inc	2752	575
Shawmut Corp	2295	6
Shawmut Design and Construction	1542	34
Shawmut Metal Products Inc	3312	108
Shawndra Products Inc	3564	27
Shawnee Development Inc	6552	60
Shawnee Lighting Systems Inc	1731	2443
Shawnee Systems Inc	2761	56
Shawnee Terminal Railway Co	4011	38
Shawntech Communications Inc	5065	276
Shaw's Fiberglass And Plastics Inc	1799	142
Shaw's Supermarkets Inc	5411	37
Shaw's Supermarkets Inc Northern Div	5411	60
Shawsheen Rubber Company Inc	2672	60
Shawver and Son Inc	1731	140
Shay Investment Services Inc	8742	171
Shaztec (USA) Inc	5063	671
Shc Holding Inc	8051	28
Shea Architects Inc	8712	292
Shea Homes	1531	7
Shealy Electrical Wholesalers Inc	5063	111
Shealy Sales and Vending Inc	5194	24
Shealy's Truck Center Inc	5511	1164
Shear Tool Inc	3324	22
Shearer Printing Service Inc	2752	1331
Shearer's Foods Inc	2096	3
Shearman and Sterling	8111	21
Shearman Corp	2711	256
Shear-Rite Steel Corp	5051	386
Shebesta Abest Inc	7373	985
Shechtman Marks Devor PC	8721	431
Shee Atika Inc	6799	161
Shee Atika Inc	6514	1
Sheehan Phinney Bass and Green	8111	289
Sheehan Pipe Line Construction Co	1623	53
Sheehy Auto Stores	5511	37
Sheehy Ford Inc	5511	223
Sheehy Ware And Pappas PC	8111	454
SheerVision Inc	3827	121
Sheetz Inc	5331	8
Sheffield Audio-Video Production	7812	55
Sheffield Bronze Paint Corp	2851	156
Sheffield Cutting Equipment	3541	232
Sheffield Homes	1521	108
Sheffield Plastics Inc	3081	34
Sheffield Press Printers And Lithographers	2752	1656
Shefsky and Froelich	8111	301
Sheid's Corp	5712	110
Sheinman Provision Company Inc	2013	231
Shekinah Studios	7372	4553
Sheladia Associates Inc	8712	144
Shelba D Johnson Trucking Inc	4213	1976
Shelburne Farms	8299	71
Shelburne Sherr Court Reporters Inc	7338	41
Shelby Contracting Company Inc	2951	26
Shelby County Bank	6035	260
Shelby County Community Services Inc	8331	105
Shelby Elastics Of North Carolina LLC	2259	2
Shelby Electric Company Inc	1731	27
Shelby Electric Cooperative Inc	4911	317
Shelby Electric Inc	1731	2086
Shelby Enterprises Inc	3498	52
Shelby Gravel Inc	3273	26
Shelby Industries LLC	3531	130
Shelby Singleton Enterprises Inc	5735	20
Shelby Systems Inc	7372	1604
Shelby Williams Industries Inc	2521	9
Shelbyville Newspapers Inc	2711	500
Shelbyville Pencil Company Inc	2499	53
Shelbyville Publishing Company Inc	2711	689
Shelco Inc	1541	106
Sheldon Good and Co	6531	89
Sheldon Laboratory Systems Inc	3821	29
Sheldon Miller and Associates	8111	594
Sheler Corp	3567	122
ShelfGenie	2434	77
Shelko Consulting LLC	7372	4439
Shell Chemical Co	2821	16
Shell Energy Trading North America	4923	9
Shell Factory Museum Inc	5947	23
Shell Oil Co	2911	7
Shell Packaging Corp	2631	28
Shell Vacations Inc	6552	5
Shellenberger Gregg Inc	3559	354
Shelley's Septic Tank Inc	1711	171
Shelly And Sands Inc	1611	84
Shelly Associates Inc	3679	509
Shelly Co	2951	7
Shelly Daniels Asphalt	1611	111
Shelly Electric Company Inc	1731	661
Shelly Fisher	3089	977
Shelly Moving and Storage Inc	4213	1523
Shelly Ward Enterprises Inc	4213	2977
Shelter Distribution Inc	5033	64
Shelter Enterprises Inc	3086	63

Company Name	SIC	Rank	Company Name	SIC	Rank	Company Name	SIC	Rank
Shelter Financial Bank	6141	64	Shetler Moving and Storage Inc	4213	793	Shop Ideas Network LLC	4813	689
Shelter Harbor Inn Inc	5812	433	Shew Electric Inc	1731	453	Shop Systems Inc	7371	534
Shelter Mortgage Corp	6162	83	Sheyenne Tooling And Manufacturing Inc	3423	50	Shop Vac Corp	3589	18
Shelter Mutual Insurance Co	6331	188				ShopKeeper Software	7372	2205
Shelter Products Inc	5031	39	Shg Services Inc	7363	50	Shopko Operating	5311	23
Shelter Systems Corp	2439	13	SHI International	7389	40	ShopKo Stores Operating Co LLC	5311	18
Shelter Systems Ltd	2439	26	Shibuya Hoppmann Corp	3565	51	ShoploopCom Inc	4813	358
Sheltered Workshop For Disabled Inc	3315	38	Shick Tube-Veyor Corp	3535	36	Shopper's Food Warehouse Corp	5411	73
Shelterlogic Holdings LLC	7389	866	Shickel Corp	3499	83	Shopper's Press Of Memphis	2741	332
Shelton Pontiac-Buick Inc	5511	926	Shiel Sexton Company Inc	1542	139	Shopping Center Group Inc	6552	86
Shelton Technologies Inc	5065	438	Shiel Sexton Company Inc Interiors Div	7389	553	Shoppingcom Ltd	7375	98
Shelton Winnelson Co	5074	105	Shield Manufactoring Inc	3931	18	Shopsite Inc	7372	490
Shelton's Poultry Inc	2015	54	Shield Packaging Company Inc	7389	884	Shopsmith Inc	3559	151
Shelton-Turnbull Printers Inc	2752	457	Shield Packaging of California Inc	2844	64	Shopsmith Woodworking Centers Limited Co	3546	12
Shelving Depot Inc	5046	256	Shield Pattern Works Inc	3544	556			
Shenandoah Engineering Services Inc	8711	564	Shields and Company Inc	6211	301	Shopsmith Woodworking Promotions Inc	3546	13
Shenandoah Life Insurance Co	6311	108	Shields Enterprises Inc	3541	106			
Shenandoah Mills Inc	2045	16	Shields Environmental Inc	5065	148	Shore Bancshares Inc	6712	286
Shenandoah Sand Inc	5032	190	Shields MRI	6324	69	Shore Bank (Onley Virginia)	6036	73
Shenandoah Telecommunications Co	4813	64	Shieldtech Systems LLC	5065	919	Shore Connection Inc	1623	841
Shenandoah Valley Educational Television Corp	4833	212	Shiflet Imaging Inc	7384	14	Shore Consultants Ltd	5734	369
			Shiflett Transport Services Inc	4213	2847	Shore Corp	2842	158
Shenandoah Valley Electric Cooperative Inc	4911	221	Shift Communications LLC	8743	51	Shore Holders	3643	160
			Shift4 Corp	7372	324	Shore Line Newspapers	2711	228
Shenango Inc	3312	67	Shifting Sands Stereo Distributors Inc	5064	162	Shore Liquidations Inc	3523	269
Shep Company LLC	2891	88	Shigamo Development Inc	3621	115	Shore Manufacturing Co	5113	72
Shepard Brothers Inc	2842	70	Shigemura and Harakal	8111	470	Shore Seafood Inc	5146	51
Shepard Industries Inc	7349	171	Shillington Box Company LLC	2653	92	Shore To Shore Inc	2679	8
Shepard Steel Company Inc	3441	104	Shilo Corporation Management Offices	7011	20	Shore Trucking Company Inc	4213	2180
Shepard Thomason Co	3714	430	Shilo Inns Co	7011	21	Shore Western Manufacturing Inc	3826	102
Shepard's Industrial Training Systems Inc	8331	207	Shiloh Industries Inc	3469	6	Shorebank (Bellwood Illinois)	6712	490
			Shiloh Industries Wellington Stamping	3469	12	Shorebank Corp	6712	197
Shepardson Stern and Kaminsky	8742	349	Shiloh Technologies LLC	5045	724	Shorebank Development Corp	6552	297
Shepher Distributors and Sales Corp	5092	10	Shilstone Companies Inc	7372	4752	Shoreham Graphics Inc	8711	658
Shepherd Caster Corp	3429	77	Shimada Enterprises Inc	3648	58	Shoreline Creations Ltd	2721	261
Shepherd Electric Supply Company Inc	5063	157	Shimadzu Scientific Instruments Inc	5049	13	Shoreline Glass Company Inc	1793	10
Shepherd of the Hills Homestead and Outdoor Theatre	7996	26	Shimano American Corp	5091	19	Shorlinc Recycling and Supply	5093	218
			Shimaya Shoten Ltd	5141	204	Shoreline Sprinkling Inc	5087	195
Shepherd Products Co	5131	21	Shims Bargain Inc	5199	9	Shorenstein Asset Services East LP	6531	316
Shepherd's Co	7349	324	Shin Shin America	7372	3061	Shorenstein Company LP	6531	63
Shepherd-Will Inc	4213	2597	Shincor Silicones Inc	2822	16	Shorenstein Realty Services LP	6531	67
Shepler's Equipment Company Inc	5072	18	Shindengen America Inc	5065	142	Shores and Ruark Seafood Inc	5146	67
Sheplers Inc	5699	8	Shine Brothers Corp	5093	102	Shoretel Inc	3613	14
Sheppard International Inc	5049	165	Shin-Etsu Handotai America Inc	3339	2	Shorett Printing Inc	2752	664
Sheppard Motors Ltd	5511	592	Shin-Etsu MicroSi Inc	2821	210	Shorewood Display Co	3993	45
Sheppard Trucking Ltd	4213	2697	Shingle Belting	3535	132	Shorewood Realtors Inc	6531	442
Sherborne Group Inc	3651	16	Shining Ocean Inc	2092	33	Short and Paulk Supply Co	5251	14
Sherbrooke Metals	3624	30	Shining Technology Inc	3572	107	Short and Son Paving Company Incorporated B P	1611	194
Sherburn Electronics Inc	5063	171	Shinko Technologies Inc	5045	444			
Sheriar Press Inc	2752	1030	Shinn Fu Company Of America Inc	5013	101	Short Circuits Inc	3672	437
Sheridan Books Inc	2732	2	Shinsei Corp	3089	1172	Short Company Inc	5087	90
Sheridan Corp	1541	225	Shinsho American Corp	5051	67	Short Freight Lines Inc	4213	1305
Sheridan Electric Cooperative Inc	4911	460	Shintech Inc	2821	53	Short Mountain Silica Co	1446	3
Sheridan Electric Inc	1731	2056	Shintone USA Inc	3523	156	Short Mountain Trucking Inc	4213	1694
Sheridan Engineering Corp	3823	384	Shioleno Metal Products Inc	3441	127	Shortcuts Software Inc	7372	2188
Sheridan Group (Hunt Valley Maryland)	2731	115	Shionogi USA Inc	8731	76	Shortridge Instruments Inc	3829	235
Sheridan Group Ltd	8743	189	Shipbuilders Of Wisconsin Inc	3732	36	Shorty's Truck and Railroad Car Parts Inc	5088	86
Sheridan Healthcare Inc	8741	104	Shipley Company LLC	2899	17			
Sheridan Newspapers Inc	2711	918	Shipley Transport	4213	1135	Shostak Iron And Metal Company Inc	5093	231
Sheridan Optical Company Inc	3851	108	Shipman Elevator Co	5191	57	Shotcrete Systems Inc	1771	30
Sheridan Press Inc	2752	47	Shipman Printing Industries Inc	2752	937	Shoto Corp	2599	25
Sheridan Printing Co	2741	216	Shipman-Ward Inc	5044	140	Shotspotter Inc	5045	221
Sherline Products Inc	3553	14	Shippers Express Inc	4213	1387	Shott Capital Management LLC	6282	554
Sherlock Systems	5046	69	Shippers Supply Corp	5113	28	Shoulders Corp	7372	4138
Sherm Edwards Candies Inc	2064	138	Shipper's Transport Co	4213	373	Shoun Trucking Company Inc	4213	882
Sherman and Associates Inc	5013	273	Shipyard Brewing Company LLC	2082	96	Shouse Tool Inc	3545	373
Sherman and Howard LLC	8111	357	Shire Us Inc	5122	44	Show Management Inc	7389	550
Sherman and Reilly Inc	3644	21	Shirlee Wenzel and Company Inc	7311	387	Show Me Trucking and Freight	4213	2856
Sherman Brothers Heavy Trucking	4213	351	Shirley Oberg Services	7374	251	Show Media	7311	589
Sherman Clay and Co	5736	11	Shirley Oil and Supply Company Inc	5541	18	Show Michigan Corp	7389	855
Sherman Corp	3599	1573	Shirley's Cookie Company Inc	2052	40	Show Pros Entertainment Services Inc	7363	108
Sherman Gabus Inc	7389	1133	Shir-Omar Inc	1731	2516	Showa Aluminum Corporation Of America	3714	196
Sherman Industries Inc	3273	104	Shiseido Cosmetics Ltd (Oakland New Jersey)	2844	46			
Sherman Machine Inc	3599	1917				Showalter Incorporated F L	1629	104
Sherman Printing Company Inc	2752	1158	Shively Brothers Inc	5084	185	Showbest Fixture Corp	2542	29
Sherman Publications Inc	2711	482	Shivtron Inc	3672	423	ShowCase Inc	7372	826
Sherman Textile Co	2211	28	Shivvers Manufacturing Inc	3523	105	ShowerTek Inc	3231	27
Sherman Wire	3315	2	Shiya-Strephans Contracting Co	1623	88	ShowHomes of America	7389	1449
Shermantic Computer Service	7378	30	Shl Inc	8742	458	Show-Me Software LLC	7372	3742
Sherm's Thunderbird Markets Inc	5411	176	Shoals Electric Company Inc	1731	873	Showroom Solutions Inc	5734	112
Shernoff Bidart and Darras LLP	8111	424	Shoals Technologies Group Inc	3679	563	Showscan Entertainment Inc	7812	148
Sherpa's Pet Trading Co	3999	151	Shockey Precast Group	3273	9	Showstopper Exhibits Inc	7389	1827
Sherrill Furniture Company Inc	2512	15	Shoe Carnival Inc	5661	7	Shps Holdings Inc	6411	95
Sherrill Industries Inc	3552	31	Shoe Metro	5661	16	SHPS Inc	7389	44
Sherry Manufacturing Company Inc	2261	15	Shoemaker Inc	5074	114	Shrader Electric Company Inc	1731	748
Sherry Matthews Advocacy Marketing Inc	7311	229	Shoemaker Manufacturing Co	3446	36	Shrager Spivey and Sachs	8111	544
			Shoffnerkalthoff Mechanical Electrical Service Inc	1711	64	Shredding Systems Inc	3559	114
Sherry-Lehmann Corp	5921	8				Shredfast Mobile Data Destruction Inc	3589	163
Sherwin Industries Inc	2951	48	Shofu Dental Corp	5047	253	Shred-Pac Inc	3589	174
Sherwin-Williams Co	2851	2	Shokai Far East Ltd	3825	56	Shreve Printing LLC	2752	1696
Sherwood	3491	58	Sho-Me Power Electric Coop	4911	188	Shrieve Chemical Co	5169	31
Sherwood America Inc	3651	118	Shonan USA Inc	2086	114	Shrin Corp	3714	272
Sherwood Automotive Group Inc	5511	1215	Shoney's North America Corp	5812	100	Shrink Nanotechnologies Inc	7372	5047
Sherwood Brands Inc	2064	28	Shonfeld's USA Inc	5141	136	Shubert Theater Organization Inc	7922	2
Sherwood Community Services	8322	239	Shook and Fletcher Insulation Co	5033	9	Shuffle Master Inc	3999	19
Sherwood Construction Company Inc	1629	25	Shook Inc	1542	303	Shuford Mills LLC	2221	36
Sherwood Engineering Inc	7373	1210	Shook Mobile Technology LP	3663	183	Shugoll Research Inc	8742	409
Sherwood Food Distributors	5142	8	Shook National Corp	1629	22	Shultz Steel Co	3325	10
Sherwood Iss LLC	5045	390	Shoosmith Brothers Inc	1794	23	Shumaker Enterprises Inc	1442	40
Sherwood Printing Inc	2752	1678	Shooting Star Solutions LLC	7379	925	Shumaker Loop and Kendrick LLP	8111	422
Sherwood Studios Inc	7389	583	Shop Acquisitions LLC	3599	1051	Shumaker Trucking Company Inc	4213	1192
Sherwood Technologies Inc	7372	4751	Shop Auto Parts Inc	5013	94	Shuman Healthcare Of Waycross Inc	5999	220
Sherwood-Turner Corp	5075	102	Shop By Design Inc	5065	135	Shuman Plastics Inc	7389	668
Shesam Inc	5169	130	Shop For Bags Inc	5621	44			

Company Name	SIC	Rank
Shumar's Welding and Machine Service Inc	3532	26
Shumate Air Conditioning and Heating Company Inc	1711	15
Shumsky Enterprises Inc	7319	38
Shunra Software Ltd	7372	3252
Shupeco LLC	3569	252
Shuqualak Lumber Company Inc	2421	31
Shur Fit Distributors Inc	2541	59
Shurclose Seal Rubber and Plastic	2822	15
Shur-Co LLC	3429	57
Shure Electronics	3651	155
SHURflo LLC	3561	50
Shurgard Storage Centers Inc	6798	81
Shur-Line Inc	3089	685
Shurtape Technologies LLC	2672	8
Shuster-Mettler Corp	3549	117
Shuster's Builders Supplies Inc	5031	95
Shutterfly Inc	7384	1
Shuttle Computer Group Inc	3571	71
Shuttlelift Inc	3999	59
Shuttlewagon Inc	3743	22
Shuttleworth Inc	3535	72
Shutts and Bowen LLP	8111	251
Shw Group LLP	8712	41
SI Financial Group Inc	6035	83
SI Goldman Co	1711	101
Si Industrial Instruments Inc	3823	383
SI Industries Inc	3555	65
SI Manufacturing Inc	3677	40
Si Roller	3555	106
Si Stainless International Inc	5046	320
SI Tech Inc	3357	82
SIA Computer Corp	3571	169
SIAM	2731	158
Sibex Inc	3672	151
Sibling Entertainment Group Holdings Inc	7922	102
Sibson Consulting Group	8742	197
Si-Cal Inc	2759	439
Sicel Technologies Inc	8731	144
SICK Inc	3577	123
Sicola Martin	7311	390
Sicoli and Massaro Inc	1542	365
Sicon International	3577	75
Sicor Inc	2834	67
Sicor Pharmaceuticals Sales Inc	2834	10
Sicpa Securink Corp	2893	12
Sid Greenberg Inc	2341	2
Sid Harvey Industries Inc	3433	50
Sid Paterson Advertising Inc	7311	766
Sid Richardson Carbon and Gasoline Co	2895	2
Sidaris Italian Foods	2099	219
Sidco Filter Corp	3569	246
Siddall Inc	7311	457
Side Eight Software	2741	510
Sidebar Inc	7372	2690
Sidehill Copper Works Inc	3443	241
Siderean Software Inc	7371	591
Sides and Associates Inc	7311	296
Sidley Austin LLP	8111	18
Sidley Diamond Tool Co	3291	24
Sidney B Bowne and Son LLP	8711	377
Sidney D Torres III Law Offices	8111	534
Sidney Electric Co	1731	615
Sidney Manufacturing Company Inc	3556	134
Sidney Transportation Services	4213	921
Sidumpr Trailer Company Inc	3716	16
Sidwell Co	7299	33
Sieb and Meyer America Inc	3625	293
Siebert Brandford Shank and Company LLC	6159	58
Siebert Financial Corp	6211	310
Siegal Steel Co	5051	322
Siegel Oil Co	5172	105
Siegelgale	7311	450
Sieger Engineering Inc	3599	152
Siegfried Companies Inc	6799	314
Siegfried Group LLP	8721	271
Siegwerk USA Inc	2893	11
Sieler Design Products	8711	677
Siematic Corp	2434	78
Siemens Applied Automation Inc	3826	13
Siemens Audio Inc	5049	29
Siemens Building Technologies Fire Safety	3669	17
Siemens Corporate Research Inc	8731	103
Siemens Corp	3674	2
Siemens Energy Inc	1629	6
Siemens Healthcare Diagnostics Inc	5047	25
Siemens Hearing Inc	3842	132
Siemens Industrial Automation Inc	3714	40
Siemens Information and Communication Networks Inc	8731	2
Siemens IT Solutions and Services Inc	3571	4
Siemens Manufacturing Company Inc	3672	60
Siemens Medical Solutions USA Inc (Malvern Pennsylvania)	7372	4
Siemens Medical Systems Inc	3841	9
Siemens Oil Gas And Marine	8711	298
Siemens PLM Software	7371	11
Siemens Power Transmission and Distribution Inc	3613	3

Company Name	SIC	Rank
Siemens Water Technologies	1629	4
Siemon Co	3643	25
Siena Marble and Granite Inc	5032	103
Sienko Precision LLC	3599	1839
Sierra Alloys Co	3463	22
Sierra Aluminum Co	3354	24
Sierra Atlantic Inc	7379	533
Sierra Automated Systems and Engineering Corp	3663	258
Sierra Bancorp	6712	262
Sierra Bravo Corp	7371	601
Sierra Cheese Manufacturing Co	2022	26
Sierra Chemical Co	5169	100
Sierra Circuits Inc	3672	119
Sierra Communications Inc	4813	546
Sierra Computers Ltd	7379	841
Sierra Corp	7379	1563
Sierra Custom Electronics Inc	3674	449
Sierra Design Manufacturing Inc	3647	23
Sierra Electric Inc	1731	2448
Sierra Electric LLC	1731	2505
Sierra Financial Services Inc	8742	360
Sierra Forest Products Inc	2421	92
Sierra Industries Inc	1731	1545
Sierra Laboratories Inc	3841	324
Sierra Lumber Manufacturers	2431	20
Sierra Machinery Inc	3569	187
Sierra Madre Foods Inc	2038	43
Sierra Meat Company Inc	5147	21
Sierra Medical Center	8071	11
Sierra Microwave Technology Inc	3679	398
Sierra Midwest Inc	3672	184
Sierra Mining and Crushing Company LLC	5032	153
Sierra Monitor Corp	3829	96
Sierra National Corp	3578	31
Sierra Nevada Corp	3812	9
Sierra Office Systems And Products Inc	2752	208
Sierra Pacific Home and Comfort Inc	1711	206
Sierra Pacific Industries	2421	5
Sierra Pacific Packaging Inc	2759	139
Sierra Point Lumber And Plywood Company Inc	5211	143
Sierra Precast Inc	3272	19
Sierra Research Inc	8731	156
Sierra Resources LLC	1311	192
Sierra Seafood Specialties LLC	5146	45
Sierra Solutions	7372	1930
Sierra Summit Mountain Resort Inc	7011	194
Sierra Systems	7372	4753
Sierra Tech Computers	7379	770
Sierra Technologies LLC	3674	329
Sierra Tel Internet	7379	852
Sierra Therm Production Furnaces Inc	3567	15
Sierra Ventures	6799	29
Sierra Video Systems	3651	116
Sierra View Company Inc	1542	397
Sierra Vista Herald	2711	156
Sierra Wireless America Inc	4812	72
Sierra-Pacific Software	7372	5126
Sierrapine A California LP	2431	12
Sievers Security Systems Inc	1731	1004
SIFCO Selective Plating	3471	58
SIGA Technologies Inc	2834	270
Sigal Construction Corp	1542	126
SiGe Semiconductor Inc (Andover Massachusetts)	4812	26
Sigel Feed and Grain Inc	5999	200
Sight Software Inc	7372	4754
Sightline Health LLC	7349	62
Sightline Payments	7389	516
SightLine Systems Corp	7371	149
Sigler Companies Inc	2752	147
Sigma Corporation of America	5043	14
Sigma Data Systems Inc	7373	1153
Sigma Design	7372	2064
Sigma Designs Inc	3674	71
Sigma Engineering and Consulting Inc	3599	2143
Sigma Environmental Services Inc	4953	68
Sigma Extruding Corp	2673	20
Sigma Four LP	3679	535
Sigma Group	7311	212
Sigma International General Medical Apparatus LLC	3841	127
Sigma Manufacturing Industries Inc	3599	2313
Sigma Marketing Group LLC	7311	403
Sigma Micro Corp	7372	2039
Sigma Plastics Group	3089	21
Sigma Plating Company Inc	3471	26
Sigma Probe Inc	3675	34
Sigma Six Corp	7372	4011
Sigma Supply Inc	5084	115
Sigma Switches Plus Inc	3625	394
Sigma Systems Inc (Denver Colorado)	7372	2862
Sigma Systems Inc (Marlborough Massachusetts)	7372	465
Sigma Technology Services	7379	1556
Sigma Tek Inc	3728	135
Sigma Temps Inc	7361	72
Sigma-Aldrich Biotechnology Holding Company Inc	2899	20
Sigma-Aldrich Chemical Co	2869	19
Sigma-Aldrich Corp	5169	9

Company Name	SIC	Rank
Sigma-Aldrich Lancaster Inc	2899	21
Sigma-Genosys of Texas Inc	2899	58
Sigma-Tau Pharmaceuticals Inc	5122	75
Sigmatech Inc	7371	780
SigmaTech Software	7372	2210
Sigmation Inc	3825	355
SigmaTron International Inc	3672	18
Sigmedics Inc	3841	253
Sigmund Cohn Corporation Of California	3356	24
Sign Boys LLC	2752	539
Sign Faces LLC	3993	74
Sign On A Sign Language Interpreting Resource Inc	7389	1604
Sign Source USA Ino	5085	324
Sign Systems Of Maine Inc	7373	1211
Signa Inc	3663	328
Signacert Inc	7371	448
Signal Advertising	7311	914
Signal Communications Corp	3669	192
Signal Engineering Corp	1731	2318
Signal Engineering Inc	8711	657
Signal Hill Petroleum Inc	1311	120
Signal International LLC	7699	9
Signal Machine Company Inc	7699	126
Signal Metal Industries Inc	3441	69
Signal Newspapers Inc	2711	378
Signal One Fire And Communication LLC	5084	789
Signal Plating Inc	3471	96
Signal Securities Inc	6211	365
Signal Service Co	1731	1365
Signal Service Inc	5063	530
Signal Service Industries Inc	1731	954
Signal Systems International	3823	386
Signal Technology Corp	3679	17
Signalcom Systems Inc	3661	232
Signalert Corp	6799	261
Signalogic Inc	7372	3375
Signatec Inc	3577	552
Signatrol Inc	3625	358
Signature Advertising LLC	7311	555
Signature Automotive Group	5511	1049
Signature Bank	6022	817
Signature Bank (Chicago Illinois)	6022	758
Signature Bank of Arkansas	6022	728
Signature Building Maintenance Inc	7349	256
Signature Cable Manufacturing Technology Inc	4841	149
Signature Cleaning Services Inc	7349	134
Signature Consultants LLC	7363	70
Signature Engraving Systems Inc	3577	409
Signature Envelope Inc	7331	132
Signature Eyewear Inc	3851	24
Signature Flight Support Corp	4581	7
Signature Foods Inc	2099	91
Signature Genomic Laboratories LLC	8071	38
Signature Graphics Inc	7336	42
Signature Group Holdings Inc	6022	613
Signature Insurance Group	6411	145
Signature Mortgage	6162	134
Signature Print Services	7389	2264
Signature Printing	2752	283
Signature Printing And Graphics Company Inc	2752	991
Signature Skylights LLC	3444	154
Signature Software Inc	7371	1656
Signature Systems Inc	7373	904
Signature Technologies Inc	3669	151
Signature Technology Group Inc	7378	19
Signcraft Inc	3993	69
SIGNERA	7371	1732
Signet Armorlite Inc	3851	12
Signet International Holdings Inc	4833	259
Signiant Inc	5045	153
Signius Communications Inc	7389	843
Sign-Lite Corp	3993	99
Signmark Div	3993	2
Signode Packaging Systems	3499	9
Signologies Inc	3993	161
Signs and Shapes International Inc	3312	113
Signs Now Corp	3993	148
Signs Plus New Ideas-New Technology Inc	5046	135
Sign-Tech Electric LLC	1731	2185
Signum Inc	5162	60
Signum Systems Corp	3825	256
Sigtronics Corp	3669	254
Sihi Pumps Inc	3561	71
Sika Corp	3272	38
Sika Sarnafil Inc	2952	10
Sikama International Inc	3548	66
Siko Products Inc	3829	252
Sikorsky Aircraft Corp	3721	10
Sikorsky Military Completions Center	3721	24
SIL Inc	2013	78
Silarx Pharmaceuticals Inc	2834	360
Silas White Construction Inc	1623	627
Silberline Manufacturing Company Inc	2816	4
Silbrico Corp	3296	9
Silco Oil Co	5541	31
Silent Partner Security Systems Inc	7382	145
Silent Technology LLC	3625	422
Silent World Dive Center Inc	7999	156

Company Name	SIC	Rank
Siler Studios	8999	218
Silex Interiors Inc	5999	197
Silgan Closures	3579	26
Silgan Containers Corp	3441	3
Silgan Holdings Inc	3089	9
Silgan Plastics Corp	3089	60
Silhouette Management Services LLC	7379	1626
Silica Transport Inc	4213	1848
Silico Corp	8742	572
Silicom Inc (Mahwah New Jersey)	3577	343
Silicomp America	7372	5108
Silicon Designs Inc	8711	610
Silicon Graphics International Corp	3571	15
Silicon Heights Computers Inc	5045	636
Silicon Image Inc	3679	65
Silicon Interfaces America Inc	7379	1298
Silicon Laboratories Inc	3669	12
Silicon Light Machines	3674	260
Silicon Microstructures Inc	3625	85
Silicon Mountain Holdings Inc	7812	105
Silicon Turnkey Solutions Inc	5065	277
Silicon Valley Bank	6211	256
Silicon Valley Cable Company Inc	7389	2131
Silicon Valley Industries Inc	2752	1838
Silicon Valley Securities Inc	6211	315
Silicon Valley Security and Patrol Inc	7381	69
Silicon Valley Staffing Group Inc	7363	141
Silicon Valley World Trade Corp	3613	108
Silicone Plastics Inc	3089	990
Silicone Products and Technology	3544	90
Siliconians Inc	3674	425
Siliconix Inc	3674	28
Silicor Technologies Inc	7372	2176
Silitronics Inc	3679	586
Silk Road Transport Inc	4213	1776
Silkey Trucking Inc	4213	2743
SilkRoad Equity LLC	6719	84
SilkRoad Technology Inc	7372	434
Silkworm Inc	7336	87
Siller Brothers Inc	2411	9
Sillery and Partners	7311	419
Silliker Inc	8071	3
SiloSmashers Inc	8742	129
Silsam Inc	7359	188
Silsbee Ford Lincoln Mercury Inc	5511	1193
Siltech Inc	3089	1864
Silterra Malaysia Sdn Bhd	3339	8
Siltronic AG (San Jose California)	3674	9
Silva Construction Company Inc	1623	644
Silvaco Inc	7372	3785
Silvan Industries Inc	3443	94
Silvanus Products Inc	2782	32
Silva's Express Inc	4213	3122
Silvas Oil Company Inc	5172	76
Silva's Pipeline Inc	1023	579
Silvatech Corp	3625	256
Silver Bell Mining LLC	3331	1
Silver Bullet Technology Inc	5045	262
Silver City Brewing Company Inc	2082	87
Silver Communications Corp	2759	214
Silver Creek Brewing Corp	2082	52
Silver Creek Communications Inc	1623	788
Silver Creek Farms Inc	2092	78
Silver Creek Specialty Meats Inc	2013	228
Silver Creek Technology Investors	6799	130
Silver Diner Inc	5812	308
Silver Dollar City Inc	7996	16
Silver Fox Productions Inc	7336	119
Silver Freedman and Taff LLP	8111	551
Silver Harris And Sons Inc	5093	245
Silver Horn Mining Ltd	3612	138
Silver Lake Cookie Company Inc	2052	21
Silver Lake Partners	6719	146
Silver Peak Systems Inc	7379	85
Silver Platter Productions Inc	7319	177
Silver Quick Associates Inc	7336	139
Silver Screen Design Inc	2261	26
Silver Soft Inc	7372	4755
Silver Software Inc	7371	1891
Silver Springs Citrus Inc	2037	20
Silver Springs Farm Inc	2011	128
Silver Star Meats Inc	2013	122
Silver Star Telephone Company Inc	4813	330
Silver State Materials Corp	3273	3
Silver State Merchandisers	2752	747
Silverado Cable Co	3679	391
Silverado Vineyards	2084	98
Silvercarrot Inc	7313	25
Silverchair Science Communications Inc	2721	287
Silvercrest Asset Management Group LLC	6282	83
Silvergate Bank	6035	141
Silverleaf Resorts Inc	6531	115
Silver-Line Plastics Corp	3084	9
Silverlink Communications Inc	7372	2177
Silverman Brothers Inc	5311	50
Silverman Heller Associates	8743	192
Silverman Media and Marketing Group Inc	8743	137
Silveron Industries Inc	3625	257
Silverpop Systems Inc	7371	84
Silvers Brothers Construction	4213	1646
Silver's Metal Co	5093	199

Company Name	SIC	Rank
Silverscape LLC	7374	308
Silversmith Inc	3824	27
Silverstone Adkins and Breit Inc	7311	523
Silverstone Technology	3571	160
Silversun Technologies Inc	7389	934
SilverTech Inc	7379	450
Silverthorne Motors	5015	15
Silverton Marine Corp	3732	46
Silverwood Products Inc	3231	28
Silvestri Studio Inc	3999	86
Silvestri Sweets Inc	2064	137
Silvine Inc	5063	535
Silvon Software Inc	7372	2042
Simacor LLC	7379	560
Simantel Group	7311	879
SIMBA Information Inc	2741	290
Simclar Inc	3679	82
SIMCO Drilling Equipment	3531	186
SIMCO Electronics	7629	3
Simco Erectors Inc	1796	35
Sim-Co Fabricators Inc	1799	97
Simco Technology Inc	5084	813
Simcona Electronics Corp	5065	225
Simeus Foods International Inc	2038	15
SimGraphics Corp	2741	486
Simi Components Inc	5065	949
Simkar LLC	3646	9
Simkins Corp	2652	9
Simkins Industries Inc	2652	5
Simmons Co (Atlanta Georgia)	2515	4
Simmons Electronics Inc	3679	718
Simmons Farm Raised Catfish Inc	2092	29
Simmons First Bank of Jonesboro	6022	746
Simmons First Mortgage Co	6162	62
Simmons First National Bank	6021	377
Simmons First National Corp (Pine Bluff Arkansas)	6712	148
Simmons Machine Tool Corp	3541	50
Simmons Outdoor Corp	5091	18
Simmonsteen Inc	3559	510
Simms Capital Management Inc	6282	393
Simon and Schuster Inc	2731	14
Simon Contractors Co	1611	91
Simon Hubig Company Inc	2051	229
Simon Lever and Co	8721	28
Simon Martin-Vegue Winkelstein Moris	8712	206
Simon Pearce US Inc	3229	12
Simon Printing Co	2752	681
Simon Property Group Inc	6798	9
Simon Systems Inc	5045	1018
Simon Worldwide Inc	2389	41
Simonds Inc	3546	37
Simonds International Corp	3425	2
Simonini Builders Inc	1521	22
Simons Specialty Cheese	2022	52
Simons-Michelson-Zieve Inc	7311	469
Simonton Holdings Inc	3089	88
Simpla Fax Inc	7371	1907
Simple Simon	7372	4012
Simple Solution Enterprises LLC	7378	146
SimplePons Inc	7941	44
SimpleSoft Inc	7379	974
SimpleTuition Inc	7371	449
Simplex Healthcare Inc	8099	23
Simplex Industries Inc	1521	109
Simplex Manufacturing Co	3569	188
Simplex Strip Doors Inc	3081	142
Simplexity Health Inc	2099	136
Simplicity Consulting Inc	8742	373
Simplicity Group LLC	7371	902
Simplicity Pattern Company Inc	2741	146
Simplicity Systems Inc	7372	3023
Simplicti Software Solutions	7372	2520
Simplified Business Solutions Inc	8721	163
Simplified Logistics LLC	8999	60
Simplomatic Manufacturing Co	3469	272
Simplot Employees Credit Union	6061	143
Simplot Phosphates LLC	2874	2
Simply Canvas	7221	10
Simply Certificates Inc	5961	145
Simply Smucker's Inc	2033	84
Simply Wireless Inc	4813	37
Simpson and Simpson CPA	8721	133
Simpson Buick Pontiac GMC	5511	976
Simpson Coatings Group Inc	2851	136
Simpson Dura-Vent	3564	8
Simpson Gumpertz and Heger Inc	8711	324
Simpson Investment Co	2411	1
Simpson Manufacturing Company Inc	2499	5
Simpson Norton Corp	0781	10
Simpson Organization Inc	6798	216
Simpson Performance Products Inc	3842	94
Simpson Strong-Tie Company Inc	3429	6
Simpson Strong-Tie International Inc	2499	20
Simpson Tacoma Kraft Company LLC	2621	24
Simpson Technologies Corp	3599	244
Simpson Thacher and Bartlett	8111	28
Simpsons Enterprises Inc	3544	323
Sims Consulting Group Inc	8742	643
Sims Financial Group Inc	6211	100
Sims Group USA Holdings Corp	5093	60
Sims Machine and Controls Inc	3569	248
Sims Machinery Company Inc	3599	1496
Sims Machining	3599	1987

Company Name	SIC	Rank
Sims Metal Management - USA	5093	21
Sim's Press Inc	2752	1034
Sims Pump Valve Company Inc	3494	74
Sims Recycling Solutions Holdings Inc	4953	90
SIMS Software	7372	1014
Simsbury Bank and Trust Co	6022	489
Simtek Inc	3699	115
Simtrol Inc	7372	4958
SimuFlite Training International	8299	21
Simul8 Corp	7372	2007
Simulations Inc	7812	306
Simulations Plus Inc	7373	371
Simultaneous Solutions Inc	7371	955
Simulyze Inc	7372	4110
Simunet Corp	7372	1013
Simutronics Corp	7372	2360
Sinaloa Hawaiian Tortillas Inc	2099	301
Sinauer Associates Inc	2731	272
Sinca Industries Inc	3523	287
Sincell Publishing Company Inc	2711	227
Sincere Design	7379	1506
Sincere Orient Commercial Corp	2099	202
Sinclair and Valentine Div	2844	128
Sinclair Broadcast Group Inc	4833	26
Sinclair Buick-GMC Trucks Inc	5511	280
Sinclair Cartage Inc	4213	686
Sinclair International Co	3496	72
Sinclair Manufacturing Co	3679	382
Sinclair Media I Inc	4833	39
Sinclair Media III Inc	4833	45
Sinclair Oil Corp	2911	16
Sinclair Optics Inc	7372	4554
Sinclair Printing Co	2752	150
Sinclair Radio of St Louis Inc	4833	138
Sinclair Television of Charleston Inc	4833	63
Sindall Transport Inc	4213	2205
Sine Patterns LLC	3827	161
Sine Qua Non	2084	39
Sinecera Inc	3492	27
Sinful Colors Inc	2844	117
Singapore Fund Inc	6726	73
Singapore Telecom USA Inc	4813	382
Singer Data Products Inc	3577	369
Singer Equipment Company Inc	5046	27
Singer Sewing Co	3552	2
Singer Showroom	5231	10
SingerLewak	8721	279
Singing Machine Company Inc	3652	20
Singing River Health System	8062	206
Single Digits Inc	4899	163
Single Path LLC	8999	133
Single Source Systems Inc	7373	265
Single Source Technologies Inc	5084	473
Single Touch Interactive Inc	4899	134
Singlebrook Technology Inc	7336	125
SingleHop Inc	4899	136
SinglePoint	7379	406
SingleSource Property Solutions	8741	141
SinglesourceitCom Inc	5045	1069
Singleton Corp	3559	393
Singleton Seafood Co	2091	5
Singular Solutions Inc	5734	125
Sinicrope and Sons Inc	2541	65
Sinn-Tech Inc	3599	1176
Sino Global Shipping America Ltd	4731	55
SinoFresh HealthCare Inc	2834	482
Sinskey Vineyards Inc	5921	14
Sintering Technologies Inc	3714	214
Sinton Dairy Foods Company LLC	2026	49
Siny Corp	2257	6
Sioux Automation Center Inc	5083	54
Sioux City Brick and Tile Co	3251	10
Sioux City Compressed Steel Inc	5093	152
Sioux City Ford Lincoln Mercury	5511	730
Sioux City Foundry Co	5051	143
Sioux City Newspapers Inc	2711	252
Sioux City Night Patrol Inc	7381	223
Sioux City Stationery Company Inc	5044	121
Sioux Corp	3589	165
Sioux Falls Kenworth Inc	5012	133
Sioux Falls Monument Company Inc	3281	58
Sioux Falls Shopping News Inc	2752	1024
Sioux Manufacturing Corp	3795	4
Sioux Tools Inc	3546	5
Sioux Valley Energy	5171	37
Siouxpreme Egg Products Inc	2015	59
Sioux-Preme Packing Co	2011	26
Sioux's Transportation Inc/STI	4213	2630
Sipco Inc	3544	92
Siphron Capital Management	6282	482
Sipi Metals Corp	3339	18
Sippel Company Inc	3441	92
Sipper Products Inc	3544	632
Sippican Inc	3669	57
Sir Bounce A Lot Inc	7359	276
Sir Speedy Inc	6794	80
Sirenic Inc	5734	156
SiRF Technology Holdings Inc	3674	83
Sirius Computer Solutions Inc	7373	38
Sirius Enterprise Systems Group LLC	5045	152
Sirius GT Inc	7372	3805
Sirius Information Inc	2741	336
Sirius Systems Inc	7382	183
Sirius Technology Corp	8748	426

Company Name	SIC	Rank
Sirius Telecommunications Inc	4813	305
Sirius XM Radio Inc	4832	2
Sirloin Saloon Inc	5812	294
Sirois Tool Company Inc	3544	272
Sirona Dental Systems Inc	3843	3
SironaHealth	8099	102
Sirote and Permutt PC	8111	222
Sirsai Multisourcing	7361	160
SirsiDynix	7371	1920
Sirus inc	4899	166
SIRVA Inc	4213	26
SIS Enterprises Inc	2392	40
SIS - G Ltd	7379	684
Sisam Electric Inc	1731	2140
Siscom Inc	5045	1071
Sisk Fulfillment Service Inc	4783	13
Siskiyou Design Inc	3827	62
Siskiyou Telephone Co	4813	406
Siso International USA Corp	5045	840
Sisson and Ryan Inc	1429	12
Sisson Engineering Corp	3599	2358
Sisson Transportation Inc	4213	2216
Sisters Of Charity Hospital Of Buffalo New York	8062	100
Sisters of Providence Health of Washington	6324	4
Sisterson and Company LLP	8999	74
SIS-USA Inc	5021	83
Sit Investment Associates Inc	6282	403
Sitca Corp	3949	21
Sitcur Analysis	7372	5036
Site Development Inc	1541	158
Site Maintenance Inc	7389	1088
Site Rite Construction Company Inc	1623	722
Site Security Solutions Inc	7382	99
Site Solution Contractors LLC	1623	548
Site Specific Inc	7336	256
Sitech Software	7372	5112
Sitehawk	6411	197
Sitehawk Retail Real Estate	6531	436
Siteit Web Design	7379	992
Sitek Process Solutions	3674	435
Sitel	7389	29
SITEL Insurance Marketing Services Inc	7389	137
Sitespring Inc	7379	999
Sitestar Corp	7374	172
SiteTech Inc	8711	630
Sitetech LLC	1623	860
Siteworx Inc	7371	542
Si-Tex Marine Electronics Inc	5065	206
SiTime Corp	3674	156
Sitler Electric Supply Inc	5063	546
Sittema-Bullock Realty Partners	6531	410
Sittercity Inc	8743	211
Situs Cos	6531	68
Siuslaw Financial Group Inc	6712	568
Siuslaw Valley Bank	6022	573
Sivalls Inc	3443	40
SiVance LLC	2869	29
Sivers Auctions Inc	7389	2492
Sivon Manufacturers Co	3567	123
Sivyer Steel Corp	3325	26
Siwek Lumber and Millwork Inc	5211	190
Siwel Consulting Inc	7373	195
Six Flags California	7996	14
Six Flags Entertainment Corp	7996	6
Six Flags Over Texas Inc	7996	13
Six Flags St Louis Inc	7996	18
Six Flags Services of Texas Inc	7996	10
Six Flags Theme Parks Inc	7996	9
Six Robblees Inc	5013	78
Six Sigma Inc	3549	75
Six-B Manufacturing Company Inc	3599	2063
SIXNET LLC	7372	2806
Siya Inc	5072	176
Size Reduction Specialists Corp	3559	552
Size Wise Rentals	5047	221
Sizeler Property Investors Inc	6798	169
Sizeler Thompson Brown Architects	8712	168
Sizzler Restaurants International Inc	5812	106
SJ Amoroso Construction Company Inc	1541	40
SJ Bashen Corp	7389	592
SJ Manufacturing Inc	7389	1709
Sj Services Inc	7349	82
SJB Group LLC	7372	3105
SJControls Inc	3823	364
SJE - Rhombus	3829	50
Sjf Material Handling Inc	5084	317
Sjh Inc	5063	278
SJM Engineering Inc	5084	665
Sjoberg Tool And Manufacturing Corp	3469	209
Sjogren Industries Inc	3541	225
Sjs Cadd Inc	7373	1209
SJW Corp	4941	6
SJW Land Co	7521	8
SK Communications LLC	8743	81
SK Electric Inc	1731	2457
SK Foods LP	2033	28
SK Max Inc	7379	1236
S-K Mold and Tool Co	3544	141
SK Plastic Molding Inc	3089	834
SK Textiles Inc	2392	7
Skach Manufacturing Company Inc	3452	87

Company Name	SIC	Rank
Skadden Arps Slate Meagher and Flom LLP and Affiliates	8111	1
Skaf Construction Co	1542	366
Skagfield Corp	2591	8
Skaggs And Gruber Ltd	5048	31
Skaggs Companies Inc	5049	19
Skagit River Brewing Co	2082	33
Skagit State Bank	6022	330
Skagit Transportation Inc	4213	1871
Skagit Valley Casino Resort	7999	36
Skagway Department Stores	5311	46
Skalli Corp	2084	43
Skally's Old World Bakery Inc	5149	149
Skanska Koch Inc	1622	26
Skanska USA Building Inc	1541	5
Skanska USA Civil Inc	1629	3
Skanska USA Civil Southeast Inc	1629	42
Skanska USA Civil West California District Inc	1611	35
Skarshaug Testing Laboratory Inc	5063	609
Skasol Inc	2899	236
SKB Corp	3089	260
SKBA Capital Management	6282	478
SKC Communication Products Inc	5065	40
Skc Inc	3821	28
Skechers USA Inc	3021	1
Skee Ball Inc	3599	191
Skeels Electric Co	1731	656
Skeeter Enterprises LLC	5013	398
Skeeter Products Inc	3732	38
Skehan Communications Group Inc	7812	329
Skeletech Inc	7389	1364
Skelly and Loy Inc	8711	87
Skelly Oil and Land Co	7353	99
Skeoch Waron Inc	5731	265
Skerbeck Brothers Shows Inc	7999	61
SKF Condition Monitoring Inc	3829	82
SKF International Inc	5094	76
Skf Polyseal Inc	3053	16
SKF USA Inc	3562	20
SKH Management Co	5148	2
Ski and Sea International Inc	5023	137
Ski Roundtop Operating Corp	7011	130
Skidmore Owings and Merrill LLP	8712	12
Skier's Choice Inc	3732	40
Skild Manufacturing Inc	3599	1352
Skilled Healthcare Group Inc	8051	11
Skillman Corp	8741	138
Skillpath Seminars Inc	7389	780
Skills Unlimited Inc	8331	167
Skillsnet Commercial Ltd	7373	580
SkillSource Staffing LLC	7363	373
Skillstorm Inc	7379	153
SkinCare Rx	2834	280
Skinder-Strauss Associates	2721	161
SkinMedica Inc	2834	166
Skinner and Kennedy Co	2752	640
Skinner Electrical Sales Inc	5063	607
Skinner Inc	5932	10
Skinner Printing Company Inc	2752	1431
Skinner Transfer Corp	4213	1013
Skinner Transportation Inc	4213	1384
skinnyCorp LLC	2339	19
Skinstore Inc	2844	82
Skip Hop Inc	2389	11
Skipco Financial Adjusters Inc	7389	1100
Skipper Rota Corp	3556	162
Skipping Stone Inc	8999	97
Skippy's Trucking Inc	4213	1125
Skip's Cutting Inc	2253	7
Skirges Corp	2891	124
Skjonberg Controls Inc	3625	308
Skkn Inc	5045	696
Skl Prime Equipment Services Inc	3312	91
Sklar Corp	5047	142
Sklar Instruments Corp	3841	167
SKM Systems Analysis Inc	7372	2863
Skoda Minotti and Co	8721	300
Skokie Valley Beverage Co	5181	71
Skrl Die Casting Inc	3365	33
Sks Bottle and Packaging Inc	5085	178
Sks Die Casting And Machining Inc	3363	43
Sks Machine Inc	3599	1654
Skullcandy Inc	3577	73
Skurka Aerospace Inc	3621	36
Skutch Electronics Inc	3661	241
Skutt Ceramic Products Inc	3567	58
Skuttle Manufacturing Co	3564	111
Sky Blue Agency Inc	7311	749
Sky Blue Broadcasting Inc	4832	155
Sky Blue Factory Inc	7373	839
Sky Blue Industries Inc	2841	42
Sky Blue Satellite Services Inc	5731	39
Sky Capital LLC	7389	925
Sky Climber LLC	3446	48
Sky Computer Services LLC	7379	549
SKY Computers Inc	3672	189
Sky Helicopters Inc	4581	48
Sky Portraits Inc	7335	16
Sky Probes Inc	3812	136
SKY Software	7372	2728
Sky Trekking Alaska Fiskehauk	4725	30
Sky Ute Sand and Gravel LLC	1442	25
Skybar	7389	1885

Company Name	SIC	Rank
SkyBitz Inc	7373	238
Skyblue Sewing Manufacturing Inc	7389	1645
SkyBox Inc	5961	152
Skybox Security Inc	7372	1431
SkyCross Inc	3663	175
SkyDance SkyDiving Inc	7999	153
Skye International Inc	3443	246
Skyhook Wireless Inc	4899	124
Skyhound	7372	4635
Skyjack Corp	5082	168
Skyland Grain LLC	5153	19
Skylands Community Bank	6022	435
Skylark Meats LLC	2013	61
Skylawn Corp	6553	3
Skyler Electric Company Inc	1731	1019
Skyler Technology Inc	7371	586
Skylight Publishing	7372	4993
Skyline Building Maintenance Inc	7349	270
Skyline Center Inc	8331	106
Skyline Chili Inc	5812	319
Skyline Corp	2451	9
Skyline Corp Nomad Div	3792	6
Skyline Exhibits West Inc	7389	2452
Skyline Homes Inc	2451	35
Skyline Multimedia Entertainment Inc	7999	117
Skyline Network Engineering LLC	7373	260
Skyline Office Solutions	7389	980
SkyLine Tools Imaging	7372	2655
Skyline Windows LLC	8711	210
SkyMall Inc	5961	93
SkyMira LLC	4899	144
Skypilot Networks	4899	243
SkyPoint Communications Inc	4899	176
Skyriver Communications Inc	4813	240
Skyscape Inc	7371	225
Sky-Skan Inc	3861	61
SkyTel Communications Inc	4812	7
Skytop Lodges Inc	7011	82
Skyvantage Corp	5045	996
Skyway Luggage Co	3161	11
Skyway Precision Inc	3599	125
Skyway Technology Group Inc	5044	123
Skywest Airlines Inc	4512	21
Skywest Inc	4512	14
Skywire Software	7371	237
Skyy Spirits LLC	2085	11
SL Cable Construction Inc	1623	390
SL Corp	7372	1547
SL Discount Distributor Corp	5049	110
SL Fusco Inc	3545	48
SL Green Realty Corp	6798	25
SL Industries Inc	3679	70
SL Montevideo Technology Inc	3621	50
SL Power Electronics	3679	168
SL Surface Technologies	3471	111
Slabe Machine Products Co	3451	59
Slack and Co	7319	36
Slack Associates	3823	426
Slade Gorton and Company Inc	5146	13
Slade Inc	3053	112
Slade's Ferry Bancorp	6712	427
Slagle Jack L Fire Equipment And Supply Company Inc	7538	14
Slakey Brothers Inc	5074	8
Slane Hosiery Mills Inc	2251	4
Slant/Fin Corp	3433	21
Slash Pine Electric Membership	4911	301
Slate Security Systems Inc	3442	130
Slater Precision Cutting Tool Manufacturing Inc	3599	2038
Slattery Skanska Inc	1629	18
Slaughter Hanson and Associates Inc	7311	853
Slay Industries Inc	4212	4
Slay Transportation Company Inc	4213	178
Slbs LLC	1731	1005
Sleep Disorders Center of Georgia	8099	66
Sleepcare Diagnostics Inc	8082	62
Sleepnet Corp	3845	115
Sletten Construction Co	1542	129
Sletten Construction of Nevada	1541	84
Sletten Inc	1541	42
Slh Manufacturing Inc	5072	143
SLIC Dotcom	4813	405
SLICE Technologies	7372	2623
Slickbar Products Corp	3412	10
Slickedit Inc	7372	1910
Slickfish Studios	7373	1175
Slide Products Inc	2842	119
Slide Works Inc	2759	407
Slidematic Industries Inc	3452	64
Slifer Designs Inc	7389	1205
Slifer Smith and Frampton Real Estate	6531	202
Slim Goodbody Corp	7812	313
Slim Haney Inc	3599	1531
Slim-Fast Foods Co	2032	14
S-Line	2241	4
Sling Media Inc	3699	32
SlingShot Entertainment Inc	7819	96
Slingshot SEO Inc	8742	549
Slingshot Software Inc	7372	1756
Slipmate Co	3479	101
SlipNot Metal Safety Flooring	3069	69
Slivnik Machining Inc	3949	154
SLM Corp	6141	2

Company Name	SIC	Rank
SLM Manufacturing Corp	3089	1683
Slo Cellular Inc	4812	118
SLO Revo Inc	7372	5150
Sloan Advertising Inc	7311	543
Sloan and Company Inc	1751	5
Sloan Implement Company Inc	5083	9
Sloan Industries Inc	3599	1251
Sloan Limited Partners LLC	7379	697
Sloan Utility Contracting Inc	1623	565
Sloan Valve Co	3494	21
Sloane Moving and Storage Company Inc	4213	2530
Slocum Adhesives Corp	2891	68
Slone Partners	7361	358
Slope Electric Cooperative Inc	4911	441
Sloss Industries Corp	3312	45
Slot 1 Recording Studios Inc	7389	1467
Slovacek Foods LLP	5147	87
Slowboy Racing Inc	5599	18
Slp Limited LLC	3672	477
SLPowers	7373	1127
SLR Contracting and Service Company Inc	3433	43
SludgeBuster International Corp	3714	358
Slumber Parties By Cari	5963	33
Sly Inc	3564	66
SM and A	8742	131
SM Energy Co	1311	26
SM Lawrence Co	1731	246
SM Wilson and Co	1542	142
Sma Behavioral Health Services Inc	8093	25
Smaato Inc	4899	76
Small Assemblies Company Inc	3621	117
Small Business Advisory Group Inc	8742	611
Small Business Computers of New England Inc	7371	838
Small Business Technology And Communications Corp	7379	1080
Small Cities Cable Television	4841	133
Small Engine Warehouse Inc	5261	23
Small Newspaper Group	2711	121
Small Parts Inc	3443	26
Small Planet Communications Inc	2731	371
Small Planet Foods Inc	2043	3
Small Precision Tools Inc	3559	65
Small Sand and Gravel Inc	1442	55
Small Wonder Inflatables Inc	5199	116
Small Wonders Preschool Childc	7389	1328
Small World Kids Inc	3944	19
Small World Toys Inc	3944	26
Small World Wireless	5999	228
Smallcomb Wiring Inc	1731	1582
Smalley Manufactring Company Inc	3535	50
Smalley Steel Ring Co	3493	5
Smalley Trucking Company Inc	4213	2886
Smalls Electrical Construction Inc	8999	108
Smallwood Reynolds Stewart Stewart and Associates Inc	8712	118
Smallwood Reynolds Stewart Stewart Interiors Inc	7389	2150
Smallworld Systems Inc	7372	521
Smarketing Business Systems Inc	5044	158
Smarsh Inc	8741	213
Smart and Final Inc	5141	32
Smart Automation Systems Inc	3711	71
Smart Balance Inc	6799	151
Smart Bear Software Inc	7371	477
Smart Bomb	7372	3097
Smart Cable Co	3577	599
Smart Cabling Solutions Inc	4899	178
Smart Carpet	5099	44
Smart City	4813	655
Smart City Holdings LLC	4813	54
Smart Communications Inc	7372	1799
Smart Controls LLC	3822	78
Smart Courier Inc	7389	1034
Smart DB Corp	5045	80
Smart Design Inc	8742	469
Smart Destinations Inc	8999	101
Smart Electronics And Assembly Inc	3699	63
Smart Engineering Tools Inc	7371	1702
Smart Financial Credit Union	6062	66
Smart Funding Corp	4813	142
Smart Industries Corp	3999	155
Smart Machine Technologies Inc	3599	331
Smart Management and Cos	8741	196
SMART Modular Technologies Inc	3572	7
Smart Move Transportation LLC	4213	2108
Smart Office Services LLC	5961	157
Smart Online Inc	7372	4143
Smart Papers LLC	2621	45
Smart Pipe Company Inc	1623	797
Smart Power Systems Inc	3679	501
Smart Pumps Inc	3561	124
Smart Refrigerated Transport	4213	1122
Smart Relay Technology Inc	3625	348
Smart Software Inc	7372	2864
Smart Solutions and Services Inc	7371	1570
Smart Solutions LLC	7372	4332
Smart Source Corp	7372	3743
Smart Web Design Corp	7374	410
Smartanalyst Inc	8732	75
SmartBargains Inc	5961	47
Smartcop Inc	7372	2513

Company Name	SIC	Rank
SmartDrive Systems Inc	7379	77
Smarte Carte Inc	7299	43
Smarter Security Systems Ltd	5063	1010
Smarter Sprinklers Inc	5083	149
Smarter Travel Media LLC	4724	91
Smarterkidscom Inc	7372	1659
SmartForce Ireland Ltd	7371	76
Smarthome Inc	7372	828
Smarthome Solutions Inc	5731	273
Smartit Staffing Inc	7361	244
Smartops Corp	7372	2212
Smartpak Equine LLC	0742	3
Smartphone Experts Inc	5699	12
SmartPrice Sales and Marketing Inc	2099	198
SmartPros Ltd	7389	575
Smartronix Inc	3577	58
Smartset Automation LLC	3823	450
Smartsoft Software Inc	5961	189
SmartSound Software Inc	7372	3676
SmartSource Computer and Audio Visual Rentals	7377	5
SmartSynch Inc	7371	367
Smart-Tek Solutions Inc	2834	336
Smartwatch Security and Sound LLC	1731	1857
Smartworks Inc	1731	1628
SmartZip Analytics Inc	7389	543
SMB and T Financial Services Inc	6022	321
Smb Electrical Contractors Inc	1731	2048
SMC Corp (Bend Oregon)	3716	11
Smc Corporation Of America	3625	16
Smc Data Systems Inc	7379	1314
Smc Electrical Corp	1731	916
Smc Electrical Products Inc	3643	47
SMC Networks Inc	7379	132
Smc Technologies Inc	2899	237
SMC3 Atlanta	7372	2757
Smci Inc	3441	142
Smd Enterprises Inc	5063	665
Smd Software Inc	7371	1557
SMDK Inc	3577	211
Sme Incorporated Of Seattle	1731	255
Sme Industries Inc	1791	5
Smead Manufacturing Co	2679	1
Smeal Fire Apparatus Co	3711	42
Smede-Son Steel And Supply Company Inc	3441	153
Smeltzer Companies Inc	2037	28
SMF Energy Corp	5172	42
SMF Inc	4213	633
Smg Circuits Corp	3672	268
Smg Security Systems Inc	7382	78
SMG Supply Inc	5085	395
SMH Capital Advisors Inc	6282	181
SMI Companies Inc	3441	65
SMI Crankshaft LLC	3714	160
SMI Export Industries Ltd	5065	488
Smi Manufacturing Inc	3533	54
SMI Seller Inc	3714	64
SMI Steel Alabama	3312	36
Smico Manufacturing Company Inc	3569	169
Smile Brands Group Inc	8099	16
SmileCare Dental Group	8021	1
Smiley Brothers Inc	7011	192
Smiley Media Inc	7319	31
Smink Electric Inc	1731	1485
Smith Affiliated Capital Corp	6799	255
Smith and Associates International Inc	5065	24
Smith and Associates Realtors Inc	6531	144
Smith and Bell Insurance Agency	6411	255
Smith and Butterfield Inc	5943	6
Smith and Green Construction Company Inc	1541	269
Smith and Just PS	8721	226
Smith and Keene Electric Service Inc	1731	245
Smith and Kraus Publishers Inc	2732	58
Smith and Loveless Inc	3589	31
Smith and Nephew Inc	3842	326
Smith and Nephew Inc Wound Management Div	3842	51
Smith and Richardson Manufacturing Company Inc	3559	100
Smith and Sons Foods Inc	5141	220
Smith and Vandiver Corp	2844	129
Smith and Waters Inc	4213	1823
Smith and Watson	2512	86
Smith and Wesson Corp	3484	6
Smith and Wesson Holding Corp	3484	5
Smith and Wollensky Restaurant Group Inc	5812	222
Smith Anderson Blount Dorsett Mitchell and Jernigan LLP	8111	278
Smith Auto Parts Inc	5084	242
Smith Bagley Inc	4812	32
Smith Barney Inc	6211	58
Smith Breeden Associates Inc	6282	489
Smith Brodcasting Of Vermont LLC	3663	264
Smith Brooks Bolshoun and Company LLP	8721	151
Smith Brothers Electric Inc	1731	909
Smith Brothers Farms Inc	2026	55
Smith Brothers Of Berne Inc	2514	8
Smith Brothers Tool Co	3543	9
Smith Brothers Trucking Inc	4213	2197
Smith Carney and Company PC	8721	166

Company Name	SIC	Rank
Smith Chevrolet Cadillac Co	5511	1051
Smith Contractors Inc	1623	85
Smith Control Systems Inc	3613	136
Smith Cookie Co	2052	28
Smith Corona Corp	3579	16
Smith County Memorial Hospital LLC	8062	233
Smith Currie and Hancock LLP	8111	260
Smith Dale T And Sons Meat Packing Corp	5147	44
Smith Elliott Kearns and Co	8721	79
Smith Engines Inc	5084	567
Smith Equipment	3548	18
Smith Equipment and Supply Co	3991	17
Smith Filter Corp	1711	219
Smith Flooring Inc	2426	26
Smith Frozen Foods Inc	2037	22
Smith Gambrell and Russell	8111	298
Smith Graham and Company Investment Advisors LP	6282	295
Smith Group Inc	8712	52
Smith Grover Manufacturing Corp	3569	180
Smith Hamilton Shop Inc	7699	141
Smith Hulsey and Busey	8111	398
Smith International Enterprise Ltd	3672	321
Smith International Inc	3533	3
Smith Jackson Boyer and Bovard PLLC	8721	134
Smith Janitorial Service Inc	7349	492
Smith/Junger/Wellman Inc	7311	977
Smith Kaplan Allen and Reynolds Advertising Agency Inc	7311	278
Smith Kramer Inc	2449	16
Smith McDonald Corp	3499	115
Smith Micro Software Inc	7372	650
Smith Moore and Co	6211	350
Smith Motors of Hammond Inc	5511	923
Smith Murphy and Schoepperle LLP	8111	502
Smith Myers U S A Inc	5065	696
Smith Packing Company Inc	5147	60
Smith Pipeline Inc	1623	326
Smith Plumbing Company Inc	5074	98
Smith Power Products Inc	5084	68
Smith Pre-Cast Inc	3272	20
Smith Precision Products Co	3561	173
Smith Print Inc	2752	1121
Smith Provision Company Inc	2013	132
Smith Roberts Baldischwiler LLC	8711	118
Smith RPM Corp	3555	122
Smith Services Inc	5075	64
Smith Southside Feed and Grain Inc	2048	142
Smith Supply Company LLC	5087	85
Smith System Inc (Plano Texas)	2531	37
Smith Television Of Ny Inc	4833	179
Smith Temporary Office Service Inc	7363	262
Smith Temps Inc	7363	193
Smith Transport Inc	4213	221
Smith Truck Service Inc	4213	2454
Smith Trucking Inc	4213	1734
Smith Whiley and Co	6799	160
Smithbates Printing and Design LLC	2752	1493
Smithbilt Industries Inc	3448	35
SmithBucklin Corp	8741	174
SmithCFI	5712	69
Smithco Engineering Inc	3443	117
Smithco West Inc	3524	21
Smith-Emery Co	8742	135
Smithereen Company Del	7342	15
Smithers Viscient North America	8734	35
Smithey Environmental Services LLC	4212	77
Smithfield Companies Ham and Products Company Inc	2035	19
Smithfield Foods Inc	2011	2
Smithfield Manufacturing	3599	2376
Smithfield Packing Company Inc	2013	7
Smithfields Lykes Div	2011	18
Smithgroup Companies Inc	8712	17
SmithLee Productions Inc	2741	250
Smith-Midland Corp	3272	56
Smith's Action Plastic Inc	3088	16
Smith's Construction Inc	1623	850
Smith's Food and Drug Centers Inc	5912	31
Smith's Machine And Grinding Inc	3599	1761
Smith's Machine and Welding Company Inc	1541	289
Smiths South-Central Sales Co	5083	69
Smiths Tubular Systems-Laconia Inc	3463	11
Smith-System Driver Improvement Institute Inc	7549	8
Smithway Inc	3715	62
Smitty Bilt Inc	3714	160
Smk Electronics Corporation USA	5063	269
Smock Materials Handling Company Inc	3535	207
Smoke Detectors Inc	5063	960
Smokestack Records	7389	2427
Smokey Mountain Chew Inc	2131	7
Smokey Point Buick GMC	5511	815
Smoky Mountain Internet Services Inc	7379	1232
Smoky Mountain Machining Inc	3599	495
Smoky Mountain Systems Inc	1731	1761
Smoot Co	3535	70
Smoot Construction	1541	140
Smooth Corp	5961	110
Smooth Technologies LLC	1731	2543

Company Name	SIC	Rank
SMP Inc	4213	1165
Smp Services	5063	923
SMPC Architects PA	8712	278
SMR Research Corp	2721	115
Sms Cleaning Inc	7349	488
Sms Communications Inc	2759	447
SMS Data Products Group Inc	7373	63
Sms Direct Inc	7331	79
Sms Industries Inc	7389	1210
Sms Moderns Hard Chrome LLC	3471	87
Sms Productions Inc	7311	818
Sms Research and Marketing Services Inc	8732	114
SmsmemoryCom	3577	505
Smsonline Net LLC	4813	588
Smt LLC	3089	1142
Smt Machine and Tool Inc	3599	1659
SMTEK International Inc	3672	25
Smucker Natural Foods Inc	2033	55
Smucker Specialty Foods Co	2033	33
Smuckers Quality Beverages of Havre de Grace	2033	48
Smulekoff Furniture Company Inc	5712	71
Smx Services and Consulting Inc	7379	781
Smy Media Inc	7319	167
Smyth and Helwys Publishing Inc	2741	320
Smyth Systems Inc	7372	3197
Smythe European Inc	5511	219
Smythe Masterson and Judd Inc	8111	587
SN Phelps and Co	6211	371
SNACC Distributing Co	8999	117
Snack Factory Inc	2099	304
Snader And Associates Inc	5065	118
Snag Proof Manufacturing Inc	3949	138
Snake River Brewing Co	2082	41
Snake River Electrical	1731	1350
Snak-Time Foods Inc	2099	348
Snap Defense Systems LLC	7382	81
Snap Fitness	7997	11
Snap Print Of Hopkins Inc	7334	82
SnapAV	3651	52
Snapco Manufacturing Corp	2241	28
Snap-On Inc	3423	2
Snapp Tool and Die Inc	3544	488
Snapper Inc	3524	5
Snapple Beverage Group Inc	2086	7
Snappy Air Distribution Products	3444	9
Snappy Snack Vending	2086	91
Snap-Tite Inc	3494	20
Snaptron Inc	3625	161
Snavely Forest Products Inc	5031	32
Snavely King Majoros O'Connor and Lee Inc	6282	622
Snavely's Machine and Manufacturing Company Inc	3599	784
Snbl USA Ltd	8731	113
SNC Manufacturing Company Inc	3612	35
SNC-Lavalin America Inc	8711	46
SNC-Lavalin Constructors Inc	1629	20
Snd Electronics LLC	5065	123
Sne Enterprises Inc	2431	4
Snead Agricultural Supply and Services Inc	5082	134
Sneakers Software Inc	7372	2265
Snee Chemical Co	2841	35
Snell and Wilmer	8111	139
Snelling Co	1711	261
Snell-Northcutt Electric Inc	1731	1511
Snelson Companies Inc	1629	24
Snet Springwich Inc	4812	63
Snethkamp Chrysler Jeep Inc	5511	643
Snider Industries Inc	2421	105
Snider Mold Company Inc	3544	459
Snider Motors Inc	5511	352
Snk America Inc	5084	477
SNL Financial LC	2721	24
Sno Pac Foods Inc	2037	36
Snodgrass and Sons Construction Inc	1791	13
Snohomish Publishing Company Inc	2731	269
Snoke Special Products Company Inc	3585	104
Snoozie Shavings Inc	4213	1813
Snorgrass Auction Co	7389	2050
Snow Brothers Inc	5013	377
Snow Christensen and Martineau	8111	373
Snow Craft Company Inc	3086	125
Snow International Corp (Clearwater Florida)	7371	1925
Snow Lion Publications Inc	2731	337
Snow Time Inc	7011	205
Sno-Way International Inc	5013	236
Snowbound Software Corp	7372	1490
Snowden Electric Company Inc	1731	834
Snowhite Bakery	5461	53
Snowshoe Brewing Co	2082	35
SNS Investment Co	6159	51
SNS Logistics Inc	4731	84
Sns One Inc	7379	728
Snug Seat Inc	3842	261
Snugl Div	3559	311
SNVC	7373	396
SNX Inc	7372	5113
Snyder Capital Management	6722	283
Snyder Chevrolet Oldsmobile Inc	5511	1046
Snyder Cohn Collyer Hamilton and Associates PC	8721	335
Snyder Cos	1521	114
Snyder Electronics	3699	295
Snyder Insurance Agency Inc	6411	244
Snyder Machine Company Inc	3599	2041
Snyder Manufacturing Company Ltd	7359	279
Snyder Manufacturing Corp	2899	245
Snyder Printing And Design	7336	192
Snyder Roofing and Sheet Metal Inc	1761	30
Snyder-Langston Real Estate and Construction Services Inc	1542	304
Snyder's Of Hanover Inc	2052	8
Snyder's-Lance Inc	2052	5
So Cal Air and Electric Inc	1731	2232
So Cal Soft-Pak Inc	7372	3080
So Cal Tractor Sales Company Inc	5082	183
So Cool Events Inc	7389	2172
So Do It LLC	8748	222
SOA Software Inc	2741	125
Soap Transcription Services	7338	26
Soaring Eagle Inc	7373	516
Soave Enterprises LLC	6799	33
Sobe Electronics	5731	187
Sobel Corrugated Containers Inc	2653	54
Sobel Westex Inc	7213	6
Sobot Tool and Manufacturing Co	3599	1729
SoBran Inc	2741	51
Sobul Prime and Schenkel	8721	463
Socco Plastic Coating Co	3479	96
Social Smoke Inc	5993	2
Societe Intertionale De Telecm	7389	1496
Society of Automotive Engineers	2741	30
Socket Holding Corp	4812	68
Socket Mobile Inc	3571	89
Socket Source Inc	5085	384
Socomatic Inc	3089	1364
SoDel Concepts	5812	396
Soderberg Inc	3851	22
Sodexo Inc	8744	1
Sodrel Truck Lines Inc	4213	383
Soehnlen Piping Company Inc	1711	207
Soest and Associates Inc	7389	2184
Soex West USA LLC	5136	16
SofDesign International Inc	7372	4636
Soffa Industries Inc	5065	961
Soffront Software Inc	7372	2350
Soffseal Inc	3069	183
Soflex Corp	7371	1657
Sofradir Ec Inc	3845	104
Soft Computer Consultants Inc	7372	604
Soft Gel Technologies Inc	2834	267
Soft Line Interior Design Inc	7389	1561
Soft Pretzel Franchise Systems Inc	2068	7
Soft Pros Inc	7371	703
Soft Sheen-Carson	2844	40
Soft Solutions Inc	7371	467
Soft Switching Technologies Corp	3621	109
Soft Tech Consulting Inc	8748	254
Soft USE Inc	7372	4555
SoftArtisans Inc	7372	3144
Softbank Capital Partners Inc	6799	116
Softbank Inc	6799	108
Softbase Systems Inc	7372	1985
Softchoice Optimus Solutions Inc	3572	19
Softdocs Inc	5045	597
Softech and Associates Inc	7379	921
Softech Consulting Inc	7379	1349
SofTech Inc	7373	460
Softech Solutions Inc	7379	1553
SofTechnics Inc	7371	412
Softek Business Systems Inc	7372	4637
Softel Systems Inc	5045	1063
Softel USA	5045	857
Softeq Development Ltd	7372	2555
SofterWare Inc	7372	869
SoftLanding Systems Inc	7372	1851
Softlayer Technologies Inc	7373	41
Softlink America Inc	7372	574
SoftLinx Inc	7372	3198
Soft-Lite LLC	3442	21
Softmems LLC	5734	269
SoftNice Inc	7361	355
Softpacific	5734	182
Softplan Systems Inc	7371	1122
SoftPLC Corp	7372	1626
SoftPress Systems Inc	7372	619
SoftPro Corp	7372	2225
Softpro Itechnology Partners	7379	1051
SoftQuest Corp	7372	3744
SOFTRAX Corp	7372	1211
Softronics Inc	7373	492
Softshare Inc	7371	869
Softsoap Enterprises Inc	2841	10
Softsol Resources Inc	7372	2038
Softsort Systems Inc	3625	128
SoftSource LLC	7372	3677
Softstar Systems	7372	5101
Softsystems Inc (Fort Worth Texas)	7372	2865
SoftTech Solutions LLC	7372	4473
Softtek Consultants	7379	1106
Soft-Train Inc	8243	12
Softub Inc	3999	95
SoftVelocity Corp	7372	1319
Softvu LLC	7371	1173
Software 21 Inc	7371	1780
Software Abroad LLC	7372	2914
Software AG Inc	7372	497
Software AG USA Inc	7371	30
Software And Engineering Associates Inc	7371	1669
Software and Management Associates	7372	3553
Software Anywhere Inc	7372	3024
Software Architects Inc	7371	615
Software Art Consulting	7372	4638
Software Arts Inc	7372	4013
Software Bisque Inc	7372	4440
Software Business Systems Inc	7371	839
Software Computer Group Inc	7372	4474
Software Concepts Inc	7372	4014
Software Consulting Associates Inc	7372	3286
Software Consulting Network Inc	7371	1364
Software Consulting Services LLC	7372	2568
Software Co-Op Inc	7372	4639
Software Data Design Inc	7371	817
Software Decisions Inc	7373	495
Software Development Inc	7372	4390
Software Development Inc (Roseville California)	7372	2178
Software Diversified Services Inc	7372	1911
Software Earnings Inc	7372	1420
Software Engineering Associates Inc	7371	1317
Software Engineering of America Inc	7372	284
Software Exchange LLC	7372	2729
Software Experts Inc	7372	3414
Software Expression Inc	5734	426
Software Folks Inc	7361	416
Software FX Inc	7372	1743
Software House	7372	1533
Software House International Inc	7389	21
Software Illustrated Inc	7372	2478
Software In Vision Inc	7371	1101
Software Information Systems LLC	5045	309
Software Integrators Inc	3577	666
Software International Associates Inc	7379	887
Software International Inc	7371	459
Software Interphase Inc	7373	1139
Software Juice Inc	7371	1736
Software Labs Inc	7372	1650
Software Leverage Inc	7379	1415
Software Licensing Consultants Corp	7389	1049
Software Made Easy LLC	7371	1336
Software Magic Inc	7372	4333
Software Management Consultants Inc	7379	124
Software Marketing Associates Inc	7372	3508
Software Methods Inc	7361	316
Software North	7372	2106
Software North LLC	7371	1859
Software On Contact Corp	7372	2746
Software One Inc (Troy Michigan)	7372	3304
Software Options Inc	7372	1651
Software Packaging Inc	7371	1828
Software Paradigms International Inc	7379	66
Software Partners/32 Inc	7372	4441
Software Power Inc	5045	584
Software Productivity Research Inc	7372	2589
Software Productivity Strategists Inc	7379	520
Software Professionals Inc (Irving Texas)	7372	1656
Software Pronto Inc	7371	1737
Software Pursuits Inc	7372	3199
Software Quality Leaders Inc	7371	321
Software Quality Management Services Inc	7379	1059
Software Reproduction Technologies Inc	7373	965
Software Research Inc (San Francisco California)	7372	3630
Software Science Inc (San Rafael California)	7379	771
Software Services Group Inc	5045	435
Software Services of Delaware Inc	7372	3161
Software Shelf International Inc	7372	3228
Software Solutions (Evansville Indiana)	7372	4391
Software Solutions Group Inc	7371	1216
Software Solutions Inc (Lebanon Ohio)	7372	1189
Software Solutions Unlimited Inc	7372	2777
Software Sourcery Systems Inc	7372	3025
Software Spectra Inc	7372	5083
Software Store Products Inc	7372	4756
Software System and Solutions Inc	7371	918
Software Systems and Services International Inc	7371	1337
Software Technologies Group Inc	7372	3466
Software Technology Group Inc	7371	592
Software Technology Inc (Lincoln Nebraska)	7372	2051
Software Technology Inc (Mobile Alabama)	7372	983
Software Testing Services Inc	7379	194
Software Tool and Die Inc	7375	158
Software Unlimited Corp	7372	4015
Software UNO Ltd	7372	2256
Software Video Co	5045	637
Software602 Inc (Jacksonville Florida)	7372	4556
Softworld Inc	7361	119
Sogeti USA LLC	7379	84
SOH Distributors Network Inc	3652	30

Company Name	SIC	Rank
Sohacki Industries Inc	3544	692
Sohn Manufacturing Inc	3842	146
Soho Press Inc	2731	374
SOHO Prospecting Inc	7379	1212
Soho Solutions Inc	7379	1223
Soil Consultants Engineering Inc	8734	30
Soil Stabilization Products Company Inc	5169	135
Soileau Industries Inc	3494	69
Soilmoisture Equipment Corp	3829	267
Sojourner Trucking Inc	4213	1909
Sokkia Corp	5082	77
Sokol And Co	2099	147
Sokudo USA LLC	3674	279
Sol Alman Co	5093	168
Sol Savransky Diamonds Inc	5094	43
Sol Schwartz and Associates PC	8721	132
Sol Telecommunication Services Inc	5065	813
Solae Co	2075	3
Solae LLC	2075	7
Solana Beach Baking Co	2051	75
Solar Communications International Inc	4813	696
Solar Compounds Corp	2891	59
Solar Con Inc	3679	480
Solar Design Associates Inc	8712	273
Solar Electric Systems Inc	1731	635
Solar Group Inc	3469	36
Solar Liberty	5989	6
Solar Light Company Inc	3648	85
Solar Products Inc	3567	74
Solar Sources Inc	1221	29
Solar Technologies Inc	5065	668
Solar Technology Inc	3669	132
Solar Testing Laboratories Inc	8748	189
Solar Thin Films Inc	5082	146
Solar Turbines Inc	3511	2
Solarattic Inc	3433	66
Solarcom Capital	7373	37
SolarFlare Communications Inc	3674	510
Solaria Corp	3433	15
Solaris Paper Inc	5093	53
Solarmer Energy Inc	3674	492
Solaronics Inc	3567	54
Solarsoft Business Systems (Lombard Illinois)	7372	2556
Solarwinds Inc	7372	244
Solazyme Inc	2836	25
Solberg Aggregate Co	5032	175
Solberg Manufacturing Inc	3564	63
Solbrekk Inc	7378	64
Solbright Inc	7372	1219
Solcom Inc	7372	2790
Soldano Custom Amplification	3651	103
Soldermask Inc	3672	352
Sole Supports Inc	3021	10
Solec International Inc	3674	160
Solecon Laboratories Inc	8734	122
Solectek Corp	3661	60
Solekai Systems Corp	8711	546
Soler and Palau - USA	3564	37
Solera Holdings Inc	7372	92
Soleras Ltd	3599	336
Soles Electric Company Inc	7694	12
Solexel Inc	3674	344
Solflower Computer Inc	3571	116
Solgas Power Systems LLC	3621	27
Soliant Health Inc	7363	118
Solid Comfort Inc	5712	88
Solid Concepts Inc	7372	661
Solid Data Systems Inc	3572	66
Solid Earth Inc	7372	3287
Solid It Networks Inc	7379	333
Solid Oak Software Inc	7372	600
Solid Signal LLC	5731	62
Solid Source Realty Inc	6531	289
Solid State Chemical Info	8731	100
Solid State Devices Inc	3674	275
Solid State Equipment Corp	3559	124
Solid State Inc	5065	32
Solid State Testing Inc	3679	603
Solid Technology	7378	179
Solid Waste Technologies Inc	7373	860
Solideal USA Inc	5531	15
Solido Design Automation Inc	3674	213
Solidscape Inc	3542	49
Solid-Scope Machining Company Inc	3429	151
SolidSpace LLC	7373	579
Solidsurface Designs Inc	1751	11
Solidus Inc	5021	55
SolidWorks Corp	7372	1201
Solidyne Corp	3822	80
Soligen Inc	3559	250
Soligen Technologies Inc	3559	269
Soligenix Inc	2834	410
Solis Jr Manuel E	7389	2042
Solitario Exploration and Royalty Corp	1041	12
Solix Inc	7389	599
Solix Systems Inc	7373	147
Sollami Co	3599	1918
Solman Inc	5051	385
Solmet Technologies Inc	3462	60
Solnix	3672	439
Solo Business Group Inc	7378	105
Solo Construction Corp	1623	40
Solo Cup Co	3089	20
Solo Cup Operating Corp	3089	1658
Solo Printing Inc	2752	134
Solo Values	7331	134
Solo W-2 Inc	8721	321
SOLOCO LLC	1381	9
Soloman Friedman Advertising LLC	7311	213
Solomon Colors Inc	2816	5
Solomon Cordwell Buenz and Associates Inc	8712	146
Solomon Cordwell Buenz and Associates Inc	8712	189
Solomon Corp	3612	13
Solomon-Page Group Ltd	7361	58
Solon Industrial Grinding Inc	3599	2377
Solon Manufacturing Co	3823	128
Solon Manufacturing Company Inc	2499	13
So-Low Environmental Equipment Co	3821	40
SOLSOFT Inc	7372	4334
Solstice Technologies	5045	421
Solta Medical Inc	3845	28
Soltec Inc	5084	773
Soltech Inc	7373	968
Solterra Renewable Technologies Inc	3433	59
Solters and Digney Public Relations	8743	110
Solunet Inc	5734	8
Solusia Inc	8711	366
Solutia Inc	2899	10
Solutience Inc	8748	299
Solution Data Systems Inc	7374	420
Solution Dispersions Inc	2895	5
Solution First Inc	3086	79
Solution One	5943	9
Solution Set LLC	7379	437
Solution Systems Inc	7372	1348
Solution Technology Inc	7372	4640
Solutionary Inc	7371	166
Solutionersnet Inc	7371	1614
Solutions 2k LLC	7373	1205
Solutions by Computer Inc	7372	1051
Solutions By Design Inc	7378	167
Solutions For Everything Inc	5064	169
Solutions Group Inc	7389	304
Solutions Group LLC	7373	1044
Solutions Magazine	2721	279
Solutions Manufacturing Inc	3679	340
Solutions Software Corp	7371	1305
Solutions Staffing	7361	88
Solutions Staffing Services Inc	7389	2465
Solutions X Global	7372	5044
Solutions-II Inc	7372	836
SolutionsIQ Inc	7372	1036
Solutionsoft Inc	7372	2888
Solvang Bakery	5461	31
Solvay Advanced Polymers LLC	2821	30
Solvay Chemical Inc	2819	8
Solvay Interox Inc	2819	32
Solvay North America LLC	2821	13
Solvay Pharmaceuticals Inc	8731	84
Solvay Solexis Inc	5169	15
Solvent Systems Inc	5734	450
Solver Inc	5045	463
Solvern Innovations Inc	6531	397
Solvetech Inc	3829	450
Solyndra Inc	3674	284
Soma Magnetics Corp	3612	129
Soma Medical Inc	5047	203
Somarakis Inc	5084	541
Somat Corp	3577	462
Somatex Inc	3531	172
Somax Inc	7378	43
Somaxon Pharmaceuticals Inc	2834	417
Somer Inc	8072	31
Somers Building Maintenance Inc	7349	2
Somerset Buick GMC Truck Inc	5511	939
Somerset Community Services Inc	8361	91
Somerset Cpas PC	7299	23
Somerset Door And Column Co	2431	102
Somerset Hills Bancorp	6022	390
Somerset Plastics Company Inc	3544	713
Somerset Plastics Inc	3089	1544
Somerset Recycling Services Inc	5093	52
Somerset Rural Electric Cooperative Inc	4911	348
Somerset Tire Service Inc	7538	4
Somerset Traveller Inc	2789	85
Somerset Wood Products Co	2431	131
Somerville Cambridge Elder Services Corp	8322	73
Some's Uniforms Inc	5699	19
SomethingdigitalCom LLC	7379	878
Somic America Inc	3714	220
Somma Tool Co	3545	255
Sommer and Maca Industries Inc	5072	56
Sommer Construction Inc	1623	172
Sommer Electric Corp	5063	207
Sommer Products Company Inc	3548	63
Sommer's Inc	5511	882
Sommers Schwartz Law Offices	8111	335
Sonabank NA	6035	150
Sonak Electrical Contractors	1731	1219
Sonant Corp	3669	5
Sonata Software Ltd	7373	47
Sonatech Inc	3699	56
Sonco Electric Company Inc	1731	1476
Sondpex Corporation Of America LLC	3651	209
Sonesta International Hotels Corp	7011	151
Soneticom Inc	7372	2367
Sonetronics Inc	3661	122
Sonex Research Inc	8731	400
Sonexis Inc	3579	35
Sonfarrel Inc	3599	282
Sonford Co	3821	66
Sonford Samplers Inc	3589	259
Sonic Air Systems Inc	3564	98
Sonic And Thermal Technologies Inc	3548	57
Sonic Automotive Inc	5511	5
Sonic Corp	5812	111
Sonic Craft Inc	3651	218
Sonic Films Inc	7812	294
Sonic Financial Corp	6719	129
Sonic Foundry Inc	7372	1075
Sonic Inc	3651	235
Sonic Industries Inc (Oklahoma City Oklahoma)	6794	27
Sonic Manufacturing Technologies Inc	3672	45
Sonic Media Solutions Inc	7374	212
Sonic Restaurants Inc	5812	252
Sonic Software Corp	7372	1145
Sonic Solutions	7373	95
Sonic Studios	5065	1003
Sonic Systems International Inc	7363	206
Sonic Technology Products Inc	3674	494
Sonicbids Corp	8999	139
Sonicor Inc	3699	210
Sonicron Systems Corp	3559	367
Sonics and Materials Inc	3699	89
Sonicwall Inc	7389	146
Sonin Inc	3824	16
Sonitrol Communications Corp	7382	49
Sonitrol Of Hawaii Inc	7382	123
Sonitrol Of Southern Oregon Inc	1731	1539
Sonitrol Of Tallahassee Inc	7382	54
Sonitrol Security Systems Of Hartford Inc	1731	466
Sonix Inc	3674	277
Sonnar Internet Inc	7379	1213
Sonneborn Brothers Inc	4213	2917
Sonnen Enterprises Inc	5511	941
Sonnenschein Nath and Rosenthal LLP	8111	132
Sonnet Industries Inc	5064	143
SONNET Networking LLC	4899	131
Sonnet Software Inc	7372	3162
Sonnet Technologies Inc	3577	199
Sonnet-NewMarkets International Inc	7389	446
Sonneys Photography	7335	29
Sonnhalter Inc	7311	516
Sonny Hancock Chevrolet Olds Cadillac Inc	5511	458
Sonny Peterson Trucking Inc	4213	2433
Sonny's Home Center Inc	5074	118
Sonobond Ultrasonics Inc	3699	241
Sonoco Crellin Inc	3089	386
Sonoco Products Baker Div	3499	98
Sonoco Products Co	2631	3
Sonoco Products Co Industrial Products Div	2655	13
Sonolite Plastics Corp	3089	1801
Sonoma County Fairgrounds-Santa Rosa	7389	1620
Sonoma County Indian Health Project Inc	8011	104
Sonoma Index Tribune Corp	2711	670
Sonoma Overhead Doors	5211	200
Sonoma Precision Manufacturing Co	3599	1223
Sonoma Scientific Inc	3679	615
Sonoma Software Solutions Inc	7371	1676
Sonoma Valley Bancorp	6712	538
Sonoma Valley Bank	6022	401
Sonomed Inc	3845	82
Sonoscan Inc	3829	135
SonoSite Inc	3845	13
Sono-Tek Corp	3699	123
Sono-Tek Inc	3589	200
Sonotronics Inc	3699	284
Sonrise Metal	3441	275
Sons Acura	5511	196
Son's Supermarket Inc	5411	267
Sonstegard Foods Co	5144	5
Sonsub Inc	4499	4
Sonus Networks Inc	7373	49
Sony Broadcast and Business Solutions Co	3845	93
Sony Computer Entertainment America Inc	3944	5
Sony Disc Manufacturing	3652	8
Sony Electronics Inc	3651	1
Sony Electronics/Info Technology	3571	11
Sony Ericsson Mobile Communications (USA) Inc	3663	17
Sony Music Entertainment Inc	3652	1
Sony Pictures Entertainment Inc	7812	5
Sony Pictures Imageworks	7379	1646
Sony Precision Technology America Inc	5049	4
Sony USA Inc	3651	3
Soo Tractor Sweeprake Co	3523	70
Soogatech Corp	7379	1592
Sooner Pipe LLC	5084	170

Company Name	SIC	Rank
Sooner Scale Inc	3596	29
Sooner Technology Applications Inc	7379	1452
Sooner Trailer Manufacturing Co	3715	21
Sooner Trailer Manufacturing Co	3799	6
Sooner Trucking and Oilfield Services	4213	1549
Sopark Corp	3672	64
Sophie's Choice Inc	5411	288
Sophisticated Data Research Inc	7374	342
Sophisticated Systems Inc	7379	270
Sophos Inc	7372	3068
Sophos Software Ltd	7372	4955
Soph-Ware Associates Inc	7371	1586
Soporcel North America Inc	5113	5
Sopp Chevrolet	5511	581
Sorb Technology Inc	3841	347
SorcityCom Inc	7389	1716
Sordoni Construction Services Inc	1542	395
Sorensen Electric Inc	1731	736
Sorensen Transportation Company Inc	4213	2574
Sorenson Engineering Inc	3451	21
Sorenson Media Inc	7371	49
Sorenson Transportation Co	4213	1111
Sorin Group	3842	53
Sormani Calendars	5961	194
Soroc Products Inc	3089	1275
Sorrento Capital Inc	6722	260
Sortiumusa	5046	234
Sort-Rite International Inc	3556	126
Sorvive Technologies Inc	4899	184
SOS Associates Inc	5064	47
SOS Computers LLC	5045	527
SOS Electric Inc	1731	636
Sos Engineering Inc	3469	368
SOS Food Lab Inc	2099	352
SOS Gases Inc	5169	117
SOS Inc	3663	271
Sos Manufacturing Inc	3679	602
Sos Printing Inc	2752	958
Sos Products Company Inc	2899	170
SOS Security Inc	7381	23
SOS Staffing Services Inc	7363	49
Sos Systems Inc	7382	76
SOS Video Communications Inc	7812	210
Soski S Piroeff Inc	5963	29
Sosmetal Products Inc	5013	111
Sossner Sales Corp	3469	358
Sotcher Measurement Inc	3825	121
Sotek Inc	3599	576
Sotera Defense Solutions Inc	8711	73
Sotera Engineered Solutions Inc	3661	52
Soterra LLC	2411	12
Sotheby's	7389	50
Sotheby's Financial Services Inc	6163	27
Sotis Business Equipment Ltd	7629	34
Soudan Metals Company Inc	5051	272
Souders Industries Inc	3714	334
Soul Co	5199	63
Soult Wholesale Co	5031	116
Sound and Communication Inc	1731	2096
Sound and Signal Inc	4841	156
Sound and Signal Systems Of New Mexico Inc	1731	764
Sound and Vision Of Orland Park Inc	5731	152
Sound Banking Co	6022	799
Sound Chamber Mastering	3695	90
Sound Chek Music	7359	40
Sound City Entertainment Group Inc	7389	1808
Sound Com Corp	5064	42
Sound Community Bank	6035	108
Sound Components Inc	5731	51
Sound Connections International Inc	3679	848
Sound Control Technologies Inc	3661	233
Sound Delivery Service	4213	2046
Sound Designs Inc	5731	209
Sound Enhancement Products Inc	3651	133
Sound Financial Inc	6035	150
Sound Ford Inc	5511	1146
Sound Ideas Inc	5731	172
Sound Ideas of America Inc	7372	4757
Sound Image Audio and Video Design Group Ltd	5731	244
Sound Inc	5065	214
Sound Manufacturing Inc	3089	1279
Sound Masters Inc	1731	2525
Sound Minds LLC	5731	260
Sound Ocean Systems Inc	3812	170
Sound of Market Street	5735	11
Sound Propeller Services Inc	3366	12
Sound Publishing Inc	2711	206
Sound Refining Inc	2911	60
Sound Room Ii Inc	5731	79
Sound Security Inc	1731	2069
Sound Shop Inc	5731	154
Sound Shore Medical Center Of Westchester	8062	133
Sound Surgical Technologies LL	5047	227
Sound Surgical Technologies LLC	3841	390
Sound Technology Corp	3825	237
Sound Transportation Inc	4213	1138
Sound/Video Impressions Inc	7389	2286
Sound Visions Corp	8748	432
Sound Waves Audio Video Interiors Inc	5731	210
SoundBite Communications Inc	7389	399
Soundcoat Company Inc	3086	57

Company Name	SIC	Rank
Soundcraft Inc	3699	144
Sound-Craft Systems Inc	2517	3
Soundelux Entertainment Group	7819	12
SoundImage NY	7389	1056
Soundquest Inc	5731	173
Sounds True Inc	7812	191
Soundscapes Inc	7922	73
Soundtrek	7372	4047
Soundtube Entertainment Inc	3651	129
Soundview Technologies Inc	3663	82
Soundwerks	5731	258
Source Abroad Inc	8999	184
Source Code Corp	5045	358
Source Communications Inc	7311	530
Source Communications LLP	3577	455
Source D/M Inc	7331	164
Source Dynamics Inc	7372	3026
Source Enterprises Inc	2721	226
Source Fluid Power Inc	3599	841
Source III Inc	7372	3950
Source Inc	5999	60
Source Interlink Companies Inc	7331	1
Source Medical Solutions Inc	7373	373
Source of Future Technology Inc	7371	791
Source Office Products	5045	328
Source One Computer Products Inc	5045	450
Source One Distributors Inc	5063	746
Source One Solutions Inc	7373	1017
Source One Spares Inc	5088	117
Source One Staffing LLC	7363	45
Source One Technologies Inc	3679	279
Source Photonics	3357	18
Source Research Inc	5065	577
Source Systems Inc	7389	2351
Source Technologies Inc	5045	392
Source Technologies LLC	4953	170
Sourcebooks Inc	2731	112
Sourcecode Inc	7373	599
SOURCECORP BPS Inc	7389	81
SOURCECORP HealthSERVE Radiology Inc	7389	443
SOURCECORP Inc	7389	100
Sourcefire Inc	7372	287
SourceGear LLC	7372	1920
Sourcelink Carolina LLC	7331	67
SourceMedia Inc	2731	387
Sourcentra Inc	8999	182
Sourceone Graphics Inc	2759	469
Sourcetech Medical LLC	5047	182
Sourcewave Inc	7361	170
Sourdough Mining Company An Alaska Restaurant Inc	5812	423
Souriau USA Inc	3643	33
Souris River Television Coop	4841	63
Sousa Electric Corp	1731	2097
South Alabama Electric Cooperative Inc	4911	403
South Arkansas Business Solutions Inc	5044	124
South Atlantic Controls Inc	3629	96
South Atlantic Forest Products Inc	5031	159
South Atlantic Services Inc	7389	1294
South Banking Co	6712	608
South Bay Alcoholism Services	7363	285
South Bay Cable	3315	5
South Bay Custom Plastic Extruders	3089	1684
South Bay Solutions Inc	3599	446
South Bend Form Tool Company Inc	3544	717
South Bend Modern Molding In	3069	153
South Bend Motor Freight	4213	378
South Boston News Inc	2711	910
South Camden Iron Works Inc	5039	48
South Carolina Bank and Trust NA	6021	149
South Carolina Black Media Group	2711	883
South Carolina Community Bank	6022	634
South Carolina Electric and Gas Co	4931	16
South Carolina Federal Credit Union	6061	13
South Carolina Logos Inc	3993	167
South Carolina Research Authority Inc	8733	1
South Carolina Tel-Con Inc	1623	173
South Central Arkansas Electric Cooperative Inc	4911	393
South Central Company Inc	5063	202
South Central Electric Association	4911	580
South Central Maintenance	7349	304
South Central Power Co	4911	163
South Central Power Co Belmont Div	4911	559
South Central Printing Inc	2752	1708
South Central Rural Telephone Cooperative Corporation Inc	4813	168
South Coast Circuits Inc	3672	159
South Coast Controls Corp	5084	884
South Coast Head Start	8351	37
South Coast Lumber Co	2436	10
South Coast Recycling Inc	5093	33
South Coast Technology Inc	3679	771
South Corporation Packaging USA	3089	67
South County Newspaper Inc	2711	567
South Cypress Floors	5713	22
South Dade Lighting Inc	5063	181
South Dakota Achieve	6513	35
South Dakota Soybean Processors LLC	2075	6
South Dakota State University	8221	20

Company Name	SIC	Rank
South Dakota Wheat Growers Association	2873	7
South Denver Endoscopy Center	8011	81
South East Carriers Inc	4213	1356
South East Industrial Sales And Service Inc	7359	96
South East Personnel Leasing Inc	7363	179
South End	2711	759
South Everson Lumber Company Inc	2421	81
South Florida Bakery Inc	2051	97
South Florida Goline Inc	4813	727
South Florida New Holland Equipment Corp	5083	191
South Fork Industries Inc	2257	11
South Georgia Pecan Company Inc	2096	14
South Haven Coil Inc	3677	9
South Holland Metal Finishing Company Inc	3471	93
South Jersey Energy	1311	57
South Jersey Gas Co	4924	28
South Jersey Industries Inc	4924	16
South Jersey Medical Equipment Ltd	5047	213
South Jersey Metal Inc	2514	21
South Kohala Management Corp	6531	463
South Louisiana Electric Cooperative Association	4911	380
South Mississippi Electric Power Association	4911	158
South Mississippi Home Health Inc	8082	83
South Mountain Moulding Inc	5023	188
South Park East	8059	7
South Peninsula Sales Inc	5962	19
South Pier Fish Company Inc	5146	50
South Pointe Center Inc	7389	1691
South St Paul Steel Supply Company Inc	5051	439
South Sales Liquidations Inc	5731	36
South Seas Aquatics	7999	158
South Shore Distributing LC	5091	82
South Shore Elder Services Inc	8322	76
South Shore Harbour Development Ltd	6552	224
South Shore Hospital	8062	60
South Shore Packing	5084	881
South Shore Tool and Die Inc	3545	139
South Shore Transportation Company Inc	4213	281
South Side Electric Inc	1731	630
South Side Machine Works Inc	3599	263
South Sound Broadcasting LLC	4832	274
South State Inc	2951	34
South Street Financial Corp	6712	563
South Tacoma Honda	5511	604
South Tech Plastics Inc	3083	38
South Tennessee Oil Company Inc	5541	20
South Tex Beauty Distributors Inc	5087	120
South Texas Lighthouse For The Blind	8331	181
South Texas Oil Co	1382	58
South Valley Internet Inc	4899	78
South Valley National Bank	6021	369
South West Sonitrol Inc	7382	126
Southampton Tile and Stone LLC	5032	173
Southanchor Manufacturing LLC	3545	362
Southard Implement Co	5083	76
Southbend	3556	89
Southbend Sporting Goods Inc	3949	96
Southboro Medical Group Inc	8069	19
Southbridge Tool and Manufacturing Inc	3544	465
Southbrook Corp	6211	298
Southco Inc	3429	158
Southco Industries Inc	3713	37
Southcoast Cabinet Inc	2434	74
Southcoast Financial Corp	6712	461
Southcoast Health System	8062	30
Southconn Technologies Inc	3625	195
Southeast Alaska Smoked Salmon Company Inc	5146	22
Southeast Assemblies Inc	5065	660
Southeast Broach Company LLC	3545	153
Southeast Colorado Power Association	4911	398
Southeast Community Work Center Inc	8331	62
Southeast Cooler Corp	3585	224
Southeast Cooperative Service Co	5191	118
Southeast Dairy Processors Inc	2026	66
Southeast Electric Of Central Florida Inc	1731	242
Southeast Enterprises Inc	8331	218
Southeast Enterprises Package	8331	34
Southeast Frozen Food Co	5142	7
Southeast Fuels Inc	5052	17
Southeast Gravel Company Inc	1442	65
Southeast Industrial Components LLC	5084	644
Southeast Industries Inc	3822	41
Southeast Power Corp	1731	491
Southeast Publications USa Inc	2741	203
Southeast Shopping Centers Corp	6552	225
Southeast Steel Sales Co	5722	13
Southeast Texas Industries Inc	3312	50
Southeast Toyota Distributors LLC	5012	4
Southeast Toyota Port Processing	5012	60
Southeast Worldwide Manufacturers	5013	183
Southeastern Asset Management Inc	6282	465
Southeastern Automotive Warehouse Inc	5013	127

Company Name	SIC	Rank
Southeastern Bank	6022	315
Southeastern Bank Financial Corp	6712	224
Southeastern Banking Corp	6712	498
Southeastern Bolt And Screw Inc	3965	19
Southeastern Bottling Company Of Arizona Inc	2086	86
Southeastern Cellular Inc	5999	216
Southeastern Chemical and Solvent Co	4953	103
Southeastern Computer Consultants Inc	7379	297
Southeastern Container Inc	3085	6
Southeastern Converting Inc	2296	2
Southeastern Dock and Door Inc	5031	287
Southeastern Electric Cooperative Inc	4911	320
Southeastern Electrical Contractors Inc	1731	2041
Southeastern Electronic Assembly Services Inc	3679	534
Southeastern Engineering Inc	3663	233
Southeastern Equipment Company Inc (Cambridge Ohio)	5082	51
Southeastern Fiberglass Products Inc	2519	9
Southeastern Forge Inc	3462	71
Southeastern Freight Lines	4213	54
Southeastern Indiana Rural Electric Membership Corp	4911	455
Southeastern Industrial Inc	3599	689
Southeastern Installation Inc	3559	282
Southeastern Kentucky Rehabilitation Industries Inc	8331	19
Southeastern Liquid Analyzers	3823	341
Southeastern Machine and Tool Inc	3444	303
Southeastern Machine and Welding Company Inc	3443	195
Southeastern Machining and Field Service Inc	3599	1313
Southeastern Materials Inc	2439	30
Southeastern Microwave Inc	5046	274
Southeastern Mills Inc	2099	87
Southeastern Ocularists Inc	3851	117
Southeastern Ohio Regional Medical Center	8062	202
Southeastern Orthotics Prosthetics Inc	3842	286
Southeastern Printing Company Inc	2752	102
Southeastern Process Equipment and Controls Inc	3823	308
Southeastern Products Inc	1799	69
Southeastern Rubber Company Inc	3061	44
Southeastern Sash and Door Inc	5211	316
Southeastern Sea Products Inc	2092	93
Southeastern Shirt Corp	2326	24
Southeastern Steel Co	3441	154
Southeastern Technology Group Inc	7379	904
Southeastern Technology Inc	3842	156
Southeastern Tool And Die Inc	3544	218
Southeastern Tool Company Inc	3544	516
Southeastern Trailer and Container Repairs Inc	7539	3
Southeastern Transfer and Storage Co	4213	2668
Southeastern Utilities Contractors Inc	1623	718
Southern Accounting Systems Inc	5943	41
Southern Adjustment Services Inc	7381	114
Southern Advantage Company Inc	5065	777
Southern Ag Carriers Inc	4213	216
Southern Agricultural Insecticides Inc	5191	54
Southern Air Inc	1711	54
Southern Alloy Corp	3325	37
Southern Amusement Co	7993	22
Southern Anesthesia and Surgical Inc	5047	136
Southern Arizona Community Bank	6022	673
Southern Arizona Graphic Associates Inc	2752	605
Southern Atlantic Label Company Inc	2752	261
Southern Audio Services Inc	3651	84
Southern Audio Visual Inc	7359	70
Southern Automotive Inc	3714	380
Southern Automotive Wholesalers Inc	3621	126
Southern Avionics and Communications Inc	5088	107
Southern Avionics Co	3812	144
Southern Bancorp	6021	233
Southern Bancorp	6022	561
Southern Bancshares Inc	6712	277
Southern Bancshares NC Inc	6712	252
Southern Bank	6022	823
Southern Bank Co	6035	231
Southern Beverage Company Inc	5149	27
Southern Beverage Packers Inc	2086	137
Southern Bindery Inc	2789	66
Southern Cal Microwave	3663	174
Southern Cal Transport Co	4213	2030
Southern California Association Of Governments	8748	180
Southern California Aviation Inc	5088	23
Southern California Braiding Company Inc	3679	388
Southern California Car Transfer Inc	4789	23
Southern California Carbide	3541	230
Southern California Edison Co	4911	15
Southern California Gas Co	4923	8
Southern California Grading Inc	6141	63
Southern California Graphics Inc	2752	242
Southern California Hydraulic Engineering Corp	5084	608
Southern California Illumination	5063	361

Company Name	SIC	Rank
Southern California Soil And Testing Inc	8711	333
Southern California Sound Image Inc	3629	85
Southern California Technical Arts Inc	3599	1322
Southern Carbide Specialists Inc	3545	310
Southern Cleaning Service Inc	7349	70
Southern Coating and Name Plates Inc	3083	47
Southern Colortype Company Inc	2752	920
Southern Commercial Bank	6022	311
Southern Communication Corp	4832	116
Southern Community Bancshares Inc	6712	708
Southern Community Bank and Trust (Pilot Mountain North Carolina)	6022	187
Southern Community Financial Corp	6712	222
Southern Co	4911	3
Southern Company Enterprise Inc	2752	1232
Southern Connecticut Gas Co	4924	46
Southern Connecticut Newspapers Inc	2711	43
Southern Converting Machinery Erectors Inc	1796	26
Southern Coos Hospital and Health Center	8062	239
Southern Copper Corporation USA	1021	2
Southern Corrections Systems	8744	19
Southern Crafts Inc	5094	45
Southern Cross Corp	3829	39
Southern Cross Systems LLC	5112	64
Southern Dallas Development Corp	6159	95
Southern Data Solutions	8742	686
Southern Datacom Inc	4813	499
Southern Design	7379	424
Southern Design Services Inc	7389	685
Southern Diversified Technologies Inc	1623	116
Southern Eagle Distributing LLC	2082	37
Southern Electric and Machine Company Inc	7694	30
Southern Electric Generating Co	4911	211
Southern Electric Service Company Inc	3625	124
Southern Electrical Equipment Company Inc	3613	59
Southern Electrical Services Inc	1731	2329
Southern Electricom Co	1731	1096
Southern Electronics Distributors Inc	5045	31
Southern Elevator Company Inc	7699	42
Southern Elevator Group Inc	7699	17
Southern Energy Homes Inc	2451	6
Southern Engineering and Automation Inc	3549	89
Southern Enterprises Of Southeast Louisiana Inc	3449	25
Southern Entertainment USA Inc	5813	4
Southern Environmental Inc	3822	8
Southern Equipment Manufacturing Inc	3523	267
Southern Erectors Inc	1791	9
Southern Exhibits Inc	5046	283
Southern Exposure Inc	7812	243
Southern Fabricators Inc	3444	172
Southern Fabricators Inc (Memphis Tennessee)	3441	29
Southern Film Extruders Inc	3081	59
Southern Finished Inc	2759	323
Southern Finishing Company Inc	2499	16
Southern Flair Builders Inc	1521	143
Southern Flavoring Company Inc	2087	79
Southern Flow Companies Inc	3826	61
Southern Folder and Index Company Incorporated Del	2675	21
Southern Food Concepts Inc	5141	186
Southern Foods Group LP	2026	2
Southern Forest Products LLC	2421	89
Southern Freight Inc	4213	186
Southern Furniture Company Of Conover Inc	2512	88
Southern Glove Manufacturing Company Inc	2381	3
Southern Graphic Systems Inc	2752	364
Southern Graphics and Systems Inc	5112	94
Southern Green Inc	3524	36
Southern Grouts and Mortars Inc	2891	49
Southern Hardware Company Inc	5072	90
Southern Health Services Inc	6411	155
Southern Healthcare Agency Inc	7363	138
Southern Heat Exchanger Corp	3443	9
Southern Hens Inc	2015	27
Southern Historical News Inc	2711	806
Southern Holdings Inc	5093	31
Southern Homes and Remodelling Inc	1521	86
Southern Hydraulic Cylinder Inc	3593	39
Southern Illinois Electric Coop	4911	530
Southern Illinois Machinery Company Inc	3555	31
Southern Illinois Power Cooperative Inc	4911	198
Southern Imperial Inc	3452	43
Southern Indiana Properties Inc	2865	23
Southern Indiana REC Inc	4911	488
Southern Indiana Resource Solutions Inc	8331	114
Southern Industrial Constructors Inc	7363	243
Southern Installations Inc	1731	1265
Southern Intermodal Xpress Inc	4213	401
Southern Ionics Inc	2819	57
Southern Iowa Electric Cooperative Inc	4911	428
Southern Iowa Resources For Families Inc	8361	182

Company Name	SIC	Rank
Southern Iron Works Inc	3441	126
Southern L and R Maintenance Inc	3582	20
Southern Lakes Newspapers LLC	2711	431
Southern Light LLC	4812	51
Southern Link Of Georgia Inc	5199	104
Southern Lithoplate Inc	2796	2
Southern LNG Inc	5172	139
Southern LP Gas Inc	5984	17
Southern Lumber Company Inc	2421	41
Southern Machine and Fabrication Company Inc	3599	887
Southern Manufacturing Company LLC	3089	1726
Southern Manufacturing Technologies Inc	3599	289
Southern Maryland Oil	5172	4
Southern Mechanical Systems Co	1711	242
Southern Media Systems Inc	1731	2491
Southern Metal Processing Company Inc	7699	62
Southern Metals Co	3356	31
Southern Metals Company Inc	3354	38
Southern Michigan Bancorp Inc	6712	472
Southern Michigan Bank and Trust	6022	190
Southern Microwave Inc	3679	682
Southern Mills Inc	2221	17
Southern Minnesota Beet Sugar Coop	2063	2
Southern Missouri Bancorp Inc	6712	395
Southern Missouri Bank and Trust Co	6035	249
Southern Missouri Containers Inc	2671	14
Southern Mold Builders	3069	157
Southern Motion Inc	2512	30
Southern Music Company Inc	5736	14
Southern National Bancorp of Virginia Inc	6712	433
Southern National Life Insurance Co	6311	190
Southern New England Telecommunications Corp	4813	13
Southern Ohio Manufacturing Inc	3599	2156
Southern Packaging Inc	2448	32
Southern Packaging Machinery Corp	3565	124
Southern Packing Corp	2011	129
Southern Perfection Fabrication Holdings Inc	6719	172
Southern Petroleum Laboratory Inc	8734	22
Southern Pine Electric Cooperative Inc	4911	303
Southern Plastics and Rubber Co	3061	62
Southern Plastics Company Inc	3949	135
Southern Poverty Law Center Inc	8111	344
Southern Pride Catfish LLC	2092	99
Southern Printing Company Inc	2752	1585
Southern Products Company Inc	3295	21
Southern Progress Corp	2721	27
Southern Provision Company Inc	5147	129
Southern Pump and Tank Co	5013	51
Southern Quality Meats Inc	2011	73
Southern Refrigerated Transport	4213	356
Southern Refrigeration Corp	5078	7
Southern Reprographics Inc	2752	1061
Southern Research Company Inc	7381	263
Southern Resin Inc	2891	86
Southern Retail Systems LLC	5999	204
Southern RI Newspapers	2711	138
Southern Rivers Energy	4911	271
Southern Rubber Company Inc	3053	84
Southern Sales and Marketing Group Inc	5021	4
Southern Sales Inc	5013	348
Southern Sand And Stone Inc	3281	33
Southern Screen Products Ltd	2431	107
Southern Security And Investigation Inc	7381	128
Southern Security Life Insurance Co	6311	243
Southern Siskiyou Newspapers Inc	2711	863
Southern Soil Environmental Inc	8734	93
Southern Soldier Mercantile Inc	2389	34
Southern Source Inc	3312	86
Southern Sports Network Inc	4832	132
Southern Stainless Equipment	3585	217
Southern Stainless Equipment Company Inc	7699	83
Southern Staircase Inc	2431	22
Southern States Buick Dodge Mazda	5511	207
Southern States Cooperative Inc	5191	5
Southern States Holdings Inc	5191	26
Southern States Hopkinsville Coop	2048	86
Southern States Imports Inc	5511	982
Southern States Packaging Co	2679	10
Southern Steel and Wire Company Inc	3496	27
Southern Sun Electric Corp	1731	1593
Southern Supply Inc	5031	435
Southern Sweets	5046	362
Southern Systems Inc	3535	52
Southern Tank and Manufacturing Company Inc	3443	202
Southern Tea LLC	2099	97
Southern Technology and Services Inc	3533	58
Southern Technology Group	7372	4048
Southern Telecheck Inc	6099	24
Southern Telephone Corp	5065	711
Southern Tennessee Medical Center LLC	8062	219
Southern Tier Express Inc	4213	883
Southern Tier Hide and Tallow Inc	5159	30
Southern Tier Plastics Inc	3089	819
Southern Tire Mart	5014	71

Company Name	SIC	Rank
Southern Tire Sales Of Jackson LLC	5014	37
Southern Tool and Machine Co	3679	155
Southern Tool Steel Inc	5051	262
Southern Truck and Equipment Inc	5085	408
Southern Trust Securities Holding Corp	6282	575
Southern Tubular Products Inc	5051	430
Southern Union Co	4924	2
Southern Vinyle Window Manufacturing Inc	3089	1427
Southern Water Consultants Inc	2819	108
Southern Weaving Co	2241	12
Southern Wine and Spirits of America Inc	5182	1
Southern Yarn Dyers Inc	2281	24
Southfield Machining Services Inc	3599	1947
SouthFirst Bancshares Inc	6712	676
Southfirst Bank	6035	213
Southgate At Shrewsbury Inc	8322	165
Southgate Automotive Group Inc	5511	364
Southgate Group Inc	2752	496
Southgate Process Equipment Inc	5049	226
SouthGroup Insurance and Financial Services	6411	173
Southland Bank	6022	720
South-Land Carbon Products Inc	3624	31
Southland CNC Inc	3599	1683
Southland Container Corp	2653	6
Southland Electric Company Inc	1731	867
Southland Electric Inc	1731	188
Southland Electrical Supply Inc	5063	262
Southland Equipment Service Inc	5084	826
Southland Erectors And Riggers Inc	1791	25
Southland Plumbing Supply Inc	5074	134
Southland Precision Inc	3444	299
Southland Printing Inc	2752	1096
Southland Racing Corp	7948	16
Southland Technologies Inc	3577	366
Southland Transportation	4213	1047
Southland Tube Inc	3317	19
Southpaw Enterprises Inc	3842	225
SouthPeak Interactive Corp	7372	809
Southport Electrical Service Inc	1731	2064
Southport Industries Inc	3643	164
Southprint	2752	1551
Southside Bancshares Inc	6712	151
Southside Bank	6022	640
Southside Financial Group LLC	6163	26
South-Side Machine Shop Inc	3599	1501
Southside Mall LLC	6531	385
Southside Recycling Inc	5093	115
Southtowne Machining Inc	3599	2189
Southwall Technologies Inc	3081	26
SouthWare Innovations Inc	7372	3163
Southwest Ag Inc	5999	85
Southwest Alarm Systems	1731	2198
Southwest Ambulance of Casa Grande Inc	4119	5
Southwest Bancorp Inc (Stillwater Oklahoma)	6712	158
Southwest Bio-Labs Inc	7389	1575
Southwest Brake and Parts Inc	5013	48
Southwest Business Machines Inc	5734	133
Southwest Canners Inc	2086	71
Southwest Community Services Inc	8331	149
Southwest Contracting Inc	1623	350
Southwest Corporate Federal Credit Union	6061	4
Southwest Cyberport Inc	4813	580
Southwest Daily Times	2741	428
Southwest Diversified Inc	6552	248
Southwest Electric Coop	4911	197
Southwest Electronic Energy Corp	5063	217
Southwest Energy Distributors Inc	5541	61
Southwest Express Inc	4213	2567
Southwest Fab Inc	7363	348
Southwest Fastener LLC	5085	292
Southwest Ford Lincoln-Mercury Inc	5511	961
Southwest Freight Inc	4213	1115
Southwest Freightlines	4213	606
Southwest Funding LP	6162	128
Southwest Galvanizing Inc	3479	54
Southwest Gas Corp	4924	7
Southwest Gem and Minerals	7389	1345
Southwest Georgia Bank	6022	519
Southwest Georgia Financial Corp	6712	570
Southwest Glassware Co	5023	203
Southwest Grain Div	5153	35
Southwest Human Development Inc	8322	32
Southwest Image and Graphics Inc	8711	645
Southwest Impreglon R Inc	3479	99
Southwest Industrial Motors Inc	7699	189
Southwest Industrial Rigging	4213	1526
Southwest Industrial Services Inc	3599	1680
Southwest Inspection And Testing	7389	1107
Southwest International Trucks Inc	5012	30
Southwest Int'l Freight Services	4213	1007
Southwest Louisiana Electric Membership Corp	4911	120
Southwest Machine and Plastic Company Inc	3728	179
Southwest Materials Handling Company Inc	5084	583
Southwest Microwave Inc	3663	94
Southwest Modern Data Systems	5045	823
Southwest Mold Inc	3544	422
Southwest Newspapers	2711	321
Southwest Office Systems Inc	5044	53
Southwest Offset Printing Co	2752	23
Southwest Plastic Binding Co	2789	31
Southwest Precision Printers Inc	2752	268
Southwest Productions Inc	7812	314
Southwest Publisher LLC	2711	742
Southwest Quality Molding Corp	3089	1650
Southwest Research Institute	7371	26
Southwest Rural Electric Association Inc	4911	485
Southwest Securities Group Inc	6211	121
Southwest Sign Group Inc	3993	92
Southwest Signal Supply Inc	3669	233
Southwest Stars Corp	7379	195
Southwest Steel Casting Co	3312	80
Southwest Stone Supply Inc	5099	138
Southwest Surveillance Systems Inc	1731	549
Southwest Technologies Inc	3842	220
Southwest Telecom Services Inc	1731	489
Southwest Telephone and Computer Inc	5065	112
Southwest Tel-Supply LLC	5065	241
Southwest Tennessee Electric Membership Corp	4911	299
Southwest Texas Electrical Cooperative Company Inc	4911	375
Southwest Trails Inc	4213	1605
Southwest Truck Service Inc	4213	3020
Southwest United Industries Inc	3471	8
Southwest Water Co	4941	14
Southwest Window And Door Inc	5031	223
Southwest Windpower Inc	3621	54
Southwest Wire Rope Inc	3496	42
Southwestern Building Maintenance	7349	493
Southwestern Computer Technologies	7378	96
Southwestern Electric Supply Company Inc	5063	390
Southwestern Electrical Company Inc	1731	438
Southwestern Energy Co	4923	5
Southwestern Energy Production Co	1311	15
Southwestern/Great American Inc	2731	27
Southwestern Industries Inc	3541	41
Southwestern Interior Contracting Company Inc	5021	90
Southwestern Minnesota Radio Inc	4832	147
Southwestern Motor Transport	4213	229
Southwestern Pennsylvania Area Agency On Aging Inc	8322	58
Southwestern Petroleum Corp	2952	16
Southwestern Precision Company Inc	3599	1700
Southwestern Public Service Co	4911	88
Southwestern Scale Company Inc	5046	139
Southwestern Stationery And Bank Supply Inc	2752	369
Southwestern Stringed Instruments Inc	5099	113
Southwestern Suppliers Inc	5082	87
Southwestern Telecom Inc	5065	789
Southwestern Textile Restoration Inc	7389	2384
Southwestern Vermont Health Care Corp	8741	88
Southwestern Wire Inc	3315	10
Southwick and Meister Inc	3545	68
Southwick Clothing LLC	2311	21
Southwire Co	3357	3
Southwire Co NSA Div	3334	12
Southwood Furniture Corp	2512	47
Southworth International Group Inc	3537	25
Southworth Products Corp	3537	55
Southworth Tool and Gage Company Inc	3599	1470
Sovena USA Inc	5149	16
Sovereign Bank	6035	3
Sovereign Bank FSB	6035	9
Sovereign Bank NA	6021	216
Sovereign Commercial Group Inc	2891	19
Sovereign Motor Cars Ltd	5511	676
Sovereign Scientific Inc	5049	43
Sovran Acquisition LP	6531	26
Sowell and Co	6211	247
Sozio Corp	5722	20
SP Industries Inc (Warminster Pennsylvania)	3821	56
SP M Inc	3053	146
SP Morell Co	5162	48
SP Mount Printing Company Inc	2752	1078
SP Newsprint Co	2621	20
S-P Products Inc	3646	101
SP Richards Co	5112	13
SP Systems Inc (Greenbelt Maryland)	7373	422
SP Systems LLC	5064	204
SP Wholesale Meat Co	5147	92
SpA At Riverfront LLC	5091	122
SpA Manufacturing Inc	5091	99
Spaan Tech Inc	8711	489
Spaans Cookie Company Inc	2052	69
Spacatomic Fireworks	2899	212
Space Age Electronics Inc	3669	129
Space Age Laminating And Bindery Company Inc	2782	50
Space Age Plastic Fabricators Inc	3089	1786
Space Coast Credit Union	6062	45
Space Coast Credit Union	6061	20
Space Computer Corp	3571	146
Space Connections Inc	5731	128
Space Design and Display Inc	5046	192
Space Div	7812	220
Space Machine and Engineering Corp	3679	776
Space Machine Company Inc	3544	799
Space Projects Ltd	7371	1577
Space Sales Inc	7313	36
Space Services Inc	7261	13
Space Systems/Loral Inc	3663	14
Spaceage Control Inc	3728	199
Spaceage Synthetics Inc	3089	1885
Spaceage Tool and Manufacturing Inc	3469	336
Spaceclaim Corp	8711	418
Spacecom	5065	718
Spacecraft Components Corp	5065	317
Spacecraft Machine Products Inc	3469	207
SpaceDev Inc	3761	5
Spacenet Corp	4841	50
Spacesaver Northwest LLC	5021	121
Spacesonics Inc	3444	148
Spacetrack Travel Solutions	7372	2262
SPADAC Inc	7373	342
Spadone Hypex Inc	3559	221
Spaghetti Warehouse Inc	5812	260
Spahn and Rose Lumber Co	5211	149
Spain Agility First Support LLC	7349	321
Spalding Automotive Inc	3714	332
Spalding Group Inc	7311	737
Spalding Software Inc	7372	4159
Spal-Usa Inc	5013	307
Span Inc	3691	42
Span-America Medical Systems Inc	3842	70
Spancrete Industries Inc	3272	55
Spancrete Machinery Corp	3272	46
Spangler and Associates	7311	549
Spangler Racing	3711	64
Spangler Valve Co	3824	15
Spanish Broadcasting System Inc	4832	20
Spanish Gardens Food Manufacturing Company Inc	2032	46
Spanish House Inc	2731	235
Spanish Tiles Ltd	5211	249
Spanlink Communications Inc	7372	1521
Span-O-Matic Inc	3444	234
SpanPro Inc	8711	126
Spansion Inc	3674	34
Spanx Inc	5137	6
SPAR Associates Inc	7372	4883
SPAR Group Inc	7389	299
Sparcon Import Corp	5072	181
Spare Backup Inc	6719	192
Sparhawk Laboratories Inc	2834	303
Sparhawk Trucking Inc	4213	1381
Spark Networks Inc	7389	393
Spark Technologies Inc	3544	839
Sparkart Group Inc	7373	695
Sparkle Performance Joint Venture Ii	7349	348
Sparkler Group Inc	3569	203
Sparknotes LLC	8748	414
Sparkology	7372	5151
Sparks Electrical Inc	1731	2121
Sparks Marketing Group Inc	7389	252
Sparling Instruments LLC	5084	680
Sparqtron Corp	3629	50
Sparrer Sausage Company Inc	2013	92
Sparrevohn Engineering	3661	242
Sparrow Corp (Daytona Beach Florida)	7372	4758
Sparrow Health System	8062	46
Sparrow Manufacturing Co	8748	150
Sparta Consulting Inc	7379	532
Sparta Inc	8748	50
Spartan Asphalt Paving Co	1611	235
Spartan Carbide Inc	3545	133
Spartan Chemical Co (Toledo Ohio)	2842	16
Spartan Communications Inc	4833	253
Spartan Computer Services Inc	7378	12
Spartan Corp	5045	398
Spartan Distributors Inc	5083	37
Spartan Foods Of America Inc	2041	15
Spartan Graphics Inc	2752	330
Spartan Inc	7381	110
Spartan Light Metal Products Inc	3363	9
Spartan Manufacturing Co	3451	121
Spartan Motors Chassis Inc	3711	19
Spartan Motors Inc	3711	24
Spartan Precision Machining Corp	3599	1847
Spartan Printing Inc	2752	1018
Spartan Staffing	7363	86
Spartan Stores Fuel LLC	5541	24
Spartan Stores Inc	5141	30
Spartan Ultrasonics Inc	6799	359
Spartan Warehouse and Distribution	4213	1921
Spartanburg Automotive Steel Inc	3465	20
Spartanburg Stainless Products Inc	3412	3
Spartanics Ltd	3577	324
Sparta-Tomah Broadcasting Company Inc	4832	164
Spartech Corp	3083	2
Spartech Polycast	2821	37
Spartek Inc	3089	623
Sparton Corp	3812	24
Sparton Electronics	3679	8
Sparton Technology Corp	3599	406

Company Name	SIC	Rank
Sparton Technology Inc	3823	25
Spates Family Consulting Inc	2439	14
Spati Industries Inc	3549	123
Spatial Integrated Systems Inc	8748	350
Spatial Technologies	7372	2054
Spatializer Audio Laboratories Inc	3674	509
Spaulding and Rogers Manufacturing Inc	3952	13
Spaulding Machine Company Inc	3599	1695
Spaulding Press Inc	2752	1835
Spaw-Glass Construction Corp	1541	173
Spawr Industries Inc	3827	158
SPC Graphics	2752	1832
SPCO Credit Union	6062	112
SPD Technologies Inc	3613	26
SPDR Gold Trust	1041	7
Speaker Factory	3651	250
Speaker Shop Inc	5731	249
Speakercraft LLC	3651	89
Speaking Roses International Inc	5999	277
Speakman Co	3432	26
Spear Corp	7389	803
Spear Group Inc	8742	431
Spear/Hall and Associates Inc	7311	524
Spear Leeds and Kellogg LP	6211	62
Spear USA LLC	2759	58
Speared Peanut Design Studio	7336	174
Spearin Preston Burrows Inc	1629	80
Speastech Inc	7379	1304
Specht Newspapers Inc	2711	591
Special Design Products Inc	3086	115
Special Dispatch Inc	4213	252
Special Drill And Reamer Corp	3545	387
Special Electronics Inc	5731	142
Special Fab and Machine Inc	3599	671
Special Hermetic Products Inc	3679	712
Special Metals Corp	3313	3
Special Metals Inc	5051	229
Special Mine Services Inc	3643	41
Special Optics Inc	3851	89
Special Plastic Systems Inc	5074	227
Special Products and Manufacturing Inc	3444	65
Special Projects Inc	3711	72
Special Service Freight-Carolinas	4213	2103
Special Service Plastic Company Inc	3089	1895
Special Service Systems Inc	7389	2459
Special Services Corp	7389	968
Special Tee Golf of Florida Inc	5941	43
Special Tool and Engineering Inc	3544	102
Specialists In Custom Software Inc	7372	1361
Speciality Incentives Inc	5199	48
Specialized Bicycle Components Inc	3751	6
Specialized Building Products LLC	5032	164
Specialized Business Software Inc	7372	4105
Specialized Business Solutions	7372	4335
Specialized Health Management Co	8742	267
Specialized Housing Inc	7389	694
Specialized Loan Servicing LLC	7374	56
Specialized Machinery Transport	4213	2076
Specialized Packaging Radisson LLC	2653	57
Specialized Plastics Inc	3081	151
Specialized Products Co	3825	53
Specialized Products Ltd	3599	290
Specialized Rail Service Inc	4213	2029
Specialized Screen Printing	2759	357
Specialized Services and Personnel	8742	347
Specialized Services Inc	5172	88
Specialized Systems Inc	3823	70
Specialized Technology Resources Inc	8731	90
Specialized Technology Resources Inc (Canton Massachusetts)	8734	56
Specialized Transportation for Outpatient Services Inc	4119	16
Specialized Transportation Services	4213	1273
Specialized Turning Inc	3823	319
Specialized Vehicles Inc	8734	185
Special-Lite Inc	3442	85
Specialties Clutch Inc	7537	1
Specialties Engineering Company Inc	3599	1350
Specialties Research Inc	3577	232
Specialties Steel Rule Dies Inc	3544	489
Specialties Technologies Inc	3599	642
Specialties Tool Co	3545	82
Specialty Baking Inc	5149	138
Specialty Bar Products Co	3499	4
Specialty Bottle LLC	5099	149
Specialty Brace and Limb	3842	269
Specialty Cable Corp	3357	49
Specialty Catalog Corp	5961	83
Specialty Coating Systems Inc	3479	24
Specialty Coatings Co	2851	86
Specialty Communications And Electronics Inc	1731	1108
Specialty Compressor and Engine Company Inc	5084	634
Specialty Concepts Inc	3613	165
Specialty Control Systems Inc	5063	805
Specialty Design and Manufacturing Company Inc	3599	978
Specialty Engineering Corp	7692	31
Specialty Enterprise Inc	5734	117
Specialty Feeds Inc	2047	35
Specialty Fertilizer Products LLC	2875	23

Company Name	SIC	Rank
Specialty Fibres LLC	5093	113
Specialty Gases Inc	5169	146
Specialty Graphics Inc	2789	132
Specialty Group	6163	38
Specialty Industries Inc	2653	50
Specialty Ink Company Inc	2899	184
Specialty Lens Corp	3851	91
Specialty Lighting Industries Inc	3646	73
Specialty Machine and Supply Inc	7699	46
Specialty Manufacturing Co	3494	41
Specialty Manufacturing Inc	3081	117
Specialty Manufacturing Of Indiana Inc	3082	32
Specialty Merchandise Corp	5199	28
Specialty Metals Corp	5051	316
Specialty Microwave Corp	3663	305
Specialty Optical Systems Inc	5063	863
Specialty Organics Inc	2869	127
Specialty Paper Mills Inc	2621	51
Specialty Photo Lab LLC	7384	45
Specialty Pipe and Tube Inc	5051	389
Specialty Piping Corp	1542	383
Specialty Polymers Inc	2821	38
Specialty Printing Inc	2791	27
Specialty Products and Insulation Co	5033	5
Specialty Promotions Inc	2752	30
Specialty Rehab Management Inc	8099	8
Specialty Resources Inc	5085	189
Specialty Restaurants Corp	5812	141
Specialty Retailers Inc	5651	13
Specialty Rice Inc	2099	291
Specialty Risk Services LLC	8744	50
Specialty Screw Corp	3452	66
Specialty Shearing and Dyeing Inc	2261	22
Specialty Silicone Fabricators Inc	3841	82
Specialty Silicone Products Inc	2891	73
Specialty Software Inc	7372	2179
Specialty Sports Venture	5091	4
Specialty Steel Company Inc	5051	481
Specialty Steel Service Colnc	5051	185
Specialty Store Services Inc	5046	64
Specialty Supply LP	3533	69
Specialty Surgical Instrumentation Inc	5047	75
Specialty Systems Inc (Louisville Kentucky)	7372	4978
Specialty Tile Products Inc	5032	74
Specialty Tool and Die Company Inc	3544	857
Specialty Tool and Machine Company Inc	3444	208
Specialty Tool Inc	5084	580
Specialty Tower Lighting Ltd	1623	600
Specialty Trade Shows Inc	7389	1243
Specialty Underwriters Alliance Inc	6331	213
Specific Systems Ltd	1711	150
Specification Rubber Products Inc	3053	27
Specified Technologies Inc	2899	111
Speck Plastics Inc	3081	153
Speck Product Design Inc	8711	415
Speck Products Inc	2394	6
Speck Sales Inc	5014	51
Speco Inc	3421	18
Specpub Inc	2721	343
Spec's Family Partner's	5921	3
Specs Liquor Warehouse	7319	145
Spectator Management Group	7941	2
Spec-Tech Industrial Electric Inc	5065	602
Spectera Inc	5995	9
SpecterwebCom LLC	4813	737
Spector Group	8712	235
Spectorsoft Corp	7372	2083
Spectra Energy Corp	1311	5
Spectra Energy Partners LP	4922	13
Spectra Engineering Inc	3533	118
Spectra Enterprises Corp	7361	27
Spectra Hardware Inc	5049	224
Spectra LMP LLC	3316	25
Spectra Logic Corp	3572	37
Spectra Marketing Systems Inc	8742	532
Spectra Measuring Systems Inc	2752	1005
Spectra Merchandising International Inc	3661	83
Spectra Symbol Corp	3679	625
Spectra Systems Corp	3651	61
SpectraCare Inc	8082	31
SpectraCell Laboratories Inc	8071	47
Spectracom Corp	3829	131
Spectracom Inc	4812	117
SpectraCom Inc (Milwaukee Wisconsin)	7371	13
Spectracomp Inc	2791	67
Spectraflex Inc	3679	833
Spectraforce Technologies Inc	8742	308
Spectral Dynamics Inc	3825	114
Spectral Instruments Inc	3861	84
Spectral Response LLC	3679	104
Spectralytics Inc	3599	1404
Spectra-Mat Inc	3671	18
Spectranetics Corp	3845	27
Spectra-Physics Lasers Inc	3845	19
SpectraScience Inc	3845	140
Spectracorv Inc	4063	132
Spectra-Strip Cable Products	3351	18
Spectra-Tech Inc	7389	1339
Spectrex Inc	3669	293
Spectro Alloys Corp	3316	11

Company Name	SIC	Rank
Spectro Coating Corp	2299	17
Spectrolab Inc	3674	272
Spectron Corp	7299	46
Spectron Glass and Electronics Inc	3679	893
Spectronics Corp	3823	58
Spectronics Inc	3826	163
Spectrotape Corp	3695	174
Spectrum Advisory Services Inc	6282	672
Spectrum Analytical Inc	8734	48
Spectrum Asset Management Inc (Newport Beach California)	6282	483
Spectrum Associates Inc	3592	26
Spectrum Automation Co	3535	168
Spectrum Bank	6022	767
Spectrum Batteries Inc	3533	83
Spectrum Brands Holdings Inc	3691	1
Spectrum Business Solutions	7331	186
Spectrum Club Co	7991	11
Spectrum Communications Cabling Services Inc	5045	323
Spectrum Company International Ltd	3823	342
Spectrum Computer Corp	5734	43
Spectrum Control Inc	3679	75
Spectrum Controls Inc	3823	65
Spectrum Diagnostics Imaging	8093	22
Spectrum Digital Services LLC	3565	128
Spectrum Engineers Inc	8711	453
Spectrum Equity Investors	6722	133
Spectrum Financial System Inc	5999	57
Spectrum FSY Microwave Inc	3679	62
Spectrum Graphic Services Inc	2752	1039
Spectrum Group International Inc	7389	7
Spectrum Healthcare Resources	7363	25
Spectrum Human Resource Systems Corp	7372	1534
Spectrum Industries Inc	2531	20
Spectrum Industries Inc (Grand Rapids Michigan)	3471	1
Spectrum Informatics Inc	7379	1240
Spectrum Instruments Inc	3825	310
Spectrum Label Corp	2759	172
Spectrum Laboratories Inc	3829	107
Spectrum Laser and Technologies Inc	3699	245
Spectrum Lighting Group Inc	5063	771
Spectrum Lighting Inc	5063	741
Spectrum Lighting Ltd	5063	744
Spectrum Marketing Inc	8742	640
Spectrum Monthly Inc	7331	31
Spectrum Organic Products LLC	2033	37
Spectrum Paper Company Inc	5087	74
Spectrum Pharmaceuticals Inc	2834	154
Spectrum Plastics Molding Resources Inc	3089	560
Spectrum Preferred Meats Inc	2011	112
Spectrum Press Inc	2752	1101
Spectrum Printers Inc	2752	1033
Spectrum Printing Company LLC	2752	909
Spectrum Properties Inc	6552	136
Spectrum Sensors And Controls Inc	3829	284
Spectrum Software	7372	4264
Spectrum Software Technology Inc	7372	4016
Spectrum Staffing and Software Solutions Inc	7363	321
Spectrum Systems Inc	3826	54
Spectrum Systems Integration Inc	1731	1907
Spectrum Technologies USA Inc	8999	159
Spectrum Technology Services LLC	7379	611
Spectrum Transportation	4789	27
Spectrum Unlimited	7375	274
Spede Technologies	7372	4557
Spee Dee Delivery Service	4213	207
Speech Cycle Inc	7372	1367
Speech Design International Inc	7371	199
SpeechSoft Inc	7372	4558
Speed I/O Technologies	3577	671
Speed Industrial Service Of Texas LLC	7363	353
Speed Link	4813	533
Speed Queen Co	3633	1
SpeeDee Oil Change and Tune-Up	7538	8
Spee-Dee Packaging Machinery Inc	3565	100
Speedemissions Inc	7549	18
Speed-Fab-Crete Corporation International	1542	284
Speedflo Business Forms Inc	2759	446
Speedflo Inc	2761	60
Speedline Athletic Wear Inc	2329	21
Speedline Technologies	3577	77
Speedling Inc	0181	17
Speed-O-Tach Inc	7699	89
Speedotron Corp	3861	111
Speedus Corp	7371	1807
Speedway Motorsports Inc	7948	5
Speedway SuperAmerica LLC	5541	2
Speedway Transportation	4213	1692
Speedwell Machine Works Inc	3599	1623
Speedy Auto Glass Inc	7536	4
Speegle Construction Inc	1541	239
Speer Concrete Inc	5032	166
Speer Cushion Co	3523	279
Spoor Equipment Inc	3625	277
Spego Inc	5084	741
Speidel LLC	5094	11
Spell LLC	2321	27
Spellbinders Paper Arts LLC	5943	13

Company Name	SIC	Rank
Spellex Corp	7372	3569
Spelling Communications	8743	169
Spellman High Voltage Electric Corp	3612	14
Spenard Builders Supply Inc	5211	169
Spence and Company Ltd	2091	22
Spence Engineering Company Inc	3491	5
Spence Industries Inc	3545	434
Spencer and Associates Inc	6411	245
Spencer Building Maintenance Inc	7349	127
Spencer Evening World	2752	845
Spencer Fane Britt and Browne LLP	8111	281
Spencer Farm Equip	5083	212
Spencer Grant Inc	3695	167
Spencer Group	7336	108
Spencer Industries Inc	3679	557
Spencer Industries Incorporated of Seattle	5085	31
Spencer Products Co	3965	9
Spencer Reed Group Inc	7361	48
Spencer Stuart and Associates Inc	7361	25
Spencer Stuart Management Consultants NV	8742	52
Spencer Technologies Inc	1731	169
Spencer Turbine Co	3564	4
Spencer-Harris Of Arkansas Inc	3599	1743
Spencers Inc	2369	3
Spenco Medical Corp	3842	98
Spenser Communications Inc	1731	161
Spentech Inc	8731	313
Spen-Tech Machine Engineering Corp	3549	63
Sper Scientific Ltd	5049	161
Sperian Protection Optical Inc	3851	9
Sperian Respiratory Protection USA LLC	3842	82
Speridian Technologies LLC	8748	293
Sperry and Hutchinson Company Inc	7389	438
Sperry and Rice Manufacturing Company LLC	3052	10
Sperry Automatics Company Inc	3451	128
Sperry Graphic Inc	2782	53
Sperry Marine	3812	23
Sperry Van Ness	6531	11
Spex Certiprep Inc	3821	39
Spex Sample Prep LLC	3821	42
Spf North America Inc	2047	24
Spg Graphics Inc	2752	191
Spg Solar Inc	1731	248
Sphere Health Systems Inc	7372	4183
Spherion of Central Kentucky Inc	7363	214
Spherix Inc	8734	197
Sphero Trading Corp	5031	188
Sphinx International Inc	7373	816
Sphs Corp	8741	71
Spi Binding Company Inc	2789	67
SPI Communications Inc	2759	101
Spi Healthcare	7338	3
SPI Healthcare Documentation LLC	7338	13
Spi Lighting Inc	3646	25
Spi/Mobile Pulley Works Inc	3441	77
SPI Publisher Services	2731	257
Spice King Corp	2099	224
Spice World Inc	5149	39
Spiceco Inc	5149	154
Spicer Productions Inc	7812	333
Spicers Paper Inc	5111	16
Spiceworks Inc	7371	547
Spicy Pickle Franchising Inc	5812	415
Spider Staging Corp	3446	9
Spie Tool Co	3545	168
Spiegel Brands Inc	5137	9
Spieler and Ricca Electrical Company Inc	1731	209
Spielman Koenigsberg and Parker LLP	8721	186
Spiers Concrete Sysmtem And Excavation LLC	5032	176
Spiers McDonald Bharucha and Royal Inc	8712	306
Spiess Construction Company Inc	1623	218
Spike/DDB LLC	7311	226
Spike Electric Inc	1731	2157
Spike Enterprise Inc	7353	82
Spiker Communications Inc	7311	972
Spillman Technologies Inc	7372	1380
Spin Inc	5099	118
Spin Magnetics	3677	48
Spin Systems Inc	7379	717
Spinco Metal Products Inc	3498	56
Spindler Co	5149	215
Spindletop Oil and Gas Co	1311	209
Spindustries LLC	3469	295
Spindustry Systems Inc	7379	943
Spine and Sport	8099	93
Spinitar	5731	85
Spinks H C Clay Company Inc	1455	5
Spinks Scale Company Inc	3596	24
Spinks Technologies	7371	1475
Spinnaker Coating LLC	2672	42
Spinnaker Contract Manufacturing Inc	3699	120
Spinnaker Inc	4213	2066
Spinnaker Industries Inc	3313	5
Spinnaker Management Group LLC	8748	241
Spinnaker Microwave Inc	3679	713
Spinnaker Networks Inc	5045	161
Spinner Printing Co	2759	347

Company Name	SIC	Rank
Spinneret Inc	3679	320
Spinning Wheels Express	4213	3124
SpinWeb Internet Media Inc	7379	672
Spira Manufacturing Corp	3053	95
Spiracle Technology LLC	3829	398
Spiral Binding Company Inc	2789	7
Spiral Designs Inc	3671	26
Spiral Industries Inc	3492	24
Spiral Software	7372	2206
Spiralfx Interactive LLC	7374	402
Spiral-Matic Inc	3556	187
Spire Biomedical Inc	8731	229
Spire Corp	3559	49
Spirent Communications	3825	14
Spireon Inc	3820	215
Spirit AeroSystems Holdings Inc	3728	2
Spirit Aerosystems Inc	3728	9
Spirit Airlines Inc	4512	25
Spirit Bank	6021	127
Spirit Finance Corp	6798	86
Spirit Foodservice Inc	3089	272
Spirit Ford Inc	5511	997
Spirit Manufacturing Inc	3949	53
Spirit Telecom LLC	4813	88
Spirit Truck Lines Inc	4213	697
Spirit Trucking Co	4213	1515
Spiroflow Systems Inc	5084	834
Spirol International Corp	3452	52
Spitz Inc	3827	80
Spitzer Industries Inc	3498	5
Spitzer Management Inc	5511	50
Spiva Construction Inc	1623	727
SPL Holdings Inc	6719	128
Splash Graphics Inc	7389	1128
Splawn Belting Inc	5085	256
Splice Communications Inc	7379	370
Splitrock Properties Inc	4813	442
Splyce Inc	7371	1217
Spm Corp	3599	1201
SPM Flow Control Inc	3533	9
Spm Industries Inc	3599	327
Spohn Associates Inc	5039	11
Spokane Computer Inc	7371	1097
Spokane County Title Insurance Co	6361	23
Spokane Machinery Co	5082	176
Spokane Recycling Products Inc	5093	162
Spokane Seed Co	5153	73
Spokane Transfer and Storage Co	4213	2364
Spokes Inc	5013	368
Spongecell	7373	658
Spongex Foam Products LLC	3089	1071
Sponsor Direct LLC	7371	1587
Spoon River Electric Cooperative Inc	4911	551
Spooner's Building Products	5031	344
Spoontiques Inc	5099	63
Sporicidin International Inc	2834	427
Sporn Group Inc	7361	406
Sport Brands International LLC	3949	22
Sport Chalet Inc	5941	12
Sport Chevrolet Company Inc	5511	405
Sport Clinic of Greater Milwaukee Inc	8049	33
Sport Clips Inc	6794	67
Sport Dimension Inc	5091	78
Sport Graphics Inc	7336	43
Sport Honda	5511	406
Sport Mitsubishi	5511	1180
Sport Obermeyer Ltd	5137	14
Sport Supply Group Inc	5961	55
Sport Truck USA Inc	5013	303
Sportchassis LLC	3711	49
Sportek International Inc	5699	16
Sport-Haley Inc	2321	19
Sportif USA Inc	5136	7
Sportika Export Inc	5122	65
Sports and Exhibition Authority Of Pittsburgh And Allegheny County	7389	2014
Sports Authority Inc	5941	2
Sports Club Company Inc	7997	8
Sports Coverage Inc	2392	26
Sports Design And Development Inc	3949	170
Sports Display Inc	7319	140
Sports Endeavors Inc	5941	20
Sports Equipment Specialists Inc	5091	147
Sports Health Home Care Corp	5211	268
Sports Management Network Inc	7941	40
Sports Mania	5941	42
Sports Molding Inc	3089	824
Sports South Inc	5091	43
Sports Technology Inc	3829	474
Sportsgraphics Inc	3949	164
Sportsman Manufacturing Co	3599	1730
Sportsman's Guide Inc	5941	14
Sportsmedia Technology Corp	7371	635
SportsQuest International LLC	7812	323
Sportsystems Corp	7948	8
Sportvision Of Delaware	7812	207
Spot Image Corp	2741	74
Spot Master Inc	3599	2164
Spot Mobile International Ltd	4813	219
Spotfire Inc	7372	971
Spotless Cleaning Co	7363	389
Spotless Enterprises Inc	3089	207
SpotMagic Inc	7372	3027
Spotts Stevens and McCoy Inc	8711	435

Company Name	SIC	Rank
Spradley Barr of Greeley	5511	593
Sprague Energy Corp	5172	20
Spragues' Rock And Sand Co	3273	81
Spratronics Inc	7389	2512
Spray Equipment and Service Center Inc	5084	357
Spray Force Manufacturing Inc	3561	154
Spray Gould and Bowers LLP	8111	547
Spray Products Corp	2899	68
Spraying Systems Co	3499	18
Spraylat Corp	2851	10
Spraymation Inc	3999	203
Spray-N-Grow Inc	2873	25
Sprecher Brewing Company Inc	2082	74
Spreen Saturn Inc	5511	990
Sprenger Midwest Inc	5031	74
Spreuer and Son Inc	3799	28
Sprig Electric Co	1731	111
Spring Air Mattress Corp	2515	18
Spring Arbor Distribution Company Inc	5192	16
Spring City Electrical Manufacturing Co	3648	23
Spring Dell Center Inc	8331	103
Spring Draco Manufacturing Co	3493	7
Spring Exacto Corp	3493	9
Spring Fourslide And Stamping Inc	3493	14
Spring Glen Fresh Foods Inc	2032	9
Spring Grove Resource Recovery Inc	4953	79
Spring Hill Laser Services Corp	2759	568
Spring Meadows Health Care Center LLC	8361	148
Spring Micromatic And Stamping Company Inc	3495	22
Spring Mid-Continent Co	3495	14
Spring Napoleon Works Inc	3493	2
Spring Novi Inc	3493	13
Spring Oak Winery Inc	2084	137
Spring Of Tampa Bay Inc	8322	178
Spring Overhead Door Inc	5031	360
Spring Rowley and Stamping Corp	3495	13
Spring Silver Foods Inc	2035	15
Spring Spiller Co	2515	16
Spring Stanley And Stamping Corp	3469	189
Spring Suhm Works Inc	3495	15
Spring Tampa Co	5531	40
Spring Wesco Co	3496	81
SpringBoard Inc	8099	74
Springboro IGA Inc	5411	269
Springbridge Rehab and Wellness Ctr	8361	118
Springbrook Software Inc	7372	1614
Springco Metal Coating	3471	45
Springdale Ford Inc	5511	960
Springdale Specialty Plastics Inc	3085	38
Springdot Inc	2752	414
Springer Bush and Perry	8111	497
Springer Electric Cooperative Inc	4911	508
Springer Equipment Company Inc	5084	445
Springer Thomas W Inc	3599	1489
Springer-Miller Systems Inc	7372	1379
Springfield Business Equipment Co	5021	106
Springfield Business Journal	2711	239
Springfield Coca-Cola Bottling Co	2086	61
Springfield Creamery Inc	2026	56
Springfield Electric Supply Company Inc	5063	808
Springfield Electric Supply Company Inc (Springfield Ilinois)	5063	16
Springfield Engineering Company Inc	1711	191
Springfield Grocer Company Inc	5141	144
Springfield Inc	3484	18
Springfield LLC	2221	7
Springfield Mold And Die Inc	3599	2294
Springfield Parts Warehouse LLC	5013	409
Springfield Pepsi-Cola Bottling Co	5149	53
Springfield Precision Instruments	3829	25
Springfield Printing Corp	2752	816
Springfield Products Inc	2821	65
Springfield Public Works	7342	79
Springfield Ready Mix Co	3273	6
Springfield Remanufacturing Corp	3599	88
Springfield Terminal Railway Co	4011	24
Springfield Tool And Die Inc	3544	442
Springfield Underground Inc	6552	293
Springfield Workshop Inc	8331	165
Spring-Green Lawn Care Corp	0782	10
Springhill Services Inc	4213	2130
Springhouse Inc	8361	138
Springleaf Finance Corp	6141	16
Springs Global US Inc	2392	2
Springs Window Fashions LLC	2591	2
Springside Cheese Corp	2022	67
Springville Manufacturing Company Inc	3593	52
Springwood Industrial Inc	5084	797
Sprinkler World Of Arizona Inc	5087	35
Sprint Healthcare Systems Inc	4899	145
Sprint Missouri Inc	4812	71
Sprint Nextel Corp	4812	2
Sprint Print Inc	2752	1218
Sprint-Denver Inc	2752	463
Sprinter Services Inc	4213	2322
Sprite Industries Inc	3826	121
Sprocket Specialties	3568	84
Sprout Group (New York New York)	6799	239
SproutLoud Media Networks LLC	7319	72
Sprowl and Associates Inc	7311	711

Company Name	SIC	Rank
Spruce Computer Systems Inc	7372	3148
Spruce Environmental Technologies Inc	3634	25
Spruce Pine Mica Co	3679	764
Spryance Inc	7338	30
SPS Commerce Inc	7372	1941
SPS Tech Corp	3672	433
SPS Technologies LLC	3452	4
SPS Technologies Waterford Co	3452	35
SPSS Inc	7372	174
Spudnik Equipment Company LLC	3523	40
Spuncast Inc	3325	29
Spur Support Services LLC	3577	417
Spurlock Inc	1623	154
Spurrier Chemical Companies Inc	2869	79
SPX Corp	3621	3
SPX Corporation Kent Moore	3559	14
SPX Corporation Service Solutions	3825	44
SPX Fluid Power	3561	60
SPX Precision Components	3542	6
SPX Valves and Controls	3492	12
Spyco Industries Inc	3599	1016
Spyder Byte Web Design LLC	7379	1000
Spyderco Inc	3421	19
Spyrus Inc	3577	155
SQN Banking Systems Inc	7371	322
SQN Signature Systems	7372	1438
Squab Producers Of Calif Inc	5144	24
Squaglia Manufacturing	3599	1290
Square 1 Bank	6022	132
Square H Brands Inc	2013	89
Square One	7372	2642
Square Peg Packaging and Printing LLC	7389	940
Square Stamping Manufacturing Corp	3469	291
Square Tree Software	7379	601
Square V Electric Co	1731	1386
Squarerigger Inc	7372	4257
Squarespace Inc	7372	1752
Squaw Valley Ski Corp	7011	113
Squeaky Clean LLC	7349	340
Squeegee Supply Inc	5099	89
Squibb-Taylor Inc	5084	260
Squid Ink Manufacturing Inc	2899	146
Squire Corrugated Container Corp	2653	62
Squire Sanders and Dempsey LLP	8111	56
Squires Timber Co	5099	91
Squires-Belt Material Co	5211	197
Squirrel Brand Co	2064	70
Sqwincher Corp	2087	55
S-R Broadcasting Co	4832	197
SR Components Inc	5065	931
SR Door Inc	2431	81
SR Holdings Inc (Lexington Massachusetts)	3149	9
SR Instruments Inc	3825	146
Sr Metals Inc	5051	203
SR One Ltd	6799	317
SR Smith LLC	3949	98
SRA International Inc	7372	37
SRA/McGraw-Hill	2741	46
SRAM Corp	3751	3
Src Cables Inc	3679	515
Src Computers LLC	3571	130
Src Elastomerics Inc	2822	12
Src Inc	5078	34
Src Medical Inc	3089	964
Src Milling Company LLC	2077	9
SRCG/Ecom Inc	3149	4
SRE Specialty Restaurant Equipment Inc	5046	336
Srf Consulting Group Inc	8711	245
SRG Global Inc	3714	49
Sri Connector Gage Company Inc	3678	61
Sri Inc	7389	2047
SRI International	8732	10
Sri Monogramming Inc	7389	1610
SRI Surgical Express Inc	7299	12
SRI Systems Inc	7371	1140
Srisys Inc	7371	1464
SRK Architects	8712	317
SRL Inc (Lexington Massachusetts)	3149	10
SRM Insurance Brokerage LLC	6331	42
Sroka Industries Inc	3599	1966
Sroufe Healthcare Products LLC	3842	266
SRP M Inc	3599	1124
SRR Inc (Lexington Massachusetts)	3149	11
Srs Computers Inc	5045	680
Srs Crisafulli Inc	3561	147
SRS Inc (Gallatin Tennessee)	7349	54
SRS Labs Inc	3674	182
SRS Trucking and Excavating Inc	4213	2721
SRSA Commercial Real Estate Inc	6531	368
SRT Communications Inc	4813	145
Srw Products Inc	5083	105
SS and C Technologies Inc	7372	162
SS Designs Inc	2396	12
SS Electric and Service Company LLC	1731	2535
SS Industrial Cable Corp	5063	655
SS White Technologies Inc	3568	27
SS8 Networks Inc	7373	182
SSA Marine Inc	4491	1
SSA-Cooper LLC	4491	17
SSB Inc	2741	88
SSB Service Inc	5099	34

Company Name	SIC	Rank
SSCI Inc	5051	197
Ssco Manufacturing Inc	3548	59
SSD Control Technology Inc	3599	1166
SSE Inc	5065	628
SSH Communications Security Inc	7379	183
Ssi Cable Corp	5063	631
Ssi Electronics Inc	3679	474
SSI Group Inc	7372	342
SSI Inc	1541	150
SSI Investment Management Inc	6282	540
Ssi Manufacturing Technologies Corp	3599	861
SSI Services Inc	8744	15
Ssi Systems Inc	1731	1962
Ssi Technology Inc	3829	132
Ssm Employee Health Care Fund	8099	33
SSOE Inc	8712	4
SSOE Systems Inc	7373	1106
Ssp Fittings Corp	3494	42
SSP Offshore (USA) Inc	8711	425
SSP Solutions Inc	3679	256
SSS Co	2834	239
Sst Conveyor Components Inc	3535	194
SST Corp	5122	46
SST Systems Inc	7372	4475
Ssttech Inc	7334	92
St Acquisitions LLC	3829	467
St Albans Window Manufacturing Inc	3089	1178
St Ann's Home	8051	73
St Associates Inc	2741	318
St Barnabas Community Enterprises	8062	208
St Charles Hospital Of Oregon Ohio Inc	8062	155
St Charles Sand Company Inc	5032	191
St Clair Jack Inc	1623	433
St Consulting International	7379	914
St Elizabeth Hospital	8062	96
St Francis Hospital Inc	8062	109
St George Steel Fabrication	3441	177
St Henry Tile Company Inc	3273	71
S-T Industries Inc	3545	192
St Joe Tool Co	3451	120
St John Associates Inc	3826	164
St Johns County Council On Aging Inc	8322	153
St Johns Mercy Health Care	8741	79
St Joseph Catholic Orphan Society	8361	126
St Joseph Hospital	8062	106
St Joseph Preferred Healthcare Inc	8741	160
St Lawrence County Newspapers	2711	98
St Louis Antique Lighting Company Inc	3646	72
St Louis Argus Newspaper	2711	894
St Louis Metallizing Co	3479	48
St Luke's Health System	8062	201
St Marys Hospital	8062	143
St Marys Tool and Die Company Inc	3544	899
St Media Group International Inc	2721	200
St Michaels Hospital Inc	8062	101
St Mobile Aerospace Engineering Inc	4581	11
St Partners LLC	2015	56
St Paul's Home For The Aged Inc	8051	70
ST Specialty Foods Inc	2099	162
St Vincent Depaul Rehabililation Services Of Texas Inc	7363	201
St Vincent Health Services Inc	8741	277
Sta Elements Inc	2844	169
STA Inc	3571	114
Staab Battery Manufacturing Company Inc	5063	479
STAAR Surgical Co	3851	13
Staber Industries Inc	3633	5
Stabilt America Inc	3089	669
Stabler Companies Inc	1442	4
Staci Corp	3672	171
Stack Container Service Inc	4213	2384
Stack On Products Co	3469	35
Stackpole Electronics Inc	3676	8
Stacks	5999	79
Staco Energy Products Co	3677	36
Staco Systems Inc	3613	52
Sta-Con Inc	3625	112
Stadco Corp	3545	21
Stadelman Fruit LLC	0723	3
Stafast Products Inc	3452	18
Staff Electric Company Inc	1731	96
Staff Force Inc	7363	111
Staff One Ltd	7361	343
Staff Quest	8049	27
Staff Tech Inc	7363	273
Staffall Inc	3679	488
Staffelbach Inc	7389	1269
Staffing Alternatives Inc	7373	549
Staffing Plus Inc	7361	227
Staffing Resources Of Miami Inc	7361	372
Staffing Source Personnel Inc	7363	242
Staffing Tree LLC	7363	221
StaffMark Inc	7363	28
Stafford Building Products Inc	5031	396
Stafford County Flour Mills Company Inc	2041	18
Stafford Equipment Co	5599	14
Stafford Media Solutions Inc	2701	9
Stafford Pluming	5087	174
Stag/Parkway Inc	5013	60
Stage Directions Inc	7812	303
Stage Equipment and Lighting Inc	7389	1027

Company Name	SIC	Rank
Stage Hands Local 2 Retirement Plan	6371	12
Stage Stores Inc	5651	10
Stagecraft Industries Inc	3999	99
Stage-Kolstad Associates	5046	378
Stageline Express Inc	4213	2940
Stageright Corp	3999	79
Stagnito Publishing Co	2721	66
Stagno's Bakery Inc	2051	200
Stag's Leap Wine Cellars	2084	37
Stags' Leap Winery Inc	2084	73
Stahl	3713	22
Stahl Electric Inc	1731	2465
Stahl Equipment Inc	3441	208
Stahl Gear and Machine Co	3566	34
Stahl Oil Company Inc	5172	104
Stahl Specialty Co	5051	19
Stahl (USA) Inc	2891	47
Stahl's Bakery Inc	5149	168
Stahly Cartage Co	4213	2034
Stahmann Farms Inc	2068	14
Staiman Recycling Corp	5093	50
Stainless Design Concepts Ltd	3569	257
Stainless Fabrication Inc	3443	96
Stainless Fabricators Inc	3443	242
Stainless Foundry and Engineering Inc	3599	65
Stainless Metals Inc	3443	245
Stainless Sales Corp	5051	291
Stainless Specialists Inc	1761	26
Stairway 9 LLC	7389	1187
Stairways Inc	3446	42
Stake Center Locating Inc	4899	170
Staker Paving and Construction Company Inc	1611	33
Stalco Inc	1731	1165
Stallard Technologies Inc	5734	39
Stallion Oilfield Services Inc	1389	26
Stamar Inc	1711	233
Stambaugh Ness PC	8721	22
Stamco Industries Inc	3465	61
Stamford Motors Inc	5511	915
Stamler Rfi	3599	1948
Stamm-Scheele Inc	1781	2
Stamor Corp	5611	20
Stampede Meat Inc	2013	39
Stampede Technologies Inc	7372	1964
Stampscom Inc	5961	88
Stan Bonham Company Inc	5083	140
Stan Clothier Co	5065	482
Stan Creech Properties Inc	6531	407
Stan Koch and Sons Trucking Inc	4213	130
Stan Sax Corp	3291	22
Stan Suarez Trucking Inc	4213	989
Stan The Tire Man Inc	5531	58
Stanadyne Corp	3714	92
Stanbury Uniforms Inc	2311	16
Stancills Inc	1442	81
Stanco Metal Products Inc	3465	12
Stanco Tool and Die Inc	3544	819
StanCorp Financial Group Inc	6321	8
Stancorp Mortgage Investors LLC	6162	138
Stand Aid Of Iowa Inc	3842	304
Stand Alone Inc	7372	4559
Standale Lumber and Supply Co	5211	137
Standard Aero Alliance Inc	3724	26
Standard Air and Lite Corp	5075	36
Standard and Poor's Compustat	2741	21
Standard and Poor's Financial Services LLC	2741	3
Standard and Poor's Securities Evaluations Inc	7323	10
Standard Bancshares Inc	6712	346
Standard Bank and Trust Co	6022	163
Standard Bank PaSB	6036	54
Standard Bellows Co	3599	1066
Standard Beverage Corp	5182	21
Standard Candy Company Inc	2023	15
Standard Casing Company Inc	3589	94
Standard Casualty Co	6399	16
Standard Communications Group LLC	1731	1461
Standard Communications LLC	3663	381
Standard Companies Inc	5211	53
Standard Companies Inc	5087	34
Standard Computer Inc	7373	889
Standard Construction Company Inc	1611	54
Standard Construction Corp	1623	159
Standard Crystal Corp	3679	813
Standard Data Corp	7374	93
Standard Data Resources Inc	5065	721
Standard Die and Fabricating Inc	3544	136
Standard Die Supply Of Indiana Inc	5085	73
Standard Drug Co (St Charles Missouri)	5912	65
Standard Duplicating Machine Corp	5044	41
Standard Electric Co	5063	15
Standard Electric Company Inc	1731	1376
Standard Electric Supply Co	5063	128
Standard Electronics Corp	5065	279
Standard Fiber LLC	5131	6
Standard Filter Corp	3564	99
Standard Forms Company of Tennessee	2752	1750
Standard Forwarding Company Inc	4213	189
Standard Fruit and Vegetable Company Inc	5148	8

Company Name	SIC	Rank
Standard Furniture Manufacturing Company Inc	2511	27
Standard Glass Corp	3231	60
Standard Gravel Company Inc	5032	171
Standard Group Inc	2657	8
Standard Homeopathic Co	2834	257
Standard Imaging Inc	3829	169
Standard Industrial Corp	3542	40
Standard Industrial Manufacturing Partners Ltd	3561	101
Standard Insurance Agency Inc	6399	17
Standard Iron and Metals Co	5093	136
Standard Jig Boring Service LLC	3599	259
Standard Life and Accident Insurance Co	6311	193
Standard Life Insurance Company of Indiana	6311	207
Standard Locknut LLC	3562	23
Standard Machine and Manufacturing Company Inc	3491	23
Standard Machine Inc	3599	1167
Standard Machine Works Inc	3533	120
Standard Magneto Sales Company Inc	5063	857
Standard Mattress Co	2515	23
Standard Meat Company LP	2013	121
Standard Microsystems Corp	3674	60
Standard Motor Products Inc	3699	9
Standard Offset Printing Company Inc	2752	101
Standard Pacific Corp	1531	20
Standard Pacific Of Orange County Inc	6552	78
Standard Paper Box Machine Company Inc	3554	56
Standard Parking Corp	7521	2
Standard Parts Corporation Inc	5013	162
Standard Pennant Company Inc	2759	511
Standard Performance Evaluation Corp	7372	3376
Standard Precision Manufacturing	3544	621
Standard Press Inc	2752	509
Standard Printing and Mail Services Inc	2752	1722
Standard Printing Co	2761	65
Standard Process Inc	5499	16
Standard Publishing	2752	65
Standard Publishing Company Inc	2711	557
Standard Rate and Data Service	2741	34
Standard Register Co	2761	3
Standard Roofings Inc	5033	15
Standard Rubber Products Co	3069	148
Standard Rubber Products Inc	3069	191
Standard Sand and Silica Co	1446	6
Standard Security Life Insurance Company of New York	6311	179
Standard Services Company Inc	5085	111
Standard Solar Inc	3612	37
Standard Southern Corp	4222	19
Standard Steel and Wire	3325	1
Standard Steel Specialty Co	3446	22
Standard Supplies Inc	5031	80
Standard Supply Electronics Co	3679	301
Standard Tar Products Company Inc	2851	94
Standard Testing Equipment Co	3829	513
Standard Textile Company Inc	2389	7
Standard Tool and Die Inc	3544	112
Standard Washer and Mat Inc	3069	260
Standard-Knapp Inc	3565	16
Standards Testing Laboratories Inc	3829	175
Standard-Taylor Industries Inc	1761	37
Standardware Inc	7372	4560
Standby Screw Machine Products Co	3451	11
Standco Industries Inc	3292	2
Standex International Corp	3585	19
Standish Group International Inc	2741	309
Standish Steel Inc	3599	2339
Standley Brothers Machine Company Inc	3599	1840
Standridge Color Corp	2865	7
Standridge Granite Corp	3281	40
Standwill Packaging Inc	2752	910
Staneco Corp	8711	567
Stanek E F And Associates Inc	3089	541
Stanford Bettendorf Inc	3556	108
Stanford Business Software Inc	7372	4641
Stanford Electronics Manufacturing and Sales	3575	55
Stanford Federal Credit Union	6061	59
Stanford Furniture Corp	2512	76
Stanford Home Centers	5031	54
Stanford Lumber Company Inc	5211	158
Stanford Ranch Capital Corp	6799	307
Stanford Ranch I LLC	6552	274
Stanford Research Systems Inc	3826	122
Stanfordville Machine and Manufacturing Company Inc	3599	560
Stangenes Industries Inc	3612	58
Stanhope Tool Inc	3545	348
Stanion Wholesale Electric Company Inc	5063	17
Stanislaus County Office Of Education	8299	9
Stanislaus Farm Supply Co	5191	13
Stanislaus Food Products Co	2033	59
Stanker and Galetto Inc	1541	196
Stanko Products Inc	3599	2384
Stanley Access Technologies	3699	44
Stanley Alarm Systems Inc	1731	1804

Company Name	SIC	Rank
Stanley Assembly Technologies	3546	8
Stanley Associates Inc	7379	34
Stanley Black and Decker Inc	3423	1
Stanley Brothers LLC	4213	2836
Stanley Consultants Inc	8711	226
Stanley Convergent Security Solutions Inc	7382	5
Stanley Engineering / Alpha Analytical Laboratories	8731	184
Stanley Engineering Company Inc	3599	377
Stanley Fastening Systems LP	3452	72
Stanley Furniture Company Inc	2511	13
Stanley Group	8711	24
Stanley Hand Tools	3423	6
Stanley Hydraulic Tools	3531	45
Stanley Industries Inc	3599	1774
Stanley Kessler and Co	5085	398
Stanley M Proctor Co	5084	302
Stanley Machining and Tool Corp	3599	251
Stanley Martin Companies Inc	6552	112
Stanley Mechanics Tools	3423	12
Stanley Refrigerated Express	4213	1449
Stanley Roberts Inc	5094	18
Stanley Steemer International Inc	7217	1
Stanley Stephens Company Inc	5023	116
Stanley T Naudus Corp	1521	166
Stanley Vidmar Storage Technologies	2522	9
Stanley-Bostitch Inc	3452	2
Stanly Fixtures Acquisition LLC	2541	48
Stanmar Inc	1629	95
Stansfeld and Fairbrother Inc	7311	1008
Stansley Mineral Resources Inc	1442	32
Stanson Corp	2841	29
Stantec Consulting Corp	8711	149
Stanton's Inc	7363	212
Stapels Manufacturing LLC	3545	354
Stapla Ultrasonics Corp	3699	145
Staplcotn Cooperative Association	5159	4
Staples Business Advantage	5112	12
Staples Inc	5943	1
Stapleton Communications Inc	8743	231
Stapleton Services and Manufacturing Inc	1623	409
Stapleton - Spence Packing Co	5149	112
Stapleton Technologies Inc	2899	247
Staplex Company Inc	3579	49
Stapling Machines Inc	3553	33
Star 3 Corp	1731	1711
Star America Inc	2251	5
Star and Son Electric Supply Company Inc	5063	800
Star Automation Inc	3569	137
Star Blue Auto Stores Inc	5531	57
Star Buffet Inc	5812	243
Star Children's Dress Company Inc	2361	8
Star Circuits Inc	3672	88
Star Clippers Ltd	4481	10
Star CNC Machine Tool Corp	5084	127
Star Computer Group Inc	5045	103
Star Construction LLC	1623	19
Star Copy Printing and Promotion Center Inc	2752	1432
Star Detective and Security Agency	7381	83
Star Dynamic Corp	3661	156
Star Electronic Sales Inc	5064	85
Star Electronics Corp	3672	277
Star Engineering Inc	3679	513
Star Envirotech Inc	5013	382
Star Equipment Corp	1623	832
Star Extruded Shapes Inc	3354	26
STAR Financial Bank Columbia City	6022	391
STAR Financial Bank New Castle	6022	105
STAR Financial Group Inc	6712	342
Star Food Products Inc	5147	32
Star Forge Inc	3523	89
Star Furniture Co	5712	94
Star Gas Partners LP	5984	4
Star Headlight and Lantern Company Inc	3669	92
Star Incorporated Lighting The Way	8331	67
Star Installations Inc	1731	568
Star Insurance Co	6331	76
Star Journal Publishing Co	2711	649
Star Kay White Inc	2087	51
Star Kitchen and Bath	5023	177
Star Lake Consulting Inc	7376	54
Star Leasing Inc	4213	1382
Star Line Trucking Corp	4213	1166
Star Lumber and Supply Company Inc	5211	47
Star Machine and Tool Co	3541	212
Star Metal Products Company Inc	3545	63
Star Metals Inc	5051	445
Star Milling Co	2048	52
Star Multi Care Services Inc	8082	63
Star Nail Products Inc	5122	89
Star Of The West Milling Co	2041	8
Star Oil Company Inc	5171	40
Star Packaging Corp	2673	18
Star Panel Technologies Inc	3577	587
Star Plastic Design	3086	88
Star Printing Co	2711	478
Star Printing Company Inc	2752	1346
Star Printing Company LLC	2752	1813
Star Printing Corp	2752	1053

Company Name	SIC	Rank
Star Publishing Co	2711	32
Star Publishing Company Inc	2711	470
Star Ravioli Manufacturing Company Inc	2098	30
Star Sales Company Of Knoxville Inc	5199	100
Star Satellite Products Inc	5065	526
Star Scientific Inc	2111	11
Star Stainless Screw Co	5072	35
Star Struck Ltd	5063	253
Star System Inc	6099	26
Star Systems Filtration Div	3569	221
Star Technologies Inc (Potomac Maryland)	7372	5114
Star Technology Inc	2891	84
Star Tel Systems Inc	1731	2401
Star Tickets Inc	7922	67
Star Trac	3949	51
Star Transportation Co	4213	1016
Star Transportation Inc	4213	301
Star Trax Inc	7389	370
Star Tribune Co	2711	60
Star Tribune Media Company LLC	2711	85
Star Truck Rentals Inc	7513	8
Star Video Duplicating	3695	78
Star Warehouse Inc	3663	398
Star West Satellite Inc	5731	14
Star X-Ray Company Inc	3844	25
Starbak Communications Inc	3577	205
Starboard TCN Worldwide Real Estate Services	6531	222
Starbrook Industries Inc	3089	1571
Starbucks Corp	5812	6
Star-Byte Inc	3695	67
StarchefsCom Inc	2721	409
StarCite Inc	7389	168
Starck H C Inc	3339	4
Starck Van Lines Inc	4213	2750
Starco Enterprises Inc	3559	156
Starcom Mediavest Group Inc	7313	11
Starcon International Inc	1711	126
Starcraft RV Inc	3792	4
Stardock Systems Inc	7372	1432
StarDot Technologies	3861	120
Stardust Cruisers Inc	3732	45
Starfire Computer Solutions	7372	3365
Starfire Lighting Inc	3646	59
Starflex Corp	3556	135
Stargatemobile LLC	5731	86
Stargel Office Solutions	5044	18
Star-Glo Industries LLC	3069	105
StarGuide Digital Networks Inc	7389	270
Sta-Rite Industries Inc	3561	29
Stark and Stark	8111	192
Stark Bank Group Ltd	6712	219
Stark Brothers Nurseries	0181	3
Stark Carpet Corp	5023	5
Stark County Community Action Agency	8399	7
Stark Encapsulation Inc	6794	150
Stark Industrial Inc	3599	28
Stark Metal Sales Inc	5051	344
Stark Raving Solutions	3695	109
Stark Truss Of Summerville Limited LLC	2439	46
Starke Machine Co	3599	412
Starkel Poultry Inc	2015	68
Starkey Inc	8093	28
Starkey Machinery Inc	3559	372
Starkey Printing Company Inc	8999	200
StarKist Foods Inc	2091	2
Starkor Manufacturing Inc	2399	34
Starled Inc	3679	711
Starlift Equipment Company Inc	5084	624
Starlight	5063	943
Starlight Enterprises Inc	8331	243
Starlight Networks Inc	7371	700
Starline Manufacturing Company Inc	3432	14
Starline Printing Inc	2752	725
Starline USA Inc	2396	18
Starlite Industries Inc	3545	232
Star-Lite Manufacturing Company Inc	7389	1278
Starlite Trailers Inc	3537	74
Starliteworld Trading Co	5047	275
Starmark	2434	20
Starmark International Inc	7311	560
Starmine Corp	7372	2351
Starn Tool and Manufacturing Co	3544	248
StarNet Communications Corp	7372	3229
Starnet Data Design Inc	7373	540
Starnet Digital Publishing Co	2791	45
StarNet Inc	4899	103
Starnet Technologies Inc	3823	320
Starpoint Solutions	7363	81
Starpower Home Entertainment Systems Inc	5731	67
Starprint Publications Inc	2752	1387
Starr Aircraft Products Inc	2393	6
Starr Burn Enterprises Inc	5093	132
Starr Electric Company Inc	1731	75
Starrete Trucking Company Inc	4213	1516
Starrfoam Manufacturing Inc	2821	102
Starshak Winzenburg	6211	331
Starship Industries	5046	356
Starside Security and Investigation Inc	7381	53

Company Name	SIC	Rank
Starsoft Technologies Inc	7371	1877
Start Wireless Group Inc	4813	276
Startech Software Systems Inc	7372	3230
StarTek Inc	7389	128
StarTek USA Inc	7389	526
STARTEL Corp	3661	96
Star-Telegram Newspaper Inc	2711	65
StarTex Power	4931	55
Starting Line Products Inc	3599	769
Starting USA Corp	3549	21
Startly Technologies LLC	7372	5048
Startspot Mediaworks Inc	7379	1035
Starvaggi Industries Inc	3273	83
Starving Students Inc	4213	741
Starwest Botanicals Inc	5149	100
Starwood Hotels and Resorts Worldwide Inc	7011	9
Starwood Property Trust	6798	214
Starwood Vacation Ownership Inc	6552	3
Starwood Vacation Services Inc	7041	1
Starz Entertainment Group LLC	4841	28
Starz LLC	4841	48
Stat Medical Supply Co	5047	266
Stat Nursing Services Inc	7361	153
STAT Pharmaceuticals Inc	5122	67
Stat Products Inc	2761	70
STAT! Systems Inc	7372	2866
StataCorp LP	7372	2033
Statco Engineering and Fabricators Inc	5084	222
Stat-Comp Inc	5063	930
State Auto Financial Corp	6331	119
State Auto Insurance Co	6331	219
State Auto Mutual Insurance Co	6331	51
State Auto Property and Casualty Insurance Co	6331	183
State Automobile Insurance Co	6331	212
State Bancorp Inc	6712	230
State Bank and Trust Co	6022	13
State Bank Financial Corp	6712	157
State Bank of Cochran	6022	575
State Bank of Cross Plains	6022	345
State Bank of Faribault	6022	648
State Bank of Ledyard	6022	802
State Bank of Long Island	6022	715
State Bank of Viroqua	6022	556
State Beauty Supply Of Louisville Inc	5087	150
State Cleaning Service Inc	7349	319
State Compensation Insurance Fund	6331	78
State Electric Co	5063	460
State Electric Supply Co	5063	8
State Electrical and Motor Service Inc	1731	939
State Electrical Supply Inc	5063	809
State Electronics Parts Corp	5065	418
State Employee's Credit Union	6062	5
State Employees Credit Union of Maryland Inc	6062	34
State Employees Federal Credit Union	6061	14
State Fair Foods Inc	2038	14
State Farm Fire and Casualty Co	6331	15
State Farm General Insurance Co	6331	225
State Farm Life Insurance Co	6311	8
State Farm Mutual Automobile Insurance Co	6331	12
State Hornet	2711	475
State House Press	2731	379
State Industrial Products Corp	2841	8
State Industrial Supply Inc	5065	585
State Industries Inc	3639	6
State Life Insurance Co	6311	71
State Line Scrap Company Inc	3999	135
State Line Scrap Metal Recycling Inc	5093	236
State National Bancshares	6712	712
State National Bank and Trust	6021	382
STATE NET	7379	254
State of the Art Inc	3676	9
State Restaurant Equipment Inc	5046	96
State Seal Co	5085	120
State Service Systems Inc	5087	20
State Steel Supply Co	5051	243
State Stone Corporation Inc	5211	254
State Street Bank and Trust Co	6022	4
State Street Corp	6712	9
State Supply Co	5074	126
State Systems Inc	5063	443
State Tool and Manufacturing Co	3643	54
State Wide Aluminum Inc	3714	246
State Wide Investors Inc	6531	276
Stat-Ease Inc	7372	4258
Stateco Financial Services Inc	6331	291
Statek Corp	3679	190
Stateline Ag Service Inc	4213	2535
Stateline Coop	5191	96
Stately Contractors Inc	1623	408
Stater Brothers Holdings Inc	6719	30
Stater Brothers Markets	5411	43
States Manufacturing Corp	3613	75
Statewide Electrical Contractors Inc	3669	197
Statewide Enterprises Inc	7381	215
Statewide Express Inc	4213	1256
Statewide Safety and Signs Inc	7359	136
Statewide Tax Recovery Inc	7322	148
Statewide Tire Distributors Inc	5014	22
Statewide Wholesale Inc	5033	48
Static Control Components Inc	3629	15

Company Name	SIC	Rank
Static Controls Corp	3625	200
Static Electric Co	1731	1448
Static Solutions Inc	3822	83
Static Technologies Corp	3822	87
Staticworx Inc	1752	13
Statimate Systems Inc	5734	427
Station 1 Internet Services Inc	7379	1386
Station Casinos Inc	7011	35
Station Holdings Inc	7999	24
Station Online Inc	7999	25
Station Technology LLC	7999	26
Station The Web Inc	7374	349
Stationary Power Services Inc	8711	420
Stationers Inc (Huntington West Virginia)	5112	5
Statistical Designs	7372	4884
Statistical Graphics Corp	7372	2643
Statistical Plastics Corp	3089	948
Statland Security Systems	7382	10
Staton Institute Inc	7389	2385
StatPac Inc	7372	1931
StatPoint LLC	7372	5058
STATS Inc	2731	204
StatSoft Inc	7372	1415
Statton Industries Inc	2511	84
Stature Electric Inc	3621	43
Staub Machine Company Inc	3599	1675
Stauble Machine and Tool Company Inc	3544	56
Staubli Corp	5084	192
Stauch Vetromile and Mitchell Advertising Inc	7311	1041
Stauffer Acquisition Corp	2752	828
Staunton Foods LLC	5149	169
Staurt Mill Capital Acquisition Partners	7389	1547
Stave Island LP	6719	154
Stavis Seafoods Inc	5146	3
Stavo Industries Inc	3569	148
Stavros Center For Independent Living Inc	8322	10
Stay In Front	7372	365
StayHealthy Inc	7379	474
StayinFront Inc	7372	297
Stayton Cooperative Telephone Company Inc	4813	331
StayWell Health Management Systems Inc	8099	17
STAZ Software Inc	7372	5152
STB Electrical Test Equipment	3825	303
Stc Aviation Inc	4581	46
Stc Inc	3677	54
Std Med Inc	3841	160
Std Precision Gear and Instrument Inc	3566	43
STE Electrical Systems Inc	1731	681
Steakley and Gilbert PC	8721	227
Steak-Out Franchising Inc	6794	52
Stealth Concealment Solutions Inc	1799	94
Stealth Ltd	1731	1900
Stealth Systems Inc	5063	518
StealthCom Solutions Inc	1731	2480
Steam Turbine Alternative Resources	3511	31
Steamatic Inc	6794	116
Steamboat Ski and Resort Corp	7999	55
Steamist Inc	3569	99
Steamworks Brewing Co	2082	23
Stearly's Motor Freight Inc	4213	2967
Stearns	3625	51
Stearns Bank NA	6021	78
Stearns Conrad and Schmidt Engineers Inc	8748	53
Stearns Financial Services Inc	6712	646
Stearns Packaging Corp	2841	16
Stearns Plumbing Inc	5074	187
Stearns Weaver Miller Weissler Alhadeff and Sitterson PA	8111	258
Stebbins Five Cos	8051	74
Stebco Products Corp	3199	8
Stec Enterprizes Inc	1731	1608
STEC Inc	3572	13
Steck Manufacturing Company Inc	3714	385
Steck-Vaughn Publishing Corp	2741	40
Ste-Del Services Inc	7359	221
Stedham Electronics Corp	3674	409
Steel and Alloy Utility Products Inc	3569	145
Steel and Machinery Transport	4213	1703
Steel and Pipe Supply Company Inc	5051	21
Steel Beach Productions Inc	7379	1042
Steel Cities Steels Inc	5051	157
Steel City Bolt and Screw LLC	3452	85
Steel City Corp	2678	18
Steel City Lighting Co	5063	939
Steel Craft Corporation of Hartford	3499	30
Steel Dust Recycling LLC	5093	173
Steel Dynamics Inc	3312	3
Steel Electric Products Company Inc	3644	43
Steel Engineers Inc	5051	103
Steel Etc Holding Co	5051	190
Steel Excel Inc	3577	128
Steel Fabricators LLC	5051	167
Steel Improvement and Forge Co	3724	15
Steel LLC	3441	35
Steel Master LLC	3535	122
Steel of West Virginia Inc	2439	5
Steel Partners Holdings LP	6712	298

Company Name	SIC	Rank
Steel Processing Inc	5093	157
Steel Products Corp	2821	174
Steel Products Corporation of Akron	3599	1898
Steel Related Industries Quality System Registrar Inc	8742	630
Steel Service Corp	3441	47
Steel Services Inc	5051	133
Steel Slitting Company Inc	7389	2185
Steel Solutions Inc	7372	4642
Steel Structures Technology Center Inc	8748	463
Steel Supply and Engineering Co	1791	19
Steel Supply Co	5051	271
Steel Tank and Fabricating Co	3443	100
Steel Technologies Inc	3316	3
Steel Transport Inc	4213	825
Steel Transport Inc	4213	1941
Steel Vault Corp	7373	930
Steel Ventures LLC	3312	66
Steel Warehouse Inc	4213	336
Steel Warehouse Quad City LLC	5051	286
Steel Works LLC	5051	366
Steel Yard Inc	5051	414
Steelcase Inc	2522	1
SteelCloud Inc	3571	179
Steelcote Manufacturing Co	2851	113
Steelcraft Inc	3599	2366
Steelcraft Manufacturing Co	3442	22
Steelcraft Tool Company Inc	3545	271
Steele and Freeman Inc	1542	340
Steele Plastics Inc	2221	44
Steele Realty and Investment Company Inc	6531	215
Steele Systems Inc	7372	2479
Steele Truck Center Inc	5511	1139
Steele Waseca Cooperative Electric	4911	537
Steelflex Electro Corp	3357	55
Steelhead Data LLC	7371	637
Steel-King Industries Inc	3441	50
Steelman Industries Inc	3567	64
Steelman Transportation Inc	4213	1112
Steelmaster Buildings Inc	5211	328
Steelpoint Capital Partners LP	6799	230
Steelscape Inc	3356	15
Steeltech Ltd	3325	35
Steelville Manufacturing Co	3599	300
Steelweld Equipment Co	3713	30
Steen Armament Research Company Inc	5091	87
Steenberg Homes Inc	5271	2
Steenhoek Implement Co	5083	193
Steeplechase Tool and Die Inc	3544	377
Steerforth Press LLC	2731	376
Stefanini Techteam	7379	69
Stefanini TechTeam Inc	7363	47
Steffen Publishing Inc	2711	380
Steffes Corp	3441	119
Stegall Metal Industries Inc	1711	47
Stegall Milling Company Inc	4213	2918
Stegeman and Kastner Inc	8741	283
Stegman Tool Company Inc	3369	28
Steimer And Company Inc	3549	113
Stein and Lubin LLP	8111	461
Stein and Partners	7311	300
Stein Garden and Gifts	5261	6
Stein Industries Inc	3679	407
Stein Mart Inc	5651	12
Stein Seal Co	3724	34
Stein Trending Branding Design LLC	8748	367
Steinbauer Associates Inc	6531	323
Steinbeck Brewing Co	2082	46
Steiner Corp	7213	1
Steiner Electric Co	5063	39
Steiner Electric Inc	1731	1140
Steiner Tractor Parts Inc	3523	206
Steinerfilm Inc	3675	19
Steinert Industries Inc	3559	490
Steinhafels Inc	5712	9
Steinhauser Inc	2752	998
Steinmetz Inc	2821	127
Stein's Inc	5169	99
Steinwall Properties LLC	3089	713
Steinway Musical Instruments Inc	3931	1
Steiny and Company Inc	1731	91
Stelbar Oil Corp	1311	234
Stelera Wireless LLC	4899	93
Stella and Dot	5944	18
Stella D' Oro Biscuit Company Inc	2052	16
Stella Golden Inc	5094	52
Stellar Business Bank	6022	693
Stellar Concepts Inc	7336	225
Stellar Distribution LLC	5531	35
Stellar Express Inc	4213	2385
Stellar Forge Products Inc	3544	693
Stellar Group Inc	1541	34
Stellar Industries Corp	3674	320
Stellar Industries Inc	3559	101
Stellar Materials Inc	3272	116
Stellar Micro Devices Inc	3671	23
Stellar Microelectronics Inc	5065	102
Stellar Mold and Tool Inc	3544	652
Stellar One Corp	3663	252
Stellar Precision Components Ltd	3599	357
Stellar Printing Inc	2759	166
Stellar Recognition Inc	3914	8

Company Name	SIC	Rank
Stellar Software Inc	7372	4885
Stellar Srkg Acquisition LLC	5013	274
Stellar Systems Inc	7371	1795
StellarOne Corp	6712	153
Stellartech Research Corp	8731	233
Stella's Kitchen And Bakery	2051	263
Stellent Inc	7372	363
Stellex Aerospace	3728	15
Stellos Electric Supply Inc	1731	653
Stelrema Corp	3089	441
Stelron Components Inc	3545	138
Stelter And Brinck Inc	3564	104
Stem Brothers Inc	5984	27
StemCells Inc	2836	79
Stemco Inc	3053	15
Stemco LLC	1731	2179
Stemmerich Inc	3559	335
Stempihar Brothers Distributing	4213	2537
Stems and Vines	5992	9
Sten Corp	3841	147
Stenerson Brothers Lumber Co	5211	59
Stenner Sales Inc	3561	127
Stenner USA Ltd	5084	900
Stenograph LLC	7371	457
Step Industries Inc	7361	260
Step Saver Inc	2741	288
STEP Tools Inc	7372	2274
Step2 Company LLC	3089	147
Stepan Co	2843	1
Stephan and Brady Inc	7311	249
Stephan Co	2844	87
Stephen A Manoogian Inc	3559	480
Stephen Chelbay Co	6411	106
Stephen Computer Services Inc	7372	3951
Stephen Douglas Plastics Inc	3089	547
Stephen L Gangi Commercial Printing Inc	2752	1567
Stephen Paul Audio Inc	3651	251
Stephens and Associates Advertising Inc	7311	789
Stephens and Michaels Associates Inc	7322	65
Stephens Carriers Inc	4213	2839
Stephens Electric Company Inc	1731	1356
Stephens Inc	6211	50
Stephens Machine Inc	3599	1508
Stephens Manufacturing Company Inc	3531	149
Stephens Media Group	2711	154
Stephens Pneumatics Inc	3443	168
Stephens Precision Inc	3469	378
Stephen's-Nu-Ad Inc	2752	1576
Stephenson Electric Co	1731	1036
Stephenson Equipment Inc	5082	80
Stephenson Printing Inc	2752	429
Stephenville Printing Company Inc	2752	1281
Stephenz Group Inc	7311	822
Stepone Systems LLC	7371	1442
Stepp Manufacturing Company Inc	3531	205
Stepper Equipment Inc	5049	144
Stepstone LLC	6799	105
Stepstone Solutions Inc	7372	4074
Steptoe and Johnson LLP	8111	67
Steren Electronics International LLC	3679	35
Stereo Lab Service Inc	7699	37
Stereographics Corp	3827	31
Stereoland	5731	108
Stereotaxis Inc	3841	79
Stereotypes Inc	5731	251
StereoVision Entertainment Inc	5731	277
Stericycle Inc	4959	1
Sterigenics International Inc	8099	22
Sterilchek Sterilizer Management Services	8734	187
Sterilite Corp	3089	58
STERIS Corp	3842	11
Sterling and Tucker	8721	190
Sterling Area Services Inc	8322	150
Sterling Bancorp (New York New York)	6712	182
Sterling Bancorporation Inc	6022	58
Sterling Bancshares Inc	6712	113
Sterling Bank and Trust FSB	6035	122
Sterling Bank (Montgomery Alabama)	6022	671
Sterling Blower Co	3535	80
Sterling BMW	5511	365
Sterling Boiler And Mechanical Inc	1711	5
Sterling Breen Crushing Inc	1429	10
Sterling Business Forms Inc	2761	26
Sterling C Sommer Inc	2752	609
Sterling Cabinets Inc	5031	411
Sterling Capital Management Co	6282	110
Sterling Chemicals Inc	2821	40
Sterling Clark Lurton Corp	2851	175
Sterling Commerce Inc	7372	89
Sterling Communications Inc	8743	84
Sterling Computer Consultants Inc	7379	1276
Sterling Computer Sales LLC	5734	311
Sterling Construction Company A Colorado Corp	1623	642
Sterling Construction Company Inc	1629	8
Sterling Creative	8743	266
Sterling Culturally Diversified Services Inc	7363	300
Sterling Cut Glass Company Inc	5023	77
Sterling Die and Engineering Inc	3544	598
Sterling Distributing Co	5182	31

Company Name	SIC	Rank
Sterling Electric Corp	5063	654
Sterling Electric Inc	3566	25
Sterling Engineering Corp	3599	288
Sterling Excavation Inc	1623	424
Sterling Express Ltd	4213	1973
Sterling Financial Corp	6712	76
Sterling Financial Investment Group Inc	6211	302
Sterling Finishing Inc	2796	72
Sterling Fluid Systems LLC (Indianapolis Indiana)	3561	36
Sterling Foods LLC	2051	36
Sterling Forest LLC	0811	4
Sterling Handling Systems Inc	3549	90
Sterling Healthcare	8741	91
Sterling Inc	3823	5
Sterling Infosystems Inc	7375	79
Sterling Investment Partners LP	6798	164
Sterling Jewelers Inc	5944	2
Sterling Lacquer Manufacturing Co	2851	97
Sterling Lumber and Investment Co	5211	98
Sterling Machine Company Inc	3599	613
Sterling Machinery Inc	3599	374
Sterling Manufacturing and Engineering Inc	3545	258
Sterling Manufacturing Company Inc	3089	1445
Sterling Medical Associates Inc	8099	44
Sterling Medical Products Inc	5047	154
Sterling Molded Products Inc	3089	1396
Sterling National Bank	6021	39
Sterling National Mortgage Company Inc	6162	69
Sterling Of Ohio Inc	5944	10
Sterling Office Systems	5734	370
Sterling Optical	5995	7
Sterling Paper Co	2657	39
Sterling Partners	6799	154
Sterling Pierce Company Inc	2789	95
Sterling Pipe and Tube Inc	3317	46
Sterling Press Inc	2732	49
Sterling Publishing Company Inc	2731	99
Sterling Rack Inc	2542	73
Sterling Resources Inc	6282	310
Sterling Savings Bank	6036	8
Sterling Scale Co	3596	19
Sterling Staffing Inc	8711	272
Sterling Sugars Inc	2061	7
Sterling Systems and Controls Inc	3625	238
Sterling Systems Sales Corp	3559	456
Sterling Transport Company Inc	4213	2361
Sterling Vision Kenoha Inc	5995	12
Sterling Vision Westminster Inc	5995	15
Sterling-Detroit Co	3569	241
Sterling-Rice Group Inc	7311	583
Sterlingwear Of Boston Inc	2311	17
Stern Agee	6282	16
Stern and Associates	8742	336
Stern and Stern Industries Inc	2221	31
Stern Brothers Plumbing Inc	5074	222
Stern Cardiovascular Center	8071	19
Stern/Leach Co	5094	28
Sterne Agee and Leach Inc	6211	280
Sterngold Dental LLC	3843	64
Stero Co	3589	117
Sterris Energy Systems Inc	5063	461
Stertil Alm Corp	3537	83
Sterwart and Stevenson	3563	31
Sterzing Food Co	2096	57
Stetron International Inc	3679	550
Stetson Convention Services Inc	7389	1177
Stetson Electric LLC	1731	964
Stettler Supply Co	5083	120
Stettner Inc	4213	3108
STEU Inc	3648	54
Steuben	3229	7
Steuben Foods Inc	2032	4
Steuby Manufacturing Co	3494	71
Steve Ford Music Inc	7389	1778
Steve Hopkins Inc	5511	653
Steve Jackson Games Inc	2731	76
Steve Kent Trucking Inc	4213	1910
Steve Klein Custom Builders	1521	80
Steve Madden Retail Inc	5661	11
Steve P Rados Inc	1622	19
Steve Rosenquist LLC	3569	301
Steve Rotfeld Productions Inc	7812	267
Steve Schollnick Advertising	7311	735
Steve Shannon Tire Company Inc	5014	33
Steve Skelton	7373	1165
Steven Charles Capital Ltd	6282	662
Steven E Douglas	7371	1856
Steven James Media Inc	2752	1705
Steven K Smith	1731	2481
Steven Madden Ltd	3144	1
Steven Roberts Original Deserts LLC	2051	18
Steven Scott Orchestra Inc	7929	6
Steven Scott Productions	7922	63
Steven Soemer	7378	176
Steven Willand Inc	5083	106
Steven-Robert Originals LLC	2052	29
Stevens and Layton Inc	1623	229
Stevens and Tate Inc	7311	695
Stevens Appliance Truck Co	3537	86
Stevens Aviation Inc	4581	21
Stevens Baron Communications Inc	7311	227

Company Name	SIC	Rank
Steven's Creek Buick Pontiac BMC	5511	299
Stevens Creek Software LLC	7371	1926
Stevens Decal Company Inc	2759	410
Stevens Desposole	7359	242
Stevens Electric Of Quincy Inc	1731	1629
Stevens Enterprises Inc	7359	192
Stevens Graphics Inc	2741	41
Stevens Group Inc	7372	3631
Stevens Inc	7311	846
Stevens Industries Inc	2531	11
Stevens Instrument Co	3825	329
Stevens Linen Associates Inc	2392	42
Stevens Manufacturing Company Inc	3599	1033
Stevens Office Interiors	5712	68
Stevens Painton Corp	1541	149
Stevens Point Brewery	2082	43
Stevens Sales Co	5065	593
Stevens Sausage Company Inc	2013	130
Stevens Technology LLC	3555	88
Stevens Transport Inc	4213	88
Stevens Travel Management Inc	4724	40
Stevens Trucking Co	4213	966
Stevensen and Neal Realtors	6531	183
Steven-Sharon Corp	3441	174
Stevenson Photo Color Company Inc	2796	17
Stevenson Tractor Inc	5082	193
Stever-Locke Industries Inc	3469	246
Steverson and Company Inc	7363	184
Steves Equipment Service Inc	5082	106
Steve's Plating Corp	2542	26
Steve's Wholesale Distributors Inc	5251	26
Stevies Inc	5139	22
Stevinson Automotive	5511	1241
Steward Carney Hospital Inc	2599	2
Steward Inc	3264	1
Steward Machine Company Inc	3566	26
Stewardship Financial Corp	6712	396
Stewart Acoustical Consultants	8999	147
Stewart Agency	8743	117
Stewart Builders Ltd	1771	4
Stewart EFI Texas LLC	3469	44
Stewart Electric Supply Inc	5063	565
Stewart Enterprises Inc	7261	2
Stewart Ergonomics Inc	3625	395
Stewart Filmscreen Corp	3861	28
Stewart Geo Technologies	8713	6
Stewart Graphics Inc	5112	52
Stewart Industries Inc (Seattle Washington)	3089	740
Stewart Information Services Corp	6361	8
Stewart Instrument Company Inc	5084	752
Stewart Manufacturing Company Inc	3599	326
Stewart Manufacturing LLC	3599	366
Stewart Mining Industries Inc	1442	45
Stewart Santa Fe Abstract Ltd	6541	21
Stewart Stone Inc	1422	34
Stewart Sutherland Inc	2671	30
Stewart Systems Inc	3556	57
Stewart Technologies Inc	7372	2730
Stewart Title Company of California Inc	6361	18
Stewart Title Company of Houston	6361	7
Stewart Title Guaranty Co	6361	9
Stewart Title of Louisiana	6541	22
Stewart Title of Pinellas Inc	6541	23
Stewart Tool Co	3545	103
Stewart's Cleaning Service LLC	7349	501
Stewart's Electrical Contractors Inc	1731	952
Stewarts Of America Inc	3552	33
Stewarts Private Blend Foods Inc	2095	43
Stewart's Restaurants Supply	6794	155
Stewart's Shops Corp	5411	183
Stewart-Taylor Co	2752	1016
Stf Services Inc	2731	229
STF Technologies Inc	7371	792
STI Automation Sensor Div	3829	338
STI Electronics Inc	3548	31
STI Group Inc	7373	601
Sti Holdings Inc	3715	12
Sti Inc	3613	150
Sti Management LLC	4813	566
STI Optronics Inc	8731	342
STI Tech Inc	7372	4017
Stibo Systems Inc	7372	3554
Stichler Products Inc	5145	31
Sticker Corp	3585	237
Sti-Co Industries Inc	3663	202
Stiefel Laboratories Inc	8731	46
Stiegler Company Inc	1731	972
Stiegler Wells Brunswick and Roth Inc	7311	680
Stifel Financial Corp	6211	57
Stifel Nicolaus and Company Inc	6211	194
Stifel Nicolaus Insurance Agency Inc	6331	209
Stiles Construction Co	1542	288
Stiles Corp	6552	62
Stiles Custom Metal Inc	3442	114
Stiles Enterprises Inc	5085	452
Stiles Machinery Inc	5084	20
Stiles Realty Co	6531	270
Stiles Truck Line Inc	4213	1388
Stiles Unlimited Inc	3089	1600
Stilian Electric Inc	1731	651
Still Current Development Inc	7371	846
Still River Systems Inc	5047	115
Still Transfer Company Inc	4213	2835

Company Name Index

Company Name	SIC	Rank
Still Waters Design/Build Group	1531	91
Stillwater Milling Co	2048	19
Stillwater Mining Co	1099	1
Stillwater Motor Company Inc	5511	407
Stillwater National Bank and Trust Co	6035	61
Stillwater Technologies Inc	3544	145
Stilsing Electric Inc	1731	793
Stilson/Die-Draulic	3537	81
Stimple and Ward Co	3621	108
Stimson Lumber Co	2421	2
Stine Enterprises Inc	5734	384
Stinehour Press	2759	383
Sting Surveillance LLC	7382	42
Stinger Medical	2522	32
Stinson Morrison Hecker LLP	8111	63
Stion Corp	3691	38
Stir Foods LLC	2032	28
Stirling And Associates Of Flager Inc	1731	1836
Stirling Properties Inc	6531	33
Stitch Wire Systems Corp	3678	72
Stitches Embroidery Inc	7389	1903
Stites and Harbison	8111	79
Stl Enterprises Inc	3728	83
Stl Office Solutions Inc	7363	239
STLtodaycom	7375	238
Stm Inc	3089	1740
Stm Manufacturing Inc	3544	212
STM Networks Inc	5045	92
STM Russell Manufacturing Co	3993	177
STMicroelectronics	3577	55
Stmicroelectronics (North America) Holding Inc	3674	89
Stobs Brothers Construction	1542	290
Stochos Inc	7379	1233
Stock Building Supply Inc	5031	1
Stock Components Systems Inc	2439	43
Stock Equipment Co	3532	15
Stock Media Corp	7336	257
Stock Transport Inc	4213	657
Stock Yard Bank and Trust Co	6022	727
Stockbridge Manufacturing Co	3451	137
Stocker Sand and Gravel Co	1442	72
Stockgrowers State Bank	6035	194
Stockmens Financial Corp	6712	488
Stockton Bates LLP	8721	408
Stockton Enterprises Inc	5087	141
Stockton Graham and Co	5046	185
Stockton Newspapers Inc	2711	67
Stockton Oil Co	5172	98
Stockton Rubber ManufacturingCoInc	3069	204
Stockton Tri-Industries Inc	3535	76
Stocktrans Inc	6289	31
Sto-Cote Products Inc	5169	161
Stoddard Imported Cars Inc	5511	720
Stoel Rives LLP	8111	91
Stoess Manor	5712	72
Stoffel Seals Corp	3089	438
Stoiber Electric Company Inc	1731	1097
Stok Software Inc	7373	1128
Stokes Dock Co	1799	113
Stokes Electric Co	5063	82
Stokes Electric Of Central Florida Inc	1731	1077
Stokes Electrical Service Inc	1731	1449
Stokes Fish Co	5146	43
Stokes Publishing Co	7372	3382
Stokley's Services Inc	1711	280
Stolar Partnership	8111	325
Stoll Metalcraft Inc	3444	124
Stolle Machinery Company LLC	3542	25
Stolt Parcel Tankers Inc	4412	31
Stolt-Nielsen Transportation Group Ltd	4412	3
Stoltz Enterprises Inc	7372	1141
Stoltz Management of Delaware Inc	6512	56
Stoltzfus Trailer Sales Inc	5561	14
Stone and Company Entertainment	7812	47
Stone and Simons Advertising Inc	7311	496
Stone and Ward Inc	7311	380
Stone and Webster Construction Inc	1542	116
Stone and Youngberg LLC	6211	95
Stone Appliances Inc	5064	53
Stone Belt Freight Lines Inc	4213	1359
Stone Brewing Co	2082	44
Stone Bridge Press	2731	185
Stone Brook	6513	17
Stone Carlie and Company LLC	8721	12
Stone Center Of Indiana Inc	5032	139
Stone City Attractions Inc	7922	92
Stone City Bank of Bedford Indiana	6022	756
Stone Coffman Company LLC	5032	137
Stone Construction Equipment Inc	3531	53
Stone County Garment Inc	2325	16
Stone Design Corp	7372	3066
Stone Electric Company Inc	1731	1705
Stone Hill Contracting Company Inc	1629	84
Stone Hill Wine Company Inc	2084	40
Stone Mountain Accessories Inc	3171	4
Stone Mountain Chrysler Jeep Dodge	5511	644
Stone Mountain Contracting Inc	1623	505
Stone Mountain Tool Inc	3599	1562
Stone Plastics Inc	3089	759
Stone Point Capital	6799	131
Stone Rudolph and Henry CPA	8721	187
Stone Soap Company Inc	2841	24
Stone Street Capital LLC	7389	1010

Company Name	SIC	Rank
Stone Technologies Corp	3699	294
Stone Technologies Inc	7373	517
Stone Timber River LLC	7372	1444
Stoneage Inc	3589	144
Stonebranch Inc	7371	333
Stonebridge Builders Inc	1521	74
Stonebridge Press Inc	2711	503
Stonebridge Technologies Inc	7372	545
Stonebridge Technologies Oklahoma	7373	377
Stonecipher Corp	1731	1433
Stone-Circle Underground Inc	1623	675
Stonecraft Inc	3281	52
StoneEagle Insurance Systems Inc	7372	2791
Stonegate Bank	6022	194
StoneGate Transport	4213	2289
Stonehenge Partners	6799	59
Stonehouse Building Products LLC	3251	14
Stonehouse Marketing Services LLC	3089	368
Stoneman Avenue Corp	5015	37
StoneMor Partners LP	6553	1
Stoner Bunting Advertising	7311	301
Stoneridge Control Devices Inc	3714	73
Stoneridge Electronics Inc	3714	62
Stoneridge Inc	3714	51
Stones Inc	5211	32
Stonesoft Inc	7379	83
StoneTech Professional Inc	2899	171
Stonewall Cable Inc	3357	72
Stonewall Kitchen LLC	2033	49
Stonewall Materials Inc	1411	15
Stonewall Products Inc	5032	97
Stoneway Electric Supply Co	5063	70
Stoney Creek Roadhouse	7389	1399
Stonhard Inc	3444	48
Stonington Cooperative Grain Co	5153	107
Stonington Insurance Co	6411	129
Stonington Partners Inc	6211	251
Stony Apparel Corp	2339	28
Stony Point Electronics Inc	3679	720
Stoody Co	3548	1
Stopka and Associates	8742	406
Stopol Inc	5084	140
Storage Battery Systems Inc	3691	19
Storage Control Systems Inc	3829	463
Storage Engine Inc	3572	85
Storage Inc	7371	22
Storage International Inc	8741	111
Storage Machine	3599	1375
Storage Solutions Inc	5046	12
Storandt Pann Margolis Inc	7311	327
Storbase Corp	7379	1622
Storch Products Company Inc	3695	135
Storck of the Americas Inc	2066	23
Store and Haul Inc	4214	31
Store Kraft Manufacturing Co	2542	13
Store Supply Warehouse LLC	5046	80
StoreBoard Media LLC	7311	772
Stored Energy Systems A LLC	3679	376
StoredIQ Inc (Austin Texas)	5045	227
StorePerform Technologies Inc	7372	802
Stores Online International Inc	5961	74
StoresOnlinecom Inc	7376	8
Storewide Delivery Company Inc	4213	2302
Storey Publishing LLC	2731	105
Storey Trucking Company Inc	4213	1452
Storflex Fixture Corp	3585	103
Storis Inc	7371	504
Stork Climax Research Services Inc	8711	534
Stork East-West Technology Corp	8734	130
Stork Fabricators Inc	3565	74
Stork H and E Turbo Blading Inc	3511	20
Stork Veco International Inc	3577	76
Storm Cat Energy Corp	1311	178
Storm Communications	1731	2434
Storm Crankshaft Grinding And Welding Corp	7389	2470
Storm Management Inc	3523	63
Storm Products Inc	3949	69
Storm Ridge South LLC	7363	381
Storm Smart Building Systems	1521	111
Stormans Inc	5411	95
Storming Media LLC	5199	23
Stormtech LLC	3589	186
Stormwise Concepts Inc	4813	401
Storopack Inc	3089	288
Storr Office Environments Inc	7389	226
Storr Office Environments of Florida Inc	7389	328
Storsoft Technology Corp	7379	1224
Story Construction Co	1542	251
Story Electrical Service Inc	1731	1972
Story Oldsmobile Inc	5511	408
Story Teller Too LLC	5192	43
Storyopolis	5942	29
Story-Wright Inc	5112	69
Stottler Stagg and Associates Architects Engineers Planners Inc	8712	248
Stoudt Brewing Co	2082	66
Stoudt Co	6799	304
Stoughton Printing Co	2752	1141
Stoughton Trucking Inc	4213	1448
Stouse Inc	2752	177
Stout Industries Inc	3993	72
Stout's Cider Mill	2099	373

Company Name	SIC	Rank
Stow Co	2511	58
Stowe Woodward AG	3069	194
Stowers Machinery Corp	5082	16
Stowers Manufacturing Company Inc	3444	300
Stow's Office Furniture Inc	5021	120
Stoyles Printing Co	2754	30
Stp Bindery Services Inc	2789	94
STR Holdings Inc	3083	5
Stracon Inc	3699	226
Strada Architecture LLC	8712	312
Strada Capital Corp	7352	17
Straddick Electric and Systems Inc	1731	1450
Stradley Ronon Stevens and Young	8111	158
Strafford Technology Inc	7371	1923
Strahl and Pitsch Inc	2842	111
Straight Cable And Tower Service Corp	4841	112
Straight Line Construction Inc	1623	109
Straight River Cable Inc	3643	137
Straightline International Inc	7311	727
Strain Measurement Devices Inc	3829	238
Strainsense Enterprises Inc	3629	115
Strainsert Co	3829	244
Straits Steel And Wire Co	3479	52
Stranco Inc	4213	2594
Strand Associates Inc	8711	48
Strand Hunt Construction Inc	1542	268
Strand Inc	5093	207
Strandberg Engineering Labs	3625	152
Strands Incorporated A Delaware Corp	7371	855
Strasburger and Price LLP	8111	84
Strata Design Inc	2434	58
Strata Inc	5065	68
Strata Marketing Inc	7371	604
Strata Technologies	3629	81
Stratacache	7372	2180
StrataCare Inc	7372	501
Strataglass LLC	3081	155
Stratapult Studios	7319	24
Stratasoft Inc	7372	2181
Stratasys Inc	3577	92
Stratatech Group LLC	5734	437
StrataVia Corp	7371	403
Stratco Inc	3533	85
Stratedge Corp	3674	315
Strategic Alliance Group	7389	1437
Strategic Analysis Inc	8732	92
Strategic Business Solutions Inc	7371	1182
Strategic Business Systems of Virginia Inc	7373	179
Strategic Capital Resources Inc	6531	390
Strategic Data and Telecom Inc	7372	3745
Strategic Data Systems	7373	375
Strategic Decisions Group	8742	476
Strategic Diagnostics Inc	2899	94
Strategic Distribution Inc	5049	7
Strategic Enterprise Technology Inc	7379	1428
Strategic Equipment and Supply Corp	5046	1
Strategic Equity Group Inc	8748	165
Strategic Financial Designs Inc	6282	547
Strategic Fixed Income LP	6282	567
Strategic Hotel Capital Inc	6798	103
Strategic Industries LLC	3724	11
Strategic Information Group Inc	7379	782
Strategic Insurance Software LLC	7372	1912
Strategic Investment Group	6282	208
Strategic Link Consulting Inc	7373	785
Strategic Logistics Staffing LLC (Jenkintown Pennsylvania)	7363	308
Strategic Management Group Inc	7372	2078
Strategic Market Solutions Inc	7331	242
Strategic Marketing and Media	7311	842
Strategic Minerals Corp	3339	10
Strategic Outsourcing Inc	8741	41
Strategic Partners Inc	2326	11
Strategic Power Systems Inc	8711	582
Strategic Products and Services	7373	72
Strategic Products Inc	3631	13
Strategic Reporting Systems Inc	5734	305
Strategic Resources International Inc	7375	181
Strategic Software Technologies Inc	7372	5084
Strategic Solutions Inc	5734	309
Strategic Staffing Solutions LC	7371	91
Strategic Support Systems Inc	7371	1543
Strategic Systems Inc	8748	207
Strategic Value Partners LLC	6733	13
Strategic Vision Inc	8732	88
Strategies A Marketing Communications Corp	8743	185
Strategies Stern International LLC	7381	249
Strategy 7 Corp	5734	252
Strategy Electronics Inc	3672	350
Strategy XXI Group Ltd	8743	30
Stratford Advisory Group Inc	6282	326
Stratford Financial Group Ltd	6159	97
Stratford Homes LP	2452	49
Stratford Software Inc	7372	2495
Stratham Tire Inc	5531	22
Strathmore Co	2752	462
Strathmore Press Inc	2752	213
Strathmore Products Inc	2851	77
Stratify Inc	7372	1181
Stratix Corp	2671	46
Straton Industries Inc	7629	23
Stratos International Inc	3674	120

Company Name	SIC	Rank
Stratos Offshore Services Co	4841	96
Stratos Optical Technologies	3679	19
Stratos Product Development LLC	8711	535
Stratosphere Corp	7011	24
Strattec Security Corp	3714	85
Stratton Corp	7011	54
Stratton Monthly Dividend Shares Inc	6722	239
Stratton Seed Co	5191	70
Stratus Media Group Inc	7929	11
Stratus Properties Inc	6552	259
Stratus Technologies Inc	7371	23
Stratus Technology Services LLC	7361	233
Straub Clinic and Hospital Inc	8062	48
Straub Design Co	3559	222
Straub Honda Hyundai	5511	1205
Straub International Inc	5083	21
Straube Associates Inc	5065	709
Straub's Inventory Control Inc	7389	2322
Straub's Markets	5411	234
Straughn Computer Management Inc	7373	1177
Straus Systems Inc	1711	187
Strauss Acquisition Corp	5072	115
Strauss and Troy	8111	306
Strauss Discount Auto	5531	14
Strauss Engineering Company Inc	3089	901
Strauss Feeds LLC	2048	107
Strauss Veal Feeds Inc	2048	61
Strayer Education Inc	8221	6
Strayer University Inc	8221	4
StrayLight Corp	7372	4442
Stream Cos	7311	414
Stream Energy	4931	39
Stream Global Services Inc	7363	21
Streambase Systems Inc	7371	1018
Streambox Inc	7371	840
Streamfeeder LLC	3579	7
Streaming Media Inc	7375	76
Streaming21 Inc (San Jose California)	3669	74
Streamlight Inc	3648	15
Streamline Design and Silkscreen Inc	2329	31
Streamline Electronics Manufacturing Inc	3672	320
Streamline Health Solutions Inc	7373	291
Streamline Inc	7331	274
Streamline Plastics Company Inc	3951	6
Streamline Wireless Inc	4812	79
Streamlite Inc	7331	45
Streams Online Media Development Corp	7371	1662
Streator Industrial Handling Inc	3443	80
Streck Inc	2835	17
Street Glow Inc	3647	16
Street Legal Industries Inc	7389	1218
Street Software Technology Inc	7375	276
StreetdeliveryCom Inc	4813	237
Streeter Associates Inc	1522	12
Streeter Printing and Graphics Inc	2752	1483
Streff Electric Inc	1731	1027
Streich Brothers Inc	3599	629
Streimer Sheet Metal Works Inc	1761	12
Strem Chemicals Inc	2819	81
Stremicks Heritage Foods LLC	2026	15
Stress Con Inc	5051	343
Stresscon Corp	3272	69
Stress-Tek Inc	3545	136
Stretch Devices Inc	3552	39
Stretch Forming Corp	3714	391
Stretchtape Inc	2672	68
Stribling Equipment LLC	5082	46
Strick Corp	3715	5
Strickland Nick Quick Print Inc	2752	1461
Strickland Packaging Company Inc	7389	800
Strictly Business Computer Systems Inc	5045	269
Stride Contractors Inc	7363	355
Stride Rite Corp	3149	12
Stride Rite Sourcing International Inc	3149	5
Stride Tool Inc	3423	42
Strieter Motor Co	5511	887
Strike Construction LLC	1623	30
Strike Force Maintenance Corp	5085	162
Strike Technology Inc	3679	507
Strikeforce Bowling LLC	3949	162
Strine Printing Company Inc	2752	98
String Real Estate Information Services	8999	176
Stringer Construction Company LLC	1623	747
Stringer Industries Inc	3553	43
Stringer's Oilfield Service	4213	1067
Stringfellow Lumber Co	5031	75
Strings Inc	6794	37
Striping Technology LP	1611	37
Stripmatic Products Inc	3469	283
Strippit Inc	3542	7
Stritt and Priebe Inc	5085	234
Strobel Industries Inc	3523	265
Strober Organization Inc	5211	29
Strobic Air Corp	3564	32
Stroh Die Casting Company Inc	3363	17
Stroheim and Romann Inc	5198	6
Strohl Systems Group Inc	7372	1114
Strohmeyer and Arpe Co	5141	216
Strohwig Industries Inc	3321	25
Strom Manufacturing	3599	1471
Stromag Inc	3568	77
Stroman Beauty Supply Inc	5087	147
Stromberg LLC	7371	482
Stromberg Sheet Metal Works Inc	1711	16
Stromberg Tool and Machine Company Inc	3469	339
Stron International Inc	8742	261
Strong Audiovisual Inc	2741	84
Strong Built Inc	3499	112
Strong Environmental Inc	4953	147
Strong Forge and Fabrication LLC	3599	1956
Strong Group Inc	3993	126
Strong Inc	5511	1044
Strong Industries Inc	3949	110
Strong Software Inc	7372	4886
Strong Travel Services	4724	137
StrongGo LLC	2821	124
Stronghold Engineering Inc	8711	556
Strongmail Systems Inc	7372	735
Strongwell Corp	3089	178
Stroock and Stroock and Lavan	8111	42
Strossner's Bakery Inc	5461	20
Stroud Diving and Hydrography Div	7389	2291
Stroud Mall LLC	6531	236
Stroudsburg Electric Supply Company Inc	5063	211
Strouse Electric Company Inc	1731	2049
Stroz Friedberg LLC	7373	301
Strube Inc	5088	113
Structural	8711	223
Structural Analysis Inc	7372	3952
Structural Associates Inc	1541	153
Structural Component Systems Inc	2439	20
Structural Composites Industries	3443	142
Structural Concepts Corp	2541	5
Structural Data Inc	7372	4887
Structural Industries Inc	2499	21
Structural Integrity Associates Inc	8711	660
Structural Research and Analysis Corp	7334	16
Structural Steel Services Inc	3441	25
Structural Systems Inc	2452	17
Structure Interactive	7311	392
Structure Medical LLC	3842	141
Structure Tone Organization	1542	4
Structurecast	3272	106
Structured Cable Products Inc	5063	528
Structured Communication Systems Inc	5065	345
Structured Finance Advisors Inc	6282	523
Structured Healthcare Management Inc	7372	3400
Structured Information Inc	8743	285
Structured Programming Services Inc	7371	853
Structured Software Systems Inc	7372	3393
Struktol Company Of America	2869	66
Strunk Brothers Inc	5084	605
Struve Distributing Company Inc	5046	55
Stryker Corp	3841	6
Stryker Endoscopy	3841	76
Stryker Howmedica Osteonics	3842	6
Stryker Medical	2599	5
Stryker Puerto Rico Ltd	3841	44
Stryker Sustainability Solutions	3841	66
Stryker Winery	2084	134
Stry-Lenkoff Company LLC	2731	177
Sts Instruments Inc	3825	249
STS LLC	1623	13
Sts Telecom LLC	4813	332
STSN Inc	7375	37
Stt Video Partners LP	4841	75
Stuart C Irby Co	5063	31
Stuart Electric Supply Inc	5063	896
Stuart Flooring Corp	2426	17
Stuart M Perry Inc	1422	11
Stuart Manufacturing Inc	3679	171
Stuart Maue Mitchell and James Ltd	8721	128
Stuart Newman Associates	8743	166
Stuart Steel Protection Corp	3599	1775
Stuart Web Inc	2752	834
Stuart's Household Furn Moving and Storage	4213	2303
Stuart's of Eldorado Inc	5943	38
Stuarts' Petroleum Corp	5171	43
Stubbins Associates Inc	8712	98
Stubhub Inc	7999	45
Stuckey Diamonds Inc	5094	21
Stuckey's Corp	5812	438
Studdard Moving and Storage	4213	2545
Student Advantage Inc	7374	70
Student Book Corp	5942	23
Student Broadcasting Inc	4832	152
Student Lifeline Inc	2741	314
Student Loan Corp	6141	10
Student Transportation of America Inc	4151	4
Students Publications Inc	2711	642
Studeo Inc	7311	637
Studeo Interactive Direct	8742	177
Studio 13	7311	690
Studio B Productions Inc	7389	915
Studio Bard Inc	7819	92
Studio Imports Limited Inc	5137	31
Studio Magnetics Company Inc	3695	59
Studio Melizo	7379	1237
Studio North Inc	7336	71
Studio One Media Inc	2752	1833
Studio One Midwest Inc	3999	208
Studio Productions Inc	8249	14
Studio Red Inc	8711	605
Studio Visia Inc	7372	2830
STUDIOS Architecture	8712	40
Studios at Las Colinas Ltd	7812	124
Studley Inc	6531	266
Studley Press Inc	2752	1117
Study Dog	3695	166
Study Island LLC	8748	38
Stueber Beverages Inc	2086	133
Stuebing Automatic Machine Company Inc	3469	323
Stuedle Spears and Francke PSC	8721	204
Stuffwholesale	5094	93
Stull and Lee Inc	8712	123
Stull Closure Technologies	3089	51
Stull Enterprises Inc	5083	38
Stuller Inc	5094	17
Stulmaker Kohn and Richardson LLP	8721	206
Stulz Investment Corporation Of America	3822	17
Stulz-Sickles Steel Company Inc	5051	325
StumbleUpon	7379	648
Stump Equipment Co	5046	327
Stump Printing Company Inc	5199	40
Stumpf Motor Company Inc	5511	231
Stupp Bridge Co	3441	19
Stupp Corp	3317	13
Sturdy Grinding And Machining Inc	3599	2228
Sturdy Memorial Hospital Inc	8062	145
Sturdy Oil Company Inc	5172	25
Sturges and Word Communications and Design Inc	8743	260
Sturges Electronics Products Company Inc	3679	420
Sturges Manufacturing Company Inc	2241	23
Sturgis Bancorp Inc	6021	247
Sturgis Falls Braodcasting	4832	258
Sturgis Molded Products Co	3089	102
Sturgis Tool And Die Inc	3544	626
Sturm Ruger and Company Inc	3489	9
Sturman Industries Inc	8711	573
Sturtevant Inc	3559	277
Stusser Electric Co	5063	68
Stutts Corporation Inc	1731	850
Stutz Candy Co	2064	91
STV Architects	8712	26
STV Environmental	8711	49
STV Group Inc	8711	84
STW Composites Inc	3721	38
Styer Transportation Co	4213	1492
Style Craft Prototype Inc	3465	67
Stylecraft Home Collection Inc	3645	16
Stylefish Inc	7379	1507
Style-Line Furn Inc	2512	56
Stylemark Inc	5099	115
Styles A E Manufacturing Company Inc	5087	161
Stylex Inc	2522	31
Styline Transportation Inc	4213	928
Stylmark Inc	2542	20
Stylors Inc	2844	138
Styrene Products Inc	2865	25
Styro Tek Inc	2821	68
Styrotech Inc	3086	107
Su America Inc	5084	755
Su Printing Services	2752	1440
Suarez Corporation Industries	7311	37
Suarez Housing Corp	6552	135
Sub Pop Ltd	8999	157
Sub Source Inc	7389	1652
Sub Station Specialists	1731	1793
Sub Systems Inc	7372	5037
Sub Zero Transportation Inc	4213	2217
Suba Manufacturing Inc	2541	54
Subaru of America Inc	5012	10
Subaru Of Indiana Automotive Inc	3711	32
SubCom	3669	69
Subcon Tool/Accutool Machine Group Inc	3599	658
Subconn Inc	5051	399
Suben Dougherty Partnership	7389	2211
Subjex Corp	7389	2523
Sublette Cooperative Inc	5153	118
Subon Data Co	5044	51
Subsea Video Systems Inc	3861	127
Substation K Inc	7812	265
Subsystem Technologies Inc	7373	199
Subtle Impressions Inc	2759	457
Sub-Tronics Inc	3677	84
Suburban Cadilac Buick Inc	5511	848
Suburban Chevrolet Cadillac Ann Arbor	5511	838
Suburban Contract Cleaning Inc	7349	53
Suburban Credit Corporation Of Va Inc	7322	96
Suburban Electric Supply Inc	5063	1101
Suburban Electrical Engineers/ Contractors Inc	1731	312
Suburban Exterminating Service Inc	7342	41
Suburban Grading and Utilities Inc (Norfolk Virginia)	1623	130
Suburban Grinding Co	7389	2051
Suburban Hospital Integrated Physician Service LLC	7389	1178
Suburban Journal Newspapers	2711	38
Suburban Journals	2711	456
Suburban Machine Company Inc	3599	1073

Company Name	SIC	Rank	Company Name	SIC	Rank	Company Name	SIC	Rank
Suburban Mailing Services Inc	7331	174	Sullivan Manufacturing Corp	3599	1744	Summit Northstar Inc	5072	163
Suburban Manufacturing Co	3599	1023	Sullivan Mechanical Contractors Inc	1711	199	Summit Packaging Systems Inc	3499	29
Suburban Marble and Granite Inc	5032	84	Sullivan Paper Company Inc	2679	18	Summit Pipeline Inc	1623	472
Suburban Materials Co	5031	399	Sullivan Screen Print Company Inc	2759	459	Summit Plastic Co	3081	84
Suburban Metal Products Inc	3599	2170	Sullivan-Palatek Inc	3563	23	Summit Plastic Molding Inc	3089	1079
Suburban Newspapers Inc	2711	595	Sullivans	5199	20	Summit Polymers Inc	3089	91
Suburban Oil Company Inc	4213	996	Sully and Son Hydraulics Inc	5084	728	Summit Press Inc (Fort Worth Texas)	2752	775
Suburban Pipeline Company Inc	1623	96	Sully Transport Inc	4213	2681	Summit Primary Care PLLC	7389	1935
Suburban Plastics Co	3089	258	Sulphur Carriers Inc	4412	7	Summit Private Investments	6282	479
Suburban Plumbing Supply Co	5074	22	Sulphur Electric Company Inc	1731	479	Summit Products Inc	3944	13
Suburban Press Inc	2752	1239	Sulzer Chemtech USA Inc	3441	20	Summit Pump Inc	5084	673
Suburban Propane LP	5984	5	Sulzer Machine and Manufacturing Inc	3599	962	Summit Research Associates Inc	8999	186
Suburban Propane Partners LP	5999	9	Sulzer Process Pumps Inc (Easley South Carolina)	3561	49	Summit Rubber Company Inc	3069	181
Suburban Publishing Corp	2711	522				Summit Sales Inc	5074	189
Suburban Publishing Inc	2721	468	Sulzer Pumps Inc (Brookshire Texas)	3594	9	Summit Software Co	7372	2591
Suburban Software Systems Inc	5045	835	Suma Distributors LLC	5065	950	Summit Software Inc	7372	4392
Suburban Surgical Co	3821	8	Sumaria Systems Inc	7373	77	Summit Sportswear Inc	7389	870
Suburban Tool and Die Company Inc	3544	418	Sumatech Inc	3599	570	Summit State Bank	6022	380
Suburban Water Systems	4941	25	Sumatron Inc	3829	523	Summit Tech Consulting	8748	243
Subuthi Overseas Inc	7371	1151	Sumer Inc	5065	611	Summit Technologies Inc	7373	324
Subway Restaurants	5812	3	Sumerset Acquisition LLC	3732	52	Summit Tool Co	3423	43
Suby Von Haden and Associates SC	8721	258	Sumida America Components Inc	3679	154	Summit Trailer Sales Inc	3715	47
SubZero Constructors Inc	1541	253	Sumitomo Corporation of America	3679	40	Summit Underground Companies Inc	1623	524
Sub-Zero Inc	3632	2	Sumitomo Cryogenics of America Inc	3823	108	Summitek Inc	5047	265
Sucampo Pharmaceuticals Inc	2834	168	Sumitomo Electric Light Wave	3827	10	Summitek Instruments Inc	3825	151
Succeed Corp	7379	283	Sumitomo Electric USA Inc	3577	282	Summits 7 Inc	5999	177
Success Communications Group	7319	22	Sumitomo Electric Wintec America Inc	3496	46	Summitt Molding and Engineering Inc	3089	1731
Success Printing and Mailing Inc	2752	1142	Sumitomo Electric Wiring Systems Inc	3714	52	Summitt Publishing Co	2721	345
Success Projects Inc	8748	267	Sumitomo Heavy Industries (USA) Inc	3565	4	Summitville Tiles Inc	3253	4
Successabilities Inc	8721	365	Sumitomo Machinery Corporation Of America	5063	314	SummitWorks Technologies Inc	7371	78
SuccessFactors Inc	7372	240				Summore Plastics Inc	3089	1618
Successfulcom	7319	166	Sumiton Machine Inc	7692	29	Sumner Communications Inc	2721	104
Successories Inc	5999	36	Summa Health System	8062	113	Sumter Coatings Inc	2821	119
Su-Dan Co	3465	38	Summa Holdings Inc	3441	233	Sumter Electric Cooperative Inc	4911	210
Sudbury Transportation Inc	4213	2962	Summary Systems Inc	3663	363	Sumter Machinery Co	5085	412
Sud-Chemie Inc	2891	7	Summatec Computer Corp	3572	82	Sumter Packaging Corp	2653	66
Suddath Cos	4213	147	Summation Technology LLC	3669	210	Sumter Textile Machinery	5046	384
Suddath International	4213	1182	Summer Infant Inc	3999	17	Sumter Utilities Inc	1731	307
Sudden Printing Inc	2752	567	Summer Street Press LLC	2731	329	SumTotal Systems Inc	7389	203
Suddenlink Communications	4899	7	Summerlot Engineered Products Inc	5051	444	Sun and Skin Care Research Inc	2844	66
Sudenga Industries Inc	3523	43	Summerour Lamps	5023	206	Sun Automation Inc	3554	9
Sudhko Inc	7371	426	Summers Fuel Inc	5052	6	Sun Badge Co	3999	175
Sudler and Hennessey	7311	74	Summers Rubber Co	5085	194	Sun Bancorp Inc	6712	138
Sudmo North America Inc	5085	377	Summers-Taylor Inc	1611	81	Sun Belt Transportation Inc	4213	1757
Sud's Motor Car Company Inc	5511	1026	Summerville Communications Inc	2711	818	Sun Belt Water Inc	4941	58
Suel Printing Company Inc	2711	679	Summerville Ford Mercury Inc	5511	979	Sun Builders Co	1541	141
Sue-Lynn Textiles Inc	2251	11	Summit Aviation	2741	406	Sun Capital Partners Inc	6722	74
Sues Young and Brown Inc	5064	24	Summit Aviation Inc	5088	45	Sun Chemical Corp	2893	1
Suffield Oxygen Sales Inc	7352	33	Summit Bancshares Inc (Oakland California)	6712	632	Sun Coast Calamari Inc	2092	38
Suffolk Bancorp	6712	223				Sun Coast Media Group Inc	2711	276
Suffolk Capital Management	6282	426	Summit Bank and Trust	6022	735	Sun Coast Merchandise Corp	5199	27
Suffolk Cement Products Inc	4213	559	Summit Bank (Oakland California)	6022	436	Sun Coast Resources Inc	4213	745
Suffolk Construction Company Inc	1542	15	Summit Brands	2899	208	Sun Coast Underground Utility Construction Corp	1623	291
Suffolk County National Bank	6021	76	Summit Brewing Co	2082	47			
Suffolk Iron Works Inc	5084	497	Summit Brokerage Services Inc	6211	362	Sun Communication Technologies Inc	5731	126
Suffolk Life Newspapers	2711	371	Summit Builders Construction Co	1541	159	Sun Communities Inc	6798	120
Sugar Beach Interiors Inc	7389	1767	Summit Building Services	7349	434	Sun Construction and Design Services Inc	1541	268
Sugar Cane Growers Cooperative Of Florida	2061	6	Summit Catalog Co	2741	446			
			Summit Chemical Co	2879	49	Sun Devil Fire Equipment Inc	5999	91
Sugar Creek Designs Inc	2396	27	Summit Childrens Residence	8361	90	Sun Dial and Panel Corp	3812	158
Sugar Creek Foods International Inc	2024	58	Summit City Chevrolet	5511	916	Sun Drop Bottling Company Of Concord	5149	179
Sugar Creek Packing Co	2013	32	Summit City Electric Company Inc	1731	2233			
Sugar Foods Corp	5149	49	Summit Construction Company Inc	1542	350	Sun Eagle Corp	1542	214
Sugar Hill Records Inc	6794	126	Summit Corporate Car Inc	4899	213	Sun Elect	1731	2520
Sugar House Van Lines	4213	3131	Summit Corporation Of America	3471	57	Sun Electric Inc	1731	1434
Sugar Jeanerette Company Inc	2061	14	Summit Credit Services Inc	7322	188	Sun Engineering Inc	3599	893
Sugar Loaf Quarries Inc	3281	45	Summit Design Inc (Burlington Massachusetts)	5045	824	Sun Express Inc	4213	2238
Sugar Plum Inc	8322	244				Sun Fab Industrial Contracting Inc	2911	59
Sugar Services Corp	4214	34	Summit Document Services Of Atlanta LLC	7334	65	Sun Gro Horticulture Inc	2873	4
Sugar Steel Corp	5051	383				Sun Groves Inc	5961	177
Sugar Vermont Maple Company Inc	2099	220	Summit Electric Inc	1731	1295	Sun Health Medison Inc	6324	127
Sugarcreek Cartage Company Inc	4213	2428	Summit Electric Supply	5065	54	Sun Healthcare Group Inc	8051	4
Sugarloaf Mountain Works Inc	8742	384	Summit Electric Supply Inc	5063	25	Sun Hydraulics Corp	3499	10
Sugaro Corp	3599	2144	Summit Electrical Construction Inc	1731	987	Sun Inc	2752	339
Sugartown Worldwide Inc	2339	25	Summit Electrical Contractors Inc	1731	725	Sun Inventory Company Inc	7389	1921
Sugino Corp	5085	230	Summit Electronics Corp	5065	237	Sun Islands Hawaii	4725	44
Sugiyo USA Inc	2092	47	Summit Energy Services Inc	7389	22	Sun Lakes Construction Company Inc	1521	40
Sugo Music Co	3652	23	Summit Engineering Corp	8711	472	Sun Lakes of Robson Communities	6552	17
Suhaimi Inc	5063	751	Summit Equipment Inc	3559	430	Sun Life Assurance Company of Canada US	6311	34
Suhner Manufacturing Inc	5084	86	Summit Filter Corp	3569	172			
Suhrco Residential Properties	6531	124	Summit Financial Group Inc	6712	239	Sun Litho Print Inc	2752	1719
Suite 224 Internet	7373	779	Summit Financial Services Group Inc	6211	246	Sun Lithographing And Printing Co	2752	586
Suite Solutions Inc	7372	3499	Summit Foundry Systems Inc	3559	289	Sun Management Inc	5734	323
Suite Sounds Inc	5731	267	Summit Funding Group Inc	6159	82	Sun Marble At Fresno Inc	5032	200
Suit-Kote Corp	2951	6	Summit Gear Inc	3949	178	Sun Media Productions	7389	815
Suitt Construction Company Inc	1542	21	Summit Graphics Inc	2789	37	Sun Microstamping Technologies	3089	874
Sujac Sewing Contractors	7389	2289	Summit Group	8748	152	Sun Moon Star	5045	948
Sukup Manufacturing Co	3523	33	Summit Habitats Inc	1521	171	Sun Mountain Sports Inc	3949	112
Sukut Construction Inc	1794	29	Summit Hotel Properties Inc	6798	156	Sun National Bank	6029	8
Sullair Corp	3563	10	Summit Imaging Products LLC	3955	13	Sun News Inc	2711	536
Sullens Transport LLC	4213	2596	Summit Import Corp	5141	172	Sun News (Myrtle Beach South Carolina)	2711	220
Sullins Electronics Corp	3643	67	Summit Inspection Services Inc	7389	1060			
Sullivan and Cromwell LLP	8111	87	Summit Laboratories Inc	2844	99	Sun Newspapers Of Lincoln Inc	2791	34
Sullivan Brothers Inc	1742	9	Summit Logistics International Inc	4491	4	Sun Nuclear Corp	3829	151
Sullivan Corp	7389	2212	Summit Lubricants Inc	2911	58	Sun Optics	5048	21
Sullivan Corp (Noblesville Indiana)	1542	329	Summit Machine Inc	3451	34	Sun Orchard Inc	2033	56
Sullivan County Chapter Of The Nys Association For Retarded Children Inc	8052	11	Summit Machine Tool	3541	9	Sun Pharmaceuticals Corp	2844	111
			Summit Machine Tool Manufacturing Corp	3541	10	Sun Press Inc	2752	1132
Sullivan Electric Group Inc	7373	1168				Sun Process Converting Inc	2891	50
Sullivan Fire Protection LLC	7389	1990	Summit Manufacturing Corp	3559	533	Sun Products Corp	2841	4
Sullivan Higdon and Sink	7311	163	Summit Media Inc	7833	3	Sun Publishing Corp	2711	405
Sullivan International Inc	8742	665	Summit Medical Inc	3842	290	Sun Rams Products Inc	3851	23
Sullivan Investment Company Inc	5531	13	Summit Motor Works Inc	5013	342	Sun Rich LLC	2041	24
			Summit National Inc	7372	4126			

Company Name	SIC	Rank
Sun Road Interprises	6712	672
Sun Sierra Software Inc	7371	1616
Sun Star Inc	3089	1322
Sun State International Trucks LLC	5599	10
Sun State Plastics Inc	3089	1143
Sun State Systems Inc	3625	299
Sun Steel Company LLC	5051	93
Sun Studio	7389	1771
Sun Suites Interests LLLP	6719	96
Sun Sun Trading Company Inc	5087	110
Sun Tech Circuits Inc	5065	752
Sun Tech Industries	3089	1884
Sun Technologies Inc	5099	99
Sun Ten Labs Liquidation Co	5149	146
Sun Valley Company Inc	7011	187
Sun Valley Lighting Standards Inc	3646	15
Sun Valley Masonry Inc	1741	5
Sun Water Systems Inc	3589	112
Sunair International Sales Corp	3663	76
Sunair Services Corp	7349	32
Sunalliance Healthcare Services Inc	8082	39
SunAmerica Asset Management Corp	6282	53
Sunbeam Television Corp	4833	78
Sunbeam Trailer Products Inc	3647	24
Sunbelt Auto Carriers Inc	4213	884
Sunbelt Chemicals	2899	108
Sunbelt Computer Systems Inc	7372	1402
Sunbelt Crane Construction and Hauling	4213	1958
Sunbelt Electronic Representative Associates Inc	5064	110
Sunbelt Express Services Inc	4213	1347
Sunbelt Furniture Xpress Inc	4213	1008
Sunbelt Human Advancement Resources Inc	8322	30
Sunbelt Import	5046	289
Sunbelt Innovative Plastics Inc	3084	33
Sunbelt Machine Works	3599	975
Sunbelt Metal Service Inc	5051	321
Sunbelt Multimedia Co	4833	196
Sunbelt Plastic Extrusions Inc	3089	966
Sunbelt Plastics Tooling Inc	3089	1334
Sunbelt Rentals Inc	7353	4
Sunbelt Title Agency and Lending Services	6531	294
Sunbelt Transfomer Ltd	3612	84
Sunbelt USA Inc	5099	109
Sunbelt-Turret Steel Inc	5051	362
Sunbird Industries Inc	5065	781
Sunbird Transport Inc	4213	1887
Sunbright Services Building Maintenance Specialists Corp	7349	146
Sunburst Chemicals Inc	2842	71
Sunburst Hospitality Corp	6531	119
Sunburst Optics Inc	5048	30
Sunburst Sensors LLC	3695	172
Sunburst Shutters Corp	3084	3
Sunburst Technology Corp	7372	2378
Sunbury Broadcasting Corp	4832	124
Suncall America Inc	5012	99
Suncare Respiratory Services Inc	8099	39
Suncast Corp	2519	3
Sunco Carriers Inc	4213	302
Suncoast Automotive Products Inc	3694	29
Suncoast Bakeries Inc	2051	105
Suncoast Coffee Inc	5149	122
Suncoast Communications and Electronics Inc	5731	97
Suncoast Electric Inc	1731	1283
Suncoast Endoscopy ASC LP	8011	141
Suncoast Identification Technologies Inc	3083	89
Suncoast Medical Clinic	3827	14
Suncoast Medicare Supply Co	7352	32
Suncoast Molders Inc	3089	1545
Suncoast Schools Federal Credit Union	6061	7
Suncoast Systems Inc	3661	221
Suncoast Tool and Gage Industries Inc	3829	401
Suncom Industries Inc	8331	118
SunCor Development Co	6531	21
Suncos Corp	2834	74
Suncraft Technologies Inc	2752	237
Suncrest Farms Country Hams Inc	2013	135
Sund Manufacturing Company Inc	3523	223
Sundance Catalog Company Ltd	5961	105
Sundance Digital Inc	5046	16
Sundance Enterprises	7011	77
Sundance Food Service Inc	2082	68
Sundance Graphic Enterprises Inc	2732	51
Sundance/Newbridge Educational Publishing LLC	2741	110
Sundance Products Inc	5162	22
Sundance Staffing Minnesota LLC	7363	307
Sundance Travel Service	4724	138
Sunday News	5192	45
Sunday Productions Inc	7389	2399
Sunday River Skiway Corp	7011	134
Sundayriver Brewing Company Inc	2082	63
Sundberg-Ferar Inc	7389	2043
Sunderland Chevrolet	5511	1089
Sundew Technologies LLC	3674	476
Sundia Corp	0161	18
Sundial Orchards Hulling and Drying	2068	32
Sundog Interative	3577	140

Company Name	SIC	Rank
Sun-Drop Bottling Company Of Rocky Mount NC Inc	2086	122
Sundstrom Pressed Steel Co	3469	292
Sundt Corp	1542	30
SunDurance Energy LLC	1711	75
Sundyne Corp	3561	37
Sunelco	5961	178
Sunesis Pharmaceuticals Inc	2834	441
Sunfish Express Inc	7389	2000
Sunflower Electric Power Corp	4911	200
Sunflower Manufacturing Co	3523	17
Sunflower Manufacturing Inc	3678	82
Sunflower Restaurant Supply Inc	5149	45
Sunflower Telephone Co	4813	239
Sunfresh Citrus and Flavors Inc	2095	60
SunGard Bi-Tech Inc	7372	653
SunGard Corbel Inc	7372	111
SunGard Data Systems Inc	7374	4
SunGard Employee Benefit Systems	7372	1076
Sungard EXP	7372	1335
SunGard HTE Inc	7373	134
Sungard Institutional Brokerage Inc	7389	2437
SunGard iWorks LLC	7372	1237
SunGard Market Data Services	7375	156
SunGard Recovery Services LP	7372	278
SunGard Securities Processing	7372	1526
SunGard Trading and Risk Systems (Boston Massachusetts)	7371	432
Sun-Gazette Co	2711	130
Sunglass Hut International Inc	5999	11
Sungrow Horticulture Canada Inc	0782	3
Sunguard Availability Services	7373	140
Suniland Press Inc	2752	572
Suniva Inc	3674	104
Sunkist Bakery Company Inc	5149	206
Sunkist Graphics Inc	2752	768
Sunkist Growers Inc	5148	4
Sunland Chemical and Research Corp	2899	172
Sunland Fabricating Inc	3498	8
Sunland Inc	2099	112
Sunland Optical Company Inc	5995	14
Sunland Park Racetrack	7948	21
Sunlife Systems International Inc	2952	19
SunLink Health Systems Inc	8062	79
Sunlink Systems Inc	7379	1602
Sunlite Plastics Inc	3089	606
Sun-Maid Growers Of California	2034	3
SunMax Corp	3577	537
Sunnen Products Co	3549	3
Sunniland Corp	5033	6
Sunnking Inc	5734	135
Sunny Components Inc	5065	900
Sunny Dell Foods Inc	5148	64
Sunny Maid Corp	2086	143
Sunny Sun Glasses Of Miami Inc	5085	396
Sunnybrook Golf Bowl	7011	227
Sunnydale Industries Inc	7389	2507
Sunnyland Farms	5961	111
Sunnyside Janitorial Service	7349	393
Sunnyside Motor Company Inc	5511	800
Sunnyside Rehabilitation And Nursing Center Inc	8051	58
Sunnyside Unified School District 12	8211	69
Sunnytech	5045	862
Sunnytech Inc	5045	468
Sunnyvale Lumber Inc	5211	94
Sunnyvalley Smoked Meats Inc	2013	80
Sunoco Inc	2911	4
Sunoco Logistics Partners LP	4619	1
Sunol Sciences Corp	3663	340
Sunon Inc	5063	552
Sunops Inc	5734	295
Sunopta Aseptic Inc	4783	12
Sunopta Fruit Group Inc	2087	52
SunOpta Sunflower	2099	119
Sunoptic Technologies LLC	3827	41
Sunovion Pharmaceuticals Inc	2834	41
Sunpower Corp (San Jose California)	3674	21
Sunprene Co	2821	111
Sunpress Inc	2741	261
Sunpro Inc	1731	387
Sunray Coop	5153	61
Sunray Electric Supply Co	5063	74
SunRay Enterprise Inc	7361	192
Sunray Printing Solutions Inc	2752	881
Sun-Re Cheese Corp	2022	42
Sun-Reporter Publishing Co	2711	355
Sunridge Corp	5734	393
Sunrise AG Coop	5143	20
Sunrise AG Service Co	5159	5
Sunrise Bakery Inc	2051	306
Sunrise Baking Company LLC	2051	99
Sunrise Bank of Albuquerque	6022	749
Sunrise Bank of Arizona	6022	647
Sunrise Chevrolet	5511	161
Sunrise Co	1531	46
Sunrise Cooperative Inc	5153	152
Sunrise Credit Services Inc	7389	614
Sunrise Electric Of Central Florida Inc	1731	1402
Sunrise Enterprises Of Roseburg	5932	12
Sunrise Express Inc	4213	1369
Sunrise Fiberglass Corp	3083	52
Sunrise Financial Group Inc	6282	552
Sunrise Foods Inc	2099	158

Company Name	SIC	Rank
Sunrise Foods LLC	2015	31
Sunrise Greetings	2771	10
Sunrise Hamilton Assisted Living LLC	8051	56
Sunrise Hitek Service Inc	2759	325
Sunrise House Foundation Inc	8093	41
Sunrise Imaging Inc	3861	121
Sunrise International Leasing Corp	7374	60
Sunrise Jewelry Manufacturing Corp	3911	30
Sunrise Machine and Tool Inc	3842	252
Sunrise Medical Inc	3842	17
Sunrise Medical Inc Mobility Products Div	3842	69
Sunrise North Farmington Hills Assisted Living LLC	8051	60
Sunrise Packaging Inc	3089	1438
Sunrise Pest Control Inc	7342	46
Sunrise Riverside Assisted Living LP	8051	52
Sunrise Senior Living Inc	8051	6
Sunrise Shaker Heights Assisted Living LLC	8051	55
Sunrise Solar Corp	7011	239
Sunrise Systems Inc	3674	324
Sunrise Telecom Inc	4813	114
Sunrise Willow Lake Assisted Living LLC	8051	54
Sunriver Resorts	7011	186
Sunroc Corp	3585	255
Sunrooms Plus Inc	1521	126
Sunrx Inc	5122	41
Sun-Rys Distributing Corp	5099	106
Suns Legacy Partners LLC	7941	33
Sunsation Inc	2037	45
Sun-Sentinel Co	2711	42
Sunset Building Maintance Inc	7349	409
Sunset Excavating Inc	1623	147
Sunset Farm	7389	1592
Sunset Financial Services Inc	6211	154
Sunset Ice Cream	2024	75
Sunset Industries Inc	3599	1552
Sunset Life Insurance Company of America	6311	194
Sunset Manufacturing Co	3599	1004
Sunset Net LLC	4899	167
Sunset Pacific Transportation	4213	198
Sunset Printing And Engraving Corp	2759	211
Sunset Publishing Corp	2721	78
Sunset Sound Recorders Inc	7389	2239
Sunset Station Inc	7999	9
Sunset Transportation	4215	11
Sunset Transportation Inc	4213	1144
Sunset Waste Services	4953	47
Sunsetter Products LP	2394	14
Sunshine Apparel Inc	5099	86
Sunshine Buick Pontiac GMC	5511	1064
Sunshine Drapery Company Inc	5714	3
Sunshine Electronic Display Corp	3993	38
Sunshine Equipment Company Inc	5083	28
Sunshine Fifty Inc	3541	85
Sunshine Filters Of Pinellas Inc	3599	1762
Sunshine Flag Car Service	7389	2070
Sunshine Makers Inc	2842	23
Sunshine Manufactured Structures Inc	2452	46
Sunshine Market Inc	5411	205
Sunshine Permit Service	7389	1828
Sunshine Rock Inc	5032	92
Sunshine Savings Bank	6022	611
Sunshine Software Sales Inc	5734	333
Sunshine Supply Company Inc	5039	29
Sunshine Trucking Inc	4213	2037
Sunshine Wireless Inc	5999	168
Sunstar Americas Inc	2844	22
Sunstar Optical Inc	5995	21
Sunstar SpA Covers Inc	3999	128
Sunstone Hotel Investors Inc	7011	25
Sunstone Hotel Properties Inc	7011	43
Sunstrand Electric Company Inc	1731	660
Sunstream Corp	3536	15
Sunstream Inc	1731	1592
Sunsweet Growers Inc	2034	2
Suntec Industries Inc	3586	19
Sunteca Systems Inc	5023	196
Sunteck Transport Company Inc	4119	13
Suntel Services LLC	5045	401
Sunterra Coconut Palms	7011	231
Sunterrace Casual Furniture Inc	2519	5
Suntide Homes Development Inc	1521	162
Sun-Times Media Holdings LLC	2711	56
Suntiva Executive Consulting LLC	8742	306
Suntree LLC	2068	5
Suntron Corp	5065	34
Suntronic Inc	3671	16
SunTrust Banks Inc	6712	8
SunTrust Mortgage Inc	6162	5
Sunup Design Systems Inc	7371	859
Sunward Trucking Inc	4213	2821
Sunwest Bank	6022	256
Sunwest Electric Inc	1731	175
Sunwest Engineering Constructors Inc	1799	143
Sunwest Metals Inc	5093	194
Sunwest Peo Of Florida Vi Inc	7361	313
SunWize Technologies Inc	3674	163
Supelco Inc	5049	5
Super 8 Motels Inc	7011	22
Super Auctions Inc	7389	1977

Company Name	SIC	Rank
Super Bakery Inc	2051	155
Super Cartage Company Inc	4213	1684
Super Conductor Materials Inc	3674	433
Super Electric Construction Co	1731	490
Super Excavators Inc	1623	138
Super Fair Cellular Inc	4812	101
Super Glue Corp/Pacer Technology	2891	28
Super Lopez Food Products And Tortilla Factory Inc	2099	187
Super Market Services Corp	5141	70
Super Micro Computer Inc	3571	14
Super Pallet Recycling Corp	5031	185
Super Products LLC	3711	44
Super Sack Bag Inc	2673	10
Super Seer Corp	3842	256
Super Service Inc	4213	231
Super Service LLC	4213	89
Super Sky Products Inc	3444	160
Super Software Inc	5734	371
Super Steel LLC	3443	51
Super Steel Treating Inc	3398	13
Super Vacuum Manufacturing Company Inc	3711	51
Super Wash Inc	7542	2
Super Web Inc	3555	79
Superbase Developers Inc	7372	2217
Superchips Inc	3674	258
Supercircuits Inc	5043	10
Superclone Corp	5045	657
Superconductor Technologies Inc	3663	154
Supercuts Inc	6794	42
Superfeet Worldwide LLC	5139	20
Supergroup Creative Omnimedia Inc	7336	221
Superion	3423	57
Superior Adjusting Inc	6411	60
Superior Advertising and Marketing Inc	2759	535
Superior Amusements and Vending Inc	5092	37
Superior Aqua Enterprises Inc	5074	228
Superior Asphalt Of Central Florida Inc	1611	231
Superior Auto Sales Inc	5012	102
Superior Automatic Sprinkler Co	1711	179
Superior Automotive Group	5511	151
Superior Baking Company Inc	2051	182
Superior Bancorp	6712	145
Superior Battery Manufacturing Company Inc	3691	24
Superior Binding Inc	2789	33
Superior Buick Cadillac Inc	5511	616
Superior Building Maintenance Inc	7349	186
Superior Bulk Logistics Inc	4213	166
Superior Business Forms Inc	2752	821
Superior Cake Products Inc	2051	212
Superior Cam Inc	3465	56
Superior Carriers Inc	4213	371
Superior Cedar Products Inc	3524	29
Superior Clay Corp	3259	5
Superior Cleaning Inc	7349	314
Superior Colour Graphics Inc	2752	580
Superior Commercial Roofing Inc	1761	61
Superior Companies Inc	3599	143
Superior Concrete Materials Inc	3272	22
Superior Controls Inc	3613	41
Superior Crane Corp	5084	323
Superior Dairy Products Co	2024	50
Superior Dental and Surgical Manufacturing Inc	3843	81
Superior Die Set Corp	3544	18
Superior Diesel Inc	5084	432
Superior Dry Kilns Inc	3559	381
Superior Electric Service Co	1731	737
Superior Electric Supply Co (Elyria Ohio)	5063	169
Superior Electrical and Electronic Distributors Co	5063	910
Superior Electrical Contractors Inc	1731	976
Superior Energy Services Inc	1389	6
Superior Engineered Products Corp	3089	268
Superior Engineering Company Inc	3544	480
Superior Environmental Corp	8748	153
Superior Essex Inc	3369	1
Superior Expo Ltd	7389	1287
Superior Fabricators Inc	3443	193
Superior Financial Corp	6712	68
Superior Floor Covering Inc	1752	10
Superior Flux and Manufacturing Co	2899	234
Superior Foods Inc	5142	23
Superior Ford Lincoln Mercury (Morgantown West Virginia)	5511	888
Superior Forge and Steel Corp	3312	89
Superior Gearbox Co	3566	21
Superior Glass Fibers Inc	2221	30
Superior Graphite Co	3295	1
Superior Group	1731	254
Superior Group Inc	3317	9
Superior Gunite	1771	7
Superior Heating and Cooling Corp	1711	256
Superior Holding Inc	3443	39
Superior Home Services	7363	329
Superior Home Services Inc	7389	528
Superior Homes LLC	2452	47
Superior Industrial Sales and Service Inc	5084	602
Superior Industries International Inc	3714	44
Superior Information Systems Inc	7379	1264

Company Name	SIC	Rank
Superior International Corp	5087	71
Superior International Industries Inc	3089	160
Superior Internet Solutions	7311	903
Superior Iron Works Inc	3441	140
Superior Jig Inc	3544	491
Superior Lamp Inc	3641	31
Superior Light and Sign Maintenance Company Inc	1731	335
Superior Lithographics Inc	2752	281
Superior Machine and Pattern Inc	3599	2171
Superior Machine Inc	3599	666
Superior Maintenance Co	0782	6
Superior Manufacturing and Hydraulics Inc	3561	100
Superior Manufacturing Group - Europe Inc	3069	240
Superior Materials Inc	3272	21
Superior Metal Products Inc	3469	279
Superior Mold and Die Co	3544	317
Superior Motors Inc (Orangeburg South Carolina)	5511	985
Superior Moulding Inc	5211	276
Superior Nut Company Inc	2068	25
Superior Pipelines Inc	1623	743
Superior Plastic LLC	3089	16
Superior Plastics Extrusion Company Inc	3081	115
Superior Pool Products LLC	5091	73
Superior Print Inc	2752	1040
Superior Printers Inc	2752	606
Superior Printing Company Inc	2752	1568
Superior Printing Inc	2759	76
Superior Products International II Inc	2821	168
Superior Protection Service Inc	7381	45
Superior Quality Foods Inc	2032	26
Superior Quartz Products Inc	3641	20
Superior Ready Mix Concrete LP	3273	7
Superior Sample Company Inc	2789	104
Superior Satellite Engineers Inc	3663	372
Superior Scaffold Services Inc	7353	30
Superior Scale Inc	5046	351
Superior Search Group Inc	7361	332
Superior Services Inc	7349	22
Superior Signal Company LLC	3489	22
Superior Silica Sands LLC	1429	20
Superior Slides Inc	7336	113
Superior Software Inc	7372	1109
Superior Software Systems Inc	3577	664
Superior Solvents and Chemicals	4213	148
Superior Steel Inc	3441	58
Superior Technical Ceramics Corp	3644	26
Superior Tire and Rubber Corp	3011	17
Superior Tool and Die Co	3544	542
Superior Tool and Machining Co	3544	401
Superior Transmission Parts Inc	8731	340
Superior Transportation Inc	4213	1417
Superior Travel	4724	118
Superior Truck Lines	4213	1957
Superior Tube Company Inc	3317	29
Superior Uniform Group Inc	2399	6
Superior Uniform Group Worldwide Distribution Center	2326	7
Superior Washer and Gasket Corp	3452	67
Superior Water And Air Inc	5999	105
Superior Water Light and Power Co	4931	51
Superior Well Services Inc	1389	15
Superior Window Manufacturing Inc	3089	1839
Superior Wireless Communication Inc	5065	605
Superior-Brookdale Ford Inc	5511	445
Superior-Lidgerwood-Mundy Corp	3556	117
Superlative Technologies Inc	5734	89
Superlon Plastics Company Inc	5074	204
SuperMarkets Online Inc	7389	457
SuperMedia LLC	2741	5
Supernews Inc	7375	172
Supernova Systems Inc	4813	521
Superpac Inc	2671	25
Superseal Manufacturing Company Inc	3089	782
SuperShuttle International Inc	4141	1
SuperSpeed Software Inc	7372	4933
Superstition Springs Chrysler Jeep Inc	5511	828
Supertech Inc	5063	742
Super-Tek Products Inc	2891	71
Supertek USA Corp	5084	777
Supertrapp Industries Inc	3714	327
SUPERVALU Champaign Distribution Center	5141	45
SUPERVALU Inc	5411	4
Supervan Service Company Inc	4213	564
Supervised Lifestyles Inc	8093	44
Superwinch LLC	3531	103
Supfina Machine Company Inc	3541	125
Supplemental Health Care Services Ltd	8082	66
Supplemental Medical Services Inc	7363	225
Suppliers To Wholesalers Inc	3444	244
Supplies Distributors Inc	5045	340
Supply Chain Edge	8742	317
Supply Chain Management Inc	7372	4971
Supply House Inc	5032	51
Supply King Inc	5087	187
Supply One Corp	2434	81
Supply Room Companies Inc	5112	19
Supply Room Inc	5099	42
Supply Technologies	5085	70

Company Name	SIC	Rank
Supply Technologies LLC	3452	5
SupplyCore Inc	7389	153
SupplyforceCom LLC	5085	124
Supplyframe Inc	7379	871
Supplynet Inc	3678	69
Supplyone Weyers Cave Inc	2653	41
SupplyPro Inc	7372	1125
Supplyworks Inc	7372	412
Support Associates Inc	8744	32
Support Construction Inc	1799	76
Support Of Microcomputers Associates Inc	7378	38
Support Services of America Inc	7349	136
Support Technology Inc	7363	304
Suppressions Systems Inc	1731	376
Supra Alloys Inc	5051	296
Supracor Systems Inc	3089	727
Sup-R-Die Inc	5085	331
Supreme Builders	1522	60
Supreme Building Messengers Inc	7389	1084
Supreme Cable Technology Inc	3679	440
Supreme Contractors LLC	1381	25
Supreme Cores Transport Inc	4213	3125
Supreme Corp	3713	12
Supreme Custom Fabricators Inc	5046	89
Supreme Electronics Corp	3823	45
Supreme Felt and Abrasives Inc	3053	102
Supreme Foods Inc	5141	185
Supreme Industries Inc	3713	10
Supreme Insulation Inc	3296	10
Supreme Machined Products Company Inc	3451	4
Supreme Manufacturing Co	3599	958
Supreme Manufacturing Company Inc	2086	111
Supreme Oil Company Inc	5172	156
Supreme Products Inc	3499	85
Supreme Radio Communications Inc	5731	81
Supreme Saw and Service Co	3425	14
Supreme Securities Services	5063	424
Supress Products LLC	2439	53
Sur La Table Inc	5719	12
Surabian Advertising	7311	959
Surado Solutions Inc	7372	1794
Surbuban Floor Covering Inc	5023	153
Sure Cast Inc	3324	18
Sure Fit Inc	5023	15
Sure Fold Company Inc	2789	124
Sure Foot Corp	3842	235
Sure Grip International Inc	3949	81
Sure Heat Manufacturing Inc	3433	33
Sure Power Industries Inc	3629	44
Sure Save Supermarket Ltd	5411	216
Sure Scan Inc	5045	890
Sure Solutions Inc	7372	693
Sure Sound and Lighting Inc	7359	217
Sure Tool and Manufacturing Company Inc	3544	740
Sure Winner Foods Inc	5143	18
Surefed Ltd	5191	169
Sure-Feed Engineering Inc	3554	14
Sureflex Inc	3677	71
Surefoot LC	5139	23
Surelite Products Company Inc	3643	165
Sure-Lock-Homes Security and Communications Inc	1731	1896
Surepayroll Inc	8721	74
Surequest Systems Inc	7372	4106
Surescript Systems Inc	7375	74
SureScripts Inc	7375	111
Surety Capital Corp	6712	716
Surety Group Inc	6351	53
Surety LLC	7389	475
SureWest Communications	4813	59
Surf City Squeeze Inc	5149	6
Surf Cowboy Inc	5136	19
Surf Electronics Inc	5065	975
Surf Investment Ltd	7378	78
Surface Blasting Systems LLC	3559	523
Surface Combustion Inc	3567	20
Surface Engineering Specialties Inc	3552	29
Surface Manufacturing Inc	3599	2047
Surface Mount Co	3672	63
Surface Mount Depot Inc	3679	267
Surface Mount Technology Corp	3559	110
Surface Mountable Electronic Components Inc	5065	641
Surface Protection Industries Inc	2851	36
Surfaces Research and Applications Inc	8734	191
Surfaces Transport Inc	4213	2239
Surfas Inc	5046	120
Sur-Flo Plastics And Engineering Inc	3089	419
Surfside East Inc	2741	254
Surfside Software Inc	7372	3786
Surf-Tech Manufacturing Corp	3672	416
Surfware Inc	7372	2249
Surge Components Inc	5065	252
Surge Global Energy Inc	1311	274
Surgery and Laser Center	8011	112
Surgery Center of Coral Gables LLC	8011	136
Surgical Appliance Industries Inc	3842	55
Surgical Eye Care Ltd	8011	152
Surgical Information Systems LLC	7371	379
Surgical Instrument Manufacturers Inc	3841	258

Company Name	SIC	Rank
Surgical Specialties Corp	3841	115
Surgical Technologies Inc	7389	2464
Surgient Inc	3577	251
Surgimed Inc	7363	379
Surgistar Inc	3841	325
Surlean Meat Co	2013	62
SurModics Inc	2834	161
Surner Heating Company Inc	5172	51
Surpass Chemical Company Inc	5169	108
SurphoriaCom Inc	7371	865
Surplus Sourcing Group Inc	7822	24
SurpluseqCom Inc	5734	378
Surprise Plastics Inc	3089	595
Surry Chemicals Inc	2843	12
Sur-Seal Gasket And Packing Co	3053	31
Surtec Inc	2842	92
Surtronics Inc	3471	98
Suruga USA Corp	3544	546
Survey Analytics LLC	8743	270
Survey Technologies Inc	3669	313
SurveyConnect Inc	7371	1658
Surveyors Materials Inc	5049	213
Survivor Industries Inc	2099	271
Survivor Software Ltd	7372	4888
Susag Sand And Gravel Inc	1442	60
Susan Magrino Agency	8743	302
Susan Marinello Interiors	7389	1050
Susan Watson	7379	1645
Susan's Florist Inc	5992	10
Suscon Inc	3085	24
Susman Godfrey LLP	8111	395
Suspa Inc	3593	12
Susque-Bancshares Leasing Company Inc	6141	68
Susque-Bancshares Life Insurance Co	6311	233
Susquehanna Bancshares Inc	6712	55
Susquehanna Bank	6022	819
Susquehanna Glass Co	5399	23
Sussek Machine Corp	3599	215
Susser Holdings Corp	5541	7
Sussex Bancorp	6712	474
Sussex IM	3089	108
Sussex Printing Corp	2741	273
Sussex Publishers Inc	2721	353
Sussex Semiconductor Inc	3674	361
Sussman-Automatic Corp	3569	104
Sustain Technologies Inc	2711	188
Sustainable Oils LLC	2869	114
Sustainable Softworks Inc	7372	4759
SustainX Inc	8731	265
Sustane Natural Fertilizer Inc	2873	26
Suther Feeds Inc	2833	27
Sutherland Asbill and Brennan (Washington DC)	8111	46
Sutherland Foodservice Inc	5144	1
Sutherland Global Services	7361	1
Sutherland Lumber Company LP	5211	8
Sutherlin Optical Co	3851	69
Sutliff Capital Ford Inc	7515	10
Sutphen Corp	3711	40
Sutro Tower Inc	4833	201
Sutron Corp	3829	66
Sutta Co	5093	107
Sutter Group (Lanham Maryland)	8743	228
Sutter Health	8049	1
Sutter Hill Ventures	6799	142
Sutter Home Winery Inc	2084	7
Suttle Apparatus Corp	3661	73
Suttle-Straus Inc	2752	74
Sutton Designs Inc	3612	64
Sutton Ford Inc	5511	266
Sutton Reid Advertising Inc	7311	568
Sutton Wj Company Inc	1623	825
Suwannee Lumber Manufacturing Co	5211	102
Suwannee Valley Electric Cooperative Inc	4911	217
Suzanna's Kitchen Inc	2015	29
Suzanne Chalet Foods Inc	2032	51
Suzanne L Kilmer	5049	77
Suzio York Hill	3273	29
Suzuki Garphyttan Corp	3496	3
Suzy Systems Inc	7372	1194
SV Investment Partners	6799	191
SV Microwave Inc	3674	309
Svam International Inc	7379	304
SVB Financial Group	6712	42
Sven And Ole's Fishing Company Inc	2084	62
Svenhard's Swedish Bakery	5149	37
Svi International Inc	5013	169
SVM Group Inc	3599	2277
Svr Group Inc	7379	916
Svrc Industries Inc	8331	50
Svt Associates Inc	3674	376
Svz USA Washington Inc	2033	95
SW Electronics and Manufacturing Corp	3577	316
Sw Florida Regional Mri Inc	8099	101
SW Marketing Associates Inc	5065	281
SW Rawls Inc	5983	20
SW Resources Inc	8331	6
SWA Group	0781	6
SwaddleDesigns LLC	5137	30
Swagelok Co	3494	5
Swagelok Hy-Level Co	3451	25

Company Name	SIC	Rank
Swaggerty Sausage Company Inc	2011	100
Swaim Inc	2514	10
Swan Associates Inc	5084	556
Swan Black Manufacturing Co	2851	164
Swan Cleaners Inc	7216	2
Swan Corp	3088	2
Swan Engineering and Machine Co	3544	298
Swan Finishing Company Inc	2231	4
Swan Industries Inc	3544	582
Swan Packing Inc	2011	67
Swanagon Inc	3651	134
Swanberg Construction Inc	1623	212
Swander Pace Capital	6799	166
Swaner Hardwood Company Inc	5031	122
Swank Inc	3199	3
Swanke Hayden Connell and Partners LLP	7389	598
Swanke Hayden Connell Ltd	8712	30
Swanner Transfer and Storage Co	4213	1936
Swanson and Youngdale Inc	1721	4
Swanson Contracting Co	1629	47
Swanson Enterprises Inc	1731	2426
Swanson Group Inc	2421	18
Swanson Group Manufacturing LLC	2435	15
Swanson Hardware Supply Inc	5072	127
Swanson Midgley LLC	8111	590
Swanson Pickle Company Inc	2035	43
Swanson Sinkey Ellis Inc	8742	151
Swanson Systems Inc	3559	199
Swanson Tool Manufacturing Inc	3545	135
Swanson Trucking Inc	4213	1789
Swanson Vineyards and Winery	0172	14
Swanson-Flosystems Co	5085	170
Swanson's Die Company Inc	3423	68
Swanson's Repair Inc	3559	382
Swantech LLC	3699	191
Swanton Welding and Machining Company Inc	3446	19
Swany America Corp	5136	13
Swarco America Inc	3069	24
SwarmBuilder Inc	7312	10
Swarovski North America Ltd	3961	2
Swarthmore Group Inc	6282	369
Swartz Moving and Storage Co	4213	1547
Swatch Group Inc (Weehawken New Jersey)	3873	4
Swatchworks Inc	2299	25
Swayzer's Inc	7349	328
SWC Technology Partners	7372	1611
Swce Inc	7372	2016
SWD Corp	5145	8
Swd Inc	3471	52
Swds Inc	7361	256
Swearingen Advertising Agency Inc	7311	1025
Swebco Manufacturing Inc	3599	548
Sweco Fab Inc	3494	56
Sweco Products Inc	7699	112
Sweda Company LLC	5094	22
Swede-O Inc	3842	204
Swedish Hill Vineyard Inc	2084	89
Swedish Match North America	2131	4
Sweed Machinery Inc	3559	214
Sweeney Buick GMC Truck Co	5511	382
Sweeney Cleaning And Restoration Inc	7349	507
Sweeney Enterprises Inc	3523	282
Sweeney Hotels International Inc	8741	202
Sweeney Industries Inc	7349	271
Sweeney Steel Service Corp	7389	1491
Sweeney Transportation Inc	4213	1505
Sweet Candy Co	2064	8
Sweet Data Concepts	7374	173
Sweet Dreams Inc	2392	30
Sweet Dreams Music Productions Inc	7812	256
Sweet Factory Inc	5441	1
Sweet Harvest Foods Management Co	2099	229
Sweet Manufacturing Co	3535	120
Sweet Shop Candies Inc	2064	57
Sweet Street Desserts Inc	2053	3
Sweet Water Trucking Company Inc	4213	1543
Sweetbay Supermarket	5411	86
Sweetspot Media Group Inc	7312	36
Sweetwater Electronic Construction and Maintenance Inc	1731	1897
Sweetwater Lumber and Land Inc	5031	381
Sweetwater Paperboard Company Inc	2631	20
Sweetwater Television Co	4841	137
Sweitzer and Associates Landscape Architects Inc	0781	20
Swenke Company Inc	1623	322
Swenson Company Inc	3089	1751
Swenson Granite Company LLC	3281	5
Swepco Tube LLC	3356	20
Swerdlow Group	1542	150
Swetman Security Service Inc	7381	97
Swets Blackwell North America	5961	39
SWF Cos	3565	10
SWH Corp	5812	149
SWI Trading Inc	5046	280
SWI Transportation Inc	4213	3074
SWIBCO Inc	3231	59
Swick Broadcasting Co	4832	110
Swift Air Delivery Inc	4213	1795
Swift Aviation Services Inc	5172	40
Swift Communications	2711	180

Company Name	SIC	Rank
Swift Computers Inc	3663	256
Swift Electrical Supply Co	5063	88
Swift Energy Co	1311	50
Swift Energy International Inc	1311	58
Swift Glass Company Inc	3231	42
Swift Lumber Inc	2421	57
Swift Office Solutions Inc	5734	122
Swift Print Communication Services LLC	2752	647
Swift Print Inc	2752	1233
Swift Saw and Tool Supply Company Inc	5085	445
Swift Spinning Inc	2281	9
Swift Technologies Inc	7379	1437
Swift Technologiescom Inc	7374	163
Swift Textile Metalizing LLC	2295	22
Swift Transportation Co	4213	9
Swiftships Shipbuilders LLC	3731	16
SwiftView Inc	7372	2386
Swifty Printing and Digital Imaging Inc	2752	1347
Swifty Transportation Inc	4213	2409
Swiger Coil Systems LLC	3621	46
Swim 'N Sport	5699	11
Swimline Corp	3949	105
Swimways Corp	3089	662
Swimwear Anywhere Inc	2339	32
Swimwise Inc	5091	103
Swindell-Dressler International Co	1541	244
Swine Graphics Enterprises LP	0213	5
Swineford National Bank	6021	245
Swinerton Builders Inc	1542	181
Swinerton Inc	1542	12
Swing Electrical Company Inc	1731	1946
Swing Transport Inc	4213	895
Swing-A-Way Products LLC	3423	58
Swinney Brothers Excavating Inc	1794	34
Swire Coca-Cola	5149	109
Swire Coca-Cola USA	2086	15
Swirl Inc	7311	502
Swisher Electric Cooperative Inc	4911	473
Swisher Hygiene Inc	7342	3
Swisher International Inc	6719	119
Swisher International Inc (Jacksonville Florida)	2121	1
Swisher Mower and Machine Company Inc	3524	14
Swiss American Screw Products Inc	3451	136
Swiss Colony Inc	2022	7
Swiss Food Products LP	2034	29
Swiss Gotham	5047	98
Swiss Oven Bakery	2051	247
Swiss Premium Dairy Inc	2026	41
Swiss Productions Inc	3083	59
Swiss Re Underwriters	6331	372
Swiss Screw Products Inc	3599	1587
Swiss Technologies Inc	3599	1432
Swiss Technology Inc	3672	312
Swiss Valley Farms Coop	5143	21
Swiss Watch International Inc	5094	19
Swiss Woodcraft Inc	2431	128
Swissbit NA Inc	3674	283
Swissline Products Inc	3599	378
Swisslog Logistics Inc	7389	292
Swiss-Micron Inc	3599	565
Swissport USA Inc	8742	28
SwissRay International Inc	3841	85
Swiss-Tech LLC	3451	39
Swiss-Tex Inc	3089	1425
Swissway Inc	3599	1472
Switchboard Inc	7375	174
Switchcraft Inc	3678	14
Switching Power Inc	3613	61
Switchnet Technologies	4813	749
Switchroom Design LLC	4813	306
Switzer Group Inc	7389	429
Switzers Inc	5141	215
Swivelier Company Inc	3646	53
SWK Holdings Corp	7372	5062
Swn Communications Inc	4822	11
Swoboda Inc	3429	93
Swope Motors Inc	5511	781
Sword AgencyPort	5045	438
Sword and Shield Enterprise Security	7382	15
Sword Intech Inc	7379	67
Swp Inc	3577	450
Sws Electronics Inc	5065	603
SWS Financial Services Inc	6289	3
SWS Systems Inc	3613	183
SWT Inc	4213	2146
SXC Health Solutions Corp	6411	13
SXC Health Solutions Corp (Lisle Illinois)	7372	1112
SY Bancorp Capital Trust I	6022	757
SY Bancorp Inc	6712	198
Sy Kessler Sales Inc	5063	195
SyApps LLC	8748	119
Sybar Press Inc	2759	556
Sybase Application Support Div	7379	17
Sybase Inc	7372	51
Sybex Inc	2731	96
Sybra LLC	5812	209
Sybron Chemicals Inc	2819	58
Sybron Dental Specialties Inc	3843	4
Sycamore Chevrolet Nissan Inc	5511	959

Company Name	SIC	Rank
Sycamore Networks Inc	3661	54
Sycamore Precision Machine Inc	3599	323
SyChip Inc	4899	88
Syclo LLC	7372	1007
SYColeman Corp	7372	18
SyCom Services Inc	7372	40
Sycon Instruments Inc	8711	642
Sy-Con Systems Inc	7371	1715
Sycor Americas Inc	7379	1164
Sycron Technologies Inc	5084	942
SYCS Productions	7372	4065
Sycuan Gaming Center	7993	3
Sydex Inc	7372	4760
Sydnor Hydrodynamics Inc	5084	79
Syfrett Feed Company Inc	2048	106
Sygenex Inc	7379	822
SYGMA Network Inc	5141	21
Sykes Enterprises Inc	7373	14
Sy-Klone Co	3564	110
Syllogisteks Co	7371	531
Syltone Marine Inc	3531	203
Sylva Herald Publishing Company Inc	2711	816
Sylvan America Inc	0182	8
Sylvan Ascent Inc	7372	4761
Sylvan Inc	0182	3
Sylvania Yarn Systems Inc	2281	17
Sylvest Farms Inc	0251	3
Sylvester Sheet Metal Corp	1761	53
Sylvia's Food Products Inc	5812	303
Sylvin Technologies Inc	3087	18
Symantec Corp	7372	6
Symbian Inc USA	7379	514
Symbion Inc	8011	12
Symbiont Inc	7373	805
Symbolic Displays	3577	166
Symbolic Sound Corp	7372	4018
Symbollon Pharmaceuticals Inc	2836	90
Symbology Inc	2759	471
Symcom Inc	3625	95
Syme Inc	3412	9
Symerix Business Essentials Inc	5045	933
Symetra Financial Corp	6311	40
Symetrics Industries Inc	3672	51
Symetrics Industries LLC	3699	109
Symetrix Inc	3679	302
Symitar Systems Inc	7371	160
Symmco Inc	3399	11
Symmetric Research	3674	472
SymmetriCom Inc	3661	18
Symmetricom Puerto Rico Ltd	3669	29
Symmetry Creative Production Inc	7336	120
Symmetry Medical Inc	3842	32
Symmetry Software Corp	7372	2480
Symmons Industries Inc	3432	11
Symms Fruit Ranch Inc	0172	1
Symon Communications Inc	7372	1764
Symorex Ltd	5085	397
Symphony Fabrics Corp	5131	15
Symphony Service Corp	7371	66
Symphony Services	7372	1461
Symphony Technology Group LLC	8742	2
Symprotek Co	3672	255
Symrise Inc	2869	22
Syms Corp	5651	16
Symtech Corp	3559	487
Symtech Corporation International	3511	39
Symtech Inc	5084	218
Synacor Inc	7372	972
Syna-Flex Rubber Products Company Inc	3053	59
Synageva BioPharma Corp	2836	30
Synagro Technologies Inc	4953	22
Synalloy Corp	3317	20
Synalloy Metals Inc	3494	2
Synamco LLC	7372	512
Syn-Apps LLC	7371	1175
SynApps Software Inc	7371	1769
Synapse Wireless Inc	3679	108
Synapsis Enterprise LLC	7371	1145
Synapsis LLC	7372	2915
Synapsis Technology Inc	7371	568
Synaptec Software Inc	7372	4393
Synaptic Decisions Inc	8742	573
SynaptiCAD Inc	7373	1060
Synaptics Inc	3577	31
Synatronic Inc	7373	1152
Synavant Inc	8742	87
Synbiotics Corp	2835	32
Sync Sound Inc	7389	562
Synchris Inc	7372	4019
Synchron Communications Inc	7389	902
Synchronicity Mastering Services LLC	3652	45
Synchronicity Systems Solutions	7371	1547
Synchronized Networking Solutions LLC	1731	2581
Synchronoss Technologies Inc	7372	223
Synchrony Inc	3699	82
Syncom Electronics Corp	5065	436
Syncom Pharmaceuticals Inc	7389	1051
SYNCOM Venture Partners	6799	185
Syncro Corp	3714	202
Syncro Technologies Inc	7371	781
Syncro Technology Corp	7371	899
Syncronex Inc	7372	2094
Syncrotech Software Corp	7372	2525
Syncsort Inc	7372	433
Synctronics	3575	53
Synder Inc	3677	59
Syndero	5999	45
Syndesis Corp	7372	5042
Syndevco Inc	3612	93
Syndicate Sales Inc	3089	304
Syndrome Distribution Inc	5091	54
Synechron Inc	8748	85
Synehi Castings Inc	3599	749
Synergetic Communications Inc	7322	83
Synergetic Data Systems Inc	7372	4643
Synergetics Co	3672	125
Synergetics Diversified Computer Services Inc	7379	372
Synergetics USA Inc	3845	47
Synergetix	3672	50
Synergex International Corp	7372	1612
Synergics Energy Development Inc	4911	590
Synergis	7361	188
Synergis Group LLC	7371	1388
Synergis Technologies Inc	7373	349
Synergistic Systems Inc	7372	4762
Synergistic Systems Inc	8742	696
Synergistic Systems Inc (Neptune Beach Florida)	7372	3200
Synergistic Technology Solutions Inc	3629	58
Synergistics Inc	3577	509
Synergon Solutions Inc	7373	271
Synergx Systems Inc	3669	105
Synergy Brands Inc	7389	222
Synergy Contracting Services LLC	3699	206
Synergy Corporate Technologies Ltd	7379	789
Synergy Development Systems Inc	7372	3366
Synergy Direct Mortgage	6163	17
Synergy Electric Inc	3699	246
Synergy Films	7819	62
Synergy Flavors Inc	2087	27
Synergy Foods LLC	5141	165
Synergy Graphics Inc	2752	126
Synergy Industries LP	3533	61
Synergy Investment Inc	8748	309
Synergy Market Systems Inc	7374	341
Synergy Microwave Corp	3679	310
Synergy Software (Reading Pennsylvania)	7372	3288
Synergy Software Technologies Inc	7371	496
Synergy Steel Inc	5051	200
Synergystex International Inc	3577	539
Synerprise Consulting Services	7322	176
Synetics Solutions Inc	3679	37
Syn-Fab Inc	3663	251
Synfora Inc	3674	235
Synful LLC	7371	1908
Syngenta Crop Protection Inc	8731	9
Syngenta Seeds Incorporated - NK	5191	6
Syniverse Holdings Inc	4899	19
SYNNEX Corp	3571	6
Synopsys Inc	7372	39
Synoptek Inc	7389	887
Synova Inc	7371	98
Synovate	8732	27
Synovate Inc	8732	20
Synovics Pharmaceuticals	2833	39
Synovis Life Technologies Inc	3842	57
Synovis Micro Companies Alliance Inc	3842	85
Synovus Financial Corp	6021	10
Synq Solutions Inc	2731	73
Synqor Inc	3679	142
Synrad Inc	3699	33
Synsor Corp	2541	20
Synta Pharmaceuticals Corp	2834	332
Syntact Solutions Inc	7372	4889
Syntech Chemicals Inc	2819	105
Syntech Development And Manufacturing Inc	3089	1483
Syn-Tech Systems Inc	3571	54
Syntecos Inc	7349	107
Syntel Inc	7371	20
SynTel LLC	5045	289
Syntellect Inc	3661	67
Synteractive	7379	795
Syntes Language Groups Inc	7389	772
Synthesis	2721	413
Synthesis Energy Systems Inc	2999	5
Synthesis Industries Inc	3599	2507
Synthetech Inc	2869	81
Synthetic Aperture	7371	178
Synthetik Software Inc	7371	1338
Syntonic Systems Inc	7371	1130
Syntrio Inc	7371	1588
Syntroleum Corp	1311	203
Syntron Bioresearch Inc	2835	21
Synutra International Inc	2023	5
Synygy Inc	7372	238
Sypamore Inc	7373	939
Syphermedia International Inc	7374	136
Sypris Data Systems Inc	3695	18
Sypris Electronics LLC	3669	35
Sypris Solutions Inc	3823	12
Sypris Technologies Inc	3463	1
Sypris Technologies Marion LLC	3714	19
Syqwest Inc	3812	203
Syraco Products Inc	3429	117
Syracuse Blueprint Company Inc	5999	150
Syracuse Computer Store Inc	5734	65
Syracuse Label Company Inc	2672	52
Syracuse Letter Company Inc	2759	562
Syracuse Office Equipment Corp	5021	105
Syracuse Online LLC	4813	667
Syracuse Plastics LLC	3089	474
Syracuse Relocation Services	4213	1942
Syratech Corp	3914	2
Syringa Bancorp	6712	604
Syringa Bank	6022	430
Syringa Networks LLC	4813	166
Syrinx Consulting Corp	7379	713
Syron Industries Inc	3089	1240
SYS International Inc	3571	69
Sy's Supplies Inc	5072	130
Sys-10 Inc	7371	1870
SysArc	7373	732
Sysco Atlanta LLC	5141	4
SYSCO Corp	5142	1
Sysco Eastern Maryland LLC	5141	58
Sysco Food Service of Jamestown	5141	127
Sysco Food Service of Seattle Inc	5141	86
Sysco Food Services Baltimore	5141	18
SYSCO Food Services Los Angeles Inc	5141	61
Sysco Food Services of Arkansas Inc	5141	128
Sysco Food Services of Austin Inc	5141	114
Sysco Food Services of Baraboo LLC	5141	71
Sysco Food Services of Central California Inc	5141	131
Sysco Food Services of Cleveland Inc	5812	128
Sysco Food Services of Detroit LLC	5141	93
SYSCO Food Services of Grand Rapids LLC	5141	123
SYSCO Food Services of Hampton Roads	2013	38
SYSCO Food Services of Idaho Inc	5141	140
SYSCO Food Services of Indianapolis LLC	5141	15
Sysco Food Services of Kansas City Inc	5141	55
SYSCO Food Services of Metro New York LLC	5141	54
Sysco Food Services of Pittsburgh Inc	5141	132
Sysco Food Services of San Francisco Inc	5141	42
Sysco Food Services of South Florida Inc	5141	28
Sysco Food Services-Chicago Inc	5141	74
Sysco Food Services-Jacksonville Inc	5141	52
Sysco Guest Supply Inc	2844	47
Sysco Intermountain Food Services Inc	5141	85
Sysco Lincoln Inc	5141	121
SYSCO/Louisville Food Services Co	5141	88
SYSCO Minnesota Inc	5141	53
Sysco Nashville LLC	5141	63
Sysco Philadelphia LLC	5141	83
Sys-Com Inc	7372	1433
Syscom Inc (Baltimore Maryland)	7371	147
Syscom Services Inc	7373	481
Syscomp Inc	7373	1045
Syscon Computers Inc	7372	2434
Syscon Inc	7373	720
Syscon International Inc	3823	92
SYSCON International Inc PlantStar Div	3577	218
SYS-CON Media Inc	2741	53
Sysconnect International Inc	7379	941
Syscore Solutions International Inc	7379	605
Sysintegrators LLC	7379	1468
Syska and Hennessy Inc	8711	113
Syslink Computer Corp	5045	386
Syslogic Inc	7371	1439
Sysmex America Inc	5047	83
Sysmind LLC	8748	70
Sysnet Technologies LLC	7373	1018
Syspro Impact Software Inc	7372	620
Systalex Corp	7371	208
Systar Inc	7372	2737
Systat Software Inc	7372	2301
Systec Corp	3535	59
Systech Computers	7379	1239
Systech Environmental Corp	4953	85
Systech Handling Inc	3599	2359
Systech Software Products Inc	7372	4069
Systech Solutions Inc	7372	151
Systech Synergy Inc	5045	647
Systecon Inc	3561	74
SYSTEK Technologies Inc	7372	1815
System Automation Corp	7371	132
System Component Sales Co	5049	76
System Components Inc	3568	65
System Concepts Inc	7372	2302
System Design Group Inc	7371	1074
System Development Integration LLC	7373	228
System Dynamics International Inc	7372	962
System Energy Resources Inc	4911	115
System Engineering International Inc	3669	119
System Essentials Inc	7372	1369
System Fabric Works Inc	7373	1178
System Freight Inc	4213	842
System Innovators Inc	7372	2607

Company Name	SIC	Rank	Company Name	SIC	Rank	Company Name	SIC	Rank
System Management Arts Inc	7372	2358	T And B Equipment Company Inc	7359	57	T-3 Energy Services Inc	3533	21
System Management Software Inc	7372	2834	T and B Foundry Co	3321	51	T3 Inc (Austin Texas)	7311	105
System One International Inc	5045	888	T and B Trucking Inc	4213	2120	T4 Inc	7374	372
System Planning Corp	8748	55	T and C Graphics Inc	2752	868	TA Association Realty	6552	88
System Services Integration Corp	7373	770	T and C Power Conversion Inc	3825	281	TA Loving Co	1542	452
System Studies Inc	7372	2563	T and C Systems Inc	5734	399	TA Pelsue Co	3357	15
System Support Inc	5045	768	T and D Machine	3599	2181	TA Systems Inc	3549	20
System Technical Support Corp	3625	149	T And D Metal Products LLC	2542	39	TA Tool and Molding Inc	3089	1598
System/Technology Development Corp	7371	1759	T and E Industries Inc	3679	449	Taap Corp	3714	411
System Transport Inc	4213	1336	T and F Inc	1731	1451	Tab Boards International Inc	8742	551
System13	8099	89	T and G Constructors Inc	1542	152	Tab Computer Systems Inc	7373	487
Systematic Automation Inc	3552	43	T and G Controls Inc	3625	144	Tab Consulting Inc	5734	286
Systematic Controls Corp	3823	351	T and H Lemont	3547	7	TAB Products Co	2522	6
Systematic Impressions Inc	5099	131	T and J Electric Company Inc	1731	1881	Tabasco Drilling Corp	4959	11
Systematix Controls Inc	3625	146	T and J Electric Corp	1731	1706	Tabb Textiles Company Inc	5023	88
Systemax Inc	5961	9	T and K Holdings Inc	5734	136	TABC Inc	3713	14
Systemetrics Inc (Cambridge Massachusetts)	7372	3953	T and K Specialty Products Inc	3599	979	Tabco Business Forms Inc	5112	56
Systemguru Inc	7379	582	T and L Automatics Inc	3451	41	Tabco Machines Inc	3599	1681
SystemOne Technologies Inc	3569	83	T and L Companions Inc	7361	376	TABcom LLC	7379	78
Systems 3 Inc	3489	14	T and L Foundry Inc	3363	45	Taber Extrusions LLC	3354	39
Systems Alternatives International Inc	7371	1073	T and L Manufacturing Corp	3441	245	Tabernus LLC	7372	3201
Systems Analysis and Integration Inc	3829	186	T and L Sharpening Inc	7699	218	Tabet Manufacturing Company Inc	3669	184
Systems and Communications Sciences Inc	7371	1496	T and L Specialty Company Inc	2899	213	Table Bluff Brewing Inc	2082	72
Systems and Products Engineering Co	3861	113	T and M Controls Inc	3625	306	Table Talk Pies Inc	2051	30
Systems and Software Consortium	7372	1212	T and M Electric Of Clay County Inc	1731	665	Table Trac Inc	7999	136
Systems And Software Enterprises Inc	7371	509	T And M Engineering and Manufacturing Inc	3531	239	Tableland Services Inc	8322	145
Systems and Synchronous Inc	7372	4094	T and M Machining Inc	3599	1885	TableTopics Inc	5092	44
Systems and System Software Solutions LLC	7371	1494	T And M Research Products Inc	3676	30	Tabloid Graphic Services Inc	2711	461
Systems Application Information Network Inc	7379	920	T and M Rubber Inc	3053	105	Tabor Communications Inc	7379	476
Systems Associates Inc (Bowling Green Ohio)	7372	2916	T and M Services Inc	7349	238	Tabor Machine Co	3532	13
Systems Consultants	7372	4136	T and M Trucking Inc	4213	2792	Tabor Machine Company Inc	3599	2412
Systems Consulting Services Inc	7372	884	T and N Manufacturing Company Inc	3053	125	Tabor Plastics Co	3089	1557
Systems Control	3613	32	T and R Chemicals Inc	2861	5	TABS Direct	7331	41
Systems Conversion Ltd	7371	706	T and R Lumber Co	2449	10	TAC Computer Inc	5045	1006
Systems Design and Development Inc	7372	2587	T and R Properties Inc	1521	45	TAC Worldwide Cos	7361	5
Systems Design Northwest Inc	7371	1514	T and S Brass and Bronze Works Inc	3432	20	Tacala Inc	5812	232
Systems Design Simplified Inc	7371	1253	T and S Die Cutting	3544	807	Tacher Co	4899	96
Systems Duplicating Company Inc	2752	1777	T and S Electric Inc	1731	1741	Tachi-S Engineering USA Inc	2531	12
Systems Effectiveness Associates Inc	7372	4644	T and S Equipment Co	3448	52	Tachyon Inc	3669	75
Systems Electrical Services Inc	1731	2345	T and S Fire And Security Inc	1731	1731	Tackett Volume Press Inc	2759	232
Systems Electro Coating LLC	3599	18	T and T Automation Inc	3625	314	Tacki Mac Grips	3069	282
Systems Engineering and Management Co	8711	247	T and T Computer Products Inc	3577	620	Tackle Construction Inc	1623	628
Systems Engineering Associates Inc	3625	323	T and T Equipment Inc	1731	1387	Tackman Pilla Arnone and Company PC	8721	447
Systems Engineering Inc	7699	263	T and T G and S Electrical Contractors	1731	612	Tacna International Corp	8742	453
Systems Engineering Services Corp	7379	282	T and T Graphics Inc	2671	50	Taco Bell Corp	5812	12
Systems Engineering Solutions Inc	8711	132	T and T Int'l Inc	5734	277	Taco Cabana Inc	5812	213
Systems Engineering Technologies Corp	8711	488	T and T Machine Products Inc	3643	153	Taco Inc	3433	11
Systems Equipment Corp	3625	267	T and T Marine Salvage Inc	4959	22	Taco John's International Inc	5812	244
Systems Group Inc	7371	169	T and T Pump Company Inc	3561	102	Taco Metals Inc	5051	191
Systems Group Inc (Galstonbury Connecticut)	7371	155	T and T Staff Management Inc	7361	231	Taco Via Franchise Systems Inc	5812	436
Systems House Inc	5045	278	T and T Tool Inc	3544	33	Tacoma Fixture Company Inc	2434	56
Systems II Transport Inc	4213	1656	T and T Transit Products	7389	1663	Tacoma Metals Inc	4953	167
Systems Implementation Inc	7371	946	T and T Transport Inc	7331	259	Tacoma Recycling Company Inc	7389	862
Systems Integrated LLC	3829	205	T and T Truck and Crane Service Inc	4213	1262	Tacoma Transload Inc	4213	1337
Systems Integration Inc	8742	589	T and T Trucking Inc	4213	872	Tacony Corp	3634	9
Systems Integration Specialists Company Inc	7372	1316	T and V Rental Company Inc	7359	39	Tactara LLC	4813	419
Systems Interface Inc	3823	175	T and W Forge Inc	3462	24	Tactical Power Systems Corp	3613	133
Systems Logistics	4213	1565	T and W Sales Inc	5064	86	Tactical Protection Corp	7382	101
Systems Machines Automation Components Corp	3625	49	T and W Textile Machinery Inc	3552	48	Tactical Technologies Inc	3699	224
Systems Made Simple Inc	7371	235	T and W Tool and Die Corp	3544	249	Tactical TeleSolutions Inc	8713	7
Systems Management Group	7379	939	T C Dunham Paint Company Inc	2851	124	Tactician Corp	7372	2382
Systems Methodologies Inc	7374	247	T C Service Co	3546	28	Tactile Systems Technology Inc	5047	92
Systems People Inc	7379	475	T Cast Holdings LLC	3324	17	Tadin Inc	5499	14
Systems Plus Telecom Inc	5065	300	T/CCI Manufacturing LLC	3069	19	Tadiran Ltd	3639	4
Systems Products International Inc	7372	3632	T Coombs and Associates LLC	8999	91	Tadiran Telecom Inc	5045	123
Systems Resource Management Inc	7371	784	T D M Corp	3599	1660	TAE Trans Atlantic Electronics Inc	3692	9
Systems Sales Corp	5063	329	T Di Russo Electric Contractor Inc	1731	2293	Taeus International Corp	8711	443
Systems Service Enterprises Inc	7379	460	T G Mercer Consulting Services Inc	1623	278	Taft Stettinius and Hollister LLP	8111	233
Systems Services of America	5141	65	T G Schmeiser Company Inc	3523	199	TAG	8721	280
Systems/Software Engineering	7371	270	T Gene Edwards Inc	1541	306	Tag Allen-Bailey and Label Inc	2679	41
Systems Solutions Inc	7379	1158	T Gray Electric Company Inc	5063	532	Tag Diamond and Label	7389	2256
System's South Inc	3599	1776	T G's Supply And Support LLC	3577	645	Tag Easy Corp	7371	1501
Systems Supply Inc	7378	68	T H Stemper Company Inc	5049	109	TAG Employer Services LLC	8721	257
Systems Technology Group Inc	7371	289	T J Snow Company Inc	5084	372	TAG Holdings LLC	3011	8
Systems Technology Inc	7389	1527	T Js Catv Inc	4841	119	Tag Name Inc	2759	489
Systems Technology International Inc	8742	498	T K O Distributors Inc	2752	674	TAG Online Inc	7372	2917
Systems Unlimited Inc	3541	138	T L Wallace Construction Inc	1611	53	Tag Plastics Inc	3089	1347
SystemsNet Inc	7372	3678	T M Electronics Inc	3545	323	Tag Trade Associates Group Ltd	3263	1
SystemSoft Corp	7372	2090	T M Tire Company Inc	5014	38	Taggart Management and Real Estate Services LLC	6531	338
Systemware Inc (Dallas Texas)	7372	2034	T/Maker Research Co	7372	4921	Tagged Inc	7379	210
Systex Inc	7371	1144	T Marzetti Co	2035	2	Tagmar Inc	4813	558
Systex Products Corp	3089	171	T/O Printing Inc	2752	1779	Tag's Bakery Inc	5461	50
Systime Computer Corp	7379	358	T P Supply Company Inc	5084	617	Tague Technologies Inc	2099	366
Systran Software Inc	7372	3118	T Precision Machining Inc	3599	1949	Tahas Technologies Inc	7379	1568
Systrand Manufacturing Corp	3714	193	T R Rizzuto Pizza Crust Inc	2045	11	Tahmc Associates	8331	139
Systron Donner Inertial Div	3812	30	T Rowe Price Group Inc	6211	44	Tahoe Partners LLC	8748	320
Systronix Inc	7373	1201	T Rowe Price Growth and Income Fund Inc	6722	130	Tahoe Rf Semiconductor Inc	3825	252
Sytron Corp	3678	83	T Rowe Price Growth Stock Fund Inc	6722	55	Tahoma Technology Inc	3577	608
Sytronics Inc	7373	507	T Rowe Price International Stock Fund	6722	56	Tai Ham Heon	5063	148
Syvox Corp	3679	442	T Rowe Price Investment Services Inc	6289	11	TAI Inc (Orland Park Illinois)	7372	3231
Syware Inc	7372	4336	T Rowe Price New Era Fund Inc	6722	64	Taif Inc	2032	31
Syzygy Media Works Inc	3695	125	T Rowe Price New Horizons Fund Inc	6722	59	Taiho Corporation Of America	3714	317
Szanca Solutions Inc	7379	714	T Rowe Price Science and Technology Fund Inc	6722	89	Taikan Company Inc	3679	862
T 3 Corp	7373	987	T Sammi Inc	7334	52	Tailor Cut Wood Products Inc	2435	28
			T Skorman Productions Inc	7922	70	Tailor Made Products Inc	3089	747
			T Stats Supply Inc	5063	354	Tailor Made Software Ltd	7379	1535
			T Stephen Johnson and Associates	6211	161	Tailored Chemical Products Inc	2891	26
			T Ultra Equipment Co	3559	377	Tait Machine Tool Inc	3599	2475
			T Volt Inc	1731	2141	Tait Weller and Baker	8721	143
			T W Burleson and Son Inc	2099	339	Taitem Engineering	3433	51
			T2 Systems Inc	7372	1658	Taitron Components Inc	5065	315
						Taiyo Yuden (USA) Inc	3677	7

Company Name	SIC	Rank
Taxware Systems Inc	5734	180
Tayco Engineering Inc	3823	78
Taycor Financial	6159	46
Taycorp Inc	3677	34
Taylor and Fenn Co	3321	12
Taylor and Fulton Inc	0161	4
Taylor and Hill Inc	8711	294
Taylor and Ives Inc	2741	365
Taylor Athletic Wear Inc	2759	553
Taylor Bean and Whitaker Mortgage Corp	6163	19
Taylor Brothers Architectural Products Inc	5031	172
Taylor Building Products Inc	3442	108
Taylor Cable Products Inc	3694	31
Taylor Capital Group Inc	6712	121
Taylor Chair Co	2521	28
Taylor Cheese Corp	2022	82
Taylor Chevrolet Inc	5511	646
Taylor Communications Inc	4832	236
Taylor Co (Rockton Illinois)	3586	5
Taylor Corp	2771	4
Taylor Cos	5511	768
Taylor Courier Service	4215	20
Taylor Desk Co	2521	35
Taylor Devices Inc	3569	70
Taylor Distributing Co	4213	1313
Taylor Elevator Corp	1796	20
Taylor Energy Co	1311	112
Taylor Forbes Equipment Company Inc	5083	141
Taylor Forge Engineered Systems Inc	3443	35
Taylor Forge Stainless Inc	3494	61
Taylor Graphics Inc	2759	369
Taylor King Furniture Inc	2512	60
Taylor Lumber Inc	2421	40
Taylor Machine Works Inc	3537	18
Taylor Made Graphics	7336	262
Taylor Made Group Inc	3732	5
Taylor Made Oil Tools Inc	7353	84
Taylor Made Security Inc	7381	189
Taylor Manufacturing Company Inc	3599	2374
Taylor Manufacturing Inc	3523	78
Taylor Metal Products Co	3469	91
Taylor Metal Works and Pipe Company Inc	3444	207
Taylor Metalworks Inc	3365	19
Taylor Morse Ltd	7334	72
Taylor Packaging Corp	3081	149
Taylor Pittsburgh Co	3523	172
Taylor Press Products Co	3469	241
Taylor Products Company Inc	3565	98
Taylor Properties	6552	209
Taylor Provision Company Inc	2013	65
Taylor Publishing Inc	2731	50
Taylor Services Inc	4213	2328
Taylor Studios Inc	7389	610
Taylor Systems Engineering Corp	7373	879
Taylor Technology Inc	5045	915
Taylor Tool and Machine Company Inc	3599	2323
Taylor Transfer Inc	5012	168
Taylor Truck Line Inc	4213	696
Taylor Trucking Inc	4213	3034
Taylor Turning Inc	3544	14
Taylor Utlimate Services Co	5046	87
Taylor/West Advertising Inc	7311	517
Taylor - Winfield Corp	3548	22
Taylor Woodrow Inc	1531	16
Taylor-Dunn Corp	3523	30
Taylor-Dunn Manufacturing Co	3537	35
Taylored Systems Inc	7389	1070
Taylor-Listug Inc	3931	15
Taylor-Made Transportation	4213	1548
Taylor-Oden Enterprises Inc	7379	1286
Taylor-Ramsey Corp	2421	17
Taylor's Oilfield Manufacturing Inc	7699	87
Taylorsville Times	2711	915
Taylor-Wharton	3443	56
Taymark Inc	5961	77
Tazewell County Resource Centers Inc	8331	102
Tazewell Machine Works Inc	3365	15
TB and P Express Inc	4213	1459
TB Wood's Corp	3569	7
Tba LLC	5074	46
Tbb Inc	2051	60
TBC Corporation Inc	5014	2
TBD Consulting	8742	662
Tbd Networks Inc	7371	1374
TBDN Tennessee Co	3564	17
TBF Graphics	2752	778
TBG Partners Inc	0781	13
TBI Construction and Construction Management Inc	1542	238
TBI Inc	4213	1831
TBM Consulting Group Inc	8742	206
TBM Hardwoods	5031	57
Tbm Inc	5172	87
Tbmc Inc	3061	35
Tbr Marble and Granite Inc	5032	186
TBS Automation Systems Inc	7372	4337
TBSP Inc	7372	4394
TBWA Chiat Day New York	7311	69
TC/American Monorail Inc (Saint Michael Minnesota)	3537	24
Tc Communications Inc	3669	186

Company Name	SIC	Rank
Tc Cosmotronic Inc	3672	122
Tc Electric Company Inc	1731	790
TC Electronic	3669	82
T-C Oil Co	1381	64
TC PipeLines LP	4922	15
TC Transportation Inc	4213	2487
TCA Reservoir Engineering Services Inc	7372	3954
Tcb Systems Inc	7349	122
TCBY Enterprises Inc	2024	7
TCC Dalton Inc	4213	3050
Tcc Printing And Imaging Inc	2759	526
TCDFW Inc	6531	200
TCE Inc	8999	107
Tce/Turbo Components and Engineering Inc	3053	72
TCF Bank Wisconsin FSB	6035	41
TCF Financial Corp	6712	44
TCF National Bank	6035	23
TCF National Bank Illinois	6035	256
TCF National Bank (Wayzata Minnesota)	6021	17
TCH Industries Inc	3364	3
Tch Pediatric Associates Inc	8011	46
Tci Aluminum/North Inc	5051	248
Tci America	5169	131
TCI Companies Inc	8742	598
Tci Electric Inc	1731	1558
TCI International Inc	3663	90
TCI Mobility Inc	3559	414
TCI Powder Coatings	3479	23
TCI Trucking and Warehousing Services	4213	2429
TCI Vacuum Forming Company Inc	3089	1122
TCIM Services Inc	7389	78
TCM Progressive Inc	5084	520
Tcn Behavioral Health Services Inc	8322	123
Tcom Limited Partnership A/K/A Tcom LP	8711	144
Tcp Business System Inc	1731	2142
TCP Inc	3641	6
TCP Reliable Inc	2834	98
TCS Consultants Inc	7372	1581
Tcs International Inc	5045	674
TCS Tele Communication Systems Inc	5999	311
TCSI Inc	4213	1141
TCSN Inc	7379	352
TcsnNet Inc	5734	144
TCT Stainless Steel Inc	5051	509
TCT Trucking Inc	4213	2375
T-Cubed Systems Inc	7372	4561
Tcw Computer Systems Inc	5734	115
TCW Funds Management Inc	6282	19
TCW Group Inc	6282	3
TCW Investment Funds Inc	6722	192
TCW Management Co	6282	76
TCWeiser Construction Co	1542	423
TCX Inc	4213	1660
TD AmeriTrade Holding Corp	6211	38
TD Ameritrade Inc	6289	5
Td Auto Finance LLC	6153	35
TD Banknorth Inc	6712	27
TD Banknorth Wealth Management Group	6722	46
TD Controls Inc	3625	359
TD Express Inc	4213	2682
Td Service Financial Corp	7322	23
TD Williamson Inc	3533	17
TDC Group Inc	7371	1339
TDC Systems Integration	7373	330
Tdi Technologies Inc	7371	1615
Tdi2 Custom Packaging Inc	2673	73
TDI-Halter LP	3731	5
TDIndustries Inc	1711	13
TDK Corporation of America	3675	11
TDK Electronics Corp	5065	360
Tdk Technologies LLC	7371	574
Tdl Inc	3675	41
Tdl Tool Inc	3599	1817
Tdnet Inc	7375	292
Tds Investments Inc	5031	293
TDS METROCOM LLC	4813	7
TDS Telecom Inc	4813	34
TDS Telecommunications Corp	4813	43
TDX Tech	5734	21
TE Connectivity Ltd	5065	4
TE Ibberson Co	1541	95
TE Lott and Co	8721	369
TE Technology Inc	3822	65
Tea Collection	5137	27
TEAC America Inc Data Storage Products Div	3572	34
Teach America Corp	2731	289
Teach Enterprises Inc	3086	40
TEACH Services Inc	2731	344
Teacher Access Inc	5049	197
Teachers Health Trust	6733	11
Teachers Insurance and Annuity Assoc College Retirement Equities Fund	6311	14
Teachers Insurance Co	6331	371
Teacher's Pal Inc	7372	4214
Teachey Mechanical Inc	1711	221
Teagle and Little Inc	2752	595
Teak Isle Inc	2821	60

Company Name	SIC	Rank
Teal Becker and Chiaramonte	8721	90
Teal Becker and Chiaramonte CPA's PC	8721	358
Teal Construction Co	1542	353
Teal Construction Inc	1611	204
Teal Electric Company Inc	5063	275
Teal Electronics Corp	3612	59
Teal's Express Inc	4213	602
Team Apparel Inc	2339	53
Team Chevrolet Oldsmobile Geo Inc	5511	442
Team Concept Printing And Thermography Inc	2759	208
Team Construction LLC	1623	201
Team Corp	3829	157
Team Electric Inc	1731	2258
Team Health Holdings Inc	8099	3
Team Inc	7389	83
Team Industries Inc	3498	16
Team Industries Park Rapids - DI Inc	3599	101
Team Litho Inc	2752	1418
Team Marathon Fitness Inc	5091	96
Team Mazda Hyundai	5511	1073
Team Motor Sales Inc	5511	909
Team Oil Tools LLC	3533	97
Team One Advertising	7311	75
Team One Transport Inc	4213	1230
Team Orthopaedics	5047	235
Team Printing Plus Inc	2752	1160
Team Resources Inc	6531	192
Team Safety Apparel Inc	2326	25
Team Schierl Cos	5983	8
Team Technologies Inc	3991	1
TEAM Technologies Inc (Cedar Falls Iowa)	7382	121
Team Towing and Recovery Inc	7549	25
Team Tsi Corp	7374	239
Team Valor Inc	7948	38
Teamf1 Inc	7371	1386
Teammark International Inc	5734	69
Teammates Commercial Interiors Inc	7389	760
TeamPlay USA	7389	1432
TeamSoft Inc (Middleton Wisconsin)	7371	983
TeamStaff Inc	7363	99
TeamStudio Inc	7372	2252
Teamvantage Molding LLC	3089	710
Teamwork Telecom Inc	4813	514
Teamworks USA Inc	7363	208
Tebben Enterprises Inc	3523	205
Tec Color Craft	2759	242
TEC Communications Inc	5065	727
Tec Electronic Component Inc	5734	104
Tec Engineering Corp	3535	209
Tec Engineering Inc	8711	612
Tec Enterprises Inc	1623	856
Tec Foods Inc	2034	30
Tec Inc	3661	224
TEC Industrial Inc	5085	354
Tec Laboratories Inc	2834	376
TEC Mechanical Service Co	1711	272
Tec South Sales Inc	5065	620
TEC Specialty Products Inc	2891	128
Tec Tec Inc	5734	332
Tec Tran Holding Corp	5088	95
Teca Inc	7372	5068
Tec-Air Inc	3089	264
Tecan Systems	3821	21
Teca-Print USA Corp	3555	120
Teccon Inc	7371	708
Tecdia Inc	5065	945
Tec-Ed Inc	2741	205
Tech Advanced Computers Inc	5734	103
Tech Circuits Inc	3672	246
Tech Color Graphics Inc	2752	392
Tech Communication Inc	3663	272
Tech Conferences Inc	8999	86
Tech Craft Inc	3599	2266
Tech Data Corp	5045	2
Tech Depot Inc	5734	85
Tech Development Inc	3511	27
Tech Electric Company Inc	5063	296
Tech Five Inc	7372	5069
Tech Group Inc	3089	70
Tech Heads Inc	7379	1110
Tech Medical Plastics Inc	3089	1223
Tech Mold Inc	3544	93
Tech Molded Plastics Inc	3089	700
Tech Nh Inc	3089	800
Tech/Ops Sevcon Inc	3625	39
Tech Packaging Inc	4783	10
Tech Pro Inc	7699	156
Tech Products Corp	3625	175
Tech Quip Inc	5084	490
Tech Ridge Inc	3544	641
Tech Spectrum It Consulting Inc	7379	1373
Tech Spray LP	2842	21
Tech Superpowers Inc	5045	697
Tech Supply Inc	5014	14
Tech Time Inc	7372	2931
Tech Tool and Molded Plastics	3544	341
Tech Tool Plastics Inc	3089	1619
Tech Transportation	4213	2423
Tech West Vacuum Inc	3843	62
Tech101 - Arcus Inc	5045	369
Tec-Hackett Inc	5084	449

Company Name	SIC	Rank
TechArts	7371	1322
Techatlantic Inc	3089	888
Techcess Solutions Inc	5045	639
TechCFO	8742	560
Techdemocracy LLC	7371	609
TechDisposal	7389	1110
Techdrive Inc	7379	1292
Teche Electric Supply Inc	5063	286
Teche Holding Co	6712	368
Tech-Energy Co	5084	760
Tech-Etch Inc	3469	56
TechExcel Inc	7372	1865
Techfarm Inc	5045	626
Techflex Inc	5063	525
Techflow Inc	7371	293
Techknow Inc	3679	793
Techlan Inc	5045	863
TechLaw Inc	8748	132
Techline Studio Furniture That Fits Inc	5021	149
Techlink Northwest Inc	7361	98
Techlink Systems Inc	7361	420
Tech-Lite Inc	3669	256
Techlogix Inc	7373	94
Techma USA Inc	8711	344
Tech-Mark Inc	3556	125
Techmart Computer Products Inc	5045	774
Techmaster Inc	5084	642
Techmation Inc	3823	373
Tech-Max Machine Inc	3599	2025
Tech-Med Inc	3469	360
Techmer Pm LLC	2821	48
Techna Plastic Services Inc	3089	1423
Technalithics Inc	8711	685
TECHNALOCK Computer Security	3429	139
Technalysis Inc	7372	469
Technatomy Corp	7379	500
Techne Corp	2836	9
Technell Inc	7311	1031
Technet Resources Inc	8748	107
Techniart Inc	7389	2455
Technic Inc	2899	70
Technica Corp	7373	154
Technical Advisors Group Inc	7372	1932
Technical Analysis Inc	2721	64
Technical and Assembly Services Corp	3672	438
Technical and Project Engineering LLC	7379	279
Technical and Scientific Application Inc	5045	320
Technical Assistance Inc	5731	198
Technical Automation Services Company Ltd	8711	289
Technical Building Services Inc	5063	280
Technical Chemical Co	2819	37
Technical Coating International Inc	3089	1110
Technical Communications Corp	3663	119
Technical Communities Inc	5734	10
Technical Connection Inc	7361	365
Technical Controls Inc	3674	351
Technical Devices Co	3548	41
Technical Die-Casting Inc	3363	41
Technical Education Research Centers Inc	8748	160
Technical Education Solutions LLC	5045	1025
Technical Fabrication Inc	3672	390
Technical Film Systems Inc	3861	101
Technical Glass Products Inc	3559	256
Technical Group Inc	7363	296
Technical Hardfacing And Machining Inc	3599	2190
Technical Heaters Inc	3052	33
Technical Instrument San Francisco	5049	65
Technical Machine Products Inc	3559	477
Technical Management Associates Inc	1731	510
Technical Manufacturing Corp	3672	332
Technical Marine Service Inc	3731	55
Technical Material Corp	3663	399
Technical Metals Inc	3469	180
Technical Methods Inc	3543	47
Technical Ordnance Inc	2899	83
Technical Precision Inc	3544	729
Technical Precision Plastics Inc	3089	599
Technical Programming Services Inc	7374	233
Technical Reality Inc	5045	602
Technical Rubber Company Inc	3011	15
Technical Sales And Services Inc	3999	143
Technical Screen Printing Inc	2759	344
Technical Service Corp	5065	839
Technical Services for Electronics Inc	3679	31
Technical Services Group Inc	5065	528
Technical Services Labs Inc	3672	444
Technical Software Consulting Inc	7379	929
Technical Software Services Inc	2741	95
Technical Solutions And Maintenance Inc	7371	984
Technical Solutions Inc	7363	171
Technical Sound Development	3651	262
Technical Support Inc	3672	240
Technical Support International	7379	1387
Technical Systems Inc	3823	106
Technical Telephone Systems Inc	5065	145
Technical Training Inc	2731	71
Technicair Inc	5531	20
Techniche International	5099	143
Technicolor Creative Services	7371	714
Technicolor Inc	7819	20
Technicolor Video Services Inc	7819	4
Technicolor Videocassette	3652	2
Technicolor Videocassette Of Michigan Inc	7819	16
Technicom Services Inc	7389	1484
TechniCon Computer Services	7372	3028
Technicon Industries Inc	3086	76
Technicraft Inc	7373	1156
Technidrill Systems Inc	3541	136
Technidyne Corp	3823	184
Technifab Inc	3086	177
Technifab Products Inc	3559	185
TechniFoam Inc	3089	743
Techniform Industries Inc	3089	1267
Techni-Glass Inc	3231	58
Technigraphics Inc	7334	80
Technigraphics Of Maryland Inc	3479	94
Techniku Inc	2591	17
Technimark LLC	3089	112
Technintel Systems Inc	7382	146
Technipaq Inc	3089	507
Technipower LLC	3679	413
Technipower Systems Inc	3625	118
Techni-Products Inc	3599	1031
Technique Consulting Group Inc	7379	1655
TechniScan Inc	5047	288
Techniserv Inc	3822	44
Techni-Soft	7372	3367
Technisonic Studios Inc	7812	199
TechniSource Inc	7371	55
Technisphere	3669	179
Technitool Inc	3089	1385
Techni-Tool Inc	5072	41
Technitrol Delaware Inc	3679	1
Techno - Graphics and Translations Inc	2741	292
Techno Inc	3824	19
Techno-Aide Inc	3841	248
Technocean Inc	3699	296
Techno-Coat Inc	3479	25
Technodrill Inc	3672	494
Technofan Inc	3812	183
Technological Artisans Inc	3679	799
Technologies/Typography	2791	66
Technology Advancement Group Inc	3571	91
Technology Alternatives Corp	3575	41
Technology and Management Services Inc	7363	121
Technology Assessment And Transfer Inc	8731	267
Technology Associates Inc	7372	3385
Technology Concepts Group Inc	7379	1305
Technology Dynamics Inc	3679	323
Technology For Energy Corp	3829	137
Technology for Productivity	7371	1919
Technology Integration Group Inc	7371	63
Technology Investment Partners LLC	7377	14
Technology Management Resources Inc	7371	1589
Technology Partners	6799	281
Technology Planning Inc	7371	1206
Technology Project Finance LLC	7359	173
Technology Publishing Co	2731	248
Technology Recovery Group Ltd	7379	933
Technology Research Corp	3613	33
Technology Resource Center Inc	5045	433
Technology Resources Inc	7361	163
Technology Solutions Inc	7371	965
Technology Solutions of SC Inc	7379	994
Technology Specialist Inc	7378	56
Technology Specialists Inc	5045	653
Technology Systems Inc	7371	1094
Technology Transfer	5045	387
Technology Upgrade Corp	5045	488
Technology Ventures Inc	7379	229
Techno-Sciences Inc	8711	183
Technosoft Corp	7371	27
Technotape USA Inc	5043	37
Technotel Inc	7371	1670
technotrans america Inc	3669	40
Technova Group Inc	7372	3029
Technovant Inc	8748	355
TechNovation Software	7372	4987
Technovative Applications Inc	3812	146
Technox Machine and Manufacturing Inc	3541	157
Techny Plastics Corp	3089	1405
Techone Trading Company Inc	5045	1051
Techpack America Cosmetic Packaging Inc	3089	85
TECHPLAN Corp	8731	151
TechPool Software	7372	4763
TechPrecision Corp	3449	3
Tech-Pro	8748	39
TechQuest Inc	5045	580
Techquest International Inc	7379	1098
TechRack Systems	2542	72
TechRadium Inc	7372	2014
Techrep Components Inc	5063	1053
Techshot	8711	360
TechSkills LLC	7372	295
TechSmith Corp	7372	1601
Techsoft Inc	5045	997
TechSoft Systems Inc	7379	652
TechSpace Inc	7373	245
Techsquare Inc	7379	1445
Tech-Star Industries Inc	3599	2340
Techstructures LLC	7371	1184
Tech-Styles Window Covering Products Inc	5023	170
Techsys Advanced Resources LLC	7379	931
TechTarget Inc	7379	104
Techtel Marketing Inc	5065	401
Techtele Communications LLC	1731	1858
Techteriors LLC	1731	2122
Tech-Time Communication Inc	1731	2377
Techtrol Cyclonetics Inc	3679	569
Techtron Corp	3825	216
Techtron Products Inc	3645	47
Techtron Systems Inc	3672	190
Techtronics LLC	3651	227
Techturn Ltd	7373	189
Tech-Way Industries Inc	3089	959
Techwood Industrial Gases LLC	5169	153
TechWorks Inc	3572	32
Teck Solutions Inc	5734	292
Teclab Inc	3821	37
Tecma Group LP	4225	1
Tecmag Inc	3679	639
Tecmark	5045	821
Tec-Masters Inc	7372	1306
Tecmer Inc	8742	492
TECMO KOEI AMERICA CORP	7372	1577
Tecnetics Industries Inc	3535	144
Tecnico Corp	3446	11
Tecniflex Inc	7699	31
Tecnifoam Inc	3086	148
Tecnocap LLC	3354	7
Tecnolux Inc	3993	186
Tecnomasium Inc	3699	268
Tecnomatic Corp	5063	1079
Teco Coal Corp	1241	3
Teco Corp	6531	458
Teco Diagnostics	2835	45
TECO Diversified Inc	6719	18
Teco Electric Motors Inc	5063	821
TECO Energy Inc	4911	46
Teco Holdings USA Inc	6719	79
Te-Co Manufacturing LLC	3545	98
Tecogen Inc	7623	8
Tecolote Research Inc	6282	79
Tecom Industries Inc	3663	98
Tecore Inc	5065	204
Tecplot Inc	7372	2783
Tecra Systems Inc	7372	3396
Tecre Company Inc	3542	65
Tecsol Manufacturing Inc	3599	2240
TECSYS US Inc	7372	1206
Tect Aerospace Wellington Inc	3728	44
Tecta America Corp	1761	2
Tecton Industries Inc	3599	643
Tectonics Inc	3599	2457
Tectrix Inc	8249	18
Tectron Engineering	3669	272
Tectum Inc	2493	4
Tecumseh Packaging Solutions Inc	2653	104
Tecumseh Products Co	3585	16
Ted Britt Ford	5511	86
Ted Chin and Company Inc	7311	700
Ted Gruber Software Inc	7372	4890
Ted Levine Drum Co	7699	60
Ted Manufacturing Corp	3643	85
TEDCO Construction Corp	1542	275
TEdec System Inc	7372	997
Tedeschi Vineyards Ltd	2084	31
Tedia Company Inc	2869	77
Teds Supply Inc	5085	421
Ted's Trash Service Inc	4953	135
Tee Group Films Inc	3081	97
Tee Lee Popcorn Inc	2099	331
Tee Tool Inc	3089	1880
TeeBerry Express Inc	4213	1364
Teeco Products Inc	5074	38
Teejet Technologies Illinois LLC	3679	375
Teel Plastics Inc	3089	239
Teeny Foods	2051	152
Tefen USA Ltd	8748	310
Teflex Inc	2821	206
Teg Corp	2752	941
Tegal Corp	3559	589
Tegam Inc	3829	208
Tegrant Corp	3086	5
Tei Electronics Inc	3931	34
TEI Engineered Products Inc	5084	746
Teichman Enterprises Inc	2542	58
Teijin Kaisei America Inc	3679	150
Teijin Kasei America Inc	3679	207
Tejas Inc	6211	306
Tejas Machines Inc	1389	59
Tejas Supreme Meat	7389	1978
Tejas Warehouse Transportation	4213	2572
Tejon Ranch Co	6519	21
Tek Data Systems Co	7372	3246
TEK Industries Inc	3571	132
Tek Pak Inc	2672	61
Tek Resource Service Corp	3577	582
Tek-Air Systems Inc	3829	174
Tekcast Industries Inc	3544	627
Tekelec	3669	13

Company Name	SIC	Rank
Tekena USA LLC	5065	468
Tekever Corp	7372	2743
Teklinks Inc	7371	172
Teklynx International	7372	955
Tekmark Global Solutions LLC	7379	125
Tekmate LLC	1731	868
Tekmethods LLC	7379	512
Teknational Thermal Insulation And Hardware Inc	3679	837
Teknetix Inc	3672	70
Teknic Inc	3625	153
Teknicote Inc	3479	44
Teknion Data Solutions Ltd	7379	1088
Tekno Books Inc	5999	201
Tekno Inc	3535	182
Teknol Inc	2899	102
Teknon Corp	1731	282
Teknon Inc	7372	3679
Teknor Apex Co	3087	2
Teknowledge Corp	7371	1340
Tekota Electric Inc	1731	1610
Tekquest Inc	3679	553
Tekquest Industries Corp	3564	163
Teksavers Inc	8999	88
Tekscan Inc	3812	114
TekScape	7373	142
Teksell Inc	7379	545
Tekserve Corp	7378	10
Teksolutions Inc	1731	1388
Tek-Star Computer Service Inc	7371	949
Teksun Inc	3089	1811
Teksync Inc	7371	1143
TekSystems Inc	7376	1
Tektest Inc	3678	63
Tektone Sound and Signal Manufacturing Inc	3669	150
Tek-Tools Inc	7371	401
Tektronix Development Co	6799	5
Tektronix Inc	3825	6
Tektronix Service Solutions	8734	50
Tektube Group LLC	3052	30
Tekvisions Inc	3829	202
TekVizion PVS Inc	5045	246
Tel Systems	7812	115
Tel Tech International	7372	3119
Tela Innovations Inc	3674	333
TELACU Industries Inc	6036	17
Tel-Adjust Inc	8721	250
Telaid Industries Inc	3661	38
Telair International Inc	3537	6
Telairity Semiconductor Inc	3674	206
Telamon Corp	7373	65
Telan Corp	3679	514
Telarus Inc	7389	705
Telassist Inc	5045	705
Telatemp Corp	3829	350
Telco Communications Inc	8743	80
Telco Intercontinental Corp	5063	581
Telco Machine and Manufacturing Inc	3599	1237
Telco Systems Inc	3661	107
Telcom Construction Inc	1623	72
Telcom Corp	1731	2492
Tel-Communication Inc	1731	596
Telcon LLC	3599	384
Tel-Conn Manufacturing Inc	3663	287
Telcordia Technologies Inc	7372	38
Teldata Communications Inc	1731	1351
Tele Data Contractors Inc	1731	2533
Tele Type Co Inc	7372	3746
TeleBright Corp	4899	48
Telebright Software Corp	7371	1407
Telebyte Inc	3577	266
Telecable Systems Inc	1731	1230
Telecare Corp	8063	11
Telecentre Of Indiana Inc	4813	638
Telecheck Services Inc (Houston Texas)	7389	87
Telechem International Inc	3674	287
TeleChoice Inc (Richmond Virginia)	8742	615
Teleco Inc	5065	136
Telecoast Communications LLC	7373	765
Telecom Assemblies Plus Inc	4841	103
Telecom Decision Makers Inc	4813	700
Telecom Electric Supply Co	5063	433
Telecom Enterprises Inc	1731	1237
Telecom Industries LLC	3661	115
Telecom Management Inc	5065	460
Telecom Networking Systems Inc	1731	825
Telecom Solutions Div	3663	34
Telecomm Research Associates	8331	117
Tele-Communication Installation and Technology	1623	597
Telecommunication Resources Inc	5063	323
TeleCommunication Systems Inc	7372	141
Telecommunications Concepts Inc	5065	131
Telecommunications Contracting Company Inc	1623	309
Telecommunications Management Solutions Inc	1731	496
Telecommunity Credit Union	6062	89
Telecomp Inc	7389	1069
Telecorp Products Inc	7372	1954
Telect Inc	3661	17
Teledata Communications Inc	7374	214

Company Name	SIC	Rank
Teledata Communications LLC	4813	489
Teledata Inc	5734	424
Teledata Technology Solutions Inc	7371	209
TeleDirect International Inc	7372	2246
Teledraft Inc	7374	151
Teledynamics Communications Service Corp	1731	818
Teledyne Advanced Pollution Instrumentation Inc	3823	115
Teledyne Analytical Instruments	3826	43
Teledyne Benthos	3999	69
Teledyne Brown Engineering Inc	3812	26
Teledyne Continental Motors Battery Products	3691	27
Teledyne Continental Motors Inc	3724	16
Teledyne Controls	8731	86
Teledyne Cougar Inc	3679	132
Teledyne Electronic Technology	3577	131
Teledyne Hastings Instruments Div	3545	4
Teledyne Interconnect Devices	3577	200
Teledyne Odom Hydrographic Inc	3829	6
Teledyne Relays	3679	137
Teledyne TapTone	3823	113
Teledyne Technologies Inc	8711	17
Teledyne Webb Research	3732	53
Teleflex Inc	3841	14
Teleflex Marine Inc	3714	211
Teleflex Medical OEM	3082	1
Teleflora LLC	7389	397
Telefonix Inc	3661	131
Telefutura 49 Kstr	4833	204
Telefutura Houston LLC	4833	40
Telefutura Tampa LLC	4833	104
Telegartner Inc	3643	108
Telegenix Inc	3669	260
Telegraph Herald Inc	2711	251
Telegraph Publishing Co	2711	237
Telegroup Business Unit (Fairfield Iowa)	4813	68
Telehouse International Corporation of America	7376	28
Telekenex	4899	36
Telelink Communications Inc	1731	1418
Telemac Corp	7373	626
Telemach Information International Inc	5734	212
Telematch Inc	7375	162
TelemateNet Software Inc	7372	1594
TeleMatrix Equipment LLC	7011	207
Telemechanics Inc	3577	237
Telemed Inc	7389	1485
Tele-Media Corporation of Delaware	4841	56
Telemet America Inc	7311	882
Telemetrics Inc	3663	248
Telemetrix Inc	3663	407
Telemetry And Process Controls Inc	3589	217
Telemundo Group Inc	4833	80
Telenaut Communications	7336	334
TeleNav Inc	3669	26
Telenity Inc	4899	33
Telenomics Inc	7372	4562
Telenotes Inc	7373	597
Telepartner International Inc	7372	4477
Telephone and Data Systems Inc	4813	10
Telephone Answering	7389	2269
Telephone Associates Inc	5065	375
Telephone Electronics Corp	4813	155
Telephone Equipment Supply Inc	3661	207
Telephone Exchange	7389	1852
Telephone Look-Up Service Co	7389	1129
Telephone Man Inc	1731	1120
Telephone Service Co	4813	134
Telephone Technical Services Inc	1731	2497
Telephone Tools Of Georgia Inc	3423	84
TelephoneBiz Inc	4813	572
Telephonetics Inc	5099	95
Telephonics Corp	3669	18
Telephonics Large Scale Integration	3674	268
Telepoint Communications Inc	7389	357
Telepress Inc	2752	667
TeleProductions International Ltd	7812	261
Telequest Communications Inc	7361	407
Teleran Technologies Inc	7372	1424
Telerent Leasing Corp	7359	23
Telerx Marketing Inc	7389	291
Telesavers Inc	5065	939
Telescan Corp	4813	563
Telescope Inc	2711	911
Telescript Inc	3663	299
Teleshuttle Corp	7375	221
Telesight Inc	7389	1011
Telesis Corp	7371	511
Telesis Technologies Inc	3953	5
Telesodt Technologies Inc	5065	782
Telesoft Corp	7373	318
TeleSoft International Inc	7372	3232
Tele-Solutions Inc	1731	1691
Telesource Inc	7389	428
TeleSpectrum Worldwide Inc	7389	176
Telesphere Networks Inc	4899	114
Telestream Inc	7372	682
TeleSynthesis Inc	7371	234
Teletec Communications LLC	7629	48
Teletec Corp	8748	337
TeleTech Holdings Inc	7363	16

Company Name	SIC	Rank
Teletechnologies Inc	5065	932
Tele-Tector Of Maryland Inc	5999	164
Teletime Video Productions Inc	7812	215
Teletouch Communications Inc	4812	40
Teletracking Technologies Inc	7373	229
Teletrol Systems Inc	3829	183
Teletypesetting Company Inc	7372	4117
Televerde	8748	19
TeleVideo Inc	3575	19
Television Equipment Associates	3669	141
Television Food Network	4841	17
Television Measurement Services	3825	356
Television Production Service Inc	7922	55
Television-Electronics Co	7622	4
Tele-Vue Optics Inc	3827	132
Tele-Vue Service Company Inc	5045	445
Telewave Inc	3663	143
Telewizja Polska USA Inc	4833	244
Telework Analytics International Inc	7372	3955
Telex Communications Inc	3663	26
Telhio Credit Union Inc	6062	48
Teligent Inc	4812	9
Teligentems LLC	3672	144
Telik Inc	2834	459
Tel-Instrument Electronics Corp	3679	246
Telios Tech LLC	5045	830
Teliris Ltd	5045	101
Telisimo International	4899	152
Telkonet Inc	4899	138
Tell Steel Inc	5051	107
Tell Tool Inc	3728	124
Tella Tool and Manufacturing Co	3544	66
Tellabs Inc	3661	3
Tellabs (Naperville Illinois)	3661	37
Tellabs Operations Inc	3663	9
Tellpsen Builders LP	1541	59
Tellico Electric Co	4911	319
Tellme Networks Inc	7372	87
Tellurex Corp	3674	321
Tellurian Technologies Inc	3679	732
Telma Retarder Inc	3714	299
Telmar Information Services Corp (New York New York)	7379	365
Telmex USA LLC	5999	136
Tel-Net Group Inc	1731	1794
Telnet USA Inc	5065	398
Telnet Worldwide Inc	4813	460
Telog Instruments Inc	3829	258
Telogis Inc	7373	233
Telogy Inc	6159	79
Telogy Networks Inc	7372	782
Telonics Inc	3663	144
Telophase Corp	7379	934
Telos Corp	7373	57
Telos Online Inc	7379	674
Telovations Inc	7379	689
Telpage Inc	4812	86
Tel-Phone Resources Co	5065	778
Tel-Power Inc	1623	231
Telquest International Corp	5065	167
Telrad Connegy	4813	94
Telrepco Inc	5045	559
Telrex	7389	472
Telscape International Inc	4813	176
Telsco Industries Inc	3432	31
Telsmith Inc	3531	37
Telsource Corp	7373	122
TelStar Associates Inc	7372	1274
Telstar Instruments	1731	561
Telstrat International Ltd	7389	861
Teltec Corp	3672	94
Tel-Tech Systems	1731	2176
Tel-Tron Technologies Corp	3625	222
Teltronics Inc	3661	61
Tel-Tru Inc	3823	169
Telular Corp	3663	62
TelVue Corp	3661	159
Telwares Communications LLC	8742	235
Telx Group Inc	7376	11
Tema Systems Inc	3532	59
Tembec Bllsr Inc	2821	90
Temco Service Industries Inc	7349	17
Temco Tool Company Inc	3544	399
Temcor	3355	8
Temic Semiconductors	3674	73
Temo Inc	3448	26
Tempaco Inc	5084	407
Temp-Air Inc	3585	99
Temp-Cal Enterprises LLC	3829	507
Tempcare Homehealth Services Inc	7363	297
Tempco Electric Heater Corp	3567	10
Tempco Engineering Inc	8711	197
Tempco Manufacturing Co	3469	142
Tempco Products Co	3089	760
Temp-Control Mechanical Corp	1711	81
Temp-Distribution of Maryland Inc	4213	990
Tempe Mission Palms	7011	91
Tempe St Luke's Hospital LP	8062	58
Tempel Steel Co	3469	13
Temper Corp	3493	15
Temperature Control Specialties Company Inc	3822	57
Temperature Corporation Inc	3625	209

Company Name	SIC	Rank
Temperature Equipment Corp	5075	14
Temperature Systems Inc	5075	25
Temp-Flex Cable Inc	3357	14
Tempico Inc	3999	152
Temple Bottling Company Ltd	2086	97
Temple Machine Shop Inc	3593	33
Temple Systems Inc	8711	686
Temple Tag Ii Ltd	3089	987
Temple Trucking Inc	4213	1488
Temple-Inland Forest Products Corp	2421	11
Temple-Inland Inc	2631	4
Templeton Coal Company Inc	5074	61
Templeton Foreign Smaller Companies Fund	6722	200
Templeton Investment Counsel Inc	6282	56
Templeton Paving LLC	1611	221
Templeton Russia and East European Fund Inc	6726	83
Templeton Worldwide Inc	6282	210
Templex Inc	3083	74
Templock Enterprises LLC	3086	170
Tempmate Inc	7361	201
Tempo Glove Manufacturing Inc	2381	8
Tempo Graphics Inc	2752	672
Tempo Industries Inc	3646	10
Tempo Lighting Inc	3645	30
Tempo Plastic Co	3086	157
Temporary Housing Directory Inc	7299	19
Temporary Solutions Inc	7361	100
TemPositions Group of Cos	7363	197
Temp-Pro Inc	3823	232
Temprel Inc	3829	270
Temps Inc	7363	191
Temps Today Inc	7363	189
Tempt Instore Productions	2752	1153
Temptek Inc	3822	93
TempTime	3823	99
Tempur-Pedic International Inc	2515	2
Tempus It Staffing LLC	7361	268
TempWorks Software Inc	7372	990
Temrex Corp	3843	58
Temtex Temperature Systems Inc	3599	2396
Ten Brink Underground	1623	501
Ten Cate Enbi Inc (Shelbyville Indiana)	3069	102
Ten Technology	3651	208
Tenable Network Security Inc	7372	846
Tenacious Cleaning Services Inc	7349	239
Tenant Advisors Inc	6531	50
Tenaska Gas Co	4923	10
Tenaska Inc	4911	74
Tenax Corp	3089	216
Tenax Finishing Products Co	2851	165
Tenberry Software Inc	7372	5049
Tencarva Machinery Co	5084	52
Ienco Assemblies Inc	7331	94
Tend Business Services Inc	7322	192
Tender Corp	2879	22
Tender Loving Care Health Care Services Inc	8082	48
Tendercare Inc	8051	26
Tenderloin Neighborhood Development Corp	8748	155
Tenebril Inc	7372	1422
Tenenbaum's Vacation Stores Inc	4724	98
Tenenblatt Corp	2257	7
Tenere Inc	3444	31
Tenet Healthcare Corp	8062	8
Tenet HealthSystem Holdings Inc	8062	4
Tenetix Inc	1623	247
Tenex Corp	3089	148
Tenex Systems Inc	7371	870
TenFold (Oakland California)	7379	1214
Tengasco Inc	1311	186
Tengion Inc	3841	410
Tenibac-Graphion Inc	3469	144
Tenino Telephone Co	4813	304
Ten-Lab	3651	104
Tenmast Software Inc	7372	3333
Tenn Tom Publishing Inc	2711	769
Tennant Co	3589	5
Tennant Printing Company Inc	2752	901
Tenneco Inc	3714	7
Tennessee Apparel Corp	2311	15
Tennessee Building Stone Inc	5032	122
Tennessee Bun Co	2051	115
Tennessee Commerce Bancorp Inc	6712	242
Tennessee Commercial Warehouse Inc	4213	595
Tennessee Cummins Mid-South LLC	3599	35
Tennessee Electric Motor Co	5063	204
Tennessee Endoscopy Center	8011	93
Tennessee Farmers Cooperative Inc	5191	50
Tennessee Gas Pipeline Co	4922	46
Tennessee Industrial Printing Services Inc	2752	1082
Tennessee Marketing Association Inc	5046	299
Tennessee Mat Company Inc	3069	83
Tennessee Metal Works Inc	3599	2150
Tennessee Motor Co	5511	706
Tennessee Precision Inc	3544	683
Tennessee Scale Works Inc	5046	257
Tennessee Sewing Machine Attachment Company Inc	3559	443
Tennessee Stone Products LLC	5032	146
Tennessee Technical Coatings Corp	2851	157

Company Name	SIC	Rank
Tennessee Tool And Engineering Inc	3544	149
Tennessee Traders and Technicians	4213	2771
Tennessee Valley Authority	4911	6
Tennessee Valley Electric Coop	4911	467
Tennessee Valley Press Inc	2759	455
Tennessee Valley Recycling LLC	5093	84
Tennessee Wire Technologies LLC	5063	422
Tennis Channel Inc	4841	54
Tennis Corporation of America	8741	45
Tennsco Corp	2522	7
Tennsmith Inc	3549	34
Tenn-Tex Plastics Inc	3089	1788
Tennyson Electric Inc	1731	640
Tennyson Maxwell Information Systems Inc	7372	3956
Tenon Intersystems	7372	4361
Tenrox Inc	7372	2026
Tensar Corp	3089	75
Tensas Delta Exploration Company LLC	1382	14
Tensilica Inc	3674	184
Tension Envelope Corp	2677	24
Tensitron Inc	3829	442
Tensor Group Inc	3555	46
Tensor Systems Corp	7371	1371
Tente Casters Inc	3562	26
Ten-Tec Inc	3663	223
Tenth City LLC	6531	134
Tentina Window Fashions Inc	2591	15
Teoco Corp	7372	1602
Teogas Inc	5734	106
Tepco Corp	2844	191
Teplis Travel Service	4724	74
Tepper Electric Supply Inc	5063	368
Tepper Galleries Inc	7389	2299
Tepro Florida Inc	3676	17
Tepro Inc	3061	12
Tepro Vacuum Products Inc	3563	60
Teq Digital	7372	4091
Teq Solutions Inc	7371	1659
Ter Precision Machining Inc	3599	1745
Tera Research Inc	8711	593
TERA Technologies Inc	7371	402
Teraco Inc	3089	464
Teracore	7379	702
Teradata Corp	3571	10
Teradyne Inc	3825	4
Teragon Financial Corp	6035	76
Terahertz Technologies Inc	3825	296
Tera-Lite Inc	1752	12
Terasoff International Inc	7371	778
Teratech Corp	3845	91
TeraTech Inc	7372	3217
TeraThink Corp	8742	506
Teratron Inc	7371	1785
Tercica Inc	2834	486
Terco Inc	3565	138
Teres Audio Inc	3651	256
Teres Solutions Inc	5734	86
Teresa Foods Inc	2038	86
Teresa Rhoades	3572	105
Teresi Trucking Inc	4213	1768
Terex Corp	3715	1
Terex Mining	3531	46
Terex Utilities Inc	5084	130
Terhorst Manufacturing Co	3089	926
Termax Corp	3965	10
Terme Bancorp Inc	6712	681
Terminal Amusement Co	5962	23
Terminal Consolidation Co	4213	1527
Terminal Corp	4214	17
Terminal Manufacturing Company LLC	3441	223
Terminal Rexall Pharmacy	3873	20
Terminal Transport Inc	4213	1863
Terminal Transportation Service	4213	2198
Terminal Trucking Co	4212	28
Terminella and Associates	6531	284
Termini Brothers Inc	2051	171
Terminix Service Inc	7342	5
Terminus Design Inc	7371	1783
Ternion Inc	5046	145
Tero Tek International Inc	7389	1726
Terocelo Inc	7371	785
Terog Manufacturing Co	3523	149
Teron Lighting Inc	3646	60
Teros Inc	7373	282
Terpening Trucking Company Inc	4213	1812
Terphane Inc	2821	120
Terra Chips	2096	29
Terra Communications Inc	7373	522
Terra Comp Technology	3571	229
Terra Data Inc	7372	4563
Terra Firm Inc	1623	404
Terra Furniture Inc	2511	96
Terra Infosystems Inc	7379	885
Terra Infotech Inc	7379	415
Terra Innova Investments Inc	3585	167
Terra Networks Operations Inc	4813	309
Terra Point USA Inc	7389	1979
Terra Technology	5045	287
Terra Technology LLC	7379	867
Terrabank Holding Corp	6712	301
Terrabank NA	6021	229
Terrace Security Co	7381	81

Company Name	SIC	Rank
Terrace Supply Co	5013	188
Terracon Consultants Inc	8711	74
Terracon Corp	3089	1401
TerraCycle Inc	5093	142
Terradigm Inc	8742	477
Terrafina Inc	3843	60
Terrahealth Inc	7361	21
Terral Riverservice Inc	5191	100
Terra-Mar Resource Information Services Inc	7371	1677
Terranetti's Italian Bakery	5149	173
Terranomics Retail Services LP	6531	174
Terranova Of California Inc	2022	39
Terratek Inc	8731	194
Terre Haute Grain Co	5153	106
Terre Hill Silo Company Inc	3272	78
Terrell Manufacturing Inc	3599	1184
Terrell's Potato Chip Company Inc	2096	36
Terremark Dallas	7379	148
Terremark Worldwide Inc	4813	53
TerreNAP Data Centers Inc	4813	579
Terreno Realty Corp	6798	172
TerreStar Corp	4899	236
Terri Lynn Inc	2068	17
Terrier Transportation Inc	4213	2691
Terrill Transportation Inc	4213	1924
Territorial Newspapers	2711	141
Teronics Development Corp	8731	376
Terry Fryer Music Inc	7819	93
Terry Heffernan Films	7335	32
Terry Hines and Assoc	7311	752
Terry J Martin Associates	8712	320
Terry L Marion	5082	179
Terry Laboratories Inc	2869	123
Terry M Harden Architects	8712	302
Terry Palecek Inc	4213	2683
Terry Print Solutions	2752	1357
Terry Spell Mechanical Services Inc	1731	1116
Terry Tree Service LLC	0783	4
Terryberry Company LLC	3911	19
Terry-Durin Co	5063	508
Terry's Machine and Manufacturing Inc	3599	2191
Terumo Cardiovascular Systems Corp	3845	14
Tervela	3577	164
Tervis Tumbler Co	3089	439
Tes Electrical Construction Inc	1731	1250
Tesa Tape Inc	2672	29
Tescan USA Inc	5049	201
Tesco Industries Inc	2521	15
Tesco South Inc	5083	74
Tescom Inc	5065	665
Tescom (USA) Software Systems Testing Inc	8999	51
TesComm Inc	7379	76
Tescor Inc	3826	85
Tescor Technology Inc	3648	94
Teseda Corp	5045	608
Tesla Motors Inc	5012	39
Tesla Vineyards LP	2084	118
Tesora Hawaii Corp	2911	32
Tesoro Alaska Co	2911	48
Tesoro Corp	2911	10
Tesoro Corp	1541	194
Tesoro Electronics Inc	3812	153
Tesoro Enterprises Inc	5099	151
Tess Data Systems Inc	7372	3957
Tessa Precision Products Inc	3599	1088
Tessco Technologies Inc	5065	21
Tessenderlo Kerley Inc	2819	71
Tessera Technologies Inc	3674	78
Tessler and Weiss/Premesco Inc	3911	16
Tessolvedts Inc	7371	683
Tessy Plastics Corp	3089	203
Test America Analytical Testing Corp	8734	77
Test and Controls International Inc	3825	203
Test and Experimentation Services Co	8711	317
Test And Measurement Instrumentation Inc	3672	309
Test and Measurement Systems Inc	3695	83
Test And Repair Services	3571	249
Test Country	8099	79
Test Equipment Remarketers Inc	5065	335
Test Equipment Solution Today	5065	446
Test Laboratories Inc	2099	360
Test Logic Inc	3825	254
Test Products Inc	3825	171
Test Switch	3825	361
Test Systems Inc	3825	357
Test Technology Inc	7629	14
Testa Communications	2721	60
Testa Consulting Services Inc	7379	1416
Testa Machine Company Inc	3599	839
Testek Inc	3829	62
Testers Inc	3533	96
Testing Engineers Inc	8734	111
Testing Machines Inc	3829	80
Testmasters Inc	7372	3747
Testmetrix Inc	3825	196
Testor Corp	2891	12
TestPak Inc	7389	756
TestQuest Inc	7372	1065
Testrite Instrument Company Inc	2542	25
Testron Inc	3829	362
Testronic Labs	8999	131

Company Name	SIC	Rank
Testware Associates Inc	7379	667
Tetco Inc	4213	324
Teter's Faucet Parts Corp	5074	178
Tethers Unlimited Inc	3724	73
Teton Machine Co	3599	602
Teton Transportation Inc	4213	191
TETRA Financial Services Inc	6289	2
Tetra Pak Americas Inc	3565	64
TETRA Process Services LC	2819	44
TETRA Production Testing GP LLC	1389	21
TETRA Real Estate LLC	6531	10
Tetra Tech FW Inc	8748	42
Tetra Tech HEI	7389	2288
Tetra Tech Inc	8711	12
Tetra Tech Inc (Kansas City Kansas)	8734	169
Tetra Technologies Inc	2819	15
Tetra Technologies Inc Specialty Chemicals Recycling Div	4953	73
Tetra Tool Co	3089	1818
Tetrad Computer Applications Inc	7372	3748
Tetrad Electronics Inc	3672	115
Tetrad Inc	3699	303
Tetradyne Software Inc	7372	3847
Tetragenics Co	3625	105
Tetrahedron Associates Inc	3542	100
Tettmar and Associates Inc	3823	485
Teva Animal Health Inc	2834	94
Teva Pharmaceuticals	2834	11
TEVA Pharmaceuticals USA	2834	58
Teva Respiratory LLC	2834	31
Tewell-Warren Printing Co	2752	578
Tewl Brothers Machine Inc	5084	896
Tex Flock Inc	2262	4
Tex Isle Supply Inc	5051	159
Tex Robbins Transportation LLC	4213	150
Tex Tan Western Leather Co	3111	9
Tex Trend Inc	3089	1303
Texacable Inc	1623	731
Texacone Co	3053	93
Tex-Am Industries Inc	3621	105
Texan Waste Equipment Inc	5064	96
Texarkana Behavioral Associates LC	8063	18
Texas Aerospace Services Limited LLP	4581	44
Texas Arai	3498	66
Texas Architectural Aggregate Inc	5032	26
Texas Art Supply Co	5199	18
Texas Auto Carriers Inc	4213	1899
Texas Bank and Trust	6035	247
Texas Brine Company LLC	4619	2
Texas Cad Inc	7373	1182
Texas Capital Bancshares Inc	6712	102
Texas Cement Products Inc	3272	124
Texas Circuitry Inc	3672	245
Texas Citrus Exchange	2033	46
Texas Coffee Company Inc	5961	170
Texas Communications Inc	4813	539
Texas Communications Of Brownwood Inc	5731	204
Texas Community Newspapers Inc	2711	257
Texas Concrete Co	3272	89
Texas Contractors Supply Co	5082	103
Texas Crating Inc	2449	18
Texas Crude Energy Inc	1382	46
Texas Crushed Stone Company Inc	1422	20
Texas Diamond Tools Inc	3425	13
Texas Disposal Systems Landfill Inc	4953	30
Texas Door and Trim Inc	5211	181
Texas Electric Cooperatives Inc	2491	10
Texas Electric Cooperatives Inc Treating Div	3479	20
Texas Electronics Inc	3829	380
Texas Energy Holdings Inc	4925	6
Texas Exclusive Five Star Enterprises Inc	7389	1275
Texas Extrusion Service Inc	3542	85
Texas Farm LLC	0213	14
Texas Farm Products Co	2048	33
Texas Foam Inc	3086	153
Texas French Bread Inc	2051	95
Texas Furnace LLC	3585	221
Texas Gas Service Co	4922	18
Texas Gas Transmission LLC	4922	28
Texas Genco Services LP	3621	29
Texas Govlink Inc	7379	687
Texas Health Resources Inc	8062	26
Texas Honing Inc	3599	313
Texas Hotel and Restaurant Equipment Inc	5046	159
Texas Independent Bank	6022	222
Texas Industries Inc	3312	20
Texas Ingredient Corp	2082	67
Texas Instruments Inc	3674	3
Texas Lawyers Insurance Exchange	6351	54
Texas Life Insurance Co	6311	140
Texas Light Bulb Supply Co	5063	185
Texas Maintenance Systems Inc	7349	41
Texas Manufactured Marble Inc	3089	1639
Texas Media Systems Ltd	5045	1026
Texas Medical Industries Inc	3842	274
Texas Metal Casting Co	3365	40
Texas Metal Equipment Company Ltd	3821	44
Texas Meter and Device Co	3825	71
Texas Molecular LP	4953	61
Texas Monthly Inc	2721	44

Company Name	SIC	Rank
Texas Motors Ford	5511	466
Texas Moving Co	4213	1346
Texas Nova-Chem Corp	2842	167
Texas Oil and Chemical Company II Inc	2911	37
Texas Pacific Film Video	7819	43
Texas Pacific Land Trust	6531	352
Texas Pack Inc	2091	4
Texas Petrochemicals Holdings Inc	2869	15
Texas Petrochemicals LP	2822	1
Texas Physical Therapy Specialists	8099	86
Texas Pipe and Supply Company Inc	5051	92
Texas Pipe Fabricators Inc	3443	215
Texas Plywood And Lumber Company Inc	5031	140
Texas Podiatry Group LLC	8043	1
Texas Process Equipment Co	5084	138
Texas Publishing Co	2741	387
Texas Recreation Corp	3086	36
Texas Refinery Corp	2992	28
Texas Research International Inc	8734	112
Texas Roadhouse Inc	5812	56
Texas Sales And Marketing Inc	5064	142
Texas Shines Inc	3589	184
Texas Skyways Inc	4581	50
Texas Spectrum Electronic Inc	3569	283
Texas Star Document Services Inc	7389	1898
Texas Star Express	4213	554
Texas State Directory Press Inc	2741	500
Texas Station LLC	7999	13
Texas Steel Conversion Inc	3498	28
Texas Technical Services Inc	1731	2065
Texas Test Fleet Inc	8748	219
Texas Toolmakers Inc	3599	1261
Texas Transeastern Inc	4213	957
Texas True Choice Inc	6324	102
Texas Vanguard Oil Co	1311	219
Texas Video and Post	7812	69
Texas-New Mexico Power Co	4911	189
TexaSoft Mission Technologies	7372	4564
Texatronics Inc	3672	100
Texco Trim Inc	3561	162
TexCom Inc	1731	144
Texeira Inc	7389	1244
Texguard Security Network Inc	7382	143
Texican Turbines and Technology	5084	647
Texland Petroleum Inc	1382	49
Texlon Plastics Corp	3089	1377
Tex-Mastic International Inc	2951	29
Tex-Mex Cold Storage Inc	4222	9
Texollini Inc	2221	13
Texoma Contracting Inc	1799	95
Texoma Peanut Co	5159	19
Texoma Underground Utilities	1623	372
Texoma Web Offset Printing Ltd	2711	546
Texor Petroleum Co	5172	14
Texre Inc	3069	110
Textape Inc	5113	52
Textco BioSoftware Inc (West Lebanon New Hampshire)	7372	4764
Textfyre Inc	7372	5016
Textile Graphics Inc	2261	25
Textile Import LLC	5131	22
Textile Parts And Machine Company Inc	3552	58
Textile Piece Dyeing Company Inc	2253	10
Textile Rubber And Chemical Company Inc	5169	81
Textileather Corp	3069	48
Textilemaster LLC	7389	1661
Textrol Inc	3625	243
Textron Defense Systems	3812	16
Textron Financial Corp	6159	15
Textron Inc	3721	4
Textron Turf Care and Specialty Products	3524	6
Text-Trieve Inc	2741	353
Tex-Tube Co	3317	43
Textured Design Furniture Inc	2511	89
Texturing Services Inc	2282	3
Textwise LLC	8732	124
Texzon Utilities Ltd	4932	11
TF Financial Corp	6712	387
TF Hudgins Inc	5085	44
TF Investments Corp	6211	47
Tfc Associates LLC	7322	14
Tfc Automation Inc	5075	70
Tfd Inc	3827	126
Tfe Company Inc	3053	96
TFH Publications Inc	2731	87
TFI LLC	3089	1136
Tfi Telemark	3671	13
Tfmcomm Inc	7622	7
TFP Data Systems	2754	22
TFS Financial Corp	6035	17
Tft Inc	3663	257
TFX Inc	4213	1090
TG Industries Inc	3536	51
Tg Kentucky Inc	3089	187
TG Lee Foods Inc	2026	27
TG Madison Inc	7311	279
Tg Missouri Corp	3089	139
TG Stegall Trucking Company Inc	4213	1911
TGaS Advisors	8748	354

Company Name	SIC	Rank
TGC Industries Inc	2673	5
TGC Transportation Inc	4213	2730
TGFIN Holdings Inc	7372	5102
TGG Inc	3599	1011
TGI Friday's Inc	5812	86
TGI Fund I LC	6722	4
Tgs Plastics Inc	3089	1415
TGS Transportation Inc	4213	1798
Tgz Acquisition Company LLC	7352	47
TH Enterprises Inc	8742	489
TH Evans Enterprises Inc	5511	967
TH Fitzgerald and Co	6282	458
Th Foods Inc	2052	17
TH Grogan and Associates Inc	3699	281
TH Hellg Inc	4214	32
TH Hill Associates Inc	8711	338
TH Lee Putnam Ventures	6799	61
TH Lee Putnum Ventures LP	6799	119
Th Plastics Inc	3089	402
TH Properties	1521	48
TH Rogers Lumber Co	5211	54
TH Ryan Cartage Co	4213	256
Thacker and Company LLC	7338	50
Thaddeus Computing Inc	2721	388
Thai Trade Development Corp	5023	195
Thaler Corp	3674	446
Thaler Machine Co	3545	80
Thaler Oil Company Inc	5171	38
Thales ATM	3812	25
Thales Communications Inc	3663	67
Thales Components Corp	3671	2
Thales Computers Inc	3577	495
Thalheimer Brothers Inc	5093	34
Thames America Trading Company Ltd	5181	107
Thames Printing Company Inc	2752	334
Thane Hawkins Polar Chevrolet Inc	5511	455
Thar Technologies Inc	8711	463
Tharco	2653	10
Tharo Systems Inc	3577	295
Tharperobbins Company Inc	5199	15
THasegawa USAInc	2087	58
That Corp	3679	435
Thatcher Engineering Corp	1741	13
Thaumaturgix Inc	7371	397
Thayer Capital Partners	6719	135
Thayer Capital Partners LP	6211	191
Thayer Medical Corp	3845	113
The Adler Network Inc	8743	235
The Allegiant Group Inc	7372	1970
The Amacore Group Inc	7389	458
The Amend Group	8742	543
The American News The Farm Form	2711	365
The Ardell Group	8743	45
The Art of Framing	5999	80
The Aspire Group	7363	51
The Bank of Harlan	6712	487
The Bohle Co	8743	174
the bounce agency	7311	204
The Brickman Group	0781	1
The Brookside Group	3089	38
The C and L Group LLC	8748	172
The Complex Studios	7389	444
The Daily Herald Co	2711	202
The Elf on the Shelf	5945	14
The Ellman Cos	6282	319
The Ewbank Group PC	8721	464
The Filta Group Inc	3589	28
The Fletcher Group	7311	933
The Ford Store San Leandro-Lincoln Mercury	5511	383
The Fresh Diet	5499	12
The Gadsden Times	2711	387
The Gas Co	4924	42
The Gear Group Inc	1521	173
The Generations Network Inc	7379	134
The Henried Center	8099	61
The History Factory	7389	456
The Home Depot Inc	5211	1
The Humanities Computing Laboratory	7372	5052
The Intersect Group Inc	8748	130
The JAR Group	7319	150
The Job Seeker	7375	283
The Jones Group Inc	2337	1
The Ledger	2711	116
The Long Co	8741	122
The M and P Lab	8734	120
The March Group LLP	7389	459
The Margolis Law Firm	8111	530
The Marketing Arm	8743	17
The Matlet Group LLC	2759	19
The Meltzer Group	6311	169
The Miller Group	2541	17
The Motz Group	3996	5
The Muller Group Inc	7389	1052
The Mushroom Co	2033	73
The New Patcraft and Designweave	2273	8
The New World Power Corp	4911	587
The O'Brien's Group	7389	795
The Ohio State Bank	6022	549
The Penna Group LLC	1531	85
The Property Group of Connecticut Inc	6531	223
The Providence Journal Co	2711	158
The Randall Group Inc	6531	60
The Retail Outsource Inc	8748	272

Company Name	SIC	Rank
The St Joe Co	6552	77
The Salt Group	8721	97
The Scarecrow Press Inc	2731	147
The Smithfield Herald	2711	437
The STAR Group	7311	190
The State Bank and Trust Co	6022	831
The Stop and Shop Supermarket Co	5411	15
The Testing Group	8734	75
The Third Rail	7372	4891
The Thomas Kinkade Co	2741	136
The Trademark Co	8111	566
The Transition Cos	6799	278
The TransVantage Group	4213	209
The Travel Team Inc	4724	44
The Way ? Group	7311	353
The1stMovement	7319	158
Thea Dispeker Artists Management	7922	93
Theatre Vision Inc	5731	221
Theda Clark Memorial Hospital	8062	128
Thedra Technologies Inc	7372	3958
TheFind Inc	7375	129
theglobecom Inc	7319	180
Theis Precision Steel Corp	3316	19
Thelab LLC	7311	630
Thelamco Inc	7389	1909
Thelen Graphics Inc	2759	149
Thelen Plus	7311	939
Thelen Sand and Gravel Inc	1442	9
THEM International Inc	3089	806
THEM Of Maryland Inc	7389	2213
TheMarketscom LLC	8732	34
Theme Creations LLC	7336	272
Themenaps LLC	3577	481
Themis Computer	3577	146
TheNextRound Inc	7371	314
Theochem Laboratories Inc	2819	63
Theodore E Tiaga Sr	3599	2461
Theodore Presser Co	2741	233
Theodoro Baking Company Inc	2051	133
Theory Development Corp	3829	390
THEOS Software Corp	7372	1744
thePlatform Inc	3577	110
ThePowerXChange LLC	5734	130
theprinterscom	2752	1312
Theracare Of New York Inc	8093	15
Therafirm Compression Products	3842	242
Theragenics Corp	3825	24
Therapeias Health Management	7371	1860
Thera-Test Laboratories Inc	8071	57
Therm Inc	3724	39
Therma Corp	1711	30
Thermacal Inc	3829	333
Thermacore Inc	8999	38
Thermadyne Holdings Corp	3541	8
Thermadyne Industries Inc	3548	2
Thermafiber Inc	3296	8
Therma-Flow Inc	3443	205
Therma-Kleen Inc	3559	520
Thermal Analysis Systems Co	7372	4645
Thermal Circuits Inc	3699	81
Thermal Conductive Bonding Inc	5051	415
Thermal Designs Inc	3479	89
Thermal Dynamics Corp	3548	3
Thermal Electronics Inc	3679	439
Thermal Energy Storage Inc	8711	700
Thermal Engineering Corp	3613	58
Thermal Equipment Corp	3567	47
Thermal Foams/Syracuse Inc	3086	118
Thermal Industries Inc	3442	41
Thermal Instrument Company Inc	3823	335
Thermal Plastic Design Inc	3089	1057
Thermal Process Construction Company Inc	3567	97
Thermal Solutions Inc (Hampton New Hampshire)	8711	51
Thermal Solutions Products LLC	3433	20
Thermal Specialties Inc	1741	9
Thermal Structures Inc	3462	6
Thermal Supply Inc	5078	10
Thermal Transfer Products Ltd	3443	66
Thermal Windows Inc	3442	30
Thermalogic Corp	3829	311
Thermasys Corp	3443	11
Thermatool Corp	3548	20
Therma-Tron-X Inc	3567	30
Therma-Tru Corp	3442	8
Thermco Instrument Corp	3823	362
Thermech Corp	2671	65
Thermeon Corp	7372	4215
Thermet Inc	3398	26
Thermik Corp	3822	72
Thermo CIDTEC	3651	77
Thermo Cos	6722	150
Thermo Craft Engineering Corp	3599	632
Thermo Credit LLC	6153	36
Thermo Door Co	5211	294
Thermo Electric Company Inc	3829	188
Thermo Energy Corp	4952	8
Thermo Fisher Scientific Inc	3829	1
Thermo Fisher Scientific LLC	3567	17
Thermo Fluids Inc	5093	35
Thermo King Christensen Inc	5078	16
Thermo King Corp	3585	7
Thermo King East Inc	5078	29

Company Name	SIC	Rank
Thermo King Of Houston LP	5078	20
Thermo Plastic Tech Inc	3089	1397
Thermo Plastics Corp	3089	1546
Thermo/Probes Inc	3823	428
Thermo Products LLC	3585	134
Thermo Ramsey	3596	5
Thermo Sensors Corp	3829	257
Thermocarbon Inc	3545	247
Thermocoax Inc	5063	1040
Thermocouple Technology Inc	3829	316
Therm-O-Disc Inc	3822	4
Thermodyne Food Service Products Inc	3589	216
Thermodynetics Inc	3499	135
ThermoEnergy Corp	4952	10
Thermo-Fab Corp	3089	1289
Thermofast LLC	2752	1509
Thermoforming Systems LLC	3565	132
ThermoGenesis Corp	3821	12
Thermold Corp	3089	218
Therm-O-Link Inc	3357	39
Thermometrics Corp	3823	396
Thermon Industries Inc	3643	40
Thermo-Pak	7389	1271
Thermopatch Corp	3953	6
Thermoplastic Services Inc	5162	33
Thermoplastics Company Inc	3559	365
Thermoptics Inc	3674	447
Therm-O-Rock East Inc	3295	5
Thermoscan Inc	3829	113
Thermoseal Industries LLC	3231	48
Thermo-Serv Inc	3089	120
Thermospas Inc	3999	39
Thermotech Inc	3829	494
Thermotek Inc	3841	193
Thermotest Inc	7389	1874
Thermo-Trol Systems Inc	5075	79
Thermo-Twin Industries Inc	3442	68
Therm-O-Type Corp	3555	39
Therm-O-Web Inc	2891	81
Therm-Tec Inc	3567	44
Thermtech Inc	3564	128
Thermtrol Corp	3822	16
Thermwell Products Company Inc	3442	27
Thermwood Corp	3559	162
TherOx Inc	3841	414
Therrell Alarm Protection Service Inc	1731	2378
Ther-Rx Corp	2834	247
Thesaurus Linguae Graecae	2741	304
TheStreet Inc	2711	139
Theta Corp	3669	309
Theta Industries Inc	3821	78
Thetford Corp	3632	6
TheTravel Society Inc	4724	101
Thexton Manufacturing Co	3423	78
THF Inc	6541	3
Thg Corp	5085	75
Thibaut Inc	2221	33
Thibiant International Inc	2844	24
Thief River Falls Times Inc	2711	663
Thiel Cheese Inc	2022	57
Thiel Electric Inc	1731	1121
Thiele Kaolin Co	1455	2
Thielenhaus Microfinish Corp	3541	30
Thieman Stamping Co	3499	100
Thieme Medical Publishers Inc	5192	29
Thiessen Products Inc	3751	15
Thilmany Nicolet Mill	2621	33
Thin Film Concepts Inc	3679	821
Thin Film Technology Corp	3679	719
Things Remembered Inc	3479	4
Think 1 Software	7372	3368
Think Computer Products	3577	219
Think Development Systems Inc	7371	972
Think Mutual Bank	6035	55
THINK Solutions Inc	7372	4765
Think Subscription Inc	7371	499
Thinkgate LLC	7374	186
Thinking Cap Solutions Inc	2721	396
Thinking Systems Corp	3841	333
Thinking Tools LLC	3545	435
Thinkmate - East Coast	7373	193
Thinknicity LLC	7363	199
Thinkom Solutions Inc	4899	130
Thinkorswim Inc	6211	130
Thinkstream Inc	7372	854
ThinkTank Holdings LLC	8999	163
Thin-Lite Corp	3646	56
Thinsolutions LLC	7373	627
Third Dimension Inc	7389	1073
Third Federal Bank	6035	89
Third Federal Savings and Loan Association of Cleveland	6035	18
Third Street Sportswear Manufacturing Inc	2369	5
Thirdwave Corp	7373	1065
Thirteen	4833	84
Thirteen / WNET	4833	260
Thirty-One Gifts LLC	5947	6
Thirty-Three Queen Realty Inc	5085	228
Thistle Foundry and Machine Company Inc	3599	1532
THK America Inc	3699	54
Thobe Group Inc	8742	192

Company Name	SIC	Rank
Thoma Cressey Bravo	6799	9
Thoma Inc	5049	50
Thomas A Despres Inc	3599	2229
Thomas and Betts Caribe Corp	3643	1
Thomas and Betts Corp	3678	4
Thomas and Herbert Consulting LLC	7373	358
Thomas and King Inc	5812	32
Thomas And King Of Arizona Inc	5812	210
Thomas and Proetz Lumber Co	5031	78
Thomas and Skinner Inc	3499	16
Thomas and Sons Distributing	4213	1641
Thomas and Thomas Inc	4213	2314
Thomas Bearden Co	6531	378
Thomas Built Buses Inc	3713	7
Thomas C Merritts Land Surveyor PC	8713	8
Thomas C Wilson Inc	3546	19
Thomas Chevrolet Subaru Cadillac Inc	5511	914
Thomas Concrete of Georgia Inc	3273	18
Thomas D Wood and Co	6162	94
Thomas Direct Sales Inc	5961	121
Thomas Door Controls Inc	5063	382
Thomas Electric Inc	1522	48
Thomas Electronics of New York Inc	3671	9
Thomas Electronics of New York Inc	3671	6
Thomas Energy Systems Inc	3563	33
Thomas Engineering Co	3577	263
Thomas Engineering Inc	3559	112
Thomas/Euclid Industries Inc	3599	491
Thomas Ferguson Associates	7311	66
Thomas G Faria Corp	3824	13
Thomas/Gont Enterprises Inc	7379	1350
Thomas Green LLC	3589	270
Thomas Group Inc	8742	581
Thomas H Ireland Inc	4213	627
Thomas Hardware Co	5661	20
Thomas Ho Co	7371	1892
Thomas Hughes	1731	1525
Thomas Industries Inc	3563	7
Thomas Instrument and Machine Inc	3599	120
Thomas Instruments Inc	3629	120
Thomas Interior Systems Inc	5021	38
Thomas Investigative Publications Inc	5999	134
Thomas J Herzfeld Advisors Inc	6282	564
Thomas J Madden and Associates Inc	5063	757
Thomas L Snarey and Associates Inc	3599	542
Thomas Laboratories Inc	2834	383
Thomas Leonardini	2084	128
Thomas Losinski	5085	441
Thomas M Leonard Inc	3554	63
Thomas M Niland Co	3089	1141
Thomas Monahan Co	5159	17
Thomas Nelson Inc	2731	23
Thomas P Reynolds Securities Inc	6282	512
Thomas P Wilbur	5145	41
Thomas Plastics Inc	3085	31
Thomas Precision Machining Inc	3599	1338
Thomas Printing	2752	1084
Thomas Products Ltd	3625	249
Thomas Properties Group Inc	6531	77
Thomas Publishing Company LLC	2741	100
Thomas Reprographics Inc	7334	4
Thomas Roofing Supply Co	5033	65
Thomas S Klise Co	2741	209
Thomas Scientific	5049	21
Thomas Sign and Awning Company Inc	3993	23
Thomas Steel Strip Corp	3316	5
Thomas Supply Inc	5031	256
Thomas Technology Solutions Inc	7371	136
Thomas Thomas and Hafer	8111	365
Thomas Toscas	2752	1549
Thomas Tran	5045	1024
Thomas Transcription Services Inc	7389	1790
Thomas Trucking Inc	4213	517
Thomas V Sobczak Consultants	7372	3334
Thomas W Ruff and Company of Florida Inc	5021	49
Thomason Auto Group	5012	23
Thomaston Manufacturing LLC	2211	8
Thomasville Furniture Industries Inc	2511	32
Thomasville Furniture Industries Inc Thomasville Upholstery Div	2512	25
Thombert Inc	3089	666
Thom-Dobson-Womack Inc	8721	301
Thompson Agency	7311	1032
Thompson and Co	8743	193
Thompson and Company Inc	7311	250
Thompson and Knight LLP	8111	153
Thompson Brands LLC	2064	56
Thompson Brooks Inc	1521	137
Thompson Candy Co	2064	51
Thompson Clive Inc	6799	347
Thompson Cobb Bazilio and Associates PC	8721	262
Thompson Coburn LLP	8111	124
Thompson Coe Cousins and Irons	8111	372
Thompson Communications and Electronics	5731	35
Thompson Co	6282	470
Thompson Creek Window Co	3089	551
Thompson Dunavant PLC	8721	14
Thompson Electric Inc	1731	147
Thompson Electric Service Inc	7629	21
Thompson Equipment Company Inc	5084	535

Company Name	SIC	Rank
Thompson Equipment Supply Inc	5046	271
Thompson Fabricating LLC	3446	38
Thompson Group Inc	6211	340
Thompson Gundrilling Inc	3321	67
Thompson Hancock Witte and Associates Inc	8712	251
Thompson Hardwoods Inc	2421	82
Thompson Hine LLP	8111	216
Thompson Hospitality Corporation Inc	5812	181
Thompson Inc	4213	2300
Thompson Lift Truck Co	5599	2
Thompson Lightning Protection Inc	3643	109
Thompson Machine Company Inc	3599	690
Thompson Mahogany Co	5031	246
Thompson Marketing	7311	416
Thompson Moving and Storage Inc	4213	2857
Thompson National Properties LLC	6798	167
Thompson Norampac Inc	2653	87
Thompson Oil Co	5171	86
Thompson Olde Inc	5023	47
Thompson Packers Inc	5147	47
Thompson Plumb Funds Inc	6282	550
Thompson Press Inc	2752	1179
Thompson Publishing Group Inc	2731	70
Thompson Pump And Manufacturing Company Inc	3561	51
Thompson/Rubinstein Investment Management Inc	6282	549
Thompson Sales Company Inc	5511	249
Thompson Steel Company Inc	5051	134
Thompson Street Capital Partners	6722	128
Thompson Suburban Dental Laboratories Inc	8072	28
Thompson Team Inc	5099	101
Thompson Technologies Inc	7361	125
Thompson Telephone Inc	5999	271
Thompson Trucking Company Inc	4213	1967
Thompsons Auto Centers	5511	1253
Thompsons Farm Supply Inc	5191	173
Thompsons Toyota of Placerville	5511	1130
Thoms Proestler Co	5141	96
Thom's Transport Company Inc	4213	305
Thomsen Greenhouses and Garden Center Inc	0181	14
THOMSON Consumer Electronics Inc/ RCA	3651	10
Thomson Elite	7373	73
Thomson Financial Inc	7375	7
Thomson Grass Valley	3999	132
Thomson Grass Valley (San Jose California)	7372	1790
Thomson/Health Care Data	7372	3030
Thomson Horstmann and Bryant Inc	6282	417
Thomson MacConnell Cadillac Inc	5511	538
THOMSON Multimedia	5046	20
Thomson Multimedia Inc	3651	2
Thomson North American Legal	2741	17
Thomson PDR	2731	74
Thomson Plastics Inc	3089	373
Thomson Professional and Regulatory Inc	7371	176
Thomson Reuters Corp	2721	2
Thomson Reuters (Markets) LLC	7383	5
Thomson Scientific IP Management Services	7372	1608
Thomson-Shore Inc	2732	14
Thor Construction Inc	1522	32
Thor Guard Inc	3643	111
Thor Industries Inc	3711	13
Thor Solutions Inc	7379	908
Thor USA	7371	200
Thoratec Corp	3845	10
Thoreau Janitorial Services Inc	7349	156
Thoren Caging Systems Inc	3821	34
Thoreson McCosh Inc	3535	235
Thorgren Tool and Molding Company Inc	3089	586
Thorlabs Inc	3826	23
ThorLo Inc	2252	6
Thornberry Consulting LLC	7379	1322
Thornberry Ltd	7372	4338
Thornburg Brothers Inc	4213	2566
Thornburg Machine and Supply Company Inc	7692	38
Thorndike Corp	3679	751
Thorndike Press	2731	174
Thorne Electric Co	3589	65
Thorne Printing And Office Supplies Inc	2752	1494
Thornhill Securities Inc	6211	342
Thornton Winery	2084	54
Thorntons Inc	5411	87
Thornton-Tomasetti Group Inc	8711	38
Thornwell Home For Children	8361	164
Thoro-Packaging Inc	2657	30
Thoroughbred Research Group Inc	8732	80
Thoroughbred Software International Inc (Somerset New Jersey)	7372	2379
Thoroughbred Technology and Telecommunications Inc	8711	525
Thoroughbred Times Company Inc	2759	265
Thorp and Co	8743	183
Thorp Equipment Inc	3523	178
Thorpe Technologies Inc	3567	76
Thorson Company Southwest	5065	766

Company Name	SIC	Rank
Thorson Manufacturing Co	3643	86
Thorstad Construction Company Inc	5083	202
Thorud Inc	3599	292
Thos S Byrne Ltd	1542	164
Thos Somerville Co	5074	10
Thot Technologies Inc	3695	144
Thought Communications Inc	7372	3959
Thought Convergence Inc	7371	939
Thought Inc	7372	2303
Thoughtworks Inc	7373	111
Thousand Oaks Micro Systems Inc	3674	428
Thousand Trails Inc	7033	1
Thousand Value Limited Corp	5065	910
Thp Graphics Group Inc	2752	738
THQ Inc	7372	93
Thrace-Linq Inc	2221	39
Thrall Enterprises Inc	2893	35
Thrasher Printing Inc	2752	1823
Thrasher Termite and Pest Control	7342	77
Threaded Products Inc	3965	28
Threadtex Inc	5131	18
Threds Inc	2759	222
Three Bond International Inc	2891	33
Three Cities Research Inc	6799	188
Three D Graphics Inc	7372	3233
Three D Metals Inc	5051	222
Three D Plastics Inc	3089	607
Three Daughters Corp	3599	1779
Three Dimensional Chemical Corp	2893	29
Three Dog Bakery Inc	2047	31
Three Dog Logistics	4731	68
Three G Enterprises Inc	3589	233
Three Hands Corp	5023	60
Three M Holding Company Inc	3599	451
Three Man Corp	2752	1433
Three Marketeers Advertising Inc	7311	402
Three Phase Electric and Controls LLC	7373	997
Three Phase Electric Inc	1731	1864
Three Pillar Global Inc	7371	470
Three Rivers Aluminum	3442	15
Three Rivers Bottling LLC	2086	149
Three Rivers Commercial News	2711	634
Three Rivers Fs Co	5984	10
Three Rivers Optical Co	3827	55
Three Rivers Trucking Inc	4213	2308
Three Seasons Corp	6531	261
Three Sons Inc	5147	38
Three Sons LLC	1623	257
Three Stage Media Inc	7371	641
Three Star Drilling and Producing Corp	1311	236
Three Star Refrigeration Engineering Inc	3585	153
Three States Supply Co	5075	20
Three Vee Food and Syrup Products Inc	2087	63
Three Way Transfer of Arkansas	4213	2332
Three-C Body Shop Inc	7532	1
Three-Dimensional Services Inc	7389	831
Threefold Janitorial Services Inc	7349	373
Threespot Media LLC	7336	93
Threewill LLC	7373	1046
Three-Z Printing Co	2752	87
Thresher Industries Inc	3363	53
Threshold Audio Inc	3651	261
Threshold Communications Inc	4813	739
Threshold Data Technology Inc	7371	1596
Threshold Pharmaceuticals Inc	2834	453
Threshold Rehabilitation Services Inc	8322	78
Thrifty Car and Truck Rental	7514	8
Thrifty Drug Stores	5912	12
Thrillistcom	7379	438
Thrivent Financial for Lutherans	6733	1
Thrivent Investment Management Inc	6722	5
Thrivent Large Cap Growth Fund	6722	227
Thrivent Large Cap Value Fund	6722	208
Thrivent Money Market Fund	6722	73
Thrivent Small Cap Stock A	6722	144
Thrombovision Inc	8099	95
Throttle Up Corp	3679	839
Through The Barn Door Properties Inc	2511	100
Thru The Bible Radio Network	4832	47
Thrun Manufacturing Inc	3724	43
ThruPoint Inc	4899	37
ThruPort Technologies	3669	49
Thrush Aircraft Inc	3721	32
Thrush Company Inc	3561	133
Thrust Industries Inc	3089	1161
Thrustmaster Of Texas Inc	3531	48
Thruway Fasteners Inc	5072	40
Thruway Food Market and Shopping Center	5411	217
THT Presses Inc	3542	72
Thul Machine Works	3599	586
Thule Inc	3714	200
Thumann Inc	2013	37
Thumb Electric Cooperative Inc	4911	547
Thumb Industries Inc	8331	224
Thumb Truck And Trailer Co	3715	63
Thumbs-Up Telemarketing Inc	7389	481
Thums Long Beach Co	1311	61
Thunder Projects Inc	2752	701
Thunderbird International Corp	3829	313
Thunderbird Supply Co	5094	30
Thunderco Inc	3625	275

Company Name	SIC	Rank
Thunderhawk Internet Systems	7379	984
Thunderhorse Investments	1731	683
Thunderline-Z Inc	3679	405
Thunderstone Expansion Programs International Inc	7372	4080
Thurel Mason Trucking Inc	4213	1198
Thuridion	7379	706
Thursby Software Systems Inc	7372	1795
Thurston County Fire Protection District 3	7389	774
Thurston Manufacturing Co	3523	140
Thurston North Public Schools	8211	56
THW Design	7389	487
Thwing-Albert Instrument Company Inc	3829	136
Thybar Corp	3444	16
Thymes Ltd	5199	138
Thymly Products Inc	2041	13
Thyssenkrupp AST USA Inc	3312	94
ThyssenKrupp Budd Co	2821	11
ThyssenKrupp Elevator	3534	3
ThyssenKrupp Robins Inc	3535	17
Thyssenkrupp Waupaca Inc	3321	49
TI Automotive - North America	3498	11
Tia Rosa Bakery	2099	10
TIAA-CREF Social Choice Eq Retire	6722	182
TIB Bank	6022	102
TIB Financial Corp	6712	213
TIB Inc	3544	766
Tibbetts Electric Inc	1731	1869
TIBCO Software Inc	7372	64
Tibor Inc	3544	374
Tibor Machine Products Inc	3599	209
TIC Corp	3651	117
TIC General	3663	404
TIC Holdings Inc	1541	13
Tic Properties LLC	6531	182
TIC - The Industrial Co	1541	18
TICC Capital Corp	6799	128
Tice Brunell and Baker CPA's PC	8721	275
TIC-Industrial Company Southeast Inc	1629	2
Ticket Software LLC	7371	124
Ticketing Technologies Corp	7389	1326
Ticketmaster Group Inc	7999	51
Ticketreturn LLC	7371	1417
Ticketsage Inc	7922	88
Ticketscom Inc	7999	71
TicketsNowcom	5961	87
Tickle Inc	7375	103
Tico Electric Inc	1731	1530
Ticor Title Insurance Co	6361	14
Tidal Communication LLC	1731	2576
Tidal Software Inc	7371	579
Tide Water Pulication LLC	2711	530
Tideland Signal Corp	3812	58
Tidelands Bancshares Inc	6021	161
Tidelands Bank	6022	604
Tidelands Oil Production Co	1311	163
Tidelands Royalty Trust B	6792	11
Tideport Distributing Inc	4213	2181
Tides Marine Inc	3053	138
Tidewater Air Filter Fabrication Company Inc	5075	73
Tidewater Communications and Electronics Inc	5065	502
Tidewater Inc	4499	1
Tidewater Newspapers Inc	2711	709
Tidewater Physicians Multispecialty Group	8011	105
Tidewater Transit Company Inc	4213	729
Tidewater Workshop	2511	94
Tideworks Technology Inc	7372	988
Tidwell And Associates Construction Company Inc	1622	46
Tidyman's LLC	5411	189
TIE Commerce	7372	2835
Tie Down Inc	3714	201
Tiede's Line Construction Inc	1623	275
Tiegel Manufacturing Co	3542	119
Tien Tien Food Company Inc	2038	79
Tiepet Inc	2821	115
Tier Technologies Inc	7373	81
TiER1 Performance Solutions	7371	450
Tiernan Aeration Inc	3564	135
Tierney Brothers Inc	5049	35
Tierney Communications Inc	7311	65
Tierpoint LLC	7374	250
Tierra Innovation Inc	7371	1323
TIES	7372	946
Tietje Mullet and Klink Inc	5153	197
Tiffany and Co	5944	1
Tiffen Acquisition LLC	3861	48
Tiffin Motor Homes Inc	3716	2
Tifton Aluminum Company Inc	3354	9
Tifton Machine Works Inc	7692	37
Tigar Hare Studios Inc	7374	309
Tiger Business Forms Inc	2752	1340
Tiger Communications	7311	992
Tiger Corp	3523	46
Tiger Electric Inc	1731	428
Tiger Equipment Inc	7359	48
Tiger Hawk Profiles	3082	28
Tiger International Resources Inc	1499	11
Tiger Lines LLC	4213	143
Tiger Management Corp	6282	77

Company Name	SIC	Rank	Company Name	SIC	Rank	Company Name	SIC	Rank
Tiger Manufacturing Corp	3537	54	Time Warner Inc	7375	1	Titan Construction Organization	1542	64
Tiger Personnel Services Inc	7361	280	Time Warner Telecom Inc	4813	18	Titan Electrical Construction and	1731	1947
Tiger Rock	1422	63	Time4 Media	2731	46	Design Inc		
Tiger Software	7372	4020	TimeCentre Inc	7371	323	Titan Energy Worldwide Inc	3612	46
Tiger Trucking Inc	4213	2816	Timecruiser Computing Corp	7371	497	Titan Fabricators Inc	3443	170
TigerDirect Inc	5961	52	TimeKeeping Systems Inc	7372	2403	Titan Formworks Systems LLC	5051	401
Tigerflex Corp	3052	6	Time-Life Customer Service Inc	7389	141	Titan Freight Systems Inc	4213	1844
TigerLogic Corp	7372	1592	Timeline Inc	2261	14	Titan Global Distribution	7011	198
Tigernet Systems Inc	7379	1288	Timemed Labeling Systems Inc	2672	28	Titan Global Holdings Inc	3669	14
TigerPAW Inc	7372	1365	Timeout Devices Inc	3577	653	Titan Industrial Corp	5051	64
Tigerpoly Manufacturing Inc	3089	163	Timepayment Corp	6153	47	Titan Industries Inc	3535	115
Tigerstop LLC	3823	215	Times And News Publishing Co	2711	348	TITAN Insurance Co	6331	317
Tigerton Lumber Co	2421	136	Times Daily Inc	2711	366	Titan International Inc	3312	13
Tigertronics	3577	624	Times Fiber Communications Inc	3357	59	Titan International Security Services	7381	165
Tigg Corp	3564	108	Times Herald Co	2711	224	Titan Machine Corp	7699	80
Tighe and Bond Inc	8711	325	Times Herald Publishing Co	2711	131	Titan Machine Products Inc	3599	411
TIGHE Trucking Inc	4213	1119	Times Of Trenton Publishing Corp	7313	8	Titan Machinery	5083	4
Tight Security Inc	7381	209	Times Picayune Publishing Corp	2711	245	Titan Medical Group LLC	7363	164
Tightrope Media Systems Inc	7371	1167	Times Publishing Co	2711	20	Titan Pharmaceuticals Inc	2836	49
Tigra Organization	7379	1595	Times Publishing Co	2711	214	Titan Photonics Inc	5065	802
Tigrent Inc	8299	14	Times Republic	2711	332	Titan Plastics Group	3089	78
Tigrett Steel and Supply Company Inc	5051	456	Times Review Newspaper Corp	2711	608	Titan Power Inc	3577	370
Tihati Productions Ltd	7922	4	Times Square Stage Lighting Company	3648	39	Titan Propane	5984	2
TII Network Technologies Inc	3613	23	Inc			Titan Rail Inc	5088	104
Tilcon Connecticut Inc	2951	5	Times-Argus Association Inc	2711	394	Titan Technologies Inc	3011	28
Tilcon New York Inc	1429	3	TimeSaver Software	7372	3680	Titan Textile	5199	87
Tilden Mining Company LC	1011	8	Timesavers Inc	3553	13	Titan Tire Corp	3011	13
Tilden Park Software Inc	7371	1341	Times-Citizen Communications Inc	2711	128	Titan Tool Co	3545	401
Tilden-Coil Constructors Inc	1542	400	Timeshare Relief Inc	7389	366	Titan Tool Supply Inc	3825	168
Tile and Design Concepts Inc	5032	157	Times-Herald Publishing Company Inc	2711	621	Titan Trucks Inc	4213	3117
Tile and Stone Accents Inc	5023	92	Times-Shamrock Commuciations	2711	316	Titan West Inc	3523	192
Tile Collection Granite LLC	1411	23	TimeTrak Systems Inc	7371	1095	Titanium Fabrication Corp	3356	18
Tile Market Of Delaware Inc	5032	46	TimeValue Software	7372	2275	Titanium Holdings Group Inc	5084	463
Tilework Reinhardt Brothers	5032	184	Timeworks Inc	3873	14	Titanium Metals Corp	3341	2
Till Photography	7372	4565	Timken Aerospace and Super Preci-	3562	11	Titanium Solutions Inc	7389	404
Tillamook Country Smoker Inc	5147	58	sion Bearings - MPB Div			Titertek Instruments Inc	3841	261
Tillamook County Creamery Associa-	2022	25	Timken Bearing Inspection Inc	7699	38	Tithe Corp	3585	230
tion			Timken Boring Specialties LLC	3599	64	Title 9 Sports Inc	5961	99
Tiller Corp	1442	24	Timken Co	3562	2	Title Boxing LLC	3949	114
Tillges Certified Orthotic Prosthetic Inc	3842	260	Timm Electric Inc	1731	1419	Title Check LLC	7389	1941
Tillie's Flower Shop	5992	13	Timm Medical Technologies Inc	5047	62	Titletown Express Inc	4213	2722
Tillman and Deal Farm Services Inc	4221	9	Timmerman Starlite Trucking	4213	1965	Titronics Research and Development	5047	283
Tilson HR Inc	7363	77	Timmerman Supper Club	7389	2081	Co		
Tilson Landscape Co	0781	21	Timmer's Express Inc	4213	1199	Titus Inc	7692	60
Tilton Rack and Basket Co	3559	398	Timmins Kroll Jacobson LLP	8721	188	Titus Tool Company Inc	5085	133
Tiltrac	5065	599	Timmons Electric Company Inc	1731	1300	Titus Transportation LLC	4213	350
Tim Brown Electric Inc	1731	1766	Timothy R Winters Architect	8712	325	Titusville Dairy Products Co	2024	56
Tim Hofer Inc	7349	260	Tim's Cascade Style Potato Chips	2096	26	TiVo Inc	4841	37
Tim Hoover Enterprises	3663	197	Timsco Inc	2759	386	Tivoli Jewelers	5094	41
Tim Inc	1731	2430	TIMTangel Inc	3631	19	Tivoly Inc	3545	33
Tim Jones	7389	1532	Tincher Dental Laboratory	8072	24	Tiw Corp	3533	32
Tim Reinhold Enterprises LLC	1731	1783	Tindall Haul and Erect Inc	4213	2329	TIW Technology Inc	7372	3555
Tim-Bar Corp	2652	4	Tindell's Inc	5211	75	Tix Corp	7812	49
Timber Blind Manufacturing Ltd	2431	41	Tingley Network Services Corp	7373	613	Tiziani Whitmyre Inc	7311	458
Timber Creek Resource LLC	2448	14	Tingley Rubber Corp	3021	9	Tizor Systems Inc	7371	386
Timber Energy Resources Inc	4911	548	Tini Aerospace Inc	3663	165	TJ Assemblies Inc	2655	14
Timber Holdings Intl	5211	168	Tink Inc	3531	163	Tj Cross Engineers Inc	8711	328
Timber Press Inc	2731	265	Tinker and Rasor	3599	271	Tj Grinding Inc	3545	332
Timber Products Co	2436	3	Tin-Mar Inc	3599	731	Tj Machine and Tool Ltd	3599	538
Timber Truss Housing Systems Inc	2439	23	Tinnerman Palnut Engineered Products	3452	13	TJ Marquart and Sons Inc	4213	1627
Timberco Inc	8742	642	LLC			TJ Metzgers Inc	2791	18
Timberlake Co	7352	8	Tinny Corp	3569	214	TJ Pizza's Inc	2038	81
Timberlake Fire Protection District	7389	2027	Tinplate Purchasing Corp	5051	225	TJ Potter Trucking Inc	4213	1517
Timberland Bancorp Inc	6712	381	Tinsley Advertising Inc	7311	171	Tj Printing Inc	2752	1462
Timberland Bank	6022	137	Tiny Prints	2759	315	TJ Ronan Paint Corp	2851	144
Timberland Co	3143	1	Tiodize Company Inc	3479	58	TJ Stidham Inc	4213	2887
Timberland Group Inc	7389	2001	Tioga Publishing Co	2711	555	Tj Truss Corp	3448	43
Timberland Home Center Inc	5211	162	Tioga Technologies Inc	3674	305	Tjc Holdings Inc	1731	1197
Timberland Homes Inc	2452	54	Tip Products Inc	3643	117	Tjernlund Products Inc	3564	68
Timberland Trucking Company Inc	4213	1338	Tip Quiet Entertainment Co	7929	12	Tjm Electronic Associates Inc	8711	579
Timberlane Woodcrafters Inc	2499	14	TIP Rural Electric Coop	4911	512	Tjm Electronics West Inc	5731	119
Timberline Corp	2759	496	Tip Top Canning Co	2033	64	TJ's Trucking Inc	4213	2398
Timberline Instruments LLC	3826	151	Tip Top Poultry Inc	2015	48	TJT Inc	3799	25
Timberline Interactive Inc	7374	355	Tipco Punch Inc	3544	537	TJX Companies Inc	5651	1
Timberline International Inc	5084	514	Tipco Technologies Inc	5085	163	TK I Inc	3621	122
Timberline Manufacturing Inc	3679	393	Tipmont Rural Electric Membership	4911	504	Tk Pacific Inc	5211	232
Timberline Pvf Inc	5051	477	Corp			TK Stanley Inc	4213	43
Timbertech Inc	2752	1476	Tipp Enterprises Inc	5149	46	TK W Inc	5211	226
Timblin Transit Inc	4213	730	Tippman Industrial Products Inc	5084	903	Tkc Optical Inc	3851	66
Timbucktoo Manufacturing Inc	3589	172	Tipton Cole Co	7372	5085	Tkk USA Inc	3429	2
TIMCO Aviation Services Inc	4581	8	Tipton Interests Inc	6552	299	TKL Research Inc	8731	81
Timco Rubber Products Inc	5085	386	Tipton Motors Inc	5511	422	Tkm Technologies Inc	3651	204
Time Advertising Inc	7311	875	Tipton Trucking Company Inc	4213	2393	Tko Manufacturing Services Inc	3714	404
Time America Inc	7372	4766	Tire Distribution Systems Inc	7534	1	TKO/Real Estate Advisory Group	2721	444
Time Auto Transportation Inc	4213	2553	Tire Kingdom Inc	5531	9	Tks Industrial Co	3559	70
Time Critical Freight Inc	4213	1246	Tire Sales and Service Inc	5014	66	TL Ashford and Associates Inc	7372	4216
Time Cycles Research	7372	4922	Tire Service Equipment Mfg Co Inc	5013	218	TL Data Corp	7372	4217
Time Domain Inc	7372	4145	Tire Town Inc	5014	70	TL Industries Inc	8711	424
Time Equities Inc	6512	44	Tire Tread Development Inc	3089	1761	T-L Irrigation Co	3479	10
Time Gathering Systems	7372	3960	Tire Warehouse Inc	5531	12	TL Krieg Offset Inc	2752	1073
Time Inc	2721	3	Tires Plus Total Car Care	7538	10	Tl Machine Inc	3451	61
Time Machine Inc	3599	825	Tirex Corp	3559	584	TL Properties Inc	2821	19
Time Mark Inc	5065	329	TIS Communications of El Paso	7378	102	TL Sparton Enterprises Inc	3069	236
Time Moving and Storage Inc	4213	2218	Tisdale Air Conditioning and Heating	3585	192	TL Trucking Inc	4213	2804
Time Passages Ltd	5961	166	Co			TL Ventures	6799	36
Time Pilot Corp	7372	4998	Tishman Realty and Construction	1541	7	TLC Communications Inc	7371	1829
Time Products Inc	3674	391	Company Inc			Tlc Electronics Inc	3679	378
Time Savers Inc	7353	65	Tishman Speyer Properties LP	6552	65	Tlc Nursing Services Inc	7361	306
Time Sharing Resources Inc (Haup-	7371	212	Titan Air Inc	3585	159	Tlc Precision Wafer Technology Inc	3674	369
pauge New York)			Titan America Inc	1442	8	TLC Staffing	7361	221
Time Sight Systems	5065	645	Titan Armored Car and Courier Inc	4213	2067	TLC Staffing	8744	51
Time Square Development Corp	2395	15	Titan Coatings Inc	2851	132	TLD (USA) Inc	3585	3
Time Systems International	3873	17	Titan Concrete Industries Inc	3272	23	Tlic Worldwide Inc	5045	654
Time Warner Cable Inc	4841	2				Tlk Industries Inc	7389	1300

Company Name	SIC	Rank
Tlm Inc	7371	513
TLogic Inc	7372	5006
TLS Corp	3663	184
TLS Marketing Consultants	8742	700
TLW Productions	7311	712
TM Advertising LP	7311	70
TM Brown Trucking Inc	4213	980
TM Byxbee Co	8721	196
TM Hopkins Operating Co	1311	217
TM Industries Inc	3599	385
TM Machine and Tool Inc	3544	872
TM Microscopes	3826	60
TM Morley Inc	4213	2510
TM Poly-Film Inc	3081	42
TM Smith Tool International Corp	3545	242
TM Studios	8999	137
TM Systems Inc	3672	445
TM Technology Partners Inc	8748	200
TM Vacuum Products	3567	65
TMA Inc	3679	129
TMA Resources Inc	7372	1083
TMA Systems LLC	7372	1307
T-Mart Enterprises Inc	5399	24
TMB Industries	6799	253
TMC Orthopedic LP	7352	10
TMC Software Inc	7371	662
TMCI Inc	4213	617
Tmd Friction Inc	5013	76
Tmd Machining Inc	3544	269
T-Metrics Inc	3663	312
Tmf Center Inc	3531	80
TMG Health	8099	107
Tmi Systems Design Corp	2511	25
Tml Intergovernmental Risk Pool	6411	82
T-Mobile USA Inc	4812	3
Tmp Acquisition Inc	3535	201
TMP/Hudson Global Resources	8721	310
TMP Interactive Inc	7311	170
Tmp Manufacturing Company Inc	3585	132
Tmp Technologies Inc	3069	96
TMP Worldwide Marketing	7379	133
Tmr-West Inc	8732	46
TMS International Corp	6719	39
TMSI Transport	4213	2435
TMT Software Co	7372	3410
TMU Inc	3469	354
Tmv Properties Inc	5731	123
TMW Systems Inc	7372	1290
Tmx Engineering/Manufacturing Crp	3599	1076
Tnco Inc	3841	226
Tnemec Company Inc	2851	22
Tng Utility Corp	1623	676
Tni Partners	2711	151
TNI USA	4213	1035
Tno-Madymo North America Inc	7377	22
Tnp Instruments Inc	3679	739
Tnr Machine Inc	3544	751
TNR Technical Inc	3699	129
TNS Prognostics	7379	1159
TNT Crane and Rigging Inc	7353	20
TNT Crust Inc	2045	4
TNT Custom Marine Inc	3731	58
Tnt Information Services	7375	229
Tnt Plastic Molding Divison Of Artistic Plastics Inc	3089	557
T-N-T Plastics Inc	2673	51
TNT Software Inc	7372	4049
Tnt Steel Industries Inc	3559	155
Tnt Technologies Inc	5045	798
Tnt Underground Contracting Inc	1623	821
Tnt-Edm Inc	3544	300
Toa Electronics Inc	5065	347
Toad-Ally Snax Inc	2064	99
TOASTnet Internet Service	7379	349
Tobacco Technology Inc	2869	107
Tobay Printing Company Inc	2732	43
Tobe Associates Inc	2721	191
Tobii Assistive Technology Inc	7371	735
Tobin and Tobin John H Hall Esq	8111	506
Tobin Machining Inc	3599	1717
Tobin Productions Inc	3695	91
Tobosa Development Services	8331	113
Tobul Accumulator Inc	3443	126
Toby Sexton Tire Company Inc	5014	56
Toby's Family Foods	2099	365
TOC Holdings Co	5541	57
Tocci Building Corp	1542	200
Tocco Designs Inc	7336	121
Tocco Inc	3433	24
Toce Brothers Inc	5531	51
Tocos America Inc	5065	285
Today Enterprises Inc	2711	786
Today Video Inc	7819	99
Today's Graphics Inc	2752	591
Today's Office Inc	5943	10
Today's Technology	5734	126
Todd Co	7311	934
Todd Enterprises Systems Inc	3572	65
Todd Grinding Co	3599	1082
Todd Holding Co	5411	68
Todd Industries Inc	3549	54
Todd Investment Advisors Inc	6282	650
Todd Services Inc	7389	1915
Todd Systems Inc	3677	14

Company Name	SIC	Rank
Todd Transit Inc	4213	533
Todd-AO Studios	7819	24
Todd-AO Studios East Inc	7819	2
Todd-AO Studios West Inc	7819	47
Todd's Ltd	7389	2002
Todd's Snax Inc	2052	24
Todd-Wadena Electric Coop	4911	562
Toefco Engineering Inc	3479	85
Tofa Enterprises Corp	5094	91
Toft Dairy Inc	2026	57
Tofte Management Company LLC	8741	236
Tofutti Brands Inc	2024	31
Tog Manufacturing Company Inc	3429	128
Tohatsu America Corp	5091	108
Tokheim Company Inc	3823	439
Tokico (USA) Inc	3714	422
Toko America Inc	3672	445
Tokumoto Yamamoto and Ichishita Inc	8721	225
Tokusen USA Inc	3315	19
Tokyo Electron America Inc	3559	20
Tokyo Electron US Holdings Inc	6719	43
Tolbert Beadle and Musgrave LLC	8111	548
Tolco Corp	5085	160
Toledo and Associates Inc	7372	1745
Toledo Automated Concepts	3559	231
Toledo Edison Co	4911	78
Toledo Engineering Company Inc	1541	98
Toledo Gearmotor Co	3566	40
Toledo Metal Spinning Co	3469	234
Toledo Molding and Die Inc	3089	138
Toledo Oil and Gas Services Inc	1389	16
Toledo Optical Laboratory Inc	3851	56
Toledo Physical Education Supply Inc	5091	79
Toledo Ticket Co	2752	618
Toledo Transducers Inc	3823	315
Tolerance Masters Inc	3599	662
Tolerance Tool and Engineering Ltd	3544	663
TolerRx Inc	2834	260
TOLIS Group Inc	7371	818
Toll Brothers Inc	1531	12
Toll Compaction Service Inc	2833	64
Toll Packaging Group LLC	7389	1016
Tolleson Lumber Company Inc	2421	137
Tollgrade Communications Inc	7389	364
Tolloti Plastic Pipe Inc	3084	43
Tol-O-Matic Inc	3593	8
Toltec Co	3646	106
Tom and Jerry Printcraft Forms Inc	2752	1234
Tom and Zee Hunt Inc	7349	508
Tom Barrow Co	5075	41
Tom Branighan Inc	1731	1198
Tom Cat Bakery	5149	23
Tom Collins Enterprises Inc	7941	37
Tom Crites and Associates International Inc	7338	31
Tom Daenen Inc	3519	31
Tom Endicott Buick Inc	5511	418
Tom Growney Equipment Inc	5082	40
Tom Hagan Enterprises Inc	1731	276
Tom Harris Inc	2099	251
Tom Johnson Construction	1521	31
Tom Johnson Investment Management Inc	6282	248
Tom Joy and Son Inc	4213	1628
Tom Kelly	7379	1062
Tom Langhals	5084	667
Tom Matson Dodge Inc	5511	910
Tom Naquin Chevrolet Nissan Inc	5511	839
Tom Raper Inc	5561	8
Tom Richards Inc	3559	89
Tom Saliga	8711	690
Tom Sawyer Software Corp	7372	1622
Tom Scott Lumber Yard Inc	5251	38
Tom Sexton and Associates Inc	5021	79
Tom Shuster Electrical Inc	1731	2143
Tom Smith Electrical Service Inc	1731	2392
Tom Smith Industries Inc	3544	23
Tom Snyder Productions Inc	7372	1037
Tom Stinnett RV Freedom Center	5561	17
Tom Sturgis Pretzels Inc	2052	61
Tom Synnott Associates Inc	8711	519
Tom Tech Systems Inc	5065	840
Tom Watson Inc	1731	989
Tom White The Printer Inc	2752	1526
Tom York Enterprises Inc	3089	1529
Toma Metals Inc	5051	505
Tomahawk Leader Inc	2711	912
Tomahawk Manufacturing Inc	5084	724
Tomahawk Sand and Gravel Company Inc	1442	90
Toman Tool Corp	3544	902
Tomanetti Food Products Inc	2099	336
Tomantron Inc	3823	432
Tomar Electronics Inc	3669	130
Tomar Inc	4213	853
Tomasello Inc	7342	52
Tomasello Winery Inc	2084	95
Tomato Enterprises Book Publishing	2731	385
Tomax Corp	7372	1518
Tomba Communications and Electronics Inc	5045	217
Tombigbee Electric Cooperative Inc	4911	511
Tombigbee Electric Power Association	4911	362
Tombigbee Tooling Inc	3599	1854

Company Name	SIC	Rank
Tombigbee Transport Corp	4213	622
Tombstone Exploration Corp	5141	234
Tomco Auto Products Inc	3592	13
Tomco Electric Inc	1731	402
Tomco2 Equipment Co	3443	70
Tomcyndi Inc	5147	108
Tomenson Machine Works Inc	3599	474
Tomi Engineering Inc	3599	610
TOMI Environmental Solutions Inc	7342	100
Tomita Electric Corp	3585	102
Tomita USA Inc	5084	189
Tomken Plastic Technologies Inc	3089	1173
Tomkins Corp	3625	240
Tomlin Trucking and Brokerage Inc	4213	2095
Tomlinson-Hawley-Patterson Inc	1542	362
Tommie Vaughn Motors	5511	648
Tommy Beasley Construction Company Inc	1623	237
Tommy Boy Music	7389	460
Tommy Dew Design Inc	7379	1225
Tommy Hilfiger Footwear Inc	3149	6
Tommy Hilfiger USA Inc	2311	1
Tomorrow's Solutions Today Inc	7379	646
Tompkins Builders Inc	1542	74
Tompkins Financial Corp	6712	147
Tompkins Insurance Agencies Inc	6411	131
Tompkins McGuire Wachenfeld and Barry LLP	8111	389
Tompkins Metal Finishing Inc	3559	164
Tompkins Trust Co	6022	123
Toms Enterprises Inc	2752	656
Tom's Food Markets Inc	5411	241
Tom's Installation Company Inc	7389	1749
Tom's of Maine Inc	2844	70
Tom's Pole Buildings Inc	7389	2099
Tom's Printing Inc	2752	1684
Toms Quality Millwork And Hardwoods Inc	2431	75
Tomson Steel Co	5051	160
Tomtec Inc	3845	88
Tomz Corp	3451	35
Ton Ken Fabricators Inc	2434	76
Tonar Industries Inc	5065	417
Tonawanda Coke Corp	3312	52
Tonawanda Tank Transport Service	4213	2488
Tone Brothers Inc	2099	30
Tone Software Corp	7372	1834
Toner Plastics Inc	3081	150
Toner Sales Inc	5044	132
TonerStore Inc	5999	305
Tongxin International Ltd	3714	120
Tonini Church Supply Co	5049	66
Tonka Equipment Co	3589	102
Tonn and Blank Construction	1541	61
Tonner Doll Company Inc	3942	14
Tonoga Inc	2295	4
Tony Abiecunas	5065	952
Tony Angelo Cement Construction Co	1611	213
Tony Downs Foods Co	2015	35
Tony R Crisalli Inc	7353	45
Tonyan Brothers Inc	4213	313
Tony's Express Inc	4213	393
Tony's Fine Foods	5147	15
Tony's Seafood Ltd	5421	3
Tonyson Financial Group LLC	7389	1936
Tooele Transcript-Bulletin Publishing Company Inc	2711	485
Tooh Dineh Industries Inc	3679	208
Tool Automation Enterprises Corp	3544	775
Tool Fabrication Corp	3545	308
Tool Grinding Inc	3599	2318
Tool Mate Corporation Inc	5084	946
Tool North Inc	3569	132
Tool Service Company Inc	3545	392
Tool Specialties Inc	3469	349
Tool Systems Inc	5083	151
Tool Technologies Van Dyke	3829	448
Tool Technology Corp	3599	1841
Tool Ventures International	3544	270
Tool-All Inc	3544	260
Toolbarncom	5399	10
Toolbold Corp	3599	1281
Toolco Industrial Corp	3553	46
Toolcraft Company Inc	3599	994
Toolcraft Incorporated Of North Carolina	3545	125
Toolcraft LLC	3544	797
Toolcraft Products Inc	3544	194
Toolex Inc	3599	1811
Tool-Flo Manufacturing Inc	3541	46
Tooling and Equipment International Corp	3499	60
Tooling Connection	3599	2418
Tooling Research Inc	3555	119
Tooling Science Inc	3544	527
Tooling Specialists Inc	3599	450
Toolkraft Inc	3599	607
Toolmasters LLC	3545	299
Toolmex Corp	5084	150
Toolroom Express Inc	3089	1004
Toolroom Inc	3544	237
Tools and Production Inc	3544	664
Tools For Bending Inc	3542	50
Tools Inc	3544	142

Company Name	SIC	Rank
Tools International Corp	3533	87
Tooltech Machinery Inc	3545	390
Tooltex Inc	3559	446
Toolwire Inc	7375	235
ToolWorx Information Products Inc	7374	225
Tootsie Roll Industries Inc	2064	6
Tootsies Inc	5621	34
Top Catch Inc	2092	68
Top Copi Reproductions Inc	2752	1495
Top Down Systems Corp	7372	2831
Top Flight Inc	2678	2
Top Graphics Inc	2752	1396
Top Guard Inc	7381	150
Top Master Inc	3281	6
Top Microsystems Corp	3577	621
Top Notch Distributors Of Missouri Inc	5072	191
Top Quality Maintenance Inc	7349	117
Top South Inc	3281	14
TOP Tobacco LP	2131	5
Top Tool Co	3469	270
Topa Equities Ltd	5181	2
TOPA Insurance Co	6411	123
Topanga Lumber and Hardware Company Inc	5211	283
Topaz Lighting Corp	5063	85
Topaz Publications Inc	8999	201
Topaz Systems Inc	3577	336
Topaz Tool and Die Inc	3544	505
Topco Associates Inc	5141	39
Topco Inc	7349	370
Topcoder Inc	3571	72
Topcon Lasers By Branco	5049	160
Topcon Positioning Systems Inc	3829	63
Topcraft Precision Molders Inc	3089	565
Topeka Television Corp	4832	33
Topeka Unified School District 501	8211	40
Topflight Grain Co	5153	154
Top-Flite Golf Co	3949	7
Topform Data Inc	5112	75
Topgrade Technology Corp	7379	1006
Topics Entertainment Inc	7372	947
Topiderm Inc	2844	25
Topifram Laboratories Inc	2834	242
Topitzes and Associates Inc	7389	593
Topline Building Inc	1542	405
Topline Federal Credit Union	6061	63
Topmost Chemical and Paper Corp	5087	123
Topnotch Foods Inc	2047	13
Topos Mondial Warehouse Corp	5046	212
Topower Computer USA Inc	5045	573
Topp Industries Inc	3089	716
TOPP Portable Air	4924	40
Toppan Photomasks Inc	3559	21
Toppan Printing Company (America) Inc	2752	117
Topper and Griggs Inc	3441	179
Topper Plastics Inc	3086	158
Topps Company Inc	2759	12
TOPS Engineering Corp	7372	4566
Tops Markets Inc	5411	67
Tops Printing Inc	2752	1285
Topsall Machine Tool Company Inc	3621	161
Top-Shelf Fixtures LLC	3496	33
Topson Downs Of California Inc	5621	41
Topsville Inc	5137	15
Top-Tier Technologies Inc	5045	585
Top-Vu Technology Inc	8711	664
Topy America Inc	3714	182
Tor CA M Industries Inc	3592	24
TOR Minerals International Inc	2819	61
Tor Rey USA Inc	5046	352
Toray Composites Inc	2821	26
Toray Industries America Inc	8732	66
Toray Marketing and Sales Inc (New York New York)	5047	175
Toray Plastics (America) Inc	3081	21
Torch Energy Advisors Inc	6282	37
Torch Energy Services	1381	42
Torco Inc	3451	42
Toreador Exploration and Production Inc	1311	134
Torelli Imports	3751	24
Toresco Enterprises Inc	5511	57
Torfino Enterprises Inc	3829	433
Torgerson's LLC	5084	588
Torin Products Inc	3541	210
Torion Technologies Inc	3826	117
Torke Coffee Company Inc	2095	56
Torkildson Katz MooreHetherington and Harris	8111	453
Torlex Inc	3679	869
Torn and Glasser Inc	5141	153
Toro Co	3524	1
Toroid Corp	3821	65
Toron Inc	2782	35
Toronto Dominion Securities Inc	6211	41
Torotel Inc	3677	22
Torotel Products Inc	3677	19
Torpedo Specialty Wire Inc	3315	25
Torq Corp	3643	123
Torqmaster Inc	3499	106
Torque-A-Matic Inc	7699	160
Torrefazione Italia LLC	2095	9
Torrential Data Solutions Inc	7371	1642

Company Name	SIC	Rank
Torres Advanced Enterprise Solutions	8748	58
Torrey Hills Technologies LLC	3568	88
Torrid Technologies Inc	7372	4646
Torrington Distributors Inc	2531	45
Torrington Supply Company Inc	5074	62
Torrisi Electric Inc	1731	2147
Tortillas Mexico Mexico Inc	2099	176
Tortilleria El Maizal Inc	2099	79
Tortilleria La California Inc	2099	327
Tortoise Energy Infrastructure Corp	6726	15
Tortoise North American Energy Corp	6799	172
Tortran Inc	3612	130
Torys LLP	8111	243
TOSC International Inc	7372	3760
Tosca Ltd	2449	9
Tosco - Tool Specialty Co	3545	250
Toshiba America Business Solutions Inc	5044	10
Toshiba America Consumer Products Inc	5064	21
Toshiba America Electronic Components Inc	3651	31
Toshiba America Inc	3651	5
Toshiba America Information Systems Inc	3579	9
Toshiba America Medical Systems Inc	5047	286
Toshiba International Corp	3621	17
Toshiba Machine Company America	5084	1
Toshiba TEC America Inc	5046	39
Toski and Co Inc	8721	220
Tosoh Smd Inc	3499	33
Tosone Electric Inc	1731	1286
Toss Inc	7363	344
Total Apparel Group Inc	6719	91
Total Attorneys Inc	7371	274
Total Automotive Warehouse Inc	5013	202
Total Bancshares Corp	6712	410
Total Beverage Solution and Vino Importers	5182	40
Total Business Services Inc	8742	697
Total Business Systems Inc	2761	41
Total Care Health Industries Inc	7352	42
Total Cleaning Systems	7699	50
Total Communications Inc	3661	93
Total Component Solutions Corp	3545	38
Total Compression and Measurement Systems LP	3563	35
Total Computer Systems Inc	5734	224
Total Containment Inc	3084	35
Total Containment Systems LP	1629	114
Total Control Solutions Inc	3679	544
Total Electric Construction Co	1731	2152
Total Electric Contracting Inc	1731	910
Total Electric Distributors Inc	5063	397
Total Electric Service Inc	1731	352
Total Electronics Corp	5065	753
Total Electronics LLC	3672	32
Total Employment Company Inc	7363	158
Total Energy Concepts Inc	3643	90
Total Equipment Suppliers Inc	5046	275
Total Express	4213	1707
Total Filtration Services Inc	3714	93
Total Fire and Safety Inc	5063	392
Total Fire Systems Inc	3699	278
Total Graphics Inc	2752	1480
Total Health Care Inc	8011	9
Total Integration Inc	7379	1454
Total Lighting Concepts Inc	5063	651
Total Machine Solutions Inc	5063	682
Total Manufacturing Company Inc	3599	1637
Total Marketing Outbound Inc	7389	2016
Total Measurement Solutions LLC	3674	450
Total Mechanical	1711	34
Total Media Technologies Inc	7389	2190
Total Medical Systems Inc	5961	186
Total Metal Services Trucking	4213	2251
Total Molding Solutions Inc	2821	169
Total Package Systems Ga LLC	5085	427
Total Petrochemicals USA Inc	2911	45
Total Pharmacy Supply Inc	5047	93
Total Plastic Services Inc	3089	1156
Total Plastics Inc	3089	354
Total Printing Company Inc	2752	1472
Total Protection Services Carolinas LLC	7381	59
Total Quality Instrumentation	3643	146
Total Quality Logistics Inc	4731	9
Total Quality Machining Inc	3599	2273
Total Quality Maintenance Systems Inc	7349	422
Total Quality Plastics Inc	3089	1116
Total Quality Systems Inc	7371	886
Total Recall Corp	5064	123
Total Reclaim Inc	7389	1635
Total Recoil Magnetics Inc	3612	106
Total Resource Management Inc	8744	31
Total Resources International Inc	3842	153
Total Safety US Inc	8748	24
Total Security Solutions	1731	602
Total Supply Inc	5075	5
Total Support Tooling Inc	3544	719
Total System Services Inc	7374	12
Total Systems Approach Inc	7373	1090
Total Systems Control Inc	5046	306
Total Systems Integration Inc	1731	1923

Company Name	SIC	Rank
Total Systems Technology Inc	2821	112
Total Video Products	1731	738
Total Vinyl Products Inc	3081	158
Total Vision Of The Gulf States LLC	4841	122
Total Warehousing Inc	4213	1725
Total Wine and More	5921	5
Totalbank	6022	174
Totalcom Management Inc	1731	1707
Totalcomp Inc	3596	15
Totally Chocolate Inc	2066	26
Totally You Inc	7378	163
TotalRewards Software Inc	7372	4259
TotalView Technologies LLC	3674	342
Totalworks Inc	2741	333
Tote Cart Co	3496	47
Totem Electric Of Tacoma Inc	1731	330
Totem Ocean Trailer Express Inc	4424	9
Toter Inc	3089	244
Totes-Isotoner Corp	3021	4
Toth Inc	7311	374
Toth Industries Inc	3599	160
Totman Enterprises Inc	1623	683
Totten Tubes Inc	5051	251
Touch International Inc	3841	310
Touch N Go Systems Inc	7372	1509
Touch Scientific Inc	8731	411
Touch Screens Inc	3577	550
Touch Stone Solutions Inc	1731	1494
Touch Technologies Inc	7372	2867
Touchdown Machining Inc	3599	1452
TouchNet Information Systems Inc	3577	184
Touchpaper	7372	1199
TouchPoint Networks	4813	211
Touchstone Technologies Inc	5045	877
Touchstone Technology Inc	3577	513
TouchSystems Inc	3577	308
Touchtable Inc	3669	291
Touchton Electric Inc	1731	2385
Touchtone Corp	7372	3289
Touchtunes Music Corp	3651	46
Toudouze Market Inc	5149	157
Toufayan Bakery Inc	2051	71
TOURCO Inc	4725	17
Tourist Bureau Marketing Inc	7389	1980
Tourmobile Sightseeing Inc	4725	6
TourScan Inc	2741	397
Tousimis Research Corp	8731	337
Toussaint Capital Partners LLC	6799	223
Tova Industries LLC	2023	22
Tow Electric Company Inc	1731	2330
Towa Intercon Technology Inc	3674	200
Towe Iron Works Inc	3441	163
Tower Automotive Operations USA I LLC	3465	7
Tower Bancorp Inc	6712	163
Tower Bank	6021	61
Tower Cleaning Systems	6794	24
Tower Distributing Inc	5013	383
Tower Extrusions Ltd	3354	41
Tower Financial Corp	6712	411
Tower Group Inc	6331	98
Tower Industries Inc	3599	127
Tower Inspection Inc	7389	1219
Tower International Inc	3465	2
Tower Isles Frozen Foods Ltd	2013	124
Tower Laboratories Ltd	2834	227
Tower Manufacturing Corp	3643	66
Tower Media Inc	2711	108
Tower Plastics Manufacturing Inc	2782	76
Tower Properties Co	6512	55
Tower Publishing	7375	266
Tower Systems Inc	1799	49
Tower Tech Inc	3089	1272
Tower Tool and Manufacturing Company Inc	3599	2317
Tower Travel Management Corp	4724	115
Tower Works Inc	3663	308
TowerBrook Capital Partners	6799	88
TowerCo	4899	43
Towers Fire Apparatus Company Inc	5999	229
Towers Perrin Reinsurance	8748	118
Towers Watson Inc	8742	10
Towle Manufacturing Co	3914	3
Towlift Inc	5084	187
Town and Country Chrysler Jeep	5511	326
Town And Country Coop	5191	93
Town and Country Electric Inc	1731	51
Town and Country Food Stores Inc	5411	167
Town and Country Ford Inc	5511	128
Town and Country Homes Inc	1521	25
Town and Country Industries Inc	2752	1199
Town and Country Linen Corp	5023	74
Town and Country Mortgage Co	6162	74
Town and Country Underground Utility Construction Inc	1623	226
Town Crier Ltd	2752	1006
Town Cryer	2711	579
Town East Ford Sales Inc	5511	211
Town House Home Furnishings LLC	2231	6
Town Motors Inc	5511	840
Town Of Cumberland	7389	2173
Town Of Weaverville	7389	1148
Town Pump Incorporated and Affiliates	5541	22
Town Shop	1623	748

Company Name	SIC	Rank
Town Talk Manufacturing Company Inc	2353	18
Towne Air Freight LLC	4213	115
Towne Machine Tool Co	3556	167
Towne Realty Inc	6531	64
TowneBank	6022	50
Towneley Capital Management Inc	6282	157
Townley Engineering And Manufacturing Company Inc	3532	12
Townsend Analytics Ltd	7372	1026
Townsend Assets Group Inc	5734	326
Townsend Ford Inc	5511	560
Townsend Holdings Inc	5039	47
Townsend Industries Inc	3555	85
Townsend Polymer Services and Information	7375	171
Townsend Raimundo Besler and Usher	8743	261
Townsend Supply Co	5063	143
Townsends Inc	2015	75
Township Builders Inc	1623	255
Townsquare Electric Inc	1731	942
Townsquare Media LLC	4832	25
Towson University	8221	26
Toxguard Fluid Technologies Inc	7389	1780
Toxics Targeting Inc	8731	357
Toy Tips Inc	8734	188
Toy Wonders Inc	5092	21
Toyal America Inc	3399	19
Toye Corp	3577	578
Toyo Seal America Corp	3053	22
Toyo Seat USA Corp	2531	21
Toyo Tire Corp (Cypress California)	5014	16
Toyo USA Inc	5085	284
Toyoda Machinery USA Inc	3541	27
Toyota Material Handling USA Inc	3537	15
Toyota Motor Corporate Services of North America Inc	8999	73
Toyota Motor Credit Corp	6141	6
Toyota Motor Distributors Inc	5013	129
Toyota Motor Manufacturing Alabama Inc	3714	81
Toyota Motor Manufacturing Indiana Inc	3713	2
Toyota Motor Manufacturing Kentucky Inc	3711	22
Toyota Motor Manufacturing North America Inc	3711	23
Toyota Motor Manufacturing West Virginia Inc	3711	20
Toyota Motor North America Inc	7319	30
Toyota Motor Sales USA Inc	5012	84
Toyota of Bedford	5511	708
Toyota of Fort Worth	5511	994
Toyota Of Melbourne	5511	159
Toyota of North Hollywood	5511	452
Toyota of Orange Inc	5511	465
Toyotalift Inc	5084	136
Toyotalift Of Arizona Inc	5084	246
Toys "R" Us Inc	5945	1
TP Composites Inc	3089	1042
TP Franklin Inc	2671	68
TP Freight Lines Inc	4213	2104
TP Tools and Equipment	3559	278
TP Trucking	4213	1241
TPB Holdings Inc	6022	709
tpbs LLP	8721	77
Tpc Technologies Inc	1731	2374
TPF Inc	3823	410
TPG Architecture LLP	8712	45
TPG Capital	6799	2
Tpg Companies Inc	8748	190
TPi Billing Solutions	7389	305
Tpi Billing Solutions LLC	7379	518
Tpi Composites Inc	3083	28
Tpi Corp	3567	5
TPI Inc	8748	25
TPL Communications Inc	3663	224
T-Plastech Corp	3089	1207
TPR Enterprises Ltd	5063	1054
TPS Enterprises Inc	2732	42
Tps International Inc	5084	778
TPS Systems Inc	7372	3681
TPT Technologies Inc	7372	3441
T-R Associates Inc	5063	389
TR Bryant Associates Inc	7363	106
TR Desktop Publishing	2791	69
TR Encoder Solutions Inc	5084	872
TR Manufacturing Inc	3699	65
TR Toppers Inc	2066	5
TR Wallis Graphics Inc	2752	1443
TR Winston and Co	6211	229
TRA Inc	8732	49
Trabon Printing Company Inc	2752	226
Trac-A-Chec Inc	7322	82
Trace Communications LLC	7334	14
Trace Die Cast Inc	3363	16
Trace laboratories Inc	8734	131
Tracer Corp	5088	55
Tracer Technologies	7372	861
Tracer Technologies Inc (York Pennsylvania)	7372	4567
Tracewell Systems Inc	3053	19
TracFone Wireless Inc	4899	20
Trachel Inc	7381	241
Trachte Building Systems Inc	3448	19

Company Name	SIC	Rank
Track Data Corp	6289	22
Trackmaster Inc	3695	126
Tracks Brewing Co	2082	49
Trackwise Inc	7389	2319
Traco Manufacturing Inc	3565	73
TRACOM Corp	8299	63
Tractor and Equipment Co	5084	9
Tractor Place Inc	5083	80
Tractor Supply Co	5261	1
Tracy Auto LLC	5511	378
Tracy Electric Inc	1731	1352
Tracy Press Inc	2711	454
Tracy Printing Inc	2752	1689
Tracy's Karate Studios	7999	103
TRad North America Inc	3433	16
Trade American Card Corp	7373	1057
Trade Center Management Associates LLC	8741	186
Trade Dimensions USA	2741	339
Trade Exchange of America Inc	7389	1222
Trade Graphics Inc	2752	1486
Trade Line Fabricating Inc	3599	1234
Trade Net Corp	7381	228
Trade Network Inc	4813	319
Trade Press Media Group Inc	2721	151
Trade Publishing Inc	2721	321
Trade Quotes Inc	7371	1515
Trade Ranger Us Inc	8742	494
Trade Ship Inc	7379	780
Trade Show Alliance Inc	7389	2466
Trade Show Solution Center LLC	7389	2530
Trade Union International Inc	3942	8
Trade Winds Transit Inc	4213	1231
Trade Winds Trucking	4213	246
Trade Wings Inc	5065	219
TradeBeam Inc	7372	683
TradeCard Inc	7372	705
Tradehome Shoe Stores Inc	5661	13
Tradelynx International	5065	477
Trademark Cosmetic Inc	2844	144
Trademark Die and Engineering Inc	3544	466
Trademark Express	7389	2334
Trademark Nitrogen Corp	2813	15
Trademark Telecom Inc	4813	701
TradeMaven Group LLC	6289	27
Tradenet Publishing Inc	3993	46
Tradeone Marketing Inc	7311	470
Tradepaq Corp	7372	447
Trader Bay Ltd	2091	30
Trader Bud's Westside Dodge	5511	818
Trader Carolina Bargain Inc	2741	451
Trader Joe's Co	5411	34
Trades Publishing Inc	2721	429
Tradeshow Equipment Rentals Inc	7359	135
TradeStar Investments Inc	6211	286
TradeStation Group Inc	7372	333
TradeStation Securities Inc	7372	84
TradeStation Technologies Inc	7372	776
Tradestone Software Inc	7372	1359
Tradewind Enterprises Inc	4213	2811
Tradewind Software Inc	7372	3031
Tradewind Turbines Corp	3724	70
Tradewinds Engine Services LLC	5088	88
Tradewinds Services Inc	8093	46
TradeWinds Software Corp	7371	1717
Trading Technologies International Inc	7372	34
Tradinter Development Company Inc	5063	735
Tradition Software Inc	7372	1275
Traditional Baking Inc	2052	44
Traeger Inc	5734	256
Traeger Pellet Grills LLC	3631	8
Traer Manufacturing	3465	18
Trafalgar Ltd	2387	2
Traffic Builders Inc	7389	1260
Traffic Control Products Company Inc	5084	266
Traffic Control Service Inc	7359	45
Traffic Management Inc	4731	86
Traffic Operations Signal Shop	3669	235
Traffic Safety Service LLC	5099	90
Traffic Safety Solutions	3669	219
Traffic Signal Hardware Inc	3669	317
Traffic Systems and Technology LLC	3648	93
Traffic Works Inc	3081	156
Trafficcom Inc	4899	85
Traffiq	2741	186
Traffix Inc	7389	287
Trafon Group Inc	5142	11
Trahan Burden and Charles Inc	7331	64
Trahide Co	5084	908
Trail King Industries Inc	3715	14
TrailBlazer Studios	7372	4184
Trailblazer Technologies	7389	1189
Trailboss Enterprises Inc	3728	117
Trailer Bridge Inc	4412	20
Trailer Convoys Inc	4213	2312
Trailer Equipment Inc	5012	137
Trailer Sales Of Tennessee Inc	5531	60
Trailer Space Inc	7359	256
Trailer Transit Inc	4213	566
Trailiner Corp	4213	362
Trailmobile Inc	3715	10
Trailstar Manufacturing Corp	7549	22
Trailsteaks LLC	2013	249
Training and Development Systems Inc	8748	257

Company Name	SIC	Rank
Training and Seminar Locators Inc	7375	249
Training Associates Corp	8742	283
Training Associates (Westborough Massachusetts)	8299	34
Training Education Development Solutions Inc	7379	788
training etc Inc	8243	7
Trainor Fairbrook	8111	476
Trainor Grain and Supply Co	5153	94
Trak Microwave Corp	3663	38
!Trak-It Solutions Inc	7372	4568
Traknet	4813	540
Tram Inc	3714	159
T-Ram Semiconductor Inc	3674	148
Tramac Corp	5082	195
Trambeam Corp	3536	33
Tramco Pump Co	3561	141
Tramcor Corp	4213	1663
Tramex Travel Inc	4724	92
Trammell Crow Co	6519	6
Trammell Crow Company (Dallas Texas)	8741	86
TRAMS Inc	7372	358
Tram-Tek Inc	3599	335
Tran Electronics Corp	3672	280
Tran Tek Automation Corp	3552	16
Trancos Inc	7319	85
Trandes Corp	7371	230
Trane Inc	3585	256
Tranex Inc	3677	64
Tranoco Inc	3559	496
Trans/Air Manufacturing Corp	3585	73
Trans American Trucking Services	4213	1319
Trans Continental Transport Inc	4213	1121
Trans Cosmos America Inc	7371	1065
Trans East Inc	7629	25
Trans Electric Inc	1731	819
Trans Energy Inc	1311	220
Trans Form Plastics Corp	3089	1530
Trans Global Communication Enterprises Inc	4813	573
Trans Gulf Transportation	4213	3098
Trans Harbor Services LLC	4731	78
Trans International Company Inc	7372	1475
Trans International LLC	5045	831
TRANS International System	4213	235
Trans Mag Corp	3612	132
Trans National Communications International Inc	4813	177
Trans National Group Services LLC	6719	98
Trans Pacific National Bank Corp	6712	657
Trans Petro of California	4213	2199
Trans Power Inc	5511	1255
Trans States Airlines Inc	4512	38
Trans Technical Leasing Inc	4213	2022
Trans Technical Logistics Inc	4213	1820
Trans Texas Gas Corp	4922	8
Trans Valley Transport Inc	4213	1467
Trans West Truck Inc	5012	98
Trans Western Polymers Inc	2673	13
Trans World Assurance Co	6311	271
Trans World Connections Ltd	3679	777
Trans World Corp	7999	82
Trans World Entertainment Corp	5735	1
Trans World Radio	4832	37
Trans World Services Inc	5162	59
TranS1 Inc	3841	112
Transact Communications Inc	7371	1199
TransAct Technologies Inc	3577	138
Transaction Network Services	7389	79
Transaction Technology Corp	1799	32
Trans-Alarm Inc	1731	414
TransAm Trucking Inc	4213	205
Transamerica Corp	6311	20
Transamerica Financial Life Insurance Co	6311	255
Transamerica Financial Services	6141	18
Transamerica Income Shares Inc	6726	70
Transamerica Investment Services Inc	6282	648
Transamerica Life and Protection	7372	780
Transamerica Occidental Life Insurance Co	6311	33
Transamerican Underground Ltd	1623	553
Transammonia Inc	5191	1
Transarctic Of North Carolina Inc	3585	236
Transaria Inc	4899	219
Transatlantic Holdings Inc	6331	48
Transatlantic Reinsurance Co	6331	81
Transbotics Corp	3629	68
Trans-Cal Industries Inc	3728	198
TransCare Pennsylvania	4119	4
Transcat Inc	3825	22
Transcend Business Solutions LLC	7371	1318
Transcend Services Inc	7389	246
Transcendent LLC	7371	1195
Transcendent Management	8742	703
Transcendent Sound Inc	3651	258
Transcept Pharmaceuticals Inc	8731	82
TransChemical Inc	2899	118
Transco Lines Inc	4213	594
Transco Northwest Inc	5085	277
Transco Products Corp	3652	43
Transco Products Inc	3479	47
Transco Suppliers Corp	5084	500

Company Name	SIC	Rank
Trans-Coil Inc	3825	39
Transcom Communications Inc	1311	187
Transcon Inc	3535	193
Transcon Shipping Specialists	4213	1796
Transcon Technologies Inc	3677	44
Transcontinental Direct USA Inc	2752	2
Transcontinental Insurance Co	6331	272
Transcontinental Realty Investors Inc	6798	118
Transcontinental Security Inc	7382	162
Trans-Continental Systems	4213	956
Transcontinents Record Sales Inc	8999	168
TransCor America Inc	4729	4
TransCorr LLC	4212	83
Transcraft Corp	3715	8
Transcribing Unlimited 2000 Inc	7338	33
Transcript Press Inc	2752	1014
Transcription Express Inc	7338	16
Transdevelopment Corp	6552	202
Transdigm Group Inc	5088	3
Transdigm Inc	3561	40
Transducer Techniques Inc	3679	519
Transdyn Controls Inc	3625	30
Transecur Inc	4813	669
Transel Elevator and Electric Inc	1731	1635
Transend Corp	7372	2698
Transene Company Inc	2819	115
Transentric	7372	790
TransEra Corp	7372	1663
Transfer Express Inc	2759	122
Transfer Graphics Inc	7334	93
Transfer West Duplication	3695	100
Transfield Services North America	1611	11
Transfirst Holdings Inc	6289	4
Transform Automotive LLC	3714	252
Transform Trucking Co	4213	2528
Transformer Engineering LLC	3612	68
Transformer Manufacturers Inc	3612	105
Transformer Technology Inc	3679	684
Transformyx Inc	2741	420
Transgenomic Inc	3826	44
Transguard General Insurance Agency Inc	6321	45
Transhealth LLC	7338	5
Transhumance Colorado Inc	2011	39
Transilwrap Company Inc	3081	11
Transistor Devices Inc	3612	9
Transit Air Inc	3585	228
Transit America Las Vegas LLC	7312	11
Transit Mix Concrete and Materials Co	3273	96
Transit Mix Concrete Co	3273	5
Transit Mix of Pueblo Inc	3273	106
Transit Services Inc	4213	2285
Transite Technology Inc	7389	675
Transition Management	7373	1147
Transition Networks Inc	3661	80
Transition Products Inc	5044	84
Transitional Living Communities	8322	147
Transitional Living Services Inc	8361	64
Transitions Optical Inc	3851	8
Transko Electronics Inc	3679	752
Translab Inc	3565	147
Transland Inc	4213	905
Translation LLC	7311	344
Translations Incorporated Corporate	7389	1886
Translationscom Inc	7372	143
Translatus Inc	7389	2292
Transline Technology Inc	3672	382
Translogic Corp	3535	5
Trans-Lux Corp	3999	64
Trans-Lux West	3993	95
TransMarket Group LLC	6211	40
Transmatic Inc	3647	14
Trans-Matic Manufacturing Co	3469	23
TransMedia Public Relations	8743	94
Transmedics Inc	3845	97
Trans-Micro Inc	7372	1986
Transmission and Fluid Equipment Inc	5085	125
Transmission Equipment International Inc	5063	660
TransMontaigne Inc	4612	3
TransMontaigne Partners LP	4612	11
TransMontaigne Product Services Inc	5172	53
Transnational Computer Technology	7372	2036
TransNet Corp	5045	339
Transnuclear Inc	8711	220
Transocean International Trading Inc	5065	414
Transoft Networks	7372	4148
TranSolutions Inc	7372	4339
Transoma Medical Inc	3845	76
Transource Inc	5511	1094
Transource Services Corp	3571	47
Transpak Corp	2759	207
Trans-Pak Inc	7389	358
Transparent Container Company Inc	3089	359
Transparent Devices Inc	3089	1609
Transparent Language Inc	7372	1718
Transparent Products Inc	3575	24
Transparent Protection Systems Inc	3081	161
Transparent Technologies Inc	7379	1111
Transperfect Translations Inc	7389	20
Transplace Texas LP	4731	11
Transplant Connect Inc	7372	3418
Transply Inc	5085	79
Transpo Trading Inc	3491	34

Company Name	SIC	Rank
Transport Corporation of America Inc	4213	112
Transport Cranes LLC	3531	221
Transport Diesel Service Inc	5013	240
Transport Distribution Co	4213	811
Transport Investments Inc	4213	214
Transport Refrigeration Sales and Service Inc	5078	11
Transport Service Co	4213	200
Transportation Control Systems Inc	3669	196
Transportation Costing Group Inc	7372	3686
Transportation Equipment Inc	2394	23
Transportation Financial Systems Inc	7361	55
Transportation Personnel Services Inc	7363	104
Transportation Resource Partners LP	6799	238
Transportation Systems Consulting Corp	7372	3032
Transportation Technical Services Inc	5063	1077
Transportation Unlimited Inc	7363	56
Transporter Inc	4213	2858
Transpower Corp	7372	2499
Transpower Technologies Inc	3572	23
Transprint USA Inc	2754	6
Transpro Contract Carriers Inc	4213	2692
Trans-Resources Inc	2899	19
Transtar Autobody Technologies Inc	7213	7
Transtar Electric Inc	1731	377
Transtar Industries Inc	3714	233
Transtar Productions Inc	7812	230
Trans-Tec Machine Ltd	3599	592
Trans-Tec Services Inc	5172	30
Transtech LLC	7379	809
TransTech of SC LP	3621	95
Transtector Systems Inc	3643	43
Trans-Tel Central Inc	1731	181
Transtel Group Inc	7629	55
Transunion Corp	7323	9
TransUnion LLC	7323	6
Transunion Title Insurance Co	6361	29
Trans-United Inc	4213	767
Transus Intermodal LLC	4213	545
Transvideo Studios	7812	90
Transvirtual Systems LLC	7371	1242
Transwall	2542	48
TransWare Enterprises Inc	7372	4569
Transweb LLC	3564	91
Transwestern Commercial Services	6531	23
Transwestern Commercial Services (Bethesda Maryland)	6531	106
TransWestern Publishing Company LP	2741	12
TranSwitch Corp	3674	144
Transwood Inc	4213	1418
Transylvania Vocational Services Inc	8093	32
Transystems Inc	4213	457
Transzap Inc	7371	678
Tran-Tec Corp	3499	124
TranTech Inc	7373	107
Tranter PHE Inc	3443	77
Trantham Services Inc	4213	2919
Tranxition Corp	7372	4444
Tranzact Technologies Inc	7372	818
Tranzon Asset Strategies	5734	6
Trap Rock Industries Inc	3272	39
Trapeze Networks	7372	1150
Trapeze Software Group Inc	7371	338
Trapeze Software Inc	7372	3076
Trapp Cadillac Chevrolet Inc	5511	232
Trappistine Nuns Inc	2064	115
Trasys LLC	7363	175
Traton Corp	1522	29
Travaini Pumps USA Inc	5084	575
Travamerica Inc	7389	2186
Travco Inc	7379	231
Travel Ad Network	7311	482
Travel Agency Management Systems Inc	7372	1603
Travel America Inc	7033	5
Travel and Transport Inc	4724	8
Travel Authority	4724	14
Travel Beyond	4724	85
Travel Company Inc	4724	133
Travel Computer Systems Inc	7372	2629
Travel Destinations Management Group Inc	4724	25
Travel Duet Inc	4724	62
Travel Dynamics International	4481	11
Travel Holdings Inc	4724	54
Travel House Corp (Mobile Alabama)	4724	142
Travel Impressions Ltd	4725	9
Travel Insurance Services	6411	73
Travel Leaders/Bentley Hedges Travel Inc	4724	94
Travel Resource Center Inc	8249	19
Travel Software Consultants	7372	4892
Travel Tags Inc	2396	2
Travel Trade Publications Inc	2721	377
TravelCenters of America LLC	6719	22
Travelclick Inc	8742	247
Travelers Haven	8361	74
Travelers Indemnity Co (Hartford Connecticut)	6331	214
Travelers Investment Management Co	6282	363
Travelers' Tales	2731	285
Travelite Inc	7699	252
Travelmore/Carlson Wagonlit Travel	4724	48

Company Name	SIC	Rank
Travelocitycom LP	7375	21
Travelodge Hotels Inc	7011	145
Travel-On Ltd	4724	88
Travelong Inc	4724	120
Travelore Travel Service	4724	132
Travelport	4724	6
Travelport Ltd	7375	4
TravelStore (Sacramento California)	4724	19
Traveltime Services Inc	4724	119
Travelview International Inc	7812	249
Travelzoo Inc	7373	71
Travers Printing Inc	2752	1434
Travers Tool Company Inc	3429	60
Traverse City Products Inc	3465	44
Travidia Inc	7372	163
Travis Associates Inc	7361	334
Travis Credit Union	6061	22
Travis Lumber Company Inc	2421	109
Travis Machine Company Inc	3599	2484
Travis Meats Inc	5142	22
Travis Pattern and Foundry Inc	3523	28
Travis Pest Management Inc	7342	73
Travis Software Corp	7372	3500
Travisa Inc	7389	539
TravisWolff Independent Advisors and Accountants	8721	294
Travizon Inc	4724	11
Trawick and Associates	7371	692
Trax Company Inc	1623	353
Trax Distributors	5065	140
Trax International Corp	8744	13
Trax Softworks Inc	7372	3633
Traxys North America LLC	5051	68
Traycon Manufacturing Company Inc	3535	167
Trayer Engineering Corp	3613	46
Traylor Brothers Inc	1622	8
Traylor Chemical and Supply Co	5191	67
Traylor Electric Company Inc	1731	611
Traylor Trucking Services	2875	29
Tray-Pak Corp	3089	445
TRC Alton Geoscience Inc	4953	27
TRC Circuits Inc	3672	426
TRC Companies Inc	4959	4
TRC Electrical Construction Services Inc	1731	329
TRC Environmental Corp	8748	16
Trc Group Inc	5153	33
Trc Manufacturing Inc	3089	1035
TRE Communications Ltd	8742	622
Tread Corp	3499	65
Treadway Electric Company Inc	5063	135
Treadway Industries LLC	3069	184
Treadwell Corp	3731	49
Treadwell Electric Contractors Inc	1731	637
Treasure Island Foods Inc	5411	184
Treasure Island Inc (Red Wing Minnesota)	7999	42
Treasure State Bank Inc	6022	708
Treatco Inc	2047	32
Treatment Products Ltd	2842	107
Treatment Systems Inc	5047	125
Treaty City Industries Inc	3053	128
Treaty Oak Bancorp	6712	686
Trebnick Systems Inc	2759	88
Trebor Instrument Corp	3599	2463
Trebor International	3561	119
Trec Industries Inc	3599	1669
Trece Corp	2879	33
Trecom Safety Corp	3851	50
Tredegar Corp	3354	6
Tredegar Film Products - Lake Zurich LLC	3081	1
Tredent Data Systems Inc	5065	125
Tree City Tool and Engineering Company Inc	3599	1228
Tree Line Transportion Inc	4213	2376
Tree of Life Inc	5141	11
Tree Star Inc	7372	1725
Tree Top Inc	2033	11
Tree Top Industries Inc	7371	1909
Tree Towns Reprographics Inc	7334	40
TreeAge Software Inc	7372	4570
Treecom Inc	6163	48
TreeCon Resources Inc	5082	62
Tree-D Inc	7371	1767
TreeHouse Foods Inc	2032	3
Treehouse Productions Management Inc	1731	1203
Treehouse Software Inc	7372	3202
Treeland Nursery Co	0811	1
Treetop Technologies Inc	7379	493
TREEV	7372	1839
Trefethen Vineyards Winery	5921	16
Trega Foods Ltd	2022	32
Trek America Tours	4725	19
Trek Bicycle Corp	3751	5
Trek Digital Products Inc	5049	120
Trek Equipment Corp	5045	500
TREK Inc	3679	361
Trek Resources Inc	1382	50
Trekk Design	7379	281
Trelleborg Automotive Molding Div	3061	8
Trelleborg Offshore Boston Inc	3086	67
Trelleborg Sealing Solutions Americas	3569	4

Company Name	SIC	Rank
Trelleborg Sealing Solutions Great Lakes	2821	39
Trelleborg YSH Inc	3061	6
Trellis Network Services Inc	7372	3556
Tremco Inc	2851	11
Tremont Capital Management Inc	6282	441
Tremont Credit Union	6061	109
Tremont LLC	6719	70
Tremont Partners Inc	6282	65
Trenam Kemker Scharf Barkin Frye O'Neill and Mullis	8111	413
Trench and Marine Pump Company Inc	3561	176
Trenchless Pipe Company Inc	3084	46
Trencor Inc	3531	55
Trend Enterprises Inc	3999	57
Trend Machinery Inc	3625	374
Trend Manor Furniture Manufacturing Company Inc	2511	87
Trend Plastics Inc	3089	1128
Trend Publishing Inc	2721	338
Trend Technologies LLC	3444	41
Trendco Supply Inc	5046	84
Trendex Inc	2782	20
Trendler Inc	3499	72
Trendsetter Software Inc	7372	3961
TRENDware International Inc	3577	287
Trendway Corp	2522	26
Trendwood Inc	2511	48
Trenor Motor Co	5511	1225
Trent Inc	3567	114
Trenton Forging Co	3462	44
Trenton Group Inc	3273	84
Trenton Systems Inc	7373	840
Trenwyth Industries Inc	3271	5
Trepanning Specialty A California Corp	3599	1928
Trepte Construction Co	1542	265
Tres Design Group Inc	8748	359
Tresch Electrical Company Inc	3645	10
Trese Inc	2752	1332
Treske Precision Machining Inc	3599	510
Tressa Inc	2844	137
Tressler Soderstrom Maloney and Priess	8111	348
Tresu Royse Inc	3555	63
Trevett's Mailing Service LLC	7331	196
Trevis Berry Transportation Inc	4213	2723
Trevose Electronics Inc	5731	94
Trex Company Inc	2499	7
T-Rex Consulting Corp	7373	497
Trex Enterprises Corp	3571	65
Trexel Inc	3089	1254
Trexler Rubber Company Inc	3069	257
Trexler Trucking Inc	4213	1389
Treyarch Corp	7372	135
Treynor Bancshares Inc	6712	423
Treynor State Bank	6022	729
Trg Products Inc	5045	652
Tri Aerospace LLC	3724	66
Tri -Auto Enterprises Inc	7311	375
Tri Bms LLC	3564	109
Tri Central Co-op	5153	132
Tri City Bankshares Corp	6712	299
Tri City H P	5046	258
Tri City Marble Inc	3281	43
Tri City Steel and Fabricating Inc	3441	206
TRI Commercial Real Estate Services Inc	6531	380
Tri Counties Bank	6022	155
Tri County Beverage Co	5181	55
Tri County Communications Inc	5731	114
Tri County Electric Co	1731	1232
Tri County Electric Coop (Lancaster Missouri)	4911	377
Tri County Feed And Grain Inc	3523	259
Tri County Industries Inc	8331	206
Tri County Publishing Inc	2711	923
Tri County Tower Service	1623	474
Tri Dal Ltd	1623	870
Tri Electronics Inc	5999	132
TRI Environmental Inc	8734	152
Tri Green Interstate Equipment Inc	7389	1981
Tri Isle Inc	4213	423
Tri M Graphics Co	2752	911
Tri Magnetics Corp	3572	101
Tri Map International Inc	3571	141
Tri Mark United East	5046	28
Tri Medica International Inc	5122	91
Tri Power Mpt Inc	5063	632
Tri R Tooling Inc	3599	2360
TRI Realtors	6531	15
Tri Seal Holdings Inc	3081	66
Tri Source Inc	3679	109
Tri Star Cabinet And Top Company Inc	2434	60
Tri Star Cnc Services LLC	3575	58
Tri Star Freight System Inc	4213	864
Tri Star Industrial Lighting Inc	5063	931
Tri Star Tool and Machine Inc	3544	579
Tri State Business Machines Inc	7699	111
Tri State Electric Inc	1731	1032
Tri State Machinery Co	5082	197
Tri State Metrovision Inc	7819	64
Tri State Parts Co	5075	83
Tri State Pest Control Inc	7342	45
Tri State Tower Inc	1623	364

Company Name	SIC	Rank
Tri State Vending	5962	21
Tri Steel Inc	5082	186
Tri Synergy Inc	7379	1265
Tri Tec Systems Inc	3679	660
Tri Tech Equipment Inc	3599	2487
Tri Tech Tool and Design Company Inc	3089	1418
Tri Technologies Inc	3559	511
Tri Tek Electronics Inc	3679	436
Tri Tel Inc	5999	170
Tri Tool Inc	3541	28
Tri Valley Coop	5153	148
Tri W-G Inc	3842	297
Triad Broadcasting	4832	108
Triad Business Products Inc	2752	1697
Triad Circuits Inc	3672	270
Triad Container Inc	2789	117
Triad Corp	1541	272
Triad Creative Group Inc	7311	750
Triad Digital Media LLC	7311	164
Triad Energy Resources Inc	2875	35
Triad Engineering Inc	8734	41
Triad Enterprises Inc	2752	453
Triad Equipment Services Of Colorado	5087	186
Triad Fastener Corp	3965	8
Triad Financial Corp	6141	19
Triad Freightliner of Greensboro Inc	5511	891
Triad Governmental Systems Inc	7371	1126
Triad Guaranty Inc	6351	22
Triad Guaranty Insurance Corp	6351	34
TRIAD Inc	8743	262
Triad Industries Inc	3589	268
Triad Interactive Inc	7371	1155
Triad Machine Inc	3599	1631
Triad Machinery Inc	5082	53
Triad Manufacturing Inc	2599	13
Triad Medical Disposables Inc/H and P Industries	3089	125
Triad Metal Products Co	3469	149
Triad Personnel Services Inc	7361	56
Triad Precision Products Inc	3053	86
Triad Solutions	7379	905
Triad Solutions Inc	8742	702
Triad Speakers Inc	3651	99
Triad Systems Engineering Inc	7379	735
Triad Tool and Die Company Inc	3599	1032
Triad Tooling Inc	5084	738
Triad Transport Inc	4213	668
Triad Web Design	7379	937
Tri-Ag Corp	5083	210
Triage Consulting Group	8742	179
Trialco Inc	3341	17
Trialon Corp	7363	125
Triana Industries Inc	3679	251
Tri-Analytics Inc	7379	831
Triangle Blueprint Co	5999	106
Triangle Brass Manufacturing Company Inc	3429	79
Triangle Broach Co	3545	391
Triangle Building Supplies And Services Inc	5211	212
Triangle Communications Group Inc	2791	32
Triangle Communications Inc	5731	89
Triangle Co	2752	1618
Triangle Construction Inc	1542	415
Triangle Dies And Supplies Inc	3544	118
Triangle Direct Media	7319	128
Triangle Electric Corp	1731	2190
Triangle Electric Inc	1731	1296
Triangle Electric Supply Co	5063	431
Triangle Engineering Corp	3599	926
Triangle Equipment Company Inc	5082	138
Triangle Ice Company Of Beaufort Inc	2097	9
Triangle Industries Inc	3469	110
Triangle Manufacturing Co	3568	61
Triangle Microsystems Inc	3822	77
Triangle Package Machinery Co	3556	18
Triangle Packing Inc	2011	153
Triangle Precision Industries Inc	3599	531
Triangle Press Inc	2732	50
Triangle Printers Inc	2752	732
Triangle Real Estate Services Inc	6552	101
Triangle Reprographics Inc	7374	158
Triangle Research and Development Corp	8731	251
Triangle Rubber Company Inc	3069	222
Triangle Rubber Company LLC	2821	107
Triangle Sales Co	7389	1779
Triangle Talent Inc	7922	52
Triangle Telephone Cooperative Association	4813	198
Triangle Tool Corp	3544	32
Triangle Transportation and Distribution Service	4213	2345
Triangle Trucking Inc	4213	2455
TrianglecablesCom LLC	5734	492
Triarch Industries Inc	2851	116
Triaxis Inc	5045	942
Tri-B Inc	4213	2557
Tribal Core	7379	1525
Tribar Manufacturing LLC	3089	496
Tribble and Stephens Co	1542	226
Tribeam Inc	3663	353
Tribology Inc	2992	54
Triboro Bagel Company Inc	2051	298

Company Name	SIC	Rank
Triboro Bar and Restaurant Supply Company Inc	5046	315
Triboro Coach Corp	4111	3
Tribune Broadcasting Co	4833	15
Tribune Co	2711	7
Tribune Company Holdings Inc	2711	3
Tribune Corp	2711	770
Tribune Entertainment Co	4833	96
Tribune Media Services Inc	7383	10
Tribune Publishing Company Inc	2711	335
Tribuzio Hilliard Studio Inc	7335	5
Tri-C Machine Corp	3599	1886
Tri-C Resources Inc	1311	166
Tri-Century Corp	2893	30
Tricerat Inc	7372	3074
Tri-Cities Manufacturing Inc	3089	1386
Tri-City Automotive Warehouse Corp	5013	257
Tri-City Electric Service Inc	1731	1776
Tri-City Electrical Contractors Inc	1731	174
Tri-City Fuel and Heating Company Inc	5983	17
Tri-City Meats Inc	5147	37
Tri-City Rentals	6531	38
Tri-City Wood Works Inc	5031	426
Trick Flow Specialties	3714	396
TriCo Bancshares	6712	189
Trico Belting and Supply Co	5084	422
Trico Contracting Inc	1623	203
Trico Corp	3569	111
Trico Electric Cooperative Inc	4911	154
Trico Electric Corp	1731	2245
Trico Marine Services Inc	4489	2
Trico Nonferrous Metal Products Inc	3599	29
Trico Opportunities Inc	8331	184
Trico Products Corp	3714	434
Tricom Communications Inc	8999	199
Tri-Com LLC	4813	629
Tri-Com Technical Services	7363	112
Tricomm Services Corp	1731	259
Tricon Chemical Corp	5169	154
Tri-Con Industries Ltd	3751	29
Tricon Systems Corp	7372	4982
Tri-Continent Scientific Inc	3824	17
Tri-Continental Corp	6726	19
Tricor America	4731	15
Tricor America	4731	23
TRI-COR Industries Inc	7373	46
Tricor International Inc	3699	236
Tricor Systems Inc	3829	138
TricorBraun	5162	14
Tri-Cord Healthcare Information Systems Inc	7371	485
Tri-County Aggregate Inc	5032	177
Tricounty Business Machines	7629	53
Tri-County Care Center	8051	71
Tri-County Chemical Inc	2873	20
Tri-County Custom Sports Inc	5091	110
Tri-County Electric Coop (St Matthews South Carolina)	4911	241
Tri-County Electric Cooperative Inc (Madison Florida)	4911	288
Tri-County Electrical Supply Inc	5063	879
TriCounty Farm Service Inc	5984	22
Tri-County Ford-Mercury Inc	5511	1032
Tri-County Implement Inc	5083	189
Tricounty Maintenance Inc	7349	227
Tri-County Parts and Equipment	5531	55
Tricounty Rural Electric Cooperative Inc	4911	581
Tri-Craft Inc	3089	1370
Tridan Intl	3562	14
Tri-Data Inc	7389	1390
Trident Building Systems Inc	3448	24
Trident Capital LP	6799	254
Trident Computer Resources Inc	7373	436
Trident Insurance Services LLC	6411	94
Trident Investments Inc	6798	165
Trident Manufacturing Inc	3679	455
Trident Medical Center LLC	8062	178
Trident One Stop Career Center	8742	575
Trident Plastics Inc	5162	50
Trident Precision Manufacturing Inc	3469	63
Trident Seafoods Corp	2092	8
Trident Services	7372	2304
Trident Software Inc (Hamden Connecticut)	7372	1933
Trident Software Inc (Sausalito California)	7372	4953
Trident Systems Inc	3577	174
Tridia Corp	7372	3290
Tri-Digital Software Inc	7372	3033
Tri-Dim Filter Corp	3564	51
Triebold Implement Inc	5083	134
Trienda LLC	3089	98
Trier Software Inc	7372	3962
Trifecta Technologies Inc	7372	3145
Trifox Inc	7372	4767
Trigen Energy Corp	4961	1
Trigen-Baltimore Energy Corp	4961	4
Trigen-Boston Energy Corp	4961	2
Trigen-Nassau Energy Corp	4961	3
Trigen-Oklahoma Energy Corp	4961	5
Trigen-St Louis Energy Corp	4939	16
Trigon Corp	2819	104
Tri-Gon Precision Inc	7539	17

Company Name	SIC	Rank
Trigyn Technologies Inc	7371	174
Trihealth Inc	8741	274
Tri-Hi Transportation Inc	4213	2011
Trijicon Inc	3827	13
Trikaya Solutions LLC	7379	1071
Trikinetics Inc	3599	2424
Tri-Kris Co	3599	1539
Tri-L Data Systems Inc	3571	125
Tri-Lakes Newspapers Inc	2711	367
Triland Foods Inc	2099	249
Trilectron Industries Inc	3812	49
Tri-Line Automation Corp	5084	685
Trilithic Inc	3826	36
Trilix Marketing Group	7319	54
Trillacorpe Construction	1522	41
Trillion Communications Corp	3661	28
Trillion Digital Communication Inc	4813	279
TRILLIUM FINANCIAL SERVICES PC	8721	252
Trillium Management Inc	6531	398
Trillium Us Inc	5087	58
Trilobyte Software Systems	7372	1143
Trilogy Communications Inc	3357	41
Trilogy Consulting	7379	668
Trilogy Design	7372	2207
Trilogy Health Services LLC	8051	36
Trilogy International Associates Inc	3812	180
Trilogy Plastics Inc	3089	636
Trim Parts Inc	3714	363
Trim Seal USA Inc	2782	15
Tri-Mac Manufacturing And Services Co	3714	412
Trimac Transport Inc	4212	14
Trimac Transportation Services USA	4213	1083
Trimac USA (Houston Texas)	4213	1010
Trimark Computer Systems Inc	5734	177
Trimark Corp	3429	62
TriMark Raygal Inc	1796	5
Trimars Delaware	5094	29
TriMas Corp	3443	4
Trimble (Corvallis Oregon)	7372	2226
Trimble Navigation Ltd	3829	4
Tri-Media Inc	7311	205
Trimedx LLC	7699	11
Trimedyne Inc	3845	90
Tri-Mer Corp	3564	74
Trimfit Inc	2252	26
Trimfoot Company LLC (Farmington Missouri)	3149	24
TriMin Systems Inc	7372	1360
Trimline Die Corp	3544	780
Trimline Medical Products Corp	3841	111
Trim-Lok Inc	3089	643
Trimm International Inc	3661	216
Tri-Modal Distribution Services	4213	353
Trimol Group Inc	3679	897
Trimold LLC	3089	346
Trim-Rite Food Corporation Inc	5147	24
Trims	2241	32
TrimTabs Investment Research	8732	91
Trim-Tex Inc	3089	593
Trinary Systems Inc	7372	2582
Trinchero Family Estates	2084	5
Trind Co	2542	62
Trine Construction Corp	1531	90
TriNet Communications Inc	5065	95
Trinet Construction Inc	1623	363
TriNet Group Inc	7389	302
Trinet Solutions Group Inc	7373	957
TriNET Systems Inc	4899	112
Trinidad/Benham Corp	5149	63
Trinidad Builders Supply Inc	5211	322
Trinidad Management Inc	8741	128
Trinity	3498	7
Trinity Animation Inc	7372	4943
Trinity Biotech USA	3841	166
Trinity Brand Industries Inc	3829	449
Trinity Broadcasting Network Inc	4833	100
Trinity Broadcasting Of Arizona	4833	250
Trinity Building Services	7349	91
Trinity Consultants Inc	7372	904
Trinity Forge Inc	3462	37
Trinity Furniture Inc	2511	70
Trinity Government Systems A Private Company Inc	7373	999
Trinity Health Care Services Inc	7361	283
Trinity Health System	8741	64
Trinity Healthcare Staffing Group Inc	7361	138
Trinity Homecare LLC	8082	59
Trinity Industries Inc	3743	2
Trinity Marketing Inc	8742	569
Trinity Mechanical Systems Inc	1711	21
Trinity Millennium Group Inc	7379	36
Trinity Outdoor LLC	7312	26
Trinity Packaging Corp	2673	6
Trinity Rail Group	3743	16
Trinity Senior Living Community	8361	6
Trinity Tool Co	3569	217
Trinity Tools Inc	3544	695
Trinity Trailer Manufacturing Inc	3715	39
Trinity Ventures	6722	177
Trinity Video Communications Inc	5999	206
Trinity Village Inc	8051	75
Trinity Wholesale Distributors Inc	5074	202
Trinity Yachts LLC	3732	11

Company Name	SIC	Rank
Trinkle Sales Inc	5065	89
TRInternational Trading Company Inc	5169	67
Trio Electrical Contracting Company Inc	1731	900
Trio Packaging Corp	5084	451
Trio Systems LLC	7372	4964
Trio Trucking Inc	4213	2242
TriOak Foods Inc	2048	17
Trioh Consulting Group Inc	7379	1094
Trion Technology	3559	178
Trion World Network Inc	2741	37
Trionics LLC	5065	433
Trioptics Inc	3851	102
Trio-Tech International	3825	51
Triournph Outdoor Rhode Island LLC	7312	17
Tri-Pacific Software Inc	7372	963
Tripada Inc	8351	40
TripAdvisor Inc	4724	10
Tri-Pak Machinery Inc	3556	114
Tri-Parish Co-Operative	5999	63
Triphase Automation Inc	5063	292
Tri-Phase Inc	3672	83
Tripi Engraving Company Inc	2759	425
Tripifoods Inc	5141	102
Triple C Technologies Inc	5046	284
Triple Canopy Inc	7381	47
Triple Crown Nutrition Inc	2048	117
Triple Crown Services Co	4213	8
Triple D Equipment Inc	5083	197
Triple D Publishing Inc	2721	274
Triple D Supply LLC	4213	2963
Triple Dot Corp	3085	36
Triple Five Industries LLC	3829	408
Triple G Express Inc	4213	656
Triple H Food Processors Inc	2033	85
Triple J Communications LLC	4813	611
Triple J Community Broadcasting	4841	144
Triple "j" Custom Interiors Inc	5023	182
Triple J Tomato Company LLC	7389	1114
Triple L Transport Inc	4213	797
Triple P Trucking Inc	4213	1340
Triple Point Technology	7372	2056
Triple Point Technology Inc	7372	592
Triple R Electric Inc	1731	525
Triple R Trucking	4213	2775
Triple R Trucking Inc	4213	2309
Triple/S Dynamics Inc	3599	261
Triple S Hauling Inc	4213	2463
Triple S Produce and Orchards	0723	24
Triple S Trucking Company Inc	4214	25
Triple Sondae Enterprises	2024	54
Triple - T Foods Inc	2047	27
Triple-B Truck Body and Metal Fabricating Co	3713	62
Triplefin LLC	7389	309
Triple-I Corp	8742	184
Triple-S Management Corp	8099	2
Triple-S Propiedad Inc	6411	111
Triple-S Steel Holdings Inc	5051	46
Triplet Tool And Die Company Inc	3544	752
Triplett Corp	3613	110
Triplett Machine Inc	3599	388
Triplett Office Essentials	8712	199
Triplex Inc	3498	20
Triplex Manufacturing Co	3714	353
Tripoli Bakery Inc	2051	206
Tripower Resources Inc	6792	2
Tripp Lite	3679	73
Tripp Nyc Inc	2339	40
Tripp Scott	8111	375
Tripwire Inc	7372	535
TriQuint Semiconductor Inc	3674	43
Tri-R Dies Inc	3544	548
Tri-R Telecommunications Inc	1731	2473
Tri-R Trucking Inc	4213	1657
Trireme Manufacturing Company Inc	3511	37
Tri-S Security Corp	7381	21
Tris USA Inc	3624	18
Trisco Resources Inc	5045	427
Triseal Corp	3713	59
Trisect Engineering and Consulting Corp	8711	570
Trisect Inc	7311	698
Trisep Corp	3589	118
Trisept Corp	7371	569
Tri-Serv Inc	7363	313
Trispec Offshore Corp	7389	1156
Trisquare Communications Inc	3663	349
TriSquare Inc	3577	412
Tristan Rubber Molding Inc	3069	210
Tri-Star Electric Inc	1731	977
Tri-Star Electronics International Inc	3643	16
Tri-Star Engineering Inc	3544	481
Tristar Fire Protection Inc	8711	413
Tristar Graphics Group Inc	2752	758
Tristar Group Inc	7389	1964
Tristar Inc	5734	138
Tristar Of America Inc	1795	9
Tri-Star Offset Corp	2752	1187
Tri-Star Plastics Inc	3089	661
Tristar Systems Corp	3549	83
Tri-Star Transport Inc	4213	1249
Tristar Web Graphics Inc	2752	328
Tri-State 1st Banc Inc	6712	677

Company Name	SIC	Rank
Tri-State Aluminium Inc	5051	330
Tri-State Armature and Electrical Works Inc	5063	154
Tri-State Automatic Sprinkler Corp	1711	264
Tri-State Bank Of Memphis	6022	619
Tri-State Beef Company Inc	2011	133
Tristate Bellcom Corp	4813	567
Tristate Blue Printing Inc	2752	1556
Tri-State Brick and Stone Of New York Inc	5032	21
Tri-State Brick and Tile Company Inc	3251	12
Tri-State Camera Exch Inc	5961	174
Tristate Capital Bank	6022	118
Tri-State Coating And Machine Company Inc	3561	136
Tri-State Consulting Services	7389	2428
Tri-State Cut Stone Co	3281	31
Tri-State Delivery Inc	4213	1289
Tri-State Design Construction Inc	1542	291
Tri-State Disposal Inc	4213	1647
Tri-State Electric And Machine Co	3599	2042
Tri-State Electric Membership Corp	4911	284
Tristate Electronic Manufacturing Inc	3679	698
Tri-State Envelope Corp	2677	26
Tri-State Expedited Service	4213	587
Tri-State Family Broadcasting Inc	4833	247
Tri-State Fire Protection Inc	1711	217
Tri-State Generation and Transmission Association Inc	4911	68
Tri-State Industries Inc	3548	46
Tri-State Insulation Co	3086	143
Tri-State Iron and Metal Co	4953	145
Tri-State Lighting and Supply Company Inc	5063	429
Tri-State Machine Inc	3599	238
Tri-State Motor Transit Co	4213	109
Tristate Network Integrators	7379	1191
Tri-State Publishing Co	2752	972
Tri-State Roofing and Sheet Metal Company Of West Virginia	1761	8
Tri-State Roofing and Siding Wholesale Inc	5033	39
Tri-State Surgical Supply and Equipment Ltd	5047	99
Tri-State Technical Services Inc	5087	38
Tri-State Truck and Equipment Inc	5082	55
Tri-State Utilities Co	1623	311
Tri-State Video Services	5046	52
Tri-Supreme Optical LLC	3851	35
TRISYS TELECOM Inc	7372	1240
Tri-Tech Electric Inc	1731	901
Tritech Electronics Inc	5065	790
Tri-Tech Electronics Inc	3728	129
Tri-Tech Engineering Inc	3600	1997
Tritech Graphics Inc	5045	451
Tri-Tech Laboratories Inc	2085	13
Tritech Manufacturing Inc	3672	346
Tri-Tech Molded Products Inc	3089	1727
Tritech Software Systems	7372	845
Tritech Solution	7378	71
Triteck Inc	7379	893
Tritek Solutions Inc	7373	312
Tritek Technologies Inc	3579	58
Triticom	7371	554
Triton Boat LLC	3732	9
Triton Corp	3799	18
Triton Distribution Systems Inc	1382	75
Triton Diving Services Inc	7389	1206
Triton Engineering Services Co	1389	61
Triton Industries Inc	3469	101
Triton Infosys Inc	3699	222
Triton Manufacturing Company Inc	3643	50
Triton Marketing Inc	5172	103
Triton Media Group LLC	4832	26
Triton Products LLC	3089	1162
Triton Services Inc	3825	21
Triton Systems of Delaware LLC	3578	8
Triton Technologies Inc	7372	2581
Tritone Development	3695	182
Tri-Tool Inc	3559	565
Tri-Town News Inc	2752	1501
Tri-Town Precision Plastics Inc	3089	596
Tri-Tronics Inc	3699	91
Tritronics Inc	5065	185
Tri-Tube Inc	3599	228
Tri-Turn Technologies	3541	245
Triumph Accessory Services	3728	139
Triumph Aerospace Systems - Newport News	8711	152
Triumph Aerostructures - Vought Aircraft Division	3728	5
Triumph Air Repairs Inc	7699	3
Triumph Apparel Corp	2339	15
Triumph Engines - Tempe	3599	47
Triumph Enterprises Inc (Fairfax Virginia)	8742	415
Triumph Fabrication	3728	110
Triumph Fabrications Hot Springs Inc	3728	42
Triumph Fabrications-Shelbyville	3444	80
Triumph Foods LLC	2015	19
Triumph Gear Systems	3566	5
Triumph Gear Systems - Macomb Inc	3599	74
Triumph Group Inc	3728	4
Triumph Instruments and Avionics	5084	44

Company Name Index

Company Name	SIC	Rank
Triumph Learning LLC	7372	3749
Triumph Motorcycles America Ltd	5012	47
Triumph Packaging Georgia LLC	4783	19
Triumph Processing Inc	3471	35
Triumph Structures - Kansas City	3599	10
Triumph Structures-Long Island LLC	3728	49
Triumph Technologies Inc	7373	299
Triumph Twist Drill Company Inc	3545	13
Triumvirate Environmental	8741	176
Triune Color Inc	2752	486
Tri-Union Express Inc	4213	308
Tri-Union Seafood LLC	2091	3
TRIUS Inc	7372	1401
Trius Therapeutics Inc	2834	326
Tri-V Tool and Manufacturing Co	3544	101
Trivak Inc	3599	974
Trivalent Group Inc	7373	274
Tri-Valley Bank	6022	816
Tri-Valley Corp	1311	229
Tri-Valley Oil and Gas Co	1311	213
Tri-Valley Supply Inc	5033	37
Trivec-Avant Corp	3663	169
Trivest Partners LP	6282	508
Trivision Executive Travel Inc	4724	63
Trivision Group Inc	7371	1611
TriVium Systems Inc	7372	2079
Tri-Wall A Weyerhaeuser Co	2653	16
Tri-Way Industries Inc	2531	36
Tri-Way Manufacturing Inc	3599	1390
Triweb Solutions LLC	7372	346
Tri-Win Outsourcing Inc	7331	136
Tri-Worth Solutions LLC	7361	366
Trix Systems Inc	7372	4647
TriZetto Group Inc	7374	23
Trj Inc	3599	916
Trm Manufacturing Inc	3081	33
Tro Manufacturing Company Inc	3469	243
Tro-Cal Inc	5082	156
Troconi Segarra and Associates LLP	8721	130
Trod Nossel Productions and Recording Studios Inc	7389	2486
Trofholz Technologies Inc	7379	413
Trogdon Publishing Inc	2741	278
Troika Company Inc	7922	47
Trojan Battery Co	3691	15
Trojan Electric Inc	1731	861
Trojan Inc	3544	25
Trojan Lithograph Corp	2671	27
Trojan Press Inc	2752	1266
Trojan Professional Services Inc	7375	151
Trojon Gear Inc	3599	1560
Trola-Dyne Inc	3444	286
Trolex Corp	3822	51
Troll Systems Corp	7371	850
Troll Touch	3577	545
Trolley Tours of Cleveland Inc	4111	15
Troma Inc	7812	221
Tronair Inc	3728	120
Trondent Development Corp	7371	772
Tronox Inc	2899	12
Tronser Inc	3675	42
Tron-Tek Inc	3663	318
Troon Company LLC	7322	161
Troon Construction	1799	28
Troop Construction and Electric Inc	1611	239
Tropaion Inc	8243	17
Tropar Trophy Manufacturing Company Inc	3499	77
Trophy Nut Co	2068	15
Tropian Inc	3674	138
Tropic Tool and Mold Inc	3089	1757
Tropical Assemblies Inc	3672	259
Tropical Blossom Honey Co	2099	361
Tropical Communications Inc	1731	2458
Tropical Ford Inc	5511	258
Tropical Nut and Fruit Co	5149	72
Tropical Oasis LLC	2023	28
Tropical Preserving Company Inc	2033	108
Tropical Shipping and Construction Company Ltd	4213	104
Tropical Tents Inc	7359	257
Tropicana Products Inc	2037	4
Tropicana Station Inc	7999	21
Tropic-Kool Engineering Corp	1711	252
Tropitone Furniture Company Inc	2514	5
Tropos Networks Inc	4899	46
Trotter Nathan and Company Inc	5051	280
Trotter's Of Alexandria Inc	5731	93
Trotwood Corp	3599	1202
Trout and Partners Ltd	8742	345
Trout Ebersole and Groff LLC	8721	75
Troutman and Sanders LLP	8111	65
Troutman Brothers Inc	5147	115
Troutman Machine Shop Inc	3842	211
Troux Technologies	5045	85
TrovaGene Inc	2836	98
Trover Solutions Inc	7322	20
Troxel Co	3317	21
Troxel Equipment Company LLC	5083	84
Troxler Electronic Laboratories Inc	8731	191
Troy Belting Supply Co	5085	110
Troy Chemical Industries Inc	2842	143
Troy Construction LLP	1623	58
Troy Corp	2869	50

Company Name	SIC	Rank
Troy Group Inc	7373	244
Troy International Products Inc	3451	144
Troy Manufacturing Co	3841	387
Troy Manufacturing New York Inc	3564	165
TROY Systems Inc (Santa Ana California)	2782	13
Troyer Foods Inc	5144	9
Troyer's Trail Bologna Inc	2011	127
Troyk Screen Printing Corp	2759	311
Troyke Manufacturing Co	3545	251
Troy-Onic Inc	3671	20
Troy's Contracting Inc	1731	1353
Trozzolo Creative Resources Inc	2741	360
TRP Machine Inc	3599	1533
TRS-RenTelco	7359	31
TRT Holdings Inc	7011	49
Tru Color Litho Inc	2752	902
Tru Corp	3643	68
Tru Kut Door Corp	5031	394
Tru Line Lithographing Inc	2752	482
Tru Manufacturing Corp	3599	1543
Tru Square Metal Products Inc	3559	448
Tru Temperature Sensors Inc	3823	451
Tru Vue Inc	3211	9
Truan Family Partnership	2671	67
Truan's Candies Inc	2064	141
Truarc Company LLC	3465	51
Truax Printing Inc	2711	926
Tru-Bamboo LLC	5023	132
Trubiquity	7372	1276
Truby's Writers Studio	8249	13
Trucast Inc	3599	1732
Truck Accessories Group Inc	3792	1
Truck Air of the Carolinas	4213	1992
Truck And Auto Supply Inc	5013	313
Truck and Trailer Equipment Company Inc	5013	197
Truck Equipment Inc	5012	68
Truck Equipment Service Co	3715	36
Truck Lease Services Inc	4213	2294
Truck 'N I Inc	4213	1524
Truck One Inc	4213	1366
Truck Service Inc	4213	1597
Truck Specialties LLC	5013	285
Truck Towne Plaza	5172	140
Truck Transport Inc	4213	959
Truck Underwriters Association	8111	107
Truckee Donner Public Utility District	4911	297
Truckee Meadows Electric Inc	1731	798
Truckers Express Inc	4213	227
TruckersB2B Inc	4213	1677
Trucking Unlimited	4213	1925
Truck-Lite Company Inc	3647	4
Truck-Rite Distribution Systems	4213	1345
Trucks and Parts Of Tampa Inc	5012	79
Trucks Inc	4213	171
Truckstaff LLC	4212	54
Truco Inc	2851	61
TruColor Visions Systems Inc	3555	58
Tru-Contour Inc	3087	21
Trucut Inc	3544	203
Trudy Corp	2731	380
True Audio	7372	4768
True BASIC Inc	7372	3034
True Commerce Inc	7371	240
True Fitness Technology Inc	3949	74
True House Inc	2439	31
True Industries Inc	3544	257
True Ld LLC	4813	402
True Line Mold And Engineering Corp	3089	1663
True Manufacturing Company Inc	3585	56
True North Trucking	4213	2340
True Position Technologies Inc	3599	314
True Precision Machining LLC	3448	51
True Product ID Inc	7389	2506
True Religion Apparel Inc	2325	5
True Temper Sports Inc	3949	41
True Temper Sports LLC	3949	42
True Value Co	5072	2
True Value Manufacturing Co	2851	23
True Wireless Inc	4812	102
TrueBlue Inc	7363	12
TrueDemand Software Inc	7372	1913
Truefit Solutions Inc	7371	1005
Truelink	7372	1126
Truelove and MacLean Inc	3469	29
TrueNorth Steel	5051	60
Trueposition Inc	3679	26
Truesdail Laboratories Inc	8734	113
Truesoups LLC	2032	8
Truetandem LLC	7379	1053
True-Tech Corp	3599	175
Truetoniqs LLC	2086	142
Tru-Fit Frame and Door Corp	5031	110
Tru-Flex Real Estate Holdings Inc	3599	364
TruFoods LLC	5812	366
Truform Machine Inc	3599	1097
Tru-Form Plastics Inc	3089	1465
TruGreen Inc	0782	8
TruGreen LandCare LLC	0782	1
Truitt and White Lumber Co	5211	99
Tru-Kay Manufacturing Co	3911	22
Trukmann's Inc	2759	341
Truland Service Corp	1731	216

Company Name	SIC	Rank
Truland Systems Corp	1731	71
Truliant Federal Credit Union	6061	26
Trulife	3842	240
Truline Corp	4213	1012
Truline Industries Inc	3728	157
Truly Nolen of America Inc	7342	7
Truman Arnold Companies Inc	5171	9
Truman Bank	6022	259
Trumark Industries Inc	5031	313
TRUMATCH Inc	2752	1809
Trumbull Industries Inc	5074	36
Trumbull-Nelson Construction Company Inc	1542	95
Trump Entertainment Resorts Inc	7011	45
Trump Hotels and Casino Resorts Holdings LP	7011	18
Trump Marina Hotel And Casino Inc	7011	117
Trump Taj Mahal Casino Resort	7011	28
Trumpf Inc	3542	2
Trunkline Gas Company LLC	4922	29
Trupar LLC	5084	596
Tru-Part Manufacturing Corp	5083	31
Tru-Power Inc	5083	127
TruProtect	3086	144
Trusco Manufacturing Company Inc	3563	62
Truscott Inc	4213	2183
Truskill Machining Inc	3544	640
Truss Partners LLC	2439	54
Truss Specialists Inc	2439	32
Truss-Tech Industries Inc	2439	33
Trussway Manufacturing Inc	2439	4
Trust Company of Lehigh Valley	6282	425
Trust Drum and Freight	5085	404
Trust For The Employee Welfare Benefi	6733	4
Trust Marketing and Communications Consortium	7389	969
Trust One Bank	6022	325
Trust Ownership Group Inc	7371	607
Trust Pipe Inc	1623	202
Trust Service Company Inc	7372	3848
TrustCo Bank Corporation of New York	6712	133
Trustco Bank NA	6021	56
Trusted Tool Manufacturing Inc	3545	418
Trustedid Inc	4813	559
Trustfile	7291	12
Trustin Technology LLC	5065	84
Trustmark Corp	6712	74
Trustmark Insurance Co	6311	61
Trustmark Life Insurance Co	6311	55
Trustmark Mutual Holding Co	6411	23
Trustmark National Bank	6021	25
Tru-Stone Technologies	3499	91
TrustTone Communications Inc	7389	517
TrustWave Corp	7372	2263
Trusty Warns Inc	3561	169
Trusty-Cook Inc	5169	170
Tru-Tech Tool and Machinery Corp	3547	11
Tru-Tex International Corp	3544	685
Truth Hardware Corp	2431	17
Truth Publishing Company Inc	2711	271
Truth Seeker Company Inc	2721	394
Trutone Inc	3695	47
Trutron Corp	3544	386
Tru-Truss Engineering	7372	5000
Tru-Val Electric Corp	1731	125
TruWest Credit Union	6062	15
Tru-Wood Cabinets Inc	2434	19
Trv Inc	3599	1282
TRW Automotive Holdings Corp	3714	4
TRW Vehicle Safety Systems Inc	2399	2
TRX Inc	7389	321
Try Green Equipment	7353	103
Trycera Financial Inc	6141	72
Trylon SMR Inc	8743	267
Tryon Trucking Inc	4213	612
Try-Us Trucking Inc	4213	2776
TS Boyd Grain Inc	4213	1720
TS C Inc	1711	248
T-S Display Systems Inc	3669	169
TS Electric Inc	1731	1006
TS Microtech Inc	3577	579
TS Partners Inc	7372	4266
Ts Steel Inc	5051	367
Ts Tech Enterprises Inc	7371	1574
TS Traker Systems	7371	809
Tsa Systems Ltd	3829	133
TSC America Inc	3577	444
Tsc Electronics Ltd	5065	397
Tsc Pyroferric International Inc	3264	14
TSC Solutions LLC	7372	246
Tsc Television Inc	4841	116
Tschiggfrie Excavating	1794	21
Tscm Corp	7349	168
TSE and Associates	3812	215
TSE Industries Inc	3089	229
TSE Sports and Entertainment	7311	640
Tsf Investments Inc	1799	58
Tsf Products Inc	2821	113
TSF Sportswear LLC	2321	20
TSG Consumer Partners	6799	170
TSG Equity Partners LLC	6799	292
Tsgc Inc	3823	361
TSH Inc	5734	463

Company Name	SIC	Rank
Tsi Accessory Group Inc	3961	5
TSI Inc	3829	22
Tsi Plastics Inc	3089	1149
TSi POWER Corp	3679	680
TSI Prism Inc	3812	175
Tsk Holdings LLC	5082	187
Tsm Corp	3599	475
Tsoi/Kobus and Associates Inc	8712	57
T-Square	3663	302
Tsr Solutions Inc	7373	828
Tss Distributions Services	7389	2257
TSS Facility Services	7349	300
Tss Technologies Inc	3599	13
Tssco Inc	5999	291
TSS-Radio LLC	3663	211
TST Impreso Inc	2621	47
Tst Inc	3341	12
Tsubaki Conveyor Of America Inc	3535	93
Tsue Chong Company Inc	2098	21
Tsukazaki Yeh and Moore	8111	545
TSV ELMA Inc	3625	2
Tsw Industries Inc	3599	852
Tsymmetry Inc	7379	707
TSYS Acquiring Solutions	7374	90
TSYS Debt Management	7374	42
TT and E Enterprises Inc	1731	739
Tt and E Iron and Metal Inc	5093	151
TT Group Inc	5139	24
Ttc Trammell Company Inc	2759	477
Tt-Dav LLC	5045	822
T-Tech Inc	3825	262
TTG Acquisition Corp	3661	24
TTG Inc	7372	3787
Tti Floor Care North America Inc	3052	3
Tti Holding International Inc	5023	104
Ttj Enterprises LP	7389	1862
TTM Technologies Inc	3072	5
TTSI Holdings Inc	4213	2377
TTSS Interactive Products Inc	7373	850
TTX Co	4741	3
TU Parks Construction Co	1541	254
Tualatin Valley Workshop Inc	8331	23
Tualatin Vineyards	2084	50
Tubacex Inc	3312	102
Tubari Inc	3999	198
Tubby's Inc	6794	114
Tube Art Displays Inc	3993	42
Tube City IMS Corp	5093	6
Tube Fab/Roman Engineering Company Inc	3498	51
Tube Forgings Of America Inc	3498	36
Tube Forming And Machin Inc	3498	84
Tube Methods Inc	3317	48
Tube Specialties Company Inc	3498	29
Tube-Tainer Inc	2655	8
Tubetech Inc	3317	62
Tubro Company Inc	3089	1651
Tubular Products Co	3317	35
Tubular Services LLC	1389	40
Tubular Steel Inc	5051	58
Tubular Textile Machinery Inc	5084	102
Tucci and Sons Inc	1611	104
Tuckahoe Sand and Gravel Company Inc	1442	51
Tucker Arensberg PC	8111	417
Tucker Automotive Corp	5013	345
Tucker Electronics Co	5065	684
Tucker Enterprises	4213	2580
Tucker Induction Systems Ltd	8711	640
Tucker Printers Inc	2752	504
Tucker Rocky Distributor Inc	5013	18
Tucker Technologies Inc	3533	70
Tucker Technology Inc	3544	584
Tucker Technology Inc (Oakland California)	1623	66
Tucker-Castleberry Printing Inc	2752	376
Tucker-Davis Technologies Inc	3829	237
Tucker's Machine and Steel Service Inc	3441	148
Tucknott Electrical Co	1731	1968
Tu-Co Peat	5191	137
TUCS Cleaning Service Inc	7349	59
Tucs Equipment Inc	3586	16
Tucson Alternator Exchange Service Inc	3694	44
Tucson Community Cable Corp	4841	163
Tucson Electric Power Co	4911	89
Tucson Realty and Trust Co	6531	427
Tucson Tallow Company Inc	2077	15
Tucson Truck Terminal Inc	5541	48
Tudor Investment Corp	6282	265
Tuerff-Davis Enviromedia Inc	7311	468
Tufco Technologies Inc	2679	9
Tuff Automation Inc	3599	2368
Tuff Torq Corp	3524	12
Tuffaloy Products Inc	3625	143
Tuffer Manufacturing Company Inc	3599	914
Tuffi Products Inc	5082	157
Tuff-Kote Company Inc	2899	233
Tuftco Corp	3552	3
Tuftco Finishing Systems Inc	3552	11
Tufting Machine Company Inc	3552	12
Tufts Associated Health Plans Inc	6324	54

Company Name	SIC	Rank
Tug River Armature and Machine Company Inc	3442	113
Tugaloo Pipeline Inc	1623	475
Tugboat Software Inc	7372	3035
Tujayar Enterprises Inc	3646	94
Tujays Janitorial Service Inc	7349	366
Tu-K Industries Inc	2844	158
Tukman Grossman Capital Management Inc	6282	630
Tukuru Technologies LLC	7379	1438
Tulare Dairy Center Inc	5083	185
Tularosa Basin Telephone Company Inc	4813	280
Tulco Oils Inc	5172	127
Tull Forsberg and Olson PLLC	8721	171
Tulnoy Lumber Inc	5072	48
Tulox Plastics Corp	3089	913
Tulsa Aircraft Engines	7699	146
Tulsa Baking Inc	5461	44
Tulsa Beef and Provision Inc	5147	82
Tulsa Centerless Bar Processing Inc	3999	174
Tulsa Communications LLC	4833	224
Tulsa Dynaspan Inc	3272	41
Tulsa Heaters Inc	3433	29
Tulsa Metal Processing Co	1099	6
Tulsa Power LLC	3549	58
Tulsa Rubber Co	3069	278
Tulsa Winch Group	3531	5
Tulsat Corp	5063	252
Tulstar Products Inc	5169	59
Tumac Lumber Company Inc	5031	33
Tum-A-Lum Lumber Co	5211	151
Tumbler Technologies Inc	3679	692
Tumlare Travel Organization Inc	4725	71
Tundra Specialties Inc	5046	58
Tung Hsin Trading Corp	5046	117
Tungsten Industries Inc	3545	260
Tunheim Group	8743	146
Tunmore Auto Center	5511	1242
Tunnell Hill Plastics Inc	3089	1378
Tunnessen's Inc	5013	372
Tunstall Consulting Inc	6282	281
Tuohy Furniture Corp	2521	26
Tupelo Furniture Market Inc	7999	86
Tuplex Corp	3996	4
Tuppas Software Corp	3829	73
Tupperware Brands Corp	3089	13
Tupperware US Inc	3089	387
Turano Baking Co	2051	34
Turbine Controls Inc	4581	38
Turbine Engine Components Technologies	3694	18
Turbine Tool and Gage Inc	3545	270
Turbine Trend Analysis Inc	8734	156
Turbo City Inc	3511	43
Turbo Diesel and Electric Systems Inc	5084	332
Turbo Dynamics Corp	5084	690
Turbo Electrical Contractors Inc	1731	1985
Tur-Bo Jet Products Company Inc	3677	17
Turbo Refrigeration LLC	3585	203
Turbo Resources International Inc	5088	42
Turbocam Inc	3599	211
Turbocare Gas Turbine Services	3479	56
Turbocare Inc	3511	19
TurboChef Technologies Inc	3556	6
Turbodyne Technologies Inc	3714	432
Turbomeca Engine Corp	3724	6
Turbon USA Inc	3955	3
Turbotec Products Inc	3443	133
Turbowave Inc	4813	557
Turchan Technologies Group Inc	3441	167
Turec Advertising Associates Inc	7311	617
Turelk Inc	1542	232
Turett Collaborative Architects	8712	307
Turf Equipment And Supply Company Inc	5083	83
Turf Paradise Inc	7948	26
Turf Products LLC	3524	9
TurfstoreCom Inc	0781	17
Turgeon Engineering Inc	3825	346
Turing Smi LLC	7379	176
Turk Manufacturing Inc	3599	1102
Turkel	7311	441
Turkey Creek Pork Skins Inc	2096	52
Turkish Investment Fund Inc	6726	92
Turley Publications Inc	2711	242
Turlock Machine Works	3593	36
Turmatic Systems Inc	3545	301
Turmoil Inc	3822	84
Turn Key Technologies Inc	7379	1536
Turn Tech Inc	3599	1604
Turnage Corp	1731	2429
Turnamatic Machine Inc	3599	369
Turnaround Computing Inc	7372	2691
Turnberry Associates	6552	51
Turnberry SLA	6036	92
Turnbo Motor Express Inc	4213	2307
Turnbull Bakeries Incorporated Of La	2051	195
Turnbull Wine Cellars	2084	130
Turner Bellows Inc	3861	68
Turner Broadcasting System Inc	4841	10
Turner Brothers LLC	4213	129
Turner Collie and Braden Inc	8711	62
Turner Construction Co	1541	2

Company Name	SIC	Rank
Turner Consulting Group Inc	7371	1270
Turner Corp	1542	2
Turner Dairy Farms Inc	2022	33
Turner Designs Inc	3829	248
Turner Holdings LLC	2024	13
Turner Industries Ltd	1541	12
Turner Laboratories Inc	8734	182
Turner Marketing Inc	7331	249
Turner New Zealand Inc	5142	40
Turner Publishing Company LLC	2731	267
Turner Pump	7353	71
Turner Roofing And Sheet Metal Inc	1761	31
Turner Staffing Ltd	7363	185
Turner Steel Company Inc	5051	365
Turner Steiner International Inc	1542	314
Turner Trucking and Salvage Company Inc	5093	170
Turner Trucking Co	4213	999
Turner White Communications Inc	2721	431
Turning Basin Service Inc	8748	265
Turning Inc	3599	1930
Turning Point Enterprises Inc	8322	175
Turning Technologies LLC	7372	674
Turn-Key Business Systems Inc	7371	1301
Turnkey Computer Systems Inc	5734	189
Turnkey Technology Corp	7371	1868
Turnkey Technology LLC	7373	789
Turnpike Ford Inc	5511	1200
Turnstile Publishing Company Inc	2721	184
Turn-Tech Inc	3599	814
Turnure Telecom LLC	1623	439
Tur-Pak Foods Inc	2015	36
Turpin Inc	1623	538
Turri Inc	1731	1134
Tursso Companies Inc	2752	467
Turtle and Hughes Inc	6063	21
Turtle Creek Software	7372	4769
Turtle Mountain Communications	4813	634
Turtle Mountain LLC	2099	146
Turtle Wax Inc	2842	8
Turtledove Clemens Inc	7311	665
Turvac Inc	7373	740
Tusca Construction	1542	198
Tuscaloosa Coca-Cola Inc	2086	38
Tuscaloosa Computer Systems Inc	7379	1351
Tuscarora Corp	5091	75
Tuscarora Hardwoods Inc	2421	122
Tuscarora Yarns Inc	2281	10
Tusco Grocers Inc	5141	167
Tuscola County Advertiser Inc	2711	285
Tusker Group LLC	7374	185
Tussey Trucking Inc	4213	1769
Tustin Cars Inc	5511	962
Tutco Inc	3634	1
Tuthill Corp	3511	10
Tuthill Transport Technologies	3493	1
Tuthill Vaccums And Blowers Systems	3363	5
Tutor Perini Corp	1542	1
Tutor-Saliba Corp	1629	15
Tutt and Associates Inc	2752	1403
Tuttle Agency LLC	7361	229
Tuttle Aluminum and Bronze Inc	3499	107
Tuttle Construction Inc	1541	148
Tuttle Family Enterprises Inc	7349	106
Tuttle Inc	3535	140
Tuttle Law Print Inc	2752	629
Tuttle-Click Automotive Group of Dealerships	5511	29
TUV Product Services	8734	44
TuVox Inc	7372	2482
Tuxis Corp	6722	279
Tuzze Trucking Inc	4213	2616
TV Allen's Cable Service Inc	4841	138
TV Data Technologies LP	2741	57
Tv Ears Inc	3651	78
Tv Guide Distribution Inc	2721	117
TV Guide Magazine Group Inc	2721	16
TV One Multimedia Solutions Inc	7372	2002
Tv Options	4841	115
TV Specialists Inc	7371	451
Tv Station	4833	242
TV Woods Inc	5731	250
Tvc Inc	7373	861
Tvd Inc	1623	833
Tvmax Holdings Inc	4841	26
TVN Entertainment Corp	4841	43
TVS Inc	4213	719
Tvt Die Casting and Manufacturing Inc	3599	691
TVT Records Inc	6794	55
TW Currie Precision Tool Company Inc	3089	1484
Tw Design And Manufacturing LLC	3599	634
TW Garner Food Co	2033	68
TW Hager Lumber Company Inc	5031	133
TW Medical Veterinary Supply	5049	39
Tw Metals Inc	5051	127
TW Phillips Gas and Oil Co	4923	26
Tw Stamping and Tool Inc	3544	599
TW Telecom Inc	4899	8
T-W Truck Equippers Of Central New York Inc	5012	176
Twa Industries Inc	1731	1813
TWB Inc	3672	149
TWC Group	8742	186
Tweddle Group Inc	2732	5

Company Name	SIC	Rank
Tween Brands Inc	5641	2
Tweeter Home Entertainment Group Inc	5731	7
Tweet-Garot Mechanical Inc	1711	58
Twelve Signs Inc	2721	205
Twentieth Century Fox Film Corp	7812	17
Twentieth Century Fox Licensing and Merchandising Corp	7313	27
Twentieth Century Giftrust Investors	6722	140
Twentieth Century Vista Investors	6722	105
Twentyfirst Century Auction	7389	1475
Twenty-First Century Computer Systems Inc	7372	2868
Twenty-First Century Laboratories Inc	2834	371
Twentymile Coal Co	1222	6
Twenty-Six Juice Inc	5149	200
twentysix New York	7371	360
Twi Industries Inc	2759	230
Twi Of South Florida Inc	7389	1318
Twigg Corp	3724	41
Twin Associates LC	7319	103
Twin Bridge Capital Partners	6799	175
Twin Brothers Marine LLC	3731	35
Twin Cities and Western Railroad Co	4011	50
Twin Cities Digital Inc	5734	131
Twin Cities Public Television Inc	4833	117
Twin City Bagel Inc	2051	68
Twin City Die Castings Co	3363	7
Twin City EDM Inc	3599	1481
Twin City Electric Company Inc	1731	988
Twin City Electric Inc	1731	1762
Twin City Engraving Company Inc	7389	2463
Twin City Fire Insurance Co	6331	245
Twin City Foods Inc	2037	10
Twin City Hide International Inc	3111	7
Twin City Knitting Company Inc	2252	5
Twin City Mold Engineering Co	3599	750
Twin City Optical Inc	3851	15
Twin City Printing and Litho Inc	2759	256
Twin City Security Inc	7381	111
Twin City Tile and Marble Co	1743	1
Twin City Tractor and Equipment Inc	5082	88
Twin City Transportation Inc	4213	1065
Twin County Dairy Inc	2022	50
Twin County Electric Power Association	4911	273
Twin Data Corp	5045	502
Twin Disc Inc	3566	3
Twin Disc SouthEast Inc	3566	1
Twin Dragon Marketing Inc	5131	48
Twin Express Inc	4213	1412
Twin Falls Tractor And Implement Co	5083	154
Twin Lakes Pool Corp	7389	2290
Twin Lakes Quarrys Inc	2951	45
Twin Lakes Telephone Cooperative Corp	4813	203
Twin Marquis Inc	2098	12
Twin Med LLC	5047	13
Twin Mills Timber and Tie Company Inc	3537	98
Twin Oaks Industries Inc	3443	185
Twin Oaks Software Development Inc	7371	1214
Twin Otter International Ltd	7359	199
Twin Peaks Computer Inc	7378	169
Twin Peaks Mall Associates Ltd	6531	297
Twin Peaks Winery Inc	2084	100
Twin River Casino	7948	13
Twin River Financial Corp	6712	573
Twin River National Bank	6021	378
Twin Rivers Technologies Us Inc	2819	34
Twin Star Electronics Inc	3672	479
Twin State Inc	2875	4
Twin Tower Erection And Maintenance Inc	7353	43
Twin Valley Developmental Services Inc	8361	165
Twin Valleys Public Power District	4911	591
Twinbridge Software Corp	7372	4571
Twinco Manufacturing Company Inc	3669	178
Twinco Romax LLC	5013	131
Twining Laboratories Of Southern California Inc	8734	27
Twinlab Corp	2099	33
Twinplex Manufacturing Co	3469	293
Twinsource LLC	3822	98
TwinStar Credit Union	6062	46
Twinstar Inc	7371	1832
Twin-State Tech Services Inc	7373	1027
Twism Promotions Inc	5199	119
Twist Inc	3495	6
Twisted Pair/BT Services Inc	5065	885
Twitchell Corp	2221	5
TWL Corp	4213	2579
TWL Inc	4213	2173
Two Brothers Travel Inc	4724	136
Two Chefs On A Roll Inc	2051	53
Two College Guys	7353	80
Two Day Corp	3577	521
Two Guys and A Truck	4213	1133
Two Harbors Investment Corp	6798	33
Two Harbors Machine Shop Inc	3599	533
Two In One Manufacturing Inc	3674	360
Two M Precision Company Inc	3599	828
Two Maids and A Mop	7389	381
Two Men and A Truck International Inc	4212	76
Two Men and A Truck of Charlotte	4213	2807

Company Name	SIC	Rank
Two River Community Bank	6021	246
Two Rivers Associates LLC	6799	305
Two Rivers Coop	5153	64
Two Rivers Enterprises Inc	5051	340
Two Rivers Head Start Agency	8351	14
Two Rivers Marketing Group	7311	504
Two Rivers Pipeline and Construction Company Inc	1623	187
Two Technologies Inc	3571	112
Two Thirty Two Productins Inc	3861	103
Two-L Electric Co	1731	1435
Twomey Co	5191	59
Twoway Communications Inc	5731	229
Two-Way Radio Service Inc	5731	96
TWP Enterprises Inc	5031	17
TWR Framing	7361	286
TWR Lighting	3646	36
TWS Holdings Inc	7375	96
TWT Distributing Inc	5087	153
TX Holdings Inc	1311	275
Tx Rx Systems Inc	3669	128
TX Technology Corp	3669	244
TXCO Resources Inc	1311	98
TXI Riverside Cement Co	3241	27
TXU Energy Retail Company LLC	4911	42
Txu Energy Services Company LLC	3679	81
TXU Energy Trading Co	4932	12
Txvia Inc	7371	1045
Ty Inc	3942	3
TY Lin International (San Francisco California)	8712	46
Ty Miles Inc	3541	170
Tyan Computer USA	3672	33
TYBRIN Corp	7371	19
Tyco Electronics Corp	3441	1
Tyco Electronics Federal Credit Union	6061	131
Tyco Electronics Integrated Cable Systems LLC	3357	17
Tyco Fire and Security Services	7382	1
Tyco Fire Products CPVC Div	2821	47
Tyco Fire Products LP	3569	18
Tyco Valves and Controls Inc	3491	6
Tyde Group Worldwide LLC	3592	5
TydenBrooks	3089	173
Tygh Silicon Inc	5065	146
Tyk America Inc	3255	8
Tykon Inc	7372	2483
Tyler Candy Company LLC	2064	94
Tyler Cole Enterprises Inc	3534	31
Tyler Equipment Corp	5082	30
Tyler Griffin Company Inc	5065	646
Tyler Iron and Metal Inc	5093	230
Tyler Martin Company Inc	3577	648
Tyler Meat Co	5147	74
Tyler Mountain Water Company Inc	5149	98
Tyler Perry Company Inc	7812	258
Tyler Retail Systems Inc	7372	3120
Tyler Technologies Inc	7372	172
Tyler Tool Company Inc	5085	341
Tympanium Corp	3625	81
Tyndale House Publishers Inc	2731	54
Tyne Plastics LLC	3087	19
Type and Design	7336	304
Typecraft Inc	2752	814
Typecraft Press Inc	2752	625
Typed Letters Corp	7331	65
Typhoon Inc	5812	299
Tyr Sport Inc	5137	24
Tyree Organization Inc	8734	7
Tyrell Software Corp	7372	3036
Tyronza Bancshares	6712	705
Tyrrell Electrical Contractors Inc	1731	1871
Tyrrell-Doyle Auto Centers	5511	824
Tyson Foods Inc	2015	1
Tyson Fresh Meats Inc	2011	1
Tyson Nutraceutical Inc	2834	342
TYX Corp	7372	1825
Tzell Travel Group of PA	4724	77
Tzeng Long USA Inc	5093	122
U and S Services Inc	5045	413
U and X Group Inc	7375	228
U E Systems Inc	3829	225
U Edit Video	7389	856
U P Machine and Engineering Co	3599	1295
U S Airmotive Inc	3679	131
U S Asphalt Co	1611	202
U S Circuit Inc	3679	276
U S Dairy Systems Inc	5083	75
U S Equipment Co	3541	155
U S Ice Corp	2097	20
U S Internet Corp	7375	107
U S Machine and Tool Inc	3544	815
U S Marine Inc	3731	7
U S Medical Instruments Inc	3841	215
U S Merchandising Inc	8742	392
U S Natural Resources Inc Friedrich Air Conditioning Div	3585	43
U S Pattern Company Inc	3543	43
U S Plastics Inc	3083	58
U S Tool Grinding Inc	7699	10
U Tellurian CA N Inc	8322	130
UA Systems Inc	7372	1588
UAI Inc	8711	540
UAI Technology Inc	7372	1959

Company Name	SIC	Rank
Uam Technologies Corp	3669	238
UAN Cultural and Creative Company Ltd	6799	358
Uas Automation Systems Inc	3567	116
Uaw-Chrysler Skill Development And Training Program	8299	56
UB Corp	3663	276
UB Machine Inc	3711	76
Ube Machinery Inc	3559	183
Ubi Soft Entertainment Inc	7372	1323
Ubicom Inc	5045	137
UBICS Inc	7371	286
Ubio Inc	3961	13
Ubisoft Red Storm	2741	508
UBMatrix	7371	452
UBS Asset Management Inc	6282	296
UBS Financial Services Inc	6211	14
UC4 Software	7373	426
Ucb Chemicals Corp	5169	20
UCB Pharma	2834	102
Ucg Information Services LLC	2731	141
Uchida Enterprises Inc	6799	342
Uchiyama America Inc	5085	107
Uci Acquisition Holdings (No1) Corp	6719	107
UCI International Inc	3714	37
UCI Medical Affiliates Inc	8093	17
Ucm Magnesia Inc	2819	97
UCM Partners	6282	129
uData Net Corp	3661	176
UDATAnet	7372	4021
Udenberg and Associates Inc	7372	3211
UDT Instruments	3829	344
Ue Systems International Corp	5065	563
Uebelhor and Sons Inc	5511	782
UEC Electronics LLC	3679	322
Uei Inc	3469	273
UFE Inc	3089	54
Uff Machine Co	3554	49
U-Fix-It Appliance Parts Inc	7389	1256
Uflex USA Inc	3531	201
UFO Inc	3089	1088
Ufood Restaurant Group Inc	5812	413
UFP Technologies Inc	3086	9
Ugcom Inc	3663	28
UGI Corp	4932	4
UGI Utilities Inc	4923	32
UGI Utilities Inc Electric Div	4911	113
UGI Utilities Inc Gas Utility Div	4924	34
UGM Enterprises Inc	7379	1577
UGM Mailing Service Inc	7331	236
UGO Entertainment Inc	7389	594
UHF Associates	3651	230
Uhimchuk and Associates	7372	4770
UHL Truck Sales Inc	5511	707
Uhlig LLC	2721	162
Uhlmann Co	2041	65
Uhrden Inc	3535	117
Uhrichsville Carbide Inc	3545	378
UIL Holdings Corp	6719	27
Uintah Basin Standard Inc	2711	264
Uintah Machine And Manufacturing Co	3599	1108
UIS Inc	2064	3
Ukasik Electric	1731	1859
UKI Supreme Corp	2284	2
Ukiah Ford-Lincoln-Mercury Inc	5511	829
Ukpeagvik Inupiat Corp	6531	233
Ukrop's Super Markets Inc	5411	103
UL Wholesale Lighting Fixtures Corp	5063	686
Uland Supply Co	5085	387
Ulbrich of California Inc	5051	165
Ulbrich Stainless Steels and Special Metals Inc	3499	5
Ulbrich's IGA Super Market	5411	264
U-Line Corp	3632	7
Ulink Technology Inc	7371	1516
Ulinski Electric Inc	1731	1763
ULLICO Inc	6311	86
Ulmas	3672	496
Ulmer and Berne LLP	8111	201
Ulrich Chemical Inc	5169	50
Ulta Salon Cosmetics and Fragrance Inc	5122	13
Ultera Systems Inc	3669	173
Ulticom Inc	3661	42
Ultima Nashua Industrial Corp	7692	49
Ultimate Automotive Group LLC	5511	1236
Ultimate Building Systems Ltd	2821	88
Ultimate Electronics Inc	5731	8
Ultimate Entertainment Marketing Inc	5065	457
Ultimate Group Corp	5065	971
Ulti-Mate Highway Products Inc	3449	41
Ultimate Image Marketing Inc	5045	560
Ultimate Juice Co	2033	19
Ultimate Linings Ltd	5013	380
Ultimate Machining and Engineering Inc	3599	862
Ultimate Medical Services Inc	7361	333
Ultimate Pontiac Buick GMC Isuzu	5511	1161
Ultimate Software Group Inc	7372	188
Ultimate Solutions LLC	1541	305
Ultimate Sound Inc	3651	130
Ultimate Systems Inc	4813	714
Ultimate Technical Solutions	5734	57
Ultimate Technology Corp	3575	9

Company Name	SIC	Rank
Ultimate Technology Inc	3823	337
Ultimate Windows Inc	2431	138
Ultimatecare Services Inc	3842	308
ULTIMED Inc	5047	267
Ultimizer's Inc	3553	35
Ultimo Software Solutions Inc	7371	608
Ultimus Inc (Carey North Carolina)	7372	886
Ultra Additives	2851	83
Ultra Aluminum Manufacturing Inc	3312	88
Ultra Clean Holdings Inc	3674	57
Ultra Electronics Criticom	4812	50
Ultra Electronics Precision Air Systems Inc	3629	94
Ultra Flex Packaging Corp	2759	36
Ultra Imaging Soltuions	5044	96
Ultra Petroleum Corp	1311	40
Ultra Power Battery Inc	5065	466
Ultra Precision Inc	3544	372
Ultra Punch Of Dayton Inc	3544	278
Ultra Pure Water Technologies Inc	3589	15
Ultra Radio LLC	4832	283
Ultra Safe Inc	5084	771
Ultra Safety Systems Inc	3531	240
Ultra Scientific Inc	8731	296
Ultra Seal Corp	7389	942
Ultra Sonic Seal Co	3548	29
Ultra Specialty Holdings Inc	3599	1474
Ultra Stores Inc	5944	12
Ultra Tech Extrustions Of Tennessee Inc	3089	1192
Ultra Wheel Co	3714	229
Ultrablend LLC	3559	153
Ultrablend Systems Inc	3559	322
Ultra-Carbide Grinding Corp	3544	893
Ultra-Cool Corp	3585	144
Ultra-Dex Inc	3545	104
Ultrafab Inc	2201	11
Ultra-Fab Products Inc	3429	154
Ultraguard Protective Systems Inc	7382	52
Ultra-Kool Inc	3559	474
Ultralife Corp	3692	3
Ultramarine Inc	7372	4478
Ultra-Mek Inc	3429	106
Ultramet	3471	75
Ultra-Metric Tool Co	3599	2145
Ultrapak Printing and Packaging Inc	2759	319
Ultrapanel Marine Inc	3613	47
Ultra-Poly Corp	2821	123
ULTRAsafe Security Specialists	7373	1140
Ultrasil Corp	3471	120
Ultra-Sonic Extrusion Dies Inc	3544	618
Ultrasonic Power Corp	3829	255
Ultrasonic Sciences Inc	3829	210
Ultrasonic Systems Inc	3559	308
Ultrasource Inc	3674	263
UltraStaff	8082	92
Ultra-Stereo Labs Inc	3699	86
Ultratec Inc	3661	108
Ultra-Tech Enterprises Inc	3679	669
Ultra-Tech Inc	3599	1712
Ultratech Inc	3559	34
UltraTech International Inc	3599	1192
Ultratest International Inc	8734	193
Ultraview Corp	3571	151
Ultraviolet Devices Inc	5074	124
Ultravolt Inc	3679	272
Ultra-X Inc	7372	4648
Ultron	3365	52
Ultron Systems Inc	3559	394
Ulvac Technologies Inc	5084	144
Ulysses Group Associates Inc	7371	1443
UM Holdings Inc	8099	52
Uma Inc	3841	210
Umass M R I and Imaging Center	3826	129
UMass Memorial Health Care	8062	249
Umatilla Electric Cooperative Association	4911	283
UMB Bank Colorado NA (Denver Colorado)	6021	110
UMB Financial Corp	6712	58
UMB National Bank of America	6021	144
UMB Oklahoma Bank	6022	560
Umbergers Of Fontana Inc	5083	160
UMBRA LLC	2599	8
UmbrellaBank FSB	6035	162
UMC Acquisition Corp	3356	14
UMC Healthcare Solutions	6411	285
UMC Inc	3599	153
Umeya Inc	2052	68
UMH Properties Inc	6798	188
Umhs Physician Services	8011	159
UMI Publications Inc	2721	432
Umpqua Bank	6022	23
Umpqua Bank (Arcata California)	6022	825
Umpqua Dairy Products Co	2026	38
Umpqua Holdings Corp	6712	67
Umpqua Research Co	8731	362
Un Communications Inc	2752	973
Unaka Company Inc	3631	2
Unapen Inc	7373	659
Unarco Industries	3496	30
Unarco Material Handling Inc	5084	28
Unas Grinding Corp	3599	1405
U-Nav Microelectronics Corp	7379	688

Company Name	SIC	Rank
Unavision	4833	174
Unbeatable Cellular and Beeper Accessories Inc	4812	48
Unbeaten Path International Ltd	7372	3037
UnboundID Corp	7372	1394
UNC Partners Inc	6799	90
Uncas Manufacturing Co	3961	1
Uncle Charley's Sausage Co	2013	137
Uncle Charlie's Meats Inc	2013	136
Uncle Dave's Kitchens Inc	2032	40
Uncle Harry's Fine Food Products	2024	81
Uncle Henry's Pretzel Bakery	2052	72
Uncle Lee's Tea Inc	2099	277
Uncle Ralph's Cookie Co	2052	63
Uncle Rays LLC	2096	9
Under Armour Inc	3949	8
Under-Communication Inc	4813	606
UndercoverWear Inc	5963	10
Underground Atlanta Inc	6512	57
Underground Construction Company Inc	1623	27
Underground Industries Inc	1623	846
Underground Services Inc	8711	585
Underground Systems Construction Inc	1623	610
Underriner Motors	5511	563
Undersea Systems International Inc	3699	133
Undertone Networks Inc	7379	338
Underwood and Weld Company Inc	4213	1996
Underwood Machinery Transport Inc	4213	2656
Underwood Memorial Hospital Inc	8062	85
Underwood Mold Company Inc	3089	530
Uneeda Enterprizes Inc	3291	12
Unelko Corp	2899	216
Unet 2 Corp	7375	279
Unette Corp	3089	735
Unety Systems Inc	7379	540
Uniex Manufacturing Inc	3535	75
Ungaretti and Harris LLP	8111	168
Unger Co	5113	34
Unger Enterprises Inc	2711	664
Unger Fabrik LLC	2339	30
Ungerboeck Systems International Inc	7373	141
Unholtz-Dickie Corp	3829	71
Uni/Care Systems Inc	7371	760
Uni Global Container Service Corp	5085	415
UniBar Inc	7372	4267
UNIBAR Maintenance Services Inc	7349	50
Unibased Systems Architecture Inc	7372	1719
Unibilt Industries Inc	2452	56
Unibox Enclosures Inc	3089	1164
Unibridge Systems Inc	3596	13
Uni-Bulk Inc	4213	1946
Unica Corp	7372	428
Unical Aviation Inc	5088	29
Unical Enterprises Inc	5045	459
Unicast Communications Corp	7371	182
Unicast Co	3321	56
Unicast Inc	3069	178
Uni-Cast Inc	3365	16
Unicco Service Co	7349	12
UNICEF	3999	14
Unicep Packaging Inc	3843	17
Unichem Corp	2841	55
Unicircuit Inc	3672	65
Unicity International Inc	2834	107
Unico American Corp	6719	102
UNICO Inc	1081	2
Unico Inc	3625	24
Unico Inc (Lake Worth Florida)	2099	31
Unico Properties LLC	6531	110
Unicom Electric Inc	3577	377
Unicom Grafix Inc	2752	1383
Unicom Marketing Group Inc	7311	767
Unicon International Inc	7371	475
Unicontrol Inc	3823	145
UNICOR	2392	3
Unicore LLC	2821	187
Unicorn HRO	7372	906
Unicorp Inc	3678	56
Unicover Corp	5999	120
Unicru Inc	7372	1081
Uni-Data And Communications Inc	7379	412
Uniden America Corp	5064	9
Unidesk Corp	7372	1366
Unidex Corporation of Western NY	3549	103
Unidine Corp	8741	148
Uniek Inc	3944	9
Unifax Insurance Systems Inc	6331	349
Unifi Inc	2221	3
Unifi Manufacturing Inc	2281	4
UNIFI Mutual Holding Co	6311	264
Unified Brands	3556	179
Unified Enterprises Corp	5078	43
Unified Grocers Inc	5142	2
Unified Management Corp	6211	72
Unified Testing Services Inc	8734	15
Unifilt Corp	3677	117
Unifirst Corp	7299	4
UniFirst Holdings Inc	6719	168
Uniflex Holdings	2673	15
Unifoil Corp	2672	55
Uniforce Services Inc	7363	71
Unifrax I LLC	3264	5
Unifuse LLC	3089	1787

Company Name	SIC	Rank
Unigard Insurance Co	6331	129
Unigard Insurance Group	6411	49
Unigearusa Inc	5063	1069
Unigene Laboratories Inc	2833	52
Uni-Glide Manufacturing Company Inc	3715	50
Uni-Graphic Inc	2752	112
Unigraphic-Color Corp	2752	1313
UniGroup Inc	4213	20
Unigroup Worldwide Inc	4213	181
Uniguest Inc	2741	217
Uni-Hydro Inc	3541	130
Unilan Network Inc	7373	1101
Unilava Corp	7379	692
Unilens Corporation USA	3851	81
Unilens Vision Inc	3851	47
Unilever Bestfoods North America	2099	5
Unilever United States Inc	2841	5
Unilight Corp	5063	953
Uniloy Milacron Inc	3559	51
Unilux Inc	3648	60
Unimar Inc	3625	191
Unimark Inc	3577	221
Unimatic Inc	3599	1599
Unimax Systems Corp	7372	2832
Unimeasure Inc	3829	457
Unimed Pharmaceuticals Inc	2834	243
Unimed Surgical Products Inc	3841	278
Unimeddirect LLC	7389	2100
Uninterruptible Power Products Inc	3629	110
Union Acceptance Corp	6141	60
Union Apparel Inc	2311	10
Union Asphalt Inc	2951	49
Union Bank and Trust Co (Lincoln Nebraska)	6022	78
Union Bank and Trust Co (Minneapolis Minnesota)	6022	750
Union Bank and Trust Co (Pottsville Pennsylvania)	6022	651
Union Bank Co	6022	488
Union Bank (Kansas City Missouri)	6022	1
Union Bank NA	6022	712
Union Bank of California NA	6021	9
Union Bankshares Inc	6022	293
Union Bankshares Inc (Kansas City Missouri)	6712	385
Union Biometrica Inc	3826	27
Union Broadcasting Inc	4832	144
Union Building Services Inc	7349	243
Union Carbide Corp	2869	13
Union Center National Bank	6021	91
Union Chemical Industries Corp	2851	173
Union Child Day Care Center Inc	8351	31
Union City Coca-Cola Bottling Company LLC	2086	125
Union City Daily Messenger Inc	2711	565
Union City Filament Corp	3356	35
Union City Mirror and Table Company Inc	2511	88
Union Computer International	5734	477
Union Concrete Construction Corp	5032	187
Union County Livestock Inc	2011	144
Union Democrat Corp	2711	150
Union Dental Holdings Inc	8021	22
Union Drilling Inc	1381	30
Union Electric Contracting Co	1731	434
Union Electric Inc	1731	1115
Union Electric Steel Corp	3312	28
Union Electronics Inc	5065	272
Union Elevator and Warehouse Co	5153	143
Union Grocery Company Inc	5141	181
Union Grove Feed LLC	2048	115
Union Health Services Inc	6324	129
Union Insurance Co	6331	326
Union International Systems Inc	7371	1830
Union Iron Inc	3523	175
Union Labor Life Insurance Co	6311	197
Union Leader Corp	2711	289
Union Lightning Protection Installers Inc	1731	1977
Union Machinery	4213	775
Union Metal Corp	3648	7
Union Pacific Corp	4011	2
Union Pacific Railroad Co	4011	4
Union Park Buick GMC	5511	613
Union Planters Bank of Louisiana	6022	266
Union Planters Bank of North Central Tennessee	6022	804
Union Planters (Monticello Iowa)	6022	807
Union Power Coop	4911	195
Union Printers Inc	2752	1671
Union Process Inc	3541	83
Union Rural Electric Coop	4911	399
Union Savings Bank (Cincinnati Ohio)	6712	404
Union Special LLC	3559	134
Union Spring and Manufacturing Corp	3493	6
Union Square Hospitality Group	5812	251
Union Standard Equipment Co	3556	123
Union Standard Insurance Co	6331	300
Union State Bank (Arkansas City Kansas)	6022	771
Union State Bank (Kewaunee Wisconsin)	6022	763
Union Technology Corp	5065	349
Union Tool and Mold Company Inc	3544	580

Company Name	SIC	Rank
Union Tool Corp	3599	1299
Union Wadding Co	2299	7
UnionBanCal Corp	6712	16
Union-Hoermann Press Inc	2752	1150
Uniontown Newspapers Inc	2711	231
Unipac Inc	2782	57
Uni-Pak Corp	3535	184
Unipar Inc	3089	1176
Unipec Inc	3089	1636
Uniphase Inc	3089	1040
Uni-Pixel Inc	3081	175
Uniplast Industries Inc	3089	1080
Uniplex Software Inc	5045	493
Uniplus Consultants Inc	7372	2763
Unipres Southeast USA Inc	3465	45
Unipres USA Inc	3465	29
Unipress Corp	3582	7
UniPrise	7372	1434
Unipsych Corp	8093	53
Uniqema	2899	67
Unique Business Systems Corp	7372	1766
Unique Communications Inc	5065	124
Unique Computer Inc	5734	446
Unique Coupons Inc	3555	114
Unique Electronics Inc	3679	236
Unique Environmental Concepts Inc	0781	8
Unique Express Inc	4213	1309
Unique Fabricating Inc	3053	21
Unique Functional Products	3715	34
Unique Industry Corp	5013	379
Unique Lamps By K W Bertschinger Inc	3499	117
Unique Lighting Systems Inc	3612	52
Unique Machine and Tool Co	3553	3
Unique Machine Co	3599	1842
Unique Machine Shop Inc	3599	1625
Unique Mailing Services Inc	7331	48
Unique Management Services Inc	7322	94
Unique Media Inc	3695	79
Unique/Multidec	7389	1959
Unique Originals Inc	2512	66
Unique Personnel Consultants	7361	287
Unique Pretzel Bakery Inc	2096	45
Unique Printers And Lithographers Inc	2752	439
Unique Products LLC	3554	46
Unique Tool and Bending Inc	3542	67
Unique Tool And Manufacturing Company Inc	3545	199
Unique Tool and Manufacturing Company Inc	3465	63
Unique Wholesale Distributors Inc	5023	64
Unique World Travel Inc	4481	12
Unirec Inc	7389	1053
Unirex Corp	5064	172
Unisea Inc	2092	16
Unisec Inc	3669	306
Uniserve Corp	8744	14
UniShippers Association Inc	6794	54
Unisoft Corp	7371	1927
Unisol International Corp	5064	165
UniSolutions Associates	7372	4022
Unison Engine Components Inc	3724	12
Unison Partners LLC	4899	229
Unisorb Corp	3564	153
UNI-SOURCE 2000 Inc	7372	4572
UniSource Energy Corp	4911	64
UniSource Energy Inc	5172	130
Unisource Group Inc	5169	165
Unisource Midwest Inc	5111	17
Unisource Worldwide Inc	5111	2
Unist Inc	3523	150
Unistaff Inc	7361	311
Unistar-Sparco Computers Inc	5045	307
Unisteel LLC	5051	426
Unistress Corp	3272	33
Unistrut Corp	3429	96
Unisun Corp	7372	2692
Uni-Sun Inc	3089	675
Unisys Corp	3571	8
Unisys Electric Inc	1731	1235
Unit Chemical Corp	2842	175
Unit Corp	1311	34
Unit Drilling Co	1381	11
Unit Drop Forge Company Inc	3462	41
Unit Liner Co	3081	108
Unit Manufacturing Co	3679	895
Unit Pack Company Inc	3089	1354
Unit Packaging Corp	7331	227
Unit Petroleum Co	1382	26
Unit Texas Drilling LLC	1311	146
Unit4 Coda Inc	7379	1086
Unite Private Networks LLC	4813	437
Unitec Inc	3679	338
Unitech America Inc	5045	128
Unitech Copy Center Inc	7334	95
Unitech Deco Inc	2759	354
UniTech Services Group Inc	7218	5
Unitech Solutions Inc	7389	1145
Unitech Tool and Machine Inc	3599	1553
United Abrasives Inc	3291	8
United Ad Label	2672	18
United Administrative Services Co	6411	243
United Agencies Insurance Group	6411	165
United Air Filter Co	3564	129
United Air Lines Inc	4512	1
United Air Specialists Inc	3564	13
United Aluminum Corp	3353	8
United American Bank	6022	400
United American Corporation Inc	6719	180
United American Election Supply Inc	3579	54
United American Healthcare Corp	6719	197
United American Insurance Co	6321	42
United Artists Theatre Circuit Inc	7832	7
United Asset Coverage Inc	7378	7
United Audio Video Group Inc	3695	58
United Auto Parts Inc	3519	29
United Auto Sales Of Utica Inc	5012	161
United Automation LLC	1731	1486
United Automobile Insurance Co	6331	215
United Avionics Inc	3728	156
United Bakery Equipment Company Inc	3565	49
United Bakery Inc	2051	234
United Bancorp Inc (Martins Ferry Ohio)	6712	558
United Bancshares Inc	6712	670
United Bancshares Inc (Columbus Grove Ohio)	6712	425
United Bank and Trust Co (Versailles Kentucky)	6022	260
United Bank and Trust (Tecumseh Michigan)	6022	384
United Bank (Arlington Virginia)	6022	808
United Bank (Atmore Alabama)	6712	576
United Bank Card Inc	5962	11
United Bank NA	6035	217
United Bank of Philadelphia	6021	374
United Bankshares Inc	6712	82
United Basket	2449	17
United Behavioral Health	8093	18
United Bindery Service	2789	63
United Biomedical Inc	2836	16
United BioSource Corp	7372	235
United Brass Works Inc	3491	36
United Building Centers	5211	10
United Burglar Alarm Inc	7382	105
United Business Forms Inc	2761	55
United Business Media LLC	2721	14
United Business Service of NY	7389	2504
United Cabinet Company LLC	2434	44
United Cable Systems Inc	4841	102
United Calibration Corp	3829	240
United Capital Corp	3499	15
United Carburetor Inc	3592	20
United Central Control Inc	7382	112
United Central Industrial Supply Company LLC	5085	41
United Central Station	5063	737
United Cerebral Palsy Of Queens Inc	8211	101
United Changers Inc	7699	205
United Chemical Technologies Inc	2819	49
United Chemi-Con Inc	5065	7
United Chiropractic Clinics of Uptown Inc	8041	3
United Circuit Technology Inc	3672	361
United Coin Machine Co	7359	5
United Collection Service Company Inc	7322	140
United Comb and Novelty Corp	3089	686
United Commercial Development Inc	6552	192
United Commercial Realty Co	6531	147
United Communications Group	2741	15
United Community Bancorp	6035	123
United Community Bank	6036	68
United Community Banks Inc	6712	91
United Community Financial Corp	6712	186
United Components Inc	3499	1
United Computer Products Company Inc	3577	424
United Computer Sales And Services Inc	7373	536
United Construction Co	1751	13
United Construction Corp	1542	382
United Consulting Group Ltd	8711	369
United Continental Holdings Inc	6719	8
United Contractors Midwest Inc	1794	8
United Conveyor Corp	3535	10
United Coolair Corp	3585	126
United Cooperative Bank	6062	39
United Corporate Furnishings Inc	5021	54
United Crane Rentals Inc	7353	48
United Dairy Farmers Inc	5411	35
United Dairy Inc	2026	13
United Dairy Machinery Corp	5084	476
United Dairymen Of Arizona	2026	9
United Data Inc	7372	1746
United Dental Laboratories Inc	8072	9
United Developers LLC	7371	1421
United Die Company Inc	3544	285
United Digital Integrators Inc	5999	306
United Digital Technologies LLC	5065	737
United Distributing Company LLC	2082	82
United Distributors Inc (Wichita Kansas)	5046	262
United Dominion Realty Trust Inc	6798	52
United Drill Bushing Corp	3545	47
United Drilling Co	3599	940
United Egg Marketing Corp	5144	16
United Elastic Corp Stuart Div	2241	7
United Electric Company Inc	1623	168
United Electric Contractors Inc	1731	2234
United Electric Cooperative Inc	4911	286
United Electric Enterprise Ltd	1731	165
United Electric Of Wheeling Inc	1731	592
United Electric Supply Co	5063	448
United Electric Supply Inc	5063	11
United Electrical Sales Ltd	5063	779
United Electrical Services Inc	1731	1487
United Embroidery Inc	2397	1
United Engine and Machine Co	3592	6
United Engineered Tooling Inc	3559	384
United Engines LLC	5084	46
United Enterprise Co	7389	1562
United Enterprise Fund LP	6722	210
United Envelope LLC	2677	20
United Enviromental Network	8711	631
United Equipment Accessories Inc	3625	106
United eSystems Inc	6099	35
United Express System Inc	4213	927
United Fabricants Strainrite Corp	3569	60
United Fabricating Inc	3441	237
United Fabricators Inc	3589	198
United Farmers Coop (Lafayette Minnesota)	5153	54
United Farmers Coop (Shelby Nebraska)	5153	52
United Farmers Mercantile Coop	5211	145
United Farmers Supply	5083	206
United Feature Syndicate Inc	7383	12
United Feed Screws Ltd	3061	66
United Fidelity Bank FSB	6035	166
United Fidelity Life Insurance Co	6311	118
United Financial Bancorp Inc	6035	50
United Financial Banking Companies Inc	6712	618
United Fire and Casualty Co	6331	117
United Fixtures Holdings	3449	6
United Food Group LLC	2011	37
United Ford LLC	5511	163
United Forms Finishing Corp	7331	240
United Freight and Transport Inc	4212	61
United Galvanizing Inc	3479	33
United Gasket Corp	3651	95
United Gear and Assembly Inc	3812	82
United General Financial Services	6541	24
United Gilsonite Laboratories	2851	47
United Graphics Inc	2732	25
United Graphics Of Louisville Inc	5112	76
United Grinding And Machine Co	3599	416
United Group Services Inc	1711	109
United Guaranty Residential Insurance Co	6351	27
United Hardware Distributing Co	5072	32
United Health Care of Arizona	6324	79
United Health Care Services Inc	7352	11
United Health Services Inc	8062	56
United Heartland Inc	6331	171
United Home Care Services Inc	8322	24
United Home Life Insurance Co	6311	191
United Illuminating Co	4911	126
United Industrial Corp	3699	12
United Industrial Engineering Corp	7363	316
United Industrial Services Inc	5084	550
United Industries Inc	3086	25
United Industries Inc (Beloit Wisconsin)	3499	23
United Information Services Inc	7389	356
United Insurance Company of America	6311	104
United Insurance Group	6311	198
United Interior Resources Inc	1542	58
United International Engineering Inc	8711	663
United Knitting Limited Partnership I	2257	5
United Knitting Machine Company Inc	3743	24
United Labor Bank	6035	178
United Laboratories Inc	2899	34
United Laminations Inc	3081	157
United Leasing Corp	6159	92
United Lens Company Inc	3229	11
United Letter Service Inc	7331	153
United Life Insurance Co	6311	124
United Lighting Company Inc	5063	539
United Liquors Ltd	5182	12
United Litho Inc	2752	157
United Loose Leaf Inc	2782	54
United Machine Shop Inc	3599	1190
United Machine Works Inc	3599	370
United Mailing Inc	7331	7
United Manufacturing Assembly Inc	3672	111
United Manufacturing Corp	7359	267
United Manufacturing Inc	3699	188
United Marketing Inc (Bellevue Washington)	6531	205
United Marketing Solutions Inc	2741	201
United Meat Company Inc	5147	10
United Media	3663	415
United Media Licensing Co	6794	92
United Medical Enterprise Inc	3841	202
United Medical Equipment Co	7352	9
United Medical Resources Inc	8741	170
United Memories Inc	8731	235
United Merchant Services of California Inc	7389	1207
United Metal Fabricators Inc	2599	29
United Metal Products Inc	3444	115
United Microsystems Inc	5045	501

Company Name Index UNITROL

Company Name	SIC	Rank
United Microwave Products Inc	3315	37
United Missouri Bank NA	6021	20
United Missouri Bank of St Louis NA	6021	24
United Motor Freight Inc	4213	2200
United Multi Media Inc	2759	317
United Natural Foods Inc	5141	14
United Noodles	5149	213
United Nursing International LLC	8051	76
United of Omaha Life Insurance Co	6311	30
United Oil Company Corp	2992	65
United Oil Company Inc	2992	56
United Online Inc	7375	10
United Optical Co	3827	44
United Pacific Pet LLC	5199	22
United Paint And Chemical Corp	2851	76
United Pallet Services Inc	2448	18
United PanAm Financial Corp	6712	367
United Parcel Service Inc	4213	1
United Performance Metals	3312	83
United Petroleum Transports	4213	392
United Pickle Products Corp	2035	32
United Pioneer Corp	2326	10
United Pipe And Steel Corp	5074	95
United Pipe and Supply Company Inc	5074	12
United Pipeline Systems USA Inc	1623	368
United Plastic Fabricating Inc	3089	190
United Plastic Molders Inc	3089	1060
United Plastic Recycling Inc	4953	124
United Plastics Corp	3082	9
United Plastics Group Inc	3089	24
United Plastics Machinery Inc	3559	300
United Plating Inc	3471	37
United Plumbing and Heating Supply Co	5074	64
United Plywood and Lumber Inc	5031	49
United Precast Inc	3272	67
United Precision Machine and Engineering Co	3599	1477
United Press Inc	2752	1605
United Press International Inc	7383	3
United Printed Circuits Inc	3672	323
United Printing Inc	2752	894
United Process Inc	3229	16
United Producers Inc	5154	2
United Products and Instruments Inc	5049	186
United Property and Casualty Insurance Co	6331	303
United Publications Inc	2721	340
United Radio Inc	5046	49
United Record Pressing	3652	42
United Recovery Systems Inc	7322	22
United Refining Co	2911	23
United Rentals Aerial	3537	38
United Rentals Inc	7513	4
United Reprographic Services Inc	7334	01
United Resources Information Inc	7311	830
United Retail Group Inc	5621	18
United Retirement Plan Consultants Inc	6282	313
United Reynolds	7359	166
United Road Services Inc	7549	3
United Rural Electric Membership Corp	4911	499
United Sales	5051	230
United Salt Corp	1479	4
United Sample Inc	7372	1436
United Satcom Inc	3663	321
United Scientific Inc	3451	100
United Seal and Rubber Company Inc	3061	56
United Security Associates Ltd	1731	1088
United Security Bancshares Inc	6712	400
United Security Bank (Fresno California)	6022	373
United Security Bankshares Inc	6712	424
United Security Inc	7381	37
United Security Products Inc	3679	399
United Service Equipment Co	3589	44
United Services Associates Inc	7349	531
United Services Automobile Association Inc	6331	13
United Sheet Metal Inc	1761	11
United Shellfish Company Inc	5146	15
United Shoe Machinery Corp	7699	56
United Silica Products Inc	3229	36
United Silicone Inc	3559	83
United Skates of America Inc	7999	64
United Solar Ovonic LLC	3692	4
United Solutions And Services LLC	7379	930
United Solutions Inc	5045	728
United Southern Industries Inc	3089	526
United Space Alliance LLC	7389	174
United Space Alliance Pension	3812	27
United Staffing Systems Inc	7363	110
United Standard Industries Inc	3469	244
United Starters And Alternators Industries Inc	3621	148
US Acrylic LLC	3089	927
US Adhesives	2891	121
US Aerospace Inc	3728	188
US Airweld Inc	5251	36
US Alliance Paper Inc	2676	5
United States Aluminum Corp	3442	95
United States Aluminum Corporation - Texas	3442	139
US Aluminum Services Corp	1799	132

Company Name	SIC	Rank
United States Alumoweld Company LLC	3496	87
United States Antimony Corp	3339	19
United States Arbitration and Mediation Inc	6794	113
US Armor Corp	3842	171
US Axle Inc	3714	351
US Bancorp	6712	4
US Bancorp Insurance Services	6411	292
US Bank Trust Company NA	6021	266
US Bank (Woodland California)	6022	759
US Bindery Inc	2789	102
United States Box Corp	2631	29
United States Brass and Copper Company Inc	5099	25
US Bronze Foundry And Machine Inc	3341	32
US Bronze Powders Inc	3399	2
US Business Interiors Inc	5021	67
US Button Corp	3965	15
United States Cargo Service Corp	4215	18
US Cavalry Inc	5961	71
United States Cellular Corp	4812	6
US Central	6062	7
US Chemicals Inc	5169	160
United States Cold Storage Inc	4222	4
US Concrete Inc	3272	30
United States Construction Corp	6552	273
United States Container Corp	5085	62
US Conveyor Technologies Manufacturing Inc	3535	73
US Cosmetics Corp	3295	11
United States Crane Certification Bureau Inc	7389	1897
United States Credit Bureau	7322	123
US Credit-Service Corp	7323	13
US Data Security Corp	7375	207
US Dismantlement LLC	1795	6
United States Distilled Products Co	2085	17
United States Drill Head Co	3545	209
United States Drug Testing Laboratories Inc	8734	135
US Durum Products Ltd	2098	24
US Electrical Motors Div	3621	18
United States Endoscopy Group Inc	3841	108
United States Energy Corp	3694	51
US Energy Corp	1311	156
US Energy Development Corp	4923	19
US Energy Service	4931	48
US Energy Services Inc	8741	184
US Engineering Co	1542	25
US Enrichment Corp	1422	1
US Epson Inc	3577	91
US Financial Services Inc	7377	17
United States Fire Arms Manufacturing Co	3489	21
US Fitness Products	5941	27
US Foodservice Inc	5141	3
US Foundry and Manufacturing Corp	3321	7
US Franchise Systems Inc	6794	122
US Frontline News Inc	2721	341
US Futaba Inc	5072	154
US Games Systems Inc	2741	317
US Gas and Electric Inc	4923	21
United States Gear Corp	3714	94
US Global Investors Inc	6282	327
US Group Inc	3541	39
United States Gypsum Co	3275	4
US Healthworks Inc	8011	36
US Home Corp	1521	2
US Home Systems Inc	5999	23
US Industrial Products Corp	5072	87
US Inspect LLC	8744	29
United States Intelligence Agency Inc	7382	177
US Internet Corp	7373	272
US Iol Inc	3851	98
US Jetting LLC	3589	105
US Kids Golf LLC	5091	92
US Laboratories Inc	8734	20
United States Life Insurance Company in the City of New York	6311	125
United States Lime and Minerals Inc	1422	2
US Lock Corp	5072	13
US Machine and Tool LLC	3544	665
United States Machine Tools Corp	3541	174
US Manufacturing Inc	3449	32
United States Marble Inc	3281	28
US Media Corp	1731	2421
US Metals and Supply Inc	5051	161
US Metro Group Inc	7349	68
US Micro PC Inc	5734	128
US Mills Inc	2099	324
United States Mineral Products Company Inc	3296	7
US Monitoring Inc	7381	262
US Municipal Supply Inc	5082	128
US Music Corp	3931	27
US Neurosurgical Inc	8093	51
US Paint Corp	2851	72
US Paper Counters	3824	40
US Para Plate Corp	3491	16
US Physical Therapy Inc	8049	2
US Pioneer LLC	3357	65
United States Pipe and Foundry Co	3498	3
United States Playing Card Co	3944	14

Company Name	SIC	Rank
United States Postal Service	4513	1
US Precast Corp	3272	51
US RE Corp	8742	313
US Realty Consultants Inc	6531	175
US Remodelers Inc	2434	8
US Rents It	7513	20
US Robotics Corp	3661	6
United States Roller Works Inc	3069	165
US Satellite Corp	4899	56
US Security Associates Inc	7381	3
US Shipping Corp	4449	9
US Silica Co	1446	1
United States Smokeless Tobacco Co	2131	2
US Steel- Bellville Operations Div	3317	5
United States Steel Corp	3312	1
US Sterling Capital Corp	6211	167
United States Stove Co	3631	9
United States Strong Tool Co	5084	85
United States Sugar Corp	2061	2
US Surf Company Inc	7359	131
US Tape Company Inc	3999	197
US Tax Advantage LLC	7291	14
US Tile	3259	3
US Timberlands Company LP	0851	3
US Tire Recycling	5093	78
US Trailer Parts Inc	5013	253
US Transport	4213	1298
US Trust Bank of America Private Wealth Management	6282	2
United States Trust Company of New York	6022	34
US Trust Company of Texas NA	6021	57
US Tsubaki Inc	3568	4
US Voice and Data	1731	308
US Window and Door	2431	123
US Window Factory Inc	5031	204
US Xpress Enterprises Inc	4213	29
US Xpress Inc	4212	11
US Zinc Corp	1031	2
United Stationers Inc	5112	1
United Stationers Supply Co	5113	1
United Steel Inc	3441	91
United Steel Products Co	3429	15
United Steel Service LLC	5051	135
United Structures Of America Inc	3448	18
United Subcontractors Inc	5033	55
United Supermarkets LLC	5411	32
United Supermarkets of Oklahoma Inc	5411	173
United Supply Inc	5051	478
United Surgical Partners International Inc	8062	53
United Systems Access Inc	4899	153
United Systems and Software Inc	7371	387
United Systems Integrators Corp	6531	286
United Systems of Arkansas Inc	2752	1085
United Systems Technology Inc	7372	3082
United Talent Agency Inc	7922	31
United Taxi Cab Company Inc	5012	192
United Technologies Corp	3534	1
United Technology	7373	174
United Therapeutics Corp	2834	50
United Titanium Inc	3369	15
United Tool and Die Company Inc	3469	367
United Tool And Engineering Co	3544	163
United Tool and Engineering Inc	3544	331
United Tool and Mold Inc	3599	907
United Tool and Plastics Inc	3089	1882
United Tool Company Inc	3599	2172
United Tote Co	3999	217
United Transmission Exchange Inc	5013	161
United Universal Industries Inc	3643	122
United Van Lines Inc	4213	14
United Water Idaho Inc	4941	38
United Water Inc	4971	1
United Water New York Inc	4941	48
United Way Of Central Oklahoma Inc	8399	19
United Way Of Genesee County	8399	24
United Way Of Lancaster County	7389	952
United Welding And Manufacturing Co	3399	33
United Western Bank	6035	95
United Western Industries Inc	3544	250
United Wholesale Flooring Inc	5023	171
United Window and Door Manufacturing Inc	3089	446
United Wire Hanger Corp	3496	43
United World Life Insurance Co	6311	244
United-County Industries Corp	3398	18
United-Guardian Inc	2834	295
UnitedHealth Group Inc	6324	1
UniTek Global Services Inc	1623	10
Unitek Inc	7373	414
Uni-Tek LLC	3599	547
Unitek Technology Inc	3571	177
Unitex Textile Rental Services	7213	4
Unitherm Food Systems Inc	3556	132
Unitil Corp	4931	41
Unitime Systems Inc	7372	194
Unitone Communication Systems Inc	3669	298
Unitra Inc	3561	145
Unitrack Industries Inc	8711	595
Unitrend Inc	3577	549
UniTrends Software Corp	7372	3849
Unitrin Specialty Lines Insurance	6331	210
Unitrol Inc	3669	203

Company Name Index

Ward's Business Directory of U.S. Private and Public Companies, 55th Edition / Volume 5 1721

Company Name	SIC	Rank
Unitron Products Inc	3449	21
Unittool Punch and Die Company Inc	5084	672
Unitus Community Credit Union	6062	55
Unity Bancorp Inc	6712	348
Unity Bank Crosby Minnesota	6021	316
Unity Building Services Inc	7349	108
Unity Construction Company Inc	1623	406
Unity Courier Service	4215	16
Unity Graphics and Engraving Company Inc	2752	882
Unity Health Plans Insurance Corp	6324	75
Unity Mutual Life Insurance Co	6311	212
Unity One Federal Credit Union	6061	97
Unity Printing Company Inc	5943	36
Unity Tool Inc	3599	1988
Univa UD	7372	1914
Univar Inc	5169	6
Univenture Inc	3089	237
Univera Inc	8731	51
Universal Accounting Center	8721	112
Universal Accounting Software Inc	7372	3038
Universal Air Filter Co	3564	47
Universal Air Products Corp	3563	40
Universal Am-Can Ltd	4213	215
Universal American Corp	6311	100
Universal Analyzers Inc	3823	209
Universal Athletic Services Inc	5139	13
Universal Atlantic Systems Inc	1731	531
Universal Automation Labs Solutions Group	7371	1431
Universal Avionics Systems Corp	3812	33
Universal Beauty Products Inc	2844	96
Universal Blanchers LLC	0723	2
Universal Blower Pac Inc	3564	139
Universal Builders Supply Inc	1799	51
Universal Building Services And Supply Co	7349	61
Universal Business Computing Co	7372	3039
Universal Business Matrix LLC	5045	187
Universal Business Solutions Inc	8748	278
Universal Care Inc	6324	65
Universal Cargo Management Inc	4731	85
Universal Certificate Group LLC	7379	860
Universal Chemical And Supply Corp	5084	635
Universal Chemicals And Coatings Inc	2851	90
Universal Circuits Inc	3672	147
Universal Collection Systems	7322	104
Universal Concept	7336	146
Universal Construction Company Inc	1542	273
Universal Construction Software Inc	7372	3963
Universal Consulting Services Inc	7379	429
Universal Container Company LLC	3085	48
Universal Controls Systems	3625	378
Universal Conversion Technologies LLP	7379	872
Universal Cooperative Inc	5013	14
Universal Corp	5159	1
Universal Data Inc	5734	227
Universal Delivery Systems Inc	4213	3062
Universal Demolishing and Recycling Inc	5093	228
Universal Detection Technology	3823	489
Universal Diecutters Corp	2675	9
Universal Directory Publishing Corp	2741	357
Universal Display Corp	3679	111
Universal Distribution Inc	4213	2823
Universal Dove Corp	7359	205
Universal Electric LLC	1731	2282
Universal Electrical Service Inc	1731	580
Universal Electronics Company Inc	3661	188
Universal Electronics Inc	3651	19
Universal Energy Systems	8731	150
Universal Engineering Sciences Inc	8734	34
Universal Engraving Inc	2796	13
Universal Enterprises Inc	1711	131
Universal Environmental Nevada	4213	2077
Universal Equipment Inc	5084	516
Universal Exhibits	7389	809
Universal Fibers Inc	2824	7
Universal Fidelity LP	7322	145
Universal Filters Inc	3569	247
Universal Fire Protection Ltd	3569	210
Universal Flow Monitors Inc	3823	167
Universal Ford Inc	5511	750
Universal Forest Products Inc	2421	4
Universal Fremont Packaging	5082	70
Universal Guaranty Life Insurance Co	6311	201
Universal Health Realty Income Trust	6798	176
Universal Health Services Inc	8062	18
Universal Hi-Tech Development Inc	7373	139
Universal Hospital Services Inc	7352	2
Universal Image Productions Inc	7374	178
Universal Imports Parts Inc	5013	229
Universal Instruments Corp	3559	19
Universal Label Printers Inc	2759	438
Universal Labeling Systems Inc	3565	82
Universal Laminating Ltd	7389	1357
Universal Land Title Inc	6541	10
Universal Land Title of Colorado Inc	6541	9
Universal Land Title of the Palm Beaches Ltd	6541	12
Universal Laser Systems Inc	3699	108
Universal Lending Corp	6162	35
Universal Level Company Inc	2431	139

Company Name	SIC	Rank
Universal Lighting Technologies Inc	3612	40
Universal Lithographers Inc	2752	693
Universal Lubricants LLC	2992	14
Universal Machine and Engineering Corp	3599	514
Universal Magnetics Inc	3559	549
Universal Manufacturing Co	5015	5
Universal Manufacturing Co (Kansas City Missouri)	3944	25
Universal Manufacturing Corp	3446	40
Universal Map Enterprises Inc	2741	97
Universal Marine Medical Supply Co	5047	157
Universal Maritime	4491	16
Universal Medical Supply Corp	5047	263
Universal Meeting Management Inc	7389	1381
Universal Merchandise Inc	2311	32
Universal Metal Corp	5093	242
Universal Metal Products Inc	3429	52
Universal Metal Service Corp	3316	26
Universal Metalcraft Inc	3444	238
Universal Millennium Inc	2752	129
Universal Mind Inc	7373	513
Universal Music Group	3652	3
Universal Music Publishing Group Nashville	2741	389
Universal Orlando	7812	7
Universal Overall Co	2326	27
Universal Paragon Corp	6552	20
Universal Pharmaceutical Medical Supply Company Inc	5047	190
Universal Photonics Inc	5049	26
Universal Pig Genes Inc	0751	12
Universal Pipe and Steel Supply Inc	5051	395
Universal Plastics Corp	3089	691
Universal Plastics Inc	3082	29
Universal Polymer and Rubber Ltd	3069	54
Universal Power Group Inc	5063	57
Universal Precision Products Inc	3554	35
Universal Presentation Concepts Inc	2541	32
Universal Printing and Publishing	2752	421
Universal Printing Company Inc	2752	50
Universal Productions International Inc	7371	1347
Universal Products Inc	2759	63
Universal Promotions Inc	7389	912
Universal Protection Service LP	7381	12
Universal Protection Services Inc	7381	9
Universal Protective Packaging Inc	3089	797
Universal Protein Supplements Corp	2834	125
Universal Pultrusions LLC	3089	1302
Universal Punch Corp	3542	41
Universal Quartz Inc	3679	819
Universal Refractories Inc	3255	4
Universal Remote Control Inc	3625	425
Universal Reproductions Inc	7334	41
Universal Rubber and Plastics Corp	5199	90
Universal Satellite Communications Inc	3651	231
Universal Scrap Metals Inc	5093	103
Universal Screen Graphics Inc	2759	448
Universal Screw Products Inc	3451	122
Universal Security Instruments Inc	5065	220
Universal Security Systems Inc	1731	689
Universal Semiconductor Inc	3674	483
Universal Sewing Machine Company Inc	5084	877
Universal Slate Exports	3281	50
Universal Software Corp	7372	1292
Universal Software Inc	7372	3634
Universal Stainless and Alloy Products Inc	3312	32
Universal Steel Buildings Inc	1791	14
Universal Steel Co	5093	13
Universal Strap Inc	2241	21
Universal Strapping Inc	3089	1746
Universal Studios Home Video	7819	21
Universal Studios Inc	7819	1
Universal Surveillance Corp	3699	181
Universal Synaptics Inc	3825	343
Universal System Technologies Inc	7371	1134
Universal Tax Systems Inc	7372	764
Universal Technical Institute Inc	8299	4
Universal Technical Resource Services Inc	8741	34
Universal Technical Systems Inc	7372	3444
Universal Technologies Inc	3728	131
Universal Test Equipment Inc	3823	314
Universal Toner Plus	5044	143
Universal Tooling Corp	3544	816
Universal Trailer Holdings Corp	3715	9
Universal Truck Equipment Inc	3531	150
Universal Truckload Services Inc	4213	51
Universal Tube Inc	3498	26
Universal Urethane Inc	3714	323
Universal Urethane Products Inc	3069	155
Universal Used Pallets Inc	5031	441
Universal Veneer Mill Corp	6512	64
Universal Wearparts Inc	3599	2103
Universal Work Force Development Center	7361	340
Universal-Automatic Corp	3541	108
Universe Company Inc	4213	1687
Universe Kogaku America Inc	5049	198
Universe Moving Company Inc	4213	2582
Universities Research Association Inc	8733	32

Company Name	SIC	Rank
University and State Employees Credit Union	6062	57
University Bancorp Inc	6022	617
University Bank	6022	674
University Book Store	5942	26
University Book Store Inc	5942	18
University Business Interiors Inc	7389	1950
University City Housing Co	6513	32
University Cooperative Society Inc	5942	25
University Endoscopy Center	8011	118
University Health Inc	8062	67
University Health Plans Inc	6324	33
University Language Services Inc	7389	1310
University Motors Ltd	5511	605
University of Arkansas for Medical Sciences	8062	248
University Of Florida Mail Document Services	7331	258
University Of Hawaii Press	2731	280
University Of Maryland Baltimore County	8221	15
University Of Nebraska Foundation	7389	182
University Of New Mexico Press	2731	41
University of North Carolina Press	2731	237
University of Pennsylvania Health System	6324	28
University of Phoenix Inc	8221	40
University of Pittsburgh Medical Center	8062	9
University Of Southern Mississippi	8221	12
University of Texas MD Anderson Cancer Center	8069	3
University Of Wyoming Research Corp	8731	192
University Physicians Services Inc	8741	228
University Press of America Inc	2731	100
University Products Inc	2541	16
University Reader Co	7334	46
University Research Company LLC	8742	144
University Research Glassware Company Inc	5084	858
University Settlement Society Of New York Inc	8322	53
University Subscription Service Inc	7389	908
University Transplant Program	3523	251
University Travel Service Inc	4724	143
Univertical Corp	2899	54
Univest Corporation of Pennsylvania	6712	193
Univest Financial Group Inc	6282	493
Univest National Bank and Trust Co	6029	3
Univex Corp	3556	85
Univision Communications Inc	4833	14
Univision Music Inc	3652	16
Univision Radio	4832	10
Uniweb Inc	2542	36
Uniweld Products Inc	3548	13
Uniworld Group Inc	7311	100
Unkefer Homer Farm Equipment Company Inc	5083	152
Unlimited Care Inc	8059	8
Unlimited Flexible Plastics Inc	5162	28
Unlimited Horizons Inc	6531	157
Unlimited Manufacturing Services Inc	5065	654
Unlimited Reprographics	7334	24
Unlimited Seams Industrial Services LLC	3714	417
Unlimited Security Systems	5063	1103
Unlimited Services Available	7363	385
Unlimited Services Group - Hawaii LLC	8742	457
Unlimited Services Inc	3679	165
Unlimited Services (Rockford)	3629	77
Unmc Physicians	8011	15
Uno Foods Inc	2099	124
Uno Restaurant Holdings Corp	5812	98
Unocal Pipeline Co	4612	12
Unotron Inc	5045	922
Untangle Inc	7371	1125
Unum Group	6311	21
UNUM Holding Co	6321	11
UNX Inc	6289	10
Unytite Inc	3452	63
UOP LLC	3823	1
UP Electric/Wittock Supply Co	5074	179
Up Software Inc	7372	4893
UP Special Delivery Inc	4213	1079
Upa Technology Inc	3829	417
UPACO Adhesives Div	2891	46
UpAgainstthe Wallcom	5611	12
Upco Graphics Inc	2657	44
Upco Inc	3533	53
Updata Capital Inc	6211	307
Update Software Inc	7372	4894
Update Systems Inc	3625	185
Upek Inc	3674	124
UPF Corp	3296	22
UPI Of Alabama Inc	3599	1969
Upl International Inc	3089	1634
Upm Inc	3089	364
UpNet Technologies Inc	7372	1915
Upper Cumberland Electric Membership Corp	4911	359
Upper Darby School District	8211	49
Upper Deck Company LLC	2752	88
Upper East Tennessee Human Development Agency	8399	17
Upper Peninsula Power Corp	4911	347

Company Name	SIC	Rank
Upper Peninsula Telephone Co	4813	144
Upper Room	2721	102
Upper Valley Press Inc	2752	551
Uppercase Living LLC	5719	22
UPS Capital Business Credit	6021	237
Ups Capital Trade Protection Services Inc	6411	100
UPS Logistics Technologies Inc	7373	316
UPS Supply Chain Solutions Inc	4212	10
Upscale Foods Inc	2038	92
Upshaw and Associates	8999	214
UPSHOT Direct Inc	3993	15
Upson Electric Membership Corp	4911	500
Upstanding LLC	7372	1975
Upstate Auto Body Warehouse Inc	5013	219
Upstate Detailing Inc	7389	1937
Upstate Network Solutions Inc	5999	207
Upstate Systems Inc	5075	98
Upstream Technologies LLC	7372	1916
Uptime Solutions Associates Inc	5045	528
Uptime Solutions Professional Services Group Inc	7373	990
Uptime Sports Nutrition Medical Industries Inc	2834	408
Uptime Studios	5065	888
Uptime Technology Inc	7371	1803
UpToDate TM Inc	2741	71
Upton Industries Inc	3567	87
Uptown Publications Inc	2721	402
UQM Technologies Inc	3679	824
UR West Linn Thriftway Inc	5411	134
Urania Engineering Company Inc	3599	1339
Uranium Resources Inc	5051	513
Uraseal Inc	3661	189
Urban Ag Corp	3842	330
Urban Child Institute	8069	23
Urban Communications Transport Corp	4841	158
Urban Contractors Inc	1623	345
Urban Corps Of San Diego	8331	84
Urban Electric Co	3648	61
Urban Electrical Services Inc	1623	391
Urban Engineers Inc	8711	265
Urban Express	4213	2489
Urban League Of Philadelphia Inc	8322	21
Urban Lending Solutions	6162	97
Urban Manufacturing Inc	3599	203
Urban Ministries Inc	2731	213
Urban Outfitters Inc	5611	4
Urban Outfitters Wholesale Inc	5651	21
Urban Renewal Corp	8322	176
Urban Science Applications Inc	7372	669
Urban Settlement Services LLC	6552	70
Urban Telecommunications Inc	1623	387
Urbana Software Inc	7372	3964
UrbanAmerica Advisors LLC	6722	209
Urbancode Inc	7371	1292
uReach Technologies Inc	4899	70
U'ren Sound and Power Systems Inc	7353	69
UREP Inc	7336	117
Uresil LLC	3841	264
Urethane Products Corp	3089	1828
Urethane Roller Specialist Inc	3569	253
Urgent Care Holdings Inc	8011	50
Urgent Design and Manufacturing Inc	3549	64
Urgent Nursing Resource Inc	7361	377
Uri Tech Inc	3672	430
Urigen NA Inc	2834	428
Urish Popeck and Company LLC	8111	471
URM Stores Inc	5141	36
Urner-Barry Publications Inc	2721	224
Urologix Inc	3845	79
Uromed Inc	5047	185
Urooj LLC	7361	419
Uroplasty Inc	3841	171
Urpan Technologies	7361	383
URS Construction Services Inc	8741	109
URS Corp	8711	4
Urs Electronics Inc	5065	496
Urs Gores Holdings Corp	4213	158
Ursa Farmers Cooperative Company Inc	5153	173
Urschel Laboratories Inc	3556	23
Urschel Manufacturing Inc	3599	1252
Urstadt Biddle Properties Inc	6798	150
Ursula Of Switzerland Inc	2335	13
Urwiler Oil and Fertilizer Inc	5191	106
US 1 Industries Inc	4213	132
US Airways Group Inc	4512	6
US Airways Inc	4512	7
Us Alert LLC	5065	972
US Aluminum Inc	3399	34
US Art Company Inc	4213	1888
Us Auctions Live Corp	8711	243
US Avionics Inc	3545	368
US Bank	6712	616
US Billing Inc	7376	33
Us Biomaterials Corp	3842	277
Us Breaker Inc	3661	202
US Cable Corp	4841	29
US Central Express Inc	4213	1811
Us Chemical Storage LLC	5084	478
Us Communications And Electric Inc	1731	483
Us Conec Ltd	3357	54
Us Connection	5012	171

Company Name	SIC	Rank
US Contractors Ltd	1629	33
Us Corrugated Inc	2653	9
US Co-Tronics Corp	3621	107
US Dataworks Inc	7374	147
US Development Corp	3089	754
Us Digital Designs Inc	8711	653
US DigitalMedia	3565	27
US Ecology Idaho Inc	4953	31
US Ecology Inc	4953	34
US Electric and Telecom	1731	1860
US Electronics Inc	3679	670
US Energy Controls Inc	3822	97
US Energy Corp	1731	1089
US Farathane Corp	5013	15
Us Farms Inc	0191	4
Us Federal Properties Trust Inc	6798	197
US Filter Wheelabrator Corp	3589	8
US First Energy	1731	1086
US Flange and Fittings Corp	5085	161
US FoodService Inc Carolina Div	5141	59
US Geological Servey	3822	69
US Global Brokerage Inc	6211	132
US Global Investors All American Equity Fund	6722	269
US Global Investors China Reg Opp	6722	250
US Global Investors Eastern European Fund	6722	176
US Global Investors Global Resources Fund	6722	153
US Global Investors Gold and Precious Metals Fund	6722	202
US Global Investors Near-Term Tax Free Fund	6722	265
US Global Investors Tax Free Fund	6722	266
Us Granite-Nevada Inc	5032	142
US Hybrid	3621	55
US Interactive Corp	7336	83
Us Interior Surface Mining Reclamation and Enforcement	7389	1202
US Inter-Mex Transportation	4213	1409
Us Investigations Services LLC	7381	13
US Laser	2759	461
US Laser Corp	3699	253
US Lighting Tech	3641	13
US Logistics Inc	7538	3
US Lumber Co	5031	413
US Machine And Tool	3469	381
US Machines Inc	7699	185
US Manufacturing Corp	3714	133
US Media Consulting	7311	498
US Media Inc	7311	1042
US Medical Group Inc	8011	167
US Molding Machinery Company Inc	3559	325
Us Motion Inc	3569	202
Us Netcom Corp	7371	978
US Oil and Refining Co	2911	53
US Oil Company Petroleum Operation	5171	6
US Oncology Inc	8093	1
US Poly Enterprises Inc	2822	10
Us Polymers-Accurez LLC	2851	105
Us Positioning Group	5045	846
US Power Generating Co	4911	56
US Ring Binder LP	3429	114
US Risk Insurance Group Inc	6411	136
US Rubber Corp	3496	96
US Rubber Reclaiming Inc	3069	98
Us Safetygear Inc	5084	388
US Script Inc	7389	352
US Searchcom Inc	7389	403
US Spine	3842	100
US Steel (Houston Texas)	3317	8
US Steel Rule Dies Inc	3544	402
US Tech Services Inc	5084	512
Us Tech Solutions Inc	7379	200
Us Technical Ceramics Inc	5032	60
Us Tel Inc	5065	498
Us Telmanagement LLC	4813	242
US Tool and Cutter Co	3541	237
US Tool and Manufacturing Co	3714	418
Us Travel Northwest Inc	7372	378
Us Ultratek Inc	3829	405
Us Vantage Company LLC	7532	7
US Vision Inc	5995	5
Us1Com Inc	2759	597
USA 800	7389	1093
USA Cartage Inc	4213	3129
USA Central Station Alarm Corp	7382	102
USA Datafax Inc	5044	93
USA Datanet Corp	4813	86
USA Digital Inc	5999	218
USA Distributors Inc	2711	466
USA Electrical Construction Contractors Inc	1731	1259
USA Environmental Management Inc	8734	52
USA Gym Supply	5091	117
USA Harness Inc	3694	30
USA Hosts	4724	78
USA Instruments Inc	3677	5
USA Jet Airlines Inc	4512	53
USA Knit Inc	2251	8
USA Lending Group	6163	42
USA Managed Care Organization Inc	6324	64
USA Microcraft Inc	5045	515
USA Mobility Inc	4812	15

Company Name	SIC	Rank
USA Notebook Inc	5045	456
USA Parking Systems Inc	7521	15
USA Printing Corp	2711	647
USA Products Group Inc	2399	22
USA Scientific Inc	5199	68
USA Services Inc	7699	169
USA Studios	3695	28
USA Technologies Inc	3578	17
USA Transport Inc	4213	1413
USA Truck Inc	4213	62
USA Video Interactive Corp	7372	5059
USA Workers' Injury Network Inc	6324	40
USA X-Tractions Inc	3559	422
USAA FSB	6035	2
Usability Sciences Corp	7379	708
USAble Life Inc	6311	237
Usach Technologies Inc	3541	116
USADATA Inc	7331	128
USAgencies Credit Union	6062	108
Usakd Enterprise Inc	5734	394
USANA Health Sciences Inc	2833	7
US-Analytics Solutions Group LLC	5045	251
USANET Inc	4822	6
Usapex Corp	3678	84
USAV Group	7812	203
U-Save Auto Rental of America Inc	6794	100
USBid Inc	7379	442
USC Atlantic Inc	3272	24
USC GP Inc	3272	25
USC Limited Partnership Inc	3272	26
USC Management Company LLC	3272	27
USC Michigan Inc	3272	28
USE Federal Credit Union	6061	114
UsedLaptopsCom Inc	5961	173
Usedroutercom Inc	5961	153
Useful Products LLC	2759	108
User Solutions Inc	7372	4260
Users Inc	7389	348
Userthink Inc	7371	1185
USF Bestway Inc	4213	182
USF Fabrication Inc	3441	55
USF Glen Moore Transport Inc	4212	7
USF Holland Inc	4213	48
USF Logistics Services Inc	4213	64
USF Reddaway	4213	2
USfalcon Inc	7389	231
USG Corp	3275	2
Usglobalsat Inc	3663	229
Usgs Water Resources Discipline	7389	1834
USHEALTH Group Inc	6321	66
Usher Enterprises Inc	5093	145
Usher Precision Manufacturing Inc	3728	205
Usher Transport Inc	4213	643
Uohcro Machine And Tool Company Inc	3599	1780
Usherwood Business Equipment Inc	7629	24
Ushio America Inc	3699	70
uShip Inc	4731	74
USI Affinity	6351	38
Usi Cable Corp	1623	632
USI Consulting Group	8748	37
USI Holdings Corp	6411	45
USI Inc (Madison Connecticut)	5044	49
USI Insurance Services LLC	6331	230
Usibelli Coal Mine Inc	1221	27
USinternetworking Inc	7373	70
USLIFE Corp	6311	74
Usm Inc	3999	142
Usm Manufacturing LLC	2099	288
Usm Precision Products Inc	3599	286
USNI Tech LLC	3559	360
Uson LP	3823	7
Usp LLC	7379	1635
Uspar Enterprises Inc	3645	53
Usr Optonix Inc	5169	132
Uss Posco Industries	3312	18
USSensor Corp	3676	10
Ussery Printing Company Inc	2752	527
UST LLC	2131	1
Uster Technologies Inc	3829	120
U-Store-It Trust	6519	5
Usui International Corp	3714	153
Ut Medicine San Antonio	8099	30
Utah Bank Note Company Inc	2752	1767
Utah Fabrication Inc	3325	38
Utah Logos Inc	3993	166
Utah Medical Products Inc	3841	114
Utah Medical Products Texas Inc	3841	105
Utah Metal Works Inc	5093	39
Utah Pacific Construction Co	1623	279
Utah Paper Box Co	2657	15
Utah Scientific Inc	3663	113
Utahamerican Energy Inc	1222	1
Utc Associates Inc	7379	1429
Ute City Tea Party Ltd	2711	870
Ute Microwave Inc	3679	671
U-Tec Construction Inc	4813	496
Utec Metals Inc	3599	1845
U-Tech Environmental Manufacturing Supply Inc	3589	139
Utek-Ekms Inc	8742	544
Utex Industries Inc	3053	1
UTG Inc	6311	186
Uti Inc	7379	1417

Company Name	SIC	Rank	Company Name	SIC	Rank	Company Name	SIC	Rank
UTi Worldwide Inc	4731	6	Vacuum Technology Of Tennessee Inc	3829	168	Valley Electrical Consolidated Inc	1731	148
Utica Corp	3724	8	Vacuum Tube Logic Of America Inc	3671	22	Valley Electrical Contracting Inc	1731	658
Utica Cutlery Co	3914	10	Vadis Quo Editions Inc	2782	47	Valley Emergency Communication	8322	174
Utica First Insurance Co	6331	341	Vador Ventures Inc	7349	58	Center		
Utica Metal Products Inc	3465	57	Vae Nortrak Inc	3312	37	Valley Endoscopy Center LP	8011	88
Utica Mutual Insurance Co	6331	136	Vagabond Inns Inc	7011	177	Valley Energy	4924	55
Utica Valley Electric Supply Company	5063	634	Vail Clinic Inc	8062	163	Valley Enterprises Building	7349	277
Inc			Vail Industries Inc	2653	113	Maintenance Inc		
Utilicor Corp	5063	79	Vail Resorts Inc	7999	15	Valley Equipment Co	5084	493
Utility Communications Inc	5999	126	Vail-Ballou Press Inc	2732	11	Valley Exposition Service Inc	7389	2106
Utility Constructors Inc	1623	222	Vailiant Communication Inc	7374	161	Valley Express Inc	4213	1735
Utility Contractors Inc	1623	103	Val Rollers Inc	3728	224	Valley Express LLC	4213	2378
Utility Integration Solutions Inc	8742	418	Valassis 1 to 1 Solutions	7372	616	Valley Family Health Center LLC	8041	4
Utility Pipe Sales Company Inc	5074	72	Valassis Communications Inc	2752	1	Valley Farmers Coop	5261	13
Utility Products Of Arizona Inc	5063	1059	Valco Cincinnati Inc	3586	11	Valley Farmers Coop (Natchitoches	5191	154
Utility Relay Company Ltd	3625	207	Valco Manufacturing Company Inc	3728	147	Louisiana)		
Utility Sales And Engineering Services	5063	819	Val-Co Pax Inc	3523	75	Valley Feed Mill Incorporated Of Paris	2048	93
LLC			Valco Plastics Inc	3443	216	Valley Fertilizer And Chemical	5999	97
Utility Sales And Service Inc	5511	1219	Valco Precision Works Inc	3599	2053	Company Inc		
Utility Systems Construction and	1623	545	Valcom Enterprises Inc	1742	14	Valley Financial Corp	6712	377
Engineering LLC			Val-Com Field Services Inc	1623	745	Valley Fine Foods Company Inc	2038	27
Utility Tool and Trailer Inc	3523	138	Valcom Inc	3661	86	Valley Flood Lite Service Inc	1731	2260
Utility Tool Company Inc	3812	185	Valcom Technology	5734	421	Valley Forge Life Insurance Co	6331	275
Utility Trailer Manufacturing Co	3715	3	Valcor Engineering Corp	3625	42	Valley Forge Press Inc	7389	1664
Utility Trailer Sales Company of	5599	11	Valcor Inc	3429	13	Valley Grain Products	2041	25
Arizona			Valdada Enterprises LLC	5049	229	Valley Grinding Service and Supply Inc	3545	218
Utility Vault Company Inc	3272	102	Valdese Textiles Inc	2221	40	Valley Header Die Inc	3544	500
Utilityworks Inc	1623	778	Valdez Corp	5149	177	Valley Healthcare Systems Inc	8011	62
UTILX Corp	1623	36	Valdor Fiber Optics	3678	23	Valley Honda Madza Volkswagen	5511	1021
Utley Brothers Inc	2752	1027	Vale Coventry Winery Inc	2084	78	Valley Imaging Partners Inc	8093	43
Utley Inc	4213	1301	Valeda Company LLC	5047	133	Valley Implement and Motor Company	5083	64
Utopia Software Solutions Inc	7372	4649	Valence Technology Inc	3691	16	Inc		
UTS Transportation Services	4213	1696	Valencia Systems Inc	7372	1747	Valley Innovative Management	5812	114
UTSI International Corp	7371	1624	Valencia Water Co	4941	45	Services Inc		
Utterback Electrical Inc	1731	2269	Valenite Inc	3541	13	Valley Instrument Company Inc	3823	323
Uusco Of Illinois Inc	5063	841	Valent Aerostructures - St Louis Inc	3599	1119	Valley Inventory Service Inc	7389	994
UV Aetek Systems Inc	3826	131	Valent USA Corp	2879	5	Valley Joist Inc	3441	114
UV Process Supply Inc	5043	27	Valente Builders Inc	1521	167	Valley Joist/Western Div	3441	41
UVEST Financial Services Group Inc	6211	374	Valenti Brothers Graphics Ltd	2752	694	Valley Labor Service Inc	7361	277
Uvex Safety Manufacturing Ltd	3851	18	Valenti Mid South Management LLC	6794	9	Valley Lahvosh Baking Co	2051	120
Uvexs Inc	2893	41	Valenti Mid-Atlantic Management LLC	8741	63	Valley Lighting LLC	5063	376
uVuMobile Inc	7389	2493	Valentine Enterprises Inc	2023	16	Valley Lightsource Inc	5063	664
UW Marx Inc	1542	212	Valentine LLC	3829	233	Valley Litho Supply	3565	116
UW Trust Co	6091	23	Valentine Research Inc	3812	125	Valley Lumber and Building Supply Inc	5211	192
uWink Inc	5812	431	Valentine Transcribing Service	7338	42	Valley Machine Company Inc	5051	342
UXB International Inc	4953	93	Valentour English Bodnar and Howell	8712	254	Valley Machine Shop Inc	3599	953
UxPro Consulting Services Inc	4813	472	Valeo	2399	23	Valley Machine Tool Company Inc	3599	992
V And F Transformer Corp	3612	56	Valeo Radar Systems Inc	5731	37	Valley Machine Works Inc	3599	1225
V and H Electric Company Inc	1731	2259	Valerio Dewalt Train Associates Inc	8712	164	Valley Machining Co	3451	67
V and J Holding Companies Inc	5812	452	Valero Energy Corp	2911	3	Valley Manufactured Housing Inc	2451	23
V and L Tool Inc	3599	2429	Valerus Compression Services	5084	10	Valley Markets Inc	5411	150
V and M Corp	5093	114	Valet Parking Service	7299	1	Valley Mechanical Inc	1711	137
V and M Star LP	3317	36	Valex Corp	3494	26	Valley Metals LLC	3317	55
V and P Hydraulic Products LLC	3593	31	Valhalla Corp	4213	2099	Valley Mills Inc	2252	14
V and S Clark Substations LLC	3264	17	Valhi Inc	2816	1	Valley Mine Service Inc	3599	1017
V and S Midwest Carriers Corp	4213	812	Valiant Industries Inc	3568	66	Valley Mining Inc	1221	37
V and W Supply Company Inc	5074	68	Valiant Products Inc	3443	214	Valley National Bancorp	6712	57
V Brothers Machine Co	3599	1651	Valiant Yachts	5551	10	Valley National Bank (Wayne New	6712	69
V Communications Inc	7372	2070	Valianti ca Inc	7372	3234	Jersey)		
V Dolan Trucking Inc	4213	1425	Valid Data Inc	7372	1589	Valley National Gases Inc	5169	54
V E Enterprises Inc	3715	4	Valid Electric Corp	3634	37	Valley Network Solutions Inc	7373	385
V E Power Door Company Inc	3699	132	Validation Experts Inc	7389	1288	Valley Newspaper Inc	2711	654
V E Products Inc	3643	166	Valjean Corp	2844	160	Valley Packaging Indutries Inc	7389	1162
V F Grace Inc	5091	26	Valk Industries Inc	7389	1065	Valley Pallet Trucking Inc	4213	2335
V J Mattson Co	1741	12	Valk Manufacturing Co	3531	96	Valley Perforating Co	3599	23
V Maslov and Company Inc	3669	212	Valkyrie Broadcasting Inc	4832	182	Valley Plastics Company Inc	3089	1771
V Richard's Market Inc	5411	258	Valkyrie Company Inc	3172	12	Valley Power Inc	5063	205
V/S Networks Inc	3679	782	Vallco Fashion Park	6512	78	Valley Power Systems Inc	3561	32
V Santoni and Co	5181	86	Vallee Electrical Services Inc	1731	1049	Valley Precision Inc	3599	1083
V Sattui Winery	5921	10	Vallejo City Unified School District	8211	63	Valley Precision Metal Product	3444	232
V Soft Inc	8711	553	Vallejo Electric Inc	1731	40	Valley Precision Plastics Corp	3089	1802
V! Studios	2741	241	Vallen Corp	5047	67	Valley Precision Tool Inc	3678	52
V Tech Industrial Corp	5734	203	Valley Agricultural Software Inc	7372	1720	Valley Press Inc	2752	1496
V Van Dyke Inc	4213	1920	Valley Apparel LLC	2311	8	Valley Processing Inc	2033	51
V-1 Oil Co	4924	47	Valley Auto Parts Co	5013	390	Valley Products Co	2841	17
V2soft Inc	7371	480	Valley Bank and Trust	6712	652	Valley Proteins Inc	2048	8
V3 Printing Corp	2752	347	Valley Bank (Roanoke Virginia)	6021	143	Valley Queen Cheese Factory Inc	2022	36
Va Associates LLC	7373	1193	Valley Biomedical Products and	2835	66	Valley Republic Bank	6022	563
Va Hospital	8011	24	Services Inc			Valley Roller Company Inc	3069	129
Vaagen Brothers Lumber Inc	2421	55	Valley Building Supply Inc	3272	91	Valley Rubber LLC	3069	123
Vaagen Brothers Lumber Inc Ione Div	2421	37	Valley Bulk Inc	4213	1722	Valley Rural Electric Cooperative Inc	4911	456
VAALCO Energy Inc	1311	101	Valley Business Bank	6022	706	Valley Sales Corp	2752	260
VAALCO Energy USA Inc	1311	127	Valley Business Printers Inc	2752	201	Valley Satellite	5731	211
VAALCO Gabon Etame Inc	1311	102	Valley Cabinet Inc	2434	34	Valley Screen Process Company Inc	2759	145
Vaassen Inc	2759	114	Valley Cadillac Corp	5511	529	Valley Services Inc	7359	247
Vac Pac Inc	2673	70	Valley Caliche Products Inc	5032	57	Valley Spreader Inc	4213	1031
Vacation Express Inc	4725	33	Valley Casework Inc	2434	67	Valley State Bank	6022	514
Vacation Internationale Ltd	6531	349	Valley Cheese Inc	2022	83	Valley Stream Motors Inc	5511	900
Vacation Outlet	4724	95	Valley Circuits	3672	293	Valley Technologies Inc	3672	179
Vacationland Vendors Inc	7993	21	Valley Collection Service	7322	205	Valley Tool and Die Inc	3451	80
Vacava Inc	7371	483	Valley Commerce Bancorp	6712	545	Valley Tool and Die Stampings Inc	3469	330
Vaccaro's Inc	2051	276	Valley Communications Inc	1731	131	Valley Tool And Machine Company Inc	3599	997
Vaccon Company Inc	3563	54	Valley Community Bancshares Inc	6712	634	Valley Tool and ManufacturingCoInc	3599	954
Vac-Con Inc	3711	33	Valley Community Bank	6022	548	Valley Tool Inc	3089	1547
Vaco (Brentwood Tennessee)	7361	37	Valley Construction Co	1611	144	Valley Truck Parts and Service Inc	5013	305
Vacuflo Of Kentucky Inc	5064	196	Valley Controls Inc	3823	367	Valley Truck Parts Inc	5013	88
Vac-U-Max	3494	63	Valley Courier Newspaper	2711	665	Valley Trucking Company Inc	4213	824
Vacumet Corp (Franklin Mas-	3399	9	Valley Craft Products Inc	3537	26	Valley Us Inc	7379	622
sachusetts)			Valley Credit Union	6062	35	Valley View Building Services Inc	1542	278
Vacuum Barrier Corp	3559	130	Valley Crest Landscape Maintenance	0782	4	Valley View Industries HC Inc	3271	21
Vacuum Dealers Trade Association	2721	420	Valley Crest Tree Co	5193	14	Valley View Industries Inc	1422	41
Vacuum Furnace Systems Corp	3567	63	Valley Decorating Inc	3089	1652	Valley View Packing Company Inc	2034	6
Vacuum Instrument Corp	3823	69	Valley Dodge Inc (Van Nuys California)	5511	120	Valley Welders Supply Inc	5084	26
Vacuum Process Technology Inc	3231	32	Valley Electric Supply Corp	5063	203	Valley Wholesale Supply Corp	5023	75

Company Name	SIC	Rank
Varolii Corp	7372	1692
Varra Companies Inc	1442	68
Varrow Inc	7379	197
Varsity Brands Inc	3949	31
Varsity Clubs of America Inc	7011	223
Varsity Communications Inc	2721	398
Varsity Ford Lincoln Mercury Inc	5511	652
Varsity Logistics Inc	7372	3467
Varsity Spirit Corp	2389	12
Varsity Spirit Fashions and Supplies Inc	2389	8
Varta Batteries Inc	5063	147
Vartech Systems Inc	5045	514
Vartek Corp	3674	463
VARtek Services Inc	7379	419
Vas Engineering Inc	3679	400
Vasamed Inc	3841	320
Vasco Corp	7389	646
VASCO Data Security Inc	7372	1016
Vasco Data Security International Inc	7373	93
Vascular Associates Laboratory Inc	8734	133
Vascular Care International Inc	5047	248
Vascular Solutions Inc	3841	59
Vasira Inc	3661	225
Vasomedical Inc	3845	70
Vasque Outdoor Footwear Div	3143	2
Vasquez Group Inc	6531	445
Vassar College	8221	23
Vast Data Systems Inc	5734	300
Vast Resources Inc	5099	29
Va-Tran Systems Inc	3559	497
Vatterott Educational Centers Inc	8249	5
Vaughan Company Inc	3561	103
Vaughan Contractors Inc	4213	2973
Vaughan Electric Company Inc	1731	693
Vaughan Foods Inc	2099	42
Vaughan Printing Inc	2732	33
Vaughan Transport Inc	4213	1554
Vaughn Industries LLC	1731	65
Vaughn Manufacturing Company Inc	3544	187
Vaughn Manufacturing Corp	3639	14
Vault Communications Inc	7311	1016
Vaultcom Inc	7379	718
Vaultus Mobile Technologies Inc	7372	1253
Vaupell Inc	3543	1
Vaupell Midwest Molding and Tooling	3089	482
VayTek Inc	7372	3042
Vazzana Underground Construction Inc	1623	272
Vb Computer Consulting Inc	7379	1033
VB Hook and Company Inc	4213	1000
VB Ross Corp	3669	270
V-Blox Corp	3679	584
Vbnet Inc	4813	515
VBrick Systems Inc	3661	58
Vbs Inc	5046	142
VC P Inc	2752	1487
VCA Antech Inc	0742	1
VCA Tucson Inc	7011	148
Vcc LLC	1622	9
Vcc Of Lima Inc	5045	648
VCE Inc	7812	271
VCG Holding Corp	7999	72
VCI Entertainment	5099	15
Vci Group Inc	7334	21
Vcommerce Corp	7372	1308
Vcp International Inc	5064	89
Vcst Inc	8742	202
vCustomer Corp	7389	401
Vdi Communications Inc	1623	558
Vdl Inc	4813	360
VDP Inc	7372	4218
Veach Oil Co	5171	15
Vec Technology LLC	3089	755
Veca Electric Company Inc	1731	180
Vecellio and Grogan Inc	1611	3
Vecellio Contracting Corp	1611	26
Vecmar Corp	5045	594
Veco Printing Inc	2679	77
Vecta	2521	22
Vector Capital Group	6799	156
Vector Computer Systems Inc	7374	385
Vector Electric And Controls Inc	1731	228
Vector Electronics and Technology Inc	3672	327
Vector Engineering And Manufacturing Corp	3599	1781
Vector Fabrication Inc	3672	342
Vector Fields Inc	7372	1721
Vector Group Ltd	2111	8
Vector Internet Services Inc	4813	164
Vector Networks Inc	7372	1971
Vector Systems Inc	3625	125
Vector Technologies Ltd	3589	143
Vector Technology Inc	7373	1042
Vector Tool and Manufacturing Inc	3599	1386
Vector Wealth Management	6282	235
Vectordyne Inc	1731	2402
Vectorply Corp	2211	27
Vectors Inc	5049	105
Vectorsite	7371	1414
Vectra Bank	6022	283
Vectra Bank Colorado	6022	67
Vectra Fitness Inc	3949	102
Vectre Corp	4953	159
Vectren Corp	4932	5

Company Name	SIC	Rank
Vectren Utility Holdings Inc	4932	3
Vectron Inc	3599	350
Vectron International Inc	3679	223
VED Software Services Inc	7372	659
Veda System Solutions Corp	7371	1014
Vedder Price Kaufman and Kammholz	8111	309
Vedder Software Group	7372	4895
Vedicsoft Solutions Inc	7372	2231
Veeco Instruments Inc	3559	9
Veeco Metrology Group	3825	163
Veeco Services Inc	4213	2055
Veeder-Root Co	3569	11
VeenendaalCave Inc	7389	531
Veetronix Inc	3679	779
Vegas Golf Inc	5941	46
Vege - Kurl Inc	2844	126
Vegetable Juices Inc	7389	1003
Vehicle Lighting Solutions Inc	5063	844
Vehicle Monitor Corp	3714	376
Vehicle Research And Development Inc	8731	417
Vehicle Safety Manufacturing LLC	6512	45
VEIL Interactive Technologies	7371	516
Veit Cos	1795	5
Veitch Machine Company Inc	3599	2370
Veka Inc	3089	247
Vektek Inc	3545	66
Vektrex Electronic Systems Inc	7371	1186
Vektron Corp	3625	415
Vela Research LP	3577	311
Velan Valve Corp	3491	4
Veldheer Tulip Garden Inc	0181	19
Veldona USA Inc	8731	328
Vella Cheese Company Of California Inc	5451	5
Vellano Brothers Inc	5085	51
Velle and Associates Inc	5065	556
Vellumoid Inc	3053	77
Vellus Products Inc	2844	206
Velmex Inc	3545	162
Velo Corporation Of America	7389	1074
Velocenet Inc	4813	609
Velocitie Integration Inc	7379	1542
Velocity Express	4213	87
Velocity Express Corp	4513	6
Velocity Group LLC	7371	1039
Velocity Networks Inc	8999	142
Velocity Solutions Inc	8742	552
Velodyne Acoustics Inc	3651	83
Velos Inc	7372	797
Veloxion Inc	3599	1195
Velquest Corp	7373	546
Veltec Inc	3089	903
Veltek Associates Inc	2842	93
Velter Products Inc	3429	143
Veltri Electric Inc	1731	1746
Velux-America Inc	5039	26
Velvac Inc	3231	18
Velvet Hammer Music Group	7389	2277
Vemco Drafting Products Corp	3829	220
Venable LLP	8111	171
Venango Machine Company Inc	3069	208
Venango Training and Development Center	7349	351
Venator Holdings LLC	8742	579
Venchurs Inc	2671	24
Venco Manufacturing Inc	3714	349
Venda Ravioli Inc	2098	9
Vendavo Inc	7372	2778
Vendely Communications Inc	5045	399
Vendig Software Services Inc	7372	5086
Vendome Copper and Brass Works Inc	3556	88
Vendor Managed Solutions Inc	7389	1497
Vendormate Inc	7372	1372
Vendors Equipment Inc	5046	246
Vendura Industries Inc	3281	21
Veneer Products Acquisitions LLC	2436	17
Veneer Stone LP	3272	31
Vengroff Williams and Associates Inc	7322	21
Venice Amusement Corp	7996	27
Venice Baking Co	2051	201
Venice Trading Company Inc	5087	190
Venkel Corp	3571	52
Venoco Inc	1311	69
Venoscope LLC	3841	408
Vensai Technologies Inc	7379	637
Ventamatic Ltd	3564	44
Ventana Distributing Company Inc	5046	149
Ventana Health Services Inc	7379	477
Ventana Medical Systems Inc	3841	35
Ventana Research	8742	130
Ventana Systems Inc	7372	4340
Ventana USA	3089	310
Ventas Inc	6798	48
Ventcon Inc	3444	106
Ventech Engineers Inc	8711	400
Ventech Engineers International Corp	1629	32
Ventech Solutions Inc	7371	648
Ven-Tel Plastics Corp	3089	289
Ventera Corp	8748	169
Ventex Technology Corp	3612	90
Ventiv Health Inc	8742	99
Ventline	3564	48
Ventraq Inc	8999	41

Company Name	SIC	Rank
Ventrus Biosciences Inc	2834	489
Ventura Associates Inc	7389	533
Ventura Coastal LLC	2037	31
Ventura Educational Systems	7372	4053
Ventura Foods LLC	2079	3
Ventura Poole Inc	3563	61
Ventura Protection Inc	5063	864
Ventura Unified School District	8211	47
Venture Capital Fund of New England	6726	10
Venture Communications Inc	4813	508
Venture Direct Worldwide Inc	7331	57
Venture Electric Co	1731	1708
Venture Electronics International Inc	3672	381
Venture Encoding Service LLC	2759	71
Venture Express	4213	485
Venture Foods Inc	2099	362
Venture Group Enterprises Inc	4813	631
Venture Homes Inc	1521	50
Venture Industries Inc	2759	478
Venture Investors LLC	6799	158
Venture Lighting International	3641	4
Venture Logistics Inc	4213	1662
Venture Measurement Company LLC	3823	98
Venture Netcomm Inc	7373	598
Venture Plastics Inc	3089	410
Venture Precision Tool Inc	3089	1840
Venture Technology Groups	5023	125
Venture Travel LLC	4512	60
Venture Up Inc	7999	99
Venturedyne Ltd	3564	11
Ventyx	7372	119
Venue Management Services Inc	8748	135
Venus Controls Inc	3625	259
Venus Exploration Inc	1311	171
Venus Foods Inc	2011	160
Venus Fuel Sales Inc	5511	1113
Venus Wafers Inc	2052	74
Venustar Software and Engineering Inc	7372	3965
Veolia Environmental Serivces North America Corp	8999	10
Veolia Es Alaron LLC	1799	90
Veolia Transportation Inc	4111	16
VeraCentra	8748	465
Veraciti Inc	7379	772
Veramark Technologies Inc	3661	112
Veranda Preston Hollow	8361	177
Verari Systems Inc	5045	48
Veraxx Engineering Corp	7373	309
Vercom Software Inc	7373	811
Verdasys Inc	5045	178
Verde Valley Medical Center	8062	158
Verde Valley Newspapers Inc	2711	144
Verdi Devito Inc	7311	528
Verdiem Corp	5045	317
Verdigris Fire Protection District	7389	1928
Verdigris Valley Electric Cooperative Inc	4911	466
Verecloud Inc	7379	681
Verendrye Electric Cooperative Inc	4911	427
Verenium Corp	2869	39
VergeTech Inc	7372	2035
VerHalen Inc	5031	27
Verhoff Machine and Welding Inc	3599	135
Vericept Corp	3577	172
Vericomm	5044	148
Vericore LLC	7322	135
Veridiam Medical	3599	183
Veridian Credit Union	6062	6
Veridien Corp	2842	147
Veridyne Inc	7373	600
Verifacts Automotive LLC	7379	157
Verifi Inc	7374	104
Verifiber LLC	3661	184
Verific Design Automation Inc	7372	3291
Verifier Inc	5063	721
Verifine Dairy Products Corporation of Sheboygan Inc	2026	83
VeriFone Inc	3578	7
VeriFone Systems Inc	7372	45
Verilogix Inc	7372	4073
Verinform Systems Inc	7371	621
Verinon Technology Solutions Ltd	7379	314
Verint Systems Inc	7373	22
Verio Inc	7379	15
Veris Inc	3823	205
Veris Industries Inc	3674	276
Verisae Inc	8999	95
VeriSign Inc	7371	18
Verisilicon Inc	3674	322
Verisk Analytics Inc	7374	15
Verisurf Software Inc	7372	2656
Veritas Capital Fund LP	6799	282
Verite Inc	2741	160
Veritec Inc	3679	809
Veritec Technologies Inc	3569	5
VeriTest Inc	7379	218
Veritext/Florida Reporting Company LLC	7338	7
Veritools Inc	7372	2869
Veritude Inc	7363	128
Verity Credit Union	6061	74
Verity Instruments Inc	3825	115
VerityThree Inc	5045	352
Verizon Avenue Corp	4813	57

Company Name	SIC	Rank
Verizon Business	4813	3
Verizon Communications Inc	4813	2
Verizon Washington	4813	27
Verizon Wireless	4812	1
Ver-Mac Industries Inc	3599	993
Vermat Corp	3452	84
Vermeer Equipment Of Texas Inc	5082	35
Vermeer Manufacturing Company Inc	3531	13
Vermeer Mid Atlantic Inc	5082	215
Vermes Machine Company Inc	3599	1534
Vermette Machine Company Inc	3537	109
Vermillion Inc	8731	385
Vermont Aerospace Manufacturing Inc	3599	105
Vermont American Corp Multi-Metals Div	3356	38
Vermont Circuits Inc	3672	166
Vermont Composites Inc	3089	329
Vermont Country Store	5961	57
Vermont Creative Software Inc	7371	1718
Vermont Electric Cooperative Inc	4911	16
Vermont Flexible Tubing Inc	3599	2241
Vermont Gas Systems Inc	4923	29
Vermont Graphics Inc	2752	1598
Vermont Heating and Ventilating Company Inc	1711	127
Vermont Information Processing Inc	7371	503
Vermont Machine Tool Corp	3542	51
Vermont Media Corp	7311	62
Vermont Municipal Bond Bank	6211	381
Vermont Panurgy Corp	5734	274
Vermont Photonics Inc	3829	195
Vermont Precision Tools Inc	3545	45
Vermont Publishing Corp	2711	602
Vermont Ski Safety Equipment Inc	3949	174
Vermont Systems Inc	7372	1349
Vermont Teddy Bear Company Inc	3942	9
Vermont Transit Company Inc	4131	10
Vermont Ware Inc	3524	42
Vern Dale Products Inc	2023	24
Vernier Software and Technology	7372	804
Vernon Auto Parts Inc	3714	280
Vernon Co	5199	25
Vernon Milling Company Inc	4213	3130
Vernon Publications LLC	2721	456
Vernon Publishing Inc	2711	690
Vernon Telephone Co-Operatives Inc	4813	283
Vern's Electric Inc	1731	1998
Vern's Machine Company Inc	3541	176
Vero Group	6211	180
Vero International Inc	7373	51
Vero Machine Industries Inc	3599	1406
Vero Systems Inc	4899	45
Veronica Foods Co	5149	35
Veronis Suhler Stevenson Partners LLC	6722	110
Veros Software Inc	7372	3406
Verplank Trucking Inc	4213	1321
Verrex Corp	3663	61
Versa Capital Management	6799	189
Versa Capital Management Inc	6799	203
Versa Co	5065	42
Versa Handling Co	3535	61
Versa Press Inc	2732	19
Versa Products Company Inc	3492	19
Versaco Manufacturing Inc	3556	176
VersaForm Systems Corp	7372	3750
Versalift East Inc	3534	25
Versalign Inc	7373	359
Versalogic Corp	3571	88
Versa-Matic Tool Inc	3561	86
Versant Corp	7372	1407
Versant Inc	7311	641
Versar Inc	8711	109
Versata Inc	7372	552
Versata Software Inc	7372	201
Versa-Tags Inc	2752	444
Versatech Inc	3599	325
Versa-Tech Inc	3599	2438
Versatile Card Technology Inc	3089	379
Versatile Construction Inc	1623	285
Versatile Distributors Inc	3089	945
Versatile Engineering Corp	3599	938
Versatile Group Inc	7372	3203
Versatile Manufacturing Inc	3444	233
Versatile Mobile Systems Inc	5045	503
Versatile Mold and Design Inc	3544	522
Versatile Systems Inc	7373	156
Versatility Software Inc	7373	1129
Versatility Tool Works And Manufacturing Company Inc	3541	236
Versatool and Die Machining and Engineering Inc	3544	590
Versatube Corp	3465	70
Verschoor Meats Inc	2011	105
Versevo Inc	3544	209
Versitron Co	3663	58
Verso Paper Corp	2621	9
Verso Technologies Inc	7373	158
Versura Inc	7374	347
Versys Corp	7372	3635
Vertec Tool Inc	3599	656
Ver-Tech Inc	5084	757
Vertechs Associates Inc	7372	2731
Vertellus Specialties Inc	2865	5

Company Name	SIC	Rank
Vertex Chemical Corp	2819	25
Vertex Data Utility Services LLC	7389	195
Vertex Diamond Tool Co	3541	67
Vertex Energy Inc	4953	66
Vertex Engineering Services Inc	8711	191
Vertex Inc	7372	564
Vertex Pharmaceuticals Inc	2834	37
Vertex Solutions Inc	7373	288
Vertex Systems Corp	7371	1380
Vertex Trading Corp	5065	857
VertexRSI Inc	3663	421
Vertica Systems Inc	5045	149
Vertical Circuits Inc	3674	306
Vertical Communications Inc	7372	541
Vertical Computer Systems Inc	7372	2501
Vertical Inc	8732	85
Vertical Software Inc (Houston Texas)	7373	885
Vertical Software Inc (Peoria Illinois)	7372	4227
Vertical Solutions Inc	7372	4771
Vertical Systems International LLC	3535	216
Vertical Television Inc	4841	134
Vertical Turbine Specialists Inc	3561	114
Verticent Inc	7372	2182
Vertiflo Pump Company Inc	3594	32
Vertiglo	7371	469
Vertigo Software Inc	7371	968
Verti-Mark Group Inc	7311	790
Vertique Inc	5084	402
Vertis Communications	7311	19
Vertis Holdings Inc	7311	10
Vertis Inc	7372	71
Vertitron Midwest Inc	3674	430
VertMarkets Inc	7389	281
Vertox Co	3825	324
Vertro Inc	7389	415
Vertrue Inc	7389	53
Vertseek Inc	4813	255
Vertu Americas Inc	5065	489
VerusMed	7375	191
Vervelife	7389	673
Very Special Chocolats Inc	2066	18
Very Special Events Inc	7389	1441
Vesbridge Partners LLC	6799	182
Vescio Threading Co	3599	386
Vesco Inc	5075	106
Vesco Material Handling Equipment Inc	5084	368
Vesco Oil Corp	5172	63
Vesco Specialized Carriers LLC	4213	2686
Vest Inc	3317	49
Vesta Corp	7374	38
Vesta Intermediate Funding Inc	2869	40
Vesta Medical LLC	3841	284
Vesta-Camden Urban Renewal LLC	8748	239
Vestal Electronic Devices Inc	3679	784
Vestal Manufacturing Enterprises Inc	3441	76
Vestar Capital Partners LP	6211	322
Vestas Americas	3511	9
Vestcom International Inc	7389	199
Vestil Manufacturing Corp	3999	61
Vestin Group Inc	6162	126
Vestin Realty Mortgage I Inc	6798	204
Vestin Realty Mortgage II Inc	6798	193
Vestper Corp	2992	47
Vesture Corp	2399	15
Vesuvius Inc	5013	79
Vet Pharm Inc	2834	262
VETECH Software Services Inc	7372	3377
Veteran Corps of America	8748	140
Veteran Solutions Inc	7361	350
Veterans Distribution of Chicago	4215	12
Veterans Enterprise Technology Solutions Inc	8748	300
Veterans Of Foreign Wars National Home For Children	8361	163
Veterans Tech LLC	7371	1918
Veterinary Pet Insurance Co	6399	22
Veterinary Pharmaceuticals Inc	2834	231
Vetline Larson Labs Inc	5912	77
Vetoquinol USA Inc	2834	261
Vetra Systems Corp	3823	444
Vetronix Corp	3714	216
Vetter Electric Inc	1731	926
Vexcel Corp	7372	1018
Vexillum Inc	1731	215
VF Corp	2325	1
Vf Imagewear Inc (Martinsville Virginia)	2253	4
VF Jeanswear LP	2325	7
VF Playwear Inc	2361	2
Vf Sportswear Inc	2329	7
VFA Inc	7372	1039
VFL Technology Corp	4953	70
Vfp Inc	2452	16
VG Reed and Sons Inc	2752	229
Vgm Golf Inc	7389	935
VG's Food Center Inc	5411	164
Vgs Systems Engineering USA Inc	7373	472
Vgu Industries Inc	3993	136
VH Associates Inc	5153	89
VH Blackinton and Company Inc	2399	17
VHA Inc	8741	308
Vha Yu Technologies Corp	5045	173
Vhayu Technologies Corp	2741	92
Vhc Ltd	3559	253
Vhg Labs Inc	5049	108

Company Name	SIC	Rank
VHGI Holdings Inc	7373	1188
VHR Broadcasting of Springfield Inc	4833	137
Vhs Huron Valley-Sinai Hospital Inc	8062	94
Vhs Sinai-Grace Hospital Inc	8062	90
Vht Amplification Inc	3651	196
Vi Casa	8361	142
VI Laboratories Inc	7372	3057
VI Technology Inc	7372	3682
Via Cheese LLC	2022	80
Via Christi Health System Inc	8062	64
ViA Marketing Design	7389	95
Via Networks USA	7374	209
VIA Pharmaceuticals Inc	2836	102
Viacell International Inc	5065	946
Viacom Inc	4841	3
Viacom International Inc	4841	14
Viacom New Media (New York New York)	2741	45
Viacore Inc	7372	1458
Viacyte	8731	159
Viad Corp	7389	42
Viade Products Inc	3843	80
Viador Inc	7372	2588
Vialanguage Inc	7389	1944
ViaLogy Corp	7372	601
Viam Manufacturing Inc	2273	32
Viamedia LLC	7313	16
Viansa Winery and Tuscan Club	2084	23
ViaSat Inc	3663	13
Viaserv Inc	7372	1230
VIASYS Healthcare Inc	3841	21
Viasystems Group Inc	3672	498
Viatech Publishing Solutions Inc	2782	5
Viatech Systems Inc	7373	285
Viatical Settlements Inc	6311	267
Viatronix Inc	7371	1406
Vibco Inc	3531	113
Vibcon Corp	3559	534
Vibes Media	7372	942
Vibgyor Optical Systems Corp	3827	104
Vibgyor Optics Inc	5049	126
Vibra Screw Inc	3535	124
Vibrac Corp	3829	342
Vibracraft Inc	3569	218
Vibrant Technologies Inc	7373	633
Vibra-Pro Company Inc	3535	136
Vibration and Noise Engineering Corp	3625	260
Vibration Control Technologies LLC	3714	95
Vibro Dynamics Corp	3499	121
Vic Bailey Imports	5511	1224
Vic Canever Chevrolet Co	5511	598
VIC Hi-Tech Corp	3571	198
Vical Inc	2836	51
Vicam LP	2835	43
Vicart Precision Fabricators Inc	3444	218
Vicas Manufacturing Company Inc	3089	862
Viccaro Equipment Corp	5084	415
Viccs Inc	7373	284
Vicente Foods Inc	5411	239
Vi-Chem Corp	3087	3
Vici Metronics Inc	3823	311
Vickers Distribution and Transfer	4213	2865
Vickers Engineering Inc	3599	168
Vickrey Ovresat Awsumb Associates Inc	8712	54
Vicksburg Printing And Publishing Co	2711	463
Vicom Inc	2741	207
Vicom Systems Inc	3577	254
ViComp Management Inc	7372	4772
Vicon (Centennial Colorado)	7373	386
Vicon Industries Inc	3669	60
Vicor Corp	3679	56
Vicor Industries Inc	3674	415
VICORP Restaurants Inc	6794	20
Vicount Industries Inc	3544	229
VICR Securities Corp	3629	3
Victaulic Co	3494	11
Victor Envelope Manufacturing Corp	2759	67
Victor Graphics Inc	2731	131
Victor Insulators Inc	3264	12
Victor L Phillips Co	5082	36
Victor Martin Inc	2514	14
Victor Microwave Inc	3679	758
Victor O Schinnerer and Company Inc	6351	29
Victor Packing Inc	2034	25
Victor Printing Inc	2761	34
Victor Products Corp	5145	36
Victor-Balata Belting Co	3728	189
Victoria Advocate Publishing Co	2711	324
Victoria Air Conditioning Inc	1711	111
Victoria Electric Company Inc	1731	2264
Victoria Financial Corp	6331	329
Victoria Home For Retired Men And Women Inc	8361	114
Victoria Packing Corp	2099	64
Victoria Partners	7011	101
Victoria Skimboards	3949	172
Victoria's Candies Inc	2064	135
Victoria's Secret Direct LLC	5961	27
Victoria's Secret Stores LLC	5632	1
Victorinox Swiss Army Inc	5094	12
Victors Three-D Inc	3915	9
Victory America Inc	5063	979
Victory Box Corp	2653	128

Company Name	SIC	Rank
Victory Brewing Co	2082	69
Victory Foam Inc	5085	171
Victory Foods Inc	5149	178
Victory Industrial Products LLC	3621	66
Victory Industries Inc	3599	1445
Victory Land Group Inc	5021	111
Victory Layne Chevrolet Inc	5511	284
Victory Of West Virginia Inc	3532	6
Victory Sign Industries Ltd	3993	111
Victory Sound Communications Inc	5731	236
Victory State Bank	6022	615
Victory Studios	3695	44
Victory Tool Inc	3599	1755
Victory Tube Company Inc	5051	246
Victory White Metal Co	5085	106
VictorystoreCom Inc	2759	194
Victron Inc	3672	43
Vida Health Communications Inc	7812	244
Vid-Air Services Inc	7622	8
Vidal Partnership	7311	112
Vidalia Naval Stores Co	5211	27
Vidar Systems Corp	3577	261
Videk Inc	3827	76
Video Accessory Corp	5064	177
Video Artists International Inc	7812	288
Video Associates Labs Inc	3577	524
Video Automation Systems Inc	3663	411
Video Collage Inc	7372	4896
Video Communications Inc	7819	77
Video Control Systems Inc	3625	336
Video Depot Inc	5735	9
Video Display Corp	3679	116
Video Excellence	7812	187
Video I-D	3695	104
Video Learning Library LLC	7822	39
Video Masters Inc	5065	849
Video Max Inc	5731	118
Video Media Productions	7812	242
Video Monitoring Services of America LP	7819	30
Video Movie Magic	3695	93
Video Network Services Inc	3577	422
Video Placement Worldwide	7822	36
Video Post and Transfer Inc	7819	28
Video Products Inc	3577	459
Video Replay Inc	3695	71
Video Service Of America Inc	5065	738
Video Systems and Security Inc	5731	174
Video Tape Associates	7819	39
Video Tape Library Ltd	7336	180
Video Technics Inc	7812	134
Video Technology Services Inc	3651	181
Video Transfer Inc	3577	384
Video Walls USA Inc	7389	2518
Videocenters Inc	8748	455
Video-Codes Inc	3651	238
Videocom Satellite Associates Inc	4899	182
Videoconferencing Center	5731	163
Videoconferencing Systems Inc	3669	190
Vide-O-Go Inc/That's Infotainment!	7822	33
Videojet Technologies Inc	3577	14
Videomasters	7812	280
VideoPropulsion Inc	7373	841
Videotape Products Inc	5099	39
Videotex Systems Inc	7371	555
Videotronix Inc	7382	20
Videssence Inc	3646	103
Videx Inc	3577	355
Vidipax LLC	7371	517
Vidisolutions Inc	7371	1477
Vidon Plastics Inc	3089	973
Vidsys Inc	7371	191
Vidtech Audio Visual Inc	7359	246
Viecore Inc	7379	100
Vie-Del Co	2033	50
Viega LLC	5074	97
Vienna Beauty Products Co	2844	185
Viet Hai Ngoai-Television Corp	4833	236
Vieux Carre Creation Inc	5046	354
View by View Inc	7379	1463
VIEW Micro-Metrology	7372	2294
View Rite Manufacturing	2541	50
View Systems Inc	7389	2438
VIEW Video Inc	7822	30
ViewCastcom Inc	3663	102
Viewlocity Inc	7372	233
Viewpoint Bank	6035	48
Viewpoint Construction Software	7372	544
Viewpoint Corp	7372	1320
ViewPoint Financial Group	6712	154
Viewpointe Archive Services LLC	7374	118
ViewSonic Corp	3577	42
ViewstreamCom Inc	7379	1570
Vigicomm Inc	3663	368
Vigilant LLC	7371	297
Vigilant Services Corp	7371	670
Vigilant Video Inc	7382	147
Vigilante Electric Cooperative Inc	4911	569
Vigo Coal Operating Company Inc	1221	36
Vigo Importing Co	2099	111
Vigor Shipyards	3731	10
Vi-Jon Laboratories Inc	2834	59
Viking Acoustical Corp	2521	41
Viking Aluminum Products Inc	3442	35
Viking Automatic Sprinkler Company Inc	1711	104
Viking Collection Service Southwest Inc	7322	85
Viking Corp	3569	16
Viking Drill and Tool Inc	3545	44
Viking Electrical Contracting Incorporated LLC	1731	2272
Viking Energy Of Lincoln Inc	1731	2033
Viking Engineering and Development Inc	3553	21
Viking Explosives and Supply Inc	2892	4
Viking Industrial Center Inc	5085	323
Viking Industrial Corp	5051	408
Viking Industrial Electric Inc	5063	927
Viking Industrial Products	3621	137
Viking Insurance Co	6331	173
Viking Label And Packaging Inc	2672	71
Viking Land Transportation Systems	4213	1681
Viking Lifts Inc	3537	107
Viking Machine And Design Inc	3565	182
Viking Packaging Machinery Inc	3564	116
Viking Pump Inc	3561	44
Viking Range Corp	3631	1
Viking Recreational Vehicles LLC	3716	14
Viking Representatives Inc	5063	693
Viking RV LLC	3792	22
Viking Seafoods LLC	2092	18
Viking Sink Company LLC	3088	30
Viking Software	7372	5087
Viking Software Solutions	7372	2387
Viking Systems Inc	7389	905
Viking Technologies Ltd	3629	59
Viking Tension Products Corp	5085	311
Viking Tool and Engineering Inc	3544	274
Viking Tool and Gage Inc	3365	25
Viking Tool Co	3541	154
Viking Yacht Co	3732	16
Vikmere Software Inc	7372	1277
Vilden Associates Inc	7372	2619
Villa Enterprises Ltd	5812	97
Villa Lagoon Tile	5211	319
Villa Lighting Supply Company Inc	5063	118
Villa Ranch	5144	18
Village At Duxbury Homeowners Cooperative Corp	8322	158
Village At Waterman Lake Ltd	8361	63
Village Bank and Trust	6022	697
Village Bank and Trust Financial Corp	6022	267
Village Candle Inc	3999	100
Village Farms LP	0182	2
Village For Families and Children	8399	16
Village Ford Inc	5511	200
Village Homes of Colorado Inc	6552	125
Village Instant Printing Inc	2752	841
Village News Inc	2711	488
Village Of Northfield	7389	1616
Village Pantries LLC	5411	135
Village ProfileCom Inc	7313	15
Village Publishing Company Inc	2711	771
Village Shop Inc	2721	214
Village Software Inc (Boston Massachusetts)	7372	470
Village Square Realty Inc	6531	383
Village Super Market Inc	5411	72
VillageEDOCS Inc	7389	923
Villages of Lake Sumter Inc	1531	24
Villani and Sons Printers Inc	2752	583
Villarreal Electric Company Inc	5063	485
Villas of Hickory Hills Inc	7011	212
Vilter Manufacturing LLC	3585	59
Vinakom Inc	8748	312
Vinatekco Corp	3577	398
Vincent Commodities Corp	6221	13
Vincent Corp	3556	91
Vincent Fister Inc	4213	1257
Vincent Giordano Corp	2013	107
Vincent Graphics LLC	7331	117
Vincent Lighting Systems Co	5063	306
Vincent Piazza Jr and Sons Seafood Inc	5146	63
Vincent Porcaro Inc	5113	41
Vincent Printing Company Inc	2759	131
Vinci Stone Products Inc	1411	16
Vinculum Solutions Inc	7371	627
Vinculums	8748	256
Vindee Industries Inc	3498	77
Vindigo Inc	7372	1254
Vin-Dotco Inc	2842	75
Vineburg Machining Inc	3451	150
Vineland Syrup Inc	2087	67
Viner's Inc	4213	2736
Vineyard Gazette Inc	2711	713
Vingtech Corp	3827	115
Vinimaya Inc	7373	662
Vining-Sparks IBG LP	6211	204
Vinitech	7371	862
Vinland Corp	3699	280
VinSolutions LLC	7372	1374
Vinson and Elkins LLP	8111	600
Vinson Electric Supply Inc	4911	597
Vinson Guard Service Inc	7381	30
Vintage Air Inc	3585	131
Vintage at Plantation Bay Apartments LLC The	6513	28
Vintage Electric Inc	1731	1076
Vintage Health Resources Inc	8742	390
Vintage Performance LLC	3651	257
Vintage Pharmaceutical Inc	2834	85
Vin-Tex Sealers Inc	3089	1903
Vinton Arcelormittal Inc	3312	60
Vintwood International Ltd	5182	38
Vinyard Fruit And Vegetable Company Inc	5148	58
Vinyl Art Inc	3089	1157
Vinyl Pak Inc	3081	76
Vinyl Tech Window Systems Inc	3089	1559
Vinyl Technologies Inc	3599	1052
Vinyl Technology Inc	2671	33
Vinyl Window Technologies Inc	3089	416
Vinylast Inc	3089	1686
Vinylex Corp	3089	308
Vinylmax LLC	3089	14
Vinylplex Inc	3084	41
Vinyl-Pro Inc	3089	1548
Vinyltech Corp	3084	20
Vinyltech Inc	3544	517
Vinylume Products Inc	3089	832
Vinylux Products Inc	3089	812
Vinzant Inc	7372	2784
Viola Brothers Inc	5211	173
Violet Blue Networks	5065	425
VIP Foodservice	5148	19
VIP Holdings Inc	7349	332
VIP Honda	5511	1097
VIP Industries Inc	3679	659
VIP Nails and Tans Inc	5087	106
Vip Office Furniture And Supply Inc	5943	14
Vip Rubber Company Inc	3069	85
VIP Sales Company Inc	5142	18
VIP Samples Inc	2782	12
Vip Services Inc	8331	124
VIP Tooling Inc	3545	329
VIPdeskcom Inc	7319	94
Viper Logic Corp	3651	173
Viper Motorcycle Co	5012	93
Viper Networks Inc	7389	2015
Viper Northwest Inc	3599	683
Viper Technologies LLC	3841	156
Vipertech Corp	7373	958
VIPS Inc	7372	74
VIPS Industries Inc	5812	370
Vira Corp	3532	23
Vira Manufacturing Inc	2542	2
Viracon/Curvlite Inc	3231	4
Viracon Georgia Inc	3231	10
Viracon Inc	3231	11
Virco Manufacturing Corp	2531	6
Virgil and Brothers Inc	5211	301
Virgil Geary	5082	207
Virgil Walker Inc	3675	30
Virgin Media Inc	6719	20
Virgin Mobile USA Inc	4812	10
Virgin Records America Inc	3652	19
Virginia American Water Co	4941	61
Virginia Beach Beverages	5149	131
Virginia Beach Educational Broadcast Foundation Inc	4832	296
Virginia Beach Marble Co	5032	193
Virginia Broadcasting Corp	4833	164
Virginia Chaparral Inc	3312	25
Virginia Commerce Bancorp Inc	6712	165
Virginia Commerce Bank	6021	332
Virginia Commonwealth Trust Co	6712	290
Virginia Concrete Company Inc	3273	13
Virginia Contractors' Supply Inc	5032	20
Virginia Controls Inc	3679	643
Virginia Dare Extract Company Inc	2087	25
Virginia Diodes Inc	3679	672
Virginia Distributing Company Inc	5181	72
Virginia Electric and Power Co	4911	21
Virginia Electrical Services Inc	1731	1824
Virginia Escape Ltd	4724	128
Virginia Fdp Inc	3714	283
Virginia Financial Group Inc	6712	229
Virginia Gas Co	4923	27
Virginia Gazette Companies LLC	2711	91
Virginia Glass Products Corp	3211	13
Virginia Harbor Services Inc	3069	1
Virginia Hardwood Co	5031	58
Virginia Heritage Bank	6022	327
Virginia Home For Boys And Girls	8361	178
Virginia Homes Manufacturing Corp	2452	43
Virginia Industries Inc	3562	6
Virginia Interactive LLC	7374	297
Virginia Kik Inc	2842	4
Virginia Lab Supply Corp	5049	149
Virginia Logos LLC	3993	162
Virginia Marble Manufacturers Inc	3281	11
Virginia Mirror Company Inc	3231	39
Virginia Panel Corp	3678	19
Virginia Quilting Inc	2391	11
Virginia Radiology Associates Inc	8071	44
Virginia Semiconductor Inc	3339	20
Virginia Storage Services	4213	3078
Virginia Systems Software Services Inc	7372	4773

Company Name	SIC	Rank
Virginia Tech Corporate Research Center Inc	8733	5
Virginia Tech Intellectual Properties Inc	6794	147
Virginia Transformer Corp	3612	125
Virginia Vermiculite LLC	3295	17
Virginia West Educational Broadcasting	4833	155
Virginia West Electric Supply Co	5063	114
Virginia West Pipeline Inc	1629	107
Virgo Publishing LLC	2741	87
Virnetx Holding Corp	7371	1872
Viron International Corp	3564	57
ViroPharma Inc	8731	30
Virpie Inc	7361	130
Virtela Communications Inc	4899	71
Virtium Technology Inc	3674	254
Virtual Boardwalk	7372	2219
Virtual Care Provider Inc	7379	312
Virtual Chip Exchange Inc	7389	115
Virtual Clinic Inc	4813	554
Virtual Enterprises Inc	7373	67
Virtual Impact Productions Inc	7371	1836
Virtual Information Systems	7371	1098
Virtual Kreation Inc	7378	32
Virtual Medical International Inc	3999	218
Virtual Meeting Strategies Inc	8741	48
Virtual Office Inc (Burbank California)	7379	1175
Virtual Radiologic Corp	8099	37
Virtual Resource Management Corp	7363	190
Virtual Services Inc	7372	699
Virtual Supply Inc	5065	486
Virtual Technology Services LLC	7379	888
Virtual Training Company Inc	7372	4396
Virtual Vision Inc	3679	685
Virtual World Technologies	5734	312
Virtual-Agent Services	7389	662
Virtualosity Solutions LLC	7372	3086
VirtualScopics Inc	3841	173
Virtue Group	8744	41
Virtus Insight Money Market Fund	6722	19
Virtusa Corp	7371	56
Virtutech Inc	5045	37
ViryaNet Inc	7372	4163
ViryaNet Ltd	7372	1760
Visa Inc	7389	4
Visa USA Inc	7389	27
Visage Image Systems	7372	4967
Visage Mobile Inc	7389	747
Visalia Newspapers Inc	2711	253
Visalia Sales Yard Inc	7389	2110
Visant Corp	3911	1
Visara Inc	3577	217
Vischer Funeral Supplies Inc	5087	114
Visco Inc	3646	97
Vishay Americas Inc	3679	299
Vishay Dale Electronics Inc	3823	18
Vishay General Semiconductor Inc	3674	58
Vishay Intertechnology Inc	3829	3
Vishay Measurement Group Inc	3823	33
Vishay Precision Group	3596	28
Vishay Thin Film Inc	3679	188
Vishay Vitramon Inc	3675	1
Vishion Tool And Machine Co	3544	741
Vishnu Inc	1623	397
Visibility Factor Inc	8999	175
Visibility Inc	7372	760
Visible Productions	2741	151
Visible Systems Corp	7372	2359
Visible Technologies Inc	7371	539
Visiblenet Inc	8742	719
Visics Corp	5065	901
Visicu Inc	7379	223
Visidaq Solutions Inc	7372	2732
Visidyne Inc	8731	323
Vision Accomplished Inc	4899	223
Vision Communications Inc	1731	1653
Vision Controls and Automation	3625	360
Vision Craft Inc	3851	75
Vision Data Equipment Corp	7372	3121
Vision Electronics Inc	5065	441
Vision Ford Lincoln Mercury Inc	5511	977
Vision Gaming and Technology Inc	3999	178
Vision Graphics Inc	2754	8
Vision International Inc	2752	530
Vision Lighting Inc	3645	81
Vision Machine Works Inc	3599	2274
Vision Net Inc	4813	192
Vision Plastics Inc	3089	423
Vision Pro Inc	5065	998
Vision Products Inc	2431	54
Vision Quest Industries Inc	3842	83
Vision Research Corp	3841	380
Vision Sciences Research Corp	8733	38
Vision Software Technologies Inc	7372	2633
Vision Solutions Inc (Irvine California)	7372	999
Vision Systems Group Inc	7371	300
Vision Technical Molding LLC	3089	880
Vision Training Products Inc	3827	113
Vision Wise Inc	2741	189
Vision Woodworking Inc	2542	21
Visionael Corp	7372	2526
Visionair Inc	7372	1754
Visionaire Group	7311	764
Visionary Baths and More	5074	30
Visionary Consulting	7374	404

Company Name	SIC	Rank
Visionary Enterprises Inc	6531	142
Visionary Integration Professionals LLC	8742	166
Visionary Legal Technologies	7372	4341
Visionary Medical Systems Inc	7371	858
Visionary Services Inc	8999	64
Visionary Solutions Inc	7372	4445
Visionary Solutions LLC	8742	218
Visioncor Inc	7371	975
Visioneer Inc	7372	1491
Visionet Systems Inc	7372	2368
Visionia Ltd	7371	1268
VisionIT	7363	67
VisionPs LLC	2752	1361
VisionQuest National Ltd	8331	17
Vision's Edge Inc	7372	2190
Visions USA Inc	7311	14
Vision-Sciences Inc	3845	83
VisionShape Inc	3577	410
Visionspring Inc	5049	122
Visiontek Products LLC	3577	127
VisionTree Software Inc	7372	3369
Visiontron Corp	3669	218
Visionweb Holdings LLC	5048	15
Visiting Nurse and Homemaker Service Inc	8322	192
Visiting Nurse and Hospice Care Of South West CT	8082	61
Visiting Nurse Service Inc	8082	64
Visiting Nurses Association	8322	188
Visiting Nursing Association of Western New York Inc	8059	13
Visitor Center Of Lexington	7389	2447
Visi-Trak Worldwide LLC	3823	271
Visits Plus Inc	4725	54
Visix Inc	3577	411
Viskase Companies Inc	3089	62
Viskase Films Inc	3081	2
Visko Federal Systems Inc	7373	905
Viskon-Aire Corp	3564	96
VIST Financial Corp	6712	243
Vista Color Corp	2752	370
Vista Color Imaging Inc	7384	43
Vista Control Systems Inc	7372	4342
Vista Equity Partners	6719	160
Vista Ford	5511	304
Vista Gold Corp	1041	21
Vista Graphic Communications LLC	2671	62
Vista Group (Van Nuys California)	8743	156
Vista Holdings LLC	7999	27
Vista Imaging Inc	3577	592
Vista Imaging Services Inc	8071	40
Vista International Inc	3999	209
Vista Lexus	5511	760
Vista Manufacturing Co	3444	281
Vista Maria	8361	34
Vista Metals Inc	3545	58
Vista Paint Corp	5231	1
Vista Satellite Communications Inc	4813	355
Vista Solutions Inc	3585	187
Vista Training Inc	8748	400
VistaCare Inc	8399	6
Vistacraft Inc	2759	486
Vistage International Inc	8742	375
Vista-Graphics Inc	2741	228
Vistalab Technologies Inc	3821	52
Vista-Pro Automotive LLC	3643	3
Vi-Star Gear Company Inc	3462	69
Vistar/VSA Corp	5143	1
Visteon Corp	5013	3
Visto Corp	7372	1159
Vistronix Inc	7371	280
Visual Access Technology Inc	7372	4023
Visual Analytics Inc	7371	799
Visual Apex Inc	5045	382
Visual Art Graphic Services Inc	2752	1388
Visual Comfort Corporation Of America	3645	35
Visual Communications Inc (Tempe Arizona)	7812	281
Visual Controls/Champ Inc	2752	220
Visual Database Systems	7371	1348
Visual Engineering Inc	7372	4972
Visual Image Media Consultants Inc	7311	765
Visual Image Photography Inc	7335	3
Visual Impact Products LLC	5091	126
Visual Information Inc	7373	1008
Visual Information Systems	7377	21
Visual Matrix Corp	3861	82
Visual Mining Inc	7372	2402
Visual Network Design Inc	7372	1868
Visual Networks Systems	7372	690
Visual Odyssey Inc	3999	212
Visual One Systems	7372	283
Visual Products Inc	2782	66
Visual Records Consulting Inc	7379	1609
Visual Resources International Inc	7389	1829
Visual Solutions Distributing Inc	5065	239
Visual Solutions Inc	7371	812
Visual Sound Inc	5946	11
Visual Systems Inc	2752	302
Visual Systems Inc (San Luis Obispo California)	7372	3449
Visualant Inc	3829	321
Vita Buona Inc	3556	59
Vita Craft Corp	3914	7

Company Name	SIC	Rank
Vita Food Products Inc	2099	62
Vita Needle Co	5051	348
Vita Sea Products International Inc	2833	71
Vita-Charge	5045	1032
Vitachrome Graphics Group Inc	2759	257
Vitacostcom Inc	5961	63
Vital Communication Inc	5731	268
Vital Energy Inc	1731	2565
Vital Images Inc	7372	632
VITAL Inc (Plano Texas)	7372	3806
Vital Link Trucking Services	4212	80
Vital Network Services	7373	276
Vital Networks inc	7379	935
Vital Plastics Inc	3089	381
Vital Presentation Concepts Inc	3579	63
Vital Records Inc	7371	428
Vital Signs Inc	3841	39
VITAL Soft Inc	7372	3292
Vital Systems Corp	3663	132
Vitalect Inc	7373	760
Vitalink	7373	962
Vitality Beverages Inc	2037	11
Vitality Foodservice Inc	5149	56
Vitalix Inc	2048	80
Vitalsmarts LLC	8742	172
VitalWear Inc	3842	173
Vitamin Power Incororated	2023	35
Vitamin Shoppe Inc	5999	10
Vitaminerals Inc	2834	440
Vitamins Inc	2834	172
VitaminShoppecom	7375	160
VitaminSpice	3829	518
Vita-Pakt Citrus Products Co	2033	58
Vitaquest International LLC	2834	36
VITAS Healthcare Corp	8082	12
Vitatech International Inc	2834	205
Vitco Steel Supply Corp	5051	381
Vitec Electronics Corp	5065	638
Vitec LLC	3089	231
VITEC Multimedia USA	7372	4024
Vitec Solutions	7371	171
Vitek Industrial Video Products Inc	3861	104
Vitel Communications Inc	1731	1764
Vit-E-Men Company Inc	2048	82
Vitesse Semiconductor Corp	3674	98
VITETTA Architects and Engineers	8712	96
Vitols Tool and Machine Corp	3544	394
Vito's Express Inc	4213	3082
Vitran Express Inc	4213	75
Vitria Technology Inc	7372	678
Vitro America Inc	3231	3
Vitro Diagnostics Inc	2836	91
Vitro Seating Products	2599	30
Vitron Acquisition LLC	3812	83
Vitronics Soltec Corp	3567	26
Vitsur Industries Inc	3429	149
Vitta Corp	3443	226
Vittetoe Slat Flooring Inc	3523	197
Vittoria North America LLC	5091	137
Vitus Electric Supply Co	5063	1027
Viva Chevrolet	5511	714
Viva International Group	3851	116
Viva Vision	7371	922
Vivax Medical Corp	2599	41
Vivax Pro Painting	1721	10
Vivek Systems Inc	5045	969
Vivendi Universal Interactive Publishing	7372	214
Viverae	8742	437
Vivian-Nichols Associates Inc	7389	847
Vivid Impact Corp	2752	298
Vividata Inc	7372	4774
Vivo Inc (Pleasanton California)	7361	166
Vivolac Cultures Corp	2099	306
VIVUS Inc	2834	451
Viwinco Inc	3089	350
Viyya Technologies Inc	7372	1513
Viz Plastic Products Ltd	3089	1070
Vizdom Software Inc	7372	4775
Viziflex Seels Inc	3089	222
Vizio Inc	3651	7
VizSeek	7372	2697
VJ Associates Incorporated Of Suffolk	7389	1139
VJ Dolan and Company Inc	2851	140
VJ Provision Inc	2011	126
VJ Smith	7312	37
VJ Studio Inc	7379	404
Vl Electronics Inc	5065	158
VL Watkins Transport Co	4213	904
VLetter Inc	7372	3043
V-Link Solutions Inc	7379	817
Vlj Inc	3444	245
VLK Architects Inc	8712	148
VLP Holding Co	5082	60
VLPS Lighting Services International Inc	7359	41
Vls Construction Inc	1623	662
VLSI Research Inc	8731	353
VLSI Standards Inc	3829	77
Vlsip Technologies Inc	3674	203
VLSystems Inc	7372	2435
VM Leasing Inc	1731	2066
Vm Services Inc	7371	331
Vm Solutions Inc	3825	332
Vmc Technologies Inc	5084	920

Company Name	SIC	Rank
Vmg Engineering Inc	3599	2211
VMG Equity Partners	6799	82
Vmi Americas Inc	6719	181
VML Inc	7311	245
VMLogix Inc	7371	1116
VMP Inc	8059	10
VMR International Inc	2741	469
Vms Construction Co	1623	236
VMware Inc	7372	16
Vna Holding Inc	6159	64
Vna Home Health Services Inc	8741	229
VndirectNet LLC	4813	397
Vocalocity Inc	5045	64
VocalTec Communication Inc	3651	67
Vocation Plus Inc	8331	210
Vocational Biographies Inc	2731	377
Vocational Services Inc	2391	16
Vocational Visions	8331	121
Vocera Communications Inc	3669	78
Vocollect Inc	3571	26
Vocus Inc	7372	393
Vodium	7379	116
Voertman's	5942	16
Voestalpine Rotec Inc	5051	226
Vogel Communications Inc	2721	382
Vogel Group	7311	1038
Vogelin Optical Company Inc	3211	16
Vogform Tool and Die Company Inc	3545	413
Vogler Ford Lincoln Mercury	5511	460
Voice And Data Cable Specialists Inc	1731	2158
Voice Communications Corp	2711	707
Voice Data Solutions Inc	7379	1283
Voice Documentation Systems LLC	7372	928
Voice Genesis Inc	7389	1607
Voice Information Systems Inc	7372	3378
Voice Link Of Columbus Inc	7389	2151
Voice Of God Recording Inc	5961	155
Voice Poll Communications Inc	7371	1561
Voice Products LLC	3669	213
Voice Publishing Company Inc	2711	852
Voice Solutions Inc	3661	238
Voice Stream Wireless	4812	94
Voice Systems Engineering Inc	7371	689
Voiceboard Corp (Camarillo California)	3661	135
VoiceLog LLC	7389	698
Voice-Tech Inc	3661	166
Voicings Publications Inc	2721	217
Voigt and Schweitzer LLC	3479	16
Voip Carriers Inc	7374	159
Voip Group Inc	7371	1354
VolP Logic LLC	3669	90
VolP Supply LLC	5734	24
Vois Inc	7389	2524
Voisard Tool Service	3544	538
Voit Cos	6531	102
Voith Fabrics Florence Inc	2231	9
Voith Fabrics Waycross Sales Inc	2231	8
Voith Hydro Inc	3511	12
Voith Paper Inc	3554	2
Voith Paper Rolls West Inc	3599	680
Volant Aerospace LLC	4581	40
Volcano Communications Group	4813	287
Volcano Corp	3845	12
Volcano Telephone Company Inc	4813	368
Volchok Consulting Inc	7371	588
Volckening Inc	3565	110
Volcom Inc	2389	4
Volcot America Inc	6221	10
Volex Inc	3089	96
Volk Packaging Corp	3086	68
Volkoptical Inc	3851	60
Volkswagen of America Inc	5012	5
Volkswagen Santa Monica Inc	5511	647
Vollmer Associates LLP	8711	161
Vollmer Electric Company Inc	1731	1091
Vollmer Public Relations	8743	209
Vollrath Associates Inc	8743	204
Volpe Express Inc	4213	1317
Volt Delta Resources Inc	7371	356
Volt Directory Services	2731	44
Volt Industrial Plastics Inc	3089	1204
Volt Information Sciences Inc	7363	8
Volt Services Group Div	7363	2
Volt Telecommunications Group Inc	1731	24
Volta Corp	3643	113
Voltage Multipliers Inc	3674	244
Volterra Semiconductor Corp	3674	94
Voltronics Corp	3675	25
Volumatic Inc	3728	193
Volumecocomo Apparel Inc	2335	12
Voluntary Purchasing Group Inc	2875	13
Volunteer Circuits Inc	3672	386
Volunteer Electric Inc	1731	350
Volunteer Energy Coop	4911	219
Volunteer International Inc	5084	508
Volunteer Knit Apparel Inc	2253	12
Volunteer Trucking Inc	4213	1264
Volunteers Of America Colorado	8322	59
Volunteers Of America National Services	8051	25
Volusion Inc	5734	28
Volvo Cars of North America Inc	5012	16
Volvo Construction Equipment North America Inc	3531	39

Company Name	SIC	Rank
Volvo Finance North America Inc	6159	6
Volvo Motor Graders Inc	3462	66
Volvo of Westport	5511	864
Volvo Road Machinery Inc	3531	26
Volvo Trucks North America Inc	3537	3
Volz Electric Inc	1731	2286
Vomela Specialty Company Inc	2396	4
Von Briesen and Roper SC	8111	368
Von Gunten Engineering Software Inc	7372	4573
Von Maur Inc	5311	40
Von Schrader Co	3589	81
Von Stiehl Winery	2084	139
Von Sydow's Moving and Storage	4213	2763
Von Tobel Lumber and Home Center Inc	5211	204
Vonage Holdings Corp	4813	25
Voncannon Trucking Co	4213	2978
Vondrak Publishing Company Inc	2711	656
Vons Companies Inc	5411	33
Vontobel USA Inc	6722	282
Vontronics Inc	5734	358
Voorhees International Inc	1542	320
Voorwood Co	3553	38
Vopak North America Inc	4226	3
Vordermeier Management Co	6531	360
Voris Communication Company Inc	2752	1074
Vormittag Associates Inc	7372	1770
Vornado/Charles E Smith Realty	6512	23
Vornado Realty Trust	6798	12
Vorne Industries Inc	3823	206
Vortex Industries Inc	7699	7
Vortex Tool Company Inc	3545	137
Vorys Brothers Inc	5075	75
Vorys Sater Seymour and Pease LLP	8111	113
Vosges Chocolates Inc	2066	25
Voss Belting and Specialty Co	3052	23
Voss Engineering Inc	3463	20
Voss Equipment Inc	5084	55
Voss Industries Inc	3429	50
Voss Manufacturing Inc	3444	162
Voss Signs LLC	2759	494
Voss Village Cadillac	5511	948
Vostrom Holdings Inc	7371	1408
Votara Corp	7371	1234
Votaw Precision Technologies Inc	3545	32
Vouge Body Shop Inc	5621	36
Vovici Corp	7371	173
Vox Medica Inc	2752	37
VOX Network Solutions	7379	409
Vox Printing Inc	2752	383
Vox Technologies Corp	5045	354
Voxel Dot Net Inc	7374	221
Voxeo Corp	7389	96
Voxiva Inc	7373	768
Voxware Inc	7373	348
VOXX International	5065	23
Voyager Aluminum Inc	3353	13
Voyager Components Inc	5065	853
Voyager Computer Corp	3571	232
Voyager Oil and Gas Inc	1311	257
Voyager Pharmaceutical Corp	2834	276
Voyageur Asset Management Inc	6282	80
Voyetra Turtle Beach Inc	3577	144
Vpc Computers Inc	3571	180
VPE Public Relations Inc	8743	317
Vpg Integrated Media Inc	7371	786
Vpisystems Corp	7371	330
VPL Transport Inc	4213	449
Vpp Technologies Inc	7311	957
Vps Control Systems Inc	5085	463
VQS Enterprises Inc	2752	203
Vqs Inc	7372	4950
Vr Industries Inc	3599	630
VR Metro LLC	4813	725
Vrakas Blum and Co	8721	125
Vratsinas Construction Co	1542	49
VrboCom LLC	7311	831
VRC Insurance Systems	7372	2592
VRex Inc	3679	681
VRH Construction Corp	1541	123
Vrolyk and Company LLC	6211	235
VS Holdings Inc	5912	13
V-S Industries Inc	3451	28
V's Italiano Ristorante	5812	437
VS Software	7372	1590
VSA Partners Inc	7336	7
VSB Bancorp Inc	6022	497
Vs-Communication Inc	1731	2331
VSE Corp	8711	23
Vsecure Technoliges	7371	1355
VSM Abrasives Corp	3291	11
V-Soft Consulting Group Inc	7379	355
VSoft Corp	7371	183
Vss LLC	5045	404
Vssi Inc	5047	194
VST Consulting Inc	8999	134
VSV Group	3711	37
VT Hatler Marine	3441	130
VT Inc	5511	8
V-T Industries Inc	3089	273
Vt Leeboy Inc	3531	85
Vt Milcom Inc	8711	98
VTA Management Services Inc	8051	61
Vte Inc	3069	218

Company Name	SIC	Rank
Vtech Communications Inc	5065	10
V-Tech Services Inc	7349	81
V-Technologies LLC	7372	4574
V-Tek Inc	3699	113
Vtel Products Corp	3669	152
V-Tip Inc	8742	685
Vti-Valtronics Inc	3812	181
Vtl Amplifiers Inc	3651	152
VTLS Inc	7372	3439
VTN Victory Television Network	4833	229
Vtr Inc	7359	266
V-Tron Electronics Corp	3357	58
Vtv Varsity Television Inc	4833	243
Vu1 Corp	5063	1102
Vucovich Inc	5083	58
Vuemetrix	3825	298
Vulcan Company Inc	3531	145
Vulcan Corp	3069	60
Vulcan Corp Rubber Products Div	3131	1
Vulcan Electric Co	3255	12
Vulcan Energy Corp	5172	132
Vulcan Engineering Co	3541	141
Vulcan Global Manufacturing Solutions Inc	3463	17
Vulcan Inc	3469	21
Vulcan Industries Inc (Moody Alabama)	2542	44
Vulcan Information Packaging Inc	2782	11
Vulcan International Corp	3069	168
Vulcan Machine Inc	3599	802
Vulcan Machinery Corp	3559	347
Vulcan Materials Co	1429	1
Vulcan Radiator Corp	3634	17
Vulcan Tool Co	3544	905
Vulcan Tool Company Inc	3469	352
Vulcan Ventures Inc	6799	37
Vulcanium Metals Inc	5051	76
VulcanSoft Ltd	7372	5103
Vutec Corp	3861	37
Vvm Inc	7371	1361
VW Broaching Services	3599	2031
Vwm-Republic Inc	2816	14
VWR Funding Inc	5047	4
VWR International LLC	5047	3
VXI Corp	3661	69
Vycera Communications Inc	4813	139
Vycon Inc	4931	57
Vynckier Enclosure Systems Inc	3699	162
Vysym Corp	7373	714
VYTA Corp	3672	497
Vyteris Holdings Inc	2834	466
Vytex Corp	5031	174
Vytran Corp	3661	146
Vyyo Inc	3669	168
Vz Solutions Inc	5065	794
W A Baum Company Inc	3841	198
W A Benjamin Electric Co	3613	74
W A Kates Co	3823	253
W and A Distribution Services	4213	1604
W and C Printing Company Inc	2752	1133
W and G Flavors Inc	2034	38
W and G Machine Works Inc	3541	145
W and H Systems Inc	3535	19
W and J Schafer Enterprises Inc	7349	157
W and K Express Inc	4213	1291
W and K Steel LLC	3441	222
W and M Welding Inc	7692	35
W and S Trucking Inc	4213	2227
W and T Offshore Inc	1382	10
W and W Fiberglass Tank Co	3089	1043
W and W Manufacturing Company Inc	3621	133
W and W Specialities Inc	2675	26
W Atlee Burpee Co	0181	6
W B Porter and Co	5046	285
W B Rogers Printing Co	2711	889
W B Young Company Inc	5083	115
W Bradley Electric Inc	7373	113
W C Laikam Co	3663	359
W C Machine and Tool Inc	3599	1067
W Capital Partners	6799	83
W Colston Leigh Inc	7929	10
W D Lee and Co	3599	2176
W D Machinery Company Inc	5084	542
W D Wright Contracting Inc	1623	310
W David Scott Inc	7372	3636
W E Neal Slate Co	1799	130
W E Plemons Machinery Services Inc	3565	123
W Flying Plastics Inc	3084	16
W G Benjey Inc	3559	285
W G Holt Inc	3674	228
W H Bagshaw Company Inc	3965	23
W H Basnight And Company Inc	5039	38
W Hall Ford Co	3589	71
W Haut Specialty Company Inc	3599	1887
W Holding Company Inc	6712	52
W I Clark Co	5082	102
W J Whatley Inc	3648	24
W K Hillquist Inc	3089	1050
W K Jennings Electric Company Inc	1731	354
W Kintz Plastics Inc	3089	582
W Kost Inc	2439	44
W Kost Manufacturing Company Inc	2439	15
W - L Construction and Paving Inc	1611	118
W L Doffing Co	3599	376
W L Fuller Inc	3545	330

Company Name	SIC	Rank
W L Hall Co	5031	130
W L Rubottom Co	2434	72
W L Streich Equipment Company Inc	5046	85
W L Walker Company Inc	5084	591
W Lee Flowers and Company Inc	5141	157
W M Lyles Co	1623	24
W M Plastics Inc	3089	617
W Meyer William And Sons Inc	3535	57
W N L Inc	5064	126
W P Law Inc	5083	91
W Peter Ronson Jr and Sons Inc	4213	3066
W Plastics Inc	3081	143
W R Cobb Co	3915	4
W R Vermillion Company Inc	2499	23
W Ray Wallace and Associates	7389	1428
W/S Packaging Group Inc	2679	6
W Schmidt Karl and Associates Inc	3559	331
W Seitchik and Sons Inc	2311	31
W Silver Inc	3312	81
W Silver Recycling Inc	5093	66
W Smith Cartage Company Inc	4213	1614
W Strahl's Software Consulting Corp	7372	5153
W Thomas Company Inc	2325	14
W W Norton and Company Inc	2731	59
W W Payton Corp	1623	117
W - W Trailer Manufacturers Inc	3799	14
W Walsh Company Inc	1623	304
W Y Shugart and Sons Inc	2252	19
WA Butler Co	5122	9
WA Chester LLC	1731	779
WA Cleary Corp	2075	10
WA Dehart Inc	2064	73
WA Hammond Drierite Company Ltd	2879	39
WA Klinger Inc	1541	45
WA Rogers Software Engineering	7379	1001
WA Roosevelt Co	5078	8
WA Whitney Co	3542	11
WA Wilde Co	8742	176
WA Wilson Glass Inc	5039	7
Waat Media Wireless Entertainment	4813	100
Waatti and Sons Electric Co	1731	2381
Wabash Area Vocational Enterprises Inc	8331	225
Wabash Asphalt Company Inc	2951	38
Wabash Instrument Corp	3821	72
Wabash Metal Products Inc	3542	24
Wabash National Corp	3715	2
Wabash Power Equipment Co	5063	246
Wabash Trailer Sales LLC	5012	198
Wabash Transformer Inc	3612	111
Wabash Valley Services Co	5999	38
WABCO Holdings Inc	3711	12
Wabel Tool Co	3599	692
Waber Tool and Engineering Company Inc	3541	221
Waccamaw Bankshares Inc	6022	275
Waccamaw Transport Inc	4213	2402
Wachovia Corp	6712	3
Wachovia Insurance	6411	224
Wachovia Securities Inc	6211	103
Wachtel and Company Inc	6211	402
Wachtell Lipton Rosen and Katz	8111	209
Wachter Inc	1731	36
Wachusett Programming	7371	1352
Wackenhut Corp	7381	2
Wackenhut Services Inc	7381	84
Wacker Chemical Corp	5169	10
Wacker Neuson Corp	3531	25
Waco Boom Company Ltd	3089	1568
Waco Independent School District	8211	28
Waco Meat Service Inc	5147	20
Waco Oil and Gas Company Inc	1311	225
Waco Scaffoldng	5541	60
Wacom Technology Corp	5045	40
Waconia Manufacturing Inc	3535	97
Wacor Electronic Systems Inc	1731	1734
Wacosa	8322	144
Wadal Plastics Inc	3089	967
Waddell and Reed Financial Inc	6211	66
Waddell Smith Magoon and Freeman	8721	165
Waddell Transfer Inc	4213	1443
Waddington North America Inc	3086	73
Wade Agricultural Products Inc	1422	44
Wade Construction	1541	229
Wade Electric Company Inc	1731	1001
Wade Electric Inc	1731	234
Wade Ford Inc	5511	272
Wade Inc	5083	67
Wade Sand and Gravel Company Inc	1411	12
Wadeken Industries Inc	0254	5
Wades Dairy Inc	5143	39
Wade-Trim	8711	227
Wadler Manufacturing Company Inc	3568	73
Wadsworth and Associates Inc	5075	97
Wadsworth Control Systems Inc	3822	63
Wadsworth-Phillips Contractors Inc	1794	35
Wafer Process Systems Inc	3559	525
Wafer Reclaim Services LLC	3674	262
Wafer Works Corp	5065	648
Wafer World Inc	3674	434
Wafertech LLC	3674	92
Waffle House Inc	5812	112
Waffle-Crete International Inc	1791	23
Wafl Wyus Broadcasting Inc	4832	233
Wag Corp	3585	252
Wagamon Brothers Inc	7538	37
Wagers Inc	2064	100
Wageworks Inc	7389	402
Waggoner Edstrom Worldwide Inc	8743	15
Waggoner Frutiger and Daub	8721	460
Waggoner Manufacturing Company Inc	7692	51
Waggoners Trucking	4213	46
Wagman Metal Products Inc	3531	188
Wagner and Brown Ltd	1311	123
Wagner and Sons Machine Shop Inc	3599	2476
Wagner Die Supply	3544	231
Wagner Electric And Construction LLC	1731	1861
Wagner Electric Company Inc	1731	643
Wagner Electric Of Fort Wayne Inc	5063	734
Wagner Electronic Products Inc	3823	235
Wagner Machine Inc	3599	1068
Wagner Moving and Storage Inc	4213	973
Wagner Oil Co	1311	148
Wagner Printing Co	2789	65
Wagner Spray Tech Corp	3563	14
Wagner Supply Company Inc	5087	56
Wagner Vineyards and Brewing Co	2084	97
Wago Corp	5063	215
Wagstaff Inc	3559	37
Wahkiakum West Telephone Inc	4813	504
Wahl Clipper Corp	3999	27
Wahlco Inc	3564	45
Wahlcometroflex Inc	3441	157
Wahlstrom Group LLC	7311	89
Wahltek Inc	5046	162
Wailea Golf LLC	7011	156
Wailuku Water Company LLC	0173	2
Waimea Plantation Cottages	7011	171
Wain Industries	3679	780
Waiters on Wheels Inc	5963	21
Wake Stone Corp	1423	1
Wakefern Food Corp	5141	1
Wakefield Item Co	2711	619
Wakefield Pork Inc	0213	15
Wakefield Thermal Solutions Inc	2899	9
Wakley and Roberton Inc	6282	612
Wal Greens	7378	86
Wal Inc	5013	104
Walbon and Company Inc	4213	969
Walbridge Aldinger Co	1541	4
Walbro Corp	3592	2
Walco Electric Co	7629	12
Walco Linck Co	2879	51
WALCO Tool and Engineering	7692	8
Walco Tool and Engineering Corp	3599	254
Wal-Con Construction Co	1623	554
Wald Relocation Services Ltd	4214	19
Waldemar S Nelson And Company Inc	8712	42
Walden Energy LLC	4924	70
Walden Farms Inc	2035	53
Walden Federal Savings and Loan Assoc	6035	220
Walden Lang In-Pak Service	2782	67
Walden Structures Inc	2452	13
Walden's Division	3599	157
Waldinger Corp	1711	19
Waldman Inc	8111	539
Waldner Business Environment	5021	3
Waldo Brothers Co	5039	24
Waldom Electronics Corp	5065	198
Waldorf Endoscopy ASC LLC	8011	116
Walerko Tool And Engineering Corp	3599	819
Wales Industrial Service Inc	7353	18
Walex Products Company Inc	2842	134
Walgreen Arizona Drug Co	5122	133
Walgreen Co	5912	2
Walgreens Infusion Services Inc	8082	21
Walker 360 Inc	7311	827
Walker and Associates Inc	5063	65
Walker and Associates Inc (Memphis Tennessee)	7311	427
Walker and Co (Winter Park Florida)	1542	185
Walker and Dunlop Inc	6163	11
Walker and Zanger Inc	5032	6
Walker Automotive	5511	328
Walker B-C Inc	1771	36
Walker Brothers Inc	5999	225
Walker Brothers Machinery Moving Inc	7389	1286
Walker Business Machines LLC	2759	564
Walker Communications Inc	2741	355
Walker Component Group	5065	224
Walker Corp	3469	69
Walker Die Casting Inc	3363	13
Walker Edison Furniture Company LLC	5021	59
Walker Electric Company Inc	1731	892
Walker Electric Inc	1731	1626
Walker Equipment Corp	3661	110
Walker Foil Stamping and Embossing Inc	2759	351
Walker Foods Inc	2099	188
Walker Ford Company Inc	5511	201
Walker Forge Inc	3462	5
Walker Group Inc	7389	1213
Walker Information Inc	8732	71
Walker International Transportation LLC	4731	18
Walker Manufacturing Co (Fort Collins Colorado)	3524	13
Walker Meats Corp	5147	99
Walker Power Systems Inc	3621	98
Walker Products	3592	7
Walker Racing Inc	7948	33
Walker Systems Support Inc	7379	609
Walker Tool and Die Inc	3544	45
Walker Tool and Machine Co	3544	870
Walker Utilities Inc	1623	336
WalkerGroup/CNI	8712	216
Walker's Food Products Co	2099	289
Walkerton Tool and Die Inc	2759	374
Walking Company Holdings Inc	5699	7
Walklett Group Inc	7371	667
Walkmed Infusion LLC	3841	345
Wall Colmonoy Corp	3398	1
Wall Drug Store Inc	5912	41
Wall Rope/Yale Technology	2298	10
Wall Street Business Products Inc	2752	1411
Wall Street Deli Inc	5812	288
Wall Street Group Inc	2759	183
Wall Street Group Inc (New York New York)	8743	102
Wall Street Mission	8331	66
Wall Street Reporter Magazine Inc	2721	288
Wall Street Software	7372	2208
Wall Street Strategies Inc	6282	170
Wall Street Transcript Corp	2721	311
Walla Walla Farmers Co-op Inc	5541	38
Wallace and Associates Inc	8721	448
Wallace and Owens Store Inc	5411	224
Wallace Buick Jeep	5511	786
Wallace Carlson Co	2752	658
Wallace Construction Inc	1611	250
Wallace County Cooperative Equity Exchange	4221	8
Wallace Electrical Incorporated Tommy	1731	588
Wallace Electronics Inc	3679	77
Wallace Graphics Inc	2759	226
Wallace Hardware Co	5072	17
Wallace Supply Co	5074	108
Wallace Supply Company Inc	5072	168
Wallace Theater Holdings Inc	7832	14
Wallace Transport Inc	4213	2252
Wallace Transportation Inc	4213	2410
Wallace Welch and Willingham Inc	6399	12
Wallach Surgical Devices Inc	3841	233
Walle Corp	2759	48
Waller Brothers Stone Company Inc	3281	26
Waller Business Forms Inc	5112	96
Waller Truck Company Inc	4213	598
Wallis Oil Co	5131	1
Wallner Tooling/Expac Inc	3542	27
Wallover Enterprises Inc	2992	26
Walls Printing Company Inc	2752	477
Wallside Inc	1751	17
Wall-Ties and Forms Inc	5082	79
Walluski Western Ltd	3523	252
Wally McCarthy's Cadillac Inc	5511	841
Walman Optical Co	5048	2
Wal-Mart Stores Inc	5331	1
Wal-Martcom USA LLC	5961	49
Walnut Circle Press Inc	2752	579
Walnut Creek Heartscan LLC	8071	60
Walnut Street Securities Inc	6211	189
Walpole Feed And Supply Co	5999	257
Walpole Inc	4213	732
Walpole Leasing Inc	4213	626
Walpole Woodworkers Inc	2499	18
Walsh Construction	1541	32
Walsh Electric Company Inc	1731	385
Walsh Electrical Contracting Inc	1731	478
Walsh Group Ltd	1542	10
Walsh Manning Corp	6531	143
Walsh Manufacturing Corp	3564	147
Walsmith Productions	7812	253
Walsworth Franklin and Bevins and McCall LLP	8111	286
Walt A O'brien	3679	389
Walt and Co	8743	89
Walt Disney Co	7812	2
Walt Disney Parks and Resorts	7996	3
Walt Disney Publications Inc	2731	81
Walt Disney Records Direct	7812	40
Walt Disney World Co	7996	4
Walt Sweeney Automotive Inc	5511	381
Waltco Lift Corp	3537	37
Walter A Wood Supply Company Inc	5085	114
Walter Associates Inc	7379	628
Walter C Brooks Company Inc	3621	113
Walter Craig Inc	5941	49
Walter Dorwin Teague Inc	8711	385
Walter Drake Inc	3089	1314
Walter E Smithe Furniture Inc	2511	12
Walter Energy Inc	3312	12
Walter Flagstone Inc	4213	2070
Walter Foster Publishing Inc	2731	179
Walter G Anderson Inc	2631	15
Walter G Legge Company Inc	2842	165
Walter Garson Jr and Associates Inc	7331	219
Walter H Hopkins Company Inc	5021	103
Walter Haas Graphics Inc	2759	495
Walter J Sheets and Son Inc	4213	2182
Walter Kidde Portable Equipment Inc	3999	34
Walter Lasley and Sons Inc	0211	10

Company Name	SIC	Rank
Walter Lewis and Son Inc	3599	2287
Walter Lorenz Surgical Inc	3841	134
Walter Machine Company Inc	3566	35
Walter Meier Inc	3423	24
Walter Oil and Gas Corp	1382	44
Walter P Dolle Insurance Agency Inc	6411	166
Walter R Earle Corp	2951	44
Walter T Kelley Company LLC	2499	47
Walter Toebe Construction	1611	108
Walters Electric Inc	1731	1680
Walters Metal Fabrication Inc	3441	129
Walter's Precision Service Inc	3545	248
Walters Tire Service Inc	5014	53
Waltex Inc	3548	60
Waltham Committee Inc	8331	69
Walther Pilot North America LLC	5084	945
Walton Feed Inc	5149	176
Walton Hauling and Warehouse Corp	4213	995
Walton Tribune	2711	839
Walton-Stout Inc	3559	152
Walt's Drive-A-Way Service Inc	4213	898
Walt's Radiator and Muffler Inc	7539	1
Waltz Brothers Inc	3556	99
Walz Group Inc	7375	104
Walz Tetrick Advertising Inc	7311	829
Walzcraft Industries Inc	2434	30
Wal-Zon Transfer Inc	4213	1791
WAM U/Rehm Show	4832	101
WAMC	4832	15
Wamco Electric Inc	1731	2007
Wamego Telephone Company Inc	4813	277
Wampler's Farm Sausage Company Inc	2011	123
Wampole Laboratories LLC	3841	13
Wand Corp	3699	94
Wand Partners LP	6799	313
Wand Special Equipment and Design Company Inc	3549	49
Wandel Press	2759	375
Wandering WiFi LLC	5045	230
Wang Electric Inc	1731	927
Wang Jing	8733	4
Wanger Asset Management	6282	560
Wangerin Trucking Company Inc	4213	2635
Wangs Alliance Corp	5063	285
Wanke Cascade	5023	32
Wanko Electric Inc	1731	951
Wannemacher Enterprises Inc	4213	843
Wanner Engineering Inc	3561	99
Want Ads Of Fort Worth Inc	2741	363
Want Ads Of Omaha Inc	2711	603
Want Ads Of Pensacola Inc	7319	119
Wantage Avenue Holding Company Inc	6331	43
Wantagh Seaford Police Boys Club	8322	183
Wappingers Falls Shopper Inc	2711	596
Wappoo Wood Products Inc	5031	443
Wapsie Produce Inc	2015	57
War Eagle Mill Inc	2041	66
Warburg Pincus Emerging Growth Fund	6722	52
Warburg Pincus LLC	6799	41
Warco Manufacturing Company Inc	3612	92
Ward and Jacobs Inc	5063	839
Ward Electric Inc	1731	2093
Ward/Hall Associates AIA PLC	8712	314
Ward Leonard Electric Company Inc	3621	69
Ward Manufacturing LLC	3321	14
Ward Mclaughlin and Co	3544	615
Ward Media Inc	7311	574
Ward North Center Inc	8351	9
Ward Petroleum Corp	1311	94
Ward Process Inc	3086	45
Ward Systems Group Inc	7372	4343
Ward Technologies Inc	3559	356
Ward Trucking Corp	4213	274
Ward-Henshaw Construction Company Inc	1623	160
Ward-Kraft Inc	2761	22
Ward's Cabinetry Inc	2499	52
Ward's Marine Electric Inc	1731	346
Ward's Systems Inc	5943	42
Ware Inc	3585	47
Ware Malcomb	8712	140
Warehouse Demo Services Inc	7389	186
Warehouse One Inc	5084	417
Warehouse Optimization LLC	7372	3966
Wareing Athon and Co	3272	72
Warfel Construction Co	1542	313
Warfield Electric Company Inc	7694	11
Waring Products Inc	3552	57
Warinner Gesinger and Associates LLC	8721	211
Warkentine Inc	5045	511
Warlick Paint Company Inc	2851	153
Warm Haven Enterprises	8748	446
Warm Springs Forest Products Industries	2421	38
Warm Thoughts Communications Inc	8742	628
Warman-Lowe and Associates Inc	7322	202
Warmington Group	1521	10
Warmka Transport Inc	4213	2268
Warnaco Group Inc	2341	1
Warnaco Inc	2329	4
Warneke Paper Box Co	2657	40
Warner Brothers	7812	4

Company Name	SIC	Rank
Warner Brothers Records Inc	6794	62
Warner Electric	3621	12
Warner Enterprises Inc	5063	165
Warner Fertilizer Company Inc	5191	81
Warner Instruments	3823	453
Warner Instruments LLC	3826	69
Warner Jewelry Case Co	3172	10
Warner Manufacturing Co	3423	17
Warner Music Group Corp	7929	1
Warner Offset Inc	2752	1279
Warner Power LLC	8748	141
Warner Press Inc	2731	194
Warner Robins Supply Company Inc	5211	123
Warner Smith and Harris PLC	8111	480
Warner Vineyards Inc	2084	127
Warner-Elektra-Atlantic Corp	5099	1
Warners Moving and Storage Inc	4213	2274
Warning Lites Incorporated Of Colorado	8748	290
Warnock Automotive Group Inc	5511	145
Warnock Food Products Inc	2096	32
Warp 9 Inc	5999	308
Warrantech Automotive Inc	7389	314
Warrantech Corp	7389	208
Warrantech Direct Inc	7389	179
Warranty Direct Inc	6411	88
Warrco Inc	1623	320
Warrell Corp	2064	10
Warren and Baerg Manufacturing Inc	3523	201
Warren Associates Incorporated Of Colorado	8721	486
Warren Broach and Machine Corp	3545	274
Warren C Sauers Company Inc	4213	1588
Warren Cheese Plant Inc	2022	70
Warren Communications Inc	4813	681
Warren Computer Center	7372	3067
Warren Distribution Inc	2992	2
Warren E and P Inc	5172	146
Warren Electric Cooperative Inc	4911	539
Warren Electric Supply Inc	5063	332
Warren Elevator Corp	7699	188
Warren Equipment Co	5082	38
Warren Equities Inc	5171	1
Warren Fabricating Corp	3441	31
Warren Fire Equipment Inc	5999	212
Warren Industries Inc	3829	271
Warren Manufacturing Inc	3715	41
Warren Miller Entertainment	7812	120
Warren Publishing Inc	2731	122
Warren Resources Inc	1382	38
Warren Rupp Inc	3561	69
Warren Rural Electric Cooperative Corp	4911	292
Warren Technology Inc	3585	82
Warren Transport Inc	4213	294
Warren Trask Co	5031	183
Warren Trucking Company Inc	4213	1060
Warren-Forthought Inc	7372	2792
Warrior and Gulf Navigation LLC	4449	22
Warrior Custom Golf Inc	5091	32
Warrior Group Inc	1542	242
Warrior Manufacturing LLC	3523	185
Warsaw Chemical Company Inc	5169	94
Warsaw Coil Company Inc	3677	23
Warsaw Foundry Company Inc	3321	59
Warshaw Inc	5063	689
Warsteiner Importers Agency Inc	5181	92
Wartburg Tool and Die Inc	3599	1967
Wartian Lock Co	3429	132
Wartrom Machine Systems Inc	3569	163
Wartsila North America Inc	5084	42
Warwick Communications Inc	7359	130
Warwick Group Inc	6211	368
Warwick Hanger Company Inc	5074	210
Warwick Ice Cream Co	2024	70
Warwick Machine and Tool Company Inc	3599	1746
Warwick Plumbing and Heating Corp	1711	28
Warwick Public Schools	8211	33
Warwick Publishing Co	2752	323
Warwick Valley Telephone Co	4813	175
Warwood Tool Co	3546	46
Warzyn Sales Inc	5049	162
Wasa Electrical Service Inc	1731	54
Wasabi Inc	7374	321
Wasatch Computer Technology Inc	7336	46
Wasatch Metal Recycling	4953	157
Wasco Hardfacing Co	3523	118
Wasco Inc	1741	8
Wasco Products Inc	3441	121
Washburn Ellingwood Sheeler Thaisz and Pinnsley CPA's PC	8721	156
Washburn's Dairy Inc	2024	52
Washers Inc	3452	59
Washex Inc	3552	6
Washington Agricultural Development Inc	2011	46
Washington Alarm Inc	7382	86
Washington Alder LLC	2421	91
Washington Area Network Services LLC	7378	162
Washington Banking Co	6712	218
Washington Chain and Supply Inc	5072	139
Washington Closure Hanford LLC	4953	175

Company Name	SIC	Rank
Washington Compost LLC	8741	294
Washington Consulting Group	7379	238
Washington County Community Residential Services Inc	8361	172
Washington County Machine Shop Inc	3599	492
Washington County Rural Telephone Cooperative Inc	4813	440
Washington County Tractor Inc	5083	55
Washington Crab Producers Inc	2092	42
Washington Crane and Hoist Company Inc	5084	525
Washington Div	3743	1
Washington Electric Cooperative Inc	4911	532
Washington Electric Membership Corp	4911	213
Washington Energy Services Co	5063	19
Washington Equipment Manufacturing Company Inc	3536	53
Washington Federal Inc	6712	59
Washington Federal Savings (Seattle Washington)	6035	20
Washington First International Bank	6022	225
Washington Gas Light Co	4924	15
Washington Group International Inc	1611	47
Washington Hardwoods Company LLC	5031	289
Washington Healthcare Mary	8741	68
Washington Information Source Co	2741	467
Washington Iron Works Inc	3599	2134
Washington Jewish Week Inc	2711	635
Washington Mills Tonawanda Inc	3291	1
Washington Mining	8711	82
Washington National Insurance Co	6321	35
Washington Nationals Baseball Club LLC	7941	9
Washington News Publishing Company Inc	2711	643
Washington North Implement Co	5083	214
Washington Ornamental Iron Works	3441	292
Washington Penn Plastic Company Inc	3087	7
Washington Post Co	2711	9
Washington Sand Company Inc	1442	91
Washington Savings Bank	6035	149
Washington Savings Bank FSB	6035	134
Washington School Employees Credit Union	6062	16
Washington Services	8721	25
Washington Services Inc	6552	307
Washington Soldier's Home and Colony	8741	232
Washington SuperMall Interest LP	6512	41
Washington Trucking Inc	4213	480
Washington Trust Bancorp Inc	6712	150
Washington Trust Bank	6022	116
Washington Trust Co	6022	77
Washington Trust Company Of Westerly	6022	545
Washington Water Service Co	4941	66
Washington Wine and Beverage Company Inc	2084	106
Washington-St Tammany Electric Coop	4911	201
Washita Refrigeration and Equipment Company Inc	5078	35
Washoe Medical Center South Meadow	8361	81
Wasik Associates Inc	3679	705
Wasmer Schroeder and Company Inc	6282	276
Wasp Inc	3537	32
Wasp Technologies Inc	5045	136
Wasser Filtration Inc	3569	105
Wasserstein Partners LP	2064	44
Wasserstrom Co	5021	1
Wasson-Ece Instrumentation Inc	3826	93
Waste Connections Inc	4953	5
Waste Conversion Technologies Inc	4953	162
Waste Industries USA Inc	4953	26
Waste Management Inc	7389	2
Waste Management Northwest Region	4953	29
Waste Management of Iowa Inc	4953	98
Waste Management of Kentucky LLC	4953	72
Waste Management of Oklahoma Inc	4953	97
Waste Management Recycle America	5093	3
Waste Microbes Inc	4953	143
Waste Minimization and Containment Services Inc	5084	911
Waste Processing Equipment Inc	3569	150
Waste Quip Inc	3443	233
Waste Solutions Group	3589	55
Waste Stream Technology Inc	0711	5
Wastren Advantage Inc	8742	216
Watanabe Ing LLP	8111	388
Watchery	3873	8
WatchGuard Technologies Inc	7372	474
WatchITcom	7373	335
Watcon Inc	2899	218
Water and Power Community Credit Union	6062	58
Water and Sewer Maintenance	7349	381
Water Bearer Films Inc	7822	28
Water Front Inc	7389	2519
Water Gremlin Co	3949	78
Water Heater Innovations Inc	3639	21
Water Pik Technologies Inc	3634	4
Water Resources International Inc	1781	3
Water Resources International Inc	3589	147
Water Saver Faucet Co	3432	27

Company Name	SIC	Rank	Company Name	SIC	Rank	Company Name	SIC	Rank
Water Services of America Inc	3585	51	Waukegan Color Supply Inc	5013	276	Wazee Company LLC	7694	4
Water Street Seafood Inc	2092	71	Waukesha Bearings Corp	3568	7	WB Cable 6	4833	233
Water Tec International Inc	3589	212	Waukesha Electric Systems Inc	3612	15	WB Capital Bond	6722	255
Water Tech Inc	5169	97	Waukesha Foundry Inc	3325	25	WB Fleming Company Inc	2048	123
Water Technology Of Pensacola	3589	260	Waukesha State Bank	6022	112	WB Mason Co	5943	3
Water Works Manufacturing LLC	3449	11	Waupaca County Publishing Company Inc	2711	516	WB Riggins Tallow Company Inc	2077	12
Waterbury Garment LLC	2341	13				W-B Supply Co	5084	314
Waterfield Technologies Inc	7373	820	Wausau Equipment Company Inc	3599	100	WB Thompson Company Inc	5082	213
Waterford Institute Inc	7372	42	Wausau Financial Systems Inc	7373	103	WB Wood Co	5021	69
Waterford Sand and Gravel Co	5032	140	Wausau Paper Corp	2621	13	WBBQ Radio	4832	106
Waterford School District	8211	88	Wausau Papers Export Corp	7389	245	Wbc Extrusion Products Inc	3081	135
Waterford-Wedgwood USA	5023	11	Wausau Tile Inc	3272	62	Wbc Inc	2759	234
WaterFurnace Renewable Energy	3433	4	Wausau Window and Wall Systems	3442	23	Wbe Network Systems Inc	5065	430
Waterhouse Inc	5946	2	Wausaukee Composites Inc	3089	238	WBH Industries	5072	85
Waterhouse Publications Inc	2759	355	Wauseon Machine And Manufacturing Inc	3599	442	Wbhg Studio	4832	239
Waterloo Coal Company Inc	1422	14				Wbhj and Wbhk Radio	4832	90
Waterloo Manufacturing Company Inc	3629	123	WAV Inc	5045	285	Wbml Radio Station	4832	121
Waterloo Manufacturing Software	7372	2004	Wave 3 Inc	4813	390	WBNA TV-Louisville	4833	105
Waterloo Mills Co	2048	65	Wave Community Newspapers	2711	135	WBNS Tv	4833	219
Waterlox Coatings Corp	2851	159	Wave Electronics Inc	5064	41	Wboc Inc	4833	146
Waterman Steamship Corp	4412	19	Wave Publishing Inc	2741	438	WBPromotions	3961	11
Watermark Books	5942	32	Wave Systems Corp	3577	223	WBPX TV-Boston	4833	106
Watermark Federal Credit Union	6061	75	Wave Systems Corp (Sunnyvale California)	8734	101	Wbt Group LLC	5199	107
Watermill Ventures Ltd	6211	326				WBWalton Enterprises Inc	3663	236
Waterous Co	3491	10	Wavecrest Computing Inc	7372	3062	WC Bradley Co	3631	3
Waterplay Manufacturing Inc	3589	226	WaveDivision Holdings LLC	4841	89	WC Branham Inc	3593	50
WaterPure International Inc	5962	24	WaveFrame Corp	7371	1637	WC Fore Trucking Inc	4213	1716
Waterra U S A Inc	3561	181	Wavefunction Inc	7372	595	WC McQuaide Inc	4213	1979
Waters Corp	3826	7	Wavelength Electronics Inc	3674	431	WC Redmon Company Inc	2511	95
Waters Equipment Company Inc	7699	152	Wavelight Inc	3699	25	WC Trucking Inc	4213	1912
Waters Industrial Supply Company Inc	5085	301	Waveline Direct LLC	2752	678	WCA Waste Corp	4953	25
Waters Network Systems LLC	3577	605	Waveline Inc	3825	182	WCB Holdings Inc	6712	695
Waters Technologies Corp	3826	172	WaveMaker Software Inc	7371	589	WCB Properties	6552	296
Waters Truck and Tractor Company Inc	5012	32	WaveMetrics Inc	7372	4397	Wcc Services Us Inc	7371	1893
Watersaver Company Inc	3069	35	Wavenet Technologies Inc	7373	563	Wcco Belting Inc	3052	17
Waterside Capital Corp	6726	99	Waverlee Homes Inc	2452	2	WCGV Licensee LLC	4833	51
Waterstone Bank	6036	32	Waverley Software Design Inc	7372	4776	Wchc Fm Radio Station	4832	76
Waterstone Financial Inc	6035	45	Waverly Group	7311	993	WCHS Licensee LLC	4833	46
Watertown Cooperative Elevator Association	5153	74	Waverly Mills Inc	2281	25	WCI Communities Inc	1531	35
			Waverly Plastics Company Inc	2673	53	WCM Investment Management	6282	203
Watertown Door and Windows Inc	5211	314	Waves Inc	7372	1350	WCP Inc	3089	587
Watertown Plastics Inc	3089	739	WaveSplitter Technologies Inc	3679	194	WCP Solutions	5111	20
Waterview Villa Inc	8051	68	Wavetech Geophysical Inc	1382	55	WCPX TV-Chicago	4833	107
Waterville Valley Resort Inc	7011	132	WaveTwo LLC	7371	556	WCRX Radio Station 881	4832	245
Water-Way Inc	3088	22	Wawa Inc	5411	38	Wcs Communications Inc	5999	251
Waterways Inc	3559	462	Wawona Frozen Foods Inc	2037	24	WCUZ 1023 FM 102	4832	149
WaterWorks America	8731	214	Waxie Sanitary Supply	5169	8	WD Burch Inc	3699	282
Waterworks District No 3	1623	566	Waxman Industries Inc	5074	21	WD Kerr and Sons Inc	4213	1932
Watford Industry Inc	3599	1535	WaxWorks Inc	7810	13	WD Larson Companies Limited Inc	5012	25
Watkins and Shepard Trucking Inc	4213	170	Way Bakery	2051	16	WD Media Inc	3695	1
Watkins and Son Inc	4213	1826	WAY Delivery Services	4213	2330	WD Music Products Inc	3931	38
Watkins Associated Developers Inc	6552	227	Way Forward Technology Inc	7371	793	WD-40 Co	2899	29
Watkins Associated Industries Inc	4213	133	Way Holding Co	1711	17	WDAY-TV-AM	4832	83
Watkins Construction Company Inc	1731	1908	Way Station Inc	8361	23	WDB Engineering Inc	8711	590
Watkins Construction Company Ltd	1623	87	Way Technology LLC	5734	50	WDBM 89 FM	4832	279
Watkins Hamilton Ross Architects Inc	8712	129	Way Transportation Company Inc	4213	2167	WDC Holdings Inc	3842	160
Watkins Inc	2099	90	Waycross Cable Company Inc	4841	142	WDEV	4832	127
Watkins Lithographic Inc	2752	537	Waycross Investment Management Co	6282	537	WDFA Marketing Inc	7319	66
Watkins Manufacturing Corp	3088	1	Waycross Journal Herald Inc	2711	614	WDKY Inc	4833	76
Watkins Manufacturing Inc	3541	171	Waymark Internet Services Inc	7336	126	WDKY Licensee LLC	4833	77
Watkins Printing Co	2752	682	Waymouth Farms Inc	2064	23	WDMLFM	4832	291
Watkins Sand Co	1442	59	Wayne Allen Ltd	7336	223	WDS Enterprises Inc	4213	2246
Watkins Security Agency Of DC Inc	7381	43	Wayne Automatic Fire Sprinklers Inc	1711	72	WDS Partners LP	4213	2057
Watkins Transportation Inc	4213	2424	Wayne Automation Corp	3565	99	Wdt World Discount Telecommunications Co	7389	1272
Watkins Trucking Company Inc	4213	2657	Wayne Board Of Education	8211	76			
Watkins Uiberall PLLC	8721	109	Wayne Burt Machine	3599	2165	WDUQ	4832	208
Watlow Electric Manufacturing Co	3822	2	Wayne Combustion Systems	3433	28	WE Aubuchon Company Inc	5251	4
Watonwan Farm Services	5191	22	Wayne County Publications Inc	2711	787	WE Blain and Sons Inc	1611	121
Watsco Inc	5075	2	Wayne County Rubber Inc	2822	21	We Buy Houses Home Services LLC	6799	353
Watson and Chalin Holding Corp	3714	269	Wayne Crouse Inc	1711	97	We Care Physicals LLC	8099	115
Watson Clinic LLP	8093	13	Wayne D Enterprises Inc	5136	15	WE Curling Welding Service Inc	1623	170
Watson Coatings Inc	2851	163	Wayne Dairy Products Inc	2026	16	We Imagine Inc	3672	203
Watson Foods Company Inc	2045	6	Wayne Densch Performing Arts Center	5181	64	WE O'Neil Construction Co	1541	81
Watson Furniture Group	2522	24	Wayne Hummer Wealth Management	6211	293	We R Signs International Inc	5046	279
Watson Gravel Inc	1442	28	Wayne Lumber Company Inc	2421	125	We Sell Cellular Inc	5065	149
Watson Grinding and Manufacturing Co	3499	90	Wayne Manufacturing Industries LLC	3086	154	Wea Electrical Contractor Inc	1731	1742
			Wayne McCall and Associates	7372	998	WEA Manufacturing Inc	3652	5
Watson Industries Inc	3812	197	Wayne Metals LLC	3443	83	Weaber Inc	2426	2
Watson Label Products Corp	2759	9	Wayne Mills Company Inc	2221	38	Weaks Martin Implement Co	5083	33
Watson Laboratories Inc	2834	153	Wayne Pak Inc	3081	121	WealthTrust Inc	6282	239
Watson Laboratories Inc (Groveport Ohio)	2834	212	Wayne Pipe and Supply Inc	5074	85	Wear Licensee LLC	4833	36
			Wayne Printing Co	2752	668	Wear The Best Inc	7389	1427
Watson Pharma Inc	2834	134	Wayne Printing Company Inc	2711	392	Wear-Tek Inc	3364	20
Watson Pharmaceuticals Inc	2834	14	Wayne Products Inc	3569	285	Weasler Engineering Inc	3568	29
Watson Truck and Supply Inc	5084	25	Wayne Reaves Computer Systems Inc	5734	145	Weastec Inc	3714	91
Watson-Hopper Inc	3533	43	Wayne Savings Bancshares Inc	6712	510	Weather Decision Technologies Inc	7373	475
Watson-Standard Co	2851	46	Wayne Savings Community Bank	6011	11	Weather Makers Inc	1711	209
Watsontown Trucking Company Inc	4213	541	Wayne Smith Trucking Inc	4213	1836	Weather Metrics Inc	3829	351
Watsonville Bureau Of Collection Inc	7322	177	Wayne Steel Supply Inc	3449	27	Weather Port LLC	5033	53
Watt Publishing Co	2721	56	Wayne Trail Technologies Inc	3728	130	Weather Seal Products Inc	1799	149
Watt Stopper Inc	3643	27	Wayne W Sell Corp	4213	1840	Weather Services International	7389	385
Watters and Martin Inc	5072	51	Wayne Wicks and Associates Investigations	8361	193	Weather Shield Manufacturing Inc	2431	9
Wattmaster Controls Inc	3822	68				Weather Shield Transportation	4213	1629
Wattrans Inc	4213	1324	Wayne Wire Cloth Products Inc	3496	18	Weather Tec Corp	3494	77
Watts Machining Inc	3599	1177	Wayne Witt Dds Inc	8021	23	Weather Watch Inc	8999	198
Watts Premier Inc	3589	62	Wayne's Pest Control	7342	51	WeatherBank Inc	8999	49
Watts Radiant Inc	5074	49	Wayne-White Counties Electric Coop	4911	251	Weatherby Inc	3484	21
Watts Spacemaker Inc	5074	66	Waypoint Business Solutions Gp LLC	7378	88	WeatherData Services Inc	7375	232
Watts Water Technologies Inc	3494	3	Waypoint Global LLC	7372	867	Weatherflow Inc	4813	594
Wauconda Tool and Engineering Company Inc	3469	103	Waypoint Systems Inc	1731	1278	Weatherford Completion and Oilfield Systems	3533	10
			Wayron LLC	3441	195			
Waukee Engineering Company Inc	3824	42	Wayside Technology Group Inc	5045	62	Weatherford National Bank	6021	312
Waukeenah Fertilizer And Farm Supply Inc	5261	17	Waytek Inc	5063	1105	Weatherford News Inc	2711	524
			Wazee Companies LLC	5063	209	Weatherford Oil Country Manufacturing	3533	26

Company Name	SIC	Rank
Weatherford Security Services Inc	7381	252
Weathergard Window Company Inc	3089	746
Weatherly Consulting Inc	8742	508
Weatherly Truck Lines Inc	4213	2124
Weatherproof Garment Co	2329	37
Weather-Rite LLC	3585	137
Weathershield Supply Inc	5031	386
Weathertech Distributing Company Inc	5075	35
WeatherVision	4899	226
Weaver and Sons Inc	3444	212
Weaver and Tidwell LLP	8721	221
Weaver Automotive Inc	5013	228
Weaver Brothers Inc	0252	5
Weaver Brothers Insurance Associates Inc	6331	321
Weaver Cooke Construction LLC	1542	52
Weaver Distributors Inc	5013	207
Weaver Electric Inc	1731	1882
Weaver Industries Inc	3624	17
Weaver Machine and Tool Company Inc	3599	1024
Weaver-Bailey Contractors Inc	1541	129
Weaz Frn	4832	89
Web 1 Capital Inc	4813	666
Web Broadcasting Corp	7372	4066
Web Construction Inc	1623	657
Web Engineering Associates Inc	8711	669
Web Fire Communications Inc	4813	528
Web Ignite Corp	7379	1215
Web Industries Fort Wayne Inc	7389	1514
Web Media Ltd	7336	258
Web Offset Printing Company Inc	2752	345
Web Plus Inc	5734	336
Web Press Corp	3555	42
Web Printing Controls Company Inc	3555	17
Web Results Inc	7379	1226
Web Seal Inc	3053	82
Web Service Company LLC	7215	2
Web Sites by Interpol	7379	1002
Web Solutions Inc	7379	551
Web Spiders Inc	7371	114
Web Strategies Internet Solutions LLC	7379	1508
Web Systems Inc	3559	505
Web Tech Services Inc	7373	1202
Web Teks Inc	7371	1486
Web To Market Corp	7379	1003
Web Warrior Inc	5063	1070
WEB-2000 Inc	7379	1526
Webb and Sons Construction Company Inc	1542	399
Webb Automotive Group Inc (Farmington New Mexico)	5511	901
Webb Communications Inc	2711	426
Webb Corp	3542	69
Webb Devlam Chicago LLP	7389	2030
Webb Electronics Ltd	7812	254
Webb Sunrise Inc	5199	79
Webb Super-Gro Products Inc	2875	37
Webb Tech	3679	870
Webber Manufacturing Company Inc	3569	215
Webber Metal Products Inc	3569	72
Webber Oil Co	5983	33
Webber's World	1731	2181
Webbs Machine Design Inc	8733	36
Webb's Oil Corp	5171	31
Webb-Stiles Co	3535	33
Webcanyon Inc	4813	742
Webco Distribution Inc	5046	239
Webco Industries Inc	3317	12
Webco Machine Products Inc	3599	1536
Webcollage Inc	7371	675
Webcom Group Inc	7372	369
Webcor Builders Inc	1542	18
Webcrafters Inc	2732	9
Webdesigns-Studio	7379	669
Weber and Judd Company Inc	5912	78
Weber and Scher Manufacturing Company Inc	3549	70
Weber Chevrolet Co	5511	443
Weber Electric Inc	1731	1627
Weber Electric Manufacturing Co	3549	62
Weber Energy Corp	1382	72
Weber H G and Company Inc	3554	11
Weber International Packaging Company LLC	3085	30
Weber Manufacturing and Supplies Inc	3451	114
Weber Marking Systems Inc	3953	3
Weber Metals Inc	3463	8
Weber Printing Company Inc	2752	873
Weber Processing Plant Inc	5421	15
Weber Sensors LLC	5065	805
Weber Shandwick Inc	8743	31
Weber Stone Co	1411	13
Weber Systems Inc	7371	841
Weber-Knapp Co	3429	83
Weber-Stephen Products LLC	3631	5
WebEx Communications Inc	7389	99
Webflare Enterprises	7379	1509
WebGear Inc	3674	412
WebGecko Software	7371	1733
WebGen Systems Inc	5045	248
Webgistix Corp	4225	20
Web-Hed Technologies Inc	7373	854
WebHouse Inc	7379	280

Company Name	SIC	Rank
Webicing Inc	5045	1042
Webicity Web Designs	7336	316
Weblife Inc	7374	406
Weblogs Inc LLC	7375	125
WebloyaltyCom Inc	7319	65
WebMaster Inc	7372	4344
WebMD Health Corp	7389	72
WebMediaBrands Inc	7379	497
Webmedx Inc	7338	2
WebMessenger Inc	4899	80
webOS Global Business Unit	3575	1
Webpower Inc	7371	533
WebRecruiter LLC	7372	2436
Webroomz Inc	7371	1796
Webs Inc	4813	347
Webs Unlimited	7372	5070
WebSafe Shield Inc	7379	970
Websense Inc	7389	109
WebSine Inc	7371	947
Website Connection	7373	1072
WebsiteMGT	7379	1510
webslingerz Inc	7379	773
WebSolutions Technology Inc	7379	1216
Websource	5111	24
Websourced Inc	5045	144
Webspun Inc	7379	1313
Webspy USA Inc	7373	1231
Webstart Communications	7379	1527
Webster Bank NA	6021	22
Webster City Custom Meats Inc	2013	99
Webster City Federal Bancorp	6712	694
Webster Computer Corp	3577	595
Webster County Coal LLC	1221	23
Webster Enterprises of Jackson County Inc	3841	252
Webster Financial Corp	6712	46
Webster First Federal Credit Union	6062	67
Webster Industries Inc	3496	14
Webster Industries Inc (Peabody Massachusetts)	2673	33
Webster Kirkwood Times Inc	2711	788
Webster Preferred Capital Corp	6798	190
Webster Printing Company Inc	2752	808
Webster Veterinary Supply Inc	0742	4
Webstone Company Inc	5074	192
Websurf Internet	7379	863
Webteam Inc	7336	109
WebTrends Corp	7372	2250
Webtyme Design and Hosting	7379	1234
Webucator Inc	8243	8
WebVMC LLC	5045	431
WebWorqs Inc	7379	861
Webworx International Inc	7313	21
Wec Carolina Energy Solutions LLC	3398	6
WEC Electric Inc	1731	904
Wechsler Ross and Partners Inc	7336	88
WechTECH Inc	7373	647
Weco Industries Inc	3639	26
WECS Electric Supply Inc	5063	736
Wedbush Bank	6035	218
Wedbush Corp	6211	70
Wedbush Morgan Securities Inc	6211	212
WedBush Securities	6798	213
Wedco Inc	5063	170
WEDCO Technology Inc	3599	51
Wedding Brand Investors LLC	2389	31
Wedeco Uv Technologies Inc	3589	101
Wedge Capital Management LLP	6282	109
WEDGE Group Inc	3533	82
Wedge Products Inc	3469	43
Wedge-Mill Tool Inc	3545	340
Wedgewood Partners Inc	6211	233
Wedlake Fabricating Inc	3499	118
Wednesday Journal Inc	2711	445
Wee Bee Audio Of Lancaster Inc	5731	153
Weeden Investors LP	6799	199
Weedon Engineering Co	5088	119
Weekley Asphalt Paving Inc	1611	101
Weekley Homes LP	1531	14
Weeks Marine Inc	1629	5
Weems and Plath Inc	5088	102
Weetabix Company Inc	2043	4
WEG GP LLC	4613	6
Wegener Corp	3663	146
Wegmann-Dazet and Co	8721	360
Wegmans Food Markets Inc	5411	42
Wegner Motor Sports Inc	7539	8
Wehah Farm Inc	4221	10
WEHCO Media Inc	2711	87
Wehr Constructors Inc	1542	57
Wehrle Trucking Inc	4213	2724
Wehrli and Associates Inc	3577	627
Weibel Inc	2084	15
Weichert REO Services	6531	28
Wei-Chuan USA Inc	2038	25
Wei-Chuan USA Inc Chicago Div	2038	19
Weidenmiller Co	3556	155
Weidert Group Inc	7311	486
Weidlinger Associates Inc	8712	61
Weidt Group	2741	114
Weigardt Brothers Inc	2091	24
Weight and Test Solutions Inc	5046	171
Weight Watchers International Inc	7299	2
Weightech Inc	3596	16

Company Name	SIC	Rank
Weihe Design Group PLC	8712	121
Weikel Enterprises Inc	5411	284
Weil Brothers-Cotton Inc	5159	14
Weil Gotshal and Manges LLP	8111	11
Weil Pump Company Inc	3561	85
Weiland Financial Group Inc	7371	804
Weiler And Company Inc	3556	22
Weiler Corp	3991	5
Weiler Engineering Inc	3565	52
Weiler Welding Company Inc	5169	102
Weil-McLain	3443	24
Weil-Thoman Moving and Storage Co	4213	3010
Weiman's Bakery Inc	2051	267
Weimer Bearing and Transmission Inc	3699	45
Weimer Construction Co	1023	601
Wein Products Inc	3699	231
Weinberg and Co	8721	200
Weinbrenner Shoe Company Inc	3143	15
Weiner Iron and Metal Corp	5093	176
Weingart Center Association Inc	8322	80
Weingarten Properties Trust	6798	19
Weingarten Realty Investors	6798	54
Weinrich Bakery	5461	52
Weinrich Truck Line Inc	4213	1849
Weins Machine Company Inc	3599	2246
Weinstein and Holtzman Inc	5072	70
Weinstein Associates Ltd	6282	519
Weinstein Otterman and Associates Inc	7311	453
Weinstock Lamp Company Inc	5063	463
Weintraub and Associates Advertising	7311	442
Weintraub Construction	1522	26
Weintraub Telecomm LLC	4899	98
Weir Floway Inc	3561	15
Weir Lewis Pumps	3561	90
Weir Valves and Controls USA Inc	3491	25
Weird Stuff Inc	5734	54
Weir's Furniture Village	5712	61
Weis Markets Inc	5411	55
Weiser Lock Corp	3429	63
Weiser Security Services Inc	7381	29
Weisman Electric Co	1731	1523
Weiss and Hughes Publishing Inc	2721	416
Weiss Communications Inc	2721	320
Weiss Group Inc	6282	106
Weiss Instruments Inc	3823	104
Weiss Ltd	2082	84
Weiss Research Inc	6282	179
Weissman's Theatrical Supplies Inc	2389	28
Weitz Company Inc Denver Div	1542	213
Weitz Group LLC	1541	21
Weitzman Group	6512	53
Weitzman Inc	7311	872
WEJ Trucking Company Inc	4213	2800
WEK and Associates Inc	5091	131
Weksler Glass Thermometer Corp	3823	309
WEL Companies Inc	4213	473
WELBRO Building Corp	1542	130
Welburn Electric Inc	1731	955
Welch Allyn Protocol Inc	3841	100
Welch Brothers Inc	3272	94
Welch Fluorocarbon Inc	3089	1217
Welch Graham and Ogden Insurance Agency	6411	279
Welch Holdings Inc	1442	63
Welch PA Inc	5734	391
Welch Printing Co	2759	146
Welch Publishing Co	2711	719
Welchdry Inc	2834	397
Wel-Co Diamond Tool Corp	3545	159
Welco Gases Corp	5169	110
Welco Lumber Co	2421	36
Welco Manufacturing Co	2891	82
Welco Services Inc	7692	22
Welcom	7372	2232
Welcome Driver Inc	7371	1869
Welcome Home Inc	5712	41
Welcome Industrial Corp	1799	70
Welcome Wagon International Inc	7319	13
WelComm Inc	7311	912
Weld Tooling Corp	3548	26
Weldall Manufacturing Inc	3531	67
Weldbend Corp	3462	33
Weldco-Beales Manufacturing Corp	3531	100
Welded Ring Products Co	3724	53
Welded Tube Of Canada Inc	3317	47
Welder Services Of Fort Wayne Inc	5084	434
Weld-Fab Manufacturing Corp	3599	1056
Weldfit Corp	3599	902
Welding Alloys (USA) Inc	3548	45
Welding Apparatus Co	3317	61
Welding Technologies Inc	7692	32
Weldlogic Inc	3548	34
Weldmac Manufacturing Co	3599	114
Weldmation Inc	3548	21
Weldon Owen Inc	2731	186
Weldon Parts Inc	5013	138
Weldon Tool Co	3541	51
Weldotron Inc	3565	184
Weldstar Co	5084	141
Weleda Inc	5122	80
Welex Inc	3559	30
Welfab Inc	3441	215
Welfare and Pension Administration Service Inc	6371	14

Company Name	SIC	Rank
Welis LLC	7371	1797
Welker Inc	3823	102
Wellborn Cabinet Inc	2434	12
WellCare Health Plans Inc	6324	22
WellCare Management Group Inc	6324	104
WellCare of New York Inc	6324	99
Wellco Enterprises Inc	3149	22
Well-Don Inc	7349	509
Wellfount Pharmacy Inc	7379	643
Wellhead Control Products	3533	115
Wellington Development Corp	3567	90
Wellington Industries Inc	3465	22
Wellington Management Company LLP	6282	189
Wellington Tile and Marble	5032	172
Welliver and Sons Inc	3546	41
Wellman and Griffith Inc	5731	66
Wellman Holding Co	3842	178
Wellman Inc	2824	3
Wellman Products Group	3399	1
Wellness Plan	6324	46
Wellness Power Management LLC	8742	136
Wellons Inc	3559	73
Wellpet LLC	2047	26
WellPoint Inc	6311	23
WellQuest Medical and Wellness Corp	8011	2
Wells Aircraft Inc	4512	57
Wells and Kimich Inc	5021	61
Wells Cargo Inc	3715	25
Wells Compression Inc	3568	92
Wells' Dairy Inc	2024	4
Wells Dental Inc	3843	83
Wells Design Group	7389	816
Wells Fargo Advantage Municipal Bond Fund Inc	6722	87
Wells Fargo Advantage Opportunity Fund	6722	97
Wells Fargo Advantage Short-Term	6722	157
Wells Fargo and Co	6712	2
Wells Fargo Bank Ltd	6021	12
Wells Fargo Bank Northwest NA	6021	121
Wells Fargo Equipment Finance Inc	6159	26
Wells Fargo Financial Inc	6141	8
Wells Fargo Financial Leasing Inc	6159	12
Wells Fargo Foothill LLC	6153	12
Wells Fargo Insurance Inc	6411	188
Wells Fargo Insurance Services	6411	50
Wells Fargo Insurance Services of California	6411	41
Wells Fargo Insurance Services of Michigan Inc	6411	268
Wells Fargo Insurance Services of North Carolina	6411	57
Wells Fargo Insurance Services of Ohio LLC	6411	254
Wells Fargo Insurance Services Southeast Inc	6411	66
Wells Fargo (New Boston Texas)	6021	80
Wells Fargo Private Bank	6211	223
Wells Financial Corp	6712	598
Wells Johnson Co	3841	296
Wells Legal Supply Inc	2754	40
Wells Manufacturing Co (Woodstock Illinois)	3316	12
Wells Print and Digital Services Inc	2752	1381
Wells Printing Company Inc	2752	584
Wells Rural Electric Co	4911	281
Wellsco Field Services LLC	7389	689
Wells-Gardner Electronics Corp	3663	66
Wellsoft Corp	7372	1440
Wellsource Inc	7371	582
Wellspan Medical Group	8011	23
Wellspring Media Inc	7822	19
Wellston Aerosol Manufacturing Company Inc	2813	26
Well-Tempered Music Library	2741	447
Welocalize Inc	7389	135
Welpak Corp	4213	2964
Welsch Furnace Co	1711	173
Welsh Gold Stampers Inc	3999	191
Weltronics Corp	5091	145
Welty Custom Exteriors Inc	5033	44
Welz Tool Machine and Boring Company Inc	3599	745
Wem Automation Inc	3625	132
Wema USA Inc	3812	196
Wemco Casting LLC	3369	22
Wemco Inc	3556	178
Wems Inc	3564	53
Wendel Aquisition Inc	2013	185
Wendel Energy Services LLC	8999	103
Wendel Rosen Black and Dean LLP	8111	312
Wendell August Forge Inc	5947	22
Wendells Woodwork Inc	5084	889
Wendle Motors Inc	5511	107
Wendling Printing Co	2752	506
Wendling Quarries Inc	1422	6
Wendon Company Inc	3599	418
Wendt Corp	5084	338
Wendt Pharmaceuticals Inc	5122	117
Wendtco Web Printing Inc	2752	930
Wendy Howard	7379	1674
Wendy's Co	5812	23
Wenger Corp	2541	10
Wenger Manufacturing Inc	3556	16
Wenger Truck Line Inc	4213	960
Wenn/Soft Inc	7372	2028
Wenner Bread Products Inc	2051	42
Wenner Media LLC	2721	33
Wente Brothers	2084	4
Wentworth Chevrolet Subaru	5511	279
Wentworth Hauser and Violich	6282	398
Wentworth Mold Incorporated Central USA Div	3544	193
Wentworth Printing Corp	2759	153
Wenvy Technologies Inc	3679	838
Weny Inc	4833	189
Wenzel Associates Inc	3679	254
Wenzel Plumbing and Heating Inc	1711	55
Wenzl and Co	5046	237
Weokie Credit Union	6062	26
WePackItAll	7389	405
Wepak Corp	2841	47
Wepco Plastics Inc	3089	1602
Wepco Vintek LLC	8743	244
Wer Corp	3365	23
Werco Manufacturing Inc	3599	679
Wercs Ltd	7372	2066
Werdco BC Inc	4213	1689
Werecon Inc	3822	94
Werhane Enterprises Ltd	4213	721
Werk-Brau Co	3531	79
Werlatone Inc	3679	667
Wermer Rogers Doran and Ruzon CPA	8721	458
Werner Electric Supply Co	3629	22
Werner Electric Ventures LLC	5063	214
Werner Enterprises Inc	4213	21
Werner Gourmet Meat Snacks Inc	2013	144
Werner-Donaldson Moving Services Inc	4214	21
Wernick Marketing Group	8743	242
Werres Corp	5084	158
Wert Bookbinding Inc	2789	54
Werthan Packaging Inc	2674	6
Wertheim Inc	7373	1012
Wes Lasher Acura/Isuzu Inc	5511	256
Wes Olson Trucking Inc	4213	2820
Wesanco Inc	3429	124
WesBanco Bank (Fairmont West Virginia)	6022	305
WesBanco Bank South Hills	6022	237
WesBanco Bank Wheeling	6022	172
WesBanco Inc	6712	108
WesBanco of Parkersburg	6022	346
WESCAP Management Group Inc	6282	419
Wesco Cedar Inc	5033	57
Wesco Fabrics Inc	2391	7
Wesco Financial LLC	6331	184
Wesco Industrial Products Inc	3537	39
WESCO International Inc	5063	2
Wesco Machine Products Inc	3599	863
Wesco Mounting and Finishing Inc	2789	119
Wesco Valve and Manufacturing Co	3592	16
Wesco-Financial Insurance Co	6331	135
Wescom Credit Union	6061	8
Wescor Inc	3826	77
Weseloh Chevrolet Co	5511	313
Wes-Flo Company Inc	4213	2436
Weslaco Independent School District	8211	13
Wesley Crow Electric Inc	1731	327
Wesley Hall Inc	2512	43
Wesley International Corp	3537	94
Wesolve LLC	7379	1005
Wessel Fragrances Inc	2869	60
Wesselmans Div	5411	209
Wesseln Construction Company Inc	1521	54
West 1 Catv Supplies Inc	5063	379
West Agro Inc	2879	17
West Alabama Capital Corp	6712	234
West and Barker Inc	3089	1158
West Bancorporation Inc	6022	129
West Bank (West Des Moines Iowa)	6712	462
West Bay Electric Inc	1731	1180
West Bend Co	3634	8
West Bend Mutual Insurance Co	3537	8
West Bend Transit and Service	4213	2456
West Bond Inc	3569	143
West Brothers Transfer and Storage	4213	778
West Brothers Transportation Services	4213	387
West Central Coop	5153	14
West Central Electric Coop	4911	306
West Central Electric Cooperative Inc	4911	334
West Central Indiana Economic Development District Inc	8748	250
West Central Industries Inc	8331	146
West Central Iowa Sheltered Workshop	8331	178
West Central Telephone Association Inc	4813	329
West Central Turkeys Inc	2015	3
West Chester University Of Pennsylvania Of The System Of Higher Education	8221	28
West Coast Bancorp	6712	177
West Coast Bank	6022	108
West Coast Copper and Supply Inc	5075	67
West Coast Courier	7389	2227
West Coast Detectives Group International Inc	7381	234
West Coast Event Productions Inc	5947	20
West Coast Fab Inc	3444	237
West Coast Gasket Co	3053	48
West Coast Graphics Inc	2752	1624
West Coast Industrial Systems Inc	3553	20
West Coast Laboratories Inc	2834	345
West Coast Life Insurance Co	6311	196
West Coast Now Inc	7389	1586
West Coast Plastics Inc	3089	490
West Coast Quartz Corp	3229	15
West Coast Tube and Pipe	5051	511
West Coast Vinyl Inc	3089	652
West Coast Wire and Steel Inc	3441	75
West Coast Wire Rope and Rigging Inc	5051	96
West Coast-Accudyne Inc	3542	89
West Code	3559	553
West Colonial Hyundai Inc	5012	145
West Corp	7389	15
West County Journals	2711	292
West Courier Express Inc	7389	1951
West Craft Manufacturing Inc	3593	26
West Creative Inc	7311	854
West Des Moines State Bank	6022	212
West Electric Inc	1731	2496
West Electronics Inc (Burlington New Jersey)	3663	297
West End Electric Inc	1731	2459
West End Machine and Welding	3599	2242
West End Milling Company Inc	2048	132
West Florida Electric Cooperative Association	4911	175
West Florida Hospital	8062	83
West Florida Urology PLC	8049	29
West Glen Communications Inc	7812	160
West Haven Foundation	8361	197
West Haven Lumber Co	5031	255
West Houston Volkswagen LLC	5012	118
West Interactive Corp	7389	253
West LA Music	5736	13
West Lake Food Corp	2011	98
West LEGALworks	2731	66
West Liberty Foods LLC	2015	20
West LiveNote (San Francisco California)	7372	2918
West Machine and Tool Inc	3599	2118
West Machine Products Inc	3599	1782
West Manufacturing	3429	133
West Marine Inc	5551	1
West Meade Pool Inc	7389	2048
West Michigan Internet Services Inc	4813	524
West Michigan Railroad Co	4011	40
West Michigan Tool and Die Co	3544	672
West Mountain Brewing Co	2082	86
West Mountain Systems Inc	7379	1675
West Northwest Transportation	4213	501
West Office Exhibition Design	7389	2082
West Orange Healthcare District Inc	8062	174
West Penn Non-Destructive Testing Inc	8734	106
West Penn Power Co	4911	229
West Penn Wire (Washington Pennsylvania)	3496	15
West Pharmaceutical Services Inc	3069	4
West Plains Electric Motor Service Inc	3613	90
West Point Foundry And Machine Company Inc	8711	461
West Point Products LLC	3861	21
West Point Veneer LLC	2435	26
West Portal Software Corp	7372	3967
West Pro	8243	14
West Publishing Corp	7375	14
West River Telecommunications Coop	4813	122
West Seattle Herald Inc	2711	797
West Shore Printing And Distribution Corp	2752	1384
West Side Communications Inc	5065	385
West Side Electric Company Inc	1731	930
West Side Industrial Supply Inc	5084	694
West Side Telephone Co	4813	380
West Side Tractor Sales Inc	5082	91
West Side Transport Inc	4213	290
West Star Aviation Inc	3724	10
West Star Electric Inc	1731	1827
West Star Electrical Contractors Inc	1731	697
West Suburban Bancorp Inc	6712	276
West Suburban Bank	6035	54
West Suburban Medical Center	8011	22
West Tennessee Express Inc	4213	1481
West Texas National Bank	6712	261
West Texas Printing Co	2752	832
West Tower Communications	1799	91
West Trading Co	5147	57
West Troy Tool and Machine Inc	5051	324
West USA Commercial Realty Inc	6531	13
West Valley Construction Company Inc	1794	27
West View Health Care Center	8051	33
West View Savings Bank	6036	81
West Virginia Glass Company Inc	3442	137
West Virginia Newspaper Publishing Co	2711	334
West Virginia Pcs Alliance LC	4899	201
West Virginia Signal and Light Inc	1731	1178
West Virginia-American Water Co	4941	30
West Virginia-Ohio Motor Sales Inc	5511	1189
West Wind Litho Inc	2732	45
West Window Corp	3442	31

Company Name	SIC	Rank
West Wisconsin Telcom Cooperative Inc	4813	394
West Wisconsin Transport Inc	4213	768
West Wood Products Inc	2499	39
Westaff Support Inc	7363	89
Westaff USA Inc	7363	90
Westak Inc	3672	74
Westamerica Bancorp	6712	115
Westamerica Bank	6022	16
Westamerica Graphics Inc	2752	415
Westar Capital LLC	6799	184
Westar Contract Kitchen and Bath Corp	5074	96
Westar Energy Inc	4931	18
Westar Graphics Inc	2752	1802
Westar Medical Products Inc	3843	76
Westat Inc	8732	1
Westborough Buick Pontiac GMC Inc	5511	965
Westbridge Realty	6531	386
Westbridge Research Group	2879	53
Westbrook Electric Construction LLC	1731	2235
Westbrook Jr Howard Wayne	7349	418
Westbrook Manufacturing Inc	3599	140
Westbrook Pharmaceutical and Surgical Supply Co	5122	81
Westbrook Technologies Inc	7371	413
Westburgh Electric Inc	5063	706
Westburne Credit Department	5084	949
Westbury Logistics	4213	2323
Westby Co-Operative Creamery	2022	63
West-Camp Press Inc	2752	399
Westcast Inc	3433	8
Westchester Book/Rainsford Type Inc	2791	14
Westchester Capital Management Inc	6282	252
Westchester Employment Agency Inc	7361	294
Westchester Modular Homes Inc	2452	30
Westcliffe Publishers Inc	2731	369
Westco Chemicals Inc	2899	90
Westco Systems Inc	5065	621
Westcoast Helicopter and Accessories	7699	251
West-Com Nurse Call Systems Inc	3663	177
Westcon	5045	102
Westcon Group Inc	7379	10
Westcor	3679	233
Westcor Partners	6552	28
Westec Industries Inc	5084	489
Westec Intelligence Surveillance	7382	18
Westec Plastics Corp	3089	1012
Westech Computer Systems Inc	7378	110
Westech Engineering Inc	3589	16
Westech Recyclers Inc	5045	867
Westech Seal Inc	2891	112
Westek Electronics Inc	3669	187
Westel Communications Inc	5065	920
Westel Inc	4813	108
Westell Inc	3661	19
Westell Technologies Inc	3661	21
Westendorf Manufacturing Company Inc	3523	115
Westerbeke Corp	3621	62
Westerly Inc	3552	24
Western Ag Enterprises Inc	2394	21
Western Air Limbach	1711	59
Western Aircraft Inc	4581	28
Western Alliance Bancorp	6719	21
Western Allied Mechanical Inc	1711	74
Western Allied Service Co	7623	6
Western American Inc	2891	72
Western American Mailers Inc	7331	146
Western Analytical Products Inc	5049	106
Western and Southern Financial Group	6311	28
Western and Southern Life Insurance Co	6311	95
Western Asset Managed High Income Fund Inc	6726	57
Western Asset Managed Municipals Fund Inc	6726	28
Western Asset Management Co	6282	679
Western Automation Inc	5063	124
Western Bank (Alamogordo New Mexico)	6022	780
Western Beef Inc	5411	121
Western Bowl Inc	7933	6
Western Box Meat Distributors Inc	4213	560
Western Branch Diesel Inc	5084	87
Western Branch Metals LC	5051	349
Western Building Specialties Of Sacramento	5031	331
Western Bus Sales Inc	5012	85
Western Carolina Electrical Supply Co	5063	432
Western Carolina Publishing Company Inc	2711	746
Western Case Inc	3089	924
Western Cnc Inc	3599	283
Western Commercial Bank	6029	30
Western Communications Inc	2711	203
Western Computer	3571	104
Western Computer Service Inc	7374	333
Western Conference Of Teamsters Pension Trust Fund	6733	10
Western Construction Components Inc	3799	27
Western Construction Group	1799	15
Western Construction Inc	1611	244

Company Name	SIC	Rank
Western Contract Furnishers of Sacramento	5712	26
Western Contract Interiors	7389	1443
Western Cooperative Co	5261	14
Western Cooperative Electric Association Inc	4911	503
Western Corporate Federal Credit Union	6061	145
Western Cutterheads Inc	5084	901
Western Dairy Products Inc	5143	14
Western DataCom Company Inc	3661	196
Western Design Center Inc	6794	156
Western Development Corp	6531	269
Western Diesel Services Inc	3519	17
Western Digital Corp	3572	3
Western Distributing Co	5182	14
Western Distributing Transportation Corp	4213	567
Western District Warehousing Corp	5159	20
Western Electronic Components Corp	3823	461
Western Energy Co	1221	17
Western Engineering Supply Company Inc	5049	134
Western Engravers Supply Inc	5087	59
Western Enterprises	3548	5
Western Environmental Services and Testing Inc	8734	98
Western Express Holdings Inc	4213	123
Western Exterminator Co	7342	4
Western Extralite Co	5063	18
Western Falcon Inc	3069	187
Western Family Foods Inc	5141	66
Western Farmers Electric Coop	4911	132
Western Filament Inc	2298	6
Western Folder Distributing Company Inc	7375	150
Western Forms Inc	3444	23
Western Gage Corp	3545	259
Western Gas Partners LP	4922	14
Western Golf Inc	5091	120
Western Graphics Inc	2752	432
Western Hydrostatics Inc	3594	18
Western Illinois Electrical Coop	4911	434
Western Industrial Tooling Inc	3599	1359
Western Industries Corp	3086	37
Western Industries Inc	3444	12
Western Integrated Technologies Inc	5084	165
Western International Gas and Cylinders Inc	5169	98
Western Iowa Coop	5153	134
Western Kentucky Plastics Inc	3089	1398
Western Lighting Industries Inc	3645	72
Western Lithograph Of Texas	2752	356
Western Livestock Reporter Inc	5192	33
Western Machine Works Inc	3549	120
Western Magnum Corp	3599	2397
Western Mailing Lists	7331	262
Western Mass Rendering Company Inc	2077	13
Western Massachusetts Electric Co	4911	109
Western Medical Management LLC	8741	286
Western Metal Lath	3449	13
Western Methods Machinery Corp	3728	106
Western Micro Services Inc	7374	226
Western Mobile Denver Paving Div	1611	63
Western Natural Gas Co	5984	28
Western Nevada Supply Co	5074	9
Western New Mexico Telephone Co	4813	289
Western New York Independent Living Inc	8322	115
Western Oil Spreading Services Inc	2951	43
Western Ophthalmics Corp	5995	23
Western Oregon Web Press Inc	2752	1465
Western Pacific Building Materials Inc	5031	157
Western Pacific Packaging Inc	7389	1290
Western Pacific Storage Solutions Inc	2542	24
Western Paging And Voice Mail Systems I LP	4812	113
Western Paving Contractors Inc	1611	132
Western Pennsylvania Steel Fabricating Inc	3443	197
Western Petroleum Co	5172	24
Western Pioneer Inc	4142	1
Western Plains Regional Hospital LLC	8062	200
Western Plastics Inc	3081	77
Western Pneumatic Tube Company LLC	3317	40
Western Pneumatics Inc	3535	28
Western Polymer Corp	2046	8
Western Ports Transportation	4213	1475
Western Pottery LLC	5074	206
Western Power Products Inc	5084	456
Western Precision Aero	3599	1140
Western Precooling Systems	7359	46
Western Printing Co	2752	466
Western Printing Company Inc	2752	907
Western Printing Ink Corp	2893	37
Western Printing Machinery Co	3555	51
Western Products Inc (Fargo North Dakota)	5033	17
Western Products (Milwaukee Wisconsin)	3531	75
Western Professional Group Inc	3564	145
Western Quality Food Products LC	2026	64
Western Refining Inc	2911	15

Company Name	SIC	Rank
Western Reflections LLC	5031	241
Western Refrigerated Freight System	4213	2457
Western Regional Off-Track Betting Corp	7999	48
Western Reserve Care System	7389	165
Western Reserve Controls Inc	3679	409
Western Reserve Farm Cooperative Inc	5191	48
Western Reserve Life Assurance Company of Ohio	6311	134
Western Reserve Metals Inc	5051	449
Western Rivers Boat Management Inc	4449	15
Western Robidoux Inc	2752	1569
Western Rubber and Supply Inc	5085	420
Western Saw Manufacturers Inc	3425	11
Western Scrap Processing Company Inc	3341	35
Western Screen Print Corp	2759	282
Western Screw Products Inc	3599	614
Western Securities Company of Delaware	3537	33
Western Select Properties LP	6552	242
Western Semi Solutions Inc	3674	486
Western Shield Acquisitions LLC	2754	24
Western Sizzlin Corp	5812	356
Western Slate Co	3821	22
Western Slope Auto Inc	5511	935
Western Springs National Bank and Trust	6021	309
Western States Envelope Co	2677	5
Western States Equipment	5013	59
Western States Fire Protection Company Inc	1711	20
Western States Machine Co	7694	3
Western States Manufacturing Company Inc	5014	65
Western States Minerals Corp	1041	18
Western States Oil Company Inc	5172	111
Western States Petroleum Inc	5172	114
Western States Tool and Supply Corp	5085	346
Western Steel Cutting Inc	5051	492
Western Steel Inc	1389	46
Western Sugar Coop	2063	3
Western Summit Manufacturing Corp	3081	118
Western Supermarkets Inc	5411	201
Western Supplies Co	3544	810
Western Supply Corp	5072	5
Western Systems and Fabrication Inc	3444	221
Western Technolgy Investments	6799	84
Western Technologies Inc	3547	24
Western Telematic Inc	3661	114
Western Textile Products Co	2396	35
Western Tire Centers Inc	5531	23
Western Titanium Inc	5051	193
Western Tool Supply Inc	5082	14
Western Trailer Co	3715	28
Western Trailer Equipment and Manufacturing Company Of Abilene	5013	299
Western Transport	4213	684
Western Transport Inc	4213	873
Western Truck Parts and Equipment	7513	9
Western Trucking	4213	2773
Western Tube and Conduit Corp	3317	22
Western Union Co	6099	3
Western United Electric Supply Corp	5063	69
Western Wares LLC	7372	4777
Western Washington University	8221	30
Western Water Co	6799	155
Western Water Constructors Inc	1623	50
Western Water Products Inc	3589	257
Western Window Systems	3442	48
Western Wire Works Inc	3496	17
Western Wood Preserving Co	5031	341
Western Wood Products Inc	5099	120
Western Woods Inc	5031	71
Western Yeast Company Inc	2048	129
Western-Cullen-Hayes Inc	3669	88
Western-Southern Enterprises	6311	88
Westerra Management LLC	6552	231
Westervelt Co	0831	1
Westest Engineering Corp	8748	255
West-Fair Electric Contractors Inc	1731	360
Westfall GMC Truck Inc	5511	391
Westfield America Inc	6798	65
Westfield Electric Inc	1731	598
Westfield Financial Inc	6712	268
Westfield Group	6331	180
Westfield Group USA	6512	39
Westfield Homes USA Inc	1531	66
Westfield News Publishing Inc	2711	307
Westfield Savings Bank	6022	175
Westfield Sheet Metal Works Inc	3444	202
Westfield Steel Inc	5051	224
Westfloor Inc	5023	67
Westford Group Inc	8741	189
Westgate Chevrolet Inc	5511	444
Westgate Fabrics Inc	5198	3
Westgate Inc	1731	319
Westgate Interiors LLC	5131	25
Westgate Mall LP	6531	298
Westgood Manufacturing Co	3544	789
WESTGROUP Management LLC	6552	245
Westheffer Company Inc	3523	193
Westin Automotive Products Inc	3714	241

Company Name	SIC	Rank
Westin Inc	2013	34
Westin Industries Inc	1731	2337
Westinghouse Air Brake Technologies Corp	3743	3
Westinghouse Lighting Corp	5063	213
Westinghouse Solar Inc	3433	48
Westlake Chemical Corp	2869	5
Westlake Hardware Inc	5251	28
Westlake Plastics Co	3081	31
Westland Electric Inc	1731	2303
Westland Enterprises Inc	2759	330
Westland International Corp	5084	810
Westland Printers Inc	2752	183
Westland Technologies Inc	3061	19
Westlaw Business	7375	18
Westlie Motor Co	5511	309
Westlock Controls Corp	3592	14
Westmaas Electric Co	1731	1109
Westman Freightliner Inc	3799	12
Westmark Industries Inc	2672	46
Westmark Products Inc	2541	9
Westmed Inc	3841	187
Westminster Capital Inc	6719	150
Westminster Cracker Company Inc	2052	22
Westminster Village Muncie Inc	8361	80
Westmont Hospitality Group	6531	199
Westmont Industries	3536	28
Westmoor Manufacturing Co	2321	25
Westmoreland Coal Co	1221	13
Westmoreland Coal Sales Co	1221	6
Westmoreland Mechanical Testing and Research Inc	8734	46
Westmoreland Telephone Co	5065	892
WestNet Inc	2731	97
Westoak Industries Inc	3679	627
Weston and Muir	7372	4778
Weston Buick GMC	5511	285
Weston Builders Supply Co	5211	213
Weston Presidio Capital Ii LP	5192	12
Weston Solutions Inc	4959	7
Weston Transportation Inc	4213	2039
Weston Woods Studio Inc	7812	98
Weston-Mason And Associates Inc	7311	876
Westosha Tool Company Inc	3544	595
Westover Consultants Inc	8742	479
Westover Scientific Inc	3826	42
Westpeak Investment Advisors LP	6282	298
Westphal Electric Inc	1731	2405
WestPoint Home Inc	2392	1
Westport Axle Corp	3463	7
Westport Consulting Group Inc	6282	657
Westport Environmental Systems LP	3564	95
Westport Hardness and Gaging Corp	5084	783
Westport Precision LLC	3444	192
Westport Research Associates Inc	3575	38
Westport Resources Management Inc	6282	526
Westport Shipyard Inc	3732	25
Westra Construction Corp	1623	81
Westrec Marina Management Inc	4493	3
Westrex International	3577	349
Westrock Group Inc	6211	77
WestRogers Advertising	7311	618
Westron Corp	3641	26
Westserve Inc	7381	152
Westshore Data Inc	1731	2578
West-Specialties Partners	5085	247
Weststar Construction Inc	1611	224
Weststar Financial Services Corp	6035	172
WestStart-CALSTART	8733	8
Westtower Communications	1623	473
Westtown Consulting Group Inc	7379	1380
Westview Capital Partners	6799	139
West-Ward Pharmaceutical Corp	2834	210
Westward Seafoods Inc	2092	27
Westway Electric Systems Inc	1731	1650
Westway Ford Inc	5511	870
Westway Holdings Corp	6719	123
Westwind Computing Inc	5734	153
Westwind Technologies Inc	3728	119
Westwood Associates Inc	5065	311
Westwood Cartage Inc	4213	1113
Westwood Computers LLC	5045	904
Westwood Corp	3613	42
Westwood Corp (Tulsa Oklahoma)	3613	25
Westwood Group	3827	145
Westwood Group Inc	7948	27
Westwood Holdings Group Inc	6282	288
Westwood Homestead Financial Corp	6712	685
Westwood Industries Inc	2512	81
Westwood Insurance Agency	6411	203
Westwood Machine and Tool Co	3544	762
Westwood Millwork Inc	5031	372
Westwood Precision Inc	3599	915
Westwood Shipping Lines	4412	21
WestWorld Productions Inc	2721	142
Westye Group - South Central LP	5064	32
Westye Group - Southeast Inc	5064	77
Wet Planet Beverage Co	5149	83
Wet Seal Inc	5621	15
Wetherill Associates Inc	5013	134
Wetmore Tool And Engineering Co	3545	61
Wet-N-Stick LLC	2679	70
Wetpaintcom Inc	7372	1363
Wetsel Inc	5193	10

Company Name	SIC	Rank
Wettekin Electronics	8711	689
Wetzel Brothers Inc	2752	451
Wetzel's Pretzels LLC	6794	101
Wexford Capital LLC	6799	11
Wexford Collection	2511	18
Wexford Group International Inc	8742	114
Wexford Health Sources Inc	8741	72
Wexford Sand Co	1446	12
Wexler and Walker Public Policy Associates	8743	119
Wexley School for Girls LLC	7311	759
Wexpro Co	1311	83
Weyand Fisheries Inc	5146	57
Weyauwega Star Dairy Inc	2022	16
Weyco Group Inc	3143	5
Weydman Electric Inc	1731	806
Weyerhaeuser Co	2611	1
Weyerhaeuser Paper Co Containerboard Packaging Div	2631	7
Weyerhaeuser Real Estate Co	1531	9
WF Anderson Electric Inc	1731	1949
WF Gormley and Sons Funeral Home	7261	7
WF Lake Corp	3052	31
WF Meyers Company Inc	3545	123
WF Saunders and Sons Inc	3273	80
WF Young Inc	5122	58
WFC Company Inc	3089	889
WFMY Television Corp	4833	126
WFP Inc	3559	405
WFPX TV-Fayetteville	4833	177
Wfs Services Inc	8742	470
Wft Communications Inc	1731	1213
WFXG TV	4833	235
WG Block Co	3272	54
Wg Stang LLC	1623	696
WG Yates and Sons Construction Co	1541	24
WGBC-TV LLC	4833	241
WGCHAM 1490	4832	268
WGGB Inc	4833	30
WGI Corp	2731	327
WGL Holdings Inc	4924	9
Wgl Talk Studio Line	4832	207
WGME Licensee LLC	4833	37
WGPX TV- Greensboro	4833	127
WGRX Thunder 1045	4832	226
WH Autopilots Inc	3625	349
WH Braum Inc	5451	2
WH C Inc	1623	185
WH Cooke and Company Inc	3823	245
WH Fay Co	4213	2556
WH Fetzer and Sons Manufacturing Inc	3312	116
Wh Industries Inc	3714	212
WH Pacific Inc	8711	215
WH Paige and Company Inc	7359	76
WH Reaves and Company Inc	6282	494
Whalen and Co	8721	432
Whalen Co	3585	113
Whalen Furniture Manufacturing Inc	2511	8
Whalen/Stoddard Inc	6531	394
Whalen Trucking Inc	4213	1030
Whalewalk Inn	7011	229
Whaley Construction Company Inc	1542	186
Whaley Pecan Company Inc	5159	24
Whaling City Ford	5511	656
Whaling Distributors Inc	2385	3
Whallon Machinery Inc	3565	96
Wham-O Inc	3949	59
Whan Bob and Son Electronics Inc	3679	863
Wharton Jeep	5511	502
Whataburger Inc	5812	99
Whatcom Educational Credit Union	6062	12
Whatcom Electric Company Inc	5013	291
Whatcom Farmers Co-Op	5191	52
Whatever It Takes Transmissions and Parts Inc	5015	4
Whatman Inc	3826	51
Whayne And Sons Enterprises Inc	7349	161
Whayne Supply Co	5082	4
WHDFT V-15	4833	217
Wheat Energy Services	5171	75
Wheat Systems Integration LLC	7373	666
Wheatbelt Public Power District	4911	404
Wheatland Bank	6022	501
Wheatland Bank (Naperville Illinois)	6022	308
Wheatland Electric Cooperative Inc	4911	279
Wheatland Rural Electric Association	4911	579
Wheatland Systems Inc	7371	1250
Wheatland Tube Co	3317	15
Wheatmark Inc	2731	196
Wheaton Dumont Cooperative Elevator Inc	2875	28
Wheaton Franciscan Healthcare	8741	40
Wheaton Franciscan Services Inc	8062	44
Wheaton Science Products Inc	3221	8
Wheaton Van Lines Inc	4213	165
Wheaton World Wide Moving	4213	289
Wheatstone Corp	3663	112
Whec-Tv LLC	4899	156
Wheel Creations Plus Inc	5013	421
Wheel Repair By Adam Inc	5013	246
Wheelabrator Technologies Inc	4953	15
Wheelchairs Of Kansas	3842	124
Wheelchairs Plus Inc	5999	210

Company Name	SIC	Rank
Wheeled Coach Industries Corp	3711	29
Wheeler Arts	7372	2733
Wheeler Brothers Grain Company Inc	5153	30
Wheeler Brothers Inc	5013	114
Wheeler Consolidated Inc	5085	121
Wheeler Inc	7379	1330
Wheeler Industries Inc	3599	1895
Wheeler Manufacturing Company Inc	3911	40
Wheeler Oil Co	1311	206
Wheeler's Corp	5031	41
Wheeler's Las Vegas RV	5561	21
Wheeling Coffee and Spice Company Inc	2095	64
Wheelock Manufacturing Inc	3679	608
Wheels Clipper	4213	644
Wheels Inc	7515	3
WheelWorks	5014	4
Wheelwright Lumber Co	5211	112
Wheelwright Trucking Company Inc	4213	2684
Whelan Capital Management	6282	640
Whelan Communications Inc	8743	321
Whelan's Inc	5211	91
Whelen Engineering Company Inc	3647	7
Where Inc	4899	122
Whereoware LLC	7389	2320
Wherley Moving and Storage Inc	4213	2058
Whf Electrical Contractors Inc	1731	862
Whicker Asset Management LLC	3089	836
Whidbey Island Bank	6022	341
Whidbey Telecom	4813	178
Whimsy Inc	4213	2458
Whink Products Co	2842	109
Whip City Tool and Die Corp	3544	545
Whip-Mix Corp	3843	16
Whipple and Company PC	8721	364
Whirl-Air-Flow Corp	3535	121
Whirley - DrinkWorks Inc	3089	137
Whirley Industries Inc	3089	193
Whirlpool Corp	3632	1
Whirltronics	3524	24
Whirlwind Holding Company Inc	3448	9
Whirlwind Music Distributors Inc	3651	87
Whisco Component Engineering Inc	3812	172
Whiskey Hill Electric Inc	1731	2177
Whispering Pines West	8361	184
Whistler Machine Works Inc	3599	803
Whit Holdings Inc	3991	19
Whitaker Bank Corp	6712	112
Whitaker Brothers Business Machines Inc	5044	107
Whitaker Buick Jeep Eagle Co	5511	842
Whitaker Corp	5192	23
Whitaker Furniture Company Inc	2511	73
Whitaker Oil Co	5172	45
Whitaker Physician Billing Services Inc	8721	363
Whitaker Security Inc	5063	988
Whitaker Transportation Co	4213	2024
Whitbread Management Inc	8741	270
Whitcom Partners Inc	6282	484
Whitcomb Trucking Inc	4213	2240
Whitcraft LLC	3443	59
White and Baldacci	8742	382
White and Case LLP	8111	9
White and Steele PC	8111	382
White and Williams LLP	8111	308
White Apron Inc	5147	29
White Birch Paper Co	2621	40
White Brothers Auto Supply Inc	5013	150
White Brothers Trucking Co	4213	2134
White Cap Industries Inc	5072	6
White Castle System Inc	5812	82
White Cloud Grain Company Inc	5191	75
White Cloud Mountain Company Inc	5149	192
White Coffee Corp	2095	22
White Coffee Pot Family Inns Inc	5812	392
White Construction Company Inc	1611	87
White County Rural Electric Membership Coop	4911	451
White Crane Systems Inc	7372	4779
White Drive Products Inc	3594	14
White Eagle Printing Company Inc	2752	1235
White Electric Inc	1731	1287
White Electric Supply Co (Lincoln Nebraska)	5063	804
White Electronic Designs Corp	3674	128
White Engineering Associates Inc	8711	550
White Engineering Surfaces Corp	3479	41
White Glove Janitorial and Building Maintenance Inc	7349	379
White Glove Janitorial Services and Supply Inc	7349	455
White Glove Placement Inc	7361	76
White Glove Service Inc	8742	496
White Graphics Inc	2761	80
White Hardware Company Inc	5211	252
White Hawk Pictures Inc	7812	87
White House / Black Market	5621	33
White Industries LLC	3559	79
White Instruments	3651	200
White James C Company Inc	3679	570
White Lodging Services Corp	7011	144
White Mountain Apache Tribe	8741	120
White Mountain Cable	1731	15
White Mountain Publishing Co	2711	243

Company Name	SIC	Rank
White Mountains Capital Inc	6331	281
White Mountains Holdings Inc	6331	261
White Mountains Insurance Group Ltd	6331	53
White Nelson and Co	8721	34
White Oak Group Inc	2752	829
White Oak Landscape Company Inc	0782	12
White Oak Mills Inc	2048	31
White Outdoor Products Co	5072	19
White Pines Corp	2752	1149
White River Capital Inc	6141	58
White River Hardwoods-Woodworks Inc	2499	22
White River Health System Inc	8062	126
White Rock Products Corp	5149	188
White Rock Quarry LP	1422	12
White Rose Food Inc	5141	12
White Rose Paper Co	5111	18
White Sewing Machine Co	5064	38
White Star Machinery and Supply Company Inc	5082	49
White Star Steel Inc	5051	304
White Star Video	7812	78
White Stone Group Inc	7372	2247
White Transportation Services	4213	2336
White Water Valley Rural Electric Membership Corp	4911	538
White Way Sign and Maintenance Company Inc	3993	44
White William D Company Inc	1731	2246
White Wing Resource Centre	5942	28
White Wolf Software Inc	7372	4897
Whitebirch Enterprises Inc	6552	24
Whiteboard Labs LLC	7336	110
White-Brook Inc	3599	1855
Whiteco Inc	3728	213
Whitegold Solutions Inc	7379	870
WhiteGyr	7379	1217
Whitehall Furniture LLC	2521	38
Whitehall Products LLC	3599	477
Whitehouse Post Productions	7812	151
Whitehurst Transport Inc	4213	854
Whiteline Express Ltd	4213	810
White-Rodgers Div	3822	102
White's Boots Inc	5661	15
White's Bridge Tooling Inc	3569	256
White's Frontier Motors	5511	709
White's Old Mill Garden Center	5261	15
White's Tractor and Truck Inc	5084	112
Whitesell Construction Company Inc	1541	130
Whitesell Corp	3965	4
Whitesides Construction Inc	1623	531
Whitestone Acquisition Corp	2676	4
Whitestone Group Inc	7382	36
Whitestone REIT	6798	171
Whitewater Manufacturing Inc	3069	273
Whitewater Processing Co	2015	50
WhiteWave Foods Co	2099	2
Whitfield and Eddy PLC	8111	434
Whitfield Foods Inc	2087	33
Whitfield R A Manufacturing Company Inc	3523	276
Whithner Corp	2759	444
Whiting Construction Company Inc	1623	365
Whiting Corp	3536	14
Whiting Door Manufacturing Corp	3714	167
Whiting Petroleum Corp	1311	28
Whiting Systems Inc	3589	116
Whiting-Turner Contracting Co	1542	7
Whitlam Label Company Inc	2759	68
Whitley Manufacturing Company Inc	1542	393
Whitley Mobile Homes Inc	4213	769
Whitley Printing Company LLC	2759	112
Whitley Products Inc	3498	34
Whitlock Brothers Inc	5031	278
Whitlock Business Systems Inc	5112	60
Whitlock Group	5045	5
Whitman Communications Inc	2752	1477
Whitman Controls Corp	3643	134
Whitman Exterminating Co	7342	86
Whitman Ford Company Inc	5511	825
Whitman Mold Inc	3599	2206
Whitman Products Company Inc	3672	264
Whitman Truss and Lumber Inc	5211	309
Whitman Vault Inc	5087	134
Whitmer Fuels Inc	4932	10
Whitmor Company Inc	3613	155
Whitmore Group	2899	88
Whitmore Manufacturing Co	2992	10
Whitmore Print And Imaging Inc	2752	190
Whitney and Company LLC	6799	286
Whitney and Son Inc	3559	337
Whitney and Whitney Inc	8748	443
Whitney Blake Co	5051	232
Whitney Electric Co	1731	628
Whitney National Bank	6021	28
Whitney Originals Inc	3999	111
Whitney Partners LLC	7361	118
Whitney Printing Corp	2759	490
Whitney Products Inc	3842	327
Whitney Tool Company Inc	3545	334
Whitney Trucking Inc	4213	3120
Whitney Worldwide Inc	5045	473
Whitridge Associates Inc	7361	141
Whitson Lumber Company Inc	2426	32
Whittaker and Gooding Trucking Co	4212	62
Whittaker Clark and Daniels	2865	16
Whittemore Dowen and Ricciardelli LLP	8721	158
Whitten Pumps Inc	3561	109
Whittet-Higgins Co	3568	50
Whittier Fertilizer Co	2875	20
Whittier Mailing Service Inc	7331	218
Whittier Wood Products Co	2511	39
Whittington Service Group Inc	7349	252
Whittle Realty	6531	255
Whittlesea Blue Cab Co	4121	1
Whittmanhart	8744	17
Whitworth Tool Inc	3599	200
Whiz Integrated Systems Software Incorporated	7372	4025
WHMETV and Radio	4832	107
Whmx Fm 1057	4832	294
WHO Manufacturing Company Inc	3546	36
Whole Foods Market Inc	5411	13
Whole Internet LLC	7379	1004
Whole Systems International	2741	458
Wholesale Carrier Services Inc	4812	76
Wholesale East Coast Phone Card Express	4813	624
Wholesale Electric Supply Company Inc (Bowling Green Kentucky)	5063	556
Wholesale Electric Supply Company Inc (Texarkana Texas)	5063	189
Wholesale Electric Supply Company of Houston Inc	5063	56
Wholesale Envelope Inc	2752	1397
Wholesale Interiors Inc	5712	75
Wholesale Lighting Inc	5063	878
Wholesale Printers Inc	2752	1419
Wholesale Roofing Supply Inc	5033	51
Wholesale Sheet Metal Inc	5051	293
Wholesale Supply Group Inc	5074	45
Wholesale Tape and Supply Co	3577	364
WHP Electronics Inc	5731	31
WHY USA Financial Group Inc	6531	452
Whyte Hirschboeck Dudek SC	8111	176
WI Simonson Inc	5511	1010
Wicc Ltd	3612	72
WICD Licensee LLC	4833	61
Wichita Bindery Inc	2789	126
Wichita Eagle	2711	187
Wichita Falls Freightliner LP	5013	293
Wichita Falls Manufacturing Inc	3364	23
Wichita Falls Nunn Electrical Supply	5063	110
Wichita Restaurant Supply Company Inc	5046	291
Wichita Steel Fabricators Inc	3443	165
Wick Communications Co	2711	927
Wicked Sportswear/Footwear LLC	5139	26
Wickenburg Pest Control	7342	38
Wicker Machine Co	3531	230
Wicker Services Inc	4213	1477
Wicker Smith Tutan O'Hara McCoy and Ford PA	8111	250
Wicker's Food Products Inc	2033	115
Wickersham Construction and Engineering Inc	1541	160
Wickett and Craig Of America Inc	3111	6
Wickford Inc	5013	223
Wickland Oil Co	6719	176
Wicks Group of Companies LLC	6719	67
Wicks Pies Inc	2053	19
Wico Metal Products Company Inc	3465	40
WICOR Inc	3561	22
WICS Licensee LLC	4833	43
Widearea Systems	4899	198
WideBand Corp	3577	510
Widener-Burrows and Associates Inc	8732	67
Wideorbit Inc	7371	476
Widepoint Corp	8742	190
Widman Construction Inc	1623	346
Widmer's Cheese Cellars Inc	2022	78
Widmeyer Communications	8743	39
Widoffs Modern Bakery Inc	5149	151
Widom Wein Cohen O'Leary Terasawa	8712	174
Wiegand and Storrer Inc	1623	459
Wiegold and Sons Inc	7623	10
Wieland Copper Products LLC	3351	17
Wieland Electric Inc	5063	224
Wieland Metals Inc	3351	23
Wiemuth and Son Company Inc	5194	10
Wienmar Inc	3281	12
Wiese Industries Inc	3523	125
Wiesen Edm Inc	3312	135
Wiesner Publications LLC	2721	91
Wiesnermedia LLC	2721	238
Wiest Truck Line Inc	4213	1593
Wifco Steel Products Inc	3446	43
Wigdahl Electric Co	1731	349
Wiggin and Dana LLP	8111	145
Wiggins Airways Inc	5088	12
Wiggins Lift Company Inc	3537	57
Wiggins Telephone Association	4813	411
Wight and Co	8712	28
Wightman Enterprises Inc	7363	301
Wiginton Corp	1711	11
WII Components Inc	2441	1
Wika Holding Corp	3823	44
Wikler and Company Inc	8748	247
Wikoff Color Corp	2893	4
Wilbanks International Inc	5083	18
Wilbedone Inc	2541	56
Wilber Corp	6712	421
Wilber National Bank (Oneonta New York)	6021	89
Wilbert Burial Vault Corp	5087	167
Wilbert Funeral Services Inc	3272	109
Wilbert Inc	3272	6
Wilbrecht Electronics Inc Elecpac Div	3679	401
Wilbrecht Ledco Inc	3676	24
Wilbur Smith Associates Inc	8711	120
Wilbur-Ellis Co	5191	3
Wil-Cal Lighting Management Company Inc	1731	1110
Wilcas Wire Co	3694	26
Wilco Corp	3677	96
Wilco Electrical LLC	1731	912
Wilco Machine and Fab Inc	3599	212
Wilco Molding Inc	3089	1772
Wilco Supply	5072	66
Wilcom America Inc	2211	37
Wilcom Inc	3825	126
Wilcon Corp	1542	327
Wilcorp Enterprises	7389	2214
Wilcorp Industries Inc	7389	1140
Wilco-Winfield LLC	2879	8
Wilcox Frozen Foods Inc	5142	17
Wilcox Industries Corp	3827	38
Wilcox Machine Co	3599	476
Wild Berry Incense Inc	2899	223
Wild Bird Centers of America Inc	6794	106
Wild Birds Unlimited Inc	5999	83
Wild Brain Inc	7379	1677
Wild Child Editorial Inc	7812	171
Wild Horse Industrial Corp	3565	161
Wild RecordsCom Inc	5099	146
Wild Rice Electric Cooperative Inc	4911	480
Wild West Lighting Inc	5063	783
Wild West Sound Company Inc	5731	159
WildBlue Communications Inc	4833	70
Wildcat Connectors Inc	3678	81
Wildcat Manufacturing Company Inc	3523	157
Wilde Automotive Group	5511	414
Wilde Of West Allis Inc	5511	169
Wildeck Inc	3441	128
Wilden Pump and Engineering Company Inc	3561	42
Wilderness Inspirations	5961	190
Wildfire Studios	7389	739
Wildish Land Co	1521	63
Wildland Adventures Inc	4725	24
Wildlife Pharmaceuticals Inc	2834	404
Wildman Harrold Attorneys and Counselors	8111	245
Wildon Solutions LLC	7379	1170
WildPackets Inc	7372	1384
Wildridge Machine LLC	3599	1843
Wildside Press / Judson Rosebush Co	2741	398
WildTangent Inc	7372	205
Wildwood Cabinets Inc	5031	336
Wildwood Electronics Inc	3613	81
Wildwood Lamps and Accents Inc	3645	54
Wilen Press LLC	7389	943
Wilentz Goldman and Spitzer PA	8111	99
Wiley Davis Electrical Inc	1731	1560
Wiley Publishing Services Inc	2731	2
Wiley Rein LLP	8111	202
Wiley Sanders Truck Lines	4213	237
Wilfred's Sea Food Inc	5146	41
Wilhelm Construction Inc	1542	133
Wilhelmina International Inc	8742	330
Wilhelmsen Callenberg Inc	7629	4
Wilke International Inc	5141	149
Wilke/Thornton Inc	7372	3164
Wilkens-Anderson Co	5049	31
Wilkerson Guthmann and Johnson Ltd	8721	380
Wilkerson Inc	3089	1728
Wilkerson Instrument Company Inc	3679	673
Wilkes and Mclean Ltd	3625	193
Wilkes Barre Window Cleaning Inc	7349	394
Wilkie Brothers Conveyors Inc	3535	104
Wilkins Electric Company Inc	1731	1135
Wilkins Kaiser and Olsen Inc	2421	74
Wilkins Research Services Inc	8732	65
Wilkinson Banking Corp	6712	282
Wilkinson Chemical Corp	2819	129
Wilkinson Industries LLC	3089	127
Wilkins-Rogers Inc	0723	15
Wilks Publications Inc	2721	325
Will Good Industries Inc	8331	116
Will Poultry Company Inc	5144	15
Willamette Broadband LLC	4841	130
Willamette Electric Inc	1731	1488
Willamette Graystone Inc	5211	119
Willamette Pattern Works	3543	52
Willamette Plastics	3089	1654
Willamette Valley Bank	6036	91
Willamette Valley Co	5085	30
Willamette Valley Rehabilitation Center Inc	7349	268
Willamette Valley Vineyards Inc	2084	33
Willard Dunham Construction Co	1541	261

Company Name	SIC	Rank
Willard J Stearns and Sons Inc	2026	79
Willard Machine	3599	2390
Willard Marine Inc	3732	66
Willard Milling Inc	2047	44
Willard Packaging Company Inc	2653	89
Willbros Engineers Inc	8742	334
Willbros Group Inc	1389	9
Will-Burt Co	3599	61
Willcare Inc	8082	16
Willco Sales and Services Inc	5046	106
Willco Technologies Inc	7379	1131
Willdan Group Inc	8711	153
Wille Brothers Co	1771	18
Wille Brothers Company Concrete Div	2951	36
Wille Electric Supply Co	5063	48
Willer Tool Corp	3544	215
Willert Home Products Inc	3089	297
Willet Hauser Architectural Glass Inc	1793	8
Willett Lumber Co	5031	438
Willey Printing Company Inc	2752	1554
William A Fraser Inc	5999	127
William A Grunnah Jr	7379	1596
William A Hazel Inc	6552	121
William A Moddrel	3599	2510
William Arthur Inc	2678	5
William B Altman Inc	4213	1758
William B Eerdmans Publishing Co	2731	56
William B Hopke Company Inc	1623	113
William Barnet and Son Inc Southern Div	2824	6
William Barnet and Son LLC	5199	38
William Beaumont Hospital	8062	33
William Beson Interior Design	7389	1231
William Blair and Company LLC	6211	169
William Blanchard Co	1542	162
William Bolthouse Farms Inc	0161	5
William Boyd Printing Company Inc	2711	375
William Breman Jewish Home Inc	8361	98
William Bunch H Auctioneers and Appraiser LLC	7389	2412
William Charles Printing Company Inc	2752	952
William D Witter Inc	6282	307
William Doyle Galleries Inc	5999	41
William E Baldwin	7353	53
William E Buchan Inc	1521	60
William E Gottfred	8111	588
William E Johnson Associates Inc	8712	281
William E Smith Trucking Inc	4213	2806
William E Walter Inc	1711	143
William Exline Inc	2782	40
William F Cosulich Associates PC	8711	336
William Frick and Co	3993	137
William G Berlin	7336	145
William G Tomko and Son Inc	1711	88
William George Company Inc	5148	65
William H Buckpitt	5045	781
William H Harvey Co	3089	527
William H Lane Inc	1542	311
William H Sadlier Inc	2731	106
William Hezmalhalch Architects Inc	8712	188
William Ho	3577	588
William J Kline and Son Inc	2711	423
William J Labb Sons Inc	3599	1540
William J Schultz Inc	1623	99
William J Shaeffer's Sons Inc	1731	257
William James and Associates Ltd	7379	1067
William Jones and Son Inc	5085	337
William K Bradford Publishing Co	5045	362
William Kenyon and Sons Inc	3599	1888
William L Bonnell Company Inc	3354	8
William L Lyon and Associates Inc	6531	150
William Lyon Homes	1521	27
William M Bird and Company Inc	5023	38
William M Mercer Companies Inc	8742	21
William M Mercer Inc	2741	35
William M Wetmore Inc	1731	2332
William M Young Co	5031	70
William Mills and Associates Inc	7311	345
William Morris Agency Inc	7922	7
William N Cann Inc	2752	1373
William P Gelberg Inc	3993	103
William P Hearne Produce Co	5148	86
William Pattison Moblie Welding	1623	749
William Penn Life Insurance Company of New York	6311	145
William R Hague Inc	3589	59
William R Sharpe Inc	1731	1596
William R Smith Co	2752	1478
William/Reid Ltd	5169	156
William Reisner Corp	5051	151
William Rondina Inc	2335	10
William S Hein and Company Inc	2731	37
William S Trimble Company Inc	5031	142
William Smith Enterprises Inc	3444	225
William Stucky and Associates Inc	7372	2817
William T Peters LLC	2653	125
William Thomas Trucking Inc	4213	1737
William Trotter Co	1521	98
Williams Alaska Petroleum Inc	4922	3
Williams and Anderson LLP	8111	349
Williams and Heintz Map Corp	2752	771
Williams and Wells Co	5088	47
Williams Benator and Libby	8721	33
Williams Brothers Construction	1623	52
Williams Brothers Trucking	4213	743
WILLIAMS Cadco	7372	4650
Williams Capital Group LP	6722	121
Williams Cheese Co	5143	35
Williams Coal Seam Gas Royalty Trust Inc	6792	9
Williams Cohen and Gray Inc	7322	55
Williams Comfort Products	3433	12
Williams Companies Inc	4922	2
Williams Co (Orlando Florida)	1541	136
Williams Construction	1623	444
Williams Controls Inc	3714	152
Williams Corp	5064	74
Williams Dental Laboratory Inc	8072	26
Williams Development and Construction Inc	1541	114
Williams Die and Mold Inc	3089	728
Williams Distributing Co	5075	22
Williams Electronics LLC	1731	1570
Williams Enterprise of Georgia Inc	3443	2
Williams Fire and Hazard Control Inc	8711	229
Williams Flooring Sales Inc	5023	175
Williams Foods Inc	2099	82
Williams Furnace Co	3585	32
Williams Group (Grand Rapids Michigan)	7311	332
Williams Health Care Systems	3842	165
Williams Import Company Inc	5021	114
Williams Incorporated T O	2013	233
Williams Industrial Service Inc	3567	59
Williams Industries Inc	3089	494
Williams Industries Inc (Manassas Virginia)	3441	45
Williams International Company LLC	3764	2
Williams Kastner and Gibbs PLLC	8111	169
Williams Machine And Tool Company Inc	3451	133
Williams Machine Works Inc	3599	1889
Williams Maintenance Inc	7349	410
Williams Manufacturing Corp	3599	2166
Williams Montgomery and John Ltd	8111	487
Williams Oil Filter Service Company Of Tacoma Inc	5085	296
Williams Partners LP	1321	2
Williams Patent Crusher and Pulverizer Company Inc	3532	29
Williams Pipe Line Co	4612	7
Williams Pipelines Partners LP	4922	31
Williams R Manufacturing Inc	3083	77
Williams Sausage Company Inc	2013	50
Williams Scotsman Inc	7359	16
Williams Scotsman International Inc	7359	11
Williams Service Inc	5511	1222
Williams Sound LLC	3842	181
Williams Stationery Company Inc	2759	605
Williams Steel Rule Die Company Inc	3544	869
Williams Supply Inc	5063	271
Williams Tank Lines	4213	650
Williams Thin Film Products	3674	259
Williams Tool Company Inc	3546	4
Williams Tool Inc	3599	1696
Williams Tooling and Manufacturing Inc	3544	863
Williams Tractor Inc	5083	36
Williams Typesetting Company Inc	2791	6
Williams Vyvx Services	4833	53
Williams Welding Inc	1623	200
Williams White And Co	3542	16
Williams Whittle Associates Inc	7311	443
Williams Wholesale Supply Of Nashville Inc	3825	148
Williamsburg Millwork Corp	2448	33
Williamsburg National Insurance Co	6331	166
Williamsburg Plumbing Inc	5031	353
Williamsburg Travel Management Cos	4724	56
Williamsburg Winery Ltd	2084	64
Williams-Helde Inc	7311	285
Williamson Cadillac Co	5511	552
Williamson Company Incorporated SL	1611	158
Williamson Corp	3826	118
Williamson County Hospital District Inc	8062	207
Williamson County Sun Inc	2711	658
Williamson Electrical Company Inc	1731	1613
Williamson Law Book Co	2761	77
Williamson Printing Corp	5111	28
Williamson-Dickie Manufacturing Co	2326	4
Williamsport Barber and Beauty Corp	5961	163
Williamsport Hospital	8062	105
Williams-Pyro Inc	3812	98
Williams-Sonoma Inc	5719	2
Willick Engineering Company Inc	3844	30
Willie Washer Manufacturing Co	3469	134
Willies Computer Software Co	7372	4575
Willies Grain Inc	4213	1960
Willimantic Waste Paper Company Inc	5093	87
Willis Case Harwood Inc	7311	979
Willis Construction CoInc	3272	95
Willis Faber North America Inc	6321	47
Willis Financial Planning Services Inc	6282	447
Willis Henry Auctions Inc	7389	1809
Willis HRH Illinois	6331	268
Willis HRH Upstate New York	6331	264
Willis Lease Finance Corp	5088	10
Willis Lumber Co	5031	445
Willis Management Vermont Ltd	6411	264
Willis North America Inc	8742	56
Willis of New Hampshire Inc	6321	75
Willis of Texas Inc	6411	158
Willis of Virginia Inc	6411	37
Willis of Wisconsin Inc	6411	124
Willis Shaw Express	4213	173
Williston Basin Interstate Pipeline Co	4922	37
Willkie Farr and Gallagher LLP	8111	45
Will-Light Inc	3645	33
Willman Industries Inc	3321	34
Willmar Cookie and Nut Co	2052	34
Willmar Electric Service Inc	1731	66
Will-Mor Engineering Company Inc	3545	99
Willoughby Brewing Co	2082	60
Willow Bend Communications Inc	7389	791
Willow Brook Foods Inc	2013	9
Willow Creek Press Inc	2731	247
Willow Tree Poultry Farm Inc	5499	13
Willowbrook Feeds Inc	2048	28
Willowood Industries Inc	8211	107
Wills Brothers Muncie Auto Auction	5012	148
Wills Group Inc	5411	219
Wills Trucking Inc	4213	565
Will-Tech Inc	4213	2923
Willy Bietak Productions Inc	7922	79
Wilmac Business Equipment Company Inc	5044	85
Wilmac Corp	6513	2
Wilmanco	3663	324
Wilmay Inc	7389	1346
Wilmer Cutler Pickering Hale and Dorr LLP	8111	22
Wilmer Service Line	2761	7
Wilmes Window Manufacturing Company Inc	3089	1660
Wilmington Fibre Specialty Co	3089	1416
Wilmington Health Associates PA	6324	67
Wilmington Machine Inc	3599	2232
Wilmington Machinery Inc	3559	327
Wilmington Public Treatment Sw	3589	238
Wilmington Research and Development Corp	3625	365
Wilmington Sales LLC	5051	470
Wilmington Savings Fund Society FSB	6035	263
Wilmington Star-News Inc	2711	407
Wilmington Trust FSB	6035	245
Wilmot Engineering Co	3532	43
Wilmur Communications Inc	4813	542
Wil-Rich LLC	3523	34
Wil's Electrical Service Contractors Inc	1731	1563
Wilsbach Distributors Inc	5181	67
Wilsey Tool Company Inc	3599	472
Wilshire Asset Management	6282	225
Wilshire Associates Inc	6282	474
Wilshire Bancorp Inc	6022	65
Wilshire Court Productions Inc	7812	250
Wilshire Enterprises Inc	6513	40
Wilshire Insurance Co	6351	51
Wilshire Precision Products Inc	3599	1122
Wilshire State Bank	6022	133
Wilson and Company Incorporated Engineers and Architects	8711	163
Wilson Audio Specialties Inc	3651	105
Wilson Bancshares Inc	6712	713
Wilson Brothers Construction Company Inc	1623	108
Wilson Building Maintenance	7349	219
Wilson Care Inc	8361	150
Wilson Co (Addison Texas)	5084	274
Wilson Construction Co	1623	49
Wilson County Board Of Education	8211	46
Wilson Electric Co	1731	318
Wilson Electronics Inc	3669	142
Wilson Elser Moskowitz Edelman and Dicker LLP	8111	24
Wilson Enterprises of Illinois Inc	5033	29
Wilson Entertainment Inc	5731	256
Wilson Farms Inc	0161	7
Wilson Graphics Inc	7336	335
Wilson Group Communications Inc	8743	273
Wilson Group Ltd	5021	18
Wilson Hauling Inc	4213	2888
Wilson John S Company Of Baltimore County	5031	171
Wilson Kc and Associates	7389	2152
Wilson Learning Corp	8742	281
Wilson Lines Inc	4213	671
Wilson Lumber Company Inc	5211	49
Wilson Manufacturing And Design Inc	3535	163
Wilson Manufacturing Co	3544	98
Wilson Media Group Inc	7319	127
Wilson of Wallingford Inc	1711	234
Wilson Office Interiors LLC	1721	12
Wilson Optical Laboratory Inc	3827	88
Wilson Pest Control Company Inc	7342	18
Wilson Photofinishing Corp	7384	22
Wilson Plywood and Door Inc	5031	194
Wilson Printing	2752	1083
Wilson Sonsini Goodrich and Rosati	8111	19
Wilson Sporting Goods Co Clothing and Pad Div	2329	26
Wilson Technology Associates Inc	7379	906
Wilson Tool Corp	3599	1588
Wilson Trailer Co	3715	13

Company Name	SIC	Rank	Company Name	SIC	Rank	Company Name	SIC	Rank
Wilson Truck Service	4212	81	WindyCityJay Truck Sales	5511	1245	Winston Resources Inc	7361	51
Wilson Trucking Corp	4213	31	Wine Cellar Innovations	2511	54	Winston Trails GCLlc	5091	84
Wilson WindowWare Inc	7372	3761	Wine Club Inc	5921	15	Winston Weaver Company Inc	2873	19
Wilson-Davis and Co	6211	361	Wine Country Chef LLC	5182	47	Winston-Salem Industries For The	2515	8
Wilson-Hurd Manufacturing Co	3089	558	Wine Technologies	7372	5155	Blind Inc		
Wilson's Corn Products Inc	2041	61	WineCommune LLC	5182	17	Winsystems Inc	3571	76
Wilson's Machine Products Inc	3728	182	Winegar Inc	3451	68	Wintec Industries Inc	3572	8
Wilspec Technologies Inc	5075	101	Winegard Co	3663	89	Wintegra Inc	3674	187
Wiltec	8711	597	Winegars Supermarkets Inc	5411	286	Wintek Corp	7375	197
Wiltec Inc	3577	611	Winesellers Ltd	5182	46	Wintel	3661	208
Wilton Products Inc	5099	7	WinEstimator Inc	7372	3150	Wintel Corp	5045	902
Wilwood Engineering	3714	293	Winetastingcom	5961	128	Wintenna Inc	3663	374
Wily Technology Inc	7372	1022	WineWare Software Corp	7372	3969	Winter Associates Inc	7389	1800
Wimbley Group Inc	7311	666	Winfield Brooks Company Inc	2842	172	Winter Corp	7379	1593
Wimmer Cookbooks (Memphis Tennessee)	2732	53	Winfield Community Volunteer Fire Company Inc	7389	1911	Winter Garden Times Inc	2711	875
Wimsatt Brothers Inc	5033	19	Winfield Consumer Products Inc	5531	27	Winter Gardens Quality Foods Inc	2099	84
Win Energy REMC	4911	363	Winfield Publishing Company Inc	2711	695	Winter Group of Cos	1541	68
Win Enterprises Inc	3571	85	Winfield Rubber Manufacturing	3061	51	Winter Kloman Moter and Repp SC	8721	149
Winamac Coil Spring Inc	3495	16	Company Inc			Winter Park Blueprint Company Inc	7334	15
Winar 1 Sales Inc	5063	602	Winfrey's Olde English Fudge Inc	2064	130	Winter Park Construction Co	1522	38
Winbco Tank Co	3443	153	Wing Enterprises Inc	3354	25	Winter People Inc	7389	1307
Wincal Technology Corp	3823	437	Wing Hing Noodles Co	2098	7	Winter Sports Inc	7999	97
Winchendon Furniture Inc	5021	163	Wing Memorial Hospital	8741	209	Winter Truck Line Inc	4213	2552
Winchester Cold Storage Company Inc	4222	15	Wingate Partners LP	6799	224	Winter Wyman and Company Inc	7361	198
Winchester Electronics	3643	14	Winger Contracting Co	5075	38	Winters Oil Partners LP	5172	35
Winchester Evening Star Inc	2711	391	Wingfield Engineering Company Inc	3613	77	Winterville Machine Works Inc	3471	89
Winchester Ford Mazda Subaru Inc	5511	944	Wingfield Scale Company Inc	5046	179	Winter-Wolff International Inc	5085	462
Winchester Homes Inc	6552	113	Wingfoot Commercial Tire Systems	7534	2	Winthrop Realty Trust	6798	155
Winchester Industries Inc	3442	106	LLC			Winthrop Resources Corp	7377	8
Winchester Metals Inc	5051	276	Wingra Stone Company Inc	3273	15	Wintriss Engineering Corp	3577	432
Winchester Optical Co	3851	31	Wings Wildlife Production Inc	7819	83	Wintron Tech LLC	3677	77
Winchester Pacific Batteries USA Inc	5013	370	Win-Holt Equipment Corp	3312	58	Wintronics Inc	3672	262
Winchester Precision Technologies Ltd	3547	15	Winkenwerder Company LLC	8748	311	Wintronix Inc	7372	472
Winchester Printers Inc	2752	1097	Winkie Manufacturing Company Inc	2339	51	Wintrust Financial Corp	6712	51
Winchester Repeating Arms	3484	7	Winkler And Chimniak Ltd	7338	52	Winvale Group	8742	481
Winchester Sun Co	2711	583	Winkler Films Inc	7812	127	Winware Inc	7371	639
Winchester Systems Inc	3572	49	Winkler Inc	5141	169	WinWay Corp	7372	4186
Winchester Tool LLC	3599	1950	Winland Electronics Inc	3823	267	WinWholesale Inc	6722	98
Wincite Systems	7372	4576	Winly Enterprises Inc	7261	17	WinWin Solutions Inc	7372	2889
Winco Distributors Inc	5031	66	Winmark Corp	5932	5	Winworks Software	7372	4577
WinCo Foods Inc	5411	53	Winmill and Company Inc	6282	163	Winzeler Inc	3089	971
Winco Identification Corp	7372	2251	Winn Design LLC	1521	158	Winzen Film Inc	2673	56
Winco Manufacturing Inc	3442	64	Winncom Technologies Corp	3663	104	Winzler and Kelly Consulting Engineers	8712	92
Winco Window Company Inc	5031	356	Winn-Dixie Louisiana Inc	5411	293	Inc		
Wincraft Inc	3499	34	Winn-Dixie Stores Inc	5411	24	Wipb Tv Channel 49	4833	167
Wincup Holdings LP	8731	60	Winnebago Color Press Inc	2752	875	Wipfli Ullrich Bertelson LLP	8721	237
Wind and Willow Inc	2045	17	Winnebago Industries Inc	3716	3	Wire Belt Company Of America Inc	3496	57
Wind Corp	3429	121	Winnemucca Farms Inc	2034	16	Wire Cut Company Inc	3541	147
Wind Energy America Inc	3575	14	Winnemucca Publishing Company Inc	2711	657	Wire Cut E D M Inc	3544	628
Wind Mill Woodworking Inc	2541	45	Winner Aviation Corp	4581	41	Wire Mesh Products Inc	3496	82
Wind River Sales Company Inc	7371	51	Winner City Shop	5087	180	Wire Products Company Inc	3495	25
Wind River Services Inc	7371	52	Winner International	3669	189	Wire Products Manufacturing Corp	3496	84
Wind River Systems Inc	7371	32	Winner Press Inc	2752	1236	Wire Sales Inc	5051	387
Windamatic Systems Inc	3621	144	Winners Circle Systems	5045	414	Wire Shop Inc	3544	696
Winder Farms	2026	51	Winnertech Corp	7379	830	Wire Tech Inc	3569	211
Windermere Associates	8742	658	WinNet Business Internet	7375	170	Wire Tech Ltd	3694	28
Windes and McClaughry Accountancy	8721	82	WinNet Internet	7375	189	Wire Technologies Inc	3357	20
Corp			Winnfield Life Insurance Company Inc	6311	268	Wire Technology Corp	3357	69
Windfield Alloy Inc	3559	225	Winnov LP	3674	312	Wire To Wire Communications Inc	7389	2215
Windgate Vineyards Inc	2084	121	Winnsboro Specialty Parts International	5083	162	Wirebenders Inc	3612	133
Windham House Inc	7389	2125	Inc			Wireco Worldgroup Inc	3496	9
Windham Machine Company Inc	3599	1407	Winnsboro State Bank and Trust Co	6712	596	Wired Accessories Inc	5065	676
Windham Sand And Stone Inc	3273	86	Winntech Digital Systems Inc	3663	126	Wired City	7374	418
Windhover Industries	5065	701	Winona Health Services	8062	175	Wired Investment Group Inc	5063	504
Windhover Information Inc	2721	220	Winona Heating and Ventilating	1761	20	Wiredrive	7389	970
Winding Specialists Company Inc	3728	217	Company Inc			Wiregrass Electric Cooperative Inc	4911	225
Windmill Group Inc	6211	349	Winona Lighting Inc	3646	19	Wireless Advanced Communications	1731	472
Windmill Inns of America Inc	7011	188	Winona ORC Industries Inc	8331	169	Inc		
Windmill International Inc	7379	131	Winona Post Inc	2711	897	Wireless Communications Unlimited	4812	126
Windmoeller and Hoelscher Corp	5084	54	Winona Powder Coating Inc	3479	53	Wireless Computing Inc	3577	394
Window Classics Corp	5031	137	Winona Printing Co	2752	805	Wireless Connection Corp	4812	99
Window Technology Inc	3442	104	Winona Printing Company Inc (Winona	2759	254	Wireless Construction Services Corp	5093	237
Window to the World Communications	4833	118	Minnesota)			Wireless Generation Inc	7373	177
Inc			Winona Production Services Inc	3543	17	Wireless Innovations LLC	4813	432
WindoWare Inc	7372	3968	Winona River and Rail Inc	5191	46	Wireless Matrix Corp (Reston Virginia)	4899	91
Windowmaster Products	3442	69	Winona Watlow Inc	3613	35	Wireless One World	5999	181
WindowPRO	5031	72	Winpak Films Inc	3081	24	Wireless Outreach LLC	4812	134
Windows Support Group	7372	3204	Winpak Portion Packaging Inc	3565	20	Wireless Ronin Technologies Inc	7373	439
Windrock Inc	3829	160	Winreal Operating Company LP	6798	215	Wireless Technologies Inc	5731	259
Windsor Airmotive	2821	46	Winroc Corp (Minneapolis Minnesota)	5032	37	Wireless Technology Inc	3651	73
Windsor Beach Technologies Inc	3599	1226	Winrock Enterprises Inc	6552	300	Wireless Telecom Group Inc	3825	66
Windsor Consultants Inc	7361	216	Win-Sam Inc	1731	787	Wireless Ventures LLC	4812	83
Windsor Electric Contracting Inc	1731	1709	Winsby Group LLC	7372	5071	Wireless Works	4812	104
Windsor Fashions Inc	5621	26	Winsert Inc	3325	16	Wireless Xcessories Group Inc	3699	71
Windsor House Investments Inc	2675	24	Winshuttle Inc	7372	3146	Wireline Technologies Inc	5082	143
Windsor Marketing Group Inc	3993	54	Winslow Automatics Inc	3841	180	Wiremasters Inc	2542	56
Windsor Mold USA Inc	3089	1733	Winslow Automation Inc	3674	282	Wiremold Co	3644	6
Windsor Republic Doors	3442	6	Winslow BMW	5511	761	Wirenetics Co	5063	192
Windsor Technologies Inc	7372	5154	Winslow Capital Management Inc	6282	533	Wire-Rite Fabrication Inc	3643	157
Windsor-Press Inc	2711	599	Winslow Group Inc	7389	2363	Wire's Electrical Shop Inc	1731	2247
Windstar Cruises Lines	4481	8	Winslow Management Co	6282	237	WireSpring Technologies Inc	7372	1987
Windstone Editions Inc	3089	1280	Winslow Marine Products Corp	3069	127	Wirestone (Boise Idaho)	7311	304
Windstone Medical Packaging Inc	3841	244	WinSoft Corp	7372	4219	Wiretech Inc	3315	23
Windstream Corp	4813	12	Winstanley Associates	7311	394	Wireway/Husky Corp	3496	31
Windtrax Inc	5087	60	Winstead Sechrest and Minick PC	8111	81	Wirewise Inc	3699	286
W-Industries Inc	3625	36	Winsted Precision Ball Co	3562	30	Wireworks Corp	3679	645
W-Industries of Louisiana LLC	7373	280	Winsted Thermographers Inc	2759	367	Wiring Unlimited Inc	1731	2294
Windward Petroleum Inc	2992	6	Winstin Ventures LLC	8748	263	Wirtz Beverage Distribution Nevada	5182	22
Windward Print Star Inc	2752	82	Winston and Strawn	8111	36	Wirtz Corp	5181	3
Windway Capital Corp	3262	3	Winston Brothers Iron and Metal Inc	5093	22	Wirtz Electric Inc	1731	1512
Windy City Amusements Inc	7999	129	Winston Hotels Inc	6798	184	Wirtz Manufacturing Company Inc	3559	135
Windy City Cutting Die Inc	3544	477	Winston Industries LLC	3589	51	Wirz and Associates Inc	8743	330
Windy Hill Foliage Inc	4213	2168	Winston Printing Co	2631	22	Wis - Pak Inc	2086	11
						Wis Seaming Equipment Inc	3552	59

Company Name	SIC	Rank
Wisage Technology Inc	7379	1397
WISCO Computing	7372	4026
Wisco Envelope Company Inc	2677	8
Wisco Industries Inc	3469	68
Wisco Supply Inc	5074	137
Wisco-Moran Drilling Company Inc	1381	56
Wiscomp Systems Inc	5045	534
Wiscon Products Inc	3451	130
Wisconsin Aluminum Foundry Company Inc	3369	5
Wisconsin Aviation Inc	4581	18
Wisconsin Community Bank (Cottage Grove Wisconsin)	6029	16
Wisconsin Distributors Inc	5181	32
Wisconsin Ear Mold Co	6513	46
Wisconsin Education Association Credit Union	6062	105
Wisconsin Energy Corp	4931	7
Wisconsin Engraving Company Inc	3479	91
Wisconsin Film and Bag Inc	2673	12
Wisconsin Free Press	2711	761
Wisconsin Gas Co	4924	26
Wisconsin Homes Inc	2452	42
Wisconsin Hydraulics Inc	7699	175
Wisconsin Industrial Machine Service Inc	3599	1756
Wisconsin Knife Works Inc	3541	58
Wisconsin Lift Truck Corp	5084	23
Wisconsin Machine Tool Corporation Inc	3545	56
Wisconsin Metal Parts Inc	3544	213
Wisconsin Metal Products Co	3469	225
Wisconsin Physicians Service Insurance Corp	6321	9
Wisconsin Plastic Products Inc	3089	1214
Wisconsin Plating Works Inc	3471	95
Wisconsin Public Service Corp	4931	37
Wisconsin Sausage Co	2013	196
Wisconsin Spice Inc	2099	140
Wisconsin Steel and Tube Corp	5051	284
Wisconsin Supply Corp	5074	56
Wisconsin Thermoset Molding Inc	3089	898
Wisconsin Tool and Mold Company Inc	3089	1577
Wisconsin Tool and Stamping Co	3469	54
Wisconsin Truss Inc	2439	58
Wisconsin Tubing Inc	5074	184
Wisconsin Veneer And Plywood Inc	2421	72
Wiscraft Inc	7389	2440
Wisdom Infotech Ltd	7371	327
Wisdom Way LLC	5045	926
Wisdomtools Enterprises Inc	7371	1357
WisdomTree Investments Inc	6282	328
Wise Company Inc	2531	4
Wise Components Inc	5065	251
Wise El Santo Company Inc	5136	8
Wise Electric Cooperative Inc	4911	509
Wise Incentives	7311	1009
Wise Machine Company Inc	3559	239
Wise Men Inc	7373	225
Wise Metals Group LLC	3353	3
Wise Payment Systems Inc	7389	1273
Wise Software and Computer Products Inc	7372	2932
Wise Software Solutions Inc	7372	3751
Wise Tag and Label Company Inc	2679	37
Wise Trucking Inc	4213	1314
Wisecarver Communications Inc	4899	221
Wisenbaker Production Co	1311	212
Wiseoutlook Ii LLC	7379	1357
Wishart Safety Training Inc	8299	65
Wishbone Systems Inc	7371	731
Wishoo Inc	3993	64
Wisne Automation And Engineering Co	7363	258
Wiss and Company LLC	8721	10
Wiss Janney Elstner Associates Inc	8712	19
Wissco Irrigation Co	1711	245
Wissota Manufacturing Co	5091	146
Wist Enterprises Inc	3677	115
Witbro Inc	3531	170
Witco Inc	3545	95
Witham Truck Center	5511	826
Withers and Ravenel Holdings PA	8711	396
Withers Broadcasting Company Of West Virginia	4832	87
Withers Corp	3544	679
Withers Tool Die and Manufacturing Co	3544	452
Witherspoon and Associates	7311	647
Withmomentum LLC	7379	1464
Withum Smith and Brown LLC	8721	103
WITN-TV Inc	4833	72
Witron Integrated Logistics Inc	3535	40
Wits Basin Precious Minerals Inc	1041	25
Wits' End Productions Inc	7812	222
Wit-Son Carbide Tool Inc	3545	244
Witt Co	5043	8
Witt Fiala Flannery and Associates	8744	37
Witt Industries Inc	3479	30
Witt Mares and Company PLC	8721	488
Wittco Foodservice Equipment Inc	3589	156
Witte Brothers Exchange Inc	4213	1221
Witte Company Inc	3559	261
Wittemann Company LLC	3569	222
Witter Manufacturing Inc	3679	674
Wittern Group Inc	7389	1157

Company Name	SIC	Rank
Wittichen Supply Co	5078	3
Wixom Technologies LLC	5031	348
Wizard Technologies Inc	5065	986
Wizard's Cauldron Ltd	2033	66
Wizards Of The Coast Inc	2731	55
Wizdom Systems Inc	7372	3557
WizSoft Inc	7372	1110
Wizults LLC	7336	261
Wizzard Software Corp	7372	2510
WJ Bullock Inc	3341	38
WJ Dillner Transfer Co	4213	2394
Wj Electric Company Inc	1731	1453
WJ Hagerty and Sons Limited Inc	2842	112
WJ Kinney and Company Inc	7371	1854
WJ Pence Company Inc	5141	155
WJ Roberts Company Inc	3599	1697
WJ Savage Company Inc	3541	120
WJAC Inc	4833	125
WJLA Inc	4833	160
Wjlp Company Inc	3677	74
WJLS Inc	3089	1309
WJPZ Radio Inc	4832	54
WJS Enterprises Inc	5044	23
WK Dickson and Company Inc	8711	129
WKA LLC	1455	7
WKEF Licensee LP	4833	34
WKI Holding Company Inc	3229	2
WKP-Spier LLC	7311	376
WKPW	4832	286
WL Butler Construction Inc	1542	453
WL Davis Trucking	4213	2924
WL Gore and Associates Inc	2821	12
WL Hailey	1623	63
WL Halsey Company Inc	5141	179
WL Homes LLC	1521	4
WL Jenkins Co	3699	247
WL Leonhardt Company Inc	5013	418
WL Logan Trucking Co	4213	236
W-L Molding Co	3089	227
WL Plastics Corp	3084	17
W-L Research Inc	8731	196
WL Ross and Company LLC	8742	256
WL Sturm Electric Inc	1731	585
WLA Inc	4213	3128
WLBT Inc	4833	157
WLFL Inc	4833	47
WLINC Inc	2752	1550
Wlm Enterprises Inc	3569	227
WLOX Inc	4833	261
WLPX TV-Charleston	4833	114
Wls Inc	5063	231
WLS Stamping Co	3469	113
WLT Software of Florida Inc	7372	3468
WLTZ NBC 38	7311	960
WLW Construction Inc	1623	405
WM Berg Inc	3568	34
Wm C Anderson Inc	3599	598
WM Dewey and Son Inc	4213	1099
Wm E Martin And Sons Company Inc	2099	296
WM Gulliksen Manufacturing Company Inc	3089	1614
Wm H Clinger Corp	1731	570
Wm H Leahy Associates Inc	5141	197
WM Jordan Company Inc	1542	98
Wm K Walthers Inc	5092	7
WM Lyles Co	1629	55
Wm Ohs Inc	2434	55
WM Schlosser Company Inc	1542	351
WM Sheppard Lumber Company Inc	2421	115
WM Software Inc	7372	4027
WM Sprinkman Corp	6799	80
Wm Steinen Manufacturing Co	3494	47
Wm T Burnett Holding LLC	2299	1
WM Tinder Inc	5031	31
Wm Wrigley Jr Co	2067	1
Wmbd 1470 Am	4832	145
Wmg Enterprises Ii Inc	5084	864
Wmg Pso LLC	4813	635
Wmh Fluidpower Inc	5084	795
WMI Auto Auction LLC	5012	149
WMMP Licensee LP	4833	64
WMOG Inc	1542	72
Wmr Contracting Inc	1731	1999
WMS Gaming Inc	3999	12
WMS Industries Inc	3999	8
WMVG Inc	4832	285
WMVO 1300 Am	4832	240
WN Cooper And Son Inc	5083	118
WN de Sherbinin Products Inc	5063	541
WN Morehouse Truck Line Inc	4213	1114
Wna American Plastic Industries Inc	3089	232
WNAB-TV Channel 58	4833	87
WNDV U93 FM	4832	200
WNPX TV-Nashville	4833	108
WnR Inc	1761	54
Wnst 1570 Am	4832	253
WNSW AM 1430	4832	170
WNTR-1079 FM	4832	122
WNY Bus Parts Inc	5013	227
Wnyc Radio	4832	36
WO Hickok Manufacturing Co	3569	195
WO Operating Co	1381	28
Woeber Mustard Manufacturing Co	2099	137
Woerner Turf Inc	4213	1989

Company Name	SIC	Rank
WOHL Tv Fox 25 And Metro Video Inc	4833	199
Wohler Technologies Inc	3663	145
Wohlsen Construction Co	1542	45
Wohlt Cheese Corp	2022	47
Wohrle's Foods Inc	2013	175
WOKQ 975 FM Stereo Inc	4832	143
Wolberg Lighting Design and Electrical Supply	5063	173
Wolcott Architecture and Interiors	7389	796
Wolf and Company PC	8721	307
Wolf Colorprint Inc	2752	568
Wolf Creek Products Inc	2499	67
Wolf Glass and Paint Company Inc	5039	51
Wolf Industries LP	5063	553
Wolf Landscape Co	1623	383
Wolf Manufacturing Company Inc	2211	31
Wolf Manufacturing Inc	3714	355
Wolf Range Co	3589	34
Wolf Robotics Inc	3548	17
Wolf Technical Services Inc	8748	225
Wolf Technologies LLC	3324	21
Wolfchase Toyota	5511	210
Wolfe And Swickard Machine Company Inc	3599	312
Wolfe and Travis Electric Company Inc	1731	156
Wolfe Dye And Bleach Works Inc	2269	10
Wolfe Industrial Inc	3599	298
Wolfe Machinery Co	7699	137
Wolfe Nilges Nahorski PC	8721	398
Wolfe Rf And Associates Inc	5734	225
Wolfe Security Group	7389	1916
Wolferman's Inc	2051	74
Wolff Associates Inc	7311	942
Wolff Brothers Supply Inc	5074	31
Wolff Controls Corp	3625	310
Wolff Shoe Co	5139	9
Wolfhouse Radio Group Inc	4832	175
Wolfington Body Company Inc	5012	18
Wolfkill Feed and Fertilizer Corp	2875	21
Wolford and Wethington Lumber Co	4213	508
Wolfram Research Inc	7372	949
Wolf's Run Transport	4213	2599
Wolfsen Land and Cattle Co	0191	6
Wolfson Casing Corp	5149	73
Wolftec Inc	3556	73
Woll2Woll Software	7372	4898
Wollaston Alloys Inc	3325	5
Wollmann Video Production Ltd	4833	215
Wolohan Capital Strategies	6531	382
Wolstenholme Machine Inc	3679	727
Wolters Kluwer Financial Services	2752	22
Wolters Kluwer Health	2741	24
Wolters Kluwer Health Inc	7372	313
Wolverine Brass Inc	5074	18
Wolverine Broach Company Inc	3545	273
Wolverine Building Group	1541	101
Wolverine Carbide and Tool Inc	3544	367
Wolverine Carbide Die Co	3599	1018
Wolverine Crane and Service Inc	3536	31
Wolverine Gas and Oil Corp	4922	40
Wolverine Metal Stamping Inc	3469	145
Wolverine Packing Co	2011	36
Wolverine Plastics Inc	3089	1202
Wolverine Power Systems Inc	4911	349
Wolverine Printing Company LLC	2752	1168
Wolverine Proctor	3567	14
Wolverine Production and Engineering Inc	3599	2173
Wolverine Software Corp	7372	2734
Wolverine Tool and Engineering Co	3544	395
Wolverine Tractor and Equipment Co	5082	25
Wolverine Tube Inc	3351	4
Wolverine World Wide Inc	3149	8
Womack Electric and Supply Company Inc	5063	234
Womack Industries Inc	7342	92
Womack Machine Supply	5084	16
Womack Material Handling Systems Inc	7359	53
Womble Carlyle Sandridge and Rice PLLC	8111	32
Womble Company Inc	3479	18
Women S Enterprise	2741	450
Womencom	7379	164
Women's Bean Project	3556	182
Women's Center	8093	52
Women's Center Of Tarrant County Inc	7361	319
Women's Golf Unlimited Inc	3949	92
Womens Law Center	8322	218
Women's Specialists of Houston	8011	173
Women's Treatment Center	8361	77
Wonalancet Co	5159	33
Wonder Machine Services Inc	3599	1227
Wonderfoil Inc	3469	385
Wondergem Consulting Inc	8743	194
Wonderlic Inc	7372	2229
Wonderware Corp	7372	227
Won-Door Corp	3446	21
Wondra Construction Inc	1623	866
Wong's Advanced Technologies Inc	5734	232
Wonton Food Corp	2032	29
Wonton Food Inc	2099	94
Wood and Hyde Leather Company Inc	3111	11
Wood Feathers Inc	5033	25

Company Name	SIC	Rank
Wood Flooring International Inc	5031	169
Wood Group ESP	3533	41
Wood Group Inc	8748	364
Wood Group Pratt and Whitney Industrial Turbine Services LLC	8711	195
Wood Group Production Services Inc	7389	683
Wood Group Turbopower LLC	4581	37
Wood Herron and Evans LLP	8111	343
Wood Masonry Supply Inc	5082	198
Wood Patel and Associates Inc	8711	312
Wood Resources LP	2499	9
Wood River Printing and Publishing Co	2752	1727
Wood River Technologies Inc	7379	550
Wood Snodgrass Inc	6411	246
Wood Stone Corp	3556	52
Wood Termite and Pest Control Inc	7342	85
Wood Trucking Corp	4213	2065
Wood Ventures	2499	55
Woodbine Agency Inc	7311	579
Woodbourne Solutions Inc	7379	786
Woodbridge Foam Fabricating Inc	3086	43
Woodbridge Group LLC	8748	197
Woodbridge Holdings Corp (Fort Lauderdale Florida)	1531	84
Woodbridge Sales and Engineering Inc	5162	2
Woodburn Diamond Die Company Inc	3544	79
Woodbury Cement Products Company Inc	5072	118
Woodbury Products Inc	5999	243
Woodbury Roof Truss Inc	2439	42
Woodbury Telephone Co	4813	248
Woodcase Fine Cabinetry Inc	2434	25
Woodcraft Inc	2426	33
Woodcraft Industries Inc	2434	4
Woodcraft Supply LLC	5251	11
Woodcrest Manufacturing Inc	2511	64
Wooden Pallets Gp LLC	2448	17
Woodenboat Publications Inc	2721	282
Woodend Nessel and Friends Inc	8742	652
Woodex Bearing Company Inc	3053	87
Woodford Feed Company Inc	5999	86
Woodforest Financial Group Inc	6021	79
Woodgrain Millwork Inc	2431	8
Woodharbor Doors and Cabinetry Inc	2434	28
Woodhaven Homes Inc	1521	136
Woodhaven National Bank	6021	349
Woodhead Industries Inc	3679	67
Woodhead LP	3643	69
Woodhill Supply Inc	5074	110
Wooding Design Ltd	7389	1830
Woodinville Fire and Life Safety	7389	944
Woodlan Tool And Machine Company Inc	3599	1042
Woodland Avenue Fire Protection District	7389	2022
Woodland Aviation Inc	5599	8
Woodland Health Care	8011	16
Woodlands Mailing and Fulfillment	7331	157
Woodlands Operating Company LP	6552	68
Woodlane Environmental Technology Inc	3823	310
Woodlawn Manufacturing Ltd	3541	40
Woodlawn Rubber Co	3069	261
Woodlines	2511	97
Woodlist Inc	7389	965
Woodmack Products Inc	3498	57
Woodman Agitator Inc	3559	439
Woodman Company Inc	3565	30
Woodman's Food Market Inc	5411	161
Wood-Mizer Products Inc	3553	7
Wood-Mode Inc	2434	11
Woodpecker Truck and Equipment Inc	5012	17
Woodpro Cabinetry Inc	2434	63
Woodridge Press Inc	2752	759
Woodruff Agency	7389	1372
Woodruff and Sons Inc	1623	57
Woodruff Electric Coop	4911	196
Woodruff Energy Co	5983	15
Woodruff Supply Company Inc	5085	286
Woodruff-Sawyer and Co	6411	205
Woods and Poole Economics Inc	2741	347
Woods Communication Corp	4833	198
Woods End Research Laboratory Inc	8732	131
Woods Industries Inc	3699	26
Woods Lumber Of Independence Ks Inc	5211	176
Woods Management Corporation of Florida	6531	335
Woods Precision Products Inc	3599	815
Woodside Group Inc (Las Vegas Nevada)	1531	19
Woodson and Bozeman Inc	5064	48
Woodstock Corp	6289	28
Woodstock Percussion Inc	5099	85
Woodstream Corp	3429	45
Woodward Broadcasting Inc	4832	130
Woodward Communications Inc	2711	195
Woodward Financial Corp	6211	403
Woodward FST Inc	3728	58
Woodward HRT	3812	19
Woodward Inc (Fort Collins Colorado)	3629	2
Woodward Industrial Controls Branch Plant	3625	40
Woodward Mccoach Inc	3672	213

Company Name	SIC	Rank
Woodward Publishing Company Inc	2711	627
Woodward Sharf and Associates Inc	7361	140
Woodworkers of Denver Inc	2541	62
Woodworker's Supply Inc	5084	124
Woodworth Capital Inc	6799	284
Woody Anderson Ford Inc	5511	208
Woody Bogler Trucking Co	4213	325
Woody Nelson and Company Inc	6531	432
Woody Sander Ford Inc	5511	734
Woody's Feed And Grain	2048	148
Woolery Enterprises Inc	2099	242
Woolpert LLP	8712	34
Woolrich Inc	2311	4
Wools of New Zealand	8743	331
Woolslayer Companies Inc	3533	62
Woolverton Printing Co	2752	610
Woonsocket Health and Rehabilitation Center	8051	48
Woori USA Inc	7389	396
Wooster Daily Record Inc	2711	63
Wooster Motor Ways Inc	4213	961
Wooster Printing and Litho Inc	2752	1435
Wooster Products Inc	3446	35
Wooster Republican Printing Co	2711	928
Woot Inc	5045	165
Wooten Graphics Inc	2759	329
Wooten Oil Co	5171	67
Wooten Transports Inc	4213	2395
Worcester Electrical Associates Inc	1731	1614
Worcester Envelope Co	2677	9
Worcester Magazine Inc	2721	177
Worcester Publishing Ltd	2711	388
Worcester Sand And Gravel Company Inc	5032	77
Worcester Scale Company Inc	5046	218
Worcester Telegram and Gazette	2711	25
Word Constructors LLC	1622	18
Word Handlers	7331	97
Word Industries Pipe Fabricators Inc	3498	22
Word Pictures Inc	7812	335
Word Processing Services Inc	7629	27
Word Processing Supplies Inc	5734	328
Word Systems Inc	5044	74
Word Tech Corp	2791	43
Word Up Publications Inc	2721	269
Worden Brothers Inc	7372	1278
Worden Co	2531	28
Wordingham Machine Company Inc	3599	816
Wordman Inc	8743	343
Wordmark Associates Inc	8748	425
Words and Images	7319	81
WordSmart Corp	7372	2027
Wordsprint Inc	2752	1213
Word-Tech Inc	7378	93
Work Area Protection Corp	3993	35
Work Force Development Board Incorporated Bcvb	8331	189
Work Opportunities Inc	8331	195
Work Opportunity Center Inc	8331	201
Work Services Corp	8331	32
Work Skills Corp	8331	109
Work Technology Corp	7372	3637
Workable Programs and Systems Inc	4813	632
Workblades Inc	3545	303
Workday Inc	7372	282
WorkDynamics Technologies Inc	7372	1180
Workers Compensation Fund	6331	289
Workers' Credit Union	6062	61
Workflow Holdings LLC	2752	19
Workforce 2000 Staffing Inc	7361	186
Workforce ROI Corp	7372	3092
Workforce Software Inc	7374	79
Workforce Solutions Group Inc	8748	335
Workforce Solutions Group Of Montgomery County Inc	7361	312
Workhouse Publicity	7389	743
Working Assets Funding Service	4812	19
Working Class Inc	7311	994
Working Media Group	7311	492
Working Person's Store	5699	13
Working World Inc	7363	195
Worklogix Management Inc	7371	882
Workman Electronic Products Inc	3679	696
Workman Publishing Company Inc	2731	104
WorkMovr Corp	7372	2404
Worknet Inc	7379	403
Workplace Systems Inc	2522	49
WorkRite Ergonomic Accessories Inc	3577	333
Workrite Inc	3553	65
Workrite Machine and Tool Inc	3541	187
Workrite Uniform Company Inc	2326	13
Works Computing Inc	7373	220
Worksafe Iowa	1731	1430
Workscape Inc	7372	292
Workshare Technology Inc	5734	68
Workshop And Rehabilitation Facilities For The Blind And Disabled Inc	8331	208
Workshop Inc	8331	97
Worksmart Promotions Inc	7319	157
Worksource Enterprises	8331	182
Workspace Development LLC	5021	26
Workspeed Inc	5045	330
Workspot Inc	7373	690
Worksquared of Northern Michigan	5021	133

Company Name	SIC	Rank
WorksRight Software Inc	7372	4651
Workstation Group	7372	4446
Workstream Inc (Maitland Florida)	7389	931
WorkZone LLC	7372	2657
World Acceptance Corp	6141	35
World Acceptance Corporation of Missouri Inc	6141	44
World Access Service Corp	6411	65
World Airways Holding Inc	4522	6
World Book Inc	2731	25
World Business Brokers Inc	6282	136
World Candies Intl Ltd	2064	83
World Cinema Inc	4841	71
World Class Manufacturing Group Inc	3451	44
World Class Plastics Inc	3089	762
World Classic Productions Inc	7929	5
World Communications Inc (Seattle Washington)	4812	70
World Computer Inc	5045	993
World Data Products Inc	5045	194
World Dryer Corp	3634	30
World Electronics Inc	3671	21
World Electronics Sales And Service Inc	3672	42
World Emblem International Inc	2395	5
World Evangelistic Enterprise Corp	4832	275
World Eyecam Inc	5065	818
World Fiber Technologies Inc	1731	154
World Finance Corporation of Georgia Inc	6141	45
World Finance Corporation of Illinois Inc	6141	46
World Finance Corporation of Kentucky Inc	6141	17
World Finance Corporation of Louisiana Inc	6141	47
World Finance Corporation of New Mexico Inc	6141	48
World Finance Corporation of Tennessee Inc	6141	49
World Finance Corporation of Texas Inc	6141	50
World Flavors Inc	2099	143
World Fuel Services Corp	5172	1
World Gym Licensing Ltd	6794	148
World Harbors Inc	2035	27
World Heart Corp	3845	118
World Hotels AG	7389	133
World Image Corp	5023	141
World Information Systems Inc	7372	3762
World Information Technology Solutions LLC	7361	266
World Insulation and Chemicals Inc	5045	1066
World Journal LLC	2711	315
World Kitchen LLC	3421	3
World Library Publications Inc	2741	121
World Link Electronics LLC	5065	783
World Links Development Inc	4724	153
World Magnetics Co	3829	310
World Manufacturing Inc	3083	85
World Market Supply Inc	5084	220
World Marketing Of America Incorporated A Close Corp	5074	60
World Minerals Inc	1499	1
World Net Services Inc	4813	560
World News Saturday/Sunday	4833	207
World Newspaper Inc	2711	422
World Of Cd-Rom	5734	458
World of Good Tastes Inc	5812	453
World of Reading Ltd	7372	4780
World of Travel	4724	81
World Omni Financial Corp	6141	20
World Online Inc	4813	541
World Outdoors	4725	35
World Pac Paper LLC	5112	22
World Pacific Ullenberg Inc	3911	43
World Plastic Extruders Inc	3089	963
World Precision Instruments Inc	3826	15
World Press Inc	2752	1348
World Private Security Inc	7381	121
World Racing Group Inc	7948	25
World Savings Bank FSB	6035	1
World Security and Electric Inc	1731	1217
World Sharp Inc	7372	4578
World Software Corp	7372	2276
World Surveillance Group Inc	4813	743
World Tariff Ltd	2741	337
World Technologies Ltd	3679	715
World Technology Solutions Corp	7379	1238
World Telecommunications	4813	625
World Tower Company Inc	4899	162
World Trade Printing Co	2752	776
World Video Sales Company Inc	3841	400
World Wide Acquisitions and Sales Inc	3577	454
World Wide Mailing LLC	7331	287
World Wide Motors Inc	5511	606
World Wide Packets Inc	3577	97
World Wide Plastics Inc	3823	131
World Wide Technology Holding Company Inc	7379	5
World Wide Technology Inc	5045	6
World Wide Wadio Inc	7311	969
World Wrestling Entertainment Inc	7812	21
World Yacht Inc	4489	3

Company Name	SIC	Rank
Worldata Inc	7331	28
Worldclass Processing Corp	3479	74
Worldcom Exchange Inc	5045	239
Worlddoc Inc	4813	338
WorldGate Communications Inc	4841	79
World-Link Group Inc	7379	1686
Worldlink Logistics Inc	4412	29
WorldNet Services Corp	6411	130
WorldRes Inc	7389	1097
World's Finest Chocolate Inc	2066	13
World's Foremost Bank	6022	378
World's Smallest Ad Agency Inc	7311	1033
Worldscan Intelligence Services Ltd	7319	154
Worldstrides	4725	5
Worldtex Inc	2241	1
WorldView Software	7372	2919
Worldvision Home Video Inc	7812	83
Worldviz LLC	5065	623
Worldwide Circuit Technologies	5045	422
Worldwide Energy and Manufacturing USA Inc	3991	2
Worldwide Entertainment Corp	7812	188
Worldwide Exporters Inc	5084	707
World-Wide Holdings Corp	6719	112
Worldwide Information Network Systems Inc	7379	180
Worldwide Oilfield Machine Inc	3533	29
Worldwide Partners Inc	7311	1010
World-Wide Power Co	5734	330
World-Wide Printing Co	2731	162
Worldwide Refractories Inc	3297	8
Worldwide Technology Inc	3564	143
Worldwide Techservices LLC	7373	54
Worldwide Travel Staffing	7361	137
Worley Machine Enterprises Inc	3451	125
WorleyParsons	1623	73
Woroco Management LLC	5172	55
Worrell Brothers Inc	5199	123
Worth Data Inc	3577	327
Worth Ethic Corp	8742	612
Worth Higgins and Associates Inc	2752	71
Worth Inc	3949	43
Worth Love Finding Inc	5735	14
Worth Media	2721	59
Worth Nickel's Publications Inc	2741	441
Worth Publishers Inc	2731	163
Worthen Industries Inc	2671	17
WorthGroup	8712	99
Worthington Biochemical Corp	2835	51
Worthington Ford Inc	5511	341
Worthington Industries Inc	3316	1
Worthington Specialty Processing	3316	9
Worthington Steel Co	5051	26
WorxAudio Technologies Inc	3651	171
Wotco	3441	71
Wotkun Group Inc	3599	2444
Wottfm	4832	231
Wound Management Technologies Inc	5045	995
Woven Electronics LLC	3679	209
Wow! Business Solutions	7375	45
WOW Global Corporation LLC	7372	336
WOW! Internet Cable and Phone	4899	13
Wow-Bow Distributors Ltd	2047	38
Wowk Tv	4833	238
Wozniak Industries Inc	3469	76
Wozniak Machinery Co	3565	173
WP and RS Mars Co	5085	67
WP Carey and Company LLC	6519	12
WP Instruments Inc	3599	2413
WPCS International Inc	4899	50
WPGH Licensee LLC	4833	31
WPKN Inc	4832	292
WPL Associates Inc	2721	454
Wpp Dough Company Inc	2041	63
WPP Group USA Inc	7311	5
WPPA Inc	6324	108
Wpromote Inc	7319	107
WPS Community Bank FSB	6035	228
WPX Delivery Solutions LLC	4215	14
WPXA TV-Atlanta	4833	115
WPXD TV-Detroit	4833	263
WPXJ TV-Buffalo	4833	111
WPXX TV-Memphis	4833	109
Wqed Multimedia	4833	141
WQN Inc	7389	500
WQXR FM	4832	98
WR Berkley Corp	6331	41
WR Case and Sons Cutlery Co	3421	7
WR Chesnut Engineering Inc	3555	110
WR Foods	5148	88
WR Grace and Co	2819	9
WR Hambrecht and Co	6211	98
WR Hodgson Company LP	1623	114
WR Meadows Inc	2951	20
WR Medical Electronics Co	3841	291
WR Sharples Company Inc	3544	753
WR Townsend Contracting Inc	1629	94
Wrabacon Inc	3565	158
Wrag-Time Air Freight Inc	4213	547
Wrap-Ade Machine Company Inc	3565	179
Wrap-Ups Inc	2789	60
Wray Ford Inc	5511	409
Wrb Communications Inc	8748	289
WRBS Inc	1623	465

Company Name	SIC	Rank
WRDW-TV Inc	4833	67
Wrek Radio Station	4832	172
Wren Associates Ltd	3699	128
Wrena LLC	3465	35
Wrench Limited Co	5082	111
Wrenn Enterprises Inc	7342	11
Wrentham Tool Products	3544	610
Wrex Products Inc	3089	778
WRG Services Inc	7378	14
Wrh Holdings LLC	3556	96
Wrico International LLC	5063	1060
Wright 1 Electric	1731	1297
Wright and Filippis Inc	3842	89
Wright and Kimbrough/Cotton	6411	251
Wright and McGill Co	3949	37
Wright Brothers Electric Company Inc	1731	2510
Wright Business Graphics Of California Inc	5112	48
Wright Capacitors Inc	3675	35
Wright Construction Group	1541	152
Wright Do It Center	5211	52
Wright Engineered Plastics Inc	3544	478
Wright Express Corp	7389	75
Wright Images	5946	9
Wright Industries Inc	3549	4
Wright Larco Inc	2752	824
Wright Lindsey and Jennings LLP	8111	380
Wright Machine and Tool Company Inc	3599	483
Wright Machine Tool Company Inc	3549	86
Wright Manufacturing Inc	3524	18
Wright Medical Group Inc	3842	22
Wright Metal Products Inc	3599	299
Wright Motor Lines Inc	4213	2367
Wright Motors Inc	5511	1201
Wright Packaging Inc	2674	13
Wright Plastic Products Company LLC	3089	415
Wright Printing Co	2752	49
Wright Pump Inc	3561	2
Wright Runstad and Co	6552	160
Wright Solutions Inc	7379	629
Wright Tool Co	3423	35
Wright Transportation Inc	4213	1832
Wright Travel Inc	4724	38
Wright Tree Service Inc	0783	3
Wright Trucking Inc	4213	2647
Wright Williams and Kelly	5045	480
Wright Wisner Distributing Corp	5181	39
Wright-K Technology Inc	3541	57
Wright's Dairy Farm Inc	0241	8
Wrightsoft Corp	7372	3638
Wriglesworth and Willock Metal Fab Inc	3444	44
Wristbandfactorycom	3172	5
Write Brothers Inc	7372	3122
WritePro Corp	7372	4579
Writers House Inc	7389	1112
Wrk Technologies Inc	5045	1033
WRLH Licensee LLC	4833	93
Wrni Radio	4832	227
Wrnj Radio Inc	4832	241
Wrr Environmental Services Company Inc	4953	112
WRS Group Ltd	2741	134
WRS Motion Picture and Video Laboratory	3695	9
Wrymark Inc	5047	91
WS Anderson Associates Inc	3599	924
Ws Atkins Inc	8711	315
WS Badcock Corp	5023	9
WS Bellows Construction Corp	1542	158
WS Deans Co	3677	121
WS Dodge Oil Company Inc	2992	49
WS Emrian Trucking Inc	4213	1136
Ws Incorporated Of Manmouth	3269	17
WS Thomas Transfer Inc	4213	1476
WS Wilson Corp	5088	34
Wsa Group Inc	8711	88
WSA Sales Company Inc	3625	340
Wsa Systems-Boca Inc	5063	547
WSB Financial Group Inc	6022	374
WSB Holding Inc	6712	518
Wsb Inc	3532	53
WSFS Financial Corp	6712	131
Wsg Parent Golf Iv LP	7992	3
Wsg Pecan Grove Iv LP	7997	6
WSI Industries Inc	3549	9
Wsi Machine and Supply LLC	3599	787
Wsj Worldwide Inc	5013	210
WSJM Inc	4832	78
Wsjv Television Inc	4833	158
WSM Inc	4832	128
WSMH Inc	4833	69
WSMH Licensee LLC	4833	65
Wspy 1071 Fm	4832	244
Wst Liq Corp	3089	942
WSYT Licensee LP	4833	56
WSYX Licensee Inc	4833	21
WT Cox Subscriptions	7822	7
WT Harvey Lumber Co	5211	44
WT Pettit and Sons Company Inc	3469	363
WT Ruark and Company Inc	2092	95
WTAG 580 AM Stereo	4832	163
WTB Financial Corp	6712	201
WTBC 1230	4833	101

Company Name	SIC	Rank
WTBF-AM	4832	169
Wtc Machinery LLC	3531	226
Wtcc Radio Station Request Line	4832	70
Wtd Supply Inc	5013	144
wTe Corp	5093	18
WTech Inc	8748	68
WTI Inc (Phoenix Arizona)	8711	273
WTI Systems Ltd	7373	132
WTI Transport Inc	4213	488
Wtop	4832	158
WTPA FM 93 5	4832	277
Wts Inc	7374	156
WTSN Channel 63	4833	231
WTTO Inc	4833	41
WTTO Licensee LLC	4833	50
WTVZ Inc	4833	48
WTWC Inc	4833	59
WTWC Licensee LLC	4833	42
WUBU 1063 FM	4832	252
Wubz105 9	3663	326
Wuesthoff Health Systems Inc	8062	124
Wuethrich Brothers-Nebraska LLC	2021	6
WUHU 107 1 FM	4832	188
Wulco Inc	5085	72
Wulff Enterprise	5045	795
Wunder Mold Inc	3089	1580
Wunderlich Securities Inc	6211	35
Wunderman	7311	55
WUPX TV-Lexington	4833	116
Wurm's Janitorial Service Inc	7349	398
Wurts and Associates Inc	6282	339
WuXi AppTec Inc	8734	14
Wvpn 88 5	4832	115
Wvrt Inc	4832	242
WVS Financial Corp	6712	603
WW Cross Industries Inc	3315	9
WW Enterprises Inc	1731	345
WW Gay Fire Protection Inc	1711	114
WW Gay Mechanical Contractor Inc	1711	48
WW Grainger Inc	5075	1
WW Metal Products Inc	3443	217
WW Owens and Sons Moving and Storage	4213	1536
Ww Painting And Construction Solutions Inc	7349	331
WW Patterson Co	3429	145
WW Products Inc	3069	150
WW Promotions Inc	7311	955
WW Rowland Trucking Company Inc	4213	835
WW Transport Inc	4213	3138
WW Wallwork Inc	5511	194
WW Williams Co	5084	90
WWA Group Inc	7389	437
Wwj 950 Am	4832	67
WWL Industries	1389	22
WWM S Inc	5021	91
WWR International	4212	65
WWW Electronics Inc	3672	415
Wxrl 1300 Am	4832	165
WY Campbell and Co	6211	173
Wyandot Inc	2096	20
Wyant Data Systems Inc	7379	1171
Wyant Inc	7373	1220
Wyatt Compressor Service Inc	7359	121
Wyatt Field Service Co	7349	33
Wyatt Technology Corp	3826	59
Wyatt Transfer Inc	4213	716
Wyav Wave 1041	4832	220
Wycen Foods Inc	2013	229
Wyckoff Farms Inc	0723	1
Wycomp Technology Inc	5734	349
Wyep 913 Fm	4832	276
Wykle Research Inc	3843	88
Wyko Inc	3559	228
Wylaco Construction Supply Co	5084	454
Wyle Information System Group	7371	31
Wyle Laboratories Inc	8734	9
Wylie and Son Inc	3523	103
Wylie Musser Chevrolet Oldsmobile Cadillac	5511	1188
Wyman-Gordon Co	3463	3
Wynalda Litho Inc	2752	62
Wyndham Worldwide Corp	7011	15
Wyndmoor Industries Inc	2281	15
Wyngate International Inc	7319	148
Wynkoop Brewing Co	5812	365
Wynn Fire Equipment LLC	5099	107
Wynn Resorts Ltd	7999	3
Wynnchurch Capital Ltd	6722	257
WynnCom	7376	23
WynnComm (Statesville North Carolina)	7371	1935
Wynne Systems	7372	494
Wynne Transport Service Inc	4213	217
Wyo-Ben Inc	1459	3
Wyomedia Corp	4833	225
Wyoming Beverages Inc	5149	153
Wyoming Building Supply Inc	5031	346
Wyoming Electric Inc	1731	920
Wyoming Ethanol LLC	2869	80
Wyoming Financial Publications	2759	525
Wyoming Gas Co	4924	67
Wyoming Machine Inc	3444	151
Wyoming Machinery Co	5084	53

Company Name	SIC	Rank
Wyoming Newspapers	2711	566
Wyoming Retirement System	6371	11
Wyoming Sand and Stone Co	1442	11
Wyoming Test Fixtures Inc	3829	437
WYPX TV-Albany	4833	128
Wyre-Wynd	3357	32
Wyrulec Co	4911	376
Wyse Advertising Inc	7311	137
Wyse Technology Inc	3575	2
WYSIWYG Corp	7372	4028
Wysong and Miles Company Inc	3542	21
Wyssmont Company Inc	3567	85
Wythe Power Equipment Company Inc	3625	252
Wyvern Consulting Ltd	8748	233
Wyvern Technologies Inc	3679	520
WYZZ Inc	4833	49
WYZZ Licensee Inc	7383	17
Wzup	4833	203
X Brand Networks Inc	4813	391
X Factory Entertainment LLC	5092	52
X Inc	5734	151
X Strategy Inc	7382	135
X Tend Communications Inc	4813	281
X Wiley Inc	5048	12
X1	5045	321
X-10 Wireless Technology Inc	7372	1309
X2 Digital Wireless Systems Inc	3577	559
Xact Wire Edm Corp	3599	793
Xactly Corp	7371	564
Xactra Technologies Inc	3545	120
Xaktsoft Inc	7372	4118
Xaloy Inc	3544	13
Xanadoo LLC	4813	364
Xanadu Alpacas	7379	1676
Xandex Inc	3825	91
Xanodyne Pharmaceuticals Inc	2834	147
Xante California	7372	3205
Xante Corp	3577	107
Xanthus Inc	5084	570
XATA Corp	3571	37
Xavier Electronics Inc	7372	4946
X-Bar Automation Inc	3613	113
Xc Networks	7373	554
Xcable Company Corp	5731	188
Xceed	7379	97
XCel Brands Inc	7389	2490
Xcel Communications Intl	8748	329
Xcel Controls Inc	7372	3558
Xcel Energy Inc	4931	4
X-Cel Feeds Inc	5191	148
Xcel Mold And Machine Inc	3544	915
X-Cel Optical Co	3229	6
XCEL Solutions Corp	7371	701
X-Cel Tooling Inc	3544	121
Xcell International Corp	3089	715
Xcellerex Inc	2834	201
XCEND Group	8742	540
Xchange Telecom Corp	4813	346
Xchanger	2741	423
Xco International Inc	3823	469
XCOR Aerospace	3812	145
Xcorporeal Inc	3845	143
Xduce Corp	7379	1580
Xdx Inc	3845	107
Xebec Corp	6719	158
Xeco Inc	3679	721
Xedar Corp (Englewood Colorado)	7375	206
Xelerated Inc	5045	294
Xelic Inc	7373	736
Xemplar Models LLC	7363	232
Xenergy Inc	8748	69
Xenetech Global Inc	3555	99
Xenia Manufacturing Inc	3694	21
Xenith Bankshares Inc	6022	453
XenoBiotic Laboratories Inc	8731	145
Xenonics Holdings Inc	3641	24
XenoPort Inc	8731	339
Xenos Group	7372	1338
Xentx Lubricants Inc	2992	55
Xerex Inc	7371	1804
Xerographic Reproduction Center Inc	7334	55
Xerographic Solutions Inc	5044	102
Xeron Inc	1382	31
Xerox Corp	3861	1
Xerox Financial Services Inc	6153	42
Xerox Global Services Inc	8742	1
Xerox Omnifax	3661	14
Xert Communications	4813	682
Xertech Inc	3949	179
Xerxes Corp	3089	23
Xeta Technologies Inc	3661	33
Xfact Inc	7379	1046
Xfmrs Inc	3677	4
Xfone Inc	4899	62
Xi Graphics Inc	7372	2874
Xia LLC	5049	112
Xifin Inc	5045	205
Xijet Inc	3577	593
Xilas Medical Inc	3823	246
Xilinx Inc	3674	20
Xinergy Microsystems	7373	875
Xinet Inc	7371	1058
Xinnix	8299	42
Xintekidel Inc	3663	357

Company Name	SIC	Rank
Xinya (USA) Electronics Inc	5045	698
Xiom Corp	5198	16
Xiosoft Inc	4813	647
Xiotech Corp	7372	56
Xirrus Inc	3663	63
Xit Activewear Inc	5199	127
Xitech Instruments Inc	3826	141
Xitron Inc	3555	23
Xitron Technologies Inc	3841	399
XIV Karats Ltd	5094	37
XKL LLC	3571	66
XL Adhesives LLC	2891	63
XI Construction Corp	1542	99
XL Environmental Inc	6331	17
X-L Machine Company Inc	3544	321
XI Parts Partnership Ltd	5013	93
X-L Plastics Inc	2673	24
XI Specialized Trailers Inc	3715	32
XI Techgroup Inc	7373	663
X-L-Engineering Corp	3451	51
Xli Corp	3544	153
XM C Inc	7373	925
XM Satellite Radio Holdings Inc	4899	11
XM Satellite Radio Inc	3663	23
X-Mark/CDT	3443	131
XMultiple Technologies	3571	87
Xnet Information System Inc	4812	108
Xnet Systems Inc	5045	529
XO Holdings Inc	4813	16
Xodus Medical Inc	3841	217
XOJET Inc	4512	54
XOMA Ltd	2834	225
Xomox Corp	3494	15
Xora Inc	5051	73
Xorbix Technologies Inc	3695	137
XOS Digital	5045	94
XP Power Ltd	5063	64
XP Systems	7373	131
Xpdent Corp	5047	256
Xpedx	5111	3
xpedx - Kirk Downey	5111	7
Xpel Technologies Corp	7372	1572
XpertRule Software Ltd	7372	3970
Xpient Solutions LLC	7372	1635
Xpitax LLC	7372	554
Xplain Corp	2721	51
Xplana Inc	2741	152
Xplore Infosystems	7372	4152
Xplore Technologies Corporation of America	3577	236
XPO Logistics Inc	4731	36
Xponential Inc	5999	53
Xponet Inc	3357	56
Xpress Air Inc	4513	4
Xpress Movers	7299	30
XPRESSCHEX Inc	7372	1722
Xpriori LLC	7372	1693
Xpto International Inc	5045	825
Xradia Inc	3827	57
X-Ray Cassette Repair Company Inc	3844	15
X-Ray Industries Inc	3829	64
X-Rite Inc	3861	13
XS Inc	7389	894
XS International Inc	5045	214
Xsell Resources Inc	7361	298
Xsis Electronics Inc	3825	240
XSynergy Software Corp	7372	4899
XT Global	8742	332
XTEC Inc	3679	151
Xtech	7379	1068
Xtek Inc	3568	14
Xtel Communications Inc	4813	271
Xtelesis Corp	4813	600
Xtellus Inc	3669	144
Xten Industries LLC	3089	568
Xtend Consulting LLC	7373	1035
Xtera Communications Inc	3572	29
Xterprise Solutions Inc	3699	83
Xtiva Financial Systems Inc	7372	1872
XTO Energy Inc	1311	13
Xto Inc	3053	39
XTRA Lease	7519	2
X-Tra Light Manufacturing Partnership Ltd	3648	25
Xtras Inc	7378	75
Xtreme Alternative Defense Systems	3812	216
Xtreme Consulting Group Inc	8742	248
Xtron Software Services Inc	7371	1507
Xttrium Laboratories Inc	2834	265
Xuron Corp	3423	64
Xvd Corp	7371	1562
Xvei Inc	8711	480
Xvionics Inc	7372	3370
Xyant Technology Inc	7371	749
Xyber Technologies Inc	7379	1632
Xybernaut Corp	3577	286
Xybernaut Solutions Inc	7372	3559
XyberNET Inc	7374	127
XYEnterprise Inc	7371	151
Xylem Flowtronex	3523	21
Xymogen	5122	83
Xymox Technologies Inc	3679	260
XYPRO Technology Corp	7371	1293
Xyquad Inc	7372	1750

Company Name	SIC	Rank
Xyratex International Inc	3825	45
Xyron Semiconductor Inc	3674	269
Xyte Inc	4813	723
Xytech Systems Corp	7372	4220
Xytel Corp	8711	620
Xytex Corp	8099	105
Xyvision Enterprise Solutions Inc	7375	173
Y and B Equipment Corp	7353	98
Y and W Sportswear Inc	2325	15
Yacht Design Software	7372	4900
Yacktman Fund	6722	218
Yacktman Funds Inc	6282	522
Yada Systems Inc	5045	489
Yadkin Valley Financial Corp	6022	89
Yadtel Telecom	4813	183
Yaffe and Co	7311	395
Yahara Materials Inc	1422	47
Yahara Software	7372	3081
Yahoo! Broadcast Services	7375	33
Yahoo! Inc	7375	2
Yahoo! Search Marketing	7389	63
Yak Pak Inc	3161	2
Yale Cordage Inc	2298	5
Yale Electric Supply Company Inc	5063	225
Yale Farmers Coop	5153	124
Yale Industrial Products Inc	3536	46
Yale Industrial Trucks Pittsburgh Inc	5084	253
Yale Materials Handling Corp	3537	82
Yale Mechanical Inc	1731	238
Yale Ogron Windows and Doors	3442	80
Yale Security Inc	3429	33
Yale-New Haven Health Services Corp	8741	83
Ya'lla Tours USA	4725	42
Yamada America Inc	5084	725
Yamada North America Inc	3714	238
Yamada Science and Art Corp	7372	3788
Yamaha Corporation of America	3931	3
Yamaha Motor Corporation USA	5012	21
Yamamoto Manufacturing Inc (San Jose California)	3672	241
Yamas Environmental Systems Inc	8711	349
Yamasa Corporation USA	2035	40
Yamasa Enterprises	2091	27
Yamato Corp	5046	161
Yamato Engine Specialists 1990 Ltd	3714	320
Yamazaki California Inc	5461	27
Yancey-Hausman and Associates	6531	415
Yancey's Fancy Inc	5143	34
Yancy and Associates Inc	7373	531
Yang-Ming International Corp	3571	153
Yank Waste Company Inc	5093	106
Yanke Bionics Inc	3842	191
Yanke Energy Inc	1629	92
Yanke Machine Shop Inc	3599	351
Yankee Candle Company Inc	3999	7
Yankee Corp	3541	98
Yankee Energy System Inc	4924	35
Yankee Gas Services Co	4924	38
Yankee Group	8742	170
Yankee Hill Brick Manufacturing Co	3251	18
Yankee Hill Machine Company Inc	3451	64
Yankee Marketers Inc	5141	134
Yankee Medical Inc	5999	143
Yankee Microwave Inc	4899	199
Yankee Printing Group Inc	2759	408
Yankee Publishing Inc	2721	210
Yanmar America Corp	5084	197
Yanni Partners Inc	6282	541
Yantis Co	1623	15
Yara North America Inc	5191	7
Yarbrough Transfer Co	4213	1310
Yardarm Marine Products Inc	3443	219
Yardi Systems Inc	7371	69
Yardney Technical Products Inc	3691	22
Yardney Water Management Systems Inc	3589	120
Yardville Supply Co	5251	24
Yarema Die and Engineering Co	3469	33
Yargus Manufacturing Inc	3523	69
Yark Automotive Group	5511	121
Yarmouth Lumber Inc	4213	2035
Yarn Sellar Inc	5949	9
Yarnell Ice Cream Company Inc	2024	21
Yas Corp	5045	990
Yash and Lujan Consulting Inc	7379	607
YASH Technologies Inc	7371	121
YaSheng Group	6531	58
Yaskawa Electric America Inc	3569	49
Yasutomi Warehousing and Distribution/YWD	4213	3041
Yasutomo and Company Inc	5112	35
Yates Bleachery Co	2261	6
Yates Companies Inc	1541	19
Yates Construction Company Inc	1623	90
Yates Electric Inc	1731	2236
Yates Electric Service Inc	1731	1420
Yates Foil USA Inc	3497	9
Yates Industries Inc	3593	23
Yates Insurance Agency Inc	6411	250
Yates Petroleum Inc	1311	72
Yates Wood and MacDonald Inc	6531	224
Yates-American Machine Company Inc	3553	32
Yates-Silverman Inc	7389	1214
Yawitz Inc	3645	45

Company Name	SIC	Rank
Yazaki North America Inc	5013	50
Yazoo Valley Electric Power Association	4911	312
Yazoo Valley Oil Mill Inc	2074	1
Ybl LLC	5031	308
Y-Delta Inc	1731	364
Yeager Manufacturing Corp	3728	160
Year One Inc	5531	21
Year-A-Round Cab Co	3599	2414
Yearout Mechanical and Engineering Inc	1711	69
Yeatts Transfer Co	4213	2563
Yeck Brothers Co	7331	178
Yelding Inc	2752	1751
Yellow Book USA Inc	2741	32
Yellow Books USA	2741	310
Yellow Cab Company Inc	4121	2
Yellow Checker Cab Company Inc	4121	3
Yellow Hair Trading and Mining Limited Inc	1499	7
Yellow Roadway Technologies Inc	7371	42
Yellow Services Inc	7375	42
Yellow Transportation Inc	4213	11
YellowBrix Inc	7379	513
YellowPepper Wireless LLC	7371	294
Yellowstone Company LLC	3949	127
Yellowstone Log Homes LLC	1521	148
YellowZone Inc	7372	1623
Yeo and Yeo Computer Consulting LLC	7373	411
Yeomans Chicago Corp	3561	82
Yeomans Distributing Co	5064	70
Yerkes and Michels CPA LLC	8721	478
Yesmailcom	7319	80
Yessick's Design Center	7389	704
Yesterday's Business Computers Inc	7379	602
Yeti Coolers	5078	19
YFF and Scholma PC	8721	116
Yh Products Corp	2041	37
Yield Engineering Systems Inc	3825	176
Yingling Aircraft Inc	5088	22
Yipes Enterprise Services Inc	4899	9
Yjcc Of Bergen County	8322	155
YK International Inc	3559	573
YKK USA Inc	3965	1
YL Communications Inc	7812	336
YMBD Inc	5147	111
YMH Torrance Inc	3621	23
Yoakum Packing Co	5147	91
Yoas Services Inc	5049	143
Yocream International Inc	2024	19
Yoder and Co	8721	240
Yoder Die Casting	3363	31
Yoder Enterprises Inc	4812	78
Yoder Industries Inc	3363	26
Yoder Lumber Company Inc	2421	69
Yoder Manufacturing Co	3547	3
Yoder Oil Company Inc	5171	52
Yodle Inc	7379	57
Yodleecom Inc	7372	251
Yofarm Co	2026	39
Yoga Journal LLC	2721	211
Yoh Services LLC	8744	21
Yohay Associates	5045	579
Yokem Toyota Inc	5511	629
Yokogawa Industrial Automation America Inc	3625	6
Yokogawa Leisure Analysis Div	3826	137
Yokohama Corporation Of North America	3011	14
Yokohama Tire Corp	3011	10
Yomega Corp	3944	46
Yon-Drake and Associates Inc	6282	557
Yonekyu USA Inc	2013	143
Yoonimex Inc	2395	19
Yoplait USA	2026	18
Yorel Integrated Solutions Inc	7373	547
York Barbell Company Inc	5091	119
York Building Maintenance Inc	7349	214
York Building Products Company Inc	3271	10
York Container Co	2653	21
York Corrugating Co	5074	89
York Electric Cooperative Inc	4911	253
York Enterprise Solutions	8748	101
York Goltens-New Corp	7699	75
York Group Inc	3995	2
York Hill Trap Rock Quarry Co	1429	17
York Hospital	8062	209
York Ice Company Inc	2097	11
York Imperial Plastics Inc	3089	1081
York International Corp	3585	5
York Pictures Inc	7822	38
York Precision Inc	3599	1952
York Printing Co	2752	1796
York River Seafood Company Inc	5146	39
York Stenographic Services Inc	7338	10
York Tape and Label Inc	2759	13
York Water Co	4941	17
Yorke Printe Shoppe Inc	2752	764
York-Seaway Industrial Products Inc	3599	408
Yorktowne Optical Co	5049	78
Yorkville Bagels Inc	2051	293
Yorozu Automotive Tennessee Inc	3465	15
Yosemite Bank	6022	580
Yoshino America Corp	3089	969

Company Name	SIC	Rank
Yost Candy Co	2064	102
Yost Dutch Maid Bakery Inc	2051	249
You and Associates LLC	7389	718
You Inc	7389	2101
YouChange Holdings Corp	7359	280
Youm-Tzib Software Solutions Inc	7372	3971
Younan Properties Inc	6531	51
Young Adult Institute Inc	8059	5
Young American Bindery	2789	130
Young Americans Bank	6022	829
Young and Associates Ltd	7372	4580
Young and Franklin Inc	3492	5
Young and Laramore Corp	7311	258
Young and Rubicam Inc	7311	6
Young and Son Inc	1794	32
Young Broadcasting of Davenport Inc	4833	89
Young Broadcasting of Lansing Inc	4833	92
Young Broadcasting of Sioux Falls Inc	4833	85
Young Chang Company Ltd	5099	125
Young Chevrolet Oldsmobile Cadillac Inc	5511	869
Young Co	7311	410
Young Computer Technologies	5045	856
Young DC Inc	2711	925
Young Dental Manufacturing LLC	3843	18
Young E F Jr Manufacturing Co	2844	148
Young Engineering and Manufacturing Inc	3823	231
Young Ford Inc	5511	389
Young Innovations Inc	3843	7
Young Isaac Inc	7311	472
Young Machine Inc	3599	2081
Young Minds Inc	7372	4398
Young Power Equipment Company Nm	5063	954
Young Supply Co	5078	5
Young Touchstone Co	3443	42
Young Transportation Inc	4213	1668
Youngberg Industries Inc	3443	157
Younger Brothers Components Inc	2439	25
Younger Brothers Door and Trim LLC	5031	201
Youngers And Sons Manufacturing Company Inc	3599	243
Youngevity Inc	2833	33
Youngman and Company Inc	8712	301
Young's Cleaning International Inc	7349	515
Young's Commercial Transfer	4213	1362
Young's Furniture Manufacturing Co	2426	22
Young's Jersey Dairy Inc	5812	412
Young's Machine Co	3532	65
Young's Market Company LLC	5182	5
Young's Valley Contax Inc	3851	100
Youngstown Arc Engraving Co	2752	1364
Youngstown Plastic Tooling and Machinery Inc	3559	266
Youngstown Tool and Die Company Inc	3544	195
Youngstown Window Cleaning Company Inc	7349	218
Youngstown-Kenworth Inc	5013	262
Youngtron Inc	3672	132
Your Home Town USA Inc	7311	832
Your Images Inc	2796	59
Your Plan B Co	7336	305
Your Recruiting Company Inc	8742	221
Your Selling Team Inc	7389	1553
Your Town Press Inc	2752	956
Your Town Transport Inc	4213	2459
Your Town Yellow Pages LLC	7389	1982
Your Vitamins Inc	2834	199
Yourchouk's Hardware Video	5731	132
Yourga Trucking Inc	4213	1232
Your-Site Virtual Servers	7379	478
yousendit Inc	4899	108
Youth Campus	8361	103
Youth Emergency Services and Shelter Of Iowa	8322	233
Youth For Tomorrow—New Life Center Inc	8361	107
Youth In Action	8322	159
Youth In Need	8351	11
Youth Services International Inc	8299	18
Yowell International	4213	1032
Yowell Transportation Services	4213	1400
Yp Inc	4813	291
Ypartnership LLC	7311	499
Ypne LLC	2741	376
Ypsilanti Equity Elevator Company Inc	5153	191
YRC Glen Moore	4213	204
YRC Regional Transportation Inc	4213	18
YRC Worldwide Inc	4731	5
YS Inc	2819	122
YS Manufacturing Inc	3599	723
YS Tech USA Inc	5065	767
Ysi Inc	3826	18
Ysk Corp	3469	18
YTB International Inc	4724	76
Y-Tex Corp	3089	537
Yuba River Moulding and Mill Work Inc	2431	109
Yucaipa Capital Partners LP	6799	301
Yucaipa Cos	5411	117
Yuhshin USA Ltd	3099	179
Yukon Equipment Inc	5082	45
Yukon Nutritional	2047	29
Yukon-Kuskokwim Health Corp	8062	214
Yule Transport Inc	4213	2083

Company Name	SIC	Rank
Yum! Brands Inc	5812	7
YUM! Restaurants International Inc	7389	103
Yuma Broadcasting Co	4833	124
Yuma Winlectric Co	5063	828
Yunker Industries Inc	2759	134
Yupi Internet Inc	7375	209
Yurcor	7372	248
Yuri Software Inc	7372	4901
Yurman Design Inc	3911	17
Yushiro Manufacturing America Inc	2992	27
Yutaka Electric International Inc	3612	124
Yves Delorme Inc	5023	46
YXLON International Inc	3844	27
YZ Enterprises Inc	2052	77
Z and L Machining Inc	3599	578
Z and M Enterprises LLC	5999	137
Z and R Corp	5143	42
Z and S Electronics Inc	5046	65
Z and Z Machine Products Inc	3599	1235
Z and Z Manufacturing Inc	3599	1784
Z Corp	3577	201
Z Infinite	7371	1882
Z Microsystems Inc	3089	488
Z Technologies Corp	2891	67
Z Technology Inc	3663	331
Z57 Inc	7374	110
Za Control Services	5063	1011
Za Management	8741	272
Zabatt Engine Services Inc	7699	68
Zabin Industries Inc	5131	45
Zaca Inc	3089	489
Zachary Confections Inc	2064	20
Zachrich Trucking Inc	4213	2744
Zachry Construction and Materials Inc	1611	46
Zachry Construction Corp	1623	3
Zachys	5999	51
Zack Electronics Inc	5065	152
Zaclon Inc	2869	95
Zaepfel Development Company Inc	6552	266
Zag Technical Services Inc	7376	39
Zagar Inc	3546	32
Zagat Survey LLC	2741	141
Zagg Inc	5999	34
Zahl-Ford Inc	8711	419
Zahn Electronics Inc	3625	343
Zahntech Advanced Technologies Inc	5094	78
Zak Designs Inc	5023	30
Zak Inc	3443	150
Zale Corp	5944	3
Zalicus Inc	2834	190
Zallie Supermarkets Inc	5411	140
Zaluzny Excavating Corp	4213	2269
Zamagias Properties	6552	211
Zamaroni Quarry Inc	5032	88
Zamperla Inc	3599	32
Zamzow Manufacturing Company Inc	2394	33
Zandar Corp	7372	4081
Zanden Communications Ltd	7372	4029
Zander Insulation	1742	20
Zander Press Inc	2752	1497
Zanders Glenn Fur and Sporting Goods Company Inc	5091	63
Zandiant Technologies Inc	3714	357
Zandri Construction Corp	1541	233
Zane Publishing Inc	2741	468
Zaner-Bloser Inc	2731	29
Zanesville Mould Div	3544	46
Zangle Inc	4813	475
Zanuck Co	7812	223
ZAP (Santa Rosa California)	3751	25
Zapata Enterprises Inc	1731	1682
Zapata Janitorial Building and General Services Inc	7349	116
Zapcom Corp	7311	1043
Zappi Oil and Gas Co	4212	50
Zapposcom Inc	5961	28
Zar Tran Inc	4213	770
Zarda Development Company Inc	5812	212
Zareba Systems Inc	3612	28
Zaremba Group LLC	6552	87
Zaro Bake Shop Inc	2051	66
Zartic Inc	2013	13
Zasio Enterprises Inc	7372	2920
Zata Corp	1731	1583
Zatec LLC	3081	114
Zateca Foods LLC	2099	231
Zatkoff Seals and Packings Co	5085	69
Zaug's Inc	5962	9
Zausner Foods Corp	2022	8
Zavala County Bank	6022	574
Zaxcom Inc	3663	336
Z-Axis Connector Co	3643	142
Zaxwear	5621	45
ZaxWerks Inc	7372	3972
Zaytran Inc	3593	40
ZBA Inc (Hillsborough New Jersey)	3577	448
Z-Band Inc	5065	692
Zbb Energy Corp	4911	595
Zbe Inc	3625	140
Zeal Group	7373	008
Zebco	3949	70
Zebco Industries Inc	3086	149
Zebec Data Systems Inc	7374	300
Zebra Imaging Inc	3827	23

Company Name	SIC	Rank
Zebra Network LLC	4813	527
Zebra Pen Corp	5112	45
Zebra Print Solutions Inc	7334	66
Zebra Technologies Corp	3577	22
Zebra Technology of Camarillo	3577	47
Zed Audio Corp	3651	245
Zed Industries Inc	3559	192
Zednem Pipeline Construction Inc	1623	264
Zee Manufacturing Ltd	2434	40
Zee Software Solutions Inc	7372	3973
Zeeco Inc	3433	34
Zeesoft Inc	7372	2693
Zefon International	3089	535
ZEH Software Inc	7372	1694
Zeig Electric Inc	1731	427
Zeiger Enterprises Inc	5012	173
Zeigler Cooper Inc	8712	111
Zeiler-Pennock Inc	7372	2484
Zeis Group Inc	7311	941
Zeit Company Inc	3914	13
Zeitgeist Publishing Inc	2721	451
Zeitner and Sons Inc	4213	1306
Zekiah Technologies Inc	7374	201
Zeks Air Drier Corp	3563	27
Zelacom Electronic Publishing	7336	317
Zeland Software Inc	7372	3044
Zelco Industries Inc	5023	180
Zelcor Media Duplication and Supplies	5046	111
Zelenka Nursery Inc	0181	8
Zelle Hofmann Voelbel Mason and Gette LLP	8111	418
Zeller Plastik Inc	3089	226
Zellmer Truck Lines Inc	4213	2603
Zellner Construction Company Inc	1541	234
Zellwin Farms Co	2671	22
Zeltex Inc	3823	356
Zemarc Corp	5084	282
Zemco Tool and Die	3089	842
Zemex Corp	1481	3
Zempleo Inc	8742	201
Zen Music Inc	7389	1261
Zen Software Inc	7372	2009
Zenar Corp	3536	20
Zendesk Inc	7372	1190
Zenger Group Inc	2752	644
Zenimax Media Inc	7372	1027
Zenion Industries Inc	3699	252
Zenith Drilling Corp	1381	59
Zenith Electronics Corp	3651	17
Zenith Engraving Company Inc	2796	45
Zenith Freight Lines LLC	4213	1150
Zenith Insurance Co	6331	208
Zenith Management Co	8741	125
Zenith National Insurance Corp	6331	124
Zenith Products Corp	2434	7
Zenith Rollers LLC	3555	82
Zenith Specialty Bag Company Inc	2673	16
Zenith Tech Inc	1771	9
Zenoss Inc	7371	324
Zenta	7389	18
Zentech Manufacturing Inc	3672	138
Zentner Transportation Inc	4213	2899
Zentrix Technologies Inc	3674	208
Zeochem LLC	1446	5
Zeolyst International	2899	80
ZeOmega LLC	7372	579
ZEON Corp	3646	63
Zeon Solutions Inc	7311	679
Zep Inc	2842	6
Zephyr Associates Inc	7372	3434
Zephyr Development Corp	7372	3585
Zephyr Environmental Corp	8748	123
Zephyr Lock LLC	3429	122
Zephyr Manufacturing Company Inc	3545	70
Zephyrus Electronics Ltd	3663	288
Zeppelin Systems USA Inc	8711	398
Zeptometrix Corp	2836	52
Zerious Electronic Publishing	7372	4581
Zero Corp	3629	4
ZERO Halliburton	3089	322
Zero Manufacturing Inc	3411	9
Zero Surge Inc	3643	154
Zero Virtual	7372	3850
Zero Zone Inc	3585	74
ZeroChaos Inc	7363	24
Zeroid and Company Inc	7373	379
Zero-Max Inc	3566	23
Zerone Inc	7379	913
Zerowait Corp	8999	78
Zesco Products Inc	5046	46
Zest Anchors Inc	5047	231
Zeta Meter Inc	3825	344
Zeta Products Inc	3861	88
Zetta Inc	7379	425
Zettacom Inc	5065	246
Zet-Tek Precision Machining	3599	1180
Zeus Concepts LLC	7372	3974
Zeus Scientific Inc	3841	218
Zevenbergen Capital Investments LLC	6282	616
ZEVEX International Inc	3845	54
Zevo Golf Company Inc	3949	111
Zezan Global Inc	4813	646
Zf Array Technology Inc	3675	23
ZF Group North American Operations	3714	59

Company Name	SIC	Rank
Zf Lemforder LLC	3714	1
Zf Sachs Automotive Of America Inc	3714	106
Zf Technologies LLC	5013	42
ZGC Inc	7359	140
ZGRAF Software Products	7372	4030
ZH Computer Inc	7371	1117
ZHA Inc (Orlando Florida)	8748	144
Zhone Technologies Inc	3661	26
Zi Solutions LLC	7361	262
Zia Enterprises Inc	5735	12
Ziamatic Corp	3569	114
Ziba Group	7379	1052
Ziba Photographs	2741	407
Zibiz Corp	7379	656
Zidell Management Company Inc	8741	273
Zidell Marine Corp	4499	8
Ziebart International Corp	7549	12
Ziegenfelder Co	2024	43
Zieger and Sons Inc	5193	16
Ziegler Asset Management Inc	6282	57
Ziegler Bolt and Parts Co	5085	128
Ziegler Chemical and Mineral Corp	2911	55
Ziegler Companies Inc	6211	241
Ziegler Leasing Corp	7352	13
Ziegner Technologies Inc	7372	3752
Ziehm Imaging Inc	3844	14
Zielinski and Associates PC	8721	168
Ziems Ford Corners Inc	5511	526
Zierden Company Inc	3714	381
Zierer Visa Service Inc	7389	390
Zierick Manufacturing Corp	3643	63
Ziff Davis Holdings Inc	6719	78
Ziff Davis Media Inc	2721	18
Ziff-Davis Inc	2721	74
Ziggity Systems Inc	3523	114
Ziggy International Inc	5046	353
Zigler Power Systems	3531	217
Zilliant Inc (Austin Texas)	7372	256
ZiLOG Inc	3674	330
Zim Chemical Company Inc	5087	142
Zimkor LLC	3441	86
Zimmer Gunsul Frasca Partnership	8712	36
Zimmer Holdings Inc	3842	4
Zimmer Orthopedic Surgical Products	3842	50
Zimmer Patient Care Div	3842	63
Zimmer Rado Group	4832	134
Zimmer Thomson Associates Inc	5047	164
Zimmerman and Co	1629	112
Zimmerman and Markman Inc	7311	1034
Zimmerman Cheese Inc	2022	73
Zimmerman Ford Inc	5511	894
Zimmerman Industries Inc	3531	168
Zimmerman Metals Inc	3441	124
Zimmerman School Equipment Inc	5049	204
Zimmerman Truck Lines Inc	4213	555
Zimmermann and Jansen Inc	3491	48
Zimmermann Printing Co	2752	669
Zim's Bagging Co	3086	65
Zin Technologies Inc	8711	142
Zina's Salads Inc	2099	319
Zinc Software Inc	7371	24
Zinfi Technologies Inc	8731	314
Zingerman's Bakehouse Inc	2051	159
Zinio Systems Inc	7375	71
Zinkan Enterprises Inc	2899	101
Zinklahoma Inc	3317	6
Zinn Polymers Inc	2821	155
Zinpro Corp	2048	41
Zin-Tech Inc	3544	525
Z-International Inc	2672	49
Zion Industries Inc	3567	80
Zion Oil and Gas Inc	1382	76
Zions Bancorp	6021	7
Zions First National Bank	6021	182
ZIOPHARM Oncology Inc	8731	405
Zip Mailing Services Inc	7331	143
Zip Tool and Die Company Inc	3599	2519
Zipcar Inc	5012	34
zipLogix	7372	1279
Zippertubing Co	3089	433
Zippi Networks Inc	7389	2497
Zippo Manufacturing Company Inc	3999	40
ZipRealty Inc	6531	172
Ziptronix Inc	3674	247
Zirc Co	3843	45
Zircon Corp	3546	18
Zircon Precision Products Inc	3599	1676
Zirmed Inc	8741	26
Ziron Environmental Services	4213	2756
Zitco Inc	5013	53
Zivco Inc	3089	1635
Zix Corp	7371	238
Zixltcom Inc	7375	135
ZKS Real Estate Partners LLC	6531	416
ZI Technologies Inc	5045	521
Z-Law Software Inc	7372	1591
Zls Corp	3829	481
ZMD America Inc	3674	313
ZMD Reining Inc	7373	851
zNET Internet Services Inc	7375	148
Z-Non Electric Inc	1731	2237
Znyx Networks Inc	3577	269
Zocalo	5021	86
Zodax LP	2511	21

Company Name	SIC	Rank
Zodiac Pool Systems Inc	3949	32
Zodiac Printing Corp	2752	1498
Zoeller Pump Company	3561	35
Zog Industries Inc	2899	227
Zogenix Inc	2834	258
ZOHO Corp	7372	30
ZOLL Medical Corp	3845	9
Zoltek Corp	3571	245
Zoltek Companies Inc	3624	3
Zomax International Inc	5045	75
Zomax US Inc	7372	242
Zombie Inc	7372	1499
Zomeworks Corp	3444	267
Zona Technology Inc	7372	3095
Zondervan Corp	2731	43
Zone Corp	4832	218
Zone Labs Inc	7372	1596
Zone Reed Industries Inc	3053	126
Zone Transportation Co	4213	454
Zonecorp Inc	7379	1656
ZonePerfect Nutrition Co	2099	149
Zones Inc	5961	31
Zontec Inc	7372	1111
Zoo Entertainment Inc	7372	4956
Zook Enterprises LLC	3559	333
Zoological Society Of San Diego	8422	1
Zoom Information Inc	7375	72
Zoom Media	7312	5
Zoom Technologies Inc	3661	16
Zooma Zooma Corp	7812	236
Zoomland Inc	5045	662
Zoomy Communications Inc	4899	154
Zoosk Inc	8999	58
Zoot Enterprises Inc	7371	364
Zoots Corp	7216	1
Zoove Corp	7375	138
Zoran Advertising and Design Inc	7311	210
Zorch International Inc	8743	49
Zordan Precision Tool Inc	3089	1579
Zoria Farms Inc	2034	4
Zortec International Inc	7371	1276
Zoup Fresh Soup Co	5812	424
Zoyto Inc	8742	362
Z-Patch Inc	3545	339
ZPAY Payroll Systems Inc	7372	2735
Zpizza International Inc	5812	417
ZRHD PC	8711	487
Zrike Co	3263	3
ZS Associates Inc	8742	35
ZT Group International Inc	7373	66
Ztar Mobile Inc	4812	92
Zte (USA) Inc	5065	248
Ztech	3585	251
Z-Tech Corp	7379	101
Ztrace Inc	5734	206
Zubeck Inc	1623	544
Zuberance Inc	7372	1988
Zubi Advertising Services Inc	7311	181
Zuckerman-Honickman Inc	5085	155
Zuern Building Products Inc	5211	55
Zuken USA Inc	7372	394
Zultner and Co	7372	4947
Zultys Technologies	3613	66
Zumasys Inc	7373	389
Zumbach Electronics Corp	3825	111
Zumiez Inc	5699	5
Zumro Manufacturing Inc	3669	257
Zunicom Inc	5063	1046
Zurich	6331	58
Zurich Kemper Life Insurance Co	6311	51
Zurich North America	6311	22
Zurn Pex Inc	3081	132
Zurn Plumbing Products Group	3432	12
Zurn Wilkins	3432	21
ZV Pate Inc	5399	5
Zvents Inc	7375	97
Zwack Inc	3541	107
Zweig White and Associates Inc	2731	182
Zweigle's Inc	2013	142
Zwicker Electric Company Inc	1731	7
Zwing Advertising and Designz Inc	7311	109
Z-Works	5111	35
Zycron Inc	7379	87
Zygo Industries Inc	3842	316
Zygo International	7373	76
Zygot Automation Inc	3565	144
Zygote Media Group Inc	7372	3753
Zykronix Inc	7373	413
ZyLAB International Inc	7373	862
Zyloware Corp	3851	43
Zyman Group LLC	8742	195
Zymequest Inc	2835	53
ZymoGenetics Inc	2836	43
Zynex Inc	3845	60
Zynga Inc	2741	8
Zypcom Inc	3661	119
ZyQuest Inc	7379	204
Zyrel Inc	3672	431
Zyrion Inc	7372	2505
Zyto Corp	7372	2818
Zyvex Instruments LLC	3545	296
ZyXEL Communications Inc	3661	142
ZZ Liner Inc	1623	750